GOD'S WORD

Complete CONCORDANCE

GOD'S™ WORD

Complete CONCORDANCE

John J. Hughes
William D. Mounce

WORLD PUBLISHING
Grand Rapids, Michigan 49418 U.S.A.

Library of Congress Catalogue Number: 95-61692

Published by: World Publishing, Inc.
Grand Rapids, MI 49418 U.S.A.
All rights reserved.

Printed in the United States of America

1 2 3 4 5 6 7 98 97 96 95

RRD-C

Contents

To the LORD of the Word

and

For all who hear his voice

Preface

While the readability and single-column format of *God's Word* make it the best Bible translation for casual reading, the scholarship of *God's Word* makes it the exceptional choice for in-depth Bible study. The translation team of God's Word to the Nations Bible Society knew the importance of a concordance for Bible students. Therefore, the Bible Society began the concordance project immediately after completing the translation of *God's Word*.

In producing this complete concordance—the first one available for studying the text of *God's Word*—the translation team focused on the same goals they had set for the translation: to be scholarly and user-friendly.

Like a phone book, a concordance is an alphabetical listing of words and addresses. In a phone book the entry "Jones" lists all the Joneses and their addresses. In a concordance each entry word lists the verses in the Bible where the entry word occurs, so that by looking under "miracle" you would see a list of all the verses in the Bible where *miracle* appears. Thus concordances are indispensable tools for studying the uses of words, for examining themes, and for locating references.

There are three basic types of concordances: exhaustive, complete, and partial. Complete and exhaustive concordances list all the occurrences of each entry word. In an exhaustive concordance, every unique word is an entry word; but in a complete concordance, only key words—significant words—are selected as entry words. Partial concordances—such as are found in the back of many study Bibles—list the most significant occurrences of selected entry words.

This concordance to *God's Word* is a complete concordance to the sixty-six books of the Old and New Testaments. With only eight exceptions, it lists all the occurrences of each of its 12,449 entry words and provides one line of intelligible context for each reference. These entry words were selected as being the most important to include in a concordance. The eight exceptions are *being, does, might, mine, on, put, well,* and *will.* Only when these words are used as nouns were they concorded. For example, when *well* refers to a cistern, it was concorded; but when *well* is used adverbially in phrases such as "do well," it was not concorded. Proofreaders and programmers took great care in creating context lines that have enough information to be helpful.

The translation team designed *God's Word Complete Concordance* to be as user-friendly as possible. Each page is visually self-explanatory. The following features enhance this volume's ease-of-use:

- The number listings occur before the alphabetical listings. Numbers are listed in figure and word style, regardless of how they appear in the text. Thus, for example, an entry word would appear as follows: "12; twelve."
- Entry words appear in lower case letters unless the entry word is a proper noun such as "Herod" or "Canaan."
- Word frequencies are listed next to the entry in parentheses.

- If a word occurs more than one time in a verse, each occurrence is given its own context line.
- Multiple-word names and phrases are listed as such, rather than forcing users to look under one or more of the component parts to locate occurrences of the item. For example, "Beth Shemesh" and "I am" are entries in the concordance, so that users can look under "Beth Shemesh," rather than looking under *Beth* or *Shemesh* to try and locate all the occurrences of "Beth Shemesh."
- To provide more context, each instance of a concorded word is reduced to its first letter, which is displayed in bold. For example, if "Pharaoh" is the entry word, a reference to Gen 40:13 might look like this: "In the next three days **P** will release you."
- *GOD'S WORD* uses half brackets (⌊ ⌋) to mark the occurrence of words that are used to assist in translation but that are not translations of original-language words. These half brackets are preserved in this concordance.
- The two-part running headers occur on the outside of each page and list the two entry words whose occurrences appear first and last on the page.
- Words were alphabetized according to the *Chicago Manual of Style* so that hyphens, apostrophes, and spaces (in multiple-word names and phrases) were not counted in the alphabetization process, for example, *daughter, daughter-in-law, daughter's, daughters, daughters-in-law.*

There are two special appendices at the end of this concordance. The appendix entitled "Words Omitted in *GOD'S WORD* Complete Concordance" lists all the words that were not concorded. This includes prepositions, articles, interjections, conjunctions, contractions, and transitional words such as *furthermore* and *therefore*. It also includes negatives, pronouns, and auxiliary verbs. Only selected numbers were concorded. Numbers that were not concorded are not listed in this appendix.

GOD'S WORD avoided using complex theological terms and archaisms by substituting words that carry the same meaning in common English. Therefore, words such as *covenant* and *cloak* do not appear in *GOD'S WORD*. The appendix entitled "Archaic Words and Uses in *GOD'S WORD* Complete Concordance" is intended to help you locate entries in *GOD'S WORD* by referring to their more archaic forms.

GOD'S WORD Complete Concordance was created by John J. Hughes, of Bits & Bytes Computer Resources, and William D. Mounce, of Teknia Software, using a specialized, Windows-based, menu-driven program, custom written by Bill Mounce. This program, whose in-house name is simply *Concorder*™, was written for producing exhaustive, complete, and partial concordances to any translation of the Bible. *Concorder* provided intelligent, full contexts for the 12,449 entry words and their 287,107 associated references and lines of concorded information, which were drawn from the 729,073-word translation. Additionally, *Concorder* tagged its output so that it could be imported, properly formatted, directly into *FrameMaker*, whose files, which consisted of 1,212 pages of the concordance proper—26,379,264 bytes of information—then were output to film. After the software was written, the concordance was produced in approximately six months. Much of this time was spent proofreading. We believe *GOD'S WORD Complete Concordance* will appear in print sooner after the publication of the translation it references (*GOD'S WORD*) than has any other printed concordance.

In an article entitled "On the Making of a Concordance," Richard M. Hohulin, an international translation consultant, asserted, "The compilation of a truly useful concordance is not for the faint of heart. It is both time-consuming and tedious. However, the end result is worth the investment of all the time and labor required." The editors and translation team of God's Word to the Nations Bible Society hope that you will find that *GOD'S WORD Complete Concordance* aids you in your personal study of God's living, saving, life-changing Word.

The Editors and the Publishers
August 1995

Acknowledgments

GOD’S WORD Complete Concordance was a team effort from start to finish.

First, we wish to thank the many scholars, pastors, and others who labored so diligently for so many years to produce *GOD’S WORD*. Without their work, this concordance would not exist.

We owe a great debt of thanks to Michael Hackbardt, Executive Director of God’s Word to the Nations Bible Society, who had the initial vision for a complete concordance that would appear shortly after the publication of *GOD’S WORD* to facilitate the study of this new translation.

We also wish to express our gratitude to Doris Rikkers at World Publishing for the encouragement, vision, and expertise she lent to this project and to David See at R.R. Donnelly & Sons for turning our *FrameMaker* files into a printed concordance.

The accuracy of *GOD’S WORD Complete Concordance* was checked by a set of custom programs, as well as by a team of highly trained individuals. In this regard, we wish to thank the following staff of Gods Word to the Nations Bible Society: Dr. Richard Gudgeon, Project Coordinator; Ronald Coulter, Assistant Coordinator; Richard Sweeney, Jr. , English Reviewer, who helped create phrase and hyphenated-word lists; Kristine Luber, English Reviewer, and Tamara Stross, English Reviewer. Ric Gudgeon provided excellent, timely, and professional assistance and support throughout the project. Ric was our day-to-day contact and the person at God’s Word to the Nations Bible Society most responsible for seeing this project through to completion. Kris, Tammy, Ron, and Ric were the best quality-control team imaginable, and much of the credit for the accuracy of the final product goes to them. Kris and Tammy meticulously created stopword and archaic-word lists, which they proofed many times. Along with Ron, they helped design the layout of the concordance and painstakingly proofed almost all the concordance’s 1,212 pages. We also thank Lara Gangloff and Claire Hughes of Bits & Bytes Computer Resources for their editorial and computer assistance, which allowed us to complete this project in a timely fashion.

John J. Hughes
William D. Mounce

Abbreviations for the Books of the Bible

Gen	Genesis	Nah	Nahum
Exo	Exodus	Hab	Habakkuk
Lev	Leviticus	Zep	Zephaniah
Num	Numbers	Hag	Haggai
Dtr	Deuteronomy	Zec	Zechariah
Jos	Joshua	Mal	Malachi
Jdg	Judges	Mat	Matthew
Rut	Ruth	Mar	Mark
1Sm	1 Samuel	Luk	Luke
2Sm	2 Samuel	Jon	John
1Ki	1 Kings	Act	Acts
2Ki	2 Kings	Rom	Romans
1Ch	1 Chronicles	1Co	1 Corinthians
2Ch	2 Chronicles	2Co	2 Corinthians
Ezr	Ezra	Gal	Galatians
Neh	Nehemiah	Eph	Ephesians
Est	Esther	Php	Philippians
Job	Job	Col	Colossians
Psa	Psalms	1Th	1 Thessalonians
Pro	Proverbs	2Th	2 Thessalonians
Ecc	Ecclesiastes	1Ti	1 Timothy
Sos	Song of Songs	2Ti	2 Timothy
Isa	Isaiah	Tit	Titus
Jer	Jeremiah	Phm	Philemon
Lam	Lamentations	Heb	Hebrews
Eze	Ezekiel	Jas	James
Dan	Daniel	1Pe	1 Peter
Hos	Hosea	2Pe	2 Peter
Joe	Joel	1Jn	1 John
Amo	Amos	2Jn	2 John
Oba	Obadiah	3Jn	3 John
Jnh	Jonah	Jud	Jude
Mic	Micah	Rev	Revelation

1/10; one-tenth; a tenth (47)

Gen 14:20 gave him a **t** of everything.
28:22 and I will surely give you a **t** of
Lev 27:30 "**O** of what comes from the
Num 18:21 "I am giving the Levites **o** of
18:24 contribute to the LORD — **o**
18:26 You will take **o** of the Israelites'
18:26 you must contribute **o** of that
18:28 So you, too, will contribute **o** of
Dtr 12:6 sacrifices, **o** of your income,
12:11 sacrifices, **o** of your income,
12:17 are: **o** of your grain, new wine,
14:22 Every year be sure to save a **t**
14:24 so much that you can't carry a **t**
14:28 end of every third year bring a **t**
26:12 the year when you will store a **t**
Jdg 20:10 We'll take **o** of all the men from
1Sm 8:15 He will take a **t** of your grain
8:17 He will take a **t** of your flocks.
9:8 I have **o** of an ounce of silver.
13:21 and **o** of an ounce of silver to
2Ch 31:5 quantities, a **t** of everything.
31:6 the cities of Judah brought a **t**
31:6 of their cattle and sheep and a **t**
31:12 the offerings of **o** of the crops,
Neh 10:37 We will bring for the Levites **o**
10:37 are the ones who collect **o**
10:38 Then the Levites should bring **o**
12:44 and a **t** of the people's money.
13:5 a **t** of all the grain harvested,
13:12 Then all Judah brought a **t** of
Eze 45:11 bath should hold the same as **o**
Amo 4:4 Bring a **t** of your income every
Mal 3:8 "When ⌊you don't bring⌋ a **t** of
3:10 "Bring **o** of your income into the
Mat 23:23 You give ⌊God⌋ **o** of your mint,
Luk 11:42 You give ⌊God⌋ **o** of your mint,
18:12 and I give you a **t** of my entire
Heb 7:2 Abraham gave Melchizedek a **t**
7:4 Abraham gave him a **t** of what
7:5 priests must receive a **t**
7:6 he received a **t** of everything
7:8 receive a **t** of everything,
7:8 received a **t** of everything,
7:9 Melchizedek a **t** of everything,
7:9 was giving a **t** of everything.
7:9 would receive a **t** of everything.
Rev 11:13 **O** of the city collapsed,

1/2; half (124)

Gen 15:10 He cut each of them in **h** and
15:10 in half and laid each **h** opposite
15:10 he did not cut the birds in **h**.
Exo 24:6 Moses took **h** of the blood and
24:6 the other **h** against the altar.
26:9 Fold the sixth sheet in **h** ⌊to
28:16 Fold it in **h** so that it's 9 inches
30:23 "Take the finest spices: 12 **1**
39:9 It was folded in **h** and was 9
Lev 6:20 He must offer **h** of it in the
6:20 morning and **h** in the evening.
Num 31:29 things from the soldiers' **h**
31:30 From the Israelites' **h** of the
31:36 **H** of it went to the soldiers who
31:42 Moses took the Israelites' **h** of
31:47 From the Israelites' **h** Moses
32:33 and **h** of the tribe of Manasseh,
34:14 and **h** of the tribe of Manasseh
Dtr 3:12 near the Arnon Valley and **h**
3:13 all of Bashan ruled by Og to **h**
3:18 tribes of Reuben and Gad and **h**
29:8 and **h** of the tribe of Manasseh
Jos 1:12 tribes of Reuben and Gad and **h**
3:4 However, stay about **h** a mile
4:12 men of Reuben, Gad, and **h**
8:33 **H** of the people were in front of
8:33 Mount Gerizim and the other **h**
12:2 of the valley and **h** of Gilead.
12:5 and **h** of Gilead to the border of
12:6 tribes of Reuben and Gad and **h**
13:7 for the nine tribes and **h**
13:8 of Reuben and Gad with **h**
13:25 and **h** of Ammon as far as
13:29 land as an inheritance to **h**
13:29 families of that **h** of the tribe.
Jos 13:31 It also included **h** of Gilead
13:31 They were given to **h** the
18:7 tribes of Gad and Reuben and **h**
21:5 of Ephraim and Dan and **h**
21:6 and **h** of the tribe of Manasseh
21:25 **H** of the tribe of Manasseh
21:27 cities with pasturelands from **h**
22:1 tribes of Reuben and Gad and **h**
22:7 inheritance to **h** of Manasseh,
22:7 Joshua had given the other **h**
22:9 tribes of Reuben and Gad and **h**
22:10 Reuben, Gad, and **h** of the tribe
22:11 Reuben, Gad, and **h** of the tribe
22:13 tribes of Reuben and Gad and **h**
22:21 tribes of Reuben and Gad and **h**
Rut 2:17 She had about **h** a bushel of
1Sm 1:24 **h** a bushel of flour,
2Sm 10:4 shaved off **h** of each man's
13:2 with his **h** sister Tamar that
13:32 the day his **h** brother raped his
18:3 about us, and if **h** of us die,
19:40 All the troops from Judah and **h**
1Ki 3:25 Give **h** to the one and half to
3:25 to the one and **h** to the other."
10:7 I wasn't even told **h** of it.
13:8 "Even if you gave me **h** of your
16:9 the general who commanded **h**
16:21 **H** of the army followed Tibni,
16:21 The ⌊other⌋ **h** followed Omri.
16:22 But the **h** which followed Omri
16:22 the **h** which followed Tibni,
2Ki 7:1 of the best flour will sell for **h**
7:1 48 cups of barley will sell for **h**
7:16 cups of the best flour sold for **h**
7:16 and 48 cups of barley sold for **h**
7:18 cups of barley will sell for **h**
7:18 of the best flour will sell for **h**
1Ch 2:52 **h** of the Manahathites,
2:54 **h** of the Manahathites,
5:18 and **h** of the tribe of Manasseh
5:22 Reuben, Gad, and **h** of the tribe
5:23 **H** of the tribe of Manasseh
5:25 But Gad, Reuben, and **h** of the
5:26 and **h** of the tribe of Manasseh
6:61 by lot from the families of **h**
6:70 From **h** of the tribe of
6:71 from the families of **h**
12:31 From **h** of the tribe of
12:37 and **h** the tribe of Manasseh,
26:32 and **h** of the tribe of Manasseh.
27:20 son of Azaziah for **h** of the tribe
27:21 for the **h** of Manasseh in
2Ch 9:6 told about **h** of the extent of
Neh 3:9 an official in charge of **h** a
3:12 an official in charge of **h** a
3:16 the official in charge of **h** the
3:17 the official in charge of **h** the
3:18 the official in charge of **h** the
4:6 which was rebuilt to about **h**
4:16 From that day on, **h** of my men
4:16 and the other **h** were wearing
4:21 **H** of us held spears from early
12:32 Hoshaiah and **h** of the leaders
12:38 I followed them with the other **h**
12:40 as did I and the **h** of the leaders
13:24 **H** their children spoke the
Est 5:3 Even if it is up to **h** of the
5:6 Even if it is up to **h** of the
7:2 Even if it is up to **h** of the
Psa 55:23 will not live out **h** their days.
Isa 44:16 **H** of the wood they burn in the
44:16 Over this **h** they roast meat that
44:19 "I burned **h** of the wood in the
Eze 16:51 "'Samaria didn't commit **h** the
Dan 7:25 a time, times, and **h** of a time.
12:7 a time, times, and **h** of a time.
Zec 14:2 **H** of the people in the city will
14:4 **H** of the mountain will move
14:4 and the other **h** will move
14:8 **h** of it to the Dead Sea and the
14:8 to the Dead Sea and the other **h**
Mar 6:23 up to **h** of my kingdom."
Luk 19:8 I'll give **h** of my property to the
Jon 7:14 When the festival was **h** over,
Act 1:12 about **h** a mile away.
18:11 in Corinth for a year and a **h**
Heb 11:37 stoned to death, sawed in **h**,
Rev 8:1 in heaven for about **h** an hour.
12:14 a time, times, and **h** a time.

2; two (589)

Gen 1:16 God made the **t** bright lights:
4:19 Lamech married **t** women,
6:19 Bring **t** of every living creature
6:20 **T** of every type of bird,
9:22 outside and told his **t** brothers.
10:25 **T** sons were born to Eber.
11:10 **T** years after the flood when
19:1 The **t** angels came to Sodom in
19:8 "Look, I have **t** daughters who
19:15 Take your wife and your **t**
19:16 and his **t** daughters by their
19:30 He and his **t** daughters settled
19:36 So Lot's **t** daughters became
21:27 and the **t** of them made an
22:3 He took with him **t** of his
22:4 **T** days later Abraham saw the
22:6 The **t** of them went on together.
22:8 The **t** of them went on together.
24:22 and **t** gold bracelets weighing
25:23 "**T** countries are in your womb.
25:23 **T** nations will go their separate
27:9 and get me **t** good young goats.
29:16 Laban had **t** daughters.
31:22 **T** days later Laban was told
31:33 and into the tent of the **t** slaves.
31:41 14 years for your **t** daughters
32:2 place Mahanaim [**T** Camps].
32:7 and the camels into **t** camps.
32:10 but now I have **t** camps.
32:22 up and gathered his **t** wives,
32:22 his **t** slaves and his eleven
33:1 Leah, Rachel, and the **t** slaves.
34:25 **T** days later, while the men
34:25 still in pain, **t** of Jacob's sons,
40:20 **T** days later, on his birthday,
41:1 After **t** full years Pharaoh had a
41:50 Joseph had **t** sons by Asenath,
42:37 "You may put my **t** sons to
44:27 wife ⌊Rachel⌋ gave me **t** sons.
45:6 has been in the land for **t** years.
46:27 Joseph had **t** sons who were
48:1 So he took his **t** sons
48:5 "So your **t** sons, who were born
Exo 2:13 he saw **t** Hebrew men fighting.
4:9 But if they won't believe these **t**
16:16 Take **t** quarts for each person
16:29 food on the sixth day for **t** days.
16:32 Take **t** quarts of manna to be
16:33 put **t** quarts of manna in it,
18:3 along with her **t** sons.
18:6 your wife and her **t** sons."
19:1 **T** months after the Israelites
19:10 and tell them they have **t** days
19:15 "Be ready **t** days from now.
21:21 the slave gets up in a day or **t**,
22:9 which **t** people claim as
25:12 **t** rings on each side.
25:18 Make **t** angels out of hammered
25:18 of hammered gold for the **t** ends
26:6 Use them to link the ⌊**t** sets of⌋
26:17 with **t** identical pegs.
26:19 **t** sockets at the bottom of each
26:19 of each frame for the **t** pegs.
26:21 **t** at the bottom of each frame.
26:23 Make **t** frames for ⌊each of⌋ the
26:25 **t** at the bottom of each frame.
28:7 It will have **t** shoulder straps
28:9 Take **t** onyx stones,
28:11 sons of Israel on the **t** stones
28:14 and **t** chains of pure gold,
28:23 Make **t** gold rings for the
28:23 Attach them to the **t** ⌊top⌋
28:24 Then fasten the **t** gold ropes to
28:25 of the ropes to the **t** settings
28:26 Make **t** gold rings, and fasten
28:26 and fasten them to the other **t**
28:27 Make **t** ⌊more⌋ gold rings,
29:1 no defects and **t** rams that have
29:3 the young bull and the **t** rams.
29:13 and the **t** kidneys with the fat
29:22 the **t** kidneys with the fat on

Exo 29:38 t one-year-old lambs.
30:4 Make t gold rings, and put them
30:34 one part fragrant spices (t kinds
31:18 Then he gave him the t tablets
32:15 mountain carrying the t tablets
34:1 "Cut t ⌊more⌋ stone tablets
34:4 So Moses cut t ⌊more⌋ stone
34:4 carrying the t stone tablets.
34:29 carrying the t tablets with
36:13 They used them to link the ⌊t
36:22 with t identical pegs.
36:24 t sockets at the bottom of each
36:24 of each frame for the t pegs.
36:26 t at the bottom of each frame.
36:28 They made t frames for ⌊each
36:30 t at the bottom of each frame.
37:3 t rings on each side.
37:7 Then he made t angels out of
37:7 of hammered gold for the t ends
37:27 He made t gold rings and put
39:4 They made t shoulder straps
39:16 They made t gold settings and
39:16 gold settings and t gold rings
39:16 rings and attached the t rings
39:16 two rings to the ⌊top⌋ t corners
39:17 They fastened the t gold ropes
39:18 of the ropes to the t settings
39:19 They made t gold rings and
39:19 them to the other t corners
39:20 They made t ⌊more⌋ gold rings
Lev 3:4 and the t kidneys with the fat
3:10 Also remove the t kidneys with
3:15 and the t kidneys with the fat
4:9 and the t kidneys with the fat
5:7 you must bring to the LORD t
5:7 mourning doves or t pigeons as
5:11 "But if you cannot afford t
5:11 mourning doves or t pigeons,
7:4 and the t kidneys with the fat
8:2 the offering for sin, the t rams,
8:16 and the t kidneys with their fat,
8:25 the t kidneys with their fat,
12:5 will be unclean for t weeks.
12:8 she must use t mourning doves
12:8 mourning doves or t pigeons.
14:4 order someone to get t living,
14:10 he must take t male lambs that
14:22 and t mourning doves or two
14:22 and two mourning doves or t
14:49 "The priest must take t birds,
15:14 he must take t mourning doves
15:14 mourning doves or t pigeons
15:29 must take t mourning doves
15:29 mourning doves or t pigeons
16:1 after Aaron's t sons had come
16:5 He will take t male goats from
16:7 He must take the t male goats
16:8 must throw lots for the t goats.
16:12 and t handfuls of finely ground,
19:19 Never plant t kinds of crops in
19:19 Never wear clothes made from t
20:14 The man and the t women
23:17 Bring t loaves of bread from
23:18 defects, one bull, and t rams.
23:19 sin and t one-year-old lambs as
23:20 All this, along with the t lambs,
24:6 Put them in t stacks of six
27:6 give 2 ounces of silver and for
27:16 Ground planted with 2 quarts of
Num 3:47 It will cost you t ounces of
6:10 he must bring t mourning doves
6:10 doves or t young pigeons
7:3 one wagon from every t leaders
7:7 He gave t wagons and four
7:17 and t bulls, five rams, five male
7:23 and t bulls, five rams, five male
7:29 and t bulls, five rams, five male
7:35 and t bulls, five rams, five male
7:41 and t bulls, five rams, five male
7:47 and t bulls, five rams, five male
7:53 and t bulls, five rams, five male
7:59 and t bulls, five rams, five male
7:65 and t bulls, five rams, five male
7:71 and t bulls, five rams, five male
7:77 and t bulls, five rams, five male
7:83 and t bulls, five rams, five male

Num 7:89 from between the t angels.
9:22 Whether it was t days,
10:2 "Make t trumpets out of
11:19 eat it just for one or t days,
11:26 T men, named Eldad and
13:23 it on a pole between t of them.
14:6 At the same time, t of those
15:9 of flour mixed with t quarts
15:10 Also give an offering of t quarts
15:25 they brought these t offerings
18:16 at the fixed price of t ounces
22:22 accompanied by his t servants.
23:2 and the t of them offered a bull
28:3 t one-year-old lambs that
28:9 "On the day of worship offer t
28:11 a burnt offering of t young bulls,
28:14 with each bull will be 2 quarts
28:19 a burnt offering of t young bulls,
28:27 to the LORD — t young bulls,
29:13 bring 13 young bulls, 2 rams,
29:14 16 cups for each of the 2 rams,
29:17 bring 12 young bulls, 2 rams,
29:20 third day bring 11 bulls, 2 rams,
29:23 day bring 10 bulls, 2 rams,
29:26 fifth day bring 9 bulls, 2 rams,
29:29 sixth day bring 8 bulls, 2 rams,
29:32 day bring 7 bulls, 2 rams,
Dtr 1:16 dispute⌋ between t Israelites
3:8 We took the land of the t
3:21 God has done to these t kings.
4:13 wrote them on t stone tablets.
4:47 the t kings of the Amorites who
5:22 on t stone tablets
9:10 Then the LORD gave me the t
9:11 the LORD gave me the t stone
9:15 I was carrying the t tablets with
9:17 I took the t tablets,
10:1 "Cut t ⌊more⌋ stone tablets like
10:3 I cut t ⌊more⌋ stone tablets like
10:3 I carried the t tablets up the
17:6 to death on the testimony of t
19:5 Suppose t people go into the
19:15 of t or three witnesses.
19:17 The t people involved must
21:15 A man might have t wives and
25:1 do whenever ⌊t⌋ people have
25:11 do when t men are fighting
25:13 Never carry t sets of weights,
25:14 Never have t kinds of
32:30 thousand or t people make ten
Jos 2:1 secretly sent out t men as
2:4 already taken the t men inside
2:10 the t kings of the Amorites,
2:23 Then the t spies came down
6:22 But Joshua said to the t spies,
9:10 everything he did to the t kings
9:17 and Kiriath Jearim t days later.
14:4 and Ephraim, formed t tribes.
15:60 The t cities of Kiriath Baal
21:13 The nine cities from those t
21:25 of Manasseh gave them t cities
21:27 t cities with pasturelands from
24:12 of you to force out the t kings
Jdg 5:30 A girl or t for each soldier,
5:30 and t pieces of colorful,
7:25 the t Midianite commanders.
9:44 The other t companies charged
11:37 Give me t months for my
11:38 and he sent her off for t months.
11:39 At the end of those t months
14:15 Did the t of you invite us ⌊just
15:13 So they tied him up with t new
15:16 I've made t piles of them.
16:25 him stand between t columns.
16:28 for at least one of my t eyes."
16:29 Samson felt the t middle
19:3 his servant and t donkeys.
19:10 He had with him t saddled
Rut 1:1 went with his wife and t sons
1:2 and the names of their t sons
1:3 was left alone with her t sons.
1:5 without her t sons or her
1:7 and her t daughters-in-law went
1:8 said to her t daughters-in-law,
1Sm 1:2 Elkanah had t wives,
1:3 Eli's t sons, Hophni and

1Sm 2:21 had three sons and t daughters.
2:34 going to happen to your t sons,
4:4 Eli's t sons, Hophni and
4:17 Your t sons, Hophni and
5:4 Dagon's head and his t hands
6:7 Now get a new cart ready for t
6:10 They took t dairy cows,
10:2 When you leave me today, t
10:4 greet you and give you t loaves
11:11 were so scattered that no t
14:49 The names of his t daughters
17:3 a ravine between the t of them.
20:5 countryside for t more nights.
20:12 "I'll find out in the next t or
25:18 of bread, 2 full wineskins,
27:3 and David had his t wives,
28:8 Saul left with t men and came
29:3 with me now for a year or t?
30:1 T days later, when David and
30:5 also captured David's t wives,
30:12 slice of fig cake and t bunches
30:18 including his t wives.
2Sm 1:1 David stayed in Ziklag t days.
2:2 went there with his t wives,
2:10 He ruled for t years,
4:2 Saul's son had t men who were
8:2 He measured t lengths which
12:1 "There were t men in a certain
13:23 T years later Absalom had
14:6 I had t sons who quarreled in
14:28 Absalom stayed in Jerusalem t
15:36 They have t sons with them:
18:24 David was sitting between the t
21:8 the t sons whom Rizpah
23:20 He killed t distinguished
1Ki 2:5 to me and to the t commanders
2:32 Joab killed t honorable men
2:39 But after three years, t of
3:16 A short time later t prostitutes
3:18 T days later this woman also
3:18 Just the t of us were in the
3:25 "Cut the living child in t.
3:26 mine or yours. Cut him ⌊in t⌋."
5:14 Lebanon and t months at home.
6:23 In the inner room he made t
6:32 The t doors were ⌊made out
6:34 He made t doors from cypress.
6:34 the doors had t folding panels.
7:15 He made t bronze pillars.
7:16 He made t capitals of cast
7:18 he made t rows ⌊of
7:24 Under the rim were t rows of
7:31 and was t feet ⌊wide⌋.
7:32 Each wheel was t feet high.
7:41 2 pillars, the bowl-shaped
7:41 capitals on top of the 2 pillars,
7:41 and 2 sets of filigree to cover
7:41 the 2 bowl-shaped capitals
7:42 400 pomegranates for the 2
7:42 for the 2 sets of filigree (2 rows
7:42 the 2 bowl-shaped capitals
8:9 the t stone tablets Moses
9:10 build the t houses (the LORD's
10:19 T lions stood beside the
11:29 The t of them were alone in the
12:12 back to Rehoboam t days later,
12:28 the king made t golden calves.
15:25 He ruled for t years.
16:8 He ruled in Tirzah for t years.
16:21 was divided into t factions.
18:23 Give us t bulls. Let the prophets
19:21 Elisha left him, took t oxen,
20:27 seemed like t newborn goats.
21:10 Have t good-for-nothing men sit
21:13 The t good-for-nothing men
22:51 Ahaziah ruled Israel for t years.
2Ki 1:14 and burned up the first t officers
2:8 and the t men crossed ⌊the
2:11 horses separated the t of them,
2:12 and tore it in t ⌊to show his
2:24 T bears came out of the woods
4:1 take my t children as slaves."
5:22 He says, 'Just now t young
5:22 of silver and t sets of clothing.'"
5:23 150 pounds of silver in t bags
5:23 of silver in two bags with t sets

2Ki 6:25 donkey's head sold for **t** pounds
6:25 manure for **t** ounces of silver.
7:14 So they took **t** chariots with
9:32 Then **t** or three eunuchs looked
10:4 They said, "If **t** kings couldn't
10:8 Jehu said, "Put them in **t** piles
11:7 Then your **t** groups who
15:23 of Israel in Samaria for **t** years.
17:16 They made **t** calves out of cast
21:5 In the **t** courtyards of the
21:19 and he ruled for **2** years in
23:12 had made in the **t** courtyards
25:4 between the **t** walls beside
25:16 The bronze from the **t** pillars,
1Ch 1:19 **T** sons were born to Eber.
4:5 had **t** wives, Helah and Naarah.
11:22 He killed **t** distinguished
26:17 **t** at each entrance.
26:18 gateway to the palace and **t** at
2Ch 3:10 he made **t** sculptured angels
3:15 He made **t** pillars for the front of
4:3 Under the rim were **t** rows of
4:12 **2** pillars, bowl-shaped capitals
4:12 capitals on top of the **2** pillars,
4:12 and **2** sets of filigree to cover
4:12 the **2** bowl-shaped capitals
4:13 400 pomegranates for the **2**
4:13 for the **2** sets of filigree (**2** rows
4:13 the **2** bowl-shaped capitals
5:10 the **t** tablets Moses placed
9:18 **T** lions stood beside the
10:12 back to Rehoboam **t** days later,
14:10 and the **t** armies set up their
21:19 **T** years later, as his life was
24:3 Jehoiada got Joash **t** wives,
27:5 same amount for **t** more years.
33:5 In the **t** courtyards of the
33:21 ruled for **2** years in Jerusalem.
Ezr 8:27 and **t** utensils of fine polished
10:13 be taken care of in a day or **t**.
Neh 12:31 and I arranged **t** large choirs to
Est 1:7 No **t** cups were alike.
2:21 **t** of the king's eunuchs who
6:2 **t** of the king's eunuchs who
9:27 these **t** days every year,
Job 13:20 "Please don't do **t** things to me
33:14 even in **t** ways without people
33:29 Truly, God does all this **t** or
42:7 with you and your **t** friends
Psa 40:6 You have dug out **t** ears for me.
46:9 He cuts spears in **t**.
107:16 gates and cut iron bars in **t**.
Pro 30:7 "I've asked you for **t** things.
30:15 The bloodsucking leech has **t**
Ecc 4:6 quiet is better than **t** handfuls
4:9 **T** people are better than one
4:11 if **t** people lie down together,
4:12 **t** people can resist one
Sos 4:5 Your breasts are like **t** fawns,
7:3 Your breasts are like **t** fawns,
Isa 5:10 and **t** quarts of seed will
6:2 With **t** they covered their faces,
6:2 with **t** they covered their feet,
6:2 and with **t** they flew.
7:4 These **t** are smoldering logs.'
7:16 the land of the **t** kings who
7:21 alive a young cow and **t** sheep.
10:13 with my own **t** powerful hands.
17:6 Only **t** or three olives are left at
22:11 a reservoir between the **t** walls
Jer 2:13 have done **t** things wrong.
3:14 one from every city and **t** from
24:1 the LORD showed me **t**
28:3 Within **t** years I will bring back
28:11 all the nations within **t** years."
33:24 has rejected the **t** families
34:18 when they cut a calf in **t**
39:4 the gate between the **t** walls,
52:7 between the **t** walls beside
52:20 The bronze from the **2** pillars,
Eze 1:11 Each creature had **t** wings with
1:11 The other **t** wings covered their
1:23 each creature had **t** wings that
1:23 Each creature had **t** wings that
21:19 "Son of man, mark **t** roads that
23:2 there were once **t** women,
35:10 "'You said, "These **t** nations,
37:22 They will no longer be **t**
37:22 or be divided into **t** kingdoms.
40:39 the gateway there were **t** tables
40:40 gateway there were **t** tables,
40:40 gateway there were **t** tables.
41:18 and each angel had **t** faces:
41:23 most holy place had **t** doors.
47:13 Joseph gets **t** parts.
Dan 2:43 So the **t** parts of the kingdom
7:4 It was made to stand on **t** feet
8:3 The ram had **t** long horns,
11:27 The **t** kings will both plan to do
12:5 I saw **t** men standing there.
Hos 6:2 After **t** days he will revive us.
12:3 to his brother's heel while the **t**
Amo 1:1 This happened **t** years before
3:3 Do **t** people ever walk together
3:12 As a shepherd rescues **t** legs
4:8 So people from **t** or three cities
Zec 4:3 There are also **t** olive trees
4:11 "What do these **t** olive trees at
4:12 "What is the meaning of the **t**
4:12 next to the **t** golden pipes that
4:14 So he said, "These are the **t**
5:9 I looked up and saw **t** women
6:1 from between the **t** mountains.
11:7 I took **t** shepherd staffs and
14:4 of Olives will be split in **t**,
Mat 2:16 to kill all the boys **t** years old
4:18 of Galilee, he saw **t** brothers,
4:21 he saw **t** other brothers,
5:41 go **t** miles with him.
6:24 "No one can serve **t** masters.
8:28 of Galilee, **t** men met him.
9:27 **t** blind men followed him.
10:29 "Aren't **t** sparrows sold for a
14:17 five loaves of bread and **t** fish."
14:19 the five loaves and the **t** fish,
18:8 or injured than to have **t** hands
18:8 than to have two hands or **t** feet
18:9 one eye than to have **t** eyes
18:15 confront him when the **t** of you
18:16 take one or **t** others with you so
18:16 verified by **t** or three witnesses.
18:19 "I can guarantee again that if **t**
18:20 Where **t** or three have come
19:5 and the **t** will be one'?
19:6 So they are no longer **t** but one.
20:20 came to Jesus with her **t** sons.
20:24 they were irritated with the **t**
20:30 **T** blind men were sitting by the
21:1 Jesus sent **t** disciples ahead of
21:28 A man had **t** sons.
21:31 "Which of the **t** sons did what
22:40 on these **t** commandments."
24:40 "At that time **t** men will be
24:41 **T** women will be working at a
26:2 will take place in **t** days.
26:37 He took Peter and Zebedee's **t**
26:60 At last **t** men came forward.
27:21 "Which of the **t** do you want me
27:38 At that time they crucified **t**
27:51 temple was split in **t** from top
Mar 5:37 Peter and the **t** brothers James
6:7 sent them out **t** by two,
6:7 sent them out two by **t**,
6:38 "Five loaves of bread and **t**
6:41 the five loaves and the **t** fish,
6:41 pieces of the **t** fish to everyone.
9:43 disabled than to have **t** hands
9:45 life lame than to have **t** feet
9:47 one eye than to have **t** eyes
10:8 and the **t** will be one.
10:8 So they are no longer **t** but one.
11:1 Jesus sent **t** of his disciples
12:42 dropped in **t** small coins,
14:1 It was **t** days before the
14:13 He sent **t** of his disciples and
15:27 They crucified **t** criminals with
15:38 temple was split in **t** from top
16:12 Later Jesus appeared to **t**
Luk 2:24 doves or **t** young pigeons."
3:11 "Whoever has **t** shirts should
5:2 Jesus saw **t** boats on the
7:18 John called **t** of his disciples
7:41 So Jesus said, "**T** men
9:13 five loaves of bread and **t** fish.
9:16 the five loaves and the **t** fish,
9:32 they saw Jesus' glory and the **t**
10:35 took out **t** silver coins
12:6 five sparrows sold for **t** cents?
12:52 Three will be divided against **t**
12:52 against two and **t** against three.
15:11 "A man had **t** sons.
15:12 property between his **t** sons.
16:13 servant cannot serve **t** masters.
17:34 that on that night if **t** people are
17:35 **T** women will be grinding grain
18:10 He said, "**T** men went into the
19:29 Jesus sent **t** of his disciples
21:2 widow drop in **t** small coins.
22:38 Here are **t** swords!"
23:32 **T** others, who were criminals,
23:45 in the temple was split in **t**.
24:4 **t** men in clothes that were as
24:13 On the same day, **t** of Jesus'
24:35 Then the **t** disciples told what
Jon 1:35 standing with **t** of his disciples.
1:37 When the **t** disciples heard
1:40 was one of the **t** disciples who
4:40 He stayed in Samaria for **t**
4:43 After spending **t** days in
6:9 barley bread and **t** small fish is
8:17 testimony of **t** people is true.
11:6 where he was for **t** more days.
11:7 Then, after the **t** days,
11:18 not quite **t** miles away.)
19:18 Jesus and **t** other men there.
19:40 These **t** men took the body of
20:4 The **t** were running side by
20:12 She saw **t** angels in white
21:2 and **t** other disciples of Jesus
Act 1:10 Suddenly, **t** men in white
1:23 The disciples determined that **t**
1:24 of these **t** you have chosen.
4:14 anything against the **t** apostles.
7:26 Moses saw **t** Israelites fighting,
7:29 In Midian he fathered **t** sons.
9:38 they sent **t** men to him.
10:7 Cornelius called **t** of his
12:6 sleeping between **t** soldiers.
12:6 were bound with **t** chains,
19:10 This continued for **t** years so
19:22 So he sent **t** of his helpers,
19:29 and they dragged the **t** men into
19:34 They kept doing this for about **t**
21:33 him to be tied up with **t** chains.
23:23 Then the officer summoned **t** of
24:27 **T** years passed. Then Porcius
28:13 and **t** days later we arrived at
28:30 Paul rented a place to live for **t**
1Co 6:16 God says, "The **t** will be one."
14:27 only **t** or three at the most
14:29 **T** or three people should speak
2Co 13:1 verified by **t** or three witnesses.
Gal 4:22 says that Abraham had **t** sons,
4:24 illustrate **t** arrangements.
Eph 5:31 and the **t** will be one.
Php 1:23 it hard to choose between the **t**.
1Ti 5:19 by **t** or three witnesses.
Heb 6:18 These **t** things can never be
9:6 That is how these **t** parts of the
10:28 If **t** or three witnesses accused
Jas 1:8 about **t** different things at
2:2 For example, **t** men come to
Rev 9:12 After these things there are **t**
11:3 I will allow my **t** witnesses
11:4 These witnesses are the **t**
11:4 and the **t** lamp stands standing
11:10 these **t** prophets had tormented
11:11 God entered the **t** witnesses,
12:14 The woman was given the **t**
13:11 and it had **t** horns like a lamb.

3; three (346)

Gen 6:10 He had **t** sons: Shem, Ham,
7:13 his **t** daughters-in-law went into
9:19 These were Noah's **t** sons.
18:2 and suddenly he saw **t** men
18:6 "get **t** measures of flour,
29:2 **T** flocks of sheep were lying

Act 27:29 they dropped **f** anchors from the
Rev 4:6 were **f** living creatures covered
4:8 Each of the **f** living creatures
5:6 with the **f** living creatures
5:8 the **f** living creatures and the 24
5:11 the **f** living creatures,
5:14 The **f** living creatures said,
6:1 I heard one of the **f** living
6:6 among the **f** living creatures,
7:1 After this I saw **f** angels
7:1 angels standing at the **f** corners
7:1 They were holding back the **f**
7:2 voice to the **f** angels who had
7:11 and the **f** living creatures.
9:13 I heard a voice from the **f** horns
9:14 "Release the **f** angels who are
9:15 The **f** angels who were ready
14:3 the **f** living creatures,
15:7 One of the **f** living creatures
19:4 The 24 leaders and the **4** living
20:8 the nations in the **f** corners of

7; seven (383)

Gen 4:15 suffer vengeance **s** times over."
4:24 If Cain is avenged **7** times,
7:2 Take with you **s** pairs of every
7:3 Also, take **s** pairs of every kind
7:4 In **s** days I will send rain to the
7:10 **S** days later the flood came on
8:10 He waited **s** more days and
8:12 He waited **s** more days and
21:28 Then Abraham set apart **s**
21:29 of these **s** female lambs you
29:18 So he offered, "I'll work **s** years
29:20 Jacob worked **s** years in return
29:21 ⌊At the end of the **s** years⌋
29:27 to work for me another **s** years."
29:30 for Laban another **s** years.
31:23 pursued Jacob for **s** days.
33:3 of them and bowed **s** times
41:2 Suddenly, **s** nice-looking,
41:3 **S** other cows came up from the
41:3 They stood behind the first **s**
41:4 skinny ate the **s** nice-looking,
41:5 **S** good, healthy heads of grain
41:6 **S** other heads of grain,
41:7 of grain swallowed the **s** full,
41:18 Suddenly, **s** nice-looking,
41:19 **S** other cows came up behind
41:20 ate up the **s** well-fed ones.
41:22 second dream I saw **s** good,
41:23 **S** other heads of grain,
41:24 swallowed the **s** good heads.
41:26 The **s** good cows are seven
41:26 seven good cows are **s** years,
41:26 and the **s** good heads of grain
41:26 heads of grain are **s** years.
41:27 The **s** thin, sickly cows that
41:27 up behind them are **s** years.
41:27 The **s** empty heads of grain
41:27 the east wind are also **s** years.
41:27 **S** years of famine are coming.
41:29 **S** years are coming when there
41:30 After them will come **s** years of
41:34 during the **s** good years.
41:36 our country during the **s** years
41:47 During the **s** good years the
41:48 in Egypt during those **s** years
41:53 The **s** years when there was
41:54 Then the **s** years of famine
46:25 for Jacob. The total was **7**.
50:10 Joseph took **s** days to mourn
Exo 2:16 **s** daughters of the priest of
7:25 **S** days passed after the LORD
12:15 For **s** days you must eat
12:19 in your houses for **s** days.
13:6 "For **s** days you must eat
13:7 be eaten during these **s** days.
22:30 stay with their mothers **s** days,
23:15 For **s** days you must eat
25:37 "Make **s** lamps, and set them
29:30 will wear them for **s** days.
29:35 Take **s** days to ordain them.
29:37 For **s** days at the altar make
34:18 unleavened bread for **s** days at
37:23 He made the **s** lamps,

Lev 4:6 some of the blood **s** times
4:17 blood and sprinkle it **s** times
8:11 of the oil on the altar **s** times
8:33 the tent of meeting for **s** days,
8:33 It will take **s** days to ordain
8:35 day and night for **s** days
12:2 she will be unclean for **s** days.
13:4 put him in isolation for **s** days.
13:5 in isolation for another **s** days.
13:21 put him in isolation for **s** days.
13:26 put him in isolation for **s** days.
13:31 disease in isolation for **s** days.
13:33 in isolation for another **s** days.
13:50 in a separate place for **s** days.
13:54 separate place for **s** more days.
14:7 He will sprinkle the blood **s**
14:8 However, for **s** days he will
14:16 sprinkle some of the oil **s** times
14:27 sprinkle some of the oil **s** times
14:38 close up the house for **s** days.
14:51 He must sprinkle the house **s**
15:13 he must wait **s** days to be
15:19 she will be unclean for **s** days.
15:24 he will be unclean for **s** days.
15:28 she must wait **s** days.
16:14 blood with his finger **s** times
16:19 some of the blood on it **s** times.
22:27 stay with its mother for **s** days.
23:6 For **s** days you must eat
23:8 a sacrifice by fire for **s** days.
23:15 "Count **s** full weeks from the
23:18 With the bread bring **s**
23:34 the LORD. It will last **s** days.
23:36 For **s** consecutive days bring a
23:39 the LORD's festival for **s** days.
23:40 the LORD your God for **s** days.
23:41 Celebrate it for **s** days each
23:42 Live in booths for **s** days.
25:8 "Count **s** of these years seven
25:8 "Count seven of these years **s**
26:18 I will discipline you **s** times for
26:21 for your sins **s** times.
26:24 I will punish you **s** times for
26:28 I will discipline you **s** times for
Num 6:9 **S** days later he must shave his
8:2 When you set up the **s** lamps
12:14 from the community for **s** days?
12:14 outside the camp for **s** days.
12:15 outside the camp for **s** days.
13:22 (Hebron was built **s** years
19:4 and sprinkle it **s** times toward
19:11 will be unclean for **s** days.
19:14 tent will be unclean for **s** days.
19:16 will be unclean for **s** days.
23:1 "Build **s** altars here,
23:1 and prepare **s** bulls and seven
23:1 seven bulls and **s** rams for me."
23:4 "I have set up **s** altars,
23:14 where he built **s** altars.
23:29 "Build **s** altars here,
23:29 and prepare **s** bulls and seven
23:29 seven bulls and **s** rams for me."
28:11 and **s** one-year-old lambs that
28:17 For **s** days you must eat only
28:19 and **s** one-year-old lambs,
28:21 and 8 cups for each of the **s**
28:24 offerings on each of the **s** days.
28:27 and **s** one-year-old lambs.
28:29 and 8 cups for each of the **s**
29:2 and **s** one-year-old lambs that
29:4 and 8 cups for each of the **s**
29:8 and **s** one-year-old lambs,
29:10 and 8 cups for each of the **s**
29:12 festival to the LORD for **s** days.
29:32 the seventh day bring **7** bulls,
29:36 and **s** one-year-old lambs that
31:19 stay outside the camp **s** days.
Dtr 7:1 and Jebusites — **s** nations
15:1 At the end of every **s** years,
16:3 Instead, for **s** days you must
16:4 in your land for **s** days.
16:9 Count **s** weeks from the time
16:13 Festival of Booths for **s** days.
16:15 For **s** days you will celebrate
28:7 away from you in **s** directions.
28:25 away from them in **s** directions.

Jos 6:4 **S** priests will carry rams' horns
6:4 around the city **s** times while
6:6 and have **s** priests carry seven
6:6 and have seven priests carry **s**
6:8 the **s** priests carrying the seven
6:8 the seven priests carrying the **s**
6:13 The **s** priests carrying the
6:13 carrying the **s** rams' horns were
6:15 They marched around the city **s**
6:15 they marched around it **s** times.
18:2 There were still **s** tribes in
18:5 will divide the land into **s** parts.
18:6 You must describe the **s** parts
18:9 The land was divided into **s**
Jdg 6:1 them over to Midian for **s** years.
6:25 a bull that is **s** years old.
12:9 He judged Israel for **s** years.
14:12 If you solve it during the **s** days
14:17 for the rest of the **s** days
16:7 "If someone ties me up with **s**
16:8 her **s** new bowstrings that
16:13 "Just weave the **s** braids of my
16:19 a man to shave off his **s** braids.
Rut 4:15 is better to you than **s** sons,
1Sm 2:5 gives birth to **s** children,
6:1 in Philistine territory **s** months
10:8 Wait **s** days until I come to tell
11:3 "Give us **s** days so that we
13:8 He waited **s** days,
16:10 So Jesse brought **s** ⌊more⌋ of
31:13 Then they fasted **s** days.
2Sm 2:11 the tribe of Judah for **s** years
5:5 In Hebron he ruled Judah for **s**
21:5 "Give us **s** of the male
21:9 All **s** died together.
24:13 "Should **s** years of famine
1Ki 2:11 He ruled for **7** years in Hebron
6:38 He spent **s** years building it.
7:17 He also made **s** rows of filigree
8:65 the LORD our God for **s** days.
16:15 Zimri ruled for **s** days in Tirzah
18:43 **S** times Elijah told him,
20:29 facing one another for **s** days,
2Ki 3:9 After **s** days they ran out of
4:35 The boy sneezed **s** times and
5:10 He said, "Wash yourself **s**
5:14 in the Jordan River **s** times,
8:1 and it will last **s** years."
8:2 in Philistine territory for **s**
8:3 At the end of **s** years,
11:21 Joash was **s** years old when
1Ch 3:4 where he ruled for **s** years and
3:24 Elioenai's **s** sons were
5:13 Their **s** relatives by families
9:25 for a period of **s** days.
10:12 Then they fasted **s** days.
15:26 they sacrificed **s** bulls and
15:26 seven bulls and **s** rams.
29:27 He ruled for **7** years in Hebron
2Ch 7:9 of the altar for **s** days
7:9 festival for ⌊another⌋ **s** days.
13:9 a young bull and **s** rams can
24:1 Joash was **7** years old when
29:21 They brought **s** bulls,
29:21 bulls, **s** rams, seven lambs,
29:21 bulls, seven rams, **s** lambs,
29:21 and **s** male goats as an offering
30:21 of Unleavened Bread for **s** days
30:22 the festival meals for **s** days,
30:23 the festival for **s** more days.
30:23 So they joyfully celebrated for **s**
35:17 Unleavened Bread for **s** days.
Ezr 6:22 So for **s** days they celebrated
7:14 I, the king, and my **s** advisers
Neh 8:18 the festival for **s** days,
Est 1:5 held a banquet lasting **s** days.
1:10 the **s** eunuchs who served
1:14 These **s** officials of the
2:9 and **s** suitable female servants
Job 1:2 He had **s** sons and three
2:13 the ground with him for **s** days
2:13 for seven days and **s** nights.
42:8 So take **s** young bulls and
42:8 seven young bulls and **s** rams.
42:13 He also had **s** sons and three
Psa 12:6 a furnace and purified **s** times.

Psa 79:12 neighbors back with **s** times
119:164 **S** times a day I praise you for
Pro 6:16 even **s** that are disgusting to
6:31 he has to repay it **s** times.
9:1 She has carved out her **s**
24:16 person may fall **s** times,
26:16 wiser than **s** people who give
26:25 of the **s** disgusting things
Ecc 11:2 what you have into **s** parts,
Isa 4:1 When that day comes, **s**
11:15 divide it into **s** streams so that
30:26 The light of the sun will be **s**
30:26 like the light of **s** days.
Jer 15:9 A mother who gives birth to **s**
32:9 field cost **s** ounces of silver.
34:14 'Every **s** years each of you
52:25 **7** men who had access to the
Eze 3:15 there among them for **s** days.
3:16 After **s** days the LORD spoke
39:9 They will burn them for **s** years.
39:12 burying them there for **s**
39:14 At the end of **s** months they
40:22 **S** steps went up to it and led to
40:26 **S** steps went up to it and led to
41:5 around the temple was **7** feet.
43:14 upper ledge it was **7** feet high
43:15 were burned was **7** feet high.
43:25 Every day for **s** days you must
43:26 For **s** days the priests should
44:26 he must wait **s** days.
45:21 a festival lasting **s** days when
45:23 Every day during the **s** days of
45:23 **s** young bulls that have no
45:23 **s** rams that have no defects,
45:25 the same as on those **s** days.
Dan 3:19 be heated **s** times hotter than
4:16 like this for **s** time periods.
4:23 wild animals for **s** time periods.'
4:25 And **s** time periods will pass
4:32 And **s** time periods will pass
4:34 At the end of the **s** time periods,
9:24 "Seventy sets of **s** time periods
9:25 **s** sets of seven time periods
9:25 seven sets of **s** time periods
9:25 sets of **s** time periods will
9:26 sets of **s** time periods,
9:27 for one set of **s** time periods.
9:27 middle of the **s** time periods,
Mic 5:5 we will attack them with **s**
Zec 3:9 That one stone has **s** eyes.
4:2 with a bowl on top and **s** lamps
4:2 There are **s** spouts for each
4:10 (These **s** eyes of the LORD
Mat 12:45 Then it goes and brings along **s**
15:34 They answered, "**S**,
15:36 He took the **s** loaves and the
15:37 and filled **s** large baskets.
16:10 Don't you remember the **s**
18:21 who wrongs me? **S** times?"
18:22 "I tell you, not just **s** times,
18:22 but seventy times **s**.
22:25 There were **s** brothers among
22:26 and the rest of the **s** brothers.
22:28 All **s** brothers had been married
Mar 8:5 They answered, "**S**."
8:6 He took the **s** loaves and gave
8:8 and filled **s** large baskets.
8:20 "When I broke the **s** loaves for
8:20 They answered him, "**S**."
12:20 There were **s** brothers.
12:22 None of the **s** brothers had any
12:23 The **s** brothers had married
16:9 from whom he had forced out **s**
Luk 2:36 Her husband had died **s** years
8:2 from whom **s** demons had gone
11:26 along **s** other spirits more
17:4 Even if he wrongs you **s** times
17:4 and comes back to you **s** times
20:29 There were **s** brothers.
20:31 In the same way all **s** brothers
20:33 The **s** brothers had married
24:13 about **s** miles from Jerusalem.
Jon 4:52 evening at **s** o'clock."
Act 6:3 choose **s** men whom the
6:6 their hands on these **s** men.
13:19 Then he destroyed **s** nations in
Act 19:14 **S** sons of Sceva, a Jewish
20:6 and stayed there for **s** days.
21:4 we stayed there for **s** days.
21:8 one of the **s** men who helped
21:27 When the **s** days were almost
Heb 11:30 around them for **s** days.
2Pe 2:5 Noah and **s** other people.
Rev 1:4 From John to the **s** churches in
1:4 from the **s** spirits who are in
1:11 and send it to the **s** churches:
1:12 I saw **s** gold lamp stands.
1:16 his right hand he held **s** stars,
1:20 The hidden meaning of the **s**
1:20 and the **s** gold lamp stands
1:20 The **s** stars are the
1:20 messengers of the **s** churches,
1:20 and the **s** lamp stands are the
1:20 stands are the **s** churches.
2:1 The one who holds the **s** stars
2:1 among the **s** gold lamp stands,
3:1 The one who has God's **s**
3:1 spirits and the **s** stars says:
4:5 **S** flaming torches were burning
4:5 These are the **s** spirits of God.
5:1 It was sealed with **s** seals.
5:5 the scroll and the **s** seals on it."
5:6 He had **s** horns and seven
5:6 had seven horns and **s** eyes,
5:6 which are the **s** spirits of God
6:1 opened the first of the **s** seals.
8:2 Then I saw the **s** angels who
8:2 and they were given **s**
8:6 The **s** angels who had the
8:6 had the **s** trumpets got ready
10:3 When he shouted, the **s**
10:4 When the **s** thunders spoke,
10:4 "Seal up what the **s** thunders
10:11 The **s** thunders told me,
12:3 fiery red serpent with **s** heads,
12:3 and **s** crowns on its heads.
13:1 It had ten horns, **s** heads,
15:1 There were **s** angels with the
15:1 the last **s** plagues which are
15:6 The **s** angels with the seven
15:6 The seven angels with the **s**
15:7 gave **s** gold bowls full
15:7 and ever, to the **s** angels.
15:8 the temple until the **s** plagues
15:8 plagues of the **s** angels came
16:1 temple saying to the **s** angels,
16:1 "Pour the **s** bowls of God's
17:1 One of the **s** angels who held
17:1 who held the **s** bowls came
17:3 It had **s** heads and ten horns.
17:7 and the beast with the **s** heads
17:9 The **s** heads are seven
17:9 The seven heads are **s**
17:10 They are also **s** kings.
17:11 It belongs with the **s** kings and
21:9 One of the **s** angels who had
21:9 who had the **s** bowls full
21:9 full of the last **s** plagues came

10; ten (136)

Gen 16:3 had lived in Canaan for **t** years,
18:32 "What if **1** are found there?"
18:32 destroy it for the sake of the **1**."
23:15 The land is worth **t** pounds of
23:16 **t** pounds of silver at the current
24:10 Then the servant took **t** of his
24:55 "Let the girl stay with us **t** days
31:7 changed my wages **t** times.
31:41 and you changed my wages **t**
32:15 40 cows and **1** bulls,
32:15 donkeys and **1** male donkeys.
42:3 **T** of Joseph's brothers went to
45:23 He sent his father **t** male
45:23 and **t** female donkeys carrying
Exo 18:21 or 100, or 50, or **1** people.
18:25 or 100, or 50, or **1** people.
26:1 "Make the inner tent with **t**
27:12 ⌊hung⌋ on **t** posts ⌊set in⌋
27:12 on ten posts ⌊set in⌋ **t** bases.
34:28 the **t** commandments.
36:8 tent with **t** sheets made from
38:12 ⌊hung⌋ on **1** posts ⌊set in⌋
Exo 38:12 on 10 posts ⌊set in⌋ **1** bases.
Lev 26:26 **T** women will need only one
Num 11:19 or five, or **t**, or twenty days,
14:22 They have tested me now **t**
29:23 fourth day bring **1** bulls,
Dtr 1:15 or 100, or 50, or **1** people.
4:13 the **t** commandments,
10:4 the **t** commandments.
23:2 of the LORD for **t** generations.
23:3 of the LORD for **t** generations.
Jos 15:55 They also received another **t**
17:5 **T** portions of land went to
21:5 received **1** cities from
21:26 In all, **t** cities with pasturelands
22:14 **T** leaders, one from each tribe
Jdg 6:27 Gideon took **t** of his servants
12:11 He judged Israel for **t** years.
17:10 I'll give you **t** pieces of silver a
Rut 1:4 They lived there for about **t**
4:2 Then Boaz chose **t** men who
1Sm 1:8 Don't I mean more to you than **t**
17:4 from Gath. He was **t** feet tall.
17:17 grain and these **t** loaves
17:18 And take these **t** cheeses to
25:5 So David sent **t** young men and
25:38 About **t** days later the LORD
2Sm 15:16 him except **t** concubines whom
18:15 Then **t** of Joab's armorbearers
19:43 "We have **t** times your interest
20:3 he took the **t** concubines he
1Ki 4:23 **1** fattened cows, 20 cows from
7:27 He made **t** bronze stands.
7:37 the way he made the **t** stands.
7:38 also made **t** bronze basins.
7:38 basin on each of the **t** stands.
7:43 **1** stands and 10 basins on the
7:43 10 stands and **1** basins on the
11:31 He told Jeroboam, "Take **1**
11:31 hands and give **t** tribes to you.
11:35 his son and give you **t** tribes.
14:3 Take **t** loaves of bread,
2Ki 5:5 and **1** sets of clothing with him.
13:7 for 50 horses, **1** chariots,
15:17 He ruled for **1** years in Samaria.
20:9 shadow to go forward **t** steps
20:9 steps or come back **t** steps?"
20:10 extend **t** ⌊more⌋ steps forward.
20:10 No, let it come back **t** steps."
20:11 stairway go back up **t** steps.
25:25 of the kings) went with **t** men
1Ch 6:61 received **1** cities chosen by
2Ch 4:6 Huram also made **t** basins for
4:7 Huram made **t** gold lamp
4:8 He made **t** tables and put them
4:14 **1** stands and 10 basins on the
4:14 10 stands and **1** basins on the
14:1 the land had peace for **t** years.
36:9 for three months and **t** days
Ezr 8:24 and **1** of their relatives.
Neh 4:12 warned us **t** times that our
5:18 Once every **t** days a supply of
11:1 lots to bring one out of every **t**
Est 9:10 These were the **t** sons of
9:12 500 men and Haman's **1** sons.
9:13 hang Haman's **t** sons on poles."
9:14 Haman's **1** sons ⌊on poles⌋.
Job 19:3 have insulted me **t** times now.
Ecc 7:19 more than **t** rulers can help
Isa 6:13 Even if one out of **t** people is
38:8 the shadow go back **t** steps."
38:8 went back up the **t** steps
Jer 41:1 king's officers) went with **t** men
41:2 and the **t** men who were with
41:8 However, **t** men from the group
42:7 After **t** days the LORD spoke
Dan 1:12 "Please test us for **t** days.
1:14 and tested them for **t** days.
1:15 After **t** days they looked
1:20 he found that they knew **t** times
7:7 had seen before. It had **t** horns.
7:20 to know about the **t** horns
7:24 The **t** horns are ten kings that
7:24 The ten horns are **t** kings that
Hos 3:2 silver and **1** bushels of barley.
Amo 5:3 to war will have ⌊only⌋ **1** left
6:9 If **t** people are left in one house,

Hag 2:16 there would be only 1.
Zec 8:23 In those days t people from
Mat 4:25 the T Cities, Jerusalem, Judea,
20:24 When the other t apostles
25:1 will be like t bridesmaids.
Mar 5:20 done for him in the T Cities.
7:31 and the territory of the T Cities
10:41 When the other t apostles
Luk 15:8 "Suppose a woman has t coins
17:12 As he went into a village, t
17:17 "Weren't t men made clean?
19:13 ⌊Before he left,⌋ he called t of
19:13 and gave them t coins.
19:16 has earned t times as much.'
19:17 Take charge of t cities.'
19:24 give it to the man who has t.'
19:25 he already has t coins.'
Jon 1:39 It was about t o'clock in the
Act 25:6 Jerusalem for eight or t days at
Rev 2:10 suffering will go on for t days.
12:3 with seven heads, t horns,
13:1 It had t horns, seven heads,
13:1 and t crowns on its horns.
17:3 It had seven heads and t horns.
17:7 and the t horns that carries
17:12 "The t horns that you saw are
17:12 you saw are t kings who have
17:16 The t horns and the beast you

11; eleven (21)

Gen 32:22 his two slaves and his e
37:9 and 1 stars bowing down to
Exo 26:7 "Make 1 sheets of goats' hair to
26:8 Each of the 1 sheets will be 45
36:14 They made 1 sheets of goats'
36:15 Each of the 1 sheets was 45
Num 29:20 "On the third day bring 1 bulls,
Dtr 1:2 (It takes 1 days to go from
Jos 15:48 they gave Judah 1 cities
2Ki 23:36 and he was king for 1 years in
24:18 and he ruled for 1 years in
2Ch 36:5 and he ruled for 1 years in
36:11 ruled for 1 years in Jerusalem.
Jer 1:3 the 1 years that Zedekiah,
52:1 and he ruled for 1 years in
Mat 28:16 The e disciples went to the
Mar 16:14 to the e apostles while they
Luk 24:9 They told everything to the e
24:33 They found the e apostles and
Act 1:26 and joined the e apostles.
2:14 stood up with the e apostles.

12; twelve (157)

Gen 14:4 For 1 years they had been
17:20 will be the father of 1 princes,
25:16 and camps — 1 leaders
35:22 Jacob had 1 sons.
42:13 "We were 1 brothers,
42:32 We were 1 brothers,
49:28 These are the 1 tribes of Israel
Exo 15:27 where there were 1 springs and
21:32 its owner must pay 1 ounces of
24:4 and ⌊set up⌋ 1 sacred stones
24:4 stones for the 1 tribes of Israel.
28:21 The stones correspond to the 1
28:21 the name of one of the 1 tribes.
39:14 They corresponded to the 1
39:14 the name of one of the 1 tribes.
Lev 24:5 "Also take flour and bake t
27:4 If it is a woman, give 1 ounces.
Num 1:44 and the 1 leaders of Israel,
7:3 six freight wagons and t oxen,
7:84 1 silver plates, 12 silver bowls,
7:84 12 silver plates, 1 silver bowls,
7:84 and 1 gold dishes.
7:86 The 1 gold dishes filled with
7:87 offerings was 1 young bulls,
7:87 was 12 young bulls, 1 rams,
7:87 1 one-year-old male lambs,
7:87 T male goats were used as
17:2 and get 1 staffs from them,
17:6 Their leaders gave him 1 staffs,
29:17 day bring 1 young bulls,
33:9 Elim had 1 springs and 70
Dtr 1:23 So I chose 1 of your men,
Jos 3:12 each of the 1 tribes of Israel.
Jos 4:2 man from each of the 1 tribes.
4:3 Order them to pick up 1 stones
4:4 Joshua called the 1 men whom
4:8 They took 1 stones,
4:9 Joshua also set 1 stones in the
4:20 At Gilgal Joshua set up the 1
18:21 These are the 1 cities with
19:15 There were 1 cities with their
21:7 descendants received 1 cities
21:40 These 1 cities were chosen by
Jdg 19:29 limb from limb into 1 pieces.
2Sm 2:15 T were from the tribe of
2:15 and t were from David's
1Ki 4:7 Solomon appointed 1 district
7:10 stones (some 1 feet long,
7:25 pool was set on 1 metal bulls.
7:44 1 pool, 1 bulls under the pool,
10:20 T lions stood on six steps,
11:30 and tore it into 1 pieces.
16:23 He ruled for 1 years,
18:31 Elijah took 1 stones,
18:32 trench that could hold 1 quarts
19:19 Elisha was plowing behind 1
2Ki 3:1 He ruled for 1 years.
2Ki 21:1 Manasseh was 1 years old
1Ch 6:63 were given 1 cities chosen by
25:9 and his relatives — 1 men.
25:10 and his relatives — 1 men.
25:11 and his relatives — 1 men.
25:12 and his relatives — 1 men.
25:13 and his relatives — 1 men.
25:14 and his relatives — 1 men.
25:15 and his relatives — 1 men.
25:16 and his relatives — 1 men.
25:17 and his relatives — 1 men.
25:18 and his relatives — 1 men.
25:19 and his relatives — 1 men.
25:20 and his relatives — 1 men.
25:21 and his relatives — 1 men.
25:22 and his relatives — 1 men.
25:23 and his relatives — 1 men.
25:24 and his relatives — 1 men.
25:25 and his relatives — 1 men.
25:26 and his relatives — 1 men.
25:27 and his relatives — 1 men.
25:28 and his relatives — 1 men.
25:29 and his relatives — 1 men.
25:30 and his relatives — 1 men.
25:31 and his relatives — 1 men.
2Ch 4:4 pool was set on 1 metal bulls.
4:15 1 pool and the 1 bulls under it,
9:19 T lions stood on six steps,
33:1 Manasseh was 1 years old
Ezr 6:17 They sacrificed 1 male goats
8:24 Then I selected 1 leaders from
8:35 1 bulls for all Israel,
8:35 and 1 male goats for an offering
Neh 5:14 During the 1 years that I was
Jer 52:20 and the 1 bronze bulls under
Eze 41:3 ½ feet high and 1 feet wide.
47:13 be divided among the 1 tribes
Dan 4:29 T months later, he was
Mat 9:20 chronic bleeding for t years.
10:1 Jesus called his t disciples
10:2 are the names of the t apostles:
10:5 Jesus sent these t out with the
11:1 After Jesus finished giving his t
14:20 they filled t baskets.
19:28 will also sit on t thrones,
19:28 judging the t tribes of Israel.
20:17 he took the t apostles aside
26:14 Then one of the t apostles,
26:20 at the table with the t apostles.
26:47 one of the t apostles,
26:53 to send more than t legions
Mar 3:14 He appointed t whom he called
3:16 He appointed these t:
4:10 followers and the t apostles,
5:25 chronic bleeding for t years.
5:42 (She was t years old.)
6:7 He called the t apostles,
6:43 they filled t baskets with bread
8:19 They told him, "T."
9:35 down and called the t apostles.
10:32 he took the t apostles aside.
11:11 with the t apostles to Bethany.
Mar 14:10 one of the t apostles,
14:17 Jesus arrived with the t
14:20 said to them, "It's one of you t,
14:43 one of the t apostles,
Luk 2:42 When he was 1 years old,
6:13 He chose t of them and called
8:1 The t apostles were with him.
8:42 who was about t years old,
8:43 bleeding for t years was
9:1 Jesus called the t apostles
9:12 the t apostles came to him.
9:17 they filled t baskets.
18:31 Jesus took the t apostles aside
22:3 one of the t apostles.
22:30 and judge the t tribes of Israel."
22:47 one of the t apostles,
Jon 6:13 of bread and filled t baskets.
6:67 So Jesus asked the t apostles,
6:70 "I chose all t of you.
6:71 who was one of the t apostles,
11:9 Aren't there t hours of daylight?
20:24 Thomas, one of the t apostles,
Act 6:2 The t apostles called all the
7:8 and Jacob did the same to his t
19:7 About t men were in the group.
24:11 no more than t days ago.
26:7 Our t tribes expect this
1Co 15:5 Next he appeared to the t
Rev 12:1 her feet and a crown of 1 stars
21:12 high wall with 1 gates.
21:12 T angels were at the gates.
21:12 The names of the 1 tribes of
21:14 of the city had 1 foundations.
21:14 The 1 names of the 12
21:14 The 12 names of the 1
21:21 The 1 gates were 12 pearls.
21:21 The 12 gates were 1 pearls.
22:2 It produced 1 kinds of fruit.

20; twenty (76)

Gen 18:31 "What if 2 are found there?"
18:31 destroy it for the sake of the 2."
31:38 "I've been with you for 2 years.
31:41 I've been with your household 2
32:14 female goats and 2 male goats,
32:14 sheep and 2 male sheep,
32:15 2 female donkeys and 10 male
Exo 16:36 at that time held 2 quarts.)
26:18 Make 2 frames for the south
26:19 at the bottom of the 2 frames,
26:20 the inner tent ⌊make⌋ 2 frames
27:10 ⌊hung⌋ on 2 posts ⌊set in⌋ 20
27:10 posts ⌊set in⌋ 2 bronze bases.
27:11 with curtains on 2 posts set in
27:11 20 posts set in 2 bronze bases.
30:14 is at least 2 years old must
36:23 They made 2 frames for the
36:24 at the bottom of the 2 frames,
36:25 tent ⌊they made⌋ 2 frames
38:10 ⌊hung⌋ on 2 posts ⌊set in⌋ 20
38:10 posts ⌊set in⌋ 2 bronze bases.
38:11 also 150 feet long with 2 posts
38:11 20 posts and 2 bronze bases.
38:26 who was at least 2 years old:
Lev 27:3 you must give for a man from 2
27:3 20 to 60 years old is 2 ounces
27:5 For a boy from 5 to 2 years old,
27:16 be worth 2 ounces of silver.
Num 1:3 who is at least 2 years old.
1:18 Each man at least 2 years old
1:20 who was at least 2 years old
1:22 who was at least 2 years old
1:24 who were at least 2 years old
1:26 who were at least 2 years old
1:28 who were at least 2 years old
1:30 who were at least 2 years old
1:32 who were at least 2 years old
1:34 who were at least 2 years old
1:36 who were at least 2 years old
1:38 who were at least 2 years old
1:40 who were at least 2 years old
1:42 who were at least 2 years old
1:45 who were at least 2 years old
11:19 days, or five, or ten, or t days,
14:29 who are at least 2 years old,
26:2 List those who are at least 2

Num 26:4 of those at least **2** years old,
32:11 'None of the people **2** years old
Jdg 4:3 oppressed Israel for **2** years.
11:33 to Abel Keramim, **2** cities in all.
15:20 Samson judged Israel for **2**
16:31 Samson had judged Israel for **2**
1Sm 7:2 For **2** years the entire nation of
14:14 killed about **t** men within about
2Sm 3:20 So Abner came with **2** men to
9:10 (Ziba had 15 sons and **2**
19:17 Ziba brought his 15 sons and **2**
24:8 after 9 months and **2** days.
1Ki 4:23 **2** cows from the pasture,
9:10 It took Solomon **2** years to
9:11 he gave King Hiram of Tyre **2**
2Ki 4:42 grain, **2** barley loaves,
15:20 Each gave **2** ounces of silver
15:27 He ruled for **2** years.
16:2 Ahaz was **2** years old when he
1Ch 23:24 was at least **2** years old.
23:27 who were at least **2** years old.
27:23 count those under **2** years old,
2Ch 3:9 gold nails weighed **2** ounces.
8:1 It took Solomon **2** years to
25:5 who were at least **2** years old
28:1 Ahaz was **2** years old when he
31:17 who were at least **2** years old.
Ezr 3:8 who were at least **2** years old
8:19 **2** of Jeshaiah's relatives and
8:27 **2** gold bowls weighing 18
Eze 45:12 shekel must weigh **2** gerahs.
Hag 2:16 of grain ⌊to get⌋ **2** measures,
2:16 there would be only **2** in it.

30; thirty (80)

Gen 11:14 Shelah was **3** years old when
11:18 Peleg was **3** years old when
11:22 Serug was **3** years old when
18:30 "What if **3** are found there?"
18:30 He answered, "If I find **3** there,
32:15 **3** female camels with their
41:46 Joseph was **3** years old when
Exo 27:16 have a **3**-foot screen made from
38:18 It was **3** feet long and 7 ½ feet
Num 4:3 the men between the ages of **3**
4:23 the men between the ages of **3**
4:30 the men between the ages of **3**
4:35 the men between the ages of **3**
4:39 the men between the ages of **3**
4:43 the men between the ages of **3**
4:47 the men between the ages of **3**
20:29 mourned for Aaron **3** days.
Dtr 34:8 the plains of Moab for **3** days.
Jdg 10:4 Jair had **3** sons who rode on 30
10:4 sons who rode on **3** donkeys.
10:4 He also had **3** towns that are
12:9 He had **3** sons and 30
12:9 had 30 sons and **3** daughters.
12:14 He had 40 sons and **3**
14:11 they chose **3** of their friends to
14:12 I'll give you **3** linen shirts and
14:12 and **3** changes of clothes.
14:19 and killed **3** men there.
20:31 They killed about **3** men from
20:39 had already killed about **3** men
1Sm 9:22 of the guests — about **3** people.
13:1 Saul was ⌊**t**⌋ years old when
2Sm 5:4 David was **3** years old when
23:13 At harvest time three of the **t**
23:18 was the leader of the **t**.
23:23 was honored more than the **t**,
23:24 One of the **t** was Joab's brother
23:24 ⌊The **t** leading men were⌋
1Ki 1:8 and David's ⌊**t**⌋ fighting men
6:2 **3** feet wide, and 45 feet high.
6:16 sectioned off a **3**-foot-long room
6:20 The inner room was **3** feet long,
6:20 **3** feet wide, and 30 feet high.
6:20 30 feet wide, and **3** feet high.
1Ch 11:15 Once three of the **t** leading men
11:20 Abishai was the leader of the **t**.
11:25 was honored more than the **t**,
11:42 his own group of **t** soldiers),
12:4 (one of the **t** fighting men
12:18 Amasai, the leader of the **t**,
23:3 was at least **3** years old was
27:6 This Benaiah was one of the **t**
27:6 commander of the **t** as well as
2Ch 3:4 room⌋ was **3** feet wide (the
3:4 of the temple) and **3** feet high.
3:8 temple was wide, **3** feet long.
3:8 It was also **3** feet wide.
3:11 of the angels' wings was **3** feet.
3:12 wingspan was **3** feet.
4:1 made a bronze altar **3** feet long,
4:1 **3** feet wide, and 15 feet high.
Ezr 1:9 **3** silver dishes: 1,000 knives:
1:10 **3** other silver bowls:
Est 4:11 presence for **3** days now."
Jer 38:10 "Take **3** men from here,
Eze 40:17 There were **3** rooms along the
41:6 There were **3** rooms on each
Dan 6:7 the next **3** days whoever asks
6:12 that for **3** days whoever asks
Zec 5:2 "It's **3** feet long and 15 feet
11:12 my wages — **3** pieces of silver.
11:13 So I took the **3** pieces of silver.
Mat 13:8 or **t** times as much as was
13:23 or **t** times as much as was
26:15 They offered him **3** silver coins.
27:3 He brought the **3** silver coins
27:9 "They took the **3** silver coins,
Mar 4:8 sprouted, and produced **t**, sixty,
4:20 and produce crops — **t**,
Luk 3:23 Jesus was about **3** years old

40; forty (86)

Gen 7:4 send rain to the earth for **4** days
7:4 earth for 40 days and **4** nights.
7:12 down on the earth for **4** days
7:12 earth for 40 days and **4** nights.
7:17 The flood continued for **4** days
8:6 After **4** more days Noah opened
18:29 "What if **4** are found there?"
18:29 "For the sake of the **4** I will not
25:20 Isaac was **4** years old when he
26:34 When Esau was **4** years old,
32:15 **4** cows and 10 bulls,
50:3 in the usual time — **4** days.
Exo 16:35 The Israelites ate manna for **4**
24:18 He stayed on the mountain **4**
24:18 mountain 40 days and **4** nights.
26:19 Then make **4** silver sockets at
26:21 and **4** silver sockets,
34:28 there with the LORD **4** days
34:28 days and **4** nights without food
36:24 Then they made **4** silver
36:26 and **4** silver sockets,
Num 13:25 **F** days later, they came back
14:33 in the desert for **4** years.
14:34 For **4** days you explored the
14:34 So for **4** years — one year for
32:13 in the desert for **4** years until
Dtr 2:7 For **4** years now the LORD
8:2 Remember that for **4** years the
8:4 didn't swell these past **4** years.
9:9 I stayed on the mountain **4**
9:9 days and **4** nights without food
9:11 At the end of the **4** days and 40
9:11 of the 40 days and **4** nights,
9:18 food and water for **4** days
9:18 water for 40 days and **4** nights
9:25 in front of the LORD for **4** days
9:25 LORD for 40 days and **4** nights
10:10 I stayed on the mountain **4**
10:10 40 days and **4** nights as
25:3 **F** lashes may be given,
29:5 For **4** years I led you through
Jos 5:6 For **4** years the Israelites
14:7 I was **4** years old when the
Jdg 3:11 peace in the land for **4** years.
5:31 So the land had peace for **4**
8:26 asked for weighed **4** pounds.
8:28 So the land had peace for **4**
12:14 He had **4** sons and 30
13:1 to the Philistines for **4** years.
1Sm 4:18 He had judged Israel for **4**
17:16 morning and evening for **4**
2Sm 2:10 Saul's son Ishbosheth was **4**
5:4 and he ruled for **4** years.
1Ki 2:11 as king of Israel for **4** years.
11:42 over all Israel was **4** years.
19:8 he traveled for **4** days and
2Ki 8:9 loaded the goods on **4** camels.
12:1 and he ruled for **4** years in
1Ch 29:27 as king of Israel for **4** years.
2Ch 9:30 over all Israel for **4** years.
24:1 and he ruled for **4** years in
Neh 9:21 them in the desert for **4** years,
Psa 95:10 For **4** years I was disgusted
Eze 4:6 the nation of Judah for **4** days,
29:11 and no one will live there for **4**
29:12 For **4** years Egypt's cities will
29:13 After **4** years I will gather the
Amo 2:10 the desert for **4** years so that
5:25 in the desert for **4** years,
Jnh 3:4 Then he said, "In **f** days
Mat 4:2 Jesus did not eat anything for **4**
4:2 for 40 days and **4** nights.
Mar 1:13 tempted by Satan for **4** days.
Luk 4:2 tempted by the devil for **4** days.
Act 1:3 For **4** days he appeared to
4:22 miracle was over **4** years old.)
7:23 When he was **4** years old,
7:30 "**F** years later, a messenger
7:36 and in the desert for **4** years.
7:42 in the desert for **4** years,
13:18 up with them for about **f** years
13:21 tribe of Benjamin. After **f** years
23:13 More than **f** men took part in
23:21 More than **f** of them are
Heb 3:10 what I had done for **4** years.
3:17 was God angry for **4** years?

99; ninety-nine (6)

Gen 17:1 When Abram was **9** years old,
17:24 Abraham was **9** years old
Mat 18:12 Won't he leave the **9** sheep in
18:13 it than about the **9** that have not
Luk 15:4 Doesn't he leave the **9** sheep
15:7 than over **9** people who already

100; one hundred; a hundred (55)

Gen 11:10 when Shem was **1** years old,
21:5 Abraham was **1** years old
26:12 harvested a **h** times as much
33:19 for **1** pieces of silver.
Exo 18:21 1,000, or **1**, or 50, or 10 people.
18:25 1,000, or **1**, or 50, or 10 people.
38:27 of silver to cast the **1** bases
Lev 26:8 of you will chase a **h** of them,
26:8 and a **h** of you will chase ten
Dtr 1:15 1,000, or **1**, or 50, or 10 people.
Jos 24:32 for **1** pieces of silver.
Jdg 7:19 Gideon and his **1** men came to
1Sm 14:14 men within about a **h** yards.
18:25 **1** Philistine foreskins so
25:18 **1** bunches of raisins,
2Sm 3:14 I made a payment of **1**
8:4 David also disabled all but **1** of
16:1 **1** bunches of raisins,
16:1 **1** pieces of ripened fruit,
24:3 the people a **h** times over,
1Ki 4:23 and **1** sheep in addition to deer,
18:4 Obadiah had hidden **1** prophets
18:13 Haven't you heard how I hid **1**
2Ki 1:14 two officers and their **1** men.
4:43 I set this in front of a **h** people?"
1Ch 12:14 one was in command of **1** men,
18:4 David also disabled all but **1** of
21:3 his people a **h** times over.
2Ch 3:16 He made **1** pomegranates and
4:8 And he made **1** gold bowls.
29:32 bulls, **1** rams, and 200 lambs.
Ezr 2:69 and **1** robes for the priests.
6:17 they sacrificed **1** bulls,
7:22 **1** measures of wheat,
8:26 **1** silver utensils weighing 150
Neh 3:1 as far as the Tower of the **H**,
12:39 and the Tower of the **H**,
Ecc 6:3 Suppose he had a **h** children
8:12 A sinner may commit a **h**
Isa 65:20 Whoever lives to be a **h** years
65:20 Whoever dies before he is a **h**
Jer 52:23 the surrounding filigree was **1**.
Amo 5:3 to war will have ⌊only⌋ **1** left.

Amo 5:3 The one that sends 1 troops off
Mat 13:8 They produced one h,
13:23 They produce one h,
18:12 Suppose a man has 1 sheep
19:29 will receive a h times more
Mar 4:8 or one h times as much as was
4:20 or one h times as much as was
10:30 will certainly receive a h times
Luk 8:8 they produced a h times as
15:4 "Suppose a man has 1 sheep
Jon 21:8 only about 1 yards.
Rom 4:19 he was about a h years old,

666; six hundred sixty-six (2)

Ezr 2:13 of Adonikam: 6
Rev 13:18 The beast's number is 6.

1,000; one thousand; a thousand (57)

Exo 18:21 them in charge of groups of 1,
18:25 them in charge of groups of 1,
Num 31:4 Send 1 men from each of the
31:5 So 1 men from each tribe were
31:6 1 men from each tribe along
Dtr 1:11 you a t times more numerous,
1:15 them in charge of groups of 1,
32:30 could one person chase a t
Jos 23:10 One of you used to chase a t.
Jdg 9:49 about a t men and women.
15:15 it up and killed 1 men with it.
15:16 I've killed a t men."
1Sm 8:12 them to be his officers over 1
13:2 and 1 were stationed with
25:2 had 3,000 sheep and 1 goats.
2Sm 10:6 of the king of Maacah (1 men),
19:17 One t people from Benjamin
1Ki 3:4 Solomon sacrificed 1 burnt
2Ki 24:16 1 craftsmen and smiths,
1Ch 12:14 best one was in command of 1.
12:20 over 1 men in Manasseh.
12:34 there were 1 commanders.
16:15 commanded for a t generations,
18:4 David took 1 chariots,
29:21 the LORD: 1 bulls, 1,000 rams,
29:21 bulls, 1 rams, 1,000 lambs,
29:21 rams, 1 lambs, wine offerings,
2Ch 1:6 and sacrificed 1 burnt offerings
30:24 of Judah provided 1 bulls
30:24 The leaders provided 1 bulls
Ezr 1:9 30 silver dishes: 1 knives: 29
1:10 bowls: 410 other utensils: 1
Job 1:3 camels, 1 oxen, 500 donkeys,
9:3 to answer one question in a t.
33:23 them, a spokesman, one in a t,
42:12 2,000 oxen, and 1 donkeys.
Psa 50:10 ⌊even⌋ the cattle on a t hills,
84:10 than a t ⌊anywhere else⌋.
90:4 Indeed, in your sight a t years
91:7 even though a t may fall dead
105:8 commanded for a t generations,
Ecc 7:28 I found one man out of a t who
Sos 4:4 A t round shields belonging to
Isa 7:23 there were 1 vines (worth 1,000
7:23 1,000 vines (worth 1 pieces
30:17 One t people will flee when
Dan 5:1 a large banquet for 1 nobles
Amo 5:3 The city that sends 1 troops off
Luk 16:7 'A t bushels of wheat.'
2Pe 3:8 with the Lord is like a t years,
3:8 and a t years are like one day.
Rev 20:2 up the serpent for 1 years.
20:3 until the 1 years were over.
20:4 ruled with Christ for 1 years.
20:5 not live until the 1 years ended.
20:6 They will rule with him for 1
20:7 When 1 years are over,

4,000; four thousand (13)

1Sm 4:2 and killed about 4 soldiers
1Ch 23:5 4 were appointed to be
23:5 and 4 were appointed to praise
2Ch 9:25 Solomon had 4 stalls for
Mat 15:38 F men had eaten.
16:10 the seven loaves for the f
25:15 another f dollars,
25:17 The one who had f dollars
25:22 "The one who received f
25:22 you gave me f dollars.
8:9 About f people were there.
8:20 the seven loaves for the f,
Act 21:38 ago and led f terrorists into

5,000; five thousand (10)

Jos 8:12 Joshua had taken about f
Jdg 20:45 But the men of Israel killed 5
2Ch 35:9 gave the Levites 5 sheep and
Mat 14:21 About f men had eaten.
16:9 the five loaves for the f
Mar 6:44 There were 5 men who had
8:19 the five loaves for the f,
Luk 9:14 (There were about f men.)
Jon 6:10 (There were about 5 men in the
Act 4:4 who believed grew to about 5.

10,000; ten thousand (33)

Lev 26:8 of you will chase t of them.
Dtr 32:30 or two people make t flee?
Jdg 1:4 They defeated 1 men at Bezek.
3:29 that time they killed about t
4:6 Take 1 men from Naphtali and
4:10 T men went to fight under
4:14 Tabor with 1 men behind him.
7:3 back home, and 1 were left.
20:34 Then 1 of Israel's best men
1Sm 15:4 soldiers and 1 men from Judah.
2Sm 18:3 But you're worth 1 of us.
1Ki 5:14 He sent a shift of 1 men to
2Ki 13:7 and 1 foot soldiers because the
14:7 Amaziah killed 1 Edomites in
24:14 all the soldiers (1 prisoners),
2Ch 25:11 he killed 1 men from Seir.
25:12 captured another 1 alive,
30:24 1,000 bulls and 1 sheep
Psa 91:7 beside you or t at your right
Sos 5:10 He stands out among 1 men.
Dan 7:10 T times ten thousand were
7:10 Ten thousand times t were
Mat 25:15 He gave one man t dollars,
25:16 "The one who received t
25:20 The one who received t
25:20 brought the additional t.
25:20 you gave me t dollars.
25:28 it to the one who has the t!
Luk 14:31 Can he and his 1 soldiers fight
1Co 14:19 be understood than t words
Rev 5:11 They numbered t times ten
5:11 ten thousand times t
9:16 numbered 20,000 times 1.

12,000; twelve thousand (23)

Num 31:5 of Israel — 1 men ready
Jos 8:25 T men and women from
Jdg 21:10 congregation sent 1 soldiers.
2Sm 10:6 and the men of Tob (1 men).
17:1 "Let me choose 1 men and
1Ki 4:26 He also had 1 chariot soldiers.
7:26 a lily's bud. It held 1 gallons.
10:26 chariots and 1 war horses.
2Ch 1:14 chariots and 1 war horses.
9:25 and chariots, and 1 war horses.
Rev 7:5 1 from the tribe of Judah were
7:5 1 from the tribe of Reuben,
7:5 1 from the tribe of Gad,
7:6 1 from the tribe of Asher,
7:6 1 from the tribe of Naphtali,
7:6 1 from the tribe of Manasseh,
7:7 1 from the tribe of Simeon,
7:7 1 from the tribe of Levi,
7:7 1 from the tribe of Issachar,
7:8 1 from the tribe of Zebulun,
7:8 1 from the tribe of Joseph,
7:8 1 from the tribe of Benjamin
21:16 It was 1 stadia long.

144,000; one hundred forty-four thousand (4)

Rev 7:4 how many were sealed: 1.
14:1 There were 1 people with him
14:3 Only the 1 people who had
14:4 These 1 virgins are pure.

A

A (3)

Rev 1:8 "I am the A and the Z," says
21:6 I am the A and the Z,
22:13 I am the A and the Z,

Aaron (305)

Exo 4:14 your brother A the Levite?
4:16 A will speak to the people for
4:27 the LORD had told A to meet
4:27 When A met Moses at the
4:28 Moses told A everything the
4:29 Then Moses and A went to
4:30 A told them everything the
5:1 Later Moses and A went to
5:4 said to them, "Moses and A,
5:20 Moses and A waiting for them.
6:13 spoke to Moses and A about
6:20 She gave birth to A and Moses.
6:23 A married Elisheba,
6:25 Eleazar, son of A, married one
6:26 This was the same A and
6:27 They — this same Moses and A
7:1 your brother A is your prophet.
7:2 Tell your brother A everything I
7:6 Moses and A did as the LORD
7:7 Moses was 80 years old and A
7:8 LORD said to Moses and A,
7:9 that God has sent you,' tell A,
7:10 Moses and A went to Pharaoh
7:10 A threw his staff down in front
7:19 LORD said to Moses, "Tell A,
7:20 Moses and A did as the LORD
7:20 A raised his staff and struck
7:22 not listen to Moses and A,
8:5 LORD said to Moses, "Tell A,
8:6 So A held his staff over the
8:8 sent for Moses and A and said,
8:12 After Moses and A left Pharaoh,
8:15 not listen to Moses and A,
8:16 LORD said to Moses, "Tell A,
8:17 When Moses told him, A held
8:19 not listen to Moses and A,
8:25 for Moses and A and said,
9:8 the LORD said to Moses and A,
9:12 wouldn't listen to Moses and A,
9:27 Pharaoh sent for Moses and A.
10:3 So Moses and A went to
10:8 So Moses and A were brought
10:11 Then Moses and A were
10:16 for Moses and A and said,
11:10 Moses and A showed Pharaoh
12:1 said to Moses and A in Egypt,
12:28 had commanded Moses and A.
12:31 called for Moses and A during
12:43 LORD said to Moses and A,
12:50 had commanded Moses and A.
16:2 about Moses and A.
16:6 So Moses and A said to all the
16:9 Moses said to A, "Tell the
16:10 While A was speaking to the
16:33 Moses said to A, "Take a jar,
16:34 A put the jar of manna in front
17:10 Amalekites, while Moses, A,
17:12 So A and Hur took a rock,
17:12 A held up one hand,
18:12 A and all the leaders of Israel
19:24 and bring A back with you.
24:1 "You and A, Nadab, Abihu,
24:9 Moses went up with A,
24:14 A and Hur are here with you.
27:21 A and his descendants must
28:1 bring your brother A and his
28:2 holy clothes for your brother A
28:4 holy clothes for your brother A
28:12 In this way A will carry their
28:29 "Whenever A goes into the
28:30 A will always be carrying over
28:35 A must wear it when he serves
28:41 these clothes on your brother A
28:43 A and his sons must wear
29:1 you must do in order to set A
29:4 "Then bring A and his sons to

Exo 29:5 and put them on **A** — the linen
29:9 belts around the waists of **A**
29:9 you will ordain **A** and his sons.
29:10 **A** and his sons will place their
29:15 Then **A** and his sons will place
29:19 Then **A** and his sons will place
29:20 put it on the right ear lobes of **A**
29:21 and sprinkle it on **A** and his
29:21 In this way **A**, his sons,
29:24 all of these in the hands of **A**
29:27 both belong to **A** and his sons.
29:28 Israelites give this portion to **A**
29:32 **A** and his sons will eat the
29:35 "Do this with **A** and his sons
29:44 I will set **A** and his sons apart
30:7 "**A** must burn sweet-smelling
30:8 Also, when **A** lights the lamps
30:10 Once a year **A** must make
30:19 **A** and his sons will use it for
30:30 Anoint **A** and his sons as well.
31:10 the holy clothes for the priest **A**
32:1 they gathered around **A**.
32:2 **A** said to them, "Have your
32:3 earrings and handed them to **A**.
32:5 When **A** saw this, he built an
32:21 Moses asked **A**, "What did
32:22 be angry, sir," **A** answered.
32:25 **A** had let the people get out of
32:35 they had **A** make the calf.
34:30 When **A** and all the Israelites
34:31 Moses called to them, so **A**
35:19 both the holy clothes for **A**
38:21 son of the priest **A**.
39:1 made the holy clothes for **A**.
39:26 the robe that is worn by **A** when
39:27 of fine linen for **A** and his sons.
39:41 the holy clothes for the priest **A**
40:12 "Bring **A** and his sons to the
40:13 Then dress **A** in the holy
40:31 Moses, **A**, and his sons used
Lev 1:7 Then the sons of the priest **A**
2:3 grain offering will belong to **A**
2:10 the grain offering belongs to **A**
6:9 "Command **A** and his sons:
6:16 **A** and his sons will eat the rest
6:18 Every male descendant of **A**
6:20 "This is the offering that **A** and
6:25 "Tell **A** and his sons:
7:31 will belong to **A** and his sons.
7:34 have given them to the priest **A**
7:35 "This is the share for **A** and his
8:2 "Take **A** and his sons,
8:6 Moses had **A** and his sons
8:7 He put the linen robe on **A** and
8:14 **A** and his sons placed their
8:18 **A** and his sons placed their
8:22 **A** and his sons placed their
8:27 these things in the hands of **A**
8:30 sprinkled it on **A** and his
8:30 In this way he dedicated **A**,
8:31 Moses told **A** and his sons:
8:31 '**A** and his sons will eat it.'
8:36 So **A** and his sons did
9:1 eighth day Moses summoned **A**
9:2 He told **A**, "Take a calf that has
9:7 Moses told **A**, "Come to the
9:8 **A** came to the altar and
9:20 **A** burned them all on the altar.
9:22 Then **A** raised his hands
9:23 Moses and **A** went into the tent
10:3 Moses said to **A**, "This is
10:3 people."' **A** was speechless.
10:6 Moses told **A** and his sons
10:8 The LORD spoke to **A**,
10:12 Moses told **A** and his surviving
10:19 **A** answered Moses,
11:1 LORD spoke to Moses and **A**,
13:1 LORD spoke to Moses and **A**,
13:2 he must be taken to the priest **A**
14:33 LORD spoke to Moses and **A**,
15:1 LORD spoke to Moses and **A**,
16:2 "Tell your brother **A** that he
16:3 "This is what **A** must do in
16:6 "**A** must sacrifice the bull as
16:8 Then **A** must throw lots for the
16:9 **A** must sacrifice the goat
16:11 "**A** will bring the bull.
16:15 "Next, **A** will slaughter the goat
16:17 meeting from the time **A** enters
Lev 16:17 **A** will make peace with the
16:21 **A** will place both hands on its
16:23 "Then **A** will go to the tent of
16:30 On this day **A** will make peace
16:34 **A** did as the LORD had
17:2 "Tell **A**, his sons, and all the
21:17 "Tell **A**: If any of your
21:21 If a descendant of the priest **A**
21:24 So Moses spoke to **A** and his
22:2 "Tell **A** and his sons that they
22:4 "No descendant of **A** who has
22:18 "Tell **A**, his sons, and all the
24:3 **A** must keep the lamps lit in
24:4 **A** must keep the lamps on the
24:9 The bread will belong to **A** and
Num 1:3 You and **A** must register
1:17 Moses and **A** took the men
1:44 Moses, **A**, and the 12 leaders
2:1 LORD spoke to Moses and **A**,
3:1 This is the list of **A** and Moses'
3:4 the lifetime of their father **A**.
3:6 of the priest **A** to assist him.
3:9 Give the Levites to **A** and his
3:10 Appoint **A** and his sons to
3:32 son of the priest **A**.
3:38 Moses, **A**, and his sons put up
3:39 that Moses and **A** counted at
3:48 Give the silver to **A** and his
3:51 the LORD said and gave **A**
4:1 LORD said to Moses and **A**,
4:5 **A** and his sons will go in and
4:15 "When **A** and his sons have
4:16 "Eleazar, son of the priest **A**,
4:17 LORD said to Moses and **A**,
4:19 **A** and his sons will go into the
4:27 be done under the direction of **A**
4:28 Ithamar, son of the priest **A**,
4:33 Ithamar, son of the priest **A**,
4:34 Moses, **A**, and the leaders of
4:37 Moses and **A** did as the LORD
4:41 Moses and **A** did as the LORD
4:45 Moses and **A** did as the LORD
4:46 all the Levites whom Moses, **A**,
6:23 "Tell **A** and his sons,
7:8 son of the priest **A**.
8:2 "Speak to **A** and tell him:
8:3 So **A** set up the lamps on the
8:11 **A** will present the Levites to
8:13 the Levites stand in front of **A**
8:19 be the only Israelites I give to **A**
8:20 Moses, **A**, and the whole
8:21 **A** presented them as an
8:22 of meeting in the presence of **A**
9:6 They came to Moses and **A**
10:8 The sons of **A**, the priests,
12:1 Miriam and **A** began to criticize
12:4 said to Moses, **A**, and Miriam,
12:5 He called to **A** and Miriam,
12:10 **A** turned to her and saw she
13:26 They came back to Moses, **A**,
14:2 complained to Moses and **A**,
14:5 Immediately, Moses and **A**
14:10 stoning Moses and **A** to death,
14:26 the LORD said to Moses and **A**,
15:33 brought him to Moses and **A**
16:3 to confront Moses and **A**
16:11 Who is **A** that you should
16:16 **A** will also be there with you.
16:17 Then you and **A** offer your
16:18 and stood with Moses and **A** at
16:19 who opposed Moses and **A** — at
16:20 LORD said to Moses and **A**,
16:37 son of the priest **A**,
16:40 descendant of **A** can come near
16:41 complained to Moses and **A**.
16:42 to confront Moses and **A**.
16:43 Then Moses and **A** went to the
16:46 Moses said to **A**, "Take your
16:47 **A** took his incense burner,
16:50 By the time **A** came back to
17:5 make against you and **A**."
18:1 The LORD said to **A**,
18:8 The LORD said to **A**,
18:20 The LORD said to **A**,
18:28 contribution to the priest **A**.
19:1 LORD said to Moses and **A**,
20:2 to confront Moses and **A**.
20:6 Moses and **A** went from the
20:8 then you and your brother **A**
Num 20:10 Then Moses and **A** assembled
20:12 the LORD said to Moses and **A**,
20:23 the LORD said to Moses and **A**,
20:24 "**A** must now join his ancestors
20:25 Bring **A** and his son Eleazar up
20:26 Then **A** will die there and join
20:28 **A** died there on top of the
20:29 saw that **A** had died,
20:29 mourned for **A** 30 days.
25:7 and grandson of the priest **A**,
25:11 and grandson of the priest **A**,
26:1 son of the priest **A**,
26:59 to Amram's children: **A**, Moses,
26:60 **A** was the father of Nadab,
26:64 and the priest **A** had counted
27:13 as your brother **A** did.
33:1 the leadership of Moses and **A**.
33:38 command the priest **A** went up
33:39 **A** was 123 years old when he
Dtr 9:20 also became very angry with **A**
9:20 But at that time I prayed for **A**,
10:6 **A** died there and was buried,
32:50 as your brother **A** died on
Jos 21:4 descendants of the priest **A**
21:13 to the descendants of **A**,
21:19 the descendants of **A**.
24:5 "Then I sent Moses and **A**,
Jdg 20:28 of Eleazar and grandson of **A**,
1Sm 12:6 LORD appointed Moses and **A**
12:8 who sent Moses and **A** to bring
1Ch 6:3 Amram's children were **A**,
6:49 **A** and his descendants offered
6:54 for the descendants of **A** from
23:13 sons were **A** and Moses.
23:13 **A** and his sons were forever
24:19 Their ancestor **A** made these
27:17 of Kemuel for the family of **A**:
Ezr 7:5 the son of **A** (the first priest).
Psa 77:20 You had Moses and **A** take
99:6 Moses and **A** were among his
105:26 servant Moses, and he sent **A**,
106:16 also became envious of **A**,
115:10 Descendants of **A**,
115:12 bless the descendants of **A**.
118:3 descendants of **A** should say,
135:19 Descendants of **A**,
Mic 6:4 I sent Moses, **A**, and Miriam to
Luk 1:5 was a descendant of **A**.
Act 7:40 They told **A**, 'We don't know
Heb 5:4 God calls him as he called **A**.
7:11 not a Levitical priest like **A**.

Aaron's (66)

Exo 7:12 But **A** staff swallowed theirs.
15:20 **A** sister, took a tambourine in
28:3 this ability — to make **A** clothes.
28:30 They, too, will be over **A** heart
28:38 It will be on **A** forehead.
28:38 be on **A** forehead so that
28:40 and turbans for **A** sons.
29:26 the ram used for **A** ordination,
29:29 "**A** holy clothes will belong to
Lev 1:5 **A** sons, the priests,
1:8 **A** sons, the priests,
1:11 **A** sons, the priests,
2:2 Then bring it to **A** sons, the
3:2 Then **A** sons, the priests,
3:5 Then **A** sons will lay them on
3:8 Then **A** sons will throw the
3:13 Then **A** sons will throw the
6:14 **A** sons must bring it into the
6:22 **A** son who is anointed to take
7:10 shared equally by all of **A** sons
7:33 When any of **A** sons offer the
8:12 of the anointing oil on **A** head
8:13 Moses had **A** sons come
8:23 and put it on **A** right ear lobe,
8:24 also brought **A** sons forward.
9:9 **A** sons brought him the blood.
9:12 **A** sons gave him the blood,
9:18 **A** sons gave him the blood,
10:1 **A** sons Nadab and Abihu each
10:4 the sons of **A** uncle, Uzziel.
10:16 and Ithamar, **A** surviving sons.
16:1 after **A** two sons had come

Lev 21:1 **A** sons: None of you should
Num 3:2 The names of **A** sons are
3:3 are the names of **A** sons,
17:3 Write **A** name on the staff for
17:6 **A** staff was among them.
17:8 He found that **A** staff for the
17:10 "Put **A** staff back in front of the
20:26 Take off **A** priestly clothes,
20:28 Moses took off **A** priestly
26:9 defied Moses and **A** authority.
Jos 21:10 that they gave **A** descendants
24:33 **A** son Eleazar also died.
1Ch 6:3 **A** sons were Nadab,
6:50 These were **A** descendants:
6:57 **A** descendants were given
6:60 **A** descendants received Geba
12:27 Jehoiada (leader of **A** families).
15:4 called together **A** descendants
23:28 to stand beside **A** descendants
23:32 **A** descendants, as they served
24:1 **A** descendants were as follows:
24:1 **A** sons were Nadab and Abihu,
24:3 **A** descendants into groups
24:31 **A** descendants, had done.
2Ch 13:9 who were **A** descendants,
13:10 the LORD are **A** descendants,
26:18 **A** descendants, who have
29:21 **A** descendants, to sacrifice the
31:19 **A** descendants, priests who lived
35:14 **A** descendants) were sacrificing
Neh 10:38 one of **A** descendants — should
12:47 for support of **A** descendants
Psa 133:2 down **A** beard — running over
Heb 9:4 **A** staff that had blossomed,

Abaddon (5)

Job 26:6 and **A** has no clothing.
31:12 be a fire that burns even in **A**.
Psa 88:11 or about your faithfulness in **A**?
Pro 15:11 If Sheol and **A** lie open in front
Rev 9:11 In Hebrew he is called **A**,

Abagtha (1)

Est 1:10 Bigtha, **A**, Zethar, and Carcas,

Abana (1)

2Ki 5:12 The **A** and Pharpar Rivers in

abandon (74)

Num 32:15 he will **a** all these people in the
Dtr 4:31 He will not **a** you, destroy you,
31:6 He won't **a** you or leave you."
31:8 He won't **a** you or leave you.
31:16 They will **a** me and reject the
31:17 I will **a** them and turn away
Jos 1:5 I will never neglect you or **a**
10:6 the camp in Gilgal: "Don't **a** us!
24:16 be unthinkable for us to **a**
24:20 If you **a** the LORD and serve
1Sm 12:22 the LORD will not **a** his people,
2Sm 11:15 Then **a** him so that he'll be
1Ki 6:13 and never **a** my people."
8:57 May he never leave us or **a** us.
2Ki 2:2 as you live, I will not **a** you."
2:4 as you live, I will not **a** you."
2:6 as you live, I will not **a** you."
21:14 I will **a** the rest of my people.
1Ch 28:9 But if you **a** him, he will reject
28:20 He will not **a** you before all the
2Ch 7:19 from me and **a** my commands
12:5 abandoned me, so I will **a** you.
15:2 But if you **a** him, he will
15:2 abandon him, he will **a** you.
Neh 9:19 you didn't **a** them in the desert.
9:31 didn't destroy them or **a** them.
Psa 16:10 because you do not **a** my soul
27:9 Do not **a** me, O God, my savior!
27:10 if my father and mother **a** me,
37:28 and he will not **a** his godly
37:33 But the LORD will not **a** him to
38:21 Do not **a** me, O LORD.
71:9 when I am old or **a** me when
71:18 and gray, do not **a** me, O God.
89:30 "If his descendants **a** my
94:14 people or **a** those who belong
119:8 obey your laws. Never **a** me.
Psa 119:53 who **a** your teachings.
119:87 not **a** your guiding principles.
Pro 2:13 from those who **a** the paths of
4:2 Do not **a** my teachings.
4:6 Do not **a** wisdom, and it will
27:10 Do not **a** your friend or your
28:4 Those who **a** (God's)
Isa 1:28 and those who **a** the LORD will
41:17 God of Israel, will not **a** them.
42:16 and I will never **a** them.
55:7 wicked people **a** their ways.
55:7 Let evil people **a** their thoughts.
Jer 2:19 and bitter it is for you if you **a**
9:2 I would **a** my people and go
14:5 give birth and **a** their young
17:13 all who **a** you will be put to
17:13 because they **a** the LORD,
23:33 I will **a** you, declares the
24:8 I will **a** King Zedekiah of
47:3 lack courage **a** their children.
48:28 People of Moab, **a** your cities.
49:11 "**A** your orphans, and I will
51:9 Let's **a** it and go to our own
Eze 20:8 They didn't **a** the disgusting
Dan 11:30 those who **a** the holy promise.
11:32 those who **a** the promise.
Jnh 2:8 idols **a** their loyalty (to
Mic 5:3 That is why the LORD will **a**
Mat 26:31 "All of you will **a** me tonight.
Mar 7:8 "You **a** the commandments of
14:27 "All of you will **a** me.
Luk 8:13 their faith is tested, they **a** it.
14:26 are not ready to **a** their fathers,
Act 2:27 because you do not **a** my soul
7:19 He made them **a** their newborn
21:21 non-Jewish people to **a** Moses.
Heb 13:5 "I will never **a** you or leave

abandoned (97)

Lev 26:43 The land, **a** by them,
Dtr 29:25 "Because they **a** the promise of
32:15 They **a** the God who made
Jdg 2:12 The Israelites **a** the LORD God
2:13 They **a** the LORD to serve the
6:13 But now the LORD has **a** us
10:6 They **a** the LORD and did not
10:10 We have **a** our God and served
10:13 But you still **a** me and served
1Sm 12:10 We have **a** the LORD and
31:7 were dead, they **a** their cities.
1Ki 9:9 'They **a** the LORD their God,
11:33 I will do this because he has **a**
19:10 have **a** your promises,
19:14 have **a** your promises,
2Ki 7:7 They **a** the camp as it was
17:16 They **a** all the commands of
21:22 He **a** the LORD God of his
22:17 this because they have **a** me
1Ch 10:7 were dead, they **a** their cities.
2Ch 7:22 'They **a** the LORD God of their
11:14 The priests **a** their land and
12:1 Israel **a** the LORD's teachings.
12:5 LORD says: You have **a** me,
13:10 We haven't **a** him.
13:11 but you have **a** him.
16:5 fortifying Ramah and **a** his work
21:10 because Jehoram had **a**
24:18 They **a** the temple of the LORD
24:20 The LORD has **a** you because
24:20 you because you have **a** him."
24:24 because Joash's soldiers had **a**
28:6 in Judah because they had **a**
34:25 this because they have **a** me
Ezr 9:9 but our God hasn't **a** us in our
9:10 have **a** your commandments!
Neh 9:17 You never **a** them,
9:28 You **a** them to their enemies,
Job 18:4 Should the earth be **a** for your
20:19 he crushed and **a** the poor.
Psa 22:1 why have you **a** me?
37:25 seen a righteous person **a**
71:11 They say, "God has **a** him.
78:60 He **a** his dwelling place in
88:5 **a** with the dead, like those who
102:17 of those who have been **a**.
Isa 1:4 They have **a** the LORD.
Isa 2:6 LORD, you have **a** your people,
6:12 the middle of the land will be **a**.
10:14 world as one gathers **a** eggs.
17:9 cities which other people **a**
17:9 Israelites will be like **a** woods
27:10 left deserted, **a** like the desert.
32:14 Noisy cities will be **a**.
49:14 "The LORD has **a** me.
54:6 if you were a wife who was **a**
54:7 "I **a** you for one brief moment,
60:15 "You have been **a** and hated;
65:11 You have **a** the LORD and
Jer 1:16 They **a** me, burned incense to
2:13 They have **a** me, the fountain
4:29 The entire city will be **a**,
5:7 Your children **a** me.
5:19 Answer them, "You have **a** me
7:29 the LORD has rejected and **a**
9:13 "They've **a** my teachings that I
12:7 "I have **a** my nation.
16:11 because your ancestors **a** me,
16:11 worshiped them, and **a** me.
19:4 the kings of Judah have **a** me.
49:25 isn't that famous, happy city **a**?
50:13 It will be completely **a**.
51:5 Israel and Judah haven't been **a**
Lam 1:6 All splendor has **a** the people
5:20 Why have you **a** us for such a
Eze 8:12 The LORD has **a** this land.'"
9:9 They think that the LORD has **a**
36:4 and to the empty ruins and **a**
Hos 1:2 prostitutes and **a** the LORD."
4:10 They have **a** the LORD.
Amo 5:2 They lie **a** in their own land.
Zec 11:17 shepherd who **a** the sheep.
Mat 23:38 Your house will be **a**,
26:56 Then all the disciples **a** him
27:46 why have you **a** me?"
Mar 14:50 Then all the disciples **a** him
15:34 why have you **a** me?"
Luk 13:35 Your house will be **a**.
Act 1:25 since Judas **a** his position to
7:21 When Moses was **a** outdoors,
2Co 4:9 persecuted, but we're not **a**.
1Ti 6:21 they have **a** the faith.
2Ti 2:18 They have **a** the truth.
4:10 Demas has **a** me.
4:16 Everyone **a** me.
Jud 1:6 but **a** their assigned place.
Rev 17:16 will leave her **a** and naked.

abandoning (4)

Dtr 28:20 evil you will do by **a** the LORD.
2Ch 32:11 misleading you and **a** you
Jer 2:17 brought this on yourself by **a**
51:5 although their land is guilty of **a**

abandons (6)

Ezr 8:22 oppose everyone who **a** him."
Job 6:14 even if he **a** the fear of the
Pro 28:13 **a** them receives compassion.
Mat 26:33 "Even if everyone else **a** you,
Mar 14:29 "Even if everyone else **a** you,
Jon 10:12 he **a** the sheep and quickly

Abarim (5)

Num 27:12 "Go up into the **A** Mountains,
33:47 camp in the **A** Mountains east
33:48 They moved from the **A**
Dtr 32:49 "Go into the **A** Mountains,
Jer 22:20 Cry out from **A**, because all

Abba (3)

Mar 14:36 He said, "**A**! Father! You can do
Rom 8:15 by which we call out, "**A**!
Gal 4:6 his Son into us to call out, "**A**!

Abda (2)

1Ki 4:6 Adoniram, son of **A**,
Neh 11:17 and so was **A** who was the

Abdeel (1)

Jer 36:26 and Shelemiah (son of **A**) to

Abdi (3)

1Ch 6:44 who was the son of **A**,

2Ch 29:12 Kish, son of **A**, and Azariah,
Ezr 10:26 Jehiel, **A**, Jeremoth, and Elijah

Abdiel (1)

1Ch 5:15 son of **A** and grandson of Guni,

Abdon (9)

Jos 19:28 **A**, Rehob, Hammon, Kanah,
21:30 the tribe of Asher: Mishal, **A**,
Jdg 12:13 After Elon, **A**, son of Hillel,
12:15 When **A** died, he was buried in
1Ch 6:74 **A** with its pastureland,
8:23 **A**, Zichri, Hanan,
8:30 His firstborn son was **A**,
9:36 His firstborn son was **A**,
2Ch 34:20 of Shaphan), **A** (son of Micah),

Abednego (15)

Dan 1:7 to Azariah he gave the name **A**.
2:49 and **A** to govern the province of
3:12 Shadrach, Meshach, and **A**.
3:13 Shadrach, Meshach, and **A**.
3:14 "Shadrach, Meshach, and **A**,
3:16 Shadrach, Meshach, and **A**
3:19 and **A** that his face turned red.
3:20 and **A** so that they could be
3:22 and **A** were killed by the
3:23 and **A** — fell into the blazing
3:26 and **A** — servants of the Most
3:26 and **A** came out of the fire.
3:28 of Shadrach, Meshach, and **A**.
3:29 and **A** will be torn limb from
3:30 and **A** to higher positions in the

Abel (16)

Gen 4:2 another child, **A**, Cain's brother.
4:2 **A** was a shepherd,
4:4 **A** also brought some choice
4:4 approved of **A** and his offering,
4:8 Cain talked to his brother **A**.
4:8 his brother **A** and killed him.
4:9 "Where is your brother **A**?"
4:25 me another child in place of **A**,
2Sm 20:14 of Israel to **A** (Beth Maacah).
20:15 him in **A** (Beth Maacah).
20:18 'Be sure to ask at **A** ⌊before
Mat 23:35 from the murder of righteous **A**
Luk 11:51 murders from **A** to Zechariah,
Heb 11:4 Faith led **A** to offer God a better
11:4 Through his faith **A** received
11:4 his faith **A** still speaks,

Abel Beth Maacah (2)

1Ki 15:20 He conquered Ijon, Dan, **A**,
2Ki 15:29 **A**, Janoah, Kedesh, Hazor,

Abel Keramim (1)

Jdg 11:33 Aroer to Minnith and on to **A**

Abel Maim (1)

2Ch 16:4 He conquered Ijon, Dan, **A**,

Abel Meholah (3)

Jdg 7:22 as the bank of the stream at **A**
1Ki 4:12 from Beth Shean to **A** and over
19:16 from **A** as prophet to take your

Abel Mizraim (1)

Gen 50:11 was named **A** [Egyptian Funeral

Abel's (1)

Heb 12:24 a better message than **A**.

Abel Shittim (1)

Num 33:49 from Beth Jeshimoth to **A**.

Abi (1)

2Ki 18:2 His mother was **A**,

Abi Albon (1)

2Sm 23:31 **A** from Beth Arabah,

Abiasaph (1)

Exo 6:24 were Assir, Elkanah, and **A**.

Abiathar (29)

1Sm 22:20 His name was **A**. He fled
22:21 **A** told David that Saul had
22:22 David told **A**, "I knew that day
23:6 When Ahimelech's son **A** fled
23:6 **A** brought a priestly ephod with
23:9 he told the priest **A**,
30:7 David told the priest **A**,
30:7 So **A** brought David the ephod.
2Sm 15:24 the ark of God beside **A** until all
15:29 So Zadok and **A** took the ark of
15:35 The priests Zadok and **A** will
15:35 it to the priests Zadok and **A**.
15:36 and **A** has Jonathan.
17:15 told the priests Zadok and **A**,
19:11 to the priests Zadok and **A**:
20:25 Zadok and **A** were priests.
1Ki 1:7 Zeruiah) and with the priest **A**,
1:19 all the king's sons, **A** the priest,
1:25 and the priest **A** ⌊to his feast⌋.
1:42 son of the priest **A**,
2:22 The priest **A** and Joab
2:26 The king told the priest **A**,
2:27 So Solomon removed **A** as the
2:35 King Solomon also replaced **A**
4:4 Zadok and **A** were priests.
1Ch 15:11 for the priests Zadok and **A**
24:6 Ahimelech (son of **A**),
27:34 and **A** succeeded Ahithophel.
Mar 2:26 of God when **A** was chief priest

Abiathar's (3)

2Sm 8:17 Ahitub's son Zadok and **A** son
15:27 Ahimaaz and **A** son Jonathan
1Ch 18:16 Ahitub's son Zadok and **A** son

Abib (5)

Exo 13:4 Today, in the month of **A**,
23:15 time in the month of **A**,
34:18 time in the month of **A**,
Dtr 16:1 Passover in the month of **A**.
16:1 In the month of **A** the LORD

Abida (2)

Gen 25:4 Epher, Hanoch, **A**, and Eldaah.
1Ch 1:33 Epher, Hanoch, **A**, and Eldaah.

Abidan (5)

Num 1:11 **A**, son of Gideoni, from the
2:22 for the people of Benjamin is **A**,
7:60 of Benjamin, **A**, son of Gideoni,
7:65 These were the gifts from **A**,
10:24 **A**, son of Gideoni,

Abiel (3)

1Sm 9:1 He was a son of **A**,
14:51 father) were the sons of **A**.
1Ch 11:32 **A** from Beth Arabah,

Abiezer (5)

Jos 17:2 to the descendants of **A**,
2Sm 23:27 **A** from Anathoth,
1Ch 7:18 birth to Ishhod, **A**, and Mahlah.
11:28 from Tekoa, **A** from Anathoth,
27:12 **A**, a member of the tribe of

Abiezer's (5)

Jdg 6:11 to Joash from **A** family.
6:24 which belongs to **A** family
6:34 ram's horn to summon **A** family
8:2 the grapes in **A** entire harvest?
8:32 the city belonging to **A** family

Abigail (18)

1Sm 25:3 and his wife's name was **A**.
25:14 One of the young men told **A**,
25:18 So **A** quickly took 200 loaves
25:23 When **A** saw David,
25:32 David said to **A**, "Blessed be
25:36 When **A** came to Nabal,
25:39 to propose marriage to **A**.
25:40 servants came to **A** at Carmel,
25:42 Then **A** quickly got up and rode
25:43 she and **A** were his wives.
27:3 Ahinoam from Jezreel and **A**
1Sm 30:5 Ahinoam from Jezreel and **A**
2Sm 2:2 Ahinoam from Jezreel and **A**
3:3 ⌊born⌋ to **A** (who had been
17:25 His mother was **A**,
1Ch 2:16 sisters were Zeruiah and **A**.
2:17 **A** was the mother of Amasa,
3:1 ⌊born⌋ to **A** from Carmel.

Abihail (6)

Num 3:35 was Zuriel, son of **A**.
1Ch 2:29 name of Abishur's wife was **A**.
5:14 These were the sons of **A**,
2Ch 11:18 was the son of David and **A**.
11:18 **A** was the daughter of Eliab,
Est 2:15 (Esther was the daughter of **A**,

Abihail's (1)

Est 9:29 A daughter Queen Esther and

Abihu (12)

Exo 6:23 She gave birth to Nadab, **A**,
24:1 "You and Aaron, Nadab, **A**,
24:9 **A**, and 70 of Israel's leaders.
28:1 **A**, Eleazar, and Ithamar to you.
Lev 10:1 Aaron's sons Nadab and **A**
Num 3:2 **A**, Eleazar, and Ithamar.
3:4 Nadab and **A** died in the
26:60 **A**, Eleazar, and Ithamar.
26:61 But Nadab and **A** had died
1Ch 6:3 Aaron's sons were Nadab, **A**,
24:1 sons were Nadab and **A**,
24:2 Nadab and **A** died before their

Abihud (1)

1Ch 8:3 sons were Addar, Gera, **A**,

Abijah (27)

1Sm 8:2 name of his second son was **A**.
1Ki 14:1 At that time **A**, son of
1Ch 2:24 Hezron's wife **A** gave birth to
3:10 Rehoboam's son was **A**.
6:28 who was his firstborn, and **A**,
7:8 **A**, Anathoth, and Alemeth.
24:10 for Hakkoz, the eighth for **A**,
2Ch 11:20 She gave birth to **A**,
11:22 Rehoboam appointed **A**,
12:16 His son **A** succeeded him as
13:1 **A** began to rule Judah.
13:2 war between **A** and Jeroboam.
13:3 **A** prepared for battle with an
13:4 Then **A** stood on Mount
13:15 Israel in front of **A** and Judah.
13:17 So **A** and his men defeated
13:19 **A** pursued Jeroboam and
13:21 But **A** became strong.
13:22 Everything else about **A** — how
14:1 **A** lay down in death with his
29:1 His mother was **A**,
Neh 10:7 Meshullam, **A**, Mijamin,
12:4 Iddo, Ginnethoi, **A**,
12:17 from **A**, Zichri; from Miniamin,
Mat 1:7 Rehoboam the father of **A**,
1:7 **A** the father of Asa,
Luk 1:5 of priests named after **A**.

Abijah's (2)

1Ch 3:10 **A** son was Asa. Asa's son was
2Ch 13:20 regained power during **A** time.

Abijam (7)

1Ki 14:31 His son **A** succeeded him as
15:1 **A** began to rule Judah.
15:4 the LORD his God made **A**
15:6 There was war between **A** and
15:7 Isn't everything else about **A** —
15:7 war between **A** and Jeroboam.
15:8 **A** lay down in death with his

Abilene (1)

Luk 3:1 Lysanias was the ruler of **A**.

ability (24)

Exo 28:3 to whom I have given this **a** —
35:34 of Dan the **a** to teach others.
Dtr 8:17 of my own **a** and strength."
Jos 24:12 your battle skills or fighting **a**.

Rut 4:13 and the LORD gave her the **a** to
1Ch 26:8 were skilled and had the **a**
Pro 12:14 as a result of his speaking **a**.
13:2 as a result of his speaking **a**,
18:20 A person's speaking **a** provides
Ecc 5:19 ⌊the **a**⌋ to accept their lot in
5:19 and ⌊the **a**⌋ to rejoice in their
Dan 1:17 and the **a** to understand all
5:12 He has the **a** to interpret
Mat 25:15 given money based on his **a**.
Mar 6:2 this kind of wisdom and the **a**
Act 2:4 Spirit gave them the **a** to speak.
21:9 daughters who had the **a**
1Co 10:13 he will also give you the **a** to
12:8 Spirit gives one person the **a**
12:8 gives another person the **a**
12:9 same Spirit gives the **a** to heal.
13:9 is incomplete and our **a**
2Co 1:8 it was beyond our **a** to endure.
8:7 your faith, your **a** to speak,

Abimael (2)

Gen 10:28 Obal, **A**, Sheba,
1Ch 1:22 Ebal, **A**, Sheba,

Abimelech (68)

Gen 20:2 So King **A** of Gerar sent men to
20:3 God came to **A** in a dream one
20:4 **A** hadn't come near her,
20:8 Early in the morning **A** called
20:9 Then **A** called for Abraham and
20:10 **A** also asked Abraham,
20:14 Then **A** took sheep,
20:15 **A** said, "Look, here's my land.
20:17 and God healed **A**,
21:22 At that time **A**, accompanied by
21:25 Then Abraham complained to **A**
21:26 **A** replied, "I don't know who
21:27 and cattle and gave them to **A**,
21:29 **A** asked him, "What is the
21:32 at Beersheba, **A** and Phicol,
26:1 So Isaac went to King **A** of the
26:8 King **A** of the Philistines
26:9 **A** called for Isaac and said,
26:10 Then **A** said, "What have you
26:11 So **A** ordered his people,
26:16 Finally, **A** said to Isaac,
26:26 **A**, his friend Ahuzzath,
Jdg 8:31 That son was named **A**.
9:1 **A**, son of Jerubbaal [Gideon],
9:3 were persuaded to follow **A**
9:4 With the silver, **A** hired
9:6 and proclaimed **A** king.
9:16 when you made **A** king,
9:18 You have made **A**,
9:19 then be happy with **A** and let
9:19 with Abimelech and let **A**
9:20 let fire come out of **A** and burn
9:20 and Beth Millo and burn up **A**."
9:21 there ⌊to avoid⌋ his brother **A**.
9:22 **A** ruled Israel for three years.
9:23 to cause problems between **A**
9:23 of Shechem turned against **A**.
9:24 70 sons would happen to **A**
9:24 helped **A** execute his brothers.
9:25 Shechem set ambushes for **A**
9:25 This was reported to **A**.
9:27 They ate, drank, and cursed **A**.
9:28 "Who's **A**, and who are we,
9:28 Why should we serve **A**?
9:29 Then I'd get rid of **A**.
9:31 secretly sent messengers to **A**.
9:34 **A** and all his troops started out
9:35 Then **A** and his troops rose
9:38 'Who's **A** that we should serve
9:39 of Shechem out to fight **A**.
9:40 **A** chased Gaal so that he ran
9:41 **A** continued to live at Arumah.
9:42 **A** was told about it.
9:44 **A** and his company charged
9:45 **A** attacked the city all day long.
9:47 When **A** was told that they had
9:48 **A** took an ax, cut some
9:49 cut brushwood and followed **A**.
9:50 Then **A** went to Thebez,
9:52 **A** came to the tower.
Jdg 9:53 a small millstone that hit **A**
9:54 'A woman killed **A**.'" His
9:54 did as he said, so **A** died.
9:55 of Israel saw that **A** was dead,
9:56 So God paid back **A** for the
10:1 After **A**, Tola, who was the son
2Sm 11:21 killed Jerubbesheth's son **A**?
1Ch 18:16 Abiathar's son **A** were priests.

Abimelech's (2)

Gen 20:18 for any woman in **A** household
21:25 which **A** servants had seized.

Abinadab (7)

1Sm 16:8 Then Jesse called **A** and
17:13 the second was **A**,
31:2 They killed Jonathan, **A**,
1Ch 2:13 **A** (his second son),
8:33 Malchishua, **A**, and Eshbaal.
9:39 Malchishua, **A**, and Eshbaal.
10:2 They killed Jonathan, **A**,

Abinadab's (6)

1Sm 7:1 ark and brought it into **A** house
7:1 They gave **A** son Eleazar the
2Sm 6:3 cart and brought it from **A**
6:3 Uzzah and Ahio, **A** sons, were
6:4 They brought it from **A** home,
1Ch 13:7 ark on a new cart from **A** home.

Abinoam (4)

Jdg 4:6 summoned Barak, son of **A**,
4:12 Sisera that Barak, son of **A**,
5:1 son of **A**, sang this song:
5:12 Take your prisoners, son of **A**.

Abiram (11)

Num 16:1 Dathan and **A** (sons of Eliab),
16:1 Dathan, **A**, and On were
16:12 Moses sent for Dathan and **A**,
16:24 tents of Korah, Dathan, and **A**."
16:25 up and went to Dathan and **A**,
16:27 tents of Korah, Dathan, and **A**.
16:27 Dathan and **A** had come out
26:9 and **A** were the sons of Eliab.
26:9 (It was Dathan and **A**,
Dtr 11:6 what he did to Dathan and **A**,
1Ki 16:34 cost him his firstborn son, **A**.

Abiram's (1)

Psa 106:17 It buried **A** followers

Abishag (5)

1Ki 1:3 They found **A** from Shunem
1:15 The king was very old, and **A**
2:17 to give me **A** from Shunem as
2:21 She replied, "Let **A** from
2:22 "Why do you ask that **A** from

Abishai (27)

1Sm 26:6 Ahimelech the Hittite and **A**,
26:6 **A** answered, "I'll go with you."
26:7 So David and **A** went among
26:8 **A** said to David, "Today God
26:9 David told **A**. "No one has ever
2Sm 2:18 there: Joab, **A**, and Asahel.
2:24 But Joab and **A** chased Abner.
3:30 (Joab and his brother **A** killed
10:10 He put his brother **A** in charge
10:10 **A** organized them for combat
10:14 the Ammonites fled from **A** and
16:9 **A**, Zeruiah's son, asked the
16:11 David told **A** and all his
18:2 brother **A** (Zeruiah's son),
18:5 The king ordered Joab, **A**,
18:12 the king gave you, **A**, and Ittai:
19:21 But **A**, Zeruiah's son, replied,
20:6 David then told **A**, "Sheba,
20:7 all the soldiers went with **A**.
20:10 his brother **A** pursued Sheba,
21:17 But **A**, son of Zeruiah, came to
23:18 Joab's brother **A**, Zeruiah's son,
1Ch 2:16 Zeruiah's three sons were **A**,
11:20 Joab's brother **A** was the leader
18:12 Zeruiah's son **A** killed 18,000
19:11 He put his brother **A** in charge
1Ch 19:15 fled from Joab's brother **A** and

Abishalom (2)

1Ki 15:2 named Maacah, daughter of **A**.
15:10 named Maacah, daughter of **A**.

Abishua (5)

1Ch 6:4 Phinehas was the father of **A**.
6:5 **A** was the father of Bukki.
6:50 Phinehas' son was **A**.
8:4 **A**, Naaman, Ahoah,
Ezr 7:5 who was the son of **A**,

Abishua's (1)

1Ch 6:51 **A** son was Bukki.

Abishur (1)

1Ch 2:28 sons were Nadab and **A**.

Abishur's (1)

1Ch 2:29 The name of **A** wife was

Abital (2)

2Sm 3:4 whose mother was **A**.
1Ch 3:3 was Shephatiah, ⌊born⌋ to **A**.

Abitub (1)

1Ch 8:11 the parents of **A** and Elpaal.

Abiud (2)

Mat 1:13 Zerubbabel the father of **A**,
1:13 **A** the father of Eliakim,

able (173)

Gen 11:30 was not **a** to have children.
14:23 that you will never be **a** to say,
15:5 if you are **a** to count them."
16:1 was not **a** to have children.
16:10 No one will be **a** to count them
19:32 bed with him so that we'll be **a**
19:34 bed with him so that we'll be **a**
32:8 camp will be **a** to escape."
32:12 No one will be **a** to count them
42:34 and you'll be **a** to move about
Exo 7:18 The Egyptians will not be **a** to
10:2 You will be **a** to tell your
18:23 you will be **a** to continue your
20:26 Otherwise, people will be **a** to
32:30 Maybe I will be **a** to make a
Lev 26:37 They will not be **a** to stand up
Num 5:28 and will be **a** to have children.
13:30 be more than **a** to conquer it."
14:16 'The LORD wasn't **a** to bring
22:6 Maybe then I'll be **a** to defeat
22:11 Maybe I'll be **a** to fight them
22:37 knew I'd be **a** to reward you."
Dtr 1:9 "I'm not **a** to take care of you by
4:1 so that you will live and be **a**
4:2 Then you will be **a** to obey the
7:14 Your men and women will be **a**
7:14 will be **a** to have offspring.
7:22 You won't be **a** to wipe them
7:24 No one will be **a** to stop you.
8:9 and you will be **a** to mine
9:28 'The LORD wasn't **a** to bring
11:15 and you will be **a** to eat all you
11:25 No one will be **a** to stop you.
24:6 The family wouldn't be **a** to
28:12 You will be **a** to make loans to
28:41 but you won't be **a** to keep
28:44 They will be **a** to make loans
28:44 but you won't be **a** to make
31:2 and I'm not **a** to lead you
32:28 They are not **a** to understand.
32:47 By these words you will be **a**
Jos 1:5 No one will be **a** to oppose you
7:12 people of Israel will not be **a**
7:13 You will not be **a** to defend
9:7 We wouldn't be **a** to make a
15:63 However, Judah was not **a** to
17:12 But Manasseh was not **a** to
23:9 Not one person has ever been **a**
Jdg 1:19 of Judah so that they were **a**
11:38 never being **a** to get married.
13:2 was not **a** to have children.
13:3 "You've never been **a** to have a

1Sm 3:14 will ever ⌊be **a** to⌋ make peace
9:13 You should be **a** to find him
24:11 you should know and be **a** to
2Sm 14:17 who is **a** to distinguish right
1Ki 9:20 the Israelites had not been **a**
11:28 that Jeroboam was a very **a**
13:6 and the king was **a** to use his
18:12 but he won't be **a** to find you.
2Ki 9:37 Jezreel so that no one will be **a**
13:5 They were **a** to live in their
1Ch 12:8 **a** to fight with shields and
12:14 The least **a** one was in
28:8 Then you will be **a** to possess
2Ch 2:6 But who is **a** to build him a
7:7 in front of the LORD was not **a**
8:7 the Israelites had not been **a**
22:9 one in Ahaziah's family was **a**
30:24 large number of priests were **a**
32:13 of these other nations ever **a**
32:14 the gods of these nations **a**
32:14 Is your God **a** to rescue you
Ezr 9:12 Then you will be strong, be **a**
9:12 and be **a** to give this land as a
Job 3:17 There the weary are **a** to rest.
5:22 "You will be **a** to laugh at
9:3 he wouldn't be **a** to answer one
11:7 or are you **a** to find the
11:15 Then you will be **a** to show
20:17 He won't be **a** to drink from the
Psa 1:5 wicked people will not be **a**
1:5 and sinners will not be **a**
64:10 are decent will be **a** to brag.
66:7 Rebels will not be **a** to oppose
76:5 None of the warriors were **a** to
94:20 the law to do unlawful things **a**
130:3 O LORD, who would be **a** to
Pro 13:23 poor people are **a** to plow,
Ecc 2:3 I was **a** to determine whether
3:13 It is a gift from God to be **a** to
5:15 They won't even be **a** to take a
7:18 one who fears God will be **a**
8:17 No one is **a** to grasp the work
8:17 he is not **a** to grasp it.
Isa 7:25 And you will no longer be **a** to
14:21 They won't be **a** to rise,
16:12 but they won't be **a** to.
26:18 We weren't **a** to bring salvation
46:2 They aren't **a** to escape with
47:11 You won't be **a** to stop it.
Jer 1:18 You will be **a** to stand up to the
1:18 You will be **a** to stand up to
4:4 will burn, and no one will be **a**
6:10 and they aren't **a** to pay
10:5 They aren't **a** to speak.
17:27 and you won't be **a** to put it
21:12 No one will be **a** to put it out
49:10 They won't be **a** to hide.
Eze 4:8 ropes so that you will not be **a**
7:19 Their silver and gold won't be **a**
17:17 Pharaoh will not be **a** to help
38:4 and be **a** to use swords.
40:46 are the only Levites who are **a**
42:9 A person was **a** to enter the
Dan 1:4 and **a** to serve in the king's
2:47 secrets because you were **a**
6:20 **a** to save you from the lions?
11:15 southern forces will not be **a**
11:16 and no one will be **a** to
11:25 the southern king won't be **a**
Hos 1:10 No one will be **a** to measure
Amo 2:14 will not be **a** to escape.
2:14 not be **a** to save themselves.
2:15 runners will not be **a** to escape.
2:15 not be **a** to save themselves.
5:15 Then you will be **a** to have
7:10 The country isn't **a** to endure
9:1 None of them will be **a** to get
9:1 of them will be **a** to escape.
Mic 2:1 plans because they are **a** to.
2:3 You won't be **a** to rescue
2:3 You will no longer be **a** to walk
Zep 1:18 and their gold will not be **a**
Zec 7:14 land so ruined that no one is **a**
11:1 so that fire will be **a** to burn
Mal 3:2 But who will be **a** to endure the
3:2 Who will be **a** to survive on the
Mat 21:21 you will be **a** to do what I did to
Luk 1:64 Zechariah was **a** to speak,
21:15 none of your enemies will be **a**
Jon 9:7 He was **a** to see.
Act 5:39 you won't be **a** to stop them.
14:8 he had never been **a** to walk.
19:40 We won't be **a** to explain this
24:8 you'll be **a** to find out from him
Rom 3:6 how would God be **a** to judge
8:4 are **a** to meet God's standards.
11:23 because God is **a** to do that.
12:2 Then you will always be **a** to
15:14 you need and that you are **a**
1Co 6:5 least one wise person who is **a**
2Co 1:4 we are **a** to comfort them by
8:12 give what they are **a** to give.
Eph 3:18 of God's people you will be **a**
6:13 Then you will be **a** to take a
6:13 you will be **a** to stand your
Php 1:10 That way you will be **a** to
Col 1:12 who has made you **a** to share
1Th 2:17 Although we may not be **a** to
5:3 They won't be **a** to escape.
1Ti 3:2 hospitable, and be **a** to teach.
2Ti 1:12 I'm convinced that he is **a** to
3:7 studying but are never **a**
Heb 2:18 he is **a** to help others when
4:15 We have a chief priest who is **a**
7:25 That is why he is always **a** to
9:15 he is **a** to bring a new promise
11:11 old and Sarah had never been **a**
Jas 3:2 He would be **a** to control
4:12 He is **a** to save or destroy you.
Rev 6:17 and who is **a** to endure it?"
7:9 No one was **a** to count how

able-bodied (1)

2Sm 24:9 In Israel there were 800,000 **a**

Abner (61)

1Sm 14:50 commander of his army was **A**,
17:55 the Philistine, he asked **A**,
17:55 the commander of the army, "**A**,
17:55 **A** answered, "I solemnly
17:57 **A** brought him to Saul.
20:25 **A** sat beside Saul,
26:5 where Saul and Ner's son **A**,
26:7 **A** and the soldiers were lying
26:14 to the troops and to Ner's son **A**.
26:14 "Won't you answer, **A**?"
26:14 is calling the king?" **A** asked.
26:15 David asked **A**, "Aren't you a
2Sm 2:8 Ner's son **A**, commander of
2:9 **A** made him king of Gilead,
2:12 Ner's son **A** and the officers of
2:14 **A** said to Joab, "Let's have the
2:17 and David's men defeated **A**
2:19 He chased **A** and refused to
2:20 When **A** looked back,
2:21 **A** told him, "Leave me alone!
2:22 So **A** spoke again to Asahel.
2:23 So **A** struck him with the butt of
2:24 Joab and Abishai chased **A**.
2:25 of Benjamin rallied behind **A**,
2:26 Then **A** called to Joab,
2:29 **A** and his men marched
2:30 Joab returned from chasing **A**.
3:6 **A** strengthened his position in
3:7 Ishbosheth asked **A**,
3:8 question made **A** very angry.
3:11 because he was afraid of **A**.
3:12 Then **A** sent messengers to
3:16 "Go home," **A** told him.
3:17 Meanwhile, **A** sent the
3:19 **A** also spoke specifically to
3:19 Then **A** went directly to David
3:20 So **A** came with 20 men to
3:20 had a feast for **A** and his men.
3:21 **A** told David, "I must go now
3:21 Then David dismissed **A**,
3:22 **A** had been dismissed,
3:23 "Ner's son **A** came to the king,
3:23 and **A** left peacefully."
3:24 **A** came to see you.
3:25 know that Ner's son **A** came
3:26 Joab sent messengers after **A**.
2Sm 3:27 When **A** returned to Hebron,
3:27 There he stabbed **A** in the
3:27 **A** died because he spilled the
3:28 the blood of Ner's son **A**.
3:30 and his brother Abishai killed **A**
3:31 on sackcloth, and mourn for **A**."
3:32 They buried **A** in Hebron.
3:33 king sang a funeral song for **A**:
3:33 Should **A** die like a godless
3:37 for killing Ner's son **A**.
4:1 heard that **A** had died
1Ki 2:5 of Israel's army — **A**,
2:32 He used his sword to kill **A**
1Ch 26:28 (son of Kish), **A** (son of Ner),
27:21 of Benjamin: Jaasiel, son of **A**

Abner's (4)

1Sm 14:51 father) and Ner (**A** father) were
2Sm 2:31 of Benjamin under **A** command
3:32 king cried loudly at **A** grave,
4:12 buried it in **A** tomb in Hebron.

aboard (3)

Psa 107:26 The sailors **a** ship rose toward
Act 21:2 so we went **a** and sailed away.
21:6 Then we went **a** the ship,

abolished (1)

Psa 119:126 people have **a** your teachings,

abolishing (1)

Rom 3:31 Are we **a** Moses' Teachings by

aborted (1)

1Co 15:8 I'm like an **a** fetus ⌊who was

Abraham (261)

Gen 17:5 but **A** [Father of Many] because
17:9 God also said to **A**,
17:15 God said to **A**, "Don't call your
17:17 Immediately, **A** bowed with his
17:18 Then **A** said to God,
17:22 God finished speaking with **A**,
17:23 So **A** took his son Ishmael,
17:24 **A** was 99 years old when he
17:26 That same day **A** and his son
18:1 The LORD appeared to **A** by
18:2 **A** looked up, and suddenly he
18:3 "Please, sir," **A** said,
18:6 So **A** hurried into the tent to find
18:7 Then **A** ran to the herd and took
18:8 **A** took cheese and milk,
18:11 **A** and Sarah were old.
18:13 The LORD asked **A**,
18:16 As **A** was walking with them to
18:17 what I am going to do from **A**.
18:18 After all, **A** is going to become
18:19 do what I have promised **A**."
18:22 but **A** remained standing in
18:23 **A** came closer and asked,
18:27 **A** asked, "Consider now, if I
18:29 **A** asked him again,
18:30 angry if I speak again," **A** said.
18:31 so bold as to ask you," **A** said.
18:32 only one more time," **A** said.
18:33 LORD finished speaking to **A**,
18:33 **A** returned home.
19:27 Early the next morning **A** came
19:29 he remembered **A**.
20:1 **A** moved to the Negev and
20:2 **A** told everyone that his wife
20:9 Then Abimelech called for **A**
20:10 Abimelech also asked **A**,
20:11 **A** said, "I thought that because
20:14 slaves and gave them to **A**.
20:17 **A** prayed to God, and God
21:2 she gave birth to a son for **A** in
21:3 **A** named his newborn son
21:4 **A** circumcised him as God had
21:5 **A** was 100 years old when his
21:7 Who would have predicted to **A**
21:8 **A** held a big feast.
21:10 She said to **A**, "Get rid of this
21:11 **A** was upset by this because
21:12 But God said to **A**,
21:14 Early the next morning **A** took

Gen 21:22 of his army, said to A,
21:24 A said, "I so swear."
21:25 Then A complained to
21:27 A took some sheep and cattle
21:28 Then A set apart seven female
21:30 A answered, "Accept these
21:33 A planted a tamarisk tree at
21:34 A lived a long time in the land
22:1 Later God tested A and called
22:1 and called to him, "A!"
22:3 Early the next morning A
22:4 Two days later A saw the
22:5 Then A said to his servants,
22:6 Then A took the wood for the
22:6 A carried the burning coals and
22:7 "Yes, Son?" A answered.
22:8 A answered, "God will provide
22:9 A built the altar and arranged
22:10 Next, A picked up the knife
22:11 him from heaven and said, "A!
22:11 A!" "Yes?" he answered.
22:13 When A looked around,
22:13 So A took the ram and
22:14 A named that place The LORD
22:15 LORD called to A from heaven
22:19 Then A returned to his
22:19 A remained in Beersheba.
22:20 Later A was told, "Milcah has
23:2 A went to mourn for Sarah and
23:3 Then A left the side of his dead
23:5 The Hittites answered A,
23:7 A got up in front of the Hittites,
23:10 He answered A so that
23:12 A bowed down again in front of
23:14 Ephron answered A,
23:16 A agreed to Ephron's terms.
23:18 to A. His property included the
23:19 After this, A buried his wife
23:20 the Hittites to A as his property
24:1 By now A was old,
24:2 So A said to the senior servant
24:6 son back there," A said to him.
24:9 as his master A commanded
24:12 God of my master A,
24:12 Show your kindness to A.
24:27 the God of my master A.
24:42 'LORD God of my master A,
24:48 the God of my master A.
25:1 A married again, and his wife's
25:2 gave birth to these sons of A:
25:5 A left everything he had to
25:6 But while he was still living, A
25:7 A lived 175 years.
25:10 This was the field that A had
25:10 There A was buried with his
25:11 After A died, God blessed his
25:12 Egyptian slave Hagar and A.
25:19 A was the father of Isaac.
26:3 that I swore to your father A.
26:5 I will bless you because A
26:24 "I am the God of your father A.
28:4 the blessing of A so that you
28:4 the land that God gave to A."
28:13 the God of your grandfather A
31:42 the God of A and the Fear of
31:53 May the God of A and Nahor —
32:9 "God of my grandfather A and
35:12 land that I gave to A and Isaac.
35:27 A and Isaac had lived there for
48:15 presence my grandfather A
48:16 the names of my grandfather A
49:30 A bought the cave that is in the
49:31 A and his wife Sarah are buried
50:13 A had bought this tomb from
50:24 swore with an oath to give to A,
Exo 2:24 remembered his promise to A,
3:6 ancestors, the God of A, Isaac,
3:15 ancestors, the God of A, Isaac,
3:16 ancestors, the God of A, Isaac,
4:5 ancestors, the God of A, Isaac,
6:3 I appeared to A, Isaac,
6:8 I solemnly swore to give to A,
32:13 Remember your servants A,
33:1 Go to the land I promised to A,
Lev 26:42 promise to Jacob, Isaac, and A.
Num 32:11 will see the land I promised A,
Dtr 1:8 to give to your ancestors A,
6:10 he swore to your ancestors A,
9:5 he swore to your ancestors A,
9:27 Remember your servants A,
29:13 he promised your ancestors A,
30:20 to give to your ancestors A,
34:4 I promised with an oath to A,
Jos 24:2 and his sons A and Nahor,
24:3 But I took your ancestor A from
1Ki 18:36 He said, "LORD God of A,
2Ki 13:23 because of his promise to A,
1Ch 1:27 Abram (that is, A).
1:34 A was the father of Isaac.
16:16 the promise that he made to A,
29:18 LORD God of our ancestors A,
2Ch 20:7 friend A to have permanently?
30:6 return to the LORD God of A,
Neh 9:7 and gave him the name A.
Psa 47:9 as the people of the God of A.
105:6 descendants of his servant A,
105:9 the promise that he made to A,
105:42 holy promise to his servant A.
Isa 29:22 what the LORD, who saved A,
41:8 the descendant of A,
51:2 Look to A, your ancestor,
51:2 When I called A, he was
63:16 Even though A doesn't know
Jer 33:26 rule the descendants of A,
Eze 33:24 'A was only one person,
Mic 7:20 You will have mercy on A as
Mat 1:1 descendant of David and A.
1:2 A was the father of Isaac,
1:17 14 generations from A to David,
3:9 'A is our ancestor.'
3:9 for A from these stones.
8:11 They will eat with A,
22:32 'I am the God of A,
Mar 12:26 'I am the God of A,
Luk 1:55 to A and his descendants."
1:73 that he swore to our ancestor A.
3:8 Don't say, 'A is our ancestor.'
3:8 for A from these stones.
3:34 Isaac, son of A, son of Terah,
13:16 here is a descendant of A.
13:28 what you'll do when you see A,
16:22 angels carried him to be with A.
16:23 he saw A and Lazarus.
16:24 He yelled, 'Father A!
16:25 "A replied, 'Remember,
16:29 "A replied, 'They have Moses'
16:30 rich man replied, 'No, Father A!
16:31 "A answered him, 'If they won't
20:37 that the Lord is the God of A,
Jon 8:39 to Jesus, "A is our father."
8:39 you would do what A did.
8:40 A wouldn't have done that.
8:52 A died, and so did the prophets,
8:53 you greater than our father A,
8:56 Your father A was pleased to
8:57 How could you have seen A?"
8:58 Before A was ever born,
Act 3:13 The God of our ancestors A,
3:25 ancestors when he said to A,
7:2 our ancestor A in Mesopotamia.
7:2 before A lived in Haran.
7:4 "Then A left the country of
7:5 "Yet, God didn't give A
7:5 even though A didn't have a
7:6 God told A that his
7:8 "God gave A circumcision to
7:8 A circumcised him on the
7:16 in the tomb that A purchased
7:17 to A had almost come,
7:32 your ancestors — the God of A,
13:26 "Brothers — descendants of A
Rom 4:1 about our ancestor A?
4:2 If A had God's approval
4:3 "A believed God, and that faith
4:3 God to be his approval of A."
4:12 Our father A had that faith
4:13 Moses' Teachings that A
4:16 by believing as A did.
4:17 A believed when he stood in
4:18 A still hoped and believed.
4:19 A didn't weaken.
9:7 or a descendant of A.
Rom 9:8 ⌊from A⌋ are not necessarily
11:1 a descendant of A from the
Gal 3:6 A serves as an example.
3:6 by God to be his approval of A.
3:8 the Good News to A ahead
3:9 are blessed together with A,
3:14 promised to A would come
3:16 promises were spoken to A
3:17 promise ⌊to A⌋ into effect didn't
3:17 cancel the promise ⌊to A⌋.
3:18 to A through a promise.
4:22 Scripture says that A had two
4:23 through a promise ⌊made to A⌋.
Heb 6:13 God made a promise to A.
6:15 So A received what God
7:1 He met A and blessed him
7:1 him when A was returning from
7:2 A gave Melchizedek a tenth of
7:4 A gave him a tenth of what he
7:4 even though A was the father
7:6 a tenth of everything from A.
7:6 Then Melchizedek blessed A,
7:9 that when A gave Melchizedek
7:10 he was in the body of A when
11:8 Faith led A to obey when God
11:8 A left his own country without
11:9 Faith led A to live as a
11:10 A was waiting for the city that
11:11 Faith enabled A to become a
11:11 A trusted that God would keep
11:12 A was as good as dead.
11:17 When God tested A,
11:17 A, the one who received the
11:19 A believed that God could
11:19 A did receive Isaac back from
Jas 2:21 Didn't our ancestor A receive
2:23 It says, "A believed God,
2:23 God to be his approval of A."
2:23 So A was called God's friend.
1Pe 3:6 Sarah obeyed A and spoke to

Abraham's (31)

Gen 20:18 because of A wife Sarah.)
21:9 Sarah saw that A son by Hagar
22:23 eight sons by A brother Nahor.
24:15 who was the wife of A brother
24:34 "I am A servant," he said.
24:52 When A servant heard their
24:59 and her nurse go with A servant
25:12 descendants of A son Ishmael.
25:19 This is the account of A son
26:1 to the earlier one during A time.
26:15 dug during his father A lifetime
26:18 dug during his father A lifetime.
26:18 had filled them in after A death.
26:24 for my servant A sake.
28:9 daughter of A son Ishmael and
1Ch 1:28 A sons were Isaac and
1:32 Keturah, A concubine, gave
Luk 19:9 are one of A descendants
Jon 8:33 "We are A descendants, and
8:37 that you're A descendants.
8:39 "If you were A children, you
Act 7:8 So when A son Isaac was
Rom 4:9 We say, "A faith was regarded
4:11 A faith was regarded as God's
9:8 are considered A descendants
2Co 11:22 Are they A descendants?
Gal 3:7 have faith are A descendants
3:29 then you are A descendants
Heb 2:16 So Jesus helps A descendants
7:5 own people, A descendants
Jas 2:22 You see that A faith and what

Abram (64)

Gen 11:26 he became the father of A,
11:27 Terah was the father of A,
11:29 Both A and Nahor married.
11:31 Terah took his son A,
11:31 Sarai, wife of his son A.
12:1 The LORD said to A,
12:4 So A left, as the LORD had told
12:4 A was 75 years old when he
12:5 A set out for Canaan.
12:6 They arrived in Canaan, and A
12:7 LORD appeared to A and said,

Gen 12:9 A kept moving toward the
12:10 A went to Egypt to stay awhile
12:11 A said to his wife Sarai,
12:14 When A arrived in Egypt,
12:16 Everything went well for A
12:18 Then Pharaoh called for A.
12:20 his men orders concerning A.
12:20 They sent A away with his
13:1 A left Egypt with his wife and
13:2 A was very rich because he
13:4 There A worshiped the LORD.
13:5 who had been traveling with A,
13:8 A said to Lot, "Please, let's not
13:12 A lived in Canaan,
13:14 the LORD said to A,
13:18 So A moved his tents and went
14:13 had escaped came and told A
14:14 When A heard that his nephew
14:17 After A came back from
14:19 He blessed A, and said,
14:19 "Blessed is A by God Most
14:20 Then A gave him a tenth of
14:21 The king of Sodom said to A,
14:22 But A said to the king of
14:23 be able to say, 'I made A rich.'
15:1 the LORD spoke his word to A
15:1 He said, "A, don't be afraid.
15:2 A asked, "Almighty LORD,
15:4 spoke his word to A again.
15:5 He took A outside and said,
15:6 Then A believed the LORD,
15:6 faith to be his approval of A.
15:8 A asked, "Almighty LORD,
15:9 He answered A, "Bring me a
15:10 So A brought all these animals
15:11 A drove them away.
15:12 deep darkness — came over A.
15:13 God said to A, "You can know
15:18 the LORD made a promise to A.
16:2 So Sarai said to A,
16:2 A agreed with Sarai.
16:3 After A had lived in Canaan for
16:3 and gave her to her husband A
16:5 So Sarai complained to A,
16:6 A answered Sarai,
16:15 A named him Ishmael.
16:16 A was 86 years old when
17:1 When A was 99 years old,
17:1 He said to A, "I am God
17:3 Immediately, A bowed with his
17:5 longer be A [Exalted Father],
1Ch 1:27 A (that is, Abraham).
Neh 9:7 the God who chose A and took

Abram's (8)

Gen 11:29 The name of A wife was Sarai,
12:17 because of Sarai, A wife
13:7 broke out between A herders
14:12 They also took A nephew Lot
14:13 (These men were A allies.
16:1 Sarai, A wife, was not able to
16:3 A wife Sarai took her Egyptian
16:15 Hagar gave birth to A son.

Abronah (2)

Num 33:34 and set up camp at A.
33:35 They moved from A and set up

Absalom (99)

2Sm 3:3 The third was A, whose mother
13:1 sister of David's son A.
13:20 Her brother A asked her,
13:20 brother A and was depressed.
13:22 A wouldn't speak at all to
13:23 Two years later A had
13:24 A went to the king and said,
13:25 Son," the king answered A.
13:25 Even when A continued to urge
13:25 he did give A his blessing.
13:26 So A said, "If you won't go,
13:27 But when A urged him,
13:28 Then A gave an order to his
13:29 did to Amnon as A had ordered.
13:30 "A has killed all the king's
13:32 A decided to do this the day
13:34 A has fled." When the servant
2Sm 13:37 A, however, fled to Geshur's
13:38 A, having fled to Geshur,
13:39 King David began to long for A
14:1 king was still thinking about A.
14:21 Bring back the young man A."
14:23 brought A back to Jerusalem.
14:24 But the king said, "A should
14:24 So A returned to his house and
14:25 good looks as much as A was.
14:27 A had three sons and one
14:28 A stayed in Jerusalem two full
14:29 So A sent for Joab in order to
14:29 A sent for him a second time,
14:30 So A said to his servants,
14:31 went to A at his home.
14:32 A answered Joab,
14:33 The king then called for A,
14:33 And the king kissed A.
15:1 A acquired a chariot,
15:2 A used to get up early and
15:2 by King David, A would ask,
15:3 A would say, "Your case is
15:5 A would reach out,
15:6 So A stole the hearts of the
15:7 Four years later A said to the
15:10 But A sent his loyal supporters
15:10 'A has become king in
15:11 from Jerusalem went with A.
15:12 While A was offering
15:12 with A kept getting larger.
15:13 the people of Israel are with A."
15:14 none of us will escape from A.
15:19 Go back, and stay with King A.
15:31 those conspiring with A."
15:34 back to the city and say to A,
15:37 as A was entering Jerusalem.
16:8 the kingship to your son A.
16:15 Meanwhile, A and all Israel's
16:16 from Archi's family came to A,
16:17 A asked Hushai. "Why didn't
16:18 Hushai answered A,
16:20 Then A asked Ahithophel,
16:21 Ahithophel told A, "Sleep with
16:22 was put up on the roof for A,
16:23 In those days both David and A
17:1 Ahithophel said to A,
17:4 A and all the leaders of Israel
17:5 A said, "Please call Hushai,
17:6 Hushai arrived, A said to him,
17:7 is no good," Hushai said to A.
17:9 support A have been defeated.'
17:14 A and all the people of Israel
17:14 be defeated in order to ruin A.)
17:15 "Ahithophel advised A and the
17:18 and Ahimaaz and told A.
17:24 to Mahanaim by the time A
17:25 A appointed Amasa to take
17:26 The Israelites and A camped in
18:5 "Treat the young man A gently
18:5 this order regarding A.
18:9 A happened to come
18:10 "I saw A hanging in a tree."
18:12 the young man A for my sake.'
18:15 armorbearers surrounded A,
18:17 They took A, threw him into a
18:18 (While he was still living,) A
18:29 "Is the young man A alright?"
18:32 "Is the young man A alright?"
18:33 "My son A!" he said as he went.
18:33 "My son, my son A!
18:33 A, my son, my son!"
19:1 is crying and mourning for A."
19:4 and cried loudly, "My son A!
19:4 A, my son, my son!"
19:6 be pleased if A were alive
19:9 but now he has fled from A and
19:10 However, A, whom we
20:6 will do us more harm than A.
1Ki 1:5 birth to him after she had A.
2:7 fleeing from your brother A.
2:28 he hadn't supported A.)
1Ch 3:2 The third was A, ⌊born⌋ to

Absalom's (13)

2Sm 13:4 in love with A sister Tamar,"
13:29 A servants did to Amnon as
2Sm 14:30 So A servants set it on fire.
14:30 "A servants have set ⌊your⌋
15:11 nothing ⌊about A plans⌋
17:20 A servants came to the woman
17:20 So A servants returned to
17:21 After A servants left,
18:9 A head became caught in the
18:14 plunged them into A heart
18:18 still called A Monument today.)
2Ch 11:20 Maacah, A granddaughter.
11:21 A granddaughter, more than all

absence (1)

1Co 16:17 They have made up for your a.

absent (2)

Php 2:12 but even more now that I'm a.
Col 2:5 Although I'm a from you

absolute (4)

Mat 20:25 have a power over people
20:25 have a authority over people.
Mar 10:42 have a power over people
10:42 have a authority over people.

abundance (1)

Dtr 33:19 They will be nourished by the a

abundant (2)

Psa 49:6 and brag about their a wealth.
Act 4:33 ⌊God's⌋ a good will was with

abuse (5)

Dtr 28:33 nothing but oppression and a.
Pro 9:7 corrects a mocker receives a.
22:10 Quarreling and a will stop.
Amo 4:1 the poor and a the needy.
1Co 4:12 When people verbally a us,

abused (7)

Jdg 19:25 They had sex with her and a
Job 31:13 "If I have a the rights of my
Isa 23:12 my dear a people Sidon."
53:7 He was a and punished,
Heb 11:37 Some were poor, a,
1Pe 2:23 Christ never verbally a those
2:23 those who verbally a him.

abusive (4)

Psa 35:16 With crude and a mockers,
1Co 5:11 use a language, get drunk,
6:10 who use a language,
2Ti 3:2 and use a language.

acacia (28)

Exo 25:5 dyed red, fine leather, a wood,
25:10 "Make an ark of a wood 45
25:13 Make poles of a wood,
25:23 "Make a table of a wood 36
25:28 Make the poles out of a wood,
26:15 "Make a framework out of a
26:26 "Make crossbars out of a wood:
26:32 four posts of a wood covered
26:37 Make five posts of a wood for
27:1 "Make an altar out of a wood.
27:6 "Make poles out of a wood for
30:1 "Build an altar out of a wood for
30:5 Make the poles out of a wood,
35:7 dyed red, fine leather, a wood,
35:24 Those who had a wood that
36:20 a framework out of a wood
36:31 made crossbars out of a wood.
36:36 They made four posts of a
37:1 Bezalel made the ark out of a
37:4 Then he made poles out of a
37:10 He made the table out of a
37:15 poles were made out of a wood
37:25 He made an altar out of a wood
37:28 He made the poles out of a
38:1 offerings out of a wood 7 ½
38:6 He made the poles out of a
Dtr 10:3 I made an ark out of a wood.
Isa 41:19 I will plant cedar, a,

Accad (1)

Gen 10:10 were Babylon, Erech, A,

accent (1)
Mat 26:73 Your a gives you away!"

accept (82)
Gen 21:30 Abraham answered, "A these
Exo 22:11 The owner must a the oath.
25:2 You must a whatever
25:3 you will a from them:
28:38 the LORD will a their offerings.
34:9 and a us as your own people."
Lev 1:3 so that the LORD will a you.
26:31 I will no longer a the soothing
26:41 hearts and a their guilt,
26:43 They must a their guilt
Num 7:5 "A these gifts from them to use
16:15 "Don't a their offering.
35:31 "Never a a cash payment in
35:32 Don't a a cash payment to
Dtr 20:11 If they a it and open ⌊their
20:12 If they won't a your offer of
29:12 You are ready to a the terms
1Sm 10:4 which you should a from them.
2Sm 24:23 "May the LORD your God a
2Ki 5:15 So please a a present from
5:16 I serve lives, I will not a it."
5:26 How could you a silver,
1Ch 28:9 to serving him, he will a you.
2Ch 15:2 to serving him, he will a you.
Est 4:4 but he refused to a it.
Job 2:10 We a the good that God gives
2:10 Shouldn't we also a the bad?"
22:22 A instruction from his mouth,
42:8 Then I will a his prayer not to
Psa 50:9 ⌊But⌋ I will not a ⌊another⌋
77:7 Will he ever a me?
119:108 Please a the praise I gladly
Pro 4:10 My son, listen and a my words,
19:20 Listen to advice and a
Ecc 5:19 ⌊the ability⌋ to a their lot in life,
Isa 29:24 and those who complain will a
Jer 6:20 I won't a your burnt offerings.
7:28 They did not a discipline.
17:23 would not listen or a discipline.
37:20 and a my plea for mercy.
Eze 16:34 and you don't a payment.
20:40 There I will a you.
20:41 I will a you as if you were a
43:27 Then I will a them,
Hos 8:13 do not a these sacrifices.
Amo 5:22 grain offerings, I won't a them.
Mic 7:3 Judges a bribes.
Zep 3:2 It does not a correction.
3:7 You will a correction!'
Mal 1:8 Would he a it from you?
1:10 "and I won't a your offerings.
1:13 should I a them from you?"
Mat 11:14 are willing to a their message,
18:19 my Father in heaven will a it.
Mar 4:16 they a it at once with joy.
4:20 They hear the word, a it,
Luk 1:17 people so that they will a
Jon 1:11 and his own people didn't a
3:11 Yet, you don't a our message.
5:41 "I don't a praise from humans.
5:43 but you don't a me.
5:43 own authority, you will a him.
5:44 when you a each other's praise
6:60 "What he says is hard to a.
14:17 The world cannot a him,
Act 16:21 customs that we can't a
22:18 The people here won't a your
Rom 15:7 Therefore, a each other in the
15:31 people in Jerusalem will a
1Co 2:14 who isn't spiritual doesn't a
6:7 Why don't you a the fact that
6:7 Why don't you a that you have
2Co 12:10 Therefore, I a weakness,
13:11 A my encouragement.
Eph 4:2 other and lovingly a each other.
Heb 13:17 and a their authority.
Jas 1:21 Humbly a the word that God
1Jn 5:9 We a human testimony.
3Jn 1:7 and they didn't a any help from
1:9 to be in charge, won't a us.
1:10 He also refuses to a the
3Jn 1:10 stop others who want to a them

acceptable (21)
Exo 5:8 fewer bricks will not be a.
30:15 make your lives a to the LORD.
Jdg 6:17 said to him, "If you find me a,
1Sm 18:26 David concluded that it was a
1Ch 6:49 sins to make Israel a to God.
2Ch 36:21 rest and was made a ⌊again⌋.
Psa 19:14 from my heart be a to you,
69:13 come to you at an a time,
Pro 21:3 what is right and fair is more a
Isa 56:7 and their sacrifices will be a
58:5 Is this an a day to the LORD?
60:7 They will be sacrificed as a
Dan 8:14 place will be made a to God."
Mal 3:3 Then they will bring a offerings
Mar 7:19 Jesus declared all foods a.)
Act 10:35 God and does what is right is a
Rom 14:20 All food is a, but it's wrong for a
15:16 nations to God as an a offering,
1Co 7:14 but now they are a to him.
2Co 6:2 Listen, now is God's a time!
Php 4:8 fair, pure, a, or commendable.

acceptance (3)
Rom 11:15 what does Israel's a mean?
1Ti 1:15 and deserves complete a:
4:9 and deserves complete a.

accepted (43)
Gen 4:7 If you do well, won't you be a?
Lev 1:4 The burnt offering will be a to
7:18 You will not be a if any meat
19:5 so that you will be a.
19:7 it is repulsive and will not be a.
22:19 or goats in order to be a.
22:20 it will not be a on your behalf.
22:21 has no defects in order to be a.
22:23 it will not be a for a vow.
22:25 A castrated animal will not be a
22:27 eighth day on it may be a as
23:11 the LORD so that you will be a.
Jdg 13:23 he would not have a our burnt
17:10 The Levite a the offer
1Sm 25:35 Then David a what she brought
2Ch 33:13 and the LORD a his prayer and
33:19 His prayer and how God a it
Est 9:23 So the Jews a as tradition
Job 42:9 And the LORD a Job's prayer.
Psa 119:158 They have not a your promise.
141:2 Let my prayer be a as
141:2 of my hands in prayer be a as
Ecc 9:7 already a what you've done.
Mal 2:14 "Why ⌊aren't our offerings a⌋?"
Luk 4:24 prophet isn't a in his hometown.
10:6 your greeting will be a.
11:37 So Jesus a the invitation.
Jon 3:33 I have a what that person said,
17:8 They have a this message,
Act 2:41 Those who a what Peter said
6:7 number of priests a the faith.
8:14 heard that the Samaritans had a
11:1 not Jewish had a God's word.
Rom 10:3 and they have not a God's way
14:3 God has a those people.
15:7 the same way that Christ a you.
2Co 8:12 ⌊remember⌋ that people are a
8:17 He a my request and eagerly
11:4 the Good News you already a,
1Th 2:13 Instead, you a it for what it
1Ti 5:12 the faith they first a.
Heb 11:2 God a our ancestors because
11:4 since God a his sacrifices.

accepting (2)
2Ki 5:20 Naaman go without a what
Jon 12:48 Those who reject me by not a

accepts (13)
Dtr 27:25 "Whoever a money to kill an
Psa 6:9 The LORD a my prayer.
Pro 10:8 who is truly wise a commands,
17:23 A wicked person secretly a a
Mal 2:13 offerings or a them from you.
Mat 13:20 who⌋ hears the word and a
Luk 10:7 Stay with the family that a you.
Jon 3:32 Yet, no one a what he says.
13:20 Whoever a me accepts the one
13:20 Whoever accepts me a the one
Php 4:18 a sacrifice that God a and with
Heb 12:6 everyone he a as his child."
1Pe 2:5 God a through Jesus Christ.

access (6)
2Ki 25:19 5 men who had a to the king
Est 1:3 provinces who had a to him.
1:14 the Persians and Medes had a
Jer 52:25 7 men who had a to the king
Amo 5:12 deny the needy a to the courts.
Zec 3:7 Then I will give you free a to

accessories (7)
Exo 30:28 for burnt offerings and all its a,
31:9 for burnt offerings and all its a,
35:16 grate, its poles, and all its a,
38:30 its bronze grate and all its a,
39:39 grate, its poles, and all its a,
Num 4:14 Next, they will put all the a
4:14 and bowls — all the altar's a.

accident (1)
1Sm 6:9 happened to us was an a."

accidentally (4)
Num 35:22 "But suppose you a kill
Dtr 19:5 The one who a killed the other
Jos 20:4 who kills someone a can run
20:9 Anyone who a kills someone

Acco (2)
Jos 19:30 Umma, A, Aphek, and Rehob.
Jdg 1:31 those who lived at A or Sidon,

accompanied (12)
Gen 21:22 time Abimelech, a by Phicol,
31:27 with songs a by tambourines
Num 22:22 a by his two servants.
1Sm 18:6 a by tambourines, joyful music,
2Ch 5:13 A by trumpets, cymbals,
23:13 a by musical instruments.
29:27 These songs were a by
29:35 and wine offerings that a
Mar 16:20 the miraculous signs that a it.
Act 1:21 be one of the men who a Jesus
20:4 the province of Asia a Paul.
21:5 with their wives and children a

accompany (5)
1Ch 16:42 that a sacred songs.
Psa 60:10 who refused to a our armies?
108:11 who refused to a our armies?
Mar 3:14 They were to a him and to be
16:17 signs that will a believers:

accomplish (7)
1Sm 26:25 You will a many things and
Ecc 2:2 What does pleasure a?"
Isa 49:4 but I didn't a anything.
55:11 but it will a whatever I want
2Co 8:11 will be matched by what you a
2Th 1:11 help you a every good desire
Heb 7:19 Moses' Teachings couldn't a

accomplished (11)
Psa 71:18 age what your strength has a,
Pro 12:14 to what his hands have a.
Ecc 2:4 I a some great things:
2:11 turned to look at all that I had a
5:6 and destroy what you've a?
Isa 41:4 Who has a this? Who has
Lam 2:17 The LORD has a what he had
4:11 LORD's fury has a his purpose.
2Co 10:16 already a by someone else.
Heb 7:28 forever a everything that God
10:14 With one sacrifice he a the

accomplishments (3)
Ecc 2:11 any of my a⌋ under the sun.
9:1 wise people, along with their a,
Gal 6:4 a without comparing yourself

accordance (1)

Neh 8:18 in **a** with the regulations.

account (29)

Gen 2:4 This is the **a** of heaven and
5:1 This is the written **a** of Adam
6:9 This is the **a** of Noah and his
10:1 This is the **a** of Noah's sons
11:10 This is the **a** of Shem and his
11:27 This is the **a** of Terah and his
25:12 This is the **a** of the
25:19 This is the **a** of Abraham's son
36:1 This is the **a** of Esau (that is,
36:9 This is the **a** of Esau and his
37:2 This is the **a** of Jacob and his
Lev 25:15 take into **a** the number of years
25:15 must sell it to you taking into **a**
25:50 and his buyer must take into **a**
25:52 he must take them into **a**.
Rut 4:18 This is the **a** of Perez and his
1Sm 23:10 and destroy the city on **a** of me.
2Ki 12:15 for the workers to give an **a**,
22:7 don't require them to **a** for the
Est 10:2 might along with the whole **a**
Job 14:3 this and call me to **a** to you.
Ecc 3:15 God will call the past to **a**.
11:9 God will make you give an **a**
Isa 10:3 called to **a** for these things,
Mat 12:36 people will have to give an **a**
18:25 had to be sold to pay off the **a**.
Luk 1:3 good idea to write an orderly **a**
Rom 14:12 All of us will have to give an **a**
1Pe 4:5 They will give an **a** to the one

accountable (2)

Mat 23:35 As a result, you will be held **a**
23:36 living now will be held **a**

accounts (2)

Mat 18:23 to settle **a** with his servants.
25:19 and settled **a** with them.

accumulate (1)

Psa 39:6 They **a** riches without knowing

accumulated (6)

Gen 12:5 all the possessions they had **a**
31:18 the possessions that he had **a**.
31:18 his own livestock that he had **a**
36:6 and everything he had **a** in
46:6 they had **a** in Canaan.
Luk 12:20 who will get what you've **a**?'

accurate (12)

Dtr 25:15 Use **a** and honest weights and
Pro 11:1 but **a** weights are pleasing to
22:21 so that you can give an **a** report
Act 23:15 more **a** information about him.
23:20 more **a** information about him.
1Ti 1:10 else is against **a** teachings.
6:3 doesn't agree with the **a** words
2Ti 1:13 to be the pattern of **a** teachings.
4:3 will not listen to **a** teachings.
Tit 1:9 Then he can use these **a**
2:1 goes along with **a** teachings.
2:8 Speak an **a** message that

accurately (2)

Act 18:25 He **a** taught about Jesus but
18:26 God's way to him more **a**.

accusation (11)

Gen 26:21 So Isaac named it Sitnah [**A**].
Ezr 4:6 which they made an **a** against
Psa 52:4 You love every destructive **a**,
Mat 18:16 with you so that every **a** may
27:37 They placed a written **a** above
Mar 15:26 notice of the **a** against him.
Jon 18:29 "What **a** are you making
Act 22:30 to find out exactly what **a**
25:16 defend himself against their **a**.'
2Co 13:1 Every **a** must be verified by
1Ti 5:19 Don't pay attention to an **a**

accusations (11)

Neh 6:8 "None of your **a** are true.
Job 13:26 write down bitter **a** against me.
Mar 15:4 Look how many **a** they're
Luk 23:10 shouted their **a** against Jesus.
Act 23:29 and found their **a** had to do with
24:8 from him that our **a** are true."
24:9 Jews supported Tertullus' **a**
24:13 even prove their **a** to you.
25:7 They made a lot of serious **a**
25:11 But if their **a** are untrue,
26:7 the Jews are making **a** against

accuse (31)

Num 5:13 were no witnesses to **a** her
Dtr 19:16 a witness takes the stand to **a**
1Ki 21:10 men sit opposite him and **a** him
Job 4:19 How much more will he **a**
27:6 My conscience won't **a** me as
Psa 38:20 and they **a** me because I try to
71:13 Let those who **a** me come to a
103:9 He will not always **a** us of
109:4 In return for my love, they **a** me,
109:20 rewards those who **a** me,
109:29 Let those who **a** me wear
Isa 57:16 I will not **a** you forever.
Jer 18:18 **A** him! Pay no attention to
Dan 6:4 to find something to **a** Daniel
6:5 find anything to **a** this man,
Hos 4:4 "No one should **a** other people
Zec 3:1 at Joshua's right side to **a** him.
Mat 12:10 so that they could **a** him
Mar 3:2 so that they could **a** him
Luk 6:7 they could find a way to **a** him
23:2 They began to **a** Jesus by
23:14 the crimes of which you **a** him.
Jon 5:45 "Don't think that I will **a** you in
Act 24:2 Tertullus began to **a** him.
24:19 in front of you to **a** me if they
24:21 They could **a** me of only one
25:5 with me and **a** him there if
25:18 they didn't **a** him of the crimes I
Rom 2:15 Their thoughts **a** them on one
8:33 Who will **a** those whom God
1Co 1:8 end so that no one can **a** you

accused (12)

Num 35:12 So anyone **a** of murder will not
35:28 **A** murderers must stay in their
35:32 "An **a** murderer who has fled to
Jos 20:6 The **a** person may remain in
1Ki 21:13 these men **a** Naboth of cursing
Eze 16:52 because you **a** your sisters.
Luk 16:1 The manager was **a** of wasting
Act 19:40 we run the risk of being **a**
23:29 He wasn't **a** of anything for
28:18 to let me go because I was **a**
Rom 3:9 We have already **a** everyone
Heb 10:28 If two or three witnesses **a**

Accuser (3)

Job 1:6 Satan the **A** came along with
2:1 Satan the **A** came along with
Zec 3:1 Satan the **A** was standing at

accusers (8)

Jer 18:19 and listen to what my **a** say.
Dan 6:15 Then Daniel's **a** gathered in
Act 23:30 I have also ordered his **a** to
23:35 your case when your **a** arrive."
24:15 for the same thing my **a** do,
24:18 My **a** found me in the temple
25:16 he must face his **a** and have a
25:18 When his **a** stood up,

accuses (4)

Job 4:18 and he **a** his angels of making
Psa 32:2 whom the LORD never **a**
Isa 50:8 Who **a** me? Let him confront
54:17 answer for anyone who **a** you.

accusing (6)

Mat 27:12 priests and leaders were **a** him,
Mar 15:3 The chief priests were **a** him of
Jon 5:45 one you trust, is already **a** you.
Act 24:20 these men who are **a** me
Rev 12:10 The one **a** our brothers and
12:10 the one **a** them day and night in

Achaicus (1)

1Co 16:17 Fortunatus, and **A** came here.

Achan (10)

Jos 7:1 **A**, son of Carmi, grandson of
7:18 and **A** was selected.
7:18 **A** from the tribe of Judah was
7:19 Joshua said to **A**, "Son,
7:20 Then **A** answered Joshua,
7:24 Joshua and all Israel took **A**
7:25 And all Israel stoned **A** and his
7:26 large pile of stones over **A** that
22:20 Didn't **A**, son of Zerah,
22:20 **A** wasn't the only one who died

Achar (1)

1Ch 2:7 Carmi's son was **A**,

Achbor (7)

Gen 36:38 died, Baal Hanan, son of **A**,
36:39 After Baal Hanan, son of **A**,
2Ki 22:12 **A** (son of Micaiah),
22:14 Hilkiah, Ahikam, **A**, Shaphan,
1Ch 1:49 died, Baal Hanan, son of **A**,
Jer 26:22 Elnathan (son of **A**) and other
36:12 Elnathan (son of **A**),

ache (1)

Pro 14:13 while laughing a heart can **a**,

achieve (1)

Isa 55:11 I want and **a** whatever

achieved (2)

Rom 11:7 It means that Israel has never **a**
11:7 God has chosen have **a** it.

achievements (1)

Pro 31:31 and let her **a** praise her at the

achieves (1)

Psa 33:16 No king **a** a victory with a large

Achim (2)

Mat 1:14 Zadok the father of **A**,
1:14 **A** the father of Eliud,

aching (1)

Job 33:19 with endless **a** in their bones

Achish (23)

1Sm 21:10 he came to King **A** of Gath.
21:12 was terrified of King **A** of Gath.
21:14 **A** said to his officers,
27:2 his 600 men to King **A** of Gath,
27:3 his men stayed with **A** in Gath.
27:5 David said to **A**, "If you will
27:6 So **A** immediately gave him
27:9 and clothing and returned to **A**.
27:10 **A** would ask, "Whom did you
27:11 He thought, "They could tell **A**
27:12 And **A** believed David.
27:12 **A** thought, "He has definitely
28:1 Then **A** said to David,
28:2 David responded to **A**,
28:2 "Very well," **A** told David,
29:2 marching in the rear with **A**.
29:3 **A** asked the Philistine officers,
29:4 officers were angry with **A**.
29:6 Then **A** called David and told
29:8 David asked **A**. "What have you
29:9 **A** answered David,
1Ki 2:39 slaves fled to Gath's King **A**,
2:40 his donkey and went to **A**

Achish's (1)

1Sm 21:11 **A** officers asked, "Isn't this

Achor (5)

Jos 7:24 to the valley of **A** [Disaster].
7:26 called the valley of **A** today.
15:7 From the valley of **A**,

Isa 65:10 The **A** Valley will be a resting
Hos 2:15 I will make the valley of **A**

Achsah (5)

Jos 15:16 "I will give my daughter **A** as a
15:17 him his daughter **A** as a wife.
Jdg 1:12 "I will give my daughter **A** as a
1:13 him his daughter **A** as a wife.
1Ch 2:49 Caleb's daughter was **A**.

Achshaph (3)

Jos 11:1 to the kings of Shimron and **A**.
12:20 Shimron Meron, the king of **A**,
19:25 Helkath, Hali, Beten, **A**,

Achzib (4)

Jos 15:44 Keilah, **A**, and Mareshah.
19:29 territory includes Meheleb, **A**,
Jdg 1:31 **A**, Helbah, Aphek, or Rehob.
Mic 1:14 The town of **A** will betray the

acknowledge (23)

Dtr 33:9 They didn't **a** their own
1Sm 11:14 and there **a** ⌊Saul's⌋ kingship."
Psa 68:34 **A** the power of God.
83:18 so that they must **a** you.
87:4 to the list of those who **a** me.
Pro 3:6 In all your ways **a** him,
Isa 26:13 but we **a** only you.
29:23 they will **a** my name as holy.
33:13 **A** my might, you people who
48:1 You **a** the God of Israel,
63:7 I will **a** the LORD's acts of
Jer 2:23 **A** what you've done.
9:6 They refuse to **a** me,"
Dan 11:39 honors to those who **a** him,
Hos 8:2 'We **a** you as our God.'
Mat 10:32 "So I will **a** in front of my
Luk 12:8 that the Son of Man will **a**
Act 2:23 who don't **a** Moses' Teachings,
Rom 1:28 it was worthless to **a** God,
1Co 14:37 gifted must **a** that what
2Th 1:8 on those who refuse to **a** God
Heb 13:15 that is, words that **a** him.
Rev 3:5 I will **a** them in the presence of

acknowledged (6)

Mar 10:42 "You know that the **a** rulers of
Jon 9:22 anyone who **a** that Jesus was
Act 26:1 Paul **a** King Agrippa and then
Gal 2:9 people) **a** that God had
1Ti 3:16 us our reverence for God is **a**
Heb 11:13 They **a** that they were living as

acknowledges (3)

Mat 10:32 heaven that person who **a** me
Luk 12:8 angels every person who **a** him
1Jn 2:23 The person who **a** the Son also

acquainted (3)

Job 24:13 They are not **a** with its ways.
Act 19:15 and I'm **a** with Paul,
Gal 1:18 personally **a** with Cephas.

acquire (9)

Gen 34:10 and **a** property here."
Lev 25:46 You may **a** them for yourselves
Pro 1:3 to **a** the discipline of wise
4:5 **A** wisdom. Acquire
4:5 **A** understanding. Do not forget.
4:7 of wisdom is to **a** wisdom.
4:7 **A** understanding with all that
8:12 I **a** knowledge and foresight.
Isa 5:8 you who **a** house after house

acquired (5)

Gen 12:5 servants they had **a** in Haran.
47:27 They **a** property there and had
2Sm 15:1 Absalom **a** a chariot,
Pro 8:9 those who have **a** knowledge.
Act 20:28 for God's church which he **a**

acquires (1)

Pro 18:15 understanding **a** knowledge.

acquit (1)

Isa 53:11 My righteous servant will **a**

acquitted (1)

Job 11:2 a good public speaker be **a**?

act (102)

Gen 34:7 **a** against Israel's family
Exo 22:25 among you — never **a** like
Num 5:13 and she wasn't caught in the **a**.
33:4 LORD had killed in a mighty **a**
Dtr 22:21 such a godless **a** in Israel:
Jos 22:16 'What is this faithless **a** you
22:20 Didn't Achan, son of Zerah, **a**
22:22 If our **a** is rebellious or
22:31 commit an unfaithful **a** against
Jdg 15:7 "If that's how you're going to **a**,
1Sm 4:9 Philistines, and **a** like men,
4:9 **A** like men and fight."
14:6 Maybe the LORD will **a** on our
20:30 ⌊You **a**⌋ as if you are your
2Sm 5:24 **a** immediately because the
7:19 you consider to be a small **a**,
13:5 **A** sick, and when your father
13:12 Don't do this godless **a**!
14:2 "Please **a** like a mourner,
14:2 but **a** like a woman who has
2Ki 5:13 you to do some extraordinary **a**,
1Ch 17:17 you consider to be a small **a**,
Psa 2:10 Now, you kings, **a** wisely.
31:23 in full those who **a** arrogantly.
37:5 and he will **a** ⌊on your behalf⌋.
64:9 "This is an **a** of God!"
119:126 It is time for you to **a**,
Pro 5:2 so that you may **a** with
12:9 a slave than to **a** important
Ecc 8:5 time and the right way ⌊to **a**⌋.
8:6 time and a right way ⌊to **a**⌋
Isa 19:16 Egyptians will **a** like women.
32:8 But honorable people **a**
32:17 Then an **a** of righteousness
58:2 They **a** as if they were a nation
Jer 6:13 to priests, **a** deceitfully.
7:3 Change the way you live and **a**,
7:5 change the way you live and **a**
8:10 to priests, **a** deceitfully.
9:24 **a** out of love, righteousness,
10:23 I know that the way humans **a**
13:27 I have seen you **a** like a
Eze 14:6 the way you think and **a**!
18:30 the way you think and **a**.
18:32 the way you think and **a**!"
33:11 the way you think and **a**!
44:24 the priests must **a** as judges
Dan 4:37 those who **a** arrogantly.
9:19 Pay attention, and **a**.
11:23 he will **a** deceitfully and rise to
Hos 4:15 "Israel, you **a** like a prostitute.
4:18 Their rulers dearly love to **a**
11:9 I will not **a** on my burning
12:2 of the way their people **a**.
Zep 3:11 never again will you **a** proud
Mal 3:3 He will **a** like a refiner and a
4:3 because on the day I **a** they
Mat 3:2 the way you think and **a**,
3:8 the way you think and **a**.
3:11 the way you think and **a**.
4:17 the way you think and **a**,
Mar 1:15 the way you think and **a**,
6:12 the way they think and **a**.
Luk 3:8 the way you think and **a**.
5:32 the way they think and **a**,
13:3 the way you think and **a**,
13:5 the way you think and **a**,
16:30 the way they think and **a**.'
20:20 The spies were to **a** like
24:47 they think and **a** so that their
Jon 8:4 this woman in the **a** of adultery.
Act 2:38 the way you think and **a**,
3:19 the way you think and **a**,
4:25 do the nations **a** arrogantly?
5:31 the way they think and **a**,
11:18 the way they think and **a**
17:30 the way they think and **a**.
20:21 the way they think and **a**
Rom 2:4 the way you think and **a**?
2:5 the way you think and **a**,
3:24 God's approval freely by an **a**
14:23 because he didn't **a** in faith.
2Co 7:9 the way you think and **a**.
7:10 the way they think and **a**
9:2 moved most of them ⌊to **a**⌋.
9:13 God through this genuine **a**
10:6 We are ready to punish every **a**
12:21 the way they think and **a** about
Gal 5:26 We can't allow ourselves to **a**
Eph 2:8 faith as an **a** of kindness.
Php 2:3 Don't **a** out of selfish ambition
Col 4:5 Be wise in the way you **a**
2Ti 2:25 the way they think and **a**
Heb 2:2 and every violation and **a** of
Jas 2:12 Talk and **a** as people who are
2Pe 3:9 the way they think and **a**.
Rev 2:5 the way you think and **a**,
2:16 the way you think and **a**,
3:3 the way you think and **a**.
3:19 the way you think and **a**.
13:5 authority to **a** for 42 months.
16:9 the way they think and **a**

acted (41)

Gen 42:7 But he **a** as if he didn't know
Exo 33:4 they **a** as if someone had died.
Jdg 2:19 ways and **a** more corruptly than
9:16 "If you **a** with sincerity and
1Sm 14:48 He **a** forcefully and defeated
21:13 and **a** insane ⌊as long
26:21 I've **a** like a fool and made a
2Sm 13:6 Amnon lay down and **a** sick,
24:10 I have **a** very foolishly."
1Ch 21:8 I have **a** very foolishly."
2Ch 16:9 You **a** foolishly in this matter.
Neh 9:16 own ancestors — **a** arrogantly.
Isa 48:3 Suddenly, I **a**, and they
48:8 I know that you've **a** very
Jer 2:20 You lay down and **a** like a
3:1 "You have **a** like a prostitute
3:6 and she **a** like a prostitute
3:8 She also **a** like a prostitute.
31:19 the way I thought and **a**.
Eze 16:16 This is where you **a** like a
20:9 But I **a** so that my name would
20:14 But I **a** so that my name would
23:5 Oholah **a** like a prostitute,
23:13 Both sisters **a** the same way.
23:31 You've **a** the same way as your
35:11 you **a** hatefully toward them.
Dan 7:7 It **a** differently from all the other
9:5 wrong, **a** wickedly, rebelled,
Hos 1:2 The people in this land have **a**
2:5 Their mother **a** like a prostitute.
Oba 1:11 You **a** like one of them.
Mat 11:20 the way they thought and **a**.
11:21 they thought and **a** long ago
12:41 and **a** when Jonah spoke
Luk 10:13 the way they thought and **a**.
11:32 and **a** when Jonah spoke
24:28 Jesus **a** as if he were going
Act 26:20 the way they thought and **a**
Gal 3:20 and God has **a** on his own.
1Ti 1:13 and **a** arrogantly toward him.
1:13 mercy because I **a** ignorantly

acting (15)

Gen 38:24 Tamar has been **a** like
Exo 23:21 He is **a** on my authority.
Jdg 9:19 So if you are now **a** with
2Sm 12:21 "Why are you **a** this way?
1Ki 1:13 Why is Adonijah **a** as king?'
Psa 37:35 seen a wicked person ⌊**a** like⌋
Isa 19:13 leaders of Zoan are **a** foolishly.
Jer 3:9 wasn't concerned about **a** like
Eze 43:7 holy name by **a** like prostitutes,
43:9 Now they must stop **a** like
Hos 2:2 Tell her to stop **a** like a
5:3 you are **a** like a prostitute,
6:10 Ephraim is **a** like a prostitute,
1Co 3:4 you **a** like ⌊sinful⌋ humans?
Rev 9:20 way they were thinking and **a**.

action (14)

1Ki 8:32 take a, and make a decision.
8:39 Forgive ⌊them⌋, and take a.
2Ch 6:23 take a, and make a decision.
Ezr 10:4 It's your duty to take a.
10:4 so be strong and take a."
Eze 8:18 So I will take a because I'm
Dan 11:28 He will take a and return to his
11:30 promise, he will return, take a,
11:32 God will be strong and take a.
Hab 3:9 You get your bow ready for a,
Luk 12:35 "Be ready for a, and have your
Act 5:17 So they took a
5:38 that if the plan they put into a is
1Pe 1:13 must be clear and ready for a.

actions (22)

Jdg 8:1 strongly protested Gideon's a.
1Sm 2:3 and he weighs ⌊our⌋ a.
2Sm 11:27 considered David's a evil.
1Ki 1:7 Adonijah had discussed his a
16:7 Baasha's a, which made the
2Ch 15:7 Your a will be rewarded."
Est 3:4 to see if Mordecai's a would
Psa 77:12 I will reflect on all your a and
Pro 5:21 and he surveys all his a.
20:11 makes himself known by his a,
Ecc 5:7 pointless a, and empty words,
Isa 43:25 to wipe away your rebellious a
66:18 Because of their a and their
Jer 17:10 him for the results of his a.
Mat 11:19 is proved right by its a."
Luk 16:15 "You try to justify your a in front
Jon 3:19 light because their a were evil.
3:20 want their a to be exposed.
Gal 6:4 you must examine your own a.
Php 2:13 desires and a that please him.
Tit 3:11 condemned by their own a.
1Jn 3:18 we must show love through a

active (4)

Num 8:25 they must retire from a service
Act 1:17 and had been given an a role
1Th 1:3 never forget that your faith is a,
Heb 4:12 God's word is living and a.

activities (4)

Act 26:12 "I was carrying out these a
Rom 8:13 nature to put to death the evil a
2Ti 2:4 get mixed up in non-military a.
Jud 1:7 and engaged in homosexual a.

activity (2)

Ecc 3:1 time for every a under heaven:
3:17 is a specific time for every a

acts (69)

Exo 6:6 and with mighty a of judgment.
Lev 16:16 they committed rebellious a.
16:21 all the rebellious a,
Dtr 3:24 the mighty a you have done?
Jos 24:19 your rebellious a and sins.
1Ki 11:41 Aren't the rest of Solomon's a—
15:23 about Asa — all his heroic a,
16:5 did and his heroic a — written
16:27 did and his heroic a — written
22:45 Jehoshaphat — the heroic a
2Ki 10:34 all his heroic a — written in the
13:8 his heroic a — written in the
13:12 his heroic a when he fought
14:15 his heroic a when he fought
14:28 his heroic a when he fought,
20:20 all his heroic a and how he
2Ch 9:29 Aren't the rest of Solomon's a
35:27 and his a from first to last — are
Est 10:2 All his a of power and might
Job 33:9 rebellious a ⌊against God⌋.
39:16 It a harshly toward its young as
Psa 14:2 there is anyone who a wisely,
39:8 me from all my rebellious a.
51:1 wipe out my rebellious a.
53:2 there is anyone who a wisely,
65:3 who forgives our rebellious a.
65:5 us with awe-inspiring a ⌊done⌋
73:6 like a necklace and a
103:12 our rebellious a from himself.
106:7 your numerous a of mercy,
119:156 Your a of compassion are
145:4 will talk about your mighty a.
150:2 Praise him for his mighty a.
Pro 13:16 person a with knowledge,
14:17 person a stupidly,
14:35 with a servant who a wisely,
14:35 with one who a shamefully.
17:2 over a son who a shamefully,
Ecc 4:1 I turned to look at all the a
Isa 44:22 I made your rebellious a
46:8 Recall your rebellious a.
53:5 wounded for our rebellious a.
59:6 have committed a of violence.
59:12 aware of our many rebellious a.
59:12 Our rebellious a are with us.
63:7 the LORD's a of mercy,
64:6 and all our righteous a are like
Jer 29:26 put any lunatic who a like
29:27 he a like a prophet among you.
Lam 1:5 suffer for its many rebellious a.
1:14 My rebellious a are a heavy
1:22 because of all my rebellious a.
Eze 16:22 and all your a of prostitution,
16:25 increased your a of prostitution.
16:29 So you increased your a of
23:43 from her a of adultery.'
37:23 or with their rebellious a.
Hos 2:2 She no longer a like my wife.
Amo 3:10 destructive a don't know how
Jnh 3:8 ways and your a of violence.
Mic 1:13 The rebellious a of Israel are
6:7 because of my rebellious a?
Zep 3:11 your rebellious a against me.
Luk 15:7 he thinks and a than over 99
15:10 the way he thinks and a."
17:3 the way he thinks and a,
Rom 1:27 commit indecent a with men,
Heb 2:4 things, other powerful a,
Rev 2:21 the way she thinks and a,

Adadah (1)

Jos 15:22 Kinah, Dimonah, A,

Adah (8)

Gen 4:19 one named A and the other
4:20 A gave birth to Jabal.
4:23 "A and Zillah, listen to me!
36:2 A, daughter of Elon the Hittite;
36:4 A gave birth to Eliphaz for
36:10 son of Esau's wife A,
36:12 the grandsons of Esau's wife A.
36:16 They were the grandsons of A.

Adaiah (9)

2Ki 22:1 daughter of A from Bozkath.
1Ch 6:41 who was the son of A,
8:21 A, Beraiah, and Shimrath.
9:12 Also from the priests were A
2Ch 23:1 son of A, and Elishaphat,
Ezr 10:29 Malluch, A, Jashub, Sheal,
10:39 Shelemiah, Nathan, A,
Neh 11:5 who was the son of A,
11:12 Also, A worked in the temple.

Adaiah's (1)

Neh 11:13 A relatives, the heads of the

Adalia (1)

Est 9:8 Poratha, A, Aridatha,

Adam (29)

Gen 3:20 A named his wife Eve [Life]
4:1 A made love to his wife Eve.
4:25 A made love to his wife again.
5:1 This is the written account of A
5:3 When A was 130 years old,
5:4 After A became the father of
5:5 A lived a total of 930 years;
11:5 of A were building.
Dtr 32:8 divided the descendants of A,
Jos 3:16 as the city of A near Zarethan.
1Ch 1:1 A, Seth, Enosh,
Job 25:6 a descendant of A — who is
31:33 my disobedience like A
35:8 only the descendants of A.
Psa 90:3 descendants of A."
115:16 earth to the descendants of A.
145:11 of A about your might
Jer 32:19 the descendants of A do.
Hos 6:7 "Like A, you rejected the
Luk 3:38 of Seth, son of A, son of God.
Rom 5:14 death ruled from the time of A
5:14 in the same way A did when
5:14 A is an image of the one who
1Co 15:22 everyone dies because of A,
15:45 A, became a living being."
15:45 The last A became a life-giving
1Ti 2:13 After all, A was formed first,
2:14 A was not deceived.
Jud 1:14 the seventh generation after A,

Adam's (18)

Psa 11:4 They examine A descendants
12:1 from among A descendants
12:8 among A descendants
14:2 from heaven on A descendants
21:10 from among A descendants
31:19 A descendants watch as you
33:13 He sees all of A descendants
36:7 that A descendants take refuge
45:2 handsome of A descendants.
53:2 from heaven on A descendants
58:1 Do you judge A descendants
66:5 deeds for A descendants
89:47 you created A descendants
107:8 his miracles for A descendants
107:15 his miracles for A descendants
107:21 his miracles for A descendants
107:31 his miracles for A descendants
Rom 5:15 ⌊God's⌋ gift and ⌊A⌋ failure.

Adamah (2)

Jos 19:36 A, Ramah, Hazor,
Isa 15:9 Moab and the survivors from A.

Adami Nekeb (1)

Jos 19:33 It continues to A, Jabneel,

Adar (9)

Ezr 6:15 the third day of the month of A
Est 3:7 until A, the twelfth month.
3:13 twelfth month, the month of A.
8:12 on the thirteenth day of A,
9:1 On the thirteenth day of A,
9:15 day of the month of A
9:17 day of the month of A.
9:19 day of the month of A
9:21 of the month of A as days they

Adbeel (2)

Gen 25:13 firstborn), Kedar, A, Mibsam,
1Ch 1:29 then Kedar, A, Mibsam,

add (32)

Gen 30:40 for himself and did not a them
32:20 And be sure to a, 'Jacob is
Lev 5:11 Never put olive oil on it or a
22:14 the priest and a one-fifth more
27:31 you must a one-fifth more to it.
Num 5:7 you did wrong, a one-fifth to it,
Dtr 4:2 Never a anything to what I
12:32 Never a anything to it or take
19:9 If this happens, you may a
2Sm 15:4 He would a, "I wish someone
1Ki 12:11 burden on you, I will a to it.
12:14 your burden heavy, I will a to it.
1Ch 22:14 and you may a to them.
2Ch 10:11 burden on you, I will a to it.
10:14 your burden heavy, I will a to it.
28:13 Do you intend to a to all our
Psa 61:6 A days upon days to the life of
87:4 ⌊The LORD says,⌋ "I will a
Pro 30:6 Do not a to his words,
Jer 7:21 A your burnt offerings to your
Amo 6:10 "Hush," he will a. "We shouldn't
Mat 6:27 "Can any of you a a single hour
Luk 12:25 "Can any of you a an hour to
Gal 2:6 as important people didn't a
3:15 a person's will or a conditions
2Pe 1:5 make every effort to a integrity

2Pe 1:5 and to integrity **a** knowledge;
1:6 to knowledge **a** self-control;
1:6 to self-control **a** endurance;
1:6 to endurance **a** godliness;
1:7 godliness **a** Christian affection;
1:7 and to Christian affection **a**

Addan (2)

Ezr 2:59 Harsha, Cherub, **A**, and Immer,
Neh 7:61 Harsha, Cherub, **A**, and Immer,

Addar (2)

Jos 15:3 up to **A**, around to Karka,
1Ch 8:3 Bela's sons were **A**,

added (50)

Exo 5:5 Then Pharaoh **a**, "Look how
32:9 The LORD **a**, "I've seen these
Num 1:44 own family, **a** up these totals.
26:63 Moses and the priest Eleazar **a**
36:3 from that of our ancestors and **a**
36:4 their land will be **a** to that of the
Jos 15:47 **A** to this were Ashdod and
Jdg 18:4 Micah had done for him and **a**,
1Sm 12:19 We have **a** ⌊another⌋ evil thing
17:10 The Philistine **a**, "I challenge
17:37 David **a**, "The LORD,
20:38 Jonathan **a**, "Quick! Hurry up!
21:3 ⌊David **a**,⌋ "Now, what do you
26:10 as the LORD lives," David **a**,
26:18 he **a**. "What have I done? What
1Ki 2:14 Then he **a**, "I have a matter ⌊to
22:19 Micaiah **a**, "Then hear the word
2Ki 20:19 He **a**, "Isn't it enough if there is
22:18 ⌊Huldah **a**,⌋ "But tell Judah's
2Ch 2:12 Huram **a**, "May the LORD God
18:18 Micaiah **a**, "Then hear the word
34:26 ⌊Huldah **a**,⌋ "Tell Judah's king
Ezr 10:10 now you have **a** to Israel's guilt.
Neh 5:9 I **a**, "What you're doing is
Pro 9:11 and years will be **a** to your life.
Ecc 3:14 Nothing can be **a** to it,
7:27 I **a** one thing to another in order
Isa 30:16 You've **a**, "We'll ride on fast
39:8 He **a**, "Just let there be peace
Jer 26:4 The LORD **a**, "Also say to
36:32 **a** many similar messages.
44:19 The women **a**, "When we
45:3 The LORD has **a** grief to my
Zec 5:6 Then he **a**, "This is what the
Mat 28:14 ⌊They **a**,⌋ "If the governor
Mar 2:27 Then he **a**, "The day of
4:9 He **a**, "Let the person who has
7:9 He **a**, "You have no trouble
Luk 3:20 So Herod **a** one more evil to all
4:24 Then Jesus **a**, "I can guarantee
6:5 Then he **a**, "The Son of Man
18:6 The Lord **a**, "Pay attention to
Jon 6:65 So he **a**, "That is why I told
Act 1:20 someone must be **a** to our
2:41 people were **a** ⌊to the group⌋.
2:47 and they were **a** to the group.
12:17 He **a**, "Tell James and the
19:19 They **a** up the cost of these
Rom 5:20 Rules were **a** to increase the
Gal 3:19 They were **a** to identify what

Addi (1)

Luk 3:28 son of Melchi, son of **A**,

addicted (2)

1Ti 3:8 be two-faced or **a** to alcohol.
Tit 2:3 Tell them not to be gossips or **a**

adding (1)

Rom 2:5 you are **a** to the anger that God

additional (3)

Jos 15:42 An **a** nine cities with their
Mat 25:20 brought the **a** ten thousand.
Act 15:28 not to place any **a** burdens

addressed (4)

Neh 2:7 let me have letters **a** to the
2:8 let me have a letter **a** to Asaph,
Dan 3:9 They **a** King Nebuchadnezzar,
Act 14:12 They **a** Barnabas as Zeus and

adds (6)

Job 34:37 He **a** disobedience to his sin.
Pro 10:22 and hard work **a** nothing to it.
19:4 Wealth **a** many friends,
Isa 3:16 The LORD **a**, "The women of
Heb 10:17 Then he **a**, "I will no longer
Rev 22:18 If anyone **a** anything to this,

Adiel (3)

1Ch 4:36 **A**, Jesimiel, Benaiah, and
9:12 and Maasai (son of **A**,
27:25 son of **A** for the goods in the

Adin (4)

Ezr 2:15 of **A**: 454
8:6 from the family of **A**:
Neh 7:20 of **A**: 655
10:16 Adonijah, Bigvai, **A**,

Adina (1)

1Ch 11:42 **A** (son of Shiza) from the tribe

Adithaim (1)

Jos 15:36 Shaaraim, **A**, Gederah,

adjourned (1)

Act 24:22 rather well, so he **a** the trial.

adjusted (1)

Lev 25:50 His sale price will be **a** based

Adlai (1)

1Ch 27:29 the valleys: Shaphat, son of **A**

Admah (5)

Gen 10:19 toward Sodom, Gomorrah, **A**,
14:2 of Gomorrah, King Shinab of **A**,
14:8 **A**, Zeboiim, and Bela (that is,
Dtr 29:23 Gomorrah, **A**, and Zeboiim,
Hos 11:8 How can I make you like **A**?

Admatha (1)

Est 1:14 **A**, Tarshish, Meres, Marsena,

Admin (1)

Luk 3:33 son of Amminadab, son of **A**,

administer (3)

Num 5:21 "Then the priest will **a** the oath
2Ch 19:8 family heads from Israel to **a**
Zec 7:9 of Armies says: **A** real justice,

administering (4)

Lev 19:15 be corrupt when **a** justice.
19:35 "Don't be corrupt when **a**
2Co 8:19 We are **a** it in a way that brings
8:20 we are **a** this generous gift.

administrator (1)

Luk 8:3 husband Chusa was Herod's **a**;

administrators (3)

Ezr 7:25 will appoint judges and **a**
Jer 37:2 But Zedekiah, his **a**,
37:18 you, your **a**, or these people?

admired (1)

2Th 1:10 holy people and **a** by all who

admit (11)

1Sm 29:9 Achish answered David, "I **a**
Job 27:5 It's unthinkable for me to **a** that
Psa 51:3 I **a** that I am rebellious.
Isa 48:6 Won't you **a** it? From now on I
Jer 3:13 **A** that you've done wrong!
Hos 5:15 place until they **a** that they are
Jon 12:42 However, they wouldn't **a** it
Act 24:14 But I'll **a** to you that I'm a
2Co 11:21 I'm ashamed to **a** it,
Gal 2:18 I **a** that I was wrong to tear it
Jas 5:16 So **a** your sins to each other,

admitted (3)

Neh 13:1 ever be **a** into God's assembly.
Luk 7:29 They **a** that God was right by
Act 19:18 Many believers openly **a** their

Adna (2)

Ezr 10:30 **A**, Chelal, Benaiah, Maaseiah,
Neh 12:15 from Harim, **A**; from Meraioth,

Adnah (2)

1Ch 12:20 **A**, Jozabad, Jediael, Michael,
2Ch 17:14 **A** (with 300,000 fighting

Adoni Bezek (6)

Jdg 1:5 they also caught up with **A**.
1:6 **A** fled. Judah's troops chased
1:7 **A** said, "Seventy kings who
1:7 troops brought **A** to Jerusalem,

Adonijah (27)

2Sm 3:4 The fourth was **A**, The fifth was
1Ki 1:5 **A**, son of Haggith, was very
1:5 **A** was boasting that he was
1:7 But **A** had discussed his
1:8 fighting men did not join **A**.
1:9 **A** sacrificed sheep,
1:11 "Haven't you heard that **A**,
1:13 Why is **A** acting as king?'
1:18 **A** has become king,
1:24 you must have said that **A** will
1:25 'Long live King **A**!'
1:41 **A** and all his guests heard this
1:42 "Come in," **A** said.
1:43 Jonathan answered **A**.
1:50 **A** was afraid of Solomon.
1:51 "**A** is afraid of you,
1:53 **A** bowed down in front of King
2:13 Then **A**, son of Haggith,
2:21 to your brother **A** as his wife."
2:22 from Shunem be given to **A**?
2:23 "May God strike me dead if **A**
2:24 that **A** will be put to death
2:25 Benaiah attacked and killed **A**.
2:28 (He had supported **A**,
1Ch 3:2 The fourth was **A**,
2Ch 17:8 **A**, Tobijah, Tob Adonijah,
Neh 10:16 **A**, Bigvai, Adin,

Adonijah's (2)

1Ki 1:49 **A** guests were frightened,
2:19 to talk to him on **A** behalf.

Adonikam (3)

Ezr 2:13 of **A**: 666
8:13 from the family of **A**:
Neh 7:18 of **A**: 667

Adoniram (2)

1Ki 4:6 **A**, son of Abda, was in charge
5:14 **A** was in charge of forced labor.

Adoni Zedek (2)

Jos 10:1 King **A** of Jerusalem heard
10:3 King **A** of Jerusalem sent

adopt (2)

Isa 44:5 and he will **a** the name of
Eph 1:5 he had already decided to **a**

adopted (9)

Gen 50:23 were **a** by Joseph at birth.
1Ki 9:9 They **a** other gods,
2Ch 7:22 They **a** other gods,
Est 2:7 Mordecai **a** her as his own
2:15 Mordecai had **a** her as his own
Act 7:21 Pharaoh's daughter **a** him and
Rom 8:15 of God's **a** children by which
9:4 are Israelites, God's **a** children.
Gal 4:5 we would be **a** as his children.

adoption (1)

Rom 8:23 as we eagerly wait for our **a**,

Adoraim (1)

2Ch 11:9 **A**, Lachish, Azekah,

Adoram (2)

2Sm 20:24 **A** was in charge of forced labor.

1Ki 12:18 Rehoboam sent **A** to Israel.

adorn (1)
Psa 144:12 be like stately columns that **a**

Adrammelech (3)
2Ki 17:31 for **A** and Anammelech,
19:37 **A** and Sharezer assassinated
Isa 37:38 **A** and Sharezer, his sons,

Adramyttium (1)
Act 27:2 sail on a ship from the city of **A**.

Adriel (2)
1Sm 18:19 was married to **A** from Meholah.
2Sm 21:8 daughter) gave birth to for **A**,

Adullam (10)
Gen 38:1 a man from **A** whose name was
38:12 he and his friend Hirah from **A**
Jos 12:15 king of Libnah, the king of **A**,
15:35 Jarmuth, **A**, Socoh, Azekah,
1Sm 22:1 place and fled to the cave at **A**.
2Sm 23:13 to David at the cave of **A** when
1Ch 11:15 rock at the cave of **A** when
2Ch 11:7 Beth Zur, Soco, **A**,
Neh 11:30 and **A** and their villages,
Mic 1:15 glory of Israel will come to **A**.

adult (4)
Joe 1:4 leave, **a** locusts will eat.
1:4 What **a** locusts leave,
2:25 mature locusts, the **a** locusts,
1Co 13:11 When I became an **a**,

adulterer (1)
Rom 7:3 she will be called an **a**.

adulterers (5)
Job 24:15 **A** watch for twilight.
Isa 57:3 of **a** and prostitutes!
Jer 9:2 They are all **a**, a mob of
23:10 The land is filled with **a**.
Mal 3:5 sorcerers, **a**, lying witnesses,

adulterous (9)
Pro 2:16 save you from an **a** woman,
5:3 The lips of an **a** woman drip
5:20 be intoxicated with an **a**
6:33 An **a** man will find disease and
7:5 yourself from an **a** woman,
22:14 The mouth of an **a** woman is a
Eze 6:9 I was hurt by their **a** hearts,
16:32 You are an **a** wife who prefers
2Pe 2:14 looking for an **a** woman.

adultery (51)
Exo 20:14 "Never commit **a**.
Lev 20:10 "If a man commits **a** with
20:10 must be put to death for their **a**.
Dtr 5:18 "Never commit **a**.
Psa 50:18 with people who commit **a**.
Pro 6:32 Whoever commits **a** with a
30:20 of a woman who commits **a**:
Jer 3:8 Israel away because of her **a**
3:9 the land and committed **a**
5:7 They committed **a**,
7:9 You steal, murder, commit **a**,
13:27 I have seen you commit **a** and
23:14 of Jerusalem commit **a**
29:23 They committed **a** with their
Eze 16:17 you committed **a** with them.
23:37 They have committed **a**.
23:37 They commit **a** with their idols.
23:43 acts of **a**.' Yet, men continued
23:45 will punish these women for **a**
23:45 women have committed **a**
Hos 3:1 by others and has committed **a**.
4:2 murdering, stealing, and **a**.
4:12 They commit **a** by giving
4:13 daughters-in-law commit **a**.
4:14 when they commit **a**.
7:4 They all commit **a**.
Mat 5:27 it was said, 'Never commit **a**.'
5:28 committed **a** in his heart.
5:32 though she has committed **a**.
5:32 as though he has committed **a**.
15:19 Evil thoughts, murder, **a**,
19:9 is committing **a** if
19:18 Never commit **a**. Never steal.
Mar 7:22 **a**, greed, wickedness,
10:11 woman is committing **a**.
10:12 she is committing **a**."
10:19 Never commit **a**. Never steal.
Luk 16:18 woman is committing **a**.
16:18 in this way is committing **a**.
18:11 I haven't committed **a**.
18:20 Never commit **a**. Never murder.
Jon 8:3 had been caught committing **a**.
8:4 this woman in the act of **a**.
Rom 2:22 you tell others not to commit **a**,
2:22 are you committing **a**?
7:3 so she is not committing **a** if
13:9 "Never commit **a**;
1Co 6:9 those who commit **a**,
Heb 13:4 those who commit **a**.
Jas 2:11 "Never commit **a**," is the same
2:11 If you do not commit **a** but you

adults (1)
Act 8:10 Everyone from children to **a**

Adummim (2)
Jos 15:7 region that faces the **A** Pass,
18:17 the region opposite the **A** Pass.

advance (3)
Num 33:52 As you **a**, force out all the
Jer 46:3 shields ready; **a** into battle.
Act 2:23 that God had determined in **a**.

advanced (3)
Jdg 20:24 troops **a** against Benjamin.
2Sm 10:13 Then Joab and his troops **a** to
1Ch 19:14 Then Joab and his troops **a** to

advancing (1)
Mat 11:12 heaven has been forcefully **a**,

advantage (27)
Exo 22:22 "Never take **a** of any widow or
Lev 25:14 don't take **a** of him.
25:17 Never take **a** of each other.
Neh 5:15 the governors' servants took **a**
Job 24:21 These men take **a** of childless
Pro 16:26 appetite works to his **a**,
Ecc 2:13 But I saw that wisdom has an **a**
2:13 light has an **a** over darkness.
2:15 then what is the **a** in being
3:19 have no **a** over animals.
5:9 Yet, a king is an **a** for a country
5:16 What **a** do they gain from
6:8 What **a** does a wise person
6:8 What **a** does a poor person
6:11 What **a** do mortals gain from
7:11 It is an **a** to everyone who sees
7:12 but the **a** of wisdom is that it
10:11 then there is no **a** in being a
Act 7:19 shrewd in the way he took **a**
Rom 3:1 Is there any **a**, then, in being a
3:9 Do we have any **a**?
2Co 12:17 Did I take **a** of you through any
12:18 Did Titus take **a** of you?
Php 2:6 did not take **a** of this equality.
1Th 4:6 No one should take **a** of or
Heb 13:17 would not be to your **a**.)
Jud 1:16 in order to take **a** of them.

advantages (1)
Rom 3:2 There are all kinds of **a**.

adversaries (2)
Psa 89:42 and made all of his **a** rejoice.
106:11 Water covered their **a**.

advice (80)
Exo 18:19 and I'll give you some **a**.
Num 24:14 I'll give you some **a**.
31:16 ones who followed Balaam's **a**
Jdg 20:7 Give me your **a** right now!"
2Sm 15:31 make Ahithophel's **a** foolish."
15:34 me by⌞ undoing Ahithophel's **a**.
16:20 Ahithophel, "What's your **a**?
16:23 Ahithophel's **a** was like getting
17:7 "This time Ahithophel's **a** is no
17:11 So my **a** is to gather all Israel's
17:14 "The **a** of Hushai from Archi's
17:14 is better than Ahithophel's **a**."
17:14 Ahithophel's good **a**
17:23 that his **a** hadn't been followed,
21:1 asked the LORD's **a** about it.
1Ki 1:12 let me give you some **a** about
12:6 King Rehoboam sought **a** from
12:8 But he ignored the **a** the older
12:8 He sought **a** from the young
12:9 asked them, "What is your **a**?
12:13 He ignored the **a** the older
12:28 After seeking **a**, the king made
20:25 He took their **a** and followed it.
2Ki 1:3 you seek **a** from Baalzebub,
1:6 to seek **a** from Baalzebub,
1:16 You sent messengers to seek **a**
6:8 he asked for **a** from his officers
18:20 You give useless **a** about
2Ch 10:6 King Rehoboam sought **a** from
10:8 But he ignored the **a** the older
10:8 He sought **a** from the young
10:9 asked them, "What is your **a**?
10:13 He ignored the older leaders' **a**.
22:3 because his mother gave him **a**
22:5 Ahaziah followed their **a** and
24:17 the king listened to their **a**.
25:16 you refuse to listen to my **a**."
25:17 After getting **a** ⌞from his
Est 1:13 the king usually asked for **a**
Job 12:13 **A** and insight are his.
29:21 quietly waiting for my **a**.
38:2 "Who is this that belittles my **a**
42:3 'Who is this that belittles my **a**
Psa 1:1 who does not follow the **a**
14:6 They put the **a** of oppressed
73:24 With your **a** you guide me,
81:12 ways and follow their own **a**.
106:13 They did not wait for his **a**.
107:11 had despised the **a** given by
Pro 1:25 You ignored all my **a**.
1:30 They refused my **a**.
3:32 The LORD's intimate **a** is with
8:14 **A** and priceless wisdom are
9:9 Give ⌞**a**⌟ to a wise person,
12:5 The **a** of wicked people is
12:15 who listens to **a** is wise.
13:10 those who take **a** gain wisdom.
15:22 Without **a** plans go wrong,
19:20 Listen to **a** and accept
19:21 but the **a** of the LORD will
20:18 are confirmed by getting **a**,
21:28 but a person who listens to **a**
21:30 and no **a** ⌞can stand up⌟
22:20 with **a** and knowledge
Ecc 4:13 who won't take **a** any longer.
Isa 11:2 the Spirit of **a** and power,
16:3 Give us **a**. Make a decision.
19:11 counselors gives stupid **a**.
36:5 You give useless **a** about
Jer 18:18 the **a** of wise people,
37:7 who sent you to get **a** from me:
38:15 If I give you **a**, you won't listen
Eze 7:26 teachings of priests and the **a**
11:2 evil and give bad **a** in this city.
Dan 4:27 my best **a** is that you stop
Mic 6:16 and you have followed their **a**.
Nah 1:11 His **a** is wicked.
Act 5:40 The council took his **a**.
21:23 So follow our **a**.
27:21 you should have followed my **a**

advise (8)
1Ki 12:6 He asked, "What do you **a**?
2Ch 10:6 He asked, "What do you **a**?
Psa 32:8 I will **a** you as my eyes watch
Pro 12:20 but joy belongs to those who **a**
Ecc 8:2 I ⌞**a**⌟ you to obey the king's
Isa 41:28 There is no one to **a** them.
Act 27:22 Now I **a** you to have courage.
Rev 3:18 I **a** you: Buy gold purified in fire

advised (15)

1Sm 19:11 But Michal, David's wife, **a** him,
2Sm 17:15 "Ahithophel **a** Absalom and the
17:15 but I **a** them to do something
17:21 has **a** against you ...."
1Ki 12:14 to them as the young men **a**.
2Ch 10:14 to them as the young men **a**.
20:21 After he had **a** the people,
22:4 After his father died, they **a** him
Ezr 10:3 of our God have **a**
10:8 and the older men had **a**,
Est 2:15 the guardian of the women, **a**.
Job 26:3 You have **a** the person who
Zec 3:6 The Messenger of the LORD **a**
Jon 18:14 was the person who had **a** the
Act 27:9 dangerous, so Paul **a** them,

adviser (10)

2Sm 15:12 sent for Ahithophel, David's **a**,
1Ki 4:5 of Nathan, was the king's **a**.
1Ch 27:32 insight, was David's **a**.
27:33 Ahithophel was the king's **a**.
2Ch 25:16 "Did we make you an **a** to the
Neh 11:24 was the king's **a** on all matters
Job 29:4 when God was an **a** in my tent.
Isa 40:13 or instructed him as his **a**?
Dan 2:27 "No wise **a**, psychic, magician,
Rom 11:34 Who can become his **a**?"

advisers (38)

Jdg 3:19 Then all his **a** left the room.
3:24 Eglon's **a** came in.
2Ch 25:17 getting advice ⌊from his **a**⌋,
Ezr 7:14 I, the king, and my seven **a** are
7:15 and his **a** willingly contributed
7:28 He made the king, his **a**,
8:25 the king, his **a**, his officials,
Est 1:3 was for all his officials and **a**,
2:18 all his officials and his **a**.
3:2 All the king's **a** were at the
3:3 Then the king's **a** at the king's
3:6 Because the king's **a** had
4:11 "All the king's **a** and the people
5:11 the officials and the king's **a**.
Job 12:20 He makes trusted **a** unable to
Pro 11:14 with many **a** there is victory.
15:22 but with many **a** they succeed.
24:6 with many **a** there is victory.
Isa 1:26 **a** like you had in the beginning.
Dan 2:12 all the wise **a** in Babylon.
2:13 issued that the wise **a** were
2:14 to kill the wise **a** in Babylon,
2:18 rest of the wise **a** in Babylon.
2:24 to destroy Babylon's wise **a**.
2:24 destroy Babylon's wise **a**.
2:48 head of all Babylon's wise **a**.
3:2 military **a**, treasurers, judges,
3:3 military **a**, treasurers, judges,
3:24 He asked his **a**, "Didn't we
3:27 and **a** gathered around
4:6 So I ordered all the wise **a** in
4:18 meaning because the wise **a**
4:36 My **a** and nobles wanted to
5:7 told these wise **a** of Babylon,
5:8 All the king's wise **a** came,
5:15 The wise **a** and the psychics
6:7 officials, governors, satraps, **a**,
Act 25:12 the appeal with his **a**

advises (2)

Psa 16:7 praise the LORD, who **a** me.
25:14 The LORD **a** those who fear

advocating (1)

Act 16:21 and they're **a** customs that we

Aeneas (4)

Act 9:33 named **A** who was paralyzed
9:34 Peter said to him, "**A**,
9:34 **A** immediately got up.
9:35 saw what had happened to **A**

Aenon (1)

Jon 3:23 John was baptizing in **A**,

affair (1)

2Sm 12:14 for the LORD by this **a**,

affect (9)

Exo 9:14 that will **a** you personally as
Job 19:4 my mistake would **a** only me.
Lam 1:12 "Doesn't this **a** all of you who
Zec 14:15 plague will also **a** horses,
14:18 nations will **a** those who won't
Act 11:28 that a severe famine would **a**
27:10 and it will **a** our lives."
1Co 6:18 commit don't **a** their bodies
8:8 Food will not **a** our relationship

affected (7)

Lev 13:21 But if the priest examines the **a**
13:21 is not white or the **a** area is not
13:25 If the hair on the **a** area has
13:25 and the **a** area looks deeper
13:26 not white and the **a** area is not
2Co 2:5 I'm not the one really **a**.
2:5 too much — it has **a** all of you.

affection (5)

Est 2:9 pleased him and won his **a**.
2Co 9:14 With deep **a** they will pray for
2Ti 3:3 and lack normal **a** for their
2Pe 1:7 to godliness add Christian **a**;
1:7 and to Christian **a** add love.

affects (2)

Job 35:8 Your wickedness **a** only
35:8 Your righteousness **a** only the

affirmed (1)

Jon 3:33 and I have **a** that God is

afflict (1)

Dtr 28:35 The LORD will **a** your knees

afford (11)

Lev 5:7 "Now, if you cannot **a** a sheep,
5:11 "But if you cannot **a** two
12:8 If she cannot **a** a lamb,
14:21 is poor and cannot **a** that much,
14:22 pigeons (whatever he can **a**).
14:30 pigeons (whichever he can **a**),
14:32 but cannot **a** what is needed
27:8 on what the person can **a**.
Num 6:21 to anything else they can **a**.
Act 11:29 whatever they could **a**
2Co 8:3 even more than they could **a**.

afraid (270)

Gen 3:10 I was **a** because I was naked,
15:1 He said, "Abram, don't be **a**.
18:15 Because she was **a**,
19:30 Lot left Zoar because he was **a**
21:17 "Don't be **a**! God has heard the
26:7 He was **a** to say "my wife."
26:24 Don't be **a**, because I am with
31:31 "I left because I was **a**.
32:11 because I'm **a** of him.
32:11 I'm **a** that he'll come and attack
35:17 midwife said to her, "Don't be **a**!
42:4 because he was **a** that
43:23 "Don't be **a**! Your God, the God
45:3 because they were **a** of him.
46:3 "Don't be **a** to go to Egypt,
50:19 said to them, "Don't be **a**!
50:21 Don't be **a**! I will provide for you
Exo 2:14 Then Moses was **a** and
3:6 hid his face because he was **a**
14:13 the people, "Don't be **a**!
15:15 of Canaan will be deathly **a**.
20:20 the people, "Don't be **a**!
34:30 they were **a** to come near him.
Num 12:8 Why weren't you **a** to criticize
14:9 and don't be **a** of the people of
14:9 So don't be **a** of them."
21:34 "Don't be **a** of him.
22:3 The Moabites were very **a**
Dtr 1:17 Never be **a** of anyone,
1:21 Don't be **a** or terrified."
1:29 Don't be **a** of them.
Dtr 2:4 They'll be **a** of you,
3:2 "Don't be **a** of him.
3:22 Don't be **a** of them,
5:5 because you were **a** of the fire
7:18 Don't be **a** of them.
7:19 to all the people you're **a** of.
7:21 Don't be **a** of them,
13:11 will hear about it and be **a**.
17:13 they will be **a** and will never
18:22 Never be **a** of him.
19:20 hear about this, they will be **a**.
20:1 Don't be **a** of them,
20:3 Don't be **a** or alarmed
20:8 "If you are **a** or have lost your
21:21 hears about it, they will be **a**.
25:18 They weren't **a** of God.
28:10 and they will be **a** of you.
31:6 Don't be **a** of them!
31:8 So don't be **a** or terrified."
Jos 2:9 country are deathly **a** of you.
2:24 live there are deathly **a** of us."
6:1 because the people were **a**
8:1 "Don't be terrified or **a**.
10:2 and his people were terribly **a**
10:8 "Don't be **a** of them.
10:25 "Don't be **a** or terrified!
11:6 "Don't be **a** of them because I
Jdg 4:18 Don't be **a**." So he went into her
6:23 Don't be **a**. You will not die."
6:27 He was too **a** of his father's
7:10 But if you're **a** to go,
8:20 He was **a** because he was
Rut 3:11 Don't be **a**, my daughter.
1Sm 3:15 But Samuel was **a** to tell Eli
4:20 helping her said, "Don't be **a**.
7:7 plan⌋ and were **a** of them.
12:20 "Don't be **a**," Samuel told the
14:26 because the troops were **a** of
15:24 I was **a** of the people and
18:12 Saul was **a** of David,
18:15 became ⌊even more⌋ **a** of him.
18:29 was even more **a** of David,
22:23 Don't be **a**.
23:3 David's men told him, "We're **a**
23:3 How much more ⌊**a** do you
23:15 David was **a** because Saul had
23:17 "Don't be **a**," he told David,
28:5 he was very **a** — terrified.
28:13 "Don't be **a**," the king said to
2Sm 1:14 "Why weren't you **a** to take it
3:11 because he was **a** of Abner.
6:9 David was **a** of the LORD that
9:7 "Don't be **a**," David told him,
10:19 And the Arameans were **a** to
12:18 But David's officials were **a** to
13:28 Don't be **a**. I've given you the
1Ki 1:50 Adonijah was **a** of Solomon.
1:51 "Adonijah is **a** of you,
17:13 Elijah told her, "Don't be **a**.
2Ki 1:15 Don't be **a** of him."
6:16 Elisha answered, "Don't be **a**.
19:6 Don't be **a** of the message that
25:24 He said, "Don't be **a** of the
25:26 they were **a** of the Babylonians.
1Ch 13:12 David was **a** of God that day.
22:13 Don't be **a** or terrified.
28:20 Don't be **a** or terrified.
2Ch 14:14 because the cities were **a**
Ezr 3:3 though they were **a** of the
4:4 them **a** to continue building.
Neh 2:2 (I was really **a**).
4:14 "Don't be **a** of our enemies.
6:16 the surrounding nations were **a**
Job 5:21 and you will not be **a** of
5:22 so do not be **a** of wild animals
6:21 terrifying, and you are **a**.
9:35 speak and not be **a** of him.
23:15 When I think of it, I'm **a** of him.
32:6 from speaking and was **a**
39:16 It is not **a** that its work is for
39:22 It laughs at fear, is **a** of nothing,
41:25 "The mighty are **a** when
Psa 3:6 I am not **a** of the tens of
27:1 Who is there to be **a** of?
27:3 my heart will not be **a**.
46:2 That is why we are not **a** even

Psa 49:5 Why should I be a in times of
49:16 Do not be a when someone
56:3 Even when I am a,
56:4 I am not a. What can mere flesh
56:11 I am not a. What can mortals do
64:9 will be a and conclude,
112:7 He is not a of bad news.
112:8 heart is steady, and he is not a.
118:6 I am not a. What can mortals do
119:120 and I am a of your regulations.
Pro 3:24 you lie down, you will not be a.
3:25 Do not be a of sudden terror or
Ecc 9:2 those who are a to take oaths.
12:5 Creator when someone is a
Isa 7:4 stay calm, and don't be a.
10:24 don't be a of the Assyrians
35:4 terrified, "Be brave; don't be a.
37:6 Don't be a of the message that
41:5 have seen him and are a.
41:10 Don't be a, because I am with
41:13 'Don't be a; I will help you.'
41:14 Don't be a, Jacob, you worm.
41:23 to intimidate us and make us a.
43:1 the LORD says: Do not be a,
43:5 Do not be a, because I am with
44:2 Don't be a, my servant Jacob,
44:8 Don't be terrified or a.
51:7 Don't be a of being insulted by
51:12 Why, then, are you a of mortals,
54:4 Don't be a, because you won't
54:14 so you will not be a.
Jer 1:8 Don't be a of people.
2:12 terribly a," declares the LORD.
3:8 Judah, her sister, wasn't a.
10:5 Don't be a of them.
17:8 It will not be a in the heat of
23:4 will no longer be a or terrified,
30:10 "Don't be a, my servant Jacob,"
33:9 They will be a and tremble
38:19 "I'm a of the Jews who have
40:9 He said, "Don't be a to serve
41:18 They were a of the
42:11 Don't be a of the king of
42:11 Don't be a of him, declares the
46:27 "Don't be a, my servant Jacob.
46:27 and no one will make them a.
46:28 Don't be a, my servant Jacob,"
51:46 Don't lose courage or be a
Lam 3:57 You told me not to be a.
Eze 2:6 Son of man, don't be a of them
2:6 Don't be a, even though thorns
3:9 Don't be a of them.
11:8 You are a of swords,
18:14 He is a, so he doesn't do such
27:35 Their kings are terribly a.
Dan 1:10 "I'm a of my master,
10:12 He told me, "Don't be a,
10:19 He said, "Don't be a.
Joe 2:21 Land, do not be a. Be glad and
2:22 Wild animals, do not be a.
Amo 3:8 Who isn't a? The Almighty
Jnh 1:5 The sailors were a,
Mic 4:4 and no one will make them a.
7:17 They will be a of you.
Zep 3:16 will be told, "Do not be a, Zion!
Hag 2:5 Don't be a.
Zec 8:13 Don't be a. Let your hands work
8:15 people of Judah. Don't be a.
9:5 will see [this] and be a.
Mat 1:20 don't be a to take Mary as your
2:22 Joseph was a to go there.
10:26 So don't be a of them.
10:28 Don't be a of those who kill the
10:31 Don't be a! You are worth more
14:5 However, he was a of the
14:26 scream because they were a.
14:27 It's me. Don't be a!"
14:30 he became a and started to
17:7 said, "Get up, and don't be a!"
21:26 we're a of what the crowd
21:46 wanted to arrest him but were a
25:25 I was a. So I hid your two
28:4 The guards were so deathly a
28:5 said to the women, "Don't be a!
28:10 said to them, "Don't be a!
Mar 5:36 synagogue leader, "Don't be a!
Mar 6:20 because Herod was a of John.
6:50 It's me. Don't be a!"
9:32 meant and were a to ask him.
10:32 others who followed were a.
11:18 They were a of him because
11:32 They were a of the people.
12:12 wanted to arrest him but were a
16:8 because they were a.
Luk 1:13 to him, "Don't be a, Zechariah!
1:30 The angel told her, "Don't be a,
2:10 angel said to them, "Don't be a!
5:10 Jesus told Simon, "Don't be a.
8:50 synagogue leader, "Don't be a!
9:45 Besides, they were a to ask
12:4 that you don't need to be a
12:5 you the one you should be a of.
12:5 Be a of the one who has the
12:5 I'm warning you to be a of him.
12:7 Don't be a! You are worth more
12:32 Don't be a, little flock.
19:21 I was a of you. You're a tough
20:19 but they were a of the people.
22:2 they were a of the people.
24:38 asked them, "Why are you a?
Jon 6:20 "It's me. Don't be a!"
7:13 they were a of the Jews.
9:22 said this because they were a
12:15 "Don't be a, people of Zion!
19:8 he became more a than ever.
19:38 but secretly because he was a
20:19 doors because they were a
Act 5:26 and his guards were a that
9:26 But everyone was a of him.
16:38 Roman citizens, they were a.
18:9 "Don't be a to speak out!
22:29 The officer was a when he
23:10 and the officer was a that they
24:25 Felix became a and said,
27:24 The angel told me, 'Don't be a,
Rom 11:20 Don't feel arrogant, but be a.
13:3 what is right don't have to be a
13:3 what is wrong should be a of it.
13:3 you like to live without being a
13:4 is wrong, you should be a.
13:5 not only because you're a of
1Co 2:3 I was a and very nervous.
16:10 doesn't have anything to be a
2Co 7:11 You were a. You wanted to see
11:3 However, I'm a that as the
12:20 I'm a that I may come and find
12:20 I'm a that there may be rivalry,
12:21 I'm a that when I come to you
Gal 2:12 He was a of those who
4:11 I'm a for you. Maybe the hard
1Ti 5:20 the other leaders will also be a.
Heb 2:15 because they were a of dying.
4:1 We are a that some of you
11:23 baby and they were not a
11:27 to leave Egypt without being a
12:21 said he was trembling and a.
13:6 I will not be a. What can mortals
1Pe 3:6 make you a to do good.
3:14 Don't be a of those who want to
2Pe 2:10 They aren't a to insult the
Jud 1:23 even though you are a that you
Rev 1:17 on me and said, "Don't be a!
2:10 Don't be a of what you are

afterbirth (1)

Dtr 28:57 with them the a from her body

afternoon (7)

Jdg 19:8 the time eating until late a.
1Ki 18:29 In the a they continued to rant
Mat 27:45 whole land until three in the a.
Mar 15:33 whole land until three in the a.
Luk 23:44 and lasted until three in the a.
Act 10:3 One day, about three in the a,
10:30 three o'clock in the a.

Agabus (3)

Act 11:28 One of them was named A.
11:28 Through the Spirit A predicted
21:10 named A arrived from Judea.

Agag (13)

Num 24:7 king will be greater than A,
1Sm 15:8 He captured King A of Amalek
15:9 Saul and the army spared A
15:20 [back] King A of Amalek,
15:32 "Bring me King A of Amalek,"
15:32 A came to him trembling.
15:32 of death is past," A said.
15:33 And Samuel cut A in pieces in
Est 3:1 Hammedatha and was from A.)
3:10 Hammedatha and was from A.)
8:3 of Haman, who was from A,
8:5 Hammedatha and was from A).
9:24 Hammedatha and was from A.)

agate (3)

Exo 28:19 In the third row put jacinth, a,
39:12 put jacinth, a, and amethyst.
Rev 21:19 the third a, the fourth emerald,

age (25)

Gen 15:15 and be buried at a very old a.
18:11 was past the a of childbearing.
21:2 a son for Abraham in his old a.
21:7 given him a son in his old a."
24:36 gave him a son in her old a,
25:8 and died at a very old a.
35:29 in death at a very old a.
37:3 had been born in Israel's old a.
48:10 was failing because of old a,
Jdg 2:8 died at the a of 110.
8:32 died at a very old a.
Rut 4:15 and support you in your old a.
1Sm 2:32 your family will live to an old a.
17:33 a warrior since he was your a."
1Ki 11:4 In his old a, his wives tempted
1Ch 29:28 He died at a very old a.
Est 9:28 and observed in every a,
Job 5:26 to your grave at a ripe old a like
32:7 I thought, 'A should speak,
42:17 Then at a very old a,
Psa 71:18 of this a what your strength
Dan 1:10 the other young men your a,
Zec 8:4 cane in hand because of old a.
Luk 1:36 with a son in her old a.
Gal 1:14 of other Jews in my a group

aged (1)

Isa 25:6 a banquet with a wines,

Agee (1)

2Sm 23:11 the son of A from Harar.

ages (10)

Gen 43:33 him according to their a — from
Num 4:3 all the men between the a
4:23 all the men between the a
4:30 all the men between the a
4:35 all the men between the a
4:39 All the men between the a of
4:43 All the men between the a of
4:47 were the men between the a
Psa 49:11 their homes for a to come,
Heb 9:26 But now, at the end of the a,

aggressive (2)

Isa 18:2 a strong and a nation,
18:7 a strong and a nation,

aging (1)

Heb 8:13 and a will soon disappear.

agony (5)

Neh 9:37 We are in a.
Psa 116:3 I experienced pain and a.
Jer 51:54 Cries of a are heard from
Mat 24:30 will cry in a when they see
Rev 12:2 pains and the a of giving birth.

agree (29)

Gen 34:17 If you won't a to be
34:23 We only need to a to do this for
44:10 "I a," he said. "We'll do what
Dtr 32:31 our enemies will a with this.
Jos 2:21 "I a," she said. So she let them

Rut 3:13 In the morning if he will **a** to
1Sm 14:7 Go ahead! I **a** with you."
1Ki 20:8 Don't **a** ⌊to his demands⌋."
22:13 Make your message **a** with
2Ch 18:12 Make your message **a** with
Job 34:4 right and **a** among ourselves as
39:9 "Will the wild ox **a** to serve
Psa 83:5 They **a** completely on their
Dan 6:7 and mayors **a** that the king
Mat 18:19 again that if two of you **a**
20:13 Didn't you **a** with me on a day's
Mar 14:56 but their statements did not **a**.
14:59 But their testimony did not **a**
Act 5:9 could you and your husband **a**
28:25 unable to **a** among themselves,
Rom 7:16 but I **a** that God's standards are
1Co 1:10 of our Lord Jesus Christ to **a**
7:5 from each other unless you **a**
9:1 Don't you **a** that I'm a free man?
9:1 Don't you **a** that I'm an apostle?
2Co 6:15 Can Christ **a** with the devil?
12:16 You **a**, then, that I haven't been
1Ti 6:3 false doctrine and doesn't **a**
1Jn 5:8 These three witnesses **a**.

agreed (25)

Gen 16:2 Abram **a** with Sarai.
23:16 Abraham **a** to Ephron's terms.
30:34 Laban answered, "**A**.
34:24 had come out to the city gate **a**
37:27 and blood." His brothers **a**.
42:20 you won't die." So they **a**.
Dtr 1:14 You **a** that this was a good
10:10 LORD listened to me and **a** not
Jdg 17:11 and **a** to live with Micah.
1Sm 20:35 place he and David had **a** on.
2Sm 2:14 men hold a contest." Joab **a**.
2Ki 12:8 The priests **a** neither to receive
1Ch 12:38 The rest of Israel also had **a** to
13:4 The whole assembly **a** to this
Job 2:11 They had **a** they would go
Jer 34:10 officials and all the people **a**
34:15 You **a** to free your neighbors,
Dan 2:9 You have **a** among yourselves
Mat 28:12 together with the leaders and **a**
Luk 22:5 They were pleased and **a** to
23:51 but he had not **a** with what they
Jon 9:22 The Jews had already **a** to put
Act 5:2 They **a** to hold back some of
12:20 They had **a** on what they
15:28 The Holy Spirit and we have **a**

agreeing (2)

Mat 20:2 After **a** to pay the workers the
Gal 2:9 **a** to be our partners.

agreement (27)

Gen 21:27 and the two of them made an **a**.
23:18 the official witnesses for the **a**.
26:28 be a solemn **a** between us.'
26:28 like to make an **a** with you
31:44 Now, let's make an **a** and let it
Jos 24:25 That day Joshua made an **a** for
1Sm 20:8 all, you forced me into an **a**
2Sm 3:12 "Make an **a** with me,"
3:13 "I'll make an **a** with you.
5:3 King David made an **a** with
19:14 people of Judah were in total **a**.
2Ki 11:4 He made an **a** with them,
1Ch 11:3 David made an **a** with them at
2Ch 15:12 They made an **a** with one
23:1 his position by making an **a**
23:3 whole assembly made an **a**
Neh 9:38 "We are making a binding **a**
10:1 following people sealed the **a**:
Job 5:23 "You will have a binding **a** with
31:1 "I have made an **a** with my
41:4 Will it make an **a** with you so
Psa 89:34 my promise or alter my own **a**.
Isa 28:15 a treaty with death and an **a**
28:18 Your **a** with the grave will not
Jer 50:5 go there to make a permanent **a**
Mat 1:19 marriage **a** with her secretly.
1Ti 1:11 were intended to be used in **a**

agreements (1)

Isa 33:8 **A** are broken. Witnesses are

agrees (2)

Act 15:15 This **a** with what the prophets
Rom 12:6 make sure what you say **a** with

Agrippa (12)

Act 25:13 Later King **A** and Bernice came
25:22 **A** told Festus, "I would like to
25:23 The next day **A** and Bernice
25:24 Then Festus said, "King **A** and
25:26 and especially to you, King **A**.
26:1 **A** said to Paul, "You're free to
26:1 Paul acknowledged King **A**
26:2 "King **A**, I think I'm fortunate
26:19 I saw from heaven, King **A**.
26:27 King **A**, do you believe the
26:28 **A** said to Paul, "Do you think
26:32 **A** told Festus, "This man could

aground (2)

Act 27:26 we will run **a** on some island."
27:41 in the water and ran the ship **a**.

Agur (1)

Pro 30:1 The words of **A**, son of Jakeh.

Agur's (1)

Pro 30:1 **A** prophetic revelation.

Ahab (76)

1Ki 16:28 His son **A** succeeded him as
16:29 **A**, son of Omri, began to rule
16:30 **A**, son of Omri, did what the
16:31 **A** then served and worshiped
16:33 **A** made poles dedicated to the
17:1 said to **A**, "I solemnly swear,
18:1 "Present yourself to **A**.
18:2 went to present himself to **A**.
18:3 **A** sent for Obadiah,
18:5 **A** told Obadiah, "Let's go
18:6 **A** went one way by himself,
18:9 hand me over to **A** to be killed?
18:12 I'll tell **A**, but he won't be able
18:15 I will present myself to **A**."
18:16 So Obadiah went to tell **A**.
18:16 **A** went to meet Elijah.
18:17 When he saw Elijah, **A** said,
18:20 **A** sent word to all the Israelites
18:41 Then Elijah told **A**,
18:42 **A** got up to eat and drink.
18:44 Elijah said, "Go and tell **A**,
18:45 **A** got into his chariot to go
18:46 ran ahead of **A** until they came
19:1 **A** told Jezebel everything
20:2 into the city to King **A** of Israel.
20:2 They told **A**, "This is what
20:5 sent messengers back ⌊to **A**⌋.
20:9 **A** told Benhadad's messengers,
20:10 Then Benhadad sent **A** the
20:13 Then a prophet came to King **A**
20:14 **A** asked, "How ⌊will this be
20:14 **A** asked. "You will," the prophet
20:15 **A** counted the young officers of
20:32 'Please let me live.'" **A** asked,
20:33 **A** said, "Bring him here."
20:33 When Benhadad arrived, **A** had
20:34 **A** said, "If you will put this into
20:34 So **A** made a treaty with
21:1 palace of King **A** of Samaria.
21:2 **A** told Naboth, "Give me your
21:3 Naboth told **A**, "The LORD has
21:4 Resentful and upset, **A** went
21:4 from my ancestors.") So **A** lay
21:15 the message and said to **A**,
21:16 **A** went to confiscate the
21:18 "Go, meet King **A** of Israel,
21:20 **A** asked Elijah, "So you've
21:25 There was no one else like **A**.
21:27 When **A** heard these things,
21:29 "Do you see how **A** is
22:20 'Who will deceive **A** so that he
22:34 **A** told his chariot driver,
22:39 Isn't everything else about **A**—
1Ki 22:40 **A** lay down in death with his
22:49 Then Ahaziah, son of **A**,
22:51 Ahaziah, son of **A**,
2Ki 1:1 After **A** died, Moab rebelled
3:1 Joram, son of **A**, became king
3:5 But when **A** died, the king of
9:7 the family of your master **A**.
9:25 chariots behind his father **A**?
10:1 **A** had 70 male heirs in
10:18 He said, "**A** served Baal a little,
21:3 the goddess Asherah as King **A**
21:3 Manasseh, like **A**,
2Ch 18:2 he went to visit **A** in Samaria.
18:2 **A** slaughtered many sheep and
18:2 And **A** persuaded Jehoshaphat
18:3 King **A** of Israel asked King
18:19 'Who will deceive King **A** of
18:33 **A** told the chariot driver,
33:3 the goddess Asherah as King **A**
33:3 Manasseh, like **A**,
Jer 29:21 says about Kolaiah's son **A**
29:22 as he cursed Zedekiah and **A**,
Mic 6:16 of the descendants of **A**,

Ahab's (38)

1Ki 16:34 In **A** time Hiel from Bethel
21:8 signed them with **A** name, and
21:21 in **A** ⌊house⌋, whether slave
21:24 If anyone from **A** ⌊house⌋ dies
22:22 **A** prophets.' "The LORD said,
22:41 Judah in **A** fourth year as king
2Ki 8:16 Joram (**A** son) was in his fifth
8:18 as **A** family had done,
8:18 his wife was **A** daughter.
8:25 Joram (**A** son) was in his
8:27 followed the ways of **A** family.
8:27 as **A** family had done,
8:27 related to **A** family by marriage.
8:28 Ahaziah went with **A** son
8:29 to Jezreel to see **A** son Joram,
9:8 **A** entire family will die.
9:8 from **A** family, whether slave
9:9 I will make **A** family like the
9:29 **A** son, was king of Israel.)
10:1 the guardians of **A** descendants
10:3 and put him on **A** throne.
10:10 spoken about **A** family will
10:11 of **A** household who was left
10:17 Jehu killed the rest of **A** family,
10:30 I wanted done to **A** family.
21:13 plumb line used for **A** dynasty.
2Ch 18:1 honorable and became **A** in-law
18:21 **A** prophets.' "The LORD said,
21:6 as **A** family had done,
21:6 his wife was **A** daughter.
21:13 You, like **A** family, have
22:3 followed the ways of **A** family,
22:4 as **A** family had done.
22:4 to do what **A** family had done.
22:5 went with **A** son King Joram
22:6 to Jezreel to see **A** son Joram,
22:7 Jehu to destroy **A** family.
22:8 judgment on **A** family,

Aharah (1)

1Ch 8:1 second son), **A** (his third son),

Aharhel (1)

1Ch 4:8 ancestor of the families of **A**,

Ahasbai (1)

2Sm 23:34 Eliphelet (son of **A** and

Ahava (3)

Ezr 8:15 by the river that flows to **A**,
8:21 fast there at the **A** River so that
8:31 Then we left the **A** River on the

Ahaz (44)

2Ki 15:38 His son **A** succeeded him as
16:1 as king of Israel when King **A**,
16:2 **A** was 20 years old when he
16:5 They blockaded **A** but couldn't
16:7 **A** sent messengers to King
16:8 **A** took the silver and gold he
16:10 Then King **A** went to

2Ki 16:10 So King **A** sent the priest Urijah
16:11 King **A** sent from Damascus.
16:11 He finished it before **A** returned
16:14 **A** put it on the north side of his
16:15 King **A** gave this command to
16:16 what King **A** had commanded.
16:17 King **A** cut off the side panels
16:18 **A** removed the covered
16:19 Isn't everything else about **A**—
16:20 **A** lay down in death with his
18:1 son of **A** of Judah,
1Ch 3:13 Jotham's son was **A**.
8:35 Pithon, Melech, Tarea, and **A**.
8:36 **A** was the father of Jehoaddah.
9:42 **A** was the father of Jarah.
2Ch 27:9 His son **A** succeeded him as
28:1 **A** was 20 years old when he
28:16 At that time King **A** sent for
28:19 because of King **A** of Israel.
28:19 **A** had spread sin throughout
28:20 Pilneser of Assyria attacked **A**.
28:20 Instead of strengthening **A**,
28:21 **A** took some of the things from
28:22 King **A** became more unfaithful
28:24 **A** collected the utensils in
28:27 **A** lay down in death with his
29:19 and all the utensils King **A**
Isa 1:1 Jotham, **A**, and Hezekiah.
7:1 When **A**, son of Jotham and
7:3 son Shear Jashub to meet **A** at
7:10 Again the LORD spoke to **A**,
7:12 But **A** answered, "I won't ask;
14:28 in the year King **A** died.
Hos 1:1 when Uzziah, Jotham, **A**,
Mic 1:1 Moresheth, when Jotham, **A**,
Mat 1:9 Jotham the father of **A**,
1:9 **A** the father of Hezekiah,

Ahaziah (41)

1Ki 22:40 His son **A** succeeded him as
22:49 Then **A**, son of Ahab, said to
22:51 **A**, son of Ahab, became king of
22:51 **A** ruled Israel for two years.
22:53 **A** served Baal, worshiped him,
2Ki 1:2 During the rebellion King **A** fell
1:17 So **A** died as the LORD had
1:17 as king because **A** had no son.
1:18 Isn't everything else about **A**—
8:24 His son **A** succeeded him as
8:25 Jehoram's son **A** became king
8:26 **A** was 22 years old when he
8:27 **A** followed the ways of Ahab's
8:28 **A** went with Ahab's son Joram
8:29 Then Jehoram's son **A** went to
9:16 (King **A** of Judah had come to
9:21 King Joram of Israel and King **A**
9:23 to flee, he said to **A**, "It's a trap,
9:23 said to Ahaziah, "It's a trap, **A**!"
9:27 When King **A** of Judah saw
9:27 **A** continued to flee until he got
9:29 (**A** had become king of Judah
10:13 relatives of King **A** of Judah.
11:2 King Jehoram and sister of **A**,
12:18 Jehoram, and **A** of Judah,
14:13 son of Joash and grandson of **A**
1Ch 3:11 Joram's son was **A**.
2Ch 20:35 himself with King **A** of Israel,
20:37 have allied yourself with **A**."
21:17 The only son left was **A**,
22:1 Jehoram's youngest son **A** king
22:1 So Jehoram's son **A** became
22:2 **A** was 42 years old when he
22:3 **A** also followed the ways of
22:5 **A** followed their advice and
22:6 Then Jehoram's son **A** went to
22:8 nephews) who were serving **A**,
22:9 He searched for **A**,
22:9 "**A** is Jehoshaphat's grandson.
22:11 of the king and sister of **A**,
25:23 son of Joash and grandson of **A**

Ahaziah's (11)

2Ki 10:13 "We're **A** relatives.
11:1 When **A** mother, Athaliah,
11:2 took **A** son Joash.
13:1 **A** son King Joash of Judah
1Ch 3:11 **A** son was Joash.
2Ch 22:7 God brought about **A** downfall
22:8 (**A** nephews) who were serving
22:9 "But no one in **A** family was
22:10 When **A** mother, Athaliah,
22:11 took **A** son Joash.
22:11 also **A** sister, she hid Joash

Ahaz's (5)

2Ki 17:1 In **A** twelfth year as king of
20:11 down on **A** stairway go back up
23:12 on the roof of **A** upstairs room,
1Ch 3:13 **A** son was Hezekiah.
Isa 38:8 the stairway of **A** upper palace.

Ahban (1)

1Ch 2:29 She gave birth to **A** and Molid.

Ahi (1)

1Ch 5:15 **A**, son of Abdiel and grandson

Ahiah (1)

Neh 10:26 **A**, Hanan, Anan,

Ahiam (2)

2Sm 23:33 **A** (son of Sharar the Hararite),
1Ch 11:35 **A** (son of Sachar the Hararite),

Ahian (1)

1Ch 7:19 Shemida's sons were **A**,

Ahiezer (6)

Num 1:12 **A**, son of Ammishaddai,
2:25 for the people of Dan is **A**,
7:66 of Dan, **A**, son of Amishaddai,
7:71 These were the gifts from **A**,
10:25 **A**, son of Ammishaddai, was in
1Ch 12:3 **A** was the leader, then Joash

Ahihud (2)

Num 34:27 **A**, son of Shelomi, the leader of
1Ch 8:7 was the father of Uzza and **A**.

Ahijah (27)

1Sm 14:3 in addition to **A**, the son of
14:3 **A** was wearing the priestly
14:18 Then Saul said to **A**,
14:18 because **A** carried the ephod in
1Ki 4:3 Elihoreph and **A**, the sons of
11:29 The prophet **A** from Shiloh met
11:29 and **A** had on new clothes.
11:30 **A** took his new garment and
12:15 son) through **A** from Shiloh.
14:2 The prophet **A**, who told me I
14:4 and came to the home of **A**.
14:4 **A** couldn't see. His eyesight had
14:5 However, the LORD had told **A**,
14:5 He also told **A** what to say to
14:6 **A** heard her footsteps when
14:18 his servant, the prophet **A**.
15:27 Then Baasha, son of **A** from
15:29 his servant **A** from Shiloh.
15:33 of Judah, Baasha, son of **A**,
21:22 the house of Baasha, son of **A**,
2Ki 9:9 the family of Baasha, son of **A**.
1Ch 2:25 Bunah, Oren, Ozem, and **A**.
8:7 Naaman, **A**, and Gera. Gera led
11:36 Mecherathite, **A** the Pelonite,
26:20 **A**, a Levite, was in charge of
2Ch 9:29 the prophecy of **A** from Shiloh,
10:15 son) through **A** from Shiloh.

Ahikam (19)

2Ki 22:12 to **A** (son of Shaphan),
22:14 So the priest Hilkiah, **A**,
25:22 son of **A** and grandson of
2Ch 34:20 **A** (son of Shaphan),
Jer 26:24 **A**, son of Shaphan,
39:14 son of **A** and grandson of
40:5 son of **A** and grandson of
40:6 went to Gedaliah, son of **A**,
40:7 appointed Gedaliah, son of **A**,
40:9 Gedaliah, son of **A** and
40:11 son of **A** and grandson of
40:14 However, Gedaliah, son of **A**,
40:16 Gedaliah, son of **A**,
Jer 41:1 Gedaliah, son of **A**, at Mizpah.
41:2 son of **A** and grandson of
41:6 "Come to Gedaliah, son of **A**."
41:10 control of Gedaliah, son of **A**.
41:16 had killed Gedaliah, son of **A**.
43:6 son of **A** and grandson of

Ahilud (3)

2Sm 20:24 Jehoshaphat, son of **A**,
1Ki 4:3 Jehoshaphat, son of **A**,
4:12 Baana, son of **A**, had Taanach,

Ahilud's (2)

2Sm 8:16 **A** son Jehoshaphat was the
1Ch 18:15 **A** son Jehoshaphat was the

Ahimaaz (18)

1Sm 14:50 Ahinoam, the daughter of **A**.
2Sm 15:27 and take your son **A** and
15:36 sons with them: Zadok has **A**,
17:17 Jonathan and **A** were waiting
17:18 man saw Jonathan and **A**
17:20 "Where are **A** and Jonathan?"
18:19 Then **A**, Zadok's son, said,
18:22 **A**, Zadok's son, spoke to Joab
18:23 I'd like to run," ⌊replied **A**.⌋
18:23 So **A** ran along the valley road
18:27 me that the first one runs like **A**,
18:28 Then **A** came up to the king,
18:28 **A** said, "May the LORD your
18:29 **A** answered, "I saw a lot of
1Ki 4:15 **A** was in charge of Naphtali.
1Ch 6:8 Zadok was the father of **A**.
6:9 **A** was the father of Azariah.
6:53 Zadok's son was **A**.

Ahiman (4)

Num 13:22 to Hebron, where **A**, Sheshai,
Jos 15:14 Caleb forced out Sheshai, **A**,
Jdg 1:10 There they killed Sheshai, **A**,
1Ch 9:17 Talmon, **A**, and their relatives.

Ahimelech (15)

1Sm 21:1 went to the priest **A** at Nob.
21:1 **A** was trembling as he went to
21:2 David answered the priest **A**,
21:8 David asked **A**, "Don't you
22:9 son when he came to **A**,
22:10 **A** prayed to the LORD for David
22:11 the king sent for the priest **A**,
22:14 **A** asked the king, "But whom
22:16 Saul said, "**A**, you and your
22:20 But **A**, Ahitub's son, had one
26:6 David asked **A** the Hittite and
2Sm 8:17 Abiathar's son **A** were priests.
1Ch 24:3 and Ithamar's descendant **A**
24:6 **A** (son of Abiathar),
24:31 front of King David, Zadok, **A**,

Ahimelech's (2)

1Sm 23:6 When **A** son Abiathar fled to
30:7 **A** son, "Please bring me the

Ahimoth (1)

1Ch 6:25 sons were Amasai and **A**.

Ahimoth's (1)

1Ch 6:26 **A** son was Elkanah.

Ahinadab (1)

1Ki 4:14 **A**, son of Iddo, was in charge

Ahinoam (7)

1Sm 14:50 name of Saul's wife was **A**,
25:43 also married **A** of Jezreel.
27:3 **A** from Jezreel and Abigail
30:5 **A** from Jezreel and Abigail
2Sm 2:2 **A** from Jezreel and Abigail
3:2 ⌊born⌋ to **A** from Jezreel.
1Ch 3:1 ⌊born⌋ to **A** from Jezreel.

Ahio (5)

2Sm 6:3 Uzzah and **A**, Abinadab's sons,
6:4 with **A** walking ahead of the
1Ch 8:31 Gedor, **A**, Zecher,
9:37 Gedor, **A**, Zechariah,

1Ch 13:7 Uzzah and A guided the cart.

Ahira (5)

Num 1:15 A, son of Enan, from the tribe of
2:29 for the people of Naphtali is A,
7:78 of Naphtali, A, son of Enan,
7:83 These were the gifts from A,
10:27 A, son of Enan,

Ahiram (1)

Num 26:38 of Ashbel, the family of A,

Ahisamach (3)

Exo 31:6 son of A, from the tribe of Dan,
35:34 Bezalel and Oholiab, son of A,
38:23 son of A, from the tribe of Dan.

Ahishahar (1)

1Ch 7:10 Zethan, Tarshish, and A.

Ahishar (1)

1Ki 4:6 A was in charge of the palace.

Ahithophel (13)

2Sm 15:12 he sent for A, David's adviser,
15:31 Then David was told, "A is
16:15 and A was with him.
16:20 Then Absalom asked A,
16:21 A told Absalom, "Sleep with
17:1 A said to Absalom,
17:6 "A has told us his plan.
17:15 "A advised Absalom and the
17:21 is what A has advised against
17:23 When A saw that his advice
23:34 Eliam (son of A) from Gilo,
1Ch 27:33 A was the king's adviser.
27:34 and Abiathar succeeded A.

Ahithophel's (6)

2Sm 15:31 make A advice foolish."
15:34 ⌊help me by⌋ undoing A advice
16:23 that A advice was like getting
17:7 "This time A advice is no
17:14 than A advice." (The LORD had
17:14 had commanded A good advice

Ahitub (10)

1Sm 14:3 the son of Ichabod's brother A,
22:12 said, "Listen here, son of A!"
1Ch 6:7 Amariah was the father of A.
6:8 A was the father of Zadok.
6:11 Amariah was the father of A.
6:12 A was the father of Zadok.
6:52 Amariah's son was A.
9:11 the son of A (the official in
Ezr 7:2 who was the son of A,
Neh 11:11 who was the son of A,

Ahitub's (6)

1Sm 22:9 to Ahimelech, A son, in Nob.
22:11 who was A son, and his entire
22:20 But Ahimelech, A son, had one
2Sm 8:17 A son Zadok and Abiathar's
1Ch 6:53 A son was Zadok.
18:16 A son Zadok and Abiathar's

Ahlab (1)

Jdg 1:31 A, Achzib, Helbah, Aphek,

Ahlai (2)

1Ch 2:31 and Sheshan's son was A.
11:41 the Hittite, Zabad (son of A),

Aho (2)

2Sm 23:9 son of Dodo and grandson of A.
1Ch 11:12 son of Dodo and grandson of A.

Ahoah (1)

1Ch 8:4 Abishua, Naaman, A,

Ahohi (2)

2Sm 23:28 Zalmon (descendant of A),
1Ch 11:29 Ilai (descendant of A),

Ahoh's (1)

1Ch 27:4 Dodai, A descendant, was in

Ahumai (1)

1Ch 4:2 was the father of A and Lahad.

Ahuzzam (1)

1Ch 4:6 Naarah gave birth to A,

Ahuzzath (1)

Gen 26:26 Abimelech, his friend A,

Ahzai (1)

Neh 11:13 who was the son of A,

Ai (38)

Gen 12:8 with Bethel on the west and A
13:3 Bethel and A where his tent
Jos 7:2 sent men from Jericho to A.
7:2 A is near Beth Aven,
7:2 the men went and looked at A.
7:3 men are needed to destroy A.
7:3 are only a few troops in A."
7:4 they fled from the men of A.
7:5 The men of A killed about
8:1 and march against A.
8:1 am about to hand the king of A,
8:2 You will do the same thing to A
8:3 started to march against A.
8:9 took their position west of A,
8:9 between Bethel and A.
8:10 of Israel led the army to A.
8:11 They camped north of A with
8:11 the ravine between them and A.
8:12 hide between Bethel and A,
8:14 When the king of A saw the
8:17 man was left in A or Bethel;
8:18 because I am handing A over
8:20 the men of A looked back,
8:21 and attacked the men of A.
8:22 The men of A were caught
8:23 But they captured the king of A
8:24 killing all the inhabitants of A
8:24 the Israelites went back to A
8:25 women from A died that day.
8:26 all the inhabitants of A.
8:28 So Joshua burned A and made
9:3 had done to Jericho and A,
10:1 that Joshua had captured A
10:2 the royal cities, larger than A.
12:9 the king of A (near Bethel),
Ezr 2:28 of Bethel and A: 223
Neh 7:32 of Bethel and A: 123
Jer 49:3 because A is destroyed.

Aiah (2)

Gen 36:24 sons of Zibeon: A and Anah.
1Ch 1:40 sons were A and Anah.

Aiah's (4)

2Sm 3:7 named Rizpah (A daughter).
21:8 Rizpah (A daughter) gave birth
21:10 Rizpah (A daughter) took
21:11 Rizpah (A daughter) had done,

Aiath (1)

Isa 10:28 They come to A.

aid (1)

Isa 30:5 That nation can't give a or help

aids (1)

1Sm 8:15 give it to his a and officials.

Aija (1)

Neh 11:31 A, Bethel and its villages,

Aijalon (10)

Jos 10:12 stand still over the valley of A!"
19:42 Shaalabbin, A, Ithlah,
21:24 A, and Gath Rimmon.
Jdg 1:35 at Har Heres, A, and Shaalbim.
12:12 he was buried in A in the
1Sm 14:31 from Michmash to A,
1Ch 6:69 A with its pastureland,
8:13 of the families who lived in A.
2Ch 11:10 Zorah, A, and Hebron.
28:18 in Beth Shemesh, A, Gederoth,

aim (5)

Psa 21:12 because you a your bow at
58:7 When they a their bows,
64:3 They a bitter words like arrows
Eze 21:22 a the battering rams against the
Gal 6:12 Their only a is to avoid

aimed (2)

1Ki 22:34 One man a his bow at random
2Ch 18:33 One man a his bow at random

aimless (1)

Lam 3:19 and my ⌊a⌋ wandering,

aimlessly (1)

Psa 59:11 Make them wander a by your

Ain (5)

Num 34:11 goes down to Riblah, east of A,
Jos 15:32 Lebaoth, Shilhim, A,
19:7 A, Rimmon, Ether, and Ashan.
21:16 A, Juttah, and Beth Shemesh.
1Ch 4:32 Their five cities were Etam, A,

air (16)

Exo 9:8 in the a as Pharaoh watches.
9:10 threw the ashes up in the a,
Job 28:21 even from the birds in the a.
38:29 given birth to the frost in the a?
Psa 144:4 Humans are like a breath of a.
Sos 1:12 fills the a with its fragrance.
Isa 3:16 walk with their noses in the a,
41:29 statues are nothing but a."
Jer 14:6 They sniff the a like jackals.
Hos 7:12 I will snatch you out of the a
Act 22:23 and throwing dirt into the a.
1Co 14:9 You will be talking into thin a.
2Co 2:14 like a fragrance that fills the a.
1Th 4:17 to meet the Lord in the a.
Rev 9:2 darkened the sun and the a.
16:17 poured his bowl into the a.

Ai's (1)

Jos 8:29 hung the king of A ⌊dead body⌋

Akan (1)

Gen 36:27 of Ezer: Bilhan, Zaavan, and A.

Akeldama (1)

Act 1:19 even call that piece of land A,

Akkub (8)

1Ch 3:24 Pelaiah, A, Johanan, Delaiah,
9:17 Shallum, A, Talmon, Ahiman,
Ezr 2:42 A, Hatita, and Shobai: 139
2:45 Lebanah, Hagabah, A,
Neh 7:45 A, Hatita, and Shobai: 138
8:7 Jamin, A, Shabbethai, Hodiah,
11:19 were the gatekeepers: A,
12:25 and A were gatekeepers

Akrabbim (3)

Num 34:4 and turns south of the A Pass.
Jos 15:3 and goes south of the A Pass.
Jdg 1:36 from the A Pass — from

alamoth (1)

1Ch 15:20 to play harps according to a.

alarm (7)

Neh 4:18 the trumpet a was with me.
Jer 4:19 horn sounding the a for war.
20:16 May he hear a cry of a in the
Hos 5:8 Sound the a at Beth Aven,
8:1 "Sound the a on the ram's horn.
Joe 2:1 Sound the a on my holy
Amo 3:6 If a ram's horn sounds an a in a

alarmed (7)

Dtr 20:3 Don't be afraid or a or tremble
2Sm 4:1 and all Israel was a.
Job 40:23 powerfully against it, it's not a.
Amo 3:6 won't the people be a?
Mat 24:6 Don't be a! These things must
Mar 13:7 and rumors of wars, don't be a!

2Th 2:2 Don't get upset right away or **a**

alcohol (2)
1Ti 3:8 be two-faced or addicted to **a**.
Tit 2:3 to be gossips or addicted to **a**,

Alemeth (4)
1Ch 6:60 **A** with its pastureland,
7:8 Abijah, Anathoth, and **A**.
8:36 Jehoaddah was the father of **A**,
9:42 Jarah was the father of **A**,

alert (13)
Psa 127:1 useless for the guard to stay **a**.
Mat 24:42 "Therefore, be **a**, because you
Mar 13:34 and ordered the guard to be **a**.
13:35 Therefore, be **a**, because you
13:37 what I'm telling you: 'Be **a**!'"
Luk 21:36 Be **a** at all times. Pray so that
Act 20:31 So be **a**! Remember that I
1Co 16:13 Be **a**. Be firm in the Christian
Eph 6:18 For the same reason be **a**.
1Pe 5:8 Keep your mind clear, and be **a**.
Rev 3:2 Be **a**, and strengthen the things
3:3 If you're not **a**, I'll come like a
16:15 is the one who remains **a**

alerted (1)
2Sm 18:25 called and **a** the king.

Alexander (7)
Mar 15:21 was the father of **A** and Rufus.
Act 4:6 Annas, Caiaphas, John, **A**,
19:33 Some people concluded that **A**
19:33 **A** motioned with his hand to
19:34 they recognized that **A** was
1Ti 1:20 people are Hymenaeus and **A**,
2Ti 4:14 **A** the metalworker did me a

Alexandria (3)
Act 6:9 from the cities of Cyrene and **A**
18:24 who had been born in **A**,
27:6 found a ship from **A** that was

Alexandrian (1)
Act 28:11 we sailed on an **A** ship that had

Aliah (1)
1Ch 1:51 Edom were Timna, **A**, Jetheth,

Alian (1)
1Ch 1:40 Shobal's sons were **A**,

alike (10)
Gen 18:25 the innocent and the guilty **a**
19:11 of the house, young and old **a**,
Exo 35:22 men and women **a** — came
Dtr 32:25 and young women **a** will die as
1Sm 30:24 They will all share **a**."
1Ch 26:13 youngest and oldest **a**,
Est 1:7 No two cups were **a**.
Psa 135:8 killed humans and animals **a**.
Isa 46:5 me so that we can be **a**?
Jer 16:6 "Old and young **a** will die in

alive (135)
Gen 6:19 order to keep them **a** with you.
6:20 will come to you to be kept **a**.
11:28 his father Terah was still **a**,
43:7 'Is your father still **a**?
43:27 How is he? Is he still **a**?"
43:28 Our father is **a** and well."
45:3 Is my father still **a**?"
45:26 told him, "Joseph is still **a**!
45:28 "My son Joseph is still **a**.
46:30 for myself that you're still **a**,
50:20 was to keep many people **a**,
Exo 4:18 like to see if they're still **a**."
22:4 if the stolen animal is found **a**
Lev 18:21 Molech ⌊by burning them **a**⌋.
Num 16:30 and they go down **a** to their
16:33 They went down **a** to their
16:48 and those who were still **a**,
Dtr 4:4 your God and are still **a** today.
5:3 all of us who are **a** here today.
18:10 daughters by burning them **a**,
24:6 prepare food in order to stay **a**.
31:27 While I am **a** and still with you,
32:39 I kill, and I make **a**.
Jos 8:23 they captured the king of Ai **a**
14:10 The LORD has kept me **a** as
24:31 had done for Israel, were **a**.
Jdg 2:18 as long as that judge was **a**.
16:30 than he had when he was **a**.
21:14 Gilead who had been kept **a**.
1Sm 14:36 not leave any of them ⌊**a**⌋."
15:8 King Agag of Amalek **a**.
25:22 of his men **a** in the morning."
27:9 he left no man or woman **a**.
27:11 man or woman back to Gath **a**.
2Sm 1:9 I'm **a**, but I'm suffering.'
12:18 "While the child was **a**,
12:21 over the child when he was **a**.
12:22 "As long as the child was **a**,
15:21 whether you're dead or **a**,
17:12 any of his men will be left ⌊**a**⌋.
18:14 while he was still **a** in the tree.
18:18 the memory of my name **a**."
19:6 be pleased if Absalom were **a**
1Ki 3:22 My son is **a** — your son is
3:22 son is dead — my son is **a**."
3:23 'My son is **a** — your son is
3:23 son is dead — my son is **a**."
3:26 was still **a** was deeply moved
12:6 Solomon while he was still **a**.
17:22 He was **a** again.
17:23 "Look! Your son is **a**."
18:4 kept them **a** by providing bread
18:5 keep the horses and mules **a**
20:18 He said, "Take them **a**,
20:32 Ahab asked, "He's still **a**?
21:29 to his family while he is **a**.
2Ki 7:4 us something to keep us **a**,
7:12 we'll capture them **a** and get
16:3 his son by burning him **a**.
17:17 daughters by burning them **a**.
2Ch 10:6 Solomon while he was still **a**.
25:12 captured another 10,000 **a**,
28:3 his son by burning him **a**,
Neh 5:2 are going⌋ to eat and stay **a**."
Job 3:13 Instead of being **a**,
Psa 22:29 even those who are barely **a**.
33:19 keep them **a** during a famine.
39:5 Certainly, everyone **a** is like a
41:2 protect him and keep him **a**.
49:18 while he is **a** (and they praise
55:15 the grave while they are still **a**,
66:9 He has kept us **a** and has not
124:3 us **a** when their anger
143:2 because there is no one **a** who
143:11 O LORD, keep me **a** for the
Pro 1:12 We'll swallow them **a** like the
27:27 to keep your servant girls **a**.
Ecc 6:3 good things ⌊while he was **a**⌋
6:12 for mortals while they are **a**,
7:2 Everyone who is **a** should take
9:3 hearts while they are still **a**.
Isa 7:21 that day a person will keep **a**
26:14 They are no longer **a**.
38:16 give me health and keep me **a**.
Jer 27:12 and you will stay **a**.
29:32 from his family will be left **a**.
49:11 and I will keep them **a**.
Lam 1:11 for food to keep themselves **a**.
1:16 comfort I need to keep me **a**.
1:19 for food to keep themselves **a**.
3:53 They threw me **a** into a pit and
Eze 20:31 sacrifices by burning them **a**.
Dan 5:19 and he kept **a** whomever he
5:19 he wanted to keep **a**.
Jnh 4:3 I'd rather be dead than **a**."
4:8 "I'd rather be dead than **a**."
Zec 1:5 the prophets — are they still **a**?
Mat 6:30 Today it's **a**, and tomorrow it's
27:63 said while he was still **a**,
Mar 16:11 when they heard that he was **a**
16:14 those who had seen him **a**.
Luk 12:28 Today it's **a**, and tomorrow it's
24:23 angels who said that he's **a**.
Jon 4:51 told him that his boy was **a**.
Act 1:3 evidence that he was **a**.
9:41 Tabitha to them. She was **a**.
20:10 "Don't worry! He's **a**!"
20:12 greatly relieved that he was **a**.
25:19 Paul claimed that Jesus is **a**.
27:20 any hope of coming out of it **a**.
27:31 you have no hope of staying **a**."
Rom 6:13 back from death and are now **a**.
7:1 only as long as they are **a**?
7:2 her husband as long as he is **a**.
7:3 while her husband is still **a**,
7:9 At one time I was **a** without
7:9 came, sin became **a**
8:10 but your spirits are **a** because
8:11 mortal bodies **a** by his Spirit
1Co 15:22 be made **a** because of Christ.
15:23 to him ⌊will be made **a**⌋.
2Co 4:11 While we are **a**, we are
Eph 2:5 but he made us **a** together with
Col 2:13 But God made you **a** with
1Th 4:15 We who are still **a** when the
4:17 we who are still **a** will be taken
1Ti 5:6 is dead although she is still **a**.
Tit 1:13 to have faith that is **a** and well.
1Pe 1:3 has a confidence which is **a**
2Pe 1:13 As long as I'm still **a**,
3:5 water and was kept **a** by water.
Rev 1:18 but now I am **a** forever.
2:8 who was dead and became **a**,
3:1 You are known for being **a**,
19:20 Both of them were thrown **a**

Allammelech (1)
Jos 19:26 **A**, Amad, and Mishal.

allegiance (3)
2Ch 36:13 Zedekiah swear an oath of **a**
Isa 19:18 of Canaan and swear **a**
45:23 every tongue will swear ⌊**a**⌋."

alley (1)
Luk 14:21 'Run to every street and **a** in

alliance (6)
Psa 83:5 They form an **a** against you:
Isa 7:2 had made an **a** with Ephraim,
Jer 50:9 I am going to stir up an **a** of
Dan 11:6 northern kings will make an **a**.
11:6 and the **a** won't last.
11:23 After an **a** has been made with

alliances (1)
Isa 30:1 They make **a** against my will.

allied (2)
2Ch 20:35 King Jehoshaphat of Judah **a**
20:37 because you have **a** yourself

allies (9)
Gen 14:5 Chedorlaomer and his **a** came
14:13 (These men were Abram's **a**.)
14:17 Chedorlaomer and his **a**,
14:24 But let my **a** Aner, Eshcol,
1Ki 20:12 as he and his **a** were drinking
20:16 the 32 kings who were his **a**.
Neh 4:2 In front of his **a** and the army
Eze 30:6 All Egypt's **a** will die.
Oba 1:7 All your **a** will force you to

Allon (1)
1Ch 4:37 (son of Shiphi, grandson of **A**,

allow (59)
Gen 12:19 'She's my sister' and **a** me to
Exo 10:25 But Moses said, "You must **a**
Lev 11:43 Never **a** yourselves to become
Num 16:5 and who it is that he will **a** to
32:16 "**A** us to build stone fences for
35:6 You must **a** murderers to
35:32 a cash payment to **a** him
Dtr 2:27 "If you **a** us to travel through
2:30 Sihon of Heshbon wouldn't **a**
Jdg 11:17 But he wouldn't **a** it,
1Sm 11:1 right eye and **a** no one
2Sm 15:25 he will **a** me to come back and
1Ki 1:27 Did you **a** this to happen
11:34 Instead, I will **a** him to be ruler
18:1 I will **a** rain to fall on the

1Ki 20:31 **A** us to dress in sackcloth,
Ezr 5:17 If it pleases Your Majesty, **a**
Neh 10:30 We will not **a** our daughters to
10:30 of the land or **a** their daughters
13:25 "We won't **a** our daughters to
13:25 and we won't **a** their daughters
Est 9:13 **a** the Jews in Susa to do
Job 20:20 He will never **a** anything he
36:6 He doesn't **a** the wicked person
Psa 16:10 to the grave or **a** your holy one
89:33 away from him or **a** my truth
107:38 and he does not **a** a shortage of
118:18 but he did not **a** me to be killed.
Pro 10:3 The LORD will not **a** a
Ecc 3:22 Who will **a** them to see what
5:12 have will not **a** them to sleep.
Jer 27:18 the LORD of Armies not to **a**
50:16 Don't **a** anyone in Babylon to
Hos 2:17 I won't **a** her to say the names
Mat 6:13 Don't **a** us to be tempted.
10:13 **a** your greeting to stand.
Mar 1:34 However, he would not **a** the
5:19 But Jesus would not **a** it.
Luk 11:4 Don't **a** us to be tempted."
Act 2:27 to the grave or **a** your holy one
4:29 and **a** us to speak your word
13:35 'You will not **a** your holy one to
16:7 Spirit of Jesus wouldn't **a** this.
Rom 14:16 Don't **a** anyone to say that what
15:5 **a** you to live in harmony with
1Co 6:4 why do you **a** people whom the
6:12 but I won't **a** anything to gain
10:13 will not **a** you to be tempted
Gal 5:2 can guarantee that if you **a**
5:26 We can't **a** ourselves to act
6:9 We can't **a** ourselves to get
Php 2:19 that the Lord Jesus will **a** me
2Th 3:13 Brothers and sisters, we can't **a**
1Ti 2:12 I don't **a** a woman to teach or to
2Ti 2:25 Maybe God will **a** them to
2Pe 2:16 a human voice and wouldn't **a**
Rev 3:21 I will **a** everyone who wins the
11:3 I will **a** my two witnesses who
11:9 bodies and will not **a** anyone

allowance (6)

1Ki 11:18 a home, a food **a**, and land.
2Ki 25:30 him a daily food **a** as long as
Neh 5:14 for by the governor's food **a**.
5:18 from the governor's food **a**,
Jer 52:34 him a daily food **a** as long as
Dan 1:5 for them to get a daily **a**

allowances (1)

2Ch 11:23 He gave them **a** and obtained

allowed (74)

Gen 3:2 "We're **a** to eat the fruit from
19:29 Lot was **a** to escape from the
31:32 has them will not be **a** to live.
34:31 "Should Shechem have been **a**
43:3 'You won't be **a** to see me
43:5 'You won't be **a** to see me
44:23 you will never be **a** to see me
Exo 19:22 Even the priests who are **a** to
Lev 11:39 any animal that you are **a**
21:2 However, you are **a** to become
Num 16:5 the LORD chooses will be **a**
27:4 should our father's name be **a**
Dtr 16:5 You're not **a** to slaughter the
24:4 her first husband is not **a** to
Jos 9:15 making a treaty which **a** them
9:21 that they should be **a** to live.
21:44 The LORD **a** them to have
Jdg 3:6 The Israelites **a** their sons and
20:36 The Israelites had **a** the men of
21:17 men who survived must be **a**
1Sm 29:4 He shouldn't ⌊be **a** to⌋ become
1Ki 13:16 "I'm not **a** to go back with you.
13:16 I'm not **a** to eat or drink with
13:22 your dead body will not be **a**
2Ch 34:11 had **a** to become run-down.
Est 5:12 Queen Esther **a** no one except
Job 8:4 he **a** them to suffer the
34:17 hates justice be **a** to govern?
Psa 66:9 alive and has not **a** us to fall.
78:61 He **a** his power to be taken
79:10 the nations ⌊be **a** to⌋ say,
125:3 A wicked ruler will not be **a** to
Ecc 2:10 I **a** myself to have any pleasure
Jer 22:27 you won't be **a** to come home."
36:5 "I'm no longer **a** to go to the
Lam 1:21 You have **a** the day to come,
Eze 14:3 Should they be **a** to ask me for
20:3 you will not be **a** to ask me for
20:25 I also **a** them to follow laws
20:31 Should you be **a** to ask me for
20:31 you won't be **a** to ask me for
31:14 and their tops were no longer **a**
Dan 7:12 but they were **a** to live for a
Mat 19:8 "Moses **a** you to divorce your
Mar 5:37 Jesus **a** no one to go with him
6:19 But she wasn't **a** to do it
10:4 They said, "Moses **a** a man to
Luk 8:51 He **a** no one to go with him
21:24 Jerusalem until the times **a**
Jon 5:10 You're not **a** to carry your cot
18:31 not **a** to execute anyone."
Act 14:16 In the past God **a** all people to
22:22 He shouldn't have been **a** to
25:24 shout that he must not be **a**
27:3 Julius treated Paul kindly and **a**
28:16 Paul was **a** to live by himself,
Rom 1:24 For this reason God **a** their
1:26 For this reason God **a** their
1:28 God **a** their own immoral minds
1Co 6:12 "I'm **a** to do anything,"
6:12 I'm **a** to do anything,
10:23 "I'm **a** to do anything,"
10:23 I'm **a** to do anything,
Eph 3:9 He **a** me to explain the way
2Th 3:10 to work shouldn't be **a** to eat."
Rev 7:2 the four angels who had been **a**
9:5 They were not **a** to kill them.
9:5 They were only **a** to torture
13:5 The beast was **a** to speak
13:7 It was **a** to wage war against
13:14 earth with the signs that it is **a**
13:15 The second beast was **a** to put
16:8 The sun was **a** to burn people
20:4 sat on them were **a** to judge.

allowing (4)

Eze 14:3 and they are **a** themselves to
14:7 to idols and by **a** himself
Luk 2:29 "Now, Lord, you are **a** your
Eph 3:8 me his kindness by **a** me

allows (4)

Exo 21:22 pay whatever fine the court **a**
Eze 14:4 devoted to idols and **a** himself
Gal 5:3 I insist that everyone who **a**
Heb 7:19 us greater confidence and **a**

Almighty (359)

Gen 15:2 Abram asked, "**A** LORD,
15:8 Abram asked, "**A** LORD,
17:1 He said to Abram, "I am God **A**.
28:3 May God **A** bless you,
35:11 also said to him, "I am God **A**.
43:14 May God **A** make him merciful
48:3 Jacob said to Joseph, "God **A**
49:25 because of the **A** who gives
Exo 6:3 and Jacob as God **A**,
Num 24:4 has a vision from the **A**,
24:16 has a vision from the **A**,
Dtr 3:24 "**A** LORD, you have ⌊only⌋
9:26 the LORD and said, "**A** LORD,
Jos 7:7 Joshua said, "**A** LORD,
Jdg 16:28 called to the LORD, "**A** LORD,
Rut 1:20 because the **A** has made my
1:21 me and the **A** has done evil
2Sm 7:18 "Who am I, **A** LORD,"
7:19 to be a small act, **A** LORD.
7:19 **A** LORD, this is the teaching
7:20 I, David, say to you, **A** LORD,
7:28 "**A** LORD, you are God,
7:29 Indeed, you, **A** LORD,
1Ki 2:26 the ark of the **A** LORD ahead
1Ch 17:26 "**A** LORD, you are God.
Job 5:17 despise discipline from the **A**.
6:4 because the arrows of the **A**
6:14 if he abandons the fear of the **A**.
8:3 the **A** distort righteousness?
8:5 and plead for mercy from the **A**,
13:3 I want to speak to the **A**,
15:25 and attacks the **A** like a warrior.
21:15 Who is the **A** that we should
21:20 drink from the wrath of the **A**.
22:3 Is the **A** pleased when you are
22:17 What can the **A** do for us?'
22:23 If you return to the **A**,
22:25 then the **A** will become your
22:26 you will be happy with the **A**
23:16 The **A** has filled me with terror.
24:1 "Why doesn't the **A** set aside
27:2 away my rights, by the **A**,
27:10 Can he be happy with the **A**?
27:11 not hide what the **A** has done.
27:13 that tyrants receive from the **A**:
29:5 When the **A** was still with me
31:2 inheritance from the **A** on high?
31:35 Let the **A** answer me.
32:8 the breath of the **A**,
33:4 breath of the **A** gives me life.
34:10 evil or that the **A** would ever do
34:12 and the **A** will never pervert
35:13 The **A** doesn't even pay
37:23 The **A**, whom we can't reach,
40:2 fault with the **A** correct him?
Psa 68:14 Meanwhile, the **A** was still
68:20 The **A** LORD is our escape
69:6 O **A** LORD of Armies.
71:5 You are my hope, O **A** LORD.
71:16 mighty deeds of the **A** LORD.
73:28 I have made the **A** LORD my
91:1 remain in the shadow of the **A**.
109:21 O LORD **A**, deal with me out of
140:7 O LORD **A**, the strong one who
141:8 My eyes look to you, LORD **A**.
Isa 3:15 The **A** LORD of Armies asks,
7:7 This is what the **A** LORD says:
10:16 That is why the **A** LORD of
10:23 The **A** LORD of Armies will
10:24 The **A** LORD of Armies says:
10:33 The **A** LORD of Armies will
13:6 like destruction from the **A**.
19:4 the **A** LORD of Armies.
22:5 The **A** LORD of Armies has
22:12 On that day the **A** LORD of
22:14 says the **A** LORD of Armies.
22:15 This is what the **A** LORD of
25:8 The **A** LORD will wipe away
28:16 This is what the **A** LORD says:
28:22 because I have heard that the **A**
30:15 This is what the **A** LORD,
40:10 The **A** LORD is coming with
48:16 Now the **A** LORD has sent me
49:22 This is what the **A** LORD says:
50:4 The **A** LORD will teach me
50:5 The **A** LORD will open my
50:7 The **A** LORD helps me.
50:9 The **A** LORD helps me.
52:4 This is what the **A** LORD says:
56:8 The **A** LORD, who gathers the
61:1 The Spirit of the **A** LORD is
61:11 so the **A** LORD will make
65:15 The **A** LORD will kill you and
Jer 1:6 I, Jeremiah, said, "**A** LORD,
2:19 the **A** LORD of Armies.
2:22 declares the **A** LORD.
4:10 I said, "**A** LORD, you certainly
7:20 is what the **A** LORD says:
14:13 Then I said, "**A** LORD,
32:17 '**A** LORD, you made heaven
32:25 Yet you, **A** LORD, told me to
44:26 "As the **A** LORD lives ..."
46:10 That day belongs to the **A**
46:10 The **A** LORD of Armies will
49:5 declares the **A** LORD of
50:25 because the **A** LORD of Armies
50:31 declares the **A** LORD of
Eze 1:24 like the thunder of the **A**,
2:4 is what the **A** LORD says.'
3:11 is what the **A** LORD says.'"
3:27 is what the **A** LORD says.'
4:14 I answered, "**A** LORD,
5:5 is what the **A** LORD says:

Eze 5:7 this is what the **A** LORD says:
5:8 this is what the **A** LORD says:
5:11 I live, declares the **A** LORD,
6:3 to the word of the **A** LORD!
6:3 This is what the **A** LORD says
6:11 is what the **A** LORD says:
7:2 "Son of man, this is what the **A**
7:5 is what the **A** LORD says:
8:1 The power of the **A** LORD
9:8 I cried, "**A** LORD, will you
10:5 It was like the sound of the **A**
11:7 this is what the **A** LORD says:
11:8 declares the **A** LORD.
11:13 down and cried out, "**A** LORD,
11:16 is what the **A** LORD says:
11:17 is what the **A** LORD says:
11:21 declares the **A** LORD.'"
12:10 is what the **A** LORD says:
12:19 'This is what the **A** LORD says
12:23 is what the **A** LORD says:
12:25 declares the **A** LORD.'"
12:28 is what the **A** LORD says:
12:28 declares the **A** LORD.'"
13:3 is what the **A** LORD says:
13:8 is what the **A** LORD says:
13:8 declares the **A** LORD.
13:13 is what the **A** LORD says:
13:16 declares the **A** LORD.'"
13:18 is what the **A** LORD says:
13:20 is what the **A** LORD says:
14:6 is what the **A** LORD says:
14:11 declares the **A** LORD.'"
14:14 declares the **A** LORD.
14:16 As I live, declares the **A** LORD,
14:18 As I live, declares the **A** LORD,
14:20 As I live, declares the **A** LORD,
14:21 is what the **A** LORD says:
14:23 declares the **A** LORD.
15:6 this is what the **A** LORD says:
15:8 declares the **A** LORD.
16:3 Tell them, 'This is what the **A**
16:8 declares the **A** LORD.
16:14 declares the **A** LORD.
16:19 declares the **A** LORD.
16:23 declares the **A** LORD.
16:30 declares the **A** LORD.
16:36 This is what the **A** LORD says:
16:43 declares the **A** LORD.
16:48 As I live, declares the **A** LORD,
16:59 is what the **A** LORD says:
16:63 declares the **A** LORD.'"
17:3 is what the **A** LORD says:
17:9 is what the **A** LORD says:
17:16 declares the **A** LORD,
17:19 this is what the **A** LORD says:
17:22 is what the **A** LORD says:
18:3 As I live, declares the **A** LORD,
18:9 declares the **A** LORD.
18:23 declares the **A** LORD.
18:30 declares the **A** LORD.
18:32 declares the **A** LORD.
20:3 is what the **A** LORD says:
20:3 As I live, declares the **A** LORD,
20:5 is what the **A** LORD says:
20:27 is what the **A** LORD says:
20:30 is what the **A** LORD says:
20:31 declares the **A** LORD,
20:33 declares the **A** LORD,
20:36 declares the **A** LORD.
20:39 this is what the **A** LORD says:
20:40 declares the **A** LORD.
20:44 declares the **A** LORD.'"
20:47 This is what the **A** LORD says:
20:49 **A** LORD, no! The people
21:7 declares the **A** LORD."
21:13 declares the **A** LORD.
21:24 is what the **A** LORD says:
21:26 This is what the **A** LORD says:
21:28 Tell them, 'This is what the **A**
22:3 is what the **A** LORD says:
22:12 declares the **A** LORD.
22:19 This is what the **A** LORD says:
22:28 is what the **A** LORD says.'
22:31 declares the **A** LORD.
23:22 this is what the **A** LORD says:
23:28 is what the **A** LORD says:

Eze 23:32 This is what the **A** LORD says:
23:34 declares the **A** LORD.
23:35 is what the **A** LORD says:
23:46 is what the **A** LORD says:
23:49 know that I am the **A** LORD."
24:3 is what the **A** LORD says:
24:6 is what the **A** LORD says:
24:9 is what the **A** LORD says:
24:14 done,'" declares the **A** LORD.
24:21 is what the **A** LORD says:
24:24 know that I am the **A** LORD.'"
25:3 to the word of the **A** LORD.
25:3 This is what the **A** LORD says:
25:6 is what the **A** LORD says:
25:8 is what the **A** LORD says:
25:12 is what the **A** LORD says:
25:13 this is what the **A** LORD says:
25:14 declares the **A** LORD.
25:15 is what the **A** LORD says:
25:16 this is what the **A** LORD says:
26:3 this is what the **A** LORD says:
26:5 declares the **A** LORD.
26:7 is what the **A** LORD says:
26:14 declares the **A** LORD.
26:15 "This is what the **A** LORD
26:19 is what the **A** LORD says:
26:21 declares the **A** LORD.
27:3 is what the **A** LORD says:
28:2 is what the **A** LORD says:
28:6 is what the **A** LORD says:
28:12 is what the **A** LORD says:
28:22 is what the **A** LORD says:
28:24 know that I am the **A** LORD.
28:25 is what the **A** LORD says:
29:3 is what the **A** LORD says:
29:8 is what the **A** LORD says:
29:13 is what the **A** LORD says:
29:16 know that I am the **A** LORD."
29:19 This is what the **A** LORD says:
29:20 declares the **A** LORD.
30:2 is what the **A** LORD says:
30:6 declares the **A** LORD.
30:10 is what the **A** LORD says:
30:13 is what the **A** LORD says:
30:22 is what the **A** LORD says:
31:10 is what the **A** LORD says:
31:15 is what the **A** LORD says:
31:18 declares the **A** LORD.'"
32:3 is what the **A** LORD says:
32:8 declares the **A** LORD.
32:11 is what the **A** LORD says:
32:14 declares the **A** LORD.
32:16 declares the **A** LORD.
32:31 declares the **A** LORD.
32:32 declares the **A** LORD.
33:11 declares the **A** LORD,
33:25 is what the **A** LORD says:
33:27 is what the **A** LORD says:
34:2 is what the **A** LORD says:
34:8 As I live, declares the **A** LORD,
34:10 This is what the **A** LORD says:
34:11 is what the **A** LORD says:
34:15 declares the **A** LORD.
34:17 this is what the **A** LORD says:
34:20 "'So this is what the **A** LORD
34:30 declares the **A** LORD.
34:31 declares the **A** LORD."
35:3 is what the **A** LORD says:
35:6 declares the **A** LORD,
35:11 declares the **A** LORD,
35:14 is what the **A** LORD says:
36:2 This is what the **A** LORD says:
36:3 is what the **A** LORD says:
36:4 to the word of the **A** LORD.
36:4 This is what the **A** LORD says
36:6 is what the **A** LORD says:
36:7 this is what the **A** LORD says:
36:13 is what the **A** LORD says:
36:14 declares the **A** LORD.
36:15 declares the **A** LORD.'"
36:22 is what the **A** LORD says:
36:23 declares the **A** LORD.
36:32 declares the **A** LORD.
36:33 is what the **A** LORD says:
36:37 is what the **A** LORD says:
37:3 "Only you know, **A** LORD."

Eze 37:5 This is what the **A** LORD says
37:9 is what the **A** LORD says:
37:12 is what the **A** LORD says:
37:19 is what the **A** LORD says:
37:21 is what the **A** LORD says:
38:3 is what the **A** LORD says:
38:10 is what the **A** LORD says:
38:14 is what the **A** LORD says:
38:17 is what the **A** LORD says:
38:18 declares the **A** LORD.
38:21 declares the **A** LORD.
39:1 is what the **A** LORD says:
39:5 declares the **A** LORD.
39:8 declares the **A** LORD.
39:10 declares the **A** LORD.
39:13 declares the **A** LORD.
39:17 this is what the **A** LORD says:
39:20 declares the **A** LORD.'
39:25 this is what the **A** LORD says:
39:29 declares the **A** LORD."
43:18 this is what the **A** LORD says:
43:27 declares the **A** LORD."
44:6 is what the **A** LORD says:
44:9 this is what the **A** LORD says:
44:15 declares the **A** LORD.
44:27 declares the **A** LORD.
45:9 is what the **A** LORD says:
45:9 declares the **A** LORD.
45:15 declares the **A** LORD.
45:18 is what the **A** LORD says:
46:1 is what the **A** LORD says:
46:16 is what the **A** LORD says:
47:13 This is what the **A** LORD says:
47:23 declares the **A** LORD.
48:29 declares the **A** LORD.
Joe 1:15 like destruction from the **A**.
Amo 1:8 The **A** LORD has said this.
3:7 Certainly, the **A** LORD doesn't
3:8 The **A** LORD has spoken.
3:11 This is what the **A** LORD says:
3:13 declares the **A** LORD,
4:2 The **A** LORD has taken an oath
4:5 The **A** LORD declares this.
5:3 This is what the **A** LORD says:
5:16 the **A** God of Armies,
6:8 The **A** LORD has sworn an
7:1 This is what the **A** LORD
7:2 "**A** LORD, please forgive us!
7:4 This is what the **A** LORD
7:4 The **A** LORD was calling for
7:5 Then I said, "**A** LORD,
7:6 either," the **A** LORD said.
8:1 This is what the **A** LORD
8:3 declares the **A** LORD.
8:9 declares the **A** LORD,
8:11 declares the **A** LORD,
9:5 The **A** LORD of Armies
9:8 I, the **A** LORD, have my eyes
Oba 1:1 This is what the **A** LORD says
Mic 1:2 The **A** LORD will be a witness
Hab 3:19 The LORD **A** is my strength.
Zep 1:7 in the presence of the **A** LORD,
Zec 9:14 The **A** LORD will blow the
Luk 1:49 because the **A** has done great
2Co 6:18 The Lord **A** says, "I will be
Rev 1:8 the one who is coming, the **A**.
4:8 holy is the Lord God **A**,
11:17 thanks to you, Lord God **A**,
15:3 and amazing, Lord God **A**.
16:7 answer, "Yes, Lord God **A**,
16:14 on the frightening day of God **A**.
19:6 The Lord our God, the **A**,
19:15 of the fierce anger of God **A**.
21:22 because the Lord God **A** and

Almighty's (1)

Job 11:7 are you able to find the **A** limits

Almodad (2)

Gen 10:26 Joktan was the father of **A**,
1Ch 1:20 Joktan was the father of **A**,

Almon (1)

Jos 21:18 Anathoth, and **A**.

almond (7)

Gen 30:37 fresh-cut branches of poplar, **a**,
Exo 25:33 cups shaped like **a** blossoms,
25:34 cups shaped like **a** blossoms,
37:19 cups shaped like **a** blossoms,
37:20 cups shaped like **a** blossoms,
Ecc 12:5 the **a** tree blossoms,
Jer 1:11 "I see a branch of an **a** tree."

Almon Diblathaim (2)

Num 33:46 and set up camp at **A**
33:47 They moved from **A** and set up

almonds (2)

Gen 43:11 myrrh, pistachio nuts, and **a**.
Num 17:8 and produced ripe **a**.

aloe (1)

Jon 19:39 of a myrrh and **a** mixture.

aloes (4)

Num 24:6 like **a** planted by the LORD,
Psa 45:8 with myrrh, **a**, and cassia.
Pro 7:17 with myrrh, **a**, and cinnamon.
Sos 4:14 **a**, and all the best spices.

alone (131)

Gen 2:18 is not good for the man to be **a**.
7:1 that you **a** are righteous among
32:24 So Jacob was left **a**.
Exo 4:26 So the LORD let him **a**.
14:12 tell you in Egypt, 'Leave us **a**!
18:14 Why do you sit here **a**,
18:18 You can't do it **a**!
29:9 They **a** are to be priests;
32:10 Now leave me **a**. I'm so angry
Num 11:17 to take care of the people **a**.
Dtr 8:3 a person cannot live on bread **a**
9:14 Leave me **a**! I'll destroy them
32:12 so the LORD **a** led his people.
33:28 Jacob's spring will be ⌊left⌋ **a**
Jdg 3:20 came up to him as he sat **a**
Rut 1:3 and she was left **a** with her two
1:5 So Naomi was left **a**,
1Sm 2:5 of many children grieves all **a**.
21:1 "Why are you **a**?" he asked
2Sm 2:19 and refused to leave him **a**.
2:21 Abner told him, "Leave me **a**!
13:2 impossible for him to be **a**
16:11 Leave him **a**. Let him curse,
18:24 he saw a man running **a**.
18:25 "If he's **a**," the king said,
18:26 ⌊another⌋ man running **a**."
1Ki 3:18 We were **a**. No one else was
8:39 because you **a** know what is in
11:29 The two of them were **a** in the
15:19 so that he will leave me **a**."
2Ki 4:27 man of God said, "Leave her **a**.
5:17 I will sacrifice to the LORD **a**.
18:14 Go away, and leave me **a**.
19:15 You **a** are God of all the
19:19 earth will know that you **a** are
2Ch 6:30 because you **a** know what is in
16:3 so that he will leave me **a**."
Ezr 4:3 We must build it **a** for the
Neh 9:6 You **a** are the LORD.
Job 7:16 Leave me **a** because my days
10:20 So stop ⌊this⌋, and leave me **a**.
15:19 (The land was given to them **a**,
21:14 they say to God, 'Leave us **a**.
22:17 They told God, 'Leave us **a**!
31:17 or have eaten my food **a**
Psa 4:8 I lie down because you **a**,
9:8 He **a** judges the world with
10:14 You **a** have been the helper of
13:2 long must I make decisions **a**
44:4 You **a** are my king,
62:1 soul waits calmly for God **a**.
62:2 He **a** is my rock and my savior
62:5 Wait calmly for God **a**,
62:6 He **a** is my rock and my savior
71:16 your righteousness, yours **a**.
72:18 who **a** does miracles.
75:7 God **a** is the judge.
76:7 You **a** must be feared!
Psa 83:18 You **a** are the Most High God of
86:10 You **a** are God.
100:3 that the LORD **a** is God.
139:2 You **a** know when I sit down
139:13 You **a** created my inner being.
139:19 people would leave me **a**.
Pro 5:17 They should be yours **a**,
9:12 you **a** will be held responsible.
Ecc 4:8 There are people who are all **a**.
4:10 for the one who is ⌊all⌋ **a** when
Sos 7:13 new and old things for you **a**,
Isa 2:11 the LORD **a** will be honored.
2:17 the LORD **a** will be honored.
26:4 the LORD, the LORD **a**,
30:17 Then you will be left **a** like a
37:16 You **a** are God of the kingdoms
37:20 know that you **a** are the LORD."
43:11 I **a** am the LORD, and there is
43:25 I **a** am the one who is going to
44:24 I spread out the earth all **a**.
45:14 "Certainly God is with you **a**,
45:24 are found in the LORD **a**."
48:15 I **a** have spoken. I have called
49:21 I was left **a**. Where have they
51:12 I **a** am the one who comforts
63:3 "I have trampled **a** in the
Jer 15:17 I sat **a** because your hand was
41:8 So he left them **a** and didn't kill
49:31 gates or bars. Its people live **a**.
Lam 3:28 They should sit **a** and remain
Eze 9:8 killing people, I was left **a**.
Dan 10:8 So I was left **a** to see this
10:13 to help me because I was left **a**
Hos 4:17 worship idols. Leave them **a**!
8:9 wild donkeys wandering off **a**.
Mic 7:14 They live **a** in the woods,
Mat 4:4 person cannot live on bread **a**
14:13 to a place where he could be **a**.
14:23 evening came, he was there **a**.
15:14 Leave them **a**! They are blind
17:1 where they could be **a**.
18:15 him when the two of you are **a**.
22:22 they left him **a** and went away.
27:19 "Leave that innocent man **a**.
27:49 The others said, "Leave him **a**!
Mar 1:35 where he could be **a** to pray.
1:45 in places where he could be **a**.
4:10 When he was **a** with his
4:34 But when he was **a** with his
6:31 to a place where we can be **a**
6:32 a place where they could be **a**.
6:47 and he was **a** on the land.
7:33 the crowd to be **a** with him.
9:2 where they could be **a**.
10:18 No one is good except God **a**.
12:12 they left him **a** and went away.
14:6 Jesus said, "Leave her **a**!
Luk 4:4 cannot live on bread **a**."
4:42 to a place where he could be **a**.
5:16 where he could be **a** for prayer.
9:10 so that they could be **a**.
9:36 they saw that Jesus was **a**.
Jon 8:9 was left **a** with the woman.
12:7 said to Judas, "Leave her **a**!
14:18 "I will not leave you all **a**.
16:32 own way and leave me all **a**.
16:32 Yet, I'm not all **a**, because the
Act 3:16 Through his power **a** this man,
5:38 We should leave them **a**.
23:19 went where they could be **a**,
Rom 12:19 After all, Scripture says, "I **a**
16:27 God **a** is wise. Glory belongs to
Heb 10:30 "I **a** have the right to take

Aloth (1)

1Ki 4:16 was in charge of Asher and **A**.

aloud (5)

Psa 3:4 I call **a** to the LORD,
27:7 Hear, O LORD, when I cry **a**.
Pro 2:3 if you ask **a** for understanding,
Isa 10:30 Cry **a**, you people in Gallim!
58:1 Cry **a**! Don't hold back! Raise

Alphaeus (5)

Mat 10:3 tax collector; James (son of **A**),
Mar 2:14 son of **A**, sitting in a tax office.
3:18 James (son of **A**), Thaddaeus,
Luk 6:15 Thomas, James (son of **A**),
Act 1:13 Matthew, James (son of **A**),

altar (390)

Gen 8:20 Noah built an **a** to the LORD.
12:7 So he built an **a** there to the
12:8 He also built an **a** to the LORD
13:4 where he had first made an **a**.
13:18 he built an **a** for the LORD.
22:9 Abraham built the **a** and
22:9 on top of the wood on the **a**.
26:25 So Isaac built an **a** there and
33:20 He set up an **a** there and
35:1 Make an **a** there. I am the God
35:3 I will make an **a** there to God,
35:7 He built an **a** there and called
Exo 17:15 Moses built an **a** and called it
20:24 "You must build an **a** for me
20:25 If you build an **a** for me made
20:26 use stairs to go up to my **a**.
21:14 must take him away from my **a**
24:4 next morning he built an **a** at
24:6 the other half against the **a**.
27:1 "Make an **a** out of acacia wood.
27:2 The four horns and the **a** must
27:5 under the ledge of the **a** so that
27:5 that it comes halfway up the **a**.
27:6 out of acacia wood for the **a**,
27:7 both sides of the **a** to carry it.
27:8 "Make the **a** out of boards so
28:43 or when they come near the **a**
29:12 and put it on the horns of the **a**
29:12 of it out at the bottom of the **a**.
29:13 and burn them on the **a**.
29:16 it against the **a** on all sides.
29:18 burn the whole ram on the **a**.
29:20 against the **a** on all sides.
29:21 of the blood that is on the **a**
29:25 and burn them on the **a** on top
29:36 this offering for sin on the **a**
29:37 For seven days at the **a** make
29:37 the LORD and set the **a** apart
29:37 Then the **a** will be most holy.
29:37 the **a** will become holy.
29:38 on the **a** regularly every day:
29:44 the tent of meeting and the **a**
30:1 "Build an **a** out of acacia wood
30:2 The horns and **a** must be made
30:6 Put the **a** in front of the canopy
30:7 on this **a** every morning when
30:9 unauthorized incense on this **a**
30:10 must be placed on the **a**
30:18 the tent of meeting and the **a**,
30:20 Before they come near the **a** to
30:27 the utensils, the **a** for incense,
30:28 the **a** for burnt offerings and all
31:8 its utensils, the **a** for incense,
31:9 the **a** for burnt offerings and all
32:5 he built an **a** in front of it and
35:15 the **a** for incense with its poles,
35:16 the **a** for burnt offerings with its
37:25 He made an **a** out of acacia
37:25 The horns and **a** were made
38:1 He made the **a** for burnt
38:2 the four horns and the **a** out
38:4 He made a grate for the **a** out of
38:4 the ledge, halfway up the **a**.
38:7 the rings on the sides of the **a**
38:7 He made the **a** out of boards so
38:30 the bronze **a** with its bronze
39:38 the gold **a**, the anointing oil,
39:39 the bronze **a** with its bronze
40:5 Put the gold **a** for incense in
40:6 "Put the **a** for burnt offerings in
40:7 the tent of meeting and the **a**,
40:10 Anoint the **a** for burnt offerings
40:10 way you will dedicate the **a**,
40:26 Moses put the gold **a** in the tent
40:29 He put the **a** for burnt offerings
40:30 the tent of meeting and the **a**
40:32 they approached the **a**.
40:33 around the tent and the **a**
Lev 1:5 all sides of the **a** that is at
1:7 Aaron will start a fire on the **a**

Lev 1:8 of the wood burning on the **a**.
1:9 priest will burn all of it on the **a**.
1:11 on the north side of the **a**.
1:11 against the **a** on all sides.
1:12 on the wood burning on the **a**.
1:13 priest will burn all of it on the **a**.
1:15 The priest must bring it to the **a**.
1:15 neck and burn the bird on the **a**.
1:15 blood against the side of the **a**.
1:16 it on the east side of the **a**
1:17 on the wood burning on the **a**.
2:2 The priest will burn it on the **a**
2:8 priest who will bring it to the **a**.
2:9 burn it as a reminder on the **a**.
2:12 must never be placed on the **a**
3:2 against the **a** on all sides.
3:8 against the **a** on all sides.
3:11 the fellowship offering on the **a**.
3:13 against the **a** on all sides.
3:16 priest will burn them on the **a**.
4:7 the blood on the horns of the **a**
4:7 blood at the bottom of the **a**
4:10 on the **a** for burnt offerings.
4:18 blood on the horns of the **a**
4:18 the blood at the bottom of the **a**
4:19 all the fat and burn it on the **a**.
4:25 and put it on the horns of the **a**
4:25 of the **a** for burnt offerings.
4:26 He will burn all the fat on the **a**
4:30 and put it on the horns of the **a**
4:30 the blood at the bottom of the **a**.
4:31 The priest will burn it on the **a**
4:34 and put it on the horns of the **a**
4:34 the blood at the bottom of the **a**.
4:35 the priest will burn it on the **a**
5:9 for sin on the side of the **a**,
5:9 drained at the bottom of the **a**.
5:12 by fire to the LORD on the **a**.
6:9 stays on the **a** overnight while
6:9 while the **a** fire is kept
6:10 the ashes left on the **a** from
6:10 and will put them next to the **a**.
6:12 always be burning on the **a**.
6:13 always be burning on the **a**.
6:14 presence in front of the **a**.
6:15 He will burn it on the **a** as a
7:2 against the **a** on all sides.
7:5 priest will burn them on the **a**.
7:31 priest will burn the fat on the **a**.
8:11 of the oil on the **a** seven times
8:11 times and anointed the **a**,
8:15 on the horns of the **a** all around
8:15 and cleansed the **a** from sins.
8:15 the blood at the bottom of the **a**
8:16 and he burned them on the **a**.
8:19 against the **a** on all sides.
8:21 the whole ram on the **a** as
8:24 against all the sides of the **a**.
8:28 of the burnt offering on the **a**.
8:30 of the blood that was on the **a**,
9:7 "Come to the **a** and sacrifice an
9:8 Aaron came to the **a** and
9:9 and put it on the horns of the **a**.
9:9 the blood at the bottom of the **a**.
9:10 On the **a** he burned the fat,
9:12 it against the **a** on all sides.
9:13 He burned it on the **a**.
9:14 of the burnt offering on the **a**.
9:17 of grain and burned it on the **a**
9:18 against the **a** on all sides.
9:20 Aaron burned them all on the **a**.
9:22 he came down ⌊from the **a**⌋.
9:24 and the pieces of fat on the **a**.
10:12 and eat it next to the **a**
14:20 and the grain offering on the **a**.
16:12 full of burning coals from the **a**,
16:18 Then he will go out to the **a**
16:18 it all around the horns of the **a**.
16:20 the tent of meeting, and the **a**,
16:25 of the offering for sin on the **a**.
16:33 the tent of meeting, and the **a**.
17:6 blood against the LORD's **a** at
17:11 make peace with me on the **a**.
21:18 may ever come near ⌊the **a**⌋.
21:23 up to the canopy or to the **a**,
22:22 in a sacrifice by fire on the **a**.

Num 3:26 the inner tent and the **a**,
4:11 a violet cloth over the gold **a**
4:13 a purple cloth over the **a**.
4:14 accessories used at the **a** on it.
4:26 around the tent and the **a**,
5:25 and bring it to the **a**.
5:26 portion and burn it on the **a**.
7:1 anointed and dedicated the **a**
7:10 for the dedication of the **a** when
7:10 their gifts in front of the **a**.
7:11 gift for the dedication of the **a**."
7:84 for the dedication of the **a** when
7:88 for the dedication of the **a** after
16:38 metal sheets to cover the **a**.
16:39 metal sheets to cover the **a**,
16:40 The bronze-covered **a** will
16:46 put burning coals from the **a**
18:3 they must not come near the **a**
18:5 at the holy place and at the **a**.
18:7 everything done at the **a**
18:17 these animals against the **a**,
23:2 a bull and a ram on each **a**.
23:4 a bull and a ram on each **a**."
23:14 a bull and a ram on each **a**.
23:30 a bull and a ram on each **a**.
Dtr 12:27 of your burnt offerings on the **a**
12:27 is to be poured out beside the **a**
16:21 When you build the **a** for the
26:4 and set it down in front of the **a**
27:5 Build an **a** of stones there
27:6 use uncut stones to build the **a**
33:10 burnt offerings on your **a**.
Jos 8:30 At that time Joshua built an **a**
8:31 He built an **a** with uncut stones
8:31 fellowship offerings on the **a**.
9:27 They served the LORD's **a**,
22:10 They built an **a** by the Jordan
22:10 The **a** was very large and
22:11 of Manasseh have built an **a** at
22:16 by building an **a** for yourselves.
22:19 or against us by building an **a**
22:19 yourselves in addition to the **a**
22:23 If we built an **a** with the
22:26 'Let's build an **a** for ourselves.
22:28 LORD's **a** our ancestors made.
22:29 the LORD by building an **a**
22:29 or sacrifices in addition to the **a**
22:34 and Gad gave the **a** a name:
Jdg 6:24 So Gideon built an **a** there to
6:25 Tear down your father's **a**
6:26 build an **a** to the LORD your
6:28 they saw that the Baal **a** had
6:28 offering on the **a** that had been
6:30 He has torn down the Baal **a**
6:31 someone tears down his **a**."
6:32 someone tears down Baal's **a**,
13:19 on a rock he used as an **a**.
13:20 up toward heaven from the **a**,
21:4 They built an **a** there and
1Sm 2:28 burnt offerings on my **a**,
2:28 of Israel burned on the **a**.
2:33 remove from my **a** will have his
7:17 he built an **a** to the LORD.
14:35 Then Saul built an **a** to the
14:35 he had built an **a** to the LORD.
2Sm 24:18 set up an **a** for the LORD at
24:21 floor from you and to build an **a**
24:25 David built an **a** for the LORD
1Ki 1:50 took hold of the horns of the **a**.
1:51 the horns of the **a** and saying,
1:53 men to take him from the **a**.
2:28 and clung to the horns of the **a**.
2:29 that Joab had fled to the **a**
3:4 1,000 burnt offerings on that **a**.
6:20 and the cedar **a** with pure gold.
6:22 He also covered the entire **a** in
7:48 the LORD's temple: the gold **a**,
8:22 stood in front of the LORD's **a**.
8:31 in front of your **a** in this temple,
8:54 stood in front of the LORD's **a**,
8:64 offerings because the bronze **a**
9:25 fellowship offerings on the **a**
9:25 He burnt them on the **a** that
12:32 He went to the **a** in Bethel to
12:33 He went to his **a** in Bethel to
13:1 was standing at the **a**

1Ki 13:2 this man condemned the **a**.
13:2 "**A**, altar! This is what the
13:2 "Altar, **a**! This is what the LORD
13:3 You will see the **a** torn apart.
13:4 condemning the **a** in Bethel,
13:4 to the man across the **a**.
13:5 The **a** was torn apart,
13:5 and the ashes from the **a** were
13:32 of the LORD against the **a**
16:32 Samaria and set up an **a** there.
18:26 around the **a** they had made.
18:30 He rebuilt the LORD's **a** that
18:32 Elijah built an **a** in the LORD's
18:32 12 quarts of grain around the **a**.
18:35 The water flowed around the **a**,
2Ki 11:11 the king and around the **a**
12:9 side of the **a** as one comes
16:10 He saw an **a** there in
16:10 priest Urijah a model of the **a**
16:11 Urijah built an **a** exactly like
16:12 from Damascus, he saw the **a**.
16:12 The king approached the **a** and
16:13 his fellowship offering on the **a**.
16:14 But he moved the bronze **a**
16:14 of the temple between his **a**
16:14 put it on the north side of his **a**.
16:15 "On this great **a** you must burn
16:15 use the bronze **a** for prayer."
18:22 at this **a** in Jerusalem.'"
23:9 to the LORD's **a** in Jerusalem.
23:15 He also tore down the **a** at
23:15 He tore down both the **a** and
23:16 tombs and burn them on the **a**
23:17 these things to the **a** of Bethel."
1Ch 6:49 offered sacrifices on the **a**
6:49 and on the **a** for incense.
16:40 This happened on the **a** of
21:18 tell David to go and set up an **a**
21:22 I'll build an **a** for the LORD on it.
21:26 David built an **a** for the LORD
21:26 on the **a** for burnt offerings.
21:29 made in the desert and the **a**
22:1 Israel's **a** for burnt offerings will
28:18 gold for the **a** of incense.
2Ch 1:5 The bronze **a** that Bezalel,
1:6 Solomon went to the bronze **a**
4:1 He made a bronze **a** 30 feet
4:19 for God's temple: the gold **a**,
5:12 east of the **a** with cymbals,
6:12 stood in front of the LORD's **a**.
6:22 in front of your **a** in this temple,
7:7 fat because the bronze **a** that
7:9 the dedication of the **a**
8:12 the LORD on the LORD's **a** that
15:8 He also repaired the LORD's **a**
23:10 the king and around the **a**
26:16 burn incense on the incense **a**.
26:19 Uzziah was at the incense **a**.
29:18 This includes the **a** for burnt
29:19 are in front of the LORD's **a**."
29:21 the animals on the LORD's **a**.
29:22 sprinkled the blood on the **a**.
29:22 sprinkled the blood on the **a**.
29:22 sprinkled the blood on the **a**.
29:24 blood an offering for sin at the **a**
29:27 of burnt offerings on the **a**.
32:12 and sacrifice at one **a**?'
33:16 He built the LORD's **a** and
35:16 the LORD's **a** as King Josiah
Ezr 3:2 and his relatives built an **a**
3:3 So they rebuilt the **a** on its
7:17 and wine to offer on the **a** of the
Neh 10:34 God's temple to burn on the **a**
Psa 26:6 I will walk around your **a**,
43:4 Then let me go to the **a** of God,
51:19 bulls will be offered on your **a**.
118:27 branches to the horns of the **a**.
Isa 6:6 taken from the **a** with tongs.
19:19 When that day comes, an **a** for
27:9 all the **a** stones into powdered
36:7 "Worship at this **a**."
56:7 will be acceptable on my **a**,
60:7 ⌊offerings⌋ on my **a**.
Lam 2:7 The Lord rejected his **a** and
Eze 8:5 to the north gate beside the **a**,
8:16 the entrance and the **a**,

Eze 9:2 in and stood by the bronze a.
40:46 the priests who serve at the a.
40:47 And the a was in front of the
41:22 There was a wooden a,
43:13 are the measurements of the a,
43:13 The base of the a was 21
43:13 All around the edge of the a
43:13 This was the height of the a:
43:17 The steps to the a faced east.
43:18 sprinkling blood on the a after
43:18 on the altar after the a is built.
43:20 rim all the way around the a.
43:20 you will remove sin from the a
43:22 Remove sin from the a as you
43:26 peace with the LORD at the a,
43:27 fellowship offerings on the a.
45:19 corners of the ledge of the a,
47:1 of the temple, south of the a.
Joe 1:13 you servants of the a.
2:17 the LORD cry between the a
Amo 2:8 Beside every a, they spread
3:14 The horns of the a will be cut
9:1 saw the Lord standing by the a,
Zec 9:15 sprinkling⌋ the corners of the a.
14:20 like the bowls in front of the a.
Mal 1:7 contaminated food on my a.
1:10 could not light fires on my a
2:13 cover the LORD's a with tears.
Mat 5:23 are offering your gift at the a
5:24 leave your gift at the a.
23:18 'To swear an oath by the a
23:18 oath by the gift on the a means
23:19 the gift or the a that makes the
23:20 To swear an oath by the a is to
23:35 between the temple and the a.
Luk 1:11 to the right of the incense a,
11:51 who was killed between the a
Act 17:23 I noticed an a with this written
1Co 9:13 Don't those who help at the a
9:13 get a share of what is on the a?
10:18 share what is on the a?
Heb 7:13 ever served as a priest at the a.
13:10 eat what is sacrificed at our a.
Jas 2:21 Isaac as a sacrifice on the a?
Rev 6:9 I saw under the a the souls of
8:3 burner and stood at the a.
8:3 of incense to offer on the gold a
8:5 filled it with fire from the a,
9:13 the four horns of the gold a
11:1 the temple of God and the a.
14:18 another angel came from the a
16:7 Then I heard the a answer,

altar's (3)

Exo 27:3 the a ashes, also shovels,
Num 4:14 bowls — all the a accessories.
Eze 43:20 and put it on the a four horns,

altars (60)

Exo 34:13 But tear down their a,
Lev 26:30 cut down your incense a,
Num 3:31 the table, the lamp stand, the a,
23:1 "Build seven a here,
23:4 "I have set up seven a,
23:14 where he built seven a.
23:29 "Build seven a here,
Dtr 7:5 Tear down their a,
12:3 Tear down their a,
Jdg 2:2 You must tear down their a.' But
1Ki 19:10 promises, torn down your a,
19:14 promises, torn down your a,
2Ki 11:18 They smashed Baal's a and
11:18 priest of Baal, in front of the a.
18:22 worship and a Hezekiah got rid
21:3 He set up a dedicated to Baal
21:4 He built a in the LORD's
21:5 he built a for the entire army of
23:12 the a that Judah's kings had
23:12 and the a Manasseh had made
23:20 illegal worship sites on their a
2Ch 14:3 He got rid of the a of foreign
14:5 places of worship and the a
23:17 They smashed Baal's a and
23:17 priest of Baal, in front of the a.
28:24 He made a for himself on every
30:14 of the ⌊idols'⌋ a in Jerusalem.
2Ch 30:14 They got rid of all the a for
31:1 and the a throughout Judah,
32:12 places of worship and a
33:3 He set up a dedicated to other
33:4 He built a in the LORD's
33:5 he built a for the entire army of
33:15 He got rid of the a he had built
34:4 He had the a of the various
34:4 He cut down the incense a that
34:5 bones of the priests on their a.
34:7 tore down the a, beat the
34:7 and cut down all the incense a
Psa 84:3 hatch their young near your a,
Isa 17:8 They won't look to the a made
17:8 or incense a which their fingers
27:9 or incense a are left standing.
36:7 worship and a Hezekiah got rid
65:3 and burnt incense on brick a.
Jer 11:13 You have set up many a ⌊in
11:13 You have as many a as there
17:1 and on the horns of their a.
17:2 their children remember their a
Eze 6:4 Your a will be destroyed,
6:5 their bones around your a.
6:6 Your a will be ruined and
6:13 beside the idols around their a.
Hos 8:11 "The more a that the people of
10:1 the more a they built.
10:2 God will tear down their a and
10:8 weeds will grow over those a.
12:11 But their a will become like
Amo 3:14 also destroy the a at Bethel.
Rom 11:3 prophets and torn down your a.

alter (1)

Psa 89:34 or a my own agreement.

alternated (1)

Exo 39:26 A gold bell a with a

alternating (1)

Exo 28:34 a gold bell a with a

altogether (1)

Job 21:23 feels a happy and contented.

Alush (2)

Num 33:13 Dophkah and set up camp at A.
33:14 They moved from A and set up

Alvah (1)

Gen 36:40 and name: Timna, A, Jetheth,

Alvan (1)

Gen 36:23 A, Manahath, Ebal, Shepho,

always (206)

Exo 13:9 teachings of the LORD are ⌊a⌋
13:22 The column of smoke was a in
13:22 of fire was a there at night.
19:9 you and will a believe you."
28:30 Aaron will a be carrying over
28:38 The medallion must a be on
34:6 a faithful and ready to forgive.
Lev 6:12 The fire must a be burning on
6:13 The fire must a be burning on
25:24 People must a have the right to
25:32 "The Levites a have the right to
Num 4:7 The bread that is a in the
9:16 The smoke a glowed this way.
18:8 contributions will a be yours.
18:11 They will a be yours.
18:19 contributions will a be yours.
22:30 You've a ridden me.
Dtr 11:1 A obey his laws, rules,
12:28 Then things will a go well for
15:11 There will a be poor people in
23:14 So your camp must a be holy.
28:13 You will a be at the top,
28:66 Your life will a be hanging by a
Jos 9:23 You will a be servants.
1Sm 2:30 your father's family would a live
2:35 and he will a live as my
23:14 Saul was a searching for him,
2Sm 2:6 May the LORD a show you
3:29 May there a be members of
2Sm 9:7 and you will a eat at my table."
9:10 Mephibosheth will a eat at my
9:13 He a ate at the king's table.
15:20 LORD⌋ a show you kindness."
19:13 Joab's place to serve me a as
1Ki 2:33 and throne a receive peace
2:45 and David's dynasty will a be
5:1 had a been David's friend.
8:52 "May your eyes a see my plea
9:3 and my heart will a be there.
10:8 because they are a stationed
11:36 my servant David will a have
11:39 suffer for this, but not a."
12:7 they will a be your servants."
17:14 and the jug will a contain oil."
17:16 and the jug a contained olive
2Ki 8:19 David that he would a give him
1Ch 16:11 A seek his presence.
23:13 and a give the blessing in his
29:18 a watch over your people's
2Ch 2:4 ⌊These festivals⌋ are a to be
7:16 and my heart will a be there.
9:7 because they are a stationed
10:7 they will a be your servants."
18:7 about me is good; it's a evil."
21:7 David that he would a give him
Neh 9:17 and a ready to forgive.
Est 2:20 Esther a did whatever
Psa 9:18 people will not a be forgotten.
10:5 He a seems to succeed.
16:8 I a keep the LORD in front of
25:15 My eyes are a on the LORD.
34:1 My mouth will a praise him.
37:26 He is a generous and lends
40:11 and your truth a protect me.
49:8 He must a give up
50:8 which are a in front of me.
51:3 My sin is a in front of me.
71:3 a place where I may a go.
71:14 But I will a have hope.
73:23 Yet, I am a with you.
84:4 They are a praising you.
86:15 a faithful and ready to forgive.
92:14 They are a healthy and fresh.
103:8 and a ready to forgive.
103:9 He will not a accuse us of
105:4 A seek his presence.
105:8 He a remembers his promise,
109:15 Let their guilt and sin a remain
109:19 a belt he a wears."
111:5 He a remembers his promise.
112:6 person will a be remembered.
115:12 who is ⌊a⌋ thinking about us,
119:98 commandments are a with me.
119:109 I a take my life into my own
119:117 and I will a respect your laws.
119:144 written instructions are a right.
145:8 and a ready to forgive.
Pro 5:19 A let her breasts satisfy you.
5:19 A be intoxicated with her love.
13:15 people is a the same.
13:25 of wicked people are a empty.
14:23 there is a something gained,
17:17 A friend a loves, and a brother
20:19 person whose mouth is a open.
21:5 but everyone who is ⌊a⌋ in a
24:21 who a insist upon change,
28:14 Blessed is the one who is a
29:14 his throne will a be secure.
Ecc 7:20 on earth that he a does what is
9:8 A wear clean clothes,
Sos 7:2 May it a be filled with spiced
Isa 26:4 Trust the LORD a,
34:10 and smoke will a go up from
47:7 You said, "I will a be a queen."
49:16 walls are a in my presence.
60:11 Your gates will a be open.
63:9 He a held them and carried
Jer 3:5 He won't a be angry.'
12:1 you would a be right.
17:25 This city will a have people
20:17 would have a been pregnant.
35:7 You must a live in tents so that
35:19 Rechab's son, will a serve me."
Eze 10:11 They a moved in the direction
35:5 "'You have a been an enemy of

Eze 37:25 David will a be their prince.
45:11 dry and liquid measures must a
46:14 rules are to be followed a.
Dan 6:10 He had a praised God this way.
6:16 whom you a worship,
6:20 God, whom you a worship,
11:12 he will not a be strong.
Hos 12:6 Be loyal and fair, and a wait
Joe 2:13 and a ready to forgive and to
3:20 People will a live in Judah.
Jnh 4:2 and a ready to forgive and to
Mic 6:14 So you will a be hungry.
Hab 1:17 nets and a kill nations without
Mal 1:4 whom the LORD is a angry.'
Mat 7:12 "A do for other people
18:10 their angels in heaven a see
26:11 You will a have the poor with
26:11 but you will not a have me with
27:55 and had a supported him.
28:20 "And remember that I am a with
Mar 14:7 You will a have the poor with
14:7 But you will not a have me
15:8 to do for them what he a did.
Luk 2:19 and a thought about them.
14:7 how the guests a chose
15:31 'My child, you're a with me.
24:53 They were a in the temple,
Jon 8:29 I a do what pleases him."
11:42 I've known that you a hear me.
12:8 You will a have the poor with
12:8 but you will not a have me with
18:20 I have a taught in synagogues
Act 2:25 'I a see the Lord in front of me.
7:51 They a opposed the Holy Spirit,
9:36 She a helped people and gave
10:2 people and a prayed to God.
14:8 He was a sitting because he
15:18 things that have a been known!'
23:1 my relationship with God has a
24:16 With this belief I a do my best
Rom 1:9 witness that I a mention you
12:2 Then you will a be able to
1Co 1:4 I a thank God for you because
11:2 I praise you for a thinking about
15:58 A excel in the work you do for
2Co 1:19 of him our message was a true.
2:14 But I thank God, who a leads
4:10 We a carry around the death of
5:6 So we are a confident.
6:10 are sad although we're a glad,
9:8 Then, when you a have
9:11 so that you can a be generous.
Gal 2:5 Good News would a be yours.
4:18 to a good cause is a good,
5:17 As a result, you don't a do what
Eph 1:16 I a remember you in my
5:20 A thank God the Father for
Php 1:20 now as a, whether I live or die.
2:12 you have a obeyed,
4:4 A be joyful in the Lord!
Col 1:3 We a thank God, the Father of
3:20 Children, a obey your parents.
3:22 a obey your earthly masters.
4:12 He a prays intensely for you.
1Th 1:2 We a thank God for all of you
2:4 Rather, we are a spreading the
2:16 The result is that those Jews a
2:17 you're a in our thoughts.
3:6 He also told us that you a have
4:17 In this way we will a be with
5:15 Instead, a try to do what is
5:16 A be joyful.
2Th 1:3 We a have to thank God for
1:11 With this in mind, we a pray
2:13 We a have to thank God for
1Ti 2:2 a quiet and peaceful life a lived
5:10 or a doing good things.
2Ti 2:8 A think about Jesus Christ.
3:7 These women are a studying
Tit 1:12 "Cretans are a liars,
1:14 who are a rejecting the truth.
2:7 A set an example by doing
Phm 1:4 Philemon, I a thank my God
Heb 7:25 That is why he is a able to
7:25 He can do this because he a
9:6 The priests a went into the first
Heb 12:11 It a seems to cause more pain
13:15 Through Jesus we should a
1Pe 3:15 A be ready to defend your
2Pe 1:12 Therefore, I will a remind you
2:14 They're a looking for an

a.m. (1)

Mat 20:3 About 9 a. he saw others

Amad (1)

Jos 19:26 Allammelech, A, and Mishal.

Amal (1)

1Ch 7:35 Zophah, Imna, Shelesh, and A.

Amalek (19)

Gen 36:12 She gave birth to A for Eliphaz.
36:16 Korah, Gatam, and A.
Num 24:20 "A was first among the nations,
Jdg 6:3 Israel planted crops, Midian, A,
6:33 All of Midian, A, and Kedem
7:12 Midian, A, and all of Kedem
12:15 in the mountains of A.
1Sm 14:48 acted forcefully and defeated A.
15:2 I will punish A for what they
15:3 Now go and attack A.
15:5 Saul went to the city of A and
15:8 captured King Agag of A alive.
15:20 brought back King Agag of A,
15:32 King Agag of A," Samuel said.
28:18 unleash his burning anger on A.
2Sm 8:12 Ammon, the Philistines, A,
1Ch 1:36 Kenaz and A, son of Timna.
18:11 Ammon, the Philistines, and A.
Psa 83:7 Gebal, Ammon, and A,

Amalekite (4)

Exo 17:13 defeated the A army in battle.
1Sm 30:13 the slave of an A," the young
2Sm 1:8 "I said to him, 'I'm an A.'
1:13 man answered, "I'm an A,

Amalekites (28)

Gen 14:7 the whole territory of the A
Exo 17:8 The A fought Israel at
17:9 Then fight the A. Tomorrow I
17:10 told him and fought the A,
17:11 the A would start to win.
17:14 of the A from the earth."
17:16 he will be at war against the A
Num 13:29 The A live in the Negev.
14:25 (The A and Canaanites are
14:43 The A and Canaanites are
14:45 The A and Canaanites who
24:20 Then Balaam saw the A and
Dtr 25:17 Remember what the A did to
25:19 memory of the A from the
Jdg 3:13 got the Ammonites and the A
10:12 the Sidonians, the A,
1Sm 15:6 "Get away from the A so that I
15:6 So the Kenites left the A.
15:7 Saul attacked the A from
15:15 army brought them from the A.
15:18 'Claim those sinners, the A,
15:20 and claimed the A for God.
27:8 the Girzites, and the A.
30:1 the A had raided the Negev,
30:5 The A also captured David's
30:18 everything the A had taken,
2Sm 1:1 returned from defeating the A,
1Ch 4:43 They killed the A who were

Amalek's (1)

Jdg 5:14 in A country came down from

Amam (1)

Jos 15:26 A, Shema, Moladah,

Amana (1)

Sos 4:8 me from the peak of Mount A,

Amariah (16)

1Ch 6:7 Meraioth was the father of A.
6:7 A was the father of Ahitub.
6:11 Azariah was the father of A.
6:11 A was the father of Ahitub.
1Ch 6:52 Meraioth's son was A.
23:19 his second was A;
24:23 A (the second of Hebron's
2Ch 19:11 Now, the chief priest A will be
31:15 Jeshua, Shemaiah, A,
Ezr 7:3 who was the son of A,
10:42 Shallum, A, and Joseph
Neh 10:3 Pashhur, A, Malchiah,
11:4 who was the son of A,
12:2 A, Malluch, Hattush,
12:13 from Ezra, Meshullam; from A,
Zep 1:1 and the great-grandson of A,

Amariah's (1)

1Ch 6:52 A son was Ahitub.

Amasa (15)

2Sm 17:25 Absalom appointed A to take
17:25 (A was the son of a man
19:13 And tell A, 'Aren't you my flesh
20:4 The king told A, "Call the
20:5 A went to call Judah together,
20:8 in Gibeon, A met them there.
20:9 Joab asked A. He took hold of
20:10 A wasn't on his guard against
20:11 men stood beside A and said,
20:12 A was wallowing in his blood
20:12 he carried A from the road to
1Ki 2:5 of Ner, and A, son of Jether.
2:32 Israel's army) and A (who was
1Ch 2:17 Abigail was the mother of A,
2Ch 28:12 son of Shallum, and A,

Amasai (5)

1Ch 6:25 sons were A and Ahimoth.
6:35 who was the son of A,
12:18 Then the Spirit gave A,
15:24 A, Zechariah, Benaiah,
2Ch 29:12 Mahath, son of A, and Joel,

Amasa's (1)

2Sm 20:9 He took hold of A beard with

Amashsai (1)

Neh 11:13 A was the son of Azarel,

Amasiah (1)

2Ch 17:16 and next to him A,

amazed (46)

Jer 4:9 will be a and astonished."
Hab 1:5 Be a and astonished.
Mat 7:28 were a at his teachings.
8:10 Jesus was a when he heard
8:27 The men were a and asked,
9:33 The crowds were a and said,
12:23 crowds were all a and said,
13:54 in a way that a them.
15:31 The crowd was a to see mute
19:25 He a his disciples more than
22:33 He a the crowds who heard his
Mar 1:22 The people were a at his
2:12 Everyone was a and praised
5:20 Ten Cities. Everyone was a.
6:2 He a many who heard him.
6:6 Their unbelief a him.
7:37 Jesus completely a the people.
10:26 This a his disciples more than
11:18 afraid of him because he a all
Luk 1:21 They were a that he was
1:63 is John." Everyone was a.
2:18 the shepherds' story was a.
2:33 Jesus' father and mother were a
4:22 They were a to hear the
4:32 The people were a at his
5:9 who was with him was a
5:10 Simon's partners, were also a.
5:26 Everyone was a and praised
7:9 Jesus was a at the officer
8:25 Frightened and a, they asked
8:56 They were a. Jesus ordered
9:43 Everyone was a to see God's
9:43 Everyone was a at all the
11:14 The people were a.
Jon 5:20 things so that you will be a.
Act 2:7 Stunned and a, the people in

Act 3:10 The people were **a** and
3:12 why are you **a** about this man?
8:9 He **a** the people of Samaria
8:11 Simon because he had **a** them
8:13 Simon was **a** to see the
9:21 who heard him was **a**.
10:45 come with Peter were **a** that
13:12 The Lord's teachings **a** him.
13:41 Be **a** and die! I am going to do
Rev 13:3 the people of the world were **a**

amazement (2)

Gen 43:33 They looked at each other in **a**.
Luk 24:41 were overcome with joy and **a**

Amaziah (43)

2Ki 12:21 His son **A** succeeded him as
13:12 when he fought against King **A**
14:1 as king of Israel when King **A**,
14:2 **A** was 25 years old when he
14:7 **A** killed 10,000 Edomites in the
14:8 Then **A** sent messengers to
14:9 message to King **A** of Judah:
14:11 But **A** wouldn't listen.
14:11 and King **A** of Judah met him in
14:13 of Israel captured King **A**,
14:15 when he fought against King **A**
14:17 Joash's son King **A** of Judah
14:18 Isn't everything else about **A**
14:21 king in place of his father **A**.
14:22 to Judah after King **A** lay down
14:23 Joash's son **A** was in his
15:3 as his father **A** had done.
1Ch 3:12 Joash's son was **A**.
4:34 Joshah (son of **A**),
6:45 who was the son of **A**,
2Ch 24:27 His son **A** succeeded him as
25:1 **A** was 25 years old when he
25:5 **A** called the people of Judah
25:9 **A** asked the man of God,
25:10 Then **A** dismissed the troops
25:11 **A** courageously led his troops.
25:13 The troops that **A** sent back so
25:14 After **A** came back from
25:15 LORD became angry with **A**.
25:17 King **A** of Judah sent
25:18 message to King **A** of Judah:
25:20 But **A** wouldn't listen.
25:21 and King **A** of Judah met him in
25:23 of Israel captured King **A**,
25:25 Joash's son King **A** of Judah
25:26 Isn't everything else about **A**,
25:27 After **A** turned away from the
25:27 **A** fled to Lachish, but they sent
26:1 king in place of his father **A**.
26:2 to Judah after King **A** lay down
26:4 as his father **A** had done.
Amo 7:10 Then **A**, the priest at Bethel,
7:12 Then **A** said to Amos,

Amaziah's (2)

2Ki 15:1 **A** son Azariah began to rule as
1Ch 3:12 **A** son was Azariah.

amazing (44)

Gen 45:7 to save your lives in an **a** way.
Exo 4:21 Pharaoh all the **a** things that
7:3 signs and **a** things in Egypt,
11:9 will do more **a** things in Egypt."
11:10 Pharaoh all these **a** things.
Dtr 4:34 signs, **a** things, and war.
6:22 signs and **a** things that were
7:19 and the **a** things the LORD did.
13:1 a miraculous sign or an **a** thing.
26:8 miraculous signs, and **a** things.
28:46 will be a sign and an **a** thing
29:3 those spectacular, **a** things.
34:11 miraculous signs and **a** things
1Ch 16:12 the **a** things he did and the
Neh 9:10 signs and did **a** things
Psa 105:5 the **a** things he did,
105:27 among them and did **a** things
118:23 and it is **a** for us to see.
135:9 He sent miraculous signs and **a**
Pro 30:18 Three things are too **a** to me,
Isa 29:14 to do something completely **a**
Jer 32:20 miraculous signs and **a** things
32:21 miraculous signs and **a** things,
Dan 4:2 miraculous signs and **a** things
4:3 uses his power to do **a** things.
6:27 miraculous signs and **a** things
11:36 He will say **a** things against
Mat 21:15 the scribes saw the **a** miracles
21:42 and it is **a** for us to see'?
Mar 12:11 and it is **a** for us to see'?"
Jon 4:48 don't see miracles and **a** things,
9:30 man replied to them, "That's **a**!
Act 2:22 did **a** things, and gave signs.
2:43 everyone as many **a** things
4:30 and doing **a** things through the
5:12 many miracles and do **a** things.
6:8 He did **a** things and performed
7:36 He is the person who did **a**
14:3 miracles and do **a** things.
15:12 miracles and **a** things that God
Rom 15:19 of miraculous and **a** signs,
Heb 2:4 **a** things, other powerful acts,
Rev 15:1 It was spectacular and **a**.
15:3 you do are spectacular and **a**,

amazingly (1)

Psa 139:14 you because I have been so **a**

ambassadors (4)

2Ch 32:31 the leaders of Babylon sent **a**
Psa 68:31 **A** will come from Egypt.
Isa 57:9 You've sent your **a** far away
Luk 14:32 If he can't, he'll send **a** to ask

ambition (5)

2Co 12:20 selfish **a**, slander, gossip,
Gal 5:20 selfish **a**, conflict, factions,
Php 1:17 about Christ out of selfish **a**
2:3 Don't act out of selfish **a** or be
Jas 3:14 and filled with self-centered **a**,

ambush (38)

Dtr 19:11 waits in **a** for him, attacks him,
Jos 8:2 Set an **a** behind the city."
8:4 "Set an **a** behind the city.
Jdg 9:32 Set an **a** ⌊for them⌋ in the
9:35 and his troops rose from their **a**.
9:43 and set an **a** in the fields.
16:2 night at the city gate to **a** him.
16:12 her bedroom waiting to **a** him.
20:29 troops in **a** around Gibeah.
20:33 Meanwhile, those waiting in **a**
20:36 those waiting in **a** near Gibeah.
20:37 The men in **a** quickly charged
20:38 waiting in **a** that they would
1Sm 15:5 and set an **a** in the valley.
22:8 my servant David to **a** me,
22:13 rise up against me and **a** me,
24:11 but you are trying to **a** me in
2Ch 13:13 But Jeroboam had set an **a** to
13:13 and the **a** was behind them.
Job 38:40 lie ready to **a** from their lairs?
Psa 10:8 He waits in **a** in the villages.
59:3 They lie in **a** for me right here!
Pro 1:11 Let's set an **a** to kill someone.
1:11 Let's hide to **a** innocent people
1:18 But these people set an **a** for
12:6 wicked people are a deadly **a**,
23:28 She is like a robber, lying in **a**.
24:15 You wicked one, do not lie in **a**
Jer 5:6 A leopard will lie in **a** outside
5:26 They lie in **a** like bird catchers.
Lam 3:10 is like a bear waiting to **a** me,
Hos 6:9 gangs of robbers who lie in **a**
7:6 like an oven while they lie in **a**.
13:7 I will wait by the road to **a** you.
Mic 7:2 All people lie in **a** to commit
Act 23:16 nephew heard about the **a**.
23:21 of them are planning to **a** him.
25:3 The Jews had a plan to **a** and

ambushed (1)

Lam 4:19 us in the mountains and **a**

ambushes (5)

Jdg 9:25 So citizens of Shechem set **a**
9:34 to set **a** around Shechem.
2Ch 20:22 the LORD set **a** against the
Ezr 8:31 and from **a** along the way.
Jer 51:12 Prepare **a**. The LORD will carry

amen (54)

Num 5:22 "Then the woman will say, '**A**,
5:22 the woman will say, 'Amen, **a**!'
Dtr 27:15 Then all the people will say **a**.
27:16 Then all the people will say **a**.
27:17 Then all the people will say **a**.
27:18 Then all the people will say **a**.
27:19 Then all the people will say **a**.
27:20 Then all the people will say **a**.
27:21 Then all the people will say **a**.
27:22 Then all the people will say **a**.
27:23 Then all the people will say **a**.
27:24 Then all the people will say **a**.
27:25 Then all the people will say **a**.
27:26 Then all the people will say **a**.
1Ch 16:36 "Then all the people said **a**
Neh 5:13 the whole congregation said **a**
8:6 All the people responded, "**A**!
8:6 **A**!" as they raised their hands
Psa 41:13 all eternity! **A** and amen!
41:13 all eternity! Amen and **a**!
72:19 with his glory. **A** and amen!
72:19 with his glory. Amen and **a**!
89:52 LORD forever. **A** and amen!
89:52 LORD forever. Amen and **a**!
106:48 Let all the people say **a**.
Jer 28:6 He said, "**A**! May the LORD do
Rom 1:25 who is blessed forever. **A**!
9:5 forever blessed. **A**.
11:36 belongs to him forever! **A**!
15:33 of peace be with you all. **A**.
16:27 Jesus Christ forever! **A**.
1Co 14:16 how can outsiders say "**A**!"
2Co 1:20 also honor God by saying, "**A**!"
Gal 1:5 our God and Father forever! **A**.
6:18 brothers and sisters! **A**.
Eph 3:21 for all time and eternity! **A**.
Php 4:20 our God and Father forever! **A**.
1Ti 1:17 and only God. **A**.
6:16 belong to him forever! **A**.
2Ti 4:18 belongs to him forever! **A**.
Heb 13:21 to Jesus Christ forever. **A**.
1Pe 4:11 Christ forever and ever! **A**.
5:11 belongs to him forever. **A**.
2Pe 3:18 and for that eternal day! **A**.
Jud 1:25 Jesus Christ our Lord. **A**.
Rev 1:6 priests for God his Father. **A**.
1:7 This is true. **A**.
3:14 in Laodicea, write: The **a**,
5:14 four living creatures said, "**A**!"
7:12 and said, "**A**! Praise, glory,
7:12 our God forever and ever! **A**!"
19:4 They said, "**A**! Hallelujah!"
22:20 **A**! Come, Lord Jesus!
22:21 Jesus be with all of you. **A**!

amethyst (3)

Exo 28:19 row put jacinth, agate, and **a**.
39:12 they put jacinth, agate, and **a**.
Rev 21:20 jacinth, and the twelfth **a**.

Ami (1)

Ezr 2:57 Pochereth Hazzebaim, and **A**.

Amishaddai (2)

Num 7:66 of Dan, Ahiezer, son of **A**,
7:71 the gifts from Ahiezer, son of **A**.

Amittai (2)

2Ki 14:25 Gath Hepher and the son of **A**.
Jnh 1:1 his word to Jonah, son of **A**.

Ammah (1)

2Sm 2:24 they came to the hill of **A**,

Ammi (1)

Hos 2:1 your brothers **A** [My People],

Ammiel (3)

Num 13:12 **A**, son of Gemalli, from the
2Sm 17:27 son of **A** from Lo Debar,
1Ch 26:5 **A** (the sixth), Issachar (the

Jos 10:6 Help us because all the A
12:2 Sihon was the A king who
13:4 as far as Aphek, the A border.
Jdg 11:22 Israel took all the A territory
1Ki 4:19 territory of King Sihon the A
Eze 16:3 Your father was an A,
16:45 and your father was an A.

Amorites (75)

Gen 10:16 also the Jebusites, the A,
14:7 and also the A who were living
15:16 because the sin of the A will
15:21 the A, the Canaanites,
48:22 I took it from the A with my
Exo 3:8 Hittites, A, Perizzites, Hivites,
3:17 Hittites, A, Perizzites, Hivites,
13:5 A, Hivites, and Jebusites.
23:23 bring you to ⌊the land of⌋ the A,
33:2 A, Hittites, Perizzites, Hivites,
34:11 Then I will force the A,
Num 13:29 The Hittites, Jebusites, and A
21:13 between Moab and the A.)
21:21 to say to King Sihon of the A,
21:26 the city of King Sihon of the A.
21:29 of King Sihon of the A.
21:30 But we shot the A full of
21:31 settled in the land of the A.
21:32 out the A who were there.
21:34 you did to King Sihon of the A,
22:2 all that Israel had done to the A.
32:33 of King Sihon of the A
32:39 out the A who were there.
Dtr 1:4 defeated King Sihon of the A,
1:7 to the mountain region of the A,
1:19 to the mountain region of the A.
1:20 to the mountain region of the A,
1:27 us over to the A so that they
1:44 The A who lived there came
3:2 you did to King Sihon of the A,
3:9 and the A call it Senir.)
4:46 the land of King Sihon of the A,
4:47 the two kings of the A who
7:1 A, Canaanites, Perizzites,
20:17 You must claim the Hittites, A,
31:4 Sihon and King Og of the A
Jos 2:10 the two kings of the A,
3:10 Perizzites, Girgashites, A,
7:7 Was it to hand us over to the A
9:2 A, Canaanites, Perizzites,
9:10 to the two kings of the A east
10:12 the LORD handed the A over
11:3 the A, Hittites, Perizzites,
12:8 A, Canaanites, Perizzites,
13:10 cities of King Sihon of the A up
13:21 kingdom of King Sihon of the A,
24:8 to the land of the A who lived
24:11 The citizens of Jericho, the A,
24:12 the two kings of the A ahead
24:15 Euphrates or the gods of the A
24:18 including the A who lived in
Jdg 1:34 The A forced the tribe of Dan
1:35 The A were determined to live
1:35 made the A do forced labor.
1:36 The territory of the A extended
3:5 Hittites, A, Perizzites, Hivites,
6:10 never fear the gods of the A
10:8 in the land of the A in Gilead.
10:11 the A, the Ammonites,
11:19 to King Sihon of the A.
11:21 land of the A who lived there.
11:23 God of Israel forced the A out
1Sm 7:14 between Israel and the A.
2Sm 21:2 but were left over from the A.
1Ki 9:20 The A, Hittites, Perizzites,
21:26 idols as the A had done.
2Ki 21:11 what the A who ⌊were here
1Ch 1:14 also the Jebusites, the A,
Ezr 9:1 Moabites, Egyptians, and A.
Neh 9:8 A, Perizzites, Jebusites,
Psa 135:11 King Sihon of the A,
136:19 King Sihon of the A — because
Amo 2:9 I destroyed the A in front of
2:9 although the A were as tall as
2:10 possession of the land of the A.

Amos (8)

Amo 1:1 These are the words of A,
7:8 me, "What do you see, A?"
7:10 It read, "A is plotting against
7:11 A says that Jeroboam will be
7:12 Then Amaziah said to A,
7:14 A responded, "I'm not a
8:2 asked, "What do you see, A?"
Luk 3:25 son of Mattathias, son of A,

amount (42)

Gen 23:16 out for Ephron the a stated
30:30 I came has grown to a large a.
Exo 5:13 They said, "Finish the same a
22:4 for the loss with double the a.
22:7 for the loss with double the a.
22:9 loss with double the a.
22:17 he must pay an a of money
38:21 This is the a of material that
38:24 The total a of gold from the
Lev 25:51 price an a equal ⌊to those
25:52 his purchase price an a equal
27:3 The a you must give for a man
27:8 pay the required a must stand
27:8 The priest will determine the a
Num 29:18 with them bring the proper a
29:21 with them bring the proper a
29:24 with them bring the proper a
29:27 with them bring the proper a
29:30 with them bring the proper a
29:33 with them bring the proper a
29:37 with them bring the proper a
35:8 must be given based on the a
Dtr 18:8 If he does, he'll get the same a
2Ch 27:5 gave him the same a
Est 4:7 He told him the exact a of
Job 28:15 gold or buy it for any a of silver.
28:19 bought for ⌊any a of⌋ pure gold.
Psa 62:9 on a scale, they a to nothing.
Pro 6:35 No a of money will change his
Isa 33:23 A large a of loot will be
40:17 All the nations a to nothing in
Zec 14:14 a very large a of gold,
Mat 13:33 a woman mixed into a large a
25:20 I've doubled the a.'
25:21 could be trusted with a small a.
25:21 put you in charge of a large a.
25:22 I've doubled the a.'
25:23 could be trusted with a small a.
25:23 put you in charge of a large a.
28:12 the soldiers a large a of money
Luk 13:21 a woman mixed into a large a
Tit 3:6 God poured a generous a of the

amounts (3)

Eze 38:13 soldiers to carry away large a
Mar 12:41 Many rich people put in large a.
Rom 2:25 a to uncircumcision.

Amoz (13)

2Ki 19:2 to the prophet Isaiah, son of A.
19:20 Then Isaiah, son of A,
20:1 The prophet Isaiah, son of A,
2Ch 26:22 by the prophet Isaiah, son of A.
32:20 the prophet Isaiah, son of A,
32:32 of the prophet Isaiah, son of A,
Isa 1:1 vision which Isaiah, son of A,
2:1 which Isaiah, son of A,
13:1 son of A, saw about Babylon.
20:2 the LORD told Isaiah, son of A,
37:2 to the prophet Isaiah, son of A.
37:21 Then Isaiah, son of A,
38:1 The prophet Isaiah, son of A,

Amphipolis (1)

Act 17:1 traveled through the cities of A

Ampliatus (1)

Rom 16:8 Greet A my dear friend in the

Amram (11)

Exo 6:18 The sons of Kohath were A,
6:20 A married his father's sister
6:20 A lived 137 years.
Num 3:19 A, Izhar, Hebron, and Uzziel
3:27 the families descended from A,
26:58 Kohath was the ancestor of A.
1Ch 6:2 Kohath's sons were A,
6:18 Kohath's sons were A,
23:12 Kohath had four sons: A,
26:23 For the descendants of A,
Ezr 10:34 of Bani: Maadai, A, Uel,

Amram's (6)

Num 26:59 The name of A wife was
26:59 gave birth to A children: Aaron,
1Ch 6:3 A children were Aaron,
23:13 A sons were Aaron and Moses.
24:20 (for A descendants through
24:21 (⌊for A⌋ descendants⌋ through

Amraphel (2)

Gen 14:1 ⌊four kings⌋ — King A of Shinar,
14:9 of Goiim, King A of Shinar,

Amzi (2)

1Ch 6:46 who was the son of A,
Neh 11:12 who was the son of A,

Anab (2)

Jos 11:21 in Hebron, Debir, and A,
15:50 A, Eshtemoh, Anim,

Anah (10)

Gen 36:2 daughter of A and
36:14 daughter of A and
36:20 land: Lotan, Shobal, Zibeon, A,
36:24 sons of Zibeon: Aiah and A.
36:24 (A found the hot springs in the
36:25 These were the children of A:
36:25 and Oholibamah, daughter of A.
36:29 Lotan, Shobal, Zibeon, A,
1Ch 1:38 A, Dishon, Ezer, and Dishan.
1:40 sons were Aiah and A.

Anaharath (1)

Jos 19:19 Hapharaim, Shion, A,

Anah's (2)

Gen 36:18 wife Oholibamah, A daughter
1Ch 1:41 A son was Dishon.

Anaiah (2)

Neh 8:4 Mattithiah, Shema, A,
10:22 Pelatiah, Hanan, A,

Anak (16)

Num 13:22 They are descendants of A.
13:28 the descendants of A there.
13:33 of A are Nephilim.)
Dtr 1:28 We even saw the people of A
2:10 and as tall as the people of A.
2:11 like the people of A,
2:21 and as tall as the people of A.
9:2 They're descendants of A.
9:2 oppose the descendants of A?"
Jos 11:21 also wiped out the people of A
11:22 None of the people of A
14:12 You heard that the people of A
14:15 man among the people of A.
15:13 Arba was the father of A.
15:14 descendants of A from Hebron.
Jdg 1:20 forced out the three sons of A.

Anak's (1)

Jos 21:11 Kiriath Arba (Arba was A father

Anamites (2)

Gen 10:13 A, Lehabites, Naphtuhites,
1Ch 1:11 A, Lehabites, Naphtuhites,

Anammelech (1)

2Ki 17:31 for Adrammelech and A,

Anan (1)

Neh 10:26 Ahiah, Hanan, A,

Anani (1)

1Ch 3:24 Johanan, Delaiah, and A.

Ananiah (2)

Neh 3:23 of Maaseiah and grandson of **A**,
11:32 in Anathoth, Nob, **A**,

Ananias (16)

Act 5:1 **A** man named **A** and his wife
5:3 Peter asked, "**A**, why did you
5:5 When **A** heard Peter say this,
9:10 A disciple named **A** lived in the
9:10 said to him in a vision, "**A**!"
9:10 **A** answered, "Yes, Lord."
9:12 man named **A** place his hands
9:13 **A** replied, "Lord, I've heard a lot
9:15 The Lord told **A**, "Go!
9:17 **A** left and entered Judas'
9:17 on Saul, **A** said, "Brother Saul,
22:12 "A man named **A** lived in
22:13 came back and I could see **A**.
22:14 "**A** said, 'The God of our
23:2 The chief priest **A** ordered the
24:1 later the chief priest **A** went

Ananias' (1)

Act 5:7 three hours later **A** wife arrived.

Anath (2)

Jdg 3:31 Ehud came Shamgar, son of **A**.
5:6 son of **A**, in the days of Jael,

Anathoth (20)

Jos 21:18 **A**, and Almon.
2Sm 23:27 Abiezer from **A**, Mebunnai (son
1Ki 2:26 "Go to your land in **A**.
1Ch 6:60 and **A** with its pastureland.
7:8 Abijah, **A**, and Alemeth.
11:28 from Tekoa, Abiezer from **A**,
12:3 Beracah and Jehu from **A**,
27:12 of the tribe of Benjamin from **A**,
Ezr 2:23 of **A**: 128
Neh 7:27 of **A**: 128
10:19 Hariph, **A**, Nebai,
11:32 in **A**, Nob, Ananiah,
Isa 10:30 in Laishah and miserable **A**!
Jer 1:1 He was one of the priests at **A**
11:21 The people of **A** want to kill
11:23 a disaster on the people of **A**.
29:27 you arrested Jeremiah from **A**?
32:7 "Buy my field that is in **A**,
32:8 buy my field that is in **A**
32:9 "So I bought the field in **A** from

ancestor (50)

Gen 10:13 Egypt was the **a** of the Ludites,
10:21 ⌊Shem was⌋ the **a** of all the
19:37 He is the **a** of the Moabites of
19:38 He is the **a** of the Ammonites of
Num 26:58 Kohath was the **a** of Amram.
Jos 17:1 the **a** of the people living in
19:47 the city Dan after their **a** Dan.
24:3 But I took your **a** Abraham from
Jdg 18:29 city Dan in honor of their **a** Dan,
1Ki 15:3 God as his **a** David had been.
15:11 as his **a** David had done.
15:24 ancestors in the city of his **a**,
22:50 them in the city of his **a** David.
2Ki 14:3 but not exactly what his **a**
15:38 them in the city of his **a** David.
16:2 as his **a** David had done.
18:3 as his **a** David had done.
20:5 God of your **a** David says:
22:2 He lived in the ways of his **a**
1Ch 1:11 Egypt was the **a** of the Ludites,
4:8 and he was the **a** of the
24:19 Their **a** Aaron made these rules
2Ch 17:3 in the old way like his **a** David.
21:12 God of your **a** David says:
28:1 as his **a** David had done.
29:2 as his **a** David had done.
34:2 He lived in the ways of his **a**
34:3 serving the God of his **a** David.
Isa 38:5 God of your **a** David says:
43:27 Your first **a** sinned,
51:2 Look to Abraham, your **a**,
58:14 the inheritance of your **a** Jacob.
Jer 35:6 because our **a** Jonadab,
Jer 35:8 have obeyed our **a** Jonadab,
35:10 our **a** Jonadab ordered
35:16 carried out the orders of their **a**,
35:18 the order of your **a** Jonadab,
Hos 12:3 Their **a** Jacob held on to his
Mat 3:9 'Abraham is our **a**.' I
Mar 11:10 Blessed is our **a** David's
Luk 1:32 him the throne of his **a** David.
1:73 the oath that he swore to our **a**
3:8 Don't say, 'Abraham is our **a**.' I
Jon 4:12 important than our **a** Jacob,
Act 2:29 that our **a** David died
4:25 your servant David (our **a**),
7:2 appeared to our **a** Abraham
Rom 4:1 about our **a** Abraham?
9:10 pregnant by our **a** Isaac.
Jas 2:21 Didn't our **a** Abraham receive

ancestor's (6)

Num 18:2 other Levites from your **a** tribe
36:6 within a family of their **a** tribe
36:8 from any family in her **a** tribe.
2Ch 17:4 dedicated his life to his **a** God
Isa 7:17 and your **a** family a time unlike
Jer 35:14 they have obeyed their **a** order.

ancestors (398)

Gen 25:8 he joined his **a** in death.
25:17 He joined his **a** in death.
31:3 "Go back to the land of your **a**
35:29 He joined his **a** in death at a
46:34 as our **a** have done.'
47:3 are shepherds, as were our **a**.
47:30 I want to rest with my **a**.
49:29 am about to join my **a** in death.
49:29 Bury me with my **a** in the cave
49:33 and joined his **a** in death.
Exo 3:6 I am the God of your **a**,
3:13 'The God of your **a** has sent
3:15 The LORD God of your **a**,
3:16 'The LORD God of your **a**,
4:5 that the LORD God of their **a**,
10:6 Your parents and **a** never saw
13:5 The LORD swore to your **a** that
13:11 as he swore to you and your **a**,
Lev 25:41 and the property of their **a**.
26:39 sins and the sins of their **a**.
26:40 sins and the sins of their **a** —
26:45 the promise to their **a**.
Num 11:12 promised their **a** with an oath?
14:22 land which I promised their **a**.
20:15 Our **a** went to Egypt,
20:15 mistreated us and our **a**.
20:24 must now join his **a** ⌊in death⌋,
20:26 will die there and join ⌊his **a**⌋."
26:55 based on the names of their **a**.
27:13 will join your **a** ⌊in death⌋,
31:2 you will join your **a** ⌊in death⌋."
32:8 That's what your **a** did when I
36:3 taken away from that of our **a**
36:7 tribal land inherited from his **a**.
36:8 the land inherited from his **a**.
Dtr 1:8 to give to your **a** Abraham,
1:11 May the LORD God of your **a**
1:21 LORD God of your **a** told you.
1:35 that I swore to give to your **a**,
4:1 God of your **a** is giving you.
4:31 or forget the promise to your **a**
4:37 Because he loved your **a** and
5:3 make this promise to our **a**,
6:3 God of your **a** promised you.
6:10 as he swore to your **a** Abraham,
6:18 to your **a** with an oath.
6:23 promised to our **a** with an oath.
7:8 the oath he swore to your **a**.
7:12 as he swore to your **a**.
7:13 as he swore to your **a**.
8:1 to your **a** with an oath.
8:3 which neither you nor your **a**
8:16 which your **a** had never seen.
8:18 which he swore to your **a**.
9:5 he swore to your **a** Abraham,
10:11 as I swore to their **a**."
10:15 LORD set his heart on your **a**
10:22 When your **a** went to Egypt,
11:9 the LORD swore to give your **a**
Dtr 11:21 to give to your **a** — as long
12:1 God of your **a** is giving you
13:6 you and your **a** never knew.
13:17 as he swore to your **a**.
19:8 borders as he promised your **a**
26:3 as he swore to our **a**."
26:5 "My **a** were wandering
26:7 out to the LORD God of our **a**,
26:15 promised with an oath to our **a**."
27:3 The LORD God of your **a** is
28:11 as he swore to your **a**.
28:36 you and your **a** never knew.
28:64 you nor your **a** ever knew.
29:13 he promised your **a** Abraham,
29:25 of the LORD God of their **a**.
30:5 you to the land your **a** owned.
30:5 numerous than your **a** were.
30:9 prosperous as he made your **a**.
30:20 to give to your **a** Abraham,
31:7 as he swore to their **a**.
31:16 lie down in death with your **a**.
31:20 that I swore to give to their **a**,
32:17 gods your **a** never worshiped.
32:50 die and join your **a** in death,
Jos 1:6 the land I swore to give their **a**.
5:6 he had sworn to give our **a**.
18:3 God of your **a** has given you?
21:43 he had sworn to give their **a**.
21:44 sworn with an oath to their **a**.
22:28 of the LORD's altar our **a** made.
24:2 of Israel says: Long ago your **a**,
24:6 When I led your **a** out of Egypt,
24:6 and horsemen chased your **a**
24:7 When your **a** cried out to the
24:14 Get rid of the gods your **a**
24:15 choose the gods your **a** served
24:17 God brought us and our **a** out
Jdg 2:1 that I swore to give to your **a**.
2:10 had joined their **a** in death.
2:12 the LORD God of their **a**,
2:17 of their **a** who had obeyed
2:17 They refused to be like their **a**.
2:20 the promise I gave their **a**
2:22 LORD's ways as their **a** did."
3:4 given their **a** through Moses.
6:13 Where are all the miracles our **a**
1Sm 2:27 I revealed myself to your **a**
2:28 I chose ⌊one of your **a**⌋ out of
2:28 And I gave your **a** the right to
12:6 brought your **a** out of Egypt.
12:7 LORD did for you and your **a**.
12:8 When your **a** went with Jacob
12:9 of them fought against your **a**.
12:15 you as he was against your **a**.
2Sm 7:12 lie down in death with your **a**,
1Ki 1:21 lie down in death with your **a**."
2:10 lay down in death with his **a**
8:21 that he made to our **a** when
8:34 land that you gave to their **a**.
8:40 the land that you gave to our **a**,
8:48 the land that you gave their **a**,
8:53 you brought our **a** out of Egypt."
8:57 with us as he was with our **a**.
8:58 commanded our **a** ⌊to keep⌋.
9:9 who brought their **a** out of
11:21 lain down in death with his **a**
11:43 lay down in death with his **a**
13:22 placed in the tomb of your **a**."
14:15 land which he gave their **a**.
14:20 lay down in death with his **a**.
14:22 than anything their **a** had done.
14:31 lay down in death with his **a**
15:8 lay down in death with his **a**
15:24 lay down in death with his **a**.
15:24 He was buried with his **a** in the
16:6 lay down in death with his **a**
16:28 lay down in death with his **a**
19:4 I'm no better than my **a**."
21:3 you what I inherited from my **a**."
21:4 from my **a**.") So Ahab lay
22:40 lay down in death with his **a**.
22:50 lay down in death with his **a**
2Ki 8:24 lay down in death with his **a**
9:28 buried him in a tomb with his **a**
10:35 lay down in death with his **a**
12:18 gifts his **a** Kings Jehoshaphat,

2Ki 12:21 They buried him with his a in
13:9 lay down in death with his a
13:13 lay down in death with his a
14:16 lay down in death with his a
14:20 in the City of David, with his a.
14:22 lay down in death with his a.
14:29 lay down in death with his a,
15:7 lay down in death with his a
15:9 as his a had done.
15:22 lay down in death with his a,
15:38 lay down in death with his a
16:20 lay down in death with his a
17:13 as I commanded your a
17:14 with as their a who refused
17:15 the promise he made to their a,
17:41 They still do whatever their a
19:12 my a destroyed rescue Gozan,
20:17 everything your a have stored
20:21 lay down in death with his a.
21:8 that I gave to their a if they will
21:15 the time their a left Egypt until
21:18 lay down in death with his a.
21:22 the LORD God of his a
22:13 us because our a did not obey
22:20 I'm going to bring you to your a.
23:32 as his a had done.
23:37 as his a had done.
24:6 lay down in death with his a,
1Ch 5:25 unfaithful to the God of their a.
9:19 as their a had been in charge of
12:17 may the God of our a see this
17:11 you to go and be with your a,
29:15 To you we are all like our a —
29:18 LORD God of our a Abraham,
29:20 the LORD God of their a
2Ch 6:25 you gave to them and their a.
6:31 the land that you gave to our a,
6:38 the land that you gave their a,
7:22 the LORD God of their a,
9:31 lay down in death with his a
11:16 to the LORD God of their a.
12:16 lay down in death with his a
13:12 the LORD God of your a.
13:18 the LORD God of their a.
14:1 lay down in death with his a
14:4 the LORD God of their a
15:12 the LORD God of their a
16:13 lay down in death with his a.
19:4 to the LORD God of their a.
20:6 He said, "LORD God of our a,
20:33 hearts set on the God of their a.
21:1 lay down in death with his a
21:10 the LORD God of his a.
21:19 as they had done for his a.
24:18 of the LORD God of their a
24:24 the LORD God of their a.
25:28 in the city of Judah with his a.
26:2 lay down in death with his a.
26:23 lay down in death with his a
27:9 lay down in death with his a,
28:6 the LORD God of their a.
28:9 "The LORD God of your a
28:25 the LORD God of his a angry.
28:27 lay down in death with his a
29:5 the LORD God of your a holy.
29:6 Our a were unfaithful and did
30:7 Don't be like your a and your
30:7 to the LORD God of their a.
30:8 to deal with like your a.
30:19 May the LORD God of their a
30:22 to the LORD God of their a.
32:15 his people from me or my a.
32:33 lay down in death with his a.
33:8 I set aside for their a if they will
33:12 in front of the God of his a.
33:20 lay down in death with his a.
34:21 us because our a did not obey
34:28 I'm going to bring you to your a.
34:32 of God, the God of their a.
34:33 the LORD God of their a.
35:24 buried in the tombs of his a.
36:15 The LORD God of their a
Ezr 5:12 But because our a made the
7:27 be to the LORD God of our a.
8:28 to the LORD God of your a.
10:11 God of your a what you have
Neh 2:3 place where my a are buried,
2:5 the city where my a are buried,
9:2 wicked things their a had done.
9:9 You saw how our a suffered in
9:10 they were treating our a.
9:16 But they — our own a — acted
9:32 leaders, priests, prophets, a,
9:34 and a didn't obey your
9:36 In the land you gave our a,
13:18 Isn't this what your a did,
Job 8:8 out what their a had learned.
15:18 not kept secret from their a.
Psa 22:4 Our a trusted you.
39:12 a stranger like all my a.
44:1 Our a have told us about the
44:2 but you planted our a ⌊there⌋.
44:2 but you set our a free.
49:19 join the generation of his a,
78:5 He commanded our a to make
78:8 they will not be like their a,
78:12 In front of their a he performed
78:57 and treacherous like their a.
79:8 the crimes of our a against us.
95:9 Your a challenged me and
106:6 have sinned, and so did our a.
106:7 When our a were in Egypt,
106:12 Then our a believed what he
109:14 remember the guilt of his a
Pro 22:28 marker that your a set in place.
Isa 37:12 my a destroyed rescue Gozan,
39:6 everything your a have stored
64:11 where our a praised you,
65:7 and for the sins of your a," says
Jer 2:5 What did your a find wrong
3:18 that I gave their a as their own
3:24 everything our a worked for,
3:25 we and our a have sinned
7:7 permanently to your a long ago.
7:14 I gave to you and to your a,
7:22 When I brought your a out of
7:25 From the time that your a left
7:26 you were worse than your a.
9:14 as their a taught them."
9:16 and their a haven't heard of.
11:4 I made this promise to your a
11:5 keep the oath I made to your a
11:7 I solemnly warned your a when
11:10 back to the evil ways of their a
11:10 promise that I made to their a.
14:20 and the wrongs done by our a.
16:11 because your a abandoned me,
16:12 have done worse than your a.
16:13 you and your a haven't heard of.
16:15 to the land that I gave their a.
16:19 "Our a have inherited lies,
17:22 as a holy day, as I told your a.
17:23 Your a did not obey me or pay
19:4 "The people, their a,
23:27 as their a forgot my name
23:39 city that I gave you and your a.
24:10 I gave to them and their a."'
25:5 gave to you and your a.
30:3 to the land that I gave their a,
31:32 that I made to their a when
32:22 with an oath to give their a,
34:5 for you as they did for your a,
34:13 promise I made to your a when
34:14 But your a refused to obey me
35:15 that I gave you and your a."
44:3 neither you nor your a heard of.
44:9 wicked things done by your a,
44:10 my decrees that I gave your a.
44:17 wine offerings to her as our a,
44:21 of Jerusalem along with your a,
50:7 the hope of their a.'
Lam 5:7 Our a sinned. Now they are
Eze 2:3 They and their a have rebelled
16:3 Your birthplace and your a
20:4 disgusting things their a did.
20:18 live by the laws of your a.
20:27 Your a insulted me again
20:30 yourselves the way your a did?
20:36 put you on trial as I put your a
20:42 that I promised to give your a.
36:28 in the land that I gave your a.
37:25 the land where their a lived.
Eze 47:14 I would give the land to your a.
Dan 2:23 God of my a, I thank and praise
9:6 a, and all the common people.
9:8 We, our kings, leaders, and a
9:16 the wicked things our a did.
11:37 no interest in the gods of his a
11:38 a god his a never heard of.
Hos 9:10 When I saw your a,
Amo 2:4 the same ones their a followed.
Mic 7:20 by an oath to our a long ago.
Zec 1:2 was very angry with your a.
1:4 Don't be like your a,
1:5 Your a — where are they now?
1:6 finally catch up with your a?
1:6 Then your a turned away from
8:14 When your a made me angry,
Mal 2:10 the promise given to our a?
3:7 Since the time of your a you
Mat 1:1 This is the list of a of Jesus
5:21 heard that it was said to your a,
5:33 heard that it was said to your a,
15:2 break the traditions of our a?
23:30 had lived at the time of our a,
23:32 finish what your a started!
Mar 7:3 follow the traditions of their a.
7:5 the traditions taught by our a?
Luk 1:55 the promise he made to our a,
1:72 has shown his mercy to our a
2:3 cities where their a had lived.
6:23 their a treated the prophets.
6:26 That's the way their a treated
11:47 your a who murdered them.
11:48 and approve of what your a did.
Jon 4:20 Our a worshiped on this
6:31 Our a ate the manna in the
6:49 Your a ate the manna in the
6:58 is not like the bread your a ate.
7:22 from Moses but from our a).
Act 3:13 The God of our a Abraham,
3:25 that God made to our a when
5:30 But the God of our a brought
7:8 sons (the a of our tribes).
7:11 Our a couldn't find any food.
7:12 he sent our a there.
7:15 and he and our a died there.
7:19 He mistreated our a.
7:32 'I am the God of your a — the
7:36 This is the man who led our a
7:38 Our a and the messenger who
7:39 but our a were not willing to
7:44 "In the desert our a had the tent
7:45 After our a received the tent,
7:51 You're just like your a.
7:52 Was there ever a prophet your a
13:17 the people of Israel chose our a
13:32 promised our a has happened.
13:36 He was laid to rest with his a,
15:10 a burden neither our a nor we
22:3 rules handed down by our a.
22:14 'The God of our a has chosen
26:6 promise that he made to our a.
28:17 handed down by our a.
28:25 Spirit spoke to your a through
Rom 9:5 from their a according
11:28 are loved because of their a.
15:8 fulfilled God's promise to the a
1Co 10:1 that all our a ⌊who left Egypt⌋
Gal 1:14 for the traditions of my a.
2Ti 1:3 clear conscience as my a did.
Heb 1:1 In the past God spoke to our a
3:9 That is where your a tested me,
4:2 Good News that your a heard.
4:7 Many years after ⌊your a failed
7:3 father, mother, or a.
8:9 that I made to their a when
11:2 God accepted our a because of
12:19 When your a heard that voice,
12:25 Your a didn't escape when they
12:26 When God spoke to your a,
1Pe 1:18 down to you from your a by
2Pe 3:4 Ever since our a died,

ancestors' (11)

Gen 47:9 fewer than my a years.
Num 1:16 the leaders of their a tribes,
13:2 from each of their a tribes.

Num 33:54 Divide it among your a tribes
36:4 of the land of our a tribe will
Ezr 9:7 From our a days until now,
Isa 14:21 sons because of their a guilt.
Eze 20:24 to their a disgusting idols
Joe 1:2 lifetime or in your a lifetime
Act 7:45 God forced out of our a way.
24:14 means that I serve our a God

ancestry (8)

1Ch 5:7 records according to their a,
7:2 grouped according to their a.
7:4 to their a and families,
7:9 according to their a (the heads
8:28 of families listed by their a.
9:9 relatives according to their a.
9:34 families according to their a.
26:31 the a of Hebron's descendants

anchor (2)

Act 27:13 They raised the a and sailed
Heb 6:19 as a sure and strong a

anchored (1)

Mar 6:53 at Gennesaret, and a there.

anchors (3)

Act 27:29 they dropped four a from the
27:30 were going to lay out the a from
27:40 They cut the a free and left

ancient (28)

Gen 49:26 and the riches of the a hills.
Dtr 33:15 the best from the a hills,
1Ch 4:22 (according to a records).
Job 12:12 "Wisdom is with the a one.
20:4 you know that from a times,
Psa 24:7 Be lifted, you a doors,
24:9 Be lifted, you a doors,
68:33 rides through the a heaven,
76:4 majestic than the a mountains.
77:11 I will remember your a
Pro 22:28 Do not move an a boundary
23:10 Do not move an a boundary
Isa 19:11 a descendant of a kings"?
58:12 Your people will rebuild the a
61:4 They will rebuild the a ruins.
Jer 5:15 It is an a nation. You don't know
18:15 along the way, on the a path.
Lam 1:7 treasures it had from a times,
Eze 26:20 the earth among the a ruins
36:2 The a worship sites now
Dan 7:9 were set up and the A One,
7:13 He came to the A One,
7:22 It did this until the A One,
Hab 3:6 The a hills sink. The ancient
3:6 The a paths belong to him.
2Pe 2:5 didn't spare the a world either.
Rev 12:9 That a snake, named Devil and
20:2 the serpent, that a snake,

Andrew (14)

Mat 4:18 Simon (called Peter) and A.
10:2 called Peter) and his brother A;
Mar 1:16 saw Simon and his brother A.
1:29 to the house of Simon and A.
3:18 A, Philip, Bartholomew,
13:3 and A asked him privately,
Luk 6:14 Peter) and Simon's brother A,
Jon 1:40 A, Simon Peter's brother,
1:41 A at once found his brother
1:42 A brought Simon to Jesus.
1:44 the hometown of A and Peter.)
6:8 One of Jesus' disciples, A,
12:22 Philip told A, and they told
Act 1:13 James, A, Philip, Thomas,

Andronicus (1)

Rom 16:7 Greet A and Junias,

Anem (1)

1Ch 6:73 and A with its pastureland.

Aner (3)

Gen 14:13 a brother of Eshcol and A.
14:24 But let my allies A,

1Ch 6:70 they were given A with its

angel (151)

Gen 19:21 The a said to him,
24:7 "God will send his a ahead of
24:40 The LORD will send his a with
Exo 26:1 and creatively work an a
26:31 Creatively work an a design
36:8 An a design was creatively
36:35 An a design was creatively
1Ki 13:18 An a spoke the word of the
19:5 An a touched him and said,
19:7 The a of the LORD came back
19:7 The a said, "Get up and eat,
2Ki 1:3 Then the a of the LORD said to
1:15 The a of the LORD told Elijah,
19:35 The LORD's a went out and
2Ch 32:21 The LORD sent an a who
Isa 37:36 The LORD's a went out and
Eze 10:7 This a put them in the hands of
10:14 The first was the face of an a,
28:14 I appointed an a to guard you.
28:16 The guardian a forced you out
41:18 and each a had two faces:
Dan 3:28 He sent his a and saved his
6:22 My God sent his a and shut the
Zec 1:9 The a who was speaking with
1:13 The LORD responded to the a
1:14 The a who was speaking with
1:19 So I asked the a who was
2:3 Then the a who was speaking
2:3 Another a came out to meet him
4:1 The a who was speaking with
4:4 I asked the a who was
4:5 Then the a asked me,
4:11 I asked the a, "What do these
5:2 The a asked me, "What do you
5:5 The a who was speaking with
5:8 The a said, "This is
5:10 I asked the a who was
6:4 I asked the a who was
6:5 The a answered, "They are the
Mat 1:20 had this in mind when an a
1:20 The a said to him,
1:24 he did what the a of the Lord
2:13 After they had left, an a of the
2:13 The a said to him,
2:19 After Herod was dead, an a of
2:20 The a said to him,
28:2 An a of the Lord had come
28:5 The a said to the women,
Luk 1:11 an a of the Lord appeared to
1:13 The a said to him,
1:18 Zechariah said to the a,
1:19 The a answered him,
1:26 God sent the a Gabriel to
1:27 The a went to a virgin
1:28 When the a entered her home,
1:29 She was startled by what the a
1:30 The a told her, "Don't be afraid,
1:34 Mary asked the a, "How can
1:35 The a answered her,
1:38 Then the a left her.
2:9 An a from the Lord suddenly
2:10 The a said to them,
2:13 of angels appeared with the a.
2:20 the way the a had told them.
2:21 This was the name the a had
22:43 Then an a from heaven
Jon 12:29 crowd said that an a had talked
20:12 One a was where Jesus' head
Act 5:19 But at night an a from the Lord
5:20 The a told them, "Stand in the
5:21 after they had listened to the a,
8:26 An a from the Lord said to
10:3 He clearly saw an a from God
10:4 He stared at the a and was
10:4 Cornelius asked the a,
10:4 The a answered him,
10:7 After saying this, the a left.
10:22 A holy a told him to summon
11:13 that he had seen an a standing
11:13 The a told him, and summon a
12:7 Suddenly, an a from the Lord
12:7 The a nudged Peter's side,
12:8 The a told him, "Put your

Act 12:8 Then the a told him,
12:9 Peter followed the a out of the
12:9 He didn't realize that what the a
12:10 The a suddenly left Peter.
12:11 I'm sure that the Lord sent his a
12:15 They said, "It has to be his a."
12:23 Immediately, an a from the Lord
23:9 Maybe a spirit or an a actually
27:23 I know this because an a from
27:24 The a told me, 'Don't be afraid,
1Co 10:10 The a of death destroyed them.
2Co 11:14 himself as an a of light.
Gal 1:8 one of us or an a from heaven.
Heb 11:28 the destroying a would not kill
Rev 1:1 this revelation through his a
5:2 I saw a powerful a calling out
7:2 I saw another a coming from
8:3 Another a came with a gold
8:5 The a took the incense burner,
8:7 When the first a blew his
8:8 When the second a blew his
8:10 When the third a blew his
8:12 When the fourth a blew his
9:1 When the fifth a blew his
9:11 who ruled them was the a from
9:13 When the sixth a blew his
9:14 The voice said to the sixth a
10:1 I saw another powerful a come
10:5 The a whom I saw standing on
10:7 In the days when the seventh a
10:8 hand of the a who is standing
10:9 I went to the a and asked him
11:15 When the seventh a blew his
14:6 I saw another a flying overhead
14:7 The a said in a loud voice,
14:8 Another a, a second one,
14:9 Another a, a third one,
14:15 Another a came out of the
14:17 Another a came out of the
14:18 Yet another a came from the
14:18 This a called out in a loud
14:18 out in a loud voice to the a
14:19 The a swung his sickle on the
16:2 The first a poured his bowl
16:3 The second a poured his bowl
16:4 The third a poured his bowl
16:5 Then I heard the a of the water
16:8 The fourth a poured his bowl
16:10 The fifth a poured his bowl on
16:12 The sixth a poured his bowl on
16:17 The seventh a poured his bowl
17:3 Then the a carried me by his
17:7 The a asked me, "Why are you
17:15 The a also said to me,
18:1 another a come from heaven.
18:21 Then a powerful a picked up a
19:9 Then the a said to me,
19:17 I saw an a standing in the sun.
20:1 I saw an a coming down from
20:2 The a chained up the serpent
20:3 The a shut and sealed the pit
21:15 The a who was talking to me
21:17 which the a was using,
22:1 The a showed me a river filled
22:6 of the prophets has sent his a
22:8 the feet of the a who had been
22:10 Then the a said to me,
22:16 "I, Jesus, have sent my a to

angel's (3)

Act 6:15 his face looked like an a face
Rev 8:4 went up from the a hand
10:10 the small scroll from the a hand

angels (171)

Gen 3:24 God placed a and a flaming
19:1 The two a came to Sodom in
19:15 the a urged Lot by saying,
19:17 one of the a said,
28:12 He saw the a of God going up
32:1 on his way, God's a met him.
Exo 25:18 Make two a out of hammered
25:19 Form the a and the throne of
25:20 The a should have their wings
25:22 mercy between the a whenever
37:7 Then he made two a out of

Exo 37:8 He formed the **a** and the throne
37:9 The **a** had their wings spread
Num 7:89 from between the two **a**.
1Sm 4:4 who is enthroned over the **a**.
2Sm 6:2 who is enthroned over the **a**.)
22:11 He rode on one of the **a** as he
1Ki 6:23 he made two 15-foot-tall **a** out
6:24 Each wing of the **a** was 7 ½
6:25 Both **a** had a 15-foot
6:27 Solomon put the **a** in the inner
6:27 The wings of the **a** extended
6:27 wing of one of the **a** touched
6:28 He covered the **a** with gold.
6:29 He carved **a**, palm trees,
6:32 He carved **a**, palm trees,
6:32 gold was hammered onto the **a**
6:35 On them he carved **a**,
7:29 were lions, oxen, and **a**.
7:36 Hiram engraved **a**,
8:6 place) under the wings of the **a**.
8:7 the **a** became a covering above
2Ki 19:15 you are enthroned over the **a**.
1Ch 13:6 is enthroned over the **a** ⌊on
28:18 the gold **a** with their wings
2Ch 3:7 and he carved **a** into the walls.
3:10 he made two sculptured **a**
3:11 A wing of one of the **a** was 7
3:12 the other one of the **a** was 7 ½
3:14 of linen and decorated it with **a**.
5:7 place) under the wings of the **a**.
5:8 ⌊rested⌋ so that the **a** became
Job 4:18 his **a** of making mistakes.
Psa 18:10 He rode on one of the **a** as he
78:49 sent an army of destroying **a**.
80:1 who is enthroned over the **a**.
91:11 He will put his **a** in charge of
99:1 He is enthroned over the **a**.
103:20 Praise the LORD, all his **a**,
104:4 You make your **a** winds and
148:2 Praise him, all his **a**.
Isa 6:2 **A** were standing above him.
6:6 Then one of the **a** flew to me.
37:16 you are enthroned over the **a**.
Eze 9:3 of Israel went up from the **a**,
10:1 dome over the heads of the **a**,
10:2 the wheels under the **a**,
10:3 The **a** were standing on the
10:4 LORD's glory rose from the **a**
10:6 the wheels beside the **a**,
10:7 One of the **a** reached into the
10:7 the fire that was between the **a**
10:8 The **a** appeared to have what
10:9 I saw four wheels beside the **a**,
10:9 wheel beside each of the **a**.
10:11 Whenever the **a** moved,
10:12 Each of the **a** had a wheel.
10:14 Each of the **a** had four faces.
10:15 The **a** rose. These were the
10:16 When the **a** moved,
10:16 When the **a** lifted their wings to
10:17 When the **a** stood still,
10:17 When the **a** rose, the wheels
10:18 entrance and stood over the **a**.
10:19 The **a** lifted their wings and
10:19 The **a** stood at the door to the
10:20 I realized that they were **a**.
11:22 Then the **a** raised their wings,
41:18 there were pictures of **a** and
41:18 between each of the **a**,
41:20 Pictures of **a** and palm trees
41:25 Pictures of **a** and palm trees
Mat 4:6 'He will put his **a** in charge of
4:11 and **a** came to take care of him.
13:39 The workers are **a**.
13:41 Son of Man will send his **a**.
13:42 The **a** will throw them into a
13:49 The **a** will go out and separate
13:50 Then the **a** will throw the evil
16:27 of Man will come with his **a**
18:10 I can guarantee that their **a** in
22:30 they are like the **a** in heaven.
24:31 He will send out his **a** with a
24:36 Even the **a** in heaven and the
25:31 in his glory and all his **a** are
25:41 prepared for the devil and his **a**!
26:53 more than twelve legions of **a**
Mar 1:13 and the **a** took care of him.
8:38 when he comes with the holy **a**
12:25 they are like the **a** in heaven.
13:27 He will send out his **a**,
13:32 Even the **a** in heaven and the
Luk 2:13 Suddenly, a large army of **a**
2:15 The **a** left them and went back
4:10 'He will put his **a** in charge of
9:26 with the Father and the holy **a**.
12:8 of God's **a** every person who
12:9 But God's **a** will be told that I
15:10 So I can guarantee that God's **a**
16:22 and the **a** carried him to be with
20:36 They are the same as the **a**.
24:23 they had seen **a** who said that
Jon 1:51 sky open and God's **a** going up
20:12 She saw two **a** in white
20:13 The **a** asked her why she was
Act 7:53 which were put into effect by **a**.
23:8 come back to life and that **a**
Rom 8:38 by death or life, by **a** or rulers,
1Co 4:9 for people and **a** to look at.
6:3 you know that we will judge **a**,
11:10 out of respect for the **a**.
13:1 languages of humans and of **a**.
Gal 3:19 It was put into effect through **a**,
Col 2:18 the worship of **a** tell you that
2Th 1:7 from heaven with his mighty **a**
1Ti 3:16 by the Spirit, was seen by **a**,
5:21 and the chosen **a** to be
Heb 1:4 greater than the **a** since
1:5 God never said to any of his **a**,
1:5 God never said to any of his **a**,
1:6 of God's **a** must worship him."
1:7 God said about the **a**,
1:13 God never said to any of the **a**,
1:14 What are all the **a**?
2:2 After all, the message that the **a**
2:7 him a little lower than the **a**.
2:9 made a little lower than the **a**,
2:16 rather than helping **a**.
9:5 Above the ark were the **a** of
12:22 of **a** joyfully gathered together
13:2 to **a** without being aware
1Pe 1:12 are things that even the **a** want
3:22 **A**, rulers, and powers have
2Pe 2:4 God didn't spare **a** who sinned.
2:11 **A**, who have more strength and
Jud 1:6 He held **a** for judgment on the
1:6 These are the **a** who didn't
1:7 that God's people and the **a** did,
1:14 thousands of his holy **a**.
Rev 3:5 of my Father and his **a**.
5:11 I heard the voices of many **a**,
7:1 After this I saw four **a** standing
7:2 to the four **a** who had been
7:11 All the **a** stood around the
8:2 Then I saw the seven **a** who
8:6 The seven **a** who had the
8:13 which the three **a** are about
9:14 "Release the four **a** who are
9:15 The four **a** who were ready for
12:7 Michael and his **a** had to fight **a**
12:7 The serpent and its **a** fought.
12:9 Its **a** were thrown down with it.
14:10 of the holy **a** and the lamb.
15:1 There were seven **a** with the
15:6 The seven **a** with the seven
15:7 and ever, to the seven **a**.
15:8 plagues of the seven **a** came
16:1 temple saying to the seven **a**,
17:1 One of the seven **a** who held
21:9 One of the seven **a** who had
21:12 Twelve **a** were at the gates.

angels' (6)

1Ki 8:7 When the **a** outstretched wings
2Ch 3:11 of the **a** wings was 30 feet.
3:12 So the **a** combined wingspan
5:8 The **a** outstretched wings were
Eze 10:5 The sound of the **a** wings was
Heb 2:5 are talking) under the **a** control

anger (241)

Gen 27:44 your brother's **a** cools down.
27:45 When your brother's **a** is gone
49:6 In their **a** they murdered men.
49:7 May their **a** be cursed because
Exo 11:8 Burning with **a**, Moses left
15:7 You sent out your burning **a**.
32:19 In a burst of **a** Moses threw
Num 16:46 The LORD is showing his **a**;
18:5 Then I won't show my **a**
25:4 LORD's **a** away from Israel."
Dtr 9:19 of the LORD's **a** and fury.
29:20 because the LORD's burning **a**
29:23 the LORD destroyed in fierce **a**.
29:28 In his fierce **a** and fury the
32:22 My **a** has started a fire that will
Jos 7:26 LORD withdrew his burning **a**.
9:20 live to avoid ⌊the LORD's⌋ **a**
1Sm 6:3 not turn his **a** away from you."
28:18 his burning **a** on Amalek.
2Sm 12:5 David burned with **a** against
2Ki 3:27 There was bitter **a** against the
5:12 he turned around and left in **a**.
22:13 The LORD's fierce **a** is
22:17 Therefore, my burning **a**
23:26 burning **a** from Judah.
2Ch 12:7 to pour my **a** on Jerusalem.
19:2 The LORD's **a** is directed
24:18 brought God's **a** upon Judah
28:9 Judah over to you in his **a**.
29:10 his burning **a** away from us.
30:8 his burning **a** away from you.
32:26 So the LORD didn't vent his **a**
34:21 The LORD's fierce **a** has been
34:25 Therefore, my **a** will be poured
Ezr 8:22 but his power and his **a** oppose
10:14 burning **a** has turned away
Est 2:1 Xerxes got over his raging **a**,
7:10 the king got over his raging **a**.
Job 4:9 kills them with a blast of his **a**.
5:2 **a** kills a stubborn fool,
9:5 and he topples them in his **a**.
9:13 God does not hold back his **a**.
10:17 increasing your **a** toward me.
14:13 hidden there until your **a** cools.
16:9 "God's **a** tore me ⌊apart⌋ and
18:4 do you rip yourself apart in **a**?
19:29 Fear death, because ⌊your **a**⌋
20:23 ⌊God⌋ throws his burning **a** at
20:28 flash flood on the day of his **a**.
21:30 day of ⌊God's⌋ **a** he is rescued.
35:15 And now ⌊you say⌋ that his **a**
40:11 Unleash your outbursts of **a**.
Psa 2:5 he speaks to them in his **a**.
2:5 In his burning **a** he terrifies
2:12 because his **a** will burst into
6:1 do not punish me in your **a** or
7:6 Arise in **a**, O LORD. Stand up
21:9 will swallow them up in his **a**.
30:5 His **a** lasts only a moment.
37:8 Let go of **a**, and leave rage
55:3 and they attack me out of **a**.
69:24 Let your burning **a** catch up
74:1 Why does your **a** smolder
76:10 wear the remainder of ⌊their⌋ **a**.
77:9 compassion because of his **a**?
78:21 Jacob and his **a** flared up at
78:31 the **a** of God flared up against
78:38 He restrained his **a** many times.
78:49 He sent his burning **a**,
78:50 He cleared a path for his **a**.
80:4 how long will you smolder in **a**
85:3 away from your burning **a**.
85:4 Put an end to your **a** against us.
85:5 Will you ever let go of your **a** in
88:16 Your burning **a** has swept over
89:46 How long will your **a** continue
90:7 Indeed, your **a** consumes us.
90:11 the power of your **a**?
102:10 because of your hostility and **a**,
106:40 The LORD burned with **a**
110:5 crush kings on the day of his **a**.
119:53 I am burning with **a** because of
124:3 their **a** exploded against us.
138:7 you guard my life against the **a**
Pro 15:1 but a harsh word stirs up **a**.
16:14 A king's **a** announces death,
21:14 gift ⌊given⌋ in secret calms **a**,
24:18 and he will turn his **a** away

Pro 27:4 **A** is cruel, and fury is
29:8 but wise people turn away **a**.
30:33 stirring up **a** produces a fight.
Ecc 7:9 because **a** is typical of fools.
Isa 5:25 That's why the **a** of the LORD
5:25 his **a** has not disappeared,
7:4 heart because of the fierce **a**
9:12 his **a** will not disappear,
9:17 his **a** will not disappear,
9:21 his **a** will not disappear,
10:4 his **a** will not disappear,
10:5 It is the rod of my **a**.
10:25 and my **a** will destroy them.
12:1 you turned your **a** away from
13:3 mighty men to carry out my **a**.
13:9 cruel day with fury and fierce **a**.
14:6 They ruled nations in **a**,
26:11 Your burning **a** will destroy
30:27 His **a** is burning. His burden is
30:30 with furious **a**, with fire storms,
42:25 So he poured out his burning **a**
48:9 I'll hold my **a** back from you,
51:17 That cup was filled with his **a**.
51:20 They experience the **a** of the
54:8 for a moment in a burst of **a**,
60:10 In my **a** I struck you,
63:3 In my **a** I trampled on people.
63:5 My **a** supported me.
63:6 In my **a** I trampled on people.
64:5 You showed your **a**,
66:15 them back with his burning **a**
Jer 2:35 God will turn his **a** from me,
4:8 burning **a** hasn't turned away
4:26 of the LORD and his burning **a**.
6:11 I am filled with the **a** of the
7:20 My **a** and fury will be poured
7:20 My **a** and fury will burn and not
7:29 because in his **a** the LORD has
12:13 of the burning **a** of the LORD.
15:14 because my **a** has started a
17:4 have stirred up the fire of my **a**.
18:20 to turn your **a** away from them.
21:5 I will fight you in **a**,
23:19 the LORD will come with his **a**.
23:20 The **a** of the LORD will not turn
25:37 by the LORD's burning **a**.
25:38 because of the fury of his **a**.
30:23 the LORD will come with his **a**.
30:24 The LORD's burning **a** will not
32:37 where I scattered them in my **a**,
33:5 own people I killed in my **a**
36:7 with his terrifying **a** and fury."
42:18 As my **a** and my fury were
44:6 That is why my fury and **a**
49:37 disaster with my burning **a**,
50:13 because of the LORD's **a**.
51:45 burning **a** of the LORD.
Lam 1:12 suffer on the day of his fierce **a**.
2:1 of Zion with the cloud of his **a**!
2:1 footstool on the day of his **a**.
2:3 In his burning **a** he cut off all of
2:6 priests because of his fierce **a**.
2:21 them on the day of your **a**.
2:22 on the day of the LORD's **a**.
3:43 You covered yourself with **a**
3:66 Pursue them in **a**, and wipe
4:11 He unleashed his burning **a**.
Eze 5:13 "I will unleash my **a**.
5:15 I punish you because of my **a**,
6:12 is how I will unleash my **a**.
7:3 I will send my **a** against you.
7:8 you and unleash my **a** on you.
7:19 on the day of the LORD's **a**.
8:3 stirs up ⌊God's⌋ **a** was located.
8:5 the idol that stirs up ⌊God's⌋ **a**.
9:8 pour out your **a** on Jerusalem?"
13:13 In my **a** rain will pour down,
16:38 in my fury and burning **a**.
19:12 But in **a** it was uprooted and
20:8 fury on them and unleash my **a**
20:21 fury on them and unleash my **a**
21:31 breathe on you with my fiery **a**.
22:20 In the same way, in my **a** and
22:21 breathe on you with my fiery **a**,
22:24 had rain during the day of my **a**.
22:31 So I will pour out my **a** on you,
Eze 22:31 and with my fiery **a** I will
23:25 I will direct my burning **a**
23:25 they will deal with you in **a**.
25:14 deal with Edom based on my **a**
36:5 In my fiery **a** I have spoken
36:6 I am speaking in my **a** and fury
38:18 I will be filled with burning **a**,
38:19 In my fiery **a** I tell you this.
43:8 So I destroyed them in my **a**.
Dan 3:13 Then, in a fit of rage and **a**,
3:19 filled with **a** toward Shadrach,
8:19 ⌊the time of God's⌋ **a**,
9:16 turn your **a** and fury away from
11:20 although not in **a** or war.
11:36 succeed until God's **a** is over,
Hos 7:6 All night long their **a** smolders,
8:5 My **a** burns against these
11:9 I will not act on my burning **a**.
11:9 and I will not come to you in **a**.
Amo 1:11 Their **a** was unstoppable.
Jnh 3:9 from his burning **a** so that we
Mic 5:15 I will take revenge with great **a**
Nah 1:2 takes revenge and is full of **a**.
1:6 Who can oppose his burning **a**?
Hab 3:12 You trample the nations in **a**.
Zep 1:18 be consumed by his fiery **a**,
2:2 before the LORD's burning **a**
2:2 of the LORD's **a** comes to you.
2:3 on the day of the LORD's **a**.
3:8 rage, my burning **a**, on them.
Zec 10:3 "My burning **a** is directed
Mat 3:7 to flee from God's coming **a**?
Luk 3:7 to flee from God's coming **a**?
Jon 3:36 he will see God's constant **a**."
Rom 1:18 God's **a** is revealed from
2:5 you are adding to the **a** that
2:5 that day when God vents his **a**.
2:8 **a** and fury on those who,
3:5 when he vents his **a** on us?
4:15 Teachings bring about **a**.
5:9 will save us from God's **a**.
9:22 wants to demonstrate his **a**
9:22 people who are objects of his **a**
12:19 let God's **a** take care of it.
13:4 an avenger to execute God's **a**
13:5 you're afraid of God's **a**
Eph 2:3 we deserved God's **a** just like
4:31 **a**, loud quarreling, cursing,
5:6 like these that God's **a** comes
Col 3:6 these sins that God's **a** comes
3:8 Also get rid of your **a**,
1Th 1:10 us from ⌊God's⌋ coming **a**.
2:16 they are receiving ⌊God's⌋ **a**.
5:9 that we experience his **a**
1Ti 2:8 prayer after putting aside their **a**
Heb 11:27 being afraid of the king's **a**.
Rev 6:16 and from the **a** of the lamb,
6:17 day of their **a** has come,
11:18 but your **a** has come.
12:12 down to them with fierce **a**,
14:10 into the cup of God's **a**.
14:19 into the winepress of God's **a**.
15:1 the final expression of God's **a**.
15:7 gold bowls full of the **a** of God,
16:1 of God's **a** over the earth."
16:19 cup of wine from his fierce **a**.
19:15 of the fierce **a** of God Almighty.

angered (5)

Gen 38:7 Er **a** the LORD. So the LORD
38:10 What Onan did **a** the LORD so
Dtr 32:16 foreign gods and **a** him
32:21 foreign gods and **a** him
Psa 7:11 a God who is **a** by injustice

Angle (5)

2Ch 26:9 Wall, Valley Gate, and the **A**,
Neh 3:19 ascent to the Armory at the **A**.
3:20 repairs on a section from the **A**
3:24 from Azariah's home to the **A**
3:25 made repairs across from the **A**

angrily (8)

Psa 27:9 Do not **a** turn me away.
38:1 O LORD, do not **a** punish me or
56:7 O God, **a** make the nations fall.
Psa 95:11 That is why I **a** took this
106:9 He **a** commanded the Red Sea,
112:10 He **a** grits his teeth and
Heb 3:11 So I **a** took a solemn oath that
4:3 As God said, "So I **a** took a

angry (220)

Gen 4:5 very **a** and was disappointed.
4:6 asked Cain, "Why are you **a**,
18:30 "Please don't be **a** if I speak
18:32 "Please don't be **a** if I speak
30:2 Jacob became **a** with Rachel
31:35 her father, "Don't be **a**, Father,
31:36 Then Jacob became **a** and
34:7 men felt outraged and very **a**
39:19 he became very **a**.
40:2 Pharaoh was **a** with his chief
41:10 time ago when Pharaoh was **a**
44:18 Don't be **a** with me,
45:5 Now, don't be sad or **a** with
Exo 4:14 Then the LORD became **a** with
16:20 So Moses was **a** with them.
21:14 someone becomes so **a** that
22:24 I will become **a** and have you
32:10 I'm so **a** with them I am going
32:11 "why are you so **a** with your
32:12 Don't be so **a**. Reconsider your
32:22 "Don't be **a**, sir," "You know that
Lev 10:6 and the LORD will become **a**
10:16 So he became **a** with Eleazar
Num 1:53 way ⌊the LORD⌋ won't be **a**
11:1 heard them, he became **a**,
11:10 The LORD became very **a**,
11:33 chew it — the LORD became **a**
12:9 The LORD was **a** with them,
16:15 Moses became **a** and said to
16:22 If one man sins, will you be **a**
22:22 God became **a** that he was
22:27 Balaam became so **a** he hit the
24:10 Balak became **a** with Balaam.
25:3 LORD became **a** with Israel.
31:14 Moses was **a** with the officers
32:10 That day the LORD became **a**
32:13 Since the LORD was **a** with
32:14 the LORD **a** with Israel again.
Dtr 1:34 he was **a** and took this oath:
1:37 The LORD became **a** with me
3:26 The LORD was **a** with me
4:21 The LORD was **a** with me
6:15 your God will become very **a**
7:4 Then the LORD will get very **a**
9:7 made the LORD your God **a**
9:8 you made the LORD so **a** that
9:19 He was so **a** he wanted to
9:20 The LORD also became very **a**
9:22 made the LORD **a** at Taberah,
11:17 LORD will become **a** with you.
13:17 the LORD will stop being **a**
29:24 to their land? Why is he so **a**?"
29:27 So the LORD became **a** with
31:17 day I will become **a** with them.
32:19 and daughters had made him **a**.
32:21 godless fools to make them **a**.
32:27 their enemies to make me **a**.
Jos 7:1 So the LORD became **a** with
22:18 and tomorrow he will be **a** with
22:20 Didn't the LORD become **a** with
23:16 the LORD will be **a** with you.
Jdg 2:12 and that made the LORD **a**.
2:14 So the LORD became **a** with
2:20 LORD became **a** with Israel.
3:8 The LORD became **a** with the
6:39 "Don't be **a** with me.
8:3 weren't **a** with him anymore.
9:30 had said, and he became **a**.
10:7 The LORD became **a** with the
14:19 He was **a**, and he went to his
1Sm 11:6 and he became very **a**.
15:11 Samuel was **a**, and he prayed
17:28 Eliab became **a** with David.
18:8 Saul became very **a** because
20:7 But if he gets really **a**,
20:30 Then Saul got **a** with Jonathan.
20:34 got up from the table very **a**
29:4 officers were **a** with Achish.
2Sm 3:8 question made Abner very **a**.

2Sm 6:7 LORD became **a** with Uzzah,
6:8 David was **a** because the
11:20 the king may become **a**.
13:21 he became very **a**.
19:42 Why are you **a** about this?
22:8 violently because he was **a**.
24:1 The LORD became **a** with
1Ki 8:46 You may become **a** with them
11:9 So the LORD became **a** with
14:22 Their sins made him more **a**
2Ki 5:11 But Naaman became **a** and left.
6:11 of Aram was very **a** about this.
13:3 So the LORD became **a** with
13:19 Then the man of God became **a**
17:18 The LORD became so **a** with
24:20 The LORD became **a** with
1Ch 13:10 The LORD became **a** with
13:11 David was **a** because the
27:24 God was **a** with Israel because
2Ch 6:36 You may become **a** with them
12:12 the LORD was no longer **a** with
16:10 He was so **a** with Hanani that
19:10 Otherwise, he will become **a**
25:15 LORD became **a** with Amaziah.
26:19 burner in his hand, became **a**.
26:19 While he was **a** with the
28:11 the LORD is very **a** with you."
28:13 The LORD is very **a** with Israel
28:25 LORD God of his ancestors **a**.
29:8 So the LORD was **a** with
32:25 The LORD became **a** with him,
36:16 until the LORD became **a**
Ezr 5:12 made the God of heaven **a**,
7:23 Why should God become **a**
9:14 you will become even more **a**
Neh 13:18 you're making him even more **a**
Est 1:12 the king became very **a**,
2:21 became **a** and planned to kill
Job 19:11 He is very **a** at me.
21:17 How often does an **a** God give
32:2 became very **a** with Job
32:3 Elihu was also very **a** with
32:5 he became very **a**.
36:13 have godless hearts remain **a**.
36:33 The storm announces his **a**
42:7 "I'm very **a** with you and your
Psa 2:12 or he will become **a** and you
18:7 violently because he was **a**.
60:1 You have been **a**. Restore us!
76:7 presence when you become **a**?
76:10 Even **a** mortals will praise you.
78:58 They made him **a** because of
79:5 Will you remain **a** forever?
85:5 Will you be **a** with us forever?
89:38 and become **a** with your
103:9 or be **a** ⌊with us⌋ forever.
106:32 They made God **a** by the water
112:10 sees this and becomes **a**.
Pro 16:32 Better to get **a** slowly than to
20:2 makes him **a** forfeits his life.
21:19 with a quarreling and **a** woman.
25:23 tongue brings **a** looks.
29:22 An **a** person stirs up a fight,
Ecc 5:6 Why should God become **a** at
7:9 Don't be quick to get **a**,
10:4 If a ruler becomes **a** with you,
Sos 1:6 My brothers were **a** with me.
Isa 12:1 you had been **a** with me,
13:13 when the LORD of Armies is **a**.
13:13 At that time he will be very **a**.
27:4 I am no longer **a**. If only thorns
34:2 The LORD is **a** with all the
41:11 "Everyone who is **a** with you
45:24 All who are **a** with him will
47:6 I was **a** with my people.
54:9 now I swear an oath not to be **a**
57:16 I will not be **a** with you forever.
57:17 I was **a** because of their sinful
57:17 ⌊from them⌋, and remained **a**.
59:15 The LORD sees it, and he's **a**
64:9 Don't be too **a**, LORD.
Jer 3:5 He won't always be **a**.' You
3:12 'I will no longer be **a** with you.
10:10 earth trembles when he is **a**.
10:24 Don't correct me when you're **a**.
18:23 Deal with them when you get **a**.
Jer 32:31 in this city have made me so **a**
37:15 The officials were so **a** with
44:3 and they made me **a**.
44:8 Why do you make me **a** by
52:3 The LORD became **a** with
Lam 5:22 us ⌊and⌋ are very **a** with us."
Eze 3:14 went away feeling bitter and **a**.
5:13 spoke to you while I was **a**.
8:18 I will take action because I'm **a**,
16:26 your prostitution to make me **a**.
16:42 and I will stop being **a**.
16:42 I will no longer be **a**.
16:43 and you made me very **a** with
20:28 offerings there to make me **a**.
35:11 When you were **a** and jealous,
Dan 2:12 This made the king so **a** and
8:7 The goat was extremely **a** with
11:30 **A** at the holy promise,
11:44 He will leave very **a** to destroy
Hos 13:11 gave you a king when I was **a**,
14:4 I will no longer be **a** with them.
Jnh 4:1 about this, and he became **a**.
4:4 right do you have to be **a**?"
4:9 "What right do you have to be **a**
4:9 "I have every right to be **a** — so
4:9 right to be angry — so **a** that
Mic 7:18 You will not be **a** forever,
Hab 3:8 The LORD is not **a** with the
3:8 If you are **a** with the rivers,
Zec 1:2 very **a** with your ancestors.
1:12 You've been **a** with them for 70
1:15 and I'm very **a** with the nations
1:15 I was only a little **a**,
7:12 of Armies became very **a**.
8:14 your ancestors made me **a**,
Mal 1:4 whom the LORD is always **a**.'
Mat 5:22 guarantee that whoever is **a**
18:34 "His master was so **a** that he
22:7 "The king became **a**.
Mar 3:5 Jesus was **a** as he looked
Luk 14:21 master of the house became **a**.
15:28 "Then the older son became **a**
Jon 7:23 why are you **a** with me
Act 12:20 Herod was very **a** with the
Rom 10:19 I will make you **a** about a
Gal 5:20 **a** outbursts, selfish ambition,
Eph 4:26 Be **a** without sinning.
4:26 Don't go to bed **a**.
Heb 3:10 That is why I was **a** with those
3:17 With whom was God **a** for 40
3:17 He was **a** with those who
Jas 1:19 and should not get **a** easily.
1:20 An **a** person doesn't do what
Rev 11:18 "The nations were **a**,
12:17 The serpent became **a** with the

anguish (21)

Exo 15:14 people of Philistia will be in **a**.
Job 15:24 Distress and **a** terrify him like a
Pro 1:27 trouble and **a** come to you.
Isa 8:22 They will go in **a** and be forced
13:8 Pain and **a** will seize them.
Jer 4:19 My **a**, my anguish! I writhe in
4:19 My anguish, my **a**!
4:31 I hear the woman cry with **a** as
6:24 We are gripped by **a** and pain
15:8 I will suddenly bring **a** and
49:24 **A** and pain grip them like a
50:43 **A** will grip him as pain grips a
Eze 7:25 **A** is coming. People will look
30:4 war in Egypt and **a** in Ethiopia.
30:9 will be in **a** when Egypt is
Dan 6:20 the king called to Daniel with **a**
Mat 26:37 was beginning to feel deep **a**.
26:38 Then he said to them, "My **a** is
Mar 14:34 He said to them, "My **a** is so
Luk 22:44 So he prayed very hard in **a**.
Rev 16:10 gnawed on their tongues in **a**

anguished (2)

Mar 14:33 began to feel distressed and **a**.
2Co 2:4 I was deeply troubled and **a**.

Aniam (1)

1Ch 7:19 Ahian, Shechem, Likhi, and **A**.

Anim (1)

Jos 15:50 Anab, Eshtemoh, **A**,

animal (152)

Gen 1:24 every type of domestic **a**,
1:24 crawling **a**, and wild animal."
1:24 crawling animal, and wild **a**."
1:25 God made every type of wild **a**,
1:25 every type of domestic **a**,
1:30 plants as food to every land **a**,
1:30 and every **a** that crawls on the
1:30 every living, breathing **a**."
3:21 God made clothes from **a** skins
6:20 every type of domestic **a**,
7:2 of every kind of clean **a** (a male
7:2 every kind of unclean **a** (a male
7:3 each) to preserve **a** life all over
7:14 with them every type of wild **a**,
7:14 every type of domestic **a**,
7:15 breathing **a** came to Noah to go
7:16 A male and a female of every **a**
8:17 Bring out every **a** that's with
8:19 Every **a**, crawling creature,
8:20 type of clean **a** and clean bird.
9:5 I will demand it from any **a** or
9:15 to you and every living **a**.
9:16 to every living **a** on earth."
15:17 passed between the **a** pieces.
37:20 and say that a wild **a** has eaten
37:33 A wild **a** has eaten him!
43:16 Butcher an **a**, and prepare a
Exo 10:26 Not one **a** must be left behind.
11:5 every firstborn domestic **a**.
11:7 be startled by any person or **a**.
12:3 family — one **a** per household.
12:4 be too small to eat a whole **a**.
12:4 one next door can share one **a**.
12:4 Choose your **a** based on the
12:5 Your **a** must be a one-year-old
12:9 roast the whole **a** over a fire.
12:12 both human and **a**.
12:21 and kill the Passover **a**.
12:29 and also every firstborn **a**.
13:2 whether human or **a**."
13:15 male in Egypt — human and **a**.
19:13 No matter whether it's an **a** or a
21:34 and then the dead **a** will be his.
22:4 But if the stolen **a** is found
22:10 or any other kind of **a** to keep
22:11 not take the other person's **a**.
22:12 But if the **a** was stolen from the
22:13 If it was killed by a wild **a**,
22:13 make up for an **a** that has been
22:14 borrows an **a** from his neighbor,
22:15 If the owner is with the **a**,
22:19 intercourse with an **a** must
22:31 Never eat the meat of an **a** that
23:5 Be sure to help him with his **a**.
Lev 1:2 you must offer an **a** from your
3:1 it must be a male or female **a**
3:6 a male or female **a** that has no
5:2 dead body of a wild or tame **a**
7:21 anything unclean, human or **a**,
7:24 The fat from an **a** that dies
7:25 Those who eat the fat from an **a**
7:26 of any bird or **a** no matter where
9:12 He slaughtered the **a** for the
11:20 a four-legged **a** is disgusting
11:23 a four-legged **a** is disgusting
11:39 "When any **a** that you are
11:42 the ground like a four-legged **a**,
17:4 Bring the **a** to the entrance of
17:13 or foreigners hunt any **a**
17:15 body of an **a** that dies naturally
17:15 by another **a** must wash their
18:23 sexual intercourse with any **a**
18:23 must never offer herself to an **a**
20:15 intercourse with an **a** must
20:15 You must kill the **a**,
20:16 offers herself sexually to any **a**,
20:16 kill both the woman and the **a**.
20:25 disgusting by eating any **a**
22:8 meat of an **a** that dies naturally
22:20 Never bring any **a** with a
22:21 it must be an **a** that has no

Lev 22:21 never be an **a** that has defects.
22:22 Never bring the LORD an **a** that
22:24 Never bring the LORD an **a** that
22:24 things to an **a** in your land.
22:25 of castrated **a** received from
22:25 A castrated **a** will not be
24:18 Whoever kills an **a** must
24:21 Whoever kills an **a** must
27:9 the kind of **a** that people offer
27:10 do exchange one **a** for another,
27:11 If it is an unclean **a** that cannot
27:26 "A firstborn **a** already belongs
27:27 But if it is an unclean **a**,
27:28 destruction — a person, an **a**,
27:33 both the first **a** and its
Num 3:13 whether human or **a**.
8:17 whether human or **a**,
9:11 You must eat the Passover **a**
15:12 Do it for each **a**, however many
18:15 firstborn male, human or **a**,
18:15 firstborn male of any unclean **a**.
31:30 and every other kind of **a**.
Dtr 4:17 any **a** on earth, any creature
12:21 you may slaughter an **a** from
15:21 But if an **a** is lame or blind or
16:2 Slaughter an **a** from your flock
22:2 take the **a** home with you.
27:21 intercourse with any **a** will
2Ki 14:9 but a wild **a** from Lebanon
2Ch 25:18 but a wild **a** from Lebanon
Neh 2:12 The only **a** I had was the one I
2:14 but the **a** I was riding couldn't
Job 24:6 They harvest **a** food in the field
39:15 or a wild **a** may trample them.
Psa 73:22 like a dumb **a** in your presence.
104:11 Every wild **a** drinks ⌊from⌋
Pro 12:1 hates correction is a dumb **a**.
30:2 I'm more ⌊like⌋ a dumb **a** than
Ecc 3:21 an **a** spirit goes downward
Isa 1:11 "What do your many **a**
Jer 51:62 no person or **a** will live here,
Eze 4:14 I have never eaten an **a** that
8:10 every kind of disgusting **a**,
21:21 and examine **a** livers.
29:11 No human or **a** will walk
34:5 became food for every wild **a**.
34:8 become food for every wild **a**.
39:4 of prey and for every wild **a**.
39:17 kind of bird and every wild **a**,
44:31 eat any bird or **a** that has died
Dan 4:16 and give it the mind of an **a**.
7:4 The first **a** was like a lion,
7:5 I saw a second **a**. It looked like
7:6 After this, I saw another **a**.
7:6 The **a** also had four heads.
7:7 After this, I saw a fourth **a** in
7:11 watched until the **a** was killed.
7:19 the truth about the fourth **a**,
7:23 He said, "The fourth **a** will be
8:4 No other **a** could stand in front
Hos 13:8 Like a wild **a** I will tear you
Jnh 3:8 Every person and **a** must put
Zec 1:18 I looked up and saw four **a**
8:10 money to hire any person or **a**.
9:9 on a colt, a young pack **a**.
Mal 1:8 you bring a blind **a** to sacrifice,
1:8 you bring a lame or a sick **a**,
Mat 21:5 on a colt, a young pack **a**."
Luk 10:34 Then he put him on his own **a**,
Act 23:24 Provide an **a** for Paul to ride,
Heb 12:20 "If even an **a** touches the

animal's (9)

Exo 21:34 pay money to the **a** owner,
Lev 1:4 Place your hand on the **a** head.
3:2 Place your hand on the **a** head.
3:8 Place your hand on the **a** head.
4:29 place his hand on the **a** head
4:33 place his hand on the **a** head
17:13 they must pour out the **a** blood
Num 9:12 or break any of the **a** bones.
Dan 5:21 was changed into an **a** mind.

animals (273)

Gen 1:26 the domestic **a** all over the
1:26 and all the **a** that crawl on the
1:28 and all the **a** that crawl on the
2:19 God had formed all the wild **a**
2:20 man named all the domestic **a**,
2:20 all the birds, and all the wild **a**.
3:1 more clever than all the wild **a**
3:14 than all the wild or domestic **a**.
3:14 You will be the lowest of **a** as
4:4 of the firstborn **a** from his flock.
6:7 but also domestic **a**,
6:7 animals, crawling **a**, and birds.
6:21 will be food for you and the **a**."
7:8 Clean and unclean **a**,
7:21 domestic and wild **a**,
7:23 Humans, domestic **a**,
8:1 and all the wild and domestic **a**
8:17 with you: birds, domestic **a**,
9:2 All the wild **a** and all the birds
9:10 is with you — birds, domestic **a**,
9:10 animals, and all the wild **a**,
15:10 brought all these **a** to him.
25:28 liked to eat the meat of wild **a**,
31:39 flock that was killed by wild **a**.
32:17 and whose **a** are these ahead
33:8 group ⌊of people and **a**⌋ I met?"
34:23 and all their **a** be ours?
45:17 your brothers, 'Load up your **a**,
Exo 8:17 into gnats that bit people and **a**.
8:18 The gnats bit people and **a**.
9:4 No **a** belonging to the Israelites
9:6 but none of the Israelites' **a**
9:7 one of the Israelites' **a** had died.
9:9 and **a** throughout Egypt."
9:10 open sores on people and **a**.
9:19 All people and **a** still outside
9:21 left their servants and **a** out
9:22 and hail will fall on people, **a**,
9:25 It struck down people, **a**,
10:25 must allow us to take ⌊our **a**⌋
12:6 of Israel must slaughter their **a**.
12:7 where they will eat the **a**.
13:12 of each of your **a** belongs
22:31 has been killed by wild **a** out
23:11 and wild **a** may eat what the
23:29 and wild **a** would take over.
Lev 4:24 where he slaughters **a**
4:29 head and slaughter it where **a**
4:33 slaughters **a** for burnt offerings.
7:24 or is killed by wild **a** you may
11:2 kinds of land **a** you may eat:
11:3 all **a** that have completely
11:8 Never eat the meat of these **a**
11:26 All **a** whose hoofs are not
11:27 All four-legged **a** that walk on
11:28 any of these **a** must wash their
11:28 These **a** are unclean for you.
11:46 are the instructions about **a**,
11:47 the **a** you may eat and those
16:27 These **a** were the offering for
16:27 from the **a** must be burned.
19:19 crossbreed different kinds of **a**.
20:25 clean and unclean **a** and birds.
22:8 naturally or is killed by wild **a**.
25:7 your **a** and the wild animals in
25:7 your animals and the wild **a** in
26:6 I will remove dangerous **a**,
26:22 I will send wild **a** among you.
27:10 Don't exchange or substitute **a**,
27:10 then both **a** will be holy.
Num 3:41 Also take the **a** of the Levites
3:41 all firstborn **a** of the Israelites."
3:45 the firstborn Israelites and the **a**
3:45 to be substitutes for their **a**.
6:14 All of these **a** must have no
7:87 The total number of **a** for the
7:88 The total number of **a** for
18:17 Throw the blood from these **a**
20:4 to have us and our **a** die here?
20:8 for them and their **a** to drink."
20:11 and all the people and their **a**
28:31 Offer these **a** that have no
31:9 They also took all their **a**,
31:11 including all the people and **a**,
31:26 the people and **a** you captured.
31:47 including people and **a**,
32:26 and all our other **a** will stay
35:3 and any other **a** they have.
Dtr 5:14 your donkeys — all of your **a** —
7:14 and your **a** will be able to have
7:22 would be overrun with wild **a**.
11:15 grass in the fields for your **a**,
13:15 everyone in it, including the **a**,
14:4 Here are the ⌊kinds of⌋ **a** you
14:6 You may eat all **a** that have
14:7 But some **a** chew their cud,
14:7 may not eat these ⌊kinds of⌋ **a**.
15:20 your family must eat these **a**
16:5 not allowed to slaughter the **a**
16:6 Instead, slaughter your **a** for
28:4 Your **a** will have offspring.
28:11 Your **a** will have many
28:26 food for all the birds and wild **a**.
28:51 eat the offspring of your **a**
30:9 Your **a** will have many
32:10 in a barren place where **a** howl.
32:24 I will send vicious **a** against
32:24 with poisonous **a** that crawl
1Sm 13:9 Saul said, "Bring me the **a**
15:9 the fattened **a**, the lambs,
17:46 to the birds and the wild **a**.
30:20 His men drove the **a** ahead of
2Sm 21:10 or any wild **a** come near them
1Ki 4:33 He described and classified **a**,
18:5 alive and not lose any **a**."
2Ki 3:9 of water for the army and the **a**.
3:17 and your other **a** will drink.
2Ch 29:21 to sacrifice the **a** on the
29:33 The **a** dedicated as holy
35:7 (These **a** were the king's
35:8 officials also voluntarily gave **a**
35:14 Later, they prepared ⌊the **a**⌋ for
35:14 So the Levites prepared ⌊the **a**⌋
35:15 prepared ⌊**a**⌋ for them.
Ezr 8:35 All of these **a** were burnt
Job 5:22 be afraid of wild **a** on the earth.
5:23 and wild **a** will be at peace
12:7 "Instead, ask the **a**,
35:11 us more than he teaches the **a**
37:8 **A** go into their dens and stay in
40:20 and all the wild **a** play there.
Psa 8:7 sheep and cattle, the wild **a**,
36:6 You save people and **a**,
49:12 They are like **a** that die.
49:20 They are like **a** that die.
74:19 the soul of your dove to wild **a**.
79:2 of your godly ones to the **a**.
80:13 graze on it. Wild **a** devour it.
104:20 when all the wild **a** in the forest
135:8 He killed humans and **a** alike.
147:9 is the one who gives food to **a**
148:10 wild **a** and all domestic
148:10 animals and all domestic **a**,
148:10 crawling **a** and birds,
Pro 12:10 ⌊even⌋ about the life of his **a**,
30:30 a lion, mightiest among **a**,
Ecc 3:18 them that they are ⌊like⌋ **a**."
3:19 Humans and **a** have the same
3:19 have no advantage over **a**.
Isa 13:21 Desert **a** will lie down there.
18:6 the mountains and the wild **a**.
18:6 and all the wild **a** on earth will
23:13 gave this land to the desert **a**.
30:6 divine revelation about the **a**
34:16 Not one of these **a** will be
35:9 Wild **a** won't go on it.
40:16 Its wild **a** are not enough for a
43:20 Wild **a**, jackals, and ostriches
46:1 are seated on **a** and cattle.
56:9 All you **a** in the field,
56:9 all you **a** in the forest,
63:14 Like **a** going down into a
Jer 7:20 this place, on humans and **a**,
7:33 become food for birds and **a**,
12:4 The **a** and the birds are dying,
12:9 Go, gather all the **a** in the field,
15:3 and birds and **a** to devour and
16:4 will be food for birds and **a**.
19:7 as food to birds and to **a**.
21:6 both people and **a**.
27:5 with the people and the **a** on it.
27:6 even made wild **a** serve him.
28:14 even make wild **a** serve him."
31:27 and Judah with people and **a**.

Jer 32:43 without people or a living in it.
33:10 and that no people or a live
33:10 No people or a live there.
33:12 where no people or a live,
34:20 be food for birds and wild a.
36:29 and take away people and a?"
50:3 People and a will run away.
50:39 That is why desert a will live
Eze 4:14 or was killed by other wild a.
5:17 and wild a against you,
14:13 and destroy its people and a.
14:15 "Suppose I send wild a through
14:15 through it because of the a.
14:17 the people and the a in it.
14:19 killing people and destroying a.
14:21 famines, wild a, and plagues.
14:21 They will destroy people and a.
19:3 to tear apart the a he hunted.
19:6 to tear apart the a he hunted.
25:13 I will wipe out people and a.
29:5 feed you to wild a and birds.
29:8 I will kill people and a.
31:6 All the wild a gave birth to their
31:13 and all the wild a lived in its
32:4 and wild a from all over the
32:13 I will also destroy all the a
32:13 and the hoofs of a won't stir up
33:27 will become food for wild a.
34:25 I will remove the wild a from
34:28 and the wild a will no longer
36:11 of people and a that live
38:20 Fish, birds, wild a,
39:18 and all the best a of Bashan.
40:38 where the priests washed the a
40:39 On these tables the a were
40:41 on which they slaughtered a.
40:42 that were used to slaughter a
40:43 were for the meat of the a.
43:25 They must be a that have no
44:11 temple by slaughtering the a
44:31 or was killed by other wild a.
46:6 and one ram — all a that have
47:9 there will be many fish and a.
Dan 2:38 over people, wild a, and birds,
4:12 Wild a found shade under it.
4:14 Make the a under it run away,
4:15 plants on the ground with the a.
4:21 Wild a lived under it,
4:23 on the ground with the wild a
4:25 people and live with the wild a.
4:32 people and live with the wild a.
7:3 Four large a, each one different
7:7 from all the other a that
7:12 The power of the rest of the a
7:17 He said, "These four large a
Hos 2:12 and wild a will devour them.
2:18 an arrangement with the wild a,
2:18 and the a that crawl on the
4:3 Wild a, birds, and fish are
Joe 1:18 The a groan. Herds of cattle
1:20 Even wild a long for you.
2:22 Wild a, do not be afraid.
Amo 5:22 offerings of your choicest a.
Jnh 3:7 This includes all people, a,
4:11 people in it as well as many a.
Mic 5:8 will be like a lion among a
7:17 like a that crawl on the ground.
Hab 2:17 done to the a will terrify you
Zep 1:3 put an end to humans and a.
2:14 will lie down in it along with a
2:15 a resting place for wild a!
Hag 1:11 produces, on humans and a,
Zec 2:4 so many people and a in it.
11:16 he will eat the meat of the fat a
14:15 and all other a in those camps.
Mal 1:13 bring stolen, lame, and sick a.
1:14 They have male a in their
Mar 1:13 He was there with the wild a,
Luk 13:1 while they were sacrificing a.
Jon 4:12 He and his sons and his a
Act 10:12 were all kinds of four-footed a,
10:13 Kill these a, and eat them."
11:6 very closely and saw tame a,
11:6 wild a, reptiles, and birds.
11:7 Kill these a, and eat them.'
15:20 eating the meat of strangled a,
15:29 eating the meat of strangled a,
21:25 or the meat of strangled a.
Rom 1:23 humans, birds, a, and snakes.
1Co 15:32 fought with wild a in Ephesus,
15:39 kind of flesh, a have another,
Tit 1:12 savage a, and lazy gluttons."
Heb 13:11 priest brings the blood of a into
13:11 But the bodies of those a were
Jas 3:7 have tamed all kinds of a,
2Pe 2:12 They are like a, which are
2:12 So they will be destroyed like a
Jud 1:10 Like a, which are creatures of
Rev 6:8 and the wild a on the earth.

ankle (2)

Isa 3:16 jingling the a bracelets on their
3:20 hats, a bracelets, blouses,

ankles (2)

Eze 47:3 The water came up to my a.
Act 3:7 feet and a became strong.

anklets (1)

Isa 3:18 things: jingling a, headbands,

Anna (2)

Luk 2:36 A, a prophet, was also there.
2:37 A never left the temple

Annas (4)

Luk 3:2 It was at the time when A and
Jon 18:13 and took him first to A,
18:24 A sent Jesus to Caiaphas,
Act 4:6 The chief priest A,

annex (5)

1Ki 6:5 He built an a containing side
6:5 This a was next to the walls of
6:6 lowest story of the a was 7 ½
6:6 temple so that this a would not
6:10 He built ⌊each story of the⌋ a 7

annihilated (1)

2Ch 20:23 from Mount Seir and a them.

announce (52)

Exo 11:2 Now a to the people ⌊of Israel⌋
Lev 23:2 must a as holy assemblies.
23:4 which you must a at their
23:37 A them as holy assemblies for
Dtr 27:13 on Mount Ebal to a the curses:
Jdg 7:3 A to the troops, 'Whoever is
2Sm 1:20 Don't a the victory in the
20:1 He blew a ram's horn ⌊to a⌋,
1Ki 21:9 letters she wrote: "A a fast.
2Ki 23:17 from Judah to a that you would
1Ch 16:23 Day after day a that the LORD
Neh 6:7 You've appointed prophets to a
8:15 They should a this command
Psa 2:7 I will a the LORD's decree.
9:11 A to the nations what he has
40:9 I will a the good news of
50:6 The heavens a his
68:11 The women who a the good
92:2 It is good to a your mercy in the
96:2 Day after day a that the LORD
106:2 Who can a all the things for
145:7 They will a what they
Pro 10:32 The lips of a righteous person a
Isa 40:2 tenderly to Jerusalem and a
42:12 to the LORD and a his praise
48:20 Shout for joy as you tell it and a
61:1 to a that captives will be set
61:2 ⌊He has sent me⌋ to a the year
62:2 name that the LORD will a.
63:1 I am coming to a my victory.
Jer 2:2 "Go and a to Jerusalem,
7:2 and a from there this message:
11:6 The LORD said to me, "A all
19:2 A there the things I plan to do.
46:14 this in Egypt; a this in Migdol.
50:2 "A this among the nations,
50:2 Raise a flag, and a it.
51:10 Let's a in Zion what the LORD
Joe 3:9 A this among the nations:
Amo 3:9 A in the palaces of Ashdod and
Jnh 1:2 A to the people that I can no
3:2 A to the people the message I
Zec 1:14 speaking with me said, "A:
1:17 "A again: This is what the
9:10 He will a peace to the nations.
Mat 6:2 don't a it with trumpet fanfare.
12:18 and he will a justice to the
Luk 4:18 He has sent me to a
4:19 to a the year of the Lord's
10:10 leave. A in its streets,
Act 21:26 into the temple courtyard to a
Rom 10:15 who a the Good News."

announced (27)

Exo 32:5 built an altar in front of it and a,
36:6 message a all over camp:
Lev 23:24 a holy assembly a by the
1Sm 13:3 Saul a, "Listen, Hebrews!"
1Ki 13:32 The things that he a by a
21:12 They a a fast and had Naboth
2Ki 7:11 The gatekeepers a the news to
9:18 So the watchman a,
9:20 So the watchman a,
23:16 the word of the LORD a by
2Ch 20:3 He a a fast throughout Judah.
Ezr 8:21 Then I a a fast there at the
Job 28:27 then he saw it and a it.
Psa 76:8 From heaven you a a verdict.
102:21 The LORD's name is a in Zion
Isa 41:26 No one a it. No one heard
43:12 and I have a it to you.
62:11 The LORD has a to the ends of
Jer 23:22 they would have a my words to
Lam 1:21 the one that you had a.
2:17 out the threat he a long ago.
Dan 4:17 guardians have a this decision.
4:17 The holy ones have a this so
Zec 7:7 words that the LORD a through
Mar 1:7 He a, "The one who comes
Gal 3:8 So Scripture a the Good News
1Ti 3:16 was a throughout the nations,

announcement (6)

Lev 23:21 Make an a that there will be a
2Ch 30:5 So they decided to send an a
36:22 this a throughout his whole
Ezr 1:1 this a throughout his whole
Est 2:8 When the king's a and decree
Jnh 3:7 Then he made this a and sent

announces (6)

Job 36:33 The thunder a his coming.
36:33 The storm a his angry wrath.
Pro 16:14 A king's anger a death,
Isa 52:7 feet of the messenger who a
52:7 the good news, a salvation,
Nah 1:15 the feet of a messenger who a

annoyance (1)

Pro 27:3 but a caused by a stubborn fool

annoyed (2)

Act 4:2 authorities were greatly a.
16:18 Paul became a, turned to the

annoys (1)

Luk 18:4 This widow really a me.

annual (15)

1Sm 1:21 went to offer the a sacrifice
2:19 husband to offer the a sacrifice.
20:6 offering the a sacrifice there.'
2Ki 17:3 to make a payments to him.
17:4 stopped making a payments
1Ch 23:31 and on appointed a festivals.
2Ch 2:4 and during the a festivals
8:13 and on the three a festivals (the
31:3 and the a festivals,
Neh 10:33 at the appointed a festivals,
Isa 29:1 Let your a festivals go on.
Lam 1:4 one comes to the a festivals.
Eze 45:17 offerings at the a festivals,
Hos 2:11 celebrations: her a festivals,
Col 2:16 the observance of a holy days,

anoint (25)

Exo 28:41 his sons, a them, ordain them,
29:7 pour it on his head, and a him.
29:36 Then a it ⌊with olive oil⌋ in
30:26 "Use it to a the tent of meeting,
30:30 A Aaron and his sons as well.
40:9 Take the anointing oil, and a
40:10 A the altar for burnt offerings
40:11 A the basin and stand,
40:13 in the holy clothes, and a him.
40:15 A them to serve me as priests,
Lev 8:10 took the anointing oil to a
Jdg 9:8 "The trees went to a someone
9:15 'If you really want to a me to be
1Sm 9:16 A him to be ruler of my people
15:1 "The LORD sent me to a you
16:3 and you will a for me the one I
16:12 LORD said, "Go ahead, a him.
1Ki 1:34 the prophet Nathan a him king
19:15 a Hazael as king of Aram.
19:16 A Jehu, son of Nimshi, as king
19:16 And a Elisha, son of Shaphat,
Psa 23:5 You a my head with oil.
Dan 9:24 and to a the Most Holy One.
Mar 16:1 spices to go and a Jesus.
Jas 5:14 Have them pray for you and a

anointed (85)

Exo 29:29 so that they can be a
40:15 as you a their father.
Lev 4:3 "If the a priest does something
4:5 Then the a priest will take
4:16 Then the a priest will bring
6:20 on the day he is a — eight cups
6:22 Aaron's son who is a to take
7:36 it to them on the day he a them.
8:11 seven times and a the altar,
8:12 oil on Aaron's head and a him
10:7 because the LORD has a you
16:32 The priest who is a and
21:10 "The priest who is a with oil
21:13 "The a priest must marry a
Num 3:3 of Aaron's sons, the a priests,
7:1 he a it and dedicated it and all
7:1 He also a and dedicated the
7:10 of the altar when it was a.
7:84 of the altar when it was a:
7:88 of the altar after it was a.
35:25 of the high priest who was a
1Sm 2:35 will always live as my a one.
10:1 "The LORD has a you to be
10:1 sign that the LORD has a you
12:3 LORD and in front of his a king.
12:5 and his a king is a witness
15:17 The LORD a you king of Israel.
16:6 presence is his a king."
16:13 flask of olive oil and a David
24:6 the LORD's a king,
24:6 since he is the LORD's a."
24:10 because you are the LORD's a.'
26:9 attacked the LORD's a king
26:11 me to attack the LORD's a king.
26:16 the LORD's a king.
26:23 to attack the LORD's a king.
2Sm 1:14 to destroy the LORD's a king?"
1:16 'I killed the LORD's a king.'"
2:4 came to Hebron and a David
2:7 the tribe of Judah has a me to
3:39 though I'm the a king.
5:3 So they a David king of Israel.
5:17 that David had been a king
12:7 I a you king over Israel and
12:20 the ground, bathed, a himself,
19:10 whom we a to rule us,
19:21 for cursing the LORD's a king?"
22:51 He shows mercy to his a,
23:1 whom the God of Jacob a,
1Ki 1:39 oil from the tent and a Solomon.
1:45 Nathan have a him king at
5:1 that Solomon had been a king
2Ki 9:3 I have a you king of Israel.'
9:6 I have a you king of the
9:12 I have a you king of Israel.'"
23:30 Josiah's son Jehoahaz, a him,
1Ch 11:3 So they a David king of Israel,
14:8 that David had been a king
16:22 'Do not touch my a ones or
29:22 On the LORD's behalf they a
2Ch 6:42 do not reject your a one.
22:7 (The LORD had a Jehu to
Psa 18:50 He shows mercy to his a,
20:6 will give victory to his a king.
45:7 why God, your God, has a you,
84:9 favor on the face of your a one.
89:20 I a him with my holy oil.
89:38 and become angry with your a
105:15 "Do not touch my a ones or
132:10 do not reject your a one.
132:17 I will prepare a lamp for my a
132:18 crown on my a one will shine."
Isa 45:1 says about Cyrus, his a one:
61:1 because the LORD has a me
Lam 4:20 person the LORD a ⌊as king⌋,
Dan 9:25 until the a prince comes,
9:26 the A One will be cut off and
Hab 3:13 your people, to save your a.
Zec 4:14 "These are the two a ones who
Luk 4:18 He has a me to tell the Good
Act 4:27 servant Jesus, whom you a.
10:38 You know that God a Jesus
2Co 1:21 with Christ. He has also a us.
Heb 1:9 is why God, your God, a you,
1Jn 2:20 The Holy One has a you,

anointing (25)

Exo 25:6 spices for the a oil and for the
29:7 Take the a oil, pour it on his
29:21 the altar and some of the a oil,
30:25 mixture, used only for a.
30:25 will be the holy oil used for a.
30:31 be my holy oil used only for a.
31:11 the a oil, and the They will
35:8 spices for the a oil and for the
35:15 with its poles, the a oil,
35:28 olive oil for the lamps, the a oil,
37:29 the holy oil to be used for a
39:38 the gold altar, the a oil,
40:9 Take the a oil, and anoint the
40:15 Their a will begin a permanent
Lev 8:2 the priests' clothes, the a oil,
8:10 Moses took the a oil to anoint
8:12 He also poured some of the a
8:30 Moses took some of the a oil
21:12 he is dedicated with the a oil
Num 4:16 grain offering, and the a oil.
2Ki 11:12 and made him king by a him.
2Ch 23:11 sons made him king by a him.
1Jn 2:27 The a you received from Christ
2:27 Instead, Christ's a teaches you
2:27 His a is true and contains no

answer (189)

Gen 24:52 servant heard their a,
34:13 his father Hamor a misleading a
41:16 but God can give Pharaoh the a
45:3 His brothers could not a him
46:34 you must a, 'We have taken
Exo 12:27 you must a, 'It's the Passover
19:8 So Moses brought their a back
Dtr 18:19 in my name will a to me.
29:25 The a will be, "Because they
Jos 4:7 You should a, 'The water of the
22:28 in the future, we will a,
Jdg 5:29 wisest servants gave her an a.
14:16 riddle and didn't tell me the a."
14:17 seventh day he told her the a
14:17 her friends the a to the riddle.
19:28 But she did not a. So he put her
1Sm 4:20 she didn't a or pay attention.
8:18 The LORD will not a you when
14:37 But he received no a that day.
14:41 why didn't you a me today?
17:30 soldiers gave him the same a.
20:10 father gives you a harsh a?"
26:14 "Won't you a, Abner?"
27:10 And David would a,
28:6 but the LORD didn't a him
28:15 me and doesn't a me anymore
2Sm 14:18 "Please don't refuse to a the
16:23 was like getting an a from God.
22:42 but he did not a them.
24:13 it over, and decide what a
1Ki 9:9 They will a ⌊themselves⌋,
10:3 too difficult for the king to a.
18:26 They said, "Baal, a us!"
18:26 there wasn't a sound or an a.
18:29 But there was no sound, no a,
18:37 A me, LORD! Answer me!
18:37 A me! Then these people will
20:9 left to take back his a.
2Ki 4:29 don't stop to a him.
9:12 They said, "That's not an a.
18:36 commanded them not to a him.
1Ch 21:12 Decide what a I should give
2Ch 7:22 They will a ⌊themselves⌋,
9:2 too difficult for Solomon to a.
Est 4:13 Mordecai sent this a back to
5:8 And tomorrow I will a you,
Job 5:1 Is there anyone to a you?
9:3 he wouldn't be able to a one
9:14 "How can I possibly a God?
9:15 I could not a ⌊him⌋.
9:32 A human like me cannot a God,
11:2 "Shouldn't someone a this
12:4 calls on God and expects an a.
13:22 Then call, and I'll a.
13:22 I'll speak, and you'll a me.
14:15 You will call, and I will a you.
15:2 "Should a wise person a with
19:16 call my slave, but he doesn't a,
20:2 disturbing thoughts make me a,
23:5 words he would use to a me.
30:20 but you don't a me.
31:14 how could I a him?
31:35 Let the Almighty a me.
32:3 because they had found no a.
32:12 None of you has an a to what
32:14 so I won't a him with your
32:17 "I'll give my a. I'll tell you what
32:20 I must open my mouth and a.
33:5 A me if you can. Present your
33:12 I've got an a for you:
33:13 he doesn't a any questions?
33:32 If you have a response, a me.
35:4 I will a you and your friends.
35:12 but he doesn't a them because
40:2 who argues with God a him?"
40:4 How can I a you? I will put my
40:5 but I can't a — twice,
Psa 4:1 A me when I call, O God of my
13:3 A me, O LORD my God!
17:6 on you because you a me,
18:41 but he did not a them.
20:1 The LORD will a you in times
20:6 He will a him from his holy
20:9 A us when we call.
22:2 but you do not a — also at night,
27:4 to search for an a in his temple.
27:7 Have pity on me, and a me.
38:15 You will a, O Lord, my God.
55:2 Pay attention to me, and a me.
60:5 and a us so that those who are
65:5 You a us with awe-inspiring
69:13 a me with the truth of your
69:16 A me, O LORD, because your
69:17 face from me. A me quickly!
77:6 My spirit searches ⌊for an a⌋:
86:1 A me, because I am oppressed
86:7 I call out to you because you a
91:15 you call to me, I will a you.
102:2 A me quickly when I call.
108:6 and a us so that those who are
119:42 Then I will have an a for the
119:145 A me, O LORD. I want to obey
143:1 A me because you are faithful
143:7 A me quickly, O LORD.
Pro 1:28 me at that time, but I will not a.
15:1 A gentle a turns away rage,
15:23 to hear an a from his own
15:28 carefully considers how to a,
16:1 but an a on the tongue comes
18:13 Whoever gives an a before he
24:26 Giving a straight a is ⌊like⌋ a
26:4 Do not a a fool with his own
26:5 A a fool with his own stupidity,
26:16 people who give a sensible a.
27:11 I can a anyone who criticizes

Pro 29:20 a person who is quick to a?
Ecc 10:19 money is the a for everything.
Sos 5:6 but he did not a me.
Isa 14:32 How should we a the
30:19 as he hears you, he will a you.
36:21 commanded them not to a him.
41:17 I, the LORD, will a them.
41:28 will they give an a?
46:7 they cry to it for help, it can't a.
49:8 In the time of favor I will a you.
50:2 Why was no one here to a
54:17 You will have an a for anyone
58:9 and the LORD will a.
65:1 I was ready to a those who
65:12 I called, but you didn't a.
65:24 Before they call, I will a.
Jer 5:19 A them, "You have abandoned
7:13 I called you, you did not a.
18:12 "But they will a, 'It's useless!
22:9 The a will be: 'They rejected
23:35 'What is the LORD's a?' and
23:37 was the LORD's a to you?'
33:3 Call to me, and I will a you.
35:17 to them, but they didn't a."
38:15 "If I a you, you'll kill me.
48:20 They will a, 'Moab is
Eze 14:4 will give that Israelite an a,
14:4 the a that his many idols
14:7 will give him an a.
Dan 2:23 You told me the a to our
3:16 need to a your last question.
Hos 2:21 day I will a your ⌊prayers⌋,"
14:8 I will a them and take care of
Amo 6:10 that person will a, "No."
Mic 3:4 but he will not a you.
3:7 because God won't a them.
6:3 I tried your patience? A me!
Hab 2:1 he will say to me and what a
2:11 A beam in the roof will a it.
Zec 10:6 their God, and I will a them.
13:6 he will a, 'I was hurt at my
13:9 call on me, and I will a them.
Mat 5:21 Whoever murders will a for it in
5:22 with another believer will a
5:22 an insulting name will a
5:22 another believer a fool will a
15:23 But he did not a her at all.
21:24 If you a it for me, I'll tell you
22:46 No one could a him,
25:40 "The king will a them,
25:45 "He will a them, 'I can
26:62 "Don't you have any a to what
Mar 11:29 "I'll ask you a question. A me,
11:30 or from humans? A me!"
14:60 "Don't you have any a to what
15:4 "Don't you have any a?
Luk 11:7 Your friend might a you from
13:25 But he will a you, 'I don't know
20:26 His a surprised them,
22:68 And if I ask you, you won't a.
23:9 but Jesus wouldn't a him.
Jon 1:19 This was John's a when the
1:20 John didn't refuse to a.
1:22 so that we can take an a back
9:21 old enough to a for himself."
18:22 how you a the chief priest?"
19:9 But Jesus didn't a him.
19:10 "Aren't you going to a me?
Act 12:13 named Rhoda came to a.
18:14 Paul was about to a when
2Co 5:12 Then you can a those who are
Col 4:6 you know how to a everyone.
Heb 4:13 We must a to him.
Rev 16:7 Then I heard the altar a,

answered (547)

Gen 3:2 The woman a the snake,
3:10 He a, "I heard you in the
3:12 The man a, "That woman,
3:13 me, and I ate," the woman a.
4:9 "I don't know," he a.
15:9 He a Abram, "Bring me a
16:6 Abram a Sarai, "Here,
16:8 She a, "I'm running away from
18:5 They a, "That's fine. Do as you
18:9 He a, "Over there, in the tent."
Gen 18:28 The LORD a, "I will not destroy
18:29 He a, "For the sake of the 40 I
18:30 He a, "If I find 30 there, I will
18:31 He a, "I will not destroy it for
18:32 He a, "I will not destroy it for
19:2 "No," they a, "we'd rather
19:18 Lot a, "Oh no!
21:30 Abraham a, "Accept these
22:1 here I am!" he a.
22:7 Abraham a. Isaac asked, "We
22:8 Abraham a, "God will provide a
22:11 "Yes?" he a.
23:5 The Hittites a Abraham,
23:10 He a Abraham so that everyone
23:14 Ephron a Abraham,
24:24 She a him, "I'm the daughter of
24:40 "He a me, 'I have been living
24:47 "She a, 'The daughter of
24:50 Laban and Bethuel a,
24:65 is my master," the servant a.
25:21 The LORD a his prayer,
26:7 Isaac a, "She's my sister."
26:9 Isaac a him, "I thought I would
26:28 They a, "We have seen that
27:1 Esau a, "Here I am."
27:18 he a. "Who are you, Son?"
27:19 Jacob a his father,
27:20 God brought it to me," he a.
27:24 he asked him. "I am," Jacob a.
27:32 your firstborn son Esau," he a.
27:37 Isaac a Esau, "I have made
27:39 His father Isaac a him,
29:5 grandson?" They a, "We do."
29:6 "He's fine," they a.
29:26 Laban a, "It's not our custom to
30:17 God a Leah's prayer.
30:22 God a her prayer and made it
30:31 give me anything," Jacob a.
30:34 Laban a, "Agreed. We'll do as
31:11 And I a, 'Yes, here I am.'
31:14 Rachel and Leah a him,
31:31 Jacob a Laban, I thought you
31:43 Then Laban a Jacob,
32:26 But Jacob a, "I won't let you go
32:27 your name?" "Jacob," he a.
32:29 The man a, "Why do you ask
33:5 given me, sir," Jacob a.
33:8 He a, "To win your favor, sir."
35:3 who a me when I was troubled
38:17 goat from the flock," he a.
38:18 staff that's in your hand," she a.
38:21 no prostitute here," they a.
40:8 both had dreams," they a him,
41:16 Joseph a Pharaoh,
42:7 Canaan, to buy food," they a.
42:10 they a him. "We've come to buy
42:13 They a him, "We were 12
43:7 They a, "The man kept asking
43:7 We simply a his questions.
43:28 They a, "Yes, sir. Our father is
44:7 They a him, "Sir, how can you
44:20 We a, 'We have a father who is
44:26 We a, 'We can't go back.
46:2 Jacob!" "Here I am," he a.
47:3 They a Pharaoh, "We are
47:9 Jacob a Pharaoh, "The length
47:30 will do as you say," Joseph a.
48:9 Joseph a his father.
Exo 1:19 The midwives a Pharaoh,
2:8 She a, "Yes!" So the girl
2:19 They a, "An Egyptian rescued
3:4 Moses a, "Here I am!"
3:12 God a, "I will be with you.
3:14 God a Moses, "I Am Who I Am.
4:2 He a, "A shepherd's staff."
5:17 Pharaoh a. "That's why you
7:1 The LORD a Moses,
8:9 Moses a Pharaoh,
8:29 Moses a, "As soon as I leave
10:9 Moses a, "Everyone! We'll be
10:29 Moses a. "You'll never see my
14:13 Moses a the people,
17:5 The LORD a Moses,
18:15 Moses a his father-in-law,
19:8 All the people a together,
19:19 and the voice of God a him.
Exo 20:20 Moses a the people,
24:3 Then all the people a with one
32:22 "Don't be angry, sir," Aaron a.
32:33 The LORD a Moses,
33:14 The LORD a, "My presence
33:17 The LORD a Moses,
Lev 10:19 Aaron a Moses, "Today they
Num 9:8 Moses a them,
10:30 Hobab a, "No, I won't go. I want
11:16 The LORD a Moses,
20:18 But the Edomites a,
22:10 Balaam a, "Balak, son of King
22:18 But Balaam a Balak's servants,
22:29 Balaam a, "You've made a fool
22:30 this to you before?" "No," he a.
23:12 Balaam a, "I must say what the
23:26 Balaam a,
24:12 Balaam a Balak, "I told the
32:20 Moses a, "Do what you have
32:31 tribes of Gad and Reuben a,
Jos 5:14 He a, "Neither one! I am here
7:20 Then Achan a Joshua,
9:9 They a him, "We came from a
9:24 They a Joshua, "We were told
15:19 She a, "Give me a blessing.
22:21 half of the tribe of Manasseh a
24:19 But Joshua a the people,
24:21 The people a Joshua,
24:22 They a, "Yes, we have!"
Jdg 1:2 The LORD a, "Judah's troops
1:15 She a, "Give me a blessing.
8:18 They a, "They were like you.
8:25 The men of Israel a,
11:8 Gilead's leaders a Jephthah,
11:13 a Jephthah's messengers,
12:2 Jephthah a, "My people and I
12:5 from Ephraim?" If he a, "No,"
13:11 to my wife?" "Yes," he a.
13:13 of the LORD a Manoah,
15:10 to fight us?" The Philistines a,
18:24 Micah a, "You've taken away
20:4 of the murdered woman, a,
20:18 The LORD a, "Judah will go
20:23 The LORD a, "Go fight them!"
20:28 The LORD a, "Go! Tomorrow I
Rut 1:16 But Ruth a, "Don't force me to
1:20 She a them, "Don't call me
2:4 They a him, "May the LORD
2:6 The young man a,
2:11 Boaz a her, "People have told
3:5 Ruth a her, "I will do whatever
3:9 She a, "I am Ruth. Spread the
1Sm 4:17 Philistines," the messenger a.
6:3 The priests a, "If you're
6:4 The priests a, "Five gold
7:9 and the LORD a him.
9:8 The servant again a Saul,
9:12 The girls a, "He's there ahead
10:14 Saul a, "To look for the
10:16 been found," Saul a his uncle.
10:22 The LORD a, "He's hiding
12:4 They a, "You didn't cheat us,
12:5 "He is a witness," they a.
14:7 His armorbearer a him,
14:29 Jonathan a, "My father has
15:15 Saul a, "The army brought
16:11 the youngest one," Jesse a.
17:55 Abner a, "I solemnly swear,
17:58 Jesse of Bethlehem," David a.
19:17 Michal a, "He told me, 'Let me
20:2 Jonathan a, You're not going to
20:9 Jonathan a, If I knew for sure
20:28 Jonathan a Saul,
21:2 David a the priest Ahimelech,
21:4 the chief priest a David.
21:5 David a the priest,
21:9 The chief priest a,
22:9 with Saul's officials, a him,
23:4 and the LORD a him.
23:11 "He will come," the LORD a.
23:12 hand you over," the LORD a.
25:10 Nabal a David's servants.
26:6 Abishai a, "I'll go with you."
26:17 Your Royal Majesty," David a.
28:11 up Samuel for me," he a.
28:13 from the ground," the woman a.

1Sm 28:14 She **a**, "An old man is coming
28:15 Saul **a**, "I'm in serious trouble.
29:9 Achish **a** David, "I admit that in
30:13 Amalekite," the young man **a**.
30:15 He **a**, "Take an oath in front of
2Sm 1:3 from the camp of Israel," he **a**.
1:4 The man **a**, "The army fled
1:6 The young man **a**,
1:13 And the young man **a**,
2:1 "Go," the LORD **a** him.
2:20 you Asahel?" "Yes," Asahel **a**.
2:27 Joab **a**, "I solemnly swear,
3:13 David **a**. "I'll make
5:19 The LORD **a** David,
5:23 and he **a**, "Don't attack now,
6:21 David **a** Michal, "⌊I didn't
9:2 "⌊Yes,⌋ I am," he **a**.
9:3 a son who is disabled," Ziba **a**.
9:6 said to him. "Yes, sir," he **a**.
9:8 bowed down ⌊again⌋ and **a**,
11:11 Uriah **a** David, "The ark and
12:19 "⌊Yes,⌋ he is dead," they **a**.
12:22 David **a**, "As long as the child
13:4 Absalom's sister Tamar," he **a**.
13:25 "No, Son," the king **a** Absalom.
14:5 She **a**, "I'm a widow;
14:19 The woman **a**, "I solemnly
14:32 Absalom **a** Joab, "I sent
15:21 But Ittai **a** the king,
16:2 family to ride on," Ziba **a**.
16:3 in Jerusalem," Ziba **a** the king.
16:18 Hushai **a** Absalom,
18:29 Ahimaaz **a**, "I saw a lot of
18:32 The Sudanese messenger **a**,
19:26 He **a**, "My servant deceived
19:42 All the people of Judah **a** the
19:43 The people of Israel **a** the
20:17 "I am," he **a**. "Listen to what I
20:17 "I'm listening," he **a**.
20:20 Joab **a**, "That's unthinkable!
21:1 The LORD **a**, "It's because of
21:4 the Gibeonites **a** him.
21:5 They **a** the king, "Give us
21:14 God **a** the prayers for the land.
24:21 David **a**, "To buy the threshing
1Ki 1:17 "Sir," she **a**, "You took an oath
1:28 Then King David **a**,
1:36 son of Jehoiada, **a** the king.
1:43 Jonathan **a** Adonijah.
2:13 she asked. "Yes," he **a**.
2:18 "Very well," Bathsheba **a**.
2:30 "No," Joab **a**, "I'll die here."
2:30 had said and how he had **a**.
2:31 The king **a**, "Do as he said.
2:38 "Very well," Shimei **a**.
10:3 Solomon **a** all her questions.
12:10 who had grown up with him **a**,
12:13 The king **a** the people harshly.
12:16 the people **a** the king,
13:14 from Judah?" "Yes," he **a**.
18:8 "Yes," Elijah **a** him.
18:18 Elijah **a**, "I haven't troubled
18:24 All the people **a**, "That's fine."
19:10 He **a**, "LORD God of Armies,
19:14 He **a**, "LORD God of Armies,
19:20 "Go back," Elijah **a** him.
20:4 The king of Israel **a**,
20:11 The king of Israel **a**,
20:14 The prophet **a**, "This is what
20:14 "You will," the prophet **a**.
21:20 Elijah **a**, "I found you.
22:8 Jehoshaphat **a**, "The king must
22:14 Micaiah **a**, "I solemnly swear,
22:20 Some **a** one way, while others
22:22 "The Spirit **a**, 'I will go out and
22:25 Micaiah **a**, "You will find out on
2Ki 1:8 Elijah from Tishbe," the king **a**.
1:10 Elijah **a** the officer,
1:12 Elijah **a** the officer,
2:2 Elisha **a**, "I solemnly swear,
2:3 He **a**, "Yes, I know. Be quiet."
2:4 Elisha **a**, "I solemnly swear,
2:5 He **a**, "Yes, I know. Be quiet."
2:6 Elisha **a**, "I solemnly swear,
2:9 Elisha **a**, "Let me inherit a
2:16 Elisha **a**, "Don't send them ⌊to

2Ki 3:7 Jehoshaphat **a**, "I'll go. I will do
3:8 Jehoshaphat **a**, "The road
3:11 officials of the king of Israel **a**,
3:13 The king of Israel **a** him,
3:14 Elisha **a**, "I solemnly swear,
4:2 She **a**, "I have nothing in the
4:13 She **a**, "I'm already living
4:14 Gehazi **a**, "Well, she has no
4:16 She **a**, "Don't say that, sir.
4:26 "Everyone's fine," she **a**.
5:22 Gehazi **a**, "No. My master has
5:25 "I didn't go anywhere," he **a**.
6:3 with us?" Elisha **a**, "I'll go."
6:12 One of his officers **a**,
6:16 Elisha **a**, "Don't be afraid.
6:22 Elisha **a**, "Don't kill them.
6:27 He **a**, "If the LORD doesn't help
6:28 She **a**, "This woman told me,
7:1 Elisha **a**, "Listen to the word of
7:2 arm the king was leaning **a**
7:19 Then the servant **a** the man of
7:19 Elisha **a**, "You will see it with
8:12 Elisha **a**, "I know the evil you
8:13 Elisha **a**, "The LORD has
8:14 Hazael **a**, "He told me that you
9:5 He **a**, "You, General!"
9:11 He **a**, "You know the man and
9:22 Jehu **a**, "How can everything
10:13 They **a**, "We're Ahaziah's
10:15 "I am," Jehonadab **a**.
19:6 Isaiah **a** them, "Say this to your
20:14 Hezekiah **a**, "They came to me
20:15 Hezekiah **a**, "They saw
23:17 The people of the city **a** him,
1Ch 5:20 and he **a** their prayers because
14:10 The LORD **a** him, "Attack!
14:14 God **a** him, "Don't go after
21:26 and the LORD **a** him by
21:28 saw the LORD had **a** him at
2Ch 9:2 Solomon **a** all her questions.
10:10 who had grown up with him **a**,
10:13 The king **a** them harshly.
10:16 the people **a** the king,
18:7 Jehoshaphat **a**, "The king must
18:13 Micaiah **a**, "I solemnly swear,
18:19 Some **a** one way, while others
18:21 "The Spirit **a**, 'I will go out and
18:24 Micaiah **a**, "You will find out on
25:9 The man of God **a**,
32:24 He prayed to the LORD, who **a**
Ezr 8:23 and he **a** our prayer.
Neh 2:20 will give us success," I **a** them.
6:4 and I **a** them the same way.
Est 5:4 So Esther **a**, "If it pleases you,
5:7 Esther **a**, "My request?
6:5 The king's staff **a** him,
7:3 Then Queen Esther **a**,
7:6 Esther **a**, "Our vicious enemy
Job 1:7 Satan **a** the LORD,
1:9 Satan **a** the LORD,
2:2 Satan **a** the LORD,
2:4 Satan **a** the LORD,
6:8 prayer would be **a** — that God
9:16 If I cried out and he **a** me,
38:1 Then the LORD **a** Job out of
40:3 Job **a** the LORD,
42:1 Then Job **a** the LORD,
Psa 22:21 of wild oxen. You have **a** me.
34:4 He **a** me and rescued me from
81:7 hidden in thunder, but I **a** you.
99:6 to the LORD, and he **a** them.
99:8 O LORD, our God, you **a** them.
118:5 The LORD **a** me ⌊and⌋ set me
118:21 because you have **a** me.
119:26 I have done, and you **a** me.
120:1 out to the LORD, and he **a** me.
138:3 When I called, you **a** me.
Pro 21:13 the poor will call and not be **a**.
Isa 7:12 But Ahaz **a**, "I won't ask;
37:6 Isaiah **a** them, "Say this to your
39:3 Hezekiah **a**, "They came to me
39:4 Hezekiah **a**, "They saw
66:4 I called, but no one **a**.
Jer 1:11 I **a**, "I see a branch of an
1:13 I **a**, "I see a boiling pot, and its
9:13 The LORD **a**, They didn't obey

Jer 11:5 land you still have today."'" I **a**,
24:3 I **a**, "Figs. Figs that are very
35:6 They **a**, "We don't drink wine,
36:18 Baruch **a**, "He dictated
37:14 Jeremiah **a**, "That's a lie!
37:17 Jeremiah **a**, "Yes! There is a
38:5 King Zedekiah **a**, "He's in your
38:15 Jeremiah **a** Zedekiah,
38:19 King Zedekiah **a** Jeremiah,
42:4 The prophet Jeremiah **a** them,
44:15 at Pathros in Egypt **a** Jeremiah.
44:20 to everyone who **a** him,
Eze 4:14 I **a**, "Almighty LORD, I have
9:9 He **a** me, "The wickedness of
37:3 I **a**, "Only you know,
Dan 2:5 The king **a** the astrologers,
2:10 The astrologers **a** the king,
2:27 Daniel **a** the king, "No wise
3:16 **a** King Nebuchadnezzar,
3:24 true, Your Majesty," they **a**.
4:19 Belteshazzar **a**, "Sir, I wish
6:12 The king **a**, "That's true.
Amo 7:8 I **a**, "A plumb line." Then the
8:2 of ripe summer fruit," I **a**.
Jnh 1:9 Jonah **a** them, "I'm a Hebrew.
2:2 in my distress, and he **a** me.
4:9 Jonah **a**, "I have every right to
Hab 2:2 Then the LORD **a** me,
Hag 2:12 The priests **a**, "No."
2:13 The priests **a**, "That makes
2:14 Then Haggai **a**, "In the same
Zec 1:9 who was speaking with me **a**,
1:21 He **a**, "Those horns scattered
2:2 He **a**, "I am going to measure
4:2 I **a**, "I see a solid gold lamp
4:5 they mean?" "No, sir," I **a**.
4:13 things mean?" "No, sir," I **a**.
5:2 "I see a flying scroll," I **a**.
5:11 He **a** me, "They are going to
6:5 The angel **a**, "They are the four
Mat 3:15 Jesus **a** him, "This is the way
4:4 Jesus **a**, "Scripture says,
9:28 "Yes, Lord," they **a**.
11:4 Jesus **a** John's disciples,
13:11 Jesus **a**, "Knowledge about the
13:37 He **a**, "The one who plants the
13:51 all of this?" "Yes," they **a**.
14:28 Peter **a**, "Lord, if it is you,
15:3 He **a** them, "Why do you break
15:13 He **a**, "Any plant that my
15:28 Then Jesus **a** her,
15:34 They **a**, "Seven, and a few
16:14 They **a**, "Some say you are
16:16 Simon Peter **a**, "You are the
17:11 Jesus **a**, "Elijah is coming and
17:25 "Certainly," he **a**. Peter went
17:26 "From other people," Peter **a**.
18:22 Jesus **a** him, "I tell you,
19:4 Jesus **a**, "Haven't you read that
19:8 Jesus **a** them, "Moses allowed
19:11 He **a** them, "Not everyone can
20:7 one has hired us,' they **a** him.
21:11 The crowd **a**, "This is the
21:21 Jesus **a** them, "I can guarantee
21:24 Jesus **a** them, "I, too, have a
21:27 So they **a** Jesus, "We don't
21:31 "The first," they **a**.
21:41 They **a**, "He will destroy those
22:29 Jesus **a**, "You're mistaken
22:37 Jesus **a** him, "'Love the Lord
22:42 They **a** him, "David's."
24:4 Jesus **a** them, "Be careful not
25:12 "But he **a** them, 'I don't even
26:23 Jesus **a**, "Someone who has
26:64 Jesus **a** him, "Yes, I am. But I
26:66 They **a**, "He deserves the
27:11 "Yes, I am," Jesus **a**.
27:25 All the people **a**,
Mar 7:28 She **a** him, "Lord, even the
8:5 you have?" They **a**, "Seven."
8:20 They **a** him, "Seven."
8:28 They **a** him, "Some say you
8:29 Peter **a** him, "You are the
9:17 A man in the crowd **a**,
10:3 Jesus **a** them, "What command
10:11 He **a** them, "Whoever divorces

Mar 11:6 The disciples **a** them as Jesus
11:33 So they **a** Jesus, "We don't
12:28 saw how well Jesus **a** them,
12:29 Jesus **a**, "The most important
12:34 heard how wisely the man **a**,
13:5 Jesus **a** them, "Be careful not
14:62 Jesus **a**, "Yes, I am, and you
15:2 "Yes, I am," Jesus **a** him.
15:5 But Jesus no longer **a** anything,
15:9 Pilate **a** them, "Do you want
Luk 1:19 The angel **a** him, "I'm Gabriel!
1:35 The angel **a** her, "The Holy
1:38 Mary **a**, "I am the Lord's
3:11 He **a** them, "Whoever has two
4:4 Jesus **a** him, "Scripture says,
4:8 Jesus **a** him, "Scripture says,
4:12 Jesus **a** him, "It has been said,
5:5 Simon **a**, "Teacher, we worked
5:31 Jesus **a** them, "Healthy people
6:3 Jesus **a** them, "Haven't you
7:22 Jesus **a** John's disciples,
7:43 Simon **a**, "I suppose the one
8:10 Jesus **a**, "Knowledge about the
8:21 He **a** them, "My mother and my
8:30 He **a**, "Legion [Six Thousand]."
9:19 They **a**, "Some say you are
9:20 Peter **a**, "You are the Messiah,
9:41 Jesus **a**, "You unbelieving and
10:26 Jesus **a** him, "What is written
10:27 He **a**, "'Love the Lord your God
10:41 The Lord **a** her, "Martha,
13:23 going to be saved?" He **a**,
15:29 But he **a** his father,
16:31 "Abraham **a** him, 'If they won't
17:20 He **a** them, "People can't
19:34 The disciples **a**, "The Lord
20:3 Jesus **a** them, "I, too, have a
20:7 So they **a** that they didn't know
20:24 They **a**, "The emperor's."
22:35 "Not a thing!" they **a**.
22:70 Jesus **a** them, "You're right to
23:3 "Yes, I am," Jesus **a**.
Jon 1:21 John **a**, "No, I'm not."
1:26 John **a** them, "I baptize with
1:48 Jesus **a** him, "I saw you under
3:5 Jesus **a** Nicodemus,
3:27 John **a**, "People can't receive
4:13 Jesus **a** her, "Everyone who
5:7 The sick man **a** Jesus,
6:7 Philip **a**, "We would need
6:68 Simon Peter **a** Jesus,
7:20 The crowd **a**, Who wants to kill
7:21 Jesus **a** them, "I performed one
7:46 The temple guards **a**,
8:11 The woman **a**, "No one, sir."
8:34 Jesus **a** them, "I can guarantee
8:49 Jesus **a**, "I'm not possessed.
9:3 Jesus **a**, "Neither this man nor
9:12 The man **a**, "I don't know."
9:17 The man **a**, "He's a prophet."
9:34 The Jews **a** him, "You were
10:25 Jesus **a** them, "I've told you,
10:33 The Jews **a** Jesus,
11:9 Jesus **a**, "Aren't there twelve
11:24 Martha **a** Jesus, "I know that
11:34 They **a** him, "Lord, come and
12:35 Jesus **a** the crowd,
13:7 Jesus **a** Peter, "You don't know
13:26 Jesus **a**, "He's the one to
13:36 Jesus **a** him, "You can't follow
14:6 Jesus **a** him, "I am the way,
14:23 Jesus **a** him, "Those who love
18:5 They **a** him, "Jesus from
18:17 Peter **a**, "No, I'm not!"
18:20 Jesus **a** him, "I have spoken
18:30 The Jews **a** Pilate,
18:31 The Jews **a** him, "We're not
18:35 Pilate **a**, "Am I a Jew?
18:36 Jesus **a**, "My kingdom doesn't
19:7 The Jews **a** Pilate,
19:11 Jesus **a** Pilate, "You wouldn't
21:5 They **a** him, "No, we haven't."
21:15 Peter **a** him, "Yes, Lord,
21:16 Peter **a** him "Yes, Lord,
Act 2:38 Peter **a** them, "All of you must
4:19 Peter and John **a** them,
Act 5:8 She **a**, "Yes, that was the
5:29 Peter and the other apostles **a**,
7:2 Stephen **a**, "Brothers and
8:24 Simon **a**, "Pray to the Lord for
8:31 The official **a**, "How can I
9:10 Ananias **a**, "Yes, Lord."
10:4 The angel **a** him, "God is
10:14 Peter **a**, "I can't do that, Lord!
10:30 Cornelius **a**, "Four days ago I
11:8 "But I **a**, 'I can't do that, Lord!
16:31 They **a**, "Believe in the Lord
19:2 They **a** him, "No, we've never
19:3 They **a**, "John's baptism."
19:15 But the evil spirit **a** them,
21:39 Paul **a**, "I'm a Jew, a citizen
22:8 "I **a**, 'Who are you, sir?'
22:27 citizen?" Paul **a**, "Yes."
23:5 Paul **a**, "Brothers, I didn't know
23:20 The young man **a**,
26:15 "The Lord **a**, 'I am Jesus,
Rev 7:14 I **a** him, "Sir, you know."

answering (2)

Job 16:3 you that you keep on **a** ⌊me⌋?
32:1 These three men stopped **a**

answers (13)

Gen 24:14 If she **a**, 'Have a drink, and I'll
1Ki 18:24 The god who **a** by fire is the
Job 13:12 Your **a** are absolutely useless.
20:3 my understanding gives me **a**.
21:34 when your **a** continue
32:15 and don't have any more **a**.
32:16 and don't have any more **a**?
34:36 for giving **a** like wicked people
Psa 3:4 and he **a** me from his holy
Isa 21:12 The watchman **a**, "Morning is
29:11 He **a**, "I can't read it.
29:12 He **a**, "I can't read."
Luk 2:47 His understanding and his **a**

ant (2)

Dtr 28:56 step on an **a** — will become
Pro 6:6 Consider the **a**, you lazy bum.

antelope (2)

Dtr 14:5 goats, **a**, and mountain sheep.
Isa 51:20 They are like an **a** caught in a

Anthothijah (1)

1Ch 8:24 Hananiah, Elam, **A**,

antichrist (4)

1Jn 2:18 heard that an **a** is coming.
2:22 the Father and the Son is an **a**.
4:3 This is the spirit of the **a** that
2Jn 1:7 mark of a deceiver and an **a**.

antichrists (1)

1Jn 2:18 many **a** are already here.

Antioch (29)

Act 6:5 to Judaism in the city of **A**.
11:19 Cyprus, and the city of **A**.
11:20 and Cyrene, arrived in **A**.
11:22 After the news about **A**
11:22 Barnabas was sent to **A**.
11:25 Then Barnabas left **A** to go to
11:26 brought him back to **A**.
11:26 Saul met with the church in **A**
11:26 for the first time in the city of **A**.
11:27 from Jerusalem to the city of **A**.
11:29 All the disciples in **A** decided
12:25 returned ⌊to **A**⌋ from Jerusalem.
13:1 and teachers in the church in **A**.
13:3 them ⌊from their work in **A**⌋.
13:14 left Perga and arrived in **A**,
13:52 the disciples ⌊in **A**⌋ continued
14:19 Jews from the cities of **A** and
14:21 and **A** (which is in Pisidia).
14:26 to the city of **A** ⌊in Syria⌋.
14:26 (In **A** they had been entrusted
15:22 and Barnabas to the city of **A**.
15:23 brothers and sisters in **A**,
15:30 way and arrived in the city of **A**.
15:33 and Silas had stayed in **A**
Act 15:35 Paul and Barnabas stayed in **A**.
18:22 and went back to the city of **A**.
18:23 After spending some time in **A**,
Gal 2:11 When Cephas came to **A**,
2Ti 3:11 to me in the cities of **A**,

Antipas (1)

Rev 2:13 even in the days of **A**.

Antipatris (1)

Act 23:31 to the city of **A** during the night.

antiphonally (2)

Ezr 3:11 they sang **a**: "He is good;
Neh 12:24 and thanksgiving **a** as David,

ants (1)

Pro 30:25 **A** are not a strong species,

Anub (1)

1Ch 4:8 the father of **A** and Zobebah,

anvils (1)

Isa 41:7 who work at their **a**.

anxiety (4)

Pro 12:25 A person's **a** will weigh him
2Co 6:4 things: suffering, distress, **a**,
11:28 daily pressure of my **a** about all
1Pe 5:7 Turn all your **a** over to God

anxious (2)

Job 39:24 **A** and excited, the horse eats
Jer 17:8 It will not be **a** during droughts.

anxiously (2)

Eze 4:16 People will **a** eat rationed
Mic 1:12 Wait **a** for good, inhabitants of

apart (80)

Gen 2:3 day and set it **a** as holy,
21:28 Then Abraham set **a** seven
21:29 female lambs you have set **a**?"
Exo 13:2 "Set **a** every firstborn male for
19:10 must set themselves **a** as holy.
19:22 must set themselves **a** as holy,
20:11 and set this day **a** as holy.
28:3 These clothes will set him **a**
28:41 and set them **a** to serve me as
29:1 to set Aaron and his sons **a**
29:27 Set **a** as holy the breast that is
29:37 the LORD and set the altar **a**
29:44 I will set Aaron and his sons **a**
30:30 In this way you will set them **a**
Lev 2:3 It is very holy, set **a** from the
2:10 It is very holy, set **a** from the
8:12 and anointed him to set him **a**
20:8 LORD who sets you **a** as holy.
21:8 I set you **a** as holy.
21:15 set him **a** as holy."
21:23 set them **a** as holy."
22:2 the Israelites set **a** for me.
22:3 offerings the Israelites set **a**
22:9 who sets them **a** as holy.
22:16 who sets them **a** as holy."
22:32 who sets you **a** as holy.
24:9 It is very holy, set **a** from the
25:10 Set **a** the fiftieth year as holy,
27:26 it cannot be set **a** as holy.
Num 3:13 I set **a** as holy every firstborn in
8:17 I set them **a** as holy to me.
11:18 They must be set **a** as holy.
Dtr 10:8 At that time the LORD set **a** the
Jdg 14:6 he tore the lion **a** as if it were a
2Sm 22:10 He spread **a** the heavens and
1Ki 5:9 There I will have them taken **a**,
8:53 set them **a** from all the people
13:3 You will see the altar torn **a**.
13:5 The altar was torn **a**,
15:15 his father had set **a** as holy.
2Ki 2:24 and tore 42 of these youths **a**.
25:13 The Babylonians broke **a** the
2Ch 15:18 his father had set **a** as holy.
Job 16:9 "God's anger tore me ⌊**a**⌋ and
18:4 do you rip yourself **a** in anger?
Psa 2:3 "Let's break **a** their chains and

Psa 17:12 a lion eager to tear ⌊its prey⌋ **a**
18:9 He spread **a** the heavens and
35:15 tore me **a** without stopping.
60:2 in it because it is falling **a**.
107:14 He broke **a** their chains.
Ecc 3:7 a time to tear **a** and a time to
Isa 7:6 march against Judah, tear it **a**,
Jer 1:5 I set you **a** for my holy purpose.
2:3 Israel was set **a** for the LORD.
14:2 Judah mourns; its gates fall **a**.
52:17 The Babylonians broke **a** the
Eze 19:3 He learned to tear **a** the
19:6 He learned to tear **a** the
20:20 Set **a** certain holy days to
37:28 have set Israel **a** as holy,
48:11 This land that has been set **a**
Hos 13:8 a wild animal I will tear you **a**.
Mic 1:4 Valleys will split **a** like water
Hab 3:6 The oldest mountains break **a**.
Mat 14:19 He broke the loaves **a**,
Mar 6:41 He broke the loaves **a** and kept
Luk 2:23 boy is to be set **a** as holy
9:16 He broke the loaves **a** and kept
Jon 10:36 God set me **a** for this holy
19:24 to each other, "Let's not rip it **a**.
Act 13:2 Barnabas and Saul **a** for me.
Eph 2:14 of hostility that kept them **a**.
1Ti 4:5 God and prayer set it **a** as holy.
2Ti 2:21 They will be set **a** for the
Heb 6:2 setting people **a** for holy tasks,
7:26 set **a** from sinners,
10:10 We have been set **a** as holy
10:14 setting them **a** for God forever.
Jas 2:18 Show me your faith **a** from the

Apelles (1)

Rom 16:10 Greet **A**, a true Christian.

apes (2)

1Ki 10:22 silver, ivory, **a**, and monkeys.
2Ch 9:21 silver, ivory, **a**, and monkeys.

Aphek (9)

Jos 12:18 the king of **A**, the king of
13:4 belongs to Sidon as far as **A**,
19:30 Umma, Acco, **A**, and Rehob.
Jdg 1:31 Achzib, Helbah, **A**, or Rehob.
1Sm 4:1 the Philistines camped at **A**.
29:1 their whole army at **A**,
1Ki 20:26 and went to **A** to fight Israel.
20:30 The survivors fled to **A**,
2Ki 13:17 defeat the Arameans at **A**."

Aphekah (1)

Jos 15:53 Janim, Beth Tappuah, **A**,

Aphiah (1)

1Sm 9:1 whose father was **A**,

Apollonia (1)

Act 17:1 the cities of Amphipolis and **A**

Apollos (12)

Act 18:24 A Jew named **A**, who had been
18:27 When **A** wanted to travel to
18:28 In public **A** helped them by
19:1 While **A** was in Corinth,
1Co 1:12 or "I follow **A**," or "I follow
3:4 "I follow **A**," aren't you acting
3:5 Who is **A**? Who is Paul? They
3:6 I planted, and **A** watered,
3:22 Whether it is Paul, **A**,
4:6 I have applied this to **A** and
16:12 Concerning **A**, our brother in
Tit 3:13 Give Zenas the lawyer and **A**

Apollyon (1)

Rev 9:11 and in Greek he is called **A**.

apologized (1)

Act 16:39 officials went to the jail and **a**

apostle (26)

Act 1:25 the place of Judas as an **a**,
1:26 drew names to choose an **a**.
Rom 1:1 called to be an **a** and appointed
11:13 As long as I am an **a** sent to
1Co 1:1 From Paul, called to be an **a** of
9:1 Don't you agree that I'm an **a**?
9:2 If I'm not an **a** to other people,
9:2 at least I'm an **a** to you.
9:2 proves that I am the Lord's **a**.
15:9 I'm not even fit to be called an **a**
2Co 1:1 From Paul, an **a** of Christ
12:12 which prove that I'm an **a**.
Gal 1:1 From Paul — an **a** ⌊chosen⌋ not
1:19 I didn't see any other **a**.
2:8 The one who made Peter an **a**
2:8 people also made me an **a**
Eph 1:1 From Paul, an **a** of Christ
Col 1:1 From Paul, an **a** of Christ
1Ti 1:1 From Paul, an **a** of Christ
2:7 this Good News and to be an **a**
2Ti 1:1 From Paul, an **a** of Christ
1:11 I was appointed to be an **a** and
Tit 1:1 a servant of God and an **a** of
Heb 3:1 look carefully at Jesus, the **a**
1Pe 1:1 an **a** of Jesus Christ.
2Pe 1:1 a servant and **a** of Jesus Christ.

apostles (117)

Mat 10:2 are the names of the twelve **a**:
20:17 he took the twelve **a** aside and
20:24 When the other ten **a** heard
20:25 Jesus called the **a** and said,
26:14 Then one of the twelve **a**,
26:20 at the table with the twelve **a**.
26:47 one of the twelve **a**,
Mar 3:14 twelve whom he called **a**.
4:10 his followers and the twelve **a**,
6:7 He called the twelve **a**,
6:12 So the **a** went and told people
6:30 The **a** gathered around Jesus.
6:31 and Jesus and the **a** didn't
9:35 down and called the twelve **a**.
10:32 he took the twelve **a** aside.
10:41 When the other ten **a** heard
10:42 Jesus called the **a** and said,
11:11 with the twelve **a** to Bethany.
14:10 one of the twelve **a**,
14:17 arrived with the twelve **a**.
14:43 one of the twelve **a**,
16:14 to the eleven **a** while they were
16:19 After talking with the **a**,
Luk 6:13 of them and called them **a**.
8:1 The twelve **a** were with him.
9:1 Jesus called the twelve **a**
9:6 The **a** went from village to
9:10 The **a** came back and told
9:12 the twelve **a** came to him.
11:49 will send them prophets and **a**.
11:49 and **a** and persecute others.'
17:5 Then the **a** said to the Lord,
18:31 Jesus took the twelve **a** aside
22:3 one of the twelve **a**.
22:14 Jesus and the **a** were at the
22:31 to have you **a** for himself.
22:47 one of the twelve **a**,
24:9 told everything to the eleven **a**
24:10 They told the **a** everything.
24:11 The **a** thought that the women's
24:33 They found the eleven **a** and
Jon 6:67 So Jesus asked the twelve **a**,
6:71 who was one of the twelve **a**,
13:18 people I've chosen ⌊to be **a**⌋.
20:24 Thomas, one of the twelve **a**,
Act 1:2 through the Holy Spirit to the **a**,
1:3 his death Jesus showed the **a**
1:6 So when the **a** came together,
1:14 The **a** had a single purpose as
1:26 and joined the eleven **a**.
2:14 stood up with the eleven **a**.
2:37 asked Peter and the other **a**,
2:42 to the teachings of the **a**,
2:43 signs happened through the **a**.
4:14 say anything against the two **a**.
4:23 they went to the other **a** and
4:24 When the **a** heard this,
4:31 When the **a** had finished
4:33 With great power the **a**
4:35 to the **a**. Then the money was
4:36 The **a** called him Barnabas,
4:37 turned the money over to the **a**.
5:2 only part of it over to the **a**.
5:12 The people saw the **a** perform
5:18 by arresting the **a** and putting
5:21 the **a** went into the temple
5:21 men to the prison to get the **a**.
5:22 they didn't find the **a**.
5:26 back the **a** without using force.
5:27 When they brought back the **a**,
5:29 Peter and the other **a** answered,
5:33 and wanted to execute the **a**.
5:34 He ordered that the **a** should be
5:40 They called the **a**,
5:41 The **a** left the council room.
6:2 The twelve **a** called all the
6:6 men stand in front of the **a**,
8:1 Most believers, except the **a**,
8:14 When the **a** in Jerusalem heard
8:18 when the **a** placed their hands
9:27 Saul and brought him to the **a**.
9:27 Barnabas told the **a** how Saul
10:41 **a** he had already chosen.
10:41 We **a** are those men who ate
11:1 The **a** and the believers
14:4 while others were for the **a**.
14:14 When the **a** Barnabas and Paul
15:2 sent to Jerusalem to see the **a**
15:4 The church in Jerusalem, the **a**,
15:6 The **a** and spiritual leaders met
15:22 Then the **a**, the spiritual
15:23 From the **a** and the spiritual
16:4 about the decisions that the **a**
21:8 seven men who helped the **a**.
Rom 1:5 of being **a** who bring people
16:7 and are prominent among the **a**.
1Co 4:9 it, God has placed us **a** last
9:5 along with us like the other **a**,
12:28 God has appointed first **a**,
12:29 Not all believers are **a**,
15:5 he appeared to the twelve **a**.
15:7 Then he appeared to all the **a**.
15:9 I'm the least of the **a**.
2Co 11:5 in any way to your super-**a**.
11:13 who brag like this are false **a**.
11:13 themselves as Christ's **a**.
12:11 in any way to your super-**a**.
Gal 1:17 to see those who were **a** before
Eph 2:20 of the **a** and prophets.
3:5 it to his holy **a** and prophets.
4:11 He also gave **a**, prophets,
1Th 2:7 although as **a** of Christ we had
2Pe 1:16 When we **a** told you about the
3:2 you through your **a**.
Jud 1:17 remember what the **a** of our
Rev 2:2 those who call themselves **a**
2:2 apostles but are not **a**.
18:20 God's people, **a**, and prophets.
21:14 The 12 names of the 12 **a** of

Appaim (1)

1Ch 2:30 sons were Seled and **A**,

Appaim's (1)

1Ch 2:31 **A** son was Ishi, and Ishi's son

appalled (2)

1Ki 9:8 impressive as it is, will be **a**.
2Ch 7:21 impressive temple will be **a**.

appeal (17)

1Ki 13:6 "Please make an **a** to the
13:6 So the man of God made an **a**
2Ki 8:3 but left again to make an **a**
8:5 mother ⌊came to⌋ make an **a**
Est 4:8 and **a** to him for her people.
Pro 8:4 and my **a** is to all people.
Act 25:11 I **a** my case to the emperor!"
25:12 Festus discussed the **a** with
25:25 But since he made an **a** to His
28:19 I was forced to **a** my case to
2Co 1:23 I **a** to God as a witness on my
8:4 They made an **a** to us,
10:1 I, Paul, make my **a** to you with
Phm 1:9 I would prefer to make an **a** on
1:10 **a** to you for my child Onesimus
1Pe 5:1 I **a** to your spiritual leaders.

1Pe 5:1 I make this **a** as a spiritual

appealed (4)

Ecc 2:10 If something **a** to me,
Act 25:12 "You have **a** your case to the
25:21 But Paul **a** his case.
26:32 set free if he hadn't **a** his case

appealing (1)

2Pe 2:18 to seduce people by **a**

appear (34)

Gen 1:9 and let the dry land **a**."
9:14 a rainbow will **a** in the clouds.
31:2 that Laban did not **a** as friendly
Exo 4:1 'The LORD didn't **a** to you.'"
Lev 9:4 The LORD will **a** to you today."
14:34 mildew may **a** in a house.
16:2 because I **a** in the smoke
Jdg 13:21 of the LORD didn't **a** again
1Sm 3:21 LORD continued to **a** in Shiloh,
Est 1:19 that Vashti may never again **a**
Job 37:13 he makes the storm **a**.
Psa 21:9 When you **a**, you will make
80:2 **A** in front of Ephraim,
94:1 O God of vengeance, **a**!
102:16 he will **a** in his glory.
Sos 2:12 Blossoms **a** in the land.
Isa 1:12 When you **a** in my presence,
3:17 Lord will cause sores ⌊to **a**⌋
16:12 When the people of Moab **a** at
Amo 4:13 He makes dawn and dusk ⌊**a**⌋.
Zec 9:14 The LORD will **a** over them,
Mat 24:11 Many false prophets will **a** and
24:24 and false prophets will **a**.
24:30 sign of the Son of Man will **a**
Mar 13:22 and false prophets will **a**.
Luk 19:11 of God would **a** suddenly.
2Co 5:10 All of us must **a** in front of
Col 3:4 will **a** with him in glory.
2Ti 3:5 They will **a** to have a godly life,
Tit 3:4 and love for humanity **a**,
Heb 9:24 he went into heaven to **a** in
9:28 and after that he will **a** a
2Pe 3:3 follow their own desires will **a**.
Jud 1:18 who ridicule ⌊God⌋ will **a**.

appearance (17)

Jdg 13:6 He had a very frightening **a** like
1Sm 16:7 "Don't look at his **a** or how tall
16:12 and a handsome **a**.
Job 14:20 You change his **a** and send
Isa 52:14 His **a** will be so disfigured that
53:2 He had nothing in his **a** that
Mat 16:3 the weather by judging the **a**
17:2 Jesus' **a** changed in front of
Mar 9:2 Jesus' **a** changed in front of
Luk 9:29 the **a** of his face changed,
12:56 the weather by judging the **a**
Jon 7:24 Stop judging by outward **a**!
Rom 2:28 is not a Jew because of his **a**,
2Co 5:12 proud of their **a** rather than their
Php 2:7 by having a human **a**.
2Th 2:8 his **a** will put an end to this
Tit 2:13 what we hope for — the **a**

appearances (1)

1Sm 16:7 Humans look at outward **a**,

appeared (85)

Gen 8:5 the tops of the mountains **a**.
12:7 Then the LORD **a** to Abram and
12:7 to the LORD, who had **a** to him.
17:1 the LORD **a** to him.
18:1 The LORD **a** to Abraham by the
26:2 The LORD **a** to Isaac and said,
26:24 That night the LORD **a** to Isaac,
31:13 I am the God who **a** to you at
35:1 I am the God who **a** to you
35:9 Then God **a** once more to
40:9 with three branches **a**
48:3 "God Almighty **a** to me at Luz
Exo 3:2 The Messenger of the LORD **a**
3:16 Isaac, and Jacob, **a** to me.
4:5 Isaac, and Jacob, **a** to you."
6:3 I **a** to Abraham, Isaac,
Lev 9:23 Then the LORD's glory **a** to all
Num 16:19 the glory of the LORD **a** to the
16:42 and the glory of the LORD **a**.
20:6 glory of the LORD **a** to them.
Dtr 1:33 He **a** in a column of fire at night
31:15 Then the LORD **a** in a column
33:2 He **a** like sunshine from Mount
Jdg 6:12 The Messenger of the LORD **a**
13:3 The Messenger of the LORD **a**
13:10 day has just **a** to me ⌊again⌋."
1Ki 3:5 In Gibeon the LORD **a** to
9:2 Then the LORD **a** to him **a**
9:2 as he had **a** to him in Gibeon.
11:9 who had **a** to him twice.
2Ch 1:7 That night God **a** to Solomon.
3:1 where the LORD **a** to his father
7:12 Then the LORD **a** to him at
Jer 31:3 The LORD **a** to me in a
Eze 10:8 The angels **a** to have what
Dan 5:5 the fingers of a person's hand **a**
7:20 It **a** to be bigger than the others.
Mat 1:20 when an angel of the Lord **a**
2:7 exactly when the star had **a**.
2:13 an angel of the Lord **a** to
2:19 an angel of the Lord **a** in a
3:1 Later, John the Baptizer **a** in
3:13 Then Jesus **a**. He came from
13:26 and formed kernels, weeds **a**.
17:3 Suddenly, Moses and Elijah **a**
27:53 where they **a** to many people.
Mar 9:4 Then Elijah and Moses **a** to
16:9 he **a** first to Mary from Magdala
16:12 Later Jesus **a** to two disciples
16:14 Still later Jesus **a** to the eleven
Luk 1:11 an angel of the Lord **a** to him.
1:80 in the desert until the day he **a**
2:9 the Lord suddenly **a** to them.
2:13 a large army of angels **a** with
7:16 great prophet has **a** among us,"
9:8 Others said that Elijah had **a**,
9:31 They **a** in heavenly glory and
22:43 Then an angel from heaven **a**
24:34 to life and has **a** to Simon."
Act 1:3 For 40 days he **a** to them and
2:3 that looked like fire **a** to them.
5:36 Some time ago Theudas **a**.
5:37 Judas from Galilee **a** and led
7:2 God who reveals his glory **a**
7:30 a messenger **a** to him in the
7:35 help of the messenger who **a**
9:17 who **a** to you on your way to
13:31 and for many days he **a** to
26:16 I have **a** to you for a reason.
1Co 15:5 He **a** to Cephas. Next he
15:5 Next he **a** to the twelve
15:6 Then he **a** to more than 500
15:7 Next he **a** to James.
15:7 Then he **a** to all the apostles.
15:8 Last of all, he also **a** to me.
1Ti 3:16 He **a** in his human nature,
Tit 2:11 God's saving kindness has **a**
Heb 7:15 who is like Melchizedek **a**.
9:26 he has **a** once to remove sin by
2Pe 3:5 The earth ⌊**a**⌋ out of water and
1Jn 3:5 You know that Christ **a** in order
3:8 that the Son of God **a** was
Rev 12:1 A spectacular sign **a** in the sky:
12:3 Another sign **a** in the sky:
16:2 Horrible, painful sores **a** on the

appears (16)

Gen 9:16 Whenever the rainbow **a** in the
Lev 13:14 But if raw flesh **a**, he will be
Job 41:32 path behind it so that the sea **a**
Psa 84:7 along until each one of them **a**
Pro 27:25 the tender growth **a**,
Isa 60:2 and his glory **a** over you.
Mal 3:2 to survive on the day he **a**?
Mar 4:28 First the green blade **a**,
Col 3:4 When Christ your life **a**,
1Ti 6:14 until our Lord Jesus Christ **a**,
1Pe 1:7 when Jesus Christ **a** again.
1:13 you when Jesus Christ **a** again.
4:13 be full of joy when he **a** again
5:4 when the chief shepherd **a**,
1Jn 2:28 Then, when he **a** we will have
3:2 We do know that when Christ **a**

appetite (11)

Num 11:6 But now we've lost our **a**!
Job 33:20 hates food and they lose their **a**
Pro 6:30 when he steals to satisfy his **a**,
13:2 but the **a** of treacherous people
13:4 but the **a** of hard-working
13:25 person eats to satisfy his **a**,
16:26 A laborer's **a** works to his
23:2 your throat if you have a big **a**.
Ecc 6:7 but their **a** is never satisfied.
Isa 5:14 is why the grave's **a** increases.
Hab 2:5 He has a large **a** like the grave.

appetites (1)

Isa 56:11 These dogs have huge **a**.

Apphia (1)

Phm 1:2 our sister **A**, our fellow soldier

Appius' (1)

Act 28:15 as far as the cities of **A** Market

apple (3)

Sos 2:3 Like an **a** tree among the trees
8:5 Under the **a** tree I woke you up.
Zec 2:8 you touches the **a** of his eye.

apples (3)

Pro 25:11 ⌊Like⌋ golden **a** in silver
Sos 2:5 raisins and refresh me with **a**
7:8 of your breath be like **a**.

applied (3)

Mat 7:2 use for others will be **a** to you.
Luk 6:38 use for others will be **a** to you."
1Co 4:6 Brothers and sisters, I have **a**

applies (5)

Exo 21:31 this same ruling **a**.
Lev 24:22 The same rule **a** to every one
Ecc 12:13 because this **a** to everyone.
Jer 11:7 and the warning still **a** to you
Rom 3:19 is in Moses' Teachings **a**

apply (4)

Exo 12:49 The same instructions **a** to
Lev 7:7 "The same instructions **a** to the
Num 9:14 The same rules will **a** to
Dan 4:24 Most High has decided to **a**

applying (1)

Mal 2:9 You have been unfair when ⌊**a**⌋

appoint (26)

Gen 41:34 Make arrangements to **a**
Num 3:10 **A** Aaron and his sons to serve
27:16 Please **a** someone over the
Dtr 1:13 and I'll **a** them to be your
16:18 **A** judges and officers for your
17:15 Be sure to **a** the king the LORD
20:9 they should **a** commanders to
1Sm 2:35 Then I will **a** a faithful priest to
2:36 'Please **a** me to one of the
8:5 Now **a** a king to judge us so
8:12 He will **a** them to be his
1Ki 14:14 The LORD will **a** a king over
1Ch 15:16 the Levite leaders to **a** some
2Ch 13:9 you could **a** your own priests,
Ezr 7:25 in your hands — will **a** judges
Est 2:3 And **a** scouts in all the
Psa 109:6 "**A** the evil one to oppose him.
Isa 42:6 I will **a** you as my promise to
49:8 I will **a** you as my promise to
60:17 I will **a** peace as your governor
Jer 49:19 I will **a** over Edom whomever I
50:44 I will **a** over Babylon
51:27 **A** a commander to lead the
Dan 6:1 would be good to **a** 120 satraps
Hos 1:11 They will **a** one leader for
Luk 19:14 who was going to **a** him⌋,

appointed (148)

Exo 23:15 Do this at the **a** time in the
31:6 Also, I have **a** Oholiab,

Exo 34:18 for seven days at the a time
Lev 16:21 A man will be a to release the
23:2 These are the a festivals with
23:4 are the LORD's a festivals
23:4 must announce at their a times.
23:37 are the LORD's a festivals.
23:44 about the LORD's a festivals.
Jdg 2:18 But when the LORD a judges
1Sm 3:20 was the LORD's a prophet.
12:1 you have said to me and a
12:6 "The LORD a Moses and
13:14 The LORD has a him as ruler
2Sm 6:21 and he a me leader of Israel,
7:11 ever since I a judges to rule my
15:3 but the king hasn't a anyone to
17:25 Absalom a Amasa to take
18:1 He a commanders in charge of
1Ki 1:35 I have a him to be the leader of
2:35 The king then a Benaiah,
4:7 Solomon a 12 district
12:31 He a men who were not
12:32 Jeroboam a a festival on the
12:32 He a priests from the illegal
13:33 who were willing and a them
15:4 He a David's descendant to
2Ki 7:17 The king a the servant on
11:18 Next, the priest a officials to be
12:11 to the men who had been a
17:32 they also a all kinds of people
21:6 and a ⌊royal⌋ mediums and
23:5 whom the kings of Judah had a
25:22 of Babylon a Gedaliah,
25:23 of Babylon had a Gedaliah,
1Ch 9:22 David and the seer Samuel a
15:17 So the Levites a Heman,
15:17 from his relatives they a Asaph,
15:17 they a Ethan, son of Kushaiah.
15:18 In addition, they a their
15:18 Obed Edom and Jeiel were a
15:19 and Ethan were a to play
15:20 and Benaiah were a to play
15:21 and Azaziah were a to play
16:4 David a some Levites to serve
17:10 ever since I a judges to rule my
22:2 He a some of them to cut
23:4 Of these, 24,000 were a to
23:4 6,000 were a to be officers and
23:5 4,000 were a to be
23:5 and 4,000 were a to praise the
23:28 They were a to stand beside
23:28 They were a to be in charge of
23:30 They were a to stand to give
23:30 They were a to do the same
23:31 They were a to stand in front of
23:31 and on a annual festivals.
23:32 They were a to follow the
25:1 and the army commanders a
26:10 His father a him head.
26:30 male relatives were a to serve
26:32 King David a them to be
2Ch 2:4 during the annual festivals a by
8:14 of Levites for their a places.
11:15 Instead, Jeroboam a ⌊his own⌋
11:22 Rehoboam a Abijah,
19:5 He a judges in the country,
19:8 also a some Levites,
20:21 he a people to sing to the
23:18 Next, Jehoiada a officials to be
23:18 They were a to sacrifice burnt
23:19 Jehoiada a gatekeepers for the
31:13 a Jehiel, Azaziah, Nahath,
31:16 They were a to distribute them
31:19 Men were a to give a portion of
32:6 He a military commanders over
33:6 and a ⌊royal⌋ mediums and
35:2 Josiah a the priests to their
Ezr 8:20 David and his officials had a
Neh 6:7 You've a prophets to announce
9:17 They became stubborn and a a
10:33 and at the a annual festivals,
10:34 our God at a times every year
13:13 I a the following men to be in
13:13 the Levite, and I a Hanan,
Est 4:5 one of the king's eunuchs a to
9:27 described and at their a time.
9:31 days of Purim at the a time.

Job 20:29 inheritance God has a for him."
30:23 to the dwelling place a for all
34:13 Who a him to be over the
Psa 102:13 Indeed, the a time has come.
104:8 to the place you a for them.
Pro 8:23 I was a from everlasting from
Isa 1:14 Festivals and your a festivals.
Jer 1:5 I a you to be a prophet to the
37:1 of Babylon a Zedekiah,
40:5 whom the king of Babylon a to
40:7 of Babylon had a Gedaliah,
40:11 in Judah and had a Gedaliah,
41:2 the king of Babylon had a
41:18 the king of Babylon had a
Eze 17:16 of the king who a him king
21:15 I have a my sword to slaughter
28:14 I a an angel to guard you.
33:7 "Son of man, I have a you as a
36:38 during the a festivals.
43:21 and burn it in the place a near
45:17 and all the other a festivals of
46:9 at the time of the a festivals.
46:11 festival days and at a festivals,
Dan 2:24 whom the king had a to destroy
2:49 Daniel a Shadrach,
3:12 are certain Jews whom you a
7:25 and plan to change the a times
11:27 end must wait until the a time.
11:29 "At the a time he will again
11:35 But the a time is still to come.
Hos 2:11 days — all her a festivals.
9:5 do on the day of an a festival
12:9 you did during your a festivals.
Hab 1:12 O LORD, you have a the
2:3 will still happen at the a time.
Mar 3:14 He a twelve whom he called
3:16 He a these twelve:
Luk 10:1 After this, the Lord a 70 other
12:14 Jesus said to him, "Who a me
19:12 a distant country to be a king,
19:15 "After he was a king,
Jon 12:48 I say have a judge a for them.
15:16 I have a you to go,
Act 3:20 whom he has a to be the Christ.
10:42 'God has a Jesus to judge the
12:21 The a day came. Herod,
17:31 and he will use a man he has a
Rom 1:1 called to be an apostle and a to
8:29 people and had already a them
8:30 those whom he had already a.
1Co 4:5 anything before the a time.
12:28 God has a first apostles,
Gal 1:15 But God, who a me before I
1Ti 1:12 has trusted me and has a me
2:7 I was a to spread this Good
2Ti 1:11 I was a to be an apostle and
Tit 1:7 is a supervisor a by God,
Heb 3:2 is faithful to God, who a him,
5:10 God a him chief priest in the
8:3 Every chief priest is a to offer

appointing (4)

1Ki 13:34 A illegal priests became the
Ezr 3:8 They began by a the Levites
Act 26:16 I'm a you to be a servant and
Tit 1:5 to be done — a spiritual leaders

appreciate (2)

Pro 15:12 A mocker does not a a warning.
Act 24:3 We a what you've done in

appreciates (1)

Pro 15:5 but whoever a a warning

appreciation (3)

Job 12:5 life has no a for misfortune.
1Co 16:18 show people like these your a.
1Th 5:12 we ask you to show your a for

approach (7)

Dtr 20:10 When you a a city to attack it,
Jos 8:5 I'll a the city with the rest of the
Job 31:37 of my steps and a him like
33:22 Their souls a the pit.
41:13 Who can a it with a harness?
Rom 5:2 Through Christ we can a God

Heb 7:19 and allows us to a God.

approached (14)

Gen 38:16 he a her by the roadside and
Exo 14:10 As Pharaoh a, the Israelites
40:32 or whenever they a the altar.
1Sm 9:18 Saul a Samuel inside the
17:40 he a the Philistine.
30:21 As David a the men,
2Sm 15:5 When anyone a him and
2Ki 2:5 who were in Jericho a Elisha.
16:12 The king a the altar and went
Ezr 4:2 they a Zerubbabel and the
Mat 26:73 the men standing there a Peter
Luk 24:15 Jesus a them and began
Act 4:1 and some Sadducees a Peter
20:15 On the following day we a the

approaches (2)

Est 4:11 provinces know that no one a
Job 40:19 Its maker a it with his sword.

approaching (3)

Luk 9:31 were discussing Jesus' a death
Act 22:6 "But as I was on my way and a
27:27 suspected that we were a land.

appropriate (4)

Rom 12:1 kind of worship is a for you.
Eph 5:3 This is not a behavior for God's
Col 3:18 This is a behavior for the Lord's
1Ti 2:9 dressing in a clothes that are

approval (137)

Gen 6:9 Noah had God's a and was a
15:6 that faith to be his a of Abram.
Dtr 6:25 how we'll have the LORD's a:
Mat 5:6 hunger and thirst for God's a.
5:20 you live a life that has God's a
6:33 kingdom and what has his a.
13:43 have God's a will shine like
13:49 from people who have God's a.
23:28 as though you have God's a,
23:29 of those who had God's a.
25:37 who have God's a will reply
25:46 but those with God's a will go
Luk 1:6 and Elizabeth had God's a.
1:17 of those who have God's a.
14:14 who have God's a come back
15:7 turned to God and have his a."
18:14 went home with God's a,
23:50 a good man who had God's a.
Jon 6:27 placed his seal of a on him."
16:8 the world what has God's a,
16:10 the world what has God's a,
Act 7:52 man with God's a would come.
10:22 He's a man who has God's a
13:10 everything that has God's a.
13:38 a through Moses' Teachings.
13:39 in Jesus receives God's a.
22:14 see the one who has God's a,
24:15 that people with God's a and
24:25 the subjects of God's a,
Rom 1:17 God's a is revealed in this
1:17 This a begins and ends with
1:17 "The person who has God's a
2:13 from God don't have God's a.
2:13 demand will have God's a.
3:10 "Not one person has God's a.
3:20 God's a by following Moses'
3:21 the way to receive God's a has
3:22 has God's a through faith
3:24 They receive God's a freely by
3:25 where God's a is given through
3:26 that he could display his a at
3:28 that a person has God's a
4:2 If Abraham had God's a
4:3 God to be his a of Abraham."
4:5 faith is regarded as God's a.
4:9 regarded as God's a of him."
4:10 his faith regarded as God's a?
4:11 was regarded as God's a while
4:11 is the seal of that a.
4:11 is regarded as God's a of them.
4:13 through God's a of his faith.
4:22 regarded as God's a of him.

Rom 4:23 faith was regarded as God's **a**
4:24 will be regarded as God's **a**
4:25 that we could receive God's **a**.
5:1 Now that we have God's **a**
5:9 has now given us God's **a**,
5:16 the gift brought God's **a**.
5:17 and the gift of his **a** will rule
5:18 **a** through one verdict.
5:19 humanity will receive God's **a**.
5:21 would rule by bringing us his **a**.
6:16 your master leads to God's **a**.
8:10 because you have God's **a**.
9:30 gain God's **a** won his approval,
9:30 gain God's approval won his **a**,
9:30 an **a** based on faith.
9:31 God's **a** by obeying Moses'
9:32 rely on faith to gain God's **a**,
10:3 ⌊how to receive⌋ God's **a**.
10:3 God's way for receiving his **a**.
10:4 has faith may receive God's **a**.
10:5 God's **a** by following his
10:6 Scripture says about God's **a**
10:10 believing you receive God's **a**,
14:17 consists of God's **a** and peace,
1Co 4:4 doesn't mean I have God's **a**.
6:11 and you have received God's **a**
2Co 3:9 ministry that brings God's **a** has
5:21 receive God's **a** through him.
9:10 things you do that have his **a**.
10:18 who receives **a**,
11:15 as servants who have God's **a**.
Gal 1:10 I saying this now to win the **a**
2:16 people don't receive God's **a**
2:16 in order to receive God's **a**
2:16 People won't receive God's **a**
2:17 searching for God's **a** in Christ,
2:21 If we receive God's **a** by
3:6 by God to be his **a** of Abraham.
3:8 time that God would give his **a**
3:11 No one receives God's **a** by
3:11 "The person who has God's **a**
3:21 we would receive God's **a**
3:24 God's **a** because of faith.
5:4 to earn God's **a** by obeying his
5:5 that comes with God's **a**.
Eph 5:9 that is good, that has God's **a**,
6:14 on God's **a** as your breastplate.
Php 1:11 that God's **a** produces.
3:6 God's **a** by keeping Jewish
3:9 receive God's **a** by obeying his
3:9 I have God's **a** through faith in
3:9 This is the **a** that comes from
1Ti 1:9 for people who have God's **a**.
2Ti 2:22 Pursue what has God's **a**.
3:16 them for a life that has God's **a**.
4:8 I have God's **a** is now waiting
Tit 3:5 we had done to gain his **a**.
3:7 kindness has given us his **a**
Heb 10:38 The person who has God's **a**
11:4 his faith Abel received God's **a**,
11:7 God's **a** that comes through
12:23 of people who have God's **a**
Jas 2:21 Abraham receive God's **a** as
2:23 God to be his **a** of Abraham."
2:24 that a person receives God's **a**
2:25 She received God's **a** because
3:18 A harvest that has God's **a**
5:6 people who have God's **a**,
5:16 who have God's **a** are effective.
1Pe 2:24 live a life that has God's **a**.
4:18 for the person who has God's **a**
2Pe 1:1 a faith based on the **a** that
2:5 the kind of life that has God's **a**.
2:7 a man who had his **a**.
2:8 was a man who had God's **a**,
3:13 that has God's **a** lives.
1Jn 2:1 who has God's full **a**.
2:29 know that Christ has God's **a**,
3:7 of has God's **a** as Christ has
3:7 approval as Christ has God's **a**.
3:12 his brother did had God's **a**.
5:14 ask for anything that has his **a**.
Rev 19:8 holy people do that have his **a**.
22:11 have God's **a** go without it,
22:11 Let those who have God's **a**

approve (11)

Gen 4:5 but he didn't **a** of Cain and his
1Sm 29:6 But the rulers don't **a** of you.
29:10 because I still **a** of you.
1Ch 13:2 "If you **a** and if the LORD our
Est 3:9 If you **a**, have the orders for
Jer 44:19 think our husbands didn't **a**?"
Hos 8:4 own kings, kings I didn't **a**.
Luk 11:48 So you are witnesses and **a** of
Rom 1:32 only do these things but also **a**
Heb 10:6 You did not **a** of burnt offerings
10:8 You did not **a** of them."

approved (18)

Gen 4:4 The LORD **a** of Abel and his
Lev 10:19 would the LORD have **a**?"
Rut 4:7 was publicly **a** in Israel.)
2Sm 3:19 entire tribe of Benjamin had **a**.
3:36 understood and **a** of this,
3:36 as all the people **a** of
17:4 the leaders of Israel **a** this plan.
1Ki 11:19 Pharaoh **a** of Hadad.
Est 1:21 king and his officials **a** of this,
Luk 18:9 who were sure that God **a**
Act 8:1 Saul **a** of putting Stephen to
15:8 showed that he **a** of people
22:20 I **a** of his death and guarded the
Rom 8:30 He **a** of those whom he had
8:30 to those whom he had **a** of.
8:33 God has **a** of them.
1Ti 3:16 was **a** by the Spirit,
Heb 11:33 kingdoms, did what God **a**,

approves (19)

Jdg 18:6 The LORD **a** of your journey."
Pro 17:15 Whoever **a** of wicked people
Mat 5:10 for doing what God **a** of.
Rom 3:26 a God who **a** of people who
3:30 since it is the same God who **a**
4:5 the one who **a** ungodly people,
4:6 God **a** of a person without that
6:13 to do everything that God **a** of.
6:18 slaves who do what God **a** of.
6:19 slaves that do what God **a** of.
6:20 free from doing what God **a** of.
Eph 4:18 from the life that God **a**
1Ti 6:11 Pursue what God **a** of:
Jas 1:20 doesn't do what God **a** of.
1Pe 3:12 are on those who do what he **a**.
3:14 suffer for doing what God **a**,
2Pe 2:21 the way of life that God **a**
1Jn 2:29 who does what God **a**
3:7 Whoever does what God **a** of

apricot (1)

Joe 1:12 palm, and **a** trees, have died.

aprons (1)

Act 19:12 and **a** that had touched

Aquila (9)

Act 18:2 he met a Jewish man named **A**
18:2 **A** had been born in Pontus,
18:18 Priscilla and **A** went with him.
18:18 **A** had his hair cut,
18:19 where Paul left Priscilla and **A**.
18:26 Priscilla and **A** heard him,
Rom 16:3 Greet Prisca and **A**,
1Co 16:19 **A** and Prisca and the church
2Ti 4:19 my greetings to Prisca and **A**

Ar (6)

Num 21:15 that go down to the site of **A**
21:28 They destroyed **A** of Moab,
Dtr 2:9 I'm not giving you any of **A** as
2:18 by the border of Moab at **A**.
2:29 who live in **A**, did for us.
Isa 15:1 In a single night **A** in Moab is

Ara (1)

1Ch 7:38 were Jephunneh, Pispa, and **A**.

Arab (5)

Jos 15:52 villages: **A**, Dumah, Eshan,
1Ki 10:15 traders' profits, all the **A** kings,
2Ch 9:14 All the **A** kings and governors
Neh 2:19 and Geshem the **A** heard about
6:1 Tobiah, Geshem the **A**,

Arabah (2)

2Sm 23:35 from Carmel, Paarai from **A**,
Amo 6:14 of Hamath to the valley of **A**.

Arabia (7)

Isa 21:13 is the divine revelation about **A**.
21:13 the night in the forest of **A**.
Jer 25:24 all the kings of **A**, and all the
Eze 27:21 **A** and all the officials of Kedar
Act 2:11 Crete, and **A**. We hear these
Gal 1:17 Instead, I went to **A** and then
4:25 Hagar is Mount Sinai in **A**.

Arabs (7)

2Ch 17:11 The **A** also brought him flocks:
21:16 and the **A** who lived near
22:1 camp with the **A** had killed all
26:7 the **A** who lived in Gur Baal,
Neh 4:7 When Sanballat, Tobiah, the **A**,
Isa 13:20 **A** won't pitch their tents there.
Eze 30:5 Sudan, Put, Lud, all the **A**,

Arad (5)

Num 21:1 When the Canaanite king of **A**,
33:40 (The Canaanite king of **A**,
Jos 12:14 king of Hormah, the king of **A**,
Jdg 1:16 of Judah in the Negev near **A**.
1Ch 8:15 sons were Zebadiah, **A**, Eder,

Arah (3)

1Ch 7:39 Ulla's sons were **A**,
Ezr 2:5 of **A**: 775
Neh 7:10 of **A**: 652

Arah's (1)

Neh 6:18 of Shecaniah, **A** son.

Aram (52)

Gen 10:22 Arpachshad, Lud, and **A**.
22:21 Kemuel (father of **A**),
Num 23:7 "Balak brought me from **A**.
Jdg 10:6 Astartes — and the gods of **A**,
2Sm 15:8 I was living at Geshur in **A**.
1Ki 11:25 He ruled **A** and despised Israel.
19:15 anoint Hazael as king of **A**.
20:1 King Benhadad of **A** gathered
20:20 King Benhadad of **A** escaped
20:22 king of **A** will attack ⌊again⌋."
20:23 of King Benhadad of **A** told him,
22:1 no war between **A** and Israel.
22:3 it back from the king of **A**?"
22:31 The king of **A** had given orders
2Ki 5:1 The LORD had given **A** a
5:5 The king of **A** said,
6:8 Whenever the king of **A** was
6:11 The king of **A** was very angry
6:24 Later King Benhadad of **A**
8:7 King Benhadad of **A**,
8:9 Benhadad of **A** has sent me
8:13 you will become king of **A**."
8:28 Hazael of **A** at Ramoth Gilead.
8:29 against King Hazael of **A**.)
9:14 against King Hazael of **A**.
9:15 fighting King Hazael of **A**.)
12:17 At this time King Hazael of **A**
12:18 things to King Hazael of **A**,
13:3 the mercy of King Hazael of **A**
13:7 the king of **A** had destroyed
13:17 the arrow of victory against **A**.
13:22 King Hazael of **A** oppressed
13:24 King Hazael of **A** died,
15:37 King Rezin of **A** and Pekah,
16:5 Then King Rezin of **A** and King
16:6 At that time King Rezin of **A**
16:7 save me from the kings of **A**
1Ch 1:17 Lud, **A**, Uz, Hul, Gether,
2:23 Geshur and **A** captured
7:34 Rohgah, Jehubbah, and **A**.
2Ch 16:7 the army of the king of **A** has
18:30 The king of **A** had given orders
22:5 Hazael of **A** at Ramoth Gilead.
22:6 against King Hazael of **A**.)

2Ch 28:5 him over to the king of **A**,
28:23 "The gods of the kings of **A** are
Isa 7:4 the fierce anger of Rezin from **A**
7:5 **A**, Ephraim, and Remaliah's
7:8 The capital of **A** is Damascus,
17:3 The remaining few from **A** will
Eze 16:57 Now the daughters of **A** and
Amo 1:5 The people of **A** will go into

Aramaic (5)

2Ki 18:26 "Speak to us in **A**,
Ezr 4:7 was written with the **A** script
4:7 translated into the **A** language.
Isa 36:11 "Speak to us in **A**,
Dan 2:4 spoke to the king in **A**,

Aramean (26)

Gen 25:20 daughter of Bethuel the **A** from
25:20 Aram and sister of Laban the **A**.
28:5 son of Bethuel the **A** and
31:20 Jacob also tricked Laban the **A**
31:24 God came to Laban the **A** in a
2Sm 8:6 David put troops in the **A**
1Ki 10:29 to all the Hittite and **A** kings.
20:26 and Benhadad organized the **A**
20:29 The Israelites killed 100,000 **A**
2Ki 5:1 of the **A** king's army,
5:20 "My master let this **A** Naaman
6:23 After this, **A** troops didn't raid
7:4 So let's go to the **A** camp.
7:5 at dusk to go into the **A** camp.
7:6 (The LORD had made the **A**
7:6 The **A** soldiers said to one
7:10 "We went into the **A** camp,
7:14 sent them to follow the **A** army
7:16 out and looted the **A** camp.
13:4 how the **A** king was oppressing
1Ch 7:14 was Manasseh's **A** concubine.
18:6 David put troops in the **A**
2Ch 1:17 to all the Hittite and **A** kings.
24:23 the **A** army attacked Joash.
24:24 The **A** army had come with a
Jer 35:11 the Babylonian and **A** armies.'

Arameans (57)

Dtr 26:5 ancestors were wandering **A**.
2Sm 8:5 When the **A** from Damascus
8:6 and the **A** became his subjects
10:6 So they hired the **A** from Beth
10:8 while the **A** from Zobah and
10:9 them for combat against the **A**.
10:11 Joab said, "If the **A** are too
10:13 troops advanced to fight the **A**,
10:13 the Arameans, and the **A** fled.
10:14 saw that the **A** had fled,
10:15 **A** reassembled ⌊their troops⌋.
10:16 to get **A** from beyond
10:16 The **A** came to Helam with
10:17 The **A** formed a battle line
10:18 The **A** fled from Israel,
10:19 And the **A** were afraid to help
1Ki 20:20 The **A** fled, and Israel pursued
20:21 and decisively defeated the **A**.
20:27 while camped opposite the **A**
20:28 Because the **A** said that the
22:11 push the **A** to their destruction."
22:35 up in his chariot facing the **A**.
2Ki 5:2 when the **A** went on raids,
6:9 The **A** are hiding there."
6:18 As the **A** came down to get
7:12 officers what the **A** had planned
7:15 that the **A** had thrown away
8:28 There the **A** wounded Joram.
8:29 by the **A** at Ramah when
13:17 defeat the **A** at Aphek."
13:19 completely defeated the **A**.
13:19 only defeat the **A** three times."
24:2 of Babylonians, **A**, Moabites,
1Ch 18:5 When the **A** from Damascus
18:6 and the **A** became his subjects
19:6 chariots and horses from the **A**
19:9 while the **A** from Zobah and
19:10 them for combat against the **A**.
19:12 Joab said, "If the **A** are too
19:14 troops advanced to fight the **A**,
19:14 the Arameans, and the **A** fled.
1Ch 19:15 saw that the **A** had fled,
19:16 to get ⌊other⌋ **A** from beyond
19:17 a battle line against the **A**,
19:18 The **A** fled from Israel,
19:19 And the **A** were no longer
2Ch 18:10 push the **A** to their destruction."
18:34 facing the **A** until evening.
22:5 There the **A** wounded Joram.
22:6 by the **A** at Ramah when
24:23 The **A** sent all the loot they
24:24 So the **A** carried out ⌊the
24:25 When the **A** withdrew,
Isa 7:2 family that the **A** had made
9:12 the **A** from the east and the
Amo 1:3 The **A** have crushed ⌊the
9:7 from Crete and the **A** from Kir?

Aram Naharaim (4)

Gen 24:10 He traveled to **A**, Nahor's city.
Dtr 23:4 from Pethor in **A**, to curse you.
Jdg 3:8 King Cushan Rishathaim of **A**
3:10 Cushan Rishathaim of **A** over

Aram's (5)

Gen 10:23 **A** descendants were Uz,
1Ki 15:18 to **A** King Benhadad,
2Ki 13:5 they were freed from **A** power.
2Ch 16:2 to **A** King Benhadad.
Isa 7:1 **A** King Rezin and Israel's King

Aran (2)

Gen 36:28 the sons of Dishan: Uz and **A**.
1Ch 1:42 Dishan's sons were Uz and **A**.

Ararat (4)

Gen 8:4 to rest in the mountains of **A**.
2Ki 19:37 and escaped to the land of **A**.
Isa 37:38 and escaped to the land of **A**.
Jer 51:27 Tell the kingdoms of **A**,

Araunah (7)

2Sm 24:16 floor of **A** the Jebusite.
24:18 up an altar for the LORD at **A**
24:20 When **A** looked down and saw
24:21 **A** asked. David answered, "To
24:22 **A** said to David, "Take it,
24:23 All this **A** gave to the king and
24:24 the king said to **A**.

Arba (3)

Jos 14:15 **A** was the greatest man among
15:13 It was the city of **A** (now called
15:13 **A** was the father of Anak.

archangel (2)

1Th 4:16 with the voice of the **a**,
Jud 1:9 When the **a** Michael argued

Archelaus (1)

Mat 2:22 But when he heard that **A** had

archer (1)

Gen 21:20 desert and became a skilled **a**.

archer's (3)

2Sm 22:35 bend an ⌊**a**⌋ bow of bronze.
Psa 18:34 bend an ⌊**a**⌋ bow of bronze.
46:9 He breaks an **a** bow.

archers (15)

Gen 49:23 **A** provoked him, shot at him,
1Sm 31:3 When the **a** got him in their
2Sm 11:24 The **a** on the wall shot down at
1Ch 8:40 sons were soldiers, skilled **a**.
10:3 When the **a** got him in their
2Ch 35:23 Some **a** shot King Josiah.
Job 16:13 and his **a** surrounded me.
Isa 21:17 The remaining number of **a**,
21:17 Kedar's mighty **a**, will be few.
Jer 4:29 at the sound of riders and **a**.
49:35 to break the bows of Elam's **a**,
50:14 all you **a** with bows.
50:29 "Call together the **a**,
51:3 Have the **a** bend their bows.
Amo 2:15 **A** will not stand their ground.

Archi (1)

1Ch 27:33 Hushai, a descendant of **A**,

Archi's (4)

2Sm 15:32 Hushai from **A** family was there
16:16 Hushai from **A** family came
17:5 is descended from **A** family,
17:14 from **A** family is better than

Archippus (2)

Col 4:17 Tell **A** to complete all the work
Phm 1:2 our fellow soldier **A**,

Archites (1)

Jos 16:2 to Ataroth at the border of the **A**.

archives (2)

Ezr 5:17 someone to search the king's **a**
6:1 library where the **a** were stored

Ard (3)

Gen 46:21 Rosh, Muppim, Huppim, and **A**.
Num 26:40 of Bela ⌊through⌋ **A**
26:40 Naaman) were the family of **A**

Ardon (1)

1Ch 2:18 were Jesher, Shobab, and **A**.

area (92)

Gen 1:9 the sky come together in one **a**,
13:3 to the **a** between Bethel and Ai
13:7 were also living in that **a**.)
34:10 move about freely in this **a**,
34:21 and move about freely in the **a**.
34:30 made the people living in the **a**,
38:21 He asked the men of that **a**,
38:22 Even the men of that **a** said,
Exo 25:37 so that they light up ⌊the **a**⌋
Lev 13:2 or an irritated **a** on his skin that
13:3 If the hair in the diseased **a**
13:3 and the diseased **a** looks
13:4 But if the irritated **a** is white
13:6 If the diseased **a** has faded and
13:17 and if the diseased **a** has
13:19 is a white sore or a pink **a**,
13:21 priest examines the affected **a**
13:21 or the affected **a** is not deeper
13:22 If the **a** has spread,
13:23 But if the irritated **a** has not
13:24 into a pink or bright white **a**,
13:25 If the hair on the affected **a** has
13:25 affected **a** looks deeper than
13:26 and the affected **a** is not deeper
13:27 If the **a** has spread,
13:28 If the irritated **a** does not
13:47 if there is a green or red **a**
13:51 he will examine the **a** again.
13:53 sees that the **a** has not spread,
13:54 he must order the **a** to be
13:55 The priest will examine the **a**
13:55 be burned, whether the **a** is
13:56 If the priest sees that the **a** is
13:58 But if the **a** disappears from the
14:37 He will examine the mildew **a**
14:56 a sore, a rash, or an irritated **a**.
Num 1:52 in its own **a** under its own
8:2 they should light up the **a** in
8:3 the lamp stand to light up the **a**
Jos 9:7 "What if you're living in this **a**?
Jdg 19:1 Levite who lived in a remote **a**
19:18 in Judah to a remote **a**
1Ki 15:20 and the entire **a** around
2Ki 4:8 So whenever he was in the **a**,
2Ch 20:29 in that **a** when they heard
Neh 3:22 lived in that **a** made repairs.
8:16 in the open **a** by Water Gate,
8:16 in the open **a** at Ephraim Gate.
11:31 live in the **a** of Geba,
Job 36:16 into an open **a** where you were
Isa 4:5 the night over the whole **a**
6:12 and a large **a** in the middle of
28:25 he put barley in its own **a**
Jer 31:40 and the whole **a** to the Kidron
33:13 in the **a** around Jerusalem,

Eze 41:9 There was an open **a** between
41:11 were entrances into the open **a**.
41:11 The base of the open **a** was 9
41:12 At the far end of the open **a**,
41:13 This included the open **a** with
41:14 including the open **a**,
42:1 rooms opposite both the open **a**
42:3 courtyard was an **a** that was 35
42:10 the open **a** and the building.
42:13 face the open **a** are holy rooms.
42:14 Then they can go into the **a**
42:15 the inner part of the temple **a**,
42:15 all the way around the outer **a**.
43:12 The whole **a** all the way
45:1 Set aside an **a** 43,750 feet long
45:1 The entire **a** will be holy.
45:2 An **a** of 875 feet square will be
45:2 with an open **a** 87 ½ feet
45:3 Measure off an **a** 43,750 feet
45:3 holy place, will be in this **a**.
45:5 An **a** 43,750 feet long and
45:6 "You must designate an **a**
45:6 located alongside the holy **a**.
45:7 land on both sides of the holy **a**
45:7 western boundary of the holy **a**,
45:7 eastern boundary of the holy **a**,
48:10 This holy **a** will belong to the
48:18 of the land borders the holy **a**
48:20 The whole **a** will be 43,750
48:21 and west side of the holy **a**
48:21 eastward from the holy **a**
48:21 and the holy **a** with the holy
Dan 3:1 He set it up in a recessed **a** in
Luk 2:9 glory of the Lord filled the **a**
16:26 a wide **a** separates us.
Jon 8:20 was teaching in the treasury **a**
Act 28:7 had property around the **a**.

areas (7)

Lev 13:38 has white irritated **a** of skin,
13:39 If the irritated **a** on the skin are
14:37 red in sunken **a** that are deeper
2Ch 27:4 and towers in the wooded **a**.
Eze 48:21 Both of these **a** are as long as
48:21 These **a** belong to the prince,
48:29 and these are their **a**,

Areli (2)

Gen 46:16 Shuni, Ezbon, Eri, Arodi, and **A**.
Num 26:17 and the family of **A**.

Areopagus (1)

Act 17:19 city court, the **A**, and asked,

Aretas (1)

2Co 11:32 The governor under King **A** put

Argob (5)

Dtr 3:4 the whole territory of **A**,
3:13 (The whole territory of **A** in
3:14 took the whole territory of **A** as
1Ki 4:13 the territory of **A** in Bashan,
2Ki 15:25 Pekah attacked Pekahiah, **A**,

argue (14)

Job 13:3 and I wish to **a** my case in front
15:3 Should he **a** with words that
23:7 people could **a** with him,
Psa 50:21 I will **a** my point with you and
Ecc 6:10 Mortals cannot **a** with the one
Isa 43:26 Let us **a** our case together.
Jer 12:1 O LORD, even if I would **a** my
Mar 8:11 Jesus and began to **a** with him.
Luk 14:6 They couldn't **a** with him about
Act 6:10 They couldn't **a** with Stephen
11:2 began to **a** with him.
1Co 11:16 If anyone wants to **a** about this
1Ti 6:4 he has an unhealthy desire to **a**
Tit 2:9 masters, not to **a** with them

argued (9)

Gen 26:20 because they had **a** with him.
1Ki 3:22 So they **a** in front of the king.
Mar 9:10 but **a** among themselves what
9:34 On the road they had **a** about
Luk 22:24 They **a** about who should be
Jon 7:12 The crowds **a** about Jesus.
Act 9:29 He talked and **a** with
23:9 who **a** their position forcefully.
Jud 1:9 When the archangel Michael **a**

argues (3)

Job 40:2 Will the person who **a** with
Jer 15:10 I am a man who **a** and quarrels
30:13 No one **a** that you should be

arguing (9)

2Sm 19:9 in all the tribes of Israel were **a**
Job 13:8 favor him ⌊as⌋ if you were **a**
Mic 6:2 He is **a** his case against Israel.
Mar 9:14 scribes were **a** with them.
9:16 are you **a** about with them?"
9:33 "What were you **a** about on the
Rom 3:5 (I'm **a** the way humans would.)
Php 2:14 without complaining or **a**.
Jud 1:9 they were **a** over the body of

argument (10)

Gen 26:20 Isaac named the well Esek [**A**],
Job 13:6 Please listen to my **a**,
19:5 disgrace as an **a** against me,
Pro 17:14 so stop before the **a** gets out of
18:6 By talking, a fool gets into an **a**,
25:9 Present your **a** to your
Mar 12:28 went to Jesus during the **a**
Jon 3:25 of John's disciples had an **a**
Act 6:9 Asia started an **a** with Stephen.
Rom 14:1 but don't get into an **a** over

arguments (16)

Job 23:4 I would have a mouthful of **a**.
Psa 38:14 hear and who can offer no **a**.
Isa 2:4 settle **a** between many people.
41:21 best **a**," says Jacob's king.
59:4 People trust pointless **a** and
Mic 4:3 settle **a** between many nations
1Co 1:17 I didn't use intellectual **a**.
2:4 with persuasive intellectual **a**.
2:13 on intellectual **a** like people do.
2Co 10:4 defenses, that is, their **a**
Gal 5:8 The **a** of the person who is
Col 2:4 you with **a** that merely sound
2Ti 2:23 to do with foolish and stupid **a**.
Tit 3:9 **a** about genealogies,
Heb 6:16 what they say and end all **a**.
2Pe 2:3 they will use good-sounding **a**

arid (1)

Dtr 8:15 desert — a thirsty and **a** land,

Aridai (1)

Est 9:9 Parmashta, Arisai, **A**,

Aridatha (1)

Est 9:8 Poratha, Adalia, **A**,

Arieh (1)

2Ki 15:25 and **A** in the fortress of the

Ariel (6)

Ezr 8:16 Then I sent for Eliezer, **A**,
Isa 29:1 horrible it will be for you **A**,
29:1 it will be for you Ariel, **A**,
29:2 I will torment **A**, and the city
29:2 The city will become like **A**.
29:7 will go to war against **A**.

Arimathea (4)

Mat 27:57 He was from the city of **A** and
Mar 15:43 He was from the city of **A** and
Luk 23:51 was from the Jewish city of **A**,
Jon 19:38 Later Joseph from the city of **A**

Arioch (7)

Gen 14:1 of Shinar, King **A** of Ellasar,
14:9 and King **A** of Ellasar — four
Dan 2:14 While **A**, the captain of the
2:15 He asked **A**, the royal official,
2:15 So **A** explained everything to
2:24 Then Daniel went to **A**,
2:25 **A** immediately took Daniel to

Arisai (1)

Est 9:9 Parmashta, **A**, Aridai,

arise (25)

Num 10:35 would say, "**A**, O LORD!
2Ch 6:41 "Now **a**, and come to your
Psa 3:7 **A**, O LORD! Save me, O my
7:6 **A** in anger, O LORD. Stand up
9:19 **A**, O LORD. Do not let mortals
10:12 **A**, O LORD! Lift your hand,
12:5 I will now **a**," says the LORD.
17:13 **A**, O LORD; confront them!
21:13 **A**, O LORD, in your strength.
35:2 small and large. **A** to help me.
44:26 **A**! Help us! Rescue us because
59:5 **a** to punish all the nations.
68:1 God will **a**. His enemies will be
74:22 **A**, O God! Fight for your own
82:8 **A**, O God! Judge the earth,
94:2 **A**, O Judge of the earth.
132:8 O LORD, **a**, and come to your
Isa 33:10 The LORD says, "Now I will **a**.
60:1 **A**! Shine! Your light has come,
Jer 31:6 will call out this message: '**A**!
Hab 1:3 Quarrels and disputes **a**.
Zec 13:7 "**A**, sword, against my
Mat 18:7 people to lose their faith will **a**.
Luk 17:1 lose their faith are certain to **a**.
Tit 3:14 urgent needs **a** so that they

Aristarchus (5)

Act 19:29 They grabbed Gaius and **A**,
20:4 **A** and Secundus from
27:2 **A**, a Macedonian from the city
Col 4:10 **A**, who is a prisoner like me,
Phm 1:24 and my coworkers Mark, **A**,

Aristobulus (1)

Rom 16:10 who belong to the family of **A**.

ark (197)

Exo 25:10 "Make an **a** of acacia wood 45
25:14 the rings on the sides of the **a**
25:15 must stay in the rings of the **a**.
25:16 Then you will put into the **a** the
25:17 of mercy to cover the **a** out
25:21 After you put into the **a** the
26:33 and put the **a** containing the
26:34 throne of mercy that is on the **a**
30:6 ⌊hangs⌋ over the **a** containing
30:6 throne of mercy that is on the **a**.
30:26 the **a** containing the words of
30:36 and put it in front of ⌊the **a**
31:7 the tent of meeting, the **a**
35:12 the **a** with its poles,
37:1 Bezalel made the **a** out of
37:5 the rings on the sides of the **a**
39:34 the canopy over ⌊the **a**,
39:35 the **a** containing the words of
40:3 Place the **a** containing the
40:3 hang the canopy over the **a**.
40:5 for incense in front of the **a**.
40:20 promise and put them in the **a**.
40:20 He put the poles on the **a** and
40:20 throne of mercy on top of the **a**.
40:21 Then he brought the **a** into the
40:21 it to mark off where the **a** was.
Lev 16:2 of the throne of mercy on the **a**,
Num 3:31 They were in charge of the **a**,
4:5 hangs over the **a** containing
4:5 cover the **a** with the canopy.
7:89 of mercy on the **a** containing
10:33 The **a** of the LORD's promise
10:35 Whenever the **a** started to
14:44 even though the **a** of the
Dtr 10:1 Also make an **a** out of wood.
10:2 you will put them in the **a**."
10:3 I made an **a** out of acacia
10:5 and put the tablets in the **a**
10:8 the tribe of Levi to carry the **a**
31:9 priests who carried the **a**
31:25 to the Levites who carried the **a**
31:26 and put it next to the **a** of the
Jos 3:3 "As soon as you see the **a** of
3:6 "Take the **a** of the promise,

Jos 3:8 the priests who carry the **a**
3:11 Watch the **a** of the promise of
3:13 The priests who carry the **a** of
3:14 The priests who carried the **a**
3:15 who were carrying the **a** came
3:17 The priests who carried the **a**
4:5 the Jordan River in front of the **a**
4:7 was cut off in front of the **a**
4:7 When the **a** crossed the Jordan,
4:9 the priests who carried the **a**
4:10 The priests who carried the **a**
4:11 the priests with the LORD's **a**
4:16 the priests who carry the **a**
4:18 The priests who carried the **a**
6:4 rams' horns ahead of the **a**.
6:6 "Pick up the **a** of the promise,
6:6 horns ahead of the LORD's **a**."
6:7 march ahead of the LORD's **a**."
6:8 The **a** of the LORD's promise
6:9 The rear guard followed the **a**
6:11 So the LORD's **a** went around
6:12 priests carried the LORD's **a**.
6:13 followed the LORD's **a** while
7:6 ground in front of the LORD's **a**.
8:33 on opposite sides of the **a**.
8:33 priests who carried the **a**
Jdg 20:27 In those days the **a** of God's
1Sm 3:3 of the LORD where the **a**
4:3 Let's get the **a** of the LORD's
4:4 men who brought back the **a**
4:4 came along with God's **a**.
4:5 When the LORD's **a** came into
4:6 the LORD's **a** had come into
4:11 The **a** of God was captured.
4:13 worried about the **a** of God.
4:17 and the **a** of God has been
4:18 mentioned the **a** of God,
4:19 she heard the news that the **a**
4:21 because the **a** of God had been
4:22 glory is gone because the **a**
5:1 had captured the **a** of God,
5:3 ground in front of the LORD's **a**.
5:4 ground in front of the LORD's **a**.
5:7 "The **a** of the God of Israel
5:8 "What should we do with the **a**
5:8 "The **a** of the God of Israel
5:8 So the people took the **a** of the
5:10 the people of Gath sent the **a**
5:10 But when the **a** of God came to
5:10 "They brought the **a** of the God
5:11 "Send the **a** of the God of Israel
6:1 The **a** of the LORD had been in
6:2 "What should we do with the **a**
6:3 "If you're returning the **a** of the
6:8 Take the **a** of the LORD,
6:8 offering in a box beside the **a**.
6:11 They put the **a** of the LORD
6:13 they looked up and saw the **a**,
6:15 down ⌊from the cart⌋ the **a**
6:18 rock on which they put the **a**
6:19 they looked inside the **a**
6:21 have brought back the **a**
7:1 came to take the LORD's **a**
7:1 of guarding the LORD's **a**.
7:2 A long time passed after the **a**
2Sm 6:2 bring God's **a** ⌊to Jerusalem⌋.
6:2 (The **a** is called by the name of
6:3 David and his men put God's **a**
6:4 Ahio walking ahead of the **a**.
6:6 So Uzzah reached out for the **a**
6:7 He died beside the **a** of God.
6:9 "How can the **a** of the LORD
6:10 So David wouldn't bring the **a**
6:11 The **a** of the LORD stayed at
6:12 owns because of the **a** of God."
6:12 David joyfully went to get the **a**
6:13 When those who carried the **a**
6:15 nation of Israel brought the **a**
6:16 When the **a** of the LORD came
6:17 The men carrying the **a** set it in
7:2 while the **a** of God remains in
11:11 Uriah answered David, "The **a**
15:24 with him were carrying the **a**
15:24 They set down the **a** of God
15:25 "Take God's **a** back to the city.
15:29 Zadok and Abiathar took the **a**
1Ki 2:26 time because you carried the **a**
3:15 and stood in front of the **a**
6:19 the temple in order to put the **a**
8:1 in Jerusalem to take the **a**
8:3 priests picked up the LORD's **a**.
8:4 They brought the **a**,
8:5 sacrifices in front of the **a**.
8:6 The priests brought the **a** of the
8:7 the place where the **a** ⌊rested⌋,
8:7 above the **a** and its poles.
8:9 There was nothing in the **a**
8:21 I've made a place there for the **a**
1Ch 6:31 after the **a** was placed there
13:3 we'll bring back our God's **a**,
13:5 God's **a** from Kiriath Jearim.
13:6 bring God's **a** ⌊to Jerusalem⌋.
13:6 ⌊on the **a**⌋ where his name
13:7 David and his men put God's **a**
13:9 reached out to grab the **a**.
13:10 killed him for reaching for the **a**.
13:12 "How can I bring God's **a** to my
13:13 So he didn't bring God's **a** to
13:14 God's **a** stayed at the home of
15:1 he prepared a place for God's **a**
15:2 only the Levites carry God's **a**
15:2 had chosen them to carry his **a**
15:3 to bring the LORD's **a**
15:12 Then bring the **a** of the LORD
15:14 holy in order to move the **a**
15:15 The Levites carried God's **a** on
15:23 were gatekeepers for the **a**.
15:24 trumpets in front of God's **a**.
15:24 were doorkeepers for the **a**.
15:25 joyfully went to get the **a**
15:26 the Levites who carried the **a**
15:27 the Levites who carried the **a**,
15:28 All Israel brought the **a** of the
15:29 When the **a** of the LORD's
16:1 The men carrying the **a** set it
16:4 LORD's **a** by offering prayers,
16:6 front of the **a** of God's promise.
16:37 continually in front of the **a**
17:1 while the **a** of the LORD's
22:19 God so that you can bring the **a**
28:2 building the temple where the **a**
28:18 wings spread to cover the **a**
2Ch 1:4 God's **a** from Kiriath Jearim
5:2 to Jerusalem to take the **a**
5:4 the Levites picked up the **a**.
5:5 They brought the **a**,
5:6 sacrifices in front of the **a**.
5:7 The priests brought the **a** of the
5:8 where the **a** ⌊rested⌋ so that
5:8 above the **a** and its poles.
5:10 There was nothing in the **a**
6:11 I've put the **a** which contains
6:41 LORD God — you and the **a** of
8:11 the LORD's **a** has come are
35:3 "Put the holy **a** in the temple
Psa 132:6 we have heard about the **a** ⌊of
132:8 place with the **a** of your power.
Jer 3:16 will no longer talk about the **a**
Heb 9:4 gold incense burner and the **a**
9:4 The **a** was completely covered
9:4 In the **a** were the gold jar filled
9:5 Above the **a** were the angels of
Rev 11:19 and the **a** of his promise was

Arkites (2)

Gen 10:17 the Hivites, the **A**, the Sinites,
1Ch 1:15 the Hivites, the **A**, the Sinites,

arm (50)

Exo 6:6 rescue you with my powerful **a**
15:16 Because of the power of your **a**,
Num 31:50 each of us found — **a** bands,
Dtr 4:34 his mighty hand and powerful **a**
5:15 his mighty hand and powerful **a**
7:19 his mighty hand and powerful **a**
9:29 great strength and powerful **a**
11:2 mighty hand and powerful **a**.
26:8 his mighty hand and powerful **a**
33:20 can tear off an **a** or a head.
2Sm 1:10 and the band that was on his **a**
24:16 Messenger stretched out his **a**
1Ki 8:41 mighty hand, and powerful **a**.
1Ki 13:4 But the **a** that he used to point
13:6 so that I can use my **a** again."
13:6 was able to use his **a** again,
2Ki 5:18 to worship, leans on my **a**,
7:2 The servant on whose **a** the
7:17 the servant on whose **a**
17:36 his great power and a mighty **a**
2Ch 6:32 mighty hand, and powerful **a**.
Job 26:2 saved the **a** that isn't strong.
31:22 and let my **a** be broken at the
38:15 and an **a** raised ⌊in victory⌋ is
Psa 10:15 Break the **a** of the wicked and
44:3 It was your right hand, your **a**,
79:11 With your powerful **a** rescue
89:10 With your strong **a** you
89:13 Your **a** is mighty. Your hand is
89:21 My **a** will also give him
98:1 His right hand and his holy **a**
136:12 mighty hand and a powerful **a**
Sos 8:5 with her **a** around her beloved?
Isa 9:20 eats the flesh from his own **a**.
50:11 But all of you light fires and **a**
62:8 hand and with his mighty **a**,
63:12 one who sent his powerful **a**
Jer 21:5 hand and my mighty **a**.
27:5 strength and my powerful **a**
32:17 great strength and powerful **a**.
32:21 mighty hand and a powerful **a**,
48:25 and its **a** is broken,"
Eze 20:33 mighty hand and a powerful **a**,
20:34 mighty hand and powerful **a**.
30:21 I have broken the **a** of Pharaoh,
30:21 His **a** isn't bandaged,
Zec 11:17 A sword will strike his **a** and
11:17 His **a** will be completely
Act 13:17 He used his powerful **a** to bring
23:19 took the young man by the **a**,

Armageddon (1)

Rev 16:16 which is called **A** in Hebrew.

armed (35)

Gen 14:14 he **a** his 318 trained men,
Num 32:20 have all your **a** men get ready
32:32 We will enter Canaan as **a**
Dtr 1:41 Each of you **a** yourself for war,
Jos 4:13 About 40,000 **a** men crossed
6:7 Let the **a** men march ahead of
6:9 The **a** men went ahead of the
6:13 The **a** men were ahead of them,
Jdg 18:11 Zorah and Eshtaol **a** for war.
18:16 The 600 **a** men from Dan stood
18:17 to the city with the 600 **a** men.
20:15 That day 26,000 men **a** with
20:17 soldiers **a** with swords.
20:25 Israel who were **a** with swords.
20:35 who were **a** with swords.
20:46 men from Benjamin who were **a**
1Sm 2:4 stumble are **a** with strength.
2Sm 22:40 You **a** me with strength for
22:46 they are **a** in their fortifications.
1Ch 12:2 They were **a** with bows and
2Ch 14:8 300,000 Judeans who were **a**
14:8 Benjaminites who were **a**
17:17 Eliada (with 200,000 **a** men
17:18 an army of 180,000 **a** men).
Ezr 8:22 to ask the king for an **a** escort
Neh 4:13 people were **a** with swords,
Est 8:11 and to destroy every **a** force of
Psa 18:39 You **a** me with strength for
93:1 he has **a** himself with power.
118:10 ⌊but **a**⌋ with the name of the
118:11 ⌊but **a**⌋ with the name of the
118:12 ⌊So **a**⌋ with the name of the
Isa 15:4 Moab's **a** men cry out.
Eze 38:4 Your soldiers will be fully **a**.
Luk 11:21 "When a strong man, fully **a**,

armful (1)

Isa 17:5 bundles of grain by the **a**.

armies (333)

Num 2:3 the **a** led by Judah will camp
2:10 "On the south side the **a** led by
2:18 "On the west side the **a** led by
2:25 "On the north side the **a** led by

Num 10:14 With their flag in front, the **a** led
10:18 With their flag in front, the **a** led
10:22 With their flag in front, the **a** led
10:25 the **a** led by Dan's descendants
10:28 Israelite **a** broke camp when
Dtr 20:1 and **a** larger than yours.
Jos 10:5 and Eglon combined their **a**.
11:4 They came out with all their **a**.
11:7 and attacked the Canaanite **a**.
Jdg 6:33 and Kedem combined their **a**,
1Sm 1:3 to the LORD of **A** at Shiloh.
1:11 made this vow, "LORD of **A**,
4:4 of the LORD of **A** — who is
15:2 is what the LORD of **A** says:
17:1 assembled their **a** for war.
17:45 in the name of the LORD of **A**,
2Sm 5:10 LORD God of **A** was with him.
6:2 by the name of the LORD of **A**,
6:18 in the name of the LORD of **A**.
7:8 is what the LORD of **A** says:
7:26 'The LORD of **A** is God over
7:27 You, LORD of **A**, God of Israel,
1Ki 15:20 He sent his generals and their **a**
18:15 as the LORD of **A** whom I
19:10 He answered, "LORD God of **A**,
19:14 He answered, "LORD God of **A**,
2Ki 3:14 as the LORD of **A** whom I
19:15 "LORD of **A**, God of Israel,
19:33 declares the LORD of **A**.
1Ch 11:9 the LORD of **A** was with him.
17:7 is what the LORD of **A** says:
17:24 ⌊people⌋ say, 'The LORD of **A**,
2Ch 14:10 and the two **a** set up their battle
16:4 He sent his generals and their **a**
Neh 9:6 highest heaven, with all its **a**.
9:6 and the **a** of heaven worship
Job 10:17 bringing new **a** against me.
Psa 24:10 The LORD of **A** is the king of
44:9 not even go along with our **a**.
46:7 The LORD of **A** is with us.
46:11 The LORD of **A** is with us.
48:8 in the city of the LORD of **A**,
59:5 O LORD God of **A**,
60:10 refused to accompany our **a**?
68:12 "The kings of the **a** flee;
69:6 O Almighty LORD of **A**.
80:4 O LORD God, commander of **a**,
80:7 O God, commander of **a**,
80:14 O God, commander of **a**,
80:19 O LORD God, commander of **a**,
84:1 place is lovely, O LORD of **A**!
84:3 near your altars, O LORD of **A**,
84:8 O LORD God, commander of **a**,
84:12 O LORD of **A**, blessed is the
89:8 O LORD God of **A**,
103:21 Praise the LORD, all his **a**,
108:11 refused to accompany our **a**?
Isa 1:9 If the LORD of **A** hadn't left us
1:24 why the Lord, the LORD of **A**,
2:12 The LORD of **A** will have his
3:1 now, the Lord, the LORD of **A**,
3:15 The Almighty LORD of **A** asks,
5:7 The vineyard of the LORD of **A**
5:9 ears I heard the LORD of **A** say,
5:16 The LORD of **A** will be honored
5:24 the teachings of the LORD of **A**
6:3 holy is the LORD of **A**!
6:5 seen the king, the LORD of **A**!"
8:13 that the LORD of **A** is holy.
8:18 in Israel from the LORD of **A**,
9:7 The LORD of **A** is determined
9:13 they sought the LORD of **A**.
9:19 by the fury of the LORD of **A**,
10:16 Almighty LORD of **A** will send
10:23 The Almighty LORD of **A** will
10:24 The Almighty LORD of **A** says:
10:26 Then the LORD of **A** will raise
10:33 The Almighty LORD of **A** will
13:4 The LORD of **A** is assembling
13:13 when the LORD of **A** is angry.
14:22 declares the LORD of **A**.
14:23 declares the LORD of **A**.
14:24 The LORD of **A** has taken an
14:27 The LORD of **A** has planned it.
17:3 declares the LORD of **A**.
18:7 brought to the LORD of **A** from
Isa 18:7 the name of the LORD of **A** is.
19:4 the Almighty LORD of **A**.
19:12 LORD of **A** is planning against
19:16 the LORD of **A** will shake his
19:17 LORD of **A** is planning against
19:18 allegiance to the LORD of **A**.
19:20 a witness that the LORD of **A** is
19:25 The LORD of **A** will bless
21:10 I heard from the LORD of **A**,
22:5 The Almighty LORD of **A** has
22:12 Almighty LORD of **A** will call
22:14 The LORD of **A** revealed this to
22:14 says the Almighty LORD of **A**.
22:15 the Almighty LORD of **A** says:
22:25 The LORD of **A** declares,
23:9 The LORD of **A** planned this in
24:21 LORD will punish heaven's **a**
24:23 because the LORD of **A** will
25:6 the LORD of **A** will prepare
28:5 the LORD of **A** will be like a
28:22 of **A** has finally determined
28:29 has come from the LORD of **A**.
29:6 The LORD of **A** will punish you
29:7 The **a** from all the nations will
29:8 will happen to the **a** from all
31:4 So the LORD of **A** will come to
31:5 The LORD of **A** will defend
34:2 He is furious with all their **a**.
37:16 "LORD of **A**, God of Israel,
37:32 The LORD of **A** is determined
37:34 declares the LORD of **A**.
39:5 the word of the LORD of **A**!
44:6 He is the LORD of **A**.
45:13 says the LORD of **A**.
47:4 His name is the LORD of **A**.
48:2 His name is the LORD of **A**.
51:15 My name is the LORD of **A**.
54:5 His name is the LORD of **A**.
Jer 2:19 the Almighty LORD of **A**.
5:14 what the LORD God of **A** says:
6:6 is what the LORD of **A** says:
6:9 is what the LORD of **A** says:
7:3 This is what the LORD of **A**,
7:21 "This is what the LORD of **A**,
8:3 declares the LORD of **A**.
9:7 is what the LORD of **A** says:
9:15 This is what the LORD of **A**,
9:16 I will send **a** after them until
9:17 is what the LORD of **A** says:
10:16 His name is the LORD of **A**.
11:17 The LORD of **A** planted you.
11:20 O LORD of **A**, you judge fairly
11:22 is what the LORD of **A** says:
15:16 O LORD God of **A**.
16:9 This is what the LORD of **A**,
19:3 This is what the LORD of **A**,
19:11 is what the LORD of **A** says:
19:15 "This is what the LORD of **A**,
20:12 But the LORD of **A** examines
23:15 This is what the LORD of **A**
23:16 is what the LORD of **A** says:
23:36 God, the LORD of **A**, our God.
25:8 is what the LORD of **A** says:
25:27 'This is what the LORD of **A**,
25:28 is what the LORD of **A** says:
25:29 declares the LORD of **A**.'
25:32 is what the LORD of **A** says:
26:18 is what the LORD of **A** says:
27:4 "This is what the LORD of **A**,
27:18 they should beg the LORD of **A**
27:21 This is what the LORD of **A**,
28:2 "This is what the LORD of **A**,
28:14 This is what the LORD of **A**,
29:4 This is what the LORD of **A**,
29:8 This is what the LORD of **A**,
29:17 The LORD of **A** says:
29:21 This is what the LORD of **A**,
29:25 'This is what the LORD of **A**,
30:8 declares the LORD of **A**,
31:23 This is what the LORD of **A**,
31:35 His name is the LORD of **A**.
32:14 'This is what the LORD of **A**,
32:15 This is what the LORD of **A**,
32:18 Your name is the LORD of **A**.
33:11 'Give thanks to the LORD of **A**
33:12 is what the LORD of **A** says:
Jer 35:11 and Aramean **a**.' That's
35:13 "This is what the LORD of **A**,
35:17 is what the LORD God of **A**,
35:18 "This is what the LORD of **A**,
35:19 So this is what the LORD of **A**,
38:17 is what the LORD God of **A**,
39:16 'This is what the LORD of **A**,
42:15 This is what the LORD of **A**,
42:18 "This is what the LORD of **A**,
43:10 'This is what the LORD of **A**,
44:2 This is what the LORD of **A**,
44:7 is what the LORD God of **A**,
44:11 This is what the LORD of **A**,
44:25 This is what the LORD of **A**,
46:10 to the Almighty LORD of **A**.
46:10 The Almighty LORD of **A** will
46:18 whose name is the LORD of **A**,
46:25 The LORD of **A**, the God of
48:1 This is what the LORD of **A**,
48:15 whose name is the LORD of **A**.
49:5 the Almighty LORD of **A**.
49:7 This is what the LORD of **A**
49:26 declares the LORD of **A**.
49:35 is what the LORD of **A** says:
49:37 I'll send **a** after them until I put
50:18 "This is what the LORD of **A**,
50:25 the Almighty LORD of **A** has
50:31 the Almighty LORD of **A**.
50:33 is what the LORD of **A** says:
50:34 His name is the LORD of **A**.
51:5 by their God, the LORD of **A**,
51:14 The LORD of **A** has taken an
51:14 fill you with many enemy **a**.
51:19 His name is the LORD of **A**.
51:33 This is what the LORD of **A**,
51:57 whose name is the LORD of **A**.
51:58 is what the LORD of **A** says:
Eze 38:6 There will be many **a** with you.
38:9 Your troops and the many **a**
38:15 in the far north and many **a** will
38:22 and on the many **a** with him.
39:4 your troops and the **a** that are
Hos 10:10 **A** will gather to attack them.
12:5 The LORD is the God of **A**.
Amo 3:13 Almighty LORD, the God of **A**.
4:13 name is the LORD God of **A**.
5:14 Then the LORD God of **A** will
5:15 Maybe the LORD God of **A** will
5:16 the Almighty God of **A**,
5:27 whose name is the God of **A**.
6:8 The LORD God of **A** declares:
6:14 the LORD God of the **A**
9:5 The Almighty LORD of **A**
Mic 4:4 The LORD of **A** has spoken.
Nah 2:13 declares the LORD of **A**.
3:5 declares the LORD of **A**.
Hab 2:13 Isn't it from the LORD of **A** that
Zep 2:9 declares the LORD of **A**,
2:10 who belong to the LORD of **A**
Hag 1:2 is what the LORD of **A** says:
1:5 is what the LORD of **A** says:
1:7 is what the LORD of **A** says:
1:9 declares the LORD of **A**.
1:14 on the house of the LORD of **A**,
2:4 declares the LORD of **A**.
2:6 is what the LORD of **A** says:
2:7 says the LORD of **A**.
2:8 declares the LORD of **A**.
2:9 declares the LORD of **A**.
2:9 declares the LORD of **A**."
2:11 is what the LORD of **A** says:
2:23 declares the LORD of **A**,
2:23 declares the LORD of **A**."'
Zec 1:3 is what the LORD of **A** says:
1:3 declares the LORD of **A**,
1:3 says the LORD of **A**.'
1:4 is what the LORD of **A** says:
1:6 'The LORD of **A** has done to us
1:12 of the LORD said, "LORD of **A**,
1:14 is what the LORD of **A** says:
1:16 is what the LORD of **A** says:
1:16 declares the LORD of **A**.
1:17 is what the LORD of **A** says:
2:8 is what the LORD of **A** says:
2:9 the LORD of **A** has sent me.
2:11 that the LORD of **A** has sent me

Zec 3:7 is what the LORD of **A** says:
3:9 declares the LORD of **A**.
3:10 declares the LORD of **A**,
4:6 says the LORD of **A**.
4:9 that the LORD of **A** has sent me
5:4 declares the LORD of **A**,
6:12 is what the LORD of **A** says:
6:15 the LORD of **A** has sent me
7:3 of the LORD of **A** as well as
7:4 Then the LORD of **A** spoke his
7:9 is what the LORD of **A** says:
7:12 the words that the LORD of **A**
7:12 LORD of **A** became very angry.
7:13 says the LORD of **A**.
8:1 LORD of **A** spoke his word.
8:2 is what the LORD of **A** says:
8:3 The mountain of the LORD of **A**
8:4 is what the LORD of **A** says:
8:6 is what the LORD of **A** says:
8:6 declares the LORD of **A**.
8:7 is what the LORD of **A** says:
8:9 is what the LORD of **A** says:
8:9 of the LORD of **A** was laid.
8:11 declares the LORD of **A**.
8:14 is what the LORD of **A** says:
8:14 declares the LORD of **A**,
8:18 The LORD of **A** spoke his word
8:19 is what the LORD of **A** says:
8:20 is what the LORD of **A** says:
8:21 and to seek the LORD of **A**.
8:22 come to seek the LORD of **A**
8:23 is what the LORD of **A** says:
9:15 The LORD of **A** will defend
10:3 The LORD of **A** takes care of
12:5 because of the LORD of **A**,
13:2 declares the LORD of **A**,
13:7 declares the LORD of **A**.
14:16 the king, the LORD of **A**,
14:17 the king, the LORD of **A**,
14:21 will be holy to the LORD of **A**.
14:21 in the house of the LORD of **A**.
Mal 1:4 is what the LORD of **A** says:
1:6 is what the LORD of **A** says:
1:8 asks the LORD of **A**.
1:9 asks the LORD of **A**.
1:10 says the LORD of **A**,
1:11 says the LORD of **A**.
1:13 says the LORD of **A**.
1:14 says the LORD of **A**.
2:2 says the LORD of **A**,
2:4 says the LORD of **A**.
2:7 messenger for the LORD of **A**,
2:8 says the LORD of **A**.
2:12 offerings to the LORD of **A**.
2:16 says the LORD of **A**.
3:1 says the LORD of **A**.
3:5 says the LORD of **A**.
3:7 says the LORD of **A**.
3:10 says the LORD of **A**.
3:11 says the LORD of **A**.
3:12 says the LORD of **A**.
3:17 says the LORD of **A**.
4:1 says the LORD of **A**.
4:3 says the LORD of **A**.
Luk 19:43 come when enemy **a** will build
21:20 "When you see **a** camped
Rom 9:29 "If the Lord of **A** hadn't left us
Heb 11:34 in battle and defeated other **a**.
Jas 5:4 The Lord of **A** has heard the
Rev 19:14 The **a** of heaven, wearing pure,
19:19 and their **a** gathered to wage

Armoni (1)

2Sm 21:8 king took **A** and Mephibosheth,

armor (17)

1Sm 17:5 and he wore a bronze coat of **a**
17:38 head and dressed him in **a**.
17:54 he kept Goliath's **a** in his tent.
31:9 his head and stripped off his **a**.
31:10 They put his **a** in the temple of
1Ki 22:34 of Israel between his scale **a**
1Ch 10:9 and took his head and his **a**.
10:10 They put his **a** in the temple of
2Ch 18:33 of Israel between his scale **a**
26:14 **a**, bows, and stones for slings.
Neh 4:16 other half were wearing body **a**
Psa 91:4 His truth is your shield and **a**.
Isa 59:17 righteousness like a coat of **a**
Jer 46:4 your spears. Put on your **a**.
51:3 Have them put on their **a**.
Eph 6:11 Put on all the **a** that God
6:13 up all the **a** that God supplies.

armorbearer (21)

Jdg 9:54 He quickly called his **a**.
9:54 killed Abimelech.'" His **a** did as
1Sm 14:1 son Jonathan said to his **a**,
14:6 Jonathan said to his **a**,
14:7 His **a** answered him,
14:12 said to Jonathan and his **a**.
14:12 Jonathan told his **a**,
14:13 and his **a** followed him.
14:13 His **a**, who was behind him,
14:14 and his **a** killed about twenty
14:17 and his **a** were not there.
16:21 much and made David his **a**.
31:4 Saul told his **a**, "Draw your
31:4 But his **a** refused because he
31:5 When the **a** saw that Saul was
31:6 So Saul, his three sons, his **a**,
2Sm 23:37 **a** for Zeruiah's son Joab,
1Ch 10:4 Saul told his **a**, "Draw your
10:4 But his **a** refused because he
10:5 When the **a** saw that Saul was
11:39 **a** for Zeruiah's son Joab,

armorbearers (1)

2Sm 18:15 Joab's **a** surrounded Absalom,

armory (4)

2Ki 20:13 fine olive oil, his entire **a**,
Neh 3:19 ascent to the **A** at the Angle.
Isa 39:2 fine olive oil, his entire **a**,
Jer 50:25 The LORD will open his **a** and

armrests (4)

1Ki 10:19 There were **a** on both sides of
10:19 Two lions stood beside the **a**.
2Ch 9:18 There were **a** on both sides of
9:18 Two lions stood beside the **a**.

arms (48)

Gen 33:4 threw his **a** around him,
45:14 He threw his **a** around his
46:29 he threw his **a** around him and
49:24 and his **a** remained limber
Num 11:12 me to carry them in my **a** — as
Dtr 33:27 his everlasting **a** support you.
Jdg 15:14 The ropes on his **a** became
16:12 ropes off his **a** as though they
2Sm 4:4 and he fell ⌊from her **a**⌋ and
12:3 She rested in his **a** and was
22:33 God **a** me with strength.
22:35 for battle so that my **a** can bend
1Ki 1:2 She can lie in your **a** and keep
3:20 She held him in her **a**.
3:20 she laid her dead son in my **a**.
17:19 Elijah took him from her **a**,
2Ki 3:21 So all men old enough to bear **a**
4:16 will hold a baby boy in your **a**."
Job 22:9 and the **a** of orphans are
Psa 18:32 God **a** me with strength and
18:34 for battle so that my **a** can bend
37:17 The **a** of wicked people will be
129:7 of those who harvest or the **a**
131:2 is content in its mother's **a**.
Isa 40:11 He gathers the lambs in his **a**.
40:11 He carries them in his **a**.
44:12 them with their strong **a**.
49:22 will bring your sons in their **a**
60:4 daughters are carried in their **a**.
66:12 and be carried in Jerusalem's **a**
Jer 38:12 and torn clothes under your **a**
Lam 2:12 away in their mothers' **a**.
Eze 13:20 I will tear them from your **a** and
30:22 I will break both his **a**,
30:24 I will make the **a** of the king of
30:24 but I will break Pharaoh's **a**.
30:25 I will strengthen the **a** of the
30:25 but Pharaoh's **a** will fall.
Dan 2:32 Its chest and **a** were made of
Dan 10:6 His **a** and legs looked like
Mic 7:5 a woman is lying in your **a**.
Mar 9:36 He put his **a** around the child
10:16 Jesus put his **a** around the
Luk 2:28 Simeon took the child in his **a**
15:20 put his **a** around him,
Act 20:10 took him into his **a**,
20:37 as they put their **a** around Paul
Heb 12:12 your tired **a** and weak knees.

army (309)

Gen 21:22 the commander of his **a**,
21:32 the commander of his **a**,
26:26 the commander of his **a**,
Exo 14:4 I do to Pharaoh and his entire **a**,
14:6 chariot and took his **a** with him.
14:9 Pharaoh's **a**, including all his
14:17 his entire **a**, his chariots,
14:28 and covered Pharaoh's entire **a**,
15:4 Pharaoh's chariots and **a** into
17:13 the Amalekite **a** in battle.
Num 2:4 of men in his **a** is 74,600.
2:6 of men in his **a** is 54,400.
2:8 of men in his **a** is 57,400.
2:11 of men in his **a** is 46,500.
2:13 of men in his **a** is 59,300.
2:15 of men in his **a** is 45,650.
2:19 of men in his **a** is 40,500.
2:21 of men in his **a** is 32,200.
2:23 of men in his **a** is 35,400.
2:26 of men in his **a** is 62,700.
2:28 of men in his **a** is 41,500.
2:30 of men in his **a** is 53,400.
10:15 commanded the **a** of Issachar.
10:16 commanded the **a** of Zebulun.
10:19 commanded the **a** of Simeon.
10:20 commanded the **a** of Gad.
10:23 the **a** of Manasseh.
10:24 commanded the **a** of Benjamin.
10:26 commanded the **a** of Asher.
10:27 commanded the **a** of Naphtali.
31:14 angry with the officers of the **a**,
Dtr 11:4 what he did to the Egyptian **a**,
17:3 or the whole **a** of heaven.
Jos 5:14 commander of the LORD's **a**."
5:15 of the LORD's **a** said
8:10 leaders of Israel led the **a** to Ai.
10:21 Then the whole **a** returned
Jdg 4:2 of King Jabin's **a** was Sisera,
4:7 (the commander of Jabin's **a**),
4:15 and his whole **a** into a panic in
4:16 pursued the chariots and the **a**
4:16 So Sisera's whole **a** was killed
8:6 "We shouldn't give your **a** food."
8:10 were in Karkor with an **a**
8:10 was left of Kedem's entire **a**.
8:11 the unsuspecting Midianite **a**.
8:12 and the whole Midianite **a**
9:29 yourself a big **a** and come out.'"
11:29 in Gilead ⌊to gather an **a**⌋.
1Sm 11:11 next day Saul arranged the **a**
12:9 commander of the **a** of Hazor,
13:6 the **a** was hard-pressed,
14:15 There was panic among the **a**
14:28 the **a** was exhausted.
14:50 commander of his **a** was Abner,
14:52 Saul would enlist him in the **a**.
15:9 Saul and the **a** spared Agag
15:9 The **a** refused to claim them for
15:9 and weak the **a** did claim
15:15 Saul answered, "The **a** brought
15:21 The **a** took some of their
17:2 So Saul and the **a** of Israel
17:13 oldest sons joined Saul's **a**
17:14 three oldest joined Saul's **a**.
17:20 He went to the camp as the **a**
17:26 that he should challenge the **a**
17:36 he has challenged the **a**
17:45 the God of the **a** of Israel,
17:46 dead bodies of the Philistine **a**
17:55 the commander of the **a**,
23:3 against the Philistine **a**?"
26:5 the commander of the **a**,
28:1 Philistines had gathered their **a**
28:4 the whole Israelite **a**,
28:5 Saul looked at the Philistine **a**,

1Sm 28:19 LORD will hand Israel's a over
29:1 their whole a at Aphek,
2Sm 1:4 "The a fled from the battle,
1:12 son Jonathan, the LORD's a,
2:8 commander of Saul's a,
3:23 came back with the whole a,
5:24 you to defeat the Philistine a."
8:9 defeated Hadadezer's whole a,
8:16 Joab was in charge of the a.
10:6 ⌊the a of⌋ the king of Maacah
10:16 commander of Hadadezer's a,
10:17 he assembled Israel's a,
11:1 and Israel's a ⌊to war⌋.
11:11 "The ark and ⌊the a of⌋ Israel
17:25 place as commander of the a.
18:7 David's men defeated Israel's a,
19:13 as the commander of the a.'"
20:15 Joab's a came and attacked
20:23 in charge of Israel's whole a.
23:10 The a returned to Eleazar,
23:13 the Philistine a was camping
24:2 the commander of the a who
24:4 and the commanders of the a.
24:9 men who could serve in the a,
1Ki 1:19 of the a ⌊to his feast⌋.
2:5 of Israel's a—Abner,
2:32 the commander of Israel's a)
2:32 the commander of Judah's a).
2:35 Joab as commander of the a.
4:4 was commander of the a.
10:26 Solomon built up ⌊his a⌋ with
11:15 the commander of the a,
11:21 the commander of the a,
16:15 while the a was camped near
16:16 When the a heard that Zimri
16:16 the commander of the a,
16:21 Then the a of Israel was
16:21 Half of the a followed Tibni,
20:1 gathered together his whole a.
20:13 Have you seen this large a?
20:22 and said, "Reinforce your a.
20:25 Recruit an a with as many
20:26 organized the Aramean a
20:28 hand over their entire a to you.
22:19 and the entire a of heaven was
22:36 a cry went through the a,
2Ki 1:9 The king sent an a officer with
3:6 to prepare Israel's a for war.
3:9 water for the a and the animals.
4:13 the commander of the a
5:1 of the Aramean king's a,
6:24 Aram assembled his whole a.
7:6 Aramean a hear what sounded
7:6 chariots, horses, and a large a.
7:14 them to follow the Aramean a
10:32 a throughout Israel's territory
11:15 who were in charge of the a,
13:7 Jehoahaz had no a left except
14:12 Israel defeated the a of Judah,
17:16 to the entire a of heaven.
18:17 with a large a from Lachish
21:3 served the entire a of heaven.
21:5 altars for the entire a of heaven.
23:4 and the entire a of heaven.
23:5 and the entire a of heaven.
25:1 Jerusalem with his entire a.
25:5 The Babylonian a pursued
25:5 His entire a had deserted him.
25:10 The entire Babylonian a that
25:19 he also took an a commander,
25:23 When all the a commanders
25:26 and the a commanders left
1Ch 10:7 saw that ⌊their a⌋ had fled
11:15 the cave of Adullam when the a
12:14 of Gad were a officers.
12:19 had deserted ⌊Saul's a⌋
12:21 commanders in the a.
12:22 until he had an a as large as
12:22 an army as large as God's a.
14:15 you to defeat the Philistine a."
14:16 the Philistine a from Gibeon
18:9 David had defeated the whole a
18:15 Joab was in charge of the a.
19:7 the king of Maacah with his a.
19:16 commander of Hadadezer's a,
19:17 he assembled Israel's a,
1Ch 20:1 Joab led the a ⌊to war⌋.
21:5 men who could serve in the a,
21:5 who could serve in the a.
25:1 David and the a commanders
26:26 of the a had donated.
27:5 The third commander of the a
27:34 the commander of the royal a.
28:1 the leaders of the a units that
2Ch 1:14 Solomon built up ⌊his a⌋ with
11:11 strengthened them and put a
12:3 and an a of countless Libyans,
13:3 prepared for battle with an a
13:12 their trumpets to call ⌊the a⌋
13:13 So Jeroboam's a was in front of
13:16 Israelites fled from Judah's ⌊a⌋,
14:8 Asa had an a of 300,000
14:11 can fight against a large ⌊a⌋.
14:12 LORD attacked the Sudanese a
14:12 The Sudanese a fled.
14:13 As a result, the Sudanese a
14:13 in front of the LORD and his a.
14:13 The LORD's a captured a lot of
14:14 The a looted all the cities
16:7 the a of the king of Aram has
16:8 and Libyans a large a
17:13 in the cities of Judah and an a
17:18 Jehozabad (with him was an a
18:18 and the entire a of heaven was
23:14 were in charge of the a out ⌊of
24:23 the Aramean a attacked Joash.
24:24 The Aramean a had come with
24:24 handed Joash's large a over
25:5 of the best men for the a,
25:7 Israel's a must not go with you,
25:22 Israel defeated the a of Judah,
26:11 Uzziah had an a of
26:13 Under them was an a of
26:14 For the entire a Uzziah
28:9 He went to meet the a coming
28:12 those coming home from the a.
28:13 They said to the a,
28:14 So the a left the prisoners and
33:3 served the entire a of heaven.
33:5 altars for the entire a of heaven.
33:11 So the LORD made the a
33:14 He put a commanders in every
Neh 2:9 (The king had sent a officers
4:2 allies and the a from Samaria,
Psa 27:3 Even though an a sets up
33:16 a victory with a large a.
68:11 the good news are a large a.
78:49 sent an a of destroying angels.
110:3 when you call up your a.
136:15 He swept Pharaoh and his a
148:2 his entire heavenly a.
Pro 30:31 a king at the head of his a.
Sos 3:7 Sixty soldiers from the a of
Isa 13:4 It is like the sound of a large a.
13:4 is assembling his a for battle.
13:5 His a is coming from a distant
33:3 flee from the noise of ⌊your⌋ a.
36:2 with a large a from Lachish
43:14 I will send ⌊an a⌋ to Babylon.
43:17 an a and reinforcements.
Jer 6:22 An a is going to come from the
10:22 Its a will destroy Judah's cities
19:13 burned incense to the entire a
32:2 At that time the a of the king of
34:1 of Babylon, his entire a,
34:7 He did this when the a of the
34:21 want to kill them and to the a
34:21 the a that has withdrawn from
34:22 "I will bring that a back to this
37:5 Pharaoh's a had come from
37:7 'Pharaoh's a has come out to
37:10 entire Babylonian a so that they
37:11 The Babylonian a had retreated
37:11 Pharaoh's a was coming.
38:3 be handed over to the a
39:1 his entire a and blockaded it.
39:5 The Babylonian a pursued
40:7 All the a commanders and their
40:13 the a commanders who were
41:11 the a commanders who were
41:13 the a commanders who were
41:16 the a commanders who were
Jer 42:1 Then all the a commanders
42:8 all the a commanders who
43:4 all the a commanders,
43:5 all the a commanders took all
46:2 about the a of Pharaoh Neco,
46:2 his a at Carchemish along
51:3 Completely destroy its whole a.
52:4 Jerusalem with his entire a.
52:8 The Babylonian a pursued
52:8 His entire a had deserted him.
52:14 The entire Babylonian a that
52:25 he also took an a commander,
Lam 1:15 He called an a to defeat my
Eze 1:24 the commotion in an a camp.
17:17 Even with a large a and many
27:10 and Put were soldiers in your a.
29:18 made his a fight hard against
29:18 Yet, he and his a got no reward
29:19 That will be the pay for his a.
29:20 Nebuchadnezzar and his a
30:18 Egypt's strong a will be
32:22 is there with its whole a,
32:23 Assyria's a lies around its
32:31 "Pharaoh and his a will see
37:10 of them to form a very large a.
38:15 a large crowd and a mighty a.
39:11 Gog and his whole a will be
Dan 3:20 told some soldiers from his a
4:35 whatever he wishes with the a
8:10 until it reached the a of heaven.
8:10 threw some of the a of heaven,
8:11 the commander of the a so that
8:12 it was given an a
8:13 of the a—take place?"
11:7 He will attack the northern a,
11:11 who will raise a large a that
11:12 When that a is captured,
11:13 return and raise an a larger than
11:13 he will invade with a large a
11:25 "With a large a he will summon
11:25 for war with a large, strong a.
11:26 His a will be overwhelmed,
Hos 10:14 So your a will hear the noise of
Joe 2:2 A large and mighty a will
2:3 In front of this a a fire burns.
2:5 a mighty a prepared for battle.
2:11 shouts out orders to his a.
2:20 "I will keep the northern ⌊a⌋ far
2:25 (They are the large a that I sent
Mat 8:5 a Roman a officer came to beg
27:54 An a officer and those
Mar 6:21 for his top officials, a officers,
Luk 2:13 Suddenly, a large a of angels
7:2 There a Roman a officer's
23:47 When an a officer saw what
Jon 18:12 Then the a officer and the
Act 10:1 He was a Roman a officer in
10:22 a Roman a officer,
25:23 Roman a officers and the most
27:1 were turned over to an a officer.
1Co 9:7 ever serve in the a at his own
Rev 19:19 the rider on the horse and his a.

army's (6)

1Sm 17:4 The Philistine a champion
1Ki 1:25 the a commanders, and the
2Ki 9:5 the a generals were sitting
1Ch 15:25 and the a commanders joyfully
27:1 the king in all the a units.
27:3 was head of all of the a officers

Arnan (1)

1Ch 3:21 Rephaiah's son was A.

Arnan's (1)

1Ch 3:21 A son was Obadiah.

Arni (1)

Luk 3:33 son of A, son of Hezron,

Arnon (24)

Num 21:13 the other side of the A Valley
21:13 (The A Valley is the border
21:15 A and the slopes of the valleys
21:24 of their land from the A Valley
21:26 all his land up to the A Valley.

Num 22:36 in the region of the A Valley,
Dtr 2:24 Cross the A Valley.
2:36 From Aroer on the edge of the A
3:8 from the A Valley to Mount
3:12 north of Aroer near the A Valley
3:16 from the A Valley (the middle
4:48 on the edge of the A Valley
Jos 12:1 of their lands from the A Valley
12:2 on the edge of the A Valley
13:9 on the edge of the A Valley,
13:16 on the edge of the A Valley,
Jdg 11:13 It stretched from the A River to
11:18 of Moab — east of the A River.
11:18 They did not cross the A River
11:22 territory from the A River
11:26 and in all the cities along the A
2Ki 10:33 which is near the A River,
Isa 16:2 crossings of the A River.
Jer 48:20 Tell the news in A that Moab is

Arnon's (1)

Num 21:28 the rulers of A worship sites.

Arodi (2)

Gen 46:16 Shuni, Ezbon, Eri, A, and Areli.
Num 26:17 the family of A, and the family

Aroer (17)

Num 32:34 the cities of Dibon, Ataroth, A,
Dtr 2:36 From A on the edge of the
3:12 Gad the land north of A near
4:48 This land went from A on the
Jos 12:2 His rule extended from A on
13:9 The border extended from A on
13:16 Their territory extended from A
13:25 and half of Ammon as far as A,
Jdg 11:26 Heshbon, A, all their villages,
11:33 He defeated them from A to
1Sm 30:28 A, Siphmoth, Eshtemoa,
2Sm 24:5 Jordan River and camped at A,
2Ki 10:33 and Manasseh) from A,
1Ch 5:8 lived in A as far as
11:44 Jeiel (sons of Hotham from A),
Isa 17:2 The cities of A will be
Jer 48:19 Stand by the road in A,

aroma (43)

Gen 8:21 LORD smelled the soothing a.
Exo 29:18 a burnt offering, a soothing a,
29:25 It's a soothing a in the LORD's
29:41 This is a soothing a,
Lev 1:9 a soothing a to the LORD.
1:13 a soothing a to the LORD.
1:17 a soothing a to the LORD."
2:2 a soothing a to the LORD.
2:9 a soothing a to the LORD.
2:12 the altar to make a soothing a.
3:5 a soothing a to the LORD.
3:16 It is a soothing a. All the fat
4:31 it on the altar for a soothing a
6:15 It is a soothing a to the LORD.
6:21 as a soothing a to the LORD.
8:21 a burnt offering, a soothing a,
8:28 a soothing a to the LORD.
17:6 as a soothing a to the LORD.
23:13 to the LORD, a soothing a.
23:18 a soothing a to the LORD.
26:31 soothing a from your sacrifices.
Num 15:3 are a soothing a to the LORD.
15:7 as a soothing a to the LORD.
15:10 a soothing a to the LORD.
15:13 a soothing a to the LORD.
15:14 a soothing a to the LORD,
15:24 a soothing a to the LORD,
18:17 a soothing a to the LORD.
28:2 offerings by fire, a soothing a.
28:6 This offering is a soothing a,
28:8 a soothing a to the LORD.
28:13 is a burnt offering, a soothing a,
28:24 a soothing a to the LORD.
28:27 a burnt offering as a soothing a
29:2 a soothing a to the LORD,
29:6 They are a soothing a,
29:8 a burnt offering, a soothing a,
29:13 a soothing a to the LORD,
29:36 a soothing a to the LORD,
Jer 48:11 and its a hasn't changed.
2Co 2:15 To God we are the a of Christ
Eph 5:2 a soothing a to God.
Php 4:18 Your gifts are a soothing a,

aromatic (1)

Exo 30:34 resin and a mollusk shells),

arouse (3)

Sos 2:7 love or a love before its
3:5 love or a love before its
8:4 love or a love before its

arouses (1)

Pro 6:34 because jealousy a a

Arpachshad (9)

Gen 10:22 Asshur, A, Lud, and Aram.
10:24 A was the father of Shelah,
11:10 he became the father of A.
11:11 After he became the father of A,
11:12 A was 35 years old when he
11:13 A lived 403 years and had
1Ch 1:17 A, Lud, Aram, Uz, Hul, Gether,
1:18 A was the father of Shelah,
1:24 Shem, A, Shelah,

Arpad (6)

2Ki 18:34 are the gods of Hamath and A?
19:13 king of Hamath, the king of A,
Isa 10:9 Isn't Hamath like A?
36:19 are the gods of Hamath and A?
37:13 king of Hamath, the king of A,
Jer 49:23 "Hamath and A are worried

Arphaxad (1)

Luk 3:36 son of Cainan, son of A,

arrange (3)

Exo 40:4 and a everything on it.
Lev 24:8 of worship (a priest) must a
Luk 9:52 into a Samaritan village to a

arranged (17)

Gen 22:9 Abraham built the altar and a
Exo 40:23 He a the bread on the table in
Jdg 20:38 The men of Israel had a with
1Sm 11:11 The next day Saul a the army
2Sm 23:5 every detail a and assured.
1Ki 18:33 He a the wood, cut up the bull,
2Ch 13:3 while Jeroboam a to oppose
23:18 (David had a them in divisions
35:16 So everything was a that day
Neh 5:7 I a for a large meeting to deal
12:31 and I a two large choirs to give
13:31 I also a for delivering wood at
Ecc 12:9 and a it in many proverbs.
Eze 41:6 The rooms were a on three
Dan 1:5 The king a for them to get a
Act 2:3 The tongues a themselves so
22:10 you'll be told everything I've a

arrangement (8)

1Ki 10:5 his officers' seating a,
2Ch 9:4 his officers' seating a,
Jer 33:20 Suppose you could break my a
33:21 Then my a with my servant
33:21 The a with my servants the
33:25 Suppose I hadn't made an a
Hos 2:18 "On that day I will make an a
Gal 4:24 is the a made on Mount Sinai.

arrangements (5)

Gen 41:34 Make a to appoint supervisors
Eze 43:11 the design of the temple, its a,
Act 20:13 He had made these a,
2Co 9:5 you before I do and make a
Gal 4:24 The women illustrate two a.

arrest (27)

1Ki 13:4 "A him," he said. But the arm
Neh 13:21 "If you do it again, I'll a you."
Isa 1:17 A oppressors. Defend orphans.
Jer 36:26 Shelemiah (son of Abdeel) to a
Mat 21:46 They wanted to a him but were
26:4 They made plans to a Jesus in
Mat 26:5 But they said, "We shouldn't a
26:48 is the man you want. A him!"
26:55 swords and clubs to a me as if
26:55 But you didn't a me then.
Mar 12:12 They wanted to a him but were
14:1 underhanded way to a Jesus
14:2 "We shouldn't a him during the
14:44 A him, and guard him closely
14:48 swords and clubs to a me as if
14:49 But you didn't a me then.
14:51 They tried to a him,
Luk 20:19 wanted to a him right there,
21:12 people will a and persecute
22:53 day and you didn't try to a me.
Jon 7:30 The Jews tried to a him but
7:32 sent temple guards to a Jesus.
7:44 Some of them wanted to a him,
10:39 Jews tried to a Jesus again,
11:57 them so that they could a him.)
Act 1:16 Judas led the men to a Jesus.
9:2 Saul wanted to a any man or

arrested (21)

Gen 39:20 So Joseph's master a him and
42:24 Simeon and had him a right
2Ki 11:16 So they a her as she came to
17:4 So the king of Assyria a him
2Ch 23:15 So they a her as she entered
Isa 53:8 He was a, taken away,
Jer 29:27 Now, why haven't you a
37:13 a the prophet Jeremiah.
37:14 Irijah a Jeremiah and took him
39:5 They a him and brought him to
Mat 14:3 Herod had a John,
26:50 took hold of Jesus, and a him.
26:57 Those who had a Jesus took
Mar 6:17 had sent men who had a John,
14:46 took hold of Jesus and a him.
Luk 22:54 So they a Jesus and led him
Jon 8:20 No one a him, because his
18:12 the Jewish guards a Jesus.
Act 4:3 So the temple guards a them.
12:3 the Jews, he a Peter too.
24:6 our tradition. So we a him.

arresting (1)

Act 5:18 by a the apostles and putting

arrival (2)

Act 28:16 After our a, Paul was allowed
2Co 7:7 comforted not only by his a

arrive (10)

Dtr 31:3 destroy those nations as you a,
1Sm 10:5 When you a at the city,
2Ki 9:2 When you a there,
Neh 2:7 safe conduct until I a in Judah.
Isa 40:10 he has won a ahead of him.
62:11 he has won a ahead of him."
Mar 9:1 kingdom of God a with power."
Act 23:35 case when your accusers a."
1Co 16:11 I'm expecting him to a with the
2Co 10:14 is that we were the first to a

arrived (120)

Gen 12:6 They a in Canaan,
12:14 When Abram a in Egypt,
29:9 Rachel a with her father's
42:6 So when Joseph's brothers a,
44:14 Judah and his brothers a at
46:6 and all his family a in Egypt.
46:8 descendants) who a in Egypt.
46:28 When Israel's family a in the
47:1 brothers have a from Canaan
Num 10:21 By the time they a,
Jos 11:7 Joshua and all his troops a
22:15 When they a these leaders
Jdg 3:27 When he a there, he blew a
16:18 So the Philistine rulers a with
19:14 by the time they a at Gibeah.
19:29 When he a home, he got a
1Sm 4:13 When he a, Eli was sitting on a
10:22 "Has he a here yet?"
18:6 As they a, David was returning
26:4 to confirm that Saul had a.
2Sm 2:32 all night and a at Hebron by

2Sm 11:7 When Uriah **a**, David asked
11:22 messenger left, and when he **a**,
13:36 the king's sons **a** and cried
16:14 finally **a** ⌊at their destination⌋
17:6 When Hushai **a**, Absalom said
1Ki 1:22 the prophet Nathan **a**.
1:42 son of the priest Abiathar, **a**.
8:3 all the leaders of Israel had **a**,
10:2 She **a** in Jerusalem with a
13:1 When he **a**, Jeroboam was
20:33 When Benhadad **a**,
2Ki 5:22 in the hills of Ephraim have **a**.
6:32 But before the messenger **a**,
6:33 to them, the messenger **a**.
9:5 When he **a** there, the army's
9:30 When Jehu **a** in Jezreel,
10:17 When they **a** in Samaria,
21:9 the Israelites **a** in the land.
24:11 of Babylon **a** while his officers
1Ch 5:25 people as the Israelites **a**.
21:21 When David **a**, Ornan looked
2Ch 5:4 all the leaders of Israel had **a**,
9:1 She **a** with a large group of
33:9 the Israelites **a** in the land.
Ezr 7:8 Ezra **a** in Jerusalem.
7:9 he **a** in Jerusalem,
8:13 who **a** later with 60 males
Neh 1:2 **a** with some men from Judah.
2:14 Gate, I **a** at King's Pool,
Est 6:14 the king's eunuchs **a** and
8:17 king's message and decree **a**,
Sos 2:12 The time of the songbird has **a**.
Jer 10:22 The report has **a**. A tremendous
41:5 80 men **a** from Shechem,
Eze 23:40 When the men **a**, they washed
33:22 evening before the refugee **a**,
33:22 On the morning the refugee **a**,
Zec 6:10 who have **a** from Babylon.
Mat 2:1 from the east **a** in Jerusalem.
8:28 When he **a** in the territory
25:10 were buying oil, the groom **a**.
25:11 other bridesmaids **a** and said,
26:47 one of the twelve apostles, **a**.
27:57 a rich man named Joseph **a**.
Mar 3:31 his mother and his brothers **a**.
5:1 They **a** in the territory of the
5:22 leader named Jairus also **a**.
6:33 the cities and **a** ahead of them.
14:17 When evening came, Jesus **a**
14:43 one of the twelve apostles, **a**.
15:43 when Joseph **a**. He was from
Luk 8:41 **a** and quickly bowed down in
22:40 When he **a**, he said to them,
22:47 to the disciples, a crowd **a**.
Jon 4:5 He **a** at a city in Samaria called
4:45 But when Jesus **a** in Galilee,
6:23 Other boats from Tiberias **a**
11:17 When Jesus **a**, he found that
11:32 When Mary **a** where Jesus
12:1 Jesus **a** in Bethany.
20:6 Simon Peter **a** after him and
20:8 who **a** at the tomb first,
Act 5:7 hours later Ananias' wife **a**.
5:22 When the temple guards **a** at
9:26 After Saul **a** in Jerusalem,
9:39 When he **a**, he was taken
10:24 day they **a** in Caesarea.
11:11 "At that moment three men **a** at
11:20 and Cyrene, **a** in Antioch.
11:23 When he **a** there, he was
13:13 from Paphos and **a** in Perga,
13:14 left Perga and **a** in Antioch,
14:19 cities of Antioch and Iconium **a**
14:27 When they **a**, they called the
15:4 and Barnabas when they **a**.
15:30 were sent on their way and **a**
16:1 Paul **a** in the city of Derbe and
17:10 When Paul and Silas **a** in the
18:5 and Timothy **a** from Macedonia,
18:19 and **a** in the city of Ephesus,
18:22 and **a** in the city of Caesarea.
18:24 **a** in the city of Ephesus.
18:27 When he **a** in Greece,
20:15 and on the next day we **a** at
20:18 with you from the first day I **a**
21:10 named Agabus **a** from Judea.
Act 21:17 When we **a** in Jerusalem,
23:33 When the soldiers **a** in the city
24:24 Some days later Felix **a** with
27:3 The next day we **a** at the city
27:5 Cilicia and Pamphylia and **a** at
28:13 We sailed from Syracuse and **a**
28:13 and two days later we **a** at the
28:15 So we finally **a** in the city of
2Co 7:5 Ever since we **a** in the
7:6 comforted us when Titus **a**.
Gal 2:12 had sent ⌊from Jerusalem⌋ **a**.
1Th 1:9 you welcomed us when we **a**.
2Ti 1:17 When he **a** in Rome,

arrives (4)

Exo 1:19 babies before a midwife **a**."
Ecc 6:4 A stillborn baby **a** in a
Mat 12:44 When it **a**, it finds the house
Act 24:22 "When the officer Lysias **a**,

arriving (2)

Job 6:20 **A** there, they are disappointed.
Act 13:5 **A** in the city of Salamis,

arrogance (30)

Lev 26:19 I will crush your **a**.
1Sm 2:3 "Do not boast ⌊or⌋ let **a** come
15:23 Wickedness and idolatry are **a**.
Job 35:12 answer them because of the **a**
Psa 31:18 people with **a** and contempt.
59:12 them be trapped by their own **a**
73:6 That is why they wear **a** like a
Pro 8:13 I hate pride, **a**, evil behavior,
11:2 **A** comes, then comes shame,
13:10 **A** produces only quarreling,
21:24 His **a** knows no limits.
Isa 10:12 all his boasting and all his **a**.
16:6 We've heard of the **a** of Moab's
16:6 heard of their boasting, **a**,
Jer 13:9 is how I will destroy Judah's **a**
13:9 and Jerusalem's extreme **a**.
13:17 I will cry secretly over your **a**.
48:29 "We have heard about the **a** of
49:16 Your **a** has deceived you.
Eze 7:10 blossomed. **A** has flourished.
28:2 In your **a** you say, "I'm a god.
Hos 5:5 The people of Israel's **a**
7:10 your **a** testifies against you,
Oba 1:3 Your **a** has deceived you.
Zep 3:11 Then I will remove your **a** and
Zec 9:6 I will cut off the Philistines' **a**.
Mar 7:22 lust, envy, cursing, **a**,
2Co 10:5 and all their intellectual **a** that
12:20 **a**, and disorderly conduct.
Col 2:18 sinful mind fills him with **a**,

arrogant (82)

Dtr 8:14 careful that you don't become **a**
2Sm 22:28 but your eyes bring down **a**
2Ki 14:10 and now you have become **a**.
2Ch 25:19 and now you've become **a**
Neh 9:29 but they became **a** and would
Job 33:17 ⌊wrong⌋ and to stop being **a**.
40:11 Look at all who are **a**,
40:12 Look at all who are **a**,
41:34 It is king of everyone who is **a**."
Psa 36:11 Do not let the feet of **a** people
40:4 and does not rely on **a** people
73:3 because I was envious of **a**
86:14 O God, **a** people attack me,
94:2 Give **a** people what they
101:5 a conceited look or **a** heart.
119:21 You threaten **a** people,
119:51 **A** people have mocked me
119:69 **A** people have smeared me
119:78 Let **a** people be put to shame
119:85 **A** people have dug pits to trap
119:122 Do not let **a** people oppress me.
123:4 contempt from those who are **a**.
138:6 and he recognizes **a** people
140:5 **A** people have laid a trap for
140:8 ⌊or⌋ they will become **a**.
Pro 6:17 **a** eyes, a lying tongue,
15:25 down the house of an **a** person,
16:18 and an **a** attitude precedes a
16:19 stolen goods with **a** people.
Pro 18:12 a person's heart is **a**,
21:4 look and an **a** attitude,
21:24 An **a**, conceited person is
Ecc 7:8 It is better to be patient than **a**.
Isa 2:11 The eyes of **a** people will be
2:12 his day against all who are **a**
2:17 Then **a** people will be brought
3:16 "The women of Zion are **a**.
5:15 And the eyes of **a** people will
9:9 With **a** and conceited hearts
13:11 I will put an end to **a** people
16:6 They are very **a**. We've heard of
23:9 in order to dishonor all **a** people
25:11 humble those **a** people despite
28:1 How horrible it will be for the **a**
28:3 The **a** drunks of Ephraim will
Jer 13:15 Don't be **a**. The LORD has
43:2 and all the **a** people said to
48:29 They are very **a**. They are very
48:29 They are very **a**, conceited,
48:30 I know how **a** they are,"
50:31 "I'm against you, you **a** city,"
50:32 Those **a** people will stumble
Eze 16:50 They were **a** and did
16:56 sister Sodom when you were **a**.
28:5 You have become **a** because
31:10 It became **a** because it was so
31:14 were kept from becoming **a**
Dan 5:20 But when he became so **a** and
Hos 13:6 you were full, you became **a**.
Hab 2:5 wine is treacherous he is **a**
3:14 They are **a** like those who
Zep 2:15 Is this the **a** city? Is this the city
Mal 3:15 now we call **a** people blessed.
4:1 All **a** people and all evildoers
Rom 1:30 God, haughty, **a**, and boastful.
11:20 Don't feel **a**, but be afraid.
11:25 so that you won't become **a**.
12:16 Don't be **a**, but be friendly to
1Co 4:18 Some of you have become **a**
4:19 Then I'll know what these **a**
5:2 You're being **a** when you
8:1 Knowledge makes people **a**,
13:4 sing its own praises. It isn't **a**.
1Ti 3:6 or he might become **a** like the
6:17 riches of this world not to be **a**
2Ti 3:2 They will brag, be **a**,
Jas 4:6 "God opposes **a** people,
4:16 you brag because you're **a**.
1Pe 5:5 because God opposes the **a**
2Pe 2:10 false teachers are bold and **a**.
Jud 1:16 their own desires, say **a** things,
Rev 13:5 beast was allowed to speak **a**

arrogantly (17)

2Ki 19:22 Who are you looking at so **a**?
Neh 9:10 knew how **a** they were treating
9:16 our own ancestors — acted **a**.
Job 36:9 and that they've behaved **a**.
Psa 10:2 The wicked person **a** pursues
17:10 Their mouths have spoken **a**.
31:23 back in full those who act **a**.
73:8 speak **a** about oppression.
94:4 They speak **a**.
Pro 30:13 around **a** and is conceited.
Isa 37:23 Who are you looking at so **a**?
Dan 4:37 can humiliate those who act **a**.
Act 4:25 'Why do the nations act **a**?
1Co 4:6 Then you won't **a** place one of
Gal 5:26 can't allow ourselves to act **a**
1Ti 1:13 and acted **a** toward him.
2Pe 2:18 They **a** use nonsense to

arrow (18)

Gen 21:16 about as far away as an **a** can
1Sm 20:36 Jonathan shot the **a** over him.
20:37 Jonathan's **a** ⌊had landed⌋,
2Ki 9:24 The **a** came out of his chest,
13:17 Elisha said, "That is the **a**
13:17 the **a** of victory against Aram.
19:32 into this city, shoot an **a** here,
Job 34:6 been wounded by a deadly **a**,
41:28 An **a** won't make it run away.
Psa 64:7 God will shoot them with an **a**.
Pro 7:23 until an **a** pierces his heart,
25:18 and a sword and a sharp **a**,

Isa 37:33 into this city, shoot an **a** here,
49:2 He made me like a sharpened **a**
Jer 5:16 Their **a** quivers are like open
Lam 2:4 right hand held the **a** steady.
Zec 9:13 bow with Ephraim ⌊as its **a**⌋.
9:14 and his **a** will go out like

arrows (62)

Exo 19:13 must be stoned or shot with **a**.
Num 21:30 we shot the Amorites full of **a**.
24:8 and pierce them with **a**.
Dtr 32:23 I will use up all my **a** on them.
32:42 My **a** will drip with blood from
1Sm 20:20 I will shoot three **a** from beside
20:21 find the **a**.' Now, if I tell the boy,
20:21 the **a** are next to you;
20:22 'The **a** are next to you,'
20:36 "please find the **a** I shoot."
20:37 "The **a** are next to you!"
20:38 young servant gathered the **a**
2Sm 22:15 He shot **a** and scattered them.
2Ki 13:15 "Get a bow and some **a**."
13:15 So he got a bow and some **a**.
13:18 Then Elisha said, "Take the **a**."
1Ch 5:18 and swords and shoot **a**.
12:2 could sling stones or shoot **a**
2Ch 26:15 towers and corners to shoot **a**
Job 6:4 because the **a** of the Almighty
39:23 A quiver of **a** rattles on it along
Psa 7:13 and turns them into flaming **a**.
11:2 They set their **a** against the
18:14 He shot his **a** and scattered
38:2 Your **a** have struck me.
45:5 Your **a** are sharp in the heart of
57:4 Their teeth are spears and **a**.
58:7 let their **a** miss the target.
60:4 attacked by bows ⌊and **a**⌋.
64:3 They aim bitter words like **a**
76:3 There he destroyed flaming **a**,
77:17 Even your **a** flashed in every
78:9 with bows ⌊and **a**⌋,
78:57 They were like **a** shot from a
91:5 **a** that fly during the day,
120:4 sharpened **a** and red-hot coals.
127:4 when he is young are like **a**
144:6 Shoot your **a**, and throw them
Pro 26:18 madman who shoots flaming **a**,
26:18 flaming arrows, **a**, and death,
Isa 5:28 Their **a** are sharpened;
7:24 with bows and **a** ⌊to hunt⌋
22:3 without their bows and **a**.
22:6 Elam takes its quiver of **a**,
Jer 9:3 tongues like bows that shoot **a**.
9:8 Their tongues are like deadly **a**.
46:9 Lydia who use bows and **a**.
50:9 Its enemy's **a** will be like
50:14 Shoot at it; don't save any **a**,
51:11 Sharpen the **a**; fill the quivers.
51:56 and their bows and **a** will be
Lam 3:12 made me the target for his **a**.
3:13 He has shot the **a** from his
Eze 5:16 When I shoot my destructive **a**
21:21 He will shake some **a**,
39:3 hand and make you drop the **a**
39:9 and large shields, bows and **a**,
Hos 1:5 I will break Israel's bows and **a**
Hab 3:9 for the **a** ⌊you⌋ promised.
3:11 scatter at the light of your **a**,
3:14 of his gang with his own **a**.
Eph 6:16 can put out all the flaming **a**

Artaxerxes (10)

Ezr 4:7 wrote to him when **A** was king
4:8 of⌋ Jerusalem to King **A**.
4:11 To King **A**, From your servants,
6:14 and **A** (the kings of Persia) had
7:1 the reign of King **A** of Persia,
7:11 the letter that King **A** gave Ezra
7:12 From: **A**, king of kings To:
7:21 I, King **A**, order all the
8:1 me during the reign of King **A**:
Neh 1:11 and make this man, King **A**,

Artaxerxes' (6)

Ezr 4:23 hearing a copy of King **A** letter.
7:7 in **A** seventh year as king.
Neh 1:1 in **A** twentieth year as king,
2:1 in **A** twentieth year as king,
5:14 twentieth year of King **A** reign
13:6 year of King **A** reign

Artemas (1)

Tit 3:12 When I send **A** or Tychicus to

Artemis (5)

Act 19:24 models of the temple of **A**.
19:27 the great goddess **A** is nothing.
19:28 "**A** of the Ephesians is great!"
19:34 "**A** of the Ephesians is great!"
19:35 of the temple of the great **A**.

article (7)

Exo 22:9 a sheep, an **a** of clothing,
Lev 11:32 It may be a wooden **a**,
13:48 or wool or on any leather **a**,
13:52 of clothing or the leather **a**
13:57 the clothing or the leather **a**.
13:58 clothing or any leather **a** when
13:59 or in any leather **a** is clean

articles (12)

Num 4:12 "They will take all the **a** that
4:15 come to carry all the holy **a**.
31:6 took with him the holy **a**
31:51 hand-crafted gold **a** from them.
2Sm 8:10 Joram brought **a** of gold,
8:11 King David dedicated these **a**
1Ki 10:25 **a** of silver and gold,
1Ch 18:11 dedicated all the **a** of gold,
2Ch 9:24 **a** of silver and gold,
Ezr 1:6 them with **a** made from silver
Act 9:39 crying and showing Peter the **a**
Rev 18:12 **a** made of ivory and very costly

artist (2)

Exo 31:4 He's a master **a** familiar with
35:32 He's a master **a** familiar with

artist's (1)

Sos 7:1 like the work of an **a** hands

artists (1)

Exo 35:35 They are master **a**."

Arubboth (1)

1Ki 4:10 who was in charge of **A**,

Arumah (1)

Jdg 9:41 continued to live at **A**.

Arvad (2)

Eze 27:8 "People from Sidon and **A**
27:11 "People from **A** and Helech

Arvadites (2)

Gen 10:18 the **A**, the Zemarites, and the
1Ch 1:16 the **A**, the Zemarites, and the

Arza (1)

1Ki 16:9 (**A** was in charge of the palace

Arza's (2)

1Ki 16:9 drunk in Tirzah at **A** house.
16:10 Zimri entered **A** house,

Asa (54)

1Ki 15:8 His son **A** succeeded him as
15:9 **A** began to rule as king of
15:11 **A** did what the LORD
15:13 **A** cut the statue down and
15:14 **A** remained committed to the
15:16 There was war between **A** and
15:17 coming from King **A** of Judah.
15:18 Then **A** took all the silver and
15:18 King **A** sent them to Damascus
15:20 did what King **A** requested.
15:22 Then King **A** drafted everyone
15:22 King **A** used the materials to
15:23 Isn't everything else about **A**—
15:24 **A** lay down in death with his
15:32 There was war between **A** and
22:41 Jehoshaphat, son of **A**,
1Ki 22:43 example his father **A** had set
22:46 from the time of his father **A**.
1Ch 3:10 Abijah's son was **A**.
9:16 and Berechiah (son of **A** and
2Ch 14:1 His son **A** succeeded him as
14:2 **A** did what the LORD his God
14:7 So **A** told Judah, "Let's build
14:8 **A** had an army of 300,000
14:9 and 300 chariots to attack **A**.
14:10 **A** went to confront him,
14:11 **A** called on the LORD his God.
14:12 army in front of **A** and Judah.
14:13 **A** and his troops pursued them
15:2 Azariah went to **A** and said to
15:2 **A** and all you men from Judah
15:8 When **A** heard the prophet
15:9 Then **A** gathered all the people
15:14 **A** and the people swore their
15:16 King **A** also removed his
15:16 **A** cut the statue down,
15:17 **A** remained committed ⌊to the
16:1 coming from King **A** of Judah.
16:2 Then **A** brought out all the
16:4 did what King **A** requested.
16:6 Then King **A** took everyone in
16:6 **A** used the materials to fortify
16:7 the seer Hanani came to King **A**
16:10 **A** was furious at the seer.
16:10 **A** also oppressed some of the
16:11 Everything about **A** from first to
16:12 **A** got a foot disease that
16:13 **A** lay down in death with his
17:2 that his father **A** had captured.
20:32 example his father **A** had set
21:12 or the ways of King **A** of Judah.
Jer 41:9 same one that King **A** made as
Mat 1:7 Abijah the father of **A**,
1:8 **A** the father of Jehoshaphat,

Asahel (18)

2Sm 2:18 there: Joab, Abishai, and **A**.
2:18 **A** was as fast on his feet as a
2:20 back, he asked, "Are you **A**?"
2:20 "Yes," **A** answered.
2:21 But **A** refused to turn away from
2:22 So Abner spoke again to **A**.
2:23 But **A** refused to turn away.
2:23 came to the place where **A** fell
2:30 officers and **A** were missing.
2:32 They took **A** and buried him in
3:27 the blood of Joab's brother **A**.
3:30 he had killed their brother **A**
23:24 the thirty was Joab's brother **A**.
1Ch 2:16 were Abishai, Joab, and **A**.
11:26 men were Joab's brother **A**,
27:7 **A**, Joab's brother, was in
2Ch 17:8 **A**, Shemiramoth, Jehonathan,
31:13 **A**, Jerimoth, Jozabad, Eliel,

Asahel's (1)

Ezr 10:15 **A** son, and Jahzeiah,

Asaiah (8)

2Ki 22:12 and the royal official **A**.
22:14 and **A** went to talk to the
1Ch 4:36 **A**, Adiel, Jesimiel, Benaiah,
6:30 Haggiah's son was **A**.
9:5 of Shilah were **A** (the firstborn)
15:6 Merari's descendants was **A**,
15:11 Uriel, **A**, Joel, Shemaiah, Eliel,
2Ch 34:20 and the royal official **A**.

Asaph (28)

2Ki 18:18 royal historian and the son of **A**,
18:37 royal historian and the son of **A**,
1Ch 6:39 Heman's relative **A** stood on
9:15 and great-grandson of **A**),
15:17 his relatives they appointed **A**,
15:19 The musicians Heman, **A**,
16:5 **A** was the head; then Jeiel,
16:5 **A** played the cymbals.
16:7 the first time David entrusted **A**
16:37 David left **A** and his relatives to
25:1 appointed the sons of **A**,
25:2 the sons of **A** were Zaccur,
25:2 (They were directed by **A**,

1Ch 25:6 the direction of their fathers **A**,
25:9 chose Joseph, the son of **A**.
26:1 from the descendants of **A**.
2Ch 5:12 who were musicians — **A**,
20:14 a Levite descended from **A**.)
29:30 words of David and the seer **A**.
35:15 places as David, **A**, Heman,
Ezr 2:41 the descendants of **A**:
Neh 2:8 have a letter addressed to **A**,
7:44 the descendants of **A**:
11:17 who was the son of **A**,
12:35 who was the son of **A**.
12:46 ago in the time of David and **A**,
Isa 36:3 royal historian and the son of **A**,
36:22 royal historian and the son of **A**,

Asaph's (4)

2Ch 29:13 From **A** descendants were
35:15 The singers (**A** descendants)
Ezr 3:10 **A** descendants took their places
Neh 11:22 from **A** descendants who were

Asarel (1)

1Ch 4:16 Ziph, Ziphah, Tiria, and **A**.

Asa's (15)

1Ki 15:25 began to rule Israel in **A** second
15:28 in **A** third year as king
15:33 In **A** third year as king of Judah,
16:8 **A** twenty-sixth year as Judah's
16:10 **A** twenty-seventh year as king
16:15 In **A** twenty-seventh year as
16:23 in **A** thirty-first year as king
16:29 in **A** thirty-eighth year as king
1Ch 3:10 **A** son was Jehoshaphat.
2Ch 14:1 In **A** time the land had peace
15:9 when they saw that **A** God,
15:10 year of **A** reign, they gathered
15:19 the thirty-fifth year of **A** reign
16:1 year of **A** reign, King Baasha
17:1 **A** son Jehoshaphat succeeded

ascends (3)

Jos 11:17 from Mount Halak which **a**
19:11 Toward the west the border **a**
19:12 and then **a** toward Japhia.

ascent (1)

Neh 3:19 a section across from the **a**

Asenath (3)

Gen 41:45 and gave him **A** as his wife.
41:50 Joseph had two sons by **A**,
46:20 were born to Joseph by **A**,

ashamed (97)

Gen 2:25 but they weren't **a** of it.
2Sm 19:3 fled from battle and were **a** of it.
19:5 all your men feel **a**," he said.
2Ki 19:26 are weak, discouraged, and **a**.
2Ch 30:15 The priests and Levites were **a**,
Ezr 8:22 I was **a** to ask the king for an
9:6 and said, "I am **a**, my God.
Job 6:20 They are **a** because they relied
11:15 your face without being **a**,
19:3 not even **a** of mistreating me.
20:3 criticism that makes me **a**,
Psa 109:28 Let those who attack me be **a**,
119:6 Then I will never feel **a** when I
119:46 of kings and not feel **a**.
Pro 25:22 will make him feel guilty and **a**,
Isa 1:29 You will be **a** of the oaks that
19:9 and weavers will be **a**.
20:5 people will be shattered and **a**
23:4 Be **a**, Sidon, because the
24:23 The sun will be **a**,
29:22 Jacob will no longer be **a**.
33:9 Lebanon is **a** and is decaying.
37:27 are weak, discouraged, and **a**.
41:11 you will be **a** and disgraced.
44:11 They will be frightened and **a**
45:16 idols will be **a** and disgraced.
45:17 never again be **a** or disgraced.
45:24 him will come to him and be **a**.
50:7 That is why I will not be **a**.
65:13 will be glad, but you will be **a**.
Jer 2:26 "As a thief feels **a** when he's
2:26 the nation of Israel will feel **a**.
2:26 and prophets will also feel **a**.
6:15 Are they **a** when they do
6:15 No, they're not **a**. They don't
8:12 Are they **a** that they do
8:12 No, they're not **a**. They don't
9:19 We're very **a**. We must leave our
14:3 they are **a** and disgraced.
15:9 She will die, **a** and humiliated,
20:11 They will be very **a** that they
22:22 Then you will be **a** and
31:19 I was so **a** and humiliated,
48:13 Then Moab will be **a** of
48:13 the nation of Israel was **a** when
50:12 your mother will be greatly **a**.
Eze 16:27 who were **a** of what you had
16:52 Be **a** of yourself and suffer
16:54 to suffer disgrace and be **a**
16:61 You will be **a** when I return
16:63 You will remember and be **a**.
36:32 Be **a** and disgraced because of
43:10 Then they will be **a** because of
43:11 Suppose they are **a** of
Dan 9:7 near and far — are still **a**
9:8 and ancestors are **a** because
12:2 to be **a** and disgraced forever.
Hos 10:6 Israel will be **a** because of its
Joe 2:26 My people will never be **a**
2:27 My people will never be **a**
Mic 1:11 Pass by, naked and **a**,
7:16 Nations will see this and be **a**
Zep 3:11 that day you will no longer be **a**
3:19 though they had been **a**.
Zec 13:4 that day every prophet will be **a**
Mar 8:38 If people are **a** of me and what I
8:38 the Son of Man will be **a** of
Luk 9:26 If people are **a** of me and what I
9:26 the Son of Man will be **a** of
13:17 who opposed him felt **a**.
16:3 enough to dig, and I'm **a** to beg.
Rom 1:16 I'm not **a** of the Good News.
5:5 We're not **a** to have this
6:21 You're **a** of what you used to do
9:33 believes in him will not be **a**."
10:11 believes in him will not be **a**."
12:20 make him feel guilty and **a**."
1Co 4:14 writing this to make you feel **a**
6:5 You should be **a** of yourselves!
15:34 You should be **a** of yourselves.
2Co 7:14 I didn't have to be **a** of anything
10:8 the Lord gave us, I'm not **a**.
11:21 I'm **a** to admit it, but Timothy
Php 1:20 I will have nothing to be **a** of.
2Th 3:14 them so that they will feel **a**.
2Ti 1:8 So never be **a** to tell others
1:8 about our Lord or be **a** of me,
1:12 However, I'm not **a**.
1:16 of my needs and wasn't **a** that
2:15 worker who isn't **a**
Tit 2:8 those who oppose us will be **a**
Heb 2:11 That is why Jesus isn't **a** to
11:16 That is why God is not **a** to be
1Pe 2:6 in him will never be **a**."
3:16 will feel **a** that they have
4:16 being a Christian, don't feel **a**,
Jud 1:12 eat with you and don't feel **a**.

Ashan (4)

Jos 15:42 to Judah: Libnah, Ether, **A**,
19:7 Ain, Rimmon, Ether, and **A**.
1Ch 4:32 Ain, Rimmon, Tochen, and **A**.
6:59 **A** with its pastureland,

Asharelah (1)

1Ch 25:2 Joseph, Nethaniah, and **A**.

Ashbel (3)

Gen 46:21 **A**, Gera, Naaman, Ehi, Rosh,
Num 26:38 family of Bela, the family of **A**,
1Ch 8:1 **A** (his second son),

Ashdod (23)

Jos 11:22 were left in Gaza, Gath, and **A**.
13:3 **A**, Ashkelon, Gath, and Ekron,
15:46 Sea and alongside **A**.
Jos 15:47 Added to this were **A** and Gaza
1Sm 5:1 brought it from Ebenezer to **A**.
5:3 the people of **A** saw that Dagon
5:5 temple in **A** still don't step
5:6 harshly with the people of **A**.
5:6 in the vicinity of **A** with tumors.
5:7 When the people of **A** realized
5:8 The people of **A** called
6:17 LORD were for the cities of **A**,
2Ch 26:6 walls of Gath, Jabneh, and **A**.
26:6 He built cities near **A** and
Neh 4:7 and the people from **A** heard
13:23 had married women from **A**,
13:24 spoke the language of **A**
Isa 20:1 to fight against **A**,
Jer 25:20 and the people left in **A**;
Amo 1:8 I will cut off those living in **A**
3:9 Announce in the palaces of **A**
Zep 2:4 **A** will be driven out at noon,
Zec 9:6 A mixed race will live in **A**,

Asher (43)

Gen 30:13 So she named him **A**
35:26 slave Zilpah were Gad and **A**.
46:17 The sons of **A** were Imnah,
Exo 1:4 Dan and Naphtali; Gad and **A**.
Num 1:13 from the tribe of **A**;
1:40 for the descendants of **A** listed
1:41 for the tribe of **A** was 41,500.
2:27 to them will be the tribe of **A**.
2:27 for the people of **A** is Pagiel,
7:72 leader of the descendants of **A**,
10:26 commanded the army of **A**.
13:13 from the tribe of **A**;
26:44 The families descended from **A**
26:46 (**A** had a daughter named
34:27 the leader of the tribe of **A**;
Dtr 27:13 **A**, Zebulun, Dan, and Naphtali.
33:24 About the tribe of **A** he said,
33:24 "The people of **A** are the most
Jos 17:7 from **A** to Michmethath,
17:10 **A** its northern border,
17:11 In Issachar and **A**,
19:24 for the families of the tribe of **A**.
19:31 for the families of the tribe of **A**.
19:34 in the south, **A** in the west,
21:6 tribes of Issachar, **A**, Naphtali,
21:30 to them from the tribe of **A**:
Jdg 1:31 The tribe of **A** did not force out
1:32 So the tribe of **A** continued to
5:17 **A** sat on the seashore and
6:35 The tribes of **A**, Zebulun,
7:23 summoned from Naphtali, **A**,
2Sm 2:9 of Gilead, **A**, Jezreel, Ephraim,
1Ki 4:16 was in charge of **A** and Aloth.
1Ch 2:2 Naphtali, Gad, and **A**.
6:62 tribes of Issachar, **A**, Naphtali,
6:74 From the tribe of **A**,
12:36 From **A** there were 40,000
2Ch 30:11 However, some people from **A**,
Eze 48:2 **A** will have one part of the land
48:3 part of the land and border **A**
48:34 **A** Gate, and Naphtali Gate.
Luk 2:36 of Phanuel from the tribe of **A**.
Rev 7:6 12,000 from the tribe of **A**,

Asherah (39)

Exo 34:13 dedicated to the goddess **A**.
Dtr 7:5 dedicated to the goddess **A**,
12:3 dedicated to the goddess **A**,
16:21 dedicated to the goddess **A**.
Jdg 6:25 to the goddess **A** that is next
6:26 wood from the **A** pole that you
6:28 The **A** pole next to it had also
6:30 cut down the **A** pole that was
1Ki 14:15 poles to the goddess **A**
14:23 up large stones and **A** poles
15:13 of the repulsive goddess **A**.
16:33 dedicated to the goddess **A**.
18:19 400 prophets of **A** who eat at
2Ki 13:6 goddess **A** remained standing
17:10 dedicated to the goddess **A**
17:16 dedicated to the goddess **A**.
18:4 dedicated to the goddess **A**.
21:3 to the goddess **A** as King Ahab
21:7 had an idol of **A** made.

2Ki 23:4 that had been made for Baal, A,
23:6 to the goddess A from
23:7 women did weaving for A.
23:14 down the poles dedicated to A,
23:15 burning the pole dedicated to A.
2Ch 14:3 dedicated to the goddess A.
15:16 of the repulsive goddess A.
17:6 to the goddess A in Judah.
19:3 You've burned the A poles in
24:18 dedicated to the goddess A.
31:1 dedicated to the goddess A,
33:3 to the goddess A as King Ahab
33:19 dedicated to the goddess A.
34:3 dedicated to the goddess A,
34:4 He destroyed the A poles,
34:7 tore down the altars, beat the A
Isa 17:8 by their hands or to the A poles
27:9 dedicated to the goddess A
Jer 17:2 goddess A beside large trees
Mic 5:14 dedicated to the goddess A.

Asherahs (2)

Jdg 3:7 the Baals and the A.
1Sm 31:10 of their goddesses — the A —

Asher's (4)

Gen 49:20 "A food will be rich.
Num 26:47 the families of A descendants.
1Ch 7:30 A sons were Imnah,
7:40 were A descendants — heads

ashes (39)

Gen 18:27 although I'm ⌊only⌋ dust and a,
Exo 9:8 "Take a handful of a from a
9:10 They took a from a kiln and
9:10 Moses threw the a up in the air,
27:3 for taking away the altar's a,
Lev 1:16 the altar on the place for the a.
4:12 camp where the a are dumped.
6:10 Then he will remove the a left
6:11 He will take the a to a clean
Num 4:13 "After they take the a away,
19:9 is clean will collect the a from
19:10 The person who collected the a
19:17 Put some of the a from the red
2Sm 13:19 Tamar put a on her head,
1Ki 13:3 The a on it will be poured ⌊on
13:5 and the a from the altar were
2Ki 23:4 he carried their a to Bethel.
23:6 and threw its a on the tombs of
Est 4:1 and put on sackcloth and a.
4:3 Many put on sackcloth and a.
Job 2:8 himself as he sat in the a.
30:19 that I become like dust and a."
42:6 and I sit in dust and a to show
Psa 102:9 I eat a like bread and my tears
147:16 wool and scatters frost like a.
Isa 44:20 They eat a because they are
58:5 your bed from sackcloth and a?
61:3 give them crowns instead of a,
Jer 6:26 and roll around in a,
31:40 with its dead bodies and a,
Eze 27:30 covered themselves with a.
28:18 I turned you into a on the
Dan 9:3 and fasted in sackcloth and a.
Jnh 3:6 put on sackcloth, and sat in a.
Mal 4:3 day I act they will be a under
Mat 11:21 long ago in sackcloth and a.
Luk 10:13 worn sackcloth and sat in a.
Heb 9:13 of goats and bulls and the a
2Pe 2:6 them by burning them to a.

Ashhur (2)

1Ch 2:24 wife Abijah gave birth to A,
4:5 A, who first settled Tekoa,

Ashima (1)

2Ki 17:30 people from Hamath made A.

Ashimah (1)

Amo 8:14 be for⌋ those who swear by A,

Ashkelon (13)

Jos 13:3 Ashdod, A, Gath, and Ekron,
Jdg 1:18 Judah also captured Gaza, A,
14:19 he went to A and killed 30 men
1Sm 6:17 Gaza, A, Gath, and Ekron.
2Sm 1:20 the victory in the streets of A,
Jer 25:20 those from the cities of A,
47:5 A will be destroyed.
47:7 LORD has ordered it to attack A
Amo 1:8 one who holds the scepter in A.
Zep 2:4 and A will be destroyed.
2:7 lie down in the houses of A.
Zec 9:5 A will see ⌊this⌋ and be afraid.
9:5 A will no longer be lived in.

Ashkenaz (3)

Gen 10:3 Gomer's descendants were A,
1Ch 1:6 Gomer's descendants were A,
Jer 51:27 Ararat, Minni, and A to attack it.

Ashnah (2)

Jos 15:33 villages: Eshtaol, Zorah, A,
15:43 Iphtah, A, Nezib,

ashore (4)

Jon 21:9 When they went a,
21:11 the boat and pulled the net a.
Act 27:39 decided to try to run the ship a.
27:43 overboard first and swim a.

Ashpenaz (1)

Dan 1:3 The king told A, to bring some

Ashtaroth (7)

Dtr 1:4 who ruled in A and in Edrei.
Jos 9:10 and King Og of Bashan in A.
12:4 Og of Bashan who lived in A
13:12 Og ruled in A and Edrei.
13:31 half of Gilead with A and Edrei,
21:27 of refuge for murderers) and A.
1Ch 6:71 with its pastureland and A

Ashteroth (1)

1Ch 11:44 Uzzia from A, Shama and Jeiel

Ashteroth Karnaim (1)

Gen 14:5 and defeated the Rephaim at A,

Ashvath (1)

1Ch 7:33 were Pasach, Bimhal, and A.

Asia (20)

Act 2:9 Pontus, the province of A,
6:9 of Cilicia and A started
16:6 the word in the province of A.
19:10 lived in the province of A heard
19:22 longer in the province of A.
19:26 throughout the province of A.
19:27 Then she whom all A and the
19:31 were from the province of A
20:4 of A accompanied Paul.
20:16 time in the province of A.
20:18 I arrived in the province of A.
21:27 the Jews from the province of A
24:19 the province of A were there.
27:2 the coast of the province of A.
Rom 16:5 first person in the province of A
1Co 16:19 in the province of A greet you.
2Co 1:8 in the province of A.
2Ti 1:15 province of A has deserted me,
1Pe 1:1 Cappadocia, A, and Bithynia.
Rev 1:4 churches in the province of A.

aside (36)

Exo 21:13 to a place I will set a for you.
Dtr 4:41 Then Moses set a three cities
19:2 When all this is done, set a
19:7 you to set a three cities
1Sm 9:23 gave you and told you to put a."
9:24 to the feast, I set it a for you."
2Sm 3:27 Joab took him a in the gateway
18:30 "Step a, and stand here,"
18:30 He stepped a and stood there.
2Ki 4:4 When one is full, set it a."
2Ch 31:3 He set a part of the king's
33:8 Israel from the land that I set a
35:12 They set a the burnt offerings
Neh 12:47 They set a holy gifts for ⌊the
12:47 and the Levites set a holy gifts
Job 24:1 set a times ⌊for punishment⌋?
Psa 85:3 You laid a all your fury.
125:3 to govern the land set a
Jer 5:23 They have turned a and
40:2 of the guard took Jeremiah a
Eze 45:1 Set a an area 43,750 feet long
48:8 The land that you set a as a
48:9 This special land that you set a
Hag 2:12 a person carries meat set a
Mat 5:17 to set a Moses' Teachings
5:17 I didn't come to set them a but
5:19 So whoever sets a any
16:22 Peter took him a and objected
20:17 he took the twelve apostles a
Mar 8:32 Peter took him a and objected
10:32 he took the twelve apostles a.
Luk 18:31 took the twelve apostles a
Act 7:27 of the men pushed Moses a.
7:39 Instead, they pushed him a,
1Co 16:2 each of you should set a some
1Ti 2:8 prayer after putting a their anger

Asiel (1)

1Ch 4:35 and great-grandson of A),

ask (282)

Gen 18:27 if I may be so bold as to a you,
18:31 if I may be so bold as to a you,"
24:14 I will a a girl, 'May I please
24:57 "We'll call the girl and a her."
25:22 So she went to a the LORD.
32:29 "Why do you a for my name?"
34:11 I'll give you whatever you a.
Exo 3:13 sent me to you,' and they a me,
3:22 should a her Egyptian neighbor
11:2 each man and woman must a
12:26 When your children a you what
13:14 your children a you what this
Lev 25:20 You may a, 'What will we eat
Num 22:17 and I will do whatever you a.
Dtr 6:20 future your children will a you,
12:30 Don't even a about their gods
17:9 A for their opinion,
18:11 a ghosts or spirits for help,
29:24 nations in the world will a,
30:12 You don't have to a,
30:13 You don't have to a,
31:17 On that day they will a,
32:7 A your fathers to remind you,
32:37 Then he will a, "Where are
Jos 4:6 the future your children will a,
4:21 when children a their parents,
9:14 but they did not a the LORD
15:18 she persuaded him to a her
Jdg 1:14 she persuaded him to a her
6:39 But let me a one more thing.
9:2 He said, "Please a all citizens
12:5 the men of Gilead would a,
13:6 So I didn't a him where he
13:18 "Why do you a for my name?
18:3 So they stopped to a him,
1Sm 1:8 husband Elkanah would a her,
7:8 A him to save us from the
9:9 when a person went to a God
17:29 I ⌊merely⌋ a a question?"
25:8 A your young men,
27:10 Achish would a, "Whom did
28:7 Then I'll go to her and a for her
2Sm 7:7 did I ever a any of the judges of
11:3 David sent someone to a about
11:20 He might a you, 'Why did you
14:18 question I'm going to a you."
14:32 you to the king to a him why
15:2 Absalom would a,
16:10 'Curse David,' should anyone a,
19:11 "A the leaders of Judah,
20:18 'Be sure to a at Abel ⌊before
1Ki 1:13 Go to King David and a him,
2:16 Now I want to a you for one
2:17 He said, "Please a King
2:20 "A, Mother," the king told her.
2:22 "Why do you a that Abishag
5:6 pay you whatever wages you a
8:43 Do everything they a you so
9:8 They will gasp and a,
14:5 is coming to a you about her
22:7 the LORD whom we could a?"

1Ki 22:8 "We can **a** the LORD through
2Ki 1:2 told them, "Go **a** Baalzebub,
1:3 king of Samaria, and **a** them,
3:11 the LORD whom we could **a**?"
4:13 "**A** her what we can do for her,
4:26 Run to meet her and **a** her how
4:28 "I didn't **a** you for a son.
8:8 **A** the LORD through him,
9:17 and **a**, 'Is everything alright?'"
22:13 **a** the LORD about the words in
22:18 king who sent you to me to **a**
1Ch 17:6 did I ever **a** any of the judges of
2Ch 1:11 You didn't **a** for riches,
1:11 You didn't even **a** for a long life.
6:33 Do everything they **a** you so
7:21 They will **a**, 'Why did the
18:6 the LORD whom we could **a**?"
18:7 "We can **a** the LORD through
20:3 Jehoshaphat decided to **a** for
32:31 ambassadors to **a** him about
34:21 **a** the LORD about the words in
34:26 king who sent you to me to **a**
Ezr 8:21 presence of our God to **a** him
8:22 I was ashamed to **a** the king for
Est 5:14 and in the morning **a** the king to
6:4 to the king's palace to **a**
7:3 That is what I **a** for.
Job 7:4 When I lie down, I **a**,
8:8 "**A** the people of past
9:12 Who is going to **a** him,
12:7 "Instead, **a** the animals,
12:7 **A** the birds, and they will tell
20:10 His children will have to **a** the
21:28 because you **a**, 'Where is the
22:13 You **a**, 'What does God know?
35:3 when you **a**, 'What benefit is it
38:3 I will **a** you, and you will teach
40:7 I will **a** you, and you will teach
42:4 I will **a** you, and you will teach
Psa 2:8 **A** me, and I will give you the
35:11 They **a** me things I know
40:6 You did not **a** for burnt offerings
42:3 People **a** me all day long,
42:9 I will **a** God, my rock,
42:10 They **a** me all day long,
73:11 Then wicked people **a**,
119:82 I **a**, "When will you comfort
Pro 2:3 you **a** aloud for understanding,
Ecc 4:8 But ⌊they never **a** themselves⌋
7:10 Don't **a**, "Why were things
7:10 that leads you to **a** this!
8:4 no one can **a** him what he is
Isa 7:11 "**A** the LORD your God for a
7:12 But Ahaz answered, "I won't **a**;
8:19 People will say to you, "**A** for
8:19 Shouldn't people **a** their God for
8:19 Why should they **a** the dead to
10:8 They **a**, 'Aren't all our
21:12 If you need to **a**, come back
21:12 come back and **a**."
41:28 When I **a** them a question,
44:20 themselves or **a** themselves,
45:9 Does the clay **a** the one who
45:11 This is what the LORD says: **A**
49:21 Then you will **a** yourself,
58:2 They **a** me for just decrees.
65:1 to answer those who didn't **a**.
Jer 2:6 They didn't **a**, "Where is the
2:8 The priests didn't **a**,
2:27 you **a** me to come and rescue
5:19 They will **a**, "Why has the
6:16 **A** which paths are the old,
6:16 **A** which way leads to
7:31 I did not **a** for this. It never
8:6 from their wickedness and **a**,
13:22 If you **a** yourself, "Why do
15:2 When they **a** you where they
15:5 No one will bother to **a** how
16:10 these things, they will **a** you,
18:13 the LORD says: **A** among
19:5 I didn't **a** them or command
21:13 "But you **a**, "Who can attack
22:8 by this city and **a** each other,
23:33 or the priests **a** you,
23:35 They should **a** their neighbors
30:6 **A** now, and see: Can a man

Jer 32:35 I didn't **a** them to do this.
38:14 "I'm going to **a** you a question,"
48:19 **A** those who are fleeing and
50:5 They will **a** which road goes to
Eze 7:26 People will **a** for a vision from
12:9 nation of Israel **a** you what you
13:12 people will **a** them,
14:3 be allowed to **a** me for help?
14:4 he goes to a prophet ⌊to **a**
14:7 If he goes to a prophet to **a** for
14:10 are when you **a** for his help.
17:12 "**A** these rebellious people,
18:19 "But you **a**, 'Why isn't the son
20:1 the leaders of Israel came to **a**
20:3 Are you coming to **a** me for
20:3 not be allowed to **a** me for help.'
20:31 Should you be allowed to **a** me
20:31 be allowed to **a** me for help.
21:7 When they **a** you why you are
21:21 **a** his household gods for help,
36:37 let the people of Israel **a** me
38:13 and all their villages will **a** you,
Dan 2:11 What you **a** is difficult,
2:18 He told them to **a** the God of
4:35 who can oppose him or **a** him,
Hos 4:12 My people **a** their wooden idols
5:13 Ephraim went to Assyria to **a**
Joe 2:17 Why should people **a**,
Mic 7:3 Officials **a** for gifts.
Zep 1:6 the LORD or **a** him for help."
Hag 2:3 **A** them, 'Is there anyone
2:11 **A** the priests for a decision.
Zec 7:2 Melech with their men to **a**
8:21 make a habit of going to **a**
8:22 of Armies in Jerusalem and to **a**
10:1 **A** the LORD for rain in the
Mal 1:2 "But you **a**, 'How did you love
1:6 "But you **a**, 'How have we
1:7 "But you **a**, 'Then how have
2:14 But you **a**, "Why ⌊aren't our
2:17 But you **a**, "How have we tried
3:7 "But you **a**, 'How can we
3:8 "But you **a**, 'How are we
3:13 "You **a**, 'How have we spoken
Mat 6:8 you need before you **a** him.
7:7 "**A**, and you will receive.
7:11 things to those who **a** him?
9:38 So **a** the Lord who gives this
11:3 to **a** Jesus, "Are you the one
19:17 "Why do you **a** me about what
20:20 down in front of him to **a** him
21:22 whatever you **a** for in prayer."
21:25 'from heaven,' he will **a** us,
22:46 to **a** him another question.
25:44 "They, too, will **a**, 'Lord,
27:20 persuaded the crowd to **a**
Mar 3:31 and sent someone to **a** him
5:31 said to him, "How can you **a**,
6:22 "**A** me for anything you want,
6:23 "I'll give you anything you **a** for,
6:24 "What should I **a** for?"
6:24 Her mother said, "**A** for the
9:32 meant and were afraid to **a** him.
11:29 "I'll **a** you a question.
11:31 say, 'from heaven,' he will **a**,
12:34 to **a** him another question.
15:43 went to Pilate's quarters to **a**
15:44 the officer to **a** him if Jesus
Luk 6:9 Then Jesus said to them, "I **a**
7:3 They were to **a** Jesus to come
7:19 and sent them to **a** the Lord,
7:20 the Baptizer sent us to **a** you,
9:45 Besides, they were afraid to **a**
10:2 So **a** the Lord who gives this
11:9 "So I tell you to **a**, and you will
11:13 Spirit to those who **a** him?"
14:32 he'll send ambassadors to **a** for
16:27 'Then I **a** you, Father,
20:5 say, 'from heaven,' he will **a**,
20:40 to **a** him another question.
22:68 And if I **a** you, you won't
Jon 1:19 from Jerusalem to **a** him,
4:9 can a Jewish man like you **a**
9:21 You'll have to **a** him.
9:23 "You'll have to **a** him.
11:22 give you whatever you **a** him."

Jon 13:24 "**A** Jesus whom he's talking
14:13 I will do anything you **a** ⌊the
14:14 If you **a** me to do something,
14:16 I will **a** the Father,
15:7 then **a** for anything you want,
15:16 and to **a** the Father in my name
15:16 to give you whatever you **a** for.
16:19 wanted to **a** him something.
16:23 you won't **a** me any more
16:23 If you **a** the Father for anything
16:24 **A** and you will receive so that
16:26 you will **a** for what you want in
16:26 telling you that I won't have to **a**
21:12 None of the disciples dared to **a**
Act 8:22 and **a** the Lord if he will forgive
9:11 and **a** for a man named Saul
12:20 the help of Blastus to **a** Herod
23:20 "The Jews have planned to **a**
26:3 So I **a** you to listen patiently to
Rom 1:10 I **a** that somehow God will now
9:19 You may **a** me, "Why does
10:6 "Don't **a** yourself who will go
10:7 "Don't **a** who will go down into
10:18 But I **a**, "Didn't they hear that
10:19 Again I **a**, "Didn't Israel
11:1 So I **a**, "Has God rejected his
11:11 So I **a**, "Has Israel stumbled so
12:3 I **a** you not to think of
1Co 1:22 Jews **a** for miraculous signs,
4:3 I don't even **a** myself questions.
14:35 they should **a** their husbands at
15:35 But someone will **a**,
2Co 8:12 God doesn't **a** for what they
Eph 3:13 So then, I **a** you not to become
3:20 more than we can **a** or imagine.
Php 4:3 Yes, I also **a** you, Syzugus,
Col 1:9 We **a** ⌊God⌋ to fill you with the
1:10 We **a** this so that you will live
1:11 We **a** him to strengthen you by
1Th 4:1 of the Lord Jesus we **a**
5:12 Brothers and sisters, we **a** you
5:13 We **a** you to love them and
Phm 1:21 you will do even more than I **a**.
Heb 13:19 I especially **a** for your prayers
Jas 1:5 you should **a** God,
1:6 When you **a** for something,
1Jn 3:22 from him anything we **a**.
5:14 that God listens to us if we **a**
5:15 have what we **a** him for.

asked (788)

Gen 3:1 He **a** the woman, "Did God
3:9 called to the man and **a** him,
3:11 God **a**, "Who told you that you
3:13 the LORD God **a** the woman,
4:6 Then the LORD **a** Cain,
4:9 The LORD **a** Cain,
4:10 The LORD **a**, "What have you
12:18 he **a**. "Why didn't you tell me
15:2 Abram **a**, "Almighty LORD,
15:8 Abram **a**, "Almighty LORD,
18:9 They **a** him, "Where is your
18:13 The LORD **a** Abraham,
18:23 Abraham came closer and **a**,
18:27 Abraham **a**, "Consider now, if I
18:29 Abraham **a** him again,
19:12 Then the men **a** Lot,
20:4 come near her, so he **a**, "Lord,
20:9 called for Abraham and **a** him,
20:10 Abimelech also **a** Abraham,
21:17 he **a** her. "Don't be afraid! God
21:29 Abimelech **a** him, "What is the
22:7 Isaac **a**, "We have the burning
24:5 The servant **a** him,
24:23 He **a**, "Whose daughter are
24:39 "I **a** my master, 'What if the
24:45 "So I **a** her, 'May I have a
24:47 "Then I **a** her, 'Whose daughter
24:58 called for Rebekah and **a** her,
24:65 She **a** the servant,
26:7 When the men of that place **a**
26:27 Isaac **a** them, "Why have you
27:20 Isaac **a** his son, "How did you
27:24 he **a** him. "I am," Jacob
27:32 his father Isaac **a** him.
27:33 violently all over, Isaac **a**,

Gen 27:36 So he **a**, "Haven't you saved a
27:38 Esau **a**, "Do you have only one
29:4 Jacob **a** some people,
29:5 He **a** them, "Do you know
29:6 Jacob **a** them. "He's fine," they
29:25 Jacob **a** Laban. "Didn't I work
30:2 angry with Rachel and **a**,
30:31 Laban **a**, "What should I give
31:26 Then Laban **a** Jacob,
32:27 So the man **a** him,
33:5 women and children, Esau **a**,
33:8 Then Esau **a**, "Why did you
33:15 Jacob **a**. "I only want to win
34:31 Simeon and Levi **a**,
37:8 Then his brothers **a** him,
37:15 you looking for?" the man **a**.
37:26 Judah **a** his brothers,
38:16 She **a**, "What will you pay to
38:18 he **a**. "Your signet ring, its cord,
38:21 He **a** the men of that area,
40:7 So he **a** these officials of
40:8 Joseph **a** them. "Why don't you
41:38 So Pharaoh **a** his servants,
42:7 he **a** them. "From Canaan, to
42:28 and turned to each other and **a**,
43:6 Israel **a**, "Why have you made
43:27 He **a** them how they were.
43:29 he **a**. "God be gracious to you,
44:15 Joseph **a** them, "What have
44:16 Judah **a**. "How else can we
44:19 Sir, you **a** us, 'Do you have a
47:3 Pharaoh **a** the brothers,
47:8 Pharaoh **a** him, "How old are
48:8 sons, he **a**, "Who are they?"
Exo 1:18 He **a** them, "Why have you
2:7 sister **a** Pharaoh's daughter,
2:13 He **a** the one who started the
2:14 The man **a**, "Who made you
2:18 to their father Reuel, he **a** them,
2:20 Reuel **a** his daughters,
4:2 Then the LORD **a** him,
4:11 The LORD **a** him, "Who gave
4:14 angry with Moses and **a**,
5:2 Pharaoh **a**, "Who is the LORD?
5:15 They **a**, "Why are you treating
5:22 went back to the LORD and **a**,
8:13 The LORD did what Moses **a**.
8:31 The LORD did what Moses **a**.
10:7 Then Pharaoh's officials **a** him,
12:31 worship the LORD as you **a**.
12:32 flocks and herds, too, as you **a**.
12:35 Moses had told them and **a**
12:36 they gave them what they **a** for.
16:15 saw it, they **a** each other,
17:3 complained to Moses and **a**,
18:7 After they **a** each other how
18:14 was doing for the people, he **a**,
32:21 Moses **a** Aaron, "What did
33:17 "I will do what you have **a**,
Lev 10:17 He **a** them, "Why didn't you eat
Num 11:11 So he **a**, "LORD, why have you
11:23 The LORD **a** Moses,
11:29 But Moses **a** him, "Do you
12:2 They **a**, "Did the LORD speak
14:20 "I forgive them, as you have **a**.
14:41 But Moses **a**, "Why are you
22:9 God came to Balaam and **a**,
22:28 speak, and it **a** Balaam,
22:32 Messenger of the LORD **a** him,
23:17 Balak **a** him, "What did the
31:15 the women live?" he **a** them.
32:6 Moses **a** the tribes of Gad and
Dtr 18:16 This is what you **a** the LORD
Jos 5:13 Joshua went up to him and **a**,
5:14 He **a**, "Sir, what do you want to
9:8 Joshua **a** them, "Who are you,
9:22 for the people of Gibeon and **a**,
15:18 from her donkey, Caleb **a** her,
17:14 descendants **a** Joshua,
18:3 So Joshua **a** the Israelites,
19:50 They gave him the city he **a** for,
Jdg 1:1 the Israelites **a** the LORD,
1:14 from her donkey, Caleb **a** her,
5:25 Sisera **a** for water.
6:29 They **a** each other,
6:40 God did what Gideon **a**.

Jdg 8:8 Gideon went to Penuel and **a**
8:18 He **a** Zebah and Zalmunna,
8:26 The gold earrings Gideon had **a**
11:12 They **a** the king, "Why did you
12:2 I **a** you for help, but you didn't
13:9 God did what Manoah **a**.
13:11 he came to the man, he **a** him,
13:12 Then Manoah **a**, "When your
13:17 Then Manoah **a** the Messenger
13:18 Messenger of the LORD **a** him,
14:3 His father and mother **a** him,
15:6 Some Philistines **a**,
15:10 The men of Judah **a**,
17:9 Micah **a** him, "Where do you
18:8 Their relatives **a** them,
18:18 metal idol, the priest **a** them,
19:17 So the old man **a**, "Where do
20:12 They **a**, "How could such an
20:18 They **a** God, "Who will go first
20:23 They **a** the LORD,
20:28 people of Israel **a** the LORD,
21:5 The people **a**, "Is there any
21:8 Then they **a**, "Is there any
21:16 leaders of the congregation **a**,
Rut 1:19 can it?" the women **a**.
2:5 Boaz **a** the young man in
2:19 Her mother-in-law **a** her,
3:9 he **a**. She answered, "I am Ruth.
3:16 her mother-in-law Naomi **a**,
1Sm 1:14 Eli **a** her. "Get rid of your wine."
1:20 "I **a** the LORD for him."
2:23 So he **a** them, "Why are you
3:17 he **a**. "Please don't hide
4:3 the leaders of Israel **a**,
4:6 heard the noise, they **a**,
4:14 Hearing the cry, Eli **a**,
4:16 son?" Eli **a**.
5:8 they **a**. "The ark of the God of
6:2 The Philistines **a**, Tell us how
6:4 The Philistines **a**, "What kind
6:20 The people of Beth Shemesh **a**,
8:10 told the people who had **a** him
9:7 "If we go," Saul **a** his servant,
9:11 They **a** the girls, "Is the seer
10:11 the people **a** one another,
10:12 But a man from that place **a**,
10:14 Saul's uncle **a** him and his
10:22 They **a** the LORD again,
10:24 Samuel **a** the people,
10:27 good-for-nothing people **a**,
11:5 Saul **a**. So they told him the
11:12 Then the people **a** Samuel,
12:13 have chosen, the one you **a** for.
12:17 when you **a** for a king."
13:11 Samuel **a**, "What have you
14:37 Then Saul **a** God, "Should I
14:43 "Tell me," Saul **a** Jonathan.
14:45 The troops **a** Saul,
15:14 However, Samuel **a**,
16:1 The LORD **a** Samuel,
16:2 Samuel **a**. "When Saul hears
17:26 David **a** the men who were
17:28 did you come here," he **a** him,
17:30 to face another man and **a**
17:43 The Philistine **a** David,
17:55 the Philistine, he **a** Abner,
17:58 Saul **a** him, "Whose son are
18:18 David **a** Saul. "And how
18:23 it a point to say this, David **a**,
19:17 Saul **a** Michal, "Why did you
19:22 in Secu and **a** ⌊the people⌋,
20:1 and **a**, "What have I done?
20:10 Then David **a**, "Who will tell
20:27 Saul **a** his son Jonathan,
20:32 Jonathan **a** his father,
21:1 he **a** David. "Why is no one
21:8 David **a** Ahimelech,
21:11 Achish's officers **a**,
22:3 He **a** the king of Moab,
22:13 Saul **a** him, "Why did you and
22:14 Ahimelech **a** the king,
23:1 David was **a**, "Did you know
23:2 David **a** the LORD,
23:4 David **a** the LORD again,
23:12 David **a**. "They will hand you
24:9 David **a** Saul, "Why do you

1Sm 24:16 Saul **a**, "Is that you speaking,
26:6 David **a** Ahimelech the Hittite
26:14 he **a**. "Who is calling the king?"
26:14 is calling the king?" Abner **a**.
26:15 David **a** Abner, "Aren't you a
26:17 he **a**. "It is my voice, Your Royal
28:11 the woman **a**. "Conjure up
28:12 she cried out loudly and **a**,
28:14 he **a** her. She answered, "An old
28:15 Samuel **a** Saul, "Why did you
29:3 The Philistine officers **a**,
29:3 Achish **a** the Philistine officers,
29:8 David **a** Achish. "What have
30:8 Then David **a** the LORD,
30:13 David **a** him, "To whom do you
30:15 David **a** him. He answered,
2Sm 1:3 David **a** him. "I escaped
1:4 David **a** him. "Please tell me."
1:5 David **a** the young man who
1:8 "He **a** me, 'Who are you?'
1:13 David **a** the young man who
1:14 David **a**, "Why weren't you
2:1 After this, David **a** the LORD,
2:1 David **a**. "To Hebron,"
2:20 When Abner looked back, he **a**,
3:7 Ishbosheth **a** Abner,
3:8 he **a**. "Until now I've been
3:12 he **a**. "Make an agreement with
3:24 Joab went to the king and **a**,
5:19 David **a** the LORD,
5:23 David **a** the LORD,
6:9 come to my ⌊city⌋?" he **a**.
7:18 am I, Almighty LORD," he **a**,
9:1 David **a**, "Is there anyone left in
9:2 the king **a** him. "⌊Yes,⌋ I am,"
9:3 David **a**, "Is there someone left
9:4 the king **a**. Ziba replied, "He is
10:3 the Ammonite princes **a** their
11:7 When Uriah arrived, David **a**
11:10 didn't go home," David **a** Uriah,
12:19 David **a** them. "⌊Yes,⌋ he is
12:20 he went home and **a** for food.
12:21 His officials **a** him,
13:4 He **a** Amnon, "Why are you,
13:6 Amnon **a** the king,
13:20 Her brother Absalom **a** her,
13:26 go with you?" the king **a** him.
14:5 The king **a** her, "What can I do
14:19 the king **a**. The woman
14:31 set my field on fire?" he **a**.
15:19 The king **a** Ittai from Gath,
15:27 the king **a** Zadok the priest.
16:2 David **a** Ziba. "The donkeys are
16:3 the king **a**. "He's staying in
16:9 Zeruiah's son, **a** the king,
16:17 Absalom **a** Hushai.
16:20 Then Absalom **a** Ahithophel,
17:20 they **a**. The woman said,
18:22 Joab **a**. "You won't be rewarded
18:29 the king **a**. Ahimaaz answered,
18:32 the king **a**. The Sudanese
19:25 meet the king, the king **a** him,
19:29 The king **a** him, "Why do you
19:41 They **a**, "Why did our cousins,
20:9 Joab **a** Amasa. He took hold of
20:17 He came near, and she **a**,
21:1 and David **a** the LORD's
21:3 and **a** them, "What can I do for
21:4 The king **a**, "What are you
24:13 he told David this and **a**,
24:21 Araunah **a**. David answered,
1Ki 1:11 Then Nathan **a** Solomon's
1:16 do you want?" the king **a**.
1:41 the sound of the horn, he **a**,
2:13 she **a**. "Yes," he answered.
2:14 "What is it?" she **a**.
2:16 "What is it?" she **a**.
2:42 Solomon **a** him, "Didn't I make
3:10 pleased that Solomon **a** for this.
3:11 God replied, "You've **a** for this
3:11 Instead, you've **a** for
3:12 I'm going to do what you've **a**.
3:13 giving you what you haven't **a**
9:13 he **a**. So he named it the region
10:13 whatever she **a** for,
11:22 Pharaoh **a** him, "What don't you

1Ki 12:6 He **a**, "What do you advise?
12:9 He **a** them, "What is your
13:6 Then the king **a** the man of
13:14 The old prophet **a** him,
17:18 The woman **a** Elijah,
18:7 my master Elijah?" he **a**.
18:9 Obadiah **a**, "What have I done
18:21 of all the people and **a** them,
19:9 He **a**, "What are you doing
20:14 Ahab **a**, "How ⌊will this be
20:14 Ahab **a**. "You will," the prophet
20:32 'Please let me live.'" Ahab **a**,
21:5 Jezebel came to him and **a**,
21:11 did what Jezebel **a** them
21:20 Ahab **a** Elijah, "So you've
22:3 The king of Israel **a** his staff,
22:4 Then he **a** Jehoshaphat,
22:6 He **a** them, "Should I go to war
22:7 But Jehoshaphat **a**,
22:15 king, the king **a** him, "Micaiah,
22:16 The king **a** him, "How many
22:20 The LORD **a**, 'Who will
22:21 "'How?' the LORD **a**.
22:24 leave me to talk to you?" he **a**.
2Ki 1:5 returned, the king **a** them,
1:7 The king **a** them, "What was
2:3 They **a** him, "Do you know that
2:5 They **a**, "Do you know that the
2:9 were crossing, Elijah **a** Elisha,
2:10 Elijah said, "You have **a** for
2:14 He **a**, "Where is the LORD God
3:8 Joram **a**, "Which road should
3:11 But Jehoshaphat **a**,
3:13 Elisha **a** the king of Israel,
4:2 Elisha **a** her, "What should I do
4:14 Elisha **a**. Gehazi answered,
4:23 Her husband **a**, "Why are you
4:43 But his servant **a**, "How can I
5:7 He **a**, "Am I God? Can I kill
5:8 He **a**, "Why did you tear your
5:13 if the prophet had **a** you to do
5:21 "Is something wrong?" he **a**.
5:25 Elisha **a** him, "Where were
6:3 Then one of the disciples **a**,
6:6 The man of God **a**,
6:8 he **a** for advice from his officers
6:11 called his officers and **a** them,
6:15 Elisha's servant **a**,
6:18 blindness, as Elisha had **a**.
6:21 them, he **a** Elisha, "Master,
6:28 Then the king **a** her,
6:32 Elisha **a** the leaders,
7:3 One of them **a**, "Why are we
8:6 When the king **a** the woman
8:12 Hazael **a**. Elisha answered, "I
8:13 But Hazael **a**, "How can a dog
8:14 who **a** him what Elisha had
9:5 Jehu **a**, "Which one of us?"
9:11 One of them **a** him,
9:22 When Joram saw Jehu, he **a**,
9:31 she **a**, "Is everything alright,
9:32 up at the window, he **a**,
10:13 he **a**. They answered, "We're
10:15 Jehu greeted him and **a**,
12:7 the other priests and **a** them,
18:27 the field commander **a** them,
20:8 Hezekiah **a** Isaiah,
20:14 came to King Hezekiah and **a**,
20:15 Isaiah **a**, "What did they see in
23:17 Then he **a**, "What is this
1Ch 10:13 He **a** a medium to request
13:12 God's ark to my ⌊city⌋?" he **a**.
14:10 David **a** God, "Should I attack
14:14 Once more David **a** God.
17:16 "Who am I, LORD God," he **a**,
19:3 the Ammonite princes **a** Hanun,
2Ch 1:11 Instead, you've **a** for wisdom
9:12 whatever she **a** for,
10:6 He **a**, "What do you advise?
10:9 He **a** them, "What is your
18:3 King Ahab of Israel **a** King
18:5 He **a** them, "Should we go to
18:6 But Jehoshaphat **a**,
18:14 king, the king **a** him, "Micaiah,
18:15 The king **a** him, "How many
18:19 The LORD **a**, 'Who will
2Ch 18:20 "'How?' the LORD **a**.
18:23 he left me to talk to you?" he **a**.
19:2 **a** King Jehoshaphat,
24:6 priest Jehoiada and **a** him,
25:9 Amaziah **a** the man of God,
25:15 sent him a prophet who **a** him,
25:16 he was talking, the king **a** him,
31:9 Hezekiah **a** the priests and the
Ezr 5:3 went to the Jews and **a** them,
5:4 They also **a** the Jews for the
5:9 We **a** their leaders the
5:10 For your information, we also **a**
8:23 So we fasted and **a** our God for
Neh 1:2 I **a** them about the Jews who
2:2 The king **a** me, "Why do you
2:4 the king **a** me. So I prayed to the
2:5 and I **a** the king, "If it pleases
2:6 beside him, the king **a** me,
2:7 I also **a** the king, "If it pleases
2:19 They **a**, "What are you doing?
6:11 But I **a**, "Should a man like me
13:6 Later, I **a** the king for
13:11 I **a**. So I brought the Levites
13:17 nobles of Judah and **a** them,
13:21 I **a** them. "If you do it again, I'll
Est 1:13 Now, the king usually **a** for
1:14 The king **a** these wise men
2:15 she **a** only for what the king's
3:3 at the king's gate **a** Mordecai,
3:4 Although they **a** him day after
5:3 Then the king **a** her,
5:6 wine, the king **a** Esther,
6:3 The king **a**, "How did I reward
6:4 The king **a**, "Who is in the
6:6 The king then **a** him,
7:2 wine, the king **a** Esther,
Job 1:7 The LORD **a** Satan,
1:8 The LORD **a** Satan,
2:2 The LORD **a** Satan,
2:3 The LORD **a** Satan,
2:9 His wife **a** him, "Are you still
21:29 Haven't you **a** travelers?
Psa 21:4 He **a** you for life. You gave him
27:4 I have **a** one thing from the
105:40 The Israelites **a**, and he
106:15 He gave them what they **a** for.
Pro 30:7 "I've **a** you for two things.
Sos 3:3 ⌊I **a**,⌋ "Have you seen the one I
Isa 1:12 who **a** you to trample on my
6:11 I **a**, "How long, O Lord?"
36:12 But the field commander **a**,
38:22 Hezekiah **a**, "What is the sign
39:3 came to King Hezekiah and **a**,
39:4 Isaiah **a**, "What did they see in
40:6 I **a**, "What should I call out?"
Jer 1:11 spoke his word to me and **a**,
1:13 spoke his word to me and **a**,
3:6 was king, the LORD **a** me,
18:5 his word to me. The LORD **a**,
24:3 Then the LORD **a** me,
32:3 up Jeremiah, Zedekiah **a** him,
36:17 Then they **a** Baruch,
36:29 and you **a** Jeremiah,
37:3 They **a** him, "Please pray to
37:17 and the king **a** him privately in
37:18 Jeremiah **a** King Zedekiah,
38:26 'I **a** the king not to send me
40:14 They **a** him, "Do you know that
40:15 secretly **a** Gedaliah at Mizpah,
Eze 8:6 He **a** me, "Son of man, do you
8:12 God **a** me, "Son of man, do you
8:15 He **a** me, "Son of man, do you
8:17 He **a** me, "Son of man, do you
20:29 Then I **a** them, "What is this
24:19 The people **a** me, "Tell us,
37:3 Then he **a** me, "Son of man,
47:6 Then he **a** me, "Son of man,
Dan 1:8 So he **a** the chief-of-staff for
1:20 Whenever the king **a** them
2:10 has ever **a** such a thing of any
2:15 He **a** Arioch, the royal official,
2:16 Daniel went and **a** the king to
2:26 The king **a** Daniel (who had
3:14 Nebuchadnezzar **a** them,
3:24 He **a** his advisers,
5:13 The king **a** him, "Are you
Dan 6:12 ⌊They **a**,⌋ "Didn't you sign a
7:16 was standing there and **a** him
10:20 He **a**, "Do you know why I
12:6 One of them **a** the man dressed
12:8 So I **a** him, "Sir, how will these
Amo 7:8 He **a** me, "What do you see,
8:2 He **a**, "What do you see,
Jnh 1:6 of the ship went to him and **a**,
1:8 They **a** him, "Tell us, why has
1:10 They **a** Jonah, "Why have you
1:11 So they **a** Jonah, "What should
4:4 The LORD **a**, "What right do
4:9 Then God **a** Jonah,
Mic 2:7 the descendants of Jacob be **a**:
7:10 because they **a** me,
Hag 2:13 Haggai **a**, "Suppose a person
Zec 1:9 I **a**. The angel who was
1:19 So I **a** the angel who was
1:21 I **a**, "What are they going to
2:2 I **a** him, "Where are you
4:2 He **a** me, "What do you see?"
4:4 I **a** the angel who was
4:5 Then the angel **a** me,
4:11 I **a** the angel, "What do these
4:12 Again I **a** him, "What is the
4:13 He **a** me, "Don't you know what
5:2 The angel **a** me, "What do you
5:6 I **a**. "A basket is coming," he
5:10 I **a** the angel who was
6:4 I **a** the angel who was
7:3 They **a** the priests from the
Mat 2:2 They **a**, "Where is the one who
8:27 The men were amazed and **a**,
9:4 He **a** them, "Why are you
9:11 saw this and **a** his disciples,
12:3 Jesus **a** them, "Haven't you
12:10 The people **a** Jesus whether it
13:10 The disciples **a** him,
13:27 workers came to him and **a**,
13:28 "His workers **a** him,
15:1 Jerusalem to Jesus. They **a**,
15:33 His disciples **a** him,
15:34 Jesus **a** them, "How many
16:1 So they **a** him to show them a
16:8 about their conversation and **a**,
16:13 he **a** his disciples,
16:15 He **a** them, "But who do you
17:10 So the disciples **a** him,
17:19 came to Jesus privately and **a**,
17:24 They **a** him, "Doesn't your
17:25 he could speak, Jesus **a** him,
18:1 disciples came to Jesus and **a**,
18:21 Peter came to Jesus and **a** him,
19:3 They **a**, "Can a man divorce
19:7 The Pharisees **a** him,
19:18 the man **a**. Jesus said, "Never
19:25 who can be saved?" they **a**.
20:21 he **a** her. She said to him,
20:32 want me to do for you?" he **a**.
21:20 They **a**, "How did the fig tree
21:23 They **a**, "What gives you the
21:42 Jesus **a** them, "Have you never
22:18 so he **a**, "Why do you test me,
22:23 came to Jesus. They **a** him,
22:41 still gathered, Jesus **a** them,
26:8 They **a**, "Why did she waste it
26:15 He **a**, They offered him 30 silver
26:17 They **a**, "Where do you want
26:22 they **a** him one by one,
26:25 **a**, "You don't mean me, do you,
27:11 The governor **a** him,
27:13 Then Pilate **a** him,
27:17 people gathered, Pilate **a** them,
27:21 The governor **a** them,
27:22 Pilate **a** them, "Then what
27:23 Pilate **a**, "Why? What has he
27:58 He went to Pilate and **a** for the
Mar 2:8 He **a** them, "Why do you have
2:16 they **a** his disciples,
2:24 The Pharisees **a** him,
2:25 Jesus **a** them, "Haven't you
3:4 Then he **a** them, "Is it right to
4:10 they **a** him about the stories.
4:13 Jesus **a** them, "Don't you
4:30 Jesus **a**, "How can we show
4:40 He **a** them, "Why are you such

Mar 4:41 with fear and **a** each other,
5:9 Jesus **a** him, "What is your
5:30 around in the crowd and **a**,
5:39 into the house, he **a** them,
6:2 They **a**, "Where did this man
6:24 she went out and **a** her mother,
7:5 and the scribes **a** Jesus,
7:17 his disciples **a** him about this
7:26 She **a** him to force the demon
8:4 His disciples **a** him,
8:5 Jesus **a** them, "How many
8:12 With a deep sigh he **a**,
8:17 they were saying and **a** them,
8:21 He **a** them, "Don't you catch on
8:23 Jesus **a** him, "Can you see
8:27 On the way he **a** his disciples,
8:29 He **a** them, "But who do you
9:11 So they **a** him, "Don't the
9:16 Jesus **a** the scribes,
9:18 I **a** your disciples to force the
9:21 Jesus **a** his father,
9:28 his disciples **a** him privately,
9:33 he **a** the disciples,
10:2 They **a**, "Can a husband
10:10 the disciples **a** him about this.
10:17 He **a** Jesus, "Good Teacher,
10:26 They **a** each other,
10:36 me to do for you?" he **a** them.
10:51 Jesus **a** him, "What do you
11:5 men standing there **a** them,
11:28 They **a** him, "What gives you
12:15 their hypocrisy, so he **a** them,
12:18 came to Jesus. They **a** him,
12:28 answered them, so he **a** him,
12:35 in the temple courtyard, he **a**,
13:3 and Andrew **a** him privately,
14:12 The disciples **a** Jesus,
14:19 they **a** him one by one,
14:48 Jesus **a** them, "Have you come
14:60 up in the center and **a** Jesus,
14:61 The chief priest **a** him again,
15:2 Pilate **a** him, "Are you the king
15:4 So Pilate **a** him again,
15:6 prisoner whom the people **a** for.
15:8 The crowd **a** Pilate to do for
15:12 So Pilate again **a** them,
Luk 1:34 Mary **a** the angel, "How can
1:63 Zechariah **a** for a writing tablet
1:66 seriously thought it over and **a**,
2:48 His mother **a** him, "Son,
3:10 The crowds **a** him,
3:12 They **a** him, "Teacher,
3:14 Some soldiers **a** him,
4:38 They **a** Jesus to help her.
5:3 belonged to Simon and **a** him
5:30 They **a**, "Why do you eat and
5:34 Jesus **a** them, "Can you force
6:2 Some of the Pharisees **a**,
8:9 His disciples **a** him what this
8:25 He **a** them, "Where is your
8:25 and amazed, they **a** each other,
8:30 Jesus **a** him, "What is your
8:37 of the Gerasenes **a** Jesus
8:45 Jesus **a**, "Who touched me?"
9:18 were with him, he **a** them,
9:20 He **a** them, "But who do you
9:54 They **a**, "Lord, do you want us
10:25 He **a**, "Teacher, what must I do
10:29 So he **a** Jesus, "Who is my
10:40 So she **a**, "Lord, don't you care
12:41 Peter **a**, "Lord, did you use this
12:42 The Lord **a**, "Who, then, is the
13:18 Jesus **a**, "What is the kingdom
13:20 He **a** again, "What can I
13:23 Someone **a** him, "Sir, are only
14:5 Jesus **a** them, "If your son or
14:18 "Everyone **a** to be excused.
15:26 and **a** what was happening.
16:7 "Then he **a** another debtor,
17:17 Jesus **a**, "Weren't ten men
17:20 The Pharisees **a** Jesus when
17:37 They **a** him, "Where, Lord?"
18:18 An official **a** Jesus,
18:26 Those who heard him **a**,
18:40 man came near, Jesus **a** him,
19:33 its owners **a** them,
Luk 20:2 They **a** him, "Tell us,
20:17 looked straight at them and **a**,
20:21 They **a** him, "Teacher,
20:27 came to Jesus. They **a** him,
21:7 The disciples **a** him,
22:9 They **a** him, "Where do you
22:49 So they **a** him, "Lord,
22:66 of their highest court and **a** him,
23:3 Pilate **a** him, "Are you the king
23:6 When Pilate heard that, he **a** if
23:9 Herod **a** Jesus many questions,
23:22 He **a**, "Why? What has he done
23:52 He went to Pilate and **a** for the
24:5 The men **a** the women,
24:17 He **a** them, "What are you
24:19 he **a**. They said to him, "We
24:38 He **a** them, "Why are you
24:41 Then Jesus **a** them,
Jon 1:21 They **a** him, "Well, are you
1:21 Then they **a**, "Are you the
1:22 So they **a** him, "Who are you?
1:25 They **a** John, "Why do you
1:38 He **a** them, "What are you
1:48 Nathanael **a** Jesus,
3:4 Nicodemus **a** him,
3:26 they went to John and **a** him,
4:9 The Samaritan woman **a** him,
4:10 you would have **a** him for a
4:27 But none of them **a** him,
4:33 The disciples **a** each other,
4:40 they **a** him to stay with them.
4:47 So he went to Jesus and **a** him
4:52 The official **a** them at what
5:6 So Jesus **a** the man,
5:12 The Jews **a** him, "Who is the
6:6 Jesus **a** this question to test
6:25 of the sea, they **a** him, "Rabbi,
6:28 The people **a** Jesus,
6:30 The people **a** him,
6:42 They **a**, "Isn't this man Jesus,
6:61 So Jesus **a** them, "Did what I
6:67 So Jesus **a** the twelve
7:15 Jews were surprised and **a**,
7:31 They **a**, "When the Messiah
7:41 Still other people **a**,
7:45 priests and Pharisees **a** them,
7:47 The Pharisees **a** the temple
7:50 Nicodemus **a** them,
7:52 They **a** Nicodemus,
8:4 and **a** Jesus, "Teacher,
8:6 They **a** this to test him.
8:10 straightened up and **a** her,
8:19 The Pharisees **a** him,
8:22 Then the Jews **a**, "Is he going
8:25 The Jews **a** him, "Who did you
9:2 His disciples **a** him,
9:8 previously seen him begging **a**,
9:10 So they **a** him, "How did you
9:12 They **a** him, "Where is that
9:15 So the Pharisees **a** the man
9:16 Other Pharisees **a**,
9:17 They **a** the man who had been
9:19 They **a** his parents,
9:26 The Jews **a** him, "What did he
9:35 Jesus found the man, he **a** him,
9:40 So they **a** him, "Do you think
10:24 They **a** him, "How long will
11:34 So Jesus **a**, "Where did you
11:37 But some of the Jews **a**,
11:47 They **a**, "What are we doing?
11:56 for Jesus and **a** each other,
12:4 was going to betray him, **a**,
13:6 Peter, Peter **a** him, "Lord,
13:12 Then he **a** his disciples,
13:25 to Jesus, that disciple **a**, "Lord,
13:36 Simon Peter **a** him,
14:22 Judas (not Iscariot) **a** Jesus,
16:24 So far you haven't **a** for
16:30 to wait for questions to be **a**.
18:4 So he went to meet them and **a**,
18:7 Jesus **a** them again,
18:17 The gatekeeper **a** Peter,
18:25 Some men **a** him, "Aren't you,
18:26 ear Peter had cut off, **a** him,
18:29 Pilate came out to them and **a**,
18:33 called for Jesus, and **a** him,
Jon 18:37 Pilate **a** him, "So you are a
19:9 the palace again and **a** Jesus,
19:15 Pilate **a** them, "Should I crucify
19:31 So they **a** Pilate to have the
19:38 the city of Arimathea **a** Pilate
20:13 The angels **a** her why she was
20:15 Jesus **a** her, "Why are you
21:5 Jesus **a** them, "Friends,
21:15 Jesus **a** Simon Peter,
21:16 Jesus **a** him again,
21:17 Jesus **a** him a third time,
21:17 sad because Jesus had **a** him
21:20 chest at the supper and **a**,
21:21 saw him, he **a** Jesus, "Lord,
Act 1:6 together, they **a** him, "Lord,
1:11 They **a**, "Why are you men
2:12 They **a** each other,
2:37 They **a** Peter and the other
3:3 he **a** them for a handout.
3:14 You **a** to have a murderer given
4:7 in front of them and then **a**,
5:3 Peter **a**, "Ananias, why did you
5:8 So Peter **a** her, "Tell me,
7:1 the chief priest **a** Stephen,
7:27 He **a** Moses, 'Who made you
7:46 David **a** that he might provide a
8:30 Philip **a** him, "Do you
9:2 and **a** him to write letters of
9:5 Saul **a**, "Who are you, sir?"
9:21 They **a**, "Isn't this the man who
10:4 Cornelius **a** the angel,
10:18 They **a** if Simon Peter was
10:23 Peter **a** the men to come into
10:48 Then they **a** Peter to stay with
13:28 they **a** Pilate to have him
16:29 The jailer **a** for torches and
16:30 Paul and Silas outside and **a**,
16:39 they **a** them to leave the city.
17:18 Some **a**, "What is this babbling
17:19 court, the Areopagus, and **a**,
18:20 The Jews **a** him to stay longer,
19:2 and **a** them, "Did you receive
19:3 Paul **a** them, "What kind of
21:33 The officer **a** who Paul was
21:37 the barracks, he **a** the officer,
22:10 "Then I **a**, 'What do you want
22:25 Paul **a** the sergeant who was
22:26 The sergeant **a** him,
22:27 officer went to Paul and **a** him,
23:12 They **a** God to curse them if
23:14 "We've **a** God to curse us if we
23:18 He **a** me to bring this young
23:19 they could be alone, and **a** him,
23:21 They have **a** God to curse
23:34 he **a** Paul which province he
25:9 So he **a** Paul, "Are you willing
25:15 information about him and **a** me
25:20 So I **a** Paul if he would like to
25:21 He **a** to be held in prison and to
26:15 "I **a**, 'Who are you, sir?'
28:20 That's why I **a** to see you and
Gal 2:10 The only thing they **a** us to do
Rev 7:13 One of the leaders **a** me,
10:9 I went to the angel and **a** him to
17:7 The angel **a** me, "Why are you

asking (40)

Gen 37:10 his father criticized him by **a**,
39:10 Although she kept **a** Joseph
43:7 "The man kept **a** about us and
Exo 10:11 that's what you've been **a** for."
15:24 complained about Moses by **a**,
17:7 they tested the LORD, **a**,
Num 11:12 Are you really **a** me to carry
11:20 and cried in front of him, **a**,
Jos 22:16 the LORD's congregation is **a**,
1Sm 10:2 He keeps **a**, "What can I do to
12:19 our other sins by **a** for a king."
28:16 Samuel said, "Why are you **a**
1Ki 1:6 never confronted him by **a** why
2:20 "I'm **a** you for one little thing,"
12:9 to these people who are **a** me
2Ch 10:9 to these people who are **a** me
16:12 Instead of **a** the LORD for help,
Isa 30:2 They go to Egypt without **a** me.
Jer 17:15 People keep **a** me,

Lam 2:12 They're **a** their mothers for
Mal 1:9 "Now try **a** God to be kind to
Mat 13:54 People were **a**, "Where did this
20:22 don't realize what you're **a**.
21:10 People were **a**, "Who is this?"
22:35 tested Jesus by **a**,
Mar 10:38 don't realize what you're **a**.
Luk 2:46 and **a** them questions.
14:3 Jesus reacted by **a** the
Jon 2:18 The Jews reacted by **a** Jesus,
4:10 God's gift is and who is **a** you
7:11 They kept **a**, "Where is that
8:7 persisted in **a** him questions,
16:18 So they were **a** each other,
17:15 I'm not **a** you to take them out
Act 21:39 I'm **a** you to let me talk to the
22:7 ground and heard a voice **a** me,
26:14 and I heard a voice **a** me in
Rom 10:20 to those who weren't **a** for me."
Eph 3:16 I'm **a** God to give you a gift
1Ti 5:5 in God by praying and **a**

asks (48)

Gen 32:17 Esau meets you and **a** you,
46:33 Pharaoh calls for you and **a**,
Jdg 4:20 If anyone comes and **a** if there
2Sm 11:21 If the king **a** this, then say,
1Ki 21:19 'This is what the LORD **a**:
2Ki 8:9 He **a** whether he will recover
9:18 Jehu, and said, "The king **a**,
9:19 to them, he said, "The king **a**,
Ezr 7:21 God of Heaven, **a** you to do.
Est 5:5 and do whatever Esther **a**."
Job 15:23 wanders around for food and **a**,
35:10 But no one **a**, 'Where is God,
Isa 1:11 The LORD **a**, "What do your
3:15 Almighty LORD of Armies **a**,
40:25 is my equal?" **a** the Holy One.
52:5 **a** the LORD. My people are
65:16 Whoever **a** for a blessing in the
66:9 **a** the LORD. "Do I cause a
66:9 to have children?" **a** your God.
Jer 5:22 **a** the LORD. "Don't you tremble
22:16 to know me?" **a** the LORD.
23:28 do with straw?" **a** the LORD.
23:29 shatters a rock?" **a** the LORD.
30:21 come near me?" **a** the LORD.
39:12 but do for him whatever he **a**."
Dan 2:10 can tell the king what he **a**.
6:7 for the next 30 days whoever **a**
6:12 that for 30 days whoever **a**
Amo 6:10 house and **a** someone who is
Zec 13:6 "When someone **a** him,
Mal 1:8 **a** the LORD of Armies.
1:9 **a** the LORD of Armies.
1:13 them from you?" **a** the LORD.
Mat 5:42 Give to everyone who **a** you for
7:8 Everyone who **a** will receive.
7:9 "If your child **a** you for bread,
7:10 Or if your child **a** for a fish,
Mar 11:3 If anyone **a** you what you are
14:14 the owner that the teacher **a**,
Luk 6:30 Give to everyone who **a** you for
11:10 Everyone who **a** will receive.
11:11 "If your child **a** you,
11:12 Or if your child **a** you for an
19:31 If anyone **a** you why you are
22:11 of the house that the teacher **a**,
Jon 16:5 Yet, none of you **a** me where
Rom 10:16 Isaiah **a**, "Lord, who has
1Pe 3:15 ⌊in God⌋ when anyone **a** you

asleep (29)

Gen 41:5 He fell **a** again and had a
Jos 2:8 Before the spies fell **a**,
Jdg 4:21 fallen sound **a** from exhaustion,
1Sm 3:3 and Samuel was **a** in the
26:7 Saul was lying **a** inside the
26:12 All of them were **a**.
1Ki 3:20 was beside me, while I was **a**.
Psa 4:8 I fall **a** in peace the moment I
121:3 Your guardian will not fall **a**.
Dan 2:1 was troubled, but he stayed **a**.
2:28 you had while you were **a**:
4:5 The visions I had while I was **a**
4:10 the visions I had while I was **a**:
4:13 these visions as I was **a**.
7:1 saw a vision while he was **a**.
Jnh 1:5 and was lying there sound **a**.
Mat 13:25 But while people were **a**,
25:5 became drowsy and fell **a**.
26:40 the disciples, he found them **a**.
26:43 He found them **a** again
Mar 13:36 come suddenly and find you **a**.
14:37 went back and found them **a**.
14:40 He found them **a** because they
Luk 8:23 sailing along, Jesus fell **a**.
22:45 He found them **a** and overcome
Act 20:9 was gradually falling **a**.
1Th 5:6 Therefore, we must not fall **a**
5:10 awake in this life or **a** in death,
2Pe 2:3 and their destruction is not **a**.

Asnah (1)

Ezr 2:50 **A**, Meunim, Nephusim,

Aspatha (1)

Est 9:7 Parshandatha, Dalphon, **A**,

aspect (1)

1Pe 1:15 be holy in every **a** of your life.

Asriel (3)

Num 26:31 the family of **A**, the family of
Jos 17:2 Helek, **A**, Shechem, Hepher,
1Ch 7:14 sons were **A** and Machir.

assassinated (6)

1Ki 15:27 Baasha **a** him in the Philistine
2Ki 19:7 I'll have him **a** in his own
19:37 Adrammelech and Sharezer **a**
Isa 37:7 I'll have him **a** in his own
37:38 **a** him and escaped to the land
Jer 41:2 So they **a** the man whom the

assassination (1)

1Ki 15:28 The **a** happened in Asa's third

assault (4)

Dtr 17:8 It may involve murder, **a**,
21:5 a disagreement or an **a**.
Jdg 4:15 in front of Barak's deadly **a**.
Job 30:21 With your mighty hand you **a**

assaults (1)

Pro 19:26 A son who **a** his father ⌊and⌋

assemble (17)

Exo 3:16 "Go, **a** the leaders of Israel.
Num 8:9 and **a** the whole community of
Dtr 4:10 "**A** the people in front of me,
31:12 **A** the men, women,
31:28 **A** all the leaders of your tribes
Neh 4:20 hear the trumpet, **a** around me.
Est 4:16 "**A** all the Jews in Susa.
8:11 for the Jews in every city to **a**,
Job 19:12 His troops **a** against me.
Isa 14:13 in the north where the gods **a**.
60:4 All of your people **a** and come
Jer 49:14 to say, "**A**, and attack Edom.
Eze 38:13 Did you **a** all these soldiers to
39:17 bird and every wild animal, '**A**,
Dan 3:2 messengers to **a** the satraps,
11:10 They will **a** a large number of
Joe 2:16 **A** the leaders. Gather the

assembled (38)

Exo 4:29 went ⌊to Egypt⌋ and **a** all
12:6 Then at dusk, all the **a** people
35:1 Moses **a** the whole Israelite
Num 1:18 and **a** the whole community on
14:5 community of Israel **a** there.
20:10 Then Moses and Aaron **a** the
Dtr 33:5 leaders of the people **a** together
Jos 8:10 in the morning and **a** the troops.
Jdg 11:20 Sihon **a** all his troops.
20:11 So all the men of Israel **a**.
20:14 their towns and **a** at Gibeah
1Sm 13:5 The Philistines **a** to fight
14:20 and all the troops with him **a**
17:1 The Philistines **a** their armies
17:1 They **a** at Socoh, which is in
1Sm 17:2 Saul and the army of Israel **a**
28:4 The Philistines **a** and camped
28:4 Saul also **a** the whole Israelite
29:1 The Philistines **a** their whole
2Sm 6:1 David again **a** all the best
10:17 he **a** Israel's army,
1Ki 8:1 Then Solomon **a** the respected
2Ki 6:24 Later King Benhadad of Aram **a**
1Ch 19:17 he **a** Israel's army,
2Ch 5:2 Then Solomon **a** the respected
Neh 9:1 When the Israelites **a** on the
Est 9:2 The Jews **a** in their cities
9:15 The Jews in Susa also **a** on
9:16 the king's provinces had also **a**
9:18 But the Jews in Susa had **a** on
Psa 22:25 am among those **a** for worship.
40:9 among those **a** for worship.
40:10 truth from those **a** for worship.
Isa 43:9 and people have **a**.
Eze 38:7 all the soldiers **a** around you.
Dan 3:3 the other provincial officials **a**
Mic 6:9 "Listen, you tribe **a** in the city.
Act 28:17 When they **a**, he said to them,

assemblies (6)

Lev 23:2 you must announce as holy **a**.
23:4 appointed festivals with holy **a**,
23:37 Announce them as holy **a** for
Isa 1:13 and the **a** you call.
1:13 I can't stand your evil **a**.
Amo 5:21 pleased with your religious **a**.

assembling (2)

1Sm 13:11 were **a** at Michmash.
Isa 13:4 The LORD of Armies is **a** his

assembly (102)

Gen 49:6 Do not let me join their **a**.
Exo 12:16 You must have a holy **a** on the
Lev 4:13 without the **a** being aware of it,
16:17 the sins of the entire **a** of Israel.
23:3 when you don't work, a holy **a**.
23:7 first day there will be a holy **a**.
23:8 day there will be a holy **a**.
23:21 that there will be a holy **a**
23:24 a holy **a** announced by the
23:27 There will be a holy **a**.
23:35 first day there will be a holy **a**.
23:36 day there will be a holy **a**.
Num 10:7 But when you gather the **a**,
15:15 is one law for the whole **a**:
16:2 community, chosen by the **a**.
16:3 above the LORD's **a**?"
16:33 so they disappeared from the **a**.
16:47 and ran into the middle of the **a**,
19:20 must be excluded from the **a**.
20:4 Did you bring the LORD's **a**
20:6 and Aaron went from the **a**
25:7 So he left the **a**, took a spear in
28:18 first day there will be a holy **a**.
28:25 day you must have a holy **a**.
28:26 you must have a holy **a**.
29:1 month you must have a holy **a**.
29:7 month you must have a holy **a**.
29:12 month you must have a holy **a**.
29:35 you must hold a religious **a**.
Dtr 5:22 LORD spoke to your whole **a**
9:10 mountain on the day of the **a**.
10:4 mountain on the day of the **a**.
16:8 hold a religious **a** dedicated
18:16 the day of the **a** at Mount Horeb.
23:1 never join the **a** of the LORD.
23:2 illicit union may not join the **a**
23:2 of his may join the **a**
23:3 or Moabites may not join the **a**
23:3 of theirs may join the **a**
23:8 may join the **a** of the LORD.
33:4 They belong to the **a** of Jacob.
Jos 8:35 in front of the whole **a** of Israel,
Jdg 21:5 that did not take part in the **a**
21:8 had come to the **a** in the camp.
1Ki 8:5 the whole **a** from Israel were
8:14 and blessed the whole **a**
8:22 of the entire **a** of Israel,
8:55 blessed the entire **a** of Israel,
12:3 Jeroboam and the entire **a** of

1Ki 12:20 sent men to invite him to the **a**.
2Ki 10:20 "Call a holy **a** to honor Baal."
1Ch 13:2 he told the whole **a** of Israel,
13:4 The whole **a** agreed to this
29:1 King David said to the whole **a**,
29:10 while the whole **a** watched.
29:20 David said to the whole **a**,
29:20 So the whole **a** praised the
2Ch 1:3 Then Solomon and the entire **a**
1:5 and the **a** worshiped the LORD.
5:6 the whole **a** from Israel were
6:3 the whole **a** from Israel while
6:12 of the entire **a** of Israel,
6:13 knelt in front of the entire **a**,
7:9 the eighth day there was an **a**.
23:3 The whole **a** made an
24:6 and the **a** had required Israel
28:14 of the leaders and the whole **a**.
29:23 in front of the king and the **a**,
29:28 The whole **a** bowed down with
29:31 The **a** brought sacrifices and
29:32 by the **a** totaled 70 bulls,
30:2 and the whole **a** in Jerusalem
30:4 The king and the whole **a**
30:13 They formed a large **a**.
30:17 Many people in the **a** had not
30:23 Then the whole **a** decided to
30:24 sheep as sacrifices for the **a**.
30:24 and 10,000 sheep for the **a**.
30:25 The whole **a** from Judah,
30:25 the whole **a** from Israel,
Ezr 2:64 The whole **a** totaled 42,360.
10:12 Then the whole **a** shouted in
Neh 7:66 The whole **a** totaled 42,360.
8:2 the Teachings in front of the **a**.
8:17 The whole **a** that had come
8:18 they had a closing festival **a** in
13:1 ever be admitted into God's **a**.
Psa 7:7 Let an **a** of people gather
82:1 takes his place in his own **a**.
89:5 and your faithfulness in the **a**
149:1 praise in the **a** of godly people.
Pro 5:14 reached total ruin in the **a**
21:16 will rest in the **a** of the dead.
Isa 4:5 of Mount Zion and over the **a**.
Joe 1:14 Call for an **a**! Gather the leaders
2:15 a time to fast. Call for an **a**.
Mic 2:5 in the LORD's **a** will draw lots
Luk 23:1 Then the entire **a** stood up and
Act 7:38 is the Moses who was in the **a**
19:39 settle the matter in a legal **a**.
19:41 he dismissed the **a**.
Heb 12:23 and to the **a** of God's firstborn

asserted (1)

Act 24:9 and **a** that everything Tertullus

Asshur (2)

Gen 10:22 **A**, Arpachshad, Lud, and Aram.
1Ch 1:17 **A**, Arpachshad, Lud, Aram, Uz,

assign (3)

Eze 44:14 I will **a** them all of the less
Mat 24:51 severely punish him and **a** him
Luk 12:46 punish him severely and **a** him

assigned (22)

Gen 40:4 The captain of the guard **a**
1Sm 29:4 him to the place you **a** him.
29:10 go to the place I have **a** to you.
2Ki 8:6 So the king **a** to her an
1Ch 6:48 were **a** all the other duties in
9:23 and their descendants were **a**
26:12 their head men were **a** duties
26:29 and his sons were **a** duties.
2Ch 25:5 together and **a** them by families
31:2 Hezekiah **a** the priests and the
Ezr 6:18 The priests were **a** to their
Neh 4:23 and the guards **a** to me never
7:1 and the Levites were **a** their
9:22 and **a** them their boundaries.
11:36 in Judah were **a** to Benjamin.
13:30 I **a** duties to the priests and
Job 38:12 orders to the morning or **a**
Eze 4:5 I have **a** to you one day for
4:6 for each year I have **a** to you.

Dan 9:24 time periods have been **a**
Mar 13:34 He **a** work to each one and
Jud 1:6 but abandoned their **a** place.

assignment (4)

1Ch 23:11 were given an **a** as one family.
25:8 drew lots for their **a** of duties,
Neh 13:30 Each one had his own **a**.
2Co 10:15 we need to carry out our **a**—

Assir (4)

Exo 6:24 The sons of Korah were **A**,
1Ch 6:22 Korah's son was **A**.
6:23 Ebiasaph's son was **A**.
6:37 who was the son of **A**,

Assir's (2)

1Ch 6:23 **A** son was Elkanah.
6:24 **A** son was Tahath.

assist (4)

Num 3:6 of the priest Aaron to **a** him.
8:26 They may **a** the other Levites
1Ki 19:21 Then he left to follow and **a**
2Ch 13:10 and the Levites **a** them.

assistance (5)

Neh 2:10 the people of Israel so much **a**.
Job 26:3 wisdom and offered so much **a**.
Psa 60:11 because human **a** is worthless.
108:12 because human **a** is worthless.
Act 6:1 and other **a** was distributed.

assistant (8)

Exo 24:13 set out with his **a** Joshua,
33:11 but his **a**, Joshua, son of Nun,
38:23 His **a** was Oholiab,
Num 11:28 who had been Moses' **a** ever
Dtr 1:38 But your **a** Joshua,
Jos 1:1 LORD said to Moses' **a** Joshua,
2Ki 3:11 He used to be Elijah's **a**."
2Ch 31:12 his brother Shimei was his **a**.

assistants (3)

2Ki 19:6 king's **a** slandered me.
Isa 37:6 king's **a** slandered me.
Jer 14:3 Important people send their **a**

assisted (2)

Ezr 8:33 Binnui's son Noadiah, **a** them.
Est 9:3 and the king's treasurers **a** the

associate (12)

Jos 23:12 with them or **a** with them,
Pro 20:19 Do not **a** with a person whose
23:20 Do not **a** with those who drink
24:21 Do not **a** with those who
Jon 4:9 don't **a** with Samaritans.)
Act 10:28 it is for a Jewish man to **a**
1Co 5:9 letter to you I told you not to **a**
5:11 was that you should not **a**
Gal 2:12 drew back and would not **a**
4:17 They don't want you to **a** with
2Th 3:6 Christ we order you not to **a**
3:14 Take note of them and don't **a**

associated (8)

Isa 44:11 Everyone **a** with the gods will
Eze 37:16 the Israelites who are **a** with it.'
37:16 all the people of Israel **a** with it.'
37:19 and the tribes of Israel **a** with it,
Act 13:7 He was **a** with an intelligent
Rom 1:5 obedience that is **a** with faith.
16:26 obedience that is **a** with faith.
Heb 10:33 At times you **a** with people

associates (3)

Job 34:8 and **a** with evil people?
Pro 13:20 but whoever **a** with fools will
28:7 Whoever **a** with gluttons

associating (2)

1Co 15:33 **A** with bad people will ruin
2Ti 2:21 Those who stop **a** with

Assos (4)

Act 20:13 ship and sailed for the city of **A**.
20:13 At **A**, we were going to pick up
20:13 planned to walk overland to **A**.
20:14 When Paul met us in **A**,

assume (5)

Lev 25:25 one who can **a** responsibility,
Rut 4:5 you will also **a** responsibility
4:6 "In that case I cannot **a**
4:6 I cannot **a** that responsibility."
Gal 6:5 **A** your own responsibility.

Assurbanipal (2)

Ezr 4:10 the great and noble **A** deported.
4:10 (**A** settled them in the cities of

assure (4)

Rom 10:2 I can **a** you that they are
2Co 2:8 That is why I urge you to **a** him
8:3 I **a** you that by their own free
Col 4:13 I **a** you that he works hard for

assured (4)

1Sm 10:16 "He **a** us the donkeys had been
2Sm 23:5 every detail arranged and **a**.
Mar 15:45 When the officer had **a** him that
Act 18:5 He **a** the Jews that Jesus is

assures (1)

Heb 11:1 Faith **a** us of things we expect

assuring (1)

Psa 94:19 your **a** words soothed my soul.

Assyria (133)

Gen 2:14 is the one that flows east of **A**.
10:11 He went from that land to **A**
25:18 in the direction of **A**.
Num 24:22 when **A** takes you as prisoners
24:24 They will conquer **A** and Eber.
2Ki 15:19 King Pul of **A** came to ⌊attack⌋
15:20 of silver for the king of **A**.
15:20 the king of **A** left the country.
15:29 Tiglath Pileser of **A** took Ijon,
15:29 people away to **A** as captives.
16:7 Tiglath Pileser of **A** to say,
16:8 to the king of **A** as a present.
16:9 The king of **A** listened to him
16:10 meet King Tiglath Pileser of **A**.
16:18 did this to please the king of **A**.
17:3 of **A** defeated Hoshea,
17:4 The king of **A** found Hoshea to
17:4 payments to the king of **A**.)
17:4 So the king of **A** arrested him
17:5 Then the king of **A** attacked the
17:6 the king of **A** captured Samaria
17:6 the Israelites to **A** as captives.
17:23 from their land to **A** as captives,
17:24 The king of **A** brought people
17:26 someone said to the king of **A**,
17:27 The king of **A** gave this
18:7 rebelled against the king of **A**
18:9 of **A** attacked Samaria,
18:11 The king of **A** took the
18:11 the Israelites to **A** as captives.
18:13 King Sennacherib of **A**
18:14 to the king of **A** at Lachish:
18:14 So the king of **A** demanded that
18:16 gave the gold to the king of **A**.
18:17 Then the king of **A** sent his
18:19 great king, the king of **A**, says:
18:23 with my master, the king of **A**.
18:28 to the great king, the king of **A**.
18:30 the control of the king of **A**.'
18:31 this is what the king of **A** says:
18:33 countries from the king of **A**?
19:4 His master, the king of **A**,
19:8 of **A** fighting against Libnah.
19:10 the control of the king of **A**.
19:11 You heard what the kings of **A**
19:17 of **A** have leveled nations.
19:20 about King Sennacherib of **A**.
19:32 LORD says about the king of **A**:
19:36 King Sennacherib of **A** left.

2Ki 20:6 from the control of the king of **A**
23:29 came to help the king of **A** at
1Ch 5:6 King Tiglath Pilneser of **A** took
5:26 Pul of **A** (King Tiglath Pilneser
5:26 (King Tiglath Pilneser of **A**)
2Ch 28:16 for help from the kings of **A**.
28:20 Pilneser of **A** attacked Ahaz.
28:21 he gave them to the king of **A**.
30:6 the power of the kings of **A**.
32:1 King Sennacherib of **A** came to
32:4 "Why should the kings of **A**
32:7 or terrified by the king of **A**
32:8 The king of **A** has human
32:9 while King Sennacherib of **A**
32:10 King Sennacherib of **A** says:
32:11 rescue us from the king of **A**?'
32:22 from King Sennacherib of **A**
33:11 of the king of **A** invade Judah.
Ezr 4:2 time of King Esarhaddon of **A**,
6:22 the king of **A** change his mind
Neh 9:32 time of the kings of **A** until now.
Psa 83:8 Even **A** has joined them.
Isa 7:17 ⌊He will bring⌋ the king of **A**.
7:18 and for the bees that are in **A**.
7:20 hire the king of **A** from beyond
8:4 carried away to the king of **A**."
8:7 Euphrates River — the king of **A**
10:5 "How horrible it will be for **A**!
10:12 he will punish the king of **A** for
11:11 remains of his people in **A**,
11:16 people left in **A** like there was
14:25 I'll crush **A** on my land.
19:23 will run from Egypt to **A**.
19:23 Egypt and the Egyptians to **A**,
19:24 along with Egypt and **A**.
19:25 the work of my hands **A**,
20:1 **A** sent his commander-in-chief
20:4 The king of **A** will lead away
20:6 be rescued from the king of **A**.
23:13 **A** gave this land to the desert
23:13 **A** set up battle towers,
27:13 Those who are dying in **A** and
30:31 the people of **A** will be
36:1 King Sennacherib of **A**
36:2 Then the king of **A** sent his
36:4 great king, the king of **A**, says:
36:8 with my master, the king of **A**.
36:13 to the great king, the king of **A**.
36:15 the control of the king of **A**.'
36:16 this is what the king of **A** says:
36:18 countries from the king of **A**?
37:4 His master, the king of **A**,
37:8 of **A** fighting against Libnah.
37:10 the control of the king of **A**.
37:11 You heard what the kings of **A**
37:18 that the kings of **A** have
37:21 about King Sennacherib of **A**.
37:33 LORD says about the king of **A**:
37:37 King Sennacherib of **A** left.
38:6 the control of the king of **A**.'"
Jer 2:18 gain anything by going to **A**
2:36 as you were put to shame by **A**.
50:17 devour them was the king of **A**.
50:18 as I punished the king of **A**.
Lam 5:6 to beg Egypt and **A** for food.
Eze 23:7 for all the important men in **A**.
27:23 **A**, and Kilmad traded with you.
31:3 What about **A**? It was a cedar in
32:22 "**A** is there with its whole army,
Hos 5:13 Ephraim went to **A** to ask the
7:11 for Egypt and run to **A** for help.
8:9 "The people of Israel went to **A**.
9:3 they will eat unclean food in **A**.
10:6 itself will be carried to **A** as
11:5 Instead, **A** will rule them
11:11 Egypt and like doves from **A**.
12:1 They make treaties with **A** and
14:3 **A** cannot save us.
Mic 5:6 They will rule **A** with their
7:12 people will come to you from **A**
Nah 3:18 Your shepherds, king of **A**,
Zep 2:13 against the north and destroy **A**.
Zec 10:10 I will gather them from **A**.
10:11 The pride of **A** will be

Assyrian (6)

2Ki 19:6 **A** king's assistants slandered
19:35 ⌊soldiers⌋ in the **A** camp.
2Ch 32:21 in the **A** king's camp.
Isa 37:6 **A** king's assistants slandered
37:36 ⌊soldiers⌋ in the **A** camp.
Eze 23:5 She lusted after her **A** lovers

Assyrians (15)

Gen 25:3 descendants were the **A**,
2Ki 19:18 So the **A** have destroyed them.
1Ch 5:22 land until the **A** captured them.
Isa 10:24 don't be afraid of the **A** when
19:23 The **A** will come to Egypt and
19:23 will worship with the **A**.
31:8 Then **A** will be killed with
37:19 So the **A** have destroyed them.
52:4 Later the **A** oppressed them for
Eze 16:28 "'You had sex with the **A**
23:9 to the **A** whom she lusted after.
23:12 She lusted after the **A** who
23:23 as well as all the **A**.
Mic 5:5 When the **A** invade our land
5:6 They will rescue us from the **A**

Assyrians' (1)

Isa 10:5 fury is the staff in the **A** hands

Assyria's (3)

2Ki 19:19 rescue us from **A** control so
Isa 37:20 rescue us from **A** control so
Eze 32:23 **A** army lies around its grave.

Astarte (6)

Jdg 2:13 god Baal and the goddess **A**.
1Sm 7:3 the statues of the goddess **A**.
7:4 rid of the statues of Baal and **A**
1Ki 11:5 Solomon followed **A** (the
11:33 and worshiped **A** (the goddess
2Ki 23:13 for **A** (the disgusting goddess

Astartes (2)

Jdg 10:6 the Baals and the **A** —
1Sm 12:10 the Baals and the **A**.

astonished (5)

Job 26:11 heaven tremble and are **a** when
Psa 48:5 ⌊Mount Zion⌋, they were **a**.
Jer 4:9 will be amazed and **a**."
Hab 1:5 Be amazed and **a**.
Mar 5:42 years old.) They were **a**.

astonishing (1)

2Ch 2:9 to build will be large and **a**.

astonishment (1)

Isa 13:8 They'll look at one another in **a**.

astounded (3)

Isa 59:16 He's **a** that there's no one to
63:5 I was **a** that there was no
Mar 6:51 The disciples were **a**.

astounding (1)

Dan 8:24 He will cause **a** destruction

astray (16)

2Ch 21:11 So he led Judah **a**.
Job 36:18 Be careful that you are not led **a**
Psa 58:3 From their birth liars go **a**.
Pro 12:26 wicked people leads others **a**.
Isa 9:16 these people lead them **a**.
19:13 leaders of Memphis are led **a**.
19:14 So they lead the Egyptians **a**
30:28 of the people to lead them **a**.
44:20 misguided minds lead them **a**.
47:10 and knowledge have led you **a**,
Jer 23:13 and led my people Israel **a**.
23:32 made up and lead my people **a**
50:6 shepherds have led them **a**.
Hos 4:12 of prostitution leads them **a**.
Amo 2:4 They have been led **a** by false
Eph 4:14 clever strategies to lead us **a**.

astrologer (3)

Dan 2:10 of any magician, psychic, or **a**.
Act 13:6 He was an **a** who claimed to
13:8 Elymas, whose name means **a**,

astrologers (9)

Isa 47:13 Let your **a** and your stargazers,
Dan 2:2 and **a** so that they could tell
2:4 The **a** spoke to the king in
2:5 The king answered the **a**,
2:10 The **a** answered the king,
3:8 After that happened, some **a**
4:7 The magicians, psychics, **a**,
5:7 screamed for the psychics, **a**,
5:11 psychics, **a**, and fortunetellers.

Asyncritus (1)

Rom 16:14 Greet **A**, Phlegon, Hermes,

Atad (2)

Gen 50:10 came to the threshing floor of **A**,
50:11 at the threshing floor of **A**,

Atarah (1)

1Ch 2:26 Her name was **A**, and she was

Ataroth (4)

Num 32:3 "**A**, Dibon, Jazer, Nimrah,
32:34 the cities of Dibon, **A**, Aroer,
Jos 16:2 goes to Luz and over to **A** at
16:7 it descends to **A** and Naarah,

Ataroth Addar (2)

Jos 16:5 the land they inherited is from **A**
18:13 the border goes down to **A** over

ate (108)

Gen 3:6 took some of the fruit and **a** it.
3:6 who was with her, and he **a** it.
3:12 fruit from the tree, and I **a** it."
3:13 and I **a**," the woman answered.
3:17 to your wife and **a** fruit from
18:8 them under the tree as they **a**.
19:3 unleavened bread, and they **a**.
24:54 the men who were with him **a**
25:34 He **a** and drank, and then he
26:30 and they **a** and drank.
27:25 brought it to Isaac, and he **a** it.
27:33 I **a** it before you came in.
31:38 and I never **a** any rams from
31:46 and **a** there by the pile of
31:54 They **a** with him and spent the
39:6 anything except the food he **a**.
41:4 that were sickly and skinny **a**
41:20 The thin, sickly cows **a** up the
43:34 So they **a** and drank with
Exo 10:15 They **a** all the plants and all
16:3 by our pots of meat and **a** all
16:35 The Israelites **a** manna for 40
16:35 They **a** manna until they came
24:11 and then they **a** and drank.
Num 11:5 Remember all the free fish we **a**
25:2 The people **a** the meat from the
Dtr 29:6 You **a** no bread and drank no
32:14 They **a** cheese from cows and
32:38 Where are the gods who **a** the
Jos 5:11 they **a** some of the produce of
24:13 So you **a** all you wanted!
Jdg 9:27 They **a**, drank, and cursed
14:9 honey⌋ into his hands and **a**
19:6 So they both sat down and **a**
19:21 they washed, they **a** and drank.
Rut 2:14 She **a** all she wanted and had
1Sm 1:18 woman went her way and **a**.
9:24 Saul **a** with Samuel that day.
14:32 The troops **a** the meat with
20:34 and **a** nothing that second
28:25 They **a** and left that ⌊same⌋
2Sm 9:11 From then on, Mephibosheth **a**
9:13 He always **a** at the king's table.
11:13 **a** and drank with him,
12:20 food in front of him, and he **a**.
12:21 you got up and **a**."
1Ki 4:20 They **a** and drank and lived
4:27 and all who **a** at his table.

1Ki 13:19 God went back with him and a
13:22 You came back, a,
19:6 So he a, drank, and went to
19:8 He got up, a, and drank.
2Ki 4:44 They a and had some left over,
6:23 They a and drank,
6:29 we boiled my son and a him.
7:8 went into a tent, a and drank,
9:34 He went inside, a,
23:9 Instead, they a their
25:29 and he a his meals in the
1Ch 12:39 They a and drank with David
29:22 That day they a and drank as
2Ch 30:18 So they a the Passover,
30:22 They a the festival meals for
Neh 5:14 my brothers and I never a any
9:25 So they a and were satisfied
Job 42:11 They a with him at his house,
Psa 41:9 the one who a my bread,
78:25 Humans a the bread of the
78:29 They a more than enough.
106:28 and they a what was sacrificed
Isa 44:19 I roasted meat and a it.
65:4 They a pork and in their pots
Jer 22:15 Your father a and drank and did
41:1 As they a together at Mizpah,
52:33 and he a his meals in the
Eze 3:3 So I a it, and it tasted as sweet
19:3 he hunted. He a people.
19:6 he hunted. He a people.
Dan 4:33 people and a grass like cattle.
5:21 a grass like cattle,
Joe 2:25 the young locusts a your crops.
Zec 7:6 When you a and drank,
Mat 12:4 into the house of God and a
14:20 All of them a as much as they
15:37 All of them a as much as they
Mar 1:6 around his waist and a locusts
2:26 Abiathar was chief priest and a
6:42 All of them a as much as they
7:2 they a without washing their
8:8 The people a as much as they
Luk 4:2 those days Jesus a nothing,
6:4 a the bread of the presence,
9:17 All of them a as much as they
13:26 'We a and drank with you,
24:43 He took it and a it while they
Jon 6:11 All the people a as much as
6:26 for me because you a as much
6:31 Our ancestors a the manna in
6:49 Your ancestors a the manna in
6:58 like the bread your ancestors a.
Act 2:46 as they a at each other's
10:41 apostles are those men who a
11:3 and you even a with them."
20:11 again, broke the bread, and a.
23:12 God to curse them if they a
1Co 10:3 All of them a the same spiritual
Gal 2:12 He a with people who were not
Rev 10:10 from the angel's hand and a it.

Ater (5)

Ezr 2:16 of A, that is, Hezekiah: 98
2:42 A, Talmon, Akkub, Hatita,
Neh 7:21 of A, that is, Hezekiah: 98
7:45 A, Talmon, Akkub, Hatita,
10:17 A, Hezekiah, Azzur,

Athach (1)

1Sm 30:30 Hormah, Borashan, A,

Athaiah (1)

Neh 11:4 descendants of Judah were A,

Athaliah (17)

2Ki 8:26 His mother was A,
11:1 When Ahaziah's mother, A,
11:2 hid him and his nurse from A.
11:3 years while A ruled the country.
11:13 When A heard the noise made
11:14 As A tore her clothes ⌊in
11:20 quiet because they had killed A
1Ch 8:26 Shamsherai, Shehariah, A,
2Ch 22:2 His mother was A,
22:10 When Ahaziah's mother, A,
22:11 she hid Joash from A.
22:12 years while A ruled the country.
23:12 When A heard the people
23:13 As A tore her clothes ⌊in
23:21 they had killed A with a sword.
24:7 woman A had broken into
Ezr 8:7 son of A, with 70 males

Athaliah's (2)

2Ki 11:4 In the seventh year of A reign,
2Ch 23:1 In the seventh year of A reign,

Atharim (1)

Num 21:1 were coming on the road to A,

Athens (7)

Act 17:15 him all the way to the city of A.
17:15 When the men left A,
17:16 for Silas and Timothy in A,
17:21 Everyone who lived in A
17:22 the court and said, "Men of A,
18:1 After this, Paul left A and went
1Th 3:1 to remain in A by ourselves.

Athlai (1)

Ezr 10:28 Hananiah, Zabbai, and A

athletic (2)

1Co 9:25 Everyone who enters an a
2Ti 2:5 Whoever enters an a

Atroth (1)

1Ch 2:54 were the Netophathites, A,

Atroth Shophan (1)

Num 32:35 A, Jazer, Jogbehah,

attach (2)

Exo 28:23 A them to the two ⌊top⌋
28:28 This will a it just above the

attached (17)

Gen 29:34 last my husband will become a
29:34 So she named him Levi [A].
32:32 eat the muscle of the thigh a
Exo 28:7 have two shoulder straps a at
28:8 Make the belt that is a to the
39:4 made two shoulder straps a at
39:5 They made the belt that is a to
39:16 and two gold rings and a
39:21 So the breastplate was a just
1Ki 6:10 beams were a to the temple.
7:32 and the axles were a to the
2Ch 9:18 had a gold footstool a to it.
Est 1:6 These curtains were a to silver
Psa 41:8 "A devilish disease has a itself
Pro 22:15 Foolishness is firmly a to a
Eze 40:43 were a to the wall all around
Jon 15:4 It has to stay a to the vine.

attaching (1)

Eze 37:7 one bone ⌊a itself⌋ to another.

attack (215)

Gen 4:7 outside your door ready to a.
14:15 He split up his men to a them
32:11 I'm afraid that he'll come and a
34:30 forces against me and a me,
43:18 They're going to a us,
Num 13:31 "We can't a those people!
20:18 we'll come out and a you."
21:23 out into the desert to a Israel.
Dtr 20:10 you approach a city to a it,
28:7 your enemies when they a you.
28:7 They will a you from one
28:25 You will a them from one
33:11 Break the backs of those who a
Jos 8:5 When they come out to a us as
8:14 the city waiting to a him.
Jdg 4:14 Deborah said to Barak, "A!
5:12 Barak, a! Take your prisoners,
7:9 the LORD said to Gideon, "A!
7:11 to go into the camp and a it."
7:15 the camp of Israel and said, "A!
9:33 and his men come out to a you,
9:43 Then he began to a them.
11:29 Jephthah went to a Ammon.
Jdg 18:9 replied, "Get up, let's a Laish.
18:23 neighbors together to a us?"
18:25 or some violent men will a you.
20:5 of Gibeah came to a me.
20:9 decide by lot who should a it.
20:31 went out to a Israel's troops
20:48 men of Israel went back to a
1Sm 7:7 rulers came to a Israel.
12:12 of Ammon coming to a you,
14:4 for a way to cross over to a
14:36 Saul said ⌊to his men⌋, "Let's a
14:37 "Should I a the Philistines?
15:3 Now go and a Amalek.
17:43 a dog that you come to ⌊a⌋ me
17:48 moved closer in order to a,
17:48 battle line to a the Philistine.
22:17 "But the king's men refused to a
22:18 "You turn and a the priests."
23:2 I go and a these Philistines?"
23:2 told David, "a the Philistines,
24:7 them and didn't let them a Saul.
26:11 be unthinkable for me to a
26:23 but I refused to a the LORD's
2Sm 1:15 "Come here and a him."
5:6 Jerusalem to a the Jebusites,
5:17 all of them came to a David.
5:19 "Should I a the Philistines?
5:19 LORD answered David, "A!
5:23 and he answered, "Don't a now,
10:9 Joab saw he was under a
11:23 overpowered us and came to a
11:25 Strengthen your a against the
13:28 wine, I'll tell you, 'A Amnon.'
17:2 I'll a him while he's tired and
17:9 are killed in the initial a,
17:12 Then we'll a him wherever we
22:30 With you I can a a line of
1Ki 2:46 He went to a and kill Shimei.
15:20 generals and their armies to a
20:12 they got ready ⌊to a⌋ the city.
20:19 the district governors led an a,
20:22 the king of Aram will a
22:12 "A Ramoth in Gilead,
22:15 "A and you will win.
22:20 deceive Ahab so that he will a
2Ki 7:6 and Egyptian kings to a us!
8:21 took all his chariots to a Zair.
12:17 He was also determined to a
12:18 called off the a on Jerusalem.
15:19 came to ⌊a⌋ the country.
15:37 son of Remaliah, to a Judah.
18:25 'A this country, and destroy it.'"
19:32 or put up dirt ramps to a it.
23:29 King Josiah went to a Necoh.
1Ch 12:19 with the Philistines to a Saul.
14:8 all of them came to a David.
14:10 "Should I a the Philistines?
14:10 The LORD answered him, "A!
19:10 Joab saw he was under a
20:1 and came to Rabbah to a it,
21:1 Satan attempted to a Israel by
2Ch 11:4 back from their a on Jeroboam.
13:13 ambush to a them from behind.
14:9 men and 300 chariots to a Asa.
16:4 generals and their armies to a
18:2 Jehoshaphat to a Ramoth
18:11 "A Ramoth in Gilead,
18:14 "A and you will win.
18:19 Ahab of Israel so that he will a
21:9 his chariot commanders to a.
21:16 people of Sudan to a Jehoram.
32:1 He set up camp ⌊to a⌋ the
35:20 Josiah went to a him.
35:22 Josiah would not stop his a.
36:17 had the Babylonian king a them
Ezr 8:22 to help us against an enemy a
Neh 4:8 All of them plotted to a
4:12 times that our enemies would a
Job 19:12 They build a ramp to a me and
33:10 looking for an excuse to a me.
Psa 7:4 who has no reason to a me —
17:7 side from those who a them.
17:9 people who violently a me,
18:29 With you I can a a line of
22:13 mouths to a me like ferocious,
31:21 of his mercy in a city under a.

Psa 35:1 a those who attack me.
35:1 attack those who a me.
44:5 can trample those who a us.
55:3 and they a me out of anger.
55:21 they are like swords ready to a.
56:6 They a, and then they hide.
59:1 Protect me from those who a
59:3 Fierce men a me, O LORD,
62:3 long will all of you a a person?
73:9 They verbally a heaven,
74:23 made by those who a you.
86:14 O God, arrogant people a me,
109:28 Let those who a me be
139:21 with those who a you?
Ecc 9:14 a powerful king came to a it.
Isa 1:8 like a city under a."
7:1 went to Jerusalem to a it,
9:21 Together they a Judah.
10:15 Can an ax a the person who
14:8 no lumberjack has come to a
15:9 A lion will a the fugitives from
33:3 Nations scatter when you a.
36:10 'A this country, and destroy it.'"
37:33 or put up dirt ramps to a it.
41:25 He will a rulers as if they were
Jer 1:15 They will a all the walls
5:6 lion from the forest will a them.
5:15 a nation from far away to a you,
6:4 Let's a at noon! How horrible it
6:5 Let's a at night and destroy its
6:6 up dirt mounds to a Jerusalem.
6:26 The destroyer will suddenly a
21:13 "'But you ask, "Who can a us?
25:9 from the north to a this land,
34:22 army back to this city to a it,
37:8 They will a the city,
37:19 king of Babylon wouldn't a you
46:20 horsefly from the north will a it.
46:22 They will a it with axes like
47:7 The LORD has ordered it to a
48:15 The enemy will a Moab and
48:18 destroyers of Moab will a you.
49:4 You think, "Who would a me?"
49:14 say, "Assemble, and a Edom.
49:28 says: Get ready, a Kedar,
49:30 you and intends to a you.
49:31 A the nation living peacefully
50:3 A nation from the north will a
50:21 "A the land of Merathaim and
50:26 A them from a distance,
50:42 ready for war, ready to a you,
51:2 They will a it from every
51:27 Prepare nations to a Babylon.
51:27 and Ashkenaz to a it.
51:27 a commander to lead the a.
51:28 Prepare nations to a Babylon.
51:48 from the north will a it,"
51:56 A destroyer will a Babylon,
Lam 3:62 of those who a me are directed
Eze 4:2 build a walls around it,
4:2 have troops ready to a it,
4:3 city as if you were going to a it,
4:3 going to attack it, and then a it.
6:3 I am going to a you with a
11:8 so I will bring swords to a you,
23:24 They will a you from the north,
23:24 They will a you from all around
28:23 People with swords will a you
29:8 I am going to a you with a
30:11 draw their swords to a Egypt
32:11 the king of Babylon will a you.
33:3 enemy coming to a the country,
38:8 In the years to come, you will a
38:9 You will a like a storm and
38:11 You will say, "I'll a a land with
38:11 I will a peaceful people who
38:16 You will a my people Israel
38:16 I will let you a my land so that
38:17 I would bring you to a them.
39:2 the far north and have you a
Dan 11:7 He will a the northern army,
11:15 will come, build dirt a ramps,
11:16 will be able to withstand his a.
11:30 come from the west to a him,
11:40 the southern king will a him.
Hos 10:10 Armies will gather to a them.
Hos 13:8 has lost her cubs, I will a you.
Joe 3:9 the warriors come near and a.
Amo 6:14 going to lead a nation to a you,
7:9 I will a Jeroboam's heirs with
Jnh 4:7 God sent a worm to a the plant
Mic 5:1 We are under a. Enemies will
5:5 we will a them with seven
Nah 2:1 scatter you is coming to a you.
3:16 ⌊They are⌋ like locusts that a
Hab 3:16 to the people who will a us.
Zec 12:2 They will a Judah along with
12:9 the nations who a Jerusalem.
14:13 and one will a the other.
Luk 11:22 man than he may a him
Act 14:5 their rulers planned to a them
16:22 The crowd joined in the a
18:10 No one will a you or harm you.
2Co 6:8 what is right to a what is wrong
Gal 5:15 you criticize and a each other,
1Pe 2:11 These desires constantly a

attacked (107)

Gen 4:8 Cain a his brother Abel and
34:25 swords and boldly a the city.
49:19 "Gad will be a by a band of
49:23 him, shot at him, and a him.
Exo 15:7 destroyed those who a you.
Num 14:45 mountains, a the Israelites,
20:20 Then they came out and a with
Dtr 1:44 lived there came out and a you
25:18 They a you when you were
Jos 8:21 they turned and a the men of Ai.
8:22 city also came out and a them.
8:22 So Israel a them on both sides.
10:5 Gibeon, camped there, and a it.
10:29 Makkedah to Libnah and a it.
10:31 camped there, and a it.
10:34 Eglon, camped there, and a it.
10:36 from Eglon to Hebron and a it.
10:38 went back to Debir and a it.
11:7 and a the Canaanite armies.
19:47 went up and a Leshem,
Jdg 1:8 The men of Judah a Jerusalem
9:18 But today you have a my
9:44 in the fields and a them.
9:45 Abimelech a the city all day
11:5 When the Ammonites a Israel,
11:20 He camped at Jahaz and a
15:8 So he a them violently and
18:27 They a a peaceful and secure
20:34 of Israel's best men a Gibeah.
1Sm 15:7 Saul a the Amalekites from
17:35 If it a me, I took hold of its
22:18 Edom turned and a the priests,
26:9 "No one has ever a the LORD's
27:9 Whenever David a the territory,
30:1 They had a Ziklag and burned
30:17 the next day, David a them.
30:23 us and handed the troops that a
2Sm 5:22 The Philistines again a and
11:1 the Ammonites and a Rabbah,
18:15 a him, and killed him.
20:15 Joab's army came and a him in
21:17 He a the Philistine and killed
23:10 he a and killed Philistines until
1Ki 2:25 Benaiah a and killed Adonijah.
2:34 went and a Joab, killed him,
14:25 King Shishak of Egypt a
16:10 entered Arza's house, a Elah,
16:17 left Gibbethon and a Tirzah.
20:16 They a at noon,
2Ki 3:24 the Israelites a them,
3:25 surrounded Kir Hareseth and a
14:11 So King Jehoash of Israel a,
15:10 a him at Kabal Am,
15:14 a Shallum (son of Jabesh),
15:16 Then Menahem a Tiphsah,
15:16 he a it and ripped open all its
15:25 Pekah a Pekahiah,
15:30 Hoshea a him and killed him.
16:9 to him and a Damascus.
17:5 Then the king of Assyria a the
17:5 He a Samaria and blockaded it
18:9 of Assyria a Samaria,
18:13 King Sennacherib of Assyria a
24:1 of Babylon a Judah,
2Ki 24:10 of Babylon a Jerusalem.
25:1 of Babylon a Jerusalem
1Ch 14:11 So David ⌊and his men⌋ a and
2Ch 12:2 Shishak of Egypt a Jerusalem.
12:9 King Shishak of Egypt a
13:15 When they shouted, God a
14:12 The LORD a the Sudanese
14:14 It a all the cities around Gerar
14:15 It also a those who were letting
20:23 the Ammonites and Moabites a
24:23 the Aramean army a Joash.
25:21 So King Jehoash of Israel a,
26:7 him when he a the Philistines,
28:20 Pilneser of Assyria a Ahaz.
36:6 of Babylon a Jehoiakim
Est 9:5 the Jews a all their enemies,
Job 1:15 men from Sheba a.
16:9 tore me ⌊apart⌋ and a me.
19:7 I'm being a!' but I get no
30:12 They have a me on my right
Psa 54:3 Strangers have a me.
55:12 who hated me had a me,
60:4 rally to it when a by bows ⌊and
124:2 on our side when people a us,
129:1 people have a me ..."
129:2 people have a me,
Isa 36:1 King Sennacherib of Assyria a
Jer 39:1 of Babylon a Jerusalem
52:4 of Babylon a Jerusalem
Lam 3:5 He has a me and surrounded
Dan 1:1 came to Jerusalem and a it.
6:24 the lions a them and crushed
8:7 with the ram, so it a the ram.
8:11 Then it a the commander of the
Joe 1:6 A strong nation a my land.
Amo 5:19 flees from a lion only to be a by
Zec 14:16 that a Jerusalem will come
Luk 10:36 man who was a by robbers?"
Jon 18:10 a the chief priest's servant,
Act 17:5 They a Jason's home and
18:12 They a Paul and brought him to
19:16 by the evil spirit a them.
1Co 4:13 When our reputations are a,

attackers (2)

Psa 7:6 up against the fury of my a.
35:15 Unknown a tore me apart

attacking (21)

Jdg 16:9 the Philistines are a!"
16:12 the Philistines are a!"
16:14 the Philistines are a!"
16:20 the Philistines are a!"
1Ki 15:27 the Israelite forces were a it.
2Ki 16:7 Aram and Israel who are a me."
25:4 While the Babylonians were a
2Ch 20:12 this large crowd that is a us.
32:9 royal forces were a Lachish,
35:21 I'm not a you. I've come to fight
Psa 3:1 increased! Many are a me.
92:11 ⌊the cries⌋ of evildoers a me.
Jer 21:2 of Babylon is a us.
32:24 to the Babylonians who are a it.
32:29 "The Babylonians who are a
34:1 that he ruled were a Jerusalem
34:7 of Babylon was a Jerusalem
52:7 While the Babylonians were a
Eze 4:8 have finished a ⌊Jerusalem⌋.
7:9 and that I am the one a ⌊you⌋.
Dan 11:24 new ways of a fortifications.

attacks (13)

Gen 32:8 "If Esau a the one camp,
Num 23:24 Here is a nation that a like a
Dtr 19:11 for him, a him, takes his life,
22:26 the case of someone who a
Jos 15:16 to anyone who a Kiriath Sepher
Job 15:25 out his hand against God and a
27:7 Let anyone who a me be
Psa 35:17 Rescue me from their a.
Pro 21:22 A wise man a a city of warriors
Isa 14:4 How his a have come to an
54:15 "If anyone a you, it will not be
54:15 Whoever a you will be
Eze 38:18 On the day that Gog a the land

Attai (4)

1Ch 2:35 She gave birth to **A**.
2:36 **A** was the father of Nathan.
12:11 The sixth was **A**. The seventh
2Ch 11:20 She gave birth to Abijah, **A**,

Attalia (2)

Act 14:25 Perga and went to the city of **A**.
14:26 From **A** they took a boat and

attempted (2)

1Ch 21:1 Satan **a** to attack Israel by
Luk 1:1 Many have **a** to write about

attempts (1)

3Jn 1:10 who want to accept them and **a**

attend (1)

Gen 49:6 Do not let me **a** their secret

attendant (4)

2Ki 8:6 the king assigned to her an **a**
9:25 Then Jehu said to his **a** Bidkar,
Luk 4:17 The **a** gave him the book of the
4:20 gave it back to the **a**,

attendants (4)

2Ki 10:25 Jehu said to the guards and **a**,
10:25 until the guards and **a** came
Jer 36:24 The king and all his **a** didn't
36:31 and his **a** for their wickedness.

attended (1)

Jon 4:45 they, too, had **a** the festival.

attention (145)

Gen 39:23 The warden paid no **a** to
40:20 his servants he gave special **a**
Exo 3:16 He said, "I have paid close **a** to
4:8 they won't believe you or pay **a**
15:26 if you pay **a** to his commands
23:21 Pay **a** to him, and listen to him.
Dtr 32:46 he said to them, "Pay **a** to all
Jos 23:14 "Pay **a**, because I will soon die
Rut 2:10 Why are you paying **a** to me?
2:19 May the man who paid **a** to you
1Sm 4:20 But she didn't answer or pay **a**.
14:52 fighting man came to Saul's **a**,
30:24 Besides, who is going to pay **a**
1Ki 8:28 please pay **a** to my prayer for
18:29 no **a** given to them.
22:28 Pay **a** to this, everyone!"
2Ch 6:19 please pay **a** to my prayer for
7:15 and my ears will pay **a** to those
18:27 Pay **a** to this, everyone!"
19:6 "Pay **a** to what you're doing.
20:15 Jahaziel said, "Pay **a** to me,
33:10 they wouldn't even pay **a**.
Neh 1:6 and pay close **a** with your ears
1:11 Lord, please pay **a** to my prayer
9:34 They didn't pay **a** to your
Est 3:4 he paid no **a** to them.
9:25 when this came to the king's **a**,
Job 4:20 without anyone paying **a**.
11:11 doesn't he pay **a** to it?
13:6 and pay **a** to my plea.
21:29 didn't pay **a** to their directions.
24:12 God pays no **a** to their prayers.
32:12 I've paid close **a** to you,
33:31 "Pay **a**, Job! Listen to me!
35:13 doesn't even pay **a** to them.
35:14 you say that you pay **a** to him,
Psa 5:2 Pay **a** to my cry for help,
10:17 You pay close **a** to them
17:1 Pay **a** to my cry. Open your ears
17:11 They have focused their **a** on
49:4 I will turn my **a** to a proverb.
55:2 Pay **a** to me, and answer me.
61:1 Pay **a** to my prayer.
66:19 He has paid **a** to my prayer.
86:6 Pay **a** when I plead for mercy.
94:7 Jacob doesn't even pay **a** to it."
94:8 Pay **a**, you stupid people!
102:17 He will turn his **a** to the prayers
107:43 ⌊think⌋ they are wise pay **a**
Psa 142:6 Pay **a** to my cry for help
Pro 1:24 and no one paid **a**.
2:2 if you pay close **a** to wisdom,
4:1 and pay **a** in order to gain
4:20 My son, pay **a** to my words.
5:1 My son, pay **a** to my wisdom.
7:1 My son, pay **a** to my words.
7:24 Pay **a** to the words from my
13:8 does not pay **a** to threats.
13:18 but whoever pays **a** to
16:20 Whoever gives **a** to the LORD's
17:4 An evildoer pays **a** to wicked
23:1 pay close **a** to what is in front
27:23 and pay close **a** to your herds.
29:12 If a ruler pays **a** to lies,
Ecc 2:12 Then I turned ⌊my **a**⌋ to
7:25 I turned my **a** to study,
9:17 One should pay more **a** to calm
Isa 1:2 Listen, heaven, and pay **a**,
1:10 Pay **a** to the teachings from our
5:12 Yet, they don't pay **a** to what
10:30 Pay **a**, you people in Laishah
28:23 Pay **a**, and hear me!
32:3 those who can hear will pay **a**.
34:1 Pay **a**, you people. The earth,
42:23 Is there anyone who will pay **a**
49:1 Pay **a**, you people far away.
51:4 Pay **a** to me, my people.
58:3 on ourselves if you don't pay **a**?
63:16 and Israel doesn't pay **a** to us,
64:4 no one has paid **a**,
66:2 I will pay **a** to those who are
Jer 4:16 them to the **a** of Jerusalem.
6:8 Pay **a** to my warning,
6:10 and they aren't able to pay **a**.
6:17 Pay **a** to the sound of the ram's
6:17 said that you wouldn't pay **a**.
6:19 because they won't pay **a** to
7:24 didn't obey me or pay **a** to me.
7:26 didn't obey me or pay **a** to me.
8:6 I have paid **a** and listened,
11:8 didn't obey me or pay **a** to me.
13:15 Listen, and pay **a**! Don't be
17:23 did not obey me or pay **a** to me.
18:18 Pay no **a** to anything he says."
18:19 Pay **a** to me, O LORD,
23:18 Who pays **a** and listens to his
25:4 listened or paid **a** to them.
44:5 you wouldn't listen or pay **a**.
Eze 40:4 Pay close **a** to everything I'm
44:5 me, "Son of man, pay close **a**.
44:5 Pay close **a** to everyone who
Dan 9:19 Pay **a**, and act. Don't delay!
10:11 Pay **a** to my words.
11:18 Then he will turn his **a** to the
Hos 5:1 Pay **a**, nation of Israel!
Mic 1:2 Pay **a**, earth and all who are on
Zec 1:4 they didn't listen or pay **a** to me,
7:11 "But people refused to pay **a**.
Mal 2:13 because he no longer pays **a**
3:16 the LORD paid **a** and listened.
Mat 6:1 in public in order to attract **a**.
22:5 "But they paid no **a** and went
23:5 everything to attract people's **a**.
Mar 4:24 He went on to say, "Pay **a** to
4:24 the measure ⌊of **a**⌋ you give.
Luk 8:18 "So pay **a** to how you listen!
18:6 The Lord added, "Pay **a** to
19:11 Jesus had the people's **a**,
Act 2:14 so pay **a** to what I say.
2:22 whom God brought to your **a**.
4:29 pay **a** to their threats now,
8:6 The crowds paid close **a** to
8:10 children to adults paid **a** to him.
8:11 They paid **a** to Simon because
12:1 time King Herod devoted his **a**
16:14 Lord made her willing to pay **a**
20:28 Pay **a** to yourselves and to the
26:26 things has escaped his **a**.
1Co 7:34 His **a** is divided. An unmarried
Php 3:17 and pay **a** to those who live by
Col 4:2 Pay **a** when you offer prayers
2Th 3:12 the Lord Jesus Christ to pay **a**
1Ti 5:19 Don't pay **a** to an accusation
2Ti 2:16 People who ⌊pay **a** to these
Tit 1:14 They shouldn't pay **a** to Jewish
Heb 2:1 reason we must pay closer **a**
5:11 have become too lazy to pay **a**,
12:5 pay **a** when the Lord
Jas 2:3 Suppose you give special **a** to
4:13 Pay **a** to this! You're saying,
5:1 Pay **a** to this if you're rich.
2Pe 1:19 You're doing well by paying **a**
1:19 Continue to pay **a** as you
Rev 1:3 of this prophecy and pay **a**
3:8 but you have paid **a** to my word

attentive (1)

2Ch 6:40 eyes be open and your ears **a**

attitude (23)

Num 14:24 servant Caleb has a different **a**
1Sm 10:9 God changed Saul's **a**.
1Ki 8:48 if they change their **a** toward
11:11 "Because this is your **a** and
2Ch 6:38 if they change their **a** toward
Pro 15:7 but a foolish **a** does not.
16:18 an arrogant **a** precedes a fall.
21:4 look and an arrogant **a**,
Jer 32:39 I will give them the same **a**
Rom 8:5 have the corrupt nature's **a**.
8:5 have the spiritual nature's **a**.
8:6 The corrupt nature's **a** leads to
8:6 But the spiritual nature's **a**
8:7 has a hostile **a** toward God.
2Co 13:11 Share the same **a** and live in
Gal 4:15 happened to your positive **a**?
Eph 4:23 were taught to have a new **a**.
Php 2:2 with joy by having the same **a**
2:5 Have the same **a** that Christ
4:2 and Syntyche to have the **a**
Col 1:21 you did showed your hostile **a**.
1Pe 3:4 quiet **a** which God considers
4:1 take the same **a** that he had.

attitudes (3)

Mal 4:6 He will change parents' **a**
4:6 **a** toward their parents.
Luk 1:17 He will change parents' **a**

attorney (1)

Act 24:1 and an **a** named Tertullus.

attract (2)

Mat 6:1 in public in order to **a** attention.
23:5 to **a** people's attention.

attractive (8)

Gen 24:16 The girl was a very **a** virgin.
26:7 because she was an **a** woman.
29:17 Leah had **a** eyes, but Rachel
1Sm 16:12 a healthy complexion, **a** eyes,
Est 1:11 because she was very **a**.
2:2 "Search for **a** young virgins for
2:3 to gather all the **a** young virgins
2:7 beautiful figure and was very **a**.

audience (1)

Pro 29:26 Many seek an **a** with a ruler,

auditorium (3)

Act 25:23 and Bernice entered the **a**
25:23 city entered the **a** with them.
25:23 Paul was brought into the **a**.

Augustus (1)

Luk 2:1 At that time the Emperor **A**

aunt (3)

Lev 18:12 She is your paternal **a**.
18:13 She is your maternal **a**.
18:14 She, too, is your **a**.

authorities (15)

Ecc 5:8 have **a** watching over them.
Mat 10:19 they hand you over ⌊to the **a**⌋,
Mar 13:11 away to hand you over to the **a**,
Luk 12:11 or in front of rulers and **a**,
Act 4:2 These religious **a** were greatly
4:21 The **a** threatened them even
4:21 the **a** couldn't find any way to
16:19 Silas and dragged them to the **a**

Act 25:5 He told them, "Have your **a**
28:17 handed over to the Roman **a**.
28:18 The Roman **a** cross-examined
Eph 1:21 He is far above all rulers, **a**,
3:10 he could let the rulers and **a** in
6:12 We are wrestling with rulers, **a**,
Col 2:15 He stripped the rulers and **a** ⌊of

authority (138)

Gen 16:9 and place yourself under her **a**."
Exo 23:21 He is acting on my **a**.
Num 26:9 defied Moses and Aaron's **a**.
26:9 when they defied the LORD's **a**.
27:20 Give him some of your **a** so
Dtr 18:22 has spoken on his own **a**.
19:6 rage the relative who has the **a**
19:12 to the relative who has the **a**
Jos 1:18 Whoever rebels against your **a**
1Sm 21:13 long as he was⌋ under their **a**.
2Sm 22:48 He brings people under my **a**.
Neh 3:7 They did this under the **a** of the
Est 1:22 own house and speak with **a**."
3:1 a position higher in **a** than all
9:29 the Jew wrote with full **a**
Job 25:2 "**A** and terror belong to God.
Psa 18:47 He brings people under my **a**.
47:3 He brings people under our **a**
75:6 The ⌊**a**⌋ to reward someone
144:2 who brings people under my **a**.
Ecc 5:8 One **a** is watching over
8:9 one person has **a** to hurt others.
Isa 22:21 I will give him your **a**,
40:10 with power to rule with **a**.
Amo 9:12 nations that were under my **a**,
Mat 7:22 the power and **a** of your name?'
7:29 he taught them with **a**.
9:6 know that the Son of Man has **a**
9:8 for giving such **a** to humans.
10:1 disciples and gave them **a**
12:8 "The Son of Man has **a** over
15:6 destroyed the **a** of God's word.
20:23 But I don't have the **a** to grant
20:25 have absolute **a** over people.
23:2 Pharisees teach with Moses' **a**.
28:18 He said, "All **a** in heaven and
Mar 1:22 he taught them with **a**.
1:27 teaching that has **a** behind it!
2:10 know that the Son of Man has **a**
2:28 the Son of Man has **a** over
3:15 They also had the **a** to force
6:7 gave them **a** over evil spirits.
7:13 you have destroyed the **a**
9:38 by using the power and **a**
10:40 But I don't have the **a** to grant
10:42 have absolute **a** over people.
16:17 They will use the power and **a**
Luk 4:32 because he spoke with **a**.
4:36 With **a** and power he gives
5:24 know that the Son of Man has **a**
6:5 "The Son of Man has **a** over
9:1 power and **a** over every demon
9:1 power and **a** to cure diseases.
9:49 by using the power and **a**
10:17 the power and **a** of your name!"
10:19 I have given you the **a** to
22:25 and those in **a** call themselves
24:47 also says that by the **a**
Jon 5:27 "He has also given the Son **a**
5:43 I have come with the **a** my
5:43 else comes with his own **a**,
10:18 I have the **a** to give my life,
10:18 and I have the **a** to take my life
17:2 After all, you've given him **a**
19:10 you know that I have the **a**
19:11 "You wouldn't have any **a** over
Act 1:7 has determined by his own **a**.
7:55 position of **a** that God gives.
7:56 the position of **a** that God has
9:14 here to Damascus with **a** from
9:28 the power and **a** of the Lord.
26:10 By the **a** I received from the
26:12 I had the power and **a** of the
Rom 8:7 to place itself under the **a**
1Co 7:4 A wife doesn't have **a** over her
7:4 a husband doesn't have **a** over
11:3 Christ has **a** over every man,
1Co 11:3 a husband has **a** over his wife,
11:3 and God has **a** over Christ.
11:4 the one who has **a** over him.
11:5 the one who has **a** over her.
11:10 she is under ⌊someone's⌋ **a**,
15:24 every ruler, **a**, and power.
15:27 put everything under Christ's **a**.
15:27 has been put under Christ's **a**,
15:27 put everything under Christ's **a**.
15:28 everything under Christ's **a**,
15:28 will put himself under God's **a**,
15:28 everything under the Son's **a**.
2Co 10:8 too much about the **a** which
10:8 The Lord gave us this **a** to help
13:10 to be harsh by using the **a** that
13:10 The Lord gave us this **a** to help
Eph 5:21 under each other's **a** out
5:22 your husbands' **a** as you have
5:22 yourselves under the Lord's **a**.
5:24 the church is under Christ's **a**,
5:24 their husbands' **a** in everything.
6:9 in heaven who has **a** over both
Php 3:21 to bring everything under his **a**,
Col 2:10 in charge of every ruler and **a**.
3:18 under your husbands' **a**.
1Th 4:8 not rejecting human **a** but God,
1Ti 2:2 everyone who has **a** over us.
2:12 to teach or to have **a** over
Tit 2:5 under their husbands' **a**.
2:9 under their masters' **a**
2:15 correct them, using your full **a**.
3:1 place themselves under the **a**
Heb 12:9 ourselves under the **a** of God,
13:17 and accept their **a**.
Jas 2:8 this law from the highest **a**:
4:7 yourselves under God's **a**.
1Pe 2:13 Place yourselves under the **a**
2:13 holds the highest position of **a**.
2:18 place yourselves under the **a** of
3:1 under your husbands' **a**.
3:5 under their husbands' **a**
3:22 have been placed under his **a**.
5:5 place yourselves under the **a** of
2Pe 2:10 and who despise the Lord's **a**.
Jud 1:6 didn't keep their position of **a**
1:8 reject the Lord's **a**,
1:25 and **a** belong to the only God,
Rev 2:26 I have received **a** from my
2:26 I will give **a** over the nations to
11:6 These witnesses have **a** to
11:6 They have **a** to turn water into
12:10 and the **a** of his Messiah have
13:2 and far-reaching **a** to the beast.
13:4 serpent because it had given **a**
13:5 It was given **a** to act for 42
13:7 It was also given **a** over every
13:12 second beast uses all the **a**
14:18 from the altar with **a** over fire.
16:9 who has the **a** over these
17:12 They will receive **a** to rule as
17:13 their power and **a** to the beast.

authorization (1)

Act 9:2 asked him to write letters of **a**

authorize (1)

Act 15:24 We did not **a** these men ⌊to

authorized (1)

Ezr 3:7 of Persia had **a** them to do.

autumn (3)

Jer 5:24 the **a** rain and the spring rain.
Hos 6:3 He will come to us like the **a**
Joe 2:23 He has sent the **a** rain and the

available (2)

Gen 47:6 All of Egypt is **a** to you.
1Ki 7:36 and designs in every **a** space

Aven (2)

Hos 10:8 The illegal worship sites of **A**
Amo 1:5 I will cut off those living in **A**

avenge (12)

Num 35:12 relative who can **a** the death.
Num 35:19 The relative who can **a** the
35:21 The relative who can **a** the
35:24 relative can **a** the death.
35:27 If the relative who can **a** the
Dtr 19:6 who has the authority to **a**
19:12 has the authority to **a** the death.
Jos 20:3 relative who can **a** the death.
20:5 "'If the relative who can **a** the
20:9 over to the relative who can **a**
Isa 1:24 I will **a** myself against my
Jer 51:11 The LORD will **a** his temple.

avenged (1)

Gen 4:24 If Cain is **a** 7 times,

avenger (4)

2Sm 14:11 to keep an **a** from doing more
Psa 8:2 to silence the enemy and the **a**.
44:16 of the enemy and the **a**.
Rom 13:4 It is God's servant, an **a** to

avenges (1)

Psa 9:12 The one who **a** murder has

Avith (2)

Gen 36:35 name of his capital city was **A**.
1Ch 1:46 of his ⌊capital⌋ city was **A**.

avoid (29)

Gen 38:9 ground to **a** giving his brother
Exo 23:7 **A** telling lies. Don't kill innocent
Dtr 5:20 "Never **a** the truth when you
23:21 your God, don't **a** keeping it.
Jos 9:20 We must let them live to **a** ⌊the
Jdg 9:21 ⌊to **a**⌋ his brother Abimelech.
Psa 37:27 **A** evil, do good, and live
Pro 4:15 **A** it. Do not walk near it.
Ecc 7:18 will be able to **a** both extremes.
7:29 ways ⌊to **a** being decent⌋."
8:5 his commands will **a** trouble.
8:8 There is no way to **a** the war
Amo 7:11 cannot **a** being taken from
7:17 Israel cannot **a** being taken
Luk 6:22 hate you, **a** you, insult you,
Jon 11:56 "Do you think that he'll **a**
Act 15:29 If you **a** these things,
20:16 Ephesus to **a** spending time
20:20 I didn't **a** telling you anything
20:20 and I didn't **a** teaching you
20:27 I didn't **a** telling you the whole
Rom 14:21 thing to do is to **a** eating meat,
16:19 is good and to **a** what is evil.
1Co 7:2 But in order to **a** sexual sins,
Gal 6:12 Their only aim is to **a**
1Ti 6:11 must **a** these things.
2Ti 2:16 **A** pointless discussions.
Tit 2:12 It trains us to **a** ungodly lives
3:9 **A** foolish controversies,

avoided (3)

Psa 17:4 I have **a** cruelty because of
Pro 16:6 the fear of the LORD, evil is **a**.
Act 27:21 You would have **a** this disaster

avoiding (1)

Pro 20:3 **A** a quarrel is honorable.

Avva (2)

2Ki 17:24 Babylon, Cuthah, **A**, Hamath,
17:31 The people from **A** made

Avvim (2)

Jos 13:3 as well as the **A** people
18:23 **A**, Parah, Ophrah,

Avvites (1)

Dtr 2:23 happened to the **A** who lived

await (1)

Psa 32:10 heartaches **a** wicked people,

awake (17)

Psa 44:23 **A**! Do not reject us forever!
102:7 I lie **a**. I am like a lonely bird on
Sos 4:16 **A**, north wind! Come,
5:2 I sleep, but my mind is **a**.

Mat 24:43 he would have stayed **a**.
25:13 "So stay **a**, because you don't
26:38 Wait here, and stay **a** with me."
26:40 "Couldn't you stay **a** with me
26:41 Stay **a**, and pray that you won't
Mar 4:27 He sleeps at night and is **a**
14:34 Wait here, and stay **a**."
14:37 you stay **a** for one hour?
14:38 Stay **a**, and pray that you won't
Luk 12:37 whom the master finds **a** when
12:38 morning and finds them **a**.
1Th 5:6 we must stay **a** and be sober.
5:10 whether we are **a** in this life or

awaken (3)
Sos 2:7 the field that you will not **a** love
3:5 that you will not **a** love or
8:4 swear to me that you will not **a**

awakened (1)
Job 14:12 He is not **a** from his sleep.

awards (2)
Dan 2:6 you gifts, **a**, and high honors.
5:17 Give your gifts and **a** to

aware (14)
Lev 4:13 the assembly being **a** of it,
Job 13:23 Make me **a** of my disobedience
Psa 38:17 I am continually **a** of my pain.
139:14 and my soul is fully **a** of this.
Pro 23:35 beat me, but I'm not **a** of it.
27:23 Be fully **a** of the condition of
Isa 58:3 we fasted if you are not **a** of it?
59:12 You are **a** of our many
Mat 24:39 They were not **a** of what was
Jon 6:61 Jesus was **a** that his disciples
Act 10:4 "God is **a** of your prayers and
1Co 5:1 Your own members are **a** that
Heb 13:2 to angels without being **a** of it.
1Pe 2:19 God is pleased if a person is **a**

awe (11)
Gen 28:17 Filled with **a**, he said,
Exo 20:20 so that you will be in **a** of him
Psa 22:23 Stand in **a** of him, all you
33:8 in the world stand in **a** of him.
65:8 at the ends of the earth are in **a**
Mal 2:5 He respected me and stood in **a**
Mat 9:8 they were filled with **a** and
Luk 1:65 neighbors were filled with **a**.
5:26 were filled with **a** and said,
Act 19:17 All of them were filled with **a**
Heb 12:28 must serve God with fear and **a**

awe-inspiring (21)
Gen 28:17 "How **a** this place is!
Exo 15:11 because of your holiness and **a**
Dtr 4:34 He did his great and **a** deeds in
7:21 He is a great and **a** God.
10:17 the great, powerful, and **a** God.
10:21 and **a** deeds you saw
26:8 used spectacular and **a** deeds,
28:58 fear this glorious and **a** name:
34:12 and **a** deeds that were
Neh 1:5 of heaven, great and **a** God,
4:14 Remember how great and **a** the
9:32 the great, mighty, and **a** God.
Psa 45:4 Let your right hand teach you **a**
65:5 You answer us with **a** acts
66:3 "How **a** are your deeds!
66:5 God has done — his **a** deeds
68:35 is **a** in his holy place.
89:7 He is greater and more **a** than
Sos 6:4 **a** like those great cities.
6:10 **a** like those heavenly bodies.
Isa 64:3 When you did **a** things that we

awesome (1)
Exo 34:10 see how **a** these miracles are

awful (1)
Num 21:5 and we can't stand this **a** food!"

awl (2)
Exo 21:6 and pierce his ear with an **a**.
Dtr 15:17 Then take an **a** and pierce it

awnings (1)
Eze 27:7 Your **a** were violet and purple.

ax (11)
Dtr 19:5 As one of them swings the **a** to
20:19 any of its fruit trees with an **a**.
Jdg 9:48 Abimelech took an **a**,
1Sm 13:20 plow, his mattock, **a**, or sickle.
2Ki 6:5 the **a** head fell into the water.
6:6 and made the **a** head float.
Ecc 10:10 If an **a** is blunt and the edge
Isa 10:15 Can an **a** attack the person
10:34 of the forest with an **a**.
Mat 3:10 The **a** is now ready to cut the
Luk 3:9 The **a** is now ready to cut the

axes (6)
2Sm 12:31 work with saws, hoes, and **a**.
1Ch 20:3 work with saws, hoes, and **a**.
Psa 74:6 paneling with **a** and hatchets.
Jer 10:3 craftsmen prepare them with **a**.
46:22 They will attack it with **a** like
Eze 26:9 down your towers with his **a**.

axles (3)
1Ki 7:30 four bronze wheels on bronze **a**
7:32 and the **a** were attached to the
7:33 The **a**, rims, spokes, and hubs

Azaliah (2)
2Ki 22:3 son of **A** and grandson of
2Ch 34:8 Shaphan, son of **A**, Maaseiah,

Azaniah (1)
Neh 10:9 Jeshua (son of **A**),

Azarel (6)
1Ch 12:6 Elkanah, Isshiah, **A**,
25:18 The eleventh chose **A**,
27:22 for the tribe of Dan: **A**,
Ezr 10:41 **A**, Shelemiah, Shemariah,
Neh 11:13 Amashsai was the son of **A**,
12:36 **A**, Milalai, Gilalai, Maai,

Azariah (48)
1Ki 4:2 these were his officials: **A**,
4:5 **A**, son of Nathan, was in
2Ki 14:21 All the people of Judah took **A**,
14:22 **A** rebuilt Elath and returned it
15:1 Amaziah's son **A** began to rule
15:6 Isn't everything else about **A** —
15:7 **A** lay down in death with his
15:30 in the twentieth year that **A**,
15:32 ruled Israel, Jotham, son of **A**,
15:34 as his father **A** had done.
1Ch 2:8 Ethan's son was **A**.
2:38 Jehu was the father of **A**.
2:39 **A** was the father of Helez.
3:12 Amaziah's son was **A**.
6:9 Ahimaaz was the father of **A**.
6:9 **A** was the father of Johanan.
6:10 Johanan was the father of **A**.
6:11 **A** was the father of Amariah.
6:13 Hilkiah was the father of **A**.
6:14 **A** was the father of Seraiah.
6:36 who was the son of **A**,
9:11 and **A**. Azariah was the son of
9:11 **A** was the son of Hilkiah,
2Ch 15:1 God's Spirit came to **A**,
15:2 **A** went to Asa and said to him,
21:2 **A**, Jehiel, Zechariah, Azariahu,
23:1 **A**, son of Jeroham, Ishmael,
23:1 **A**, son of Obed, Maaseiah,
26:17 The priest **A** went in after him
26:20 When the chief priest **A** and all
28:12 Then **A**, son of Jehohan,
29:12 of Amasai, and Joel, son of **A**.
29:12 Abdi, and **A**, son of Jehallelel.
31:10 The chief priest **A** from Zadok's
31:13 King Hezekiah and **A**,
Ezr 7:1 who was the son of **A**,
7:3 who was the son of **A**,
Neh 3:23 After them **A**, son of Maaseiah
7:7 **A**, Raamiah, Nahamani,
Neh 8:7 Kelita, **A**, Jozabad, Hanan,
10:2 Seraiah, **A**, Jeremiah,
12:33 **A**, Ezra, Meshullam,
Jer 43:2 **A** (son of Hoshaiah),
Dan 1:6 Hananiah, Mishael, and **A**.
1:7 And to **A** he gave the name
1:11 Hananiah, Mishael, and **A**.
1:19 and **A** among all of them.
2:17 and **A** about this matter.

Azariah's (7)
2Ki 15:8 In **A** thirty-eighth year as king
15:13 became king in **A** thirty-ninth
15:17 In **A** thirty-ninth year as king of
15:23 In **A** fiftieth year as king of
15:27 In **A** fifty-second year as king
1Ch 3:12 **A** son was Jotham.
Neh 3:24 on a section from **A** home

Azariahu (1)
2Ch 21:2 **A**, Michael, and Shephatiah.

Azaz (1)
1Ch 5:8 and Bela (son of **A**,

Azazel (4)
Lev 16:8 the LORD and the other for **A**.
16:10 the goat chosen by lot for **A** into
16:10 will release it in the desert to **A**
16:26 the goat to **A** must wash his

Azaziah (3)
1Ch 15:21 and **A** were appointed to play
27:20 son of **A** for half of the tribe of
2Ch 31:13 **A**, Nahath, Asahel, Jerimoth,

Azbuk's (1)
Neh 3:16 After him Nehemiah, **A** son, the

Azekah (7)
Jos 10:10 all the way to **A** and Makkedah.
10:11 slope of Beth Horon toward **A**,
15:35 Jarmuth, Adullam, Socoh, **A**,
1Sm 17:1 and **A** at Ephes Dammim.
2Ch 11:9 Adoraim, Lachish, **A**,
Neh 11:30 and in **A** and its villages.
Jer 34:7 and the cities of Lachish and **A**.

Azel (5)
1Ch 8:37 Eleasah's son was **A**.
8:38 **A** had six sons. Their names
9:43 Eleasah's son was **A**.
9:44 **A** had six sons. Their names
Zec 14:5 mountains will go as far as **A**.

Azel's (2)
1Ch 8:38 All of these men were **A** sons
9:44 All of these men were **A** sons

Azgad (4)
Ezr 2:12 of **A**: 1,222
8:12 from the family of **A**:
Neh 7:17 of **A**: 2,322
10:15 Bunni, **A**, Bebai,

Aziza (1)
Ezr 10:27 Jeremoth, Zabad, and **A**

Azmaveth (7)
2Sm 23:31 Beth Arabah, **A** from Bahurim,
1Ch 8:36 father of Alemeth, **A**, and Zimri.
9:42 father of Alemeth, **A**, and Zimri.
11:33 **A** from Bahurim, Eliahba from
27:25 for the royal treasuries: **A**,
Ezr 2:24 of **A**: 42
Neh 12:29 from the region of Geba and **A**.

Azmaveth's (1)
1Ch 12:3 **A** sons Jeziel and Pelet,

Azmon (3)
Num 34:4 to Hazar Addar and on to **A**.
34:5 From **A** it turns toward the
Jos 15:4 and on to **A**. It comes out at the

Aznoth Tabor (1)
Jos 19:34 The border turns west to **A**,

Azor (2)
Mat 1:13 Eliakim the father of **A**,
1:14 **A** the father of Zadok,

Azotus (1)
Act 8:40 found himself in the city of **A**.

Azriel (3)
1Ch 5:24 Eliel, **A**, Jeremiah, Hodaviah,
27:19 of Naphtali: Jerimoth, son of **A**
Jer 36:26 Seraiah (son of **A**),

Azrikam (6)
1Ch 3:23 were Elioenai, Hizkiah, and **A**.
8:38 Their names were **A**,
9:14 of Hasshub, grandson of **A**,
9:44 Their names were **A**,
2Ch 28:7 who was the king's son, **A**,
Neh 11:15 who was the son of **A**,

Azubah (4)
1Ki 22:42 His mother's name was **A**,
1Ch 2:18 Caleb and his wife **A** had a son
2:19 After **A** died, Caleb married
2Ch 20:31 His mother's name was **A**,

Azzan (1)
Num 34:26 Paltiel, son of **A**, the leader of

Azzur (2)
Neh 10:17 Ater, Hezekiah, **A**,
Jer 28:1 son of **A**, from Gibeon,

Azzur's (1)
Eze 11:1 I saw among them **A** son

B

Baal (72)
Num 25:3 worshiping the god **B** of Peor,
25:5 worshiping the god **B** of Peor."
4:3 the god **B** while you were
Jdg 2:13 the LORD to serve the god **B**
6:25 altar dedicated to the god **B**
6:28 they saw that the **B** altar had
6:30 He has torn down the **B** altar
6:31 "You're not going to defend **B**,
6:32 [Let **B** Defend Himself],
6:32 let **B** defend himself."
1Sm 7:4 got rid of the statues of **B**
1Ki 16:31 then served and worshiped **B**.
16:32 He built the temple of **B** in
18:18 following the various **B** gods.
18:19 And bring the 450 prophets of **B**
18:21 him; if **B** is God, follow him."
18:22 but there are 450 prophets of **B**.
18:23 Let the prophets of **B** choose
18:25 Elijah told the prophets of **B**,
18:26 and called on the name of **B**
18:26 They said, "**B**, answer us!"
18:40 "Seize the prophets of **B**.
19:18 have not knelt to worship **B**
22:53 Ahaziah served **B**,
2Ki 3:2 had set up and dedicated to **B**.
10:18 said, "Ahab served **B** a little,
10:19 servants, and priests of **B**.
10:19 have a great sacrifice to offer **B**.
10:19 those who worshiped **B**.)
10:20 a holy assembly to honor **B**."
10:21 All the worshipers of **B** came,
10:21 They went into the temple of **B**
10:22 for all the worshipers of **B**."
10:23 went into the temple of **B** and
10:23 and said to the worshipers of **B**,
10:23 of **B** should be here."
10:25 swords to kill the **B** worshipers
10:25 stronghold in the temple of **B**.
10:26 of the temple of **B** and burned it.
10:27 destroyed the sacred stone of **B**
2Ki 10:27 of Baal and the temple of **B**
10:28 of **B** worship throughout Israel.
11:18 the land went to the temple of **B**
11:18 killed Mattan, the priest of **B**,
17:16 They worshiped **B**.
21:3 He set up altars dedicated to **B**
23:4 that had been made for **B**,
23:5 They had been sacrificing to **B**,
1Ch 4:33 cities as far as the city of **B**.
5:5 Reaiah's son was **B**.
8:30 then Zur, Kish, **B**, Nadab,
9:36 then Zur, Kish, **B**, Nadab,
2Ch 23:17 people went to the temple of **B**
23:17 killed Mattan, the priest of **B**,
34:4 the various **B** gods torn down.
Psa 106:28 the god **B** while they were
Jer 2:8 prophesied in the name of **B**
3:24 the shameful worship of **B**
7:9 incense as an offering to **B**,
11:13 Jerusalem to sacrifice to **B**.
11:17 incense as an offering to **B**.
12:16 an oath in the name of **B**.
19:5 their children as sacrifices to **B**.
23:13 of Samaria prophesied by **B**
23:27 forgot my name because of **B**.
32:29 to the roofs to burn incense to **B**
32:35 they built worship sites for **B**
Hos 2:8 used it to make statues of **B**.
2:17 names of other gods called **B**.
13:1 became guilty of worshiping **B**,
Zep 1:4 faithful few of **B** from this place
Rom 11:4 have not knelt to worship **B**."

Baalah (6)
Jos 15:9 around to **B** (now called Kiriath
15:10 From **B** the border turns west
15:11 to Shikkeron, on to Mount **B**,
15:29 **B**, Iim, Ezem,
2Sm 6:2 all the people with him left **B**
1Ch 13:6 David and all Israel went to **B**

Baalath (3)
Jos 19:44 Eltekeh, Gibbethon, **B**,
1Ki 9:18 **B**, Tadmor in the desert (inside
2Ch 8:6 He also rebuilt **B** and all the

Baalath Beer (1)
Jos 19:8 around these cities as far as **B**

Baal Berith (2)
Jdg 8:33 They made **B** their god.
9:4 of silver from the temple of **B**.

Baal Gad (3)
Jos 11:17 to Seir as far as **B**
12:7 Their lands extended from **B**
13:5 all Lebanon eastward from **B**

Baal Hamon (1)
Sos 8:11 Solomon had a vineyard at **B**.

Baal Hanan (5)
Gen 36:38 Shaul died, **B**, son of Achbor
36:39 After **B**, son of Achbor, died
1Ch 1:49 Shaul died, **B**,son of Achbor
1:50 After **B** died, Hadad succeeded
27:28 **B** from Gedor for storing olive

Baal Hazor (1)
2Sm 13:23 sheepshears at **B** near Ephraim.

Baal Hermon (2)
Jdg 3:3 Mount Lebanon from Mount **B**
1Ch 5:23 land from Bashan to **B**, Senir

Baalis (1)
Jer 40:14 "Do you know that King **B** of

Baal Meon (3)
Num 32:38 Nebo, **B** (whose names were
1Ch 5:8 Aroer as far as Nebo and **B**.
Eze 25:9 Beth Jeshimoth, **B**, and

Baal Peor (2)
Dtr 4:3 saw what the LORD did at **B**.
Hos 9:10 went to **B** and worshipped

Baal Perazim (4)
2Sm 5:20 So David went to **B** and
5:20 is why that place is called **B**.
1Ch 14:11 Philistines at **B**
14:11 they call that place **B**.

Baal's (5)
Jdg 6:32 down **B** altar, let Baal defend
1Ki 19:2 took the lives of **B** prophets.
2Ki 11:18 They smashed **B** altars and his
1Ch 5:6 **B** son was Beerah.
2Ch 23:17 They smashed **B** altars and his

Baals (14)
Jdg 2:11 to serve other gods — the **B**.
3:7 the **B** and the Asherahs.
8:33 other gods — the **B** —
10:6 gods and goddesses — the **B**
10:10 served other gods — the **B**."
1Sm 12:10 gods and goddesses — the **B**
2Ch 17:3 to serving other gods — the **B**.
24:7 worship other gods — the **B**.)
28:2 worshiping other gods — the **B**.
33:3 to other gods — the **B** —
Jer 2:23 followed other gods — the **B**?
9:14 ways and other gods — the **B**,
Hos 2:13 offering to other gods — the **B**.
11:2 sacrificed to other gods — the **B**

Baal Shalisha (1)
2Ki 4:42 A man from **B** brought bread

Baal Tamar (1)
Jdg 20:33 formed their battle line at **B**.

Baalzebub (4)
2Ki 1:2 He had told them, "Go ask **B**,
1:3 'Do you seek advice from **B**,
1:6 to seek advice from **B**,
1:16 to seek advice from **B**,

Baal Zephon (1)
Num 33:7 back to Pi Hahiroth, east of **B**,

Baana (3)
1Ki 4:12 **B**, son of Ahilud, had Taanach,
4:16 **B**, son of Hushai, was in
Neh 3:4 Next to them Zadok, son of **B**,

Baanah (10)
2Sm 4:2 One was named **B**,
4:5 Rechab and **B**, the sons of
4:6 Then Rechab and his brother **B**
4:9 to Rechab and his brother **B**,
4:12 who executed Rechab and **B**,
23:29 Heleb (son of **B**)
1Ch 11:30 Heled (son of **B**)
Ezr 2:2 Mispar, Bigvai, Rehum, and **B**.
Neh 7:7 Bigvai, Nehum, and **B**.
10:27 Malluch, Harim, and **B**.

Baara (1)
1Ch 8:8 his wives Hushim and **B**.

Baaseiah (1)
1Ch 6:40 who was the son of **B**,

Baasha (26)
1Ki 15:16 war between Asa and King **B**
15:17 King **B** of Israel invaded Judah
15:19 break your treaty with King **B**
15:21 When **B** heard the news,
15:22 **B** had been using those to
15:27 Then **B**, son of Ahijah from the
15:27 **B** assassinated him in the
15:28 **B** succeeded Nadab as king of
15:32 between Asa and **B** as long as
15:33 king of Judah, **B**, son of Ahijah,
16:1 Jehu, Hanani's son, against **B**.
16:3 So I will destroy **B** and his
16:5 Isn't everything else about **B** —
16:6 **B** lay down in death with his
16:7 against **B** and his family
16:7 of all the things **B** did which
16:7 **B** destroyed Jeroboam's family.

1Ki 16:8 Elah, son of **B**, began to rule
16:13 for all the sins committed by **B**
21:22 son) and like the house of **B**,
2Ki 9:9 son) and like the family of **B**,
2Ch 16:1 King **B** of Israel invaded Judah
16:3 break your treaty with King **B**
16:5 When **B** heard the news,
16:6 **B** had been using those to
Jer 41:9 against King **B** of Israel.

Baasha's (5)

1Ki 16:4 from **B** ⌊family⌋ who dies
16:7 **B** actions, which made the
16:11 he killed **B** entire family.
16:11 He didn't spare any of **B** male
16:12 Zimri destroyed **B** entire family,

babble (1)

Gen 11:9 of the whole earth into **b**.

babbling (1)

Act 17:18 Some asked, "What is this **b**

Babel (1)

Gen 11:9 This is why it was named **B**,

babies (13)

Exo 1:19 that they have their **b** before
Dtr 32:25 nursing **b** and gray-haired men.
Isa 13:18 have no compassion for **b**,
Jer 44:7 and **b** from Judah until none are
Hos 9:11 more pregnancies, births, or **b**.
9:14 them unable to nurse their **b**.
Mat 24:19 are nursing **b** in those days.
Mar 13:17 are nursing **b** in those days.
Luk 21:23 pregnant or who are nursing **b**
Act 7:19 their newborn **b** outdoors,
1Co 14:20 it comes to evil, be like **b**,
Heb 5:13 what is right. They are still **b**.
1Pe 2:2 word as newborn **b** desire milk.

baby (17)

Exo 2:3 She put the **b** in it and set it
2:6 the basket, looked at the **b**,
2:7 women to nurse the **b** for you?"
Num 11:12 as a nurse carries a **b** — all
12:12 Don't let her be like a stillborn **b**
2Sm 12:25 the **b** Jedidiah [The LORD's
2Ki 4:16 you will hold a **b** boy in your
Job 3:16 be buried like a stillborn **b**.
24:9 a poor woman's **b** as security
Ecc 6:4 A stillborn **b** arrives in a
6:5 the **b** finds more rest than the
Jer 20:15 become the father of a **b** boy.
Hos 13:13 They are like a **b** who is about
Luk 1:41 she felt the **b** kick.
1:44 I felt the **b** jump for joy.
2:16 Mary and Joseph with the **b**,
Heb 11:23 that Moses was a beautiful **b**

Babylon (326)

Gen 10:10 ⌊cities⌋ in his kingdom were **B**,
2Ki 17:24 Assyria brought people from **B**,
17:30 The people from **B** made
20:12 King Merodach Baladan of **B**,
20:14 from the distant country of **B**."
20:17 will be taken away to **B**.
20:18 in the palace of the king of **B**.'"
24:1 of **B** attacked ⌊Judah⌋,
24:7 the king of **B** had taken all
24:10 of **B** attacked Jerusalem.
24:11 King Nebuchadnezzar of **B**
24:12 surrendered to the king of **B**.
24:12 king of **B** captured Jehoiakin.
24:15 He took Jehoiakin to **B** as a
24:15 Jerusalem as captives to **B**.
24:16 The king of **B** brought all 7,000
24:16 fight in war as captives to **B**.
24:17 The king of **B** made King
24:20 rebelled against the king of **B**.
25:1 King Nebuchadnezzar of **B**
25:6 him to the king of **B** at Riblah,
25:7 shackles and took him to **B**.
25:8 nineteenth year as king of **B**,
25:8 and an officer of the king of **B**,
25:11 surrendered to the king of **B**,
2Ki 25:13 They shipped the bronze to **B**.
25:20 them to the king of **B** at Riblah.
25:21 The king of **B** executed them
25:22 of **B** appointed Gedaliah,
25:23 of **B** had appointed Gedaliah,
25:24 serve the king of **B**,
25:27 King Evil Merodach of **B**,
25:28 kings who were with him in **B**.
25:30 The king of **B** gave him a daily
1Ch 9:1 taken away to **B** as captives
2Ch 32:31 When the leaders of **B** sent
33:11 and brought him to **B**.
36:6 King Nebuchadnezzar of **B**
36:6 shackles to take him to **B**.
36:7 of the LORD's temple to **B**.
36:7 He put them in his palace in **B**.
36:10 Jehoiakin and brought him to **B**
36:18 He brought to **B** each of the
36:18 the king and his officials to **B**.
36:20 The king of **B** took those who
36:20 who weren't executed to **B**
Ezr 1:11 with him when the exiles left **B**
2:1 (King Nebuchadnezzar of **B**
2:1 Babylon had taken them to **B**.)
4:9 Persia, Erech, **B**, Susa, (that is,
5:12 of **B** (a Chaldean).
5:12 and deported its people to **B**.
5:13 of the reign of King Cyrus of **B**,
5:14 Cyrus took out of a temple in **B**
5:14 them into a temple in **B**.)
5:17 search the king's archives in **B**
6:1 the archives were stored in **B**.
6:5 Cyrus took out of a temple in **B**
6:5 them into a temple in **B**.)
7:1 of Persia, Ezra left **B**.
7:9 He had left **B** on the first day of
7:16 province of **B** when you take
8:1 genealogy of those who left **B**
9:8 leave us a few survivors from **B**
Neh 7:6 King Nebuchadnezzar of **B** had
13:6 of King Artaxerxes' reign in **B**,
Est 2:6 of **B** had carried away.)
Psa 87:4 "I will add Egypt and **B** as well
137:1 By the rivers of **B**, we sat down
137:8 You destructive people of **B**,
Isa 13:1 son of Amoz, saw about **B**.
13:19 **B**, the jewel of the kingdoms,
14:4 you will mock the king of **B**
14:22 name of the survivors from **B**,
21:9 Then he said, "**B** has fallen!
39:1 King Merodach Baladan of **B**,
39:3 from the distant country of **B**."
39:6 will be taken away to **B**.
39:7 in the palace of the king of **B**.'"
43:14 I will send ⌊an army⌋ to **B**.
47:1 virgin princess of **B**!
48:14 out the LORD's plan against **B**.
48:20 Leave **B**; flee from the
Jer 20:4 of Judah over to the king of **B**.
20:4 people away as captives to **B**
20:5 and bring them to **B**.
20:6 You will go to **B**, and you will
21:2 of **B** is attacking us.
21:4 to fight the king of **B** as well as
21:7 to King Nebuchadnezzar of **B**
21:10 be handed over to the king of **B**,
22:25 of **B** and the Babylonians.
24:1 King Nebuchadnezzar of **B**
24:1 and brought them to **B**.
24:5 I sent away from here to **B**,
25:1 was king of **B**.)
25:9 King Nebuchadnezzar of **B**,
25:11 serve the king of **B** for 70 years.
25:12 I will punish the king of **B** and
25:12 I will turn **B** into a permanent
25:14 make slaves of the people of **B**,
27:6 King Nebuchadnezzar of **B**.
27:7 grandson until **B** is defeated.
27:8 to King Nebuchadnezzar of **B**.
27:9 you'll never serve the king of **B**.
27:11 surrenders to the king of **B**
27:12 "Surrender to the king of **B**,
27:13 that don't serve the king of **B**.
27:14 you'll never serve the king of **B**.
27:16 be brought back from **B** soon.
27:17 Instead, serve the king of **B**,
Jer 27:18 to be taken away to **B**.
27:19 from Jerusalem to **B** along
27:22 They will be taken to **B** and
28:2 break the yoke of the king of **B**.
28:3 of **B** took from this
28:3 this place and carried off to **B**.
28:4 of Judah who went to **B**,
28:4 the yoke of the king of **B**."
28:6 captives from **B** to this place.
28:11 King Nebuchadnezzar of **B** off
28:14 King Nebuchadnezzar of **B**.
29:1 captives from Jerusalem to **B**.
29:3 to King Nebuchadnezzar in **B**.
29:4 captive from Jerusalem to **B**:
29:15 has given you prophets in **B**.
29:20 sent away from Jerusalem to **B**.
29:21 to King Nebuchadnezzar of **B**.
29:22 from Judah who are in **B** will
29:22 the king of **B** burned to death.
29:28 sent this message to us in **B**:
32:2 **B** was blockading Jerusalem.
32:3 this city over to the king of **B**,
32:4 be handed over to the king of **B**.
32:5 will take Zedekiah to **B**,
32:28 and King Nebuchadnezzar of **B**.
32:36 over to the king of **B**.' Now
34:1 King Nebuchadnezzar of **B**,
34:2 this city over to the king of **B**,
34:3 You will see the king of **B** with
34:3 Then you will go to **B**.
34:7 of **B** was attacking Jerusalem
34:21 and to the army of the king of **B**,
35:11 of **B** invaded this land,
36:29 king of **B** will certainly come
37:1 of **B** appointed Zedekiah,
37:17 handed over to the king of **B**."
37:19 king of **B** wouldn't attack you
38:3 to the army of the king of **B**,
38:17 to the officers of the king of **B**,
38:18 to the officers of the king of **B**,
38:22 to the officers of the king of **B**.
38:23 be captured by the king of **B**,
39:1 King Nebuchadnezzar of **B**
39:3 officers of the king of **B** came
39:3 of the officers of the king of **B**.
39:5 The king of **B** passed
39:6 The king of **B** slaughtered
39:7 and took him to **B**.
39:11 King Nebuchadnezzar of **B**
39:13 the king of **B** sent for Jeremiah.
40:1 who were being taken to **B**.
40:4 like to come with me to **B**,
40:4 want to come with me to **B**,
40:5 whom the king of **B** appointed
40:7 of **B** had appointed Gedaliah,
40:7 had not been taken away to **B**.
40:9 serve the king of **B**,
40:11 heard that the king of **B** had left
41:2 the king of **B** had appointed
41:18 the king of **B** had appointed
42:11 Don't be afraid of the king of **B**,
43:3 us or take us as captives to **B**."
43:10 King Nebuchadnezzar of **B**.
44:30 to King Nebuchadnezzar of **B**
46:2 King Nebuchadnezzar of **B**
46:13 of King Nebuchadnezzar of **B**,
46:26 to King Nebuchadnezzar of **B**
49:28 Nebuchadnezzar of **B** defeated.
49:30 King Nebuchadnezzar of **B** has
50:1 that the LORD spoke about **B**
50:2 Say, '**B** will be captured.
50:3 from the north will attack **B**
50:8 "Run away from **B**.
50:9 the north and bring it against **B**.
50:9 take up positions against **B**.
50:9 **B** will be captured from the
50:12 **B**, you will be the least
50:13 No one will live in **B** because
50:13 Everyone who passes by **B**
50:14 up your positions around **B**,
50:14 because the people of **B** have
50:16 Don't allow anyone in **B** to
50:17 King Nebuchadnezzar of **B**.
50:18 going to punish the king of **B**
50:23 See how desolate **B** is of all
50:24 I will set traps for you, **B**.

Jer 50:28 Fugitives and refugees from **B**
50:29 soldiers with bows, against **B**.
50:29 Pay the people of **B** back for
50:34 to the people who live in **B**.
50:35 who lives in **B**," declares
50:38 **B** is a land of idols,
50:40 **B** will be like Sodom,
50:42 to attack you, people of **B**.
50:43 The king of **B** has heard
50:44 I will appoint over **B** whomever
50:45 the LORD is making against **B**
50:46 news that **B** has been captured.
51:1 up a destructive wind against **B**
51:2 I will send people to winnow **B**,
51:6 Run away from **B**! Run for your
51:6 He will pay the people of **B**
51:7 **B** was a golden cup in the
51:8 **B** will suddenly fall and be
51:9 We wanted to heal **B**,
51:9 God has judged **B**.
51:11 his plan is to destroy **B**.
51:12 flag in front of the walls of **B**.
51:12 the people who live in **B**.
51:13 **B**, you live beside many rivers
51:24 your presence I will pay back **B**
51:24 and all the people who live in **B**
51:25 "I am against you, **B**,
51:27 Prepare nations to attack **B**.
51:28 Prepare nations to attack **B**.
51:29 carries out his plans against **B**
51:29 against Babylon to make **B**
51:30 The warriors of **B** have stopped
51:31 They inform the king of **B** that
51:33 The people of **B** are like a
51:34 King Nebuchadnezzar of **B** has
51:35 done to us be done to **B**."
51:35 "May the people of **B** be held
51:37 **B** will become piles of rubble.
51:41 **B**, the city that the whole world
51:42 What a horrifying sight **B** will
51:42 The sea will rise over **B**,
51:44 I will punish Bel in **B**.
51:44 will no longer stream to **B**,
51:48 in them will rejoice over **B**,
51:49 Because the people of **B** have
51:49 the earth, **B** must fall.
51:53 The people of **B** might go up to
51:54 of agony are heard from **B**.
51:55 The LORD will destroy **B**.
51:56 A destroyer will attack **B**,
51:58 The thick walls of **B** will be
51:59 when Seraiah went to **B** with
51:60 that would happen to **B**.
51:60 that have been written about **B**.
51:61 "When you come to **B**,
51:64 '**B** will sink like this scroll.
52:3 rebelled against the king of **B**.
52:4 King Nebuchadnezzar of **B**
52:9 him to the king of **B** at Riblah
52:9 where the king of **B** passed
52:10 The king of **B** slaughtered
52:11 The king of **B** took him to
52:11 king of Babylon took him to **B**
52:12 nineteenth year as king of **B**,
52:12 and an officer of the king of **B**,
52:15 surrendered to the king of **B**,
52:17 shipped all the bronze to **B**.
52:26 them to the king of **B** at Riblah.
52:27 The king of **B** executed them
52:31 King Evil Merodach of **B**,
52:32 kings who were with him in **B**.
52:34 The king of **B** gave him a daily
Eze 1:3 in **B** by the Chebar River.
12:13 I will bring him to **B**,
17:12 Tell them, 'The king of **B** came
17:12 them home with him to **B**.
17:15 the king of **B** by sending his
17:16 his treaty with the king of **B**.
17:20 I will take you to **B** and judge
19:9 brought him to the king of **B**.
21:19 two roads that the king of **B**
21:21 The king of **B** will stop where
21:23 But the king of **B** will remind
23:15 officers who were born in **B**.
23:17 So these men came from **B**,
23:23 I will bring men from **B** and
Eze 24:2 The king of **B** has surrounded
26:7 of **B** against you,
29:18 King Nebuchadnezzar of **B**
29:19 to King Nebuchadnezzar of **B**.
30:10 use King Nebuchadnezzar of **B**
30:24 the arms of the king of **B** strong.
30:25 the arms of the king of **B**,
30:25 in the hand of the king of **B**.
32:11 of the king of **B** will attack you.
Dan 1:1 King Nebuchadnezzar of **B**
2:12 all the wise advisers in **B**.
2:14 to kill the wise advisers in **B**,
2:18 rest of the wise advisers in **B**.
2:48 of the whole province of **B**
2:49 to govern the province of **B**.
3:1 in the wall in the province of **B**.
3:12 to govern the province of **B**:
3:30 positions in the province of **B**.
4:6 all the wise advisers in **B**
4:29 around the royal palace in **B**.
4:30 "Look how great **B** is!
5:7 told these wise advisers of **B**,
5:30 Belshazzar of **B** was killed.
7:1 first year as king of **B**,
9:1 made ruler of the kingdom of **B**.
Mic 4:10 in the open fields, and go to **B**.
Hag 1:12 who returned from **B** obeyed
1:14 returned from **B** began working
2:2 few who returned from **B**.
Zec 2:7 Escape, you inhabitants of **B**!
6:10 who have arrived from **B**.
Mat 1:11 the people were exiled to **B**.
1:12 After the exile to **B**,
1:17 from David until the exile to **B**,
Act 7:43 into exile beyond the city of **B**.'
1Pe 5:13 Your sister church in **B**,
Rev 14:8 **B** the Great has fallen!
16:19 God remembered to give **B** the
17:5 was Mystery: **B** the Great,
18:2 **B** the Great has fallen!
18:4 "Come out of **B**, my people,
18:10 the powerful city **B**!
18:21 "The important city **B** will be

Babylonia (10)

Gen 10:10 and Calneh in Shinar [**B**].
11:2 in Shinar [**B**] and settled there.
Jos 7:21 I saw a fine robe from **B**,
Isa 11:11 Sudan, Elam, **B**, Hamath,
Eze 11:24 brought me to the exiles in **B**.
17:16 the king of Judah will die in **B**.
23:16 sent messengers to them in **B**.
23:23 from Babylon and from all **B**,
Dan 1:2 to the temple of his god in **B**
Zec 5:11 a house for it in Shinar [**B**].

Babylonian (15)

2Ki 25:5 The **B** army pursued King
25:10 The entire **B** army that was
25:24 be afraid of the **B** officers.
2Ch 36:17 So he had the **B** king attack
Isa 43:14 I will bring back all the **B**
Jer 35:11 to Jerusalem (to escape) the **B**
37:10 defeat the entire **B** army so that
37:11 The **B** army had retreated from
39:5 The **B** army pursued them and
41:3 as well as the **B** soldiers that
52:8 The **B** army pursued King
52:14 The entire **B** army that was
Eze 23:14 They were figures of **B** men,
23:15 All of them looked like **B**
Dan 1:7 gave them (**B**) names:

Babylonians (57)

2Ki 24:2 LORD sent raiding parties of **B**,
25:4 While the **B** were attacking the
25:6 The **B** captured the king,
25:13 The **B** broke apart the bronze
25:25 the Judeans and **B** who were
25:26 they were afraid of the **B**.
Isa 23:13 Look at the land of the **B**.
47:1 on a throne, princess of the **B**!
47:5 sit in silence, princess of the **B**!
48:14 use his strength against the **B**.
48:20 Leave Babylon; flee from the **B**!
Jer 21:4 as well as the **B** who are now
Jer 21:4 will bring the **B** inside this city.
21:9 and surrender to the **B** will live.
22:25 of Babylon and the **B**.
32:4 will not escape from the **B**.
32:5 When you fight the **B**,
32:24 over to the **B** who are attacking
32:25 was handed over to the **B**.'"
32:28 to hand this city over to the **B**
32:29 "The **B** who are attacking this
32:43 has been handed over to the **B**.
33:4 ramps and weapons of the **B**.
33:5 people of Israel fought the **B**.
37:5 and when the **B** who were
37:8 Then the **B** will return.
37:9 that the **B** will leave you.
37:13 "You're deserting to the **B**!"
37:14 I'm not deserting to the **B**."
38:2 who surrender to the **B** will live.
38:18 will be handed over to the **B**.
38:19 who have deserted to the **B**.
38:19 The **B** may hand me over to
38:23 will be brought to the **B**.
39:8 The **B** burned down the royal
40:9 "Don't be afraid to serve the **B**.
40:10 represent you when the **B** come
41:18 They were afraid of the **B**
43:3 order to hand us over to the **B**.
50:1 and the land of the **B** through
50:8 Leave the land of the **B**.
50:10 The **B** will become the prize.
50:25 a job to do in the land of the **B**.
50:35 "A sword will kill the **B** and
50:45 to do to the land of the **B**.
50:45 the pasture because of the **B**.
51:54 heard from the land of the **B**.
52:7 While the **B** were attacking the
52:9 The **B** captured the king and
52:17 The **B** broke apart the bronze
Eze 12:13 to Babylon, the land of the **B**,
16:29 land of the merchants, the **B**.
17:17 in battle when the **B** put up dirt
Dan 1:4 language and literature of the **B**.
Hab 1:6 I am going to send the **B**,
1:12 you have appointed the **B** to
1:15 The **B** pull them all up with

Babylon's (14)

Isa 13:22 will howl in **B** strongholds,
Jer 27:19 "**B** King Nebuchadnezzar took
29:10 When **B** 70 years are over,
39:5 King Nebuchadnezzar at Riblah
39:9 **B** captain of the guard,
50:2 **B** statues will be put to shame.
51:3 Don't spare **B** young men.
51:4 **B** soldiers will fall down badly
51:6 die because of **B** crimes.
51:36 I will dry up **B** sea and make
51:47 when I will punish **B** idols.
Dan 2:24 to destroy **B** wise advisers.
2:24 "Don't destroy **B** wise advisers.
2:48 head of all **B** wise advisers.

baby's (4)

Exo 2:4 The **b** sister stood at a
2:7 Then the **b** sister asked
2:8 So the girl brought the **b** mother
Luk 1:62 So they motioned to the **b** father

back-breaking (3)

Exo 1:14 their lives bitter with **b** work
Dtr 26:6 made us do **b** work for them.
Rom 11:10 them carry **b** burdens forever."

backed (1)

Jon 18:6 the crowd **b** away and fell to

background (2)

Est 2:10 her nationality or her family **b**,
2:20 her family **b** or nationality,

backs (19)

Dtr 33:11 Break the **b** of those who
33:29 and you will stomp on their **b**."
2Sm 22:41 my enemies turn their **b** to me,
2Ch 29:6 tent and turned their **b** on him.
Psa 18:40 my enemies turn their **b** to me,

Psa 21:12 They turn their **b** ⌊and flee⌋
66:11 You have laid burdens on our **b**.
145:14 He straightens ⌊the **b**⌋ of those
146:8 The LORD straightens ⌊the **b**⌋
Pro 19:29 and beatings for the **b** of fools.
26:3 and a rod is for the **b** of fools.
Isa 1:4 have turned their **b** on him.
30:6 They carry their riches on the **b**
Jer 2:27 You've turned your **b**,
32:33 have turned their **b**,
Eze 8:16 25 men who had their **b** turned
10:12 Their entire bodies, their **b**,
29:7 and they wrenched their **b**.
2Pe 2:21 than to know it and turn their **b**

bad (48)

Gen 37:2 about the **b** things his brothers
Exo 7:21 and it smelled so **b** that the
16:20 full of worms and smelled **b**.
33:4 the people heard this **b** news,
Lev 27:10 a good one for a **b** one or a bad
27:10 a good one for a bad one or a **b**
27:33 not look to see if it is good or **b**
Num 13:19 the land they live in good or **b**?
24:13 no matter how good or **b**
2Ki 2:19 But the water is **b**,
Neh 6:13 Then they could give me a **b**
Job 2:10 we also accept the **b**?"
Psa 112:7 He is not afraid of **b** news.
Pro 20:14 "**B**! Bad!" says the buyer.
20:14 **B**!" says the buyer.Then as he
22:24 of one who has a **b** temper,
30:9 name of my God a **b** reputation.
Ecc 5:14 then lost in **b** business deals.
7:14 But when times are **b**,
12:14 whether it is good or **b**.
Isa 24:9 Liquor tastes **b** to its drinkers.
Jer 5:12 Nothing **b** will happen to us.
23:17 "Nothing **b** will happen to you."
24:2 other basket had very **b** figs.
24:2 These figs were so **b** that they
24:3 I also see figs that are very **b**,
24:3 so **b** that they can't be eaten."
24:8 says about the **b** figs that are
24:8 figs that are so **b** that they can't
24:8 LORD says, 'Like these **b** figs,
29:17 figs that are so **b** that they can't
42:6 whether it's good or **b**.
49:23 they heard the **b** news.
Lam 3:38 Both good and **b** come from the
Eze 8:17 Isn't it **b** enough that the people
11:2 plan evil and give **b** advice
36:31 ways and the **b** things that you
Mic 3:11 Nothing **b** will happen to us."
Zep 1:12 won't do anything — good or **b**.
Mat 7:17 but a rotten tree produces **b**
7:18 tree cannot produce **b** fruit,
13:48 and threw the **b** ones away.
Act 6:13 stops saying **b** things about
28:21 anything **b** about you.
Rom 9:11 or had done anything good or **b**,
1Co 15:33 Associating with **b** people will
2Ti 3:13 phony preachers will go from **b**
Tit 2:8 say anything **b** about us.

badgers (5)

Lev 11:5 You must never eat rock **b**.
11:5 (Rock **b** are unclean because
Dtr 14:7 camels, rabbits, and rock **b**.
Psa 104:18 The rocks are a refuge for **b**.
Pro 30:26 Rock **b** are not a mighty

badly (12)

1Sm 24:17 me well while I treated you **b**.
31:3 he was **b** wounded by them.
1Ki 22:34 these troops. I'm **b** wounded."
2Ch 18:33 these troops. I'm **b** wounded."
35:23 "Take me away because I'm **b**
Psa 18:38 I wounded them so **b** that they
106:32 Things turned out **b** for Moses
Jer 37:10 only a few **b** wounded men left
51:4 will fall down **b** wounded
Mar 12:27 You're **b** mistaken!"
Act 19:16 He beat them up so **b** that they
Rom 11:11 "Has Israel stumbled so **b** that

bag (11)

Gen 42:35 each man found his **b** of
1Sm 17:40 put them in his shepherd's **b**.
17:49 Then David reached into his **b**,
Job 14:17 will be closed up in a **b**,
Psa 126:6 carrying his **b** of seed,
Mat 10:10 Don't take a traveling **b** for the
Mar 6:8 to take any food, a traveling **b**,
Luk 9:3 traveling **b**, any food, money,
10:4 a traveling **b**, or sandals,
22:35 wallet, traveling **b**, or sandals,
22:36 a traveling **b** should take them

baggage (1)

1Sm 10:22 "He's hiding among the **b**."

bags (16)

Gen 42:25 orders to fill their **b** with grain.
42:25 After their **b** were filled,
42:35 their father saw the **b** of money,
43:11 products of the land in your **b**.
2Ki 5:23 150 pounds of silver in two **b**
Isa 46:6 People pour gold out of their **b**
Jer 10:17 Pick up your **b**. You are being
46:19 Pack your **b**, inhabitants of
Eze 12:3 "Son of man, pack your **b** as if
12:4 Bring out your **b** as if you were
12:6 Let them see you put your **b** on
12:7 During the day I brought out **b**
12:7 I brought out my **b** in the dark.
12:7 I carried my **b** on my shoulders.
12:12 is among you will put his **b**
Mic 6:11 dishonest scales and **b** filled

Bahurim (7)

2Sm 3:16 cried over her all the way to **B**.
16:5 When King David came to **B**,
17:18 home of a man in **B** who had
19:16 of Benjamin and the town of **B**,
23:31 Beth Arabah, Azmaveth from **B**,
1Ki 2:8 of Gera from **B** in Benjamin,
1Ch 11:33 Azmaveth from **B**, Eliahba from

bail (1)

Job 17:3 guarantee my **b** yourself.

bait (2)

Pro 29:6 To an evil person sin is **b** in a
Amo 3:5 the ground if there's no **b** in it?

Bakbakkar (1)

1Ch 9:15 **B**, Heresh, Galal, grandson of

Bakbuk (2)

Ezr 2:51 **B**, Hakupha, Harhur,
Neh 7:53 **B**, Hakupha, Harhur,

Bakbukiah (3)

Neh 11:17 The Levite leader **B** was the
12:9 Their relatives **B** and Unno
12:25 Mattaniah, **B**, Obadiah,

bake (14)

Gen 11:3 bricks and **b** them thoroughly."
Exo 16:23 **B** what you want to bake,
16:23 Bake what you want to **b**,
29:2 and **b** some loaves of bread,
Lev 23:17 **B** them with four quarts of flour.
24:5 "Also take flour and **b** twelve
Dtr 28:5 bread you **b** will be blessed.
28:17 the bread you **b** will be cursed.
1Sm 8:13 make perfumes, cook, and **b**.
1Ki 17:12 I didn't **b** any bread.
Isa 44:15 They start fires and **b** bread.
Eze 4:12 **B** the bread in front of people,
4:15 **B** your bread over it."
46:20 they must **b** grain offerings so

baked (11)

Gen 19:3 **b** some unleavened bread,
40:16 baskets of white **b** goods were
40:17 contained all kinds of **b** goods
Exo 12:39 Egypt, they **b** round, flat bread.
Lev 2:4 grain offering which has been **b**
6:21 Offer **b** pieces of the grain
7:9 Every grain offering, whether **b**
1Sm 28:24 and **b** some unleavened bread.
1Ki 19:6 near his head some bread **b**
Isa 44:19 I also **b** bread over its coals.
Eze 27:17 **b** goods, honey, olive oil,

baker (9)

Gen 40:1 and his **b** offended their master,
40:2 chief cupbearer and his chief **b**.
40:5 the cupbearer and the **b**
40:16 The chief **b** saw that the
40:20 chief cupbearer and the chief **b**.
40:22 But he hung the chief **b** just as
41:10 he confined me and the chief **b**
41:13 but he hung the **b** on a pole."
Hos 7:4 an oven so hot that a **b** doesn't

bakers' (1)

Jer 37:21 day from the **b** street until all

baking (2)

Lev 6:17 Don't use yeast in **b** the bread.
Pro 25:20 or pouring vinegar on **b** soda,

Balaam (69)

Num 22:5 sent messengers to summon **B**,
22:7 They came to **B** and told him
22:8 the night here," **B** said to them,
22:8 princes of Moab stayed with **B**.
22:9 God came to **B** and asked,
22:10 **B** answered, "Balak, son of
22:12 But God said to **B**,
22:13 When **B** got up in the morning,
22:14 "**B** refused to come with us."
22:16 When they came to **B**,
22:18 But **B** answered Balak's
22:20 night God came to **B** and said,
22:21 When **B** got up in the morning,
22:22 **B** was riding on his donkey,
22:23 **B** hit the donkey to get it back
22:25 So **B** hit the donkey again.
22:27 it lay down under **B**.
22:27 **B** became so angry he hit the
22:28 donkey speak, and it asked **B**,
22:29 **B** answered, "You've made a
22:30 The donkey said to **B**,
22:31 Then the LORD let **B** see the
22:31 So **B** knelt, bowing with his
22:34 **B** said to the Messenger of the
22:35 of the LORD said to **B**,
22:35 So **B** went with Balak's
22:36 Balak heard that **B** had come,
22:37 Balak said to **B**, "Why didn't
22:38 **B** replied, "Well, I've come to
22:39 **B** went with Balak to Kiriath
22:40 and sent some of the meat to **B**
22:41 The next morning Balak took **B**
23:1 **B** said to Balak, "Build seven
23:2 Balak did what **B** told him,
23:3 **B** said to Balak, "Stay here
23:3 Then **B** went off to a higher
23:4 God came to him, and **B** said,
23:5 The LORD told **B**, "Go back to
23:7 Then **B** delivered this
23:11 Balak said to **B**, "What have
23:12 **B** answered, "I must say what
23:15 Then **B** said to Balak,
23:16 The LORD came to **B** and told
23:18 Then **B** delivered this
23:25 Balak said to **B**, "If you won't
23:26 **B** answered, "Didn't I tell you
23:27 Balak said to **B**, "Come, let me
23:28 So Balak took **B** to the top of
23:29 **B** said to Balak, "Build seven
23:30 Balak did what **B** told him,
24:1 When **B** saw that the LORD
24:3 "This is the message of **B**,
24:10 Balak became angry with **B**.
24:12 **B** answered Balak,
24:15 Then **B** delivered this
24:15 "This is the message of **B**,
24:20 Then **B** saw the Amalekites
24:25 Then **B** got up and went back
31:8 They also killed **B**,
Dtr 23:4 They even hired **B**,
23:5 your God refused to listen to **B**.

Jos 13:22 people of Israel also killed **B**,
24:9 He summoned **B**, son of Beor,
24:10 But I refused to listen to **B**.
Neh 13:2 Instead, they hired **B** to curse
Mic 6:5 ⌊to do to you⌋ and how **B**,
2Pe 2:15 off to follow the path of **B**,
2:15 **B** loved what his wrongdoing
Rev 2:14 follow what **B** taught Balak.

Balaam's (5)

Num 22:7 with them to pay for **B** services.
22:25 it moved over and pinned **B** foot
31:16 ones who followed **B** advice
Dtr 23:5 Instead, he turned **B** curse into
Jud 1:11 They have rushed into **B** error

Baladan's (2)

2Ki 20:12 At that time **B** son, King
Isa 39:1 At that time **B** son, King

Balah (1)

Jos 19:3 Hazar Shual, **B**, Ezem,

Balak (40)

Num 22:2 **B**, son of Zippor, saw all that
22:4 At that time **B**, son of Zippor,
22:7 and told him what **B** had said.
22:10 Balaam answered, "**B**,
22:14 went back to **B** and said,
22:15 **B** sent a larger group of more
22:16 "This is what **B**, son of Zippor,
22:18 "Even if **B** gave me his palace
22:36 When **B** heard that Balaam had
22:37 **B** said to Balaam, "Why didn't
22:39 went with **B** to Kiriath Huzoth.
22:40 **B** sacrificed cattle,
22:41 The next morning **B** took
23:1 Balaam said to **B**, "Build seven
23:2 **B** did what Balaam told him,
23:3 Balaam said to **B**, "Stay here
23:5 told Balaam, "Go back to **B**,
23:6 So he went back to **B** and
23:7 "**B** brought me from Aram.
23:11 **B** said to Balaam, "What have
23:13 Then **B** said to him,
23:15 Then Balaam said to **B**,
23:16 and told him, "Go back to **B**,
23:17 He came to **B** and found him
23:17 **B** asked him, "What did the
23:18 up, **B**, and listen! Hear me,
23:25 **B** said to Balaam, "If you won't
23:27 **B** said to Balaam, "Come,
23:28 So **B** took Balaam to the top of
23:29 Balaam said to **B**, "Build seven
23:30 **B** did what Balaam told him,
24:10 **B** became angry with Balaam.
24:12 Balaam answered **B**,
24:13 'Even if **B** would give me his
24:25 and **B** also went on his way.
Jos 24:9 Then **B**, son of King Zippor of
Jdg 11:25 You're not any better than **B**,
Mic 6:5 what King **B** of Moab
Rev 2:14 follow what Balaam taught **B**.
2:14 **B** trapped the people of Israel

Balak's (4)

Num 22:5 **B** message was, "A nation has
22:13 he said to **B** princes, "Go back
22:18 **B** servants, "Even if Balak
22:35 So Balaam went with **B** princes

balance (3)

Isa 40:12 on a scale and the hills on a **b**?
2Co 8:13 it's a matter of striking a **b**.
8:14 In this way things **b** out.

balances (1)

Pro 16:11 Honest **b** and scales belong to

bald (10)

Lev 13:40 even though he is **b**.
13:41 though he is **b** on the forehead.
13:42 is a pink patch on the **b** places
13:43 the disease in the **b** places
21:5 mourn by shaving **b** spots
Dtr 14:1 yourselves or shaving **b** spots
Isa 3:24 They will have **b** heads
15:2 Every head is shaved **b**,
Eze 29:18 soldier's head was worn **b**,
Mic 1:16 Make yourselves as **b** as

baldy (1)

2Ki 2:23 They said, "Go away, **b**!

balm (1)

Gen 43:11 Take a little **b**, a little honey,

balsam (8)

2Sm 5:23 at them in front of the **b** trees.
5:24 in the tops of the **b** trees,
2Ki 20:13 the silver, gold, **b**, fine olive oil,
1Ch 14:14 at them in front of the **b** trees.
14:15 in the tops of the **b** trees,
Psa 84:6 a valley where **b** trees grow,
Isa 39:2 the silver, gold, **b**, fine olive oil,
Eze 27:17 and **b** for your goods.

Bamoth (2)

Num 21:19 and from Nahaliel to **B**,
21:20 and from **B** to the valley in

Bamoth Baal (2)

Num 22:41 Balak took Balaam up to **B**.
Jos 13:17 Dibon, **B**, Beth Baal Meon,

band (4)

Gen 49:19 be attacked by a **b** of raiders,
Exo 13:16 on your hand and ⌊like⌋ a **b**
2Sm 1:10 on his head and the **b** that was
1Ki 7:35 had a round, nine-inch-high **b**.

bandage (5)

1Ki 20:38 disguised with a **b** over his
20:41 Then he quickly took the **b** off
Isa 30:26 the LORD will **b** his people's
Eze 34:16 **b** those that are injured,
Hos 6:1 he will **b** our wounds.

bandaged (4)

Isa 1:6 They haven't been cleansed, **b**,
Eze 30:21 His arm isn't **b**, so it can't heal
34:4 or **b** those that were injured.
Luk 10:34 and cleaned and **b** his wounds.

bandages (2)

Job 5:18 God injures, but he **b**.
Psa 147:3 is the one who **b** their wounds.

banding (1)

2Sm 2:25 **b** together and taking their

bandit (2)

Pro 6:11 will come ⌊to you⌋ like a **b**.
24:34 your need will come like a **b**.

bands (12)

Exo 27:10 The hooks and **b** on the posts
27:11 The hooks and **b** on the posts
27:17 courtyard should have silver **b**,
36:38 the posts and the **b** with gold,
38:10 The hooks and **b** on the posts
38:11 The hooks and **b** on the posts
38:12 The hooks and **b** on the posts
38:17 The hooks and **b** on the posts
38:17 And the **b** on all the posts of
38:19 The hooks and **b** on the posts
38:28 silver to make the hooks and **b**
Num 31:50 that each of us found — arm **b**,

Bani (14)

2Sm 23:36 **B** from the tribe of Gad,
1Ch 6:46 who was the son of **B**,
9:4 (Imri's father was **B**.)
Ezr 2:10 of **B**: 642
8:10 from the family of **B**:
10:29 From the descendants of **B**:
10:34 From the descendants of **B**:
Neh 8:7 The Levites — Jeshua, **B**,
9:4 Then Jeshua, **B**, Kadmiel,
9:4 Bunni, Sherebiah, **B**,
9:5 **B**, Hashabneiah, Sherebiah,
10:13 Hodiah, **B**, and Beninu.
10:14 Pahath Moab, Elam, Zattu, **B**,
11:22 who was the son of **B**,

Bani's (1)

Neh 3:17 including Rehum (**B** son), made

banish (1)

Jer 7:34 I will **b** the sounds of joy and

banished (6)

2Sm 14:13 brought back the one you **b**!
14:14 to keep a **b** person in exile.
1Ch 12:1 Ziklag when he was **b** by Saul,
Isa 24:11 and the earth's happiness is **b**.
27:13 in Assyria and those who are **b**
Jnh 2:4 'I have been **b** from your sight.

bank (9)

Gen 41:17 standing on the **b** of the Nile.
Exo 2:3 the papyrus plants near the **b**
2:5 servants walked along the **b**
7:15 Wait for him on the **b** of the
Dtr 2:37 didn't enter the land along the **b**
Jdg 7:22 and as far as the **b** of the
2Ki 2:13 and stood on the **b** of the
Eze 47:7 man led me back along the **b**
Luk 19:23 you put my money in the **b**?

bankers (1)

Mat 25:27 invested my money with the **b**.

bankrupt (1)

Gal 4:9 the powerless and **b** principles

banks (5)

Jos 3:15 (The Jordan overflows all its **b**
1Ch 12:15 when it was flooding its **b**.
Isa 8:7 channels and go over all its **b**.
Jer 46:8 river quickly overflowing its **b**.
Zec 11:3 because the lush **b** of the

banner (4)

Exo 17:15 called it The LORD Is My **B**.
Isa 11:10 root of Jesse will stand as a **b**
11:12 He will raise a **b** for the nations
13:2 Raise a **b** on the bare

banquet (28)

1Sm 9:22 and his servant to the **b** hall
20:29 why he hasn't come to your **b**."
25:36 he was holding a **b** in his
25:36 It was like a king's **b**.
1Ki 3:15 offerings and held a **b**
2Ch 18:2 many sheep and cattle for a **b**
Est 1:3 he held a **b** in the third year of
1:3 The **b** was for all his officials
1:5 the king held a **b** lasting seven
1:5 This **b** was held in the
1:9 Queen Vashti also held a **b** for
2:18 king held a great **b** for Esther.
Psa 23:5 You prepare a **b** for me while
78:19 God prepare a **b** in the desert?
Ecc 7:2 to go to a funeral than to a **b**
Sos 2:4 He leads me into a **b** room and
Isa 25:6 a **b** with aged wines,
Jer 16:8 into a home where there is a **b**.
Dan 5:1 Belshazzar threw a large **b**
5:10 queen herself into the **b** hall.
Amo 6:7 around the **b** table will stop.
Luk 14:13 Instead, when you give a **b**,
14:15 person who will be at the **b**
14:16 "A man gave a large **b** and
14:17 When it was time for the **b**,
14:24 will taste any food at my **b**."'
Rev 19:9 wedding **b**.'" He also told me,
19:17 Gather for the great **b** of God.

banquets (1)

Ecc 7:4 minds of fools think about **b**.

baptism (19)

Mar 1:4 desert telling people about a **b**
10:38 Can you be baptized with the **b**
10:39 You will be baptized with the **b**
Luk 3:3 He told people about a **b** of
12:50 I have a **b** to go through,

Act 10:37 John spread the news about **b**.
13:24 about the **b** of repentance.
18:25 about the **b** John performed.
19:3 "What kind of **b** did you have?"
19:3 They answered, "John's **b**."
19:4 Paul said, "John's **b** was a
19:4 baptism was a **b** of repentance.
1Co 10:2 all united with Moses by **b**
Eph 4:5 is one Lord, one faith, one **b**,
Col 2:12 the tomb with Christ through **b**.
2:12 In **b** you were also brought
1Pe 3:21 **B**, which is like that water,
3:21 **B** doesn't save by removing dirt
3:21 Rather, **b** is a request to God

baptisms (1)

Heb 6:2 about such things as **b**,

baptize (18)

Mat 3:11 I **b** you with water so that you
3:11 He will **b** you with the Holy
21:25 Did John's right to **b** come from
28:19 **B** them in the name of the
Mar 1:8 but he will **b** you with the Holy
11:30 Did John's right to **b** come from
Luk 3:16 "I **b** you with water.
3:16 He will **b** you with the Holy
7:29 right by letting John **b** them.
20:4 did John's right to **b** come from
20:7 who gave John the right to **b**.
Jon 1:25 "Why do you **b** if you're not the
1:26 them, "I **b** with water.
1:31 However, I came to **b** with
1:33 who sent me to **b** with water,
Act 10:47 "No one can refuse to **b** these
1Co 1:14 I thank God that I didn't **b** any
1:17 Christ didn't send me to **b**.

baptized (48)

Mat 3:6 he **b** them in the Jordan River.
3:7 and Sadducees coming to be **b**,
3:13 Jordan River to be **b** by John.
3:14 "I need to be **b** by you.
3:16 After Jesus was **b**,
Mar 1:5 he **b** them in the Jordan River.
1:8 I have **b** you with water,
1:9 in Galilee and was **b** by John
10:38 Can you be **b** with the baptism
10:39 You will be **b** with the baptism
16:16 Whoever believes and is **b** will
Luk 3:7 were coming to be **b** by John.
3:12 tax collectors came to be **b**.
3:21 When all the people were **b**,
3:21 baptized, Jesus, too, was **b**.
7:30 They refused to be **b**.
Jon 3:22 time with them and **b** people.
3:23 (People came to John to be **b**,
10:40 where John first **b** people.
Act 1:5 John **b** with water,
1:5 but in a few days you will be **b**
2:38 and each of you must be **b** in
2:41 what Peter said were **b**.
8:12 believed him and were **b**.
8:13 and after he was **b**,
8:16 They had only been **b** in the
8:36 can keep me from being **b**?"
8:38 into the water, and Philip **b** him.
9:18 Then Saul stood up and was **b**.
10:48 ordered that they should be **b**
11:16 'John **b** with water,
11:16 but you will be **b** by the Holy
16:15 Lydia and her family were **b**,
16:33 family were **b** immediately.
18:8 Paul believed and were **b**.
19:5 they were **b** in the name of the
22:16 Be **b**, and have your sins
Rom 6:3 who were **b** into Christ Jesus
6:3 Jesus were **b** into his death?
6:4 When we were **b** into his death,
1Co 1:13 Were you **b** in Paul's name?
1:15 say you were **b** in my name.
1:16 I also **b** Stephanas and his
1:16 sure whether I **b** anyone else.
12:13 By one Spirit we were all **b**
15:29 However, people are **b**
15:29 why do people get **b** as if they
Gal 3:27 Clearly, all of you who were **b**

Baptizer (17)

Mat 3:1 Later, John the **B** appeared in
11:11 one is greater than John the **B**.
11:12 time of John the **B** until now,
14:2 "This is John the **B**!
14:8 of John the **B** on a platter."
16:14 "Some say you are John the **B**,
17:13 was talking about John the **B**.
Mar 1:4 John the **B** was in the desert
6:14 "John the **B** has come back to
6:24 for the head of John the **B**."
6:25 give me the head of John the **B**
8:28 "Some say you are John the **B**,
Luk 7:20 "John the **B** sent us to ask you,
7:33 John the **B** has come neither
9:19 "Some say you are John the **B**,
Jon 5:33 sent people to John ⌊the **B**⌋,
Act 13:24 John ⌊the **B**⌋ told everyone in

baptizes (1)

Jon 1:33 that person is the one who **b**

baptizing (6)

Jon 1:28 where John was **b**.
3:23 John was **b** in Aenon,
3:26 Well, he's **b**, and everyone is
4:1 and **b** more disciples than
4:2 Jesus was not **b** people.
Act 1:22 time that John was **b** people

bar (6)

Jos 7:21 and a **b** of gold weighing about
7:24 silver, the robe, the **b** of gold,
Jdg 16:3 and **b** of the city gate and
1Sm 23:7 door ⌊held shut by⌋ a **b**."
Neh 7:3 shut the doors and **b** them.
Isa 9:4 the **b** that is across their

Barabbas (13)

Mat 27:16 prisoner by the name of **B**.
27:17 you want me to free **B** or Jesus,
27:20 to ask for the release of **B**
27:21 free for you?" They said, "**B**."
27:26 Then Pilate freed **B** for the
Mar 15:7 was a man named **B** in prison.
15:11 would free **B** for them instead.
15:15 so he freed **B** for them.
Luk 23:18 him away! Free **B** for us."
23:19 (**B** had been thrown into prison
23:25 He freed **B**, who had been put
Jon 18:40 Free **B**!" (Barabbas was a
18:40 (**B** was a political

Barachel (2)

Job 32:2 Then Elihu, son of **B**,
32:6 So Elihu, son of **B**,

Barachiah (1)

Mat 23:35 to that of Zechariah, son of **B**,

Barak (14)

Jdg 4:6 Deborah summoned **B**,
4:8 **B** said to her, "If you go with
4:9 started out for Kedesh with **B**.
4:10 **B** called the tribes of Zebulun
4:12 report reached Sisera that **B**,
4:14 Then Deborah said to **B**,
4:14 So **B** came down from Mount
4:16 **B** pursued the chariots and the
4:22 **B** was still pursuing Sisera.
4:22 So **B** went into her tent.
5:1 On that day Deborah and **B**,
5:12 **B**, attack! Take your prisoners,
5:15 They were also with **B**,
Heb 11:32 **B**, Samson, Jephthah, David,

Barak's (1)

Jdg 4:15 in front of **B** deadly assault.

barbarian (1)

Col 3:11 **b**, uncivilized person, slave,

barber's (1)

Eze 5:1 and use it as a **b** razor to shave

bare (27)

Num 35:21 to death with your **b** hands,
Jdg 14:6 With his **b** hands, he tore the
2Sm 22:16 of the earth were laid **b** at
Psa 18:15 earth were laid **b** at your stern
29:9 ⌊the trees of⌋ the forests **b**.
Isa 3:17 will make their foreheads **b**.
13:2 a banner on the **b** mountaintop.
23:13 stripped palaces **b**,
41:18 make rivers flow on **b** hilltops.
49:9 find pastures on every **b** hill.
Jer 2:25 Don't run until your feet are **b**
3:2 "Look at the **b** hills,
7:29 song of mourning on the **b** hills,
12:12 Looters swarm all over the **b**
13:22 torn off and your limbs are **b**.
14:6 donkeys stand on the **b** hills.
51:2 winnow it and strip its land **b**.
Eze 16:7 Yet, you were naked and **b**.
16:22 when you were naked and **b**,
16:39 and leave you naked and **b**.
23:29 will leave you naked and **b**.
24:7 blood was poured on a **b** rock.
24:8 blood of its victims on a **b** rock.
26:4 dust and turn Tyre into a **b** rock.
26:14 I will turn you into **b** rock.
Joe 1:7 and left the branches **b**.
Hab 3:13 stripping him **b** from head to

barefoot (7)

2Sm 15:30 his head and walked **b**.
Job 12:17 He leads counselors away **b**
12:19 He leads priests away **b** and
Isa 20:2 walked around **b** and naked.
20:3 "My servant Isaiah has gone **b**
20:4 They will be **b** and naked.
Mic 1:8 I will walk around **b** and naked.

bargain (2)

Job 41:6 Will traders **b** over it and divide
Pro 20:14 he brags ⌊about his **b**⌋.

Bariah (1)

1Ch 3:22 Igal, **B**, Neariah, and Shaphat.

Barjesus (1)

Act 13:6 met a Jewish man named **B**.

bark (3)

Gen 30:37 plane trees and peeled the **b**
Isa 56:10 like dogs that are unable to **b**.
Lam 4:8 It has become as dry as **b**.

Barkos (2)

Ezr 2:53 **B**, Sisera, Temah,
Neh 7:55 **B**, Sisera, Temah,

barley (35)

Exo 9:31 flax and the **b** were ruined,
9:31 because the **b** had formed
Lev 27:16 planted with 2 quarts of **b** will
Num 5:15 with eight cups of **b** flour as
Dtr 8:8 The land has wheat and **b**,
Jdg 7:13 There was a loaf of **b** bread
Rut 1:22 just when the **b** harvest began.
2:17 had about half a bushel of **b**.
2:23 grain until both the **b** harvest
3:2 He will be separating the **b**
3:15 out six measures of **b**.
3:17 me these six measures of **b**
2Sm 14:30 He has **b** in it. Go and set it on
17:28 **b**, flour, roasted grain, beans,
21:9 people started harvesting **b**.
1Ki 4:28 They brought their quota of **b**
2Ki 4:42 harvested grain, 20 **b** loaves,
7:1 And 48 cups of **b** will sell for
7:16 and 48 cups of **b** sold for half
7:18 "Forty-eight cups of **b** will sell
1Ch 11:13 There was a field of ripe **b**.
2Ch 2:10 120,000 bushels of **b**,
2:15 send the wheat, **b**, olive oil,
27:5 and 60,000 bushels of **b**.
Job 31:40 weeds instead of **b**."
Isa 28:25 Doesn't he put **b** in its own area
Jer 41:8 We have wheat, **b**,

Eze 4:9 "Then take wheat, **b**,
4:12 as you would eat **b** loaves.
13:19 people for a few handfuls of **b**
45:13 seventeen percent of your **b**.
Hos 3:2 of silver and 10 bushels of **b**.
Joe 1:11 Mourn for the wheat and the **b**.
Jon 6:9 who has five loaves of **b** bread
Rev 6:6 a day's pay or three quarts of **b**

barn (7)

Lev 11:18 **b** owls, pelicans, ospreys,
Dtr 14:16 little owls, great owls, **b** owls,
Hag 2:19 Is there any seed left in the **b**?
Mat 3:12 will gather his wheat into a **b**,
13:30 bring the wheat into my **b**.'"
Luk 3:17 will gather the wheat into his **b**,
12:24 even have a storeroom or a **b**.

Barnabas (52)

Act 4:36 The apostles called him **B**,
9:27 Then **B** took an interest in Saul
9:27 **B** told the apostles how Saul
9:27 **B** also told them how boldly
11:22 **B** was sent to Antioch.
11:24 **B** was a dependable man,
11:25 Then **B** left Antioch to go to the
11:26 **B** brought him back to Antioch.
11:26 **B** and Saul met with the church
11:30 sent their contribution with **B**
12:25 After **B** and Saul delivered the
13:1 **B**, Simeon (called the Black),
13:2 "Set **B** and Saul apart for me.
13:3 their hands on **B** and Saul,
13:4 After **B** and Saul were sent by
13:7 The governor sent for **B** and
13:14 Paul and **B** left Perga and
13:15 ⌊a message⌋ to Paul and **B**.
13:42 As Paul and **B** were leaving
13:43 Judaism followed Paul and **B**.
13:43 Paul and **B** talked with them
13:46 Paul and **B** told them boldly,
13:50 started to persecute Paul and **B**
13:51 Paul and **B** shook the dust off
14:1 Paul and **B** went into the
14:3 Paul and **B** stayed in the city of
14:5 In the meantime, Paul and **B**
14:12 They addressed **B** as Zeus
14:13 a sacrifice ⌊to Paul and **B**⌋.
14:14 When the apostles **B** and Paul
14:18 Although Paul and **B** said
14:20 The next day Paul and **B** left
14:22 Paul and **B** told them,
15:2 Paul and **B** had a fierce dispute
15:2 So Paul and **B** and some of the
15:3 Paul and **B** ⌊to Jerusalem⌋.
15:4 Paul and **B** when they arrived.
15:4 Paul and **B** reported everything
15:12 They listened to **B** and Paul
15:22 men to send with Paul and **B**
15:25 you with our dear **B** and Paul.
15:26 **B** and Paul have dedicated
15:35 Paul and **B** stayed in Antioch.
15:36 After a while Paul said to **B**,
15:37 **B** wanted to take John Mark
15:39 Paul and **B** disagreed so
15:39 **B** took Mark with him and
1Co 9:6 Or is it only **B** and I who don't
Gal 2:1 to Jerusalem again with **B**.
2:9 shook hands with **B** and me,
2:13 Even **B** was swept along with
Col 4:10 So does Mark, the cousin of **B**.

barns (8)

Dtr 28:8 The LORD will bless your **b**
2Ch 32:28 and he made **b** for all his cattle
Psa 129:7 It will never fill the **b** of those
144:13 May our **b** be filled with all
Pro 3:10 Then your **b** will be full,
Joe 1:17 **B** are ruined. The grain has
Mat 6:26 or gather the harvest into **b**.
Luk 12:18 I'll tear down my **b** and build

barracks (9)

Neh 3:16 as the pool and the soldiers' **b**.
Act 21:34 Paul to be taken into the **b**.
21:35 Paul came to the stairs of the **b**,
21:37 about to take Paul into the **b**,
21:40 Paul stood on the stairs of the **b**
22:24 soldiers to take Paul into the **b**
23:10 to drag Paul back to the **b**.
23:16 He entered the **b** and told Paul.
23:32 They returned to their **b** the

barred (4)

Jos 6:1 Jericho was bolted and **b** shut
2Ch 14:7 towers and doors that can be **b**.
26:21 separate house and was **b** from
Isa 24:10 to every house is **b** shut.

barren (10)

Dtr 32:10 in a **b** place where animals
Job 30:3 they gnaw at the dry and **b**
Pro 30:16 the grave, a **b** womb,
Eze 33:28 the land into a **b** wasteland.
33:29 when I make the land a **b**
35:7 Mount Seir into a **b** wasteland,
Hos 2:3 turn her into a dry and **b** land,
Joe 2:3 it the land is like a **b** desert.
2:20 force it into a dry and **b** land.
3:19 Edom will become a **b** desert.

barricade (1)

Sos 8:9 If she is a door, we will **b** her

barricades (2)

2Sm 22:30 my God I can break through **b**.
Psa 18:29 my God I can break through **b**.

barrier (3)

Sos 8:9 will build a silver **b** around her.
Jer 5:22 a permanent **b** that it cannot
Eze 40:12 There was a **b** about 21 inches

bars (20)

Dtr 3:5 gates with **b** across
1Ki 4:13 bronze **b** across their gates.
2Ch 8:5 double-door gates, and **b**.
Neh 3:3 its doors, locks, and **b** in place.
3:6 its doors, locks, and **b** in place.
3:13 its doors, locks, and **b** in place,
3:14 its doors, locks, and **b** in place.
3:15 its doors, locks, and **b** in place.
Job 38:10 for it and put up **b** and gates,
40:18 They are like iron **b**.
Psa 107:16 gates and cut iron **b** in two.
147:13 He makes the **b** across your
Isa 45:2 and cut through the iron **b**.
Jer 49:31 It is a nation with no gates or **b**.
51:30 The **b** across their gates are
Lam 2:9 the **b** across its ⌊gates⌋.
Eze 34:27 because I will break off the **b**
Amo 1:5 I will break the **b** ⌊on the
Jnh 2:6 where **b** held me forever.
Nah 3:13 destroyed the **b** of your gates.

Barsabbas (2)

Act 1:23 Joseph (who was called **B**
15:22 Judas (called **B**) and Silas,

Bartholomew (4)

Mat 10:3 Philip and **B**; Thomas and
Mar 3:18 Andrew, Philip, **B**,
Luk 6:14 James, John, Philip, **B**,
Act 1:13 Philip, Thomas, **B**, Matthew,

Bartimaeus (1)

Mar 10:46 a blind beggar named **B**,

Baruch (34)

Neh 3:20 After him **B**, Zabbai's son,
10:6 Daniel, Ginnethon, **B**,
11:5 Maaseiah was the son of **B**,
Jer 32:12 the copies of the deeds to **B**,
32:13 Then I gave **B** these orders:
32:16 I had given the copies to **B**,
36:4 Then Jeremiah called **B**,
36:4 and **B** wrote it all down on a
36:5 Jeremiah told **B**, "I'm no longer
36:8 **B**, son of Neriah, did as the
36:10 Then **B** read the scroll
36:10 **B** read it to all the people in the
36:11 heard **B** read from the scroll
36:13 everything he heard **B** read
36:14 great-grandson of Cushi, to **B**.
36:14 Jehudi said to **B**, "Bring the
36:14 **B**, son of Neriah, took the scroll
36:15 They said to **B**, "Please sit
36:15 So **B** read it to them.
36:16 They said to **B**, "We must tell
36:17 Then they asked **B**,
36:18 **B** answered, "He dictated
36:19 The officials said to **B**,
36:26 of Abdeel) to arrest the scribe **B**
36:26 had hidden **B** and Jeremiah.
36:27 up the scroll that **B** had written
36:32 and gave it to the scribe **B**,
36:32 As Jeremiah dictated, **B** wrote
43:3 But **B**, son of Neriah,
43:6 the prophet Jeremiah and **B**,
45:1 prophet Jeremiah spoke to **B**,
45:1 **B** wrote these things on a
45:2 God of Israel says to you, **B**:
45:4 "Say this to **B**, 'This is what

Barzillai (13)

2Sm 17:27 and **B** from Rogelim in Gilead
19:31 **B**, the man from Gilead,
19:32 **B** was an elderly man,
19:33 The king told **B**, "Cross the
19:34 **B** replied, "I don't have much
19:39 The king kissed **B** and blessed
19:39 Then **B** went back home.
21:8 son of **B** from Meholah.
1Ki 2:7 to the sons of **B** from Gilead.
Ezr 2:61 and **B** (who had married one of
2:61 the daughters of **B** from Gilead
Neh 7:63 and **B** (who had married one of
7:63 the daughters of **B** from Gilead

base (15)

Exo 25:31 The lamp stand, its **b**,
37:17 The lamp stand, its **b**,
38:27 This was 75 pounds per **b**.
2Ki 16:17 under it and set it on a stone **b**.
Job 28:9 overturn mountains at their **b**.
Eze 41:8 I also saw a raised **b** all around
41:8 This **b** was the foundation for
41:11 The **b** of the open area was 9
41:22 Its corners, its **b**, and its sides
43:13 The **b** of the altar was 21
43:14 From the **b** on the ground to the
43:17 Its **b** was 21 inches.
Heb 6:13 greater on whom to **b** his oath,
6:16 When people take oaths, they **b**
2Pe 1:16 we didn't **b** our message on

Basemath (7)

Gen 26:34 He also married **B**,
36:3 also **B**, daughter of Ishmael
36:4 and **B** gave birth to Reuel.
36:10 son of Esau's wife **B**.
36:13 the grandsons of Esau's wife **B**.
36:17 the grandsons of Esau's wife **B**.
1Ki 4:15 married Solomon's daughter **B**

basement (2)

Jdg 9:46 about it and went into the **b**
9:49 the brushwood on top of the **b**

bases (25)

Exo 26:37 five bronze **b** for the posts."
27:10 20 posts ⌊set in⌋ 20 bronze **b**.
27:11 on 20 posts set in 20 bronze **b**.
27:12 on ten posts ⌊set in⌋ ten **b**.
27:14 three posts ⌊set in⌋ three **b**.
27:16 on four posts ⌊set in⌋ four **b**.
27:17 silver hooks, and bronze **b**.
27:18 linen yarn and with bronze **b**.
35:17 for the courtyard, the posts, **b**,
36:36 they cast four silver **b** for them.
36:38 but the five **b** for the posts were
38:10 20 posts ⌊set in⌋ 20 bronze **b**.
38:11 with 20 posts and 20 bronze **b**.
38:12 on 10 posts ⌊set in⌋ 10 **b**.
38:14 on three posts ⌊set in⌋ three **b**.
38:17 The **b** for the posts were made
38:19 posts ⌊set in⌋ four bronze **b**.
38:27 of silver to cast the 100 **b**

Exo 38:30 With this he made the **b** for the
38:31 the **b** all around the courtyard,
38:31 the **b** for the entrance to the
39:40 for the courtyard, the posts, **b**,
Num 3:37 the **b**, pegs, and ropes.
4:32 the **b**, pegs, and ropes.
Sos 5:15 are columns of marble set on **b**

Bashan (60)

Num 21:33 the road that goes to **B**.
21:33 King Og of **B** and all his troops
32:33 Amorites and King Og of **B** —
Dtr 1:4 in Heshbon, and King Og of **B**,
3:1 the road that goes to **B**.
3:1 King Og of **B** and all his troops
3:3 God also handed King Og of **B**
3:4 the kingdom of Og in **B**.
3:10 and all of **B** as far as Salcah
3:10 cities of Og's kingdom in **B**.
3:11 only King Og of **B** was left.
3:13 Gilead and all of **B** ruled by Og
3:13 territory of Argob in **B** used
3:14 The settlements in **B** he named
4:43 and Golan in **B** for the tribe of
4:47 and the land of King Og of **B**,
29:7 and King Og of **B** came out
32:14 rams from the stock of **B**,
33:22 Out of **B** they pounce ⌊on their
Jos 9:10 and King Og of **B** in Ashtaroth.
12:4 The territory of King Og of **B**
12:5 all of **B** to the border of Geshur
13:11 and all of **B** as far as Salecah
13:12 (whole kingdom of Og in **B**).
13:30 all of **B** (the whole kingdom
13:30 kingdom of King Og of **B**)
13:30 of Jair that were in **B**.
13:31 the royal cities of Og in **B**.
17:1 had received Gilead and **B**
17:5 the land of Gilead and **B** east
20:8 and Golan in **B** from the tribe of
21:6 of the tribe of Manasseh in **B**.
21:27 Golan in **B** (a city of refuge for
22:7 Moses had given land in **B** as
1Ki 4:13 had the territory of Argob in **B**,
4:19 the Amorite and King Og of **B**.
2Ki 10:33 Arnon River, to Gilead and **B**.
1Ch 5:11 descendants in **B** as far ⌊east⌋
5:12 sons Janai and Shaphat in **B**.
5:16 in **B** and its villages,
5:23 lived in the land from **B**
6:62 of Manasseh that lived in **B**.
6:71 received Golan in **B**
Neh 9:22 and the land of King Og of **B**.
Psa 22:12 bulls from **B** have encircled me.
68:15 The mountain of **B** is the
68:15 The mountain of **B** is the
68:22 "I will bring them back from **B**.
135:11 of the Amorites, King Og of **B**,
136:20 and King Og of **B** — because
Isa 2:13 Lebanon and all the oaks of **B**,
33:9 **B** and Carmel are shaken.
Jer 22:20 Raise your voice in **B**!
50:19 on Mount Carmel and Mount **B**.
Eze 27:6 made your oars from oaks in **B**.
39:18 and all the best animals of **B**.
Amo 4:1 you cows of **B** who live on
Mic 7:14 Let them feed in **B** and Gilead
Nah 1:4 **B** and Carmel wither.
Zec 11:2 Cry, oak trees of **B**,

basic (1)

Heb 6:2 We shouldn't repeat the **b**

basics (2)

Heb 6:1 We shouldn't repeat the **b** about
6:1 we did and the **b** about faith

basin (16)

Exo 30:18 "Make a bronze **b** with a
30:28 and the **b** with its stand.
31:9 the **b** with its stand,
35:16 the **b** with its stand,
38:8 He made the **b** and stand out of
39:39 the **b** with its stand,
40:7 Put the **b** between the tent of
40:11 Anoint the **b** and stand,
Exo 40:30 He put the **b** between the tent
Lev 8:11 and the **b** with its stand to
1Ki 7:30 four supports beneath the **b**.
7:38 Each **b** held 240 gallons.
7:38 Every **b** was six feet ⌊wide⌋.
7:38 There was one **b** on each of
2Ki 16:17 and removed the **b** from each
Jon 13:5 Then he poured water into a **b**

basins (5)

1Ki 7:38 Hiram also made ten bronze **b**.
7:43 stands and 10 **b** on the stands,
2Ch 4:6 Huram also made ten **b** for
4:14 stands and 10 **b** on the stands,
4:22 snuffers, **b**, dishes,

basis (12)

Exo 34:27 because on the **b** of these
Ezr 2:59 they were Israelites on the **b**
7:14 Judah and Jerusalem on the **b**
Neh 7:61 they were Israelites on the **b**
Psa 89:49 on ⌊the **b** of⌋ your faithfulness.
Pro 20:7 righteous person lives on the **b**
Dan 1:13 Decide how to treat us on the **b**
Rom 3:27 On what **b** was it eliminated?
3:27 On the **b** of our own efforts?
3:27 it is eliminated on the **b** of faith.
Phm 1:9 an appeal on the **b** of love.
Rev 20:12 The dead were judged on the **b**

basket (38)

Gen 40:17 The top **b** contained all kinds
40:17 them out of the **b** on my head."
Exo 2:3 she took a **b** made of papyrus
2:5 She saw the **b** among the
2:6 daughter opened the **b**,
29:3 Put the bread in a **b**,
29:3 and bring the **b** along with the
29:23 From the **b** of unleavened
29:32 and the bread ⌊left⌋ in the **b**.
Lev 8:2 and the **b** of unleavened bread.
8:26 and a wafer from the **b** of
8:31 the meat and the bread in the **b**
Num 6:15 They must also bring a **b** of
6:17 offer the **b** of unleavened bread
6:19 of unleavened bread from the **b**,
Dtr 23:24 But never put any in your **b**.
26:2 is giving you, and put it in a **b**.
26:4 Then the priest will take the **b**
26:10 You will place the **b** in the
Jdg 6:19 He put the meat in a **b** and the
Psa 81:6 hands were freed from the **b**.
Isa 40:12 dust of the earth in a bushel **b**
Jer 24:2 One **b** had very good figs,
24:2 The other **b** had very bad figs.
Amo 8:1 a **b** of ripe summer fruit.
8:2 "A **b** of ripe summer fruit,"
Zec 5:6 "A **b** is coming," he said.
5:7 cover ⌊on the **b**⌋ was raised,
5:7 a woman was sitting in the **b**.
5:8 he pushed her back into the **b**
5:9 They carried the **b** into the sky.
5:10 "Where are they taking the **b**?"
5:11 they will set the **b** there on a
Mat 5:15 a lamp and puts it under a **b**.
Mar 4:21 into a room to put it under a **b**
Luk 11:33 and hides it or puts it under a **b**.
Act 9:25 him in a large **b** through
2Co 11:33 So I was let down in a **b**

baskets (15)

Gen 40:16 In my dream three **b** of white
40:18 "The three **b** are three days.
2Ki 10:7 They put the heads in **b** and
Jer 24:1 the LORD showed me two **b** of
Amo 8:5 shrink the size of the bushel **b**,
Mat 14:20 they filled twelve **b**.
15:37 pieces and filled seven large **b**.
16:9 and how many **b** you filled?
16:10 how many large **b** you filled?
Mar 6:43 they filled twelve **b** with bread
8:8 pieces and filled seven large **b**.
8:19 how many **b** did you fill with
8:20 how many large **b** did you fill
Luk 9:17 they filled twelve **b**.
Jon 6:13 of bread and filled twelve **b**.

batch (4)

Rom 11:16 the whole **b** of dough is holy.
1Co 5:6 through the whole **b** of dough?
5:7 you may be a new **b** of dough,
Gal 5:9 through the whole **b** of dough.

bath (2)

Exo 2:5 came to the Nile to take a **b**,
Eze 45:11 The ephah and the **b** should

bathe (3)

Lev 15:16 he must **b** his whole body.
2Ch 28:15 to eat and drink, and let them **b**.
Psa 68:23 may **b** your feet in blood and

bathed (4)

2Sm 12:20 the ground, **b**, anointed himself,
1Ki 22:38 where the prostitutes **b**.
Job 29:6 my steps were **b** in buttermilk,
Eze 16:9 "'Then I **b** you with water,

bathing (2)

2Sm 11:2 the roof he saw a woman **b**,
Sos 5:12 are set like doves **b** in milk.

Bath Rabbim (1)

Sos 7:4 pools by the gate of **B**.

Bathsheba (12)

2Sm 11:3 The man said, "She's **B**,
12:24 David comforted his wife **B**.
1Ki 1:11 asked Solomon's mother **B**,
1:12 **B**, let me give you some
1:15 **B** went to the king in his
1:16 **B** knelt and bowed down in
1:28 answered, "Call **B** in here."
1:31 Then **B** bowed down with her
2:13 went to **B**, Solomon's mother.
2:18 "Very well," **B** answered.
2:19 **B** went to King Solomon to talk
Mat 1:6 David and Uriah's wife ⌊**B**⌋

Bathshua (2)

1Ch 2:3 three were born to him by **B**,
3:5 four was Ammiel's daughter **B**)

bats (3)

Lev 11:19 of herons, hoopoes, and **b**.
Dtr 14:18 of herons, hoopoes, and **b**.
Isa 2:20 throw to the moles and the **b**

battalion (4)

1Sm 22:7 a regiment or a **b** of soldiers?
1Ch 13:1 commanded a regiment or **b**.
27:1 regiment and **b** commanders,
2Ch 25:5 to regiment and **b** commanders

battalions (8)

Num 31:14 of the companies and **b**,
31:48 of the companies and **b** of men,
2Sm 18:1 in charge of regiments and **b**.
18:4 out by **b** and regiments.
1Ch 26:26 of regiments and **b**,
28:1 of regiments and **b**,
29:6 of regiments and **b**,
2Ch 1:2 of regiments and **b**,

battered (1)

Isa 24:12 Its gate is **b** to pieces.

battering (5)

Eze 4:2 and place **b** rams all around it.
21:22 he will set up his **b** rams there,
21:22 aim the **b** rams against the city
26:9 He will direct his **b** rams
Nah 2:5 has been set up for the **b** ram.

battle (251)

Gen 14:8 marched out and prepared for **b**
Exo 13:18 The Israelites were ready for **b**
17:13 the Amalekite army in **b**.
Num 14:3 land — just to have us die in **b**?
14:43 and you will die in **b**.
21:24 But Israel defeated them in **b**
27:17 them in and out ⌊of **b**⌋ so that

Num 27:21 of Israel will go into **b**.
31:8 Balaam, son of Beor, in **b**.
31:14 who were returning from **b**.
31:21 soldiers who had gone into **b**,
32:17 march⌋ in **b** formation ahead
32:20 armed men get ready for **b**.
32:27 we will all get ready for **b**
32:29 Gad and Reuben get ready for **b**
32:30 If they don't get ready for **b** and
Dtr 2:32 out to meet us in **b** at Jahaz.
3:18 be ready for **b** when they cross
20:2 Before the **b** starts,
20:3 today you're going into **b**
20:5 Otherwise, you might die in **b**,
20:6 Otherwise, you might die in **b**,
20:7 Otherwise, you might die in **b**,
Jos 1:14 march in **b** formation ahead
4:12 They marched across in **b**
4:13 to the plains of Jericho for **b**.
8:14 the plains to meet Israel for **b**,
8:22 caught between the **b** lines
11:6 that they cannot be used in **b**.
11:19 Israel captured everything in **b**.
24:12 because of your **b** skills
Jdg 1:4 Judah's troops went into **b**,
1:22 also went into **b** against Bethel,
5:13 The LORD's people went into **b**
5:14 from Machir went into **b**.
6:35 went to meet the enemy in **b**.
7:24 "Go into **b** against Midian.
8:10 In the **b**, 120,000 soldiers died.
8:13 returned from the **b** through
20:15 cities and organized for **b** along
20:20 their **b** line facing Gibeah.
20:22 They formed their **b** line where
20:30 They formed their **b** line facing
20:33 They formed their **b** line at Baal
20:34 The **b** was fierce.
20:39 would turn around in the **b**.
20:39 just like in the first **b**."
20:42 But the **b** caught up with the
20:44 from Benjamin who died in **b**.
21:22 a wife for each man in the **b**.
1Sm 4:2 their troops to meet Israel in **b**.
4:2 in battle. As the **b** spread,
4:12 ran from the front line of the **b**.
4:16 the one who came from the **b**.
11:7 Saul and Samuel ⌊into **b** ⌋."
13:22 So on the day of **b**,
14:20 assembled and went into **b**.
14:22 pursued the Philistines in **b**.
14:23 Now, the **b** moved beyond Beth
17:2 They formed a **b** line to fight
17:8 "Why do you form a **b** line?
17:10 the Israelite **b** line today.
17:13 joined Saul's army for the **b**.
17:20 out to the **b** line shouting their
17:21 formed their **b** lines facing each
17:22 quartermaster, ran to the **b** line,
17:23 came from the **b** lines of the
17:28 came here just to see the **b**."
17:38 Saul put his **b** tunic on David;
17:48 ran toward the opposing **b** line
17:52 Judah rose up, shouted a **b** cry,
18:4 to David along with his **b** tunic,
18:13 out ⌊to **b**⌋ and back again.
18:16 he led them in and out ⌊of **b**⌋.
26:10 or he'll go into **b** and be swept
28:1 will be going with me into **b**."
29:4 He shouldn't go with us into **b**.
29:4 our enemy during the **b**.
29:9 'He shouldn't go into **b** with us.'
30:24 of those who go into **b** must
31:1 killed in **b** on Mount Gilboa.
2Sm 1:4 "The army fled from the **b**,
1:12 Israel had been defeated in **b**.
1:25 the mighty have fallen in **b**!
3:29 work a spindle, who die in **b**,
3:30 Asahel in the **b** at Gibeon.)
5:2 the one who led Israel in **b**.
10:8 The Ammonites formed a **b**
10:17 The Arameans formed a **b** line
11:1 time when kings go out to **b**,
11:18 to David all the details of the **b**.
11:19 telling the king about the **b**,
12:9 had Uriah the Hittite killed in **b**.
2Sm 17:11 Lead them into **b** yourself.
18:2 "I am going ⌊into **b**⌋ with you,"
18:8 more people than the **b**.
19:3 city as if they had fled from **b**
19:10 to rule us, has died in **b**.
21:15 Once again there was a **b**
21:17 "You'll never go into **b** with us
21:18 After this, there was another **b**
21:20 In another **b** at Gath,
22:35 He trains my hands for **b** so
22:40 armed me with strength for **b**.
23:9 Philistines gathered there for **b**.
1Ki 11:15 went to bury those killed in **b**
20:11 you have even dressed for **b**.'"
20:14 "Who will start the **b**?"
20:29 the seventh day the **b** started.
20:39 "I went to fight in the **b**.
22:30 disguise myself and go into **b**,
22:30 himself and went into **b**.
22:35 But the **b** got worse that day,
2Ki 3:26 Moab saw he was losing the **b**,
14:7 and took the city of Sela in **b**.
14:11 met him in **b** at Beth Shemesh
1Ch 5:20 called out to God during the **b**,
5:22 Many were killed in **b** because
10:1 killed in **b** on Mount Gilboa.
11:13 Philistines gathered there for **b**.
12:1 who went into **b** with David.
12:33 They were equipped for **b** with
12:35 there were 28,600 ready for **b**.
12:36 soldiers ready for **b**.
12:38 who were prepared for **b**,
19:7 for the **b** from their cities.
19:9 The Ammonites formed a **b**
19:17 David formed a **b** line against
20:1 time when kings go out to **b**,
20:6 In another **b** at Gath,
26:27 some of the loot taken in **b**
2Ch 13:3 Abijah prepared for **b** with an
13:14 the **b** was in front of them and
14:10 two armies set up their **b** lines
14:13 of the Sudanese died in **b**.
18:3 ⌊We will join⌋ your troops in **b**.
18:29 disguise myself and go into **b**,
18:29 himself and went into **b**.
18:34 But the **b** got worse that day,
20:15 The **b** isn't yours. It's God's.
20:16 go into **b** against them.
20:17 You won't fight this **b**.
25:8 If you go into **b** with them,
25:13 go with him into **b** raided
25:21 met him in **b** at Beth Shemesh
29:9 Our fathers were killed in **b**,
35:20 to fight a **b** at Carchemish at
35:22 himself as he went into **b**.
Job 6:4 terrors line up in **b** against me.
15:24 him like a king ready for **b**.
38:23 for the day of **b** and war?
39:21 in its power. It charges into **b**.
39:25 and it smells the **b** far away —
39:25 of the captains and the **b** cries.
Psa 18:34 He trains my hands for **b** so
18:39 armed me with strength for **b**.
24:8 The LORD, heroic in **b**!
78:9 ⌊and ran⌋ on the day of **b**.
89:43 and failed to support him in **b**.
140:7 my head in the day of **b**.
144:1 to fight and my fingers to do **b**,
Pro 21:31 is made ready for the day of **b**,
Ecc 9:11 or the **b** by heroes.
Isa 3:25 Your mighty men will die in **b**.
8:9 Prepare for **b**, but be terrified.
8:9 Prepare for **b**, but be terrified.
8:10 Make plans for **b**, but they will
9:4 did in the **b** against⌋ Midian.
9:5 boot marching to the sound of **b**
13:4 is assembling his army for **b**.
14:19 those who were killed in **b**.
21:5 Prepare your shields for **b**!
21:15 and from the thick of **b**.
22:2 Your dead didn't die in **b**.
23:13 Assyria set up **b** towers,
27:4 I would fight them in **b** and set
28:6 who defend the city gates in **b**.
30:32 He will fight them in **b**,
31:8 They will flee from **b**,
Isa 31:9 at ⌊the sight of⌋ the **b** flag.
42:13 He prepares himself for **b** like a
42:13 He shouts, gives the **b** cry,
Jer 4:16 They are shouting **b** cries
4:21 How long must I see the **b** flag
6:23 ready for **b** against my people
8:6 like horses charging into **b**.
18:21 men will be struck down in **b**.
20:16 morning and a **b** cry at noon.
43:11 He will kill in **b** those who are
43:11 are supposed to be killed in **b**.
46:3 shields ready; advance into **b**.
46:9 Go into **b**, you horsemen.
46:9 March into **b**, you warriors,
49:2 when I will sound the **b** cry
49:14 attack Edom. Get ready for **b**."
50:22 The noise of **b** and great
51:12 Raise your **b** flag in front of the
51:20 war club and my weapon for **b**.
51:27 Raise your **b** flag throughout
Eze 6:8 Some people will escape the **b**
7:14 But no one will go into **b**,
7:15 is in a field will die in **b**.
11:10 You will die in **b**. I will judge
13:5 Israel will not be protected in **b**
17:17 be able to help him in **b** when
17:21 best of your troops will die in **b**.
21:22 the order to kill, raise a **b** cry,
24:21 you left behind will die in **b**.
25:13 People will die in **b**.
26:6 on the mainland will die in **b**.
26:11 He will kill your people in **b**,
29:18 hard-fought **b** against Tyre.
30:5 the promised land will die in **b**.
30:17 and Bubastis will die in **b**,
31:17 grave to join others killed in **b**.
31:18 people who were killed in **b**,
32:20 those who were killed in **b**.
32:21 people who were killed in **b**.'
32:22 They have been killed in **b**.
32:23 They have been killed in **b**.
32:24 They have been killed in **b**.
32:25 They were killed in **b** because
32:26 They were killed in **b** because
32:28 those who were killed in **b**.
32:29 those who were killed in **b**.
32:30 those who were killed in **b**.
32:31 who have been killed in **b**,
32:32 who were killed in **b**," declares
33:27 ruined cities will be killed in **b**.
35:5 of Israel in **b** when they were
35:8 Those killed in **b** will fall on
39:23 They were killed in **b**.
Dan 11:26 and many will die in **b**.
Hos 7:7 All their kings die in **b**,
7:16 Their officials will die in **b**
10:14 army will hear the noise of **b**.
10:14 destroyed Beth Arbel in **b**.
Joe 2:5 a mighty army prepared for **b**.
Amo 1:14 are shouting on the day of **b**
2:2 the noise of **b** while troops are
Nah 2:1 Prepare for **b**!
2:3 on the day he prepares for **b**.
Zep 1:16 a day of rams' horns and **b**
Zec 9:10 There will be no **b** bows.
10:4 from them a **b** bow,
14:2 the nations to Jerusalem for **b**.
14:3 as he does when he fights a **b**.
1Co 14:8 who will get ready for **b**?
Heb 11:34 They were powerful in **b** and
Rev 9:7 like horses prepared for **b**.
9:9 many horses rushing into **b**.

battlefield (1)

Jdg 5:18 Naphtali risked his life on the **b**.

battle's (1)

1Sm 17:47 determines every **b** outcome.

battles (6)

1Sm 8:20 out ⌊to war⌋, and fight our **b**."
18:17 for me and fight the LORD's **b**."
25:28 you are fighting the LORD's **b**.
2Ch 32:8 side to help us and fight our **b**."
Eze 5:12 Another third will die in **b**
Rev 6:2 rode off as a warrior to win **b**.

bay (2)
Jos 18:19 and ends at the northern **b**
Act 27:39 but they could see a **b** with a

Bazlith (1)
Neh 7:54 **B**, Mehida, Harsha,

Bazluth (1)
Ezr 2:52 **B**, Mehida, Harsha,

bdellium (1)
Gen 2:12 **B** and onyx are also ⌊found⌋

beach (2)
Act 21:5 We knelt on the **b**,
27:39 they could see a bay with a **b**.

beads (1)
Sos 1:11 ornaments with silver **b** for you.

beak (1)
Gen 8:11 and in its **b** was a freshly

Bealiah (1)
1Ch 12:5 Eluzai, Jerimoth, **B**,

Bealoth (1)
Jos 15:24 Ziph, Telem, **B**,

beam (12)
1Sm 17:7 like the **b** used by weavers.
2Sm 21:19 was like a **b** used by weavers.)
1Ch 11:23 had a spear like a weaver's **b**
20:5 was like a **b** used by weavers.)
Ezr 6:11 be impaled on a **b** torn from his
Hab 2:11 A **b** in the roof will answer it.
Mat 7:3 and not notice the wooden **b**
7:4 when you have a **b** in your own
7:5 First remove the **b** from your
Luk 6:41 and not notice the wooden **b**
6:42 when you don't see the **b** in
6:42 First remove the **b** from your

beams (13)
1Ki 6:9 rows of cedar **b** and planks.
6:10 Its cedar **b** were attached to the
6:36 a course of finished cedar **b**.
7:2 pillars supporting cedar **b**.
7:11 ⌊the foundation⌋ were cedar **b**
7:12 blocks and a layer of cedar **b**,
2Ch 34:11 and wood for the fittings and **b**
Ezr 5:8 stones and with wooden **b** laid
Neh 3:3 They laid its **b** and set its
3:6 They laid its **b** and set its
Psa 104:3 You lay the **b** of your home in
Pro 13:9 of righteous people **b** brightly,
Zep 2:14 LORD will expose the cedar **b**.

beans (2)
2Sm 17:28 flour, roasted grain, **b**, lentils,
Eze 4:9 "Then take wheat, barley, **b**,

bear (37)
Gen 44:34 I couldn't **b** to see my father's
Jdg 10:16 So the LORD could not **b** to
1Sm 17:34 Whenever a lion or a **b** came
17:37 me from the lion and the **b**,
2Sm 17:8 as a wild **b** whose cubs have
2Ki 3:21 So all men old enough to **b**
Est 8:6 I cannot **b** to see my people
8:6 And I simply cannot **b** to see
Job 7:13 bed may help me **b** my pain,'
21:3 **B** with me while I speak.
Psa 38:4 it is more than I can **b**.
55:12 insulted me, then I could **b** it.
92:14 they are old, they still **b** fruit.
Pro 3:35 but fools will **b** disgrace.
17:12 Better to meet a **b** robbed of its
18:14 but who can **b** a broken spirit?
27:6 kisses are too much to **b**.
28:15 a roaring lion and a charging **b**,
30:21 even four it cannot **b** up under:
Sos 4:2 All of them **b** twins,
6:6 All of them **b** twins,
Isa 11:1 branch from its roots will **b**
11:3 He will gladly **b** the fear of the
64:12 us suffer more than we can **b**?
Jer 10:19 my punishment, and I will **b** it.
44:22 The LORD could no longer **b**
Lam 3:10 He is like a **b** waiting to
Eze 4:4 You will **b** its punishment as
4:5 So for 390 days, you will **b** the
4:6 You will **b** the punishment for
17:8 it could grow branches, **b** fruit,
36:8 will grow branches and **b** fruit
Dan 7:5 It looked like a **b**. It was raised
Hos 13:8 Like a **b** that has lost her cubs,
Amo 5:19 lion only to be attacked by a **b**.
Mic 6:16 You will **b** the disgrace of my
Zep 3:18 They **b** a burden of disgrace.

beard (13)
Lev 14:9 head, his **b**, and his eyebrows,
19:27 never cut the edges of your **b**.
1Sm 21:13 and let his spit run down his **b**.
2Sm 10:4 shaved off half of each man's **b**,
20:9 He took hold of Amasa's **b** with
Ezr 9:3 hair from my scalp and my **b**,
Psa 133:2 running down the **b** — down
133:2 down Aaron's **b** — running over
Isa 7:20 on your legs, and even your **b**.
15:2 and every **b** is cut off.
50:6 who pluck hairs out of my **b**.
Jer 48:37 and every **b** is cut off.
Eze 5:1 razor to shave your head and **b**.

bearded (2)
Lev 11:13 They are eagles, **b** vultures,
Dtr 14:12 **b** vultures, black vultures,

beards (4)
Lev 21:5 shaving the edges of your **b**,
2Sm 10:5 "Stay in Jericho until your **b**
1Ch 19:5 "Stay in Jericho until your **b**
Jer 41:5 Their **b** were shaved off,

bearing (5)
Gen 1:11 vegetation: plants **b** seeds,
1:11 and fruit trees **b** fruit with
1:12 vegetation: plants **b** seeds,
1:12 and trees **b** fruit with seeds,
Isa 32:12 for the vines **b** grapes.

bear's (1)
Rev 13:2 Its feet were like **b** feet.

bears (7)
1Sm 17:36 I have killed lions and **b**,
1Ki 8:43 which I built **b** your name.
2Ki 2:24 Two **b** came out of the woods
2Ch 6:33 which I built **b** your name.
Psa 103:14 He **b** in mind that we are dust.
Isa 11:7 Cows and **b** will eat together.
59:11 We all growl like **b**.

beast (46)
Job 28:8 No proud **b** has ever walked on
Psa 68:30 Threaten the **b** who is among
Rev 11:7 the **b** which comes from the
13:1 I saw a **b** coming out of the
13:2 The **b** that I saw was like a
13:2 far-reaching authority to the **b**.
13:3 amazed and followed the **b**.
13:4 it had given authority to the **b**.
13:4 also worshiped the **b** and said,
13:4 "Who is like the **b**?
13:5 The **b** was allowed to speak
13:11 I saw another **b** come from the
13:12 The second **b** uses all the
13:12 all the authority of the first **b**
13:12 The second **b** makes the earth
13:12 living on it worship the first **b**,
13:13 The second **b** performs
13:14 to do in front of the ⌊first⌋ **b**.
13:14 for the **b** who was wounded
13:15 The second **b** was allowed to
13:15 into the statue of the ⌊first⌋ **b**.
13:15 Then the statue of the ⌊first⌋ **b**
13:16 The second **b** forces all people
13:18 figure out the number of the **b**,
14:9 "Whoever worships the **b** or its
Rev 14:11 for those who worship the **b**
15:2 had won the victory over the **b**,
16:2 who had the brand of the **b**
16:10 his bowl on the throne of the **b**.
16:13 the **b**, and the false prophet.
17:3 sitting on a bright red **b** covered
17:7 of the woman and the **b**
17:8 "You saw the **b** which once
17:8 surprised when they see the **b**
17:11 The **b** that was and is no
17:12 kings with the **b** for one hour.
17:13 power and authority to the **b**.
17:16 The ten horns and the **b** you
17:17 to the **b** until God's words
18:2 and every unclean and hated **b**.
19:19 I saw the **b**, the kings of the
19:20 The **b** and the false prophet
19:20 for the **b** were captured.
19:20 who had the brand of the **b**
20:4 They had not worshiped the **b**
20:10 where the **b** and the false

beast's (3)
Rev 13:3 One of the **b** heads looked like
13:17 which is the **b** name or the
13:18 The **b** number is 666.

beat (31)
Exo 2:12 he **b** the Egyptian to death and
5:14 The slave drivers **b** the
Num 35:21 or if you **b** your enemy to death
2Sm 22:43 I **b** them into a powder as fine
2Ch 34:7 tore down the altars, **b** the
Neh 13:25 cursed them, **b** some of them,
Psa 18:42 I **b** them into a powder as fine
121:6 The sun will not **b** down on
Pro 23:35 They **b** me, but I'm not aware of
Isa 32:12 **B** your breasts as you mourn
53:4 him, **b** him, and punished him.
58:4 and fight and **b** your workers?
Jer 37:15 with Jeremiah that they **b** him
Lam 3:3 He **b** me again and again all
Eze 21:12 So **b** your breast, and grieve.
Jnh 4:8 The sun **b** down on Jonah's
Nah 2:7 doves as they **b** their breasts."
Mat 7:25 Winds blew and **b** against that
21:35 took his servants and **b** one,
24:49 The servant may begin to **b** the
Mar 12:3 took the servant, **b** him,
12:5 Some of these they **b**,
Luk 10:30 **b** him, and left him for dead.
12:45 The servant may begin to **b** the
20:10 But the workers **b** the servant
20:11 The workers **b** him,
22:63 made fun of him as they **b** him.
Act 5:40 called the apostles, **b** them,
16:22 guards⌋ to **b** them with sticks.
18:17 and **b** him in front of the court.
19:16 He **b** them up so badly that

beaten (13)
Exo 2:11 being **b** by an Egyptian.
5:16 We're being **b**, but your men are
Dtr 25:2 in the wrong deserves to be **b**,
25:2 Then the judge will have him **b**
Psa 102:4 My heart is **b** down and
Isa 1:5 "Why do you still want to be **b**?
17:6 an olive tree that has been **b**.
28:27 Black cumin is **b** with a rod
Mal 1:4 'We have been **b** down,
Act 16:37 "Roman officials have had us **b**
2Co 11:23 been **b** more severely,
11:24 had me **b** with 39 lashes;
11:25 officials had me **b** with clubs.

beating (11)
Exo 2:13 are you **b** another Hebrew?"
21:20 that the slave dies from the **b**,
Dtr 25:11 from the man who is **b** him.
Jdg 6:11 Joash's son Gideon was **b** out
Psa 68:25 The young women **b**
Pro 18:6 and his mouth invites a **b**.
Jer 4:19 My heart is **b** wildly!
Luk 12:47 to do it will receive a hard **b**.
12:48 will receive a light **b**.
Act 21:32 they stopped **b** Paul.

1Pe 2:20 you deserve if you endure a **b**

beatings (5)

Psa 89:32 and their crimes with **b**.
Pro 19:29 are set for mockers and **b**
20:30 Brutal **b** cleanse away
20:30 Such **b** cleanse the innermost
2Co 6:5 **b**, imprisonments, riots,

beats (2)

Job 5:18 He **b** you up, but his hands
19:10 He **b** me down on every side

beautiful (101)

Gen 6:2 of other humans were **b**.
12:11 "I know that you're a **b** woman.
12:14 saw how very **b** his wife was.
29:17 but Rachel had a **b** figure and
29:17 beautiful figure and **b** features.
30:20 presented me with a **b** present.
49:21 a doe set free that has **b** fawns.
Exo 2:2 She saw how **b** he was and
39:28 and the other **b** turbans out
Num 24:5 How **b** are your tents,
Dtr 3:25 me go over and see the **b** land
3:25 those **b** mountains in Lebanon."
21:11 If you see a **b** woman among
1Sm 25:3 She was sensible and **b**,
2Sm 13:1 the **b** sister of David's son
14:27 His daughter Tamar was a **b**
1Ki 1:3 throughout Israel for a **b**,
1:4 The woman was very **b**.
Ezr 7:27 LORD's temple in Jerusalem **b**.
Est 2:7 The young woman had a **b**
Job 42:15 were as **b** as Job's daughters.
Psa 16:6 my inheritance is something **b**.
48:2 Its **b** peak is the joy of the
93:5 is what makes your house **b**
135:3 name because his name is **b**.
Pro 4:9 It will hand you a **b** crown."
11:22 ⌊so⌋ is a **b** woman who lacks
16:31 Silver hair is a **b** crown found
Ecc 3:11 It is **b** how God has done
5:18 have seen what is good and **b**:
Sos 1:1 The most **b** song of Solomon.
1:8 do not know, most **b** of women,
1:15 You are **b**, my true love!
1:15 You are so **b**!
2:10 my **b** one, and come with me.
2:13 Get up, my true love, my **b** one,
4:1 You are **b**, my true love.
4:1 You are so **b**. Your eyes behind
4:7 You are **b** in every way,
4:10 How **b** are your expressions of
5:9 Most **b** of women, what makes
6:1 most **b** of women?
6:4 You are **b**, my true love,
6:10 She is **b** like the moon,
7:1 How **b** are your feet in their
7:6 How **b** and charming you are,
Isa 2:16 of Tarshish and all the **b** boats.
3:24 bald heads instead of **b** hair.
4:2 LORD will be **b** and wonderful.
5:9 Large, **b** houses will be without
44:13 into forms of people, **b** people,
52:1 Put on your **b** clothes,
52:7 How **b** on the mountains are
60:7 So I will honor my **b** temple.
62:3 Then you will be a **b** crown in
63:15 from your holy and **b** dwelling.
64:11 Our holy and **b** temple,
Jer 3:19 the most **b** property among the
4:30 making yourself **b** for nothing.
11:16 a large olive tree that has **b** fruit
13:20 given to you — your **b** sheep?
46:20 "Egypt is like a **b** cow,
48:17 staff, the **b** rod, that is broken!'
Lam 2:4 He killed all the **b** people.
2:15 they used to call absolutely **b**,
Eze 7:20 They were proud of their **b**
16:12 and a **b** crown on your head.
16:13 and olive oil. You were very **b**,
16:17 You took your **b** gold and silver
16:39 take away your **b** jewelry,
20:6 This land is the most **b** land,
20:15 This land is the most **b** land,
Eze 23:26 and take away your **b** jewels.
23:42 women's wrists and **b** crowns
25:9 They are the **b** cities of Beth
27:24 they traded for **b** clothes,
31:7 So the tree was big and **b** with
31:9 I was the one who made it **b**
32:19 "⌊Tell them,⌋ 'Are you more **b**
33:32 with a **b** voice who sings
Dan 4:12 It had **b** leaves and plenty of
4:21 It had **b** leaves and plenty of
8:9 south, the east, and the **b** land.
11:16 He will rise to power in the **b**
11:41 He will invade the **b** land,
11:45 the seas at a **b** holy mountain.
Hos 10:11 I will put a yoke on its **b** neck.
14:6 They will be **b** like olive trees.
Amo 5:11 You plant **b** vineyards,
8:13 On that day **b** young women
Zec 9:17 They will be **b** and lovely.
Mat 23:27 graves that look **b**
26:10 She has done a **b** thing for me.
Mar 13:1 stones and these **b** buildings!"
14:6 She has done a **b** thing for me.
Luk 21:5 and decorated with **b** gifts.
Act 3:2 The gate was called **B** Gate.
3:10 and beg at the temple's **B** Gate.
7:20 and he was a very **b** child.
Rom 10:15 As Scripture says, "How **b** are
Heb 11:23 saw that Moses was a **b** baby

beautifully (3)

Psa 33:3 Play **b** and joyfully on stringed
147:1 pleasant to sing ⌊his⌋ praise **b**.
Rev 21:19 the city wall were **b** decorated

beautifully-designed (1)

Sos 4:4 neck is like David's **b** tower.

beautify (2)

2Ch 3:6 the building with gems to **b**
Isa 60:13 will come to **b** my holy place,

beauty (39)

2Ch 20:21 LORD and praise him for the **b**
Est 1:11 especially the officials, her **b**,
2:3 they will have their **b** treatment.
2:9 her with the **b** treatment,
2:12 The time of **b** treatment was
Psa 27:4 in order to gaze at the LORD's **b**
45:11 The king longs for your **b**.
50:2 the perfection of **b**.
96:6 Strength and **b** are in his holy
Pro 6:25 Do not desire her **b** in your
31:30 is deceptive, and **b** evaporates,
Sos 7:5 Your dangling curls are royal **b**.
Isa 3:24 Their **b** will be scarred.
13:19 the proud **b** of the Chaldeans,
20:5 hope and Egypt was their **b**.
28:1 Their glorious **b** is ⌊like⌋ a
28:4 Their glorious **b** is ⌊like⌋ a
40:6 and all their **b** is like a flower in
Lam 2:1 He has thrown down Israel's **b**
Eze 16:14 every nation because of your **b**.
16:14 Your **b** was perfect because I
16:15 "'But you trusted your **b**,
16:25 You used your **b** to seduce
27:3 to brag about your perfect **b**.
27:4 "'Your builders made your **b**
27:11 making your **b** perfect.
28:12 full of wisdom and perfect in **b**.
28:17 too proud because of your **b**.
31:8 garden couldn't match its **b**.
1Ti 2:9 I want women to show their **b**
2:9 Their **b** will be shown by what
Tit 2:10 Then they will show the **b** of
Jas 1:11 drop off, and the **b** is gone.
1Pe 1:24 and all their **b** is like a flower of
3:3 Wives must not let their **b** be
3:3 **B** doesn't come from hairstyles,
3:4 Rather, **b** is something internal
3:4 **B** expresses itself in a gentle
3:5 in God expressed their **b**

Bebai (6)

Ezr 2:11 of **B**: 623
8:11 from the family of **B**:
Ezr 8:11 son of **B**, with 38 males
10:28 From the descendants of **B**:
Neh 7:16 of **B**: 628
10:15 Bunni, Azgad, **B**,

Becher (1)

1Ch 7:6 sons: Bela, **B**, and Jediael.

Becher's (2)

1Ch 7:8 **B** sons were Zemirah,
7:8 These were all of **B** sons

Becorath (1)

1Sm 9:1 and great-grandson of **B**,

bed (102)

Gen 19:4 Before they had gone to **b**,
19:32 Then we'll go to **b** with him so
19:33 Then the older one went to **b**
19:33 know when she came to **b**
19:34 Last night I went to **b** with my
19:34 Then you go to **b** with him so
19:35 Then the younger one went to **b**
19:35 know when she came to **b**
26:10 might have easily gone to **b**
30:15 Jacob can go to **b** with you
30:16 "So he went to **b** with her that
35:22 Reuben went to **b** with his
39:7 "Come to **b** with me."
39:10 he refused to go to **b** with her or
39:12 "Come to **b** with me!
39:14 in and tried to go to **b** with me,
47:31 his face at the head of his **b**.
48:2 his strength and sat up in **b**.
49:4 you climbed into your father's **b**.
49:33 he pulled his feet into his **b**.
Exo 8:3 into your bedroom, on your **b**,
21:18 him so that he has to stay in **b**.
Lev 15:5 Those who touch his **b** must
15:21 Those who touch her **b** must
15:23 touches anything on the **b**
15:24 Any **b** he lies on will become
15:26 any **b** she lies on or anything
Num 31:17 who has gone to **b** with a man.
31:18 never gone to **b** with a man.
31:35 never gone to **b** with a man.
Dtr 3:11 His **b** was made of iron and
24:13 his coat to **b** ⌊that night,⌋
Jdg 16:3 But Samson was in **b** ⌊with the
21:11 female who has gone to **b**
21:12 who had never gone to **b**
1Sm 3:5 "Go back to **b**." So Samuel
3:6 he responded. "Go back to **b**."
3:15 remained in **b** until morning.
19:13 some idols, laid them in the **b**,
19:15 "Bring him here to me in his **b**
19:16 and there in the **b** were the
28:23 the ground and sat on the **b**.
2Sm 4:7 was sleeping on his **b**
4:11 an innocent man on his own **b**
11:2 David got up from his **b** and
11:4 and he went to **b** with her.
11:11 to eat and drink and go to **b**
11:13 on his **b** among his superior's
12:11 He will go to **b** with your wives
12:24 He went to **b** with her,
13:5 "Lie down on your **b**.
13:11 "Come to **b** with me,
1Ki 1:47 himself bowed down on his **b**
17:19 and laid him on his own **b**.
2Ki 1:4 You will not get up from the **b**
1:6 You will not get up from the **b**
1:16 You will not get up from the **b**
4:10 room on the roof and put a **b**,
4:21 upstairs and laid him on the **b**
4:32 boy was lying on Elisha's **b**.
4:35 and then got back on the **b** and
9:16 Joram was lying in **b** there.
1Ch 5:1 he dishonored his father's **b**.
2Ch 16:14 They laid him on a **b** full of
24:25 They killed Joash in his **b**.
Job 7:13 My **b** may help me bear my
17:13 make my **b** in the darkness,
27:19 He may go to **b** rich,
Psa 4:4 Think about this on your **b** and
6:6 eyes flood my **b** every night.

Psa 36:4 trouble while lying on his **b**
63:6 As I lie on my **b**, I remember
127:2 up early and going to **b** late.
132:4 get into my **b**, shut my eyes,
139:8 If I make my **b** in hell,
Pro 7:16 I've made my **b**, with colored
7:17 I've sprinkled my **b** with myrrh,
22:27 should your **b** be repossessed?
26:14 the lazy person turns on his **b**.
Sos 3:1 Night after night on my **b** I
Isa 14:11 out like a **b** under you,
28:20 The **b** is too short to stretch out
57:2 honestly will rest on his own **b**.
57:7 You've made your **b** on a high
57:8 You've made your **b** with them.
57:8 you have pleasure with in **b**.
58:5 making your **b** from sackcloth
Eze 23:8 men went to **b** with her,
23:17 went to **b** with her,
32:25 A **b** has been made for Elam
Dan 2:29 while you were lying in **b**,
Amo 3:12 having only a corner of a **b** or
Mic 2:1 plans for disaster while in **b**.
Mat 8:14 mother-in-law in **b** with a fever.
Mar 1:30 Simon's mother-in-law was in **b**
4:21 it under a basket or under a **b**?
7:30 the little child lying on her **b**,
Luk 8:16 a bowl or puts it under a **b**.
11:7 and my children are in **b**.
17:34 night if two people are in one **b**,
Act 28:8 father happened to be sick in **b**.
Eph 4:26 Don't go to **b** angry.

Bedad (2)

Gen 36:35 son of **B** succeeded him as
1Ch 1:46 Husham died, Hadad, son of **B**,

Bedan (2)

1Sm 12:11 sent Jerubbaal, **B**, Jephthah,
1Ch 7:17 Ulam's son was **B**.

Bedan's (1)

1Ch 7:18 **B** sister Hammolecheth gave

bedding (1)

2Sm 17:28 **b**, bowls, pots, wheat, barley,

Bedeiah (1)

Ezr 10:35 Benaiah, **B**, Cheluhi,

bedrock (1)

Luk 6:48 a person who dug down to **b**

bedroom (12)

Exo 8:3 into your **b**, on your bed,
Jdg 15:1 to sleep with my wife in her **b**."
16:9 Some men were hiding in the **b**
16:12 Some men were in her **b**
2Sm 4:7 sleeping on his bed in his **b**.
13:10 "Bring the food into the **b** so
13:10 to her brother Amnon in the **b**.
2Ki 6:12 even what you say in your **b**."
11:2 and in a **b** she hid him and his
2Ch 22:11 put him and his nurse in a **b**.
Ecc 10:20 rich people even in your **b**.
Sos 3:4 into the **b** of the one who

bedrooms (1)

Psa 105:30 even in the kings' **b**.

beds (5)

Job 33:15 when they sleep on their **b**,
Psa 149:5 Let them sing for joy on their **b**.
Sos 6:2 his garden, to the **b** of spices,
Hos 7:14 even though they cry in their **b**
Amo 6:4 for those who sleep on ivory **b**.

Beeliada (1)

1Ch 14:7 Elishama, **B**, and Eliphelet.

Beelzebul (7)

Mat 10:25 the owner of the house **B**,
12:24 people only with the help of **B**,
12:27 out of people with the help of **B**,
Mar 3:22 Jerusalem said, "**B** is in him,"
Luk 11:15 people only with the help of **B**,
Luk 11:18 I say this because you say **B**
11:19 demons out with the help of **B**,

Beer (1)

Num 21:16 there they went to **B** [Well].

Beera (1)

1Ch 7:37 Shilsha, Ithran, and **B**.

Beerah (2)

Jdg 9:21 He went to **B** and lived there
1Ch 5:6 Baal's son was **B**.

Beerah's (1)

1Ch 5:7 **B** brothers according to their

Beer Elim (1)

Isa 15:8 Their wailing echoes as far as **B**.

Beeri (2)

Gen 26:34 daughter of **B** the Hittite.
Hos 1:1 Hosea, son of **B**, when Uzziah,

Beer Lahai Roi (3)

Gen 16:14 is named **B** [Well of the Living
24:62 come back from **B**, since he was
25:11 son Isaac, who settled near **B**.

Beeroth (10)

Jos 9:17 cities of Gibeon, Chephirah, **B**,
18:25 villages: Gibeon, Ramah, **B**,
2Sm 4:2 sons of Rimmon from **B** from
4:2 (**B** was considered a part of
4:3 even though the people of **B**
4:5 the sons of Rimmon from **B**,
4:9 the sons of Rimmon from **B**,
23:37 from Ammon, Naharai from **B**,
Ezr 2:25 Jearim, Chephirah, and **B**: 743
Neh 7:29 Jearim, Chephirah, and **B**: 743

Beersheba (34)

Gen 21:14 around in the desert near **B**.
21:31 is why that place is called **B**,
21:32 After they made the treaty at **B**,
21:33 planted a tamarisk tree at **B**
22:19 and together they left for **B**.
22:19 Abraham remained in **B**.
26:23 He went from there to **B**.
26:33 name of the city is still **B** today.
28:10 Jacob left **B** and traveled
46:1 When he came to **B**,
46:5 So Jacob left **B**. Israel's sons
Jos 15:28 Hazar Shual, **B**, Biziothiah,
19:2 villages: **B** (Sheba), Moladah,
Jdg 20:1 people of Israel from Dan to **B**
1Sm 3:20 All Israel from Dan to **B** knew
8:2 They were judges in **B**.
2Sm 3:10 and Judah from Dan to **B**.'"
17:11 all Israel's troops from Dan to **B**,
24:2 tribes of Israel from Dan to **B**
24:7 Then they went to **B** in the
24:15 Of the people from Dan to **B**,
1Ki 4:25 (from Dan to **B**) lived securely,
19:3 He came to **B** in Judah and left
2Ki 12:1 His mother was Zibiah from **B**.
23:8 cities of Judah from Geba to **B**
1Ch 4:28 descendants lived in **B**,
21:2 count Israel from **B** to Dan.
2Ch 19:4 went to the people between **B**
24:1 His mother was Zibiah from **B**.
30:5 throughout Israel from **B** to
Neh 11:27 in **B** and its villages,
11:30 they settled in the land from **B**
Amo 5:5 Don't travel to **B**. Gilgal will
8:14 long as there is a road to **B** ...."

bees (4)

Dtr 1:44 chased you like a swarm of **b**.
Jdg 14:8 He saw a swarm of **b** and
Psa 118:12 swarmed around me like **b**,
Isa 7:18 in Egypt and for the **b** that are

beg (21)

Est 4:8 go to the king, **b** him for mercy,
7:7 But Haman stayed to **b** Queen
Job 19:16 doesn't answer, though I **b** him.
Psa 109:10 children wander around and **b**.
118:25 We **b** you, O LORD, save us!
118:25 We **b** you, O LORD, give us
Jer 27:18 they should **b** the LORD of
Lam 1:11 groaning as they **b** for bread.
4:4 Little children **b** for bread,
5:6 We had to **b** Egypt and Assyria
Mat 8:5 a Roman army officer came to **b**
Mar 5:17 Then the people began to **b**
Luk 8:28 I **b** you not to torture me!"
9:38 I **b** you to look at my son.
16:3 and I'm ashamed to **b**.
Jon 9:8 man who used to sit and **b**?"
Act 3:2 There he would **b** for handouts
3:10 man who used to sit and **b** at
2Co 5:20 We **b** you on behalf of Christ to
10:2 I **b** you that when I am with you
Gal 4:12 I **b** you to become like me.

began (233)

Gen 4:26 At that time people **b** to
8:3 The water **b** to recede from the
16:4 she **b** to be disrespectful to
39:7 a while his master's wife **b**
41:2 came up from the river and **b**
41:18 came up from the river and **b**
41:54 of famine **b** as Joseph had
41:55 When everyone in Egypt **b** to
44:12 He **b** with the oldest and ended
50:10 they **b** a great and solemn
Exo 1:8 Joseph, **b** to rule in Egypt.
8:14 and the land **b** to stink because
Lev 24:11 The Israelite woman's son **b**
Num 11:1 The people **b** complaining out
11:1 and fire from the LORD **b** to
12:1 Miriam and Aaron **b** to criticize
13:32 So they **b** to spread lies among
25:1 the men **b** to have sex with
Dtr 1:5 River in Moab when Moses **b**
Jos 5:12 That year they **b** to eat the
Jdg 2:4 they **b** to cry loudly.
2:11 They **b** to serve other gods —
7:21 in the Midianite camp **b**
9:43 Then he **b** to attack them.
9:52 He **b** to fight against it and
10:6 They **b** to serve other gods and
11:39 So the custom **b** in Israel
13:25 The LORD's Spirit **b** to stir in
16:19 Then she **b** to torture him
Rut 1:7 They **b** to walk back along the
1:9 they **b** to cry loudly.
1:14 They **b** to cry loudly again.
1:22 just when the barley harvest **b**.
1Sm 13:8 and the troops **b** to scatter.
18:10 He **b** to prophesy in his house
2Sm 13:39 King David **b** to long for
1Ki 6:1 Solomon **b** to build the LORD's
6:1 He **b** building in the month of
6:15 he **b** to line the inside walls of
14:21 He was 41 years old when he **b**
15:1 Abijam **b** to rule Judah.
15:9 Asa **b** to rule as king of Judah.
15:25 Nadab, son of Jeroboam, **b** to
15:33 **b** to rule Israel in Tirzah.
16:8 Elah, son of Baasha, **b** to rule
16:23 Omri **b** to rule Israel in Asa's
16:29 Ahab, son of Omri, **b** to rule
22:42 35 years old when he **b** to rule,
2Ki 6:4 came to the Jordan River and **b**
8:11 Then the man of God **b** to cry.
8:16 of Judah, **b** to rule.
8:17 He was 32 years old when he **b**
8:26 22 years old when he **b** to rule,
10:32 So in those days the LORD **b**
11:1 she **b** to destroy the entire royal
11:21 years old when he **b** to rule.
12:1 Joash **b** to rule in Jehu's
13:1 **b** to rule in Samaria as king of
13:10 Jehoahaz's son Jehoash **b** to
14:1 of Joash of Judah, **b** to rule.
14:2 25 years old when he **b** to rule,
14:23 son King Jeroboam of Israel **b**
15:1 Amaziah's son Azariah **b** to
15:2 He was 16 years old when he **b**
15:17 **b** to rule as king of Israel.
15:23 son Pekahiah **b** to rule.

2Ki 15:27 **b** to rule Israel in Samaria.
15:30 Hoshea **b** to rule as king in his
15:32 **b** to rule as king of Judah.
15:33 He was 25 years old when he **b**
15:37 In those days the LORD **b** to
16:1 **b** to rule as king of Judah.
16:2 20 years old when he **b** to rule.
17:1 **b** to rule as king of Israel in
18:1 of Judah, **b** to rule as king.
18:2 25 years old when he **b** to rule,
21:1 12 years old when he **b** to rule,
21:19 22 years old when he **b** to rule,
22:1 8 years old when he **b** to rule,
23:36 25 years old when he **b** to rule,
24:8 was 18 years old when he **b**
24:18 21 years old when he **b** to rule,
2Ch 3:1 Solomon **b** to build the LORD's
3:2 He **b** to build on the second
12:13 He was 41 years old when he **b**
13:1 Abijah **b** to rule Judah.
20:31 He was 35 years old when he **b**
22:2 42 years old when he **b** to rule,
22:10 she **b** to destroy the entire royal
24:1 7 years old when he **b** to rule,
25:1 25 years old when he **b** to rule,
26:3 16 years old when he **b** to rule,
27:1 25 years old when he **b** to rule.
27:8 He was 25 years old when he **b**
28:1 20 years old when he **b** to rule.
28:18 They captured and **b** living in
29:1 Hezekiah **b** to rule as king
29:28 the ground, singers **b** to sing,
33:1 12 years old when he **b** to rule,
33:21 22 years old when he **b** to rule,
34:1 8 years old when he **b** to rule,
34:3 he **b** to dedicate his life to
34:3 In his twelfth year as king, he **b**
36:5 25 years old when he **b** to rule,
36:9 was eight years old when he **b**
36:11 21 years old when he **b** to rule,
36:20 the Persian Empire **b** to rule.
Ezr 3:8 back from exile to Jerusalem) **b**
3:8 They **b** by appointing the
3:12 temple with their own eyes **b**
4:6 When Xerxes **b** to rule,
5:2 **b** to rebuild God's temple in
10:1 They also **b** to cry bitterly.
Neh 9:27 When they **b** to suffer,
Est 5:11 Then Haman **b** to relate in
6:13 There, Haman **b** to relate in
Psa 32:3 my bones **b** to weaken
107:5 They **b** to lose hope.
107:25 and a storm **b** to blow,
Pro 8:22 me long ago, when his way **b**,
8:23 the first, before the earth **b**.
Ecc 1:7 the place where the streams **b**
Jer 26:1 son of Josiah, **b** to rule.
27:1 King Josiah of Judah, **b** to rule,
52:1 21 years old when he **b** to rule,
Eze 23:27 which you **b** in Egypt.
36:3 and people **b** to talk and gossip
Dan 9:23 As soon as you **b** to make your
10:16 opened my mouth and **b** to talk.
Hos 9:15 wickedness **b** in Gilgal;
Jnh 1:5 They **b** to throw the cargo
Hab 1:12 Didn't you exist before time **b**,
Hag 1:14 from Babylon **b** working
1:15 They **b** on the twenty-fourth
Zec 4:10 when little things **b** to happen?
Mat 4:17 Jesus **b** to tell people,
5:2 and he **b** to teach them:
9:33 the man **b** to speak.
12:1 disciples were hungry and **b**
14:26 and **b** to scream because they
15:22 came ⌊to him⌋ and **b** to shout,
16:21 From that time on Jesus **b** to
18:24 When he **b** to do this,
18:28 the servant he found and **b**
20:11 they **b** to protest to the owner.
21:23 courtyard and **b** to teach.
26:74 Then Peter **b** to curse and
27:23 But they **b** to shout loudly,
Mar 1:21 the synagogue and **b** to teach.
1:45 the man left, he **b** to talk freely.
2:23 they **b** to pick the heads of
4:1 Jesus **b** to teach again by the
Mar 5:17 Then the people **b** to beg
5:20 He **b** to tell how much Jesus
6:2 he **b** to teach in the synagogue.
6:49 and they **b** to scream.
6:55 all over the countryside and **b**
8:11 Pharisees went to Jesus and **b**
8:31 Then he **b** to teach them that
10:32 He **b** to tell them what was
10:47 by⌋, he **b** to shout, "Jesus,
11:15 into the temple courtyard and **b**
14:33 and John with him and **b** to feel
14:65 Some of them **b** to spit on him.
14:71 Then Peter **b** to curse and
14:72 Then Peter **b** to cry very hard.
15:18 Then they **b** to greet him,
Luk 1:64 and he **b** to praise God.
2:38 up to Mary and Joseph and **b**
3:23 old when he **b** ⌊his ministry⌋.
5:6 of fish that their nets **b** to tear.
6:11 Pharisees were furious and **b**
7:15 dead man sat up and **b** to talk,
11:14 had gone out, the man **b** to talk.
15:24 Then they **b** to celebrate.
19:7 But the people who saw this **b**
19:37 the whole crowd of disciples **b**
19:41 and saw the city, he **b** to cry.
19:45 into the temple courtyard and **b**
22:23 So they **b** to discuss with each
23:2 They **b** to accuse Jesus by
23:21 They **b** yelling, "Crucify him!
24:15 them and **b** walking with them.
24:27 Then he **b** with Moses'
Jon 2:11 was the place where Jesus **b**
5:16 The Jews **b** to persecute
6:41 The Jews **b** to criticize Jesus
6:52 The Jews **b** to quarrel with
7:14 courtyard and **b** to teach.
8:2 sat down and **b** to teach them.
13:5 poured water into a basin and **b**
13:22 The disciples **b** looking at
Act 1:1 I wrote about what Jesus **b** to
2:4 filled with the Holy Spirit and **b**
3:7 of the man's right hand and **b**
4:15 to leave the council room and **b**
5:14 men and women than ever **b**
5:21 courtyard and **b** to teach.
7:18 Joseph, **b** to rule in Egypt.
7:32 Moses **b** to tremble and didn't
7:58 they **b** to stone him to death.
9:20 He immediately **b** to spread the
10:37 Everything **b** in Galilee after
11:2 who insisted on circumcision **b**
11:4 Then Peter **b** to explain to
11:15 "When I **b** to speak,
12:21 sat on his throne and **b** making
13:5 they **b** to spread God's word in
13:24 Before Jesus **b** his ministry,
14:10 man jumped up and **b** to walk.
16:13 We sat down and **b** talking to
17:32 some **b** joking about it,
18:26 He **b** to speak boldly in the
19:6 and they **b** to talk in other
19:17 name of the Lord Jesus and **b**
19:28 became furious and **b** shouting,
21:28 Then they **b** shouting,
22:22 Then they **b** to shout,
23:7 and Sadducees **b** to quarrel,
24:2 Tertullus **b** to accuse him.
26:1 Agrippa and then **b** his defense.
27:7 Our difficulties **b** along the
27:13 When a gentle breeze **b** to
27:18 that the next day the men **b**
27:20 was so severe that we finally **b**
27:35 everyone, broke it, and **b** to eat.
28:13 day a south wind **b** to blow,
1Co 2:7 for our glory before the world **b**.
2Co 8:11 So finish what you **b** to do.
Php 1:6 who **b** this good work in you,
2Ti 1:9 Before the world **b**,
Tit 1:2 eternal life before the world **b**.
Jud 1:25 Before time **b**, now, and for

beggar (3)

Mar 10:46 a blind **b** named Bartimaeus,
Luk 16:20 There was also a **b** named
16:22 "One day the **b** died,

beggars (1)

2Co 6:10 that we're **b** although we make

begged (33)

Exo 12:33 The Egyptians **b** the people to
1Sm 20:6 'David repeatedly **b** me to let
20:28 "David repeatedly **b** me ⌊to let
2Ki 1:13 The officer **b** him, "Man of God,
2Ch 33:12 he **b** the LORD his God to be
Est 8:3 at his feet crying and **b** him
Mat 8:31 The demons **b** Jesus,
8:34 When they saw him, they **b**
14:36 They **b** him to let them touch
18:29 fell at his feet and **b** him,
18:32 because you **b** me.
Mar 1:40 The man fell to his knees and **b**
5:10 He **b** Jesus not to send them
5:12 The demons **b** him,
5:18 been demon-possessed **b** him,
5:23 He **b** Jesus, "My little daughter
6:56 They **b** him to let them touch
7:32 They **b** Jesus to lay his hand
8:22 They **b** Jesus to touch him.
Luk 5:12 He **b** Jesus, "Sir, if you want
7:4 They came to Jesus and **b**,
8:31 The demons **b** Jesus not to
8:32 The demons **b** Jesus to let
8:38 demons had gone out **b** him,
8:41 He **b** Jesus to come to his
9:40 I **b** your disciples to force the
15:28 His father came out and **b** him
Act 9:38 They **b** Peter, "Hurry to Joppa!
21:12 who lived there **b** Paul not
28:14 some believers who **b**
2Co 12:8 I **b** the Lord three times to take
Heb 12:17 Even though he **b** and cried for
12:19 they **b** not to hear it say another

begging (6)

Gen 50:17 "I'm **b** you to forgive the crime
Psa 37:25 or his descendants **b** for food.
Pro 18:23 A poor person is timid when **b**,
Luk 18:35 was sitting and **b** by the road.
Jon 9:8 previously seen him **b** asked,
2Co 8:4 They made an appeal to us, **b**

begin (23)

Exo 40:15 Their anointing will **b** a
Num 17:5 man I choose will **b** to grow.
Jos 3:7 "Today I will **b** to honor you in
Jdg 13:5 He will **b** to rescue Israel from
2Ch 2:1 Solomon gave orders to **b**
Neh 2:18 "Let's **b** to rebuild."
2:18 to **b** this God-pleasing work.
Psa 61:2 I call to you when I **b** to lose
75:3 who lives on it **b** to melt,
77:3 I **b** to lose hope as I think about
81:2 **B** a psalm, and strike a
142:3 When I **b** to lose hope,
143:4 That is why I **b** to lose hope
Isa 27:12 On that day the LORD will **b**
32:4 reckless will **b** to understand,
Jer 16:14 "when people will no longer **b**
Eze 39:14 months they will **b** their search.
Mat 24:49 The servant may **b** to beat the
Luk 12:45 The servant may **b** to beat the
21:28 these things **b** to happen,
Gal 3:3 Did you **b** in a spiritual way
1Pe 4:17 has come for the judgment to **b**,
4:17 and it will **b** with God's family.

beginning (72)

Gen 1:1 In the beginning **G** created
11:6 This is only the **b** of what they
Exo 9:18 Egypt since the **b** of its history.
Num 13:20 when grapes were **b** to ripen.)
Jos 8:33 Right from the **b**, the LORD's
Jdg 7:19 It was the **b** of the midnight
1Sm 3:12 everything I said from **b** to end.
2Sm 21:9 They were killed at the **b** of the
21:10 the rock for herself from the **b**
1Ki 16:11 At the **b** of Zimri's reign,
2Ki 17:34 as they've done from the **b**.
17:40 as they had done from the **b**.
2Ch 25:26 about Amaziah, from **b** to end,

2Ch 26:22 about Uzziah, from **b** to end,
28:26 about him — everything from **b**
Psa 55:19 enthroned from the **b** will deal
111:10 the LORD is the **b** of wisdom.
Pro 1:7 LORD is the **b** of knowledge.
4:7 The **b** of wisdom is to acquire
9:10 the LORD is the **b** of wisdom.
20:21 obtained in the **b** will never
Ecc 3:11 what God is doing from the **b**
7:8 something is better than its **b**.
Isa 1:26 advisers like you had in the **b**.
40:21 you been told from the **b**?
41:4 course of history from the **b**?
41:26 Who revealed this from the **b**
46:10 From the **b** I revealed the end.
48:3 From the **b** I revealed to you
48:16 Listen to this: From the **b** I
52:4 In the **b** my people went to
Jer 17:12 highly honored from the **b**.
Eze 40:1 tenth day of the month in the **b**
48:1 **B** at the northern border,
Mat 19:4 them male and female in the **b**
19:8 It was never this way in the **b**.
24:8 All of these are only the **b**
24:21 has not happened from the **b**
26:37 He was **b** to feel deep anguish.
Mar 1:1 This is the **b** of the Good News
10:6 them male and female in the **b**,
13:8 These are only the **b** pains ⌊of
13:19 has not happened from the **b**
Luk 1:2 of God's word from the **b**,
1:3 everything closely from the **b**.
23:54 the day of worship was just **b**.
24:47 **b** in the city of Jerusalem.
Jon 1:1 In the **b** the Word already
1:2 was already with God in the **b**.
6:64 "Jesus knew from the **b** those
8:9 **b** with the older men,
8:25 whom I said I was from the **b**.
8:44 was a murderer from the **b**.
9:32 Since the **b** of time,
15:27 have been with me from the **b**."
Act 1:1 from the **b** ⌊of his life⌋
11:15 that happened to us in the **b**.
Col 1:18 He is the **b**, the first to come
2Th 2:13 and we thank God that in the **b**
Heb 1:10 God also said, "Lord, in the **b**
2Pe 3:4 it did from the **b** of the world."
1Jn 1:1 Word of life existed from the **b**.
2:7 that you've had from the **b**.
2:13 who has existed from the **b**.
2:14 who has existed from the **b**.
2:24 you heard from the **b** lives
3:8 committing sin since the **b**.
3:11 you have heard from the **b** is
2Jn 1:5 Rather, from the **b** we were
1:6 you have heard this from the **b**.
Rev 21:6 A and the Z, the **b** and the end.
22:13 and the last, the **b** and the end.

begins (4)

Jos 18:15 The southern border **b** just
2Sm 13:28 "When Amnon **b** to feel good
Psa 73:14 my punishment ⌊**b** again⌋.
Rom 1:17 This approval **b** and ends with

begun (9)

Num 16:47 plague had already **b** among
17:8 of Levi had not only **b** to grow,
Dtr 2:31 LORD said to me, "I have **b**
3:24 you have ⌊only⌋ **b** to show me
1Sm 3:2 His eyesight had **b** to fail so
Est 9:23 as tradition what they had **b**,
Job 30:21 You have **b** to treat me cruelly.
Mic 6:13 I have **b** to strike you with
Rev 11:17 and have **b** ruling as king.

behalf (40)

Lev 22:20 will not be accepted on your **b**.
22:25 will not be accepted on your **b**
Num 3:38 in charge of the holy place on **b**
1Sm 7:9 to the LORD on **b** of Israel,
14:6 the LORD will act on our **b**.
25:39 David sent men ⌊on his **b**⌋
2Sm 3:12 to David to speak on his **b**.
1Ki 2:19 to talk to him on Adonijah's **b**.
2Ki 11:17 a promise to the LORD on **b**
22:13 "On **b** of the people,
1Ch 29:22 On the LORD's **b** they anointed
2Ch 9:8 on his throne to be king on **b**
23:16 a promise to the LORD on **b**
34:21 "On **b** of those who are left in
Est 2:22 told the king, on **b** of Mordecai.
Job 8:6 then he will rise up on your **b**
13:7 and talk deceitfully on his **b**?
13:8 arguing in court on God's **b**?
Psa 37:5 and he will act ⌊on your **b**⌋.
Pro 20:16 a loan on **b** of a foreigner.
27:13 a loan in **b** of a foreigner.
Dan 12:1 will stand up on **b** of the
Jon 5:31 "If I testify on my own **b**,
5:32 else testifies on my **b**,
5:36 on my **b** than John's testimony.
5:36 I perform, testify on my **b**.
5:37 who sent me testifies on my **b**.
5:39 Scriptures testify on my **b**.
8:13 "You testify on your own **b**,
8:14 "Even if I testify on my own **b**,
8:18 I testify on my own **b**,
10:25 Father's name testify on my **b**.
Rom 10:1 desire and prayer to God on **b**
2Co 1:23 to God as a witness on my **b**,
5:20 We beg you on **b** of Christ to
Col 1:24 I am doing this on **b** of his
Heb 2:9 he died on **b** of everyone.
6:20 Jesus went before us on our **b**.
9:24 in God's presence on our **b**.
1Jn 2:1 He speaks on our **b** when we

behave (1)

1Ki 1:52 Solomon said, "If he will **b** like

behaved (4)

2Ki 17:15 They **b** like the nations around
Job 36:9 and that they've **b** arrogantly.
Psa 106:39 They **b** like prostitutes.
Jer 2:23 Look how you've **b** in the

behaves (1)

Pro 13:5 but a wicked person **b** with

behaving (1)

2Sm 3:8 "Have I been **b** like some

behavior (12)

1Sm 21:13 So he changed his **b** ⌊when he
Job 13:15 I will defend my **b** to his face.
34:31 I will stop my immoral **b**.
Pro 1:3 of wise **b** — righteousness
8:13 I hate pride, arrogance, evil **b**,
21:8 but the **b** of those who are pure
21:16 from the way of wise **b** will rest
Eze 28:15 Your **b** was perfect from the
Eph 5:3 This is not appropriate **b** for
Col 3:18 This is appropriate **b** for the
1Ti 4:12 Instead, make your speech, **b**,
Jas 1:21 So get rid of all immoral **b** and

Behemoth (2)

Job 40:15 "Look at **B**, which I made along
40:19 **B** is the first of God's

being (21)

Gen 2:7 The man became a living **b**.
9:10 and every living **b** that is with
9:12 to you and every living **b** that is
Num 19:11 dead body of any human **b** will
19:13 the dead body of a human **b**
Job 4:17 Can ⌊any⌋ human **b** be pure to
28:21 from the eyes of every living **b**,
33:20 so that their whole **b** hates food
Psa 139:13 You alone created my inner **b**.
Pro 18:8 into a person's innermost **b**.
20:27 his entire innermost **b**.
20:30 cleanse the innermost **b**.
26:22 into a person's innermost **b**.
30:2 a dumb animal than a human **b**.
Dan 4:13 I saw a guardian, a holy **b**,
4:23 You saw a guardian, a holy **b**,
Act 17:29 think that the divine **b** is like
Rom 7:22 God's standards in my inner **b**.
1Co 15:45 became a living **b**."
1Th 5:23 he keep your whole **b** — spirit,
Heb 1:3 the exact likeness of God's **b**.

beings (7)

Job 30:23 place appointed for all living **b**."
34:15 all living **b** would die together,
Psa 29:1 to the LORD, you heavenly **b**.
89:6 Who among the heavenly **b** is
103:20 you mighty **b** who carry out his
Isa 13:12 and human **b** more rare than
Act 14:15 We're human **b** like you.

Beker (2)

Gen 46:21 **B**, Ashbel, Gera, Naaman, Ehi,
Num 26:35 of Shuthelah, the family of **B**,

Bel (5)

Isa 46:1 The god **B** bows down;
Jer 50:2 **B** will be put to shame.
51:44 I will punish **B** in Babylon.
51:44 I will make **B** spit out
Dan 4:8 after my god ⌊**B**⌋.)

Bela (12)

Gen 14:2 and the king of **B** (that is,
14:8 Admah, Zeboiim, and **B** (that is,
36:32 **B**, son of Beor, ruled Edom.
36:33 After **B** died, Jobab, son of
46:21 The sons of Benjamin were **B**,
Num 26:38 Benjamin were the family of **B**,
26:40 The descendants of **B**
1Ch 1:43 people of Israel: **B**, son of Beor,
1:44 After **B** died, Jobab, son of
5:8 and **B** (son of Azaz,
7:6 Benjamin had three sons: **B**,
8:1 the father of **B** (his firstborn),

Bela's (2)

1Ch 7:7 **B** five sons were Ezbon,
8:3 **B** sons were Addar,

belief (2)

Act 24:16 With this **b** I always do my
Rev 2:13 have not denied your **b** in me,

believe (192)

Gen 45:26 Jacob was stunned and didn't **b**
Exo 4:1 "They will never **b** me or listen
4:8 "If they won't **b** you or pay
4:8 they may **b** the second.
4:9 But if they won't **b** these two
19:9 you and will always **b** you."
Dtr 9:23 You didn't **b** him or obey him.
1Ki 10:7 But I didn't **b** the reports until I
2Ch 9:6 But I didn't **b** the reports until I
20:20 the LORD your God, and **b**.
20:20 **B** his prophets, and you will
32:15 Don't **b** him. No god of any
Job 9:16 I do not **b** that he would listen
15:22 He doesn't **b** he'll return from
29:24 they could hardly **b** it,
Psa 27:13 I **b** that I will see the goodness
78:22 because they did not **b** God or
106:24 They did not **b** what he said.
119:66 I **b** in your commandments.
Isa 43:10 so that you can know and **b**
Jer 28:15 made these people **b** a lie.
29:31 He has made you **b** a lie.
40:14 son of Ahikam, didn't **b** them.
Lam 4:12 on earth could **b** that enemies
Eze 21:23 The people won't **b** this
Hos 2:8 "She doesn't **b** that I gave her
Hab 1:5 that you would not **b** even if
Mat 9:28 "Do you **b** that I can do this?"
18:6 "These little ones **b** in me.
21:25 'Then why didn't you **b** him?'
21:32 but you didn't **b** him.
21:32 change your minds and **b** him.
24:23 "At that time don't **b** anyone
24:26 And don't **b** anyone who says,
27:42 the cross now, and we'll **b** him.
Mar 1:15 and **b** the Good News."
5:36 "Don't be afraid! Just **b**."
9:24 father cried out at once, "I **b**!
9:42 "These little ones **b** in me.
11:31 'Then why didn't you **b** him?'

Mar 13:21 "At that time don't **b** anyone
15:32 so that we may see and **b**."
16:11 They didn't **b** her when they
16:13 who did not **b** them either.
16:14 stubborn to **b** those who had
16:16 does not **b** will be condemned.
Luk 1:20 But because you didn't **b** what I
5:26 things today we can hardly **b**!"
8:12 they don't **b** and become saved.
8:13 They **b** for a while,
8:50 Just **b**, and she will get well."
20:5 'Why didn't you **b** him?'
22:67 "If I tell you, you won't **b** me.
24:11 and they didn't **b** them.
24:25 You're so slow to **b** everything
Jon 1:50 Jesus replied, "You **b** because
3:12 If you don't **b** me when I tell
3:12 how will you **b** me when I tell
3:18 Those who **b** in him won't be
3:18 But those who don't **b** are
3:18 because they don't **b**
4:21 Jesus told her, "**B** me.
4:48 amazing things, they won't **b**."
5:24 who listen to what I say and **b**
5:38 because you don't **b** in the
5:44 How can you **b** when you
5:46 Moses, you would **b** me.
5:47 If you don't **b** what Moses
5:47 will you ever **b** what I say?"
6:29 something for you so that you **b**
6:30 we can see it and **b** in you?
6:36 However, you don't **b** in me.
6:40 those who see the Son and **b**
6:64 But some of you don't **b**.
6:64 beginning those who wouldn't **b**
6:69 Besides, we **b** and know that
7:5 his brothers didn't **b** in him.
8:24 If you don't **b** that I am the one,
8:45 So you don't **b** me because I
8:46 why don't you **b** me?
9:18 the Jews didn't **b** that the man
9:35 "Do you **b** in the Son of Man?"
9:36 he is so that I can **b** in him."
9:38 of Jesus and said, "I **b**, Lord."
10:25 but you don't **b** me.
10:26 However, you don't **b** because
10:37 my Father does, don't **b** me.
10:38 things and you refuse to **b** me,
10:38 then at least **b** the things that
11:25 Those who **b** in me will live
11:26 will never die. Do you **b** that?"
11:27 I **b** that you are the Messiah,
11:40 "Didn't I tell you that if you **b**,
11:42 around me will **b** that you sent
11:48 everyone will **b** in him.
12:36 While you have the light, **b** in
12:37 they wouldn't **b** in him.
12:39 the people couldn't **b** because,
13:19 you will **b** that I am the one.
14:1 **B** in God, and believe in me.
14:1 Believe in God, and **b** in me.
14:10 Don't you **b** that I am in the
14:11 **B** me when I say that I am in
14:11 Otherwise, **b** me because of
14:12 Those who **b** in me will do the
14:29 it does happen, you will **b**.
16:9 because people don't **b** in me.
16:30 Because of this, we **b** that you
16:31 replied to them, "Now you **b**.
17:20 praying for those who will **b**
17:21 the world will **b** that you have
19:35 the truth so that you, too, will **b**.
20:25 them, "I refuse to **b** this unless
20:27 Stop doubting, and **b**."
20:29 Jesus said to Thomas, "You **b**
20:29 who haven't seen me but **b**."
20:31 so that you will **b** that Jesus is
Act 3:16 We **b** in the one named Jesus.
5:14 ever began to **b** in the Lord.
9:26 They wouldn't **b** that he was a
10:43 testify that people who **b**
13:8 so that the governor wouldn't **b**.
13:41 that you would not **b** even if
14:2 But the Jews who refused to **b**
14:27 not Jewish the opportunity to **b**.
15:7 hear the Good News and **b**.
Act 15:11 We certainly **b** that the Lord
16:15 "If you're convinced that I **b** in
16:31 "**B** in the Lord Jesus,
19:4 John told people to **b** in Jesus,
19:9 became stubborn, refused to **b**,
20:21 way they think and act and to **b**
22:19 and whip those who **b** in you.
23:8 The Pharisees **b** in all these
24:14 God and **b** everything written
24:21 front of you because ⌊I **b** that⌋
26:8 Why do all of you refuse to **b**
26:27 do you **b** the prophets?
26:27 I know you **b** them!"
Rom 2:8 refuse to **b** the truth and who
3:26 of people who **b** in Jesus.
4:5 people don't work but **b** God,
4:24 as God's approval of us who **b**
6:8 we **b** that we will also live with
10:9 and **b** that God brought him
10:14 How can they **b** in him if they
11:20 off because they didn't **b**,
11:20 on the tree because you do **b**.
14:2 Some people **b** that they can
14:2 Other people with weak faith **b**
14:22 So whatever you **b** about these
15:31 in Judea who refuse to **b**.
1Co 1:21 we speak to save those who **b**.
7:26 of the present crisis I **b**
8:7 gods that they **b** they are eating
11:18 I **b** some of what I hear.
2Co 4:4 the minds of those who don't **b**.
4:13 We also **b**; therefore, we also
Gal 3:9 So people who **b** are blessed
3:22 could be given to those who **b**.
Php 1:29 you the privilege not only to **b**
1Th 4:14 We **b** that Jesus died and
4:14 We also **b** that, through Jesus,
2Th 2:11 so that they will **b** a lie.
2:12 who did not **b** the truth,
1Ti 1:16 example for those who would **b**
4:1 and they will **b** the teachings of
4:3 of thanks by those who **b**
4:10 especially of those who **b**.
6:1 All slaves who **b** must give
6:2 Slaves whose masters also **b**
2Ti 3:12 live a godly life because they **b**
Tit 3:8 things so that those who **b**
Heb 3:19 of rest because they didn't **b**.
4:2 the past because they didn't **b**.
4:3 We who **b** are entering that
11:6 Whoever goes to God must **b**
Jas 2:19 You **b** that there is one God.
2:19 The demons also **b** that,
1Pe 1:8 see him now, but you **b** in him.
1:21 Through him you **b** in God who
2:7 honor belongs to those who **b**.
2:7 But to those who don't **b**:
2:8 because they refused to **b** it.
2Pe 2:14 who aren't sure of what they **b**.
3:16 of what they **b** distort what Paul
1Jn 3:23 commandment: to **b** in his Son,
4:1 Dear friends, don't **b** all people
5:10 Those who **b** in the Son of God
5:10 Those who don't **b** God have
5:13 I've written this to those who **b**
Jud 1:5 destroyed those who didn't **b**.

believed (67)

Gen 15:6 Then Abram **b** the LORD,
Exo 4:31 and the people **b** them.
14:31 they feared the LORD and **b** in
Jos 9:14 The men **b** the evidence they
1Sm 27:12 And Achish **b** David.
Psa 78:32 no longer **b** in his miracles.
106:12 Then our ancestors **b** what he
Isa 53:1 Who has **b** our message?
Jnh 3:5 The people of Nineveh **b** God.
Mat 8:13 What you **b** will be done for
9:29 "What you have **b** will be done
21:32 and prostitutes **b** him.
Jon 1:12 to everyone who **b** in him.
2:11 and his disciples **b** in him.
2:22 So they **b** the Scripture and
2:23 many people **b** in him because
4:39 Many Samaritans in that city **b**
4:41 Many more Samaritans **b**
Jon 4:50 The man **b** what Jesus told
5:46 If you really **b** Moses,
7:31 people in the crowd **b** in him.
7:48 ruler or any Pharisee **b** in him?
8:30 many people **b** in him.
8:31 to those Jews who **b** in him,
10:42 Many people there **b** in Jesus.
11:45 what Jesus had done **b** in him.
12:38 who has **b** our message?
12:42 Many rulers **b** in Jesus.
16:27 have loved me and have **b** that
17:8 They have **b** that you sent me.
20:8 went inside. He saw and **b**.
Act 4:4 so the number of men who **b**
8:12 men and women **b** him and
8:13 Even Simon **b**, and after he
9:42 many people **b** in the Lord.
11:17 When they **b**, God gave them
11:17 gift that he gave us when we **b**
11:21 and a large number of people **b**
11:24 A large crowd **b** in the Lord.
13:12 saw what had happened, he **b**.
13:48 prepared for everlasting life **b**.
14:1 crowd of Jews and Greeks **b**.
14:9 closely and saw that the man **b**
14:23 to the Lord in whom they **b**.
18:8 Crispus and his whole family **b**
18:8 Paul **b** and were baptized.
Rom 4:3 "Abraham **b** God, and that faith
4:17 Abraham **b** when he stood in
4:18 Abraham still hoped and **b**.
10:14 him if they have not **b** in him?
10:16 But not everyone has **b** the
10:16 who has **b** our message?"
1Co 15:2 unless you **b** it without thinking
15:11 and this is what you **b**.
2Co 4:13 The following is written, "I **b**;
Gal 2:16 So we also **b** in Jesus Christ in
3:6 He **b** God, and that faith was
Eph 1:13 You heard and **b** the message
Php 1:5 the first day ⌊you **b**⌋ until now.
1Th 4:16 First, the dead who **b** in Christ
2Th 1:10 by all who have **b** in him.
1:10 includes you because you **b**
1Ti 3:16 was **b** in the world,
Heb 11:19 Abraham **b** that God could
Jas 2:23 It says, "Abraham **b** God,
1Jn 4:16 We have known and **b** that
5:10 They haven't **b** the testimony

believer (30)

Mat 5:22 with another **b** will answer
5:22 Whoever calls another **b** an
5:22 Whoever calls another **b** a fool
5:23 **b** has something against
7:4 How can you say to another **b**,
18:15 "If a **b** does something wrong,
18:15 you have won back that **b**.
18:21 to forgive a **b** who wrongs me?
Luk 6:42 How can you say to another **b**,
17:3 "If a **b** sins, correct him.
Jon 6:47 Every **b** has eternal life.
Act 2:3 one came to rest on each **b**.
16:1 mother was a Jewish **b**,
Rom 4:11 he is the father of every **b** who
16:5 of Asia to become a **b** in Christ.
1Co 6:6 Instead, one **b** goes to court
6:6 goes to court against another **b**,
8:9 make a **b** who is weak
8:11 your knowledge is ruining a **b**
8:11 a **b** for whom Christ died.
2Co 5:17 Whoever is a **b** in Christ is a
6:15 Can a **b** share life with an
2Th 3:6 with any **b** who doesn't live
1Ti 5:16 If any woman is a **b** and has
Jas 2:15 Suppose a **b**, whether a man or
1Jn 3:15 Everyone who hates another **b**
3:17 and notices another **b** in need.
3:17 bother to help the other **b**?
4:20 but hates another **b** is a liar.
5:16 If you see another **b** committing

believer's (4)

Mat 7:3 of sawdust in another **b** eye
7:5 of sawdust from another **b** eye
Luk 6:41 of sawdust in another **b** eye

Luk 6:42 of sawdust from another **b** eye

believers (117)

Mat 18:17 tell it to the community of **b**.
18:35 not sincerely forgive other **b**."
Mar 16:17 signs that will accompany **b**:
Jon 1:7 **b** through his message.
2:24 was wary of these **b**.
4:53 and his entire family became **b**.
7:39 whom his **b** would receive.
Act 2:1 all the **b** were together in one
2:4 All the **b** were filled with the
2:44 All the **b** kept meeting together,
2:46 The **b** had a single purpose
4:4 heard the message became **b**,
4:32 The whole group of **b** lived in
5:12 The **b** had a common faith in
8:1 Most **b**, except the apostles,
8:4 The **b** who were scattered
9:41 After he called the **b**,
10:45 All the **b** who were
11:1 The apostles and the **b**
11:2 the **b** who insisted on
11:12 Six **b** ⌊from Joppa⌋ went with
11:19 Some of the **b** who were
11:20 But other **b**, who were from
11:29 to help the **b** living in Judea.
12:17 and the other **b** about this."
14:2 their minds against the **b**.
15:1 to teach **b** that people can't
15:3 brought great joy to all the **b**.
15:5 But some **b** from the party of
15:22 who were leaders among the **b**.
15:32 and strengthen the **b**.
15:36 We'll visit the **b** to see how
15:40 left after the **b** entrusted him
16:2 The **b** in Lystra and Iconium
16:34 were thrilled to be **b** in God.
16:40 They met with the **b**,
17:6 Jason and some other **b**
17:10 the **b** sent Paul and Silas to the
17:12 Many of them became **b**,
17:14 The **b** immediately sent Paul to
17:34 men joined him and became **b**.
18:27 the **b** ⌊in Ephesus⌋
18:27 him to help the **b** a great deal.
19:2 Spirit when you became **b**?"
19:18 Many **b** openly admitted their
21:7 We greeted the **b** in Ptolemais
21:12 we and the **b** who lived there
21:17 the **b** welcomed us warmly.
21:20 thousands of Jews are now **b**,
21:25 we have written non-Jewish **b**
22:5 I was going there to tie up **b**
26:11 each synagogue, punished **b**,
28:14 some **b** who begged
28:15 **B** in Rome heard that we were
Rom 8:1 So those who are **b** in Christ
12:3 has given each of you as **b**.
13:11 than when we first became **b**.
15:26 Because the **b** in Macedonia
1Co 6:5 disagreements between **b**?
6:8 and you do this to other **b**.
8:12 When you sin against other **b**
8:13 to false gods⌋ causes other **b**
8:13 make other **b** lose their faith.
11:11 Yet, as **b** in the Lord,
11:19 the genuine **b** among you are.
12:29 Not all **b** are apostles,
14:22 a sign for unbelievers, not for **b**.
14:22 had revealed is a sign for **b**,
15:6 to more than 500 **b** at one time.
15:18 Then those who have died as **b**
2Co 9:2 and I brag about you to the **b** in
11:26 and from **b** who turned out to be
Gal 1:2 and all the **b** who are with me.
6:10 especially for the family of **b**.
Eph 1:19 might and strength for us, the **b**.
1Th 1:7 became a model for all the **b**
2:10 in our dealings with you **b**.
2:13 This word is at work in you **b**.
4:6 of or exploit other **b** that way.
4:10 We encourage you as **b** to
1Ti 4:1 later times some **b** will desert
4:12 purity an example for other **b**.
6:2 though their masters are also **b**.
1Ti 6:2 As a result, **b** who are slaves
6:2 work are **b** whom they love.
2Ti 2:14 Remind **b** about these things,
Tit 1:6 and have children who are **b**.
1:10 There are many **b**,
1:13 sharply correct **b** so that they
2:1 Tell **b** to live the kind of life
2:9 Tell slaves who are **b** to place
2:15 Tell these things to the **b**.
3:1 Remind **b** to willingly place
3:1 **B** should obey them and be
3:2 **B** shouldn't curse anyone or be
Heb 10:25 gathering together with other **b**,
11:35 Other **b** were brutally tortured
13:2 hospitality to **b** you don't know.
13:2 By doing this some **b** have
Jas 1:9 Humble **b** should be proud
1:10 Rich **b** should be proud
4:11 and judge other **b** slander
1Pe 5:9 knowing that other **b**
1Jn 2:9 light but hate other **b** are still
2:10 Those who love other **b** live in
2:11 Those who hate other **b** are in
3:10 or love other **b** isn't God's child.
3:14 because we love other **b**.
3:16 must give our lives for other **b**.
4:20 People who don't love other **b**,
4:21 God must also love other **b**.
3Jn 1:3 I was very happy when some **b**
1:5 in whatever you do for other **b**,
1:6 These **b** have told the
1:8 We must support **b** who go on
1:10 He also refuses to accept the **b**
Jud 1:12 meals you share with other **b**.

believers' (1)

1Ti 5:10 taking care of **b** needs, helping

believes (24)

Pro 14:15 A gullible person **b** anything,
Isa 28:16 Whoever **b** ⌊in him⌋ will not
Mar 9:23 possible for the person who **b**."
11:23 who doesn't doubt but **b** what
16:16 Whoever **b** and is baptized will
Jon 3:15 Then everyone who **b** in him
3:16 Son so that everyone who **b**
3:36 Whoever **b** in the Son has
6:35 and whoever **b** in me will never
7:38 the person who **b** in me.'"
11:26 Everyone who lives and **b** in
12:44 "Whoever **b** in me believes not
12:44 "Whoever believes in me **b** not
12:46 world so that everyone who **b**
Act 13:39 However, everyone who **b** in
Rom 1:16 power to save everyone who **b**,
3:22 Everyone who **b** has God's
9:33 Whoever **b** in him will not be
10:11 Scripture says, "Whoever **b** in
Php 4:21 Greet everyone who **b** in Christ
Jas 2:24 not only because of what he **b**.
1Pe 2:6 and the person who **b** in him
1Jn 5:1 Everyone who **b** that Jesus is
5:5 Isn't it the person who **b** that

believing (13)

Luk 1:45 You are blessed for **b** that the
Jon 12:11 the Jews and **b** in Jesus.
20:31 you will have life by **b** in him.
Act 26:18 who are made holy by **b** in me.'
Rom 4:16 by **b** as Abraham did.
10:10 By **b** you receive God's
1Co 13:7 being patient, never stops **b**,
Gal 2:16 but only by **b** in Jesus Christ.
2:20 The life I now live I live by **b** in
3:2 or by **b** what you heard?
3:5 or through **b** what you heard?
3:26 children by **b** in Christ Jesus.
Rev 14:13 From now on those who die **b**

belittles (2)

Job 38:2 "Who is this that **b** my advice
42:3 "⌊You said,⌋ 'Who is this that **b**

bell (2)

Exo 28:34 a gold **b** alternating with a
39:26 A gold **b** alternated with a

bellies (2)

Psa 17:14 You fill their **b** with your
Pro 13:25 but the **b** of wicked people are

bellows (1)

Jer 6:29 The **b** of the blast furnace blow

bells (4)

Exo 28:33 yarn with gold **b** in between —
28:35 The sound of the **b** must be
39:25 They made **b** out of pure gold
Zec 14:20 LORD" will be written on the **b**

belly (12)

Gen 3:14 You will crawl on your **b**.
Lev 11:42 many legs that goes on its **b**
Jdg 3:21 and plunged it into Eglon's **b**.
2Sm 2:23 The spear went into his **b** and
3:27 he stabbed Abner in the **b**.
4:6 they stabbed him in the **b**.
Job 20:14 the food in his **b** turns sour.
20:23 Let that misery fill his **b**.
31:15 in my mother's **b** make them?
32:19 My **b** is like ⌊a bottle of⌋ wine
Jer 51:34 He has filled his **b** with our
Mat 12:40 Just as Jonah was in the **b** of

belong (141)

Gen 20:7 you and all who **b** to you are
32:17 'To whom do you **b**,
32:18 they **b** to your servant Jacob.
38:9 descendant wouldn't **b** to him,
45:11 and all who **b** to you won't lose
47:26 the priests didn't **b** to Pharaoh.
Exo 21:4 the wife and her children **b** to
29:27 They both **b** to Aaron and his
29:29 "Aaron's holy clothes will **b** to
Lev 2:3 rest of the grain offering will **b**
5:13 The offering will **b** to the priest
7:7 Both offerings **b** to the priest to
7:14 It will **b** to the priest who
7:31 However, the breast will **b** to
7:33 the right thigh will **b** to him as
10:15 These parts will **b** to you and
23:20 will be holy and will **b** to the
24:9 The bread will **b** to Aaron and
25:55 "The Israelites **b** to me as
Num 5:9 to the priest will **b** to the priest.
5:10 person's holy offerings will **b**
5:10 to the priest will **b** to the priest."
6:20 They are holy and **b** to the
18:9 as a most holy offering will **b**
Dtr 7:6 who **b** to the LORD your God.
9:26 They **b** to you. You saved them
9:29 They **b** to you. You used your
10:14 and everything it contains **b**
20:15 that are far away which don't **b**
21:15 and the firstborn son might **b** to
22:1 or sheep out where it doesn't **b**,
29:29 They **b** to the LORD our God.
29:29 revealed in these teachings **b**
33:4 They **b** to the assembly of
33:8 "Your Thummim and Urim **b** to
Jos 6:19 bronze and iron are holy and **b**
13:2 includes all the districts that **b**
15:12 Judah that **b** to their families.
17:9 These cities **b** to Ephraim,
18:21 cities with their villages that **b**
Jdg 11:31 safely from Ammon will **b**
1Sm 30:13 "To whom do you **b**?
Neh 5:5 and vineyards **b** to others."
Job 25:2 "Authority and terror **b** to God.
Psa 28:9 and bless those who **b** to you.
30:4 faithful people who **b** to him.
34:9 you holy people who **b** to him.
47:9 rulers of the earth **b** to God.
82:8 all the nations **b** to you.
94:5 those who **b** to you suffer.
94:14 or abandon those who **b** to him.
106:5 with the people who **b** to you.
Pro 16:1 plans of the heart **b** to humans,
16:11 Honest balances and scales **b**
23:10 or enter fields that **b** to orphans,
Isa 23:18 Her merchandise will **b** to
44:5 will say, "I **b** to the LORD."

Isa 45:14 They will **b** to you.
47:6 dishonored those who **b** to me.
63:17 are the tribes that **b** to you.
Jer 5:10 they don't **b** to the LORD.
14:10 keep their feet where they **b**.
32:8 of the closest relative **b** to you.
50:11 looted the people who **b** to me.
Eze 18:4 and their children **b** to me.
35:10 along with their land, **b** to us.
36:2 worship sites now **b** to us.'"
44:28 The priests **b** to me.
44:29 to the LORD will **b** to them.
45:4 This holy part of the land will **b**
45:5 and 17,500 feet wide will **b**
45:6 It will **b** to all the people of
45:8 This land will **b** to the prince in
46:16 The gift will **b** to his
46:17 The gift will **b** to the servant
48:10 This holy area will **b** to the
48:11 that has been set apart will **b**
48:21 area and the city property will **b**
48:21 These areas **b** to the prince,
48:22 boundaries will **b** to the prince.
Hos 5:7 their children do not **b** to him.
Joe 2:17 Don't let the people who **b** to
3:2 the people who **b** to me,
Oba 1:21 kingdom will **b** to the LORD."
Mic 7:14 the sheep that **b** to you.
Hab 1:6 of lands that don't **b** to them.
3:6 The ancient paths **b** to him.
Zep 2:7 The coast will **b** to the faithful
2:10 they insulted the people who **b**
Mal 2:15 Your flesh and spirit **b** to him.
Mat 13:38 good seeds are those who **b**
13:38 The weeds are those who **b** to
Mar 9:41 of water to drink because you **b**
Jon 8:47 because you don't **b** to God."
13:8 you don't **b** to me."
17:14 them because they don't **b**
17:14 any more than I **b** to the world.
17:16 They don't **b** to the world any
17:16 any more than I **b** to the world.
18:36 "My kingdom doesn't **b** to this
Act 27:23 angel from the God to whom I **b**
Rom 1:6 called to **b** to Jesus Christ.)
7:4 You **b** to someone else,
8:9 Spirit of Christ doesn't **b** to him.
11:24 onto the olive tree they **b** to?
13:12 get rid of the things that **b**
13:12 the weapons that **b** to the light.
14:8 we live or die, we **b** to the Lord.
16:10 Greet those who **b** to the family
16:11 Greet those Christians who **b**
1Co 2:6 It is a wisdom that doesn't **b** to
3:23 You **b** to Christ, and Christ
6:19 You don't **b** to yourselves.
9:18 way I won't use the rights that **b**
15:23 those who **b** to him ⌊will be
2Co 10:7 note that we also **b** to Christ.
Gal 3:29 If you **b** to Christ, then you are
5:24 Those who **b** to Christ Jesus
Eph 1:14 until we are set free to **b** to him.
3:6 They **b** to the same body and
6:6 like slaves who **b** to Christ,
Col 1:10 kind of lives that prove you **b**
1Th 2:12 live in a way that proves you **b**
5:5 You **b** to the day and the light
5:8 Since we **b** to the day,
1Ti 1:17 Worship and glory **b** forever to
6:16 Honor and power **b** to him
2Ti 2:19 knows those who **b** to him,"
Heb 10:39 We don't **b** with those who turn
10:39 Instead, we **b** with those who
1Pe 2:9 people who **b** to God.
4:11 Glory and power **b** to Jesus
1Jn 3:19 is how we will know that we **b**
4:4 Dear children, you **b** to God.
4:5 These people **b** to the world.
4:6 We **b** to God. The person who
4:6 Whoever doesn't **b** to God
3Jn 1:6 way that proves you **b** to God.
Jud 1:25 and authority **b** to the only God,
Rev 1:5 and power forever and ever **b**
19:1 and power **b** to our God.

belonged (44)

Gen 30:42 So the weaker ones **b** to Laban
31:1 has taken everything that **b**
31:21 in a hurry with all that **b** to him.
36:24 care of the donkeys that **b**
Num 3:21 To Gershon **b** the families
3:27 To Kohath **b** the families
3:33 To Merari **b** the families
16:33 with everything that **b** to them.
27:1 **b** to the families of Manasseh,
Jos 17:6 while Gilead **b** to Manasseh's
21:40 All these cities **b** to the
Jdg 6:11 the oak tree in Ophrah that **b**
18:28 city was in the valley that **b**
19:14 (Gibeah **b** to the tribe of
Rut 2:3 part of the field that **b** to Boaz,
4:3 is selling the field that **b** to our
4:9 bought from Naomi all that **b**
4:9 to Elimelech and all that **b**
1Sm 2:14 fork brought up ⌊from the pot⌋ **b**
2Sm 8:7 took the gold shields that **b**
9:9 grandson everything that **b**
16:4 "In that case everything that **b**
1Ki 7:51 the holy things that had **b**
2Ki 9:21 found him in the field that **b**
9:25 throw him into the field that **b**
11:10 and the shields that had **b**
12:16 It **b** to the priests.
24:7 This territory had **b** to the king
2Ch 5:1 the holy things that had **b**
23:9 and large shields that had **b**
26:23 a field containing tombs that **b**
Ezr 5:14 gold and silver utensils that **b**
6:5 gold and silver utensils that **b**
Neh 13:5 These things **b** by law to the
Psa 78:62 with those who **b** to him.
78:71 the people who **b** to the LORD.
106:40 with those who **b** to him.
Eze 16:20 and daughters, who **b** to me,
Luk 1:5 who **b** to the division of priests
5:3 Jesus got into the boat that **b**
Jon 17:6 They **b** to you, and you gave
18:36 If my kingdom **b** to this world,
Act 6:9 They **b** to a synagogue called
27:1 His name was Julius, and he **b**

belonging (27)

Gen 12:6 the land to the oak tree **b**
13:18 went to live by the oak trees **b**
14:13 living next to the oak trees **b**
18:1 to Abraham by the oak trees **b**
Exo 9:4 No animals **b** to the Israelites
Lev 25:31 without walls are regarded as **b**
27:23 something holy, **b** to the LORD.
Dtr 11:23 of ⌊the land **b** to⌋ people taller
Jdg 8:32 the city **b** to Abiezer's family.
11:15 didn't take away the land **b**
1Sm 6:18 the number of Philistine cities **b**
9:3 When some donkeys **b** to
30:29 Racal, the cities **b** to the
30:29 the cities **b** to the Kenites,
1Ki 21:7 I'll give you the vineyard **b** to
2Ki 10:33 of Gilead (the territory **b** to
1Ch 6:56 but the fields **b** to the city and
9:16 villages **b** to the Netophathites).
28:1 all the property and livestock **b**
2Ch 31:15 served under him in the cities **b**
Ezr 1:7 brought out the utensils **b**
Pro 24:30 the vineyard **b** to a person
Sos 4:4 A thousand round shields **b** to
Eze 45:7 on both sides of the property **b**
48:12 to the land **b** to the Levites.
48:13 Alongside the land **b** to the
48:13 to the priests will be the land **b**

belongings (7)

Gen 45:20 Don't worry about your **b**
1Sm 14:32 troops seized the Philistines' **b**.
15:19 Why have you taken their **b**
15:21 The army took some of their **b**
Isa 10:6 the people to take their **b**,
Eze 22:25 their treasures and precious **b**.
Luk 17:31 come down to get their **b** out

belongs (98)

Gen 31:16 took away from our father **b**
47:26 ⌊of the produce⌋ **b** to Pharaoh.
Exo 9:29 that the earth **b** to the LORD.
13:12 of your animals **b** to the LORD.
20:17 or anything else that **b** to him."
Lev 2:10 The rest of the grain offering **b**
3:16 All the fat **b** to the LORD.
7:8 The skin of the burnt offering **b**
7:9 **b** to the priest who offers it.
10:13 by fire to the LORD that **b**
14:13 offering for sin, **b** to the priest.
25:30 the house in the city **b** to the
25:34 But a field that **b** to their cities
27:24 to whom it **b** as family property.
27:26 "A firstborn animal already **b** to
27:26 or a sheep, it **b** to the LORD.
27:28 or a field that **b** to you — must
27:28 is very holy. It **b** to the LORD.
27:30 is holy and **b** to the LORD.
27:32 is holy and **b** to the LORD.
Num 16:5 LORD will show who **b** to him,
16:26 touch anything that **b** to them,
16:30 and everything that **b** to them,
18:9 which is not burned **b** to you.
Dtr 5:21 or anything else that **b** to him."
Jos 6:17 Everything in it **b** to the LORD.
13:4 as well as Mearah which **b**
17:8 of Tappuah **b** to Manasseh,
17:8 of Manasseh, **b** to Ephraim.)
17:10 ⌊of the river⌋ **b** to Ephraim,
17:10 is north ⌊of it⌋ **b** to Manasseh.
Jdg 6:24 which **b** to Abiezer's family.
17:7 (Bethlehem **b** to the family of
1Sm 27:6 (This is why Ziklag still **b** to
2Sm 16:4 to Mephibosheth now **b** to you."
20:19 up what **b** to the LORD?"
21:3 bless what **b** to the LORD?"
1Ki 17:9 Zarephath (which **b** to Sidon),
22:3 that Ramoth in Gilead **b** to us,
2Ch 26:18 That right **b** to the priests,
Job 41:11 under heaven **b** to me!
Psa 3:8 Victory **b** to the LORD!
22:28 because the kingdom **b** to the
61:5 given me the inheritance that **b**
62:11 ⌊said⌋ twice: "Power **b** to God.
62:12 Mercy **b** to you, O Lord.
79:1 invaded the land that **b** to you.
89:18 Our shield **b** to the LORD.
89:18 Our king **b** to the Holy One of
103:17 His righteousness **b** to their
115:16 The highest heaven **b** to the
149:9 This is an honor that **b** to all
Pro 12:20 but joy **b** to those who advise
21:31 but the victory **b** to the LORD.
25:6 spot that **b** to notable people,
Jer 10:16 Israel is the tribe that **b** to him.
46:10 That day **b** to the Almighty
51:19 Israel is the tribe that **b** to him.
Eze 18:4 life of every person **b** to me.
Jnh 2:9 Victory **b** to the LORD!"
Mat 5:3 kingdom of heaven **b** to them.
5:10 kingdom of heaven **b** to them.
22:21 give the emperor what **b** to the
22:21 and give God what **b** to God."
Mar 12:17 "Give the emperor what **b** to
12:17 and give God what **b** to God."
Luk 20:25 then give the emperor what **b** to
20:25 and give God what **b** to God."
Jon 3:29 the person to whom the bride **b**.
8:47 The person who **b** to God
18:37 Everyone who **b** to the truth
Act 1:25 to go to the place where he **b**."
2:39 This promise **b** to you and to
2:39 It **b** to everyone who worships
Rom 11:36 Glory **b** to him forever!
16:27 Glory **b** to him through Jesus
1Co 2:12 didn't receive the spirit that **b**
3:21 Everything **b** to you.
3:22 everything **b** to you.
3:23 and Christ **b** to God.
6:19 your body is a temple that **b**
2Co 4:7 power of this treasure **b**
10:7 is confident he **b** to Christ,
Gal 1:5 Glory **b** to our God and Father

Eph 3:20 Glory **b** to God, whose power
3:21 Glory **b** to God in the church
Php 4:20 Glory **b** to our God and Father
Col 2:17 casts the shadow **b** to Christ.
2Ti 4:18 Glory **b** to him forever!
Heb 13:21 Glory **b** to Jesus Christ forever.
Jas 3:15 It **b** to this world.
1Pe 2:7 This honor **b** to those who
5:11 Power **b** to him forever.
2Pe 3:18 Glory **b** to him now and for that
1Jn 3:8 person who lives a sinful life **b**
Rev 7:10 "Salvation **b** to our God,
13:8 That book **b** to the lamb who
17:11 It **b** with the seven kings and

beloved (37)

Dtr 33:12 "The LORD's **b** people will live
2Sm 12:25 baby Jedidiah [The LORD's **B**].
1Ki 20:3 Your **b** wives and children are
Sos 1:13 My **b** is a pouch of myrrh that
1:14 My **b** is a bouquet of henna
1:16 You are handsome, my **b**,
2:3 so is my **b** among the young
2:9 My **b** is like a gazelle or a
2:10 My **b** said to me, "Get up,
2:16 My **b** is mine, and I am his.
2:17 flee, turn around, my **b**.
4:16 Let my **b** come to his garden,
5:2 My **b** is knocking. Open to me,
5:4 My **b** put his hand through the
5:5 I got up to open for my **b**.
5:6 I opened for my **b**, but my
5:6 but my **b** had turned away.
5:8 if you find my **b** you will tell
5:9 what makes your **b** better than
5:9 better than any other **b**?
5:9 What makes your **b** better than
5:9 than any other **b** that you make
5:10 My **b** is dazzling yet ruddy.
5:16 This is my **b**, and this is my
6:1 Where did your **b** go,
6:1 Where did your **b** turn?
6:2 My **b** went to his garden,
6:3 beloved's, and my **b** is mine.
7:9 goes down smoothly to my **b**
7:11 Come, my **b**. Let's go into the
7:13 old things for you alone, my **b**.
8:5 with her arm around her **b**?
8:14 Come away quickly, my **b**.
Isa 5:1 Let me sing a lovesong to my **b**
5:1 My **b** had a vineyard on a fertile
Lam 2:13 comfort you, **b** people of Zion?
Rev 20:9 holy people and the **b** city.

beloved's (3)

Sos 2:8 I hear my **b** voice. Look!
6:3 I am my **b**, and my beloved is
7:10 I am my **b**, and he longs for me.

Belshazzar (6)

Dan 5:1 King **B** threw a large banquet
5:2 **B** ordered that the gold and
5:9 King **B** was terrified,
5:22 "**B**, you are one of You didn't
5:29 Then **B** ordered that Daniel be
5:30 That night King **B** of Babylon

Belshazzar's (2)

Dan 7:1 In **B** first year as king of
8:1 In **B** third year as king,

belt (42)

Exo 12:11 you eat it: with your **b** on,
28:4 priest's turban, and a cloth **b**.
28:8 Make the **b** that is attached to
28:27 just above the **b** of the ephod.
28:28 will attach it just above the **b**
28:39 but the **b** should be
29:5 Use the **b** to tie it on him tightly.
39:5 They made the **b** that is
39:20 just above the **b** of the ephod.
39:21 was attached just above the **b**
39:28 the undergarments and **b** out
39:29 The **b** was embroidered with
Lev 8:7 and fastened the **b** around him.
16:4 must wear a linen **b** and turban.
1Sm 18:4 his sword, his bow, and his **b**.
2Sm 18:11 four ounces of silver and a **b**."
21:16 which he wore on a new **b**,
1Ki 2:5 stained the **b** around his waist
2Ki 1:8 a leather **b** around his waist."
4:29 God told Gehazi, "Put on a **b**,
9:1 He said, "Put on your **b**.
Job 12:21 unbuckles the **b** of the mighty.
Psa 109:19 a **b** he always wears."
Pro 31:17 She puts on strength like a **b**
Isa 11:5 Justice will be the **b** around his
11:5 will be the **b** around his hips.
22:21 robe and fasten it with your **b**.
Jer 13:1 said to me: "Buy a linen **b**.
13:2 So I bought the **b**, as the LORD
13:4 "Take the **b** that you bought,
13:6 and get the **b** from where I told
13:7 I got the **b** from where I had
13:7 Now the **b** was ruined.
13:10 are like this good-for-nothing **b**.
13:11 As a **b** clings to a person's
Dan 10:5 and he had a **b** made of gold
Mat 3:4 a leather **b** around his waist.
Mar 1:6 He wore a leather **b** around his
Act 21:11 During his visit he took Paul's **b**
21:11 up the man who owns this **b**.
Eph 6:14 truth around your waist like a **b**.
Rev 1:13 wore a gold **b** around his waist.

Belteshazzar (10)

Dan 1:7 To Daniel he gave the name **B**.
2:26 (who had been renamed **B**),
4:8 (He had been renamed **B** after
4:9 "**B**, head of the magicians,
4:18 Now you, **B**, tell me its
4:19 **B**) was momentarily stunned.
4:19 I told him, "**B**, don't let the
4:19 **B** answered, "Sir, I wish that
5:12 been renamed **B**) was found
10:1 (who had been renamed **B**).

belts (9)

Exo 28:40 "Also make linen robes, **b**,
29:9 Tie **b** around the waists of
Lev 8:13 fastened their **b** around them,
Job 12:18 He loosens kings' **b** and strips
Pro 31:24 delivers **b** to the merchants.
Isa 3:24 will wear ropes instead of **b**.
5:27 The **b** on their waists aren't
Eze 23:15 The men had **b** around their
Rev 15:6 with gold **b** around their waists.

Benabinadab (1)

1Ki 4:11 **B** had the entire region of Dor.

Benaiah (43)

2Sm 8:18 Jehoiada's son **B** was
20:23 **B**, son of Jehoiada, was in
23:20 **B**, son of Jehoiada, was from
23:21 **B** went to him with a club,
23:22 These are the things that **B**,
23:30 **B** from Pirathon, Hiddai from
1Ki 1:8 **B** (son of Jehoiada),
1:10 Nathan, **B**, the fighting men,
1:26 me or the priest Zadok or **B**,
1:32 and **B**, son of Jehoiada."
1:36 **B**, son of Jehoiada,
1:38 **B** (son of Jehoiada),
1:44 **B** (son of Jehoiada),
2:25 Solomon gave this task to **B**,
2:25 **B** attacked and killed Adonijah.
2:29 of the LORD, Solomon sent **B**,
2:30 When **B** came to the tent of the
2:30 So **B** reported to the king what
2:34 Then **B**, son of Jehoiada,
2:35 The king then appointed **B**,
2:46 Then the king gave orders to **B**,
4:4 **B**, son of Jehoiada,
1Ch 4:36 Asaiah, Adiel, Jesimiel, **B**, and
11:22 **B**, son of Jehoiada, was from
11:23 But **B** went to him with a club,
11:24 These are the things that **B**,
11:31 in Benjamin, **B** from Pirathon,
15:18 Eliab, **B**, Maaseiah, Mattithiah,
15:20 and **B** were appointed to play
15:24 Amasai, Zechariah, **B**,
1Ch 16:5 Eliab, **B**, Obed Edom,
16:6 The priests **B** and Jahaziel
18:17 Jehoiada's son **B** was
27:5 during the third month was **B**,
27:6 This **B** was one of the thirty
27:14 **B**, a member of the tribe of
27:34 Jehoiada (son of **B**) and
2Ch 20:14 of Zechariah, grandson of **B**,
31:13 and **B** to serve under Conaniah
Ezr 10:25 Eleazar, Malchiah, and **B**
10:30 **B**, Maaseiah, Mattaniah,
10:35 **B**, Bedeiah, Cheluhi,
10:43 Zebina, Jaddai, Joel, and **B**

Benaiah's (2)

Eze 11:1 Jaazaniah and **B** son Pelatiah.
11:13 **B** son Pelatiah died.

Ben Ammi (1)

Gen 19:38 birth to a son and named him **B**.

bend (11)

Gen 49:15 he will **b** his back to the burden
2Sm 22:35 for battle so that my arms can **b**
1Ki 8:58 May he **b** our hearts toward
Psa 11:2 Wicked people **b** their bows.
18:34 for battle so that my arms can **b**
37:14 their swords and **b** their bows
144:5 O LORD, **b** your heaven low,
Pro 29:1 A person who will not **b** after
Jer 51:3 Have the archers **b** their bows.
Zec 9:13 I will **b** Judah as my bow and
Mar 1:7 I am not worthy to **b** down and

Bendeker (1)

1Ki 4:9 **B**, who was in charge of

bending (1)

Psa 7:12 By **b** his bow, he makes it

bends (1)

Psa 113:6 He **b** down to look at heaven

Bene Berak (1)

Jos 19:45 Jehud, **B**, Gath Rimmon,

benefit (20)

Jdg 17:3 to the LORD for my son's **b**.
Neh 13:31 me, my God, for my **b**."
Job 35:3 'What **b** is it to you?'
Pro 5:10 or strangers will **b** from your
Hab 2:18 "What **b** is there in a carved
2:18 What **b** is there in a molded
Zec 7:6 didn't you do it to **b** yourselves?
Jon 12:30 wasn't for my **b** but for yours.
Act 24:2 and reforms that **b** the people.
1Co 7:35 I'm saying this for your **b**,
9:10 he speaking entirely for our **b**?
9:10 This was written for our **b** so
9:11 seed that has been of **b** to you,
2Co 1:15 you so that you could **b** twice.
2:10 presence of Christ for your **b**.
12:19 do, dear friends, is for your **b**.
Gal 5:2 Christ will be of no **b** to you.
1Ti 6:2 those who receive the **b**
Tit 2:11 appeared for the **b** of all people.
1Pe 1:12 spoken were not for their own **b**

benefits (1)

Gal 5:1 we may enjoy the **b** of freedom.

Bene Hashem (1)

1Ch 11:34 **B** from Gizon, Jonathan

Bene Jaakan (2)

Num 33:31 and set up camp at **B**.
33:32 They moved from **B** and set up

Bene Jashen (1)

2Sm 23:32 Elihba from Shaalbon, **B**,

Bengeber (1)

1Ki 4:13 **B** was in charge of Ramoth

Ben Hadad (1)

Amo 1:4 down the palaces of **B**.

Benhadad (29)

1Ki 15:18 to Damascus to Aram's King B,
15:20 B did what King Asa requested.
20:1 King B of Aram gathered
20:2 "This is what B says:
20:5 But B sent messengers back
20:5 They said, "B has sent this
20:10 Then B sent Ahab the
20:12 B heard this as he and his
20:16 They attacked at noon, when B
20:17 B had sent men ⌊to watch the
20:20 King B of Aram escaped on a
20:23 the officers of King B of Aram
20:26 Spring came, and B organized
20:30 B had also fled. He came to the
20:32 "Your servant B says,
20:33 "B is your brother,"
20:33 When B arrived, Ahab had him
20:34 B told him, "I will give back the
20:34 So Ahab made a treaty with B
2Ki 6:24 Later King B of Aram
8:7 King B of Aram, who was sick,
8:9 "Your humble servant King B of
8:14 and went to his master B,
13:3 and Hazael's son B as long as
13:24 and his son B succeeded him
13:25 reconquered the cities that B
13:25 Jehoash defeated B three
2Ch 16:2 to Damascus to Aram's King B.
16:4 B did what King Asa requested.

Benhadad's (2)

1Ki 20:9 Ahab told B messengers, "Tell
Jer 49:27 and burn down B palaces.

Ben Hail (1)

2Ch 17:7 he sent his officers B,

Ben Hanan (1)

1Ch 4:20 Amnon, Rinnah, B, and Tilon.

Benhesed (1)

1Ki 4:10 B, who was in charge of

Ben Hinnom (10)

Jos 15:8 It continues up the valley of B
18:16 overlooks the valley of B,
2Ki 23:10 in the valley of B unclean so
2Ch 28:3 sacrifices in the valley of B
33:6 in the valley of B,
Jer 7:31 in the valley of B
7:32 or the valley of B.
19:2 Go to the valley of B at
19:6 or the valley of B.
32:35 In the valley of B they

Benhur (1)

1Ki 4:8 Their names were B,

Beninu (1)

Neh 10:13 Hodiah, Bani, and B.

Benjamin (173)

Gen 35:18 but his father named him B
35:24 of Rachel were Joseph and B.
42:4 send Joseph's brother B
42:36 and now you want to take B.
43:14 other brother and B ⌊home⌋
43:15 twice as much money, and B.
43:16 Joseph saw B with them,
43:29 he saw his brother B,
45:12 "You and my brother B can see
45:14 his arms around his brother B
45:14 Benjamin and cried with B,
45:22 but he gave B three hundred
46:19 Rachel were Joseph and B.
46:21 The sons of B were Bela,
49:27 "B is a ravenous wolf.
Exo 1:3 Issachar, Zebulun, and B;
Num 1:11 from the tribe of B;
1:36 for the descendants of B listed
1:37 for the tribe of B was 35,400.
2:22 "Then ⌊will be⌋ the tribe of B.
2:22 for the people of B is Abidan,
7:60 leader of the descendants of B,
Num 10:24 commanded the army of B.
13:9 from the tribe of B;
26:38 The families descended from B
26:41 the families descended from B.
34:21 from the tribe of B;
Dtr 27:12 Issachar, Joseph, and B.
33:12 About the tribe of B he said,
Jos 18:11 for the families of the tribe of B.
18:20 given to B for its families.
18:21 that belong to the tribe of B
21:4 tribes of Judah, Simeon, and B.
21:17 The tribe of B also gave them
Jdg 1:21 The men of B did not force out
1:21 tribe of B in Jerusalem today.
3:15 man from the tribe of B.
5:14 B came with its troops after
10:9 of Judah, B, and Ephraim.
19:14 belonged to the tribe of B.)
19:16 there were from the tribe of B.
20:3 The people of B heard that
20:4 and I went to Gibeah in B
20:10 territory of B they can punish
20:12 men throughout the tribe of B.
20:13 But the men of B refused to
20:14 So the men of B went from their
20:17 The men of Israel (B not
20:18 "Who will go first to fight B?"
20:20 went to war with the men of B.
20:21 That day the men of B came
20:23 close relatives, the men of B?"
20:24 troops advanced against B.
20:25 B went out from Gibeah to
20:28 close relatives, the men of B?
20:30 went to fight the men of B.
20:31 The men of B went out to
20:32 The men of B shouted,
20:35 men from B who were armed
20:36 Then the men of B realized
20:36 had allowed the men of B
20:39 The men of B had already
20:40 the men of B turned around and
20:41 and the men of B panicked.
20:42 caught up with the men of B.
20:43 They closed in on the men of B
20:44 men from B who died
20:46 In all, 25,000 men from B who
20:48 the rest of the territory of B.
21:1 marry anyone from B."
21:6 close relatives, the men of B.
21:13 the men of B at Rimmon Rock
21:14 So the men of B came back at
21:15 felt sorry for the people of B
21:16 women in B have been killed?"
21:18 wives to the men of B is under
21:20 So they told the men of B,
21:21 go back to the territory of B.
21:23 The men of B did just that.
1Sm 4:12 A man from the tribe of B ran
9:1 the tribe of B whose name was
9:1 a descendant of B.
9:4 went through the territory of B
9:16 a man from the territory of B.
9:21 "I am a man from the tribe of B,
9:21 all the families of the tribe of B.
10:2 on the border of B at Zelzah.
10:20 the tribe of B was chosen.
10:21 When he had the tribe of B
13:2 with Jonathan at Gibeah in B.
13:15 from Gilgal to Gibeah in B,
13:16 them stayed at Geba in B while
14:16 at Gibeah in B could see
22:7 "Listen here, men of B!
2Sm 2:9 and B, that is, all Israel.
2:15 Twelve were from the tribe of B
2:25 The men of B rallied behind
2:31 of B under Abner's command.
3:19 specifically to the people of B.
3:19 entire tribe of B had approved.
4:2 Beeroth from the tribe of B.
4:2 was considered a part of B,
19:16 Gera's son from the tribe of B
19:17 One thousand people from B
20:1 from the tribe of B happened to
21:14 son Jonathan in the land of B,
23:29 (son of Ribai) from Gibeah in B,
1Ki 2:8 son of Gera from Bahurim in B,
1Ki 4:18 was in charge of B.
12:21 of Judah and the tribe of B,
12:23 all the people of Judah and B,
15:22 to fortify Geba in B and Mizpah.
1Ch 2:2 Dan, Joseph, B, Naphtali, Gad,
6:60 From the tribe of B,
6:65 tribes of Judah, Simeon, and B.
7:6 B had three sons: Bela, Becher,
7:10 Bilhan's sons were Jeush, B,
8:1 B was the father of Bela (his
9:3 B, Ephraim, and Manasseh:
9:7 From the descendants of B
11:31 (son of Ribai) from Gibeah in B,
12:2 ⌊from the tribe of⌋ B.
12:16 Some of the men of B and
21:6 Joab didn't include Levi and B
27:12 of the tribe of B from Anathoth,
27:21 of Zechariah for the tribe of B:
2Ch 11:1 the people of Judah and B,
11:3 and all Israel in Judah and B.
11:10 fortified cities in Judah and B.
11:12 held on to Judah and B.
11:23 in every region of Judah and B,
15:2 all you men from Judah and B.
15:8 idols from all of Judah, B,
15:9 all the people from Judah and B
16:6 to fortify Geba in B and Mizpah.
17:17 From B there was the fighting
25:5 for all of Judah and B.
31:1 B, Ephraim, and Manasseh.
34:9 in the tribes of Judah and B,
34:32 found in Jerusalem and B join
Ezr 1:5 of the families of Judah and B,
4:1 of Judah and B heard that
10:9 and B gathered within three
10:32 B, Malluch, and Shemariah
Neh 3:23 After them B and Hasshub
11:4 of Judah and of B settled
11:7 are the descendants of B:
11:36 in Judah were assigned to B.
12:34 Judah, B, Shemaiah,
Est 2:5 the tribe of B named Mordecai.
Psa 68:27 B, the youngest, is leading
80:2 Appear in front of Ephraim, B,
Jer 1:1 Anathoth in the territory of B.
6:1 "Take cover, people of B!
17:26 from the territory of B,
20:2 at Upper B Gate that was
32:8 Anathoth in the territory of B.
32:44 will happen in the territory of B,
33:13 in the territory of B,
37:12 and go to the territory of B
37:13 But when he came to B Gate,
38:7 to be sitting at B Gate.
38:8 spoke to the king at B Gate.
Eze 48:23 B will have one part of the land.
48:24 part of the land and border B
48:32 Gate, B Gate, and Dan Gate.
Hos 5:8 you descendants of B.
Oba 1:19 and ⌊the descendants of⌋ B
Zec 14:10 from B Gate to the place of
Act 13:21 from the tribe of B.
Rom 11:1 of Abraham from the tribe of B.
Php 3:5 I'm from the tribe of B.
Rev 7:8 from the tribe of B were sealed.

Benjaminite (1)

2Sm 16:11 shouldn't this B do this?

Benjaminites (1)

2Ch 14:8 and 280,000 B who were armed

Benjamin's (11)

Gen 43:34 but B portion was five times
44:12 The cup was found in B sack
Jos 18:28 This is B inheritance for its
Jdg 20:15 with swords came from B cities
20:34 But B men didn't realize their
21:17 Some said, "B men who
1Ch 8:40 these men were B descendants
12:29 From B descendants, Saul's
Neh 11:8 of B descendants⌋ totaled 928.
11:31 B descendants live in the area
Eze 48:22 and B boundaries will belong

Benob (1)
2Sm 21:16 of Haraphah named **B**,

Benoni (1)
Gen 35:18 she named her son **B** [Son of

bent (14)
Psa 35:14 I was **b** over as if I were
38:6 I am **b** over and bowed down
145:14 of those who are **b** over.
146:8 of those who are **b** over.
Ecc 1:15 one can straighten what is **b**.
7:13 straighten what God has **b**?
Lam 2:4 Like an enemy he **b** his bow.
Hos 11:4 I **b** down and fed them.
Luk 4:39 He **b** over her, ordered the fever
24:12 He **b** down to look inside and
Jon 8:6 Jesus **b** down and used his
8:8 Then he **b** down again and
20:5 He **b** over and looked inside
20:11 she **b** over and looked inside.

Ben Zoheth (1)
1Ch 4:20 Ishi's sons were Zoheth and **B**

Beon (1)
Num 32:3 Elealeh, Sebam, Nebo, and **B**,

Beor (11)
Gen 36:32 Bela, son of **B**, ruled Edom.
Num 22:5 son of **B**, who was at Pethor,
24:3 message of Balaam, son of **B**.
24:15 message of Balaam, son of **B**.
31:8 Balaam, son of **B**, in battle.
Dtr 23:4 even hired Balaam, son of **B**,
Jos 13:22 also killed Balaam, son of **B**,
24:9 Balaam, son of **B**, to curse you.
1Ch 1:43 people of Israel: Bela, son of **B**,
Mic 6:5 son of **B**, responded to him.
2Pe 2:15 the path of Balaam, son of **B**.

Bera (1)
Gen 14:2 kings⌋ — King **B** of Sodom,

Beracah (3)
1Ch 12:3 **B** and Jehu from Anathoth,
2Ch 20:26 in the valley of **B** [Thanks].
20:26 called the valley of **B** today.

Beraiah (1)
1Ch 8:21 Adaiah, **B**, and Shimrath.

Berea (6)
Act 17:10 Paul and Silas to the city of **B**.
17:10 Silas arrived in the city of **B**,
17:11 The people of **B** were more
17:13 spreading God's word in **B**,
17:14 Silas and Timothy stayed in **B**.
20:4 (son of Pyrrhus) from **B**,

Berechiah (8)
1Ch 3:20 Hashubah, Ohel, **B**, Hasadiah,
6:39 He was the son of **B**,
9:16 and **B** (son of Asa and
15:23 **B** and Elkanah were
2Ch 28:12 **B**, son of Meshillemoth,
Neh 3:4 son of **B** and grandson of
Zec 1:1 who was the son of **B** and the
1:7 who was the son of **B** and the

Berechiah's (3)
1Ch 15:17 they appointed Asaph, **B** son.
Neh 3:30 After him Meshullam, **B** son,
6:18 daughter of Meshullam, **B** son

Bered (2)
Gen 16:14 there between Kadesh and **B**.
1Ch 7:20 Shuthelah's son was **B**.

Bered's (1)
1Ch 7:20 **B** son was Tahath.

Beri (1)
1Ch 7:36 Harnepher, Shual, **B**, Imrah,

Beriah (9)
Gen 46:17 Imnah, Ishvah, Ishvi, and **B**.
46:17 The sons of **B** were Heber and
Num 26:44 and the family of **B**.
26:45 The descendants **B** were the
1Ch 7:23 named him **B** [Tragedy],
7:30 Imnah, Ishvah, Ishvi, and **B**.
8:13 **B** and Shema were the heads
23:10 Jahath, Zina, Jeush, and **B**.
23:11 Jeush and **B** didn't have many

Beriah's (4)
1Ch 7:24 **B** daughter was Sheerah,
7:25 **B** son was Rephah.
7:31 **B** sons were Heber and
8:15 **B** sons were Zebadiah,

Berites (1)
2Sm 20:14 All the **B** were gathered

Bernice (3)
Act 25:13 Later King Agrippa and **B** came
25:23 The next day Agrippa and **B**
26:30 The king, the governor, **B**,

Beroth (1)
1Ch 11:39 from Ammon, Naharai from **B**,

Berothah (1)
Eze 47:16 **B** and Sibraim, which are

Berothai (1)
2Sm 8:8 of bronze from Betah and **B**,

beryl (7)
Exo 28:20 In the fourth row put **b**,
39:13 In the fourth row they put **b**,
Eze 1:16 They looked like **b**.
10:9 The wheels looked like **b**.
28:13 **b**, onyx, gray quartz, sapphire,
Dan 10:6 His body was like **b**.
Rev 21:20 the eighth **b**, the ninth topaz,

Besai (2)
Ezr 2:49 Uzza, Paseah, **B**,
Neh 7:52 **B**, Meunim, Nephusheshim,

Besodeiah's (1)
Neh 3:6 **B** son, made repairs on Old

Besor (3)
1Sm 30:9 600 men went to the **B** Valley,
30:10 the **B** Valley stayed behind.
30:21 and had stayed in the **B** Valley.

best (139)
Gen 4:12 no longer yield its **b** for you.
18:7 and took one of his **b** calves.
23:6 dead in one of our **b** tombs.
24:10 him all of his master's **b** things.
43:11 Put some of the **b** products of
45:18 I will give you the **b** land in
45:18 Then you can enjoy the **b** food
45:20 your belongings because the **b**
45:23 carrying Egypt's **b** products
47:6 your brothers live in the **b** part
47:11 his brothers live in the **b** part
49:11 his colt to the **b** vine.
Exo 14:7 He took 600 of his **b** chariots
15:4 Pharaoh's **b** officers were
22:5 loss with the **b** from his field
22:29 "Never withhold your **b** wine
23:19 "You must bring the **b** of the
34:26 "You must bring the first and **b**
Lev 23:40 the first day take the **b** fruits,
Num 13:20 Do your **b** to bring back some
18:12 the **b** of all the olive oil and the
18:12 of all the olive oil and the **b**
18:29 you must contribute the **b** and
18:30 When you contribute the **b** part,
18:32 When you contribute the **b** part,
24:7 will be considered the **b**.
Dtr 12:11 and all the **b** offerings you vow
13:6 or your **b** friend may secretly
23:16 your cities that seems **b** to him.
Dtr 32:14 male goats, and the **b** wheat.
33:13 the **b** gift heaven can send,
33:14 the **b** gift the sun can give,
33:14 the **b** produce of each month,
33:15 the **b** from the ancient hills,
33:21 They chose the **b** land for
Jos 1:14 However, all your **b** soldiers
8:3 Joshua picked 30,000 of his **b**
10:7 all his soldiers and **b** warriors,
Jdg 3:29 of Moab's **b** fighting men.
9:2 'What seems **b** to you?
14:20 wife was given to his **b** man.
15:2 So I gave her to your **b** man.
15:6 and gave her to his **b** man."
20:15 with 700 of Gibeah's **b** men.
20:16 the **b** 700 were left-handed.
20:34 Then 10,000 of Israel's **b** men
1Sm 1:23 "Do what you think is **b**," her
2:29 making yourselves fat on the **b**
8:14 He will take the **b** of your fields,
8:16 female slaves, your **b** cattle,
14:36 you think is **b**," they responded.
14:40 "Do whatever you think is **b**,"
15:9 spared Agag and the **b** sheep
15:9 and all the **b** ⌊property⌋.
15:15 They spared the **b** sheep and
15:21 their belongings — the **b** sheep
27:1 The **b** thing for me to do is to
2Sm 6:1 assembled all the **b** soldiers
18:4 "I'll do what you think **b**," the
20:6 take the **b** ones for himself."
1Ki 12:21 180,000 of the **b** soldiers,
2Ki 7:1 24 cups of the **b** flour will sell
7:16 Then 24 cups of the **b** flour
7:18 And twenty-four cups of the **b**
8:12 kill their **b** young men,
10:3 choose the **b** and most honest
10:5 Do what you think is **b**."
1Ch 12:14 and the **b** one was in command
2Ch 11:1 180,000 of the **b** soldiers,
13:3 of 400,000 of the **b** soldiers,
13:3 of the **b** professional soldiers.
13:17 and 500 of the **b** men of Israel
25:5 he had 300,000 of the **b** men
36:17 and execute their **b** young men
36:17 He didn't spare the **b** men or the
Neh 5:8 "We have done our **b** to buy
5:16 Instead, I put my **b** effort into
10:37 decide who should bring the **b**
Est 2:9 and her servants to the **b** place
8:8 You write what you think is **b**
Psa 37:20 will vanish like the **b** part
47:7 Make your **b** music for him!
55:13 it is you, my equal, my **b** friend,
55:20 ⌊My **b** friend⌋ has betrayed his
78:31 slaughtered the **b** young men
78:63 consumed his **b** young men,
90:10 But the **b** of them ⌊bring⌋
119:24 They are my **b** friends.
Pro 3:9 and with the first and **b** part
Sos 4:13 pomegranates and the **b** fruits,
4:14 and all the **b** spices.
7:9 mouth taste like the **b** wine ...
Isa 1:19 you will eat the **b** from the land.
17:10 Instead, you have planted the **b**
25:6 people a feast with the **b** foods,
25:6 with the **b** foods and the finest
41:21 forward your **b** arguments,"
43:24 or satisfy me with the **b** part
48:17 I teach you what is **b** for you.
55:2 and enjoy the **b** foods.
Jer 2:3 It was the **b** part of the harvest.
2:21 grapevine from the very **b** seed.
Eze 17:21 The **b** of your troops will die in
20:40 for your offerings, your **b** gifts,
24:4 into pieces, all the **b** pieces,
24:5 selected from the **b** sheep.
31:16 the choicest and **b** trees of
34:3 You eat the **b** parts of the
34:14 and they will feed on the **b**
39:18 all the **b** animals of Bashan.
39:19 You can eat the **b** meat until
44:30 The priests should have the **b**
44:30 The **b** of every gift from all your
44:30 The **b** of your dough must go to
48:14 not let others have the **b** part

Dan 4:27 my **b** advice is that you stop
11:15 Even their **b** troops will not be
Amo 4:10 With swords I killed your **b**
Mic 7:4 The **b** of them is like a briar.
Nah 2:5 remembers his **b** fighting men.
3:10 and all her **b** men were bound
3:18 Your **b** fighting men are at rest.
Mat 18:6 It would be **b** for the person
Mar 9:42 It would be **b** for the person
Luk 12:58 do your **b** to settle with him
15:22 Bring out the **b** robe,
17:2 It would be **b** for that person to
Jon 2:10 serves the **b** wine first.
2:10 saved the **b** wine for now."
3:29 The **b** man, who stands and
Act 24:16 this belief I always do my **b**
1Co 12:31 will show you the **b** thing to do.
13:13 But the **b** one of these is love.
Eph 4:3 do your **b** to maintain the unity
Php 1:10 be able to determine what is **b**
1Th 3:1 We thought it **b** to remain in
2Ti 2:15 Do your **b** to present yourself to
Tit 3:13 and Apollos your **b** support
Heb 12:10 us as they thought **b**.

best-trained (2)

1Sm 24:2 Then Saul took 3,000 of the **b**
26:2 with him 3,000 of Israel's **b** men

bet (2)

Job 1:11 I **b** he'll curse you to your face."
2:5 I **b** he'll curse you to your face."

Betah (1)

2Sm 8:8 of bronze from **B** and Berothai,

Beten (1)

Jos 19:25 Helkath, Hali, **B**, Achshaph,

Beth Anath (3)

Jos 19:38 **B**, and Beth Shemeth.
Jdg 1:33 lived at Beth Shemesh or **B**
1:33 Shemesh and **B** were made

Bethanoth (1)

Jos 15:59 Maarath, **B**, and Eltekon were

Bethany (16)

Mat 21:17 and went out of the city to **B**
26:6 Jesus was in **B** in the home of
Mar 11:1 to Bethphage and **B**,
11:11 with the twelve apostles to **B**.
11:12 The next day, when they left **B**,
14:3 Jesus was in **B** at the home of
Luk 19:29 came near Bethphage and **B** at
24:50 took them to a place near **B**.
Jon 1:28 This happened in **B** on the east
11:1 Lazarus, who lived in **B**,
11:11 I'm going to **B** to wake him."
11:18 (**B** was near Jerusalem,
11:54 Instead, he left **B** and went to
12:1 Jesus arrived in **B**.
12:2 was prepared for Jesus in **B**.
12:9 found out that Jesus was in **B**.

Beth Arabah (5)

Jos 15:6 It then passes north to **B**
15:61 villages: **B**, Middin, Secacah,
18:22 **B**, Zemaraim, Bethel,
2Sm 23:31 Abi Albon from **B**,
1Ch 11:32 Abiel from **B**,

Beth Arbel (1)

Hos 10:14 Shalman destroyed **B** in battle

Beth Ashbea (1)

1Ch 4:21 guild of linen workers at **B**,

Beth Aven (7)

Jos 7:2 Ai is near **B**, east of Bethel
18:12 and ends at the desert of **B**
1Sm 13:5 camped at Michmash, east of **B**.
14:23 the battle moved beyond **B**
Hos 4:15 Don't go to **B**.
5:8 Sound the alarm at **B**,
10:5 fear the calf-shaped idol at **B**.

Beth Azmaveth (1)

Neh 7:28 of **B**: 42

Beth Baal Meon (1)

Jos 13:17 Dibon, Bamoth Baal, **B**,

Beth Barah (2)

Jdg 7:24 watering holes as far as **B**
7:24 watering holes as far as **B**

Beth Biri (1)

1Ch 4:31 Hazar Susim, **B**, and Shaaraim.

Beth Car (1)

1Sm 7:11 and killed them as far as **B**.

Beth Dagon (2)

Jos 15:41 Gederoth, **B**, Naamah,
19:27 Then it turns east to **B**

Beth Diblathaim (1)

Jer 48:22 Dibon, Nebo, **B**,

Beth Eden (1)

Amo 1:5 who holds the scepter in **B**.

Beth Eked (2)

2Ki 10:12 When he came to **B**
10:14 42 of them at a cistern near **B**.

Bethel (73)

Gen 12:8 moved on to the hills east of **B**,
12:8 and he put up his tent — with **B**
13:3 from the Negev as far as **B**,
13:3 to the area between **B** and Ai
28:19 He named that place **B** [House
31:13 God who appeared to you at **B**,
35:1 "Go to **B** and live there.
35:3 Then let's go to **B**.
35:6 **B**) in the land of Canaan.
35:8 under the oak tree outside **B**.
35:15 with him **B** [House of God].
35:16 Then they moved on from **B**.
Jos 7:2 Ai is near Beth Aven, east of **B**.
8:9 between **B** and Ai.
8:12 them hide between **B** and Ai,
8:17 Not one man was left in Ai or **B**;
12:9 the king of Ai (near **B**),
12:16 of Makkedah, the king of **B**,
16:1 through the mountains to **B**.
16:2 From **B** the border goes to Luz
18:13 slope of Luz (now called **B**).
18:22 Beth Arabah, Zemaraim, **B**,
Jdg 1:22 also went into battle against **B**,
1:23 They sent men to spy on **B**.
4:5 Deborah between Ramah and **B**
20:18 The men of Israel went to **B**.
20:26 and all the troops went to **B**.
20:27 ark of God's promise was at **B**.
20:31 on the roads to **B** and Gibeah.
21:2 The people went to **B** and sat
21:19 Shiloh is north of **B**,
21:19 going from **B** to Shechem,
1Sm 7:16 year he went around to **B**,
10:3 their way to worship God at **B**:
13:2 and in the mountains of **B**,
30:27 were shares for those in **B**,
1Ki 12:29 He put one in **B** and the other in
12:32 He went to the altar in **B** to
12:32 worship sites ⌊to serve⌋ in **B**.
12:33 He went to his altar in **B** to burn
13:1 God from Judah had come to **B**.
13:4 God condemning the altar in **B**,
13:10 on the road he had taken to **B**.
13:11 An old prophet was living in **B**.
13:11 man of God did in **B** that day
13:32 the LORD against the altar in **B**
16:34 Hiel from **B** rebuilt Jericho.
2Ki 2:2 the LORD is sending me to **B**."
2:2 So they went to **B**.
2:3 of the prophets at **B** came
2:23 From there he went to **B**.
10:29 calves that were at **B** and Dan.
17:28 from Samaria went to live in **B**.
23:4 he carried their ashes to **B**.
23:15 He also tore down the altar at **B**
23:17 these things to the altar of **B**."
23:19 to the worship places at **B**.
1Ch 7:28 descendants were in **B**
2Ch 13:19 **B** and its villages,
Ezr 2:28 of **B** and Ai: 223
Neh 7:32 of **B** and Ai: 123
11:31 **B** and its villages,
Jer 48:13 ashamed when it trusted **B**.
Hos 10:15 is what will happen to you, **B**,
12:4 Jacob found him at **B**,
Amo 3:14 will also destroy the altars at **B**.
4:4 Go to **B** and sin. Go to Gilgal
5:5 But don't search ⌊for me⌋ at **B**.
5:5 **B** will come to nothing.
5:6 **B** will have no one to put it out.
7:10 Then Amaziah, the priest at **B**,
7:13 ⌊ever⌋ prophesy again in **B**,
Zec 7:2 Now, ⌊the people from⌋ **B** sent

Beth Emek (1)

Jos 19:27 north and goes to **B** and Neiel

Bethesda (1)

Jon 5:2 was a pool called **B** in Hebrew.

Beth Ezel (1)

Mic 1:11 **B** is in mourning.

Beth Gadar (1)

1Ch 2:51 who first settled **B**.

Beth Gamul (1)

Jer 48:23 Kiriathaim, **B**, Beth Meon,

Beth Gilgal (1)

Neh 12:29 from **B**, and from the region

Beth Haggan (1)

2Ki 9:27 fled on the road leading to **B**.

Beth Hakkerem (2)

Neh 3:14 charge of the district of **B**.
Jer 6:1 Raise the flag over **B**,

Beth Haram (1)

Jos 13:27 Valley it included **B**,

Beth Haran (1)

Num 32:36 and **B** as walled cities.

Beth Hoglah (3)

Jos 15:6 and goes up to **B**.
18:19 to the north slope of **B**
18:21 Jericho, **B**, Emek Keziz,

Beth Horon (15)

Jos 10:10 that goes to the slope of **B**
10:11 slope of **B** toward Azekah,
16:3 of Japhlet and Lower **B**,
16:5 Ataroth Addar to Upper **B**.
18:13 mountains south of Lower **B**.
18:14 the mountain that faces **B**,
21:22 Kibzaim, and **B**.
1Sm 13:18 turned onto the road to **B**.
1Ki 9:17 rebuilt Gezer, Lower **B**,
1Ch 6:68 **B** with its pastureland,
7:24 who built Upper and Lower **B**
2Ch 8:5 He rebuilt Upper **B** and
8:5 and Lower **B** into cities
2Ch 25:13 Judah from Samaria to **B**.
Neh 13:28 son-in-law of Sanballat from **B**.

Beth Jeshimoth (4)

Num 33:49 Their camp extended from **B**
Jos 12:3 road that goes south from **B**
13:20 slopes of Pisgah, and **B**.
Eze 25:9 the beautiful cities of **B**,

Beth Joab (1)

1Ch 2:54 Atroth, ⌊who first settled⌋ **B**,

Beth Leaphrah (1)

Mic 1:10 Roll in the dust of **B**.

Beth Lebaoth (1)
Jos 19:6 **B**, and Sharuhen.

Bethlehem (56)
Gen 35:19 the way to Ephrath (that is, **B**).
48:7 the way to Ephrath" (that is, **B**).
Jos 19:15 Shimron, Idalah, and **B**.
Jdg 12:8 Ibzan from **B** judged Israel.
12:10 he was buried in **B**.
17:7 a young man from **B** in Judah.
17:7 (**B** belongs to the family of
17:7 a Levite but was living in **B**.
17:8 This man left **B** in Judah to live
17:9 "I'm a Levite from **B** in Judah.
19:1 He took a woman from **B** in
19:2 father's home, to **B** in Judah.
19:18 "We're on our way from **B** in
19:18 I had gone to **B** in Judah.
Rut 1:1 A man from **B** in Judah went
1:2 of Ephrathah from **B**
1:19 went on until they came to **B**.
1:19 When they entered **B**,
1:22 They happened to enter **B** just
2:4 Boaz was coming from **B**,
4:11 make a name for yourself in **B**.
1Sm 16:1 I'm sending you to Jesse in **B**
16:4 When he came to **B**,
16:18 sons from **B** who can play
17:12 and the city of **B** in Judah.
17:15 and forth from Saul's camp to **B**,
17:58 Jesse of **B**," David answered.
20:6 begged me to let him run to **B**,
20:28 begged me ⌊to let him go⌋ to **B**.
2Sm 2:32 him in his father's tomb in **B**.
21:19 son of Jaare Oregim from **B**,
23:14 Philistine troops were at **B**.
23:15 the well at the city gate of **B**."
23:24 Elhanan (son of Dodo) from **B**,
1Ch 2:51 Salma, who first settled **B**,
2:54 ⌊who first settled⌋ **B**,
4:4 who first settled **B**.
11:16 Philistine troops were in **B**.
11:17 cistern at the city gate of **B**."
11:26 Elhanan (son of Dodo) from **B**,
2Ch 11:6 He rebuilt **B**, Etam, Tekoa,
Ezr 2:21 The people of **B**: 123
Neh 7:26 the people of **B** and Netophah:
Jer 41:17 they stayed near **B** at Geruth
Mic 5:2 You, **B** Ephrathah,
Mat 2:1 Jesus was born in **B** in Judea
2:5 They told him, "In **B** in Judea.
2:6 **B** in the land of Judah,
2:8 As he sent them to **B**,
2:16 old and younger in or near **B**.
Luk 2:4 to a Judean city called **B**.
2:4 went to **B** because David had
2:6 While they were in **B**,
2:8 were in the fields near **B**.
2:15 "Let's go to **B** and see what the
Jon 7:42 David and from the village of **B**,

Beth Maacah (3)
2Sm 20:14 tribes of Israel to Abel (**B**).
20:15 attacked him in Abel (**B**).
2Ki 25:23 and Jaazaniah from **B**

Beth Marcaboth (2)
Jos 19:5 Ziklag, **B**, Hazar Susah
1Ch 4:31 **B**, Hazar Susim, Beth Biri

Beth Meon (1)
Jer 48:23 Kiriathaim, Beth Gamul, **B**,

Beth Millo (4)
Jdg 9:6 from Shechem and **B** united.
9:20 citizens of Shechem and **B**.
9:20 citizens of Shechem and **B**
2Ki 12:20 against him and killed him at **B**

Beth Nimrah (2)
Num 32:36 **B**, and Beth Haran as walled
Jos 13:27 Beth Haram, **B**, Succoth,

Beth Pazzez (1)
Jos 19:21 En Gannim, En Haddah, and **B**.

Beth Pelet (2)
Jos 15:27 Hazar Gaddah, Heshmon, **B**,
Neh 11:26 in Jeshua, Moladah, and **B**,

Beth Peor (4)
Dtr 3:29 stayed in the valley near **B**.
4:46 River in the valley near **B**,
34:6 a valley in Moab, near **B**.
Jos 13:20 **B**, the slopes of Pisgah,

Bethphage (3)
Mat 21:1 Jerusalem and had reached **B**
Mar 11:1 Jerusalem, to **B** and Bethany,
Luk 19:29 When he came near **B** and

Beth Rapha (1)
1Ch 4:12 was the first to settle **B**.

Beth Rechab (1)
1Ch 2:55 They first settled **B**.

Beth Rehob (2)
Jdg 18:28 valley that belonged to **B**.
2Sm 10:6 hired the Arameans from **B**

Bethsaida (7)
Mat 11:21 horrible it will be for you, **B**!
Mar 6:45 a boat and cross to **B** ahead
8:22 As they came to **B**,
Luk 9:10 to a city called **B** so that they
10:13 horrible it will be for you, **B**!
Jon 1:44 (Philip was from **B**,
12:21 went to Philip (who was from **B**

Beth Shan (2)
1Sm 31:10 corpse to the wall of **B**.
31:12 sons from the wall of **B**.

Beth Shean (7)
Jos 17:11 Manasseh possessed **B**
17:16 in **B** and its villages,
Jdg 1:27 force out the people of **B**,
2Sm 21:12 the public square of **B**,
1Ki 4:12 and all of **B**.
4:12 from **B** to Abel Meholah
1Ch 7:29 Next to Manasseh were **B**

Beth Shemesh (22)
Jos 15:10 Then it goes down to **B**
19:22 and **B** and ends at the Jordan
21:16 Ain, Juttah, and **B**.
Jdg 1:33 those who lived at **B**
1:33 But the people of **B**
1Sm 6:9 own country toward **B**,
6:12 up the road to **B**.
6:12 to the border of **B**.
6:13 The people of **B**
6:14 field of Joshua of **B**
6:15 The people of **B**
6:18 field of Joshua of **B**.
6:19 of the people from **B**
6:20 people of **B** asked,
1Ki 4:9 Makaz, Shaalbim, **B**,
2Ki 14:11 battle at **B** in Judah.
14:13 at **B** and went to
1Ch 6:59 and **B** with its pasturland
2Ch 25:21 battle at **B** in Judah.
25:23 at **B** and brought him
28:18 began living in **B**,
Jer 43:13 At **B** he will break

Beth Shemeth (1)
Jos 19:38 Beth Anath, and **B**.

Beth Shittah (1)
Jdg 7:22 They fled as far as **B**,

Beth Tappuah (1)
Jos 15:53 Janim, **B**, Aphekah

Beth Togarmah (1)
Eze 27:14 People from **B** exchanged

Bethuel (10)
Gen 22:22 Hazo, Pildash, Jidlaph, and **B**.
22:23 **B** is the father of Rebekah.
24:15 She was the daughter of **B**,
24:24 "I'm the daughter of **B**,
24:47 'The daughter of **B**,
24:50 Laban and **B** answered,
25:20 daughter of **B** the Aramean
28:2 Go to the home of **B**,
28:5 son of **B** the Aramean and
1Ch 4:30 **B**, Hormah, Ziklag,

Bethul (1)
Jos 19:4 Elto Lad, **B**, Hormah,

Beth Zur (3)
1Ch 2:45 who first settled **B**.
2Ch 11:7 **B**, Soco, Adullam,
Neh 3:16 of half the district of **B**,

Bethzur (1)
Jos 15:58 Halhul, **B**, Gedor,

Betonim (1)
Jos 13:26 to Ramath Mizpeh and **B**,

betray (25)
1Sm 19:17 "Why did you **b** me by sending
1Ch 12:17 But if you've come to **b** me to
Job 21:34 answers continue to **b** me?"
Isa 16:3 Don't **b** the refugees.
24:16 Traitors continue to **b**,
Jer 12:6 your father's household **b** you.
Mic 1:14 The town of Achzib will **b** the
Mat 24:10 They will **b** and hate each
26:16 he looked for a chance to **b**
26:21 One of you is going to **b** me."
26:23 the bowl with me will **b** me.
Mar 14:10 went to the chief priests to **b**
14:11 for a chance to **b** Jesus.
14:18 One of you is going to **b** me,
Luk 21:16 and friends will **b** you and kill
22:4 them how he could **b** Jesus.
22:6 for an opportunity to **b** Jesus
22:21 of the one who will **b** me is
22:48 do you intend to **b** the Son of
Jon 6:64 and the one who would **b** him.
6:71 would later **b** Jesus.
12:4 who was going to **b** him,
13:11 knew who was going to **b** him.
13:21 One of you is going to **b** me!"
21:20 who is going to **b** you?"

betrayed (20)
Psa 55:20 best friend⌋ has **b** his friends.
73:15 I would have **b** God's people.
Isa 33:1 although you haven't been **b**.
33:1 being a traitor, you will be **b**.
Jer 3:20 **b** me," declares the LORD.
Lam 1:2 of Jerusalem's friends have **b**
1:19 who love me, but they **b** me.
Mat 10:4 who later **b** Jesus.
17:22 "The Son of Man will be **b** and
20:18 There the Son of Man will be **b**
26:25 Then Judas, who **b** him,
27:3 Then Judas, who had **b** Jesus,
Mar 3:19 and Judas Iscariot (who later **b**
9:31 "The Son of Man will be **b** and
10:33 There the Son of Man will be **b**
Luk 9:44 The Son of Man will be **b** and
Jon 18:2 Judas, who **b** him,
18:5 Judas, who **b** him,
Act 7:52 now become the people who **b**
1Co 11:23 On the night he was **b**,

betraying (4)
Mat 26:46 The one who is **b** me is near."
27:4 He said, "I've sinned by **b** an
Mar 14:42 The one who is **b** me is near."
Jon 13:2 put the idea of **b** Jesus into

betrays (5)
Isa 21:2 The traitor **b**. The destroyer
Jer 3:20 like a wife who **b** her husband,
Mat 26:24 it will be for that person who **b**
Mar 14:21 it will be for that person who **b**
Luk 22:22 be for that person who **b** him."

better (150)

Gen 29:19 Laban responded, "It's **b** that I
37:32 You **b** examine it to see
Exo 14:12 It would have been **b** for us to
Num 11:18 We were **b** off in Egypt!'
14:3 Wouldn't it be **b** for us to go
Dtr 17:20 Then he won't think he's **b** than
Jdg 8:2 after the harvest **b** than all
11:25 You're not any **b** than Balak,
15:2 her younger sister **b** looking?
18:19 Is it **b** for you to be a priest for
Rut 3:10 rich or poor — is **b** than
4:15 who loves you is **b**
1Sm 15:22 To follow instructions is **b** than
15:22 To obey is **b** than sacrificing
15:28 neighbor who is **b** than you.
16:16 strum a tune, and you'll feel **b**."
16:23 ⌊from his terror⌋ and felt **b**,
2Sm 14:32 It would be **b** for me if I were
17:14 is **b** than Ahithophel's advice."
18:3 It's **b** for you to be ready to
1Ki 2:32 men who were **b** than
19:4 I'm no **b** than my ancestors."
21:2 I will give you a **b** vineyard for
2Ki 5:12 have **b** water than any
8:10 "Tell him that he will get **b**,
8:14 "He told me that you will get **b**."
2Ch 21:13 Your brothers were **b** than you.
Job 19:5 yourselves look **b** than me by
Psa 37:16 righteous person has is **b** than
63:3 mercy is **b** than life ⌊itself⌋.
84:10 One day in your courtyards is **b**
90:11 he **b** understands your fury.
118:8 It is **b** to depend on the LORD
118:9 It is **b** to depend on the LORD
Pro 3:14 Its yield is **b** than fine gold.
8:11 wisdom is **b** than jewels.
8:19 What I produce is **b** than gold,
8:19 I yield is **b** than fine silver.
12:9 **B** to be unimportant and have a
15:16 **B** to have a little with the fear
15:17 **B** to have a dish of vegetables
16:8 **B** a few ⌊possessions⌋ gained
16:16 How much **b** it is to gain
16:19 **B** to be humble with lowly
16:32 **B** to get angry slowly than to
16:32 **B** to be even-tempered than to
17:1 **B** a bite of dry bread ⌊eaten⌋ in
17:12 **B** to meet a bear robbed of its
19:1 **B** to be a poor person who
19:22 and it is **b** to be poor than a liar.
21:9 **B** to live on a corner of a roof
21:19 **B** to live in a desert than with a
22:1 Respect is **b** than silver or gold.
25:7 because it is **b** to be told,
25:24 **B** to live on a corner of a roof
27:5 is **b** than unexpressed love.
27:10 A neighbor living nearby is **b**
28:6 **B** to be a poor person who has
30:32 you had **b** put your hand over
Ecc 2:3 myself feel **b** by drinking wine.
2:24 There is nothing **b** for people to
3:12 I realize that there's nothing **b**
3:22 I saw that there's nothing **b** for
4:3 been born yet is **b** off than both
4:6 quiet is **b** than two handfuls
4:9 Two people are **b** than one
4:13 who is poor and wise is **b** than
5:1 It is **b** to go there and listen
5:5 It is **b** not to make a promise
6:3 it ⌊still⌋ would have been **b** for
6:9 It is **b** to look at what is in front
7:1 A good name is **b** than
7:1 and the day you die is **b** than
7:2 It is **b** to go to a funeral than to
7:3 Sorrow is **b** than laughter
7:5 It is **b** to listen to wise people
7:8 The end of something is **b** than
7:8 It is **b** to be patient than
7:10 Don't ask, "Why were things **b**
8:15 People have nothing **b** to do
9:4 because a living dog is **b** than
9:16 "Wisdom is **b** than strength,"
9:18 Wisdom is **b** than weapons of
Sos 1:2 of love are **b** than wine,
Sos 1:3 **b** than the fragrance of cologne.
4:10 How much **b** are your
5:9 what makes your beloved **b**
5:9 What makes your beloved **b**
Isa 29:16 Is the potter no **b** than his clay?
56:5 I will give them something **b**
56:12 will be like today, only **b**."
Jer 22:15 Do you think you're a **b** king
Lam 2:14 in order to make things **b** again.
4:9 swords are **b** off than those
Eze 15:2 Is it **b** than the wood from a tree
36:11 and I will make you **b** off than
Hos 2:7 Things were **b** for me than they
Amo 6:2 Are you **b** than these
Nah 3:8 Are you **b** than No-amon,
Mat 5:29 It is **b** for you to lose a part of
5:30 It is **b** for you to lose a part of
10:15 Judgment day will be **b** for
10:24 "A student is not **b** than his
10:24 Nor is a slave **b** than his owner.
11:22 that judgment day will be **b**
11:24 that judgment day will be **b**
18:8 It is **b** for you to enter life
18:9 It is **b** for you to enter life with
19:10 it's **b** not to get married."
26:24 It would have been **b** for that
Mar 9:43 It is **b** for you to enter life
9:45 It is **b** for you to enter life lame
9:47 It is **b** for you to enter the
14:21 It would have been **b** for that
Luk 5:39 He says, 'The old wine is **b**!'"
6:40 A student is no **b** than his
10:14 Judgment day will be **b** for
Jon 4:52 at what time his son got **b**.
11:50 It is **b** for one man to die for the
18:14 advised the Jews that it was **b**
Act 17:30 when people didn't know any **b**.
Rom 11:18 So don't brag about being **b**
1Co 4:7 Who says that you are any **b**
7:9 It is **b** for you to marry than to
7:38 in marriage does even **b**.
8:8 ⌊that food⌋ and no **b** off if we
12:31 You ⌊only⌋ want the **b** gifts,
2Co 11:23 but I'm a far **b** one.
Gal 4:1 he is no **b** off than a slave,
Eph 1:17 as you come to know Christ **b**.
Php 1:23 That's by far the **b** choice.
1:24 But for your sake it's **b** that I
2:3 as being **b** than yourselves.
3:8 I'm much **b** off knowing Christ
1Ti 6:2 serve their masters even **b**
Phm 1:16 no longer as a slave but **b** than
Heb 6:9 we are still convinced that **b**
7:22 the guarantee of a **b** promise.
8:6 He also brings a **b** promise
8:6 that is based on **b** guarantees.
9:11 Christ went through a **b**,
9:23 to be cleansed by **b** sacrifices.
10:34 you know that you have a **b**
11:4 Faith led Abel to offer God a **b**
11:16 these men were longing for a **b**
11:26 Christ would be **b** than having
12:24 a **b** message than Abel's.
1Pe 1:14 because you didn't know any **b**.
3:17 After all, if it is God's will, it's **b**
2Pe 2:21 It would have been **b** for them

beware (6)

Jer 9:4 "**B** of your neighbors.
Mat 7:15 "**B** of false prophets.
Luk 20:46 "**B** of the scribes! They like to
Php 3:2 **B** of dogs! Beware of those who
3:2 **B** of those who do evil things.
3:2 **B** of those who insist on

Bezai (3)

Ezr 2:17 of **B**: 323
Neh 7:23 of **B**: 324
10:18 Hodiah, Hashum, **B**,

Bezalel (12)

Exo 31:2 "I have chosen **B**, son of Uri
31:3 I have filled **B** with the Spirit of
35:30 "The LORD has chosen **B**,
35:31 The LORD has filled **B** with the
35:34 has given **B** and Oholiab,
Exo 36:1 ⌊Moses continued,⌋ "So **B** and
36:2 Moses called **B** and Oholiab
37:1 **B** made the ark out of acacia
38:22 Now **B**, son of Uri and
1Ch 2:20 and Uri was the father of **B**.
2Ch 1:5 The bronze altar that **B**,
Ezr 10:30 **B**, Binnui, and Manasseh

Bezek (3)

Jdg 1:4 defeated 10,000 men at **B**.
1:5 At **B** they also caught up with
1Sm 11:8 When Saul counted them at **B**,

Bezer (5)

Dtr 4:43 The cities were **B** on the desert
Jos 20:8 **B** on the desert plateau from
21:36 with pasturelands: **B**, Jahaz,
1Ch 6:78 **B** in the wilderness with its
7:37 **B**, Hod, Shamma, Shilsha,

Bichri (3)

2Sm 20:6 told Abishai, "Sheba, son of **B**,
20:10 pursued Sheba, son of **B**.
20:21 the name of Sheba, son of **B**,

Bichri's (4)

2Sm 20:1 **B** son, from the tribe of
20:2 David to follow Sheba, **B** son.
20:7 to pursue Sheba, **B** son
20:13 and pursued Sheba, **B** son

Bidkar (1)

2Ki 9:25 Jehu said to his attendant **B**,

big (33)

Gen 21:8 Abraham held a **b** feast.
Exo 29:20 and on the **b** toes of their right
Lev 8:23 and on the **b** toe of his right
8:24 and on the **b** toes of their right
14:14 and on the **b** toe of the right foot
14:17 and on the **b** toe of the right foot
14:25 and on the **b** toe of the right foot
14:28 and on the **b** toe of the right foot
Num 35:23 Or suppose you drop a **b** stone,
Dtr 1:28 The cities are **b** with sky-high
9:1 with **b** cities that have sky-high
Jdg 1:6 and cut off his thumbs and **b**
1:7 their thumbs and **b** toes cut off
9:29 'Get yourself a **b** army and
9:38 "Where is your **b** mouth now?
20:38 they would make a **b** column
1Sm 19:22 He went as far as the **b** cistern
Neh 8:12 send portions. They had a **b**,
8:17 not done this. There was a **b**,
Psa 35:21 They open their **b** mouths and
104:25 The sea is so **b** and wide with
131:1 am not involved in things too **b**
Pro 13:3 Whoever has a **b** mouth comes
23:2 throat if you have a **b** appetite.
Isa 30:14 No piece will be **b** enough to
Jer 5:28 They grow **b** and fat.
22:14 for myself with **b** upper rooms.'
46:17 king of Egypt, is a **b** windbag.
Eze 31:7 So the tree was **b** and beautiful
Amo 6:11 the command to level **b** houses
Jnh 1:17 The LORD sent a **b** fish to
Gal 6:12 who want to make a **b** deal out
Jas 3:4 They are very **b** and are driven

bigger (3)

Jer 26:19 a **b** disaster on ourselves."
Dan 7:20 to be **b** than the others.
Luk 12:18 barns and build **b** ones so that

Bigtha (1)

Est 1:10 Harbona, **B**, Abagtha, Zethar,

Bigthan (3)

Est 2:21 the king's gate, **B** and Teresh,
2:23 the dead bodies of **B** and
6:2 him that **B** and Teresh,

Bigvai (6)

Ezr 2:2 **B**, Rehum, and Baanah.
2:14 of **B**: 2,056
8:14 from the family of **B**:

Neh 7:7 **B**, Nehum, and Baanah.
7:19 of **B**: 2,067
10:16 Adonijah, **B**, Adin,

Bildad (5)

Job 2:11 **B** of Shuah, Zophar of Naama.
8:1 Then **B** from Shuah replied ⌊to
18:1 Then **B** from Shuah replied ⌊to
25:1 Then **B** from Shuah replied ⌊to
42:9 Eliphaz of Teman, **B** of Shuah,

Bileam (1)

1Ch 6:70 Aner with its pastureland and **B**

Bilgah (3)

1Ch 24:14 the fifteenth for **B**, the sixteenth
Neh 12:5 Mijamin, Maadiah, **B**,
12:18 from **B**, Shammua;

Bilgai (1)

Neh 10:8 Maaziah, **B**, and Shemaiah.

Bilhah (10)

Gen 29:29 (Laban had given his slave **B**
30:3 She said, "Here's my servant **B**.
30:4 So she gave him her slave **B**
30:5 **B** became pregnant,
30:7 Rachel's slave **B** became
35:22 with his father's concubine **B**,
35:25 The sons of Rachel's slave **B**
37:2 with the sons of **B** and Zilpah,
46:25 were the descendants of **B**,
1Ch 4:29 **B**, Ezem, Tolad,

Bilhah's (1)

1Ch 7:13 They were **B** grandsons

Bilhan (3)

Gen 36:27 were the sons of Ezer: **B**,
1Ch 1:42 Ezer's sons were **B**,
7:10 Jediael's son was **B**.

Bilhan's (1)

1Ch 7:10 **B** sons were Jeush,

Bilshan (2)

Ezr 2:2 **B**, Mispar, Bigvai, Rehum,
Neh 7:7 **B**, Mispereth, Bigvai, Nehum,

Bimhal (1)

1Ch 7:33 Japhlet's sons were Pasach, **B**,

binding (3)

Neh 9:38 "We are making a **b** agreement
10:29 in **b** themselves with a curse
Job 5:23 "You will have a **b** agreement

Binea (2)

1Ch 8:37 Moza was the father of **B**.
9:43 Moza was the father of **B**.

Binea's (2)

1Ch 8:37 **B** son was Raphah.
9:43 **B** son was Rephaiah.

Binnui (7)

Ezr 10:30 Bezalel, **B**, and Manasseh
10:38 From the descendants of **B**:
Neh 3:18 This included **B**, the official in
3:24 After him **B**, Henadad's son,
7:15 of **B**: 648
10:9 **B** (of the sons of Henadad),
12:8 The Levites were Jeshua, **B**,

Binnui's (1)

Ezr 8:33 and **B** son Noadiah,

bird (57)

Gen 1:21 and every type of flying **b**.
1:30 every **b** in the sky,
6:20 Two of every type of **b**,
7:3 pairs of every kind of **b** (a male
7:14 and every type of **b** (every
8:19 and **b** — everything that moves
8:20 of clean animal and clean **b**.
Lev 1:14 offering to the LORD is a **b**,
1:15 break its neck and burn the **b**
1:17 bird's wings to tear the **b** open,
1:17 Then the priest will lay the **b**
5:10 he will sacrifice the second **b**
7:26 "Never eat the blood of any **b** or
14:5 someone to kill one **b** over
14:6 The priest will take the living **b**,
14:6 and dip them and the living **b**
14:6 blood of the **b** that was killed
14:7 Then he will let the living **b** fly
14:50 He must kill the one **b** over a
14:51 and the living **b** and dip them in
14:51 blood of the **b** that was killed.
14:52 the living **b**, the cedar wood,
14:53 Then he will let the living **b** fly
17:13 hunt any animal or **b** that may
20:25 by eating any animal or **b**
Dtr 14:11 You may eat any clean **b**.
22:6 If the mother **b** is sitting on the
Job 28:7 No **b** of prey knows the way to
39:26 your understanding make a **b**
41:5 Can you play with it like a **b** or
Psa 11:1 to your mountain like a **b**?
50:11 I know every **b** in the
102:7 am like a lonely **b** on a rooftop.
124:7 We escaped like a **b** caught in
Pro 1:17 a net within the sight of any **b**.
6:5 of a hunter and like a **b** from
7:23 like a **b** darting into a trap.
27:8 Like a **b** wandering from its
Ecc 10:20 A **b** may carry your words,
12:4 are startled at the sound of a **b**,
Isa 31:5 Jerusalem like a hovering **b**.
46:11 I will call a **b** of prey from the
Jer 4:25 and every **b** has flown away.
5:26 lie in ambush like **b** catchers.
12:9 are like a colorful **b** of prey.
Lam 3:52 no reason hunted me like a **b**.
Eze 17:23 Every kind of **b** will nest in it
39:4 let you become food for every **b**
39:17 Tell every kind of **b** and every
44:31 priests must never eat any **b**
Dan 7:6 like the wings of a **b**.
Hos 7:12 you out of the air like a **b**.
9:11 glory will fly away like a **b**.
Amo 3:5 Does a **b** land in a trap on the
Zep 2:14 A **b** will sing in a window.
Luk 21:35 like a trap that catches a **b**.
Rev 18:2 evil spirit, every unclean **b**,

bird's (3)

Lev 1:17 Then pull on the **b** wings to
5:8 He will break the **b** neck
14:52 So he must use the **b** blood,

birds (87)

Gen 1:20 and let **b** fly through the sky
1:22 there be many **b** on the earth."
1:26 fish in the sea, the **b** in the sky,
1:28 fish in the sea, the **b** in the sky,
2:19 wild animals and all the **b** out
2:20 the domestic animals, all the **b**,
6:7 crawling animals, and **b**.
7:8 Clean and unclean animals, **b**,
7:21 on the earth died, including **b**,
7:23 and **b** were wiped off the earth.
8:17 with you: **b**, domestic animals,
9:2 and all the **b** will fear you
9:10 being that is with you — **b**,
15:10 he did not cut the **b** in half.
15:11 When **b** of prey came down
40:17 but the **b** were eating them out
40:19 The **b** will eat the flesh from
Lev 11:13 "Here are the kinds of **b** you
11:46 instructions about animals, **b**,
14:4 clean **b**, some cedar wood,
14:49 "The priest must take two **b**,
15:14 will give these **b** to the priest.
20:25 and unclean animals and **b**.
Dtr 14:12 But here are the **b** that you
28:26 bodies will be food for all the **b**
1Sm 17:44 I'll give your body to the **b**."
17:46 of the Philistine army to the **b**
2Sm 21:10 She wouldn't let any **b** land on
1Ki 4:23 fallow deer, and fattened **b**.
4:33 animals, **b**, reptiles, and fish.
14:11 in the country, **b** will eat him.'
16:4 **B** will eat anyone from his
21:24 in the country, **b** will eat him."
Job 12:7 Ask the **b**, and they will tell
28:21 even from the **b** in the air.
35:11 us wiser than the **b** in the sky?'
Psa 8:8 the **b**, the fish, whatever swims
78:27 **b** like the sand on the
78:28 He made the **b** fall in the
79:2 your servants to the **b** for food.
104:12 The **b** live by the streams.
104:17 **B** build their nests in them.
148:10 crawling animals and **b**,
Ecc 9:12 in a cruel net or **b** caught
Isa 16:2 daughters are like fluttering **b**,
18:6 They will be left for the **b** of
18:6 The **b** of prey will feed on them
Jer 5:27 Like cages filled with **b**,
7:33 become food for **b** and animals,
9:10 **B** and cattle have fled.
12:4 animals and the **b** are dying,
12:9 Other **b** of prey surround it.
15:3 and **b** and animals to devour
16:4 will be food for **b** and animals.
19:7 as food to **b** and to animals.
34:20 be food for **b** and wild animals.
Eze 13:20 you use to trap people like **b**.
29:5 feed you to wild animals and **b**.
31:6 All the **b** made their nests in its
31:13 All the **b** perched on the fallen
32:4 I will make **b** perch on you,
38:20 Fish, **b**, wild animals,
Dan 2:38 and **b**, wherever they live.
4:12 **B** came to live in its branches.
4:14 and make the **b** fly from its
4:21 and **b** made their homes in its
Hos 2:18 with the wild animals, the **b**,
4:3 Wild animals, **b**, and fish are
11:11 They will come trembling like **b**
Zep 1:3 I will put an end to the **b** in the
Mat 6:26 "Look at the **b**. They don't plant,
8:20 have holes, and **b** have nests,
13:4 and **b** came and devoured
13:32 a tree that is large enough for **b**
Mar 4:4 and **b** came and devoured
4:32 large branches that **b** can nest
Luk 8:5 and were devoured by **b**.
9:58 have holes, and **b** have nests,
12:24 are worth much more than **b**.
13:19 and the **b** nested in its
Act 10:12 animals, reptiles, and **b**.
11:6 wild animals, reptiles, and **b**.
Rom 1:23 **b**, animals, and snakes.
1Co 15:39 have another, **b** have another,
Jas 3:7 **b**, reptiles, and sea creatures.
Rev 19:17 to all the **b** flying overhead,
19:21 All the **b** gorged themselves on

birds' (1)

Dan 4:33 nails grew as long as **b** claws

Birsha (1)

Gen 14:2 King **B** of Gomorrah,

birth (184)

Gen 3:16 when you give **b** to children.
4:1 pregnant and gave **b** to Cain.
4:2 Then she gave **b** to another
4:17 pregnant and gave **b** to Enoch.
4:20 Adah gave **b** to Jabal.
4:25 She gave **b** to a son and
8:21 even though from **b** their hearts
16:11 and you will give **b** to a son.
16:15 Hagar gave **b** to Abram's son.
16:16 when Hagar gave **b** to Ishmael.
17:21 Sarah will give **b** to him at this
19:37 The older one gave **b** to a son
19:38 younger daughter also gave **b**
21:2 she gave **b** to a son for
22:20 "Milcah has given **b** to these
25:2 Keturah gave **b** to these sons
25:13 listed in the order of their **b**:
25:23 go their separate ways from **b**.
25:24 the time came for her to give **b**,
29:32 became pregnant and gave **b**
29:33 pregnant again and gave **b**

Gen 29:34 pregnant again and gave **b**
29:35 pregnant again and gave **b**
30:5 and she gave **b** to a son for
30:7 pregnant again and gave **b**
30:10 Leah's slave Zilpah gave **b** to
30:12 Leah's slave Zilpah gave **b** to
30:17 became pregnant and gave **b**
30:19 pregnant again and gave **b**
30:21 Later she gave **b** to a daughter
30:23 became pregnant and gave **b**
30:25 After Rachel gave **b** to Joseph,
30:39 Then they gave **b** to young that
31:8 all the flocks gave **b** to
31:8 flocks gave **b** to striped young.
36:4 Adah gave **b** to Eliphaz for
36:4 and Basemath gave **b** to Reuel.
36:5 Oholibamah gave **b** to Jeush,
36:12 She gave **b** to Amalek for
36:14 She gave **b** to Jeush,
38:3 became pregnant and gave **b**
38:4 pregnant again and gave **b**
38:5 pregnant again and gave **b**
38:27 time came for Tamar to give **b**,
38:28 When she was giving **b**,
46:18 She gave **b** to these children
46:25 She gave **b** to these sons for
50:23 were adopted by Joseph at **b**.
Exo 2:22 She gave **b** to a son.
6:16 sons of Levi listed in **b** order:
6:19 from Levi listed in **b** order.
6:20 She gave **b** to Aaron and
6:23 She gave **b** to Nadab,
6:25 She gave **b** to Phinehas.
21:4 him a wife and she gives **b**
21:22 that she gives **b** prematurely.
28:10 in **b** order — six of their names
Lev 12:2 When a woman gives **b** to a
12:5 "When a woman gives **b** to a
12:7 for the woman who gives **b**
Num 11:12 Did I give **b** to them?
26:59 She gave **b** to Amram's
Dtr 28:57 and the children she gives **b** to.
Jdg 8:31 at Shechem also gave **b**
11:2 wife also gave **b** to sons.
13:5 dedicated to God from **b**.
Rut 1:12 And even if I gave **b** to sons,
4:12 Tamar gave **b** to for Judah."
4:13 So she gave **b** to a son.
4:15 because she has given **b**."
1Sm 1:20 became pregnant and gave **b**
2:5 who was childless gives **b**
4:19 and gave **b** to a son.
4:20 You've given **b** to a son."
2Sm 11:27 Then she gave **b** to a son.
12:15 that Uriah's wife had given **b**
12:24 and she later gave **b** to a son.
21:8 Rizpah (Aiah's daughter) gave **b**
21:8 Merab (Saul's daughter) gave **b**
1Ki 1:5 His mother gave **b** to him after
3:17 I gave **b** ⌊to a son⌋ while she
3:18 this woman also gave **b** ⌊to
2Ki 19:3 woman who is about to give **b**
1Ch 1:32 gave **b** to the following sons:
2:4 gave **b** to Judah's sons Perez
2:19 She gave **b** to Hur.
2:21 She gave **b** to Segub.
2:24 wife Abijah gave **b** to Ashhur,
2:29 She gave **b** to Ahban and
2:35 She gave **b** to Attai.
4:6 Naarah gave **b** to Ahuzzam,
4:9 she said that his **b** was painful.
4:17 His wife gave **b** to Miriam,
7:18 gave **b** to Ishhod,
7:23 She gave **b** to a son,
2Ch 11:19 Mahalath gave **b** to the
11:20 She gave **b** to Abijah,
Ezr 10:44 women had given **b** to children.
Job 15:35 trouble and give **b** to evil.
21:10 Their cows give **b** to calves
31:18 and from my **b** I treated the
38:28 Who gave **b** to the dewdrops?
38:29 and who has given **b** to the
39:1 the mountain goats give **b**?
39:2 the time when they'll give **b**?
39:3 They kneel down to give **b** and
39:3 the pain of giving **b** is over.
Psa 7:14 and gives **b** to lies.
22:10 was placed in your care from **b**.
58:3 From their **b** liars go astray.
90:2 before you gave **b** to the earth
144:13 May our sheep give **b** to
Pro 23:25 she who gave **b** to you rejoice.
31:2 What, son to whom I gave **b**?
Ecc 6:4 baby arrives in a pointless **b**
Sos 6:9 to the one who gave **b** to her.
8:5 into labor and gave **b** to you!
Isa 7:14 become pregnant and give **b**
8:3 became pregnant and gave **b**
13:8 writhe like a woman giving **b**
23:4 never been in labor or given **b**.
26:17 women ready to give **b**.
26:18 with labor pains only to give **b**
33:11 You will give **b** to straw.
37:3 woman who is about to give **b**
46:3 I've carried you since your **b**.
51:18 all the children she gave **b** to,
54:1 who never gave **b** to children.
54:1 women who never had **b** pains.
59:4 trouble and give **b** to evil.
65:23 They will never again give **b** to
66:7 goes into labor, she gives **b**.
66:8 she also gave **b** to her children.
66:9 a mother to the moment of **b**
Jer 4:31 with anguish as she gives **b**
6:24 a woman giving **b** to a child.
14:5 Even deer in the fields give **b**
15:9 A mother who gives **b** to seven
15:10 did my mother give **b** to me?
20:14 that my mother gave **b** to me.
22:23 a woman giving **b** to a child.
30:6 Can a man give **b** to a child?
30:6 in pain like a woman giving **b**
50:12 The woman who gave **b** to you
Eze 23:4 I married them, and they gave **b**
23:37 the children they gave **b**
31:6 All the wild animals gave **b** to
47:22 among you and have given **b**
Dan 9:1 who was a Mede by **b**,
Zec 13:3 who gave **b** to him,
13:3 who gave **b** to him,
Mat 1:18 The **b** of Jesus Christ took
1:21 She will give **b** to a son,
1:23 become pregnant and give **b**
1:25 with her before she gave **b**
2:1 After Jesus' **b** wise men from
Luk 1:31 pregnant, give **b** to a son,
1:57 she gave **b** to a son.
2:7 She gave **b** to her firstborn son.
2:21 Eight days after his **b**,
11:27 is the mother who gave **b**
23:29 who couldn't give **b**,
Jon 1:13 Their **b** was from God.
3:6 Flesh and blood give **b** to flesh
3:6 but the Spirit gives **b** to things
16:21 when her time to give **b** comes.
Act 3:2 lame from **b** was being carried
Rom 9:3 who, like me, are Jewish by **b**.
16:7 who are Jewish by **b** like me.
16:11 who is Jewish by **b** like me.
16:21 who are Jewish by **b** like me.
Gal 2:15 We are Jewish by **b**,
4:4 A woman gave **b** to him,
4:19 My children, I am suffering **b**
4:27 who cannot give **b** to any
1Ti 2:15 will be saved through the **b**
Tit 3:5 gives us new **b** and renewal.
Jas 1:15 pregnant and gives **b** to sin.
1:15 it gives **b** to death.
1Pe 1:3 God has given us a new **b**
Rev 12:2 and the agony of giving **b**.
12:4 was going to give **b** so that
12:5 She gave **b** to a son,
12:13 who had given **b** to the boy.

birthday (3)

Gen 40:20 Two days later, on his **b**,
Mat 14:6 When Herod celebrated his **b**,
Mar 6:21 finally came on Herod's **b**.

birthplace (1)

Eze 16:3 Your **b** and your ancestors

births (1)

Hos 9:11 more pregnancies, **b**, or babies.

Birzaith (1)

1Ch 7:31 who first settled **B**.

Bishlam (1)

Ezr 4:7 **B**, Mithredath, Tabeel, and the

bishop (4)

1Ti 3:1 sets his heart on being a **b**,
3:2 A **b** must have a good
Tit 1:7 Because a **b** is a supervisor
1Pe 2:25 shepherd and **b** of your lives.

bishops (2)

Act 20:28 Holy Spirit has placed you as **b**
Php 1:1 in the city of Philippi and their **b**

bit (9)

Exo 5:11 load will not be reduced one **b**."
8:17 It turned into gnats that **b**
8:18 gnats **b** people and animals.
Num 21:6 They **b** the people,
Psa 32:9 ⌊They need⌋ a **b** and bridle in
78:45 He sent a swarm of flies that **b**
Pro 23:8 You will vomit the little **b** you
Isa 30:28 placing a **b** in the mouths of the
Act 28:3 The snake **b** Paul's hand and

bite (3)

Pro 17:1 Better a **b** of dry bread ⌊eaten⌋
Jer 8:17 They will **b** you," declares the
Amo 9:3 a sea snake to **b** them.

bites (4)

Gen 49:17 that **b** a horse's heels so that
Pro 16:30 Whoever **b** his lips has
23:32 Later it **b** like a snake and
Ecc 10:11 If a snake **b** before it has been

Bithron (1)

2Sm 2:29 the entire **B** until they came

Bithynia (2)

Act 16:7 of Mysia and tried to enter **B**,
1Pe 1:1 Cappadocia, Asia, and **B**.

biting (1)

Job 13:14 I am **b** off more than I can chew

bits (1)

Jas 3:3 We put **b** in the mouths of

bitten (4)

Num 21:8 Anyone who is **b** can look at it
21:9 bronze snake after they were **b**,
Ecc 10:8 wall may be **b** by a snake.
Amo 5:19 wall only to be **b** by a snake.

bitter (51)

Gen 27:34 out a very loud and **b** cry
Exo 1:14 They made their lives **b** with
12:8 a fire and eaten with **b** herbs
15:23 they came to Marah [**B** Place],
15:23 the water because it tasted **b**.
Num 5:18 his hands the **b** water that can
5:19 This **b** water that can bring a
5:23 wash them off into the **b** water.
5:24 drink the **b** water that can
5:24 go into her ⌊and⌋ become **b**.
5:27 will go into her and become **b**.
9:11 unleavened bread and **b** herbs.
Dtr 29:18 source of this kind of **b** poison.
32:32 and their clusters are **b**.
Rut 1:20 Call me Mara [**B**] because the
1:20 has made my life very **b**.
1Sm 22:2 or **b** about life joined him,
2Ki 3:27 There was **b** anger against the
4:27 She is **b**. The LORD has hidden
Job 3:20 life to those who find it so **b**,
13:26 You write down **b** accusations
21:25 dies with a **b** soul.
23:2 "My complaint is **b** again today.
27:2 who has made my life **b**:

Psa 64:3 They aim **b** words like arrows
106:33 since they made him **b** so that
Pro 5:4 end she is as **b** as wormwood,
17:25 to his father and **b** grief
27:7 even **b** food tastes sweet.
Ecc 7:26 is more **b** than death itself.
Isa 5:20 who turn what is **b** into
5:20 is sweet into something **b**.
38:15 because of my **b** experience.
38:17 Now my **b** experience turns
Jer 2:19 know and see how evil and **b**
4:18 It is **b**. It breaks your heart."
31:15 the sound of crying in **b** grief.
Lam 1:4 are made to suffer. Zion is **b**.
1:20 because I've been very **b**.
Eze 3:14 went away feeling **b** and angry.
21:6 heart and with **b** crying while
27:31 and with **b** mourning.
Hos 12:14 of Ephraim made the LORD **b**.
Amo 8:10 and its end will be **b**.
Mat 2:18 the sound of crying in **b** grief.
Act 8:23 I can see that you are **b** with
Rom 3:14 full of curses and **b** resentment.
Eph 6:4 make your children **b** about life.
Rev 8:11 water because it had turned **b**.
10:9 It will be **b** in your stomach,
10:10 it was **b** in my stomach.

bitterly (23)

Num 14:39 the people mourned **b**,
Jdg 5:23 "**B** curse those who live there!
2Sm 13:36 all his men also cried very **b**.
2Ki 14:26 he saw how **b** everyone
20:3 consider right. "And he cried **b**.
Ezr 10:1 They also began to cry **b**.
Est 4:1 the city and cried loudly and **b**.
Job 10:1 I will speak as **b** as I feel.
Isa 22:4 from me so that I can cry **b**.
33:7 Messengers of peace cry **b**.
38:3 consider right. "And he cried **b**.
Jer 6:26 lost your only child, and cry **b**.
13:17 I will cry **b**, and my eyes will
22:10 Cry **b** for those who are taken
48:5 crying **b** as they go.
Lam 1:2 Jerusalem cries **b** at night with
Eze 27:30 cried loudly and **b** over you.
Zep 1:14 Warriors will cry out **b** on the
Zec 12:10 and they will cry **b** for him as
Mat 26:75 Peter went outside and cried **b**.
Luk 22:62 Peter went outside and cried **b**.
Jas 3:14 But if you are **b** jealous and
Rev 5:4 I cried **b** because no one was

bitterness (14)

Rut 1:13 My **b** is much worse than yours
1Sm 15:32 "Surely, the **b** of death is past,"
30:6 the people in their **b** said
2Sm 2:26 you know this will end in **b**?
Job 7:11 about the **b** in my soul."
9:18 He fills me with **b**.
Psa 73:21 my heart was filled with **b**
Pro 14:10 The heart knows its own **b**,
Jer 9:15 going to feed these people **b**
Lam 3:5 me with **b** and hardship.
3:15 He has filled me with **b**.
Eze 27:31 They cried over you with **b** and
Eph 4:31 Get rid of your **b**, hot tempers,
Heb 12:15 God so that **b** doesn't take root

Biziothiah (1)

Jos 15:28 Hazar Shual, Beersheba, **B**,

Biztha (1)

Est 1:10 **B**, Harbona, Bigtha, Abagtha,

black (28)

Gen 30:32 or spotted sheep, every **b** lamb,
30:33 or any lamb that isn't **b** will
30:35 white on it), and every **b** lamb.
30:40 face any that were striped or **b**
Exo 10:15 until it was **b** ⌊with them⌋.
Lev 11:13 bearded vultures, **b** vultures,
13:31 the skin and there is no **b** hair
13:37 hasn't spread and **b** hair grows
Dtr 14:12 bearded vultures, **b** vultures,
18:10 them alive, practice **b** magic,
18:14 to those who practice **b** magic.
Jos 13:22 who used **b** magic.
1Sm 15:23 The sin of **b** magic is rebellion.
2Ki 17:17 They practiced **b** magic and
1Ch 29:2 stones and settings, **b** stones,
Est 1:6 pearl-like stone, and **b** marble.
Job 3:4 That day—let it be pitch-**b**.
28:3 the gloomy, pitch-**b** rock.
Sos 5:11 His hair is wavy, **b** as a raven.
Isa 28:25 doesn't he scatter **b** cumin
28:27 **B** cumin isn't threshed with a
28:27 **B** cumin is beaten with a rod
Jer 4:28 and the sky will grow **b**.
Amo 5:20 It is pitch-**b**, with no light.
Zec 6:2 The second had **b** horses.
6:6 The chariot with the **b** horses
Mat 5:36 make one hair **b** or white.
Act 13:1 Simeon (called the **B**),
Rev 6:5 and there was a **b** horse,
6:12 The sun turned as **b** as

blacker (1)

Lam 4:8 faces are ⌊now⌋ **b** than soot.

blackmail (1)

Luk 3:14 and never use threats or **b** to

blackness (1)

Job 3:6 "That night — let the **b** take it

blacksmith (1)

1Sm 13:19 No **b** could be found in the

blacksmiths (3)

Isa 41:7 Metalsmiths encourage **b** who
44:12 **B** shape iron into tools.
54:16 I've created **b** to fan the coals

blade (8)

Jdg 3:22 the handle went in after the **b**.
3:22 Eglon's fat covered the **b**
3:22 The **b** stuck out in back.
1Sm 13:20 the Philistines to sharpen the **b**
Eze 5:1 "Son of man, take a sharp **b**,
5:2 and cut it up with a **b** around
21:16 or wherever your **b** is turned.
Mar 4:28 First the green **b** appears,

blades (1)

1Sm 13:21 a pim for plow **b** and mattocks,

blame (7)

Gen 43:9 you can **b** me the rest of my
44:32 then you can **b** me the rest of
1Sm 22:15 You shouldn't **b** me or anyone
2Sm 3:29 May the **b** fall on the head of
Job 1:22 all this Job did not sin or **b** God
Psa 73:13 washing my hands of any **b**.
Col 1:22 without sin, fault, or **b**.

blamed (2)

Exo 28:38 He's the one to be **b** for
1Ti 6:14 Then you cannot be **b** for doing

blameless (9)

Exo 28:43 Then they will be **b** and won't
Psa 19:13 Then I will be **b**, and I will be
51:4 and you are **b** when you judge.
Php 1:10 is best and be pure and **b** until
2:15 you will be **b** and innocent.
1Th 2:10 and **b** we were in our dealings
3:13 Then you will be **b** in the
5:23 and body — **b** when our Lord
Rev 14:5 never told a lie. They are **b**.

blanket (5)

Gen 9:23 Shem and Japheth took a **b**
1Sm 19:13 put a goat-hair **b** at its head,
19:16 with the goat-hair **b** at its head.
2Ki 8:15 the next day Hazael took a **b**,
Isa 28:20 The **b** is too narrow to serve as

blankets (4)

Jdg 5:10 who sit on saddle **b**,
1Sm 9:25 They spread **b** on the roof for
1Ki 1:1 he was covered with **b**,
Eze 27:20 traded saddle **b** with you.

blast (14)

Exo 15:8 With a **b** from your nostrils,
19:13 ram's horn sounds a long **b**."
19:16 and a very loud **b** from a ram's
20:18 They heard the **b** of the ram's
Jos 6:5 When you hear a long **b** on the
6:20 loudly when they heard the **b**
2Sm 22:16 at the **b** of the breath from his
Job 4:9 kills them with a **b** of his anger.
Psa 18:15 at the **b** of the breath from your
147:17 can withstand his chilling **b**?
Isa 27:8 He removed it with a fierce **b**
Jer 6:29 The bellows of the **b** furnace
Eze 22:20 to melt them with a fiery **b**.
Heb 12:19 to a trumpet's **b**, and to a voice.

blasts (1)

Rev 8:13 the remaining trumpet **b** which

Blastus (2)

Act 12:20 They enlisted the help of **B** to
12:20 (**B** was in charge of the king's

blazing (18)

Dtr 5:23 saw the mountain **b** with fire,
Psa 21:9 them ⌊burn⌋ like a **b** furnace.
Isa 34:9 Its land will become **b** tar.
Eze 20:47 The **b** fire will not be put out.
Dan 3:6 be thrown into a **b** furnace."
3:11 will be thrown into a **b** furnace.
3:15 be thrown into a **b** furnace.
3:17 can save us from a **b** furnace
3:20 be thrown into the **b** furnace.
3:21 were thrown into the **b** furnace.
3:23 fell into the **b** furnace.
3:26 to the door of the **b** furnace
Joe 2:3 Behind it flames are **b**.
Mat 13:42 throw them into a **b** furnace.
13:50 the evil people into a **b** furnace.
20:12 hard all day under a **b** sun.'
2Th 1:7 his mighty angels in a **b** fire.
Heb 12:18 feel, to a **b** fire, to darkness,

bleach (3)

Job 9:30 and cleanse my hands with **b**,
Isa 1:25 remove your impurities with **b**.
Mar 9:3 anyone on earth could **b** them.

bled (1)

Lam 4:9 who were stabbed **b** to death.

bleeding (7)

Lev 12:4 to be made clean from her **b**.
12:5 to be made clean from her **b**.
Mat 9:20 from chronic **b** for twelve years.
Mar 5:25 from chronic **b** for twelve years.
5:29 Her **b** stopped immediately.
Luk 8:43 been suffering from chronic **b**
8:44 and her **b** stopped at once.

blemish (2)

2Sm 14:25 He had no **b** from head to toe.
Sos 4:7 There is no **b** on you.

blemishes (2)

2Pe 2:13 false teachers are stains and **b**.
3:14 without ⌊spiritual⌋ stains or **b**.

blended (1)

2Ch 16:14 full of spices and **b** perfumes.

bless (122)

Gen 12:2 you a great nation, I will **b** you.
12:3 I will **b** those who bless you,
12:3 I will bless those who **b** you,
17:16 I will **b** her, and I will also give
17:16 I will **b** her, and she will
17:20 Yes, I will **b** him, make him
22:17 I will certainly **b** you and make
26:3 I will be with you and **b** you.
26:5 I will **b** you because Abraham
26:24 I will **b** you and increase the
27:4 to eat so that I will **b** you before
27:7 for me to eat so that I will **b** you

Gen 27:10 eat so that he will **b** you before
27:19 for you so that you may **b** me."
27:25 so that I will **b** you."
27:29 those who **b** you be blessed."
27:31 for you so that you will **b** me."
27:34 his father, "**B** me too, Father!"
27:38 **B** me too, Father!" And Esau
28:3 May God Almighty **b** you,
32:26 "I won't let you go until you **b**
48:9 to me so that I may **b** them."
48:16 me from all evil, **b** these boys.
Exo 12:32 Just go! And **b** me, too!"
20:24 I will come to you and **b** you.
23:25 and he will **b** your food and
Num 6:23 is how you will **b** the Israelites.
6:24 The LORD will **b** you and
6:27 my name to **b** the Israelites,
6:27 the Israelites, I will **b** them."
22:6 I know that whomever you **b** is
23:11 but all you've done is **b** them!"
23:20 have received a command to **b**.
23:25 then at least don't **b** them!"
24:1 the LORD wanted to **b** Israel,
24:9 Those who **b** you will be
Dtr 1:11 and may he **b** you as he has
7:13 He will love you, **b** you,
7:13 He will **b** you with children.
7:13 He will **b** your land with
7:13 He will **b** your herds with
14:24 He may **b** you with so much
14:29 Then the LORD your God will **b**
15:4 your God will certainly **b** you
15:5 He will **b** you only if you listen
15:6 The LORD your God will **b** you,
15:10 the LORD your God will **b** you
15:18 the LORD your God will **b** you
16:15 your God will **b** all your harvest
21:5 him as priests and to **b** people
23:20 Then the LORD your God will **b**
24:13 to bed ⌊that night⌋, he'll **b** you.
24:19 Then the LORD your God will **b**
26:15 **B** your people Israel and the
27:12 Mount Gerizim to **b** the people:
28:8 The LORD will **b** your barns
28:8 The LORD your God will **b** you
28:12 time and **b** everything you do.
30:16 and the LORD your God will **b**
33:11 LORD, **b** them with strength
33:13 "May the LORD **b** their land
33:14 May the LORD **b** their land with
33:16 May the LORD **b** their land with
Jos 8:33 commanded the priests to **b**
24:10 All he could do was **b** you.
Jdg 17:2 "The LORD **b** you,
Rut 2:4 "May the LORD **b** you!"
2:20 "May the LORD **b** him.
3:10 "May the LORD **b** you,
1Sm 2:20 Eli would **b** Elkanah (and his
15:13 "The LORD **b** you.
23:21 Saul responded, "The LORD **b**
2Sm 2:5 "May the LORD **b** you because
6:20 David returned to **b** his family,
7:29 Now, please **b** my house so
21:3 so that you will **b** what belongs
1Ch 4:10 "Please **b** me and give me
16:43 went back to **b** his family.
17:27 Now, you were pleased to **b**
Job 31:20 (If his body didn't **b** me,
Psa 5:12 You **b** righteous people,
28:9 and **b** those who belong to you.
29:11 The LORD will **b** his people
62:4 They **b** with their mouths,
65:10 showers and **b** what grows
67:1 God have pity on us and **b** us!
67:6 May God, our God, **b** us.
67:7 May God **b** us, and may all the
109:17 He did not like to **b** ⌊others⌋,
109:28 They may curse, but you will **b**.
115:12 thinking about us, will **b** us.
115:12 He will **b** the descendants of
115:12 He will **b** the descendants of
115:13 He will **b** those who fear the
115:14 May the LORD continue to **b**
118:26 We **b** you from the LORD's
128:4 This is how the LORD will **b**
128:5 May the LORD **b** you from Zion
Psa 129:8 by the LORD" or "We **b** you
132:15 I will certainly **b** all that Zion
134:3 and earth, **b** you from Zion.
145:1 I will **b** your name forever and
145:2 I will **b** you every day.
Pro 30:11 and does not **b** his mother.
31:28 husband stand up and **b** her.
Isa 19:25 LORD of Armies will **b** them,
65:23 The LORD will **b** their
Jer 31:23 "The LORD **b** you,
Eze 34:26 I will **b** them and the places
Hag 2:19 But from now on I will **b** you."
Mat 19:13 to Jesus to have him **b** them
Luk 6:28 **B** those who curse you.
Act 3:26 God did this to **b** you by turning
Rom 12:14 **B** those who persecute you.
12:14 **B** them, and don't curse them.
1Co 4:12 verbally abuse us, we **b** them.
10:16 When we **b** the cup of blessing
Heb 6:14 He said, "I will certainly **b** you
11:20 led Isaac to **b** Jacob and Esau.
11:21 faith led him to **b** each of
Jas 2:7 the name that was used to **b**
1Pe 3:9 Instead, **b** them, because you

blessed (257)

Gen 1:22 God **b** them and said,
1:28 God **b** them and said,
2:3 Then God **b** the seventh day
5:2 He **b** them and called them
9:1 God **b** Noah and his sons and
10:9 hunter whom the LORD **b**.
10:9 hunter whom the LORD **b**."
12:3 every family on earth will be **b**."
14:19 He **b** Abram, and said,
14:19 "**B** is Abram by God Most High,
14:20 **B** is God Most High,
18:18 nations of the earth will be **b**.
22:18 nations of the earth will be **b**,
24:1 and the LORD had **b** him in
24:31 you whom the LORD has **b**.
24:35 "The LORD has **b** my master,
25:11 God **b** his son Isaac,
26:4 nations of the earth will be **b**.
26:12 because the LORD had **b** him.
26:29 Now you are **b** by the LORD."
27:23 Esau's hands. So he **b** him.
27:27 he **b** him and said,
27:27 country that the LORD has **b**.
27:29 those who bless you be **b**."
27:33 I **b** him, and he will stay
27:33 and he will stay **b**."
28:1 called for Jacob and **b** him.
28:6 Esau learned that Isaac had **b**
28:6 He learned that Isaac had **b**
28:14 every family on earth will be **b**.
30:13 Leah said, "I've been **b**!
30:13 Women will call me **b**."
30:27 seen that the LORD has **b** me
30:30 The LORD has **b** you wherever
31:55 and his daughters and **b** them.
32:29 Then he **b** Jacob there.
35:9 Paddan Aram, and he **b** him.
39:5 From that time on the LORD **b**
41:52 second son Ephraim [**B** Twice
47:7 Jacob **b** Pharaoh.
47:10 Then Jacob **b** Pharaoh and left.
48:3 me at Luz in Canaan and **b** me.
48:15 Then Jacob **b** Joseph,
48:20 That day he **b** them.
Exo 20:11 That's why the LORD **b** the day
39:43 So Moses **b** them.
Lev 9:22 toward the people and **b** them.
9:23 came out, they **b** the people.
Num 22:6 that whomever you bless is **b**
22:12 because they are **b**."
23:20 He has **b**, and I can't change it.
24:9 Those who bless you will be **b**!
24:10 you have **b** them three times.
Dtr 2:7 The LORD your God has **b** you
7:14 You will be **b** more than any
11:27 You'll be **b** if you obey the
12:7 the LORD your God has **b** you.
12:15 your God has **b** you with.
28:3 You will be **b** in the city and
28:3 in the city and **b** in the country.
Dtr 28:4 You will be **b**. You will have
28:5 the bread you bake will be **b**.
28:6 You will be **b** when you come
28:6 you come and **b** when you go.
29:19 He may think that he is so **b**
33:1 Moses, the man of God, **b** the
33:20 "**B** is the one who gives the
33:24 people of Asher are the most **b**
33:29 You are **b**, Israel! Who is like
Jos 14:13 So Joshua **b** Caleb,
17:14 because the LORD has **b** us."
22:6 Then Joshua **b** them.
22:7 sent them home, he **b** them.
Jdg 5:24 should be the most **b** woman,
5:24 the most **b** woman living in a
13:24 and the LORD **b** him.
Rut 2:19 who paid attention to you be **b**."
1Sm 25:32 "**B** be the LORD God of Israel,
25:33 May your good judgment be **b**.
25:33 Also, may you be **b** for keeping
25:39 dead, he said, "**B** be the LORD,
26:25 Then Saul said, "**B** are you,
2Sm 6:11 and the LORD **b** Obed Edom
6:12 "The LORD has **b** Obed
6:18 he **b** the people in the name of
7:29 my house will be **b** forever."
14:22 the ground, and he **b** the king.
19:39 king kissed Barzillai and **b** him.
1Ki 2:45 But King Solomon is **b**,
8:14 the king turned around and **b**
8:55 he stood and in a loud voice **b**
8:66 They **b** the king and went to
10:8 How **b** your men must be!
10:8 How **b** these servants of yours
1Ch 13:14 and the LORD **b** Obed Edom's
16:2 he **b** the people in the name of
17:27 Indeed, you, LORD, have **b** it.
17:27 It will be **b** forever."
26:5 God had **b** Obed Edom.
2Ch 6:3 the king turned around and **b**
9:7 How **b** your men must be!
9:7 How **b** these servants of yours
30:27 Levitical priests **b** the people.
31:10 The LORD has **b** his people,
Neh 11:2 The people **b** everyone who
Job 1:10 You have **b** everything he does.
5:17 "**B** is the person whom God
29:11 ears that heard me **b** me.
42:12 The LORD **b** the latter years of
Psa 1:1 **B** is the person who does not
2:12 **B** is everyone who takes
32:1 **B** is the person whose
32:2 **B** is the person whom the
33:12 **B** is the nation whose God is
33:12 **B** are the people he has
34:8 **B** is the person who takes
37:22 Those who are **b** by him will
40:4 **B** is the person who places his
41:1 **B** is the one who has concern
41:2 He will be **b** in the land.
45:2 is why God has **b** you forever.
65:4 **B** is the person you choose
72:17 May all nations be **b** through
72:17 through him and call him **b**.
84:4 **B** are those who live in your
84:5 **B** are those who find strength
84:12 **b** is the person who trusts you.
89:15 **B** are the people who know
94:12 O LORD, **b** is the person whom
106:3 **B** are those who defend justice
112:1 **B** is the person who fears the
112:2 of a decent person will be **b**.
115:15 You will be **b** by the LORD,
118:26 **B** is the one who comes in the
119:1 **B** are those whose lives have
119:2 **B** are those who obey his
127:5 **B** is the man who has filled his
128:1 **B** are all who fear the LORD
129:8 "May you be **b** by the LORD" or
137:8 **b** is the one who pays you
137:9 **B** is the one who grabs your
144:15 **B** are the people who have
144:15 **B** are the people whose God is
146:5 **B** are those who receive help
Pro 3:13 **B** is the one who finds wisdom
3:18 Those who cling to it are **b**.

Pro 5:18 Let your own fountain be **b**,
8:32 **B** are those who follow my
8:34 **B** is the person who listens to
10:7 a righteous person remains **b**,
14:21 but **b** is the one who is kind to
16:20 and **b** is the person who trusts
20:7 **B** are his children after he is
20:21 will never be **b** in the end.
22:9 Whoever is generous will be **b**
28:14 **B** is the one who is always
29:18 but **b** are those who follow
Ecc 10:17 A country is **b** when the king is
Sos 6:9 Her sisters saw her and **b** her.
Isa 19:25 my possession Israel are **b**."
30:18 **B** are all those who wait for
32:20 **B** are those who plant beside
51:2 I **b** him and gave him many
56:2 **B** is the one who does these
56:2 **B** is the one who keeps the
61:9 whom the LORD has **b**.
65:16 in the land will be **b** by
65:23 they will be offspring **b** by
Jer 4:2 then the nations will be **b**,
17:7 **B** is the person who trusts the
20:14 birth to me. May it not be **b**.
Eze 3:12 "**B** is the LORD's glory,
Dan 12:12 **B** are those who wait until they
Mal 3:12 "All nations will call you **b**
3:15 now we call arrogant people **b**.
Mat 5:3 "**B** are those who recognize
5:4 **B** are those who mourn.
5:5 **B** are those who are gentle.
5:6 **B** are those who hunger and
5:7 **B** are those who show mercy.
5:8 **B** are those whose thoughts
5:9 **B** are those who make peace.
5:10 **B** are those who are
5:11 "**B** are you when people insult
11:6 his faith in me is indeed **b**."
13:16 "**B** are your eyes because they
14:19 up to heaven and **b** the food.
16:17 son of Jonah, you are **b**!
19:15 After Jesus **b** them,
21:9 **B** is the one who comes in the
23:39 '**B** is the one who comes in the
24:46 That servant will be **b** if his
25:34 my Father has **b** you!
26:26 Jesus took bread and **b** it.
Mar 6:41 up to heaven and **b** the food.
8:7 He **b** them and said that the
10:16 children and **b** them by placing
11:9 **B** is the one who comes in the
11:10 **B** is our ancestor David's
14:22 Jesus took bread and **b** it.
14:61 the Son of the **B** One?"
Luk 1:42 "You are the most **b** of all
1:42 and **b** is the child that you will
1:43 I feel **b** that the mother of my
1:45 You are **b** for believing that the
1:48 all people will call me **b**
2:34 Then Simeon **b** them and said
6:20 "**B** are those who are poor.
6:21 **B** are those who are hungry.
6:21 **B** are those who are crying.
6:22 **B** are you when people hate
7:23 his faith in me is indeed **b**."
9:16 up to heaven, and **b** the food.
10:23 "How **b** you are to see what
11:27 "How **b** is the mother who gave
11:28 Jesus replied, "Rather, how **b**
12:37 **B** are those servants whom the
12:38 They will be **b** if he comes in
12:43 That servant will be **b** if his
13:35 '**B** is the one who comes in the
14:14 Then you will be **b** because
14:15 in the kingdom of God is **b**."
19:38 They shouted joyfully, "**B** is
23:29 '**B** are the women who couldn't
24:30 he took bread and **b** it.
24:50 raised his hands and **b** them.
Jon 12:13 **B** is the one who comes in the
13:17 you are **b** whenever you follow
20:29 **B** are those who haven't seen
Act 3:25 all people on earth will be **b**.'
Rom 1:25 the Creator, who is **b** forever.
4:7 "**B** are those whose
Rom 4:8 **B** is the person whom the Lord
4:9 only the circumcised people **b**,
4:9 people **b** as well?
9:5 God over everything, forever **b**.
14:22 shouldn't feel guilty. He is **b**.
1Co 7:40 However, she will be more **b** if
Gal 3:8 people of the world will be **b**."
3:9 So people who believe are **b**
Eph 1:3 Through Christ, God has **b** us
1Ti 1:11 contains the glory of the **b** God.
6:15 God is the **b** and only ruler.
Heb 7:1 He met Abraham and **b** him
7:6 Then Melchizedek **b** Abraham,
Jas 1:12 **B** are those who endure when
1:25 committed to them will be **b**.
5:11 those who endure to be **b**.
1Pe 3:14 what God approves, you are **b**.
4:14 you are **b** because the Spirit of
Rev 1:3 **B** is the one who reads,
14:13 die believing in the Lord are **b**."
16:15 **B** is the one who remains alert
19:9 '**B** are those who are invited to
20:6 **B** and holy are those who are
22:7 **B** is the one who follows the
22:14 "**B** are those who wash their

blesses (9)

1Sm 9:13 since he **b** the sacrifice.
Psa 10:3 He **b** robbers, but he curses the
49:18 Even though he **b** himself
107:38 He **b** them, and their numbers
147:13 He **b** the children within you.
Pro 3:33 but he **b** the home of righteous
27:14 Whoever **b** his friend early in
Heb 6:7 God **b** the earth. So rain often
7:7 the more important person **b**

blessing (67)

Gen 12:2 and you will be a **b**:
24:60 They gave Rebekah a **b**:
27:12 curse on myself instead of a **b**."
27:30 Isaac finished **b** Jacob.
27:35 and has taken away your **b**."
27:36 and now he's taken my **b**."
27:36 you saved a **b** for me?"
27:38 "Do you have only one **b**,
27:41 because of the **b** that his father
28:4 and your descendants the **b**
30:13 So she named him Asher [**B**].
39:5 Therefore, the LORD's **b** was
48:20 Israel will speak this **b**,
49:28 each of them his special **b**.
Exo 32:29 God gave you a **b** today
Lev 25:21 I will give you my **b** in the
Dtr 11:26 the choice of a **b** or a curse.
11:29 recite the **b** from Mount
23:5 turned Balaam's curse into a **b**
33:1 with this **b** before he died.
Jos 15:19 She answered, "Give me a **b**.
Jdg 1:15 She answered, "Give me a **b**.
2Sm 7:29 With your **b** my house will be
13:25 he did give Absalom his **b**.
16:12 his curse into a **b** for me today."
1Ch 23:13 always give the **b** in his name.
Neh 9:5 high above all **b** and praise.
13:2 God turned the curse into a **b**.)
Job 29:13 I received a **b** from the dying.
Psa 3:8 May your **b** rest on your people.
21:6 Yes, you made him a **b** forever.
24:5 ⌊This person⌋ will receive a **b**
37:26 His descendants are a **b**.
84:11 He does not hold back any **b**
109:17 so he never received a **b**.
133:3 promised the **b** of eternal life.
Pro 10:22 It is the LORD's **b** that makes a
11:11 With the **b** of decent people a
11:26 but a **b** will be upon the head of
24:25 and a great **b** will come to
27:14 voice — his **b** is considered
Isa 19:24 They will be a **b** on the earth.
44:3 and my **b** on your descendants.
65:8 because there's a **b** in it."
65:16 Whoever asks for a **b** in the
Jer 32:40 that I will never stop **b** them.
32:41 I will enjoy **b** them.
Eze 34:26 showers will be a **b** to them.
Eze 44:30 This will cause a **b** to rest on
Joe 2:14 his plan and leave a **b** for you.
Zec 7:2 men to ask the LORD for a **b**.
8:13 and you will become a **b**.
8:21 going to ask the LORD for a **b**
8:22 and to ask the LORD for a **b**.
12:10 "I will pour out the Spirit of **b**
Luk 24:51 While he was **b** them,
Rom 1:11 to see you to share a spiritual **b**
4:6 thing when he speaks this **b**:
15:29 I will bring the full **b** of Christ.
1Co 10:16 When we bless the cup of **b**
2Co 9:5 Then it will be the **b** it was
Gal 3:14 price⌋ so that the **b** promised
Eph 1:3 spiritual **b** that heaven has
Phm 1:6 knowledge of every **b** we have
Heb 12:17 he wanted to receive the **b** that
12:17 he begged and cried for the **b**,
1Pe 3:9 you were called to inherit a **b**.

blessings (47)

Gen 49:25 Almighty who gives you **b** from
49:25 **b** from the deep springs below
49:25 **b** from breasts and womb.
49:26 The **b** of your father are greater
49:26 father are greater than the **b**
49:26 May these **b** rest on the head of
Dtr 16:10 offering in proportion to the **b**
16:17 a gift in proportion to the **b**
28:2 These are all the **b** that will
28:11 LORD will give you plenty of **b**:
30:1 All these **b** and curses I have
30:9 your God will give you many **b**
30:19 you life or death, **b** or curses.
33:16 May these **b** come to the tribes
33:23 are filled with the LORD's **b**.
Jos 8:34 read all the Teachings — the **b**
1Ki 8:66 with cheerful hearts for all the **b**
2Ch 7:10 with cheerful hearts for all the **b**
Psa 21:3 You welcomed him with the **b**
84:6 The early rains cover it with **b**.
87:7 "Zion is the source of all our **b**."
103:5 fills your life with **b** so that you
104:28 and they are filled with **b**.
107:43 may understand the LORD's **b**.
119:41 Let your **b** reach me,
128:2 **B** to you! May things go well
144:15 the people who have these **b**!
Pro 10:6 **B** cover the head of a righteous
28:20 trustworthy person has many **b**,
Isa 3:10 Tell the righteous that **b** will
45:7 I make **b** and create disasters.
55:3 promise to you — the **b**
Jer 6:16 Ask which way leads to **b**.
29:32 He will not see the **b** that I'm
31:12 to it to enjoy the LORD's **b**:
31:14 with my **b**," declares the LORD.
32:42 bring on them all these **b** that
33:9 will hear about all the **b** that
44:27 them to bring disasters, not **b**.
Hos 3:5 trembling to the LORD for his **b**
Zec 4:7 stone with shouts of '**B**,
4:7 shouts of 'Blessings, **b** on it!'"
9:12 I will return to you double ⌊**b**⌋.
Mal 2:2 and I'll curse the **b** you give.
3:10 for you and flood you with **b**.
2Co 9:6 received God's **b** will receive
9:6 a harvest of God's **b** in return.

blew (32)

Gen 2:7 from the dust of the earth and **b**
Exo 10:19 It picked up the locusts and **b**
15:10 Your breath **b** the sea over
Jos 6:8 off as they **b** their horns.
6:9 the priests, who **b** their horns.
6:13 The priests **b** their horns as
6:13 while the horns **b** continually.
6:16 the priests **b** their rams' horns.
Jdg 3:27 When he arrived there, he **b** a
6:34 So Gideon **b** the ram's horn to
7:19 They **b** their rams' horns and
7:20 The three companies also **b**
2Sm 2:28 So Joab **b** a ram's horn,
18:16 Joab **b** the ram's horn to stop
20:1 He **b** a ram's horn ⌊to
20:22 He **b** the ram's horn,

1Ki 1:39 They **b** the ram's horn,
1:40 people followed him, **b** flutes,
2Ki 9:13 They **b** a ram's horn and said,
1Ch 15:24 and Eliezer **b** trumpets in front
2Ch 13:14 the priests **b** the trumpets,
29:28 and the trumpets **b** until the
Mat 7:25 Winds **b** and beat against that
7:27 Winds **b** and struck that house.
Act 27:14 northeaster) **b** from the island.
Rev 8:7 the first angel **b** his trumpet,
8:8 the second angel **b** his trumpet,
8:10 the third angel **b** his trumpet,
8:12 the fourth angel **b** his trumpet,
9:1 the fifth angel **b** his trumpet,
9:13 the sixth angel **b** his trumpet,
11:15 seventh angel **b** his trumpet,

blight (2)

Amo 4:9 ⌊crops⌋ with **b** and mildew.
Hag 2:17 I infested all your work with **b**

blind (90)

Gen 27:1 Isaac was old and going **b**,
Exo 4:11 them sight or makes them **b**?
23:8 because bribes **b** those who
Lev 19:14 anything in the way of **b** people
21:18 anyone who is **b** or lame,
22:22 the LORD an animal that is **b**,
Dtr 15:21 But if an animal is lame or **b** or
16:19 because bribes **b** wise people
27:18 "Whoever leads **b** people in the
28:29 daylight as **b** people grope
2Sm 5:6 Even the **b** and the lame could
5:8 lame and the **b** who hate me
5:8 So there is a saying, "The **b**
Job 29:15 I was eyes for the **b** person.
40:24 Can anyone **b** its eyes or
Psa 146:8 LORD gives sight to **b** people.
Isa 29:9 If you **b** yourselves,
29:18 The **b** will see out of their
35:5 Then the eyes of the **b** will be
42:7 You will give sight to the **b**,
42:16 I will lead the **b** on unfamiliar
42:18 Look, you **b** people,
42:19 Who is **b** except my servant or
42:19 Who is **b** like the one who has
42:19 one who has my trust or **b** like
43:8 Bring the people who are **b** but
56:10 ⌊Israel's⌋ watchmen are **b**.
59:10 We grope like **b** men along a
Jer 31:8 **B** people and lame people will
Zep 1:17 they will walk like they are **b**,
Zec 11:17 right eye will be completely **b**."
12:4 all the horses of the nations **b**.
Mal 1:8 When you bring a **b** animal to
Mat 9:27 two **b** men followed him.
9:28 and the **b** men followed him.
11:5 **B** people see again,
12:22 The demon made the man **b**
13:13 They see, but they're **b**.
15:14 They are **b** leaders.
15:14 When one **b** person leads
15:30 them the lame, **b**, disabled,
15:31 walking, and the **b** seeing.
20:30 Two **b** men were sitting by the
21:14 **B** and lame people came to
23:16 it will be for you, you **b** guides!
23:17 You **b** fools! What is more
23:19 You **b** men! What is more
23:24 You **b** guides! You strain gnats
23:26 You **b** Pharisees! First clean the
Mar 8:18 Are you **b** and deaf?
8:22 some people brought a **b** man
8:23 Jesus took the **b** man's hand
10:46 a **b** beggar named Bartimaeus,
10:49 They called the **b** man and told
10:50 The **b** man threw off his coat,
10:51 The **b** man said, "Teacher,
Luk 4:18 the restoring of sight to the **b**,
6:39 "Can one **b** person lead
7:21 sight to many who were **b**.
7:22 **B** people see again,
14:13 the lame, and the **b**.
14:21 the **b**, and the lame.'
18:35 a **b** man was sitting and
18:38 Then the **b** man shouted,
Luk 18:39 of the crowd told the **b** man
18:41 The **b** man said, "Lord, I want
Jon 5:3 people — people who were **b**,
9:1 a man who had been born **b**.
9:2 why was this man born **b**?
9:3 Instead, he was born **b** so that
9:7 (Siloam means "sent.") The **b**
9:13 had been **b** to the Pharisees.
9:17 been born **b** another question:
9:18 that the man had been **b**
9:19 the one you say was born **b**?
9:20 our son and that he was born **b**.
9:24 the man who had been **b**.
9:25 I used to be **b**, but now I can
9:32 giving sight to a person born **b**.
9:39 **B** people will be given sight,
9:39 who can see will become **b**."
9:40 "Do you think we're **b**?"
9:41 Jesus told them, "If you were **b**,
10:21 a demon give sight to the **b**?"
11:37 who gave a **b** man sight keep
Act 9:8 he opened his eyes, he was **b**.
13:11 For a while you will be **b**,
22:11 "I was **b** because the light had
Rom 2:19 that you are a guide for the **b**,
Rev 3:17 pitiful, poor, **b**, and naked.

blinded (7)

Exo 21:26 in the eye and the slave is **b**,
2Ki 25:7 and then they **b** Zedekiah.
Isa 29:9 blind yourselves, you will be **b**.
Jer 39:7 Then he **b** Zedekiah,
52:11 Then he **b** Zedekiah and put
Jon 12:40 "God **b** them and made them
2Co 4:4 The god of this world has **b** the

blindfolded (1)

Luk 22:64 They **b** him and said to him,

blindly (1)

Lam 4:14 My people staggered **b** through

blindness (5)

Gen 19:11 with **b** so that they gave up
Dtr 28:28 with madness, **b**, and panic.
28:29 as blind people grope in their **b**.
2Ki 6:18 strike these people with **b**."
6:18 The LORD struck them with **b**,

bloated (1)

Job 15:27 "His face is **b** with fat,

block (6)

Psa 35:3 Hold your spear to **b** the way of
Sos 5:14 His chest is a **b** of ivory
Isa 8:14 people trip and a stumbling **b**
44:19 and bowing to a **b** of wood."
Eze 39:11 It will **b** those who travel
Hos 2:6 "That is why I will **b** her way

blockade (21)

Dtr 20:12 set up a **b** around the city.
20:19 you must do whenever you **b**
20:19 not people you have come to **b**.
20:20 them in your **b** until you capture
28:52 They will **b** all your cities until
28:52 They'll **b** all the cities
28:53 make you suffer during the **b**,
28:55 make you suffer during the **b**
28:57 during the **b** of your cities.
1Sm 23:8 to go to war and **b** Keilah,
1Ki 8:37 Enemies may **b** Israel's city
20:1 He went to **b** Samaria and fight
2Ki 6:25 The shortages caused by the **b**
25:2 The **b** of the city lasted until
2Ch 6:28 Enemies may **b** Israel's city
Isa 29:3 I will **b** you with towers.
29:7 against it, **b** it, and torment it.
Jer 52:5 The **b** of the city lasted until
Lam 4:10 were being destroyed ⌊by a **b**⌋.
Eze 4:2 Set up a **b** against it,
5:2 When the **b** is over,

blockaded (11)

1Sm 11:1 the Ammonite **b** Jabesh Gilead.
2Ki 6:24 They went to Samaria and **b** it.
2Ki 16:5 They **b** Ahaz but couldn't get
17:5 He attacked Samaria and **b** it
18:9 Assyria attacked Samaria, **b** it,
24:10 Jerusalem. (The city was **b**.)
2Ch 32:10 live in Jerusalem while it is **b**?
Ecc 9:14 He surrounded it and **b** it.
Jer 10:17 up your bags. You are being **b**.
39:1 with his entire army and **b** it.
Eze 4:7 face toward the **b** Jerusalem.

blockades (5)

Jer 19:9 eat each other's flesh during **b**
50:29 Set up **b** around it.
Eze 17:17 put up dirt ramps and set up **b**
21:22 put up ramps, and set up **b**.
26:8 He will set up **b**, put up dirt

blockading (4)

2Ki 24:11 his officers were **b** the city.
Jer 21:4 who are now **b** you outside
32:2 of Babylon was **b** Jerusalem.
37:5 were **b** Jerusalem heard this

blocked (4)

1Sm 15:2 They **b** Israel's way after the
Job 19:8 "God has **b** my path so that I
Lam 3:7 He has **b** me so that I can't get
3:9 He has **b** my way with cut

blocking (3)

Exo 9:17 You are still **b** my people from
14:3 The desert is **b** their escape.'
Isa 30:11 Stop **b** our path! Get the Holy

blocks (10)

Exo 20:25 never make it with cut stone **b**.
1Ki 5:17 expensive **b** of stone in order
6:7 with stone **b** that were finished
7:9 built with high-grade stone **b**.
7:9 The stone **b** were cut to size
7:11 beams and high-grade stone **b**,
7:12 had three layers of cut stone **b**
Psa 33:10 The LORD **b** the plans of the
Isa 44:13 Carpenters measure **b** of wood
Jer 6:21 I'm going to lay stumbling **b** in

blood (326)

Gen 4:10 Your brother's **b** is crying out to
4:11 which has received the **b** of
6:3 because they are flesh and **b**.
9:4 are not to eat meat with **b** in it.
9:4 meat with blood in it. (**B** is life.)
9:5 addition, I will demand your **b**
9:6 Whoever sheds human **b**,
9:6 by humans his **b** will be shed,
29:14 "You are my own flesh and **b**."
37:27 our own flesh and **b**."
37:31 and dipped the robe in the **b**.
49:11 his garments in the **b** of grapes.
Exo 4:9 will turn into **b** on the ground."
4:25 are a bridegroom of **b** to me!"
4:26 "You are a bridegroom of **b**!
7:17 and the water will turn into **b**.
7:19 so that they turn into **b**.
7:19 There will be **b** everywhere in
7:20 water in the river turned into **b**.
7:21 was **b** everywhere in Egypt.
12:7 They must take some of the **b**
12:13 But the **b** on your houses will
12:13 When I see the **b**, I will pass
12:22 dip it in the **b** which is in a
12:22 and put some of the **b** on the
12:23 When he sees the **b** on the top
23:18 "Never offer the **b** of a sacrifice
24:6 Moses took half of the **b** and
24:8 Moses took the **b** and sprinkled
24:8 "Here is the **b** which seals the
29:12 Take some of the bull's **b**,
29:16 Slaughter it, take the **b**,
29:20 Slaughter it, take some of the **b**,
29:20 Throw the ⌊rest of the⌋ **b**
29:21 Take some of the **b** that is on
30:10 with the LORD by putting **b**
30:10 generations to come — **b** from
34:25 "Never offer the **b** of a sacrifice
Lev 1:5 the priests, will offer the **b**.

Lev 1:11 will throw the **b** against the
1:15 First, he will drain the **b**
3:2 will throw the **b** against the
3:8 sons will throw the **b** against
3:13 sons will throw the **b** against
3:17 Never eat any fat or **b**."
4:5 will take some of the bull's **b**
4:6 some of the **b** seven times
4:7 the priest will put some of the **b**
4:7 pour the rest of the bull's **b** at
4:16 bring some of the bull's **b** into
4:17 dip his finger in some of the **b**
4:18 He will also put some **b** on the
4:18 He will pour the rest of the **b** at
4:25 priest will take some of the **b**
4:25 He will pour the rest of the **b** at
4:30 priest will take some of the **b**
4:30 He will pour the rest of the **b** at
4:34 will take some of the **b** from
4:34 He will pour the rest of the **b** at
5:9 He will sprinkle some of the **b**
5:9 and the rest of the **b** will be
6:27 If **b** gets on someone's clothes,
6:30 some of the **b** was brought into
7:2 ⌊A priest⌋ will throw the **b**
7:14 to the priest who throws the **b**
7:26 "Never eat the **b** of any bird or
7:27 Those who eat any **b** must be
7:33 any of Aaron's sons offer the **b**
8:15 Moses took the **b** and put it on
8:15 He poured the rest of the **b** at
8:19 it and threw the **b** against
8:23 took some of the **b**,
8:24 He put some of the **b** on their
8:24 Moses threw the rest of the **b**
8:30 oil and some of the **b** that was
9:9 Aaron's sons brought him the **b**.
9:9 He dipped his finger in the **b**
9:9 Then he poured out the **b** at the
9:12 Aaron's sons gave him the **b**,
9:18 Aaron's sons gave him the **b**,
10:18 Since its **b** was not brought
12:7 will be clean from her flow of **b**.
14:6 them and the living bird in the **b**
14:7 He will sprinkle the **b** seven
14:14 will take some of the **b** from
14:17 same places he had put the **b**
14:25 priest will take some of the **b**
14:28 same places he had put the **b**
14:51 the fresh water containing the **b**
14:52 So he must use the bird's **b**,
15:23 If her **b** touches anything on the
15:25 a woman has a discharge of **b**
16:14 will take some of the bull's **b**
16:14 he will sprinkle some of the **b**
16:15 He will take the **b** inside,
16:15 as he did with the bull's **b**.
16:18 He will take some of the **b** from
16:18 bull and some of the goat's **b**
16:19 he will sprinkle some of the **b**
16:27 sin whose **b** was brought into
17:4 He has shed **b** and must be
17:6 The priest will pour the **b**
17:10 or foreigners eat any **b**,
17:11 because **b** contains life.
17:11 I have given this **b** to you to
17:11 **B** is needed to make peace
17:12 foreigners should ever eat **b**.
17:13 must pour out the animal's **b**
17:14 life of any creature is in its **b**.
17:14 of Israel: Never eat any **b**,
17:14 life of any creature is in its **b**.
17:14 Whoever eats **b** must be
18:6 anyone related to you by **b**.
19:26 "Never eat any meat with **b**
20:18 had sexual intercourse in **b**.
Num 18:17 Throw the **b** from these
19:4 Eleazar will take some of the **b**
19:5 entire cow (the skin, meat, **b**,
23:24 and drinks the **b** of its victim."
Dtr 12:16 But never eat the **b**.
12:23 be sure you never eat **b**,
12:23 because **b** contains life.
12:24 Never eat **b**. Pour it on the
12:25 If you don't eat **b**, things will go
12:27 Sacrifice the meat and the **b** of

Dtr 12:27 The **b** of your sacrifices is to
15:23 But never eat the **b**.
32:42 My arrows will drip with **b** from
Jdg 9:2 I'm your own flesh and **b**.'"
1Sm 14:32 ate the meat with **b** still in it.
14:33 by eating meat with **b** in it."
14:34 LORD by eating meat with **b**
19:5 innocent **b** for no reason?"
25:26 you from spilling innocent **b**
25:31 because you spilled **b**
26:20 Don't let my **b** fall to the ground,
2Sm 1:16 for spilling your own **b**.
1:22 From the **b** of those killed and
3:27 died because he spilled the **b**
3:28 innocent of spilling the **b**
5:1 own flesh and **b**," they said.
16:8 back for all the **b** you spilled
16:11 my own flesh and **b**,
19:12 my own flesh and **b**.
19:13 'Aren't you my flesh and **b**?
20:12 Amasa was wallowing in his **b**
23:17 This is the **b** of men who
1Ki 2:5 he shed **b** as if it were wartime.
2:5 With their **b** he stained the belt
2:31 You can remove the innocent **b**
2:31 blood — the **b** which Joab shed
2:33 The responsibility for their **b**
18:28 and spears until their **b** flowed.
21:19 the dogs licked up Naboth's **b**,
21:19 the dogs will lick up your **b**.'"
22:35 The **b** from the wound had
22:38 The dogs licked up his **b**,
2Ki 3:22 It was as red as **b**.
3:23 They said, "It's **b**! The kings
9:7 on Jezebel for shedding the **b**
9:26 'Just as I saw the **b** of Naboth
9:33 and some of her **b** splattered on
16:13 and sprinkled the **b** of his
16:15 Sprinkle all the **b** of the burnt
24:4 including the innocent **b** he had
1Ch 11:1 own flesh and **b**," they said.
11:19 Should I drink the **b** of these
2Ch 29:22 and the priests sprinkled the **b**
29:22 the rams and sprinkled the **b**
29:22 and sprinkled the **b** on the altar.
29:24 the goats and made their **b**
30:16 The priests sprinkled the **b**
35:11 The priests sprinkled the **b**
Neh 5:5 We have the same flesh and **b**
Job 16:13 and spills my **b** on the ground.
16:18 "Earth, don't cover my **b**.
39:30 Its young ones feed on **b**.
Psa 16:4 their sacrificial offerings of **b**
30:9 will you profit if my **b** is shed,
50:13 of bulls or drink the **b** of goats?
56:4 mere flesh ⌊and **b**⌋ do to me?
58:10 feet in the **b** of wicked people.
68:23 may bathe your feet in **b** and
68:23 lick the **b** of your enemies."
72:14 Their **b** will be precious in his
78:39 that they were only flesh and **b**,
78:44 He turned their rivers into **b** so
79:3 They have shed the **b** of your
79:10 the **b** of your servants.
105:29 He turned their water into **b** and
106:38 They shed innocent **b**,
106:38 shed innocent blood, the **b**
106:38 land became polluted with **b**.
Pro 1:16 to do evil and hurry to shed **b**.
30:33 punching a nose produces **b**,
Isa 1:11 not pleased with the **b** of bulls,
1:15 your hands are covered with **b**.
9:5 every garment rolled in **b** will
15:9 water in Dimon is red with **b**,
26:21 The earth will uncover the **b**
31:3 Their horses are flesh and **b**,
34:3 will be red with their **b**.
34:5 my sword is covered ⌊with **b**⌋
34:6 sword is covered with **b**.
34:6 with the **b** of lambs and goats,
34:7 land will be drenched with **b**.
49:26 drunk on their own **b** as though
52:15 many nations ⌊with his **b**⌋.
59:3 Your hands are stained with **b**,
59:7 They hurry to shed innocent **b**.
63:3 Their **b** splattered my clothes

Isa 63:6 poured their **b** on the ground."
66:3 someone who ⌊offers⌋ pig's **b**.
Jer 2:34 You have the **b** from poor and
17:5 who makes flesh and **b** his
18:21 Pour out their ⌊**b**⌋ by using
19:4 with the **b** of innocent people.
46:10 and it will drink their **b** until it's
Lam 4:13 who spilled the **b** of righteous
Eze 16:6 kicking around in your own **b**.
16:9 and I washed off your **b**.
16:22 kicking around in your own **b**.
16:36 sacrificed their **b** to these idols.
23:37 Their hands are covered with **b**.
23:45 their hands are covered with **b**.
24:7 **B** is still in that city.
24:7 The **b** was poured on a bare
24:8 I put the **b** of its victims on a
24:8 Now that **b** can't be covered.
28:23 against you and make **b** flow
32:6 the earth with your flowing **b** all
33:25 You eat meat with **b** in it.
36:18 because they poured out **b**
39:17 You can eat meat and drink **b**
39:18 meat of warriors and drink the **b**
39:19 are full and drink **b** until you are
43:18 offerings and for sprinkling **b**
43:20 Take some of the bull's **b**,
44:7 you offered fat and **b** to me.
44:15 They may bring fat and **b** to me,
45:19 The priest must take some **b**
Joe 2:30 **b**, fire, and clouds of smoke.
2:31 will become as red as **b** before
Zep 1:17 Their **b** will be poured out like
Zec 9:7 I will remove the **b** from their
9:11 of the **b** that sealed my
Mat 23:35 for all the innocent **b**
26:28 This is my **b**, the blood of the
26:28 the **b** of the promise.
27:6 because it's **b** money."
27:8 the Field of **B** ever since.
Mar 14:24 He said to them, "This is my **b**,
14:24 the **b** of the promise.
Luk 22:20 new promise made with my **b**."
22:44 became like drops of **b** falling
Jon 3:6 Flesh and **b** give birth to flesh
3:6 blood give birth to flesh and **b**,
6:53 the Son of Man and drink his **b**,
6:54 drink my **b** have eternal life,
6:55 and my **b** is true drink.
6:56 my flesh and drink my **b** live
19:34 and **b** and water immediately
Act 1:19 'Field of **B**' in their dialect.
2:19 **b**, fire, and clouds of smoke.
2:20 will become as red as **b** before
20:28 he acquired with his own **b**.
Rom 3:25 through faith in Christ's **b**.
5:9 Since Christ's **b** has now given
1Co 10:16 we sharing the **b** of Christ?
11:25 new promise made with my **b**.
11:27 for the Lord's body and **b**.
15:50 Flesh and **b** cannot inherit the
Eph 1:7 Through the **b** of his Son,
2:13 brought near by the **b** of Christ.
Col 1:20 through Christ's **b** sacrificed
Heb 2:14 daughters have flesh and **b**,
2:14 Jesus took on flesh and **b** to be
9:7 he entered and brought **b** that
9:12 He used his own **b**,
9:12 not the **b** of goats and bulls,
9:13 The **b** of goats and bulls and
9:14 The **b** of Christ, who had no
9:18 first promise was made with **b**.
9:19 Then he took the **b** of calves
9:20 He said, "Here is the **b** that
9:21 Moses sprinkled **b** on the tent
9:22 As Moses' Teachings tell us, **b**
9:22 because if no **b** is shed,
9:25 a sacrifice with **b** that isn't his
10:4 (The **b** of bulls and goats
10:19 because of the **b** of Jesus we
10:22 been sprinkled ⌊with his **b**⌋
10:29 That person looks at the **b** of
10:29 promise (the **b** that made him
10:29 different from other people's **b**,
11:28 Passover and spread the **b** ⌊on
12:24 and to the sprinkled **b** that

Heb 13:11 The chief priest brings the **b** of
13:12 the people holy with his own **b**.
13:20 back to life through the **b** of an
1Pe 1:2 and are sprinkled with his **b**.
1:19 was the precious **b** of Christ,
1Jn 1:7 And the **b** of his Son Jesus
5:6 who came by water and **b**.
5:6 but with water and with **b**.
5:8 the Spirit, the water, and the **b**.
2Jn 1:7 Christ came in flesh and **b**.
Rev 1:5 freed us from our sins by his **b**
5:9 You bought people with your **b**
6:10 on earth who shed our **b**?"
6:12 full moon turned as red as **b**.
7:14 them white in the **b** of the lamb.
8:7 hail and fire were mixed with **b**,
8:8 of the sea turned into **b**,
11:6 authority to turn water into **b**
12:11 over him because of the **b**
14:20 **B** flowed out of the winepress
16:3 The sea turned into **b** like the
16:3 sea turned into blood like the **b**
16:4 They turned into **b**.
16:6 You have given them **b** to drink
16:6 they have poured out the **b**
17:6 woman was drunk with the **b**
18:24 "The **b** of prophets,
19:2 on her for the **b** of his servants."
19:13 He wears clothes dipped in **b**,

blood-red (1)

Dtr 32:14 drank the **b** wine of grapes.

bloodshed (8)

Gen 37:22 "Let's not have any **b**.
42:22 Now we must pay for this **b**."
Lev 17:4 is guilty of **b**. He has shed blood
1Ch 22:8 'You have caused a lot of **b**
22:8 so much **b** in my presence.
28:3 fought wars and caused **b**.'
2Ch 19:10 case involves **b** or commands,
Mic 3:10 You build Zion on **b** and

bloodshot (1)

Pro 23:29 no reason? Who has **b** eyes?

bloodstains (2)

Isa 4:4 He will clean **b** from Jerusalem
Lam 4:14 with **b** that no one

bloodsucking (1)

Pro 30:15 The **b** leech has two daughters

bloodthirsty (8)

2Sm 16:7 Get out, you **b** man!
16:8 because you're a **b** man."
Psa 5:6 with **b** and deceitful people.
26:9 or my life along with **b** people.
55:23 **B** and deceitful people will not
59:2 Save me from **b** people.
139:19 and that **b** people would leave
Pro 29:10 **B** people hate an innocent

bloody (6)

Jdg 9:24 God did this so that the **b**
Hos 6:8 It is stained with **b** footprints.
Nah 3:1 be for that city of **b** violence!
Act 15:20 and from eating **b** meat.
15:29 from eating **b** meat,
21:25 to false gods, **b** meat,

bloom (5)

Exo 9:31 heads and the flax was in **b**.
Sos 2:13 The grapevines **b** and give off
6:11 if the pomegranates were in **b**.
7:12 if the pomegranates are in **b**.
Hab 3:17 Even if the fig tree does not **b**

blooming (1)

Sos 2:15 Our vineyards are **b**.

blossom (9)

Psa 72:7 May righteous people **b** in his
90:6 the morning they **b** and sprout.
92:7 troublemakers **b** ⌊like flowers⌋,
92:13 They **b** in our God's courtyards.
Isa 27:6 Israel will **b**, bud, and fill the
35:1 wilderness will rejoice and **b**.
35:2 Like a lily the land will **b**.
Hos 14:5 They will **b** like flowers.
14:7 They will **b** like grapevines.

blossomed (4)

Gen 40:10 Soon after it sprouted it **b**.
Num 17:8 but it had also **b** and produced
Eze 7:10 Wrongdoing has **b**.
Heb 9:4 Aaron's staff that had **b**,

blossoms (13)

Exo 25:33 cups shaped like almond **b**,
25:34 cups shaped like almond **b**,
37:19 cups shaped like almond **b**,
37:20 cups shaped like almond **b**,
Job 15:33 a vine and throw off his **b** like
Psa 103:15 It **b** like a flower in the field.
Ecc 12:5 the road, the almond tree **b**,
Sos 2:12 **B** appear in the land.
6:11 walnut grove to look at the **b**
7:12 if the grape **b** have opened,
Isa 5:24 and their **b** will blow away like
18:5 Before the harvest, when **b** are
18:5 and grapes are ripening from **b**,

blotted (1)

Pro 6:33 and his disgrace will not be **b**

blouses (1)

Isa 3:20 hats, ankle bracelets, **b**,

blow (48)

Gen 8:1 So God made a wind **b** over
Exo 10:13 a wind from the east **b** over
Num 10:3 When you **b** both trumpets,
10:7 the trumpets will **b** without
10:8 will **b** the trumpets.
10:10 **b** the trumpets when you
Jos 6:4 while the priests **b** their horns.
6:9 continued to **b** their horns.
Jdg 7:18 When I and those with me **b**
7:20 so that they could **b** them.
1Sm 6:19 them with such a great **b**.
1Ki 1:34 Then **b** the ram's horn and say,
2Ch 21:14 The LORD will strike a great **b**
Job 30:15 They **b** away my dignity like
Psa 42:10 With a shattering **b** to my
68:2 **B** them away like smoke.
78:26 He made the east wind **b** in the
81:3 **B** the ram's horn on the day of
83:13 O my God, **b** them away like
107:25 and a storm began to **b**,
140:11 people with one **b** after another.
147:18 wind **b** ⌊and⌋ water flow.
Sos 4:16 **B** on my garden! Let its spices
Isa 5:24 and their blossoms will **b** away
Jer 4:5 Say, "**B** the ram's horn
4:11 hot wind from the heights will **b**
6:1 **B** the ram's horn in Tekoa.
6:29 of the blast furnace **b** fiercely
14:17 It will be a very serious **b**.'"
22:22 The wind will **b** away all your
51:27 **B** the ram's horn among the
Eze 24:16 "Son of man, with one **b** I'm
33:3 he will **b** his horn to warn the
33:6 coming and doesn't **b** his horn
Hos 5:8 "**B** the ram's horn in Gibeah.
5:8 **B** the trumpet in Ramah.
13:15 It will **b** out of the desert.
Joe 2:1 **B** the ram's horn in Zion.
2:15 **B** the ram's horn in Zion.
Jnh 4:8 God made a hot east wind **b**.
Hag 1:9 something home, I **b** it away.
Zec 9:14 The Almighty LORD will **b** the
Jon 6:18 A strong wind started to **b** and
Act 27:13 a gentle breeze began to **b** from
28:13 day a south wind began to **b**,
Rev 8:6 trumpets got ready to **b** them.
8:13 the three angels are about to **b**."
10:7 angel is ready to **b** his trumpet,

blowing (14)

Lev 23:24 by the **b** of rams' horns.
Jdg 7:22 The 300 men kept on **b** their
2Ki 11:14 were rejoicing and **b** trumpets.
2Ch 5:12 were 120 priests **b** trumpets.
7:6 the Levites **b** trumpets while all
15:14 and the **b** of trumpets and rams'
23:13 were rejoicing and **b** trumpets.
Amo 2:2 shouting and rams' horns are **b**.
Mat 14:32 the wind stopped **b**.
Mar 4:39 The wind stopped **b**,
6:51 and the wind stopped **b**.
Luk 12:55 When you see a south wind **b**,
Act 2:2 a sound like a violently **b** wind
Rev 7:1 the earth to keep them from **b**

blown (16)

Job 15:30 He will be **b** away by his own
37:21 clouds or after the wind has **b**
Psa 18:42 powder as fine as the dust **b** by
35:5 Let them be like husks **b** by the
Isa 17:13 on the mountains being **b** by
17:13 dust being **b** by a storm.
19:7 up, be **b** away, and disappear.
27:13 a ram's horn will be **b** loudly.
29:5 foes will be like husks **b** by
41:2 them into straw **b** by the wind.
Jer 13:24 like straw that is **b** away by
Eze 7:14 They have **b** a ram's horn,
Hos 13:3 They will be like straw **b** away
Jas 1:6 is like a wave that is **b** by
2Pe 2:17 They are a mist **b** around by a
Jud 1:12 They are dry clouds **b** around

blows (16)

Num 10:4 If only one trumpet **b**,
2Sm 7:14 and with **b** inflicted by people.
Psa 1:4 husks that the wind **b** away.
78:39 a breeze that **b** and does not
103:16 When the wind **b** over the
Ecc 1:6 The wind **b** toward the south
1:6 Round and round it **b**.
1:6 it blows. It **b** in a full circle.
Isa 14:6 with **b** that didn't stop.
18:3 Listen when someone **b** a
40:7 the LORD's breath **b** on them.
40:24 Then he **b** on them and they
Eze 17:10 when the east wind **b** on it.
17:21 every direction that the wind **b**.
Mic 6:13 to strike you with heavy **b**
Jon 3:8 The wind **b** wherever it

blue (3)

Exo 24:10 of sapphire as clear and **b** as
Jer 10:9 for the idols is **b** and purple,
Rev 9:17 fiery red, pale **b**, and yellow.

blunt (2)

Pro 18:23 rich person is **b** when replying.
Ecc 10:10 If an ax is **b** and the edge isn't

blur (1)

Psa 6:7 My eyes **b** from grief.

blurred (3)

Job 17:7 Now my eyes are **b** from grief.
Isa 32:3 those who can see won't be **b**,
1Co 13:12 Now we see a **b** image in a

blush (4)

Psa 83:16 Let their faces **b** with shame,
Jer 3:3 and you refuse to **b**.
6:15 don't even know how to **b**.
8:12 don't even know how to **b**.

Boanerges (1)

Mar 3:17 sons whom Jesus named **B**,

board (6)

Jdg 17:10 and your room and **b**."
Eze 27:27 everyone else on **b** sank into
Jnh 1:3 paid for the trip and went on **b**.
Act 20:3 When Paul was going to **b** a
20:14 we took him on **b** and went to
28:10 put whatever we needed on **b**.

boarded (1)

Act 20:6 we **b** a ship at Philippi.

boards (6)

Exo 27:8 "Make the altar out of **b** so that
38:7 He made the altar out of **b** so
1Ki 6:15 of the temple with cedar **b**.
6:16 of the temple with cedar **b** from
Sos 8:9 will barricade her with cedar **b**.
Eze 27:5 Your builders made all your **b**

boars (1)

Psa 80:13 Wild **b** from the forest graze on

boast (6)

1Sm 2:3 "Do not **b** (or) let arrogance
Psa 20:7 but we will **b** in the name of the
34:2 My soul will **b** about the LORD.
Isa 3:9 They **b** about their sins,
61:6 You will **b** in their splendor.
Amo 4:5 Brag and **b** about your freewill

boastful (2)

Jer 48:29 very arrogant, conceited, and **b**.
Rom 1:30 God, haughty, arrogant, and **b**.

boasting (5)

1Ki 1:5 Adonijah was **b** that he was
2Ki 19:28 me and your **b** has reached my
Isa 10:12 the king of Assyria for all his **b**
16:6 We've heard of their **b**,
37:29 me and your **b** has reached my

boasts (2)

Psa 10:3 The wicked person **b** about his
Isa 16:6 but their **b** aren't true.

boat (55)

Mat 4:21 They were in a **b** with their
4:22 and they immediately left the **b**
8:23 went with him as he left in a **b**.
8:24 waves were covering the **b**.
9:1 Jesus got into a **b**,
13:2 so large that he got into a **b**.
13:2 He sat in the **b** while the entire
14:13 he left in a **b** and went to a
14:14 When Jesus got out of the **b**,
14:22 made his disciples get into a **b**
14:24 The **b**, now hundreds of yards
14:29 So Peter got out of the **b** and
14:32 When they got into the **b**,
14:33 The men in the **b** bowed down
15:39 Jesus stepped into the **b** and
Mar 1:19 They were in a **b** preparing
1:20 in the **b** and followed Jesus.
3:9 to have a **b** ready so that
4:1 so he got into a **b** and sat in it.
4:1 The **b** was in the water while
4:36 they took Jesus along in a **b**
4:37 were breaking into the **b** so that
4:38 a cushion in the back of the **b**.
5:2 As Jesus stepped out of the **b**,
5:18 As Jesus stepped into the **b**,
5:21 of the Sea of Galilee in a **b**.
6:32 So they went away in a **b** to a
6:34 When Jesus got out of the **b**,
6:45 made his disciples get into a **b**
6:47 When evening came, the **b**
6:51 He got into the **b** with them,
6:54 as they stepped out of the **b**,
8:10 and his disciples got into a **b**
8:13 He got into a **b** again and
8:14 one loaf with them in the **b**.
Luk 5:3 So Jesus got into the **b** that
5:3 taught the crowd from the **b**.
5:4 "Take the **b** into deep water,
5:7 to their partners in the other **b**
8:22 and his disciples got into a **b**.
8:23 The **b** was taking on water,
8:37 got into a **b** and started back.
Jon 6:17 They got into a **b** and started to
6:19 He was coming near the **b**,
6:21 willing to help Jesus into the **b**.
6:21 Immediately, the **b** reached the
6:22 They noticed that only one **b**
6:22 had not stepped into that **b**
21:3 They went out in a **b** but didn't
21:6 out on the right side of the **b**,
Jon 21:8 other disciples came with the **b**
21:11 Simon Peter got into the **b** and
Act 14:26 From Attalia they took a **b** and
18:18 they took a **b** headed for Syria
18:21 Paul took a **b** from Ephesus

boats (10)

Job 9:26 They pass by quickly like **b**
Isa 2:16 Tarshish and all the beautiful **b**.
18:2 messengers by sea in **b** made
Mar 4:36 Other **b** were with him.
Luk 5:2 Jesus saw two **b** on the shore.
5:7 came and filled both **b** until
5:7 boats until the **b** nearly sank.
5:11 partners brought the **b** to shore,
Jon 6:23 Other **b** from Tiberias arrived
6:24 they got into these **b** and went

Boaz (32)

Rut 2:1 character named **B**.
2:3 of the field that belonged to **B**,
2:4 **B** was coming from Bethlehem,
2:5 **B** asked the young man in
2:8 **B** said to Ruth, "Listen,
2:11 **B** answered her, "People have
2:14 to eat, **B** told her, "Come here.
2:15 **B** ordered his servants,
2:19 with today is named **B**."
2:23 who were working for **B**.
3:2 Isn't **B**, whose young women
3:7 **B** had eaten and drunk to his
3:10 **B** replied, "May the LORD
3:14 At that moment **B** thought to
3:15 Then **B** told Ruth, "Stretch out
4:1 **B** went to the city gate and sat
4:1 **B** said, "Please come over
4:2 Then **B** chose ten men who
4:3 **B** said to the man,
4:5 **B** continued, "When you buy
4:8 So when the man said to **B**,
4:9 Then **B** said to the leaders and
4:13 Then **B** took Ruth home,
4:21 Salmon was the father of **B**.
4:21 **B** was the father of Obed.
1Ki 7:21 left and named it **B** [In Him Is
1Ch 2:11 and Salma was the father of **B**.
2:12 **B** was the father of Obed,
2Ch 3:17 the one on the left **B** [In Him Is
Mat 1:5 the father and mother of **B**.
1:5 **B** and Ruth were the father and
Luk 3:32 Obed, son of **B**, son of Salmon,

Bocheru (2)

1Ch 8:38 Their names were Azrikam, **B**,
9:44 Their names were Azrikam, **B**,

Bochim (2)

Jdg 2:1 LORD went from Gilgal to **B**.
2:5 So they called that place **B**

bodies (113)

Gen 47:18 you except our **b** and our land.
Exo 30:32 must never be poured on the **b**
Lev 11:8 animals or touch their dead **b**.
11:11 Consider their dead **b**
11:24 Whoever touches their dead **b**
11:25 of their dead **b** must wash his
11:27 Whoever touches their dead **b**
11:31 Whoever touches their dead **b**
11:35 Anything on which their dead **b**
11:36 their dead **b** will be unclean.
11:37 If their dead **b** fall on seed that
11:38 the seed and their dead **b** fall
15:5 wash their clothes and their **b**.
15:6 wash their clothes and their **b**.
15:7 wash their clothes and their **b**.
15:10 wash their clothes and their **b**.
15:21 wash their clothes and their **b**.
15:22 wash their clothes and their **b**.
15:27 wash their clothes and their **b**.
17:15 wash their clothes and their **b**.
17:16 wash their clothes and their **b**,
21:5 or slashing your **b**.
21:11 must never go near any dead **b**
26:29 You will eat the **b** of your sons
26:30 and pile your dead **b** on top of
Num 8:7 Make them shave their whole **b**
14:29 Your **b** will drop dead in this
14:32 However, your **b** will drop dead
14:33 until the last of your **b** lies dead
19:19 must wash their clothes and **b**,
Dtr 14:8 their meat or touch their dead **b**.
28:26 Your dead **b** will be food for all
Jos 7:25 Then they burned the **b** and
10:26 them to death and hung their **b**
Jdg 8:7 I'll whip your **b** with thorns and
1Sm 17:46 this day I will give the dead **b**
21:5 The young men's **b** are kept
21:5 then will their **b** be holy today?"
31:12 all night and took the dead **b**
31:12 Jabesh and burned the **b** there.
2Sm 4:12 and hung their dead **b** by the
21:10 the sky rained on the dead **b**.
2Ki 10:25 and threw out the **b** until
1Ch 10:12 and took away the dead **b**
Neh 9:37 kings have control over our **b**,
Est 2:23 the dead **b** of Bigthan and
Job 39:30 wherever there are dead **b**."
Psa 44:25 Our **b** cling to the ground.
63:10 Their dead **b** will be left as
73:4 Their **b** are healthy.
79:2 They have given the dead **b** of
110:6 and fill them with dead **b**.
Sos 6:10 like those heavenly **b**.
Isa 5:25 The hills tremble, and dead **b**
26:21 no longer cover up its dead **b**.
34:3 Their dead **b** will be thrown out.
Jer 7:33 The dead **b** of these people
9:22 Dead **b** will fall like manure on
16:4 Their **b** will be food for birds
19:7 I will give their **b** as food to
31:40 with its dead **b** and ashes,
33:5 houses are filled with the **b**
41:5 and cuts were on their **b**.
41:9 where Ishmael threw all the **b**
41:9 Nethaniah, filled it with the **b**.
Lam 4:7 Their **b** were more pink than
Eze 1:11 two wings covered their **b**.
6:5 I will lay the dead **b** of the
10:12 Their entire **b**, their backs,
30:11 and fill the land with dead **b**.
43:7 it with the dead **b** of their kings.
43:9 prostitutes and take the dead **b**
Dan 3:27 the fire had not harmed their **b**.
Hos 7:14 cuts on their **b** while praying
Joe 2:20 odor will rise from the dead **b**.
Amo 6:10 comes to take the dead **b** out
8:3 dead **b** scattered everywhere.
Nah 3:3 Dead **b** pile up! There is no end
Mat 27:52 and the **b** of many holy people
Jon 19:31 the Jews didn't want the **b** to
19:31 broken and their **b** removed.
Rom 1:24 dishonor their **b** by sexual
6:6 to put an end to sin in our **b**.
7:5 were at work throughout our **b**.
8:10 your **b** are dead because of sin,
8:11 make your mortal **b** alive by his
8:23 the freeing of our **b** (from sin).
12:1 I encourage you to offer your **b**
12:4 Our **b** have many parts,
1Co 6:15 Don't you realize that your **b** are
6:18 commit don't affect their **b**
6:18 sin against their own **b**.
10:5 so their dead **b** were scattered
15:40 There are heavenly **b** and
15:40 heavenly bodies and earthly **b**.
15:40 Heavenly **b** don't all have the
15:40 neither do earthly **b**.
2Co 4:7 Our **b** are made of clay,
4:10 death of Jesus in our **b** so that
4:10 Jesus is also shown in our **b**.
5:6 as we are living in these **b**,
5:10 done while living in their **b**.
Eph 2:11 done to their **b** called you "the
5:28 wives as they love their own **b**.
Php 3:21 he will change our humble **b**
Heb 9:13 made their **b** holy and clean.
10:22 and our **b** have been washed
13:11 But the **b** of those animals
Jas 3:6 of evil among the parts of our **b**,
3:6 completely contaminates our **b**.
Jud 1:8 contaminate their **b** with sin,

Rev 11:8 Their dead **b** will lie on the
11:9 look at the witnesses' dead **b**

body (291)

Gen 9:23 covered their father's naked **b**.
25:25 His whole **b** was covered with
40:19 head and hang your dead **b**
50:26 His **b** was embalmed and
Exo 2:12 death and hid the **b** in the sand.
4:7 again like the rest of his **b**.
22:13 in the dead **b** as evidence.
22:27 clothes he has to cover his **b**.
Lev 5:2 unclean — the unclean dead **b**
5:2 a wild or tame animal or the **b**
11:28 Those who carry the dead **b** of
11:32 When the dead **b** of one of
11:39 whoever touches its dead **b**
11:40 of its dead **b** must wash their
11:40 Those who carry its dead **b**
13:13 does cover his whole **b**,
13:13 His **b** has turned white.
13:43 somewhere else on the **b**,
14:9 must wash his clothes and **b**.
15:8 wash his clothes and his **b**.
15:11 wash his clothes and his **b**.
15:13 wash his clothes and his **b**
15:16 he must bathe his whole **b**.
16:4 He must wash his **b** and put
16:24 He will wash his **b** in the holy
16:26 wash his clothes and his **b**.
16:28 wash his clothes and his **b**.
17:15 or foreigners who eat the **b**
19:28 Never slash your **b** to mourn
22:4 of semen or touches a dead **b**,
Num 5:2 from touching a dead **b**.
5:22 can bring a curse go into your **b**
6:6 must never go near a dead **b**.
6:11 who touched the dead **b**.
9:6 from touching a dead **b**,
9:7 because we touched a dead **b**.
9:10 unclean from touching a dead **b**
19:7 wash his clothes and his **b**.
19:8 wash his clothes and his **b**.
19:11 "Whoever touches the dead **b**
19:13 Whoever touches the dead **b** of
19:17 from touching a dead **b**.
19:18 in the tent ⌊with the dead **b**⌋.
25:8 man and into the woman's **b**.
31:19 a dead **b** must stay outside
Dtr 21:2 the distance from the **b**
21:3 which city is nearest the **b**,
21:23 never leave his dead **b** hung on
21:23 because anyone whose **b** is
28:35 will cover your whole **b** from
28:57 them the afterbirth from her **b**
Jos 8:29 hung the king of Ai's ⌊dead **b**⌋
8:29 the order to take his **b** down.
Jdg 14:8 honey in the lion's dead **b**.
14:9 it out of the lion's dead **b**.
1Sm 5:4 rest of Dagon's **b** was intact.
17:44 I'll give your **b** to the birds."
2Sm 20:12 stopped as they came to the **b**,
1Ki 12:10 than my father's whole **b**.
13:22 That is why your dead **b** will
13:24 His dead **b** was thrown on the
13:24 the lion were standing by the **b**.
13:25 who passed by saw the **b** lying
13:25 and the lion standing by the **b**.
13:28 He found the **b** of the man
13:28 The lion had not eaten the **b**,
13:29 The old prophet picked up the **b**
13:30 He laid the **b** of the man of God
2Ki 4:34 He crouched over the boy's **b**,
6:31 stays on his ⌊**b**⌋ today."
9:35 they couldn't find any of her **b**
9:36 'Dogs will eat Jezebel's **b**
13:21 But when the **b** touched
23:30 His officers put his dead **b** in a
2Ch 10:10 than my father's whole **b**.
Neh 4:16 half were wearing **b** armor
Est 5:14 have Mordecai's ⌊dead **b**⌋ hung
7:10 hung Haman's ⌊dead **b**⌋
8:7 and Haman's ⌊dead **b**⌋ was
Job 6:12 Does my **b** have the strength of
7:5 My **b** is covered with maggots
7:15 My **b** would prefer death ⌊to

Job 12:10 the spirit in every human **b** are
16:8 My frail **b** rises up and testifies
18:13 eats away at the limbs of his **b**.
19:26 has been stripped off my **b**,
21:6 and shuddering seizes my **b**.
30:17 my bones. My **b** doesn't rest.
30:30 My **b** burns with fever.
31:20 (If his **b** didn't bless me,
Psa 16:9 My **b** rests securely
30:9 Will the dust ⌊of my **b**⌋ give
31:9 My eyes, my soul, and my **b**
38:3 No healthy spot is left on my **b**
38:7 no healthy spot is left on my **b**.
63:1 My **b** longs for you in a dry,
73:26 My **b** and mind may waste
84:2 My whole **b** shouts for joy to
109:18 so cursing entered his **b** like
109:24 My **b** has become lean,
119:120 My **b** shudders in fear of you,
Pro 3:8 ⌊Then⌋ your **b** will be healed,
4:22 and they heal the whole **b**.
5:11 when your **b** and flesh are
14:30 heart makes for a healthy **b**,
15:30 Good news refreshes the **b**.
16:24 the spirit and healthy for the **b**.
Ecc 11:10 you or wears down your **b**,
12:12 studying will wear out your **b**.
Isa 1:6 left on your ⌊**b**⌋ — only bruises,
10:18 will destroy both **b** and soul.
21:3 That is why my **b** is full of
Jer 16:6 No one will cut his own **b** or
26:23 Uriah and threw his **b** into
Eze 1:23 two wings that covered its **b**.
8:2 From the waist down its **b**
8:2 and from the waist up its **b**
16:8 and covered your naked **b**.
16:25 You offered your **b** to everyone
16:36 your naked **b** when you gave
16:37 I will uncover your **b** for them,
23:34 and tear your breasts off your **b**.
32:6 will be filled with your dead **b**.
44:25 by going near a dead **b**.
Dan 4:33 Dew from the sky made his **b**
5:21 and his **b** became wet with
7:11 Its **b** was destroyed and put
10:6 His **b** was like beryl.
Hos 2:9 I gave her to cover her naked **b**.
2:10 I will show her naked **b** to her
Nah 3:5 will show nations your naked **b**
Mat 5:29 you to lose a part of your **b** than
5:30 you to lose a part of your **b** than
6:22 "The eye is the lamp of the **b**.
6:22 your whole **b** will be full of
6:23 your whole **b** will be full of
6:25 and the **b** more than clothes?
10:28 be afraid of those who kill the **b**
10:28 the one who can destroy both **b**
14:12 John's disciples came for the **b**
24:28 wherever there is a dead **b**.
26:12 this perfume on my **b** before
26:26 and eat it. This is my **b**."
27:58 and asked for the **b** of Jesus.
27:59 Joseph took the **b** and wrapped
28:13 stolen his **b** while they were
Mar 6:29 they came for his **b** and laid it
9:48 worms that eat the **b** never die,
14:8 to pour perfume on my **b** before
14:22 "Take this. This is my **b**."
15:43 to ask for the **b** of Jesus.
15:46 He took the **b** down from the
15:46 Then he laid the **b** in a tomb,
Luk 11:34 "Your eye is the lamp of your **b**.
11:34 your whole **b** is full of light.
11:34 your **b** is full of darkness.
11:36 If your whole **b** is full of light
12:4 afraid of those who kill the **b**.
12:23 and the **b** is more than clothes.
14:2 A man whose **b** was swollen
17:37 wherever there is a dead **b**."
22:19 them, and said, "This is my **b**,
23:52 and asked for the **b** of Jesus.
23:53 Then he laid the **b** in a tomb
23:55 tomb and how his **b** was laid
24:3 they did not find the **b** of the
24:23 and didn't find his **b**.
Jon 2:21 spoke about was his own **b**.

Jon 19:38 to let him remove Jesus' **b**.
19:38 permission to remove Jesus' **b**.
19:40 These two men took the **b** of
20:12 They were sitting where the **b**
Act 1:18 His **b** split open, and all his
2:26 My **b** also rests securely
2:31 and that his **b** wouldn't decay.
4:10 your presence with a healthy **b**
5:6 wrapped his **b** in a sheet,
9:37 Her **b** was prepared for burial
9:40 turned toward the **b** and said,
13:34 that Jesus' **b** never decayed.
13:36 but his **b** decayed.
13:37 to life had a **b** that didn't decay.
Rom 2:28 a matter of how the **b** looks.
4:19 His **b** was already as good as
6:12 rule your physical **b** so that you
6:13 Never offer any part of your **b** to
6:13 No part of your **b** should ever
6:13 all the parts of your **b** to God.
6:19 all the parts of your **b** as slaves
6:19 offer all the parts of your **b** as
7:4 Teachings through Christ's **b**.
7:23 ⌊at work⌋ throughout my **b**.
7:23 still exist throughout my **b**.
7:24 rescue me from my dying **b**?
8:13 the evil activities of the **b**,
12:5 Christ makes us one **b** and
1Co 6:13 However, the **b** is not for
6:13 and the Lord is for the **b**.
6:15 bodies are parts of Christ's **b**?
6:15 I take the parts of Christ's **b**
6:15 them parts of a prostitute's **b**?
6:16 becomes one **b** with her?
6:19 Don't you know that your **b** is a
6:20 God in the way you use your **b**.
7:4 have authority over her own **b**,
7:4 have authority over his own **b**,
7:34 so that she may be holy in **b**
9:27 Rather, I toughen my **b** with
10:16 we sharing the **b** of Christ?
10:17 there is one loaf, we are one **b**,
11:24 bread and said, "This is my **b**,
11:27 for the Lord's **b** and blood.
11:29 doesn't recognize the Lord's **b**.
12:12 For example, the **b** is one unit
12:12 As all the parts form one **b**,
12:13 were all baptized into one **b**.
12:14 As you know, the human **b** is
12:15 so I'm not part of the **b**!"
12:15 it's no longer part of the **b**?
12:16 so I'm not a part of the **b**!"
12:16 it's no longer part of the **b**?
12:17 If the whole **b** were an eye,
12:17 If the whole **b** were an ear,
12:18 every part of the **b** together as
12:19 How could it be a **b** if it only
12:20 there are many parts but one **b**.
12:22 The parts of the **b** that we think
12:23 The parts of the **b** that we think
12:24 God has put the **b** together and
12:25 God's purpose was that the **b**
12:26 If one part of the **b** suffers,
12:27 You are Christ's **b** and each of
13:3 all that I have and give up my **b**
15:35 With what kind of **b** will they
15:42 When the **b** is planted,
15:43 When the **b** is planted,
15:44 It is planted as a physical **b**.
15:44 back to life as a spiritual **b**.
15:44 As there is a physical **b**,
15:44 so there is also a spiritual **b**.
15:53 This **b** that decays must be
15:53 into a **b** that cannot decay.
15:53 This mortal **b** must be changed
15:53 changed into a **b** that will live
15:54 When this **b** that decays is
15:54 into a **b** that cannot decay,
15:54 and this mortal **b** is changed
15:54 changed into a **b** that will live
2Co 5:8 prefer to live away from this **b**
5:9 Whether we live in the **b** or
7:1 everything that contaminates **b**
Gal 6:13 about what was done to your **b**.
6:17 the scars of Jesus on my **b**.
Eph 1:23 The church is Christ's **b** and

Eph 2:14 In his **b** he has made Jewish
2:16 to God in one **b** by his cross,
3:6 They belong to the same **b** and
4:4 There is one **b** and one Spirit.
4:12 and to build up the **b** of Christ.
4:16 He makes the whole **b** fit
4:16 he makes the **b** grow so that it
4:25 are all members of the same **b**.
5:23 It is his **b**, and he is its Savior.
5:29 No one ever hated his own **b**.
5:30 We are parts of his **b**.
Php 1:20 boldly and honor Christ in my **b**,
3:21 make them like his glorified **b**.
Col 1:18 of the church, which is his **b**.
1:22 God by dying in his physical **b**.
1:24 In my **b** I am completing
1:24 doing this on behalf of his **b**,
2:9 All of God lives in Christ's **b**,
2:17 but the **b** ⌊that casts the
2:19 Christ makes the whole **b** grow
2:23 and harsh treatment of the **b**.
3:15 by bringing you into one **b**.
1Th 5:23 and **b** — blameless when our
1Ti 4:8 Training the **b** helps a little,
Heb 7:10 he was in the **b** of Abraham
9:10 for the **b** until God would
10:5 but you prepared a **b** for me.
10:10 to do by sacrificing his **b** once
10:20 (The curtain is his own **b**.)
Jas 2:26 A **b** that doesn't breathe is
3:5 tongue is a small part of the **b**,
5:3 Like fire, it will destroy your **b**.
1Pe 2:24 Christ carried our sins in his **b**
3:18 His **b** was put to death,
3:21 by removing dirt from the **b**.
Jud 1:9 arguing over the **b** of Moses.
Rev 3:18 naked **b** from showing.

bodyguard (2)
1Sm 22:14 the commander of your **b**.
28:2 "I will make you my **b** for life."

bodyguards (2)
2Sm 23:23 put him in charge of his **b**.
1Ch 11:25 put him in charge of his **b**.

body's (1)
Job 14:22 He feels only his **b** pain.

Bohan (2)
Jos 15:6 and goes up to the Rock of **B**,
18:17 It descends to the Rock of **B**,

boil (13)
Exo 16:23 and **b** what you want to boil.
16:23 and boil what you want to **b**.
29:31 and **b** its meat in a holy place.
Lev 13:18 "If a **b** on the skin has healed
13:20 has developed in the **b**.
13:23 it is a scar caused by the **b**.
2Ki 20:7 and put it on the **b** so that the
Job 41:31 It makes the deep sea **b** like a
Isa 38:21 and place it over the **b** so that
64:2 brushwood and makes water **b**.
Eze 24:5 the mixture in the pot to a **b**.
46:20 place where the priests must **b**
46:24 must **b** the people's sacrifices."

boiled (7)
Exo 12:9 Don't eat any of it raw or **b** but
Num 6:19 of the shoulders from a **b** ram,
1Sm 2:15 He doesn't want **b** meat from
1Ki 19:21 He **b** the meat, using the
2Ki 6:29 So we **b** my son and ate him.
2Ch 35:13 They **b** the holy offerings in
Hag 2:12 touch bread, **b** food, wine, oil,

boiling (4)
1Sm 2:13 While the meat was **b**,
Job 41:20 nostrils like a **b** pot heated over
41:31 It stirs up the ocean like a **b**
Jer 1:13 I answered, "I see a **b** pot,

boils (7)
Exo 9:9 The dust will cause **b** to break
9:10 and they caused **b** to break into
9:11 because they had **b** like all
Dtr 28:27 with the same **b** that plagued
28:35 legs with severe **b** that can't
28:35 The **b** will cover your whole
Job 2:7 struck Job with painful **b** from

bold (12)
Gen 18:27 if I may be so **b** as to ask you,
18:31 if I may be so **b** as to ask you,"
Psa 138:3 You made me **b** by
Pro 21:29 person puts up a **b** front,
28:1 people are as **b** as lions.
Luk 11:8 and because you were so **b**.
Rom 15:15 parts of which are rather **b**,
15:18 I'm **b** enough to tell you only
2Co 10:12 to those who are **b** enough
Eph 3:12 We can go to God with **b**
Phm 1:8 Christ makes me **b** enough to
2Pe 2:10 teachers are **b** and arrogant.

boldly (22)
Gen 34:25 took their swords and **b**
Exo 14:8 who were **b** leaving Egypt.
Num 33:3 The Israelites **b** left in full view
Mar 15:43 Joseph **b** went to Pilate's
Act 4:13 to see how **b** they spoke.
4:29 allow us to speak your word **b**.
4:31 to speak the word of God **b**.
8:25 After they had **b** spoken about
9:27 Barnabas also told them how **b**
9:28 He spoke **b** with the power and
13:46 Paul and Barnabas told them **b**,
14:3 They spoke **b** about the Lord,
18:26 He began to speak **b** in the
19:8 the synagogue and speak **b**.
28:31 and taught very **b** about
Rom 10:20 Isaiah said very **b**,
2Co 3:12 promise⌋, we speak very **b**.
Eph 6:19 Then I will speak **b** when I
6:20 about this Good News as **b** as
Php 1:14 to speak God's word more **b**
1:20 I will speak very **b** and honor
1Jn 3:21 we can **b** look to God

bolt (1)
2Sm 13:17 and **b** the door behind her."

bolted (2)
Jos 6:1 Jericho was **b** and barred shut
2Sm 13:18 his servant took her out and **b**

bolts (3)
Dtr 33:25 May the locks and **b** of your
Psa 78:48 the hail strike their cattle and **b**
144:6 Hurl **b** of lightning,

bond (1)
Act 17:9 Jason and the others post **b**,

bone (10)
Gen 2:23 The man said, "This is now **b**
Lev 24:20 a broken **b** for a broken bone,
24:20 a broken bone for a broken **b**,
Num 19:16 who touches a human **b**
19:18 who has touched a human **b**
Pro 12:4 disgraces him is like **b** cancer.
14:30 but jealousy is ⌊like⌋ **b** cancer.
Eze 37:7 one **b** ⌊attaching itself⌋ to
39:15 the land and see a human **b**,
39:15 diggers have buried that **b**

bones (89)
Gen 2:23 "This is now bone of my **b** and
40:19 will eat the flesh from your **b**."
50:25 to carry my **b** back with you."
Exo 12:46 "Never break any of the **b**.
13:19 Moses took the **b** of Joseph
13:19 take my **b** with you."
Lev 22:22 has broken **b**, cuts, warts,
Num 9:12 or break any of the animal's **b**.
24:8 are his enemies, crush their **b**,
Jos 24:32 Joseph's **b**, which the people
1Sm 31:13 They took the **b** and buried
2Sm 21:12 David went and took the **b** of
21:13 When David brought up the **b** of
21:13 his men gathered the **b** of those
21:14 Then they buried the **b** of Saul
1Ki 13:2 Human **b** will be burned on
13:31 Lay my **b** beside his bones.
13:31 Lay my bones beside his **b**.
2Ki 13:21 the body touched Elisha's **b**,
23:14 their places with human **b**.
23:16 he sent men to take the **b** out of
23:18 Don't disturb his **b**."
23:18 So they left his **b** with the
23:18 they left his bones with the **b**
23:20 then burned human **b** on them.
1Ch 10:12 They buried the **b** under the
2Ch 34:5 He burned the **b** of the priests
Job 2:5 and strike his flesh and **b**.
4:14 and all my **b** shook.
10:11 together with **b** and tendons?
19:20 I am skin and **b**, and I have
20:11 His **b**, once full of youthful
21:24 and his **b** are strong and
30:17 At night God pierces my **b**.
33:19 with endless aching in their **b**
33:21 Their **b**, not seen before,
40:18 Its **b** are bronze tubes.
Psa 6:2 my **b** shake with terror.
22:14 and all my **b** are out of joint.
22:17 I can count all my **b**.
31:10 and my **b** waste away.
32:3 my **b** began to weaken
34:20 The LORD guards all of his **b**.
35:10 All my **b** will say, "O LORD,
38:3 There is no peace in my **b**
42:10 With a shattering blow to my **b**,
51:8 Let the **b** that you have broken
53:5 God has scattered the **b**
102:3 My **b** burn like hot coals.
102:5 I am nothing but skin and **b**
109:18 like water and his **b** like oil.
139:15 My **b** were not hidden from you
141:7 so our **b** will be planted at the
Pro 3:8 your **b** will have nourishment.
25:15 and a soft tongue can break **b**.
Isa 17:4 they will become skin and **b**.
38:13 if a lion had crushed all my **b**.
58:11 He will strengthen your **b**.
Jer 8:1 "At that time the **b** of the kings
8:1 the **b** of the priests and the
8:1 and the **b** of the others who
8:2 Their **b** will not be gathered or
20:9 a burning fire shut up in my **b**.
23:9 All my **b** tremble. I am like a
50:17 The last to gnaw at their **b** was
Lam 1:13 He made it go deep into my **b**.
3:4 He has broken my **b**.
4:8 skin has shriveled on their **b**.
Eze 6:5 their **b** around your altars.
24:4 Fill the pot with the meatiest **b**
24:5 Cook the **b** that are in it well.
24:10 the mixture, and let the **b** burn.
32:27 shields were placed on their **b**
37:1 The valley was filled with **b**.
37:2 that there were very many **b** at
37:3 can these **b** live?"
37:4 "Prophesy to these **b**.
37:4 Tell them, 'Dry **b**, listen to the
37:5 LORD says to these **b**:
37:7 and the **b** came together,
37:11 of Israel are like these **b**.
37:11 The people say, 'Our **b** are dry,
Dan 6:24 them and crushed all their **b**.
Mic 3:2 people and the flesh off their **b**.
3:3 You break their **b** to pieces.
Mat 23:27 are full of dead people's **b**
Luk 24:39 Ghosts don't have flesh and **b**,
Jon 19:36 "None of his **b** will be broken."
Heb 11:22 about burying his **b**.

bonfire (2)
2Ch 16:14 they burned a **b** in his honor.
21:19 His people did not make a **b** in

book (104)
Exo 24:7 Then he took the **B** of the
32:32 out of the **b** you have written."
32:33 "I will wipe out of my **b**
Num 21:14 is how it's described in the **B**
Dtr 28:58 that are written in this **b**.

Dtr 28:61 written in this **B** of Teachings.
29:20 described in this **b** will happen
29:21 in this **B** of the Teachings.
29:27 the curses described in this **b**.
30:10 laws that are written in this **B**
31:24 of these teachings in a **b**.
31:26 "Take this **B** of Teachings,
Jos 8:31 the people of Israel in the **b**
10:13 recorded in the **B** of Jashar?
18:9 They described it in a **b**.
23:6 do everything written in the **B**
24:26 wrote these things in the **B**
2Sm 1:18 is recorded in the **B** of Jashar.)
2Ki 14:6 command written in the **B**
22:8 "I have found the **b** of Moses'
22:8 Hilkiah gave the **b** to Shaphan,
22:10 Hilkiah has given me a **b**."
22:11 When the king heard what the **b**
22:13 words in this **b** that has been
22:13 did not obey the things in this **b**
22:16 everything written in the **b** that
23:2 read everything written in the **B**
23:3 of the promise written in this **b**.
23:21 written in this **B** of the Promise.
23:24 Teachings written in the **b** that
1Ch 9:1 in the genealogies in the **B**
2Ch 16:11 first to last is written in the **B**
17:9 They had the **B** of the LORD's
20:34 which is included in the **B** of
24:27 is in the notes made in the **B**
25:4 command written in the **B**
25:26 written in the **B** of the Kings of
27:7 and his life — is written in the **B**
28:26 to end — is written in the **B**
34:14 the priest Hilkiah found the **b** of
34:15 "I have found the **b** of the
34:15 Hilkiah gave the **b** to Shaphan.
34:16 Shaphan took the **b** to the king
34:18 Hilkiah has given me a **b**."
34:21 words in this **b** that was found.
34:21 everything written in this **b**."
34:24 written in the **b** that was read
34:30 read everything written in the **B**
34:31 of the promise written in this **b**.
35:12 as written in the **B** of Moses.
35:25 They are written in ⌞the **B** of⌟
36:8 him — is written in the **B**
Ezr 6:18 written in the **B** of Moses.
Neh 7:5 I found the **b** with the
8:1 Ezra the scribe to bring the **B**
8:3 to the **B** of Moses' Teachings.
8:5 opened the **b** in front of all the
8:8 They read the **B** of God's
8:18 continued to read from the **B**
9:3 ⌞they listened as⌟ the **B** of the
12:23 Levites were recorded in the **B**
13:1 On that day the **B** of Moses
Est 9:32 and they are written in a **b**.
Psa 40:7 about me in the scroll of the **b**.)
56:8 They are already in your **b**.)
69:28 be erased from the **B** of Life.
87:6 record this in the **B** of Nations:
139:16 recorded in your **b** before one
Isa 29:11 like words in a **b** that is closed
29:11 You give this **b** to someone
29:12 Then you give the **b** to
29:18 hear the words written in the **b**.
30:8 and inscribe it in a **b** so that it
34:16 Search the LORD's **b**,
Jer 25:13 everything written in this **b**.
30:2 Write in a **b** everything that I
Dan 12:1 everyone written in the **b**,
12:4 and seal the **b** until the end
Nah 1:1 This **b** contains the vision of
Mal 3:16 A **b** was written in his
Mar 12:26 Haven't you read in the **b** of
Luk 3:4 prophet Isaiah wrote in his **b**,
4:17 The attendant gave him the **b**
4:20 Jesus closed the **b**,
20:42 David says in the **b** of Psalms,
Jon 20:30 are not written in this **b**.
Act 1:1 In my first **b**, Theophilus,
7:42 This is written in the **b** of the
Php 4:3 names are in the **B** of Life.
Heb 10:7 about me in the scroll of the **b**.)
Rev 3:5 their names from the **B** of Life.
Rev 13:8 is not written in the **B** of Life.
13:8 That **b** belongs to the lamb
17:8 names were not written in the **B**
20:12 including the **B** of Life.
20:15 names were not found in the **B**
21:27 are written in the lamb's **B**
22:7 of the prophecy in this **b**."
22:9 who follow the words in this **b**.
22:10 words of the prophecy in this **b**
22:18 words of the prophecy in this **b**:
22:18 that are written in this **b**.
22:19 words from this **b** of prophecy,
22:19 city that are described in this **b**.

books (9)

Ecc 12:12 People never stop writing **b**.
Dan 7:10 and the **b** were opened.
Luk 16:2 Let me examine your **b**.
Jon 21:25 room for the **b** that would
Act 19:19 in the occult gathered their **b**
19:19 added up the cost of these **b**
2Co 3:15 when they read the **b** of Moses,
Rev 20:12 **B** were opened, including the
20:12 as recorded in the **b**.

boot (1)

Isa 9:5 Every warrior's **b** marching to

booth (1)

Lam 2:6 He stripped his own **b** as if it

booths (23)

Lev 23:34 month is the Festival of **B**
23:42 Live in **b** for seven days.
23:42 born in Israel must live in **b**
23:43 people of Israel live in **b** when
Dtr 16:13 Festival of **B** for seven days.
16:16 and the Festival of **B**.
31:10 during the Festival of **B**,
1Ki 8:2 Solomon at the Festival ⌞of **B**⌟
8:65 celebrated the Festival ⌞of **B**⌟.
2Ch 5:3 the king at the Festival ⌞of **B**⌟
7:8 celebrated the Festival ⌞of **B**⌟.
8:13 and the Festival of **B**) as
Ezr 3:4 celebrated the Festival of **B**.
Neh 8:14 of Israel should live in **b** during
8:15 branches — to make **b** as
8:16 to make **b** for themselves.
8:16 Some made **b** on their roofs,
8:17 come back from exile made **b**
Eze 45:25 at the Festival of **B**,
Zec 14:16 to celebrate the Festival of **B**.
14:18 to celebrate the Festival of **B**.
14:19 to celebrate the Festival of **B**.
Jon 7:2 Jewish Festival of **B** was near.

Borashan (1)

1Sm 30:30 Hormah, **B**, Athach,

border (162)

Gen 10:19 The **b** of the Canaanites
49:13 His **b** will go as far as Sidon.
Exo 16:35 they came to the **b** of Canaan.
Num 13:21 of Zin to the **b** of Hamath.
20:23 near the **b** of Edom,
21:13 (The Arnon Valley is the **b**
21:15 and lie along the **b** of Moab ...."
21:24 ⌞They stopped at⌟ the **b** of the
22:36 right on the **b** of Moab.
33:37 at Mount Hor on the **b** of Edom.
33:44 at Iye Abarim on the **b** of Moab.
34:3 of Zin along the **b** of Edom.
34:3 In the east the southern **b** starts
34:5 of Egypt so that the **b** ends at
34:6 "The western **b** is the coastline
34:7 "The northern **b** extends from
34:8 and from Mount Hor to the **b** of
34:9 From there the **b** goes to
34:10 "The eastern **b** extends from
34:11 From Shepham the **b** goes
34:12 Then the **b** goes along the
Dtr 2:18 you are going to pass by the **b**
3:14 territory of Argob as far as the **b**
3:16 middle of the valley is the **b**)
3:16 which is the **b** of Ammon.
3:17 The western **b** was the river,
Jos 12:2 which is the **b** of Ammon.
12:5 all of Bashan to the **b** of
12:5 and half of Gilead to the **b** of
13:3 as far as the **b** of Ekron.
13:4 as far as Aphek, the Amorite **b**.
13:5 Hermon to the **b** of Hamath.
13:9 The **b** extended from Aroer on
13:10 Amorites up to the **b** of Ammon.
13:23 The **b** of Reuben's territory was
13:26 as far as the **b** of Lidbir.
13:27 River served as its western **b**,
15:2 The southern **b** starts from the
15:4 of Egypt so that the **b** ends at
15:4 This is the southern **b**.
15:5 The eastern **b** is the Dead Sea
15:5 The northern **b** starts from the
15:7 From the valley of Achor, the **b**
15:7 Then the **b** passes the Springs
15:9 mountain the **b** goes around
15:10 From Baalah the **b** turns west
15:11 From there the **b** goes on the
15:11 The **b** ends at the
15:12 The western **b** is the coastline
15:21 of the Negev, on the **b** of Edom,
16:1 The **b** of Joseph's territory goes
16:2 From Bethel the **b** goes to Luz
16:2 Ataroth at the **b** of the Archites.
16:3 Then it descends west to the **b**
16:5 The eastern **b** of the land they
16:6 From there the **b** goes west,
16:6 The **b** then turns east to
16:8 At Tappuah the **b** goes west
17:7 Manasseh's **b** extends from
17:7 Then the **b** goes south toward
17:8 on the **b** of Manasseh,
17:9 The **b** then descends
17:9 Manasseh's ⌞southern⌟ **b** is
17:10 Sea ⌞is its western **b**⌟,
17:10 Asher its northern **b**,
17:10 and Issachar its eastern **b**.
18:12 Their northern **b** starts at the
18:13 From there the **b** goes to the
18:13 Then the **b** goes down to
18:14 The **b** turns and goes around
18:15 The southern **b** begins just
18:16 Then the **b** descends to the
18:19 The **b** continues to the north
18:19 This is its southern **b**.
18:20 Jordan River is its eastern **b**.
19:10 The **b** of their inheritance goes
19:11 Toward the west the **b**
19:12 turns directly east toward the **b**
19:14 There the **b** turns north to
19:22 The **b** touches Tabor,
19:26 The **b** touches Carmel and
19:29 The **b** then turns to Hosah and
19:33 Their **b** starts from Heleph at
19:34 The **b** turns west to Aznoth
19:46 with the **b** passing in front of
19:47 The **b** of Dan extended beyond
22:11 built an altar at the **b** of Canaan.
Jdg 3:3 Hermon to the **b** of Hamath.
11:18 River because it was Moab's **b**.
1Sm 6:12 them to the **b** of Beth Shemesh.
10:2 be at Rachel's grave on the **b**
24:4 and cut off the **b** of Saul's robe.
24:5 had cut off the **b** of Saul's robe.
24:11 The **b** of your robe is in my
24:11 Since I cut off the **b** of your
1Ki 4:21 and as far as the Egyptian **b**.
8:65 ⌞the territory between⌟ the **b**
2Ki 3:21 They stood at the **b**.
14:25 Israel's boundaries from the **b**
1Ch 13:5 Shihor River near Egypt to the **b**
2Ch 7:8 ⌞the territory between⌟ the **b**
9:26 and as far as the Egyptian **b**.
26:8 and his fame spread to the **b** of
Isa 19:19 for the LORD will be near its **b**.
Eze 29:10 all the way to the **b** of Sudan.
45:7 will extend to the eastern **b** ⌞of
47:15 This is the northern **b** for the
47:15 On the north side the **b** will run
47:16 which is on the **b** of Hauran.
47:17 So the **b** will run from the
47:17 Enon on the **b** of Damascus.
47:17 The **b** of Hamath will lie to the

Eze 47:18 On the east side the **b** will run
47:18 serve as the **b** between Gilead
47:18 The **b** will continue from the
47:19 On the south side the **b** will run
47:19 This is the southern **b**.
47:20 Mediterranean Sea is the **b** up
48:1 Beginning at the northern **b**,
48:1 on the northern **b** of Damascus
48:1 from the eastern **b** to the
48:1 border to the western **b**.
48:2 one part of the land and **b** Dan
48:2 It will extend from the eastern **b**
48:2 border to the western **b**.
48:3 one part of the land and **b** Asher
48:3 It will extend from the eastern **b**
48:3 border to the western **b**.
48:4 part of the land and **b** Naphtali
48:4 It will extend from the eastern **b**
48:4 border to the western **b**.
48:5 of the land and **b** Manasseh
48:5 It will extend from the eastern **b**
48:5 border to the western **b**.
48:6 part of the land and **b** Ephraim
48:6 It will extend from the eastern **b**
48:6 border to the western **b**.
48:7 part of the land and **b** Reuben
48:7 It will extend from the eastern **b**
48:7 border to the western **b**.
48:8 gift for the LORD will **b** Judah
48:8 It will extend from the eastern **b**
48:8 border to the western **b**,
48:21 the holy area to the eastern **b**,
48:21 westward to the western **b**.
48:23 It will extend from the eastern **b**
48:23 border to the western **b**.
48:24 part of the land and **b** Benjamin
48:24 It will extend from the eastern **b**
48:24 border to the western **b**.
48:25 part of the land and **b** Simeon
48:25 It will extend from the eastern **b**
48:25 border to the western **b**.
48:26 part of the land and **b** Issachar
48:26 It will extend from the eastern **b**
48:26 border to the western **b**.
48:27 part of the land and **b** Zebulun
48:27 It will extend from the eastern **b**
48:27 border to the western **b**.
48:28 The southern **b** of Gad will run
Amo 6:14 will oppress you from the **b**
Luk 17:11 Jesus traveled along the **b**

borders (27)

Exo 23:31 "I will establish your **b** from the
34:24 expand ⌊your country's⌋ **b**.
Num 34:2 your inheritance has these **b**:
34:12 your land and the **b** around it."
Dtr 11:24 Your **b** will be from the desert
12:20 expand your ⌊country's⌋ **b** as
19:8 expand your country's **b** as
32:8 he set up **b** for the tribes
Jos 1:4 Your **b** will be the desert ⌊on
15:12 These are the **b** around Judah
18:4 ⌊the **b** of⌋ their inheritance.
18:20 These are the **b** surrounding
19:9 its inheritance inside Judah's **b**.
23:12 other nations within your ⌊**b**⌋,
2Ki 19:23 I'll come to its most distant **b**
Psa 147:14 one who brings peace to your **b**
Isa 28:25 area and winter wheat at its **b**?
60:18 and destruction within your **b**.
Eze 11:10 I will judge you at Israel's **b**.
11:11 I will judge you at Israel's **b**.
25:9 the cities that protect Moab's **b**.
47:13 These are the **b** of the land that
47:16 which are between the **b** of
48:18 The rest of the land **b** the holy
Mic 7:11 extending your **b** is coming.
Zec 9:2 and also Hamath, which **b** on it,
Mal 1:5 'Even outside the **b** of Israel

bored (1)

Pro 14:14 turns ⌊from God⌋ becomes **b**

born (169)

Gen 4:18 To Enoch was **b** Irad.
4:26 A son was also **b** to Seth,
6:1 and daughters were **b** to them.
10:25 Two sons were **b** to Eber.
14:14 **b** in his own household,
17:12 whether he is **b** in your
17:13 Every male **b** in your
17:17 "Can a son be **b** to a
17:23 everyone **b** in his household,
17:27 whether **b** in the household or
21:5 old when his son Isaac was **b**.
25:25 The first one **b** was red.
25:26 Afterwards, his brother was **b**
25:26 60 years old when they were **b**.
35:26 who were **b** in Paddan Aram.
36:5 of Esau who were **b** in Canaan.
37:3 because Joseph had been **b**
38:5 He was **b** at Kezib.
38:29 his hand, his brother was **b**.
38:30 After that his brother was **b**
44:20 is old and a younger brother **b**
46:20 Manasseh and Ephraim were **b**
46:22 of Rachel who were **b** to Jacob.
46:27 two sons who were **b** in Egypt.
48:5 "So your two sons, who were **b**
Exo 1:22 ⌊Hebrew⌋ boy that was **b**,
23:12 The slaves **b** in your
Lev 18:9 or not she was **b** in your house.
22:11 the slave and anyone **b** in his
22:27 a calf, a lamb, or a goat is **b**,
23:42 Everyone **b** in Israel must live
25:45 you and from their families **b**
27:26 LORD because it was **b** first.
Num 26:59 who was **b** in Egypt.
Dtr 23:2 A man **b** from an illicit union
Jos 5:5 However, the men **b** later,
Jdg 13:7 the time he is **b** until he dies.'"
13:8 do for the boy who will be **b**."
16:17 to God before I was **b**.
Rut 2:11 the country where you were **b**.
2Sm 3:2 Sons were **b** to David while he
3:2 ⌊**b**⌋ to Ahinoam from Jezreel.
3:3 The second was Chileab, ⌊**b**⌋
3:5 ⌊**b**⌋ to David's wife Eglah.
3:5 These sons were **b** to David
5:14 are the names of the children **b**
12:14 the son that is **b** to you must
1Ki 13:2 There will be a son **b** in
1Ch 1:19 Two sons were **b** to Eber.
2:3 These three were **b** to him by
2:9 The sons **b** to Hezron were
3:1 were David's sons who were **b**
3:1 ⌊**b**⌋ to Ahinoam from Jezreel.
3:1 ⌊**b**⌋ to Abigail from Carmel.
3:2 The third was Absalom, ⌊**b**⌋ to
3:3 was Shephatiah, ⌊**b**⌋ to Abital.
3:3 ⌊**b**⌋ to David's wife Eglah.
3:4 Six sons were **b** to him in
3:5 These ⌊children⌋ were **b** to
14:4 of the children who were **b**
Ezr 10:3 and the children **b** from them,
Job 3:1 and cursed the day he was **b**.
3:3 "Scratch out the day I was **b**
3:11 didn't I die as soon as I was **b**
5:7 But a person is **b** for trouble as
11:12 when a wild donkey is **b** tame.
14:1 "A person who is **b** of a woman
15:7 you the first human to be **b**?
15:14 faultless or someone **b**
25:4 How can anyone **b** of a woman
38:21 know because you were **b** then
Psa 22:31 They will tell people yet to be **b**
51:5 Indeed, I was **b** guilty.
71:6 on you before I was **b**.
78:6 Children yet to be **b** ⌊would
78:51 the ones **b** in the tents of Ham
87:4 claim that it⌋ was **b** there."
87:5 "Every race is **b** in it.
87:6 ⌊claims that it⌋ was **b** there."
90:2 Before the mountains were **b**,
105:36 the first ones **b** in the land
127:4 The children **b** to a man when
Pro 8:24 I was **b** before there were
8:25 I was **b** before the mountains
17:17 a brother is **b** to share trouble.
Ecc 2:7 In addition, slaves were **b** in
3:2 a time to be **b** and a time to die,
4:3 who hasn't been **b** yet is better
Ecc 4:14 even though he had been **b** in
6:3 for him to have been **b** dead.
7:1 is better than the day you're **b**.
Isa 9:6 A child will be **b** for us.
26:18 no new people were **b** on earth.
46:3 you from the time you were **b**.
48:8 a rebel since you were **b**.
49:1 Before I was **b**, the LORD
66:8 Can a country be **b** in one day?
66:8 Can a nation be **b** in a moment?
Jer 1:5 Before you were **b**,
2:14 Were they **b** into slavery?
16:3 about the sons and daughters **b**
20:14 Cursed is the day that I was **b**,
22:26 You weren't **b** there,
46:16 to the land where we were **b**,
Eze 16:4 When you were **b**,
16:5 rejected when you were **b**.
21:30 in the land where you were **b**,
23:15 officers who were **b** in Babylon.
Hos 2:3 naked as the day she was **b**.
13:13 a baby who is about to be **b**
Mat 2:1 Jesus was **b** in Bethlehem in
2:2 "Where is the one who was **b**
2:4 was supposed to be **b**.
11:11 Of all the people ever **b**,
19:12 because they were **b** that way.
26:24 person if he had never been **b**."
Mar 7:26 **b** in Phoenicia in Syria.
14:21 person if he had never been **b**."
Luk 1:14 will be glad that he was **b**.
1:15 Holy Spirit even before he is **b**.
2:4 David had been **b** there.
2:11 was **b** in David's city.
7:28 that of all the people ever **b**,
Jon 1:13 are people who haven't been **b**
3:3 without being **b** from above."
3:4 "How can anyone be **b** when
3:4 mother a second time to be **b**,
3:5 of God without being **b**
3:7 of you must be **b** from above.
3:8 with everyone **b** of the Spirit."
8:58 Before Abraham was ever **b**,
9:1 he saw a man who had been **b**
9:2 why was this man **b** blind?
9:3 Instead, he was **b** blind so that
9:17 been **b** blind another question:
9:19 the one you say was **b** blind?
9:20 son and that he was **b** blind.
9:32 giving sight to a person **b** blind.
9:34 "You were **b** full of sin.
16:21 But after the child is **b**,
18:37 I have been **b** and have come
Act 4:36 had been **b** on the island of
7:8 Abraham's son Isaac was **b**,
7:20 "At that time Moses was **b**,
14:8 A man who was **b** lame was in
18:2 Aquila had been **b** in Pontus,
18:24 who had been **b** in Alexandria,
22:3 I was **b** and raised in the city of
22:28 "But I was **b** a Roman citizen."
Rom 9:8 This means that children **b** by
9:8 Instead, children **b** by the
9:11 Before the children had been **b**
Gal 1:15 appointed me before I was **b**
4:24 Her children are **b** into slavery.
Heb 7:3 No one knows when he was **b**
7:10 though Levi had not yet been **b**,
11:23 for three months after he was **b**.
1Pe 1:3 We have been **b** into a new life
1:4 We have been **b** into a new life
1:23 You have been **b** again,
2Pe 2:12 creatures of instinct that are **b**
1Jn 2:29 of has been **b** from God.
3:9 Those who have been **b** from
3:9 They have been **b** from God.
4:7 loves has been **b** from God
5:1 Messiah has been **b** from God.
5:4 who has been **b** from God has
5:18 have been **b** from God don't
Rev 12:4 devour her child when it was **b**.

borrow (6)

Dtr 15:6 but you will not have to **b** from
28:12 but won't need to **b** from any.
2Ki 4:3 Elisha said, "**B** many empty

Neh 5:4 Others said, "We've had to **b**
Mat 5:42 wants to **b** something from you.
Luk 11:5 let me **b** three loaves of bread.

borrowed (3)

Dtr 23:19 or anything else that is **b**.
2Ki 6:5 master! It was **b**!"
Jer 15:10 I have never lent or **b** anything.

borrower (4)

Exo 22:14 the **b** must make up for the
22:15 the **b** doesn't have to make up
Pro 22:7 and a **b** is a slave to a lender.
Eze 18:7 He returns what a **b** gives him

borrowers (1)

Isa 24:2 and sellers, lenders and **b**,

borrows (2)

Exo 22:14 "Whenever someone **b** an
Psa 37:21 A wicked person **b**,

bother (17)

Num 9:13 and not on a trip and yet don't **b**
Dtr 2:9 The LORD said to me, "Don't **b**
2:19 don't **b** them or start a fight with
1Sm 20:8 Why **b** taking me to your
1Ki 8:38 whose consciences **b** them,
2Ki 3:14 I wouldn't even **b** to look at you
Isa 3:9 They don't even **b** to hide them.
Jer 15:5 No one will **b** to ask how you
Mar 5:35 Why **b** the teacher anymore?"
Luk 7:6 to tell Jesus, "Sir, don't **b**.
8:49 Don't **b** the teacher anymore."
11:7 inside his house, 'Don't **b** me!
1Co 7:21 That shouldn't **b** you.
2Co 11:9 I didn't **b** any of you for help.
12:13 except that I didn't **b** you for
12:14 and I won't **b** you for help.
1Jn 3:17 be in that person if he doesn't **b**

bothered (1)

1Sm 24:5 David's conscience **b** him

bothering (5)

Mat 8:29 "Why are you **b** us now,
26:10 "Why are you **b** this woman?
Mar 5:7 "Why are you **b** me now,
14:6 Why are you **b** her?
Luk 8:28 "Why are you **b** me,

bottle (10)

Job 32:19 My belly is like ⌊a **b** of⌋ wine
Psa 56:8 Put my tears in your **b**.
Ecc 10:1 Dead flies will make a **b** of
Jer 13:12 Every **b** will be filled with
13:12 'We know that every **b** will be
Mat 26:7 a woman went to him with a **b**
Mar 14:3 She had a **b** of very expensive
14:3 She opened the **b** and poured
Luk 7:37 So she took a **b** of perfume
Jon 12:3 Mary took a **b** of very

bottles (1)

Jer 13:14 Then I will smash them like **b**

bottom (35)

Exo 15:5 They sank to the **b** like a rock.
26:19 make 40 silver sockets at the **b**
26:19 two sockets at the **b** of each
26:21 two at the **b** of each frame.
26:24 will be held together at the **b**
26:25 two at the **b** of each frame.
28:27 and fasten them to the **b** of the
29:12 rest of it out at the **b** of the altar.
36:24 made 40 silver sockets at the **b**
36:24 two sockets at the **b** of each
36:26 two at the **b** of each frame.
36:29 were held together at the **b**
36:30 two at the **b** of each frame.
39:20 and fastened them to the **b**
Lev 4:7 rest of the bull's blood at the **b**
4:18 the rest of the blood at the **b**
4:25 the rest of the blood at the **b**
4:30 of the blood at the **b** of the altar.
4:34 of the blood at the **b** of the altar.
Lev 5:9 blood will be drained at the **b**
8:15 the rest of the blood at the **b**
9:9 the blood at the **b** of the altar.
Num 8:4 lamp stand, from top to **b**,
Dtr 28:13 be at the top, never at the **b**,
Psa 88:6 You have put me in the **b** of the
Isa 1:6 From the **b** of your feet to the
6:1 The **b** of his robe filled the
Eze 27:34 at the **b** of the sea.
37:2 were very many bones at the **b**
Dan 6:24 Before they reached the **b** of
Amo 9:3 if they hide from me at the **b**
Jnh 2:6 I sank to the **b**, where bars held
Mat 27:51 was split in two from top to **b**.
Mar 15:38 was split in two from top to **b**.
Jon 19:23 in one piece from top to **b**.

bottomless (8)

Luk 8:31 order them to go into the **b** pit.
Rev 9:1 the key to the shaft of the **b** pit.
9:2 It opened the shaft of the **b** pit,
9:11 was the angel from the **b** pit.
11:7 comes from the **b** pit will fight
17:8 and will come from the **b** pit
20:1 holding the key to the **b** pit and
20:3 He threw it into the **b** pit.

bought (59)

Gen 17:12 is born in your household or **b**
17:13 born in your household or **b**
17:23 and everyone **b** with money—
17:27 born in the household or **b**
25:10 field that Abraham had **b** from
33:19 Then he **b** the piece of land on
33:19 He **b** it from the sons of Hamor,
39:1 **b** him from the Ishmaelites who
47:14 payment for the grain people **b**.
47:20 Joseph **b** all the land in Egypt
47:23 "Now that I have **b** you and
49:30 Abraham **b** the cave that is in
49:32 in it were **b** from the Hittites."
50:5 Bury me in the tomb I **b** for
50:13 Abraham had **b** this tomb from
Exo 12:44 "Any male slave you have **b**
21:8 he must let her be **b** back by
Lev 19:20 and if her freedom was never **b**
25:31 They can be **b** back.
25:48 he has the right to be **b** back.
25:50 from the year he was **b** until
27:22 You may give a field you **b** (not
27:24 the person from whom it was **b**,
27:27 animal, it must be **b** back.
27:27 If it is not **b** back, it must be
27:28 must not be sold or **b** back.
27:29 this way cannot be **b** back.
27:33 They cannot be **b** back."
Jos 24:32 plot of ground Jacob had **b** from
Rut 4:9 that I have **b** from Naomi all
4:10 In addition, I have **b** as my wife
2Sm 12:3 little female lamb that he had **b**.
24:24 So David **b** the threshing floor
1Ki 10:28 The king's traders **b** them from
16:24 Omri **b** a hill from Shemer for
2Ch 1:16 The king's traders **b** them from
Neh 5:16 on this wall, and we **b** no land.
Job 28:16 It can't be **b** with the gold from
28:19 It cannot be **b** for ⌊any amount
Psa 74:2 You **b** this tribe to be your
Ecc 2:7 I **b** male and female slaves.
Isa 52:3 You will be **b** back,
Jer 13:2 So I **b** the belt, as the LORD
13:4 "Take the belt that you **b**,
32:9 "So I **b** the field in Anathoth
Hos 3:2 So I **b** her for 23 ounces of
Amo 2:8 the wine that they **b** with fines.
Mat 13:44 he had, and **b** that field.
13:46 everything he had, and **b** it.
Mar 16:1 and Salome **b** spices to go and
Luk 14:18 The first said to him, 'I **b** a field,
14:19 'I **b** five pairs of oxen,
Act 1:18 he **b** a piece of land where he
1Co 6:20 You were **b** for a price.
7:23 You were **b** for a price.
2Pe 2:1 deny the Lord, who has **b** them,
Rev 5:9 You **b** people with your blood
14:3 people who had been **b**
Rev 14:4 They were **b** from among

boulder (1)

Job 18:4 your sake or a **b** be dislodged?

bounce (1)

Nah 3:2 gallop! Chariots **b** along!

bound (11)

Neh 10:29 They also **b** themselves to
Job 36:8 if righteous people are **b** in
Psa 56:12 I am **b** by my vows to you,
Isa 45:23 I have **b** myself with an oath.
Nah 3:10 her best men were **b** in chains.
Jon 19:40 took the body of Jesus and **b**
Act 12:6 His hands were **b** with two
Rom 7:2 a married woman is **b** by law to
7:6 died to those laws that **b** us.
1Co 7:15 or Christian woman is not **b** ⌊by
Jud 1:6 **b** by eternal chains.

boundaries (8)

Gen 23:18 as all the trees inside the **b**
2Ki 14:25 He restored Israel's **b** from the
Neh 9:22 and assigned them their **b**.
Psa 74:17 You determined all the **b** of the
Isa 10:13 I've eliminated the **b** of nations.
26:15 have extended all the land's **b**.
Eze 48:22 and Benjamin's **b** will belong
Act 17:26 the year and the **b** within which

boundary (16)

Exo 19:12 Mark off a **b** around the
19:21 force their way through ⌊the **b**⌋
19:23 yourself to mark off a **b** around
19:24 force their way through the **b**
Dtr 19:14 neighbor's original **b** marker
27:17 his neighbor's **b** marker will
Job 24:2 "⌊People⌋ move **b** markers.
26:10 at the **b** where light meets
Psa 16:6 Your **b** lines mark out pleasant
104:9 Water cannot cross the **b** you
Pro 22:28 Do not move an ancient **b**
23:10 Do not move an ancient **b**
Jer 5:22 I made the sand a **b** for the sea,
Eze 45:7 From the western **b** of the holy
45:7 From the eastern **b** of the holy
Hos 5:10 those who move **b** markers.

bouquet (1)

Sos 1:14 My beloved is a **b** of henna

bow (85)

Gen 27:3 equipment, your quiver and **b**,
27:29 May people **b** down to you.
27:29 the sons of your mother **b** down
37:10 your brothers come and **b** down
48:22 with my own sword and **b**."
49:8 sons will **b** down to you.
49:24 But his **b** stayed steady,
Exo 11:8 come, **b** down to me, and say,
33:10 they would all **b** with their
Dtr 8:19 and if you serve them and **b**
11:16 other gods and **b** down to them.
26:10 LORD your God and **b** down
30:17 You might be tempted to **b**
33:3 They **b** at your feet to receive
Jos 23:7 their gods or **b** down to them.
23:16 serve them and **b** down to
1Sm 2:36 your household will **b** down
18:4 his sword, his **b**, and his belt.
2Sm 1:22 Jonathan's **b** did not turn away,
22:35 bend an ⌊archer's⌋ **b** of bronze.
22:40 my opponents **b** at my feet.
1Ki 22:34 One man aimed his **b** at
2Ki 5:18 and I have to **b** down in the
9:24 But Jehu took his **b** and shot
13:15 "Get a **b** and some arrows."
13:15 So he got a **b** and some arrows.
13:16 "Take the **b** in your hand."
13:16 So the king picked up the **b**.
17:35 **b** down to them, serve them,
17:36 **B** down to the LORD,
2Ch 18:33 One man aimed his **b** at
Est 3:2 would not kneel and **b** to him.
3:5 did not kneel and **b** to him,

Job 9:13 Even Rahab's helpers **b**
20:24 a bronze **b** will pierce him.
29:20 and the **b** in my hand will
Psa 5:7 for you, I will **b** toward your holy
7:12 By bending his **b**, he makes it
18:34 bend an ⌊archer's⌋ **b** of bronze.
18:39 my opponents **b** at my feet.
21:12 you aim your **b** at their faces.
44:6 I do not rely on my **b**,
46:9 He breaks an archer's **b**.
78:57 arrows shot from a defective **b**.
86:9 that you have made will **b**
95:6 let's worship and **b** down.
97:7 All the gods will **b** to him.
99:5 **B** down at his footstool.
99:9 **B** at his holy mountain.
138:2 I will **b** toward your holy
Pro 14:19 Evil people will **b** to good
14:19 Wicked people will **b** at the
Isa 41:2 With his **b** he turns them into
44:15 them into carved statues and **b**
44:17 They **b** to them and worship
45:14 They will **b** to you and pray to
45:23 "Every knee will **b** to me and
46:2 stoop low and **b** down together.
46:6 They **b** down and worship it.
49:7 Princes will see ⌊you⌋ and **b**.
49:23 They will **b** in front of you with
60:14 those who oppress you will **b**
60:14 All who despise you will **b** at
65:12 All of you will **b** to be
Lam 2:4 Like an enemy he bent his **b**.
2:10 of Jerusalem **b** their heads
3:12 He has drawn his **b** and made
Eze 39:3 Then I will knock the **b** out of
Dan 3:5 **b** down and worship the gold
3:6 Whoever doesn't **b** down and
3:10 of instruments should **b** down
3:11 that⌋ whoever doesn't **b** down
3:15 will you **b** down and worship
Hos 7:16 They are like a defective **b**.
Mic 6:6 when I **b** in front of the God of
Hab 3:9 You get your **b** ready for action,
Zep 2:11 coast and nation will **b** to him.
Zec 9:13 I will bend Judah as my **b** and
9:13 as my bow and draw my **b**
10:4 from them a battle **b**,
Mat 4:9 you all this if you will **b** down
1Co 14:25 in this way they will quickly **b**
Rev 3:9 come and **b** at your feet
4:10 the 24 leaders **b** in front of the
6:2 and its rider had a **b**.

bowed (106)

Gen 17:3 Immediately, Abram **b** with his
17:17 Immediately, Abraham **b** with
18:2 and he **b** with his face touching
19:1 he got up to meet them and **b**
23:7 and **b** with his face touching
23:12 Abraham **b** down again in front
24:52 he **b** down to the LORD.
33:3 of them and **b** seven times
33:6 came forward and **b** down.
33:7 came forward and **b** down.
33:7 came forward and **b** down.
37:7 my bundle and **b** down to it."
42:6 they **b** in front of him with their
43:26 Then they **b** to him with their
44:14 Immediately, they **b** with their
47:31 Then Israel **b** down in prayer
48:12 them off his father's lap and **b**
50:18 came and immediately **b** down
Exo 18:7 Moses **b** with his face touching
32:8 They've **b** down to it and
Lev 9:24 they shouted and **b** with their
Num 14:5 Moses and Aaron **b** with their
16:4 he **b** with his face touching the
16:22 Immediately, they **b** with their
16:45 Immediately, they **b** with their
20:6 Immediately, they **b** with their
Dtr 29:26 other gods and **b** down
Jos 5:14 Immediately, Joshua **b** with his
7:6 dust on their heads and **b** down
Jdg 13:20 they immediately **b** down with
Rut 2:10 Ruth immediately **b** down to
1Sm 20:41 and quickly **b** down three times
1Sm 25:23 She immediately **b** down in
25:24 After she **b** at his feet,
25:41 She **b** down with her face
2Sm 1:2 he immediately **b** down with
9:6 he quickly **b** down with his
9:8 Mephibosheth **b** down ⌊again⌋
14:4 king and immediately **b** down
14:22 Joab quickly **b** down with his
14:33 who came to the king and **b**
15:5 approached him and **b** down,
18:21 The messenger **b** down with
18:28 and **b** down in front of him.
19:18 Shimei, Gera's son, **b** down in
24:20 he went out and **b** down with
1Ki 1:16 Bathsheba knelt and **b** down in
1:23 he **b** down in front of him.
1:31 Then Bathsheba **b** down with
1:47 The king himself **b** down on
1:53 Adonijah **b** down in front of
2:19 got up to meet her and **b** down
18:7 him and immediately **b** down
18:39 saw it and immediately **b** down
18:42 to the top of Carmel and **b** down
2Ki 2:15 they went to meet him and **b**
4:37 Then she immediately **b** at his
1Ch 21:16 They **b** down with their faces
21:21 the threshing floor and **b** down
2Ch 20:18 Jehoshaphat **b** down with his
20:18 Jerusalem immediately **b** down
24:17 the officials of Judah **b** in front
25:14 as his gods, **b** down to them,
29:28 The whole assembly **b** down
29:29 with him kneeled and **b** down.
29:30 **b** down, and worshiped.
Neh 8:6 raised their hands and then **b**
Psa 38:6 I am bent over and **b** down very
57:6 (My soul is **b** down.)
Eze 1:28 I immediately **b** down,
3:23 and I immediately **b** down.
9:8 So I immediately **b** down.
11:13 I immediately **b** down and cried
43:3 I immediately **b** down.
44:4 I immediately **b** down.
Dan 2:46 immediately **b** down
3:7 and language **b** down and
10:15 When he said this to me, I **b**
Mat 2:11 So they **b** down and worshiped
8:2 skin disease came and **b** down
9:18 He **b** down in front of Jesus
14:33 The men in the boat **b** down in
15:25 She came to him, **b** down,
20:20 She **b** down in front of him to
26:39 he quickly **b** with his face to
28:9 **b** down to worship him,
28:17 they **b** down in worship,
Mar 5:6 **b** down in front of him,
5:22 he quickly **b** down in front of
5:33 So she quickly **b** in front of him
7:25 She went to him and **b** down.
Luk 5:12 When the man saw Jesus, he **b**
8:41 arrived and quickly **b** down in
8:47 she quickly **b** in front of him.
17:16 He quickly **b** at Jesus' feet and
24:5 The women were terrified and **b**
Jon 9:38 The man **b** in front of Jesus
19:30 Then he **b** his head and died.
Act 10:25 **b** down, and worshiped Peter.
Rev 5:8 creatures and the 24 leaders **b**
5:14 the leaders **b** and worshiped.
7:11 They **b** in front of the throne
11:16 immediately **b**, worshiped God,
19:4 and the 4 living creatures **b**
19:10 I **b** at his feet to worship him.
22:8 I **b** to worship at the feet of the

bowing (14)

Gen 24:26 The man knelt, **b** to the LORD
24:48 I knelt, **b** down to the LORD.
37:9 and 11 stars **b** down to me."
43:28 Then they knelt, **b** down.
Exo 4:31 **b** with their faces touching the
12:27 **b** with their faces touching the
34:8 Immediately, Moses knelt, **b**
Num 22:31 So Balaam knelt, **b** with his
Dtr 17:3 by worshiping and **b** down to
Jos 7:10 are you doing **b** on the ground?
Est 3:2 kneeling and **b** to Haman with
Psa 44:25 Our souls are **b** in the dust.
Isa 44:19 into a disgusting thing and **b**
58:5 Is fasting just **b** your head like

bowl (39)

Exo 12:22 it in the blood which is in a **b**,
Lev 14:5 a clay **b** containing fresh water.
14:50 a clay **b** containing fresh water.
Num 7:13 and a silver **b** that weighed 1
7:19 and a silver **b** that weighed 1
7:25 and a silver **b** that weighed 1
7:31 and a silver **b** that weighed 1
7:37 and a silver **b** that weighed 1
7:43 and a silver **b** that weighed 1
7:49 and a silver **b** that weighed 1
7:55 and a silver **b** that weighed 1
7:61 and a silver **b** that weighed 1
7:67 and a silver **b** that weighed 1
7:73 and a silver **b** that weighed 1
7:79 and a silver **b** that weighed 1
7:85 and each **b** weighed 1 ¾
Jdg 5:25 him buttermilk in a royal **b**.
6:38 He squeezed out a **b** full of
1Ch 28:17 the weight of each gold **b**,
28:17 the weight of each silver **b**,
Ecc 12:6 the golden **b** is broken,
Sos 7:2 Your navel is a round **b**.
Isa 51:17 You drank from the **b**,
51:22 the **b**, the cup of my fury.
Hab 2:15 his neighbor drink from the **b**
Zec 4:2 solid gold lamp stand with a **b**
4:3 one on the right of the **b** and the
9:15 filled like a sacrificial **b** ⌊used
Mat 26:23 has dipped his hand into the **b**
Mar 14:20 his hand into the **b** with me.
Luk 8:16 a lamp and hides it under a **b**
Rev 5:8 Each held a harp and a gold **b**
16:2 The first angel poured his **b**
16:3 The second angel poured his **b**
16:4 The third angel poured his **b**
16:8 The fourth angel poured his **b**
16:10 The fifth angel poured his **b** on
16:12 The sixth angel poured his **b**
16:17 The seventh angel poured his **b**

bowls (33)

Exo 8:3 ovens and into your mixing **b**.
12:34 it on their shoulders in **b**,
24:6 of the blood and put it into **b**,
25:29 as well as pitchers and **b** to be
27:3 **b**, forks, and incense burners.
37:16 he made plates, dishes, **b**,
38:3 **b**, forks, and incense burners.
Num 4:7 put on it the plates, dishes, **b**,
4:14 and **b** — all the altar's
7:84 12 silver **b**, and 12 gold dishes.
2Sm 17:28 **b**, pots, wheat, barley, flour,
1Ki 7:40 made pots, shovels, and **b**.
7:45 pots, shovels, and **b**.
7:50 dishes, snuffers, **b**,
2Ki 12:13 But no silver **b**, snuffers,
25:15 burners and **b** that were made
1Ch 28:17 the pure gold for the forks, **b**,
2Ch 4:8 And he made 100 gold **b**.
4:11 made the pots, shovels, and **b**.
Ezr 1:10 gold **b**: 30 other silver bowls:
1:10 gold bowls: 30 other silver **b**:
8:27 20 gold **b** weighing 18 pounds
Neh 7:70 nearly 18 pounds of gold, 50 **b**,
Isa 22:24 from **b** to jars of every kind."
Jer 52:18 shovels, snuffers, **b**, dishes,
52:19 **b**, pots, lamp stands, dishes,
52:19 and the **b** used for wine
52:19 the trays and **b** that were made
Zec 14:20 of the LORD will be like the **b**
Rev 15:7 gave seven gold **b** full
16:1 "Pour the seven **b** of God's
17:1 who held the seven **b** came
21:9 who had the seven **b** full

bowl-shaped (7)

1Ki 7:20 above the **b** parts around
7:41 2 pillars, the **b** capitals on top
7:41 filigree to cover the 2 **b** capitals
7:42 filigree to cover the 2 **b** capitals

2Ch 4:12 2 pillars, **b** capitals on top of
4:12 filigree to cover the 2 **b** capitals
4:13 filigree to cover the 2 **b** capitals

bows (33)

1Sm 2:4 "The **b** of the warriors are
1Ch 12:2 They were armed with **b** and
2Ch 14:8 with small shields and **b**.
17:17 armed men with **b** and shields),
26:14 armor, **b**, and stones for slings.
Neh 4:13 with swords, spears, and **b**.
4:16 holding spears, shields, and **b**.
Psa 11:2 Wicked people bend their **b**.
37:14 their swords and bend their **b**
37:15 and their **b** will be broken.
58:7 When they aim their **b**,
60:4 attacked by **b** ⌊and arrows⌋.
78:9 with **b** ⌊and arrows⌋,
Isa 5:28 all their **b** are ready to shoot.
7:24 People will come there with **b**
13:18 But their **b** will smash the
21:15 from **b** ready to shoot,
22:3 without their **b** and arrows.
46:1 The god Bel **b** down;
Jer 6:23 take hold of **b** and spears.
9:3 They use their tongues like **b**
46:9 Lydia who use **b** and arrows.
49:35 I'm going to break the **b** of
50:14 all you archers with **b**.
50:29 the soldiers with **b**,
50:42 will take hold of **b** and spears.
51:3 Have the archers bend their **b**.
51:56 and their **b** and arrows will be
Eze 39:9 large shields, **b** and arrows,
Hos 1:5 that day I will break Israel's **b**
1:7 I won't use **b**, swords, wars,
2:18 I will destroy all the **b**,
Zec 9:10 There will be no battle **b**.

bowstrings (3)

Jdg 16:7 with seven new **b** that are not
16:8 her seven new **b** that were not
16:9 Samson snapped the **b** as a

box (13)

1Sm 6:8 as a guilt offering in a **b** beside
6:11 the LORD and the **b** containing
6:15 and the **b** which contained
2Ki 12:9 the priest Jehoiada took a **b**,
12:9 to the LORD's temple in the **b**.
12:10 saw a lot of money in the **b**,
2Ch 24:8 and they made a **b** and placed
24:10 and dropped it into the **b** until
24:11 the Levites brought the **b**
24:11 officer would empty the **b**
Mar 12:41 sat facing the temple offering **b**,
Luk 21:1 gifts into the temple offering **b**.
1Co 9:26 So I **b** — but not as if I were just

boxes (1)

Isa 3:20 blouses, perfume **b**, charms,

boxing (1)

1Co 9:26 not as if I were just shadow **b**.

boy (98)

Gen 21:12 "Don't be upset about the **b** and
21:14 He also gave her the **b** and
21:15 she put the **b** under one of the
21:16 don't want to watch the **b** die."
21:17 God heard the **b** crying,
21:17 God has heard the **b** crying
21:18 Come on, help the **b** up!
21:19 water and gave the **b** a drink.
21:20 God was with the **b** as he grew
22:5 with the donkey while the **b**
22:12 lay a hand on the **b**," he said.
37:30 and said, "The **b** isn't there!
42:22 you not to sin against the **b**?
43:8 "Send the **b** along with me.
44:22 'The **b** can't leave his father.
44:22 If the **b** leaves him,
44:30 If I come ⌊home⌋ without the **b**
44:31 and he sees that the **b** isn't
44:32 that the **b** would come back.
44:33 and let the **b** go back with his
Gen 44:34 back to my father if the **b** isn't
Exo 1:16 If it's a **b**, kill it, but if it's a girl,
1:22 ⌊Hebrew⌋ **b** that was born,
2:6 and saw it was a **b**.
Lev 12:2 a woman gives birth to a **b**,
12:3 The **b** must be circumcised
12:7 who gives birth to a **b** or a girl.
27:5 For a **b** from 5 to 20 years old,
27:6 For a **b** from one month to five
Jdg 13:5 cut his hair because the **b** will
13:7 food because the **b** will
13:8 we must do for the **b** who will
13:12 how should the **b** live and what
13:24 The **b** grew up, and the LORD
1Sm 1:11 remember me, and give me a **b**,
1:22 "I'll wait until the **b** is weaned.
1:24 Shiloh while the **b** was ⌊still⌋
2:11 But the **b** ⌊Samuel⌋ served the
2:18 As a **b** he was ⌊already⌋
2:21 Meanwhile, the **b** Samuel grew
2:26 The **b** Samuel continued to
3:1 The **b** Samuel was serving the
3:8 the LORD was calling the **b**.
4:21 She called the **b** Ichabod [No
17:33 You're just a **b**, but he's been a
20:21 I will send out a **b** and say,
20:21 Now, if I tell the **b**,
20:22 But if I tell the **b**, 'The arrows
20:35 had a young **b** with him.
20:36 "Run," he told the **b**,
20:36 The **b** ran, and Jonathan shot
20:37 When the **b** reached the place
20:39 The **b** had no idea what was
20:40 gave his weapons to the **b**.
20:40 He told the **b**, "Take them back
20:41 When the **b** had left,
2Sm 4:4 When the **b** was five years old,
1Ki 11:17 Hadad was a young **b** at the
11:20 Tahpenes presented the **b** to
14:3 you what will happen to the **b**."
14:17 of her home, the **b** died.
17:21 himself over the **b** three times
2Ki 4:16 you will hold a baby **b** in your
4:18 Several years later the **b** went
4:20 The **b** sat on her lap until noon,
4:26 and the **b** are doing."
4:31 "The **b** didn't wake up."
4:32 the dead **b** was lying on
4:34 Then he lay on the **b**,
4:35 The **b** sneezed seven times
2Ch 34:3 while he was still a **b**,
Job 3:3 'A **b** has been conceived!'
Psa 89:19 "I set a **b** above warriors.
Pro 4:3 When I was a **b** ⌊learning⌋
Isa 7:16 Indeed, before the **b** knows
8:4 Before the **b** knows how to say
Jer 1:6 how to speak. I am only a **b**!"
1:7 "Don't say that you are only a **b**.
20:15 become the father of a baby **b**.
Mat 17:18 the demon to come out of the **b**.
17:18 that moment the **b** was cured.
17:19 force the demon out of the **b**?"
Mar 9:20 They brought the **b** to him.
9:20 it threw the **b** into convulsions.
9:26 The **b** looked as if he were
9:28 we force the spirit out of the **b**?"
10:20 since I was a **b**."
Luk 2:23 "Every firstborn **b** is to be set
2:43 The **b** Jesus stayed behind in
9:42 the demon knocked the **b** to the
9:42 He cured the **b** and gave him
18:21 since I was a **b**."
Jon 4:49 come with me before my little **b**
4:51 told him that his **b** was alive.
6:9 "A **b** who has five loaves of
Act 20:12 The people took the **b** home.
Rev 12:5 She gave birth to a son, a **b**,
12:13 who had given birth to the **b**.

boy's (11)

Gen 44:20 The **b** brother is dead,
44:30 is wrapped up with the **b** life.
44:33 be your slave in the **b** place,
2Ki 4:29 Lay my staff on the **b** face.
4:30 The **b** mother said,
4:31 and put the staff on the **b** face,
2Ki 4:34 mouth on the **b** mouth, his eyes
4:34 his eyes on the **b** eyes, his
4:34 his hands on the **b** hands.
4:34 He crouched over the **b** body,
Jon 4:53 Then the **b** father realized that

boys (12)

Gen 38:27 and she had twin **b**.
48:16 me from all evil, bless these **b**.
Exo 1:17 They let the **b** live.
1:18 Why have you let the **b** live?"
Num 31:17 So kill all the Midianite **b** and
2Ki 2:23 some **b** came out of the city
2Ch 28:8 captured 200,000 women, **b**,
Isa 3:4 "I will make **b** their leaders.
Lam 5:13 and ⌊our⌋ **b** stagger under
Joe 3:3 They traded **b** for prostitutes.
Zec 8:5 The city will be filled with **b**
Mat 2:16 He sent soldiers to kill all the **b**

Bozez (1)

1Sm 14:4 The name of one ⌊cliff⌋ was **B**,

Bozkath (2)

Jos 15:39 Lachish, **B**, Eglon,
2Ki 22:1 daughter of Adaiah from **B**.

Bozrah (8)

Gen 36:33 son of Zerah from **B**,
1Ch 1:44 son of Zerah from **B**,
Isa 34:6 will receive a sacrifice in **B**,
63:1 Who is this coming from **B** in
Jer 48:24 Kerioth, **B**, and on all the cities
49:13 that **B** will become a pile of
49:22 and spread their wings over **B**.
Amo 1:12 burn down the palaces of **B**.

brace (3)

Job 38:3 **B** yourself like a man!
40:7 "**B** yourself like a man!
Jer 1:17 **B** yourself, Jeremiah! Stand up,

bracelets (9)

Gen 24:22 gold **b** weighing four ounces.
24:30 He saw the nose ring and the **b**
24:47 nose and the **b** on her wrists.
Num 31:50 bands, **b**, signet rings, earrings,
Isa 3:16 the ankle **b** on their feet."
3:19 pendants, **b**, scarfs,
3:20 hats, ankle **b**, blouses,
Eze 16:11 I put **b** on your wrists and a
23:42 and they put **b** on the women's

brag (75)

Jdg 7:2 Israel might **b** and say,
1Ki 20:11 'Don't **b** about a victory before
1Ch 16:10 **B** about his holy name.
Psa 5:5 Those who **b** cannot stand in
49:6 They trust their riches and **b**
52:1 Why do you **b** about the evil
63:11 takes an oath by God will **b**,
64:10 are decent will be able to **b**.
75:4 I said to those who **b**,
75:4 "Don't **b**," and to wicked
94:4 **b** about themselves.
105:3 **B** about his holy name.
106:5 and **b** with the people who
Pro 25:6 Do not **b** about yourself in front
27:1 Do not **b** about tomorrow,
Jer 9:23 Don't let wise people **b** about
9:23 Don't let strong people **b** about
9:23 rich people **b** about their riches.
9:24 If they want to **b**, they should
9:24 they should **b** that they
9:24 They should **b** that I,
48:30 They **b** and don't do what they
49:4 Why do you **b** about your
Eze 24:21 You **b** that my holy place gives
27:3 you used to **b** about your
33:28 People will no longer **b** about
Amo 4:5 **B** and boast about your freewill
Oba 1:12 Don't **b** so much when they're
Rom 2:17 Teachings, **b** about your God,
2:23 As you **b** about the laws in
3:27 we have anything to **b** about?
4:2 would have had a reason to **b**.

Rom 4:2 But he could not **b** to God
5:2 So we **b** because of our
5:3 We also **b** when we are
5:11 us continue to **b** about God.
11:18 So don't **b** about being better
11:18 If you **b**, remember that you
15:17 me the right to **b** about what I'm
1Co 1:29 one can **b** in God's presence.
1:31 "Whoever brags must **b** about
3:21 So don't **b** about people.
5:6 It's not good for you to **b**.
9:16 I have nothing to **b** about
2Co 9:2 and I **b** about you to the
9:3 when we **b** that you're ready,
10:8 So, if I **b** a little too much about
10:13 How can we **b** about things
10:13 Instead, we will only **b** about
10:15 How can we **b** about things
10:16 We won't **b** about things
10:17 "Whoever brags should **b** about
11:12 of those people who want to **b**
11:13 People who **b** like this are
11:16 fool so that I can also **b** a little.
11:18 it's common for people to **b**,
11:21 Whatever other people dare to **b**
11:21 I, like a fool, can also **b** about.
11:30 If I must **b**, I will brag about the
11:30 If I must brag, I will **b** about the
12:1 I must **b**, although it doesn't do
12:5 I'll **b** about this person,
12:5 but I won't **b** about myself
12:6 If I ever wanted to **b**,
12:9 So I will **b** even more about my
Gal 6:13 that they can **b** about what was
6:14 ever **b** about anything except
Eph 2:9 so no one can **b** about it.
Php 2:16 Then I can **b** on the day of
1Th 2:19 or prize that we can **b** about in
2Th 1:4 That's why we **b** in God's
2Ti 3:2 They will **b**, be arrogant,
Jas 3:5 but it can **b** about doing
3:14 self-centered ambition, don't **b**.
4:16 you **b** because you're arrogant.

bragged (3)

Eze 35:13 You **b** and continually talked
Zep 2:8 and **b** about their territory.
2Co 7:14 said to him when I **b** about you.

bragging (9)

Psa 12:3 flattering lip and every **b** tongue
Jer 9:24 This kind of **b** pleases me,
Rom 3:27 **B** has been eliminated.
1Co 4:7 why are you **b** as if it weren't a
9:15 my **b** into meaningless words.
2Co 7:14 our **b** to Titus has also proved
11:10 my **b** will not be silenced
11:17 I say as I start **b** is foolishness.
Jas 4:16 arrogant. All such **b** is evil.

brags (5)

Psa 97:7 idols and **b** about false gods
Pro 20:14 he **b** ⌊about his bargain⌋.
25:14 ⌊so⌋ is a person who **b** about a
1Co 1:31 As Scripture says, "Whoever **b**
2Co 10:17 "Whoever **b** should brag about

braids (4)

Jdg 16:13 "Just weave the seven **b** of my
16:14 So Delilah tied his **b** to the
16:14 Samson woke up and tore his **b**
16:19 a man to shave off his seven **b**.

branch (22)

Exo 12:22 Take the **b** of a hyssop plant,
Num 13:23 they cut off a **b** with only one
Job 15:32 and his **b** will not become
Isa 4:2 When that day comes, the **b** of
11:1 and a **b** from its roots will bear
14:19 of your tomb like a rejected **b**.
17:6 left at the top of the highest **b**,
Jer 1:11 "I see a **b** of an almond tree."
23:5 grow a righteous **b** for David.
33:15 I will cause a righteous **b** to
Eze 19:14 spread from the vine's main **b**.
21:21 will stop where the roads **b** off,
Zec 3:8 to bring my servant, the **B**.
6:12 is the man whose name is **B**.
6:12 He will **b** out from where he is,
Mal 4:1 won't leave a single root or **b**.
Mat 24:32 When its **b** becomes tender
Mar 13:28 When its **b** becomes tender
Jon 15:2 He also prunes every **b** that
15:4 A **b** cannot produce any fruit by
15:6 in me is thrown away like a **b**
Rom 11:17 off, and you, a wild olive **b**,

branches (93)

Gen 30:37 took fresh-cut **b** of poplar,
30:37 the white which was on the **b**.
30:38 He placed the peeled **b** in the
30:39 they mated in front of the **b**.
30:41 Jacob would lay the **b** in the
30:41 that they would mate by the **b**.
30:42 he didn't lay down the **b**.
40:9 with three **b** appeared
40:12 "The three **b** are three days.
49:22 with **b** climbing over a wall.
Exo 25:32 Six **b** are to come out of the
25:32 three **b** on one side and three
25:33 Each of the six **b** coming out of
25:35 the three pairs of **b** coming out
25:36 The buds and **b** should also be
37:18 Six **b** came out of its sides,
37:18 three **b** on one side and three
37:19 Each of the six **b** coming out of
37:21 the three pairs of **b** coming out
37:22 The buds and **b** were
Lev 23:40 day take the best fruits, palm **b**,
23:40 the **b** of leafy trees and poplars,
2Sm 18:9 mule went under the tangled **b**
Neh 8:15 and get **b** — olive and wild
8:15 and other thick-leaved **b** — to
8:16 So the people went to get **b** to
Job 14:9 sprout and grow **b** like a plant.
15:30 A flame will shrivel his **b**.
18:16 His **b** wither over him.
29:19 dew will lie on my **b** all night.
Psa 80:10 Its **b** covered the mighty
80:11 It reached out with its **b** to the
104:12 They sing among the **b**.
118:27 in a festival procession with **b**
Isa 7:18 the flies that are at the distant **b**
9:14 both palm **b** and cattails.
10:33 LORD of Armies will trim the **b**
17:6 on the rest of the **b**," declares
18:5 and chop off the spreading **b**.
27:10 They will feed on the **b**.
27:11 When the **b** are dried up,
Jer 5:10 Cut off the **b** because they don't
6:9 pass your hand over its **b**
11:16 and your **b** will be broken.
48:32 Your **b** ⌊once⌋ spread as far as
Eze 17:6 Its **b** turned upward toward the
17:6 **b** and growing shoots.
17:7 this eagle and sent its **b** toward
17:8 of water so that it could grow **b**,
17:9 the leaves on its **b** will wither.
17:23 It will grow **b** and produce fruit.
17:23 a home in the shelter of its **b**.
19:10 It had a lot of fruit and many **b**
19:11 Its **b** were strong. They were
19:11 to be tall with many **b** around it,
19:11 saw it because of its many **b**.
19:12 Its strong **b** broke off.
19:14 It no longer has any strong **b**
31:3 with fine **b** that shaded
31:5 Its **b** became large and long
31:6 birds made their nests in its **b**.
31:7 and beautiful with its long **b**.
31:8 pine trees couldn't equal its **b**.
31:8 couldn't measure up to its **b**.
31:9 it beautiful with its many **b**.
31:12 Its **b** fell on the mountains and
31:12 Its broken **b** fell in every ravine
31:13 the wild animals lived in its **b**.
36:8 will grow **b** and bear fruit for my
Dan 4:12 Birds came to live in its **b**.
4:14 Cut off its **b**! Strip off its leaves!
4:14 make the birds fly from its **b**.
4:21 birds made their homes in its **b**.
Hos 14:6 They will be like growing **b**.
Joe 1:7 and left the **b** bare.
Zec 4:12 the meaning of the two **b** from
Mat 13:32 for birds to nest in its **b**."
21:8 Others cut **b** from the trees and
Mar 4:32 It grows such large **b** that birds
11:8 Others cut leafy **b** in the fields
Luk 13:19 and the birds nested in its **b**."
Jon 12:13 So they took palm **b** and went
15:2 He removes every one of my **b**
15:5 You are the **b**. Those who live in
15:6 **B** like this are gathered,
19:2 twisted some thorny **b** into
Rom 11:16 the root is holy, the **b** are holy.
11:17 But some of the olive **b** have
11:18 being better than the other **b**.
11:19 "Well," you say, "**B** were cut
11:21 If God didn't spare the natural **b**,
11:24 it be easier for these natural **b**
Rev 7:9 holding palm **b** in their hands,

brand (3)

Rev 13:17 buy or sell unless he has the **b**,
16:2 on the people who had the **b**
19:20 deceived those who had the **b**

branded (5)

1Ti 4:2 have been scarred as if **b** by
Rev 13:16 people and slaves — to be **b**
14:9 whoever is **b** on his forehead or
14:11 or for anyone **b** with its name."
20:4 or its statue and were not **b**

brass (1)

Mar 7:4 jars, **b** pots, and dinner tables.)

brave (13)

Jdg 6:12 LORD is with you, **b** man."
2Sm 17:10 and the men with him are **b**.
23:20 was from Kabzeel and was a **b**
1Ch 11:22 was from Kabzeel and was a **b**
Job 36:5 He is mighty and **b**.
41:10 No one is **b** enough to provoke
Psa 76:5 **B** people were robbed.
147:10 nor is he pleased by **b** soldiers.
Isa 10:16 disease against **b** men.
35:4 terrified, "Be **b**; don't be afraid.
41:6 say to their relatives, "Be **b**!"
Eze 22:14 Will you still be **b**?
Amo 2:16 **B** soldiers will run away naked

bravest (1)

2Sm 17:10 Even the **b** man with a heart

bray (1)

Job 6:5 "Does a wild donkey **b** when

brazenly (1)

Pro 7:13 kisses him and **b** says to him,

bread (270)

Gen 14:18 Salem brought out **b** and wine.
18:5 Let me bring some **b** so that
18:6 of flour, knead it, and make **b**."
19:3 baked some unleavened **b**,
21:14 next morning Abraham took **b**
25:34 Esau a meal of **b** and lentils.
27:17 and the **b** she had prepared.
45:23 **b**, and food for his father's trip.
Exo 12:8 bitter herbs and unleavened **b**.
12:15 you must eat unleavened **b**.
12:17 the Festival of Unleavened **B**
12:18 you must eat unleavened **b**.
12:20 must eat ⌊only⌋ unleavened **b**."
12:34 So the people picked up their **b**
12:39 Egypt, they baked round, flat **b**.
13:6 you must eat unleavened **b**.
13:7 Only unleavened **b** should be
23:15 the Festival of Unleavened **B**:
23:15 you must eat unleavened **b**,
25:30 Put the **b** of the presence on
29:2 and bake some loaves of **b**,
29:2 some rings of **b** made with
29:3 Put the **b** in a basket,
29:23 of unleavened **b** which is
29:23 take a round loaf of **b**,
29:23 a ring of **b** made with olive oil,

Exo 29:32 meat of the ram and the **b** ⌊left⌋
29:34 If any meat or **b** from the
34:18 the Festival of Unleavened **B.**
34:18 you must eat unleavened **b** for
35:13 the **b** of the presence,
39:36 the **b** of the presence,
40:23 He arranged the **b** on the table
Lev 2:4 be rings of unleavened **b** made
2:4 of unleavened **b** brushed
2:5 will be unleavened **b** made of
6:16 They will eat unleavened **b** in
6:17 Don't use yeast in baking the **b.**
7:12 rings of unleavened **b** mixed
7:12 wafers of unleavened **b**
7:13 In addition to these rings of **b,**
7:13 you must bring **b** with yeast
8:2 the basket of unleavened **b.**
8:26 He took a loaf of unleavened **b,**
8:26 a ring of **b** made with olive oil,
8:26 of unleavened **b** which was
8:31 Take the meat and the **b** in the
8:32 You must burn any meat or **b**
10:12 Make unleavened **b,**
23:6 Festival of Unleavened **B.**
23:6 you must eat unleavened **b.**
23:14 Don't eat **b,** roasted grain,
23:17 Bring two loaves of **b** from your
23:18 With the **b** bring seven
23:20 present them along with the **b**
24:5 and bake twelve rings of **b.**
24:7 The incense on the **b** will be a
24:8 ⌊a priest⌋ must arrange the **b**
24:9 The **b** will belong to Aaron and
Num 4:7 The **b** that is always in the
6:15 **b** containing some rings
6:15 some rings of **b** made
6:15 of unleavened **b** brushed
6:17 basket of unleavened **b** along
6:19 one ring of unleavened **b** from
6:19 and one wafer of unleavened **b**
9:11 unleavened **b** and bitter herbs.
11:8 or make round loaves of **b** out
14:9 We will devour them like **b.**
21:5 There's no **b** or water,
28:17 must eat only unleavened **b.**
Dtr 8:3 a person cannot live on **b** alone
16:3 Never eat leavened **b** with the
16:3 unleavened **b** at this festival.
16:3 (It is the **b** of misery because
16:3 Eat this **b** so that, as long as
16:8 For six days eat unleavened **b,**
16:16 the Festival of Unleavened **B,**
28:5 The grain you harvest and the **b**
28:17 The grain you harvest and the **b**
29:6 You ate no **b** and drank no
Jos 5:11 **b** and roasted grain.
9:5 All their **b** was dried out and
9:12 Our **b** was warm when we left
Jdg 6:19 goat and unleavened **b** made
6:20 the meat and the unleavened **b,**
6:21 touched the meat and the **b**
6:21 and burned the meat and the **b.**
7:13 There was a loaf of barley **b**
7:13 the loaf of **b** hit that tent so hard
19:19 I even have **b** and wine for
Rut 2:14 Have some **b,** and dip it into
1Sm 2:5 themselves out for a piece of **b,**
2:36 a coin or a loaf of **b** and say,
2:36 so that I may eat a piece of **b.**'"
10:3 be carrying three loaves of **b,**
10:4 and give you two loaves of **b,**
16:20 Jesse took six bushels of **b,**
17:17 grain and these ten loaves of **b**
21:3 Give me five loaves of **b** or
21:4 "I don't have any ordinary **b,**"
21:4 "But there is holy **b** for the
21:6 So the priest gave him holy ⌊**b**⌋
21:6 because he only had the **b**
21:6 replaced with warm **b** that day.
22:13 You gave him **b** and a sword
25:11 Should I take my **b,**
25:18 quickly took 200 loaves of **b,**
28:24 and baked some unleavened **b.**
2Sm 6:19 and women — one loaf of **b,**
13:6 Tamar come and make some **b**
13:8 made flat **b** in front of him,

2Sm 13:9 pan and served him ⌊the **b**⌋.
13:10 Tamar took the **b** she had
16:1 loaded with 200 loaves of **b,**
16:2 "The **b** and the ripe fruit are for
1Ki 7:48 the gold table on which the **b** of
14:3 Take ten loaves of **b,**
17:6 Ravens brought him **b** and
17:11 "Please bring me a piece of **b**
17:12 I didn't bake any **b.**
18:4 kept them alive by providing **b**
18:13 in each cave and provided **b**
19:6 he saw near his head some **b**
22:27 and feed him nothing but **b** and
2Ki 4:42 Shalisha brought **b** made from
18:32 a country with **b** and vineyards,
23:9 they ate their unleavened **b**
1Ch 9:31 with preparing the flat **b.**
9:32 responsible for setting the **b** out
16:3 men and women — a loaf of **b,**
23:29 responsible for the rows of **b,**
23:29 the unleavened **b** wafers,
23:29 and the **b** made in frying pans.
28:16 each table with the rows of **b,**
2Ch 2:4 rows of **b** there continually.
4:19 the gold tables on which the **b**
8:13 (the Festival of Unleavened **B,**
13:11 incense and rows of **b**
18:26 and feed him nothing but **b** and
29:18 the table for the rows of **b** and
30:13 the Festival of Unleavened **B**
30:21 the Festival of Unleavened **B**
35:17 Unleavened **B** for seven days.
Ezr 6:22 the Festival of Unleavened **B**
Neh 9:15 You gave them **b** from heaven
10:33 for rows of the **b** of the
Psa 41:9 the one who ate my **b,**
78:20 But can he also give us **b** or
78:25 Humans ate the **b** of the mighty
102:9 I eat ashes like **b** and my tears
104:15 and **b** to strengthen human
105:40 filled them with **b** from heaven.
Pro 6:26 price is ⌊only⌋ a loaf of **b,**
9:5 "Come, eat my **b,** and drink the
17:1 Better a bite of dry **b** ⌊eaten⌋ in
28:21 on you even for a piece of **b.**
31:27 does not eat the **b** of idleness.
Ecc 11:1 Throw your **b** on the surface of
Isa 36:17 a country with **b** and vineyards.
44:15 They start fires and bake **b.**
44:19 I also baked **b** over its coals.
Jer 37:21 He gave him a loaf of **b** every
37:21 the bakers' street until all the **b**
38:9 there's no more **b** in the city."
Lam 1:11 are groaning as they beg for **b.**
2:12 asking their mothers for some **b**
4:4 Little children beg for **b,**
Eze 4:9 them to make **b** for yourself.
4:12 Eat the **b** as you would eat
4:12 Bake the **b** in front of people,
4:13 Israel will eat unclean **b** among
4:15 Bake your **b** over it."
4:16 I am going to cut off the **b**
4:16 will anxiously eat rationed **b**
13:19 of barley and a few pieces of **b.**
45:21 when unleavened **b** is eaten.
Hos 7:4 its flames when he makes **b.**
7:8 are like a half-baked loaf of **b.**
Amo 4:5 Burn **b** as a thank offering.
Hag 2:12 If his clothes touch **b,**
Mat 4:3 stones to become loaves of **b.**"
4:4 'A person cannot live on **b**
6:11 Give us our daily **b** today.
7:9 "If your child asks you for **b,**
12:4 the house of God and ate the **b**
14:17 five loaves of **b** and two fish."
15:33 "Where could we get enough **b**
15:34 "How many loaves of **b** do you
15:36 Then he broke the **b** and gave
15:36 and they gave the **b** and fish to
16:5 to take any **b** along when they
16:7 they had not taken any **b** along.
16:8 that you don't have any **b**?
16:11 I wasn't talking to you about **b**?
16:12 to watch out for the yeast in **b,**
26:17 the Festival of Unleavened **B,**
26:26 Jesus took **b** and blessed it.

Mat 26:26 He broke the **b,** gave it to his
Mar 2:26 was chief priest and ate the **b**
6:37 wages on **b** to feed them?"
6:38 "Five loaves of **b** and two fish."
6:43 twelve baskets with **b** and fish.
6:44 men who had eaten the **b.**
6:52 happened with the loaves of **b.**
8:4 could anyone get enough **b**
8:5 "How many loaves of **b** do you
8:6 Then he broke the **b** and gave
8:14 forgotten to take any **b** along
8:16 that they didn't have any **b.**
8:17 fact that you don't have any **b**?
14:1 the Festival of Unleavened **B.**
14:12 the Festival of Unleavened **B.**
14:22 Jesus took **b** and blessed it.
14:22 He broke the **b,** gave it to them,
Luk 4:3 stone to become a loaf of **b.**"
4:4 'A person cannot live on **b**
6:4 ate the **b** of the presence,
7:33 eating **b** nor drinking wine,
9:13 "We have five loaves of **b** and
11:3 Give us our **b** day by day.
11:5 let me borrow three loaves of **b.**
22:1 The Festival of Unleavened **B,**
22:7 Festival of Unleavened **B** when
22:19 Then Jesus took **b** and spoke
22:19 He broke the **b,** gave it to them,
24:30 he took **b** and blessed it.
24:30 He broke the **b** and gave it to
24:35 Jesus when he broke the **b.**
Jon 6:5 "Where can we buy **b** for these
6:7 a year's wages to buy enough **b**
6:9 who has five loaves of barley **b**
6:13 the leftover pieces of **b**
6:23 they had eaten the **b** after
6:31 'He gave them **b** from heaven
6:32 didn't give you **b** from heaven,
6:32 you the true **b** from heaven.
6:33 God's **b** is the man who comes
6:34 give us this **b** all the time."
6:35 told them, "I am the **b** of life.
6:41 "I am the **b** that came from
6:48 "I am the **b** of life.
6:50 This is the **b** that comes from
6:51 I am the living **b** that came from
6:51 Whoever eats this **b** will live
6:51 The **b** I will give to bring life to
6:58 This is the **b** that came from
6:58 It is not like the **b** your
6:58 who eat this **b** will live forever."
13:18 eats my **b** has turned against
13:26 this piece of **b** after I've dipped
13:26 So Jesus dipped the **b** and
13:27 after Judas took the piece of **b,**
13:30 Judas took the piece of **b** and
21:9 and they saw a loaf of **b.**
21:13 Jesus took the **b,** gave it to
Act 2:42 to the breaking of **b,**
12:3 the days of Unleavened **B.**
20:6 the Festival of Unleavened **B,**
20:7 On Sunday we met to break **b.**
20:11 again, broke the **b,** and ate.
27:35 Paul said this, he took some **b,**
1Co 5:8 we must celebrate it with the **b**
10:16 When we break the **b** aren't we
11:23 the Lord Jesus took **b**
11:24 He broke the **b** and said,
11:26 Every time you eat this **b** and
11:27 Therefore, whoever eats the **b**
11:28 is proper when they eat the **b**
Heb 9:2 and the **b** of the presence were

breadcrumbs (1)

Psa 147:17 throws his hailstones like **b.**

break (122)

Gen 19:9 forward to **b** down the door.
27:40 your freedom and **b** his yoke off
Exo 9:9 The dust will cause boils to **b**
9:10 and they caused boils to **b** into
12:46 "Never **b** any of the bones.
13:13 then you must **b** the donkey's
34:20 then you must **b** the donkey's
40:36 the Israelites would **b** camp.
40:37 they wouldn't **b** camp.

Lev 1:15 He will **b** its neck and burn the
2:6 **B** it into pieces and pour olive
5:8 He will **b** the bird's neck
11:33 **b** the pottery because
Num 9:12 the meat until morning or **b** any
9:17 the Israelites would **b** camp,
9:18 the Israelites would **b** camp,
9:19 command and wouldn't **b** camp.
9:20 command they would **b** camp.
9:22 same place and not **b** camp.
9:22 they would **b** camp.
10:2 and as a signal to **b** camp.
10:5 the east side will **b** camp first.
10:6 on the south will **b** camp.
10:6 The fanfare is the signal to **b**
12:15 The people didn't **b** camp until
30:2 he must not **b** his word.
Dtr 1:7 **B** camp, and get ready! Go to
2:24 continued,⌋ "Now **b** camp.
21:4 they must **b** the heifer's neck.
33:11 **B** the backs of those who
Jos 3:3 **b** camp and follow them.
Jdg 2:1 I said, 'I will never **b** my
11:35 to the LORD. Now I can't **b** it."
1Sm 2:31 when I will **b** your strength
2Sm 22:30 God I can **b** through barricades.
1Ki 11:27 the Millo and repairing a **b**
15:19 Now **b** your treaty with King
2Ki 3:26 swordsmen to try to **b** through
11:8 Kill anyone who tries to **b**
2Ch 16:3 Now **b** your treaty with King
Ezr 9:14 If we **b** your commandments
Job 24:16 In the dark, they **b** into houses,
Psa 2:3 "Let's **b** apart their chains and
2:9 You will **b** them with an iron
10:15 **B** the arm of the wicked and
15:4 a promise and does not **b** it,
18:29 God I can **b** through barricades.
46:5 will help it at the **b** of dawn.
58:6 **B** the young lions' teeth,
80:12 Why did you **b** down the stone
98:4 **B** out into joyful singing,
144:14 May no one **b** in, and may no
148:6 it a law that no one can **b**.
Pro 25:15 and a soft tongue can **b** bones.
Isa 9:4 You will **b** the yoke that
28:24 Does he continue to **b** up the
30:14 It will **b** like pottery.
42:3 He will not **b** off a damaged
44:23 **B** into shouts of joy,
45:2 I will **b** down the bronze doors
49:13 **B** into shouts of joy,
52:9 **B** out into shouts of joy,
54:1 **B** into shouts of joy,
55:12 and the hills will **b** into songs
58:6 go free, and **b** every yoke.
58:8 Then your light will **b** through
Jer 5:22 they can't **b** through.
14:21 your promise to us; don't **b** it.
15:12 (No one can **b** iron,
18:7 threaten to tear up, **b** down,
21:12 Otherwise, my fury will **b** out
25:34 and you will **b** like fine pottery.
28:2 I will **b** the yoke of the king of
28:4 So I will **b** the yoke of the king
28:11 I will **b** the yoke of King
30:8 "I will **b** the yokes off your
32:29 are attacking this city will **b** in,
33:20 Suppose you could **b** my
43:13 At Beth Shemesh he will **b** the
48:38 because I will **b** Moab like a jar
49:35 I'm going to **b** the bows of
Lam 4:4 but no one will **b** off a piece for
Eze 13:11 winds will **b** it to pieces.
13:13 In my fury I'll cause a storm to **b**
17:15 He can't **b** a treaty and go
17:22 I will **b** off the highest twig and
23:34 You will **b** it into pieces and
30:18 dark when I **b** Egypt's power.
30:22 I will **b** both his arms,
30:24 but I will **b** Pharaoh's arms.
34:27 because I will **b** off the bars on
Hos 1:5 On that day I will **b** Israel's
4:2 People **b** ⌊my laws⌋,
7:1 They **b** into houses and steal.
10:11 Jacob must **b** up the ground.
Hos 10:12 "**B** new ground. Plant
Joe 2:8 Even when they **b** through the
2:8 they do not **b** their ranks.
Amo 1:5 I will **b** the bars ⌊on the gates⌋
Mic 2:13 They will **b** out, go through the
3:3 You **b** their bones to pieces.
Nah 1:13 But now I will **b** Nineveh's
Hab 3:6 The oldest mountains **b** apart.
Zec 11:10 to **b** the promise that I had
11:14 to **b** off the brotherhood
Mat 1:19 So he decided to **b** the
5:33 'Never **b** your oath,
6:19 and thieves **b** in and steal.
6:20 and thieves don't **b** in and steal.
12:20 He will not **b** off a damaged
15:2 "Why do your disciples **b** the
15:3 "Why do you **b** the
24:43 let the thief **b** into his house.
Luk 8:29 But he would **b** the chains.
12:39 have let him **b** into his house.
Jon 5:18 Not only did he **b** the laws
19:33 they didn't **b** his legs.
Act 20:7 On Sunday we met to **b** bread.
23:3 yet you **b** those teachings by
1Co 10:16 When we **b** the bread aren't we
Gal 4:27 **B** into shouting, those who feel
Rev 5:2 to open the scroll and **b**

breakdown (1)

2Ch 17:14 The following is a **b** of these

breakfast (2)

Jon 21:12 told them, "Come, have **b**."
21:15 After they had eaten **b**,

breaking (11)

Exo 22:2 "If anyone catches a thief **b** in
2Ch 24:20 Why are you **b** the LORD's
Jer 2:34 You didn't kill them for **b** in to
Eze 21:6 "So, son of man, groan with a **b**
Jnh 1:4 the ship was in danger of **b** up.
Mat 27:24 Instead, a riot was **b** out.
Mar 4:37 The waves were **b** into the
Act 2:42 to the **b** of bread, and to prayer.
21:13 crying like this and **b** my heart?
Eph 2:14 people one by **b** down
Jas 2:10 person is guilty of **b** all of them.

breaks (12)

Exo 1:10 Then, if war **b** out,
Job 34:24 He **b** mighty people into pieces
Psa 27:3 Even though a war **b** out
29:5 of the LORD **b** the cedars.
46:9 He **b** an archer's bow.
141:7 As someone plows and **b** up
Pro 15:4 a deceitful tongue **b** the spirit.
Ecc 10:8 Whoever **b** through a stone
Isa 14:7 It **b** out into shouts of joy.
66:3 a lamb is like someone who **b**
Jer 4:18 It is bitter. It **b** your heart."
Amo 4:3 will leave ⌊the city⌋ through **b**

breast (14)

Exo 29:26 "Take the **b** from the ram used
29:27 Set apart as holy the **b** that is
Lev 7:30 Bring the fat with the **b**.
7:30 Take the **b** and present it to the
7:31 However, the **b** will belong to
7:34 I have taken the **b** that was
8:29 Moses also took the **b** from the
10:14 Also eat the **b** presented ⌊to
10:15 the **b** presented ⌊to the LORD⌋,
Num 6:20 along with the ram's **b** that is
18:18 But the meat is yours, like the **b**
Job 24:9 the ⌊nursing⌋ orphan from a **b**
Pro 5:20 and fondle a loose woman's **b**?
Eze 21:12 So beat your **b**, and grieve.

breastplate (29)

Exo 25:7 priest's⌋ ephod and his **b**.
28:4 the clothes they will make: a **b**,
28:15 "Make the **b** for
28:22 "For the **b** make chains out of
28:23 Make two gold rings for the **b**.
28:23 the two ⌊top⌋ corners of the **b**.
28:24 at the ⌊top⌋ corners of the **b**.
Exo 28:25 ephod ⌊so that the **b** hangs⌋
28:26 to the other two corners of the **b**
28:28 Then the **b** should be fastened
28:28 and will hold the **b** in place.
28:29 the **b** for decision-making.
28:30 into the **b** for decision-making.
29:5 that is worn with it, and the **b**.
35:9 ⌊chief priest's⌋ ephod and **b**.
35:27 ⌊chief priest's⌋ ephod and **b**.
39:8 They made the **b** as creatively
39:15 For the **b** they made chains out
39:16 the ⌊top⌋ two corners of the **b**.
39:17 at the ⌊top⌋ corners of the **b**.
39:18 the ephod ⌊so that the **b** hung⌋
39:19 to the other two corners of the **b**
39:21 Then they fastened the **b** by its
39:21 So the **b** was attached just
Lev 8:8 Then he put the **b** on him,
1Ki 22:34 his scale armor and his **b**.
2Ch 18:33 his scale armor and his **b**.
Eph 6:14 on God's approval as your **b**.
1Th 5:8 put on faith and love as a **b**

breastplates (2)

Rev 9:9 They had **b** like iron.
9:17 The riders had **b** that were fiery

breasts (28)

Gen 49:25 blessings from **b** and womb.
Lev 9:20 they placed on the **b**.
9:21 However, he first took the **b**
Job 3:12 Why did **b** let me nurse?
Psa 22:9 me feel safe at my mother's **b**.
Pro 5:19 Always let her **b** satisfy you.
Sos 1:13 that lies at night between my **b**.
4:5 Your **b** are like two fawns,
7:3 Your **b** are like two fawns,
7:7 and your **b** are like its clusters.
7:8 May your **b** be like clusters on
8:1 who nursed at my mother's **b**.
8:8 a little sister, and she has no **b**.
8:10 and my **b** are like towers.
Isa 28:9 taken from their ⌊mother's⌋ **b**?
32:12 Beat your **b** as you mourn for
60:16 nations and nurse at royal **b**.
66:11 satisfied from her comforting **b**.
66:11 your heart's delight at her full **b**.
Lam 4:3 Even jackals offer their **b** to
Eze 16:7 Your **b** developed,
23:3 fondled and caressed their **b**.
23:8 to bed with her, caressed her **b**,
23:21 caressed and fondled her **b**.
23:34 and tear your **b** off your body.
Hos 2:2 the lovers from between her **b**.
Nah 2:7 like doves as they beat their **b**."
Luk 11:27 you and the **b** that nursed you."

breath (57)

Gen 2:7 dust of the earth and blew the **b**
25:8 Then he took his last **b**,
25:17 he took his last **b** and died.
35:18 As she took her last **b**,
35:29 he took his last **b** and died.
49:33 He took his last **b** and joined
Exo 15:10 Your **b** blew the sea over them.
Num 16:22 are the God who gives the **b**
27:16 are the God who gives the **b**
2Sm 22:16 blast of the **b** from his nostrils.
Job 3:11 and breathe my last **b** when
4:9 God destroys them with his **b**
7:7 Remember, my life is only a **b**,
9:18 would not let me catch my **b**.
10:18 I wish I had breathed my last **b**
11:20 hope is to take their last **b**."
14:10 A person breathes his last **b**,
15:30 be blown away by his own **b**.
19:17 My **b** offends my wife.
27:3 'As long as there is one **b**
27:3 and God's **b** fills my nostrils,
27:5 Until I breathe my last **b**,
32:8 the **b** of the Almighty,
33:4 The **b** of the Almighty gives me
34:14 withdrew his Spirit and his **b**,
37:10 God's **b** produces ice,
41:21 Its **b** sets coals on fire,
Psa 18:15 blast of the **b** from your nostrils.

Psa 33:6 the stars by the **b** of his mouth.
104:29 You take away their **b**,
144:4 Humans are like a **b** of air.
146:4 When they breathe their last **b**,
Ecc 3:19 them have the same **b** ⌊of life⌋.
11:5 as you don't know how the **b**
12:7 and the **b** of life goes back to
Sos 7:8 of your **b** be like apples.
Isa 11:4 wicked with the **b** from his lips.
25:4 (A tyrant's **b** is like a rainstorm
30:28 His **b** is like an overflowing
30:33 The LORD's **b** will be like a
33:11 Your **b** will be a fire which will
40:7 when the LORD's **b** blows
42:5 the people who are on it and **b**
57:13 A **b** will take them away.
Jer 4:31 people Zion are gasping for **b**.
Lam 1:19 leaders breathed their last **b**
4:20 who is the **b** of our life,
Eze 37:5 I will cause **b** to enter you,
37:6 I will put **b** in you, and you will
37:8 Yet, there was no **b** in them.
37:9 "Prophesy to the **b**!
37:9 Tell the **b**, 'This is what the
37:9 Come from the four winds, **B**,
37:10 and the **b** entered them.
Act 17:25 He gives everyone life, **b**,
Rev 11:11 After 3 ½ days the **b** of life
13:15 beast was allowed to put **b** into

breathe (13)

Job 3:11 I was born and **b** my last breath
27:5 Until I **b** my last breath,
31:39 made its owners **b** their last,
Psa 27:12 They **b** out violence.
135:17 cannot hear. They cannot **b**.
146:4 When they **b** their last breath,
Jer 10:14 are false ⌊gods⌋. They can't **b**.
15:9 will grow faint and **b** her last.
51:18 They can't **b**. They are
Eze 21:31 pour out my fury on you and **b**
22:21 **b** on you with my fiery anger,
37:9 and **b** on these people who
Jas 2:26 A body that doesn't **b** is dead.

breathed (3)

Job 10:18 I wish I had **b** my last breath
Lam 1:19 My priests and leaders **b** their
Jon 20:22 he **b** on the disciples and said,

breathes (3)

Job 14:10 A person **b** his last breath,
Psa 150:6 Let everything that **b** praise the
Pro 14:5 but a dishonest witness **b** lies.

breathing (5)

Gen 1:30 earth — every living, **b** animal."
6:17 sky — every living, **b** human.
7:15 A pair of every living, **b** animal
7:22 (every living, **b** creature) died.
Lam 5:5 ⌊Our enemies⌋ are **b** down our

breathless (2)

1Ki 10:5 the LORD's temple, she was **b**.
2Ch 9:4 the LORD's temple, she was **b**.

bred (1)

Est 8:10 special horses **b** for speed.

breed (1)

Job 21:10 bulls are fertile when they **b**.

breeze (5)

Psa 72:16 May it wave ⌊in the **b**⌋ on the
78:39 a **b** that blows and does not
Sos 2:17 the day brings a cooling **b**
4:6 When the day brings a cool **b**
Act 27:13 When a gentle **b** began to blow

brewing (1)

Jer 25:32 A great storm is **b** from the

briar (1)

Mic 7:4 The best of them is like a **b**.

briars (8)

Isa 7:23 there will be **b** and thorns.
7:24 will be filled with **b** and thorns.
7:25 will be filled with **b** and thorns.
9:18 It burns up **b** and thorns.
27:4 If only thorns and **b** would
32:13 where thorns and **b** will grow.
55:13 trees will grow where **b** grew.
Eze 28:24 sharp **b** from everyone around

bribe (14)

Exo 23:8 Never take a **b**, because bribes
Dtr 10:17 favorites and never takes a **b**.
16:19 Never take a **b**, because bribes
1Sm 12:3 Did I take a **b** from anyone to
Job 6:22 'Offer me a **b** from your wealth,'
36:18 Don't let a large **b** turn you ⌊to
Psa 15:5 on a loan or take a **b** against
Pro 6:35 The largest **b** will not satisfy
17:8 A **b** seems ⌊like⌋ a jewel to
17:23 person secretly accepts a **b**
21:14 and a secret **b** calms great fury.
Ecc 7:7 and a **b** can corrupt the mind.
Isa 5:23 the guilty innocent for a **b**,
Eze 16:33 to all your lovers and **b** them

bribed (2)

Ezr 4:5 They **b** officials to keep the
Act 6:11 Then they **b** some men to lie.

bribes (13)

Exo 23:8 Never take a bribe, because **b**
Dtr 16:19 Never take a bribe, because **b**
1Sm 8:3 They took **b** and denied people
2Ch 19:7 is impartial and never takes **b**."
Job 15:34 the tents of those who offer **b**.
Psa 26:10 Their right hands are full of **b**.
Pro 15:27 but whoever hates **b** will live.
Isa 1:23 They all love **b** and run after
33:15 extortion and refuses to take **b**.
Eze 22:12 Other people take **b** to murder
Amo 5:12 the righteous by taking **b**.
Mic 3:11 leaders exchange justice for **b**.
7:3 Judges accept **b**.

brick (3)

Isa 65:3 and burnt incense on **b** altars.
Jer 43:9 and bury them under the **b**
Nah 3:14 the clay! Grab the **b** mold!

bricks (11)

Gen 11:3 "Let's make **b** and bake them
11:3 They used **b** as stones and tar
Exo 1:14 work in mortar and **b**
5:7 straw to make **b** as you have
5:8 number of **b** they were making
5:8 Making fewer **b** will not be
5:14 "You didn't finish all the **b** you
5:16 and yet we're told to make **b**.
5:18 make the same number of **b**."
5:19 "Don't make fewer **b** each day
Isa 9:10 "**B** have fallen, but we will

bride (19)

Gen 34:12 the price I must pay for the **b**
1Sm 18:25 for the **b** except 100 Philistine
2Sm 17:3 people to you as a **b** is returned
Sos 4:8 from Lebanon as my **b**.
4:9 My **b**, my sister, you have
4:10 of love, my **b**, my sister!
4:11 Your lips drip honey, my **b**.
4:12 My **b**, my sister is a garden that
5:1 My **b**, my sister, I will come to
Isa 49:18 them on yourself as a **b** would."
61:10 like a **b** with her jewels.
62:5 bridegroom rejoices over his **b**,
Jer 2:2 the love you had for me as a **b**.
2:32 her jewelry or a **b** her veils.
Jon 3:29 person to whom the **b** belongs.
Rev 19:7 His **b** has made herself ready.
21:2 dressed like a **b** ready for her
21:9 I will show you the **b**,
22:17 The Spirit and the **b** say,

bridegroom (5)

Exo 4:25 "You are a **b** of blood to me!"
4:26 "You are a **b** of blood!
Psa 19:5 out of its chamber like a **b**.
Isa 61:10 robe of righteousness like a **b**
62:5 As a **b** rejoices over his bride,

bride-price (2)

Exo 22:16 must pay the **b** and marry her.
22:17 equal to the **b** for virgins.

brides (6)

Jer 7:34 the sounds of **b** and grooms,
16:9 happiness and the sounds of **b**
25:10 the sounds of **b** and grooms,
33:11 the sounds of **b** and grooms.
Joe 2:16 **B** leave their chambers.
Rev 18:23 Voices of **b** and grooms will

bridesmaids (9)

Psa 45:14 Her **b** follow her. They will be
Mat 25:1 of heaven will be like ten **b**.
25:3 The foolish **b** took their lamps,
25:4 The wise **b**, however,
25:5 all the **b** became drowsy and
25:7 Then all the **b** woke up and got
25:9 "But the wise **b** replied,
25:10 The **b** who were ready went
25:11 "Later the other **b** arrived and

bridle (6)

2Ki 19:28 my hook in your nose and my **b**
Psa 32:9 ⌊They need⌋ a bit and **b** in
39:1 I will **b** my mouth while wicked
Pro 26:3 a **b** is for the donkey,
Isa 37:29 my hook in your nose and my **b**
Rev 14:20 as a horse's **b** for 1,600 stadia.

brief (10)

Ezr 9:8 And now, for a **b** moment,
Job 7:16 because my days are so **b**.
Ecc 2:3 their **b** lives under heaven.
5:18 during the **b** lives God gives
5:20 much thought to their **b** lives
6:12 they are alive, during the **b**,
8:15 during their **b** lives which God
9:9 during all your **b**, pointless life.
Isa 54:7 you for one **b** moment,
Act 24:4 listen to us. We will be **b**.

briefly (2)

1Co 16:7 all I could do is visit you **b**,
Eph 3:3 written to you about this **b**.

bright (55)

Gen 1:16 God made the two **b** lights:
Exo 25:4 violet, purple, and **b** red yarn,
26:1 violet, purple, and **b** red yarn,
26:31 of violet, purple, and **b** red yarn.
26:36 violet, purple, and **b** red yarn.
27:16 violet, purple, and **b** red yarn,
28:5 and **b** red yarn, and fine linen.
28:6 and **b** red yarn into the fabric.
28:15 and **b** red yarn and out of fine
28:33 and **b** red yarn with gold bells
35:6 violet, purple, and **b** red yarn,
35:23 purple, or **b** red yarn, fine linen,
35:25 and **b** red yarn, and fine linen,
35:35 purple and **b** red yarn on fine
36:8 violet, purple, and **b** red yarn.
36:35 and **b** red yarn and fine linen
36:37 violet, purple, and **b** red yarn.
38:18 and **b** red yarn embroidered on
38:23 and **b** red yarn on fine linen.
39:1 From the violet, purple, and **b**
39:2 violet, purple, and **b** red yarn.
39:3 violet, purple, and **b** red yarn,
39:8 violet, purple, and **b** red yarn,
39:24 and **b** red yarn, and fine yarn.
39:29 violet, purple, and **b** red yarn.
Lev 13:24 into a pink or **b** white area,
Num 4:8 They will spread a **b** red cloth
Job 10:22 light is as **b** as darkness.
25:5 Even the moon isn't **b**,
37:21 at the sun when it's **b** among

Psa 139:12 Night is as **b** as day.
Isa 1:18 "Though your sins are **b** red,
9:2 in darkness will see a **b** light.
58:10 darkness will become as **b** as
63:1 with his clothes stained **b** red?
Eze 1:4 surrounded by a **b** light.
1:13 The fire was **b**, and lightning
1:27 A **b** light surrounded him.
23:14 men, painted in **b** red.
Dan 2:31 This statue was very **b**.
Hab 3:11 at the **b** lightning of your spear.
Mat 4:16 darkness have seen a **b** light.
17:2 His face became as **b** as the
17:5 He was still speaking when a **b**
27:28 clothes and put a **b** red cape
28:3 He was as **b** as lightning,
Luk 11:36 it will be as **b** as a lamp
24:4 as **b** as lightning suddenly
Act 22:6 a **b** light from heaven suddenly
22:11 the light had been so **b**.
Rev 17:3 I saw a woman sitting on a **b**
17:4 **b** red clothes, gold jewelry,
18:12 purple cloth, silk, **b** red cloth,
18:16 **b** red clothes, gold jewelry,
22:16 I am the **b** morning star."

brighter (4)

Job 11:17 Then your life will be **b** than
Pro 4:18 light of dawn that becomes **b**
4:18 becomes brighter and **b** until
Act 26:13 I saw a light that was **b** than

brightly (2)

Pro 13:9 of righteous people beams **b**,
Isa 62:1 salvation burns **b** like a torch.

brightness (12)

Jdg 5:31 sun when it rises in all its **b**.
2Sm 22:13 Out of the **b** in front of him,
23:4 like the **b** after a rainstorm.
Psa 18:12 Out of the **b** in front of him,
Isa 59:9 We hope for **b**, but we walk in
60:3 come to the **b** of your dawn.
60:19 nor will the **b** of the moon give
Eze 1:28 The **b** all around him looked
10:4 and the **b** of the LORD's glory
Dan 12:3 are wise will shine like the **b**
Hab 3:4 His **b** is like the sunlight.
Rev 1:16 sun when it shines in all its **b**.

brilliant (2)

Jon 5:35 a lamp that gave off **b** light.
1Co 2:1 kind of **b** message or wisdom.

brim (1)

Jon 2:7 servers filled the jars to the **b**.

bring (841)

Gen 5:29 "This child will **b** us relief from
6:19 **B** two of every living creature
8:17 **B** out every animal that's with
15:9 "**B** me a three-year-old heifer,
18:4 Why don't we let someone **b** a
18:5 Let me **b** some bread so that
19:5 **B** them out to us so that we
19:8 Why don't you let me **b** them
20:9 you that you would **b** such
27:4 **B** it to me to eat so that I will
27:5 for some wild game to **b** back,
27:7 '**B** me some wild game,
27:12 Then I'll **b** a curse on myself
27:25 "**B** me some of the game,
28:15 I will also **b** you back to this
37:14 and **b** some news back to me."
37:22 from them and **b** him back
38:24 "**B** her out to be burned."
42:20 But you must **b** me your
42:34 **b** me your youngest brother.
42:37 to death if I don't **b** him back
42:37 and I'll **b** him back to you."
43:7 '**B** your brother here'?"
43:9 If I don't **b** him back to you and
44:21 "Then you said to us, '**B** him
44:32 'If I don't **b** him back to you,
45:13 Hurry and **b** my father here!"
45:19 **B** your father, and come back.
Gen 45:27 Joseph had sent to **b** him back,
46:5 had sent to **b** him back.
47:18 There's nothing left to **b** you
48:9 Then Israel said, "Please **b**
48:21 He will **b** you back to the land
Exo 3:8 and to **b** them from that
3:10 that you can **b** my people Israel
3:11 I should go to Pharaoh and **b**
3:12 When you **b** the people out of
6:6 I will **b** you out from under the
6:8 I will **b** you to the land I
6:13 He commanded them to **b** the
6:26 "**B** the Israelites out of Egypt in
7:4 and I will **b** my people,
7:5 my power against Egypt and **b**
8:2 I will **b** a plague of frogs on
8:5 This will **b** frogs onto the land.'"
9:3 the LORD will **b** a terrible
9:19 Now, send ⌊servants⌋ to **b**
10:4 tomorrow I will **b** locusts into
10:12 hand over Egypt to **b** locusts.
11:1 "I will **b** one more plague on
13:3 his mighty hand to **b** you out
13:9 his mighty hand to **b** you out
13:14 used his mighty hand to **b**
13:16 used his mighty hand to **b**
14:11 They said to Moses, "Did you **b**
15:17 You will **b** them and plant them
16:5 they prepare what they **b** home,
17:3 "Why did you **b** us out of
17:5 LORD answered Moses, "**B**
18:16 have a disagreement and **b**
18:19 God and **b** their disagreements
18:22 They should **b** all important
18:26 They would **b** difficult cases to
19:24 and **b** Aaron back with you.
21:6 then his master must **b** him to
21:6 The master must **b** him to the
22:9 both people must **b** their case
22:13 he must **b** in the dead body as
23:19 "You must **b** the best of the first
23:20 you on your trip and **b** you
23:23 go ahead of you and will **b** you
27:20 the Israelites to **b** you pure,
28:1 **b** your brother Aaron and his
28:38 Israelites **b** their holy offerings
29:3 Put the bread in a basket, and **b**
29:4 "Then **b** Aaron and his sons to
29:10 "Then **b** the young bull to the
32:2 and **b** them to me."
32:12 Reconsider your decision to **b**
34:26 "You must **b** the first and best
35:5 Let everyone who is willing **b**
40:4 **B** in the table, and arrange
40:4 **B** in the lamp stand,
40:12 "**B** Aaron and his sons to the
Lev 1:2 If any of you **b** a sacrifice to the
1:3 "If you **b** a burnt offering from
1:10 you must **b** a male that has no
1:15 The priest must **b** it to the altar.
2:1 if any of you **b** a grain offering
2:2 Then **b** it to Aaron's sons,
2:4 "If you **b** a grain offering which
2:8 "**B** the LORD the grain offering
2:8 Offer it to the priest who will **b**
2:11 "Every grain offering that you **b**
2:12 You may **b** them to the LORD
2:14 "If you **b** a grain offering to the
3:6 you must **b** a male or female
3:7 you must **b** it to the LORD.
3:12 you must **b** it to the LORD.
3:14 Then **b** the fat that covers the
4:3 he must **b** a bull that has no
4:4 He must **b** the bull into the
4:5 some of the bull's blood and **b**
4:14 They must **b** it in front of the
4:16 Then the anointed priest will **b**
4:23 he must **b** a male goat that has
4:28 he must **b** a female goat that
4:32 he must **b** a female that has no
5:6 **B** your guilt offering to the
5:7 you must **b** to the LORD two
5:8 **B** them to the priest,
5:11 then **b** eight cups of flour as an
5:12 **B** it to the priest. The priest will
5:15 **b** a guilt offering to the LORD.
Lev 5:18 You must **b** the priest a ram
6:5 day you **b** your guilt offering.
6:6 Then **b** the LORD your guilt
6:6 in money. **B** it to the priest.
6:14 Aaron's sons must **b** it into the
6:20 that Aaron and his sons must **b**
7:11 that you must **b** to the LORD.
7:12 you must also **b** rings of
7:13 you must **b** bread with yeast
7:14 From every offering you must **b**
7:29 a fellowship offering must **b**
7:30 **B** the sacrifices by fire made to
7:30 **B** the fat with the breast.
7:38 the Israelites to **b** their offerings
10:15 They will **b** the thigh given as
12:6 she must **b** a one-year-old lamb
12:6 She must **b** them to the priest
14:11 will declare him clean must **b**
15:29 or two pigeons and **b** them
16:7 two male goats and **b** them into
16:10 But he must **b** the goat chosen
16:11 "Aaron will **b** the bull.
16:12 He will **b** them up to the
16:20 he will **b** the living goat
17:4 **B** the animal to the entrance of
17:5 in the open fields and **b** them
17:5 They must **b** them to the priest
17:9 but do not **b** them to the
19:5 "When you **b** a fellowship
19:6 your sacrifice on the day you **b**
19:21 He must **b** a ram for his guilt
21:6 Be holy because you **b**
21:17 he must never **b** food to offer to
21:21 he must never **b** sacrifices by
21:21 He must never **b** food to offer to
22:9 or their sin will **b** them death
22:18 Israelites or foreigners may **b**
22:20 Never **b** any animal with a
22:21 A person may **b** the LORD a
22:22 Never **b** the LORD an animal
22:24 Never **b** the LORD an animal
22:25 Never **b** any kind of castrated
23:8 **B** the LORD a sacrifice by fire
23:10 **b** the priest a bundle of the first
23:13 **B** a grain offering of four quarts
23:14 when you **b** the offering to your
23:15 after Passover (the day you **b**
23:16 Then **b** a new grain offering to
23:17 **B** two loaves of bread from
23:18 With the bread **b** seven
23:18 With these offerings also **b**
23:25 **B** a sacrifice by fire to the
23:27 Humble yourselves, and **b** the
23:36 For seven consecutive days **b**
23:36 **B** the LORD a sacrifice by fire.
23:37 **B** burnt offerings, other
24:2 the Israelites to **b** you pure,
25:20 do not plant or **b** in our crops?'
26:6 "I will **b** peace to your land.
26:25 I will **b** war on you to get
26:41 I will oppose them and **b** them
27:11 **b** it in front of the priest.
Num 3:6 "**B** the tribe of Levi,
5:9 offerings that the Israelites **b**
5:18 The priest will **b** the woman
5:18 bitter water that can **b** a curse.
5:19 This bitter water that can **b** a
5:22 'May this water that can **b** a
5:24 water that can **b** the curse.
5:25 and **b** it to the altar.
5:27 the water that can **b** the curse
6:10 On the eighth day he must **b**
6:12 He must **b** a one-year-old male
6:14 They must **b** these offerings to
6:15 They must also **b** a basket of
6:16 "The priest will **b** these
6:21 have vowed to **b** their offerings
6:21 They must **b** these offerings in
7:11 a different leader will **b** his gift
8:9 **B** the Levites to the front of the
8:10 Then **b** the Levites into the
9:7 Why won't you let us **b** our
9:7 the Israelites **b** their offerings?"
9:13 You didn't **b** your offering to the
11:16 LORD answered Moses, "**B** me
13:20 Do your best to **b** back some

Num 14:8 he will **b** us into this land and
14:16 The LORD wasn't able to **b**
14:24 I'll **b** him to the land he already
14:31 Instead, I will **b** them into the
15:3 you may **b** offerings by fire to
15:13 do it this way when they **b**
15:14 If they **b** an offering by fire,
18:2 **B** the other Levites from your
18:13 in their land that they **b**
18:19 contributions the Israelites **b**
19:2 Tell the Israelites to **b** you a
20:4 Did you **b** the LORD's
20:5 you make us leave Egypt and **b**
20:10 must we **b** water out of this
20:12 So you will not **b** this
20:25 **B** Aaron and his son Eleazar
28:2 Be sure to **b** me my offerings at
28:3 offerings by fire that you must **b**
28:3 Every day you must **b** as a
28:5 ⌊With each of them⌋ also **b** a
28:7 Also **b** a wine offering of one
28:11 "On the first of every month **b**
28:19 **b** the LORD an offering by fire,
28:20 Along with them **b** grain
28:20 **B** 24 cups for each bull,
28:22 Also **b** one male goat as an
28:24 **B** all these offerings on each of
28:26 **B** the LORD your new grain
28:27 **B** a burnt offering as a soothing
28:28 Along with them **b** grain
28:28 **B** 24 cups for each bull,
28:30 Also **b** one male goat to make
29:2 **b** one young bull, one ram,
29:3 Along with them **b** grain
29:3 **B** 24 cups for each bull,
29:5 Also **b** one male goat as an
29:8 **b** one young bull, one ram,
29:9 Along with them **b** grain
29:9 **B** 24 cups for each bull,
29:11 Also **b** one male goat as an
29:13 **b** 13 young bulls, 2 rams,
29:14 Along with them **b** grain
29:14 **B** 24 cups for each of the 13
29:16 Also **b** one male goat as an
29:17 "On the second day **b** 12
29:18 Along with them **b** the proper
29:19 Also **b** one male goat as an
29:20 "On the third day **b** 11 bulls,
29:21 Along with them **b** the proper
29:22 Also **b** one male goat as an
29:23 "On the fourth day **b** 10 bulls,
29:24 Along with them **b** the proper
29:25 Also **b** one male goat as an
29:26 "On the fifth day **b** 9 bulls,
29:27 Along with them **b** the proper
29:28 Also **b** one male goat as an
29:29 "On the sixth day **b** 8 bulls,
29:30 Along with them **b** the proper
29:31 Also **b** one male goat as an
29:32 "On the seventh day **b** 7 bulls,
29:33 Along with them **b** the proper
29:34 Also **b** one male goat as an
29:36 the LORD, **b** one bull, one ram,
29:37 Along with them **b** the proper
29:38 Also **b** one male goat as an
29:39 are the offerings you must **b**
29:39 are the offerings you must **b**
Dtr 1:16 the cases that your people **b**.
1:17 You may **b** me any case that's
4:38 of your way to **b** you into their
5:15 and powerful arm to **b** you out
6:10 The LORD your God will **b** you
6:21 used his mighty hand to **b**
6:23 LORD led us out of there to **b**
7:1 The LORD your God will **b** you
7:8 his mighty hand to **b** you out.
7:19 and powerful arm to **b** you out.
7:26 Never **b** a disgusting idol into
9:26 your mighty hand to **b** them out
9:28 "The LORD wasn't able to **b**
9:29 powerful arm to **b** them out ⌊of
12:6 **B** him your burnt offerings,
12:6 the offerings you vow to **b**,
12:11 You must **b** everything I
12:11 **B** your burnt offerings,
12:11 you vow to **b** to the LORD.

Dtr 12:17 the offerings you vow to **b**;
12:26 offerings you have vowed to **b**,
14:28 At the end of every third year **b**
16:10 **B** a freewill offering in
16:17 Each man must **b** a gift in
17:5 then **b** the man or woman who
21:4 The leaders of that city will **b**
21:12 **B** her into your home.
23:18 Never **b** gifts or money earned
24:11 you're making the loan will **b**
24:13 Make sure you **b** it back to him
24:19 If you forget to **b** in one of the
26:8 hand and powerful arm to **b**
28:49 The LORD will **b** against you a
28:60 He will again **b** all the
28:61 The LORD will also **b** you
28:68 The LORD will **b** you back to
30:4 gather you and **b** you back from
30:5 The LORD your God will **b** you
31:20 I will **b** them into the land that I
31:21 even now before I **b** them into
31:23 because you will **b** the
32:23 I will **b** one disaster after
33:7 and **b** them to their people.
Jos 2:3 "**B** out the men who came to
6:18 you will **b** destruction and
6:22 **B** the woman out, along with
7:7 why did you **b** these people
7:25 "Why did you **b** this disaster on
7:25 The LORD will **b** disaster on
10:22 and **b** me the five kings!"
23:15 LORD will **b** about every evil
24:20 he will turn and **b** disaster on
Jdg 6:18 I want to **b** my gift and set it in
6:30 told Joash, "**B** your son out.
7:4 **B** them down to the water,
19:22 "**B** out the man who came to
19:24 Here, let me **b** out my virgin
Rut 4:15 He will **b** you a new life and
1Sm 1:22 Then I'll **b** him and present him
2:19 would make him a robe and **b**
9:7 "what could we **b** the man
9:7 There's no present we can **b**
9:23 Samuel said to the cook, "**B**
10:27 and wouldn't **b** him presents,
11:2 right eye and **b** disgrace
12:8 who sent Moses and Aaron to **b**
13:9 Then Saul said, "**B** me the
14:18 "**B** the priestly ephod,"
14:34 **b** me your ox or your sheep,
15:32 "**B** me King Agag of Amalek,"
16:17 can play well and **b** him to me."
17:18 and **b** back some news about
19:15 Saul told them, "**B** him here to
20:3 It will **b** him distress.'
20:31 send some men to **b** him to me.
21:14 Why **b** him to me?
21:15 lunatics that you **b** this man so
23:9 priest Abiathar, "**B** the ephod."
27:11 He did not **b** a single man or
30:7 "Please **b** me the priestly
2Sm 3:12 "I'll support you and **b** all Israel
3:13 to see me unless you **b** Michal,
6:2 in Judah to **b** God's ark ⌊to
6:10 So David wouldn't **b** the ark of
6:12 from Obed Edom's house and **b**
12:23 Can I **b** him back?
13:10 Amnon told Tamar, "**B** the food
14:10 against you, **b** him to me.
14:21 **B** back the young man
15:8 I said, 'If the LORD will **b** me
15:14 or he'll catch up to us and **b**
16:2 "Why did you **b** these?"
17:13 all Israel will **b** ropes to that
18:19 "Let me run and **b** the king the
19:11 you be the last ⌊tribe⌋ to **b**
19:12 Why should you be the last to **b**
19:15 meet the king and **b** him across
19:18 They crossed the river to **b**
19:41 kidnap you and **b** Your Majesty
22:28 eyes **b** down arrogant people.
1Ki 3:24 king told his servants to **b** him
5:9 My workers will **b** logs from
8:34 and **b** them back to the land
10:22 the Tarshish fleet would **b** gold,
13:18 He said, '**B** him home with you

1Ki 14:10 "'That is why I will **b** disaster
17:10 "Please **b** me a drink of water."
17:11 "Please **b** me a piece of bread
17:13 first make a small loaf and **b**
18:19 And **b** the 450 prophets of Baal
20:33 Ahab said, "**B** him here."
21:21 So I am going to **b** evil on you.
21:29 I will **b** evil on it during his
2Ki 2:20 Elisha said, "**B** me a new jar,
4:6 "**B** me another container."
4:41 Elisha said, "**B** some flour."
5:7 Can I kill someone and then **b**
7:9 Let's **b** the news to the royal
10:6 **b** the heads of your master's
10:22 "**B** out the robes for all the
12:4 is currently required to **b**
17:27 "**B** one of the priests you
17:36 and a mighty arm to **b** you out
20:20 pool and tunnel to **b** water into
21:12 I'm going to **b** such a disaster
22:16 I'm going to **b** disaster on this
22:20 That is why I'm going to **b** you
22:20 I'm going to **b** you to your grave
22:20 of the disaster I'm going to **b**
1Ch 13:3 Then we'll **b** back our God's
13:5 in order to **b** God's ark from
13:6 to **b** God's ark ⌊to Jerusalem⌋.
13:12 "How can I **b** God's ark to my
13:13 So he didn't **b** God's ark to his
15:3 all Israel at Jerusalem to **b**
15:12 Then **b** the ark of the LORD
16:29 **B** an offering, and come to him.
21:2 **B** me ⌊the results⌋ so that I
22:19 LORD God so that you can **b**
2Ch 6:25 and **b** them back to the land
9:21 Tarshish ships would **b** gold,
19:10 about every case they **b** to you,
24:6 you require the Levites to **b**
24:19 them prophets to **b** them back
28:13 "Don't **b** the prisoners here.
29:31 Come, **b** sacrifices and thank
31:10 "Since the people started to **b**
32:23 went to Jerusalem to **b** gifts
34:24 I'm going to **b** disaster on this
34:28 That is why I'm going to **b** you
34:28 I'm going to **b** you to your grave
34:28 of the disaster I'm going to **b**
Ezr 3:6 They started to **b** these burnt
3:7 which the men would **b** by sea
8:17 that they should **b** us men who
Neh 1:9 get you from there and **b** you
4:11 We'll kill them and **b** the work
8:1 They told Ezra the scribe to **b**
9:29 You warned them in order to **b**
10:31 If the inhabitants of the land **b**
10:34 of our families should **b** wood
10:35 lots to decide who should **b**
10:36 lots to decide who should **b**
10:37 lots to decide who should **b**
10:37 We will **b** for the Levites
10:38 Then the Levites should **b**
10:39 and the Levites should **b** into
10:39 They should **b** these products
11:1 people drew lots to **b** one out
Est 1:11 to **b** Queen Vashti in front of the
2:3 young virgins and **b** them
5:5 "**B** Haman right away,
6:1 So he told ⌊a servant⌋ to **b** the
6:8 ⌊The servants⌋ should **b** a
Job 22:4 Does God correct you and **b**
28:3 ⌊Humans⌋ **b** an end to
28:11 so that they **b** hidden treasures
34:23 for a person in order to **b** him
38:26 to **b** rain on a land where no
38:32 Can you **b** out the
39:12 Can you rely on it to **b** your
40:20 The hills **b** it food,
Psa 15:3 or **b** disgrace on his neighbor.
17:13 **B** them to their knees!
18:27 but you **b** down a conceited
25:17 and **b** me out of my distress.
35:11 Malicious people **b** charges
43:3 Let them **b** me to your holy
46:4 is a river whose streams **b** joy
50:14 **B** ⌊your⌋ thanks to God as a
55:3 They **b** misery crashing down

Psa	59:11	**B** them down, O Lord,
	60:9	Who will **b** me into the fortified
	68:22	The Lord said, "I will **b** them
	68:22	I will **b** them back from the
	68:29	Kings will **b** you gifts because
	71:20	You **b** me back from the depths
	72:3	May the mountains **b** peace to
	72:3	and the hills **b** righteousness.
	72:10	and the islands **b** presents.
	72:10	from Sheba and Seba **b** gifts.
	76:11	Let everyone around him **b** gifts
	90:10	But the best of them ⌊**b**⌋
	96:8	**B** an offering, and come into
	107:22	Let them **b** songs of
	108:10	Who will **b** me into the fortified
	116:17	I will **b** a song of thanksgiving
	119:84	When will you **b** those who
Pro	3:2	because they will **b** you long
	4:8	It will **b** you honor when you
	10:4	Lazy hands **b** poverty,
	10:4	but hard-working hands **b**
	12:18	but the words of wise people **b**
	19:24	He doesn't even **b** it back to his
	21:27	especially if they **b** it with evil
	24:22	what misery both may **b**?
	27:1	know what another day may **b**.
	29:17	He will **b** delight to your soul.
Ecc	5:1	to go there and listen than to **b**
	5:1	to bring the sacrifices fools **b**.
	8:7	know what the future will **b**.
	10:14	knows what the future will **b**,
Sos	8:2	I would **b** you into my mother's
	8:11	Each one was to **b** 25 pounds
Isa	1:13	Don't **b** any more worthless
	7:17	"The LORD will **b** on you,
	7:17	⌊He will **b**⌋ the king of Assyria.
	8:7	Lord is going to **b** against them
	9:1	But in the future he will **b** glory
	11:12	of Israel and **b** together
	14:2	People will take them and **b**
	15:9	yet I will **b** even more on
	21:14	**B** water for the thirsty,
	21:14	**B** food to the fugitives.
	25:12	He will **b** down Moab's high
	26:18	We weren't able to **b** salvation
	31:2	wise and can **b** about disaster.
	32:17	will **b** about peace,
	41:21	"**B** forward your best
	41:22	"**B** ⌊your idols⌋ so they can tell
	42:1	He will **b** justice to the nations.
	42:3	will faithfully **b** about justice.
	42:7	**b** prisoners out of prisons,
	42:7	and **b** those who live in
	43:5	I will **b** your descendants from
	43:6	**B** my sons from far away and
	43:7	**B** everyone who is called by
	43:8	**B** the people who are blind but
	43:9	They should **b** their witnesses
	43:14	I will **b** back all the Babylonian
	43:23	You did not **b** me sheep for
	46:11	and I will **b** it about.
	46:13	I'll **b** my righteousness near;
	46:13	for Zion and **b** my glory
	48:15	I will **b** him here, and he will
	49:5	in order to **b** Jacob back
	49:22	They will **b** your sons in their
	50:8	Who will **b** a case against me?
	51:5	I will **b** justice to people.
	54:7	but I will **b** you back with
	54:16	I've also created destroyers to **b**
	56:7	Then I will **b** them to my holy
	60:6	They will **b** gold and incense.
	60:9	the first to **b** your children from
	60:11	night so that people may **b** you
	60:17	I will **b** gold instead of bronze.
	60:17	I will **b** silver instead of iron,
	65:9	I will **b** ⌊with me⌋ Jacob's
	66:4	harsh treatment for them and **b**
	66:9	"Do I **b** a mother to the moment
	66:20	They will **b** all your relatives
	66:20	who **b** their grain offerings
Jer	3:14	and **b** you to Zion.
	4:16	**B** them to the attention of
	5:15	Nation of Israel, I'm going to **b**
	6:19	I'm going to **b** disaster on these
	11:11	I'm going to **b** a disaster on
Jer	11:23	I will **b** a disaster on the
	12:9	and **b** them to devour it.
	13:11	be my people and **b** fame,
	14:15	Wars and famines will **b** an
	15:8	I will suddenly **b** anguish and
	16:4	Wars and famines will **b** them
	16:15	this because I will **b** them back
	17:18	**B** the day of disaster on them,
	17:21	on the day of worship or **b**
	17:22	Do not **b** anything out of your
	17:24	me and not **b** anything through
	17:26	They will **b** burnt offerings,
	17:26	They will also **b** thank
	19:3	I'm going to **b** such a disaster
	19:15	I'm going to **b** on this city and
	20:5	and **b** them to Babylon.
	21:4	I will **b** the Babylonians inside
	23:3	I will **b** them back to their
	23:12	I will **b** disaster on them.
	23:40	I will **b** eternal disgrace and
	24:6	and I will **b** them back to this
	25:9	I will **b** the families from the
	25:13	I will **b** on that land all the
	25:29	I am going to **b** disaster on the
	26:3	about the disaster I intend to **b**
	26:13	that he intends to **b** on you.
	26:19	he intended to **b** on them.
	26:19	But we are about to **b** a bigger
	27:22	from there and **b** them back
	28:3	Within two years I will **b** back
	28:4	I will also **b** back to this place
	28:6	prophecy come true and **b** back
	29:10	promise to you and **b** you back
	29:14	I will **b** you back from captivity.
	29:14	I will **b** you back from the place
	30:3	"when I will **b** my people Israel
	30:3	I will **b** them back to the land
	30:18	I'm going to **b** the captives
	30:19	I'll **b** them honor, and they
	30:21	I'll **b** him near, and he will
	31:8	"I will **b** them from the land of
	31:9	will pray as I **b** them back.
	32:37	I will **b** them back to this place
	32:42	so I will **b** on them all these
	32:44	I will **b** them back from
	33:11	You will hear those who **b**
	34:22	"I will **b** that army back to this
	35:17	I am going to **b** on Judah and
	36:3	that I plan to **b** on them,
	36:14	Jehudi said to Baruch, "**B** the
	36:31	So I will **b** on them,
	40:2	threatened to **b** this disaster
	42:17	the disasters I will **b** on them.
	43:11	He will **b** death to those who
	44:7	Why do you **b** this terrible
	44:11	I'm going to **b** disaster on you
	44:27	watch over them to **b** disasters,
	45:5	because I'm going to **b** disaster
	48:35	those who **b** offerings to their
	48:44	I will **b** a year of punishment to
	49:5	I am going to **b** terror on you
	49:8	When I punish them, I will **b**
	49:16	I will **b** you down from there,"
	49:32	I will **b** disaster on them from
	49:36	I'll **b** the four winds from the
	49:37	I'll **b** disaster with my burning
	50:9	nations from the north and **b**
	50:19	I will **b** the people of Israel
	50:25	will open his armory and **b** out
	50:34	up their cause in order to **b** rest
	51:8	**B** medicine for its pain.
	51:27	**B** up horses like a swarm of
	51:64	of the disasters that I will **b**
Lam	3:33	He does not willingly **b**
	5:21	O LORD, **b** us back to you,
Eze	5:16	I will **b** more and more famines
	9:1	Each of you should **b** your
	11:8	so I will **b** swords to attack
	11:17	I will **b** them together from the
	12:4	**B** out your bags as if you were
	12:13	I will **b** him to Babylon,
	14:17	"Suppose I **b** a war against that
	14:22	that I will **b** on Jerusalem,
	14:22	disaster that I will **b** against it.
	16:40	They will also **b** a mob against
	20:6	At that time I promised to **b**
Eze	20:14	nations who had watched me **b**
	20:15	I swore that I would not **b** them
	20:22	nations who had watched me **b**
	20:34	I will **b** you out from the nations
	20:35	I will **b** you into the desert of
	20:38	I will **b** you out of the land
	20:41	When I **b** you out from the
	20:42	because I will **b** you to the land
	23:22	I will **b** them against you from
	23:23	I will **b** men from Babylon and
	23:46	**B** together a mob ⌊against the
	24:5	**B** the mixture in the pot to a
	26:3	I will **b** many nations against
	26:7	From the north I'm going to **b**
	26:7	He will **b** horses, chariots,
	26:19	I will **b** the deep ocean over
	26:20	I will **b** you down with those
	28:7	That is why I am going to **b**
	29:14	I will **b** back the Egyptian
	30:10	of Babylon to **b**
	30:14	and **b** punishment on Thebes.
	30:19	I will **b** punishment on Egypt.'"
	32:8	I will **b** darkness over your
	32:18	**B** them down along with the
	33:2	Tell them, 'Suppose I **b** war on
	34:13	I will **b** them out from the
	34:13	and **b** them to their own land.
	34:16	**b** back those that have strayed
	36:12	I will **b** people, my people
	36:24	I will **b** you back to your own
	37:12	I will **b** you to Israel.
	37:13	open your graves and **b** you out
	37:21	from everywhere and **b** them
	38:17	those days that I would **b** you
	39:2	I will **b** you from the far north
	39:25	Now I will **b** back Jacob's
	39:27	I will **b** them back from the
	43:22	"On the second day **b** a male
	44:15	They may **b** fat and blood to
	44:27	he must **b** his offering for sin,
	46:5	be whatever the prince can **b**.
	46:7	whatever the prince wants to **b**.
	46:11	the prince may **b** whatever he
	46:11	bring whatever he wants to **b**.
	46:20	so that they don't have to **b**
	47:9	the river flows, it will **b** life.
Dan	1:3	to **b** some of the Israelites,
	5:26	of your kingdom and will **b**
	9:14	So you were prepared to **b** this
	9:24	time periods will serve to **b**
Hos	4:4	or **b** charges against them.
	4:19	sacrifices will **b** them shame.
	6:11	you when I **b** my people back
	9:12	Even if they **b** up children,
	9:13	Ephraim will **b** out their
	12:13	The LORD used a prophet to **b**
Joe	1:14	**B** them to the temple of the
	3:1	I will **b** back the captives of
	3:2	I will **b** them down to the valley
	3:11	O LORD, **b** your soldiers.
Amo	4:4	**B** your sacrifices every
	4:4	**B** a tenth of your income every
	5:22	Even though you **b** me burnt
	5:25	Did you **b** me sacrifices and
	6:3	They **b** the reign of violence
	9:2	I will **b** them down from there.
	9:4	on them so that I can **b** disaster
	9:7	Didn't I **b** Israel from Egypt?
	9:7	Didn't I **b** the Philistines from
Oba	1:3	'No one can **b** me down to
	1:4	I will **b** you down from there,"
Mic	1:15	I will again **b** a conqueror
	2:12	I will surely **b** together the few
	4:6	I will **b** together those who are
	4:12	He will **b** them together like cut
	6:6	What should I **b** when I come
	6:6	Should I **b** him year-old calves
	7:9	He will **b** me into the light,
Nah	1:9	He is the one who will **b**
Hab	1:12	the Babylonians to **b** judgment.
Zep	1:17	"I will **b** such distress on
	3:8	to **b** kingdoms together,
	3:10	people, will **b** my offering.
	3:20	that time I will **b** you ⌊home⌋.
Hag	1:9	When you **b** something home,
	2:14	offering they **b** is unclean.

Zec 3:8 I'm going to **b** my servant,
4:7 He will **b** out the topmost stone
8:8 I will **b** them back,
10:6 I will **b** them back,
10:10 I will **b** them back from Egypt.
10:10 I will **b** them to Gilead and to
13:9 I will **b** this third ⌊of the
Mal 1:8 When you **b** a blind animal to
1:8 When you **b** a lame or a sick
1:13 "You **b** stolen, lame, and sick
1:13 When you **b** such offerings,
3:3 Then they will **b** acceptable
3:8 "When ⌊you don't **b**⌋ a tenth of
3:10 "**B** one-tenth of your income
Mat 10:8 **b** the dead back to life,
10:34 "Don't think that I came to **b**
10:34 come to **b** peace but conflict.
13:30 But I'll have them **b** the wheat
14:18 Jesus said, "**B** them to me."
17:17 **B** him here to me!"
21:2 Untie them, and **b** them to me.
Mar 2:4 Since they could not **b** him to
4:21 "Does anyone **b** a lamp into a
6:27 ordered him to **b** John's head.
9:19 put up with you? **B** him to me!"
11:2 ever sat on it. Untie it, and **b** it.
12:15 **B** me a coin so that I can look
Luk 1:16 He will **b** many people in Israel
2:32 to the nations and **b** glory
8:15 good despite what life may **b**.
9:41 up with you? **B** your son here!"
12:51 "Do you think I came to **b**
12:51 came to **b** nothing but division.
14:21 **B** back the poor, the blind, and
15:22 **B** out the best robe,
15:23 **B** the fattened calf,
18:40 stopped and ordered them to **b**
19:27 **B** my enemies, who didn't want
19:30 ever sat on it. Untie it, and **b** it.
19:42 today what would **b** you peace!
Jon 4:16 your husband, and **b** him here."
4:33 "Did someone **b** him something
6:39 He wants me to **b** them back to
6:40 He wants me to **b** them back to
6:44 I will **b** these people back to
6:51 The bread I will give to **b** life to
6:54 and I will **b** them back to life on
7:18 But the man who wants to **b**
7:45 "Why didn't you **b** Jesus?"
8:6 to **b** charges against him.
8:54 "If I **b** glory to myself,
11:4 Instead, this sickness will **b**
11:52 but that Jesus would die to **b**
14:3 Then I will **b** you into my
21:10 Jesus told them, "**B** some of
21:19 of death Peter would **b** glory
Act 5:16 They would **b** their sick and
5:26 with some of his men to **b** back
7:42 'Did you **b** me sacrifices and
9:15 I've chosen this man to **b** my
12:4 Herod wanted to **b** Peter to trial
12:6 Herod was going to **b** Peter
13:17 He used his powerful arm to **b**
17:5 and Silas in order to **b** them out
19:38 That's where they should **b**
22:5 up believers and **b** them back
23:18 He asked me to **b** this young
23:20 planned to ask you to **b** Paul
23:21 ⌊that you will **b** Paul⌋."
26:8 God can **b** dead people back
28:19 charges to **b** against my own
Rom 1:5 who **b** people from every
2:7 what is good. But he will **b**
4:15 Teachings **b** about anger.
7:10 intended to **b** me life actually
10:6 (that is, to **b** Christ down).
10:7 to **b** Christ back from the dead).
11:13 I **b** honor to my ministry.
13:2 **b** punishment on themselves.
14:19 those things which **b** peace
15:7 He did this to **b** glory to God.
15:16 I do this in order that I might **b**
15:18 through me to **b** people who are
15:25 I'm going to Jerusalem to **b** help
15:29 that when I come to you I will **b**
15:31 will accept the help I **b**.
Rom 16:26 of every nation to **b** them
1Co 4:5 He will also **b** to light what is
6:20 So **b** glory to God in the way
15:15 then God didn't **b** Christ back to
2Co 4:6 For that reason we **b** to light
4:14 Jesus back to life will also **b**
8:19 to travel with us and **b** this gift
8:23 churches and **b** glory to Christ.
Gal 3:13 laws **b** by becoming cursed
Eph 1:10 He planned to **b** all of history to
3:13 In fact, my troubles **b** you glory.
6:4 Instead, **b** them up in Christian
Php 1:11 Your lives will then **b** glory and
3:21 Through his power to **b**
Col 1:20 God was also pleased to **b**
1Th 2:9 and day so that we could **b** you
4:14 God will **b** back those who
1Ti 6:7 We didn't **b** anything into the
2Ti 4:11 Get Mark and **b** him with you.
4:13 When you come, **b** the warm
4:13 Also **b** the scrolls and
Heb 2:10 it was the right time to **b** Jesus,
7:27 have to **b** daily sacrifices as
9:15 he is able to **b** a new promise
10:35 It will **b** you a great reward.
11:19 God could **b** Isaac back from
13:15 we should always **b** God
Jas 2:12 judged by laws that **b** freedom.
5:19 can **b** that person back.
1Pe 1:13 will **b** you when Jesus
3:18 people so that he could **b** you
2Pe 2:1 They will secretly **b** in their
2:1 **b** themselves swift destruction.
2:11 don't **b** an insulting judgment
2Jn 1:10 and doesn't **b** these teachings,
3Jn 1:10 when I come I will **b** up what
Rev 21:24 and the kings of the earth will **b**
21:26 They will **b** the glory and
22:12 I will **b** my reward with me to

bringing (45)

Exo 14:11 Look what you've done by **b** us
18:6 ⌊and I'm **b**⌋ your wife and her
36:3 But the people still kept **b** him
36:5 They said, "The people are **b**
36:6 Then the people stopped **b**
Lev 18:3 I am **b** you to Canaan.
20:22 the land I am **b** you to live in
23:37 for **b** sacrifices by fire
Num 14:3 Why is the LORD **b** us to this
Dtr 8:7 The LORD your God is **b** you
1Sm 25:27 Here is a gift I am **b** to you.
2Sm 4:10 thought he was **b** good news.
18:26 one is also **b** good news."
19:10 talking about **b** back the king?"
19:43 to suggest **b** back our king?"
1Ki 1:42 so you must be **b** good news."
2Ki 4:5 The children kept **b** containers
Ezr 1:8 in charge of **b** them out.
8:30 They were responsible for **b**
Neh 13:15 I saw them **b** in loads of wine,
13:16 who lived in Jerusalem were **b**
13:31 wood at regular times and for **b**
Job 10:17 You keep **b** new armies
Pro 16:15 is like a cloud **b** spring rain.
17:9 but whoever keeps **b** up the
Jer 2:9 "That is why I am **b** charges
2:9 "and I am **b** charges against
4:6 I'm **b** disaster and widespread
39:16 against this city by **b** disaster
Eze 20:9 myself known to them by **b**
Dan 9:12 do to us and our rulers by **b**
Jnh 1:7 responsible for **b** this disaster
Mal 2:12 tents and from **b** offerings
Mat 15:30 **b** with them the lame,
27:13 charges they're **b** against you?"
Mar 15:4 they're **b** against you!"
Luk 2:27 Mary and Joseph were **b** the
Jon 19:4 "I'm **b** him out to you to let you
Act 13:33 by **b** Jesus back to life.
17:31 will do this by **b** that man back
Rom 5:21 As sin ruled by **b** death,
5:21 God's kindness would rule by **b**
Eph 3:2 responsibility of **b** his kindness
Col 3:15 this peace by **b** you into one
Heb 2:10 Therefore, while God was **b**

brings (68)

Exo 13:5 When he **b** you into that land
13:11 "When the LORD **b** you to the
Lev 4:3 something wrong and **b** guilt
4:32 "If someone **b** a lamb as his
Num 15:4 Whoever **b** the offering must
Dtr 11:29 When the LORD your God **b**
2Sm 22:48 He **b** people under my
Job 9:23 a sudden disaster **b** death,
12:22 the darkness and **b** gloom into
Psa 18:47 He **b** people under my
47:3 He **b** people under our authority
104:20 He **b** darkness, and it is
135:7 and who **b** wind out of his
144:2 and the one who **b** people
146:7 He **b** about justice for those
147:6 He **b** wicked people down to
147:14 He is the one who **b** peace to
Pro 10:1 but a foolish son **b** grief to his
10:5 at harvest time **b** shame.
11:29 Whoever **b** trouble upon his
13:15 Good sense **b** favor,
13:17 but a dependable envoy **b**
15:27 greedy for unjust gain **b** trouble
18:16 one who gives it and **b** him into
19:26 mother **b** shame and disgrace.
25:23 ⌊As⌋ the north wind **b** rain,
25:23 tongue **b** angry looks.
26:6 and **b** violence upon himself.
26:15 He wears himself out as he **b** it
31:14 She **b** her food from far away.
Sos 2:17 When the day **b** a cooling
4:6 When the day **b** a cool breeze
Isa 28:19 this message **b** only terror.
40:26 Who **b** out the stars one by
49:6 of Jacob and **b** back those
52:7 He **b** the good news,
52:8 When the LORD **b** Zion back,
61:11 Like the ground that **b** forth its
Jer 10:13 He **b** wind out of his
51:16 He **b** wind out of his
Hos 12:2 The LORD **b** charges against
Amo 5:20 The day of the LORD **b**
Zep 3:5 He **b** his judgment to light
Mat 12:45 Then it goes and **b** along
13:52 He **b** new and old things out of
Mar 9:18 Whenever the spirit **b** on a
Luk 11:26 Then the spirit goes and **b**
12:58 when an opponent **b** you to
Jon 5:21 way that the Father **b** back
6:44 the Father who sent me **b** them
11:25 "I am the one who **b** people
1Co 11:34 a gathering that **b** judgment
2Co 1:6 it **b** you comfort and salvation.
1:9 who **b** the dead back to life.
3:6 what was written **b** death,
3:6 but the Spirit **b** life.
3:8 Won't the ministry that **b** the
3:9 If the ministry that **b**
3:9 then the ministry that **b** God's
3:10 In fact, the ministry that **b**
7:10 the world causes **b** only death.
8:19 it in a way that **b** glory
Php 1:27 the faith that the Good News **b**.
1Ti 6:6 A godly life **b** huge profits to
Heb 8:6 He also **b** a better promise from
12:24 have come to Jesus, who **b**
13:11 The chief priest **b** the blood of
Jas 5:20 Realize that whoever **b** a

brittle (1)

Dan 2:42 be strong, and part will be **b**.

broad (9)

Num 25:4 and execute them in **b** daylight
Dtr 28:29 You will grope in **b** daylight as
2Sm 12:11 with your wives in **b** daylight.
12:12 but I will make this happen in **b**
Neh 3:8 of Jerusalem as far as **B** Wall.
12:38 of the Ovens, as far as **B** Wall,
Amo 8:9 darken the earth in **b** daylight.
2Pe 2:13 wild parties in **b** daylight.
Rev 20:9 they spread over the **b** expanse

broiled (1)

Luk 24:42 They gave him a piece of **b**

broke (72)

Gen 13:7 Quarrels **b** out between
Num 9:21 in the morning, they **b** camp.
9:21 smoke moved, they **b** camp.
9:23 at his command they **b** camp.
10:14 descendants **b** camp first.
10:17 who carried it, **b** camp.
10:18 descendants **b** camp next.
10:21 carried the holy things, **b** camp.
10:22 descendants **b** camp next.
10:25 Dan's descendants **b** camp last
10:28 armies **b** camp when they
Jos 3:14 So they **b** camp to cross the
9:17 The Israelites **b** camp.
Jdg 5:8 war **b** out inside the city gates.
7:20 rams' horns and **b** their jars.
1Sm 4:18 He **b** his neck, and he died.
19:8 When war **b** out again,
2Sm 2:17 Fierce fighting **b** out that day,
21:19 When more fighting **b** out with
2Ki 8:21 **b** through their lines,
25:4 The enemy **b** through the city
25:13 The Babylonians **b** apart the
1Ch 20:4 After this, war **b** out with the
20:5 When more fighting **b** out with
2Ch 14:3 **b** down the sacred stones,
21:9 night and **b** through their lines.
21:17 Judah, **b** into the country,
26:19 a skin disease **b** out on his
Job 29:17 I **b** the teeth of the wicked
Psa 106:18 A fire **b** out among their
106:29 a plague **b** out among them.
107:14 He **b** apart their chains.
Isa 7:17 Ephraim **b** away from Judah.
Jer 2:20 "Long ago you **b** off your yoke,
28:10 the prophet Jeremiah and **b** it.
28:12 After the prophet Hananiah **b**
39:2 they **b** into the city.
52:7 The enemy **b** through the city
52:17 The Babylonians **b** apart the
Eze 17:4 It **b** off the highest twig and
17:16 The king of Judah **b** his
17:18 The king of Judah **b** the
19:12 Its strong branches **b** off.
29:7 they leaned on you, you **b**,
Dan 8:7 It **b** both of the ram's horns.
8:8 his large horn **b** off.
8:22 The horn **b** off, and four horns
Zec 11:10 my staff called Favor and **b**
11:14 Then I **b** my second staff,
Mat 14:19 He **b** the loaves apart,
15:36 Then he **b** the bread and gave
26:26 He **b** the bread, gave it to his
Mar 5:4 the chains off his hands and **b**
6:41 He **b** the loaves apart and kept
8:6 Then he **b** the bread and gave
8:19 When I **b** the five loaves for the
8:20 "When I **b** the seven loaves for
14:22 He **b** the bread, gave it to them,
Luk 9:16 He **b** the loaves apart and kept
22:19 He **b** the bread, gave it to them,
22:24 Then a quarrel **b** out among the
24:30 He **b** the bread and gave it to
24:35 Jesus when he **b** the bread.
Jon 19:32 The soldiers **b** the legs of the
Act 8:1 persecution **b** out against
11:19 that **b** out following Stephen's
13:43 meeting of the synagogue **b** up,
19:23 the way ⌊of Christ⌋ **b** out
20:11 again, **b** the bread, and ate.
27:35 **b** it, and began to eat.
1Co 11:24 He **b** the bread and said,
Rev 12:7 Then a war **b** out in heaven.

broken (88)

Lev 6:28 cooked must be **b** into pieces.
15:12 touches pottery, it must be **b**,
22:22 blind, has **b** bones, cuts, warts,
24:20 a **b** bone for a broken bone,
24:20 a broken bone for a **b** bone,
26:13 I have **b** their power over you
Num 15:31 the word of the LORD and **b**
Jdg 21:15 because the LORD had **b**
1Sm 2:4 bows of the warriors are **b**,
2:10 the LORD are **b** into pieces.
2Ki 18:21 you're trusting a **b** stick for a
2Ch 24:7 had **b** into God's temple
32:5 He rebuilt all the **b** sections of
Neh 1:3 of Jerusalem has been **b** down,
2:13 of Jerusalem were **b** down
Job 2:8 Job took a piece of **b** pottery to
17:1 "My spirit is **b**. My days have
17:11 My plans are **b**. My dreams ape
22:9 and the arms of orphans are **b**.
31:22 let my arm be **b** at the elbow.
38:15 an arm raised ⌊in victory⌋ is **b**.
41:25 **B** down, they draw back.
41:30 like sharp pieces of **b** pottery.
Psa 22:15 up like pieces of **b** pottery.
31:12 like a piece of **b** pottery.
34:20 Not one of them is **b**.
37:15 and their bows will be **b**.
37:17 of wicked people will be **b**,
51:8 Let the bones that you have **b**
51:17 pleasing to God is a **b** spirit.
51:17 a **b** and sorrowful heart.
55:20 He has **b** his solemn promise.
60:1 You have **b** down our defenses.
69:20 Insults have **b** my heart,
89:40 You have **b** through all his
124:7 The trap was **b**, and we
Pro 18:14 but who can bear a **b** spirit?
25:19 ⌊Like⌋ a **b** tooth and a lame
25:28 ⌊Like⌋ a city **b** into ⌊and⌋ left
29:1 suddenly be **b** beyond repair.
Ecc 4:12 rope is not easily **b**.
12:6 the golden bowl is **b**,
12:6 water wheel is **b** at the cistern.
Isa 5:27 loose or their sandal straps **b**.
8:9 Be **b**, you people. Be terrified.
8:15 They will fall and be **b**.
14:5 The LORD has **b** the staff of
14:29 of the one who struck you is **b**,
22:9 places in David's wall are **b**.
24:19 The earth will be completely **b**.
27:11 are dried up, they will be **b** off.
33:8 Agreements are **b**.
33:20 and none of its ropes will be **b**.
36:6 you're trusting a **b** stick for a
58:12 called the Rebuilder of **B** Walls
Jer 2:13 **b** cisterns that can't hold water.
5:5 But they, too, had **b** off their
10:20 and all my ropes are **b**.
11:16 and your branches will be **b**.
22:28 like a rejected and **b** pot that no
28:13 You have **b** the wooden yoke,
33:21 my servant David could be **b**,
33:21 priests could also be **b**.
48:4 Moab will be **b**. Its little ones
48:17 staff, the beautiful rod, that is **b**!'
48:25 arm is **b**," declares the LORD.
50:23 whole earth is **b** and shattered.
51:30 bars across their gates are **b**.
51:56 bows and arrows will be **b**.
Lam 3:4 He has **b** my bones.
Eze 29:6 you have become like a ⌊**b**⌋
30:16 Thebes will be **b** into pieces,
30:21 I have **b** the arm of Pharaoh,
30:22 the healthy one and the **b** one.
31:12 Its **b** branches fell in every
Dan 11:4 his kingdom will be **b** into
Zec 11:11 So it was **b** on that day,
11:16 those that have **b** their legs
Mat 21:44 falls on this stone will be **b**.
Luk 20:18 falls on that stone will be **b**.
Jon 19:31 Pilate to have the men's legs **b**
19:36 "None of his bones will be **b**."
Act 25:8 "I haven't **b** any Jewish law or
27:41 the back of the ship was **b**
Rom 4:15 don't exist, they can't be **b**.
7:6 God has **b** their effect on us so
11:17 olive branches have been **b** off,
11:20 They were **b** off because they

brokenhearted (3)

Psa 109:16 and **b** people to their graves.
147:3 He is the healer of the **b**.
Isa 61:1 me to heal those who are **b**,

bronze (154)

Gen 4:22 who made **b** and iron tools.
Exo 25:3 from them: gold, silver, and **b**,
26:11 Make 50 **b** fasteners,
26:37 Cast five **b** bases for the
27:2 ⌊of wood⌋ covered with **b**.
27:3 all the utensils for it out of **b**:
27:4 a grate for it out of **b** mesh,
27:4 and make a **b** ring for ⌊each of⌋
27:6 and cover them with **b**.
27:10 20 posts ⌊set in⌋ 20 **b** bases.
27:11 on 20 posts set in 20 **b** bases.
27:17 silver hooks, and **b** bases.
27:18 linen yarn and with **b** bases.
27:19 must be made of **b**.
30:18 "Make a **b** basin with a bronze
30:18 "Make a bronze basin with a **b**
31:4 familiar with gold, silver, and **b**.
35:5 the LORD: gold, silver, and **b**,
35:16 burnt offerings with its **b** grate,
35:24 could give silver or **b** brought
35:32 familiar with gold, silver, and **b**.
36:18 They also made 50 **b** fasteners
36:38 for the posts were made of **b**.
38:2 ⌊of wood⌋ covered with **b**.
38:3 made all the utensils out of **b**:
38:4 grate for the altar out of **b** mesh,
38:5 the four corners of the **b** grate).
38:6 wood and covered them with **b**.
38:8 out of the **b** mirrors given by
38:10 20 posts ⌊set in⌋ 20 **b** bases.
38:11 with 20 posts and 20 **b** bases.
38:17 for the posts were made of **b**.
38:19 posts ⌊set in⌋ four **b** bases.
38:20 courtyard were made of **b**.
38:29 The **b** from the offerings
38:30 the **b** altar with its bronze grate
38:30 the bronze altar with its **b** grate
39:39 the **b** altar with its bronze grate,
39:39 the bronze altar with its **b** grate,
Num 16:39 So the priest Eleazar took the **b**
21:9 So Moses made a **b** snake and
21:9 People looked at the **b** snake
31:22 Any gold, silver, **b**,
Dtr 28:23 The sky above will look like **b**,
Jos 6:19 gold and everything made of **b**
6:24 gold and everything made of **b**
22:8 **b**, iron, and loads of clothing.
1Sm 17:5 He had a **b** helmet on his head,
17:5 and he wore a **b** coat of armor
17:6 On his legs he had **b** shin
17:6 and on his back a **b** javelin.
17:38 he put a **b** helmet on David's
2Sm 8:8 a large quantity of **b** from Betah
8:10 of gold, silver, and **b** with him.
21:16 who had a **b** spear weighing 7
22:35 bend an ⌊archer's⌋ bow of **b**.
1Ki 4:13 60 large cities with walls and **b**
7:14 was a skilled **b** craftsman.
7:14 all kinds of **b** craftsmanship.
7:14 and did all his ⌊**b**⌋ work.
7:15 He made two **b** pillars.
7:16 He made two capitals of cast **b**
7:27 He made ten **b** stands.
7:30 Each stand had four **b** wheels
7:30 four bronze wheels on **b** axles
7:38 Hiram also made ten **b** basins.
7:45 these utensils out of polished **b**
7:47 because so much **b** was used.
7:47 how much the **b** weighed.
8:64 offerings because the **b** altar
14:27 So King Rehoboam made **b**
2Ki 16:14 But he moved the **b** altar
16:15 I will use the **b** altar for prayer."
16:17 panels of the ⌊**b**⌋ stands ⌊used
16:17 He took the **b** pool down from
16:17 down from the **b** bulls that were
18:4 He even crushed the **b** snake
25:7 They put him in **b** shackles
25:13 broke apart the **b** pillars
25:13 and the **b** pool in the LORD's
25:13 They shipped the **b** to Babylon.
25:14 and all the **b** utensils used in
25:16 The **b** from the two pillars,
25:17 27 feet high and had a **b** capital

2Ki 25:17 the capital were all made of **b**.
1Ch 15:19 appointed to play **b** cymbals.
18:8 large quantity of **b** from Tibhath
18:11 and **b** to the LORD,
22:3 He also prepared so much **b**
22:14 and so much **b** and iron that it
22:16 The gold, silver, **b**,
29:2 **b** for bronze objects,
29:2 bronze for **b** objects,
29:7 135,000 pounds of **b**,
2Ch 1:5 The **b** altar that Bezalel,
1:6 Solomon went to the **b** altar
2:7 **b**, and iron as well as purple,
2:14 **b**, iron, stone, wood, purple,
4:1 He made a **b** altar 30 feet long,
4:9 He covered the doors with **b**.
4:16 all of them out of polished **b**
4:18 how much the **b** weighed.
6:13 (Solomon had made a **b**
7:7 and the fat because the **b** altar
12:10 So King Rehoboam made **b**
24:12 who worked with iron and **b**
33:11 put him in **b** shackles,
36:6 and put him in **b** shackles
Ezr 8:27 of fine polished **b** that were as
Job 6:12 body have the strength of **b**?
20:24 a **b** bow will pierce him.
40:18 Its bones are **b** tubes.
41:27 iron to be like straw and **b**
Psa 18:34 bend an ⌊archer's⌋ bow of **b**.
107:16 He shattered **b** gates and cut
Isa 45:2 I will break down the **b** doors
48:4 Like **b**, nothing gets through
60:17 I will bring gold instead of **b**.
60:17 **b** instead of wood,
Jer 1:18 city, an iron pillar, and a **b** wall.
6:28 They are all like **b** and iron.
15:12 iron, iron from the north, or **b**.)
15:20 I will make you like a solid **b**
27:19 pillars, the **b** pool, the stands,
39:7 put him in **b** shackles,
52:11 and put him in **b** shackles.
52:17 broke apart the **b** pillars
52:17 and the **b** pool in the LORD's
52:17 shipped all the **b** to Babylon.
52:18 and all the **b** utensils used in
52:20 The **b** from the 2 pillars,
52:20 and the 12 **b** bulls under the
52:22 They were all made of **b**.
Eze 1:7 they glittered like polished **b**.
1:27 He looked like glowing **b** with
9:2 in and stood by the **b** altar.
27:13 They exchanged slaves and **b**
40:3 like he was covered with **b**.
Dan 2:32 and hips were made of **b**.
2:35 at once, the iron, clay, **b**, silver,
2:39 third kingdom, a kingdom of **b**,
2:45 It smashed the iron, **b**,
4:15 Secure it with an iron and **b**
4:23 Secure it with an iron and **b**
5:4 silver, **b**, iron, wood, or stone.
5:23 gold, **b**, iron, wood, or stone.
7:19 and had iron teeth and **b** claws.
10:6 legs looked like polished **b**.
Mic 4:13 and your hoofs as hard as **b**.
Zec 6:1 They were mountains of **b**.
Rev 1:15 His feet were like glowing **b**
2:18 whose feet are like glowing **b**,
9:20 silver, **b**, stone, and wood,
18:12 costly wood, **b**, iron, marble,

bronze-covered (1)

Num 16:40 The **b** altar will remind Israel

brook (8)

1Ki 2:37 day you leave and cross the **b**
2Ki 23:4 an open field near the Kidron **B**.
2Ch 29:16 outside the city to the Kidron **B**.
32:4 and the **b** that flowed through
Psa 110:7 He will drink from the **b** along
Isa 15:6 The Nimrim **B** has run dry!
27:12 River to the **b** of Egypt.
Eze 48:28 and it will run along the **B** of

brooks (3)

Psa 74:15 You opened the springs and **b**.
Isa 30:25 There will be **b** and streams on
Joe 3:18 will flow in all the **b** of Judah.

broom (4)

1Ki 19:4 He sat down under a **b** plant
19:5 and slept under the **b** plant.
Job 30:4 and the roots of the **b** plant are
Isa 14:23 it with the **b** of destruction,"

broth (3)

Jdg 6:19 the meat in a basket and the **b**
6:20 and pour the **b** over them."
Isa 65:4 made **b** from unclean foods.

brother (238)

Gen 4:2 to another child, Abel, Cain's **b**.
4:8 Cain talked to his **b** Abel.
4:8 Cain attacked his **b** Abel and
4:9 "Where is your **b** Abel?"
4:9 to take care of my **b**?"
4:11 of your **b** whom you killed.
10:21 Shem, Japheth's older **b**,
14:13 a **b** of Eshcol and Aner.
20:5 she even say, 'He's my **b**'?
20:13 say that I'm your **b**."'
20:16 I've given your **b** 25 pounds of
22:20 these children of your **b** Nahor:
22:21 Uz (the firstborn), Buz (his **b**),
22:23 sons by Abraham's **b** Nahor.
24:15 the wife of Abraham's **b** Nahor.
24:29 Rebekah had a **b** whose name
24:53 presents to her **b** and mother.
24:55 Her **b** and mother replied,
25:26 Afterwards, his **b** was born
27:6 father speaking to your **b** Esau.
27:11 "My **b** Esau is a hairy man,
27:23 hairy like his **b** Esau's hands.
27:30 left when his **b** Esau came
27:35 Isaac said, "Your **b** came and
27:40 and you will serve your **b**.
27:41 Then I'll kill my **b** Jacob."
27:42 Your **b** Esau is comforting
27:43 away to my **b** Laban in Haran.
28:5 the Aramean and **b** of Rebekah.
32:3 ahead of him to his **b** Esau
32:6 "We went to your **b** Esau.
32:11 save me from my **b** Esau,
32:13 Then he prepared a gift for his **b**
32:17 "When my **b** Esau meets you
33:3 ground as he came near his **b**.
33:9 Keep what you have, **B**."
35:1 were fleeing from your **b** Esau."
35:7 he was fleeing from his **b**.
36:6 land away from his **b** Jacob.
37:26 will we gain by killing our **b**
37:27 because he is our **b**,
38:8 a descendant for your **b**."
38:9 giving his **b** a descendant.
38:29 back his hand, his **b** was born.
38:30 After that his **b** was born with
42:4 send Joseph's **b** Benjamin
42:13 The youngest **b** stayed with
42:15 your youngest **b** comes here.
42:16 be sent to get your **b** while
42:20 must bring me your youngest **b**.
42:21 for what we did to our **b**.
42:32 The youngest **b** stayed with
42:34 But bring me your youngest **b**.
42:34 I'll give your **b** back to you,
42:38 His **b** is dead, and he's the only
43:3 unless your **b** is with you.'
43:4 If you let our **b** go with us,
43:5 unless your **b** is with you."'
43:6 the man you had another **b**?"
43:7 Do you have another **b**?' We
43:7 'Bring your **b** here'?"
43:13 Take your **b**, and go back to
43:14 that he will send your other **b**
43:29 he saw his **b** Benjamin,
43:29 "Is this your youngest **b**,
43:30 moved at the sight of his **b**,
44:19 'Do you have a father or a **b**?'
44:20 is old and a younger **b** born
44:20 The boy's **b** is dead,
44:23 'If your youngest **b** doesn't
44:26 go back if our youngest **b** is
Gen 44:26 our youngest **b** is with us.'
45:4 the **b** you sold into slavery in
45:12 "You and my **b** Benjamin can
45:14 He threw his arms around his **b**
48:19 Nevertheless, his younger **b**
Exo 4:14 "What about your **b** Aaron the
7:1 and your **b** Aaron is your
7:2 Tell your **b** Aaron everything I
28:1 bring your **b** Aaron and his
28:2 Make holy clothes for your **b**
28:4 holy clothes for your **b** Aaron
28:41 Put these clothes on your **b**
Lev 16:2 The LORD said, "Tell your **b**
18:14 with the wife of your father's **b**.
21:2 father, son, daughter, or **b**,
25:25 If your **b** becomes poor and
Num 6:7 father, mother, **b**, or sister dies,
20:8 then you and your **b** Aaron
20:14 is what your **b** Israel says:
27:13 as your **b** Aaron did.
Dtr 13:6 Your own **b**, son, or daughter,
25:5 Her husband's **b** must marry
28:54 become stingy toward his **b**,
32:50 as your **b** Aaron died on Mount
Jos 15:17 son of Caleb's **b** Kenaz,
Jdg 1:13 of Caleb's younger **b** Kenaz,
3:9 son of Caleb's younger **b**
9:18 just because he's your **b**.
9:21 ⌊to avoid⌋ his **b** Abimelech.
1Sm 14:3 the son of Ichabod's **b** Ahitub,
17:28 Eliab, David's oldest **b**,
20:29 and my **b** ordered me to be
26:6 Zeruiah's son and Joab's **b**,
2Sm 1:26 over you, my **b** Jonathan.
2:22 How could I look your **b** Joab
3:27 the blood of Joab's **b** Asahel.
3:30 (Joab and his **b** Abishai killed
3:30 he had killed their **b** Asahel
4:6 and his **b** Baanah escaped.
4:9 to Rechab and his **b** Baanah,
10:10 He put his **b** Abishai in charge
13:3 a son of David's **b** Shimea.
13:7 go to your **b** Amnon's home,"
13:8 went to her **b** Amnon's home.
13:10 and brought it to her **b** Amnon
13:20 Her **b** Absalom asked her,
13:20 "Has your **b** Amnon been with
13:20 He's your **b**. Don't dwell on this
13:20 at the home of her **b** Absalom
13:26 then please let my **b** Amnon go
13:32 the son of David's **b** Shimea,
13:32 day his half **b** raped his sister
14:7 who killed his **b** so that we
18:2 another third under Joab's **b**
20:9 "How are you, my **b**?"
20:10 Then Joab and his **b** Abishai
21:21 son of David's **b** Shimei,
23:18 Joab's **b** Abishai, was the
23:24 the thirty was Joab's **b** Asahel.
1Ki 1:10 fighting men, or his **b** Solomon.
2:7 fleeing from your **b** Absalom.
2:15 has been turned over to my **b**
2:21 given to your **b** Adonijah as his
2:22 After all, he is my older **b**.
9:13 cities have you given me, **b**?"
13:30 "Oh no, my **b**, my brother!"
13:30 "Oh no, my brother, my **b**!"
20:32 "He's still alive? He's my **b**."
20:33 is your **b**," they said.
1Ch 2:32 (Shammai's **b**) were Jether
2:42 **b**) were his firstborn
4:11 Chelub, Shuhah's **b**,
7:34 The sons of his **b** Shomer were
7:35 His **b** Helem's sons were
8:39 His **b** Eshek's sons were Ulam
11:20 Joab's **b** Abishai was the
11:26 men were Joab's **b** Asahel,
11:45 and his **b** Joha the Tizite,
19:11 He put his **b** Abishai in charge
19:15 fled from Joab's **b** Abishai and
20:5 the **b** of Goliath from Gath.
20:7 son of David's **b** Shimea,
24:25 through Micah's **b** Isshiah).
24:31 The families of the oldest **b**
27:7 Asahel, Joab's **b**, was in
2Ch 31:12 and his **b** Shimei was his

2Ch 31:13 Conaniah and his **b** Shimei.
36:4 Jehoahaz's **b** Eliakim king
Neh 7:2 I put my **b** Hanani and
Job 1:4 (Each **b** took his turn having a
30:29 I'm a **b** to jackals and a
Psa 35:14 mourning for my friend or my **b**.
50:20 sit and talk against your own **b**.
Pro 17:17 and a **b** is born to share trouble.
18:19 An offended **b** is more
Sos 8:1 If only you were my **b**,
Isa 19:2 will fight — **b** against brother,
19:2 will fight — brother against **b**,
Jer 22:18 it is for my **b** and sister!"
Eze 44:25 daughter, **b**, or unmarried
Mal 1:2 "Wasn't Esau Jacob's **b**?"
Mat 10:2 called Peter) and his **b** Andrew;
10:2 James and his **b** John,
10:21 "**B** will hand over brother to
10:21 will hand over **b** to death;
12:50 Father in heaven wants is my **b**
14:3 the wife of his **b** Philip.
17:1 and John (the **b** of James) and
22:24 his **b** should marry his widow
22:24 and have children for his **b**.'
22:25 he left his widow to his **b**.
22:26 The second **b** also died,
Mar 1:16 saw Simon and his **b** Andrew.
3:17 James and his **b** John
3:35 does what God wants is my **b**
6:3 and the **b** of James,
6:17 used to be his **b** Philip's wife.)
12:19 his **b** should marry his widow
12:19 and have children for his **b**.'
13:12 "**B** will hand over brother to
13:12 will hand over **b** to death;
Luk 3:1 Herod ruled Galilee, and his **b**
6:14 Peter) and Simon's **b** Andrew,
12:13 tell my **b** to give me my share
15:27 'Your **b** has come home.
15:32 This **b** of yours was dead but
20:28 his **b** should marry his widow
20:28 and have children for his **b**.'
20:30 second **b** married the widow,
Jon 1:40 Andrew, Simon Peter's **b**,
1:41 Andrew at once found his **b**
6:8 who was Simon Peter's **b**,
11:2 Her **b** Lazarus was the one
11:19 to comfort them about their **b**.
11:21 my **b** would not have died.
11:23 "Your **b** will come back to life."
11:32 my **b** would not have died."
Act 7:9 were jealous of their **b** Joseph.
9:17 said, "**B** Saul, the Lord Jesus,
12:2 He had James, the **b** of John,
21:20 They said to Paul, "You see, **b**,
22:13 '**B** Saul, receive your sight!'
Rom 16:23 our **b** in the Christian faith,
1Co 1:1 our **b** in the Christian faith.
16:12 our **b** in the Christian faith:
2Co 1:1 and from Timothy our **b**.
2:13 couldn't find Titus, our **b**, there.
8:18 sent our Christian **b** whom all
8:22 our Christian **b** whom we have
Gal 1:19 I only saw James, the Lord's **b**.
Eph 6:21 He is our dear **b** and a faithful
Php 2:25 send Epaphroditus — my **b**,
Col 1:1 and from our **b** Timothy.
4:7 He is our dear **b**, and partner in
4:9 and is our faithful and dear **b**.
1Th 3:2 we sent our **b** Timothy to you.
Phm 1:1 and our **b** Timothy.
1:7 You, **b**, have comforted God's
1:16 than a slave — as a dear **b**.
Heb 13:23 You know that Timothy, our **b**,
1Pe 5:12 whom I regard as a faithful **b**.
2Pe 3:15 This is what our dear **b** Paul
1Jn 3:12 evil one and murdered his **b**.
3:12 why did Cain murder his **b**?
3:12 the things his **b** did had God's
Jud 1:1 of Jesus Christ and **b** of James.
Rev 1:9 I am John, your **b**. I share your

brotherhood (1)

Zec 11:14 to break off the **b** between

brother-in-law (5)

Gen 38:8 Do your duty for her as a **b**,
Num 10:29 Moses said to his **b** Hobab,
Dtr 25:5 He must do his duty as her **b**.
25:7 She must say, "My **b** refuses to
25:7 want to do his duty as my **b**."

brother's (24)

Gen 4:10 Your **b** blood is crying out to
4:21 His **b** name was Jubal.
10:25 His **b** name was Joktan.
27:44 until your **b** anger cools down.
27:45 When your **b** anger is gone and
38:8 "Go sleep with your **b** widow.
38:9 he slept with his **b** widow,
44:2 in the youngest **b** sack along
Lev 18:16 She is your **b** wife
20:21 Whoever marries his **b** wife
20:21 wife violates his **b** marriage
Dtr 25:6 the dead **b** name so that his
25:7 his **b** widow, she must go
25:7 to let his **b** name continue
25:9 his **b** widow must go up to him
25:9 to continue his **b** family line."
2Sm 14:7 him because he took his **b** life.
1Ch 1:19 His **b** name was Joktan.
7:16 His **b** name was Sheresh,
Job 1:13 wine in their oldest **b** home,
1:18 wine at their oldest **b** home
Hos 12:3 held on to his **b** heel while
Mar 6:18 to be married to your **b** wife.
Luk 15:27 to celebrate your **b** safe return.'

brothers (302)

Gen 9:22 outside and told his two **b**.
9:25 be the lowest slave to his **b**.
27:29 Be the master of your **b**,
27:37 have made all his **b** serve him.
34:11 said to Dinah's father and her **b**,
34:25 Simeon and Levi, Dinah's **b**,
37:2 bad things his **b** were doing.
37:4 Joseph's **b** saw that their father
37:5 dream and when he told his **b**,
37:8 Then his **b** asked him,
37:9 and he told it to his **b**.
37:10 he told his father and his **b**,
37:10 mother and I and your **b** come
37:11 So his **b** were jealous of him,
37:12 His **b** had gone to take care of
37:13 "Your **b** are taking care of the
37:14 So Israel said, "See how your **b**
37:16 "I'm looking for my **b**.
37:17 So Joseph went after his **b**
37:23 So when Joseph reached his **b**,
37:26 Judah asked his **b**,
37:27 flesh and blood." His **b** agreed.
37:28 the **b** pulled Joseph out of the
37:30 He went back to his **b** and said,
38:1 About that time Judah left his **b**
38:11 might die like his **b**.
42:3 Ten of Joseph's **b** went to buy
42:4 Benjamin with the other **b**,
42:6 So when Joseph's **b** arrived,
42:7 As soon as Joseph saw his **b**,
42:8 Joseph recognized his **b**,
42:13 answered him, "We were 12 **b**,
42:19 you will let one of your **b** stay
42:28 He said to his **b**, "My money
42:32 We were 12 **b**, sons of the
42:33 Leave one of your **b** with me.
43:24 The man took the **b** into
43:32 served separately from his **b**.
43:33 The **b** were seated facing him
44:14 Judah and his **b** arrived at
44:33 let the boy go back with his **b**.
45:1 Joseph told his **b** who he was.
45:3 Joseph said to his **b**,
45:3 His **b** could not answer him
45:4 Joseph said to his **b**.
45:15 He kissed all his **b** and cried
45:15 After that his **b** talked with him.
45:16 that Joseph's **b** had come,
45:17 said to Joseph, "Say to your **b**,
45:24 So Joseph sent his **b** on their
46:31 Then Joseph said to his **b** and
Gen 46:31 'My **b** and my father's family,
47:1 "My father and my **b** have
47:2 Since he had taken five of his **b**
47:3 Pharaoh asked the **b**,
47:5 "Your father and your **b** have
47:6 Have your father and your **b**
47:11 Joseph had his father and his **b**
47:12 also provided his father, his **b**,
48:22 mountain ridge than your **b**.
49:5 "Simeon and Levi are **b**.
49:8 "Judah, your **b** will praise you.
49:26 of the prince among his **b**.
50:8 Joseph's household, his **b**,
50:14 back to Egypt along with his **b**
50:15 Joseph's **b** realized what their
50:17 your **b** committed against you.
50:18 Then his **b** also came and
50:24 At last Joseph said to his **b**,
Exo 1:6 Eventually, Joseph, all his **b**,
32:29 with your own sons and **b**."
Lev 21:10 clothes is chief over his **b**.
25:48 One of his **b** may buy him
Num 25:6 a Midianite woman to his **b**.
27:9 give his property to his **b**.
27:10 If he has no **b**, give his property
Dtr 25:5 When **b** live together and one
33:9 didn't recognize their own **b**.
Jos 2:13 my father, mother, **b**, sisters,
2:18 gather your father, mother, **b**,
6:23 mother, **b**, everything she had,
Jdg 8:19 replied, "They were my **b**,
9:5 There he executed his 70 **b**,
9:24 Abimelech execute his **b**.
9:26 and his **b** moved into Shechem.
9:31 Gaal (son of Ebed) and his **b**
9:41 Zebul threw Gaal and his **b** out
9:56 father when he killed his 70 **b**.
11:3 Jephthah fled from his **b**.
21:22 When their fathers or **b** come to
1Sm 16:13 David in the presence of his **b**.
17:17 ten loaves of bread to your **b**.
17:17 Take them to your **b** in the
17:18 See how your **b** are doing,
17:22 battle line, and greeted his **b**.
20:29 let me go to see my **b**.' This
22:1 When his **b** and all ⌊the rest⌋
30:23 But David said, "My **b**,
1Ki 1:9 He had invited all his **b**,
1Ch 4:9 was more honorable than his **b**.
4:27 But his **b** didn't have many
5:2 was more prominent than his **b**
5:7 Beerah's **b** according to their
7:22 even though his **b** tried to
8:14 Their **b** were Shashak and
25:3 (The six **b** were directed by
26:7 and Othni's skilled **b** Rephael,
27:18 one of David's **b** for the tribe of
2Ch 11:22 head and prince among his **b**.
21:2 He had the following **b**,
21:4 and then executed all his **b**
21:13 You have killed your **b**,
21:13 Your **b** were better than you.
35:9 Conaniah and his **b** Shemaiah
Ezr 10:18 was Jozadak's son) and his **b**.
Neh 1:2 one of my **b**, Hanani,
4:14 Fight for your **b**, your sons,
4:23 My **b**, my servants, and the
5:10 My **b**, my servants, and I are
5:14 my **b** and I never ate any food
Job 6:15 My **b** have been as deceptive
19:13 "My **b** stay far away from me.
42:11 Then all his **b** and sisters and
42:15 them and their **b** an inheritance.
Psa 69:8 a stranger to my ⌊own⌋ **b**,
133:1 good and pleasant it is when **b**
Pro 17:2 the inheritance with the **b**.
Sos 1:6 My **b** were angry with me.
Jer 35:3 and I took Jaazaniah's **b** and
Hos 2:1 "So call your **b** Ammi [My
Mat 1:2 the father of Judah and his **b**.
1:11 father of Jechoniah and his **b**.
4:18 Sea of Galilee, he saw two **b**,
4:21 he saw two other **b**,
12:46 his mother and **b** were standing
12:47 "Your mother and your **b** are
12:48 and who are my **b**?"

Mat 12:49 here are my mother and my **b**.
19:29 **b** or sisters, father, mother,
20:24 were irritated with the two **b**.
22:25 There were seven **b** among us.
22:26 and the rest of the seven **b**.
22:28 All seven **b** had been married
25:40 did for one of my **b** or sisters,
25:45 to do for one of my **b** or sisters,
Mar 3:31 his mother and his **b** arrived.
3:32 "Your mother and your **b** are
3:33 and who are my **b**?"
3:34 here are my mother and my **b**.
5:37 and the two **b** James and John.
10:29 home, **b**, sisters, mother, father,
10:30 homes, **b**, sisters, mothers,
12:20 There were seven **b**.
12:22 None of the seven **b** had any
12:23 The seven **b** had married her."
Luk 8:19 His mother and his **b** came to
8:20 "Your mother and your **b** are
8:21 "My mother and my **b** are those
14:26 wives, children, **b**, and sisters,
16:28 I have five **b**. He can warn them
16:29 Your **b** should listen to them!'
18:29 up his home, wife, **b**, parents,
20:29 There were seven **b**.
20:31 In the same way all seven **b**
20:33 The seven **b** had married her."
21:16 "Even parents, **b**, relatives,
Jon 2:12 After this, Jesus, his mother, **b**,
7:3 So Jesus' **b** told him,
7:5 Even his **b** didn't believe in
7:10 But after his **b** had gone to the
20:17 But go to my **b** and sisters and
Act 1:14 and they were joined by his **b**.
1:16 "**B**, what the Holy Spirit
2:29 "**B**, I can tell you confidently
2:37 "**B**, what should we do?"
3:17 "And now, **b**, I know that like
6:3 So, **b** and sisters, We will put
7:2 "**B** and fathers, listen to me.
7:13 Joseph told his **b** who he was,
7:26 said to them, 'Men, you are **b**.
13:15 The message said, "**B**,
13:26 "**B** — descendants of Abraham
13:38 "So, **b**, I'm telling you that
15:7 stood up and said to them, "**B**,
15:13 responded, "**B**, listen to me.
15:23 the spiritual leaders, your **b**.
15:23 To their non-Jewish **b** and
15:23 Dear **b** and sisters,
22:1 "**B** and fathers, listen as I now
23:1 Jewish council and said, "**B**,
23:5 Paul answered, "**B**,
23:6 he shouted in the council, "**B**,
28:17 he said to them, "**B**,
Rom 1:13 you to know, **b** and sisters,
7:1 Don't you realize, **b** and sisters,
7:4 In the same way, **b** and sisters,
8:12 So, **b** and sisters, we have no
10:1 **B** and sisters, my heart's desire
11:25 **B** and sisters, I want you to
12:1 **B** and sisters, because of
15:14 I'm convinced, **b** and sisters,
15:30 **B** and sisters, I encourage you
16:14 and the **b** and sisters who are
16:17 **B** and sisters, I urge you to
1Co 1:10 **B** and sisters, I encourage all
1:11 **B** and sisters, some people
1:26 **B** and sisters, consider what
2:1 **B** and sisters, when I came to
3:1 **B** and sisters, I couldn't talk to
4:6 **B** and sisters, I have applied
5:11 people who call themselves **b**
7:24 **B** and sisters, you should
7:29 is what I mean, **b** and sisters:
9:5 the Lord's **b**, and Cephas do?
10:1 you to know, **b** and sisters,
11:33 Therefore, **b** and sisters,
12:1 **B** and sisters, I don't want there
14:6 **B** and sisters, it wouldn't do
14:20 **B** and sisters, don't think like
14:26 does this mean, **b** and sisters?
14:39 So, **b** and sisters, desire to
15:1 **B** and sisters, I'm making
15:31 **B** and sisters, I swear to you
1Co 15:50 **B** and sisters, this is what I
15:58 So, then, **b** and sisters,
16:15 I encourage you, **b** and sisters,
16:20 All the **b** and sisters ⌊here⌋
2Co 1:8 **B** and sisters, we don't want
8:1 **B** and sisters, we want you to
13:11 With that, **b** and sisters,
Gal 1:11 you to know, **b** and sisters,
3:15 **B** and sisters, let me use an
4:12 **B** and sisters, I beg you to
4:28 Now you, **b** and sisters,
4:31 **B** and sisters, we are not
5:11 **B** and sisters, if I am still
5:13 called to be free, **b** and sisters.
6:1 **B** and sisters, if a person gets
6:18 with your spirit, **b** and sisters!
Eph 6:23 the Lord Jesus Christ give our **b**
Php 1:12 you to know, **b** and sisters,
1:14 Lord has given most of our **b**
3:1 Now then, **b** and sisters,
3:13 **B** and sisters, I can't consider
3:17 **B** and sisters, imitate me,
4:1 So, **b** and sisters, I love you
4:8 Finally, **b** and sisters,
4:21 The **b** and sisters who are with
Col 1:2 our **b** and sisters who are
4:15 Greet our **b** and sisters in
1Th 1:4 **B** and sisters, we never forget
2:1 You know, **b** and sisters,
2:9 You remember, **b** and sisters,
2:14 You, **b** and sisters,
2:17 **B** and sisters, we have been
3:7 So **b** and sisters, your faith has
4:1 Now then, **b** and sisters,
4:13 **B** and sisters, we don't want
5:1 **B** and sisters, you don't need
5:4 But, **b** and sisters,
5:12 **B** and sisters, we ask you to
5:14 encourage you, **b** and sisters,
5:25 **B** and sisters, pray for us.
5:26 Greet all the **b** and sisters with
5:27 letter to all the **b** and sisters.
2Th 1:3 God for you, **b** and sisters.
2:1 **B** and sisters, we have this
2:13 God for you, **b** and sisters.
2:15 Then, **b** and sisters,
3:1 Finally, **b** and sisters,
3:6 **B** and sisters, in the name of
3:13 **B** and sisters, we can't allow
3:15 instruct them like **b** and sisters.
1Ti 4:6 things out to our **b** and sisters.
5:1 men as if they were your **b**,
2Ti 4:21 Claudia and all the **b** and
Phm 1:20 because we're **b** in the Lord,
Heb 2:11 to call them **b** and sisters.
2:17 he had to become like his **b**
3:1 **B** and sisters, you are holy
3:12 Be careful, **b** and sisters,
10:19 **B** and sisters, because of the
13:22 I urge you, **b** and sisters,
Jas 1:2 My **b** and sisters, be very
1:16 My dear **b** and sisters,
1:19 my dear **b** and sisters:
2:1 My **b** and sisters, practice your
2:5 Listen, my dear **b** and sisters!
2:14 My **b** and sisters, what good
3:1 **B** and sisters, not many of you
3:10 My **b** and sisters, this should
3:12 My **b** and sisters, can a fig tree
4:11 **B** and sisters, stop slandering
5:7 **B** and sisters, be patient until
5:9 **B** and sisters, or you will be
5:10 **B** and sisters, follow the
5:12 all things, my **b** and sisters,
5:19 My **b** and sisters, if one of you
1Pe 2:17 Love your **b** and sisters in the
2Pe 1:10 Therefore, **b** and sisters,
1Jn 3:13 **B** and sisters, don't be
Rev 12:10 one accusing our **b** and sisters,

brothers' (3)

Gen 48:6 land listed under their **b** names
Job 22:6 take your **b** goods as security
Mat 13:55 Aren't his **b** names James,

brought (733)

Gen 2:19 Then he **b** them to the man to
2:22 He **b** her to the man.
4:3 Later Cain **b** some crops from
4:4 Abel also **b** some choice parts
8:9 He reached out and **b** the dove
14:16 He **b** back everything they had,
14:16 He also **b** back his relative Lot
14:18 of Salem **b** out bread
15:7 who **b** you out of Ur of the
15:10 So Abram **b** all these animals
19:16 They **b** them safely outside the
21:6 "God has **b** me laughter,
24:32 Then water was **b** for him and
26:35 These women **b** Isaac and
27:14 He went and got them and **b**
27:20 "The LORD your God **b** it to
27:25 Jacob **b** it to Isaac,
27:25 Jacob also **b** him wine,
27:31 a good-tasting meal and **b**
27:33 "Who hunted game and **b** it to
29:13 kissed him and **b** him into his
29:23 his daughter Leah and **b** her
30:14 He **b** them to his mother Leah.
31:39 I never **b** you any of the flock
32:13 from what he had **b** with him:
33:11 take the present I've **b** you,
37:32 Then they **b** the special robe
38:25 As she was **b** out,
39:14 My husband **b** this Hebrew
39:17 "The Hebrew slave you **b** here
41:14 and immediately he was **b** from
43:2 grain they had **b** from Egypt,
43:18 because they had been **b** to
43:18 They thought, "We've been **b**
43:21 So we **b** it back with us.
43:22 We also **b** more money to buy
43:23 Then he **b** Simeon out to them.
43:26 gave him the gifts they had **b**
43:34 Joseph had portions of food **b**
44:8 We **b** the money we found in
46:7 He had **b** his sons,
46:32 They've **b** their flocks and
47:7 Then Joseph **b** his father
47:17 So they **b** their livestock to
48:10 So Joseph **b** his sons close to
48:13 and **b** them close to him.
Exo 2:8 So the girl **b** the baby's mother.
2:10 she **b** him to Pharaoh's
4:20 He also **b** with him the staff
5:22 "Why have you **b** this trouble
6:7 who **b** you out from under the
8:7 magic spells and **b** frogs onto
8:12 the frogs he had **b** on Pharaoh.
9:19 animals still outside and not **b**
9:20 warning **b** their servants
10:8 So Moses and Aaron were **b**
10:13 By morning the east wind had **b**
12:17 on this very day that I **b** you out
12:39 dough they had **b** from Egypt,
12:51 That very day the LORD **b** all
16:3 You **b** us out into this desert to
16:6 it was the LORD who **b** you out
16:32 in the desert when I **b** you out
18:1 how the LORD had **b** Israel out
18:5 Moses' father-in-law Jethro **b**
18:12 **b** a burnt offering and other
19:4 you on eagles' wings and **b** you
19:8 So Moses **b** their answer back
20:2 who **b** you out of slavery in
22:8 owner of the house must be **b**
29:46 I **b** them out of Egypt so that I
32:4 here are your gods who **b** you
32:6 and **b** fellowship offerings.
32:7 Your people whom you **b** out of
32:8 here are your gods who **b** you
32:11 your people whom you **b** out
32:12 That's why he **b** them out ⌊of
32:23 happened to this Moses who **b**
33:1 "You and the people you **b** out
35:21 came and **b** their contributions
35:22 alike — came and **b** all kinds
35:23 or fine leather **b** them.
35:24 could give silver or bronze **b**
35:24 be used in the construction **b** it.

Exo 35:25 in spinning yarn **b** violet,
35:27 The leaders **b** onyx stones and
35:28 They also **b** the spices and the
35:29 was willing **b** all these items
35:29 They **b** these items to be used
36:3 the Israelites had **b**
39:33 Then they **b** everything to
40:21 Then he **b** the ark into the tent
Lev 6:30 if some of the blood was **b** into
8:14 He **b** the bull that was the
8:18 He **b** forward the ram for the
8:22 He **b** forward the second ram
8:24 Moses also **b** Aaron's sons
9:5 Moses commanded and **b** them
9:9 Aaron's sons **b** him the blood.
9:15 He **b** the people's offerings.
9:16 he **b** forward the burnt offering
9:17 He also **b** the grain offering.
10:18 Since its blood was not **b**
11:45 I **b** you out of Egypt to be your
16:27 for sin whose blood was **b** into
19:36 I am the LORD your God who **b**
22:33 I **b** you out of Egypt to be your
23:43 in booths when I **b** them out
24:11 So they **b** him to Moses.
25:38 LORD your God, who **b** you out
25:42 I **b** them out of Egypt.
25:55 I **b** them out of Egypt.
26:13 I **b** you out of Egypt so that you
26:45 I **b** them out of Egypt to be their
27:11 animal that cannot be **b**
Num 5:15 since it is a grain offering **b**
5:18 the grain offering **b** because of
7:3 They **b** these gifts to the LORD:
7:3 They **b** them in front of the tent.
7:10 The leaders also **b** offerings for
7:12 The one who **b** his gifts on the
7:13 He **b** a silver plate that
7:14 He also **b** a gold dish that
7:18 the tribe of Issachar, **b** his gifts.
7:19 He **b** a silver plate that
7:20 He also **b** a gold dish that
7:25 **b** his gifts: a silver plate that
7:26 He also **b** a gold dish that
7:31 **b** his gifts: a silver plate that
7:32 He also **b** a gold dish that
7:37 **b** his gifts: a silver plate that
7:38 He also **b** a gold dish that
7:43 **b** his gifts: a silver plate that
7:44 He also **b** a gold dish that
7:49 **b** his gifts: a silver plate that
7:50 He also **b** a gold dish that
7:55 **b** his gifts: a silver plate that
7:56 He also **b** a gold dish that
7:61 **b** his gifts: a silver plate that
7:62 He also **b** a gold dish that
7:67 **b** his gifts: a silver plate that
7:68 He also **b** a gold dish that
7:73 **b** his gifts: a silver plate that
7:74 He also **b** a gold dish that
7:79 **b** his gifts: a silver plate that
7:80 He also **b** a gold dish that
11:11 why have you **b** me this
11:31 wind from the sea that **b** quails
12:14 Then she can be **b** back."
12:15 camp until she was **b** back.
13:23 They also **b** some
15:25 and they **b** these two offerings
15:33 him gathering wood **b** him
15:41 the LORD your God, who **b** you
16:9 The LORD has **b** you near
16:10 He has **b** you and all the other
16:13 Isn't it enough that you **b** us out
16:14 Certainly you haven't **b** us into
16:39 had been **b** by those who
17:9 Moses **b** out the staffs from the
18:9 Whatever is **b** to me as a most
18:15 that is **b** to the LORD is yours.
20:16 and **b** us out of Egypt.
23:7 "Balak **b** me from Aram.
23:11 I **b** you here to curse my
23:22 The God who **b** them out of
24:8 The God who **b** them out of
25:6 One of the Israelite men **b** a
27:5 So Moses **b** their case to the
28:8 and wine offering as you **b**
Num 31:12 and **b** the prisoners of war,
31:50 So we have **b** as gifts to the
31:54 from the commanders and **b**
32:17 Israelites until we have **b** them
Dtr 1:25 region's fruit with them and **b**
1:27 That's why he **b** us out of
4:20 are the people the LORD **b** out
4:37 he was with you as he **b** you
5:6 who **b** you out of slavery in
6:12 who **b** you out of slavery in
8:14 who **b** you out of slavery in
9:4 the LORD **b** us here to take
9:12 Your people whom you **b** out of
9:28 That's why he **b** them out — to
13:5 who **b** you out of Egypt and
13:10 who **b** you out of slavery in
16:1 the LORD your God **b** you out
17:8 any case which may be **b**
20:1 who **b** you out of Egypt,
25:1 that is **b** into court.
26:9 He **b** us to this place and gave
26:10 So now I've **b** the first produce
29:25 to them when he **b** them out
29:27 angry with this land and **b**
Jos 6:23 spies went and **b** out Rahab,
7:23 took the loot from the tent and **b**
7:24 he had — and **b** them
8:23 of Ai alive and **b** him to Joshua.
10:23 So they **b** him the kings of
10:24 When they **b** them to Joshua,
24:8 "After that I **b** you to the land of
24:17 The LORD our God **b** us and
24:32 of Israel had **b** from Egypt,
Jdg 1:7 Judah's troops **b** Adoni Bezek
2:1 He said, "I **b** you out of Egypt
2:12 the God who **b** them out of
2:15 the power of the LORD **b**
3:17 Then he **b** the tax payment to
6:8 I **b** you out of Egypt.
6:13 'The LORD **b** us out of Egypt?'
7:25 Then they **b** the severed heads
11:35 You've **b** me to my knees!
11:35 What disaster you've **b** me!
15:13 new ropes and **b** him back from
16:8 The Philistine rulers **b** her
18:3 to ask him, "Who **b** you here?
21:12 They **b** them to the camp at
Rut 1:21 but the LORD has **b** me back
1Sm 1:24 She also **b** a three-year-old bull,
1:24 She **b** him to the LORD's house
1:25 butchered the bull and **b**
2:14 Whatever the fork **b** up ⌊from
4:4 sent some men who **b** back
5:1 they **b** it from Ebenezer to
5:2 They **b** it into the temple of
5:10 "They **b** the ark of the God of
6:21 "The Philistines have **b** back
7:1 to take the LORD's ark and **b**
9:22 Samuel **b** Saul and his servant
10:18 I **b** Israel out of Egypt and
12:6 Aaron and **b** your ancestors out
14:29 "My father has **b** trouble to the
14:34 each of the soldiers **b** his ox
15:15 Saul answered, "The army **b**
15:20 **b** ⌊back⌋ King Agag of Amalek,
16:8 called Abinadab and **b** him
16:10 So Jesse **b** seven ⌊more⌋ of
17:54 took the Philistine's head and **b**
17:57 Abner **b** him to Saul.
18:27 David **b** the foreskins,
22:4 He **b** them to the king of Moab,
23:6 Abiathar **b** a priestly ephod
25:35 David accepted what she **b** him
30:7 So Abiathar **b** David the ephod.
30:19 David **b** back everything.
2Sm 1:5 man who had **b** him the news.
1:10 on his arm and **b** them here
1:13 the young man who had **b** him
2:8 and **b** him to Mahanaim.
3:26 They **b** him back from the
4:8 They **b** Ishbosheth's head to
6:3 God's ark on a new cart and **b**
6:4 They **b** it from Abinadab's
6:15 and the entire nation of Israel **b**
7:18 that you have **b** me this far?
8:7 and he **b** them to Jerusalem.
2Sm 8:10 Joram **b** articles of gold,
11:27 David sent for her and **b** her to
12:31 He **b** out the troops who were
13:10 bread she had prepared and **b**
14:13 because you haven't **b** back
14:23 So Joab went to Geshur and **b**
17:28 **b** ⌊supplies⌋ and food for
17:29 They **b** these things because
19:17 Ziba **b** his 15 sons and 20
19:40 from Israel **b** the king across.
21:13 When David **b** up the bones of
22:20 He **b** me out to a wide-open
23:16 They **b** it to David,
1Ki 1:3 from Shunem and **b** her
1:38 mule and **b** him to Gihon.
2:19 He had a throne **b** for his
3:1 Solomon **b** her to the City of
3:24 him a sword. When they **b** it,
4:28 They **b** their quota of barley
7:13 had Hiram **b** from Tyre.
7:51 He **b** the holy things that had
8:4 They **b** the ark, the tent of
8:6 The priests **b** the ark of the
8:16 'Ever since I **b** my people
8:21 ancestors when he **b** them out
8:51 own people whom you **b** out
8:53 when you **b** our ancestors out
9:9 who **b** their ancestors out of
9:9 That is why the LORD **b** this
9:28 and **b** it to King Solomon.
10:10 of spices **b** ⌊into Israel⌋ as
10:11 Hiram's fleet that **b** gold from
10:11 brought gold from Ophir also **b**
10:25 who came **b** him gifts:
12:28 are your gods who **b** you out
13:20 the old prophet who had **b** back
13:23 prophet whom he had **b** back.
13:26 the old prophet who had **b**
13:29 it on the donkey, and **b** it back.
15:15 He **b** into the LORD's temple
17:6 Ravens **b** him bread and meat
17:20 have you **b** misery on the
17:23 Elijah took the child, **b** him
18:20 word to all the Israelites and **b**
20:39 A man turned around and **b** a
22:37 he was **b** to Samaria to be
2Ki 2:20 put salt in it." They **b** it to him.
4:20 picked him up and **b** him
4:42 A man from Baal Shalisha **b**
5:2 they had **b** back a little girl from
5:6 He **b** the letter to the king of
5:20 accepting what he had **b**.
8:1 whose son he had **b** back
8:5 telling the king how Elisha **b**
8:5 whom Elisha **b** back to life."
9:28 His servants **b** him in a chariot
10:8 "They've **b** the heads of the
10:18 Then Jehu **b** all the people
10:22 So he **b** out robes for them.
10:26 Then they **b** out the large
11:12 Then Jehoiada **b** out the king's
11:19 and they **b** the king from the
12:4 contributions that are **b** into
12:4 and all the money **b** voluntarily
12:9 put the money that was **b**
12:13 with the money that was **b**.
12:16 offerings for sin was not **b** into
14:20 They **b** him back by horse,
17:7 who **b** them out of Egypt ⌊and
17:24 The king of Assyria **b** people
22:4 the money that has been **b** into
23:8 He **b** all the priests out of the
23:30 dead body in a chariot and **b**
24:16 The king of Babylon **b** all 7,000
25:6 **b** him to the king of Babylon at
25:20 took them and **b** them to the
1Ch 5:26 He **b** them to Halah,
9:28 count them when they **b** them
10:12 Saul and his sons and **b** them
11:18 They **b** it to David,
12:40 and Naphtali **b** food on
15:28 All Israel **b** the ark of the
17:5 from the day I **b** Israel out ⌊of
17:16 that you have **b** me this far?
18:7 and he **b** them to Jerusalem.
20:3 He **b** out the troops who were

1Ch 22:4 The men of Sidon and Tyre **b**
2Ch 1:4 David had ⌊already⌋ **b** God's
5:1 He **b** the holy things that had
5:5 They **b** the ark, the tent of
5:7 The priests **b** the ark of the
6:5 'Ever since I **b** my people
7:22 who **b** them out of Egypt.
7:22 That is why he **b** this disaster
8:11 Solomon **b** Pharaoh's daughter
8:18 and **b** it to King Solomon.
9:10 servants who **b** gold from Ophir
9:10 from Ophir also **b** sandalwood
9:12 more than what she had **b** him.
9:14 the merchants and traders **b**.
9:14 of the land also **b** gold
9:24 who came **b** him gifts:
15:11 the loot they had **b** with them:
15:18 He **b** into God's temple the
16:2 Then Asa **b** out all the silver
17:11 Some of the Philistines **b** gifts
17:11 The Arabs also **b** him flocks:
19:4 He **b** the people back to the
20:28 So they **b** harps, lyres,
22:7 God **b** about Ahaziah's
22:9 They **b** him to Jehu and killed
23:11 Then they **b** out the king's son,
23:14 Then the priest Jehoiada **b** the
23:20 and they **b** the king from the
24:9 the contributions should be **b**
24:10 They **b** the money and dropped
24:11 Whenever the Levites **b** the
24:14 When they finished, they **b** the
24:18 This offense of theirs **b** God's
25:14 he **b** the gods of the people of
25:23 at Beth Shemesh and **b** him to
25:28 They **b** him back by horse and
28:5 and **b** them to Damascus.
28:8 Judah and **b** them to Samaria.
28:15 on donkeys and **b** them
29:4 He **b** the priests and Levites
29:21 They **b** seven bulls,
29:23 Then they **b** the male goats for
29:31 The assembly **b** sacrifices and
29:31 was willing **b** burnt offerings.
29:32 The burnt offerings **b** by the
30:15 Then they **b** burnt offerings to
31:5 the Israelites **b** plenty of
31:5 They **b** large quantities,
31:6 living in the cities of Judah **b**
31:12 they faithfully **b** in the
33:11 and **b** him to Babylon.
33:13 The LORD **b** him back to his
34:9 him the money that had been **b**
34:14 When they **b** out the money
35:24 him out of the chariot and **b** him
36:7 Nebuchadnezzar also **b** some
36:10 sent for Jehoiakin and **b** him
36:18 He **b** to Babylon each of the
Ezr 1:7 King Cyrus **b** out the utensils
3:5 offerings **b** to the LORD.
4:2 of Assyria, who **b** us here."
5:14 in Jerusalem and **b** them into
6:5 in Jerusalem and **b** them into
8:18 so Iddo and his relatives **b** us
8:18 They **b** us 18 of Sherebiah's
8:19 They also **b** Hashabiah,
Neh 2:1 after some wine was **b** for the
8:2 Then Ezra the priest **b** the
9:23 You **b** them into the land you
13:11 So I **b** the Levites back
13:12 Then all Judah **b** a tenth of all
13:15 and **b** them into Jerusalem
13:18 with the results that our God **b**
13:19 sure that no loads could be **b**
Est 1:17 Queen Vashti to be **b** to him,
2:8 were gathered together and **b**
Job 24:24 They are **b** down low and
29:16 cases **b** by strangers.
42:11 the evil the LORD had **b** to him.
Psa 18:19 He **b** me out to a wide-open
22:9 Indeed, you are the one who **b**
30:3 you **b** me up from the grave.
37:33 him when he is **b** to trial.
45:14 she is **b** to the king.
45:14 They will be **b** to you.
45:15 joy and delight they are **b** in.

Psa 46:8 he has **b** to the earth.
66:12 but then you **b** us out and
78:33 He **b** their days to an end like a
78:33 He **b** their years to an end in
78:54 He **b** them into his holy land,
78:71 He **b** him from tending the
80:8 You **b** a vine from Egypt.
81:10 the one who **b** you out of Egypt.
105:16 He **b** famine to the land.
105:37 He **b** Israel out with silver and
105:40 The Israelites asked, and he **b**
105:43 He **b** his people out with joy,
107:14 He **b** them out of the dark,
136:11 He **b** Israel out from among
Pro 7:26 because she has **b** down many
15:8 A sacrifice **b** by wicked people
Sos 1:4 The king has **b** me into his
3:4 him go until I had **b** him into my
Isa 2:9 People will be **b** down.
2:11 mighty people will be **b** down.
2:17 arrogant people will be **b** down,
3:9 have **b** disaster on themselves.
5:15 People will be **b** down.
10:13 I've **b** down people like a
10:33 The tallest ones will be **b**
14:11 Your pride has been **b** down to
14:15 But you've been **b** down to
18:7 At that time gifts will be **b** to
18:7 They will be **b** to Mount Zion,
22:4 destruction **b** on my people."
23:3 of the Nile River is **b** to Tyre.
23:4 I've **b** up no daughters."
26:5 He has **b** down those who live
32:10 will fail and no fruit will be **b**
60:5 of the sea will be **b** to you.
63:11 Where is the one who **b** them
Jer 2:6 who **b** us from Egypt?
2:7 I **b** them into a fertile land to eat
2:17 You have **b** this on yourself by
4:18 "You **b** this on yourself.
6:15 They will be **b** down when I
7:22 When I **b** your ancestors out of
8:12 They will be **b** down when I
10:9 Hammered silver is **b** from
11:4 ancestors when I **b** them out
11:7 ancestors when I **b** them out
11:19 I was like a trusting lamb **b** to
11:20 because I've **b** my case to you.
16:14 'The LORD **b** the people of
16:15 But they will say, 'The LORD **b**
20:12 because I've **b** my case to you.
23:7 'The LORD **b** the people of
23:8 'The LORD **b** the descendants
24:1 into captivity and **b** them
25:7 **b**⌋ harm upon yourselves.'
25:31 LORD has **b** charges against
26:23 They **b** Uriah from Egypt and
27:16 will be **b** back from Babylon
31:23 When I have **b** them back from
31:32 by the hand and **b** them out
32:21 You **b** your people from Egypt
32:23 so you **b** all this disaster on
32:42 As I **b** all these disasters on
34:13 when I **b** them from Egypt,
34:16 You **b** back the male and
35:4 I **b** them into the LORD's
38:14 the prophet Jeremiah and **b** him
38:22 of Judah's king will be **b** out
38:23 wives and children will be **b**
39:5 They arrested him and **b** him to
41:5 They **b** grain offerings and
41:16 who were with him **b** back
41:16 Johanan **b** back men,
42:10 about the disaster I've **b** on you.
44:2 have seen all the disasters I **b**
44:12 will die in wars or be **b** to an
51:10 The LORD has **b** about our
52:9 captured the king and **b** him
52:26 took them and **b** them to the
Lam 2:2 He **b** the kingdom ⌊of Judah⌋
Eze 8:14 He **b** me to the entrance of the
8:16 Then he **b** me into the inner
9:2 Each one **b** a deadly weapon
11:24 the Spirit lifted me and **b** me to
12:7 During the day I **b** out bags as
12:7 I **b** out my bags in the dark.

Eze 13:22 even though I hadn't **b** them
14:22 and daughters will be **b** out.
17:12 He **b** them home with him to
19:4 and **b** him with hooks to Egypt.
19:9 put him in a cage and **b** him
20:10 "'So I **b** the Israelites out of
20:28 I **b** them to the land that I
20:28 they made sacrifices and **b**
22:4 You have **b** an end to your
27:15 and they **b** you ivory and ebony
30:11 will be **b** to destroy the land.
31:16 I **b** the tree down to the grave to
31:18 But you will be **b** down below
34:4 You have not **b** back those that
37:1 The LORD **b** me out by his
38:8 from many nations and **b**
38:8 These people were **b** there
39:28 and I **b** them back again to their
40:1 and he **b** me to Jerusalem.
40:2 In visions, God **b** me to Israel
40:3 He **b** me closer. I saw a man
40:4 You were **b** here to be shown
40:17 Then the man **b** me into the
40:28 Then the man **b** me to the inner
40:32 Then the man **b** me to the east
40:35 Then the man **b** me to the north
40:48 Then the man **b** me to the
41:1 Then the man **b** me into the
42:1 He **b** me to the side rooms
43:5 The Spirit lifted me and **b** me
44:4 The man **b** me through the
44:7 You **b** godless foreigners into
46:5 The grain offering that is to be **b**
46:5 the grain offering that is to be **b**
46:5 gallon of olive oil must be **b**
46:11 of a half-bushel must be **b**
46:11 and a half-bushel must be **b**
46:11 gallon of olive oil must be **b**
46:19 The man **b** me through a
Dan 1:18 the chief-of-staff **b** all the young
3:8 forward and **b** charges against
3:13 they were **b** to the king.
4:6 advisers in Babylon to be **b**
5:2 in Jerusalem be **b** to him.
5:3 So the servants **b** the gold
5:7 fortunetellers to be **b** to him.
5:10 the king and his nobles **b**
5:13 my grandfather **b** from Judah?
5:15 and the psychics were **b**
5:23 from his temple **b** to you.
6:16 and Daniel was **b** to him and
6:17 A stone was **b** and placed over
6:24 had **b** charges against Daniel
6:24 against Daniel to be **b** to him.
9:11 So you **b** on us the curses you
9:15 "Lord our God, you **b** your
Hos 4:1 The LORD has **b** these
9:4 It will not be **b** ⌊as an offering⌋
12:9 I **b** you out of Egypt.
13:4 I **b** you out of Egypt.
Joe 1:9 wine offerings are no longer **b**
3:5 You **b** my finest treasures to
Amo 2:10 I **b** you out of Egypt.
3:1 family that I **b** out of Egypt.
Jnh 2:6 But you **b** me back from the pit,
Mic 6:4 I **b** you out of Egypt and freed
Mat 4:24 People **b** him everyone who
4:24 They also **b** epileptics,
8:16 In the evening the people **b**
9:2 Some people **b** him a
9:32 some people **b** a man to Jesus.
10:18 of me you will even be **b**
11:5 dead people are **b** back to life,
12:22 Then some people **b** Jesus a
14:11 So the head was **b** on a platter
14:35 The people **b** him everyone
16:21 day he would be **b** back to life.
17:9 of Man has been **b** back to life."
17:16 I **b** him to your disciples,
17:23 but on the third day he will be **b**
18:24 of dollars was **b** to him.
19:13 Then some people **b** little
20:19 But on the third day he will be **b**
21:7 They **b** the donkey and the colt
22:10 went into the streets and **b**
22:19 They **b** him a coin.

Mat 25:20 received ten thousand dollars **b**
26:32 "But after I am **b** back to life,
27:3 He **b** the 30 silver coins back
27:63 days I will be **b** back to life.'
27:64 'He has been **b** back to life.'
28:6 He has been **b** back to life as
28:7 that he has been **b** back
Mar 1:12 At once the Spirit **b** him into the
1:32 people **b** to him everyone who
6:28 Then he **b** the head on a platter
7:32 Some people **b** to him a man
8:22 some people **b** a blind man to
9:17 "Teacher, I **b** you my son.
9:20 They **b** the boy to him.
10:13 Some people **b** little children to
11:7 They **b** the donkey to Jesus,
12:16 They **b** a coin. He said to them,
14:28 "But after I am **b** back to life,
16:6 He has been **b** back to life.
Luk 2:27 They **b** him so that they could
4:16 where he had been **b** up.
4:40 from various diseases **b** them
5:11 Simon and his partners **b** the
5:18 Some men **b** a paralyzed man
7:22 dead people are **b** back to life,
10:34 own animal, **b** him to an inn,
16:20 Lazarus who was regularly **b**
18:15 Some people **b** infants to
19:35 They **b** the donkey to Jesus,
22:66 They **b** Jesus in front of their
23:14 He told them, "You **b** me this
24:6 He has been **b** back to life!
Jon 1:42 Andrew **b** Simon to Jesus.
8:3 scribes and the Pharisees **b**
9:13 Some people **b** the man who
10:4 After he has **b** out all his sheep,
10:31 The Jews had again **b** some
12:1 whom Jesus had **b** back to life,
12:9 whom Jesus had **b** back to life.
12:17 from the tomb and **b** him back
16:21 child has been **b** into the world.
18:16 the gatekeeper and **b** Peter into
19:39 went with Joseph and **b** 75
Act 2:22 was a man whom God **b**
2:32 "God **b** this man Jesus back to
3:15 But God **b** him back to life,
3:26 God has **b** his servant back to
4:10 but God has **b** him back to life.
4:34 or houses and **b** the money
5:27 When they **b** back the apostles,
5:30 But the God of our ancestors **b**
6:12 and **b** him in front of the Jewish
7:11 throughout Egypt and Canaan **b**
7:45 they **b** it into this land.
9:27 an interest in Saul and **b** him
10:36 the people of Israel and **b** them
10:40 but God **b** him back to life on
11:26 After finding Saul, Barnabas **b**
12:25 They **b** John Mark with them.
13:30 But God **b** him back to life,
13:34 "God stated that he **b** Jesus
13:37 However, the man God **b** back
14:13 The priest of the god Zeus **b**
15:3 This story **b** great joy to all the
15:31 the encouragement it **b** them.
17:19 Then they **b** Paul to the city
18:12 Paul and **b** him to court.
19:24 His business **b** a huge profit for
19:37 The men you **b** here don't rob
21:28 He has even **b** Greeks into the
22:30 Then the officer **b** Paul and had
24:17 back to my people and **b** gifts
25:3 of having Paul **b** to Jerusalem.
25:15 leaders **b** me some information
25:23 Paul was **b** into the auditorium.
25:26 So I have **b** him to all of you,
26:2 that the Jews **b** against me.
Rom 3:19 The whole world is **b** under the
4:24 in the one who **b** Jesus,
4:25 of our failures and was **b** back
5:16 the gift **b** God's approval.
6:4 As Christ was **b** back from
6:9 who was **b** back to life,
7:4 the one who was **b** back to life.
7:10 me life actually **b** me death.
8:11 of the one who **b** Jesus back
Rom 8:11 Then the one who **b** Christ
8:34 he was **b** back to life.
10:9 and believe that God **b** him
11:15 that the world has been **b** back
1Co 15:4 He was **b** back to life on the
15:11 this is the message we **b** you,
15:12 you that Christ has been **b** back
15:13 If the dead can't be **b** back to
15:15 testified that he **b** Christ back
15:21 Since a man **b** death,
15:21 a man also **b** life back from
2Co 3:7 The ministry that **b** death was
4:14 We know that the one who **b**
5:15 man who died and was **b** back
Gal 1:1 God the Father who **b** him back
2:4 False Christians were **b** in.
4:13 You know that the first time I **b**
Eph 1:20 in Christ when he **b** him back
2:6 God has **b** us back to life
2:13 have been **b** near by the blood
2:15 He **b** an end to the
2:16 He also **b** them back to God in
Php 4:18 Now that Epaphroditus has **b**
Col 1:13 power of darkness and has **b**
1:22 But now Christ has **b** you back
2:12 In baptism you were also **b**
2:12 who **b** him back to life.
2:14 the charges that were **b** against
3:1 Since you were **b** back to life
1Th 1:5 the Good News we **b** came
1:10 whom he **b** back to life.
1Ti 1:14 Through his kindness he **b** me
2:14 was deceived and **b** sin into
2Ti 1:10 News he has **b** eternal life into
2:8 He was **b** back to life and is a
Heb 2:2 that the angels **b** was reliable,
7:27 First they **b** sacrifices for their
7:27 and then they **b** sacrifices for
7:27 Jesus **b** the sacrifice for the
8:9 by the hand and **b** them out
9:7 Once a year he entered and **b**
9:9 that were **b** there could not
12:2 ignored the disgrace it **b** him.
13:20 The God of peace **b** the great
1Pe 1:21 in God who **b** Christ back
3:18 but he was **b** to life through his
2Pe 2:5 He **b** the flood on the world of

brow (1)

Gen 3:19 By the sweat of your **b**,

brown (2)

Jdg 5:10 people who ride on **b** donkeys,
Amo 1:2 of the shepherds are turning **b**,

bruise (4)

Gen 3:15 and you will **b** his heel."
Exo 21:25 burn for a burn, a **b** for a bruise,
21:25 burn for a burn, a bruise for a **b**,
Job 9:17 with a storm and **b** me without

bruised (1)

Lev 22:24 the LORD an animal that has **b**,

bruises (1)

Isa 1:6 left on your ⌊body⌋ — only **b**,

bruising (1)

Gen 4:23 I killed a man for **b** me,

brush (1)

Neh 5:13 may God **b** off from home and

brushed (6)

Exo 29:2 some wafers **b** with olive oil.
Lev 2:4 bread **b** with olive oil.
7:12 wafers of unleavened bread **b**
Num 6:15 wafers of unleavened bread **b**
Neh 5:13 I **b** off my clothes and said,
5:13 may everyone be **b** off and left

brushwood (7)

Jdg 9:48 took an ax, cut some **b**,
9:49 So all his troops also cut **b** and
9:49 They piled the **b** on top of the
Job 41:20 like a boiling pot heated over **b**.
Isa 64:2 Be like the fire that kindles **b**
Act 28:3 Paul gathered a bundle of **b**
28:3 a poisonous snake out of the **b**.

brutal (2)

Pro 20:30 **B** beatings cleanse away
2Ti 3:3 lack self-control, be **b**,

brutally (2)

Exo 1:14 gave them were **b** hard.
Heb 11:35 Other believers were **b** tortured

Bubastis (1)

Eze 30:17 from Heliopolis and **B** will die

bucket (2)

Lev 15:12 and any wooden **b** he touches
Isa 40:15 nations are like a drop in a **b**

buckets (1)

Num 24:7 Water will flow from their **b**,

bud (6)

Exo 25:35 There should be a **b** under
37:20 each with a **b** and petals.
37:21 There was a **b** under each of
1Ki 7:26 shaped like a lily's **b**.
2Ch 4:5 shaped like a lily's **b**.
Isa 27:6 Israel will blossom, **b**,

budded (2)

Sos 6:11 to see if the grapevine had **b**
7:12 Let's see if the vines have **b**,

buds (7)

Exo 25:31 as well as the flower cups, **b**,
25:33 blossoms, with **b** and petals.
25:34 blossoms, with **b** and petals.
25:36 The **b** and branches should
37:17 as well as the flower cups, **b**,
37:19 blossoms, with **b** and petals.
37:22 The **b** and branches were

build (142)

Gen 6:15 This is how you should **b** it:
6:16 **B** the ship with lower,
11:4 Then they said, "Let's **b** a city
16:2 Maybe I can **b** a family through
30:3 and I can **b** a family for myself
Exo 20:24 "You must **b** an altar for me
20:25 If you **b** an altar for me made
30:1 ⌊The LORD continued,⌋ "**B** an
Num 23:1 "**B** seven altars here,
23:29 "**B** seven altars here,
32:16 "Allow us to **b** stone fences for
32:24 **B** cities for your families and
Dtr 6:10 cities that you didn't **b**.
8:12 You will **b** nice houses and
16:21 When you **b** the altar for the
22:8 Whenever you **b** a new house,
27:5 **B** an altar of stones there
27:6 You must use uncut stones to **b**
28:30 You will **b** a house,
Jos 22:26 'Let's **b** an altar for ourselves.
Jdg 6:26 Then, in the proper way, **b** an
2Sm 7:5 Are you the one who will **b** me
7:7 Israel why they didn't **b** me
7:13 He will **b** a house for my name,
7:27 'I will **b** a house for you.'
24:21 floor from you and to **b**
1Ki 2:36 "**B** a house for yourself in
5:3 He couldn't **b** a temple for the
5:5 will **b** a temple for my name.'
5:18 logs and stone to **b** the temple.
6:1 Solomon began to **b** the
8:16 tribes of Israel as a place to **b**
8:19 But you must not **b** the temple.
8:19 Instead, your own son will **b**
9:1 ⌊else⌋ he wanted to **b**.
9:10 It took Solomon 20 years to **b**
9:15 King Solomon drafted to **b**
9:19 he wanted to **b** in Jerusalem,
11:38 I will **b** a permanent dynasty
1Ch 14:1 and carpenters to **b** a palace for
17:4 You must not **b** this house for
17:6 my people why they didn't **b** me

1Ch 17:10 will **b** a house for you.
17:12 He will **b** a house for me,
17:25 to me that you will **b** me
21:22 I'll **b** an altar for the LORD on it.
22:2 to cut stones to **b** God's temple.
22:6 and commanded him to **b**
22:8 You must not **b** a temple for my
22:10 He will **b** a temple for my name.
22:11 and you will **b** the temple of the
28:2 have made preparations to **b** it.
28:3 'You must not **b** the temple for
28:6 'Your son Solomon will **b** my
28:10 the LORD has chosen you to **b**
29:16 wealth that we gathered to **b**
29:19 laws and do everything to **b**
2Ch 2:3 him cedar so that he could **b**
2:4 I want to **b** the temple for the
2:6 But who is able to **b** him a
2:6 Who am I to **b** him a temple
2:9 because the temple I want to **b**
2:12 and intelligence and can **b**
3:1 Solomon began to **b** the
3:2 He began to **b** on the second
3:3 foundation to **b** God's temple.
6:5 tribes of Israel as a place to **b**
6:9 But you must not **b** the temple.
6:9 Instead, your own son will **b**
8:1 It took Solomon 20 years to **b**
8:6 he wanted to **b** in Jerusalem,
14:7 So Asa told Judah, "Let's **b**
36:23 Then he ordered me to **b** a
Ezr 1:2 Then he ordered me to **b** a
1:3 (which is in Judah) and **b**
4:2 "We want to help you **b**
4:3 your people and our people to **b**
4:3 We must **b** it alone for the
Job 19:12 They **b** a ramp to attack me
20:19 force a house that he didn't **b**.
Psa 28:5 and never **b** them up again,
104:17 Birds **b** their nests in them.
107:36 and they **b** cities to live in.
127:1 LORD does not **b** the house,
Pro 24:27 Afterwards, **b** your house.
Ecc 3:3 to tear down and a time to **b** up,
Sos 8:9 If she is a wall, we will **b** a
Isa 22:11 You will **b** a reservoir between
27:11 Women will come and **b** a fire
45:13 He will **b** my city and let my
57:14 It will be said: "**B** a road!
57:14 **B** a road! Prepare the way!
62:10 **B** up! Build up the highway!
62:10 **B** up the highway!
65:21 They will **b** houses and live
65:22 They will not **b** homes and
66:1 Where can you **b** a house or
Jer 1:10 You will **b** and plant."
6:6 **B** up dirt mounds to attack
12:16 Then they will **b** homes among
18:9 another time I may promise to **b**
22:14 He says, 'I will **b** a large house
24:6 I will **b** them up and not tear
29:5 **B** houses, and live in them.
29:28 **B** houses, and live in them.
31:4 Once again I will **b** you up,
31:28 Now I will watch over them to **b**
35:7 Never **b** any houses or plant
42:10 Then I will **b** you up and not
49:16 Even though you **b** your nest
Eze 4:2 **b** attack walls around it,
16:31 You **b** your platforms at the
22:30 among you who could **b** walls
28:26 They will **b** homes and plant
Dan 11:15 **b** dirt attack ramps,
Hos 2:6 way with thornbushes and **b**
8:11 that the people of Ephraim **b**
Amo 5:11 That is why you **b** houses from
Oba 1:4 eagle and **b** your nest among
Mic 3:10 You **b** Zion on bloodshed and
Hab 1:10 at every fortified city and **b**
Zep 1:13 They will **b** houses,
Hag 1:8 get lumber, and **b** the house.
Zec 5:11 "They are going to **b** a house
Mat 16:18 on this rock I will **b** my church.
23:29 You **b** tombs for the prophets
27:40 tear down God's temple and **b**
Mar 14:58 three days I'll **b** another temple,
Mar 15:29 tear down God's temple and **b**
Luk 11:47 You **b** the monuments for the
11:48 for whom you **b** monuments.
12:18 I'll tear down my barns and **b**
14:28 you want to **b** a tower.
14:30 'This person started to **b** but
19:43 when enemy armies will **b**
Jon 2:20 forty-six years to **b** this temple.
Act 7:49 are you going to **b** for me?
Rom 15:2 good things that will **b** his faith.
15:20 I didn't want to **b** on a
1Co 3:12 People may **b** on this
Eph 4:12 and to **b** up the body of Christ.
Col 2:7 your roots in him and **b** on him.

builder (6)

Neh 4:18 and each **b** had his sword
Psa 147:2 LORD is the **b** of Jerusalem.
1Co 3:10 a skilled and experienced **b**,
Heb 3:3 in the same way that the **b**
3:4 After all, every house has a **b**,
3:4 but the **b** of everything is God.

builders (16)

2Ki 12:11 used it to pay the carpenters, **b**,
22:6 **b**, and masons.) Also,
2Ch 34:11 included carpenters and **b**.)
Ezr 3:10 The **b** laid the foundation of the
5:8 The **b** are doing an excellent
Neh 4:5 insulted you in front of these **b**."
Psa 118:22 The stone that the **b** rejected
127:1 it is useless for the **b** to work
Jer 24:1 and the **b** from Jerusalem into
Eze 27:4 "'Your **b** made your beauty
27:5 Your **b** made all your boards
Mat 21:42 'The stone that the **b** rejected
Mar 12:10 'The stone that the **b** rejected
Luk 20:17 'The stone that the **b** rejected
Act 4:11 is the stone that the **b** rejected,
1Pe 2:7 "The stone that the **b** rejected

building (61)

Gen 4:17 Cain was **b** a city,
11:5 descendants of Adam were **b**.
11:8 and they stopped **b** the city.
Exo 38:24 to the LORD used in **b**
Jos 22:16 from following the LORD by **b**
22:19 the LORD or against us by **b**
22:29 from following the LORD by **b**
Jdg 16:26 on which the **b** stands so that
16:27 The **b** was filled with people.
16:29 columns on which the **b** stood.
16:30 and the **b** fell on the rulers and
1Ki 3:1 he finished **b** his own house,
5:5 Now I'm thinking of **b** a temple
6:1 He began **b** in the month of Ziv
6:5 next to the walls of the main **b**
6:9 he had finished **b** the walls,
6:12 concerns the temple you are **b**:
6:14 finished **b** the temple's ⌊frame⌋,
6:38 He spent seven years **b** it.
7:1 13 years to finish **b** his palace.
8:17 David had his heart set on **b**
8:18 you had your heart set on **b**
9:1 Solomon finished **b** the LORD's
11:27 Solomon was **b** the Millo and
2Ki 25:9 important **b** was burned down.
1Ch 22:5 I'll prepare ⌊the **b** materials⌋ for
22:7 "I had my heart set on **b** a
22:19 Start **b** the holy place of the
28:2 I had my heart set on **b** the
2Ch 2:1 Solomon gave orders to begin **b**
2:5 The temple I am **b** will be great
3:5 the larger **b** with cypress,
3:6 He covered the **b** with gems to
3:7 He also overlaid the **b**,
3:11 and touched the wall of the **b**.
3:12 touched the other wall of the **b**.
6:7 David had his heart set on **b**
6:8 you had your heart set on **b**
27:3 temple and did extensive **b**
Ezr 4:1 who returned from exile were **b**
4:4 made them afraid to continue **b**.
5:4 who were working on this **b**.
6:14 They finished **b** as the God of
Neh 3:31 made repairs as far as the **b**
Neh 4:3 on top of what they're **b**!"
Jer 52:13 important **b** was burned down.
Eze 41:12 was a **b** 122 ½ feet wide.
41:12 The wall of the **b** was 9 feet
41:13 the open area with the **b**
41:15 the length of the **b** facing
42:1 open area and the northern **b**.
42:2 The **b** that faced north was 175
42:5 first or second stories of the **b**
42:10 faced the open area and the **b**.
Luk 14:29 and can't finish the **b**,
17:28 and selling, planting and **b**.
1Co 3:9 God's field. You are God's **b**.
3:10 lay the foundation ⌊for that **b**⌋.
3:10 someone else is **b** on it.
2Co 5:1 we still have a **b** from God.
Eph 2:21 In him all the parts of the **b** fit

buildings (12)

1Ki 7:9 to the roof, all these **b**,
1Ch 15:1 After David constructed **b** for
29:4 to cover the walls of the **b**,
2Ch 34:11 fittings and beams of the **b** that
Jer 51:30 Their **b** are set on fire.
Eze 40:2 were some **b** that looked like
Mat 24:1 pointed out to him the temple **b**.
24:2 "You see all these **b**,
Mar 13:1 stones and these beautiful **b**!"
13:2 "Do you see these large **b**?
13:3 of Olives facing the temple **b**,
Luk 21:6 "About these **b** that you see —

builds (12)

Job 27:18 He **b** his house like a moth,
Psa 102:16 When the LORD **b** Zion,
Pro 14:1 The wisest of women **b** up her
17:19 Whoever **b** his city gate high
29:4 a king **b** up a country,
Jer 22:13 who **b** his house dishonestly
Eze 13:10 When someone **b** a flimsy wall,
Amo 9:6 The one who **b** stairs up to
Hab 2:12 it will be for the one who **b**
1Co 3:10 must be careful how he **b** on it.
8:1 but love **b** them up.
Eph 4:16 body grow so that it **b** itself up

built (173)

Gen 8:20 Noah **b** an altar to the LORD.
10:11 land to Assyria and **b** Nineveh,
12:7 So he **b** an altar there to the
12:8 He also **b** an altar to the LORD
13:18 There he **b** an altar for the
22:9 Abraham **b** the altar and
26:25 So Isaac **b** an altar there and
33:17 where he **b** a house for himself
35:7 He **b** an altar there and called
Exo 1:11 They **b** Pithom and Rameses
15:17 the holy place that you **b** with
17:15 Moses **b** an altar and called it
24:4 Early the next morning he **b** an
32:5 When Aaron saw this, he **b** an
Num 13:22 (Hebron was **b** seven years
23:14 where he **b** seven altars.
24:21 Your nest is **b** in a rock.
32:36 They also **b** stone fences for
Dtr 20:5 "If you have **b** a new house but
Jos 2:15 since her house was **b** into
8:30 At that time Joshua **b** an altar
8:31 He **b** an altar with uncut stones
11:13 not burn cities **b** on mounds.
22:10 They **b** an altar by the Jordan
22:11 of the tribe of Manasseh have **b**
22:23 If we **b** an altar with the
22:23 and if we **b** it for making burnt
24:13 to live in that you hadn't **b**,
Jdg 1:26 There he **b** a city and called it
6:24 So Gideon **b** an altar there to
6:28 on the altar that had been **b**.
21:4 They **b** an altar there and
Rut 4:11 both of whom **b** our family of
1Sm 7:17 And in Ramah he **b** an altar to
14:35 Then Saul **b** an altar to the
14:35 it was the first time he had **b**
2Sm 5:9 He **b** the city ⌊of Jerusalem⌋
5:11 They **b** a palace for David.
24:25 David **b** an altar for the LORD

1Ki 3:2 the LORD had not yet been **b**.
6:2 temple that King Solomon **b**
6:5 He **b** an annex containing side
6:7 The temple was **b** with stone
6:10 He **b** ⌊each story of the⌋ annex
6:16 He **b** it to serve as an inner
6:36 He **b** the inner courtyard with
7:2 He **b** a hall ⌊named⌋ the Forest
7:8 Solomon also **b** private
7:9 were **b** with high-grade stone
8:13 I certainly have **b** you a high
8:20 I've **b** the temple for the name
8:27 can this temple that I have **b**?
8:43 which I **b** bears your name.
8:44 the temple I **b** for your name,
8:48 temple I have **b** for your name,
9:3 which you have **b** is holy so
9:19 He also **b** cities for his chariots,
9:24 that Solomon had **b** for her.
9:24 Then he **b** the Millo.
9:25 offerings on the altar he **b**
9:26 King Solomon also **b** a fleet
10:4 wisdom, the palace he **b**,
10:26 Solomon **b** up ⌊his army⌋ with
11:7 Then Solomon **b** an illegal
12:25 Then he left that place and **b**
12:31 Jeroboam **b** worship sites on
14:23 They **b** worship sites for
16:24 He fortified the hill and **b** the
16:32 He **b** the temple of Baal in
18:32 Elijah **b** an altar in the LORD's
22:39 the ivory palace he **b**,
2Ki 15:35 Jotham **b** the Upper Gate of the
16:11 Urijah **b** an altar exactly like
16:18 This walkway had been **b** in
17:9 They **b** for themselves illegal
21:4 He **b** altars in the LORD's
21:5 he **b** altars for the entire army of
23:13 King Solomon of Israel had **b**
23:19 The kings of Israel had **b** these
25:1 They set up camp and **b** dirt
1Ch 6:10 Solomon **b** in Jerusalem.)
6:32 tent of meeting until Solomon **b**
7:24 who **b** Upper and Lower Beth
8:12 and Shemed (who **b** Ono,
11:8 He **b** the city ⌊of Jerusalem⌋
21:26 David **b** an altar for the LORD
22:5 and the temple that will be **b**
22:19 into the temple that will be **b**
2Ch 1:14 Solomon **b** up ⌊his army⌋ with
6:2 But I have **b** you a high temple,
6:10 I've **b** the temple for the name
6:18 can this temple that I have **b**?
6:33 which I **b** bears your name.
6:34 the temple I **b** for your name,
6:38 temple I have **b** for your name,
8:4 Tadmor in the desert and **b** all
8:6 He **b** all the cities for his
8:11 to a palace he had **b** for her.
8:12 on the LORD's altar that he **b**
9:3 wisdom, the palace he **b**,
11:5 Jerusalem and **b** fortified cities
14:6 He **b** fortified cities in Judah
14:7 "So they **b** the cities,
17:12 He **b** fortresses and cities
20:8 have lived in it and **b**
26:6 He **b** cities near Ashdod and
26:9 Uzziah **b** towers in Jerusalem
26:10 He **b** towers in the desert.
27:3 Jotham **b** the Upper Gate of the
27:4 He **b** cities in the hills of Judah,
27:4 and he **b** forts and towers in the
32:5 **b** another wall outside ⌊the city
33:4 He **b** altars in the LORD's
33:5 he **b** altars for the entire army of
33:14 and he **b** it very high.
33:15 He got rid of the altars he had **b**
33:16 He **b** the LORD's altar and
33:19 he **b** illegal worship sites
35:3 of David and king of Israel, **b**.
Ezr 3:2 Zerubbabel and his relatives **b**
3:2 They **b** it in order to sacrifice
5:8 The temple is being **b** with
5:11 originally **b** many years ago
Neh 7:4 and no houses were being **b**.
9:4 Chanani stood on the stairs **b**
Neh 12:29 The singers had **b** villages for
Job 3:14 counselors of the world who **b**
Psa 8:2 you have **b** a fortress against
78:69 He **b** his holy place to be like
89:4 I **b** your throne to last
122:3 Jerusalem is **b** to be a city
Pro 9:1 Wisdom has **b** her house.
24:3 With wisdom a house is **b**.
Ecc 2:4 I **b** houses for myself.
Isa 5:2 **b** a watchtower in it,
Jer 7:31 They have **b** worship sites at
19:5 They have **b** worship sites to
30:18 Cities will be **b** on the ruins,
30:18 and fortified palaces will be **b**
32:24 ramps have been **b** up around
32:31 and furious from the day they **b**
32:35 Hinnom they **b** worship sites
35:9 **b** houses to live in,
45:4 I will tear down what I have **b**.
52:4 They set up camp and **b** dirt
Eze 16:24 you **b** yourself platforms and
16:25 You also **b** worship sites at the
43:18 on the altar after the altar is **b**.
Dan 4:30 I **b** the royal palace by my own
Hos 8:14 of Israel have **b** palaces,
8:14 The people of Judah have **b**
10:1 the more altars they **b**.
Amo 7:7 Lord was standing by a wall **b**
Zec 9:3 Tyre **b** itself a fortress.
Mat 7:24 be like a wise person who **b**
7:26 be like a foolish person who **b**
21:33 and **b** a watchtower.
Mar 12:1 and **b** a watchtower.
Luk 4:29 Their city was **b** on a hill with
6:49 obey it is like someone who **b**
7:5 He loves our people and **b** our
21:5 They noted that it was **b** with
Jon 18:18 around a fire they had **b**
Act 7:44 Moses **b** this tent exactly as
7:47 Solomon was the one who **b**
7:48 live in a house **b** by humans,
1Co 3:14 what a person has **b** survives,
Eph 2:20 You are **b** on the foundation of
2:22 are being **b** in the Spirit
Heb 11:7 He obeyed God and **b** a ship to
11:10 that God had designed and **b**,
1Pe 2:5 a spiritual house that is being **b**
3:20 patiently while Noah **b** the ship.

Bukki (5)

Num 34:22 **B**, son of Jogli, the leader of
1Ch 6:5 Abishua was the father of **B**.
6:5 **B** was the father of Uzzi.
6:51 Abishua's son was **B**.
Ezr 7:4 who was the son of **B**,

Bukkiah (2)

1Ch 25:4 the sons of Heman were **B**,
25:13 The sixth chose **B**,

Bukki's (1)

1Ch 6:51 **B** son was Uzzi. Uzzi's son was

Bul (1)

1Ki 6:38 In the month of **B** (the eighth

bulging (1)

Isa 30:13 like a high wall with a **b** crack,

bull (119)

Exo 21:28 "Whenever a **b** gores a man or
21:28 the **b** must be stoned to death,
21:29 But if the **b** has had the habit of
21:29 then the **b** must be stoned and
21:31 If the **b** gores someone's son or
21:32 If the **b** gores a male or female
21:32 and the **b** must be stoned.
21:33 one and doesn't cover it and a **b**
21:35 "Whenever one person's **b** kills
21:35 bull kills another person's **b**,
21:35 they must sell the live **b** and
21:35 They must divide the dead **b**,
21:36 if it was known that the **b** had
21:36 must make up for the loss — **b**
21:36 up for the loss — bull for **b** —
21:36 then the dead **b** will be his."
Exo 22:1 "Whenever someone steals a **b**
22:1 head of cattle to replace the **b**
22:4 whether it's a **b**, donkey,
22:9 over the ownership of a **b**,
22:10 a donkey, a **b**, a sheep,
29:1 "Take a young **b** that has no
29:3 basket along with the young **b**
29:10 "Then bring the young **b** to the
29:11 Slaughter the **b** in the LORD's
29:36 Each day sacrifice a young **b**
Lev 1:5 Then slaughter the **b** in the
4:3 he must bring a **b** that has no
4:4 He must bring the **b** into the
4:4 He will then slaughter the **b** in
4:8 all of the fat from the **b** that is
4:10 were removed from the **b** used
4:11 will take the entire **b** (the skin,
4:14 must sacrifice a **b** as
4:20 the same thing with this **b** that
4:20 that he did with the **b** used as
4:21 Then he will take the **b** outside
4:21 same way he burned the first **b**.
8:2 the **b** that will be the offering for
8:14 He brought the **b** that was the
8:17 He burned the rest of the **b**,
9:4 a **b** and a ram as a fellowship
9:18 He slaughtered the **b** and the
9:19 However, the fat from the **b** and
16:3 He must take a **b** as an offering
16:6 "Aaron must sacrifice the **b** as
16:11 "Aaron will bring the **b**.
16:18 some of the blood from the **b**
16:27 He must take the **b** and the
17:3 Israelite who slaughters a **b**,
22:23 You may use a **b** or a sheep
23:18 defects, one **b**, and two rams.
27:26 Whether it is a **b** or a sheep,
Num 7:15 a young **b**, a ram, and a
7:21 a young **b**, a ram, and a
7:27 a young **b**, a ram, and a
7:33 a young **b**, a ram, and a
7:39 a young **b**, a ram, and a
7:45 a young **b**, a ram, and a
7:51 a young **b**, a ram, and a
7:57 a young **b**, a ram, and a
7:63 a young **b**, a ram, and a
7:69 a young **b**, a ram, and a
7:75 a young **b**, a ram, and a
7:81 a young **b**, a ram, and a
8:8 Next, they must take a young **b**
8:8 must take a second young **b** as
15:8 you sacrifice a young **b** as
15:9 Offer with the young **b** a grain
15:11 Do this for each **b**,
15:24 must sacrifice a young **b** as
23:2 and the two of them offered a **b**
23:4 and I offered a **b** and a ram on
23:14 He offered a **b** and a ram on
23:22 has the strength of a wild **b**.
23:30 and he offered a **b** and a ram on
24:8 has the strength of a wild **b**.
28:12 With each **b** there will be a
28:14 that goes with each **b** will
28:20 Bring 24 cups for each **b**,
28:28 Bring 24 cups for each **b**,
29:2 bring one young **b**,
29:3 Bring 24 cups for each **b**,
29:8 bring one young **b**,
29:9 Bring 24 cups for each **b**,
29:36 LORD, bring one **b**, one ram,
29:37 and wine offerings for the **b**,
Dtr 33:17 be as majestic as a firstborn **b**.
Jdg 6:25 "Take a **b** from your father's
6:25 a **b** that is seven years old.
6:26 Take this second **b** and
6:28 They saw that the second **b**
1Sm 1:24 also brought a three-year-old **b**,
1:25 the parents butchered the **b**
2Sm 6:13 David sacrificed a **b** and a
1Ki 18:23 I'll do the same with the other **b**.
18:25 "Choose one **b** for yourselves.
18:26 They took the **b** he gave them,
18:33 the wood, cut up the **b**,
2Ch 13:9 Anyone who has a young **b**
Psa 50:9 young **b** from your household
69:31 than ⌊sacrificing⌋ an ox or a **b**

Psa 92:10 make me as strong as a wild **b**,
106:20 statue of a **b** that eats grass.
Isa 66:3 Whoever kills a **b** is like
Eze 1:10 each one had the face of a **b**.
43:19 Give a young **b** to the priests
43:21 Then take a young **b** as an
43:22 as you did with the young **b**.
43:23 offer a young **b** and a ram that
43:25 sacrifice a goat, a young **b**,
45:18 take a young **b** that has no
45:22 common people a young **b** as
45:24 a half-bushel for each young **b**
46:6 offering must be one young **b**,
46:7 With each young **b** and each
46:11 be brought with each young **b**,
Hos 4:16 of Israel are as stubborn as a **b**.
Rev 4:7 the second was like a young **b**,

bull's (12)

Exo 21:28 The **b** owner is free from any
21:30 the **b** owner may save his life
29:12 Take some of the **b** blood, and
29:14 But burn the **b** meat, skin,
Lev 4:4 place his hand on the **b** head.
4:5 will take some of the **b** blood
4:7 pour the rest of the **b** blood at
4:15 place their hands on the **b** head
4:16 bring some of the **b** blood into
16:14 will take some of the **b** blood
16:15 as he did with the **b** blood
Eze 43:20 Take some of the **b** blood, and

bulls (83)

Gen 32:15 40 cows and 10 **b**,
Exo 24:5 and they sacrificed **b** as burnt
Lev 7:23 Never eat any fat from **b**,
Num 7:17 and two **b**, five rams, five male
7:23 and two **b**, five rams, five male
7:29 and two **b**, five rams, five male
7:35 and two **b**, five rams, five male
7:41 and two **b**, five rams, five male
7:47 and two **b**, five rams, five male
7:53 and two **b**, five rams, five male
7:59 and two **b**, five rams, five male
7:65 and two **b**, five rams, five male
7:71 and two **b**, five rams, five male
7:77 and two **b**, five rams, five male
7:83 and two **b**, five rams, five male
7:87 burnt offerings was 12 young **b**,
7:88 fellowship offerings was 24 **b**,
8:12 on the heads of the young **b**.
23:1 and prepare seven **b** and seven
23:29 and prepare seven **b** and seven
28:11 a burnt offering of two young **b**,
28:19 a burnt offering of two young **b**,
28:27 to the LORD — two young **b**,
29:13 bring 13 young **b**, 2 rams,
29:14 24 cups for each of the 13 **b**,
29:17 second day bring 12 young **b**,
29:18 wine offerings for each of the **b**,
29:20 "On the third day bring 11 **b**,
29:21 wine offerings for each of the **b**,
29:23 "On the fourth day bring 10 **b**,
29:24 wine offerings for each of the **b**,
29:26 "On the fifth day bring 9 **b**,
29:27 wine offerings for each of the **b**,
29:29 "On the sixth day bring 8 **b**,
29:30 wine offerings for each of the **b**,
29:32 "On the seventh day bring 7 **b**,
29:33 wine offerings for each of the **b**,
1Ki 1:19 fattened calves, **b**, and sheep.
1:25 he went and sacrificed many **b**,
7:25 pool was set on 12 metal **b**.
7:25 Three **b** faced north,
7:44 1 pool, 12 **b** under the pool,
18:23 Give us two **b**. Let the prophets
2Ki 16:17 the bronze **b** that were under
1Ch 15:26 seven **b** and seven rams.
29:21 the LORD: 1,000 **b**, 1,000 rams,
2Ch 4:3 shaped like **b** all around
4:4 pool was set on 12 metal **b**.
4:4 Three **b** faced north,
4:15 1 pool and the 12 **b** under it,
29:21 They brought seven **b**,
29:22 So they slaughtered the **b**,
29:32 by the assembly totaled 70 **b**,
2Ch 29:33 were 600 **b** and 3,000 sheep.
30:24 of Judah provided 1,000 **b**
30:24 The leaders provided 1,000 **b**
35:7 addition, he provided 3,000 **b**.
35:8 300 **b** for Passover sacrifices.
35:9 500 **b** as Passover sacrifices.
35:12 did the same with the **b**.
Ezr 6:9 the God of heaven — young **b**,
6:17 they sacrificed 100 **b**,
7:17 must use this money to buy **b**,
8:35 12 **b** for all Israel, 96 rams,
Job 21:10 Their **b** are fertile when they
42:8 So take seven young **b** and
Psa 22:12 Many **b** have surrounded me.
22:12 Strong **b** from Bashan have
50:13 Do I eat the meat of **b** or drink
51:19 Young **b** will be offered on your
68:30 the herd of **b** with the calves of
Isa 1:11 not pleased with the blood of **b**,
34:7 young **b** along with rams.
Jer 50:27 Kill all their young **b**.
52:20 and the 12 bronze **b** under the
Eze 39:18 **b** and all the best animals of
45:23 seven young **b** that have no
Hos 12:11 They sacrifice **b** in Gilgal.
Mat 22:4 My **b** and fattened calves have
Act 14:13 priest of the god Zeus brought **b**
Heb 9:12 not the blood of goats and **b**,
9:13 The blood of goats and **b** and
10:4 (The blood of **b** and goats

bum (2)

Pro 6:6 Consider the ant, you lazy **b**.
6:9 will you lie there, you lazy **b**?

Bunah (1)

1Ch 2:25 firstborn), then **B**, Oren, Ozem,

bunch (4)

Num 13:23 cut off a branch with only one **b**
13:24 called that valley Eshcol [**B**
13:24 of Grapes] because of the **b**
32:14 You're a **b** of sinners trying to

bunches (4)

1Sm 25:18 roasted grain, 100 **b** of raisins,
30:12 of fig cake and two **b** of raisins.
2Sm 16:1 of bread, 100 **b** of raisins,
Rev 14:18 and gather the **b** of grapes from

bundle (7)

Gen 37:7 bundles gathered around my **b**
Lev 23:10 bring the priest a **b** of the first
23:12 On the day you present the **b**,
23:15 (the day you bring the **b**
1Sm 25:29 your life is wrapped in the **b** of
Sos 7:2 Your waist is a **b** of wheat
Act 28:3 Paul gathered a **b** of

bundles (11)

Gen 37:7 We were tying grain into **b** out
37:7 your **b** gathered around my
Dtr 24:19 bring in one of the **b** of wheat,
Rut 2:7 I will only gather among the **b**
2:15 gather grain even among the **b**.
2:16 pull some grain out of the **b**
Job 24:10 yet they carry **b** of grain.
Psa 126:6 carrying his **b** of grain.
129:7 the arms of those who gather **b**.
Isa 17:5 time will be like harvesting **b**
Mat 13:30 weeds first and tie them in **b**

Bunni (3)

Neh 9:4 Shebaniah, **B**, Sherebiah, Bani,
10:15 **B**, Azgad, Bebai,
11:15 who was the son of **B**.

burden (41)

Gen 49:15 he will bend his back to the **b**
Num 11:11 you that you put the **b**
Dtr 28:48 The LORD will put a heavy **b**
2Sm 13:25 we'll be a **b** to you."
13:33 You shouldn't **b** your heart with
15:33 you will only be a **b** to me.
19:35 I now become a **b** to you,
1Ki 12:4 father made us carry a heavy **b**.
1Ki 12:4 work and lighten the heavy **b**
12:9 to lighten the **b** my father put
12:11 my father put a heavy **b** on you,
12:14 my father made your **b** heavy,
2Ch 10:4 father made us carry a heavy **b**.
10:4 work and lighten the heavy **b**
10:9 to lighten the **b** my father put
10:11 my father put a heavy **b** on you,
10:14 my father made your **b** heavy,
Job 7:20 I've become a **b** even to myself.
Psa 81:6 "I removed the **b** from his
Pro 15:10 Discipline is a terrible ⌊**b**⌋ to
Ecc 1:13 with a terrible **b** that God has
3:10 down with a **b** that God has
Isa 1:14 They've become a **b** to me,
10:27 At that time their **b** will be
14:25 and its **b** will be removed from
30:27 His **b** is heavy. His lips are
43:23 I did not **b** you by requiring
47:6 a heavy **b** on old people.
53:11 He will carry their sins as a **b**.
Jer 23:33 say to them, 'You are the **b**!
Lam 1:14 acts are a heavy **b** for me.
Zep 3:18 They bear a **b** of disgrace.
Mat 11:30 yoke is easy and my **b** is light."
Luk 11:46 You **b** people with loads that
Act 15:10 You're putting a **b** on the
15:10 a **b** neither our ancestors nor
2Co 11:9 myself from being a financial **b**
12:16 that I haven't been a **b** to you.
1Th 2:9 News of God without being a **b**
2Th 3:8 and day in order not to be a **b**
Rev 2:24 things of Satan — I won't **b** you

burdened (5)

Pro 28:17 A person **b** with the guilt of
Isa 43:24 Rather, you **b** me with your
Jer 23:33 revelation has the LORD **b** you
1Ti 5:16 In this way the church is not **b**
2Ti 3:6 women who are **b**

burdens (11)

Psa 55:22 Turn your **b** over to the LORD,
66:11 You have laid **b** on our backs.
68:19 who daily carries our **b** for us.
Isa 9:4 will break the yoke that **b** them,
46:1 The gods that you carry are **b**,
Lam 3:27 to endure **b** when they're
3:28 has laid these **b** on them.
Hos 8:10 suffer for a while under the **b**
Act 15:28 place any additional **b** on you.
Rom 11:10 Let them carry back-breaking **b**
Gal 6:2 Help carry each other's **b**.

burial (10)

Ecc 6:3 even get an honorable **b** ⌊after
8:10 people given an ⌊honorable⌋ **b**.
Jer 22:19 He will receive a donkey's **b**.
26:23 his body into the **b** ground
Eze 39:11 I will give Gog a **b** place in
Mat 27:7 field for the **b** of strangers.
Jon 19:40 was the Jewish custom for **b**.
Act 5:9 will carry you outside for **b**."
7:16 were taken to Shechem for **b**
9:37 Her body was prepared for **b**

buried (114)

Gen 15:15 will die in peace and be **b** at
23:19 After this, Abraham **b** his wife
25:9 His sons Isaac and Ishmael **b**
25:10 There Abraham was **b** with his
35:4 Jacob **b** these things under the
35:8 Deborah died and was **b** under
35:19 Rachel died and was **b** on the
35:29 His sons Esau and Jacob **b**
48:7 So I **b** her there on the way to
49:31 and his wife Sarah are **b** there.
49:31 his wife Rebekah are **b** there.
49:31 I also **b** Leah there.
50:13 him back to Canaan and **b** him
50:14 After Joseph had **b** his father,
Num 11:34 ⌊Meat⌋ because there they **b**
20:1 Miriam died and was **b** there.
Dtr 10:6 Aaron died there and was **b**,
34:6 He was **b** in a valley in Moab,
Jos 7:21 You will find them **b** inside my

Jos 7:22 The loot was **b** inside with the
24:30 He was **b** on his own land at
24:32 were **b** at Shechem.
24:33 He was **b** on the hill that had
Jdg 2:9 He was **b** at Timnath Heres
8:32 He was **b** in the tomb of his
10:2 Tola died and was **b** in Shamir.
10:5 Jair died and was **b** in Kamon.
12:7 of Gilead died and was **b**
12:10 he was **b** in Bethlehem.
12:12 When Elon died, he was **b** in
12:15 he was **b** in Pirathon,
16:31 They took Samson and **b** him
Rut 1:17 and I will be **b** there with you.
1Sm 25:1 They **b** him at his home in
28:3 had mourned for him and **b** him
31:13 They took the bones and **b**
2Sm 2:4 were the ones who **b** Saul."
2:32 They took Asahel and **b** him in
3:32 They **b** Abner in Hebron.
4:12 took Ishbosheth's head and **b**
17:23 and was **b** in his father's tomb.
21:14 Then they **b** the bones of Saul
1Ki 2:10 with his ancestors and was **b**
2:34 and **b** him at his home in the
11:43 with his ancestors and was **b**
13:31 After he had **b** the man of God,
13:31 where the man of God was **b**.
14:13 who will be ⌊properly⌋ **b**.
14:18 All Israel **b** him and mourned
14:31 with his ancestors and was **b**
15:8 with his ancestors and was **b**
15:24 He was **b** with his ancestors in
16:6 ancestors and was **b** in Tirzah.
16:28 and was **b** in Samaria.
22:37 was brought to Samaria to be **b**.
22:50 with his ancestors and was **b**
2Ki 8:24 with his ancestors and was **b**
9:28 They **b** him in a tomb with his
10:35 and was **b** in Samaria.
12:21 They **b** him with his ancestors
13:9 and was **b** in Samaria.
13:13 with his ancestors and was **b**
13:20 Elisha died and was **b**.
14:16 with his ancestors and was **b**
14:20 and he was **b** in Jerusalem,
15:7 with his ancestors and was **b**
15:38 with his ancestors and was **b**
16:20 with his ancestors and was **b**
21:18 He was **b** in the garden of his
21:26 He was **b** in his tomb in the
23:30 They **b** Josiah in his tomb.
1Ch 10:12 They **b** the bones under the
2Ch 9:31 with his ancestors and was **b**
12:16 with his ancestors and was **b**
14:1 with his ancestors and was **b**
16:14 They **b** him in the tomb that he
21:1 with his ancestors and was **b**
21:20 He was **b** in the City of David
22:9 Then they **b** him.
24:16 He was **b** in the City of David
24:25 they **b** him in the City of David,
25:28 him back by horse and **b** him
26:23 with his ancestors and was **b**
27:9 and they **b** him in the City of
28:27 with his ancestors and was **b**
32:33 He was **b** in the upper tombs of
33:20 They **b** him in his own palace.
35:24 He died and was **b** in the
Neh 2:3 where my ancestors are **b**,
2:5 city where my ancestors are **b**,
Job 3:16 I would be **b** like a stillborn
3:21 for it more than for **b** treasure?
27:15 who survive him will be **b** by
Psa 40:10 I have not **b** your righteousness
106:17 It **b** Abiram's followers.
Isa 14:18 have been **b** with honor,
Jer 8:2 bones will not be gathered or **b**,
13:5 So I went and **b** it by the
13:7 the belt from where I had **b** it.
20:6 You will be **b** there together
25:33 be mourned, taken away, or **b**.
43:10 over these stones that I **b**,
Eze 39:11 his whole army will be **b** there.
39:15 grave diggers have **b** that bone
Mat 13:44 of heaven is like a treasure **b**
13:44 discovered it, he **b** it again.
14:12 came for the body and **b** it.
Luk 16:22 rich man also died and was **b**.
23:53 which no one had ever been **b**.
Act 2:29 ancestor David died and was **b**
5:6 carried him outside, and **b** him.
5:9 Those who **b** your husband are
5:10 her outside and **b** her next
8:2 Devout men **b** Stephen as they

burn (174)

Exo 21:25 a **b** for a burn, a bruise for a
21:25 a burn for a **b**, a bruise for a
29:13 and **b** them on the altar.
29:14 But **b** the bull's meat,
29:18 Then **b** the whole ram on the
29:25 and **b** them on the altar on top
29:34 left over until morning, **b** it up.
30:7 "Aaron must **b** sweet-smelling
30:8 he must **b** incense.
30:8 offering must **b** constantly
30:9 "Never **b** any unauthorized
30:20 altar to serve as priests and **b**
Lev 1:9 Then the priest will **b** all of it
1:13 Then the priest will **b** all of it
1:15 He will break its neck and **b**
2:2 The priest will **b** it on the altar
2:9 part of the grain offering and **b**
2:11 Never **b** yeast or honey as an
2:16 The priest will **b** the flour,
3:11 Then the priest will **b** the
3:16 Then the priest will **b** them on
4:12 He will **b** it there on a wood fire.
4:19 He will remove all the fat and **b**
4:21 outside the camp and will **b**
4:26 He will **b** all the fat on the altar
4:31 The priest will **b** it on the altar
4:35 Then the priest will **b** it on the
5:12 He will **b** it as a reminder on
6:12 The priest will **b** wood on it
6:12 burnt offering on the fire and **b**
6:15 He will **b** it on the altar as a
7:5 The priest will **b** them on the
7:31 "The priest will **b** the fat on the
8:32 You must **b** any meat or bread
13:24 "If anyone has a **b** on his skin
13:24 the raw flesh of the **b** turns into
13:25 has developed in the **b**.
13:28 is only a sore caused by the **b**.
13:28 it is a scar caused by the **b**.
13:52 He must **b** the piece of clothing
13:57 you must **b** the clothing or the
16:25 He will **b** the fat of the offering
17:6 He will **b** the fat as a soothing
19:6 On the third day **b** whatever is
Num 5:26 as a memorial portion and **b**
11:1 LORD began to **b** among them.
16:40 can come near to **b** incense
18:17 and **b** the fat as an offering by
31:23 anything that won't **b** — must
31:23 Whatever might **b** must ⌊only⌋
Dtr 7:5 Asherah, and **b** their idols.
7:25 **B** their idols. Don't ever long for
12:3 **b** their poles dedicated to the
12:31 They even **b** their sons and
13:16 Then **b** their city and all their
32:22 has started a fire that will **b**
33:10 They **b** incense for you to
Jos 11:6 You must **b** their chariots."
11:13 Israel did not **b** cities built on
Jdg 9:15 out of the thornbush and **b** up
9:20 of Abimelech and **b** up citizens
9:20 Millo and **b** up Abimelech."
9:52 of the tower to **b** it down.
12:1 Now we're going to **b** your
14:15 If you don't, we'll **b** you and
1Sm 2:28 on my altar, to **b** incense,
2Sm 23:7 Fire will **b** them up completely
1Ki 12:33 went to his altar in Bethel to **b**
14:10 I will **b** down Jeroboam's
14:10 It will **b** like manure until it is
22:44 and **b** incense at these
2Ki 1:10 from heaven and **b** up you
1:12 from heaven and **b** up you
12:3 and **b** incense at these
14:4 and **b** incense at these
15:4 and **b** incense at these
15:35 and **b** incense at these
16:15 "On this great altar you must **b**
23:16 out of the tombs and **b** them
2Ch 2:4 I want to dedicate it to him, **b**
4:20 of pure gold (to **b** as directed
13:11 lamp stand **b** every evening.
26:16 the LORD's temple to **b** incense
26:18 you have no right to **b** incense
29:7 and didn't **b** incense or
29:11 his servants, and **b** sacrifices."
Neh 10:34 wood to our God's temple to **b**
Job 20:26 fire that no one fans will **b** him.
Psa 21:9 you will make them ⌊**b**⌋ like a
79:5 your fury continue to **b** like fire?
89:46 anger continue to **b** like fire?
102:3 My bones **b** like hot coals.
Isa 1:31 Both of them will **b** together,
5:24 As flames **b** up straw and dry
10:17 He will **b** up and devour the
33:11 be a fire which will **b** you up.
40:16 are not enough to **b** an offering.
44:15 become ⌊fuel⌋ for people to **b**.
44:16 Half of the wood they **b** in the
57:5 You **b** with lust under oak trees
Jer 4:4 It will **b**, and no one will be
5:14 My words will **b** them up.
7:9 **b** incense as an offering to
7:20 My anger and fury will **b** and
7:31 Hinnom in order to **b** their sons
15:14 has started a fire. It will **b** you."
17:4 of my anger. It will **b** forever.
17:27 The fire will **b** down the
18:15 They **b** incense as an offering
19:5 sites to **b** their children as
21:10 and he will **b** it down.'
21:12 will break out and **b** like fire.
21:14 and it will **b** up everything
32:29 this city on fire, and **b** it down.
32:29 They will **b** down the houses
32:29 up to the roofs to **b** incense
33:18 to **b** grain offerings,
34:2 and he will **b** it down.
34:5 People will **b** ⌊funeral⌋ fires for
34:22 it, capture it, and **b** it down.
36:25 the king not to **b** the scroll,
37:8 city, capture it, and **b** it down.
37:10 get up and **b** down this city.'"
38:18 They will **b** it down,
43:12 He will **b** down the temples
43:13 in Egypt and **b** down
44:3 They went to **b** incense and
44:6 poured out and continued to **b**
44:17 We will **b** incense to the queen
44:25 We will **b** incense to the queen
48:45 It will **b** the foreheads of the
49:27 **b** down Benhadad's palaces."
50:32 that will **b** up everything around
Eze 5:2 When the blockade is over, **b**
5:4 them in a fire and **b** them up.
15:7 another fire will **b** them.
16:41 They will **b** your houses and
20:47 It will **b** the whole land from the
23:25 and **b** down whatever is
23:47 daughters and **b** their homes.
24:10 and let the bones **b**.
24:11 and its tarnish will **b** off.
28:18 So I set fire to you to **b** you up.
39:9 set fire to weapons and **b** them.
39:9 They will **b** small and large
39:9 They will **b** them for seven
43:21 and **b** it in the place appointed
Hos 4:13 and they **b** incense on the hills
8:14 and **b** down their palaces."
Amo 1:4 house of Hazael and **b** down
1:7 Gaza and **b** down its palaces.
1:10 of Tyre and **b** down its palaces.
1:12 a fire on Teman and **b** down
1:14 Rabbah and **b** down its palaces
2:2 I will send a fire on Moab and **b**
2:5 a fire on Judah and **b** down
4:5 **B** bread as a thank offering.
5:6 house of Joseph and **b** it down.
Hab 1:16 to their nets and **b** incense
Zec 9:4 the sea and **b** the city down.
11:1 be able to **b** down your cedars.

Zec 12:6 They will **b** up all the
Mal 4:1 It will **b** like a furnace.
4:1 The day that is coming will **b**
Mat 3:12 but he will **b** the husks in a fire
Luk 1:9 the Lord's temple to **b** incense.
3:17 but he will **b** the husks in a fire
9:54 fire from heaven to **b** them up?"
Rom 1:27 relations with women and **b**
1Co 7:9 than to **b** ⌊with sexual desire⌋.
2Pe 3:10 makes up the universe will **b**
3:12 up the universe will **b** and melt.
Rev 16:8 allowed to **b** people with fire.
17:16 They will eat her flesh and **b**

burned (163)

Gen 38:24 "Bring her out to be **b**."
Exo 12:10 in the morning must be **b** up.
15:7 It **b** them up like straw.
32:20 **b** it, ground it into powder,
40:27 He **b** sweet-smelling incense
Lev 4:21 will burn it the same way he **b**
4:26 of the fellowship offering is **b**.
6:22 It must be completely **b**.
6:23 a priest must be completely **b**.
6:30 with the LORD. It must be **b**."
7:17 from the sacrifice must be **b**.
7:19 It must be **b**. Anyone who is
8:16 and he **b** them on the altar.
8:17 He **b** the rest of the bull,
8:20 Moses **b** the head with the
8:21 Then Moses **b** the whole ram
8:28 from their hands and **b** them
9:10 On the altar he **b** the fat,
9:11 He **b** the meat and the skin
9:13 He **b** it on the altar.
9:17 He took a handful of grain and **b**
9:20 Aaron **b** them all on the altar.
10:2 from the LORD and **b** them,
10:15 and the fat that is to be **b** and
10:16 it had already been **b**.
13:55 It must be **b**, whether the area
16:27 from the animals must be **b**.
20:14 and the two women must be **b**.
21:9 her father. She must be **b**.
Num 11:3 the LORD **b** among them there.
16:39 those who had been **b** to death.
18:9 which is not **b** belongs
19:5 will be **b** while he watches.
19:8 The person who **b** the calf
19:17 from the red cow that was **b** as
24:22 But it is destined to be **b**,
31:10 They **b** all the cities where the
Dtr 9:21 sinful calf you made and **b** it.
Jos 6:24 Then Israel **b** the city and
7:15 must be **b** because he has
7:25 Then they **b** the bodies and
8:28 So Joshua **b** Ai and made it a
11:9 horses and **b** their chariots,
11:11 Joshua also **b** Hazor.
11:13 an exception and **b** Hazor.
Jdg 6:21 flared up from the rock and **b**
15:6 So the Philistines **b** Samson's
15:14 his arms became like strings **b**
18:27 with swords, and **b** their city.
20:48 They also **b** down every city
1Sm 2:15 before the people **b** the fat,
2:16 "First let the fat be **b**,
2:28 people of Israel **b** on the altar.
30:1 had attacked Ziklag and **b** it.
30:3 it had been **b** down,
30:14 and we **b** down Ziklag."
31:12 Jabesh and **b** the bodies there.
2Sm 12:5 David **b** with anger against the
1Ki 3:3 he still sacrificed and **b**
9:16 captured Gezer, **b** it down,
11:8 foreign wives who **b** incense
13:2 bones will be **b** on you."
15:13 Asa cut the statue down and **b**
16:18 in the royal palace and **b** down
2Ki 1:10 fire came from heaven and **b** up
1:12 fire came from heaven and **b** up
1:14 come from heaven and **b** up
10:26 of the temple of Baal and **b** it.
16:4 He offered sacrifices and **b**
17:31 The people from Sepharvaim **b**
21:6 He **b** his son as a sacrifice,
2Ki 23:4 Josiah **b** the utensils outside
23:6 He **b** it in the Kidron Valley,
23:11 He also **b** the chariots of the
23:15 They **b** the worship site,
23:20 altars and then **b** human bones
25:9 He **b** down the LORD's temple,
25:9 Every important building was **b**
1Ch 14:12 ordered that the gods be **b**.
2Ch 15:16 and **b** it in the Kidron Valley.
16:14 And they **b** a bonfire in his
19:3 You've **b** the Asherah poles in
25:14 and **b** sacrifices to them.
28:3 He **b** sacrifices in the valley of
28:4 He offered sacrifices and **b**
33:6 He **b** his son as a sacrifice in
34:5 He **b** the bones of the priests
36:19 They **b** God's temple,
36:19 **b** down all its palaces,
Neh 2:3 is in ruins and its gates are **b**
2:13 where its gates had been **b**.
2:17 and its gates are **b** down.
4:2 **b** as these stones are,
Est 1:12 and his rage **b** inside him.
Job 1:16 and completely **b** your flocks
22:20 and a fire has **b** up what ⌊little⌋
28:5 decays as if ⌊it were **b**⌋ by fire.
Psa 39:3 My heart **b** like a fire flaring up
74:7 They **b** your holy place to the
74:8 They **b** every meeting place of
78:21 His fire **b** against Jacob and
80:16 vine has been cut down and **b**.
106:18 Flames **b** up wicked people.
106:40 The LORD **b** with anger
Isa 1:7 Your cities are **b** down.
3:14 "You have **b** down the
6:13 the land will be **b** again.
9:5 rolled in blood will be **b** as fuel
24:6 who live on the earth are **b** up,
42:25 It **b** them, but they did not take
43:2 through fire, you will not be **b**,
44:19 "I **b** half of the wood in the fire.
64:11 has been **b** to the ground.
Jer 1:16 **b** incense to other gods,
2:15 The cities have been **b** down,
19:13 This is because people **b**
29:22 the king of Babylon **b** to death.
36:23 until the whole scroll was **b** up.
36:27 After the king **b** up the scroll
36:28 that King Jehoiakim of Judah **b**.
36:29 LORD says: You **b** this scroll,
36:32 King Jehoiakim of Judah had **b**.
38:17 and this city will not be **b**.
38:23 and this city will be **b** down."
39:8 The Babylonians **b** down the
44:19 added, "When we **b** incense
44:21 remember that you **b** incense
44:23 You **b** incense as offerings to
49:2 Its villages will be **b** down.
51:32 The enemy has **b** its marshes,
52:13 He **b** down the LORD's temple,
52:13 Every important building was **b**
Lam 2:3 He **b** like a raging fire in ⌊the
4:11 that even **b** its foundations.
Eze 15:5 the fire has **b** and charred it?
19:12 They withered and were **b**.
43:15 sacrifices were **b** was 7 feet
Dan 3:27 their clothes weren't **b**,
Hos 2:13 all the times she **b** incense as
11:2 and they **b** incense to idols.
Joe 1:19 Fire has **b** up the open
1:19 Flames have **b** up all the trees
1:20 Fire has **b** up the open
Amo 7:4 up the ocean and **b** up the land.
Oba 1:18 They will be **b** and destroyed.
Mic 1:7 for being a prostitute will be **b**.
Nah 1:10 They will be completely **b** up
Mat 13:30 and tie them in bundles to be **b**.
13:40 as weeds are gathered and **b**,
22:7 murderers, and **b** their city.
Jon 15:6 thrown into a fire, and **b**.
Act 19:19 their books and **b** them
1Co 3:15 If his work is **b** up,
13:3 and give up my body to be **b**.
Heb 6:8 In the end it will be **b**.
13:11 those animals were **b** outside
2Pe 3:7 earth are designated to be **b**.
Rev 8:7 One-third of the earth was **b** up,
8:7 one-third of the trees was **b** up,
8:7 and all the green grass was **b**
16:9 They were severely **b**.
18:8 She will be **b** up in a fire,
20:9 from heaven and **b** them up.

burner (12)

Lev 10:1 Abihu each took an incense **b**
16:12 He will take an incense **b** full
Num 16:17 man will take his incense **b**
16:18 each man took his incense **b**,
16:46 "Take your incense **b**,
16:47 Aaron took his incense **b**,
16:47 put incense on the incense **b**
2Ch 26:19 Uzziah, who held an incense **b**
Eze 8:11 them was holding an incense **b**
Heb 9:4 It contained the gold incense **b**
Rev 8:3 came with a gold incense **b**
8:5 The angel took the incense **b**,

burners (18)

Exo 25:38 The tongs and incense **b** must
27:3 bowls, forks, and incense **b**.
37:23 and the incense **b** out of pure
38:3 bowls, forks, and incense **b**.
Num 16:6 this tomorrow: Take incense **b**,
16:17 will offer all 250 incense **b**
16:17 Aaron offer your incense **b**."
16:37 to take the incense **b** out of the
16:37 incense **b** have become holy.
16:38 The incense **b** of these men
16:39 incense **b** which had been
16:39 The incense **b** were then
1Ki 7:50 incense **b** of pure gold,
2Ki 25:15 guard took all of the incense **b**
2Ch 4:22 incense **b** of pure gold,
Jer 52:19 pans, incense **b**, bowls, pots,
Eze 6:4 and your incense **b** will be
6:6 Your incense **b** will be cut

burning (115)

Gen 19:24 Then the LORD made **b** sulfur
22:6 Abraham carried the **b** coals
22:7 Isaac asked, "We have the **b**
Exo 3:2 was on fire, it was not **b** up.
3:3 "Why isn't this bush **b** up?
11:8 **B** with anger, Moses left
15:7 You sent out your **b** anger.
30:1 of acacia wood for **b** incense.
37:25 of acacia wood for **b** incense.
Lev 1:8 top of the wood **b** on the altar.
1:12 fat on the wood **b** on the altar.
1:17 will lay the bird on the wood **b**
3:5 burnt offering on the **b** wood.
6:9 while the altar fire is kept **b**.
6:12 The fire must always be **b** on
6:13 The fire must always be **b** on
10:1 incense burner and put **b** coals
16:12 burner full of **b** coals from
18:21 god Molech ⌊by **b** them alive⌋.
Num 16:7 and put **b** coals and incense in
16:18 put **b** coals and incense in it,
16:46 put **b** coals from the altar and
19:6 and throw them onto the **b** cow.
Dtr 9:15 while it was still **b** with fire.
18:10 or daughters by **b** them alive,
29:20 because the LORD's **b** anger
33:16 the one who was in the **b** bush.
Jos 7:26 LORD withdrew his **b** anger.
1Sm 28:18 unleash his **b** anger on Amalek.
2Sm 14:7 the ⌊one⌋ **b** coal that is
2Ki 16:3 his son by **b** him alive.
17:17 and daughters by **b** them alive.
18:4 Israelites had been **b** incense
22:17 Therefore, my **b** anger directed
23:10 sons or daughters by **b** them
23:15 crushing it to powder and **b** the
23:26 **b** anger from Judah.
2Ch 26:18 the holy task of **b** incense.
28:3 his son by **b** him alive,
29:10 may turn his **b** anger away from
30:8 and he will turn his **b** anger
Ezr 10:14 our God's **b** anger has turned
Job 20:23 ⌊God⌋ throws his **b** anger at
Psa 2:5 In his **b** anger he terrifies them

Psa 11:6 He rains down fire and **b** sulfur
38:7 insides are filled with **b** pain,
58:9 pot is heated by **b** twigs.
69:24 Let your **b** anger catch up with
78:49 He sent his **b** anger,
85:3 You turned away from your **b**
88:16 Your **b** anger has swept over
118:12 like **b** thornbushes.
119:53 I am **b** with anger because of
140:10 Let **b** coals fall on them.
Pro 6:27 his lap without **b** his clothes?
6:28 coals without **b** his feet?
16:27 and his speech is like a **b** fire.
26:21 ⌊As⌋ charcoal fuels **b** coals
Ecc 7:6 the crackling of thorns **b** under
Isa 4:4 of judgment and a spirit of **b**.
6:6 In his hand was a **b** coal that
13:8 Their faces will be **b** red.
26:11 Your **b** anger will destroy your
30:27 His anger is **b**. His burden is
30:33 piled high with plenty of **b** logs.
30:33 will be like a flood of **b** sulfur,
34:9 soil will be turned to **b** sulfur.
42:25 So he poured out his **b** anger
49:10 nor will the sun or the **b**,
66:15 pay them back with his **b** anger
Jer 4:8 and cry because the LORD's **b**
4:26 of the LORD and his **b** anger.
11:17 him furious by **b** incense as
12:13 because of the **b** anger
19:4 by **b** incense as
20:9 inside me like a **b** fire shut up
25:37 by the LORD's **b** anger.
30:24 The LORD's **b** anger will not
44:5 and wouldn't stop **b** incense as
44:8 make me angry by **b** incense
44:15 that their wives were **b** incense
44:18 But since we stopped **b**
49:37 bring disaster with my **b** anger,
51:45 Run from the **b** anger of the
Lam 2:3 In his **b** anger he cut off all of
4:11 He unleashed his **b** anger.
5:10 from the **b** heat of starvation.
Eze 1:13 creatures looked like **b** coals
10:2 fill your hands with **b** coals.
10:6 to take **b** coals from between
16:38 penalty in my fury and **b** anger.
20:31 as sacrifices by **b** them alive.
23:25 I will direct my **b** anger against
38:18 I will be filled with **b** anger,
38:22 and **b** sulfur on his troops and
Dan 7:9 and its wheels were **b** fire.
Hos 11:9 I will not act on my **b** anger.
Joe 2:5 like crackling fire **b** up straw,
Amo 4:11 You were like a **b** log snatched
Jnh 3:9 turn from his **b** anger so that
Nah 1:6 Who can oppose his **b** anger?
Zep 2:2 before the LORD's **b** anger
3:8 my rage, my **b** anger, on them.
Zec 3:2 Isn't this man like a **b** log
10:3 "My **b** anger is directed against
12:6 like a **b** torch among freshly
Luk 1:10 while he was **b** incense.
12:35 and have your lamps **b**.
Act 7:30 to him in the flames of a **b** bush
2Pe 2:6 and destroyed them by **b** them
Rev 4:5 Seven flaming torches were **b**
7:16 Neither the sun nor any **b** heat
8:8 like a huge mountain **b**
19:20 into the fiery lake of **b** sulfur.
21:8 in the fiery lake of **b** sulfur.

burns (22)

Exo 22:6 so that it **b** up stacked
Lev 16:28 Whoever **b** them must wash
Job 15:34 and fire **b** up the tents of those
30:30 My body **b** with fever.
31:12 It would be a fire that **b** even in
Psa 46:9 spears in two. He **b** chariots.
83:15 the way fire **b** a forest and
97:3 It **b** his enemies who surround
Pro 31:18 Her lamp **b** late at night.
Isa 5:25 of the LORD **b** hot against his
9:18 Surely wickedness **b** like fire.
9:18 It **b** up briars and thorns.
33:14 through a fire that **b** forever?
Isa 47:14 Fire **b** them. They can't rescue
62:1 and its salvation **b** brightly like
66:3 Whoever **b** incense is like
66:24 The fire that **b** them will not go
Eze 15:4 The fire **b** up both its ends and
Hos 7:6 but in the morning it **b** like a
8:5 My anger **b** against these
Joe 2:3 In front of this army a fire **b**.
Rev 11:5 mouths and **b** up their enemies.

burnt (296)

Gen 8:20 On it he made a **b** offering of
22:2 Sacrifice him there as a **b**
22:3 cut the wood for the **b** offering,
22:6 took the wood for the **b** offering
22:7 but where is the lamb for the **b**
22:8 a lamb for the **b** offering,
22:13 and sacrificed it as a **b** offering
Exo 10:25 and **b** offerings we have
18:12 brought a **b** offering and other
20:24 Sacrifice your **b** offerings and
24:5 and they sacrificed bulls as **b**
29:18 It's a **b** offering, a soothing
29:25 the altar on top of the **b** offering.
29:42 be the daily **b** offering ⌊made⌋
30:9 on this altar or any **b** offerings
30:28 the altar for **b** offerings and all
31:9 the altar for **b** offerings and all
32:6 people sacrificed **b** offerings
35:16 the altar for **b** offerings with its
38:1 He made the altar for **b**
40:6 "Put the altar for **b** offerings in
40:10 Anoint the altar for **b** offerings
40:29 He put the altar for **b** offerings
40:29 He sacrificed **b** offerings and
Lev 1:3 "If you bring a **b** offering from
1:4 The **b** offering will be accepted
1:6 Skin the **b** offering,
1:9 It is a **b** offering, an offering by
1:13 It is a **b** offering, an offering by
1:17 It is a **b** offering, an offering by
3:5 lay them on top of the **b** offering
4:7 of the altar for **b** offerings at
4:10 on the altar for **b** offerings.
4:18 of the altar for **b** offerings at
4:24 animals for **b** offerings.
4:25 horns of the altar for **b**
4:25 of the altar for **b** offerings.
4:29 for **b** offerings are slaughtered.
4:30 horns of the altar for **b**
4:33 animals for **b** offerings.
4:34 horns of the altar for **b**
5:7 the other a **b** offering.
5:10 the second bird as a **b** offering.
6:9 for the **b** offering that stays
6:10 that consumed the **b** offering
6:12 He will lay the **b** offering on the
6:25 the **b** offering is slaughtered.
7:2 the **b** offering is slaughtered.
7:8 The skin of the **b** offering
7:37 instructions for the **b** offering,
8:18 the ram for the **b** offering.
8:21 It was a **b** offering,
8:28 them on top of the **b** offering
9:2 has no defects as a **b** offering.
9:3 without defects) as a **b** offering,
9:7 offering for sin and a **b** offering
9:12 the animal for the **b** offering.
9:13 also gave him the **b** offering,
9:14 them on top of the **b** offering
9:16 he brought forward the **b**
9:17 to the morning **b** offering.
9:22 offering for sin, the **b** offering,
9:24 and consumed the **b** offering
10:19 for sin and their **b** offering
12:6 lamb for a **b** offering
12:8 One will be the **b** offering and
14:13 for sin and the **b** offering.
14:19 he will slaughter the **b** offering.
14:20 The priest will sacrifice the **b**
14:22 sin and the other a **b** offering.
14:31 it as a **b** offering together
15:15 and the other as a **b** offering.
15:30 and the other as a **b** offering.
16:3 sin and a ram as a **b** offering.
16:5 sin and a ram as a **b** offering.
Lev 16:24 out and sacrifice the **b** offering
17:8 make **b** offerings or sacrifices
22:18 foreigners may bring **b**
23:12 has no defects as a **b** offering
23:18 They will be a **b** offering to the
23:37 Bring **b** offerings, other
Num 6:11 the other one as a **b** offering.
6:14 male lamb as a **b** offering,
6:16 for sin and the **b** offering.
7:15 male lamb as a **b** offering;
7:21 male lamb as a **b** offering;
7:27 male lamb as a **b** offering;
7:33 male lamb as a **b** offering;
7:39 male lamb as a **b** offering;
7:45 male lamb as a **b** offering;
7:51 male lamb as a **b** offering;
7:57 male lamb as a **b** offering;
7:63 male lamb as a **b** offering;
7:69 male lamb as a **b** offering;
7:75 male lamb as a **b** offering;
7:81 male lamb as a **b** offering;
7:87 for the **b** offerings was 12
8:12 the other one as a **b** offering
10:10 you sacrifice your **b** offerings
15:3 They may be **b** offerings or any
15:5 sheep or goat for the **b** offering
15:8 a young bull as a **b** offering
15:24 a young bull as a **b** offering,
23:3 "Stay here beside your **b**
23:6 standing beside his **b** offering
23:15 "Stay here beside your **b**
23:17 standing beside his **b** offering
28:3 **b** offering two one-year-old
28:6 This is the daily **b** offering
28:10 This **b** offering is for every day
28:10 addition to the daily **b** offerings
28:11 bring the LORD a **b** offering
28:13 This is a **b** offering,
28:14 This will be the monthly **b**
28:15 In addition to the daily **b**
28:19 a **b** offering of two young bulls,
28:23 to the morning **b** offering.
28:24 addition to the daily **b** offering
28:27 Bring a **b** offering as a soothing
28:31 in addition to the daily **b**
29:2 As a **b** offering, a soothing
29:6 to the monthly **b** offering
29:6 and the daily **b** offerings with
29:8 As a **b** offering, a soothing
29:11 LORD) and the daily **b** offerings
29:13 As a **b** offering, an offering by
29:16 addition to the daily **b** offerings
29:19 addition to the daily **b** offerings
29:22 addition to the daily **b** offerings
29:25 addition to the daily **b** offerings
29:28 addition to the daily **b** offerings
29:31 addition to the daily **b** offerings
29:34 addition to the daily **b** offerings
29:36 As a **b** offering, an offering by
29:38 addition to the daily **b** offerings
29:39 offerings, your **b** offerings,
Dtr 12:6 Bring him your **b** offerings,
12:11 Bring your **b** offerings,
12:13 your **b** offerings wherever you
12:27 the blood of your **b** offerings
13:16 all their goods as a **b** offering
27:6 Sacrifice **b** offerings on it to the
33:10 smell and sacrifice **b** offerings
Jos 8:31 They made **b** offerings to the
22:23 built it for making **b** offerings,
22:26 be for **b** offerings or sacrifices,
22:27 the LORD with our **b** offerings,
22:28 They didn't make it for **b**
22:29 building an altar for **b** offerings,
Jdg 6:26 and sacrifice it as a **b** offering
6:28 been sacrificed as a **b** offering
11:31 I will sacrifice it as a **b**
13:16 But if you make a **b** offering,
13:23 have accepted our **b** offering
20:26 Then they sacrificed **b**
21:4 there and sacrificed **b** offerings
1Sm 2:28 to sacrifice **b** offerings on my
6:14 the cows as a **b** offering
6:15 Shemesh presented **b** offerings
7:9 and sacrificed it as a **b** offering
7:10 was sacrificing the **b** offering,

1Sm 10:8 Then I will come to sacrifice **b**
13:9 "Bring me the animals for the **b**
13:9 So he sacrificed the **b** offering.
13:10 sacrificing the **b** offering,
13:12 into sacrificing the **b** offering."
15:22 as delighted with **b** offerings
2Sm 6:17 David sacrificed **b** offerings
6:18 sacrificing the **b** offerings
24:22 are oxen for the **b** offering,
24:24 my God **b** sacrifices that cost
24:25 there and sacrificed **b** offerings
1Ki 3:4 Solomon sacrificed 1,000 **b**
3:15 He sacrificed **b** offerings and
8:64 He sacrificed the **b** offerings,
9:25 Solomon sacrificed **b** offerings
9:25 He **b** them on the altar that was
10:5 and the **b** offerings that he
18:38 and consumed the **b** offering,
2Ki 3:27 him on the wall as a **b** offering.
5:17 I will not offer any **b** offering or
10:24 offer sacrifices and **b** offerings.
10:25 When the **b** offerings had been
16:13 He sacrificed his **b** offering and
16:15 burn the morning **b** offerings
16:15 the king's **b** offerings and grain
16:15 and the **b** offerings,
16:15 Sprinkle all the blood of the **b**
1Ch 6:49 on the altar for **b** offerings
16:1 They presented **b** offerings and
16:2 finished sacrificing **b** offerings
16:40 ordered to sacrifice **b** offerings
16:40 altar of **b** offerings continually,
21:23 give you oxen for the **b** offering,
21:24 and offer **b** sacrifices that cost
21:26 there and sacrificed **b** offerings
21:26 on the altar for **b** offerings.
21:29 the altar for **b** offerings were at
22:1 Israel's altar for **b** offerings will
23:31 **b** offerings were made
29:21 They sacrificed **b** offerings to
2Ch 1:6 1,000 **b** offerings on it.
2:4 I want to ⌊sacrifice⌋ **b** offerings
4:6 prepared for the **b** offerings
7:1 and consumed the **b** offerings
7:7 He sacrificed the **b** offerings,
8:12 Then Solomon sacrificed **b**
9:4 and the **b** offerings that he
13:11 They sacrifice **b** offerings to
23:18 to sacrifice **b** offerings
24:14 they sacrificed **b** offerings in
29:7 incense or sacrifice **b** offerings
29:18 the altar for **b** offerings,
29:24 The king had said that the **b**
29:27 the sacrificing of **b** offerings
29:27 When the **b** offerings started,
29:28 the **b** offering was finished.
29:29 When the **b** offerings were
29:31 was willing brought **b** offerings.
29:32 The **b** offerings brought by the
29:32 All of these were **b** offerings to
29:34 help to skin all the **b** offerings.
29:35 There were many **b** offerings in
29:35 accompanied the **b** offerings.
30:15 Then they brought **b** offerings
31:2 sacrificing **b** offerings,
31:3 king's property for **b** offerings,
31:3 **b** offerings on the weekly
35:12 They set aside the **b** offerings
35:14 were sacrificing the **b** offerings
35:16 and the **b** offerings were
Ezr 3:2 in order to sacrifice **b** offerings.
3:3 They sacrificed **b** offerings on
3:4 required number of **b** offerings.
3:5 sacrificed the daily **b** offerings,
3:6 They started to bring these **b**
6:9 Jerusalem need for **b** offerings
8:35 captivity sacrificed **b** offerings
8:35 All of these animals were **b**
Neh 10:33 offerings and daily **b** offerings,
Job 1:5 and sacrifice **b** offerings
42:8 and make a **b** offering for
Psa 20:3 with favor on your **b** offerings.
40:6 You did not ask for **b** offerings
50:8 your sacrifices or **b** offerings,
51:16 You are not pleased with **b**
51:19 right spirit — with **b** offerings
Psa 51:19 offerings and whole **b** offerings.
66:13 your temple with **b** offerings.
66:15 livestock for **b** offerings
Isa 1:11 I've had enough of your **b**
40:16 enough for a single **b** offering.
43:23 me sheep for your **b** offerings
56:7 Their **b** offerings and their
65:3 in gardens and **b** incense
65:7 They **b** incense on the
Jer 6:20 I won't accept your **b** offerings.
7:21 Add your **b** offerings to your
7:22 **b** offerings and sacrifices.
14:12 Even if they sacrifice **b**
17:26 They will bring **b** offerings,
33:18 to sacrifice **b** offerings,
Eze 16:21 them as **b** offerings to idols.
23:37 to for me as **b** offerings to idols.
40:38 the animals for the **b** offerings.
40:39 slaughtered for **b** offerings,
40:42 of cut stone for **b** offerings.
40:42 for **b** offerings and sacrifices.
43:18 rules for sacrificing **b** offerings
43:24 and offer them as **b** offerings
43:27 the priests must sacrifice **b**
44:11 the animals for the **b** offerings
45:15 with grain offerings, **b**
45:17 to provide **b** offerings,
45:17 sin, grain offerings, **b** offerings,
45:23 he must prepare **b** offerings for
45:25 sin, **b** offerings, grain offerings,
46:2 prepare the prince's **b** offerings
46:4 has no defects as a **b** offering
46:6 the **b** offering must be one
46:12 prepares a freewill **b** offering,
46:12 either a **b** offering or a
46:12 He must sacrifice **b** offerings
46:13 every day as a **b** offering
46:15 morning as a daily **b** offering.
Dan 8:11 the daily **b** offering from him
8:12 a stop to the daily **b** offering.
8:13 vision — the daily **b** offering,
11:31 take away the daily **b** offering,
12:11 From the time the daily **b**
Hos 6:6 not to give me **b** offerings.
Amo 5:22 Even though you bring me **b**
Mic 6:6 year-old calves as **b** offerings?
Mar 12:33 the **b** offerings and sacrifices."
Heb 10:6 You did not approve of **b**
10:8 offerings, **b** offerings,

burst (13)

Gen 7:11 all the deep springs **b** open.
38:29 So she said, "Is this how you **b**
Exo 32:19 In a **b** of anger Moses threw
Jdg 5:4 the sky poured, the clouds **b**,
2Sm 23:16 So the three fighting men **b** into
1Ch 11:18 So the three **b** into the
Job 32:19 wineskins that are ready to **b**.
38:8 behind gates when it **b** through
Psa 2:12 his anger will **b** into flames.
Isa 54:8 for a moment in a **b** of anger,
Mat 9:17 If they do, the skins **b**,
Mar 2:22 the wine will make the skins **b**,
Luk 5:37 wine will make the skins **b**.

bursting (1)

Gen 38:29 He was named Perez [**B** Into].

bury (41)

Gen 23:4 so that I can **b** my dead wife."
23:6 **B** your dead in one of our best
23:8 are willing to let me **b** my wife,
23:11 giving it to you. **B** your wife!"
23:13 so that I can **b** my wife there."
23:15 that between us? **B** your wife!"
47:29 Please don't **b** me here.
47:30 and **b** me in their tomb."
49:29 **B** me with my ancestors in the
50:5 **B** me in the tomb I bought for
50:5 let me go there and **b** my father;
50:6 "Go and **b** your father,
50:7 So Joseph left to **b** his father.
50:14 there with him to **b** his father.
Dtr 21:23 Be sure to **b** him that same day,
1Ki 2:31 Kill him, and **b** him.
11:15 went to **b** those killed in battle
1Ki 13:29 to mourn for him and to **b** him.
13:31 **b** me in the tomb where the
14:13 will mourn for him and **b** him.
2Ki 9:10 and no one will **b** her."
9:35 when they went out to **b** her,
2Ch 24:25 but they didn't **b** him in the
Psa 79:3 is no one to **b** your people.
Jer 7:32 They will **b** ⌊people⌋ at
13:4 and **b** it there in a crack in the
13:6 from where I told you to **b** it."
14:16 No one will **b** them,
16:4 will mourn for them or **b** them.
16:6 will mourn for them or **b** them.
19:11 They will **b** ⌊the dead⌋ in
19:11 there's no other place to **b** them.
43:9 large stones, and **b** them under
Eze 29:5 one will pick you up or **b** you.
39:14 the help of others they will **b**
Hos 9:6 them and Memphis will **b** them.
Mat 8:21 first let me go to **b** my father."
8:22 let the dead **b** their own dead."
Luk 9:59 first let me go to **b** my father."
9:60 "Let the dead **b** their own dead.
Rev 11:9 not allow anyone to **b** them.

burying (7)

Gen 23:6 you his tomb for **b** your dead."
Num 33:4 The Egyptians were **b** all their
2Sm 2:5 to your master Saul by **b** him.
2Ki 13:21 day some people who were **b**
Eze 39:12 The people of Israel will be **b**
39:13 common people will be **b** them.
Heb 11:22 instructions about **b** his bones.

bush (14)

Gen 22:13 him caught by its horns in a **b**.
Exo 3:2 flames of fire coming out of a **b**.
3:2 and although the **b** was on fire,
3:3 "Why isn't this **b** burning up?
3:4 God called to him from the **b**,
Dtr 33:16 one who was in the burning **b**.
Ecc 12:5 ⌊and⌋ the caper **b** has ⌊no⌋
Jer 17:6 He will be like a **b** in the
Mar 12:26 It's in the passage about the **b**,
Luk 20:37 in the passage about the **b** that
Act 7:30 him in the flames of a burning **b**
7:31 he went closer to look at the **b**,
7:32 and didn't dare to look at the **b**.
7:35 who appeared to him in the **b**.

bushel (5)

Rut 2:17 had about half a **b** of barley.
1Sm 1:24 bull, half a **b** of flour,
25:18 a **b** of roasted grain,
Isa 40:12 dust of the earth in a **b** basket
Amo 8:5 the size of the **b** baskets,

bushels (11)

Num 11:32 No one gathered less than 60 **b**.
1Sm 16:20 Jesse took six **b** of bread,
1Ki 4:22 for one day was 180 **b** of flour,
4:22 360 **b** of coarse flour,
5:11 Solomon gave Hiram 120,000 **b**
2Ch 2:10 your lumberjacks 120,000 **b**
2:10 120,000 **b** of barley,
27:5 60,000 **b** of wheat,
27:5 and 60,000 **b** of barley.
Hos 3:2 of silver and 10 **b** of barley.
Luk 16:7 'A thousand **b** of wheat.'

bushes (4)

Gen 2:5 Wild **b** and plants were not on
21:15 put the boy under one of the **b**.
21:17 the boy crying from the **b**.
Job 30:7 They howl in **b** and huddle

business (14)

1Sm 21:8 the king's **b** was urgent."
25:2 a man in Maon whose **b** was
Job 20:18 no joy from the profits of his **b**
Psa 107:23 who do **b** on the high seas,
Pro 9:15 those minding their own **b**,
Ecc 5:14 were then lost in bad **b** deals.
Luk 16:1 "A rich man had a **b** manager.
Act 19:24 was in the **b** of making silver
19:24 His **b** brought a huge profit for

Act 19:25 a good income from this **b**,
1Co 5:12 After all, do I have any **b**
5:12 Isn't it your **b** to judge those
1Ti 5:13 get involved in other people's **b**,
Jas 4:13 conduct **b**, and make money."

businesses (1)

Mat 22:5 and others went to their **b**.

businessmen (1)

Nah 3:16 You have produced more **b**

bustling (1)

Isa 23:7 Is this your **b** city founded in

busy (5)

Exo 5:9 so that they will be too **b**
1Ki 20:40 But while I was **b** doing other
Psa 39:6 They are **b** for no reason.
Hag 1:9 while each of you is **b** working
Jas 1:11 While they are **b**, they will die.

butcher (4)

Gen 43:16 **B** an animal, and prepare a
1Sm 14:34 sheep, and **b** it here, and eat.
Isa 22:13 slaughter cattle, and **b** sheep.
Eze 34:3 and **b** the finest sheep.

butchered (11)

Num 11:22 and herds were **b** for them?
Dtr 28:31 Your ox will be **b** as you
1Sm 1:25 Then the parents **b** the bull and
14:32 and **b** them on the ground.
14:34 him that night and **b** it there.
25:11 and my meat that I **b** for my
25:18 2 full wineskins, 5 **b** sheep,
28:24 The woman immediately **b** a
1Ki 19:21 took two oxen, and **b** them.
Psa 44:11 You hand us over to be **b** like
Mat 22:4 fattened calves have been **b**.

butchers (1)

Exo 22:1 steals a bull or a sheep and **b**

butt (1)

2Sm 2:23 So Abner struck him with the **b**

butter (2)

Psa 55:21 His speech is smoother than **b**,
Pro 30:33 As churning milk produces **b**

buttermilk (4)

Jdg 5:25 She offered him **b** in a royal
2Sm 17:29 honey, **b**, sheep, and calves.
Job 20:17 from the rivers of honey and **b**.
29:6 my steps were bathed in **b**,

buttocks (1)

Isa 20:4 Their **b** will be exposed in

buy (111)

Gen 41:57 to Joseph in Egypt to **b** grain,
42:2 Go there and **b** some for us so
42:3 went to **b** grain in Egypt.
42:5 who were going to **b** grain,
42:7 "From Canaan, to **b** food,"
42:10 "We've come to **b** food.
43:2 "Go back and **b** us a little more
43:4 we'll go and **b** food for you.
43:20 here to **b** food once before.
43:22 brought more money to **b** food.
44:25 'Go back and **b** us a little more
47:22 But he didn't **b** the priests' land
Exo 13:13 a goat to **b** any firstborn donkey
13:13 If you don't **b** it back,
13:13 You must also **b** every firstborn
13:15 LORD and **b** every firstborn son
21:2 "Whenever you **b** a Hebrew
34:20 you a sheep or a goat to **b** back
34:20 If you don't **b** it back,
34:20 You must **b** back every
Lev 25:14 or **b** anything from him,
25:15 When you **b** property from your
25:24 right to **b** their property back.
25:25 must **b** back what he sold.
25:26 a man doesn't have anyone to **b**
Lev 25:26 enough to **b** it back himself,
25:28 earn enough to **b** it back,
25:29 it he has the right to **b** it back.
25:29 He may **b** it back only within
25:30 If he does not **b** it back during
25:32 right to **b** back their property
25:44 but **b** them from the nations
25:45 You may also **b** them from the
25:48 of his brothers may **b** him back.
25:49 relative could also **b** him back.
25:49 he could **b** his own freedom.
25:54 If he cannot **b** his freedom in
27:13 If you want to **b** it back,
27:15 If you want to **b** it back,
27:19 If you want to **b** it back,
27:20 But if you don't **b** it back and it
27:20 you cannot **b** it back.
27:31 If you **b** back any part of it,
Num 3:47 the holy place) to **b** them back.
3:48 It will **b** back those Israelites
18:15 But you must **b** back every
18:16 you must **b** them back at the
18:17 "But you must never **b** back a
Dtr 14:26 Use the silver to **b** whatever
28:68 but no one will **b** you.
Rut 4:4 **B** it in the presence of these
4:4 If you wish to **b** back the
4:4 you can **b** back the property.
4:4 But if you do not wish to **b**
4:4 "I'll **b** back the property."
4:5 Boaz continued, "When you **b**
4:6 Take all my rights to **b** back
4:8 said to Boaz, "**B** it for yourself,"
2Sm 24:21 David answered, "To **b** the
24:24 "I must **b** it from you at a ⌊fair⌋
2Ki 12:12 They also used it to **b** wood
12:12 and to **b** anything else that
22:6 rest of⌋ the money to **b** lumber
2Ch 34:11 They were to **b** quarried stones
Ezr 7:17 must use this money to **b** bulls,
Neh 5:8 "We have done our best to **b**
5:8 we have to **b** them back again!"
10:31 we won't **b** anything from them
Job 6:27 Would you **b** and sell your
28:15 obtain it with solid gold or **b**
Psa 49:7 No one can ever **b** back
49:15 But God will **b** me back from
Pro 17:16 in his hand to **b** wisdom when
23:23 **B** truth (and do not sell it),
23:23 ⌊that is,⌋ **b** wisdom, discipline,
27:26 the male goats will **b** a field.
Isa 5:8 house and **b** field after field
43:24 You did not **b** me any sugar
55:1 can come, **b**, and eat! Come,
55:1 Come, **b** wine and milk.
Jer 13:1 said to me: "**B** a linen belt.
19:1 Go and **b** a clay jar from a
32:7 "**B** my field that is in Anathoth,
32:7 it is your responsibility to **b** it.'"
32:8 He said to me, 'Please **b** my
32:8 **B** it for yourself.' Then I knew
32:15 My people will again **b** houses,
32:25 told me to **b** a field with money
32:43 But people will once again **b**
32:44 They will **b** fields for money,
Eze 7:13 enough to **b** back what they
Dan 2:8 "I'm sure you're trying to **b**
Joe 3:3 that they could **b** wine to drink.
Amo 8:6 We can **b** the poor with money
Zec 11:5 Those who **b** them will kill
Mat 14:15 to **b** food for themselves."
27:7 So they decided to use it to **b** a
27:10 and used the coins to **b** a
Mar 6:36 to **b** themselves something
Luk 9:13 Unless we go to **b** food for all
22:36 should sell his coat and **b** one.
Jon 4:8 into the city to **b** some food.)
6:5 "Where can we **b** bread for
6:7 year's wages to **b** enough bread
13:29 him to **b** what they needed
Act 8:20 thought you could **b** God's gift.
1Co 7:30 Those who **b** something
Rev 3:18 I advise you: **B** gold purified in
3:18 **B** white clothes from me.
3:18 **B** ointment to put on your eyes
13:17 does this so that no one may **b**

buyer (7)

Lev 25:28 stays in the hands of the **b** until
25:30 in the city belongs to the **b**
25:50 Then he and his **b** must take
25:50 of years he was with his **b**,
25:53 years he should serve his **b** as
25:53 His **b** should not treat him
Pro 20:14 says the **b**. Then, as he goes

buyers (2)

Isa 24:2 and masters, **b** and sellers,
Eze 7:12 **B** will not rejoice, and sellers

buying (6)

Rut 4:7 concerning **b** back property
1Ch 21:24 "I insist on **b** it for the full price.
Mat 21:12 threw out everyone who was **b**
25:10 "While they were **b** oil,
Mar 11:15 to throw out those who were **b**
Luk 17:28 eating, drinking, **b** and selling,

buys (5)

Lev 22:11 But if a priest **b** a slave,
25:33 If any Levite **b** back ⌊a house⌋,
Pro 31:16 "She picks out a field and **b** it.
Rev 18:11 no one **b** their cargo anymore.
18:12 No one **b** their cargo of gold,

Buz (5)

Gen 22:21 (the firstborn), **B** (his brother),
1Ch 5:14 and great-great-grandson of **B**.
Job 32:2 a descendant of **B** from the
32:6 the descendant of **B**,
Jer 25:23 Dedan, Tema, **B**, and all who

Buzi (1)

Eze 1:3 to the priest Ezekiel, son of **B**,

buzzards (2)

Lev 11:14 kites, all types of **b**,
Dtr 14:13 **b**, all types of kites,

by-passing (1)

Jdg 11:18 **b** Edom and Moab.

bystander (1)

Pro 26:17 ⌊so⌋ is a **b** who gets involved

C

Cabbon (1)

Jos 15:40 **C**, Lahmas, Chitlish,

Cabul (2)

Jos 19:27 there it goes northward to **C**,
1Ki 9:13 So he named it the region of **C**

Caesarea (19)

Act 8:40 until he came to the city of **C**.
9:30 they took Saul to **C** and sent
10:1 Cornelius lived in the city of **C**.
10:24 following day they arrived in **C**.
11:11 been sent from **C** to find me.
12:19 Herod left Judea and went to **C**,
18:22 and arrived in the city of **C**.
21:8 we went to Philip's home in **C**
21:16 Some of the disciples from **C**
23:23 Have them ready to go to **C** at
23:33 in the city of **C** with Paul,
24:1 Ananias went to the city of **C**
25:1 from the city of **C** to Jerusalem.
25:4 he would be returning to **C** soon
25:5 your authorities come to **C**
25:6 most and then returned to **C**.
25:13 city of **C** to welcome Festus.
25:17 leaders came to **C** with me.
25:24 in Jerusalem and **C** have talked

Caesarea Philippi (2)

Mat 16:13 Jesus came to the region of **C**,
Mar 8:27 went to the villages around **C**.

cage (1)

Eze 19:9 With hooks they put him in a c

cages (1)

Jer 5:27 Like c filled with birds,

Caiaphas (9)

Mat 26:3 the palace of the chief priest C.
26:57 arrested Jesus took him to C,
Luk 3:2 Annas and C were chief priests
Jon 11:49 One of them, C, who was chief
11:51 C didn't say this on his own.
18:13 the father-in-law of C.
18:13 C, the chief priest that year,
18:24 Annas sent Jesus to C,
Act 4:6 The chief priest Annas, C,

Caiaphas' (1)

Jon 18:28 Jesus was taken from C house

Cain (22)

Gen 4:1 pregnant and gave birth to C.
4:2 and C was a farmer.
4:3 Later C brought some crops
4:5 but he didn't approve of C and
4:5 So C became very angry and
4:6 Then the LORD asked C,
4:8 C talked to his brother Abel.
4:8 C attacked his brother Abel and
4:9 The LORD asked C,
4:13 But C said to the LORD,
4:15 Anyone who kills C will suffer
4:15 The LORD gave C a sign so
4:16 Then C left the LORD's
4:17 C made love to his wife.
4:17 C was building a city,
4:24 If C is avenged 7 times,
4:25 since C killed him."
Num 24:22 you ⌊descendants of⌋ C,
1Jn 3:12 Don't be like C. He was a child
3:12 And why did C murder his
3:12 Because the things C did were
Jud 1:11 have followed the path of C.

Cainan (2)

Luk 3:36 son of C, son of Arphaxad,
3:37 son of Mahalaleel, son of C,

Cain's (2)

Gen 4:2 another child, Abel, C brother.
Heb 11:4 better sacrifice than C sacrifice.

cake (7)

1Sm 30:12 They gave him a slice of fig c
2Sm 6:19 one loaf of bread, one date c,
6:19 date cake, and one raisin c.
2Ki 20:7 Then Isaiah said, "Get a fig c,
1Ch 16:3 a date c, and a raisin cake.
16:3 a date cake, and a raisin c.
Isa 38:21 Then Isaiah said, "Take a fig c,

cakes (6)

1Sm 25:18 and 200 fig c and loaded them
1Ch 12:40 There was plenty of flour, fig c,
Isa 16:7 the raisin c of Kir Hareseth.
Jer 7:18 women knead dough to make c
44:19 and made c for her with her
Hos 3:1 gods and love to eat raisin c."

Calah (2)

Gen 10:11 built Nineveh, Rehoboth Ir, C,
10:12 city between Nineveh and C.

calamity (3)

Pro 1:26 I will laugh at your c.
1:27 when c strikes you like a wind
Jer 30:7 It will be a time of c for the

calamus (1)

Sos 4:14 nard and saffron, c,

Calcol (2)

1Ki 4:31 C, or Darda, Mahol's sons.
1Ch 2:6 C, and Dara — five in all.

calculates (1)

Pro 23:7 As he c the cost to himself,

Caleb (37)

Num 13:6 C, son of Jephunneh, from the
13:30 C told the people to be quiet
13:30 C said, "Let's go now and take
14:6 Joshua (son of Nun) and C (son
14:24 But because my servant C has
14:30 you will enter it except C (son
14:38 only Joshua (son of Nun) and C
26:65 The only ones left were C (son
32:12 Only C (son of Jephunneh the
34:19 These are their names: C,
Dtr 1:36 except C, son of Jephunneh.
Jos 14:6 C, son of Jephunneh and
14:13 So Joshua blessed C,
14:14 is still the inheritance of C,
14:14 because C was completely
15:13 Joshua gave C, son of
15:14 C forced out Sheshai,
15:16 C said, "I will give my daughter
15:17 So C gave him his daughter
15:18 from her donkey, C asked her,
15:19 So C gave her the upper and
21:12 its fields and villages to C,
Jdg 1:12 C said, "I will give my daughter
1:13 So C gave him his daughter
1:14 from her donkey, C asked her,
1:15 So C gave her the upper and
1:20 Hebron was given to C,
1Sm 25:3 He was a descendant of C.
30:14 of the Negev where C settled,
1Ch 2:18 Hezron's son was C.
2:18 C and his wife Azubah had a
2:19 C married Ephrath.
2:24 Hezron died in C Ephrathah,
2:42 The descendants of C
2:50 were the descendants of C.
4:15 The sons of C, son of
6:56 its villages were given to C,

Caleb's (6)

Jos 15:17 son of C brother Kenaz,
Jdg 1:13 Then Othniel, son of C younger
3:9 son of C younger brother
1Ch 2:46 Ephah, C concubine, was the
2:48 Maacah, C concubine, was the
2:49 C daughter was Achsah.

calf (28)

Exo 32:4 he made it into a statue of a c.
32:8 a statue of a c for themselves.
32:19 he saw the c and the dancing.
32:20 Then he took the c they had
32:24 and out came this c!
32:35 they had Aaron make the c.
Lev 9:2 He told Aaron, "Take a c that
9:3 a c and a lamb (each
9:8 slaughtered the c as his own
22:27 "When a c, a lamb, or a goat is
Num 19:8 The person who burned the c
Dtr 9:16 a statue of a c for yourselves.
9:21 I took that sinful c you made
1Sm 28:24 a fattened c that she owned.
2Sm 6:13 a bull and a fattened c.
1Ki 12:30 far as Dan to worship the one c.
2Ch 11:15 and the goat and c statues
Neh 9:18 they made a metal statue of a c
Psa 29:6 Lebanon skip along like a c
106:19 they made ⌊a statue of⌋ a c.
Jer 31:18 I was like a young, untrained c.
34:18 my presence when they cut a c
34:19 between the pieces of the c.
Hos 10:11 "Ephraim is like a trained c
Luk 15:23 Bring the fattened c,
15:27 father has killed the fattened c
15:30 killed the fattened c for him.'
Act 7:41 was the time they made a c.

calf's (1)

1Ki 10:19 of the throne was a c head.

calf-shaped (4)

Hos 8:5 Get rid of your c idol,
8:6 Samaria's c idol was made in
10:5 Samaria fear the c idol at Beth
13:2 sacrifices and kiss c idols."

call (203)

Gen 2:19 to see what he would c them.
17:15 God said to Abraham, "Don't c
24:57 "We'll c the girl and ask her."
30:13 Women will c me blessed."
Exo 33:19 and there I will c out my name
Lev 13:45 cover their upper lips and c out,
Num 10:2 Use them to c the community
Dtr 3:9 (The Sidonians c Mount
3:9 and the Amorites c it Senir.)
4:25 I c heaven and earth as
28:65 no place to c your own.
30:19 I c on heaven and earth as
31:14 C for Joshua. Both of you come
31:28 I will speak these words and c
Jdg 16:25 "C Samson in to entertain us."
18:23 Why did you c your neighbors
Rut 1:20 "Don't c me Naomi [Sweet].
1:20 C me Mara [Bitter] because the
1:21 Why do you c me Naomi when
1Sm 3:5 "I didn't c ⌊you,⌋" Eli replied.
3:6 "I didn't c ⌊you,⌋ son,"
9:9 because a person we now c a
12:17 I will c on the LORD,
2Sm 2:26 before you will c off your troops
17:5 "Please c Hushai,
20:4 The king told Amasa, "C the
20:5 went to c Judah together,
1Ki 1:28 "C Bathsheba in here."
8:52 them whenever they c on you.
18:24 "You c on the name of your
18:24 but I will c on the name of the
18:25 C on the name of your god,
22:13 The messenger who went to c
2Ki 4:12 "C this Shunem woman."
4:15 Elisha said, "C her."
4:36 "C the Shunem woman.
5:11 c on the name of the LORD his
10:20 Jehu said, "C a holy assembly
1Ch 14:11 That is why they c that place
16:8 C on his name. Make known
2Ch 13:12 their trumpets to c ⌊the army⌋
18:12 The messenger who went to c
Job 13:22 Then c, and I'll answer.
14:3 You observe this and c me to
14:15 You will c, and I will answer
19:7 I c for help, but there is no
19:16 I c my slave, but he doesn't
27:10 Can he c on God at all times?
30:20 "I c to you for help,
30:28 up in public and c for help.
35:9 people makes them c for help.
36:13 They don't even c for help
38:34 Can you c to the clouds and
Psa 3:4 I c aloud to the LORD,
4:1 Answer me when I c,
4:3 hears me when I c to him.
14:4 they do not c on the LORD?
20:9 Answer us when we c.
28:1 O LORD, I c to you.
28:2 my prayer for mercy when I c
50:15 C on me in times of trouble.
53:4 that they do not c on God?
55:16 But I c on God, and the LORD
56:9 will retreat when I c ⌊to you⌋.
57:2 I c to God Most High,
61:2 From the ends of the earth, I c
72:17 through him and c him blessed.
80:18 and we will c on you.
86:3 because I c out to you all day
86:7 When I am in trouble, I c out to
88:9 All day long I c out to you,
89:26 He will c out to me,
91:15 When you c to me,
102:2 Answer me quickly when I c.
105:1 C on him. Make known among
110:3 when you c up your army.
116:2 I will c on him as long as I live
116:13 take the cup of salvation and c
116:17 I will c on the name of the
130:1 out of the depths I c to you.
142:5 I c out to you, O LORD. I say,

Psa	147:9	young ravens when they **c** out.
Pro	1:28	"They will **c** to me at that time,
	2:3	if indeed you **c** out for insight,
	8:1	Does not wisdom **c** out?
	21:13	ear to the cry of the poor will **c**
Ecc	3:15	God will **c** the past to account.
Isa	1:13	and the assemblies you **c**.
	5:20	be for those who **c** evil good
	8:12	that everything these people **c**
	12:4	**C** on his name. Make his deeds
	13:2	**C** loudly to them. Signal them
	22:12	LORD of Armies will **c**
	22:20	I will **c** my servant Eliakim,
	24:11	People in the streets **c** for wine.
	30:7	That is why I **c** it, 'Rahab who
	34:14	Male goats will **c** to their
	40:6	A voice called, "**C** out!"
	40:6	I asked, "What should I **c** out?"
	40:6	"**C** out: All people are like
	40:9	**C** out with a loud voice,
	41:25	He will **c** on my name from the
	44:5	Another will **c** on the name of
	46:11	I will **c** a bird of prey from the
	46:11	I will **c** someone for my plan
	48:2	You **c** yourselves ⌊citizens⌋ of
	48:13	When I **c** for them,
	55:6	**C** on him while he is near.
	58:5	Is this what you **c** fasting?
	58:9	Then you will **c**, and the LORD
	58:13	if you **c** the day of worship a
	60:14	They will **c** you the city of the
	60:18	You will **c** your walls Salvation
	65:15	kill you and **c** his servants by
	65:24	Before they **c**, I will answer.
Jer	1:15	I am going to **c** every family
	2:27	You **c** wood your father.
	2:27	You **c** stone your mother.
	3:17	At that time they will **c**
	3:19	I thought that you would **c** me
	6:30	⌊People⌋ will **c** them useless
	7:27	You will **c** to them,
	9:17	**C** for the women who cry at
	11:14	I won't listen when they **c** to
	20:3	LORD doesn't **c** you Pashhur,
	29:12	Then you will **c** to me.
	30:17	"People **c** you an outcast:
	31:6	will **c** out this message:
	33:3	**C** to me, and I will answer you.
	44:26	in Egypt will ever again **c**
	50:29	"**C** together the archers,
Lam	2:15	used to **c** absolutely beautiful,
	3:8	Even when I cry and **c** for help,
	3:55	"I **c** your name from the
	3:57	close at hand when I **c** to you.
Eze	9:1	Then I heard the LORD **c** out
Dan	5:12	Now, **c** Daniel, and he will tell
	8:16	a man in Ulai ⌊Gate⌋ **c** loudly,
Hos	2:1	"So **c** your brothers Ammi [My
	2:1	and **c** your sisters Ruhamah
	2:16	"On that day she will **c** me her
	2:16	will no longer **c** me her master.
	2:17	never again **c** out their names.
	2:23	loved I will **c** my loved ones.
	2:23	my people I will **c** my people.
	7:11	You **c** for Egypt and run to
	11:7	Even if they **c** to the Most High,
Joe	1:14	**C** for an assembly!
	2:15	**C** for an assembly.
Amo	5:16	They will **c** on farmers to
Zec	7:13	So now when they **c**,
	13:9	They will **c** on me,
Mal	3:12	"All nations will **c** you blessed
	3:15	So now we **c** arrogant people
Mat	9:13	I've come to **c** sinners,
	10:25	they will certainly **c** the family
	20:8	the supervisor, '**C** the workers,
	22:43	by the Spirit, **c** him Lord?
	23:7	to have people **c** them Rabbi.
	23:8	don't make others **c** you Rabbi,
	23:9	And don't **c** anyone on earth
	23:10	Don't make others **c** you a
	24:31	angels with a loud trumpet **c**,
	26:53	Don't you think that I could **c**
Mar	2:17	I've come to **c** sinners,
	10:18	"Why do you **c** me good?
	10:49	stopped and said, "**C** him!"
Luk	1:48	all people will **c** me blessed
	5:32	I've come to **c** sinners to
	5:32	not to **c** people who think they
	6:46	"Why do you **c** me Lord but
	9:54	do you want us to **c** down fire
	18:19	"Why do you **c** me good?
	19:15	Then he said, '**C** those
	22:25	and those in authority **c**
Jon	9:11	He replied, "The man people **c**
	13:13	You **c** me teacher and Lord,
	15:15	I don't **c** you servants anymore,
Act	1:19	They even **c** that piece of land
	7:5	in this land to **c** his own,
	10:28	no longer **c** anyone impure
	22:16	away as you **c** on his name.'
	24:14	which they **c** a sect.
Rom	2:17	You **c** yourself a Jew,
	8:15	children by which we **c** out,
	9:12	a choice based on God's **c** and
	9:25	my people I will **c** my people.
	9:25	loved I will **c** my loved ones.
1Co	1:2	to people everywhere who **c**
	5:11	who **c** themselves brothers
	8:5	as they would **c** them.
	14:8	trumpet doesn't sound a clear **c**,
Gal	4:6	of his Son into us to **c** out,
Php	3:14	that God's heavenly **c** offers
1Th	4:7	God didn't **c** us to be sexually
	4:16	with the trumpet ⌊**c**⌋ of God.
2Th	1:11	will make you worthy of his **c**.
1Ti	5:21	I solemnly **c** on you in the sight
2Ti	4:1	I solemnly **c** on you in the
Heb	2:11	ashamed to **c** them brothers
Jas	5:14	**c** for the church leaders.
1Pe	1:17	So if you **c** God your Father,
Rev	2:2	You have tested those who **c**

called (471)

Gen	2:19	Whatever the man **c** each
	3:9	The LORD God **c** to the man
	5:2	He blessed them and **c** them
	12:18	Then Pharaoh **c** for Abram.
	19:5	They **c** to Lot, "Where are the
	20:8	Abimelech **c** together all his
	20:9	Then Abimelech **c** for Abraham
	21:17	and the Messenger of God **c** to
	21:31	why that place is **c** Beersheba,
	22:1	tested Abraham and **c** to him,
	22:11	the Messenger of the LORD **c**
	22:15	the Messenger of the LORD **c**
	24:58	They **c** for Rebekah and asked
	25:30	This is why he was **c** Edom.
	26:9	Abimelech **c** for Isaac and said,
	27:1	he **c** his older son Esau and
	28:1	Isaac **c** for Jacob and blessed
	30:11	So she **c** him Gad [Luck].
	31:11	the Messenger of God **c** to me,
	31:47	⌊In his language⌋ Laban **c** it
	31:47	but Jacob **c** it Galeed.
	35:7	He built an altar there and **c**
	35:8	So Jacob **c** it the Tree of
	35:10	You will no longer be **c** Jacob,
	39:14	she **c** her household servants
	47:29	He **c** for his son Joseph and
	48:16	May they be **c** by my name and
	49:1	Jacob **c** for his sons and said,
Exo	1:18	So the king of Egypt **c** for the
	3:4	God **c** to him from the bush,
	8:25	Pharaoh **c** for Moses and Aaron
	10:16	Then Pharaoh quickly **c** for
	10:24	Then Pharaoh **c** for Moses and
	12:21	Then Moses **c** for all the
	12:31	Pharaoh **c** for Moses and Aaron
	15:23	That's why the place was **c**
	16:31	The Israelites **c** the food
	17:15	Moses built an altar and **c** it
	19:3	and the LORD **c** to him from the
	19:7	So Moses went down and **c** for
	19:20	top of Mount Sinai and **c** Moses
	24:16	on the seventh day the LORD **c**
	33:7	He **c** it the tent of meeting.
	34:5	with him and **c** out his name
	34:31	Moses **c** to them, so Aaron and
	36:2	Moses **c** Bezalel and Oholiab
Lev	1:1	The LORD **c** Moses and spoke
	10:4	Moses **c** Mishael and
Num	11:3	That place was **c** Taberah
	11:34	That place was **c** Kibroth
	12:5	He **c** to Aaron and Miriam,
	13:24	So they **c** that valley Eshcol
	21:3	So they **c** the place Hormah
	32:41	He **c** them Havvoth Jair
Dtr	2:11	the Moabites **c** them Emites.
	2:20	**c** them Zamzummim.
	3:13	Argob in Bashan used to be **c**
	25:10	in Israel his family will be **c**
	31:7	Then Moses **c** for Joshua and
Jos	4:4	Joshua **c** the 12 men whom he
	7:26	this reason that place is still **c**
	8:16	All the troops in the city were **c**
	10:24	he **c** for all the men of Israel.
	14:15	past Hebron was **c** Kiriath Arba.
	15:9	Baalah (now **c** Kiriath Jearim).
	15:10	Jearim (now **c** Chesalon).
	15:13	the city of Arba (now **c** Hebron).
	15:15	Debir was **c** Kiriath Sepher.)
	15:25	Kerioth Hezron (now **c** Hazor),
	15:49	Kiriath Sannah (now **c** Debir),
	15:54	Kiriath Arba (now **c** Hebron),
	15:60	Baal (now **c** Kiriath Jearim)
	18:13	slope of Luz (now **c** Bethel).
	18:14	Baal (now **c** Kiriath Jearim),
	18:28	Jebus (now **c** Jerusalem),
	20:7	and Kiriath Arba (now **c**
	23:2	So he **c** all the leaders,
	24:1	He **c** together Israel's leaders,
Jdg	1:10	Hebron was **c** Kiriath Arba.)
	1:11	Debir was **c** Kiriath Sepher.)
	1:17	So the city was **c** Hormah
	1:23	(In the past the city was **c** Luz.)
	1:26	he built a city and **c** it Luz.
	2:5	So they **c** that place Bochim
	4:10	Barak **c** the tribes of Zebulun
	6:24	He **c** it The LORD Calms.
	9:54	He quickly **c** his armorbearer.
	10:4	that are still **c** Havvoth Jair
	15:17	He **c** that place Ramath Lehi
	15:18	So he **c** out to the LORD and
	15:19	So he **c** the place En Hakkore
	16:19	She **c** for a man to shave off
	16:25	Samson was **c** from the prison,
	16:28	Then Samson **c** to the LORD,
	18:12	is still **c** Mahaneh Dan [The
	18:22	Micah's neighbors were **c**
	18:29	the city was **c** Laish.
	19:10	as Jebus (now **c** Jerusalem).
1Sm	3:4	Then the LORD **c** Samuel.
	3:5	You **c** me." "I didn't call ⌊you⌋,"
	3:6	The LORD **c** Samuel again.
	3:6	You **c** me." "I didn't call ⌊you⌋,
	3:8	The LORD **c** Samuel a third
	3:8	You **c** me." Then Eli realized
	3:10	He **c** as he had called the other
	3:10	He called as he had **c** the other
	3:16	Then Eli **c** Samuel.
	4:21	She **c** the boy Ichabod [No
	5:8	The people of Ashdod **c**
	5:11	They **c** together all the
	6:2	when the Philistines **c** for
	9:9	a prophet used to be **c** a seer.)
	9:26	At dawn Samuel **c** to Saul on
	10:17	Samuel **c** the people to ⌊come
	12:18	Then Samuel **c** on the LORD.
	16:8	Then Jesse **c** Abinadab and
	17:8	Goliath stood and **c** to the
	17:43	So the Philistine **c** on his gods
	20:30	he **c** Jonathan. "I know you've
	20:37	Jonathan **c** after him,
	23:8	So Saul **c** together all the
	23:28	place was **c** Slippery Rock.
	24:8	and **c** to Saul, "Your Majesty!"
	26:14	Then David **c** to the troops and
	28:15	So I've **c** on you to tell me what
	29:6	Then Achish **c** David and told
2Sm	1:7	he **c** to me, and I said, 'Yes?'"
	1:15	Then David **c** one of ⌊his⌋
	2:16	that place in Gibeon is **c** the
	2:26	Then Abner **c** to Joab,
	5:9	David lived in the fortress and **c**
	5:20	that place is **c** Baal Perazim.
	6:2	(The ark is **c** by the name of
	6:8	(That place is still **c** Perez

2Sm	9:9	Then the king **c** for Ziba,
	13:17	Then he **c** his personal servant
	14:33	The king then **c** for Absalom,
	18:1	David **c** together the troops that
	18:18	He **c** the rock by his name,
	18:18	**c** Absalom's Monument today.)
	18:25	The watchman **c** and alerted
	18:26	man running, the watchman **c**,
	20:16	Then a clever woman **c** from
	21:2	The king **c** the Gibeonites
	22:4	I **c** on him, and I was saved
	22:7	I **c** on the LORD in my distress.
	22:7	I **c** to my God for help.
1Ki	9:13	(⌊They're⌋ still ⌊**c**⌋ that today.)
	10:17	them in the hall ⌊which he **c**⌋
	10:21	for the hall ⌊which he **c**⌋
	13:21	The LORD also **c** to the man of
	17:10	He **c** to her, "Please bring me a
	17:11	to get it, he **c** to her again,
	17:20	Then he **c** to the LORD,
	17:21	over the boy three times and **c**
	18:26	and **c** on the name of Baal from
	18:28	(This is what their ritual **c** for.)
	20:7	Then the king of Israel **c** for all
	20:39	the disciple **c** to him.
	22:6	So the king of Israel **c** 400
	22:9	The king of Israel **c** for an
2Ki	3:13	The LORD has **c** the three of
	3:21	to bear arms were **c** to fight.
	4:1	of the prophets **c** to Elisha,
	4:12	Gehazi **c** her, and she stood in
	4:15	So Gehazi **c** her, and she
	4:22	She **c** her husband and said,
	4:36	Elisha **c** Gehazi and said,
	4:36	"Gehazi **c** her. When she came
	6:11	He **c** his officers and asked
	7:10	So they **c** the city gatekeepers
	9:1	The prophet Elisha **c** one of the
	12:7	So King Joash **c** for Jehoiada
	12:18	who **c** off the attack on
	18:4	They **c** it Nehushtan.
	18:18	When they **c** for King Hezekiah,
	20:11	Then the prophet Isaiah **c** on
1Ch	5:20	They had **c** out to God during
	11:7	so it was **c** the City of David.
	13:11	(That place is still **c** Perez
	15:3	David **c** together all Israel at
	15:4	David also **c** together Aaron's
	15:11	David **c** for the priests Zadok
	21:26	He **c** on the LORD,
2Ch	7:14	who are **c** by my name,
	13:4	He **c** out, "Jeroboam and all
	14:11	Asa **c** on the LORD his God.
	18:5	So the king of Israel **c** 400
	18:8	The king of Israel **c** for an
	20:2	Tamar" (also **c** En Gedi).
	20:26	that place is still **c** the valley of
	24:6	So the king **c** for the chief
	25:5	Amaziah **c** the people of Judah
	32:20	about this and **c** to heaven.
Neh	5:12	Then I **c** the priests and made
Est	4:5	Then Esther **c** for Hathach,
	9:26	So the Jews **c** these days
Job	29:12	the poor who **c** ⌊for help⌋
Psa	17:6	I have **c** on you because you
	18:3	I **c** on him, and I was saved
	18:6	I **c** on the LORD in my distress.
	30:3	You **c** me back to life from
	31:17	O LORD, I have **c** on you,
	34:6	Here is a poor man who **c** out.
	79:6	kingdoms that have not **c** you.
	81:7	you **c** out ⌊to me⌋,
	99:6	They **c** to the LORD,
	118:5	During times of trouble I **c** on
	119:145	I have **c** out with all my heart.
	119:146	I have **c** out. Save me, so that I
	138:3	When I **c**, you answered me.
Pro	1:24	"I **c**, and you refused to listen.
	16:21	truly wise is **c** understanding,
	21:24	person is **c** a mocker.
Sos	5:6	I **c** for him, but he did not
Isa	1:26	After that you will be **c** the
	4:3	in Jerusalem will be **c** holy,
	6:3	They **c** to each other and said,
	10:3	you do on the day you are **c**
	13:3	I've **c** my mighty men to carry
Isa	19:18	One of the cities will be **c**
	21:8	The watchman **c**, "Sir, I stand
	31:4	a crowd of shepherds is **c**
	32:5	will no longer be **c** nobles,
	35:8	It will be **c** the Holy Road.
	40:6	A voice **c**, "Call out!" I asked,
	41:9	of the earth and **c** you from its
	42:6	have **c** you to do what is right.
	43:1	I have **c** you by name;
	43:7	Bring everyone who is **c** by my
	45:3	have **c** you by name.
	45:4	I have **c** you by name.
	47:1	longer be **c** soft and delicate.
	47:5	You will no longer be **c** the
	48:8	and that you have been **c**
	48:12	Jacob, Israel, whom I have **c**.
	48:15	I have **c** him. I will bring him
	50:2	one here to answer when I **c**?
	51:2	When I **c** Abraham,
	54:5	He is **c** the God of the whole
	54:6	"The LORD has **c** you as if you
	56:7	because my house will be **c** a
	58:12	You will be **c** the Rebuilder of
	61:3	They will be **c** Oaks of
	61:6	You will be **c** the priests of the
	61:6	You will be **c** the servants of
	62:4	will no longer be **c** Deserted,
	62:4	will no longer be **c** Destroyed.
	62:12	They will be **c** Holy People,
	62:12	and you will be **c** Sought After,
	63:19	who are not **c** by your name.
	65:12	I **c**, but you didn't answer.
	66:4	I **c**, but no one answered.
Jer	7:10	house that is **c** by my name.
	7:11	The house that is **c** by my
	7:13	When I **c** you, you did not
	7:14	house that is **c** by my name.
	7:30	house that is **c** by my name.
	11:16	The LORD **c** you a large olive
	14:9	We are **c** by your name.
	15:16	because I am **c** by your name,
	19:6	will no longer be **c** Topheth
	19:6	it will be **c** Slaughter Valley.
	32:34	temple that is **c** by my name,
	33:16	Jerusalem will be **c** The LORD
	34:15	temple that is **c** by my name.
	35:17	I **c** to them, but they didn't
	36:4	Then Jeremiah **c** Baruch,
	36:9	a time for fasting was **c**.
	42:8	So Jeremiah **c** Kareah's son
Lam	1:15	He **c** an army to defeat my
	1:19	I **c** for those who love me,
Eze	9:3	The LORD **c** to the person
	10:13	were **c** the whirling wheels.
	20:29	it is still **c** 'worship site' today.)
	38:8	time you will be **c** to service.
	39:11	So it will be **c** the valley of
Dan	3:4	The herald **c** out loudly,
	6:20	the king **c** to Daniel with
	9:18	and at the city **c** by your name.
	9:19	people are **c** by your name."
Hos	2:17	the names of other gods **c** Baal.
	11:1	and I **c** my son out of Egypt.
	11:2	The more I **c** them,
Jnh	2:2	Jonah prayed: "I **c** to the LORD
Hag	1:11	I **c** for a drought on the land,
Zec	6:8	Then he **c** out to me,
	7:13	"When I **c**, they wouldn't listen.
	8:3	Jerusalem will be **c** the City of
	8:3	will be **c** the holy mountain.
	11:10	Then I took my staff **c** Favor
	11:14	staff, **c** Unity, in pieces,
Mal	1:4	They will be **c** 'the Wicked
Mat	1:16	of Jesus, who is **c** Christ.
	2:4	He **c** together all the chief
	2:7	Then Herod secretly **c** the wise
	2:15	"I have **c** my son out of Egypt."
	2:23	his home in a city **c** Nazareth.
	2:23	"He will be **c** a Nazarene."
	4:18	Simon (**c** Peter) and Andrew.
	4:21	nets to go fishing. He **c** them,
	5:9	They will be **c** God's children.
	5:19	commands say will be **c** great
	10:1	Jesus **c** his twelve disciples
	10:2	Simon (who is **c** Peter) and his
	10:25	If they have **c** the owner of the
Mat	15:10	Then he **c** the crowd and said
	15:32	Jesus **c** his disciples and said,
	18:2	He **c** a little child and had him
	20:25	Jesus **c** the apostles and said,
	20:32	Jesus stopped and **c** them.
	21:13	'My house will be **c** a house of
	25:14	He **c** his servants and
	26:36	to a place **c** Gethsemane.
	27:8	why that field has been **c**
	27:17	or Jesus, who is **c** Christ?"
	27:22	with Jesus, who is **c** Christ?"
	27:33	They came to a place **c**
	27:34	wine mixed with a drug **c** gall.
Mar	1:20	He immediately **c** them,
	3:13	**c** those whom he wanted,
	3:14	twelve whom he **c** apostles.
	3:23	Jesus **c** them together and
	6:7	He **c** the twelve apostles,
	7:14	Then he **c** the crowd again and
	8:1	Jesus **c** his disciples and said
	8:34	Then Jesus **c** the crowd to
	9:35	He sat down and **c** the twelve
	10:42	Jesus **c** the apostles and said,
	10:49	They **c** the blind man and told
	11:17	'My house will be **c** a house of
	12:43	He **c** his disciples and said to
	14:32	to a place **c** Gethsemane.
	15:16	of the palace and **c** together
	15:23	mixed with a drug **c** myrrh,
Luk	1:32	be a great man and will be **c**
	1:35	developing inside you will be **c**
	1:76	"You, child, will be **c** a prophet
	2:4	to a Judean city **c** Bethlehem.
	6:13	he **c** his disciples.
	6:13	of them and **c** them apostles.
	6:15	Simon (who was **c** the Zealot),
	7:11	Jesus went to a city **c** Nain.
	7:18	Then John **c** two of his
	8:2	also **c** Magdalene,
	8:8	After he had said this, he **c** out,
	8:54	Jesus took her hand and **c** out,
	9:1	Jesus **c** the twelve apostles
	9:10	to a city **c** Bethsaida so that
	13:12	When Jesus saw her, he **c** her
	15:19	I don't deserve to be **c** your son
	15:21	to be **c** your son anymore.'
	15:26	He **c** to one of the servants and
	16:2	So the rich man **c** for his
	16:5	"So the manager **c** for each one
	18:16	But Jesus **c** the infants to him
	19:13	⌊Before he left,⌋ he **c** ten of his
	19:29	Mount of Olives (as it was **c**),
	21:37	Mount of Olives (as it was **c**)
	22:1	Bread, **c** Passover, was near.
	22:47	The man **c** Judas,
	23:13	Then Pilate **c** together the chief
	23:33	came to the place **c** The Skull,
	24:13	going to a village **c** Emmaus.
Jon	1:48	the fig tree before Philip **c** you."
	2:9	person in charge **c** the groom
	4:5	at a city in Samaria **c** Sychar.
	4:25	(Messiah is the one **c** Christ.)
	5:2	was a pool **c** Bethesda
	9:24	So once again the Jews **c** the
	11:16	Thomas, who was **c** Didymus,
	11:47	priests and the Pharisees **c**
	11:54	to a city **c** Ephraim,
	12:17	Jesus when he **c** Lazarus from
	15:15	But I've **c** you friends because
	18:33	**c** for Jesus, and asked him,
	19:13	in a place **c** Stone Pavement.
	19:13	(In Hebrew it is **c** Gabbatha.)
	19:17	city⌋ to a location **c** The Skull.
	19:17	(In Hebrew this place is **c**
	20:24	who was **c** Didymus,
	21:2	Thomas (**c** Didymus),
Act	1:12	Jerusalem from the mountain **c**
	1:23	Joseph (who was **c** Barsabbas
	3:2	The gate was **c** Beautiful Gate.
	3:11	at the place **c** Solomon's Porch.
	4:18	They **c** Peter and John and
	4:32	No one **c** any of his
	4:36	The apostles **c** him Barnabas,
	5:21	who were with him **c** together
	5:40	They **c** the apostles,
	6:2	The twelve apostles **c** all the

Act 6:9 c Freedmen's Synagogue.
7:59 Stephen, he c out, "Lord Jesus,
8:10 and that power is c great."
9:41 After he c the believers,
10:7 Cornelius c two of his
10:24 them and had c his relatives
11:26 The disciples were c
13:1 Simeon (c the Black),
13:2 do the work for which I c them."
14:27 When they arrived, they c the
15:22 They chose Judas (c
16:10 We concluded that God had c
19:25 He c a meeting of his workers
20:17 to the city of Ephesus and c
23:17 Then Paul c one of the
23:18 "The prisoner Paul c me.
27:8 came to a port c Fair Harbors.
27:14 Soon a powerful wind (c a
27:16 side of a small island c Cauda,
28:1 out that the island was c Malta.
Rom 1:1 c to be an apostle and
1:6 among those who have been c
1:7 whom God loves and has c
7:3 she will be c an adulterer.
8:28 whom he has c according
8:30 He also c those whom he had
8:30 of those whom he had c,
9:24 for us whom he c — whether we
9:26 they will be c children of the
1Co 1:1 From Paul, c to be an apostle
1:2 holy by Christ Jesus and c
1:9 He c you to be partners with
1:24 Jews and Greeks who are c,
1:26 you were when God c you
7:15 God has c you to live in peace.
7:17 gave him when God c him.
7:18 circumcised when he was c
7:18 uncircumcised when he was c
7:20 they were when they were c.
7:21 you a slave when you were c?
7:22 If the Lord c you when you
7:22 were free when you were c,
7:24 you were in when God c you.
15:9 I'm not even fit to be c an
Gal 1:6 who c you in his kindness,
1:15 was born and who c me by his
5:13 You were indeed c to be free,
Eph 2:11 Those who c themselves "the
2:11 c you "the uncircumcised."
4:1 proves that God has c you.
4:4 In the same way you were c to
Col 3:15 God has c you into this peace
4:11 Jesus, c Justus, also greets
2Th 2:14 With this in mind he c you by
1Ti 6:12 life to which you were c
2Ti 1:9 God saved us and c us to be
Heb 5:4 God calls him as he c Aaron.
7:2 He is also c king of Salem
9:2 The first part of this tent was c
9:3 was the part of the tent c
9:15 so that those who are c can
11:8 to obey when God c him
11:16 not ashamed to be c their God.
Jas 2:23 Abraham was c God's friend.
1Pe 1:15 But because the God who c
2:9 who c you out of darkness into
2:21 God c you to endure suffering
3:9 because you were c to inherit
4:16 God for being c that name.
5:10 who has c you through Christ
2Pe 1:3 knowledge of the one who c
1Jn 3:1 actually c God's dear children.
Jud 1:1 To those who have been c,
Rev 2:24 who haven't learned what are c
9:11 In Hebrew he is c Abaddon,
9:11 and in Greek he is c Apollyon.
14:18 This angel c out in a loud
16:16 is c Armageddon in Hebrew.
17:14 Those who are c, chosen,

calling (20)

Exo 34:6 c out, "The LORD, the LORD,
1Sm 3:8 that the LORD was c the boy.
26:14 "Who is c the king?"
Job 31:30 didn't speak sinfully by c down
Psa 116:4 But I kept c on the name of the
Pro 8:4 "I am c to all of you,
Isa 21:11 Someone is c to me from Seir,
Jer 3:4 But now you are c to me.
Amo 7:4 The Almighty LORD was c for
Mat 27:47 that, they said, "He's c Elijah."
Mar 10:49 Get up! He's c you."
15:35 "Listen! He's c Elijah."
Jon 11:28 and he is c for you."
2Co 5:20 and through us God is c you.
Gal 1:7 But what some people are c
5:8 from the one who is c you.
Heb 3:1 holy partners in a heavenly c.
2Pe 1:10 use more effort to make God's c
Rev 5:2 I saw a powerful angel c out in
11:12 voice from heaven c to them,

calls (40)

Gen 46:33 Now, when Pharaoh c for you
Jdg 15:19 [Spring of the One Who C Out].
1Sm 3:9 "When he c you, say, 'Speak,
Job 11:10 ⌊someone⌋ and then c
12:4 I am one who c on God and
30:24 is ruined when that person c
Psa 42:7 One deep sea c to another at
86:5 everyone who c out to you.
Pro 1:21 of noisy streets she c out.
9:3 She c from the highest places
9:15 and c to those who pass by,
Isa 40:26 He c them all by name.
59:4 No one c for justice,
62:6 Whoever c on the LORD,
64:7 No one c on your name or tries
Jer 20:3 he c you Terror Everywhere.
Hos 7:7 and none of them c to me.
Joe 2:32 Then whoever c on the name
2:32 be those whom the LORD c,
Amo 5:8 He c for water from the sea to
9:6 the one who c for the water in
Mic 6:9 The voice of the LORD c out to
Mat 5:22 Whoever c another believer an
5:22 Whoever c another believer a
22:45 If David c him Lord,
Mar 12:37 David c him Lord. So how can
Luk 15:6 Then he c his friends and
15:9 When she finds it, she c her
20:44 David c him Lord. So how can
Jon 10:3 He c his sheep by name and
10:35 So if God c people gods (and
Act 2:21 Then whoever c on the name
9:14 priests to put anyone who c
Rom 4:17 and c into existence nations
11:29 gifts or when he c someone.
Eph 1:18 the confidence that he c you
1Th 2:12 to the God who c you into his
5:24 The one who c you is faithful,
Heb 5:4 God c him as he called Aaron.
Rev 2:20 who c herself a prophet.

calm (18)

Jdg 6:23 LORD said to him, "C down!
Job 30:27 are churning and won't c down.
37:17 when the earth is c under a
Psa 107:29 He made the storm c down,
131:2 have kept my soul c and quiet.
Ecc 9:17 attention to c words from wise
10:4 If you remain c, you can make
Isa 7:4 Say to him, 'Be careful, stay c,
25:5 You c the uproar of foreigners.
32:17 peace, c, and safety forever.
Jnh 1:11 we do with you to c the sea?"
1:12 Then the sea will become c.
1:15 and the sea became c.
Mat 8:26 and the sea became very c.
14:27 Jesus said, "C down!
Mar 4:39 and the sea became very c.
6:50 Immediately, he said, "C down!
Luk 8:24 and the sea became c.

calmed (3)

Neh 8:11 So the Levites c all the people
Job 26:12 With his power he c the sea.
Jer 49:23 like a sea that can't be c.

calmly (2)

Psa 62:1 My soul waits c for God alone.
62:5 Wait c for God alone,

calms (5)

Jdg 6:24 He called it The LORD C.
Psa 65:7 the one who c the roar of the
Pro 15:18 but one who holds his temper c
21:14 A gift ⌊given⌋ in secret c anger,
21:14 and a secret bribe c great fury.

Calneh (2)

Gen 10:10 and C in Shinar [Babylonia].
Amo 6:2 Go to C and look. Go from there

Calno (1)

Isa 10:9 Isn't C like Carchemish?

calves (32)

Gen 18:7 herd and took one of his best c.
Dtr 7:13 He will bless your herds with c,
28:4 Your cattle will have c,
28:18 will be cursed with few c,
28:51 no c from your herds,
1Sm 6:7 Take their c away,
6:10 and shut the c in the stall.
14:32 They took sheep, cows, and c,
2Sm 17:29 buttermilk, sheep, and c.
1Ki 1:9 and fattened c at Zoheleth
1:19 has sacrificed many fattened c,
1:25 bulls, fattened c, and sheep.
12:28 the king made two golden c.
12:32 in Bethel to sacrifice to the c
2Ki 10:29 of⌋ the golden c that were at
17:16 They made two c out of cast
2Ch 13:8 and you have the gold c that
Job 21:10 birth to c and never miscarry.
Psa 68:30 the herd of bulls with the c of
144:14 May our cattle have many c.
Isa 1:11 enough fat from your fattened c.
11:6 C, young lions, and year-old
27:10 C will graze there.
Jer 31:12 and olive oil, lambs and c.
46:21 soldiers are like fattened c.
50:11 You dance around like c on the
Eze 1:7 their feet were like those of c,
Amo 6:4 flocks and c from their stalls.
Mic 6:6 year-old c as burnt offerings?
Mal 4:2 You will go out and leap like c
Mat 22:4 My bulls and fattened c have
Heb 9:19 Then he took the blood of c

camel (5)

Gen 24:64 she got down from her c.
Jer 2:23 You are like a young c that
Mat 19:24 again that it is easier for a c
Mar 10:25 It is easier for a c to go through
Luk 18:25 Indeed, it is easier for a c to go

camel's (3)

Gen 31:34 put them in her c saddle-bag
Mat 3:4 wore clothes made from c hair
Mar 1:6 in clothes made from c hair.

camels (54)

Gen 12:16 male and female slaves, and c.
24:10 ten of his master's c and left,
24:11 The servant had the c kneel
24:14 and I'll also water your c,' let
24:19 for your c until they've had
24:20 and drew enough for all his c.
24:22 When the c had finished
24:25 of straw and feed ⌊for your c⌋
24:30 with the c by the spring.
24:31 and made a place for the c."
24:32 The c were unloaded and
24:35 female slaves, c and donkeys.
24:44 draw water for your c," let her
24:46 and I'll water your c too.'
24:46 and she also watered the c.
24:61 Riding on c, they followed the
24:63 looked up, he saw c coming.
30:43 female slaves, c, and donkeys.
31:17 children and his wives on c.
32:7 and the c into two camps.
32:15 30 female c with their young,
37:25 Their c were carrying the
Exo 9:3 c, cattle, sheep, and goats.
Lev 11:4 You must never eat c.

Lev 11:4 (C are unclean because they
Dtr 14:7 They include c, rabbits,
Jdg 6:5 They and their c could not be
7:12 There were so many c that
1Sm 15:3 and sheep, c and donkeys."
27:9 took sheep, cattle, donkeys, c,
30:17 men who rode away on c.
1Ki 10:2 with c carrying spices,
2Ki 8:9 had loaded the goods on 40 c.
1Ch 5:21 livestock: 50,000 of their c,
12:40 donkeys, c, mules, and oxen.
27:30 for the c: Obil, a descendant of
2Ch 9:1 with c carrying spices,
14:15 captured many sheep and c.
Ezr 2:67 435 c, and 6,720 donkeys.
Neh 7:69 435 c, and 6,720 donkeys.
Job 1:3 and goats, 3,000 c, 1,000 oxen,
1:17 and made a raid on the c.
1:17 They took the c and
42:12 and goats, 6,000 c, 2,000 oxen,
Isa 21:7 on donkeys, and riders on c.
30:6 treasures on the humps of c
60:6 "Many c will cover your ⌊land⌋,
60:6 young c from Midian and
66:20 on mules and c to my holy
Jer 49:29 and c will be carried away.
49:32 Their c will be taken as prizes.
Eze 25:5 turn Rabbah into a pasture for c,
Zec 14:15 horses, mules, c, donkeys,
Mat 23:24 but you swallow c.

camels' (2)

Jdg 8:21 that were on their c necks
8:26 the chains from their c necks

camp (278)

Gen 32:2 Jacob said, "This is God's c!"
32:8 "If Esau attacks the one c,
32:8 then the other c will be able to
32:21 he stayed in the c that night.
Exo 14:2 up their c facing Pi Hahiroth,
14:2 Set up your c facing north — by
14:9 they were setting up their c by
14:20 between the Egyptian c and
14:20 camp and the Israelite c.
14:24 the Egyptian c into a panic.
16:13 quails came and covered the c,
16:13 a layer of dew around the c.
19:2 They had set up c there in front
19:16 people in the c shook with fear.
19:17 led the people out of the c
29:14 and excrement outside the c.
32:17 "It's the sound of war in the c!"
32:19 When he came near the c,
32:26 the entrance to the c and said,
32:27 and forth from one end of the c
33:7 and set it up far outside the c.
33:7 will used to go outside the c
33:11 would come back to the c,
36:6 message announced all over c:
40:36 the Israelites would break c.
40:37 they wouldn't break c.
Lev 4:12 to a clean place outside the c
4:21 will take the bull outside the c
6:11 to a clean place outside the c.
8:17 and excrement outside the c,
9:11 and the skin outside the c.
10:4 Take them outside the c."
10:5 away to a place outside the c,
13:46 They must live outside the c.
14:3 The priest will go outside the c
14:8 After that he may go into the c.
16:26 Then he may return to the c.
16:27 bull and the goat outside the c.
16:28 Then he may return to the c.
17:3 or goat inside or outside the c
24:10 with an Israelite in the c.
24:14 must be taken outside the c.
24:23 name was taken outside the c.
Num 1:50 care of the tent and c around it.
1:51 When we c, they will set it up.
1:52 "The other Israelites will c with
1:53 The Levites will c all around
2:3 the armies led by Judah will c
2:9 troops in Judah's c is 186,400.
2:10 Reuben will c under their flag.
Num 2:16 in Reuben's c is 151,450.
2:17 same order as they are in the c,
2:18 Ephraim will c under their flag.
2:24 in Ephraim's c is 108,100.
2:25 by Dan will c under their flag.
2:31 the men in Dan's c is 157,600.
2:34 They set up c under their flags,
4:5 When the c is supposed to
4:15 holy things and the c is ready
5:2 outside the c anyone who has
5:3 men and women outside the c.
5:3 They must not make this c
5:4 unclean people outside the c.
9:17 the Israelites would break c,
9:17 the Israelites would set up c.
9:18 the Israelites would break c,
9:18 command they would set up c.
9:19 command and wouldn't break c.
9:20 command they would set up c,
9:20 command they would break c.
9:21 in the morning, they broke c.
9:21 smoke moved, they broke c.
9:22 same place and not break c.
9:22 they would break c.
9:23 command they set up c,
9:23 at his command they broke c.
10:2 and as a signal to break c.
10:5 the east side will break c first.
10:6 on the south will break c.
10:6 fanfare is the signal to break c.
10:14 descendants broke c first.
10:17 who carried it, broke c.
10:18 descendants broke c next.
10:21 carried the holy things, broke c.
10:22 descendants broke c next.
10:25 As a rear guard for the whole c,
10:25 Dan's descendants broke c last
10:28 armies broke c when they went
10:31 know where we can set up c
10:34 by day when they moved the c.
11:1 people on the outskirts of the c.
11:9 When dew fell on the c at night,
11:26 had stayed in the c.
11:26 and they prophesied in the c.
11:27 are prophesying in the c."
11:30 the leaders went back to the c.
11:31 dropped them all around the c.
11:32 the quails out all around the c.
12:14 be put in isolation outside the c
12:15 put in isolation outside the c
12:15 The people didn't break c until
12:16 from Hazeroth and set up c
14:44 and Moses stayed in the c.
15:35 outside the c and stone him."
15:36 took him outside the c
19:3 It must be taken outside the c
19:7 After that, he may go into the c.
19:9 in a clean place outside the c.
21:10 moved and set up c at Oboth.
21:11 and set up c at Iye Abarim
21:12 they moved and set up c at
21:13 moved from there and set up c
22:1 set up c across from Jericho,
22:5 and are setting up their c here
22:41 the outskirts of the Israelites' c.
24:2 looked up, and saw Israel's c
31:12 the community of Israel at the c
31:13 outside the c to meet them.
31:19 stay outside the c seven days.
31:24 you may come into the c."
33:1 Israelites set up c after they left
33:5 and set up c at Succoth.
33:6 Succoth and set up c at Etham,
33:7 and set up c near Migdol.
33:8 they set up c at Marah.
33:9 so they set up c there.
33:10 from Elim and set up c by
33:11 from the Red Sea and set up c
33:12 of Sin and set up c at Dophkah.
33:13 Dophkah and set up c at Alush.
33:14 and set up c at Rephidim,
33:15 from Rephidim and set up c
33:16 set up c at Kibroth Hattaavah.
33:17 and set up c at Hazeroth.
33:18 and set up c at Rithmah.
33:19 and set up c at Rimmon Perez.
Num 33:20 Perez and set up c at Libnah.
33:21 Libnah and set up c at Rissah.
33:22 and set up c at Kehelathah.
33:23 and set up c at Mount Shepher.
33:24 and set up c at Haradah.
33:25 and set up c at Makheloth.
33:26 and set up c at Tahath.
33:27 Tahath and set up c at Terah.
33:28 Terah and set up c at Mithcah.
33:29 and set up c at Hashmonah.
33:30 and set up c at Moseroth.
33:31 and set up c at Bene Jaakan.
33:32 and set up c at Hor Haggidgad.
33:33 and set up c at Jotbathah.
33:34 and set up c at Abronah.
33:35 and set up c at Ezion Geber.
33:36 Geber and set up c at Kadesh
33:37 and set up c at Mount Hor
33:41 Hor and set up c at Zalmonah.
33:42 and set up c at Punon.
33:43 Punon and set up c at Oboth.
33:44 and set up c at Iye Abarim
33:45 Iyim and set up c at Dibon Gad.
33:46 set up c at Almon Diblathaim.
33:47 Almon Diblathaim and set up c
33:48 Abarim Mountains and set up c
33:49 They set up c on the plains of
33:49 Their c extended from Beth
Dtr 1:7 Break c, and get ready! Go to
1:33 you to find places for you to c.
2:15 until none were left in the c.
2:24 continued,⌋ "Now break c.
23:9 you're at war and have set up c
23:10 go outside the c and stay there.
23:11 sunset he may come back to c.
23:12 Choose a place outside the c
23:14 God moves around in your c
23:14 So your c must always be holy.
29:11 water in your c are also here.
Jos 1:11 "Go through the c.
3:2 the officers went through the c.
3:3 break c and follow them.
3:14 So they broke c to cross the
4:3 down where you will c tonight."
4:8 They carried them to the c and
4:19 They made their c at Gilgal,
5:8 in the c until they recovered.
6:11 Then they went back to the c
6:14 day and returned to the c.
6:18 and disaster on the c of Israel.
6:23 a place outside the c of Israel.
8:13 The main c was north of the
8:14 the king of Ai saw the main c,
9:6 to Joshua in the c at Gilgal.
9:17 The Israelites broke c.
10:6 to Joshua at the c in Gilgal:
10:15 returned to the c at Gilgal.
10:21 Joshua in the c at Makkedah.
10:43 returned to the c at Gilgal.
18:9 to Joshua at the c at Shiloh.
Jdg 6:4 The enemy used to c on the
7:1 Midian's c was north of him at
7:8 The c of Midian was below
7:9 Go into the c! I will hand it over
7:10 take your servant Purah to the c
7:11 the courage to go into the c
7:11 Purah went to the edge of the c.
7:13 around in the c of Midian.
7:14 and the whole c over to him."
7:15 Then he went back to the c of
7:15 hand Midian's c over to you."
7:17 I come to the edge of the c,
7:18 the rest of you around the c do
7:19 men came to the edge of the c.
7:21 kept his position around the c,
7:21 everyone in the Midianite c
7:22 the LORD caused the whole c
18:12 Dan [The C of Dan] today.
21:8 come to the assembly in the c.
21:12 They brought them to the c at
1Sm 4:3 the troops came back to the c,
4:5 the LORD's ark came into the c,
4:6 this shouting in the Hebrew c?"
4:6 ark had come into the c.
4:7 god has come into ⌊their⌋ c."
11:11 into the ⌊Ammonite⌋ c during

1Sm 13:17 parties left the Philistine c
14:16 ⌊in the Philistine c⌋ dispersing
14:17 "and see who has left ⌊our c⌋."
14:19 the confusion in the Philistine c
14:21 stationed in the c now joined
17:4 champion came out of their c.
17:15 from Saul's c to Bethlehem,
17:17 brothers in the c right away.
17:20 He went to the c as the army
17:53 all the goods in the Philistine c.
22:4 was living in his fortified c.
22:5 "Don't live in your fortified c,"
24:22 his men went to their fortified c.
26:5 Saul was lying in the c,
26:6 go with me to Saul in the c?"
26:7 was lying asleep inside the c
2Sm 1:2 day a man came from Saul's c.
1:3 "I escaped from the c of Israel,"
17:8 He will not c with the troops
23:14 David was in the fortified c,
23:16 men burst into the Philistine c
1Ki 16:16 troops in the c made Omri,
2Ki 3:24 the Moabites came to Israel's c,
6:8 about where they were to c.
7:4 So let's go to the Aramean c.
7:5 dusk to go into the Aramean c.
7:5 they came to the edge of the c,
7:7 They abandoned the c as it
7:8 came to the edge of the c,
7:10 "We went into the Aramean c,
7:12 so they've left the c to hide in
7:16 out and looted the Aramean c.
19:35 ⌊soldiers⌋ in the Assyrian c.
25:1 They set up c and built dirt
1Ch 9:19 the entrances to the LORD's c.
11:16 David was in the fortified c,
11:18 three burst into the Philistine c
12:8 to join David at the fortified c
12:16 came to David at the fortified c.
2Ch 22:1 the raiders who came to the c
31:2 the gates of the LORD's c.
32:1 He set up c ⌊to attack⌋ the
32:21 in the Assyrian king's c.
Job 19:12 me and c around my tent.
Psa 27:3 an army sets up c against me,
53:5 who set up c against you.
69:25 Let their c be deserted and their
78:28 birds fall in the middle of his c,
106:16 In the c certain men became
Isa 37:36 ⌊soldiers⌋ in the Assyrian c.
Jer 52:4 They set up c and built dirt
Eze 1:24 the commotion in an army c.
Zec 9:8 I will c in front of my house as
Heb 13:11 burned outside the Israelite c.
13:13 must go to him outside the c
Rev 20:9 the earth and surrounded the c

campaign (4)

Jos 10:42 and their territories in one c
1Sm 18:6 David was returning from a c
23:13 So he gave up the c.
2Sm 10:14 So Joab stopped his c against

campaigning (1)

1Sm 29:6 I consider your c with me a

campaigns (2)

1Sm 21:5 kept holy even on ordinary c.
1Ch 11:2 who led Israel on its c to war.

camped (45)

Gen 33:18 He c within sight of the city.
Exo 13:20 from Succoth and c at Etham,
15:27 They c there by the water.
17:1 They c at Rephidim,
18:5 the desert where he was c near
Num 10:5 the tribes that are c on the east
10:6 the tribes that are c on the
Jos 3:1 where they c before crossing.
5:10 The people of Israel c at Gilgal
8:11 They c north of Ai with the
10:5 c there, and attacked it.
10:31 c there, and attacked it.
10:34 Eglon, c there, and attacked it.
11:5 All these kings c together by
Jdg 6:33 and c in the valley of Jezreel.
Jdg 7:1 up early and c above En Harod.
9:50 c there, and captured it.
10:17 and they c at Gilead.
10:17 together and c at Mizpah.
11:18 They c east of Moab — east of
11:20 He c at Jahaz and attacked
15:9 c in Judah, and overran Lehi.
18:12 They c at Kiriath Jearim in
20:19 in the morning and c at Gibeah.
1Sm 4:1 and c near Ebenezer while
4:1 the Philistines c at Aphek.
13:5 They c at Michmash,
13:16 the Philistines c at Michmash.
17:1 and c between Socoh and
17:2 army of Israel assembled and c
26:3 Saul c by the road at the hill of
26:5 to the place where Saul had c.
26:5 the troops were c around him.
28:4 assembled and c in Shunem.
28:4 and they c at Gilboa.
29:1 and Israel c at the spring in
2Sm 17:26 The Israelites and Absalom c
24:5 the Jordan River and c at Aroer,
1Ki 16:15 while the army was c near
20:27 The Israelites, while c
20:29 They c facing one another for
1Ch 19:7 They c near Medeba.
Ezr 8:15 and we c there for three days.
Isa 29:1 the city where David c.
Luk 21:20 armies c around Jerusalem,

camping (2)

2Sm 23:13 from the Philistine army was c
1Ch 11:15 army of the Philistines was c

camps (14)

Gen 25:16 settlements and c — 12 leaders
32:2 that place Mahanaim [Two C].
32:7 and the camels into two c.
32:10 but now I have two c.
Num 2:32 troops in the c was 603,550.
1Sm 23:14 David lived in fortified c in the
23:14 and he lived in fortified c in the
23:19 with us in fortified c at Horesh
23:29 in the fortified c of En Gedi.
Psa 34:7 The Messenger of the LORD c
Isa 29:3 I will set up war c all around
Eze 25:4 They will set up their c and
Amo 4:10 I made the stench from your c
Zec 14:15 all other animals in those c.

Cana (5)

Jon 2:1 place in the city of C in Galilee.
2:11 C in Galilee was the place
4:46 to the city of C in Galilee,
4:46 A government official was in C.
21:2 Nathanael from C in Galilee,

Canaan (85)

Gen 9:19 Ham was the father of C.
9:22 Ham, father of C, saw his father
9:25 So he said, "C is cursed!
9:26 C will be his slave.
9:27 C will be his slave."
10:6 were Cush, Egypt, Put, and C.
10:15 C was the father of Sidon his
11:31 Ur of the Chaldeans to go to C.
12:5 Abram set out for C.
12:6 They arrived in C, and Abram
13:12 Abram lived in C, while Lot
16:3 After Abram had lived in C for
17:8 where you are living — all of C
23:2 Arba (that is, Hebron) in C.
31:18 back to his father Isaac in C.
33:18 to the city of Shechem in C.
35:6 Bethel) in the land of C.
36:2 his wives from the women of C:
36:5 of Esau who were born in C.
36:6 he had accumulated in C
37:1 to live in the land of C,
42:5 there was also famine in C.
42:7 "From C, to buy food,"
42:13 sons of one man in C.
42:29 came to their father Jacob in C,
42:32 stayed with our father in C.'
44:8 found in our sacks back from C.
Gen 45:17 animals, and go back to C.
45:25 came to their father Jacob in C.
46:6 they had accumulated in C.
46:12 (Er and Onan had died in C.)
46:31 father's family, who were in C,
47:1 brothers have arrived from C
47:4 The famine is so severe in C
47:13 Neither Egypt nor C were
47:14 in Egypt and in C as payment
47:15 in Egypt and C was gone,
48:3 me at Luz in C and blessed me.
48:7 Rachel died in C when we
49:30 east of Mamre in C,
50:5 tomb I bought for myself in C."
50:13 They carried him back to C
Exo 6:4 made a promise to give them C,
15:15 The people of C will be deathly
16:35 they came to the border of C.
Lev 14:34 "When you come to C that I am
18:3 I am bringing you to C.
25:38 you out of Egypt to give you C
Num 13:2 "Send men to explore C,
13:17 Moses sent them to explore C,
26:19 but they died in C.
32:30 of must be in C with yours."
32:32 We will enter C as armed
33:40 in the Negev, which was in C,
33:51 Jordan River and entering C.
34:2 When you enter C,
34:29 to divide C for the Israelites.
35:10 the Jordan River and enter C,
35:14 the Jordan River and three in C.
Dtr 32:49 Take a look at the land of C
Jos 5:12 to eat the crops that grew in C.
14:1 people of Israel inherited in C.
21:2 at Shiloh in C. They said to
22:9 of the Israelites at Shiloh in C.
22:10 of the Jordan that was still in C.
22:11 built an altar at the border of C.
22:32 and Gad in Gilead to Israel in C
24:3 I led him through all of C and
Jdg 1:3 we will fight the people of C.
3:1 not experienced any war in C.
4:2 LORD used King Jabin of C,
4:23 the power of King Jabin of C.
5:19 Then the kings of C fought.
21:12 to the camp at Shiloh in C.
1Ch 1:8 were Cush, Egypt, Put, and C.
1:13 C was the father of Sidon his
16:18 by saying, 'I will give you C.
Psa 105:11 "I will give you the land of C.
106:38 they sacrificed to the idols of C.
135:11 and all the kingdoms in C.
Isa 19:18 that speak the language of C
Oba 1:20 will take possession of C.
Zep 2:5 C, the land of the Philistines:
Act 7:11 throughout Egypt and C
13:19 destroyed seven nations in C

Canaan's (1)

Isa 23:11 C fortifications be destroyed.

Canaanite (17)

Gen 10:18 Later the C families scattered.
28:1 to marry any of the C women.
28:6 to marry any of the C women.
28:8 Isaac disapproved of C women.
34:1 went out to visit some of the C
38:2 of a C man whose name
46:10 the son of a C woman.
Exo 6:15 the son of a C woman.
Num 21:1 When the C king of Arad,
33:40 (The C king of Arad,
Jos 5:1 River and all the C kings along
11:7 and attacked the C armies.
13:3 is considered to be C territory,
1Ch 2:3 him by Bathshua, a C woman.
Neh 9:24 You handed the C kings and
Zec 14:21 there will no longer be any C
Mat 15:22 A C woman from that territory

Canaanites (63)

Gen 10:19 The border of the C extended
12:6 At that time the C were in the
13:7 (C and Perizzites were also
15:21 the Amorites, the C,

Gen 24:3 of the **C** among whom I'm
24:37 son from the daughters of the **C**,
34:30 the **C** and the Perizzites,
50:11 When the **C** living there saw
Exo 3:8 milk and honey where the **C**,
3:17 in Egypt to the land of the **C**,
13:5 give you the land of the **C**,
13:11 brings you to the land of the **C**
23:23 **C**, Hivites, and Jebusites.
23:28 **C**, and Hittites out of your way.
33:2 and I will force out the **C**,
34:11 **C**, Hittites, Perizzites, Hivites,
Lev 18:3 Don't live the way the **C** do.
Num 13:29 And the **C** live along the coast
14:25 (The Amalekites and **C** are
14:43 Amalekites and **C** are there,
14:45 The Amalekites and **C** who
21:3 and handed the **C** over
21:3 They destroyed the **C** and their
Dtr 1:7 coast (the land of the **C**),
7:1 **C**, Perizzites, Hivites,
11:30 in the region of the **C** who live
20:17 **C**, Perizzites, Hivites,
Jos 3:10 he will certainly force the **C**,
7:9 When the **C** and everyone who
9:2 **C**, Perizzites, Hivites,
11:3 the **C** from east and west,
12:8 **C**, Perizzites, Hivites,
13:4 all the land of the **C** as well as
16:10 they did not force out the **C**
16:10 So the **C** still live in Ephraim
17:12 since the **C** were determined
17:13 they made the **C** do forced
17:16 all the **C** living in the valley,
17:18 But you must force out the **C**,
24:11 **C**, Hittites, Girgashites, Hivites,
Jdg 1:1 go first to fight the **C** for us?"
1:2 to hand the **C** over to you."
1:4 and the LORD handed the **C**
1:5 defeated the **C** and Perizzites.
1:9 went to fight the **C** who lived
1:10 Then they went to fight the **C**
1:17 They defeated the **C** who lived
1:27 The **C** were determined to live
1:28 they made the **C** do forced
1:29 not force out the **C** who lived
1:29 So the **C** continued to live with
1:30 So the **C** continued to live with
1:32 continued to live with the **C**
1:33 continued to live with the **C**.
3:3 all the **C**, the Sidonians,
3:5 of Israel lived among the **C**,
2Sm 24:7 cities of the Hivites and the **C**.
1Ki 9:16 and killed the **C** living there.
Ezr 9:1 disgusting practices of the **C**,
Neh 9:8 to him to give the land of the **C**,
9:24 You defeated for them the **C**,
9:24 they wanted with the **C**.
Eze 16:3 were in the land of the **C**.

canals (3)

Exo 7:19 of Egypt — its rivers, **c**, ponds,
8:5 over the rivers, **c**, and ponds.
Isa 19:6 The **c** will stink. Egypt's

cancel (9)

Lev 26:44 I will not reject or **c** my promise
Num 30:8 he can **c** the vow or promise
Dtr 15:1 seven years, you must **c** debts.
31:10 seventh year you must **c** debts.
Est 8:5 **c** the official orders
Luk 7:42 kind enough to **c** their debts.
Rom 3:3 **c** God's faithfulness?
Gal 3:15 No one can **c** a person's will or
3:17 Abraham⌋ into effect didn't **c**

canceled (7)

Num 30:12 Her husband has **c** it,
Dtr 15:9 on debts are **c** — is near,
Est 8:8 king's signet ring cannot be **c**."
Psa 77:8 **c** throughout every generation?
Mat 18:27 freed him, and **c** his debt.
18:32 I **c** your entire debt,
Luk 7:43 who had the largest debt **c**."

cancels (2)

Num 30:12 But if her husband **c** it when he
30:15 But if he **c** it later, he will suffer

cancer (3)

Pro 12:4 disgraces him is like bone **c**.
14:30 but jealousy is ⌊like⌋ bone **c**.
2Ti 2:17 they say will spread like **c**.

Candace (1)

Act 8:27 of Queen **C** of Ethiopia.

cane (6)

Exo 21:19 walk around outside with a **c**,
30:23 6 ¼ pounds of fragrant **c**;
Isa 43:24 You did not buy me any sugar **c**
Jer 6:20 Sugar **c** that comes from a
Eze 27:19 and sugar **c** for your goods.
Zec 8:4 Each will have a **c** in hand

Canneh (1)

Eze 27:23 Haran, **C**, Eden, the merchants

canopy (27)

Exo 26:31 "Make a **c** of violet,
26:33 Hang the **c** from the fasteners
26:33 The **c** will mark off the most
26:35 "Place the table outside the **c**
27:21 of meeting outside the **c** where
30:6 Put the altar in front of the **c**
35:12 of mercy and the **c** over it,
36:35 They made the **c** out of violet,
38:27 for the holy place and the **c**.
39:34 the **c** over ⌊the ark⌋,
40:3 and hang the **c** over the ark.
40:21 the tent and hung the **c** over
40:22 side of the tent outside the **c**.
40:26 tent of meeting in front of the **c**.
Lev 4:6 LORD's presence facing the **c**
4:17 LORD's presence facing the **c**.
16:2 If he goes up to the **c** and
16:12 He will bring them up to the **c**.
16:15 the blood inside, go up to the **c**,
21:23 he must never come up to the **c**
24:3 outside the **c** where the words
Num 4:5 down the **c** that hangs over
4:5 will cover the ark with the **c**.
18:7 at the altar and under the **c**.
2Ch 3:14 Solomon made the **c** of violet,
Isa 40:22 stretches out the sky like a **c**
Jer 43:10 spread his royal **c** above them.

capable (4)

Exo 18:21 "But choose **c** men from all the
18:25 Moses chose **c** men from all
Neh 10:28 and everyone who is **c** of
1Co 6:2 aren't you **c** of judging

cape (7)

Rut 3:15 "Stretch out the **c** you're
Mat 27:28 and put a bright red **c** on him.
27:31 they took off the **c** and put his
Mar 15:20 they took off the purple **c** and
Jon 19:2 and put a purple **c** on him.
19:5 of thorns and the purple **c**.
Act 27:7 So at **C** Salmone, we started to

caper (1)

Ecc 12:5 ⌊and⌋ the **c** bush has ⌊no⌋

Capernaum (18)

Mat 4:13 and made his home in **C**
8:5 When Jesus went to **C**,
11:23 And you, **C**, will you be lifted to
17:24 When they came to **C**,
Mar 1:21 Then they went to **C**.
2:1 later Jesus came back to **C**.
9:33 Then they came to **C**.
Luk 4:23 we've heard you've done in **C**.'"
4:31 Jesus went to **C**, a city in
7:1 say to the people, he went to **C**.
10:15 And you, **C**, will you be lifted to
Jon 2:12 disciples went to the city of **C**
4:46 His son was sick in **C**.
4:47 Jesus and asked him to go to **C**
Jon 4:51 official was on his way to **C**,
6:17 to cross the sea to the city of **C**.
6:24 boats and went to the city of **C**
6:59 teaching in a synagogue in **C**.

Caphtorites (3)

Gen 10:14 Philistines came), and the **C**.
Dtr 2:23 The **C**, who came from Crete,
1Ch 1:12 Philistines came), and the **C**.

capital (15)

Gen 36:32 of his ⌊**c**⌋ city was Dinhabah.
36:35 name of his **c** city was Avith.
36:39 and the name of his **c** city was
Jos 13:10 Sihon's **c** was Heshbon.
1Ki 7:16 Each **c** was 7 ½ feet high.
7:17 filigree and chains for each **c**.
2Ki 25:17 27 feet high and had a bronze **c**
25:17 around the **c** were all made
1Ch 1:43 of his ⌊**c**⌋ city was Dinhabah.
1:46 name of his ⌊**c**⌋ city was Avith.
1:50 and the name of his ⌊**c**⌋ city
2Ch 3:15 and the **c** on each pillar was 7
Isa 7:8 The **c** of Aram is Damascus,
7:9 The **c** of Ephraim is Samaria,
Jer 52:22 The **c** that was on it was 7 ½

capitals (13)

1Ki 7:16 He made two **c** of cast bronze
7:18 cover the **c** which were above
7:18 He made the **c** identical to
7:19 The **c** on top of the pillars in
7:20 filigree on the **c** on both pillars.
7:22 There were lily-shaped **c** at the
7:41 2 pillars, the bowl-shaped **c** on
7:41 to cover the 2 bowl-shaped **c**
7:42 2 bowl-shaped **c** on the pillars),
2Ch 3:16 and ⌊also⌋ put them on the **c**.
4:12 2 pillars, bowl-shaped **c** on top
4:12 to cover the 2 bowl-shaped **c**
4:13 2 bowl-shaped **c** on the pillars),

Cappadocia (2)

Act 2:9 Elamites. Judea, **C**, Pontus,
1Pe 1:1 Galatia, **C**, Asia, and Bithynia.

captain (38)

Gen 37:36 officials and **c** of the guard.
39:1 Egyptian officials and **c**
40:3 put them in the prison of the **c**
40:4 The **c** of the guard assigned
41:10 me and the chief baker to the **c**
41:12 a slave of the **c** of the guard,
1Sm 17:18 take these ten cheeses to the **c**
18:13 He made David **c** of a regiment.
2Sm 23:19 So he became their **c**,
2Ki 25:8 who was the **c** of the guard and
25:10 army that was with the **c**
25:11 the **c** of the guard,
25:12 The **c** of the guard left some of
25:15 The **c** of the guard took all of
25:18 The **c** of the guard took the
25:20 the **c** of the guard,
1Ch 11:21 So he became their **c** but didn't
Jer 37:13 the **c** of the guard there,
39:9 Babylon's **c** of the guard,
39:10 the **c** of the guard, At that time
39:13 Nebuzaradan (the **c** of the
40:1 the **c** of the guard, Nebuzaradan
40:2 The **c** of the guard took
40:5 The **c** of the guard gave
41:10 the **c** of the guard, son of
43:6 the **c** of the guard, son of
52:12 who was the **c** of the guard and
52:14 army that was with the **c**
52:15 the **c** of the guard,
52:16 the **c** of the guard,
52:19 The **c** of the guard also took
52:19 The **c** of the guard took all of
52:24 The **c** of the guard took the
52:26 the **c** of the guard,
52:30 the **c** of the guard, In all, 4,600
Dan 2:14 the **c** of the royal guard,
Jnh 1:6 The **c** of the ship went to him
Rev 18:17 Every ship's **c**, everyone who

captains (4)

2Sm 4:2 son had two men who were **c**
1Ki 14:27 where the **c** of the guards were
2Ch 12:10 where the **c** of the guards were
Job 39:25 the thundering ⌊orders⌋ of the **c**

captive (39)

Dtr 21:10 you may take them **c**.
32:42 who were killed and taken **c**.
Jdg 18:30 living in that land were taken **c**.
1Sm 30:3 daughters had been taken **c**.
2Ki 6:22 Do you kill everyone you take **c**
24:15 Jehoiakin to Babylon as a **c**.
1Ch 5:6 Assyria took him away as a **c**.
6:15 Jehozadak was taken **c** when
2Ch 33:11 They took Manasseh **c**,
Ezr 2:1 the exiles had been taken **c**.
9:7 We have been taken **c**,
Neh 7:6 the exiles had been taken **c**.
7:6 of Babylon had taken them **c**.
Est 2:6 (Kish had been taken **c** from
Psa 68:18 You took prisoners **c**.
78:61 his power to be taken **c**
106:46 from all those who held them **c**.
Sos 7:5 locks could hold a king **c**.
Isa 14:2 They will take their captors **c**
52:2 Get up, **c** Jerusalem.
52:2 your neck, **c** people of Zion.
Jer 13:17 LORD's flock will be taken **c**.
22:12 place where he was taken **c**,
29:4 were taken **c** from Jerusalem
29:14 where you are being held **c**.
41:10 Then Ishmael took **c** the rest of
41:10 took them **c** and left for Ammon.
41:14 had taken **c** at Mizpah turned
43:12 temples and take their gods **c**.
51:41 praised, has been taken **c**.
52:28 people Nebuchadnezzar took **c**:
Eze 6:9 nations where they are taken **c**.
12:3 March like a **c** from your place
12:4 leave like a **c** going into exile.
21:24 So you will be taken **c**.
Amo 1:6 have taken all the people **c**
Rom 7:23 sets and tries to take me **c**
2Co 10:5 We take every thought **c** so
Eph 4:8 he took **c** those who had

captives (55)

Dtr 21:11 a beautiful woman among the **c**
1Sm 30:8 up with them and rescue the **c**."
1Ki 8:46 them to ⌊another⌋ country as **c**,
8:47 in the land where they are **c**,
8:48 their enemies where they are **c**,
2Ki 15:29 people away to Assyria as **c**.
16:9 took the people to Kir as **c**,
17:6 the Israelites to Assyria as **c**.
17:23 from their land to Assyria as **c**,
17:26 "The people you took as **c** and
18:11 the Israelites to Assyria as **c**.
24:15 Jerusalem as **c** to Babylon.
24:16 fight in war as **c** to Babylon.
25:21 So the people of Judah were **c**
1Ch 8:6 taken away as **c** to Manahath:
8:7 led the rest of them away as **c**.
9:1 taken away to Babylon as **c**
2Ch 6:36 them to ⌊another⌋ country as **c**,
6:37 in the land where they are **c**,
6:38 in the land where they are **c**,
36:20 They remained **c** until the
Job 3:18 There the **c** have no troubles at
Pro 24:11 Rescue **c** condemned to death,
Isa 20:4 and the old — **c** from Egypt
61:1 to announce that **c** will be set
Jer 20:4 will take the people away as **c**
24:5 of Israel says: The **c** of Judah,
28:4 and all the **c** of Judah who
28:6 and all the **c** from Babylon
29:1 rest of the leaders among the **c**.
29:1 took away as **c** from Jerusalem
29:7 city where I've taken you as **c**,
29:16 who weren't taken away as **c**:
29:20 all you **c** who were sent away
29:22 Because of them, all the **c** from
29:28 You will be **c** a long time.
29:31 this message to all the **c**:
Jer 30:10 from where they are **c**.
30:16 will be taken away as **c**.
30:18 I'm going to bring the **c** back to
40:1 in chains along with the **c**
43:3 us or take us as **c** to Babylon."
46:19 you will be taken away as **c**.
46:27 from the land where you are **c**.
49:6 I will return the **c** of Ammon,
49:39 I'll return the **c** of Elam,
52:27 So the people of Judah were **c**
Eze 29:14 I will bring back the Egyptian **c**
39:25 Now I will bring back Jacob's **c**
Dan 2:25 "I've found one of the **c** from
5:13 one of the **c** that my grandfather
6:13 one of the **c** from Judah,
Joe 3:1 I will bring back the **c** of Judah
Zec 9:11 I will set your **c** free from the
9:12 you **c** who have hope.

captivity (35)

1Ch 5:26 of the tribe of Manasseh into **c**.
6:15 and Jerusalem away into **c**.
Ezr 8:35 from **c** sacrificed burnt
Neh 1:2 **c** and about Jerusalem.
1:3 "Those who survived **c** are in
Pro 7:22 like a ram hobbling into **c**
Isa 46:2 They go away into **c**.
Jer 1:3 were taken away into **c**
13:19 will be taken away into **c**.
15:2 are destined to die in **c** will die
15:2 to die in captivity will die in **c**.'
20:6 in your house will go into **c**.
22:22 and your lovers will go into **c**.
24:1 builders from Jerusalem into **c**
27:19 into **c** from Jerusalem to
29:14 I will bring you back from **c**.
30:3 Israel and Judah back from **c**.
31:23 have brought them back from **c**,
32:44 their **c**," declares the LORD.
48:7 Chemosh will go into **c** with all
48:11 They haven't gone into **c**.
48:46 will be taken away into **c**.
49:3 will be taken away into **c**
Lam 1:5 ahead of their opponents into **c**.
1:18 young men have gone into **c**.
Eze 12:11 will go into exile and into **c**.
33:21 in the twelfth year of our **c**,
39:23 the people of Israel went into **c**
39:28 I sent them into **c** among the
40:1 of the twenty-fifth year of our **c**
Hos 6:11 I bring my people back from **c**.
10:5 glory will be taken away into **c**.
Amo 1:5 of Aram will go into **c** at Kir.
1:15 Their king will go into **c** along
Nah 3:10 Even she went into **c** and was

captors (2)

Isa 14:2 They will take their **c** captive
Mic 2:4 divides our fields among our **c**."

capture (28)

Dtr 2:37 bank of the Jabbok River or **c**
20:19 city for a long time in order to **c**
20:20 blockade until you **c** the city.
Jos 8:7 out of hiding and **c** the city.
Jdg 7:24 **C** the watering holes as far as
1Sm 23:14 but God didn't let him **c** David.
23:26 and his men, trying to **c** them.
2Sm 12:28 surround the city, and **c** it.
12:28 Otherwise, I will **c** the city,
2Ki 6:13 Then I will send men to **c** him."
7:12 we'll **c** them alive and get into
10:14 Jehu ordered, "**C** them!"
21:14 property that their enemies **c**.
2Ch 32:18 so that they could **c** the city.
Pro 16:32 even-tempered than to **c** a city.
Jer 32:3 of Babylon, and he will **c** it.
32:24 built up around the city to **c** it!
32:28 of Babylon. They will **c** it.
34:22 attack it, **c** it, and burn it down.
37:8 They will attack the city, **c** it,
38:3 and it will **c** the city."
43:11 He will **c** those who are
Dan 11:15 and **c** a fortified city.
11:18 to the coastlands and **c** many
Hos 9:6 Egypt will **c** them and
Amo 6:13 to **c** Karnaim by ourselves."
9:12 They will **c** the few survivors
Hab 1:10 city and build a dirt ramp to **c** it.

captured (140)

Gen 14:14 that his nephew had been **c**,
Exo 22:10 it dies, is injured, or is **c** in war,
Num 21:32 the Israelites **c** its cities and
31:26 the people and animals you **c**.
32:39 Manasseh, went to Gilead, **c** it,
32:41 **c** the settlements in Gilead.
32:42 Nobah **c** Kenath and its
Dtr 1:39 children would be **c** in war,
2:34 At that time we **c** all his cities
2:35 we did loot the cities that we **c**,
3:4 At that time we **c** all of his
3:4 We **c** a total of 60 cities — the
3:5 We also **c** a large number of
21:13 was wearing when you **c** her.
Jos 6:20 straight ahead and **c** the city.
8:8 When you have **c** the city,
8:19 They entered the city, **c** it,
8:21 who had been hiding had **c**
8:22 The men who had **c** the city
8:23 But they **c** the king of Ai alive
10:1 heard that Joshua had **c** Ai
10:28 same day Joshua **c** Makkedah,
10:32 He **c** it on the next day and
10:32 the same way he had **c** Libnah.
10:35 They **c** it that day and killed
10:37 They **c** it and its neighboring
10:39 He **c** it and its king and all its
10:40 So Joshua **c** the whole land —
10:42 Joshua **c** all these kings and
11:10 Then Joshua turned back and **c**
11:12 So Joshua **c** all these cities
11:17 He **c** all their kings and killed
11:19 Israel **c** everything in battle.
11:23 Joshua **c** the whole land as the
12:4 in Ashtaroth and Edrei was **c**.
15:17 of Caleb's brother Kenaz, **c** it.
19:47 **c** it, and killed everyone there.
22:9 which they had **c** as
Jdg 1:8 attacked Jerusalem and **c** it.
1:13 younger brother Kenaz, **c** it.
1:18 Judah also **c** Gaza,
3:28 They followed him and **c** the
7:24 They **c** the watering holes as
7:25 They also **c** Oreb and Zeeb,
8:6 You haven't **c** Zebah and
8:12 He **c** King Zebah and King
8:14 and **c** a young man from
8:15 **c** Zebah and Zalmunna."'
9:44 the city and **c** its entrance.
9:45 He **c** the city and killed the
9:50 camped there, and **c** it.
12:5 The men of Gilead **c** the
21:23 They **c** the number of wives
1Sm 4:11 The ark of God was **c**.
4:17 and the ark of God has been **c**."
4:19 that the ark of God had been **c**
4:21 the ark of God had been **c**
4:22 of God has been **c**," she said.
5:1 After the Philistines had **c** the
15:8 He **c** King Agag of Amalek
30:2 Although they **c** the young and
30:5 The Amalekites also **c** David's
2Sm 5:7 But David **c** the fortress Zion
12:26 Rabbah and **c** its royal fortress.
12:27 "I fought against Rabbah and **c**
12:29 He fought against the city and **c**
21:16 **c** David and intended to kill
1Ki 8:50 and cause those who **c** them to
9:16 (The king of Egypt **c** Gezer,
16:18 saw that the city had been **c**,
2Ki 10:14 ⌊Jehu's men⌋ **c** and
14:13 of Israel **c** King Amaziah,
16:9 He **c** it, took the people to Kir
17:6 the king of Assyria **c** Samaria
17:27 of the priests you **c** from there.
18:10 and **c** it at the end of three
18:13 cities of Judah and **c** them.
24:12 the king of Babylon **c**
24:14 He **c** all Jerusalem,
25:6 The Babylonians **c** the king,
25:11 **c** the few people left in the city,

1Ch 2:23 Geshur and Aram c Havvoth
5:21 They c 100,000 people.
5:22 land until the Assyrians c them.
11:5 But David c the fortress Zion
2Ch 12:4 He c the fortified cities in
13:19 Abijah pursued Jeroboam and c
14:13 The LORD's army c a lot of
14:15 cattle graze and c many sheep
15:8 and the cities he had c in the
17:2 that his father Asa had c.
22:9 and Jehu's men c him while he
25:12 The Judeans c another 10,000
25:23 of Israel c King Amaziah,
28:5 him, c many prisoners,
28:8 Israelites c 200,000 women,
28:11 you have c from your relatives,
28:17 Judah and c prisoners.
28:18 They c and began living in
30:9 from those who c them.
Neh 9:25 The Israelites c fortified cities
Psa 137:3 was there that those who had c
137:7 the day Jerusalem ⌊was c⌋.
Isa 13:15 Whoever is c will be executed.
20:1 to fight against Ashdod, he c it.
22:3 and were c without their bows
28:13 will be hurt, trapped, and c.
36:1 cities of Judah and c them.
Jer 34:3 You will certainly be c and
38:23 You will be c by the king of
38:28 until the day Jerusalem was c.
39:9 c the few people left in the city,
41:10 He c the king's daughters and
43:11 who are supposed to be c.
48:1 be put to shame; it will be c.
48:7 your treasures, you will be c.
48:41 the fortified places will be c.
50:2 Say, 'Babylon will be c.
50:9 Babylon will be c from the
50:24 You will be found and c
50:33 All their enemies have c them.
50:46 news that Babylon has been c.
51:31 Babylon that his entire city is c.
51:41 "Sheshach has been c.
51:56 its soldiers will be c,
52:9 The Babylonians c the king
52:15 c the few people left in the city,
Eze 17:12 to Jerusalem and c its king
21:23 and they will be c.
33:21 He said, "The city has been c."
40:1 years after Jerusalem was c.
Dan 11:12 When that army is c,
11:33 They will be c and looted.
Amo 4:10 men along with your c horses.
Zec 14:2 The city will be c,
2Co 4:9 We're c, but we're not killed.
Eph 4:8 took captive those who had c
Heb 7:2 a tenth of everything he had c.
7:4 him a tenth of what he had c,
Rev 19:20 miracles for the beast were c.

captures (2)

Jos 15:16 attacks Kiriath Sepher and c it."
Jdg 1:12 defeats Kiriath Sepher and c it."

capturing (1)

Act 12:4 After c Peter, Herod had him

caravan (2)

Gen 37:25 they saw a c of Ishmaelites
Isa 21:13 You c of travelers from the

caravans (1)

Job 6:19 C from Tema look for them.

Carcas (1)

Est 1:10 Bigtha, Abagtha, Zethar, and C,

carcasses (2)

Gen 15:11 of prey came down upon the c,
Nah 2:12 used to fill its caves with torn c

Carchemish (3)

2Ch 35:20 came to fight a battle at C at
Isa 10:9 Isn't Calno like C?
Jer 46:2 defeated his army at C along

care (161)

Gen 2:15 farm the land and to take c of it.
4:9 to take c of my brother?"
30:29 to your livestock under my c.
30:31 then I'll go back to taking c of
30:36 Jacob continued to take c of
33:13 frail and that I have to take c
36:24 desert while he was taking c
37:2 He took c of the flocks with the
37:12 His brothers had gone to take c
37:13 "Your brothers are taking c of
37:16 they're taking c of their flocks."
39:6 all that he owned in Joseph's c.
39:23 to anything under Joseph's c
40:4 and he took c of them.
42:37 Let me take c of him,
46:32 They take c of livestock.
46:34 'We have taken c of herds all
50:24 God will definitely take c of
50:25 will definitely take c of you.
Exo 3:1 Moses was taking c of the
12:6 Take c of it until the fourteenth
30:7 when he takes c of the lamps.
Lev 6:2 you were supposed to take c
6:4 were supposed to take c of,
Num 1:50 They will take c of the tent and
3:8 They will take c of all the
3:26 They took c of all these things.
3:31 They took c of all these things.
3:36 They took c of all these things.
3:37 They also took c of the posts
4:4 They will take c of the most
4:32 They must take c of all this
7:9 because they took c of the holy
11:14 I can't take c of all these
11:17 They will help you take c of
11:17 You won't have to take c of the
Dtr 1:9 "I'm not able to take c of you
1:12 How can I take c of your
12:19 Don't forget to take c of the
14:27 Never forget to take c of the
28:39 vineyards and take c of them,
32:10 guarded them, took c of them,
Jdg 18:7 people there lived without a c.
19:20 Let me take c of your needs.
Rut 2:20 responsible for taking c of us."
3:9 relative who can take c of me."
3:13 if he will agree to take c of you,
3:13 He can take c of you.
3:13 does not wish to take c of you,
3:13 I will take c of you myself.
4:14 who will take c of you.
1Sm 2:25 God will take c of him.
2Sm 14:8 to take c of this matter."
15:16 behind to take c of the palace.
16:21 whom he left to take c
18:3 they won't c about us,
18:3 they won't c either.
1Ki 1:4 servant and took c of him,
1:15 Shunem was taking c of him.
2Ki 9:34 Then he said, "Take c of this
2Ch 31:14 at East Gate and had to take c
Ezr 10:13 We can't take c of this outside.
10:13 this sin that it can't be taken c
Est 2:3 There, in the c of the king's
2:8 were placed in the c of Hegai.
2:8 and placed in the c of Hegai,
2:14 There she would be in the c of
Job 3:4 above not ⌊even⌋ c about it.
Psa 8:4 of Man that you take c of him?
10:4 ⌊and says⌋, "God doesn't c."
10:13 to himself, "God doesn't c"?
22:10 was placed in your c from birth.
27:10 the LORD will take c of me.
55:22 and he will take c of you.
65:9 You take c of the earth,
74:1 against the sheep in your c?
80:15 Take c of what your right hand
95:7 and we are the people in his c,
100:3 people and the sheep in his c.
144:3 that you should c about them?
Pro 27:18 Whoever takes c of a fig tree
31:13 out wool and linen ⌊with c⌋
Sos 1:6 I have not even taken c of my
8:12 to those who take c of its fruit.
Isa 13:17 They don't c for silver and
40:11 Like a shepherd he takes c of
46:3 I've taken c of you from the
46:4 you're old, I'll take c of you.
46:4 and will continue to c for you.
Jer 15:15 Remember me, take c of me,
21:7 compassion, or c for them.'
23:1 in my c," declares the LORD.
23:2 to the shepherds who take c
23:2 You have not taken c of them,
23:2 so now I will take c of you by
23:4 shepherds will take c of them.
Eze 34:2 Israel who have been taking c
34:2 shepherds take c of the sheep?
34:3 you don't take c of the sheep.
34:8 They have taken c of only
34:10 I won't let them take c of my
34:10 and they will no longer take c
34:13 I will take c of them on the
34:15 I will take c of my sheep and
34:16 I will take c of my sheep fairly.
34:23 and he will take c of them.
34:23 He will take c of them and be
44:8 You didn't take c of my holy
44:15 descendants of Zadok took c
44:16 and take c of everything I gave
48:11 They took c of my holy place.
Hos 12:12 he took c of sheep to pay for
12:13 a prophet to take c of them.
13:5 I took c of you in the desert,
14:8 them and take c of them.
Mic 2:8 by without a c as they return
7:14 take c of your people,
Zep 2:7 The LORD their God will take c
Zec 10:3 The LORD of Armies takes c of
11:4 Take c of the sheep that are
11:7 And I took c of the sheep.
11:16 He will not take c of those that
Mat 4:11 angels came to take c of him.
8:33 Those who took c of the pigs
25:36 and you took c of me.
25:43 and you didn't take c of me.'
27:4 They replied, "What do we c?
28:14 hears about it, we'll take c of it,
Mar 1:13 and the angels took c of him.
4:38 don't you c that we're going to
5:14 Those who took c of the pigs
5:26 she had been under the c
Luk 1:68 He has come to take c of his
7:16 has taken c of his people."
8:34 When those who had taken c
10:34 to an inn, and took c of him.
10:35 the innkeeper, 'Take c of him.
10:40 "Lord, don't you c that my sister
Jon 15:1 Father takes c of the vineyard.
21:16 "Take c of my sheep."
Act 7:20 His parents took c of him for
14:26 had been entrusted to God's c
15:40 entrusted him to the Lord's c.
18:15 you'll have to take c of that
24:23 his friends take c of his needs.
27:3 and receive any c he needed.
Rom 12:19 let God's anger take c of it.
1Co 9:7 Does anyone take c of a flock
Eph 5:29 he feeds and takes c of it,
5:29 as Christ takes c of the church.
1Th 2:7 mother taking c of her children.
1Ti 3:5 can he take c of God's church?)
5:8 If anyone doesn't take c of his
5:10 taking c of believers' needs,
2Ti 1:16 He often took c of my needs
Heb 2:6 of Man that you take c of him?
13:17 They take c of you because
Jas 1:27 is to take c of orphans and
Jud 1:12 They are shepherds who c
Rev 12:6 so that she might be taken c
12:14 where she could be taken c of

cared (3)

Isa 57:11 remembered me or c about me.
Jon 12:6 say this because he c about
Act 18:17 But Gallio couldn't have c less.

carefree (2)

Psa 123:4 ridicule from those who are c.
Eze 23:42 heard the noise from a c crowd.

careful (57)

Gen 31:24 "Be **c** not to say anything at all
31:29 'Be **c** not to say anything at all
Exo 23:13 "Be **c** ⌊to do⌋ everything I told
34:12 Be **c** not to make a treaty with
34:15 Be **c** not to make a treaty with
Dtr 2:4 be afraid of you, but be very **c**.
4:9 However, be **c**, and watch
4:15 at Mount Horeb. So be very **c**
4:23 Be **c** that you don't forget the
5:32 So be **c** to do what the LORD
6:3 and be **c** to obey these laws.
6:12 be **c** that you don't forget the
8:1 Be **c** to obey every command I
8:11 Be **c** that you don't forget the
8:14 When this happens, be **c** that
11:16 Be **c**, or you'll be tempted to
11:32 be **c** to obey all the laws and
12:13 Be **c** that you don't sacrifice
12:30 be **c** you aren't tempted to
15:9 Be **c** not to think these
24:8 Be very **c** to do exactly as the
Jos 23:11 Be very **c** to love the LORD
Jdg 13:4 Now you must be **c**.
13:13 "Your wife must be **c** to do
13:14 She must be **c** to do everything
1Sm 19:2 Please be **c** tomorrow morning.
2Ki 6:9 "Be **c** not to go by that place.
1Ch 28:10 So be **c**, because the LORD
2Ch 19:7 Be **c** about what you do.
Ezr 4:22 Be **c** not to neglect your duty in
Job 36:18 Be **c** that you are not led astray
36:21 Be **c**! Don't turn to evil, because
Isa 7:4 Say to him, 'Be **c**, stay calm,
38:15 I will be **c** the rest of my life
Mal 2:15 So be **c** not to be unfaithful to
2:16 "Be **c** not to be unfaithful."
Mat 6:1 "Be **c** not to do your good
16:6 Jesus said to them, "Be **c**!
18:10 "Be **c** not to despise these little
23:3 So be **c** to do everything they
24:4 Jesus answered them, "Be **c**
Mar 8:15 Jesus warned them, "Be **c**!
13:5 Jesus answered them, "Be **c**
13:33 Be **c**! Watch! You don't know
Luk 11:35 So be **c** that the light in you
12:15 He told the people, "Be **c** to
21:8 Jesus said, "Be **c** that you are
Act 13:40 "Be **c**, or what the prophets
1Co 3:10 Each person must be **c** how he
8:9 But be **c** that by using your
10:12 should be **c** that they don't
Gal 5:15 be **c** that you don't destroy
Eph 5:15 then, be very **c** how you live.
Col 2:8 Be **c** not to let anyone rob you
Heb 3:12 Be **c**, brothers and sisters,
12:25 Be **c** that you do not refuse to
2Jn 1:8 Be **c** that you don't destroy

carefully (56)

Exo 15:26 He said, "If you will listen **c** to
19:5 If you **c** obey me and are
Lev 20:22 "If you **c** obey all my laws and
22:31 "**C** obey my commands.
25:18 and **c** follow my rules.
26:3 and **c** obey my commands:
Dtr 15:5 bless you only if you listen **c**
16:12 and obey these laws **c**.
17:10 Follow all their instructions **c**,
27:8 Write clearly and **c** all the
28:1 **C** obey the LORD your God,
Jos 22:3 You have **c** kept the
22:5 **C** follow the commands and
Jdg 2:22 or not they will **c** follow
1Ki 22:43 Jehoshaphat **c** followed the
1Ch 22:13 will succeed if you will **c** obey
2Ch 20:32 Jehoshaphat **c** followed the
Ezr 8:29 Guard them **c**. In Jerusalem,
Job 13:17 "Listen **c** to my words.
21:2 "Listen **c** to my words,
29:16 I **c** investigated cases brought
Psa 37:10 Then you can **c** examine
48:9 Inside your temple we **c** reflect
49:3 the insights I have **c**
119:4 principles be **c** followed.
Psa 143:5 I **c** consider what your hands
Pro 4:26 **C** walk a straight path,
15:28 person **c** considers how
23:12 and listen **c** to words of
Ecc 8:9 and I have **c** considered all that
8:16 When I **c** considered how to
9:1 I have **c** thought about all this,
12:9 He very **c** thought about it,
12:10 wrote the words of truth very **c**.
Isa 21:7 Let him watch **c**, very carefully.
21:7 Let him watch carefully, very **c**.
47:7 You didn't **c** consider these
55:2 Listen **c** to me: Eat what is
Jer 2:33 You **c** planned ways to look for
12:16 Suppose they learn **c** the ways
Hag 1:5 **C** consider your ways!
1:7 **C** consider your ways!
2:15 from now on, **c** consider this.
2:18 **C** consider from now on,
2:18 LORD was laid. **C** consider:
Mal 2:2 you don't **c** consider this.
Mat 2:8 "Go and search **c** for the child.
Luk 4:10 of you to watch over you **c**.
9:44 "Listen **c** to what I say.
15:8 and look for the coin **c** until she
Act 5:35 consider **c** what you do with
17:11 and every day they **c**
21:24 **c** follow Moses' Teachings.
1Co 11:2 about me and for **c** following
Heb 3:1 So look **c** at Jesus,
1Pe 1:10 The prophets **c** researched and

careless (4)

Pro 12:18 **C** words stab like a sword,
14:16 a fool is **c** and overconfident.
Ecc 5:3 **C** speaking comes when there
Mat 12:36 of every **c** word they say.

carelessly (6)

Exo 20:7 name of the LORD your God **c**.
20:7 anyone who **c** uses his name
Num 30:6 or **c** promise that she
Dtr 5:11 name of the LORD your God **c**.
5:11 his name **c** will be punished.
Job 6:3 sand of the seas. I spoke **c**

cares (7)

Dtr 11:12 the LORD your God **c** about.
1Sm 10:2 father no longer **c** about them.
Psa 142:4 No one **c** about me.
Pro 12:10 A righteous person **c** ⌊even⌋
Isa 57:1 people die, and no one **c**.
Jer 30:17 outcast: Zion, no one **c** for you.
1Pe 5:7 to God because he **c** for you.

caressed (3)

Eze 23:3 fondled and **c** their breasts.
23:8 to bed with her, **c** her breasts,
23:21 when young men **c** and fondled

caresses (2)

Sos 2:6 His right hand **c** me.
8:3 His right hand **c** me.

caressing (1)

Gen 26:8 saw Isaac **c** his wife Rebekah.

caretaker (1)

Sos 1:6 They made me the **c** of the

caretakers (1)

Sos 8:11 He entrusted that vineyard to **c**.

cargo (7)

Eze 27:25 filled with heavy **c** in the sea.
Jnh 1:5 They began to throw the **c**
Act 21:3 the ship was to unload its **c**.
27:10 will cause damage to the **c**
27:18 began to throw the **c** overboard.
Rev 18:11 because no one buys their **c**
18:12 No one buys their **c** of gold,

Carites (2)

2Ki 11:4 company commanders of the **C**
11:19 company commanders of the **C**

Carmel (30)

Jos 12:22 the king of Jokneam in **C**,
15:55 villages: Maon, **C**, Ziph, Juttah,
19:26 The border touches **C** and
1Sm 15:12 "Saul went to **C** to set up a
25:2 whose business was in **C**.
25:2 was shearing his sheep in **C**.
25:5 told them, "Go to **C**, visit Nabal,
25:7 as long as they've been in **C**.
25:40 servants came to Abigail at **C**,
27:3 had been Nabal's wife) from **C**.
30:5 had been Nabal's wife) from **C**.
2Sm 2:2 had been Nabal's wife) from **C**.
3:3 had been Nabal's wife) from **C**.
23:35 Hezrai from **C**, Paarai from
1Ki 18:19 gather around me on Mount **C**.
18:20 prophets together on Mount **C**.
18:42 Elijah went to the top of **C** and
18:43 "Please go back to ⌊Mount **C**⌋.
2Ki 2:25 that place, went to Mount **C**,
4:25 to the man of God at Mount **C**.
1Ch 3:1 ⌊born⌋ to Abigail from **C**.
11:37 Hezro from **C**, Naari (son of
Sos 7:5 your head as high as Mount **C**.
Isa 33:9 Bashan and **C** are shaken.
35:2 the majesty of **C** and Sharon.
Jer 46:18 Someone who is like Mount **C**
50:19 They will eat on Mount **C** and
Amo 1:2 top of ⌊Mount⌋ **C** is dried up.
9:3 if they hide on top of Mount **C**,
Nah 1:4 Bashan and **C** wither.

Carmi (7)

Gen 46:9 Hanoch, Pallu, Hezron, and **C**.
Exo 6:14 Hanoch, Pallu, Hezron, and **C**.
Num 26:6 and the family of **C**.
Jos 7:1 Achan, son of **C**, grandson of
7:18 tribe of Judah was the son of **C**,
1Ch 4:1 Hezron, **C**, Hur, and Shobal.
5:3 Hanoch, Pallu, Hezron, and **C**.

Carmi's (1)

1Ch 2:7 **C** son was Achar, who caused

carpenter (2)

Exo 38:23 He was a jeweler, **c**,
Mar 6:3 Isn't this the **c**, the son of Mary,

carpenter's (1)

Mat 13:55 Isn't this the **c** son?

carpenters (10)

Exo 35:35 of jewelers, **c**, and designers.
2Sm 5:11 **c**, and stonemasons.
2Ki 12:11 They used it to pay the **c**,
22:6 (These workers include the **c**,
1Ch 14:1 and **c** to build a palace for
22:15 stonecutters, masons, **c**,
2Ch 24:12 and they hired masons and **c** to
34:11 included **c** and builders.)
Ezr 3:7 to the stonecutters and **c**.
Isa 44:13 **C** measure blocks of wood

carpeted (1)

Psa 65:13 The valleys are **c** with grain.

Carpus (1)

2Ti 4:13 bring the warm coat I left with **C**

carriage (6)

Sos 3:9 King Solomon had a **c** made for
Act 8:28 the official rode along in his **c**,
8:29 said to Philip, "Go to that **c**,
8:30 Philip ran to the **c** and could
8:31 Philip to sit with him in his **c**.
8:38 official ordered the **c** to stop.

carried (125)

Gen 22:6 Abraham **c** the burning coals
31:26 You've **c** off all my daughters like
34:29 They **c** off all the wealth and
50:13 They **c** him back to Canaan
Exo 12:34 dough before it had risen and **c**
19:4 I did to Egypt and how I **c** you
38:21 ordered by Moses and **c** out by

Num 4:47 the work of serving and who **c**
10:17 who **c** it, broke camp.
10:21 who **c** the holy things,
13:23 They **c** it on a pole between
Dtr 1:31 how the LORD your God **c** you,
1:31 He **c** you wherever you went
10:3 I **c** the two tablets up the
31:9 to the Levitical priests who **c**
31:25 command to the Levites who **c**
Jos 3:14 The priests who **c** the ark of
3:17 The priests who **c** the ark of
4:8 They **c** them to the camp and
4:9 where the priests who **c** the ark
4:10 The priests who **c** the ark
4:10 tell the people had been **c** out.
4:18 The priests who **c** the ark of
6:12 The priests **c** the LORD's ark.
8:33 the Levitical priests who **c**
11:15 So Joshua **c** out what the
Jdg 3:18 back the men who had **c** it.
9:48 and **c** it on his shoulder.
16:3 He **c** them on his shoulders to
1Sm 14:18 because Ahijah **c** the ephod in
15:13 I **c** out the LORD's
17:7 The man who **c** his shield
17:34 a lion or a bear came and **c** off
2Sm 5:21 and his men **c** the idols away.
6:13 When those who **c** the ark of
20:12 he **c** Amasa from the road to
1Ki 2:26 you at this time because you **c**
5:15 men who **c** heavy loads,
8:4 The priests and the Levites **c**
8:15 with his hand he **c** it out.
8:24 With your hand you **c** it out as
14:28 guards **c** the shields and then
17:19 took him from her arms, **c**
2Ki 7:8 and **c** off the silver,
7:8 **c** off its contents, went away,
23:4 Then he **c** their ashes to
1Ch 12:24 They **c** shields and spears.
15:15 The Levites **c** God's ark on
15:26 God helped the Levites who **c**
15:27 all the Levites who **c** the ark,
18:7 that Hadadezer's servants **c**,
2Ch 5:5 The priests and the Levites **c**
6:4 with his hand he **c** it out.
6:15 With your hand you **c** it out as
8:16 All of Solomon's work was **c**
12:11 guards **c** the shields and then
24:24 So the Arameans **c** out ⌊the
29:16 They **c** into the courtyard every
35:3 It shouldn't be **c** on your
Ezr 6:12 It's to be **c** out exactly as
7:23 has commanded must be **c** out
Est 2:6 of Babylon had **c** away.)
9:1 and decree were to be **c** out.
Job 10:19 as if I had been **c** from the
15:12 your emotions **c** you away?
21:32 He is **c** to the cemetery,
Psa 9:16 by the judgment he has **c** out.
89:50 Remember how I have **c** in my
111:8 They are **c** out with truth and
119:166 **c** out your commandments.
Pro 17:12 its cubs than a fool ⌊**c** away⌋
Ecc 8:11 a crime isn't **c** out quickly,
Isa 8:4 from Samaria will be **c** away
8:10 but they won't be **c** out,
46:3 I've **c** you since your birth.
53:4 our suffering and **c** our
53:12 He **c** the sins of many.
60:4 daughters are **c** in their arms.
63:9 He always held them and **c**
66:12 You will nurse and be **c** in
Jer 10:5 They have to be **c**,
28:3 this place and **c** off to Babylon.
35:14 This order has been **c** out.
35:16 have **c** out the orders of their
40:3 He has **c** out his threat.
49:29 and camels will be **c** away.
Lam 2:17 He **c** out the threat he
Eze 8:3 the Spirit **c** me between
12:7 I let the people see me as I **c**
17:4 broke off the highest twig and **c**
23:14 Yet, she **c** her prostitution even
23:18 "She **c** out her prostitution
27:25 from Tarshish **c** your goods.
Dan 2:35 The wind **c** them away,
3:22 that the men who **c** Shadrach,
Hos 10:6 The thing itself will be **c** to
10:7 The king of Samaria will be **c**
Amo 5:26 You **c** along the statues of ⌊the
Oba 1:11 strangers **c** off Jacob's wealth.
Nah 2:7 It will be **c** away. Its young
Hab 1:4 and justice is never **c** out.
1:4 so that when justice is **c** out,
Zep 2:2 before the decree is **c** out
Zec 5:9 They **c** the basket into the sky.
Luk 16:22 and the angels **c** him to be with
21:24 and they will be **c** off into all
Jon 12:6 and **c** the contributions.)
19:17 He **c** his own cross and went
20:15 if you **c** him away,
Act 3:2 was being **c** by some men.
5:6 **c** him outside, and buried him.
5:10 So they **c** her outside and
5:15 As a result, people **c** their sick
7:43 You **c** along the shrine of
27:15 The wind **c** the ship away,
27:15 so we were **c** along by the
27:17 the sail and were **c** along by
Eph 3:11 which he **c** out through Christ
4:14 tossed and **c** about by all kinds
Heb 13:9 Don't get **c** away by all kinds of
1Pe 2:24 Christ **c** our sins in his body on
2Pe 3:17 So be on your guard not to be **c**
Rev 17:3 Then the angel **c** me by his
17:17 until God's words are **c** out.
21:10 He **c** me by his power away to

carriers (3)

Jos 9:21 woodcutters and water **c**
9:23 be woodcutters and water **c**
9:27 them woodcutters and water **c**

carries (12)

Lev 11:25 Whoever **c** any part of their
Num 11:12 them in my arms — as a nurse **c**
Dtr 32:11 and **c** them on its feathers,
Job 27:21 The east wind **c** him away,
Psa 37:7 when he **c** out his schemes.
68:19 who daily **c** our burdens for us.
Pro 10:23 laughter of a fool when he **c** out
Isa 40:11 He **c** them in his arms.
Jer 51:29 The LORD **c** out his plans
Hag 2:12 Suppose a person **c** meat set
Rom 2:27 The uncircumcised man who **c**
Rev 17:7 and the ten horns that **c** her.

carry (140)

Gen 21:12 will **c** on your name.
44:1 as much food as they can **c**.
50:25 So be sure to **c** my bones back
Exo 25:14 sides of the ark in order to **c** it.
25:28 and use them to **c** the table.
27:7 on both sides of the altar to **c** it.
28:12 In this way Aaron will **c** their
37:5 sides of the ark in order to **c** it.
38:7 on the sides of the altar to **c** it.
Lev 11:28 Those who **c** the dead body of
11:40 Those who **c** its dead body
15:10 Those who **c** such things must
Num 1:50 The Levites will **c** the tent and
4:10 put them on a frame to **c** them.
4:12 and put them on a frame to **c**
4:15 the Kohathites will come to **c**
4:15 The Kohathites will **c** all the
4:19 he will do and what he will **c**.
4:24 will do and what they will **c**:
4:25 They will **c** the sheets that are
4:25 They will also **c** the inner
4:27 All their work, whatever they **c**
4:27 they're supposed to **c**.
4:31 They will **c** the framework for
4:32 by name the things he will **c**.
4:49 told what to do and what to **c**.
7:9 They had to **c** the holy things
11:12 Are you really asking me to **c**
Dtr 1:31 as parents **c** their children.
10:8 set apart the tribe of Levi to **c**
14:24 with so much that you can't **c**
23:13 You must **c** a pointed stick as
25:6 the first son she has will **c**
Dtr 25:13 Never **c** two sets of weights,
29:11 who cut wood and **c** water
Jos 3:3 the Levitical priests who **c** it,
3:8 Order the priests who **c** the ark
3:13 The priests who **c** the ark of
4:16 "Order the priests who **c** the
6:4 Seven priests will **c** rams'
6:6 and have seven priests **c**
Jdg 5:19 But they didn't **c** off any rich
17:8 of Ephraim to **c** on his work.
1Sm 15:11 did not **c** out my instructions."
2Sm 18:20 You can **c** the news some
1Ki 12:4 "Your father made us **c** a heavy
12:15 directing these events to **c** out
15:22 He made them **c** the stones
2Ki 4:19 "**C** him to his mother."
5:17 dirt as a pair of mules can **c**.
5:23 couple of his own servants to **c**
1Ch 5:18 fighters who could **c** shields
15:2 only the Levites **c** God's ark
15:2 had chosen them to **c** his ark
23:26 Levites will no longer have to **c**
2Ch 2:2 70,000 men to **c** heavy loads,
2:18 70,000 of them **c** heavy loads,
10:4 "Your father made us **c** a heavy
10:15 directing these events to **c** out
16:6 He made them **c** the stones
20:25 found more than they could **c**.
30:12 so that they united to **c** out
Job 23:14 He will **c** out ⌊his⌋ orders
24:10 yet they **c** bundles of grain.
30:22 up and let the wind **c** me away.
31:36 I would certainly **c** it on my
32:22 maker would soon **c** me away.
Psa 20:4 heart's desire and **c** out all your
28:9 and **c** them forever.
91:12 They will **c** you in their hands
103:20 you mighty beings who **c** out
103:21 his servants who **c** out his will.
119:150 Those who **c** out plots against
149:9 to **c** out the judgment that is
Pro 6:27 Can a man **c** fire in his lap
Ecc 4:2 who still have to **c** on.
10:20 A bird may **c** your words,
Isa 5:29 as they snatch their prey and **c**
10:23 will **c** out this destruction
13:3 I've called my mighty men to **c**
15:7 That is why they **c** the wealth
19:21 to the LORD and **c** them out.
30:1 They **c** out plans, but not mine.
30:6 They **c** their riches on the
30:14 big enough to **c** live coals from
33:23 people will **c** off your loot.
41:16 The wind will **c** them away.
45:20 Ignorant people **c** wooden idols
46:1 gods that you **c** are burdens,
46:7 lift it on their shoulders and **c** it.
48:14 He will **c** out the LORD's plan
49:22 their arms and **c** your daughters
52:11 you Levites who **c** the utensils
53:11 He will **c** their sins as a burden.
57:13 A wind will **c** them all away.
64:6 and our sins **c** us away like the
Jer 17:21 If you value your lives, do not **c**
39:16 I'm going to **c** out my threat
46:9 Sudan and Put who **c** shields,
51:12 The LORD will **c** out his plans
Eze 12:6 your shoulders and **c** them out
29:19 He will **c** off its wealth,
38:4 They will **c** large and small
38:13 to **c** away large amounts
Hos 4:19 The wind will **c** them away in
5:14 I will **c** ⌊them⌋ off,
Joe 2:11 The troops that **c** out his
Mic 2:1 they **c** out their plans because
Nah 1:14 longer have descendants to **c**
Hab 1:7 They will **c** out their own kind
Zep 2:3 the land who **c** out his justice.
Mat 4:6 They will **c** you in their hands
23:4 make loads that are hard to **c**
27:32 forced him to **c** Jesus' cross.
Mar 6:55 the countryside and began to **c**
11:16 He would not let anyone **c**
15:21 forced him to **c** Jesus' cross.
Luk 4:11 They will **c** you in their hands
10:4 Don't **c** a wallet, a traveling

Luk 11:46 with loads that are hard to **c**.
11:46 But you won't lift a finger to **c**
14:27 So those who do not **c** their
23:26 made him **c** it behind Jesus.
Jon 5:10 allowed to **c** your cot today."
5:36 the Father gave me to **c** out,
Act 5:9 and they will **c** you outside for
15:10 our ancestors nor we can **c**.
20:24 I want to **c** out the mission I
21:35 that the soldiers had to **c** him.
Rom 9:7 will **c** on your name."
9:28 The Lord will **c** out his
11:10 **c** back-breaking burdens
13:4 has the right to **c** out
2Co 4:10 We always **c** around the death
10:15 need to **c** out our assignment
Gal 6:2 Help **c** each other's burdens.
6:17 After all, I **c** the scars of Jesus
Php 1:6 will **c** it through to completion
Heb 11:18 will **c** on your name."
Jas 4:15 will live and **c** out our plans."

carrying (48)

Gen 37:25 Their camels were **c** the
45:23 **c** Egypt's best products
45:23 ten female donkeys **c** grain,
Exo 25:27 to hold the poles for **c** the table.
28:29 he will be **c** the names of the
28:30 Aaron will always be **c** over
30:4 sides to hold the poles for **c** it.
32:15 and went down the mountain **c**
34:4 **c** the two stone tablets.
34:29 **c** the two tablets with God's
37:14 to hold the poles for **c** the table.
37:27 sides to hold the poles for **c** it.
Dtr 9:15 I was **c** the two tablets with the
Jos 3:15 When the priests who were **c**
6:8 the seven priests **c** the seven
6:13 The seven priests **c** the seven
1Sm 10:3 One will be **c** three young
10:3 one will be **c** three loaves of
10:3 one will be **c** a ⌊full⌋ wineskin.
17:41 by the man **c** his shield,
2Sm 6:17 The men **c** the ark set it in its
15:24 all the Levites with him were **c**
18:20 "You won't be the man **c** good
1Ki 10:2 with camels **c** spices,
1Ch 16:1 The men **c** the ark set it inside
2Ch 9:1 with camels **c** spices,
Ezr 4:5 of Judah from **c** out their plans
Neh 4:17 The workers who were **c** loads
5:18 were already **c** a heavy load.
Job 5:12 He keeps shrewd people from **c**
Psa 126:6 out weeping, **c** his bag of seed,
126:6 **c** his bundles of grain.
Isa 25:1 reliable in **c** out your plans
Jer 17:27 day by not **c** anything through
Eze 9:2 in linen who was **c** paper
9:3 who was **c** paper and pen.
9:11 in linen who was **c** paper
Mat 11:28 are tired from **c** heavy loads,
26:47 A large crowd **c** swords and
Mar 2:3 to him **c** a paralyzed man.
14:13 You will meet a man **c** a jug of
14:43 A crowd **c** swords and clubs
Luk 7:14 the men who were **c** it stopped.
22:10 and you will meet a man **c** a
24:1 They were **c** the spices that
Jon 18:3 They were **c** lanterns,
Act 26:12 "I was **c** out these activities
27:43 soldiers from **c** out their plan.

Carshena (1)

Est 1:14 from those closest to him — **C**,

cart (14)

1Sm 6:7 Now get a new **c** ready for two
6:7 Hitch the cows to the **c**.
6:8 and put it on the **c**.
6:8 Send the **c** on its way,
6:10 hitched them to a **c**,
6:11 of their hemorrhoids on the **c**.
6:14 The **c** came into the field of
6:14 chopped up the wood of the **c**
6:15 taken down ⌊from the **c**⌋
2Sm 6:3 men put God's ark on a new **c**
2Sm 6:3 were guiding the new **c**.
1Ch 13:7 a new **c** from Abinadab's home.
13:7 Uzzah and Ahio guided the **c**.
Isa 28:28 The wheels of his **c** will roll

carve (3)

Isa 22:16 What right do you have to **c** out
44:13 They **c** them with chisels and
44:13 They **c** them into forms of

carved (42)

Exo 20:4 Never make your own **c** idols
Lev 26:1 idols or set up a **c** statue
Dtr 4:16 and make your own **c** idols.
4:23 Don't make your own **c** idols or
4:25 corrupt and make **c** idols
5:8 Never make your own **c** idols
27:15 "Whoever has a **c** or metal
Jdg 17:3 I want to make a **c** idol and a
17:4 He made a **c** idol and a metal
18:14 an ephod, a **c** idol, a metal idol,
18:17 They took the **c** idol,
18:18 house and took the **c** idol,
18:20 and the **c** idol and went with
18:30 The people of Dan set up the **c**
18:31 the **c** idol Micah had
1Ki 6:18 Gourds and flowers were **c**
6:29 He **c** angels, palm trees,
6:32 He **c** angels, palm trees,
6:35 On them he **c** angels,
10:19 **C** into the back of the throne
2Ch 3:7 and he **c** angels into the walls.
33:7 Manasseh had a **c** idol made.
34:3 **c** idols, and metal idols.
34:4 poles, **c** idols, and metal idols.
Psa 74:6 They smashed all its **c**
Pro 9:1 She has **c** out her seven pillars.
Isa 10:10 They had more **c** statues than
44:15 They make them into **c** statues
44:17 they make into gods, **c** statues.
48:5 My **c** idols and my metal idols
Eze 23:14 pictures of men **c** on walls.
40:16 Pictures of palm trees were **c**
40:26 Pictures of palm trees were **c**
40:31 Pictures of palm trees were **c**
40:34 Pictures of palm trees were **c**
40:37 Pictures of palm trees were **c**
41:19 These pictures were **c** all
41:20 angels and palm trees were **c**
41:25 angels and palm trees were **c**
Hab 2:18 "What benefit is there in a **c**
2:18 idol when its maker has **c** it?
Act 28:11 Castor and Pollux **c** on its front.

case (81)

Exo 22:9 must bring their **c** to God.
22:11 The **c** between them must be
Num 5:8 In that **c**, the payment for what
27:5 brought their **c** to the LORD,
Dtr 1:16 Judge each **c** fairly,
1:17 You may bring me any **c** that's
15:4 In any **c**, there shouldn't be any
17:8 There may be a **c** that is too
17:8 or a dispute — any **c** which may
17:8 Take this **c** to the place that
22:26 This is like the **c** of someone
25:1 The judges will hear the **c** and
Jos 20:4 and present his **c** to the leaders
Jdg 9:20 But if that's not the **c**,
11:25 ever have a **c** against Israel?
Rut 4:6 The man replied, "In that **c** I
1Sm 2:15 But ⌊in the **c** of Eli's sons,⌋
2Sm 15:2 When anyone had a **c** to be
15:3 "Your **c** is good and proper,
15:4 Then anyone who had a **c** to
15:6 the king to have him try their **c**.
16:4 The king told Ziba, "In that **c**
20:21 That isn't the **c**. A man from the
2Ch 19:6 be with you when you hear a **c**.
19:10 cities about every **c** they bring
19:10 even if the **c** involves
Job 5:8 help and present my **c** to him.
9:32 'Let's take our **c** to court.'
13:3 and I wish to argue my **c** in
13:18 I have prepared my **c**.
13:19 Who can make a **c** against me?
Job 23:4 I would present ⌊my⌋ **c** to him.
33:5 Present your **c** to me,
35:2 'My **c** is more just than God's,'
35:14 your **c** is in front of him,
37:19 ⌊a **c**⌋ because of darkness.
Psa 35:23 Plead my **c**, O my God and my
43:1 and plead my **c** against an
119:154 Plead my **c** ⌊for me⌋,
Pro 18:17 The first to state his **c** seems
22:23 the LORD will plead their **c**
23:11 will plead their **c** against you.
Isa 1:17 Plead the **c** of widows."
3:14 The LORD presents his **c** to
41:21 "Present your **c**," says the
43:26 Let us argue our **c** together.
43:26 State your **c** so that you can
45:21 Speak and present your **c**.
49:4 Yet, certainly my **c** is in the
50:8 Who will bring a **c** against me?
59:4 no one pleads his **c** truthfully.
Jer 11:20 I've brought my **c** to you.
12:1 if I would argue my **c** with you,
20:12 I've brought my **c** to you.
42:9 sent me to humbly plead your **c**
Lam 3:58 Plead my **c** for me,
Hos 4:4 My **c** is against you priests.
Mic 6:1 Plead your **c** in front of the
6:2 is arguing his **c** against Israel.
7:9 up my cause and wins my **c**.
Mat 27:19 While Pilate was judging the **c**,
Luk 10:6 But if that's not the **c**,
Act 22:1 as I now present my **c** to you."
23:30 to state their **c** against him
23:35 he said, "I'll hear your **c** when
24:10 pleased to present my **c** to you.
24:22 arrives, I'll decide your **c**."
25:11 I appeal my **c** to the emperor!"
25:12 "You have appealed your **c** to
25:14 told the king about Paul's **c**.
25:20 to have his **c** heard there.
25:21 But Paul appealed his **c**.
25:21 the Emperor decide his **c**.
26:32 appealed his **c** to the emperor."
27:24 You must present your **c** to the
28:19 I was forced to appeal my **c** to
Rom 3:4 and you win your **c** in court."
1Co 5:10 If that were the **c**, you would
8:11 In that **c**, your knowledge is
Gal 5:11 In that **c** the cross wouldn't be
1Ti 3:15 in **c** I'm delayed. I want you to

cases (10)

Exo 18:22 bring all important **c** to you,
18:22 settle all minor **c** themselves.
18:26 bring difficult **c** to Moses,
Dtr 1:16 "Hear the **c** that your people
19:15 **C** must be settled based on the
21:5 Their decision is final in all **c**
2Ch 19:8 the LORD's laws and decide **c**.
Job 29:16 **c** brought by strangers.
1Co 6:2 of judging insignificant **c**?
6:4 When you have **c** dealing with

cash (3)

Exo 21:30 However, if only a **c** settlement
Num 35:31 "Never accept a **c** payment in
35:32 Don't accept a **c** payment to

Casiphia (2)

Ezr 8:17 them to Iddo, the leader in **C**.
8:17 the temple servants in **C**,

casket (1)

2Sm 3:31 David followed the open **c**.

Casluhites (2)

Gen 10:14 Pathrusites, **C** (from whom the
1Ch 1:12 Pathrusites, **C** (from whom the

cassia (4)

Exo 30:24 12 ½ pounds of **c** — all
Job 42:14 Jemimah, the second **C**,
Psa 45:8 with myrrh, aloes, and **c**.
Eze 27:19 exchanged wrought iron, **c**,

cast (29)

Exo 25:12 C four gold rings for it,
26:37 C five bronze bases for the
36:36 and they c four silver bases for
37:3 He c four gold rings for its four
37:13 He c four gold rings for it and
38:5 He c four rings to hold the
38:27 7,500 pounds of silver to c
Lev 19:4 gods or c metal idols.
19:26 "Never c evil spells,
Dtr 18:11 c spells, ask ghosts or spirits
1Ki 7:16 He made two capitals of c
7:23 made a pool from c metal.
7:24 They were c in metal when the
7:24 in metal when the pool was c.
7:30 The supports were made of c
7:33 and hubs were all c metal.
7:37 All of them were c in the same
7:46 The king c them in foundries in
2Ki 17:16 two calves out of c metal.
17:17 black magic and c evil spells.
21:6 fortunetellers, c evil spells,
2Ch 4:2 made a pool from c metal.
4:3 They were c in metal when the
4:3 in metal when the pool was c.
4:17 The king c them in foundries in
33:6 fortunetellers, c evil spells,
Psa 58:5 or of anyone trained to c spells.
Isa 19:8 All who c their lines into the
Jer 22:28 out and c into another land

casting (1)

Isa 44:10 making gods or c metal idols.

castle (1)

Pro 18:19 the locked gate of a c tower.

Castor (1)

Act 28:11 The ship had the gods C and

castrate (1)

Gal 5:12 would c themselves.

castrated (5)

Lev 22:25 Never bring any kind of c
22:25 A c animal will not be
Isa 56:3 C men should not say,
56:4 ⌊I will remember⌋ the c men
Mat 19:12 celibate because they were c.

castration (1)

Lev 22:25 on your behalf because c is

casts (2)

Hab 3:6 He c a glance and startles the
Col 2:17 but the body ⌊that c the

casualties (2)

Jdg 20:31 started to inflict c as before.
1Sm 4:17 "Our troops suffered heavy c.

catastrophe (6)

Rev 8:13 a loud voice, "C, catastrophe,
8:13 a loud voice, "Catastrophe, c,
8:13 c for those living on earth,
9:12 The first c is over.
11:14 The second c is over.
11:14 The third c will soon be here.

catastrophes (2)

Job 31:3 Aren't there c for wicked people
Rev 9:12 are two more c yet to come.

catch (58)

Gen 44:4 and when you c up with them,
Exo 15:9 I'll c up with them!
Dtr 19:6 the relative may c up with him
32:11 spreads its wings to c them,
Jos 2:5 you'll c up with them."
Jdg 18:22 called together to help him c up
21:21 Each of you c a woman from
1Sm 30:8 Will I c up with them?"
30:8 "You will certainly c up with
2Sm 2:21 C one of the young men,
15:14 Let's leave right away, or he'll c
1Ch 21:12 away when their swords c up
Job 9:18 would not let me c my breath.
18:10 A trap is on his path ⌊to c⌋ him.
Psa 7:5 the enemy chase me and c me.
10:9 there to c oppressed people.
35:8 Let the net that they hid c them.
57:6 spread out a net to c me.
69:24 burning anger c up with them.
Pro 6:25 Do not let her c you with her
12:27 lazy hunter does not c his prey,
23:5 Will you c only a fleeting
Ecc 1:14 ⌊It's like⌋ trying to c the wind.
1:17 is ⌊like⌋ trying to c the wind.
2:11 was ⌊like⌋ trying to c the wind.
2:17 was ⌊like⌋ trying to c the wind.
2:26 ⌊It's like⌋ trying to c the wind.
4:4 ⌊It's like⌋ trying to c the wind.
4:6 and of trying to c the wind.
4:16 ⌊It's like⌋ trying to c the wind.
6:9 ⌊It's like⌋ trying to c the wind.
7:26 but she will c whoever
12:1 come and the years c up
Sos 2:15 C the foxes for us,
Jer 5:26 They set traps and c people.
16:16 "and they will c the people of
18:22 because they dug a pit to c me
42:16 Then the wars you fear will c
Eze 17:20 my net over you to c you
Hos 2:7 but she won't c them.
12:1 The people of Ephraim try to c
Amo 9:10 "Destruction will not c up to us
9:13 when the one who plows will c
9:13 stomps on grapes will c up
Zec 1:6 finally c up with your
Mat 4:19 I will teach you how to c
17:27 Take the first fish that you c.
Mar 1:17 I will teach you how to c
8:17 Don't you c on? Are your minds
8:21 "Don't you c on yet?"
Luk 5:4 lower your nets to c some fish."
5:10 From now on you will c people
20:20 They wanted to c him saying
21:34 Then that day could suddenly c
Jon 21:3 went out in a boat but didn't c
21:6 and you'll c some."
Act 27:40 they raised the top sail to c
2Co 11:32 the city of Damascus to c me.

catchers (1)

Jer 5:26 They lie in ambush like bird c.

catches (8)

Exo 22:2 "If anyone c a thief breaking in
Num 35:19 When he c up with the
35:21 must kill you when he c up
Job 5:13 He c the wise with their own
18:9 A trap c his heel. A snare holds
Psa 10:9 He c oppressed people when
Luk 21:35 like a trap that c a bird.
1Co 3:19 "God c the wise in their

catching (1)

2Sm 1:6 horsemen were c up with him.

cattail (3)

Isa 42:3 will not break off a damaged c.
58:5 just bowing your head like a c
Mat 12:20 will not break off a damaged c.

cattails (5)

1Ki 14:15 strike Israel like c which shake
Psa 68:30 the beast who is among the c,
Isa 9:14 both palm branches and c.
19:6 The reeds and c will wither.
35:7 Grass will become c and

cattle (100)

Gen 12:16 was given sheep, c, donkeys,
13:5 his own sheep, c, and tents.
20:14 Then Abimelech took sheep, c,
21:27 took some sheep and c
24:35 has given him sheep and c,
32:5 I have c and donkeys,
32:7 the sheep and goats, the c,
33:13 flocks and c that are nursing
34:28 sheep and goats, c, donkeys,
Gen 36:6 his possessions, all his c,
47:17 sheep, goats, c, and donkeys.
49:6 At their whim they crippled c.
50:8 and their c were left in
Exo 9:3 camels, c, sheep, and goats.
9:20 servants and c indoors quickly.
12:38 of sheep, goats, and c.
20:10 and female slaves, your c,
20:24 your sheep, goats, and c on it.
22:1 for the loss with five head of c
22:30 must do the same with your c
34:19 whether c, sheep, or goats.
Lev 1:2 offer an animal from your c,
1:3 a burnt offering from your c,
3:1 is a fellowship offering of c
22:19 that has no defects from your c,
22:21 Whether it is from the c,
26:22 of your children, destroy your c,
27:32 Every tenth head of c or sheep
Num 15:3 They may be c, sheep,
22:40 Balak sacrificed c,
31:28 This includes people, c,
31:30 This includes people, c,
31:33 72,000 c,
31:38 Of the 36,000 c they received,
31:44 36,000 c,
35:3 in and pastureland for their c,
Dtr 2:35 taking the c and goods.
3:7 taking all of the c and goods.
12:6 and the firstborn of your c,
12:17 the firstborn of your c,
14:23 and eat the firstborn of your c,
14:26 want: c, sheep, goats, wine,
20:14 the c and everything else in the
28:4 Your c will have calves,
28:18 Your c will be cursed with few
Jos 6:21 and old, as well as c, sheep,
7:24 his c, his donkeys, his sheep,
14:4 in with pasturelands for their c
Jdg 20:48 They killed all the people and c
1Sm 8:16 and female slaves, your best c,
27:9 He also took sheep, c,
30:20 He took all the sheep and the c.
2Sm 12:4 take one of his own sheep or c
1Ki 1:9 Adonijah sacrificed sheep, c,
7:29 the c were engraved designs.
8:5 sheep and c sacrifices
8:63 Solomon sacrificed 22,000 c
2Ki 3:17 You, your c, and your other
5:26 vineyards, sheep, c, or slaves?
1Ch 12:40 wine, olive oil, c, and sheep,
2Ch 5:6 sheep and c sacrifices
7:5 King Solomon offered 22,000 c
14:15 who were letting their c graze
15:11 700 c and 7,000 sheep.
18:2 slaughtered many sheep and c
31:6 Judah brought a tenth of their c
32:28 and he made barns for all his c
32:29 he had many sheep and c.
Neh 10:36 the firstborn of our sons, our c,
Job 1:10 His c have spread out over the
18:3 Why do you think of us as c?
40:15 It eats grass as c do.
Psa 8:7 all the sheep and c,
50:10 ⌊even⌋ the c on a thousand
66:15 I will offer c and goats.
78:48 He let the hail strike their c and
104:14 You make grass grow for c and
107:38 does not allow a shortage of c.
144:14 May our c have many calves.
Pro 14:4 Where there are no c,
Isa 22:13 slaughter c, and butcher sheep.
30:23 When that day comes, your c
46:1 are seated on animals and c.
65:10 will be a resting place for c
Jer 5:17 devour your flocks and your c.
9:10 No one can hear the sound of c.
9:10 Birds and c have fled.
Eze 38:12 people have c and property,
38:13 and to take c and property?"'
Dan 4:25 You will eat grass like c.
4:32 You will eat grass like c.
4:33 people and ate grass like c.
5:21 wild donkeys, ate grass like c,
Hos 5:6 go with their sheep and their c
Joe 1:18 Herds of c wander around

Jnh 3:7 people, animals, c, and sheep.
Hab 3:17 and the stalls have no c —
Jon 2:14 those who were selling c,
2:15 with their sheep and c out
Rev 18:13 c, sheep, horses, wagons,

cattle-prod (1)

1Sm 13:21 or set a metal point on a c.

Cauda (1)

Act 27:16 side of a small island called C,

caught (59)

Gen 22:13 he saw a ram behind him c by
31:23 Laban c up with him in the
31:25 When Laban finally c up with
44:6 When he c up with them,
Exo 14:9 c up with them as they were
22:7 person's house: If the thief is c,
22:8 If the thief is not c,
Num 5:13 her and she wasn't c in the act.
11:22 in the sea were c for them?"
Dtr 22:22 If a man is c having sexual
Jos 8:22 The men of Ai were c between
Jdg 1:5 At Bezek they also c up with
1:6 troops chased him, c him,
15:4 So Samson c 300 foxes.
15:5 olive orchards also c on fire.
20:42 But the battle c up with the
20:45 They c up with another 2,000
1Sm 31:2 The Philistines c up to Saul
2Sm 18:9 Absalom's head became c in
2Ki 25:5 King Zedekiah and c up
1Ch 10:2 The Philistines c up to Saul
Psa 9:15 Their feet are c in the net they
10:2 He will be c in the schemes
18:37 I chased my enemies and c up
40:12 My sins have c up with me so
124:7 We escaped like a bird c in a
Pro 3:26 keep your foot from getting c.
5:22 and he will be c in the ropes of
6:2 c by your own promise.
6:31 but when he is c, he has to
Ecc 9:12 Like fish that are c in a cruel
9:12 caught in a cruel net or birds c
Isa 8:15 They will be trapped and c.
24:18 climbs out of that pit will be c
51:20 They are like an antelope c in
Jer 2:26 feels ashamed when he's c,
39:5 army pursued them and c up
41:12 They c up with him at the large
48:27 Were they c among thieves?
48:44 climbs out of the pit will be c
50:24 You will be c, but you won't
52:8 King Zedekiah and c up
Lam 1:3 Those who chased them c up
4:20 was c in their pits.
Eze 12:13 and he will be c in my net.
19:4 about him, c him in their pit,
19:8 their net over him and c him
Amo 3:4 den unless it has c something?
3:5 unless it has c something?
Mat 14:31 out, c hold of him, and said,
Luk 5:5 hard all night and c nothing.
5:6 they c such a large number of
5:9 large number of fish they had c.
Jon 8:3 been c committing adultery.
8:4 we c this woman in the act of
21:5 haven't you c any fish?"
21:10 some of the fish you've just c."
2Co 11:29 When anyone is c in a trap,
2Pe 2:12 that are born to be c and killed.

cauldron (1)

1Sm 2:14 it into the pot, kettle, c, or pan.

caulk (1)

Eze 27:9 inside you to c your seams.

caulkers (1)

Eze 27:27 your c and your merchants,

cause (49)

Exo 9:9 The dust will c boils to break
Jdg 9:23 c problems between Abimelech
2Sm 17:2 and I'll c him to panic.
1Ki 8:50 and c those who captured them
Ezr 6:12 name is worshiped there c
Est 8:5 if you consider my c to be
Psa 9:4 You have defended my just c:
37:6 your just c like the noonday
45:4 your majesty for the c of truth,
45:17 I will c your name to be
74:22 Fight for your own c!
140:12 who are oppressed and the c
Pro 29:7 person knows the just c
30:21 Three things c the earth to
Isa 3:17 The Lord will c sores ⌊to
44:25 I c the signs of false prophets
47:12 succeed. You may c terror.
66:9 "Do I c a mother to deliver and
Jer 10:18 land at this time and c trouble
22:16 He defended the c of the poor
27:10 They will c you to be taken far
33:15 I will c a righteous branch to
50:34 He will certainly take up their c
51:36 I am going to take up your c
Eze 13:13 In my fury I'll c a storm to break
36:33 I will c your cities to be lived in
37:5 I will c breath to enter you,
44:30 This will c a blessing to rest
Dan 8:24 He will c astounding
9:27 that c destruction until ⌊those
Mic 7:9 his fury until he takes up my c
Mat 18:7 Situations that c people to lose
24:15 will c destruction will stand
Mar 13:14 c destruction standing where
Luk 17:1 "Situations that c people to
17:2 his neck than for him to c one
Act 19:33 that Alexander was the c,
27:10 This disaster will c damage to
Rom 7:13 something good c my death?
1Co 10:32 Don't c others to stumble,
Gal 4:18 (Devotion to a good c is
2Th 1:6 to those who c you to suffer.
2Ti 2:23 You know they c quarrels.
Heb 12:11 It always seems to c more pain
12:15 up to c trouble that corrupts
Jas 2:17 itself is dead if it doesn't c you
2Pe 1:4 sinful desires c in the world.
2:2 freedom and will c others
Jud 1:19 are the people who c divisions.

caused (34)

Gen 2:21 So the LORD God c him to fall
34:30 "You have c me a lot of trouble!
Exo 9:10 and they c boils to break into
Lev 13:23 it is a scar c by the boil.
13:28 it is only a sore c by the burn.
13:28 it is a scar c by the burn.
Num 25:18 on the day of the plague c by
31:16 Balaam's advice and c
Jdg 7:22 and the LORD c the whole
1Ki 2:32 him for the slaughter he c.
11:25 to the trouble that Hadad c,
2Ki 6:25 The shortages c by the
1Ch 2:7 Carmi's son was Achar, who c
22:8 'You have c a lot of bloodshed
22:8 you have c so much bloodshed
28:3 You have fought wars and c
2Ch 13:20 The LORD c Jeroboam to
21:11 This c the inhabitants of
21:13 You, like Ahab's family, have c
Psa 78:40 How often they c him grief in
105:29 water into blood and c their fish
Pro 27:3 but annoyance c by a stubborn
Lam 1:12 pain that the LORD has c me,
Eze 5:7 you have c more trouble than
7:19 Their silver and gold c them to
Mal 2:8 the ⌊correct⌋ path and c many
Rom 7:13 Rather, my death was c by sin
2Co 2:5 If someone c distress,
7:9 but because the distress I c
7:11 look at how much devotion it c
1Ti 6:10 faith and have c themselves
Heb 11:29 Faith c the people to go
11:30 Faith c the walls of Jericho to
Jas 4:1 Aren't they c by the selfish

causes (25)

1Sm 2:7 The LORD c poverty and
Job 39:20 when its snorting c terror?
Pro 10:10 with his eye c heartache.
26:28 and a flattering mouth c ruin.
Dan 11:31 thing that c destruction.
12:11 thing that c destruction is set
Mat 5:29 "So if your right eye c you to
13:41 in his kingdom that c people
18:6 best for the person who c one
18:7 the world because it c people
18:7 for the person who c someone
18:8 "If your hand or your foot c you
18:9 If your eye c you to lose your
Mar 9:42 best for the person who c one
9:43 "So if your hand c you to lose
9:45 If your foot c you to lose your
9:47 If your eye c you to lose your
Luk 17:1 for the person who c someone
Rom 14:20 something if it c someone else
14:21 or doing anything else that c
1Co 8:13 to false gods⌋ c other believers
2Co 7:10 in a godly way c people
7:10 But the distress that the world c
Gal 5:5 faith c us to wait eagerly for the
Jas 4:1 What c fights and quarrels

causing (1)

Heb 13:17 (C them to complain would not

cautious (1)

Pro 14:16 A wise person is c and turns

cavalry (12)

Exo 14:9 his horse-drawn chariots and c,
14:17 entire army, his chariots, and c.
14:18 his chariots, and his c."
14:23 and c followed them into the
14:26 their chariots, and their c."
14:28 and the c that had followed
15:19 and c went into the sea,
1Ki 9:22 of his chariot and c units.
20:20 escaped on a horse with the c.
2Ch 8:9 of his chariot and c units.
Ezr 8:22 king for an armed escort with c
Neh 2:9 had sent army officers and c

cave (34)

Gen 19:30 where they lived in a c.
23:9 to let me have the c of
23:11 field together with the c that is
23:18 included the field with the c
23:19 buried his wife Sarah in the c
23:20 So the field and its c were sold
25:9 and Ishmael buried him in the c
25:9 The c is east of Mamre.
49:29 me with my ancestors in the c
49:30 Abraham bought the c that is in
49:32 The field and the c in it were
50:13 Canaan and buried him in the c
Jos 10:16 and hid in the c at Makkedah.
10:17 hiding in the c at Makkedah."
10:18 against the mouth of the c,
10:22 Joshua said, "Open the c,
10:27 Then they threw them into the c
10:27 stones over the mouth of the c.
Jdg 15:8 Then he went to live in a c in
15:11 men from Judah went to the c
1Sm 22:1 and fled to the c at Adullam.
24:3 the road where there was a c.
24:3 sitting further back in the c.
24:7 Saul left the c and went out
24:8 Later, David got up, left the c,
24:10 handed you over to me in the c.
2Sm 23:13 men came to David at the c
1Ki 18:4 He put 50 prophets in each c
18:13 I hid 50 prophets in each c and
19:9 There he went into a c and
19:13 stood at the entrance of the c.
1Ch 11:15 down to David's rock at the c
Jer 48:28 nests at the entrance of a c.
Jon 11:38 It was a c with a stone

caves (13)

Jdg 6:2 places in the mountains, c,
1Sm 13:6 they hid in c, in thorny thickets,
1Ki 18:4 had hidden 100 prophets in c.
18:13 of the LORD's prophets in c?
Isa 2:19 People will go into c in the

Isa 2:21 They will go into **c** in the rocks
32:14 will become permanent **c**.
65:4 and spent their nights in **c**.
Jer 49:8 Hide in deep **c**, inhabitants of
Eze 33:27 places and **c** will die from
Nah 2:12 It used to fill its **c** with torn
Heb 11:38 and mountains and lived in **c**
Rev 6:15 free people hid themselves in **c**

cease (4)

Job 8:22 of the wicked will **c** to exist."
14:6 and he will **c** to be.
14:12 until the heavens **c** to exist.
Isa 24:8 Noisy celebrations **c**.

cedar (51)

Lev 14:4 birds, some **c** wood, red yarn,
14:6 bird, the **c** wood, the red yarn,
14:49 two birds, **c** wood, red yarn,
14:51 He must take the **c** wood,
14:52 bird, the **c** wood, the hyssop,
Num 19:6 priest will take some **c** wood,
2Sm 7:2 I'm living in a house made of **c**,
7:7 didn't build me a house of **c**?'
1Ki 4:33 classified trees — from the **c**
5:8 to the **c** and cypress logs.
5:10 Hiram gave Solomon all the **c**
6:9 rows of **c** beams and planks.
6:10 Its **c** beams were attached to
6:15 of the temple with **c** boards.
6:16 the temple with **c** boards from
6:18 into the **c** paneling inside
6:18 was ⌞covered with⌟ **c**.
6:20 Solomon covered it and the **c**
6:36 a course of finished **c** beams.
7:2 It had four rows of **c** pillars
7:2 pillars supporting **c** beams.
7:3 The hall was covered with **c**
7:7 The hall was covered with **c**
7:11 Above ⌞the foundation⌟ were **c**
7:12 blocks and a layer of **c** beams,
9:11 Solomon with as much **c**
2Ki 14:9 a message to a **c** in Lebanon.
1Ch 17:1 living in a house made of **c**,
17:6 didn't build me a house of **c**?'
22:4 David so many **c** logs that
2Ch 2:3 You sent him **c** so that he
2:8 Send me **c**, cypress,
25:18 a message to a **c** in Lebanon.
Ezr 3:7 and Tyre in exchange for **c**,
Job 40:17 It makes its tail stiff like a **c**.
Psa 37:35 himself out like a large **c** tree.
148:9 fruit trees and all **c** trees,
Sos 8:9 we will barricade her with **c**
Isa 41:19 I will plant **c**, acacia, myrtle,
41:19 I will place **c**, fir, and cypress
60:13 glory will come to you: **C**, fir,
Jer 22:7 cut down your finest **c** trees
22:14 panels the rooms with **c**,
22:15 because you use more **c**?
Eze 17:3 It took hold of the top of a **c**
17:22 take hold of the top of a **c** tree.
17:23 become a magnificent **c** tree.
27:5 They took **c** trees from
31:3 It was a **c** in Lebanon with fine
31:8 The **c** trees in God's garden
Zep 2:14 will expose the **c** beams.

cedars (26)

Num 24:6 like **c** by the water.
Jdg 9:15 and burn up the **c** of Lebanon.'
1Ki 5:6 So order men to cut down **c**
10:27 and he made **c** as plentiful as
2Ki 19:23 I'll cut down its tallest **c** and its
2Ch 1:15 and he made **c** as plentiful as
9:27 and he made **c** as plentiful as
Psa 29:5 of the LORD breaks the **c**.
29:5 splinters the **c** of Lebanon.
80:10 branches covered the mighty **c**.
92:12 grow tall like the **c** in Lebanon.
104:16 The LORD's trees, the **c** in
Sos 1:17 The **c** will be the walls of our
5:15 like Lebanon, choice as the **c**.
Isa 2:13 all the towering and mighty **c**
9:10 we will replace them with **c**."
14:8 The **c** of Lebanon say,
Isa 37:24 I'll cut down its tallest **c** and its
44:14 cut down **c** for themselves.
44:14 Then they plant **c**,
Jer 22:23 and have your nest in the **c**.
Hos 14:5 They will be firmly rooted like **c**
14:6 be fragrant like **c** from Lebanon.
Amo 2:9 the Amorites were as tall as **c**
Zec 11:1 be able to burn down your **c**.
11:2 because the **c** have fallen and

cedarwood (2)

2Sm 5:11 David, along with **c**, carpenters,
1Ch 14:1 David, along with **c**, masons,

ceiling (3)

Exo 26:33 from the fasteners in the **c**,
1Ki 6:15 with wood from floor to **c**.
7:7 with cedar from floor to **c**.

celebrate (67)

Exo 5:1 people go into the desert to **c**
12:14 You will **c** this day as a
12:17 You must **c** the Festival of
12:17 You must **c** this day.
12:47 of Israel must **c** the Passover.
12:48 "Foreigners may want to **c** the
12:48 Then they may **c** the Passover
23:14 "Three times a year you must **c**
23:15 "**C** the Festival of Unleavened
23:16 "**C** the Festival of the Harvest
23:16 "**C** the Festival of the Final
34:18 "You must **c** the Festival of
34:22 "You must **c** the Festival of
Lev 23:39 **c** the LORD's festival for seven
23:40 and **c** in the presence of the
23:41 **C** it for seven days each year.
23:41 **C** this festival in the seventh
25:2 the land will **c** a year to honor
26:34 Then the land will joyfully **c** its
26:35 it will **c** the time ⌞to honor the
Num 9:2 "The Israelites must **c** the
9:3 You must **c** it on the fourteenth
9:4 the Israelites to **c** the Passover,
9:6 and they couldn't **c** the
9:10 You may still **c** the Passover.
9:11 You will **c** it on the fourteenth
9:12 for the Passover when you **c** it.
9:13 don't bother to **c** the Passover,
9:14 living with you may want to **c**
29:12 Instead, **c** a festival to the
Dtr 16:10 Then **c** the Festival of Weeks
16:13 **c** the Festival of Booths for
16:15 For seven days you will **c** this
Jdg 16:23 to their god Dagon and to **c**.
2Sm 1:20 of godless men will **c**.
6:21 I will **c** in the LORD's presence,
2Ki 23:21 king ordered all the people to **c**
2Ch 30:1 temple in Jerusalem to **c**
30:2 in Jerusalem decided to **c**
30:3 They couldn't **c** it at the regular
30:5 to come to Jerusalem to **c**
30:13 gathered in Jerusalem to **c**
30:23 whole assembly decided to **c**
35:18 They did not **c** the Passover as
Neh 12:27 them come to Jerusalem to **c**
Psa 68:3 Let them **c** in God's presence.
68:4 **C** in his presence.
Sos 1:4 We will **c** and rejoice with you.
Isa 9:3 your presence like those who **c**
22:13 Instead, you will rejoice, **c**,
Eze 45:21 you will **c** the Passover,
Hos 9:1 Don't **c** as other nations do.
Nah 1:15 **C** your festivals, Judah!
Zep 3:14 **C** and rejoice with all your
Zec 14:16 and to **c** the Festival of Booths.
14:18 those who won't come to **c**
14:19 all the nations that won't go to **c**
Mat 26:18 I will **c** the Passover with my
Luk 15:6 and says to them, 'Let's **c**!
15:9 together and says, 'Let's **c**!
15:23 and let's **c** with a feast.
15:24 Then they began to **c**.
15:27 calf to **c** your brother's safe
15:32 But we have something to **c**,
1Co 5:8 So we must not **c** our festival
5:8 Instead, we must **c** it with the
Rev 11:10 They will **c** and send gifts to

celebrated (31)

Lev 26:35 it never **c** while you lived
Num 9:5 and they **c** it on the fourteenth
Jos 5:10 There they **c** the Passover on
1Sm 11:15 and all of Israel's soldiers **c**.
1Ki 1:40 and **c** so loudly that their
8:65 time Solomon and all Israel **c**
2Ki 23:22 never been **c** like this during
23:23 this Passover was **c** in
1Ch 29:22 ate and drank as they joyfully **c**
2Ch 2:4 are always to be **c** by Israel.)
7:8 time Solomon and all Israel **c**
7:9 the altar for seven days and **c**
30:5 These people had not **c** it in
30:21 So the Israelites in Jerusalem **c**
30:23 So they joyfully **c** for seven
35:1 Josiah **c** the Passover for the
35:16 The Passover was **c**,
35:17 Israelites who were present **c**
35:17 They also **c** the Festival of
35:18 had a Passover like this been **c**
35:18 the Passover as Josiah **c**
35:19 this Passover was **c**.
Ezr 3:4 they **c** the Festival of Booths.
6:16 had returned from exile **c** at
6:19 from exile **c** the Passover.
6:22 So for seven days they **c** the
Neh 8:18 The people **c** the festival for
Job 31:29 enemy or **c** when harm came
Psa 42:4 crowds of people **c** a festival.
Mat 14:6 When Herod **c** his birthday,
Col 2:15 of them as he **c** his victory

celebrates (1)

Zep 3:17 and **c** over you with shouts of

celebrating (14)

Exo 31:16 **c** it for generations to come as
Dtr 16:1 Honor the LORD your God by **c**
Jdg 19:4 there with him, **c** for three days.
1Sm 18:7 The women who were **c** sang,
30:16 They were **c** because they had
2Sm 6:5 entire nation of Israel were **c**
1Ki 1:45 They have come from there **c**,
2Ki 11:20 the people of the land were **c**.
1Ch 12:40 because Israel was **c**.
13:8 David and all Israel were **c** in
15:29 saw King David dancing and **c**,
2Ch 23:21 the people of the land were **c**.
Est 9:22 to be days for feasting and **c**
Amo 6:7 The **c** of those sprawled

celebration (11)

Exo 32:18 sound of a wild **c** that I hear."
Num 9:3 for the **c** of the Passover."
2Ch 23:13 The singers were leading the **c**
Neh 8:12 They had a big, joyful **c**
8:17 There was a big, joyful **c**.
Est 9:17 made it a day of feasting and **c**.
9:18 made it a day of feasting and **c**.
9:19 a holiday for feasting and **c**.
9:29 the well-known **c** of Purim.
Hos 7:5 On the day of the king's **c**,
Luk 15:29 goat for a **c** with my friends.

celebrations (2)

Isa 24:8 Noisy **c** cease. Joyful harp
Hos 2:11 I will put an end to all her **c**:

celibate (3)

Mat 19:12 For example, some men are **c**
19:12 Others are **c** because they
19:12 others have decided to be **c**

cell (4)

Jer 37:16 Jeremiah went into a prison **c**,
Act 5:19 Lord opened the doors to their **c**
12:7 and his **c** was filled with light.
12:9 followed the angel out of the **c**.

cement (1)

Lev 26:19 your land will be as hard as **c**.

cemetery (2)
Job 17:1 The c ⌊is waiting⌋ for me.
21:32 He is carried to the c,

Cenchrea (3)
Act 18:18 In the city of C, Aquila had his
18:18 From C they took a boat
Rom 16:1 of the church in the city of C.

census (17)
Exo 30:12 "When you take a c of the
38:25 The silver collected when the c
Num 1:2 "Take a c of the whole
1:49 of Levi or include them in the c
4:2 "Take a c of the Levites who
4:22 "Also take a c of the
7:2 who helped in the c — came
26:2 "Take a c of the whole
26:4 "Take a c of those at least 20
26:53 the list of names ⌊from the c⌋.
26:54 Use the totals ⌊from the c⌋ in
2Sm 24:9 Joab reported the c figures to
1Ch 21:5 Joab reported the c figures to
21:7 God considered the c to be
Luk 2:1 Emperor Augustus ordered a c
2:2 This was the first c taken
Act 5:37 at the time of the c,

cent (1)
Mar 12:42 worth less than a c.

center (15)
Exo 28:32 an opening for the head in the c
39:23 The opening in the c of the
Num 35:5 with the city in the c.
1Ki 6:27 each other in the c of the room.
7:25 toward the c ⌊of the pool⌋.
7:31 opening in t center
2Ch 4:4 toward the c ⌊of the pool⌋.
Eze 1:5 In the c of the cloud I saw what
5:5 I have placed it in the c of the
Mar 3:3 in the c ⌊of the synagogue⌋."
14:60 chief priest stood up in the c
Luk 6:8 and stand in the c ⌊of the
Rev 4:6 In the c near the throne and
5:6 I saw a lamb standing in the c
7:17 The lamb in the c near the

centers (2)
1Ki 20:34 You may set up trading c in
1Ti 1:4 God's plan, which c in faith.

cents (1)
Luk 12:6 five sparrows sold for two c?

Cephas (10)
Jon 1:42 be C" (which means "Peter").
1Co 1:12 or "I follow C," or "I follow
3:22 Whether it is Paul, Apollos, C,
9:5 the Lord's brothers, and C do?
15:5 He appeared to C. Next he
Gal 1:18 personally acquainted with C.
2:9 James, C, and John (who were
2:11 When C came to Antioch,
2:12 Then C drew back and would
2:14 So I told C in front of everyone,

ceremonies (21)
Gen 50:11 living there saw the funeral c at
50:11 "These funeral c are taken very
50:11 Mizraim[Egyptian Funeral C].
Num 8:21 The Levites performed the c to
Jos 3:5 "Perform the c to make
7:13 tomorrow by performing the c
1Sm 16:5 Perform the c to make
16:5 He performed the c for Jesse
1Ch 15:12 relatives must perform the c
2Ch 5:11 present had performed the c
29:5 Perform the c to make the
29:15 relatives and performed the c
29:17 eight days they performed the c
30:3 priests had performed the c
30:15 so they performed the c to
30:24 were able to perform the c
35:3 all Israel and performed c
2Ch 35:6 perform the c to make
Jon 3:25 with a Jew about purification c.
Heb 9:10 used in various purification c.
9:10 These c were required for the

ceremony (7)
Gen 50:10 began a great and solemn c
Exo 12:25 as he promised, observe this c.
12:26 you what this c means to you,
13:5 observe this c in this month.
Act 21:24 the purification c with them,
21:26 the purification c with them.
24:18 gone through the purification c.

certain (34)
Gen 15:8 how can I be c that I will take
28:11 When he came to a c place,
Exo 11:1 When he does, he will be c to
Num 35:11 select c cities to be places of
1Sm 17:51 and made c the Philistine was
21:2 my young men at a c place.'"
22:22 was there that he would be c
2Sm 12:1 were two men in a c city.
1Ki 2:37 you can be c that you will die.
2:42 you could be c that you would
Est 3:8 there is a c nationality
Psa 106:16 In the camp c men became
Pro 30:11 A c kind of person curses his
30:12 A c kind of person thinks he is
30:13 A c kind of person looks
30:14 A c kind of person,
Jer 26:15 But know for c that if you put
Eze 20:12 I also gave them c days to
20:20 Set apart c holy days to
Dan 3:12 There are c Jews whom you
Mat 20:23 these positions for c people."
26:18 "Go to a c man in the city,
Mar 10:40 been prepared for c people."
14:51 A c young man was following
Luk 8:27 a c man from the city met him.
11:1 was praying in a c place.
17:1 to lose their faith are c to arise.
Act 12:1 to mistreating c members
Rom 5:9 we are even more c that Christ
5:10 we are even more c that,
5:17 It is c that death ruled because
5:17 It's even more c that those who
1Ti 1:3 That way you could order c
4:3 and from eating c foods.

certainty (2)
Ecc 8:12 Still, I know with c that it will
1Th 1:5 and with complete c.

certificate (1)
Dtr 24:1 writes out a c of divorce,

chain (11)
Gen 41:42 put a gold c around his neck.
Pro 1:9 a ⌊golden⌋ c around your neck.
Dan 4:15 it with an iron and bronze c
4:23 it with an iron and bronze c
5:7 wear a gold c on his neck,
5:16 wear a gold c on your neck,
5:29 in purple and wear a gold c
Mat 8:9 As you know, I'm in a c of
Mar 5:3 any longer, not even with a c.
Luk 7:8 As you know, I'm in a c of
Rev 20:1 pit and a large c in his hand.

chained (6)
2Sm 3:34 Your feet were not c.
Isa 51:14 C prisoners will be set free.
Mar 5:4 He had often been c hand and
Luk 8:29 He was c hand and foot.
Heb 11:36 and some were c and put in
Rev 20:2 The angel c up the serpent for

chains (43)
Exo 28:14 and two c of pure gold,
28:14 fasten these c to the settings.
28:22 "For the breastplate make c out
39:15 For the breastplate they made c
Jdg 8:26 and the c from their camels'
16:21 They tied him up with double c
1Ki 6:21 He put golden c across the
1Ki 7:17 filigree and c for each capital.
2Ch 3:5 the form of palm trees and c.
3:16 He made c for the inner room
3:16 and put them on the c.
Job 36:8 righteous people are bound in c
36:13 for help when he c them up.
38:31 "Can you connect the c of the
Psa 2:3 "Let's break apart their c and
107:10 They were held in iron c
107:14 He broke apart their c.
116:16 You have freed me from my c.
149:8 to put their kings in c and their
Ecc 7:26 Even her hands are ⌊like⌋ c.
Isa 28:22 or your c will be tightened,
40:19 make silver c for them.
45:14 They will come to you in c.
52:2 Free yourself from the c around
58:6 Loosen the c of wickedness,
Jer 2:20 off your yoke, tore off your c,
5:5 their yokes and torn off their c.
40:1 found Jeremiah in c along
40:4 Today I'm removing the c from
Lam 3:7 He has put heavy c on me.
Eze 7:23 "Get the c ready! The land is
Nah 1:13 of you and tear its c from you.
3:10 her best men were bound in c.
Mar 5:4 However, he snapped the c off
5:4 and broke the c from his feet.
Luk 8:29 But he would break the c.
Act 12:6 hands were bound with two c,
12:7 At that moment the c fell from
16:26 all the prisoners' c came loose.
21:33 him to be tied up with two c.
28:20 I'm wearing these c because of
2Pe 2:4 he has secured them with c
Jud 1:6 bound by eternal c.

chair (5)
1Sm 1:9 priest Eli was sitting on a c by
4:13 Eli was sitting on a c beside
4:18 Eli fell from his c backwards
2Ki 4:10 c, and lamp stand there for him.
Sos 3:7 Solomon's sedan c!

chairs (2)
Mat 21:12 tables and the c
Mar 11:15 tables and the c

Chaldea (1)
Act 7:4 Abraham left the country of C

Chaldean (1)
Ezr 5:12 of Babylon (a C).

Chaldeans (6)
Gen 11:28 Haran died in Ur of the C,
11:31 out together from Ur of the C
15:7 brought you out of Ur of the C
Neh 9:7 and took him from Ur of the C
Job 1:17 "The C formed three
Isa 13:19 the proud beauty of the C,

chalk (2)
Isa 27:9 altar stones into powdered c
44:13 blocks of wood with ⌊c⌋ lines.

challenge (9)
Num 16:1 of Peleth) dared to c Moses.
1Sm 17:10 The Philistine added, "I c the
17:16 came forward and made his c.
17:25 He keeps coming to c Israel.
17:26 Philistine that he should c
2Ch 13:7 and inexperienced to c them.
13:8 Do you now intend to c the
Jer 49:19 Who can c me? Is there any
50:44 Who can c me? Is there any

challenged (4)
1Sm 17:36 one of them because he has c
2Sm 21:21 When he c Israel, Jonathan,
1Ch 20:7 When he c Israel, Jonathan,
Psa 95:9 Your ancestors c me and

chamber (2)
Job 37:9 A storm comes out of its c.
Psa 19:5 which comes out of its c like a

chambers (1)
Joe 2:16 Brides leave their **c**.

chameleons (1)
Lev 11:30 lizards, skinks, and **c**.

champion (3)
1Sm 17:4 The Philistine army's **c** came
17:23 to them, the Philistine **c**,
Psa 19:5 Like a **c**, it is eager to run its

champions (1)
Isa 5:22 who are **c** at mixing drinks,

Chanani (1)
Neh 9:4 and **C** stood on the stairs built

chance (9)
Num 11:33 before they had even had a **c**
Jer 46:17 He has missed his **c**.'
Mat 26:16 looked for a **c** to betray Jesus.
Mar 6:31 didn't even have a **c** to eat.
14:11 looking for a **c** to betray Jesus.
Luk 10:31 "By **c**, a priest was traveling
Act 25:16 face his accusers and have a **c**
1Co 7:21 if you have a **c** to become free,
1Ti 5:14 enemy any **c** to ridicule them.

change (125)
Gen 35:2 and **c** your clothes.
45:22 each of them a **c** of clothes,
Exo 13:17 they may **c** their minds and go
Num 23:19 He doesn't **c** his mind.
23:20 He has blessed, and I can't **c** it.
Jdg 7:19 the midnight watch just at the **c**
1Sm 15:29 does not lie or **c** his mind,
1Ki 8:48 if they **c** their attitude toward
13:33 Jeroboam didn't **c** his evil
2Ki 22:19 You had a **c** of heart and
2Ch 6:38 if they **c** their attitude toward
34:27 You had a **c** of heart and
Ezr 6:22 king of Assyria **c** his mind so
Job 6:18 They **c** their course.
6:29 Please **c** your mind.
6:29 **C** your mind because I am still
9:27 I will **c** my expression and
14:20 You **c** his appearance and
23:13 Who can make him **c** his mind?
29:24 on my face did not **c**.
Psa 7:12 If a person does not **c**,
55:19 Selah They never **c**.
90:13 **C** your plans about ⌊us,⌋
102:26 You will **c** them like clothes,
110:4 an oath and will not **c** his mind:
Pro 6:35 of money will **c** his mind.
24:21 who always insist upon **c**,
31:5 what they have decreed and **c**
Isa 54:10 of peace will never **c**," says
Jer 2:36 You **c** your mind so easily.
4:28 I won't **c** my plans,
7:3 **C** the way you live and act,
7:5 "'Suppose you really **c** the way
13:16 into the shadow of death and **c**
13:23 Can Ethiopians **c** the color of
13:23 skin or leopards **c** their spots?
15:7 they will not **c** their ways.
18:8 Then I will **c** my plans about
18:10 Then I will **c** my plans about
18:11 **c** your lives, and do good.'
26:3 Then I'll **c** my plan about the
26:13 Now, **c** your ways and what
26:13 Then the LORD will **c** his plan
42:10 I will **c** my plans about the
Eze 3:18 they can **c** their wicked ways
7:13 against that crowd will not **c**.
14:6 **C** the way you think and act!
18:30 "**C** the way you think and act.
18:32 "**C** the way you think and act!"
21:26 Things are going to **c**.
24:14 you, pity you, or **c** my plans.
33:8 to warn him to **c** his ways.
33:11 **C** the way you think and act!
Dan 2:9 hoping that things will **c**.
6:8 and Persians no one could **c**
7:25 and plan to **c** the appointed
Hos 10:9 You never **c**. War will overtake
Joe 2:13 forgive and to **c** his plans about
2:14 He may reconsider and **c** his
Amo 1:3 I will not **c** my plans.
1:6 I will not **c** my plans.
1:9 I will not **c** my plans.
1:11 I will not **c** my plans.
1:13 I will not **c** my plans.
2:1 I will not **c** my plans.
2:4 I will not **c** my plans.
2:6 I will not **c** my plans.
Mic 4:7 I will **c** those who are lame into
4:7 I will **c** those who are forced
Zec 8:14 and I didn't **c** my plans.
Mal 3:6 "I, the LORD, never **c**.
4:6 He will **c** parents' attitudes
Mat 3:2 "Turn to God and **c** the way
3:11 with water so that you will **c**
4:17 "Turn to God and **c** the way
10:10 the trip, a **c** of clothes, sandals,
18:3 Unless you **c** and become like
21:32 you didn't **c** your minds and
Mar 1:15 **C** the way you think and act,
6:9 not take along a **c** of clothes.
6:12 they should turn to God and **c**
Luk 1:17 He will **c** parents' attitudes
1:17 He will **c** disobedient people
5:32 I've come to call sinners to **c**
9:3 food, money, or a **c** of clothes.
12:37 He will **c** his clothes,
13:3 if you don't turn to God and **c**
13:5 if you don't turn to God and **c**
16:30 they will turn to God and **c** the
24:47 be told to turn to God and **c**
Act 2:38 of you must turn to God and **c**
3:19 So **c** the way you think and act,
5:31 to **c** the way they think and act,
6:14 will destroy the temple and **c**
8:22 So **c** your wicked thoughts,
11:18 to turn to him so that they can **c**
17:30 everywhere to turn to him and **c**
20:21 I warned Jews and Greeks to **c**
26:20 groups were expected to **c**
Rom 2:4 trying to lead you to him and **c**
2:5 are stubborn and don't want to **c**
12:2 Instead, **c** the way you think.
2Co 7:9 I caused you has led you to **c**
7:10 godly way causes people to **c**
Gal 4:20 you right now so that I could **c**
Eph 4:14 kinds of teachings that **c** like
4:22 You were taught to **c** the way
Php 3:21 he will **c** our humble bodies
2Ti 2:25 God will allow them to **c**
3:5 will not let its power **c** them.
Heb 1:12 You will **c** them like clothes.
6:17 God wouldn't **c** his plan.
7:21 an oath and will not **c** his mind.
12:17 to **c** what had happened.
12:27 clearly that God will **c** what
Jas 1:17 The Father doesn't **c** like the
2Pe 3:9 opportunity to turn to him and **c**
Rev 2:5 Return to me and **c** the way
2:5 from its place if you don't **c**.
2:16 So return to me and **c** the way
2:21 her time to turn to me and **c**
3:3 Obey, and **c** the way you think
3:19 Take this seriously, and **c** the
9:20 still did not turn to me and **c**
16:9 They would not **c** the way they

changed (56)
Gen 31:7 He has **c** my wages ten times.
31:41 and you **c** my wages ten times.
41:14 had shaved and **c** his clothes,
Exo 10:19 Then the LORD **c** the wind to a
14:5 he and his officials **c** their
Num 32:38 Meon (whose names were **c**),
1Sm 10:9 God **c** Saul's attitude.
21:13 So he **c** his behavior ⌊when he
2Sm 12:20 himself, and **c** his clothes.
24:16 the LORD **c** his mind about the
2Ki 23:34 Josiah and **c** Eliakim's name
24:17 place and **c** Mattaniah's name
1Ch 21:15 the LORD reconsidered and **c**
2Ch 36:4 and **c** Eliakim's name
Neh 4:23 to me never **c** their clothes.
Psa 30:11 You have **c** my sobbing into
105:25 He **c** their minds so that they
106:45 his rich mercy, he **c** his plans.
Isa 26:3 whose minds cannot be **c**,
Jer 26:19 So the LORD **c** his plan about
31:19 I **c** the way I thought and acted.
34:11 But afterwards, they **c** their
34:15 Recently, you **c** and did what I
34:16 Now you have **c** again and
48:11 and its aroma hasn't **c**.
Lam 4:1 The fine gold has **c**!
Dan 4:16 Let its human mind be **c**,
5:21 and his mind was **c** into an
6:15 the king makes can be **c**."
6:17 situation could not be **c**.
Hos 11:8 I have **c** my mind. I am deeply
Amo 7:3 The LORD **c** his plans about
7:6 The LORD **c** his plans about
Mat 3:8 have turned to God and have **c**
11:20 because they had not **c**
11:21 they would have **c** the way
12:41 they turned to God and **c**
17:2 Jesus' appearance **c** in front of
21:29 But later he **c** his mind and
Mar 9:2 Jesus' appearance **c** in front of
Luk 3:8 have turned to God and have **c**
9:29 the appearance of his face **c**,
10:13 they would have **c** the way
11:32 of Nineveh turned to God and **c**
Jon 4:46 where he had **c** water into
Act 26:20 prove they had **c** their lives.
28:6 they **c** their minds and said he
1Co 15:51 but we will all be **c**.
15:52 They will be **c** so that they can
15:53 that decays must be **c** into
15:53 This mortal body must be **c**
15:54 this body that decays is **c** into
15:54 and this mortal body is **c** into a
2Co 3:18 we are being **c** into his image
12:21 led sinful lives and have not **c**
Heb 6:18 two things can never be **c**.

changes (12)
Gen 45:22 of silver and five **c** of clothes.
Jdg 14:12 linen shirts and 30 **c** of clothes.
1Sm 15:29 is not a mortal who **c** his mind."
Job 38:14 The earth **c** like clay stamped
Psa 107:33 He **c** rivers into a desert,
107:35 He **c** deserts into lakes and dry
Ecc 8:1 and it **c** one's grim look.
Dan 2:21 He **c** times and periods of
Luk 15:7 person who turns to God and **c**
15:10 person who turns to God and **c**
17:3 If he **c** the way he thinks and
Rom 11:29 God never **c** his mind when he

changing (1)
Hos 13:14 even think of **c** my plans."

channel (3)
2Ki 18:17 came there and stood at the **c**
Job 38:25 "Who made a **c** for the flooding
Isa 36:2 He stood at the **c** for the Upper

channeled (1)
2Ch 32:30 He **c** the water directly

channels (1)
Isa 8:7 It will overflow all its **c** and go

chaos (3)
Isa 34:11 stretch the measuring line of **c**
Hab 3:2 In all this **c**, remember to be
Act 21:30 The whole city was in **c**,

character (12)
Rut 2:1 of outstanding **c** named Boaz.
3:11 woman who has strength of **c**.
4:11 So show your strength of **c** in
Pro 12:4 A wife with strength of **c** is the
31:10 can find a wife with a strong **c**?
Rom 5:4 endurance creates **c**,
5:4 and **c** creates confidence.
2Co 5:12 appearance rather than their **c**.
Eph 5:13 the true **c** of everything
1Ti 3:8 must also be of good **c**.

1Ti 3:11 wives must also be of good **c**.
Tit 2:2 Tell them to be men of good **c**,

characters (1)

Act 17:5 They took some low-class **c**

charcoal (1)

Pro 26:21 ⌊As⌋ **c** fuels burning coals and

charge (197)

Gen 24:2 of his household who was in **c**
30:35 He had his sons take **c** of them.
32:16 He placed servants in **c** of
39:4 He put him in **c** of his
39:22 the warden placed Joseph in **c**
41:33 man and put him in **c** of Egypt.
41:40 You will be in **c** of my palace,
41:41 "I now put you in **c** of Egypt."
41:43 put Joseph in **c** of Egypt.
43:16 he said to the man in **c** of his
43:19 So they came to the man in **c**
44:1 commanded the man in **c**
44:4 Joseph said to the man in **c**
47:6 put them in **c** of my livestock."
Exo 1:11 Egyptians put slave drivers in **c**
5:14 placed Israelite foremen in **c**
18:21 Put them in **c** of groups of
18:25 the Israelites and put them in **c**
22:25 a moneylender. **C** no interest.
Num 1:50 Put the Levites in **c** of the tent
1:53 So the Levites will be in **c** of
3:25 the Gershonites were in **c**
3:28 They were in **c** of the holy
3:31 They were in **c** of the ark,
3:32 supervise those who were in **c**
3:36 duty of the Merarites to be in **c**
3:38 They were in **c** of the holy
4:16 will be in **c** of the oil for the
4:16 He is in **c** of the whole tent and
4:27 You are in **c** of telling them
4:28 will be in **c** of them.
4:33 will be in **c** of them."
18:5 "You must be in **c** of the work
18:8 "I am putting you in **c** of all the
31:30 to the Levites who are in **c**
31:47 to the Levites who were in **c**
Dtr 1:15 I put them in **c** of groups of
22:20 But if the **c** is true,
23:19 Never **c** another Israelite any
23:20 You may **c** a foreigner interest,
Jos 6:5 Then the troops must **c** straight
Rut 2:5 Boaz asked the young man in **c**
1Sm 18:5 Saul put him in **c** of the fighting
2Sm 3:8 But now you **c** me with a crime
8:16 Zeruiah's son Joab was in **c** of
10:10 He put his brother Abishai in **c**
18:1 He appointed commanders in **c**
20:23 Now, Joab was put in **c** of
20:23 was in **c** of the Cherethites and
20:24 Adoram was in **c** of forced
23:23 put him in **c** of his bodyguards.
1Ki 4:5 was in **c** of the district
4:6 Ahishar was in **c** of the palace.
4:6 was in **c** of forced labor.
4:8 who was in **c** of the hills of
4:9 who was in **c** of Makaz,
4:10 who was in **c** of Arubboth,
4:13 Bengeber was in **c** of Ramoth
4:14 was in **c** of Mahanaim.
4:15 Ahimaaz was in **c** of Naphtali.
4:16 was in **c** of Asher and Aloth.
4:17 was in **c** of Issachar.
4:18 was in **c** of Benjamin.
4:19 was in **c** of Gilead,
5:14 was in **c** of forced labor.
5:16 who were in **c** of the workers.
9:23 These were the officers in **c** of
11:28 So he put Jeroboam in **c** of all
12:18 He was in **c** of forced labor,
16:9 (Arza was in **c** of the palace in
18:3 who was in **c** of the palace.
2Ki 7:17 arm he used to lean to be in **c**
10:5 So the official in **c** of the
10:22 Then Jehu told the man in **c** of
11:15 commanders who were in **c**
11:18 appointed officials to be in **c**
2Ki 15:5 king's son Jotham was in **c**
18:18 who was in **c** of the palace and
18:37 Then Eliakim, who was in **c** of
19:2 who was in **c** of the palace,
22:5 it to the foremen who are in **c**
22:9 it to the workmen who are in **c**
22:14 Shallum was in **c** of the
25:19 the scribe who was in **c** of the
1Ch 6:31 David put men in **c** of the
9:11 official in **c** of God's temple).
9:17 (Shallum was in **c**.)
9:19 their ancestors had been in **c**
9:20 had been the official in **c** of the
9:26 Levite gatekeepers were in **c**
9:28 Some of them were in **c** of the
9:29 of Korah were placed in **c**
11:25 put him in **c** of his bodyguards.
18:15 Zeruiah's son Joab was in **c** of
19:11 He put his brother Abishai in **c**
22:12 as he commands you to take **c**
23:28 They were appointed to be in **c**
26:20 Ahijah, a Levite, was in **c** of
26:22 They were in **c** of the
26:24 official in **c** of the treasuries.
26:26 He and his relatives were in **c**
27:2 was in **c** of the first unit,
27:4 was in **c** of the unit during the
27:7 Joab's brother, was in **c**
27:9 was in **c** of the sixth unit
27:10 was in **c** of the seventh unit
27:11 was in **c** of the eighth unit
27:12 was in **c** of the ninth unit during
27:13 was in **c** of the tenth unit during
27:14 was in **c** of the eleventh unit
27:16 The following officers were in **c**
27:25 were all the commanders in **c**
27:32 were in **c** of the king's sons.
28:1 the officials in **c** of all the
29:6 and the officials in **c** of the
2Ch 8:10 These were the officers in **c** of
10:18 He was in **c** of forced labor,
19:11 chief priest Amariah will be in **c**
19:11 will be in **c** of every matter
23:14 commanders who were in **c**
23:18 appointed officials to be in **c**
26:21 His son Jotham was in **c** of the
28:7 who was in **c** of the palace,
28:15 mentioned by name took **c**
31:12 The Levite Conaniah was in **c**
31:13 who was in **c** of God's temple,
34:10 to the foremen who were in **c**
34:22 Shallum was in **c** of the
35:8 the men in **c** of God's temple,
Ezr 1:8 the treasurer Mithredath in **c**
8:30 priests and the Levites took **c**
Neh 3:9 an official in **c** of half a district
3:12 an official in **c** of half a district
3:14 the official in **c** of the district of
3:15 the official in **c** of the district of
3:16 the official in **c** of half the
3:17 the official in **c** of half the
3:18 the official in **c** of half the
3:19 the official in **c** of Mizpah,
7:2 the fortress, in **c** of Jerusalem.
11:9 Joel, son of Zichri, was in **c**,
11:14 The man in **c** of them was
11:16 who were in **c** of the work
11:21 Ziha and Gishpa in **c** of them.
11:22 The man in **c** of the Levites in
11:22 who were the singers in **c**
12:8 who with his relatives was in **c**
12:44 On that day men were put in **c**
13:4 to Tobiah and had been put in **c**
13:13 the following men to be in **c**
Est 8:2 in **c** of Haman's property.
Job 9:19 who will **c** me with a crime?
34:13 Who put him in **c** of the earth?
Psa 69:27 **C** them with one crime after
91:11 He will put his angels in **c** of
Isa 22:15 the man in **c** of the palace,
36:3 Eliakim, who was in **c** of the
36:22 Then Eliakim, who was in **c** of
37:2 who was in **c** of the palace,
Jer 1:10 Today I have put you in **c** of
6:27 "Jeremiah, I have put you in **c**
52:25 the scribe who was in **c** of the
Eze 18:17 He doesn't **c** interest or make
44:8 foreigners in **c** of my temple.
Dan 1:11 put a supervisor in **c** of Daniel,
4:17 lowest of people in **c** of them.'"
5:21 he wishes in **c** of them.
6:3 thought about putting him in **c**
Nah 3:3 Horses **c**! Swords flash! Spears
Mat 4:6 will put his angels in **c** of you.
24:45 master will put that person in **c**
24:47 He will put that servant in **c** of
25:21 I will put you in **c** of a large
25:23 I will put you in **c** of a large
Mar 13:34 he put his servants in **c**.
Luk 4:10 'He will put his angels in **c** of
12:42 that the master will put in **c**
12:44 He will put that servant in **c** of
19:17 Take **c** of ten cities.'
19:19 'You take **c** of five cities.'
Jon 2:8 and take it to the person in **c**.
2:9 The person in **c** tasted the
2:9 person in **c** called the groom
12:6 He was in **c** of the moneybag
Act 4:1 Some priests, the officer in **c** of
6:3 put them in **c** of this problem.
8:27 a high-ranking official in **c** of all
12:20 (Blastus was in **c** of the king's
21:31 the officer in **c** of the Roman
26:2 myself against every **c** that
1Co 9:18 the Good News free of **c**.
2Co 11:7 of God free of **c** so that you
Col 2:10 Christ is in **c** of every ruler and
Phm 1:18 owes you anything, **c** it to me.
Heb 3:6 But Christ is a faithful son in **c**
10:21 priest in **c** of God's house.
3Jn 1:9 who loves to be in **c**,

charged (8)

Jos 6:20 The troops **c** straight ahead
Jdg 9:44 Abimelech and his company **c**
9:44 The other two companies **c** at
20:37 quickly **c** toward Gibeah.
Hos 13:16 of Samaria are guilty as **c**
Luk 11:50 the people living now will be **c**
Act 21:32 and officers and **c** the crowd.
24:20 me should tell what I was **c**

charges (26)

Dtr 22:14 Then he might make up **c**
22:17 he has made up **c** against her.
2Ch 36:8 did and all the **c** against him —
Job 15:26 He stubbornly **c** at him with a
23:6 would press **c** against me.
39:21 joy in its power. It **c** into battle.
Psa 35:11 people bring **c** against me.
Jer 2:9 I am bringing **c** against you,"
2:9 **c** against your grandchildren.
25:31 LORD has brought **c** against
Dan 3:8 brought **c** against the Jews.
6:24 had brought **c** against Daniel
Hos 4:1 The LORD has brought these **c**
4:4 people or bring **c** against them.
12:2 The LORD brings **c** against
Mat 27:13 "Don't you hear how many **c**
Jon 8:6 a reason to bring **c** against him.
Act 19:38 bring **c** against each other.
24:1 governor their **c** against Paul.
25:2 about their **c** against Paul.
25:9 to be tried there on these **c**
25:27 specify any **c** against him."
28:19 That doesn't mean I have any **c**
2Co 7:11 of the **c** against you.
Col 2:14 He did this by erasing the **c**
2:14 He took the **c** away by nailing

charging (7)

Neh 5:7 I told them, "You are **c** interest
5:10 we must stop **c** them interest.
5:11 and olive oil you've been **c**
Pro 28:15 a roaring lion and a **c** bear,
Jer 8:6 ways like horses **c** into battle.
Dan 8:4 I saw the ram **c** west,
Mat 10:8 Give these things without **c**,

chariot (67)

Gen 41:43 He had him ride in the **c** of the
46:29 Joseph prepared his **c** and

Exo 14:6 So Pharaoh prepared his **c** and
Jdg 4:15 Sisera got down from his **c** and
5:28 "Why is his **c** taking so long?
2Sm 10:18 and David killed 700 **c** drivers
15:1 Absalom acquired a **c**,
1Ki 1:5 So he got a **c** and horses and
4:26 Solomon had stalls for 40,000 **c**
4:26 He also had 12,000 **c** soldiers.
4:28 and straw for the **c** horses
7:33 were made like **c** wheels.
9:22 of his **c** and cavalry units.
10:26 He stationed ⌊some⌋ in **c**
10:29 Each **c** was imported from
12:18 So King Rehoboam got on his **c**
18:44 'Prepare ⌊your **c**⌋,
18:45 Ahab got into his **c** to go back
20:33 Ahab had him come up on the **c**
22:31 orders to the 32 **c** commanders.
22:32 When the **c** commanders saw
22:33 the **c** commanders realized that
22:34 Ahab told his **c** driver,
22:35 kept propped up in his **c** facing
22:35 wound had flowed into the **c**.
22:38 His **c** was washed at the pool
2Ki 2:11 a fiery **c** with fiery horses
2:12 Israel's **c** and horses!"
5:9 came with his horses and **c**
5:21 he got down from his **c** to
5:26 the man turned around in his **c**
8:21 The Edomites and their **c**
9:16 So Jehu got on his **c** and drove
9:17 Joram said, "Take a **c** driver,
9:18 So a **c** driver rode off,
9:21 horses to the **c**," Joram ordered.
9:21 each in his own **c**.
9:23 As Joram turned his **c** around
9:24 and he slumped over in his **c**.
9:27 "Shoot him down in his **c**."
9:28 him in a **c** to Jerusalem.
10:15 Jehu helped him up into the **c**.
10:16 had Jehonadab ride on his **c**.
13:14 Israel's **c** and horses!"
23:30 put his dead body in a **c**
1Ch 19:18 and David killed 7,000 **c**
28:18 Solomon the plans for the **c**,
2Ch 1:14 He stationed ⌊some⌋ in **c**
1:17 They imported each **c** from
8:9 of his **c** and cavalry units.
9:25 He stationed ⌊some⌋ in **c**
10:18 So King Rehoboam got on his **c**
18:30 orders to the **c** commanders.
18:31 When the **c** commanders saw
18:32 and the **c** commanders realized
18:33 Ahab told the **c** driver,
18:34 himself up in his **c** facing
21:9 Jehoram took all his **c**
21:9 The Edomites and their **c**
35:24 officers took him out of the **c**
35:24 him to Jerusalem in his other **c**.
Psa 76:6 **c** riders and horses were put to
104:3 You use the clouds for your **c**.
Isa 5:28 Their **c** wheels are as quick as
Jer 46:9 Drive wildly, you **c** drivers.
Zec 6:2 The first **c** had red horses.
6:6 The **c** with the black horses is

chariots (102)

Gen 50:9 **C** and horsemen went with him.
Exo 14:7 He took 600 of his best **c** as
14:7 well as all the other **c** in Egypt,
14:9 his horse-drawn **c** and cavalry,
14:17 entire army, his **c**, and cavalry.
14:18 his **c**, and his cavalry."
14:23 and all Pharaoh's horses, **c**,
14:25 He made the wheels of their **c**
14:26 their **c**, and their cavalry."
14:28 as well as the **c** and the
15:4 He has thrown Pharaoh's **c** and
15:19 When Pharaoh's horses, **c**,
Dtr 11:4 army, its horses and **c**.
20:1 **c**, and armies larger than yours.
Jos 11:4 They also had horses and **c**.
11:6 You must burn their **c**."
11:9 their horses and burned their **c**,
17:16 of Jezreel have **c** made of iron."
17:18 and have **c** made of iron."
Jos 24:6 The Egyptians with their **c** and
Jdg 1:19 valley who had **c** made of iron.
4:3 King Jabin had 900 **c** made of
4:7 of Jabin's army), his **c**,
4:13 So Sisera summoned all his **c**
4:13 all his chariots (900 **c** made
4:15 LORD threw Sisera, all his **c**,
4:16 Barak pursued the **c** and the
5:28 don't I hear the clatter of his **c**?"
1Sm 8:11 serve on his **c** and horses,
8:11 make them run ahead of his **c**.
8:12 and equipment for his **c**.
13:5 They had 30,000 **c**,
2Sm 1:6 and the **c** and horsemen were
8:4 so that they couldn't pull **c**.
1Ki 9:19 He also built cities for his **c**,
10:26 built up ⌊his army⌋ with **c**
10:26 He had 1,400 **c** and 12,000 war
16:9 commanded half of Elah's **c**,
20:1 along with their horses and **c**.
20:21 and destroyed the horses and **c**
20:25 with as many horses and **c** as
2Ki 6:14 So the king sent horses and **c**
6:15 and **c** surrounding the city.
6:17 was full of fiery horses and **c**.
7:6 army hear what sounded like **c**,
7:14 So they took two **c** with horses,
8:21 Jehoram took all his **c** to attack
9:25 driving our **c** behind his father
10:2 you, and you have **c**, horses,
13:7 left except for 50 horses, 10 **c**,
18:24 trust Egypt for **c** and horses?
19:23 "With my many **c** I'll ride up the
23:11 He also burned the **c** of the sun
1Ch 18:4 David took 1,000 **c**,
18:4 so that they couldn't pull **c**.
19:6 pounds of silver to hire **c**
19:7 They hired 32,000 **c** and the
2Ch 1:14 built up ⌊his army⌋ with **c**
1:14 He had 1,400 **c** and 12,000 war
8:6 He built all the cities for his **c**,
9:25 4,000 stalls for horses and **c**,
12:3 Shishak had 1,200 **c**,
14:9 with 1,000,000 men and 300 **c**
16:8 army with many **c** and drivers?
Psa 20:7 Some ⌊rely⌋ on **c** and others
46:9 spears in two. He burns **c**.
68:17 The **c** of God are twenty
Sos 6:12 that I had become like the **c**
Isa 2:7 and there is no end to their **c**.
21:7 He will see **c**, pairs of
21:9 Here come **c** and horsemen in
22:6 manned **c**, and horsemen.
22:7 valleys will be filled with **c**,
22:18 your splendid **c** will remain.
31:1 who depend on many **c**,
36:9 trust Egypt for **c** and horses?
37:24 "With my many **c** I'll ride up the
43:17 He leads **c** and horses,
66:15 with fire and with his **c** like
66:20 on horses, in **c**, in wagons,
Jer 4:13 His **c** are like a raging wind.
17:25 and their princes will ride in **c**
22:4 the gates of this palace in **c**
47:3 the rattling of enemy **c**,
50:37 will kill their horses, their **c**,
51:21 you to crush **c** and their drivers.
Eze 23:24 with **c** and wagons and with a
26:7 He will bring horses, **c**,
26:10 and **c** will shake your walls
Dan 11:40 rush at him like a storm with **c**,
Joe 2:5 they sound like rattling **c**,
Mic 1:13 Harness the horses to the **c**,
5:10 horses and demolish your **c**.
Nah 2:3 The metal on his **c** flashes
2:4 **C** are racing madly through the
2:13 "I will send your **c** up in smoke,
3:2 gallop! **C** bounce along!
Hab 3:8 your **c** of salvation?
Hag 2:22 I will overthrow **c** and their
Zec 6:1 and saw four **c** going out from
9:10 will make sure there are no **c**
Rev 9:9 wings was like the roar of **c**

charm (1)

Pro 31:30 "**C** is deceptive, and beauty

charmed (4)

Ecc 10:11 bites before it has been **c**,
Sos 4:9 my sister, you have **c** me.
4:9 You have **c** me with a single
Jer 8:17 vipers that can't be **c**.

charmer (2)

Psa 58:5 hear the voice of a snake **c**
Ecc 10:11 advantage in being a snake **c**.

charming (2)

Sos 7:6 How beautiful and **c** you are,
Nah 3:4 this very **c** mistress of evil

charmingly (1)

Pro 26:25 When he talks **c**, do not trust

charms (4)

Pro 7:21 With all her seductive **c**,
Isa 3:20 blouses, perfume boxes, **c**,
Eze 13:18 for women who sew magic **c**
13:20 I'm against the magic **c** that

charred (1)

Eze 15:5 the fire has burned and **c** it?

chars (1)

Eze 15:4 both its ends and **c** its middle.

chase (28)

Exo 34:15 When they **c** after their gods as
34:16 When their daughters **c** after
Lev 20:6 psychics and **c** after them as
26:7 You will **c** your enemies,
26:8 Five of you will **c** a hundred of
26:8 and a hundred of you will **c** ten
Dtr 31:16 they will **c** after foreign gods as
32:30 How could one person **c** a
Jos 8:16 city were called out to **c** them.
10:19 **C** your enemies! Cut off their
23:10 of you used to **c** a thousand.
2Sm 2:28 They didn't **c** or fight Israel
1Ch 21:12 enemies will **c** you away when
2Ch 21:11 to **c** after foreign gods
21:13 to **c** after foreign gods
Job 13:25 or trying to **c** dry husks?
18:11 side and **c** him every step
Psa 7:5 then let the enemy **c** me and
16:4 Those who quickly **c** after
Isa 30:16 So those who **c** you will also
Jer 29:18 I will **c** them with wars,
49:19 "I will suddenly **c** them from
50:44 I will suddenly **c** them from
Eze 20:30 Will you **c** their detestable
33:31 hearts they **c** dishonest profits.
Hos 2:5 She said, 'I'll **c** after my lovers.
5:11 are determined to **c** idols.
12:1 to catch the wind and try to **c**

chased (31)

Exo 2:17 came and **c** them away.
Dtr 1:44 attacked you and **c** you like
Jos 8:16 As they **c** Joshua,
8:17 unprotected as they **c** Israel.
10:10 He **c** them along the road that
11:8 The Israelites **c** them as far as
24:6 and horsemen **c** your ancestors
Jdg 1:6 Judah's troops **c** him,
2:17 The Israelites **c** after other
8:27 All Israel **c** after it there as
8:33 the people of Israel **c** after other
9:40 Abimelech **c** Gaal so that he
2Sm 2:19 He **c** Abner and refused to
2:24 But Joab and Abishai **c** Abner.
22:38 I **c** my enemies and destroyed
1Ch 5:25 They **c** after the gods of the
12:15 They **c** away all the people in
Neh 13:28 I **c** Joiada's son away from me.
Job 18:18 the light into the dark and **c** out
20:8 He will be **c** away like a vision
Psa 18:37 I **c** my enemies and caught up
Isa 17:13 They will be **c** away like
Jer 23:2 my sheep and **c** them away.
23:3 the countries where I **c** them.
23:12 They will be **c** away,

Jer 50:17 sheep that lions have **c**.
Lam 1:3 Those who **c** them caught up
4:19 They **c** us in the mountains
Eze 20:16 their hearts **c** disgusting idols.
Dan 5:21 He was **c** away from people,
Hos 2:13 and she **c** after her lovers.

chases (6)
Lev 20:5 who **c** after Molech as
Psa 35:5 of the LORD **c** them.
Pro 12:11 but the one who **c** unrealistic
19:7 When he **c** them with words,
28:19 Whoever **c** unrealistic dreams
Isa 41:3 He **c** them, marching by safely

chasing (11)
Gen 31:36 that you have come **c** after me?
Lev 17:7 goat idols and **c** after them as
26:17 even when no one is **c** you.
26:36 but no one will be **c** them.
Num 15:39 if you were **c** after prostitutes.
Dtr 1:44 They defeated you, **c** you from
Jos 7:5 **c** them from the city gate to the
2Sm 2:26 troops from **c** their relatives?"
2:27 stopped **c** their relatives until
2:30 Joab returned from **c** Abner.
Pro 28:1 flees when no one is **c** him,

chatter (1)
Job 27:12 Why then do you **c** on about

cheap (2)
Pro 26:23 clay pot covered with **c** silver,
Jon 2:10 the host serves **c** wine.

cheat (12)
Gen 21:23 God that you will never **c** me,
29:25 Why did you **c** me?"
1Sm 12:3 Did I **c** or oppress anyone?
12:4 "You didn't **c** us, oppress us,
Hos 7:1 People **c** each other.
12:7 They love to **c** people.
Amo 8:5 and **c** with dishonest scales.
Mic 2:2 They **c** a man and his family,
Mal 3:5 and those who **c** workers out of
3:8 "Can a person **c** God?
Mar 10:19 Never **c**. Honor your father and
1Co 6:8 Instead, you do wrong and **c**,

cheated (6)
Gen 27:36 He's **c** me twice already:
31:7 Your father has **c** me.
Dan 6:2 so that the king wouldn't be **c**.
Luk 19:8 to those I have **c** in any way."
1Co 6:7 accept that you have been **c**?
2Co 7:2 ruined anyone, or **c** anyone.

cheaters (1)
Mal 1:14 "**C** are under a curse.

cheating (4)
Mal 3:8 Yet, you are **c** me!
3:8 'How are we **c** you?'
3:9 the whole nation is **c** me!
Mar 7:22 adultery, greed, wickedness, **c**,

cheats (2)
Jer 9:4 Every relative **c**.
9:5 Everyone **c** his neighbor.

Chebar (8)
Eze 1:1 the exiles by the **C** River,
1:3 in Babylon by the **C** River.
3:15 who lived by the **C** River.
3:23 the glory I saw by the **C** River,
10:15 that I saw at the **C** River.
10:20 the God of Israel at the **C** River.
10:22 faces that I saw by the **C** River.
43:3 the one I saw by the **C** River.

check (2)
Gen 30:33 itself whenever you come to **c**
Neh 7:5 they could **c** their genealogy.

Chedorlaomer (5)
Gen 14:1 of Ellasar, King **C** of Elam,
14:4 they had been subject to **C**,
14:5 In the fourteenth year **C** and his
14:9 fought against King **C** of Elam,
14:17 came back from defeating **C**

cheek (7)
1Ki 22:24 and struck him on the **c**.
2Ch 18:23 and struck him on the **c**.
Mic 5:1 of Israel on the **c** with a stick.
Mat 5:39 slaps you on your right **c**,
5:39 turn your other **c** to him as well.
Luk 6:29 someone strikes you on the **c**,
6:29 offer the other **c** as well.

cheeks (6)
Job 16:10 In scorn they slapped my **c**.
Sos 1:10 Your **c** are lovely with
5:13 His **c** are like a garden of
Isa 50:6 those who whip me and my **c**
Lam 1:2 with tears running down its **c**.
3:30 They should turn their **c** to the

cheer (8)
1Ki 21:7 Get up, eat, and **c** up.
Job 22:29 you will say, '**C** up!'
Psa 104:15 make wine to **c** human hearts,
Mat 9:2 said to the man, "**C** up, friend!
9:22 her he said, "**C** up, daughter!
Mar 10:49 blind man and told him, "**C** up!
Jon 16:33 But **c** up! I have overcome
1Th 5:14 **c** up those who are

cheered (2)
Est 8:15 the city of Susa **c** and rejoiced.
2Co 2:2 how could you have **c** me up

cheerful (9)
1Ki 8:66 They rejoiced with **c** hearts for
2Ch 7:10 They rejoiced with **c** hearts for
Est 8:16 So the Jews were **c**,
Pro 15:13 A joyful heart makes a **c** face,
15:15 but a **c** heart has a continual
16:15 When the king is **c**,
Ecc 3:12 for them to do than to be **c**
2Co 9:7 since God loves a **c** giver.
Heb 10:34 You were **c** even though your

cheerfully (3)
Psa 100:2 Serve the LORD **c**.
Ecc 9:7 and drink your wine **c**,
Rom 12:8 people in need, help them **c**.

cheese (6)
Gen 18:8 Abraham took **c** and milk,
Dtr 32:14 They ate **c** from cows and
Job 10:10 like milk and curdle me like **c**?
Isa 7:15 He will eat **c** and honey until
7:22 That person will eat **c**,
7:22 the land will eat **c** and honey.

cheeses (1)
1Sm 17:18 And take these ten **c** to the

Chelal (1)
Ezr 10:30 Adna, **C**, Benaiah, Maaseiah,

Chelub (2)
1Ch 4:11 **C**, Shuhah's brother, was the
27:26 in the fields: Ezri, son of **C**

Chelubai (1)
1Ch 2:9 were Jerahmeel, Ram, and **C**.

Cheluhi (1)
Ezr 10:35 Benaiah, Bedeiah, **C**,

Chemosh (9)
Num 21:29 you people of the god **C**.
21:29 **C** let his sons become
Jdg 11:24 of what your god **C** took
1Ki 11:7 for **C** (the disgusting idol
11:33 **C** (the god of Moab),
2Ki 23:13 **C** (the disgusting god of Moab),
Jer 48:7 **C** will go into captivity with all
48:13 Moab will be ashamed of **C** as
48:46 You people of **C** will die.

Chenaanah (5)
1Ki 22:11 Zedekiah, son of **C**,
22:24 Then Zedekiah, son of **C**,
1Ch 7:10 Ehud, **C**, Zethan, Tarshish,
2Ch 18:10 Zedekiah, son of **C**,
18:23 Zedekiah, son of **C**,

Chenaniah (3)
1Ch 15:22 **C**, a Levite leader,
15:27 who were singers, and **C**,
26:29 From Izhar's descendants **C**

Chephar Ammoni (1)
Jos 18:24 **C**, Ophni, and Geba.

Chephirah (4)
Jos 9:17 cities of Gibeon, **C**, Beeroth,
18:26 Mizpeh, **C**, Mozah,
Ezr 2:25 of Kiriath Jearim, **C**,
Neh 7:29 of Kiriath Jearim, **C**,

Cheran (2)
Gen 36:26 Hemdan, Eshban, Ithran, and **C**.
1Ch 1:41 Hamran, Eshban, Ithran, and **C**.

Cherethites (9)
1Sm 30:14 of the Negev where the **C** live,
2Sm 8:18 was commander of the **C**
15:18 all the **C**, all the Pelethites,
20:7 So Joab's men, the **C**,
20:23 charge of the **C** and Pelethites.
1Ki 1:38 (son of Jehoiada), the **C**,
1:44 (son of Jehoiada), the **C**,
1Ch 18:17 was commander of the **C**
Eze 25:16 the Philistines, cut off the **C**,

cherish (1)
Pro 4:8 **C** wisdom. It will raise you up. It

Cherith (2)
1Ki 17:3 and hide beside the **C** River,
17:5 He went to live by the **C** River,

Cherub (2)
Ezr 2:59 Harsha, **C**, Addan, and Immer,
Neh 7:61 Harsha, **C**, Addan, and Immer,

Chesalon (1)
Jos 15:10 of Mount Jearim (now called **C**).

Chesil (1)
Jos 15:30 Eltolad, **C**, Hormah,

chest (7)
2Ki 9:24 The arrow came out of his **c**,
Job 41:24 Its **c** is solid like a rock,
Sos 5:14 His **c** is a block of ivory
Dan 2:32 Its **c** and arms were made of
Zec 13:6 are these scars on your **c**?' he
Mat 13:52 old things out of his treasure **c**."
Jon 21:20 who leaned against Jesus' **c** at

chestnut (1)
Zec 1:8 Behind him were red, **c**,

chests (1)
Mat 2:11 they opened their treasure **c**

Chesulloth (1)
Jos 19:18 included Jezreel, **C**, Shunem,

chew (13)
Lev 11:3 hoofs and that also **c** their cud.
11:4 from those that either **c** their
11:4 because they **c** their cud
11:5 because they **c** their cud
11:6 because they **c** their cud
11:7 hoofs but do not **c** their cud,
11:26 or that don't **c** their cud are
Num 11:33 had even had a chance to **c**
Dtr 14:6 hoofs and that also **c** their cud.
14:7 But some animals **c** their cud,
14:7 (Although they **c** their cud,
14:8 they don't **c** their cud.)
Job 13:14 I am biting off more than I can **c**

chicks (5)

Dtr 22:6 a nest containing c or eggs,
22:6 never take her with the c.
22:7 You may take the c,
Mat 23:37 gathers her c under her wings!
Luk 13:34 gathers her c under her wings!

Chidon's (1)

1Ch 13:9 they came to C threshing floor,

chief (187)

Gen 40:2 Pharaoh was angry with his c
40:2 cupbearer and his c baker.
40:9 So the c cupbearer told Joseph
40:16 The c baker saw that the
40:20 attention to the c cupbearer
40:20 cupbearer and the c baker.
40:21 He restored the c cupbearer to
40:22 But he hung the c baker just as
40:23 Nevertheless, the c cupbearer
41:9 Then the c cupbearer spoke to
41:10 he confined me and the c baker
Exo 25:7 be set in the ⌊c priest's⌋ ephod
28:4 the c priest's turban,
35:9 be set in the ⌊c priest's⌋ ephod
35:27 be set in the ⌊c priest's⌋ ephod
39:28 They also made the c priest's
Lev 16:32 ordained to serve as c priest
21:10 wears the c priest's clothes is
21:10 clothes is c over his brothers.
Num 3:32 The c leader of the Levites
Jos 20:6 until whoever is c priest at that
1Sm 10:12 "But who's the c prophet?"
21:4 the c priest answered David.
21:9 The c priest answered,
1Ki 4:2 was the ⌊c⌋ priest.
2Ki 12:10 the king's scribe and the c
22:4 "Go to the c priest Hilkiah.
22:8 The c priest Hilkiah told the
23:4 ordered the c priest Hilkiah,
25:18 guard took the c priest Seraiah,
1Ch 9:26 The four c Levite gatekeepers
2Ch 19:11 Now, the c priest Amariah will
24:6 So the king called for the c
24:11 the king's scribe and the c
26:20 When the c priest Azariah and
31:10 The c priest Azariah from
34:9 They came to the c priest
Ezr 8:29 Do this in front of the c priests,
Neh 3:1 The c priest Eliashib and his
3:20 house of the c priest Eliashib.
13:28 the son of the c priest Eliashib.)
Jer 20:1 the c officer of the LORD's
39:3 Samgar Nebo (the c officer),
39:3 and the c fortuneteller),
39:13 Nebushazban (the c official),
39:13 and the c fortuneteller),
52:24 guard took the c priest Seraiah,
Eze 38:2 He is the c prince of the
38:3 c prince of Meshech and Tubal.
39:1 the c prince of Meshech and
Dan 10:13 one of the c commanders,
Hag 1:1 and to the c priest Joshua (who
1:12 the c priest Joshua (who was
1:14 the c priest Joshua (who was
2:2 the c priest Joshua (who is the
2:4 "C Priest Joshua (son of
Zec 3:1 me Joshua, the c priest,
3:8 "Listen, C Priest Joshua and
6:11 on the head of C Priest Joshua,
Mat 2:4 He called together all the c
16:21 leaders, c priests, and scribes.
20:18 will be betrayed to the c priests
21:15 When the c priests and the
21:23 The c priests and the leaders
21:45 When the c priests and the
26:3 Then the c priests and the
26:3 palace of the c priest Caiaphas.
26:14 went to the c priests.
26:47 They were from the c priests
26:51 the ear of the c priest's servant.
26:57 him to Caiaphas, the c priest,
26:58 came to the c priest's courtyard.
26:59 The c priests and the whole
26:62 The c priest stood up and said
Mat 26:63 Then the c priest said to him,
26:65 Then the c priest tore his robes
27:1 Early in the morning all the c
27:3 to the c priests and leaders.
27:6 The c priests took the money
27:12 While the c priests and leaders
27:20 But the c priests and leaders
27:41 The c priests together with the
27:62 the c priests and Pharisees
28:11 They told the c priests
28:12 The c priests gathered together
Mar 2:26 when Abiathar was c priest
8:31 the c priests, and the scribes.
10:33 will be betrayed to the c priests
11:18 When the c priests and scribes
11:27 the c priests, the scribes,
14:1 The c priests and the scribes
14:10 went to the c priests to betray
14:43 They were from the c priests,
14:47 the ear of the c priest's servant.
14:53 men took Jesus to the c priest.
14:53 All the c priests, leaders,
14:54 into the c priest's courtyard.
14:55 The c priests and the whole
14:60 So the c priest stood up in the
14:61 The c priest asked him again,
14:63 The c priest tore his clothes
14:66 of the c priest's female servants
15:1 Early in the morning the c
15:3 The c priests were accusing
15:10 Pilate knew that the c priests
15:11 The c priests stirred up the
15:31 The c priests and the scribes
Luk 3:2 were c priests that God
9:22 the c priests, and the scribes.
19:47 The c priests, the scribes,
20:1 The c priests, scribes,
20:19 The scribes and the c priests
22:2 The c priests and the scribes
22:4 Judas went to the c priests and
22:50 ear of the c priest's servant.
22:52 Jesus said to the c priests,
22:54 away to the c priest's house.
22:66 the c priests and the scribes,
23:4 Pilate said to the c priests and
23:10 Meanwhile, the c priests and
23:13 called together the c priests,
24:20 Our c priests and rulers had
Jon 7:32 So the c priests and the
7:45 the c priests and Pharisees
11:47 So the c priests and the
11:49 who was c priest that year,
11:51 As c priest that year,
11:57 (The c priests and the
12:10 The c priests planned to kill
18:3 the guards from the c priests
18:10 attacked the c priest's servant,
18:13 Caiaphas, the c priest that year,
18:15 was well-known to the c priest.
18:15 into the c priest's courtyard.
18:19 The c priest questioned Jesus
18:22 "Is that how you answer the c
18:24 to Caiaphas, the c priest.
18:26 One of the c priest's servants,
18:35 Your own people and the c
19:6 When the c priests and the
19:15 The c priests responded,
19:21 The c priests of the Jewish
Act 4:6 The c priest Annas,
4:6 and the rest of the c priest's
4:23 them everything the c priests
5:17 The c priest and the whole
5:21 The c priest and those who
5:24 and the c priests heard this,
5:27 The c priest questioned them.
7:1 Then the c priest asked
9:1 He went to the c priest
9:14 with authority from the c priests
9:21 to the c priests ⌊in Jerusalem
19:14 of Sceva, a Jewish c priest,
22:5 The c priest and the entire
22:30 day and ordered the c priests
23:2 The c priest Ananias ordered
23:4 "You're insulting God's c
23:5 know that he is the c priest.
23:14 They went to the c priests and
Act 24:1 Five days later the c priest
25:2 The c priests and the other
25:15 went to Jerusalem, the c priests
26:10 I received from the c priests,
26:12 and authority of the c priests.
Heb 2:17 serve as a faithful c priest
3:1 the apostle and c priest about
4:14 We have a superior c priest
4:15 We have a c priest who is able
5:1 Every c priest is chosen from
5:2 The c priest can be gentle with
5:5 the glory of being a c priest
5:10 God appointed him c priest in
6:20 He has become the c priest
7:26 We need a c priest who is holy,
7:27 as those c priests did.
7:28 as c priests even though
8:1 do have this kind of c priest.
8:1 This c priest has received the
8:3 Every c priest is appointed to
8:3 Therefore, this c priest had to
9:7 But only the c priest went into
9:11 But Christ came as a c priest of
9:25 Every year the c priest went
10:12 However, this c priest made
13:11 The c priest brings the blood of
1Pe 5:4 when the c shepherd appears,

chief-of-staff (7)

Dan 1:3 The king told Ashpenaz, the c,
1:7 The c gave them ⌊Babylonian⌋
1:8 So he asked the c for
1:9 God made the c kind and
1:10 The c told Daniel, "I'm afraid of
1:11 The c put a supervisor in
1:18 the c brought all the young men

chiefs (2)

Jos 23:2 So he called all the leaders, c,
24:1 leaders, c, judges, and officers,

child (151)

Gen 4:2 she gave birth to another c,
4:25 "God has given me another c
5:29 "This c will bring us relief from
17:12 every male c who is eight
17:17 woman, have a c?"
18:13 'Can I really have a c now that
21:8 The c grew and was weaned.
21:13 because he is your c."
Exo 1:16 look at the c when you deliver
2:9 "Take this c, nurse him for me,
2:9 She took the c and nursed him.
2:10 When the c was old enough,
Jdg 11:34 She was his only c.
13:3 never been able to have a c,
Rut 4:16 Naomi took the c, held him on
1Sm 1:24 while the boy was ⌊still⌋ a c.
1:25 the bull and brought the c to Eli.
1:27 I prayed for this c, and the
2Sm 12:15 The LORD struck the c that
12:15 so that the c became sick.
12:16 pleaded with God for the c;
12:18 On the seventh day the c died.
12:18 to tell him that the c was dead.
12:18 "While the c was alive,
12:18 can we tell him the c is dead?
12:19 realized that the c was dead.
12:19 "Is the c dead?" David asked
12:21 You fasted and cried over the c
12:21 But as soon as the c died,
12:22 "As long as the c was alive,
12:22 to me and let the c live.'
12:24 The LORD loved the c
1Ki 3:25 said, "Cut the living c in two.
3:26 moved by her love for the c.
3:26 give her the living c.
3:27 "Give the living c to the first
14:12 foot in the city the c will die.
17:23 Elijah took the c, brought him
18:12 to the LORD since I was a c.
2Ki 8:5 Elisha brought a dead c back
Est 2:20 as she did when she was a c.
Psa 58:8 a stillborn c who never sees
131:2 as a weaned c is content
Pro 4:3 tender and only c of my mother,

Pro 15:20 a foolish **c** despises its mother.
20:11 Even a **c** makes himself
22:6 Train a **c** in the way he should
23:13 not hesitate to discipline a **c**.
29:15 **c** disgraces his mother.
Ecc 11:5 limbs of a **c** within its mother's
Isa 9:6 A **c** will be born for us.
10:19 few that a **c** could count them.
13:8 a woman giving birth to a **c**.
49:15 a woman forget her nursing **c**?
49:15 on the **c** from her womb?
66:7 labor pains, she delivers a **c**.
66:13 As a mother comforts her **c**,
Jer 4:31 as she gives birth to her first **c**.
6:24 a woman giving birth to a **c**.
6:26 as if you have lost your only **c**,
22:23 a woman giving birth to a **c**.
30:6 Can a man give birth to a **c**?
30:6 a woman giving birth to a **c**?
31:20 Is he a pleasant **c**?
Hos 11:1 "When Israel was a **c**,
Amo 8:10 like a funeral for an only **c**,
Mic 5:3 until the time a mother has a **c**.
5:4 The **c** will become the
6:7 Should I give him my firstborn **c**
6:7 him my young **c** for my sin?
Zec 13:5 this land since I was a **c**.'
Mat 1:25 Joseph named the **c** Jesus.
2:8 and search carefully for the **c**.
2:9 the place where the **c** was.
2:11 they saw the **c** with his mother
2:13 take the **c** and his mother,
2:13 to search for the **c** and kill him."
2:14 took the **c** and his mother,
2:20 take the **c** and his mother,
2:20 who tried to kill the **c** are dead."
2:21 took the **c** and his mother,
7:9 "If your **c** asks you for bread,
7:10 Or if your **c** asks for a fish,
10:21 a father will hand over his **c**.
18:2 He called a little **c** and had him
18:4 becomes like this little **c** is
18:5 And whoever welcomes a **c**
Mar 5:39 The **c** isn't dead. She's just
5:40 disciples and went to the **c**.
7:30 and found the little **c** lying
9:21 this way since he was a **c**.
9:26 shook the **c** violently,
9:36 Then he took a little **c** and had
9:36 He put his arms around the **c**
9:37 "Whoever welcomes a **c** like
10:15 of God as a little **c** receives
12:19 and leaves a wife but no **c**,
13:12 a father will hand over his **c**.
Luk 1:35 Therefore, the holy **c**
1:36 said she couldn't have a **c**.
1:42 and blessed is the **c** that you
1:57 for Elizabeth to have her **c**,
1:59 When the **c** was eight days old,
1:62 what he wanted to name the **c**.
1:66 does the future hold for this **c**?"
1:76 "You, **c**, will be called a
1:80 The **c** John grew and became
2:6 came for Mary to have her **c**.
2:17 When they saw the **c**,
2:21 Eight days after his birth, the **c**
2:27 were bringing the **c** Jesus into
2:28 Then Simeon took the **c** in his
2:34 "This **c** is the reason that many
2:40 The **c** grew and became strong.
7:12 man was a widow's only **c**.
8:54 and called out, "**C**, get up!"
9:38 at my son. He's my only **c**.
9:39 leaving the **c** worn out.
9:47 So he took a little **c** and had
9:48 welcomes this little **c**
11:11 "If your **c** asks you,
11:12 Or if your **c** asks you for an
15:31 "His father said to him, 'My **c**,
16:25 replied, 'Remember, my **c**,
18:17 of God as a little **c** receives
23:29 and who couldn't nurse a **c**.'
Jon 1:13 husband's desire (to have a **c**).
16:21 But after the **c** is born,
16:21 that a **c** has been brought
Act 7:5 Abraham didn't have a **c**.
7:20 and he was a very beautiful **c**.
Rom 9:11 that the older **c** would serve
1Co 4:17 Timothy is my dear **c**,
13:11 When I was a **c**, I spoke like a
13:11 I was a child, I spoke like a **c**,
13:11 like a child, thought like a **c**,
13:11 and reasoned like a **c**.
Gal 4:1 As long as an heir is a **c**,
1Ti 1:2 a genuine **c** in faith.
1:18 Timothy, my **c**, I'm giving you
2:15 saved through the birth of the **c**,
2Ti 1:2 To Timothy, my dear **c**.
2:1 My **c**, find your source of
Tit 1:4 To Titus, a genuine **c** in the
Phm 1:10 for my **c** Onesimus [Useful].
Heb 12:5 to you as his children: "My **c**,
12:6 everyone he accepts as his **c**."
1Jn 3:10 other believers isn't God's **c**.
3:12 He was a **c** of the evil one and
Rev 12:4 that it could devour her **c** when
12:5 Her **c** was snatched away and

childbearing (2)

Gen 18:11 Sarah was past the age of **c**.
Luk 1:18 and my wife is beyond her **c**

childbirth (7)

Exo 1:16 help the Hebrew women in **c**,
Isa 21:3 Pain grips me like the pain of **c**.
42:14 But like a woman in **c** I will cry
Jer 48:41 will be like women in **c**.
49:22 will be like women in **c**.
Rom 8:22 groaning with the pains of **c** up
Gal 4:27 those who feel no pains of **c**!

childhood (3)

Pro 29:21 Pamper a slave from **c**,
Ecc 11:10 because **c** and youth are
Act 13:1 close friend of Herod since **c**),

childish (1)

1Co 13:11 I no longer used **c** ways.

childless (15)

Gen 25:21 his wife because she was **c**.
1Sm 2:5 Even the woman who was **c**
15:33 your sword made women **c**,
15:33 will be made **c** among women."
2Sm 6:23 Michal was **c** her entire life.
Job 24:21 These men take advantage of **c**
Psa 113:9 a woman who is in a **c** home
Isa 49:21 I was **c** and unable to have
51:2 I called Abraham, he was **c**.
54:1 Sing with joy, you **c** women
Jer 15:7 I will make them **c**.
18:21 Then their wives will become **c**
22:30 about Jehoiakin: He will be **c**.
Eze 14:15 that country and they make it **c**
Mat 22:24 Moses said, 'If a man dies **c**,

children (534)

Gen 3:16 labor when you give birth to **c**.
6:4 humans and had **c** by them.
6:4 These **c** were famous long ago.
10:1 Japheth had **c** after the flood.
10:21 older brother, also had **c**.
11:30 Sarai was not able to have **c**.
15:2 I'm going to die without **c**,
15:3 You have given me no **c**,
16:1 was not able to have **c**.
16:2 has kept me from having **c**.
18:19 him so that he will direct his **c**
20:17 so that they could have **c**.
20:18 household to have **c**
21:7 that Sarah would nurse **c**?
21:23 me, my **c**, or my descendants.
22:20 has given birth to these **c**
22:24 had the following **c**:
24:60 mother of many thousands of **c**.
25:22 When the **c** inside her were
29:31 it possible for her to have **c**,
29:35 Then she stopped having **c**.
30:1 she could not have **c** for Jacob,
30:1 She said to Jacob, "Give me **c**,
30:2 has kept you from having **c**?"
30:3 She can have **c** for me,
Gen 30:9 that she had stopped having **c**,
30:22 it possible for her to have **c**.
30:26 Give me my wives and my **c**
31:16 father belongs to us and our **c**.
31:17 Then Jacob put his **c** and his
31:43 for my daughters or for their **c**?
32:11 me and the mothers and **c** too.
32:22 two slaves and his eleven **c**
33:1 he divided the **c** among Leah,
33:2 the slaves and their **c** in front,
33:2 Leah and her **c** after them,
33:5 he saw the women and **c**,
33:5 "The **c** God has graciously
33:6 Then the slaves and their **c**
33:7 Likewise, Leah and her **c** came
33:13 you know that the **c** are frail
34:29 and all the women and **c**
36:25 These were the **c** of Anah:
41:52 [Blessed Twice with **C**],
41:52 because God gave him **c** in the
42:36 to make me lose all my **c**!
43:14 If I lose my **c**, I lose my
43:14 lose my children, I lose my **c**."
45:10 Live there with your **c** and your
45:19 with you from Egypt for your **c**
46:5 put their father Jacob, their **c**,
46:18 gave birth to these **c** for Jacob.
47:12 on the number of **c** they had.
47:27 property there and had many **c**.
48:6 Any other **c** you have after
48:16 they have many **c** on the earth."
50:8 (Only their **c**, their flocks,
50:21 will provide for you and your **c**."
50:23 his grandchildren, Ephraim's **c**.
50:23 Even the **c** of Machir,
Exo 1:7 of Israel had many **c**.
2:6 "This is one of the Hebrew **c**."
10:2 You will be able to tell your **c**
10:10 take your women and **c** along.
10:24 Even your women and **c** may
11:5 to the firstborn **c** of female
12:24 law for you and your **c**.
12:26 When your **c** ask you what this
12:37 plus all the women and **c**.
13:8 On that day tell your **c**,
13:14 "In the future when your **c** ask
17:3 Was it to make us, our **c**,
20:5 I punish **c** for their parents' sins
21:4 the wife and her **c** belong to the
21:5 my master, my wife, and my **c**.
22:24 Then your wives and **c** will
23:26 or be unable to have **c**.
34:7 punishing **c** and grandchildren
Lev 10:13 that belongs to you and your **c**.
10:15 will belong to you and your **c**.
18:21 Never give your **c** as sacrifices
20:2 you give one of their **c** as
20:3 gave one of their **c** to Molech,
20:4 ignore those who give their **c**
20:20 They will die without **c**.
20:21 and woman will have no **c**.
21:15 He must not dishonor his **c**
22:13 doesn't have any **c**,
25:41 you will release him and his **c**
25:54 he and his **c** will be released in
26:22 They will rob you of your **c**,
Num 3:4 They had no **c**. So only Eleazar
5:28 and will be able to have **c**.
14:3 Our wives and **c** will be taken
14:18 go unpunished, punishing **c** ...
14:31 You said your **c** would be
14:33 Your **c** will be shepherds in the
16:27 tents with their wives and **c**.
26:59 She gave birth to Amram's **c**:
31:9 women and **c** as prisoners
32:26 Our **c**, our wives, our livestock,
Dtr 1:31 as parents carry their **c**.
1:39 you thought the little **c**
1:39 be captured in war, your **c**,
2:34 destroying men, women, and **c**.
3:6 and **c** — as we did to King
3:19 Your wives, **c**, and livestock
4:9 to your **c** and grandchildren.
4:10 teach their **c** the same thing."
4:25 Even when you have **c** and
5:9 I punish **c** for their parents' sins

Dtr 5:29 for them and their **c** forever.
6:2 long as you live, you, your **c**,
6:7 Repeat them to your **c**.
6:20 In the future your **c** will ask
7:4 These people will turn your **c**
7:13 He will bless you with **c**.
7:14 women will be able to have **c**,
8:5 as parents discipline their **c**.
11:2 ⌊I'm not talking⌋ to your **c**.
11:19 Teach them to your **c**,
11:21 Then you and your **c** will live
14:1 You are the **c** of the LORD your
20:14 But take the women and **c**,
21:15 Both wives might have **c**,
24:16 death for the crimes of their **c**,
24:16 and **c** must never be put to
28:4 You will have **c**. Your land will
28:11 You will have many **c**.
28:18 You will have few **c**.
28:53 will eat the flesh of your own **c**,
28:54 and the **c** he still has left.
28:55 any of the flesh of his **c** that
28:57 body and the **c** she gives birth
29:11 Your **c**, your wives, and the
29:22 the next generation of your **c**
29:29 to us and to our **c** forever.
30:2 If you and your **c** return to the
30:9 You will have many **c**.
31:12 the men, women, and **c**,
31:13 Their **c**, who don't know these
32:5 shame they are no longer his **c**.
32:20 **c** who can't be trusted.
32:25 Foreign wars will kill off their **c**,
32:46 Then you will command your **c**
33:9 didn't acknowledge their own **c**.
Jos 1:14 Your wives, **c**, and livestock
4:6 In the future your **c** will ask,
4:21 "In the future when **c** ask their
4:22 the **c** should be told that Israel
8:35 of Israel, including women, **c**,
22:24 in the future your **c** might say
22:24 children might say to our **c**,
Jdg 13:2 wife was not able to have **c**.
18:21 When they left, they put their **c**,
21:10 including the women and **c**.
1Sm 1:2 Peninnah had **c**, but Hannah
1:5 had kept her from having **c**.
1:6 had made her unable to have **c**,
2:5 gives birth to seven **c**,
2:5 of many **c** grieves all alone.
2:20 "May the LORD give you **c**
15:3 infants and **c**, cows and sheep,
22:19 **c** and infants, cows, donkeys,
30:22 only his wife and **c** and leave."
2Sm 5:14 These are the names of the **c**
12:3 grew up in his home with his **c**.
1Ki 11:20 the palace among Pharaoh's **c**.
20:3 beloved wives and **c** are mine."
20:5 gold, wives, and **c** are mine.
20:7 When he sent for my wives, **c**,
2Ki 4:1 to take my two **c** as slaves."
4:4 the door behind you and your **c**,
4:5 the door behind her and her **c**.
4:5 The **c** kept bringing containers
4:7 The rest is for you and your **c**."
8:12 smash their little **c**,
14:6 But he didn't execute their **c**.
14:6 death for the crimes of their **c**,
14:6 and **c** must never be put to
16:3 Sacrificing ⌊**c**⌋ was one of the
17:31 Sepharvaim burned their **c**
17:41 So did their **c** and their
1Ch 2:30 but Seled died without **c**.
2:32 Jether died without **c**.
3:5 These ⌊**c**⌋ were born to David
4:27 his brothers didn't have many **c**,
6:3 Amram's **c** were Aaron,
7:4 They had many wives and **c**.
14:4 These are the names of the **c**
24:2 and neither had any **c**.
2Ch 20:13 and **c** were standing in front of
25:4 But he didn't execute their **c**.
25:4 death for the crimes of their **c**,
25:4 and **c** must never be put to
30:9 your relatives and **c** will find
Ezr 9:12 inheritance to your **c**.'
Ezr 10:1 and **c** gathered around him.
10:3 and the **c** born from them,
10:44 women had given birth to **c**.
Neh 5:5 Our **c** are just like theirs.
8:2 and any ⌊**c**⌋ who could
8:3 and ⌊**c**⌋ who could understand
9:23 You made their **c** as numerous
9:24 Their **c** took possession of the
12:43 The women and **c** rejoiced as
13:24 Half their **c** spoke the language
Est 3:13 women and **c** — on a single
8:11 even women and **c**,
Job 1:5 Job thought, "My **c** may have
5:4 His **c** are far from help.
5:25 "You will find that your **c** are
8:4 If your **c** sinned against him,
18:19 He will not have any **c** or
19:17 I stink to my own **c**.
19:18 Even young **c** despise me.
20:10 His **c** will have to ask the poor
21:8 They see their **c** firmly
21:11 They send their little **c** out ⌊to
21:11 and their **c** dance around.
21:19 punishment for his **c**.' God
24:5 plains provide food for their **c**.
27:14 If he has many **c**, swords will
29:5 me and my **c** were around me,
42:16 He saw his **c**, grandchildren,
Psa 8:2 mouths of little **c** and infants,
17:14 Their **c** are satisfied ⌊with it⌋,
17:14 leave what remains to their **c**.
21:10 You will destroy their **c** from
34:11 Come, **c**, listen to me. I will
72:4 May he save the **c** of needy
78:4 will not hide them from our **c**.
78:5 to make them known to their **c**
78:6 **C** yet to be born ⌊would learn
78:6 will grow up and tell their **c**
90:16 Let our **c** see your glorious
102:28 The **c** of your servants will go
103:13 has compassion for his **c**,
103:17 to their **c** and grandchildren,
109:9 "Let his **c** become fatherless
109:10 Let his **c** wander around and
109:12 any pity to his fatherless **c**.
115:14 to bless you and your **c**.
127:3 **C** are an inheritance from the
127:4 The **c** born to a man when he
128:3 Your **c** will be like young olive
128:6 live to see your children's **c**.
137:9 the one who grabs your little **c**
147:13 He blesses the **c** within you.
Pro 14:26 and his **c** will have a place of
17:6 parents are the glory of their **c**.
20:7 Blessed are his **c** after he is
31:28 Her **c** and her husband stand
Ecc 4:8 They have no **c** or other family
5:14 The owners had **c**,
6:3 Suppose he had a hundred **c**
12:12 Be warned, my **c**, People never
Isa 1:2 "I raised ⌊my⌋ **c** and helped
1:4 of evildoers and destructive **c**.
3:4 **C** will govern them."
3:12 "**C** will oppress my people.
8:18 I am here with the **c** that the
11:6 and little **c** will lead them.
13:16 Their little **c** will be smashed
13:18 will they look with pity on **c**.
28:9 To **c** just weaned from milk?
29:23 When they see all their **c**,
29:23 the **c** I made with my hands,
30:1 it will be for those rebellious **c**.
30:9 are rebellious and deceitful **c**,
30:9 **c** who refuse to listen to the
38:19 faithfulness known to their **c**.
45:11 is going to happen to my **c**!
47:8 I won't suffer the loss of **c**."
47:9 the loss of your **c** and your
48:19 Your **c** would be like its grains.
49:17 Your **c** will hurry back.
49:18 All of your **c** are gathering
49:20 The **c** taken from you will say
49:21 has fathered these ⌊**c**⌋ for me?
49:21 childless and unable to have **c**.
49:21 Who raised these ⌊**c** for me⌋?
49:25 and I will save your **c**.
Isa 51:18 From all the **c** she gave birth to,
51:18 From all the **c** she raised,
51:20 Your **c** have fainted.
54:1 who never gave birth to **c**.
54:1 "There will be more **c** of
54:1 been deserted than there are **c**
54:13 All your **c** will be taught by the
54:13 and your **c** will have unlimited
57:3 come here, you **c** of witches,
57:4 Aren't you rebellious **c**,
57:5 You slaughter **c** in the valleys
59:21 They will be with your **c** and
60:9 to bring your **c** from far away.
61:5 and **c** of foreigners will work
63:8 **c** who will not lie to me."
65:23 give birth to **c** who die young,
66:8 she also gave birth to her **c**.
66:9 make her unable to have **c**?"
Jer 2:30 your **c** without results.
3:19 "I wanted to treat you like **c**
5:7 Your **c** abandoned me.
6:11 "Pour it out on the **c** in the
6:21 Parents and **c** will stumble
7:18 **C** gather wood, fathers light
9:21 Death has cut down the **c** in
10:20 My **c** have left me and have
13:14 smash parents and **c** together,
16:3 fathers who have **c** in this land:
17:2 Even their **c** remember their
18:21 hand their **c** over to famine.
19:5 to burn their **c** as sacrifices
30:20 Their **c** will be like they were
31:15 Rachel is crying for her **c**.
31:17 Your **c** will return to their own
32:18 However, you punish **c** for the
32:39 good and for the good of their **c**.
38:23 "All your wives and **c** will be
40:7 and **c** who had not been taken
41:16 back men, women, **c**, soldiers,
43:6 They took men, women, **c**,
44:7 destroying men, women, **c**,
47:3 lack courage abandon their **c**.
49:1 Doesn't Israel have any **c**?
49:10 Their **c** and relatives will be
Lam 1:5 Its **c** go ahead of their
1:16 My **c** are devastated because
1:20 In the streets swords kill my **c**.
2:11 Little **c** and infants faint in the
2:19 of your little **c** who faint from
2:20 Should women eat their own **c**,
2:20 the **c** they have nursed?
2:22 My enemy has murdered the **c** I
4:2 "Zion's precious **c**,
4:4 Little **c** beg for bread,
4:10 mothers cooked their own **c**.
4:10 The **c** were used for food by
Eze 2:4 to these defiant and stubborn **c**.
5:10 is why parents will eat their **c**,
5:10 and **c** will eat their parents.
5:17 and they will rob you of your **c**.
9:6 women, young women, and **c**.
16:21 You slaughtered my **c** and
16:36 You also killed your **c** and
16:45 rejected her husband and her **c**.
16:45 their husbands and their **c**.
18:4 Fathers and their **c** belong to
20:18 I said to their **c** in the desert,
20:31 You offer your **c** as sacrifices
23:37 They have sacrificed the **c**
23:39 When they sacrificed their **c** to
36:12 take their **c** away from them.
36:13 and take the **c** away from your
36:14 or take the **c** away from your
36:15 You will never again take the **c**
37:25 They, their **c**, and their
47:22 given birth to **c** while they lived
Dan 6:24 They, their wives, and their **c**
Hos 1:2 and have **c** with that prostitute.
1:10 'You are the **c** of the living
2:4 I won't love her **c**,
2:4 they are **c** of a prostitute.
4:6 so I will forget your **c**.
4:10 but they'll never have **c**.
5:7 because their **c** do not belong
9:12 Even if they bring up **c**,
9:12 I will take those **c** away before

children's (9)

child's (10)

Chileab (1)

Chilion (3)

chilling (1)

Chimham (3)

chimneys (1)

chin (2)

Chinnereth (1)

Chinneroth (2)

Chios (1)

chirped (1)

chisel (3)

chisels (2)

Chislev (2)

Chisloth Tabor (1)

Chitlish (1)

Chloe's (1)

choice (14)

Rom 9:12 a **c** based on God's call and
9:16 Therefore, God's **c** does not
11:28 But by God's **c** they are loved
Php 1:23 That's by far the better **c**.

choices (2)
2Sm 24:12 I'm offering you three **c**.
1Ch 21:10 I'm offering you three **c**.

choicest (3)
Isa 5:2 planted it with the **c** vines,
Eze 31:16 all the trees in Eden, the **c**
Amo 5:22 offerings of your **c** animals.

choir (4)
Neh 12:31 One **c** went to the right on the
12:38 The other **c** went to the left.
12:39 The **c** stopped at Guard's Gate.
Hab 3:19 For the **c** director; on stringed

choirs (4)
Neh 12:31 and I arranged two large **c** to
12:40 So both **c** stood in God's
Psa 26:12 LORD with the **c** in worship.
68:26 the source of Israel, with the **c**.

choke (4)
Mat 13:22 deceitful pleasures of riches **c**
18:28 he found and began to **c** him.
Mar 4:19 They **c** the word so that it can't
Luk 8:14 and pleasures of life **c** them.

choked (4)
Job 7:15 My throat would rather be **c**.
Mat 13:7 grew up and **c** them.
Mar 4:7 The thornbushes grew up and **c**
Luk 8:7 grew up with them and **c** them.

choose (88)
Exo 12:4 **C** your animal based on the
12:5 You may **c** a lamb or a young
17:9 "**C** some of our men.
18:21 "But **c** capable men from all the
20:24 Wherever I **c** to have my name
25:2 "Tell the Israelites to **c**
35:5 **C** something of your own to
Num 14:4 said to each other, "Let's **c**
16:7 Then the LORD will **c** the man
17:5 The staff from the man I **c** will
Dtr 1:13 **c** some men who are wise,
12:5 The LORD your God will **c** a
12:11 Then the LORD your God will **c**
12:14 the place that the LORD will **c**
12:18 your God at the place he will **c**.
12:26 to the place the LORD will **c**.
14:23 your God in the place he will **c**
14:24 the LORD your God will **c**
14:25 the LORD your God will **c**.
14:26 liquor — whatever you **c**.
15:20 in the place the LORD will **c**.
16:2 place where the LORD will **c**
16:6 the LORD your God will **c**
16:7 the LORD your God will **c**.
16:11 the LORD your God will **c**
16:15 your God in the place he will **c**.
16:16 your God at the place he will **c**:
17:8 that the LORD your God will **c**.
17:10 the place that the LORD will **c**.
17:15 king the LORD your God will **c**.
18:6 to the place the LORD will **c**.
21:3 leaders from that city must **c**
23:12 **C** a place outside the camp
26:2 the LORD your God will **c**
28:36 lead you and the king you **c**
30:19 **C** life so that you and your
31:11 your God at the place he will **c**.
Jos 3:12 **C** one man from each of the 12
4:2 "**C** one man from each of the 12
18:4 **C** three men from each tribe,
20:2 'Now **c** for yourselves the
20:3 **C** them so that anyone who
24:15 then **c** today whom you will
24:15 Even if you **c** the gods your
1Sm 14:42 "**C** between me and my son
17:8 **C** a man, and let him come
2Sm 17:1 "Let me **c** 12,000 men and
2Sm 24:12 **C** one of them for me to do to
1Ki 8:16 I didn't **c** any city in any of the
11:37 "I will **c** you so that you can
18:23 Let the prophets of Baal **c** one
18:25 "**C** one bull for yourselves.
2Ki 10:3 **c** the best and most honest of
1Ch 21:10 **C** one of them for me to do to
2Ch 6:5 I didn't **c** any city from the
6:5 And I didn't **c** any man to be
Ezr 1:4 All who ⌊**c** to⌋ remain behind,
Job 15:5 You **c** ⌊to talk with⌋ a sly
32:14 Job did not **c** his words to
34:33 You must **c**, not I. Tell me what
Psa 25:12 will teach which path to **c**.
65:4 Blessed is the person you **c**
75:2 When I **c** the right time,
78:67 He did not **c** the tribe of
Pro 1:29 hated knowledge and did not **c**
3:31 Do not **c** any of his ways.
Isa 7:15 how to reject evil and **c** good.
7:16 how to reject evil and **c** good,
14:1 for Jacob and again **c** Israel.
40:20 The poorest people **c** wood
44:14 Then they **c** fir trees or oaks.
56:4 **c** what pleases me,
66:4 So I will **c** harsh treatment for
Jer 49:19 over Edom whomever I **c**.
50:44 over Babylon whomever I **c**.
Eze 33:2 and the people of this country **c**
Zec 1:17 and will again **c** Jerusalem."
2:12 and will again **c** Jerusalem.
Jon 15:16 You didn't **c** me, but I chose
Act 1:26 drew names to **c** an apostle.
6:3 So, brothers and sisters, **c**
14:23 each church **c** spiritual leaders,
15:22 church decided to **c** some
15:25 decision that we should **c** men
1Co 16:3 to the people whom you **c**.
Eph 1:11 also decided ahead of time to **c**
Php 1:23 I find it hard to **c** between the
Jas 2:5 Didn't God **c** poor people in the

chooses (9)
Num 16:5 Only the person the LORD **c**
Dtr 10:15 of this, today he **c** you,
12:21 the place the LORD your God **c**
23:16 your people wherever he **c**,
Psa 36:4 while lying on his bed and **c**
47:4 He **c** our inheritance for us,
Pro 21:1 them in any direction he **c**.
Isa 41:24 Whoever **c** you is disgusting.
Jon 5:21 Son gives life to anyone he **c**.

choosing (3)
Exo 8:9 "You may have the honor of **c**
Eze 24:6 without **c** any particular piece.
2Pe 1:10 to make God's calling and **c**

chop (4)
Isa 18:5 with pruning shears and **c** off
Jer 46:22 axes like those who **c** wood.
Lam 5:4 have to pay to **c** our own wood.
Mic 3:3 You **c** them up like meat for a

chopped (1)
1Sm 6:14 The people **c** up the wood of

Chorazin (2)
Mat 11:21 horrible it will be for you, **C**!
Luk 10:13 horrible it will be for you, **C**!

chose (89)
Gen 6:2 married any woman they **c**.
13:11 Lot **c** the whole Jordan Plain
36:2 Esau **c** his wives from the
38:6 Judah **c** a wife for his firstborn
Exo 18:25 Moses **c** capable men from all
Dtr 1:23 So I **c** 12 of your men,
4:37 and **c** their descendants,
7:6 He **c** you to be his own special
7:7 set his heart on you and **c** you,
23:23 You freely **c** to make your vow
33:21 They **c** the best land for
Jos 9:27 wherever he **c** to put it.
Jdg 5:8 When the people **c** new gods,
10:14 out for help to the gods you **c**.
Jdg 14:11 they **c** 30 of their friends to be
Rut 4:2 Then Boaz **c** ten men who
1Sm 2:28 I **c** ⌊one of your ancestors⌋ out
13:2 Saul **c** 3,000 men from Israel;
2Sm 6:21 He **c** me rather than your father
1Ki 11:13 ⌊the city⌋ that I **c**."
11:34 of my servant David whom I **c**,
11:36 the city where I **c** to place my
14:21 the city that the LORD **c** from
2Ki 8:20 Judah and **c** its own king.
23:27 Jerusalem, the city that I **c**,
1Ch 25:9 The first lot drawn **c** Joseph,
25:9 The second **c** Gedaliah,
25:10 The third **c** Zaccur,
25:11 The fourth **c** Izri, his sons,
25:12 The fifth **c** Nethaniah,
25:13 The sixth **c** Bukkiah,
25:14 The seventh **c** Jesarelah,
25:15 The eighth **c** Jeshaiah,
25:16 The ninth **c** Mattaniah,
25:17 The tenth **c** Shimei,
25:18 The eleventh **c** Azarel,
25:19 The twelfth **c** Hashabiah,
25:20 The thirteenth **c** Shubael,
25:21 The fourteenth **c** Mattithiah,
25:22 The fifteenth **c** Jeremoth,
25:23 The sixteenth **c** Hananiah,
25:24 seventeenth **c** Joshbekashah,
25:25 The eighteenth **c** Hanani,
25:26 The nineteenth **c** Mallothi,
25:27 The twentieth **c** Eliathah,
25:28 The twenty-first **c** Hothir,
25:29 The twenty-second **c** Giddalti,
25:30 The twenty-third **c** Mahazioth,
25:31 twenty-fourth **c** Romamti Ezer,
28:4 the LORD God of Israel **c** me
28:4 From the families of Judah he **c**
28:5 sons) he **c** my son Solomon
2Ch 12:13 the city that the LORD **c** from
21:8 Judah and **c** its own king.
Ezr 10:16 Ezra the priest **c** men who
10:16 He **c** one from each family
Neh 1:9 bring you to the place where I **c**
9:7 the God who **c** Abram and took
Psa 78:68 but he **c** the tribe of Judah,
78:70 He **c** his servant David.
135:4 The LORD **c** Jacob to be his
135:4 to be his own and **c** Israel
Isa 49:1 I was born, the LORD **c** me.
65:2 They **c** to go the wrong
65:12 You **c** what I don't like.
66:4 They **c** what I don't like.
Eze 20:5 LORD says: When I **c** Israel,
Hos 8:4 "They **c** their own kings,
8:4 They **c** their own princes,
8:4 They **c** to make idols with their
Luk 6:13 He **c** twelve of them and called
14:7 how the guests always **c**
Jon 6:70 "I **c** all twelve of you.
15:16 didn't choose me, but I **c** you.
15:19 I **c** you from the world,
Act 6:5 So they **c** Stephen,
6:5 and they **c** Philip, Prochorus,
13:17 people of Israel **c** our ancestors
15:7 God **c** me so that people who
15:22 They **c** Judas (called
15:40 Paul **c** Silas and left after the
1Co 1:27 But God **c** what the world
1:27 God **c** what the world
1:28 God **c** what the world
Eph 1:4 he **c** us through Christ to be
1:5 He freely **c** to do this
2Th 2:13 that in the beginning he **c** you
Heb 11:25 He **c** to suffer with God's
1Pe 1:2 knew you long ago and **c** you

chosen (151)
Gen 18:19 I have **c** him so that he will
24:14 let her be the one you have **c**
24:44 be the woman the LORD has **c**
Exo 21:8 the master who has **c** her as
21:9 But if he has **c** her for his son,
31:2 "I have **c** Bezalel, son of Uri
35:30 "The LORD has **c** Bezalel,
Lev 16:9 Aaron must sacrifice the goat **c**
16:10 But he must bring the goat **c** by

Num 1:16 These were the men **c** from the
16:2 **c** by the assembly.
18:6 I have **c** the other Levites from
26:9 men **c** by the community,
Dtr 7:8 You were **c** because the LORD
14:2 the LORD has **c** you to be his
18:5 the LORD your God has **c** the
21:5 The LORD your God has **c**
Jos 20:7 of Judah were **c** as cities
20:8 of Manasseh were **c** as cities
20:9 These are the cities **c** as cities
21:4 that were **c** by drawing lots.
21:20 Cities were **c** by lot from the
21:40 These 12 cities were **c** by lot.
24:22 have testified that you have **c**
1Sm 8:18 you have **c** for yourselves.
10:20 the tribe of Benjamin was **c**.
10:21 the family of Matri was **c**.
10:21 Saul, the son of Kish, was **c**.
10:24 see whom the LORD has **c**?
12:13 here is the king you have **c**,
14:41 Jonathan and Saul were **c**,
14:42 Then Jonathan was **c**.
16:8 has not **c** this one either."
16:9 "The LORD has not **c** this one
16:10 has not **c** ⌊any of⌋ these.
2Sm 16:18 and all Israel have **c**.
21:6 Saul whom the LORD had **c**.)
24:15 morning until the time he had **c**.
1Ki 3:8 your people whom you have **c**.
8:16 But now I've **c** David to rule my
8:44 toward the city you have **c** and
8:48 and the city you have **c**,
11:32 the city I have **c** from all the
2Ki 21:7 "I have **c** this temple and
1Ch 6:54 they settled in the territory **c**
6:61 received 10 cities **c** by lot from
6:62 given 13 cities **c** by lot from
6:63 given 12 cities **c** by lot from
6:65 They gave ⌊them⌋ the cities **c**
6:66 had cities **c** by lot from
9:22 The men **c** to be gatekeepers
15:2 because the LORD had **c** them
16:13 of Jacob, his **c** ones.
16:41 had been selected, **c** by name,
24:6 One family was **c** for Eleazar,
26:14 Shelemiah was **c** for the east
26:14 was **c** for the north side.
26:15 Obed Edom was **c** for the
26:15 sons were **c** for the storerooms.
26:16 Shuppim and Hosah were **c** for
28:4 He had **c** the tribe of Judah to
28:6 because I have **c** him
28:10 because the LORD has **c** you
29:1 the one whom God has **c**,
2Ch 6:6 But now I've **c** Jerusalem to be
6:6 I've **c** David to rule my people
6:34 you toward this city you have **c**
6:38 and the city you have **c**,
7:12 prayer and have **c** this place
7:16 I have **c** and declared this
29:11 The LORD has **c** you to stand
33:7 "I have **c** this temple and
Job 36:21 because you have **c** evil
Psa 33:12 people he has **c** as his own.
68:16 where God has **c** to live?
80:17 rest on the man you have **c**,
89:3 "I have made a promise to my **c**
89:19 up one **c** from the people.
105:6 of Jacob, his **c** ones.
105:26 he sent Aaron, whom he had **c**.
105:43 his **c** ones with a song of joy.
106:5 the prosperity of your **c** ones,
106:23 them, but Moses, his **c** one,
119:30 I have **c** a life of faithfulness.
119:173 I have **c** ⌊to follow⌋ your
132:13 The LORD has **c** Zion.
Pro 16:16 should be **c** over silver.
Isa 1:29 that you have **c** for your gods.
22:5 LORD of Armies has **c**
41:8 Israel, Jacob, whom I have **c**,
41:9 I've **c** you; I haven't rejected
42:1 Here is my **c** one, with whom I
43:10 "I have **c** you as my servant so
43:20 land for my **c** people to drink.
44:1 Jacob, Israel, whom I have **c**.
Isa 44:2 Jeshurun, whom I have **c**.
45:4 Jacob, Israel, my **c** one,
49:7 The Holy One of Israel has **c**
58:5 the kind of fasting I have **c**?
58:6 is the kind of fasting I have **c**:
65:9 My **c** ones will inherit them.
65:15 used as a curse by my **c** ones.
65:22 and my **c** ones will enjoy what
66:3 People have certainly **c** their
Jer 33:24 the two families he has **c**.
Eze 20:6 to a land that I had **c** for them.
39:14 "'People will be **c** to go through
Hos 4:17 The people of Ephraim have **c**
Hag 2:23 because I have **c** you,
Zec 3:2 who has **c** Jerusalem,
Mat 12:18 is my servant whom I have **c**,
22:14 but few of those are **c** to stay."
24:22 of those whom God has **c**.
24:24 even those whom God has **c**.
24:31 gather those whom God has **c**.
Mar 13:20 of those whom God has **c**.
13:22 those whom God has **c**.
13:27 gather those whom God has **c**.
Luk 1:9 he was **c** by priestly custom to
9:35 is my Son, whom I have **c**.
18:7 Won't God give his **c** people
23:35 the Messiah that God has **c**,
Jon 13:18 I know the people I've **c** ⌊to be
Act 1:2 the apostles, whom he had **c**.
1:24 which of these two you have **c**.
1:26 Matthias was **c** and joined the
9:15 I've **c** this man to bring my
10:41 apostles he had already **c**.
22:14 God of our ancestors has **c** you
Rom 8:33 those whom God has **c**?
11:5 God has **c** by his kindness.
11:6 If they were **c** by God's
11:6 they weren't **c** because of
11:7 those whom God has **c** have
Gal 1:1 From Paul — an apostle ⌊**c**⌋ not
Col 3:12 whom God has **c** and loved,
1Th 1:4 God loves you and has **c** you.
1Ti 5:21 and the **c** angels to be impartial
2Ti 2:10 who have been **c** so that they,
Tit 1:1 I was sent to lead God's **c**
Heb 5:1 Every chief priest is **c** from
7:4 was the father of the **c** people.
1Pe 1:1 To God's **c** people who are
2:4 but was **c** as precious by
2:6 "I am laying a **c** and precious
2:9 However, you are **c** people,
2:9 You were **c** to tell about the
5:13 church in Babylon, **c** by God,
2Jn 1:1 To the **c** lady and her children,
1:13 of your **c** sister greet you.
Rev 17:14 Those who are called, **c**,

Christ (526)

Mat 1:1 the list of ancestors of Jesus **C**,
1:16 of Jesus, who is called **C**.
1:18 The birth of Jesus **C** took place
11:2 about the things **C** had done.
26:68 They said, "You **C**,
27:17 or Jesus, who is called **C**?"
27:22 with Jesus, who is called **C**?"
Mar 1:1 the Good News about Jesus **C**,
9:41 belong to **C** will certainly not
Luk 2:11 Today your Savior, **C** the Lord,
23:2 and he says that he is **C**,
Jon 1:17 existence through Jesus **C**.
1:41 Messiah" (which means "**C**").
4:25 (Messiah is the one called **C**.)
7:27 When the **C** comes,
9:22 that Jesus was the **C** out
17:3 and Jesus **C**, whom you sent.
Act 2:36 you crucified, both Lord and **C**."
2:38 name of Jesus **C** so that your
3:6 of Jesus **C** from Nazareth,
3:20 he has appointed to be the **C**.
4:10 of Jesus **C** from Nazareth.
4:10 You crucified Jesus **C**,
5:20 everything about life ⌊in **C**⌋."
8:12 and the one named Jesus **C**,
9:2 who followed the way ⌊of **C**⌋
9:34 Jesus **C** makes you well.
10:36 of peace through Jesus **C**.
Act 10:36 Jesus **C** is everyone's Lord.
10:48 in the name of Jesus **C**.
11:17 believed in the Lord Jesus **C**.
15:26 the one named Jesus **C**.
16:18 you in the name of Jesus **C**
19:9 crowd about the way ⌊of **C**⌋,
19:23 the way ⌊of **C**⌋ broke out
22:4 who followed the way ⌊of **C**⌋:
24:14 a follower of the way ⌊of **C**⌋,
24:22 the way ⌊of **C**⌋ rather well,
24:24 him talk about faith in **C** Jesus.
28:31 boldly about the Lord Jesus **C**.
Rom 1:1 a servant of Jesus **C**,
1:3 his Son, our Lord Jesus **C**.
1:6 called to belong to Jesus **C**.)
1:7 and the Lord Jesus **C** are yours.
1:8 thank my God through Jesus **C**
2:16 when God, through **C** Jesus,
3:22 through faith in Jesus **C**.
3:24 through the price **C** Jesus paid
3:25 God showed that **C** is the
5:1 our Lord Jesus **C** has done.
5:2 Through **C** we can approach
5:6 **C** died for ungodly people.
5:8 **C** died for us while we were
5:9 we are even more certain that **C**
5:11 In addition, our Lord Jesus **C**
5:11 After all, it is through **C** that we
5:15 of one person, Jesus **C**,
5:17 of one person, Jesus **C**.
5:21 because of Jesus **C** our Lord.
6:3 into **C** Jesus were baptized
6:4 As **C** was brought back from
6:8 If we have died with **C**,
6:9 We know that **C**, who was
6:11 the power **C** Jesus gives you.
6:23 life found in **C** Jesus our Lord.
7:25 our Lord Jesus **C** rescues me!
8:1 are believers in **C** Jesus can no
8:2 who gives life through **C** Jesus,
8:9 the Spirit of **C** doesn't belong
8:10 However, if **C** lives in you,
8:11 Then the one who brought **C**
8:34 **C** has died, and more
8:34 **C** has the highest position in
8:34 **C** also intercedes for us.
8:35 separate us from the love **C** has
8:38 love which **C** Jesus our Lord
9:3 condemned and cut off from **C**
10:4 **C** is the fulfillment of Moses'
10:6 (that is, to bring **C** down).
10:7 to bring **C** back from the dead).
10:17 that is heard is what **C** spoke.
12:5 **C** makes us one body and
13:14 live like the Lord Jesus **C** did,
14:9 For this reason **C** died and
14:15 **C** died for that person.
14:18 The person who serves **C** with
15:3 **C** did not think only of himself.
15:5 the example of **C** Jesus.
15:6 and Father of our Lord Jesus **C**.
15:7 same way that **C** accepted you.
15:8 **C** became a servant for the
15:16 to be a servant of **C** Jesus to
15:17 So **C** Jesus gives me the right
15:18 only what **C** has done through
15:19 News about **C** from Jerusalem
15:20 the name of **C** was not known.
15:29 will bring the full blessing of **C**.
15:30 you through our Lord Jesus **C**
16:3 in the service of **C** Jesus.
16:5 Asia to become a believer in **C**.
16:9 coworker in the service of **C**,
16:16 All the churches of **C** greet you.
16:18 are not serving **C** our Lord.
16:25 message I tell about Jesus **C**.
16:27 to him through Jesus **C** forever!
1Co 1:1 called to be an apostle of **C**
1:2 that was made holy by **C** Jesus
1:2 the name of our Lord Jesus **C**.
1:3 and the Lord Jesus **C** are yours!
1:4 because **C** Jesus has shown
1:5 Through **C** Jesus you have
1:6 Our message about **C** has
1:7 Lord Jesus **C** to be revealed.
1:8 on the day of our Lord Jesus **C**.

1Co 1:9 with his Son Jesus C our Lord.
1:10 in the name of our Lord Jesus C
1:12 follow Cephas," or "I follow C."
1:13 Has C been divided?
1:17 C didn't send me to baptize.
1:17 the cross of C lose its meaning.
1:23 is that C was crucified.
1:24 who are called, he is C,
1:30 You are partners with C Jesus
2:2 only one subject — Jesus C,
2:16 we have the mind of C.
3:1 were infants in your faith in C.
3:11 and that foundation is Jesus C.
3:23 You belong to C, and Christ
3:23 and C belongs to God.
4:1 think of us as servants of C
4:10 given up our wisdom for C,
4:10 you have insight because of C.
4:15 the Good News about C Jesus.
5:7 C, our Passover lamb,
6:11 in the name of the Lord Jesus C
8:6 is only one Lord, Jesus C.
8:11 a believer for whom C died.
8:12 you are sinning against C.
9:12 Good News of C in any way.
10:4 and that rock was C.
10:16 we sharing the blood of C?
10:16 we sharing the body of C?
11:1 Imitate me as I imitate C.
11:3 I want you to realize that C has
11:3 and God has authority over C.
12:12 form one body, so it is with C.
15:3 C died to take away our sins
15:12 If we have told you that C has
15:13 then C hasn't come back to life.
15:14 If C hasn't come back to life,
15:15 testified that he brought C back
15:15 God didn't bring C back to life.
15:16 then C hasn't come back to life
15:17 If C hasn't come back to life,
15:18 believers in C no longer exist.
15:19 If C is our hope in this life only,
15:20 But now C has come back from
15:22 be made alive because of C.
15:23 C is the first, then at his
15:24 C will hand over the kingdom
15:25 C must rule until God has put
15:31 in you which C Jesus our Lord
15:57 through our Lord Jesus C.
16:15 to be won ⌊for C⌋ in Greece.
16:24 Through C Jesus my love is
2Co 1:1 From Paul, an apostle of C
1:2 and the Lord Jesus C are yours!
1:3 and Father of our Lord Jesus C!
1:5 Because C suffered so much
1:19 God's Son, Jesus C,
1:20 Certainly, C made God's many
1:21 in a relationship with C.
2:10 presence of C for your benefit.
2:12 the Good News about C.
2:14 us in victory because of C.
2:14 clear what it means to know C.
2:15 To God we are the aroma of C
2:16 is qualified to tell about C?
3:4 C gives us confidence about
3:14 because only C can remove it.
4:4 It is C who is God's image.
4:5 It is about Jesus C as the Lord.
5:16 If we did think of C from a
5:17 Whoever is a believer in C is a
5:18 with him through C,
5:19 God was using C to restore his
5:20 We beg you on behalf of C to
5:21 God had C, who was sinless,
6:15 Can C agree with the devil?
8:9 kindness of our Lord Jesus C.
8:23 churches and bring glory to C.
9:13 to spread the Good News of C
10:1 gentleness and kindness of C.
10:5 so that it is obedient to C.
10:7 is confident he belongs to C,
10:7 note that we also belong to C.
10:14 with the Good News about C.
11:2 in marriage to one man — C.
11:3 sincere and pure devotion to C.
12:2 I know a follower of C who
2Co 12:10 and difficulties suffered for C.
13:3 Since you want proof that C is
13:3 C isn't weak in dealing with
13:5 people in whom Jesus C lives?
Gal 1:1 or individual but by Jesus C
1:3 Father and our Lord Jesus C!
1:4 C took the punishment for our
1:6 you're so quickly deserting C,
1:7 distort the Good News about C.
1:12 but Jesus C revealed it to me.
1:22 The churches of C in Judea
2:4 the freedom C Jesus gives us.
2:16 only by believing in Jesus C.
2:16 we also believed in Jesus C
2:16 approval because of faith in C
2:17 for God's approval in C,
2:17 does that mean that C
2:19 I have been crucified with C.
2:20 longer live, but C lives in me.
3:1 Wasn't C Jesus' crucifixion
3:13 C paid the price to free us from
3:14 ⌊C paid the price⌋ so that the
3:14 of the world through Jesus C
3:16 That descendant is C.
3:22 based on faith in Jesus C could
3:24 Before C came, Moses' laws
3:24 C came so that we could
3:26 by believing in C Jesus.
3:27 clothed yourselves with C.
3:28 You are all the same in C
3:29 If you belong to C,
4:14 messenger or C Jesus himself.
4:19 for you again until C is formed
5:1 C has freed us so that we may
5:2 C will be of no benefit to you.
5:4 laws have been cut off from C.
5:6 As far as our relationship to C
5:24 Those who belong to C Jesus
6:12 because of the cross of C.
6:14 the cross of our Lord Jesus C.
6:18 good will of our Lord Jesus C
Eph 1:1 From Paul, an apostle of C
1:1 people who are united with C
1:2 and the Lord Jesus C are yours!
1:3 and Father of our Lord Jesus C!
1:3 Through C, God has blessed
1:4 he chose us through C to be
1:5 to adopt us through Jesus C.
1:9 decided to do this through C.
1:10 all of history to its goal in C.
1:10 Then C would be the head of
1:11 choose us through C according
1:12 our hope on C would praise him
1:17 the God of our Lord Jesus C,
1:17 as you come to know C better.
1:20 that same power in C when
1:22 under the control of C.
1:22 He has made C the head of
2:5 made us alive together with C.
2:6 to life together with C Jesus
2:7 He did this through C Jesus out
2:10 He has created us in C Jesus
2:12 at that time you were without C.
2:13 But now through C Jesus you,
2:13 brought near by the blood of C.
2:20 C Jesus himself is the
3:1 am the prisoner of C Jesus for
3:4 the mystery about C.
3:6 that God made in C Jesus.
3:8 the immeasurable wealth of C
3:11 out through C Jesus our Lord.
3:12 confidence through faith in C.
3:17 Then C will live in you through
3:21 in the church and in C Jesus
4:7 out to us by C who gave it.
4:12 and to build up the body of C.
4:13 until we measure up to C,
4:15 in our relationship to C,
4:32 has forgiven you through C.
5:2 Live in love as C also loved us.
5:5 in the kingdom of C and of God.
5:14 and C will shine on you."
5:20 the name of our Lord Jesus C.
5:21 authority out of respect for C.
5:23 is the head of his wife as C is
5:25 love your wives as C loved the
Eph 5:29 as C takes care of the church.
6:5 as you are when you obey C.
6:6 like slaves who belong to C,
6:23 Lord Jesus C give our brothers
6:24 love for our Lord Jesus C.
Php 1:1 servants of C Jesus.
1:1 who is united with C Jesus.
1:2 and the Lord Jesus C are yours!
1:6 on the day of C Jesus.
1:8 all the compassion of C Jesus,
1:10 blameless until the day of C.
1:11 Jesus C will fill your lives with
1:13 I am in prison because of C.
1:15 tell the message about C
1:16 tell the message about C out
1:17 They tell the message about C
1:18 are told the message about C,
1:19 from the Spirit of Jesus C.
1:20 speak very boldly and honor C
1:21 C means everything to me in
1:23 to leave this life and be with C.
1:26 have pride in C Jesus with me.
1:27 reflect the Good News about C.
1:29 not only to believe in C
2:5 same attitude that C Jesus had.
2:11 and confess that Jesus C is
2:16 Then I can brag on the day of C
2:21 not after those of Jesus C.
2:30 almost died for the work of C
3:3 and take pride in C Jesus.
3:7 I now consider worthless for C.
3:8 off knowing C Jesus my Lord.
3:8 it all away in order to gain C
3:9 approval through faith in C.
3:10 that knows C. Faith knows the
3:12 Jesus C has already won
3:14 heavenly call offers in C Jesus.
3:18 the enemies of the cross of C.
3:20 Jesus C coming from heaven
4:7 and emotions through C Jesus.
4:13 through C who strengthens me.
4:19 glorious way through C Jesus.
4:21 who believes in C Jesus.
4:23 our Lord Jesus C be with you.
Col 1:1 From Paul, an apostle of C
1:2 sisters who are united with C
1:3 the Father of our Lord Jesus C,
1:4 about your faith in C Jesus
1:7 as a trustworthy deacon for C
1:19 to have all of himself live in C.
1:20 back to himself through C.
1:22 But now C has brought you
1:27 this mystery — which is C
1:28 about C as we instruct
2:2 a complete understanding of C.
2:3 of wisdom and knowledge in C.
2:5 and how firm your faith in C is.
2:6 You received C Jesus the Lord,
2:8 things rather than following C.
2:10 has made you complete in C.
2:10 C is in charge of every ruler
2:11 circumcision performed by C.
2:12 tomb with C through baptism.
2:12 back to life with C through faith
2:13 But God made you alive with C
2:15 he celebrated his victory in C.
2:17 the shadow⌋ belongs to C.
2:19 hold on to ⌊C,⌋ the head.
2:19 C makes the whole body grow
2:20 If you have died with C to the
3:1 brought back to life with C,
3:1 that are above — where C holds
3:3 life is hidden with C in God.
3:4 When C your life appears,
3:11 Instead, C is everything and in
3:24 It is C, your real master,
4:3 may tell the mystery about C.
4:12 Epaphras, a servant of C Jesus
1Th 1:1 Father and the Lord Jesus C.
1:3 in our Lord Jesus C is enduring.
2:7 although as apostles of C we
2:14 that are united with C Jesus.
3:2 the Good News about C.
4:16 the dead who believed in C
5:9 through our Lord Jesus C.
5:18 because it is God's will in C

1Th 5:23 when our Lord Jesus C comes.
5:28 our Lord Jesus C be with you.
2Th 1:1 Father and the Lord Jesus C.
1:2 and the Lord Jesus C are yours!
1:12 of the good will of Jesus C,
2:14 the glory of our Lord Jesus C.
2:16 with our Lord Jesus C,
3:6 in the name of our Lord Jesus C
3:12 people by the Lord Jesus C
3:18 good will of our Lord Jesus C
1Ti 1:1 From Paul, an apostle of C
1:1 and C Jesus our confidence.
1:2 Father and C Jesus our Lord
1:12 I thank C Jesus our Lord that
1:14 that C Jesus shows people.
1:15 C Jesus came into the world to
1:16 mercy so that C Jesus could
2:5 humans — a human, C Jesus.
3:13 a result of their faith in C Jesus.
4:6 You are a good servant of C
5:11 than their devotion to C,
5:21 in the sight of God, C Jesus,
6:3 Jesus C and godly teachings
6:13 and in the sight of C Jesus,
6:14 until our Lord Jesus C appears,
2Ti 1:1 From Paul, an apostle of C
1:1 that contains C Jesus' promise
1:2 Father and C Jesus our Lord.
1:9 God planned that C Jesus
1:10 coming of our Savior C Jesus,
1:10 C has destroyed death,
1:13 With faith and love for C Jesus,
2:1 in the kindness of C Jesus.
2:3 like a good soldier of C Jesus.
2:8 Always think about Jesus C.
2:10 may receive salvation from C
3:12 they believe in C Jesus will
3:15 saved through faith in C Jesus.
4:1 presence of God and C Jesus,
4:1 I do this because C Jesus will
Tit 1:1 God and an apostle of Jesus C.
1:4 and from C Jesus our Savior
2:13 great God and Savior, Jesus C.
3:6 us through Jesus C our Savior.
Phm 1:1 who is a prisoner for C Jesus,
1:3 and the Lord Jesus C are yours!
1:6 of every blessing we have in C.
1:8 C makes me bold enough to
1:9 and now a prisoner for C Jesus,
1:20 me some comfort because of C.
1:23 who is a prisoner because of C
1:25 of our Lord Jesus C be yours.
Heb 3:6 But C is a faithful son in charge
5:5 So C did not take the glory of
6:1 the elementary truths about C
6:6 Yet, they have deserted ⌊C⌋.
9:11 But C came as a chief priest of
9:11 C went through a better,
9:14 The blood of C, who had no
9:15 Because C offered himself to
9:24 C didn't go into a holy place
9:25 However, C didn't go into
9:28 Likewise, C was sacrificed
10:5 when C came into the world,
10:8 In this passage C first said,
10:9 Then C says, "I have come to
10:10 because Jesus C did what God
11:26 that being insulted for C would
13:8 Jesus C is the same yesterday,
13:21 he work in us through Jesus C
13:21 belongs to Jesus C forever.
Jas 1:1 of God and of the Lord Jesus C.
2:1 Lord Jesus C by not favoring
1Pe 1:1 an apostle of Jesus C.
1:2 you are obedient to Jesus C
1:3 and Father of our Lord Jesus C!
1:3 Jesus C has come back
1:7 when Jesus C appears again.
1:8 you have never seen C,
1:11 the Spirit of C kept referring
1:13 when Jesus C appears again.
1:19 was the precious blood of C,
1:21 in God who brought C back
2:4 You are coming to C,
2:5 God accepts through Jesus C.
2:21 suffering because C suffered
1Pe 2:22 C never committed any sin.
2:23 C never verbally abused those
2:24 C carried our sins in his body
3:1 could win these men ⌊for C⌋ by
3:15 your lives to C as Lord.
3:18 This is true because C
3:21 It saves you through Jesus C,
3:22 C has gone to heaven where
4:1 Since C has suffered
4:11 receives glory through Jesus C.
4:11 belong to Jesus C forever
4:14 because of the name of C,
5:10 has called you through C Jesus
5:14 to all of you who are in C.
2Pe 1:1 servant and apostle of Jesus C.
1:1 our God and Savior, Jesus C.
1:8 about our Lord Jesus C is living
1:11 of our Lord and Savior Jesus C.
1:14 Our Lord Jesus C has made
1:16 coming of our Lord Jesus C,
2:20 our Lord and Savior Jesus C
3:18 of our Lord and Savior Jesus C.
1Jn 1:3 and with his Son Jesus C.
1:5 the message we heard from C
2:1 we have Jesus C,
2:3 We are sure that we know C if
2:5 But whoever obeys what C
2:5 how we know we are in C.
2:8 It's a truth that exists in C and
2:12 sins are forgiven through C.
2:13 because you know C who has
2:14 because you know C,
2:25 C has given us the promise of
2:27 you received from C lives
2:27 So live in C as he taught you to
2:28 Now, dear children, live in C.
2:29 If you know that C has God's
3:2 We do know that when C
3:3 in C keep themselves pure,
3:3 themselves pure, as C is pure.
3:5 You know that C appeared in
3:6 Those who live in C don't go
3:6 haven't seen or known C.
3:7 as C has God's approval.
3:16 we realize that C gave his life
3:23 the one named Jesus C,
4:2 that Jesus C has come as
4:3 that Jesus C has come as
4:21 C has given us this
5:6 This Son of God is Jesus C,
5:20 who is real, his Son Jesus C.
5:20 This Jesus C is the real God
2Jn 1:3 the Father and from Jesus C,
1:7 to declare that Jesus C came
1:9 what C taught doesn't have
1:9 to teach what C taught has both
3Jn 1:7 trip to serve the one named C,
Jud 1:1 a servant of Jesus C and
1:1 who are kept safe for Jesus C.
1:4 only Master and Lord, Jesus C.
1:17 of our Lord Jesus C told you
1:21 the mercy of our Lord Jesus C
1:25 through Jesus C our Lord.
Rev 1:1 is the revelation of Jesus C.
1:2 the testimony about Jesus C.
1:5 and from Jesus C,
20:4 ruled with C for 1,000 years.
20:6 to be priests of God and C.

Christian (53)

Act 26:28 persuade me to become a C?"
Rom 9:1 As a C, I'm telling you the truth.
12:6 you say agrees with the C faith.
14:15 if what you eat hurts another C,
14:21 another C to have doubts.
16:1 She is our sister in the C faith
16:2 Give her a C welcome that
16:10 Greet Apelles, a true C.
16:13 Rufus, that outstanding C,
16:17 ⌊from the C faith⌋ by teaching
16:22 send you C greetings.
16:23 our brother in the C faith,
1Co 1:1 our brother in the C faith.
4:15 have countless C guardians,
4:15 I became your father in the C
4:17 help you remember my C way
1Co 5:11 brothers or sisters in the C faith
5:12 who are outside ⌊the C faith⌋?
7:12 If any C man is married to a
7:13 If any C woman is married to a
7:15 Under these circumstances a C
7:15 man or C woman is not
7:18 to be a C shouldn't undo his
7:18 a C shouldn't get circumcised.
7:39 but only if the man is a C.
16:12 our brother in the C faith:
16:13 Be firm in the C faith.
16:19 send their warmest C greetings.
2Co 1:24 have control over your C faith.
1:24 firmly established in the C faith.
8:18 With him we have sent our C
8:22 them our C brother whom we
13:5 you are still in the C faith.
Eph 6:4 in C discipline and instruction.
6:16 take the C faith as your shield.
Php 2:29 Give him a joyful C welcome.
Col 1:28 everyone as mature C people.
4:5 who are outside ⌊the C faith⌋.
1Ti 3:6 He must not be a new C,
3:9 the mystery of the C faith.
4:1 believers will desert the C faith.
4:6 by the words of the C faith
5:8 he has denied the C faith and
5:12 by rejecting the C faith,
6:10 wandered away from the C faith
6:12 the good fight for the C faith.
6:20 use to oppose ⌊the C faith⌋.
Phm 1:16 both as a person and as a C.
1Pe 3:16 treat the good C life you live
4:16 If you suffer for being a C,
2Pe 1:7 to godliness add C affection;
1:7 and to C affection add love.
Jud 1:3 fight for the C faith that was

Christians (25)

Act 11:26 The disciples were called C
26:10 I locked many C in prison.
Rom 14:10 criticize or despise other C?
14:13 make other C have doubts
15:25 to bring help to the C there.
15:26 a debt to the C in Jerusalem,
15:26 poor among the C in Jerusalem.
15:27 wealth of the C in Jerusalem.
15:28 over to the C in Jerusalem,
16:7 They also were C before I was.
16:11 Greet those C who belong to
1Co 1:26 when God called you to be C.
16:11 him to arrive with the other C.
16:12 to visit you with the other C.
2Co 9:1 helping the C ⌊in Jerusalem⌋.
Gal 2:4 False C were brought in.
2:13 The other Jewish C also joined
Eph 6:1 parents because you are C.
Php 2:1 So then, as C, do you have any
1Th 4:9 the way C should love each
4:10 love to all the C throughout
1Ti 3:7 People who are not C must
Rev 6:11 all their coworkers, the other C,
19:10 a coworker of the C who hold
22:9 I work with other C,

Christ's (50)

Rom 3:25 given through faith in C blood.
5:9 Since C blood has now given
7:4 Teachings through C body.
8:17 If we share in C suffering in
1Co 6:15 bodies are parts of C body?
6:15 I take the parts of C body
7:22 were called, you are C slave
9:21 really subject to C teachings
12:27 You are C body and each of
15:27 everything under C authority.
15:27 C authority, this clearly excludes
15:27 everything under C authority
15:28 everything under C authority,
2Co 2:17 As C spokesmen and in God's
3:3 It's clear that you are C letter,
4:4 the Good News about C glory.
4:6 glory which shines from C face
5:10 in front of C judgment seat.
5:14 Clearly, C love guides us.
5:20 we are C representatives, and

2Co 11:10 As surely as I have C truth, my
11:13 themselves as C apostles
11:23 Are they C servants?
12:9 in order that C power will live
12:19 We speak as C people in
13:13 the Lord Jesus C good will,
Gal 1:10 I would not be C servant
2:21 then C death was pointless.
3:27 C name have clothed yourselves
6:2 you will follow C teachings
Eph 1:23 The church is C body and
3:19 You will know C love, which
4:20 you learned from C teachings
5:24 under C authority, so wives are
5:32 (I'm talking about C
6:20 doing this as C representative,
Col 1:20 through C blood sacrificed
1:24 remains of C sufferings.
2:6 so continue to live as C people
2:9 All of God lives in C body,
3:15 Also, let C peace control you.
3:16 Let C word with all its wisdom
2Th 2:1 about our Lord Jesus C coming
3:5 God's love and C endurance
Heb 3:14 we will remain C partners only
1Pe 1:11 he predicted C sufferings
4:13 as you share C sufferings.
5:1 also witnessed C sufferings
1Jn 2:27 Instead, C anointing teaches
3:24 obey C commandments live

christs (2)

Mat 24:24 False c and false prophets will
Mar 13:22 False c and false prophets will

chronic (6)

Lev 13:11 he has a c skin disease.
15:3 Whether it is c or not makes no
2Ch 21:15 You will suffer from a c
Mat 9:20 She had been suffering from c
Mar 5:25 been suffering from c bleeding
Luk 8:43 been suffering from c bleeding

Chronicles (1)

Neh 12:23 recorded in the Book of C until

church (76)

Mat 16:18 on this rock I will build my c.
Act 5:11 The whole c and everyone
8:1 out against the c in Jerusalem.
8:3 Saul tried to destroy the c.
9:31 Then the c throughout Judea,
11:22 reached the c in Jerusalem,
11:26 and Saul met with the c
12:1 certain members of the c.
12:5 but the c was praying very hard
13:1 teachers in the c in Antioch.
14:23 c choose spiritual leaders,
14:27 the members of the c together.
15:3 The c sent Paul and Barnabas
15:4 The c in Jerusalem,
15:22 and the whole c decided to
18:22 ⌊to Jerusalem⌋, greeted the c,
20:17 the spiritual leaders of the c
20:28 be shepherds for God's c which
Rom 16:1 faith and a deacon of the c
16:5 Also greet the c that meets in
16:23 is host to me and the whole c.
1Co 1:2 To God's c that was made holy
4:17 teach it everywhere in every c.
6:4 allow people whom the c has
7:17 the guideline I use in every c.
10:32 or members of God's c.
11:18 you gather as a c you split up
11:22 Do you despise God's c and
12:28 In the c God has appointed first
14:4 he helps the c grow.
14:5 he says to help the c grow.
14:12 so that you help the c grow.
14:19 in order to teach others in c,
14:28 should remain silent in c.
14:35 for a woman to speak in c.
15:9 because I persecuted God's c.
16:19 Aquila and Prisca and the c
2Co 1:1 To God's c in the city of
Gal 1:13 I violently persecuted God's c
Eph 1:22 everything for the good of the c.
1:23 The c is Christ's body and
3:10 this so that now, through the c,
3:21 Glory belongs to God in the c
4:11 teachers as gifts ⌊to his c⌋.
5:23 as Christ is the head of the c.
5:24 As the c is under Christ's
5:25 wives as Christ loved the c
5:26 He did this to make the c holy
5:27 it to himself as a glorious c,
5:29 as Christ takes care of the c.
5:32 Christ's relationship to the c.)
Php 3:6 I was a persecutor of the c.
4:15 you were the only c to share
Col 1:18 He is also the head of the c,
1:24 on behalf of his body, the c.
1:25 I became a servant of the c
4:15 especially Nympha and the c
4:16 read it in the c at Laodicea.
1Th 1:1 To the c at Thessalonica
4:12 from those outside ⌊the c⌋,
2Th 1:1 To the c at Thessalonica
1Ti 3:5 can he take care of God's c?)
3:15 God's family is the c of the
5:16 In this way the c is not
Phm 1:2 and the c that meets in your
Jas 5:14 call for the c leaders.
1Pe 5:13 Your sister c in Babylon,
2Jn 1:1 From the c leader.
3Jn 1:1 From the c leader.
Rev 2:1 messenger of the c in Ephesus,
2:8 messenger of the c in Smyrna,
2:12 of the c in Pergamum,
2:18 messenger of the c in Thyatira,
3:1 messenger of the c in Sardis,
3:7 of the c in Philadelphia,
3:14 of the c in Laodicea,

churches (33)

Act 15:41 Cilicia and strengthened the c.
16:5 So the c were strengthened in
Rom 16:4 are all the c among the nations.
16:16 All the c of Christ greet you.
1Co 11:16 nor do any of the c of God.
14:33 As in all the c of God's holy
16:1 as I directed the c in Galatia.
16:19 The c in the province of Asia
2Co 8:1 showed his kindness to the c
8:18 brother whom all the c praise
8:19 More than that, the c elected
8:23 are representatives of the c
11:8 I robbed other c by taking pay
11:28 of my anxiety about all the c.
12:13 treated worse than the other c,
Gal 1:2 To the c in Galatia.
1:22 The c of Christ in Judea didn't
1Th 2:14 were like the c of God in Judea
2:14 country as those c did from
2Th 1:4 That's why we brag in God's c
Rev 1:4 From John to the seven c in
1:11 and send it to the seven c:
1:20 the messengers of the seven c,
1:20 lamp stands are the seven c.
2:7 to what the Spirit says to the c.
2:11 to what the Spirit says to the c.
2:17 to what the Spirit says to the c.
2:23 Then all the c will know that I
2:29 to what the Spirit says to the c.
3:6 to what the Spirit says to the c.
3:13 to what the Spirit says to the c.
3:22 what the Spirit says to the c."
22:16 this testimony to you for the c.

churn (1)

Job 37:12 He guides the clouds as they c

churning (5)

Job 30:27 My insides are c and won't
Pro 30:33 As c milk produces butter and
Isa 57:20 the wicked are like the c sea.
Lam 1:20 My stomach is c. My heart is
2:11 My stomach is c. My heart is

Chusa (1)

Luk 8:3 Joanna, whose husband C

Cilicia (8)

Act 6:9 and the provinces of C
15:23 in Antioch, Syria, and C.
15:41 the provinces of Syria and C
21:39 well-known city of Tarsus in C.
22:3 raised in the city of Tarsus in C
23:34 was from the province of C,
27:5 the coast of the provinces of C
Gal 1:21 to the regions of Syria and C.

cinnamon (4)

Exo 30:23 6 ¼ pounds of fragrant c;
Pro 7:17 bed with myrrh, aloes, and c.
Sos 4:14 nard and saffron, calamus, c,
Rev 18:13 c, spices, incense, perfume,

circle (6)

2Sm 5:23 but c around behind them,
1Ch 14:14 C around, and come at them in
Ecc 1:6 It blows in a full c.
Jer 23:18 Who is in the LORD's inner c
23:22 If they had been in my inner c,
Mar 3:34 who sat in a c around him,

circles (1)

Psa 19:6 It c around to the other.

circuit (1)

1Ch 11:8 Millo and making a complete c.

circular (1)

1Ki 7:31 in the center to t circular frame

circumcise (7)

Dtr 10:16 So c your uncircumcised
30:6 The LORD your God will c
Jos 5:2 and c the men of Israel."
Luk 1:59 went ⌊to the temple⌋ to c him.
Jon 7:22 So you c a male on a day of
7:23 If you c a male on the day of
Act 21:21 tell them not to c their children

circumcised (60)

Gen 17:10 male among you is to be c.
17:11 All of you must be c.
17:12 is eight days old must be c,
17:13 is to be c without exception.
17:23 and c them that day,
17:24 99 years old when he was c.
17:25 13 years old when he was c.
17:26 and his son Ishmael were c.
17:27 a foreigner, were c with him.
21:4 Abraham c him as God had
34:15 male must be c as we are.
34:17 If you won't agree to be c,
34:22 male must be c as they are.
34:24 So they were all c at the city
Exo 12:44 may eat it after you have c him.
12:48 in the household must be c.
Lev 12:3 The boy must be c when he is
Jos 5:3 Joshua made flint knives and c
5:4 is the reason Joshua c them:
5:5 men who left Egypt had been c.
5:5 through the desert, were not c.
5:7 took their place had not been c
5:7 So Joshua c them.
5:8 When all the men had been c,
Jer 4:4 Be c by the LORD,
9:25 I will punish all who are c.
9:26 though these nations are c,
Luk 2:21 the child was c and named
Act 7:8 Abraham c him on the eighth
10:45 All the believers who were c
15:1 are c as Moses' Teachings
15:5 who are not Jewish must be c
16:3 So he c him because of the
Rom 2:26 won't he be considered c even
2:27 spite of the fact that you are c
3:1 is there any value in being c?
3:30 God who approves c people
4:9 Are only the c people blessed,
4:10 Was he c or was he
4:10 He had not been c.
4:11 of every believer who is not c,
4:12 of those who not only are c

Rom 4:12 had that faith before he was **c**.
1Co 7:18 Any man who was already **c**
7:18 be a Christian shouldn't get **c**.
Gal 2:3 no one forced him to be **c**.
2:7 who are not **c** as Peter had
2:7 to tell it to those who are **c**.
5:2 if you allow yourselves to be **c**,
5:3 to be **c** must realize that
5:6 matter whether we are **c** or not.
6:12 are trying to force you to be **c**.
6:13 who had themselves **c** did this
6:13 Yet, they want you to be **c** so
6:15 whether a person is **c** or not.
Eph 2:11 who called themselves "the **c**"
Php 3:3 We are the ⌊true⌋ **c** people ⌊of
3:5 I was **c** on the eighth day.
Col 2:11 In him you were also **c**.
3:11 **c** or uncircumcised,

circumcision (18)

Exo 4:26 It was because of the **c** that
Jos 5:3 men of Israel at the Hill of **C**.
Jon 7:22 the teaching about **c** (although
Act 7:8 "God gave Abraham **c** to
11:2 the believers who insisted on **c**
Rom 2:25 For example, **c** is valuable if
2:25 **c** amounts to uncircumcision.
2:28 nor is **c** a matter of how the
2:29 and **c** is something that
2:29 **C** is spiritual, not just a written
4:11 The mark of **c** is the seal of
1Co 7:18 Christian shouldn't undo his **c**.
7:19 **C** is nothing, and the lack of it
Gal 2:12 insisted that **c** was necessary.
5:11 preaching that **c** is necessary,
Php 3:2 of those who insist on **c**.
Col 2:11 It was not a **c** performed by
2:11 in the **c** performed by Christ.

circumference (6)

1Ki 7:15 27 feet high and 18 feet in **c**.
7:23 and had a **c** of 45 feet.
7:24 gourds all around the 45-foot **c**
2Ch 4:2 and had a **c** of 45 feet.
4:3 bulls all around the 45-foot **c**
Jer 52:21 27 feet high and 18 feet in **c**.

circumstances (3)

1Co 7:15 Under these **c** a Christian man
7:24 remain in whatever **c** you were
7:24 God is with you in those **c**.

cistern (30)

Gen 37:22 Put him into that **c** that's out in
37:24 and put him into an empty **c**.
37:28 pulled Joseph out of the **c**.
37:29 Reuben came back to the **c**
Exo 21:33 someone opens up a **c**
21:34 the owner of the **c** must make
Lev 11:36 However, a spring or a **c**
1Sm 19:22 He went as far as the big **c** in
2Sm 3:26 brought him back from the **c**
17:18 a man in Bahurim who had a **c**
17:19 spread it over the top of the **c**,
17:21 both men came out of the **c**
2Ki 10:14 of them at a **c** near Beth Eked.
18:31 tree and drink from his own **c**.
1Ch 11:17 a drink of water from the **c** at
11:18 and drew water from the **c**.
11:22 He also went into a **c** and
Pro 5:15 Drink water out of your own **c**
Ecc 12:6 water wheel is broken at the **c**.
Isa 36:16 tree and drink from his own **c**.
Jer 38:6 him into the **c** of Malchiah,
38:6 to lower Jeremiah into the **c**.
38:6 There was no water in the **c**,
38:7 they had put Jeremiah in the **c**.
38:9 have thrown him into the **c**,
38:10 out of the **c** before he dies."
38:11 with ropes to Jeremiah in the **c**.
38:13 up and lift him out of the **c**.
41:7 them and threw them into a **c**.
41:9 Now, the **c** where Ishmael

cisterns (8)

Gen 37:20 throw him into one of the **c**,
Dtr 6:11 You will have **c** that you didn't
1Sm 13:6 among rocks, in pits, and in **c**.
2Ch 26:10 He dug many **c** because he
Neh 9:25 **c**, vineyards, olive trees,
Jer 2:13 have also dug their own **c**,
2:13 broken **c** that can't hold water.
14:3 They go to the **c**, but they don't

cite (1)

1Sm 12:7 in front of the LORD and **c** all

cities (502)

Gen 10:10 The first ⌊**c**⌋ in his kingdom
13:12 while Lot lived among the **c** of
19:25 He destroyed those **c**,
19:25 all who lived in the **c**,
19:29 When God destroyed the **c** on
19:29 that came to the **c** where
22:17 possession of their enemies' **c**.
24:60 of their enemies' **c**."
35:5 God made the people of the **c**
41:35 to be kept for food in the **c**.
41:48 years and put this food in the **c**.
47:21 moved the people to the **c**.
Exo 1:11 as supply **c** for Pharaoh.
Lev 25:32 their property in the **c** they own.
25:33 in the Levite **c** are their
25:34 that belongs to their **c** must not
26:25 When you gather in your **c**,
26:31 I will make your **c** deserted and
26:33 Your **c** will be deserted.
Num 13:19 Do their **c** have walls around
13:28 and the **c** have walls and are
21:2 we'll destroy their **c** because
21:3 the Canaanites and their **c**.
21:25 Israel took all those Amorite **c**,
21:32 the Israelites captured its **c**
24:19 whoever is left in their **c**."
31:10 They burned all the **c** where
32:16 fences for our livestock and **c**
32:17 families will live in walled **c**,
32:24 Build **c** for your families and
32:26 stay here in the **c** of Gilead.
32:33 the whole land with its **c**
32:34 of Gad rebuilt the **c** of Dibon,
32:36 and Beth Haran as walled **c**.
32:37 rebuilt the **c** of Heshbon,
32:38 they gave the **c** they rebuilt.
35:2 Levites some **c** from their own
35:2 the pastureland around those **c**.
35:3 Then the Levites will have **c** to
35:4 "The land around the **c** that you
35:6 "Six of the **c** you give the
35:6 the Levites will be **c** of refuge.
35:6 murderers to escape to these **c**.
35:6 give the Levites 42 other **c**.
35:7 So you will give a total of 48 **c**
35:8 The **c** you give the Levites
35:8 Take more **c** from larger tribes
35:11 select certain **c** to be places of
35:12 These **c** will be places of
35:13 There will be six **c** you select
35:15 These six **c** will be places of
35:15 person may flee to these **c**.
Dtr 1:22 take and the **c** we'll come to."
1:28 The **c** are big with sky-high
2:34 that time we captured all his **c**
2:35 However, we did loot the **c** that
2:37 capture the **c** in the mountains.
3:4 time we captured all of his **c**.
3:4 We captured a total of 60 **c** —
3:5 All of these **c** were fortified
3:7 However, we did loot the **c**,
3:10 We took all of the **c** of the
3:10 **c** of Og's kingdom in Bashan.
3:12 region of Gilead with its **c**.
3:19 must stay here in the **c** that
4:41 Then Moses set aside three **c**
4:42 could flee to one of these **c**
4:43 The **c** were Bezer on the desert
6:10 prosperous **c** that you didn't
9:1 with big **c** that have sky-high
12:12 (The Levites live in your **c**
12:17 LORD's offerings⌋ in your **c**.
12:18 live in your **c** must eat these
13:12 residents in one of the **c** which
Dtr 14:21 foreigners who live in your **c**,
14:27 the Levites who live in your **c**.
14:28 and store it in your **c**.
14:29 and widows who live in your **c**
15:7 poor Israelites in one of your **c**
16:5 for Passover in any of the **c**
16:11 the Levites who live in your **c**,
16:14 and widows who live in your **c**.
17:2 In one of the **c** the LORD your
17:8 be brought to court in your **c**.
18:6 A Levite from any of your **c** in
19:1 and live in their **c** and houses.
19:2 set aside three **c** in the land
19:3 a route to each of these **c**
19:3 may run to one of these **c**.
19:4 past may run to one of these **c**
19:5 may run to one of these **c**
19:7 aside three **c** for yourselves.
19:9 you may add three more **c** of
19:11 and runs to one of these **c**.
20:15 must do to all the **c** that are far
20:16 not spare anyone's life in the **c**
21:2 to each of the neighboring **c**.
23:16 in any of your **c** that seems
24:14 living in one of your **c**.
26:12 and widows in your **c**,
28:52 They will blockade all your **c**
28:52 They'll blockade all the **c**
28:55 the blockade of all your **c**.
28:57 during the blockade of your **c**.
29:23 **c** the LORD destroyed in fierce
31:12 foreigners who live in your **c**.
Jos 9:17 They came to the **c** of Gibeon,
10:2 It was like one of the royal **c**,
10:19 them get back into their own **c**,
10:20 got back into the fortified **c**.
11:12 So Joshua captured all these **c**
11:13 Israel did not burn **c** built on
11:14 loot and livestock from these **c**.
11:21 by destroying them and their **c**.
13:10 It included all the **c** of King
13:17 included Heshbon and all its **c**
13:21 It also included all the **c** of the
13:23 It included **c** with their villages.
13:25 all the **c** of Gilead,
13:28 It included **c** with their villages.
13:31 the royal **c** of Og in Bashan.
14:4 gave the Levites **c**
14:12 that they have large, fortified **c**.
15:9 From there it goes to the **c** of
15:21 gave the tribe of Judah 29 **c**
15:33 foothills they gave Judah 14 **c**
15:37 also gave Judah 16 other **c**
15:42 An additional nine **c** with their
15:45 Ekron with its **c** and villages.
15:46 This included all the **c** with
15:47 Ashdod and Gaza with their **c**
15:48 they gave Judah 11 **c**
15:52 also gave Judah nine other **c**
15:55 also received another ten **c**
15:59 and Eltekon were six other **c**
15:60 The two **c** of Kiriath Baal (now
15:61 desert Judah was given six **c**
16:9 with all the **c** and their villages
17:9 These **c** belong to Ephraim,
17:9 they are among Manasseh's **c**.
17:12 possession of these **c** since
18:9 seven parts according to its **c**.
18:21 These are the 12 **c** with their
18:25 There were 14 other **c** with
19:2 inheritance they received 13 **c**
19:7 There were four other **c** with
19:8 All the villages around these **c**
19:15 were 12 **c** with their villages.
19:16 These **c** with their villages are
19:22 were 16 **c** with their villages.
19:23 These **c** with their villages are
19:30 were 22 **c** with their villages.
19:31 These **c** with their villages are
19:35 The fortified **c** were Ziddim,
19:38 were 19 **c** with their villages.
19:39 These **c** with their villages are
19:48 These **c** with their villages are
20:2 choose for yourselves the **c**
20:4 can run to one of these **c**.
20:7 were chosen as **c** of refuge.

Jos 20:8 of Manasseh were chosen as **c**
20:9 These are the **c** chosen as
20:9 are the cities chosen as **c**
20:9 may escape to these **c**.
21:2 that we should receive **c**
21:3 were given the following **c**
21:4 These are the **c** for the families
21:4 the Levite received 13 **c** from
21:5 received 10 **c** from
21:6 received 13 **c** from
21:7 descendants received 12 **c**
21:8 The Israelites gave these **c**
21:9 These are the names of the **c**
21:13 So they gave the following **c**
21:13 The nine **c** from those two
21:17 also gave them four **c**:
21:19 In all, 13 **c** with pasturelands
21:20 **C** were chosen by lot from the
21:21 These four **c** with pasturelands
21:23 tribe of Dan gave them four **c**:
21:25 them two **c** with pasturelands:
21:26 In all, ten **c** with pasturelands
21:27 two **c** with pasturelands from
21:28 Four **c** with pasturelands were
21:30 Another four **c** with
21:32 Also three **c** with pasturelands
21:33 In all, 13 **c** with pasturelands
21:34 gave four **c** with pasturelands:
21:36 them four **c** with pasturelands:
21:38 them four **c** with pasturelands:
21:40 All these **c** belonged to the
21:40 These 12 **c** were chosen by lot.
21:41 the Israelites there were 48 **c**
21:42 Each of these **c** had its own
24:13 **c** to live in that you hadn't built,
Jdg 11:26 and in all the **c** along the Arnon
11:26 these **c** during that time?
11:33 on to Abel Keramim, 20 **c** in all.
12:7 buried in one of the **c** of Gilead.
20:15 came from Benjamin's **c**
20:42 whoever came out of the **c**
21:23 So they rebuilt their **c** and lived
1Sm 6:17 LORD were for the **c** of Ashdod,
6:18 of Philistine **c** belonging
6:18 including walled **c** and farm
7:14 The **c** between Ekron and Gath
7:14 controlled by these **c** from
8:22 "Go ⌊back⌋ to your own **c**."
18:6 Women from all of Israel's **c**
30:29 Racal, the **c** belonging to the
30:29 the **c** belonging to the Kenites,
31:7 they abandoned their **c**.
31:7 came to live in these **c**.
2Sm 2:1 I go to one of the **c** of Judah?"
8:8 and Berothai, Hadadezer's **c**.
10:12 for our people and for the **c**
12:31 the same to all the Ammonite **c**.
20:6 or he will find some fortified **c**
24:7 city of Tyre and all the **c**
1Ki 4:13 60 large **c** with walls and
9:11 Hiram of Tyre 20 **c** in Galilee.
9:12 Hiram left Tyre to see the **c**
9:13 "What kind of **c** have you given
9:15 and ⌊the **c** of⌋ Hazor,
9:19 all the storage **c** that he owned.
9:19 He also built **c** for his chariots,
9:19 **c** for his war horses,
10:26 stationed ⌊some⌋ in chariot **c**
12:17 who lived in the **c** of Judah.
13:32 illegal worship sites in the **c**
15:20 armies to attack the **c** of Israel.
15:23 and the **c** he fortified — written
22:39 and all the **c** he fortified —
2Ki 3:25 Then Israel tore down the **c**,
10:2 fortified **c**, and weapons.
13:25 reconquered the **c** that
13:25 and recovered those **c** of Israel.
17:6 and in the **c** of the Medes.
17:9 of worship in all of their **c**,
17:24 and settled them in the **c**
17:24 over Samaria and lived in its **c**.
17:26 as captives and settled in the **c**
17:29 this in the **c** where they lived:
18:11 and in the **c** of the Medes.
18:13 attacked all the fortified **c**
19:13 the king of the **c** of Sepharvaim,

2Ki 19:25 will turn fortified **c** into piles
19:26 who live in these **c** are weak,
23:5 places of worship in the **c**
23:8 all the priests out of the **c**
23:19 of worship in the **c** of Samaria.
1Ch 2:23 and its villages (60 **c** in all).
4:31 These were their **c** until David
4:32 Their five **c** were Etam,
4:33 around these **c** as far as
6:60 a total of 13 **c** for their families.
6:61 received 10 **c** chosen by lot
6:62 were given 13 **c** chosen by lot
6:63 were given 12 **c** chosen by lot
6:64 the **c** with their pasturelands.
6:65 They gave ⌊them⌋ the **c**
6:66 had **c** chosen by lot
6:67 were given these **c** of refuge:
7:29 son of Israel, live in these **c**.
9:2 own **c** were ⌊some⌋ Israelites,
10:7 they abandoned their **c**.
10:7 came to live in these **c**.
13:2 priests and Levites in their **c**
18:8 and Cun, Hadadezer's **c**.
19:7 for the battle from their **c**.
19:13 for our people and for the **c**
20:3 the same to all the Ammonite **c**.
27:25 **c**, villages, and watchtowers:
2Ch 1:14 stationed ⌊some⌋ in chariot **c**
8:2 He rebuilt the **c** Huram gave
8:4 all the storage **c** in Hamath.
8:5 Beth Horon into **c** fortified
8:6 and all the storage **c** that
8:6 He built all the **c** for his
8:6 all the **c** for his war horses,
9:25 stationed ⌊some⌋ in chariot **c**
10:17 who lived in the **c** of Judah.
11:5 and built fortified **c** in Judah.
11:10 These were fortified **c** in Judah
11:12 He made the **c** very secure.
12:4 He captured the fortified **c** in
13:19 and captured some of his **c**:
14:5 incense in all the **c** of Judah.
14:6 He built fortified **c** in Judah
14:7 "Let's build these **c** and make
14:7 "So they built the **c**,
14:14 It attacked all the **c** around
14:14 because the **c** were afraid
14:14 The army looted all the **c**
15:8 and the **c** he had captured in
16:4 armies to attack the **c** of Israel.
16:4 and all the storage **c** in the
17:2 put troops in all the fortified **c**
17:2 posts in Judah and in the **c**
17:7 to teach in the **c** of Judah.
17:9 the people in all the **c** of Judah.
17:12 He built fortresses and **c** where
17:13 large supplies of food in the **c**
17:19 fortified **c** throughout Judah.
19:10 in other **c** about every case
21:3 along with fortified **c** in Judah.
23:2 the Levites from all the **c**
24:5 "Go to the **c** of Judah,
26:6 He built **c** near Ashdod and
27:4 He built **c** in the hills of Judah,
31:1 there went to the **c** in Judah.
31:1 returned to their own **c**.
31:6 Judah who were living in the **c**
31:15 under him in the **c** belonging
32:1 camp ⌊to attack⌋ the fortified **c**.
32:29 He made **c** for himself because
34:6 In the **c** of Manasseh,
Ezr 2:1 All of them went to their own **c**.
2:70 servants settled in their own **c**.
2:70 Israelites settled in their own **c**.
3:1 had already settled in their **c**.)
4:10 settled them in the **c**
Neh 7:6 All of them went to their own **c**.
7:73 of Israel settled in their own **c**.
7:73 of Israel were in their own **c**.
8:15 all their **c** and Jerusalem:
9:25 Israelites captured fortified **c**
11:1 supposed to live in the other **c**.
11:3 settled in the **c** of Judah.
11:3 own property in their own **c**.
11:20 lived in all the **c** of Judah.
12:44 from the fields around the **c**.

Est 9:2 The Jews assembled in their **c**
Job 15:28 He lives in ruined **c** where no
Psa 9:6 You have uprooted their **c**.
48:11 Mount Zion be glad and the **c**
69:35 he will rebuild the **c** of Judah.
89:40 have laid his fortified **c** in ruins.
107:36 and they build **c** to live in.
Sos 6:4 like those great **c**.
Isa 1:7 Your **c** are burned down.
6:11 And he replied, "Until the **c** lie
14:17 a desert and tore down its **c**,
14:21 and rebuild **c** all over it.
17:2 The **c** of Aroer will be deserted.
17:2 These **c** will be used for sheep,
17:3 Fortified **c** will disappear from
17:9 the fortified **c** which other
19:18 When that day comes, five **c** in
19:18 One of the **c** will be called
25:2 You have turned **c** into ruins,
25:2 fortified **c** into piles of rubble,
25:2 and foreigners' palaces into **c**
25:3 and **c** ruled by the world's
32:14 Noisy **c** will be abandoned.
36:1 attacked all the fortified **c**
37:13 the king of the **c** of Sepharvaim,
37:26 will turn fortified **c** into piles
37:27 who live in these **c** are weak,
40:9 Tell the **c** of Judah:
42:11 and its **c** raise their voices.
44:26 He says about the **c** of Judah,
54:3 they will resettle deserted **c**.
61:4 They will renew the ruined **c**,
64:10 Your holy **c** have become a
Jer 1:15 the city and all the **c** of Judah.
2:15 The **c** have been burned down,
2:28 as many gods as you have **c**,
4:5 Let's go into the fortified **c**."
4:7 Your **c** will be ruined,
4:16 cries against the **c** of Judah.
4:26 and all its **c** are torn down
5:6 lie in ambush outside their **c**.
5:6 All who leave the **c** will be torn
5:17 destroy the fortified **c** you trust.
7:17 what they are doing in the **c**
7:34 In the **c** of Judah and in the
8:14 Let's go into the fortified **c** and
9:11 I will destroy the **c** of Judah so
10:22 Its army will destroy Judah's **c**
11:6 all these things in the **c**
11:12 Then the **c** of Judah and those
11:13 as many gods as you have **c**.
13:19 The **c** in the Negev will be
17:26 will come from the **c** of Judah,
20:16 May that man be like the **c** that
22:6 into **c** that no one lives in.
25:18 Jerusalem and the **c** of Judah
25:20 those from the **c** of Ashkelon,
26:2 people who come from the **c**
30:18 **C** will be built on the ruins,
31:21 come back to your **c**.
31:23 saying in Judah and in its **c**:
31:24 Judah and all its **c** will live
32:44 of Jerusalem, in the **c** of Judah,
32:44 in the **c** on the mountains,
33:10 The **c** of Judah and the streets
33:12 or animals live, and in all its **c**,
33:13 In the **c** on the mountains,
33:13 and in the **c** of Judah,
34:1 Jerusalem and all its **c**.
34:7 attacking Jerusalem and the **c**
34:7 These were the only fortified **c**
34:22 I will destroy the **c** of Judah so
36:6 when they come from their **c**.
40:5 to govern the **c** of Judah.
40:10 Live in the **c** you have taken
44:2 and on all the **c** of Judah.
44:6 and continued to burn in the **c**
44:17 and our officials did in the **c** of
44:21 you burned incense in the **c**
46:8 I will destroy **c** and the people
47:2 the **c** and those who live in
48:9 Its **c** will become deserted
48:15 attack Moab and destroy its **c**.
48:21 has come to all the **c**
48:24 and on all the **c** of Moab,
48:28 of Moab, abandon your **c**.

Jer 48:41 The **c** will be taken,
49:1 people live in Gad's **c**?
49:13 All its **c** will lie in ruins
49:18 and their neighboring **c** when
50:32 I will light a fire in their **c** that
50:40 and their neighboring **c** when I,
51:30 They stay in their fortified **c**.
51:43 Its **c** will be ruined.
Lam 2:2 He tore down the fortified **c** of
5:11 are the girls in the **c** of Judah.
Eze 6:6 the **c** will be ruined,
12:20 The **c** where people live will
19:7 and turned **c** into wastelands.
21:19 roads start to fork toward the **c**.
25:9 up the **c** that protect Moab's
25:9 They are the beautiful **c** of Beth
26:19 into ruins like **c** that have no
29:12 For 40 years Egypt's **c** will lie
30:7 and Egypt's **c** will lie in ruins.
30:7 be ruined more than other **c**.
30:17 and people from these **c** will go
33:24 those who live in the ruined **c**
33:27 whoever is in the ruined **c** will
35:4 I will turn your **c** into ruins,
35:9 Your **c** will not be lived in.
36:4 abandoned **c** that have become
36:10 The **c** will be inhabited,
36:33 I will cause your **c** to be lived
36:35 The **c** were destroyed.
36:38 Their ruined **c** will be filled
39:9 Those living in the **c** of Israel
45:5 so that they have **c** to live in.
48:15 long, will be left for **c**, homes,
Hos 8:14 have built many fortified **c**.
8:14 I will send a fire on their **c** and
11:6 War will sweep through their **c**,
13:10 Where in all your **c** are your
Amo 4:6 nothing to eat in any of your **c**.
4:8 So people from two or three **c**
9:14 They will rebuild the ruined **c**
Oba 1:20 of the **c** in the Negev.
Mic 5:2 be included among Judah's **c**.
5:11 I will destroy the **c** in your land
5:14 I will wipe out your **c**.
7:12 Assyria and the **c** of Egypt,
Hab 2:8 **c**, and all their inhabitants.
2:17 **c**, and all their inhabitants.
Zep 1:16 cries against the fortified **c**
3:6 Their **c** will be completely
Zec 1:12 Jerusalem and the **c** of Judah?
1:17 My **c** will overflow with
7:7 surrounding **c** were inhabited
8:20 citizens from many **c** are going
Mat 4:25 the Ten **C**, Jerusalem, Judea,
11:1 to teach his message in their **c**.
11:20 Then Jesus denounced the **c**
14:13 followed him on foot from the **c**.
Mar 5:20 had done for him in the Ten **C**.
6:33 The people ran from all the **c**
6:56 go into villages, **c**, or farms,
7:31 and the territory of the Ten **C**
Luk 2:3 in the **c** where their ancestors
4:43 kingdom of God in other **c** also.
10:13 If the miracles worked in your **c**
19:17 Take charge of ten **c**.'
19:19 'You take charge of five **c**.'
Act 5:16 Crowds from the **c** around
6:9 day⌋ some men from the **c**
8:40 He traveled through all the **c**
12:20 This was because their **c**
14:6 and Derbe, **c** of Lycaonia,
14:19 However, Jews from the **c** of
14:21 went back to the **c** of Lystra,
14:22 the disciples in these **c**
16:4 As they went through the **c**,
17:1 and Silas traveled through the **c**
26:11 in **c** outside ⌊Jerusalem⌋.
28:15 so they came as far as the **c** of
2Ti 3:11 to me in the **c** of Antioch,
2Pe 2:6 God condemned the **c** of
2:6 He made those **c** an example
Jud 1:7 and the **c** near them is
1:7 The people of these **c** suffered
Rev 16:19 and the **c** of the nations fell.

citizen (8)

Act 21:39 Paul answered, "I'm a Jew, a **c**
22:25 a Roman **c** who hasn't had
22:26 This man is a Roman **c**."
22:27 are you a Roman **c**?"
22:28 money to become a Roman **c**."
22:28 "But I was born a Roman **c**."
22:29 that he had tied up a Roman **c**.
23:27 out that he was a Roman **c**,

citizens (38)

Gen 19:4 all the young and old male **c** of
Jos 24:11 The **c** of Jericho, the Amorites,
Jdg 9:2 "Please ask all **c** of Shechem,
9:3 he said to all **c** of Shechem.
9:6 All the **c** from Shechem and
9:7 you **c** of Shechem,
9:18 king over the **c** of Shechem
9:20 out of Abimelech and burn up **c**
9:20 Also let fire come out of **c** of
9:23 Abimelech and **c** of Shechem.
9:23 So **c** of Shechem turned
9:24 Abimelech and **c** of Shechem.
9:24 **C** of Shechem had helped
9:25 So **c** of Shechem set
9:26 **C** of Shechem trusted him.
9:39 Then Gaal led **c** of Shechem
9:46 All the **c** of Shechem's Tower
20:5 The **c** of Gibeah came to
20:6 I did this because the **c** of
20:10 Benjamin they can punish the **c**
1Sm 23:11 Will the **c** of Keilah hand me
23:12 "Will the **c** of Keilah hand me
2Sm 21:12 of his son Jonathan from the **c**
2Ki 24:15 and the leading **c** of the land
Isa 48:2 You call yourselves ⌊**c**⌋ of the
Eze 17:13 away the leading **c** from Judah
Dan 9:7 the **c** of Jerusalem,
Zec 8:20 People and **c** from many cities
8:21 The **c** of one city will come to
Mat 8:12 The **c** of that kingdom will be
Luk 19:14 "The **c** of his own country
Act 16:21 or practice as Roman **c**."
16:37 even though we're Roman **c**.
16:38 Paul and Silas were Roman **c**,
19:35 Then he said, "**C** of Ephesus,
Eph 2:19 and outsiders but **c** together
Php 1:27 Live as **c** who reflect the Good
3:20 We, however, are **c** of heaven.

citizenship (1)

Eph 2:12 were excluded from **c** in Israel,

citron (1)

Rev 18:12 all kinds of **c** wood,

city (1068)

Gen 4:17 Cain was building a **c**,
10:12 and Resen, the great **c**
11:4 Then they said, "Let's build a **c**
11:5 LORD came down to see the **c**
11:8 they stopped building the **c**.
18:24 50 innocent people in the **c**?
18:26 people inside the **c** of Sodom,
18:28 Will you destroy the whole **c**
19:2 the night in the **c** square."
19:12 or any other relatives in the **c**?
19:14 is going to destroy the **c**."
19:15 away when the **c** is punished."
19:16 them safely outside the **c**.
19:20 Look, there's a **c** near enough
19:21 the **c** you're talking about.
19:22 (The **c** is named Zoar [Small].)
23:10 entering the **c** gate could hear
23:18 had entered the **c** gate were
24:10 to Aram Naharaim, Nahor's **c**.
24:11 kneel down outside the **c** by
24:13 and the girls of the **c** are
26:33 That is why the name of the **c**
28:19 the name of the **c** was Luz.
33:18 Jacob came safely to the **c** of
33:18 camped within sight of the **c**.
34:20 Shechem went to their **c** gate
34:20 to speak to the men of their **c**.
34:24 come out to the **c** gate agreed
Gen 34:24 all circumcised at the **c** gate.
34:25 and boldly attacked the **c**.
34:27 looted the **c** where their sister
34:28 and whatever else was in the **c**
35:27 to his father Isaac to Mamre's **c**,
36:32 his ⌊capital⌋ **c** was Dinhabah.
36:35 of his capital **c** was Avith.
36:39 name of his capital **c** was Pau.
41:45 priest from the **c** of On.
41:48 In each **c** he put the food from
41:50 priest from the **c** of On.
44:4 from the **c** when Joseph said
44:13 and went back into the **c**.
46:20 priest from the **c** of On.
Exo 9:29 "As soon as I'm out of the **c**,
9:33 Pharaoh and went out of the **c**,
20:10 living in your **c** must never do
Lev 14:40 out and thrown outside the **c**
14:41 an unclean place outside the **c**.
14:45 an unclean place outside the **c**.
14:53 the living bird fly from the **c** into
25:29 sells a home in a walled **c**,
25:30 the house in the **c** belongs to
25:33 purchased house in the **c** will
Num 20:16 a **c** on the edge of your
21:26 Heshbon was the **c** of King
21:27 Restore Sihon's **c**!
21:28 flames from Sihon's **c**.
35:4 1,500 feet from the **c** wall.
35:5 Outside the **c** measure off
35:5 with the **c** in the center.
35:5 their pastureland around the **c**.
35:25 must take you back to the **c**
35:26 "But don't go outside the **c** of
35:27 death finds you outside the **c**
35:28 murderers must stay in their **c**
35:32 murderer who has fled to a **c**
Dtr 2:36 of the Arnon Valley and the **c**
2:36 no **c** had walls that could keep
3:4 There wasn't a **c** we didn't take.
3:6 destroying every **c**,
3:11 in the Ammonite **c** of Rabbah.)
5:14 living in your **c** must never do
12:15 In whatever **c** you live,
12:21 as much as you want in your **c**.
13:15 must kill the residents of that **c**
13:15 with swords and destroy that **c**
13:16 into the middle of the **c** square.
13:16 Then burn their **c** and all their
15:22 Eat it in your **c**. Clean and
16:18 for your tribes in every **c** that
17:5 evil thing to the gates of your **c**,
19:12 the leaders of your **c** must send
19:12 They must take him from that **c**
20:10 When you approach a **c** to
20:12 set up a blockade around the **c**.
20:13 your God hands the **c** over
20:13 man in that **c** with your swords.
20:14 and everything else in the **c**,
20:19 do whenever you blockade a **c**
20:20 until you capture the **c**.
21:3 determined which **c** is nearest
21:3 the leaders from that **c** must
21:4 The leaders of that **c** will bring
21:6 All the leaders from the **c**
21:19 him to the leaders of the **c** at
21:19 leaders of the city at the **c** gate.
21:20 will say to the leaders of the **c**,
21:21 All the men of the **c** should
22:15 must go to the **c** gate where
22:15 where the leaders of the **c** are
22:17 in front of the leaders of the **c**.
22:18 The leaders of that **c** must take
22:21 The men of her **c** must stone
22:23 If this happens in a **c**,
22:24 take them to the gate of the **c**
22:24 die because she was in a **c**
25:7 go to the leaders of the **c** at
25:7 leaders of the city at the **c** gate.
25:8 Then the leaders of the **c** must
28:3 You will be blessed in the **c**
28:16 You will be cursed in the **c** and
34:3 the valley of Jericho (the **C**
Jos 2:1 especially the **c** of Jericho."
2:2 have entered the **c** tonight.
2:15 house was built into the **c** wall.

Jos 2:15 (She lived in the **c** wall.)
3:16 like a dam as far away as the **c**
6:3 will march around the **c** once
6:4 around the **c** seven times while
6:5 wall around the **c** will collapse.
6:5 straight ahead into the **c**."
6:7 "March around the **c**.
6:11 ark went around the **c** once.
6:14 They went around the **c** once
6:15 They marched around the **c**
6:16 the LORD has given you the **c**!
6:17 The **c** has been claimed by the
6:20 ahead and captured the **c**.
6:24 Then Israel burned the **c** and
6:26 to rebuild the **c** of Jericho.
6:26 son to set up the **c** doors."
7:5 chasing them from the **c** gate to
8:1 people, **c**, and land over to you.
8:2 Set an ambush behind the **c**."
8:4 "Set an ambush behind the **c**.
8:4 go very far away from the **c**.
8:5 I'll approach the **c** with the rest
8:6 will lure them away from the **c**.
8:7 out of hiding and capture the **c**.
8:8 When you have captured the **c**,
8:11 until they were near the **c**.
8:12 Bethel and Ai, west of the **c**.
8:13 main camp was north of the **c**,
8:13 were hiding west of the **c**.
8:14 troops behind the **c** waiting
8:16 All the troops in the **c** were
8:16 were lured away from the **c**.
8:17 So the **c** was left unprotected
8:18 in your hand toward the **c**,
8:19 They entered the **c**,
8:20 they could see the **c** going up
8:21 been hiding had captured the **c**
8:22 captured the **c** also came out
8:27 of that **c** for themselves,
8:29 threw it in the entrance of the **c**
10:2 because Gibeon was a large **c**.
10:37 He claimed the **c** and all its
11:19 Not one **c** had made a peace
13:9 including the **c** in the middle of
13:16 including the **c** in the middle of
15:8 of the Jebusite **c** Jerusalem.
15:13 It was the **c** of Arba (now
18:14 Kiriath Jearim), a **c** of Judah.
18:16 south slope of the **c** of Jebus,
19:29 on to the fortified **c** of Tyre.
19:47 and renamed the **c** Dan after
19:50 They gave him the **c** he asked
19:50 He rebuilt the **c** and lived there.
20:4 stand at the entrance to the **c**,
20:4 case to the leaders of that **c**.
20:4 they will take him into their **c**
20:6 may remain in that **c** until
20:6 to his home in the **c** from which
21:11 This is the **c** of Hebron located
21:13 two tribes were Hebron (a **c**
21:21 were Shechem (a **c**
21:27 Golan in Bashan (a **c** of refuge
21:32 Kedesh in Galilee (a **c** of
21:38 Ramoth in Gilead (a **c** of refuge
Jdg 1:8 there and set the **c** on fire.
1:16 the people of Judah from the **C**
1:17 So the **c** was called Hormah
1:23 the past the **c** was called Luz.)
1:24 saw a man coming out of the **c**.
1:24 us how we can get into the **c**,
1:25 So they got into the **c** and
1:26 There he built a **c** and called it
1:26 The **c** still has that name today.
3:13 and occupied the **C** of Palms.
5:8 broke out inside the **c** gates.
5:11 went down to the **c** gates.
6:27 family and the men of the **c**,
6:28 When the men of the **c** got up
6:30 the men of the **c** told Joash,
8:16 took the leaders of the **c**
8:17 and killed the men of that **c**.
8:32 the **c** belonging to Abiezer's
9:31 have turned the **c** against you.
9:33 get up quickly and raid the **c**.
9:35 stood at the entrance to the **c**.
9:40 killed at the entrance of the **c**.
Jdg 9:43 the people coming out of the **c**.
9:44 and his company charged the **c**
9:45 Abimelech attacked the **c** all
9:45 He captured the **c** and killed
9:45 He also tore down the **c** and
14:18 the men of the **c** said to him,
16:2 waited all night at the **c** gate
16:3 and bar of the **c** gate and pulled
18:7 and came to the **c** of Laish.
18:16 stood at the entrance to the **c**.
18:17 stood at the entrance to the **c**
18:27 and went to the **c** of Laish.
18:27 and burned their **c**.
18:28 because their **c** was far from
18:28 The **c** was in the valley that
18:28 The people of Dan rebuilt the **c**
18:29 They named the **c** Dan in honor
18:29 the **c** was called Laish.
19:12 never go into a **c** of foreigners.
19:15 and sat down in the **c** square,
19:16 came into the **c** from his work
19:17 the traveler in the **c** square.
19:20 the night in the **c** square."
19:22 some worthless men from the **c**
20:11 stood united against the **c**.
20:31 and were led away from the **c**.
20:32 them from the **c** to the roads."
20:37 in the **c** and killed everyone.
20:38 rise from the **c** as a signal.
20:40 started to rise from the **c**.
20:40 and saw the whole **c** going up
20:48 cattle they found in every **c**.
20:48 They also burned down every **c**
Rut 4:1 Boaz went to the **c** gate and
4:2 were leaders of that **c** and said,
1Sm 1:3 man would go from his own **c**
4:13 The man went into the **c** to tell
4:13 The whole **c** cried out.
5:9 the LORD threw the **c** into a
5:9 unimportant people in the **c**,
5:11 a fear of death throughout the **c**,
5:12 So the cry of the **c** went up to
9:6 "There's a man of God in this **c**,
9:10 They went to the **c** where the
9:11 were going up the hill to the **c**,
9:12 He ⌊just⌋ went into the **c** today
9:13 As you go into the **c**,
9:14 and his servant went to the **c**.
9:25 left the worship site for the **c**.
9:27 were going toward the **c** limits,
10:5 When you arrive at the **c**,
15:5 Saul went to the **c** of Amalek
16:4 the leaders of the **c**,
17:12 the region of Ephrath and the **c**
20:29 will offer a sacrifice in the **c**,
20:42 and Jonathan went into the **c**.
21:13 on the doors of the **c** gate
22:19 the **c** of the priests.
23:7 by going into a **c** which has ⌊a
23:10 to Keilah and destroy the **c**
27:5 I live in the royal **c** with you?"
2Sm 5:7 Zion (that is, the **C** of David).
5:9 and called it the **C** of David.
5:9 He built the **c** ⌊of Jerusalem⌋
6:9 of the LORD come to my ⌊**c**⌋?"
6:10 with him to the **C** of David.
6:12 and bring it to the **C** of David.
6:16 LORD came to the **C** of David,
8:1 the main Philistine **c** from them.
10:3 sent his men to explore the **c**,
10:8 at the entrance of the ⌊**c**⌋ gate,
10:14 Abishai and went into the **c**.
11:16 kept the **c** under observation,
11:17 The men of the **c** came out and
11:20 go so close to the **c** to fight?
11:23 to the entrance of the **c** gate.
11:25 your attack against the **c**,
12:1 were two men in a certain **c**.
12:26 fought against the Ammonite **c**
12:28 surround the **c**, and capture it.
12:28 Otherwise, I will capture the **c**,
12:29 against the **c** and captured it.
12:30 took a lot of goods from the **c**.
15:2 the road leading to the **c** gate.
15:2 "Which **c** are you from?"
15:14 us when he massacres the **c**."
2Sm 15:17 were leaving the **c** on foot,
15:24 had withdrawn from the **c**.
15:25 "Take God's ark back to the **c**.
15:27 "Go back to the **c** peacefully,
15:34 But if you go back to the **c** and
15:37 went to the **c** as Absalom was
17:13 If he retreats into a **c**,
17:13 Israel will bring ropes to that **c**
17:17 being seen coming into the **c**,
17:23 and went home to his own **c**.
18:3 to send us help from the **c**."
19:3 sneaked into the **c** as if they
19:37 so that I can die in my **c** near
20:14 and followed him to the **c**.
20:15 put up a dirt ramp against the **c**,
20:16 woman called from the **c**,
20:19 to destroy a mother **c** in Israel?
20:21 and I'll withdraw from the **c**."
20:22 and withdrew from the **c**
23:15 at the **c** gate of Bethlehem."
24:5 south of the **c** in the middle of
24:7 They went to the fortified **c** of
1Ki 1:41 reason for the noise in the **c**?"
1:45 so the **c** is excited.
2:10 was buried in the **C** of David.
2:36 Don't leave ⌊the **c**⌋ to go
2:42 warn you that if you left ⌊the **c**⌋
3:1 Solomon brought her to the **C** of
8:1 the LORD's promise from the **C**
8:16 I didn't choose any **c** in any of
8:37 may blockade Israel's **c** gates.
8:44 toward the **c** you have chosen
8:48 and the **c** you have chosen,
9:24 daughter moved from the **C**
11:13 ⌊the **c**⌋ that I chose."
11:27 in the ⌊wall of⌋ the **C** of David.
11:32 the **c** I have chosen from all the
11:36 the **c** where I chose to place
11:43 was buried in the **C** of David.
13:25 They talked about it in the **c**
13:29 He came to his own **c** to mourn
14:11 Jeroboam's house dies in the **c**,
14:12 moment you set foot in the **c**
14:21 the **c** that the LORD chose from
14:21 the **c** where the LORD put his
14:31 with them in the **C** of David.
15:8 was buried in the **C** of David.
15:22 using those to fortify the **c**.
15:24 with his ancestors in the **c**
15:27 him in the Philistine **c**
16:4 ⌊family⌋ who dies in the **c**.
16:15 the Philistine **c** of Gibbethon.
16:18 When Zimri saw that the **c** had
16:24 fortified the hill and built the **c**
16:24 He named the **c** after its former
16:34 Setting up the **c** doors cost him
20:2 He sent messengers into the **c**
20:12 got ready ⌊to attack⌋ the **c**.
20:17 had sent men ⌊to watch the **c**⌋.
20:30 the **c** where the wall fell on
20:30 He came to the **c** and hid in an
21:8 and nobles living in Naboth's **c**.
21:10 him to death outside the **c**."
21:11 The men in Naboth's **c** — the
21:13 him to death outside the **c**.
21:24 Ahab's ⌊house⌋ dies in the **c**,
22:26 the governor of the **c**,
22:36 "Every man to his own **c**!
22:50 was buried with them in the **c**
2Ki 2:19 The people of the **c** ⌊of
2:23 some boys came out of the **c**
3:19 You will defeat every walled **c**
3:19 city and every important **c**.
6:14 at night and surrounded the **c**.
6:15 and chariots surrounding the **c**.
6:19 This isn't the **c**. Follow me, and
6:26 was walking on the **c** wall,
6:30 he was walking on the **c** wall,
7:3 at the entrance of the **c** gate.
7:4 If we go into the **c**,
7:10 So they called the **c**
7:12 'When they've left the **c**,
7:12 them alive and get into the **c**.'"
8:24 with them in the **C** of David.
9:15 let anyone escape from the **c**
9:28 his ancestors in the **C** of David.

2Ki 10:5 the mayor of the **c**,
11:20 But the **c** was quiet because
12:21 his ancestors in the **C** of David.
14:7 Dead Sea region and took the **c**
14:20 in Jerusalem, in the **C** of David,
15:7 with them in the **C** of David.
15:16 Because the **c** didn't open its
15:38 was buried with them in the **c**
16:20 with them in the **C** of David.
17:9 to the ⌊largest⌋ fortified **c**.
18:8 to the ⌊largest⌋ fortified **c** all
18:30 and this **c** will not be put under
19:32 He will never come into this **c**,
19:33 and he won't come into this **c**,"
19:34 "I will shield this **c** to rescue it
20:6 I'll rescue you and defend this **c**
20:20 tunnel to bring water into the **c**,
23:8 named after the mayor of the **c**.
23:8 going through the **c** gate.)
23:17 people of the **c** answered him,
23:27 Jerusalem, the **c** that I chose,
24:10 (The **c** was blockaded.)
24:11 officers were blockading the **c**.
25:1 dirt ramps around the **c** walls.
25:2 The blockade of the **c** lasted
25:3 the famine in the **c** became so
25:4 The enemy broke through the **c**
25:4 attacking the **c** from all sides,
25:11 the few people left in the **c**,
25:19 From the **c** he also took an
25:19 king whom he found in the **c**,
25:19 people whom he found in the **c**.
1Ch 1:43 his ⌊capital⌋ **c** was Dinhabah.
1:46 of his ⌊capital⌋ **c** was Avith.
1:50 of his ⌊capital⌋ **c** was Pai.
4:12 first settled the **c** of Nahash.
4:33 cities as far as the **c** of Baal.
6:56 but the fields belonging to the **c**
6:57 given Hebron as a **c** of refuge,
11:5 Zion (that is, the **C** of David).
11:7 so it was called the **C** of David.
11:8 He built the **c** ⌊of Jerusalem⌋
11:8 Joab rebuilt the rest of the **c**.
11:17 at the **c** gate of Bethlehem."
13:12 I bring God's ark to my ⌊**c**⌋?"
13:13 to his ⌊home⌋, the **C** of David.
15:1 for himself in the **C** of David,
15:29 came to the **C** of David,
19:9 line at the entrance of the **c**,
19:15 Abishai and went into the **c**.
20:2 took a lot of goods from the **c**.
2Ch 5:2 the LORD's promise from the **C**
6:5 I didn't choose any **c** from the
6:28 may blockade Israel's **c** gates.
6:34 toward this **c** you have chosen
6:38 and the **c** you have chosen,
8:11 Pharaoh's daughter from the **C**
9:31 was buried in the **C** of David.
11:12 In each **c** he stored shields and
11:23 in every fortified **c**.
12:13 the **c** that the LORD chose from
12:13 the **c** where the LORD put his
12:16 was buried in the **C** of David.
14:1 was buried in the **C** of David.
15:6 one **c** crushed another.
16:6 using those to fortify the **c**.
16:14 for himself in the **C** of David.
18:25 the governor of the **c**,
19:5 in each fortified **c** of Judah.
20:4 came from every **c** in Judah.
21:1 with them in the **C** of David.
21:20 He was buried in the **C** of
23:21 But the **c** was quiet because
24:16 He was buried in the **C** of
24:25 buried him in the **C** of David,
25:28 horse and buried him in the **c**
27:9 buried him in the **C** of David.
28:15 brought them to Jericho (the **C**
28:25 And in each **c** of Judah,
28:27 and was buried in the **c**
29:16 the unclean items outside the **c**
29:20 gathered the leaders of the **c**
30:10 So the messengers went from **c**
30:10 messengers went from city to **c**
30:26 The **c** of Jerusalem was filled
31:19 pasturelands of every Levite **c**.

2Ch 32:3 out of the springs outside the **c**.
32:5 wall outside ⌊the **c** wall⌋,
32:5 the Millo in the **C** of David,
32:6 in the square by the **c** gate.
32:18 that they could capture the **c**.
32:30 the west side of the **C** of David.
33:14 rebuilt the outer wall of the **C**
33:14 in every fortified **c** in Judah.
34:8 the mayor of the **c**,
Ezr 4:12 that rebellious and wicked **c**.
4:13 know that if this **c** is rebuilt
4:15 that this **c** has been rebellious
4:15 This **c** has a history of
4:15 why this **c** was destroyed.
4:16 to know that if this **c** is rebuilt
4:19 I discovered that this **c** has a
4:21 Keep this **c** from being rebuilt
10:14 judges of each **c** until our God's
Neh 2:3 shouldn't I look sad when the **c**,
2:5 to the **c** where my ancestors
2:8 near the temple, for the **c** wall,
3:15 down from the **C** of David.
6:1 hung the doors in the **c** gates).
7:4 The **c** was large and
11:1 to live in Jerusalem, the holy **c**.
11:9 second-in-command over the **c**.
11:18 in the holy **c** totaled 284.
12:37 up the stairs of the **C** of David.
13:18 evils on us and on this **c**?
Est 3:15 but the **c** of Susa was in
4:1 He went into the middle of the **c**
4:6 out to Mordecai in the **c** square
6:9 on the horse in the **c** square.
6:11 had him ride in the **c** square,
8:11 Jews in every **c** to assemble,
8:15 And the **c** of Susa cheered and
8:17 In every province and every **c**
9:28 age, family, province, and **c**.
Job 5:4 They are crushed at the **c** gate,
24:12 Those dying in the **c** groan.
29:7 When I went through the **c** gate
39:7 It laughs at the noise of the **c**
Psa 31:21 his mercy in a **c** under attack.
46:4 bring joy to the **c** of God,
46:5 God is in that **c**. It cannot fall.
48:1 mountain is in the **c** of our God.
48:2 It is the **c** of the great king.
48:8 we have now seen in the **c** of
48:8 in the **c** of our God.
55:9 violence and conflict in the **c**.
55:10 around on ⌊top of⌋ the **c** walls.
59:6 like dogs. They prowl the **c**.
59:14 like dogs. They prowl the **c**.
60:9 bring me into the fortified **c**?
72:16 May those from the **c** flourish
87:1 ⌊The **c**⌋ the LORD has
87:2 The LORD loves the **c** of Zion
87:3 are said about you, O **c** of God!
101:8 LORD's **c** of all troublemakers.
107:4 without finding an inhabited **c**.
107:7 went straight to an inhabited **c**.
108:10 bring me into the fortified **c**?
122:3 Jerusalem is built to be a **c**
122:4 of the LORD's tribes go to that **c**
127:1 the LORD does not protect a **c**,
127:5 with his enemies in the **c** gate.
Pro 1:21 At the entrances to the **c** she
8:3 near the gates to the **c**.
9:3 the highest places in the **c**,
9:14 on the high ground of the **c**
10:15 wealth is ⌊his⌋ strong **c**.
11:10 people prosper, a **c** is glad.
11:11 decent people a **c** is raised up,
16:32 than to capture a **c**.
17:19 Whoever builds his **c** gate high
18:11 person's wealth is his strong **c**
18:19 ⌊resistant⌋ than a strong **c**,
21:22 A wise man attacks a **c** of
22:22 oppressed person at the **c** gate,
24:7 At the **c** gate he does not open
25:28 ⌊Like⌋ a **c** broken into ⌊and⌋
29:8 create an uproar in a **c**,
31:23 "Her husband is known at the **c**
31:31 praise her at the **c** gates."
Ecc 7:19 than ten rulers can help a **c**.
8:10 They were praised in the **c** for

Sos 3:2 up now and roam around the **c**,
3:3 their rounds in the **c** found me.
5:7 their rounds in the **c** found me.
Isa 1:8 like a **c** under attack."
1:26 will be called the Righteous **C**,
14:31 Cry out in the **c**! Be frightened,
15:3 On their roofs and in their **c**
17:1 will no longer be a **c**.
19:2 neighbor, **c** against city,
19:2 neighbor, city against **c**,
22:2 You are a **c** filled with shouting,
23:7 Is this your bustling **c** founded
23:7 Is this the **c** that sent its people
23:8 the **c** that produced kings?
23:16 Go around in the **c**,
24:10 The ruined **c** lies desolate.
24:12 The **c** is left in ruins.
26:1 We have a strong **c**.
26:5 who live high in the towering **c**.
27:10 The fortified **c** is isolated.
28:6 defend the **c** gates in battle.
29:1 the **c** where David camped.
29:2 I will torment Ariel, and the **c**
29:2 The **c** will become like Ariel.
32:13 the happy homes in a joyful **c**.
32:19 and the **c** will be completely
33:20 the **c** of our festivals.
36:15 and this **c** will not be put under
37:33 He will never come into this **c**,
37:34 and he won't come into this **c**,"
37:35 "I will shield this **c** to rescue it
38:6 I'll rescue you and defend this **c**
45:13 He will build my **c** and let my
48:2 ⌊citizens⌋ of the holy **c**.
52:1 holy **c** of Jerusalem.
54:11 comfortless, storm-ravaged **c**!
54:11 I will rebuild your **c** with
60:14 They will call you the **c** of the
60:14 the **c** of the Holy One of Israel.
62:12 Sought After, a **C** Not Deserted.
65:19 will no longer be heard in the **c**.
66:6 Listen to the uproar from the **c**.
Jer 1:15 all the walls around the **c**
1:18 made you like a fortified **c**,
3:14 will take you, one from every **c**
4:29 All the people in the **c** will flee
4:29 The entire **c** will be abandoned,
5:1 Search the **c** squares.
6:6 This **c** must be punished.
8:16 the **c** and its people.
14:18 If I go to the **c**, I see those sick
15:7 shovel at the **c** gates.
17:24 through the gates of this **c**
17:25 through the gates of this **c**.
17:25 This **c** will always have
19:8 I will devastate this **c**.
19:11 and this **c** as this potter's
19:12 I will make this **c** like Topheth.
19:13 be unclean like this **c** Topheth.
19:15 I'm going to bring on this **c** and
20:5 all the riches of this **c** over
21:4 the Babylonians inside this **c**.
21:6 defeat those who live in this **c**,
21:7 and everyone else in this **c**
21:9 Those who live in this **c** will
21:10 I've decided to harm this **c**,
21:13 You are the **c** that is in the
22:8 nations will pass by this **c**
22:8 done this to this important **c**?'
23:39 presence and out of the **c** that
25:29 disaster on the **c** that is named
26:6 I will turn this **c** into something
26:9 Shiloh and this **c** will become
26:11 this **c** as you yourselves
26:12 this temple and against this **c**.
26:15 put me to death, you, this **c**,
26:20 He prophesied against this **c**
27:17 Why should this **c** be turned
27:19 utensils that are left in this **c**.
29:7 Work for the good of the **c**
29:7 and pray to the LORD for that **c**.
29:16 the people who live in this **c**,
31:38 "when the **c** will be rebuilt for
32:3 I'm going to hand this **c** over to
32:24 have been built up around the **c**
32:24 the **c** will be handed over to the

Jer	32:25	although the **c** was handed
	32:28	I'm going to hand this **c** over to
	32:29	attacking this **c** will break in,
	32:29	will break in, set this **c** on fire,
	32:31	"The people in this **c** have
	32:31	this **c** from my presence.
	32:36	have said this about the **c**,
	33:4	The houses in this **c** and the
	33:5	I will hide my face from this **c**
	33:6	"But I will heal this **c** and
	34:2	I'm going to hand this **c** over to
	34:22	bring that army back to this **c**
	36:9	who was coming from any **c**
	37:8	They will attack the **c**,
	37:10	get up and burn down this **c**.'"
	37:21	all the bread in the **c** was gone.
	38:2	Those who stay in this **c** will
	38:3	This **c** will certainly be handed
	38:3	and it will capture the **c**."
	38:4	soldiers who are left in this **c**
	38:9	there's no more bread in the **c**."
	38:17	and this **c** will not be burned.
	38:18	this **c** will be handed over to
	38:23	and this **c** will be burned
	39:2	they broke into the **c**.
	39:4	They left the **c** at night by way
	39:9	the few people left in the **c**,
	39:16	this **c** by bringing disaster
	41:7	When they came into the **c**,
	48:2	will be silenced, **c** of Madmen.
	48:8	destroyer will come to every **c**,
	48:8	and no **c** will escape.
	49:25	happy **c** abandoned?
	50:31	you arrogant **c**," declares the
	51:31	that his entire **c** is captured.
	51:41	Babylon, the **c** that the whole
	52:4	dirt ramps around the **c** walls.
	52:5	The blockade of the **c** lasted
	52:6	the famine in the **c** became so
	52:7	broke through the **c** walls,
	52:7	They left the **c** at night through
	52:7	attacking the **c** from all sides,
	52:15	the few people left in the **c**,
	52:25	From the **c** he also took an
	52:25	king whom he found in the **c**,
	52:25	people whom he found in the **c**.
Lam	1:1	Once the **c** was crowded with
	1:2	Out of all those who love the **c**,
	1:19	their last breath in the **c**,
	2:11	infants faint in the **c** streets.
	2:12	people in the **c** streets.
	2:15	'Is this the **c** they used to call
	3:51	all the young women in my **c**.
	5:14	stopped meeting at the **c** gate,
Eze	4:3	a wall between you and the **c**.
	4:3	Turn your face toward the **c** as
	5:2	in a fire in the middle of the **c**.
	5:2	it up with a blade around the **c**.
	7:15	Whoever is in the **c** will be
	7:23	and the **c** is filled with
	9:1	who are going to punish this **c**.
	9:4	throughout the **c** of Jerusalem,
	9:4	that are being done in the **c**."
	9:5	him throughout the **c** and kill.
	9:7	and killed the people in the **c**.
	9:9	and the **c** is filled with
	10:2	Then scatter them over the **c**."
	11:2	and give bad advice in this **c**.
	11:3	This **c** is a cooking pot,
	11:6	killed many people in this **c**
	11:7	put in the middle of the **c** are
	11:7	and the **c** is the cooking pot.
	11:7	I will force you out of the **c**.
	11:9	I will force you out of the **c**.
	11:11	The **c** will not be your cooking
	11:23	glory left the middle of the **c**
	11:23	the mountain east of the **c**.
	13:4	foxes among the ruins ⌊of a **c**⌋.
	16:24	sites in every **c** square.
	17:4	the twig in a **c** of merchants.
	21:20	to the Ammonite **c** of Rabbah,
	21:20	and the fortified **c** of Jerusalem.
	21:22	rams against the **c** gates,
	22:2	you judge the **c** of murderers?
	22:3	you are the **c** that murders
	22:20	gather you and put you in the **c**.
Eze	22:21	and melt you in the **c**.
	22:22	You will be melted in the **c** like
	22:24	"Son of man, tell the **c**,
	24:6	it will be for that **c** of murderers,
	24:7	Blood is still in that **c**.
	24:8	so that I would pay that **c** back,
	24:9	it will be for that **c** of murderers.
	26:2	'The **c** that was the gateway
	26:10	as people enter a conquered **c**.
	26:17	for you: Tyre, you famous **c**,
	26:19	I will turn your **c** into ruins like
	27:3	Tyre is the **c** at the entrance to
	27:32	the **c** destroyed in the sea?"
	29:12	ruined more than any other **c**.
	33:21	"The **c** has been captured."
	39:16	(A **c** named Hamonah will also
	40:2	that looked like those in a **c**.
	45:7	the property belonging to the **c**.
	47:15	It will run through the **c** of
	48:15	The **c** will be in the middle of it.
	48:16	be the measurements for the **c**:
	48:18	provide food for the **c** workers.
	48:19	**C** workers from all the tribes in
	48:20	along with the **c** property.
	48:21	and the **c** property will belong
	48:30	will be the exits for the **c**:
	48:31	The gates of the **c** will be
	48:35	The **c** will measure about
Dan	9:16	and fury away from your **c**,
	9:18	and at the **c** called by your
	9:19	because your **c** and your
	9:24	for your people and your holy **c**.
	9:25	and rebuilt with a **c** square
	9:26	The **c** and the holy place will
	9:27	to those who destroy ⌊the **c**⌋."
	11:15	and capture a fortified **c**.
Hos	6:8	Gilead is a **c** filled with
	11:6	demolish their **c** gates,
Joe	2:9	They rush into the **c**.
Amo	3:6	horn sounds an alarm in a **c**,
	3:6	If there is a disaster in a **c**,
	4:3	Each of you will leave ⌊the **c**⌋
	4:7	I sent rain on one **c** and not on
	4:8	as they walked to another **c**
	5:3	The **c** that sends 1,000 troops
	5:16	loud crying in every **c** square,
	6:2	there to the great **c** of Hamath.
	6:2	the **c** of the Philistines.
	6:8	So I will hand over the **c** and
	7:17	become a prostitute in the **c**,
Jnh	1:2	at once for the important **c**,
	3:2	at once for the important **c**,
	3:3	Nineveh was a very large **c**.
	3:4	Jonah entered the **c** and
	3:7	and sent it throughout the **c**:
	4:5	Jonah left the **c** and sat down
	4:5	what would happen to the **c**.
	4:11	I feel sorry for this important **c**,
Mic	4:10	Now you will leave the **c**,
	5:1	your troops, you **c** of troops.
	6:9	of the LORD calls out to the **c**.
	6:9	you tribe assembled in the **c**.
	6:12	rich people in the **c** are violent.
	6:12	who live in the **c** speak lies,
Nah	2:4	way and that in the **c** squares.
	3:1	How horrible it will be for that **c**
Hab	1:10	will laugh at every fortified **c**
	2:12	who builds a **c** by slaughter
Zep	1:10	from the Second Part of the **c**,
	2:15	Is this the arrogant **c**?
	2:15	Is this the **c** that used to live
	2:15	the **c** that used to think to itself,
	3:1	corrupt place, the **c** of violence.
	3:5	righteous LORD is in that **c**.
Zec	8:3	will be called the **C** of Truth.
	8:5	The **c** will be filled with boys
	8:21	The citizens of one **c** will
	8:21	one city will come to another **c**,
	9:4	the sea and burn the **c** down.
	14:2	The **c** will be captured,
	14:2	Half of the people in the **c** will
	14:2	won't be taken from the **c**.
Mat	2:23	home in a **c** called Nazareth.
	4:5	devil took him into the holy **c**
	5:14	A **c** cannot be hidden when it
	5:35	which is the **c** of the great King.
Mat	8:33	care of the pigs ran into the **c**.
	8:34	Everyone from the **c** went to
	9:1	and came to his own **c**.
	10:5	Jewish or into any Samaritan **c**.
	10:11	you go into a **c** or village,
	10:14	leave that house or **c**,
	10:15	and Gomorrah than for that **c**.
	10:23	they persecute you in one **c**,
	10:23	gone through every **c** in Israel,
	12:25	And every **c** or household
	21:10	the whole **c** was in an uproar.
	21:17	left them and went out of the **c**
	21:18	as Jesus returned to the **c**,
	22:7	and burned their **c**.
	22:9	where the roads leave the **c**.
	23:34	and persecute from **c** to city.
	23:34	and persecute from city to **c**.
	26:18	"Go to a certain man in the **c**,
	27:32	He was from the **c** of Cyrene.
	27:53	and they went into the holy **c**
	27:57	He was from the **c** of Arimathea
	28:11	of the guards went into the **c**.
Mar	1:33	The whole **c** had gathered at
	1:45	no longer enter any **c** openly.
	5:14	In the **c** and countryside they
	11:19	disciples would leave the **c**.)
	14:13	and told them, "Go into the **c**.
	14:16	They went into the **c** and found
	15:21	A man named Simon from the **c**
	15:43	He was from the **c** of Arimathea
Luk	1:26	to Nazareth, a **c** in Galilee.
	1:39	Mary hurried to a **c** in the
	2:4	from Nazareth, a **c** in Galilee,
	2:4	a Judean **c** called Bethlehem.
	2:11	was born in David's **c**.
	4:29	Their **c** was built on a hill with
	4:29	forced Jesus out of the **c**,
	4:31	to Capernaum, a **c** in Galilee,
	5:12	One day Jesus was in a **c**
	7:11	Jesus went to a **c** called Nain.
	7:12	near the entrance to the **c**,
	7:12	crowd from the **c** was with her.
	7:37	life in that **c** found out that
	8:1	Jesus traveled from one **c** and
	8:4	come to Jesus from every **c**,
	8:27	certain man from the **c** met him.
	8:34	in the **c** and countryside.
	8:39	He went through the whole **c**
	9:5	welcome you, leave that **c**,
	9:10	He took them with him to a **c**
	10:1	to go ahead of him to every **c**
	10:8	Whenever you go into a **c** and
	10:10	"But whenever you go into a **c**
	10:12	easier for Sodom than for that **c**.
	13:22	traveled and taught in one **c**
	14:21	every street and alley in the **c**!
	18:2	He said, "In a **c** there was a
	18:3	In that **c** there was also a
	19:41	he came closer and saw the **c**,
	22:10	He told them, "Go into the **c**,
	22:39	Jesus went out ⌊of the **c**⌋ to
	23:19	place in the **c** and for murder.)
	23:26	who was from the **c** of Cyrene.
	23:48	they cried and returned to the **c**.
	23:51	from the Jewish **c** of Arimathea,
	23:56	Then they went back to the **c**
	24:9	tomb and went back to the **c**.
	24:47	in the **c** of Jerusalem.
	24:49	Wait here in the **c** until you
Jon	1:45	from the **c** of Nazareth."
	2:1	a wedding took place in the **c**
	2:12	and disciples went to the **c** of
	4:5	He arrived at a **c** in Samaria
	4:8	disciples had gone into the **c**
	4:28	jar and went back into the **c**.
	4:30	The people left the **c** and went
	4:39	Many Samaritans in that **c**
	4:46	Jesus returned to the **c** of Cana
	6:17	the sea to the **c** of Capernaum.
	6:24	these boats and went to the **c**
	11:54	to a **c** called Ephraim,
	19:17	cross and went out ⌊of the **c**⌋
	19:20	was crucified was near the **c**.
	19:38	Later Joseph from the **c** of
Act	1:13	When they came into the **c**,
	4:27	"In this **c** Herod and Pontius

Act 5:18 and putting them in the c jail.
6:5 to Judaism in the c of Antioch.
7:4 and lived in the c of Haran.
7:43 exile beyond the c of Babylon.'
7:58 had thrown him out of the c,
8:5 Philip went to the c of Samaria
8:8 that c was extremely happy.
8:9 named Simon lived in that c.
8:40 himself in the c of Azotus.
8:40 he came to the c of Caesarea.
9:2 leaders in the c of Damascus.
9:3 near the c of Damascus,
9:6 Go into the c, and you'll be told
9:10 lived in the c of Damascus.
9:11 Saul from the c of Tarsus.
9:19 was with the disciples in the c
9:24 They were watching the c
9:27 Jesus in the c of Damascus.
9:32 who lived in the c of Lydda.
9:35 Everyone who lived in the c of
9:36 Tabitha lived in the c of Joppa.
9:38 Lydda is near the c of Joppa.
9:42 throughout the c of Joppa,
10:1 lived in the c of Caesarea.
10:5 now to the c of Joppa,
11:5 "I was praying in the c of
11:19 and the c of Antioch.
11:25 left Antioch to go to the c
11:26 the first time in the c of Antioch.
11:27 Jerusalem to the c of Antioch.
12:10 the iron gate that led into the c.
13:4 they went to the c of Seleucia
13:5 Arriving in the c of Salamis,
13:6 as far as the c of Paphos.
13:13 in Perga, a c in Pamphylia.
13:14 in Antioch, a c near Pisidia.
13:44 almost the whole c gathered to
13:50 and the officials of the c.
13:51 and went to the c of Iconium.
14:1 happened in the c of Iconium.
14:3 and Barnabas stayed in the c
14:13 was at the entrance to the c.
14:19 out of the c when they thought
14:20 up and went back into the c.
14:20 Barnabas left for the c of Derbe.
14:21 spread the Good News in that c
14:25 spoke the message in the c
14:25 and went to the c of Attalia.
14:26 boat and headed home to the c
15:21 to every c for generations.
15:22 Barnabas to the c of Antioch.
15:30 and arrived in the c of Antioch.
15:36 "Let's go back to every c where
16:1 Paul arrived in the c of Derbe
16:8 and went to the c of Troas.
16:11 we sailed to the c of Neapolis,
16:12 we went to the c of Philippi.
16:12 Philippi is a leading c in that
16:12 We were in this c for a number
16:13 of worship we went out of the c
16:14 a convert to Judaism from the c
16:20 up a lot of trouble in our c.
16:39 they asked them to leave the c.
17:1 came to the c of Thessalonica,
17:5 and started a riot in the c.
17:6 in front of the c officials.
17:10 and Silas to the c of Berea.
17:10 Silas arrived in the c of Berea,
17:15 all the way to the c of Athens.
17:16 he saw that the c had statues
17:19 brought Paul to the c court,
17:23 As I was going through your c
18:1 and went to the c of Corinth.
18:10 I have many people in this c."
18:18 In the c of Cenchrea,
18:19 and arrived in the c of Ephesus,
18:22 arrived in the c of Caesarea.
18:22 went back to the c of Antioch.
18:24 arrived in the c of Ephesus.
19:1 to get to the c of Ephesus.
19:17 and Greeks living in the c
19:23 broke out in the c of Ephesus.
19:29 spread throughout the c,
19:35 The c clerk finally quieted the
19:35 everyone knows that this c of
20:13 and sailed for the c of Assos.
Act 20:14 and went to the c of Mitylene.
20:15 we arrived at the c of Miletus.
20:17 Paul sent messengers to the c
20:23 in every c that imprisonment
21:1 from there to the c of Patara.
21:3 We landed at the c of Tyre,
21:5 accompanied us out of the c.
21:7 from Tyre to the c of Ptolemais.
21:29 with him in the c earlier
21:30 The whole c was in chaos,
21:39 a citizen from the well-known c
22:3 I was born and raised in the c
22:5 in the c of Damascus.
22:6 my way and approaching the c
22:10 Go into the c of Damascus,
22:11 led me into the c of Damascus.
23:31 They took Paul to the c of
23:33 the soldiers arrived in the c
24:1 priest Ananias went to the c
24:12 synagogues throughout the c.
25:1 he went from the c of Caesarea
25:13 and Bernice came to the c
25:23 important men of the c entered
26:12 I went to the c of Damascus.
27:2 We set sail on a ship from the c
27:2 from the c of Thessalonica,
27:3 we arrived at the c of Sidon.
27:5 Pamphylia and arrived at the c
27:7 began along the coast of the c
27:8 port was near the c of Lasea.
27:12 They hoped to reach the c of
28:12 We stopped at the c of
28:13 and arrived at the c of Rhegium.
28:13 we arrived at the c of Puteoli.
28:15 finally arrived in the c of Rome.
Rom 16:1 the church in the c of Cenchrea.
16:23 Erastus, the c treasurer,
1Co 1:2 to be God's holy people in the c
2Co 1:1 To God's church in the c of
1:16 plans had been to go from the c
2:12 When I went to the c of Troas,
10:13 us to do — coming to ⌊the c
11:26 I've faced dangers in the c,
11:32 Aretas put guards around the c
Eph 1:1 with Christ in the c of Ephesus.
Php 1:1 To God's people in the c of
Col 1:2 Christ in the c of Colossae.
4:9 Onesimus is from your c and is
4:12 of Christ Jesus from your c,
1Ti 1:3 you to stay in the c of Ephesus.
2Ti 4:10 went to the c of Thessalonica.
4:12 I'm sending Tychicus to the c
4:13 with Carpus in the c of Troas.
4:20 Erastus stayed in the c of
4:20 and I left Trophimus in the c
Tit 1:5 spiritual leaders in every c as
3:12 to visit me in the c of Nicopolis.
Heb 11:10 Abraham was waiting for the c
11:10 c with permanent foundations.
11:16 He has prepared a c for them.
12:22 to the c of the living God,
13:14 We don't have a permanent c
13:14 but we are looking for the c
Jas 4:13 we will go into some c,
Rev 3:12 the name of the c of my God
11:2 the holy c for 42 months.
11:8 important c where their Lord
11:8 The spiritual names of that c
11:13 One-tenth of the c collapsed,
14:20 in the winepress outside the c.
16:19 The important c split into three
17:18 important c which dominates
18:10 horrible it is for that important c
18:10 the powerful c Babylon!
18:16 horrible for that important c
18:18 'Was there ever a c as
18:19 horrible for that important c.
18:21 "The important c Babylon will
20:9 holy people and the beloved c.
21:2 Then I saw the holy c,
21:10 He showed me the holy c,
21:14 The wall of the c had 12
21:15 stick to measure the c,
21:16 The c was square.
21:16 He measured the c with the
21:18 The c was made of pure gold,
Rev 21:19 The foundations of the c wall
21:21 The street of the c was made
21:23 The c doesn't need any sun or
21:26 of the nations into the holy c.
22:2 Between the street of the c and
22:3 and the lamb will be in the c.
22:14 go through the gates into the c.
22:19 the holy c that are described

city's (10)

2Ki 2:19 "This c location is as good as
6:32 his home with the ⌊c⌋ leaders.
10:6 with the c most powerful men.
Lam 1:10 hands on all of the c treasures.
Eze 45:6 feet long as the c property.
48:17 The c pastureland will be
48:22 property and the c property will
48:35 From then on the c name will
Luk 10:11 'We are wiping your c dust
Rev 18:19 because of that c high prices.

civilian (1)

Isa 3:3 military leaders and c leaders,

civilization (1)

Job 28:4 open up a mineshaft far from c,

civilized (1)

Rom 1:14 obligation to those who are c

claim (33)

Exo 22:9 two people c as their own,
Dtr 20:17 You must c the Hittites,
Jos 11:20 so that he could c them all
Jdg 21:11 These are your directions: C
21:11 with a man, and c every male.
21:11 C them for the LORD by
1Sm 15:3 C everything they have for God
15:9 The army refused to c them for
15:9 and weak the army did c
15:18 He said, 'C those sinners,
2Sm 19:43 in the king and a greater c
1Ki 9:20 had not been able to c them
Neh 2:20 You have no property or c or
Job 3:5 darkness and long shadows c
27:5 never give up my c of integrity.
Psa 87:4 Each nation ⌊will c that it⌋
Isa 43:28 I will c Jacob for destruction.
Jer 14:14 They c that I sent them,
50:21 C them for me by killing them
50:26 c them for me by destroying
Mic 4:13 You will c their loot for the
Zec 2:12 The LORD will c Judah as his
Jon 10:33 God. You c to be God,
Act 15:2 spiritual leaders about this c.
21:21 They c that you tell them not to
Rom 3:8 Some slander us and c that
2Co 3:5 in any way to c that we can
Php 3:4 I can c even more.
1Ti 2:10 is proper for women who c
6:21 Although some c to have
Tit 1:16 They c to know God,
Rev 2:9 I also know that those who c to
3:9 They c that they are Jewish,

claimed (54)

Lev 27:21 it will be holy like a field c by
Num 18:14 "Anything in Israel that is c by
21:2 cities because you've c them."
21:3 Hormah [C for Destruction].
Dtr 2:12 of Esau c their land,
2:21 that the Ammonites c their land
2:22 descendants c their land
2:34 all his cities and c them
3:6 We c them all for God,
7:2 because they have been c by
13:15 because they are c by God.
13:17 of the things c for destruction.
Jos 6:17 The city has been c by the
6:18 away from what has been c by
6:18 If you take anything that is c
6:21 They c everything in it for the
7:1 disloyal about the things c by
7:1 took something that had been c
7:11 They have taken what I c for
7:12 Israel are now c for destruction.

Jos 7:12 what I have **c** for myself.
7:13 You have what I **c** for myself,
7:13 you get rid of what I have **c**.
7:15 ⌊stolen⌋ what the LORD has **c**.
10:1 Joshua had captured Ai and **c**
10:28 He **c** them for the LORD by
10:35 He **c** it for the LORD by
10:37 He **c** the city and all its people
10:39 So they **c** them all for the
10:40 He **c** every living creature for
11:11 They **c** everyone for the LORD
11:12 He **c** them for the LORD by
11:21 Joshua **c** them for the LORD by
22:20 act faithlessly with the things **c**
Jdg 1:17 who lived in Zephath and **c**
1:17 Hormah [**C** for Destruction].
1Sm 15:8 But he **c** all the people for God
15:15 But the rest they **c** for God and
15:20 and **c** the Amalekites for God.
15:21 best sheep and cows were **c**
25:31 reason and **c** your own victory.
1Ki 20:42 He was **c** by God and should
2Ki 13:13 Then Jeroboam **c** the throne.
1Ch 2:7 goods that were **c** by God.
4:41 They **c** the Meunites for God
2Ch 32:14 My predecessors **c** and
Isa 34:2 He has **c** them for destruction.
34:5 the people I've **c** for destruction.
Jon 19:7 law he must die because he **c**
Act 5:36 He **c** that he was important,
6:1 The Greek-speaking Jews **c**
8:9 He **c** that he was great.
13:6 He was an astrologer who **c** to
25:19 But Paul **c** that Jesus is alive.

claiming (4)

Gen 26:20 herders, **c**, "This water is ours!"
Dtr 13:1 One of your people, **c** to be a
Rom 1:22 While **c** to be wise,
2Th 2:4 God's temple and **c** to be God.

claims (6)

Psa 87:6 "Every race ⌊**c** that it⌋ was
Ecc 8:17 a wise person **c** to know,
Jon 19:12 Anyone who **c** to be a king is
2Th 2:2 when someone **c** that we said
1Ti 6:20 discussions and the **c**
Jas 2:14 good does it do if someone **c**

clap (7)

Psa 47:1 **C** your hands, all you people.
98:8 Let the rivers **c** their hands and
Isa 55:12 all the trees will **c** their hands.
Eze 6:11 **C** your hands, stomp your feet,
21:14 **C** your hands! Let the sword
21:17 I will also **c** my hands and rest
Nah 3:19 about you will **c** their hands.

clapped (3)

Num 24:10 He **c** his hands and said,
2Ki 11:12 As the guards **c** their hands,
Eze 25:6 You **c** your hands and stomped

claps (2)

Job 27:23 It **c** its hands over him.
34:37 He **c** his hands to insult us.

clarify (1)

Act 21:25 ⌊To **c** this matter⌋ we have

clashing (1)

1Co 13:1 I am a loud gong or a **c** cymbal.

class (1)

2Co 10:12 put ourselves in the same **c**

classes (3)

1Sm 2:36 to one of the priestly **c** so that
2Ki 25:26 Then people of all **c** and the
1Co 1:26 or in the upper social **c**.

classified (2)

1Ki 4:33 He described and **c** trees—
4:33 He described and **c** animals,

clatter (1)

Jdg 5:28 I hear the **c** of his chariots?"

Claudia (1)

2Ti 4:21 Eubulus, Pudens, Linus, **C** and

Claudius (2)

Act 11:28 while **C** was emperor.
18:2 Italy because **C** had ordered all

Claudius Lysias (1)

Act 23:26 **C** sends greetings to Your

claws (2)

Dan 4:33 nails grew as long as birds' **c**.
7:19 had iron teeth and bronze **c**.

clay (33)

Lev 14:5 over a **c** bowl containing fresh
14:50 over a **c** bowl containing fresh
Job 4:19 who live in **c** houses that have
10:9 that you made me out of **c**
33:6 was formed from a piece of **c**.
38:14 The earth changes like **c**
Psa 40:2 out of the mud and **c**.
Pro 26:23 ⌊Like⌋ a **c** pot covered with
Isa 29:16 the potter no better than his **c**?
41:25 were treading on **c** like a potter.
45:9 Does the **c** ask the one who
64:8 We are the **c**, and you are our
Jer 18:4 Whenever a **c** pot he was
18:4 he would rework it into a new **c**
18:6 you as this potter does with **c**?
18:6 you are like the **c** in the potter's
19:1 Go and buy a **c** jar from a
32:14 Put them in a **c** jar so that they
Lam 4:2 are now treated like **c** pots,
Eze 4:1 take **c**, put it in front of you,
Dan 2:33 partly of iron and partly of **c**.
2:35 Then all at once, the iron, **c**,
2:41 They were partly potters' **c** and
2:41 iron was mixed with **c**.
2:42 were partly iron and partly **c**.
2:43 iron was mixed with **c**.
2:43 more than iron can mix with **c**.
2:45 It smashed the iron, bronze, **c**,
Nah 3:14 the claypits and trample the **c**!
Rom 9:21 whatever he wants with his **c**.
9:21 use from the same lump of **c**.
2Co 4:7 Our bodies are made of **c**,
2Ti 2:20 those made of wood and **c**.

claypits (1)

Nah 3:14 Step into the **c** and trample the

clean (173)

Gen 7:2 every kind of **c** animal (a male
7:8 **C** and unclean animals,
8:20 of each type of **c** animal
8:20 type of clean animal and **c** bird.
35:2 until you are ritually **c**,
Lev 4:12 to a **c** place outside the camp
6:11 He will take the ashes to a **c**
7:19 Anyone who is **c** may eat from
10:10 what is **c** and what is unclean.
10:14 may eat them in a **c** place
11:32 Then it will be **c** ⌊again⌋.
11:36 holding water will remain **c**.
11:37 is to be planted, the seed is **c**.
11:47 between **c** and unclean,
12:4 to be made **c** from her bleeding.
12:4 needed to make her **c** are over.
12:5 to be made **c** from her bleeding.
12:6 needed to make her **c** are over,
12:7 Then she will be **c** from her
12:8 and she will be **c**."
13:6 the priest must declare him **c**.
13:6 wash his clothes and will be **c**.
13:7 to the priest to be declared **c**,
13:13 declare the diseased person **c**.
13:13 turned white. The person is **c**.
13:17 declare the diseased person **c**.
13:17 person clean. He is **c**.
13:23 The priest must declare him **c**.
13:28 The priest must declare him **c**,
Lev 13:34 the priest must declare him **c**.
13:34 his clothes, he will be **c**.
13:35 person has been declared **c**,
13:37 The person is **c**, so the priest
13:37 the priest must declare him **c**.
13:39 on the skin. The person is **c**.
13:40 "If a man loses his hair, he is **c**,
13:41 on the front of his head, he is **c**,
13:58 wash it again, and it will be **c**.
13:59 leather article is **c** or unclean."
14:2 for making a person **c** after
14:4 **c** birds, some cedar wood,
14:7 and will declare that person **c**.
14:8 Then he will be **c**.
14:9 Then he will be **c**.
14:11 will declare him **c** must bring
14:20 had the skin disease will be **c**.
14:48 must declare the house **c**.
14:49 use them to make the house **c**.
14:52 red yarn to make the house **c**.
14:53 for the house, and it will be **c**.
14:57 distinguish between what is **c**
15:8 spits on anyone who is **c**,
15:13 Then he will be **c**.
15:28 After that, she will be **c**.
16:30 with the LORD to make you **c**.
16:30 Then you will be **c** from all
17:15 Then they will be **c**.
20:25 Separate **c** and unclean
22:4 the holy offerings until he is **c**.
22:7 the sun has set, he will be **c**.
Num 6:9 head in order to be declared **c**.
8:6 Israelites, and make them **c**.
8:7 you must do to make them **c**:
8:7 Then they will be **c**.
8:15 "Once you have made them **c**
8:21 them in order to make them **c**.
9:13 But if you are **c** and not on a
18:11 who is **c** may eat them.
18:13 household who is **c** may eat it.
19:9 "A man who is **c** will collect
19:9 put them in a **c** place outside
19:12 Then he will be **c**.
19:12 seventh day, he will not be **c**.
19:18 A person who is **c** will take a
19:19 A person who is **c** will sprinkle
19:19 On the seventh day the **c**
19:19 in the evening they will be **c**.
31:23 fire in order to make it **c**.
31:24 your clothes, and you will be **c**.
Dtr 12:15 **C** and unclean people may eat
12:22 **C** and unclean people may eat
14:11 You may eat any **c** bird.
14:20 of⌋ flying creature that is **c**.
15:22 **C** and unclean people may eat
2Sm 22:21 because my hands are **c**.
22:25 he can see that I am **c**.
2Ki 5:10 skin will be healthy and **c**."
5:12 I wash in them and be **c**?"
5:13 'Wash and be **c**'?"
1Ch 23:28 that all the holy things were **c**,
2Ch 13:11 rows of bread on the **c** table.
29:15 entered the temple to make it **c**.
29:16 the LORD's temple to make it **c**.
29:18 all of the LORD's temple **c**.
30:17 lambs for all who weren't **c**
30:18 had not made themselves **c**.
30:19 those who are not **c** as required
34:3 and Jerusalem **c** by destroying
34:5 made Judah and Jerusalem **c**.
34:8 the land and the temple **c**,
Ezr 6:20 all of them were ⌊now⌋ **c**.
Job 14:4 person could become **c**!
17:9 with **c** hands grows stronger.
33:9 I'm **c**; I have no sin.
Psa 18:20 because my hands are **c**.
18:24 can see that my hands are **c**.
24:4 ⌊The one who⌋ has **c** hands
51:7 with hyssop, and I will be **c**.
51:10 Create a **c** heart in me,
Ecc 9:2 wicked, or good, **c** or unclean,
9:8 Always wear **c** clothes,
Isa 1:16 Become **c**! Get your evil deeds
4:4 He will **c** bloodstains from
28:8 There isn't a **c** place left.
66:20 their grain offerings in **c** dishes

Jer 13:27 Will you ever be **c**?"
Eze 16:4 with water to make you **c**.
22:24 You have not been made **c**.
22:26 difference between what is **c**
24:12 myself out trying to **c** this pot.
24:13 I tried to **c** you of your filthy
24:13 but you wouldn't **c** yourself
24:13 You will never be **c** until I
34:18 You drink **c** water.
36:25 I will sprinkle **c** water on you
36:25 on you and make you **c** instead
39:12 months to make the land **c**.
39:14 through the land and make it **c**.
44:23 difference between what is **c**
44:26 After a priest is made **c**,
Zec 3:5 "Put a **c** turban on his head."
3:5 They put a **c** turban on his
Mat 3:12 and he will **c** up his threshing
8:2 you can make me **c**."
8:3 So be **c**!" Immediately, his skin
8:3 went away, and he was **c**.
8:4 proof to people that you are **c**."
11:5 with skin diseases are made **c**,
12:44 swept **c**, and in order.
23:25 You **c** the outside of cups and
23:26 First **c** the inside of the cups
23:26 that the outside may also be **c**.
27:59 wrapped it in a **c** linen cloth.
Mar 1:40 you can make me **c**."
1:41 "I'm willing. So be **c**!"
1:42 went away, and he was **c**.
1:44 proof to people that you are **c**."
Luk 2:22 make a mother **c** had passed,
3:17 his hand to **c** up his threshing
5:12 you can make me **c**."
5:13 So be **c**!" Immediately, his skin
5:14 proof to people that you are **c**."
7:22 with skin diseases are made **c**,
11:25 the house swept **c** and in order.
11:39 "You Pharisees **c** the outside
11:41 everything will be **c** for you.
17:14 they were made **c**.
17:17 "Weren't ten men made **c**?
Jon 13:10 have washed are completely **c**.
13:10 of you, except for one, are **c**."
13:11 of you, except for one, are **c**.")
15:3 "You are already **c** because of
Act 10:15 God has made **c** are impure."
11:9 God has made **c** are impure.'
Tit 1:15 Everything is **c** to those who
1:15 is clean to those who are **c**.
1:15 But nothing is **c** to corrupt
Heb 9:13 made their bodies holy and **c**.
10:22 been washed with **c** water.
Jas 3:11 Do **c** and polluted water flow
4:8 **C** up your lives, you sinners,
Rev 3:4 who have kept their clothes **c**.
15:6 out of the temple wearing **c**,

cleaned (1)

Luk 10:34 went to him, and **c** and

cleanse (19)

Lev 16:19 he will **c** it and declare it holy.
Jos 22:17 Didn't we **c** ourselves from it?
Neh 13:9 Then I told them to **c** the rooms,
13:22 Then I told the Levites to **c**
Job 1:5 in order to **c** them from sin.
9:30 with lye soap and **c** my hands
Psa 51:2 and **c** me from my sin.
Pro 20:30 beatings **c** away wickedness.
20:30 beatings **c** the innermost being.
Isa 52:15 He will **c** many nations ⌊with
Jer 33:8 I will **c** them from all the sins
Eze 36:25 Then I will **c** you from all your
36:33 On the day that I **c** you from all
37:23 I will **c** them so that they will
39:16 In this way they will **c** the land.'
Mat 10:8 **c** those with skin diseases,
2Co 7:1 we need to **c** ourselves from
Tit 2:14 us free from every sin and to **c**
Heb 9:22 used to **c** almost everything,

cleansed (29)

Lev 8:15 all around with his finger and **c**
14:7 seven times on the one to be **c**
14:8 "The one to be **c** must wash
14:14 the right foot of the one to be **c**.
14:17 the right foot of the one to be **c**.
14:18 on the head of the one to be **c**.
14:19 is being **c** from his impurity.
14:21 "But if the one to be **c** is poor
14:25 the right foot of the one to be **c**.
14:28 the right foot of the one to be **c**.
14:29 on the head of the one to be **c**
14:30 Then the one to be **c** must take
14:31 for the one who is being **c**.
15:13 must wait seven days to be **c**.
2Sm 11:4 (She had just **c** herself after her
Ezr 6:20 and Levites had **c** themselves,
Neh 12:30 and the Levites **c** themselves.
12:30 Then they **c** the people,
13:30 So I **c** them from everything
Pro 20:9 I'm **c** from my sin"?
Isa 1:6 They haven't been **c**,
Act 15:9 He has **c** non-Jewish people
15:9 faith as he has **c** us Jews.
Heb 1:3 After he had **c** people from their
9:14 and **c** our consciences from
9:23 had to be **c** by these sacrifices.
9:23 had to be **c** by better sacrifices.
10:2 would have been **c** once
2Pe 1:9 that you were **c** from your past

cleanses (3)

Jer 4:11 be a wind that winnows or **c**.
1Jn 1:7 the blood of his Son Jesus **c**
1:9 he forgives them and **c** us from

cleansing (6)

Lev 14:4 a hyssop sprig to use for the **c**.
14:23 them to the priest for his **c** at
14:32 afford what is needed for his **c**."
Neh 12:45 what needed to be done for **c**.
Mal 3:2 purifying fire and like a **c** soap.
Eph 5:26 to make the church holy by **c** it,

clear (63)

Gen 20:5 and with a **c** conscience."
20:6 did this with a **c** conscience,"
Exo 24:10 made out of sapphire as **c**
Lev 26:10 You will **c** out old food
Num 24:3 the man whose eyesight is **c**.
24:15 the man whose eyesight is **c**.
Jos 17:15 **C** ground for yourselves there
17:18 so you will have to **c** it.
Rut 3:4 He will make it **c** what you
2Sm 19:6 Today, you have made it **c** that
1Ch 28:19 the details of the plan **c** to me."
Pro 8:9 All of it is **c** to a person who
Isa 40:3 "**C** a way for the LORD.
43:19 I will **c** a way in the desert.
62:10 **C** away the stones!
Eze 32:14 Then I will make its water **c**
Hab 2:2 Make it **c** on tablets so that
Mal 3:1 and he will **c** the way ahead of
Luk 1:66 It was **c** that the Lord was with
Act 23:1 me a perfectly **c** conscience."
24:16 best to have a **c** conscience
Rom 1:19 can be known about God is **c**
1:19 he has made it **c** to them.
14:7 It's **c** that we don't live to honor
1Co 1:11 Chloe's family have made it **c**
4:4 I have a **c** conscience,
7:31 It is **c** that this world in its
9:26 So I run — but not without a **c**
11:19 exist in order to make it **c** who
14:8 trumpet doesn't sound a **c** call,
2Co 1:12 proud that our conscience is **c**.
2:14 God uses us to make **c** what it
3:3 It's **c** that you are Christ's letter,
7:11 You were ready to **c**
11:6 Timothy and I have made this **c**
12:10 It's **c** that when I'm weak,
Gal 6:13 It's **c** that not even those who
Php 1:13 As a result, it has become **c** to
Col 4:4 this mystery as **c** as possible.
1Ti 1:5 from a **c** conscience,
1:18 faith and with a **c** conscience
3:9 They must have **c**
2Ti 1:3 whom I serve with a **c**
4:5 But you must keep a **c** head in
Heb 6:17 wanted to make this perfectly **c**
7:15 This became **c** when a
9:9 the worshiper a **c** conscience.
11:14 things make it **c** that they are
13:18 sure that our consciences are **c**
Jas 4:8 you sinners, and **c** your minds,
1Pe 1:13 your minds must be **c**
3:16 Keep your conscience **c**.
3:21 to God for a **c** conscience.
4:7 and keep your minds **c** so that
5:8 Keep your mind **c**,
2Pe 1:14 Christ has made that **c** to me.
1Jn 2:19 But by leaving they made it **c**
3:2 will be isn't completely **c** yet.
Rev 4:6 a sea of glass as **c** as crystal.
21:11 gray quartz, as **c** as crystal.
21:18 of pure gold, as **c** as glass.
21:21 of pure gold, as **c** as glass.
22:1 water of life, as **c** as crystal.

cleared (6)

Gen 20:16 You're completely **c**."
Neh 13:19 of Jerusalem were **c** of traffic,
Job 26:13 With his wind the sky was **c**.
37:21 and **c** those clouds away.
Psa 78:50 He **c** a path for his anger.
80:9 You **c** the ground for it so that it

Clement (1)

Php 4:3 the Good News along with **C**

Cleopas (1)

Luk 24:18 One of them, **C**, replied,

clerk (1)

Act 19:35 The city **c** finally quieted the

clever (17)

Gen 3:1 The snake was more **c** than all
1Sm 23:22 I'm told he's very **c**.
2Sm 13:3 Jonadab was a very **c** man.
14:2 to get a **c** woman from there.
20:16 Then a **c** woman called from
20:22 all the people with her **c** plan.
22:27 with devious people you are **c**.
Psa 18:26 with devious people you are **c**.
Pro 1:6 a proverb and a **c** saying,
Isa 5:21 consider themselves to be **c**.
10:13 because I am so **c**.
Hab 2:6 directing **c** sayings and riddles
Luk 16:8 manager for being so **c**.
16:8 Worldly people are more **c** than
2Co 12:16 Was I a **c** person who trapped
Eph 4:14 use cunning and **c** strategies
2Pe 1:16 message on **c** myths that we

cleverly (1)

Dan 8:25 He will **c** use his power to

cleverness (1)

1Co 3:19 catches the wise in their **c**."

cliff (18)

Exo 33:21 Stand by this rocky **c**.
33:22 put you in a crevice in the **c**
Jdg 15:8 live in a cave in the **c** at Etam.
15:11 to the cave in the **c** at Etam.
15:13 brought him back from the **c**.
1Sm 14:4 There was a **c** on each side of
14:4 name of one ⌊**c**⌋ was Bozez,
14:5 One **c** stood like a pillar on the
14:13 Jonathan climbed up ⌊the **c**⌋,
2Ch 25:12 took them to the top of a **c**,
25:12 off the top of the **c** so that they
Job 39:28 It perches for the night on a **c**.
Psa 141:6 their judges are thrown off a **c**,
Mat 8:32 herd rushed down the **c** into
Mar 5:13 pigs rushed down the **c** into
Luk 4:29 city was built on a hill with a **c**.
4:29 and led him to the **c**.
8:33 the herd rushed down the **c** into

cliffs (10)

Num 23:9 them from the top of rocky **c**,
Sos 2:14 in the secret places of the **c**,
Isa 2:21 rocks and into cracks in the **c**

Isa 7:19 in the cracks in the **c**,
Jer 48:28 Live among the **c**. Be like doves
49:16 You live on rocky **c** and
51:25 against you, roll you off the **c**,
Eze 38:20 the **c** will crumble,
Oba 1:3 You live on rocky **c**.
Nah 1:6 fire and smashes the rocky **c**.

climb (5)

Psa 139:9 If I **c** upward on the rays of the
Sos 7:8 I thought, "I will **c** the palm tree
Jer 4:29 into the thickets and **c** among
Joe 2:7 They **c** walls like soldiers.
2:9 They **c** into houses.

climbed (4)

Gen 49:4 and you **c** into your father's
49:4 He **c** up on my couch.
1Sm 14:13 Jonathan **c** up ⌊the cliff⌋,
Luk 19:4 So Zacchaeus ran ahead and **c**

climbing (1)

Gen 49:22 with branches **c** over a wall.

climbs (3)

Isa 24:18 Whoever **c** out of that pit will
Jer 48:44 Whoever **c** out of the pit will be
Jon 10:1 pen through the gate but **c**

cling (12)

Dtr 28:60 and they will **c** to you.
2Ki 5:27 Naaman's skin disease will **c**
Job 8:17 They **c** to a stone house.
27:6 I **c** to my righteousness and
Psa 25:10 mercy and truth for those who **c**
31:6 I hate those who **c** to false
44:25 Our bodies **c** to the ground.
Pro 3:18 Those who **c** to it are blessed.
4:4 "**C** to my words
4:13 **C** to discipline. Do not relax
Jer 8:5 They still **c** to deceit.
13:11 entire nation of Judah **c** to me,"

clings (4)

Job 17:9 Yet, the righteous person **c** to
38:38 clumps and the soil **c** together?
Psa 63:8 My soul **c** to you. Your right
Jer 13:11 As a belt **c** to a person's waist,

Clopas (1)

Jon 19:25 Mary (the wife of **C**),

close (73)

Gen 46:4 Joseph will **c** your eyes
48:10 So Joseph brought his sons **c**
48:13 and brought them **c** to him.
Exo 3:16 He said, "I have paid **c**
21:8 back by one of her **c** relatives.
25:27 The rings are to be **c** to the rim.
28:27 This will be **c** to the seam just
37:14 The rings were put **c** to the rim
39:20 This was **c** to the seam just
Lev 14:38 the door of the house and **c** up
20:19 with a **c** relative must
21:3 sister who is still **c** to you.
Dtr 28:2 will come to you and stay **c**
28:15 come to you and stay **c** to you:
28:45 will pursue you and stay **c**
Jos 2:5 the gate was just about to **c**,
Jdg 1:17 of Simeon, their **c** relatives.
20:23 war against our **c** relatives,
20:28 war against our **c** relatives,
21:6 felt sorry for their **c** relatives,
Rut 2:20 He is a **c** relative, one of those
3:9 you are a **c** relative who can
3:12 It is true that I am a **c** relative of
2Sm 11:20 'Why did you go so **c** to the
11:21 Why did you go so **c** to the
12:11 give them to someone **c** to you.
2Ki 4:4 Then **c** the door behind you
6:32 messenger comes, **c** the door.
Ezr 4:12 They are **c** to finishing the
Neh 1:6 Open your eyes, and pay **c**
6:10 and **c** the temple doors.
Job 15:23 that his ruin is **c** at hand.
24:1 Why don't those who are **c** to
32:12 I've paid **c** attention to you,
33:22 Their lives come **c** to those
41:16 One is so **c** to the other that
Psa 10:17 You pay **c** attention to them
23:6 and mercy will stay **c**
40:9 I will not **c** my lips.
69:15 or the pit **c** its mouth over me.
69:18 Come **c**, and defend my soul.
119:25 I am **c** to death. Give me a new
132:4 shut my eyes, or **c** my eyelids
138:6 he sees humble people ⌊**c** up⌋,
148:14 the people who are **c** to him.
Pro 2:2 if you pay **c** attention to
6:4 eyes rest or your eyelids **c**.
23:1 pay **c** attention to what is in
27:23 and pay **c** attention to your
31:27 She keeps a **c** eye on the
Isa 34:1 Come **c**, you nations,
Jer 30:21 and he will come **c** to me.
Lam 3:56 Don't **c** your ears when I cry out
3:57 Be **c** at hand when I call to you.
Eze 40:4 Pay **c** attention to everything
44:5 "Son of man, pay **c** attention.
44:5 Pay **c** attention to everyone
Zep 3:2 It does not draw **c** to its God.
Mat 6:6 go to your room and **c** the door.
Luk 12:33 and moths can't get **c** enough
19:43 wall to surround you and **c** you
22:47 He came **c** to Jesus to kiss
Jon 11:3 your **c** friend is sick."
13:25 Leaning **c** to Jesus,
Act 8:6 The crowds paid **c** attention to
8:29 that carriage, and stay **c** to it."
10:9 way and coming **c** to Joppa,
10:24 relatives and **c** friends together.
13:1 Manaen (a **c** friend of Herod
27:13 raised the anchor and sailed **c**
Jas 4:8 Come **c** to God, and he will
4:8 and he will come **c** to you.
Rev 21:25 They will never **c** because

closed (27)

Gen 2:21 one of the man's ribs and **c** up
7:16 Then the LORD **c** the door
Lev 14:46 house any time it is **c** up will
Jos 2:7 men had left, the gate was **c**.
Jdg 3:23 (He had **c** and locked the doors
20:43 They **c** in on the men of
2Ki 4:5 So she left him and **c** the door
4:33 went into the room, **c** the door,
2Ch 28:24 and **c** the doors to the LORD's
Job 11:20 Their escape route will be **c**.
14:17 My disobedience will be **c** up
17:4 You have **c** their minds so that
41:14 Who can open its **c** mouth?
Psa 27:2 Evildoers **c** in on me to tear me
Ecc 12:4 the doors to the street are **c**,
Isa 29:11 in a book that is **c** and sealed.
44:18 And their minds are **c**,
60:11 They will never be **c** day or
Eze 46:1 courtyard must be **c** during
46:2 must not be **c** until evening.
Mar 3:5 because their minds were **c**.
6:52 Instead, their minds were **c**.)
8:17 Are your minds **c**?
Luk 4:20 Jesus **c** the book, gave it back
Rom 11:7 of the rest of Israel were **c**,
11:25 have become **c** until all
2Co 3:14 their minds became **c**.

close-minded (4)

Isa 6:10 Make these people **c**.
Mat 13:15 These people have become **c**
Jon 12:40 and made them **c** so that their
Act 28:27 These people have become **c**

closer (20)

Gen 18:23 Abraham came **c** and asked,
45:4 "Please come **c** to me,"
Exo 3:5 God said, "Don't come any **c**!
20:21 distance while Moses went **c**
Jos 3:4 Don't come any **c** to them so
Rut 3:12 but there is a relative **c** than I.
1Sm 17:41 was coming **c** and closer to
17:41 coming closer and **c** to David.
17:48 When the Philistine moved **c** in
2Sm 18:25 runner continued to come **c**.
Psa 88:3 my life comes **c** to the grave.
Pro 18:24 friend can stick **c** than family.
Eze 40:3 He brought me **c**. I saw a man
Dan 8:7 I saw it come **c** to the ram.
Amo 6:3 bring the reign of violence **c**.
Luk 9:51 The time was coming **c** for
19:11 was getting **c** to Jerusalem,
19:41 When he came **c** and saw the
Act 7:31 As he went **c** to look at the
Heb 2:1 For this reason we must pay **c**

closes (2)

Pro 17:18 A person without good sense **c**
Luk 13:25 gets up and **c** the door,

closest (14)

1Sm 18:1 became David's **c** friend.
Est 1:14 those **c** to him — Carshena,
Job 19:14 My relatives and my **c** friends
19:19 All my **c** friends are disgusted
Psa 41:9 Even my **c** friend whom I
Pro 2:17 the **c** friend of her youth,
16:28 separates the **c** of friends.
17:9 separates the **c** of friends.
Jer 20:10 All my **c** friends are waiting to
32:7 because as the **c** relative it is
32:8 because the rights of the **c**
Mar 6:36 Send the people to the **c** farms
Luk 9:12 "Send the crowd to the **c**
Jon 1:18 the one who is **c** to the Father's

closing (3)

Neh 8:18 they had a **c** festival assembly
Pro 11:15 but whoever hates the **c** of a
1Co 10:11 living in the **c** days of history.

cloth (35)

Exo 28:4 priest's turban, and a **c** belt.
Num 4:6 will spread a **c** made entirely
4:7 "They will spread a violet **c**
4:8 They will spread a bright red **c**
4:9 "They will take a violet **c** and
4:11 "They will spread a violet **c**
4:11 the gold altar and cover the **c**
4:12 put them in a violet **c**,
4:13 spread a purple **c** over the altar.
Dtr 22:17 parents must spread out the **c**
Jdg 5:30 embroidered **c** for the neck of
1Sm 21:9 It is wrapped in a **c** behind the
2Ch 2:7 purple, dark red, and violet **c**.
2:14 and dark red **c**, and linen.
3:14 and dark red **c** and of linen and
Pro 31:22 ⌊made of⌋ linen and purple **c**.
Eze 16:4 with salt or wrapped in **c**.
27:16 purple **c**, richly woven cloth,
27:16 richly woven **c**, linen, coral,
27:24 purple robes, embroidered **c**,
Mat 9:16 new piece of **c** that will shrink.
27:59 wrapped it in a clean linen **c**.
Mar 2:21 new piece of **c** that will shrink.
2:21 and rip away some of the old **c**,
15:46 had purchased some linen **c**.
15:46 cross and wrapped it in the **c**.
Luk 2:7 She wrapped him in strips of **c**
2:12 an infant wrapped in strips of **c**
5:36 "No one tears a piece of **c** from
5:36 the new **c** will tear the old.
19:20 in a **c** for safekeeping because
Jon 11:44 Strips of **c** were wound around
20:7 He also saw the **c** that had
Rev 18:12 purple **c**, silk, bright red cloth,
18:12 purple cloth, silk, bright red **c**,

clothe (10)

2Ch 6:41 **C** your priests, LORD God,
Job 40:10 **C** yourself in splendor and
Psa 132:9 **C** your priests with
132:16 I will **c** its priests with
132:18 I will **c** his enemies with
Isa 50:3 I **c** the heavens in darkness
51:9 **C** yourself with strength,
52:1 **C** yourself with strength,
Mat 6:30 So how much more will he **c**
Luk 12:28 So how much more will he **c**

clothed (12)

2Ki 19:2 of the priests, **c** in sackcloth,
Job 8:22 hate you will be **c** with shame,
38:9 when I **c** it with clouds and
Psa 30:11 sackcloth and **c** me with joy
35:26 at my expense be **c**
65:6 the one who is **c** with power,
93:1 He is **c** with majesty.
93:1 The LORD has **c** himself;
104:1 You are **c** with splendor and
Isa 37:2 of the priests, **c** in sackcloth,
Eze 23:6 and commanders **c** in purple.
Gal 3:27 have **c** yourselves with Christ.

clothes (329)

Gen 3:7 and made **c** for themselves.
3:21 The LORD God made **c** from
24:53 gold and silver jewelry and **c**
27:15 her older son Esau's good **c**,
27:27 When Isaac smelled his **c**,
28:20 me food to eat and **c** to wear,
35:2 and change your **c**.
37:29 he tore his **c** in grief.
37:34 his grief, Jacob tore his **c**,
38:14 she took off her widow's **c**,
38:19 and put her widow's **c** back on.
39:12 grabbed him by his **c** and said,
39:12 and left his **c** in her hand.
39:13 gone but had left his **c** behind,
39:15 outside and left his **c** with me."
39:16 She kept Joseph's **c** with her
39:18 outside and left his **c** with me."
41:14 had shaved and changed his **c**,
44:13 they tore their **c** in grief.
45:22 each of them a change of **c**,
45:22 of silver and five changes of **c**.
49:11 He will wash his **c** in wine,
Exo 3:22 and gold jewelry and for **c**.
12:34 wrapped up in their **c**.
12:35 and silver jewelry and for **c**.
19:10 Have them wash their **c**
19:14 and they washed their **c**.
20:26 be able to see under your **c**."
21:10 the first wife of food, **c**, or sex.
22:26 your neighbor's **c** as collateral,
22:27 It may be the only **c** he has to
28:2 Make holy **c** for your brother
28:3 this ability — to make Aaron's **c**.
28:3 These **c** will set him apart as
28:4 These are the **c** they will make:
28:4 They will make these holy **c**
28:40 These **c** will give them dignity
28:41 Put these **c** on your brother
29:5 Take the **c**, and put them on
29:21 sprinkle it on Aaron and his **c**
29:21 and on his sons and their **c**.
29:21 and their **c** will be holy.
29:29 "Aaron's holy **c** will belong to
31:10 the special **c** — the holy clothes
31:10 the special clothes — the holy **c**
31:10 for the priest Aaron and the **c**
35:19 the special **c** worn for official
35:19 the holy place — both the holy **c**
35:19 for Aaron the priest and the **c**
35:21 and to make the holy **c**.
39:1 yarn they made special **c** worn
39:1 also made the holy **c** for Aaron.
39:41 the special **c** worn when
39:41 the holy place — both the holy **c**
39:41 for the priest Aaron and the **c**
40:13 Then dress Aaron in the holy **c**,
Lev 6:10 priest must put on his linen **c**,
6:11 Then he will take off these **c**
6:27 If blood gets on someone's **c**,
8:2 the priests' **c**, the anointing oil,
8:30 sprinkled it on Aaron and his **c**
8:30 and on his sons and their **c**.
8:30 Aaron, his **c**, his sons,
8:30 clothes, his sons, and their **c**.
10:6 uncombed or tearing your **c**.
11:25 dead bodies must wash his **c**.
11:28 animals must wash their **c**
11:40 dead body must wash their **c**
11:40 body away will wash their **c**
13:6 The person must wash his **c**
Lev 13:34 When he has washed his **c**,
13:45 skin disease must wear torn **c**
14:8 be cleansed must wash his **c**,
14:9 he must wash his **c** and body.
14:47 in the house must wash his **c**.
15:5 his bed must wash their **c**
15:6 he sat on must wash their **c**
15:7 a discharge must wash their **c**
15:8 he spits on must wash his **c**
15:10 such things must wash their **c**
15:11 he touched must wash his **c**
15:13 He must wash his **c** and his
15:17 Any **c** or any leather with
15:21 her bed must wash their **c**
15:22 she sits on must wash their **c**
15:27 unclean and must wash their **c**
16:4 These are holy **c**. He must
16:23 take off the linen **c** he had put
16:24 place and put on his other **c**.
16:26 goat to Azazel must wash his **c**
16:28 burns them must wash his **c**
16:32 He will put on the holy linen **c**
17:15 animal must wash their **c**
17:16 If they don't wash their **c** and
19:19 Never wear **c** made from two
21:10 the chief priest's **c** is chief over
21:10 uncombed or by tearing his **c**.
Num 8:7 whole bodies and wash their **c**.
8:21 their sins and washed their **c**.
14:6 tore their **c** in despair.
15:38 tassels on the corners of their **c**
19:7 priest must then wash his **c**
19:8 the calf must also wash his **c**
19:10 the cow must also wash his **c**.
19:19 must wash their **c** and bodies,
19:21 uncleanness must wash his **c**.
20:26 Take off Aaron's priestly **c**,
20:28 took off Aaron's priestly **c**
31:20 Do the same for all the **c** and
31:24 the seventh day wash your **c**,
Dtr 8:4 Your **c** didn't wear out,
10:18 and gives them food and **c**.
21:13 and no longer wear the **c** she
22:3 if you find a donkey, some **c**,
22:5 must never wear women's **c**.
22:11 Never wear **c** made of wool
22:12 shawl you wear over your **c**.
24:17 And never take widows' **c** to
29:5 During that time your **c** and
Jos 7:6 of Israel tore their **c** in grief.
9:5 and their **c** were tattered.
9:13 Our **c** and sandals are also
Jdg 3:16 it to his right side under his **c**.
5:30 colorful **c** for Sisera,
5:30 Sisera, colorful, embroidered **c**,
8:26 the purple **c** worn by the kings
11:35 he tore his **c** in grief and said,
14:12 shirts and 30 changes of **c**.
14:19 He took their **c** and gave them
17:10 of silver a year, a set of **c**,
1Sm 4:12 Shiloh that day with his **c** torn
17:39 Saul's sword over his **c**
19:24 He even took off his **c** as he
28:8 himself by putting on other **c**,
2Sm 1:2 His **c** were torn, and he had dirt
1:11 Then David grabbed his own **c**
1:24 you in decorated, red **c**,
1:24 who put gold jewelry on your **c**.
3:31 "Tear your **c**, put on sackcloth,
10:4 cut off their **c** from the waist
12:20 and changed his **c**.
13:31 The king stood up, tore his **c**,
13:31 him with their **c** torn ⌊to show
14:2 and dress in mourning **c**.
15:32 His **c** were torn, and he had dirt
19:24 or washed his **c** from the day
1Ki 11:29 and Ahijah had on new **c**.
21:27 he tore his **c** ⌊in distress⌋ and
2Ki 4:39 He filled his **c** with wild gourds.
5:7 he tore his **c** ⌊in distress⌋.
5:8 the king of Israel had torn his **c**,
5:8 "Why did you tear your **c**?
5:26 How could you accept silver, **c**,
6:30 he tore his **c** ⌊in distress⌋.
6:30 wearing sackcloth under his **c**.
7:8 and **c** they found in that tent.
2Ki 7:15 whole road was littered with **c**
11:14 tore her **c** ⌊in distress⌋,
18:37 went to Hezekiah with their **c**
19:1 he tore his **c** in grief,
22:11 he tore his **c** ⌊in distress⌋.
22:19 You also tore your **c** ⌊in
25:29 no longer wore prison **c**,
1Ch 19:4 cut off their **c** from the waist
2Ch 20:25 lot of goods, **c**, and valuables.
23:13 tore her **c** ⌊in distress⌋,
28:15 the prisoners and gave **c** from
28:15 They provided **c** for them,
34:19 he tore his **c** ⌊in distress⌋.
34:27 tore your **c** ⌊in distress⌋,
Ezr 9:3 I tore my **c** ⌊in distress⌋,
9:5 and with my **c** torn,
Neh 4:23 to me never changed their **c**.
5:13 I brushed off my **c** and said,
9:21 Their **c** didn't wear out,
Est 4:1 he tore his **c** and put on
Job 2:12 them tore his own **c** ⌊in grief⌋.
9:31 and my own **c** would find me
13:28 wineskins, like moth-eaten **c**.
22:6 a loan and strip them of their **c**.
30:18 great strength he grabs my **c**.
31:19 die because he had no **c**
37:17 you whose **c** are hot and
Psa 22:18 my **c** among themselves.
102:26 You will change them like **c**,
Pro 6:27 his lap without burning his **c**?
31:22 Her **c** are ⌊made of⌋ linen and
Ecc 9:8 Always wear clean **c**,
Sos 5:3 I have taken off my **c**!
Isa 3:24 instead of expensive **c**.
4:1 food and provide our own **c**.
32:11 Take off your **c**, walk around
36:22 went to Hezekiah with their **c**
37:1 he tore his **c** in grief,
52:1 Put on your beautiful **c**,
58:7 and cover them with **c** when
59:6 Their webs can't be used for **c**,
59:17 He wears **c** of vengeance.
61:3 and **c** of praise instead of a
61:10 me in the **c** of salvation.
63:1 with his **c** stained bright red?
63:2 Why are your **c** red and your
63:3 Their blood splattered my **c** so
Jer 2:34 and innocent people on your **c**.
13:22 Your **c** have been torn off and
13:26 I will also tear off your **c**,
36:24 show any fear or tear their **c**
38:11 He took rags and torn **c** from
38:12 "Put these rags and torn **c**
41:5 shaved off, their **c** were torn,
52:33 no longer wore prison **c**,
Lam 1:9 own filth ⌊covers⌋ its **c**.
4:5 expensive **c** now pick through
4:14 that no one would touch their **c**.
4:21 drunk and take off all your **c**.
Eze 5:3 wrap them in the hem of your **c**.
16:13 and embroidered **c**.
16:16 You took some of your **c** and
16:18 took off your embroidered **c**
16:39 They will tear off your **c**,
18:7 and he gives **c** to those who
18:16 and he gives **c** to those who
23:26 They will rip off your **c** and
26:16 take off their embroidered **c**.
27:24 they traded for beautiful **c**,
42:14 behind the **c** that they wore
42:14 These **c** are holy. The priests
42:14 The priests must put on other **c**.
44:17 they must wear linen **c**.
44:19 they must take off the **c** that
44:19 They must leave their **c** in the
44:19 and put on other **c** so that they
44:19 from their **c** to the people.
Dan 3:21 They were wearing their **c**,
3:27 their **c** weren't burned,
7:9 His **c** were as white as snow
12:6 in linen **c** who was above
12:7 in linen **c** who was above
Joe 2:13 Tear your hearts, not your **c**.
Amo 2:8 out on **c** taken as security.
Hag 2:12 and he folds it up in his **c**.
2:12 If his **c** touch bread,

Zec 3:3 Joshua was wearing filthy **c**
3:4 "Remove Joshua's filthy **c**.
8:23 nations will take hold of the **c**
14:14 amount of gold, silver, and **c**.
Mat 3:4 John wore **c** made from
6:25 food and the body more than **c**?
6:28 "And why worry about **c**?
6:28 never work or spin yarn for **c**.
6:30 That's the way God **c** the grass
9:20 and touched the edge of his **c**.
9:21 "If I only touch his **c**,
10:10 the trip, a change of **c**, sandals,
11:8 A man dressed in fine **c**?
11:8 Those who wear fine **c** are in
14:36 touch just the edge of his **c**.
14:36 touched his **c** was made well.
17:2 the sun and his **c** as white as
22:11 in the wedding **c** ⌊provided
22:12 proper wedding **c**?' "The
25:36 I needed **c**, and you gave me
25:38 homes or see you in need of **c**
25:43 I needed **c**, and you didn't give
25:44 or as a stranger or in need of **c**
27:28 They took off his **c** and put a
27:31 cape and put his own **c** back
27:35 they divided his **c** among
28:3 and his **c** were as white as
Mar 1:6 John was dressed in **c** made
5:27 in the crowd and touched his **c**.
5:28 "If I can just touch his **c**,
5:30 "Who touched my **c**?"
6:9 not take along a change of **c**.
6:56 them touch the edge of his **c**.
6:56 touched his **c** was made well.
9:3 His **c** became dazzling white,
14:63 The chief priest tore his **c** ⌊in
15:20 cape and put his own **c** back
15:24 Then they divided his **c** among
Luk 7:25 A man dressed in fine **c**?
7:25 Those who wear splendid **c**
8:27 by demons and had not worn **c**
8:44 touched the edge of his **c**,
9:3 food, money, or a change of **c**.
9:29 his **c** became dazzling white.
12:23 and the body is more than **c**.
12:27 never work or spin yarn for **c**.
12:28 That's the way God **c** the grass
12:37 He will change his **c**,
16:19 man who wore expensive **c**.
23:34 the soldiers divided his **c**
24:4 two men in **c** that were as
Jon 13:4 removed his outer **c**,
13:12 their feet and put on his outer **c**,
19:23 they took his **c** and divided
19:24 my **c** among themselves.
20:12 She saw two angels in white **c**.
21:7 he put back on the **c** that he
Act 1:10 in white **c** stood near them.
10:30 a man dressed in radiant **c**
12:21 Herod, wearing his royal **c**,
16:22 Then the officials tore the **c** off
18:6 Paul shook the dust from his **c**
20:33 anyone's silver, gold, or **c**.
2Co 11:27 proper **c** during cold weather.
1Ti 2:9 in appropriate **c** that are modest
2:9 or expensive **c** they wear.
6:8 As long as we have food and **c**,
Heb 1:11 They will all wear out like **c**.
1:12 You will change them like **c**.
Jas 2:2 wearing gold rings and fine **c**;
2:2 is wearing shabby **c**.
2:3 to the man wearing fine **c**
2:15 or a woman, needs **c** or food
5:2 and your **c** have been eaten by
1Pe 3:3 hairstyles, gold jewelry, or **c**.
Rev 3:4 who have kept their **c** clean.
3:4 will walk with me in white **c**
3:5 this way will wear white **c**.
3:18 Buy white **c** from me.
4:4 sat 24 leaders wearing white **c**.
16:15 alert and doesn't lose his **c**.
17:4 The woman wore purple **c**,
17:4 bright red **c**, gold jewelry,
18:16 purple **c**, bright red clothes,
18:16 bright red **c**, gold jewelry,
19:13 He wears **c** dipped in blood,
Rev 19:16 On his **c** and his thigh he has a

clothing (46)

Exo 22:9 a sheep, an article of **c**,
Lev 11:32 It may be a wooden article, **c**,
13:47 "Now about **c** — if there is a
13:47 or red area on a piece of **c**
13:50 the mildew and will put the **c**
13:52 He must burn the piece of **c** or
13:54 to be washed and put the **c**
13:56 tear it out of the **c** or the leather.
13:57 you must burn the **c** or the
13:58 from the woven or knitted **c**
13:59 mildew in **c** that is woven
14:55 that infects **c** or houses
Jos 22:8 bronze, iron, and loads of **c**.
1Sm 27:9 and **c** and returned to Achish.
1Ki 10:25 **c**, weapons, spices, horses,
2Ki 5:5 and 10 sets of **c** with him.
5:22 of silver and two sets of **c**."
5:23 in two bags with two sets of **c**.
2Ch 9:24 **c**, weapons, spices, horses,
Est 4:4 She sent **c** for Mordecai to put
Job 26:6 and Abaddon has no **c**.
27:16 dust and piles up **c** like dirt,
29:14 and it was my **c**. I practiced
38:14 it⌋ stand out like ⌊folds in⌋ **c**.
Psa 22:18 They throw dice for my **c**.
73:6 and acts of violence like **c**.
102:26 They will all wear out like **c**.
109:18 cursing as though it were **c**,
109:19 Let cursing be his **c**,
109:29 disgrace as though it were **c**.
Pro 27:26 ⌊will provide⌋ you with **c**,
31:21 family has a double layer of **c**.
Sos 4:11 The fragrance of your **c** is like
Isa 23:18 plenty of food and expensive **c**.
30:22 away like **c** ruined by stains.
51:6 The earth will wear out like **c**,
51:8 Moths will eat them like **c**.
63:3 so all my **c** has been stained.
Jer 10:9 The **c** for the idols is blue and
Dan 3:21 their clothes, hats, and other **c**.
Hos 5:12 Ephraim as a moth destroys **c**.
Zep 1:8 and all who dress in foreign **c**.
Hag 1:6 You wear **c**, but you never
Zec 3:4 and I will dress you in fine **c**."
Jon 19:24 They threw dice for my **c**."
Act 9:39 the articles of **c** that Dorcas had

cloud (58)

Exo 19:9 to you in a storm **c** so that
19:16 lightning with a heavy **c** over
20:21 to the dark **c** where God was.
24:15 and the **c** covered it.
24:16 For six days the **c** covered it,
24:16 to Moses from inside the **c**.
24:18 Moses entered the **c** as he
34:5 The LORD came down in a **c**
Lev 16:13 The **c** of incense will cover the
Dtr 5:22 a loud voice from the fire, the **c**,
2Sm 22:10 with a dark **c** under his feet.
1Ki 8:10 a **c** filled the LORD's temple.
8:11 couldn't serve because of the **c**.
8:12 said he would live in a dark **c**.
18:44 "A little **c** like a man's hand is
2Ch 5:13 temple was filled with a **c**.
5:14 couldn't serve because of the **c**.
6:1 said he would live in a dark **c**.
Job 3:5 Let a dark **c** hang over it.
7:9 As a **c** fades away and
22:13 from behind a dark **c**?
26:9 by spreading his **c** over it.
30:15 prosperity vanishes like a **c**.
Psa 18:9 with a dark **c** under his feet.
78:14 He guided them by a **c** during
105:39 He spread out a **c** as a
Pro 16:15 is like a **c** bringing spring rain.
Isa 4:5 The LORD will create a **c** of
19:1 is riding on a fast-moving **c**
25:5 by the shadow of a **c**.
44:22 acts disappear like a thick **c**
Lam 2:1 the people of Zion with the **c**
3:44 You covered yourself with a **c**
Eze 1:4 There was an immense **c** with
1:5 In the center of the **c** I saw
Eze 8:11 and a **c** of incense went up.
10:3 A **c** filled the inner courtyard.
10:4 the **c** filled the temple,
38:9 and cover the land like a **c**.
38:16 Israel like a **c** that covers
Mat 17:5 a bright **c** overshadowed them.
17:5 came out of the **c** and said,
Mar 9:7 Then a **c** overshadowed them.
9:7 came out of the **c** and said,
Luk 9:34 a **c** overshadowed them.
9:34 as they went into the **c**.
9:35 came out of the **c** and said,
12:54 "When you see a **c** coming up
21:27 the Son of Man coming in a **c**
Act 1:9 A **c** hid him so that they could
1Co 10:1 left Egypt⌋ were under the **c**,
10:2 with Moses by baptism in the **c**
Rev 10:1 He was dressed in a **c**,
11:12 They went up to heaven in a **c**,
14:14 and there was a white **c**,
14:14 and on the **c** sat someone who
14:15 to the one who sat on the **c**,
14:16 The one who sat on the **c**

clouded (2)

Psa 69:23 Let their vision become **c** so
Rom 11:10 Let their vision become **c** so

clouds (67)

Gen 9:13 I will put my rainbow in the **c** to
9:14 Whenever I form **c** over the
9:14 a rainbow will appear in the **c**.
9:16 the rainbow appears in the **c**,
Dtr 33:26 majesty he rides through the **c**.
Jdg 5:4 the sky poured, the **c** burst,
2Sm 22:12 the dark rain **c** his covering.
23:4 like a morning without **c**,
1Ki 18:45 grew darker with **c** and wind,
Job 20:6 and his head touches the **c**,
22:14 Thick **c** surround him so that
22:14 He walks above the **c**.'
26:8 holds the water in his thick **c**,
26:8 and the **c** don't ⌊even⌋ split
35:5 Observe the **c** high above you.
36:28 which then drips from the **c**.
36:29 understand how **c** spread out
37:11 Yes, he loads the thick **c** with
37:11 his lightning from the **c**.
37:12 He guides the **c** as they churn
37:15 the lightning flash from his **c**?
37:16 Do you know how the **c** drift
37:21 when it's bright among the **c**
37:21 and cleared those **c** away.
38:9 when I clothed it with **c** and
38:9 and wrapped it up in dark **c**,
38:34 Can you call to the **c** and have
38:37 is wise enough to count the **c**
Psa 18:11 the dark rain **c** his covering.
18:12 those rain **c** passed by with
77:17 The **c** poured out water.
78:23 he commanded the **c** above
97:2 **C** and darkness surround him.
104:3 You use the **c** for your chariot.
135:7 He is the one who makes the **c**
147:8 He covers the sky with **c**.
Ecc 11:3 If the **c** are full of rain,
11:4 at the **c** will never harvest.
12:2 ⌊and⌋ the **c** come back with
Sos 3:6 wilderness like **c** of smoke?
Isa 5:6 and I will command the **c** not to
5:30 will be darkened by thick **c**.
9:18 it whirls upward in **c** of smoke.
14:14 I'll go above the top of the **c**.
60:8 these people that fly by like **c**,
Jer 4:13 The enemy comes up like **c**.
10:13 He makes **c** rise from the ends
51:16 He makes **c** rise from the ends
Eze 1:28 looked like a rainbow in the **c**.
30:18 **C** will cover Egypt,
31:3 Its top was among the **c**.
31:10 and its top reached the **c**.
31:14 longer allowed to reach the **c**.
32:7 I will cover the sun with **c**,
Dan 7:13 I saw among the **c** in heaven
Joe 2:2 a day of **c** and overcast skies.
2:30 blood, fire, and **c** of smoke.

Nah 1:3 and c are the dust from his feet.
Zep 1:15 a day of c and overcast skies,
Mat 24:30 the Son of Man coming on the c
26:64 be coming on the c of heaven."
Mar 13:26 see the Son of Man coming in c
14:62 coming with the c of heaven."
Act 2:19 blood, fire, and c of smoke.
1Th 4:17 still alive will be taken in the c
Jud 1:12 They are dry c blown around
Rev 1:7 He is coming in the c.

cloudy (2)

Dtr 4:11 It was dark, c, and gloomy.
Eze 34:12 I will rescue them on a c and

club (4)

2Sm 23:21 Benaiah went to him with a c,
1Ch 11:23 Benaiah went to him with a c,
Pro 25:18 ⌊Like⌋ a c and a sword and a
Jer 51:20 "You are my war c and my

clubs (8)

Job 41:29 It considers c to be like
Eze 39:9 and war c and spears.
Mat 26:47 carrying swords and c was
26:55 come out with swords and c
Mar 14:43 A crowd carrying swords and c
14:48 come out with swords and c
Luk 22:52 out with swords and c as if
2Co 11:25 officials had me beaten with c.

clumps (2)

Job 38:38 when the dirt hardens into c
Psa 65:10 rain⌋ and level their c of soil.

clung (2)

1Ki 2:28 fled to the LORD's tent and c
Psa 119:31 I have c tightly to your written

cluster (1)

Isa 65:8 for new wine in a c of grapes,

clusters (5)

Gen 40:10 Then its c ripened into grapes.
Dtr 32:32 and their c are bitter.
Job 9:9 and the c of stars in the south.
Sos 7:7 and your breasts are like its c.
7:8 May your breasts be like c on

clutches (2)

2Sm 22:6 The c of death had confronted
Psa 18:5 The c of death had confronted

Cnidus (1)

Act 27:7 along the coast of the city of C

coal (2)

2Sm 14:7 the ⌊one⌋ burning c that is left
Isa 6:6 In his hand was a burning c

coals (27)

Gen 22:6 Abraham carried the burning c
22:7 "We have the burning c and the
Lev 10:1 burner and put burning c
16:12 burner full of burning c from
Num 16:7 and put burning c and incense
16:18 put burning c and incense in it,
16:37 out of the fire and scatter the c
16:46 put burning c from the altar and
2Sm 22:9 Glowing c flared up from it.
Job 41:21 Its breath sets c on fire,
Psa 18:8 Glowing c flared up from it.
102:3 My bones burn like hot c.
120:4 arrows and red-hot c.
140:10 Let burning c fall on them.
Pro 6:28 Can anyone walk on red-hot c
26:21 ⌊As⌋ charcoal fuels burning c
Isa 30:14 big enough to carry live c from
44:12 They work them over the c and
44:19 I also baked bread over its c.
47:14 There are no glowing c to keep
54:16 to fan the c into flames
Eze 1:13 like burning c and torches.
10:2 fill your hands with burning c.
10:6 to take burning c from between
10:7 angels and took out some c.

Eze 24:11 Then set the empty pot on the c
Jon 21:9 a fire with a fish lying on the c,

coarse (2)

1Ki 4:22 360 bushels of c flour,
Neh 10:37 bring the best of our c flour,

coast (19)

Gen 49:13 "Zebulun will live by the c.
49:13 He will have ships by the c.
Num 13:29 the Canaanites live along the c
Dtr 1:7 on the whole Mediterranean c
Jos 9:2 Mediterranean c as far as
15:47 as the River of Egypt and the c
1Ki 9:26 the Red Sea c at Ezion Geber
2Ch 8:17 Then Solomon went to the c
Jer 47:7 it to attack Ashkelon and the c.
Eze 25:16 the people that are left on the c.
26:15 The people who live on the c
26:16 Then the princes from the c
26:17 those who lived by the c.
26:18 who live by the c tremble.
Zep 2:7 The c will belong to the faithful
2:11 So every person from every c
Act 27:2 going to stop at ports on the c
27:5 We sailed along the c of the
27:7 difficulties began along the c

coastal (1)

Act 9:35 city of Lydda and the c region

coastland (2)

Isa 20:6 who live on this c will say,
23:2 you inhabitants of the c,

coastlands (12)

Gen 10:5 people of the c spread into their
Isa 24:15 God of Israel along the c.
41:1 silent and listen to me, you c.
41:5 The c have seen him and are
42:4 The c will wait for his
42:10 you c and all who live on them.
42:12 announce his praise on the c.
51:5 The c put their hope in me,
59:18 the people who live on the c.
60:9 the c wait with hope for me.
66:19 and to the distant c who have
Dan 11:18 will turn his attention to the c

coastline (2)

Num 34:6 "The western border is the c of
Jos 15:12 The western border is the c of

coasts (5)

Jer 2:10 Go over to the c of Cyprus,
Eze 27:7 came from the c of Elishah.
27:15 with many people on the c,
27:35 All those who live on the c are
39:6 those who live safely on the c.

coat (32)

Gen 6:14 Make rooms in the ship and c
Dtr 24:12 don't keep the c you took as a
24:13 When he wears his c to bed
Jdg 8:25 So they spread out a c.
1Sm 17:5 and he wore a bronze c of
18:4 Jonathan took off the c he had
1Ki 19:13 he wrapped his face in his c,
19:19 Elijah took off his c and put it
2Ki 2:8 Elijah took his c, rolled it up,
2:13 Then he picked up Elijah's c
2:14 He took the c and struck the
9:13 them immediately took off his c
Pro 25:20 ⌊Like⌋ taking off a c on a cold
Isa 3:6 family and say, "You have a c.
3:7 I don't have any food or a c in
59:17 puts on righteousness like a c
59:17 wraps himself with fury as a c.
Jer 43:12 will put on Egypt as his c as
43:12 as a shepherd puts on his c.
Zec 13:4 a prophet⌋ in a c made of hair.
Mat 5:40 let him have your c too.
9:16 "No one patches an old c with
9:16 it will rip away from the c,
Mar 2:21 "No one patches an old c with
10:50 The blind man threw off his c,

Luk 5:36 a piece of cloth from a new c
5:36 a new coat to patch an old c.
6:29 If someone takes your c,
22:36 should sell his c and buy one.
Act 12:8 "Put your c on, and follow me."
2Ti 4:13 bring the warm c I left with
Heb 1:12 They will be taken off like a c.

coated (1)

Exo 2:3 made of papyrus plants and c

coats (13)

Isa 3:22 fine robes, c, shawls, purses,
Mic 2:8 You take c from those who
Mat 21:7 and the colt and put their c
21:8 of the people spread their c
24:18 not turn back to get their c.
Mar 11:7 to Jesus, put their c on it,
11:8 Many spread their c on the
13:16 not turn back to get their c.
Luk 19:35 to Jesus, put their c on it,
19:36 spread their c on the road.
Act 7:58 The witnesses left their c with
22:20 of his death and guarded the c
22:23 was yelling, taking off their c,

cobra (1)

Psa 58:4 They are like a deaf c that

cobras (2)

Dtr 32:33 the deadly poison of c.
Psa 91:13 You will step on lions and c.

cobras' (1)

Isa 11:8 Infants will play near c holes.

coffin (2)

Gen 50:26 and placed in a c in Egypt.
Luk 7:14 He went up to the open c,

coin (15)

1Sm 2:36 down in front of him to get a c
Pro 18:18 Flipping a c ends quarrels and
Mat 17:27 and you will find a c.
17:27 Give that c to them for you and
22:19 Show me a c used to pay
22:19 They brought him a c.
Mar 12:15 Bring me a c so that I can look
12:16 They brought a c. He said to
Luk 15:8 and look for the c carefully until
15:9 I've found the c that I lost.'
19:16 the c you gave me has earned
19:18 'The c you gave me,
19:20 Here's your c. I've kept it in a
19:24 'Take his c away,
20:24 "Show me a c. Whose face and

coincidence (1)

Est 7:9 with the king, said, "What a c!

coins (14)

Mat 10:9 even copper c in your pockets.
26:15 They offered him 30 silver c.
27:3 He brought the 30 silver c back
27:9 "They took the 30 silver c,
27:10 and used the c to buy a potter's
Mar 12:42 widow dropped in two small c,
Luk 7:41 owed him five hundred silver c,
10:35 Samaritan took out two silver c
15:8 "Suppose a woman has ten c
19:13 servants and gave them ten c.
19:25 he already has ten c.'
21:2 widow drop in two small c.
Jon 2:15 dumped the moneychangers' c
Act 19:19 were worth 50,000 silver c.

cold (19)

Gen 8:22 c and heat, summer and winter,
31:40 the day and the c at night wore
Neh 9:29 they gave you the c shoulder,
Job 24:7 without a covering from the c.
37:9 It is c because of the strong
Psa 119:70 hearts are c and insensitive,
Pro 25:20 ⌊Like⌋ taking off a coat on a c
25:25 ⌊Like⌋ c water to a thirsty soul,
Jer 36:30 heat of day and the c of night.

Nah 3:17 on the fences when it is c.
Zec 14:6 be neither heat nor freezing c.
Mat 10:42 followers a cup of c water
24:12 most people's love will grow c.
Jon 18:18 themselves because it was c.
Act 28:2 it because of the rain and the c.
2Co 11:27 clothes during c weather.
Rev 3:15 that you are neither c nor hot.
3:15 I wish you were c or hot.
3:16 are lukewarm and not hot or c,

Col Hozeh (1)

Neh 11:5 who was the son of C,

Col Hozeh's (1)

Neh 3:15 Shallun, C's son, the official in

collapse (5)

Jos 6:5 The wall around the city will c.
Neh 4:3 make their stone wall c if
Psa 10:10 They c, and they fall under
Nah 3:19 There is no relief for your c.
Mat 7:25 But it did not c, because its

collapsed (7)

Exo 23:5 hates you has c under its load,
Jos 6:20 the rams' horns, and the wall c.
Jdg 7:13 that tent so hard that the tent c,
19:26 where her husband was and c.
Mat 7:27 It c, and the result was a total
Luk 6:49 quickly c and was destroyed."
Rev 11:13 One-tenth of the city c,

collapses (1)

Job 8:15 If one leans on his house, it c.

collar (5)

Exo 28:32 (like a leather c) all around
39:23 (like a leather c) all around
Job 30:18 seizes me by the c of my robe.
Psa 105:18 cut into his neck with an iron c.
133:2 running over the c of his robes.

collateral (1)

Exo 22:26 of your neighbor's clothes as c,

collect (25)

Gen 41:35 Have them c all the food during
Lev 25:36 Don't c interest or make any
25:37 Never c any kind of interest on
Num 19:9 "A man who is clean will c the
31:28 C a tax for the LORD.
31:28 served in the war c one out
31:29 C all these things from the
31:30 c one out of every 50 things.
Dtr 15:2 don't c payment on the debt
15:3 but don't c payment on the debt
2Ki 12:4 Joash told the priests, "⌊C⌋ all
12:10 and the chief priest would c
2Ch 24:5 and c money throughout Israel
Neh 10:31 plant the fields or c any debts.
10:37 are the ones who c one-tenth
10:38 Levites when they c the tenth.
Psa 15:5 The one who does not c
Eze 22:12 You c interest and make
Amo 3:10 Those who c profits in their
Mat 17:25 do the kings of the world c fees
21:34 to the workers to c his share
Mar 12:2 to the workers to c from them
Luk 3:13 He told them, "Don't c more
3:13 than you are ordered to c."
Heb 7:5 The priests c it from their own

collected (16)

Gen 41:48 Joseph c all the food grown in
47:14 Joseph c all the money that
Exo 38:25 The silver c when the census
Num 3:50 The silver Moses c for the
19:10 The person who c the ashes
31:47 Israelites' half Moses c one out
2Ki 22:4 have c from the people.
2Ch 24:11 so they c a lot of money.
28:24 Ahaz c the utensils in God's
34:9 Levite doorkeepers had c from
Ecc 12:11 Their c sayings are like nails
Mic 1:7 Samaria c its wages for being
Zec 14:14 surrounding nations will be c,
Luk 19:23 I could have c it with interest.'
1Co 16:1 concerning the money to be c
16:2 have to be c when I come.

collecting (2)

2Ch 20:25 spent three days c the loot.
Ecc 2:26 of gathering and c ⌊wealth⌋.

collection (5)

Isa 57:13 let your c of idols save you.
Rom 15:26 have decided to take up a c
15:28 When the c is completed and I
2Co 8:10 not only willing ⌊to take a c⌋
9:2 send their c⌋ since last year,"

collector (7)

Mat 10:3 and Matthew the tax c;
18:17 you would a heathen or a tax c.
Luk 5:27 He saw a tax c named Levi
18:10 and the other was a tax c.
18:11 I'm not even like this tax c.
18:13 "But the tax c was standing at
18:14 "I can guarantee that this tax c

collectors (18)

Isa 33:18 Where are the tax c?
Mat 5:46 Even the tax c do that!
9:10 Many tax c and sinners came
9:11 eat with tax c and sinners?"
11:19 a friend of tax c and sinners!'
17:24 the c of the temple tax came to
21:31 Tax c and prostitutes are going
21:32 The tax c and prostitutes
Mar 2:15 Many tax c and sinners who
2:16 eating with sinners and tax c,
2:16 he eat with tax c and sinners?"
Luk 3:12 Some tax c came to be
5:29 A huge crowd of tax c and
5:30 drink with tax c and sinners?"
7:29 "All the people, including tax c,
7:34 a friend of tax c and sinners!'
15:1 All the tax c and sinners came
19:2 He was the director of tax c,

collects (5)

Job 27:16 Though he c silver like dust
36:27 He c drops of water.
Psa 41:6 His heart c gossip.
Pro 28:8 loans and interest c them
Hab 2:5 He c all the people to himself.

cologne (2)

Sos 1:3 better than the fragrance of c.
1:3 (C should be named after you.)

colony (1)

Act 16:12 and it is a Roman c.

color (1)

Jer 13:23 Can Ethiopians change the c of

colored (2)

Exo 28:39 be embroidered with c yarn.
Pro 7:16 with c sheets of Egyptian linen.

colorful (8)

Jdg 5:30 c clothes for Sisera,
5:30 Sisera, c, embroidered clothes,
5:30 and two pieces of c,
Psa 45:14 Wearing a c gown,
Jer 12:9 My people are like a c bird of
Eze 16:16 and made your worship sites c.
17:3 wings with long, c feathers.
Luk 23:11 They put a c robe on him and

colors (1)

1Ch 29:2 stones of different c,

Colossae (1)

Col 1:2 with Christ in the city of C.

colt (6)

Gen 49:11 his c to the best vine.
Zec 9:9 on a c, a young pack animal.
Mat 21:2 tied there and a c with it.
Mat 21:5 on a c, a young pack animal.'"
21:7 brought the donkey and the c
Jon 12:15 He is riding on a donkey's c."

column (42)

Gen 19:26 back and turned into a c of salt.
Exo 13:21 went ahead of them in a c
13:21 he went ahead of them in a c
13:22 The c of smoke was always in
13:22 The c of fire was always there
14:19 So the c of smoke moved from
14:20 The ⌊c of⌋ smoke was there
14:24 LORD looked down from the c
16:10 the LORD in the ⌊c of⌋ smoke.
33:9 the c of smoke would come
33:10 When all the people saw the c
40:34 Then the ⌊c of⌋ smoke
40:36 whenever the ⌊c of⌋ smoke
40:37 But if the c didn't move,
40:38 So the LORD's c stayed over
40:38 the c throughout their travels.
Num 9:15 the ⌊c of⌋ smoke covered it.
9:18 As long as the ⌊c of⌋ smoke
9:21 Sometimes the ⌊c of⌋ smoke
9:22 as long as the ⌊c of⌋ smoke
10:11 the ⌊c of⌋ smoke left the tent of
10:12 until the ⌊c of⌋ smoke stopped
10:34 The LORD's ⌊c of⌋ smoke was
11:25 down in the ⌊c of⌋ smoke
12:5 the LORD came down in the c
14:14 that your c of smoke stays over
14:14 you go ahead of them in a c
14:14 of smoke by day and in a c
Dtr 1:33 He appeared in a c of fire at
1:33 of fire at night and in a c
4:36 him speak from the c of fire.
31:15 Then the LORD appeared in a c
Jdg 16:29 With his right hand on one c
20:38 that they would make a big c
20:40 But when the c of smoke
1Sm 13:17 One c turned onto the road to
13:18 Another c turned onto the road
Neh 9:12 led them during the day by a c
9:12 and during the night by a c
9:19 The c of smoke didn't leave
9:19 The c of fire didn't leave them
Psa 99:7 to them from a c of smoke.

columns (9)

Jdg 16:25 him stand between two c.
16:26 Let me touch the c on which
16:29 Samson felt the two middle c
1Sm 13:17 the Philistine camp in three c.
Psa 144:12 be like stately c that adorn
Sos 5:15 His legs are c of marble set on
Jer 36:23 As Jehudi read three or four c,
Zep 2:14 herons will nest on top of its c.
Rev 10:1 and his feet were like c of fire.

comb (1)

Mat 6:17 wash your face and c your hair.

combat (9)

Exo 22:24 angry and have you killed in c.
Jdg 4:16 whole army was killed in c.
2Sm 10:9 for c against the Arameans.
10:10 for c against the Ammonites.
2Ki 6:22 you take captive in c?
1Ch 19:10 for c against the Arameans.
19:11 for c against the Ammonites.
Sos 3:8 swords, experienced in c.
Isa 3:25 your warriors will die in c.

combined (4)

Jos 10:5 and Eglon c their armies.
Jdg 6:33 and Kedem c their armies,
2Ch 3:11 The c length of the angels'
3:12 So the angels' c wingspan was

comfort (62)

Gen 37:35 and daughters came to c him,
2Sm 10:2 servants to c Hanun after his
10:3 because he sent men to c you?
1Ch 7:22 his brothers tried to c him.
19:2 to c Hanun after his
19:2 Ammonite territory to c Nahash

1Ch 19:3 because he sent men to **c** you?
Job 2:11 with Job and **c** him.
6:10 Then I would still have **c**.
7:13 'My couch may give me **c**.
15:11 Isn't God's **c** enough for you,
21:2 let that be the **c** you offer me.
21:34 How can you **c** me with this
36:11 prosperity and their years in **c**.
Psa 69:20 I looked for people to **c** me,
71:21 You **c** me and make me greater
119:50 This is my **c** in my misery:
119:52 and I found **c** ⌊in them⌋.
119:76 Let your mercy **c** me as you
119:82 I ask, "When will you **c** me?"
Ecc 4:1 No one can **c** them.
4:1 No one can **c** those who suffer.
Isa 22:4 Don't try to **c** me because of the
28:12 "This is a place for **c**.
40:1 "**C** my people! Comfort them!"
40:1 **C** them!" says your God.
51:3 So the LORD will **c** Zion.
51:3 He will **c** all those who live
51:19 to you. Who will **c** you?
52:9 The LORD will **c** his people.
57:18 I'll **c** them and their mourners.
61:2 to **c** all those who grieve.
66:13 her child, so will I **c** you.
Jer 16:7 No one will offer food to **c**
31:13 I will **c** them. I will give them
Lam 1:2 love the city, no one offers it **c**.
1:9 No one offers it **c**. 'O LORD,
1:16 No one can give me the **c** I
1:17 No one offers it **c**. The LORD
1:21 No one offers me **c**.
2:13 can I make that will **c** you,
Nah 3:7 Where can I find anyone to **c**
Zec 1:17 The LORD will again **c** Zion
10:2 They give useless **c**.
Luk 2:25 for the one who would **c** Israel.
6:24 They have had their **c**.
Jon 11:19 and Mary to **c** them about their
Act 9:31 in the fear of the Lord and the **c**
1Co 14:3 encourage them, and to **c** them.
2Co 1:3 and the God who gives **c**.
1:4 we are able to **c** them by using
1:4 the same **c** we have received
1:5 receive so much **c** from him.
1:6 it brings you **c** and salvation.
1:6 we can effectively **c** you when
1:7 you also share our **c**.
2:7 So now forgive and **c** him.
7:7 but also by learning about the **c**
Php 2:1 Do you have any **c** from love?
Col 4:11 They have provided me with **c**.
1Th 4:18 **c** each other with these words!
Phm 1:20 me some **c** because of Christ.

comfortable (2)

Psa 49:14 far away from their **c** homes.
Jnh 4:6 shade and make him more **c**.

comfortably (2)

Jer 44:17 and we lived **c** and saw no
Dan 4:4 was living **c** at home.

comforted (27)

Gen 24:67 So Isaac was **c** after his
37:35 but he refused to be **c**.
Rut 2:13 You have **c** me and reassured
2Sm 12:24 Then David **c** his wife
Job 42:11 and **c** him for all the evil the
Psa 77:2 Yet, my soul refused to be **c**.
86:17 have helped me and **c** me.
Isa 12:1 away from me, and you **c** me.
49:13 The LORD has **c** his people
66:13 You will be **c** in Jerusalem.
Jer 31:15 She refuses to be **c**,
Eze 14:22 Then you will be **c** after the
14:23 You will be **c** when you see
31:16 were **c** below the earth.
32:31 these things and be **c** over all
Mat 2:18 She refused to be **c** because
5:4 who mourn. They will be **c**.
1Co 16:18 They have **c** me, and they
16:18 and they have **c** you.
2Co 1:6 If we are **c**, we can effectively
2Co 2:7 that if he's not forgiven and **c**.
7:6 **c** us when Titus arrived.
7:7 We were **c** not only by his
7:13 This is what has **c** us.
7:13 In addition to being **c**,
1Th 2:11 We **c** you and encouraged you.
Phm 1:7 have **c** God's people.

comforting (6)

Gen 27:42 Your brother Esau is **c** himself
Job 16:2 You are all pathetic at **c** me.
Isa 66:11 be satisfied from her **c** breasts.
Eze 16:54 have done, including **c** them.
Zec 1:13 using kind and **c** words.
Jon 11:31 The Jews who were **c** Mary in

comfortless (1)

Isa 54:11 "You suffering, **c**, I will rebuild

comforts (5)

Job 29:25 like one who **c** mourners.
Isa 51:12 I alone am the one who **c** you.
66:13 As a mother **c** her child,
2Co 1:4 He **c** us whenever we suffer.
7:6 who **c** those who are dejected,

coming (278)

Gen 24:13 and the girls of the city are **c**
24:63 looked up, he saw camels **c**.
24:65 "Who is that man over there **c**
28:12 God going up and **c** down on it.
30:16 As Jacob was **c** in from the
32:6 He is **c** to meet you with 400
33:1 Jacob saw Esau **c** with 400
37:25 of Ishmaelites **c** from Gilead.
41:27 Seven years of famine are **c**.
41:29 Seven years are **c** when there
41:31 because the **c** famine will be
48:7 As I was **c** back from Paddan,
Exo 3:2 him there as flames of fire **c** out
14:10 Egyptians were **c** after them.
18:6 "I'm **c** to ⌊visit⌋ you,
19:9 "I am **c** to you in a storm cloud
25:33 Each of the six branches **c** out
25:35 three pairs of branches **c** out
32:1 Moses delayed **c** down from
37:19 Each of the six branches **c** out
37:21 three pairs of branches **c** out
Num 21:1 heard that the Israelites were **c**
22:16 keep you from **c** to me.
33:40 that the Israelites were **c**.)
Dtr 5:23 But when you heard the voice **c**
31:14 time of your death is **c** soon.
32:35 Their doom is **c** quickly.
Jdg 1:24 The spies saw a man **c** out of
9:36 troops are **c** down from the
9:37 there are troops **c** down from
9:37 One company is **c** along the
9:43 and saw the people **c** out
11:7 So why are you **c** to me now
11:34 he saw his daughter **c** out to
14:5 When they were **c** to the
19:25 her go when the sun was **c** up.
Rut 2:4 Boaz was **c** from Bethlehem,
4:11 who is **c** into your home,
1Sm 2:31 The time is **c** when I will break
9:11 they met girls **c** out to get
9:14 Samuel was **c** toward them on
11:5 Just then Saul was **c** from the
12:12 saw King Nahash of Ammon **c**
14:11 some Hebrews are **c** out of the
17:25 "Did you see that man **c** ⌊from
17:25 He keeps **c** to challenge Israel.
17:41 was **c** closer and closer to
25:11 them to men **c** from who knows
25:20 and his men **c** toward her.
28:14 "An old man is **c** up,
2Sm 3:22 and Joab were **c** home from
13:34 he saw many people **c** down
17:17 could not risk being seen **c** into
18:27 must be **c** with good news."
19:41 all the people of Israel kept **c**
24:20 king and his men **c** toward him,
1Ki 14:5 "Jeroboam's wife is **c** to ask
15:17 going to or **c** from King Asa
18:41 like a heavy rain ⌊is **c**⌋."
1Ki 18:44 like a man's hand is **c** from
2Ki 4:25 When he saw her **c** at a
9:17 in Jezreel saw Jehu's troops **c**.
9:18 but he isn't **c** back."
9:20 but he isn't **c** back.
10:15 who was **c** to meet him.
11:9 took his men who were **c**
19:9 King Tirhakah of Sudan was **c**
2Ch 16:1 going to or **c** from King Asa
20:2 "A large crowd is **c** against you
20:11 are now paying us back by **c**
20:16 They will be **c** up the Ziz Pass.
21:19 as his life was **c** to an end,
23:8 Each took his men who were **c**
28:9 He went to meet the army **c**
28:12 opposed those **c** home from
Neh 6:10 Some men are **c** at night to kill
Job 3:26 And trouble keeps **c**!"
19:14 closest friends have stopped **c**.
36:33 The thunder announces his **c**.
Psa 37:13 he has seen that his time is **c**.
96:13 presence because he is **c**.
96:13 He is **c** to judge the earth.
98:9 presence because he is **c**
Ecc 11:8 that is **c** is pointless.
Sos 3:6 Who is this young woman **c** up
8:5 Who is this young woman **c**
Isa 5:26 Look, they are **c** very quickly!
13:5 His army is **c** from a distant
13:5 The LORD is **c** with the
19:1 cloud and is **c** to Egypt.
21:12 answers, "Morning is **c**,
37:9 King Tirhakah of Sudan was **c**
40:10 The Almighty LORD is **c** with
62:11 people Zion, 'Your Savior is **c**.
63:1 Who is this **c** from Bozrah in
63:1 I am **c** to announce my victory.
66:18 I am **c** to gather the nations of
Jer 4:16 "Hostile troops are **c** from a
6:1 destruction are **c** from the
7:32 "That is why the days are **c**,"
8:16 They are **c** to devour the land
9:25 "The days are **c**," declares the
10:22 A tremendous uproar is **c** from
13:20 and see those who are **c** from
16:14 "That is why the days are **c**,"
19:6 "That is why the days are **c**,
23:5 "The days are **c**," declares the
23:7 "That is why the days are **c**,"
30:3 The days are **c**," declares the
31:27 "The days are **c**," declares the
31:31 "The days are **c**," declares the
31:38 "The days are **c**," declares the
33:14 "The days are **c**," declares the
36:9 who was **c** from any city
37:11 Pharaoh's army was **c**.
46:13 prophet Jeremiah about the **c**
46:21 The day of destruction is **c**.
48:12 That is why the days are **c**,"
48:16 "Moab's destruction is **c** near;
48:16 disaster is **c** quickly.
49:2 That is why the days are **c**,
49:19 their places like a lion **c** out
50:28 refugees from Babylon are **c**
50:44 their places like a lion **c** out
51:47 That is why the days are **c**
51:52 "That is why the days are **c**,"
51:55 He will silence the loud noise **c**
Eze 1:4 I saw a storm **c** from the north.
7:2 the land of Israel: The end is **c**!
7:2 The end is **c** to the four corners
7:3 Now the end is **c** for you.
7:5 One disaster after another is **c**.
7:6 The end is **c**. The end is
7:6 The end is **c**. It is stirring itself
7:6 itself up against you. It is **c**!
7:7 Destruction is **c** to you,
7:7 The time is **c**. The day is near.
7:10 It is **c**! Destruction is coming!
7:10 Destruction is **c**! Wrongdoing
7:12 The time is **c**. The day is near.
7:25 Anguish is **c**. People will look
20:3 Are you **c** to ask me for help?
21:7 It's **c**! It will surely take place!'
30:9 is in trouble. That day is **c**!
33:3 If he sees the enemy **c** to

Eze 33:6 watchman sees the enemy **c**
39:8 "It's **c**! It will happen! declares
43:2 glory of the God of Israel **c** from
Dan 8:5 I saw a male goat **c** from the
8:6 The goat was **c** toward the
Joe 2:1 the day of the LORD is **c**.
Mic 7:11 extending your borders is **c**.
Nah 2:1 one who will scatter you is **c**
Zep 1:14 It is near and **c** very quickly.
Zec 5:5 and see what's **c**."
5:6 "A basket is **c**," he said.
5:9 and saw two women **c** forward
9:9 Your King is **c** to you:
Mal 4:1 "Certainly the day is **c**!
4:1 The day that is **c** will burn
Mat 3:7 Pharisees and Sadducees **c**
3:7 how to flee from God's **c** anger?
3:14 Why are you **c** to me?"
3:16 and he saw the Spirit of God **c**
11:3 "Are you the one who is **c**,
16:28 Son of Man **c** in his kingdom."
17:11 Jesus answered, "Elijah is **c**
19:14 stop children from **c** to me!
21:5 'Your king is **c** to you.
22:31 told you about the dead **c** back
24:3 the sign that you are **c** again,
24:30 they see the Son of Man **c**
24:43 time of the night a thief was **c**,
26:64 He will be **c** on the clouds of
Mar 1:10 split open and the Spirit **c** down
1:45 But people still kept **c** to him
6:31 Many people were **c** and going,
9:12 Jesus said to them, "Elijah is **c**
10:14 stop the children from **c** to me.
10:17 As Jesus was **c** out to the road,
11:10 David's kingdom that is **c**!
13:26 will see the Son of Man **c**
14:62 He will be **c** with the clouds of
15:21 was **c** ⌊into Jerusalem⌋ from
Luk 3:7 Crowds of people were **c** to be
3:7 how to flee from God's **c** anger?
3:16 is more powerful than I is **c**.
6:19 because power was **c** from him
7:19 "Are you the one who is **c**,
7:20 'Are you the one who is **c**,
9:42 While he was **c** ⌊to Jesus⌋,
9:51 The time was **c** closer for
12:39 at what hour the thief was **c**,
12:54 "When you see a cloud **c** up in
15:25 As he was **c** back to the house,
17:20 "People can't observe the **c** of
18:3 was also a widow who kept **c**
18:5 Otherwise, she'll keep **c** to me
18:16 stop the children from **c** to me!
19:4 who was **c** that way.
19:37 By this time he was **c** near the
21:27 will see the Son of Man **c**
23:26 Simon was **c** into Jerusalem.
23:29 The time is **c** when people will
Jon 1:9 was **c** into the world.
1:29 John saw Jesus **c** toward him
1:47 Jesus saw Nathanael **c** toward
1:51 angels going up and **c** down
4:21 A time is **c** when you
4:23 Indeed, the time is **c**,
4:25 "I know that the Messiah is **c**.
5:25 A time is **c** (and is now here)
5:28 A time is **c** when all the dead
6:5 saw a large crowd **c** to him,
6:19 He was **c** near the boat,
8:56 to see that my day was **c**.
9:4 no one can do anything is **c**.
10:12 When he sees a wolf **c**,
11:20 Martha heard that Jesus was **c**,
11:56 he'll avoid **c** to the festival?"
12:12 that Jesus was **c** to Jerusalem.
12:15 Your king is **c**. He is riding on a
14:28 but I'm **c** back to you.'
14:30 But he's **c**, so I won't talk with
16:2 Certainly, the time is **c** when
16:25 The time is **c** when I won't use
16:32 The time is **c**, and is already
17:11 and I'm **c** back to you.
17:13 ⌊Father,⌋ I'm **c** back to you.
Act 9:3 As Saul was **c** near the city of
10:9 were on their way and **c** close
Act 10:29 That is why I didn't object to **c**
10:33 Thank you for **c**. All of us are
19:4 in Jesus, who was **c** later."
24:25 and the **c** judgment,
27:20 began to lose any hope of **c** out
28:15 in Rome heard that we were **c**,
1Co 15:12 of you say that **c** back from
15:23 Christ is the first, then at his **c**,
2Co 10:13 God has given us to do — **c**
Php 1:26 So by **c** to you again,
3:10 the power that his **c** back
3:20 Jesus Christ **c** from heaven as
1Th 1:10 us from ⌊God's⌋ **c** anger.
2Th 1:7 ⌊**c**⌋ from heaven with his
2:1 about our Lord Jesus Christ's **c**
1Ti 1:18 that are still **c** to you:
2Ti 1:10 Now with the **c** of our Savior
4:6 My life is **c** to an end,
Heb 6:2 dead people **c** back to life,
7:14 about priests **c** from that tribe.
8:8 "The days are **c**, says the Lord,
10:25 we see the day of the Lord **c**.
10:37 "Yet, the one who is **c** will
11:13 but they saw these things **c** in
Jas 5:1 the misery that is **c** to you.
1Pe 2:4 You are **c** to Christ,
4:12 by the fiery troubles that are **c**
2Pe 1:16 told you about the powerful **c**
1Jn 2:18 heard that an antichrist is **c**.
4:3 that you have heard is **c**.
Rev 1:4 and the one who is **c**,
1:7 He is **c** in the clouds.
1:8 and the one who is **c**,
3:10 the time of testing which is **c**
3:11 I am **c** soon! Hold on to what
3:12 (the New Jerusalem **c** down out
4:8 was, who is, and who is **c**."
7:2 I saw another angel **c** from the
7:14 are the people who are **c** out
13:1 I saw a beast **c** out of the sea.
16:15 "See, I am **c** like a thief.
20:1 I saw an angel **c** down from
21:2 **c** down from God out of
21:10 **c** down from God out of
22:7 I'm **c** soon! Blessed is the one
22:12 "I'm **c** soon! I will bring my
22:20 things says, "Yes, I'm **c** soon!"

comma (2)

Mat 5:18 neither a period nor a **c** will
Luk 16:17 a **c** from Moses' Teachings.

command (143)

Exo 7:2 Aaron everything I **c** you,
27:20 "For the lighting, you must **c**
34:11 Do everything that I **c** today.
Lev 6:9 "**C** Aaron and his sons:
10:13 That is the **c** I received.
24:2 "**C** the Israelites to bring you
Num 3:39 Aaron counted at the LORD's **c**,
4:49 At the LORD's **c** through
5:2 "**C** the Israelites to send
9:18 At the LORD's **c** the Israelites
9:18 and at his **c** they would set up
9:19 Israelites obeyed the LORD's **c**
9:20 At the LORD's **c** they would set
9:20 and at his **c** they would break
9:23 At the LORD's **c** they set up
9:23 and at his **c** they broke camp.
9:23 They obeyed the **c** that the
10:13 following the **c** that the LORD
10:14 son of Amminadab, was in **c**.
10:18 son of Shedeur, was in **c**.
10:22 son of Ammihud, was in **c**.
10:25 son of Ammishaddai, was in **c**.
13:3 So at the LORD's **c**,
14:41 you disobeying the LORD's **c**?
15:31 and broken the LORD's **c**.
16:40 following the **c** that the LORD
20:24 both rebelled against my **c** at
22:18 I couldn't disobey the **c** of the
23:20 I have received a **c** to bless.
24:13 I couldn't disobey the LORD's **c**
27:14 You both rebelled against my **c**
27:21 At his **c** Joshua and the whole
27:21 And at his **c** they will return."
Num 28:2 "Give this **c** to the Israelites:
31:49 all the soldiers under our **c**,
32:25 we will do as you **c**.
33:2 At the LORD's **c** Moses wrote
33:38 At the LORD's **c** the priest
36:5 gave the Israelites a **c** from
Dtr 1:26 But you rebelled against the **c**
1:43 You defied the LORD's **c** and
3:18 of the tribe of Manasseh this **c**:
3:21 I also gave Joshua this **c**:
4:2 add anything to what I **c** you,
8:1 Be careful to obey every **c** I
12:11 You must bring everything I **c**
12:14 you must do everything I **c** you.
12:32 sure to do everything I **c** you.
15:11 That's why I **c** you to be
15:15 That's why I'm giving you this **c**
18:18 He will tell them everything I **c**
18:20 in my name that I didn't **c** him
27:1 "Obey every **c** I'm giving you
27:4 following the **c** I'm giving you
27:11 Moses gave the people this **c**:
30:2 doing everything I **c** you today,
30:11 This **c** I'm giving you today
30:12 will go to heaven to get this **c**
30:13 This **c** isn't on the other side of
31:23 LORD gave this **c** to Joshua,
31:25 He gave this **c** to the Levites
32:46 Then you will **c** your children
Jdg 4:10 men went to fight under his **c**.
5:15 sent into the valley under his **c**.
7:13 When it got to the **c** post,
8:5 food for the men under my **c**.
1Sm 13:13 "You didn't follow the **c** of the
13:14 follow the **c** of the LORD."
15:24 by not following the LORD's **c**
16:16 Your Majesty, why don't you **c**
2Sm 2:31 of Benjamin under Abner's **c**.
18:2 of the troops under Joab's **c**,
1Ki 2:43 and obey the **c** I gave you?
9:4 heart), do everything I **c**,
11:10 Solomon did not obey God's **c**.
11:38 If you will do all I **c** you,
13:2 By a **c** of the LORD,
13:5 God performed at the LORD's **c**.
13:21 mouth and didn't obey the **c** that
13:32 that he announced by a **c**
2Ki 14:6 He obeyed the LORD's **c**
16:15 King Ahaz gave this **c** to the
17:27 king of Assyria gave this **c**:
1Ch 12:14 The least able one was in **c** of
12:14 the best one was in **c** of 1,000.
12:32 relatives were under their **c**.
28:21 and people are at your **c**."
2Ch 7:13 or **c** grasshoppers to devour the
7:17 David was, do everything I **c**,
25:4 He obeyed the LORD's **c**
29:25 This **c** came from the LORD
30:12 united to carry out the **c** which
Neh 8:15 They should announce this **c**
Est 1:12 Vashti refused the king's **c** that
1:15 did not obey King Xerxes' **c**,
3:3 do you ignore the king's **c**?"
4:3 by the king's **c** and decree,
4:8 it to Esther to inform and **c** her
8:14 in keeping with the king's **c**.
9:1 the king's **c** and decree were to
9:32 Esther's **c** had established
Psa 19:8 The **c** of the LORD is radiant.
148:5 they were created by his **c**.
Pro 6:20 Obey the **c** of your father,
6:23 because the **c** is a lamp,
8:29 would not overstep his **c**,
Isa 5:6 and I will **c** the clouds not to
50:2 I dry up the sea with my **c**,
Jer 1:7 say whatever I **c** you to say.
19:5 I didn't ask them or **c** them to
23:32 I didn't send them or **c** them to
26:2 Tell them everything that I **c**
29:23 I didn't **c** them to do this.
34:22 I am going to give a **c**,"
37:21 King Zedekiah gave the **c** to
38:10 Melech from Sudan this **c**:
Dan 9:25 that from the time the **c** is given
Amo 6:11 LORD is going to give the **c**
9:3 I will **c** a sea snake to bite

Amo 9:4 I will **c** a sword to kill them.
Nah 1:14 has given this **c** about you,
Mat 5:19 So whoever sets aside any **c**
8:8 But just give a **c**, and my
8:9 you know, I'm in a chain of **c**
8:9 and have soldiers at my **c**.
8:16 spirits out of people with a **c**
Mar 9:25 I **c** you to come out of him and
10:3 "What **c** did Moses give you?"
10:5 "He wrote this **c** for you
Luk 4:36 "What kind of **c** is this?
7:7 But just give a **c**, and let my
7:8 you know, I'm in a chain of **c**
7:8 and have soldiers at my **c**.
Act 16:18 "I **c** you in the name of Jesus
1Co 7:6 just said is not meant as a **c**
7:10 I pass this **c** along (not really I,
7:25 Even though I don't have any **c**
1Th 4:16 come from heaven with a **c**,
1Ti 1:1 apostle of Christ Jesus by the **c**
6:14 you obey this **c** completely.
Tit 1:3 with this word by the **c**
Heb 12:20 They couldn't obey the **c** that
Rev 3:10 have obeyed my **c** to endure,

commanded (245)

Gen 2:16 The LORD God **c** the man.
3:11 you eat fruit from the tree I **c**
3:17 from the tree, although I **c** you,
6:22 everything that God had **c** him.
7:5 that the LORD **c** him.
7:9 of each) as God had **c** Noah.
7:16 went in as God had **c** Noah.
21:4 circumcised him as God had **c**.
24:9 did as his master Abraham **c**
28:1 Then he **c** him, "You are not to
28:6 Jacob and had **c** him not
32:4 He **c** them to give this
32:17 He **c** the first servant,
32:19 He also **c** the second servant,
44:1 Joseph **c** the man in charge of
50:16 your father died, he **c** us,
Exo 1:22 Then Pharaoh **c** all his people
4:28 the LORD had **c** him to do.
6:13 He **c** them to bring the
7:6 did as the LORD had **c** them.
7:10 and did as the LORD had **c**.
7:20 Aaron did as the LORD had **c**.
12:28 LORD had **c** Moses and Aaron.
12:50 LORD had **c** Moses and Aaron.
16:16 This is what the LORD has **c**:
16:24 next morning as Moses had **c**,
16:28 you refuse to do what I have **c**
16:32 "This is what the LORD has **c**:
16:34 as the LORD **c** Moses.
17:1 to place as the LORD **c** them.
19:7 that the LORD had **c** him.
23:15 unleavened bread, as I **c** you.
29:35 sons exactly as I have **c** you.
31:6 make everything I have **c** you:
31:11 all these things as I **c** you."
32:8 turned from the way I **c** them
34:4 as the LORD had **c** him,
34:18 As I **c** you, you must eat
34:32 and he **c** them to do everything
34:34 Israelites what he had been **c**,
35:1 the LORD has **c** you to do:
35:4 "This is what the LORD has **c**:
35:10 everything the LORD has **c**:
35:29 LORD had **c** through Moses.
36:1 the work as the LORD has **c**.
36:5 the work the LORD **c** us to do."
38:22 the LORD had **c** Moses.
40:16 everything as the LORD **c** him.
Lev 7:36 The LORD **c** the Israelites to
7:38 at the same time that he **c**
8:4 Moses did as the LORD **c** him,
8:5 "The LORD has **c** that this is
8:9 as the LORD had **c** Moses.
8:13 as the LORD had **c** Moses.
8:17 as the LORD **c** him.
8:21 on the altar as the LORD **c** him.
8:29 as the LORD had **c**.
8:31 Eat them there as I **c** when I
8:34 I did today what the LORD **c**
8:35 This is what I was **c**."
Lev 8:36 the LORD **c** through Moses.
9:5 they took the things Moses **c**
9:6 Moses said, "The LORD has **c**
9:7 LORD for them as the LORD **c**."
9:10 sin as the LORD had **c** Moses.
9:21 them to the LORD as Moses **c**.
10:15 as the LORD has **c**."
10:18 have eaten it there, as I **c**."
16:34 Aaron did as the LORD had **c**
17:2 this is what the LORD has **c**:
24:23 to death as the LORD **c** Moses.
24:23 did as the LORD **c** Moses.
Num 1:19 Sinai as the LORD had **c** him.
1:54 as the LORD **c** Moses.
2:33 As the LORD had **c** Moses,
2:34 as the LORD had **c** Moses.
3:16 them as he had been **c**.
3:42 Israelites as the LORD **c** him.
3:51 money as he had been **c**.
4:37 did as the LORD had **c** Moses
4:41 did as the LORD had **c** Moses
4:45 did as the LORD had **c** Moses
4:49 as the LORD **c** Moses.
8:3 as the LORD **c** Moses.
8:20 did what the LORD **c** Moses
8:22 They did as the LORD had **c**
9:5 as the LORD had **c** Moses.
10:15 **c** the army of Issachar.
10:16 **c** the army of Zebulun.
10:19 **c** the army of Simeon.
10:20 **c** the army of Gad.
10:23 **c** the army of Manasseh.
10:24 **c** the army of Benjamin.
10:26 **c** the army of Asher.
10:27 **c** the army of Naphtali.
15:23 (Everything the LORD **c** you
15:36 as the LORD **c** Moses.
17:11 what the LORD **c** him to do.
19:2 the LORD's teachings have **c**:
20:9 presence as he had been **c**.
20:27 Moses did as the Lord **c**.
26:4 as the LORD **c** Moses."
27:11 as the LORD **c** Moses."
27:22 Moses did as the LORD **c** him.
29:40 the LORD had **c** him.
30:1 the LORD has **c** ⌊about vows⌋:
31:7 as the LORD **c** Moses,
31:31 did as the LORD **c** Moses.
31:41 as the LORD had **c** him.
31:47 as the LORD **c** him.
34:13 Moses **c** the Israelites,
34:13 The LORD has **c** that this land
34:29 These are the men the LORD **c**
36:2 They said, "Sir, the LORD **c**
36:2 The LORD also **c** you to give
36:10 did as the LORD **c** Moses.
Dtr 1:3 everything the LORD had **c** him
1:19 as the LORD our God had **c**.
1:41 as the LORD our God **c** us to
4:5 as the LORD my God **c** me.
4:13 which he **c** you to do.
4:14 The LORD also **c** me to teach
5:12 the LORD your God has **c** you.
5:15 the LORD your God has **c** you
5:16 the LORD your God has **c** you.
5:32 the LORD your God has **c** you.
6:1 and rules the LORD your God **c**
6:20 the LORD our God **c** you mean
6:24 The LORD our God **c** us to
6:25 our God, as he has **c** us."
9:12 turned from the way I **c** them
9:16 way the LORD **c** you to live.
10:5 where the LORD **c** me to put
12:21 I have **c** you to do this.
20:17 as the LORD your God has **c**
24:8 Make sure you do what I **c**
26:13 and widows as you **c** me.
26:13 I didn't forget to do what you **c**.
26:14 I have done everything you **c**
29:1 that the LORD **c** Moses
31:5 to them everything that I **c** you.
31:10 Then Moses **c** them,
31:29 turn from the way I have **c** you
34:9 LORD had **c** through Moses.
Jos 1:7 that my servant Moses **c** you.
1:9 "I have **c** you, 'Be strong and
Jos 1:13 LORD's servant Moses **c** you.
8:27 as the LORD had **c** Joshua.
8:31 LORD's servant Moses had **c**
8:33 LORD's servant Moses had **c**
8:35 from everything Moses had **c**.
9:24 your God **c** his servant Moses
10:40 the LORD God of Israel had **c**.
11:12 servant Moses had **c** him.
11:15 LORD had **c** his servant Moses
11:15 and what Moses had **c** him.
11:15 the LORD had **c** Moses.
11:20 as he had **c** Moses.
13:6 by drawing lots, as I **c** you.
14:2 LORD had **c** through Moses.
14:5 as the LORD had **c** Moses.
17:4 They said, "The LORD **c**
21:2 "The LORD **c** through Moses
21:8 LORD had **c** through Moses.
22:2 LORD's servant Moses **c** you.
22:2 me in everything I **c** you.
Jdg 13:14 be careful to do everything I **c**."
1Sm 2:29 offerings that I have **c** people
2Sm 9:11 "I will do everything you've **c**,
11:19 And he **c** the messenger,
17:14 (The LORD had **c** Ahithophel's
24:19 and as the LORD had **c** him.
1Ki 5:17 The king **c** them to quarry
8:58 which he **c** our ancestors ⌊to
11:11 or my laws that I **c** you
13:9 he **c** me not to eat or drink or go
15:5 to do anything the LORD **c** him
16:9 But Zimri, the general who **c**
17:4 and I've **c** ravens to feed you
17:9 I've **c** a widow there to feed
2Ki 16:16 did what King Ahaz had **c**.
17:13 decrees as I **c** your ancestors
17:15 although the LORD had **c** them
17:35 made a promise to Israel, he **c**,
18:12 the LORD's servant, had **c**.
18:36 because the king **c** them not
24:3 because the LORD had **c**
1Ch 6:49 God's servant Moses had **c**.
13:1 with every officer who **c**
15:15 as Moses had **c** according
16:15 the word that he **c** for a
22:6 his son Solomon and **c** him
22:13 decrees the LORD **c** Moses
24:19 LORD God of Israel had **c** him.
27:15 the twelfth unit was **c** by
28:8 the LORD your God has **c**.
2Ch 8:13 of Booths) as Moses had **c**.
8:14 David, the man of God, had **c**.
26:11 They were **c** by Hananiah,
35:15 the king's seer Jeduthun had **c**.
35:16 altar as King Josiah had **c**.
Ezr 7:23 the God of heaven has **c** must
Neh 8:1 Lord had **c** Israel ⌊to follow⌋.
Est 3:2 because the king had **c** it.
4:5 She **c** him to go to Mordecai
4:10 Esther spoke to Hathach and **c**
4:17 did just as Esther had **c** him.
9:14 The king **c** this, issuing a
Psa 78:5 He **c** our ancestors to make
78:23 In spite of that, he **c** the clouds
105:8 the word that he **c** for a
106:9 He angrily **c** the Red Sea,
119:4 You have **c** that your guiding
Isa 13:3 I've **c** my holy ones.
23:11 He has **c** that Canaan's
34:16 because the LORD has **c** it,
36:21 because the king **c** them not
45:12 I **c** all the stars ⌊to shine⌋.
48:5 idols have **c** them to happen."
Jer 11:8 the terms that I **c** them to keep."
14:14 **c** them, and spoke to them.
23:38 even though I **c** you not to
26:8 that the LORD had **c** him
32:23 They didn't do anything you **c**
36:8 as the prophet Jeremiah **c** him.
36:26 The king **c** Jerahmeel (the
50:21 "Do everything I **c** you.
Eze 9:11 "I did everything you **c**."
10:6 After the LORD had **c** the
37:7 So I prophesied as I was **c**.
37:10 So I prophesied as he **c** me,
Amo 2:12 You **c** the prophets to stop

Zec 1:6 which I've **c** my servants the
Mat 1:24 the angel of the Lord had **c** him
8:4 the sacrifice Moses **c** as proof
28:20 to do everything I have **c** you.
Mar 1:44 which Moses **c** as proof
Luk 5:14 sacrifice as Moses **c** as proof
Jon 14:31 what the Father has **c** me
1Co 9:14 the Lord has **c** that those who
2Pe 3:2 and Savior **c** you through your
1Jn 3:23 and to love each other as he **c**
2Jn 1:4 the truth as the Father has **c** us.
1:5 from the beginning we were **c**
1:6 We were **c** to live in love,

commander (79)

Gen 21:22 by Phicol, the **c** of his army,
21:32 and Phicol, the **c** of his army,
26:26 and Phicol, the **c** of his army,
Jos 5:14 I am here as the **c** of the
5:15 The **c** of the LORD's army said
Jdg 4:2 The **c** of King Jabin's army
4:7 I will lead Sisera (the **c** of
11:6 "Come and be our **c** so that we
11:11 made him their leader and **c**.
1Sm 12:9 who was the **c** of the army of
14:50 The name of the **c** of his army
17:55 the **c** of the army, "Abner,
22:2 and he became their **c**.
22:14 the **c** of your bodyguard.
26:5 the **c** of the army, were lying.
2Sm 2:8 son Abner, **c** of Saul's army,
8:18 Jehoiada's son Benaiah was **c**
10:16 the **c** of Hadadezer's army,
11:11 and my **c** Joab and Your
17:25 to take Joab's place as **c**
19:13 always as the **c** of the army.'"
24:2 King David said to Joab, the **c**
1Ki 1:19 and Joab the **c** of the army ⌊to
2:32 was the son of Ner and the **c**
2:32 was the son of Jether and the **c**
2:35 to replace Joab as **c** of the
4:4 was **c** of the army.
11:15 Edom, Joab, the **c** of the army,
11:21 the **c** of the army, had died,
16:16 the **c** of the army, king of Israel.
2Ki 4:13 us to speak to the king or the **c**
5:1 Naaman, the **c** of the Aramean
11:9 Each **c** took his men who were
18:17 and his field **c** with a large
18:18 went out to the field **c**.
18:26 and Joah said to the field **c**,
18:27 But the field **c** asked them,
18:28 Then the field **c** stood and
18:37 the message from the field **c**.
19:4 all the words of the field **c**.
19:8 The field **c** returned and found
25:19 the city he also took an army **c**,
1Ch 18:17 Jehoiada's son Benaiah was **c**
19:16 the **c** of Hadadezer's army,
27:5 The third **c** of the army during
27:6 of the thirty fighting men and **c**
27:8 was **c** of the fifth unit during the
27:34 Joab was the **c** of the royal
2Ch 17:14 were **C** Adnah (with 300,000
17:15 **C** Jehohanan (with 280,000),
Ezr 4:8 Rehum the **c** and Shimshai the
4:9 At that time, Rehum the **c** and
4:17 this reply: To Rehum the **c**,
4:23 Rehum the **c**, Shimshai the
Neh 7:2 the **c** of the fortress,
Psa 80:4 O LORD God, **c** of armies,
80:7 O God, **c** of armies,
80:14 O God, **c** of armies,
80:19 O LORD God, **c** of armies,
84:8 O LORD God, **c** of armies,
Isa 36:2 king of Assyria sent his field **c**
36:3 went out to the field **c**.
36:11 and Joah said to the field **c**,
36:12 But the field **c** asked,
36:13 Then the field **c** stood and
36:22 the message from the field **c**.
37:4 heard the words of the field **c**.
37:8 The field **c** returned and found
55:4 a leader and a **c** for people.
Jer 51:27 Appoint a **c** to lead the attack.
52:25 the city he also took an army **c**,
Dan 8:11 Then it attacked the **c** of the
8:25 oppose the **C** of Commanders,
10:13 The **c** of the Persian kingdom
10:20 return to fight the **c** of Persia.
10:20 the **c** of Greece will come.
10:21 commanders except your **c**,
11:18 But a **c** will silence the insults
12:1 that time Michael, the great **c**,

commander-in-chief (2)

2Ki 18:17 the king of Assyria sent his **c**,
Isa 20:1 Sargon of Assyria sent his **c**

commander's (1)

Dtr 33:21 Indeed, a **c** piece of land was

commanders (79)

Num 31:14 the **c** of the companies and
31:48 the **c** of the companies and
31:52 by the **c** weighed about 420
31:54 Eleazar took the gold from the **c**
Dtr 20:9 should appoint **c** to lead them.
Jdg 5:9 My heart goes out to Israel's **c**,
5:14 **C** from Machir went into battle.
5:15 Issachar's **c** were with
7:25 the two Midianite **c**.
8:3 Zeeb, Midian's **c**, over to you.
2Sm 18:1 He appointed **c** in charge of
18:5 all the **c** this order regarding
19:6 have made it clear that your **c**
24:4 king overruled Joab and the **c**
1Ki 1:25 the king's sons, the army's **c**,
2:5 son) did to me and to the two **c**
9:22 and **c** of his chariot and cavalry
22:31 given orders to the 32 chariot **c**.
22:32 the chariot **c** saw Jehoshaphat,
22:33 the chariot **c** realized that he
2Ki 8:21 their chariot **c** surrounded him,
11:4 sent for the company **c**
11:9 The company **c** did as the
11:10 He gave the **c** the spears and
11:14 The **c** and the trumpeters were
11:15 the company **c** who were
11:19 He took the company **c** of the
25:23 When all the army **c** and their
25:26 all classes and the army **c** left
1Ch 11:10 Now, these were the **c** of
12:21 were all warriors, **c** in the army.
12:34 Naphtali there were 1,000 **c**.
15:25 and the army's **c** joyfully went
25:1 David and the army **c**
26:26 the **c** of regiments and
26:26 and the **c** of the army had
27:1 regiment and battalion **c**,
27:22 were the **c** of Israel's tribes.
27:25 These were all the **c** in charge
28:1 the **c** of regiments and
29:6 the **c** of regiments and
2Ch 1:2 spoke to all Israel — to the **c**
8:9 and **c** of his chariot and cavalry
12:6 Then the **c** of Israel and the
17:14 Judah's regimental **c** were
18:30 given orders to the chariot **c**.
18:31 the chariot **c** saw Jehoshaphat,
18:32 and the chariot **c** realized that
21:9 took all his chariot **c** to attack.
21:9 their chariot **c** surrounded him,
23:1 agreement with the company **c**:
23:9 Jehoiada gave the **c** the
23:13 The **c** and the trumpeters were
23:14 the company **c** who were
23:20 He took the company **c**,
25:5 to regiment and battalion **c**
32:6 He appointed military **c** over
32:6 the troops and gathered the **c**
32:21 and **c** in the Assyrian king's
33:11 So the LORD made the army **c**
33:14 He put army **c** in every fortified
Isa 10:8 'Aren't all our **c** kings?
Jer 40:7 All the army **c** and their men
40:8 These are the **c** who went with
40:13 all the army **c** who were still
41:11 and all the army **c** who were
41:13 and all the army **c** who were
41:16 and all the army **c** who were
41:16 and **c** from Gibeon.
Jer 42:1 Then all the army **c** along with
42:8 all the army **c** who were with
43:4 (son of Kareah), all the army **c**,
43:5 and all the army **c** took all
Eze 23:6 They were governors and **c**
23:12 They were governors and **c** in
23:23 young men, governors and **c**,
Dan 8:25 oppose the Commander of **C**,
10:13 Michael, one of the chief **c**,
10:21 **c** except your commander,

commanding (12)

Dtr 11:28 if you turn from the way I'm **c**
19:7 This is why I'm **c** you to set
24:18 So I'm **c** you to do this.
24:22 So I'm **c** you to do this.
26:16 Today the LORD your God is **c**
28:14 Do everything I'm **c** you today.
30:16 This is what I'm **c** you today:
Jon 15:12 This is what I'm **c** you to do.
15:17 This is what I'm **c** you to do.
Act 22:26 he reported it to his **c** officer.
2Co 8:8 I'm not **c** you, but I'm testing
2Ti 2:4 This pleases his **c** officer.

commandment (24)

Mat 15:3 "Why do you break the **c** of
22:36 "Teacher, which **c** is the
22:38 greatest and most important **c**.
Mar 12:28 "Which **c** is the most important
12:31 most important **c** is this:
12:31 No other **c** is greater than
Luk 23:56 they rested according to the **c**.
Jon 13:34 "I'm giving you a new **c**:
Rom 7:8 opportunity provided by this **c**
7:9 But when this **c** came,
7:10 I found that the **c** which was
7:11 opportunity provided by this **c**,
7:12 holy, and the **c** is holy, right,
7:13 Through a **c** sin became more
13:9 and every other **c** are summed
Eph 6:3 an important **c** with a promise.
Heb 9:19 told all the people every **c**.
1Jn 2:7 I'm writing to give you a new **c**.
2:7 Rather, I'm giving you an old **c**
2:7 the old **c** you've already heard.
2:8 I'm writing to give you a new **c**.
3:23 This is his **c**: to believe in his
4:21 Christ has given us this **c**:
2Jn 1:5 I'm writing to give you a new **c**.

commandments (72)

Exo 20:6 who love me and obey my **c**.
24:12 with the teachings and the **c**
34:28 words of the promise, the ten **c**.
Dtr 4:13 terms of his promise, the ten **c**,
4:45 These are the **c**, laws,
5:10 who love me and obey my **c**.
5:22 These are the **c** the LORD
5:22 He wrote the **c** on two stone
5:29 and obey all my **c** as long as
10:4 words as before, the ten **c**.
Ezr 9:10 We have abandoned your **c**!
9:11 The **c** you gave us through
9:14 If we break your **c** again and
10:3 the others who tremble at the **c**
Neh 1:5 who love you and obey your **c**.
1:7 We haven't obeyed the **c**,
1:9 me and continue to obey my **c**,
9:13 and good laws and **c**.
9:14 You gave them **c**, laws,
9:29 and would not obey your **c**.
9:34 didn't pay attention to your **c**
10:29 themselves to follow all the **c**,
Psa 89:31 my laws and do not obey my **c**,
119:6 when I study all your **c**.
119:10 me wander away from your **c**.
119:19 Do not hide your **c** from me.
119:21 and wander away from your **c**.
119:32 I will eagerly pursue your **c**
119:35 Lead me on the path of your **c**,
119:47 Your **c**, which I love, make me
119:48 ⌊in prayer⌋ because of your **c**,
119:60 I hurry to obey your **c**.
119:66 because I believe in your **c**.
119:73 so that I may learn your **c**.

Psa 119:86 (All your **c** are reliable.)
119:96 ⌊but⌋ your **c** have no limit.
119:98 Your **c** make me wiser than my
119:98 because your **c** are always
119:115 I can obey the **c** of my God.
119:127 I love your **c** more than gold,
119:131 pant because I long for your **c**.
119:143 but your **c** ⌊still⌋ make me
119:151 and all your **c** are reliable.
119:166 I have carried out your **c**.
119:172 because all your **c** are fair.
119:176 I have never forgotten your **c**.
Dan 9:4 who love you and obey your **c**.
9:5 away from your **c** and laws.
Mat 19:17 to enter into life, obey the **c**."
19:18 "Which **c**?" the man asked.
19:20 "I have obeyed all these **c**.
22:40 depend on these two **c**."
Mar 7:8 "You abandon the **c** of God to
7:9 have no trouble rejecting the **c**
10:19 You know the **c**: Never murder.
10:20 I've obeyed all these **c** since I
Luk 18:20 You know the **c**: Never commit
18:21 "I've obeyed all these **c** since I
Jon 14:15 you will obey my **c**.
14:21 knows and obeys my **c** is
15:10 If you obey my **c**, you will live
15:10 I have obeyed my Father's **c**,
15:14 my friends if you obey my **c**.
Rom 13:9 The **c**, "Never commit adultery;
Eph 2:15 He brought an end to the **c** and
1Jn 2:3 know Christ if we obey his **c**.
2:4 but doesn't obey his **c** is a liar.
3:22 it because we obey his **c**
3:24 Those who obey Christ's **c** live
5:2 we love God by obeying his **c**.
5:3 God means that we obey his **c**.
5:3 Obeying his **c** isn't difficult

commands (124)

Gen 26:5 completed the duties, **c**, laws,
Exo 15:26 if you pay attention to his **c**
18:23 If God **c** you, and you do this,
25:22 you all my **c** for the Israelites.
Lev 4:2 by any of the LORD's **c** — this is
4:13 by any of the LORD's **c**,
4:22 that is forbidden by any of the **c**
4:27 forbidden by the LORD's **c** —
5:17 by any of the LORD's **c**,
7:38 Moses **c** about these offerings
22:31 "Carefully obey my **c**.
26:3 laws and carefully obey my **c**:
26:14 to me and obey all these **c**,
26:15 promise by disobeying my **c**,
27:34 These are the **c** the LORD
Num 9:8 what the LORD **c** you to do."
15:22 by not obeying all these **c**
15:23 the day the LORD gave the **c**.)
15:39 will remember all the LORD's **c**
15:40 will remember to obey all my **c**,
36:6 This is what the LORD **c** for
36:13 These are the **c** and rules the
Dtr 4:2 you will be able to obey the **c**
4:40 Obey his laws and **c** which I'm
5:31 I will give you all the **c**,
6:1 These are the **c**, laws,
6:2 his laws and **c** that I'm giving
6:17 Be sure to obey the **c** of the
7:9 who love him and obey his **c**.
7:11 So obey the **c**, laws, and rules
8:2 wholeheartedly obey his **c**.
8:6 Obey the **c** of the LORD your
8:11 Don't fail to obey his **c**,
10:13 LORD wants you to obey his **c**
11:1 obey his laws, rules, and **c**.
11:8 Obey all the **c** I'm giving you
11:13 If you faithfully obey the **c** that
11:22 Faithfully obey all these **c** I'm
11:27 be blessed if you obey the **c**
11:28 be cursed if you disobey the **c**
13:4 your God, fear him, obey his **c**,
13:18 obey all the **c** that I'm giving
15:5 obey all these **c** I'm giving you
17:20 and he won't disobey these **c**
19:9 you faithfully obey all these **c**
26:13 I disobeyed none of your **c**,
Dtr 26:17 **c**, and rules, and listen to him.
26:18 you must be sure to obey his **c**.
27:10 your God and follow his **c**
28:1 and faithfully follow all his **c**
28:9 He will do this if you obey the **c**
28:13 if you faithfully obey the **c** of
28:15 and faithfully follow all his **c**
28:45 God or follow his **c** and laws,
30:8 follow all his **c** that I'm giving
30:10 you obey him and follow his **c**
30:16 and obey his **c**, laws,
Jos 22:3 You have carefully kept the **c**
22:5 Carefully follow the **c** and
22:5 his directions, and keep his **c**.
Jdg 2:17 who had obeyed the LORD's **c**.
3:4 out if they would obey the **c**
1Ki 2:3 Obey his directions, laws, **c**,
3:14 my laws and **c** as your father
6:12 my rules, and keep my **c**,
8:58 will follow him and keep his **c**,
8:61 and keep his **c** as you have
9:6 from me and do not keep my **c**
11:10 had given him **c** about this.
11:34 who obeyed my **c** and laws.
11:38 my laws and **c** as my servant
14:8 He obeyed my **c** and faithfully
18:18 it by disobeying the LORD's **c**
2Ki 17:13 and obey my **c** and decrees as
17:13 the **c** I sent to you through my
17:16 They abandoned all the **c** of
17:19 Even Judah didn't obey the **c** of
17:34 or **c** that the LORD gave to the
17:37 and **c** that he wrote for you:
18:6 He obeyed the **c** that the LORD
21:8 if they will obey all the **c**
23:3 the LORD and obey his **c**,
1Ch 22:12 and understanding as he **c** you
28:7 to obey my **c** and laws,
29:19 so that he will obey your **c**,
2Ch 7:19 from me and abandon my **c**
14:4 and follow his teachings and **c**.
17:4 God and lived by God's **c**.
19:10 case involves bloodshed or **c**,
24:20 are you breaking the LORD's **c**?
31:21 Teachings and **c** into worship
33:8 if they will obey all the **c**,
34:31 the LORD and obey his **c**,
Ezr 7:11 knowledge of the LORD's **c**
Neh 9:16 and wouldn't obey your **c**.
Job 9:7 He **c** the sun not to rise.
23:12 I have not left his **c** behind.
Psa 42:8 The LORD **c** his mercy during
78:7 he has done, and to obey his **c**.
112:1 and is happy to obey his **c**.
148:8 strong winds that obey his **c**,
Pro 2:1 and treasure my **c** within you,
3:1 and keep my **c** in mind,
4:4 Obey my **c** so that you may
7:1 Treasure my **c** that are within
7:2 Obey my **c** so that you may
10:8 who is truly wise accepts **c**,
13:13 ⌊God's⌋ **c** will be rewarded.
Ecc 8:2 you to obey the king's **c**
8:5 Whoever obeys his **c** will
12:13 Fear God, and keep his **c**,
Isa 48:18 only you had listened to my **c**!
Joe 2:11 that carry out his **c** are mighty.
Mat 5:19 teaches what the **c** say will
Luk 1:6 **c** and regulations perfectly.
15:29 never disobeyed one of your **c**.
Jon 12:50 I know that what he **c** is
Act 17:30 But now he **c** everyone
1Co 7:19 what God **c** is everything.
14:37 write to you is what the Lord **c**.
Tit 1:14 myths or **c** given by people
2Jn 1:6 we live by doing what he **c**.
Rev 12:17 the ones who keep God's **c**
14:12 who obey his **c** and keep their

commendable (1)

Php 4:8 fair, pure, acceptable, or **c**.

commit (62)

Exo 20:14 "Never **c** adultery.
32:21 you encouraged them to **c** such
Lev 6:3 or **c** any other sin like this,
Num 18:1 any sins you **c** when you work
Dtr 5:18 "Never **c** adultery.
21:7 "We didn't **c** this murder,
Jos 22:31 because you did not **c** an
1Sm 19:4 "You should not **c** a sin against
1Ki 14:16 sins which he led Israel to **c**."
15:30 sins which he led Israel to **c**.
2Ki 3:3 (Nebat's son) led Israel to **c**.
10:29 led Israel to **c** — ⌊the worship
10:31 that Jeroboam led Israel to **c**.
13:2 He continued to **c** the sins that
13:2 (Nebat's son) led Israel to **c**.
13:6 and his dynasty led Israel to **c**.
13:6 They continued to **c** those sins.
13:11 that Jeroboam led Israel to **c**.
13:11 He continued to **c** them.
14:24 (Nebat's son) led Israel to **c**.
15:9 (Nebat's son) led Israel to **c**.
15:18 (Nebat's son) led Israel to **c**.
15:24 (Nebat's son) led Israel to **c**.
15:28 (Nebat's son) led Israel to **c**.
17:21 and led them to **c** a serious sin.
21:16 to his sin that he led Judah to **c**
Neh 13:27 **c** such a serious crime against
Psa 50:18 with people who **c** adultery.
Ecc 8:11 people are encouraged to **c**
8:12 A sinner may **c** a hundred
Jer 7:9 You steal, murder, **c** adultery,
13:27 I have seen you **c** adultery and
23:14 The prophets of Jerusalem **c**
Eze 16:51 "'Samaria didn't **c** half the sins
23:37 They **c** adultery with their idols.
Hos 4:12 They **c** adultery by giving
4:13 and your daughters-in-law **c**
4:14 when they **c** adultery.
7:4 They all **c** adultery.
Mic 7:2 lie in ambush to **c** murder.
Mat 5:27 it was said, 'Never **c** adultery.'
19:18 Never **c** adultery. Never steal.
Mar 10:19 Never **c** adultery. Never steal.
Luk 18:20 Never **c** adultery.
Act 21:25 also should not **c** sexual sins."
Rom 1:27 Men **c** indecent acts with men,
2:22 you tell others not to **c** adultery,
13:9 "Never **c** adultery; never steal;
1Co 5:9 who continue to **c** sexual sins.
5:10 unbelievers who **c** sexual sins,
6:9 who continue to **c** sexual sins,
6:9 those who **c** adultery,
6:18 Other sins that people **c** don't
2Co 11:7 Did I **c** a sin when I humbled
1Th 2:16 Jews always **c** as many sins
Heb 13:4 judge those who **c** sexual sins,
13:4 especially those who **c**
Jas 2:11 "Never **c** adultery,"
2:11 If you do not **c** adultery but you
4:2 don't have, so you **c** murder.
1Jn 5:16 This is true for those who **c**
Rev 2:22 Those who **c** sexual sins with

commitment (3)

1Sm 7:3 Make a **c** to the LORD,
1Ki 3:6 truth, righteousness, and **c**.
2Co 9:13 of service because of your **c**

commits (4)

Lev 20:10 "If a man **c** adultery with
Pro 6:32 Whoever **c** adultery with a
30:20 of a woman who **c** adultery:
Heb 12:16 Make sure that no one **c**

committed (90)

Gen 13:13 They **c** terrible sins against the
34:7 because Shechem had **c** such
50:17 sin your brothers **c** against you.
Exo 32:30 "You have **c** a serious sin.
32:31 "These people have **c** such a
Lev 5:6 to the LORD for the sin you **c**.
5:7 a guilt offering for the sin you **c**.
5:11 as an offering for the sin you **c**.
16:16 the sins the Israelites **c** against
16:16 because they **c** rebellious acts.
16:18 the LORD there for the sins **c**.
16:34 for all the sins the Israelites **c**."
Num 5:15 someone of a sin that was **c**.
12:11 us for this foolish sin we **c**.

Num 35:33 The land where a murder was **c**
Dtr 9:18 because of the sin you **c**.
19:15 or sin he may have **c**.
21:1 one knows who **c** the murder,
22:21 death because she has **c** such
22:26 She has not **c** a sin for which
Jos 22:16 act you have **c** against
22:17 Does the sin we **c** at Peor
Jdg 9:24 **c** against Jerubbaal's 70
1Sm 3:14 for the sins that Eli's family **c**."
14:38 Find out what sin was **c** today.
20:1 What sin have I **c** against your
20:8 If I have **c** any crime,
26:18 What crime have I **c**?
2Sm 19:19 "Don't remember the crime I **c**
24:10 "I have **c** a terrible sin by what
1Ki 8:61 May your hearts be **c** to the
11:4 He was no longer **c** to the
15:3 his father had set and wasn't **c**
15:14 Asa remained **c** to the LORD
16:13 This was for all the sins **c** by
16:19 because of the sins he had **c** —
16:31 It wasn't enough that he **c** the
2Ki 17:22 all the sins Jeroboam **c**
21:17 the sins he **c** — written in the
1Ch 12:17 even though I haven't **c** a crime,
21:8 David said to God, "I have **c** a
29:19 completely **c** ⌊to you⌋ so
2Ch 15:17 Asa remained **c** ⌊to the LORD⌋
16:9 find those whose hearts are **c**
Neh 1:6 have **c** against you as
1:6 my father's family and I have **c**.
9:18 They **c** outrageous sins.
9:26 They **c** outrageous sins.
Job 13:23 crimes and sins have I **c**?
Isa 59:6 hands have **c** acts of violence.
Jer 3:9 she polluted the land and **c**
5:7 They **c** adultery, even though I
15:13 have **c** throughout your
29:23 They **c** adultery with their
33:8 that they have **c** against me.
33:8 that they have **c** against me
37:18 crime have I **c** against you,
Eze 16:17 Then you **c** adultery with them.
22:13 and the murders you have **c**.
23:37 They have **c** adultery.
23:45 because these women have **c**
Dan 6:22 I haven't **c** any crime."
Hos 3:1 by others and has **c** adultery.
6:9 Certainly, they have **c** a crime.
Amo 1:3 Damascus has **c** three crimes,
1:6 Gaza has **c** three crimes,
1:9 Tyre has **c** three crimes,
1:11 Edom has **c** three crimes,
1:13 Ammon has **c** three crimes,
2:1 Moab has **c** three crimes,
2:4 Judah has **c** three crimes,
2:6 Israel has **c** three crimes,
Mat 5:28 her has already **c** adultery
5:32 as though she has **c** adultery.
5:32 as though he has **c** adultery.
10:22 you because you are **c** to me.
24:9 you because you are **c** to me.
Mar 13:13 you because you are **c** to me.
15:7 rebels who had **c** murder
Luk 6:22 slander you because you are **c**
18:11 I haven't **c** adultery.
21:17 you because you are **c** to me.
Jon 15:21 you because you are **c** to me,
Act 11:23 to remain solidly **c** to the Lord.
21:20 deeply **c** to Moses' Teachings.
Rom 3:25 to deal with sins **c** in the past.
Heb 9:15 free from the sins they **c** under
Jas 1:25 people free and who remains **c**
1Pe 2:22 Christ never **c** any sin.
Jud 1:7 because they **c** sexual sins

committing (17)

1Ki 15:34 Israel into **c** the ⌊same⌋ sins.
2Ki 13:2 He never gave up **c** those sins.
13:11 evil and never gave up **c**
Ecc 5:6 mouth talk you into **c** a sin.
Dan 4:27 Stop **c** the same errors,
Mat 19:9 unfaithfulness is **c** adultery if
Mar 10:11 another woman is **c** adultery.
10:12 she is **c** adultery."
Luk 16:18 another woman is **c** adultery.
16:18 in this way is **c** adultery.
Jon 8:3 had been caught **c** adultery.
8:46 of you convict me of **c** a sin?
Rom 2:22 are you **c** adultery?
7:3 so she is not **c** adultery if she
1Jn 3:8 because the devil has been **c**
5:16 If you see another believer **c** a
Rev 9:21 not turn away from **c** murder,

common (40)

Gen 11:1 language with a **c** vocabulary.
Lev 4:27 "If a **c** person unintentionally
20:2 The **c** people must stone them
20:4 If the **c** people ignore those
1Ki 10:27 The king made silver as **c** in
17:18 "What do you and I have in **c**,
2Ki 23:6 on the tombs of the **c** people.
25:3 severe that the **c** people had no
25:19 and 60 of the **c** people whom
2Ch 1:15 king made silver and gold as **c**
9:27 The king made silver as **c** in
Est 8:17 Then many **c** people pretended
Job 12:24 He takes away the **c** sense of
Psa 49:2 **c** people and important ones,
62:9 **C** people are only a whisper in
Pro 22:2 rich and the poor have this in **c**:
29:13 an oppressor have this in **c**:
Isa 3:5 and **c** people will make fun of
5:13 Honored men will starve, and **c**
5:14 people and **c** people will go
Jer 1:18 and ⌊all⌋ the **c** people.
26:23 burial ground for the **c** people.
34:19 and all the **c** people who
37:2 and the **c** people didn't listen to
52:6 severe that the **c** people had no
52:25 and 60 **c** people whom he
Eze 7:27 The **c** people will lose their
22:29 The **c** people oppress and rob
39:13 All the **c** people will be burying
45:16 All the **c** people must give this
45:22 himself and for all the **c** people
46:3 The **c** people must worship at
Dan 9:6 and all the **c** people.
Jon 15:19 If you had anything in **c** with
15:19 you don't have anything in **c**
Act 5:12 The believers had a **c** faith in
1Co 12:7 for the **c** good of everyone.
2Co 6:14 anything in **c** with darkness?
11:18 Since it's **c** for people to brag,
Phm 1:6 faith you have in **c** with others,

commotion (2)

1Sm 4:14 Eli asked, "What is this **c**?"
Eze 1:24 like the **c** in an army camp.

communities (1)

Neh 10:37 the produce from all our farm **c**.

community (93)

Gen 28:3 you will become a **c** of people.
35:11 A nation and a **c** of nations will
48:4 you will become a **c** of people.
Exo 12:3 Tell the whole **c** of Israel:
12:6 assembled people from the **c**
12:19 excluded from the **c** of Israel,
12:47 "The whole **c** of Israel must
16:1 The whole **c** of Israelites
16:2 In the desert the whole **c**
16:9 "Tell the whole **c** of Israelites,
16:10 to the whole **c** of Israelites,
16:22 All the leaders of the **c** came to
17:1 The whole **c** of Israelites left
34:31 the leaders of the **c** came back
35:1 the whole Israelite **c**
35:4 said to the whole Israelite **c**,
35:20 whole Israelite **c** left Moses.
38:25 of the **c** was taken weighed
Lev 4:21 It is an offering for sin for the **c**.
Num 1:2 "Take a census of the whole **c**
1:16 the men chosen from the **c**,
1:18 and assembled the whole **c** on
1:53 be angry with the **c** of Israel.
3:7 work for him and the whole **c**
4:34 and the leaders of the **c**
8:9 assemble the whole **c** of Israel.
8:20 Moses, Aaron, and the whole **c**
10:2 Use them to call the **c** together
10:3 the whole **c** will meet with you
12:14 she be excluded from the **c**
13:26 and the whole **c** of Israel at
14:1 Israelite **c** raised their voices
14:5 ground in front of the whole **c**
14:7 said to the whole **c** of Israel,
14:10 But when the whole **c** of Israel
14:27 **c** that keeps complaining
14:35 wicked **c** who have joined
14:37 whole **c** complain about Moses
15:24 the whole **c** must sacrifice a
15:25 LORD for the whole **c** of Israel.
15:26 So the whole **c** of Israel will be
15:33 and Aaron and the whole **c**.
15:35 The whole **c** must take him
15:36 So the whole **c** took him
16:2 well-known leaders of the **c**,
16:3 in the whole **c** is holy,
16:9 from the rest of the **c** of Israel?
16:9 in front of the **c** to serve them.
16:22 be angry with the whole **c**?"
16:24 "Tell the **c**: Move away from
16:26 He said to the **c**, "Move away
16:41 The next day the whole **c** of
16:42 The **c** came together to
16:46 and go quickly into the **c** to
19:9 They will be kept by the **c** of
20:1 In the first month the whole **c** of
20:2 Since the **c** was without water,
20:8 brother Aaron gather the **c**.
20:8 In this way you will give the **c**
20:10 and Aaron assembled the **c**
20:22 The whole **c** of Israel left
20:27 The whole **c** saw them go up
20:29 The whole **c** saw that Aaron
25:6 front of Moses and the whole **c**
26:2 "Take a census of the whole **c**
26:9 men chosen by the **c**,
27:2 and the whole **c** at the entrance
27:16 appoint someone over the **c**
27:17 so that the LORD's **c** will not
27:19 priest Eleazar and the whole **c**,
27:20 authority so that the whole **c**
27:21 Joshua and the whole **c**
27:22 priest Eleazar and the whole **c**.
31:12 and the **c** of Israel at the camp
31:13 and all the leaders of the **c**
31:16 The LORD's **c** experienced a
31:26 of the families of the **c** need
31:27 in the war and the rest of the **c**.
31:43 The **c** received 337,500 sheep
32:2 and the leaders of the **c**,
32:4 LORD won for the **c** of Israel,
35:12 has had a trial in front of the **c**.
35:24 Then the **c** must use these
35:25 ⌊If you are innocent,⌋ the **c**
2Ch 31:18 on them — the whole **c**.
Ezr 10:8 from the **c** of former exiles.
10:14 leaders represent the whole **c**.
Job 30:5 They are driven from the **c**.
Pro 26:26 will be revealed to the **c**.
Jer 30:20 Their **c** will be established in
Mat 18:17 tell it to the **c** of believers.
18:17 If he also ignores the **c**,
Act 22:5 letters to take to the Jewish **c**

companies (10)

Num 31:14 of the **c** and battalions,
31:48 the commanders of the **c** and
Jdg 7:16 the 300 men into three **c**.
7:20 The three **c** also blew their
9:34 He used four **c** to set
9:43 divided them into three **c**,
9:44 The other two **c** charged at
1Sm 29:2 by with their **c** and regiments.
2Ch 26:11 to go to war in their **c** based
Job 1:17 "The Chaldeans formed three **c**

companion (4)

Job 30:29 to jackals and a **c** of ostriches.
Pro 28:24 isn't wrong!" is a **c** to a vandal.
Jer 3:4 You have been my **c** ever
Mal 2:14 Yet, she is your **c**,

companions (6)

Jos 14:8 But my **c** discouraged the
2Ki 9:2 him get up and leave his **c**.
Psa 45:7 you, rather than your **c**,
Sos 1:7 among the flocks of your **c**.
Act 9:8 So his **c** led him into
Heb 1:9 you, rather than your **c**,

company (17)

Jdg 9:37 One **c** is coming along the road
9:44 Abimelech and his **c** charged
2Ki 11:4 Jehoiada sent for the **c**
11:9 The **c** commanders did as the
11:15 the **c** commanders who were
11:19 He took the **c** commanders of
2Ch 23:1 with the **c** commanders:
23:14 the **c** commanders who were
23:20 He took the **c** commanders,
Psa 1:1 or join the **c** of mockers.
50:18 You keep **c** with people who
107:32 in the **c** of respected leaders.
111:1 LORD with all my heart in the **c**
Pro 22:24 never keep **c** with a hothead,
Jer 15:17 I didn't keep **c** with those who
Dan 6:18 the night without food or **c**.
Rom 15:24 After I have enjoyed your **c** for

compare (16)

Job 41:33 Nothing on land can **c** to it.
Psa 35:10 who can **c** with you?
89:6 Who in the skies can **c** with
Sos 1:9 My true love, I **c** you to a mare
Isa 40:18 whom, then, can you **c** God?
40:18 To what statue can you **c** him?
40:25 whom, then, can you **c** me?
46:5 To whom will you **c** me and
46:5 To whom will you **c** me so that
Eze 31:8 in God's garden couldn't **c** to it.
Dan 1:13 Then **c** us to the young men
Mar 4:30 To what can we **c** it?
Luk 13:18 What can I **c** it to?
13:20 He asked again, "What can I **c**
2Co 10:12 same class with or **c** ourselves
10:12 themselves and **c** themselves

compared (7)

Jdg 8:2 "I haven't done anything **c** with
8:3 What have I done **c** with that?"
Job 8:7 in the past will seem small **c**
Psa 39:5 life span is nothing **c** to yours.
Eze 16:52 like they are innocent **c** to you.
Dan 4:35 on earth is nothing **c** to him.
Rom 8:18 sufferings insignificant **c**

compares (1)

Psa 40:5 No one **c** to you! I will tell others

comparing (1)

Gal 6:4 without **c** yourself to others.

comparison (3)

Lam 2:13 What **c** can I make that will
Rom 5:15 There is no **c** between ⌊God's⌋
5:16 There is also no **c** between

compasses (1)

Isa 44:13 chisels and mark them with **c**.

compassion (70)

Dtr 32:36 judge his people and have **c**
2Ch 30:9 will find **c** from those who
Neh 1:11 King Artaxerxes, show me **c**."
9:19 But because of your endless **c**,
9:27 because of your endless **c**.
9:28 many times because of your **c**.
9:31 But your **c** is endless.
Psa 40:11 Do not withhold your **c**
51:1 keeping with your unlimited **c**,
69:16 Out of your unlimited **c**,
77:9 Has he locked up his **c**
79:8 out to us soon with your **c**,
102:13 will rise and have **c** on Zion,
103:4 crowns you with mercy and **c**,
103:13 As a father has **c** for his
103:13 so the LORD has **c** for those
Psa 106:46 He let them find **c** from all
119:77 Let your **c** reach me so that I
119:156 Your acts of **c** are many in
135:14 and have **c** on his servants.
145:9 is good to everyone and has **c**
Pro 12:10 but the **c** of wicked people is
28:13 and abandons them receives **c**.
Isa 9:17 nor will he show **c** for their
13:18 They'll have no **c** for babies,
14:1 The LORD will have **c** for
27:11 Maker won't have **c** on them,
30:18 He rises to have **c** on you.
49:10 The one who has **c** on them
49:13 his people and will have **c**
49:15 Will she have no **c** on the child
54:7 you back with unlimited **c**.
54:8 but I will have **c** on you with
54:10 who has **c** on you.
55:7 and he will show **c** to them.
60:10 but in my favor I have **c** on you.
63:7 of Israel because of his **c**
63:9 In his love and **c** he reclaimed
63:15 of your heart and your **c**?
Jer 6:23 They are cruel and have no **c**.
12:15 I will have **c** on them again.
13:14 or **c** when I destroy them.'"
15:6 I'm tired of showing **c** to you.
16:5 and **c** away from these people,"
21:7 show them **c**, or care for them.'
30:18 to Jacob's tents and show **c**
31:20 I will certainly have **c** on him,"
42:12 I will have **c** on you.
42:12 I will make him have **c** on you
50:42 will be cruel and have no **c**.
Lam 3:22 His **c** is never limited.
3:32 he will have **c** in keeping with
Eze 5:11 I will not have **c** for you or feel
7:4 I will not have **c** for you or feel
7:9 I will not have **c** or feel sorry.
8:18 and I won't have **c** for them or
9:5 Don't have any **c**, and don't feel
9:10 But I will not have **c** or feel
20:17 But I had **c** on them.
39:25 Jacob's captives and have **c**
Hos 2:19 I will show you my love and **c**.
Amo 1:11 refused to show any **c** to them.
Mic 7:19 You will again have **c** on us.
Zec 1:12 much longer until you show **c**
1:16 returned to Jerusalem with **c**.
10:6 because I have **c** for them.
Rom 12:1 because of God's **c** toward us,
Php 1:8 with all the **c** of Christ Jesus,
2:1 you have any sympathy and **c**?
1Pe 3:8 other, have **c**, and be humble.

compassionate (21)

Exo 22:27 I will listen because I am **c**.
34:6 a **c** and merciful God,
2Ch 30:9 your God is merciful and **c**.
Neh 9:17 one who is **c**, merciful, patient,
9:31 You are a merciful and **c** God.
Psa 25:6 your **c** and merciful deeds.
78:38 But he is **c**. He forgave their sin.
86:15 are a **c** and merciful God.
103:8 The LORD is **c**, merciful,
111:4 The LORD is merciful and **c**.
112:4 He is merciful, **c**, and fair.
116:5 and righteous. Our God is **c**.
145:8 The LORD is merciful, **c**,
Dan 1:9 kind and **c** toward Daniel.
9:9 are **c** and forgiving,
9:18 but because you are very **c**.
Joe 2:13 He is merciful and **c**,
Jnh 4:2 you are a merciful and **c** God,
Zec 7:9 and be **c** and kind to each
2Co 1:3 He is the Father who is **c** and
Jas 5:11 the Lord is **c** and merciful.

compete (2)

Exo 9:11 The magicians couldn't **c** with
Jer 12:5 how can you **c** with horses?

competent (2)

Ezr 8:18 brought us someone **c**,
2Ti 2:2 who will be **c** to teach others.

competition (1)

2Ti 2:5 Whoever enters an athletic **c**

complain (17)

Num 14:37 community **c** about Moses by
16:11 that you should **c** about him?"
Dtr 15:9 The poor will **c** to the LORD
24:15 Otherwise, they will **c** to the
Jdg 21:22 or brothers come to us to **c**,
2Sm 19:28 have the right to **c** to the king."
Job 7:11 that is in my spirit and **c** about
Psa 55:17 and night I **c** and groan,
64:1 my voice, O God, when I **c**.
Isa 29:24 who **c** will accept instruction.
40:27 Jacob, why do you **c**?
Jer 2:29 "Why do you **c** about me?
Lam 3:39 person) **c** about being punished
1Co 10:10 Don't **c** as some of them did.
Heb 13:17 joyfully and not **c** about you.
13:17 (Causing them to **c** would not
Jud 1:16 These people **c**, find fault,

complained (20)

Gen 16:5 So Sarai **c** to Abram,
21:25 Then Abraham **c** to Abimelech
Exo 5:15 Israelite foremen **c** to Pharaoh.
15:24 The people **c** about Moses by
16:2 community **c** about Moses
17:2 So they **c** to Moses by saying,
17:3 They **c** to Moses and asked,
17:7 because the Israelites **c**
Num 14:2 They **c** to Moses and Aaron,
14:29 and who **c** about me will die.
16:41 whole community of Israel **c**
20:3 The people **c** to Moses and
20:13 where the Israelites **c** about the
Dtr 1:27 You **c** in your tents and said,
Jos 9:18 **c** about the leaders.
Neh 5:1 **c** publicly about their Jewish
Psa 106:25 They **c** in their tents.
Luk 5:30 Pharisees and their scribes **c**
15:2 Pharisees and the scribes **c**,
Act 6:1 Greek-speaking Jews **c** about

complaining (17)

Exo 16:7 he has heard you **c** about him.
16:7 Why are you **c** about us?"
16:8 has heard you **c** about him.
16:8 You're not **c** about us but about
16:9 He has heard you **c**.'"
16:12 "I've heard the Israelites **c**.
17:2 "Why are you **c** to me?
17:7 [Testing] and Meribah [**C**]
Num 11:1 The people began **c** out loud to
14:27 that keeps **c** about me?
20:13 was the oasis of Meribah [**C**],
27:14 holy I am when they were **c** at
Job 9:27 if I say, 'I will forget my **c**;
21:4 Am I **c** about a person?
Php 2:14 without **c** or arguing.
Jas 5:9 stop **c** about each other,
1Pe 4:9 each other as guests without **c**.

complains (1)

Rom 11:2 Scripture passage when he **c**

complaint (10)

Num 12:2 The LORD heard their **c**.
Neh 5:6 furious when I heard their **c**
Job 10:1 I will freely express my **c**.
23:2 "My **c** is bitter again today.
31:35 write ⌊his **c**⌋ on a scroll.
Pro 23:29 Who has a **c**? Who has wounds
Hab 2:1 what answer I will get to my **c**.
Act 19:38 have a legal **c** against anyone,
1Co 6:1 of you has a **c** against another,
Col 3:13 each other if anyone has a **c**.

complaints (8)

Gen 18:20 have many **c** against them,
18:21 see whether these **c** are true.
19:13 The **c** to the LORD against its
Num 14:27 I've heard the **c** the Israelites
17:5 I will silence the frequent **c**
17:10 you will stop their **c** about me,

Job 35:13 God doesn't listen to idle **c**.
Psa 142:2 I pour out my **c** in his presence

complete (24)

Num 6:13 for Nazirites who **c** their vows:
1Ch 11:8 Millo and making a **c** circuit.
Job 19:13 friends are **c** strangers to me.
Psa 16:11 **C** joy is in your presence.
55:14 to each other in **c** confidence
Isa 10:22 Destruction will be **c** and fair.
Jer 10:8 They are **c** idiots. They learn
51:9 Babylon. Its judgment is **c**.
Eze 36:5 joy and with **c** scorn.
Jon 15:11 and your joy will be **c**.
Act 2:28 In your presence there is **c** joy.'
1Co 13:10 But when what is **c** comes,
13:12 Then I will have **c** knowledge
13:12 God has **c** knowledge of me.
Col 2:2 come from a **c** understanding
2:10 God has made you **c** in Christ.
4:17 Tell Archippus to **c** all the work
1Th 1:5 and with **c** certainty.
1Ti 1:15 and deserves **c** acceptance:
4:9 and deserves **c** acceptance.
6:1 believe must give **c** respect
Phm 1:6 come to have a **c** knowledge
Jas 1:4 Then you will be mature and **c**,
1Pe 2:18 and show them **c** respect.

completed (12)

Gen 26:5 obeyed me and **c** the duties,
50:3 The embalming was **c** in the
2Ch 7:11 royal palace and **c** everything
8:16 temple was laid until it was **c**.
29:34 them until the work was **c**
Est 2:12 to King Xerxes after she had **c**
Rom 15:28 When the collection is **c** and I
Php 3:12 or have already **c** the course.
2Ti 4:7 I have **c** the race. I have kept
Rev 3:2 you are doing has not been **c**
10:7 the mystery of God will be **c**,
14:16 harvesting of the earth was **c**.

completes (1)

Eph 1:23 is Christ's body and **c** him as

completing (1)

Col 1:24 In my body I am **c** whatever

completion (1)

Php 1:6 will carry it through to **c** on the

complex (1)

Luk 21:5 talking about the temple **c**.

complexion (2)

1Sm 16:12 He had a healthy **c**,
17:42 a healthy **c** and good looks.

comprehend (3)

Ecc 1:8 can express, **c**, or understand.
Mat 13:14 will see clearly but never **c**.
Act 28:26 will see clearly but never **c**.

Conaniah (3)

2Ch 31:12 The Levite **C** was in charge of
31:13 and Benaiah to serve under **C**
35:9 **C** and his brothers Shemaiah

conceal (1)

Pro 10:11 of wicked people **c** violence.

concealed (2)

Jon 8:59 However, Jesus was **c**,
12:36 he was **c** as he left.

conceals (1)

Pro 10:18 Whoever **c** hatred has lying

conceit (1)

Isa 16:6 boasting, arrogance, and **c**,

conceited (19)

2Ch 32:25 But Hezekiah was **c**,
32:26 realized they had become **c**.
Psa 18:27 but you bring down a **c** look.
Psa 101:5 tolerate anyone with a **c** look
131:1 O LORD, my heart is not **c**.
Pro 16:5 Everyone with a **c** heart is
21:4 A **c** look and an arrogant
21:24 **c** person is called a mocker.
30:13 around arrogantly and is **c**.
Isa 2:12 all who are arrogant and **c**
9:9 With arrogant and **c** hearts they
Jer 48:29 They are very arrogant, **c**,
Dan 5:20 became so arrogant and **c** that
11:12 southern king will become **c**.
2Co 12:7 to keep me from becoming **c**,
12:7 me to keep me from being **c**.
Php 2:3 out of selfish ambition or be **c**.
1Ti 6:4 is a **c** person. He shows that he
2Ti 3:4 They will be reckless and **c**.

conceive (3)

Job 15:35 They **c** trouble and give birth to
Isa 45:10 "Why did you **c** me?"
59:4 They **c** trouble and give birth to

conceived (8)

Job 3:3 'A boy has been **c**!'
Psa 51:5 a sinner when my mother **c** me.
Sos 3:4 bedroom of the one who **c** me.
Isa 59:13 We have **c** and uttered lies in
Gal 4:23 son of the slave woman was **c**
4:23 the free woman was **c** through
4:29 at that time the son who was **c**
4:29 way persecuted the son **c**

conceives (1)

Psa 7:14 See how that person **c** evil,

concentrate (2)

1Ti 4:13 Until I get there, **c** on reading
Tit 3:8 who believe in God can **c**

concern (10)

Gen 39:8 "My master doesn't **c** himself
Psa 41:1 Blessed is the one who has **c**
Isa 9:19 No one shows **c** for others:
Luk 12:29 "Don't **c** yourself about what
Jon 21:22 how does that **c** you?
21:23 how does that **c** you?"
Act 15:14 showed his **c** by taking from
1Co 9:9 God's **c** isn't for oxen.
12:25 feel the same **c** for each other.
2Co 7:11 wanted to show your **c** for us.

concerned (33)

Gen 39:6 He wasn't **c** about anything
Exo 2:25 and was **c** about them.
4:31 that the LORD was **c** about
Lev 5:19 guilty as far as the LORD is **c**."
Num 15:15 As far as the LORD is **c**,
2Sm 3:28 "As far as the LORD is **c**,
22:24 innocent as far as he was **c**.
Job 7:17 you should be **c** about him?
35:15 and he isn't too **c** about evil.
Psa 18:23 innocent as far as he was **c**.
Jer 3:9 Because she wasn't **c** about
Eze 36:21 I became **c** about my holy
Joe 2:18 Then the LORD became **c**
Mat 6:32 Everyone is **c** about these
6:33 But first, be **c** about his
Luk 1:15 As far as the Lord is **c**,
12:30 Everyone in the world is **c**
12:31 Rather, be **c** about his kingdom.
Jon 10:13 The hired hand is **c** about what
12:43 They were more **c** about what
Rom 6:2 As far as sin is **c**, we have
15:2 We should all be **c** about our
1Co 7:32 An unmarried man is **c** about
7:33 But the married man is **c** about
7:34 woman or a virgin is **c** about
7:34 But the married woman is **c**
10:24 People should be **c** about
2Co 7:7 and how **c** you are about me.
Gal 5:6 to Christ Jesus is **c**,
Php 2:4 Don't be **c** only about your own
2:4 but also be **c** about the
Heb 12:16 or is as **c** about earthly things
Jud 1:19 They are **c** about physical

concerning (25)

Gen 12:20 gave his men orders **c** Abram.
24:9 swore the oath to him **c** this.
47:26 Joseph made a law **c** the land
Lev 19:35 administering justice **c** length,
Rut 4:7 in Israel **c** buying back property
1Sm 3:14 an oath **c** Eli's family line:
10:25 Samuel explained the laws **c**
1Ki 14:19 Everything else **c** Jeroboam,
14:29 Isn't everything else **c**
15:5 the matter **c** Uriah the Hittite).
2Ch 12:15 Aren't the events **c** Rehoboam
Neh 11:24 on all matters **c** the people.
Est 8:5 cancel the official orders ⌊**c**⌋
Job 23:14 He will carry out ⌊his⌋ orders **c**
Psa 139:17 are your thoughts **c** me,
Isa 45:11 me orders **c** my handiwork?
Jer 39:11 an order **c** Jeremiah.
Act 19:23 time a serious disturbance **c**
1Co 7:1 Now, **c** the things that you
7:25 **C** virgins: Even though I don't
8:1 **c** food offered to false gods:
11:34 I will give directions **c** the other
12:1 **c** spiritual gifts.
16:1 Now, **c** the money to be
16:12 **C** Apollos, our brother in the

concerns (3)

1Ki 6:12 "This **c** the temple you are
Psa 46:10 Let go ⌊of your **c**⌋!
1Co 7:32 I don't want you to have any **c**.

conclude (2)

Psa 64:9 Everyone will be afraid and **c**,
Rom 3:28 We **c** that a person has God's

concluded (4)

1Sm 18:26 David **c** that it was acceptable
Jon 19:28 that Scripture could finally be **c**.
Act 16:10 We **c** that God had called us to
19:33 Some people **c** that Alexander

concludes (1)

Psa 10:4 His every thought ⌊**c**⌋,

conclusion (1)

Ecc 12:13 it all, this is the **c**: Fear God,

concubine (22)

Gen 22:24 Nahor's **c**, whose name was
35:22 bed with his father's **c** Bilhah,
36:12 Timna was a **c** of Esau's son
Jdg 8:31 His **c** at Shechem also gave
19:1 Bethlehem in Judah to be his **c**.
19:9 started to leave with his **c**
19:10 saddled donkeys and his **c**.
19:24 daughter and this man's **c**.
19:25 So the Levite grabbed his **c**
19:27 His wife (that is, his **c**) was
19:29 He took his **c** and cut her limb
20:4 "My **c** and I went to Gibeah in
20:5 they raped my **c** until she died.
20:6 So I took my **c** and cut her into
2Sm 3:7 Saul had a **c** named Rizpah
3:7 have sex with my father's **c**?"
21:11 **c** Rizpah (Aiah's daughter)
1Ch 1:32 Keturah, Abraham's **c**,
2:46 Ephah, Caleb's **c**, was the
2:48 Maacah, Caleb's **c**,
7:14 was Manasseh's Aramean **c**.
Ecc 2:8 have with one **c** after another.

concubines (17)

Gen 25:6 given gifts to the sons of his **c**.
2Sm 5:13 David married more **c** and
15:16 him except ten **c** whom
16:21 "Sleep with your father's **c**
16:22 and he slept with his father's **c**
19:5 daughters, wives, and **c** today.
20:3 he took the ten **c** he had left to
1Ki 11:3 and 300 wives who were **c**.
1Ch 3:9 there were the sons of the **c**.
2Ch 11:21 than all his other wives and **c**.
11:21 (He had 18 wives and 60 **c**.
Est 2:14 the guardian of the **c**.

Sos 6:8 There are 60 queens, 80 **c**,
6:9 Queens and **c** saw her and
Dan 5:2 nobles, his wives, and his **c**.
5:3 and **c** drank from them.
5:23 and **c** drank wine from them.

condemn (38)

Lev 17:10 I will **c** them and exclude them
20:3 I will **c** them and exclude them
20:5 I will **c** them and their families.
20:6 "I will **c** people who turn to
26:17 I will **c** you so that you will go
Num 23:7 he said. 'Come, **c** Israel.'
23:8 How can I **c** those whom the
2Sm 14:13 "When you say this, you **c**
1Ki 8:32 **C** the guilty person with the
Job 9:20 my own mouth would **c** me.
10:2 I will say to God, 'Don't **c** me.
34:17 Will you **c** the one who is
34:29 keeps quiet, who can **c** him?
40:8 Would you **c** me so that you
Psa 5:10 **C** them, O God. Let their own
37:33 person's power or **c** him when
94:21 They **c** innocent people to
109:31 who would **c** them to death.
Isa 66:14 but he will **c** his enemies.
Mat 12:41 of judgment and will **c** you,
12:42 She will **c** you, because she
20:18 They will **c** him to death
Mar 10:33 They will **c** him to death and
Luk 11:31 She will **c** them, because she
11:32 they will **c** the people living
Jon 3:17 the world, not to **c** the world,
8:11 said, "I don't **c** you either.
8:26 you and a lot I could **c** you for.
12:47 follow them, I don't **c** them.
12:47 I didn't come to **c** the world but
Act 25:15 him and asked me to **c** him.
Rom 2:1 you **c** yourself, since you,
2:27 Teachings say will **c** you
2:27 He will **c** you in spite of the
8:34 Who will **c** them? Christ has
2Co 7:3 I'm not saying this to **c** you.
1Ti 5:12 They **c** themselves by
1Jn 3:21 if our conscience doesn't **c** us,

condemned (55)

Exo 22:20 must be **c** and destroyed.
Num 23:8 whom the LORD hasn't **c**?
Dtr 15:9 and you will be **c** for your sin.
24:15 and you will be **c** for your sin.
1Ki 13:2 this man **c** the altar.
Psa 9:5 You **c** nations. You destroyed
34:21 hate righteous people will be **c**.
34:22 refuge in him will never be **c**.
79:11 those who are **c** to death.
102:20 free those who were **c** to death.
119:21 who are **c** and wander away
Pro 24:11 Rescue captives **c** to death,
24:24 by people and **c** by nations.
Jer 8:14 The LORD our God has **c** us to
26:11 "This man is **c** to die because
26:16 man should not be **c** to die.
Mat 12:7 not have **c** innocent people.
23:33 you escape being **c** to hell?
27:3 he saw that Jesus was **c**.
Mar 14:64 All of them **c** him with the
16:16 does not believe will be **c**.
Luk 2:34 many people in Israel will be **c**
6:37 and you will never be **c**.
23:40 Can't you see that you're **c** in
24:20 priests and rulers had him **c**
Jon 3:18 who believe in him won't be **c**.
3:18 who don't believe are already **c**
3:19 This is why people are **c**:
8:10 Has anyone **c** you?"
Act 13:27 So they **c** Jesus and fulfilled
Rom 2:12 will still be **c** to destruction.
3:8 They are **c**, and that's what
5:16 one person's failure **c** everyone.
5:18 Therefore, everyone was **c**
8:1 Jesus can no longer be **c**.
8:3 That way God **c** sin in our
9:3 I wish I could be **c** and cut off
14:23 he is **c** because he didn't act in
1Co 4:9 like people **c** to die.
1Co 10:30 why am I **c** for that?
11:32 us so that we won't be **c** along
Gal 1:8 gave you should be **c** to hell,
1:9 that person should be **c** to hell.
2Th 2:12 God disapproves of, will be **c**.
1Ti 3:6 arrogant like the devil and be **c**.
Tit 2:8 message that cannot be **c**.
3:11 They are sinners **c** by their
Heb 11:7 Through faith Noah **c** the world
Jas 5:6 You have **c** and murdered
5:9 each other, or you will be **c**.
5:12 Do this so that you won't be **c**.
2Pe 2:6 God **c** the cities of Sodom and
Jud 1:4 Not long ago they were **c** in
Rev 18:20 God has **c** it for you."
19:2 He has **c** the notorious

condemning (2)

1Ki 13:4 heard the man of God **c**
Luk 6:37 Stop **c**, and you will never be

condemns (5)

Job 15:6 Your ⌊own⌋ mouth **c** you,
Pro 12:2 **c** everyone who schemes.
17:15 whoever **c** righteous people is
Rom 2:2 is right when he **c** people
1Jn 3:20 Whenever our conscience **c** us,

condition (12)

Gen 34:15 consent to you only on one **c**:
34:22 become one nation on one **c**:
1Sm 11:2 a treaty with you on this one **c**:
2Sm 3:13 But there's one **c**: You can't
2Ch 24:13 to its proper **c** and reinforced it.
Pro 27:23 Be fully aware of the **c** of your
Jer 34:13 I put a **c** on the promise I made
Eze 15:5 When the vine was in perfect **c**,
Mat 12:45 In the end the **c** of that person
Luk 11:26 In the end the **c** of that person
13:16 Satan has kept her in this **c** for
Col 1:23 This is on the **c** that you

conditions (11)

Dtr 17:2 may be disregarding the **c**
29:12 ready to accept the terms and **c**
29:14 receive this promise and its **c**.
29:19 Someone may hear the **c** of
29:21 for disaster based on all the **c**
Jos 23:16 When you ignore the **c** placed
2Ki 18:12 their God and disregarded the **c**
Isa 56:4 observe the **c** of my promise.
56:6 observe the **c** of my promise.
Jer 32:11 containing the terms and **c**,
Gal 3:15 cancel a person's will or add **c**

conduct (5)

1Ch 15:21 lyres and to **c** the sheminith.
Neh 2:7 them to grant me safe **c** until
Pro 31:27 She keeps a close eye on the **c**
2Co 12:20 arrogance, and disorderly **c**.
Jas 4:13 **c** business, and make money."

conducted (1)

Neh 13:10 who **c** the worship ⌊in the

confess (11)

Lev 5:5 of these sins, you must **c** it.
16:21 He will **c** over it all the sins,
26:40 "But if they **c** their sins and the
Num 5:7 you must **c** your sin,
Ezr 10:11 **C** to the LORD God of your
Neh 1:6 I **c** the sins that we Israelites
Psa 32:5 I decided to **c** them to you,
38:18 I **c** my guilt. My sin troubles me.
1Co 14:25 and **c** that God is truly among
Php 2:11 and **c** that Jesus Christ is Lord
1Jn 1:9 If we **c** our sins, he forgives

confessed (7)

1Sm 7:6 They **c**, "We have sinned
2Ch 30:22 and **c** their sins to the LORD
Neh 9:2 They stood and **c** their sins as
9:3 they **c** their sins and worshiped
Dan 9:4 I **c** and said, "Lord, you are
Mat 3:6 As they **c** their sins,
Mar 1:5 As they **c** their sins,

confesses (1)

Pro 28:13 Whoever **c** and abandons them

confessing (2)

Ezr 10:1 praying, **c** ⌊these sins⌋, crying,
Dan 9:20 I continued to pray, **c** my sins

confession (2)

Num 5:15 an offering used for a **c** — to
5:18 the offering used for a **c** (that is,

confidence (62)

2Ch 17:6 He had the **c** to live the way
Job 4:6 your fear of God give you **c**
8:14 His **c** is easily shattered.
31:24 "If I put my **c** in gold or said to
Psa 27:3 will still have **c** ⌊in the LORD⌋.
40:4 is the person who places his **c**
55:14 talk to each other in complete **c**
71:5 You have been my **c** ever
112:7 full of **c** in the LORD.
Pro 3:26 The LORD will be your **c**.
11:7 his **c** in strength vanishes.
14:26 of the LORD there is strong **c**,
25:19 ⌊so⌋ is **c** in an unfaithful
Jer 17:7 The LORD will be his **c**.
Mic 7:5 Don't have **c** in ⌊your⌋ friends.
Luk 21:28 begin to happen, stand with **c**!
Rom 5:2 So we brag because of our **c**
5:4 and character creates **c**.
5:5 not ashamed to have this **c**,
12:12 Be happy in your **c**,
15:4 that we would have **c** through
2Co 1:7 We have **c** in you.
3:4 Christ gives us **c** about you in
3:12 Since we have **c** ⌊in the new
7:4 I have great **c** in you,
8:22 he has so much **c** in you.
10:15 We have **c** that as your faith
Gal 5:5 eagerly for the **c** that comes
5:10 The Lord gives me **c** that you
Eph 1:18 You will know the **c** that he
3:12 We can go to God with bold **c**
Php 1:14 of our brothers and sisters **c**
2:24 But the Lord gives me **c** that I
3:3 place any **c** in physical things,
3:4 although I could have **c** in my
3:11 with the **c** that I'll come back to
1Th 1:3 and your **c** in our Lord Jesus
2Th 3:4 The Lord gives us **c** that you
1Ti 1:1 Savior and Christ Jesus our **c**.
3:13 reputation and will have **c** as
4:10 because we place our **c** in the
5:5 has no family has placed her **c**
6:17 arrogant and not to place their **c**
6:17 they should place their **c** in
Tit 1:2 My message is based on the **c**
3:7 who have the **c** that we have
Heb 3:6 to be proud of the **c** we have.
3:14 to our original **c** until the end.
6:18 hold on to the **c** we have been
6:19 We have this **c** as a sure and
6:19 This **c** goes into the ⌊holy⌋
7:19 else that gives us greater **c**
10:35 So don't lose your **c**.
1Pe 1:3 life that has a **c** which is alive
1:13 Place your **c** completely in
1:21 So your faith and **c** are in God.
3:5 is how holy women who had **c**
3:15 defend your **c** ⌊in God⌋ when
1Jn 2:28 he appears we will have **c**,
3:3 So all people who have this **c**
4:17 So we look ahead with **c** to the
Rev 13:10 people need endurance and **c**.

confident (23)

2Ki 18:19 What makes you so **c**?
2Ch 32:10 Why are you so **c** as you live
Job 11:18 You will feel **c** because there's
24:23 let them feel **c** and self-reliant,
40:23 It's **c** ⌊even⌋ when the Jordan
Psa 57:7 My heart is **c**, O God. My heart
57:7 My heart is **c**. I want to sing and
108:1 My heart is **c**, O God. I want to
Isa 12:2 I am **c** and unafraid,

Isa 36:4 What makes you so **c**?
Rom 2:19 You are **c** that you are a guide
4:21 and was absolutely **c** that God
2Co 1:10 We are **c** that he will continue
1:15 **C** of this, I had previously
2:3 I'm **c** about all of you that
5:6 So we are always **c**.
5:8 We are **c** and prefer to live
7:16 I'm pleased that I can be **c**
9:4 us for feeling so **c** as much as
10:7 If anyone is **c** he belongs to
Phm 1:21 I am **c** as I write to you that you
Heb 6:11 you will remain **c** until the end.
1Jn 5:14 We are **c** that God listens to us

confidently (5)

Act 2:29 "Brothers, I can tell you **c** that
1Ti 1:7 about which they speak so **c**.
Heb 4:16 So we can go **c** to the throne of
10:19 of Jesus we can now **c** go into
13:6 So we can **c** say, "The Lord is

confined (7)

Gen 40:4 they had been **c** for some time,
41:10 he **c** me and the chief baker to
Exo 21:29 warned but has not kept it **c**,
21:36 and its owner didn't keep it **c**,
Neh 6:10 Shemaiah who was **c** to his
Jer 39:15 While Jeremiah was still **c** in
Act 9:33 who was paralyzed and **c**

confinement (2)

2Sm 20:3 widows in **c** until they died.
Act 16:24 Paul and Silas into solitary **c**

confining (1)

Jos 17:15 of Ephraim are too **c** for you."

confirm (10)

Dtr 9:5 because the LORD wants to **c**
29:13 the LORD will **c** today that you
1Sm 26:4 David sent spies to **c** that Saul
1Ki 1:14 I'll come in and **c** what you
2Ki 23:24 He did this to **c** the words of
Psa 75:1 and your miracles **c** that.
Jer 32:25 and get witnesses to **c** it,
Dan 9:27 He will **c** his promise with
Jon 3:11 and we **c** what we've seen.
Act 7:8 circumcision to **c** his promise.

confirmed (12)

1Sm 11:15 they **c** Saul as their king.
2Ki 23:3 He **c** the terms of the promise
1Ch 16:17 He **c** it as a law for Jacob,
Neh 6:6 and Geshem has **c** it,
Job 28:27 He **c** it and examined it.
Psa 105:10 He **c** it as a law for Jacob,
Pro 20:18 Plans are **c** by getting advice,
Mar 16:20 He **c** his word by the
Act 14:3 who **c** their message about his
2Ti 2:2 and it's been **c** by many
Heb 2:3 who heard him **c** that message.
2Pe 1:19 prophets as **c** beyond all doubt.

confirming (2)

Dtr 8:18 He's **c** the promise which he
Php 1:7 I'm in prison or defending and **c**

confirms (1)

Isa 44:26 He **c** the word of his servant

confiscate (4)

1Ki 21:15 **C** the vineyard which Naboth
21:16 Ahab went to **c** the vineyard.
21:18 He went to **c** Naboth's vineyard.
21:19 just to **c** ⌞a vineyard⌟?'

confiscated (3)

1Ki 21:26 (The LORD **c** their land for
1Ch 5:21 They **c** the Hagrites' livestock:
Ezr 7:26 exiled, have his goods **c**,

confiscates (1)

Pro 29:4 but a person who **c** religious

conflict (8)

Psa 55:9 I see violence and **c** in the city.
80:6 You made us a source of **c** to
Pro 6:14 a twisted mind. He spreads **c**.
6:19 spreads **c** among relatives.
22:10 out a mocker, and **c** will leave.
Mat 10:34 come to bring peace but **c**.
Gal 5:20 selfish ambition, **c**, factions,
1Ti 6:5 and **c** between people whose

conflicts (4)

Gen 16:12 He will have **c** with all his
2Sm 22:44 You rescued me from my **c**
Psa 18:43 You rescued me from my **c**
2Co 7:5 Outwardly we have **c**,

conform (3)

Ezr 7:18 However, what you do must **c**
Gal 5:25 then our lives need to **c** to our
6:16 come to rest on all those who **c**

confront (10)

Num 16:3 They came together to **c**
16:42 came together to **c** Moses
20:2 together to **c** Moses and Aaron.
2Ch 14:10 Asa went to **c** him,
Job 41:11 Who can **c** me that I should
Psa 17:13 Arise, O LORD; **c** them!
Isa 27:4 thorns and briars would **c** me!
50:8 Let us **c** each other!
50:8 accuses me? Let him **c** me!
Mat 18:15 **c** him when the two of you are

confronted (9)

Gen 31:36 became angry and **c** Laban.
2Sm 22:6 The clutches of death had **c**
22:19 I faced disaster, they **c** me,
1Ki 1:6 His father had never **c** him by
1Ch 19:17 the Jordan, and **c** them.
Neh 5:7 I **c** the nobles and the leaders.
Psa 17:3 You have **c** me at night.
18:5 The clutches of death had **c**
18:18 I faced disaster, they **c** me,

confronts (2)

Psa 34:16 The LORD **c** those who do evil
1Pe 3:12 The Lord **c** those who do evil."

confuse (3)

Psa 55:9 Completely **c** their language,
Isa 29:9 If you **c** yourselves,
Act 17:13 there to upset and **c** the people.

confused (15)

Job 37:20 a person speak when he is **c**?
Psa 35:26 thoroughly put to shame and **c**.
40:14 who seek to end my life be **c**
55:2 are restless, and I am **c**
70:2 those who seek my life be **c**
Isa 21:4 I'm **c**. I'm shaking with terror.
28:7 and become **c** from too much
29:9 yourselves, you will be **c**.
Jer 8:9 put to shame, **c**, and trapped.
Joe 1:18 of cattle wander around **c**.
Mic 7:4 Now is the time you will be **c**.
Luk 21:25 will be deeply troubled and **c**
Act 9:22 and he **c** the Jews living in
15:24 who came from us have **c** you
19:32 The crowd was **c**.

confusing (2)

Gal 1:7 They are **c** you. They want to
5:10 However, the one who is **c** you

confusion (17)

1Sm 7:10 them into such **c** that they were
14:19 the **c** in the Philistine camp
14:20 their fellow soldiers in wild **c**.
2Sm 18:29 "I saw a lot of **c** when Joab
22:15 lightning and threw them into **c**.
Neh 4:8 to attack Jerusalem to create **c**.
Job 10:22 shadows and **c** where light is
Psa 18:14 lightning and threw them into **c**.
35:4 downfall be turned back in **c**.
144:6 and throw them into **c**.

Isa 22:5 It will be a day of **c** and
Jer 51:34 He has thrown us into **c**.
Eze 7:7 There will be **c**. There will be
22:5 and you will be filled with **c**.
Amo 3:9 See the widespread **c** and
Act 19:29 The **c** spread throughout the
21:34 because of the noise and **c**,

congratulate (4)

2Sm 8:10 to greet King David and **c** him
1Ki 1:47 come ⌞to⌟ **c** His Majesty King
1Ch 18:10 to greet King David and **c** him
Ecc 4:2 I **c** the dead, who have already

congregation (50)

Lev 4:13 "If the whole **c** of Israel
4:14 the **c** must sacrifice a bull as
4:15 The leaders of the **c** will place
8:3 Gather the whole **c** at the
8:4 and the **c** gathered at the
8:5 Moses told the **c**, "The LORD
9:5 The whole **c** came and stood
10:6 angry with the whole **c**.
10:17 to take away the sins of the **c**
16:5 take two male goats from the **c**
19:2 "Tell the whole **c** of Israel:
24:14 Then the whole **c** must stone
24:16 The whole **c** must stone them
Num 20:12 So you will not bring this **c** into
Dtr 31:30 Then, as the whole **c** of Israel
Jos 9:15 The leaders of the **c** swore to it
9:18 because the leaders of the **c**
9:18 The whole **c** complained about
9:21 water carriers for the whole **c**,
9:27 and water carriers for the **c**.
18:1 The whole **c** of Israel gathered
20:6 can stand trial in front of the **c**
20:9 he stands trial in front of the **c**.
22:12 the whole **c** of Israel gathered
22:16 "All of the LORD's **c** is asking,
22:17 was a plague on the LORD's **c**!
22:18 with the whole **c** of Israel.
22:20 with the whole **c** of Israel?
22:30 the leaders of the **c**,
Jdg 20:1 The **c** stood united in the
20:2 tribes took their places in the **c**
21:10 The **c** sent 12,000 soldiers.
21:13 Then the whole **c** sent
21:14 However, the **c** had not found
21:15 The **c** felt sorry for the people
21:16 The leaders of the **c** asked,
1Ch 28:8 sight of Israel (the LORD's **c**)
Neh 5:13 Then the whole **c** said amen
Psa 22:22 I will praise you within the **c**.
74:2 Remember your **c**.
111:1 of decent people and in the **c**.
Pro 5:14 in the assembly and in the **c**."
Lam 1:10 have forbidden to enter your **c**.'
Act 15:30 They gathered the **c** together
15:33 the **c** sent them back to
1Co 14:23 Suppose the whole **c** gathers
Heb 2:12 I will praise you within the **c**."
3Jn 1:6 These believers have told the **c**
1:9 I wrote a letter to the **c**.
1:10 throw those people out of the **c**.

congregations (1)

2Co 8:24 Show their **c** that we were right

conjure (3)

1Sm 28:8 **C** up the person I request."
28:11 "Whom should I **c** up for you?"
28:11 "**C** up Samuel for me,"

conjures (2)

1Sm 28:7 "Find me a woman who **c** up
28:7 at Endor who **c** up the dead."

conjuring (1)

1Sm 28:15 you disturb me by **c** me up?"

connect (1)

Job 38:31 "Can you **c** the chains of the

connected (2)

Eze 41:9 the side rooms **c** to the temple

Rom 12:5 who are **c** to each other.

connection (2)

Jos 22:25 You have no **c** with the LORD!'
22:27 'You have no **c** with the LORD!'

conquer (11)

Num 13:30 be more than able to **c** it."
24:24 They will **c** Assyria and Eber.
32:29 with you and you **c** the land,
2Ch 32:1 He intended to **c** them himself.
Isa 11:14 They will **c** Edom and Moab.
45:1 by his right hand so he could **c**
Rom 12:21 Don't let evil **c** you,
12:21 but **c** evil with good.
Rev 11:7 them, **c** them, and kill them.
13:7 holy people and to **c** them.
17:14 The lamb will **c** them because

conquered (17)

Gen 14:7 and they **c** the whole territory of
Num 24:18 Edom will be **c**, and Seir,
24:18 and Seir, his enemy, will be **c**.
32:22 and the land is **c**. Then you may
Jos 13:1 there is a lot of land left to be **c**.
2Sm 8:11 from all the nations he **c** —
1Ki 11:15 When David had **c** Edom,
15:20 He **c** Ijon, Dan, Abel Beth
2Ki 12:17 fought against Gath and **c** it.
18:8 He **c** the Philistines from the
1Ch 22:18 and the country has been **c** by
2Ch 8:3 went to Hamath Zobah and **c** it.
16:4 He **c** Ijon, Dan, Abel Maim,
27:5 of the Ammonites and **c** them.
Neh 9:28 to their enemies, who **c** them.
Eze 26:10 enter as people enter a **c** city.
Heb 11:33 Through faith they **c** kingdoms,

conquering (1)

Jos 18:3 are you going to waste time **c**

conqueror (2)

Isa 14:12 to the ground, you **c** of nations!
Mic 1:15 I will again bring a **c** against

conquerors (1)

Isa 49:24 or prisoners be freed from **c**?

conquests (1)

Job 40:19 is the first of God's **c**.

conscience (32)

Gen 20:5 innocence and with a clear **c**."
20:6 this with a clear **c**," God said
1Sm 24:5 But afterward, David's **c**
25:31 you shouldn't have a troubled **c**
2Sm 24:10 his **c** troubled him.
Job 27:6 My **c** won't accuse me as long
Psa 16:7 My **c** warns me at night.
Ecc 7:22 Your **c** knows that you have
Act 23:1 given me a perfectly clear **c**."
24:16 do my best to have a clear **c**
Rom 13:5 also because of your own **c**.
1Co 4:4 I have a clear **c**, but that
8:7 guilty because their **c** is weak.
8:10 with a weak **c** sees you,
10:25 letting your **c** trouble you.
10:27 letting your **c** trouble you.
10:28 informed you and because of **c**.
10:29 I'm not talking about your **c** but
10:29 but the other person's **c**.
10:29 judged by someone else's **c**?
2Co 1:12 We are proud that our **c** is clear.
1Ti 1:5 a pure heart, from a clear **c**,
1:18 in faith and with a clear **c**
1:19 to let their faith guide their **c**
2Ti 1:3 whom I serve with a clear **c** as
Heb 9:9 give the worshiper a clear **c**.
10:22 to free us from a guilty **c**,
1Pe 3:16 Keep your **c** clear.
3:21 a request to God for a clear **c**.
1Jn 3:20 Whenever our **c** condemns us,
3:20 our **c** and knows everything.
3:21 if our **c** doesn't condemn us,

consciences (9)

1Ki 8:38 whose **c** bother them,
Rom 2:15 Their **c** speak to them.
1Co 8:12 way and harm their weak **c**,
1Ti 3:9 They must have clear **c** about
4:2 Their **c** have been scarred as if
Tit 1:15 minds and their **c** are
Heb 9:14 to God and cleansed our **c** from
10:2 Their **c** would have been free
13:18 We are sure that our **c** are clear

consecrate (1)

Eze 43:26 at the altar, purify it, and **c** it.

consecutive (2)

Lev 23:36 For seven **c** days bring a
Act 17:2 On three **c** days of worship,

consent (3)

Gen 34:15 We will give our **c** to you only
34:22 These people will **c** to live
Phm 1:14 to do anything without your **c**.

consented (1)

1Ch 13:2 and if the LORD our God has **c**,

consequence (1)

Pro 22:3 go ahead and suffer ⌊the **c**⌋.

consequences (6)

Num 5:31 will suffer the **c** of her sin."
9:13 must suffer the **c** for your sin.
18:22 Otherwise, they'll suffer the **c**
18:32 you won't suffer the **c** of any
30:15 he will suffer the **c**."
Job 8:4 suffer the **c** of their sinfulness.

consider (88)

Gen 18:27 Abraham asked, "**C** now,
Exo 8:26 that they **c** disgusting,
19:23 the mountain and **c** it holy."
Lev 11:10 However, you must **c** all
11:11 **C** their dead bodies disgusting.
11:13 of birds you must **c** disgusting
11:42 **C** them disgusting.
Num 18:10 You must **c** it holy.
23:9 people who do not **c**
Dtr 7:26 **C** it detestable and disgusting.
23:7 Never **c** the Edomites
23:7 Never **c** the Egyptians
1Sm 12:24 **C** the great things he did for
15:17 you don't **c** yourself great,
25:17 Now, **c** what you should do
29:6 I **c** your campaigning with me a
2Sm 7:19 And even this you **c** to be a
1Ki 11:33 He did not do what I **c** right or
11:38 and do what I **c** right by
20:6 anything that you **c** valuable."'
20:22 **C** what you have to do.
2Ki 10:30 "You did what I **c** right,
20:3 I've done what you **c** right.
21:15 they have done what I **c** evil
1Ch 17:17 And this you **c** to be a small
Neh 5:19 **C** everything that I have done
9:32 Do not **c** all the hardships that
Est 8:5 if you **c** my cause to be
Job 13:24 me⌋ and **c** me your enemy?
19:15 My female slaves **c** me to be a
30:10 Since they **c** me disgusting,
33:1 words and **c** everything I say.
34:27 following him and didn't **c** any
37:14 Stop and **c** God's miracles.
Psa 5:1 **C** my innermost thoughts.
28:5 because they never **c** what he
50:22 **C** this, you people who forget
51:4 I have done what you **c** evil.
74:20 **C** your promise because every
137:6 if I don't **c** Jerusalem my
143:5 I carefully **c** what your hands
Pro 3:7 Do not **c** yourself wise.
6:6 **C** the ant, you lazy bum.
Ecc 7:13 **C** what God has done!
7:14 But when times are bad, **c** this:
Isa 5:21 are wise and **c** themselves
38:3 I've done what you **c** right.
41:20 Together they will **c** and
41:22 about so that we may **c** them
47:7 You didn't carefully **c** these
53:3 and we didn't **c** him to be worth
65:12 You did what I **c** evil.
66:4 They did what I **c** evil.
Jer 2:31 "**C** the word of the LORD,
7:30 Judah have done what I **c** evil,"
9:17 LORD of Armies says: **C** this:
18:10 that nation does what I **c** evil
32:30 Judah have done what I **c** evil.
33:24 they no longer **c** them a nation.
34:15 changed and did what I **c** right.
Lam 2:20 "O LORD, look and **c**:
Dan 8:25 He will **c** himself to be great
Hos 8:12 but they **c** these things strange
Hag 1:5 Carefully **c** your ways!
1:7 Carefully **c** your ways!
2:15 from now on, carefully **c** this.
2:15 **C** how things were before one
2:18 Carefully **c** from now on,
2:18 LORD was laid. Carefully **c**:
Mal 2:2 and if you won't **c** giving honor
2:2 you don't carefully **c** this.
Luk 12:24 **C** the crows. They don't plant or
12:27 **C** how the flowers grow.
Act 5:35 **c** carefully what you do with
13:46 Since you reject the word and **c**
15:6 leaders met to **c** this statement.
Rom 6:11 So **c** yourselves dead to sin's
8:18 I **c** our present sufferings
11:1 **C** this. I'm an Israelite myself, a
14:16 that what you **c** good is evil.
1Co 1:26 Brothers and sisters, **c** what
Php 3:7 I now **c** worthless for Christ.
3:8 I **c** everything else worthless
3:13 I can't **c** myself a winner yet.
2Ti 1:13 **c** what you heard me say to be
Heb 10:24 We must also **c** how to
Jas 5:11 We **c** those who endure to be
1Jn 3:1 **C** this: The Father has given

considerate (1)

Php 4:5 everyone know how **c** you are.

consideration (1)

Pro 21:10 and has no **c** for his neighbor.

considered (122)

Gen 30:33 isn't black will be **c** stolen."
Lev 27:9 to the LORD, it will be **c** holy.
Num 18:27 Your contribution will be **c** to
18:30 your contribution will be **c** to be
24:7 kingdom will be **c** the best.
Dtr 9:18 You did what the LORD **c** evil
Jos 13:3 This is **c** to be Canaanite
Jdg 2:11 did what the LORD **c** evil.
3:7 did what the LORD **c** evil.
3:12 did what the LORD **c** evil.
3:12 did what the LORD **c** evil.
4:1 did what the LORD **c** evil.
6:1 did what the LORD **c** evil.
10:6 did what the LORD **c** evil.
13:1 did what the LORD **c** evil.
17:6 Everyone did whatever he **c**
21:25 Everyone did whatever he **c**
1Sm 2:30 me will be **c** insignificant.
8:6 But Samuel **c** it wrong for them
18:8 angry because he **c** this saying
2Sm 4:2 (Beeroth was **c** a part of
11:27 LORD **c** David's actions evil.
12:9 word by doing what I **c** evil?
13:13 And you will be **c** one of the
1Ki 10:21 because it wasn't **c** valuable in
11:6 did what the LORD **c** evil.
14:8 me by doing only what I **c** right.
14:22 did what the LORD **c** evil.
15:5 did what the LORD **c** right:
15:11 Asa did what the LORD **c** right,
15:26 He did what the LORD **c** evil,
15:34 He did what the LORD **c** evil.
16:7 did which the LORD **c** evil.
16:19 the things the LORD **c** evil.
16:25 Omri did what the LORD **c** evil.
16:30 did what the LORD **c** evil.
21:25 to do what the LORD **c** evil.

1Ki 22:43 and did what the LORD **c** right.
22:52 He did what the LORD **c** evil.
2Ki 3:2 He did what the LORD **c** evil,
8:18 So he did what the LORD **c**
8:27 He did what the LORD **c** evil,
12:2 did what the LORD **c** right,
13:2 He did what the LORD **c** evil.
13:11 He did what the LORD **c** evil
14:3 He did what the LORD **c** right,
14:24 He did what the LORD **c** evil.
15:3 He did what the LORD **c** right,
15:9 He did what the LORD **c** evil,
15:18 He did what the LORD **c** evil.
15:24 He did what the LORD **c** evil.
15:28 He did what the LORD **c** evil.
15:34 He did what the LORD **c** right,
16:2 what the LORD his God **c** right,
17:2 He did what the LORD **c** evil,
17:17 by doing what the LORD **c** evil,
18:3 He did what the LORD **c** right,
21:2 He did what the LORD **c** evil
21:20 He did what the LORD **c** evil,
22:2 did what the LORD **c** right.
23:32 He did what the LORD **c** evil,
23:37 did what the LORD **c** evil,
24:9 did what the LORD **c** evil,
24:19 did what the LORD **c** evil,
1Ch 2:3 The LORD **c** Er, evil, so the
13:4 to this because the people **c**
21:7 God **c** the census to be sinful,
2Ch 9:20 (Silver wasn't **c** valuable in
14:2 his God **c** good and right.
20:32 and did what the LORD **c** right.
21:6 So he did what the LORD **c**
22:4 He did what the LORD **c** evil,
24:2 did what the LORD **c** right,
25:2 He did what the LORD **c** right,
26:4 He did what the LORD **c** right,
27:2 He did what the LORD **c** right,
28:1 didn't do what the LORD **c** right,
29:2 He did what the LORD **c** right,
29:6 what the LORD our God **c** evil.
30:4 whole assembly **c** their plan
32:23 From then on, he was **c**
33:2 He did what the LORD **c** evil
33:22 He did what the LORD **c** evil,
34:2 He did what the LORD **c** right.
35:5 Let the Levites be **c** a part of
36:5 what the LORD his God **c** evil.
36:9 He did what the LORD **c** evil.
36:12 what the LORD his God **c** evil
Ezr 2:62 For this reason they were **c**
Neh 7:64 For this reason they were **c**
9:28 again doing what you **c** evil.
Job 15:14 Why should a mortal be **c**
15:14 of a woman be **c** righteous?
18:3 Why are we **c** stupid in your
34:6 I'm **c** a liar in spite of my rights.
38:18 Have you ⌊even⌋ **c** how wide
Psa 49:3 the insights I have carefully **c**.
77:5 I have **c** the days of old,
106:31 was **c** righteous forever,
109:7 Let his prayer be **c** sinful.
Pro 17:28 He is **c** intelligent if he keeps
27:14 his blessing is **c** a curse.
Ecc 8:9 and I have carefully **c** all that is
8:16 When I carefully **c** how to
Sos 1:7 ⌊Tell me,⌋ or I will be **c** a
Isa 29:17 fertile field will be **c** a forest.
32:5 nor will scoundrels be **c**
32:15 fertile field will be **c** a forest.
40:15 a drop in a bucket and are **c**
Jer 30:19 and they won't be **c**
52:2 did what the LORD **c** evil,
Dan 6:22 this because he **c** me innocent.
Mal 2:17 "Everyone who does evil is **c**
Luk 20:35 But people who are **c** worthy to
22:24 who should be **c** the greatest.
Jon 11:50 You haven't even **c** this:
Act 5:41 happy to have been **c** worthy
Rom 2:26 won't he be **c** circumcised
9:8 are **c** Abraham's descendants.
12:17 those things that are **c** noble.
Php 3:7 things that I once **c** valuable,
2Th 1:5 right and that you are **c** worthy

considering (1)

1Ch 12:19 him away after **c** the matter.

considers (34)

Exo 15:26 God and do what he **c** right,
Dtr 4:25 that the LORD your God **c** evil,
6:18 Do what the LORD **c** right and
12:8 does whatever he **c** right.
12:25 doing what the LORD **c** right.
12:28 your God **c** good and right.
13:18 and do what he **c** right.
17:2 is doing what the LORD **c** evil.
21:9 doing what the LORD **c** right.
31:29 by doing what he **c** evil."
33:21 the LORD **c** fair and honorable."
1Sm 15:19 done what the LORD **c** evil?"
2Sm 10:12 LORD will do what he **c** right."
15:26 let him do to me what he **c**
23:5 "Truly, God **c** my house to be
1Ki 21:20 to do what the LORD **c** evil.
2Ki 3:18 The LORD **c** that an easy thing
1Ch 19:13 LORD will do what he **c** right."
Job 19:11 He **c** me to be his enemy.
33:10 He **c** me his enemy.
41:27 It **c** iron to be like straw and
41:29 It **c** clubs to be like stubble,
Pro 12:15 A stubborn fool **c** his own way
15:28 person carefully **c** how
21:12 A righteous person wisely **c**
Sos 8:10 So he **c** me to be one who has
Isa 40:17 He **c** them less than nothing
Rom 4:8 whom the Lord never **c** sinful."
1Co 1:27 what the world **c** nonsense
1:27 God chose what the world **c**
1:28 God chose what the world **c**
1:28 what it despises — what it **c**
1:28 what it **c** to be something.
1Pe 3:4 attitude which God **c** precious.

consist (1)

Rom 14:17 God's kingdom does not **c** of

consisted (2)

1Ch 27:1 Each unit **c** of 24,000 men.
Mat 3:4 His diet **c** of locusts and wild

consists (2)

Psa 122:5 It **c** of ⌊princes who are⌋
Rom 14:17 Rather, God's kingdom **c** of

consoled (1)

2Sm 13:39 people had **c** him over Amnon's

consoling (1)

Jer 16:7 No one will give a **c** drink to

conspiracy (7)

2Sm 15:12 the **c** grew stronger,
2Ki 15:15 all about his **c** — is written
Est 8:3 and his **c** against the Jews.
Isa 8:12 these people call a **c** is
8:12 people call a conspiracy is a **c**.
Jer 11:9 The LORD said to me, "**C**
Act 23:12 morning the Jews formed a **c**.

conspirators (2)

2Ki 14:19 **C** in Jerusalem plotted against
2Ch 25:27 **c** in Jerusalem plotted against

conspired (1)

2Ch 24:26 the men who **c** against him:

conspiring (1)

2Sm 15:31 among those **c** with Absalom."

constant (8)

Exo 28:29 over his heart as a **c** reminder
1Sm 18:29 and so Saul became David's **c**
Ecc 5:17 in **c** frustration, sickness,
Isa 51:13 Why should you live in **c** fear
Nah 3:4 of Nineveh's **c** prostitution,
Jon 3:36 he will see God's **c** anger."
Eph 4:19 with a **c** desire for more.
Col 2:23 for holding back the **c** desires

constellation (1)

Job 38:31 the chains of the ⌊**c**⌋ Pleiades

constellations (4)

Job 9:9 He made ⌊the **c**⌋ Ursa Major,
38:32 Can you bring out the **c** at the
Isa 13:10 The stars in the sky and their **c**
Amo 5:8 God made the ⌊**c**⌋ Pleiades

construct (1)

Exo 35:21 The gifts were used to **c** the

constructed (1)

1Ch 15:1 After David **c** buildings for

constructing (2)

Exo 36:1 the work for **c** the holy place."
36:3 had brought for the work of **c**

construction (3)

Exo 35:24 be used in the **c** brought it.
1Ki 6:7 a sound at the temple **c** site.
Ezr 5:16 The temple has been under **c**

constructive (2)

Pro 13:18 but whoever pays attention to **c**
25:12 ⌊so⌋ is **c** criticism to the ear of

consult (8)

Lev 19:26 and never **c** fortunetellers.
Dtr 18:11 or spirits for help, or **c** the dead.
1Sm 14:36 "Let's **c** God first."
28:8 He said to her, "Please **c** with
1Ch 21:30 David couldn't go there to **c**
Isa 40:14 Whom did he **c**? Who gave him
45:21 Yes, let them **c** one another.
Jer 21:2 "**C** the LORD for us,

consulted (3)

2Ki 21:6 as a sacrifice, **c** fortunetellers,
1Ch 13:1 David **c** with every officer who
2Ch 33:6 of Ben Hinnom, **c** fortunetellers

consume (10)

Dtr 5:25 This great fire will **c** us!
32:22 It will **c** the earth and its crops
Ecc 5:11 number of people who **c** them.
Isa 61:6 You will **c** the wealth of the
Eze 22:31 with my fiery anger I will **c** you.
Hos 7:7 They **c** their judges ⌊like a
Nah 3:15 Fire will **c** you there.
3:15 It will **c** you like locusts.
Jon 2:17 "Devotion for your house will **c**
Heb 10:27 fire that will **c** God's enemies.

consumed (11)

Lev 6:10 on the altar from the fire that **c**
9:24 the LORD's presence and **c**
Num 16:35 Fire came from the LORD and **c**
26:10 followers died when the fire **c**
1Ki 18:38 from the LORD fell down and **c**
2Ch 7:1 came down from heaven and **c**
Psa 69:9 for your house has **c** me,
78:63 Fire **c** his best young men,
Pro 5:11 your body and flesh are **c**.
Zep 1:18 The whole earth will be **c** by
3:8 The whole land will be **c** by

consumes (3)

Psa 90:7 Indeed, your anger **c** us.
119:139 ⌊for your words⌋ **c** me,
2Co 11:20 you slaves, **c** your wealth,

contact (1)

1Co 5:10 that you could not have any **c**

contain (4)

Lev 24:5 Each ring will **c** four quarts of
1Ki 17:14 and the jug will always **c** oil."
Rom 2:14 that Moses' Teachings **c**,
2Co 6:16 God's temple **c** false gods?

contained (5)

Gen 40:17 The top basket **c** all kinds of
1Sm 6:15 the LORD and the box which **c**

2Sm 12:30 weighed 75 pounds and **c**
1Ki 17:16 and the jug always **c** olive oil,
Heb 9:4 It **c** the gold incense burner and

container (8)

Gen 21:14 Abraham took bread and a **c**
21:15 the water in the **c** was gone,
21:19 She filled the **c** with water and
Num 19:15 Every **c** without a lid fastened
19:17 as an offering for sin into a **c**.
1Ki 1:39 The priest Zadok took the **c** of
2Ki 4:6 "Bring me another **c**."
Eze 4:9 Put them in a **c**, and use them

containers (10)

Exo 7:19 in the wooden and stone **c**.'"
16:18 measured it into two-quart **c**.
Num 4:9 and all the **c** for the olive oil
2Ki 4:3 "Borrow many empty **c** from all
4:4 and pour oil into all those **c**.
4:5 children kept bringing **c** to her,
4:6 When the **c** were full,
4:6 "There are no more **c**."
Jer 14:3 come back with their **c** empty.
Mat 13:48 gathered the good fish into **c**,

containing (23)

Exo 23:18 time you offer anything **c** yeast.
26:33 and put the ark **c** the words of
30:6 which ⌊hangs⌋ over the ark **c**
30:26 the ark **c** the words of my
30:36 and put it in front of ⌊the ark **c**⌋
31:7 the tent of meeting, the ark **c**
34:25 time you offer anything **c** yeast.
39:35 the ark **c** the words of God's
40:3 Place the ark **c** the words of
Lev 14:5 over a clay bowl **c** fresh water.
14:50 over a clay bowl **c** fresh water.
14:51 dip them in the fresh water **c**
Num 4:5 that hangs over the ark **c**
6:15 unleavened bread **c** some rings
7:89 the throne of mercy on the ark **c**
Dtr 22:6 and find a nest **c** chicks
1Sm 6:11 ark of the LORD and the box **c**
1Ki 6:5 He built an annex **c** side rooms
2Ch 24:6 for the use of the tent **c**
26:23 in a field **c** tombs that belonged
Jer 32:11 **c** the terms and conditions,
36:10 Then Baruch read the scroll **c**
Rev 15:5 that the temple of the tent **c**

contains (14)

Lev 17:11 because blood **c** life.
Dtr 10:14 the earth and everything it **c**
12:23 because blood **c** life.
1Ki 8:21 place there for the ark which **c**
2Ch 6:11 I've put the ark which **c** the
Job 28:6 are sapphire. Its dust **c** gold.
Psa 24:1 The earth and everything it **c**
50:12 world and all that it **c** are mine.
Nah 1:1 This book **c** the vision of
1Co 10:26 and everything it **c** is his."
Col 1:23 the hope that the Good News **c**.
1Ti 1:11 with the Good News that **c**
2Ti 1:1 that **c** Christ Jesus' promise
1Jn 2:27 anointing is true and **c** no lie.

contaminate (2)

Zep 3:4 Its priests **c** what is holy.
Jud 1:8 They **c** their bodies with sin,

contaminated (7)

Ezr 2:62 reason they were considered **c**
Neh 7:64 reason they were considered **c**
13:29 because they have **c** the
Lam 4:14 They were so **c** with
Mal 1:7 "You offer **c** food on my altar.
1:7 'Then how have we **c** you?'
1:12 that the Lord's table may be **c**

contaminates (2)

2Co 7:1 from everything that **c** body
Jas 3:6 and it completely **c** our bodies.

contempt (33)

Gen 25:34 is how Esau showed his **c**
Exo 18:11 who treated Israel with **c**.
Lev 24:11 name and treating it with **c**.
24:15 who treat their God with **c** will
Num 14:11 these people treat me with **c**?
14:23 who treat me with **c** will see it!
16:30 have treated the LORD with **c**."
1Sm 2:17 made to the LORD with **c**.
2Sm 12:14 since you have shown total **c**
Est 1:18 will be **c** and short tempers.
Job 12:21 He pours **c** on influential
31:34 noisy crowd and because the **c**
Psa 31:18 people with arrogance and **c**.
44:13 and an object of ridicule and **c**
79:4 an object of ridicule and **c** to
107:40 He poured **c** on their influential
119:22 Remove the insults and **c** that
123:3 more than our share of **c**.
123:4 our share of **c** from those who
Pro 18:3 comes, **c** also comes,
Jer 6:10 they show **c** for it and object to
19:8 stunned and hiss with **c** at all
20:8 of insults and **c** all day long.
48:27 you shake your heads in **c**.
48:39 held in **c** by everyone around
51:37 and an object of **c**,
Lam 1:15 inside my ⌊walls⌋ with **c**.
Eze 25:6 You rejoiced and felt **c** for the
Mic 7:6 A son treats his father with **c**.
Luk 23:11 soldiers treated Jesus with **c**
Rom 2:4 Do you have **c** for God,
1Co 16:11 no one should treat him with **c**.
1Pe 3:16 live with **c** will feel ashamed

contemptible (1)

Dan 11:21 "A **c** person will take his place.

content (8)

Jos 7:7 I wish we had been **c** to live
Jdg 18:20 The priest was **c**. He took the
Rut 3:7 eaten and drunk to his heart's **c**,
Psa 131:2 My soul is **c** as a weaned child
131:2 content as a weaned child is **c**
Rom 2:20 because you have the full **c**
Php 4:11 I've learned to be **c** in whatever
1Ti 6:6 profits to people who are **c**

contented (1)

Job 21:23 feels altogether happy and **c**.

contents (2)

Num 4:16 the holy place and its **c**."
2Ki 7:8 carried off its **c**, went away,

contest (2)

2Sm 2:14 have the young men hold a **c**."
1Co 9:25 an athletic **c** goes into strict

continual (2)

Lev 24:8 It is a **c** reminder of my promise
Pro 15:15 but a cheerful heart has a **c**

continue (104)

Gen 19:2 you can **c** your journey."
Exo 9:2 you refuse to let them go and **c**
18:23 you will be able to **c** your work,
33:13 you and so that you will **c**
Dtr 5:25 If we **c** to hear the voice of the
5:33 Then you will **c** to live,
22:19 She will **c** to be his wife,
25:7 his brother's name **c** in Israel.
25:9 refuses to **c** his brother's family
28:51 They'll **c** to do this until they've
28:61 They will **c** until you're dead.
Jos 11:20 to **c** fighting against Israel
Jdg 20:23 "Should we **c** to wage war
20:28 "Should we **c** to wage war
Rut 2:13 may your kindness to me **c**.
1Sm 1:18 "May you **c** to be kind to me,"
16:11 We won't **c** until he gets here."
2Sm 7:29 my house so that it may **c**
1Ch 17:27 my house so that it may **c**
Ezr 4:4 made them afraid to **c** building.
9:15 a few of us **c** to remain as
Neh 1:9 But if you return to me and **c** to
4:10 We can't **c** to rebuild the wall."
Job 21:34 your answers **c** to betray me?"
Psa 36:10 **C** to show your mercy to those
49:12 But mortals will not **c** here with
68:21 of those who **c** to be guilty.
72:17 May his name **c** as long as the
73:15 "I will **c** to talk like that,"
79:5 Will your fury **c** to burn like
89:4 make your dynasty **c** forever.
89:46 How long will your anger **c** to
95:10 people whose hearts **c** to stray.
102:24 Your years ⌊**c** on⌋ throughout
111:9 his promise should **c** forever.
115:14 May the LORD **c** to bless you
119:32 commandments because you **c**
119:91 All things **c** to stand today
Pro 1:5 will listen and **c** to learn,
10:30 but wicked people will not **c** to
12:7 of righteous people **c** to stand.
14:11 decent people will **c** to expand.
21:28 to advice will **c** to speak.
23:17 Instead, **c** to fear the LORD.
Isa 1:5 Why do you **c** to rebel?
24:16 Traitors **c** to betray,
28:24 Does he **c** to break up the soil
46:4 I made you and will **c** to care
66:22 that I am about to make will **c**
66:22 will also **c** in my presence.
Jer 4:14 Don't **c** making evil plans.
23:26 How long will these prophets **c**
31:3 So I will **c** to show you my
Lam 3:26 "It is good to **c** to hope and
Eze 8:17 fill the land with violence and **c**
47:18 The border will **c** from the Dead
Hos 4:18 they **c** to have sex with the
Zec 14:8 It will **c** in summer and in
Mal 2:4 promise to Levi will **c**," says
Jon 9:41 so you **c** to be sinners.
11:48 If we let him **c** what he's doing,
17:21 I pray that all of these people **c**
Act 13:43 them to **c** trusting God's good
Rom 5:11 our Lord Jesus Christ lets us **c**
6:1 Should we **c** to sin so that
11:22 but kind to you if you **c** to hold
11:23 If Jewish people do not **c** in
1Co 1:8 He will **c** to give you strength
5:9 to associate with people who **c**
6:9 People who **c** to commit
2Co 1:10 that he will **c** to rescue us,
3:11 remains **c** to be glorious?
11:9 and I will **c** to do that.
Eph 4:13 This is to **c** until all of us are
Php 1:18 Yes, I will **c** to be happy
1:22 If I **c** to live in this life,
1:25 I know that I will **c** to live and
2:12 In the same way **c** to work out
Col 1:23 is on the condition that you **c**
2:6 so **c** to live as Christ's people.
4:12 He prays that you will **c** to be
2Th 3:4 that you are doing and will **c**
1Ti 4:16 **C** to do what I've told you.
2Ti 3:14 However, **c** in what you have
Tit 1:13 correct believers so that they **c**
3:10 to do with people who **c**
Heb 3:6 We are his household if we **c**
3:10 'Their hearts **c** to stray,
3:14 Christ's partners only if we **c**
6:10 and you **c** to help them.
10:22 So we must **c** to come ⌊to
10:23 We must **c** to hold firmly to our
10:25 Instead, we must **c** to
13:1 **C** to love each other.
1Pe 4:19 to a faithful creator and **c**
2Pe 1:19 **C** to pay attention as you
2:16 the prophet to **c** his insanity.
2Jn 1:5 I'm now requesting that we **c** to
1:9 Everyone who doesn't **c** to
Jud 1:3 encourage you to **c** your fight
Rev 20:6 They will **c** to be priests of
22:11 and let filthy people **c** to be
22:11 who have God's approval **c**
22:11 let holy people **c** to be holy."

continued (114)

Gen 7:17 The flood **c** for 40 days on the
26:13 He **c** to be successful,
29:1 Jacob **c** on his trip and came to
30:36 Jacob **c** to take care of the rest

Gen 37:1 Jacob **c** to live in the land of
Exo 7:13 Yet, Pharaoh **c** to be stubborn
7:22 So Pharaoh **c** to be stubborn
8:19 Yet, Pharaoh **c** to be stubborn
9:7 Yet, Pharaoh **c** to be stubborn
9:34 his officials **c** to be stubborn.
21:1 ⌊The LORD **c**,⌋ "Here are the
22:1 ⌊The LORD **c**,⌋ "Whenever
23:1 ⌊The LORD **c**,⌋ "Never spread
26:1 ⌊The LORD **c**,⌋ "Make the
27:1 ⌊The LORD **c**,⌋ "Make an altar
28:1 ⌊The LORD **c**,⌋ "Out of all the
29:1 ⌊The LORD **c**,⌋ "Now,
30:1 ⌊The LORD **c**,⌋ "Build an altar
36:1 ⌊Moses **c**,⌋ "So Bezalel and
Lev 2:1 ⌊The LORD **c**,⌋ "Now,
3:1 ⌊The LORD **c**,⌋ "If your
5:1 ⌊The LORD **c**,⌋ "Now,
7:1 ⌊The LORD **c**,⌋ "These are the
26:1 ⌊The LORD **c**,⌋ "Never make
Num 29:1 ⌊The LORD **c**,⌋ "On the first
Dtr 2:24 ⌊The LORD **c**,⌋ "Now break
31:1 Moses **c** to speak to all the
Jos 3:10 Joshua **c**, "This is how you
6:9 the ark while the priests **c**
10:10 the slope of Beth Horon and **c**
Jdg 1:29 So the Canaanites **c** to live
1:30 So the Canaanites **c** to live
1:32 So the tribe of Asher **c** to live
1:33 So they **c** to live with the
9:41 Abimelech **c** to live at Arumah.
Rut 2:23 And she **c** to live with her
4:5 Boaz **c**, "When you buy the
1Sm 2:18 Meanwhile, Samuel **c** to serve
2:26 The boy Samuel **c** to grow and
3:21 The LORD **c** to appear in
11:11 during the morning hours and **c**
14:8 Jonathan **c**, "Listen, we'll cross
19:23 over him too. He **c** his journey,
20:12 ⌊is my witness⌋," Jonathan **c**,
2Sm 3:34 And all the people **c** to cry for
5:10 David **c** to grow more powerful
13:25 Even when Absalom **c** to urge
18:25 The runner **c** to come closer.
1Ki 3:6 And you **c** to show him your
18:29 In the afternoon they **c** to rant
22:44 The people **c** to sacrifice and
2Ki 2:11 As they **c** walking and talking,
9:27 Ahaziah **c** to flee until he got to
12:3 The people **c** to offer sacrifices
13:2 He **c** to commit the sins that
13:6 They **c** to commit those sins.
13:11 He **c** to commit them.
14:4 The people **c** to offer sacrifices
15:4 The people **c** to offer sacrifices
15:35 The people **c** to offer sacrifices
17:29 ⌊that settled in Samaria⌋ **c**
1Ch 11:9 David **c** to grow more powerful
22:11 ⌊David **c**,⌋ "Now, son,
2Ch 27:2 the people **c** their corrupt ways.
33:17 The people **c** to sacrifice at the
33:23 Instead, Amon **c** to sin.
Ezr 6:14 So the Jewish leaders **c** to
Neh 1:4 I **c** to fast and pray to the God
4:21 So we **c** to work. Half of us held
8:18 Ezra **c** to read from the Book of
Job 27:1 Job **c** his poems and said,
29:1 Job **c** his poems and said,
34:1 Elihu **c** to speak ⌊to Job and
35:1 Elihu **c** to speak ⌊to Job and
36:1 Elihu **c** to speak ⌊to Job⌋,
Psa 78:17 They **c** to sin against him,
78:32 In spite of all this, they **c** to sin,
94:18 O LORD, **c** to hold me up.
106:43 but they **c** to plot rebellion
Ecc 2:3 wisdom **c** to control my mind.
Isa 57:17 But they **c** to be sinful.
64:5 We've **c** to sin for a long time.
Jer 1:3 The LORD **c** to speak to
25:3 the LORD **c** to speak his word
44:6 anger were poured out and **c**
Eze 23:8 She **c** the prostitution that she
23:43 men **c** to have sex with her.
Dan 7:11 I **c** to watch because of the
8:4 it pleased and **c** to grow.
8:10 It **c** to gain power until it
Dan 9:20 I **c** to pray, confessing my sins
11:2 looked like a human **c**,⌋ "What
12:1 like a human **c**,⌋ "At that time
Zep 3:7 Still, they **c** to be corrupt in
Mar 7:20 He **c**, "It's what comes out of a
Luk 10:31 around him and **c** on his way.
10:32 around him and **c** on his way.
16:9 ⌊Jesus **c**,⌋ "I'm telling you that
19:28 he **c** on his way to Jerusalem.
21:10 Then Jesus **c**, "Nation will
Jon 8:8 Then he bent down again and **c**
16:1 ⌊Jesus **c**,⌋ "I have said these
18:25 Simon Peter **c** to stand and
Act 4:31 filled with the Holy Spirit and **c**
4:33 With great power the apostles **c**
6:7 The word of God **c** to spread,
8:39 The official joyfully **c** on his
12:24 But God's word **c** to spread and
13:52 the disciples ⌊in Antioch⌋ **c** to
19:10 This **c** for two years so that all
22:2 even more quiet. Then Paul **c**,
27:18 We **c** to be tossed so violently
28:24 but others **c** to disbelieve.
Heb 11:27 Moses didn't give up but **c** as if

continues (29)

Exo 34:7 He **c** to show his love to
Num 34:11 and **c** along the eastern slope
Jos 15:8 It **c** up the valley of Ben
18:18 Then it **c** on to the north side of
18:19 The border **c** to the north slope
19:33 It **c** to Adami Nekeb,
2Ki 9:22 as your mother **c** her idolatry
Job 14:14 as long as my hard labor **c**.
Psa 3:5 the LORD **c** to support me.
37:17 but the LORD **c** to support
50:23 I will let everyone who **c** in my
111:3 His righteousness **c** forever.
111:10 His praise **c** forever.
112:3 His righteousness **c** forever.
112:9 His righteousness **c** forever.
119:90 earth in place, and it **c** to stand.
Ecc 2:26 But to the person who **c** to sin,
7:26 will catch whoever **c** to sin.
Jer 32:20 for yourself that **c** to this day.
Lam 3:20 My soul **c** to remember ⌊these
5:19 **c** throughout every generation.
Dan 6:26 the living God who **c** forever.
2Co 9:9 His righteousness **c** forever."
Eph 2:2 This ruler **c** to work in people
Heb 7:3 Melchizedek **c** to be a priest
Jas 1:25 However, the person who **c** to
2Pe 3:4 everything **c** as it did from the
2Jn 1:9 The person who **c** to teach
Rev 2:26 who wins the victory and **c**

continuing (1)

Dtr 28:59 They will be terrible and **c**

contract (1)

Rut 4:7 This was the way a **c** was

contracts (2)

Isa 16:14 count the years left of their **c**.
21:16 count the years left on their **c**.

contradict (2)

Act 13:45 to **c** whatever Paul said.
Gal 3:21 to Moses **c** God's promises?

contrary (2)

Gal 5:17 your corrupt nature wants is **c**
5:17 your spiritual nature wants is **c**

contribute (9)

Lev 22:15 the Israelites **c** to the LORD.
Num 18:24 Levites what the Israelites **c**
18:26 When you do, you must **c**
18:28 So you, too, will **c** one-tenth of
18:29 you must **c** the best and holiest
18:30 When you **c** the best part,
18:32 When you **c** the best part,
Jon 6:63 physical existence doesn't **c**
Act 11:29 to **c** whatever they could

contributed (11)

Num 31:52 All the gold **c** to the LORD by
Ezr 2:68 they **c** freewill offerings to help
2:69 They **c** as much as they could
7:15 and his advisers willingly **c**
7:16 when you take the gifts **c** by
7:16 They willingly **c** these gifts for
8:25 and all the Israelites had **c** for
Neh 7:70 of the heads of the families **c**
7:70 The governor **c** the following to
7:71 of the heads of the families **c**
7:72 The rest of the people **c** 337

contribution (31)

Exo 25:2 to give me as a special **c**.
25:2 You must accept whatever **c**
25:3 This is the kind of **c** you will
29:27 and the thigh that is the **c**.
29:28 to Aaron and his sons as a **c**.
29:28 This will also be their **c** to the
30:13 of silver is a **c** to the LORD.
30:14 must give this **c** to the LORD.
30:15 This **c** is given to make peace
35:5 your own to give as a special **c**
35:5 is willing bring this kind of **c**
35:24 or bronze brought it as their **c**
36:6 more to give as their special **c**
Lev 7:14 to the LORD as a ⌊special⌋ **c**.
7:32 the priest the right thigh as a **c**.
7:34 the thigh from the **c** offering.
10:14 the thigh that was given as a **c**.
10:15 bring the thigh given as a **c**,
Num 5:9 "Any **c** over and above the holy
15:19 some of it as a **c** to the LORD.
15:20 do with the **c** you make from
15:21 your dough as a **c** to the LORD.
18:26 income as your **c** to the LORD.
18:27 Your **c** will be considered to be
18:28 You will give the LORD's **c** to
18:30 your **c** will be considered to be
31:29 Eleazar as a **c** to the LORD.
Eze 45:13 "'This is the **c** you must give to
45:16 people must give this **c**
Act 11:30 did this and sent their **c**
12:25 and Saul delivered the **c** ⌊to

contributions (29)

Exo 35:21 them came and brought their **c**
36:3 turned over to them all the **c**
Lev 22:12 the food taken from the holy **c**.
Num 18:8 you in charge of all the **c** given
18:8 These **c** will always be yours.
18:11 "The **c** that come as gifts taken
18:19 your daughters all the holy **c**
18:19 These **c** will always be yours.
Dtr 12:6 of your income, your **c**,
12:11 of your income, your **c**,
12:17 freewill offerings; and your **c**.
2Ki 12:4 "⌊Collect⌋ all the holy **c** that
2Ch 24:6 to bring the **c** from Judah
24:6 had required Israel to give **c**
24:9 Jerusalem that the **c** should
24:9 had required Israel to make **c**.)
31:12 they faithfully brought in the **c**,
Ezr 8:25 ⌊These were⌋ the **c** that the
8:26 I weighed ⌊the **c**⌋ for them to
Neh 10:37 flour, **c**, fruit from every tree,
10:39 the storerooms their **c** of grain,
12:44 of the storerooms for the **c**,
13:5 The **c** for the priests had also
Pro 29:4 religious **c** tears it down.
Eze 44:30 gift from all your **c** must go
Mal 3:8 of your income and other **c**.
Mat 6:4 Give your **c** privately.
Jon 12:6 moneybag and carried the **c**.)
2Co 8:12 with whatever **c** you have.

control (97)

Gen 4:7 It wants to **c** you, but you must
9:2 have been put under your **c**.
41:35 up grain under Pharaoh's **c**,
43:31 He was in **c** of his emotions
45:1 Joseph could no longer **c** his
49:4 because you were out of **c** like
Exo 18:10 from the **c** of the Egyptians,

Exo 23:31 living in the land under your **c**,
32:25 had let the people get out of **c**,
Lev 26:25 fall under the **c** of your enemy.
Jos 18:1 The land was under their **c**.
1Sm 2:27 under Pharaoh's **c** in Egypt.
2Sm 8:1 He took **c** of the main Philistine
8:3 went to restore his **c** ⌊over
2Ki 14:5 As soon as he had a firm **c**
18:30 city will not be put under the **c**
18:34 rescue Samaria from my **c**?
18:35 rescue them from my **c**?
18:35 rescue Jerusalem from my **c**?"
19:10 will not be put under the **c**
19:19 rescue us from Assyria's **c** so
20:6 and defend this city from the **c**
21:14 I will put them under the **c** of
1Ch 18:3 went to establish his **c** ⌊over
2Ch 25:3 As soon as he had firm **c** over
32:14 rescue their people from my **c**?
32:14 able to rescue you from my **c**?
Neh 9:37 These kings have **c** over our
Job 23:2 I try hard to **c** my sighing.
Psa 8:6 put everything under his **c**:
10:14 and placed them under your **c**.
19:13 not let anyone gain **c** over me.
119:133 and do not let any sin **c** me.
Pro 12:24 Hard-working hands gain **c**,
17:14 the argument gets out of **c**.
21:1 Both are under the LORD's **c**.
27:16 Whoever can **c** her can control
27:16 can control her can **c** the wind.
Ecc 2:3 continued to **c** my mind.
2:19 He will still have **c** over
8:8 No one has **c** over the day of
Isa 3:6 of ruins will be under your **c**."
36:15 city will not be put under the **c**
36:19 rescue Samaria from my **c**?
36:20 rescue them from my **c**?
36:20 rescue Jerusalem from my **c**?"
37:10 will not be put under the **c**
37:20 rescue us from Assyria's **c** so
38:6 and defend this city from the **c**
47:6 I put them under your **c**.
Jer 10:23 humans act is not under their **c**.
41:10 put under the **c** of Gedaliah,
Lam 1:5 Its opponents are now in **c**.
Eze 13:18 You want to **c** the lives of my
13:21 will no longer be under your **c**.
Dan 2:38 has given you **c** over people,
11:16 will be completely under his **c**.
11:43 He will **c** gold and silver
Amo 1:11 They refused to **c** their fury.
Mat 22:44 your enemies under your **c**.'"
Mar 5:4 No one could **c** him.
12:36 your enemies under your **c**.'"
Luk 9:39 a spirit takes **c** of him,
Jon 13:3 had put everything in Jesus' **c**.
Act 2:35 your enemies under your **c**.'"
26:18 and from Satan's **c** to God's.
27:16 we barely got **c** of the ship's
Rom 1:24 allowed their lusts to **c** them.
1:26 shameful passions to **c** them.
1:28 own immoral minds to **c** them.
8:8 Those who are under the **c** of
8:9 you are under the **c** of your
1Co 6:12 anything to gain **c** over my life.
7:9 if you cannot **c** your desires,
14:32 revealed must **c** themselves.
15:25 put every enemy under his **c**.
15:28 God will be in **c** of everything.
2Co 1:24 It isn't that we want to have **c**
Gal 2:4 They hoped to find a way to **c**
3:23 We were kept under **c** by
3:23 We were under their **c** until this
3:25 under the **c** of a guardian.
4:2 He is placed under the **c** of
4:4 under the **c** of God's laws.
Eph 1:22 everything under the **c** of
6:12 and spiritual forces that **c** evil
Col 3:15 Also, let Christ's peace **c** you.
1Ti 3:11 but they must **c** their tempers
Heb 2:5 are talking) under the angels' **c**.
2:8 put everything under his **c**."
2:8 everything under his Son's **c**,
2:8 everything under his Son's **c**.
Jas 1:26 religious but can't **c** his tongue,
Jas 3:2 able to **c** everything he does.
3:3 and we have **c** over everything
4:1 desires that fight to **c** you?
1Jn 5:19 the whole world is under the **c**

controlled (13)

Jdg 9:29 How I wish I **c** these people!
1Sm 7:14 the territory **c** by these cities
1Ki 4:24 He **c** all the territory west of the
Est 5:10 However, Haman **c** himself.
Mar 1:23 the synagogue who was **c** by
5:2 The man was **c** by an evil spirit
Luk 8:29 (The evil spirit had **c** the man
Rom 6:14 because you're not **c** by laws,
6:15 because we are not **c** by laws
6:15 laws but are **c** by God's favor?
Gal 3:22 that the whole world is **c** by
4:5 who were **c** by these laws
4:21 Those who want to be **c** by

controls (5)

Job 37:15 Do you know how God **c** them
Pro 13:3 Whoever **c** his mouth protects
16:23 person's heart **c** his speech,
17:27 has knowledge **c** his words,
29:11 but a wise person **c** them.

controversies (1)

Tit 3:9 Avoid foolish **c**, quarrels, and

controversy (1)

Act 26:3 custom and **c** in Judaism.

convened (2)

Dan 7:10 The court **c**, and the books
Act 25:17 The next day I immediately **c**

conversation (7)

Exo 13:9 ⌊always⌋ to be a part of your **c**.
Rut 1:18 to go with her, she ended the **c**.
Pro 23:8 and spoil your pleasant **c**.
Jer 38:24 let anyone know about this **c**,
38:27 because they hadn't heard his **c**
Mat 16:8 knew about their **c** and asked,
2Th 2:2 we said through some spirit, **c**,

conversations (1)

Act 24:26 to have friendly **c** with him.

convert (2)

Act 16:14 She was a **c** to Judaism from
18:7 who was a **c** to Judaism.

converted (3)

Act 6:5 who had **c** to Judaism in the
17:4 group of Greeks who had **c**
18:4 Greeks who had **c** to Judaism.

converts (7)

Act 2:10 Jewish people, **c** to Judaism,
13:16 of Israel and **c** to Judaism,
13:26 descendants of Abraham and **c**
13:43 many Jews and **c** to Judaism
17:17 with Jews and **c** to Judaism.
Col 4:11 They are the only **c** from the
Tit 1:10 especially **c** from Judaism,

convict (6)

Dtr 19:15 is never enough to **c** someone
Pro 24:25 be pleased with those who **c**
Jon 8:46 Can any of you **c** me of
16:8 He will come to **c** the world of
16:9 He will **c** the world of sin,
Jud 1:15 He has come to **c** all these

convicted (3)

Num 35:31 the life of a **c** murderer who has
Dtr 21:22 When a **c** person is put to
2Pe 2:16 But he was **c** for his evil.

conviction (1)

Rom 14:14 knowledge and **c** that no food

convicts (1)

Jas 2:9 and this law **c** you of being

convince (6)

Exo 4:5 "This is to **c** the people that the
Jon 16:8 and to **c** the world that God
16:11 He will **c** the world that God
Act 19:8 with people to **c** them about
28:23 He was trying to **c** them about
1Co 14:24 are wrong and **c** them that they

convinced (15)

Gen 45:28 "You have **c** me!" Israel said.
1Ki 17:24 "Now I'm **c** that you are a man
Luk 20:6 They're **c** that John was a
Act 16:15 She said, "If you're **c** that I
28:24 Some of them were **c** by what
Rom 8:38 I am **c** that nothing can ever
15:14 I'm **c**, brothers and sisters,
15:14 I'm also **c** that you have all the
2Co 5:14 We are **c** of the fact that one
Php 1:6 I'm **c** that God, who began this
1:25 Since I'm **c** of this,
Col 4:12 to be mature and completely **c**
2Ti 1:5 I'm **c** that it also lives in you.
1:12 I'm **c** that he is able to protect
Heb 6:9 we are still **c** that better things

convinces (2)

Heb 11:1 us of things we expect and **c**
11:3 Faith **c** us that God created the

convincing (1)

Act 1:3 a lot of **c** evidence that

convulsions (4)

Mar 1:26 evil spirit threw the man into **c**
9:20 it threw the boy into **c**.
Luk 9:39 of him, he shrieks, goes into **c**,
9:42 ground and threw him into **c**.

coo (1)

Isa 59:11 We **c** like doves. We hope for

cooed (1)

Isa 38:14 I **c** like doves. My eyes were

cooing (1)

Sos 2:12 The **c** of the mourning dove is

cook (13)

Exo 23:19 "Never **c** a young goat in its
34:26 "Never **c** a young goat in its
Lev 8:31 "**C** the meat at the entrance to
Num 11:8 They would **c** it in a pot or
Dtr 14:21 Never **c** a young goat in its
16:7 **C** the meat, and eat it at the
1Sm 8:13 make perfumes, **c**, and bake.
9:23 Samuel said to the **c**,
9:24 So the **c** picked up the leg and
2Ki 4:38 and **c** some stew for the
Eze 24:5 **C** the bones that are in it well.
24:10 **C** the meat thoroughly,
Zec 14:21 some of them and **c** in them.

cooked (4)

Lev 6:28 the offering for sin is **c** must
6:28 the offering for sin is **c** must
2Sm 13:8 bread in front of him, and **c** it.
Lam 4:10 The hands of loving mothers **c**

cooking (5)

Psa 58:9 faster than a **c** pot is heated
Eze 11:3 This city is a **c** pot,
11:7 and the city is the **c** pot.
11:11 The city will not be your **c** pot,
Zec 14:20 And the **c** pots in the house of

cool (4)

Gen 3:8 In the **c** of the evening,
Sos 4:6 When the day brings a **c**
Jer 18:14 The **c** mountain streams never
Luk 16:24 in water to **c** off my tongue.

cooling (1)

Sos 2:17 When the day brings a **c**

coolness (1)
Pro 25:13 Like the **c** of snow on a harvest

cools (2)
Gen 27:44 until your brother's anger **c**
Job 14:13 hidden there until your anger **c**.

copied (1)
Pro 25:1 proverbs that were **c** by

copies (4)
Jer 32:12 I gave the **c** of the deeds to
32:14 the sealed and the unsealed **c**
32:16 I had given the **c** to Baruch,
Heb 9:23 The **c** of the things in heaven

copper (8)
Lev 6:28 Any **c** kettle in which the
Dtr 8:9 and you will be able to mine **c**
33:25 gates be made of iron and **c**.
Job 28:2 rocks are melted for ⌊their⌋ **c**.
Eze 22:18 All of them are like **c**,
22:20 People gather silver, **c**,
24:11 that it gets hot and its **c** glows.
Mat 10:9 or even **c** coins in your

copy (11)
Dtr 17:18 Levitical priests make him a **c**
Jos 8:32 he wrote on stone slabs a **c**
Ezr 4:11 This is the **c** of the letter they
4:23 to Jerusalem after hearing a **c**
5:6 Here is a **c** of the letter
7:11 This is a **c** of the letter that
Est 3:14 A **c** of the document was made
4:8 He also gave him a **c** of the
8:13 The **c** of the document was
Jer 32:11 Then I took the sealed **c** of the
32:11 as well as an unsealed **c**.

copying (2)
2Ki 21:2 the LORD considered evil by **c**
2Ch 33:2 the LORD considered evil by **c**

coral (2)
Lam 4:7 bodies were more pink than **c**.
Eze 27:16 richly woven cloth, linen, **c**,

corban (1)
Mar 7:11 used to help them is **c** (that is,

cord (11)
Gen 38:18 "Your signet ring, its **c**,
38:25 recognize whose signet ring, **c**,
Exo 28:28 of the ephod with a violet **c**.
28:37 Fasten a violet **c** to it,
39:21 of the ephod with a violet **c**.
39:31 They fastened a violet **c** to it
Jos 2:18 tie this red **c** in the window
2:21 tied the red **c** in the window.
Job 30:11 Because God has untied my **c**
Ecc 12:6 before the silver **c** is snapped,
Eze 16:4 your umbilical **c** wasn't cut.

cords (3)
Est 1:6 and marble pillars by **c** made
Eze 27:24 rugs with woven and twisted **c**.
Hos 11:4 I led them with **c** of human

core (3)
Psa 14:3 have become rotten to the **c**.
53:3 have become rotten to the **c**.
Rom 3:12 have become rotten to the **c**.

coriander (2)
Exo 16:31 It was like **c** seeds.
Num 11:7 (Manna was ⌊small⌋ like **c**

Corinth (14)
Act 18:1 and went to the city of **C**.
18:2 In **C** he met a Jewish man
18:11 Paul lived in **C** for a year and a
18:18 After staying in **C** quite a while
19:1 While Apollos was in **C**,
1Co 1:2 holy people in the city of **C**
2Co 1:1 To God's church in the city of **C**
2Co 1:16 been to go from the city of **C**
1:16 to return to you again in **C**
1:23 that I stayed away from **C**
10:13 ⌊the city of **C**⌋ where you live.
10:14 we hadn't already been to **C**.
10:14 we were the first to arrive in **C**
2Ti 4:20 Erastus stayed in the city of **C**

Corinthians (2)
Act 18:8 Many **C** who heard Paul
2Co 6:11 very open in speaking to you **C**.

cormorants (2)
Lev 11:17 little owls, **c**, great owls,
Dtr 14:17 pelicans, ospreys, **c**,

Cornelius (12)
Act 10:1 A man named **C** lived in the
10:2 **C** gave many gifts to poor
10:3 God come to him and say, "**C**!"
10:4 **C** asked the angel,
10:7 **C** called two of his household
10:8 **C** explained everything to them
10:17 the men sent by **C** found
10:22 The men replied, "**C**,
10:24 **C** was expecting them and had
10:25 **C** met him, bowed down,
10:30 **C** answered, "Four days ago I
10:31 He said to me, '**C**, God has

Cornelius' (4)
Act 10:9 while **C** men were on their way
10:25 **C** house, Cornelius met him,
10:27 he entered **C** house and found
11:12 and we visited **C** home

corner (31)
Exo 26:24 Both **c** frames will be made
36:29 Both **c** frames were made this
Rut 3:9 Spread the **c** of your garment
1Ki 7:39 temple in the southeast ⌊**c**⌋.
2Ki 14:13 from Ephraim Gate to **C** Gate.
20:13 and every **c** of his kingdom.
2Ch 4:10 side in the southeast ⌊**c**⌋.
25:23 from Ephraim Gate to **C** Gate.
26:9 towers in Jerusalem at **C** Wall,
28:24 on every **c** in Jerusalem.
Neh 3:24 Angle and to the **c** of the wall.
3:31 far as the upper room at the **c**.
3:32 room at the **c** and Sheep Gate.
Job 18:17 not be known on the street **c**.
Psa 74:20 promise because every dark **c**
Pro 7:8 crossing a street near her **c**
7:12 on the prowl at every **c**.
21:9 Better to live on a **c** of a roof
25:24 Better to live on a **c** of a roof
Isa 39:2 and every **c** of his kingdom.
45:19 privately or in some dark **c**
51:20 lie sleeping at every street **c**.
Jer 31:38 Tower of Hananel to **C** Gate.
31:40 as far as the **c** of Horse Gate in
Lam 2:19 from hunger at every street **c**."
4:1 are scattered at every street **c**.
Eze 46:21 I saw that in each **c** of the
Amo 3:12 ⌊having only⌋ a **c** of a bed or a
Nah 3:10 to death at every street **c**.
Zep 1:16 and against the high **c** towers.
Zec 14:10 the place of First Gate, **C** Gate,

corners (41)
Exo 25:26 and fasten them to the four **c**,
26:23 frames for ⌊each of⌋ the **c** at
27:2 a horn at each of its four **c**.
27:4 of⌋ the four **c** of the grate.
28:7 attached at the ⌊top⌋ **c** so that
28:23 two ⌊top⌋ **c** of the breastplate.
28:24 the ⌊top⌋ **c** of the breastplate.
28:26 fasten them to the other two **c**
36:28 frames for ⌊each of⌋ the **c** at
37:13 fastened the rings to the four **c**,
38:2 a horn at each of its four **c**.
38:5 poles (one for each of the four **c**
39:4 attached at the ⌊top⌋ **c** so that
39:16 ⌊top⌋ two **c** of the breastplate.
39:17 the ⌊top⌋ **c** of the breastplate.
39:19 them to the other two **c**
Lev 19:9 don't harvest the grain in the **c**
23:22 don't harvest the grain in the **c**
Num 15:38 must wear tassels on the **c**
Dtr 22:12 Make tassels on the four **c** of
1Ki 7:34 The four supports at the four **c**
2Ch 26:15 placed on the towers and **c**
Job 1:19 the desert and struck the four **c**
Psa 144:12 that adorn the **c** of a palace.
Pro 1:21 At the **c** of noisy streets she
Isa 11:12 from the four **c** of the earth.
Jer 25:32 from the distant **c** of the earth."
49:36 the four winds from the four **c**
Eze 7:2 to the four **c** of the earth.
41:22 Its **c**, its base, and its sides
43:20 on the four **c** of the ledge,
45:19 on the four **c** of the ledge of the
46:21 and took me past the four **c**
46:22 that were in each of the four **c**
46:22 the smaller courtyards in the **c**
Zec 9:15 for sprinkling⌋ the **c** of the altar.
Mat 6:5 in synagogues and on street **c**
Act 10:11 by its four **c** to the ground.
11:5 being lowered by its four **c** from
Rev 7:1 angels standing at the four **c**
20:8 the nations in the four **c** of the

cornerstone (12)
Job 38:6 footings sunk? Who laid its **c**
Psa 118:22 rejected has become the **c**.
Isa 28:16 has been tested, a precious **c**,
Jer 51:26 stones in you to use as a **c**.
Zec 10:4 From them will come a **c**,
Mat 21:42 rejected has become the **c**.
Mar 12:10 rejected has become the **c**.
Luk 20:17 rejected has become the **c**'?
Act 4:11 stone that has become the **c**.
Eph 2:20 Christ Jesus himself is the **c**.
1Pe 2:6 chosen and precious **c** in Zion,
2:7 rejected has become the **c**,

cornerstones (1)
Isa 19:13 The leaders who are the **c** of

corpse (8)
1Sm 31:10 Asherahs — and fastened his **c**
2Ki 9:37 Jezebel's **c** will be like manure
Psa 89:10 crushed Rahab; it was like a **c**.
Isa 14:19 of the pit like a trampled **c**.
Jer 36:30 and his own **c** will be thrown
Eze 32:5 the valleys with your rotting **c**.
Hag 2:13 unclean by touching a **c**.
Mar 15:45 Pilate let Joseph have the **c**.

corpses (13)
Gen 34:27 Jacob's sons stripped the **c**
2Ki 19:35 they saw all the **c**.
2Ch 20:24 **C** were lying on the ground.
Isa 26:19 Their **c** will rise. Those who lie
34:3 A stench will rise from their **c**.
37:36 they saw all the **c**.
66:24 will go out and look at the **c**
Jer 34:20 and their **c** will be food for birds
50:26 pile up their **c** like piles of
Eze 11:6 have filled its streets with **c**.
11:7 The **c** that you put in the
Nah 3:3 There is no end to the **c**!
3:3 People trip over **c**

correct (24)
Lev 19:17 Be sure to **c** your neighbor so
Job 6:25 me, you **c** yourselves!
11:4 'My teaching is morally **c**,' and,
22:4 Does God **c** you and bring you
40:2 fault with the Almighty **c** him?
Psa 19:8 instructions of the LORD are **c**.
33:4 The word of the LORD is **c**,
141:5 may strike me or **c** me out
Pro 29:17 **C** your son, and he will give
Jer 2:19 own wickedness will **c** you,
10:24 **C** me, O LORD, but please be
10:24 Don't **c** me when you're angry.
30:11 I will **c** you with justice.
46:28 I will **c** you with justice.
Hab 1:12 you have destined them to **c**
Zec 8:16 Give **c** and fair verdicts for
Mal 2:8 have turned from the ⌊**c**⌋ path

Luk 17:3 "If a believer sins, **c** him.
Jon 18:37 Jesus replied, "You're **c** in
1Ti 5:1 use harsh words when you **c**
Tit 1:9 and **c** those who oppose
1:13 For this reason, sharply **c**
2:15 Encourage and **c** them,
Rev 3:19 I **c** and discipline everyone I

corrected (3)

Jer 5:3 but they refuse to be **c**.
30:14 I've **c** you as a cruel person
Luk 9:55 But he turned and **c** them.

correcting (3)

Job 6:25 In **c** me, you correct
2Ti 2:25 He must be gentle in **c** those
3:16 pointing out errors, **c** people,

correction (6)

Job 6:26 Do you think my words need **c**?
Pro 5:12 How my heart despised **c**!
12:1 but whoever hates **c** is a dumb
Jer 2:30 They didn't respond to **c**.
Zep 3:2 It does not accept **c**.
3:7 You will accept **c**!' Then

correctly (5)

Jdg 12:6 couldn't pronounce the word **c**,
2Ch 15:3 a priest who taught ⌊**c**⌋,
Jon 7:24 appearance! Instead, judge **c**."
1Co 11:31 If we were judging ourselves **c**,
2Ti 2:15 to teach the word of truth **c**.

corrects (5)

Job 5:17 is the person whom God **c**.
Pro 9:7 Whoever **c** a mocker receives
Heb 12:5 Don't give up when he **c** you.
12:7 God **c** you as a father corrects
12:7 you as a father **c** his children.

correspond (1)

Exo 28:21 The stones **c** to the 12 sons of

corresponded (2)

Exo 39:14 They **c** to the 12 sons of Israel,
Dan 8:8 They **c** to the four winds of

corresponding (2)

Dtr 32:8 set up borders for the tribes **c**
Eze 42:12 parallel to the **c** wall that ran

corridors (5)

Eze 41:15 the west side along with its **c**
41:16 and the **c** of all three stories
42:3 were **c** facing corridors
42:3 were corridors facing **c**
42:5 the **c** took space away

corroded (1)

Jas 5:3 Your gold and silver are **c**,

corrosion (1)

Jas 5:3 and their **c** will be used as

corrupt (65)

Gen 6:11 The world was **c** in God's sight
6:12 God saw the world and how **c**
Lev 19:15 "Don't be **c** when administering
19:35 "Don't be **c** when administering
Dtr 4:16 that you don't become **c** and
4:25 don't become **c** and make
31:29 you will become thoroughly **c**
32:5 that his people are **c**.
2Ch 27:2 the people continued their **c**
Job 9:20 It would declare that I am **c**
15:16 one who is disgusting and **c**,
Psa 14:1 They are **c**. They do disgusting
53:1 They are **c**. They do disgusting
Pro 17:23 secretly accepts a bribe to **c**
Ecc 7:7 and a bribe can **c** the mind.
Isa 43:28 That is why I will **c** the leaders
Jer 6:28 They **c** themselves.
Eze 16:47 to be more **c** than they ever
20:44 the evil and **c** things that you
Dan 11:32 With flattery he will **c** those
Zep 3:1 for that rebellious and **c** place,
Zep 3:7 Still, they continued to be **c** in
Mat 17:17 unbelieving and **c** generation!
Luk 9:41 unbelieving and **c** generation!
Act 2:40 "Save yourselves from this **c**
Rom 6:19 the weakness of your **c** nature.
7:5 the influence of our **c** nature,
7:14 but I have a **c** nature,
7:18 good lives in my **c** nature.
7:25 standards with my **c** nature.
8:3 condemned sin in our **c** nature.
8:4 who do not live by our **c** nature
8:5 Those who live by the **c** nature
8:5 have the **c** nature's attitude.
8:6 The **c** nature's attitude leads to
8:7 This is so because the **c**
8:8 of the **c** nature can't please
8:9 nature, not your **c** nature.
8:12 live the way our **c** nature wants
8:13 If you live by your **c** nature,
1Co 3:1 influenced by your **c** nature.
3:3 influenced by your **c** nature.
3:3 aren't you influenced by your **c**
5:5 to destroy his **c** nature so that
Gal 5:13 into an excuse for your **c** nature
5:16 on what your **c** nature wants.
5:17 What your **c** nature wants is
5:17 to what your **c** nature wants.
5:19 Now, the effects of the **c** nature
5:24 crucified their **c** nature along
6:8 in ⌊the soil of⌋ your **c** nature,
Eph 2:3 the desires of our **c** nature.
2:3 We did what our **c** desires and
Php 2:15 people who are crooked and **c**.
Col 2:11 But it was a removal of the **c**
2:13 your uncircumcised **c** nature.
2:23 desires of your **c** nature.
1Th 2:3 **c** practices, or deception.
1Ti 6:5 whose **c** minds have been
2Ti 3:8 Their minds are **c**,
Tit 1:15 is clean to **c** unbelievers.
3:11 that people like this are **c**.
Jas 2:4 people and using a **c** standard
1Pe 2:11 the desires of your **c** nature.
2Pe 2:10 who follow their **c** nature along

corrupted (6)

2Ch 29:5 anything that has been **c** from
Hos 9:9 People have deeply **c**
Mal 2:8 You have **c** the promise made
Tit 1:15 and their consciences are **c**.
1Pe 1:4 that can't be destroyed or **c**
Rev 19:2 the notorious prostitute who **c**

corruption (3)

Exo 18:21 you can trust, men who hate **c**.
2Pe 1:4 the **c** that sinful desires
2:19 themselves are slaves to **c**.

corruptly (1)

Jdg 2:19 acted more **c** than their parents.

corrupts (1)

Heb 12:15 trouble that **c** many of you.

Cos (1)

Act 21:1 straight to the island of **C**.

Cosam (1)

Luk 3:28 son of **C**, son of Elmadam,

cosmetics (1)

Gen 37:25 carrying the materials for **c**,

cost (18)

Exo 13:13 It will **c** you a sheep or a goat
34:20 It will **c** you a sheep or a goat
Num 3:47 It will **c** you two ounces of
Dtr 15:18 It would have **c** you twice as
Jos 6:26 It will **c** him his firstborn son to
6:26 It will **c** him his youngest son
2Sm 24:24 sacrifices that **c** me nothing."
1Ki 16:34 Laying the foundation **c** him his
16:34 Setting up the city doors **c** him
1Ch 12:19 They said, "It will **c** us our
21:24 sacrifices that **c** me nothing."
Ezr 6:8 The **c** ⌊for this⌋ should be paid
Pro 7:23 He does not realize that it will **c**
23:7 he calculates the **c** to himself,
Jer 32:9 The field **c** seven ounces of
Amo 8:5 bushel baskets, increase the **c**,
Act 19:19 They added up the **c** of these
Rev 21:6 It won't **c** anything.

costly (4)

Est 1:4 his kingdom and the **c** splendor
Psa 49:8 to be paid for his soul is too **c**.
Pro 21:20 **C** treasure and wealth are in
Rev 18:12 made of ivory and very **c** wood,

costs (1)

Luk 14:28 down and figure out what it **c**.

cot (10)

Mar 2:4 Then they lowered the **c** on
2:9 up, pick up your **c**, and walk'?
2:11 pick up your **c**, and go home!"
2:12 immediately picked up his **c**,
Jon 5:8 up, pick up your **c**, and walk."
5:9 picked up his **c**, and walked.
5:10 allowed to carry your **c** today."
5:11 me to pick up my **c** and walk."
Act 9:33 confined to a **c** for eight years.
9:34 Get up, and pick up your **c**."

cots (2)

Mar 6:55 began to carry the sick on **c**
Act 5:15 on stretchers and **c** so that at

couch (7)

Gen 49:4 He climbed up on my **c**.
1Ki 21:4 So Ahab lay on the **c**,
Est 7:8 Haman was falling on the **c**
Job 7:13 'My **c** may give me comfort.
Psa 6:6 I soak my **c** with tears.
Sos 1:16 ground will be our **c**.
Amo 3:12 of a bed or a piece of a **c**.

couches (3)

Est 1:6 Gold and silver **c** were on a
Eze 23:41 They sat on their fine **c** with
Amo 6:4 They sprawl out on their **c** and

council (31)

Job 15:8 Did you listen in on God's **c**
Psa 89:7 God is terrifying in the **c** of the
Mat 26:59 the whole **c** were searching
Mar 14:55 Jewish **c** were searching
15:1 The whole Jewish **c** decided
15:43 member of the Jewish **c**.
Luk 22:66 In the morning the **c** of the
23:50 was a member of the Jewish **c**,
Jon 3:1 and a member of the Jewish **c**.
11:47 called a meeting of the **c**.
11:53 From that day on, the Jewish **c**
Act 4:15 and John to leave the **c** room
5:21 called together the Jewish **c**,
5:27 them stand in front of the **c**.
5:33 the men on the **c** heard this,
5:35 Then he said to the **c**,
5:40 The **c** took his advice.
5:41 The apostles left the **c** room.
6:12 him in front of the Jewish **c**.
6:15 Everyone who sat in the **c**
7:54 As **c** members listened to
7:57 But the **c** members shouted
7:59 While **c** members were
22:5 The chief priest and the entire **c**
22:30 the entire Jewish **c** to meet.
23:1 at the Jewish **c** and said,
23:6 he shouted in the **c**,
23:15 Here's our plan: You and the **c**
23:20 Paul to the Jewish **c** tomorrow.
23:28 So I took him to their Jewish **c**
24:20 when I stood in front of their **c**.

counsel (1)

Isa 28:29 His **c** is wonderful,

counselor (3)

1Ch 26:14 a **c** who displayed insight,
Isa 9:6 He will be named: Wonderful **C**,
Mic 4:9 Has your **c** died? Pain grips you

counselors (5)

Est 6:13 Then his **c** and his wife Zeresh
Job 3:14 be with the kings and the **c**
12:17 He leads **c** away barefoot and
Isa 3:3 leaders, **c**, skilled workers,
19:11 The wisest of Pharaoh's **c**

count (49)

Gen 13:16 If anyone could **c** the dust of
13:16 could also **c** your descendants.
15:5 up at the sky and **c** the stars,
15:5 if you are able to **c** them."
16:10 No one will be able to **c** them
32:12 No one will be able to **c** them
Lev 23:15 "**C** seven full weeks from the
25:8 "**C** seven of these years seven
25:27 he must **c** the years from its
Num 3:15 "**C** the Levites by households
3:15 **C** every male who is at least
6:12 The first time period won't **c**.
23:10 Who can **c** them or number
31:26 of the community need to **c** all
Dtr 16:9 **C** seven weeks from the time
2Sm 24:1 **c** Israel and Judah."
24:2 to Beersheba and **c** the people.
24:4 they left the king ⌊in order⌋ to **c**
1Ki 3:8 too numerous to **c** or record.
2Ki 12:10 chief priest would collect and **c**
22:4 Have him **c** the money that has
1Ch 9:28 They would **c** them when they
21:1 David to **c** the Israelites.
21:2 **c** Israel from Beersheba to Dan.
23:27 last instructions were to **c**
27:23 David didn't **c** those under 20
27:24 started to **c** them but didn't
Job 5:9 miracles that ⌊we⌋ cannot **c**.
14:16 Though now you **c** my steps,
31:4 my ways and **c** all my steps?
38:37 Who is wise enough to **c** the
39:2 Can you **c** the months they are
Psa 22:17 I can **c** all my bones.
40:5 which are more than I can **c**.
48:12 Go around it. **C** its towers.
62:10 Do not **c** on extortion ⌊to make
139:18 If I try to **c** them, there would be
Ecc 1:15 No one can **c** what is not there.
Isa 10:19 few that a child could **c** them.
16:14 I will **c** them like workers count
16:14 I will count them like workers **c**
21:16 I will **c** it like workers count the
21:16 I will count it like workers **c** the
22:10 You will **c** the houses in
Jer 33:13 will once again **c** their sheep,"
Hos 1:10 to measure them or **c** them.
Joe 1:6 It has too many soldiers to **c**.
Rev 7:9 No one was able to **c** how
11:1 **C** those who worship there.

counted (39)

Exo 30:12 for his life when he is **c**.
30:12 to them when they are **c**.
30:13 As each person is **c**,
30:14 Everyone **c** who is at least 20
38:26 for everyone **c** who was at
Lev 27:32 or sheep that you **c** is holy
Num 2:32 of Israelites, **c** by households.
3:39 that Moses and Aaron **c** at
26:62 They were not **c** along with the
26:64 and the priest Aaron had **c**
31:49 we have **c** all the soldiers
Jdg 6:5 their camels could not be **c**.
7:12 that they could not be **c**.
1Sm 11:8 When Saul **c** them at Bezek,
13:15 where Saul **c** the troops who
15:4 and he **c** them at Telaim:
18:27 and they **c** them out for the king
2Sm 2:15 The men got up and were **c** as
24:10 After David **c** the people,
1Ki 20:15 Ahab **c** the young officers of
20:15 he **c** all the Israelite soldiers.
1Ch 21:17 who ordered the people to be **c**.
22:4 logs that the logs couldn't be **c**.
22:16 iron are more than can be **c**.
23:3 at least 30 years old was **c**.
23:14 were **c** with the tribe of Levi.
1Ch 23:24 by name as they were **c**.
2Ch 2:17 Solomon **c** all the men who
2:17 as his father David had **c** them.
2:17 Solomon **c** 153,600 foreigners.
Ezr 8:34 Everything was **c** and weighed,
Job 36:26 of his years cannot be **c**.
Isa 33:18 are those who **c** the towers?
53:12 and he was **c** with sinners.
Jer 33:22 of heaven that cannot be **c**
46:23 than locusts; they can't be **c**.
Mat 10:30 hair on your head has been **c**.
Luk 12:7 hair on your head has been **c**.
22:37 'He was **c** with criminals,'

counterfeit (1)

2Ti 3:8 and the faith they teach is **c**.

counting (3)

1Ki 10:15 not **c** ⌊the gold⌋ which came
20:15 After **c** them, he counted all the
2Ch 9:14 not **c** ⌊the gold⌋ which the

countless (14)

Exo 8:14 They were piled into **c** heaps,
Num 10:36 to the **c** thousands of Israel!"
1Ki 8:5 Israel were offering **c** sheep
2Ch 5:6 Israel were offering **c** sheep
12:3 and an army of **c** Libyans,
Job 21:33 **C** others went before him.
Psa 40:12 **C** evils have surrounded me.
104:25 big and wide with **c** creatures,
105:34 He spoke, and **c** locusts and
Sos 6:8 80 concubines, and **c** virgins,
Jer 2:32 have forgotten me for **c** days.
1Co 4:15 have **c** Christian guardians,
Heb 11:12 the stars in the sky and as **c** as
Jud 1:14 "The Lord has come with **c**

countries (51)

Gen 10:5 spread into their own **c**.
10:20 within their **c** and nations.
10:31 within their **c** according
25:23 "Two **c** are in your womb.
41:54 All the other **c** were
Dtr 29:16 how we passed through other **c**
29:22 come from distant **c** will see
1Ki 4:24 with all the neighboring **c**.
8:41 Israelites come from distant **c**
2Ki 18:33 the nations rescue their **c** from
18:35 Did the gods of those **c** rescue
19:11 the kings of Assyria did to all **c**,
19:18 the gods from these **c** into fires
1Ch 22:5 and honored in all other **c**.
2Ch 6:32 will come from distant **c**
9:28 from Egypt and from all other **c**.
13:9 as the people in foreign **c** do.
32:13 to the people of all other **c**?
32:13 able to rescue their **c** from me?
32:17 in other **c** couldn't rescue their
32:19 by the people in other **c**.
Psa 107:3 and gathered from other **c**,
Isa 36:18 the nations rescue their **c** from
36:20 Did the gods of these **c** rescue
37:11 the kings of Assyria did to all **c**,
37:19 the gods from these **c** into fires
Jer 23:3 of my flock from all the **c** where
27:6 Now I have handed all these **c**
28:8 many **c** and great kingdoms.
40:11 and in all the other **c** heard that
51:28 and all the **c** that they rule.
Eze 5:5 the nations with **c** all around it.
6:8 be scattered throughout the **c**.
11:16 scattered them among the **c**,
11:16 the **c** where they've gone.'
11:17 from the **c** where I've scattered
12:15 and force them into other **c**.
20:23 and force them into other **c**.
20:32 the different people in other **c**.
20:34 gather you from the **c** where
20:41 you from the **c** where you have
22:15 and force you into other **c**.
29:12 and force them into other **c**.
30:23 and force them into other **c**.
30:26 and force them into other **c**.
32:9 the nations to **c** that you haven't
34:13 gather them from the **c**,
Eze 39:27 and gather them from the **c**
Dan 9:7 whom you scattered in **c** near
11:40 He will invade **c**, and pass
11:42 use his power against many **c**.

country (250)

Gen 14:6 the Horites in the hill **c** of Seir,
27:3 and go out into the open **c** and
27:5 Esau went into the open **c**
27:27 is like the smell of open **c** that
30:25 "Let me go home to my own **c**.
31:4 to the open **c** where his flocks
32:3 Esau in Seir, the **c** of Edom.
34:5 his livestock out in the open **c**,
34:7 in from the open **c** as soon as
36:35 the Midianites in the **c** of Moab.
37:15 around in the open **c**.
41:36 reserve supply for our **c** during
41:56 had spread all over the **c**,
42:6 As governor of the **c**,
42:9 out where our **c** is unprotected."
42:12 out where our **c** is unprotected."
42:34 to move about freely in this **c**.'"
Exo 1:10 against us, and leave the **c**."
2:22 a foreigner living in another **c**."
6:1 he will throw them out of his **c**."
6:11 to let the Israelites leave his **c**."
7:2 to let the Israelites leave the **c**.
8:2 of frogs on your whole **c**.
8:25 to your God here in this **c**."
10:4 I will bring locusts into your **c**.
10:14 Egypt and landed all over the **c**
11:10 let the Israelites leave his **c**.
12:33 people to leave the **c** quickly.
18:3 a foreigner living in another **c**."
18:27 Jethro went back to his own **c**.
Lev 14:7 bird fly away into the open **c**.
14:53 fly from the city into the open **c**.
19:29 or the **c** will turn to prostitution
25:9 rams' horns throughout the **c**.
25:45 their families born in your **c**.
26:1 to worship them in your **c**,
26:33 Your **c** will be in ruins.
Num 10:9 go to war in your own **c** against
10:30 I want to go back to my own **c**
20:17 Please let us go through your **c**.
20:18 may not pass through our **c**.
21:22 "Let us go through your **c**.
22:6 and force them out of the **c**.
22:13 "Go back to your own **c**,
Dtr 2:24 and take possession of his **c**.
2:27 us to travel through your **c**,
2:31 to give you Sihon and his **c**.
9:28 the **c** we left will say,
11:3 of Egypt) and to his whole **c**.
22:25 an engaged girl out in the **c**,
22:27 man found the girl out in the **c**.
23:7 were foreigners living in their **c**.
28:3 in the city and blessed in the **c**.
28:16 in the city and cursed in the **c**.
28:40 trees everywhere in your **c**
29:2 and to his whole **c**.
29:28 and deported them to another **c**,
30:4 scattered to the most distant **c**
34:11 and to his whole **c**.
Jos 1:4 to the Euphrates River (the **c**
2:1 told them, "Go, look at that **c**,
2:9 All the people in this **c** are
2:24 has given us the whole **c**.
7:2 to them, "Go, look at that **c**."
9:6 have come from a distant **c**.
9:9 "We came from a **c** very far
9:11 who lives in our **c** told us,
10:41 to Gaza and from all the **c**
13:21 who lived in that **c**.
Jdg 5:4 marched from the **c** of Edom,
5:14 in Amalek's **c** came down from
9:27 They went into the **c** and
11:17 let us go through your **c**.' But
20:31 men from Israel in the open **c**
Rut 1:1 for a while in the **c** of Moab.
1:2 They went to the **c** of Moab
1:6 way back from the **c** of Moab.
1:22 came back from the **c** of Moab,
2:6 with Naomi from the **c** of Moab.
2:11 and the **c** where you were

Rut 4:3 come back from the **c** of Moab,
1Sm 6:5 which are destroying the **c**,
6:5 on you, your gods, and your **c**.
6:9 own **c** toward Beth Shemesh,
14:29 has brought trouble to the **c**.
20:11 "Let's go out into the **c**."
20:11 So they went out into the **c**.
20:35 Jonathan went out to the **c**
21:11 the king of ⌊his⌋ **c**?
23:23 and if he's in the **c**,
23:27 Philistines are raiding the **c**."
30:11 found an Egyptian in the open **c**
2Sm 3:12 "Who owns this **c**?"
10:8 by themselves in the open **c**.
15:23 The whole **c** was crying loudly
18:6 So the troops went out to the **c**
18:8 spread over the whole **c**.
19:9 from Absalom and left the **c**.
24:8 they had covered the whole **c**,
24:25 heard the prayers for the **c**,
1Ki 4:21 the Euphrates River to the **c**
8:46 to ⌊another⌋ **c** as captives,
9:18 in the desert (inside the **c**),
10:6 "What I heard in my **c** about
10:13 servants went back to her **c**.
10:15 and the governors of the **c**.
11:21 "Let me go to my own **c**."
11:29 them were alone in the open **c**,
14:11 If anyone dies in the **c**,
16:4 his ⌊family⌋ who dies in the **c**."
20:7 for all the leaders of the **c**.
20:27 the Arameans who filled the **c**,
21:24 If anyone dies in the **c**,
2Ki 3:27 they went home to their own **c**.
4:38 there was a famine in the **c**.
8:1 to send a famine on this **c**,
8:6 day she left the **c** until now."
11:3 while Athaliah ruled the **c**.
13:20 to invade the **c** in the spring.
15:5 the palace and governed the **c**.
15:19 Assyria came to ⌊attack⌋ the **c**.
15:20 the king of Assyria left the **c**.
17:5 of Assyria attacked the entire **c**.
17:26 customs of the god of that **c**,
17:26 customs of the god of this **c**."
17:27 customs of the god of that **c**."
18:25 'Attack this **c**, and destroy it.'"
18:32 you away to a **c** like your own.
18:32 It's a **c** with grain and new
18:32 a **c** with bread and vineyards,
18:32 a **c** with olive trees,
19:7 a rumor and return to his own **c**.
19:7 assassinated in his own **c**.'"
20:14 from the distant **c** of Babylon."
23:33 and fined the **c** 7,500 pounds
23:35 But he had to tax the **c** to pay
24:7 didn't leave his own **c** again
25:24 Live in this **c**, serve the king of
1Ch 1:46 the Midianites in the **c** of Moab,
19:3 and spy on the **c**?"
19:9 by themselves in the open **c**.
21:12 the whole **c** of Israel.'
22:18 live in this **c** under my power,
22:18 and the **c** has been conquered
2Ch 6:36 to ⌊another⌋ **c** as captives,
7:14 their sins, and heal their **c**.
9:5 "What I heard in my **c** about
9:12 servants went back to her **c**.
9:26 the Euphrates River to the **c**
14:7 The **c** is still ours because we
19:3 the Asherah poles in this **c**,
19:5 He appointed judges in the **c**,
20:7 who were living in this **c** out
20:7 Didn't you give this **c** to the
21:17 against Judah, broke into the **c**,
22:12 while Athaliah ruled the **c**.
26:21 palace and governed the **c**.
32:21 returned to his own **c**.
36:3 and fined the **c** 7,500 pounds
Est 10:1 Xerxes levied a tax on the **c**
Job 24:4 people of the **c** go into hiding.
42:15 Nowhere in the whole **c** could
Pro 28:2 When a **c** is in revolt,
29:4 a king builds up a **c**,
Ecc 5:9 for a **c** with cultivated fields.
10:16 How horrible it will be for any **c**
Ecc 10:17 A **c** is blessed when the king
Isa 1:7 "Your **c** is devastated.
8:8 will extend over your whole **c**,
14:1 resettle them in their own **c**.
23:10 Travel through your **c** like the
33:9 The **c** grieves and wastes
36:10 "Have I come to destroy this **c**
36:10 'Attack this **c**, and destroy it.'"
36:17 you away to a **c** like your own.
36:17 It's a **c** with grain and new
36:17 a **c** with bread and vineyards.
37:7 a rumor and return to his own **c**.
37:7 assassinated in his own **c**.'"
37:18 Assyria have leveled every **c**.
39:3 from the distant **c** of Babylon."
66:8 Can a **c** be born in one day?
Jer 4:16 are coming from a distant **c**.
12:5 If you stumble in open **c**,
17:3 on mountains in the open **c**.
32:44 on the mountains, in the hill **c**,
40:7 to govern the **c** and some of the
40:9 Live in this **c**, serve the king of
40:13 who were still in the **c** came
41:8 and honey hidden in the **c**."
51:47 The whole **c** will be put to
Lam 4:21 inhabitants of the **c** of Uz.
Eze 12:19 Their **c** will be stripped of
12:20 and the **c** will become a
14:13 "Son of man, suppose a **c** sins
14:14 and Job — were in that **c**,
14:15 wild animals through that **c**
14:16 And the **c** would become a
14:17 a war against that **c** by saying,
14:17 go throughout this **c**.' Suppose
14:19 I send a plague into that **c**
15:8 I will turn the **c** into a
17:4 carried it to a **c** of merchants.
17:5 it took a seedling from that **c**
17:14 it would remain a humiliated **c**
17:14 The **c** could only survive by
17:16 He will die in the **c** of the king
21:19 should start from the same **c**.
29:12 Egypt the most desolate **c**
30:7 become the most desolate **c**
33:2 'Suppose I bring war on this **c**,
33:2 and the people of this **c** choose
33:3 enemy coming to attack the **c**,
36:24 and gather you from every **c**.
45:7 to the eastern border ⌊of the **c**⌋.
Dan 11:9 and return to his own **c**.
11:19 the fortresses in his own **c**,
11:28 king will return to his **c**
11:28 action and return to his own **c**.
Hos 12:12 Jacob fled to the **c** of Syria.
Amo 7:10 The **c** isn't able to endure
Jnh 1:8 What **c** are you from?
4:2 when I was still in my own **c**?
Mic 5:6 with their swords and the **c**
Nah 3:13 The gates of your **c** are wide
Mat 2:12 left for their **c** by another road.
Mar 15:21 from his home in the **c**.
16:12 walking to their home in the **c**.
Luk 4:14 throughout the surrounding **c**.
4:25 severe everywhere in the **c**.
15:13 and left for a **c** far away from
15:14 spread throughout that **c**.
15:15 a job from someone in that **c**
15:16 No one in the **c** would give him
19:12 "A prince went to a distant **c** to
19:14 of his own **c** hated him.
Jon 4:44 is not honored in his own **c**.
Act 2:10 and the **c** near Cyrene in Libya.
7:4 "Then Abraham left the **c** of
7:6 be foreigners living in another **c**
7:7 After that, they will leave that **c**
26:20 the whole **c** of Judea.
2Co 11:26 city, in the open **c**, on the sea,
1Th 2:14 your own **c** as those churches
Heb 11:8 Abraham left his own **c** without
11:9 foreigner in the **c** that God had
11:14 they are looking for their own **c**.
11:15 about the **c** that they had
11:16 were longing for a better **c** —
11:16 a better country — a heavenly **c**

country's (5)

Exo 34:24 will expand ⌊your **c**⌋ borders.
Dtr 12:20 expand your ⌊**c**⌋ borders as
19:8 may expand your **c** borders as
Job 12:24 common sense of a **c** leaders
Jer 40:7 and some of the **c** poorest men,

countrymen (1)

2Sm 15:20 and take your **c** with you.

countryside (19)

Exo 22:31 by wild animals out in the **c**.
Num 22:5 spread out all over the **c**
22:11 are spreading out all over the **c**.
1Sm 20:5 But let me go and hide in the **c**
20:24 So David hid in the **c**.
1Ki 18:5 "Let's go throughout the **c** to
18:6 up in order to cover the entire **c**.
2Ki 3:20 from Edom and filled the **c**.
7:12 left the camp to hide in the **c**.
2Ch 7:13 grasshoppers to devour the **c**,
Neh 12:28 from the **c** around Jerusalem,
Mat 14:35 messengers all around the **c**.
Mar 5:14 In the city and **c** they reported
6:55 They ran all over the **c** and
Luk 8:34 everything in the city and **c**,
Jon 3:22 disciples went to the Judean **c**,
4:3 So he left the Judean **c** and
11:54 Bethany and went to the **c** near
11:55 Many people came from the **c**

couple (2)

2Ki 5:23 He gave them to a **c** of his own
Pro 7:20 be home for a **c** of weeks."

courage (31)

Dtr 20:3 Don't lose your **c**!
20:8 are afraid or have lost your **c**,
Jos 2:11 There was no **c** left in any of
5:1 So they lost heart and had no **c**
Jdg 7:11 After that, you will have the **c**
2Sm 4:1 died in Hebron, he lost his **c**,
7:27 That is why I have found the **c**
17:10 like a lion would lose his **c**,
1Ch 17:25 is why I have found ⌊the **c**⌋
Psa 23:4 rod and your staff give me **c**.
107:26 Their **c** melted in ⌊the face of⌋
Isa 13:7 and everyone's **c** will fail.
15:4 men cry out. Their **c** is gone.
19:1 presence. Egypt's **c** will fail.
19:3 The Egyptians will lose **c**.
46:8 Remember this, and take **c**.
57:15 who are humble and the **c**
Jer 4:9 the leaders will lose their **c**.
47:3 lack **c** abandon their children.
50:43 about them, and he loses **c**.
51:46 Don't lose **c** or be afraid when
Eze 7:27 people will lose their **c**.
21:7 their hearts will lose **c**,
Dan 11:25 his power and **c** against
Zep 3:16 Zion! Do not lose **c**!"
Act 23:11 "Don't lose your **c**!
27:22 Now I advise you to have **c**.
27:25 So have **c**, men! I trust God
Rom 5:7 someone would have the **c**
1Th 2:2 But our God gave us the **c** to
Heb 3:6 if we continue to have **c**

courageous (21)

Dtr 31:6 Be strong and **c**. Don't tremble!
31:7 of all Israel, "Be strong and **c**.
31:23 son of Nun: "Be strong and **c**,
Jos 1:6 Be strong and **c**, because you
1:7 "Only be strong and very **c**,
1:9 you, 'Be strong and **c**!
1:18 Just be strong and **c**!"
10:25 Be strong and **c**, because this
1Sm 16:18 He's a **c** man and a warrior.
2Sm 2:7 Now, be strong and **c**.
13:28 haven't I? Be strong and **c**."
1Ch 22:13 Be strong and **c**. Don't be afraid
28:20 son Solomon, "Be strong and **c**,
2Ch 25:8 no matter how **c** you are,
26:17 with 80 of the LORD's **c** priests.
32:7 "Be strong and **c**. Don't be

Psa 27:14 and let your heart be **c**.
31:24 and let your heart be **c**.
Nah 2:1 Prepare for battle! Be very **c**!
1Co 12:9 the same Spirit gives ⌊**c**⌋ faith.
16:13 faith. Be **c** and strong.

courageously (1)

2Ch 25:11 Amaziah **c** led his troops.

course (14)

Gen 15:16 not have run its **c** until then."
Exo 2:11 In the **c** of time Moses grew up.
1Sm 21:5 "Of **c** women have been kept
1Ki 6:36 of finished stones and a **c**
Job 6:18 They change their **c**.
Psa 19:5 it is eager to run its **c**.
Pro 2:9 fair — every good **c** ⌊in life⌋.
Isa 41:4 Who has determined the **c** of
Hab 3:2 In the **c** of the years,
3:2 In the **c** of the years,
Luk 12:39 "Of **c**, you realize that if the
Jon 4:9 (Jews, of **c**, don't associate
2Co 10:3 Of **c** we are human,
Php 3:12 have already completed the **c**.

courses (1)

1Ki 6:36 the inner courtyard with three **c**

court (46)

Exo 9:20 Those members of Pharaoh's **c**
21:22 pay whatever fine the **c** allows
23:2 When you testify in **c**,
23:3 favors to poor people in **c**.
23:6 justice to poor people in **c**.
Dtr 17:8 which may be brought to **c**
25:1 that is brought into **c**.
Jos 20:4 to the city, where **c** is held,
1Sm 19:7 to his former status in Saul's **c**.
2Ch 19:11 will serve as officers of the **c**.
Job 9:32 'Let's take our case to **c**.'
11:10 and then calls a **c** into session,
13:8 arguing in **c** on God's behalf?
22:4 you and bring you into a **c**
31:21 others would back me up in **c**,
Psa 122:5 The **c** of justice sits there.
143:2 not take me to **c** for judgment,
Pro 25:8 Do not be in a hurry to go to **c**.
29:9 When a wise person goes to **c**
Jer 29:2 and his mother, the **c** officials,
Lam 3:36 deprive people of justice in **c**.
Dan 2:49 Daniel stayed at the king's **c**.
7:10 The **c** convened, and the
Mat 5:21 murders will answer for it in **c**.'
5:22 believer will answer for it in **c**.
5:22 answer for it in the highest **c**.
5:25 are on the way to **c** with him.
Luk 12:58 an opponent brings you to **c**
22:66 their highest **c** and asked him,
Act 17:19 they brought Paul to the city **c**,
17:22 in the middle of the **c** and said,
17:32 When the people of the **c** heard
17:33 this response, Paul left the **c**.
17:34 who was a member of the **c**,
18:12 Paul and brought him to **c**.
18:16 had them forced out of his **c**.
18:17 and beat him in front of the **c**.
19:38 days and officials to hold **c**.
25:6 place in **c** and summoned Paul.
25:10 in the emperor's **c** where
25:17 day I immediately convened **c**
Rom 3:4 and you win your case in **c**."
1Co 4:3 **c** should cross-examine me.
6:1 how dare you go to **c** to settle
6:6 Instead, one believer goes to **c**
Jas 2:6 you and drag you into **c**?

courteous (1)

1Co 4:13 are attacked, we remain **c**.

courtesy (1)

Tit 3:2 gentle and show **c** to everyone.

courtroom (1)

Isa 3:13 LORD takes his place in the **c**.

courts (5)

Amo 5:12 the needy access to the **c**.
5:15 able to have justice in your **c**.
Zec 8:16 fair verdicts for peace in your **c**.
Mat 10:17 hand you over to the Jewish **c**
Mar 13:9 hand you over to the Jewish **c**

courtyard (189)

Exo 27:9 "Make a **c** for the tent.
27:9 The south side of the **c** should
27:12 "The **c** on the west end should
27:13 the **c** should also be 75 feet
27:16 "The entrance to the **c** must
27:17 All the posts around the **c**
27:18 The **c** should be 150 feet long,
27:19 the pegs for the tent and the **c**,
35:17 the curtains for the **c**,
35:17 screen for the entrance to the **c**,
35:18 tent and the **c** with their ropes,
38:9 He also made the **c**.
38:9 The south side of the **c** was
38:14 entrance to the **c** was 22 ½
38:16 All the curtains around the **c**
38:17 the posts of the **c** were made
38:18 the entrance to the **c** was made
38:18 just like the curtains of the **c**.
38:20 the surrounding **c** were made
38:31 the bases all around the **c**,
38:31 bases for the entrance to the **c**,
38:31 the pegs for the surrounding **c**.
39:40 the curtains for the **c**,
39:40 screen for the entrance to the **c**,
40:8 Set up the surrounding **c**,
40:8 screen at the entrance to the **c**.
40:33 He set up the **c** around the tent
40:33 screen at the entrance to the **c**.
Lev 6:16 in the **c** of the tent of meeting.
6:26 in the **c** of the tent of meeting.
Num 3:26 the curtains for the **c**,
3:26 entrance to the **c** that surrounds
3:37 the posts for the surrounding **c**,
4:26 the curtains for the **c** around the
4:26 screen for the entrance to the **c**,
4:32 the posts for the surrounding **c**,
2Sm 17:18 who had a cistern in his **c**,
1Ki 6:36 He built the inner **c** with three
7:9 including the large **c**,
7:12 The large **c** had three layers of
7:12 like the inner **c** of the LORD's
8:64 day the king designated the **c**
2Ki 20:4 as far as the middle **c** when
23:11 They were in the temple **c** near
1Ch 6:32 served as musicians in the **c**
26:18 At the **c** on the west there were
26:18 palace and two at the **c** itself.
2Ch 4:9 He also made the priests' **c**
4:9 courtyard and the large **c**
6:13 He put it in the middle of the **c**.
7:7 Solomon designated the **c** in
20:5 In the new **c** at the LORD's
24:21 stoned him to death in the **c**
29:16 They carried into the **c** every
Ezr 10:9 all the people sat in the **c** of
Neh 3:25 king's palace to the guards' **c**.
8:1 gathered together in the **c**
8:3 he read from it in the **c** in front
Est 2:11 back and forth in front of the **c**
5:1 She stood in the **c** of the king's
6:4 "Who is in the **c**?"
6:4 Haman came through the **c** to
6:5 to be standing in the **c**."
Jer 19:14 He stood in the **c** of the LORD's
26:2 Stand in the **c** of the LORD's
32:2 was locked up in the **c**
32:8 Hanamel came to me in the **c**
32:12 sitting in the **c** of the prison.
33:1 was still being held in the **c**
36:10 in the upper **c** at the entrance of
36:20 they went to the king in the **c**
37:21 to have Jeremiah put in the **c**
37:21 stayed in the **c** of the prison.
38:6 It was in the **c** of the prison.
38:13 stayed in the **c** of the prison.
38:28 Jeremiah stayed in the **c** of the
39:14 They took Jeremiah out of the **c**
Jer 39:15 was still confined in the **c**
Eze 8:3 to the north gate of the inner **c**
8:7 me to the entrance of the **c**.
8:16 he brought me into the inner **c**
10:3 A cloud filled the inner **c**.
10:4 of the LORD's glory filled the **c**.
10:5 was heard as far as the outer **c**.
40:14 gateway was a **c** on all sides.
40:17 brought me into the outer **c**.
40:17 and pavement all around the **c**.
40:18 The pavement in the lower **c**
40:19 to the outside of the inner **c**.
40:20 leading to the outer **c**.
40:23 The inner **c** had a gateway
40:27 The inner **c** had a gateway
40:28 me to the inner **c** through
40:30 halls all around the inner **c**.
40:31 halls faced the outer **c**.
40:32 to the east side of the inner **c**.
40:34 entrance hall faced the outer **c**.
40:37 walls faced the outer **c**.
40:44 gateways to the inner **c** were
40:47 The man measured the **c**.
41:15 of the building facing the **c**
42:1 toward the north to the outer **c**.
42:3 Opposite the inner **c** was an
42:3 outer **c** were corridors facing
42:7 the side rooms and the outer **c**.
42:8 The row of rooms in the outer **c**
42:9 enter the outer **c** through them.
42:10 parallel to the wall of the **c**
42:14 into the outer **c** until they leave
43:5 and brought me into the inner **c**.
44:17 the gateways to the inner **c**,
44:17 in the gateways to the inner **c**
44:19 the people in the outer **c**,
44:21 when they enter the inner **c**.
44:27 When he enters the inner **c** of
45:19 of the gateways of the inner **c**.
46:1 The east gate of the inner **c**
46:20 the offerings into the outer **c**.
46:21 the man led me to the outer **c**
46:21 past the four corners of the **c**.
46:21 each corner of the **c** there was
46:21 there was a smaller **c**.
46:22 corners of the **c** were 60 feet
46:22 in the corners of the **c** were
Mat 21:12 Jesus went into the temple **c**
21:14 came to him in the temple **c**,
21:15 shouting in the temple **c**,
21:23 Jesus went into the temple **c**
24:1 As Jesus left the temple **c** and
26:55 in the temple **c** every day.
26:58 he came to the chief priest's **c**.
26:69 Peter was sitting in the **c**.
Mar 11:11 and went into the temple **c**,
11:15 Jesus went into the temple **c**
11:16 anything across the temple **c**.
11:27 was walking in the temple **c**,
12:35 was teaching in the temple **c**,
13:1 was going out of the temple **c**,
14:49 in the temple **c** every day.
14:54 went into the chief priest's **c**.
14:66 Peter was in the **c**.
15:16 soldiers led Jesus into the **c**
Luk 2:27 Simeon went into the temple **c**.
2:27 the child Jesus into the **c** at
2:37 Anna never left the temple **c**
2:46 they found him in the temple **c**.
18:10 went into the temple **c** to pray.
19:45 Jesus went into the temple **c**
19:47 in the temple **c** every day.
20:1 the people in the temple **c**
21:37 would teach in the temple **c**.
21:38 hear him speak in the temple **c**.
22:53 I was with you in the temple **c**
22:55 lit a fire in the middle of the **c**.
Jon 2:14 and pigeons in the temple **c**.
2:15 and cattle out of the temple **c**.
5:14 met the man in the temple **c**
7:14 Jesus went to the temple **c**
7:28 was teaching in the temple **c**,
7:37 standing ⌊in the temple **c**⌋.
8:2 he returned to the temple **c**.
8:20 treasury area of the temple **c**.
8:59 and he left the temple **c**.

Jon 10:23 porch in the temple **c**.
11:56 As they stood in the temple **c**,
18:15 Jesus into the chief priest's **c**.
18:16 and brought Peter into the **c**.
18:20 synagogues or in the temple **c**,
Act 3:1 were going to the temple **c**
3:2 man at a gate in the temple **c**.
3:2 from people going into the **c**.
3:3 were about to go into the **c**,
3:8 and John into the temple **c**.
5:20 "Stand in the temple **c**,
5:21 apostles went into the temple **c**
5:25 are standing in the temple **c**.
5:42 Every day in the temple **c** and
21:26 Then he went into the temple **c**
21:27 Asia saw Paul in the temple **c**.
21:28 Greeks into the temple **c**
21:29 taken him into the temple **c**.
21:30 him out of the temple **c**.
21:30 The **c** doors were immediately
22:17 I was praying in the temple **c**,
24:6 He also entered the temple **c** in
24:12 with anyone in the temple **c**
24:18 the temple **c** doing these things
26:21 me prisoner in the temple **c**
Rev 11:2 do not measure the temple **c**.

courtyards (26)

2Ki 21:5 In the two **c** of the LORD's
23:12 had made in the two **c**
1Ch 23:28 to be in charge of the **c**
28:6 will build my temple and my **c**
28:12 He gave him plans for the **c** of
2Ch 23:5 All the people must be in the **c**
33:5 In the two **c** of the LORD's
Neh 8:16 on their roofs, others in their **c**,
8:16 in the **c** of God's temple,
Psa 65:4 invite to live with you in your **c**.
84:2 and yearns for the LORD's **c**.
84:10 One day in your **c** is better than
92:13 They blossom in our God's **c**.
96:8 and come into his **c**.
100:4 Come into his **c** with a song of
116:19 in the **c** of the LORD's house,
135:2 in the **c** of the house of our
Isa 1:12 asked you to trample on my **c**?
62:9 will drink wine in my holy **c**.
Eze 9:7 Fill its **c** with dead people,
40:44 for the singers in the inner **c**.
42:6 pillars like the pillars in the **c**.
46:22 The smaller **c** that were in
46:22 All four of the smaller **c** in the
46:23 Around each of the four **c** were
Zec 3:7 temple and watch over my **c**.

cousin (7)

Lev 25:49 His uncle, his **c**, or some other
2Sm 16:5 a man who was a distant **c** of
Jer 32:7 'Jeremiah, your **c** Hanamel,
32:8 my **c** Hanamel came to me in
32:9 in Anathoth from my **c** Hanamel
32:12 the presence of my **c** Hanamel
Col 4:10 the **c** of Barnabas.

cousins (3)

Num 36:11 and Noah married their **c** on
2Sm 19:41 They asked, "Why did our **c**,
1Ch 23:22 Their **c**, the sons of Kish,

cover (112)

Exo 10:5 They will **c** the land so that the
21:33 or digs a new one and doesn't **c**
22:27 clothes he has to **c** his body.
25:11 **C** it with pure gold inside and
25:13 and **c** them with gold.
25:17 "Make a throne of mercy to **c**
25:24 **C** it with pure gold,
25:28 acacia wood, **c** them with gold,
26:13 side in order to **c** the inner tent.
26:14 Make a **c** of rams' skins that
26:14 Over that put a **c** made of fine
26:29 **C** the frames with gold,
26:29 and **c** the crossbars with gold.
26:37 wood for the screen and **c** them
27:6 and **c** them with bronze.
28:42 Make linen undergarments to **c**
Exo 30:3 **C** all of it with pure gold — the
30:5 and **c** them with gold.
33:22 a crevice in the cliff and **c** you
35:11 and **c**, along with the fasteners,
36:19 They made a **c** out of rams'
36:19 and over that they put a **c** made
39:34 the **c** made of rams' skins dyed
39:34 the **c** made of fine leather,
40:19 inner tent and put the **c** on top.
Lev 13:13 If the disease does **c** his whole
13:45 They must **c** their upper lips
16:13 The cloud of incense will **c** the
17:13 animal's blood and **c** it with dirt.
Num 3:25 the outer tent and **c**,
4:5 First they will **c** the ark with
4:8 They will **c** all this with fine
4:9 will take a violet cloth and **c**
4:11 cloth over the gold altar and **c**
4:12 **c** that with fine leather,
4:25 They will also carry the inner **c**
4:25 the outer **c** of fine leather that
16:38 thin metal sheets to **c** the altar.
16:39 thin metal sheets to **c** the altar,
Dtr 23:13 **c** up your excrement.
27:2 stones and **c** them with plaster.
27:4 and **c** them with plaster,
28:35 The boils will **c** your whole
Jos 24:7 the sea flow back and **c** them.
2Sm 17:19 The man's wife took a **c**,
1Ki 7:18 around the filigree to **c**
7:41 and 2 sets of filigree to **c** the 2
7:42 for each filigree to **c**
18:6 So they split up in order to **c**
1Ch 28:18 with their wings spread to **c**
29:4 They are to be used to **c** the
2Ch 4:12 and 2 sets of filigree to **c** the 2
4:13 for each filigree to **c**
Job 14:17 and you will **c** over my sins.
16:18 "Earth, don't **c** my blood.
21:26 and worms **c** them.
24:15 as they **c** their faces.
38:34 have a flood of water **c** you?
40:13 and **c** their faces in the hidden
40:22 Lotus plants provide it with **c**.
Psa 32:5 and I did not **c** up my guilt.
84:6 early rains **c** it with blessings.
91:4 He will **c** you with his feathers,
104:2 You **c** yourself with light as
104:9 come back to **c** the earth.
Pro 10:6 Blessings **c** the head of a
Isa 4:5 His glory will **c** everything.
14:11 under you, and worms **c** you.
26:21 and will no longer **c** up its dead
28:20 is too narrow to serve as a **c**.
29:10 He will **c** your heads.
40:19 Goldsmiths **c** them with gold.
50:3 and **c** them with sackcloth.
54:9 floodwaters would never **c**
58:7 and **c** them with clothes when
59:6 nor can they **c** themselves with
60:6 camels will **c** your ⌊land⌋,
Jer 4:6 Take **c**! Don't just stand there!
6:1 "Take **c**, people of Benjamin!
14:3 They **c** their heads,
14:4 They **c** their heads.
46:8 'I will rise; I will **c** the earth.
51:42 and its roaring waves will **c** it.
Eze 7:18 and horror will **c** them.
12:6 **C** your face so that you won't
12:12 The prince will **c** his face so
13:10 the prophets **c** it up with paint.
13:11 Tell those who **c** up the wall
13:12 that you used to **c** the wall?"
22:28 Your prophets **c** up these
24:7 ground where dust would **c** it.
24:17 Don't **c** your face or eat the food
24:22 Don't **c** your faces or eat the
26:10 that their dust will **c** you.
26:19 Mediterranean Sea will **c** you.
30:18 Clouds will **c** Egypt,
32:7 I will **c** the sky and darken the
32:7 I will **c** the sun with clouds,
37:6 and **c** you with skin.
38:9 will attack like a storm and **c**
Hos 2:9 I gave her to **c** her naked body.
10:8 say to the mountains, "**C** us!"
Joe 3:18 new wine will **c** the mountains.
Mic 3:7 All of them will **c** their faces,
Hab 2:16 and disgrace will **c** your glory.
Zec 5:7 A lead **c** ⌊on the basket⌋ was
5:8 and forced the lead **c** down
Mal 2:13 You **c** the LORD's altar with
Luk 23:30 and to the hills, '**C** us!'
1Co 11:6 if a woman doesn't **c** her head,
11:6 she should **c** her head.
11:7 A man should not **c** his head.

covered (148)

Gen 1:2 and darkness **c** the deep water.
7:19 It **c** all the high mountains
9:23 and **c** their father's naked
24:65 Then she took her veil and **c**
25:25 whole body was **c** with hair,
38:14 **c** her face with a veil,
38:15 because she had **c** her face.
Exo 8:6 The frogs came up and **c** the
8:21 outside will be **c** with them.
10:15 They **c** all the ground until it
14:28 The water flowed back and **c**
15:5 The deep water **c** them.
16:13 quails came and **c** the camp,
16:14 the ground was **c** with a thin
19:18 All of Mount Sinai was **c** with
20:18 the mountain **c** with smoke.
24:15 mountain, and the cloud **c** it.
24:16 For six days the cloud **c** it,
26:32 of acacia wood **c** with gold,
27:2 piece ⌊of wood⌋ **c** with bronze.
36:34 They **c** the frames with gold
36:34 They also **c** the crossbars with
36:36 acacia wood for it and **c** them
36:38 They **c** the tops of the posts
37:2 He **c** it with pure gold inside
37:4 wood and **c** them with gold.
37:11 He **c** it with pure gold and put a
37:15 wood and were **c** with gold.
37:26 He **c** all of it with pure gold —
37:28 wood and **c** them with gold.
38:2 piece ⌊of wood⌋ **c** with bronze.
38:6 wood and **c** them with bronze.
38:17 of the posts were **c** with silver.
38:19 of the posts were **c** with silver.
40:34 Then the ⌊column of⌋ smoke **c**
Num 9:15 the ⌊column of⌋ smoke **c** it.
12:10 Miriam was **c** with an
12:10 she was **c** with the disease.
16:33 The ground **c** them,
Jos 2:6 them up to the roof and **c** them
Jdg 3:22 Eglon's fat **c** the blade because
4:19 to drink and **c** him up again.
6:39 all the ground is **c** with dew."
6:40 all the ground was **c** with dew.
1Sm 5:9 and they were **c** with tumors.
19:13 and **c** the idols with a garment.
2Sm 15:30 He **c** his head and walked
15:30 And all of the troops with him **c**
19:4 The king **c** his face and cried
24:8 When they had **c** the whole
1Ki 1:1 he was **c** with blankets,
6:15 He **c** the floor of the temple
6:18 Everything was ⌊**c** with⌋ cedar.
6:20 Solomon **c** it and the cedar
6:21 He **c** the inside of the temple
6:21 room which was **c** with gold.
6:22 He **c** the entire inside of the
6:22 He also **c** the entire altar in the
6:28 He **c** the angels with gold.
6:30 He **c** the floor of the inner and
6:32 and flowers into them and **c**
6:35 He evenly **c** them with gold.
7:3 The hall was **c** with cedar
7:7 The hall was **c** with cedar from
10:18 made a large ivory throne and **c**
2Ki 3:25 every good field until it was **c**.
16:18 Ahaz removed the **c** walkway
18:16 had them **c** ⌊with gold⌋.)
19:1 **c** himself with sackcloth,
2Ch 3:4 He **c** its inside walls with pure
3:6 He **c** the building with gems to
3:10 angels and **c** them with gold.
4:9 He **c** the doors with bronze.
9:17 made a large ivory throne and **c**

Est 6:12 was in despair and **c** his head.
7:8 and servants **c** Haman's face.
Job 7:5 My body is **c** with maggots and
31:33 "If I have **c** my disobedience
36:16 table was **c** with rich foods.
Psa 34:5 will never be **c** with shame.
44:19 us in a place for jackals and **c**
65:13 The pastures are **c** with flocks.
68:13 wings of a dove **c** with silver,
69:7 Humiliation has **c** my face.
71:13 who want my downfall be **c**
78:53 while the sea **c** their enemies.
80:10 Its shade **c** the mountains.
80:10 branches **c** the mighty cedars.
89:45 the days of his youth and **c** him
104:6 You **c** the earth with an ocean
106:11 Water **c** their adversaries.
140:7 you have **c** my head in the day
140:9 of those who surround me be **c**
Pro 24:31 The ground was **c** with weeds,
26:23 ⌊Like⌋ a clay pot **c** with cheap
Sos 5:14 block of ivory **c** with sapphires.
Isa 1:15 your hands are **c** with blood.
6:2 With two they **c** their faces,
6:2 with two they **c** their feet,
14:19 You are **c** with those who were
27:9 descendants of Jacob are **c** up.
28:8 All the tables are **c** with vomit
34:5 When my sword is **c** ⌊with
34:6 LORD's sword is **c** with blood.
34:6 It is **c** with fat, with the blood of
34:7 Their dust will be **c** with fat.
34:13 Its palaces are **c** with thorns.
37:1 **c** himself with sackcloth,
Jer 3:25 and be **c** by our disgrace.
26:18 a worship site **c** with trees.'
Lam 2:1 "Look how the Lord has **c** the
3:43 You **c** yourself with anger and
3:44 You **c** yourself with a cloud so
Eze 1:11 other two wings **c** their bodies.
1:18 They were **c** with eyes.
1:23 had two wings that **c** its body.
7:18 faces will be **c** with shame,
8:10 I saw that the walls were **c**
10:12 and wheels were **c** with eyes.
13:14 the wall that the prophets **c** up
13:15 on the wall and on those who **c**
16:8 and **c** your naked body.
16:10 fine linen and **c** you with silk.
16:18 your embroidered clothes and **c**
23:37 Their hands are **c** with blood.
23:45 their hands are **c** with blood.
24:8 Now that blood can't be **c**.
27:30 and **c** themselves with ashes.
28:13 You were **c** with every kind of
31:15 I **c** the underground springs
37:8 were on them, and skin **c** them.
40:3 like he was **c** with bronze.
Oba 1:10 you will be **c** with shame.
Jnh 2:5 deep ⌊sea⌋ **c** me completely.
Mic 3:12 a worship site **c** with trees.
7:10 and they will be **c** with shame,
Hab 2:19 It's **c** with gold and silver,
Mat 10:26 Nothing has been **c** that will
Mar 14:65 They **c** his face and hit him
Luk 5:12 a city where there was a man **c**
12:2 Nothing has been **c** that will
16:21 Lazarus was **c** with sores,
2Co 3:18 faces that are not **c** with veils,
4:3 News that we tell others is **c**
Heb 9:4 was completely **c** with gold.
Rev 4:6 were four living creatures **c**
4:8 wings and were **c** with eyes,
17:3 sitting on a bright red beast **c**

covering (21)

Gen 37:26 our brother and **c** up his death?
Lev 7:3 the fat **c** the internal organs,
Num 4:6 Over this they will put a **c** of
4:10 and all its utensils under a **c**
4:14 They will spread a **c** of fine
4:15 and his sons have finished **c**
9:16 At night the smoke **c** the tent
16:42 they saw the smoke **c** it,
2Sm 22:12 the dark rain clouds his **c**.
1Ki 8:7 the angels became a **c** above
2Ch 5:8 the angels became a **c** above
Job 24:7 without a **c** from the cold.
Psa 18:11 the dark rain clouds his **c**.
105:39 out a cloud as a protective **c**
Isa 11:9 the LORD like water **c** the sea.
25:7 the veil of grief **c** all people
25:7 and the mask **c** all nations.
Mat 8:24 The waves were **c** the boat.
Jon 11:38 with a stone **c** the entrance.
1Co 11:15 is given to her in place of a **c**.
2Co 3:13 He kept **c** his face with a veil.

coverings (1)

Exo 38:28 bands for the posts and the **c**

covers (30)

Exo 22:15 the rental fee **c** the loss.
29:13 "Then take all the fat that **c** the
29:22 the fat that **c** the internal
Lev 3:3 the fat that **c** the internal organs
3:9 fat that **c** the internal organs.
3:14 the fat that **c** the internal organs
4:8 fat that **c** the internal organs,
13:12 If skin disease develops and **c**
Job 9:24 He **c** the faces of its judges.
22:11 see and a flood of water **c** you.
23:17 thick darkness that **c** my face.
26:9 He **c** his throne by spreading
36:30 of lightning around him and **c**
Psa 44:15 front of me. Shame **c** my face
147:8 He **c** the sky with clouds.
Pro 10:6 but violence **c** the mouths of
10:12 but love **c** every wrong.
26:23 ⌊so⌋ is smooth talk that **c** up
28:13 Whoever **c** over his sins does
Isa 60:2 Darkness now **c** the earth,
60:2 thick darkness **c** the nations.
Jer 51:51 Shame **c** our faces,
Lam 1:9 own filth ⌊**c**⌋ its clothes.
Eze 38:16 like a cloud that **c** the land.
Hab 2:14 glory like the water **c** the sea.
3:3 His splendor **c** the heavens.
Mal 2:16 "I hate the person who **c**
1Co 11:4 Every man who **c** his head
2Co 3:15 a veil **c** their minds.
1Pe 4:8 because love **c** many sins.

cow (13)

Lev 22:28 Never slaughter a **c** or a sheep
Num 19:2 bring you a red **c** that is perfect,
19:5 Then the entire **c** (the skin,
19:6 throw them onto the burning **c**.
19:9 collect the ashes from the **c**
19:9 The **c** is an offering for sin.
19:10 from the **c** must also wash
19:17 from the red **c** that was burned
Jdg 6:4 not one sheep, **c**, or donkey.
14:18 you hadn't used my **c** to plow,
Isa 7:21 alive a young **c** and two sheep.
Jer 46:20 "Egypt is like a beautiful **c**,
Eze 4:15 "I will let you use **c** manure in

cowardly (3)

Jon 14:27 So don't be troubled or **c**.
2Ti 1:7 God didn't give us a **c** spirit but
Rev 21:8 But **c**, unfaithful, murderers,

cowards (2)

Mat 8:26 "Why do you **c** have so little
Mar 4:40 "Why are you such **c**?

coworker (8)

Rom 16:9 Greet Urbanus our **c** in the
16:21 Timothy my **c** greets you;
2Co 8:23 that Titus is my partner and **c**
Php 2:25 Epaphroditus — my brother, **c**,
Phm 1:1 To our dear **c** Philemon,
Rev 19:10 I am your **c** and a coworker of
19:10 I am your coworker and a **c** of
22:9 I am your **c**. I work with other

coworkers (8)

Rom 16:3 Greet Prisca and Aquila, my **c**
1Co 3:9 We are God's **c**. You are God's
2Co 6:1 Since we are God's **c**,
9:3 I've sent my **c** so that when we
2Co 9:5 that I should encourage our **c**
Php 4:3 Clement and the rest of my **c**,
Phm 1:24 and my **c** Mark, Aristarchus,
Rev 6:11 a little longer until all their **c**,

cows (34)

Gen 32:15 their young, 40 **c** and 10 bulls,
41:2 well-fed **c** came up from the
41:3 Seven other **c** came up from
41:3 These **c** were sickly and
41:3 first seven **c** on the riverbank.
41:4 The **c** that were sickly and
41:4 seven nice-looking, well-fed **c**.
41:18 well-fed **c** came up from the
41:19 Seven other **c** came up behind
41:19 These **c** were scrawny,
41:19 I've never seen such sickly **c**
41:20 The thin, sickly **c** ate up the
41:26 The seven good **c** are seven
41:27 The seven thin, sickly **c** that
Dtr 32:14 They ate cheese from **c** and
1Sm 6:7 for two dairy **c** that have never
6:7 Hitch the **c** to the cart.
6:10 They took two dairy **c**,
6:12 The **c** went straight up the road
6:14 the cart and sacrificed the **c** as
14:32 They took sheep, **c**,
15:3 and children, **c** and sheep,
15:9 Agag and the best sheep and **c**,
15:14 and this sound of **c** that I hear?"
15:15 spared the best sheep and **c**
15:21 best sheep and **c** were claimed
22:19 infants, **c**, donkeys, and sheep.
2Sm 12:2 large number of sheep and **c**,
1Ki 4:23 10 fattened **c**, 20 cows from the
4:23 20 **c** from the pasture,
Job 21:10 Their **c** give birth to calves and
Isa 11:7 **C** and bears will eat together.
Amo 4:1 Listen to this message, you **c**
Heb 9:13 and the ashes of **c** sprinkled

Cozbi (2)

Num 25:15 woman who was killed was **C**,
25:18 They used their sister **C**,

Cozeba (1)

1Ch 4:22 Saraph, and the men of **C**.

crack (2)

Isa 30:13 a high wall with a bulging **c**,
Jer 13:4 bury it there in a **c** in the rocks."

cracked (4)

Lev 2:14 roast the **c** grain over fire.
Jdg 9:53 on the head and **c** his skull.
Jer 2:16 Tahpanhes have **c** your skulls,
14:4 The ground is **c** because there

crackling (2)

Ecc 7:6 laughter of a fool is like the **c**
Joe 2:5 like **c** fire burning up straw,

cracks (5)

Psa 60:2 Heal the **c** in it because it is
Isa 2:21 caves in the rocks and into **c**
7:19 in the **c** in the cliffs,
57:5 and under the **c** in the rocks.
Jer 16:16 and even in the **c** in the rocks.

craftsman (7)

Exo 31:6 I have given every **c** the skill
36:1 with the help of every other **c**
36:2 and Oholiab and every other **c**
Dtr 27:15 LORD that was made by a **c**,
1Ki 7:14 was a skilled bronze **c**.
Pro 8:30 was beside him as a master **c**.
Rev 18:22 Skilled **c** will never be found in

craftsmanship (1)

1Ki 7:14 about all kinds of bronze **c**.

craftsmen (20)

Exo 35:10 "Have all the skilled **c** among
36:4 Finally, all the skilled **c** who
36:8 All the skilled **c** among the
2Ki 24:14 and all the **c** and smiths.

2Ki 24:16 1,000 c and smiths,
1Ch 4:14 who first settled the valley of C.
4:14 this because they were c.)
29:5 else the c will make.
Neh 11:35 and in the valley of the C.
Isa 40:19 C make idols. Goldsmiths cover
40:20 not rot and search out skillful c
41:7 C encourage goldsmiths.
44:11 The c themselves are only
Jer 10:3 The hands of c prepare them
10:4 C decorate them with silver
10:9 C and goldsmiths shape these
29:2 of Judah and Jerusalem, the c,
Hos 13:2 All of them are the work of c.
Zec 1:20 the LORD showed me four c.
1:21 But the c have come to terrify

cranes (2)

Isa 38:14 I chirped like swallows and c.
Jer 8:7 and c know when it's time to

crash (1)

Eze 31:16 fear at the sound of the tree's c.

crashing (4)

Psa 55:3 They bring misery c down on
65:7 roar of the seas, their c waves,
150:5 Praise him with c cymbals.
Zep 1:10 and a loud c sound from the

crave (4)

Pro 23:3 Do not c his delicacies,
23:6 and do not c his delicacies.
31:4 wine or for rulers to c liquor.
Mic 7:1 eat or any ripened figs that I c.

craved (3)

Num 11:34 of Those Who C ⌊Meat⌋
Psa 78:18 by demanding the food they c.
Rev 18:14 'The fruit you c is gone.

craves (2)

Pro 13:2 people ⌊c⌋ violence.
13:4 A lazy person c food and there

craving (2)

Num 11:4 the Israelites had a strong c
11:34 who had a strong c ⌊for meat⌋.

crawl (8)

Gen 1:26 the animals that c on the earth."
1:28 the animals that c on the earth."
3:14 You will c on your belly.
7:8 creatures that c on the ground
Dtr 32:24 animals that c on the ground.
Job 30:14 They c through the ruins.
Hos 2:18 and the animals that c on the
Mic 7:17 like animals that c on the

crawling (7)

Gen 1:24 c animal, and wild animal."
6:7 animals, c animals, and birds.
7:23 domestic animals, c creatures,
8:19 Every animal, c creature,
Dtr 33:29 enemies will come c to you,
Psa 148:10 c animals and birds,
Eze 8:10 of every kind of c creature,

crawls (11)

Gen 1:25 every type of creature that c
1:30 and every animal that c on the
6:20 every type of creature that c
7:14 every type of creature that c on
7:21 Every creature that c on the
8:17 and every creature that c on the
9:2 Every creature that c on the
Lev 11:44 that swarms or c on the ground.
20:25 animal or bird or anything that c
Dtr 4:18 any creature that c on the
Eze 38:20 everything that c on the ground,

crazy (9)

Ecc 10:13 up saying c things that are
Jer 50:38 statues that will go c with fear.
Hos 9:7 and that spiritual people are c.
Jon 10:20 He's c! Why do you listen to
Act 12:15 The people told her, "You're c!"
26:24 shouted, "Paul, you're c!
26:24 education is driving you c!"
26:25 Paul replied, "I'm not c,
2Co 5:13 So if we were c, it was for

create (16)

Jdg 5:12 Get up and c a song!
Neh 4:8 Jerusalem to c confusion.
Psa 51:10 C a clean heart in me,
Pro 29:8 Mockers c an uproar in a city,
Isa 4:5 The LORD will c a cloud of
45:7 I make light and c darkness.
45:7 blessings and c disasters.
45:18 He did not c it to be empty but
57:19 I'll c praise on their lips:
65:17 I will c a new heaven and a
65:18 forever in what I'm going to c,
65:18 because I'm going to c
Jer 31:22 The LORD will c something
Mat 17:27 so that we don't c a scandal,
Rom 16:17 those people who c divisions
Eph 2:15 and c one new humanity

created (57)

Gen 1:1 God created h and earth.
1:21 So God c the large sea
1:27 So God c humans in his image.
1:27 In the image of God he c them.
1:27 He c them male and female.
2:4 and earth when they were c,
5:1 When God c humans,
5:2 He c them male and female.
5:2 them humans when he c them.
6:7 the earth these humans that I c.
Dtr 4:32 Start from the very day God c
2Sm 7:24 You c the people of Israel to be
Psa 8:6 him rule what your hands c.
74:17 You c summer and winter.
89:12 You c north and south.
89:47 Have you c Adam's
94:9 God c ears. Do you think he
102:18 a people yet to be c may praise
104:19 He c the moon, which marks
104:30 out your Spirit, and they are c.
119:73 Your hands c me and made me
139:13 You alone c my inner being.
148:5 they were c by his command.
Isa 40:26 Who c these things?
41:20 the Holy One of Israel has c it.
42:5 The LORD God c the heavens
43:1 The LORD c Jacob and formed
43:7 whom I c for my glory,
45:8 I, the LORD, have c them.
45:12 I made the earth and c humans
45:18 The LORD c the heavens.
48:7 They are c now, not in the
54:16 I've c blacksmiths to fan the
54:16 I've also c destroyers to bring
Eze 21:30 In the place where you were c,
28:13 made of gold when you were c.
28:15 from the time you were c,
Mal 2:10 Hasn't the same God c us?
Mat 21:16 you have c praise'?"
Rom 1:25 and serve what is c rather than
1Co 11:9 Man wasn't c for woman but
Eph 2:10 He has c us in Christ Jesus to
3:9 God, who c all things,
4:24 to become a new person c
Col 1:16 He c all things in heaven and
1:16 has been c through him
1Ti 4:3 God c food to be received with
4:4 Everything God c is good.
Heb 4:3 his work when he c the world.
9:11 that is not part of this c world.
9:26 times since the world was c.
11:3 Faith convinces us that God c
Jas 3:9 who were c in God's likeness.
Rev 4:11 because you c everything.
4:11 came into existence and was c
10:6 who c heaven and everything
17:8 of Life when the world was c,

creates (5)

Amo 4:13 the mountains and c the wind.
Rom 5:3 We know that suffering c
5:4 endurance c character,
5:4 and character c confidence.
15:30 and by the love that the Spirit c,

creation (18)

Gen 2:3 he stopped all his work of c.
Psa 8:3 the c of your fingers,
Mat 25:34 for you from the c of the world.
Mar 10:6 female in the beginning, at c.
13:19 beginning of God's c until now,
Rom 1:20 From the c of the world,
8:19 All c is eagerly waiting for God
8:20 C was subjected to frustration
8:22 We know that all c has been
8:23 However, not only c groans.
8:39 or by anything else in c.
2Co 5:17 a believer in Christ is a new c.
Gal 6:15 what matters is being a new c.
Eph 1:4 Before the c of the world,
Col 1:15 the firstborn of all c.
1:23 throughout all c under heaven.
Rev 3:14 the source of God's c,
13:8 before the c of the world.

creatively (8)

Exo 26:1 and c work an angel design
26:31 C work an angel design into
28:6 C work gold, violet, purple,
28:15 as c as you make
36:8 An angel design was c worked
36:35 An angel design was c worked
39:3 which they c worked into each
39:8 They made the breastplate as c

creator (17)

Job 35:10 asks, 'Where is God, my C,
36:3 and prove that my C is fair.
Psa 149:2 Let Israel find joy in their c.
Ecc 12:1 Remember your C when you
12:2 Remember your C before the
12:3 Remember your C when those
12:4 Remember your C when the
12:5 Remember your C when
12:6 Remember your C before the
Isa 27:11 and their C won't have pity on
40:28 the C of the ends of the earth,
43:15 One, the C of Israel, your King.
51:13 forgotten the LORD, your C?
Mat 19:4 "Haven't you read that the C
Rom 1:25 is created rather than the C,
Col 3:10 in knowledge to be like its C.
1Pe 4:19 themselves to a faithful c

creature (55)

Gen 1:21 every type of c that swims
1:24 produce every type of living c:
1:25 and every type of c that crawls
2:19 each c became its name.
6:19 Bring two of every living c into
6:20 and every type of c that crawls
7:4 of the earth every living c that
7:14 every type of c that crawls on
7:14 of bird (every c with wings).
7:21 Every c that crawls on the
7:22 (every living, breathing c) died.
7:23 Every living c on the face of
8:17 and every c that crawls on the
8:19 Every animal, crawling c,
8:21 again kill every living c as
9:2 Every c that crawls on the
Exo 20:4 or statues that represent any c
Lev 5:2 swarming c — and then ignore
11:12 Every c in the water without
11:41 "Any c that swarms on the
11:42 Don't eat any c with many legs
11:42 or any c that swarms on the
11:46 and every living c that swims
11:46 water and every c that swarms
17:14 is because the life of any c is
17:14 because the life of any c is in
22:5 an unclean swarming c or an
Dtr 4:17 any c with wings that flies,
4:18 any c that crawls on the
5:8 or statues that represent any c
11:6 and every living c with them.

Dtr 14:9 may eat of every **c** that lives
14:9 You may eat any **c** that has
14:20 kind of⌊ flying **c** that is clean.
14:21 Never eat any **c** that dies
Jos 10:40 He claimed every living **c** for
Job 12:9 What **c** doesn't know that the
12:10 The life of every living **c** and
Psa 50:10 Every **c** in the forest,
136:25 He gives food to every living **c**
Ecc 10:20 or some winged **c** may repeat
Eze 1:10 each **c** had the face of a
1:11 Each **c** had two wings with
1:23 Under the dome, each **c** had
1:23 Each **c** had two wings that
8:10 of every kind of crawling **c**,
Dan 4:12 It fed every living **c**.
4:17 every living **c** will know that
Heb 4:13 No **c** can hide from God.
Rev 4:7 The first living **c** was like a
5:13 I heard every **c** in heaven,
5:13 Every **c** in those places was
6:3 I heard the second living **c** say,
6:5 I heard the third living **c** say,
6:7 voice of the fourth living **c** say,

creatures (60)

Gen 1:20 water swarm with swimming **c**,
1:21 So God created the large sea **c**,
7:8 and **c** that crawl on the ground
7:23 domestic animals, crawling **c**,
Lev 11:9 "Here are the kinds of **c** that
11:10 consider all swarming **c** living
11:24 the **c** mentioned above,
11:29 "The following swarming **c**
11:31 Among all the swarming **c** that
11:32 body of one of these **c** falls
11:33 "If any of these **c** falls into a
Job 26:5 and so do the **c** living there.
Psa 74:14 and gave them to the **c**
103:22 Praise the LORD, all his **c** in
104:24 The earth is filled with your **c**.
104:25 big and wide with countless **c**,
145:15 The eyes of all **c** look to you,
145:21 and all living **c** will praise his
148:7 Praise him, large sea **c** and all
Isa 42:10 the seas and all the **c** that live
Eze 1:5 what looked like four living **c**.
1:9 The **c** went straight ahead,
1:12 Each of the **c** went straight
1:13 The living **c** looked like
1:13 and forth between the living **c**.
1:14 The living **c** ran back and forth
1:15 As I looked at the living **c**,
1:19 When the living **c** moved,
1:19 When the living **c** rose from the
1:20 spirit wanted to go, the **c** went.
1:20 the spirit of the living **c** was
1:21 So whenever the **c** moved,
1:21 Whenever the **c** stood still,
1:21 And whenever the **c** rose from
1:21 the spirit of the living **c** was
1:22 over the heads of the living **c**.
1:24 When the **c** moved,
1:24 When the **c** stood still,
3:13 living **c** touching one another
10:15 These were the living **c** that I
10:17 The spirit of the living **c** was in
10:20 These are the living **c** that I
Jas 1:18 make us his most important **c**.
3:7 birds, reptiles, and sea **c**.
2Pe 2:12 which are **c** of instinct that are
Jud 1:10 which are **c** of instinct,
Rev 4:6 were four living **c** covered
4:8 Each of the four living **c** had
4:9 the living **c** give glory,
5:6 the throne with the four living **c**
5:8 the four living **c** and the 24
5:11 many angels, the four living **c**,
5:14 The four living **c** said,
6:1 I heard one of the four living **c**
6:6 from among the four living **c**,
7:11 leaders and the four living **c**.
8:9 one-third of the **c** that were
14:3 of the throne, the four living **c**,
15:7 One of the four living **c** gave
19:4 and the 4 living **c** bowed

credit (5)

Lev 7:18 You will not receive **c** for it.
1Sm 18:8 "To David they **c** tens of
18:8 "but to me they **c** ⌊only⌋ a few
Pro 19:11 and it is to his **c** that he
1Pe 2:20 What **c** do you deserve if you

creditor (2)

2Ki 4:1 Now a **c** has come to take my
Psa 109:11 Let a **c** take everything he

creditors (3)

Isa 24:2 and borrowers, debtors and **c**.
50:1 To which of my **c** did I sell
Hab 2:7 Won't your **c** suddenly rise up

creekbed (1)

Job 21:33 The soil in the **c** is sweet to

cremated (2)

Isa 33:12 People will be **c**. They will be
Amo 2:1 Moabites have **c** Edom's king.

Crescens (1)

2Ti 4:10 **C** went to the province of

crescent-shaped (1)

Isa 3:18 headbands, **c** necklaces,

crest (1)

Est 6:8 that has a royal **c** on its head.

Cretans (1)

Tit 1:12 "**C** are always liars,

Crete (11)

Dtr 2:23 who came from **C**,
Jer 47:4 who is left from the island of **C**.
Amo 9:7 I bring the Philistines from **C**
Zep 2:5 for the nation from **C**.
Act 2:11 **C**, and Arabia. We hear these
27:7 south side of the island of **C**.
27:8 sailing along the shore of **C**.
27:12 is located on the island of **C**.)
27:13 sailed close to the shore of **C**.
27:21 my advice not to sail from **C**.
Tit 1:5 I left you in **C** to do what still

crevice (1)

Exo 33:22 I will put you in a **c** in the cliff

crevices (1)

Sos 2:14 hiding places of the rocky **c**,

crew (1)

Eze 27:34 your whole **c** sank with you.

crews (1)

Neh 4:10 "The work **c** are worn out,

cricket (1)

Lev 11:22 **c**, katydid, or grasshopper.

crickets (1)

Dtr 28:42 **C** will swarm all over your

cried (134)

Gen 33:4 and kissed him. They both **c**.
37:35 how Joseph's father **c** over him.
41:55 the people **c** to Pharaoh for
43:30 his private room and **c** there.
45:1 around him, so he **c** out,
45:2 He **c** so loudly that the
45:14 Benjamin and **c** with Benjamin,
45:15 He kissed all his brothers and **c**
46:29 his arms around him and **c**
50:1 **c** over him, and kissed him.
50:17 Joseph **c** when he got their
Exo 2:23 So they **c** out, and their cries
14:10 Terrified, the Israelites **c** out to
15:25 Moses **c** out to the LORD,
17:4 So Moses **c** out to the LORD,
Num 11:2 The people **c** out to Moses,
11:20 who is here among them and **c**
12:13 So Moses **c** to the LORD,
Num 14:1 their voices and **c** out loud all
20:16 When we **c** out to the LORD,
Dtr 1:45 you **c** to the LORD,
26:7 We **c** out to the LORD God of
Jos 24:7 When your ancestors **c** out to
Jdg 3:9 Then the people of Israel **c** out
3:15 Then the people of Israel **c** out
4:3 The people of Israel **c** out to
5:28 window and **c** as she peered
6:6 because of Midian and **c** out
6:7 When the people of Israel **c** out
10:10 Then the people of Israel **c** out
10:12 you **c** out to me for help.
11:38 and she **c** about never being
14:16 So Samson's wife **c** on his
14:17 But she **c** on his shoulder for
20:23 The Israelites went and **c** in
20:26 They sat there and **c** in the
21:2 They **c** very loudly,
1Sm 1:10 to the LORD while she **c**.
4:13 The whole city **c** out.
5:10 the people of Ekron **c** out,
7:9 Samuel **c** to the LORD on
11:4 the people **c** loudly.
12:8 they **c** out to the LORD,
12:10 Then they **c** out to the LORD
20:41 each other and **c** together,
20:41 but David **c** the loudest.
24:16 and Saul **c** loudly.
28:12 she **c** out loudly and asked,
30:4 Then David and his men **c**
2Sm 1:12 They mourned, **c**, and fasted
3:16 went with her and **c** over her all
3:32 The king **c** loudly at Abner's
3:32 and all the people **c**.
12:21 You fasted and **c** over the child
12:22 child was alive, I fasted and **c**.
13:36 sons arrived and **c** loudly.
13:36 The king and all his men also **c**
15:30 David **c** as he went up the
15:30 their heads and **c** as they went.
18:33 the room above the gate and **c**.
19:4 covered his face and **c** loudly,
1Ki 22:32 But when Jehoshaphat **c** out,
2Ki 2:12 Elisha saw this, he **c** out,
4:40 eating the stew, they **c** out,
6:5 He **c** out, "Oh no, master!
6:26 a woman **c** to him,
11:14 she **c**, "Treason, treason!"
13:14 **c** over him, and said, "Master!
20:3 right." And he **c** bitterly.
22:19 clothes ⌊in distress⌋ and **c**
2Ch 13:14 They **c** out to the LORD,
18:31 But when Jehoshaphat **c** out,
34:27 and **c** in front of me.
Neh 1:4 I sat down and **c**. I mourned for
9:4 for the Levites and **c** loudly
9:27 began to suffer, they **c** to you.
9:28 They **c** to you again,
Est 4:1 city and **c** loudly and bitterly.
Job 2:12 They **c** out loud and wept,
9:16 If I **c** out and he answered me,
31:38 "If my land has **c** out against
Psa 18:6 I **c** to my God for help.
18:41 They **c** out for help,
18:41 They **c** out to the LORD,
22:5 They **c** to you and were saved.
22:24 that oppressed person **c** out
30:2 I **c** out to you for help,
31:22 pleas for mercy when I **c** out
66:17 With my mouth I **c** out to him.
69:10 I **c** and fasted, but I was
77:1 Loudly, I **c** to God.
77:1 Loudly, I **c** to God so that he
107:6 In their distress they **c** out to
107:13 In their distress they **c** out to
107:19 In their distress they **c** out to
107:28 In their distress they **c** out to
119:147 and I **c** out for help.
120:1 I **c** out to the LORD,
137:1 we sat down and **c** as we
Isa 38:3 right." And he **c** bitterly.
38:13 I **c** out until morning as if a lion
Lam 2:18 of Jerusalem's people **c** out
Eze 9:8 I **c**, "Almighty LORD, will you
11:13 bowed down and **c** out,

Eze 27:28 "When your sailors **c** out,
27:30 They **c** loudly and bitterly over
27:31 They **c** over you with
Hos 12:4 Jacob **c** and pleaded with him.
Jnh 1:5 and they **c** to their gods for
1:14 So they **c** to the LORD for help:
2:2 my ⌊watery⌋ grave I **c** for help,
Mat 26:75 Then Peter went outside and **c**
27:46 About three o'clock Jesus **c** out
27:50 Then Jesus loudly **c** out once
Mar 9:24 The child's father **c** out at once,
15:34 At three o'clock Jesus **c** out in
15:37 Then Jesus **c** out in a loud
Luk 22:62 Then Peter went outside and **c**
23:27 The women in the crowd **c** and
23:46 Jesus **c** out in a loud voice,
23:48 they **c** and returned to the city.
Jon 11:35 Jesus **c**.
20:11 stood there and **c** as she
20:11 As she **c**, she bent over and
Act 20:37 Everyone **c** a lot as they put
Heb 12:17 Even though he begged and **c**
Rev 5:4 I **c** bitterly because no one was
6:10 They **c** out in a loud voice,
7:2 He **c** out in a loud voice to the
12:2 She **c** out from labor pains and
14:15 He **c** out in a loud voice to the
18:2 He **c** out in a powerful voice,
18:18 they repeatedly **c** out,
19:17 He **c** out in a loud voice to all

cries (31)

Exo 2:23 So they cried out, and their **c**
22:27 When he **c** out to me,
Job 39:25 of the captains and the battle **c**.
Psa 9:12 He has never forgotten their **c**.
72:12 rescue the needy person who **c**
88:2 Turn your ear to hear my **c**.
92:11 My ears hear ⌊the **c**⌋ of
144:14 May there be no **c** of distress in
145:19 He hears their **c** for help and
Isa 5:7 but heard only **c** of distress.
15:3 squares everyone wails and **c**.
15:5 My heart **c** out for Moab.
15:8 **C** for help echo throughout the
16:9 of Sibmah as Jazer **c** for them.
40:3 A voice **c** out in the desert:
56:12 ⌊Each one **c**,⌋ "Let me get
Jer 4:16 They are shouting battle **c**
14:12 I won't listen to their **c** for help.
30:5 "We hear **c** of fear,
30:5 **c** of panic, not cries of peace.
30:5 cries of panic, not **c** of peace.
48:32 I will cry for you as Jazer **c**.
51:54 **C** of agony are heard from
Lam 1:2 Jerusalem **c** bitterly at night
Amo 8:3 will become loud **c**," declares
Zep 1:16 rams' horns and battle **c** against
Zec 12:10 will cry bitterly for him as one **c**
Mat 3:3 "A voice **c** out in the desert:
Mar 1:3 "A voice **c** out in the desert:
Luk 3:4 "A voice **c** out in the desert:
Jas 5:4 Lord of Armies has heard the **c**

crime (38)

Gen 31:36 "What is my **c**?" Jacob
50:17 begging you to forgive the **c**
50:17 please forgive our **c**,
Dtr 19:15 to convict someone of a **c**,
19:16 accuse a person falsely of a **c**.
22:28 When the **c** is discovered,
24:16 be put to death for his own **c**.
25:2 lashes as the **c** deserves.
1Sm 20:1 What **c** am I guilty of?
20:8 If I have committed any **c**,
26:18 What **c** have I committed?
2Sm 3:8 now you charge me with a **c**
19:19 "Don't remember the **c** I
2Ki 14:6 be put to death for his own **c**."
1Ch 12:17 though I haven't committed a **c**,
2Ch 25:4 be put to death for his own **c**."
Neh 13:27 commit such a serious **c**
Job 9:19 who will charge me with a **c**?
Psa 64:6 for the perfect **c** and say,
69:27 them with one **c** after another.
Pro 29:16 people increase, **c** increases,
Ecc 8:11 When a sentence against a **c**
Jer 37:18 "What **c** have I committed
Dan 6:22 I haven't committed any **c**."
Hos 6:9 they have committed a **c**.
Amo 1:3 and now a fourth **c**,
1:6 and now a fourth **c**,
1:9 and now a fourth **c**,
1:11 and now a fourth **c**,
1:13 and now a fourth **c**,
2:1 and now a fourth **c**,
2:4 and now a fourth **c**,
2:6 and now a fourth **c**,
Mic 1:5 All this is because of Jacob's **c**
1:5 What is Jacob's **c**?
Hab 2:12 and founds a town by **c**.'
Luk 23:4 find this man guilty of any **c**."
Act 18:14 of misdemeanor or **c** involved,

crimes (35)

Dtr 24:16 never be put to death for the **c**
24:16 never be put to death for the **c**
2Ki 14:6 never be put to death for the **c**
14:6 never be put to death for the **c**
2Ch 25:4 never be put to death for the **c**
25:4 never be put to death for the **c**
Job 13:23 How many **c** and sins have I
Psa 5:10 them out for their many **c**
39:11 discipline people for their **c**.
58:2 No, you invent new **c** on earth,
79:8 Do not hold the **c** of our
89:32 and their **c** with beatings.
107:17 and because of their **c**.
Ecc 8:11 are encouraged to commit **c**.
8:12 sinner may commit a hundred **c**
Jer 14:10 He will remember their **c** and
18:23 Don't forgive their **c**.
25:12 and that nation for their **c**,
41:11 heard about all the **c** Ishmael,
50:20 "people will look for Israel's **c**,
51:6 die because of Babylon's **c**.
Lam 4:13 Jerusalem's prophets and the **c**
Amo 1:3 has committed three **c**,
1:6 Gaza has committed three **c**,
1:9 Tyre has committed three **c**,
1:11 Edom has committed three **c**,
1:13 Ammon has committed three **c**,
2:1 Moab has committed three **c**,
2:4 Judah has committed three **c**,
2:6 Israel has committed three **c**,
5:12 I know that your **c** are
Mic 3:8 of⌋ Jacob about their **c**
Luk 23:14 found this man guilty of the **c**
Act 25:18 him of the **c** I was expecting.
Rev 18:5 God has remembered her **c**.

criminal (9)

Job 31:11 and that would be a **c** offense.
31:28 would be a **c** offense,
Mat 26:55 to arrest me as if I were a **c**?
Mar 14:48 to arrest me as if I were a **c**?
Luk 22:52 and clubs as if I were a **c**?
23:40 But the other **c** scolded him:
Jon 18:30 Pilate, "If he weren't a **c**,
2Ti 2:9 been put into prison like a **c**.
1Pe 4:15 thief, **c**, or troublemaker.

criminals (9)

1Ki 1:21 be treated like **c** when you lie
Psa 64:2 me from the secret plots of **c**,
Mat 27:38 At that time they crucified two **c**
27:44 Even the **c** crucified with him
Mar 15:27 They crucified two **c** with him,
Luk 22:37 'He was counted with **c**,' must
23:32 Two others, who were **c**,
23:33 The **c** were also crucified,
23:39 One of the **c** hanging there

cringe (4)

2Sm 22:45 Foreigners will **c** in front of me.
Psa 18:44 Foreigners will **c** in front of me.
66:3 great that your enemies will **c**
81:15 who hate the LORD would **c**

crippled (4)

Gen 49:6 At their whim they **c** cattle.
Lev 21:19 or a **c** hand or foot,
2Sm 4:4 had a son who was **c**.
Act 4:9 the good we did for a **c** man.

crisis (3)

Pro 24:10 If you faint in a **c**, you are
25:19 person in a ⌊time of⌋ **c**.
1Co 7:26 Because of the present **c** I

Crispus (2)

Act 18:8 The synagogue leader **C** and
1Co 1:14 any of you except **C** and Gaius

criticism (5)

Gen 20:16 This is to silence any **c**
Job 20:3 I have heard **c** that makes me
Pro 13:18 constructive **c** will be honored.
25:12 ⌊so⌋ is constructive **c** to the
27:5 Open **c** is better than

criticize (8)

Num 12:1 Miriam and Aaron began to **c**
12:8 afraid to **c** my servant Moses?"
Eze 3:26 so that you can't talk or **c** them,
Jon 6:41 The Jews began to **c** Jesus for
Rom 14:3 the vegetarians should not **c**
14:4 Who are you to **c** someone
14:10 Why do you **c** or despise other
Gal 5:15 But if you **c** and attack each

criticized (3)

Gen 37:10 his father **c** him by asking,
Num 21:5 and **c** God and Moses.
21:7 "We sinned when we **c** the

criticizes (2)

Pro 27:11 can answer anyone who **c** me.
28:23 Whoever **c** people will be more

criticizing (4)

Psa 50:8 I am not **c** you for your
Jon 6:43 Jesus responded, "Stop **c** me!
6:61 disciples were **c** his message.
Rom 14:13 So let's stop **c** each other.

crocodile (2)

Eze 29:3 You are like a monster **c** lying
32:2 you are like a **c** in the water.

crooked (10)

1Sm 20:30 "Son of a **c** and rebellious
Psa 125:5 But when people become **c**,
Pro 2:15 Their paths are **c**. Their ways
8:8 is nothing twisted or **c** in it.
21:8 The way of a guilty person is **c**,
Isa 59:8 They've made their paths **c**.
Jer 3:21 They have become **c** and have
Lam 3:9 stones and made my paths **c**.
Luk 3:5 The **c** ways will be made
Php 2:15 people who are **c** and corrupt.

crop (9)

Dtr 14:28 bring a tenth of that year's **c**,
22:9 This includes the **c** you
2Ki 2:21 No more deaths or **c** failures
2Ch 31:5 and every **c** from the fields.
Isa 33:4 as grasshoppers harvest a **c**.
Amo 7:1 second **c** was being harvested.
Jon 4:36 The person who harvests the **c**
4:38 I have sent you to harvest a **c**
1Co 9:10 to receive a share of the **c**.

crops (74)

Gen 4:3 Later Cain brought some **c** from
26:12 Isaac planted ⌊**c**⌋ in that land.
47:13 nor Canaan were producing **c**
47:23 Plant **c** in the land.
Exo 23:10 "For six years you may plant **c**
23:16 harvest your **c** from the fields.
Lev 19:19 Never plant two kinds of **c** in
25:3 for six years you may plant **c**
25:4 Don't plant **c** in your fields or
25:15 account the number of **c** ⌊until
25:16 you only the number of **c**.
25:20 do not plant or bring in our **c**?'
26:4 The land will produce its **c**,
26:16 You will plant your **c** and get

Lev 26:20 your land will produce no **c**
Num 20:5 This is no place to plant **c**.
24:7 and their **c** will have plenty of
Dtr 11:17 the ground won't grow any **c**,
14:22 the **c** harvested from whatever
26:12 that year's **c** ⌊in your houses⌋.
28:4 Your land will have **c**.
28:11 Your soil will produce many **c**
28:18 Your land will have few **c**.
28:22 scorching winds, and ruined **c**.
28:38 You will plant many **c** in your
28:38 locusts will destroy your **c**.
28:42 trees and the **c** in your fields.
28:51 and the **c** from your fields
30:9 Your soil will produce many **c**.
32:22 consume the earth and its **c**
33:14 LORD bless their land with **c**,
33:16 and the most plentiful **c** of the
Jos 5:12 began to eat the **c** that grew
Jdg 6:3 Whenever Israel planted **c**,
6:3 came and damaged the **c**.
6:4 the land and destroy the **c** all
1Sm 8:12 his ground and harvest his **c**,
2Sm 9:10 harvest ⌊the **c**⌋ so that your
1Ki 8:37 or grasshoppers may destroy **c**.
2Ki 2:19 and the land cannot grow **c**."
19:30 again take root and produce **c**.
2Ch 6:28 or grasshoppers may destroy **c**.
31:12 offerings of one-tenth of the **c**,
Job 31:8 and let my **c** be uprooted.
Psa 78:46 He gave their **c** to
85:12 and our land will produce **c**.
105:35 devoured the **c** in the fields.
107:37 and vineyards that produce **c**.
144:13 be filled with all kinds of **c**.
Isa 37:31 again take root and produce **c**.
61:11 ground that brings forth its **c**
Jer 7:20 and on trees and **c**.
Eze 25:4 They will eat your **c** and drink
34:27 the land will yield **c**,
34:29 that is known for its good **c**.
36:30 grow on the trees and **c** grow
36:36 the ruined places and planted **c**
Hos 2:22 You will produce many **c**,
Joe 2:25 the young locusts ate your **c**.
Amo 4:9 I struck your ⌊**c**⌋ with blight
Zec 8:12 The land will yield its **c**.
Mal 3:11 insects from eating ⌊your **c**⌋.
Mat 9:38 send workers to harvest his **c**."
13:23 This type produces **c**.
Mar 4:20 and produce **c** — thirty,
Luk 10:2 send workers to harvest his **c**.
12:16 had land that produced good **c**.
12:17 enough room to store my **c**.'
Act 14:17 you rain from heaven and **c**
2Ti 2:6 have the first share of the **c**.
Heb 6:7 it produces useful **c** for farmers.
Jas 5:4 cries of those who gather the **c**.
5:7 for their precious **c** to grow.
5:18 and the ground produced **c**.

cross (88)

Num 32:5 make us **c** the Jordan River."
32:21 Have them **c** the Jordan,
32:29 in the LORD's presence and **c**
35:10 "Tell the Israelites: When you **c**
Dtr 2:13 "Now **c** the Zered River."
2:24 **C** the Arnon Valley.
2:29 We'll keep going until we **c** the
3:18 when they **c** ⌊the Jordan River⌋
3:27 will never **c** the Jordan River.
4:14 after you **c** ⌊the Jordan River⌋
4:21 took an oath that I wouldn't **c**
4:22 to die in this land and not **c**
9:1 Listen, Israel, you're about to **c**
11:31 You're about to **c** the Jordan
12:10 But you will **c** the Jordan River
27:2 "The day you **c** the Jordan
27:4 After you **c** the Jordan River,
27:12 After you **c** the Jordan River,
30:13 "Who will **c** the sea to get it for
30:18 of when you **c** the Jordan River.
31:2 that I cannot **c** the Jordan River.
31:3 your God is the one who will **c**
31:3 Joshua will also **c** the river
31:13 when you **c** the Jordan River."
32:47 when you **c** the Jordan River."
Jos 1:2 and all these people must **c**
1:11 In three days you will **c** the
2:7 leading to a shallow place to **c**
3:14 So they broke camp to **c** the
5:1 so that the Israelites could **c**.
Jdg 3:28 and refused to let anyone **c**.
11:18 They did not **c** the Arnon River
12:5 "Let me **c**," the men of Gilead
1Sm 14:4 searched for a way to **c** over
14:8 we'll **c** over to the Philistines
30:10 who were too exhausted to **c**
2Sm 17:16 make sure you **c** ⌊the river⌋,
17:21 "**C** the river quickly because
17:22 all the troops with him left to **c**
19:18 going to **c** the Jordan River.
19:33 "**C** the river with me.
19:36 I'll just **c** the Jordan River with
1Ki 2:37 But the day you leave and **c**
Job 36:12 they will **c** the River ⌊of Death⌋
Psa 104:9 Water cannot **c** the boundary
Isa 47:2 your legs, and **c** the river.
51:23 and like a street for them to **c**.
Jer 5:22 barrier that it cannot **c**.
5:22 they roar, they can't **c** it.
Eze 47:5 a river which I couldn't **c**.
47:5 deep to **c** except by swimming.
Mat 8:18 he ordered ⌊his disciples⌋ to **c**
10:38 Whoever doesn't take up his **c**
14:22 disciples get into a boat and **c**
23:15 You **c** land and sea to recruit a
27:32 forced him to carry Jesus' **c**.
27:40 come down from the **c**."
27:42 come down from the **c** now,
Mar 4:35 "Let's **c** to the other side."
6:45 disciples get into a boat and **c**
15:21 forced him to carry Jesus' **c**.
15:30 Come down from the **c**,
15:32 come down from the **c** now so
15:46 took the body down from the **c**
Luk 8:22 He said to them, "Let's **c** to the
16:26 People couldn't **c** it in either
23:26 They laid the **c** on him and
23:53 After he took it down from the **c**,
Jon 6:17 got into a boat and started to **c**
19:17 He carried his own **c** and went
19:19 a notice and put it on the **c**.
19:25 were standing beside Jesus' **c**.
Act 5:30 Jesus by hanging him on a **c**.
10:39 hung him on a **c** and killed him,
13:29 they took him down from the **c**
1Co 1:17 That would have made the **c** of
1:18 The message about the **c** is
Gal 5:11 In that case the **c** wouldn't be
6:12 because of the **c** of Christ.
6:14 about anything except the **c**
6:14 By his **c** my relationship to the
Eph 2:16 to God in one body by his **c**,
Php 2:8 the point of death, death on a **c**.
3:18 the enemies of the **c** of Christ.
Col 1:20 blood sacrificed on the **c**.
2:14 away by nailing them to the **c**.
Heb 12:2 so he endured death on the **c**
1Pe 2:24 his body on the **c** so that freed

crossbar (2)

Exo 26:28 The middle **c** will run from one
36:33 They made the middle **c** so

crossbars (11)

Exo 26:26 "Make **c** out of acacia wood:
26:29 make gold rings to hold the **c**,
26:29 and cover the **c** with gold.
35:11 frames, **c**, posts, and sockets,
36:31 They also made **c** out of
36:34 made gold rings to hold the **c**.
36:34 also covered the **c** with gold.
39:33 frames, **c**, posts, sockets,
40:18 up the frames, inserted the **c**,
Num 3:36 tent, the **c**, posts, sockets,
4:31 tent, the **c**, posts, and sockets,

crossbreed (1)

Lev 19:19 Never **c** different kinds of

crossed (46)

Gen 31:21 He **c** the Euphrates River and
32:10 had a shepherd's staff when I **c**
32:22 his eleven children and **c** at
48:14 But Israel **c** his hands and
Dtr 2:13 So we **c** the Zered River.
2:14 left Kadesh Barnea until we **c**
11:8 you've **c** ⌊the Jordan River⌋.
Jos 2:23 **c** the Jordan River,
3:16 Then the people **c** from the
3:17 the whole nation of Israel had **c**
4:7 When the ark **c** the Jordan,
4:11 As soon as everyone had **c**,
4:11 priests with the LORD's ark **c**
4:13 About 40,000 armed men **c** the
4:22 should be told that Israel **c**
4:23 ahead of you until you had **c**,
4:23 to the Red Sea until we had **c**.
24:11 "Then you **c** the Jordan River
Jdg 6:33 **c** ⌊the Jordan River⌋,
8:4 were exhausted when they **c** it,
10:9 Ammon also **c** the Jordan River
12:1 They **c** ⌊the Jordan River⌋ to
1Sm 13:7 Some Hebrews **c** the Jordan
2Sm 2:29 They **c** the Jordan River and
10:17 **c** the Jordan River,
17:20 "They've **c** the stream."
17:22 had **c** the Jordan River.
17:24 with him **c** the Jordan River.
19:18 They **c** the river to bring over
19:39 All the troops **c** the Jordan
19:39 and then the king **c**.
19:40 The king **c** the river to Gilgal,
24:5 They **c** the Jordan River and
2Ki 2:8 and the two men **c** ⌊the river⌋
2:14 and Elisha **c** ⌊the river⌋.
1Ch 12:15 these men **c** the Jordan River
19:17 Israel's army, **c** the Jordan,
Psa 66:6 They **c** the river on foot.
Isa 23:2 messengers have **c** the sea.
Dan 8:5 It **c** the whole earth without
Mat 9:1 got into a boat, **c** the sea,
14:34 They **c** the sea and landed at
Mar 5:21 Jesus again **c** to the other side
6:53 They **c** the sea, came to shore
8:13 He got into a boat again and **c**
Jon 6:1 Jesus later **c** to the other side

crosses (5)

Mat 16:24 pick up their **c**, and follow me.
Mar 8:34 pick up their **c**, and follow me.
Luk 9:23 pick up their **c** every day,
14:27 those who do not carry their **c**
Jon 19:31 the bodies to stay on the **c**.

cross-examine (4)

Pro 18:17 his neighbor comes to **c** him.
Act 24:8 When you **c** him, you'll be able
1Co 4:3 any human court should **c** me.
9:3 myself to those who **c** me.

cross-examined (2)

Act 25:26 something to write after he is **c**.
28:18 The Roman authorities **c** me

cross-examines (2)

Job 13:9 Will it go well when he **c** you?
1Co 4:4 It is the Lord who **c** me.

cross-examining (1)

Act 4:9 today you are **c** us about the

crossing (7)

Num 33:51 'You will be **c** the Jordan River
Jos 3:1 where they camped before **c**.
4:1 The whole nation finished **c**
2Sm 15:23 The king was **c** the Kidron
2Ki 2:9 While they were **c**,
Job 33:18 the pit and their lives from **c**
Pro 7:8 He was **c** a street near her

crossings (7)

Jdg 3:28 him and captured the shallow **c**
12:5 Gilead captured the shallow **c**
12:6 and kill him at the shallow **c**

2Sm 15:28 I'll wait at the river c in the
17:16 'Don't rest tonight in the river c
Isa 16:2 at the shallow c of the Arnon
Jer 51:32 The river c have been taken.

crossroads (2)

Jer 6:16 Stand at the c and look.
Oba 1:14 Don't stand at the c to kill their

crouch (2)

Job 38:40 as they c in their dens and lie
Isa 10:4 Nothing's left but to c among

crouched (2)

2Ki 4:34 He c over the boy's body,
4:35 on the bed and c over him.

crouching (1)

Psa 17:12 a young lion c in hiding places.

crow (3)

Job 38:41 "Who provides food for the c
Luk 22:34 rooster won't c tonight until you
Jon 13:38 No rooster will c until you say

crowd (161)

Exo 23:2 Never follow a c in doing
1Sm 14:16 in Benjamin could see the c ⌊in
2Sm 6:19 to the whole c of Israelites,
1Ki 8:65 A large c had come from ⌊the
2Ch 7:8 A very large c had come from
13:8 You are a large c, and you
14:11 we go against this large c.
20:2 "A large c is coming against
20:2 The c is already in Hazazon
20:12 this large c that is attacking
20:15 or terrified by this large c.
20:24 the desert and looked for the c.
32:4 A large c gathered as they
32:7 of Assyria or the c with him.
Ezr 10:1 a large c of Israelite men,
10:13 But the c is too large,
Job 31:34 noisy c and because the
Psa 35:18 you in a c ⌊of worshipers⌋.
42:4 how I used to walk with the c
Isa 31:4 growls over its prey when a c
Jer 26:17 got up and said to the entire c,
31:8 A large c will return here.
Eze 7:11 None of that c, none of their
7:12 will be against the whole c.
7:13 The visions against that c will
7:14 fury is against their whole c.
23:42 the noise from a carefree c.
38:15 You will be a large c and a
Dan 10:6 sounded like the roar of a c.
Joe 2:8 They do not c one another.
Mat 8:18 Jesus saw a c around him,
9:8 When the c saw this,
9:23 flute players and a noisy c.
9:25 When the c had been put
13:2 The c that gathered around him
13:2 boat while the entire c stood
13:11 it has not been given to the c.
14:14 of the boat, he saw a large c.
15:10 Then he called the c and said
15:30 A large c came to him,
15:31 The c was amazed to see
15:33 enough bread to feed such a c
15:35 He ordered the c to sit down on
17:14 When they came to a c,
20:29 a large c followed Jesus.
20:31 The c told them to be quiet.
21:9 The c that went ahead of him
21:11 The c answered, "This is the
21:26 afraid of what the c might do.
26:47 A large c carrying swords and
26:55 At that time Jesus said to the c,
27:15 prisoner whom the c wanted.
27:20 and leaders persuaded the c
27:24 his hands in front of the c.
Mar 2:4 him to Jesus because of the c,
3:7 A large c from Galilee,
3:9 so that the c would not crush
3:20 Another c gathered so that
3:32 The c sitting around Jesus told
4:1 A very large c gathered around
Mar 4:1 the entire c lined the shore.
4:36 Leaving the c, they took Jesus
5:21 A large c gathered around him
5:24 A huge c followed Jesus and
5:25 In the c was a woman who had
5:27 she came from behind in the c
5:30 around in the c and asked,
5:31 when you see the c pressing
5:38 Jesus saw a noisy c there.
6:34 he saw a large c and felt sorry
7:14 Then he called the c again and
7:33 took him away from the c
8:1 there was once again a large c
8:6 He ordered the c to sit down on
8:34 Then Jesus called the c to
9:14 saw a large c around them.
9:17 A man in the c answered,
9:25 When Jesus saw that a c was
12:12 him but were afraid of the c.
12:37 The large c enjoyed listening
14:43 A c carrying swords and clubs
15:8 The c asked Pilate to do for
15:11 stirred up the c so that Pilate
Luk 5:3 and taught the c from the boat.
5:19 the house because of the c.
5:29 A huge c of tax collectors and
6:17 A large c of his disciples and
6:19 The entire c was trying to
7:9 He turned to the c following
7:11 and a large c went with him.
7:12 A large c from the city was
8:4 When a large c had gathered
8:19 with him because of the c.
8:40 a c welcomed him.
8:43 for twelve years was in the c.
9:12 They said to him, "Send the c
9:16 to the disciples to give to the c.
9:37 a large c met Jesus.
9:38 A man in the c shouted,
11:27 a woman in the c shouted,
12:13 Someone in the c said to him,
13:14 The leader told the c,
13:17 But the entire c was happy
18:36 When he heard the c going by,
18:39 The people at the front of the c
19:3 see Jesus because of the c.
19:37 Then the whole c of disciples
19:39 Some of the Pharisees in the c
22:6 to them when there was no c.
22:47 to the disciples, a c arrived.
23:4 to the chief priests and the c,
23:5 The priests and the c became
23:18 The whole c then shouted,
23:23 But the c pressured Pilate.
23:27 A large c followed Jesus.
23:27 The women in the c cried and
Jon 5:13 had withdrawn from the c.)
6:2 A large c followed him
6:5 As Jesus saw a large c
6:10 were about 5,000 men in the c.)
7:11 looking for Jesus in the c at
7:20 The c answered, Who wants to
7:31 However, many people in the c
7:32 The Pharisees heard the c
7:40 After some of the c heard
7:49 This c is cursed because it
11:42 I've said this so that the c
12:9 A large c of Jews found out
12:12 On the next day the large c
12:18 Because the c heard that
12:29 The c standing there heard the
12:29 Others in the c said that an
12:34 The c responded to him,
12:35 Jesus answered the c,
18:5 was standing with the c.
18:6 the c backed away and fell to
Act 2:7 the people in the c said,
11:24 A large c believed in the Lord.
14:1 in such a way that a large c
14:13 The priest and the c wanted to
14:14 They rushed into the c
14:18 they hardly kept the c from
15:12 The whole c was silent.
16:22 The c joined in the attack
17:5 order to bring them out to the c.
17:8 The c and the officials were
Act 19:9 to say in front of the c about
19:26 He has won over a large c that
19:30 Paul wanted to go into the c,
19:32 The c was confused.
19:35 city clerk finally quieted the c.
21:27 the whole c and grabbed Paul.
21:32 and officers and charged the c.
21:32 When the c saw the officer and
21:34 Some of the c shouted one
21:35 the c was so violent that the
24:12 courtyard or stirring up a c
24:18 No c or noisy mob was present.
Rev 7:9 a large c from every nation,
19:1 noise from a large c in heaven,
19:6 like the noise from a large c,

crowded (6)

Isa 49:19 you will be too c for ⌊your⌋
49:20 "This place is too c for me.
Jer 26:9 Then all the people c around
Lam 1:1 the city was c with people.
Luk 5:1 The people c around him as
12:1 They were so c that they

crowding (2)

Luk 8:42 the people were c around him.
8:45 the people are c you and

crowds (38)

Psa 42:4 of joy and thanksgiving while c
55:14 God's house with the festival c.
68:27 of Judah with their noisy c,
Jer 5:7 They traveled in c to the
Mat 4:25 Large c followed him.
5:1 When Jesus saw the c,
7:28 the c were amazed at his
8:1 large c followed him.
9:33 The c were amazed and said,
9:36 When he saw the c,
11:7 spoke to the c about John.
12:23 The c were all amazed and
12:46 Jesus was still talking to the c,
13:34 to tell the c all these things.
14:13 The c heard about this and
14:15 Send the c to the villages to
19:2 Large c followed him,
21:46 him but were afraid of the c,
22:33 He amazed the c who heard
23:1 Then Jesus said to the c and
Mar 2:13 Large c came to him,
10:1 C gathered around him again,
11:18 all the c with his teaching.
Luk 3:7 C of people were coming to be
3:10 The c asked him,
4:42 The c searched for him.
5:15 Large c gathered to hear him
7:24 spoke to the c about John.
9:11 But the c found out about this
12:54 Jesus said to the c,
14:25 Large c were traveling with
23:48 C had gathered to see the sight.
Jon 7:12 The c argued about Jesus.
Act 5:16 C from the cities around
8:6 The c paid close attention to
13:45 When the Jews saw the c,
14:11 The c who saw what Paul had
Rev 17:15 c, nations, and languages.

crowed (5)

Mat 26:74 Just then a rooster c.
Mar 14:68 the entrance. Then a rooster c.
14:72 Just then a rooster c a second
Luk 22:60 was still speaking, a rooster c.
Jon 18:27 and just then a rooster c.

crown (53)

Gen 49:26 on the c of the prince among
Exo 29:6 and fasten the holy c to it.
39:30 medallion (the holy c) out
Lev 8:9 the gold medallion (the holy c)
Dtr 33:16 May they c the people who are
2Sm 1:10 And I took the c that was on
12:30 He took the gold c from the
12:30 (The c weighed 75 pounds and
2Ki 11:12 gave him the c and the
1Ch 20:2 He took the gold c from the

1Ch 20:2 (The c was found to weigh 75
2Ch 23:11 gave him the c and the
Est 1:11 wearing her royal c.
2:17 So he put the royal c on her
8:15 and white robe, a large gold c,
Job 19:9 He has taken the c off my head.
31:36 place it on my head like a c.
Psa 21:3 of good things and set a c
65:11 You c the year with your
89:39 have thrown his c into the dirt.
132:18 but the c on my anointed one
Pro 4:9 It will hand you a beautiful c."
12:4 strength of character is the c
14:24 The c of wise people is their
16:31 Silver hair is a beautiful c
17:6 are the c of grandparents,
27:24 Nor does a c last from one
Sos 3:11 Look at his c, the crown his
3:11 Look at his crown, the c his
Isa 28:5 Armies will be like a glorious c
35:10 will be on their heads ⌊as a c⌋.
51:11 will be on their heads ⌊as a c⌋.
62:3 Then you will be a beautiful c
62:3 a royal c in the hand of your
Lam 5:16 The c has fallen from our head.
Eze 16:12 and a beautiful c on your head.
21:26 and get rid of your c.
Zec 6:11 the silver and gold, make a c,
6:14 The c will be a reminder to
9:16 in his land like jewels in a c.
Mat 27:29 twisted some thorns into a c,
Mar 15:17 twisted some thorns into a c,
Jon 19:2 some thorny branches into a c,
19:5 He was wearing the c of thorns
1Co 9:25 They do it to win a temporary c,
Php 4:1 You are my joy and my c.
Jas 1:12 they will receive the c of life
1Pe 5:4 you will receive the c of glory
Rev 2:10 and I will give you the c of life.
3:11 so that no one takes your c.
6:2 He was given a c and rode off
12:1 the moon under her feet and a c
14:14 He had a gold c on his head

crowned (4)

Psa 8:5 You have c him with glory and
Pro 14:18 people are c with knowledge.
Heb 2:7 You c him with glory and honor.
2:9 but we see him c with glory

crowns (11)

Psa 103:4 the one who c you with mercy
149:4 He c those who are oppressed
Isa 61:3 to give them c instead of
Jer 13:18 because your c have fallen off
Eze 23:42 and beautiful c on their heads.
Rev 4:4 They had gold c on their heads.
4:10 They place their c in front of
9:7 They seemed to have c that
12:3 and seven c on its heads.
13:1 and ten c on its horns.
19:12 On his head are many c.

crows (9)

Lev 11:15 all types of c,
Dtr 14:14 all types of c,
Isa 34:11 Owls and c will live there.
Mat 26:34 Before a rooster c tonight,
26:75 "Before a rooster c,
Mar 14:30 before a rooster c twice,
14:72 "Before a rooster c twice,
Luk 12:24 Consider the c. They don't plant
22:61 "Before a rooster c today,

crucible (2)

Pro 17:3 The c is for refining silver and
27:21 The c is for refining silver and

crucified (38)

Mat 26:2 will be handed over to be c."
27:22 "He should be c!" they all said.
27:23 shout loudly, "He should be c!"
27:26 and handed over to be c.
27:35 After they had c him,
27:38 At that time they c two
27:44 Even the criminals c with him
28:5 looking for Jesus, who was c.
Mar 15:15 and handed over to be c.
15:24 Next they c him. Then they
15:25 the morning when they c him.
15:27 They c two criminals with him,
15:32 Even those who were c with
16:6 from Nazareth, who was c.
Luk 23:23 shouted that Jesus had to be c,
23:33 called The Skull, they c him.
23:33 The criminals were also c,
24:7 over to sinful people, be c,
24:20 him condemned to death and c.
Jon 19:16 Jesus over to them to be c.
19:18 The soldiers c Jesus and two
19:20 where Jesus was c was near
19:23 When the soldiers had c Jesus,
19:32 who had been c with Jesus.
19:41 the place where Jesus was c.
Act 2:23 Teachings, you c Jesus,
2:36 God made Jesus, whom you c,
4:10 You c Jesus Christ,
Rom 6:6 person we used to be was c
1Co 1:13 Was Paul c for you?
1:23 message is that Christ was c.
2:2 Jesus Christ, who was c.
2:8 they had, they wouldn't have c
2Co 13:4 He was weak when he was c,
Gal 2:19 I have been c with Christ.
5:24 have c their corrupt nature
6:14 relationship to me have been c.
Rev 11:8 city where their Lord was c.

crucifixion (1)

Gal 3:1 Wasn't Christ Jesus' c clearly

crucify (14)

Mat 20:19 of him, whip him, and c him.
23:34 You will kill and c some of
27:31 Then they led him away to c
Mar 15:13 "C him!" they shouted back.
15:14 shouted even louder, "C him!"
15:20 Then they led him out to c him.
Luk 23:21 They began yelling, "C him!
23:21 "Crucify him! C him!"
Jon 19:6 Jesus, they shouted, "C him!
19:6 C him!" Pilate told them, "You
19:6 "You take him and c him.
19:10 to free you or to c you?"
19:15 C him!" Pilate asked them,
19:15 "Should I c your king?"

crucifying (1)

Heb 6:6 They are c the Son of God

crude (2)

Psa 35:16 With c and abusive mockers,
Eze 16:58 must suffer because of all the c

cruel (17)

Gen 49:7 be cursed because it's so c.
2Sm 3:39 sons, are too c for me.
Psa 71:4 of one who is c and unjust.
Pro 5:9 your years to some c person,
11:17 but a c person hurts himself.
17:11 Therefore, a c messenger will
27:4 Anger is c, and fury is
Ecc 9:12 Like fish that are caught in a c
Isa 13:9 It will be a c day with fury and
Jer 6:23 They are c and have no
30:14 you as a c person would.
50:42 They will be c and have no
Lam 4:3 are as c as wild ostriches.
Eze 21:31 I will hand you over to c
Dan 11:20 He will have a c official go out
Joe 3:19 the nations were c to Judah.
Rom 1:30 think up new ways to be c.

cruelly (4)

Exo 5:23 he has treated your people c,
Dtr 26:6 So the Egyptians treated us c,
Jdg 4:3 iron and had c oppressed Israel
Job 30:21 You have begun to treat me c.

cruelty (3)

Psa 17:4 I have avoided c because of
119:51 have mocked me with c,
Pro 12:10 people is ⌊nothing but⌋ c.

crumble (1)

Eze 38:20 be torn down, the cliffs will c,

crumbling (2)

Jos 9:5 their bread was dried out and c.
9:12 Look at it now! It's dry and c.

crush (49)

Gen 3:15 He will c your head,
Exo 23:24 gods and c their sacred stones.
34:13 c their sacred stones,
Lev 26:19 I will c your arrogance.
Num 11:8 then grind it in a handmill or c
24:8 are his enemies, c their bones,
24:17 He will c the heads of the
Dtr 9:3 will use you to c their power.
12:3 c their sacred stones,
Jdg 4:23 used the people of Israel to c
1Ch 17:10 I will c all your enemies.
Est 9:24 when⌋ to c and destroy them.
Job 6:9 ⌊finally⌋ be willing to c me,
39:15 It forgets that a foot may c them
40:12 C wicked people wherever
Psa 68:21 Certainly, God will c the heads
72:4 people and c their oppressor.
74:8 themselves, "We will c them."
89:23 I will c his enemies in front of
94:5 They c your people,
110:5 He will c kings on the day of
110:6 earth he will c ⌊their⌋ heads.
Pro 27:22 If you c a stubborn fool in a
Isa 3:15 "How can you c my people and
14:25 I'll c Assyria on my land.
28:28 but his horses won't c it.
41:15 the mountains and c them
53:10 Yet, it was the LORD's will to c
Jer 5:3 You c them, but they refuse to
51:20 I will use you to c nations.
51:21 I will use you to c horses and
51:21 I will use you to c chariots and
51:22 I will use you to c men and
51:22 I will use you to c the old and
51:22 I will use you to c young men
51:23 I will use you to c shepherds
51:23 I will use you to c farmers and
51:23 to c governors and officials.
Lam 3:34 c any prisoner on earth
Dan 2:40 kingdom will smash and c all
7:23 and c the whole world.
Amo 2:13 I am going to c you as an
Mic 6:15 You will c olives, but you
Hab 3:13 You c the leader of the wicked
Zec 11:6 who will c the land.
Mat 21:44 it will c that person."
Mar 3:9 that the crowd would not c him.
Luk 20:18 it will c that person."
Rom 16:20 will quickly c Satan under your

crushed (50)

Lev 21:20 skin diseases, or c testicles.
22:24 c, torn out, or cut out testicles.
Dtr 9:21 I c it, grinding it thoroughly
23:1 A man whose testicles are c or
Jdg 3:30 The power of Moab was c by
5:26 She c his head. She shattered
8:28 The power of Midian was c by
10:8 They oppressed and c the
11:33 So the Ammonites were c by
1Sm 7:13 power of the Philistines was c,
2Sm 8:1 defeated and c the Philistines.
22:43 I c them and stomped on them
2Ki 18:4 c the sacred stones,
18:4 He even c the bronze snake
23:12 them down from there, c them,
23:14 Josiah c the sacred stones,
1Ch 18:1 defeated and c the Philistines.
2Ch 14:13 It was c in front of the LORD
15:6 One nation c another nation;
15:6 one city c another.
15:16 Asa cut the statue down, c it,
31:1 They c the sacred stones,
Job 4:19 Those houses can be c
5:4 They are c at the city gate,
20:19 because he c and abandoned

Job 34:25 them at night, and they're **c**.
Psa 10:10 ⌊His⌋ victims are **c**.
34:18 those whose spirits are **c**.
44:19 Yet, you **c** us in a place for
74:14 You **c** the heads of Leviathan
89:10 You **c** Rahab; it was like a
Pro 6:15 he will be **c** beyond recovery.
Isa 1:28 Rebels and sinners will be **c** at
19:10 Egypt's weavers will be **c**.
38:13 as if a lion had **c** all my bones.
42:4 He will not be discouraged or **c**
53:5 He was **c** for our sins.
57:15 those who are **c** and humble.
57:15 the courage of those who are **c**.
59:5 When an egg is **c**,
Jer 8:21 I am **c** because my dear people
8:21 my dear people have been **c**.
Eze 32:28 "You Egyptians will be **c** with
36:3 into ruins and **c** you from every
Dan 6:24 them and **c** all their bones.
7:7 It devoured and **c** its victims
7:19 It devoured and **c** its victims,
Hos 5:11 oppressed — **c** by punishment,
Amo 1:3 The Arameans have **c** ⌊the
2Co 4:8 but we aren't **c** by our troubles.

crushes (2)

Dan 2:40 As iron **c** things, this fourth
Amo 2:13 overloaded wagon **c** a person.

crushing (1)

2Ki 23:15 They burned the worship site, **c**

crusted (1)

Job 7:5 My skin is **c** over with sores;

cry (207)

Gen 16:11 has heard your **c** of distress.
23:2 Sarah and to **c** about her death.
27:34 out a very loud and bitter **c**
42:24 stepped away from them to **c**.
43:30 looking for a place to **c**.
Exo 3:9 I have heard the **c** of the people
22:23 If you do and they **c** out to me,
22:23 be sure that I will hear their **c**.
Lev 10:6 All the other Israelites may **c**
Dtr 33:7 "Hear the **c** of Judah,
Jdg 2:4 they began to **c** loudly.
2:5 place Bochim [Those Who **C**].
10:14 **C** out for help to the gods you
Rut 1:9 they began to **c** loudly.
1:14 They began to **c** loudly again.
1Sm 1:7 Hannah would **c** and not eat.
4:14 Hearing the **c**, Eli asked,
5:12 So the **c** of the city went up to
8:18 you will **c** out because of the
9:16 and their **c** has come
17:20 battle line shouting their war **c**.
17:52 shouted a battle **c**,
30:4 have the strength to **c** anymore.
2Sm 1:24 of Israel, **c** over Saul,
3:34 people continued to **c** for him.
22:7 and my **c** for help reached his
1Ki 8:28 Listen to my **c** for help as I pray
22:36 At sundown a **c** went through
2Ki 8:11 the man of God began to **c**.
2Ch 6:19 Listen to my **c** for help as I pray
20:9 We will **c** out to you in our
Ezr 10:1 They also began to **c** bitterly.
Neh 8:9 Don't mourn or **c**."
Job 5:1 "**C** out! Is there anyone to
16:18 Don't ever let my **c** ⌊for justice⌋
19:7 Indeed, I **c**, 'Help! I'm being
24:12 Wounded people **c** for help,
27:9 Will God hear his **c** when
27:15 widows won't **c** ⌊for them⌋.
30:25 Didn't I **c** for the person whose
34:28 They forced the poor to **c** out to
34:28 and he hears the **c** of those
35:9 oppression makes them **c** out.
35:12 Then they **c** out, but he doesn't
38:41 crow when its young ones **c**
Psa 5:2 Pay attention to my **c** for help,
17:1 Pay attention to my **c**.
18:6 and my **c** for help reached his
22:2 My God, I **c** out by day,
Psa 27:7 Hear, O LORD, when I **c** aloud.
30:8 I will **c** out to you, O LORD.
34:15 His ears hear their **c** for help.
34:17 ⌊Righteous people⌋ **c** out.
39:12 Open your ear to my **c** for help.
40:1 He turned to me and heard my **c**
61:1 Listen to my **c** for help,
88:1 O LORD God, my savior, I **c**
88:13 I **c** out to you for help,
102:1 and let my **c** for help come to
106:44 when he heard their **c** for help.
119:169 Let my **c** for help come into
126:5 Those who **c** while they plant
141:1 O LORD, I **c** out to you,
141:1 ears to me when I **c** out to you.
142:1 Loudly, I **c** to the LORD.
142:6 Pay attention to my **c** for help
Pro 21:13 Whoever shuts his ear to the **c**
Ecc 3:4 a time to **c** and a time to laugh,
Isa 3:7 comes the relative will **c** out,
3:26 gates of Zion will **c** and grieve,
10:30 **C** aloud, you people in Gallim!
13:6 **C** loudly, for the day of the
14:31 **C** loudly in the gate!
14:31 **C** out in the city! Be frightened,
15:2 to the worship sites, to **c**.
15:4 and Elealeh also **c** out.
15:4 Moab's armed men **c** out.
15:5 They **c** loudly over the
16:9 I will **c** for the grapevines of
19:8 Fishermen will **c**. All who cast
19:20 When the people **c** to the
22:4 from me so that I can **c** bitterly.
23:1 **C** loudly, you ships of
23:6 **C** loudly, you inhabitants of the
23:14 **C** loudly, you ships of
26:17 They writhe and **c** out in their
30:19 You won't **c** anymore.
30:19 on you when you **c** for help.
33:7 Heroes **c** in the streets.
33:7 Messengers of peace **c** bitterly.
42:2 He will not **c** out or raise ⌊his
42:13 He shouts, gives the battle **c**,
42:14 woman in childbirth I will **c** out.
46:7 If they **c** to it for help,
57:13 When you **c** for help,
58:1 **C** aloud! Don't hold back! Raise
58:9 You will **c** for help,
65:14 But you will **c** because of your
Jer 4:8 and **c** because the LORD's
4:31 I hear the woman **c** with
6:26 your only child, and **c** bitterly.
7:16 Don't **c** or pray for them.
8:19 The **c** from my dear people
9:1 of tears so that I could **c** day
9:10 I will **c** and weep for the
9:17 the women who **c** at funerals.
9:18 come quickly and **c** for us.
9:20 Teach your daughters how to **c**.
11:11 Although they will **c** out to me,
11:12 who live in Jerusalem will **c**
11:14 Don't **c** or pray for them.
13:17 If you won't listen, I will **c**
13:17 I will **c** bitterly, and my eyes
14:2 Their **c** goes up from
18:22 Make them **c** out from their
20:8 I have to **c** out and shout,
20:16 May he hear a **c** of alarm in the
20:16 morning and a battle **c** at noon.
22:10 Don't **c** for the dead.
22:10 **C** bitterly for those who are
22:20 "Go to Lebanon and **c**!
22:20 **C** out from Abarim,
25:34 Mourn, you shepherds, and **c**.
30:15 Why do you **c** about your
31:9 They will **c** as they return.
46:12 your **c** fills the earth.
46:17 There they will **c**, 'Pharaoh,
47:2 People will **c** out and everyone
47:2 lives in the land will **c** loudly.
47:6 You **c** out, "Sword of the
48:3 People will **c** out from
48:4 Its little ones will **c** out.
48:5 the distressful **c** of destruction.
48:20 Shout loudly, and **c**.
48:31 why I will weep for Moab and **c**
Jer 48:32 I will **c** for you as Jazer cries.
48:32 I will **c** for you, grapevines of
48:34 "The **c** will be heard from
48:39 "They will **c**, 'Look how Moab
49:2 the battle **c** against Rabbah,
49:3 **C** loudly, Heshbon, because Ai
49:3 **C**, people of Rabbah, put on
50:4 and Judah will **c** as they go
50:15 Shout a war **c** against them on
50:46 Its **c** will be heard among the
51:8 **C** for it. Bring medicine for its
Lam 2:19 **C** out at night, every hour on
3:8 Even when I **c** and call for help,
3:56 Listen to my **c** ⌊for help⌋.
3:56 your ears when I **c** out for relief.
Eze 21:12 "'**C** and mourn, son of man,
21:22 the order to kill, raise a battle **c**,
24:16 But you must not mourn, **c**,
24:23 Don't grieve or **c**! You will waste
30:2 LORD says: **C** for that day!
32:18 **c** for the many people of Egypt.
Hos 7:14 even though they **c** in their
8:2 They **c** out to me,
10:5 The priests will **c** loudly
Joe 1:5 Wake up and **c**, you drunks!
1:5 **C** loudly, you wine drinkers!
1:8 **C** loudly like a young woman
1:11 **C** loudly, you grape growers!
1:13 **C** loudly, you servants of the
1:14 and **c** to the LORD for help.
1:19 O LORD, I **c** to you for help!
2:17 serve the LORD **c** between
Amo 5:16 mourners to **c** loudly.
Jnh 2:2 and you heard my **c**.
3:8 **C** loudly to God for help.
Mic 1:8 I will mourn and **c** because of
1:8 I will **c** like a jackal and mourn
1:10 Don't **c** there. Roll in the dust of
3:4 Then you will **c** to the LORD,
Hab 1:2 O LORD, am I to **c** for help,
1:2 I **c** out to you, yet you will not
2:11 A stone in the wall will **c** out.
Zep 1:10 On that day a loud **c** will come
1:14 Warriors will **c** out bitterly on
Zec 11:2 **C**, cypress trees, because the
11:2 **C**, oak trees of Bashan,
12:10 and they will **c** bitterly for him
Mat 8:12 People will **c** and be in
13:42 People will **c** and be in
13:50 They will **c** and be in extreme
22:13 People will **c** and be in
24:30 All the people on earth will **c** in
24:51 People will **c** and be in
25:30 People will **c** and be in
Mar 14:72 Peter began to **c** very hard.
Luk 6:25 They will mourn and **c**.
7:13 He said to her, "Don't **c**."
7:32 a funeral song, but you didn't **c**.'
8:52 Jesus said, "Don't **c**!
13:28 Then you will **c** and be in
18:7 people justice when they **c** out
19:40 the stones will **c** out."
19:41 saw the city, he began to **c**.
23:28 of Jerusalem, don't **c** for me!
23:28 Rather, **c** for yourselves and
Jon 11:31 she was going to the tomb to **c**.
16:20 You will **c** because you are
Jas 4:9 Be miserable, mourn, and **c**.
5:1 **C** and moan about the misery
Rev 18:9 lived in luxury with her will **c**
18:11 "The merchants of the earth **c**
18:15 They will **c** and mourn,

crying (73)

Gen 4:10 Your brother's blood is **c** out to
21:17 God heard the boy **c**,
21:17 the boy **c** from the bushes.
35:8 Jacob called it the Tree of **C**.
45:14 who was **c** on his shoulder.
Exo 2:6 He was **c**, and she felt sorry for
3:7 and I have heard them **c** out
5:8 That's why they're **c**,
11:6 will be loud **c** throughout Egypt,
12:30 There was loud **c** throughout
14:15 "Why are you **c** out to me?
32:18 It's not the sound of losers **c**.

Num 11:4 Even the Israelites started c
11:10 people from every family c at
11:13 They keep c for me to give
11:18 heard them c and saying,
25:6 of Israel while they were c at
1Sm 1:8 her, "Hannah, why are you c?
7:8 Don't stop c to the LORD our
11:5 "Why are these people c?"
2Sm 13:19 on her head, and went away c.
15:23 The whole country was c
19:1 Joab was told, "The king is c
2Ki 8:12 "Sir, why are you c?"
Ezr 10:1 confessing ⌊these sins⌋, c,
Neh 8:9 All the people were c as they
9:9 and you heard them c at the
Est 8:3 She fell down at his feet c and
Job 16:16 My face is red from c,
Psa 6:8 has heard the sound of my c.
69:3 I am exhausted from c for help.
Isa 22:5 of⌊ tearing down walls and c
22:12 LORD of Armies will call for c
65:19 Screaming and c will no longer
Jer 3:21 The sound of c is heard on the
3:21 It is the c and the pleading of
9:19 The sound of c is heard from
25:36 The shepherds are c and the
31:15 the sound of c in bitter grief.
31:15 Rachel is c for her children.
31:16 the LORD says: Stop your c,
41:6 to meet them, c as he went.
48:5 c bitterly as they go.
49:21 The sound of their c will be
Lam 1:16 I'm c because of ⌊all⌋ these
Eze 8:14 Women were sitting there and c
21:6 heart and with bitter c while
27:32 song for you with loud c:
Joe 2:12 with fasting, c, and mourning."
Amo 5:16 There will be loud c in every
5:17 There will be loud c in every
Mic 4:9 Now why are you c so loudly?
Zec 11:3 The shepherds are c,
Mat 2:18 the sound of c in bitter grief.
2:18 Rachel was c for her children.
Mar 5:38 were c and sobbing loudly.
5:39 making so much noise and c?
16:10 who were grieving and c.
Luk 6:21 Blessed are those who are c.
7:38 She was c and washed his
8:52 Everyone was c and showing
Jon 1:23 "I'm a voice c out in the desert,
11:33 When Jesus saw her c,
11:33 the Jews who were c with her,
20:13 asked her why she was c.
20:15 asked her, "Why are you c?
Act 9:39 They were c and showing
21:13 "Why are you c like this and
Heb 5:7 pleaded with loud c and tears,
Rev 5:5 the leaders said to me, "Stop c!
7:10 and c out in a loud voice,
18:19 shouted while c and mourning,
21:4 There won't be any grief, c,

crystal (8)

Exo 28:18 put turquoise, sapphire, and c.
39:11 put turquoise, sapphire, and c.
Job 28:17 gold ornaments, jewels, or c
Eze 1:22 It looked like dazzling c.
28:13 c, beryl, onyx, gray quartz,
Rev 4:6 a sea of glass as clear as c.
21:11 like gray quartz, as clear as c.
22:1 the water of life, as clear as c.

cub (3)

Gen 49:9 Judah, you are a lion c.
Dtr 33:22 "The people of Dan are a lion c.
Nah 2:11 and the lion c who moved

cubits (1)

Rev 21:17 angel was using, it was 144 c.

cubs (11)

2Sm 17:8 whose c have been stolen.
Job 4:11 and the c of the lioness are
38:32 or guide Ursa Major with its c?
38:39 and satisfy the hunger of her c
Pro 17:12 meet a bear robbed of its c than
Jer 51:38 lions and growling lion c.
Eze 19:2 the lions. She fed many c.
19:3 One of the c she raised
19:5 she took another one of her c
Hos 13:8 Like a bear that has lost her c,
Nah 2:12 its prey to pieces to feed its c.

cucumber (2)

Isa 1:8 like a shack in a c field,
Jer 10:5 like scarecrows in c gardens.

cucumbers (1)

Num 11:5 fish we ate in Egypt and the c,

cud (11)

Lev 11:3 and that also chew their c.
11:4 those that either chew their c
11:4 because they chew their c
11:5 because they chew their c
11:6 because they chew their c
11:7 hoofs but do not chew their c,
11:26 don't chew their c are unclean
Dtr 14:6 and that also chew their c.
14:7 But some animals chew their c,
14:7 (Although they chew their c,
14:8 they don't chew their c.)

cuddled (1)

Isa 66:12 arms and c on her knees.

cultivated (3)

Ecc 5:9 for a country with c fields.
Isa 7:25 all the hills which used to be c
Rom 11:24 have been grafted onto a c one.

cumin (7)

Isa 28:25 doesn't he scatter black c seed
28:25 black cumin seed and plant c?
28:27 Black c isn't threshed with a
28:27 wheels aren't rolled over c.
28:27 Black c is beaten with a rod
28:27 with a rod and c with a stick.
Mat 23:23 of your mint, dill, and c.

Cun (1)

1Ch 18:8 of bronze from Tibhath and C,

cunning (2)

Mat 10:16 So be as c as snakes but as
Eph 4:14 by people who use c

cup (68)

Gen 40:11 Pharaoh's c was in my hand,
40:11 I put the c in Pharaoh's hand."
40:13 You will put Pharaoh's c in his
40:21 put the c in Pharaoh's hand.
44:2 Then put my silver c in the
44:5 Isn't this the c that my master
44:10 The man who has the c will be
44:12 The c was found in Benjamin's
44:16 the one who had the c."
44:17 Only the man who had the c
2Sm 12:3 his food and drink from his c.
1Ki 7:26 Its rim was like the rim of a c,
2Ch 4:5 Its rim was like the rim of a c,
Neh 2:1 I picked up the c of wine and
Psa 11:6 He makes them drink from a c
16:5 is my inheritance and my c.
23:5 head with oil. My c overflows.
75:8 A c is in the LORD's hand.
116:13 I will take the c of salvation
Pro 23:31 because it sparkles in the c,
Isa 51:17 You drank from the c in the
51:17 That c was filled with his
51:17 You drank from the bowl, the c
51:22 I'm taking from your hand the c
51:22 the bowl, the c of my fury.
Jer 25:15 Take from my hand this c filled
25:17 So I took the c from the LORD's
25:26 Sheshach will drink from the c.
25:28 But if they refuse to take the c
49:12 drink from the c still drink from
51:7 Babylon was a golden c in the
Lam 4:21 The c ⌊of the LORD's fury⌋ will
Eze 23:31 I will put her c in your hand.
23:32 will drink from your sister's c,
23:32 a c that is deep and wide.
23:32 because this c holds so much.
23:33 The c of your sister Samaria
Hab 2:16 The c in the LORD's right hand
Zec 12:2 like a c ⌊of wine⌋ that
Mat 10:42 any of my humble followers a c
20:22 Can you drink the c that I'm
20:23 "You will drink my c.
26:27 Then he took a c and spoke a
26:39 let this c ⌊of suffering⌋ be
26:42 if this c cannot be taken away
Mar 9:41 Whoever gives you a c of
10:38 Can you drink the c that I'm
10:39 "You will drink the c that I'm
14:23 Then he took a c, spoke a
14:23 and gave the c to them.
14:36 Take this c ⌊of suffering⌋
Luk 22:17 Then he took a c and spoke a
22:20 he did the same with the c.
22:20 He said, "This c that is poured
22:42 take this c ⌊of suffering⌋ away
Jon 18:11 Shouldn't I drink the c ⌊of
1Co 10:16 When we bless the c of
10:21 You cannot drink the Lord's c
10:21 Lord's cup and the c of demons.
11:25 he did the same with the c.
11:25 He said, "This c is the new
11:26 this bread and drink from this c,
11:27 or drinks from the Lord's c
11:28 the bread and drink from the c.
Rev 14:10 been poured unmixed into the c
16:19 to give Babylon the Great the c
17:4 she was holding a gold c filled
18:6 Serve her a drink in her own c

cupbearer (11)

Gen 40:1 Later the king's c and his baker
40:2 was angry with his chief c
40:5 both prisoners — the c and the
40:9 So the chief c told Joseph his
40:13 to do when you were his c.
40:20 special attention to the chief c
40:21 He restored the chief c to his
40:21 So the c put the cup in
40:23 Nevertheless, the chief c didn't
41:9 Then the chief c spoke to
Neh 1:4 I was c to the king when I

cupbearer's (1)

Gen 40:16 given to the c dream was good.

cupbearers (2)

1Ki 10:5 the uniforms they wore, his c,
2Ch 9:4 his c and their uniforms,

cups (51)

Exo 25:31 as well as the flower c,
25:33 flower c shaped like almond
25:34 flower c shaped like almond
29:40 make an offering of eight c
37:17 as well as the flower c,
37:19 flower c shaped like almond
37:20 flower c shaped like almond
Lev 5:11 then bring eight c of flour as an
6:20 he is anointed — eight c of flour.
14:10 He must also take eight c of
14:21 He will take only eight c of
Num 5:15 to the priest along with eight c
15:4 LORD a grain offering of eight c
15:6 give a grain offering of 16 c of
15:9 bull a grain offering of 24 c
28:5 bring a grain offering of eight c
28:9 a grain offering of 16 c of flour
28:12 will be a grain offering of 24 c
28:12 ram a grain offering of 16 c
28:13 lamb a grain offering of 8 c
28:20 Bring 24 c for each bull,
28:20 for each bull, 16 c for each ram,
28:21 and 8 c for each of the seven
28:28 Bring 24 c for each bull,
28:28 for each bull, 16 c for each ram,
28:29 and 8 c for each of the seven
29:3 Bring 24 c for each bull,
29:3 for each bull, 16 c for each ram,
29:4 and 8 c for each of the seven
29:9 Bring 24 c for each bull,

Num 29:9 for each bull, 16 **c** for each ram,
29:10 and 8 **c** for each of the seven
29:14 Bring 24 **c** for each of the 13
29:14 16 **c** for each of the 2 rams,
29:15 and 8 **c** for each of the 14
1Ki 10:21 King Solomon's **c** were gold,
2Ki 7:1 About this time tomorrow 24 **c**
7:1 And 48 **c** of barley will sell for
7:16 Then 24 **c** of the best flour sold
7:16 and 48 **c** of barley sold for half
7:18 "Forty-eight **c** of barley will sell
7:18 And twenty-four **c** of the best
2Ch 9:20 King Solomon's **c** were gold,
Est 1:7 People drank from golden **c**.
1:7 No two **c** were alike.
Isa 65:11 good fortune and offered **c** full
Jer 35:5 Then I set **c** and pitchers filled
Mat 23:25 the outside of **c** and dishes.
23:26 First clean the inside of the **c**
Mar 7:4 they must also wash their **c**,
Luk 11:39 the outside of **c** and dishes.

curb (1)

Pro 7:12 the next she is at the **c**,

curdle (1)

Job 10:10 milk and **c** me like cheese?

cure (16)

2Ki 5:3 Then the prophet could **c** him
5:6 **C** him of his skin disease."
5:7 that I can **c** his skin disease!
Hos 5:13 But the king couldn't **c** them or
14:4 ⌊The LORD says,⌋ "I will **c**
Mat 10:1 people and to **c** every disease
10:8 **C** the sick, bring the dead back
17:16 but they couldn't **c** him."
Mar 6:5 a few sick people and **c** them.
6:13 many who were sick to **c** them.
16:18 hands on the sick and **c** them."
Luk 4:23 to me, 'Doctor, **c** yourself!'
8:43 No one could **c** her.
9:1 and authority to **c** diseases.
9:2 of God and to **c** the sick.
Jas 5:15 and the Lord will **c** them.)

cured (32)

Dtr 28:35 severe boils that can't be **c**.
Jer 30:15 your injury that can't be **c**?
46:11 without results; you can't be **c**.
Mat 4:23 He also **c** every disease and
4:24 by demons, and he **c** them all.
8:16 and **c** everyone who was
9:35 He also **c** every disease and
12:15 and he **c** all of them.
12:22 Jesus **c** him so that he could
14:14 them and **c** their sick people.
15:28 moment her daughter was **c**.
15:30 them at his feet, and he **c** them.
15:31 people talking, the disabled **c**,
17:18 At that moment the boy was **c**.
Mar 1:34 He **c** many who were sick with
3:10 He had **c** so many that
5:29 She felt **c** from her illness.
5:34 Be **c** from your illness."
Luk 4:27 But God **c** no one except
4:40 on each of them and **c** them.
5:15 him and have their diseases **c**.
6:18 wanted to hear him and be **c**
6:18 by evil spirits were **c**.
7:7 and let my servant be **c**.
8:2 They had been **c** from evil
8:47 and how she was **c** at once.
9:6 and **c** the sick everywhere.
9:11 and **c** those who were sick.
9:42 He **c** the boy and gave him
Act 5:16 and each person was **c**.
8:7 and lame people were **c**.
19:12 Their sicknesses would be **c**,

curing (2)

Luk 6:19 from him and **c** all of them.
7:21 At that time Jesus was **c** many

curls (1)

Sos 7:5 Your dangling **c** are royal

current (1)

Gen 23:16 **c** merchants' exchange rate.

currents (3)

Psa 8:8 swims in the **c** of the seas.
Pro 8:28 determined the **c** in the ocean,
Isa 43:16 and a road through the strong **c**.

curse (101)

Gen 8:21 "I will never again **c** the ground
12:3 whoever curses you, I will **c**.
27:12 Then I'll bring a **c** on myself
27:13 "Let any **c** on you fall on me,
27:29 May those who **c** you be
Exo 22:28 show disrespect for God or **c**
Lev 19:14 Never **c** deaf people or put
24:14 All who heard him **c** ⌊my
24:16 But those who **c** the LORD's
Num 5:18 bitter water that can bring a **c**.
5:19 that can bring a **c** will not harm
5:21 see what happens when the **c**
5:21 the oath and the **c** by saying:
5:22 that can bring a **c** go into your
5:24 bitter water that can bring the **c**.
5:27 the water that can bring the **c**
22:6 Please come and **c** these
22:6 whomever you **c** is cursed."
22:11 Now come and **c** them for me.
22:12 Don't **c** these people,
22:17 Please, come and **c** these
23:7 'Come, **c** Jacob for me,'
23:8 How can I **c** those whom God
23:11 you here to **c** my enemies,
23:13 **C** them for me from there."
23:23 No spell can **c** the
23:25 "If you won't **c** them,
23:27 Maybe God wants you to **c**
24:9 Those who **c** you will be
24:10 you to **c** my enemies,
Dtr 11:26 the choice of a blessing or a **c**.
11:29 and the **c** from Mount Ebal.
23:4 in Aram Naharaim, to **c** you.
23:5 Instead, he turned Balaam's **c**
Jos 6:26 time Joshua pronounced this **c**:
6:26 "The LORD will **c** whoever
9:23 You are under a **c** now.
23:15 bring about every evil **c** until
24:9 Balaam, son of Beor, to **c** you.
Jdg 5:23 "**C** Meroz!" said the Messenger
5:23 "Bitterly **c** those who live there!
9:57 So the **c** of Jotham,
17:2 heard you put a **c** on them.
21:18 men of Benjamin is under a **c**."
1Sm 14:44 me than are in this **c** if you do
17:43 called on his gods to **c** David.
2Sm 16:9 should this dead dog **c** you,
16:10 Let him **c**. If the LORD has told
16:10 '**C** David,' should anyone ask,
16:11 Let him **c**, since the LORD has
16:12 my misery and turn his **c** into
2Ki 9:34 woman who had a **c** on her.
Neh 10:29 in binding themselves with a **c**
13:2 hired Balaam to **c** the Israelites.
13:2 turned the **c** into a blessing.)
Job 1:11 I bet he'll **c** you to your face."
2:5 I bet he'll **c** you to your face."
2:9 principles? **C** God and die!"
3:8 Let those who **c** the day (those
3:8 up Leviathan) **c** that night.
31:30 sinfully by calling down a **c**
Psa 62:4 but in their hearts they **c**.
102:8 me use my name as a **c**.
109:28 They may **c**, but you will bless.
Pro 11:26 People will **c** the one who
26:2 so a hastily spoken **c** does not
27:14 his blessing is considered a **c**.
30:10 The slave will **c** you,
Ecc 10:20 Don't **c** the king even in your
10:20 and don't **c** rich people even in
Isa 24:6 That is why a **c** devours the
65:15 Your name will be used as a **c**
Jer 23:10 land mourns because of the **c**.
29:22 are in Babylon will use this **c**:
29:22 May the LORD **c** you as he
42:18 You will become a **c** word.
Lam 3:65 Let your **c** be on them.
Hos 7:16 die in battle because they **c**.
Zec 5:3 to me, "This is a **c** that will go
5:4 I will send out a **c**,
8:13 have been a **c** among the
Mal 1:14 "Cheaters are under a **c**.
2:2 "then I'll send a **c** on you,
2:2 and I'll **c** the blessings you
3:9 So a **c** is on you because the
Mat 26:74 Then Peter began to **c** and
Mar 3:28 will be forgiven for any sin or **c**.
14:71 Then Peter began to **c** and
Luk 6:28 Bless those who **c** you.
Act 23:12 They asked God to **c** them if
23:14 "We've asked God to **c** us if
23:21 They have asked God to **c**
26:11 and forced them to **c** ⌊the name
Rom 12:14 Bless them, and don't **c** them.
Gal 3:10 Certainly, there is a **c** on all
3:13 us from the **c** that God's laws
2Ti 3:2 They will **c** their parents,
Tit 3:2 Believers shouldn't **c** anyone or
Jas 2:7 Don't they **c** the good name ⌊of
3:9 the same tongues we **c** people,
Rev 22:3 There will no longer be any **c**.

cursed (90)

Gen 3:14 You are **c** more than all the
3:17 The ground is **c** because of
4:11 So now you are **c** from the
5:29 the LORD has **c** the ground."
9:25 So he said, "Canaan is **c**!
27:29 May those who curse you be **c**.
49:7 May their anger be **c** because
49:7 May their fury be **c** because it's
Lev 20:9 He has **c** his father or mother
24:14 "The man who **c** ⌊my name⌋
24:23 So the man who had **c** the
Num 5:27 become **c** among her people.
22:6 and whomever you curse is **c**."
23:8 those whom God hasn't **c**?
24:9 who curse you will be **c**!"
Dtr 11:28 You'll be **c** if you disobey the
21:23 is hung on a pole is **c** by God.
27:15 sets it up in secret will be **c**."
27:16 or mother will himself be **c**."
27:17 boundary marker will be **c**."
27:18 the wrong direction will be **c**."
27:19 or widows of justice will be **c**."
27:20 with his father's wife will be **c**.
27:21 with any animal will be **c**."
27:22 mother's daughter will be **c**."
27:23 his mother-in-law will be **c**."
27:24 person secretly will be **c**."
27:25 an innocent person will be **c**."
27:26 of these teachings will be **c**."
28:16 You will be **c** in the city and
28:16 in the city and **c** in the country.
28:17 the bread you bake will be **c**.
28:18 You will be **c**. You will have
28:18 Your cattle will be **c** with few
28:19 You will be **c** when you come
28:19 you come and **c** when you go.
Jdg 9:27 ate, drank, and **c** Abimelech.
1Sm 14:24 Saul made the troops swear, "**C**
14:28 '**C** is anyone who eats food
26:19 let them be **c** by the LORD.
2Sm 16:7 Shimei **c** and said,
16:13 Shimei **c**, hurled stones,
1Ki 2:8 He **c** me repeatedly when I
2Ki 2:24 he saw them and **c** them in the
22:19 here will be destroyed and **c**.
Neh 13:25 **c** them, beat some of them,
Job 1:5 may have sinned and **c** God
3:1 opened his mouth and **c**
5:3 but I quickly **c** his house.
24:18 Their property is **c** in the land.
Psa 37:22 Those who are **c** by him will
109:17 ⌊on others⌋, so he, too, was **c**.
Pro 22:14 The one who is **c** by the LORD
24:24 will be **c** by people and
Ecc 7:22 you have **c** others many times.
Isa 52:5 And my name is **c** all day long.
65:20 years old will be **c** as a sinner.
Jer 11:3 **C** is anyone who doesn't listen
17:5 is what the LORD says: **C** is

Jer 20:14 **C** is the day that I was born,
20:15 **C** is the man who made my
24:9 ridiculed and **c** wherever
25:18 something ridiculed and **c**,
26:6 something that will be **c** by all
29:18 They will become something **c**,
29:22 curse you as he **c** Zedekiah
42:18 ridiculed, **c**, and disgraced.
44:8 destroy yourselves and be **c**
44:12 They will become something **c**,
44:22 ruined, destroyed, and **c**.
48:10 **C** are those who neglect doing
48:10 **C** are those who keep their
49:13 ridiculed, ruined, and **c**.
Mic 6:10 I have **c** all the wicked people
Mal 2:2 Yes, I've already **c** them
Mat 25:41 God has **c** you! Go into
Mar 11:21 fig tree you **c** has dried up."
Jon 7:49 This crowd is **c** because it
Rom 2:24 "God's name is **c** among the
1Co 12:3 God's Spirit says, "Jesus is **c**."
16:22 love the Lord, let him be **c**!
Gal 3:10 in Moses' Teachings is **c**."
3:13 bring by becoming **c** instead
3:13 who is hung on a tree is **c**."
1Ti 1:13 In the past I **c** him,
Heb 6:8 and in danger of being **c**.
2Pe 2:14 on their greed. They are **c**.
Rev 16:9 They **c** the name of God,
16:11 and **c** the God of heaven for
16:21 The people **c** God because the

curses (33)

Gen 12:3 and whoever **c** you,
Exo 21:17 "Whoever **c** his father or
Lev 20:9 "Whoever **c** his father or
24:16 Whoever **c** the LORD's name
Num 5:23 "The priest will write these **c**
Dtr 27:13 Mount Ebal to announce the **c**:
27:16 "Whoever **c** his father or
28:15 If you don't, all these **c** will
28:20 The LORD will send you **c**,
28:45 All these **c** will come to you.
28:46 These **c** will be a sign and an
29:20 All the **c** described in this book
29:27 brought on it all the **c** described
30:1 All these blessings and **c** I
30:7 your God will put all these **c**
30:19 life or death, blessings or **c**.
Jos 8:34 the blessings and **c** — as they
2Ch 34:24 here according to the **c** written
Psa 10:3 but he **c** the LORD.
59:12 because they speak **c** and lies.
109:17 He loved to put **c** ⌊on others⌋,
Pro 3:33 The LORD **c** the house of
20:20 The lamp of the person who **c**
28:27 the poor receives many **c**.
30:11 A certain kind of person **c** his
Jer 15:10 Yet, everyone **c** me.
Dan 9:11 So you brought on us the **c** you
9:11 the **c** written in the Teachings
Mat 15:4 mother' and 'Whoever **c** father
Mar 3:29 But whoever **c** the Holy Spirit
7:10 mother' and 'Whoever **c** father
Rom 3:14 full of **c** and bitter resentment.
Jas 3:10 Praise and **c** come from the

cursing (21)

Lev 24:11 Israelite woman's son began **c**
1Sm 3:13 sin — that they were **c** God —
2Sm 16:5 cousin of Saul came out **c**.
19:21 Shimei be put to death for **c**
1Ki 21:10 him and accuse him of **c** God
21:13 these men accused Naboth of **c**
2Ch 32:17 Sennacherib wrote letters **c** the
Psa 10:7 His mouth is full of **c**,
109:18 He wore **c** as though it were
109:18 so **c** entered his body like
109:19 Let **c** be his clothing,
Ecc 7:21 hear your own servant **c** you.
Isa 8:21 **c** their king and God.
Hos 4:2 There is **c**, lying, murdering,
Mat 12:31 will be forgiven for any sin or **c**.
12:31 **c** the Spirit will not be forgiven.
15:19 and **c** come from within.
Mar 7:22 lust, envy, **c**, arrogance,
Eph 4:31 loud quarreling, **c**, and hatred.
Col 3:8 hatred, **c**, obscene language,
1Ti 6:4 jealousy, rivalry, **c**, suspicion,

curtain (8)

Jdg 4:18 and she hid him under a tent **c**.
Mat 27:51 Suddenly, the **c** in the temple
Mar 15:38 The **c** in the temple was split
Luk 23:45 The **c** in the temple was split
Heb 6:19 the ⌊holy⌋ place behind the **c**
9:3 Behind the second **c** was the
10:20 way for us to go through the **c**.
10:20 (The **c** is his own body.)

curtains (23)

Exo 27:9 feet long and have **c** made out
27:11 with **c** on 20 posts set in 20
27:12 feet wide and have **c** ⌊hung⌋
27:14 wide with **c** ⌊hung on⌋ three
27:18 with ⌊**c**⌋ made of fine linen
35:17 the **c** for the courtyard,
38:9 feet long and had **c** made out
38:12 75 feet long and had **c** ⌊hung⌋
38:14 22 ½ feet wide with **c** ⌊hung⌋
38:16 All the **c** around the courtyard
38:18 just like the **c** of the courtyard.
39:40 the **c** for the courtyard,
Num 3:26 the **c** for the courtyard,
4:26 the **c** for the courtyard around
4:26 equipment used to set up the **c**.
Est 1:6 had white and violet linen **c**.
1:6 These **c** were attached to
Psa 104:2 as though they were **c**.
Sos 1:5 Kedar's tents, like Solomon's **c**.
Isa 54:2 Stretch out the **c** of your tent,
Jer 4:20 Their **c** are torn in an instant.
10:20 tent again or put up my tent **c**.
49:29 Their tent **c**, utensils,

curves (1)

Sos 7:1 The **c** of your thighs are like

Cush (4)

Gen 10:6 Ham's descendants were **C**,
10:8 **C** was the father of Nimrod,
1Ch 1:8 Ham's descendants were **C**,
1:10 **C** was the father of Nimrod,

Cushan (1)

Hab 3:7 I see trouble in the tents of **C**.

Cushan Rishathaim (3)

Jdg 3:8 He used King **C** of Aram
3:8 Israel served **C** for eight years.
3:10 The LORD handed King **C** of

Cushi (2)

Jer 36:14 and the great-grandson of **C**,
Zep 1:1 who was the son of **C**,

cushion (1)

Mar 4:38 But he was sleeping on a **c** in

Cush's (2)

Gen 10:7 **C** descendants were Seba,
1Ch 1:9 **C** descendants were Seba,

custody (2)

Lev 24:12 They kept him in **c** until the
Num 15:34 They kept him in **c** until they

custom (9)

Gen 29:26 Laban answered, "It's not our **c**
Jdg 11:39 So the **c** began in Israel
1Sm 30:25 on he made this a rule and a **c**
2Ki 11:14 by the pillar according to **c**.
Luk 1:9 he was chosen by priestly **c** to
Jon 18:39 You have a **c** that I should free
19:40 was the Jewish **c** for burial.
Act 26:3 especially familiar with every **c**
1Co 11:16 because⌋ we don't have any **c**

customary (1)

Mar 14:12 the Passover lamb was **c**

customs (13)

Dtr 12:30 aren't tempted to follow their **c**.
2Ki 17:8 and lived by the **c** of the
17:19 but lived according to Israel's **c**.
17:26 of Samaria don't know the **c**
17:26 because they don't know the **c**
17:27 go back to teach them the **c**
17:33 own gods according to the **c**
17:34 they are still following their **c**,
17:34 by the decrees, **c**, teachings,
Act 6:14 change the **c** that Moses gave
16:21 and they're advocating **c** that
21:21 children or follow Jewish **c**.
28:17 violated the **c** handed down by

cut (256)

Gen 15:10 He **c** each of them in half and
15:10 he did not **c** the birds in half.
22:3 When he had **c** the wood for
30:37 Jacob took fresh-**c** branches of
40:19 Pharaoh will **c** off your head
Exo 4:25 **c** off her son's foreskin,
20:25 make it with **c** stone blocks.
29:17 **C** the ram into pieces,
31:5 He knows how to **c** and set
34:1 The LORD said to Moses, "**C**
34:4 So Moses **c** two ⌊more⌋ stone
34:13 and **c** down their poles
35:33 He knows how to **c** and set
39:3 into thin sheets and **c** them up.
Lev 1:6 and **c** it into pieces.
1:12 Then **c** it into pieces.
3:4 Also **c** off the lobe of the liver
8:20 the ram was **c** into pieces,
9:13 which was **c** in pieces and
19:27 and never **c** the edges of your
22:24 torn out, or **c** out testicles.
26:1 Never **c** figures in stone to
26:30 **c** down your incense altars,
Num 13:23 they **c** off a branch with only
13:24 grapes the Israelites **c** off there.
Dtr 7:5 **c** down their poles dedicated to
10:1 "**C** two ⌊more⌋ stone tablets
10:3 I **c** two ⌊more⌋ stone tablets
12:3 **c** down their idols,
19:5 go into the woods to **c** wood.
19:5 them swings the ax to **c** down
20:19 Never **c** those trees down,
20:20 You may **c** them down and use
21:12 shave her head, **c** her nails,
23:1 whose penis is **c** off may never
23:25 to **c** your neighbor's grain.
25:12 **c** off her hand. Have no pity
29:11 and the foreigners who **c** wood
32:26 I said that I would **c** them in
32:42 My sword will **c** off the heads
Jos 3:16 Sea) was completely **c** off.
4:7 of the Jordan River was **c** off
10:19 **C** off their rear guard.
Jdg 1:6 and **c** off his thumbs and big
1:7 thumbs and big toes **c** off used
6:25 to the god Baal and **c** down
6:26 pole that you have **c** down."
6:28 to it had also been **c** down.
6:30 down the Baal altar and **c** down
9:48 **c** some brushwood,
9:49 So all his troops also **c**
13:5 You must never **c** his hair
16:17 no one has ever **c** the hair on
19:29 He took his concubine and **c**
20:6 So I took my concubine and **c**
Rut 4:10 name will not be **c** off from his
1Sm 5:4 hands were **c** off ⌊and were
11:7 pair of oxen, **c** them in pieces,
15:33 And Samuel **c** Agag in pieces
17:46 I will strike you down and **c** off
20:16 if Jonathan's name is **c** off from
24:4 David quietly got up and **c** off
24:5 him because he had **c** off
24:11 Since I **c** off the border of your
31:9 They **c** off his head and
2Sm 4:7 and **c** off his head.)
4:12 **c** off their hands and feet,
10:4 **c** off their clothes from the
14:16 from the man who wants to **c**

2Sm 14:26 he used to **c** his hair because it
14:26 When he **c** the hair on his head
20:22 They **c** off Sheba's head and
1Ki 3:25 "**C** the living child in two.
3:26 or yours. **C** him ⌊in two⌋."
5:6 So order men to **c** down cedars
5:17 provide a foundation of **c** stone
7:9 The stone blocks were **c** to
7:11 which had been **c** to size.
7:12 three layers of **c** stone blocks
9:7 then I will **c** Israel out of the
15:13 Asa **c** the statue down and
18:23 for themselves, **c** it into pieces,
18:28 They also **c** themselves with
18:33 the wood, **c** up the bull,
2Ki 3:19 You will **c** down every good
3:25 They sealed every well and **c**
4:39 Then he **c** them into the pot of
6:4 and began to **c** down trees.
6:6 Elisha **c** off a piece of wood.
12:12 it to buy wood and **c** stones
16:17 King Ahaz **c** off the side panels
18:4 and **c** down the poles
19:23 I'll **c** down its tallest cedars
23:14 **c** down the poles dedicated to
1Ch 19:4 **c** off their clothes from the
22:2 He appointed some of them to **c**
2Ch 2:16 We will **c** all the lumber you
14:3 and **c** down the poles
15:16 Asa **c** the statue down,
28:24 in God's temple, **c** them up,
31:1 **c** down the poles dedicated to
34:4 He **c** down the incense altars
34:7 and **c** down all the incense
Job 6:9 he would reach out to **c** me off.
8:12 if they were fresh and not **c**,
14:7 for a tree when it is **c** down.
21:21 of his months is **c** short?
27:8 person have when he is **c** off,
28:10 They **c** out mineshafts in the
Psa 12:3 May the LORD **c** off every
31:22 "I have been **c** off from your
37:9 Evildoers will be **c** off ⌊from
37:22 are cursed by him will be **c** off.
37:28 of wicked people will be **c** off.
37:34 When wicked people are **c** off,
37:38 of wicked people will be **c** off.
63:10 They will be **c** down by
72:6 that falls on ⌊freshly⌋ **c** grass,
78:64 His priests were **c** down with
80:16 The vine has been **c** down and
88:5 who are **c** off from your power.
89:45 You **c** short the days of his
90:5 in the morning like **c** grass.
105:18 and **c** into his neck with an iron
107:16 bronze gates and **c** iron bars
109:13 Let his descendants be **c** off
129:4 He has **c** me loose from the
Pro 2:22 But wicked people will be **c** off
10:31 but a devious tongue will be **c**
23:18 and your hope will never be **c**
24:14 and your hope will never be **c**
27:25 ⌊When⌋ grass is **c** short,
Isa 6:13 oak or an oak is **c** down,
9:10 will rebuild with hand-**c** stones.
9:10 Fig trees have been **c** down,
9:14 So in one day the LORD will **c**
10:33 highest trees will be **c** down.
10:34 He will **c** down the underbrush
14:12 How you have been **c** down to
14:22 "I'll **c** off the name of the
15:2 and every beard is **c** off.
16:8 Rulers of the nations have **c** off
18:5 he will **c** off the shoots with
22:16 What right do you have to **c** it
22:25 It will be **c** off and will fall,
37:24 I'll **c** down its tallest cedars
38:12 You **c** me off from the loom.
44:14 They **c** down cedars for
45:2 the bronze doors and **c** through
48:19 Their names would not be **c** off
51:1 the rock from which you were **c**
51:9 Didn't you **c** Rahab into pieces
53:7 is silent when its wool is **c** off.
Jer 5:10 **C** off the branches because
6:6 Armies says: **C** down its trees.
Jer 7:29 "**C** off your hair and throw it
9:21 Death has **c** down the children
9:22 has been **c** but not gathered.
10:3 Woodcutters **c** down trees from
11:19 Let's **c** Jeremiah off from this
16:6 No one will **c** his own body or
19:7 I will **c** them down with swords
22:7 They will **c** down your finest
34:18 in my presence when they **c**
36:23 the king would **c** them off with
46:15 your soldiers be **c** down?
46:23 They will **c** down the forest,"
47:4 to **c** off from Tyre and Sidon
47:5 long will you **c** yourselves,
48:25 "Moab's horn is **c** off,
48:37 and every beard is **c** off.
51:13 of your life has been **c** off.
Lam 2:3 In his burning anger he **c** off all
2:21 men are **c** down by swords.
3:9 He has blocked my way with **c**
Eze 4:16 I am going to **c** off the bread
5:2 Take another third, and **c** it up
5:16 and I will **c** off your food
6:6 burners will be **c** down,
14:13 **c** off its food supply,
16:4 your umbilical cord wasn't **c**.
16:40 They will stone you and **c** you
17:24 I **c** down tall trees,
21:16 Sword, **c** to the right.
21:16 **C** to the left or wherever your
23:25 They will **c** off your nose and
24:4 **C** the meat into pieces,
25:16 **c** off the Cherethites,
26:9 and he will **c** down your towers
31:12 from the most ruthless nation **c**
32:12 I will **c** down your people with
39:10 from the field or **c** down trees
40:42 four tables made of **c** stone
Dan 1:10 he would have my head **c** off."
2:34 a stone was **c** out,
2:45 stone that you saw **c** out from
4:14 '**C** down the oak tree!
4:14 **C** off its branches!
4:23 He said, '**C** down the oak tree!
9:26 the Anointed One will be **c** off
Hos 6:5 That is why I **c** ⌊you⌋ down by
Joe 3:13 **C** them down like grain.
Amo 1:5 I will **c** off those living in Aven
1:8 I will **c** off those living in
3:14 The horns of the altar will be **c**
5:11 build houses from hand-**c** stones
9:1 **C** off everyone's head.
Mic 4:12 bring them together like **c** grain
Nah 1:12 they will be **c** down and die.
3:15 A sword will **c** you down.
Zep 3:6 "I will **c** off the nations.
Zec 9:6 and I will **c** off the Philistines'
12:6 torch among freshly **c** straw.
13:8 the land two-thirds will be **c** off
Mat 3:10 The ax is now ready to **c** the
3:10 good fruit will be **c** down
5:30 **c** it off and throw it away.
7:19 to produce good fruit is **c** down
13:30 When the grain is **c**,
14:10 had John's head **c** off in prison.
18:8 **c** it off and throw it away.
21:8 Others **c** branches from the
26:51 pulled out his sword and **c** off
27:60 which had been **c** in a rock.
Mar 6:16 "I had John's head **c** off,
6:27 The guard **c** off John's head in
9:43 you to lose your faith, **c** it off!
9:45 you to lose your faith, **c** it off!
11:8 Others **c** leafy branches in the
14:47 pulled out his sword and **c** off
15:46 which had been **c** out of rock,
Luk 3:9 The ax is now ready to **c** the
3:9 good fruit will be **c** down
9:9 "I had John's head **c** off.
13:7 **C** it down! Why should it use up
13:9 But if not, then **c** it down."
21:24 Swords will **c** them down,
22:50 One of the disciples **c** off the
23:53 the body in a tomb **c** in rock,
Jon 18:10 and **c** off the servant's right ear.
18:26 man whose ear Peter had **c** off,
Act 8:32 is silent when its wool is **c** off.
8:33 his life on earth being **c** short?"
18:18 Aquila had his hair **c**,
27:32 Then the soldiers **c** the ropes
27:40 They **c** the anchors free and
Rom 9:3 and **c** off from Christ
11:19 "Branches were **c** off so that I
11:22 will be **c** off ⌊from the tree⌋.
11:24 fact that you have been **c** from
1Co 11:6 she should **c** off her hair.
11:6 for a woman to **c** off her hair
2Co 6:12 We haven't **c** you off.
6:12 Your own emotions have **c** you
Gal 5:4 have been **c** off from Christ.
Rev 20:4 whose heads had been **c** off

Cuth (1)

2Ki 17:30 people from **C** made Nergal.

Cuthah (1)

2Ki 17:24 Babylon, **C**, Avva, Hamath,

cuts (10)

Lev 22:22 **c**, warts, scabs, or ringworm.
Psa 46:9 He **c** spears in two.
76:12 He **c** short the lives of
Pro 26:6 send a message **c** off his own
Isa 10:15 the person who **c** with it?
Jer 22:14 He **c** out windows in it,
41:5 and **c** were on their bodies.
Hos 7:14 cry in their beds and make **c**
Mar 4:29 he **c** it with a sickle,
Heb 4:12 sword and **c** as deep as

cutting (5)

Dtr 14:1 don't ⌊mourn⌋ by **c** yourselves
1Sm 17:51 was dead by **c** off his head.
2Ki 6:5 As one of them was **c** down a
Hab 2:10 by **c** off many people
Mar 5:5 and **c** himself with stones.

cycle (2)

Heb 10:1 Teachings with their yearly **c**
10:3 Instead, this yearly **c** of

cymbal (1)

1Co 13:1 am a loud gong or a clashing **c**.

cymbals (16)

2Sm 6:5 tambourines, sistrums, and **c**.
1Ch 13:8 tambourines, **c**, and trumpets.
15:16 and **c** to produce joyful music
15:19 appointed to play bronze **c**.
15:28 trumpets, **c**, harps, and lyres.
16:5 Asaph played the **c**.
16:42 Jeduthun played trumpets, **c**,
25:1 with lyres, harps, and **c**.
25:6 They played **c**, lyres,
2Ch 5:12 stood east of the altar with **c**,
5:13 Accompanied by trumpets, **c**,
29:25 in the LORD's temple with **c**,
Ezr 3:10 took their places with **c**
Neh 12:27 with songs and **c**,
Psa 150:5 Praise him with loud **c**.
150:5 Praise him with crashing **c**.

cypress (14)

Gen 6:14 yourself a ship of **c** wood.
2Sm 6:5 instruments made from **c** wood
1Ki 5:8 regard to the cedar and **c** logs.
5:10 cedar and **c** wood he wanted.
6:15 of the temple with **c** planks.
6:34 He made two doors from **c**.
9:11 as much cedar and **c** lumber
2Ch 2:8 Send me cedar, **c**,
3:5 the larger building with **c**,
Sos 1:17 The **c** trees will be our rafters.
Isa 41:19 I will place cedar, fir, and **c**
55:13 **C** trees will grow where
60:13 and **c** trees will come to
Zec 11:2 Cry, **c** trees, because the

cypresses (3)

2Ki 19:23 tallest cedars and its finest **c**.
Isa 14:8 Even the **c** rejoice over you.
37:24 tallest cedars and its finest **c**.

Cyprus (15)

Gen 10:4 Tarshish, **C**, and Rhodes.
Num 24:24 will come from the shores of **C**.
1Ch 1:7 Tarshish, **C**, and Rhodes.
Isa 23:1 has come to the ships from **C**.
23:12 Get up, and travel to **C**.
Jer 2:10 Go over to the coasts of **C**,
Eze 27:6 pine trees on the shores of **C**.
Act 4:36 been born on the island of **C**.
11:19 **C**, and the city of Antioch.
11:20 who were from **C** and Cyrene,
13:4 there sailed to the island of **C**.
15:39 and sailed to the island of **C**.
21:3 We could see the island of **C**
21:16 was from the island of **C**
27:4 northern side of the island of **C**

Cyrene (7)

Mat 27:32 He was from the city of **C**.
Mar 15:21 the city of **C** was coming ⌞into
Luk 23:26 who was from the city of **C**.
Act 2:10 and the country near **C** in Libya.
6:9 some men from the cities of **C**
11:20 who were from Cyprus and **C**,
13:1 the Black), Lucius (from **C**),

Cyrus (23)

2Ch 36:23 This is what King **C** of Persia
Ezr 1:2 This is what King **C** of Persia
1:7 King **C** brought out the utensils
1:8 King **C** of Persia put the
3:7 Lebanon to Joppa as King **C**
4:3 as King **C** of Persia ordered us
4:5 throughout the reign of King **C**
5:13 the reign of King **C** of Babylon,
5:13 **C** gave permission for God's
5:14 In addition, **C** took out of a
5:14 **C** gave them to a man named
5:15 **C** told him, 'Take these
5:17 King **C** gave permission
6:3 as king From: King **C** Subject:
6:5 In addition, **C** took out of a
6:14 of Israel had ordered and as **C**,
Isa 44:28 He says about **C**, "He is my
45:1 what the LORD says about **C**,
45:2 I will go ahead of you, **C**,
45:13 I prepared **C** for my righteous
48:14 The LORD loves **C**.
Dan 1:21 first year of King **C** ⌞of Persia⌟.
6:28 and the reign of **C** the Persian.

Cyrus' (4)

2Ch 36:22 come true in **C** first year as king
Ezr 1:1 come true in **C** first year as king
6:3 Date: **C** first year as king From:
Dan 10:1 In **C** third year as king of

D

Dabbesheth (1)

Jos 19:11 to Maralah and touches **D**

Daberath (3)

Jos 19:12 of Chisloth Tabor, on to **D**,
21:28 tribe of Issachar: Kishion, **D**,
1Ch 6:72 **D** with its pastureland,

daddy (1)

Isa 8:4 how to say '**D**' or 'Mommy,'

dagger (3)

Jdg 3:16 a two-edged **d** for himself.
3:21 took the **d** from his right side,
3:22 Ehud didn't pull the **d** out.

Dagon (9)

Jdg 16:23 a great sacrifice to their god **D**
1Sm 5:2 brought it into the temple of **D**
5:2 Dagon and placed it beside **D**.
5:3 saw that **D** had fallen forward
5:3 So they took **D** and put him
5:4 saw that **D** had ⌞again⌟ fallen
1Sm 5:5 This is why the priests of **D**
5:7 harshly with us and our god **D**."
1Ch 10:10 his head to the temple of **D**.

Dagon's (3)

1Sm 5:4 **D** head and his two hands
5:4 The rest of **D** body was intact.
5:5 else who comes into **D** temple

daily (46)

Exo 29:42 be the **d** burnt offering ⌞made⌟
Num 4:16 the **d** grain offering,
28:3 bring as a **d** burnt offering two
28:6 This is the **d** burnt offering
28:10 addition to the **d** burnt offerings
28:15 In addition to the **d** burnt
28:24 addition to the **d** burnt offering
28:31 in addition to the **d** burnt
29:6 and the **d** burnt offerings with
29:11 LORD) and the **d** burnt offerings
29:16 addition to the **d** burnt offerings
29:19 addition to the **d** burnt offerings
29:22 addition to the **d** burnt offerings
29:25 addition to the **d** burnt offerings
29:28 addition to the **d** burnt offerings
29:31 addition to the **d** burnt offerings
29:34 addition to the **d** burnt offerings
29:35 You must not do any **d** work.
29:38 addition to the **d** burnt offerings
2Ki 25:30 him a **d** food allowance as
1Ch 16:37 as the **d** work required.
2Ch 31:16 perform the **d** service that each
Ezr 3:5 sacrificed the **d** burnt offerings,
Neh 10:33 and for the **d** grain offerings and
10:33 offerings and **d** burnt offerings,
12:47 giving gifts for the **d** support
12:47 holy gifts for ⌞the **d** support of⌟
Est 2:9 a **d** supply of food,
2:23 his official record of **d** events.
6:1 to bring the official **d** records,
Job 7:1 like a hired hand's **d** ⌞work⌟?
Psa 37:18 The LORD knows the **d**
68:19 Thanks be to the Lord, who **d**
Jer 33:18 and to prepare **d** sacrifices."
52:34 him a **d** food allowance as
Eze 46:15 morning as a **d** burnt offering.
Dan 1:5 for them to get a **d** allowance
8:11 it took the **d** burnt offering from
8:12 a stop to the **d** burnt offering.
8:13 vision — the **d** burnt offering,
11:31 take away the **d** burnt offering,
12:11 From the time the **d** burnt
Mat 6:11 Give us our **d** bread today.
Act 19:9 and held **d** discussions
2Co 11:28 I have the **d** pressure of my
Heb 7:27 to bring **d** sacrifices as those

dairy (2)

1Sm 6:7 ready for two **d** cows that have
6:10 They took two **d** cows,

Dais (1)

2Ki 17:4 had sent messengers to King **D**

Dalmanutha (1)

Mar 8:10 and went into the region of **D**.

Dalmatia (1)

2Ti 4:10 Titus went to the province of **D**.

Dalphon (1)

Est 9:7 Parshandatha, **D**, Aspatha,

dam (4)

Exo 15:8 The waves stood up like a **d**.
Jos 3:13 will stop and stand up like a **d**."
3:16 The water rose up like a **d** as
Psa 33:7 the water in the sea like a **d**

damage (3)

2Ki 12:7 "Why aren't you repairing the **d**
Act 27:10 This disaster will cause **d** to
Rev 6:6 But do not **d** the olive oil and

damaged (5)

Exo 9:32 wheat nor the wild grain was **d**,
Exo 22:5 he must make up for what the **d**
Jdg 6:3 Kedem came and **d** the crops.
Isa 42:3 He will not break off a **d** cattail.
Mat 12:20 He will not break off a **d** cattail.

Damaris (1)

Act 17:34 and a woman named **D**,

Damascus (64)

Gen 14:15 which is north of **D**.
15:2 Eliezer of **D** will inherit my
2Sm 8:5 When the Arameans from **D**
8:6 in the Aramean kingdom of **D**,
1Ki 11:24 They went to **D**, settled there,
11:24 and ruled a kingdom in **D**.
15:18 King Asa sent them to **D** to
19:15 back to the wilderness near **D**,
20:34 centers in **D** as my father
2Ki 5:12 Rivers in **D** have better water
8:7 Elisha went to **D**. King
8:9 and all kinds of goods from **D**.
14:28 how he recovered **D** and
16:9 listened to him and attacked **D**.
16:10 Then King Ahaz went to **D** to
16:10 He saw an altar there in **D**.
16:11 model King Ahaz sent from **D**.
16:11 Ahaz returned home from **D**.
16:12 When the king came from **D**,
1Ch 18:5 When the Arameans from **D**
18:6 in the Aramean kingdom of **D**,
2Ch 16:2 He sent them to **D** to Aram's
24:23 and Jerusalem to the king of **D**.
28:5 and brought them to **D**.
28:23 He sacrificed to the gods of **D**,
Sos 7:4 like a Lebanese tower facing **D**.
Isa 7:8 The capital of Aram is **D**,
7:8 and the leader of **D** is Rezin.
8:4 the wealth of **D** and the loot
10:9 Isn't Samaria like **D**?'
17:1 is the divine revelation about **D**.
17:1 "**D** will no longer be a city.
17:3 kingdom will disappear from **D**.
Jer 49:23 This is a message about **D**.
49:24 The people of **D** are weak.
49:27 "I will set fire to the walls of **D**
Eze 27:18 People from **D** traded with you
47:16 the borders of **D** and Hamath.
47:17 Hazar Enon on the border of **D**.
47:18 will run between Hauran and **D**.
48:1 border of **D** near Hamath,
Amo 1:3 Because **D** has committed
1:5 the bars ⌞on the gates⌟ of **D**.
5:27 send you into exile beyond **D**,
Zec 9:1 of Hadrach and will rest on **D**
Act 9:2 leaders in the city of **D**.
9:3 was coming near the city of **D**,
9:8 his companions led him into **D**.
9:10 Ananias lived in the city of **D**.
9:14 Saul has come here to **D** with
9:17 to you on your way to **D**,
9:19 in the city of **D** for several days.
9:22 Jews living in **D** by proving that
9:27 named Jesus in the city of **D**.
22:5 community in the city of **D**.
22:6 the city of **D** about noon,
22:10 Go into the city of **D**,
22:11 me led me into the city of **D**.
22:12 man named Ananias lived in **D**.
22:12 All the Jews living in **D** spoke
26:12 when I went to the city of **D**.
26:20 to the ⌞Jewish⌟ people in **D**
2Co 11:32 the city of **D** to catch me.
Gal 1:17 and then came back to **D**.

Dan (74)

Gen 14:14 the four kings all the way to **D**.
30:6 she named him **D** [He Judges].
35:25 Bilhah were **D** and Naphtali.
46:23 The son of **D** was Hushim.
49:16 "**D** will hand down decisions
49:17 **D** will be a snake on a road,
Exo 1:4 **D** and Naphtali; Gad and Asher.
31:6 from the tribe of **D**
35:34 from the tribe of **D** the ability to
38:23 from the tribe of **D**.
Lev 24:10 from the tribe of **D** in Israel) and

Num 1:12 from the tribe of **D**;
1:38 for the descendants of **D** listed
1:39 for the tribe of **D** was 62,700.
2:25 led by **D** will camp under
2:25 for the people of **D** is Ahiezer,
7:66 leader of the descendants of **D**,
13:12 from the tribe of **D**;
26:42 The family descended from **D**
26:42 the family descended from **D**.
34:22 the leader of the tribe of **D**;
Dtr 27:13 Zebulun, **D**, and Naphtali.
33:22 About the tribe of **D** [He
33:22 "The people of **D** are a lion cub.
34:1 could see Gilead as far as **D**,
Jos 19:40 for the families of the tribe of **D**.
19:47 The border of **D** extended
19:47 and renamed the city **D** after
19:47 city Dan after their ancestor **D**.
19:48 for the families of the tribe of **D**.
21:5 of the tribes of Ephraim and **D**
21:23 The tribe of **D** gave them four
Jdg 1:34 forced the tribe of **D** into
5:17 And **D**...Why did he stay by the
13:2 was from the family of **D**.
18:1 And in those days the tribe of **D**
18:2 So all the families of **D** sent out
18:11 So 600 men from the tribe of **D**
18:12 [The Camp of **D**] today.
18:14 said to the other men of **D**,
18:16 The 600 armed men from **D**
18:22 him catch up to the people of **D**.
18:23 But the people of **D** turned
18:25 The people of **D** replied,
18:26 The people of **D** went on their
18:27 The people of **D** took what
18:28 The people of **D** rebuilt the city
18:29 They named the city **D** in honor
18:29 in honor of their ancestor **D**,
18:30 The people of **D** set up the
20:1 All the people of Israel from **D**
1Sm 3:20 All Israel from **D** to Beersheba
2Sm 3:10 Judah from **D** to Beersheba.'"
17:11 troops from **D** to Beersheba,
24:2 the tribes of Israel from **D**
24:15 people from **D** to Beersheba,
1Ki 4:25 Judah and Israel (from **D** to
12:29 in Bethel and the other in **D**.
12:30 The people went as far as **D** to
15:20 He conquered Ijon, **D**,
2Ki 10:29 that were at Bethel and **D**.
1Ch 2:2 **D**, Joseph, Benjamin, Naphtali,
12:35 From **D** there were 28,600
21:2 Israel from Beersheba to **D**.
27:22 for the tribe of **D**: Azarel, son of
2Ch 2:14 of a woman from the tribe of **D**,
16:4 He conquered Ijon, **D**,
30:5 Israel from Beersheba to **D**.
Jer 4:15 A message is heard from **D**,
8:16 of horses can be heard from **D**.
Eze 48:1 **D** will have one part of the land.
48:2 part of the land and border **D**
48:32 Benjamin Gate, and **D** Gate.
Amo 8:14 swear, **D**, as your god lives ...."

dance (9)

2Sm 6:21 "I didn't **d** in front of the slave
Job 21:11 and their children **d** around.
Psa 51:8 bones that you have broken **d**.
Ecc 3:4 a time to mourn and a time to **d**,
Sos 6:13 you look at the **d** of Mahanaim?
Jer 31:13 women will rejoice and **d** along
50:11 You **d** around like calves on
Mat 11:17 music for you, but you didn't **d**.
Luk 7:32 music for you, but you didn't **d**.

danced (5)

1Sm 18:6 They sang and **d**, joyful music,
2Sm 6:14 Wearing a linen ephod, David **d**
1Ki 18:26 So they **d** around the altar they
Mat 14:6 Herodias' daughter **d** for his
Mar 6:22 daughter, came in and **d**.

dancers (1)

Psa 87:7 Singers and **d** will sing,

dances (4)

Jdg 21:21 come out to take part in the **d**,
1Sm 21:11 used to sing about in the **d**:
29:5 of whom people sing in **d**:
Job 41:22 and power **d** in front of it.

dancing (12)

Exo 15:20 **d** with tambourines,
32:19 he saw the calf and the **d**.
Jdg 11:34 She was **d** with tambourines in
21:23 from the women who were **d**
2Sm 6:16 saw King David leaping and **d**
1Ch 15:29 King David **d** and celebrating,
Psa 30:11 changed my sobbing into **d**.
149:3 them praise his name with **d**.
150:4 him with tambourines and **d**.
Jer 31:4 will go **d** with happy people.
Lam 5:15 Our **d** has turned into mourning.
Luk 15:25 he heard music and **d**.

danger (7)

Jnh 1:4 ship was in **d** of breaking up.
Luk 8:23 and they were in **d**.
Act 19:27 There's a **d** that people will
19:27 and there's a **d** that people will
Rom 8:35 hunger, nakedness, **d**,
1Co 15:30 putting ourselves in **d**?
Heb 6:8 it is worthless and in **d** of being

dangerous (7)

Lev 26:6 I will remove **d** animals,
Dtr 1:19 that vast and **d** desert you saw
8:15 through that vast and **d** desert
Pro 14:25 but one who tells lies is **d**.
Ecc 10:13 saying crazy things that are **d**.
Mat 8:28 because the men were so **d**.
Act 27:9 Sailing was now **d**,

dangers (3)

Ecc 12:5 afraid of heights and of **d** along
2Co 11:26 I've faced **d** from raging rivers,
11:26 I've faced **d** in the city,

dangle (1)

Job 28:4 In this shaft men **d** and

dangling (1)

Sos 7:5 Your **d** curls are royal beauty.

Daniel (84)

1Ch 3:1 The second was **D**,
Ezr 8:2 from the family of Ithamar: **D**
Neh 10:6 **D**, Ginnethon, Baruch,
Eze 14:14 if these three men — Noah, **D**,
14:16 LORD, not even Noah, **D**,
14:18 LORD, not even Noah, **D**,
14:20 even Noah, **D**, and Job could,
28:3 think that you are wiser than **D**
Dan 1:6 **D**, Hananiah, Mishael,
1:7 To **D** he gave the name
1:8 **D** made up his mind not to
1:9 and compassionate toward **D**.
1:10 The chief-of-staff told **D**,
1:11 put a supervisor in charge of **D**,
1:11 **D** said to the supervisor,
1:17 **D** could also understand all
1:19 them and found no one like **D**,
1:21 **D** served the royal palace until
2:13 some men were sent to find **D**
2:14 **D** spoke to him using shrewd
2:15 explained everything to **D**.
2:16 **D** went and asked the king to
2:17 Then **D** went home and told his
2:19 The secret was revealed to **D**
2:19 So **D** praised the God of
2:24 Then **D** went to Arioch,
2:24 **D** told him, "Don't destroy
2:25 Arioch immediately took **D** to
2:26 The king asked **D** (who had
2:27 **D** answered the king,
2:46 on the ground in front of **D**.
2:46 and offerings be given to **D**.
2:47 The king said to **D**,
2:48 Then the king promoted **D** and
Dan 2:48 Nebuchadnezzar made **D**
2:49 **D** appointed Shadrach,
2:49 But **D** stayed at the king's court.
4:8 Finally, **D** came to me.
4:19 Then **D** (who had been
5:12 This **D** (who had been renamed
5:12 Now, call **D**, and he will tell
5:13 So **D** was taken to the king.
5:13 king asked him, "Are you **D**,
5:17 **D** told the king, "Keep your
5:29 Belshazzar ordered that **D**
5:29 He made **D** the third-highest
6:2 **D** was one of these officials.
6:3 This man, **D**, The king thought
6:4 to find something to accuse **D**
6:5 to accuse this man, **D**,
6:10 When **D** learned that the
6:11 as a group and found **D** praying
6:13 They replied, "Your Majesty, **D**,
6:14 he could think of to save **D**.
6:16 and **D** was brought to him and
6:16 The king told **D**, "May your
6:20 near the den where **D** was,
6:20 the king called to **D** with
6:20 "**D**, servant of the living God!
6:21 **D** said to the king,
6:23 overjoyed and had **D** taken out
6:23 When **D** was taken out of the
6:24 had brought charges against **D**
6:27 He saved **D** from the lions.
6:28 This man, **D**, prospered during
7:1 of Babylon, **D** had a dream.
7:2 In my visions at night I, **D**,
7:15 I, **D**, was deeply troubled,
7:28 I, **D**, was terrified by my
8:1 as king, I, **D**, saw a vision.
8:15 Now as I, **D**, watched the
8:27 I, **D**, was exhausted and sick
9:2 In the first year of his reign, I, **D**,
9:22 He informed me, "**D**,
10:1 a message was revealed to **D**
10:1 **D** understood the message
10:2 During those days I, **D**,
10:7 I, **D**, was the only one who
10:11 The man said to me, "**D**,
10:12 He told me, "Don't be afraid, **D**.
12:4 "But you, **D**, keep these words
12:5 When I, **D**, looked up, I saw
12:9 He replied, "Go, **D**.
Mat 24:15 "The prophet **D** said that the

Daniel's (3)

Dan 6:15 Then **D** accusers gathered in
6:17 so that **D** situation could not be
6:26 with terror in front of **D** God,

Danites (1)

Eze 27:19 "'**D** and Greeks from Uzal

Dan Jaan (1)

2Sm 24:6 to Tahtim Hodshi and then to **D**

Dannah (1)

Jos 15:49 **D**, Kiriath Sannah (now called

Dan's (4)

Num 2:31 the men in **D** camp is 157,600.
10:25 **D** descendants broke camp last
Jos 19:47 **D** descendants went up and
Jdg 18:30 were priests for **D** tribe until

Dara (1)

1Ch 2:6 and **D** — five in all.

Darda (1)

1Ki 4:31 Calcol, or **D**, Mahol's sons.

dare (9)

1Ki 9:6 if you and your descendants **d**
Neh 13:17 How **d** you treat the day of
Job 10:15 I **d** not lift up my head.
Psa 50:16 "How **d** you quote my decrees
Jer 30:21 Who would **d** to come near
Act 7:32 began to tremble and didn't **d**
1Co 6:1 how **d** you go to court to settle
2Co 11:21 Whatever other people **d** to

Jud 1:9 But Michael didn't **d** to hand

dared (8)

Num 16:1 and On (son of Peleth) **d** to
Jos 10:21 Not a single person **d** to speak
Est 7:5 person who has **d** to do this?"
Mat 22:46 and from that time on no one **d**
Mar 12:34 After that, no one **d** to ask him
Luk 20:40 From that time on, no one **d** to
Jon 21:12 None of the disciples **d** to ask
Act 5:13 None of the other people **d** to

dares (3)

Gen 49:9 Who **d** to disturb him?
Num 24:9 Who **d** to disturb them?
Dtr 18:20 But any prophet who **d** to say

Darius (17)

Ezr 4:5 the reign of King **D** of Persia.
5:5 be stopped until **D** received
5:6 of that river) sent to King **D**.
5:7 the following report: To King **D**,
6:1 Then King **D** gave the order to
6:12 I, **D**, have issued a decree.
6:13 what King **D** had ordered.
6:14 had ordered and as Cyrus, **D**,
Neh 12:22 until the reign of **D** the Persian.
Dan 5:31 **D** the Mede took over the
6:1 **D** decided it would be good to
6:6 "May King **D** live forever!
6:9 So **D** signed the written decree.
6:25 Then King **D** wrote to the
6:28 prospered during the reign of **D**
9:1 Xerxes' son **D**, who was a
11:1 During **D** the Mede's first year

Darius' (8)

Ezr 4:24 until **D** second year as king
6:15 in the sixth year of King **D** reign
Hag 1:1 in **D** second year as king,
1:15 in **D** second year as king.
2:10 in **D** second year as king,
Zec 1:1 the eighth month of **D** second
1:7 in **D** second year as king,
7:1 in **D** fourth year as king,

dark (102)

Gen 15:17 had gone down, and it was **d**.
Exo 20:21 to the **d** cloud where God
Dtr 4:11 It was **d**, cloudy, and gloomy.
Jos 2:5 When it was **d** and the gate
2Sm 22:10 down with a **d** cloud under his
22:12 He made the **d** rain clouds his
1Ki 8:12 said he would live in a **d** cloud.
2Ch 2:7 purple, **d** red, and violet cloth.
2:14 and **d** red cloth, and linen.
3:14 and **d** red cloth and of linen and
6:1 said he would live in a **d** cloud.
Job 3:5 Let a **d** cloud hang over it.
3:9 Let its stars turn **d** before dawn.
6:16 They are **d** with ice.
12:25 They grope in the **d** with no
15:22 believe he'll return from the **d**.
16:16 and **d** shadows encircle my
18:6 The light in his tent becomes **d**,
18:18 driven from the light into the **d**
19:8 He has made my paths **d**.
22:13 from behind a **d** cloud?
23:17 But I am not silenced by the **d**
24:16 In the **d**, they break into
26:10 boundary where light meets **d**.
29:3 through the **d** in his light.
30:28 I walk in the **d** without the sun.
30:30 My skin turns **d** and peels.
38:9 and wrapped it up in **d** clouds,
Psa 11:2 shoot in the **d** at people whose
18:9 down with a **d** cloud under his
18:11 the **d** rain clouds his covering.
23:4 I walk through the **d** valley
35:6 Let their path be **d** and slippery
74:20 because every **d** corner
82:5 As they walk around in the **d**,
88:6 of the pit — in deep, **d** places.
88:12 your miracles in that **d** place
91:6 plagues that roam the **d**,
105:28 and made ⌊their land⌋ **d**.
Psa 107:10 Those who lived in the **d**,
107:14 He brought them out of the **d**,
112:4 Light will shine in the **d** for a
139:12 darkness is not too **d** for you.
143:3 He has made me live in **d**
Pro 7:9 in the **d** hours of the night.
31:15 She wakes up while it is still **d**
Ecc 2:14 but a fool walks in the **d**.
11:8 there will be many **d** days.
12:2 and the stars turn **d**,
Sos 1:5 I am **d** and lovely like Kedar's
1:6 at me because I am so **d**.
Isa 1:18 Though they are **d** red,
13:10 The sun will be **d** when it rises.
16:3 your shadow as **d** as night.
29:15 Their deeds are done in the **d**,
45:3 I will give you treasures from **d**
45:19 privately or in some **d** corner
47:5 Go into the **d**, and sit in
58:10 then your light will rise in the **d**,
Jer 13:16 your God before it gets **d**,
23:12 like slippery paths in the **d**.
23:12 and they will fall down in the **d**.
Eze 12:6 and carry them out in the **d**.
12:7 I brought out my bags in the **d**.
12:12 shoulders in the **d** and leave.
30:18 the day will turn **d** when
Dan 2:22 He knows what is in the **d**,
Joe 2:10 The sun and the moon turn **d**,
2:31 The sun will become **d**,
3:15 sun and the moon will turn **d**.
Mic 3:6 and the day will turn **d** for them.
7:8 Although I sit in the **d**,
Mat 6:23 is darkness, how **d** it will be!
10:27 what I say to you in the **d**.
24:29 the sun will turn **d**,
Mar 13:24 the sun will turn **d**,
Luk 1:79 light to those who live in the **d**
12:3 you have said in the **d** will
Jon 1:5 The light shines in the **d**,
1:5 and the **d** has never
3:19 Yet, people loved the **d** rather
6:17 By this time it was **d**,
8:12 and will never live in the **d**."
12:35 Those who walk in the **d** don't
12:46 in me will not live in the **d**.
20:1 while it was still **d**,
Act 2:20 The sun will become **d**,
Rom 2:19 a light to those in the **d**,
13:12 the things that belong to the **d**
1Co 4:5 to light what is hidden in the **d**
Eph 4:18 because they are in the **d**.
5:8 Once you lived in the **d**,
1Th 5:4 you don't live in the **d**.
5:5 light not to the night and the **d**.
2Pe 1:19 that shines in a **d** place as you
1Jn 1:6 with God" and yet live in the **d**,
2:9 other believers are still in the **d**.
2:11 hate other believers are in the **d**
2:11 are in the dark and live in the **d**.
2:11 because they can't see in the **d**.
Rev 8:12 that one-third of them turned **d**.
16:10 Its kingdom turned **d**.

darken (3)

Eze 32:7 cover the sky and **d** the stars.
32:8 I will **d** all the lights shining in
Amo 8:9 the sun go down at noon and **d**

darkened (2)

Isa 5:30 light will be **d** by thick clouds.
Rev 9:2 The smoke **d** the sun and the

darker (2)

Gen 49:12 His eyes are **d** than wine.
1Ki 18:45 Gradually, the sky grew **d** with

darkest (1)

Pro 7:27 leads to the **d** vaults of death.

darkness (108)

Gen 1:2 and **d** covered the deep water.
1:4 separated the light from the **d**.
1:5 and the **d** he named night.
1:18 to separate the light from the **d**.
15:12 deep **d** — came over Abram.
Exo 10:21 and a **d** ⌊so thick⌋ that it can
10:22 there was total **d** for three days.
14:20 was there when **d** came,
Dtr 5:22 the cloud, and the gloomy **d**.
5:23 the voice coming from the **d**
Jos 24:7 he put **d** between you and the
1Sm 2:9 people are silenced in **d**
2Sm 22:12 He surrounded himself with **d**.
22:29 The LORD turns my **d** into light.
Job 3:5 Let the **d** and long shadows
5:14 In the daytime they meet **d** and
10:21 away to a land of **d** and gloom,
10:22 where light is as bright as **d**.
11:17 The **d** in your life will become
12:22 mysteries ⌊hidden⌋ in the **d**
15:24 "The day of **d** troubles him.
15:30 "He won't escape the **d**.
17:12 Light has nearly become **d**.
17:13 and make my bed in the **d**,
20:26 Total **d** waits in hiding for his
22:11 ⌊That is why⌋ **d** surrounds you
23:17 or by the thick **d** that covers my
24:17 because morning and deep **d**
24:17 with the terrors of deep **d**.
28:3 ⌊Humans⌋ bring an end to **d**
30:26 When I looked for light, **d** came.
34:22 There's no **d** or deep shadow
37:19 prepare ⌊a case⌋ because of **d**.
38:17 seen the gateways to total **d**?
38:19 Where is the home of **d**
Psa 18:11 He made the **d** his hiding place,
18:28 My God turns my **d** into light.
88:18 **D** is my only friend!
97:2 Clouds and **d** surround him.
104:20 He brings **d**, and it is nighttime,
105:28 He sent **d** and made ⌊their
139:11 If I say, "Let the **d** hide me and
139:12 even the **d** is not too dark for
139:12 **D** and light are the same ⌊to
Pro 2:13 to walk the ways of **d**,
4:19 wicked people is like deep **d**.
20:20 will be snuffed out in total **d**.
Ecc 2:13 light has an advantage over **d**.
5:17 spend their entire lives in **d**,
6:4 birth and goes out into the **d**.
6:4 The **d** then hides its name.
Isa 5:20 who turn **d** into light and light
5:20 into light and light into **d**,
5:30 will see only **d** and distress.
8:22 in anguish and be forced into **d**.
9:2 The people who walk in **d** will
29:18 see out of their gloom and **d**.
42:7 who live in **d** out of dungeons.
42:16 I will turn **d** into light in front of
45:7 I make light and create **d**.
49:9 and to those who are in **d**,
50:3 I clothe the heavens in **d** and
50:10 Let those who walk in **d** and
58:10 and your **d** will become as
59:9 hope for light, but we walk in **d**.
60:2 **D** now covers the earth,
60:2 and thick **d** covers the nations.
Jer 2:31 a land of thick **d**, for Israel?
13:16 and change it into deep **d**.
Lam 3:2 me walk in **d** instead of light.
3:6 He has made me live in **d**,
Eze 32:8 I will bring **d** over your land,
Joe 2:2 It is a day of **d** and gloom,
Amo 5:8 He turns deep **d** into dawn.
5:18 LORD is one of **d** and not light.
5:20 The day of the LORD brings **d**
Mic 3:6 will have **d** without revelations.
Nah 1:8 will pursue his enemies with **d**.
Zep 1:15 a day of **d** and gloom,
Mat 4:16 The people who lived in **d**
6:23 whole body will be full of **d**.
6:23 If the light in you is **d**,
8:12 be thrown outside into the **d**.
22:13 throw him outside into the **d**.
25:30 servant outside into the **d**.
27:45 At noon **d** came over the whole
Mar 15:33 At noon **d** came over the whole
Luk 11:34 your body is full of **d**.
11:35 that the light in you isn't **d**.
11:36 body is full of light and not **d**,
22:53 this is your time, when **d** rules."

Luk 23:44 Around noon **d** came over the
Jon 12:35 light so that **d** won't defeat you.
Act 26:18 their eyes and turn them from **d**
Rom 1:21 minds were plunged into **d**.
2Co 4:6 should shine out of **d** has given
6:14 anything in common with **d**?
Eph 5:11 useless works that **d** produces.
6:12 who govern this world of **d**,
Col 1:13 rescued us from the power of **d**
Heb 12:18 fire, to **d**, to gloom, to a storm,
1Pe 2:9 who called you out of **d** into his
2Pe 2:4 secured them with chains of **d**
2:17 Gloomy **d** has been kept for
1Jn 1:5 and there isn't any **d** in him.
2:8 and in you: The **d** is fading,
Jud 1:6 They were held in **d**,
1:13 whom gloomy **d** is kept forever.

Darkon (2)

Ezr 2:56 Jaalah, **D**, Giddel,
Neh 7:58 Jaala, **D**, Giddel,

dart (2)

Job 41:26 Neither will a spear, lance, or **d**.
Nah 2:4 like lightning, as they **d** about.

darting (2)

Pro 7:23 like a bird **d** into a trap.
26:2 sparrow, like a **d** swallow,

date (5)

2Sm 6:19 one loaf of bread, one **d** cake,
1Ch 16:3 a **d** cake, and a raisin cake.
Ezr 6:3 **D**: Cyrus' first year as king
Neh 2:6 When I gave him a specific **d**,
Eze 24:2 write down today's **d**.

dates (1)

1Th 5:1 write to you about times and **d**.

Dathan (11)

Num 16:1 **D** and Abiram (sons of Eliab),
16:1 **D**, Abiram, and On were
16:12 Moses sent for **D** and Abiram,
16:24 tents of Korah, **D**, and Abiram."
16:25 up and went to **D** and Abiram,
16:27 tents of Korah, **D**, and Abiram.
16:27 **D** and Abiram had come out
26:9 and Nemuel, **D**, and Abiram
26:9 (It was **D** and Abiram,
Dtr 11:6 what he did to **D** and Abiram,
Psa 106:17 split open and swallowed **D**.

daughter (210)

Gen 11:29 wife was Milcah, **d** of Haran.
19:31 The older **d** said to the younger
19:34 The next day the older **d** said
19:38 The younger **d** also gave birth
20:12 she is my sister — my father's **d**
24:15 She was the **d** of Bethuel,
24:23 He asked, "Whose **d** are you?
24:24 "I'm the **d** of Bethuel,
24:47 'Whose **d** are you?'
24:47 answered, 'The **d** of Bethuel,
24:48 the right direction to get the **d**
25:20 **d** of Bethuel the Aramean from
26:34 **d** of Beeri the Hittite.
26:34 **d** of Elon the Hittite.
28:9 **d** of Abraham's son Ishmael
29:6 "Here comes his **d** Rachel with
29:10 **d** of his uncle Laban,
29:18 for your younger **d** Rachel."
29:23 In the evening he took his **d**
29:24 Zilpah to his **d** Leah as her
29:26 younger **d** ⌊in marriage⌋ before
29:27 wedding festivities with this **d**.
29:28 Then Laban gave his **d** Rachel
29:29 Bilhah to his **d** Rachel as her
30:21 Later she gave birth to a **d** and
34:1 Dinah, **d** of Leah and Jacob,
34:3 very fond of Jacob's **d** Dinah.
34:5 had dishonored his **d** Dinah.
34:7 family by raping Jacob's **d**.
34:8 has his heart set on your **d**.
34:17 we'll take our **d** and go."
34:19 such pleasure in Jacob's **d**.
Gen 36:2 **d** of Elon the Hittite;
36:2 **d** of Anah and granddaughter of
36:3 also Basemath, **d** of Ishmael
36:14 **d** of Anah and granddaughter of
36:18 wife Oholibamah, Anah's **d**.
36:25 and Oholibamah, **d** of Anah.
36:39 **d** of Matred and granddaughter
38:2 There Judah met the **d** of a
38:12 wife, the **d** of Shua, died.
41:45 She was the **d** of Potiphera,
41:50 by Asenath, **d** of Potiphera,
46:15 in addition to his **d** Dinah.
46:18 Laban gave to his **d** Leah.
46:20 by Asenath, **d** of Potiphera,
46:25 Laban gave to his **d** Rachel.
Exo 2:5 While Pharaoh's **d** came to the
2:6 Pharaoh's **d** opened the basket,
2:7 sister asked Pharaoh's **d**,
2:9 Pharaoh's **d** said to the woman,
2:10 she brought him to Pharaoh's **d**,
2:10 Pharaoh's **d** named him Moses
2:21 So Reuel gave his **d** Zipporah
6:23 Aaron married Elisheba, **d** of
21:7 a man sells his **d** into slavery,
21:9 he must treat her like a **d**.
21:31 bull gores someone's son or **d**,
Lev 18:9 whether she is your father's **d**
18:9 daughter or your mother's **d**.
18:10 whether she is your son's **d** or
18:10 daughter or your daughter's **d**,
18:11 sexual intercourse with a **d**
18:17 with a woman and her **d**
19:29 "Never dishonor your **d** by
20:17 his father's **d** or his mother's
20:17 daughter or his mother's **d**,
21:2 father, son, **d**, or brother,
21:9 When a priest's **d** dishonors
22:12 if a priest's **d** marries a layman,
22:13 If a priest's **d** is widowed or
24:10 was Shelomith (**d** of Dibri,
Num 25:15 was killed was Cozbi, **d** of Zur.
25:18 **d** of a Midianite leader,
26:46 (Asher had a **d** named Serah.)
Dtr 13:6 Your own brother, son, or **d**,
22:15 that their **d** was a virgin.
22:16 "I gave my **d** in marriage to this
22:17 He says he found out that my **d**
27:22 with his sister, his father's **d**,
27:22 or his mother's **d** will be
28:56 or toward her own son or **d**.
Jos 15:16 Caleb said, "I will give my **d**
15:17 So Caleb gave him his **d**
Jdg 1:12 Caleb said, "I will give my **d**
1:13 So Caleb gave him his **d**
11:34 he saw his **d** coming out to
11:35 in grief and said, "Oh no, **D**!
11:40 praises of the **d** of Jephthah,
19:24 let me bring out my virgin **d**
Rut 2:2 Naomi told her, "Go, my **d**."
2:8 said to Ruth, "Listen, my **d**.
2:22 Ruth, "It's a good idea, my **d**,
3:1 said to her, "My **d**,
3:10 the LORD bless you, my **d**.
3:11 Don't be afraid, my **d**.
3:16 "How did things go, my **d**?"
3:18 replied, "Stay here, my **d**,
1Sm 14:49 were Merab (the firstborn **d**)
14:49 and Michal (the younger **d**).
14:50 Ahinoam, the **d** of Ahimaaz.
17:25 He will give his **d** to that man
18:17 "Here is my oldest **d** Merab.
18:19 came to give Saul's **d** Merab
18:20 However, Saul's **d** Michal fell
18:27 Then Saul gave him his **d**
18:28 that his **d** Michal loved David.
25:44 Saul had given his **d** Michal,
2Sm 3:3 mother was Maacah (the **d**
3:7 named Rizpah (Aiah's **d**).
3:13 Saul's **d**, when you come."
6:16 Saul's **d** Michal looked out of a
6:20 Saul's **d** Michal came out to
6:23 So Saul's **d** Michal was
11:3 **d** of Eliam and wife of Uriah the
12:3 in his arms and was like a **d**.
14:27 had three sons and one **d**.
14:27 His **d** Tamar was a beautiful
2Sm 17:25 His mother was Abigail, the **d**
21:8 Rizpah (Aiah's **d**) gave birth
21:8 Merab (Saul's **d**) gave birth
21:10 Rizpah (Aiah's **d**) took
21:11 Rizpah (Aiah's **d**) had done,
1Ki 3:1 After marrying Pharaoh's **d**,
4:11 (Solomon's **d** Taphath was his
4:15 (He also married Solomon's **d**
7:8 this for his wife, Pharaoh's **d**.
9:16 Then he gave it to his **d**,
9:24 Pharaoh's **d** moved from the
11:1 in addition to Pharaoh's **d**.
15:2 Maacah, **d** of Abishalom.
15:10 Maacah, **d** of Abishalom.
16:31 **d** of King Ethbaal of Sidon.
22:42 name was Azubah, **d** of Shilhi.
2Ki 8:18 his wife was Ahab's **d**.
9:34 After all, she was a king's **d**."
11:2 But Jehosheba, **d** of King
14:9 'Let your **d** marry my son,'
15:33 was Jerusha, **d** of Zadok.
18:2 was Abi, **d** of Zechariah.
21:19 **d** of Haruz from Jotbah.
22:1 **d** of Adaiah from Bozkath.
23:31 **d** of Jeremiah from Libnah.
23:36 **d** of Pedaiah from Rumah.
24:8 **d** of Elnathan from Jerusalem.
24:18 **d** of Jeremiah from Libnah.
1Ch 1:50 **d** of Matred and granddaughter
2:21 slept with the **d** of Machir,
2:49 Caleb's **d** was Achsah.
3:2 ⌊born⌋ to Maacah (the **d** of
3:5 was Ammiel's **d** Bathshua) and
7:24 Beriah's **d** was Sheerah,
15:29 Saul's **d** Michal looked out of a
2Ch 8:11 Solomon brought Pharaoh's **d**
11:18 Mahalath, **d** of Jerimoth.
11:18 Abihail was the **d** of Eliab,
13:2 **d** of Uriel from Gibeah.
20:31 name was Azubah, **d** of Shilhi.
21:6 his wife was Ahab's **d**.
22:11 But Jehoshebath, **d** of the king
22:11 Jehoshebath was the **d** of King
25:18 'Let your **d** marry my son,'
27:1 was Jerushah, **d** of Zadok.
29:1 was Abijah, **d** of Zechariah.
Neh 6:18 married the **d** of Meshullam,
Est 2:7 known as Esther, his uncle's **d**,
2:7 adopted her as his own **d**.
2:15 (Esther was the **d** of Abihail,
2:15 had adopted her as his own **d**.)
9:29 Abihail's **d** Queen Esther and
Job 42:14 named the first ⌊**d**⌋ Jemimah,
Psa 45:10 Listen, **d**! Look closely! Turn
45:13 The **d** of the king is glorious
Sos 7:1 feet in their sandals, noble **d**!
Jer 52:1 **d** of Jeremiah from Libnah.
Eze 16:44 you: Like mother, like **d**.
16:45 You are your mother's **d**.
44:25 **d**, brother, or unmarried sister.
Dan 11:6 The southern king's **d** will go to
11:17 give the southern king his **d** as
Hos 1:3 married Gomer, **d** of Diblaim.
1:6 pregnant again and had a **d**.
Mic 4:10 **D** of Zion, writhe in pain and
7:6 A **d** rebels against her mother.
Mat 9:18 and said, "My **d** just died.
9:22 saw her he said, "Cheer up, **d**!
10:35 a **d** against her mother,
10:37 loves a son or **d** more than me
14:6 Herodias' **d** danced for his
15:22 My **d** is tormented by a demon."
15:28 that moment her **d** was cured.
Mar 5:23 "My little **d** is dying.
5:34 Jesus told her, "**D**,
5:35 leader, "Your **d** has died.
6:22 His **d**, that is, came in and
6:22 daughter, that is, Herodias' **d**,
7:25 A woman whose little **d** had an
7:26 to force the demon out of her **d**.
7:29 The demon has left your **d**."
Luk 8:42 His only **d**, who was about
8:48 Jesus told her, "**D**,
8:49 He said, "Your **d** is dead.
12:53 A mother will be against her **d**
12:53 and a **d** against her mother.

Act 7:21 Pharaoh's **d** adopted him and
1Co 7:36 when his virgin **d** is old enough
7:37 come to a decision about his **d**.
7:38 father to give his **d** in marriage,
7:38 father who doesn't give his **d**
Heb 11:24 known as a son of Pharaoh's **d**.

daughter-in-law (16)

Gen 11:31 (son of Haran), and his **d** Sarai,
38:11 Judah said to his **d** Tamar,
38:16 he didn't know she was his **d**,
38:24 "Your **d** Tamar has been acting
Lev 18:15 sexual intercourse with your **d**.
20:12 sexual intercourse with his **d**,
Rut 1:22 of Moab, Ruth, her Moabite **d**,
2:20 Naomi said to her **d**,
2:22 Naomi told her **d** Ruth,
4:15 Your **d** who loves you is better
1Sm 4:19 His **d**, Phinehas' wife,
1Ch 2:4 Tamar, Judah's **d**, gave birth to
Mic 7:6 A **d** rebels against her
Mat 10:35 a **d** against her mother-in-law.
Luk 12:53 will be against her **d**
12:53 a **d** against her mother-in-law."

daughter's (1)

Lev 18:10 daughter or your **d** daughter,

daughters (208)

Gen 5:4 and had other sons and **d**.
5:7 and had other sons and **d**.
5:10 and had other sons and **d**.
5:13 and had other sons and **d**.
5:16 and had other sons and **d**.
5:19 and had other sons and **d**.
5:22 and had other sons and **d**.
5:26 and had other sons and **d**.
5:30 and had other sons and **d**.
6:1 and **d** were born to them.
6:2 The sons of God saw that the **d**
6:4 sons of God slept with the **d**
11:11 and had other sons and **d**.
11:13 and had other sons and **d**.
11:15 and had other sons and **d**.
11:17 and had other sons and **d**.
11:19 and had other sons and **d**.
11:21 and had other sons and **d**.
11:23 and had other sons and **d**.
11:25 and had other sons and **d**.
19:8 "Look, I have two **d** who have
19:12 here — any in-laws, sons, **d**,
19:14 to the men engaged to his **d**.
19:15 Take your wife and your two **d**
19:16 and his two **d** by their hands,
19:30 He and his two **d** settled in the
19:36 So Lot's two **d** became
24:3 get my son a wife from the **d**
24:37 get a wife for my son from the **d**
28:2 a wife from there from the **d**
29:16 Laban had two **d**. The name of
31:26 You've carried off my **d** like
31:28 my grandchildren and my **d**.
31:31 I thought you would take your **d**
31:41 for you 14 years for your two **d**
31:43 Jacob, "These are my **d**,
31:43 what can I do today for my **d** or
31:50 If you mistreat my **d** or marry
31:55 his grandchildren and his **d**
34:9 with us; give your **d** to us,
34:16 Then we'll give our **d** to you
34:21 We can marry their **d** and let
36:6 took his wives, his sons, his **d**,
37:35 All his other sons and **d** came
46:7 his sons, his grandsons, his **d**,
46:15 of these sons and **d** was 33.
Exo 2:16 seven **d** of the priest of Midian
2:20 Reuel asked his **d**,
3:22 Put them on your sons and **d**.
6:25 married one of the **d** of Putiel.
10:9 young and old, our sons and **d**,
20:10 You, your sons, your **d**,
21:4 she gives birth to sons or **d**,
32:2 and **d** take off the gold earrings
34:16 will end up marrying their **d**.
34:16 When their **d** chase after their
Lev 10:14 You and your sons and **d** may
Lev 26:29 the bodies of your sons and **d**.
Num 18:11 to you, your sons, and your **d**.
18:19 and your **d** all the holy
21:29 he let his **d** become prisoners
26:33 had no sons — only **d**.
27:1 The **d** of Zelophehad,
27:7 "Zelophehad's **d** are right.
27:8 turn his property over to his **d**.
27:9 If he has no **d**, give his property
30:16 and for fathers with young **d**
36:2 relative Zelophehad to his **d**.
36:6 commands for Zelophehad's **d**:
36:10 Zelophehad's **d** did as the
Dtr 5:14 You, your sons, your **d**,
7:3 Never let your **d** marry their
7:3 or your sons marry their **d**.
12:12 **d**, male and female slaves,
12:18 Instead, you, your sons and **d**,
12:31 their sons and **d** as sacrifices
16:11 **d**, male and female slaves,
16:14 **d**, male and female slaves,
18:10 your sons or **d** by burning them
28:32 as your sons and **d** are given
28:41 You will have sons and **d**,
28:53 own children, the sons and **d**,
32:19 because his own sons and **d**
Jos 7:24 gold, his sons and **d**, his cattle,
17:3 had no sons — only **d**.
17:6 Manasseh's **d** were given
Jdg 3:6 allowed their sons and **d**
11:34 had no other sons or **d**.
12:9 He had 30 sons and 30 **d**.
12:9 His sons and **d** married people
21:1 "None of us will ever let our **d**
21:7 not let any of our **d** marry
21:18 them any of our **d** as wives.
Rut 1:11 Naomi said, "Go back, my **d**.
1:12 Go back, my **d**. Go, because I
1:13 No, my **d**. My bitterness is
1Sm 1:4 and all her sons and **d**.
2:21 and had three sons and two **d**.
8:13 He will take your **d** and have
14:49 The names of his two **d** were
30:3 and **d** had been taken captive.
30:6 thinking of their sons and **d**.
30:19 young or old, sons or **d**,
2Sm 1:20 or the **d** of the Philistines will
1:20 and the **d** of godless men will
1:24 **D** of Israel, cry over Saul,
5:13 he fathered more sons and **d**.
13:18 The king's virgin **d** wore this
19:5 lives of your sons, **d**, wives,
2Ki 17:17 sons and **d** by burning them
23:10 their sons or **d** by burning them
1Ch 2:34 had no sons, but he had **d**.
2:35 let Jarha marry one of his **d**.
4:27 Shimei had 16 sons and 6 **d**.
7:15 Zelophehad had only **d**.
14:3 and fathered more sons and **d**.
23:22 He only had **d**. Their cousins,
25:5 gave Heman 14 sons and 3 **d**.)
2Ch 11:21 He fathered 28 sons and 60 **d**.)
13:21 and fathered 22 sons and 16 **d**.
24:3 and Joash had sons and **d**.
29:9 killed in battle, and our sons, **d**,
31:18 with their wives, sons, **d**,
Ezr 2:61 (who had married one of the **d**
9:12 So never let your **d** marry their
9:12 or your sons marry their **d**,
Neh 3:12 repairs with the help of his **d**.
4:14 your sons, your **d**, your wives,
5:5 have to force our sons and **d**
5:5 Some of our **d** have already
7:63 (who had married one of the **d**
10:28 Their wives, sons, **d**,
10:30 We will not allow our **d** to
10:30 of the land or allow their **d**
13:25 "We won't allow our **d** to marry
13:25 and we won't allow their **d** to
Job 1:2 He had seven sons and three **d**.
1:13 Job's sons and **d** were eating
1:18 "Your sons and your **d** were
42:13 had seven sons and three **d**.
42:15 were as beautiful as Job's **d**.
Psa 45:9 The **d** of kings are among your
106:37 their sons and **d** to demons.
Psa 106:38 and **d** whom they sacrificed
144:12 May our **d** be like stately
Pro 30:15 leech has two **d** — "Give!"
Isa 16:2 Moab's **d** are like fluttering
23:4 I've brought up no **d**."
32:9 you overconfident **d**.
43:6 from far away and my **d** from
49:22 carry your **d** on their shoulders.
56:5 better than sons and **d**.
60:4 Your **d** are carried in their arms.
Jer 3:24 and herds, their sons and **d**.
5:17 devour your sons and your **d**.
7:31 their sons and **d** as sacrifices.
9:20 Teach your **d** how to cry.
11:22 Their sons and **d** will die
14:16 wives, their sons, or their **d**.
16:2 any sons or **d** in this place!
16:3 says about the sons and **d** born
19:9 the flesh of their sons and **d**.
29:6 and have sons and **d**.
29:6 and let your **d** get married so
29:6 that they can have sons and **d**.
32:35 their sons and **d** to Molech.
35:8 with our wives, sons, and **d**,
41:10 He captured the king's **d** and all
43:6 children, and the king's **d**.
48:46 and your **d** will be taken away
Eze 14:16 rescue their own sons or **d**.
14:18 could rescue their sons or **d**.
14:20 rescue their sons or **d**.
14:22 Some of your sons and **d** will
16:20 "You took your sons and **d**,
16:46 She and her **d** lived north of
16:46 lives south of you with her **d**.
16:48 your sister Sodom and her **d**
16:48 you and your **d** have done.
16:49 She and her **d** were proud that
16:53 fortunes of Sodom and her **d**,
16:53 and Samaria and her **d**.
16:55 When Sodom and her **d** and
16:55 and Samaria and her **d** return
16:55 you and your **d** will return to
16:57 Now the **d** of Aram and their
16:57 The **d** of the Philistines also
16:61 I will give them to you as **d**,
22:11 their sisters, their father's **d**.
23:2 **d** of the same mother.
23:4 they gave birth to sons and **d**.
23:10 took away her sons and **d**,
23:25 will take your sons and your **d**
23:47 mob will kill their sons and **d**
24:21 So the sons and **d** that you left
24:25 take away their sons and **d**.
Hos 4:13 why your **d** become prostitutes,
4:14 Yet, I will not punish your **d**
Joe 2:28 Your sons and **d** will prophesy.
3:8 I will sell your sons and **d** to
Amo 7:17 and your sons and **d** will be
Act 2:17 Your sons and **d** will speak
21:9 Philip had four unmarried **d**
2Co 6:18 you will be my sons and **d**."
Heb 2:10 many sons and **d** to glory,
2:13 "I am here with the sons and **d**
2:14 Since all of these sons and **d**
1Pe 3:6 You became Sarah's **d** by not

daughters-in-law (7)

Gen 7:13 wife and his three **d** went into
Rut 1:6 Naomi and her **d** started on the
1:7 and her two **d** went with her.)
1:8 Then Naomi said to her two **d**,
Eze 22:11 men sexually dishonor their **d**.
Hos 4:13 and your **d** commit adultery.
4:14 or your **d** when they commit

David (960)

Rut 4:17 who was the father of **D**.
4:22 Jesse was the father of **D**.
1Sm 16:13 flask of olive oil and anointed **D**
16:13 The LORD's Spirit came over **D**
16:19 "Send me your son **D**,
16:20 them with his son **D** to Saul.
16:21 **D** came to Saul and served
16:21 and made **D** his armorbearer.
16:22 "Please let **D** stay with me
16:23 **D** took the lyre and strummed a

1Sm 17:12 **D** was a son of a man named
17:14 and **D** was the youngest.
17:15 **D** went back and forth from
17:17 Jesse told his son **D**,
17:20 **D** got up early in the morning
17:22 **D** left the supplies behind in
17:23 and **D** heard them.
17:26 **D** asked the men who were
17:27 The soldiers repeated ⌊to **D**⌋
17:28 heard **D** talking to the men.
17:28 Eliab became angry with **D**.
17:29 **D** snapped at him.
17:31 What **D** said was overheard
17:32 **D** told Saul, "No one should be
17:33 Saul responded to **D**,
17:34 **D** replied to Saul, "I am a
17:37 **D** added, "The LORD,
17:37 "Go," Saul told **D**, "and may
17:38 Saul put his battle tunic on **D**;
17:39 **D** fastened Saul's sword over
17:39 in these things," **D** told Saul.
17:39 So **D** took all those things off.
17:41 coming closer and closer to **D**.
17:42 Philistine got a good look at **D**,
17:42 After all, **D** was a young man
17:43 The Philistine asked **D**,
17:43 called on his gods to curse **D**.
17:44 on," the Philistine told **D**,
17:45 **D** told the Philistine,
17:48 **D** quickly ran toward the
17:49 Then **D** reached into his bag,
17:50 **D** proved to be stronger than
17:50 **D** struck down and killed the
17:50 even though **D** didn't have a
17:51 **D** ran and stood over the
17:54 **D** took the Philistine's head
17:55 As Saul watched **D** going out
17:57 When **D** returned from killing
17:57 **D** had the Philistine's head in
17:58 of Bethlehem," **D** answered.
18:1 **D** finished talking to Saul.
18:1 He loved **D** as much as ⌊he
18:2 (From that day on Saul kept **D**
18:3 pledge of mutual loyalty with **D**
18:4 had on and gave it to **D** along
18:5 **D** was successful wherever
18:6 As they arrived, **D** was
18:7 but **D** tens of thousands!"
18:8 "To **D** they credit tens of
18:8 thing left for **D** is my kingdom."
18:9 day on Saul kept an eye on **D**.
18:10 in his house while **D** strummed
18:11 "I'll nail **D** to the wall."
18:11 But **D** got away from him twice.
18:12 Saul was afraid of **D**,
18:12 because the LORD was with **D**
18:13 So he kept **D** away.
18:13 He made **D** captain of a
18:13 **D** led the troops out ⌊to battle⌋
18:16 in Israel and Judah loved **D**,
18:17 Finally, Saul said to **D**,
18:18 **D** asked Saul. "And how
18:19 Saul's daughter Merab to **D**,
18:20 Michal fell in love with **D**.
18:21 Saul thought, "I'll give her to **D**.
18:21 So he said to **D** a second time,
18:22 "Talk to **D** in private.
18:23 it a point to say this, **D** asked,
18:24 told Saul what **D** had said,
18:25 Saul replied, "Tell **D**,
18:25 Saul planned to have **D** fall into
18:26 When his officers told **D** this,
18:26 **D** concluded that it was
18:27 **D** and his men went out and
18:27 **D** brought the foreskins,
18:27 king so that **D** could become
18:28 that the LORD was with **D**
18:28 his daughter Michal loved **D**.
18:29 was even more afraid of **D**,
18:30 **D** was more successful than
18:30 So **D** gained a good reputation.
19:1 and all his officers to kill **D**.
19:1 Jonathan was very fond of **D**,
19:2 so he reported to **D**,
19:4 So Jonathan spoke well of **D** to
19:4 your servant **D**," he said.

1Sm 19:7 Jonathan told **D** all of this.
19:7 Then Jonathan took **D** to Saul.
19:7 So **D** was returned to his former
19:8 **D** went to fight the Philistines.
19:9 **D** was strumming a tune.
19:10 Saul tried to nail **D** to the wall
19:10 But **D** dodged it, and Saul's
19:10 **D** fled, escaping ⌊from Saul⌋
19:12 So Michal lowered **D** through a
19:14 Saul sent messengers to get **D**,
19:15 back to see **D** themselves.
19:18 **D** escaped and went to Samuel
19:19 reported to Saul that **D** was
19:20 Saul sent messengers to get **D**.
19:22 "Where are Samuel and **D**?"
20:1 **D** fled from the pastures at
20:3 But **D** took an oath,
20:4 Jonathan said to **D**,
20:5 **D** replied, "Tomorrow is the
20:6 '**D** repeatedly begged me to let
20:10 Then **D** asked, "Who will tell
20:17 Jonathan swore an oath to **D**
20:17 because of his love for **D**.
20:17 He loved **D** as much as ⌊he
20:24 So **D** hid in the countryside.
20:28 Jonathan answered Saul, "**D**
20:29 **D** said to me 'Please let me go.
20:33 father was determined to kill **D**.
20:34 He was worried sick about **D**
20:35 place he and **D** had agreed on.
20:39 but Jonathan and **D** understood.
20:41 When the boy had left, **D** came
20:41 but **D** cried the loudest.
20:42 Jonathan told **D**. "We have both
20:42 forever.'" So **D** left,
21:1 **D** went to the priest Ahimelech
21:1 trembling as he went to meet **D**.
21:1 he asked **D**. "Why is no one
21:2 **D** answered the priest
21:3 ⌊**D** added,⌋ "Now, what do you
21:4 the chief priest answered **D**.
21:5 **D** answered the priest,
21:8 **D** asked Ahimelech,
21:9 **D** said, "There's none like it.
21:10 That day **D** left. He was ⌊still⌋
21:11 officers asked, "Isn't this **D**,
21:11 but **D** tens of thousands.'"
21:12 When **D** realized what they had
22:1 So **D** escaped from that place
22:3 From there **D** went to Mizpah in
22:4 him as long as **D** was living
22:5 the prophet Gad told **D**.
22:5 So **D** went to the forest of
22:6 Saul heard that **D** and his men
22:8 has encouraged my servant **D**
22:10 prayed to the LORD for **D**
22:14 officials can you trust like **D**?
22:17 because they support **D**,"
22:17 they knew **D** was fleeing,
22:20 was Abiathar. He fled to **D**.
22:21 Abiathar told **D** that Saul had
22:22 **D** told Abiathar, "I knew that
23:1 **D** was asked, "Did you know
23:2 **D** asked the LORD,
23:2 "Go," the LORD told **D**,
23:4 **D** asked the LORD again,
23:5 **D** and his men went to Keilah,
23:5 So **D** rescued the people who
23:6 son Abiathar fled to **D** at Keilah,
23:7 When Saul was told that **D**
23:8 where **D** and his men were.
23:9 When **D** learned that Saul was
23:10 Then **D** said, "LORD God of
23:12 **D** asked. "They will hand you
23:13 So **D** and his men,
23:13 "**D** has escaped from Keilah!"
23:14 **D** lived in fortified camps in the
23:14 God didn't let him capture **D**.
23:15 **D** was afraid because Saul had
23:16 Jonathan came to **D** at Horesh.
23:17 "Don't be afraid," he told **D**,
23:18 **D** stayed in Horesh,
23:19 They said, "**D** is hiding with us
23:24 **D** and his men were in the
23:25 **D** was told the news.
23:25 about it and pursued **D** into

1Sm 23:26 and **D** and his men went on the
23:26 **D** was hurrying to get away
23:26 ⌊the mountain⌋ toward **D**
23:28 Saul gave up pursuing **D** and
23:29 From there **D** went to stay in
24:1 he was told "Now **D** is in the
24:2 Israel and went to search for **D**
24:3 ⌊it⌋ to relieve himself while **D**
24:4 think is right.'" **D** quietly got up
24:7 So **D** stopped his men by
24:8 Later, **D** got up, left the cave,
24:8 When Saul looked back, **D**
24:9 **D** asked Saul, "Why do you
24:16 When **D** finished saying this,
24:16 you speaking, my servant **D**?"
24:17 He told **D**, "You are more
24:22 So **D** swore to Saul.
24:22 Then Saul went home, and **D**
25:1 Then **D** went to the desert of
25:4 While **D** was in the desert,
25:5 So **D** sent ten young men and
25:8 Please give us and your son **D**
25:9 repeated all of this to him for **D**,
25:10 "Who is **D**?" Nabal answered
25:13 **D** told his men. And everyone,
25:13 And everyone, including **D**,
25:13 four hundred men went with **D**,
25:14 "**D** sent messengers from the
25:20 mountain path when she met **D**
25:21 **D** had thought, "I guarded this
25:23 When Abigail saw **D**,
25:23 bowed down in front of **D**
25:32 **D** said to Abigail, "Blessed be
25:35 Then **D** accepted what she
25:39 When **D** heard Nabal was dead,
25:39 Then **D** sent men ⌊on his
25:40 "**D** has sent us to you so that
25:43 **D** also married Ahinoam of
26:1 "**D** is hiding at the hill of
26:2 men to search for **D**.
26:3 but **D** stayed in the desert.
26:4 **D** sent spies to confirm that
26:5 Then **D** went to the place
26:5 **D** saw the place where Saul
26:6 **D** asked Ahimelech the Hittite
26:7 So **D** and Abishai went among
26:8 Abishai said to **D**, "Today God
26:9 **D** told Abishai. "No one has
26:10 as the LORD lives," **D** added,
26:12 **D** took the spear and the jar of
26:13 **D** went over to the other side
26:14 Then **D** called to the troops and
26:15 **D** asked Abner, "Aren't you a
26:17 that your voice, my servant **D**?"
26:17 Royal Majesty," **D** answered.
26:21 "My servant **D**," Saul said,
26:22 **D** responded, "Here's the king's
26:25 are you, my servant **D**.
26:25 So **D** went his way,
27:1 **D** said to himself, "One of
27:2 So **D** went with his 600 men to
27:3 **D** and his men stayed with
27:3 and **D** had his two wives,
27:4 When Saul was told that **D** had
27:5 **D** said to Achish, "If you will
27:7 **D** stayed in Philistine territory
27:8 Then **D** and his men went to
27:9 Whenever **D** attacked the
27:10 And **D** would answer,
27:12 And Achish believed **D**.
28:1 Then Achish said to **D**,
28:2 **D** responded to Achish,
28:2 "Very well," Achish told **D**,
28:17 it to your fellow Israelite **D**.
29:2 **D** and his men were marching
29:3 Philistine officers, "Isn't this **D**,
29:5 Isn't this **D** of whom people
29:5 but **D** tens of thousands'?"
29:6 Then Achish called **D** and told
29:8 **D** asked Achish. "What have
29:9 Achish answered **D**,
29:11 Early the next morning **D** and
30:1 Two days later, when **D** and
30:3 By the time **D** and his men
30:4 Then **D** and his men cried
30:6 **D** was in great distress

1Sm 30:6 But **D** found strength in the
30:7 **D** told the priest Abiathar,
30:7 Abiathar brought **D** the ephod.
30:8 Then **D** asked the LORD,
30:9 So **D** and his 600 men went to
30:10 **D** and 400 men went in pursuit,
30:11 country and took him to **D**.
30:13 **D** asked him, "To whom do
30:15 **D** asked him. He answered,
30:17 the next day, **D** attacked them.
30:18 **D** rescued everything the
30:19 **D** brought back everything.
30:21 **D** came to the 200 men who
30:21 They came to meet **D** and the
30:21 As **D** approached the men,
30:22 man who had gone with **D** said,
30:23 But **D** said, "My brothers,
30:26 When **D** came to Ziklag,
30:31 Hebron, and to all the places **D**
2Sm 1:1 After Saul died and **D** returned
1:1 **D** stayed in Ziklag two days.
1:2 When he came to **D**,
1:3 **D** asked him. "I escaped from
1:4 **D** asked him. "Please tell me."
1:5 **D** asked the young man who
1:11 Then **D** grabbed his own
1:13 **D** asked the young man who
1:14 **D** asked, "Why weren't you
1:15 Then **D** called one of ⌊his⌋
1:16 while **D** said, "You are
1:17 **D** wrote this song of mourning
2:1 After this, **D** asked the LORD,
2:1 **D** asked. "To Hebron," the
2:2 **D** went there with his two
2:3 **D** took his men and their
2:4 came to Hebron and anointed **D**
2:4 They told **D**, "The people of
2:5 So **D** sent messengers to the
2:10 the tribe of Judah followed **D**.
2:11 In Hebron **D** was king over the
3:1 of Saul and **D** dragged on,
3:2 Sons were born to **D** while he
3:5 These sons were born to **D**
3:6 the families of Saul and **D**,
3:8 I haven't handed you over to **D**.
3:9 me dead unless I do for **D** what
3:12 Abner sent messengers to **D**
3:13 **D** answered. "I'll make an
3:14 Then **D** sent messengers to
3:17 wanted to make **D** your king.
3:18 the LORD said about **D**:
3:18 through my servant **D**.'"
3:19 Then Abner went directly to **D**
3:20 with 20 men to **D** in Hebron,
3:20 and **D** had a feast for Abner and
3:21 Abner told **D**, "I must go now
3:21 Then **D** dismissed Abner,
3:22 no longer with **D** in Hebron.
3:23 but **D** dismissed him,
3:26 After leaving **D**, Joab sent
3:26 without **D** knowing about it.
3:28 Later when **D** heard about it,
3:31 **D** told Joab and all the people
3:31 King **D** followed the open
3:35 day all the people tried to get **D**
3:35 But **D** had taken an oath:
4:8 head to **D** at Hebron.
4:9 **D** responded to Rechab and his
4:12 So **D** gave an order to his
5:1 of Israel came to **D** at Hebron.
5:3 King **D** made an agreement
5:3 they anointed **D** king of Israel.
5:4 **D** was 30 years old when he
5:6 The Jebusites told **D**,
5:6 (meaning that **D** could never
5:7 But **D** captured the fortress
5:7 Zion (that is, the City of **D**).
5:8 That day **D** said, So there is a
5:9 **D** lived in the fortress and
5:9 and called it the City of **D**.
5:10 **D** continued to grow more
5:11 of Tyre sent messengers to **D**,
5:11 They built a palace for **D**.
5:12 So **D** realized that the LORD
5:13 **D** married more concubines
5:17 heard that **D** had been anointed
2Sm 5:17 all of them came to attack **D**.
5:17 But **D** heard about it and went
5:19 **D** asked the LORD,
5:19 The LORD answered **D**,
5:20 So **D** went to Baal Perazim
5:21 so **D** and his men carried the
5:23 **D** asked the LORD,
5:25 **D** did as the LORD ordered him
6:1 **D** again assembled all the best
6:3 **D** and his men put God's ark on
6:5 **D** and the entire nation of Israel
6:8 **D** was angry because the
6:9 **D** was afraid of the LORD that
6:10 So **D** wouldn't bring the ark of
6:10 LORD with him to the City of **D**.
6:12 King **D** was told, "The LORD
6:12 Then **D** joyfully went to get the
6:12 and bring it to the City of **D**.
6:13 **D** sacrificed a bull and a
6:14 Wearing a linen ephod, **D**
6:16 LORD came to the City of **D**,
6:16 and saw King **D** leaping
6:17 inside the tent **D** had put up
6:17 **D** sacrificed burnt offerings and
6:18 When **D** had finished
6:20 When **D** returned to bless his
6:21 **D** answered Michal,
7:1 While King **D** was living in his
7:5 "Say to my servant **D**,
7:8 you will say to my servant **D**:
7:17 Nathan told **D** all these words
7:18 King **D** went into the tent and
7:20 "What more can I, **D**,
7:26 the house of your servant **D** will
8:1 After this, **D** defeated and
8:3 When **D** went to restore his
8:4 **D** took 1,700 horsemen and
8:4 **D** also disabled all but 100 of
8:5 **D** killed 22,000 of them.
8:6 **D** put troops in the Aramean
8:6 Everywhere **D** went,
8:7 **D** took the gold shields that
8:8 King **D** also took a large
8:9 **D** had defeated Hadadezer's
8:10 his son Joram to greet King **D**
8:11 King **D** dedicated these articles
8:13 **D** made a name for himself by
8:14 Everywhere **D** went,
8:15 So **D** ruled all Israel.
9:1 **D** asked, "Is there anyone left
9:2 summoned to ⌊come to⌋ **D**.
9:3 **D** asked, "Is there someone left
9:5 So King **D** sent men to get him
9:6 grandson of Saul) came to **D**,
9:6 **D** said to him. "Yes, sir,"
9:7 "Don't be afraid," **D** told him,
10:2 **D** thought, "I will show
10:2 "So **D** sent his servants to
10:3 "Do you think **D** is honoring
10:3 Hasn't **D** sent his men to
10:5 After **D** was told ⌊what had
10:6 themselves offensive to **D**.
10:7 After **D** heard about this,
10:17 When **D** was told ⌊about this⌋,
10:18 and **D** killed 700 chariot drivers
10:18 **D** struck Shobach dead.
11:1 **D** sent Joab, his mercenaries,
11:1 while **D** stayed in Jerusalem.
11:2 Now, when evening came, **D**
11:3 **D** sent someone to ask about
11:4 So **D** sent messengers and
11:5 So she sent someone to tell **D**
11:6 Then **D** sent a messenger to
11:6 So Joab sent Uriah to **D**.
11:7 When Uriah arrived, **D** asked
11:8 "Go home," **D** said to Uriah,
11:10 When they told **D**, "Uriah didn't
11:10 didn't go home," **D** asked Uriah,
11:11 Uriah answered **D**,
11:12 **D** said to Uriah, "Then stay
11:13 **D** summoned him,
11:14 In the morning **D** wrote a letter
11:18 ⌊a messenger⌋ to report to **D** all
11:22 he reported to **D** everything
11:25 **D** said to the messenger,
11:27 her mourning was over, **D** sent
2Sm 12:1 So the LORD sent Nathan to **D**.
12:5 **D** burned with anger against
12:7 Nathan told **D**. "This is what the
12:13 Then **D** said to Nathan,
12:15 had given birth to for **D** so that
12:16 **D** pleaded with God for the
12:19 But when **D** saw that his
12:19 **D** asked them. "⌊Yes,⌋ he is
12:20 So **D** got up from the ground,
12:22 **D** answered, "As long as the
12:24 Then **D** comforted his wife
12:24 **D** named him Solomon.
12:27 he sent messengers to tell **D**,
12:29 So **D** gathered all the troops
12:30 **D** also took a lot of goods from
12:31 Then **D** and all the troops
13:7 **D** sent for Tamar at the palace.
13:21 When King **D** heard about this,
13:21 But **D** didn't punish his son
13:25 **D** did not want to go,
13:30 **D** heard this rumor:
13:39 King **D** began to long for
15:2 a case to be tried by King **D**,
15:13 Someone came to tell **D**,
15:14 **D** told all his men who were
15:22 So **D** told Ittai, "Go ahead and
15:30 **D** cried as he went up the
15:31 Then **D** was told, So David
15:31 So **D** prayed, "LORD,
15:32 When **D** came to the top ⌊of the
15:33 **D** told him, "If you go with me,
16:1 When **D** had gone over the top
16:2 **D** asked Ziba. "The donkeys
16:5 When King **D** came to Bahurim,
16:6 He threw stones at **D** and
16:6 the warriors were shielding **D**.
16:10 'Curse **D**,' should anyone ask,
16:11 **D** told Abishai and all his
16:13 As **D** and his men went along
16:13 and threw dirt at **D**.
16:23 In those days both **D** and
17:1 and leave tonight to go after **D**.
17:16 messengers quickly to tell **D**,
17:17 they were to go and tell King **D**.
17:21 and went and told King **D**.
17:21 "Leave right away," they told **D**.
17:22 **D** and all the troops with him
17:24 **D** had ⌊already⌋ come to
17:27 When **D** came to Mahanaim,
17:28 ⌊supplies⌋ and food for **D**
18:1 **D** called together the troops
18:2 **D** put a third of the troops under
18:24 **D** was sitting between the two
19:11 So King **D** sent ⌊this
19:16 of Judah to meet King **D**.
19:22 **D** responded, "Are you sure
19:43 claim on **D** than you have.
20:2 So all the people of Israel left **D**
20:3 When **D** came to his palace in
20:5 to do it than **D** had given him.
20:6 **D** then told Abishai,
20:21 has rebelled against King **D**.
20:26 of Jair, was a priest to **D**.
21:1 In the time of **D**, there was a
21:1 and **D** asked the LORD's
21:7 name between **D** and Jonathan,
21:11 When **D** was told what Saul's
21:12 **D** went and took the bones of
21:13 When **D** brought up the bones
21:15 So **D** and his men went to fight
21:15 but **D** became exhausted.
21:16 captured **D** and intended to kill
21:17 son of Zeruiah, came to help **D**.
21:22 and **D** and his men killed them.
22:1 **D** sang this song to the LORD
22:51 mercy to his anointed, to **D**,
23:1 These are the last words of **D**:
23:1 "Here is the declaration by **D**,
23:9 Eleazar was with **D** at Pas
23:13 thirty leading men came to **D** at
23:14 While **D** was in the fortified
23:15 When **D** became thirsty,
23:16 They brought it to **D**,
23:23 **D** put him in charge of his
24:1 so he provoked **D** to turn
24:2 King **D** said to Joab,

2Sm 24:10 After **D** counted the people,
24:10 **D** said to the LORD,
24:11 When **D** got up in the morning,
24:12 "Go and tell **D**, 'This is what
24:13 When Gad came to **D**,
24:13 he told **D** this and asked,
24:14 situation," **D** told Gad.
24:17 When **D** saw the Messenger
24:18 That day Gad came to **D** and
24:19 **D** went as Gad had told him
24:21 **D** answered, "To buy the
24:22 Araunah said to **D**,
24:24 So **D** bought the threshing floor
24:25 **D** built an altar for the LORD
1Ki 1:1 King **D** had grown old,
1:11 and our master **D** doesn't
1:13 Go to King **D** and ask him,
1:28 Then King **D** answered,
1:31 "May Your Majesty, King **D**,
1:32 King **D** said, "Summon the
1:37 greater king than you, King **D**."
1:43 "His Majesty King **D** has made
1:47 His Majesty King **D**,
2:1 When **D** was about to die,
2:10 **D** lay down in death with his
2:10 and was buried in the City of **D**.
2:26 LORD ahead of my father **D**
2:33 But may **D**, his descendants,
2:44 evil that you did to my father **D**.
3:1 brought her to the City of **D**
3:6 great love to my father **D**,
3:7 me king in place of my father **D**.
3:14 commands as your father **D** did,
5:3 "You know that my father **D**
5:5 the LORD spoke to my father **D**:
5:7 He has given **D** a wise son to
6:12 about you to your father **D**.
7:51 had belonged to his father **D**—
8:1 from the City of **D** (that is,
8:15 made a promise to my father **D**;
8:16 But now I've chosen **D** to rule
8:17 "My father **D** had his heart set
8:18 the LORD said to my father **D**,
8:24 your promise to my father **D**,
8:25 your promise to my father **D**,
8:26 you made to my father **D**,
8:66 LORD had given his servant **D**
9:4 me as your father **D** was (with
9:5 I promised your father **D** when
9:24 moved from the City of **D**
11:4 God as his father **D** had been.
11:6 LORD as his father **D** had done.
11:12 because of your father **D**.
11:15 When **D** had conquered Edom,
11:21 in Egypt that **D** had lain down
11:24 after **D** killed the men of Zobah.
11:27 in the ⌊wall of⌋ the City of **D**.
11:32 of my servant **D** and Jerusalem,
11:33 and decrees as his father **D** did.
11:34 because of my servant **D** whom
11:36 my servant **D** will always have
11:38 as my servant **D** did,
11:38 dynasty for you as I did for **D**.
11:43 and was buried in the City of **D**.
12:16 look after your own house, **D**!"
14:8 not been like my servant **D**.
14:31 with them in the City of **D**.
15:3 as his ancestor **D** had been.
15:5 The LORD did this because **D**
15:5 **D** never failed to do anything
15:8 and was buried in the City of **D**.
15:11 as his ancestor **D** had done.
15:24 in the city of his ancestor, **D**.
22:50 in the city of his ancestor **D**.
2Ki 8:19 The LORD had told **D** that he
8:24 with them in the City of **D**.
9:28 his ancestors in the City of **D**.
11:10 that had belonged to King **D**
12:21 his ancestors in the City of **D**.
14:3 what his ancestor **D** had done.
14:20 in Jerusalem, in the City of **D**,
15:7 with them in the City of **D**.
15:38 in the city of his ancestor **D**.
16:2 as his ancestor **D** had done.
16:20 with them in the City of **D**.
17:21 away from the family of **D**,
2Ki 18:3 as his ancestor **D** had done.
19:34 for the sake of my servant **D**."
20:5 God of your ancestor **D** says:
20:6 for the sake of my servant **D**.'"
21:7 where the LORD had said to **D**
22:2 ancestor **D** and never stopped.
1Ch 2:15 and **D** (his seventh son).
3:5 were born to **D** in Jerusalem:
4:31 their cities until **D** became king.
6:31 **D** put men in charge of the
9:22 **D** and the seer Samuel
10:14 turned the kingship over to **D**,
11:1 gathered around **D** at Hebron.
11:3 **D** made an agreement with
11:3 So they anointed **D** king of
11:4 **D** and all Israel went to
11:5 They told **D**, "You will never
11:5 But **D** captured the fortress
11:5 Zion (that is, the City of **D**).
11:6 Now, **D** said, "Whoever is the
11:7 **D** lived in the fortress,
11:7 so it was called the City of **D**.
11:9 **D** continued to grow more
11:13 Eleazar was with **D** at Pas
11:16 While **D** was in the fortified
11:17 **D** was thirsty and said,
11:18 They brought it to **D**,
11:25 **D** put him in charge of his
12:1 who came to **D** at Ziklag when
12:1 who went into battle with **D**.
12:8 Some men left Gad to join **D** at
12:16 and Judah came to **D** at
12:17 **D** went to meet them.
12:18 ⌊to say⌋, "We are yours, **D**.
12:18 So **D** welcomed them and
12:19 ⌊Saul's army⌋ to join **D** when
12:19 (However, **D** didn't help the
12:20 When **D** went to Ziklag,
12:21 They helped **D** fight raiding
12:22 men came to help **D** until he
12:23 The men joined **D** at Hebron to
12:23 turn Saul's kingship over to **D**,
12:31 by name to make **D** king.
12:38 to Hebron — to make **D** king
12:38 had agreed to make **D** king.
12:39 They ate and drank with **D** for
13:1 **D** consulted with every officer
13:5 So **D** gathered all Israel from
13:6 **D** and all Israel went to Baalah
13:7 **D** and his men put God's ark on
13:8 **D** and all Israel were
13:11 **D** was angry because the
13:12 **D** was afraid of God that day.
13:13 to his ⌊home⌋, the City of **D**.
14:1 of Tyre sent messengers to **D**,
14:1 to build a palace for **D**.
14:2 So **D** realized that the LORD
14:3 **D** married more wives in
14:8 heard that **D** had been anointed
14:8 all of them came to attack **D**.
14:8 But **D** heard about it and went
14:10 **D** asked God, "Should I attack
14:11 So **D** ⌊and his men⌋ attacked
14:11 **D** said, "Using my power like
14:12 so **D** ordered that the gods be
14:14 Once more **D** asked God.
14:16 **D** did as God ordered him,
15:1 After **D** constructed buildings
15:1 for himself in the City of **D**,
15:2 Then **D** insisted that only the
15:3 **D** called together all Israel at
15:4 **D** also called together Aaron's
15:11 **D** called for the priests Zadok
15:16 **D** told the Levite leaders to
15:25 So **D**, the leaders of Israel,
15:27 **D** was dressed in a fine linen
15:27 **D** also wore a linen ephod.
15:29 promise came to the City of **D**,
15:29 and saw King **D** dancing
16:1 it inside the tent **D** had put up
16:2 When **D** had finished
16:4 **D** appointed some Levites to
16:7 For the first time **D** entrusted
16:37 **D** left Asaph and his relatives
16:38 **D** also left Obed Edom and 68
16:39 **D** left Zadok and his priestly
1Ch 16:43 **D** went back to bless his
17:1 When **D** was living in his
17:2 Nathan told **D**, "Do everything
17:4 "Say to **D**, my servant, 'This is
17:7 you will say to my servant **D**:
17:15 Nathan told **D** all these words
17:16 Then King **D** went into the tent
17:24 And the house of **D**,
18:1 After this, **D** defeated and
18:3 When **D** went to establish his
18:4 **D** took 1,000 chariots,
18:4 **D** also disabled all but 100 of
18:5 **D** killed 22,000 of them.
18:6 **D** put troops in the Aramean
18:6 Everywhere **D** went,
18:7 **D** took the gold shields that
18:8 **D** also took a large quantity of
18:9 heard that **D** had defeated
18:10 son Hadoram to greet King **D**
18:11 King **D** dedicated all the
18:13 Everywhere **D** went,
18:14 So **D** ruled all Israel.
19:2 **D** thought, "I will show
19:2 "So **D** sent messengers to
19:3 "Do you think **D** is honoring
19:5 After people told **D** ⌊what had
19:6 themselves offensive to **D**.
19:8 After **D** heard about this,
19:17 When **D** was told ⌊about this⌋,
19:17 **D** formed a battle line against
19:18 and **D** killed 7,000 chariot
19:18 **D** also killed Shophach.
19:19 they made peace with **D** and
20:1 while **D** stayed in Jerusalem.
20:2 **D** also took a lot of goods from
20:3 Then **D** and all the troops
20:8 and **D** and his men killed them.
21:1 to attack Israel by provoking **D**
21:2 **D** said to Joab and the leaders
21:5 the census figures to **D**:
21:8 **D** said to God, "I have
21:10 "Go and tell **D**, 'This is what
21:11 When Gad came to **D**,
21:13 situation," **D** told Gad.
21:16 When **D** looked up,
21:16 **D** and the leaders were
21:17 **D** said to God, "I'm the one
21:18 Messenger told Gad to tell **D**
21:19 **D** went as Gad had told him in
21:21 When **D** arrived, Ornan looked
21:21 the ground in front of **D**.
21:22 **D** said to Ornan, "Let me have
21:23 Ornan said to **D**, "Take it,
21:24 "No," King **D** told Ornan,
21:25 So **D** gave Ornan 15 pounds of
21:26 **D** built an altar for the LORD
21:28 At that time, when **D** saw the
21:30 However, **D** couldn't go there to
22:1 Then **D** said, "This is where
22:2 **D** ordered the foreigners living
22:3 **D** prepared a large quantity of
22:4 Tyre brought **D** so many cedar
22:5 **D** thought, "My son Solomon is
22:5 So **D** prepared many materials
22:7 **D** told his son Solomon,
22:11 ⌊**D** continued,⌋ "Now, son,
22:17 **D** ordered all the leaders of
22:18 ⌊**D** said,⌋ "Isn't the LORD your
23:1 When **D** had grown old and had
23:5 the instruments **D** had made
23:6 **D** organized the Levites into
23:25 **D** had said, "The LORD God of
24:3 **D**, Eleazar's descendant
24:31 drew them in front of King **D**,
25:1 **D** and the army commanders
26:26 dedicated to God that King **D**,
26:32 King **D** appointed them to be
27:23 **D** didn't count those under 20
27:24 in the official records of King **D**.
28:1 **D** held a meeting in Jerusalem
28:2 **D** stood in front of them and
28:11 Then **D** gave his son Solomon
28:14 ⌊**D** specified⌋ the weight of
28:19 ⌊**D** said,⌋ "All this was written
28:20 **D** also told his son Solomon,
29:1 Then King **D** said to the whole

1Ch 29:9 King **D** was also overjoyed,
29:10 **D** said, "May you be praised,
29:20 Then **D** said to the whole
29:23 as king in place of his father **D**.
29:26 **D**, son of Jesse, had ruled all
29:29 Everything about King **D** from
2Ch 1:1 Solomon, son of **D**,
1:4 (However, **D** had ⌊already⌋
1:8 great love to my father **D**,
1:9 you made to my father **D**.
2:3 what you did for my father **D**.
2:7 whom my father **D** provided
2:12 the earth and has given King **D**
2:14 workmen of His Majesty **D**,
2:17 as his father **D** had counted
3:1 LORD appeared to his father **D**.
3:1 There **D** had prepared the site
5:1 had belonged to his father **D**—
5:2 from the City of **D** (that is,
6:4 made a promise to my father **D**;
6:6 I've chosen **D** to rule my
6:7 "My father **D** had his heart set
6:8 the LORD said to my father **D**,
6:15 your promise to my father **D**,
6:16 your promise to my father **D**,
6:17 the promise you made to **D**,
6:42 your mercy to your servant **D**!"
7:6 which King **D** made
7:10 the LORD had given **D**,
7:17 to me as your father **D** was,
7:18 in a promise to your father **D**,
8:11 daughter from the City of **D**
8:11 not live in the palace of King **D**
8:14 father **D** had directed,
8:14 gate because this is what **D**,
9:31 and was buried in the City of **D**.
10:16 look after your own house, **D**!"
11:17 years they lived the way **D**
11:18 was the son of **D** and Abihail.
12:16 and was buried in the City of **D**.
13:5 gave the kingdom of Israel to **D**
14:1 and was buried in the City of **D**.
16:14 for himself in the City of **D**.
17:3 the old way like his ancestor **D**.
21:1 with them in the City of **D**.
21:7 the promise he had made to **D**,
21:7 The LORD had told **D** that he
21:12 God of your ancestor **D** says:
21:20 He was buried in the City of **D**
23:9 that had belonged to King **D**
23:18 (**D** had arranged them in
23:18 and singing as **D** had directed.)
24:16 He was buried in the City of **D**
24:25 they buried him in the City of **D**,
27:9 they buried him in the City of **D**.
28:1 as his ancestor **D** had done.
29:2 as his ancestor **D** had done.
29:25 cymbals, harps, and lyres as **D**,
29:27 instruments of King **D** of Israel.
29:30 the LORD with the words of **D**
32:5 the Millo in the City of **D**,
32:30 the west side of the City of **D**.
33:7 where God had said to **D** and
33:14 wall of the City of **D** from west
34:2 in the ways of his ancestor **D**
34:3 the God of his ancestor **D**.
35:3 son of **D** and king of Israel,
35:4 listed in the records of King **D**
35:15 were in their places as **D**,
Ezr 3:10 instructions of King **D** of Israel.
8:3 from the family of **D**:
8:20 the temple servants whom **D**
Neh 3:15 going down from the City of **D**.
3:16 from the tombs of **D** as far as
12:24 thanksgiving antiphonally as **D**,
12:36 the musical instruments of **D**,
12:37 up the stairs of the City of **D**.
12:45 and the gatekeepers did what **D**
12:46 ago in the time of **D** and Asaph,
Psa 18:50 mercy to his anointed, to **D**,
72:20 The prayers by **D**, son of
78:70 He chose his servant **D**.
78:71 that had lambs so that **D** could
78:72 With unselfish devotion **D**
89:3 this oath to my servant **D**:
89:20 I found my servant **D**.
Psa 89:35 and for all: I will not lie to **D**.
89:49 You swore an oath to **D** on ⌊the
132:1 O LORD, remember **D** and all
132:10 For the sake of your servant **D**,
132:11 The LORD swore an oath to **D**.
132:17 make a horn sprout up for **D**.
144:10 your servant **D** away from
Ecc 1:1 the son of **D** and the king in
Isa 7:13 descendants of **D**," Isaiah said.
16:5 He is from the tent of **D**.
22:22 the house of **D** around his neck.
29:1 the city where **D** camped.
37:35 for the sake of my servant **D**."
38:5 God of your ancestor **D** says:
55:3 the blessings I promised to **D**.
Jer 21:12 descendants of **D**.
23:5 grow a righteous branch for **D**.
30:9 your God and **D** your king.
33:15 branch to spring up for **D**.
33:17 "This what the LORD says: **D**
33:21 with my servant **D** could
33:22 descendants of my servant **D**
33:26 of Jacob and of my servant **D**.
Eze 34:23 over them, my servant **D**,
34:24 and my servant **D** will be their
37:24 "My servant **D** will be their
37:25 My servant **D** will always be
Hos 3:5 their God and **D** their king.
Amo 6:5 Like **D**, they write all kinds of
Zec 12:8 who stumble will be like **D**,
12:12 the family of **D** by itself,
Mat 1:1 descendant of **D** and Abraham.
1:6 Jesse the father of King **D**.
1:6 **D** and Uriah's wife
1:17 generations from Abraham to **D**
1:17 14 generations from **D** until the
1:20 him, "Joseph, descendant of **D**,
9:27 "Have mercy on us, Son of **D**."
12:3 "Haven't you read what **D** did
12:23 this man be the Son of **D**?"
15:22 mercy on me, Lord, Son of **D**!
20:30 Son of **D**, have mercy on us!"
20:31 Son of **D**, have mercy on us!"
21:9 "Hosanna to the Son of **D**!
21:15 "Hosanna to the Son of **D**!"
22:43 "Then how can **D**,
22:43 call him Lord? **D** says,
22:45 If **D** calls him Lord,
Mar 2:25 "Haven't you ever read what **D**
10:47 Son of **D**, have mercy on me!"
10:48 "Son of **D**, have mercy on me!"
12:36 **D**, guided by the Holy Spirit,
12:37 **D** calls him Lord. So how can
Luk 1:27 of **D** named Joseph.
1:32 the throne of his ancestor **D**.
1:69 in the family of his servant **D**.
2:4 a descendant of King **D**,
2:4 went to Bethlehem because **D**
3:31 son of Nathan, son of **D**,
6:3 "Haven't you read what **D** did
18:38 Son of **D**, have mercy on me!"
18:39 "Son of **D**, have mercy on me!"
20:42 **D** says in the book of Psalms,
20:44 **D** calls him Lord. So how can
Jon 7:42 from the descendants of **D**
7:42 of Bethlehem, where **D** lived?
Act 1:16 Holy Spirit predicted through **D**
2:25 This is what **D** meant when he
2:29 that our ancestor **D** died
2:30 **D** was a prophet and knew that
2:31 **D** knew that the Messiah
2:34 **D** didn't go up to heaven,
4:25 your servant **D** (our ancestor),
7:45 here until the time of **D**,
7:46 **D** asked that he might provide
13:22 Saul and made **D** their king.
13:22 God spoke favorably about **D**.
13:22 He said, 'I have found that **D**,
13:34 enduring love promised to **D**.'
13:36 the people of his time, **D** died.
Rom 1:3 he was a descendant of **D**.
4:6 **D** says the same thing when
4:6 that person's earning it. **D** said,
11:9 And **D** says, "Let the table set
2Ti 2:8 to life and is a descendant of **D**.
Heb 4:7 God spoke about it through **D**
Heb 11:32 **D**, Samuel, and the prophets.
Rev 3:7 who has the key of **D**,
5:5 tribe of Judah, the Root of **D**,
22:16 the root and descendant of **D**.

David's (142)

1Sm 17:28 Eliab, **D** oldest brother,
17:38 put a bronze helmet on **D** head
18:1 became **D** closest friend.
18:29 became **D** constant enemy.
19:5 by shedding **D** innocent blood
19:11 messengers to watch **D** house
19:11 **D** wife, advised him,
20:15 will wipe each of **D** enemies off
20:16 cut off from **D** family, then may
20:16 the LORD punish **D** house.
20:25 but **D** place was empty.
20:27 **D** place was still empty.
23:3 **D** men told him, "We're afraid of
23:16 He strengthened **D** ⌊faith⌋ in
24:4 **D** men told him, "Today is the
24:5 But afterward, **D** conscience
25:9 When **D** young men came to
25:10 Nabal answered **D** servants.
25:12 **D** young men returned and told
25:40 When **D** servants came to
25:42 she went with **D** messengers
25:44 **D** wife, to Palti, Laish's son,
26:17 Saul recognized **D** voice.
30:5 also captured **D** two wives,
30:11 **D** men found an Egyptian in the
30:20 him and said, "This is **D** loot.
2Sm 1:15 **D** young man executed him
2:13 **D** officers also left ⌊Hebron⌋.
2:15 and twelve were from **D** officers
2:17 and **D** men defeated Abner and
2:30 ⌊only⌋ 19 of **D** officers and
2:31 However, **D** officers had killed
3:1 **D** family became stronger and
3:5 ⌊born⌋ to **D** wife Eglah.
3:10 establish **D** throne over Israel
3:22 Just then **D** men and Joab
8:2 Moabites became **D** subjects
8:14 the Edomites were **D** subjects.
8:18 And **D** sons were priests.
9:11 Mephibosheth ate at **D** table as
10:2 But when **D** servants entered
10:4 So Hanun took **D** men, shaved
10:17 a battle line against **D** ⌊troops⌋
11:17 some of **D** mercenaries, fell
11:27 considered **D** actions evil.
12:18 But **D** officials were afraid to
13:1 After this, **D** son Amnon fell in
13:1 the beautiful sister of **D** son
13:3 a son of **D** brother Shimea.
13:32 the son of **D** brother Shimea,
15:12 **D** adviser, to come from his
15:37 So Hushai, **D** friend, went to
16:6 and **D** servants, although all
16:16 When **D** friend Hushai from
18:7 There **D** men defeated Israel's
18:9 with some of **D** men.
20:1 have no share in **D** kingdom.
20:11 on **D** side should follow Joab."
21:17 Then **D** men swore an oath,
21:21 son of **D** brother Shimei,
23:8 the names of **D** fighting men:
24:11 word to the prophet Gad, **D** seer
1Ki 1:8 and **D** ⌊thirty⌋ fighting men did
1:38 put Solomon on King **D** mule
2:12 sat on his father **D** throne,
2:24 set me on my father **D** throne
2:45 and **D** dynasty will always be
3:3 and lived by his father **D** rules.
5:1 had always been **D** friend
8:20 I have taken my father **D** place,
11:13 one tribe for my servant **D** sake
11:39 I will make **D** descendants
12:16 do we have in **D** kingdom?
12:19 has rebelled against **D** dynasty
12:20 remained loyal to **D** dynasty
12:26 return to **D** dynasty now.
13:2 be a son born in **D** family line.
14:8 the kingdom away from **D** heirs
15:4 But for **D** sake the LORD his
15:4 He appointed **D** descendant to

2Ki 8:19 But for **D** sake the LORD didn't
1Ch 3:1 These were **D** sons who were
3:3 ⌊born⌋ to **D** wife Eglah.
3:9 All of these were **D** sons.
7:2 In **D** day there were 22,600 of
11:10 commanders of **D** fighting men,
11:11 The first of **D** fighting men was
11:15 men went down to **D** rock at
14:17 **D** fame spread through all
18:2 Moabites became **D** subjects
18:13 its people became **D** subjects.
18:17 And **D** sons were his main
19:2 But when **D** servants entered
19:4 So Hanun took **D** men, shaved
20:2 king and put it on **D** head.
20:7 son of **D** brother Shimea,
21:9 LORD spoke to Gad, **D** seer
23:27 **D** last instructions were to
26:31 In the fortieth year of **D** reign,
27:18 one of **D** brothers for the tribe
27:25 in charge of King **D** property:
27:32 **D** uncle Jonathan,
27:32 insight, was **D** adviser.
29:22 made **D** son Solomon king.
29:24 **D** sons pledged their loyalty
2Ch 6:10 I've taken my father **D** place,
10:16 do we have in **D** kingdom?
10:19 has rebelled against **D** dynasty
13:6 the servant of **D** son Solomon.
13:8 in the hands of **D** descendants?
21:7 didn't want to destroy **D** family.
23:3 said about **D** descendants
29:26 stood with **D** instruments,
32:33 upper tombs of **D** descendants.
Neh 12:37 the wall rises past **D** palace
Psa 122:5 who are⌋ **D** descendants
Pro 1:1 **D** son who was king of Israel,
Sos 4:4 **D** beautifully-designed tower.
Isa 7:2 When word reached **D** family
9:7 He will establish **D** throne and
22:9 places in **D** wall are broken.
Jer 13:13 The kings who sit on **D** throne,
17:25 on **D** throne will come through
22:2 the one sitting on **D** throne
22:4 sit on **D** throne will ride through
22:30 They won't sit on **D** throne and
29:16 the king who sits on **D** throne
33:26 let any of **D** descendants rule
36:30 have no one to sit on **D** throne,
Amo 9:11 day I will set up **D** fallen tent.
Zec 12:7 so that the honor of **D** family
12:8 and **D** family will be like God,
12:10 blessing and mercy on **D** family
13:1 will be opened for **D** family
Mat 22:42 They answered him, "**D**."
Mar 11:10 **D** kingdom that is coming!
12:35 say that the Messiah is **D** son
Luk 2:11 was born in **D** city
20:41 say that the Messiah is **D** son
Act 2:30 place one of **D** descendants
13:23 Israel from **D** descendants, as
15:16 I will set up **D** fallen tent again.

dawn (39)

Gen 19:15 As soon as it was **d**,
32:24 man wrestled with him until **d**.
32:26 said, "Let me go; it's almost **d**."
44:3 At **d** the men were sent on their
Exo 14:24 Just before **d**, the LORD
Jos 6:15 seventh day they got up at **d**.
Jdg 16:2 "We'll kill him at **d**."
1Sm 9:26 At **d** Samuel called to Saul on
14:36 possessions until the light of **d**.
25:34 had one of his men left at **d**."
25:36 didn't tell him anything until **d**.
30:17 From **d** until evening the next
2Sm 17:22 When the **d** came,
Neh 4:21 held spears from early **d** until
Job 3:9 Let its stars turn dark before **d**.
3:9 Let it not see the first light of **d**
7:4 from tossing about until **d**.
24:14 At **d** murderers rise;
38:12 or assigned a place for the **d**
41:18 are like the first rays of the **d**.
Psa 46:5 will help it at the break of **d**.
57:8 I want to wake up at **d**.
63:1 At **d** I search for you.
108:2 I want to wake up at **d**.
119:147 I got up before **d**, and I cried out
Pro 4:18 light of **d** that becomes brighter
Sos 6:10 She looks like the **d**.
Isa 8:20 is because it doesn't **d** on them.
14:12 you morning star, son of the **d**!
58:8 will break through like the **d**,
60:3 to the brightness of your **d**.
62:1 righteousness shines like the **d**
Dan 6:19 At **d**, as soon as it was light,
Joe 2:2 over the mountains like the **d**.
Amo 4:13 He makes **d** and dusk
5:8 He turns deep darkness into **d**.
Jnh 4:7 At **d** the next day, God sent a
Mar 13:35 evening or at midnight or at **d**
Luk 1:78 A new day will **d** on us from

dawned (1)

Isa 60:1 the glory of the LORD has **d**.

dawns (3)

Psa 97:11 Light **d** for righteous people and
Isa 60:2 But the LORD **d**, and his glory
Mic 2:1 When the morning **d**,

day (1341)

Gen 1:5 God named the light **d**,
1:5 then morning — the first **d**.
1:8 then morning — a second **d**.
1:13 then morning — a third **d**.
1:14 the sky to separate the **d** from
1:16 the larger light to rule the **d** and
1:18 to dominate the **d** and the night,
1:19 then morning — a fourth **d**.
1:23 then morning — a fifth **d**.
1:31 then morning — the sixth **d**.
2:2 By the seventh **d** God had
2:2 On the seventh **d** he stopped
2:3 God blessed the seventh **d**
2:3 because on that **d** he stopped
3:17 from it every **d** of your life.
6:5 All **d** long their deepest
7:11 On the seventeenth **d** of the
7:13 On that same **d** Noah and his
8:4 On the seventeenth **d** of the
8:5 On the first **d** of the tenth
8:13 By the first **d** of the first month
8:14 By the twenty-seventh **d** of the
8:22 **d** and night will never stop."
10:25 because in his **d** the earth was
17:23 and circumcised them that **d**,
17:26 That same **d** Abraham and his
18:1 during the hottest part of the **d**.
19:34 The next **d** the older daughter
21:8 On the **d** Isaac was weaned,
26:32 That same **d** Isaac's servants
27:45 I lose both of you in one **d**?"
29:7 the middle of the **d**," he said.
30:35 However, that same **d** Laban
31:39 stolen during the **d** or at night.
31:40 scorching heat during the **d**
33:13 driven too hard for even one **d**,
33:16 That **d** Esau started back to
39:10 kept asking Joseph **d** after day,
39:10 kept asking Joseph day after **d**,
39:11 One **d** he went into the house
42:18 On the third **d** Joseph said to
48:15 all my life to this very **d**,
48:20 That **d** he blessed them.
Exo 2:13 Moses went there the next **d**,
2:15 One **d**, while Moses was
5:6 That same **d** Pharaoh gave
5:13 same amount of work each **d**,
5:19 each **d** than you're supposed
8:22 But on that **d** I will treat the
9:6 The next **d** the LORD did as he
10:13 blow over the land all that **d**
10:28 The **d** I do, you will die."
12:3 On the tenth ⌊**d**⌋ of this month
12:6 of it until the fourteenth ⌊**d**⌋
12:14 "This **d** will be one for you to
12:14 You will celebrate this **d** as a
12:15 On the very first **d** you must
12:15 in it from the first **d** through
12:15 day through the seventh **d** must
Exo 12:16 a holy assembly on the first **d**
12:17 it was on this very **d** that
12:17 You must celebrate this **d**.
12:18 the evening of the fourteenth **d**
12:18 the twenty-first **d** you must eat
12:51 That very **d** the LORD brought
13:3 "Remember this **d** — the day
13:3 "Remember this day — the **d**
13:6 The seventh **d** will be a
13:8 On that **d** tell your children,
13:21 By **d** the LORD went ahead of
13:21 could travel by **d** or by night.
13:22 front of the people during the **d**.
14:30 That **d** the LORD saved Israel
16:1 This was on the fifteenth **d** of
16:4 Each **d** the people should go
16:4 only what they need for that **d**.
16:5 But on the sixth **d** when they
16:22 But on the sixth **d** they
16:23 Tomorrow is a **d** of worship,
16:23 a holy **d** of worship dedicated
16:25 "because today is a **d** of
16:26 but on the seventh **d**,
16:26 seventh day, the **d** of worship,
16:27 On the seventh **d** some people
16:29 The LORD has given you this **d**
16:29 you enough food on the sixth **d**
16:29 On the seventh **d** you may not
16:30 on the seventh **d** of the week.
18:13 The next **d** Moses was settling
19:11 ready by the **d** after tomorrow.
19:11 On that **d** the LORD will come
19:16 the morning of the second **d**,
20:8 "Remember the **d** of worship by
20:8 by observing it as a holy **d**.
20:10 The seventh **d** is the day of
20:10 The seventh day is the **d** of
20:10 never do any work ⌊on that **d**⌋.
20:11 didn't work on the seventh **d**.
20:11 why the LORD blessed the **d**
20:11 and set this **d** apart as holy.
21:21 the slave gets up in a **d** or two,
22:30 but on the eighth **d** you must
23:12 but on the seventh **d** you must
24:16 and on the seventh **d** the LORD
29:36 Each **d** sacrifice a young bull
29:38 on the altar regularly every **d**:
31:14 "'Observe the **d** of worship
31:14 treats it like any other **d** must
31:14 Whoever works on that **d** must
31:15 but the seventh **d** is a day of
31:15 seventh day is a **d** of worship,
31:15 a **d** when you don't work.
31:15 Whoever works on that **d** must
31:16 must observe this **d** of worship,
31:17 and on the seventh **d** he
32:6 Early the next **d** the people
32:28 and that **d** about 3,000 people
32:30 The next **d** Moses said to the
34:21 but on the seventh **d** you must
34:21 you must not work ⌊on this **d**⌋.
35:2 but the seventh **d** is a holy day
35:2 day is a holy **d** of worship,
35:2 a **d** when you don't work.
35:2 does any work on this **d** should
35:3 homes on this **d** of worship."
40:2 tent of meeting) on the first **d**
40:17 tent was set up on the first **d**
40:38 over the tent during the **d**,
Lev 6:5 owner on the **d** you bring your
6:20 bring to the LORD on the **d**
6:20 They must do this every **d**.
7:15 must be eaten on the **d**
7:16 it must be eaten the **d** you offer
7:16 day you offer it or the next **d**.
7:17 However, on the third **d** any
7:18 offering is eaten on the third **d**.
7:35 It was given to them on the **d**
7:36 to give it to them on the **d**
8:33 not until the last **d** of your
8:35 to the tent of meeting **d**
9:1 On the eighth **d** Moses
13:5 On the seventh **d** the priest will
13:6 On the seventh **d** the priest will
13:27 On the seventh **d** the priest will
13:32 On the seventh **d** the priest will

Lev 13:34 On the seventh **d** the priest will
13:51 On the seventh **d** he will
14:9 On the seventh **d** he must
14:10 "On the eighth **d** he must take
14:23 On the eighth **d** he will take
14:39 On the seventh **d** the priest will
15:14 On the eighth **d** he must take
15:29 On the eighth **d** she must take
16:29 On the tenth **d** of the seventh
16:30 On this **d** Aaron will make
19:6 Eat your sacrifice on the **d** you
19:6 you bring it and on the next **d**.
19:6 On the third **d** burn whatever is
19:7 you eat any of it on the third **d**,
22:27 From the eighth **d** on it may be
22:28 and its young the same **d**.
22:30 Eat it the same **d**. Never leave
23:3 But the seventh **d** is a day of
23:3 seventh day is a **d** of worship,
23:3 a **d** when you don't work,
23:3 It is the LORD's **d** of worship
23:5 "The fourteenth **d** of the first
23:6 The fifteenth **d** of this same
23:7 On the first **d** there will be a
23:8 On the seventh **d** there will be
23:11 it on the **d** after Passover.
23:12 On the **d** you present the
23:14 or fresh grain until this same **d**,
23:15 from the **d** after Passover (the
23:15 after Passover (the **d** you bring
23:16 until the **d** after the seventh
23:21 holy assembly on that same **d**.
23:24 On the first **d** of the seventh
23:24 It will be a memorial **d**,
23:27 "In addition, the tenth **d** of this
23:27 seventh month is a special **d**
23:28 Don't do any work that **d**.
23:28 It is a special **d** for the payment
23:29 themselves on that **d** will
23:30 who do any work on that **d**.
23:32 It is a **d** of worship,
23:32 a **d** when you don't work.
23:32 on the evening of the ninth **d**
23:32 observe the **d** of worship."
23:34 The fifteenth **d** of this seventh
23:35 On the first **d** there will be a
23:36 On the eighth **d** there will be a
23:37 each one on its special **d**.
23:39 "However, on the fifteenth **d** of
23:40 On the first **d** take the best
24:8 Every **d** of worship ⌊a priest⌋
25:9 On the tenth **d** of the seventh
25:9 the special **d** for the payment
27:23 You will pay its value on that **d**
Num 1:1 It was the first **d** of the second
1:18 whole community on the first **d**
3:13 The **d** I killed every firstborn
6:10 On the eighth **d** he must bring
6:11 That same **d** the person must
7:11 "Each **d** a different leader will
7:12 on the first **d** was Nahshon,
7:18 On the second **d** Nethanel,
7:24 On the third **d** the leader of the
7:30 On the fourth **d** the leader of the
7:36 On the fifth **d** the leader of the
7:42 On the sixth **d** the leader of the
7:48 On the seventh **d** the leader of
7:54 On the eighth **d** the leader of
7:60 On the ninth **d** the leader of the
7:66 On the tenth **d** the leader of the
7:72 On the eleventh **d** the leader of
7:78 On the twelfth **d** the leader of
8:17 The **d** I killed every firstborn
9:3 celebrate it on the fourteenth **d**
9:5 it on the fourteenth **d**
9:6 celebrate the Passover that **d**.
9:11 celebrate it on the fourteenth **d**
9:15 On the **d** the tent of the words
9:21 **D** or night, when the smoke
10:10 festival days and on the first **d**
10:11 On the twentieth **d** of the
10:34 them by **d** when they moved
11:31 walk in a **d** in any direction.
11:32 All that **d** and night and all the
11:32 day and night and all the next **d**
14:14 in a column of smoke by **d**

Num 14:34 one year for each **d** — you will
15:23 to come as it did the **d**
15:32 wood on the **d** of worship.
16:41 The next **d** the whole
17:8 The next **d** Moses went into
19:12 use this water on the third **d**
19:12 the third day and the seventh **d**
19:12 use this water on the third **d**
19:12 the third day and the seventh **d**,
19:19 of unclean people on the third **d**
19:19 the third day and the seventh **d**.
19:19 On the seventh **d** the clean
25:18 who was killed on the **d** of the
28:3 Every **d** you must bring as a
28:9 "On the **d** of worship offer two
28:10 burnt offering is for every **d**
28:16 "The fourteenth **d** of the first
28:18 On the first **d** there will be a
28:25 On the seventh **d** you must
28:26 On that **d** you must not do any
29:1 "On the first **d** of the seventh
29:1 It is a **d** for ⌊the trumpets to
29:7 "On the tenth **d** of the seventh
29:12 "On the fifteenth **d** of the
29:17 "On the second **d** bring 12
29:20 "On the third **d** bring 11 bulls,
29:23 "On the fourth **d** bring 10 bulls,
29:26 "On the fifth **d** bring 9 bulls,
29:29 "On the sixth **d** bring 8 bulls,
29:32 "On the seventh **d** bring 7 bulls,
29:35 "On the eighth **d** you must hold
30:14 to her about it **d** after day,
30:14 to her about it day after **d**,
31:24 On the seventh **d** wash your
32:10 That **d** the LORD became
33:3 from Rameses on the fifteenth **d**
33:3 the **d** after the Passover.
33:38 He died there on the first **d** of
Dtr 1:3 On the first **d** of the eleventh
1:33 a column of smoke during the **d**
4:10 Never forget the **d** you stood in
4:15 You didn't see the LORD the **d**
4:32 Start from the very **d** God
5:12 "Observe the **d** of worship as a
5:12 the day of worship as a holy **d**.
5:14 The seventh **d** is the day of
5:14 The seventh day is the **d** of
5:14 never do any work ⌊on that **d**⌋.
5:15 to observe the **d** of worship.
9:7 LORD from the **d** you left Egypt
9:10 on the **d** of the assembly.
10:4 fire on the mountain on the **d**
16:3 remember the **d** you left Egypt.
16:4 on the evening of the first **d**.
16:8 and on the seventh **d** hold a
16:8 Don't do any work that **d**.
18:16 your God to give you on the **d**
21:16 When the **d** comes for the
21:23 sure to bury him that same **d**,
24:15 Pay them each **d** before sunset
27:2 "The **d** you cross the Jordan
27:11 That same **d** Moses gave the
28:32 looking for them all **d** long,
28:66 will live in terror **d** and night.
29:4 But to this **d** the LORD hasn't
31:17 On that **d** I will become angry
31:17 On that **d** they will ask,
31:18 On that **d** I will certainly turn
31:22 That **d** Moses wrote down this
32:35 because their **d** of disaster is
32:48 That same **d** the LORD said to
33:12 will shelter them all **d** long,
Jos 1:8 them night and **d** so that you
4:14 On that **d** the LORD honored
4:19 On the tenth **d** of the first
4:24 your God every **d** of your life."
5:10 the fourteenth **d** of the month.
5:11 On the **d** after the Passover,
5:12 The **d** after that, the manna
6:3 the city once a **d** for six days.
6:4 But on the seventh **d** you must
6:14 the city once on the second **d**
6:15 On the seventh **d** they got up at
6:15 That was the only **d** they
8:25 and women from Ai died that **d**.
9:27 But that **d** Joshua made them

Jos 10:12 The **d** the LORD handed the
10:13 and for nearly a **d** the sun was
10:14 Never before or after this **d** was
10:28 That same **d** Joshua captured
10:32 He captured it on the next **d**
10:35 They captured it that **d** and
14:9 On that **d** Moses swore this
14:12 the LORD spoke of that **d**.
22:3 All this time, to this **d**,
24:25 That **d** Joshua made an
Jdg 3:30 was crushed by Israel that **d**.
4:14 This is the **d** the LORD will
4:23 So on that **d**, God used the
5:1 On that **d** Deborah and Barak,
6:24 To this **d** it is still in Ophrah,
6:27 didn't do anything during the **d**.
6:32 So that **d** they nicknamed
9:42 The next **d** the people ⌊of
9:45 attacked the city all **d** long.
10:4 called Havvoth Jair to this **d**.
13:10 the other **d** has just appeared
14:15 On the fourth **d** they said to
14:17 Finally, on the seventh **d** he
14:18 sundown on the seventh **d**,
16:16 Every **d** she made his life
19:5 On the fourth **d** they got up
19:8 On the morning of the fifth **d**,
19:11 it was very late in the **d**.
20:15 That **d** 26,000 men armed with
20:21 That **d** the men of Benjamin
20:22 they had formed it on the first **d**.
20:24 On the second **d** the Israelite
20:26 and fasted that **d** until evening.
20:30 On the third **d** the men of Israel
20:35 On that **d** the Israelites
20:46 with swords were killed that **d**.
21:4 The next **d** the people got up
1Sm 1:9 One **d**, after Hannah had
2:34 of them will die on the same **d**.
3:12 On that **d** I am going to do to
4:12 He went to Shiloh that **d** with
5:3 Early the next **d** the people of
6:15 sacrifices to the LORD that **d**.
6:16 back to Ekron that same **d**.
7:6 of the LORD, and fasted that **d**.
7:10 On that **d** the LORD thundered
8:18 "When that **d** comes,
8:18 you when that **d** comes."
9:15 one **d** before Saul came:
9:24 Saul ate with Samuel that **d**.
10:9 That **d** all these signs
11:11 The next **d** Saul arranged the
11:11 until it got hot that **d**.
12:2 you from my youth until this **d**.
12:18 That **d** the LORD sent thunder
13:22 So on the **d** of battle,
14:1 One **d** Saul's son Jonathan
14:18 ephod in front of Israel that **d**.
14:23 the LORD saved Israel that **d**.
14:24 were driven hard that **d**.
14:31 That **d** they struck down the
14:37 he received no answer that **d**.
16:13 stayed with him from that **d** on.
17:12 and in Saul's **d** he was an old
17:46 And this **d** I will give the dead
18:2 (From that **d** on Saul kept
18:9 From that **d** on Saul kept an
18:10 The next **d** an evil spirit from
18:10 on the lyre as he did every **d**.
19:24 and lay there naked all **d**
20:19 The **d** after tomorrow you will
20:26 Saul didn't say anything that **d**,
20:27 But on the second **d** of the
20:34 and ate nothing that second **d**
21:6 with warm bread that **d**.
21:7 That same **d** one of Saul's
21:10 That **d** David left. He was ⌊still⌋
22:18 and that **d** he killed 85 men
22:22 "I knew that **d** when Doeg from
24:4 "Today is the **d** the LORD
25:16 were a wall protecting us **d**
28:20 eaten anything all **d** or all night.
29:3 wrong with him from the **d**
29:6 with you from the **d** you came
30:17 dawn until evening the next **d**,
30:25 in Israel as it is to this **d**.

Psa 88:1 to you during the **d** and at night.
88:9 All **d** long I call out to you,
88:17 They swirl around me all **d**
89:16 They find joy in your name all **d**
90:4 years are like a single **d**,
91:5 arrows that fly during the **d**,
96:2 **D** after day announce that the
96:2 Day after **d** announce that the
102:8 All **d** long my enemies insult
110:5 kings on the **d** of his anger.
118:24 This is the **d** the LORD has
119:97 They are in my thoughts all **d**
119:164 Seven times a **d** I praise you
121:6 beat down on you during the **d**,
136:8 the sun to rule the **d** — because
137:7 Remember what they did the **d**
139:12 Night is as bright as **d**.
139:16 Every **d** ⌊of my life⌋ was
140:2 They start fights every **d**.
140:7 my head in the **d** of battle.
145:2 I will bless you every **d**.
146:4 On that **d** their plans come to
Pro 8:30 I made him happy **d** after day,
8:30 I made him happy day after **d**,
8:34 watches at my door **d** after day,
8:34 watches at my door day after **d**,
11:4 are of no help on the **d** of fury,
15:15 Every **d** is a terrible day for a
15:15 Every day is a terrible **d** for a
16:4 people for the **d** of trouble.
21:26 All **d** long he feels greedy,
21:31 made ready for the **d** of battle,
25:13 of snow on a harvest **d**,
25:20 taking off a coat on a cold **d**
27:1 what another **d** may bring.
27:15 water on a rainy **d** is like
Ecc 7:1 and the **d** you die is better than
7:1 is better than the **d** you're born.
8:8 No one has control over the **d**
8:16 without sleep **d** and night),
Sos 2:17 When the **d** brings a cooling
3:11 on him on his wedding **d**,
3:11 his **d** of joyful delight.
4:6 When the **d** brings a cool
8:8 the **d** she becomes engaged?
Isa 2:11 On that **d** the LORD alone will
2:12 will have his **d** against all who
2:17 On that **d** the LORD alone will
2:20 On that **d** people will throw to
3:7 When that **d** comes the relative
3:18 On that **d** the Lord will take
4:1 When that **d** comes,
4:2 When that **d** comes,
4:5 a cloud of smoke during the **d**
4:6 the heat during the **d** as well as
5:30 On that **d** they will roar over
7:18 On that **d** the LORD will
7:20 "On that **d** the Lord will hire the
7:21 On that **d** a person will keep
7:23 On that **d**, in every place where
9:14 So in one **d** the LORD will cut
10:3 What will you do on the **d** you
10:17 and thornbushes in one **d**.
10:32 This **d** they stopped at Nob.
13:6 for the **d** of the LORD is near.
13:9 The **d** of the LORD is going to
13:9 It will be a cruel **d** with fury and
14:3 When that **d** comes,
17:4 "When that **d** comes,
17:7 When that **d** comes,
17:9 When that **d** comes,
17:11 On the **d** you plant,
17:11 become a ⌊rotting⌋ pile on a **d**
19:18 When that **d** comes,
19:19 When that **d** comes,
19:21 the LORD when that **d** comes.
19:23 When that **d** comes,
19:24 When that **d** comes,
20:6 When that **d** comes,
21:8 on the watchtower every **d**.
22:5 Armies has chosen a special **d**.
22:5 It will be a **d** of confusion and
22:5 ⌊a **d** of⌋ tearing down walls
22:8 On that **d** the LORD will
22:12 On that **d** the Almighty LORD
22:20 When that **d** comes,
Isa 22:25 "On that **d** the peg which I
23:15 When that **d** comes,
24:21 On that **d** the LORD will
25:9 On that **d** ⌊his people⌋ will
26:1 On that **d** this song will be
27:1 On that **d** the LORD will use
27:2 On that **d** sing about a
27:3 I watch over it **d** and night so
27:12 On that **d** the LORD will begin
27:13 On that **d** a ram's horn will be
28:5 When that **d** comes,
28:19 during the **d** and during the
28:24 go on plowing every **d** so
29:18 When that **d** comes,
30:23 When that **d** comes,
30:25 When the **d** of the great
30:26 When that **d** comes,
31:7 When that **d** comes,
34:8 will have a **d** of vengeance,
34:10 not be extinguished **d** or night,
37:3 Today is a **d** filled with misery,
38:12 You ended my life in one **d**.
38:13 You ended my life in one **d**.
39:6 have stored up to this **d**,
43:13 "From the ⌊first⌋ **d** I was the
47:9 In one **d** both of these will
49:8 In the **d** of salvation I will help
52:5 And my name is cursed all **d**
52:6 When that **d** comes,
56:2 is the one who keeps the **d**
56:6 All of them will keep the **d** of
58:2 They look for me every **d** and
58:5 themselves for ⌊only⌋ a **d**?
58:5 an acceptable **d** to the LORD?
58:13 If you stop trampling on the **d** of
58:13 as you please on my holy **d**,
58:13 if you call the **d** of worship a
58:13 the LORD's holy **d** honorable,
60:11 They will never be closed **d** or
60:19 be your light during the **d**,
61:2 the LORD's good will and the **d**
62:6 will never be silent **d** or night.
63:4 I planned the **d** of vengeance.
65:2 I stretched out my hands all **d**
65:5 like a smoldering fire all **d** long.
66:8 Can a country be born in one **d**?
Jer 4:9 "When that **d** comes,"
6:4 The **d** is passing, and the
9:1 of tears so that I could cry **d**
12:3 them for the **d** of slaughter.
14:17 'My eyes flow with tears **d** and
16:13 you will serve other gods **d**
17:16 longed for the **d** of destruction.
17:17 my refuge on the **d** of disaster.
17:18 Bring the **d** of disaster on them,
17:21 do not carry anything on the **d**
17:22 homes on the **d** of worship.
17:22 but observe the **d** of worship as
17:22 the day of worship as a holy **d**,
17:24 of this city on the **d** of worship.
17:24 You must observe the **d** of
17:24 as a holy **d** by not doing
17:27 listen to me and observe the **d**
17:27 as a holy **d** by not carrying
17:27 Jerusalem on the **d** of worship.
18:17 On the **d** of their disaster,
20:3 The next **d** when Pashhur took
20:7 I've been made fun of all **d** long.
20:8 insults and contempt all **d** long.
20:14 Cursed is the **d** that I was born,
20:14 the **d** that my mother gave birth
25:33 On that **d** those killed by the
30:7 How terrible that **d** will be!
30:7 There will be no other **d** like it.
30:8 "On that **d**," declares the LORD
31:6 There will be a **d** when
31:35 sun to be a light during the **d**.
32:20 To this **d** you are still doing
32:20 that continues to this **d**.
32:31 and furious from the **d** they built
32:31 the day they built it to this **d**.
33:20 break my arrangement with **d**
33:25 made an arrangement with **d**
35:14 not drunk any wine to this **d**,
36:6 On a **d** of fasting, you must
36:30 and exposed to the heat of **d**
Jer 37:21 him a loaf of bread every **d** from
38:28 the **d** Jerusalem was captured.
39:2 On the ninth **d** of the fourth
41:4 The **d** after the murder of
44:10 yourselves even to this **d**.
46:10 That **d** belongs to the Almighty
46:10 It is a **d** of vengeance when he
46:21 The **d** of destruction is coming.
48:41 On that **d** Moab's soldiers will
49:22 On that **d** Edom's soldiers will
49:26 be silenced that **d**," declares
50:30 that **d**," declares the LORD.
50:31 "Your **d** has come,
51:2 direction on the **d** of trouble.
52:4 On the tenth **d** of the tenth
52:6 On the ninth **d** of the fourth
52:12 On the tenth **d** of the fifth month
52:31 On the twenty-fifth **d** of the
Lam 1:12 he has made me suffer on the **d**
1:13 He has made me sick all **d**
1:21 have allowed the **d** to come,
2:1 footstool on the **d** of his anger.
2:7 as though it were a festival **d**.
2:16 Yes, this is the **d** we've been
2:18 down like a river **d** and night.
2:21 You killed them on the **d** of
2:22 escaped or survived on the **d**
3:3 me again and again all **d** long.
3:14 All **d** long ⌊they make fun of
3:62 directed against me all **d** long.
Eze 1:1 On the fifth **d** of the fourth
1:2 On the fifth **d** of the month,
2:3 rebelled against me to this **d**.
4:5 I have assigned to you one **d**
4:6 one **d** for each year I have
4:10 of food every **d** at set times.
7:7 The **d** is near. There will be
7:10 "The **d** is near! It is coming!
7:12 The **d** is near. Buyers will not
7:19 be able to rescue them on the **d**
8:1 On the fifth **d** of the sixth
12:7 During the **d** I brought out bags
13:5 in battle on the **d** of the LORD.
20:1 On the tenth **d** of the fifth month
20:31 your disgusting idols to this **d**.
22:8 the **d** to worship me.
22:24 has not had rain during the **d**
24:1 On the tenth **d** of the tenth
24:2 Jerusalem this very **d**.
24:25 "Son of man, on that **d** I will
24:26 On that **d** a refugee will come
24:27 On that very **d** your mouth will
26:1 On the first **d** of the month in
29:1 On the twelfth **d** of the tenth
29:17 On the first **d** of the first month
29:21 "On that **d** I will make the
30:2 LORD says: Cry for that **d**!
30:3 The **d** is near. The day of the
30:3 The **d** of the LORD is near.
30:3 It will be a gloomy **d**,
30:9 On that **d** I will send
30:9 is in trouble. That **d** is coming!
30:16 will be in trouble every **d**.
30:18 At Tahpanhes the **d** will turn
30:20 On the seventh **d** of the first
31:1 On the first **d** of the third month
32:1 On the first **d** of the twelfth
32:17 On the fifteenth **d** of the month
33:21 On the fifth **d** of the tenth month
34:12 and gloomy **d** from every place
36:33 On the **d** that I cleanse you
38:18 On the **d** that Gog attacks the
38:19 On that **d** there will be a large
39:8 This is the **d** I have spoken
39:11 "'When that **d** comes,
39:13 Israel will be honored on the **d**
39:22 From that **d** on, the people of
40:1 It was the tenth **d** of the month
43:22 "On the second **d** bring a male
43:25 Every **d** for seven days you
43:27 days are over, on the eighth **d**,
45:18 On the first **d** of the first month,
45:20 do the same on the seventh **d**
45:21 "'On the fourteenth **d** of the first
45:23 Every **d** during the seven days
45:25 On the fifteenth **d** of the

Eze	46:1	on the weekly **d** of worship.
	46:4	offering on the **d** of worship.
	46:6	On the first **d** of the month,
	46:12	as he does on the **d** of worship.
	46:13	that has no defects every **d** as
Dan	6:10	Three times each **d** he got
	6:13	He prays three times each **d**."
	10:4	On the twenty-fourth **d** of the
	10:12	since the first **d** you decided
Hos	1:5	On that **d** I will break Israel's
	1:11	The **d** of Jezreel will be a great
	1:11	day of Jezreel will be a great **d**.
	2:3	naked as the **d** she was born.
	2:16	"On that **d** she will call me her
	2:18	"On that **d** I will make an
	2:21	"On that **d** I will answer your
	4:5	During the **d** you stumble,
	6:2	On the third **d** he will raise us
	7:5	On the **d** of the king's
	9:5	What will they do on the **d** of
	12:1	try to chase the east wind all **d**.
Joe	1:15	This will be a terrible **d**!
	1:15	The **d** of the LORD is near,
	2:1	because the **d** of the LORD is
	2:2	It is a **d** of darkness and gloom,
	2:2	a **d** of clouds and overcast
	2:11	The **d** of the LORD is
	2:31	as blood before the terrifying **d**
	3:14	The **d** of the LORD is near in
	3:18	On that **d** new wine will cover
Amo	1:14	troops are shouting on the **d**
	1:14	howling on the **d** of the storm.
	2:16	will run away naked that **d**.
	3:14	On the **d** I punish Israel for its
	5:8	He turns **d** into night.
	5:18	be for those who long for the **d**
	5:18	Why do you long for that **d**?
	5:18	The **d** of the LORD is one of
	5:20	The **d** of the LORD brings
	6:3	be for those who think that a **d**
	8:3	On that **d** the songs of the
	8:5	When will the **d** of worship be
	8:9	On that **d**, declares the
	8:10	I will make that **d** seem like a
	8:13	On that **d** beautiful young
	9:11	On that **d** I will set up David's
Oba	1:8	"On that **d** I will destroy the
	1:15	"The **d** of the LORD is near for
Jnh	3:4	city and walked for about a **d**.
	4:7	At dawn the next **d**,
Mic	2:4	When that **d** comes,
	3:6	and the **d** will turn dark for
	4:6	"When that **d** comes,"
	5:10	"When that **d** comes,"
	7:4	The **d** you thought you would
	7:11	The **d** for rebuilding your walls
	7:12	When that **d** comes,
Nah	1:7	is a fortress in the **d** of trouble.
	2:3	when they are waved on the **d**
	2:8	pool of water from its first **d** on.
Hab	3:16	I wait for the **d** of trouble to
Zep	1:7	because the **d** of the LORD is
	1:8	"On the **d** of the LORD's
	1:9	On that **d** I will punish all who
	1:10	On that **d** a loud cry will come
	1:14	The frightening **d** of the LORD
	1:14	bitterly on the **d** of the LORD.
	1:15	That **d** will be a day of
	1:15	That day will be a **d** of
	1:15	a **d** of trouble and distress,
	1:15	a **d** of devastation and
	1:15	a **d** of darkness and gloom,
	1:15	a **d** of clouds and overcast
	1:16	a **d** of rams' horns and battle
	1:18	be able to rescue them on the **d**
	2:2	the **d** passes like windblown
	2:2	before the **d** of the LORD's
	2:3	you will find shelter on the **d**
	3:8	One **d** I will stand up as a
	3:11	On that **d** you will no longer be
	3:16	On that **d** Jerusalem will be
Hag	1:1	On the first **d** of the sixth
	1:15	began on the twenty-fourth **d**
	2:1	On the twenty-first **d** of the
	2:10	On the twenty-fourth **d** of the
	2:18	from the twenty-fourth **d** of the
Hag	2:18	from the **d** when the foundation
	2:20	time on the twenty-fourth **d**
	2:23	On that **d**, declares the LORD
Zec	1:7	On the twenty-fourth **d** of the
	2:11	On that **d** many nations will
	3:9	this land's sin in a single **d**.
	3:10	On that **d**," declares the LORD
	4:10	Who despised the **d** when little
	6:10	This same **d** go to the house of
	7:1	On the fourth **d** of the ninth
	9:16	On that **d** the LORD their God
	11:11	So it was broken on that **d**,
	12:3	On that **d** I will make
	12:4	The LORD declares, "On that **d**
	12:6	"On that **d** I will make the
	12:8	On that **d** the LORD will
	12:9	"On that **d** I will seek to
	12:11	On that **d** the mourning in
	13:1	"On that **d** a fountain will be
	13:2	"On that **d**," declares the LORD
	13:4	"On that **d** every prophet will
	14:1	A **d** is going to come for the
	14:4	On that **d** his feet will stand on
	14:6	On that **d** there will be neither
	14:7	There will be one **d** — a day
	14:7	There will be one day — a **d**
	14:7	difference between **d** and night.
	14:8	On that **d** living water will flow
	14:9	On that **d** the LORD will be the
	14:13	On that **d** a large-scale panic
	14:20	On that **d** "Holy to the LORD"
	14:21	On that **d** there will no longer
Mal	3:2	able to endure the **d** he comes?
	3:2	to survive on the **d** he appears?
	3:17	"On that **d** I will make them my
	4:1	"Certainly the **d** is coming!
	4:1	The **d** that is coming will burn
	4:3	because on the **d** I act they will
	4:5	before that very terrifying **d**
Mat	6:34	Each **d** has enough trouble of
	7:22	Many will say to me on that **d**,
	10:15	Judgment **d** will be better for
	11:22	I can guarantee that judgment **d**
	11:24	I can guarantee that judgment **d**
	12:1	Then on a **d** of worship Jesus
	12:2	right to do on the **d** of worship."
	12:5	Moses' Teachings that on the **d**
	12:5	things they shouldn't on the **d**
	12:8	authority over the **d** of worship
	12:10	it was right to heal on a **d**
	12:11	into a pit on a **d** of worship,
	12:12	So it is right to do good on the **d**
	12:36	on judgment **d** people will have
	12:45	to the evil people of this **d**."
	13:1	That same **d** Jesus left the
	16:21	but on the third **d** he would be
	17:23	but on the third **d** he will be
	20:6	here all **d** long without work?'
	20:12	we worked hard all **d** under
	20:19	But on the third **d** he will be
	22:23	On that **d** some Sadducees,
	24:20	that it will not be winter or a **d**
	24:36	"No one knows when that **d** or
	24:38	and getting married until the **d**
	24:42	know on what **d** your Lord will
	25:13	don't know the **d** or the hour.
	26:17	On the first **d** of the Festival of
	26:29	wine again until that **d** when
	26:55	the temple courtyard every **d**.
	27:62	The next **d**, which was the day
	27:62	which was the **d** of worship,
	27:64	tomb secure until the third **d**.
	28:1	After the **d** of worship,
	28:15	the Jewish people to this **d**.
Mar	1:21	On the next **d** of worship,
	2:23	Once on a **d** of worship Jesus
	2:24	permitted on the **d** of worship?"
	2:27	Then he added, "The **d** of
	2:27	not people for the **d** of worship.
	2:28	authority over the **d** of worship
	3:2	he would heal the man on the **d**
	3:4	to do evil on the **d** of worship,
	4:27	and is awake during the **d**.
	5:5	Night and **d** he was among the
	6:2	When the **d** of worship came,
	9:31	but on the third **d** he will come
Mar	11:12	The next **d**, when they left
	13:32	"No one knows when that **d** or
	14:12	was customary on the first **d**
	14:25	wine again until that **d** when
	14:49	the temple courtyard every **d**.
	15:42	before the **d** of worship,
	16:1	When the **d** of worship was
Luk	1:20	to talk until the **d** this happens.
	1:78	A new **d** will dawn on us from
	1:80	He lived in the desert until the **d**
	2:37	courtyard but worshiped **d**
	2:44	After traveling for a **d**,
	4:16	synagogue on the **d** of worship.
	4:31	taught them on a **d** of worship.
	5:1	One **d** Jesus was standing by
	5:12	One **d** Jesus was in a city
	5:17	One **d** when Jesus was
	6:1	Once, on a **d** of worship,
	6:2	right to do on the **d** of worship?"
	6:5	authority over the **d** of worship
	6:6	On another **d** of worship,
	6:7	he would heal the man on the **d**
	6:9	thing to do on a **d** of worship:
	6:13	When it was **d**, he called his
	8:22	One **d** Jesus and his disciples
	9:12	Toward the end of the **d**,
	9:22	but on the third **d** he would
	9:23	pick up their crosses every **d**,
	9:37	The next **d**, when they had
	10:12	I can guarantee that judgment **d**
	10:14	Judgment **d** will be better for
	10:35	The next **d** the Samaritan took
	11:3	Give us our bread **d** by day.
	11:3	Give us our bread day by **d**.
	13:10	synagogue on the **d** of worship.
	13:14	for healing on the **d** of worship.
	13:14	come on the **d** of worship."
	13:15	or donkey on the **d** of worship?
	13:16	to free her on the **d** of worship?"
	13:32	finish my work on the third **d**.
	13:33	tomorrow, and the next **d**.
	14:1	On a **d** of worship Jesus went
	14:3	"Is it right to heal on the **d** of
	14:5	into a well on a **d** of worship,
	16:19	Every **d** was like a party to him.
	16:22	"One **d** the beggar died,
	17:4	you seven times in one **d**
	17:24	The **d** of the Son of Man will be
	17:25	rejected by the people of his **d**.
	17:27	and getting married until the **d**
	17:29	But on the **d** that Lot left
	17:30	The **d** when the Son of Man is
	17:31	"On that **d** those who are on
	18:7	out to him for help **d** and night?
	18:33	But on the third **d** he will come
	19:47	the temple courtyard every **d**.
	20:1	One **d** Jesus was teaching the
	21:34	Then that **d** could suddenly
	21:35	That **d** will surprise all people
	21:37	During the **d** Jesus would
	22:7	The **d** came during the Festival
	22:53	in the temple courtyard every **d**
	23:12	Pilate became friends that **d**.
	23:54	It was Friday, and the **d** of
	23:56	But on the **d** of worship they
	24:7	back to life on the third **d**.'"
	24:13	On the same **d**, two of Jesus'
	24:21	**d** since everything happened.
	24:29	and the **d** is almost over.
	24:46	come back to life on the third **d**.
Jon	1:29	toward him the next **d** and said,
	1:35	The next **d** John was standing
	1:39	the rest of that **d** with him.
	1:43	The next **d** Jesus wanted to go
	5:9	happened on a **d** of worship.
	5:10	"This is a **d** of worship.
	5:16	people on the **d** of worship.
	5:18	laws about the **d** of worship,
	6:22	On the next **d** the people were
	6:39	them back to life on the last **d**.
	6:40	them back to life on the last **d**."
	6:44	back to life on the last **d**.
	6:54	them back to life on the last **d**.
	7:22	a male on a **d** of worship.
	7:23	you circumcise a male on the **d**
	7:23	well on the **d** of worship?

Jon 7:37 the last and most important **d**
8:56 to see that my **d** was coming.
9:4 me wants us to do while it is **d**.
9:14 The **d** when Jesus mixed the
9:14 man sight was a **d** of worship.
9:16 traditions for the **d** of worship."
11:9 walk during the **d** don't stumble
11:24 come back to life on the last **d**,
11:53 From that **d** on, the Jewish
12:7 this to prepare me for the **d**
12:12 On the next **d** the large crowd
12:48 will judge them on the last **d**.
14:20 On that **d** you will know that I
16:23 When that **d** comes,
16:26 When that **d** comes,
19:31 was Friday and the next **d** was
19:31 important **d** of worship,
19:42 since that **d** was the Jewish
19:42 that day was the Jewish **d**
Act 1:2 until the **d** he was taken to
1:22 people to the **d** that Jesus was
2:1 the fiftieth **d** after Passover,
2:20 as blood before the terrifying **d**
2:29 that his tomb is here to this **d**.
2:41 That **d** about 3,000 people
2:46 and went to the temple every **d**.
2:47 Every **d** the Lord saved people,
3:2 Every **d** these men would put
4:3 and John in jail until the next **d**.
4:5 The next **d** the Jewish rulers,
5:42 Every **d** in the temple courtyard
6:1 neglected every **d** when food
6:9 ⌊One **d**⌋ some men from the
7:8 him on the eighth **d**.
7:26 The next **d** Moses saw two
8:1 On that **d** widespread
9:24 were watching the city gates **d**
10:3 One **d**, about three in the
10:9 Around noon the next **d**,
10:23 The next **d** Peter left with them.
10:24 The following **d** they arrived in
10:40 him back to life on the third **d**.
12:21 The appointed **d** came.
13:11 unable to see the light of **d**."
13:14 On the **d** of worship they went
13:27 are read every **d** of worship.
13:42 subject the next **d** of worship.
13:44 On the next **d** of worship,
14:20 The next **d** Paul and Barnabas
15:21 on every **d** of worship."
16:5 and grew in numbers every **d**.
16:11 The next **d** we sailed to the
16:13 On the **d** of worship we went
16:16 One **d** when we were going to
17:11 and every **d** they carefully
17:17 also held discussions every **d**
17:31 He has set a **d** when he is
18:4 On every **d** of worship,
20:7 he intended to leave the next **d**,
20:15 On the following **d** we
20:15 The next **d** we went by the
20:15 and on the next **d** we arrived at
20:16 for the **d** of Pentecost,
20:18 time with you from the first **d**
20:31 you for three years, **d** and night,
21:1 The next **d** we sailed to the
21:7 and spent the **d** with them.
21:8 The next **d** we went to Philip's
21:18 The next **d** Paul went with us
21:26 The next **d**, Paul took the men
22:30 officer released Paul the next **d**
23:32 to their barracks the next **d**
25:6 The next **d** Festus took his
25:17 The next **d** I immediately
25:23 The next **d** Agrippa and
26:7 intense devotion **d** and night.
26:22 helping me to this **d** so that
27:3 The next **d** we arrived at the
27:9 lost so much time that the **d**
27:18 by the storm that the next **d**
27:19 On the third **d** they threw the
27:33 "This is the fourteenth **d** you
28:13 The next **d** a south wind began
28:23 On a designated **d** a larger
Rom 2:5 you on that **d** when God vents
2:16 as they face the **d** when God,
Rom 8:36 "We are being killed all **d** long
10:21 "All **d** long I have stretched out
11:8 as Scripture says, "To this **d**
13:12 almost over, and the **d** is near.
13:13 who live in the light of **d**.
14:5 One person decides that one **d**
14:6 people observe a special **d**,
1Co 1:8 you of anything on the **d**
3:13 The **d** will make what each
5:5 be saved on the **d** of the Lord.
10:8 of them died on one **d**.
15:4 back to life on the third **d** as
15:31 I face death every **d**.
2Co 1:14 our reason to be proud on the **d**
3:14 In fact, to this **d** the same veil
4:16 we are renewed **d** by day.
4:16 we are renewed day by **d**.
6:2 On the **d** of salvation I helped
6:2 Now is the **d** of salvation!
11:25 on the sea for a night and a **d**.
Eph 4:30 seal on you for the **d** you will
Php 1:5 the first **d** ⌊you believed⌋ until
1:6 on the **d** of Christ Jesus.
1:10 blameless until the **d** of Christ.
2:16 Then I can brag on the **d** of
3:5 circumcised on the eighth **d**.
Col 1:6 you from the first **d** you heard it.
1:9 you since the **d** we heard about
1Th 2:9 We worked night and **d** so that
3:10 We pray very hard night and **d**
5:2 You know very well that the **d**
5:4 That **d** won't take you by
5:5 You belong to the **d** and the
5:8 Since we belong to the **d**,
2Th 1:10 ⌊This will happen⌋ on that **d**
2:2 or letter that the **d** of the Lord
2:3 ⌊That **d** cannot come unless⌋
3:8 hard and struggled night and **d**
1Ti 5:5 asking for his help night and **d**.
2Ti 1:3 in my prayers night and **d** when
1:12 had entrusted to me until that **d**.
1:18 mercy when that **d** comes.
4:8 give me that prize on that **d**.
Heb 3:13 Encourage each other every **d**
4:4 said this about the seventh **d**:
4:4 "On the seventh **d** God rested
4:7 So God set another **d**.
4:7 That **d** is today. Many years
4:8 have spoken about another **d**.
10:11 Every **d** each priest performed
10:25 even more as we see the **d**
Jas 5:5 for the **d** of slaughter.
1Pe 2:12 they will praise God on the **d**
2Pe 1:19 a dark place as you wait for **d**
2:8 Each **d** was like torture to him
2:9 on the **d** of judgment.
3:7 They are being kept until the **d**
3:8 One **d** with the Lord is like a
3:8 thousand years are like one **d**.
3:10 The **d** of the Lord will come
3:10 On that **d** heaven will pass
3:12 as you look forward to the **d** of
3:12 When that **d** comes,
3:18 him now and for that eternal **d**!
1Jn 4:17 to the **d** of judgment.
Jud 1:6 for judgment on the great **d**.
Rev 1:10 Spirit's power on the Lord's **d**.
4:8 Without stopping **d** or night
6:17 because the frightening **d** of
7:15 They serve him **d** and night in
8:12 no light for one-third of the **d**
9:15 ready for that hour, **d**, month,
12:10 the one accusing them **d** and
14:11 There will be no rest **d** or night
16:14 frightening **d** of God Almighty.
18:8 will come in a single **d**.
20:10 They will be tortured **d** and
21:25 Its gates will be open all **d**.

daybreak (8)

Exo 14:27 and at **d** the water returned to
Jdg 19:26 At **d**, the woman came to the
Rut 2:7 on her feet from **d** until now.
2Sm 2:32 and arrived at Hebron by **d**.
Neh 8:3 From **d** until noon,
Hos 10:15 At **d**, the king of Israel will be
Mat 20:1 a landowner who went out at **d**
Act 27:33 Just before **d** Paul was

daydreaming (1)

Ecc 5:3 **D** comes when there are too

daydreams (1)

Ecc 5:7 In spite of many **d**,

daylight (12)

Num 25:4 and execute them in broad **d** in
Dtr 28:29 You will grope in broad **d** as
2Sm 12:11 bed with your wives in broad **d**.
12:12 make this happen in broad **d**
Jer 15:9 humiliated, while it is still **d**.
Eze 12:3 people see you leave in the **d**.
12:4 Let them see you in the **d**.
Amo 8:9 darken the earth in broad **d**.
Mat 10:27 Tell in the **d** what I say to you
Luk 12:3 the dark will be heard in the **d**.
Jon 11:9 "Aren't there twelve hours of **d**?
2Pe 2:13 holding wild parties in broad **d**.

day's (6)

Mat 20:2 the workers the usual **d** wages,
20:9 and each received a **d** wages
20:10 of them received a **d** wages
20:13 agree with me on a **d** wages
Rev 6:6 "A quart of wheat for a **d** pay or
6:6 quarts of barley for a **d** pay.

days (533)

Gen 1:14 festivals, **d**, and years.
6:4 were on the earth in those **d**,
7:4 In seven **d** I will send rain to
7:4 send rain to the earth for 40 **d**
7:10 Seven **d** later the flood came
7:12 the earth for 40 **d** and 40 nights.
7:17 The flood continued for 40 **d** on
7:24 were on the earth for 150 **d**.
8:3 At the end of 150 **d** the water
8:6 After 40 more **d** Noah opened
8:10 He waited seven more **d** and
8:12 He waited seven more **d** and
17:12 child who is eight **d** old must
21:4 When Isaac was eight **d** old,
22:4 Two **d** later Abraham saw the
24:55 the girl stay with us ten **d** or so.
29:20 years seemed like only a few **d**
30:36 He traveled three **d** away from
31:22 Two **d** later Laban was told
31:23 pursued Jacob for seven **d**.
34:25 Two **d** later, while the men
40:12 three branches are three **d**.
40:13 In the next three **d** Pharaoh will
40:18 "The three baskets are three **d**.
40:19 In the next three **d** Pharaoh will
40:20 Two **d** later, on his birthday,
42:17 he put them in jail for three **d**.
49:1 happen to you in the **d** to come.
50:3 in the usual time — 40 **d**.
50:3 mourned for him 70 **d**.
50:10 Joseph took seven **d** to mourn
Exo 3:18 Please let us travel three **d** into
5:3 Please let us travel three **d** into
7:25 Seven **d** passed after the
8:27 We need to travel three **d** into
10:22 was total darkness for three **d**.
10:23 one went anywhere for three **d**.
12:15 For seven **d** you must eat
12:16 You must not work on these **d**
12:19 in your houses for seven **d**.
13:6 "For seven **d** you must eat
13:7 be eaten during these seven **d**.
15:22 For three **d** they traveled in the
16:5 as they gather on other **d**."
16:26 You can gather food on six **d**,
16:29 food on the sixth day for two **d**.
19:10 and tell them they have two **d**
19:15 "Be ready two **d** from now.
20:9 You have six **d** to do all your
20:11 In six **d** the LORD made
22:30 with their mothers seven **d**,
23:12 "For six **d** you will do your
23:15 For seven **d** you must eat
24:16 For six **d** the cloud covered it,

Exo 24:18 He stayed on the mountain 40 **d**
29:30 will wear them for seven **d**.
29:35 Take seven **d** to ordain them.
29:37 For seven **d** at the altar make
31:13 to observe my **d** of worship.
31:15 You may work for six **d**,
31:17 heaven and earth in six **d**,
34:18 bread for seven **d** at
34:21 "You may work six **d**,
34:28 was there with the LORD 40 **d**
35:2 You may work for six **d**,
Lev 8:33 the tent of meeting for seven **d**,
8:33 will take seven **d** to ordain you.
8:35 day and night for seven **d**
12:2 will be unclean for seven **d**.
12:2 This is the same number of **d**
12:3 when he is eight **d** old.
12:4 she must stay at home for 33 **d**
12:4 holy place until the **d** needed
12:5 she must stay at home for 66 **d**
12:6 "When the **d** needed to make
13:4 put him in isolation for seven **d**.
13:5 in isolation for another seven **d**.
13:21 put him in isolation for seven **d**.
13:26 put him in isolation for seven **d**.
13:31 in isolation for seven **d**.
13:33 in isolation for another seven **d**.
13:50 in a separate place for seven **d**.
13:54 place for seven more **d**.
14:8 However, for seven **d** he will
14:38 close up the house for seven **d**.
15:13 he must wait seven **d** to be
15:19 will be unclean for seven **d**.
15:24 he will be unclean for seven **d**.
15:25 blood for many **d** other than her
15:28 she must wait seven **d**.
19:3 Observe my **d** of worship.
19:30 "Observe my **d** of worship and
22:27 with its mother for seven **d**.
23:3 You may work for six **d**.
23:6 For seven **d** you must eat
23:8 a sacrifice by fire for seven **d**.
23:16 This is a total of fifty **d**.
23:34 It will last seven **d**.
23:36 For seven consecutive **d** bring
23:38 to the LORD's **d** of worship,
23:39 the LORD's festival for seven **d**.
23:39 The first and the eighth **d** will
23:40 LORD your God for seven **d**.
23:41 it for seven **d** each year.
23:42 Live in booths for seven **d**.
26:2 Observe my **d** of worship and
26:35 All the **d** it lies deserted,
Num 6:9 Seven **d** later he must shave
9:20 stayed only a few **d** over
9:22 Whether it was two **d**,
10:10 Also, on your festival **d** and on
10:33 LORD and traveled for three **d**.
11:19 won't eat it just for one or two **d**,
11:19 or five, or ten, or twenty **d**,
12:14 the community for seven **d**?
12:14 outside the camp for seven **d**.
12:15 outside the camp for seven **d**.
13:25 Forty **d** later, they came back
14:34 For 40 **d** you explored the land.
19:11 will be unclean for seven **d**.
19:14 will be unclean for seven **d**.
19:16 will be unclean for seven **d**.
20:29 mourned for Aaron 30 **d**.
24:14 your people in the **d** to come."
28:17 For seven **d** you must eat only
28:24 on each of the seven **d**.
29:12 to the LORD for seven **d**.
31:19 stay outside the camp seven **d**.
31:19 on the third and seventh **d**
33:8 After they traveled for three **d** in
Dtr 1:2 (It takes 11 **d** to go from Mount
5:13 You have six **d** to do all your
9:9 I stayed on the mountain 40 **d**
9:11 At the end of the 40 **d** and 40
9:18 without food and water for 40 **d**
9:25 in front of the LORD for 40 **d**
10:10 I stayed on the mountain 40 **d**
16:3 Instead, for seven **d** you must
16:4 in your land for seven **d**.
16:8 For six **d** eat unleavened

Dtr 16:13 Festival of Booths for seven **d**.
16:15 For seven **d** you will celebrate
31:29 In the **d** to come disasters will
34:8 in the plains of Moab for 30 **d**.
Jos 1:11 In three **d** you will cross the
2:16 Hide there for three **d** until they
2:22 stayed there for three **d** until
3:2 Three **d** later the officers went
6:3 the city once a day for six **d**.
6:14 They did this for six **d**.
9:16 But three **d** after the treaty was
9:17 and Kiriath Jearim two **d** later.
Jdg 5:6 In the **d** of Shamgar,
5:6 son of Anath, in the **d** of Jael,
11:40 that for four **d** every year the
14:12 you solve it during the seven **d**
14:14 For three **d** they couldn't solve
14:17 for the rest of the seven **d**
17:6 In those **d** Israel didn't have a
18:1 In those **d** Israel didn't have a
18:1 And in those **d** the tribe of Dan
19:1 In those **d** when Israel didn't
19:4 celebrating for three **d**.
20:27 In those **d** the ark of God's
21:25 In those **d** Israel didn't have a
Rut 1:1 In the **d** when the judges were
1Sm 3:1 In those **d** a prophecy from the
9:20 that were lost three **d** ago
10:8 Wait seven **d** until I come to
11:3 "Give us seven **d** so that we
13:8 He waited seven **d**,
17:16 morning and evening for 40 **d**,
20:12 two or three **d** how my father
25:38 About ten **d** later the LORD
27:1 "One of these **d** Saul will
30:1 Two **d** later, when David and
30:12 any water for three whole **d**.)
30:13 because I got sick three **d** ago.
31:13 Then they fasted seven **d**.
2Sm 1:1 David stayed in Ziklag two **d**.
16:23 In those **d** both David and
20:4 and in three **d** be here yourself."
24:8 after 9 months and 20 **d**.
1Ki 3:18 Two **d** later this woman also
8:65 the LORD our God for seven **d**.
12:12 back to Rehoboam two **d** later,
16:15 Zimri ruled for seven **d** in
19:8 he traveled for 40 **d** and nights
20:29 facing one another for seven **d**,
2Ki 2:17 for three **d** without finding him.
3:9 After seven **d** they ran out of
10:32 So in those **d** the LORD began
15:29 In the **d** of King Pekah of Israel,
15:37 In those **d** the LORD began to
20:1 In those **d** Hezekiah became
20:17 The LORD says, 'The **d** are
23:29 In Josiah's **d** Pharaoh Necoh
1Ch 4:41 In the **d** of King Hezekiah of
5:17 in genealogical records in the **d**
9:25 for a period of seven **d**.
10:12 Then they fasted seven **d**.
12:39 drank with David for three **d**
21:12 or three **d** of the LORD's sword
23:31 made — on weekly worship **d**,
29:15 Our **d** are as fleeting as
2Ch 2:4 on weekly worship **d**,
7:9 of the altar for seven **d**
7:9 festival for ⌊another⌋ seven **d**.
8:13 on weekly worship **d**,
10:12 back to Rehoboam two **d** later,
20:25 three **d** collecting the loot.
26:5 God in the **d** of Zechariah,
29:17 and for eight **d** they performed
30:21 Unleavened Bread for seven **d**
30:22 the festival meals for seven **d**,
30:23 the festival for seven more **d**.
30:23 celebrated for seven more **d**.
30:26 in Jerusalem since the **d**
31:3 on the weekly worship **d**,
32:24 In those **d** Hezekiah became
35:17 Unleavened Bread for seven **d**.
36:9 months and ten **d** in Jerusalem.
Ezr 6:22 So for seven **d** they celebrated
8:15 we camped there for three **d**.
8:32 we rested for three **d**.
9:7 our ancestors' **d** until now,

Ezr 10:8 didn't come within three **d** as
10:9 within three **d** in Jerusalem.
Neh 1:4 I mourned for **d**. I continued to
2:11 and was there for three **d**.
5:18 Once every ten **d** a supply of
6:15 The wall took 52 **d** to finish.
6:17 In those **d** the nobles of Judah
8:18 the festival for seven **d**,
10:33 on the weekly **d** of worship,
12:26 They lived in the **d** of Joiakim,
12:26 and in the **d** of Nehemiah the
13:15 In those **d** I saw people in
13:23 In those **d** I saw some Jews
Est 1:1 In the **d** of Xerxes the following
1:4 of his greatness for many **d**,
1:5 When those **d** were over,
1:5 held a banquet lasting seven **d**.
2:21 In those **d**, while Mordecai was
4:11 king's presence for 30 **d** now."
4:16 or drink at all for three entire **d**.
9:21 the fourteenth and fifteenth **d**
9:21 of Adar as **d** they must observe
9:22 them just like the **d** when
9:22 He declared that these **d** are to
9:22 that these days are to be **d**
9:26 the Jews called these **d** Purim,
9:27 these two **d** every year,
9:28 So these **d** must be
9:28 These **d** of Purim must not be
9:28 and the importance of these **d**
9:31 in order to establish these **d**
Job 2:13 the ground with him for seven **d**
3:6 Let it not be included in the **d** of
7:6 My **d** go swifter than a
7:16 because my **d** are so brief.
8:9 Our **d** on earth are only a
9:25 "My **d** go by more quickly than
10:5 Are your **d** like a mortal's days?
10:5 Are your days like a mortal's **d**?
12:12 has had many **d** has insight.
14:5 If the number of his **d** and the
15:20 person is tortured all his **d**.
17:1 My **d** have been snuffed out.
17:11 My **d** are passing by.
21:13 spend their **d** in happiness,
24:1 him see his **d** ⌊of judgment⌋?
29:2 in the **d** when God watched
29:18 but I will make my **d** as
30:16 **D** of suffering seize me.
30:25 person whose **d** were difficult?
30:27 **D** of misery are ahead of me.
33:25 go back to the **d** of their youth.
36:11 they will live out their **d** in
Psa 23:6 will stay close to me all the **d**
23:6 house for **d** without end.
27:4 in the LORD's house all the **d**
39:4 me about the number of **d**
39:5 made the length of my **d** ⌊only⌋
44:1 in their day, in **d** long ago.
55:23 will not live out half their **d**.
61:6 Add **d** upon days to the life of
61:6 Add days upon **d** to the life of
77:5 I have considered the **d** of old,
78:33 He brought their **d** to an end
81:3 the full moon, on our festival **d**.
89:29 his throne like the **d** of heaven.
89:45 You cut short the **d** of his youth
90:9 Indeed, all our **d** slip away
90:12 each of our **d** so that we
90:14 joyfully and rejoice all our **d**.
90:15 Make us rejoice for as many **d**
93:5 beautiful for **d** without end.
102:3 My **d** disappear like smoke.
102:11 My **d** are like a shadow that is
102:23 reduced ⌊the number of⌋ my **d**.
109:8 Let his **d** be few ⌊in number⌋.
128:5 prospering all the **d** of your life.
143:5 I remember the **d** long ago.
Pro 10:27 lengthens ⌊the number of⌋ **d**,
31:12 harms him all the **d** of her life.
Ecc 2:16 be forgotten in the **d** to come.
6:12 pointless **d** they live?
7:10 better in the old **d** than they are
11:1 will find it again after many **d**.
11:8 there will be many dark **d**.
12:1 before the **d** of trouble come

Isa 1:13 Festivals, your **d** of worship,
2:2 In the last **d** the mountain of the
13:22 Its **d** will not be extended.
30:26 like the light of seven **d**.
38:1 In those **d** Hezekiah became
39:6 The LORD says, 'The **d** are
51:9 up as you did in **d** long past,
53:10 his descendants for many **d**.
56:4 who keep my **d** of worship,
58:3 you see that on the **d** you fast,
60:20 and your **d** of sadness will be
65:20 who lives for only a few **d**
Jer 2:32 forgotten me for countless **d**.
3:16 In those **d** you will be fertile,
3:18 In those **d** the nation of Judah
5:18 Yet, even in those **d**,
7:32 "That is why the **d** are coming,"
9:25 "The **d** are coming,"
13:6 After many **d** the LORD said to
16:14 "That is why the **d** are coming,"
19:6 "That is why the **d** are coming,
20:18 I will finish my **d** in shame.
23:5 "The **d** are coming,"
23:7 "That is why the **d** are coming,"
23:20 In the last **d** you will
30:3 The **d** are coming,"
30:24 In the last **d** you will
31:27 "The **d** are coming,"
31:29 "When those **d** come,
31:31 "The **d** are coming,"
31:33 to Israel after those **d**," declares
31:38 "The **d** are coming,"
33:14 "The **d** are coming,"
33:15 In those **d** and at that time,
33:16 In those **d** Judah will be saved
42:7 After ten **d** the LORD spoke his
48:12 That is why the **d** are coming,"
48:47 Moab in the last **d**," declares
49:2 That is why the **d** are coming,
50:4 "In those **d** and at that time,"
50:20 In those **d** and at that time,"
51:47 That is why the **d** are coming
51:52 "That is why the **d** are coming,"
Lam 2:6 the memory of festivals and **d**
Eze 3:15 there among them for seven **d**.
3:16 After seven **d** the LORD spoke
4:4 as many **d** as you lie
4:5 So for 390 **d**, you will bear the
4:6 of the nation of Judah for 40 **d**,
4:9 Eat it during the 390 **d** that you
12:22 you have in Israel: 'D go by,
20:12 I also gave them certain **d** to
20:13 They dishonored the **d** to
20:16 They dishonored the **d** to
20:20 Set apart certain holy **d** to
20:21 They dishonored the **d** to
20:24 They dishonored the **d** to
22:4 have brought an end to your **d**,
22:26 They ignore the **d** to worship
23:38 the **d** to worship me.
38:16 In the **d** to come, I will let you
38:17 They prophesied in those **d**
43:25 Every day for seven **d** you
43:26 For seven **d** the priests should
43:27 When those **d** are over,
44:24 observe holy **d** to worship me.
44:26 he must wait seven **d**.
45:17 the weekly **d** of worship,
45:21 a festival lasting seven **d** when
45:23 Every day during the seven **d**
45:25 the same as on those seven **d**.
46:1 during the six working **d**,
46:3 of the LORD on the weekly **d**
46:11 "'On festival **d** and at
Dan 1:12 "Please test us for ten **d**.
1:14 and tested them for ten **d**.
1:15 After ten **d** they looked
2:28 to happen in the **d** to come.
5:11 In the **d** of your grandfather,
5:26 God has numbered the **d**
6:7 for the next 30 **d** whoever asks
6:12 that for 30 **d** whoever asks
8:19 what will happen in the last **d**,
8:23 "In the last **d** of those
8:27 was exhausted and sick for **d**.
10:2 During those **d** I, Daniel,
Dan 10:13 kingdom opposed me for 21 **d**.
10:14 to your people in the last **d**,
11:20 But in a few **d** the king will be
12:11 there will be 1,290 **d**.
12:12 wait until they reach 1,335 **d**.
Hos 2:11 her weekly worship **d** — all her
3:5 for his blessings in the last **d**.
6:2 After two **d** he will revive us.
9:5 or on the LORD's festival **d**?
Joe 2:29 In those **d** I will pour my Spirit
3:1 "In those **d** and at that time,
Amo 4:4 of your income every three **d**.
8:11 The **d** are going to come,
9:13 The **d** are going to come,
Jnh 1:17 fish for three **d** and three
3:3 It took three **d** to walk through
3:4 Then he said, "In forty **d**
Mic 4:1 In the last **d** the mountain of the
5:2 the distant past, to **d** long ago.
Hab 1:5 in your **d** that you would
Zep 1:1 LORD spoke his word in the **d**
Zec 8:6 remaining people in those **d**,
8:23 In those **d** ten people from
Mat 4:2 did not eat anything for 40 **d**
12:40 belly of a huge fish for three **d**
12:40 for three **d** and three nights.
15:32 have been with me three **d** now
17:1 After six **d** Jesus took Peter,
24:19 are nursing babies in those **d**.
24:22 reduce the number of those **d**,
24:22 But those **d** will be reduced
24:29 after the misery of those **d**,
24:37 be exactly like the **d** of Noah.
24:38 In the **d** before the flood,
26:2 will take place in two **d**.
26:61 temple and rebuild it in three **d**
27:40 and build it again in three **d**,
27:63 'After three **d** I will be brought
Mar 1:13 was tempted by Satan for 40 **d**.
2:1 Several **d** later Jesus came
8:2 have been with me three **d** now
8:31 but after three **d** he would come
9:2 After six **d** Jesus took only
10:34 But after three **d** he will come
13:17 are nursing babies in those **d**.
13:20 But those **d** will be reduced
13:24 after the misery of those **d**,
14:1 It was two **d** before the
14:58 and in three **d** I'll build another
15:29 and build it again in three **d**.
Luk 1:23 When the **d** of his service were
1:59 When the child was eight **d** old,
2:21 Eight **d** after his birth,
2:22 After the **d** required by Moses'
2:46 Three **d** later, they found him in
4:2 tempted by the devil for 40 **d**.
4:2 During those **d** Jesus ate
9:28 About eight **d** after he had said
13:14 "There are six **d** when work
13:14 So come on one of those **d** to
15:13 "After a few **d**, the younger son
17:22 will long to see one of the **d**
21:23 are nursing babies in those **d**.
Jon 2:1 Three **d** later a wedding took
2:12 and stayed there for a few **d**.
2:19 and I'll rebuild it in three **d**."
2:20 going to rebuild it in three **d**?"
4:40 He stayed in Samaria for two **d**.
4:43 spending two **d** in Samaria,
11:6 where he was for two more **d**.
11:7 Then, after the two **d**,
11:17 had been in the tomb for four **d**.
11:39 He's been dead for four **d**."
12:1 Six **d** before Passover,
Act 1:3 For 40 **d** he appeared to them
1:5 but in a few **d** you will be
2:17 'In the last **d**, God says, I will
2:18 In those **d** I will pour my Spirit
3:24 him spoke about these **d**.
9:9 For three **d** he couldn't see and
9:19 city of Damascus for several **d**.
9:43 for a number of **d** with Simon,
10:30 Cornelius answered, "Four **d**
10:48 to stay with them for several **d**.
12:3 the **d** of Unleavened Bread.
13:31 and for many **d** he appeared to
Act 13:41 in your **d** that you would
16:12 in this city for a number of **d**.
16:18 She kept doing this for many **d**.
17:2 three consecutive **d** of worship,
19:38 we have special **d** and officials
20:6 Five **d** later we joined them in
20:6 and stayed there for seven **d**.
21:4 we stayed there for seven **d**.
21:10 been there for a number of **d**,
21:27 When the seven **d** were almost
24:1 Five **d** later the chief priest
24:11 no more than twelve **d** ago.
24:24 Some **d** later Felix arrived with
25:1 Three **d** after Festus took over
25:6 Jerusalem for eight or ten **d** at
25:14 staying there for a number of **d**,
26:4 know how I lived the earliest **d**
27:7 slowly for a number of **d**.
27:20 For a number of **d** we couldn't
28:7 and for three **d** we were his
28:12 and stayed there for three **d**.
28:13 and two **d** later we arrived at
28:17 After three **d** Paul invited the
Rom 14:5 person decides that all **d** are
1Co 10:11 in the closing **d** of history.
Gal 1:18 I stayed with him for fifteen **d**.
4:10 You religiously observe **d**,
Eph 5:16 because these are evil **d**.
6:13 a stand during these evil **d**.
Php 4:15 also know that in the early **d**,
Col 2:16 observance of annual holy **d**,
2:16 or weekly worship **d**.
2Ti 3:1 In the last **d** there will be
Heb 1:2 In these last **d** he has spoken
8:8 "The **d** are coming,
8:10 make to Israel after those **d**,
10:16 will make to them after those **d**,
11:30 around them for seven **d**.
Jas 5:3 stored up riches in these last **d**.
1Pe 3:10 enjoy good **d** must keep their
3:20 disobeyed long ago in the **d**
2Pe 3:3 In the last **d** people who follow
Rev 2:10 suffering will go on for ten **d**.
2:13 even in the **d** of Antipas.
10:7 In the **d** when the seventh
11:3 They will speak for 1,260 **d**."
11:9 For 3 ½ **d** some members of
11:11 After 3 ½ **d** the breath of life
12:6 be taken care of for 1,260 **d**.

days' (1)

Num 10:33 a distance of three **d** journey

daytime (1)

Job 5:14 In the **d** they meet darkness

dazzling (5)

Sos 5:10 My beloved is **d** yet ruddy.
Eze 1:22 It looked like **d** crystal.
Mar 9:3 His clothes became **d** white,
Luk 9:29 and his clothes became **d**
Rev 19:8 the privilege of wearing **d**,

deacon (6)

Rom 16:1 in the Christian faith and a **d**
Eph 6:21 our dear brother and a faithful **d**
Col 1:7 as a trustworthy **d** for Christ
4:7 our dear brother, trustworthy **d**,
1Ti 3:10 he may become a **d**.
3:12 A **d** must have only one wife.

deacons (4)

Php 1:1 and their bishops and **d** —
1Ti 3:8 **D** must also be of good
3:12 **D** must manage their children
3:13 Those **d** who serve well gain

dead (356)

Gen 14:3 of Siddim (that is, the **D** Sea).
23:3 left the side of his **d** wife
23:4 so that I can bury my **d** wife."
23:6 Bury your **d** in one of our best
23:6 his tomb for burying your **d**."
40:19 head and hang your **d** body
42:38 His brother is **d**, and he's the
44:20 The boy's brother is **d**,

Exo 4:19 who wanted to kill you are **d**."
12:33 said, "Soon we'll all be **d**!"
14:30 lying **d** on the seashore.
21:34 and then the **d** animal will be
21:35 They must divide the **d** bull,
21:36 bull — and then the **d** bull will
22:13 he must bring in the **d** body as
Lev 5:2 unclean — the unclean **d** body
10:5 The **d** men were still in their
11:8 animals or touch their **d** bodies.
11:11 their **d** bodies disgusting.
11:24 Whoever touches their **d**
11:25 of their **d** bodies must wash
11:27 Whoever touches their **d**
11:28 Those who carry the **d** body of
11:31 Whoever touches their **d**
11:32 When the **d** body of one of
11:35 Anything on which their **d**
11:36 But anyone who touches their **d**
11:37 If their **d** bodies fall on seed
11:38 the seed and their **d** bodies fall
11:39 whoever touches its **d** body
11:40 Those who eat any of its **d**
11:40 Those who carry its **d** body
19:28 slash your body to mourn the **d**,
21:11 He must never go near any **d**
22:4 of semen or touches a **d** body,
26:30 and pile your **d** bodies on top of
26:30 bodies on top of your **d** idols.
Num 5:2 from touching a **d** body.
6:6 they must never go near a **d**
6:9 might suddenly drop **d** next
6:11 who touched the **d** body.
9:6 from touching a **d** body,
9:7 because we touched a **d** body.
9:10 unclean from touching a **d** body
14:29 Your bodies will drop **d** in this
14:32 will drop **d** in this desert.
14:33 your bodies lies **d** in the desert.
19:11 "Whoever touches the **d** body
19:13 Whoever touches the **d** body of
19:17 from touching a **d** body.
19:18 in the tent ⌊with the **d** body⌋.
31:19 or touched a **d** body must stay
34:3 starts from the end of the **D** Sea
34:12 so that it ends at the **D** Sea.
35:24 or if the **d** person's relative can
Dtr 3:17 Sea of the Plains (the **D** Sea),
4:49 River as far as the **D** Sea at
14:8 meat or touch their **d** bodies.
18:11 spirits for help, or consult the **d**.
21:6 their hands over the **d** heifer.
21:23 never leave his **d** body hung on
25:6 carry the **d** brother's name so
26:14 I didn't offer any of it to the **d**.
28:26 Your **d** bodies will be food for
28:61 will continue until you're **d**.
Jos 1:2 "My servant Moses is **d**.
3:16 (the **D** Sea) was completely
8:29 Joshua hung the king of Ai's ⌊**d**
11:6 tomorrow they will all be **d**.
12:3 Sea of the Plains (the **D** Sea)
15:2 from the south end of the **D** Sea
15:5 The eastern border is the **D**
15:5 the north end of the **D** Sea at
18:19 the northern bay of the **D** Sea at
Jdg 3:25 their ruler lying on the floor, **d**.
4:22 He saw Sisera lying there **d**
5:27 Where he sank, he fell **d**.
9:55 saw that Abimelech was **d**,
14:8 honey in the lion's **d** body.
14:9 it out of the lion's **d** body.
16:16 him until he wished he were **d**.
Rut 2:20 kind to people — living or **d**."
4:5 the **d** man's widow.
4:5 in the **d** man's name."
4:10 in the **d** man's name.
4:10 In this way the **d** man's name
1Sm 3:17 May God strike you **d** if you
4:17 and Phinehas, also are **d**,
4:19 and her husband were **d**,
17:46 And this day I will give the **d**
17:51 Philistine was **d** by cutting off
19:11 you'll be **d** tomorrow!"
20:31 bring him to me. He's a **d** man!"
24:14 A **d** dog? One flea?

1Sm 25:39 David heard Nabal was **d**,
26:16 the LORD lives, you are **d** men.
28:7 woman who conjures up the **d**.
28:7 Endor who conjures up the **d**."
28:8 "Please consult with a **d**
31:5 saw that Saul was **d**,
31:7 that Saul and his sons were **d**,
31:8 Philistines came to strip the **d**,
31:12 all night and took the **d** bodies
2Sm 1:4 his son Jonathan are **d** too."
1:5 and his son Jonathan are **d**?"
1:19 lies **d** on your hills.
2:7 Because your master Saul is **d**,
3:9 May God strike me **d** unless I
3:35 "May God strike me **d** if I taste
4:12 and hung their **d** bodies by the
8:13 in the **D** Sea region as
9:8 would look at a **d** dog like me?"
10:18 David struck Shobach **d**.
11:21 Uriah the Hittite is also **d**.'"
11:24 man Uriah the Hittite also is **d**."
11:26 that her husband Uriah was **d**,
12:18 to tell him that the child was **d**.
12:18 can we tell him the child is **d**?
12:19 realized that the child was **d**.
12:19 "Is the child **d**?" David asked
12:19 he is **d**," they answered.
12:23 should I fast now that he's **d**?
13:32 Only Amnon is **d**. Absalom
13:33 that all the king's sons are **d**,
13:33 Majesty. Only Amnon is **d**.
14:2 has been mourning for the **d**
14:5 "I'm a widow; my husband is **d**.
15:21 whether you're **d** or alive,
16:9 "Why should this **d** dog curse
18:20 because the king's son is **d**."
19:6 were alive and all of us were **d**.
19:13 May God strike me **d** unless
21:10 the sky rained on the **d** bodies.
23:10 only returned to strip the **d**.
1Ki 2:23 "May God strike me **d** if
3:20 Then she laid her **d** son in my
3:21 to nurse my son, he was **d**!
3:22 son is alive — your son is **d**."
3:22 Your son is **d** — my son is
3:23 son is **d**,' and that one keeps
3:23 Your son is **d** — my son is
13:22 That is why your **d** body will
13:24 His **d** body was thrown on the
19:2 "May the gods strike me **d** if by
20:10 "May the gods strike me **d** if
21:15 to sell you. He's **d** now."
22:37 When the king was **d**,
2Ki 4:1 Elisha, "Sir, my husband is **d**!
4:32 the **d** boy was lying on Elisha's
6:31 He said, "May God strike me **d**
8:5 Elisha brought a **d** child back
11:1 saw that her son was **d**,
14:7 Edomites in the **D** Sea region
14:25 of Hamath to the **D** Sea as
23:30 His officers put his **d** body in a
1Ch 10:5 saw that Saul was **d**,
10:7 that Saul and his sons were **d**,
10:8 Philistines came to strip the **d**,
10:12 and took away the **d** bodies
10:13 information ⌊from a **d** person⌋.
18:12 Edomites in the **D** Sea region.
2Ch 20:2 the other side of the **D** Sea,
22:10 saw that her son was **d**,
25:11 he came to the **D** Sea region,
Est 2:23 the **d** bodies of Bigthan and
5:14 have Mordecai's ⌊**d** body⌋ hung
7:10 So servants hung Haman's ⌊**d**
8:7 and Haman's ⌊**d** body⌋ was
Job 26:5 "The souls of the **d** tremble
33:22 come close to those already **d**.
39:30 It is found wherever there are **d**
Psa 31:12 from memory as if I were **d**
63:10 Their **d** bodies will be left as
64:7 Suddenly, they will be struck **d**.
79:2 They have given the **d** bodies
88:5 abandoned with the **d**,
88:10 miracles for those who are **d**?
88:10 Will the spirits of the **d** rise and
91:7 thousand may fall **d** beside you
106:28 what was sacrificed to the **d**.

Psa 110:6 and fill them with **d** bodies.
115:17 Those who are **d** do not praise
Pro 2:18 ways lead to the souls of the **d**.
9:18 that the souls of the **d** are there,
21:16 rest in the assembly of the **d**.
Ecc 4:2 I congratulate the **d**,
6:3 for him to have been born **d**.
9:3 After that, they join the **d**.
9:4 dog is better than a **d** lion.
9:5 but the **d** don't know anything.
9:5 no more reward for the **d** when
10:1 **D** flies will make a bottle of
Isa 5:25 The hills tremble, and **d** bodies
8:19 Why should they ask the **d** to
14:9 It wakes up the ghosts of the **d**,
22:2 Your **d** didn't die in battle.
26:14 The wicked are **d**.
26:14 The spirits of the **d** won't rise.
26:19 Your **d** will live. Their corpses
26:19 Those who lie **d** in the dust
26:19 will revive the spirits of the **d**.
26:21 no longer cover up its **d** bodies.
34:3 Their **d** bodies will be thrown
56:3 "We're only **d** trees!"
59:10 We are like **d** people among
66:16 will be struck **d** by the LORD.
Jer 7:33 The **d** bodies of these people
9:22 This is what the LORD says: **D**
16:7 comfort those who mourn the **d**
19:11 They will bury ⌊the **d**⌋ in
22:10 Don't cry for the **d**. Don't shake
31:15 because they are **d**.
31:40 filled with its **d** bodies and
51:4 They will lie **d** in their own
51:47 and all its soldiers will lie **d**.
Eze 6:5 I will lay the **d** bodies of the
9:7 its courtyards with **d** people,
28:23 Your people will fall **d**.
30:4 Many Egyptians will fall **d**.
30:11 and fill the land with **d** bodies.
32:6 will be filled with your **d** body.
32:22 All of its soldiers are **d**.
32:23 All of its soldiers are **d**.
32:24 All of its soldiers are **d**.
32:25 made for Elam among the **d**.
32:25 They lie among the **d**.
32:30 went down with the **d**.
39:11 Valley, east of the **D** Sea.
39:14 will bury the **d** soldiers that are
43:7 dishonor it with the **d** bodies
43:9 and take the **d** bodies
44:25 by going near a **d** body.
44:25 unclean if the **d** person is his
47:8 and into the **D** Sea.
47:8 the water flows into the **D** Sea,
47:9 the water in the **D** Sea fresh.
47:18 continue from the **D** Sea down
Joe 2:20 odor will rise from the **d** bodies.
Amo 6:10 comes to take the **d** bodies out
8:3 "There will be **d** bodies
Jnh 4:3 I'd rather be **d** than alive."
4:8 "I'd rather be **d** than alive."
Nah 3:3 **D** bodies pile up! There is no
Zec 14:8 half of it to the **D** Sea and the
Mat 2:18 because they were **d**."
2:19 After Herod was **d**,
2:20 who tried to kill the child are **d**."
8:22 and let the **d** bury their own
8:22 let the dead bury their own **d**."
9:24 The girl is not **d**. She's
10:8 bring the **d** back to life,
11:5 **d** people are brought back to
22:28 when the **d** come back to life,
22:31 you about the **d** coming back
22:32 He's not the God of the **d** but of
23:27 are full of **d** people's bones
24:28 wherever there is a **d** body.
Mar 5:39 The child isn't **d**. She's just
9:26 The boy looked as if he were **d**,
9:26 and everyone said, "He's **d**!"
12:23 When the **d** come back to life,
12:25 When the **d** come back to life,
12:26 of Moses that the **d** come back
12:27 He's not the God of the **d** but of
15:44 him if Jesus was, in fact, **d**.
15:45 assured him that Jesus was **d**,

Luk 7:12 The **d** man was a widow's only
7:15 The **d** man sat up and began to
7:22 **d** people are brought back to
8:49 He said, "Your daughter is **d**.
8:52 She's not **d**. She's just sleeping."
8:53 because they knew she was **d**.
9:60 "Let the **d** bury their own dead.
9:60 "Let the dead bury their own **d**.
10:30 beat him, and left him for **d**.
15:24 My son was **d** and has come
15:32 This brother of yours was **d** but
16:30 comes back to them from the **d**,
17:37 wherever there is a **d** body."
20:33 when the **d** come back to life,
20:37 the bush that the **d** come back
20:38 He's not the God of the **d** but of
24:5 are you looking among the **d**
Jon 5:21 the Father brings back the **d**
5:25 now here) when the **d** will hear
5:28 A time is coming when all the **d**
11:13 meant that Lazarus was **d**,
11:39 Martha, the **d** man's sister,
11:39 He's been **d** for four days."
11:44 The **d** man came out.
19:33 and saw that he was already **d**,
Act 4:2 that the **d** will come back
5:5 Peter say this, he dropped **d**.
5:10 she dropped **d** in front of Peter.
5:10 they found Sapphira **d**.
10:42 to judge the living and the **d**.'
14:19 they thought that he was **d**.
20:9 and was **d** when they picked
23:6 that the **d** will come back
23:8 (The Sadducees say that the **d**
24:21 that the **d** will come back
26:8 God can bring **d** people back
28:6 to swell up or suddenly drop **d**.
Rom 4:17 God who gives life to **d** people
4:19 already as good as **d** now that
6:11 So consider yourselves **d** to
7:8 Clearly, without laws sin is **d**.
8:10 your bodies are **d** because of
10:7 bring Christ back from the **d**).
14:9 of both the living and the **d**.
1Co 10:5 so their **d** bodies were
15:12 back from the **d** is impossible?
15:13 If the **d** can't be brought back to
15:15 But if it's true that the **d** don't
15:16 if the **d** don't come back to life,
15:20 has come back from the **d**.
15:29 because the **d** ⌞will come back
15:29 If the **d** can't come back to life,
15:32 If the **d** are not raised,
15:35 "How do the **d** come back to
15:42 will be when the **d** come back
15:52 and then the **d** will come back
2Co 1:9 who brings the **d** back to life.
Eph 2:1 You were once **d** because of
2:5 We were **d** because of our
5:14 Rise from the **d**, and Christ will
Php 3:11 I'll come back to life from the **d**.
Col 2:13 You were once **d** because of
1Th 4:16 First, the **d** who believed in
1Ti 5:6 pleasure is **d** although she is
2Ti 4:1 are living and those who are **d**.
Heb 6:2 **d** people coming back to life,
9:17 is used only after a person is **d**
11:4 even though he is **d**.
11:12 Abraham was as good as **d**.
11:19 bring Isaac back from the **d**.
11:19 receive Isaac back from the **d**
11:35 loved ones back from the **d**.
Jas 2:17 faith by itself is **d** if it doesn't
2:26 body that doesn't breathe is **d**.
2:26 faith that does nothing is **d**.
1Pe 4:5 to judge the living and the **d**.
4:6 although they are now **d**.
Rev 1:17 down at his feet like a **d** man.
1:18 I was **d**, but now I am alive
2:8 who was **d** and became alive,
3:1 for being alive, but you are **d**.
11:8 Their **d** bodies will lie on the
11:9 look at the witnesses' **d** bodies
11:18 The time has come for the **d** to
16:3 blood like the blood of a **d** man,
20:5 The rest of the **d** did not live
Rev 20:12 I saw the **d**, both important and
20:12 The **d** were judged on the
20:13 The sea gave up its **d**.
20:13 Death and hell gave up their **d**.

deadly (16)

Exo 10:17 to take this **d** plague away from
Dtr 32:24 by pestilence and **d** epidemics.
32:33 the **d** poison of cobras.
Jdg 4:15 in front of Barak's **d** assault.
Job 34:6 been wounded by a **d** arrow,
Psa 7:13 He prepares his **d** weapons
17:9 from my **d** enemies who
91:3 traps and from **d** plagues.
144:10 David away from a **d** sword.
Pro 12:6 wicked people are a **d** ambush,
Jer 9:8 Their tongues are like **d** arrows.
Eze 9:2 Each one brought a **d** weapon
Amo 6:12 turned justice into something **d**
Mar 16:18 and if they drink any **d** poison,
2Co 2:16 people we are a **d** fragrance,
Jas 3:8 evil filled with **d** poison.

deaf (19)

Lev 19:14 Never curse **d** people or put
1Sm 7:8 "Don't turn a **d** ear to us!
Psa 28:1 do not turn a **d** ear to me.
39:12 Do not be **d** to my tears,
58:4 They are like a **d** cobra that
83:1 Do not turn a **d** ear to me.
109:1 do not turn a **d** ear to me.
Isa 29:18 When that day comes, the **d**
35:5 ears of the **d** will be unplugged.
42:18 Listen, you **d** people.
42:19 except my servant or **d** like
43:8 the people who are **d** but still
59:1 to save or his ear too **d** to hear.
Mic 7:16 Their ears will become **d**.
Mat 11:5 **d** people hear again,
Mar 7:32 to him a man who was **d**
7:37 He makes the **d** hear and the
8:18 Are you blind and **d**?
Luk 7:22 **d** people hear again,

deal (48)

Exo 32:9 and they are impossible to **d**
33:3 you are impossible to **d** with,
33:5 'You are impossible to **d** with.
34:9 we are impossible to **d** with,
Num 5:29 for how to **d** with jealousy.
Dtr 9:6 You are impossible to **d** with!
9:13 and they are impossible to **d**
10:16 to **d** with any longer.
31:27 You are impossible to **d** with.
Jdg 2:15 he made them suffer a great **d**.
10:9 So Israel suffered a great **d**.
2Ki 17:14 became as impossible to **d**
18:23 make a **d** with my master,
2Ch 30:8 Don't be impossible to **d** with
36:13 and so impossible to **d**
Neh 5:7 a large meeting to **d** with them.
9:29 became impossible to **d** with,
Psa 55:19 the beginning will **d** with them.
109:21 O LORD Almighty, **d** with me
Pro 11:15 closing of a **d** remains secure.
17:18 without good sense closes a **d**
Isa 36:8 make a **d** with my master,
57:8 You've made a **d** with those
Jer 2:8 Those who **d** with my
7:26 became impossible to **d** with,
17:23 They were impossible to **d**
18:23 **D** with them when you get
19:15 become impossible to **d** with,
32:5 stay there until I **d** with him,
Lam 1:22 Then **d** with them as you have
Eze 20:44 because I will **d** with you for
20:44 I will not **d** with you based on
22:14 Will you remain strong when I **d**
23:25 against you so that they will **d**
25:14 My people will **d** with Edom
Dan 11:39 he will **d** with strong fortresses.
Zep 3:19 At that time I will **d** with all
Zec 8:11 But now I won't **d** with the few
Mat 18:17 **d** with him as you would a
Act 18:27 to help the believers a great **d**.
Rom 3:25 In his patience God waited to **d**
1Co 2:2 I decided to **d** with only one
2Co 10:2 you I won't have to **d** forcefully
12:7 am forced to **d** with a recurring
Gal 6:12 who want to make a big **d** out
Col 2:22 All of these things **d** with
2Ti 4:14 did me a great **d** of harm.
Heb 9:28 This time he will not **d** with sin,

dealing (11)

Dtr 18:13 You must have integrity ⌞in **d**⌟
1Sm 5:7 because their God is **d** harshly
2Sm 22:26 ⌞In **d**⌟ with faithful people you
22:27 ⌞In **d**⌟ with devious people you
Ezr 10:17 they had finished **d** with all the
Psa 18:25 ⌞In **d**⌟ with faithful people you
18:26 ⌞In **d**⌟ with devious people you
Pro 28:6 than to be rich and double-**d**
Luk 16:8 it comes to **d** with others."
1Co 6:4 When you have cases **d** with
2Co 13:3 Christ isn't weak in **d** with you.

dealings (1)

1Th 2:10 in our **d** with you believers.

deals (4)

Pro 22:26 among those who make **d**
Ecc 5:14 then lost in bad business **d**.
Isa 2:6 they make **d** with foreigners.
Rom 2:4 and **d** patiently with you?

dealt (8)

Dtr 34:10 whom the LORD **d** with face to
1Sm 2:13 this was how the priests **d**
5:6 The LORD **d** harshly with the
5:11 where God **d** ⌞with them⌟ very
Psa 105:25 and they **d** treacherously with
Lam 1:22 deal with them as you have **d**
Eze 31:11 and he surely **d** with it.
Zec 1:6 He has **d** with us as our ways

dear (79)

2Ki 19:21 'My **d** people in Zion despise
Psa 39:11 eat away at what is **d** to them.
60:5 us so that those who are **d**
108:6 us so that those who are **d**
Isa 23:12 my **d** abused people Sidon."
37:22 'My **d** people in Zion despise
41:8 of Abraham, my **d** friend.
Jer 8:11 They treat my **d** people's
8:19 The cry from my **d** people
8:21 I am crushed because my **d**
8:22 of my **d** people been restored?
9:1 night for my **d** people who have
9:7 What else can I do for my **d**
14:17 my **d** people will suffer
31:4 my **d** people Israel.
31:20 Is Ephraim my **d** son?
31:21 Come back, my **d** people Israel,
46:11 **d** people of Egypt.
Lam 3:48 over the ruin of my **d** people.
Hos 9:16 I would kill their **d** children."
Jon 13:33 Jesus said, "**D** children,
Act 15:23 **D** brothers and sisters,
15:25 with our **d** Barnabas and Paul.
Rom 12:19 Don't take revenge, **d** friends.
16:5 Greet my **d** friend Epaenetus.
16:8 Greet Ampliatus my **d** friend in
16:9 and my **d** friend Stachys.
16:12 Greet **d** Persis, who has
1Co 4:14 instruct you as my **d** children.
4:17 Timothy is my **d** child,
10:14 Therefore, my **d** friends,
2Co 7:1 have these promises, **d** friends,
12:19 Everything we do, **d** friends,
Eph 1:6 given us in his **d** Son would
6:21 He is our **d** brother and a
Php 2:12 My **d** friends, you have always
4:1 Therefore, **d** friends,
Col 1:7 our **d** fellow servant.
4:7 He is our **d** brother,
4:9 and is our faithful and **d** brother.
4:14 My **d** friend Luke, and Demas
1Th 2:8 That's how **d** you were to us!
2Ti 1:2 To Timothy, my **d** child.
Phm 1:1 To our **d** coworker Philemon,
1:16 than a slave — as a **d** brother.

Phm 1:16 He is especially **d** to me,
Heb 6:9 **D** friends, even though we say
Jas 1:16 My **d** brothers and sisters,
1:19 my **d** brothers and sisters:
2:5 my **d** brothers and sisters!
1Pe 2:11 **D** friends, since you are
4:12 **D** friends, don't be surprised by
2Pe 3:1 **D** friends, this is the second
3:8 **D** friends, don't ignore this fact:
3:14 Therefore, **d** friends,
3:15 This is what our **d** brother Paul
3:17 **D** friends, you already know
1Jn 2:1 My **d** children, I'm writing this
2:7 **D** friends, it's not as though I'm
2:12 I'm writing to you, **d** children,
2:28 Now, **d** children, live in Christ.
3:1 called God's **d** children.
3:2 **D** friends, now we are God's
3:7 **D** children, don't let anyone
3:18 **D** children, we must show love
3:21 **D** friends, if our conscience
4:1 **D** friends, don't believe all
4:4 **D** children, you belong to God.
4:7 **D** friends, we must love each
4:11 **D** friends, if this is the way
5:21 **D** children, guard yourselves
2Jn 1:5 **D** lady, I'm now requesting that
3Jn 1:1 To my **d** friend Gaius,
1:2 **D** friend, I know that you are
1:5 **D** friend, you are showing your
1:11 **D** friend, never imitate evil,
Jud 1:3 **D** friends, I had intended to
1:17 **D** friends, remember what the
1:20 **D** friends, use your most holy

dearly (1)

Hos 4:18 Their rulers **d** love to act

death (444)

Gen 23:2 for Sarah and to cry about her **d**.
24:67 comforted after his mother's **d**.
25:8 he joined his ancestors in **d**.
25:17 He joined his ancestors in **d**.
26:11 or his wife will be put to **d**."
26:18 filled them in after Abraham's **d**.
35:29 He joined his ancestors in **d** at
37:26 brother and covering up his **d**?
42:2 so that we won't starve to **d**."
42:37 "You may put my two sons to **d**
43:8 so that we won't starve to **d**.
47:19 so that we won't starve to **d**
49:29 about to join my ancestors in **d**.
49:33 and joined his ancestors in **d**.
50:10 ceremony to mourn Jacob's **d**.
50:10 days to mourn his father's **d**.
50:15 their father's **d** could mean.
Exo 2:12 he beat the Egyptian to **d** and
8:26 won't they stone us to **d**?
16:3 desert to let us all starve to **d**!"
18:4 He saved me from Pharaoh's **d**
19:12 the mountain must be put to **d**.
21:12 and kills him must be put to **d**.
21:14 from my altar and put him to **d**.
21:15 or mother must be put to **d**.
21:16 person must be put to **d**,
21:17 or mother must be put to **d**.
21:28 gores a man or a woman to **d**,
21:28 the bull must be stoned to **d**,
21:29 and its owner must be put to **d**,
22:19 an animal must be put to **d**.
31:14 any other day must be put to **d**.
31:15 on that day must be put to **d**.
35:2 on this day should be put to **d**.
Lev 19:20 they should not be put to **d**.
20:2 they must be put to **d**.
20:2 people must stone them to **d**.
20:4 and do not put them to **d**,
20:9 or mother must be put to **d**.
20:10 be put to **d** for their adultery.
20:11 father's wife must be put to **d**.
20:12 both of them must be put to **d**.
20:13 and must be put to **d**.
20:15 an animal must be put to **d**.
20:16 They must be put to **d**.
20:27 or a psychic must be put to **d**.
20:27 They must be stoned to **d**
Lev 22:9 or their sin will bring them **d**
24:14 must stone him to **d**.
24:16 LORD's name must be put to **d**.
24:16 must stone them to **d**.
24:17 person must be put to **d**.
24:21 kills a person must be put to **d**.
24:23 There they stoned him to **d** as
27:29 They must be put to **d**.
Num 1:51 near the tent will be put to **d**.
3:10 duties must be put to **d**."
3:38 duties had to be put to **d**.
14:10 stoning Moses and Aaron to **d**,
15:35 "This man must be put to **d**.
15:36 the camp and stoned him to **d**,
16:29 if they die a natural **d** — then
16:39 who had been burned to **d**.
20:24 now join his ancestors ⌊in **d**⌋,
23:10 Let me die the **d** of innocent
27:13 will join your ancestors ⌊in **d**⌋,
31:2 will join your ancestors ⌊in **d**⌋."
35:12 relative who can avenge the **d**.
35:16 Murderers must be put to **d**.
35:17 Murderers must be put to **d**.
35:18 Murderers must be put to **d**.
35:19 avenge the **d** must make sure
35:19 sure a murderer is put to **d**.
35:21 or if you beat your enemy to **d**
35:21 you must be put to **d**.
35:21 can avenge the **d** must kill you
35:24 relative can avenge the **d**.
35:25 You must live there until the **d**
35:27 avenge the **d** finds you outside
35:28 in their city of refuge until the **d**
35:28 own property only after his **d**.
35:30 person will be put to **d** as
35:30 No one can be put to **d** on the
35:31 has been given the **d** penalty.
35:31 Murderers must be put to **d**.
35:32 on his own land before the **d**
35:33 through the **d** of the murderer.
Dtr 13:5 or dreamer must be put to **d**
13:9 You must put them to **d**.
13:9 join you in putting them to **d**.
13:10 Stone them to **d** because they
17:5 and stone that person to **d**.
17:6 can only be sentenced to **d**
17:6 should ever be sentenced to **d**
17:7 them in putting the person to **d**.
19:6 avenge the **d** will pursue him.
19:6 he didn't deserve the **d** penalty,
19:12 the authority to avenge the **d**.
21:21 the city should stone him to **d**.
21:22 a convicted person is put to **d**,
22:8 for a **d** at your home
22:21 of her city must stone her to **d**
22:24 of the city and stone them to **d**.
24:16 Parents must never be put to **d**
24:16 children must never be put to **d**
24:16 Each person must be put to **d**
30:15 prosperity or **d** and destruction.
30:19 that I have offered you life or **d**,
31:14 "The time of your **d** is coming
31:16 you are going to lie down in **d**
32:43 he will take revenge for the **d**
32:50 and join your ancestors in **d**,
Jos 1:1 After the **d** of the LORD's
1:18 your orders will be put to **d**.
2:13 and that you'll save us from **d**."
7:25 Achan and his family to **d**.
8:24 They put them all to **d**;
10:26 After this, Joshua put them to **d**
11:14 But they put everyone to **d** until
20:3 relative who can avenge the **d**.
20:5 can avenge the **d** pursues him,
20:9 who can avenge a **d** before
Jdg 1:1 After Joshua's **d** the Israelites
2:10 had joined their ancestors in **d**.
5:18 But Zebulun mocked **d**,
6:31 defends him will be put to **d**
14:15 burn you and your family to **d**.
15:6 wife and her father to **d**.
20:13 We must put them to **d** to rid
21:5 at Mizpah must be put to **d**.
Rut 1:17 if anything but **d** separates you
1Sm 5:11 There was a fear of **d**
14:45 rescued Jonathan from **d**.
1Sm 15:32 the bitterness of **d** is past,"
20:3 I'm only one step away from **d**."
2Sm 4:4 the news about ⌊the **d** of⌋ Saul
7:12 comes for you to lie down in **d**
10:2 Hanun after his father's ⌊**d**⌋.
13:39 consoled him over Amnon's **d**.
19:21 "Shouldn't Shimei be put to **d**
22:5 The waves of **d** had
22:6 of **d** had confronted me.
1Ki 1:21 down in **d** with your ancestors."
2:10 David lay down in **d** with his
2:24 that Adonijah will be put to **d**
2:37 be responsible for your own **d**."
3:11 or the **d** of your enemies.
11:21 that David had lain down in **d**
11:43 Solomon lay down in **d** with
12:18 but they stoned him to **d**.
14:20 Then he lay down in **d** with his
14:31 Rehoboam lay down in **d** with
15:8 Abijam lay down in **d** with his
15:24 Asa lay down in **d** with his
16:6 Baasha lay down in **d** with his
16:28 Omri lay down in **d** with his
21:10 stone him to **d** outside the city."
21:13 him to **d** outside the city.
21:14 "Naboth has been stoned to **d**."
21:16 he heard about Naboth's **d**,
22:40 Ahab lay down in **d** with his
22:50 Jehoshaphat lay down in **d**
2Ki 4:40 "There's **d** in the pot,
7:17 the people trampled him to **d**
7:20 him to **d** in the gateway.
8:24 Jehoram lay down in **d** with his
10:35 Jehu lay down in **d** with his
13:9 Jehoahaz lay down in **d** with
13:13 Jehoash lay down in **d** with his
14:6 "Parents must never be put to **d**
14:6 children must never be put to **d**
14:6 Each person must be put to **d**
14:16 Jehoash lay down in **d** with his
14:17 Judah lived 15 years after the **d**
14:22 down in **d** with his ancestors.
14:29 Jeroboam lay down in **d** with
15:7 Azariah lay down in **d** with his
15:22 Menahem lay down in **d** with
15:38 Jotham lay down in **d** with his
16:20 Ahaz lay down in **d** with his
20:21 Hezekiah lay down in **d** with
21:18 Manasseh lay down in **d** with
24:6 Jehoiakim lay down in **d** with
1Ch 19:2 Hanun after his father's ⌊**d**⌋.
2Ch 1:11 or the **d** of those who hate you.
9:31 Solomon lay down in **d** with
10:18 but they stoned him to **d**.
12:16 Rehoboam lay down in **d** with
14:1 Abijah lay down in **d** with his
16:13 Asa lay down in **d** with his
21:1 Jehoshaphat lay down in **d**
21:19 He died a painful **d**.
24:21 order they stoned him to **d**
25:4 "Parents must never be put to **d**
25:4 children must never be put to **d**
25:4 Each person must be put to **d**
25:25 Judah lived 15 years after the **d**
26:2 down in **d** with his ancestors.
26:23 Uzziah lay down in **d** with his
27:9 Jotham lay down in **d** with his
28:27 Ahaz lay down in **d** with his
32:33 Hezekiah lay down in **d** with
33:20 Manasseh lay down in **d** with
Est 4:11 that person must be put to **d**.
Job 3:21 to those who long for **d** but it
4:7 ⌊ever⌋ died ⌊an untimely **d**⌋?
5:20 famine he will save you from **d**,
7:15 prefer **d** ⌊to these dreams⌋.
9:23 a sudden disaster brings **d**,
19:29 Fear **d**, because ⌊your anger⌋
19:29 anger⌋ is punishable by **d**.
28:22 Decay and **D** say, 'We've heard
30:23 I know you will lead me to **d**,
33:18 from crossing the River ⌊of **D**⌋.
36:12 they will cross the River ⌊of **D**⌋
38:17 Have the gateways to **d** been
Psa 6:5 In **d**, no one remembers you.
9:13 me away from the gates of **d**
18:4 The ropes of **d** had become

Psa 18:5 of **d** had confronted me.
22:15 lay me down in the dust of **d**.
23:4 through the dark valley of **d**,
33:19 to rescue their souls from **d**
44:19 us with the shadow of **d**.
48:14 He will lead us beyond **d**."
49:14 they are driven to hell with **d**
55:4 terrors of **d** have seized me.
55:15 Let **d** suddenly take ⌊wicked
56:13 You have rescued me from **d**.
68:20 LORD is our escape from **d**.
79:11 those who are condemned to **d**.
88:15 have been suffering and near **d**.
89:48 go on living and never see **d**?
94:17 quickly fallen silent ⌊in **d**⌋.
94:21 condemn innocent people to **d**.
102:20 who were condemned to **d**.
109:31 who would condemn them to **d**.
116:3 The ropes of **d** became tangled
116:8 You saved me from **d**.
116:15 the sight of the LORD is the **d**
119:25 I am close to **d**. Give me a new
Pro 2:18 Her house sinks down to **d**.
5:5 Her feet descend to **d**.
7:27 leads to the darkest vaults of **d**.
8:36 All those who hate me love **d**."
10:2 righteousness rescues from **d**.
11:4 righteousness saves from **d**.
11:7 At the **d** of a wicked person,
11:19 pursues evil finds his own **d**.
12:28 Eternal **d** is not along its path.
13:14 away from the grasp of **d**.
14:12 but eventually it ends in **d**.
14:27 away from the grasp of **d**.
14:32 but even in his **d** a righteous
16:14 A king's anger announces **d**,
16:25 but eventually it ends in **d**.
18:21 has the power of life and **d**,
19:16 LORD's ways will be put to **d**.
19:18 the one responsible for his **d**.
21:6 They are looking for **d**.
24:11 captives condemned to **d**,
26:18 flaming arrows, arrows, and **d**,
Ecc 7:26 is more bitter than **d** itself.
8:8 over the day of his own **d**.
8:8 to avoid the war ⌊against **d**⌋.
10:14 or what will happen after ⌊**d**⌋.
Sos 8:6 Love is as overpowering as **d**.
Isa 13:15 is found will be stabbed to **d**.
13:16 smashed to **d** right before their
14:30 But I will put your root to **d** with
25:8 He will swallow up **d** forever.
28:15 "We made a treaty with **d** and
28:18 Your treaty with **d** will be
38:18 **D** doesn't praise you!
53:12 he poured out his life in **d**
54:4 of your husband's **d** anymore.
65:12 Now I will destine you for **d**.
Jer 2:6 of drought and the shadow of **d**.
9:21 **D** has come through our
9:21 **D** has cut down the children in
13:16 will turn it into the shadow of **d**
15:9 from these people to **d**
18:21 Their husbands will be put to **d**.
21:8 give you the choice of life or **d**.
26:15 certain that if you put me to **d**,
26:19 of Judah put Micah to **d**?
26:21 the king wanted to put him to **d**.
26:24 to the people to be put to **d**.
29:22 the king of Babylon burned to **d**
38:4 "Have this man put to **d**.
38:9 where he'll starve to **d**,
43:11 He will bring **d** to those who
48:2 **D** will come after you.
Lam 1:20 Inside the houses it's like **d**.
4:9 who were stabbed bled to **d**.
Eze 16:38 I will give you the **d** penalty in
18:13 be responsible for his own **d**.
28:8 will die a violent **d** in the sea.
33:8 hold you responsible for his **d**.
38:22 Gog with plagues and **d**.
Hos 10:14 children were smashed to **d**.
13:14 I want to reclaim them from **d**.
13:14 **D**, I want to be a plague to you.
13:16 children will be smashed to **d**,
Amo 5:17 through your land ⌊with **d**⌋.
Jnh 1:14 hold us responsible for the **d**
Nah 3:10 smashed to **d** at every street
Hab 2:5 He is like **d** — never satisfied.
Mat 4:16 in a land overshadowed by **d**."
10:21 will hand over brother to **d**;
15:4 or mother must be put to **d**.'
20:18 They will condemn him to **d**
21:35 and stoned a third to **d**.
23:37 and stone to **d** those sent
26:66 "He deserves the **d** penalty!"
Mar 7:10 or mother must be put to **d**.'
10:33 They will condemn him to **d**
13:12 will hand over brother to **d**;
14:64 him with the **d** sentence.
Luk 7:2 slave was sick and near **d**.
9:31 Jesus' approaching **d**
13:34 and stone to **d** those sent
15:17 while I'm starving to **d** here?
20:6 everyone will stone us to **d**.
23:15 to deserve the **d** penalty.
23:22 man deserving of the **d** penalty.
24:20 condemned to **d** and crucified.
Jon 5:24 already passed from **d** to life.
8:5 to stone women like this to **d**.
8:51 what I say will never see **d**."
8:52 what I say will never taste **d**.'
10:31 rocks to stone Jesus to **d**.
10:32 do you want to stone me to **d**?"
10:33 "We're going to stone you to **d**,
11:4 "His sickness won't result in **d**.
11:8 Jews wanted to stone you to **d**.
21:19 kind of **d** Peter would bring
Act 1:3 After his **d** Jesus showed the
1:18 where he fell headfirst to his **d**.
2:23 who was given over ⌊to **d**⌋ by
2:24 But God raised him from **d** to
2:24 and destroyed the pains of **d**,
2:24 because **d** had no power to
5:5 heard about his **d** was terrified.
5:26 stone them to **d** for using force.
5:28 on us for putting that man to **d**."
7:58 they began to stone him to **d**.
8:1 of putting Stephen to **d**.
11:19 Stephen's **d** went as far
14:5 them and stone them to **d**.
14:19 They tried to stone Paul to **d**
18:6 responsible for your own **d**.
20:26 responsible for the ⌊spiritual⌋ **d**
22:20 I approved of his **d** and guarded
25:11 which I deserve the **d** penalty,
25:25 to deserve the **d** penalty.
Rom 4:25 was handed over to **d** because
5:10 If the **d** of his Son restored our
5:12 and **d** came through sin.
5:12 **D** spread to everyone,
5:14 Yet, **d** ruled from the time of
5:17 It is certain that **d** ruled
5:21 As sin ruled by bringing **d**,
6:3 were baptized into his **d**?
6:4 we were baptized into his **d**,
6:4 Christ was brought back from **d**
6:5 united with him in a **d** like his,
6:9 **D** no longer has any power
6:13 who have come back from **d**
6:16 sin be your master leads to **d**.
6:21 to do because it ended in **d**.
6:23 The reward for sin is **d**,
7:5 they did things that result in **d**.
7:10 me life actually brought me **d**.
7:13 something good cause my **d**?
7:13 Rather, my **d** was caused by
8:2 from the standards of sin and **d**.
8:6 nature's attitude leads to **d**.
8:13 your spiritual nature to put to **d**
8:32 Son but handed him over ⌊to **d**⌋
8:35 or violent **d** separate us from
8:38 can't be separated by **d** or life,
13:4 to carry out the **d** sentence.
1Co 3:22 Cephas, the world, life or **d**,
10:10 The angel of **d** destroyed them.
11:26 the Lord's **d** until he comes.
15:21 Since a man brought **d**,
15:21 also brought life back from **d**.
15:26 last enemy he will destroy is **d**.
15:31 I face **d** every day.
15:54 "**D** is turned into victory!
Amo 15:55 **D**, where is your victory?
15:55 **D**, where is your sting?"
15:56 Sin gives **d** its sting,
2Co 1:9 as if we're under a **d** sentence.
1:10 rescued us from a terrible **d**,
3:6 what was written brings **d**,
3:7 The ministry that brought **d**
4:10 We always carry around the **d**
4:11 are constantly handed over to **d**
4:12 **D** is at work in us,
7:10 the world causes brings only **d**.
11:23 and have faced **d** more often.
11:25 people tried to stone me to **d**;
Gal 2:21 then Christ's **d** was pointless.
Php 2:8 obedient to the point of **d**,
2:8 the point of death, **d** on a cross.
3:10 I'm becoming like him in his **d**,
Col 3:5 Therefore, put to **d** whatever is
1Th 5:10 in this life or asleep in **d**,
2Ti 1:10 Christ has destroyed **d**,
Heb 2:9 honor because he suffered **d**.
2:14 who had power over **d** (that is,
5:7 who could save him from **d**.
9:15 Through his **d** he paid the price
11:34 out raging fires, and escaped **d**.
11:37 Some were stoned to **d**,
12:2 so he endured **d** on the cross
12:20 it must be stoned to **d**."
Jas 1:15 sin grows up, it gives birth to **d**.
5:20 his ways will save him from **d**,
1Pe 3:18 His body was put to **d**,
3:21 who came back from **d** to life.
1Jn 3:14 we have passed from **d** to life,
3:14 grow in love remains in **d**.
5:16 a sin that doesn't lead to **d**,
5:16 commit sins that don't lead to **d**.
5:16 There is a sin that leads to **d**.
5:17 are sins that don't lead to **d**.
Rev 1:18 I have the keys of **d** and hell.
2:10 Be faithful until **d**, and I will
2:11 never be hurt by the second **d**.
6:8 and its rider's name was **D**.
9:6 that time people will look for **d**
9:6 but **d** will escape them.
11:10 will gloat over the witnesses' **d**.
13:15 and put to **d** whoever would not
18:8 this reason her plagues of **d**,
20:6 The second **d** has no power
20:13 **D** and hell gave up their dead.
20:14 **D** and hell were thrown into the
20:14 (The fiery lake is the second **d**.)
21:4 There won't be any more **d**.
21:8 This is the second **d**."

deathly (5)

Exo 15:15 The people of Canaan will be **d**
Jos 2:9 this country are **d** afraid of you.
2:24 The people who live there are **d**
Dan 10:8 My face turned **d** pale,
Mat 28:4 The guards were so **d** afraid of

death's (6)

Job 18:13 **D** firstborn son eats away at
Psa 107:10 in **d** shadow were prisoners in
107:14 of the dark, out of **d** shadow.
107:18 and they came near **d** gates
Isa 9:2 live in the land of **d** shadow
Luk 1:79 in the dark and in **d** shadow.

deaths (8)

2Ki 2:21 No more **d** or crop failures will
Jer 16:4 They will die horrible **d**.
51:35 be held responsible for our **d**."
Eze 3:18 hold you responsible for their **d**.
3:20 hold you responsible for their **d**.
33:4 be responsible for their own **d**.
33:5 are responsible for their own **d**.
33:6 hold him responsible for their **d**

debate (2)

Job 9:3 If he wished to **d** with God,
Act 25:20 Their **d** about these things left

debating (1)

Act 15:7 After a lot of **d**, Peter stood up

Debir (13)

Jos 10:3 and King **D** of Eglon:
10:38 went back to **D** and attacked it.
10:39 He did the same thing to **D** and
11:21 in Hebron, **D**, and Anab,
12:13 the king of **D**, the king of
15:7 the border goes up to **D** and
15:15 against the people living in **D**.
15:15 (In the past **D** was called
15:49 Kiriath Sannah (now called **D**),
21:15 Holon, **D**,
Jdg 1:11 to fight the people living at **D**.
1:11 (In the past **D** was called
1Ch 6:58 **D** with its pastureland,

Deborah (12)

Gen 35:8 Rebekah's nurse **D** died and
Jdg 4:4 **D**, wife of Lappidoth, was a
4:5 Tree of **D** between Ramah
4:6 **D** summoned Barak,
4:9 **D** replied, "Certainly, I'll go with
4:9 So **D** started out for Kedesh
4:10 **D** also went along with him.
4:14 Then **D** said to Barak,
5:1 On that day **D** and Barak,
5:7 deserted — deserted until I, **D**,
5:12 Get up, **D**! Get up! Get up and
5:15 commanders were with **D**.

debt (11)

Dtr 15:2 don't collect payment on the **d**
15:3 on the **d** another Israelite still
1Sm 22:2 who was in trouble, in **d**,
2Ki 4:7 "Sell the oil, and pay your **d**.
Mat 18:25 he could not pay off the **d**,
18:27 and canceled his **d**.
18:32 I canceled your entire **d**,
Luk 7:43 had the largest **d** canceled."
Rom 13:8 However, one **d** you can never
13:8 can never finish paying is the **d**
15:26 and Greece owe a **d**

debtor (3)

Luk 16:6 "The **d** replied, 'Eight hundred
16:7 "Then he asked another **d**,
16:7 "The **d** replied, 'A thousand

debtors (2)

Isa 24:2 and borrowers, **d** and creditors.
Luk 16:5 for each one of his master's **d**.

debts (7)

Dtr 15:1 you must cancel **d**.
15:2 on **d** has been proclaimed
15:9 payments on **d** are canceled —
31:10 year you must cancel **d**.
Neh 10:31 plant the fields or collect any **d**.
Luk 7:42 kind enough to cancel their **d**.
Rom 13:8 Pay your **d** as they come due.

decay (14)

Job 28:22 **D** and Death say, 'We've heard
Psa 16:10 or allow your holy one to **d**.
49:14 Their forms will **d** in the grave,
Pro 27:20 Hell and **d** are never satisfied,
Isa 3:24 there will be the smell of **d**.
Act 2:27 or allow your holy one to **d**.
2:31 and that his body wouldn't **d**.
13:35 not allow your holy one to **d**.'
13:37 to life had a body that didn't **d**.
Rom 8:21 be set free from slavery to **d**
1Co 15:42 comes back to life, it cannot **d**.
15:50 cannot inherit what doesn't **d**.
15:53 into a body that cannot **d**.
15:54 into a body that cannot **d**,

decayed (3)

Act 13:34 and that Jesus' body never **d**.
13:36 his ancestors, but his body **d**.
Jas 5:2 Your riches have **d**,

decaying (1)

Isa 33:9 Lebanon is ashamed and is **d**.

decays (5)

Job 28:5 but beneath it the food **d** as if
1Co 15:42 When the body is planted, it **d**.
15:50 What **d** cannot inherit what
15:53 This body that **d** must be
15:54 When this body that **d** is

deceit (12)

Psa 17:1 comes from lips free from **d**.
50:19 Your tongue plans **d**.
52:2 a sharp razor, you master of **d**.
Pro 12:20 **D** is in the heart of those who
26:24 but inside he holds on to **d**.
Isa 30:12 trusted oppression and **d**,
Jer 5:27 their houses are filled with **d**.
8:5 They still cling to **d**.
9:6 **D** follows deceit. They refuse to
9:6 Deceit follows **d**. They refuse to
Hos 11:12 of Israel surrounds me with **d**."
Rom 1:29 quarreling, **d**, and viciousness.

deceitful (19)

Job 27:4 will not mumble anything **d**.'
Psa 5:6 with bloodthirsty and **d** people.
32:2 sin and who has no **d** thoughts.
34:13 lips from speaking **d** things.
43:1 me from **d** and unjust people.
52:4 accusation, you **d** tongue!
55:23 Bloodthirsty and **d** people will
101:7 The one who does **d** things
109:2 Wicked and **d** people have
120:2 lying lips and from a **d** tongue.
120:3 You **d** tongue, what can the
Pro 15:4 but a **d** tongue breaks the spirit.
Isa 30:9 are rebellious and **d** children,
Jer 3:10 was **d**," declares the LORD.
17:9 "The human mind is the most **d**
17:9 one can understand how **d** it is.
Mat 13:22 But the worries of life and the **d**
Mar 4:19 the **d** pleasures of riches,
1Pe 3:10 and their lips from speaking **d**

deceitfully (9)

Job 13:7 God and talk **d** on his behalf?
Pro 12:17 but a lying witness speaks **d**.
26:26 His hatred is **d** hidden,
Jer 6:13 from prophets to priests, act **d**.
8:10 from prophets to priests, act **d**.
9:8 They speak **d**. People speak
Dan 11:23 he will act **d** and rise to power
Mic 6:12 and their tongues speak **d**.
1Pe 2:22 He never spoke **d**.

deceive (45)

Lev 19:11 or **d** your neighbor.
19:12 my name in order to **d** anyone.
Jos 9:22 "Why did you **d** us by saying,
24:27 You cannot **d** your God."
1Sm 28:12 "Why did you **d** me?
2Sm 3:25 Ner's son Abner came to **d** you,
1Ki 22:20 The LORD asked, 'Who will **d**
22:21 LORD, and said, 'I will **d** him.'
2Ki 18:29 Don't let Hezekiah **d** you.
19:10 you trust **d** you by saying
2Ch 18:19 The LORD asked, 'Who will **d**
18:20 LORD, and said, 'I will **d** him.'
32:15 Don't let Hezekiah **d** you or
Job 15:31 worthless things and **d** himself
Psa 38:12 they think of ways to **d** me.
Pro 24:28 and do not **d** with your lips.
Isa 36:14 Don't let Hezekiah **d** you.
37:10 you trust **d** you by saying
Jer 23:26 prophets continue to lie and **d**?
37:9 Don't **d** yourselves by thinking
Dan 8:25 power to **d** others successfully.
Oba 1:7 at peace with you will **d** you.
Zep 3:13 or use their tongues to **d** others.
Zec 13:4 He won't **d** people by dressing
Mat 24:4 "Be careful not to let anyone **d**
24:5 and they will **d** many people.
24:11 will appear and **d** many people.
24:24 and do wonderful things to **d**,
Mar 13:5 "Be careful not to let anyone **d**
13:6 and they will **d** many people.
13:22 and do wonderful things to **d**,
Act 5:3 with the idea that you could **d**
Rom 16:18 they **d** unsuspecting people.
1Co 3:18 Don't **d** yourselves.
15:33 Don't let anyone **d** you.
Eph 4:22 you through desires that **d** you.
5:6 Don't let anyone **d** you with
2Th 2:3 Don't let anyone **d** you about
2:10 of to **d** those who are
1Ti 4:1 They will follow spirits that **d**,
Tit 1:10 They speak nonsense and **d**
1Jn 2:26 those who are trying to **d** you.
3:7 don't let anyone **d** you.
2Jn 1:7 Many people who **d** others
Rev 20:8 He will go out to **d** Gog and

deceived (24)

Gen 3:13 "The snake **d** me, and I ate,"
27:35 "Your brother came and **d** me
Jos 9:24 We **d** you because we feared
2Sm 19:26 "My servant **d** me,
Job 12:16 and the person who is **d**.
Isa 44:20 eat ashes because they are **d**.
Jer 4:10 you certainly have **d** these
20:7 O LORD, you have **d** me,
20:7 deceived me, and I was **d**.
42:20 You only **d** yourselves when
49:16 Your arrogance has **d** you.
Eze 13:10 "'They have **d** my people by
Oba 1:3 Your arrogance has **d** you.
Luk 21:8 "Be careful that you are not **d**.
Jon 7:47 "Have you been **d** too?
Rom 7:11 **d** me and then killed me.
2Co 11:3 I'm afraid that as the snake **d**
1Ti 2:14 Besides that, Adam was not **d**.
2:14 It was the woman who was **d**
Heb 3:13 none of you will be **d** by sin
5:2 who are ignorant and easily **d**,
Rev 18:23 were **d** by its witchcraft.
19:20 prophet had **d** those who had
20:10 The devil, who **d** them,

deceiver (4)

Job 12:16 He owns both the **d** and the
Mat 27:63 we remember how that **d** said
2Jn 1:7 mark of a **d** and an antichrist.
Rev 12:9 the **d** of the whole world,

deceives (3)

Pro 23:3 because this is food that **d** you.
Jon 7:12 "No he isn't. He **d** the people."
Rev 13:14 It **d** those living on earth with

deceiving (7)

1Ki 22:22 'You will succeed in **d** him.
2Ki 10:19 (Jehu was **d** them.)
2Ch 18:21 'You will succeed in **d** him.
1Co 6:9 Stop **d** yourselves!
2Pe 2:13 They especially enjoy **d** you
1Jn 1:8 sinful" we are **d** ourselves,
Rev 20:3 the serpent to keep it from **d**

decency (1)

Psa 111:8 are carried out with truth and **d**.

decent (51)

Job 1:1 He was **d**, he feared God,
1:8 is a man of integrity: He is **d**,
2:3 is a man of integrity: He is **d**,
4:7 Find me a **d** person who has
17:8 **D** people are shocked by this,
23:7 Then **d** people could argue
Psa 7:10 those whose motives are **d**.
11:2 at people whose motives are **d**.
11:7 **D** people will see his face.
25:8 The LORD is good and **d**.
32:11 all whose motives are **d**.
33:1 LORD is proper for **d** people.
36:10 to those whose motives are **d**.
37:14 to slaughter those who are **d**.
37:37 and look at the **d** person,
49:14 (**D** people will rule them in the
64:10 Everyone whose motives are **d**
92:15 it known that the LORD is **d**.
94:15 are **d** will pursue justice.
97:11 for those whose motives are **d**.
107:42 **D** people will see this and

Psa 111:1 in the company of **d** people
112:2 The family of a **d** person will
112:4 shine in the dark for a **d** person.
125:4 to those whose motives are **d**.
140:13 **D** people will live in your
Pro 2:7 priceless wisdom for **d** people.
2:21 **D** people will live in the land.
3:32 advice is with **d** people.
4:11 I have guided you along **d**
11:3 Integrity guides **d** people,
11:6 **D** people are saved by their
11:11 With the blessing of **d** people a
12:6 the words of **d** people rescue.
14:9 is forgiveness among **d** people.
14:11 but the tents of **d** people will
15:8 prayers of **d** people please him.
15:19 but the road of **d** people is an
16:17 The highway of **d** people turns
21:18 will take the place of **d** people.
21:29 but a **d** person's way of life is
28:10 Whoever leads **d** people into
29:10 but **d** people seek ⌊to protect⌋
29:27 A **d** person is disgusting to
Ecc 7:29 God made people **d**,
7:29 ways ⌊to avoid being **d**⌋."
Dan 11:17 and some **d** men will invade
Mic 7:2 from the earth, and no one is **d**.
7:4 The most **d** person is sharper
1Co 15:33 bad people will ruin **d** people.
1Pe 2:12 Live **d** lives among

decently (1)

Rom 13:13 We should live **d**, as people

deception (10)

Job 15:35 Their wombs produce **d**."
31:5 lies or my feet have run after **d**,
Psa 10:7 His mouth is full of cursing, **d**,
36:3 are ⌊nothing but⌋ trouble and **d**.
Zep 1:9 house with violence and **d**.
Mat 27:64 Then the last **d** will be worse
Rom 3:13 Their tongues practice **d**.
1Th 2:3 corrupt practices, or **d**.
1Pe 2:1 evil, every kind of **d**, hypocrisy,
2Pe 3:17 not to be carried away by the **d**

deceptive (3)

Job 6:15 My brothers have been as **d** as
Pro 4:24 Put **d** speech far away from
31:30 "Charm is **d**, and beauty

decide (31)

Gen 16:5 May the LORD **d** who is right —
31:37 Let them **d** which one of us is
Exo 18:16 I **d** which person is right,
33:5 and I'll **d** what to do with you.'"
Num 35:24 rules in order to **d** if you ⌊are
Dtr 17:8 that is too hard for you to **d**.
22:13 and **d** he doesn't like her.
25:1 hear the case and **d** who's right
Jdg 11:27 who will **d** today whether Israel
20:9 We'll **d** by lot who should
1Sm 24:12 May the LORD **d** between you
24:15 He will **d** between you and me.
2Sm 24:13 Think it over, and **d** what
1Ch 21:12 **D** what answer I should give
2Ch 19:8 the LORD's laws and **d** cases.
Neh 10:34 laypeople have drawn lots to **d**
10:35 We have drawn lots to **d** who
10:36 we have drawn lots to **d** who
10:37 Also, we have drawn lots to **d**
Job 34:4 Let's **d** for ourselves what is
Isa 11:3 his eyes see or **d** by what his
Jer 42:17 So all the people who **d** to go
Dan 1:13 **D** how to treat us on the basis
11:17 "Then the northern king will **d**
Jon 7:28 I didn't **d** to come on my own.
Act 4:19 "**D** for yourselves whether God
24:22 Lysias arrives, I'll **d** your case."
25:21 the Emperor **d** his case.
Rom 14:13 Instead, you should **d** never to
1Co 14:29 Everyone else should **d**
16:6 wherever I **d** to go.

decided (56)

Gen 6:13 God said to Noah, "I have **d** to
41:32 has been definitely **d** by God,
Exo 2:21 Moses **d** to stay with the man.
Num 15:34 in custody until they **d** what
30:14 this means he's **d** that she
1Sm 20:7 sure that he has **d** to harm me.
20:9 for sure that my father had **d**
2Sm 13:32 Absalom **d** to do this the day
2Ki 8:1 The LORD has **d** to send a
2Ch 20:3 Frightened, Jehoshaphat **d** to
25:16 said, "I know that God has **d**
30:2 assembly in Jerusalem **d**
30:5 So they **d** to send an
30:23 Then the whole assembly **d** to
Est 2:1 what had been **d** against her.
Job 29:25 I **d** how they should live.
Psa 32:5 I **d** to confess them to you,
68:28 Your God has **d** you will be
119:112 I have **d** to obey your laws.
Jer 21:10 I've **d** to harm this city,
Dan 4:24 The Most High has **d** to apply it
6:1 Darius **d** it would be good to
10:12 ever since the first day you **d**
11:36 what has been **d** must be done.
Jnh 3:5 They **d** to fast, and everyone,
Zep 3:8 I have **d** to gather nations,
Hag 2:14 I have **d** that these people are
Mat 1:19 So he **d** to break the marriage
19:12 Still others have **d** to be
27:1 the people **d** to execute Jesus.
27:7 So they **d** to use it to buy a
Mar 15:1 The whole Jewish council **d** to
Luk 23:24 Pilate **d** to give in to their
Act 3:13 even though Pilate had **d** to let
4:28 had already **d** should be done.
7:23 he **d** to visit his own people,
11:29 All the disciples in Antioch **d** to
15:19 "So I've **d** that we shouldn't
15:22 and the whole church **d** to
19:21 Paul **d** to go to Jerusalem by
20:3 So he **d** to go back through
20:16 Paul had **d** to sail past
25:25 I have **d** to send him to Rome.
27:1 When it was **d** that we should
27:12 most of the men **d** to sail from
27:39 So they **d** to try to run the ship
Rom 15:26 they have **d** to take up a
1Co 1:21 So God **d** to use the nonsense
2:2 While I was with you, I **d** to
2Co 2:1 I **d** not to visit you again while I
9:7 give whatever you have **d**.
Eph 1:5 of his love he had already **d**
1:9 He had **d** to do this through
1:11 God also **d** ahead of time to
Tit 3:12 I have **d** to spend the winter
Jas 1:18 God **d** to give us life through

decides (7)

Gen 50:15 What if he **d** to pay us back for
Lev 27:12 will be whatever the priest **d**.
27:14 will be whatever the priest **d**.
Num 24:23 live when God **d** to do this?
30:13 "A husband **d** whether or not
Rom 14:5 One person **d** that one day is
14:5 Another person **d** that all days

deciding (1)

Lev 13:59 for **d** whether mildew

decision (21)

Exo 32:12 Reconsider your **d** to bring this
Dtr 17:11 they tell you to do in their **d**.
21:5 Their **d** is final in all cases
1Ki 3:28 All Israel heard about the **d** the
8:32 take action, and make a **d**.
2Ch 6:23 take action, and make a **d**.
Ezr 5:17 Your Majesty's **d** on this matter.
Psa 81:4 a law for Israel, a legal **d** from
Isa 16:3 Make a **d**. At high noon make
Dan 4:17 have announced this **d**.
Hos 5:1 This is my **d** about you.
Joe 3:14 many people in the valley of **d**.
3:14 LORD is near in the valley of **d**.
Hag 2:11 Ask the priests for a **d**.
Mar 15:1 immediately came to a **d**
Act 15:25 a unanimous **d** that we should
15:27 Silas to report to you on our **d**.
21:25 believers a letter with our **d**.
Rom 14:5 person must make his own **d**.
1Co 7:37 a father may have come to a **d**
7:37 If his **d** is to keep her ⌊at

decision-making (3)

Exo 28:15 "Make the breastplate for **d** as
28:29 wearing the breastplate for **d**.
28:30 into the breastplate for **d**.

decisions (20)

Gen 49:16 "Dan will hand down **d** for his
Exo 21:1 "Here are the legal **d** to be used
24:3 the LORD's words and legal **d**.
28:30 the LORD's⌋ **d** for the Israelites.
Num 27:21 will use the Urim to make **d**
Dtr 1:17 Be impartial in your **d**.
1:17 since your **d** come from God.
Jdg 4:5 would come to her for legal **d**.
Est 1:13 experts in royal decrees and **d**,
Psa 13:2 How long must I make **d** alone
19:9 The **d** of the LORD are true.
94:15 The **d** of judges will again
147:19 laws and judicial **d** to Israel.
147:20 other nations do not know the **d**
Isa 11:4 He will make fair **d** for the
Eze 13:9 will not help my people make **d**
44:24 as judges and make **d** based
Act 16:4 they told people about the **d**
Rom 2:5 will reveal that his **d** are fair.
11:33 it is impossible to explain his **d**

decisive (1)

Jdg 11:33 It was a **d** defeat. So the

deck (3)

Eze 27:6 They made your **d** from pine
Jnh 1:5 Now, Jonah had gone below **d**
Act 27:17 The men pulled it up on **d**.

decks (1)

Gen 6:16 lower, middle, and upper **d**.

declaration (7)

2Sm 23:1 "Here is the **d** by David,
23:1 son of Jesse — the **d** by the
Job 13:17 to my words. Hear my **d**.
Pro 30:1 This man's **d**: "I'm weary,
Heb 3:1 whom we make our **d** of faith.
4:14 need to hold on to our **d** of faith:
10:23 to hold firmly to our **d** of faith.

declare (46)

Exo 21:5 'I hereby **d** my love for my
23:7 never **d** guilty people innocent.
Lev 13:3 he must **d** him unclean.
13:6 the priest must **d** him clean.
13:8 the priest must **d** him unclean.
13:11 the priest must **d** him unclean
13:13 the priest must **d** the diseased
13:15 raw flesh and **d** him unclean.
13:17 the priest must **d** the diseased
13:20 the priest must **d** the person
13:22 the priest must **d** him unclean.
13:23 The priest must **d** him clean.
13:25 The priest must **d** him unclean.
13:27 the priest must **d** him unclean.
13:28 The priest must **d** him clean,
13:30 the priest must **d** the person
13:34 the priest must **d** him clean.
13:37 so the priest must **d** him clean.
13:44 The priest must **d** him unclean
14:7 and will **d** that person clean.
14:11 The priest who will **d** him
14:48 the priest must **d** the house
16:19 he will cleanse it and **d** it holy.
Dtr 20:12 your offer of peace but **d** war
26:3 "I **d** today to the LORD your
27:14 The Levites will **d** to all the
1Ki 8:32 but **d** the innocent person
2Ki 14:8 of Israel, to **d** war on Israel.
2Ch 6:23 but **d** the innocent person
25:17 of Israel, to **d** war on Israel.
Job 9:20 It would **d** that I am corrupt
9:28 that you won't **d** me innocent.
Psa 19:1 The heavens **d** the glory of

Pro 20:6 people **d** themselves loyal,
Isa 5:23 who **d** the guilty innocent for a
Eze 38:21 I will **d** war against Gog on all
Mic 3:5 But they **d** a holy war against
Jon 1:7 John came to **d** the truth about
1:8 but he came to **d** the truth about
15:26 will **d** the truth about me.
15:27 You will **d** the truth,
Act 20:26 Therefore, I **d** to you today that
Rom 10:9 If you **d** that Jesus is Lord,
1Jn 4:3 But every person who doesn't **d**
4:15 God lives in those who **d** that
2Jn 1:7 They refuse to **d** that Jesus

declared (28)

Lev 8:15 at the bottom of the altar and **d**
13:7 to the priest to be **d** clean,
13:35 the person has been **d** clean,
Num 6:9 his head in order to be **d** clean.
Dtr 26:17 Today you have **d** that the
26:18 Today the LORD has **d** that
1Ki 9:3 I have **d** that this temple which
9:7 I will reject this temple that I **d**
2Ch 7:16 I have chosen and **d** this
7:20 I will reject this temple that I **d**
Est 2:18 He also **d** that day a holiday in
9:22 He **d** that these days are to be
Job 9:2 a mortal be **d** righteous to God?
13:18 I know that I will be **d**
15:18 you what wise people have **d**
Psa 17:15 face when I am **d** innocent.
35:27 I am **d** innocent joyfully sing
Isa 45:25 of Israel will be **d** righteous,
Amo 2:11 The LORD has **d** this.
2:16 The LORD has **d** this.
Mat 12:37 words you will be **d** innocent,
12:37 or by your words you will be **d**
Mar 7:19 Jesus **d** all foods acceptable.)
Jon 1:15 (John **d** the truth about him
1:34 I have seen this and have **d**
13:21 He **d**, "I can guarantee this
Rom 1:4 holy nature he was **d** the Son
Heb 2:6 Instead, someone has **d** this

declares (353)

Gen 22:16 on my own name, **d** the LORD,
Exo 22:9 The one whom God **d** guilty
Num 14:28 them, 'As I live, **d** the LORD,
1Sm 2:30 the LORD God of Israel **d**:
2:30 "But now the LORD **d**:
2Ki 9:26 back in this field,' **d** the LORD.
19:33 **d** the LORD of Armies.
22:19 listen ⌊to you⌋, **d** the LORD.
2Ch 34:27 listen ⌊to you⌋, **d** the LORD.
Isa 14:22 **d** the LORD of Armies.
14:22 and descendants," **d** the LORD.
14:23 **d** the LORD of Armies.
17:3 **d** the LORD of Armies.
17:6 **d** the LORD God of Israel.
19:4 A strong king will rule them," **d**
22:25 The LORD of Armies **d**,
30:1 The LORD **d**, "How horrible it
31:9 The LORD **d** this. His fire is in
37:34 **d** the LORD of Armies.
41:14 **d** the LORD, your Defender,
43:10 my witnesses," **d** the LORD.
43:12 that I am God," **d** the LORD.
49:18 swear as I live," **d** the LORD,
52:5 are screaming, **d** the LORD.
54:17 comes from me," **d** the LORD.
55:8 not your ways," **d** the LORD.
56:8 scattered people of Israel, **d**,
59:20 from rebellion," **d** the LORD.
66:2 come into being," **d** the LORD.
66:17 at the same time," **d** the LORD.
66:20 Jerusalem," **d** the LORD.
66:21 and Levites," **d** the LORD.
66:22 in my presence," **d** the LORD.
66:23 to worship me," **d** the LORD.
Jer 1:8 I will rescue you," **d** the LORD.
1:15 from the north," **d** the LORD.
1:19 I will rescue you," **d** the LORD.
2:3 struck them,'" **d** the LORD.
2:9 against you," **d** the LORD,
2:12 Be terribly afraid," **d** the LORD.
2:19 **d** the Almighty LORD of
Jer 2:22 **d** the Almighty LORD.
2:29 against me," **d** the LORD.
3:1 back to me!" **d** the LORD.
3:10 was deceitful," **d** the LORD.
3:12 I'm merciful,' **d** the LORD.
3:13 not obeyed me,' **d** the LORD.
3:14 people," **d** the LORD.
3:16 in the land," **d** the LORD.
3:20 betrayed me," **d** the LORD.
4:1 The LORD **d**, "If you come
4:9 that day comes," **d** the LORD,
4:17 against me," **d** the LORD.
5:9 for these things," **d** the LORD.
5:11 unfaithful to me," **d** the LORD.
5:15 to attack you, **d** the LORD.
5:18 in those days, **d** the LORD,
5:29 for these things," **d** the LORD.
6:12 live in the land," **d** the LORD.
7:11 you are doing,'" **d** the LORD.
7:13 did at Shiloh,'" **d** the LORD.
7:19 provoking me," **d** the LORD.
7:30 I consider evil," **d** the LORD.
7:32 days are coming," **d** the LORD,
8:1 The LORD **d**, "At that time the
8:3 **d** the LORD of Armies.
8:13 their harvest,'" **d** the LORD,
8:17 will bite you," **d** the LORD.
9:3 don't know me," **d** the LORD.
9:6 deceit. me," **d** the LORD.
9:9 for these things, **d** the LORD.
9:24 pleases me, **d** the LORD.
9:25 days are coming," **d** the LORD,
12:17 and destroy it," **d** the LORD.
13:11 cling to me," **d** the LORD.
13:14 children together, **d** the LORD.
13:25 planned for you," **d** the LORD.
15:3 to punish them," **d** the LORD.
15:6 You have left me," **d** the LORD.
15:9 of their enemies," **d** the LORD.
15:20 and rescue you, **d** the LORD.
16:5 these people," **d** the LORD.
16:11 abandoned me, **d** the LORD.
16:14 days are coming," **d** the LORD,
16:16 many fishermen," **d** the LORD,
17:24 "Now," **d** the LORD,
19:6 days are coming, **d** the LORD,
19:12 who live in it, **d** the LORD.
21:7 Afterwards, **d** the LORD,
21:10 to do good to it, **d** the LORD.
21:13 rock in the plain,'" **d** the LORD.
21:14 you have done,'" **d** the LORD.
22:5 oath on myself," **d** the LORD,
22:24 "As I live," **d** the LORD,
23:1 in my care," **d** the LORD.
23:2 you have done," **d** the LORD.
23:4 will be missing," **d** the LORD.
23:5 days are coming," **d** the LORD,
23:7 days are coming," **d** the LORD,
23:11 them doing evil," **d** the LORD.
23:12 to be punished," **d** the LORD.
23:23 who is far away," **d** the LORD.
23:24 I can't see him," **d** the LORD.
23:24 and earth!" **d** the LORD.
23:30 from each other," **d** the LORD.
23:32 they made up," **d** the LORD.
23:32 people at all," **d** the LORD.
23:33 will abandon you, **d** the LORD.'
25:7 listened to me, **d** the LORD.
25:9 of Babylon, **d** the LORD.
25:12 for their crimes, **d** the LORD.
25:29 **d** the LORD of Armies.'
25:31 kill the wicked, **d** the LORD.'
27:8 power, **d** the LORD.
27:11 and live on it,'" **d** the LORD.
27:15 I didn't send them, **d** the LORD.
27:22 I come for them, **d** the LORD.
28:4 went to Babylon, **d** the LORD.
29:9 I didn't send them, **d** the LORD.
29:11 that I have for you, **d** the LORD.
29:14 let you find me, **d** the LORD.
29:14 I've scattered you, **d** the LORD.
29:19 didn't listen to me, **d** the LORD.
29:19 refused to listen, **d** the LORD.
29:23 I'm a witness, **d** the LORD.
29:32 send my people, **d** the LORD,
30:3 days are coming," **d** the LORD,
Jer 30:8 **d** the LORD of Armies,
30:10 servant Jacob," **d** the LORD.
30:11 I will rescue you," **d** the LORD.
30:17 your wounds," **d** the LORD.
31:1 "At that time," **d** the LORD,
31:14 my blessings," **d** the LORD.
31:16 for your work, **d** the LORD.
31:17 is filled with hope, **d** the LORD.
31:20 on him," **d** the LORD.
31:27 days are coming," **d** the LORD,
31:28 and to plant them," **d** the LORD.
31:31 days are coming," **d** the LORD,
31:32 husband to them," **d** the LORD.
31:33 after those days," **d** the LORD:
31:34 will know me," **d** the LORD,
31:36 stop working, **d** the LORD,
31:37 they have done, **d** the LORD.
31:38 days are coming," **d** the LORD,
32:5 I deal with him, **d** the LORD.
32:30 they've done," **d** the LORD.
32:44 their captivity," **d** the LORD.
33:14 days are coming," **d** the LORD,
34:5 spoken my word, **d** the LORD."
34:17 going to free you," **d** the LORD.
34:22 give a command," **d** the LORD.
35:13 obey my words? **d** the LORD.
39:17 I will rescue you, **d** the LORD.
39:18 you trusted me, **d** the LORD.'"
42:11 be afraid of him, **d** the LORD.
44:29 you this sign,' **d** the LORD.
45:5 on all people, **d** the LORD.
46:5 all around them," **d** the LORD.
46:18 "As I live," **d** the king,
46:23 down the forest," **d** the LORD,
46:26 did long ago," **d** the LORD.
46:28 servant Jacob," **d** the LORD.
48:12 days are coming," **d** the LORD,
48:15 will be slaughtered," **d** the king,
48:25 its arm is broken," **d** the LORD.
48:30 **d** the LORD, "but it isn't right.
48:35 to their gods," **d** the LORD.
48:38 no one wants," **d** the LORD.
48:43 live in Moab," **d** the LORD.
48:44 to Moab," **d** the LORD.
48:47 in the last days," **d** the LORD.
49:2 days are coming, **d** the LORD,
49:5 **d** the Almighty LORD of
49:6 of Ammon, **d** the LORD.
49:13 an oath on myself, **d** the LORD,
49:16 down from there," **d** the LORD.
49:26 **d** the LORD of Armies.
49:30 of Hazor, **d** the LORD.
49:31 and securely, **d** the LORD.
49:32 from every side, **d** the LORD.
49:37 my burning anger, **d** the LORD.
49:38 king and officials, **d** the LORD.
49:39 captives of Elam, **d** the LORD.
50:4 and at that time," **d** the LORD,
50:10 they want," **d** the LORD.
50:20 and at that time," **d** the LORD,
50:21 with a sword," **d** the LORD.
50:30 that day," **d** the LORD.
50:31 **d** the Almighty LORD of
50:35 lives in Babylon," **d** the LORD.
50:40 will stay there," **d** the LORD.
51:24 they did in Zion," **d** the LORD.
51:25 the whole earth," **d** the LORD.
51:26 permanent ruins," **d** the LORD.
51:39 wake up again, **d** the LORD.
51:48 will attack it," **d** the LORD.
51:52 days are coming," **d** the LORD,
51:53 me against them," **d** the LORD.
51:57 and never wake up," **d** the king,
Eze 5:11 I live, **d** the Almighty LORD,
11:8 **d** the Almighty LORD.
11:21 **d** the Almighty LORD.'"
12:25 **d** the Almighty LORD.'"
12:28 **d** the Almighty LORD.'"
13:8 **d** the Almighty LORD.
13:16 **d** the Almighty LORD.'"
14:11 **d** the Almighty LORD.'"
14:14 **d** the Almighty LORD.
14:16 As I live, **d** the Almighty LORD,
14:18 As I live, **d** the Almighty LORD,
14:20 As I live, **d** the Almighty LORD,
14:23 **d** the Almighty LORD.

Eze 15:8 **d** the Almighty LORD.
16:8 **d** the Almighty LORD.
16:14 **d** the Almighty LORD.
16:19 **d** the Almighty LORD.
16:23 **d** the Almighty LORD.
16:30 **d** the Almighty LORD.
16:43 **d** the Almighty LORD.
16:48 As I live, **d** the Almighty LORD,
16:58 you have done, **d** the LORD.
16:63 **d** the Almighty LORD.'"
17:16 **d** the Almighty LORD,
18:3 As I live, **d** the Almighty LORD,
18:9 **d** the Almighty LORD.
18:23 **d** the Almighty LORD.
18:30 **d** the Almighty LORD.
18:32 **d** the Almighty LORD.
20:3 As I live, **d** the Almighty LORD,
20:31 **d** the Almighty LORD,
20:33 **d** the Almighty LORD,
20:36 **d** the Almighty LORD.
20:40 **d** the Almighty LORD.
20:44 **d** the Almighty LORD.'"
21:7 **d** the Almighty LORD."
21:13 **d** the Almighty LORD.
22:12 **d** the Almighty LORD.
22:31 **d** the Almighty LORD.
23:34 **d** the Almighty LORD.
24:14 done,'" **d** the Almighty LORD.
25:14 **d** the Almighty LORD.
26:5 **d** the Almighty LORD.
26:14 **d** the Almighty LORD.
26:21 **d** the Almighty LORD.
28:10 I have spoken,'" **d** the LORD.
29:20 **d** the Almighty LORD.
30:6 **d** the Almighty LORD.
31:18 **d** the Almighty LORD.'"
32:8 **d** the Almighty LORD.
32:14 **d** the Almighty LORD.
32:16 **d** the Almighty LORD.
32:31 **d** the Almighty LORD.
32:32 **d** the Almighty LORD.
33:11 **d** the Almighty LORD,
34:8 As I live, **d** the Almighty LORD,
34:15 **d** the Almighty LORD.
34:30 **d** the Almighty LORD.
34:31 **d** the Almighty LORD."
35:6 **d** the Almighty LORD,
35:11 **d** the Almighty LORD,
36:14 **d** the Almighty LORD.
36:15 **d** the Almighty LORD.'"
36:23 **d** the Almighty LORD.
36:32 **d** the Almighty LORD.
37:14 I have done it, **d** the LORD.'"
38:18 **d** the Almighty LORD.
38:21 **d** the Almighty LORD.
39:5 **d** the Almighty LORD.
39:8 **d** the Almighty LORD.
39:10 **d** the Almighty LORD.
39:13 **d** the Almighty LORD.
39:20 **d** the Almighty LORD.'
39:29 **d** the Almighty LORD."
43:27 **d** the Almighty LORD."
44:12 for their sins, **d** the LORD.
44:15 **d** the Almighty LORD.
44:27 **d** the Almighty LORD.
45:9 **d** the Almighty LORD.
45:15 **d** the Almighty LORD.
47:23 **d** the Almighty LORD.
48:29 **d** the Almighty LORD.
Hos 2:13 She forgot me," **d** the LORD.
2:16 me her husband," **d** the LORD.
2:21 your ⌊prayers,⌋" **d** the LORD.
11:11 their own homes," **d** the LORD.
Joe 2:12 "But even now," **d** the LORD,
Amo 3:10 to do what is right, **d** the LORD.
3:13 **d** the Almighty LORD,
3:15 be demolished, **d** the LORD.
4:3 dump. The LORD **d** this.
4:5 The Almighty LORD **d** this.
4:6 didn't return to me, **d** the LORD.
4:8 didn't return to me, **d** the LORD.
4:9 didn't return to me, **d** the LORD.
4:10 didn't return to me, **d** the LORD.
4:11 didn't return to me, **d** the LORD.
6:8 The LORD God of Armies **d**:
6:14 **d** the LORD God of the Armies
Amo 8:3 **d** the Almighty LORD.
8:9 **d** the Almighty LORD,
8:11 **d** the Almighty LORD,
9:8 of Jacob, **d** the LORD.
9:12 my authority, **d** the LORD,
9:13 are going to come, **d** the LORD,
Oba 1:4 down from there," **d** the LORD.
1:8 Esau's mountain," **d** the LORD.
Mic 4:6 that day comes," **d** the LORD,
5:10 that day comes," **d** the LORD,
Nah 2:13 **d** the LORD of Armies.
3:5 **d** the LORD of Armies.
Zep 1:2 put an end to it," **d** the LORD.
1:3 face of the earth," **d** the LORD.
1:10 from the hills," **d** the LORD.
2:9 **d** the LORD of Armies,
3:8 The LORD **d**, "Just wait!
Hag 1:8 I will be honored," **d** the LORD.
1:9 **d** the LORD of Armies.
1:13 "I am with you, **d** the LORD."
2:4 be strong," **d** the LORD.
2:4 land, be strong," **d** the LORD.
2:4 **d** the LORD of Armies.
2:8 **d** the LORD of Armies.
2:9 **d** the LORD of Armies.
2:9 **d** the LORD of Armies."
2:14 so is this nation, **d** the LORD.
2:17 come back to me, **d** the LORD.
2:23 **d** the LORD of Armies,
2:23 (son of Shealtiel), **d** the LORD.
2:23 **d** the LORD of Armies.'"
Zec 1:3 **d** the LORD of Armies,
1:4 attention to me, **d** the LORD.
1:16 **d** the LORD of Armies.
2:5 of fire around it, **d** the LORD.
2:6 land of the north, **d** the LORD.
2:10 live among you, **d** the LORD.
3:9 **d** the LORD of Armies.
3:10 **d** the LORD of Armies,
5:4 **d** the LORD of Armies,
8:6 **d** the LORD of Armies.
8:11 **d** the LORD of Armies.
8:14 **d** the LORD of Armies,
8:17 all these things, **d** the LORD.
10:12 live in his name," **d** the LORD.
11:6 The LORD **d**, "I will no longer
12:4 The LORD **d**, "On that day I
13:1 ⌊The LORD **d**,⌋ "On that day a
13:2 **d** the LORD of Armies,
13:7 **d** the LORD of Armies.
13:8 The LORD **d**, "Throughout the
Mal 1:2 **d** the LORD. "I loved Jacob,
Act 15:17 search for the Lord, **d** the Lord.
1Jn 4:2 Every person who **d** that Jesus

declaring (2)

Jer 25:29 I'm **d** war on all those who live
Rom 10:10 and by **d** your faith you are

decorate (2)

Jer 10:4 Craftsmen **d** them with silver
Mat 23:29 tombs for the prophets and **d**

decorated (6)

2Sm 1:24 who dressed you in **d**,
2Ch 3:5 and **d** it with ⌊designs in the
3:14 of linen and **d** it with angels.
Amo 3:15 Houses ⌊**d**⌋ with ivory will be
Luk 21:5 built with fine stones and **d**
Rev 21:19 the city wall were beautifully **d**

decorations (1)

1Ki 7:18 he made two rows ⌊of **d**⌋

decrease (3)

Jer 29:6 Grow in number there; don't **d**.
30:19 and their number won't **d**.
Jon 3:30 while I must **d** in importance.

decreased (1)

Gen 8:3 of 150 days the water had **d**.

decreasing (1)

Gen 8:5 The water kept **d** until the tenth

decree (33)

Ezr 6:8 I am issuing this **d** about how
6:11 I am also issuing a **d** that if
6:12 I, Darius, have issued a **d**.
7:13 I have issued a **d** that any
Est 1:19 Your Majesty, issue a royal **d**.
1:20 When you issue your **d**,
2:8 and **d** were heard,
3:14 was made public in a **d**
3:15 The **d** was also issued at the
4:3 by the king's command and **d**,
4:8 a copy of the **d** that was issued
4:8 The **d** gave permission to
4:16 even if it is against a royal **d**.
8:13 was made public in a **d**
8:14 The **d** was issued also in the
8:17 king's message and **d** arrived,
9:1 the king's command and **d**
9:14 issuing a **d** in Susa.
Psa 2:7 I will announce the LORD's **d**.
Pro 8:15 and rulers **d** fair laws.
Dan 2:13 So a **d** was issued that the
2:15 "Why is the king's **d** so harsh?"
6:7 make a statute and enforce a **d**.
6:7 The **d** should state that for the
6:8 Your Majesty, issue this **d**,
6:9 So Darius signed the written **d**.
6:12 spoke to the king about his **d**.
6:12 "Didn't you sign a **d** which
6:12 the **d** can't be repealed."
6:13 order or the **d** that you signed.
6:15 Persians have a law that no **d**
6:26 I **d** that in every part of my
Zep 2:2 before the **d** is carried out

decreed (2)

Est 9:13 tomorrow what was **d** for today.
Pro 31:5 and forget what they have **d**

decrees (14)

1Ki 11:33 my laws and **d** as his father
2Ki 17:13 and obey my commands and **d**
17:15 They rejected his **d**,
17:34 fear the LORD or live by the **d**,
1Ch 22:13 carefully obey the laws and **d**
Est 1:13 in royal **d** and decisions,
1:15 "According to the royal **d**,
1:19 It should be recorded in the **d** of
3:8 They do not obey your **d**.
Psa 50:16 "How dare you quote my **d** and
Isa 58:2 They ask me for just **d**.
Jer 44:10 my teachings or by my **d** that
44:23 **d**, or written instructions.
Act 17:7 the emperor's **d** by saying that

Dedan (11)

Gen 10:7 were Sheba and **D**.
25:3 was the father of Sheba and **D**.
1Ch 1:9 were Sheba and **D**.
1:32 sons were Sheba and **D**.
Isa 21:13 from the people of **D** will spend
Jer 25:23 **D**, Tema, Buz, and all who
49:8 deep caves, inhabitants of **D**.
Eze 25:13 into ruins from Teman to **D**.
27:15 People from **D** traded goods
27:20 **D** traded saddle blankets with
38:13 "Sheba, **D**, the merchants from

Dedan's (1)

Gen 25:3 **D** descendants were the

dedicate (29)

Exo 29:36 ⌊with olive oil⌋ in order to **d** it.
29:44 I will **d** the tent of meeting and
30:29 In this way you will **d** them for
40:9 In this way you will **d** it and all
40:10 In this way you will **d** the altar,
40:13 In this way you will **d** him to
Lev 8:10 and everything in it and **d** them.
8:11 basin with its stand to **d** them.
Num 6:11 person must **d** his head again.
6:12 Once again he will **d** himself to
Dtr 15:19 You must **d** every firstborn
20:5 and someone else will **d** it.
Jdg 17:3 Then his mother said, "I **d** this

1Ch 22:19 So **d** your hearts and lives to
23:13 were forever designated to **d**
28:8 our God listens to **d** your lives
28:9 If you **d** your life to serving him,
29:5 make an offering and **d** himself
2Ch 2:4 I want to **d** it to him,
14:4 He told the people of Judah to **d**
15:2 If you will **d** your lives to
15:12 with one another to **d** their lives
15:13 who refused to **d** their lives
17:3 Jehoshaphat didn't **d** his life to
25:15 "Why do you **d** your life to
34:3 he began to **d** his life to serving
Dan 3:2 other provincial officials to **d**
3:3 officials assembled to **d**
1Pe 3:15 But **d** your lives to Christ as

dedicated (90)

Exo 12:42 since it is **d** to the LORD.)
16:23 a holy day of worship **d** to the
16:25 today is a day of worship **d**
20:10 day is the day of worship **d**
34:13 and cut down their poles **d** to
35:2 It is **d** to the LORD.
40:11 and they will be **d**.
Lev 8:30 In this way he **d** Aaron,
21:12 because he is **d** with the
27:28 "However, everything **d** to the
27:28 Everything **d** in that way is
27:29 People **d** this way cannot be
Num 6:2 as a Nazirite **d** to the LORD.
6:5 the entire time that they are **d**
6:6 While they are **d** to the LORD
7:1 he anointed it and **d** it and all
7:1 He also anointed and **d** the
Dtr 5:14 day is the day of worship **d**
7:5 cut down their poles **d** to the
12:3 burn their poles **d** to the
16:8 hold a religious assembly **d**
16:15 will celebrate this festival **d**
16:21 never plant beside it any tree **d**
20:5 built a new house but not **d** it,
27:5 Build an altar of stones there **d**
Jdg 6:25 Tear down your father's altar **d**
6:25 Baal and cut down the pole **d**
13:5 the boy will be a Nazirite **d**
13:7 the boy will be a Nazirite **d**
16:17 I was **d** to God before I was
1Sm 1:28 He will be **d** to the LORD for
2Sm 8:11 King David **d** these articles to
8:11 and gold he had **d** from all
1Ki 8:63 of Israel **d** the LORD's temple.
14:15 River because they **d** poles
16:33 Ahab made poles **d** to the
2Ki 3:2 father had set up and **d** to Baal.
12:18 had **d** to the LORD,
12:18 the things he had **d** to the
13:6 In addition, the pole **d** to the
16:14 But he moved the bronze altar **d**
17:10 up sacred stones and poles **d**
17:16 They made a pole **d** to the
18:4 and cut down the poles **d** to the
21:3 He set up altars **d** to Baal and
21:3 to Baal and made a pole **d**
23:6 He took the pole **d** to the
23:11 horses that Judah's kings had **d**
23:14 down the poles **d** to Asherah,
23:15 burning the pole **d** to Asherah.
1Ch 15:13 We hadn't **d** our lives to serving
18:11 King David **d** all the articles of
26:20 treasuries of the gifts **d** to God.
26:26 all the treasuries of the gifts **d**
28:12 temple and the gifts **d** to God.)
2Ch 7:5 So the king and all the people **d**
14:3 and cut down the poles **d** to the
14:7 because we have **d** our lives
14:7 We have **d** our lives to him,
17:4 Instead, he **d** his life to his
17:6 places of worship and poles **d**
19:3 and you've wholeheartedly **d**
22:9 Jehoshaphat **d** his life to
24:18 idols and the poles **d**
26:5 He **d** his life to serving God in
26:5 As long as he **d** his life to
29:31 Hezekiah said, "You have **d**
29:33 The animals **d** as holy
2Ch 31:1 cut down the poles **d** to the
31:6 of the holy things they had **d**
31:12 and the gifts **d** to God.
31:14 and the holy gifts **d** to God.
31:21 into worship and **d** his life
33:3 He set up altars **d** to other gods
33:3 the Baals — and made a pole **d**
33:19 and set up idols and poles **d**
34:3 poles **d** to the goddess
Neh 3:1 They **d** it and set its doors in
3:1 of the Hundred, which they **d**,
12:27 Jerusalem was going to be **d**,
Isa 27:9 powdered chalk and no poles **d**
Jer 17:2 their altars and their poles **d**
Eze 46:14 It will be a grain offering **d** to
Mic 5:14 I will pull out your poles **d** to
Act 15:26 Barnabas and Paul have **d** their
Rom 12:1 **d** to God and pleasing to him.
2Co 8:16 God for making Titus as **d**
8:22 and found to be a **d** worker.
8:22 We find that he is much more **d**
Tit 2:3 that shows they are **d** to God.

dedicates (1)

Ezr 8:22 good of everyone who **d** his life

dedicating (4)

2Ch 12:14 not serious about **d** himself
30:19 their hearts set on **d** their lives
Dan 9:13 our wrongs and **d** ourselves
Jon 17:19 I'm **d** myself to this holy work

dedication (11)

Num 7:10 also brought offerings for the **d**
7:11 his gift for the **d** of the altar."
7:84 the leaders of Israel for the **d**
7:88 These were the gifts for the **d**
2Ch 7:9 They had observed the **d** of the
Ezr 6:16 at the **d** of God's temple.
6:17 At the **d** of God's temple,
Neh 12:27 to celebrate the **d** joyfully
Jon 10:22 The Festival of the **D** of the
2Co 8:7 speak, your knowledge, your **d**,
8:8 by pointing out the **d** of others.

deed (7)

Pro 19:17 will repay him for his good **d**.
Jer 32:10 I signed the **d**, sealed it,
32:10 witness the signing of the **d**,
32:11 I took the sealed copy of the **d**,
32:12 who had signed the **d**
32:14 the unsealed copies of the **d**.
Mat 19:16 what good **d** should I do to gain

deeds (36)

Dtr 3:24 or on earth who can do the **d**
4:34 his great and awe-inspiring **d**
10:21 and awe-inspiring **d** you saw
11:3 the miraculous signs and **d**
26:8 and awe-inspiring **d**,
34:12 awe-inspiring **d** that were seen
2Sm 3:39 evildoer as his evil **d** deserve."
Psa 17:7 your miraculous **d** of mercy,
20:6 his holy heaven with mighty **d**
25:6 compassionate and merciful **d**.
28:4 they have done, for their evil **d**.
66:3 "How awe-inspiring are your **d**!
66:5 **d** for Adam's descendants.
71:16 I will come with the mighty **d** of
77:11 I will remember the **d** of the
78:4 the LORD's power and great **d**
99:8 who punishes their ⌊sinful⌋ **d**.
111:2 The LORD's **d** are spectacular.
141:5 is directed against evil **d**.
145:4 generation will praise your **d**
145:6 the power of your terrifying **d**,
145:12 to make known your mighty **d**
Pro 20:11 whether his **d** are pure or right.
Isa 1:16 Get your evil **d** out of my sight.
12:4 Make his **d** known among the
28:21 work, and perform his **d**,
28:21 his deeds, his mysterious **d**.
29:15 Their **d** are done in the dark,
59:18 them back according to their **d**.
Jer 5:28 Their evil **d** have no limits.
32:12 the copies of the **d** to Baruch,
Jer 32:44 for money, sign **d**, seal them,
32:44 witness the signing of the **d**.
Zec 1:4 evil ways and your evil **d**.' But
1:6 as our ways and **d** deserve."'
Jas 3:17 filled with mercy and good **d**,

deep (88)

Gen 1:2 darkness covered the **d** water.
2:21 him to fall into a **d** sleep.
7:11 all the **d** springs burst open.
7:18 water rose and became very **d**,
8:2 The **d** springs and the sky had
15:12 a **d** sleep — a dreadful,
15:12 **d** darkness — came over
49:25 blessings from the **d** springs
Exo 15:5 The **d** water covered them.
15:8 The **d** water thickened in the
Num 11:31 about three feet **d** as far as
Dtr 33:13 with dew and **d** springs below
1Sm 26:12 made them fall into a **d** sleep.
Ezr 9:7 we have been **d** in guilt.
Neh 9:11 You threw into **d** water those
Job 4:13 when **d** sleep falls on people,
24:17 because morning and **d**
24:17 with the terrors of **d** darkness.
28:14 The **d** ocean says,
33:15 when people fall into a **d** sleep,
34:22 There's no darkness or **d**
41:31 It makes the **d** sea boil like a
Psa 36:6 judgments like the **d** ocean.
39:2 While I was **d** in thought,
40:8 Your teachings are **d** within me.
40:10 not buried your righteousness **d**
42:7 One **d** sea calls to another at
51:6 **D** down inside me you teach
69:2 I am sinking in **d** mud.
69:2 I am in **d** water. A flood is
69:14 hate me and from the **d** water.
88:6 in the bottom of the pit — in **d**,
92:5 How very **d** are your thoughts!
95:4 In his hand are the **d** places of
106:9 He led them through **d** water as
Pro 1:2 to understand **d** thoughts,
3:20 By his knowledge the **d** waters
4:19 people is like **d** darkness.
4:21 Keep them **d** within your heart
18:4 mouth are like **d** waters.
19:15 throws one into a **d** sleep,
20:5 the human heart is like **d** water,
22:14 an adulterous woman is a **d** pit.
23:27 A prostitute is a **d** pit.
25:3 high heavens and the **d** earth,
Ecc 7:24 It is **d**, very deep. Who can find
7:24 It is deep, very **d**. Who can find
9:13 it made a **d** impression on me.
Isa 7:19 and settle in the **d** valleys,
29:10 out on you a spirit of **d** sleep.
30:33 It was made **d** and wide and
44:23 you **d** places of the earth.
44:27 He says to the **d** water,
63:13 led them through the **d** water?
Jer 13:16 and change it into **d** darkness.
49:8 Hide in **d** caves, inhabitants of
51:39 They will fall into a **d** sleep
51:57 They will fall into a **d** sleep
Lam 1:13 He made it go **d** into my bones.
2:13 Your wounds are as **d** as the
Eze 23:32 a cup that is **d** and wide.
26:19 I will bring the **d** ocean over
47:5 The river was too **d** to cross
Amo 5:8 He turns **d** darkness into dawn.
Jnh 2:3 You threw me into the **d**,
2:5 The **d** ⌊sea⌋ covered me
Mic 7:19 all our sins into the **d** sea.
Nah 3:18 have fallen into a **d** sleep.
Hab 3:10 The **d** ocean roars.
Zec 10:11 and dry up all the **d** places of
Mat 13:5 because the soil wasn't **d**.
13:6 their roots weren't **d** enough.
26:37 He was beginning to feel **d**
Mar 4:5 because the soil wasn't **d**.
8:12 With a **d** sigh he asked,
Luk 5:4 "Take the boat into **d** water,
22:15 "I've had a **d** desire to eat this
Jon 4:11 to get water, and the well is **d**.
7:38 water will flow from **d** within

Rom 9:2 I have **d** sorrow and endless
11:8 given them a spirit of **d** sleep.
11:33 and knowledge are so **d** that it
1Co 2:10 especially the **d** things of God.
2Co 9:14 With **d** affection they will pray
Eph 3:18 long, high, and **d** his love is.
6:6 who have a **d** desire to do what
Heb 4:12 sword and cuts as **d** as
Rev 2:24 what are called the **d** things

deeper (14)

Lev 13:3 and the diseased area looks **d**
13:4 white and does not look **d** than
13:20 If it looks **d** than the rest of the
13:21 the affected area is not **d** than
13:25 the affected area looks **d** than
13:26 the affected area is not **d** than
13:30 If it looks **d** than the rest of the
13:31 and it does not look **d** than
13:32 and the scab does not look **d**
13:34 skin and does not look **d** than
14:37 in sunken areas that are **d** than
Job 11:8 It is **d** than ⌊the depths⌋ of hell.
Psa 106:43 against him and to sink **d**
Eph 1:18 Then you will have **d** insight.

deepest (7)

Gen 6:5 All day long their **d** thoughts
1Ch 29:18 over your people's **d** thoughts.
Psa 55:23 ⌊wicked people⌋ into the **d** pit.
Isa 14:15 to the **d** part of the pit.
Lam 3:55 "I call your name from the **d** pit,
Eze 32:23 Their graves are in the **d** parts
2Co 7:15 His **d** feelings go out to you

deer (15)

Dtr 12:15 were eating a gazelle or a **d**.
12:22 you would eat a gazelle or a **d**:
14:5 **d**, gazelles, fallow deer,
14:5 deer, gazelles, fallow **d**,
15:22 were eating a gazelle or a **d**.
2Sm 22:34 makes my feet like those of a **d**
1Ki 4:23 and 100 sheep in addition to **d**,
4:23 fallow **d**, and fattened birds.
Psa 18:33 makes my feet like those of a **d**
42:1 As a **d** longs for flowing
Pro 5:19 a loving doe and a graceful **d**.
Isa 35:6 who are lame will leap like **d**,
Jer 14:5 Even **d** in the fields give birth
Lam 1:6 were like **d** that couldn't find
Hab 3:19 my feet like those of a **d**.

defeat (56)

Lev 26:7 and you will **d** them.
26:8 You will **d** your enemies,
26:17 so that you will go down in **d**
Num 22:6 Maybe then I'll be able to **d**
Dtr 7:2 them to you and you **d** them,
28:7 The LORD will **d** your enemies
28:25 will let your enemies **d** you.
32:30 used these people to **d** them
Jos 10:10 and continued to **d** them all
Jdg 2:14 around them to **d** them.
3:8 of Aram Naharaim to **d** them.
4:2 who ruled at Hazor, to **d** them.
4:9 will use a woman to **d** Sisera."
6:16 You will **d** Midian as if it were
10:7 and Ammonites to **d** them.
11:33 It was a decisive **d**.
1Sm 4:3 the Philistines to **d** us today?
4:10 It was a major **d** in which
11:11 hours and continued to **d**
23:4 the power to **d** the Philistines."
2Sm 5:8 "Whoever wants to **d** the
5:24 of you to **d** the Philistine army."
1Ki 5:3 LORD let him **d** his enemies.
8:33 "An enemy may **d** your people
2Ki 3:19 You will **d** every walled city
13:17 You will completely **d** the
13:19 But now you will only **d** the
14:10 invite disaster and your own **d**
18:24 How can you **d** my master's
1Ch 14:15 of you to **d** the Philistine army."
2Ch 6:24 "An enemy may **d** your people
25:8 will use the enemy to **d** you,
25:8 power to help you or to **d** you."
2Ch 25:19 invite disaster and your own **d**
Job 32:13 Let God, not humans, **d** him.'
Psa 44:14 You made our ⌊**d**⌋ a proverb
81:14 would quickly **d** their enemies.
89:23 of him and **d** those who hate
118:7 I will see ⌊the **d** of⌋ those who
Isa 7:1 but they couldn't **d** it.
36:9 How can you **d** my master's
Jer 1:19 but they will not **d** you.
15:20 but they will not **d** you.
21:6 I will **d** those who live in this
37:10 Even if you would **d** the entire
43:11 He will **d** Egypt. He will bring
46:13 of Babylon, who will **d** Egypt.
49:37 I'll **d** the people of Elam in the
50:36 kill their soldiers and **d** them.
Lam 1:15 He called an army to **d** my
Eze 26:15 when they hear about your **d**.
26:18 Your **d** will make the people
Dan 11:22 large forces and **d** them,
Luk 11:22 he may attack him and **d** him.
Jon 12:35 so that darkness won't **d** you.
Rev 19:15 of his mouth to **d** the nations.

defeated (114)

Gen 14:5 and his allies came and **d**
14:15 He **d** them, pursuing them all
36:35 Hadad **d** the Midianites in the
Exo 17:13 So Joshua **d** the Amalekite
Num 14:42 You will be **d** by your enemies
14:45 and **d** them at Hormah.
21:24 But Israel **d** them in battle and
21:35 The Israelites **d** him,
Dtr 1:4 This was after he had **d** King
1:42 will be **d** by your enemies.'"
1:44 They **d** you, chasing you from
2:33 to us, and we **d** him, his sons,
3:3 We **d** him, leaving no
4:46 Moses and Israel **d** him after
29:7 out to fight us, but we **d** them.
Jos 8:15 and all Israel pretended to be **d**.
10:10 Israel and **d** them decisively at
10:20 Israelites **d** them decisively,
10:41 So Joshua **d** the people from
11:8 and the Israelites **d** them.
12:1 River that the people of Israel **d**.
12:6 and the people of Israel **d** them.
12:7 and the people of Israel **d**.
13:12 Moses had **d** them and forced
13:21 Moses **d** him and Midian's
Jdg 1:4 They **d** 10,000 men at Bezek.
1:5 They fought him and **d** the
1:17 They **d** the Canaanites who
3:13 and they **d** the Israelites and
8:11 and **d** the unsuspecting
11:21 Israel **d** them and took
11:33 He **d** them from Aroer to
12:4 The men of Gilead **d** Ephraim.
20:32 "They're **d** as before!"
20:35 So the LORD **d** them in front of
20:36 Benjamin realized they were **d**.
20:39 "Israel is completely **d**,
1Sm 4:2 the Philistines **d** Israel and
4:10 Philistines fought and **d** Israel.
7:10 that they were **d** by Israel.
13:3 Jonathan **d** the Philistine
13:4 have **d** the Philistine troops,
14:48 acted forcefully and **d** Amalek.
18:7 "Saul has **d** thousands but
19:8 He **d** them so decisively that
21:11 ' Saul has **d** thousands but
23:5 and decisively **d** them.
29:5 'Saul has **d** thousands but
2Sm 1:12 of Israel had been **d** in battle.
2:17 and David's men **d** Abner and
5:20 [The Lord Overwhelms] and **d**
5:25 as the LORD ordered him and **d**
8:1 After this, David **d** and crushed
8:2 He also **d** Moab, made the
8:3 he **d** Zobah's King Hadadezer,
8:9 had **d** Hadadezer's whole army,
10:15 that Israel had **d** them,
10:19 saw that Israel had **d** them,
17:9 support Absalom have been **d**.'
17:14 good advice to be **d**
18:7 David's men **d** Israel's army,
1Ki 20:21 and decisively **d** the Arameans.
20:25 as the one which was **d**.
2Ki 3:24 after the Moabites and **d** them.
10:32 Hazael **d** Jehu's army
13:19 completely **d** the Arameans.
13:25 Jehoash **d** Benhadad three
14:10 You certainly **d** Edom,
14:12 Israel **d** the army of Judah,
17:3 of Assyria **d** Hoshea,
1Ch 1:46 who **d** the Midianites in the
5:10 against the Hagrites, **d** them,
14:11 ⌊and his men⌋ attacked and **d**
14:16 and his men **d** the Philistine
18:1 After this, David **d** and crushed
18:2 He also **d** Moab, and the
18:3 he **d** King Hadadezer at
18:9 Hamath heard that David had **d**
19:16 that Israel had **d** them,
19:19 saw that Israel had **d** them,
20:1 Joab **d** Rabbah and tore it
20:4 and the Philistines were **d**.
2Ch 13:17 and his men **d** them decisively,
20:22 into Judah. They were **d**.
25:19 You say you **d** Edom,
25:22 Israel **d** the army of Judah,
28:5 to the king of Aram, who **d** him,
28:5 who decisively **d** him.
28:17 had again invaded and **d** Judah
28:23 the gods who had **d** him.
Neh 9:24 You **d** for them the Canaanites,
Psa 118:10 name of the LORD, I **d** them.
118:11 name of the LORD, I **d** them.
118:12 name of the LORD, I **d** them.
135:10 He is the one who **d** many
136:17 Give thanks to the one who **d**
Isa 54:15 attacks you will be **d** by you.
Jer 22:20 because all your lovers are **d**."
27:7 his grandson until Babylon is **d**.
46:2 of Babylon **d** his army at
46:5 Their warriors are **d**.
47:1 before Pharaoh **d** Gaza.
48:20 'Moab is disgraced; it is **d**.
48:39 'Look how Moab is **d**!
49:28 Nebuchadnezzar of Babylon **d**.
Eze 30:18 Egypt's strong army will be **d**.
Dan 8:25 Commanders, but he will be **d**,
11:14 this vision, but they will be **d**.
11:33 But for some time they will be **d**
11:34 As they are being **d**,
11:35 of the wise people will be **d**
11:41 tens of thousands will be **d**.
1Co 6:7 You are already totally **d**
Heb 11:34 in battle and **d** other armies.

defeating (8)

Gen 14:17 After Abram came back from **d**
2Sm 1:1 returned from **d** the Amalekites
8:10 for fighting and **d** Hadadezer.
1Ch 18:10 for fighting and **d** Hadadezer.
2Ch 25:14 back from **d** the Edomites,
Job 41:9 Certainly, any hope ⌊of **d** it⌋ is
Dan 7:21 the holy people and **d** them.
Heb 7:1 was returning from **d** the kings.

defeats (2)

Jdg 1:12 to whoever **d** Kiriath Sepher
Isa 41:2 He **d** kings. With his sword he

defect (11)

Lev 21:17 generations) has a physical **d**,
21:18 no one who has a physical **d**
21:21 priest Aaron has a physical **d**,
21:21 He has a **d**. He must never bring
21:23 since he has a physical **d**.
22:20 any animal with a physical **d**,
22:25 castration is a physical **d**."
Dtr 15:21 serious **d** — never sacrifice
17:1 an ox or a sheep that has a **d**
Mar 7:32 and who also had a speech **d**.
Heb 9:14 who had no **d**, does even more.

defected (1)

1Sm 29:3 from the day he **d** until now."

defective (3)

Lev 21:20 or dwarf, who has **d** sight,

Psa 78:57 like arrows shot from a **d** bow.
Hos 7:16 They are like a **d** bow.

defects (52)

Exo 12:5 male that has no **d**.
29:1 a young bull that has no **d**
29:1 and two rams that have no **d**.
Lev 1:3 must offer a male that has no **d**.
1:10 bring a male that has no **d**.
3:1 or female animal that has no **d**.
3:6 or female animal that has no **d**.
4:3 bring a bull that has no **d** as
4:23 that has no **d** as his offering.
4:28 that has no **d** as his offering
4:32 bring a female that has no **d**.
5:15 It must be a ram that has no **d**
5:18 priest a ram that has no **d** from
6:6 a ram that has no **d** or its value
9:2 "Take a calf that has no **d** for
9:2 sin and a ram that has no **d** as
9:3 one-year-old and without **d**) as
14:10 two male lambs that have no **d**
14:10 female lamb that has no **d**.
22:19 that has no **d** from your cattle,
22:21 be an animal that has no **d**
22:21 never be an animal that has **d**.
23:12 male lamb that has no **d** as
23:18 lambs that have no **d**,
Num 6:14 these animals must have no **d**.
19:2 cow that is perfect, with no **d**.
28:3 lambs that have no **d**.
28:9 lambs that have no **d**,
28:11 lambs that have no **d**.
28:19 all of them without **d**.
28:31 animals that have no **d** along
29:2 lambs that have no **d**.
29:8 all of them without **d**.
29:13 all of them without **d**.
29:17 lambs that have no **d**.
29:20 lambs that have no **d**.
29:23 lambs that have no **d**.
29:26 lambs that have no **d**.
29:29 lambs that have no **d**.
29:32 lambs that have no **d**.
29:36 lambs that have no **d**.
Eze 43:22 a male goat that has no **d** as
43:23 bull and a ram that have no **d**.
43:25 be animals that have no **d**.
45:18 take a young bull that has no **d**
45:23 young bulls that have no **d**,
45:23 seven rams that have no **d**,
46:4 LORD six lambs that have no **d**
46:4 and one ram that has no **d** as
46:6 all animals that have no **d**.
46:13 that has no **d** every day as
1Pe 1:19 with no **d** or imperfections.

defend (40)

Dtr 33:7 They must **d** themselves.
Jos 7:12 to **d** themselves against their
7:13 You will not be able to **d**
Jdg 6:31 "You're not going to **d** Baal,
6:31 If he's a god, let him **d** himself
6:32 [Let Baal **D** Himself],
6:32 let Baal **d** himself."
2Ki 20:6 I'll rescue you and **d** this city
Est 8:11 to **d** themselves, to wipe out,
9:16 had also assembled to **d**
Job 13:10 Will he really **d** you if you
13:15 I will **d** my behavior to his face.
Psa 41:12 You **d** my integrity,
54:1 and **d** me with your might.
69:18 Come close, and **d** my soul.
82:3 **D** weak people and orphans.
106:3 Blessed are those who **d**
140:12 I know that the LORD will **d** the
Pro 31:9 Speak out, judge fairly, and **d**
Isa 1:17 **D** orphans. Plead the case of
1:23 They never **d** orphans.
28:6 give strength to those who **d**
31:5 The LORD of Armies will **d**
31:5 He will **d** it and rescue it.
38:6 I'll rescue you and **d** this city
Jer 5:28 They don't **d** the rights of the
Eze 22:30 by the gaps in the walls to **d**
Zec 9:15 LORD of Armies will **d** them.
Zec 12:8 On that day the LORD will **d**
Luk 12:11 how you will **d** yourselves
21:14 how you will **d** yourselves.
Act 19:33 he wanted to **d** himself
25:16 to **d** himself against their
26:2 you and **d** myself against every
Rom 2:15 and **d** them on another.
1Co 9:3 This is how I **d** myself to those
2Co 6:8 is wrong and to **d** the truth.
12:19 that we're trying to **d** ourselves
Php 1:16 me here to **d** the Good News.
1Pe 3:15 Always be ready to **d** your

defended (11)

1Sm 25:39 who **d** me against the insults of
2Sm 23:12 in the middle of the field and **d**
1Ch 11:14 in the middle of the field and **d**
Psa 9:4 You have **d** my just cause:
77:15 might you have **d** your people,
107:2 Let the people the LORD **d**
107:2 They are the people he **d** from
Jer 22:16 He **d** the cause of the poor and
Dan 11:1 I strengthened and **d** Michael."
Act 7:24 an Egyptian, he **d** the Israelite.
25:8 Paul **d** himself by saying,

defender (17)

Job 19:25 But I know that my **d** lives,
Psa 19:14 my rock and my **d**.
68:5 fatherless and the **d** of widows.
78:35 that the Most High was their **d**.
Isa 19:20 a savior and **d** to rescue them.
33:21 The LORD will be our mighty **d**
41:14 your **D**, the Holy One of Israel.
43:14 This is what the LORD, your **D**,
44:6 LORD is Israel's king and **d**.
47:4 Our **d** is the Holy One of Israel.
48:17 This is what the LORD, your **D**,
49:7 The LORD is the **d** of Israel,
54:5 Your **d** is the Holy One of
54:8 says the LORD your **d**.
60:16 Mighty One of Jacob, your **D**.
63:16 is our **D** From Everlasting.
Jer 50:34 Their **d** is strong. His name is

defenders (2)

Eze 30:8 and all her **d** will be killed.
32:21 'You and your **d** have come

defending (2)

Act 26:24 As Paul was **d** himself in this
Php 1:7 whether I'm in prison or **d** and

defends (2)

Jdg 6:31 Whoever **d** him will be put to
Isa 51:22 LORD your God **d** his people.

defense (11)

Exo 2:17 Moses got up, came to their **d**,
2Sm 22:19 but the LORD became my **d**.
Job 36:2 is more to be said in God's **d**.
Psa 18:18 but the LORD came to my **d**.
35:23 Wake up, and rise to my **d**.
Isa 34:8 a year of revenge in **d** of Zion.
Jer 41:9 of his **d** against King Baasha
Nah 3:8 The sea was ⌊her⌋ **d**.
Act 26:1 Agrippa and then began his **d**.
2Ti 4:16 no one stood up in my **d**.
1Pe 3:15 However, make your **d** with

defenseless (3)

Psa 116:6 The LORD protects **d** people.
141:8 Do not leave me **d**.
Jer 4:31 We're **d** in the presence of

defenses (8)

Psa 60:1 You have broken down our **d**.
Pro 21:22 and pulls down the strong **d**
Isa 22:8 will remove the **d** of Judah.
Joe 2:8 when they break through the **d**,
Amo 3:11 strip you of your **d**,
Nah 3:12 All your **d** will be like fig trees
3:14 Strengthen your **d**!
2Co 10:4 them we destroy people's **d**,

defiance (1)

Psa 119:85 trap me in **d** of your teachings.

defiant (3)

Neh 9:26 But they were **d** and rebelled
Isa 3:8 They are **d** in his honored
Eze 2:4 I am sending you to these **d**

defiantly (1)

Psa 75:5 so proudly or speak so **d**."

defied (3)

Num 26:9 who **d** Moses and Aaron's
26:9 they **d** the LORD's authority.
Dtr 1:43 You **d** the LORD's command

definite (1)

Exo 9:5 The LORD set a **d** time.

deformity (2)

Lev 21:18 who has a disfigured face, a **d**,
22:23 use a bull or a sheep with a **d**

defy (8)

Exo 23:21 Don't **d** him, because he will
Dtr 17:13 will never **d** ⌊God's law⌋ again.
2Ki 19:4 sent him to **d** the living God.
19:16 sent to **d** the living God.
19:23 Through your servants you **d**
Isa 37:4 sent him to **d** the living God.
37:17 sent to **d** the living God.
37:24 Through your servants you **d**

defying (3)

2Ki 19:22 are you **d** and slandering?
Isa 37:23 are you **d** and slandering?
Jon 19:12 to be a king is **d** the emperor."

degenerative (2)

Psa 106:15 He ⌊also⌋ gave them a **d**
Isa 10:16 send a **d** disease against brave

degrade (1)

2Sm 6:22 and I will **d** myself even more

dejected (2)

Lam 2:8 They are completely **d**.
2Co 7:6 who comforts those who are **d**,

Delaiah (7)

1Ch 3:24 Akkub, Johanan, **D**, and Anani.
24:18 the twenty-third for **D**,
Ezr 2:60 the descendants of **D**,
Neh 6:10 son of **D** and grandson of
7:62 the descendants of **D**,
Jer 36:12 **D** (son of Shemaiah),
36:25 Even when Elnathan, **D**,

delay (7)

Gen 24:56 He said to them, "Don't **d** me
Psa 40:17 O my God, do not **d**!
70:5 O LORD, do not **d**!
Eze 12:25 happen without any more **d**.
Dan 9:19 Don't **d**! Do this for your sake,
Heb 10:37 will come soon. He will not **d**.
Rev 10:6 "There will be no more **d**.

delayed (6)

Exo 32:1 Moses **d** coming down from
Pro 13:12 **D** hope makes one sick at
Isa 46:13 My salvation will not be **d**.
Eze 12:28 that I say will no longer be **d**.
Hab 2:3 If it's **d**, wait for it. It will
1Ti 3:15 in case I'm **d**. I want you to

delays (1)

1Ki 18:44 and leave before the rain **d**

deliberately (5)

Num 15:30 who **d** does something wrong
35:20 or by **d** throwing something at
Dtr 17:12 If anyone **d** disobeys the priest
Psa 78:18 They **d** tested God by
2Pe 3:5 They are **d** ignoring one fact:

delicacies (6)
Gen 49:20 He will provide **d** fit for a king.
Psa 141:4 Do not let me taste their **d**.
Pro 23:3 Do not crave his **d**,
23:6 and do not crave his **d**.
Jer 51:34 has filled his belly with our **d**.
Lam 4:5 Those who used to eat **d** are

delicate (1)
Isa 47:1 no longer be called soft and **d**.

delicious (1)
Job 33:20 lose their appetite for a **d** meal.

delight (21)
Dtr 30:9 The LORD will again **d** in
2Sm 1:26 You were my great **d**.
1Ch 29:3 I **d** in the temple of my God.
29:17 hearts and **d** in honesty.
Psa 45:15 With joy and **d** they are brought
Pro 12:22 but honest people are his **d**.
29:17 He will bring **d** to your soul.
Sos 3:11 his day of joyful **d**.
Isa 5:7 Judah are the garden of his **d**.
16:10 Joy and **d** have vanished from
32:14 They will be a **d** for wild
58:13 you call the day of worship a **d**
61:10 I will **d** in my God.
62:4 But you will be named My D,
65:18 to create Jerusalem to be a **d**
66:3 souls **d** in detestable things.
66:11 You will nurse to your heart's **d**
Jer 13:27 adultery and squeal with **d**.
15:16 are my joy and my heart's **d**,
Mat 12:18 whom I love, and in whom I **d**.
2Pe 1:17 whom I love and in whom I **d**."

delighted (17)
Exo 18:9 Jethro was **d** ⌊to hear⌋ about
1Sm 15:22 "Is the LORD as **d** with burnt
Job 3:22 **d** to find the grave.
Psa 49:13 who are **d** by what they
97:8 The people of Judah are **d** with
Pro 8:31 and **d** in the human race.
11:20 but he is **d** with those whose
14:35 A king is **d** with a servant who
15:23 A person is **d** to hear an
21:15 a righteous person is **d**,
Isa 62:4 The LORD is **d** with you,
Zec 4:10 They will be **d** when they see
Mat 13:44 He was so **d** with it that he
14:6 Herod was so **d** with her that
Mar 6:22 and his guests were **d** with her.
Act 7:41 sacrifice to that false god and **d**
2Th 2:12 but was **d** with what God

delightful (3)
Isa 27:2 On that day sing about a **d**
Eze 26:12 and tear down your **d** homes.
Mal 3:12 because you will be a **d** land,"

delights (6)
Psa 1:2 Rather, he **d** in the teachings of
37:23 and the LORD **d** in his way.
45:8 of stringed instruments **d** you.
Pro 12:12 A wicked person **d** in setting a
15:30 A twinkle in the eye **d** the heart.
Col 2:18 Let no one who **d** in ⌊false⌋

Delilah (9)
Jdg 16:4 Valley. Her name was **D**.
16:6 So **D** said to Samson,
16:10 **D** told Samson, "Look,
16:12 So **D** took some new ropes and
16:13 **D** told Samson, "You're still
16:14 So **D** tied his braids to the loom
16:15 **D** said to Samson,
16:18 When **D** realized that he had
16:19 **D** put Samson to sleep on her

deliver (9)
Gen 38:20 Judah sent his friend Hirah to **d**
Exo 1:16 look at the child when you **d** it.
2Sm 18:20 You must not **d** the news today
18:22 should you **d** the message?"
Job 39:3 to give birth and **d** their young.
Isa 61:1 anointed me to **d** good news
66:9 of birth and not let her **d**?"
66:9 "Do I cause a mother to **d** and
Act 15:23 wrote this letter for them to **d**:

delivered (15)
Num 23:7 Then Balaam **d** this message:
23:18 Then Balaam **d** this message:
24:3 and he **d** this message:
24:15 Then Balaam **d** this message:
24:20 and **d** this message:
24:21 Kenites and **d** this message:
24:23 He **d** this message:
1Sm 23:7 "God has **d** him into my hands.
Ezr 8:36 The exiles **d** the king's orders
Est 1:12 that the eunuchs **d** to her.
1:15 which the eunuchs **d**?"
Job 15:7 Were you **d** before the hills
Act 12:25 After Barnabas and Saul **d** the
15:30 together and **d** the letter.
23:33 they **d** the letter to the governor

delivering (2)
Jdg 3:18 had finished **d** the payment,
Neh 13:31 I also arranged for **d** wood at

delivers (2)
Pro 31:24 and sells them and **d** belts
Isa 66:7 has labor pains, she **d** a child.

delusion (2)
Psa 62:9 Important people are only a **d**.
2Th 2:11 them a powerful **d** so that they

demand (16)
Gen 9:5 I will **d** your blood for your life.
9:5 I will **d** it from any animal or
9:5 I will **d** the life of any person
Exo 21:22 the woman's husband to **d**.
Num 16:10 but now you **d** to be priests.
Dtr 15:2 Don't **d** that your neighbor or
15:3 You may **d** that a foreigner pay,
Eze 34:10 I will **d** that they hand over my
Mar 8:12 do these people **d** a sign?
Luk 12:20 I will **d** your life from you
23:24 decided to give in to their **d**.
Act 18:14 reason would **d** that I put up
Rom 2:13 those laws **d** will have God's
2:26 what Moses' Teachings **d**,
8:3 to do what God's standards **d**
Gal 5:3 Moses' Teachings **d**.

demanded (12)
Gen 31:36 Jacob **d** of Laban. "What is my
31:39 That's what you **d** of me when
Exo 21:30 if only a cash settlement is **d**
21:30 whatever price is **d** of him.
2Ki 18:14 So the king of Assyria **d** that
23:35 to pay the silver Pharaoh had **d**.
Neh 5:18 Yet, in spite of all this, I never **d**
Psa 137:3 had captured us **d** that we sing.
Luk 11:16 wanted to test Jesus and **d** that
12:48 More will be **d** from everyone
22:31 Satan has **d** to have you
Act 13:21 "Then the people **d** a king,

demanding (2)
Psa 78:18 deliberately tested God by **d**
Mar 8:11 They tested him by **d** that he

demands (5)
1Ki 20:8 Don't agree ⌊to his **d**⌋."
Jer 5:4 and the justice that God **d**.
5:5 and the justice that God **d**."
Eph 2:15 commandments and **d** found
Jud 1:3 It **d** that I write to you and

Demas (3)
Col 4:14 the physician, and **D** greet you.
2Ti 4:10 **D** has abandoned me.
Phm 1:24 Mark, Aristarchus, **D**,

Demetrius (4)
Act 19:24 **D**, a silversmith, was in the
19:25 **D** said, "Men, you know that
19:38 If **D** and the men who work for
3Jn 1:12 says good things about **D**.

Demetrius' (1)
Act 19:28 When **D** workers and the others

demolish (3)
Hos 11:6 their cities, **d** their city gates,
Mic 5:10 horses and **d** your chariots.
Zep 3:6 I will **d** their streets.

demolished (5)
Isa 49:19 you are destroyed and **d**
Eze 6:6 Your altars will be ruined and **d**.
Amo 3:15 Mansions will be **d**,
Nah 2:10 is destroyed, deserted, **d**.
Zep 1:13 Their homes will be **d**.

demon (27)
Mat 9:32 he was possessed by a **d**.
9:33 But as soon as the **d** was
11:18 'There's a **d** in him!'
12:22 a man possessed by a **d**.
12:22 The **d** made the man blind and
15:22 daughter is tormented by a **d**."
17:18 Jesus ordered the **d** to come
17:19 "Why couldn't we force the **d**
Mar 7:26 She asked him to force the **d**
7:29 The **d** has left your daughter."
7:30 and the **d** was gone.
9:22 The **d** has often thrown him
Luk 4:33 by a spirit, an evil **d**.
4:35 The **d** threw the man down in
7:33 'There's a **d** in him!'
8:29 Then the **d** would force him to
9:1 and authority over every **d**
9:42 the **d** knocked the boy to the
11:14 Jesus was forcing a **d** out of a
11:14 The **d** had made the man
11:14 When the **d** had gone out,
Jon 7:20 "You're possessed by a **d**!
8:48 that you're possessed by a **d**?"
8:52 that you're possessed by a **d**.
10:20 "He's possessed by a **d**!
10:21 this if he's possessed by a **d**.
10:21 Can a **d** give sight to the

demonic (1)
Jas 3:15 It is self-centered and **d**.

demon-possessed (3)
Mar 5:16 had happened to the **d** man
5:18 who had been **d** begged him,
Luk 8:36 restored the **d** man to health.

demons (55)
Dtr 32:17 They sacrificed to **d** that are
Psa 106:37 their sons and daughters to **d**.
Mat 4:24 and people possessed by **d**,
7:22 Didn't we force out **d** and do
8:16 who were possessed by **d**.
8:28 They were possessed by **d**
8:31 The **d** begged Jesus,
8:32 The **d** came out and went into
8:33 about the men possessed by **d**.
9:34 "He forces **d** out of people with
9:34 with the help of the ruler of **d**."
10:8 and force **d** out of people.
12:24 "This man can force **d** out of
12:24 of Beelzebul, the ruler of **d**."
12:27 If I force **d** out of people with
12:28 But if I force **d** out with the help
Mar 1:32 and those possessed by **d**.
1:34 and forced many **d** out
1:34 would not allow the **d** to speak.
1:39 and he forced **d** out of people.
3:15 to force **d** out of people.
3:22 and "He forces **d** out of people
3:22 with the help of the ruler of **d**."
5:12 The **d** begged him,
5:15 possessed by the legion of **d**.
6:13 They also forced many **d** out of
9:38 we saw someone forcing **d** out
16:9 he had forced out seven **d**.
16:17 of my name to force **d** out
Luk 4:41 **D** came out of many people,

Luk 8:2 whom seven **d** had gone out;
8:27 The man was possessed by **d**
8:30 (Many **d** had entered him.)
8:31 The **d** begged Jesus not to
8:32 The **d** begged Jesus to let
8:33 The **d** came out of the man and
8:35 from whom the **d** had gone out.
8:38 The man from whom the **d** had
9:49 we saw someone forcing **d** out
10:17 They said, "Lord, even **d** obey
11:15 "He can force **d** out of people
11:15 of Beelzebul, the ruler of **d**."
11:18 helps me force **d** out of people.
11:19 If I force **d** out with the help of
11:20 But if I force out **d** with the help
13:32 "Tell that fox that I will force **d**
1Co 10:20 people make are made to **d**
10:20 want you to be partners with **d**.
10:21 the Lord's cup and the cup of **d**.
10:21 of the Lord and at the table of **d**.
1Ti 4:1 will believe the teachings of **d**.
Jas 2:19 The **d** also believe that,
Rev 9:20 have stopped worshiping **d**
16:14 They are spirits of **d** that do
18:2 She has become a home for **d**.

demonstrate (5)

Rom 9:17 to **d** my power through you and
9:22 If God wants to **d** his anger and
2Co 6:4 Instead, our lives **d** that we are
6:7 We **d** that we are God's
1Ti 1:16 sinner, to **d** his patience.

demonstrated (1)

2Co 7:11 In every way you have **d** that

demonstrates (2)

Rom 5:8 This **d** God's love for us.
2Pe 1:8 it **d** that your knowledge about

demonstration (1)

2Co 8:24 So give these men a **d** of your

demote (1)

Dan 5:19 whomever he wanted to **d**.

demoted (1)

Dan 5:19 and he **d** whomever he wanted

den (13)

Psa 10:9 hiding place like a lion in his **d**.
Dan 6:7 will be thrown into a lions' **d**.
6:12 will be thrown into a lions' **d**?"
6:16 and thrown into the lions' **d**.
6:17 over the opening of the **d**.
6:19 and quickly went to the lions' **d**.
6:20 As he came near the **d** where
6:23 had Daniel taken out of the **d**.
6:23 Daniel was taken out of the **d**,
6:24 were thrown into the lions' **d**.
6:24 reached the bottom of the **d**,
Amo 3:4 Does a young lion growl in its **d**
Nah 2:11 Where is the lions' **d**,

denied (17)

Gen 18:15 Sarah **d** that she had laughed.
1Sm 8:3 bribes and **d** people justice.
Job 31:28 and I would have **d** God above.
Ecc 5:8 being oppressed, **d** justice,
5:8 or **d** their rights in any district.
Isa 59:13 have rebelled and **d** the LORD.
Mat 26:70 But Peter **d** it in front of them all
26:72 Again Peter **d** it and swore with
Mar 14:68 But Peter **d** it by saying,
14:70 Peter again **d** it. After a little
Luk 8:45 After everyone **d** touching him,
22:57 But Peter **d** it by saying,
Jon 18:25 Peter **d** it by saying,
18:27 Peter again **d** it, and just then a
1Ti 5:8 he has **d** the Christian faith and
Rev 2:13 and have not **d** your belief
3:8 word and have not **d** my name.

denies (1)

Job 8:18 ⌊the ground⌋ **d** it ⌊and says⌋,

denounced (1)

Mat 11:20 Then Jesus **d** the cities where

dens (4)

Job 37:8 Animals go into their **d** and
38:40 as they crouch in their **d** and lie
Psa 104:22 gather and lie down in their **d**.
Nah 2:12 and its **d** with torn flesh.

dense (3)

Exo 8:24 **D** swarms of flies came into
Pro 25:14 ⌊Like⌋ a **d** fog or a dust storm,
Zec 11:2 because your **d** forest has

deny (13)

Exo 23:6 "Never **d** justice to poor people
23:8 who can see and **d** justice
Dtr 16:19 blind wise people and **d** justice
Pro 30:9 or I may feel satisfied and **d**
Isa 29:21 **d** justice to people who are in
Lam 3:35 **d** people their rights in the
Amo 5:12 You **d** the needy access to the
Act 4:16 knows about. We can't **d** that.
19:36 No one can **d** this.
Tit 1:16 but they **d** him by what they do.
Heb 7:7 No one can **d** that the more
2Pe 2:1 They will **d** the Lord,
Jud 1:4 freedom and **d** our only Master

Denya (1)

Ezr 4:9 group — the people from **D**

depart (3)

Gen 49:10 A scepter will never **d** from
Isa 54:10 kindness will never **d** from you.
Zec 10:11 and the scepter of Egypt will **d**.

departed (1)

Act 1:10 staring into the sky as he **d**.

depend (19)

2Ch 16:7 the king of Syria and did not **d**
Psa 62:7 and my glory **d** on God.
62:10 increase, do not **d** on them.
118:8 It is better to **d** on the LORD
118:9 It is better to **d** on the LORD
123:2 As servants **d** on their masters,
123:2 so we **d** on the LORD our God
Isa 10:20 descendants will no longer **d**
10:20 They will only **d** on the LORD,
31:1 who **d** on many chariots,
31:1 who **d** on very strong war
48:2 You **d** on the God of Israel.
50:10 LORD and **d** upon their God.
Mat 22:40 Teachings and the Prophets **d**
Jon 5:34 But I don't **d** on human
Rom 9:16 God's choice does not **d** on a
1Co 7:31 should do so but not **d** on them.
2Co 1:18 You can **d** on God.
1Th 4:12 and you won't have to **d** on

dependable (7)

1Sm 29:6 LORD lives, you are a **d** man.
Psa 19:7 testimony of the LORD is **d**.
119:138 They are fair and completely **d**.
Pro 13:17 but a **d** envoy brings healing.
Isa 8:2 have these **d** witnesses testify:
33:16 of food and a **d** supply of water.
Act 11:24 Barnabas was a **d** man,

depended (5)

2Ch 16:7 "Because you **d** on the king of
16:8 But when you **d** on the LORD,
31:18 and other people who **d** on
Psa 71:6 I **d** on you before I was born.
Act 12:20 This was because their cities **d**

depending (1)

2Ch 14:11 because we are **d** on you.

depends (1)

Psa 123:2 as a maid **d** on her mistress,

deported (3)

Dtr 29:28 from their land and **d** them

Ezr 4:10 great and noble Assurbanipal **d**.
5:12 this temple and **d** its people

deposit (6)

Gen 38:17 as a **d** until you send
38:18 should I give you as a **d**?"
38:20 he could get back his **d** from
Dtr 24:10 his house to take a security **d**.
24:11 loan will bring the **d** out to you.
24:12 coat you took as a **d** overnight.

deposited (1)

2Ch 34:14 out the money that had been **d**

depress (1)

Job 19:2 me and **d** me with words?

depressed (3)

1Sm 1:15 responded, "I'm **d**, not drunk.
2Sm 13:20 her brother Absalom and was **d**.
1Ki 21:27 and walked around **d**.

depression (4)

Lev 26:16 suffer from eye problems and **d**.
Pro 15:13 but with a heartache comes **d**.
17:22 but **d** drains one's strength.
Isa 65:14 and wail because of your **d**.

deprive (5)

Exo 21:10 he must not **d** the first wife of
Dtr 24:17 Never **d** foreigners and orphans
Isa 10:2 They **d** the poor of justice.
Lam 3:36 or **d** people of justice in court.
Mal 3:5 against those who **d** foreigners

deprived (2)

Job 38:15 Wicked people are **d** of their
39:17 because God has **d** it of

deprives (1)

Dtr 27:19 "Whoever **d** foreigners,

depriving (2)

Pro 18:5 thereby **d** an innocent person of
Ecc 4:8 so hard and **d** themselves

depths (21)

Dtr 32:22 that will burn to the **d** of hell.
Job 11:8 It is deeper than ⌊the **d**⌋ of hell.
36:30 and covers the **d** of the sea.
38:16 the valleys of the ocean **d**?
Psa 36:1 who has rebellion in the **d**
46:2 topple into the **d** of the sea.
63:9 will go into the **d** of the earth.
68:22 them back from the **d** of the sea
71:20 me back from the **d** of the earth.
77:16 Even the **d** of the sea trembled.
86:13 rescued me from the **d** of hell.
107:24 performed in the **d** of the sea.
107:26 They plunged into the **d**.
130:1 out of the **d** I call to you.
135:6 or in all the **d** of the oceans.
148:7 creatures and all the ocean **d**,
Pro 9:18 her guests are in the **d** of hell.
Isa 51:10 You made a road in the **d** of the
Jnh 2:2 From the **d** of my ⌊watery⌋
2:3 into the **d** of the sea,
Rom 10:7 go down into the **d**," (that is,

deputies (1)

Jer 51:28 their governors, all their **d**,

deputy (1)

1Ki 22:47 in Edom; instead, a **d** ruled.

Derbe (4)

Act 14:6 they escaped to Lystra and **D**,
14:20 Barnabas left for the city of **D**.
16:1 Paul arrived in the city of **D**
20:4 Gaius from **D**, Timothy,

derived (1)

2Ch 19:10 or regulations **d** from Moses'

descend (2)

Pro 5:5 Her feet **d** to death.

Eze 26:20 you down with those who **d**

descendant (93)

Gen 3:15 and her **d** hostile toward each
22:18 Through your **d** all the nations
26:4 Through your **d** all the nations
28:14 you and through your **d**
38:8 produce a **d** for your brother."
38:9 But Onan knew that the **d**
38:9 to avoid giving his brother a **d**.
Lev 6:18 Every male **d** of Aaron may eat
21:21 If a **d** of the priest Aaron has a
22:4 "No **d** of Aaron who has a skin
Num 16:1 (Korah was a **d** of Kohath and
16:40 Israel that no one but a **d**
26:59 was Jochebed, a **d** of Levi,
27:1 of Gilead, **d** of Machir,
32:41 Then Jair, a **d** of Manasseh,
Dtr 3:14 Jair, a **d** of Manasseh,
23:2 No **d** of his may join the
23:3 Not one **d** of theirs may join the
Rut 4:12 Also, from the **d** whom the
1Sm 9:1 was Aphiah, a **d** of Benjamin.
25:3 He was a **d** of Caleb.
2Sm 17:25 named Ithra, a **d** of Ishmael.
20:26 And Ira, a **d** of Jair,
21:16 A **d** of Haraphah named Benob,
21:18 another **d** of Haraphah.
21:20 He also was a **d** of Haraphah.
22:51 and to his **d** forever.
23:28 Zalmon (**d** of Ahohi),
23:38 Ira (**d** of Ithra),
23:38 of Ithra), Gareb (**d** of Ithra),
1Ki 4:13 a **d** of Manasseh, in Gilead.
15:4 He appointed David's **d** to rule
2Ki 25:25 a **d** of the kings) went with ten
1Ch 2:17 was Jether, a **d** of Ishmael.
4:37 a **d** of Shimri and Shemaiah).
9:31 son of Shallum, Korah's **d**,
11:29 of Hushai), Ilai (**d** of Ahohi),
11:40 Ira (**d** of Ithra),
11:40 of Ithra), Gareb (**d** of Ithra),
20:4 killed Sippai, a **d** of Haraphah,
20:6 He also was a **d** of Haraphah.
24:3 David, Eleazar's **d** Zadok,
24:3 and Ithamar's **d** Ahimelech
24:6 son of Nethanel and a **d** of Levi.
26:21 for Ladan, the **d** of Gershon,
26:24 a **d** of Moses' son Gershom.
27:3 He was a **d** of Perez,
27:4 Dodai, Ahoh's **d**, was in charge
27:8 Shamhuth, Izrah's **d**,
27:11 a **d** of Zerah from Hushah,
27:13 a **d** of Zerah from Netophah,
27:15 He was Othniel's **d**.
27:30 a **d** of Ishmael for the donkeys:
27:33 Hushai, a **d** of Archi,
29:8 them to Jehiel, Gershon's **d**,
Ezr 8:18 who was a **d** of Mahli,
8:19 (who was a **d** of Merari),
10:18 a **d** of Jeshua (who was
Job 25:6 who is only a maggot — a **d**
32:2 Elihu, son of Barachel, a **d**
32:6 the **d** of Buz, replied ⌊to Job⌋,
Psa 18:50 and to his **d** forever.
Isa 14:29 and his **d** will be a flying,
19:11 "I'm a **d** of wise men,
19:11 a **d** of ancient kings"?
41:8 have chosen, the **d** of Abraham,
65:9 will bring ⌊with me⌋ Jacob's **d**,
Jer 33:17 David will never fail to have a **d**
33:18 will never fail to have a **d**
33:21 and he would not have a **d** to
35:19 A **d** of Jonadab, Rechab's son,
41:1 a **d** of the royal family and of
Mat 1:1 **d** of David and Abraham.
1:20 to him, "Joseph, **d** of David,
Luk 1:5 Elizabeth was a **d** of Aaron.
1:27 promised in marriage to a **d**
2:4 Joseph, a **d** of King David,
2:36 She was a **d** of Phanuel from
13:16 Now, here is a **d** of Abraham.
Act 3:25 'Through your **d** all people on
4:36 Joseph, a **d** of Levi,
23:6 Pharisee and a **d** of Pharisees.
Rom 1:3 nature he was a **d** of David.
Rom 4:16 is guaranteed for every **d**,
9:7 or a **d** of Abraham.
11:1 I'm an Israelite myself, a **d** of
Gal 3:16 to Abraham and to his **d**.
3:16 but "your **d**," referring to one.
3:16 to one. That **d** is Christ.
3:19 Moses' laws did this until the **d**
Php 3:5 I'm a **d** of Israel. I'm from the
2Ti 2:8 back to life and is a **d** of David.
Rev 22:16 I am the root and **d** of David.

descendants (634)

Gen 3:15 I will make your **d** and her
5:1 account of Adam and his **d**.
6:9 the account of Noah and his **d**.
9:9 my promise to you, your **d**,
10:1 Ham, and Japheth, and their **d**.
10:2 Japheth's **d** were Gomer,
10:3 Gomer's **d** were Ashkenaz,
10:4 Javan's **d** were the people from
10:5 From these **d** the people of the
10:6 Ham's **d** were Cush,
10:7 Cush's **d** were Seba,
10:7 Raamah's **d** were Sheba and
10:20 These were Ham's **d** by
10:22 Shem's **d** were Elam,
10:23 Aram's **d** were Uz,
10:31 These were Shem's **d** by
10:32 From these ⌊**d**⌋ the nations
11:5 the city and the tower that the **d**
11:10 the account of Shem and his **d**.
11:27 the account of Terah and his **d**.
12:7 to give this land to your **d**."
13:15 you see to you and to your **d**
13:16 I will also give you as many **d**
13:16 he could also count your **d**.
15:5 how many **d** you will have!"
15:13 for sure that your **d** will live
15:16 In the fourth generation your **d**
15:18 "I will give this land to your **d**.
16:10 "I will give you many **d**.
17:2 I will give you very many **d**."
17:6 I will give you many **d**.
17:7 my promise to you and your **d**
17:7 God and the God of your **d**.
17:8 and your **d** as your permanent
17:9 "You and your **d** in generations
17:19 promise to him and his **d**.
17:20 increase the number of his **d**.
21:12 through Isaac your **d** will carry
21:23 cheat me, my children, or my **d**.
22:17 make your **d** as numerous as
22:17 Your **d** will take possession of
24:7 give this land to your **d**.' "God
24:60 May your **d** take possession of
25:3 Dedan's **d** were the Assyrians,
25:4 These were the **d** of Keturah.
25:12 This is the account of the **d** of
25:18 His **d** lived as nomads from the
25:19 Abraham's son Isaac and his **d**.
26:3 these lands to you and your **d**.
26:4 I will make your **d** as numerous
26:4 give all these lands to your **d**.
26:24 increase the number of your **d**
28:3 number of your **d** so that you
28:4 May he give to you and your **d**
28:13 you are lying to you and your **d**.
28:14 Your **d** will be like the dust on
32:12 prosperous and that your **d** will
35:12 also give this land to your **d**."
36:1 Esau (that is, Edom) and his **d**.
36:9 the account of Esau and his **d**.
36:15 tribal leaders among Esau's **d**:
36:17 the tribal leaders among the **d**
36:18 the tribal leaders among the **d**
36:19 These were the **d** of Esau (that
37:2 the account of Jacob and his **d**.
45:7 sure that you would have **d**
46:8 the names of Israel's **d** (Jacob
46:8 (Jacob and his **d**) who arrived
46:15 These were the **d** of the sons
46:18 These were the **d** of Zilpah,
46:22 These were the **d** of Rachel
46:25 These were the **d** of Bilhah,
46:26 of Jacob's direct **d** who went
48:4 number of your **d** so that you
Gen 48:4 I will give this land to your **d**
48:19 and his **d** will become many
Exo 1:5 number of Jacob's **d** was 70.
1:7 But the **d** of Israel had many
16:32 of manna to be kept for your **d**.
16:33 presence to be kept for your **d**."
19:3 you must say to the **d** of Jacob.
27:21 Aaron and his **d** must keep the
28:43 law for him and his **d**."
29:29 will belong to his **d** so that they
30:21 law for him and his **d**
32:13 'I will make your **d** as
32:13 I will give to your **d** all the land
33:1 'I will give it to your **d**.'
Lev 21:17 "Tell Aaron: If any of your **d**
22:3 generations if any of your **d**,
25:46 your **d** as permanent property.
Num 1:10 and Manasseh are Joseph's **d**.)
1:20 households for the **d** of Reuben,
1:22 and households for the **d**
1:24 and households for the **d**
1:26 and households for the **d**
1:28 and households for the **d**
1:30 and households for the **d**
1:32 and households for the **d**
1:34 and households for the **d**
1:36 and households for the **d**
1:38 and households for the **d**
1:40 and households for the **d**
1:42 and households for the **d**
3:1 list of Aaron and Moses' **d** at
7:24 the leader of the **d** of Zebulun,
7:30 the leader of the **d** of Reuben,
7:36 the leader of the **d** of Simeon,
7:42 day the leader of the **d** of Gad,
7:48 the leader of the **d** of Ephraim,
7:54 leader of the **d** of Manasseh,
7:60 the leader of the **d** of Benjamin,
7:66 day the leader of the **d** of Dan,
7:72 day the leader of the **d** of Asher,
7:78 the leader of the **d** of Naphtali,
9:10 Suppose you or any of your **d**
10:8 law for you and your **d**.
10:14 the armies led by Judah's **d**
10:18 the armies led by Reuben's **d**
10:22 the armies led by Ephraim's **d**
10:25 the armies led by Dan's **d** broke
13:22 They are **d** of Anak.
13:28 even saw the **d** of Anak there.
13:33 (The **d** of Anak are Nephilim.)
14:24 His **d** will possess it.
16:1 and On were **d** of Reuben.)
18:8 I am giving you and your **d** all
18:19 presence for you and your **d**."
23:10 The **d** of Jacob are like specks
23:21 any trouble for the **d** of Jacob.
23:23 spell can curse the **d** of Jacob.
24:22 to be burned, you ⌊**d** of⌋ Cain,
25:13 My promise is that he and his **d**
26:5 The **d** of Reuben were the
26:11 But the **d** of Korah didn't die.)
26:18 were the families of Gad's **d**.
26:21 The **d** of Perez were the family
26:30 The **d** of Gilead were the
26:36 The **d** of Shuthelah were the
26:37 the families of Ephraim's **d**.
26:40 The **d** of Bela (⌊through⌋ Ard
26:45 The **d** Beriah were the family of
26:47 were the families of Asher's **d**.
32:39 The **d** of Machir, son of
32:40 of Machir (the **d** of Manasseh),
34:24 and Ephraim are Joseph's **d**.)
36:1 (families of Joseph's **d**) came
36:5 "The tribe of Joseph's **d** is right.
36:12 families of the **d** of Manasseh,
Dtr 1:8 and Jacob, and to you, their **d**."
1:36 set his feet on to him and his **d**,
2:4 the **d** of Esau, who live in Seir.
2:5 I've given Esau's **d** the region
2:8 by our relatives, the **d** of Esau,
2:9 I have given it to the **d** of Lot."
2:12 but the **d** of Esau claimed their
2:19 I have already given to the **d**
2:22 same thing for the **d** of Esau,
2:22 Before the **d** of Esau came,
2:22 that Esau's **d** claimed their land

Dtr 2:22 Esau's **d** are still there today.
2:29 as the **d** of Esau, who live in
4:37 ancestors and chose their **d**,
4:40 will go well for you and your **d**.
7:13 increase the number of your **d**.
9:2 They're **d** of Anak.
9:2 can oppose the **d** of Anak?"
10:15 today he chooses you, their **d**,
11:9 your ancestors and their **d** —
12:25 will go well for you and your **d**.
12:28 go well for you and your **d**
18:5 chosen the Levites and their **d**
21:5 The priests, the **d** of Levi,
28:46 to warn you and your **d** forever.
28:59 will strike you and your **d**
30:6 hearts and the hearts of your **d**.
30:19 so that you and your **d** will live.
31:21 never be forgotten by their **d**.
32:8 when he divided the **d** of Adam,
34:4 I said I would give it to their **d**.
Jos 14:4 because Joseph's **d**,
14:4 Joseph's **d** gave the Levites
14:9 inheritance for you and your **d**
15:14 three **d** of Anak from Hebron.
17:2 to the **d** of Abiezer,
17:2 These were the male **d** of
17:6 to Manasseh's other **d**.
17:14 Joseph's **d** asked Joshua,
17:16 Joseph's **d** responded,
17:17 Joshua said to the **d** of Joseph,
18:5 and Joseph's **d** will stay within
19:47 Dan's **d** went up and attacked
21:3 Levi's **d** were given the
21:4 These **d** of the priest Aaron the
21:5 The rest of Kohath's **d** received
21:6 Gershon's **d** received 13 cities
21:7 Merari's **d** received 12 cities for
21:8 to Levi's **d** by drawing lots,
21:10 that they gave Aaron's **d** who
21:13 pasturelands to the **d** of Aaron,
21:19 to the priests, the **d** of Aaron.
21:20 rest of Levi's **d** who were from
21:27 the families of Gershon's **d**,
21:41 were 48 cities in all for Levi's **d**.
22:25 the **d** of Reuben and Gad.
22:25 So your **d** would stop our
22:25 stop our **d** from worshiping
22:27 Then your **d** cannot say to our
22:27 cannot say to our **d**,
22:28 is made to us or to our **d**
24:3 Canaan and gave him many **d**.
24:32 was inherited by Joseph's **d**.
Jdg 1:16 The **d** of Moses' father-in-law,
1:22 The **d** of Joseph also went into
3:2 to teach Israel's **d** about war,
4:11 other Kenites (the **d** of Hobab,
9:28 Serve the **d** of Hamor,
18:30 Moses) and his **d** were priests
Rut 1:2 They were **d** of Ephrathah from
1Sm 2:33 And all your **d** will die in the
2:35 I will give him faithful **d**,
20:42 me and you and between my **d**
20:42 and your **d** forever.'" So David
24:21 that you will not wipe out my **d**
27:10 of the Negev where the **d**
2Sm 4:8 revenge on Saul and his **d**."
7:12 I will send one of your **d**,
14:7 my husband's name or **d** remain
21:5 "Give us seven of the male **d**
21:22 These four were **d** of Haraphah
1Ki 2:4 'If your **d** are faithful to me with
2:33 fall on Joab and his **d** forever.
2:33 But may David, his **d**,
8:25 of Israel if your **d** are faithful
9:6 But if you and your **d** dare to
9:21 but they had **d** who were still in
11:39 I will make David's **d** suffer for
21:21 I will destroy your **d**.
2Ki 5:27 to you and your **d** permanently!"
8:19 and his **d** a ⌊shining⌋ lamp.
10:1 of Ahab's **d** in Samaria.
10:30 generations of your **d** will sit
15:12 "Four generations of your **d**
17:20 LORD rejected all of Israel's **d**,
17:34 that the LORD gave to the **d**
20:18 Some of your own **d** will be

1Ch 1:5 Japheth's **d** were Gomer,
1:6 Gomer's **d** were Ashkenaz,
1:7 Javan's **d** were the people from
1:8 Ham's **d** were Cush,
1:9 Cush's **d** were Seba,
1:9 Raama's **d** were Sheba and
1:17 The **d** of Shem were Elam,
1:29 This is their list of **d**:
1:33 All these were **d** of Keturah.
2:23 these people were **d** of Machir,
2:33 These were the **d** of Jerahmeel.
2:42 The **d** of Caleb (Jerahmeel's
2:50 people were the **d** of Caleb.
2:52 Jearim, had these **d**: Haroeh,
2:54 The **d** of Salma, ⌊who first
3:17 The **d** of the prisoner Jeconiah
4:1 Judah's **d** were Perez,
4:21 The **d** of Shelah, son of Judah,
4:28 Simeon's **d** lived in Beersheba,
4:42 Simeon's male **d** to Mount Seir.
4:43 Simeon's **d** still live there
5:8 Reuben's **d** lived in Aroer as far
5:11 Gad's **d** lived next to Reuben's
5:11 lived next to Reuben's **d**
5:18 The **d** of Reuben, Gad, and half
5:19 Hagar's **d** (including Jetur,
5:20 Hagar's **d** and the nations with
5:20 handed over to Reuben's **d**.
6:19 These are the **d** of Levi's sons.
6:22 These were Kohath's **d**:
6:29 These were Merari's **d**:
6:33 served (their **d** also served):
6:49 Aaron and his **d** offered
6:50 These were Aaron's **d**:
6:54 the places where Levi's **d** lived,
6:54 ⌊first⌋ lot was drawn for the **d**
6:57 Aaron's **d** were given Hebron
6:60 Aaron's **d** received Geba with
6:61 The rest of Kohath's **d** received
6:62 The families of Gershom's **d**
6:63 The families of Merari's **d** were
6:66 of Kohath's **d** had cities chosen
6:70 of the rest of Kohath's **d**.
6:71 Gershom's **d** received Golan in
6:77 The rest of Merari's **d** received
6:78 Merari's **d** received land east of
7:3 The five **d** of Uzzi were
7:11 of these men were Jediael's **d**.
7:12 and Huppites were Ir's **d**.
7:12 were **d** of someone else.
7:17 **d** of Machir (son of Manasseh).
7:28 and homes of Ephraim's **d** were
7:29 The **d** of Joseph, son of Israel,
7:40 All of these men were Asher's **d**
8:40 these men were Benjamin's **d**.
9:3 was settled by **d** of Judah,
9:4 From the **d** of Perez,
9:5 From the **d** of Shilah were
9:6 And from the **d** of Zerah were
9:7 From the **d** of Benjamin were
9:19 (Korah's **d**) were responsible
9:23 So they and their **d** were
9:29 Other **d** of Korah were placed
12:6 and Jashobeam (Korah's **d**),
12:14 These **d** of Gad were army
12:24 From Judah's **d** there were
12:25 From Simeon's **d** there were
12:26 From Levi's **d** there were 4,600
12:29 From Benjamin's **d**,
12:30 From Ephraim's **d** there were
12:32 From Issachar's **d** there were
15:4 Aaron's **d** and the Levites.
15:5 Leading Kohath's **d** was Uriel,
15:6 Leading Merari's **d** was Asaiah,
15:7 Leading Gershom's **d** was Joel,
15:8 Elizaphan's **d** was Shemaiah,
15:9 Leading Hebron's **d** was Eliel,
15:10 Uzziel's **d** was Amminadab,
15:17 their own relatives, Merari's **d**,
16:13 you **d** of Israel, his servant,
16:13 his servant, you **d** of Jacob,
17:11 I will send one of your **d**.
20:8 These ⌊men⌋ were the **d** of
23:7 and Shimei were Gershon's **d**.
23:24 These were Levi's **d**,
23:28 to stand beside Aaron's **d**

1Ch 23:32 help their relatives, Aaron's **d**,
24:1 The divisions of Aaron's **d**
24:3 divided Aaron's **d** into groups
24:4 Since Eleazar's **d** had more
24:4 family heads than Ithamar's **d**,
24:4 that Eleazar's **d** had 16 family
24:4 and Ithamar's **d** had 8 family
24:5 both Eleazar's and Ithamar's **d**.
24:20 for Levi's **d** ⌊from Kohath⌋:
24:20 Amram's **d** through Shubael),
24:21 Amram's **d**⌋ through Rehabiah),
24:22 Izhar's **d** through Shelomoth),
24:23 Jeriah (for Hebron's **d**),
24:23 (the second ⌊of Hebron's **d**⌋),
24:23 (the third ⌊of Hebron's **d**⌋),
24:23 (the fourth ⌊of Hebron's **d**⌋),
24:24 (for Uzziel's **d** through Micah),
24:25 and Zechariah (for ⌊Uzziel's⌋ **d**
24:26 from Levi's **d** from Merari:
24:27 and Ibri (for Merari's **d** through
24:28 had no sons, for Mahli's **d**),
24:29 (for ⌊Mahli's⌋ **d** through Kish),
24:30 and Jerimoth (for Mushi's **d**).
24:30 These were Levi's **d** according
24:31 relatives, Aaron's **d**, had done.
26:1 For Korah's **d** there was
26:1 from the **d** of Asaph.
26:4 ⌊Also for Korah's **d**⌋ there were
26:8 people were Obed Edom's **d**.
26:10 From the **d** of Merari there
26:19 among Korah's and Merari's **d**.
26:21 were also⌋ the **d** of Ladan,
26:23 For the **d** of Amram,
26:29 From Izhar's **d** Chenaniah and
26:30 From Hebron's **d** Hashabiah
26:31 was the head of Hebron's **d**.
26:31 the ancestry of Hebron's **d** was
27:10 Pelonite from the **d** of Ephraim,
28:8 it as an inheritance to your **d**.
2Ch 6:16 of Israel if your **d** are faithful
7:19 But if you and your **d** turn away
8:8 but they had **d** who were still in
11:14 and his **d** rejected them as
13:5 Israel to David and his **d** forever
13:8 in the hands of David's **d**?
13:9 priests who were Aaron's **d**,
13:10 serve the LORD are Aaron's **d**,
20:7 you give this country to the **d**
20:8 His **d** have lived in it and built
20:19 **d** of Kohath and Korah,
21:7 and his **d** a ⌊shining⌋ lamp.
23:3 the LORD said about David's **d**.
26:18 to the priests, Aaron's **d**,
29:12 From Kohath's **d** were Mahath,
29:12 From Merari's **d** were Kish,
29:12 From Gershon's **d** were Joah,
29:13 From Elizaphan's **d** were
29:13 From Asaph's **d** were
29:14 From Heman's **d** were Jehiel
29:14 From Jeduthun's **d** were
29:21 told the priests, Aaron's **d**,
31:19 These men were Aaron's **d**,
32:33 in the upper tombs of David's **d**.
34:12 and Meshullam (**d** of Kohath).
35:14 (Aaron's **d**) were sacrificing
35:15 The singers (Asaph's **d**) were
Ezr 2:3 the **d** of Parosh: 2,172
2:36 the **d** of Jedaiah (through the
2:40 the **d** of Jeshua and Kadmiel,
2:41 from exile: the **d** of Asaph: 128
2:42 the **d** of Shallum, Ater, Talmon,
2:43 exile: the **d** of Ziha, Hasupha,
2:55 These **d** of Solomon's servants
2:55 the **d** of Sotai, Hassophereth,
2:58 The temple servants and the **d**
2:60 the **d** of Delaiah, Tobiah,
2:61 These **d** of the priests ⌊couldn't
2:61 the **d** of Hobaiah, Hakkoz,
3:9 **d** joined Henadad's family
3:10 Asaph's **d** took their places
10:2 one of the **d** of Elam,
10:18 Among the **d** of the priests,
10:20 From the **d** of Immer:
10:21 From the **d** of Harim:
10:22 From the **d** of Pashhur:
10:25 From the **d** of Parosh:

Ezr 10:26 From the **d** of Elam:
10:27 From the **d** of Zattu:
10:28 From the **d** of Bebai:
10:29 From the **d** of Bani:
10:30 From the **d** of Pahath Moab:
10:31 From the **d** of Harim:
10:33 From the **d** of Hashum:
10:34 From the **d** of Bani:
10:38 From the **d** of Binnui:
10:43 From the **d** of Nebo:
Neh 7:8 the **d** of Parosh: 2,172
7:39 the **d** of Jedaiah (through the
7:43 exile: the **d** of Jeshua, that is,
7:44 from exile: the **d** of Asaph: 148
7:45 the **d** of Shallum, Ater, Talmon,
7:46 exile: the **d** of Ziha, Hasupha,
7:57 These **d** of Solomon's servants
7:57 the **d** of Sotai, Sophereth,
7:60 The temple servants and the **d**
7:62 the **d** of Delaiah, Tobiah,
7:63 the **d** of Hobaiah, Hakkoz,
9:2 Those who were **d** of Israel
9:8 and Girgashites to his **d**.
10:38 A priest — one of Aaron's **d** —
11:3 and **d** of Solomon's servants
11:4 Some of the **d** of Judah and of
11:4 The **d** of Judah were Athaiah,
11:6 All the **d** of Perez who settled
11:7 These are the **d** of Benjamin:
11:8 of Benjamin's **d**⌋ totaled 928.
11:22 Mica from Asaph's **d** who were
11:24 one of the **d** of Zerah,
11:31 Benjamin's **d** live in the area of
12:47 gifts for support of Aaron's **d**.
Est 9:27 for themselves and their **d**
9:31 for themselves and their **d**
Job 5:25 are many and your **d** are like
18:19 children or **d** among his people
21:8 and they get to see their **d**.
27:14 and his **d** won't have enough
35:8 affects only the **d** of Adam.
Psa 11:4 They examine Adam's **d**.
12:1 from among Adam's **d**!
12:8 increases among Adam's **d**.
14:2 down from heaven on Adam's **d**
21:10 offspring from among Adam's **d**
22:23 All you **d** of Jacob,
22:23 awe of him, all you **d** of Israel.
22:30 There will be **d** who serve him,
25:13 and his **d** will inherit the land.
31:19 Adam's **d** watch as you show it
33:13 He sees all of Adam's **d**.
36:7 that Adam's **d** take refuge in the
37:25 or his **d** begging for food.
37:26 His **d** are a blessing.
37:28 but the **d** of wicked people will
45:2 most handsome of Adam's **d**.
53:2 down from heaven on Adam's **d**
58:1 Do you judge Adam's **d** fairly?
66:5 deeds for Adam's **d**.
69:36 The **d** of his servants will
77:15 the **d** of Jacob and Joseph.
80:1 the one who leads ⌊the **d** of⌋
83:8 They helped the **d** of Lot.
89:30 "If his **d** abandon my teachings
89:47 Adam's **d** for no reason?
90:3 and say, "Return, **d** of Adam."
98:3 and faithful to Israel's **d**.
102:28 Their **d** will be secure in your
105:6 you **d** of his servant Abraham,
105:6 Abraham, you **d** of Jacob,
106:27 kill their **d** among the nations,
107:8 his miracles for Adam's **d**.
107:15 his miracles for Adam's **d**.
107:21 his miracles for Adam's **d**.
107:31 his miracles for Adam's **d**.
109:13 Let his **d** be cut off and their
112:2 His **d** will grow strong on the
115:10 **D** of Aaron, trust the LORD.
115:12 He will bless the **d** of Israel.
115:12 He will bless the **d** of Aaron.
115:16 the earth to the **d** of Adam.
118:3 The **d** of Aaron should say,
122:5 of ⌊princes who are⌋ David's **d**.
132:11 of your own **d** on your throne.
132:12 then their **d** will also sit on your
Psa 135:19 **D** of Israel, praise the LORD.
135:19 **D** of Aaron, praise the LORD.
135:20 **D** of Levi, praise the LORD.
145:11 your kingdom and will tell the **d**
Pro 11:21 but the **d** of righteous people
Isa 1:4 They are **d** of evildoers and
2:5 Come, **d** of Jacob,
2:6 your people, the **d** of Jacob,
7:13 "Listen now, **d** of David,"
8:17 his face from the **d** of Jacob.
10:20 the survivors of Jacob's **d** will
14:1 and unite with the **d** of Jacob.
14:20 The **d** of the wicked will never
14:22 and **d**," declares the LORD.
22:24 **d** and offspring and all the little
27:9 way the wrongdoings of the **d**
29:22 says about the **d** of Jacob:
39:7 Some of your own **d** will be
43:5 I will bring your **d** from the east
44:3 and my blessing on your **d**.
45:19 I didn't say to Jacob's **d**,
45:25 All the **d** of Israel will be
46:3 Listen to me, **d** of Jacob,
48:1 Listen to this, **d** of Jacob!
48:19 Your **d** would be like sand.
51:2 him and gave him many **d**.
53:10 he will see his **d** for many
54:3 Your **d** will take over other
57:3 you **d** of adulterers and
57:4 rebellious children, **d** of liars?
58:1 about their rebellion and the **d**
60:14 The **d** of those who oppress
61:9 the nations and their **d** among
61:9 that they are the **d** whom
65:23 will bless their **d** as well.
66:22 "So your **d** and your name will
Jer 2:4 word of the LORD, **d** of Jacob,
5:20 "Tell this to the **d** of Jacob,
7:15 all of Ephraim's **d**.'
10:25 have devoured the **d** of Jacob.
21:12 **d** of David. This is what the
22:28 Is that why he and his **d** will be
22:30 None of his **d** will succeed him
23:8 'The LORD brought the **d** of the
29:32 I will also punish his **d**.
30:7 of calamity for the **d** of Jacob,
30:10 I'm going to rescue your **d** from
30:10 The **d** of Jacob will again have
31:11 The LORD will free the **d** of
31:36 will Israel's **d** stop being a
31:37 I ever reject all of Israel's **d**
32:19 You see everything the **d** of
33:22 I will multiply the **d** of my
33:26 Then I would reject the **d** of
33:26 I would not let any of David's **d**
33:26 rule the **d** of Abraham,
35:6 'You and your **d** must never
35:14 ordered his **d** not to drink wine.
35:14 His **d** have not drunk any wine
35:16 The **d** of Jonadab,
36:31 I will punish him, his **d**,
46:27 to rescue you and your **d** from
46:27 Then Jacob's **d** will again have
49:1 over the inheritance of Gad's **d**?
49:8 bring disaster on the **d** of Esau.
49:10 Yet, I will strip the **d** of Esau.
Eze 20:5 and swore an oath to the **d**
40:46 These priests are Zadok's **d**.
43:19 These priests are Zadok's **d**,
44:15 priests who are Levites and **d**
46:16 The gift will belong to his **d**
48:11 the priests who are **d** of Zadok.
Dan 11:4 will not be given to his **d**.
12:1 will stand up on behalf of the **d**
Hos 1:7 Yet, I will love the **d** of Judah.
5:8 you **d** of Benjamin.
Amo 3:13 testify against the **d** of Jacob,
6:6 the ruin ⌊of the **d**⌋ of Joseph.
7:2 How can ⌊the **d** of⌋ Jacob
7:5 How can ⌊the **d** of⌋ Jacob
7:16 against the **d** of Isaac.'
9:8 totally destroy the **d** of Jacob,
Oba 1:17 The **d** of Jacob will get back
1:18 The **d** of Jacob will be like a
1:18 The **d** of Joseph will be like a
1:18 But the **d** of Esau will be like
Oba 1:18 one left among the **d** of Esau."
1:19 and ⌊the **d** of⌋ Benjamin will
Mic 2:7 Should the **d** of Jacob be
3:8 So I will tell ⌊the **d** of⌋ Jacob
3:9 you leaders of the **d** of Jacob,
6:16 the practices of the **d** of Ahab,
Nah 1:14 You will no longer have **d** to
Mal 1:4 "The **d** of Esau may say,
2:3 "I'm going to punish your **d**.
2:15 ⌊God⌋ look for but godly **d**?
3:6 That is why you **d** of Jacob
Mat 3:9 that God can raise up **d**
23:31 yourselves that you are the **d**
Luk 1:55 to Abraham and his **d**."
3:8 that God can raise up **d**
19:9 are one of Abraham's **d**.
Jon 7:42 Messiah will come from the **d**
8:33 "We are Abraham's **d**,
8:37 I know that you're Abraham's **d**.
Act 2:30 one of David's **d** on his throne.
3:25 You are the **d** of the prophets
7:5 this land to him and to his **d**,
7:6 God told Abraham that his **d**
13:23 come to Israel from David's **d**,
13:26 "Brothers — **d** of Abraham and
13:33 the promise for us, their **d**,
Rom 4:13 that Abraham or his **d** received
4:16 not only for those who are **d** by
4:16 who are **d** by believing as
4:18 is how many **d** you will have."
9:7 "Through Isaac your **d** will
9:8 are considered Abraham's **d**.
9:27 "Although the **d** of Israel are as
9:29 of Armies hadn't left us some **d**,
2Co 11:22 Are they Abraham's **d**?
Gal 3:7 have faith are Abraham's **d**.
3:16 "**d**," referring to many,
3:29 you are Abraham's **d** and heirs,
Heb 2:16 So Jesus helps Abraham's **d**
6:14 you and give you many **d**."
7:5 their own people, Abraham's **d**.
7:9 Levi gave, although later his **d**
11:12 Yet, from this man came **d** as
11:18 "Through Isaac your **d** will

descended (56)

Gen 36:16 These were the tribal leaders **d**
36:17 These were the tribal leaders **d**
36:18 These were the tribal leaders **d**
36:40 the tribal leaders **d** from Esau,
Exo 6:14 the families **d** from Reuben.
6:15 the families **d** from Simeon.
6:19 These were the families **d** from
6:24 were the families **d** from Korah.
Num 3:21 the families **d** from Libni
3:21 the families **d** from Gershon.
3:23 The families **d** from Gershon
3:27 the families **d** from Amram,
3:27 the families **d** from Kohath.
3:29 The families **d** from Kohath put
3:33 the families **d** from Mahli
3:33 the families **d** from Merari.
4:2 Levites who are **d** from Kohath.
26:12 The families **d** from Simeon
26:15 The families **d** from Gad were
26:20 The families **d** from Judah
26:23 The families **d** from Issachar
26:26 The families **d** from Zebulun
26:28 The families **d** from Joseph
26:35 The families **d** from Ephraim
26:37 the families **d** from Joseph.
26:38 The families **d** from Benjamin
26:41 the families **d** from Benjamin.
26:42 The family **d** from Dan was the
26:42 was the family **d** from Dan.
26:44 The families **d** from Asher were
26:48 The families **d** from Naphtali
26:57 The families **d** from Levi were
36:1 families were **d** from Gilead,
Jos 16:5 for the families **d** from Ephraim.
17:2 the families **d** from Manasseh,
19:10 for the families **d** from Zebulun.
19:16 to the families **d** from Zebulun.
19:17 for the families **d** from Issachar.
19:32 drawn for the families **d** from
2Sm 17:5 who is **d** from Archi's family,

1Ki 12:31 men who were not **d** from Levi
1Ch 5:12 One family **d** from Gad's first
5:12 Another family **d** from Gad's
5:12 Other families **d** from Gad's
6:44 relatives **d** from Merari.
6:54 from the family **d** from Kohath.
9:14 From the Levites **d** from Merari
23:6 or Merari) they were **d** from.
26:21 who was **d** from Gershon.
2Ch 20:14 a Levite **d** from Asaph.)
34:12 (Levites **d** from Merari),
Ezr 8:20 (They were **d** from the temple
Isa 48:1 You are **d** from Judah.
51:2 from whom you are **d**.
Rom 9:5 The Messiah is **d** from their
9:6 Clearly, not everyone **d** from

descends (6)

Jos 16:3 Then it **d** west to the border of
16:7 From Janoah it **d** to Ataroth and
17:9 The border then **d** southward to
18:16 Then the border **d** to the foot of
18:16 It **d** to the valley of Hinnom,
18:17 It **d** to the Rock of Bohan,

descent (2)

Est 6:13 If Mordecai is of Jewish **d**,
Rom 9:8 natural **d** (from Abraham) are

describe (5)

Jos 18:6 You must **d** the seven parts of
Eze 43:10 "Son of man, **d** this temple to
Mat 11:16 "How can I **d** the people who
Luk 7:31 "How can I **d** the people who
2Co 9:15 for his gift that words cannot **d**.

described (9)

Num 21:14 This is how it's **d** in the Book
Dtr 29:20 All the curses **d** in this book
29:27 it all the curses **d** in this book.
Jos 18:9 They **d** it in a book.
1Ki 4:33 He **d** and classified trees —
4:33 He **d** and classified animals,
Est 9:27 as they were **d** and at their
Gal 3:1 crucifixion clearly **d** to you?
Rev 22:19 holy city that are **d** in this book.

description (3)

Jos 18:4 survey the land and write a **d**
18:8 ordered them to write a **d**
18:8 Write a **d** of it, and return to me.

desert (285)

Gen 14:6 El Paran on the edge of the **d**.
16:7 found her by a spring in the **d**,
21:14 around in the **d** near Beersheba.
21:20 He lived in the **d** and became a
21:21 He lived in the **d** of Paran,
36:24 the hot springs in the **d** while
37:22 that cistern that's out in the **d**,
47:19 the ground won't become a **d**."
Exo 3:1 sheep to the far side of the **d**,
3:18 us travel three days into the **d**
4:27 Aaron to meet Moses in the **d**.
5:1 Let my people go into the **d** to
5:3 us travel three days into the **d**
7:16 go to worship me in the **d**."
8:27 to travel three days into the **d**
8:28 to the LORD your God in the **d**
13:18 on the road through the **d**
13:20 on the edge of the **d**.
14:3 The **d** is blocking their escape.'
14:11 "Did you bring us out into the **d**
14:12 Egyptians than to die in the **d**!"
15:22 the Red Sea into the **d** of Shur.
15:22 in the **d** without finding water.
16:1 Elim and came to the **d** of Sin,
16:2 In the **d** the whole community
16:3 You brought us out into this **d**
16:10 they looked toward the **d**.
16:32 I gave you to eat in the **d** when
17:1 of Israelites left the **d**
18:5 wife to Moses in the **d** where
19:1 they came to the **d** of Sinai.
19:2 had come into the **d** of Sinai.
23:31 Sea and from the Sinai **D**
Lev 7:38 offerings to him in the Sinai **D**.
16:10 He will release it in the **d** to
16:21 to release the goat in the **d**.
16:22 must release the goat in the **d**.
Num 1:1 of meeting in the **D** of Sinai.
1:19 the men of Israel in the **D**
3:4 his presence in the **D** of Sinai.
3:14 said to Moses in the **D** of Sinai,
9:1 to Moses in the **D** of Sinai.
9:5 they were in the **D** of Sinai.
10:12 the Israelites moved from the **D**
10:12 stopped in the **D** of Paran.
10:31 we can set up camp in the **d**,
12:16 set up camp in the **D** of Paran.
13:3 these men from the **D** of Paran.
13:21 explored the land from the **D**
13:26 at Kadesh in the **D** of Paran.
14:2 we had died in Egypt or this **d**!
14:16 he slaughtered them in the **d**.'
14:22 in Egypt and in the **d** will see
14:25 go back into the **d**,
14:29 bodies will drop dead in this **d**.
14:32 bodies will drop dead in this **d**.
14:33 will be shepherds in the **d**
14:33 your bodies lies dead in the **d**.
14:35 will meet their end in this **d**.
15:32 the Israelites were in the **d**,
16:13 honey only to kill us in the **d**?
20:1 of Israel came into the **D** of Zin,
20:4 assembly into this **d** just
21:5 just to let us die in the **d**?
21:11 Abarim in the **d** west of Moab.
21:13 in the **d** that extends into
21:18 From the **d** they went to
21:23 troops and came out into the **d**
24:1 He turned toward the **d**,
26:64 had counted in the **D** of Sinai.
26:65 "They must all die in the **d**."
27:3 "Our father died in the **d**.
27:14 my command in the **D** of Zin.
27:14 at Kadesh in the **D** of Zin.)
32:13 he made them wander in the **d**
32:15 all these people in the **d**.
33:6 on the edge of the **d**.
33:8 the middle of the sea into the **d**.
33:8 three days in the **D** of Etham,
33:11 set up camp in the **D** of Sin.
33:12 They moved from the **D** of Sin
33:15 set up camp in the **D** of Sinai.
33:16 They moved from the **D** of
33:36 camp at Kadesh in the **D** of Zin.
34:3 side includes part of the **D**
Dtr 1:1 Moses gave in the **d** east
1:19 vast and dangerous **d** you saw
1:31 and in the **d**." There you saw
1:40 Turn around, go back into the **d**
2:1 We went back into the **d**,
2:7 traveled through this vast **d**.
2:8 goes through the **d** of Moab.
2:26 From the **d** of Kedemoth,
4:43 The cities were Bezer on the **d**
8:2 you on your journey in the **d**.
8:15 that vast and dangerous **d** —
8:16 fed you in the **d** with manna,
9:7 LORD your God angry in the **d**.
9:28 out — to let them die in the **d**."
11:5 for you in the **d** until you came
11:24 will be from the **d** to Lebanon,
29:5 years I led you through the **d**.
32:10 He found his people in a **d** land,
32:51 at Kadesh in the **D** of Zin.
Jos 1:4 Your borders will be the **d** (on
5:4 way through the **d** after they left
5:5 on the way through the **d**,
5:6 through the **d** until all their
8:15 They ran away toward the **d**.
8:20 had been running toward the **d**,
8:24 and in the **d** where they had
12:8 foothills, plains, slopes, **d**,
14:10 Israel wandered in the **d** when
15:1 of Edom and the **d** of Zin.
15:61 In the **d** Judah was given six
16:1 through the **d** that goes up from
18:12 and ends at the **d** of Beth Aven.
20:8 Bezer on the **d** plateau from the
24:7 Then you lived in the **d** for a
Jdg 1:16 of Palms into the **d** of Judah.
8:7 thorns and thistles from the **d**."
8:16 thorns and thistles from the **d**.
11:16 they went through the **d** to the
11:18 "Then they went through the **d**,
11:22 the Jabbok River and from the **d**
20:42 Israel toward the road to the **d**.
20:42 the cities on the road to the **d**.
20:45 others turned and fled into the **d**
20:47 men turned and fled into the **d**
1Sm 4:8 every kind of plague in the **d**.
13:18 the valley of Zeboim and the **d**.
23:14 lived in fortified camps in the **d**,
23:14 the mountains of the **d** of Ziph.
23:15 him at Horesh in the **d** of Ziph.
23:24 his men were in the **d** of Maon,
23:25 stronghold in the **d** of Maon.
23:25 David into the **d** of Maon.
24:1 David is in the **d** near En Gedi."
25:1 David went to the **d** of Paran.
25:4 While David was in the **d**,
25:14 sent messengers from the **d**
25:21 man's stuff in the **d** for nothing!
26:2 Saul went to the **d** of Ziph,
26:3 but David stayed in the **d**.
26:3 Saul had come to the **d** for him,
2Sm 2:24 the road from Gibeon to the **d**.
15:23 down the road toward the **d**.
15:28 the river crossings in the **d** until
16:2 tired and thirsty in the **d**."
17:16 in the river crossings in the **d**,
17:29 "The troops in the **d** are hungry,
1Ki 2:34 buried him at his home in the **d**.
9:18 Baalath, Tadmor in the **d**
14:16 So the LORD will **d** Israel
2Ki 3:8 road through the **d** of Edom."
1Ch 5:9 the edge of the **d** that extends
12:8 at the fortified camp in the **d**.
21:29 tent that Moses made in the **d**
2Ch 1:3 had made the tent in the **d**.
8:4 He rebuilt Tadmor in the **d** and
20:16 valley in front of the Jeruel **D**.
20:20 and went to the **d** of Tekoa.
20:24 went to the watchtower in the **d**
24:9 (In the **d** the LORD's servant
26:10 He built towers in the **d**.
Neh 9:19 didn't abandon them in the **d**.
9:21 You provided for them in the **d**
Job 1:19 great storm swept across the **d**
24:5 Like wild donkeys in the **d**,
38:26 on a **d** where there are no
39:6 I gave it the **d** to live in and the
Psa 55:7 I would stay in the **d**.
65:12 The pastures in the **d** overflow
68:7 you marched through the **d**,
72:9 May the people of the **d** kneel
74:14 the creatures of the **d** for food.
78:15 He split rocks in the **d**.
78:17 to rebel in the **d** against the
78:19 prepare a banquet in the **d**?
78:40 they caused him grief in the **d**!
94:14 The LORD will never **d** his
95:8 the time at Massah in the **d**.
102:6 I am like a **d** owl, like an owl
106:9 water as though it were a **d**.
106:14 In the **d** they tested God.
107:4 They wandered around the **d**
107:33 He changes rivers into a **d**,
107:40 stumble around in a pathless **d**.
136:16 led his people through the **d** —
Pro 21:19 Better to live in a **d** than with a
Isa 13:21 **D** animals will lie down there.
14:17 who made the world like a **d**
16:1 lambs from Sela through the **d**
16:8 and strayed out into the **d**.
21:1 divine revelation about the **d** by
21:1 invader will come from the **d**,
23:13 gave this land to the **d** animals.
27:10 abandoned like the **d**.
35:1 The **d** and the dry land will be
35:6 Water will gush out into the **d**,
40:3 A voice cries out in the **d**:
41:19 and wild olive trees in the **d**.
42:11 Let those who live in the **d** and
43:19 I will clear a way in the **d**.
43:20 I will provide water in the **d**.

Isa	51:3	He will make its **d** like Eden.
	64:10	holy cities have become a **d**.
	64:10	Zion has become a **d**.
Jer	2:2	you followed me into the **d**,
	2:6	He led us through the **d**,
	2:24	donkey that is used to the **d**,
	2:31	Haven't I been a **d**,
	3:2	for them like a nomad in the **d**.
	4:11	the heights will blow in the **d**
	4:26	the fertile land has become a **d**,
	9:2	I had a place to stay in the **d**.
	9:12	it has been ruined like the **d** so
	9:26	their foreheads or live in the **d**.
	12:12	all over the bare hills in the **d**.
	13:24	is blown away by a **d** wind.
	17:6	live in the dry places in the **d**,
	22:6	I will certainly turn it into a **d**,
	25:24	foreign people living in the **d**;
	31:2	wars have found favor in the **d**.
	48:6	like a wild donkey in the **d**."
	50:12	You will become a parched **d**.
	50:39	That is why **d** animals will live
	50:39	**D** owls will also live there.
	51:43	It will become a **d**,
Lam	5:9	our lives in the heat of the **d**.
Eze	6:14	from the **d** to Diblah.
	19:13	Now it is planted in the **d**,
	20:10	Egypt and led them into the **d**.
	20:13	rebelled against me in the **d**.
	20:13	out my fury on them in the **d**
	20:15	swore an oath to them in the **d**.
	20:17	wipe them out in the **d**.
	20:18	I said to their children in the **d**,
	20:21	my anger on them in the **d**.
	20:23	swore an oath to them in the **d**.
	20:35	I will bring you into the **d** of the
	20:36	on trial in the **d** of Egypt,
	23:42	of people came from the **d**,
	29:5	I will leave you in the **d**,
Hos	2:14	I will lead her into the **d**.
	9:10	like finding grapes in the **d**.
	13:5	I took care of you in the **d**,
	13:15	It will blow out of the **d**.
Joe	2:3	it the land is like a barren **d**.
	3:19	Edom will become a barren **d**.
Amo	2:10	I led you through the **d** for 40
	5:25	and grain offerings in the **d**
Zep	2:13	a dried up wasteland like the **d**.
Mal	1:3	to the jackals in the **d**.
Mat	3:1	appeared in the **d** of Judea.
	3:3	"A voice cries out in the **d**:
	4:1	the Spirit led Jesus into the **d**
	11:7	did you go into the **d** to see?
	24:26	'He's in the **d**!' don't
Mar	1:3	"A voice cries out in the **d**:
	1:4	John the Baptizer was in the **d**
	1:12	the Spirit brought him into the **d**
Luk	1:80	He lived in the **d** until the day
	3:2	son of Zechariah, in the **d**.
	3:4	"A voice cries out in the **d**:
	4:1	led him while he was in the **d**,
	7:24	did you go into the **d** to see?
	8:29	force him to go into the **d**.)
Jon	1:23	"I'm a voice crying out in the **d**,
	3:14	the snake ⌊on a pole⌋ in the **d**,
	6:31	ate the manna in the **d**.
	6:49	the manna in the **d** and died.
	11:54	to the countryside near the **d**,
Act	7:30	bush in the **d** of Mount Sinai.
	7:36	and in the **d** for 40 years.
	7:38	was in the assembly in the **d**.
	7:42	and grain offerings in the **d**
	7:44	"In the **d** our ancestors had the
	8:26	and take the **d** road that goes
	13:18	for about forty years in the **d**.
	21:38	thousand terrorists into the **d**?"
1Co	10:5	were scattered over the **d**.
1Ti	4:1	times some believers will **d**
Heb	3:8	rebelled and tested me in the **d**.
	3:17	who sinned and died in the **d**.

deserted (52)

Exo	23:29	the land would be **d**,
Lev	16:22	all their sins away to a **d** place.
	26:22	few that your roads will be **d**.
	26:31	I will make your cities **d** and
Lev	26:32	I will make your land so **d** that
	26:33	Your cities will be **d**.
	26:34	honor the LORD⌋ while it lies **d**
	26:35	All the days it lies **d**,
	26:43	while it lies **d** without them.
Jos	8:28	Ai and made it a **d** mound
	22:3	have never **d** your relatives.
Jdg	5:6	the days of Jael, roads were **d**.
	5:7	Villages in Israel were **d** —
	5:7	Israel were deserted — **d** until
2Ki	25:5	His entire army had **d** him.
1Ch	12:19	Manasseh had **d** ⌊Saul's army⌋
	12:20	these men from Manasseh **d** to
2Ch	29:6	They **d** him. They turned away
Psa	9:10	because you have never **d**
	69:25	Let their camp be **d** and their
	107:4	on a **d** road without finding
Isa	7:16	kings who terrify you will be **d**.
	17:2	The cities of Aroer will be **d**.
	27:10	The homestead is left **d**,
	32:14	Palaces will be **d**.
	33:8	Highways are **d**. Travelers stop
	54:1	who have been **d** than there are
	54:3	and they will resettle **d** cities.
	62:4	You will no longer be called **D**,
	62:12	Sought After, a City Not **D**.
Jer	33:10	the streets of Jerusalem are **d**.
	33:12	of Armies says: In this **d** place,
	38:19	afraid of the Jews who have **d**
	38:22	and your friends have **d** you.'
	44:2	Today they are **d** ruins.
	48:9	Its cities will become **d** ruins.
	52:8	His entire army had **d** him.
Lam	1:1	"Look how **d** Jerusalem is!
	1:4	"The roads to Zion are **d**.
Eze	14:5	They have **d** me because of
	35:5	You **d** the people of Israel in
	35:12	You said, "They have been **d**
Nah	2:10	Nineveh is destroyed, **d**,
Zep	2:4	Gaza will be **d**, and Ashkelon
	2:13	will turn Nineveh into a **d** ruin,
Mat	23:38	house will be abandoned, **d**.
Act	1:20	'Let his home be **d**,
	13:13	John Mark **d** them there and
	15:38	John Mark had **d** them in
Gal	4:27	Because the **d** woman will
2Ti	1:15	the province of Asia has **d** me,
Heb	6:6	Yet, they have **d** ⌊Christ⌋.

deserting (3)

Jer	37:13	"You're **d** to the Babylonians!"
	37:14	I'm not **d** to the Babylonians."
Gal	1:6	that you're so quickly **d** Christ,

deserts (8)

1Ch	12:19	cost us our heads when he **d**
Psa	68:4	for him to ride through the **d**.
	107:35	He changes **d** into lakes and
Isa	41:18	I will turn **d** into lakes.
	48:21	he led them through the **d**.
	50:2	and I turn rivers into **d**.
Eze	14:7	lives in Israel **d** me by devoting
Heb	11:38	Some wandered around in **d**

deserve (58)

Gen	40:15	I've done nothing to **d** being put
Lev	20:11	be put to death. They **d** to die.
	20:12	a disgusting thing and **d** to die.
	20:13	be put to death. They **d** to die.
	20:16	be put to death. They **d** to die.
	20:27	to death because they **d** to die."
Dtr	19:6	his life even though he didn't **d**
2Sm	3:39	evildoer as his evil deeds **d**."
1Ki	2:26	You **d** to die, but I won't kill you
Ezr	9:13	punished us far less than we **d**
Job	36:17	the judgment evil people **d**.
Psa	28:4	and give them what they **d**.
	94:2	arrogant people what they **d**.
	103:10	He has not treated us as we **d**
Ecc	8:14	get what the righteous **d**.
Isa	42:8	else or the praise I **d** to idols.
	66:6	back his enemies as they **d**.
Jer	10:7	This is what you **d**.
	14:16	the destruction that they **d**.
	49:12	If those who don't **d** to drink
Lam	3:64	back, O LORD, for what they **d**,
Eze	7:27	I will give them what they **d**
	14:4	answer that his many idols **d**.
	16:59	I will give you what you **d**.
Dan	9:4	you are great and **d** respect as
Hos	9:14	LORD, give them what they **d**.
Zec	1:6	us as our ways and deeds **d**.'"
	13:3	'You don't **d** to live because
Mat	5:46	do you **d** a reward?
	8:8	I don't **d** to have you come into
	10:37	more than me does not **d**
	10:37	more than me does not **d**
	10:38	cross and follow me doesn't **d**
	22:8	were invited don't **d** the honor.
Luk	6:32	do you **d** any thanks for that?
	6:33	do you **d** any thanks for that?
	6:34	do you **d** any thanks for that?
	7:6	I don't **d** to have you come into
	15:19	I don't **d** to be called your son
	15:21	I don't **d** to be called your son
	23:15	anything to **d** the death penalty.
	23:41	We're getting what we **d**.
Act	25:11	something wrong for which I **d**
	25:25	that he has done anything to **d**
Rom	1:27	they **d** for their perversion.
	1:32	who do such things **d** to die,
	3:8	and that's what they **d**.
1Co	9:12	don't we **d** even more?
	15:19	we **d** more pity than any other
2Co	5:10	people will receive what they **d**
	11:15	end they will get what they **d**.
Col	2:18	tell you that you don't **d** a prize.
Heb	11:38	The world didn't **d** these good
1Pe	2:20	What credit do you **d** if you
Rev	3:4	clothes because they **d** it.
	4:11	you **d** to receive glory,
	5:9	"You **d** to take the scroll and
	16:6	This is what they **d**."

deserved (6)

Jdg	9:16	if you treated him as he **d**,
Luk	12:48	he **d** punishment will receive
Act	23:29	of anything for which he **d**
	28:18	of nothing for which I **d** to die.
Eph	2:3	So, because of our nature, we **d**
Rev	5:4	no one was found who **d**

deserves (24)

Lev	20:9	father or mother and **d** to die.
Dtr	22:26	a sin for which she **d** to die.
	25:2	the person who's in the wrong **d**
	25:2	as many lashes as the crime **d**.
	32:3	our God the greatness he **d**!
2Sm	12:5	who did this certainly **d** to die!
1Ch	16:29	the LORD the glory his name **d**.
Job	34:11	give each person what he **d**.
Psa	29:2	the LORD the glory his name **d**.
	96:8	to the LORD the glory he **d**.
Mat	10:10	After all, the worker **d** to have
	26:66	"He **d** the death penalty!"
Luk	7:4	and begged, "He **d** your help.
	10:7	After all, the worker **d** his pay.
Act	26:31	doing anything for which he **d**
Php	4:8	on whatever is right or **d** praise:
1Ti	1:15	and **d** complete acceptance:
	4:9	and **d** complete acceptance.
	5:18	and "The worker **d** his pay."
Heb	3:3	Jesus **d** more praise than
	10:29	respect for the Son of God **d**?
	10:29	He **d** a much worse
Rev	5:2	"Who **d** to open the scroll and
	5:12	"The lamb who was slain **d** to

deserving (1)

Luk	23:22	I haven't found this man **d** of

design (8)

Exo	26:1	work an angel **d** into the fabric.
	26:31	Creatively work an angel **d** into
	36:8	An angel **d** was creatively
	36:35	An angel **d** was creatively
1Ki	7:8	but they were similar in **d**.
Eze	43:11	Then show them the **d** of the
	43:11	and entrances — its entire **d**.
	43:11	so that they can remember its **d**

designate (1)
Eze 45:6 "'You must **d** an area 8,750 feet

designated (10)
1Ki 8:64 On that day the king **d** the
1Ch 12:31 who had been **d** by name
15:13 serving him in the way ⌊he⌋ **d**."
23:13 and his sons were forever **d**
2Ch 7:7 Solomon **d** the courtyard in
Neh 12:44 gifts **d** by Moses' Teachings
Act 28:23 On a **d** day a larger number of
Heb 7:28 Moses' Teachings **d** mortals
7:28 **d** the Son who forever
2Pe 3:7 present heaven and earth are **d**

designed (4)
1Ch 28:13 He **d** all the utensils for
2Ch 26:15 **d** by inventive people.
Sos 4:4 like David's beautifully-**d** tower.
Heb 11:10 city that God had **d** and built,

designer (1)
Exo 38:23 He was a jeweler, carpenter, **d**,

designers (1)
Exo 35:35 of jewelers, carpenters, and **d**.

designs (4)
1Ki 7:29 and the cattle were engraved **d**.
7:30 cast metal with **d** on the sides.
7:36 and **d** in every available space
2Ch 3:5 and decorated it with ⌊**d** in the

desirable (8)
Gen 3:6 and **d** for making someone
1Sm 9:20 will have all that is **d** in Israel?
Psa 19:10 They are more **d** than gold,
Pro 19:22 Loyalty is **d** in a person,
22:1 A good name is more **d** than
Sos 5:16 Everything about him is **d**!
Eze 23:12 all of them **d** young men.
23:23 They are **d** young men,

desire (49)
Gen 39:7 wife began to **d** Joseph,
Exo 20:17 "Never **d** to take your
20:17 "Never **d** to take your
Dtr 5:21 "Never **d** to take your
2Sm 7:21 your promise and your own **d**.
1Ki 11:37 you can rule everything you **d**.
1Ch 17:19 for my sake and your own **d**.
Job 31:7 or my heart has followed ⌊the **d**
Psa 10:17 You have heard the **d** of
20:4 He will give you your heart's **d**
21:2 You gave him his heart's **d**.
51:6 Yet, you **d** truth and sincerity.
106:14 They had an unreasonable **d**
145:16 and you satisfy the **d** of every
Pro 6:25 Do not **d** her beauty in your
8:11 Nothing you **d** can equal it.
10:24 the **d** of righteous people.
11:23 The **d** of righteous people ends
13:19 A fulfilled **d** is sweet to the
21:25 The **d** of a lazy person will kill
Isa 53:2 that would make us **d** him.
Jer 5:8 stallions that are wild with **d**.
24:7 I will give them the **d** to know
Eze 23:27 You won't **d** these things
24:21 It's your hearts' **d**. So the sons
24:25 It is their hearts' **d** and the thing
Dan 11:37 his ancestors or **d** for women.
Mic 2:2 They **d** ⌊other people's⌋ fields,
2:2 They **d** ⌊people's⌋ houses,
Hag 2:7 all the nations **d** will come.
Luk 22:15 "I've had a deep **d** to eat this
Jon 1:13 or from a husband's **d** ⌊to have
8:44 and you **d** to do what your
Rom 7:18 Although I have the **d** to do
9:16 depend on a person's **d** or
10:1 my heart's **d** and prayer to God
1Co 7:9 than to burn ⌊with sexual **d**⌋.
10:6 so that we won't **d** what is evil,
14:1 and **d** spiritual gifts,
14:39 So, brothers and sisters, **d** to
Eph 4:19 with a constant **d** for more.
Eph 6:6 who have a deep **d** to do what
1Th 2:17 effort to fulfill our **d** to see you.
2Th 1:11 you accomplish every good **d**
1Ti 6:4 Rather, he has an unhealthy **d**
Jas 1:15 Then **d** becomes pregnant and
1Pe 2:2 **D** God's pure word as newborn
2:2 as newborn babies **d** milk.
5:2 but out of a **d** to serve.

desired (1)
Est 2:14 again unless the king **d** her

desires (45)
2Sm 3:21 rule everything your heart **d**."
Job 20:20 will never allow anything he **d**
Psa 10:3 boasts about his selfish **d**.
37:4 give you the **d** of your heart.
38:9 You know all my **d**,
Pro 3:15 and all your **d** cannot equal it.
10:3 he intentionally ignores the **d**
21:10 The mind of a wicked person **d**
Mat 5:28 a woman and **d** her has already
23:25 full of greed and uncontrolled **d**.
Mar 4:19 and the **d** for other things take
Rom 6:12 body so that you obey its **d**.
7:7 known that some **d** are sinful if
7:7 "Never have wrong **d**."
7:8 me have all kinds of wrong **d**.
13:9 never have wrong **d**," and
13:14 forget about satisfying the **d**
16:18 They are serving their own **d**.
1Co 7:9 if you cannot control your **d**,
Gal 5:24 along with its passions and **d**.
Eph 2:3 and followed the **d** of our
2:3 We did what our corrupt **d** and
4:22 you through **d** that deceive you.
Php 2:13 God who produces in you the **d**
Col 2:23 for holding back the constant **d**
1Ti 3:1 he **d** something excellent.
5:11 Whenever their natural **d**
6:9 harmful **d** which drown them
2Ti 3:6 sins and led by all kinds of **d**.
4:3 they will follow their own **d**
Tit 2:12 filled with worldly **d** so that we
Jas 1:14 by his own **d** as they lure
4:1 by the selfish **d** that fight
1Pe 1:14 you lived to satisfy your **d**
2:11 you to keep away from the **d**
2:11 These **d** constantly attack you.
4:2 by sinful human **d** as you live
4:3 had sinful **d**, got drunk,
2Pe 1:4 the corruption that sinful **d**
2:10 along the path of impure **d**
2:18 by appealing to their sexual **d**,
3:3 follow their own **d** will appear.
1Jn 2:17 the world and its evil **d** are
Jud 1:16 follow their own **d**,
1:18 follow their own ungodly **d**."

desolate (13)
Dtr 29:23 It will be as **d** as Sodom,
Job 38:27 to saturate the **d** wasteland in
Isa 6:11 and the land is completely **d**.
13:9 He will make the earth **d**.
24:1 the earth into a **d** wasteland.
24:10 The ruined city lies **d**.
49:8 them inherit the **d** inheritance.
Jer 6:8 I will make your land **d**,
18:16 Their land will become **d** and
44:6 So they became the **d** ruin that
50:23 See how **d** Babylon is of all the
Eze 29:12 I will make Egypt the most **d**
30:7 "'Egypt will become the most **d**

desolation (2)
Isa 60:18 about violence in your land or **d**
Zep 1:15 a day of devastation and **d**,

despair (7)
Lev 26:36 I will fill with **d** those who are
Num 14:6 tore their clothes in **d**.
Dtr 28:65 mind, failing eyesight, and **d**.
Est 6:12 He was in **d** and covered his
Job 9:23 fun of the **d** of innocent people.
Psa 88:15 and now I am in **d**.
Ecc 2:20 Then I fell into **d** over

desperate (3)
2Sm 24:14 "I'm in a **d** situation,"
1Ch 21:13 "I'm in a **d** situation,"
Job 6:26 Do you think they're what a **d**

despise (42)
Dtr 31:20 They will **d** me and reject my
1Sm 2:30 and those who **d** me will be
27:12 his own people in Israel **d** him.
2Sm 12:9 Why did you **d** my word by
16:21 have made your father **d** you.
19:43 Why, then, do you **d** us?
2Ki 19:21 'My dear people in Zion **d** you
Est 1:17 and they will **d** their husbands.
Job 5:17 That person should not **d**
19:18 Even young children **d** me.
36:5 He doesn't **d** anyone.
Psa 10:13 the wicked person **d** God?
51:17 O God, you do not **d** a broken
69:33 He does not **d** his own who are
74:10 Will the enemy **d** you forever?
102:17 He will not **d** their prayers.
Pro 1:7 fools **d** wisdom and discipline.
6:30 People do not **d** a thief who is
23:9 because he will **d** the wisdom
23:22 and do not **d** your mother
Sos 8:7 people would utterly **d** him.
Isa 37:22 'My dear people in Zion **d** you
60:14 All who **d** you will bow at your
Jer 14:19 Do you **d** Zion? Why have you
14:21 sake of your name, don't **d** us.
23:17 saying to those who **d** me,
33:24 They **d** my people,
Eze 16:57 Aram and their neighbors **d** you
16:57 of the Philistines also **d** you.
Amo 5:21 I hate your festivals; I **d** them.
Oba 1:2 of nations. Others will **d** you.
Mic 3:9 You **d** justice and pervert
Mal 1:6 You priests **d** my name.
Mat 6:24 to the first and **d** the second.
18:10 "Be careful not to **d** these little
Luk 16:13 to the first and **d** the second.
Rom 14:3 should not **d** people who eat
14:10 criticize or **d** other Christians?
1Co 11:22 Do you **d** God's church and
Gal 4:14 you didn't **d** or reject me.
1Th 5:20 Don't **d** what God has revealed.
2Pe 2:10 of impure desires and who **d**

despised (34)
Num 15:31 That person has **d** the word of
Jdg 9:38 troops ⌊whose ruler⌋ you **d**?
1Sm 10:27 They **d** him and wouldn't bring
17:42 a good look at David, he **d** him.
2Sm 6:16 presence, so she **d** him.
12:10 your house because you **d** me
1Ki 11:25 He ruled Aram and **d** Israel.
1Ch 15:29 and celebrating, so she **d** him.
2Ch 36:16 messengers, **d** his words,
Neh 4:4 We are **d**. Turn their insults
Psa 22:6 by humanity and **d** by people.
22:24 The LORD has not **d** or been
74:18 of godless fools **d** your name.
89:38 But you have **d**, rejected,
107:11 against God's words and had **d**
119:141 I am unimportant and **d**,
Pro 1:30 They **d** my every warning.
5:12 How my heart **d** correction!
12:8 has a twisted mind will be **d**.
Ecc 9:16 poor person's wisdom was **d**,
Isa 1:4 They have **d** the Holy One of
5:24 the LORD of Armies and have **d**
16:14 "Moab's honor will be **d** within
49:7 the LORD says to the **d** one,
53:3 He was **d** and rejected by
53:3 He was **d** like one from whom
Jer 49:15 nations and **d** among humanity.
Lam 1:11 look and see how **d** I am!"
Eze 16:59 You **d** your marriage vows and
22:8 You have **d** my holy things and
Zec 4:10 Who **d** the day when little
Mal 1:6 'How have we **d** your name?'
1:7 that the LORD's table may be **d**.
1:12 and that its food may be **d**.

despises (12)
Psa 15:4 The one who **d** those rejected
Pro 11:12 A person who **d** a neighbor has
13:13 Whoever **d** ⌊God's⌋ words will
14:2 is devious in his ways **d** him.
14:21 Whoever **d** his neighbor sins,
15:5 A stubborn fool **d** his father's
15:20 but a foolish child **d** its mother.
15:32 ignores discipline **d** himself,
19:16 ⌊but⌋ whoever **d** the LORD's
27:7 One who is full **d** honey,
Lam 1:8 who used to honor it now **d** it.
1Co 1:28 ordinary and what it **d** — what

despite (8)
Dtr 21:8 with the LORD **d** the murder.
Jdg 8:35 Gideon) **d** all the good he had
1Ch 22:14 "**D** my troubles I've made
Job 6:10 I would be happy **d** my endless
Isa 25:11 humble those arrogant people **d**
64:12 **D** these things, LORD, will you
Luk 8:15 what is good **d** what life may
2Co 3:11 ministry faded away **d** its glory,

destination (1)
2Sm 16:14 ⌊at their **d**⌋ and rested there.

destine (1)
Isa 65:12 Now I will **d** you for death.

destined (8)
Num 24:22 But it is **d** to be burned,
Job 15:22 He is **d** ⌊to be killed⌋ with a
Jer 15:2 Those who are **d** to die will die.
15:2 Those who are **d** to die in wars
15:2 Those who are **d** to die in
15:2 Those who are **d** to die in
Hab 1:12 you have **d** them to correct us.
1Th 3:3 we're **d** to suffer persecution.

destiny (10)
Psa 16:5 the one who determines my **d**.
Ecc 2:14 to realize that the same **d** waits
2:15 I thought to myself, "⌊If⌋ the **d**
3:19 and animals have the same **d**.
9:2 people will share the same **d**,
9:3 Everyone shares the same **d**.
Isa 17:14 the **d** of those who robbed us.
57:6 They are your **d**. You have
65:11 wine to the goddess of **d**.
Jer 13:25 the **d** I have planned for you,"

destitute (1)
Lam 4:5 to eat delicacies are now **d**

destroy (312)
Gen 6:13 Now I'm going to **d** them along
6:17 the earth to **d** all people under
9:15 become a flood to **d** all life.
18:28 Will you **d** the whole city
18:28 "I will not **d** it if I find 45 there."
18:31 He answered, "I will not **d** it for
18:32 He answered, "I will not **d** it for
19:13 we're going to **d** this place.
19:13 the LORD has sent us to **d** it."
19:14 LORD is going to **d** the city."
19:21 I will not **d** the city you're
20:4 will you **d** a nation even if it's
Exo 12:13 Nothing will touch or **d** you
23:24 Instead, you must **d** their gods
32:10 with them I am going to **d** them.
32:14 his threat to **d** his people.
33:3 and I would **d** you on the way."
33:5 I might **d** you at any time.
Lev 26:22 of your children, **d** your cattle,
26:26 I will **d** your food supply.
26:30 I will **d** your worship sites,
Num 14:12 them with a plague, I'll **d** them,
16:21 and I'll **d** them in an instant."
16:45 and let me **d** them in an
21:2 we'll **d** their cities because
24:17 heads of the Moabites and **d** all
24:19 He will rule from Jacob and **d**
25:11 stand up for myself and **d** them.
33:52 and **d** all their places of
Dtr 1:27 so that they could **d** us!
4:31 He will not abandon you, **d** you,
7:2 **d** every one of them because
7:4 you and will quickly **d** you.
7:16 You must **d** all the people the
7:24 You will **d** them all.
8:20 The LORD is going to **d** other
9:3 land and will quickly **d** them as
9:8 angry that he wanted to **d** you.
9:14 I'll **d** them and wipe their name
9:19 so angry he wanted to **d** you.
9:20 Aaron and wanted to **d** him.
9:25 the LORD said he would **d** you.
9:26 don't **d** your people.
10:10 to me and agreed not to **d** you.
12:2 Completely **d** all the worship
12:29 The LORD your God will **d** the
13:15 city with swords and **d** that city
19:1 The LORD your God will **d** all
20:17 LORD and completely **d** them,
20:20 You may **d** trees that you know
28:38 locusts will **d** your crops.
28:63 will be more than glad to **d** you
31:3 He will **d** those nations as you
33:27 way and tell you to **d** them.
Jos 7:3 men are needed to **d** Ai.
7:7 so that they could **d** us?
7:12 anymore unless you **d** what
9:18 The Israelites didn't **d** these
9:24 whole land and **d** all who live
10:4 "Come, help me **d** Gibeon
24:20 He will **d** you, although he has
Jdg 6:4 used to camp on the land and **d**
1Sm 15:6 so that I won't **d** you
15:9 army did claim for God and **d**.
23:10 going to come to Keilah and **d**
24:21 my descendants or **d** my name
2Sm 1:14 to take it upon yourself to **d**
10:3 the city, spy on it, and **d** it?"
11:25 against the city, and **d** it.'
14:7 We're going to **d** the one who
20:15 with Joab were trying to **d**
20:19 Are you trying to **d** a mother
20:20 to swallow ⌊it⌋ up or **d** ⌊it⌋.
21:2 tried to **d** them for Israel and
24:16 out his arm to **d** Jerusalem,
1Ki 8:37 or grasshoppers may **d** crops.
14:10 I will **d** every male in his
14:14 king will **d** Jeroboam's house.
16:3 So I will **d** Baasha and his
21:21 I will **d** your descendants.
21:21 I will **d** every male in Ahab's
2Ki 8:19 LORD didn't want to **d** Judah.
9:7 You will **d** the family of your
9:8 I will **d** every male from Ahab's
10:19 He actually wanted to **d** those
11:1 she began to **d** the entire royal
13:23 didn't want to **d** the Israelites,
18:25 "Have I come to **d** this place
18:25 'Attack this country, and **d** it.'"
24:2 Jehoiakim to **d** Judah as
1Ch 19:3 **d**, and spy on the country?"
21:15 Messenger to Jerusalem to **d** it,
2Ch 6:28 or grasshoppers may **d** crops.
8:7 had not been able to **d** them.
12:7 I will not **d** them. In a little while
12:12 and didn't completely **d** him.
20:10 from them and didn't **d** them.
20:23 they helped **d** one another.
20:37 He said, "The LORD will **d**
21:7 didn't want to **d** David's family.
22:4 They did this to **d** him.
22:7 Jehu to **d** Ahab's family.)
22:10 she began to **d** the entire royal
25:16 that God has decided to **d** you
35:21 so stop now or else he will **d**
Ezr 6:12 with my orders or tries to **d**
9:14 angry with us until you finally **d**
Neh 9:31 You didn't **d** them or abandon
Est 3:13 and **d** all the Jews — young and
4:7 king's treasury to **d** the Jews.
8:5 He signed ⌊the order⌋ to **d** the
8:11 and to **d** every armed force of
9:24 against the Jews to **d** them.
9:24 when⌋ to crush and **d** them.
Job 10:8 then you turned to **d** me.
Job 14:19 and you **d** a mortal's hope.
15:4 Yes, you **d** the fear ⌊of God⌋
30:12 and then prepare ways to **d** me.
30:13 of my path in order to **d** me.
Psa 5:6 You **d** those who tell lies.
21:10 You will **d** their children from
54:5 **D** them with your truth!
59:13 **D** them in your rage.
59:13 **D** them until not one of them is
63:9 But those who try to **d** my life
68:21 of his enemies ⌊and **d** even⌋
69:4 Those who want to **d** me are
73:27 You **d** all who are unfaithful to
74:11 your pockets. **D** your enemies!
75:10 I will **d** all the weapons of
78:38 He did not **d** them.
94:23 He will **d** them because of their
94:23 The LORD our God will **d** them.
101:5 I will **d** anyone who secretly
101:8 Every morning I will **d** all the
106:23 said he was going to **d** them,
106:34 They did not **d** the people as
119:95 waited for me in order to **d** me,
143:12 wipe out my enemies and **d** all
145:20 but he will **d** all wicked people.
Pro 1:32 Fools **d** themselves because
18:24 Friends can **d** one another,
26:10 many people who **d** everything,
Ecc 5:6 **d** what you've accomplished?
9:18 but one sinner can **d** much that
Isa 10:7 Their purpose is to **d** and put
10:18 the orchard will **d** both body
10:25 and my anger will **d** them.
11:9 They will not hurt or **d** anyone
13:5 of his fury to **d** the whole world.
13:9 He will **d** its sinners.
26:11 anger will **d** your enemies.
28:22 determined to **d** the whole land.
31:8 by human hands will **d** them.
36:10 "Have I come to **d** this country
36:10 'Attack this country, and **d** it.'"
48:9 from you, rather than **d** you.
51:13 those who are ready to **d** you?
65:8 person will say, "Don't **d** it,
65:8 I will not **d** everything.
65:25 "They will not hurt or **d** anyone
Jer 1:10 You will **d** and overthrow.
4:7 left his place to **d** your land.
4:27 I will not **d** it completely.
5:6 the wilderness will **d** them.
5:10 rows of grapevines and **d** them,
5:10 but don't **d** all of them.
5:17 With their swords they will **d**
5:18 I won't **d** all of you.
6:5 at night and **d** its palaces.'"
9:11 I will **d** the cities of Judah so
10:22 Its army will **d** Judah's cities
11:19 "Let's **d** the tree with its fruit.
12:17 will uproot that nation and **d** it,"
13:9 This is how I will **d** Judah's
13:14 or compassion when I **d** them.'"
14:12 But I will **d** these people with
15:3 and animals to devour and **d**.
15:6 power against you and **d** you.
15:7 I will **d** my people because
17:18 and **d** them completely.
18:7 and **d** a nation or a kingdom.
22:7 I will send people to **d** you.
25:9 I'm going to **d** them and turn
30:11 "I will completely **d** all the
30:11 but I will not completely **d** you.
34:22 I will **d** the cities of Judah so
36:29 certainly come to **d** this land
44:8 You will **d** yourselves and be
44:11 on you and **d** all of Judah.
46:8 I will **d** cities and the people in
46:28 I will completely **d** all the
46:28 but I will not completely **d** you.
47:4 The time has come to **d** all the
47:4 The LORD will **d** the
48:2 "Let's **d** that nation!"
48:15 attack Moab and **d** its cities.
48:18 They will **d** your fortresses.
48:32 The destroyer will **d** your
49:20 He will surely **d** the pasture
49:38 I'll set my throne in Elam and **d**

Jer 50:3 Babylon and **d** its land so
50:37 A sword will **d** their treasures,
50:45 He will surely **d** the pasture
51:3 Completely **d** its whole army.
51:11 his plan is to **d** Babylon.
51:20 I will use you to **d** kingdoms.
51:55 The LORD will **d** Babylon.
51:62 you have threatened to **d** this
Lam 2:8 The LORD planned to **d** the
Eze 6:3 and **d** your worship sites.
6:14 against them and **d** the land,
9:8 will you **d** everyone who is left
11:13 will you completely **d** all the
13:13 and hailstones will **d** the wall.
14:9 you and **d** you from among
14:13 and **d** its people and animals.
14:17 Suppose I **d** the people and the
14:21 will **d** people and animals.
16:39 They will **d** your platforms and
20:17 I didn't **d** them or completely
20:47 I am about to set fire to you to **d**
21:28 It's polished to **d** and flash like
22:27 They murder and **d** people to
25:7 you disappear, and **d** you.
25:15 to **d** their long-time enemies.
25:16 and **d** the people that are left on
26:4 They will **d** the walls of Tyre
26:8 He will **d** the villages on your
26:12 They will **d** your walls and tear
30:11 will be brought to **d** the land.
30:12 I will have foreigners **d** the land
30:13 I will **d** the statues and put an
30:14 I will **d** Pathros, set fire to
32:12 of Egypt and **d** its many people.
32:13 I will also **d** all the animals
34:16 I will **d** those that are fat and
35:7 and I will **d** everyone who
43:3 when he came to **d** Jerusalem
Dan 2:12 that he gave an order to **d** all
2:24 to **d** Babylon's wise advisers.
2:24 Daniel told him, "Don't **d**
4:23 **D** it! But leave the stump and its
8:24 He will **d** those who are
8:25 great and **d** many people when
9:27 to those who **d** ⌊the city⌋."
11:17 daughter as a wife in order to **d**
11:44 to **d** and exterminate many.
Hos 2:12 I will **d** her grapevines and fig
2:18 I will **d** all the bows,
4:5 So I will **d** your mother,
4:6 I will **d** my people because
5:12 I will **d** Ephraim as a moth
5:12 I will **d** the nation of Judah as
10:2 and **d** their stone markers.
11:9 I will not **d** Ephraim again.
13:14 Grave, I want to **d** you.
13:15 The wind will **d** every precious
Amo 3:14 I will also **d** the altars at Bethel.
9:8 But I won't totally **d** the
Oba 1:8 "On that day I will **d** the wise
Jnh 3:10 his threat to **d** them,
Mic 5:10 "I will **d** your horses and
5:11 I will **d** the cities in your land
5:12 I will **d** your sorcerers,
5:13 I will **d** your idols and your
6:14 Anything you save I will **d**.
Zep 2:5 "I will **d** you so that no one will
2:13 against the north and **d** Assyria.
Hag 2:22 the thrones of kingdoms and **d**
Zec 5:4 will stay in their houses and **d**
8:14 I made plans to **d** you,
9:15 They will **d** and trample the
12:9 "On that day I will seek to **d** all
Mal 3:11 They will not **d** the produce of
Mat 6:19 where moths and rust **d** and
6:20 where moths and rust don't **d**
10:28 Instead, fear the one who can **d**
21:41 "He will **d** those evil people.
Mar 1:24 Have you come to **d** us?
9:22 into fire or into water to **d** him.
12:9 He will come and **d** the
Luk 4:34 Have you come to **d** us?
6:9 a person his health or to **d** it?"
10:19 snakes and scorpions and to **d**
12:33 enough to **d** your treasure.
20:16 He will **d** these workers and
Jon 10:10 thief comes to steal, kill, and **d**.
12:25 love their lives will **d** them,
Act 6:14 that Jesus from Nazareth will **d**
8:3 Saul tried to **d** the church.
Rom 14:15 Don't **d** anyone by what you
1Co 1:19 Scripture says, "I will **d** the
1:28 be nothing — in order to **d** what
3:17 God will **d** him because God's
5:5 to Satan to **d** his corrupt nature
15:26 last enemy he will **d** is death.
2Co 10:4 them we **d** people's defenses,
Gal 1:13 God's church and tried to **d** it.
1:23 the faith that he once tried to **d**."
5:15 that you don't **d** each other.
2Th 2:8 Lord Jesus will **d** him by what
Heb 2:14 so that by dying he would **d**
Jas 4:12 He is able to save or **d** you.
5:3 Like fire, it will **d** your body.
2Pe 3:9 He doesn't want to **d** anyone
1Jn 2:10 Nothing will **d** the faith of those
3:8 of God appeared was to **d** what
2Jn 1:8 Be careful that you don't **d** what
Jud 1:10 they know to **d** themselves.
Rev 11:18 and to **d** those who destroy the
11:18 destroy those who **d** the earth."

destroyed (239)

Gen 13:10 LORD **d** Sodom and Gomorrah.)
19:25 He **d** those cities, the whole
19:29 When God **d** the cities on the
Exo 9:25 in the fields and **d** every tree
15:7 you **d** those who attacked you.
22:20 must be condemned and **d**.
Lev 26:38 They will be **d** among the
Num 4:18 families from Levi's tribe be **d**.
11:1 It **d** some people on the
21:3 They **d** the Canaanites and
21:28 They **d** Ar of Moab,
21:29 You are **d**, you people of the
21:30 We **d** everyone and everything
24:20 but in the end it will be **d**."
24:24 But they, too, will be totally **d**."
Dtr 4:3 The LORD your God **d**
7:23 into a great panic until they're **d**.
7:26 you and the idol will be **d**.
7:26 and disgusting. It must be **d**."
8:19 you will certainly be **d**.
8:20 You will be **d** like them if you
11:4 So the LORD **d** them forever.
12:30 After they've been **d**,
28:20 everything you do until you're **d**
28:24 you from the sky until you're **d**.
28:45 stay close to you until you're **d**,
28:51 from your fields until you're **d**.
29:23 the LORD **d** in fierce anger.
30:18 that you will certainly be **d**.
31:4 to their lands when he **d** them.
31:17 They will be **d**, and many
Jos 2:10 We've heard how you **d** them
6:18 will be **d** by the LORD.
8:26 until he had completely **d** all
10:1 the same way he had **d** Jericho
10:35 same way he had **d** Lachish.
11:14 to death until they were all **d**.
23:4 nations I have already **d** from
23:15 until he has **d** you from this
24:8 and I **d** them in front of you.
Jdg 4:24 and stronger until they **d** him.
1Sm 5:6 He **d** them by striking the
15:15 they claimed for God and **d**."
2Sm 1:27 weapons of war have been **d**!"
7:9 and I **d** all your enemies in front
11:1 They **d** the Ammonites and
22:38 my enemies and **d** them.
22:41 and I **d** those who hated me.
1Ki 11:16 until they had **d** every male
13:34 family so that it had to be **d**
16:7 Baasha **d** Jeroboam's family.
16:12 So Zimri **d** Baasha's entire
20:21 king of Israel went out and **d**
2Ki 10:27 They **d** the sacred stone of
13:7 the king of Aram had **d** the rest.
19:11 how they totally **d** them.
19:12 my ancestors **d** rescue Gozan,
19:18 So the Assyrians have **d** them.
21:3 that his father Hezekiah had **d**.
2Ki 21:9 that the LORD had **d** when
22:19 live here will be **d** and cursed.
1Ch 4:41 Meunites for God and **d** them.
5:25 God had **d** these people as the
17:8 and I **d** all your enemies in front
20:1 They **d** the Ammonites and
2Ch 24:23 Judah and Jerusalem and **d** all
26:16 powerful, his pride **d** him.
31:1 The Israelites **d** all of these
32:14 claimed and **d** those nations.
33:9 that the LORD had **d** when
34:4 He **d** the Asherah poles,
36:19 and **d** everything of value.
Ezr 4:15 That's why this city was **d**.
5:12 So Nebuchadnezzar **d** this
Neh 1:3 its gates have been **d** by fire."
Est 7:4 can be wiped out, killed, and **d**.
Job 4:7 decent person who has been **d**.
16:7 You, ⌊God,⌋ have **d** everyone
Psa 9:5 You **d** wicked people.
18:40 and I **d** those who hated me.
35:8 fall into their own pit and be **d**.
37:38 But rebels will be completely **d**.
73:19 They are suddenly **d**.
74:3 The enemy has **d** everything in
76:3 There he **d** flaming arrows,
79:7 They have **d** his home.
80:16 Let them be **d** by the
83:10 They were **d** at Endor.
88:16 Your terrors have **d** me.
92:7 only to be **d** forever.
Pro 14:11 of wicked people will be **d**,
22:8 of his own fury will be **d**.
Isa 1:7 Your fields are **d** right before
1:20 you will be **d** by swords."
9:16 are guided by them will be **d**.
13:19 Gomorrah when God **d** them.
14:20 because you have **d** your land
15:1 Ar in Moab is laid waste and **d**!
15:1 Kir in Moab is laid waste and **d**!
22:25 hanging on it will be **d**."
23:1 Your port at Tyre is **d**.
23:11 Canaan's fortifications be **d**.
23:14 because your fortress will be **d**.
26:14 have punished them, **d** them,
33:1 although you haven't been **d**.
33:1 destroying, you will be **d**.
37:11 how they totally **d** them.
37:12 my ancestors **d** rescue Gozan,
37:19 So the Assyrians have **d** them.
49:17 Those who **d** you and laid
49:19 Though you are **d** and
55:13 sign that will never be **d**.
60:12 that do not serve you will be **d**.
61:4 restore the places **d** long ago.
61:4 the places **d** generations ago.
62:4 land will no longer be called **D**.
Jer 4:13 it will be for us! We will be **d**!
4:20 My tents are suddenly **d**.
4:30 You are going to be **d**!
9:10 They are **d** so that no one can
10:20 My tent is **d**, and all my ropes
10:25 They have **d** their homes.
12:10 shepherds have **d** my vineyard.
12:11 The whole land is **d**,
20:16 that the LORD **d** without pity.
25:37 The peaceful pastures are **d** by
44:22 ruined, **d**, and cursed.
47:5 Ashkelon will be **d**.
48:1 it will be for Nebo; it will be **d**.
48:8 The valley will be **d**,
48:9 It will be **d**. Its cities will
48:20 news in Arnon that Moab is **d**.'
48:42 Moab will be **d** as a nation,
49:3 Heshbon, because Ai is **d**.
49:10 children and relatives will be **d**.
49:18 cities when they were **d**.
50:40 cities when I, God, **d** them.
51:25 You have **d** the whole earth,"
Lam 2:5 He **d** its strongholds.
2:6 garden and **d** his own festivals.
2:9 ⌊The LORD⌋ **d** and shattered
4:6 Sodom was **d** instantly,
4:10 were being **d** ⌊by a blockade⌋.
Eze 6:4 Your altars will be **d**.
6:6 be smashed and completely **d**.

Eze 12:20 where people live will be **d**,
13:14 they will be **d** by it.
19:7 He **d** fortresses and turned
19:14 Fire has **d** its fruit.
22:30 land and keep it from being **d**.
26:2 gateway for the nations is **d**,
26:17 famous city, you have been **d**.
27:32 the city **d** in the sea?"
36:35 The cities were **d**.
37:11 We are completely **d**.'
43:8 So I **d** them in my anger.
Dan 2:18 so that they would not be **d**
2:44 a kingdom that will never be **d**.
6:26 His kingdom will never be **d**.
7:11 Its body was **d** and put into a
7:14 His kingdom will never be **d**.
7:26 completely and permanently **d**.
9:26 and the holy place will be **d**
11:20 a few days the king will be **d**,
Hos 7:13 They must be **d** because
8:4 Because of this, they will be **d**.
9:6 if they escape without being **d**,
10:8 worship sites of Aven will be **d**.
10:14 All your fortresses will be **d**
10:14 the time Shalman **d** Beth Arbel
10:15 of Israel will be completely **d**.
Joe 1:7 They **d** my grapevines.
1:10 The grain has been **d**.
1:11 The harvest is **d** in the field.
1:17 Storehouses are **d**.
Amo 2:9 I **d** the Amorites in front of them
2:9 I **d** their fruit above the ground
3:15 with ivory will be **d**.
4:11 I **d** some of you as I destroyed
4:11 I destroyed some of you as I **d**
7:9 sites of Isaac will be **d**,
Oba 1:10 You will be **d** forever.
1:12 the people of Judah are **d**.
1:18 They will be burned and **d**.
Jnh 3:4 forty days Nineveh will be **d**."
Mic 2:10 It will be **d**, because it offends
2:10 be destroyed, completely **d**,
5:9 and all your enemies will be **d**.
Nah 2:2 looted it and have **d** its vines.
2:10 Nineveh is **d**, deserted,
3:7 'Nineveh has been violently **d**!
3:13 Fire has **d** the bars of your
Zep 1:11 all the merchants will be **d**
2:4 and Ashkelon will be **d**.
3:6 Their towers will be **d**.
3:6 cities will be completely **d**.
Zec 11:2 the stately trees have been **d**.
11:3 their rich pastures are **d**.
11:3 lush banks of the Jordan are **d**.
Mal 3:6 of Jacob haven't been **d** yet.
Mat 15:6 of your traditions you have **d**
Mar 7:13 of your traditions you have **d**
Luk 6:49 quickly collapsed and was **d**."
17:27 Then the flood **d** all of them.
17:29 from the sky and **d** all of them.
21:20 the time is near for it to be **d**.
Jon 11:50 for the whole nation to be **d**."
Act 2:24 him from death to life and **d**
8:20 "May your money be **d** with
9:21 "Isn't this the man who **d** those
13:19 Then he **d** seven nations in
27:22 Only the ship will be **d**.
1Co 1:18 to those who are being **d**,
10:10 The angel of death **d** them.
Php 1:28 them that they will be **d**
3:19 In the end they will be **d**.
2Th 1:9 the penalty by being **d** forever,
1Ti 1:19 and their faith has been **d** like
2Ti 1:10 Christ has **d** death,
Heb 7:16 from a life that cannot be **d**.
10:39 those who turn back and are **d**.
1Pe 1:4 an inheritance that can't be **d**
1:18 silver or gold which can be **d**.
1:23 not from a seed that can be **d**,
1:23 everlasting word that can't be **d**.
3:4 internal that can't be **d**.
2Pe 2:6 and **d** them by burning
2:12 So they will be **d** like animals
3:6 also flooded and **d** that world.
3:7 people will be judged and **d**.
3:10 the universe will burn and be **d**.
2Pe 3:11 All these things will be **d** in
3:12 will be on fire and will be **d**.
3:16 These people will be **d**.
Jud 1:5 But on another occasion he **d**
1:11 like Korah and **d** themselves.
Rev 8:9 one-third of the ships were **d**.
18:17 this wealth has been **d**!' Every
18:19 In one moment it has been **d**!'

destroyer (12)

Exo 12:23 and he will not let the **d** come
Jdg 16:24 **d** of our land and killer of so
Job 15:21 the **d** comes to him.
Isa 16:4 Be their refuge from the **d**.
21:2 The **d** destroys. Go to war,
33:1 horrible it will be for you, you **d**,
Jer 4:7 A **d** of nations has set out.
6:26 The **d** will suddenly attack us.
15:8 At noontime I will send a **d**
48:8 The **d** will come to every city,
48:32 The **d** will destroy your ripened
51:56 A **d** will attack Babylon,

destroyers (4)

Isa 54:16 created **d** to bring destruction.
Jer 48:18 The **d** of Moab will attack you.
51:48 because **d** from the north will
51:53 But **d** will still come from me

destroying (39)

Dtr 2:34 them for God by **d** men,
3:6 **d** every city, including men,
Jos 10:20 decisively, almost **d** them.
10:28 them for the LORD by **d** them.
10:35 He claimed it for the LORD by **d**
10:37 people for the LORD by **d** them.
10:39 all for the LORD by **d** them.
10:40 creature for the LORD by **d** it,
11:11 for the LORD by **d** them
11:12 them for the LORD by **d** them,
11:21 them for the LORD by **d** them
22:33 against Reuben and Gad and **d**
Jdg 1:17 claimed it for the LORD by **d** it.
21:11 Claim them for the LORD by **d**
1Sm 6:5 mice which are **d** the country,
15:3 they have for God by **d** it.
15:8 the people for God by **d** them.
15:9 claim them for God by **d** them.
15:18 Amalekites, for me by **d** them.
2Sm 14:11 doing more harm by **d** my son."
24:16 who was **d** the people.
1Ki 9:20 claim them for God by **d** them.
1Ch 21:12 the Messenger of the LORD **d**
21:15 but as he was **d** it,
21:15 he said to the **d** Messenger.
2Ch 34:3 and Jerusalem clean by **d**
Est 9:5 enemies, killing them, **d** them,
Psa 78:49 He sent an army of **d** angels.
Isa 33:1 When you've finished **d**,
Jer 23:1 be for the shepherds who are **d**
44:7 Why do you keep **d** men,
50:26 claim them for me by **d** them,
Lam 2:3 **d** everything around him.
Eze 14:19 killing people and **d** animals.
Hos 13:9 You are **d** yourself,
Mal 4:6 and reclaim my land by **d** you."
Luk 9:25 but lose their lives by **d** them?
2Ti 2:18 They are **d** the faith of others
Heb 11:28 so that the **d** angel would not

destroys (15)

Gen 9:11 be a flood that **d** the earth."
Dtr 28:48 work on you until he **d** you.
Job 4:9 God **d** them with his breath and
9:22 That is why I say, 'He **d**
12:23 important and then **d** them.
Pro 6:32 Whoever does this **d** himself.
Isa 21:2 The destroyer **d**. Go to war,
33:14 of us live through a fire that **d**?
Jer 12:12 The LORD's sword **d** them from
Hos 5:12 Ephraim as a moth **d** clothing.
5:12 nation of Judah as rot **d** wood.
Amo 5:9 He **d** strongholds and ruins
1Co 3:17 If anyone **d** God's temple,
15:24 the Father as he **d** every ruler,
2Ti 2:14 good but only **d** those who are

destruction (89)

Gen 19:29 to escape from the **d** that came
Lev 27:28 dedicated to the LORD for **d** —
Num 21:3 place Hormah [Claimed for **D**].
32:15 be responsible for their **d**."
Dtr 7:10 But he sends **d** to pay back
13:17 any of the things claimed for **d**.
30:15 and prosperity or death and **d**.
Jos 6:18 claimed by the LORD for **d**,
6:18 you will bring **d** and disaster on
7:12 of Israel are now claimed for **d**.
11:20 them all for **d** without mercy,
Jdg 1:17 called Hormah [Claimed for **D**].
2Sm 22:5 of **d** had overwhelmed me.
1Ki 22:11 push the Arameans to their **d**."
2Ki 23:13 southern part of the Hill of **D**.
2Ch 18:10 push the Arameans to their **d**."
Est 3:9 the orders for their **d** be written.
8:6 to see the **d** of my relatives."
Job 5:21 be afraid of **d** when it comes.
5:22 to laugh at **d** and starvation,
Psa 5:9 **D** comes from their hearts.
18:4 of **d** had overwhelmed me.
35:8 Let **d** surprise them.
55:11 **D** is everywhere. Oppression
Pro 3:25 of sudden terror or of the **d**
17:19 his city gate high invites **d**.
18:12 Before **d** a person's heart is
Isa 10:22 **D** will be complete and fair.
10:23 will carry out this **d** throughout
13:6 come like **d** from the Almighty.
14:23 it with the broom of **d**," declares
15:5 They cry loudly over the **d** on
16:4 The **d** will end. The one who
22:4 me because of the **d** brought
30:28 the nations with a sieve of **d**,
34:2 He has claimed them for **d**.
34:5 on the people I've claimed for **d**.
34:11 and the plumb line of **d** over it.
43:28 I will claim Jacob for **d**.
47:11 **D** will overtake you suddenly.
51:19 Violence, **d**, famine, and war
54:14 You will be far from **d**,
54:16 created destroyers to bring **d**.
59:7 Ruin and **d** are on their
60:18 and **d** within your borders.
Jer 4:6 widespread **d** from the north.
6:1 widespread **d** are coming from
6:7 Violence and **d** can be heard in
7:6 that lead you to your own **d**.
14:16 them the **d** that they deserve.
14:17 people will suffer massive **d**.
17:16 not longed for the day of **d**.
20:8 and shout, "Violence and **d**!"
46:21 The day of **d** is coming.
48:2 in Heshbon will plan Moab's **d**.
48:3 "Looting and great **d**!"
48:5 heard the distressful cry of **d**.
48:16 "Moab's **d** is coming near;
50:22 battle and great **d** fills the land.
51:54 Sounds of terrible **d** are heard
Lam 2:11 on the ground because of the **d**
3:47 so have devastation and **d**.
Eze 7:7 **D** is coming to you,
7:10 **D** is coming! Wrongdoing has
21:31 people who are skilled in **d**.
32:9 the news of your **d** among
Dan 8:24 He will cause astounding **d**
9:27 that cause **d** until those time
11:31 disgusting thing that causes **d**.
12:11 thing that causes **d** is set up,
Joe 1:15 come like **d** from the Almighty.
Amo 9:10 "**D** will not catch up to us or run
Jnh 4:2 to reconsider your threats of **d**.
Hab 1:3 **D** and violence are in front of
2:17 and the **d** done to the animals
Zec 14:11 will never be threatened with **d**.
Mat 7:13 road that lead to **d** are wide.
24:15 that will cause **d** will stand
Mar 13:14 will cause **d** standing where
Rom 2:12 will still be condemned to **d**.
9:22 because they are headed for **d**?
Gal 6:8 you will harvest **d**.
1Th 5:3 **d** will suddenly strike them.
2Th 2:3 sin, the man of **d**, is revealed.

1Ti 6:9 drown them in **d** and ruin.
2Pe 2:1 will bring themselves swift **d**.
2:3 and their **d** is not asleep.
Rev 17:8 bottomless pit and go to its **d**.
17:11 seven kings and goes to its **d**.

destructive (14)

Psa 52:4 You love every **d** accusation,
57:1 wings until **d** storms pass by.
137:8 You **d** people of Babylon,
Isa 1:4 of evildoers and **d** children.
28:2 He is like a hailstorm, a **d** wind.
Jer 51:1 I will stir up a **d** wind against
51:25 you, Babylon, you **d** mountain.
Eze 5:16 When I shoot my **d** arrows of
Dan 8:13 burnt offering, the **d** rebellion,
9:26 the end of the **d** war that has
Hos 12:1 They are very violent and **d**.
Amo 3:10 violent and **d** acts don't know
Heb 12:29 After all, our God is a **d** fire.
2Pe 2:1 bring in their own **d** teachings.

detail (6)

2Sm 23:5 with every **d** arranged and
Ezr 7:23 must be carried out in **d**
Est 5:11 Haman began to relate in **d**
6:13 Haman began to relate in **d** to
Jon 5:39 You study the Scriptures in **d**
Heb 9:5 things in **d** isn't possible now.)

detailed (1)

2Ki 16:10 of the altar and a set of **d** plans.

details (5)

2Sm 11:18 to David all the **d** of the battle.
1Ch 28:19 He made all the **d** of the plan
Job 15:2 person answer with endless **d**
Act 19:18 spells and told all the **d**.
Col 2:18 gives endless **d** of the visions

detergent (1)

Jer 2:22 Even if you wash with **d** and

determination (2)

Neh 4:6 The people worked with **d**.
Isa 63:15 Where is your **d** and might?

determine (14)

Lev 27:8 The priest will **d** the amount
27:12 The priest will **d** what its value
27:14 the priest will **d** what its value
1Ki 7:47 No one tried to **d** how much the
2Ch 4:18 that no one tried to **d** how much
Ezr 5:17 to **d** whether King Cyrus
Est 9:24 lot) thrown ⌊in order to **d** when⌋
Ecc 2:3 I was able to **d** whether this
Rom 12:2 be able to **d** what God really
14:4 The Lord will **d** whether his
1Co 3:13 That fire will **d** what kind of
11:28 individuals must **d** whether
Eph 5:10 **D** which things please the Lord.
Php 1:10 That way you will be able to **d**

determined (44)

Dtr 21:3 When it has been **d** which city
Jos 14:2 tribes was **d** by drawing lots
17:12 since the Canaanites were **d**
Jdg 1:27 The Canaanites were **d** to live
1:35 The Amorites were **d** to live at
Rut 1:18 Naomi saw that Ruth was **d**
1Sm 20:33 his father was **d** to kill David.
1Ki 20:40 You have **d** it yourself."
2Ki 12:17 also **d** to attack Jerusalem.
19:31 The LORD is **d** to do this.'
1Ch 28:7 forever if he will remain **d**
28:13 He **d** the divisions of priests
2Ch 11:16 every tribe of Israel who were **d**
27:6 powerful because he was **d**
Ezr 7:10 Ezra was **d** to study the
Neh 11:23 orders that **d** which duties they
Job 14:5 of his months are **d** by you,
38:5 Who **d** its dimensions?
Psa 17:3 I have **d** that my mouth will not
74:17 You **d** all the boundaries of the
Pro 8:28 when he **d** the currents in the
Isa 9:7 LORD of Armies is **d** to do this!
10:23 the world as he has **d**.
14:26 This is the plan **d** for the whole
28:22 LORD of Armies has finally **d**
37:32 LORD of Armies is **d** to do this.'
41:4 Who has **d** the course of
Jer 42:15 Suppose you're **d** to go to
44:12 those who were **d** to go to live
Dan 1:10 The king **d** what you should
8:19 the end time has been **d**.
9:26 war that has been **d**.
9:27 It has been **d** that this will
11:28 He will be **d** to fight against the
Hos 5:11 its people are **d** to chase idols.
11:7 My people are **d** to turn away
Nah 2:7 The LORD has **d**: "It will be
Luk 9:51 So he was **d** to go to
Act 1:7 the Father has **d** by his own
1:23 The disciples **d** that two men
2:23 that God had **d** in advance.
20:22 "I am **d** to go to Jerusalem now.
1Th 2:8 about you that we were **d**
Jas 4:2 You're **d** to have things,

determines (4)

1Sm 17:47 because the LORD **d** every
Psa 16:5 are the one who **d** my destiny.
147:4 He **d** the number of stars.
Pro 16:33 but the LORD **d** every outcome.

determining (1)

Exo 28:30 over his heart the ⌊means for **d**

detestable (26)

Dtr 7:26 Consider it **d** and disgusting.
2Ch 15:8 put away the **d** idols from all
Isa 66:3 and their souls delight in **d**
Jer 7:30 "They set up their **d** idols in the
16:18 of their **d** and disgusting idols."
32:34 They set up their **d** idols in the
44:4 not to do these **d** things that
44:22 wicked and **d** things you did.
Eze 5:9 Because of all the **d** things that
5:11 your disgusting and **d** things,
7:3 you for all the **d** things that you
7:4 and for the **d** things you have
7:8 you for all the **d** things that you
7:9 and for the **d** things that you
7:20 and **d** statues ⌊of false
11:18 disgusting and **d** things that are
11:21 minds are set on following **d**
20:7 I said to them, "Get rid of the **d**
20:8 Not one of them got rid of the **d**
20:30 Will you chase their **d** idols
37:23 with their **d** things,
Tit 1:16 They are **d**, disobedient,
Rev 17:4 holding a gold cup filled with **d**
17:5 the Mother of Prostitutes and **D**
21:8 and **d** people, murderers,
21:27 no one who does anything **d**,

Deuel (5)

Num 1:14 Eliasaph, son of **D**,
2:14 of Gad is Eliasaph, son of **D**.
7:42 of Gad, Eliasaph, son of **D**,
7:47 gifts from Eliasaph, son of **D**.
10:20 Eliasaph, son of **D**,

devastate (1)

Jer 19:8 I will **d** this city. It will become

devastated (7)

Psa 35:12 I am **d** because they pay me
38:8 I am numb and completely **d**.
Isa 1:7 "Your country is **d**.
1:7 Your fields are **d** and taken
Jer 12:11 **D**, it mourns in my presence.
Lam 1:13 He has left me **d**. He has made
1:16 My children are **d** because my

devastating (1)

Nah 1:8 end to Nineveh with a **d** flood.

devastation (3)

Psa 46:8 the **d** he has brought to the
Lam 3:47 so have **d** and destruction.
Zep 1:15 a day of **d** and desolation,

develop (3)

Mar 4:17 But they don't **d** any roots.
Luk 8:13 but they don't **d** any roots.
Heb 3:12 none of you ever **d** a wicked,

developed (6)

Lev 13:20 skin disease has **d** in the boil.
13:25 infectious skin disease has **d**
13:39 a rash has **d** on the skin.
Num 12:12 baby that's not completely **d**."
2Sm 13:15 Now, Amnon **d** an intense
Eze 16:7 Your breasts **d**, and your hair

developing (2)

Lev 13:42 disease is **d** in those places.
Luk 1:35 Therefore, the holy child **d**

develops (2)

Lev 13:12 If skin disease **d** and covers
14:43 If the mildew **d** again in the

devil (37)

Mat 4:1 desert to be tempted by the **d**.
4:5 Then the **d** took him into the
4:8 Once more the **d** took him to a
4:9 The **d** said to him,
4:11 Then the **d** left him,
13:39 who planted them is the **d**.
25:41 for the **d** and his angels!
Luk 4:2 where he was tempted by the **d**
4:3 The **d** said to him,
4:5 The **d** took him to a high place
4:6 The **d** said to him,
4:9 Then the **d** took him into
4:13 After the **d** had finished
4:13 the **d** left him until another time.
8:12 but then the **d** comes.
Jon 6:70 Yet, one of you is a **d**."
8:44 come from your father, the **d**,
8:44 The **d** was a murderer from the
13:2 the **d** had already put the idea
Act 13:10 and schemes, you son of the **d**!
2Co 6:15 Can Christ agree with the **d**?
Eph 4:27 Don't give the **d** any opportunity
1Ti 3:6 like the **d** and be condemned.
3:7 insults that the **d** sets as traps
Heb 2:14 over death (that is, the **d**).
Jas 4:7 Resist the **d**, and he will run
1Pe 5:8 Your opponent the **d** is
1Jn 3:8 a sinful life belongs to the **d**,
3:8 because the **d** has been
3:8 to destroy what the **d** does.
Jud 1:9 Michael argued with the **d**,
1:9 down a judgment against the **d**.
Rev 2:10 The **d** is going to throw some
12:9 named **D** and Satan,
12:12 because the **D** has come down
20:2 named **D** and Satan.
20:10 The **d**, who deceived them,

devilish (1)

Psa 41:8 "A **d** disease has attached

devil's (4)

Act 10:38 who was under the **d** power.
Eph 6:11 a stand against the **d** strategies
2Ti 2:26 from the **d** snare so that they
1Jn 3:10 from the **d** children.

devious (17)

Dtr 32:5 They are **d** and scheming.
32:20 They are **d** people,
2Sm 22:27 ⌊In dealing⌋ with **d** people you
Psa 18:26 ⌊In dealing⌋ with **d** people you
101:4 keep far away from **d** minds.
Pro 2:12 from the person who speaks **d**
2:15 are crooked. Their ways are **d**.
3:32 The **d** person is disgusting to
10:31 but a **d** tongue will be cut off.
10:32 mouths of wicked people are **d**.
11:20 **D** people are disgusting to the
14:2 but a person who is **d** in his
16:28 A **d** person spreads quarrels.
16:30 his eye is plotting something **d**.
17:20 and one with a **d** tongue

Pro 22:5 A **d** person has thorns and
Jer 11:15 they do so many **d** things?

deviousness (1)

Pro 2:14 who find joy in the **d** of evil.

devise (4)

Psa 2:1 their people **d** useless plots?
Isa 32:7 They **d** wicked plans in order
Jer 15:3 "I will **d** four ways to punish
Act 4:25 their people **d** useless plots?

devised (3)

Jos 9:4 they **d** a scheme. They posed
2Sm 14:13 "Why have you **d** something
Dan 11:25 of the schemes **d** against him.

devises (1)

Pro 6:14 He **d** evil all the time with a

devising (1)

Pro 6:18 a mind **d** wicked plans,

devote (8)

2Ch 31:4 that they could **d** themselves
Act 6:4 However, we will **d** ourselves
Rom 12:7 then **d** yourself to serving.
12:7 **d** yourself to teaching.
12:8 If it is encouraging others, **d**
1Co 7:5 for a set time to **d** yourselves
1Ti 4:15 **D** your life to them so that
2Ti 4:5 **D** yourself completely to your

devoted (20)

2Ki 10:16 See how **d** I am to the LORD."
Isa 26:11 They will see how **d** your
Eze 14:3 of man, these people are **d**
14:4 Suppose an Israelite is **d** to
44:29 Everything in Israel that is **d** to
Mat 6:24 or he will be **d** to the first and
Luk 16:13 or he will be **d** to the first and
Act 1:14 purpose as they **d** themselves
2:42 The disciples were **d** to the
8:13 he became **d** to Philip.
12:1 About that time King Herod **d**
18:5 Paul **d** all his time to teaching
22:3 I was as **d** to God as all of you
Rom 10:2 that they are deeply **d** to God,
12:10 Be **d** to each other like a loving
1Co 16:15 This family has **d** itself to
Gal 4:17 the Good News⌋ are **d** to you,
4:17 that you will be **d** only to them.
Tit 1:9 He must be **d** to the trustworthy
1Pe 3:13 Who will harm you if you are **d**

devoting (1)

Eze 14:7 Israel deserts me by **d** himself

devotion (20)

2Ch 32:32 including his **d** to God,
35:26 about Josiah — including his **d**
Job 15:4 God⌋ and diminish **d** to God.
Psa 69:9 Indeed, **d** for your house has
78:72 With unselfish **d** David
119:139 My **d** ⌊for your words⌋
Sos 8:6 **D** is as unyielding as the grave.
Jer 12:3 see me and test my **d** to you.
Jon 2:17 "**D** for your house will consume
Act 26:7 worship with intense **d** day
Rom 12:11 be lazy in showing your **d**.
1Co 7:35 you how to live a noble life of **d**
2Co 7:11 look at how much **d** it caused
7:12 I wanted you to show your **d**
11:3 sincere and pure **d** to Christ.
Gal 4:18 (**D** to a good cause is always
1Th 4:3 sin as a mark of your **d** to him.
2Th 2:13 through a life of spiritual **d**
1Ti 5:11 stronger than their **d** to Christ,
Heb 5:7 heard because of his **d** to God.

devour (30)

Lev 26:38 The land of their enemies will **d**
Num 14:9 We will **d** them like bread.
24:8 He will **d** nations that are his
2Ch 7:13 to **d** the countryside,
Psa 14:4 those who **d** my people as if
21:9 in his anger. Fire will **d** them.
53:4 those who **d** my people as if
80:13 graze on it. Wild animals **d** it.
Isa 9:12 They will **d** Israel with open
10:17 He will burn up and **d** the
51:8 Worms will **d** them like wool.
66:17 go into the garden and **d** pork,
Jer 5:17 They will **d** your harvest and
5:17 They will **d** your sons and your
5:17 They will **d** your flocks and
5:17 They will **d** your grapevines
8:16 They are coming to **d** the land
12:9 and bring them to **d** it.
15:3 and animals to **d** and destroy.
46:10 His sword will **d** until it has
50:17 The first to **d** them was the
Eze 36:13 People say that you **d** your
36:14 So you will no longer **d** your
Dan 7:23 It will **d**, trample, and crush the
Hos 2:12 and wild animals will **d** them.
5:7 Moon ⌊Festivals⌋ will **d** them
13:8 Like a lion I will **d** you.
Zec 11:9 those that are left **d** each other."
1Pe 5:8 as he looks for someone to **d**.
Rev 12:4 that it could **d** her child when

devoured (21)

2Sm 18:8 That day the woods **d** more
Job 20:26 is left in his tent will be **d**.
Psa 79:7 They have **d** Jacob.
105:35 They **d** all the plants in the
105:35 They **d** the crops in the fields.
Isa 5:5 its hedge so that it can be **d**
49:19 Those who **d** you will be long
Jer 2:3 All who **d** it became guilty,
10:25 They have **d** the descendants
10:25 They have **d** them completely.
15:16 were found, and I **d** them.
30:16 who devours you will be **d**,
51:34 of Babylon has **d** us.
Eze 5:12 in plagues and be **d** in famines.
7:15 Whoever is in the city will be **d**
Dan 7:7 It **d** and crushed its victims and
7:19 It **d** and crushed its victims,
Amo 4:9 repeatedly **d** your gardens,
Mat 13:4 and birds came and **d** them.
Mar 4:4 and birds came and **d** them.
Luk 8:5 and were **d** by birds.

devouring (4)

Psa 14:4 people as if they were **d** food,
50:3 A **d** fire is in front of him and a
53:4 people as if they were **d** food,
Isa 30:27 His tongue is like a **d** flame.

devours (6)

Gen 49:27 In the morning he **d** his prey.
Num 13:32 is one that **d** those who live
Pro 21:20 wise person, but a fool **d** them.
30:14 **d** oppressed people from the
Isa 24:6 That is why a curse **d** the earth,
Jer 30:16 That is why everyone who **d**

devout (10)

1Ki 18:3 Obadiah was a **d** worshiper of
Luk 2:25 lived an honorable and **d** life.
Jon 9:31 he listens to people who are **d**
Act 2:5 **D** Jewish men from every
2:12 All of these **d** men were
8:2 **D** men buried Stephen as they
10:2 everyone in his home were **d**
10:7 servants and a **d** soldier,
13:50 But Jews stirred up **d** women
22:12 He was a **d** person who

dew (35)

Gen 27:28 May God give you **d** from the
27:39 of the earth and the **d** from
Exo 16:13 a layer of **d** around the camp.
16:14 When the **d** was gone,
Num 11:9 When **d** fell on the camp at
Dtr 32:2 Let my words drip like **d**,
33:13 with **d** and deep springs below
33:28 **D** will drip from Israel's skies.
Jdg 6:37 If there is **d** on the wool while
6:39 the ground is covered with **d**."
6:40 the ground was covered with **d**.
2Sm 1:21 may there be no **d** or rain on
17:12 We'll fall on him as **d** falls on
1Ki 17:1 there will be no **d** or rain during
Job 29:19 and **d** will lie on my branches
Psa 110:3 to you in holy splendor like **d**
133:3 It is like **d** on ⌊Mount⌋ Hermon,
133:3 **d** which comes down on Zion's
Pro 3:20 and the skies dropped **d**.
19:12 his favor is like **d** on the grass.
Sos 5:2 My head is wet with **d**,
Isa 18:4 like heavy **d** in the heat of the
26:19 because your **d** is a refreshing
26:19 your dew is a refreshing **d**,
Dan 4:15 Let it get wet with the **d** from
4:23 Let it get wet with the **d** from
4:25 The **d** from the sky will make
4:33 **D** from the sky made his body
5:21 body became wet with **d** from
Hos 6:4 as quickly as the morning **d**.
13:3 **d** that disappears quickly.
14:5 I will be like **d** to the people of
Mic 5:7 among many people like **d** from
Hag 1:10 that the sky has withheld its **d**
Zec 8:12 The sky will produce its **d**.

dewdrops (2)

Job 38:28 Who gave birth to the **d**?
Sos 5:2 my hair with the **d** of night.

dialect (2)

Act 1:19 'Field of Blood' in their **d**.
2:6 to recognize his own **d** when

dialects (1)

Act 2:8 them speaking in our native **d**?

diameter (2)

1Ki 7:23 It was 15 feet in **d**.
2Ch 4:2 It was 15 feet in **d**.

diamond (2)

Jer 17:1 It is engraved with a **d** point on
Eze 3:9 I will make you as hard as a **d**,

Diblah (1)

Eze 6:14 from the desert to **D**.

Diblaim (1)

Hos 1:3 married Gomer, daughter of **D**.

Dibon (9)

Num 21:30 From Heshbon to **D** they all
32:3 "Ataroth, **D**, Jazer, Nimrah,
32:34 of Gad rebuilt the cities of **D**,
Jos 13:9 plateau from Medeba to **D**.
13:17 on the plateau, **D**, Bamoth Baal,
Neh 11:25 in **D** and its villages,
Isa 15:2 The people of **D** go to the
Jer 48:18 "People of **D**, come down from
48:22 **D**, Nebo, Beth Diblathaim,

Dibon Gad (2)

Num 33:45 Iyim and set up camp at **D**.
33:46 They moved from **D** and

Dibri (1)

Lev 24:10 was Shelomith (daughter of **D**,

dice (15)

Job 6:27 Would you also throw **d** for an
Psa 22:18 They throw **d** for my clothing.
Pro 16:33 The **d** are thrown, but the
Isa 34:17 the one who throws **d** for them,
Joe 3:3 They threw **d** for my people.
Oba 1:11 and threw **d** for Jerusalem.
Jnh 1:7 "Let's throw **d** to find out who is
1:7 So they threw **d**, and the dice
1:7 So they threw dice, and the **d**
Nah 3:10 Soldiers tossed **d** for her
Mat 27:35 themselves by throwing **d**.
Mar 15:24 themselves by throwing **d**
Luk 23:34 themselves by throwing **d**.
Jon 19:24 Let's throw **d** to see who will
19:24 They threw **d** for my clothing."

dictate (2)

Jer 36:17 Did Jeremiah **d** it to you?"
Mic 7:3 Powerful people **d** what they

dictated (8)

Jer 36:2 on it everything that I have **d**
36:4 Jeremiah **d** everything that the
36:6 message that you wrote as I **d**.
36:18 "He **d** everything to me,
36:27 and that Jeremiah had **d**,
36:32 As Jeremiah **d**, Baruch wrote
45:1 as Jeremiah **d** them during
Rom 7:6 an old way **d** by written words.

Didymus (3)

Jon 11:16 Thomas, who was called **D**,
20:24 who was called **D**,
21:2 Thomas (called **D**),

die (431)

Gen 2:17 you will certainly **d**."
3:3 If you do, you will **d**!'"
3:4 "You certainly won't **d**!"
6:17 Everything on earth will **d**.
15:2 I'm going to **d** without children,
15:15 But you will **d** in peace and be
19:19 will overtake me, and I'll **d**.
20:3 "You're going to **d** because of
20:7 belong to you are doomed to **d**."
21:16 don't want to watch the boy **d**."
25:32 "I'm about to **d**." Esau said.
27:2 don't know when I'm going to **d**.
27:4 that I will bless you before I **d**."
27:7 of the LORD before I **d**.'
27:46 I might as well **d**."
30:1 "Give me children, or I'll **d**!"
33:13 all the flocks will **d**.
37:35 will mourn for my son until I **d**."
38:11 might **d** like his brothers.
42:20 Then you won't **d**."
42:28 They wanted to **d**.
44:9 If one of us has it, he will **d**,
44:22 leaves him, his father will **d**.'
44:31 the boy isn't ⌊with me⌋, he'll **d**.
45:28 will go and see him before I **d**."
46:4 your eyes ⌊when you **d**⌋."
46:30 still alive, I'm ready to **d**."
47:15 "Do you want us to **d** right in
47:19 Do you want us to **d** right in
47:29 Israel was about to **d**.
48:21 "Now I'm about to **d**,
50:5 He said, "I'm about to **d**.
50:24 to his brothers, "I'm about to **d**.
Exo 7:18 The fish in the Nile will **d**,
9:4 to the Israelites will **d**.'"
9:19 and not brought in will **d** when
10:28 The day I do, you will **d**."
11:5 firstborn son in Egypt will **d**,
14:11 bring us out into the desert to **d**
14:12 than to **d** in the desert!"
16:3 the LORD had let us **d** in Egypt!
17:3 and our livestock **d** of thirst?"
19:21 or many of them will **d**.
20:19 let God speak to us, or we'll **d**!"
28:35 holy place so that he won't **d**.
28:43 will be blameless and won't **d**.
30:20 wash so that they will not **d**.
30:21 and feet so that they will not **d**.
Lev 8:35 Then you will not **d**.
10:6 If you do, you will **d** and the
10:7 meeting or else you, too, will **d**,
10:9 tent of meeting, or you will **d**.
15:31 Otherwise, they will **d** because
16:2 of mercy on the ark, he will **d**,
16:13 so that he will not **d**.
20:9 or mother and deserves to **d**.
20:11 They deserve to **d**.
20:12 thing and deserve to **d**.
20:13 They deserve to **d**.
20:16 They deserve to **d**.
20:20 They will **d** without children.
20:27 because they deserve to **d**."
24:16 the LORD's name must **d**.
Num 4:15 the holy things, or they will **d**.
4:19 they won't **d** when they come
Num 4:20 for a moment, or they will **d**."
14:3 just to have us **d** in battle?
14:29 complained about me will **d**.
14:35 this desert. Here they will **d**!"
14:43 and you will **d** in battle.
16:29 If these men **d** like all other
16:29 like all other people — if they **d**
16:40 Everyone else will **d** like Korah
17:10 about me, and they won't **d**."
17:12 "Now we're going to **d**!
17:13 near the LORD's tent will **d**!
17:13 Are we all going to **d**?"
18:3 or they will **d**, and you will die,
18:3 will die, and you will **d**, too.
18:7 place to do this work⌋ must **d**."
18:22 of their sin and **d**.
18:32 the Israelites, and you won't **d**."
20:4 us and our animals **d** here?
20:26 Then Aaron will **d** there and
21:5 us leave Egypt — just to let us **d**
23:10 Let me **d** the death of innocent
26:11 descendants of Korah didn't **d**.)
26:65 "They must all **d** in the desert."
27:4 name be allowed to **d** out
35:12 murder will not have to **d** until
Dtr 4:22 I'm going to **d** in this land and
5:25 Why should we **d**?
5:25 of the LORD our God, we'll **d**!
7:20 among them until they all **d**.
9:28 to let them **d** in the desert."
17:12 that person must **d**.
18:16 fire again. If we do, we'll **d**!"
18:20 the name of other gods must **d**."
19:12 avenge the death. He must **d**.
20:5 you might **d** in battle,
20:6 you might **d** in battle,
20:7 you might **d** in battle,
22:22 man and the woman must **d**.
22:24 The girl must **d** because she
22:24 The man must **d** because he
22:25 then only the man must **d**.
22:26 for which she deserves to **d**.
24:7 another Israelite must **d**.
24:7 The kidnapper must **d**,
25:6 his name won't **d** out in Israel.
28:22 will pursue you until you **d**.
31:27 rebellious will you be after I **d**?
31:29 I know that after I **d** you will
32:25 women alike will **d** as well as
32:50 you will **d** and join your
33:6 of Reuben live and not **d** out,
Jos 23:14 because I will soon **d** like
Jdg 5:31 all your enemies **d** like that,
6:23 Don't be afraid. You will not **d**."
6:30 He must **d**. He has torn down
13:22 "We will certainly **d** because
15:18 But now I'll **d** from thirst and fall
16:30 "Let me **d** with the Philistines,"
Rut 1:17 Wherever you **d**, I will die,
1:17 Wherever you die, I will **d**,
1Sm 2:33 And all your descendants will **d**
2:34 Both of them will **d** on the
5:12 The people who didn't **d** were
12:19 for us so that we will not **d**.
14:39 ⌊who did it⌋, he must **d**."
14:43 And for that I am to **d**?"
14:44 are in this curse if you do not **d**,
14:45 "Should Jonathan **d** after he
20:2 You're not going to **d**!
20:14 And even when I **d**,
22:16 entire family are going to **d**."
26:10 come when he'll **d** ⌊naturally⌋,
2Sm 3:29 work a spindle, who **d** in battle,
3:33 Should Abner **d** like a godless
11:15 he'll be struck down and **d**."
12:5 did this certainly deserves to **d**!
12:13 away your sin; you will not **d**.
12:14 son that is born to you must **d**."
14:14 We are all going to **d**;
18:3 about us, and if half of us **d**,
19:23 "You won't **d**," and the king
19:37 let me go back so that I can **d**
1Ki 1:52 ⌊anything⌋ wrong, he will **d**."
2:1 When David was about to **d**,
2:26 You deserve to **d**, but I won't
2:30 Joab answered, "I'll **d** here."
1Ki 2:37 can be certain that you will **d**.
2:42 be certain that you would **d**?
13:31 he said to his sons, "When I **d**,
14:12 foot in the city the child will **d**.
17:12 that we can eat it and then **d**."
19:4 a broom plant and wanted to **d**.
2Ki 1:4 Instead, you will **d** there."'
1:6 Instead, you will **d** there."'
1:16 Instead, you will **d** there."
7:3 we sitting here waiting to **d**?
7:4 is also there, and we'll still **d**.
7:4 But if we stay here, we'll **d**.
7:4 if they kill us, we'll **d** anyway."
8:10 that he is actually going to **d**."
9:8 Ahab's entire family will **d**.
18:32 Don't **d**! Don't listen to
20:1 sick and was about to **d**.
20:1 because you're about to **d**.
2Ch 21:20 No one was sorry to see him **d**.
32:11 you to **d** from hunger
32:24 sick and was about to **d**.
Ezr 7:26 or be sentenced to **d**.
Est 4:14 you and your relatives will **d**.
4:16 a royal decree. If I **d**, I die."
4:16 a royal decree. If I die, I **d**."
Job 2:9 Curse God and **d**!"
3:11 "Why didn't I **d** as soon as I
4:11 The old lions **d** without any
4:21 Won't they **d** without wisdom?
12:2 people, and when you **d**,
12:2 when you die, wisdom will **d**.
13:19 I'd be silent and **d**.
29:18 'I may **d** in my own house,
31:19 If I have seen anyone **d**
34:15 living beings would **d** together,
34:20 They **d** suddenly in the middle
36:12 Death⌋ and **d** like those who
36:14 They **d** while they're young,
Psa 2:12 become angry and you will **d**
9:3 and **d** in your presence.
13:3 up my eyes, or else I will **d**
41:5 about me: "When will he **d**,
49:10 can see that wise people **d**,
49:12 They are like animals that **d**.
49:20 They are like animals that **d**.
73:27 who are far from you will **d**.
82:7 You will certainly **d** like
83:17 Let them **d** in disgrace
104:29 and they **d** and return to dust.
105:29 and caused their fish to **d**.
118:17 I will not **d**, but I will live and
Pro 5:23 He will **d** for his lack of
10:21 but stubborn fools **d** because
11:10 When wicked people **d**,
15:10 who hates a warning will **d**.
19:9 One who tells lies will **d**.
21:28 A lying witness will **d**,
23:13 If you spank him, he will not **d**.
28:28 When they **d**, righteous people
30:7 keep them from me before I **d**:
Ecc 2:16 wise person and the fool will **d**.
3:2 time to be born and a time to **d**,
7:1 and the day you **d** is better than
7:15 Righteous people **d** in spite of
7:17 Why should you **d** before your
9:5 living know that they will **d**,
Isa 3:25 your warriors will **d** in combat.
3:25 mighty men will **d** in battle.
22:2 Your dead didn't **d** in battle.
22:13 tomorrow we're going to **d**."
22:14 even when you **d**," says
22:18 There you will **d**. There your
31:3 Both will **d** together.
38:1 sick and was about to **d**.
38:1 because you're about to **d**.
50:2 and people **d** of thirst.
51:6 who live there will **d** like flies.
51:12 who must **d**, of humans,
51:14 They will not **d** in prison.
57:1 Righteous people **d**,
59:5 who eat their eggs will **d**.
65:23 birth to children who **d** young,
66:24 worms that eat them will not **d**.
Jer 6:15 So they will **d** with those who
6:15 they will die with those who **d**.
6:21 and their friends will **d**.

Jer 8:3 will want to **d** rather than live
8:12 So they will **d** with those who
8:12 they will die with those who **d**.
8:14 the fortified cities and **d** there.
8:14 God has condemned us to **d**.
11:22 The young men will **d** because
11:22 Their sons and daughters will **d**
15:2 who are destined to **d** will die.
15:2 who are destined to die will **d**.
15:2 Those who are destined to **d** in
15:2 to die in wars will **d** in wars.
15:2 Those who are destined to **d** in
15:2 in famines will **d** in famines.
15:2 Those who are destined to **d** in
15:2 in captivity will **d** in captivity.'
15:9 She will **d**, ashamed and
16:4 They will **d** horrible deaths.
16:6 "Old and young alike will **d** in
20:6 and you will **d** there.
21:6 They will **d** from a terrible
21:9 who live in this city will **d**
22:12 He will **d** in the place where he
22:26 but you will **d** there.
26:8 him and said, "You must **d**!
26:11 "This man is condemned to **d**
26:16 should not be condemned to **d**.
27:10 I'll scatter you, and you will **d**.
27:13 you and your people **d** in wars,
27:15 you and the prophets will **d**."
28:16 You will **d** this year because
31:30 But each person will **d** for his
34:4 You will not **d** in war.
34:5 You will **d** peacefully.
34:17 "I will free you to **d** in wars,
37:20 house, or I will **d** there."
38:2 stay in this city will **d** in wars,
38:24 this conversation, or you will **d**.
38:26 to Jonathan's house to **d** there.'"
39:18 You will not **d** in war.
42:16 and you will **d** there.
42:17 and live in Egypt will **d** in wars,
42:22 to know that you will **d** in wars,
43:11 those who are supposed to **d**.
44:12 They will **d** in Egypt.
44:12 will **d** in wars or be brought to
44:27 the people from Judah will **d**
48:46 You people of Chemosh will **d**.
49:26 is why its young men will **d**
50:30 is why their young men will **d**
51:6 You shouldn't **d** because of
Eze 3:18 wicked people will surely **d**,
3:18 these wicked people will **d**
3:19 Then they will **d** because of
3:20 them stumble, and they will **d**.
3:20 they will **d** because of their sin,
5:12 One-third of you will **d** in
5:12 Another third will **d** in battles
6:11 So they will **d** in wars,
6:12 who are near will **d** in wars,
6:12 has escaped will **d** in famines.
7:15 is in a field will **d** in battle.
11:10 You will **d** in battle.
12:13 And that's where he'll **d**.
13:19 kill people who shouldn't **d**,
17:16 of Judah will **d** in Babylonia.
17:16 He will **d** in the country of the
17:21 of your troops will **d** in battle.
18:4 The person who sins will **d**.
18:13 So he must **d**, and he will be
18:17 He won't **d** for his father's sins.
18:18 So the father will **d** because of
18:20 The person who sins will **d**.
18:21 certainly live. He will not **d**.
18:23 don't want wicked people to **d**."
18:24 He will **d** because of them.
18:26 and does evil things, he will **d**.
18:26 He will **d** because of the evil
18:28 certainly live. He will not **d**.
18:31 Why do you want to **d**,
18:32 I don't want anyone to **d**,"
21:15 will sink and many will **d**.
21:32 You will **d** in the land.
24:21 you left behind will **d** in battle.
25:13 People will **d** in battle.
26:6 on the mainland will **d** in battle.
28:8 and you will **d** a violent death

Eze 28:10 You will **d** at the hands of
30:5 promised land will **d** in battle.
30:6 All Egypt's allies will **d**.
30:6 People will **d** in war from
30:17 and Bubastis will **d** in battle,
31:14 Every tree is going to **d** and go
32:10 When you **d**, all of them will
33:6 that watchman must **d** because
33:8 you will certainly **d**,' and you
33:8 That wicked person will **d**
33:9 then he will **d** because of his
33:11 I don't want wicked people to **d**.
33:11 Do you want to **d**, people of
33:13 He will **d** because of the evil
33:14 person that he will certainly **d**.
33:15 certainly live. He will not **d**.
33:18 he will **d** because of it.
33:27 and caves will **d** from plagues.
39:4 You will **d** on the mountains of
39:5 You will **d** in the open field
Dan 11:26 and many will **d** in battle.
Hos 2:3 and she will **d** of thirst.
7:7 All their kings **d** in battle,
7:16 Their officials will **d** in battle
13:1 Baal, so they must **d**.
Amo 1:8 rest of the Philistines will **d**.
2:2 Moab will **d** during the noise of
6:9 left in one house, they will **d**.
7:17 and you will **d** in an unclean
Jnh 1:6 will notice us, and we won't **d**."
1:14 don't let us **d** for taking this
3:9 anger so that we won't **d**."
4:8 He wanted to **d**. So he said, "I'd
4:9 so angry that I want to **d**."
Nah 1:12 they will be cut down and **d**.
Hab 1:12 We will not **d**! O LORD, you
Zep 2:12 you will also **d** by my sword."
Zec 11:9 Let those that are dying **d**.
13:8 two-thirds will be cut off and **d**.
Mat 8:25 Save us! We're going to **d**!"
16:28 here will not **d** until they see
26:24 The Son of Man is going to **d**
26:35 "Even if I have to **d** with you,
Mar 3:4 back his health or to let him **d**?"
4:38 you care that we're going to **d**?"
9:1 here will not **d** until they see
9:48 that eat the body never **d**,
14:21 The Son of Man is going to **d**
14:31 "Even if I have to **d** with you,
Luk 2:26 told him that he wouldn't **d** until
8:24 We're going to **d**!" Then he got
9:27 here will not **d** until they see
13:3 act, then you, too, will all **d**.
13:5 act, then you, too, will all **d**."
13:33 prophet to **d** outside Jerusalem.
20:36 nor **d** anymore. They are the
22:22 The Son of Man is going to **d**
22:33 with you and to **d** with you."
Jon 3:16 who believes in him will not **d**
4:47 his son who was about to **d**.
6:50 so that whoever eats it won't **d**.
8:21 But you will **d** because of your
8:24 reason I told you that you'll **d**
8:24 you'll **d** because of your sins."
11:16 can **d** with Jesus."
11:25 in me will live even if they **d**.
11:26 believes in me will never **d**.
11:50 It is better for one man to **d** for
11:51 prophesied that Jesus would **d**
11:52 that Jesus wouldn't **d** merely
11:52 but that Jesus would **d** to bring
12:33 how he was going to **d**.
18:14 have one man **d** for the people.
18:32 how he would **d** came true.
19:7 and by that law he must **d**
21:23 **d** spread among Jesus'
21:23 didn't say that he wouldn't **d**.
Act 7:19 where they would **d**.
13:41 Be amazed and **d**!
17:3 suffer, **d**, and come back to life,
21:13 in Jerusalem but also to **d** there
23:29 for which he deserved to **d**
26:31 for which he deserves to **d**
28:18 for which I deserved to **d**.
Rom 1:32 do such things deserve to **d**,
5:7 Finding someone who would **d**

Rom 5:7 would have the courage to **d**
6:9 will never **d** again.
8:13 you are going to **d**.
14:7 we don't **d** to honor ourselves.
14:8 and if we **d**, we honor the Lord.
14:8 So whether we live or **d**,
1Co 4:9 like people condemned to **d**.
9:15 I would rather **d** than have
15:32 tomorrow we're going to **d**!"
15:51 Not all of us will **d**,
2Co 7:3 that we will live and **d** together.
Php 1:20 whether I live or **d**.
1:21 and when I **d** I'll have even
1Ti 6:16 is the only one who cannot **d**.
Heb 7:8 tenth of everything, but they **d**.
9:27 People **d** once, and after that
Jas 1:11 they are busy, they will **d**.
2Pe 1:14 I know that I will **d** soon.
1:15 these things after I **d**.
Rev 3:2 are left which are about to **d**.
9:6 They will long to **d**,
14:13 From now on those who **d**

died (309)

Gen 5:5 a total of 930 years; then he **d**.
5:8 a total of 912 years; then he **d**.
5:11 a total of 905 years; then he **d**.
5:14 a total of 910 years; then he **d**.
5:17 a total of 895 years; then he **d**.
5:20 a total of 962 years; then he **d**.
5:27 a total of 969 years; then he **d**.
5:31 a total of 777 years; then he **d**.
7:21 that crawls on the earth **d**,
7:22 breathing creature) **d**.
9:29 a total of 950 years; then he **d**.
11:28 Haran **d** in Ur of the Chaldeans,
11:32 lived 205 years and **d** in Haran.
23:2 She **d** in Kiriath Arba (that is,
25:8 and **d** at a very old age.
25:11 After Abraham **d**, God blessed
25:17 he took his last breath and **d**.
35:8 Rebekah's nurse Deborah **d**
35:19 Rachel **d** and was buried on
35:29 he took his last breath and **d**.
36:33 After Bela **d**, Jobab, son of
36:34 After Jobab **d**, Husham from the
36:35 After Husham **d**, Hadad, son of
36:36 After Hadad **d**, Samlah from
36:37 After Samlah **d**, Shaul from
36:38 After Shaul **d**, Baal Hanan,
36:39 Baal Hanan, son of Achbor, **d**,
38:12 wife, the daughter of Shua, **d**.
46:12 (Er and Onan had **d** in Canaan.)
48:7 Rachel **d** in Canaan when we
50:16 "Before your father **d**,
50:26 Joseph **d** when he was 110
Exo 1:6 and that entire generation **d**.
2:23 the king of Egypt **d**.
7:21 The fish in the Nile **d**,
8:13 The frogs **d** in the houses,
9:6 livestock of the Egyptians **d**,
9:6 of the Israelites' animals **d**.
9:7 of the Israelites' animals had **d**.
12:30 in every house someone had **d**.
32:28 that day about 3,000 people **d**.
33:4 acted as if someone had **d**.
Lev 10:2 and they **d** in the presence of
16:1 the LORD's presence and **d**.
21:1 of your relatives who has **d**.
Num 3:4 Nadab and Abihu **d** in the
11:2 and the fire **d** down.
14:2 "If only we had **d** in Egypt or
14:36 sent to explore the land **d**
14:37 They **d** because they had
14:39 as if someone had **d**.
16:48 between those who had **d**
16:49 Still, 14,700 **d** from the plague
16:49 who had **d** because of Korah.
19:16 was killed or has **d** naturally
19:18 killed or who has **d** naturally.
20:1 Miriam **d** and was buried there.
20:3 "If only we had **d** when the
20:3 died when the other Israelites **d**
20:28 Aaron **d** there on top of the
20:29 saw that Aaron had **d**,
21:6 and many of the Israelites **d**.

Num 21:30 Heshbon to Dibon they all **d**.
25:9 people **d** from that plague.
26:10 They and their followers **d**
26:19 but they **d** in Canaan.
26:61 But Nadab and Abihu had **d**
27:3 "Our father **d** in the desert.
27:3 He **d** for his own sin and left no
33:38 He **d** there on the first day of
33:39 old when he **d** on Mount Hor.
Dtr 2:14 soldiers from that generation **d**,
2:16 the last of these soldiers had **d**,
10:6 Aaron **d** there and was buried,
32:50 brother Aaron **d** on Mount Hor.
33:1 with this blessing before he **d**.
34:5 servant Moses **d** in Moab.
34:7 was 120 years old when he **d**.
Jos 5:4 All the soldiers had **d** on the
5:6 their soldiers who left Egypt **d**.
5:6 They **d** because they
8:25 and women from Ai **d** that day.
10:11 More **d** from the hailstones
22:20 wasn't the only one who **d**
24:29 servant Joshua, son of Nun, **d**.
24:33 Aaron's son Eleazar also **d**.
Jdg 1:7 to Jerusalem, where he **d**.
2:8 **d** at the age of 110.
2:19 But after each judge **d**,
2:21 Joshua left behind when he **d**.
3:11 Then Othniel, son of Kenaz, **d**.
4:1 After Ehud **d**, the people of
4:21 into the ground. So Sisera **d**.
8:10 the battle, 120,000 soldiers **d**.
8:32 **d** at a very old age.
8:33 As soon as Gideon **d**,
9:49 in Shechem's Tower **d** too.
9:54 as he said, so Abimelech **d**.
10:2 Tola **d** and was buried in
10:5 Jair **d** and was buried in
12:6 42,000 men from Ephraim **d**.
12:7 Then Jephthah of Gilead **d** and
12:10 When Ibzan **d**, he was buried
12:12 When Elon **d**, he was buried in
12:15 When Abdon **d**, he was buried
15:15 from a donkey that had just **d**.
16:30 Philistines when he **d** than
20:5 my concubine until she **d**.
20:44 from Benjamin who **d** in battle.
Rut 1:3 Naomi's husband Elimelech **d**,
1:5 Mahlon and Chilion **d** as well.
1:8 to our loved ones who have **d**.
2:11 after your husband **d**.
1Sm 4:10 30,000 Israelite foot soldiers **d**.
4:11 sons, Hophni and Phinehas, **d**.
4:18 He broke his neck, and he **d**.
4:21 and her husband ⌊**d**⌋.
15:35 see Saul again before he **d**,
25:1 Samuel **d**, and all Israel
25:38 even more sick, and Nabal **d**.
28:3 Meanwhile, Samuel had **d**,
31:5 on his sword and **d** with him.
31:6 all his men **d** together that day.
2Sm 1:1 After Saul **d** and David returned
1:4 and many of the soldiers **d**.
1:23 separated even when they **d**.
2:23 He fell down there and **d** on the
2:23 Asahel fell and **d** stopped there.
3:27 Abner **d** because he spilled the
4:1 that Abner had **d** in Hebron,
4:10 who told me that Saul had **d**.
6:7 He **d** beside the ark of God.
10:1 Later the king of Ammon **d**,
11:17 fell and **d**—including Uriah the
11:24 Your Majesty's mercenaries **d**.
12:18 On the seventh day the child **d**.
12:21 But as soon as the child **d**,
17:23 Then he hanged himself, **d**,
18:33 I wish I had **d** in your place!
19:10 to rule us, has **d** in battle.
20:3 in confinement until they **d**.
20:10 (He **d** without being stabbed
21:9 All seven **d** together.
24:15 Dan to Beersheba, 70,000 **d**.
1Ki 3:19 That night this woman's son **d**
11:21 had **d**, he said to Pharaoh,
11:40 in Egypt until Solomon **d**.
14:17 of her home, the boy **d**.
1Ki 16:18 over his own head. He **d**
16:22 Tibni **d**, and Omri became
22:35 He **d** that evening.
2Ki 1:1 After Ahab **d**, Moab rebelled
1:17 So Ahaziah **d** as the LORD had
3:5 But when Ahab **d**, the king of
4:20 her lap until noon, when he **d**.
9:27 he got to Megiddo, where he **d**.
13:20 Elisha **d** and was buried.
13:24 King Hazael of Aram **d**,
15:5 lasted until the day the king **d**.
23:34 away to Egypt, where he **d**.
1Ch 1:44 After Bela **d**, Jobab, son of
1:45 After Jobab **d**, Husham from the
1:46 After Husham **d**, Hadad, son of
1:47 After Hadad **d**, Samlah from
1:48 After Samlah **d**, Shaul from
1:49 After Shaul **d**, Baal Hanan,
1:50 After Baal Hanan **d**,
1:51 Then Hadad **d**. The tribal
2:19 After Azubah **d**, Caleb married
2:24 After Hezron **d** in Caleb
2:30 but Seled **d** without children.
2:32 Jether **d** without children.
10:5 he also fell on the sword and **d**.
10:6 and his dynasty **d** together.
10:13 So Saul **d** because of his
13:10 He **d** in God's presence.
19:1 King Nahash of Ammon **d**,
21:14 and 70,000 Israelites **d**.
22:5 ⌊for Solomon⌋ before he **d**.
23:22 Eleazar **d** without having any
24:2 Nadab and Abihu **d** before their
24:2 Abihu died before their father **d**
29:28 He **d** at a very old age.
2Ch 13:20 become sick, and Jeroboam **d**.
14:13 of the Sudanese **d** in battle.
16:13 He **d** in the forty-first year of his
18:34 evening. At sundown he **d**.
21:19 He **d** a painful death.
22:4 After his father **d**, they advised
24:15 had lived out his years, he **d**.
24:15 was 130 years old when he **d**.
24:17 After he **d**, the officials of
24:22 As Zechariah **d**, he said,
24:25 When he **d**, they buried him in
26:21 skin disease until the day he **d**.
32:33 When Hezekiah **d**,
35:24 He **d** and was buried in the
Est 2:7 When her father and mother **d**,
Job 1:19 the young people, and they **d**.
4:7 ⌊ever⌋ **d** ⌊an untimely death⌋?
42:17 Then at a very old age, Job **d**.
Psa 76:5 They **d**. None of the warriors
119:92 I would have **d** in my misery.
143:3 those who have **d** long ago.
Ecc 4:2 who have already **d**,
6:3 honorable burial ⌊after he **d**⌋.
Sos 5:6 I almost **d** when he left.
Isa 6:1 In the year King Uzziah **d**,
14:28 in the year King Ahaz **d**.
53:9 there with the rich when he **d**,
Jer 28:17 So the prophet Hananiah **d** in
52:11 where he stayed until he **d**.
Lam 3:6 like those who **d** a long time
Eze 4:14 eaten an animal that **d** by itself
11:13 Benaiah's son Pelatiah **d**.
24:18 and in the evening my wife **d**.
31:14 earth to join those who have **d**
32:27 the godless warriors who **d**
44:31 or animal that has **d** naturally
Joe 1:12 trees in the orchards, have **d**.
1:12 the joy of these people has **d**
Jnh 4:10 up overnight and **d** overnight.
Mic 4:9 Has your counselor **d**?
Mat 2:15 He stayed there until Herod **d**.
8:32 into the sea and **d** in the water.
9:18 "My daughter just **d**.
22:25 The first married and **d**.
22:26 The second brother also **d**,
22:27 At last the woman **d**.
27:52 people who had **d** came back
Mar 5:35 "Your daughter has **d**.
12:20 and **d** without having children.
12:21 The second married her and **d**
12:22 Last of all, the woman **d**.
Mar 15:37 cried out in a loud voice and **d**.
15:44 if Jesus had already **d**.
Luk 2:36 Her husband had **d** seven
13:4 those 18 people who **d** when
16:22 "One day the beggar **d**,
16:22 man also **d** and was buried.
20:29 and **d** without having children.
20:31 widow, **d**, and left no children.
20:32 Finally, the woman **d**.
23:46 After he said this, he **d**.
Jon 6:49 the manna in the desert and **d**.
6:58 They eventually **d**.
8:52 Abraham **d**, and so did the
8:53 our father Abraham, who **d**?
8:53 The prophets have also **d**.
11:14 them plainly, "Lazarus has **d**,
11:21 my brother would not have **d**.
11:32 my brother would not have **d**."
19:30 Then he bowed his head and **d**.
Act 2:29 that our ancestor David **d**
5:37 He, too, **d**, and all his followers
7:4 After his father **d**, God made
7:15 and he and our ancestors **d**
7:60 After he had said this, he **d**.
9:37 She became sick and **d**.
12:23 eaten by maggots, and he **d**.
13:36 the people of his time, David **d**.
25:19 man named Jesus who had **d**.
Rom 5:6 Christ **d** for ungodly people.
5:8 Christ **d** for us while we were
5:15 If humanity **d** as the result of
6:2 sin is concerned, we have **d**.
6:7 The person who has **d** has
6:8 If we have **d** with Christ,
6:10 When he **d**, he died once and
6:10 When he died, he **d** once and
7:4 you have **d** to the laws in
7:6 But now we have **d** to those
7:10 and I **d**. I found that the
8:34 Christ has **d**, and more
14:9 For this reason Christ **d** and
14:15 Christ **d** for that person.
1Co 8:11 a believer for whom Christ **d**.
10:8 thousand of them **d** on one day.
11:30 a number ⌊of you⌋ have **d**.
15:3 Christ **d** to take away our sins
15:6 still living, but some have **d**.)
15:18 Then those who have **d** as
15:20 person of those who have **d**
2Co 5:14 of the fact that one man has **d**
5:14 Therefore, all people have **d**.
5:15 He **d** for all people so that
5:15 but for the man who **d**
Php 2:27 was so sick that he almost **d**.
2:30 He risked his life and almost **d**
Col 2:20 If you have **d** with Christ to the
3:3 You have **d**, and your life is
1Th 4:13 about those who have **d**.
4:14 We believe that Jesus **d** and
4:14 bring back those who have **d**.
4:15 of those who have already **d**.
5:10 He **d** for us so that,
2Ti 2:11 If we have **d** with him,
2:18 who have **d** have already come
Heb 2:9 Through God's kindness he **d**
3:17 who sinned and **d** in the desert.
7:3 he was born or when he **d**.
7:23 because when a priest **d**
9:16 that the one who made it has **d**.
11:13 All these people **d** having faith.
2Pe 3:4 Ever since our ancestors **d**,
Jud 1:12 As a result, they have **d** twice.
Rev 8:9 that were living in the sea **d**,
8:11 and many people **d** from this
16:3 every living thing in the sea **d**.

dies (50)

Gen 27:10 he will bless you before he **d**."
Exo 21:20 a stick so that the slave **d** from
22:2 in and hits him so that he **d**,
22:10 for him, and it **d**, is injured,
22:14 and it is injured or **d** while the
Lev 7:24 The fat from an animal that **d**
11:39 that you are allowed to eat **d**,
17:15 of an animal that **d** naturally
21:2 one of your nearest relatives **d**.

Lev 22:8 of an animal that **d** naturally
Num 6:7 mother, brother, or sister **d**,
19:14 for when a person **d**
27:8 If a man **d** and leaves no sons,
Dtr 14:1 So when someone **d**,
14:21 any creature that **d** naturally.
24:3 her and divorces her, or if he **d**,
25:5 one of them **d** without having
Jos 20:6 is chief priest at that time **d**.
Jdg 13:7 the time he is born until he **d**.'"
1Ki 14:11 from Jeroboam's house **d**
14:11 If anyone **d** in the country,
16:4 from Baasha's ⌊family⌋ who **d**
16:4 ⌊family⌋ who **d** in the country."
21:24 anyone from Ahab's ⌊house⌋ **d**
21:24 If anyone **d** in the country,
Job 8:13 The hope of the godless **d**.
14:8 and its stump **d** in the soil,
14:10 But a human **d** and is
14:14 "If a person **d**, will he go on
21:23 One person **d** in his prime and
21:25 **d** with a bitter soul.
Psa 49:17 anything with him when he **d**.
Pro 26:20 and without gossip a quarrel **d**
Ecc 3:19 One **d** just like the other.
Isa 65:20 Whoever **d** before he is a
Jer 9:12 The land **d**; it has been ruined
38:10 out of the cistern before he **d**."
Eze 24:17 grieve for the person who **d**.
Mat 22:24 'If a man **d** childless,
Mar 12:19 'If a man **d** and leaves a wife
Luk 20:28 'If a married man **d** and has no
Jon 4:49 with me before my little boy **d**."
12:24 is planted in the ground and **d**.
12:24 If it **d**, it will produce a lot of
Rom 7:2 But if her husband **d**,
7:3 But if her husband **d**,
1Co 7:39 If her husband **d**, she is free to
15:22 As everyone **d** because of
15:36 come to life unless it **d** first.
Heb 9:17 effect only when a person **d**.

diet (1)
Mat 3:4 His **d** consisted of locusts and

differ (1)
Est 3:8 Their laws **d** from those of all

difference (20)
Lev 10:10 Teach them the **d** between
15:3 it is chronic or not makes no **d**;
18:9 It makes no **d** whether or not
24:16 It makes no **d** whether they are
24:22 It makes no **d** whether you are
Dtr 1:39 to know the **d** between good
1Ki 3:9 and tell the **d** between good
2Ch 12:8 learn the **d** between serving me
Job 6:30 to tell the **d** between right
Eze 22:26 They don't teach the **d** between
44:23 people the **d** between what is
44:23 to tell the **d** between what is
Zec 14:7 LORD — with no **d** between day
Mal 3:18 Then you will again see the **d**
Rom 3:22 There is no **d** between people.
10:12 There is no **d** between Jews
1Co 12:10 can tell the **d** between spirits.
14:7 If there is no **d** in the notes,
Gal 2:6 they were makes no **d** to me,
Heb 5:14 to know the **d** between good

differences (1)
Rom 14:1 an argument over **d** of opinion.

different (47)
Exo 33:16 Then we will be **d** from all
Lev 13:55 If it doesn't look any **d** and the
19:19 Never crossbreed **d** kinds of
Num 7:11 "Each day a **d** leader will bring
14:24 servant Caleb has a **d** attitude
20:21 around and went a **d** way.
1Sm 10:6 You will be a **d** person while
2Sm 14:20 the matter in a **d** light.
1Ki 7:8 were in a **d** location than
1Ch 29:2 stones of **d** colors,
Neh 4:19 to be done in **d** places that we
Eze 16:34 You are a **d** kind of prostitute.
Eze 20:32 like the **d** people in other
41:6 arranged on three **d** stories.
Dan 7:3 each one **d** from the others,
7:19 which was so **d** from all the
7:23 It will be **d** from all other
7:24 He will be **d** from the kings
11:29 this time will be **d** from the first.
Mar 8:12 it will be far **d** than what they
Luk 20:11 So he sent a **d** servant.
Act 7:18 Then a **d** king, who knew
Rom 7:23 However, I see a **d** standard
12:6 gave each of us **d** gifts.
1Co 12:4 There are **d** spiritual gifts,
12:5 There are **d** ways of serving,
12:6 There are **d** types of work to do,
12:10 Another can speak in **d** kinds
14:10 No matter how many **d**
2Co 11:4 receive a spirit that is **d** from
11:4 you good news that is **d** from
12:20 come and find you **d** from what
12:20 and that you may find me **d**
Gal 1:6 to follow a **d** kind of good
1:8 you good news that is **d** from
1:9 you good news that is **d** from
Heb 1:1 our ancestors at many **d** times
1:1 and in many **d** ways through
7:12 When a **d** kind of priesthood is
7:12 for those priests are **d**.
7:13 was a member of a **d** tribe.
7:15 The regulations were **d**.
7:15 This became clear when a **d**
10:29 as no **d** from other people's
Jas 1:2 when you are tested in **d** ways.
1:8 thinking about two **d** things at
1Pe 1:6 you have to suffer **d** kinds

differently (3)
Exo 8:22 treat the region of Goshen **d**.
Dan 7:7 It acted **d** from all the other
Php 3:15 And if you think **d**,

differs (1)
1Co 15:41 Even one star **d** in splendor

difficult (17)
Gen 11:6 to do will be too **d** for them.
47:9 of my life have been few and **d**,
Exo 18:26 They would bring **d** cases to
1Ki 10:3 No question was too **d** for the
2Ki 2:10 have asked for something **d**.
2Ch 9:2 No question was too **d** for
Neh 5:15 before me had made life **d**
Job 7:1 "Isn't a mortal's stay on earth **d**
30:25 person whose days were **d**?
Psa 73:16 it was too **d** for me.
131:1 in things too big or too **d** for me.
Eze 3:5 to understand or **d** to speak.
3:6 hard to understand, **d** to speak,
Dan 2:11 What you ask is **d**,
Act 20:19 I served the Lord during the **d**
Gal 4:14 my illness was **d** for you,
1Jn 5:3 his commandments isn't **d**

difficulties (3)
Act 27:7 Our **d** began along the coast of
Rom 8:37 victory in all these **d**.
2Co 12:10 and **d** suffered for Christ.

difficulty (1)
Act 27:8 We had **d** sailing along the

dig (13)
Dtr 6:11 have cisterns that you didn't **d**
23:13 to squat, **d** a hole with it.
2Ki 19:24 I'll **d** wells and drink foreign
Job 3:21 it never comes — though they **d**
Isa 22:16 What right do you have to **d** a
37:25 I'll **d** wells and drink water.
Jer 18:20 They **d** a pit to take my life.
Eze 8:8 **d** through the wall."
12:5 **D** a hole through the wall of
12:12 People will **d** holes in the wall
Amo 9:2 Even if they **d** their way into
Luk 13:8 I'll **d** around it and fertilize it.
16:3 I'm not strong enough to **d**,

diggers (1)
Eze 39:15 the grave **d** have buried that

dignified (1)
2Sm 6:20 "How **d** Israel's king was today!

dignity (7)
Exo 28:2 Aaron to give him **d** and honor.
28:40 will give them **d** and honor.
Job 30:15 They blow away my **d** like the
40:10 yourself in majesty and **d**.
Pro 30:29 three things that walk with **d**,
30:29 even four that march with **d**:
Tit 2:7 example of moral purity and **d**.

digs (4)
Exo 21:33 opens up a cistern or **d**
Psa 7:15 He **d** a pit and shovels it out.
Pro 26:27 Whoever **d** a pit will fall into it.
Ecc 10:8 Whoever **d** a pit may fall into it.

Diklah (2)
Gen 10:27 Hadoram, Uzal, **D**,
1Ch 1:21 Hadoram, Uzal, **D**,

Dilean (1)
Jos 15:38 **D**, Mizpah, Joktheel,

diligent (1)
2Ch 29:34 The Levites were more **d** in

dill (1)
Mat 23:23 of your mint, **d**, and cumin.

dim (1)
Ecc 12:3 of the windows see a **d** light.

dimensions (2)
Job 38:5 Who determined its **d**?
Eze 42:11 They had the same exits, **d**,

diminish (2)
Job 15:4 God⌋ and **d** devotion to God.
Jer 50:38 A drought will **d** their water

Dimnah (1)
Jos 21:35 **D**, and Nahalal.

Dimon (2)
Isa 15:9 The water in **D** is red with
15:9 yet I will bring even more on **D**.

Dimonah (1)
Jos 15:22 Kinah, **D**, Adadah,

Dinah (7)
Gen 30:21 to a daughter and named her **D**.
34:1 **D**, daughter of Leah and Jacob,
34:3 fond of Jacob's daughter **D**.
34:5 had dishonored his daughter **D**.
34:13 had dishonored their sister **D**.
34:26 They took **D** from Shechem's
46:15 in addition to his daughter **D**.

Dinah's (2)
Gen 34:11 Then Shechem said to **D** father
34:25 **D** brothers, took their swords

Dinhabah (2)
Gen 36:32 of his ⌊capital⌋ city was **D**.
1Ch 1:43 of his ⌊capital⌋ city was **D**.

dining (1)
Est 7:8 garden to the palace **d** room,

dinner (23)
Gen 19:3 prepared a special **d** for them,
26:30 prepared a special **d** for them,
40:20 Pharaoh had a special **d**
Est 5:4 come today with Haman to a **d**
5:5 came to the **d** that Esther had
5:8 come with Haman to a **d** I will
5:12 king to the **d** she had prepared.
5:14 Then go with the king to the **d**
6:14 to the **d** Esther had prepared.

Est 7:1 to have **d** with Queen Esther.
7:7 was furious as he got up from **d**
Mat 9:10 Later Jesus was having **d** at
22:4 been invited, 'I've prepared **d**.
Mar 2:15 Later Jesus was having **d** at
6:21 Herod gave a **d** for his top
7:4 jars, brass pots, and **d** tables.)
Luk 14:12 you invite people for lunch or **d**,
17:8 'Get **d** ready for me!
17:8 After you serve me my **d**,
19:8 ⌊Later, at **d**,⌋ Zacchaeus stood
Jon 12:2 **D** was prepared for Jesus in
12:2 Martha served the **d**,
1Co 10:27 you ⌊to his house for **d**⌋,

dinners (3)
Mat 23:6 love the place of honor at **d**
Mar 12:39 and the places of honor at **d**.
Luk 20:46 and the places of honor at **d**.

Dionysius (1)
Act 17:34 With them were **D**,

Diotrephes (1)
3Jn 1:9 But **D**, who loves to be in

dip (11)
Exo 12:22 **d** it in the blood which is in a
Lev 4:6 The priest will **d** his finger in it
4:17 The priest will **d** his finger in
14:6 and the hyssop sprig and **d**
14:16 He will **d** his right finger in the
14:51 and the living bird and **d** them
Num 19:18 of hyssop, **d** it in the water,
Rut 2:14 and **d** it into the sour wine."
2Ki 5:14 So he went to **d** himself in the
Isa 30:14 a fireplace or to **d** water from
Luk 16:24 Send Lazarus to **d** the tip of his

dipped (7)
Gen 37:31 and **d** the robe in the blood.
Lev 9:9 He **d** his finger in the blood and
1Sm 14:27 staff he had in his hand and **d**
Mat 26:23 "Someone who has **d** his hand
Jon 13:26 this piece of bread after I've **d**
13:26 So Jesus **d** the bread and gave
Rev 19:13 He wears clothes **d** in blood,

dipping (1)
Mar 14:20 someone **d** his hand into the

dire (1)
Dtr 28:57 eat them out of **d** necessity,

direct (9)
Gen 18:19 so that he will **d** his children
46:26 The total number of Jacob's **d**
Ezr 3:8 were at least 20 years old to **d**
Psa 45:1 I will **d** my song to the king.
119:36 **D** my heart toward your written
Jer 10:23 Humans do not **d** their steps as
Eze 23:25 I will **d** my burning anger
26:9 He will **d** his battering rams
2Th 3:5 May the Lord **d** your lives as

directed (27)
Rut 3:6 as her mother-in-law had **d** her.
2Ki 22:13 The LORD's fierce anger is **d**
22:17 Therefore, my burning anger **d**
23:25 as **d** in Moses' Teachings.
1Ch 25:2 (They were **d** by Asaph,
25:3 (The six brothers were **d** by
29:18 Keep their hearts **d** toward you.
2Ch 4:20 lamps of pure gold (to burn as **d**
8:14 Solomon's father David had **d**,
19:2 The LORD's anger is **d** toward
23:18 and singing as David had **d**.)
34:13 the workers and **d** all
Job 30:15 Terrors are **d** toward me.
Psa 37:23 A person's steps are **d** by the
119:59 and I have **d** my feet back to
141:5 prayer is **d** against evil deeds.
Isa 40:13 Who has **d** the Spirit of the
Lam 3:62 attack me are **d** against me all
Hab 1:9 Every face will be **d** forward.
Zec 10:3 "My burning anger is **d** against
Mat 21:6 did as Jesus had **d** them.
26:19 did as Jesus had **d** them
27:10 as the Lord had **d** me."
Mar 12:12 They knew that he had **d** this
Luk 20:19 They knew that he had **d** this
1Co 16:1 I want you to do as I **d** the
Tit 1:5 leaders in every city as I **d** you.

directing (4)
1Ki 12:15 the LORD was **d** these events
2Ch 10:15 the LORD was **d** these events
Ezr 3:9 in **d** those working on God's
Hab 2:6 Won't all of them ridicule him, **d**

direction (36)
Gen 13:10 Then Lot looked in the **d** of
24:48 The LORD led me in the right **d**
25:18 in the **d** of Assyria.
Exo 38:21 Levites under the **d** of Ithamar,
Num 4:27 will be done under the **d** of
7:8 to do under the **d** of Ithamar,
11:31 could walk in a day in any **d**.
Dtr 27:18 blind people in the wrong **d** will
28:7 They will attack you from one **d**
28:25 You will attack them from one **d**
1Ch 25:2 as a prophet under the king's **d**
25:6 the LORD's temple under the **d**
25:6 temple under the **d** of the king.
2Ch 23:18 the LORD's temple under the **d**
Neh 4:12 would attack us from every **d**.
12:42 sang under the **d** of Jezrahiah.
Psa 36:4 and chooses to go the wrong **d**.
77:17 your arrows flashed in every **d**.
Pro 1:5 person will gain **d** —
11:14 will fall when there is no **d**,
21:1 them in any **d** he chooses.
23:19 your mind going in the right **d**.
Isa 65:2 They chose to go the wrong **d**.
Jer 49:36 scatter its people in every **d**.
50:5 goes to Zion and turn in that **d**.
51:2 They will attack it from every **d**
Eze 10:11 They always moved in the **d**
12:14 I will scatter in every **d** all
17:21 will be scattered in every **d** that
Dan 6:10 opened in the **d** of Jerusalem.
Joe 3:11 Hurry from every **d**,
Nah 3:17 and they scatter in every **d**.
Mat 24:31 and from every **d** under the sky,
Mar 13:27 and from every **d** under the sky,
Luk 16:26 cross it in either **d** even if they
2Pe 1:21 humans spoke under God's **d**.

directions (32)
Gen 3:24 sword that turned in all **d** east
46:28 to Joseph to get **d** to Goshen.
Dtr 5:33 Follow all the **d** the LORD your
8:6 Follow his **d**, and fear him.
10:12 him, follow all his **d**, love him,
11:22 your God, follow all his **d**,
13:5 you away from following the **d**
19:9 and follow his **d** as long as
26:17 and that you will follow his **d**,
28:7 run away from you in seven **d**.
28:9 your God and follow his **d**.
28:25 run away from them in seven **d**.
30:16 LORD your God, follow his **d**,
Jos 22:5 LORD your God, follow his **d**,
Jdg 21:11 These are your **d**: Claim every
1Sm 14:16 camp⌋ dispersing in all **d**.
1Ki 1:49 got up and scattered in all **d**.
2:3 Obey his **d**, laws, commands,
2Ch 35:13 lambs according to the **d**.
Ezr 3:2 They ⌊followed the **d**⌋ written
3:4 Following the written **d**,
6:18 by following the **d** written
Neh 10:34 to the **d** in the Teachings.
10:36 Following the **d** in the
Job 21:29 didn't pay attention to their **d**.
Psa 119:3 They follow his **d**.
Jer 5:31 rule under the prophets' **d**,
Eze 1:17 they moved in any of the four **d**
10:11 they moved in any of the four **d**
16:33 them to come to you from all **d**
Dan 11:4 into pieces and divided in the **d**
1Co 11:34 I will give **d** concerning the

director (2)
Hab 3:19 For the choir **d**; on stringed
Luk 19:2 He was the **d** of tax collectors,

directors (1)
Neh 12:46 there had been **d** for the singers

directs (3)
Pro 16:9 but the LORD **d** his steps.
20:24 The LORD is the one who **d** a
Gal 5:16 as your spiritual nature **d** you.

dirt (38)
Exo 20:24 an altar for me made out of **d**.
Lev 17:13 blood and cover it with **d**.
1Sm 4:12 clothes torn and **d** on his head.
2Sm 1:2 and he had **d** on his head.
15:32 and he had **d** on his head.
16:13 and threw **d** at David.
20:15 They put up a **d** ramp against
22:43 them like the **d** on the streets.
1Ki 18:38 offering, wood, stones, and **d**.
2Ki 5:17 give me as much **d** as
19:32 or put up **d** ramps to attack it.
25:1 They set up camp and built **d**
Neh 9:1 and threw **d** on their heads.
Job 27:16 and piles up clothing like **d**,
30:19 He throws me into the **d** so that
38:38 when the **d** hardens into
Psa 18:42 they were **d** on the streets.
89:39 thrown his crown into the **d**.
143:3 has ground my life into the **d**.
Isa 29:3 put up mounds of **d** around you.
37:33 or put up **d** ramps to attack it.
47:1 Go, sit in the **d**, virgin princess
Jer 6:6 Build up **d** mounds to attack
32:24 "'See how the **d** ramps have
33:4 to be used against the **d** ramps
52:4 They set up camp and built **d**
Lam 2:10 They throw **d** on their heads
Eze 4:2 put up **d** ramps around it,
17:17 the Babylonians put up **d** ramps
26:8 up blockades, put up **d** ramps,
Dan 11:15 build **d** attack ramps,
Hab 1:10 fortified city and build a **d** ramp
Jon 9:6 and mixed the spit with **d**.
9:11 Jesus mixed some spit with **d**,
9:14 Jesus mixed the spit and **d**
9:15 "He put a mixture of spit and **d**
Act 22:23 and throwing **d** into the air.
1Pe 3:21 save by removing **d** from

dirty (3)
Sos 5:3 Why should I get them **d**
Act 13:10 and said, "You are full of **d**
Eph 5:4 It's not right that **d** stories,

disability (1)
Luk 13:12 you are free from your **d**."

disable (1)
Jos 11:6 You must **d** their horses so that

disabled (12)
Jos 11:9 Joshua **d** their horses and
2Sm 4:4 ⌊from her arms⌋ and became **d**.
8:4 David also **d** all but 100 of their
9:3 son who is **d**," Ziba answered.
9:13 who was **d**, lived in Jerusalem.
19:26 Since I am **d**, I said,
1Ch 18:4 David also **d** all but 100 of their
Mat 15:30 blind, **d**, those unable to talk,
15:31 the **d** cured, the lame walking,
18:8 It is better for you to enter life **d**
Mar 9:43 It is better for you to enter life **d**
Luk 13:11 The spirit had **d** her for 18

disagree (1)
Gal 5:10 that you will not **d** with this.

disagreed (2)
Job 31:13 when they have **d** with me,
Act 15:39 Paul and Barnabas **d** so

disagreement (3)

Exo 18:16 Whenever they have a **d** and
Dtr 21:5 involving a **d** or an assault.
25:1 people have a **d** that is brought

disagreements (8)

Exo 18:13 Moses was settling **d** among
18:19 to God and bring their **d** to him.
18:22 who usually settle **d** among
18:23 will have their **d** settled so that
18:26 who usually settled **d** among
24:14 Take all your **d** to them."
Dtr 1:12 and your **d** all by myself?
1Co 6:5 to settle **d** between believers?

disappear (52)

Dtr 4:26 you will quickly **d** from the land
11:17 and you'll quickly **d** from this
28:20 you're destroyed and quickly **d**
Jos 23:16 Then you will quickly **d** from
Neh 4:5 and don't let their sins **d** from
Job 4:20 They will **d** forever without
6:18 go into a wasteland and **d**.
24:24 low and **d** like everything else.
36:20 people **d** from their places.
Psa 37:20 But wicked people will **d**.
41:5 when will his family name **d**?"
58:7 Let them **d** like water that
92:9 They **d**, and all troublemakers
102:3 My days **d** like smoke.
Pro 25:10 report about you will never **d**.
Isa 2:18 Then idols will **d** completely.
9:12 his anger will not **d**,
9:17 his anger will not **d**,
9:21 his anger will not **d**,
10:4 his anger will not **d**,
17:3 cities will **d** from Ephraim,
17:3 kingdom will **d** from Damascus.
19:7 dry up, be blown away, and **d**.
29:14 of their wise people will **d**.
41:11 be reduced to nothing and **d**.
44:22 I made your rebellious acts **d**
60:20 nor will your moon **d**.
Jer 10:11 These gods will **d** from the
10:15 they are punished, they **d**.
18:18 word of the prophets won't **d**.
24:10 and plagues until they **d** from
40:15 What is left of Judah would **d**."
51:18 they are punished, they will **d**.
Eze 7:26 the advice of leaders will **d**.
25:7 make you **d**, and destroy you.
30:6 Egypt's strength will **d**.
Dan 11:19 but he will stumble, fall, and **d**.
Joe 1:16 Happiness and rejoicing **d** from
Nah 3:11 You will **d**. Even you will look
Mat 5:18 the earth and the heavens **d**,
5:18 will **d** from Moses' Teachings
24:34 This generation will not **d** until
24:35 earth and the heavens will **d**,
24:35 but my words will never **d**.
Mar 13:30 This generation will not **d** until
13:31 earth and the heavens will **d**,
13:31 but my words will never **d**.
Luk 16:17 earth and the heavens to **d** than
21:32 This generation will not **d** until
21:33 earth and the heavens will **d**,
21:33 but my words will never **d**.
Heb 8:13 outdated and aging will soon **d**.

disappeared (13)

Num 16:33 so they **d** from the assembly.
Jdg 6:21 the Messenger of the LORD **d**.
Isa 5:25 his anger has not **d**,
34:12 All of its princes have **d**.
Jer 7:28 Truth has **d** and vanished from
10:20 have left me and have **d**.
48:33 Joy and gladness have **d** from
48:36 The wealth they gained has **d**.
49:7 Has wisdom **d** from your
2Co 5:17 The old way of living has **d**.
Rev 18:14 and your splendor have **d**.
21:1 first heaven and earth had **d**,
21:4 the first things have **d**."

disappears (8)

Lev 13:58 But if the area **d** from the
Job 7:9 As a cloud fades away and **d**,
Psa 103:16 blows over the flower, it **d**,
112:10 He angrily grits his teeth and **d**.
Hos 6:4 It **d** as quickly as the morning
13:3 morning dew that **d** quickly.
Joe 1:16 Food **d** right before our eyes.
Jas 4:14 seen for a moment and then **d**.

disappoint (1)

Jer 15:18 Will you **d** me like a stream

disappointed (6)

Gen 4:5 became very angry and was **d**.
4:6 and why do you look **d**?
Job 6:20 Arriving there, they are **d**.
Psa 22:5 trusted you and were never **d**.
Jer 12:13 They were **d** by their harvests
14:4 The farmers are **d**.

disappointment (1)

Psa 119:116 Do not turn my hope into **d**.

disapproval (1)

Luk 19:7 saw this began to express **d**.

disapproved (1)

Gen 28:8 Isaac **d** of Canaanite women.

disapproves (2)

2Th 2:10 will use everything that God **d**
2:12 delighted with what God **d** of,

disaster (122)

Gen 19:19 This **d** will overtake me,
Exo 32:12 to bring this **d** on your people.
Dtr 29:21 the tribes of Israel for **d** based
32:23 I will bring one **d** after another
32:35 because their day of **d** is near.
Jos 6:18 you will bring destruction and **d**
7:24 them to the valley of Achor [**D**].
7:25 did you bring this **d** on us?
7:25 The LORD will bring **d** on you
24:20 he will turn and bring **d** on you.
Jdg 2:15 of the LORD brought **d** on them.
11:35 What **d** you've brought me!
1Sm 6:9 then this **d** is the LORD's doing.
2Sm 15:14 he'll catch up to us and bring **d**
22:19 On the day when I faced **d**,
24:16 changed his mind about the **d**.
1Ki 9:9 LORD brought this **d** on them.'"
14:10 "That is why I will bring **d** on
2Ki 14:10 Why must you invite **d** and
21:12 I'm going to bring such a **d** on
22:16 I'm going to bring **d** on this
22:20 not see any of the **d** I'm going
1Ch 21:15 changed his mind about the **d**.
2Ch 7:22 he brought this **d** on them.'"
25:19 Why must you invite **d** and
34:24 I'm going to bring **d** on this
34:28 not see any of the **d** I'm going
Job 9:23 When a sudden **d** brings death,
18:12 **D** is waiting beside him.
21:17 How often does **d** happen to
21:30 On the day of **d** the wicked
30:24 person calls for help in his **d**.
31:23 "A **d** from God terrifies me.
Psa 18:18 On the day when I faced **d**,
107:26 melted in the face of **d**.
107:39 of oppression, **d**, and sorrow.
Pro 1:33 will be free from the dread of **d**."
6:15 That is why **d** will come on
13:21 **D** hunts down sinners,
16:18 Pride precedes a **d**,
24:16 in a **d** wicked people fall.
24:22 because **d** will come to them
28:14 is hard-hearted falls into **d**.
Ecc 9:12 humans are trapped by a **d**
11:2 because you don't know what **d**
Isa 3:9 have brought **d** on themselves.
3:11 **D** will strike them.
10:3 when the **d** comes from far
24:18 Whoever flees from news of a **d**
28:15 the overwhelming **d** passes by,
28:18 the overwhelming **d** passes by,
31:2 is wise and can bring about **d**.
47:11 **D** will strike you. You won't be
Jer 1:14 Then the LORD said to me, "**D**
2:3 and **d** struck them,'" declares
4:6 I'm bringing **d** and widespread
4:15 and a report of **d** comes from
4:20 One **d** follows another.
6:1 because **d** and widespread
6:19 I'm going to bring **d** on these
11:11 I'm going to bring a **d** on them
11:15 turn **d** away from them?
11:17 He has pronounced **d** on you.
11:23 I will bring a **d** on the people of
15:11 plead with you in times of **d**
17:17 are my refuge on the day of **d**.
17:18 Bring the day of **d** on them,
18:8 change my plans about the **d**
18:11 I'm going to prepare a **d** and
18:17 On the day of their **d**,
19:3 I'm going to bring such a **d** on
23:12 I will bring **d** on them.
25:29 I am going to bring **d** on the
25:32 **D** is spreading from nation to
26:3 I'll change my plan about the **d**
26:13 his plan about the **d** that
26:19 changed his plan about the **d**
26:19 bring a bigger **d** on ourselves."
29:11 are plans for peace and not **d**,
32:23 you brought all this **d** on them.
39:16 against this city by bringing **d**
40:2 to bring this **d** on this place.
42:10 plans about the **d** I've brought
44:7 this terrible **d** on yourselves?
44:11 I'm going to bring **d** on you and
44:17 comfortably and saw no **d**.
44:23 you have met with this **d** as
44:29 that my threats of **d** will happen
45:5 because I'm going to bring **d** on
48:16 **d** is coming quickly.
48:44 "Whoever flees from a **d** will
49:8 I will bring **d** on the
49:32 I will bring **d** on them from
49:37 I'll bring **d** with my burning
Lam 1:21 have heard about my **d**.
Eze 6:10 I am the LORD and that the **d**
7:5 One **d** after another is coming.
7:26 One **d** will happen after
14:22 after every **d** that I will bring
Dan 9:12 by bringing a great **d** on us.
9:13 This entire **d** happened to us,
9:14 prepared to bring this **d** on us.
Hos 2:15 make the valley of Achor [**D**]
Joe 2:13 to change his plans about **d**.
Amo 3:6 If there is a **d** in a city,
6:3 that a day of **d** is far away.
9:4 on them so that I can bring **d**
Oba 1:13 of my people when **d** strikes
1:13 their misery when **d** strikes.
1:13 Don't take their wealth when **d**
Jnh 1:7 for bringing this **d** on us."
1:8 why has this **d** happened to
Mic 1:12 From the LORD a **d** will come on
2:1 and work out plans for **d** while
2:3 I'm planning a **d** to punish your
2:3 This will be a time of **d**.
Hab 2:9 high and save himself from **d**.'
Zep 3:15 You will never fear **d** again.
Mat 7:27 and the result was a total **d**."
Act 27:10 "Men, we're going to face a **d**
27:10 This **d** will cause damage to
27:21 have avoided this **d** and loss.

disasters (25)

Dtr 31:17 and many terrible **d** will happen
31:17 'Haven't these **d** happened to
31:21 When many terrible **d** happen
31:29 In the days to come **d** will
Job 31:3 for wicked people and **d**
Pro 21:12 throws wicked people into **d**.
Isa 24:17 **D**, pits, and traps are in store
45:7 I make blessings and create **d**.
51:19 Twice as many **d** have
Jer 16:10 threaten us with all these **d**?
19:8 at all the **d** that happen
19:15 and on all its towns the **d** that

Jer 25:13 I will bring on that land all the **d**
28:8 and me prophesied wars, **d**,
32:42 As I brought all these **d** on
35:17 live in Jerusalem all the **d** that
36:3 will hear about all the **d** that
36:31 people of Judah all the **d** that
42:17 will survive or escape the **d**
44:2 You have seen all the **d** I
44:27 to watch over them to bring **d**,
48:43 **D**, pits, and traps are in store
51:60 all the **d** that would happen
51:64 rise again because of the **d** that
Eze 14:22 be comforted after the **d** that

disastrous (1)

Lam 5:16 it has been **d** for us.

disbelieve (1)

Act 28:24 but others continued to **d**.

discarded (1)

Mal 2:3 You will be **d** with it.

discharge (20)

Lev 15:2 If a man has a **d** from his penis,
15:2 his penis, his **d** is unclean.
15:3 He is unclean because of the **d**
15:4 "The man who has a **d** makes
15:7 who has a **d** must wash their
15:8 If a man who has a **d** spits on
15:9 When a man who has a **d** sits
15:11 If a man who has a **d** touches
15:12 who has a **d** touches pottery,
15:13 "When a man's **d** stops,
15:15 LORD for the man who had a **d**.
15:25 "If a woman has a **d** of blood
15:25 as long as she has a **d**.
15:26 As long as she has a **d**,
15:28 "When her **d** stops,
15:30 woman who had an unclean **d**.
15:32 for any man who has a **d**
15:33 man or woman who has a **d**,
22:4 disease or a **d** may eat any
Num 5:2 a serious skin disease or a **d**

disciple (40)

1Ki 20:35 A **d** of the prophets spoke to a
20:35 ⌊The **d** said,⌋ "Punch me,"
20:36 The **d** said, "Since you didn't
20:37 Then the **d** found another man.
20:39 the **d** called to him.
2Ki 4:1 One of the wives of a **d** of the
6:7 The **d** reached for it and picked
Amo 7:14 and I'm not a **d** of the prophets.
Mat 8:21 Another **d** said to him,
10:37 does not deserve to be my **d**.
10:37 does not deserve to be my **d**.
10:38 me doesn't deserve to be my **d**.
10:42 is my **d** will certainly never
13:52 scribe who has become a **d**
27:57 and had become a **d** of Jesus.
Jon 9:28 yelled at him, "You're his **d**,
13:23 One **d**, the one whom Jesus
13:24 motioned to that **d** and said,
13:25 that **d** asked, "Lord, who is it?"
18:15 and another **d** followed Jesus.
18:15 The other **d** was well-known to
18:15 So that **d** went with Jesus into
18:16 The other **d** talked to the
19:26 his mother and the **d** whom
19:27 Then he said to the **d**,
19:27 lived with that **d** in his home.
19:38 (Joseph was a **d** of Jesus but
20:2 to Simon Peter and the other **d**,
20:3 So Peter and the other **d**
20:4 but the other **d** ran faster than
20:8 Then the other **d**, who arrived
21:7 The **d** whom Jesus loved said
21:20 saw the **d** whom Jesus loved.
21:20 That **d** was following them.
21:23 So a rumor that that **d** wouldn't
21:24 This **d** was an eyewitness of
Act 9:10 A **d** named Ananias lived in the
9:26 believe that he was a **d**.
9:36 A **d** named Tabitha lived in the
16:1 where a **d** named Timothy

disciples (319)

2Ki 2:3 Some of the **d** of the prophets
2:5 Then some of the **d** of the
2:7 Fifty **d** of the prophets stood at
2:15 The **d** of the prophets who
2:17 But the **d** kept urging him ⌊to
4:38 ⌊One day,⌋ while the **d** of the
4:38 stew for the **d** of the prophets."
5:22 now two young men from the **d**
6:1 The **d** of the prophets said to
6:3 Then one of the **d** asked,
9:1 Elisha called one of the **d**
Isa 8:16 the teachings among my **d**.
Mat 5:1 His **d** came to him,
8:18 he ordered his **d** to cross to
8:23 Jesus' **d** went with him as he
9:10 to eat with Jesus and his **d**.
9:11 saw this and asked his **d**,
9:14 Then John's **d** came to Jesus.
9:14 fast often but your **d** never do?"
9:18 he was talking to John's **d**.
9:19 Jesus and his **d** got up and
9:37 Then he said to his **d**,
10:1 Jesus called his twelve **d** and
11:1 his twelve **d** these instructions,
11:2 had done. So he sent his **d**
11:4 Jesus answered John's **d**,
12:1 His **d** were hungry and began
12:2 Your **d** are doing something
12:49 Pointing with his hand at his **d**,
13:10 The **d** asked him, "Why do you
13:36 His **d** came to him and said,
14:12 John's **d** came for the body and
14:15 In the evening the **d** came to
14:19 gave them to the **d**,
14:22 Jesus quickly made his **d** get
14:26 When the **d** saw him walking
15:2 "Why do your **d** break the
15:12 Then the **d** came and said to
15:23 Then his **d** came to him and
15:32 Jesus called his **d** and said,
15:33 His **d** asked him, "Where could
15:36 the bread and gave it to the **d**,
15:37 The **d** picked up the leftover
16:5 The **d** had forgotten to take any
16:7 The **d** had been discussing
16:13 Philippi, he asked his **d**,
16:20 Then he strictly ordered the **d**
16:21 began to inform his **d** that
16:24 Then Jesus said to his **d**,
17:6 The **d** were terrified when they
17:10 So the **d** asked him,
17:13 Then the **d** understood that he
17:16 I brought him to your **d**,
17:19 Then the **d** came to Jesus
17:23 Then the **d** became very sad.
18:1 At that time the **d** came to
19:10 The **d** said to him,
19:13 But the **d** told the people not to
19:23 Jesus said to his **d**,
19:25 He amazed his **d** more than
21:1 Jesus sent two **d** ahead of him.
21:6 The **d** did as Jesus had
21:20 The **d** were surprised to see
22:16 They sent their **d** to him along
23:1 said to the crowds and to his **d**,
24:1 his **d** came to him.
24:3 his **d** came to him privately and
26:1 all these things, he told his **d**,
26:8 The **d** were irritated when they
26:17 the **d** went to Jesus.
26:18 with my **d** at your house.'"
26:19 The **d** did as Jesus had
26:26 gave it to his **d**, and said,
26:35 All the other **d** said the same
26:36 Then Jesus went with the **d** to
26:40 When he went back to the **d**,
26:45 Then he came back to the **d**
26:56 Then all the **d** abandoned him
27:64 Otherwise, his **d** may steal him
28:7 Then go quickly, and tell his **d**
28:8 great joy and ran to tell his **d**.
28:13 say that Jesus' **d** had come at
28:16 The eleven **d** went to the
28:19 make **d** of all nations:

Mar 2:15 were eating with him and his **d**.
2:16 collectors, they asked his **d**,
2:18 John's **d** and the Pharisees
2:18 "Why do John's **d** and the
2:18 and the Pharisees' **d** fast,
2:18 fast, but your **d** don't?"
2:23 As the **d** walked along,
2:24 Why are your **d** doing
3:7 Jesus left with his **d** for the
3:9 Jesus told his **d** to have a boat
3:20 Jesus and his **d** could not even
4:34 when he was alone with his **d**,
4:35 Jesus said to his **d**,
5:31 His **d** said to him, "How can
5:40 and his three **d** and went to the
6:1 His **d** followed him.
6:29 When John's **d** heard about
6:35 his **d** came to him.
6:41 and kept giving them to the **d**
6:45 Jesus quickly made his **d** get
6:51 The **d** were astounded.
7:2 They saw that some of his **d**
7:5 "Why don't your **d** follow the
7:17 his **d** asked him about this
8:1 Jesus called his **d** and said to
8:4 His **d** asked him, "Where could
8:6 the bread and gave it to his **d**
8:8 The **d** picked up the leftover
8:10 After that, Jesus and his **d** got
8:14 The **d** had forgotten to take any
8:27 Then Jesus and his **d** went to
8:27 On the way he asked his **d**,
8:33 Jesus turned, looked at his **d**,
8:34 to himself along with his **d**.
9:14 When they came to the other **d**,
9:18 I asked your **d** to force the spirit
9:28 his **d** asked him privately,
9:31 he was teaching his **d**.
9:32 The **d** didn't understand what
9:33 was at home, he asked the **d**,
10:10 the **d** asked him about this.
10:13 But the **d** told the people not to
10:23 around and said to his **d**,
10:24 The **d** were stunned by his
10:26 This amazed his **d** more than
10:32 Jesus and his **d** were on their
10:32 His **d** were shocked ⌊that he
10:46 As Jesus, his **d**, and many
11:1 sent two of his **d** ahead of him.
11:4 The **d** found the young donkey
11:6 The **d** answered them as
11:14 you again!" His **d** heard this.
11:19 (Every evening Jesus and his **d**
11:20 While Jesus and his **d** were
11:27 Jesus and his **d** returned to
12:43 He called his **d** and said to
13:1 one of his **d** said to him,
14:12 The **d** asked Jesus,
14:13 He sent two of his **d** and told
14:14 the Passover meal with my **d**?'
14:16 The **d** left. They went into the
14:31 All the other **d** said the same
14:32 He said to his **d**, "Stay here
14:50 Then all the **d** abandoned him
16:7 Go and tell his **d** and Peter that
16:12 Later Jesus appeared to two **d**
16:20 The **d** spread ⌊the Good
Luk 5:30 scribes complained to Jesus' **d**.
5:33 They said to him, "John's **d**
5:33 and so do the **d** of the
5:33 But your **d** eat and drink."
6:1 His **d** were picking the heads
6:2 "Why are your **d** doing
6:13 it was day, he called his **d**.
6:17 A large crowd of his **d** and
6:20 Jesus looked at his **d** and said,
7:11 His **d** and a large crowd went
7:18 John's **d** told him about all
7:18 Then John called two of his **d**
7:22 Jesus answered John's **d**,
8:3 support for Jesus and his **d**.
8:9 His **d** asked him what this
8:22 One day Jesus and his **d** got
9:14 Then he told his **d**,
9:16 and kept giving them to the **d**
9:18 privately and his **d** were

Luk 9:36 The **d** said nothing,
9:40 I begged your **d** to force the
9:43 So he said to his **d**,
9:54 James and John, his **d**,
10:1 the Lord appointed 70 other **d** to
10:17 The 70 **d** came back very
10:23 He turned to his **d** in private
11:1 one of his **d** said to him,
11:1 to pray as John taught his **d**."
11:5 Jesus said to his **d**,
12:1 Jesus spoke to his **d** and said,
12:22 Then Jesus said to his **d**,
14:26 they cannot be my **d**.
14:27 and follow me cannot be my **d**.
14:33 none of you can be my **d**
16:1 Then Jesus said to his **d**,
17:1 Jesus told his **d**, But how
17:22 Jesus said to his **d**,
18:1 used this illustration with his **d**
18:15 When the **d** saw this,
19:29 sent two of his **d** ahead of him.
19:34 The **d** answered, "The Lord
19:37 Then the whole crowd of **d**
19:39 tell your **d** to be quiet."
20:45 Jesus said to the **d**,
21:5 Some ⌊of the **d**⌋ were talking
21:7 The **d** asked him, "Teacher,
22:11 the Passover meal with my **d**?'
22:13 The **d** left. They found
22:24 quarrel broke out among the **d**.
22:32 strengthen the other **d**."
22:38 The **d** said, "Lord, look!
22:39 His **d** followed him.
22:45 he got up and went to the **d**.
22:47 he was still speaking to the **d**,
22:50 One of the **d** cut off the right ear
24:13 two of Jesus' **d** were going to a
24:35 Then the two **d** told what had
24:41 The **d** were overcome with joy
24:52 The **d** worshiped him and were
Jon 1:35 was standing with two of his **d**.
1:37 When the two **d** heard John
1:40 was one of the two **d** who
2:2 Jesus and his **d** had been
2:11 and his **d** believed in him.
2:12 and **d** went to the city of
2:17 His **d** remembered that
2:22 After he came back to life, his **d**
3:22 Later, Jesus and his **d** went to
3:25 Some of John's **d** had an
4:1 baptizing more **d** than John.
4:2 baptizing people. His **d** were.)
4:8 (His **d** had gone into the city to
4:27 At that time his **d** returned.
4:31 the **d** were urging him,
4:33 The **d** asked each other,
6:3 a mountain and sat with his **d**.
6:8 One of Jesus' **d**, Andrew,
6:12 were full, Jesus told his **d**,
6:13 The **d** gathered the leftover
6:16 his **d** went to the sea.
6:22 into that boat with his **d**.
6:22 The **d** had gone away without
6:24 Jesus nor his **d** were there,
6:60 many of Jesus' **d** heard him,
6:61 Jesus was aware that his **d**
6:66 made many of his **d** go back
7:3 and go to Judea so that your **d**
8:31 you are truly my **d**.
9:2 His **d** asked him, "Rabbi,
9:27 Do you want to become his **d**
9:28 but we're Moses' **d**.
11:7 Jesus said to his **d**,
11:8 The **d** said to him,
11:11 Jesus said this, he told his **d**,
11:12 His **d** said to him, "Lord, if he's
11:13 but the **d** thought Jesus meant
11:16 said to the rest of the **d**,
11:54 where he stayed with his **d**.
12:4 One of his **d**, Judas Iscariot,
12:16 At first Jesus' **d** didn't know
12:16 the **d** remembered that these
12:16 The **d** remembered that they
13:12 Then he asked his **d**,
13:22 The **d** began looking at each
13:35 will know that you are my **d**
Jon 15:8 show that you are my **d**.
16:17 Some of his **d** said to each
16:29 His **d** said, "Now you're talking
17:25 Yet, I knew you, and these ⌊**d**⌋
18:1 he went with his **d** to the other
18:2 and his **d** often gathered there.
18:17 you one of this man's **d** too?"
18:19 about his **d** and his teachings.
18:25 "Aren't you, too, one of his **d**?"
20:10 So the **d** went back home.
20:18 from Magdala went to the **d**
20:19 That Sunday evening, the **d**
20:20 The **d** were glad to see the
20:22 he breathed on the **d** and said,
20:25 The other **d** told him,
20:26 A week later Jesus' **d** were
20:30 other miracles that his **d** saw.
21:1 showed himself again to the **d**.
21:2 and two other **d** of Jesus were
21:4 The **d** didn't realize that it was
21:8 The other **d** came with the boat
21:12 None of the **d** dared to ask him
21:14 showed himself to the **d** after
21:15 me more than the other **d** do?"
Act 1:15 At a time when about 120 **d**
1:23 The **d** determined that two men
2:6 own dialect when the **d** spoke.
2:42 The **d** were devoted to the
6:1 as the number of **d** grew,
6:2 called all the **d** together
6:6 The **d** had these men stand in
6:7 and the number of **d** in
9:1 to murder the Lord's **d**.
9:19 Saul was with the **d** in the city
9:25 However, Saul's **d** lowered him
9:26 he tried to join the **d**.
9:28 Jerusalem with the **d**.
9:30 As soon as the **d** found out
9:38 When the **d** heard that Peter
10:23 Some **d** from Joppa went along.
11:26 The **d** were called Christians
11:29 All the **d** in Antioch decided to
11:30 The **d** did this and sent their
13:52 Meanwhile, the **d** ⌊in Antioch⌋
14:20 But when the **d** gathered
14:21 in that city and won many **d**.
14:22 They strengthened the **d** in
14:22 cities and encouraged the **d**
14:23 They had the **d** in each church
14:28 for a long time with these **d**.
15:10 putting a burden on the **d**,
18:23 ⌊the faith of⌋ all the **d**.
18:27 They wrote to the **d** in Greece
19:1 He met some **d** in Ephesus
19:9 He took his **d** and held daily
19:30 but his **d** wouldn't let him.
20:1 Paul sent for the **d**,
20:30 to lure **d** into following them.
21:4 In Tyre we searched for the **d**.
21:4 The Spirit had the **d** tell Paul
21:6 and the **d** went back home.
21:16 Some of the **d** from Caesarea
21:16 and was one of the first **d**.

disciples' (1)

Jon 13:5 and began to wash the **d** feet

discipline (45)

Lev 26:18 I will **d** you seven times for
26:23 "If this **d** does not help and you
26:28 I will **d** you seven times for
Dtr 8:5 you as parents **d** their children.
11:2 Remember today the **d** you
Job 5:17 despise **d** from the Almighty.
37:13 Whether for **d**, or for ⌊the good
Psa 6:1 me in your anger or **d** me
38:1 do not angrily punish me or **d**
39:11 With stern warnings you **d**
50:17 You hate **d**. You toss my words
94:12 is the person whom you **d**
Pro 1:2 to grasp wisdom and **d**,
1:3 to acquire the **d** of wise
1:7 fools despise wisdom and **d**.
1:8 My son, listen to your father's **d**,
1:9 because **d** and teachings are a
3:11 Do not reject the **d** of the LORD,
Pro 4:1 listen to ⌊your⌋ father's **d**,
4:13 Cling to **d**. Do not relax your
5:12 "Oh, how I hated **d**!
5:23 He will die for his lack of **d** and
6:23 and the warnings from **d** are the
8:10 Take my **d**, not silver, and my
8:33 Listen to **d**, and become wise.
10:17 Whoever practices **d** is on the
12:1 Whoever loves **d** loves to learn,
13:1 son listens to his father's **d**,
13:18 to a person who ignores **d**,
15:5 fool despises his father's **d**,
15:10 **D** is a terrible ⌊burden⌋ to
15:32 ignores **d** despises himself,
15:33 The fear of the LORD is **d**
19:18 **D** your son while there is still
19:20 Listen to advice and accept **d**
23:13 Do not hesitate to **d** a child.
23:23 wisdom, **d**, and understanding.
31:1 used by his mother to **d** him.
Isa 26:16 by your **d** upon them.
Jer 7:28 They did not accept **d**.
17:23 would not listen or accept **d**.
Eph 6:4 in Christian **d** and instruction.
Heb 12:7 Endure your **d**. God corrects
12:11 those who learn from that **d**
Rev 3:19 I correct and **d** everyone I love.

disciplined (16)

Job 33:19 they are **d** with endless aching
Psa 118:18 The LORD **d** me severely,
Pro 23:12 Live a more **d** life, and listen
29:19 slave cannot be **d** with words.
Jer 31:18 mourn and say, 'You **d** me,
31:18 disciplined me, and I was **d**.
Eze 21:10 refused to be **d** or punished.
21:13 if you refuse to be **d** again?
2Th 3:6 who doesn't live a **d** life
3:7 We lived a **d** life among you.
3:11 of you are not living **d** lives.
Heb 12:7 children are **d** by their fathers.
12:8 If you aren't **d** like the other
12:9 we have fathers who **d** us,
12:10 For a short time our fathers **d**
12:11 We don't enjoy being **d**.

disciplines (7)

Psa 94:10 He **d** nations. Do you think he
Pro 13:24 but whoever loves his son **d**
1Co 11:32 he **d** us so that we won't be
Heb 12:5 attention when the Lord **d** you.
12:6 The Lord **d** everyone he loves.
12:6 He severely **d** everyone he
12:10 Yet, God **d** us for our own good

disciplining (1)

Dtr 8:5 The LORD your God was **d**

discourage (2)

Num 32:7 That might **d** them from
Eze 21:7 has come that will **d** everyone.

discouraged (26)

Exo 6:9 they were so **d** by their back
Num 32:9 But then they **d** the rest of the
Dtr 1:28 Our own men have **d** us by
Jos 14:8 my companions **d** the people.
1Sm 17:32 "No one should be **d** because
2Ki 19:26 are weak, **d**, and ashamed.
2Ch 15:7 strong and not become **d**.
Ezr 4:4 Then the people of that region **d**
Job 22:29 When others are **d**,
23:16 God has **d** me. The Almighty
Psa 42:5 Why are you **d**, my soul?
42:6 My soul is **d**. That is why I will
42:11 Why are you **d**, my soul?
43:5 Why are you **d**, my soul?
Isa 37:27 are weak, **d**, and ashamed.
42:4 He will not be **d** or crushed
51:7 Don't be **d** by their ridicule.
54:4 Don't be **d**, because you won't
Lam 3:20 ⌊these things⌋ and is so **d**.
Eze 13:22 You have **d** righteous people
Dan 11:30 and he will be **d** and turn back.
2Co 4:1 We don't become **d**,
4:16 That is why we are not **d**.

Eph 3:13 I ask you not to become **d** by
Col 3:21 or they will become **d**.
1Th 5:14 cheer up those who are **d**,

discourages (1)

Jer 38:4 He **d** the soldiers who are left

discover (3)

Job 11:7 "Can you **d** God's hidden
Psa 21:8 Your hand will **d** all your
Act 5:39 You may even **d** that you're

discovered (8)

Dtr 22:28 When the crime is **d**,
Ezr 4:19 I **d** that this city has a long
Neh 13:7 I went to Jerusalem and **d** the
Mat 13:44 When a man **d** it, he buried it
Act 28:14 In Puteoli we **d** some believers
Rom 4:1 we have **d** about our ancestor
7:21 So I've **d** this truth:
Rev 2:2 You have **d** that they are liars.

discredit (2)

Neh 6:13 bad reputation in order to **d** me.
Act 19:27 that people will **d** our line

discredited (1)

Jon 10:35 The Scriptures cannot be **d**.

discreetly (1)

Pro 12:23 person ⌊**d**⌋ hides knowledge,

discriminate (1)

Act 15:9 God doesn't **d** between Jewish

discriminating (1)

Jas 2:4 Aren't you **d** against people and

discuss (6)

1Ki 2:14 have a matter ⌊to **d**⌋ with you."
Isa 1:18 "Come on now, let's **d** this!"
Luk 6:11 were furious and began to **d**
22:23 So they began to **d** with each
Act 4:15 council room and began to **d**
18:4 Paul would **d** ⌊Scripture⌋ in the

discussed (6)

1Ki 1:7 But Adonijah had **d** his actions
Mat 21:25 They **d** this among themselves.
Mar 11:31 They **d** this among themselves.
Luk 22:4 and the temple guards and **d**
Act 24:25 As Paul **d** the subjects of
25:12 Festus **d** the appeal with his

discussing (9)

Mat 16:7 The disciples had been **d**
16:8 "Why are you **d** among
Mar 8:16 They had been **d** with one
8:17 "Why are you **d** the fact that
Luk 9:31 **d** Jesus' approaching death
24:17 "What are you **d**?"
24:19 They said to him, "We were **d**
Act 20:7 Paul was **d** ⌊Scripture⌋ with
Heb 9:5 (**D** these things in detail isn't

discussion (5)

Job 6:25 painful an honest **d** can be!
Dan 5:10 The **d** between the king and
Luk 9:46 A **d** started among them about
Act 18:19 and had a **d** with the Jews.
24:12 No one found me having a **d**

discussions (10)

Act 17:2 he had **d** about Scripture with
17:17 He held **d** in the synagogue
17:17 He also held **d** every day in the
17:18 philosophers had **d** with him.
19:8 He had **d** with people to
19:9 his disciples and held daily **d**
1Ti 1:6 and have turned to useless **d**.
6:20 Turn away from pointless **d**
2Ti 2:16 Avoid pointless **d**.
2:16 pointless **d**⌋ will become more

disease (75)

Exo 4:6 his hand out, it had a skin **d**.
Lev 13:2 turns into an infectious skin **d**,
13:3 The priest will examine the **d**.
13:3 it is an infectious skin **d**.
13:5 If the **d** looks the same and has
13:8 It is an infectious skin **d**.
13:9 has an infectious skin **d**,
13:11 he has a chronic skin **d**.
13:12 If skin **d** develops and covers
13:13 If the **d** does cover his whole
13:15 It is an infectious skin **d**.
13:20 An infectious skin **d** has
13:22 him unclean. It is a skin **d**.
13:25 an infectious skin **d** has
13:25 It is an infectious skin **d**.
13:27 It is an infectious skin **d**.
13:29 a man or a woman has some **d**
13:30 the priest will examine the **d**.
13:30 a **d** on the head or the chin.
13:31 priest examines the scabby **d**
13:31 the person with the scabby **d**
13:32 the priest will examine the **d**.
13:42 a skin **d** is developing in those
13:43 If the sore from the **d** in the bald
13:43 like a skin **d** somewhere else
13:44 down with an infectious skin **d**.
13:44 of the skin **d** on his head.
13:45 with a skin **d** must wear torn
13:46 long as they have the skin **d**,
14:2 a person clean after a skin **d**.
14:20 had the skin **d** will be clean.
14:32 who has an infectious skin **d**
22:4 of Aaron who has a skin **d**
26:16 terrorize you with **d** and fever.
Num 5:2 who has a serious skin **d**
12:10 with an infectious skin **d**.
12:10 she was covered with the **d**.
Dtr 28:22 LORD will strike you with **d**,
1Ki 15:23 he was old, he had a foot **d**.
2Ki 5:1 but he had a skin **d**.
5:3 could cure him of his skin **d**."
5:6 Cure him of his skin **d**."
5:7 so that I can cure his skin **d**!
5:11 and heal the skin **d**.
5:27 Naaman's skin **d** will cling to
5:27 Gehazi had a **d** that made his
15:5 with a skin **d** that lasted until
2Ch 16:12 Asa got a foot **d** that became
21:15 intestinal **d** until your intestines
21:18 with an incurable intestinal **d**.
26:19 a skin **d** broke out on his
26:20 a skin **d** was on his forehead.
26:20 had inflicted him ⌊with the **d**⌋.
26:21 King Uzziah had a skin **d** until
26:21 Since he had a skin **d**,
26:23 People said, "He had a skin **d**."
Job 18:13 His skin is eaten away by **d**.
Psa 41:8 "A devilish **d** has attached
106:15 gave them a degenerative **d**.
Pro 6:33 man will find **d** and dishonor,
Isa 10:16 **d** against brave men.
Mat 4:23 He also cured every **d** and
4:24 from any kind of **d** or pain.
8:2 A man with a serious skin **d**
8:3 his skin **d** went away,
9:35 cured every **d** and sickness.
10:1 to cure every **d** and sickness.
26:6 who had suffered from a skin **d**.
Mar 1:40 with a serious skin **d** came
1:42 his skin **d** went away,
3:10 everyone with a **d** rushed up
14:3 who had suffered from a skin **d**.
Luk 5:12 covered with a serious skin **d**.
5:13 his skin **d** went away.
17:12 ten men with a skin **d** met him.

diseased (6)

Lev 13:3 If the hair in the **d** area has
13:3 and the **d** area looks deeper
13:6 If the **d** area has faded and not
13:13 declare the **d** person clean.
13:17 and if the **d** area has turned
13:17 declare the **d** person clean.

diseases (28)

Exo 15:26 make you suffer any of the **d**
Lev 14:56 and for skin **d** where there is a
14:57 These instructions for skin **d**
21:20 skin **d**, or crushed testicles.
Dtr 7:15 the terrible **d** you experienced
24:8 outbreaks of serious skin **d**.
28:59 and severe and lingering **d**.
28:60 He will again bring all the **d** of
29:22 happened in this land and the **d**
2Sm 3:29 have oozing sores and skin **d**,
1Ki 8:37 Plant **d**, heat waves, funguses,
2Ki 7:3 Four men with skin **d** were at
7:8 When the men with skin **d**
2Ch 6:28 Plant **d**, heat waves, funguses,
Psa 103:3 the one who heals all your **d**,
Hab 3:5 **D** go ahead of him.
Mat 8:17 and removed our **d**."
10:8 cleanse those with skin **d**,
11:5 those with skin **d** are made
Mar 1:34 who were sick with various **d**
Luk 4:27 also many people with skin **d**
4:40 from various **d** brought them
5:15 him and have their **d** cured.
6:18 him and be cured of their **d**.
7:21 curing many people who had **d**,
7:22 those with skin **d** are made
9:1 power and authority to cure **d**.
21:11 and dreadful **d** in various

disfigured (3)

Lev 21:18 who has a **d** face, a deformity,
Isa 52:14 His appearance will be so **d**
52:14 His looks will be so **d** that he

disgrace (67)

Gen 30:23 "God has taken away my **d**."
34:14 That would be a **d** to us!
Dtr 22:30 this would **d** his father.
Jos 5:9 "Today I have removed the **d** of
1Sm 11:2 eye and bring **d** on all Israel."
17:26 and gets rid of Israel's **d**?
2Sm 13:13 Where could I go in my **d**?
2Ki 19:3 misery, punishment, and **d**.
Job 10:15 I am filled with **d** while I look
19:5 than me by using my **d** as
Psa 15:3 or bring **d** on his neighbor.
31:11 I have become a **d** because of
35:26 be clothed with shame and **d**.
39:8 Do not **d** me in front of godless
44:13 You made us a **d** to our
44:15 All day long my **d** is in front of
71:13 covered with **d** and humiliation.
74:21 people come back in **d**.
79:4 We have become a **d** to our
83:17 forever. Let them die in **d**
109:29 accuse me wear **d** as though
Pro 3:35 but fools will bear **d**.
6:33 and his **d** will not be blotted
13:5 behaves with shame and **d**.
14:34 but sin is a **d** in any society.
18:3 and insult comes along with **d**.
19:26 his mother brings shame and **d**.
Isa 4:1 Take away our **d**."
20:4 be exposed in order to **d** Egypt.
22:18 There you will become a **d** to
25:8 and he will remove the **d** of his
30:3 Egypt's shadow will be their **d**.
30:5 It can only offer shame and **d**."
37:3 misery, punishment, and **d**.
54:4 You won't remember the **d** of
Jer 3:25 and be covered by our **d**.
23:40 I will bring eternal **d** and shame
24:9 They will be a **d** and an
29:18 and they will be a **d** among all
Lam 5:1 Take a look at our **d**!
Eze 16:52 You will have to suffer **d**
16:52 of yourself and suffer **d**,
16:54 You will have to suffer **d** and
16:63 mouth because of your **d** when
22:4 That is why I will make you a **d**
28:16 down from God's mountain in **d**.
32:24 Now they suffer **d** with those
32:25 Now they suffer **d** with those
32:30 They suffer **d** with those who
36:15 You will no longer suffer the **d**
36:30 will no longer suffer **d** among
44:13 They must suffer **d** because of
Joe 2:17 who belong to you become a **d**.

Joe 2:19 you a **d** among the nations.
Mic 2:6 **D** will never overtake us."
6:16 will bear the **d** of my people."
Nah 3:5 body and kingdoms your **d**.
Hab 2:10 You have planned **d** for your
2:16 You are filled with **d** rather than
2:16 and **d** will cover your glory.
Zep 3:18 They bear a burden of **d**.
Mat 1:19 did not want to **d** her publicly.
Luk 1:25 He has removed my public **d**."
1Co 11:6 If it's a **d** for a woman to cut off
2Ti 2:9 I'm suffering **d** for spreading
Heb 12:2 on the cross and ignored the **d**
Jud 1:12 These people are a **d** at the

disgraced (25)

Dtr 27:20 He has **d** his father."
Psa 35:4 my life be put to shame and **d**.
40:14 downfall be turned back and **d**.
44:9 you have rejected and **d** us.
70:2 downfall be turned back and **d**.
71:24 my downfall have been **d**
78:66 behind and **d** them forever.
Isa 41:11 you will be ashamed and **d**.
45:16 idols will be ashamed and **d**.
45:16 will go away completely **d**.
45:17 never again be ashamed or **d**.
54:4 because you won't be **d**.
61:7 your wealth instead of being **d**.
Jer 14:3 they are ashamed and **d**.
22:22 be ashamed and **d** by all your
42:18 ridiculed, cursed, and **d**.
44:12 cursed, ridiculed, and **d**.
48:20 They will answer, 'Moab is **d**;
50:12 who gave birth to you will be **d**.
51:51 and we have been **d**.
Eze 32:30 They are **d** because they
36:32 Be ashamed and **d** because of
Dan 12:2 to be ashamed and **d** forever.
Hos 10:6 Ephraim will be **d**.
Mic 3:7 practice witchcraft will be **d**.

disgraceful (2)

1Co 11:14 itself teach you that it is **d**
1Ti 3:7 the victim of **d** insults that

disgraces (5)

Psa 57:3 He **d** the one who is harassing
Pro 12:4 but the wife who **d** him is like
25:8 the end if your neighbor **d** you?
28:7 with gluttons **d** his father.
29:15 child **d** his mother.

disgracing (1)

Heb 6:6 God again and publicly **d** him.

disguise (5)

1Ki 14:2 but **d** yourself so that people
22:30 "I will **d** myself and go into
2Ch 18:29 "I will **d** myself and go into
2Co 11:13 since they **d** themselves as
11:15 also **d** themselves as servants

disguised (7)

Gen 38:14 face with a veil, and **d** herself.
1Ki 20:38 Then the prophet, **d** with a
22:30 So the king of Israel **d** himself
2Ch 18:29 So the king of Israel **d** himself
35:22 He **d** himself as he went into
Mat 7:15 They come to you **d** as sheep,
1Ti 4:2 will speak lies **d** as truth.

disguises (2)

Pro 26:24 Whoever is filled with hate **d** it
2Co 11:14 And no wonder, even Satan **d**

disguising (1)

1Sm 28:8 After **d** himself by putting on

disgust (12)

Lev 26:11 I will never look at you with **d**.
26:15 and look at my rules with **d**,
26:30 I will look at you with **d**.
26:43 and looked at my laws with **d**.
26:44 them or look at them with **d**.
Psa 119:158 and I am filled with **d**.
Eze 23:17 turned away from them in **d**.
23:18 I turned away from her in **d** as I
23:22 you turned away from in **d**.
23:28 you turned away from in **d**.
Mal 1:13 and you sniff at it in **d**," says
Rom 2:22 As you treat idols with **d**,

disgusted (14)

1Ch 21:6 the number because he was **d**
Job 19:19 closest friends are **d** with me.
Psa 5:6 The LORD is **d** with
22:24 has not despised or been **d**
95:10 For 40 years I was **d** with
106:40 He was **d** with those who
119:163 I hate lying; I am **d** with it.
139:21 Shouldn't I be **d** with those who
Isa 66:24 All humanity will be **d** by them.
Eze 20:43 You will be **d** by every wrong
Amo 5:10 You are **d** by anyone who
6:8 I am **d** with Jacob's pride,
Zec 11:8 they also became **d** with me.
2Co 7:11 You were **d** with the wrong that

disgusting (166)

Gen 46:34 shepherds are **d** to Egyptians."
Exo 8:26 our God are **d** to Egyptians.
8:26 sacrifices that they consider **d**,
Lev 7:21 or any other **d** uncleanness and
11:10 that have no fins or scales **d**.
11:11 They must remain **d** to you.
11:11 Consider their dead bodies **d**.
11:12 fins or scales is **d** to you.
11:13 of birds you must consider **d**
11:20 four-legged animal is **d** to you.
11:23 four-legged animal is **d** to you.
11:41 that swarms on the ground is **d**
11:42 the ground. Consider them **d**.
11:43 Don't become **d** by eating
18:22 man as with a woman. It is **d**.
18:26 ever do any of these **d** things.
18:27 you did all these **d** things.
18:29 Whoever does any of these **d**
18:30 What they do is **d**.
20:12 They have done a **d** thing and
20:13 men are doing something **d**
20:25 Never become **d** by eating any
Dtr 7:25 Besides, these idols are **d** to
7:26 Never bring a **d** idol into your
7:26 Consider it detestable and **d**.
12:31 they do for their gods is **d**
13:14 and you can prove that this **d**
14:3 anything that is **d** to the LORD.
17:1 That would be **d** to him.
17:4 that this **d** thing has been
18:9 never learn the **d** practices of
18:12 Whoever does these things is **d**
18:12 because of their **d** practices.
20:18 to do all the **d** things they do
22:5 Whoever does this is **d** to the
23:7 Never consider the Edomites **d**.
23:7 consider the Egyptians **d**.
23:18 These earnings are **d** to the
24:4 This would be **d** in the LORD's
25:16 measures is **d** to the LORD.
27:15 anything **d** to the LORD that
29:17 You saw their **d** gods and idols
1Ki 11:5 and Milcom (the **d** idol
11:7 for Chemosh (the **d** idol
11:7 and for Molech (the **d** idol
14:24 did all the **d** practices done by
21:26 He did many **d** things as a
2Ki 16:3 one of the **d** things done by
21:2 copying the **d** things done by
21:11 of Judah has done **d** things,
23:13 them for Astarte (the **d** goddess
23:13 Chemosh (the **d** god of Moab),
23:13 and Milcom (the **d** god of the
23:24 and **d** gods that could be seen
2Ch 28:3 one of the **d** things done by the
33:2 copying the **d** things done by
34:33 Josiah got rid of all the **d** idols
36:8 about Jehoiakim — the **d** things
36:14 and followed all the **d** practices
Ezr 9:1 people and from the **d** practices
9:11 by their **d** practices that have
9:14 people doing these **d** things,
Job 6:7 such things. They are **d** to me.
9:31 own clothes would find me **d**.
15:16 the one who is **d** and corrupt,
30:10 Since they consider me **d**,
Psa 14:1 They do **d** things. There is no
53:1 They do **d** things. There is no
88:8 You made me **d** to them.
107:18 All food was **d** to them,
Pro 3:32 The devious person is **d** to the
6:16 even seven that are **d** to him:
8:7 wickedness is **d** to my lips.
11:1 Dishonest scales are **d** to the
11:20 Devious people are **d** to the
12:22 Lips that lie are **d** to the LORD,
13:19 turning from evil is **d** to fools.
15:8 brought by wicked people is **d**
15:9 The way of wicked people is **d**
15:26 thoughts of evil people are **d**
16:5 with a conceited heart is **d**
16:12 Wrongdoing is **d** to kings
17:15 people is **d** to the LORD.
20:10 both are **d** to the LORD.
20:23 double standard of weights is **d**
21:27 sacrifice of wicked people is **d**,
24:9 and a mocker is **d** to everyone.
26:25 because of the seven **d** things
28:9 to ⌊God's⌋ teachings is **d**.
29:27 An unjust person is **d** to
29:27 person is **d** to wicked people.
Isa 1:13 Your incense is **d** to me,
41:24 Whoever chooses you is **d**.
44:19 rest of the wood into a **d** thing
66:17 pork, **d** things, and mice.
Jer 2:7 They made my property **d**.
4:1 if you take your **d** idols out of
5:30 "Something horrible and **d** is
6:15 when they do **d** things?
7:10 safe to do all these **d** things.
8:12 ashamed that they do **d** things?
16:18 of their detestable and **d** idols."
23:13 I saw something **d**.
Eze 5:11 worship place with all your **d**
6:9 the evil and **d** things that they
6:11 have done evil and **d** things.
6:13 made offerings to their **d** idols.
7:20 and used them to make **d**
7:20 why I will make their jewels **d**.
8:6 are doing very **d** things here,
8:6 But you will see even more **d**
8:9 **d** things that the people of
8:10 every kind of **d** animal,
8:13 "You will see even more **d**
8:15 even more **d** things than these."
8:17 done these **d** things that you
9:4 about all the **d** things that are
11:18 will come and remove all the **d**
11:21 detestable and **d** idols,
12:16 that everything they did was **d**.
14:5 me because of their **d** idols.'
14:6 and don't return to any of your **d**
16:2 the **d** things they have
16:22 With all the **d** things that you
16:36 lovers and to all your **d** idols.
16:43 addition to all your **d** practices?
16:47 You didn't do the same **d** things
16:50 They were arrogant and did **d**
16:51 You have done many more **d**
16:51 Because of all the **d** things that
16:52 sins are more **d** than theirs.
16:58 crude and **d** things you have
18:12 for help. He does **d** things.
18:13 He has done all these **d** things.
18:24 He does all the **d** things that
20:4 Tell them about the **d** things
20:7 yourselves with the **d** idols
20:8 They didn't abandon the **d** idols
20:16 because their hearts chased **d**
20:18 yourselves with their **d** idols.
20:24 their ancestors' **d** idols for help.
20:31 yourselves with all your **d** idols
20:39 Serve your **d** idols.
20:39 with your gifts and your **d** idols.
22:2 Then tell it about all the **d**
22:3 You dishonor yourself with **d**
22:4 of the **d** idols you have
22:11 Men do **d** things with their

Eze 23:36 them about their **d** practices?
33:26 You do **d** things. You dishonor
33:29 of all the **d** things that they
36:31 all these wicked and **d** things.
43:8 of the **d** things that they
44:6 I've had enough of all the **d**
44:7 you could do all your **d** things.
44:13 of the **d** things that they
Dan 9:27 This will happen along with **d**
11:31 and set up the **d** thing that
12:11 and the **d** thing that causes
Hos 9:10 They became as **d** as the
Zec 9:7 and the **d** things from between
Mal 2:9 "So I have made you **d**,
2:11 A **d** thing has been done in
Mat 24:15 said that the **d** thing that will
Mar 13:14 "When you see the **d** thing that
Luk 16:15 to humans is **d** to God.

dish (27)

Num 7:13 Each **d** was filled with flour
7:14 He also brought a gold **d** that
7:19 Each **d** was filled with flour
7:20 He also brought a gold **d** that
7:25 Each **d** was filled with flour
7:26 He also brought a gold **d** that
7:31 Each **d** was filled with flour
7:32 He also brought a gold **d** that
7:37 Each **d** was filled with flour
7:38 He also brought a gold **d** that
7:43 Each **d** was filled with flour
7:44 He also brought a gold **d** that
7:49 Each **d** was filled with flour
7:50 He also brought a gold **d** that
7:55 Each **d** was filled with flour
7:56 He also brought a gold **d** that
7:61 Each **d** was filled with flour
7:62 He also brought a gold **d** that
7:67 Each **d** was filled with flour
7:68 He also brought a gold **d** that
7:73 Each **d** was filled with flour
7:74 He also brought a gold **d** that
7:79 Each **d** was filled with flour
7:80 He also brought a gold **d** that
2Ki 4:41 "**D** it out for the people to eat."
21:13 same way that a **d** is wiped out
Pro 15:17 Better to have a **d** of

Dishan (4)

Gen 36:21 Dishon, Ezer, and **D**.
36:28 These were the sons of **D**:
36:30 Dishon, Ezer, and **D**.
1Ch 1:38 Anah, Dishon, Ezer, and **D**.

Dishan's (1)

1Ch 1:42 **D** sons were Uz and Aran.

dished (1)

2Ki 4:40 They **d** out the food for the men

dishes (24)

Exo 25:29 Make plates and **d** for the table
30:27 the table and all the **d**,
31:8 the table and the **d**,
35:13 table with its poles, all the **d**,
37:16 For the table he made plates, **d**,
39:36 the table with all the **d**,
Num 4:7 put on it the plates, **d**, bowls,
7:84 12 silver bowls, and 12 gold **d**.
7:85 Together all the silver **d**
7:86 The 12 gold **d** filled with
7:86 Together all the gold **d**
1Ki 7:50 **d**, snuffers, bowls, saucers,
2Ki 12:13 But no silver bowls, snuffers, **d**,
25:14 the pots, shovels, snuffers, **d**,
2Ch 4:22 snuffers, basins, **d**,
24:14 They made **d** and gold and
Ezr 1:9 This is the inventory: gold **d**:
1:9 30 silver **d**: 1,000 knives: 29
Isa 66:20 their grain offerings in clean **d**
Jer 52:18 shovels, snuffers, bowls, **d**,
52:19 bowls, pots, lamp stands, **d**,
Mat 23:25 the outside of cups and **d**.
23:26 inside of the cups and **d** so that
Luk 11:39 the outside of cups and **d**.

Dishon (6)

Gen 36:21 **D**, Ezer, and Dishan.
36:25 **D** and Oholibamah,
36:26 These were the sons of **D**:
36:30 **D**, Ezer, and Dishan.
1Ch 1:38 Anah, **D**, Ezer, and Dishan.
1:41 Anah's son was **D**.

dishonest (28)

Dtr 25:16 Everyone who uses **d** weights
1Sm 8:3 example but turned to **d** ways
Pro 6:12 is a person who has a **d** mouth.
6:19 a **d** witness spitting out lies,
11:1 **D** scales are disgusting to the
11:18 wicked person earns **d** wages,
14:5 but a **d** witness breathes lies.
20:23 and **d** scales are no good.
Jer 22:17 are set on nothing but **d** profits.
Eze 21:25 "You **d** and wicked prince of
21:29 be placed on the necks of **d**,
28:18 of your many sins and **d** trade.
33:31 but in their hearts they chase **d**
Hos 12:7 "The merchants use **d** scales.
Amo 8:5 and cheat with **d** scales.
Mic 6:11 I cannot tolerate **d** scales and
Luk 16:8 "The master praised the **d**
16:9 wealth is often used in **d** ways,
16:10 Whoever is **d** with very little is
16:10 with very little is **d** with a lot.
18:6 to what the **d** judge thought.
18:11 I'm not a robber or a **d** person.
Jon 7:18 and doesn't have **d** motives.
1Co 5:10 are **d**, or worship false gods.
5:11 language, get drunk, or are **d**.
2Co 6:8 We are treated as **d** although
11:13 They are **d** workers,
Php 1:18 with honest or **d** motives,

dishonestly (10)

Pro 10:2 Treasures gained **d** profit no
10:9 but whoever lives **d** will be
19:1 than to be one who talks **d**
20:17 Food gained **d** tastes sweet to
28:18 Whoever lives **d** will fall all at
Jer 6:13 are eager to make money **d**.
8:10 are eager to make money **d**.
17:11 A person who gets rich **d** is
22:13 person who builds his house **d**
Luk 16:11 wealth that is often used **d**,

dishonesty (2)

Pro 4:24 Remove **d** from your mouth.
Jer 9:3 Lies and **d** rule the land.

dishonor (51)

Lev 19:29 "Never **d** your daughter by
21:6 God's holy men, and don't **d**
21:15 He must not **d** his children
21:23 He must never **d** the holy
22:2 In this way they will not **d** my
22:15 Priests must not **d** the holy
22:32 Never **d** my holy name.
Ezr 4:14 happen that will **d** the king.
Psa 89:34 I will not **d** my promise or alter
Pro 6:33 man will find disease and **d**,
Isa 23:9 in order to **d** all arrogant people
30:22 Then you will **d** your
Jer 14:21 Don't **d** your glorious throne.
Lam 2:2 down to the ground in **d**.
Eze 7:21 These foreigners will **d** the
7:22 and foreigners will **d** my
7:22 Robbers will go in and **d** it.
9:7 He said to them, "**D** the temple!
13:19 You **d** me in front of my people
14:11 They will no longer **d** me with
18:6 He doesn't **d** his neighbor's
18:15 doesn't **d** his neighbor's wife.
20:7 Don't **d** yourselves with the
20:18 Don't obey their rules or **d**
20:26 I let them **d** themselves when
20:30 Will you **d** yourselves the way
20:31 You **d** yourselves with all your
20:39 You will no longer **d** my holy
20:43 you did to **d** yourselves.
22:3 You **d** yourself with disgusting
Eze 22:11 **d** their daughters-in-law.
22:26 and **d** my holy things.
24:21 I'm going to **d** my holy place.
28:7 wisdom and **d** your greatness.
33:26 You **d** your neighbor's wife.
37:23 They will no longer **d**
39:7 and I will never let them **d** my
43:7 will no longer **d** my holy name
43:7 nor will they **d** it with the dead
Dan 11:31 His forces will **d** the holy place
Amo 2:7 They **d** my holy name.
Mic 4:11 "Let's **d** Zion and gloat over it."
Mal 1:12 "But you **d** it when you say that
2:10 And why do we **d** the promise
Mat 26:65 You've just heard him **d** God!
Mar 14:64 You've heard him **d** God!
Jon 8:49 honor my Father, but you **d** me.
Act 5:41 considered worthy to suffer **d**
Rom 1:24 As a result, they **d** their bodies
1Ti 1:20 to teach them not to **d** God.
2Pe 2:2 and will cause others to **d**

dishonorable (1)

2Ti 2:21 associating with **d** people will

dishonored (51)

Gen 34:5 had **d** his daughter Dinah.
34:13 he had **d** their sister Dinah.
34:27 where their sister had been **d**.
49:4 Then you **d** it. He climbed up on
Lev 19:8 they have **d** what is holy
20:3 and **d** my holy name.
22:9 them death because they **d**
1Ch 5:1 because he **d** his father's bed.
Psa 74:7 They **d** the place where you
79:1 They have **d** your holy temple.
Isa 47:6 I **d** those who belong to me.
48:11 Why should my name be **d**?
Jer 2:23 that you haven't **d** yourselves
32:34 by my name, and they **d** it.
34:16 have changed again and **d** me.
Eze 4:14 I have never **d** myself.
5:11 because you have **d** my holy
7:24 and their holy places will be **d**.
20:9 name would not be **d** among
20:13 They **d** the days to worship me.
20:14 name would not be **d** among
20:16 They **d** the days to worship me,
20:21 They **d** the days to worship me.
20:22 name would not be **d** among
20:24 They **d** the days to worship me,
22:4 You are **d** because of the
22:5 Your name will be **d**,
22:8 despised my holy things and **d**
22:16 You will be **d** in the sight of the
22:26 So I am **d** among the people.
23:7 She **d** herself with the idols of
23:17 and **d** her with their lust.
23:17 After they had **d** her,
23:30 after the nations and **d** yourself
23:38 they do these things and **d**
23:39 into my holy place and **d** it.
25:3 when my holy place was **d**,
28:18 You **d** your own holy places
36:17 they **d** it by the way they lived
36:18 blood on the land and they **d**
36:20 they **d** my holy name.
36:21 name because my people **d**
36:22 which you have **d** among the
36:23 which has been **d** by the
36:23 that you have **d** among them.
43:8 They **d** my holy name because
44:7 You **d** my temple when you
Mal 2:11 Judah has **d** the holy place that
Mat 26:65 and said, "He has **d** God!
1Co 4:10 You are honored, but we are **d**.
2Co 6:8 as we are praised and **d**,

dishonoring (10)

Lev 18:21 If you do, you are **d** the name of
21:12 If he does, he will be **d** it,
Num 18:32 You won't be **d** the holy
Eze 23:13 I saw that she was **d** herself.
Mat 9:3 scribes thought, "He's **d** God."
Mar 2:7 He's **d** God. Who besides God
Luk 5:21 He's **d** God! Who besides God

Jon 10:33 you've done, but for **d** God.
10:36 why do you say that I'm **d** God
Rom 2:23 are you **d** God by ignoring

dishonors (7)
Lev 19:12 This **d** the name of your God.
21:9 When a priest's daughter **d**
21:9 a prostitute, she **d** her father.
Eze 18:11 He **d** his neighbor's wife.
Luk 12:10 But the person who **d** the Holy
1Co 11:4 what God has revealed **d**
11:5 uncovered while she speaks **d**

Dishon's (1)
1Ch 1:41 **D** sons were Hamran,

disks (1)
Sos 5:14 His hands are **d** of gold set

dislocated (1)
Gen 32:25 that it was **d** as they wrestled.

dislodged (2)
Job 14:18 mountain falls and rocks are **d**,
18:4 for your sake or a boulder be **d**?

disloyal (2)
Jos 7:1 of Israel proved to be **d** about
Psa 78:57 They were **d** and treacherous

dismal (1)
Job 10:22 to a **d** land of long shadows

dismembered (1)
2Ch 25:12 of the cliff so that they were **d**.

dismiss (1)
2Sm 3:24 Why did you **d** him and let him

dismissed (11)
Exo 7:23 He **d** the entire matter from his
2Sm 3:21 Then David **d** Abner,
3:22 Abner had been **d**,
3:23 to the king, but David **d** him,
1Ki 8:66 the eighth day he **d** the people.
2Ki 5:24 Then he **d** the men,
2Ch 7:10 Solomon **d** the people to their
23:8 had not **d** the priestly divisions.
25:10 Then Amaziah **d** the troops that
Act 19:41 he **d** the assembly.
23:22 The officer **d** the young man

disobedience (22)
Exo 23:21 he will not forgive your **d**.
34:7 wrongdoing, **d**, and sin.
Num 14:18 forgives wrongdoing and **d** ....
Job 7:21 Why don't you forgive my **d**
13:23 me aware of my **d** and my sin.
14:17 My **d** will be closed up in a
31:33 "If I have covered my **d** like
34:37 He adds **d** to his sin.
Psa 32:1 Blessed is the person whose **d**
59:3 but not because of any **d**,
107:17 suffered because of their **d**
Isa 24:20 Its **d** weighs heavy on it.
Amo 3:14 the day I punish Israel for its **d**,
Rom 4:7 "Blessed are those whose **d** is
5:19 Clearly, through one person's **d**
6:19 to sexual perversion and **d**.
11:30 to you because of the **d**
11:32 the prison of their own **d** so that
2Co 10:6 every act of **d** when you have
Heb 2:2 act of **d** was properly punished.
10:17 sins and their **d** against them."
1Jn 3:4 are disobeying God. Sin is **d**.

disobedient (9)
Job 34:6 though I haven't been **d**.'
Lam 3:42 have been **d** and rebellious.
Luk 1:17 He will change **d** people so
Act 7:51 can you be so heartless and **d**?
Rom 6:19 This led you to live **d** lives.
10:21 to **d** and rebellious people."
Tit 1:16 They are detestable, **d**,
3:3 once stupid, **d**, and misled.
Jas 2:9 law convicts you of being **d**.

disobey (7)
Num 22:18 I couldn't **d** the command of the
24:13 I couldn't **d** the LORD's
Dtr 11:28 You'll be cursed if you **d** the
17:20 and he won't **d** these
Jer 42:13 and you **d** the LORD your God.
Act 26:19 "At that point I did not **d** the
Heb 11:23 not afraid to **d** the king's order.

disobeyed (10)
Dtr 26:13 I **d** none of your commands,
Jos 5:6 died because they **d** the LORD.
Isa 24:5 live on it because they've **d**
Jer 50:29 They have **d** the LORD,
Dan 3:28 They **d** the king and risked
Luk 15:29 I've never **d** one of your
Rom 5:14 way Adam did when he **d**.
11:30 In the past, you **d** God.
11:31 the Jewish people have also **d**
1Pe 3:20 They are like those who **d** long

disobeying (4)
Lev 26:15 promise by **d** my commands,
Num 14:41 "Why are you **d** the LORD's
1Ki 18:18 father's family have done it by **d**
1Jn 3:4 who live sinful lives are **d** God.

disobeys (2)
Dtr 17:12 If anyone deliberately **d** the
Jas 2:11 a person who **d** God's laws.

disorder (3)
Jos 10:10 LORD threw the enemy into **d**
1Co 14:33 God is not a God of **d** but a
Jas 3:16 there is **d** and every kind of

disorderly (1)
2Co 12:20 arrogance, and **d** conduct.

disown (2)
2Ti 2:12 If we **d** him, he will disown us.
2:12 If we disown him, he will **d** us.

disowned (1)
Lam 2:7 his altar and **d** his holy place.

dispersing (1)
1Sm 14:16 camp⌋ **d** in all directions.

display (9)
Psa 60:12 God we will **d** great strength.
68:28 **D** your strength, O God, as you
78:38 He did not **d** all of his fury.
108:13 God we will **d** great strength.
Isa 44:23 He will **d** his glory in Israel.
49:3 I will **d** my glory through you."
49:18 of them like jewels and **d** them
61:3 so that he might **d** his glory.
Rom 3:26 He waited so that he could **d**

displayed (3)
1Ch 26:14 a counselor who **d** insight,
Psa 105:27 They **d** his miraculous signs
Luk 1:51 "He **d** his mighty power.

displays (4)
Psa 19:1 and the sky **d** what his hands
118:15 The right hand of the LORD **d**
118:16 The right hand of the LORD **d**
Pro 13:16 but a fool **d** stupidity.

displease (1)
1Sm 29:7 to **d** the Philistine rulers."

displeased (2)
Num 11:11 How have I **d** you that you put
Dan 6:14 The king was very **d** when he

displeasing (1)
1Th 2:15 They are **d** to God.

dispose (1)
1Sm 25:29 But he will **d** of the lives of

dispute (7)
Exo 22:9 If there is a **d** over the
Dtr 1:16 no matter whether it is ⌊a **d**⌋
1:16 two Israelites or ⌊a **d**⌋ between
17:8 or a **d** — any case which may
Jdg 12:2 in a legal **d** with Ammon.
Pro 26:21 a quarrelsome person fuels a **d**.
Act 15:2 and Barnabas had a fierce **d**

disputes (9)
Pro 15:18 who holds his temper calms **d**.
18:19 and **d** are like the locked gate
Isa 2:4 Then he will judge **d** between
Eze 34:17 I will judge **d** between one
34:20 I will judge **d** between the fat
44:24 In all **d** the priests must act as
Mic 4:3 Then he will judge **d** between
Hab 1:3 Quarrels and **d** arise.
Act 23:29 with **d** about Jewish teachings.

disputing (2)
Act 18:15 But since you're **d** words,
25:19 They were **d** with him about

disqualified (1)
1Co 9:27 so that I will not be **d** after

disqualify (1)
Exo 19:15 Don't **d** yourselves by having

disregard (3)
Dtr 9:27 **D** the stubbornness,
21:16 This would show a total **d** for
Pro 6:20 and do not **d** the teachings of

disregarded (2)
2Ki 18:12 obey the LORD their God and **d**
Isa 58:2 haven't **d** God's judgment ⌊on

disregarding (1)
Dtr 17:2 This person may be **d** the

disrespect (1)
Exo 22:28 "Never show **d** for God or curse

disrespectful (4)
Gen 16:4 she began to be **d** to Sarai,
16:5 she's being **d** to me.
Dtr 32:15 Jeshurun got fat and **d**.
2Pe 3:3 These **d** people will ridicule

distaff (1)
Pro 31:19 "She puts her hands on the **d**,

distance (46)
Gen 22:4 saw the place in the **d**.
32:16 keep a **d** between the herds."
35:16 were still some **d** from Ephrath,
37:18 They saw him from a **d**.
48:7 were still some **d** from Ephrath.
Exo 2:4 The baby's sister stood at a **d**
20:18 with fear and stood at a **d**.
20:21 The people kept their **d** while
24:1 to me and worship at a **d**.
Num 10:33 went ahead of them a **d**
Dtr 21:2 go and measure the **d** from
32:52 You may see the land from a **d**,
Jdg 18:22 some **d** from Micah's house,
1Sm 26:13 on top of the hill some **d** away.
1Ki 6:24 The **d** from the tip of one wing
2Ki 2:7 prophets stood at a **d** as Elijah
2:15 at Jericho saw him from a **d**.
3:22 they saw the water from a **d**.
4:25 he saw her coming at a **d**,
5:19 had left him and gone some **d**,
Job 2:12 When they saw him from a **d**,
30:10 they keep their **d** from me and
36:25 have looked at it from a **d**.
Psa 38:11 and my friends keep their **d**
138:6 arrogant people from a **d**.
Pro 19:7 friends keep their **d** from him!
Isa 33:17 a land that stretches into the **d**.
Jer 50:26 Attack them from a **d**,
Eze 40:19 The man measured the **d** from
40:23 The man measured the **d** from

Eze 40:27 The man measured the **d** from
Mat 8:30 of pigs was feeding in the **d**.
26:58 Peter followed at a **d** until he
27:55 were there watching from a **d**.
Mar 5:6 The man saw Jesus at a **d**.
8:3 of them have come a long **d**."
8:25 everything clearly even at a **d**.
11:13 In the **d** he saw a fig tree with
14:54 Peter followed him at a **d** and
15:40 were watching from a **d**.
Luk 15:20 While he was still at a **d**,
16:23 As he looked up, in the **d** he
17:12 They stood at a **d**
18:13 collector was standing at a **d**.
22:54 Peter followed at a **d**.
23:49 at a **d** and watched everything.

distanced (1)

Isa 57:8 You've **d** yourself from me.

distant (44)

Dtr 4:32 Search the **d** past,
29:22 come from **d** countries will see
30:4 scattered to the most **d** country
Jos 9:6 have come from a **d** country.
2Sm 7:19 You've also spoken about the **d**
16:5 a man who was a **d** cousin of
1Ki 8:41 come from **d** countries
2Ki 19:23 I'll come to its most **d** borders
19:25 I planned it in the **d** past.
20:14 from the **d** country of Babylon."
1Ch 17:17 You've spoken about the **d**
2Ch 6:32 will come from **d** countries
Neh 1:9 be driven to the most **d** point
Psa 10:1 Why are you so **d**,
38:21 do not be so **d** from me.
65:5 the earth and of the most **d** sea,
71:12 O God, do not be so **d** from me.
139:9 ⌊or⌋ land on the most **d** shore
Isa 7:18 flies that are at the **d** branches
8:9 all you **d** parts of the earth.
13:5 army is coming from a **d** land,
23:7 city founded in the **d** past?
23:7 its people to settle in **d** lands?
37:24 I'll come to its most **d** heights
37:26 I planned it in the **d** past.
39:3 from the **d** country of Babylon."
41:9 you from its most **d** places.
45:21 Who revealed this in the **d** past
63:11 Moses and the **d** past.
66:19 and to the **d** coastlands who
Jer 4:16 are coming from a **d** country.
6:20 Sugar cane that comes from a **d**
6:22 is preparing itself in the **d** parts
8:19 people comes from a **d** land:
16:19 to you from the most **d** parts
25:32 is brewing from the **d** corners
31:10 Tell it to the **d** islands.
51:50 the LORD in a **d** land,
Eze 12:27 will happen in the **d** future.'
Dan 4:22 Your power reaches the most **d**
8:26 that will happen in the **d** future."
Mic 5:2 origins go back to the **d** past,
Luk 19:12 He said, "A prince went to a **d**
Heb 11:13 things coming in the **d** future

distills (1)

Job 36:27 He **d** rain from his mist,

distinction (1)

Exo 11:7 shows the **d** between Egypt

distinguish (9)

Exo 8:23 I will **d** between my people and
9:4 But the LORD will **d** between
Lev 11:47 These instructions help you **d**
14:57 help you **d** between what is
2Sm 14:17 who is able to **d** right from
Ezr 3:13 No one could **d** between the
Job 12:11 Doesn't the ear **d** sounds and
Eze 22:26 They don't **d** between what is
Rom 2:18 know what he wants, and **d**

distinguished (6)

2Sm 23:20 He killed two **d** soldiers from
1Ch 7:40 men, soldiers, and **d** leaders.
1Ch 11:22 He killed two **d** soldiers from
11:26 The **d** fighting men were Joab's
Dan 6:3 This man, Daniel, **d** himself
1Jn 3:10 way God's children are **d** from

distort (10)

Job 8:3 Does God **d** justice,
8:3 or does the Almighty **d**
Act 13:8 opposed them and tried to **d** the
13:10 Quit trying to **d** the truth about
20:30 and say things that **d** the truth.
2Co 4:2 and we don't **d** God's word.
Gal 1:7 They want to **d** the Good News
4:17 These people ⌊who **d** the
2Pe 3:16 they believe **d** what Paul says
3:16 his letters the same way they **d**

distracted (1)

1Co 7:35 without being **d** by other things.

distracting (1)

Exo 5:4 why are you **d** the people from

distracts (1)

Heb 12:1 especially sin that **d** us.

distress (53)

Gen 16:11 LORD has heard your cry of **d**.
Dtr 4:30 When you're in **d** and all these
1Sm 2:32 You will see **d** in my dwelling
20:3 It will bring him **d**.' But
30:6 David was in great **d** because
2Sm 22:7 I called on the LORD in my **d**.
1Ki 21:27 he tore his clothes ⌊in **d**⌋ and
2Ki 5:7 he tore his clothes ⌊in **d**⌋.
6:30 he tore his clothes ⌊in **d**⌋.
11:14 Athaliah tore her clothes ⌊in **d**⌋,
22:11 he tore his clothes ⌊in **d**⌋.
22:19 also tore your clothes ⌊in **d**⌋
2Ch 23:13 Athaliah tore her clothes ⌊in **d**⌋,
33:12 When he experienced this **d**,
34:19 he tore his clothes ⌊in **d**⌋.
34:27 tore your clothes ⌊in **d**⌋,
Ezr 9:3 I tore my clothes ⌊in **d**⌋,
Job 7:11 but I will speak from the **d** that
15:24 **D** and anguish terrify him like a
36:15 he opens their ears through **d**.
Psa 18:6 I called on the LORD in my **d**.
25:17 and bring me out of my **d**.
31:9 because I am in **d**.
107:6 In their **d** they cried out to the
107:13 In their **d** they cried out to the
107:19 In their **d** they cried out to the
107:28 In their **d** they cried out to the
144:14 be no cries of **d** in our streets.
Pro 17:5 someone's⌋ **d** will not escape
Isa 5:7 but heard only cries of **d**.
5:30 will see only darkness and **d**.
8:22 and see only **d** and gloom.
9:1 gloom for the land that is in **d**.
25:4 a refuge for the needy in their **d**,
30:6 experience **d** and hardship.
46:7 It can't rescue them from their **d**
Jer 15:11 of disaster and in times of **d**.
Lam 1:20 "O LORD, see the **d** I'm in!
Hos 5:15 In their **d** they will eagerly look
Oba 1:12 brag so much when they're in **d**.
1:14 survivors when they're in **d**.
Jnh 2:2 "I called to the LORD in my **d**,
Zep 1:15 a day of trouble and **d**,
1:17 "I will bring such **d** on humans
Zec 10:11 will pass through a sea of **d**,
Rom 2:9 There will be suffering and **d**
8:35 Can trouble, **d**, persecution,
2Co 2:5 If someone caused **d**,
2:7 Such **d** could overwhelm
6:4 things: suffering, **d**, anxiety,
7:9 but because the **d** I caused you
7:10 But the **d** that the world causes
1Th 3:7 us in all our **d** and trouble.

distressed (10)

Gen 32:7 Jacob was terrified and **d**.
Isa 19:10 who work for money will be **d**.
Mar 14:33 began to feel **d** and anguished.
2Co 2:1 visit you again while I was **d**.
2Co 2:3 you and be **d** by those who
5:4 We feel **d** because we don't
7:9 You were **d** in a godly way,
7:10 In fact, to be **d** in a godly way
7:11 When you became **d** in a godly
2Pe 2:7 Lot was **d** by the lifestyle of

distresses (1)

1Sm 10:19 from all your troubles and **d**.

distressful (1)

Jer 48:5 heard the **d** cry of destruction.

distribute (12)

Dtr 26:12 During that year **d** what you
26:14 I didn't **d** any of it while I was
Jos 13:6 However, you must **d** the land
2Ch 31:14 His responsibility was to **d** the
31:15 They were to **d** the offerings
31:16 They were appointed to **d** them
31:16 served under Kore were to **d**
31:17 They were to **d** offerings to the
Dan 11:24 He will **d** loot and wealth to his
11:39 and **d** land for a price.
Luk 18:22 **D** the money to the poor,
Act 6:2 God's word in order to **d** food.

distributed (12)

Dtr 26:13 When you have **d** all that was
26:13 I **d** it to the Levites,
Jos 13:32 This is the land that Moses **d**
14:1 the heads of Israel's tribes **d**
17:6 These portions were **d**
2Sm 6:19 He also **d** to all the people — to
1Ch 16:3 He also **d** to every person in
Isa 33:23 A large amount of loot will be **d**.
Jon 6:11 and **d** them to the people who
Act 2:45 and other possessions and **d**
4:35 Then the money was **d** to
6:1 and other assistance was **d**.

distributing (1)

Neh 13:13 I made them responsible for **d**

distribution (1)

2Ch 31:17 **D** was based on the way they

district (15)

1Ki 4:5 in charge of the **d** governors.
4:7 Solomon appointed 12 **d**
20:14 officers of the **d** governors."
20:15 officers of the **d** governors.
20:17 The young officers of the **d**
20:19 The young officers of the **d**
Neh 3:9 charge of half a **d** of Jerusalem,
3:12 charge of half a **d** of Jerusalem,
3:14 the official in charge of the **d** of
3:15 in charge of the **d** of Mizpah,
3:16 official in charge of half the **d**
3:17 in charge of half the **d** of Keilah,
3:17 made repairs for his **d**.
3:18 in charge of half the **d** of Keilah.
Ecc 5:8 or denied their rights in any **d**.

districts (1)

Jos 13:2 includes all the **d** that belong

disturb (7)

Gen 49:9 Who dares to **d** him?
Num 24:9 Who dares to **d** them?
1Sm 28:15 "Why did you **d** me by
2Ki 23:18 Don't **d** his bones."
Isa 17:2 be no one to **d** those sheep.
Act 15:24 you with statements that **d** you.
1Th 3:3 so that these troubles don't **d**

disturbance (1)

Act 19:23 During that time a serious **d**

disturbed (5)

Isa 21:3 I'm **d** by what I hear.
31:4 by their voices or **d** by
Jer 23:9 the prophets: I am deeply **d**.
Mat 2:3 about this, they became **d**.
Mar 6:20 he would become very **d**,

disturbing (2)
Job 4:13 With **d** thoughts from visions in
20:2 "My **d** thoughts make me

disturbs (2)
Job 16:3 What **d** you that you keep on
Lam 3:51 What I see with my eyes **d** me

ditch (1)
Isa 7:3 to meet Ahaz at the end of the **d**

ditches (1)
2Ki 3:16 Make this valley full of **d**.

divide (37)
Gen 49:7 I will **d** them among ⌊the sons
Exo 14:16 over the sea, and **d** the water.
15:9 I'll **d** the loot! I'll take all I want!
21:35 must sell the live bull and **d**
21:35 They must **d** the dead bull,
Num 31:27 **D** the loot between the soldiers
33:54 **D** the land among your families
33:54 **D** it among your ancestors'
34:13 "This is the land you will **d** by
34:17 names of the men who will **d**
34:18 from each tribe to **d** the land.
34:29 LORD commanded to **d** Canaan
Dtr 19:3 to each of these cities and **d**
Jos 13:7 So **d** this land. It will be an
18:5 They will **d** the land into seven
22:8 **D** the loot from your enemies
2Sm 19:29 and Ziba should **d** the land."
Job 27:17 and the innocent will **d** the
41:6 traders bargain over it and **d**
Psa 22:18 They **d** my clothes among
60:6 I will **d** Shechem. I will measure
68:12 at home will **d** the goods.
108:7 I will **d** Shechem. I will measure
Pro 30:27 yet all of them **d** into swarms
Ecc 11:2 **D** what you have into seven
Isa 7:6 **d** it among ourselves,
11:15 with his scorching wind and **d**
53:12 and he will **d** the prize with the
Eze 5:1 scales to weigh your hair and **d**
45:1 "'**D** the land by drawing lots for
47:14 **D** the land equally.
47:21 **D** this land among yourselves
47:22 **D** it by drawing lots.
48:29 This is the land you will **d** as
Mic 2:5 draw lots to **d** your property.
Luk 11:22 man trusted and will **d** the loot.
12:14 or to **d** ⌊your inheritance⌋?"

divided (75)
Gen 2:10 the garden it **d** into four rivers.
10:25 in his day the earth was **d**.
32:7 So he **d** the people,
33:1 So he **d** the children among
Exo 14:21 into dry ground. The water **d**,
Lev 11:3 that have completely **d** hoofs
11:4 chew their cud or have **d** hoofs,
11:4 cud but do not have **d** hoofs.)
11:5 cud but do not have **d** hoofs.)
11:6 cud but do not have **d** hoofs.)
11:7 pigs have completely **d** hoofs
11:26 hoofs are not completely **d**
Num 26:53 will possess must be **d** using
26:55 But the land must be **d** by
26:56 must be **d** by drawing lots."
Dtr 14:6 that have completely **d** hoofs
14:7 have completely **d** hoofs.
14:7 they don't have **d** hoofs.
14:8 (Although their hoofs are **d**,
32:8 when he **d** the descendants of
Jos 14:5 So the people of Israel **d** the
18:9 The land was **d** into seven
18:10 There Joshua **d** the land
19:51 the leaders of the families **d**
Jdg 7:16 Gideon **d** the 300 men into
9:43 **d** them into three companies,
1Ki 16:21 Then the army of Israel was **d**
2Ki 2:8 The water **d** to their left and
2:14 it **d** to his left and his right,
1Ch 1:19 in his day the earth was **d**.
24:3 **d** Aaron's descendants into
24:4 they were **d** so that Eleazar's
24:5 Both groups were **d** impartially
Neh 9:11 You **d** the sea in front of them
Psa 78:13 He **d** the sea and led them
136:13 Give thanks to one who **d** the
Pro 3:20 the deep waters were **d**,
Isa 18:2 whose land is **d** by rivers.
18:7 whose land is **d** by rivers.
63:12 Where is the one who **d** the
Eze 37:22 or be **d** into two kingdoms.
47:13 the land that is to be **d** among
Dan 2:41 will be a **d** kingdom which has
5:25 Numbered, Weighed, and **D**.
5:28 **D** — your kingdom will be
5:28 your kingdom will be **d**
11:4 be broken into pieces and **d**
Joe 3:2 the nations. They **d** my land.
Amo 7:17 land will be surveyed and **d** up,
Zec 14:1 taken will be **d** among you.
Mat 12:25 "Every kingdom **d** against itself
12:25 And every city or household **d**
12:26 he is **d** against himself.
27:35 they **d** his clothes among
Mar 3:24 If a kingdom is **d** against itself,
3:25 a household is **d** against itself,
3:26 rebels against himself and is **d**,
15:24 Then they **d** his clothes among
Luk 11:17 "Every kingdom **d** against itself
11:17 A house **d** against itself falls.
11:18 if Satan is **d** against himself,
12:52 on a family of five will be **d**.
12:52 Three will be **d** against two
15:12 So the father **d** his property
23:34 Meanwhile, the soldiers **d** his
Jon 7:43 were **d** because of Jesus.
9:16 were **d** in their opinions.
10:19 The Jews were **d** because of
19:23 they took his clothes and **d**
19:24 "They **d** my clothes among
Act 14:4 the people of Iconium were **d**.
23:7 the men in the meeting were **d**.
1Co 1:13 Has Christ been **d**?
7:34 His attention is **d**. An unmarried
12:25 that the body should not be **d**

divides (3)
Gen 49:27 the evening he **d** the plunder."
Isa 34:17 and his hand **d** up ⌊the land⌋
Mic 2:4 He **d** our fields among our

dividing (6)
Jos 11:23 **d** it among the tribes.
12:7 **d** it among the tribes.
19:51 So they finished **d** the land.
22:25 Jordan River a **d** line between
Jdg 5:30 really finding and **d** the loot:
Isa 9:3 harvest or rejoice when **d** loot.

divine (24)
2Ch 24:27 the many **d** revelations against
Job 34:23 to bring him to **d** judgment.
Pro 16:10 When a **d** revelation is on a
Isa 13:1 This is the **d** revelation which
14:28 This was the **d** revelation in
15:1 This is the **d** revelation about
17:1 This is the **d** revelation about
19:1 This is the **d** revelation about
21:1 This is the **d** revelation about
21:11 This is the **d** revelation about
21:13 This is the **d** revelation about
22:1 This is the **d** revelation about
23:1 This is the **d** revelation about
30:6 This is the **d** revelation about
35:4 vengeance, with **d** revenge.
Eze 12:10 This is the **d** revelation about
Hab 1:1 The **d** revelation that the
Zec 9:1 This is the **d** revelation.
Mal 1:1 This is a **d** revelation.
Act 7:10 God gave Joseph **d** favor and
17:29 we shouldn't think that the **d**
Rom 1:20 his eternal power and **d** nature,
2Pe 1:3 God's **d** power has given us
1:4 you will share in the **d** nature

division (11)
Gen 10:25 name of the one was Peleg [**D**],
Jos 22:14 and head of a family **d** in Israel.
1Ch 1:19 name of the one was Peleg [**D**],
15:18 relatives from the second **d**:
2Ch 31:2 or Levite was put in a **d** based
31:16 each **d** was responsible for.
Ezr 10:16 chose one from each family **d**.
Luk 1:5 who belonged to the **d** of
1:8 on duty with his **d** of priests.
12:51 I came to bring nothing but **d**.
Act 27:1 he belonged to the emperor's **d**.

divisions (34)
Num 1:3 military duty. List them by **d**.
1:16 and heads of the **d** of Israel.
10:4 the heads of the **d** of Israel,
31:5 tribe were supplied from the **d**
31:48 the officers from the military **d**,
Jos 22:21 the heads of the **d** of Israel.
22:30 and the heads of the **d** of Israel
Jdg 5:15 Among Reuben's **d** important
5:16 Reuben's **d** of important men
1Sm 11:11 arranged the army in three **d**.
1Ch 23:6 the Levites into **d** based
24:1 The **d** of Aaron's descendants
26:1 The following were the **d** of the
26:12 These **d** of gatekeepers
26:19 These were the **d** of the
28:13 He determined the **d** of priests
28:21 Here are also the **d** of the
2Ch 5:11 regard to staying in their **d**.
8:14 he set up the **d** of priests for
8:14 service and the ⌊**d** of⌋ Levites
8:14 Solomon also set up **d** of
23:8 not dismissed the priestly **d**.
23:18 (David had arranged them in **d**
31:2 the priests and the Levites to **d**.
31:15 young and old, by their **d**.
31:17 the way they served in their **d**.
35:4 the family groups of your **d**,
35:5 place representing the family **d**
35:10 the Levites according to their **d**,
35:12 according to their family **d**.
Ezr 6:18 priests were assigned to their **d**
Neh 11:36 Some **d** of Levites in Judah
Rom 16:17 for those people who create **d**
Jud 1:19 are the people who cause **d**.

divorce (16)
Dtr 22:19 and he can never **d** her as long
22:29 he can never **d** her as long as
24:1 writes out a certificate of **d**,
Isa 50:1 are your mother's **d** papers?
Jer 3:8 that I gave Israel her **d** papers.
Mal 2:16 "I hate **d**," says the LORD God
Mat 19:3 They asked, "Can a man **d** his
19:7 wife a written notice to **d** her?"
19:8 "Moses allowed you to **d** your
19:10 a man can use to **d** his wife,
Mar 10:2 "Can a husband **d** his wife?"
10:4 wife a written notice to **d** her."
1Co 7:11 husband should not **d** his wife.
7:12 he should not **d** her.
7:13 she should not **d** her husband.
7:27 Don't seek a **d**. Are you divorced

divorced (10)
Lev 21:7 or **d** women because a priest is
21:14 marry a widow, a **d** woman,
22:13 daughter is widowed or **d**,
Num 30:9 "But a widow or a **d** woman
Dtr 24:1 (He **d** her because he found out
1Ch 8:8 Shaharaim **d** his wives Hushim
Eze 44:22 or women who have been **d**.
Mat 5:32 Whoever marries a woman **d** in
Luk 16:18 man who marries a woman **d**
1Co 7:27 Are you **d** from your wife?

divorces (8)
Dtr 24:3 doesn't love her and **d** her,
Jer 3:1 A saying: If a man **d** his wife
Mat 5:31 'Whoever **d** his wife must give
5:32 that any man who **d** his wife
19:9 I can guarantee that whoever **d**
Mar 10:11 He answered them, "Whoever **d**
10:12 If a wife **d** her husband and
Luk 16:18 "Any man who **d** his wife to

Di Zahab (1)
Dtr 1:1 near Laban, Hazeroth, and **D**.

docked (1)
Eze 27:9 their sailors **d** alongside you

doctor (5)
Isa 3:7 will cry out, "I'm not a **d**!
Mat 9:12 "Healthy people don't need a **d**;
Mar 2:17 "Healthy people don't need a **d**;
Luk 4:23 to me, '**D**, cure yourself!'
5:31 "Healthy people don't need a **d**;

doctors (5)
Gen 50:2 Then Joseph ordered the **d** in
50:2 So the **d** embalmed Israel.
2Ch 16:12 LORD for help, he went to **d**.
Jer 8:22 Aren't there **d** there?
Mar 5:26 been under the care of many **d**

doctrine (8)
Rom 16:17 faith⌋ by teaching **d** that is not
1Co 14:6 prophecy, or **d** to you.
14:26 **d**, revelation, another language,
15:2 News if you hold on to the **d**
15:3 most important points of **d** that
1Ti 1:3 people to stop teaching false **d**
6:3 Whoever teaches false **d** and
Tit 3:10 to teach false **d** after you have

document (4)
Neh 9:38 are putting their seals on the **d**."
Est 3:14 A copy of the **d** was made
8:13 The copy of the **d** was made
Dan 6:10 When Daniel learned that the **d**

documents (5)
Est 1:22 He sent official **d** to all the
3:13 were sent with official **d**
8:10 name and sealed the official **d**
9:30 Mordecai sent official **d**
Jer 32:14 Take both of these **d**,

Dodai (1)
1Ch 27:4 **D**, Ahoh's descendant, was in

Dodai's (1)
1Ch 27:4 In **D** unit there were 24,000.

Dodavahu (1)
2Ch 20:37 son of **D** from Mareshah,

dodged (1)
1Sm 19:10 But David **d** it, and Saul's spear

Dodo (5)
Jdg 10:1 son of Puah and grandson of **D**,
2Sm 23:9 He was the son of **D** and
23:24 (son of **D**) from Bethlehem,
1Ch 11:12 He was the son of **D** and
11:26 (son of **D**) from Bethlehem,

doe (2)
Gen 49:21 "Naphtali is a **d** set free that
Pro 5:19 a loving **d** and a graceful deer.

Doeg (5)
1Sm 21:7 His name was **D**. A foreman for
22:9 Then **D** from Edom,
22:18 So the king said to **D**,
22:18 **D** from Edom turned and
22:22 "I knew that day when **D** from

does (3)
Job 39:1 Do you watch the **d** when they
Sos 2:7 me by the gazelles or by the **d**
3:5 me by the gazelles or by the **d**

dog (11)
Exo 11:7 not even a **d** will be startled by
1Sm 17:43 "Am I a **d** that you come to
24:14 A dead **d**? One flea?
2Sm 3:8 behaving like some Judean **d**?"
9:8 look at a dead **d** like me?"
16:9 should this dead **d** curse you,
2Ki 8:13 "How can a **d** like me do such
Pro 26:11 As a **d** goes back to its vomit,
26:17 ⌊Like⌋ grabbing a **d** by the
Ecc 9:4 because a living **d** is better
2Pe 2:22 "A **d** goes back to its vomit,"

dog's (1)
Isa 66:3 someone who breaks a **d** neck.

dogs (28)
Exo 22:31 countryside. Throw it to the **d**."
Jdg 7:5 tongues like **d** from those who
1Ki 14:11 dies in the city, **d** will eat him.
16:4 **D** will eat anyone from
21:19 At the place where the **d** licked
21:19 the **d** will lick up your blood.'"
21:23 "The **d** will eat Jezebel inside
21:24 dies in the city, **d** will eat him.
22:38 The **d** licked up his blood,
2Ki 9:10 **D** will eat Jezebel inside the
9:36 He said, '**D** will eat Jezebel's
Job 30:1 fit to sit with the **d** of my flock.
Psa 22:16 **D** have surrounded me.
22:20 my life from vicious **d**.
59:6 They howl like **d**. They prowl
59:14 They howl like **d**. They prowl
68:23 the tongues of your **d** may lick
Isa 56:10 All of them are like **d** that are
56:11 These **d** have huge appetites.
Jer 15:3 swords to kill, **d** to drag away,
Mat 7:6 "Don't give what is holy to **d** or
15:26 food and throw it to the **d**."
15:27 But even the **d** eat scraps that
Mar 7:27 food and throw it to the **d**."
7:28 even the **d** under the table eat
Luk 16:21 and **d** would lick them.
Php 3:2 Beware of **d**! Beware of those
Rev 22:15 Outside are **d**, sorcerers,

dollars (15)
Mat 18:24 him millions of **d** was brought
18:28 who owed him hundreds of **d**.
25:15 gave one man ten thousand **d**,
25:15 another four thousand **d**,
25:15 and another two thousand **d**.
25:16 ten thousand **d** invested
25:17 who had four thousand **d** did
25:18 two thousand **d** went off,
25:20 ten thousand **d** brought
25:20 you gave me ten thousand **d**.
25:22 received four thousand **d** came
25:22 you gave me four thousand **d**.
25:24 received two thousand **d** came
25:25 So I hid your two thousand **d** in
25:28 Take the two thousand **d** away

dome (5)
Eze 1:22 Something like a **d** was spread
1:23 Under the **d**, each creature had
1:25 A voice came from above the **d**
1:26 Above the **d** over their heads
10:1 As I looked at the **d** over the

domestic (15)
Gen 1:24 every type of **d** animal,
1:25 every type of **d** animal,
1:26 the **d** animals all over the earth,
2:20 man named all the **d** animals,
3:14 than all the wild or **d** animals.
6:7 but also **d** animals,
6:20 every type of **d** animal,
7:14 every type of **d** animal,
7:21 **d** and wild animals,
7:23 Humans, **d** animals,
8:1 and all the wild and **d** animals
8:17 with you: birds, **d** animals,
9:10 is with you — birds, **d** animals,
Exo 11:5 including every firstborn **d**
Psa 148:10 wild animals and all **d** animals,

dominate (2)
Gen 1:18 to **d** the day and the night,
Dan 11:12 Although he will **d** tens of

dominates (1)
Rev 17:18 is the important city which **d**

donated (7)
2Ki 12:10 count the money that was **d**
22:9 "We have taken the money **d** in
1Ch 26:26 commanders of the army had **d**.
26:27 (They had **d** some of the loot
26:28 and Joab (son of Zeruiah) had **d**
26:28 that had been **d** — was under
2Ch 34:17 We took the money that was **d**

donkey (85)
Gen 16:12 free and wild as an untamed **d**.
22:3 Abraham saddled his **d**.
22:5 "You stay here with the **d** while
42:27 opened his sack to feed his **d**.
44:13 Then each one loaded his **d**
49:11 He will tie his **d** to a grapevine,
49:14 "Issachar is a strong **d**,
Exo 4:20 wife and sons, put them on a **d**,
13:13 to buy any firstborn **d** back from
20:17 or female slave, his ox, his **d**,
21:33 it and a bull or a **d** falls into it,
22:4 it's a bull, **d**, or a sheep,
22:9 of a bull, a **d**, a sheep,
22:10 gives his neighbor a **d**,
23:4 ox or **d** wandering loose,
23:5 Whenever you see that the **d** of
23:12 Then your ox and **d** can rest.
34:20 goat to buy back the firstborn **d**.
Num 16:15 from them, not even a **d**.
22:21 he saddled his **d** and left with
22:22 Balaam was riding on his **d**,
22:23 When the **d** saw the
22:23 the **d** turned off the road into a
22:23 Balaam hit the **d** to get it back
22:25 When the **d** saw the
22:25 So Balaam hit the **d** again.
22:27 When the **d** saw the
22:27 he hit the **d** with his stick.
22:28 the LORD made the **d** speak,
22:30 The **d** said to Balaam,
22:30 to Balaam, "I'm your own **d**.
22:32 "Why have you hit your **d** three
22:33 The **d** saw me and turned
22:33 you by now but spared the **d**."
Dtr 5:21 or female slave, his ox, his **d**,
22:3 Do the same if you find a **d**,
22:4 If you see another Israelite's **d**
22:10 ox and a **d** harnessed together.
28:31 You will watch as your **d** is
Jos 15:18 When she got down from her **d**,
Jdg 1:14 When she got down from her **d**,
6:4 on — not one sheep, cow, or **d**.
15:15 jawbone from a **d** that had just
15:16 "With a jawbone from a **d**,
15:16 With a jawbone from a **d**,
19:28 So he put her on the **d** and left
1Sm 12:3 Did I take anyone's **d**?
25:20 She was riding on her **d** down
25:23 quickly got down from her **d**.
25:42 quickly got up and rode on a **d**
2Sm 17:23 followed, he saddled his **d**, left,
19:26 'Saddle the **d** for me,
1Ki 2:40 so he saddled his **d** and went
13:13 "Saddle the **d** for me."
13:13 they had saddled the **d** for him,
13:23 he saddled the **d** for the prophet
13:24 The **d** and the lion were
13:27 sons to saddle his **d** for him.
13:28 He also found the **d** and the
13:28 nor had it torn the **d** to pieces.
13:29 the man of God, laid it on the **d**,
2Ki 4:24 She saddled the **d**.
Job 6:5 "Does a wild **d** bray when it's
11:12 when a wild **d** is born tame.
24:3 drive away the orphan's **d**.
39:5 "Who lets the wild **d** go free?
39:5 unties the ropes of the wild **d**?
Pro 26:3 a bridle is for the **d**,
Jer 2:24 You are like a wild **d** that is
48:6 Run like a wild **d** in the desert."
Zec 9:9 He is humble and rides on a **d**,
Mat 21:2 You will find a **d** tied there and
21:5 He's gentle, riding on a **d**,
21:7 They brought the **d** and the colt
Mar 11:2 will find a young **d** tied there.

Mar 11:4 disciples found the young **d**
11:5 "Why are you untying that **d**?
11:7 They brought the **d** to Jesus,
Luk 13:15 each of you free your ox or **d**
19:30 will find a young **d** tied there.
19:33 they were untying the young **d**,
19:33 "Why are you untying the **d**?"
19:35 They brought the **d** to Jesus,
Jon 12:14 Jesus obtained a **d** and sat on
2Pe 2:16 A **d**, which normally can't talk,

donkey's (5)

Exo 13:13 you must break the **d** neck.
34:20 you must break the **d** neck.
2Ki 6:25 so severe that a **d** head sold
Jer 22:19 He will receive a **d** burial.
Jon 12:15 He is riding on a **d** colt.

donkeys (75)

Gen 12:16 **d**, male and female slaves,
24:35 female slaves, camels and **d**.
30:43 female slaves, camels, and **d**.
32:5 I have cattle and **d**,
32:15 20 female **d** and 10 male
32:15 female donkeys and 10 male **d**.
34:28 the sheep and goats, cattle, **d**,
36:24 care of the **d** that belonged
42:26 their grain on their **d** and left.
43:18 us, overpower us, take our **d**,
43:24 their feet and feed for their **d**.
44:3 sent on their way with their **d**.
45:23 He sent his father ten male **d**
45:23 and ten female **d** carrying grain,
47:17 sheep, goats, cattle, and **d**.
Exo 9:3 **d**, camels, cattle, sheep,
Num 31:28 This includes people, cattle, **d**,
31:30 This includes people, cattle, **d**,
31:34 61,000 **d**, and
31:39 Of the 30,500 **d** they received,
31:45 30,500 **d**,
Dtr 5:14 your **d** — all of your animals —
Jos 6:21 as well as cattle, sheep, and **d**.
7:24 his cattle, his **d**, his sheep,
9:4 took worn-out sacks on their **d**.
Jdg 5:10 people who ride on brown **d**,
10:4 had 30 sons who rode on 30 **d**.
12:14 grandsons who rode on 70 **d**.
19:3 along his servant and two **d**.
19:10 saddled **d** and his concubine.
19:19 have straw and fodder for our **d**.
19:21 to his house and fed the **d**.
1Sm 8:16 and your **d** for his own use.
9:3 When some **d** belonging to
9:3 and go look for the **d**."
9:4 Shalisha without finding the **d**.
9:4 but the **d** weren't there.
9:5 will stop worrying about the **d**
9:8 he'll tell us where to find the **d**."
9:20 about the **d** that were lost
10:2 'We've found the **d** you went
10:14 answered, "To look for the **d**,
10:16 "He assured us the **d** had been
15:3 and sheep, camels and **d**."
22:19 infants, cows, **d**, and sheep.
25:18 cakes and loaded them on **d**.
27:9 He also took sheep, cattle, **d**,
2Sm 16:1 him with a pair of saddled **d**.
16:2 "The **d** are for the king's family
2Ki 4:22 the servants and one of the **d**.
7:7 and **d** and ran for their lives.)
7:10 The horses and **d** were still
1Ch 5:21 sheep and goats, and 2,000 **d**.
12:40 and Naphtali brought food on **d**,
27:30 of Ishmael for the **d**:
2Ch 28:15 who was exhausted on **d**
Ezr 2:67 435 camels, and 6,720 **d**.
Neh 7:69 435 camels, and 6,720 **d**.
13:15 They piled the loads on **d** and
Job 1:3 camels, 1,000 oxen, 500 **d**,
1:14 and the **d** were grazing nearby,
24:5 Like wild **d** in the desert,
42:12 2,000 oxen, and 1,000 **d**.
Psa 104:11 Wild **d** quench their thirst.
Isa 1:3 Oxen know their owners, and **d**
21:7 pairs of horsemen, riders on **d**,
30:6 riches on the backs of young **d**
Isa 30:24 The oxen and the **d** which
32:14 They will be a delight for wild **d**
32:20 who let oxen and **d** roam freely.
Jer 14:6 Wild **d** stand on the bare hills.
Eze 23:20 genitals were like those of **d**
Dan 5:21 He lived with wild **d**,
Hos 8:9 They were like wild **d**
Zec 14:15 horses, mules, camels, **d**,

donors (2)

2Ki 12:5 should receive it from the **d**
12:7 money from the **d** ⌊for your own

doom (1)

Dtr 32:35 Their **d** is coming quickly.

doomed (5)

Gen 20:7 who belong to you are **d** to die."
1Sm 25:17 and his whole household are **d**.
Job 15:28 in houses that are **d** to be piles
Pro 31:8 the rights of those who are **d**.
Isa 6:5 I'm **d**. Every word that passes

door (89)

Gen 4:7 sin is lying outside your **d**
6:16 Put a **d** in the side of the ship.
7:16 closed the **d** behind them.
19:6 and shut the **d** behind him.
19:9 forward to break down the **d**.
19:10 with them, and shut the **d**.
19:11 gave up trying to find the **d**.
43:19 and spoke to him at the **d**.
Exo 12:4 the one next **d** can share one
21:6 master must bring him to the **d**
Lev 14:38 the priest will go out to the **d** of
Dtr 3:5 with high walls and double-**d**
15:17 it through his ear lobe into a **d**,
Jdg 3:25 took the key and opened the **d**.
4:20 "Stand at the **d** of the tent.
9:51 They locked the **d** behind them
16:3 took hold of the doors, **d** posts,
19:22 house and pounded on the **d**.
19:26 the woman came to the **d** of the
19:27 concubine) was lying at the **d**
1Sm 1:9 was sitting on a chair by the **d**
23:7 a double **d** ⌊held shut by⌋
2Sm 13:17 and bolt the **d** behind her."
13:18 out and bolted the **d** behind her.
2Ki 4:4 Then close the **d** behind you
4:5 and closed the **d** behind her
4:21 and shut the **d** behind her.
4:33 into the room, closed the **d**,
6:32 messenger comes, close the **d**.
9:3 the **d** and leave immediately."
9:10 Then he opened the **d** and left.
2Ch 8:5 with walls, double-**d** gates
Neh 3:20 section from the Angle to the **d**
3:21 repairs on a section from the **d**
Job 31:9 waited near my neighbor's **d**,
31:32 I opened my **d** to the traveler.)
Psa 141:3 watch over the **d** of my lips.
Pro 5:8 Do not even go near her **d**.
8:34 watches at my **d** day after day,
26:14 ⌊As⌋ a **d** turns on its hinges,
Sos 7:13 and at our **d** are all kinds of
8:9 If she is a **d**, we will barricade
Eze 8:8 through the wall, and I saw a **d**.
10:19 The angels stood at the **d** to
40:13 It was 44 feet wide from one **d**
40:13 from one door to the opposite **d**.
40:38 There was a room with a **d** that
41:11 There was one **d** to the north
41:17 In the space above the **d** to the
41:20 floor to the space above the **d**.
46:3 people must worship at the **d**
47:1 the man took me back to the **d**
Dan 3:26 Nebuchadnezzar went to the **d**
Hos 2:15 of Achor [Disaster] a **d** of hope.
Mat 6:6 to your room and close the **d**.
7:7 Knock, and the **d** will be
7:8 the **d** will be opened.
24:33 know that he is near, at the **d**.
25:10 and the **d** was shut.
25:11 said, 'Sir, sir, open the **d** for us!'
27:60 a large stone against the **d**
Mar 1:33 city had gathered at his **d**.
Mar 2:2 even in front of the **d**.
11:4 It was tied to the **d** of a house.
13:29 know that he is near, at the **d**.
15:46 stone against the **d** of the tomb.
Luk 11:7 The **d** is already locked,
11:9 Knock, and the **d** will be
11:10 the **d** will be opened.
12:36 to open the **d** at their master's
13:24 to enter through the narrow **d**.
13:25 gets up and closes the **d**,
13:25 knock at the **d**, and say, 'Sir,
13:25 and say, 'Sir, open the **d** for us!'
Act 5:9 husband are standing at the **d**,
12:6 guards were in front of the **d**.
12:13 Peter knocked on the **d** of the
12:14 that instead of opening the **d**,
12:14 "Peter is standing at the **d**!"
12:15 insisted that Peter was at the **d**.
12:16 When they opened the **d**,
18:7 was next **d** to the synagogue.
Jas 5:9 the judge is standing at the **d**.
Rev 3:7 who opens ⌊a **d**⌋ that no one
3:7 and who shuts ⌊a **d**⌋ that no
3:8 See, I have opened a **d** in front
3:20 standing at the **d** and knocking.
3:20 to my voice and opens the **d**,
4:1 After these things I saw a **d**

doorframe (2)

Exo 12:23 on the top and sides of the **d**,
21:6 bring him to the door or the **d**

doorframes (6)

Exo 12:7 it on the sides and tops of the **d**
12:22 of the **d** ⌊of your houses⌋.
Dtr 6:9 Write them on the **d** of your
11:20 Write them on the **d** of your
1Ki 7:5 the doors and **d** were square.
Eze 41:21 The **d** in the holy place were

doorkeeper (1)

Jer 35:4 Shallum's son, the **d**.

doorkeepers (7)

2Ki 22:4 ⌊the money⌋ that the **d** have
23:4 and the **d** to take out of the
25:18 priest Zephaniah, and the 3 **d**.
1Ch 15:24 and Jehiah were **d** for the ark.
2Ch 8:14 up divisions of **d** at every gate
34:9 the money that the Levite **d**
Jer 52:24 priest Zephaniah, and the 3 **d**.

doorposts (13)

1Ki 6:31 The **d** had five sides.
6:33 way he made square **d** out
2Ki 18:16 ⌊the gold⌋ off the doors and **d**
Pro 8:34 day after day, waits by my **d**.
Isa 6:4 shook the foundations of the **d**,
57:8 your idols beside doors and **d**.
Eze 41:16 The **d**, the small windows,
43:8 and their **d** by my doorposts.
43:8 and their doorposts by my **d**.
45:19 for sin and put it on the **d**
45:19 and on the **d** of the gateways of
46:2 He must stand by the **d** of the
Heb 11:28 the blood ⌊on the **d**⌋ so that

doors (70)

Jos 6:26 son to set up the city **d**."
Jdg 3:23 had closed and locked the **d**
3:24 that the **d** were locked.
3:25 but Eglon didn't open the **d**.
11:31 whatever comes out of the **d**
16:3 took hold of the **d**, door posts,
19:27 opened the **d** of the house,
1Sm 3:15 Then he opened the **d** of the
21:13 He scribbled on the **d** of the
1Ki 6:31 He made **d** for the entrance to
6:32 The two **d** were ⌊made out of⌋
6:34 He made two **d** from cypress.
6:34 Each of the **d** had two folding
7:5 All the **d** and doorframes were
7:5 There were three **d** facing each
7:50 the gold sockets for the **d** of the
7:50 and the **d** of the temple.
16:34 Setting up the city **d** cost him

2Ki 18:16 stripped ⌊the gold⌋ off the **d**
1Ch 22:3 for nails and fittings on the **d**
2Ch 3:7 and the **d** with gold,
4:9 the large courtyard and its **d**.
4:9 He covered the **d** with bronze.
4:22 the gold **d** of the inner ⌊room⌋
4:22 and the gold **d** of the temple.
14:7 with towers and **d** that can
28:24 and closed the **d** to the LORD's
29:3 he opened the **d** of the LORD's
29:7 They also shut the **d** of the
Neh 3:1 it and set its **d** in place.
3:3 laid its beams and set its **d**,
3:6 laid its beams and set its **d**,
3:13 They rebuilt it and set its **d**,
3:14 He rebuilt it and set its **d**,
3:15 roof over it, and set its **d**, locks,
6:1 time I had not yet hung the **d**
6:10 and close the temple **d**.
7:1 rebuilt and I had hung the **d**.
7:3 they should shut the **d** and bar
13:19 I ordered the **d** to be shut and
Job 3:10 because it did not shut the **d** of
Psa 24:7 Be lifted, you ancient **d**,
24:9 Be lifted, you ancient **d**,
78:23 and opened the **d** of heaven.
Pro 18:16 A gift opens **d** for the one who
Ecc 12:4 your Creator when the **d**
Isa 26:20 and shut the **d** behind you.
45:1 and open **d** ahead of him so
45:2 I will break down the bronze **d**
57:8 idols beside **d** and doorposts.
Eze 26:2 and its **d** are swung open to
41:11 The **d** in the side rooms were
41:23 the most holy place had two **d**.
41:24 Each of the **d** were double
41:24 double **d** that swung open.
41:25 trees were carved on the **d**
42:4 The **d** of these side rooms
42:11 exits, dimensions, and **d**.
42:12 The **d** to the south rooms were
42:12 rooms were the same as the **d**
Zec 11:1 Open your **d**, Lebanon, so that
Mal 1:10 shut the **d** ⌊to my house⌋
Jon 20:19 were together behind locked **d**
20:26 Even though the **d** were locked,
Act 5:19 from the Lord opened the **d**
5:23 the guards standing at the **d**.
5:23 when we opened the **d**,
16:26 All the **d** immediately flew
16:27 up and saw the prison **d** open.
21:30 **d** were immediately shut.

doorstep (1)

Jdg 19:27 house with her hands on the **d**.

doorway (11)

Gen 19:11 all the men who were in the **d**
Exo 12:23 he will pass over that **d**,
2Ki 4:15 and she stood in the **d**.
Psa 119:130 Your word is a **d** that lets in
Pro 9:14 She sits at the **d** of her house.
Eze 42:12 There was a **d** at the other end
42:12 People entered through that **d**.
43:8 They put their **d** by my
43:8 They put their doorway by my **d**
Zep 1:9 punish all who jump over the **d**
2:14 The **d** will be in ruins,

doorways (1)

Eze 33:30 you by the walls and in the **d**

Dophkah (2)

Num 33:12 of Sin and set up camp at **D**.
33:13 They moved from **D** and set up

Dor (5)

Jos 12:23 the king of **D** in Naphoth Dor,
17:11 and the people living in **D**,
Jdg 1:27 Shean, Taanach, **D**, Ibleam,
1Ki 4:11 had the entire region of **D**.
1Ch 7:29 and **D** and its villages.

Dorcas (2)

Act 9:36 Her Greek name was **D**.
9:39 clothing that **D** had made while

Dothan (3)

Gen 37:17 'Let's go to **D**.'" So Joseph
37:17 brothers and found them at **D**.
2Ki 6:13 The king was told, "He is in **D**."

double (16)

Exo 22:4 for the loss with **d** the amount.
22:7 for the loss with **d** the amount.
22:9 loss with **d** the amount.
Dtr 21:17 He must give that son a **d**
Jdg 16:21 They tied him up with **d** chains
1Sm 23:7 gate with ⌊a **d** door⌋ held shut
2Ki 2:9 "Let me inherit a **d** share of
Pro 20:10 A **d** standard of weights and
20:23 A **d** standard of weights is
31:21 family has a **d** layer of clothing.
Isa 40:2 has received from the LORD **d**
61:7 You will receive a **d** measure
61:7 That is why you will have a **d**
Eze 41:24 Each of the doors were **d** doors
Zec 9:12 return to you **d** ⌊blessings⌋.
1Ti 5:17 Give **d** honor to spiritual

doubled (4)

Mat 25:16 at once and **d** his money.
25:17 same and also **d** his money.
25:20 dollars. I've **d** the amount.'
25:22 dollars. I've **d** the amount.'

double-dealing (1)

Pro 28:6 integrity than to be rich and **d**.

double-door (2)

Dtr 3:5 with high walls and **d** gates
2Ch 8:5 with walls, **d** gates, and bars.

double-edged (1)

Isa 41:15 sledge with sharp, **d** teeth.

double-pronged (1)

Eze 40:43 **D** hooks, three inches long,

doubt (9)

2Ki 24:3 Without a **d**, this happened to
Psa 73:27 Without a **d**, those who are far
Mat 14:31 so little faith! Why did you **d**?"
21:21 If you have faith and do not **d**,
Mar 11:23 for someone who doesn't **d**
Act 2:36 beyond a **d** that God made
Rom 4:20 He didn't **d** God's promise out
Gal 3:4 ⌊I **d**⌋ that it was for nothing!
2Pe 1:19 as confirmed beyond all **d**.

doubters (1)

Jas 4:8 and clear your minds, you **d**.

doubting (1)

Jon 20:27 Stop **d**, and believe."

doubts (11)

Mat 28:17 though some had **d**.
Luk 24:38 Why do you have **d**?
Rom 14:13 make other Christians have **d**
14:20 someone else to have **d**.
14:21 another Christian to have **d**.
14:23 But if a person has **d** and still
Jas 1:6 for something, don't have any **d**.
1:6 A person who has **d** is like a
1:7 A person who has **d** shouldn't
1:8 A person who has **d** is thinking
Jud 1:22 mercy to those who have **d**.

dough (15)

Exo 12:34 picked up their bread **d** before
12:39 With the **d** they had brought
12:39 The **d** hadn't risen because
Num 15:20 Shape one part of your **d** into a
15:21 must give one part of your **d** as
2Sm 13:8 She took **d**, kneaded it,
Jer 7:18 and women knead **d** to make
Eze 44:30 The best of your **d** must go to
Mat 13:33 its way through all the **d**."
Luk 13:21 its way through all the **d**."
Rom 11:16 If the first handful of **d** is holy,
11:16 the whole batch of **d** is holy.
1Co 5:6 through the whole batch of **d**?
5:7 you may be a new batch of **d**,
Gal 5:9 through the whole batch of **d**.

dove (22)

Gen 8:8 Next, he sent out a **d** to see if
8:9 The **d** couldn't find a place to
8:9 out and brought the **d** back into
8:10 days and again sent the **d** out
8:11 The **d** came to him in the
8:12 days and sent out the **d** again,
15:9 a mourning **d**, and a pigeon."
Lev 1:14 a mourning **d** or pigeon.
12:6 a pigeon or a mourning **d** as
2Ki 6:25 and a half-pint of **d** manure
Psa 55:6 "If only I had wings like a **d** — I
68:13 like⌋ the wings of a **d** covered
74:19 not hand over the soul of your **d**
Sos 2:12 The cooing of the mourning **d**
2:14 My **d**, in the hiding places of
5:2 sister, my **d**, my perfect one.
6:9 but she is unique, my **d**,
Hos 7:11 are like a silly, senseless **d**.
Mat 3:16 coming down as a **d** to him.
Mar 1:10 coming down to him as a **d**.
Luk 3:22 down to him in the form of a **d**.
Jon 1:32 come down as a **d** from heaven

doves (21)

Lev 5:7 to the LORD two mourning **d**
5:11 cannot afford two mourning **d**
12:8 she must use two mourning **d**
14:22 and two mourning **d** or two
14:30 take one of the mourning **d**
15:14 he must take two mourning **d**
15:29 she must take two mourning **d**
Num 6:10 he must bring two mourning **d**
Sos 1:15 Your eyes are like **d**!
4:1 behind your veil are like **d**.
5:12 are set like **d** bathing in milk.
Isa 38:14 I cooed like **d**. My eyes were
59:11 We coo like **d**. We hope for
60:8 like **d** to their nests?
Jer 8:7 Mourning **d**, swallows,
48:28 Be like **d** that make their nests
Eze 7:16 They will moan like **d** in the
Hos 11:11 Egypt and like **d** from Assyria.
Nah 2:7 be mourning like **d** as they beat
Mat 10:16 snakes but as innocent as **d**.
Luk 2:24 "a pair of mourning **d** or two

downfall (15)

2Ch 22:7 God brought about Ahaziah's **d**
Ezr 6:12 is worshiped there cause the **d**
Est 6:13 will certainly lead to your **d**."
Psa 5:10 their own schemes be their **d**.
35:4 Let those who plan my **d** be
35:26 Let those who gloat over my **d**
40:14 Let those who want my **d** be
70:2 Let those who want my **d** be
71:13 Let those who want my **d** be
71:24 my **d** have been disgraced
Pro 29:16 people will witness their **d**.
Ecc 5:13 Riches lead to the **d** of those
Jer 49:21 quake at the sound of their **d**.
Lam 1:7 they laughed at Jerusalem's **d**.
1:9 Its **d** was shocking.

downhearted (1)

1Sm 1:8 Why are you so **d**?

downstairs (1)

Act 10:20 Get up, and go **d**. Don't hesitate

downstream (1)

Job 11:16 it like water that has flowed **d**.

draft (1)

1Sm 8:11 He will **d** your sons,

drafted (5)

1Ki 9:15 laborers whom King Solomon **d**
9:21 Solomon **d** them for slave labor.
15:22 Then King Asa **d** everyone in
2Ch 2:2 Solomon **d** 70,000 men to carry
8:8 Solomon **d** them for slave labor.

drag (16)

2Sm 17:13 bring ropes to that city and **d**
Job 24:22 ⌊God⌋ will **d** away ⌊these⌋
Psa 7:2 tear me to pieces and **d** me off
28:3 Do not **d** me away with wicked
52:5 He will grab you and **d** you out
Pro 21:7 people will **d** them away since
Jer 12:3 **D** them away like sheep to be
15:3 swords to kill, dogs to **d** away,
49:20 He will surely **d** away the little
50:45 He will surely **d** away the little
Eze 32:20 **D** Egypt and all its people
Hab 1:15 **d** them away in nets,
Luk 12:58 he will **d** you in front of a judge.
21:12 They will **d** you in front of
Act 23:10 his soldiers to **d** Paul back
Jas 2:6 you and **d** you into court?

dragged (11)

2Sm 3:1 of Saul and David **d** on,
Job 18:14 He is **d** from the safety of his
Psa 144:14 and may no one be **d** out.
Jer 22:19 He will be **d** off and thrown
Jon 21:8 came with the boat and **d**
Act 8:3 He **d** men and women out of
14:19 Paul to death and **d** him out
16:19 Paul and Silas and **d** them
17:6 they **d** Jason and some other
19:29 and they **d** the two men into the
21:30 The mob grabbed Paul and **d**

dragnets (2)

Hab 1:15 and gather them in **d**.
1:16 and burn incense to their **d**.

drags (2)

Ecc 12:5 the grasshopper **d** itself along,
Jon 10:12 So the wolf **d** the sheep away

drain (2)

Lev 1:15 First, he will **d** the blood
Eze 23:34 You will drink from it and **d** it.

drained (2)

Lev 5:9 the rest of the blood will be **d** at
Isa 51:17 people stagger, and you **d** it!

drains (3)

Job 14:11 ⌊As⌋ water **d** out of a lake,
Psa 58:7 like water that **d** away.
Pro 17:22 but depression **d** one's strength.

drank (48)

Gen 9:21 He **d** some wine, got drunk,
24:46 So I **d**, and she also watered
24:54 who were with him ate and **d**
25:34 He ate and **d**, and then he got
26:30 and they ate and **d**.
27:25 brought him wine, and he **d** it.
43:34 So they ate and **d** with Joseph
Exo 24:11 and then they ate and **d**.
Num 20:11 the people and their animals **d**.
Dtr 29:6 You ate no bread and **d** no
32:14 cows and **d** milk from sheep
32:14 They **d** the blood-red wine of
32:38 fat from their sacrifices and **d**
Jdg 9:27 They ate, **d**, and cursed
15:19 Samson **d** some water.
19:6 down and ate and **d** together.
19:21 they washed, they ate and **d**.
2Sm 11:13 ate and **d** with him,
1Ki 4:20 ate and **d** and lived happily.
13:19 him and ate and **d** in his home.
13:22 You came back, ate, and **d** at
17:6 And he **d** from the stream.
19:6 So he ate, **d**, and went to sleep
19:8 He got up, ate, and **d**.
2Ki 6:23 They ate and **d**, and then he
7:8 they went into a tent, ate and **d**,
9:34 He went inside, ate, and **d**.
1Ch 12:39 They ate and **d** with David for
29:22 That day they ate and **d** as
Est 1:7 People **d** from golden cups.
Isa 51:17 You **d** from the cup in the
Isa 51:17 You **d** from the bowl,
Jer 22:15 Your father ate and **d** and did
25:18 When they **d** from it,
51:7 The nations **d** its wine.
Dan 5:1 nobles and **d** wine with them.
5:3 and concubines **d** from them.
5:4 They **d** the wine and praised
5:23 and concubines **d** wine from
Oba 1:16 **d** on my holy mountain,
Zec 7:6 When you ate and **d**,
Mar 14:23 cup to them. They all **d** from it.
Luk 13:26 'We ate and **d** with you,
Jon 4:12 his animals **d** water from it."
Act 10:41 are those men who ate and **d**
23:12 ate or **d** anything before they
1Co 10:4 and all of them **d** the same
10:4 They **d** from the spiritual rock

draw (25)

Gen 24:11 would go out to **d** water.
24:13 city are coming out to **d** water.
24:20 to the well to **d** more water,
24:43 who comes out to **d** water,
24:44 but I will also **d** water for your
Jos 18:6 I will **d** lots for you here in the
18:8 Then I will **d** lots for you in the
Jdg 8:20 But Jether didn't **d** his sword.
1Sm 14:41 ⌊let the priest⌋ **d** Urim.
14:41 ⌊let him⌋ **d** Thummim."
31:4 armorbearer, "**D** your sword!
1Ch 10:4 his armorbearer, "**D** your sword
Job 41:25 Broken down, they **d** back.
Isa 12:3 With joy you will **d** water from
Eze 4:1 and **d** a map of Jerusalem on it.
5:2 and I will **d** a sword and go
28:7 They will **d** their swords
30:11 They will **d** their swords to
47:22 They will **d** lots with you for
Mic 2:5 LORD's assembly will **d** lots
Nah 1:5 who live in it **d** back as well.
Zep 3:2 It does not **d** close to its God.
Hag 2:16 wine vat to **d** out 50 measures,
Zec 9:13 as my bow and **d** my bow
Jon 12:32 I will **d** all people toward me."

drawing (15)

Gen 24:19 "I'll also keep **d** water for your
Num 26:55 land must be divided by **d** lots.
26:56 the land must be divided by **d**
33:54 among your families by **d** lots.
33:54 given to each family by **d** lots.
34:13 land you will divide by **d** lots.
36:2 Israelites their land by **d** lots.
Jos 13:6 inheritance to Israel by **d** lots,
14:2 was determined by **d** lots as
19:51 divided the land by **d** lots.
21:4 that were chosen by **d** lots.
21:8 to Levi's descendants by **d** lots,
1Ch 24:5 impartially by **d** lots so that
Eze 45:1 "'Divide the land by **d** lots for
47:22 Divide it by **d** lots.

drawings (2)

Eze 8:10 the walls were covered with **d**
8:11 In front of these **d** stood 70 of

drawn (27)

Num 22:23 in the road with his sword **d**,
22:31 in the road with his sword **d**.
Jos 15:1 The lot was **d** for the families
16:1 The lot was **d** for Joseph.
17:1 The lot was **d** for the tribe of
18:11 The lot was **d** for the families
19:1 The second lot was **d** for the
19:10 The third lot was **d** for the
19:17 The fourth lot was **d** for the
19:24 The fifth lot was **d** for the
19:32 The sixth lot was **d** for the
19:40 The seventh lot was **d** for the
21:10 Their lot was the first one **d**.
Rut 2:9 that the young men have **d**."
1Ch 6:54 for them when lots were **d**:
6:54 The ⌊first⌋ lot was **d** for the
24:7 The first lot **d** was for Jehoiarib,
25:9 The first lot **d** chose Joseph,
2Ch 23:10 stood with their weapons **d**.
Neh 10:34 and laypeople have **d** lots to
10:35 We have **d** lots to decide who
10:36 we have **d** lots to decide who
10:37 Also, we have **d** lots to decide
Lam 3:12 He has **d** his bow and made
Eze 21:28 a sword is **d** ready to kill.
32:20 A sword has been **d**.
Mic 5:6 of Nimrod with **d** swords.

draws (3)

Psa 10:9 people when he **d** them into his
Pro 20:5 who has understanding **d** it out.
Nah 1:5 The earth **d** back in his

dread (8)

Exo 15:16 Terror and **d** will fall on them.
Job 3:25 What I **d** happens to me.
9:28 I ⌊still⌋ **d** everything I must
Psa 119:39 Take away insults, which I **d**,
Pro 1:33 be free from the **d** of disaster."
10:24 That which wicked people **d**
Isa 57:11 Whom did you **d** and fear so
Jer 42:16 The famines you **d** will follow

dreaded (3)

Dtr 28:60 diseases of Egypt that you **d**,
Job 31:34 because I **d** the large,
Psa 31:11 I have become someone **d** by

dreadful (3)

Gen 15:12 a deep sleep — a **d**,
Dan 7:7 It was terrifying, **d**,
Luk 21:11 and **d** diseases in various

dream (74)

Gen 20:3 God came to Abimelech in a **d**
20:6 God said to him in the **d**.
28:12 He had a **d** in which he saw a
31:10 the mating season I had a **d**:
31:11 In the **d** the Messenger of God
31:24 the Aramean in a **d** at night
37:5 Joseph had a **d** and when he
37:6 "Please listen to the **d** I had.
37:9 Then he had another **d**,
37:9 "I had another **d**: I saw the sun,
37:10 "What's this **d** you had?
40:5 Each man had a **d** with its own
40:9 cupbearer told Joseph his **d**.
40:9 He said "In my **d** a grapevine
40:16 to the cupbearer's **d** was good.
40:16 said to Joseph, "I had a **d** too.
40:16 In my **d** three baskets of white
41:1 two full years Pharaoh had a **d**.
41:5 again and had a second **d**.
41:7 woke up. It was only a **d**.
41:11 Each **d** had its own meaning.
41:15 said to Joseph, "I had a **d**,
41:15 that when you are told a **d**,
41:17 "In my **d** I was standing on the
41:22 "In my second **d** I saw seven
41:25 had the same **d** twice.
41:26 It's all the same **d**.
41:32 has had a recurring **d** is
Jdg 7:13 a man telling his friend a **d**.
7:13 "I had a strange **d**.
7:15 When Gideon heard the **d** and
1Ki 3:5 to Solomon in a **d** at night.
3:15 up and realized it had been a **d**.
Job 20:8 He will fly away like a **d** and
33:15 In a **d**, a prophetic vision at
Psa 73:20 As ⌊someone⌋ gets rid of a **d**
90:5 They are a **d**. They sprout again
Isa 29:7 All of this will be like a **d**,
29:8 people who **d** that they're eating
29:8 who **d** that they're drinking
Jer 23:25 They say, 'I had a **d**!
23:25 'I had a dream! I had a **d**!'
23:28 The prophet who has a **d**
23:28 has a dream should tell his **d**.
Dan 2:3 king said to them, "I had a **d**,
2:3 I want to know what the **d**
2:4 Tell us the **d**, and we'll interpret
2:5 If you don't tell me the **d** and its
2:6 But if you tell me the **d** and its
2:6 tell me the **d** and its meaning."
2:7 "Your Majesty, tell us the **d**,

Dan 2:9 If you don't tell me the **d**,
2:9 So tell me the **d**. Then I'll know
2:26 "Can you tell me the **d** I had
2:28 This is your **d**, the vision you
2:36 This is the **d**. Now we'll tell you
2:45 The **d** is true, and you can trust
4:5 I had a **d** that terrified me.
4:7 I told them the **d**, but they
4:8 gods is in him. I told him the **d**:
4:9 of the visions I had in my **d**.
4:18 ⌊I said,⌋ "This is the **d** I,
4:19 don't let the **d** and its meaning
4:19 I wish that the **d** were about
7:1 of Babylon, Daniel had a **d**.
7:1 down the main parts of the **d**.
Joe 2:28 Your old men will **d** dreams.
Mat 1:20 the Lord appeared to him in a **d**.
2:12 God warned them in a **d** not to
2:13 Lord appeared to Joseph in a **d**.
2:19 of the Lord appeared in a **d**
2:22 Warned in a **d**, he left for
27:19 upset today because of a **d**
Act 2:17 Your old men will **d** dreams.

dreamed (5)

Gen 41:1 He **d** he was standing by the
Jer 14:14 They **d** up the visions they tell
23:16 about visions that they **d** up.
Dan 2:2 could tell him what he had **d**.
2:11 No one can tell what you **d**

dreamer (3)

Gen 37:19 here comes that master **d**!
Dtr 13:2 don't listen to that prophet or **d**
13:5 That prophet or **d** must be put

dreamers (1)

Jud 1:8 slipped in among you are **d**.

dreaming (2)

Psa 126:1 it was as if we were **d**.
Isa 56:10 They lie around **d**;

dream's (4)

Dan 2:16 he could explain the **d** meaning
2:24 explain the **d** meaning to him."
2:25 who can explain the **d** meaning
4:6 to me to tell me the **d** meaning

dreams (28)

Gen 37:8 more for his **d** and his words.
37:20 see what happens to his **d**."
40:5 king of Egypt — had **d** one
40:8 "We both had **d**," they
41:8 Pharaoh told them his **d**,
41:11 We both had **d** the same night.
41:12 We told him our **d**,
42:9 Then he remembered the **d** he
Num 12:6 visions or speak to them in **d**.
Dtr 13:1 prophet or to have prophetic **d**,
1Sm 28:6 didn't answer him through **d**,
28:15 either by the prophets or in **d**.
Job 7:14 then you frighten me with **d**
7:15 prefer death ⌊to these **d**⌋.
17:11 My **d** ⌊are shattered⌋.
Pro 12:11 unrealistic **d** has no sense.
28:19 Whoever chases unrealistic **d**
Jer 23:27 tell each other the **d** they had,
23:32 who prophesy **d** they made up,"
23:32 "They tell the **d** they made up
27:9 interpreters of **d**, fortunetellers,
29:8 Don't even listen to your own **d**.
Dan 1:17 all kinds of visions and **d**.
2:1 reign, he had some **d**.
5:12 He has the ability to interpret **d**,
Joe 2:28 Your old men will dream **d**.
Zec 10:2 They speak about false **d**.
Act 2:17 Your old men will dream **d**.

dreary (1)

Jer 46:19 will become a **d** wasteland,

drench (3)

Psa 65:10 You **d** plowed fields ⌊with
Isa 16:9 I will **d** you with my tears,
Eze 32:6 I will **d** the earth with your

drenched (3)

Job 24:8 They are **d** by the rainstorms in
Sos 5:5 and my fingers were **d** with
Isa 34:7 Their land will be **d** with blood.

dress (19)

Exo 29:8 **D** them in their linen robes,
40:13 Then **d** Aaron in the holy
40:14 and **d** them in their linen robes.
Rut 3:3 up, put on some perfume, **d** up,
2Sm 14:2 and **d** in mourning clothes.
1Ki 20:31 Allow us to **d** in sackcloth,
Job 10:11 Didn't you **d** me in skin and
39:19 strength to a horse or **d** its neck
40:10 Then **d** yourself in majesty and
Psa 45:13 Her **d** is embroidered with gold.
Pro 23:21 Drowsiness will **d** a person in
Isa 22:21 I will **d** him in your linen robe
Jer 4:30 Why do you **d** in red and put on
Eze 16:10 I put an embroidered **d** on you
23:12 and commanders in full **d**.
34:3 of the sheep, **d** in the wool,
Nah 3:5 "I will lift up your **d** over your
Zep 1:8 all who **d** in foreign clothing.
Zec 3:4 and I will **d** you in fine

dressed (52)

Gen 3:21 man and his wife and **d** them.
41:42 He had Joseph **d** in robes of
Exo 12:11 This is how ⌊you should be **d**
Lev 8:7 He also **d** him in the robe that
1Sm 17:38 head and **d** him in armor.
2Sm 1:24 who **d** you in decorated,
1Ki 20:11 you have even **d** for battle.'"
20:32 So they **d** in sackcloth and put
21:27 distress⌋ and **d** in sackcloth.
22:10 Jehoshaphat of Judah were **d**
1Ch 15:27 David was **d** in a fine linen
21:16 leaders were **d** in sackcloth.
2Ch 5:12 and their relatives — were **d** in
18:9 Jehoshaphat of Judah were **d**
Ezr 3:10 Then the priests who were **d** in
Psa 69:11 I **d** myself in sackcloth,
Pro 7:10 She is **d** as a prostitute.
Isa 61:10 He has **d** me in the clothes of
63:1 Who is this **d** in splendor,
Eze 9:2 Among them was a person **d** in
9:3 LORD called to the person **d**
9:11 Then the person **d** in linen who
10:2 said to the person **d** in linen,
10:6 had commanded the person **d**
10:7 hands of the person **d** in linen.
16:10 I **d** you in fine linen and
16:13 You were **d** in fine linen,
26:16 **D** in terror, they will sit on the
Dan 5:7 its meaning will be **d** in purple,
5:16 you will be **d** in purple,
5:29 ordered that Daniel be **d**
10:5 I saw a man **d** in linen,
12:6 One of them asked the man **d**
12:7 I heard the man **d** in linen
Joe 1:8 woman who is **d** in sackcloth,
Jnh 3:5 least important, **d** in sackcloth.
Zec 3:5 on his head and **d** him while
Mat 6:29 all his majesty was **d** like one
11:8 A man **d** in fine clothes?
22:11 saw a person who was not **d**
Mar 1:6 John was **d** in clothes made
5:15 The man was sitting there **d**
15:17 They **d** him in purple,
16:5 He was **d** in a white robe and
Luk 7:25 A man **d** in fine clothes?
8:35 **D** and in his right mind,
12:27 all his majesty was **d** like one
Act 10:30 Suddenly, a man **d** in radiant
1Co 4:11 poorly **d**, roughly treated,
Rev 10:1 He was **d** in a cloud,
12:1 was a woman who was **d**
21:2 **d** like a bride ready for her

dresses (1)

Pro 31:25 She **d** with strength and

dressing (2)

Zec 13:4 He won't deceive people by **d**
1Ti 2:9 to show their beauty by **d**

drew (21)

Gen 24:20 and **d** enough for all his
24:45 down to the spring and **d** water.
Exo 2:16 They **d** water and filled the
2:19 He even **d** water for us and
Jos 18:10 So Joshua **d** lots for them in
19:51 that the tribes of Israel **d** by lot.
Jdg 1:3 given to us when we **d** lots,
1Sm 7:6 They **d** some water,
2Sm 23:16 camp and **d** water from
1Ch 11:18 camp and **d** water from
24:31 They **d** lots as their relatives,
24:31 They **d** them in front of King
25:8 They **d** lots for their
26:13 They **d** lots by families,
2Ch 18:31 God **d** them away from him,
Neh 11:1 The rest of the people **d** lots to
Jer 41:2 with him got up, **d** their swords,
Jon 18:10 He **d** it, attacked the chief
Act 1:26 They **d** names to choose an
16:27 he **d** his sword and was about
Gal 2:12 Then Cephas **d** back and

dried (38)

Gen 8:7 the water on the land had **d** up.
8:13 the water on the land had **d** up.
Jos 2:10 We've heard how the LORD **d**
4:23 The LORD your God **d** up the
5:1 heard that the LORD had **d** up
9:5 bread was **d** out and crumbling.
Jdg 16:7 bowstrings that are not **d** out,
16:8 bowstrings that were not **d** out.
1Ki 17:7 after some time the stream **d** up
18:38 The fire even **d** up the water
Psa 22:15 My strength is **d** up like pieces
74:15 You **d** up the ever-flowing
106:9 the Red Sea, and it **d** up.
119:83 a shriveled and **d** out wineskin,
Isa 19:5 in the Nile River will be **d** up,
19:6 will be emptied and **d** up.
27:11 When the branches are **d** up,
37:27 **d** up by the east wind.
Jer 8:13 and the leaves have **d** up.
12:4 in every field remain **d** up?
23:10 in the wilderness have **d** up.
Eze 19:12 The east wind **d** up its fruit.
Hos 9:16 Their roots are **d** up.
Joe 1:10 and the ground is **d** up.
1:10 The new wine has **d** up.
1:12 The grapevines are **d** up.
1:17 The grain has **d** up.
Amo 1:2 top of ⌊Mount⌋ Carmel is **d** up.
4:7 Another field had none and **d**
7:4 The fire **d** up the ocean and
Zep 2:13 a **d** up wasteland like the
Mat 21:19 At once the fig tree **d** up.
Mar 11:20 they saw that the fig tree had **d**
11:21 The fig tree you cursed has **d**
Luk 7:38 Then she **d** his feet with her
7:44 feet with her tears and **d** them
Jon 12:3 Then she **d** his feet with her
Rev 16:12 The water in the river **d** up to

dried-up (1)

2Pe 2:17 false teachers are **d** springs.

dries (12)

Job 14:11 or ⌊as⌋ a river **d** up completely,
Psa 129:6 like grass that **d** up before it
Isa 15:6 The grass **d** up, the vegetation
24:4 The earth **d** up and withers.
24:7 New wine **d** up, All happy
40:7 Grass **d** up, and flowers wither
40:8 Grass **d** up, and flowers wither,
Jer 15:18 that **d** up in summertime?
Nah 1:4 He **d** up all the rivers.
Jon 15:6 away like a branch and **d** up.
Jas 1:11 scorching heat and **d** up plants.
1Pe 1:24 The grass **d** up and the flower

drift (3)

Job 37:16 Do you know how the clouds **d**
Act 27:32 the lifeboat and let it **d** away.
Heb 2:1 Then we won't **d** away ⌊from

drifted (2)

Act 27:16 As we **d** to the sheltered side
2Co 11:25 and I **d** on the sea for a night

drifter (2)

Pro 6:11 will come ⌊to you⌋ like a **d**,
24:34 your poverty will come like a **d**,

drifters (1)

Pro 26:10 so is one who hires fools or **d**.

drifting (1)

Act 27:27 night we were still **d** through

drilled (1)

2Ki 12:9 took a box, **d** a hole in its lid,

drink (271)

Gen 19:32 Let's give our father wine to **d**.
19:33 they gave their father wine to **d**.
19:34 him wine to **d** again tonight.
19:35 their father wine to **d** again.
21:19 water and gave the boy a **d**.
24:14 'May I please have a **d** from
24:14 If she answers, 'Have a **d**,
24:17 "Please give me a **d** of water."
24:18 "**D**, sir," she said. She quickly
24:18 to her hand and gave him a **d**.
24:19 had finished giving him a **d**,
24:19 until they've had enough to **d**."
24:43 "Please give me a **d** of water."
24:44 "Not only may you have a **d**,
24:45 I asked her, 'May I have a **d**?'
24:46 her jar and said, 'Have a **d**,
30:38 where the flocks came to **d**.
30:38 were in heat and came to **d**,
Exo 7:18 not be able to **d** any water from
7:21 couldn't **d** any water from
7:24 dug along the Nile for water to **d**
7:24 because they couldn't **d** any
15:23 they couldn't **d** the water
15:24 "What are we supposed to **d**?"
17:1 no water for the people to **d**.
17:2 "Give us water to **d**!"
17:6 out of it for the people to **d**."
32:20 and made the Israelites **d** it.
Lev 10:9 "You and your sons must not **d**
11:34 Any liquid that you **d** from that
Num 5:24 Then he will have the woman **d**
5:26 Then he will have the woman **d**
6:3 Nazirites must never **d** wine,
6:20 the Nazirites may **d** wine.
20:5 And there's no water to **d**!"
20:8 for them and their animals to **d**."
20:17 or **d** any of the water from your
20:19 and if we or our livestock **d**
21:22 fields or vineyards or **d** any
33:14 no water for the people to **d**.
Dtr 2:6 you eat and the water you **d**.'"
2:28 we eat and the water we **d**.
28:39 but you won't **d** any wine or
Jdg 4:19 give me a little water to **d**.
4:19 instead she gave him milk to **d**
7:5 those who kneel down to **d**."
7:6 the men knelt down to **d** water.
13:4 Don't **d** any wine or liquor or eat
13:7 So don't **d** any wine or liquor or
13:14 **d** any wine or liquor,
Rut 2:9 go to the jars and **d** some of the
1Sm 1:9 to eat and **d** in Shiloh,
30:11 him food to eat and water to **d**.
2Sm 11:11 go to my house to eat and **d**
12:3 She would eat his food and **d**
19:35 Can I taste what I eat or **d**?
23:15 "I wish I could have a **d** of
23:16 but he refused to **d** it.
23:17 So he refused to **d** it.
1Ki 13:7 have something to eat and **d**,
13:8 go with you to eat or **d** there.
13:9 commanded me not to eat or **d**
13:16 allowed to eat or **d** with you.
13:17 he told me not to eat or **d** there
13:18 have something to eat and **d**."
13:22 'Don't eat or **d** there.'
13:23 had something to eat and **d**,
1Ki 17:4 You can **d** from the stream,
17:10 "Please bring me a **d** of water."
18:41 told Ahab, "Get up, eat, and **d**.
18:42 Ahab got up to eat and **d**.
2Ki 3:17 and your other animals will **d**.
6:22 Let them eat and **d**.
18:27 and **d** their own urine
18:31 and fig tree and **d** from his own
19:24 dig wells and **d** foreign water.
1Ch 11:17 "I wish I could have a **d** of
11:18 but he refused to **d** it.
11:19 Should I **d** the blood of these
11:19 So he refused to **d** it.
2Ch 28:15 them something to eat and **d**,
Ezr 3:7 Then they gave food, **d**,
10:6 Ezra didn't eat any food or **d**
Neh 8:10 eat rich foods, **d** sweet drinks,
8:12 all the people went to eat and **d**
Est 1:8 this rule: **D** as you please.
3:15 Haman sat down to **d** a toast,
4:16 Fast for me: Do not eat or **d** at
Job 1:4 sisters to eat and **d** with them.
20:17 He won't be able to **d** from the
21:20 He should **d** from the wrath of
22:7 give a tired person a **d** of water,
Psa 11:6 He makes them **d** from a cup
36:8 and you make them **d** from the
50:13 Do I eat the meat of bulls or **d**
69:21 they gave me vinegar to **d**.
75:8 will have to **d** every last drop.
78:15 He gave them plenty to **d**,
78:44 could not **d** from their streams.
80:5 made them **d** ⌊their own⌋ tears.
102:9 my tears are mixed with my **d**
104:16 which he planted, **d** their fill.
107:9 He gave plenty to **d** to those
110:7 He will **d** from the brook along
Pro 4:17 and **d** wine obtained through
5:15 **D** water out of your own cistern
7:18 Come, let's **d** our fill of love
9:5 and **d** the wine I have mixed.
23:7 "Eat and **d**," but he doesn't
23:20 those who **d** too much wine,
23:30 Those who **d** glass after glass
23:35 I'm going to look for another **d**."
25:21 give him some water to **d**.
31:4 It is not for kings to **d** wine or
31:5 Otherwise, they **d** and forget
Ecc 2:24 for people to do than to eat, **d**,
3:13 God to be able to eat and **d**
5:18 It is to eat and **d** and to enjoy
8:15 eat, **d**, and enjoy themselves.
9:7 and **d** your wine cheerfully,
Sos 5:1 I will **d** my wine with my milk.
5:1 **D** and become intoxicated with
8:2 you some spiced wine to **d**,
Isa 5:11 who get up early to look for a **d**,
21:5 **D**. Get up, you leaders! Prepare
22:13 You will eat meat, **d** wine,
22:13 "Let's eat and **d** because
24:9 People no longer **d** wine when
36:12 and **d** their own urine
36:16 and fig tree and **d** from his own
37:25 I'll dig wells and **d** water.
43:20 land for my chosen people to **d**.
44:12 If they don't **d** water,
51:22 You will never **d** from it again.
60:16 You will **d** milk from other
62:8 nor will foreigners **d** the new
62:9 Those who gather grapes will **d**
65:13 My servants will **d**,
Jer 2:18 going to Egypt to **d** water from
2:18 going to Assyria to **d** water from
8:14 He has given us poison to **d**
9:15 and give them poison to **d**.
16:7 No one will give a consoling **d**
16:8 Don't sit with them to eat and **d**.
23:15 to eat and poison to **d**.
25:15 whom I'm sending you **d** from
25:16 When they **d** from it,
25:17 the LORD sent me **d** from it:
25:19 made these people **d** from it:⌋
25:26 Sheshach will **d** from the cup.
25:27 **D**, get drunk, vomit, fall down,
25:28 from your hand and **d** from it,
25:28 You must **d** from it!
Jer 35:2 and offer them a **d** of wine."
35:5 I said to them, "**D** some wine."
35:6 answered, "We don't **d** wine,
35:6 must never **d** wine.
35:14 his descendants not to **d** wine.
46:10 and it will **d** their blood until it's
49:12 If those who don't deserve to **d**
49:12 drink from the cup still **d** from
49:12 You must **d** from it.
Lam 3:15 He has made me **d** wormwood.
5:4 We have to pay to **d** our own
Eze 4:11 and **d** it at set times.
4:16 and fearfully **d** rationed water.
12:18 be worried as you **d** your water.
12:19 terrified as they **d** their water.
23:32 You will **d** from your sister's
23:34 You will **d** from it and drain it.
25:4 eat your crops and **d** your milk.
34:18 You **d** clean water.
34:19 trampled and **d** what your feet
39:17 can eat meat and **d** blood there.
39:18 eat the meat of warriors and **d**
39:19 are full and **d** blood until you
44:21 None of the priests may **d** wine
Dan 1:10 what you should eat and **d**.
1:12 to eat and water to **d**.
5:2 He wanted to **d** from them with
Joe 3:3 that they could buy wine to **d**.
Amo 2:8 they **d** the wine that they
2:12 You made the Nazirites **d** wine.
4:1 "Get some wine! Let's **d**!"
4:8 city in order to get a **d** of water.
5:11 but you will not **d** their wine.
6:6 will be for those who **d** wine by
9:14 They will plant vineyards and **d**
Oba 1:16 so all nations will **d** in turn.
1:16 They will **d** and guzzle down
Jnh 3:7 No one is to eat or **d** anything.
Mic 6:15 new wine, but you won't **d** it.
Nah 1:10 people drunk on their own **d**.
Hab 2:15 who makes his neighbor **d** from
2:16 **D**! Yes you! And expose
Zep 1:13 but they won't **d** their wine."
Hag 1:6 You **d**, but you're still thirsty.
Zec 9:15 They will **d** and shout as if
10:7 if they had some wine ⌊to **d**⌋.
Mat 6:25 what you will eat, **d**, or wear.
6:31 or 'What are we going to **d**?' or
20:22 Can you **d** the cup that I'm
20:22 the cup that I'm going to **d**?"
20:23 "You will **d** my cup.
24:49 and eat and **d** with the drunks.
25:35 you gave me something to **d**.
25:37 and give you something to **d**?
25:42 and you gave me nothing to **d**.
26:27 and said, "**D** from it, all of you.
26:29 "I can guarantee that I won't **d**
26:29 that day when I **d** new wine
26:42 be taken away unless I **d** it,
27:34 They gave him a **d** of wine
27:34 he tasted it, he refused to **d** it.
27:48 a stick and offered Jesus a **d**.
Mar 9:41 gives you a cup of water to **d**
10:38 Can you **d** the cup that I'm
10:38 the cup that I'm going to **d**?
10:39 Jesus told them, "You will **d**
10:39 the cup that I'm going to **d**.
14:25 I won't **d** this wine again until
14:25 that day when I **d** new wine
15:36 a stick and offered Jesus a **d**.
16:18 and if they **d** any deadly
Luk 1:15 He will never **d** wine or any
5:30 "Why do you eat and **d** with
5:33 But your disciples eat and **d**."
10:7 Eat and **d** whatever they offer
12:19 Take life easy, eat, **d**,
12:29 about what you will eat or **d**,
12:45 and to eat, **d**, and get drunk.
13:15 stall to give it some water to **d**?
22:18 now on I won't **d** this wine until
22:30 You will eat and **d** at my table
Jon 4:7 "Give me a **d** of water."
4:9 like me for a **d** of water?"
4:10 and who is asking you for a **d**,
4:10 would have asked him for a **d**.
4:14 But those who **d** the water that

Jon 6:53 the Son of Man and **d** his blood,
6:54 Those who eat my flesh and **d**
6:55 and my blood is true **d**.
6:56 Those who eat my flesh and **d**
7:37 is thirsty must come to me to **d**.
18:11 Shouldn't I **d** the cup ⌊of
Act 9:9 couldn't see and didn't eat or **d**.
23:21 eat or **d** anything before they
Rom 12:20 If he is thirsty, give him a **d**.
1Co 3:2 I gave you milk to **d**.
9:4 we have the right to eat and **d**?
9:7 of a flock and not **d** milk from
10:4 drank the same spiritual **d**.
10:21 You cannot **d** the Lord's cup
10:31 So, whether you eat or **d**,
11:22 homes in which to eat and **d**?
11:25 Every time you **d** from it,
11:26 this bread and **d** from this cup,
11:28 the bread and **d** from the cup.
12:13 gave all of us one Spirit to **d**.
15:32 "Let's eat and **d** because
Col 2:16 because of what you eat or **d**
1Ti 3:3 He must not **d** excessively or
5:23 Instead, **d** a little wine for your
Tit 1:7 He must not **d** too much or be a
Heb 9:10 were meant to be food, **d**,
Rev 14:8 She has made all the nations **d**
14:10 will **d** the wine of God's fury,
16:6 You have given them blood to **d**
18:6 Serve her a **d** in her own cup
18:6 as the **d** she served others.
21:6 I will give a **d** from the fountain

drinkers (2)

Isa 24:9 Liquor tastes bad to its **d**.
Joe 1:5 Cry loudly, you wine **d**!

drinking (28)

Gen 24:22 the camels had finished **d**,
Rut 3:3 until he's finished eating and **d**.
1Sm 30:16 all over the land, eating, and **d**.
2Sm 13:28 good from **d** ⌊too much⌋ wine,
1Ki 1:25 They are eating and **d** with him
20:12 this as he and his allies were **d**
Est 1:8 The **d** followed this rule:
5:6 While they were **d** wine,
7:2 while they were **d** wine,
Job 1:13 were eating and **d** wine
1:18 were eating and **d** wine at their
6:4 and my spirit is **d** their poison.
Ecc 2:3 myself feel better by **d** wine.
Isa 5:22 who are heroes at **d** wine,
29:8 who dream that they're **d**
Dan 1:8 eating the king's rich food and **d**
Hos 4:18 When they're done **d** their wine,
Mat 11:18 came neither eating nor **d**,
11:19 Son of Man came eating and **d**,
24:38 flood, people were eating, **d**,
Luk 5:39 "No one who has been **d** old
7:33 neither eating bread nor **d** wine,
7:34 of Man has come eating and **d**,
17:27 People were eating, **d**,
17:28 People were eating, **d**,
Rom 14:21 is to avoid eating meat, **d** wine,
1Co 11:29 eats and drinks is eating and **d**
1Ti 5:23 Stop **d** only water.

drinks (12)

Gen 44:5 the cup that my master **d** from
Num 23:24 down until it eats its prey and **d**
Neh 8:10 eat rich foods, drink sweet **d**,
Job 15:16 who **d** wickedness like water.
34:7 who **d** scorn like water,
Psa 104:11 wild animal **d** ⌊from them⌋.
Pro 31:7 Such a person **d** and forgets
Isa 5:22 are champions at mixing **d**,
Jon 4:13 "Everyone who **d** this water
Rom 14:17 of what a person eats or **d**.
1Co 11:27 whoever eats the bread or **d**
11:29 Anyone who eats and **d** is

drip (8)

Dtr 32:2 Let my words **d** like dew,
32:42 My arrows will **d** with blood
33:28 Dew will **d** from Israel's skies.
Job 16:20 My eyes **d** ⌊with tears⌋ to God
Pro 5:3 woman **d** with honey.
Sos 4:11 Your lips **d** honey,
5:13 lips are lilies that **d** with myrrh.
Amo 9:13 New wine will **d** from the

dripped (1)

Sos 5:5 My hands **d** with myrrh,

dripping (2)

Pro 19:13 is like constantly **d** water.
27:15 Constantly **d** water on a rainy

drippings (1)

Psa 19:10 even the **d** from a honeycomb.

drips (1)

Job 36:28 which then **d** from the clouds.

drive (8)

Gen 42:38 the grief would **d** this
44:29 you'll **d** this gray-haired old
44:31 The grief would **d** our
Dtr 28:34 things you see will **d** you mad.
Job 24:3 They **d** away the orphan's
Pro 22:10 **D** out a mocker, and conflict
Isa 54:2 and **d** in the tent pegs.
Jer 46:9 **D** wildly, you chariot drivers.

driven (10)

Gen 33:13 If they're **d** too hard for even
1Sm 14:24 Israel's soldiers were **d** hard
Neh 1:9 though your people may be **d** to
Job 18:18 He will be **d** from the light into
30:5 are **d** from the community.
Psa 49:14 Like sheep, they are **d** to hell
Ecc 12:11 nails that have been **d** in firmly.
Lam 3:2 God has **d** me away and made
Zep 2:4 Ashdod will be **d** out at noon,
Jas 3:4 They are very big and are **d** by

driver (6)

1Ki 22:34 Ahab told his chariot **d**,
2Ki 9:17 Joram said, "Take a chariot **d**,
9:18 So a chariot **d** rode off,
9:19 Joram sent out a second **d**.
2Ch 18:33 Ahab told the chariot **d**,
Job 3:18 the shouting of the slave **d**.

drivers (12)

Exo 1:11 So the Egyptians put slave **d** in
3:7 out because of the slave **d**.
5:6 to the slave **d** and foremen:
5:10 The slave **d** and foreman went
5:13 The slave **d** kept hurrying
5:14 Pharaoh's slave **d** had placed
5:14 The slave **d** beat the foremen
2Sm 10:18 and David killed 700 chariot **d**
1Ch 19:18 and David killed 7,000 chariot **d**
2Ch 16:8 with many chariots and **d**?
Jer 46:9 Drive wildly, you chariot **d**.
51:21 to crush chariots and their **d**.

drives (2)

Pro 16:26 because his hunger **d** him on.
19:26 ⌊and⌋ who **d** away his mother

driving (5)

2Ki 9:20 The troop's leader is **d** like a
9:25 I were **d** our chariots behind
Pro 28:3 is like a **d** rain that leaves
Jer 30:23 Like a **d** wind, it will swirl
Act 26:24 education is **d** you crazy!"

drop (16)

Num 5:21 LORD will make your uterus **d**
5:22 swell and your uterus **d**!' "Then
5:27 will swell, her uterus will **d**,
6:9 "Someone might suddenly **d**
14:29 Your bodies will **d** dead in this
14:32 However, your bodies will **d**
35:23 Or suppose you **d** a big stone,
Job 15:33 He will **d** his unripened grapes
29:17 wicked person and made him **d**
Psa 75:8 will have to drink every last **d**.
Isa 40:15 The nations are like a **d** in a
Eze 39:3 your left hand and make you **d**
Luk 16:17 heavens to disappear than to **d**
21:2 He noticed a poor widow **d** in
Act 28:6 to swell up or suddenly **d** dead.
Jas 1:11 The flowers **d** off, and the

dropped (12)

Num 11:31 quails and **d** them all around
Jdg 8:25 from his loot and **d** them on it.
2Sm 20:8 the sword **d** ⌊into his hand⌋.
2Ki 2:16 Spirit lifted him up and **d** him
2Ch 24:10 They brought the money and **d**
Pro 3:20 and the skies **d** dew.
Mar 12:42 A poor widow **d** in two small
Luk 11:6 A friend of mine on a trip has **d**
Act 5:5 Peter say this, he **d** dead.
5:10 she **d** dead in front of Peter.
21:14 we **d** the issue and said,
27:29 they **d** four anchors from the

dropping (2)

Luk 21:1 **d** their gifts into the temple
Rev 6:13 sky to the earth like figs **d** from

drops (3)

Job 36:27 He collects **d** of water.
Luk 22:44 His sweat became like **d** of
1Pe 1:24 dries up and the flower **d** off,

drought (9)

Dtr 28:22 waves, **d**, scorching winds,
1Ki 18:1 later in the third year of the **d**,
Job 12:15 back the waters, there is a **d**.
24:19 Just as⌋ **d** and heat steal
Jer 2:6 a land of **d** and the shadow of
14:1 word to Jeremiah about the **d**.
50:38 A **d** will diminish their water
Amo 8:11 be an ordinary famine or **d**.
Hag 1:11 I called for a **d** on the land,

droughts (1)

Jer 17:8 It will not be anxious during **d**.

drove (8)

Gen 15:11 Abram **d** them away.
31:18 He **d** all his livestock ahead of
Num 25:8 He **d** the spear through the man
1Sm 23:5 **d** off their livestock,
30:20 His men **d** the animals ahead
2Ki 9:16 Jehu got on his chariot and **d**
16:6 that time King Rezin of Aram **d**
Psa 109:16 "He **d** oppressed, needy,

drown (1)

1Ti 6:9 harmful desires which **d** them

drowned (6)

Exo 15:4 Pharaoh's best officers were **d**
Dtr 11:4 He **d** them in the Red Sea
Mat 18:6 one of them to lose faith to be **d**
Mar 5:13 the cliff into the sea and **d**.
Luk 8:33 the cliff into the lake and **d**.
Heb 11:29 also tried this, but they **d**.

drowning (1)

Psa 119:28 I am **d** in tears. Strengthen me

drowsiness (1)

Pro 23:21 **D** will dress a person in rags.

drowsy (1)

Mat 25:5 became **d** and fell asleep.

drudgery (1)

Psa 73:5 They have no **d** in their lives

drug (3)

Mat 27:34 mixed with a **d** called gall.
Mar 15:23 mixed with a **d** called myrrh,
Gal 5:20 idolatry, **d** use, hatred, rivalry,

drunk (56)

Gen 9:21 He drank some wine, got **d**,
43:34 with Joseph until they were **d**.
Dtr 21:20 He eats too much and is a **d**."
Rut 3:7 Boaz had eaten and **d** to his
1Sm 1:13 Eli thought she was **d**.

1Sm 1:14 long are you going to stay **d**?"
1:15 "I'm depressed, not **d**.
25:36 in a good mood and very **d**,
30:12 (He hadn't eaten any food or **d**
2Sm 11:13 drank with him, and got him **d**.
1Ki 16:9 Elah was getting **d** in Tirzah at
20:16 was in his tent getting **d**
Est 1:10 when the king was **d** on wine,
Pro 23:21 because both a **d** and a glutton
Ecc 10:17 to get strength and not to get **d**.
Isa 5:11 late until they are **d** from wine.
19:14 astray like a **d** who staggers
24:20 The earth will stumble like a **d**
28:1 where they lie **d** from wine.
29:9 You are **d**, but not from wine.
49:26 and they will become **d** on their
51:21 you humble people who are **d**
63:6 In my wrath I made them **d** and
Jer 13:13 who lives in this land **d**.
13:13 in Jerusalem will become **d**.
23:9 I am like a **d**, like a person who
25:27 Drink, get **d**, vomit, fall down,
35:8 We have never **d** wine,
35:14 His descendants have not **d**
48:26 "Get the people of Moab **d**;
51:7 It made the whole world **d**.
51:39 and make them **d** so that they
51:57 their officials and wise men **d**,
Lam 4:21 You'll get **d** and take off all your
Eze 39:19 drink blood until you are **d** at
Hos 7:5 officials become **d** from wine,
Nah 1:10 thorns and like people **d**
3:11 will stagger like a **d**.
Hab 2:15 making him **d** in order to stare
Zec 9:15 and shout as if they were **d**.
Mat 11:19 He's a glutton and a **d**,
Luk 7:34 He's a glutton and a **d**,
12:45 and to eat, drink, and get **d**.
21:34 sure that you don't become **d**,
Jon 2:10 When people are **d**,
Act 2:13 "They're **d** on sweet wine."
2:15 These men are not **d** as you
1Co 5:11 get **d**, or are dishonest.
6:10 those who are greedy or **d**,
11:21 hungry and another gets **d**.
Eph 5:18 Don't get **d** on wine,
1Th 5:7 at night; people who get **d**,
5:7 who get drunk, get **d** at night.
1Pe 4:3 got **d**, went to wild parties,
Rev 17:2 those living on earth became **d**
17:6 I saw that the woman was **d**

drunkards (1)

Psa 69:12 and **d** make up songs about

drunkenness (3)

Eze 23:33 will be filled with **d** and sorrow.
Rom 13:13 Wild parties, **d**, promiscuity,
Gal 5:21 envy, **d**, wild partying,

drunk's (1)

Pro 26:9 a thorn stuck in a **d** hand, so is

drunks (6)

Job 12:25 he makes them stumble like **d**.
Psa 107:27 reeled and staggered like **d**,
Isa 28:1 the arrogant **d** of Ephraim.
28:3 The arrogant **d** of Ephraim will
Joe 1:5 Wake up and cry, you **d**!
Mat 24:49 and eat and drink with the **d**.

Drusilla (1)

Act 24:24 Felix arrived with his wife **D**,

dry (99)

Gen 1:9 and let the **d** land appear."
1:10 God named the **d** land earth.
7:22 Everything on **d** land (every
8:14 second month the land was **d**.
Exo 14:16 go through the sea on **d** ground.
14:21 turned the sea into **d** ground.
14:22 middle of the sea on **d** ground.
14:29 the sea on **d** ground while
15:19 through the sea on **d** ground.
16:36 (Now, the standard **d** measure
Lev 7:10 mixed with olive oil or **d**,
Dtr 8:7 land with rivers that don't **d** up.
10:7 a land with rivers that don't **d**
29:19 ground along with **d** ground."
Jos 3:17 stood firmly on **d** ground
3:17 the Jordan River on **d** ground.
4:18 their feet stepped onto **d** land,
4:22 the Jordan River on **d** ground.
9:12 It's **d** and crumbling.
15:19 you've given me some **d** land,
Jdg 1:15 you've given me some **d** land,
6:37 wool while all the ground is **d**,
6:39 Let the wool be **d** while all the
6:40 The wool was **d**, but all the
2Ki 2:8 ⌊the river⌋ on **d** ground.
19:24 I'll **d** up all the streams of Egypt
Neh 9:11 through the sea on **d** ground.
Job 6:17 In the heat their riverbeds **d** up.
13:25 or trying to chase **d** husks?
18:16 His roots **d** up under him.
30:3 they gnaw at the **d** and barren
30:6 have to live in **d** riverbeds,
Psa 37:2 They will quickly **d** up like
63:1 My body longs for you in a **d**,
66:6 He turned the sea into **d** land.
90:6 evening they wither and **d** up.
95:5 and his hands formed the **d**
105:41 a river through the **d** places.
107:35 and **d** ground into springs.
126:4 as you restore streams ⌊to **d**
Pro 17:1 Better a bite of **d** bread ⌊eaten⌋
Isa 5:24 As flames burn up straw and **d**
11:15 The LORD will **d** up the gulf of
15:6 The Nimrim Brook has run **d**!
19:5 the river will be **d** and empty.
19:7 beside the Nile will **d** up,
25:5 like heat in a **d** land.)
33:12 They will be set on fire like **d**
35:1 The desert and the **d** land will
35:7 and **d** ground will have springs.
37:25 I'll **d** up all the streams of Egypt
41:18 I will turn **d** land into springs.
42:15 I will **d** up all their vegetation.
42:15 into islands. I will **d** up ponds.
43:19 I will make rivers on **d** land.
43:20 I will make rivers on the **d** land
44:3 ground and rain on **d** land.
44:27 says to the deep water, "**D** up."
44:27 So I will **d** up your rivers.
48:18 like a river ⌊that never runs **d**⌋.
50:2 I **d** up the sea with my
51:10 Didn't you **d** up the sea,
53:2 like a root out of **d** ground.
Jer 2:25 are bare and your throats are **d**.
17:6 He will live in the **d** places in
18:14 mountain streams never **d** up.
48:18 honor and sit on the **d** ground.
48:34 the streams of Nimrim will **d** up.
50:38 water supply, and it will **d** up.
51:36 I will **d** up Babylon's sea and
51:36 sea and make its springs **d**.
Lam 4:8 It has become as **d** as bark.
Eze 17:24 I **d** up green trees, and I make
17:24 and I make **d** trees grow.
19:13 in a **d** and waterless land.
20:47 green trees and all your **d** trees.
30:12 I will **d** up the Nile River and
37:2 and they were very **d**.
37:4 Tell them, '**D** bones,
37:11 people say, 'Our bones are **d**,
45:10 honest **d** and liquid measures.
45:11 The **d** and liquid measures
Hos 2:3 I will turn her into a **d** and
13:5 of you in the desert, in a **d** land.
13:15 Then their springs will run **d**,
13:15 and their wells will **d** up.
Joe 1:20 Streams run **d**. Fire has burned
2:20 and I will force it into a **d** and
Nah 1:4 yells at the sea and makes it **d**.
1:10 burned up like very **d** straw.
Hag 2:6 the sea and the **d** land.
Zec 10:11 and **d** up all the deep places of
Mat 12:43 it goes through **d** places
21:20 the fig tree **d** up so quickly?"
Luk 11:24 it goes through **d** places
23:31 what will happen to a **d** one?"
Jon 13:5 the disciples' feet and **d** them
Heb 11:29 Red Sea as if it were **d** land.
Jud 1:12 They are **d** clouds blown

drying (1)

Hos 4:3 That is why the land is **d** up,

due (3)

Dtr 32:35 In **d** time their foot will slip,
2Ch 31:4 they were **d** so that they
Rom 13:8 Pay your debts as they come **d**.

dug (27)

Gen 21:30 may be proof that I **d** this well."
26:15 servants had **d** during his father
26:18 He **d** out the wells that had
26:18 had been **d** during his father
26:19 Isaac's servants **d** in the valley
26:21 Then they **d** another well,
26:22 from there and **d** another well.
26:25 and his servants **d** a well there.
26:32 him about a well they had **d**.
Exo 7:24 All the Egyptians **d** along the
Num 21:18 the well **d** by princes,
21:18 the well dug by princes, **d** out
2Ch 26:10 He **d** many cisterns because
Psa 35:7 For no reason they **d** the pit ⌊to
40:6 You have **d** out two ears for me.
57:6 They **d** a pit to trap me,
94:13 times of trouble while a pit is **d**
119:85 Arrogant people have **d** pits to
Isa 5:2 He **d** it up, removed its stones,
51:1 quarry from which you were **d**.
Jer 2:13 They have also **d** their own
13:7 to the Euphrates and **d** it up.
18:22 because they **d** a pit to catch
Eze 8:8 So I **d** through the wall,
12:7 In the evening I **d** a hole
Mat 25:18 **d** a hole in the ground,
Luk 6:48 He is like a person who **d**

Dumah (4)

Gen 25:14 Mishma, **D**, Massa,
Jos 15:52 their villages: Arab, **D**, Eshan,
1Ch 1:30 Mishma, **D**, Massa, Hadad,
Isa 21:11 is the divine revelation about **D**.

dumb (3)

Psa 73:22 I was like a **d** animal in your
Pro 12:1 hates correction is a **d** animal.
30:2 I'm more ⌊like⌋ a **d** animal than

dump (1)

Amo 4:3 will be thrown into a garbage **d**.

dumped (4)

Lev 4:12 camp where the ashes are **d**.
14:41 scraped off the walls must be **d**
2Ki 23:12 and **d** their rubble in the Kidron
Jon 2:15 He **d** the moneychangers' coins

dumping (2)

2Ch 30:14 the altars for incense by **d** them
Act 27:38 they lightened the ship by **d** the

dung (4)

Neh 2:13 Snake Fountain and **D** Gate
3:13 of the wall, as far as **D** Gate.
3:14 **D** Gate itself was repaired by
12:31 the right on the wall to **D** Gate.

dungeon (2)

Gen 40:15 to deserve being put in this **d**."
41:14 he was brought from the **d**.

dungeons (1)

Isa 42:7 who live in darkness out of **d**.

dusk (13)

Exo 12:6 Then at **d**, all the assembled
16:12 'At **d** you will eat meat,
29:39 the morning and the other at **d**.
29:41 Offer the other lamb at **d**,
30:8 Aaron lights the lamps at **d**,
Num 9:3 day of this month at **d**.
9:5 first month at **d** while they were
9:11 day of the second month at **d**.

Num 28:4 the morning and the other at **d**.
28:8 Offer the other lamb at **d** along
2Ki 7:5 So they started out at **d** to go
7:7 So at **d** they fled. They
Amo 4:13 makes dawn and **d** ⌊appear⌋.

dust (98)

Gen 2:7 God formed the man from the **d**
3:19 You are **d**, and you will return
3:19 and you will return to **d**."
13:16 as many descendants as the **d**
13:16 If anyone could count the **d** of
18:27 I'm ⌊only⌋ **d** and ashes,
28:14 descendants will be like the **d**
Exo 8:16 out your staff and strike the **d**
8:16 All over Egypt the **d** will turn
8:17 in his hand and struck the **d**
8:17 All the **d** on the ground
9:9 a fine **d** throughout Egypt.
9:9 The **d** will cause boils to break
Lev 14:41 The plaster **d** scraped off the
Num 5:17 of pottery and put some **d** from
23:10 of Jacob are like specks of **d**.
Dtr 28:24 The LORD will send **d** storms
Jos 7:6 They put **d** on their heads and
1Sm 2:8 He raises the poor from the **d**.
2Sm 22:43 into a powder as fine as the **d**
1Ki 16:2 said, "I raised you from the **d**
20:10 be enough **d** left from Samaria
2Ki 13:7 them like **d** that people trample.
23:6 Kidron Valley, ground it to **d**,
2Ch 1:9 as specks of **d** on the ground.
Job 2:12 They threw **d** on their heads.
4:19 have their foundation in the **d**.
7:21 Soon I'll lie down in the **d**.
10:9 will return me to the **d** again.
16:15 thrown my strength in the **d**.
17:16 my hope rest with me in the **d**?"
20:11 will lie down with him in the **d**.
21:26 Together they lie down in the **d**,
22:24 lay your gold down in the **d**,
27:16 Though he collects silver like **d**
28:6 Its **d** contains gold.
30:19 I become like **d** and ashes."
34:15 humanity would return to **d**.
39:14 and warms them in the **d**.
40:13 Hide them completely in the **d**,
41:28 from a sling turn to **d** against it.
42:6 and I sit in **d** and ashes to
Psa 7:5 Let him lay my honor in the **d**.
18:42 as fine as the **d** blown by
22:15 lay me down in the **d** of death.
22:29 All those who go down to the **d**
30:9 Will the **d** ⌊of my body⌋ give
44:25 Our souls are bowing in the **d**.
72:9 May his enemies lick the **d**.
78:27 meat down on them like **d**,
90:3 mortals back into **d** and say,
103:14 He bears in mind that we are **d**.
104:29 and they die and return to **d**.
113:7 He lifts the poor from the **d**.
Pro 8:26 fields or the first **d** of the world.
25:14 a dense fog or a **d** storm,
Ecc 12:7 Then the **d** ⌊of mortals⌋ goes
Isa 5:24 will blow away like **d**.
17:13 like whirling **d** being blown by
25:12 them into the **d** on the ground.
26:5 ground and throws it into the **d**.
26:19 Those who lie dead in the **d**
29:4 words will be muffled by the **d**.
29:4 will be whispered from the **d**.
29:5 enemies will be like fine **d**.
34:7 Their **d** will be covered with fat.
40:12 Who has held the **d** of the earth
40:15 and are considered to be like **d**
40:15 of the islands is like fine **d**.
41:2 his sword he turns them into **d**.
41:15 mountains and crush them to **d**.
49:23 They will lick the **d** at your feet.
52:2 Shake the **d** from yourselves.
65:25 and **d** will be food for snakes.
Jer 17:13 from you will be written in **d**,
25:34 Roll in the **d**, you leaders of the
Lam 3:16 He has trampled me into the **d**.
3:29 put their mouths in the **d**.
Eze 24:7 ground where **d** would cover it.
26:4 Then I will sweep up the **d** and
26:10 that their **d** will cover you.
27:30 They put **d** on their heads and
Amo 2:7 the heads of the poor into the **d**.
Mic 1:10 Roll in the **d** of Beth Leaphrah.
7:17 They will lick **d** like snakes,
Nah 1:3 clouds are the **d** from his feet.
Zep 1:17 blood will be poured out like **d**
Zec 9:3 It piled up silver like **d** and gold
Mat 10:14 and shake its **d** off your feet.
Mar 6:11 leave and shake the **d** from
Luk 9:5 and shake its **d** off your feet as
10:11 'We are wiping your city's **d**
Act 13:51 Paul and Barnabas shook the **d**
18:6 So Paul shook the **d** from his
1Co 15:47 first man was made from the **d**
15:48 man who was made from the **d**
15:49 man who was made from the **d**
Rev 18:19 Then they threw **d** on their

duties (26)

Gen 26:5 me and completed the **d**,
Exo 29:44 his sons apart for their holy **d**
30:30 set them apart for their holy **d**
35:19 clothes worn for official **d**
39:1 clothes worn for official **d**
Lev 8:12 to set him apart for his holy **d**.
Num 3:10 tries to do the priests' **d** must
3:38 tried to do the Levites' **d** had
4:27 they carry and all their **d**,
4:31 These are their **d** as they work
8:26 the other Levites in their **d** at
8:26 you will handle the Levites' **d**."
1Ch 6:32 They performed their **d**
6:48 were assigned all the other **d** in
9:33 and were free from other **d**
25:8 lots for their assignment of **d**,
26:12 head men were assigned **d**
26:29 and his sons were assigned **d**.
2Ch 35:2 appointed the priests to their **d**
Neh 7:1 were assigned their **d** after
11:23 orders that determined which **d**
13:30 I assigned **d** to the priests and
Dan 6:4 to accuse Daniel of in his **d**
Act 25:1 after Festus took over his **d**
1Ti 5:17 who handle their **d** well.
Heb 9:6 of the tent to perform their **d**.

duty (41)

Gen 38:8 Do your **d** for her as a
Lev 5:15 "If any of you fail to do your **d**
6:2 LORD by failing to do your **d**,
Num 1:3 who is eligible for military **d**.
1:20 old and eligible for military **d**.
1:22 old and eligible for military **d**.
1:24 old and eligible for military **d**.
1:26 old and eligible for military **d**.
1:28 old and eligible for military **d**.
1:30 old and eligible for military **d**.
1:32 old and eligible for military **d**.
1:34 old and eligible for military **d**.
1:36 old and eligible for military **d**.
1:38 old and eligible for military **d**.
1:40 old and eligible for military **d**.
1:42 old and eligible for military **d**.
1:45 old and eligible for military **d**
3:32 It was Eleazar's **d** to supervise
3:36 It was the **d** of the Merarites to
26:2 old and eligible for military **d**."
32:22 have fulfilled your military **d**
Dtr 24:5 will be free from military **d**
25:5 do his **d** as her brother-in-law.
25:7 do his **d** as my brother-in-law."
1Ki 2:3 Fulfill your **d** to the LORD your
2Ki 11:5 those who are on **d** on the day
11:7 groups who ⌊normally⌋ go off **d**
11:9 his men who were coming on **d**
11:9 who were about to go off **d**
1Ch 9:33 they were on **d** day and night.
2Ch 23:4 and Levites who are on **d**
23:6 who are on **d** with them.
23:8 his men who were coming on **d**
23:8 who were about to go off **d**.
Ezr 4:22 Be careful not to neglect your **d**
10:4 It's your **d** to take action.
Mat 27:65 soldiers you want for guard **d**.
Mat 27:66 posted the soldiers on guard **d**.
Luk 1:8 Zechariah was on **d** with his
17:10 We've only done our **d**.'"
Heb 10:11 performed his religious **d**.

dwarf (1)

Lev 21:20 who is a hunchback or **d**,

dwell (2)

2Sm 13:20 Don't **d** on this matter."
Isa 43:18 and do not **d** on events from

dwellers (1)

Jdg 8:11 Gideon went up Tent **D** Road,

dwelling (24)

Exo 15:13 will guide them to your holy **d**.
1Sm 2:29 people to make in my **d** place?
2:32 will see distress in my **d** place.
2Sm 15:25 both it and its **d** place again.
2Ch 36:15 his people and his **d** place.
Job 30:23 to the **d** place appointed for all
36:29 he thunders from his **d** place?
39:6 and the salt flats as its **d** place.
Psa 43:3 mountain and to your **d** place.
49:11 their **d** places throughout every
68:5 The God who is in his holy **d**
78:28 all around his **d** place.
78:60 He abandoned his **d** place in
84:1 Your **d** place is lovely,
132:5 a **d** place for the Mighty One of
132:7 Let's go to his **d** place.
Isa 18:4 and watch from my **d** place.
26:21 to come out from his **d** place
63:15 from your holy and beautiful **d**.
Jer 7:12 where I first made a **d** place for
25:30 thunders from his holy **d** place.
51:37 It will become a **d** place for
Eze 37:27 My **d** place will be with them.
Zec 2:13 out from his holy **d** place."

dwells (2)

Job 15:28 in ruined cities where no one **d**,
Psa 26:8 the place where your glory **d**.

dwindle (1)

Lam 2:12 Their lives **d** away in their

dwindles (1)

Pro 13:11 through injustice **d** away,

dye (1)

Act 16:14 of Thyatira and sold purple **d**

dyed (6)

Exo 25:5 rams' skins **d** red, fine leather,
26:14 skins that have been **d** red
35:7 rams' skins **d** red, fine leather,
35:23 goats' hair, rams' skins **d** red,
36:19 rams' skins that had been **d** red
39:34 the cover made of rams' skins **d**

dying (32)

Gen 35:18 Rachel was **d**. As she took her
1Sm 4:20 As she was **d**, the women
2Ki 7:13 rest of the Israelites who are **d**.
Job 24:12 Those **d** in the city groan.
29:13 received a blessing from the **d**.
Pro 31:6 liquor to a person who is **d**
Ecc 8:8 save wicked people ⌊from **d**⌋.
Isa 27:13 Those who are **d** in Assyria
Jer 12:4 animals and the birds are **d**,
Lam 4:9 who are **d** from starvation.
4:9 The others are **d** because there
Eze 30:24 groan like a person who is **d**.
Hos 4:3 animals, birds, and fish are **d**.
Zec 11:9 Let those that are **d** die.
11:16 take care of those that are **d**.
Mat 26:38 is so great that I feel as if I'm **d**.
Mar 5:23 "My little daughter is **d**.
14:34 is so great that I feel as if I'm **d**.
Luk 8:42 about twelve years old, was **d**.
Jon 11:37 sight keep Lazarus from **d**?"
Act 25:11 I don't reject the idea of **d**.
Rom 7:24 Who will rescue me from my **d**
2Co 2:15 and among those who are **d**.

2Co 4:3 is hidden from those who are **d**.
6:9 as **d** although, as you see,
Col 1:22 brought you back to God by **d**
2Th 2:10 of to deceive those who are **d**,
Heb 2:14 He did this so that by **d** he
2:15 because they were afraid of **d**.
11:5 Enoch to be taken instead of **d**.
11:21 While Jacob was **d**,
11:22 While Joseph was **d**,

dynasty (16)

1Sm 25:28 give you, sir, a lasting **d**,
1Ki 2:24 throne and gave me a **d** as
2:45 and David's **d** will always be
9:5 your royal **d** over Israel forever
11:38 I will build a permanent **d** for
12:19 against David's **d** to this day.
12:20 remained loyal to David's **d**.
12:26 return to David's **d** now.
2Ki 13:6 Jeroboam and his **d** led Israel
21:13 plumb line used for Ahab's **d**.
1Ch 10:6 and his **d** died together.
2Ch 7:18 I will establish your royal **d** as
10:19 against David's **d** to this day.
Psa 89:4 make your **d** continue forever.
89:29 I will make his **d** endure forever
89:36 His **d** will last forever.

dysentery (1)

Act 28:8 was suffering from fever and **d**.

E

eager (14)

1Ki 11:22 have here that makes you **e**
Job 29:23 They were as **e** to hear me as
Psa 17:12 one of them is like a lion **e**
19:5 it is **e** to run its course.
Pro 10:28 but the **e** waiting of wicked
Ecc 5:2 Don't be **e** to speak in the
Jer 6:13 are **e** to make money
8:10 are **e** to make money
Zec 6:7 they were **e** to patrol the earth.
Luk 19:48 the people were **e** to hear him.
Rom 1:15 That's why I'm **e** to tell you
1Co 14:12 In the same way, since you're **e**
Gal 2:10 very thing which I was **e** to do.
Php 2:28 So I'm especially **e** to send him

eagerly (23)

1Ki 19:10 I have **e** served you.
19:14 I have **e** served you.
Job 7:2 he **e** looks for his pay.
29:21 "People listened to me **e**,
Psa 78:34 their sins and **e** looked for God.
119:32 I will **e** pursue your
Pro 7:15 **E**, I looked for you, and I've
8:17 Those **e** looking for me will
11:27 Whoever **e** seeks good
Isa 26:9 with my spirit I **e** look for you.
51:5 and they wait **e** for me.
Hos 5:15 they will **e** look for me."
Rom 8:19 All creation is **e** waiting for
8:23 We groan as we **e** wait for our
8:25 we **e** wait for it with
1Co 1:7 don't lack any gift as you wait **e**
2Co 8:17 He accepted my request and **e**
Gal 5:5 faith causes us to wait **e** for the
Eph 6:7 Serve **e** as if you were serving
Php 1:20 I **e** expect and hope that I will
2Ti 4:8 to everyone who is **e** waiting
Heb 9:28 save those who **e** wait for him.
2Pe 3:12 to the day of God and **e** wait

eagerness (1)

2Sm 21:2 ⌊to spare them⌋, Saul, in his **e**,

eagle (25)

Dtr 28:49 swoop down on you like an **e**.
32:11 Like an **e** that stirs up its nest,
Job 9:26 like an **e** swooping down on its
39:27 Is it by your order that the **e**
Psa 103:5 become young again like an **e**.
Pro 23:5 for itself like an **e** flying into
30:19 an **e** making its way through
Jer 49:16 build your nest as high as an **e**,
Eze 1:10 each one had the face of an **e**.
10:14 the fourth was the face of an **e**.
17:3 A large **e** came to Lebanon.
17:5 The **e** planted the seedling like
17:6 turned upward toward the **e**,
17:7 "There was another large **e**
17:7 stretched its roots toward this **e**
17:7 branches toward the **e** so that
17:7 so that the **e** could water it.
17:9 Won't the first **e** uproot it and
Dan 7:4 but it had wings like an **e**.
Hos 8:1 on the LORD's temple like an **e**.
Oba 1:4 though you fly high like an **e**
Hab 1:8 They will fly like an **e** that
Rev 4:7 the fourth was like a flying **e**.
8:13 I saw an **e** flying overhead,
12:14 the two wings of the large **e**

eagles (8)

Lev 11:13 They are **e**, bearded vultures,
Dtr 14:12 never eat: **e**, bearded vultures,
2Sm 1:23 They were swifter than **e** and
Isa 40:31 They will soar on wings like **e**.
Jer 4:13 His horses are faster than **e**.
48:40 enemy will swoop down like **e**
49:22 enemy will swoop down like **e**
Lam 4:19 hunting us were faster than **e**

eagles' (2)

Exo 19:4 how I carried you on **e** wings
Dan 4:33 hair grew as long as **e** feathers

ear (44)

Exo 21:6 the doorframe and pierce his **e**
29:20 and put it on the right **e** lobes of
Lev 8:23 put it on Aaron's right **e** lobe,
8:24 the blood on their right **e** lobes,
14:14 and put it on the right **e** lobe,
14:17 in his hand on the right **e** lobe,
14:25 and put it on the right **e** lobe,
14:28 in his hand on the right **e** lobe,
Dtr 15:17 pierce it through his **e** lobe into
1Sm 7:8 "Don't turn a deaf **e** to us!
2Ki 19:16 Turn your **e** toward me,
Job 4:12 something whispered in my **e**.
12:11 Doesn't the **e** distinguish
13:1 My **e** has heard and understood
34:3 The **e** tests words like the
Psa 17:6 Turn your **e** toward me.
28:1 do not turn a deaf **e** to me.
31:2 Turn your **e** toward me.
39:12 Open your **e** to my cry for help.
45:10 Turn your **e** ⌊toward me⌋.
71:2 Turn your **e** toward me,
83:1 Do not turn a deaf **e** to me.
86:1 Turn your **e** ⌊toward me⌋,
88:2 Turn your **e** to hear my cries.
102:2 Turn your **e** toward me.
109:1 do not turn a deaf **e** to me.
116:2 he turns his **e** toward me.
Pro 5:13 nor did I keep my **e** open to my
15:31 The **e** that listens to a
20:12 The **e** that hears, the eye that
21:13 Whoever shuts his **e** to the cry
25:12 constructive criticism to the **e**
Isa 37:17 Turn your **e** toward me,
59:1 weak to save or his **e** too deaf
Amo 3:12 two legs or a piece of an **e** out
Mat 26:51 out his sword and cut off the **e**
Mar 14:47 out his sword and cut off the **e**
Luk 22:50 the disciples cut off the right **e**
22:51 the servant's **e** and healed him.
Jon 18:10 and cut off the servant's right **e**.
18:26 a relative of the man whose **e**
1Co 2:9 eye has seen, no **e** has heard,
12:16 Or suppose an **e** says,
12:17 If the whole body were an **e**,

earn (6)

Lev 25:28 However, if he cannot **e**
Hag 1:6 money as fast as you **e** it.
1Co 9:14 News should **e** their living from
Gal 5:4 Those of you who try to **e**
1Th 2:9 and what we did to **e** a living.
4:11 and **e** your own living,

earned (8)

Dtr 23:18 Never bring gifts or money **e** by
Job 20:18 He will give back what he **e**
Pro 31:16 from the profits she has **e**.
Isa 15:7 the wealth that they have **e**
Luk 19:16 the coin you gave me has **e** ten
Rom 4:4 gift but something they have **e**.
2Pe 2:13 what their wrongdoing **e** them.
2:15 what his wrongdoing **e** him.

earning (3)

Isa 23:17 Then she will go back to **e**
Act 19:25 you know that we're **e** a good
Rom 4:6 without that person's **e** it.

earnings (3)

Dtr 23:18 These **e** are disgusting to the
Ecc 5:15 able to take a handful of their **e**
Isa 23:18 Her profits and her **e** will be

earns (4)

Lev 25:26 but if he prospers and **e** enough
Psa 112:5 He **e** an honest living.
Pro 11:18 person **e** dishonest wages,
11:18 righteousness **e** honest pay.

earrings (11)

Gen 35:4 as well as the **e** that they had
Exo 32:2 off the gold **e** they are wearing,
32:3 the people took off their gold **e**
35:22 **e**, signet rings, and pendants.
Num 31:50 signet rings, **e**, and pendants.
Jdg 8:24 Each of you give me the **e** from
8:24 the Ishmaelites, wore gold **e**.)
8:25 Each man took the **e** from his
8:26 The gold **e** Gideon had asked
8:26 the half-moon ornaments, the **e**,
Eze 16:12 in your nose, **e** on your ears,

ears (102)

Num 11:20 until it comes out of their **e** and
Dtr 29:4 eyes that see, or **e** that hear.
Jdg 5:3 Open your **e**, you princes! I will
1Sm 3:11 in Israel that will make the **e**
15:14 is this sound of sheep in my **e**
2Sm 7:22 we have heard with our own **e**.
22:7 my cry for help reached his **e**.
2Ki 19:28 boasting has reached my **e**,
21:12 Jerusalem and Judah that the **e**
1Ch 17:20 we have heard with our own **e**.
2Ch 6:40 be open and your **e** attentive
7:15 and my **e** will pay attention
Neh 1:6 pay close attention with your **e**
Job 15:21 Terrifying sounds are in his **e**.
29:11 "⌊Any⌋ **e** that heard me
33:16 he opens people's **e** and
34:2 Open your **e** to me,
34:16 Open your **e** to my words!
36:15 opens their **e** through distress.
37:14 "Open your **e** to this,
42:5 about you with my own **e**,
Psa 5:1 Open your **e** to my words,
17:1 Open your **e** to my prayer,
18:6 my cry for help reached his **e**.
34:15 His **e** hear their cry for help.
40:6 You have dug out two **e** for me.
44:1 have heard it with our own **e**.
49:1 Open your **e**, all who live in the
54:2 and open your **e** to the words
55:1 Open your **e** to my prayer,
58:4 a deaf cobra that shuts its **e**
77:1 would open his **e** to ⌊hear⌋ me.
78:1 Open your **e** to my teachings,
78:1 Turn your **e** to the words from
80:1 Open your **e**, O Shepherd of
84:8 Open your **e**, O God of Jacob.
86:6 Open your **e** to my prayer,
92:11 My **e** hear ⌊the cries⌋ of
94:9 God created **e**. Do you think he
115:6 They have **e**, but they cannot
130:2 Let your **e** be open to my pleas
135:17 They have **e**, but they cannot
140:6 O LORD, open your **e** to hear

Psa 141:1 Open your e to me when I cry
143:1 Open your e to hear my urgent
Pro 4:20 Open your e to what I say.
5:1 your e to my understanding
17:4 A liar opens his e to a
18:15 The e of wise people seek
22:17 Open your e, and hear the
26:17 [Like] grabbing a dog by the e,
Isa 5:9 With my own e I heard the
6:10 Plug their e. Shut their eyes.
6:10 their eyes, hear with their e,
11:3 or decide by what his e hear.
28:23 Open your e, and listen to me!
32:3 and the e of those who can
35:5 and the e of the deaf will be
37:29 boasting has reached my e,
42:20 Your e are open, but you hear
43:8 who are deaf but still have e.
48:8 Your e have never been open
50:5 Almighty LORD will open my e.
51:4 Open your e to hear me,
55:3 Open your e, and come to me!
Jer 5:21 You have e, but you cannot
6:10 Their e are plugged,
9:20 and open your e to hear his
19:3 disaster on this place that the e
Lam 3:56 Don't close your e when I cry
Eze 8:18 Even if they shout in my e,
12:2 They have e, but they can't
16:12 earrings on your e,
23:25 will cut off your nose and e
40:4 and listen with your e.
Dan 9:18 Open your e and listen,
Hos 5:1 Open your e, royal family!
Joe 1:2 Open your e, all inhabitants of
Mic 7:16 Their e will become deaf.
Zec 7:11 me and shut their e so that they
Mat 11:15 Let the person who has e
13:9 Let the person who has e
13:15 Their e never hear.
13:16 and your e because they hear.
13:43 Let the person who has e
Mar 4:9 "Let the person who has e
4:23 Let the person who has e
7:16 Let the person who has e
7:33 put his fingers into the man's e,
Luk 8:8 "Let the person who has e
14:35 "Let the person who has e
Act 28:27 Their e never hear.
Rom 11:8 and their e don't hear!"
1Pe 3:12 His e hear their prayer.
Rev 2:7 "Let the person who has e
2:11 Let the person who has e listen
2:17 Let the person who has e listen
2:29 Let the person who has e listen
3:6 Let the person who has e listen
3:13 Let the person who has e listen
3:22 Let the person who has e listen
13:9 If anyone has e, let him listen:

earth (713)

Gen 1:1 created heaven and earth.
1:2 The e was formless and empty,
1:10 God named the dry land e.
1:11 "Let the e produce vegetation:
1:12 The e produced vegetation:
1:15 in the sky to shine on the e."
1:17 in the sky to give light to the e,
1:20 fly through the sky over the e."
1:22 there be many birds on the e."
1:24 Then God said, "Let the e
1:26 animals all over the e,
1:26 animals that crawl on the e."
1:28 fill the e, and be its master.
1:28 animals that crawl on the e."
1:29 with seeds on the face of the e
1:30 crawls on the e — every living,
2:1 Heaven and e and everything
2:4 heaven and e when they were
2:4 God made e and heaven.
2:5 plants were not on the e yet
2:5 God hadn't sent rain on the e.
2:6 would come up from the e
2:7 the man from the dust of the e
4:12 a wanderer on the e."
4:14 a wanderer on the e.
Gen 6:1 people increased all over the e,
6:4 The Nephilim were on the e in
6:5 humans had become on the e.
6:6 he had made humans on the e,
6:7 "I will wipe off the face of the e
6:12 all people on e lived evil lives.
6:13 all people because the e is full
6:13 destroy them along with the e.
6:17 about to send a flood on the e
6:17 Everything on e will die.
7:3 life all over the e after the flood.
7:4 days I will send rain to the e
7:4 I will wipe off the face of the e
7:6 when the flood came to the e.
7:10 later the flood came on the e.
7:12 came pouring down on the e
7:14 of creature that crawls on the e,
7:17 continued for 40 days on the e.
7:19 rose very high above the e.
7:21 that crawls on the e died,
7:21 that swarms over the e,
7:23 face of the e was wiped out.
7:23 and birds were wiped off the e.
7:24 were on the e for 150 days.
8:1 made a wind blow over the e,
8:9 water was still all over the e.
8:11 the water was gone from the e.
8:17 creature that crawls on the e.
8:17 and spread over the e."
8:19 that moves on the e — came out
8:22 As long as the e exists,
9:1 in number, and fill the e.
9:7 Spread over the e,
9:10 ship — every living thing on e.
9:11 be a flood that destroys the e."
9:13 a sign of my promise to the e.
9:14 I form clouds over the e,
9:16 to every living animal on e."
9:17 I am making to all life on e."
9:19 the whole e was populated.
10:8 first mighty warrior on the e.
10:25 in his day the e was divided.
10:32 over the e after the flood.
11:4 all over the face of the e."
11:8 them all over the face of the e,
11:9 of the whole e into babble.
11:9 them all over the face of the e.
12:3 family on e will be blessed."
13:16 as the dust of the e.
13:16 could count the dust of the e,
14:19 Maker of heaven and e.
14:22 Maker of heaven and e,
18:18 of the e will be blessed.
18:25 Won't the judge of the whole e
22:18 all the nations of the e will
24:3 of heaven and e that you will
26:4 of the e will be blessed.
27:28 fertile fields on the e,
27:39 lack the fertile fields of the e
28:12 saw a stairway set up on the e
28:14 will be like the dust on the e.
28:14 family on e will be blessed.
45:7 have descendants on the e
47:9 "The length of my stay on e
48:16 have many children on the e."
Exo 9:14 no one like me anywhere on e.
9:15 have wiped you off the e.
9:16 name famous throughout the e.
9:23 and lightning struck the e.
9:29 will know that the e belongs
15:12 The e swallowed them.
17:14 of the Amalekites from the e."
20:4 sky, on the e, or in the water.
20:11 made heaven, e, and the sea,
31:17 the LORD made heaven and e
32:12 wipe them off the face of the e.
33:16 people on the face of the e."
Num 12:3 humble than anyone else on e.)
14:21 of the LORD fills the whole e,
16:32 and the e opened up to
Dtr 3:24 in heaven or on e who can do
4:10 me as long as they live on e,
4:17 any animal on e, any creature
4:25 I call heaven and e as
4:32 day God created people on e.
4:36 showed you his great fire on e,
Dtr 4:39 in heaven above and here on e.
5:8 sky, on the e, or in the water.
6:15 wipe you off the face of the e,
7:6 out of all the nations on e.
7:24 and no one on e will even
9:14 and wipe their name off the e.
10:14 the e and everything it contains
11:21 as there's a sky above the e.
14:2 of all the people who live on e,
25:19 of the Amalekites from the e.
28:49 from the ends of the e.
28:64 from one end of the e to the
29:20 that person's name from the e.
30:19 I call on heaven and e as
31:28 and call on heaven and e
32:1 E, hear the words from my
32:13 ride on the heights of the e
32:22 It will consume the e and its
33:16 most plentiful crops of the e.
33:17 those at the ends of the e.
Jos 2:11 is the God of heaven and e.
3:11 of the Lord of the whole e as
3:13 the Lord of the whole e,
7:9 every memory of us from the e.
Jdg 5:4 the e quaked, the sky poured,
1Sm 2:8 "The pillars of the e are the
2:10 LORD judges the ends of the e.
4:5 that the e rang with echoes.
14:15 The e shook, and there was a
20:15 enemies off the face of the e.
20:31 long as Jesse's son lives on e,
2Sm 7:9 of the greatest people on e.
7:23 It is the one nation on e that
14:7 remain on the face of the e."
14:20 who knows everything on e."
22:8 Then the e shook and quaked.
22:16 The foundations of the e were
23:4 the grass grow from the e.'
1Ki 4:34 kings of the e who had heard
8:23 in heaven above or on e below.
8:27 "Does God really live on e?
13:34 and wiped off the face of the e.
2Ki 19:15 You made heaven and e.
19:19 kingdoms on e will know that
1Ch 1:10 first mighty warrior on the e.
1:19 in his day the e was divided.
16:14 pronounced throughout the e.
16:23 "Sing to the LORD, all the e!
16:30 in his presence, all the e!
16:30 "The e stands firm;
16:31 rejoice and the e be glad.
16:33 when he comes to judge the e.
17:8 of the greatest people on e.
17:21 It is the one nation on e that
21:16 between heaven and e.
29:11 in heaven and on e is yours.
2Ch 2:12 He made the heavens and the e
6:14 god like you in heaven or on e.
6:18 really live on e with people?
Ezr 5:11 of the God of heaven and e.
Neh 9:6 You made the e and everything
Job 1:7 wandering all over the e."
2:2 wandering all over the e."
5:10 He gives rain to the e and
5:22 afraid of wild animals on the e.
5:25 are like the grass of the e.
7:1 "Isn't a mortal's stay on e
8:9 Our days on e are only a
9:6 He shakes the e from its place,
9:24 The e is handed over to the
11:9 It is longer than the e and wider
12:8 Or speak with the e,
12:15 releases them, they flood the e.
16:18 "E, don't cover my blood.
18:4 Should the e be abandoned for
18:17 him will vanish from the e,
19:25 he will rise on the e.
20:4 time humans were placed on e,
20:27 E rises up against him.
26:7 the e on nothing whatsoever.
28:24 he can see to the ends of the e
34:13 Who put him in charge of the e?
35:11 teaches the animals of the e,
37:3 flashes to the ends of the e.
37:12 over the face of the inhabited e
37:13 or for [the good of] his e,

Job 37:17 when the **e** is calm under a
38:4 I laid the foundation of the **e**?
38:13 so that it could grab the **e** by its
38:14 The **e** changes like clay
38:18 considered how wide the **e** is?
38:24 wind is spread across the **e**?
38:33 sky or make them rule the **e**?
Psa 2:8 the ends of the **e** as your own
2:10 Be warned, you rulers of the **e**!
8:1 is your name throughout the **e**!
8:9 is your name throughout the **e**!
16:3 Those who lead holy lives on **e**
18:7 Then the **e** shook and quaked.
18:15 The foundations of the **e** were
19:4 message to the ends of the **e**.
21:10 their children from the **e**
22:27 All the ends of the **e** will
22:29 All prosperous people on **e** will
24:1 The **e** and everything it
33:5 His mercy fills the **e**.
33:8 Let all the **e** fear the LORD.
33:14 down upon all who live on **e**.
34:16 all memory of them from the **e**.
45:16 them princes over the whole **e**.
46:2 afraid even when the **e** quakes
46:6 The **e** melts at the sound of
46:8 he has brought to the **e**.
46:9 an end to wars all over the **e**.
46:10 I rule the nations. I rule the **e**.
47:2 is the great king of the whole **e**.
47:7 God is the king of the whole **e**.
47:9 The rulers of the **e** belong to
48:2 peak is the joy of the whole **e**.
48:10 ⌊reaches⌋ to the ends of the **e**.
50:1 He has summoned the **e** from
50:4 He summons heaven and **e** to
57:5 glory extend over the whole **e**.
57:11 glory extend over the whole **e**.
58:2 you invent new crimes on **e**,
58:11 is a God who judges on **e**."
59:13 Jacob to the ends of the **e**.
61:2 From the ends of the **e**,
63:9 will go into the depths of the **e**.
65:5 the hope of all the ends of the **e**
65:8 live at the ends of the **e** are
65:9 You take care of the **e**,
66:1 Shout happily to God, all the **e**!
66:4 The whole **e** will worship you.
67:2 your ways will be known on **e**,
67:4 and guide the nations on the **e**.
67:6 The **e** has yielded its harvest.
67:7 the ends of the **e** worship him.
68:8 the **e** quaked and the sky
69:34 Let heaven and **e**, the seas,
71:20 back from the depths of the **e**.
72:8 River to the ends of the **e**.
72:19 May the whole **e** be filled with
73:9 they order people around on **e**.
73:25 anyone else in heaven or on **e**.
74:12 victorious throughout the **e**.
74:17 all the boundaries of the **e**.
75:3 When the **e** and everyone who
75:8 wicked people on **e** will have
76:8 The **e** was fearful and silent
76:9 every oppressed person on **e**.
76:12 He terrifies the kings of the **e**.
77:18 The **e** trembled and shook.
78:69 like the **e** which he made to
82:5 all the foundations of the **e**
82:8 Judge the **e**, because all the
83:18 Most High God of the whole **e**.
89:11 The **e** is also yours.
89:27 Most High to the kings of the **e**.
90:2 before you gave birth to the **e**
94:2 Arise, O Judge of the **e**.
95:4 are the deep places of the **e**,
96:1 Sing to the LORD, all the **e**!
96:9 in his presence, all the **e**!
96:10 The **e** stands firm;
96:11 rejoice and the **e** be glad.
96:13 He is coming to judge the **e**.
97:1 Let the **e** rejoice. Let all the
97:4 The **e** sees them and trembles.
97:5 of the Lord of the whole **e**.
97:9 are above the whole **e**.
98:3 All the ends of the **e** have seen
Psa 98:4 happily to the LORD, all the **e**.
98:9 he is coming to judge the **e**.
99:1 the angels. Let the **e** quake.
100:1 happily to the LORD, all the **e**.
102:15 All the kings of the **e** will fear
102:19 heaven he looked at the **e**.
102:25 you laid the foundation of the **e**.
103:11 are above the **e** — that is
104:5 You set the **e** on its
104:6 You covered the **e** with an
104:9 come back to cover the **e**.
104:13 You fill the **e** with the fruits of
104:24 The **e** is filled with your
104:30 You renew the face of the **e**.
104:32 He looks at the **e**, and it
105:7 pronounced throughout the **e**.
108:5 glory extend over the whole **e**.
109:15 memory of him from the **e**,
110:6 Throughout the **e** he will crush
112:2 will grow strong on the **e**.
113:6 down to look at heaven and **e**.
114:7 **E**, tremble in the presence of
115:15 the maker of heaven and **e**.
115:16 but he has given the **e** to the
119:64 mercy, O LORD, fills the **e**.
119:87 me off ⌊the face of⌋ the **e**.
119:90 You set the **e** in place,
119:119 wicked people on **e** as if they
121:2 the maker of heaven and **e**.
124:8 the maker of heaven and **e**.
134:3 the maker of heaven and **e**,
135:6 he wants in heaven or on **e**,
135:7 rise from the ends of the **e**,
136:6 to the one who spread out the **e**
138:4 All the kings of the **e** will give
140:11 not let slanderers prosper on **e**.
146:6 who made heaven, **e**,
147:15 his promise throughout the **e**.
148:7 Praise the LORD from the **e**.
148:11 kings of the **e** and all its
148:11 and all judges on the **e**,
148:13 glory is above heaven and **e**.
Pro 3:19 laid the foundation of the **e**.
8:23 before the **e** began.
8:29 traced the foundations of the **e**,
11:31 person is rewarded on **e**,
25:3 high heavens and the deep **e**,
30:4 Who has set up the **e** from one
30:14 oppressed people from the **e**
30:21 things cause the **e** to tremble,
30:24 Four things on **e** are small,
Ecc 1:4 but the **e** lasts forever.
3:21 spirit goes downward to the **e**?
5:2 is in heaven and you are on **e**,
7:20 is no one so righteous on **e** that
8:14 done on **e** that is pointless.
8:16 done on **e** (even going without
11:2 disaster may happen on **e**.
11:3 will let it pour down on the **e**.
Isa 1:2 heaven, and pay attention, **e**!
2:19 when he rises to terrify the **e**.
2:21 when he rises to terrify the **e**.
5:26 those at the ends of the **e**.
6:3 The whole **e** is filled with his
8:9 all you distant parts of the **e**.
8:22 They will look at the **e** and see
11:4 for the humble people on **e**.
11:4 He will strike the **e** with a rod
11:12 from the four corners of the **e**.
12:5 this be known throughout the **e**.
13:9 He will make the **e** desolate.
13:13 and the **e** will be shaken from
14:7 The whole **e** rests and is
14:9 all who were leaders on **e**.
14:16 man who made the **e** tremble,
14:21 be able to rise, possess the **e**,
14:26 determined for the whole **e**.
18:3 of the world who live on the **e**.
18:6 and all the wild animals on **e**
19:24 will be a blessing on the **e**.
24:1 The LORD is going to turn the **e**
24:1 He will mar the face of the **e**
24:3 The **e** will be completely laid
24:4 The **e** dries up and withers.
24:4 leaders of the **e** waste away.
24:5 The **e** is polluted by those who
Isa 24:6 is why a curse devours the **e**,
24:6 live on the **e** are burned up,
24:13 That is the way it will be on **e**
24:16 From the ends of the **e** we hear
24:17 in store for those who live on **e**.
24:18 foundations of the **e** will shake.
24:19 The **e** will be completely
24:19 The **e** will shake back and
24:19 The **e** will stagger.
24:20 The **e** will stumble like a drunk
24:21 heaven and earth's kings on **e**.
25:8 of his people from the whole **e**.
26:9 guiding principles are on **e**,
26:18 no new people were born on **e**.
26:19 and the **e** will revive the spirits
26:21 to punish those who live on **e**
26:21 The **e** will uncover the blood
34:1 The **e**, everyone in it,
37:16 You made heaven and **e**.
37:20 kingdoms on **e** will know that
40:12 Who has held the dust of the **e**
40:21 the foundations of the **e**?
40:22 God is enthroned above the **e**,
40:28 the Creator of the ends of the **e**,
41:5 The ends of the **e** tremble.
41:9 you from the ends of the **e**
42:4 he has set up justice on the **e**.
42:5 He shaped the **e** and all that
42:10 praise from the ends of the **e**,
43:6 from the ends of the **e**.
44:23 you deep places of the **e**.
44:24 I spread out the **e** all alone.
45:8 Let the **e** open. Let salvation
45:12 I made the **e** and created
45:18 God formed the **e** and made it.
45:22 who live at the ends of the **e**,
48:13 laid the foundation of the **e**.
48:20 Shout it out to the ends of the **e**.
49:13 Rejoice, you **e**! Break into
51:6 Look at the **e** below.
51:6 The **e** will wear out like
51:13 laid the foundations of the **e**.
51:16 laid the foundations of the **e**,
52:10 All the ends of the **e** will see
54:5 called the God of the whole **e**.
54:9 would never cover the **e** again.
55:9 heavens are higher than the **e**,
55:10 again until they water the **e**.
58:14 you ride on the heights of the **e**.
60:2 Darkness now covers the **e**,
62:7 of praise throughout the **e**.
62:11 announced to the ends of the **e**:
65:17 a new heaven and a new **e**.
66:1 The **e** is my footstool.
66:22 "The new heaven and **e** that I
Jer 4:23 I see the **e**. It's formless and
4:27 The whole **e** will be ruined,
4:28 The **e** will mourn, and the sky
6:19 Listen, **e**! I'm going to bring
6:22 in the distant parts of the **e**.
9:24 and justice on the **e**.
10:10 The **e** trembles when he is
10:11 gods will disappear from the **e**
10:11 they didn't make heaven and **e**.
10:12 The LORD made the **e** by his
10:13 rise from the ends of the **e**.
15:4 to all the kingdoms on the **e**.
15:10 and quarrels with the whole **e**.
23:24 "I fill heaven and **e**!"
24:9 to all the kingdoms of the **e**.
25:26 all the kingdoms of the **e**.
25:29 war on all those who live on **e**,
25:30 against all those who live on **e**.
25:31 is echoing to the ends of the **e**
25:32 the distant corners of the **e**."
25:33 stretch from one end of the **e**
26:6 by all the nations on **e**.'"
27:5 arm to make the **e** along
28:16 you from the face of the **e**.
29:18 to all the kingdoms on the **e**.
31:8 from the farthest parts of the **e**.
31:22 create something new on **e**:
31:37 the foundations of the **e** could
32:17 you made heaven and **e** by
33:2 "I made ⌊the **e**⌋, formed it,
33:9 All the nations on **e** will hear

Jer 33:25 or made laws for heaven and **e**.
44:8 by all the nations on **e**.
45:4 I have planted throughout the **e**.
46:8 'I will rise; I will cover the **e**.
46:12 your cry fills the **e**.
49:21 The **e** will quake at the sound
50:23 The hammer of the whole **e** is
50:41 will rise from the ends of the **e**.
50:46 The **e** will quake at the news
51:15 The LORD made the **e** by his
51:16 rise from the ends of the **e**.
51:25 the whole **e**," declares
51:29 The **e** trembles and writhes in
51:48 Then heaven and **e** and
51:49 many people throughout the **e**,
Lam 2:1 beauty from heaven to **e**.
3:34 crush any prisoner on **e**
4:12 Neither the kings of the **e** nor
4:12 living on **e** could believe that
Eze 1:19 living creatures rose from the **e**,
1:21 the creatures rose from the **e**,
7:2 to the four corners of the **e**.
7:21 evil people on **e** as prizes.
8:3 me between heaven and **e**.
26:20 you live below the **e** among
27:33 You made the kings of the **e**
31:14 going to die and go below the **e**
31:16 were comforted below the **e**.
31:18 be brought down below the **e**
32:4 from all over the **e** will feed
32:6 I will drench the **e** with your
32:18 Send them down below the **e**
32:24 They went down below the **e**
34:6 throughout the whole **e**.
35:14 The whole **e** will be glad when
38:20 and every person on **e** will
39:18 blood of the princes of the **e**.
43:2 and the **e** was shining because
Dan 2:10 "No one on **e** can tell the king
4:10 oak tree in the middle of the **e**.
4:11 be seen everywhere on **e**.
4:20 be seen everywhere on **e**.
4:35 Everyone who lives on **e** is
4:35 and with those who live on **e**.
6:27 things in heaven and on **e**.
7:17 that will rise to power on the **e**.
7:23 fourth of these kingdoms on **e**.
8:5 It crossed the whole **e** without
Hos 2:21 it will speak to the **e**,
2:22 and the **e** will produce grain,
Joe 2:10 The **e** quakes in their presence,
2:30 in the sky and on the **e**:
3:16 The sky and the **e** will shake.
Amo 3:2 Out of all the families on **e**,
4:13 on the high places of the **e**.
5:8 to pour it over the face of the **e**.
8:9 darken the **e** in broad daylight.
9:5 LORD of Armies touches the **e**.
9:6 sets their foundation on the **e**,
9:6 the face of the **e** — His name
9:8 will wipe it off the face of the **e**.
Oba 1:3 one can bring me down to **e**.'
Mic 1:2 **e** and all who are on it.
1:3 on the worship places of the **e**.
4:13 for the Lord of the whole **e**.
5:4 will reach the ends of the **e**.
6:2 you strong foundations of the **e**.
7:2 people are gone from the **e**,
7:13 The **e** will become a
Nah 1:5 The **e** draws back in his
2:13 remove your prey from the **e**,
Hab 1:6 will march throughout the **e**
2:14 But the **e** will be filled with the
2:20 All the **e** should be silent in his
3:3 His praise fills the **e**.
3:6 He stands and shakes the **e**.
3:12 march through the **e** with fury.
Zep 1:2 everything on the face of the **e**
1:3 of the **e**," declares the LORD.
1:18 The whole **e** will be consumed
1:18 to those who live on **e**.
2:11 the gods of the **e** waste away.
3:20 all the people of the **e** when
Hag 1:10 dew and the **e** has withheld its
2:6 to shake the sky and the **e**,
2:21 shake the heavens and the **e**.
Zec 1:10 LORD has sent to patrol the **e**."
1:11 "We have patrolled the **e**.
4:10 the LORD roam over all the **e**.)"
4:14 beside the Lord of the whole **e**."
5:3 that will go out all over the **e**.
5:6 sins look like all over the **e**."
6:5 of the Lord of the whole **e**.
6:7 they were eager to patrol the **e**.
6:7 He said, "Go, patrol the **e**!"
6:7 And they patrolled the **e**.
9:10 River to the ends of the **e**.
12:1 laid the foundation of the **e**,
14:9 will be king over all the **e**.
14:10 The whole **e** will become like
14:17 If any of the families on the **e**
Mat 5:5 They will inherit the **e**.
5:13 "You are salt for the **e**.
5:18 Until the **e** and the heavens
5:35 or by the **e**, which is his
6:10 Let your will be done on **e** as it
6:19 treasures for yourselves on **e**,
9:6 Son of Man has authority on **e**
10:34 that I came to bring peace to **e**.
11:25 Lord of heaven and **e**,
12:40 Man will be in the heart of the **e**
12:42 came from the ends of the **e**
18:19 agree on anything here on **e**,
23:9 call anyone on **e** your father,
23:35 blood of those murdered on **e**,
24:30 All the people on **e** will cry in
24:35 The **e** and the heavens will
27:51 The **e** shook, and the rocks
28:18 and on **e** has been given
Mar 2:10 Son of Man has authority on **e**
4:31 one of the smallest seeds on **e**.
9:3 on **e** could bleach them.
13:31 The **e** and the heavens will
Luk 2:14 and on **e** peace to those who
5:24 Son of Man has authority on **e**
10:21 Lord of heaven and **e**,
11:31 came from the ends of the **e**
12:49 come to throw fire on the **e**.
12:51 I came to bring peace to **e**?
12:56 the appearance of **e** and sky.
16:17 It is easier for the **e** and the
18:8 will he find faith on **e**?"
21:25 The nations of the **e** will be
21:33 The **e** and the heavens will
21:35 all people who live on the **e**.
Jon 3:12 I tell you about things on **e**,
3:31 I, a person from the **e**,
3:31 know nothing but what is on **e**,
12:32 I have been lifted up from the **e**,
12:34 must be lifted up from the **e**'?
17:4 On **e** I have given you glory by
18:36 doesn't have its origin on **e**."
Act 1:8 and to the ends of the **e**."
2:19 sky and give signs on the **e**:
3:25 all people on **e** will be blessed.'
7:49 The **e** is my footstool.
8:33 his life on **e** being cut short?"
17:24 it is the Lord of heaven and **e**.
17:26 humanity to live all over the **e**.
Rom 9:17 my name throughout the **e**."
10:18 words to the ends of the **e**."
1Co 8:5 heaven and on **e** — many gods
10:26 Certainly, "The **e** is the Lord's
15:47 made from the dust of the **e**.
15:47 He came from the **e**.
15:48 The people on **e** are like the
15:48 made from the dust of the **e**.
15:49 made from the dust of the **e**,
2Co 5:1 we live here on **e** is ever taken
Eph 1:10 everything in heaven and on **e**.
3:15 and on **e** receives its name.
4:9 to the lowest parts of the **e**?
6:3 you may have a long life on **e**."
Php 2:10 everyone in heaven, on **e**,
Col 1:16 all things in heaven and on **e**,
1:20 to bring everything on **e**
Heb 1:10 you laid the foundation of the **e**.
5:7 During his life on **e**,
6:7 God blesses the **e**.
6:8 However, if the **e** produces
8:4 If he were on **e**, he would not
8:4 On **e** ⌊other⌋ priests offer gifts
Heb 9:1 It also had a holy place on **e**.
11:13 with no permanent home on **e**.
12:9 On **e** we have fathers who
12:25 who warned them on **e**.
12:26 his voice shook the **e**.
12:26 more I will shake not only the **e**
13:14 a permanent city here on **e**,
Jas 5:5 luxury and pleasure here on **e**.
5:12 on anything in heaven or on **e**.
1Pe 1:17 residents on **e** in fear.
4:2 live the rest of your lives on **e**.
2Pe 3:5 heaven and **e** existed a long
3:5 The **e** ⌊appeared⌋ out of water
3:7 the present heaven and **e** are
3:10 The **e** and everything that
3:13 a new heaven and a new **e** —
Rev 1:5 the ruler over the kings of the **e**.
1:7 Every tribe on **e** will mourn
3:10 world to test those living on **e**.
5:3 No one in heaven, on **e**,
5:3 or under the **e** could open the
5:10 will rule as kings on the **e**."
5:13 heaven, on **e**, under the earth,
5:13 under the **e**, and on the sea.
6:4 to take peace away from the **e**
6:8 power over one-fourth of the **e**
6:8 and the wild animals on the **e**.
6:10 those living on **e** who shed our
6:13 sky to the **e** like figs dropping
6:15 Then the kings of the **e**,
7:1 at the four corners of the **e**.
7:1 back the four winds of the **e**
8:5 and threw it on the **e**.
8:7 and were thrown on the **e**.
8:7 One-third of the **e** was burned
8:13 for those living on **e**,
9:1 I saw a star that had fallen to **e**
9:3 out of the smoke onto the **e**,
9:4 green plant, or tree on the **e**.
10:6 the **e** and everything in it,
11:4 presence of the Lord of the **e**.
11:6 into blood and to strike the **e**
11:10 Those living on **e** will gloat
11:10 tormented those living on **e**.
11:18 those who destroy the **e**."
12:4 sky and threw them down to **e**.
12:9 was thrown down to **e**.
12:12 How horrible it is for the **e** and
12:13 it had been thrown down to **e**,
12:16 The **e** helped the woman by
13:8 Everyone living on **e** will
13:11 another beast come from the **e**,
13:12 The second beast makes the **e**
13:13 come down from heaven to **e**
13:14 It deceives those living on **e**
13:14 It tells those living on **e** to
14:3 been bought on **e** could learn
14:6 spread to those who live on **e** —
14:7 one who made heaven and **e**,
14:15 harvest on the **e** is overripe."
14:16 swung his sickle over the **e**,
14:16 of the **e** was completed.
14:18 of grapes from the vine of the **e**,
14:19 swung his sickle on the **e**
14:19 grapes from the vine of the **e**.
16:1 of God's anger over the **e**."
16:2 poured his bowl over the **e**.
16:18 since humans have been on **e**.
17:2 The kings of the **e** had sex
17:2 and those living on **e** became
17:5 and Detestable Things of the **E**.
17:8 Those living on **e**,
17:18 dominates the kings of the **e**."
18:1 and his glory lit up the **e**.
18:3 The kings of the **e** had sex
18:3 the merchants of the **e** rich."
18:9 "The kings of the **e** who had
18:11 "The merchants of the **e** cry
18:24 been murdered on **e** was found
19:19 the beast, the kings of the **e**,
20:8 in the four corners of the **e**,
20:9 over the broad expanse of the **e**
20:11 The **e** and the sky fled from his
21:1 a new heaven and a new **e**,
21:1 heaven and **e** had disappeared,
21:24 and the kings of the **e** will bring

earthenware (1)
Isa 45:9 is pottery among other e pots.

earthly (12)
Isa 40:23 makes e judges worth nothing.
Rom 15:27 obligated to use their e wealth
1Co 7:33 is concerned about e things,
7:34 is concerned about e things,
9:11 the harvest from your e goods?
15:40 heavenly bodies and e bodies.
15:40 neither do e bodies.
Eph 6:5 Slaves, obey your e masters
Col 3:22 always obey your e masters.
Heb 12:16 about e things as Esau
1Pe 4:6 like humans in their e lives
Rev 9:3 like the power of e scorpions.

earthquake (16)
1Ki 19:11 After the wind came an e.
19:11 But the LORD wasn't in the e.
19:12 After the e there was a fire.
Eze 38:19 that day there will be a large e
Amo 1:1 two years before the e.
Zec 14:5 flee as you did from the e at
Mat 27:54 Jesus with him saw the e
28:2 there was a powerful e.
Act 16:26 Suddenly, a violent e shook
Rev 6:12 A powerful e struck.
8:5 noise, lightning, and an e.
11:13 moment a powerful e struck.
11:13 people were killed by the e,
11:19 thunder, an e, and heavy hail.
16:18 thunder, and a powerful e.
16:18 powerful e since humans have

earthquakes (4)
Isa 29:6 thunder, e, and loud noises,
Mat 24:7 and e in various places.
Mar 13:8 There will be e and famines in
Luk 21:11 There will be terrible e,

earth's (2)
Isa 24:11 the e happiness is banished.
24:21 in heaven and e kings on earth.

ease (6)
Gen 50:21 setting their minds at e.
Job 16:5 lips could e ⌊your pain⌋.
16:12 I was at e, and he shattered
Amo 6:1 for those who are at e in Zion,
Zec 1:15 nations who think they are at e.
2Co 7:13 All of you had put his mind at e.

eased (1)
Job 16:6 If I speak, my pain is not e.

easier (10)
Exo 18:22 Make it e for yourself by letting
Mat 9:5 Is it e to say, 'Your sins are
19:24 can guarantee again that it is e
Mar 2:9 Is it e to say to this paralyzed
10:25 It is e for a camel to go through
Luk 5:23 Is it e to say, 'Your sins are
10:12 that judgment day will be e
16:17 It is e for the earth and the
18:25 Indeed, it is e for a camel to go
Rom 11:24 So wouldn't it be e for these

easily (11)
Gen 26:10 One of the people might have e
Exo 4:10 and I become tongue-tied e."
Dtr 1:41 thinking you could e invade the
2Sm 11:25 kill one person as e as another.
Job 8:14 His confidence is e shattered.
Pro 14:6 but knowledge comes e to a
Ecc 4:12 A triple-braided rope is not e
Jer 2:36 You change your mind so e.
Act 26:26 I can e speak to a king who
Heb 5:2 are ignorant and e deceived,
Jas 1:19 and should not get angry e.

east (194)
Gen 2:8 a garden in Eden, in the e.
2:14 the one that flows e of Assyria.
3:24 that turned in all directions e
4:16 Land of Wandering], e of Eden.
11:2 As people moved toward the e,
12:8 on to the hills e of Bethel,
12:8 on the west and Ai on the e.
13:11 He moved toward the e.
13:14 e, and west of where you are.
23:17 e of Mamre, was sold
23:19 e of Mamre (that is,
25:6 his son Isaac to a land in the e.
25:9 The cave is e of Mamre.
28:14 out to the west and to the e,
29:1 and came to the land in the e.
41:6 and scorched by the e wind,
41:23 and scorched by the e wind,
41:27 by the e wind are also
49:30 e of Mamre in Canaan,
50:10 which is on the e side of the
50:11 That's why that place on the e
50:13 field of Machpelah, e of Mamre.
Exo 10:13 a wind from the e blow over
10:13 By morning the e wind had
14:21 the sea with a strong e wind
27:13 On the e end, facing the rising
38:13 The e side, facing the rising
Lev 1:16 filth and throw it on the e side
16:14 it with his finger on the e side
Num 2:3 "On the e side, facing the
3:38 put up their tents on the e side
10:5 on the e side will break
22:1 on the plains of Moab e of the
32:19 our land here, e of the Jordan."
32:32 of is here, e of the Jordan."
33:7 Pi Hahiroth, e of Baal Zephon,
33:47 Abarim Mountains e of Nebo.
34:3 In the e the southern border
34:11 goes down to Riblah, e of Ain,
34:15 tribes received land e
35:5 off 3,000 feet on the e side,
35:14 three on the e side of the
Dtr 1:1 Moses gave in the desert e
1:5 The Israelites were e of the
3:8 land of the two Amorite kings e
3:17 is near Mount Pisgah on the e.
3:27 look west, north, south, and e.
4:41 aside three cities on the e side
4:46 to the people when they were e
4:47 of the Amorites who were e
4:49 all the plains on the e side
Jos 1:14 the land that Moses gave you e
1:15 take possession of the land e
2:10 who ruled e of the Jordan River.
3:16 crossed from the e side ⌊of
4:19 at Gilgal, just e of Jericho.
7:2 is near Beth Aven, e of Bethel.
9:10 the two kings of the Amorites e
11:3 Canaanites from e and west,
11:8 the valley of Mizpah in the e.
12:1 are the kings of the land e
13:3 the Shihor River, e of Egypt,
13:8 had received their inheritance e
13:32 e of the Jordan River near
14:3 tribes their inheritance e
16:1 the springs of Jericho on the e,
16:6 The border then turns e to
16:6 Shiloh and passes e to Janoah.
17:5 land of Gilead and Bashan e
18:7 Moses gave them on the e side
19:12 from Sarid it turns directly e
19:13 From there it goes directly e to
19:27 Then it turns e to Beth Dagon
19:34 Judah in the e at the Jordan.
20:8 as cities of refuge on the e side
20:8 the Jordan River, e of Jericho.
22:4 servant Moses gave you e
24:8 who lived on the e side
Jdg 5:17 Gilead remained e of the
8:11 e of Nobah and Jogbehah,
10:8 they oppressed all who lived e
11:18 They camped e of Moab — east
11:18 They camped east of Moab — e
20:43 overtook them e of Gibeah.
21:19 Shiloh is north of Bethel, e of
1Sm 11:1 no one among the Israelites e
13:5 at Michmash, e of Beth Aven.
15:7 Havilah to Shur, e of Egypt.
1Ki 7:25 faced south, and three faced e.
11:7 illegal worship site on the hill e
17:3 "Leave here, turn e,
17:3 which is e of the Jordan River.
17:5 which is e of the Jordan River.
2Ki 10:33 e of the Jordan River:
13:17 the window that faces e."
23:13 the illegal places of worship e
1Ch 4:39 on the e side of the valley,
5:10 the entire region e of Gilead.
5:11 Bashan as far ⌊e⌋ as Salcah.
6:78 descendants received land e
7:28 its villages, Naaran to the e,
9:18 at the king's gate on the e side.
9:24 were on the four sides (e,
12:15 the valleys to the e and west.
12:37 From the e side of the Jordan
26:14 was chosen for the e side.
26:17 On the e side there were six
2Ch 4:4 faced south, and three faced e.
5:12 in fine linen and stood e
29:4 in the square on the e side ⌊of
31:14 was the gatekeeper at **E** Gate
Neh 3:26 from Water Gate toward the e
3:29 the guard at **E** Gate,
12:37 reaches Water Gate on the e.
Job 1:3 person in the Middle **E**.
15:2 his stomach with the e wind?
18:20 People in the e are seized with
23:8 However, if I go e,
27:21 The e wind carries him away,
38:24 and the e wind is spread
Psa 48:7 With the e wind you smash the
75:6 does not ⌊come⌋ from the e,
78:26 He made the e wind blow in
103:12 As far as the e is from the west
107:3 from the e and from the west,
Isa 9:12 the Arameans from the e and
11:14 will loot the people of the e.
24:15 Honor the LORD in the e.
27:8 a fierce blast from the e winds.
37:27 dried up by the e wind.
41:2 "Who has raised up from the e
41:25 call on my name from the e.
43:5 your descendants from the e
45:6 so that from the e to the west
46:11 call a bird of prey from the e.
59:19 Those in the e will fear his
Jer 18:17 Like the e wind I will scatter
31:40 corner of Horse Gate in the e,
49:28 and loot the people from the e.
Eze 8:16 They were facing e and
10:19 stood at the door to the e gate
11:1 me and took me to the e gate
11:1 (It's the gate that faces e.)
11:23 the mountain e of the city.
17:10 when the e wind blows
19:12 The e wind dried up its fruit.
25:4 you over to the people in the e.
25:10 over to the people in the e.
27:26 and an e wind wrecked you in
39:11 e of the Dead Sea.
40:6 to the gateway that faced e.
40:19 It was 175 feet from e to north.
40:21 size as those in the e gateway.
40:22 size as those in the e gateway.
40:23 gate just like the e gateway.
40:32 man brought me to the e side
42:9 had an entrance on the e side.
42:15 led me out through the e gate.
42:16 He measured the e side with a
43:1 Then the man took me to the e
43:2 of Israel coming from the e.
43:4 the temple through the e gate.
43:17 The steps to the altar faced e.
44:1 me back to the outer e gate
46:1 The e gate of the inner
46:12 the e gate must be opened for
47:1 of the temple toward the e.
47:1 (The temple faced e.)
47:2 and around to the outer e gate.
47:8 flows through the land to the e,
47:18 On the e side the border will
47:18 This is the e side.
48:10 On the e side it will be 17,500
48:16 On the e side it will be 7,875
48:17 4,375 feet on the e,

Eze 48:18 will be 17,500 feet on its **e** side
48:21 Whatever is left on the **e** side
48:32 The **e** side will be 7,875 feet
48:32 The three gates on the **e** side
Dan 8:9 the **e**, and the beautiful land.
11:44 But news from the **e** and the
Hos 12:1 try to chase the **e** wind all day.
13:15 wind will come from the **e**.
Amo 8:12 roam from the north to the **e**,
Jnh 4:5 the city and sat down **e** of it.
4:8 God made a hot **e** wind blow.
Zec 14:4 just **e** of Jerusalem.
14:4 large valley from **e** to west.
Mat 2:1 from the **e** arrived in Jerusalem.
24:27 flashes from **e** to west.
Jon 1:28 in Bethany on the **e** side
Rev 7:2 angel coming from the **e**
16:12 a road for the kings from the **e**.
21:13 were three gates on the **e**,

eastern (31)

Gen 10:30 Sephar in the **e** mountains.
Num 23:7 me from the **e** mountains.
34:10 "The **e** border extends from
34:11 and continues along the **e**
Jos 12:1 and all the **e** plains.
12:3 It included the **e** plains from the
15:5 The **e** border is the Dead Sea
16:5 The **e** border of the land they
17:10 and Issachar its **e** border.
18:20 Jordan River is its **e** border.
1Ki 4:30 than that of all the **e** people
Isa 2:6 are filled with **E** influences.
Eze 40:10 on each side of the **e** gateway.
41:14 The **e** side of the temple,
45:7 From the **e** boundary of the
45:7 his land will extend to the **e**
48:1 the **e** border to the western
48:2 It will extend from the **e** border
48:3 It will extend from the **e** border
48:4 It will extend from the **e** border
48:5 It will extend from the **e** border
48:6 It will extend from the **e** border
48:7 It will extend from the **e** border
48:8 It will extend from the **e** border
48:21 the holy area to the **e** border,
48:23 It will extend from the **e** border
48:24 It will extend from the **e** border
48:25 It will extend from the **e** border
48:26 It will extend from the **e** border
48:27 It will extend from the **e** border
Joe 2:20 will be forced into the **e** sea.

eastward (5)

Jos 13:5 all Lebanon **e** from Baal Gad at
1Ch 5:9 Some of them lived **e** as far as
Eze 42:12 corresponding wall that ran **e**.
47:3 in his hand, the man went **e**.
48:21 This land will extend **e** from

easy (9)

1Sm 18:23 "Do you think it's **e** to become
2Ki 3:18 The LORD considers that an **e**
20:10 Hezekiah replied, "It's **e** for the
Job 12:5 "A person who has an **e** life
Pro 19:23 rest **e** without suffering harm.
Isa 8:1 the Prey Will be **E**].
Mat 11:30 because my yoke is **e** and my
Luk 12:19 Take life **e**, eat, drink,
Eph 5:14 makes everything **e** to see.

eat (610)

Gen 2:9 and their fruit was good to **e**.
2:16 He said, "You are free to **e** from
2:17 But you must never **e** from the
2:17 because when you **e** from it,
3:1 'You must never **e** the fruit of
3:2 "We're allowed to **e** the fruit
3:3 'You must never **e** it or touch it.
3:5 "God knows that when you **e** it
3:6 had fruit that was good to **e**,
3:11 Did you **e** fruit from the tree I
3:11 commanded you not to **e** from?"
3:17 'You must never **e** its fruit.'
3:17 Through hard work you will **e**
3:18 and you will **e** wild plants.
Gen 3:19 you will produce food to **e** until
3:22 fruit from the tree of life and **e**.
9:4 "But you are not to **e** meat with
24:33 "I won't **e** until I've said what I
25:28 Because Isaac liked to **e** the
25:30 pot of red stuff to **e** — that red
27:4 Bring it to me to **e** so that I will
27:7 meal for me to **e** so that
27:10 Then take it to your father to **e**
27:19 Sit up and **e** this meat I've
27:25 the game, and I will **e** it, Son,
27:31 **e** some of the meat I've hunted
28:20 my trip and give me food to **e**
31:54 He invited his relatives to **e** the
32:32 the people of Israel do not **e**
37:25 As they sat down to **e**,
40:19 The birds will **e** the flesh from
43:16 because they are going to **e**
43:25 they were going to **e** there.
43:32 it offensive to **e** with Hebrews.
Exo 10:5 They will **e** everything left by
10:12 They will invade Egypt and **e**
12:4 may be too small to **e**
12:4 and what each person can **e**.
12:7 where they will **e** the animals.
12:9 Don't **e** any of it raw or boiled
12:11 be dressed when⌋ you **e** it:
12:11 You must **e** it in a hurry.
12:15 you must **e** unleavened bread.
12:18 you must **e** unleavened bread.
12:20 **E** nothing made with yeast.
12:20 must **e** ⌊only⌋ unleavened bread
12:43 may **e** the Passover meal.
12:44 slave you have bought may **e**
12:45 foreigner visiting you may **e** it.
12:45 "No hired worker may **e** it.
12:48 may ever **e** the Passover meal.
13:3 Don't **e** anything made with
13:6 you must **e** unleavened bread.
16:8 LORD will give you meat to **e**
16:12 'At dusk you will **e** meat,
16:12 and in the morning you will **e**
16:15 the LORD has given you to **e**.
16:16 gather as much as you can **e**.
16:18 as much as they could **e**.
16:21 as much food as they could **e**.
16:25 "**E** it today," Moses said,
16:32 the food that I gave you to **e**
18:12 the leaders of Israel came to **e**
22:31 Never **e** the meat of an animal
23:11 your people will have food to **e**,
23:11 and wild animals may **e** what
23:15 you must **e** unleavened bread,
29:32 Aaron and his sons will **e** the
29:33 They will **e** those offerings
29:33 No one else may **e** them
34:15 they may invite you to **e** the
34:18 you must **e** unleavened bread
Lev 3:17 Never **e** any fat or blood."
6:16 Aaron and his sons will **e** the
6:16 They will **e** unleavened bread
6:18 descendant of Aaron may **e** it.
6:26 makes the offering for sin will **e**
6:29 male among the priests may **e**
7:6 among the priests may **e** it.
7:19 may **e** from these sacrifices.
7:20 Those who **e** meat from the
7:21 uncleanness and still **e**
7:23 Never **e** any fat from bulls,
7:24 but you must never **e** it.
7:25 Those who **e** the fat from an
7:26 "Never **e** the blood of any bird
7:27 Those who **e** any blood must
8:31 **E** them there as I commanded
8:31 'Aaron and his sons will **e** it.'
10:12 Make unleavened bread, and **e**
10:13 **E** it in a holy place because it
10:14 Also **e** the breast presented ⌊to
10:14 and daughters may **e** them
10:17 "Why didn't you **e** the offering
11:2 of land animals you may **e**:
11:4 are the kinds you must never **e**:
11:4 You must never **e** camels.
11:5 You must never **e** rock badgers.
11:6 You must never **e** rabbits.
11:7 You must never **e** pigs.
Lev 11:8 Never **e** the meat of these
11:9 which you may **e** — anything
11:11 Never **e** their meat.
11:13 disgusting and must not **e**.
11:21 However, you may **e** winged
11:22 You may **e** any kind of locust,
11:39 that you are allowed to **e** dies,
11:40 Those who **e** any of its dead
11:42 Don't **e** any creature with many
11:47 the animals you may **e** and
11:47 eat and those you may not **e**."
17:10 or foreigners **e** any blood,
17:12 foreigners should ever **e** blood.
17:14 Never **e** any blood,
17:15 Israelites or foreigners who **e**
19:6 **E** your sacrifice on the day you
19:7 If you **e** any of it on the third
19:8 Those who **e** it will be
19:23 you must not **e** the fruit for ⌊the
19:25 fifth year you may **e** the fruit.
19:26 "Never **e** any meat with blood
21:22 He may **e** the food of his God —
22:4 or a discharge may **e** any
22:6 He must not **e** any of the holy
22:7 Then he may **e** the holy
22:8 He must never **e** the meat of an
22:10 "Laypeople must never **e** any
22:11 may **e** the priest's food.
22:12 she must never **e** the food
22:13 she may **e** her father's food.
22:13 But a layperson must never **e** it.
22:14 "Those who **e** a holy offering
22:30 **E** it the same day.
23:6 you must **e** unleavened bread.
23:14 Don't **e** bread, roasted grain,
24:9 They will **e** it in a holy place.
25:6 that year is for all of you to **e** —
25:7 produces will be yours to **e**.
25:12 You will **e** what the field itself
25:19 and you will **e** all you want and
25:20 You may ask, 'What will we **e**
25:22 You will **e** it, even in the ninth
26:5 You will **e** all you want and
26:16 your enemies will **e** them.
26:26 You will **e** and go away hungry.
26:29 You will **e** the bodies of your
Num 6:3 and they must never **e** fresh
6:4 they must never **e** anything that
9:11 You must **e** the Passover
11:4 "If only we had meat to **e**!
11:13 for me to give them meat to **e**.
11:18 Then they will **e** meat.
11:18 'If only we had meat to **e**!
11:19 They won't **e** it just for one or
11:21 'I will give them meat to **e** for a
15:19 and **e** any of the food from the
18:10 **E** it in a most holy place.
18:10 Any male may **e** it.
18:11 who is clean may **e** them.
18:13 who is clean may **e** it.
18:31 households may **e** it anywhere,
22:4 **e** up everything around
28:17 must **e** only unleavened bread.
Dtr 2:6 them in silver for the food you **e**
2:28 you in silver for the food we **e**
4:28 These gods can't see, hear, **e**,
8:12 You will **e** all you want.
11:15 will be able to **e** all you want.
12:7 you and your families will **e**
12:15 you may slaughter and **e** as
12:15 and unclean people may **e**
12:16 But never **e** the blood.
12:17 You may not **e** ⌊the LORD's
12:18 live in your cities must **e** these
12:20 Then **e** as much meat as you
12:21 **E** as much as you want in your
12:22 **E** it as you would eat a gazelle
12:22 Eat it as you would **e** a gazelle
12:22 people may **e** it together.
12:23 be sure you never **e** blood,
12:23 Never **e** the life with the meat.
12:24 Never **e** blood. Pour it on the
12:25 If you don't **e** blood,
12:27 but you may **e** the meat.
14:3 Never **e** anything that is
14:4 ⌊kinds of⌋ animals you may **e**:

Dtr	14:6	You may **e** all animals that
	14:7	You may not **e** these ⌊kinds
	14:8	Also, you may not **e** pigs.
	14:8	Never **e** their meat or touch
	14:9	Here's what you may **e** of every
	14:9	You may **e** any creature that
	14:10	But never **e** anything that
	14:11	You may **e** any clean bird.
	14:12	birds that you should never **e**:
	14:20	However, you may **e** any
	14:21	Never **e** any creature that dies
	14:21	your cities, and they may **e** it.
	14:23	**E** the tenth of your grain,
	14:23	and **e** the firstborn of your
	14:26	Then you and your family will **e**
	14:29	may come to **e** all they want.
	15:20	family must **e** these animals
	15:22	**E** it in your city. Clean and
	15:22	people may **e** them together as
	15:23	But never **e** the blood.
	16:3	Never **e** leavened bread with
	16:3	for seven days you must **e**
	16:3	**E** this bread so that,
	16:7	Cook the meat, and **e** it at the
	16:8	six days **e** unleavened bread,
	18:1	They will **e** what has been
	20:19	You can **e** the fruit.
	23:24	you may **e** as many grapes as
	26:12	and they may **e** all they want.
	26:14	I didn't **e** any of this holy
	27:7	offerings, **e** them there,
	28:31	but you won't **e** any of its meat.
	28:33	People you never knew will **e**
	28:39	because worms will **e** them.
	28:51	They'll **e** the offspring of your
	28:53	you will **e** the flesh of your own
	28:57	She will secretly **e** them out of
Jos	5:12	That year they began to **e** the
Jdg	13:4	or liquor or **e** any unclean food.
	13:7	or liquor or **e** any unclean food
	13:14	She must not **e** anything that
	13:14	or **e** any unclean food.
	13:15	a young goat for you to **e**."
	13:16	I will not **e** any of your food.
	14:9	them some of the honey to **e**.
	14:14	the eater came something to **e**.
	19:5	"**E** something to keep up your
	19:8	The woman's father said, "**E**
Rut	2:14	When it was time to **e**,
1Sm	1:7	Hannah would cry and not **e**.
	1:9	Hannah had something to **e**
	2:36	priestly classes so that I may **e**
	9:13	goes to the worship site to **e**.
	9:13	The people will not **e** until he
	9:13	those who are invited may **e**.
	9:19	You will **e** with me today.
	9:24	**E** it. When I invited people to
	14:34	and butcher it here, and **e**.
	20:5	when I should sit and **e** at the
	20:24	sat down to **e** the festival meal.
	21:3	what do you have ⌊to **e**⌋?
	28:22	I will serve you something to **e**.
	28:22	**E** it so that you will have
	28:23	"I don't want to **e**," he said.
	30:11	They gave him food to **e** and
2Sm	3:35	to get David to **e** some food.
	9:7	you will always **e** at my table."
	9:10	family will have food to **e**.
	9:10	will always **e** at my table."
	11:11	I then go to my house to **e**
	12:3	She would **e** his food and drink
	12:17	And he wouldn't **e** with them.
	13:9	But he refused to **e**.
	13:11	When she handed it to him to **e**,
	16:2	are for ⌊your⌋ servants to **e**.
	19:28	with those who **e** at your table.
	19:35	Can I taste what I **e** or drink?
	19:42	Did we **e** the king's food,
1Ki	2:7	Let them **e** at your table.
	13:7	have something to **e** and drink,
	13:8	go with you to **e** or drink there.
	13:9	he commanded me not to **e** or
	13:15	home with me, and **e** a meal,"
	13:16	I'm not allowed to **e** or drink
	13:17	he told me not to **e** or drink
	13:18	have something to **e** and drink."
1Ki	13:22	'Don't **e** or drink there.'
	13:23	had something to **e** and drink,
	14:11	in the city, dogs will **e** him.
	14:11	in the country, birds will **e** him.'
	16:4	Dogs will **e** anyone from
	16:4	Birds will **e** anyone from his
	17:12	and my son so that we can **e**
	18:19	who **e** at Jezebel's table."
	18:41	Ahab, "Get up, **e**, and drink.
	18:42	Ahab got up to **e** and drink.
	19:5	him and said, "Get up and **e**."
	19:7	The angel said, "Get up and **e**,
	19:21	the meat to the people to **e**.
	21:4	everyone⌋, and refused to **e**.
	21:5	Why don't you **e**?"
	21:7	Get up, **e**, and cheer up.
	21:23	"The dogs will **e** Jezebel
	21:24	in the city, dogs will **e** him.
	21:24	the country, birds will **e** him."
2Ki	4:8	had invited him to **e** ⌊with her⌋.
	4:8	he stopped in to **e**.
	4:40	out the food for the men to **e**.
	4:40	So they couldn't **e** it.
	4:41	"Dish it out for the people to **e**."
	4:42	"Give it to the people to **e**."
	4:43	"Give it to the people to **e**," the
	4:43	They will **e** and even have
	6:22	Let them **e** and drink.
	6:28	Let's **e** him today. We'll eat my
	6:28	We'll **e** my son tomorrow.'
	6:29	We'll **e** him,' but she hid her
	7:2	but you won't **e** any of it."
	7:19	but you won't **e** any of it.")
	9:10	Dogs will **e** Jezebel inside the
	9:36	He said, 'Dogs will **e** Jezebel's
	18:27	have to **e** their own excrement
	18:31	Everyone will **e** from his own
	19:29	You will **e** what grows by itself
	19:29	and **e** what is produced.
2Ch	28:15	them something to **e** and drink,
	31:10	have had all we wanted to **e**
Ezr	2:63	The governor told them not to **e**
	9:12	be able to **e** the good things the
	10:6	Ezra didn't **e** any food or drink
Neh	5:2	are going⌋ to **e** and stay alive."
	7:65	The governor told them not to **e**
	8:10	he told them, "Go, **e** rich foods,
	8:12	Then all the people went to **e**
	9:36	they could **e** its produce and
Est	4:16	Fast for me: Do not **e** or drink at
Job	1:4	to invite their three sisters to **e**
	4:11	die without any prey ⌊to **e**⌋,
	5:5	fool gathers, hungry people **e**.
	20:21	"Nothing is left for him to **e**.
	31:8	⌊then⌋ let someone else **e**
	31:17	without letting the orphan **e** any
Psa	22:26	Oppressed people will **e** until
	22:29	on earth will **e** and worship.
	39:11	Like a moth you **e** away at
	50:13	Do I **e** the meat of bulls or drink
	59:15	around to find something to **e**.
	78:24	manna down on them to **e**
	80:5	You made them **e** tears as food.
	102:9	I **e** ashes like bread and my
	127:2	for the food you **e** by getting up
	128:2	You will certainly **e** what your
Pro	1:31	They will **e** the fruit of their
	4:17	They **e** food obtained through
	9:5	"Come, **e** my bread,
	12:9	and have nothing to **e**.
	12:11	his land will have plenty to **e**,
	18:21	will have to **e** their own words.
	20:13	and you will have plenty to **e**.
	23:1	When you sit down to **e** with a
	23:6	Do not **e** the food of one who is
	23:7	He tells you, "**E** and drink,"
	23:20	those who **e** too much meat,
	24:13	**E** honey, my son, because it is
	25:16	**e** only as much as you need.
	25:21	give him some food to **e**,
	27:18	care of a fig tree can **e** its fruit,
	28:19	his land will have plenty to **e**.
	31:27	and she does not **e** the bread of
Ecc	2:24	better for people to do than to **e**,
	2:25	Who can **e** or enjoy
	3:13	a gift from God to be able to **e**
Ecc	5:12	whether they **e** a little or a lot.
	5:18	It is to **e** and drink and to enjoy
	8:15	to do under the sun than to **e**,
	10:17	and when the high officials **e** at
Sos	4:16	and let him **e** his own precious
	5:1	I will **e** my honeycomb with my
	5:1	**E**, my friends! Drink and
Isa	1:19	you will **e** the best from the
	4:1	"We'll **e** our own food and
	5:17	and foreigners will **e** among the
	7:15	He will **e** cheese and honey
	7:22	That person will **e** cheese,
	7:22	land will **e** cheese and honey.
	11:7	Cows and bears will **e** together.
	11:7	Lions will **e** straw like oxen.
	14:30	The poorest of the poor will **e**,
	21:5	**E**. Drink. Get up, you leaders!
	22:13	You will **e** meat, drink wine,
	22:13	"Let's **e** and drink because
	30:24	which work the soil will **e**
	36:12	have to **e** their own excrement
	36:16	Everyone will **e** from his own
	37:30	You will **e** what grows by itself
	37:30	and the next year you will **e**
	37:30	and **e** what is produced.
	44:16	that they can **e** until they are
	44:20	They **e** ashes because they
	49:26	I will make your oppressors **e**
	50:9	Moths will **e** them.
	51:8	Moths will **e** them like clothing.
	55:1	money can come, buy, and **e**!
	55:2	to me: **E** what is good,
	55:10	and food for people to **e**.
	56:9	in the forest, come and **e**.
	59:5	Those who **e** their eggs will
	62:8	let your enemies **e** your grain,
	62:9	Those who harvest grain will **e**
	65:13	My servants will **e**,
	65:21	They will plant vineyards and **e**
	65:22	plant and have others **e** from it.
	65:25	lions will **e** straw like oxen,
	66:24	The worms that **e** them will not
Jer	2:7	into a fertile land to **e** its fruit
	7:21	your sacrifices, and **e** the meat.
	16:8	sit with them to **e** and drink.
	19:9	I will make the people **e** the
	19:9	They will **e** each other's flesh
	23:15	I will give them wormwood to **e**
	29:5	and **e** what they produce.
	29:28	and **e** what they produce.'"
	44:17	We had plenty to **e** then,
	50:19	They will **e** on Mount Carmel
	50:19	They will **e** until they are full
Lam	2:20	Should women **e** their own
	4:5	Those who used to **e**
	4:9	is nothing in the fields to **e**.
Eze	2:8	and **e** what I am giving to you."
	3:1	"Son of man, **e** what you find.
	3:1	**E** this scroll. Then speak to the
	3:2	and he gave me the scroll to **e**.
	3:3	**e** this scroll I'm giving you,
	4:9	**E** it during the 390 days that
	4:10	The food that you **e** should be
	4:10	**E** eight ounces of food every
	4:12	**E** the bread as you would eat
	4:12	as you would **e** barley loaves.
	4:13	the people of Israel will **e**
	4:16	People will anxiously **e**
	5:10	parents will **e** their children,
	5:10	children will **e** their parents.
	12:18	shake as you **e** your food.
	12:19	They will be worried as they **e**
	16:19	all the food that I gave you to **e**.
	18:6	He doesn't **e** at the illegal
	18:15	He doesn't **e** at the illegal
	22:9	People who live in you **e** food
	22:25	They **e** people and take their
	24:17	Don't cover your face or **e** the
	24:17	or eat the food that mourners **e**
	24:22	Don't cover your faces or **e** the
	24:22	or eat the food that mourners **e**.
	25:4	They will **e** your crops and
	33:25	You **e** meat with blood in it.
	34:3	You **e** the best parts of the
	34:19	Must my sheep **e** what your
	34:28	animals will no longer **e** them.

Eze 39:17 You can e meat and drink
39:18 You can e the meat of warriors
39:19 You can e the best meat until
42:13 who come near the LORD e
44:3 prince may sit there and e food
44:29 They will e grain offerings,
44:31 The priests must never e any
Dan 1:10 what you should e and drink.
1:12 Give us only vegetables to e
4:25 You will e grass like cattle.
4:32 You will e grass like cattle.
7:5 It was told, "Get up, and e as
10:3 I didn't e any good-tasting food.
11:26 People who e the king's rich
Hos 3:1 and love to e raisin cakes."
4:10 "They will e, but they'll never
8:7 foreigners would e it all.
8:13 offer sacrifices to me and e
9:3 and they will e unclean food in
9:4 like the food that mourners e.
9:4 All who e this food will be
Joe 1:4 mature locusts will e.
1:4 adult locusts will e.
1:4 grasshoppers will e.
1:7 stripped off what they could e,
2:26 You will have plenty to e,
Amo 4:6 I left you with nothing to e in
6:4 couches and e lambs from their
7:12 E there, and prophesy there!
9:14 plant gardens and e their fruit.
Oba 1:7 Those who e food with you
Jnh 3:7 No one is to e or drink anything.
Mic 3:3 You e my people's flesh.
3:5 they have something to e,
6:14 You will e, but you won't be
7:1 But there aren't any grapes to e
Hab 3:14 who secretly e up the poor.
Hag 1:6 You e, but you're never full.
Zec 11:16 But he will e the meat of the fat
Mat 4:2 Jesus did not e anything for 40
6:25 worrying about what you will e,
6:31 'What are we going to e?' or
8:11 They will e with Abraham,
9:10 and sinners came to e
9:11 "Why does your teacher e with
12:1 to pick the heads of grain to e.
12:4 had no right to e those loaves.
14:16 You give them something to e."
15:2 their hands before they e."
15:27 But even the dogs e scraps
15:32 now and have nothing to e.
24:49 to beat the other servants and e
25:35 you gave me something to e.
25:42 and you gave me nothing to e.
26:26 and said, "Take this, and e it.
Mar 2:16 "Why does he e with tax
2:26 had no right to e those loaves.
3:20 his disciples could not even e.
5:43 the little girl something to e.
6:31 didn't even have a chance to e.
6:36 themselves something to e."
6:37 give them something to e."
7:3 don't e unless they have
7:4 they don't e unless they have
7:5 their hands before they e!"
7:27 let the children e all they want.
7:28 even the dogs under the table e
8:1 a large crowd with nothing to e.
8:2 now and have nothing to e.
9:48 In hell worms that e the body
11:14 "No one will ever e fruit from
14:14 is my room where I can e
Luk 5:30 They asked, "Why do you e
5:33 But your disciples e and drink."
6:4 had no right to e those loaves.
7:36 invited Jesus to e with him.
8:55 to give her something to e.
9:13 give them something to e."
10:7 E and drink whatever they offer
10:8 e whatever they serve you.
12:19 Take life easy, e, drink,
12:22 about what you will e or wear.
12:29 about what you will e or drink,
12:45 the other servants and to e,
13:29 all over the world and will e
14:1 of worship Jesus went to e at

Luk 15:17 more food than they can e,
17:7 'Have something to e'?
17:8 my dinner, you can e yours.'
22:8 the Passover lamb for us to e."
22:11 is the room where I can e
22:14 When it was time to e the
22:15 "I've had a deep desire to e
22:16 I can guarantee that I won't e it
22:30 You will e and drink at my
24:41 "Do you have anything to e?"
Jon 4:31 have something to e."
4:32 "I have food to e that you don't
4:33 bring him something to e?"
6:5 bread for these people to e?"
6:31 them bread from heaven to e."'
6:52 man give us his flesh to e?"
6:53 If you don't e the flesh of the
6:54 Those who e my flesh and
6:56 Those who e my flesh and
6:58 Those who e this bread will
18:28 they wanted to e the Passover.
Act 9:9 see and didn't e or drink.
9:19 After he had something to e,
10:10 hungry and wanted to e.
10:13 these animals, and e them."
11:7 Kill these animals, and e them.'
16:34 and gave them something to e.
21:25 should not e food sacrificed
23:21 God to curse them if they e
27:21 hardly anyone wanted to e,
27:33 to have something to e.
27:33 and have had nothing to e.
27:34 you to e something.
27:35 broke it, and began to e.
27:36 and had something to e.
Rom 14:2 that they can e all kinds
14:2 they can e only vegetables.
14:3 People who e all foods should
14:3 people who e only vegetables.
14:3 people who e all foods,
14:6 When people e all kinds of
14:6 they honor the Lord as they e,
14:6 honor the Lord when they e,
14:15 So if what you e hurts another
14:15 destroy anyone by what you e.
14:20 work because of what you e.
14:20 but it's wrong for a person to e
1Co 5:11 Don't e with such people.
8:8 We are no worse off if we e
8:10 that person to e food offered
8:13 I will never e that kind of food
9:4 have the right to e and drink?
9:7 vineyard and not e the grapes?
10:18 Don't those who e the
10:25 E anything that is sold in the
10:27 e anything he serves you
10:28 don't e it because of the one
10:30 thanks to God for the food I e,
10:31 So, whether you e or drink,
11:22 homes in which to e and drink?
11:22 who don't have anything to e?
11:26 Every time you e this bread
11:28 are doing is proper when they e
11:33 when you gather to e,
11:34 Whoever is hungry should e at
15:32 "Let's e and drink because
2Co 9:10 food to those who need to e.
Col 2:16 you because of what you e
2Th 3:8 We didn't e anyone's food
3:10 shouldn't be allowed to e."
Heb 13:10 no right to e what is sacrificed
Jas 2:16 and make sure you e enough."
2Pe 2:13 you while they e with you.
Jud 1:12 They e with you and don't feel
Rev 2:14 them to e food sacrificed
2:20 and to e food sacrificed
3:20 I'll come in and we'll e together.
10:9 He said to me, "Take it and e it.
17:16 They will e her flesh and burn
19:18 E the flesh of kings,

eaten (69)

Gen 6:21 every kind of food that can be e
14:24 except what my men have e.
37:20 that a wild animal has e him.
37:33 A wild animal has e him!

Gen 41:21 Even though they had e them,
41:21 one could tell they had e them.
Exo 12:8 The meat must be e that same
12:8 be roasted over a fire and e
12:46 "The meal must be e inside
13:7 should be e during these seven
21:28 and its meat may not be e.
29:34 It must not be e because it is
Lev 6:23 burned. It must not be e."
6:30 for sin must not be e if some
7:6 It will be e in a holy place.
7:15 of thanksgiving must be e
7:16 it must be e the day you offer it
7:18 from the fellowship offering is e
7:19 unclean must not be e.
10:18 certainly should have e it there,
10:19 If I had e the offering for sin
11:41 disgusting and must not be e.
17:13 animal or bird that may be e,
22:16 their guilt because they have e
Dtr 6:11 After you have e all that you
8:10 When you have e all you want,
14:19 They must never be e.
31:20 When they have e all they
Rut 3:7 Boaz had e and drunk to his
1Sm 1:8 Why haven't you e?
14:30 If only the troops had e some of
28:20 because he hadn't e anything
30:12 After he had e, he revived.
30:12 (He hadn't e any food or drunk
1Ki 13:28 The lion had not e the body,
Ezr 6:21 The lambs were e by the
Job 6:6 Is tasteless food e without salt,
18:13 His skin is e away by disease.
31:17 or have e my food alone
31:39 If I have e its produce without
Pro 9:17 and food e in secret is tasty."
17:1 Better a bite of dry bread ⌊e⌋ in
23:8 vomit the little bit you have e
30:17 valley and e by young vultures.
Isa 28:4 they will be taken and e.
Jer 24:2 so bad that they couldn't be e.
24:3 so bad that they can't be e."
24:8 are so bad that they can't be e.
29:17 are so bad that they can't be e.
31:29 'Fathers have e sour grapes,
Eze 4:14 I have never e an animal that
18:2 'Fathers have e sour grapes,
45:21 when unleavened bread is e.
Hos 10:13 You have e the fruit that your
Mat 14:21 About five thousand men had e.
14:21 and children who had e.)
15:38 Four thousand men had e.
15:38 and children who had e.)
Mar 6:44 men who had e the bread.
8:3 them home before they've e,
Luk 15:16 that he would have e what
16:21 Lazarus would have e any
Jon 6:23 the place where they had e
21:15 After they had e breakfast,
Act 10:14 I've never e anything that is
12:23 Herod was e by maggots,
27:38 After the people had e all they
Jas 5:2 clothes have been e by moths.
Rev 10:10 but when I had e it,

eater (2)

Jdg 14:14 "From the e came something to
Nah 3:12 figs fall into the mouth of the e.

eating (64)

Gen 40:17 but the birds were e them out of
43:2 When they finished e the grain
Lev 11:43 Don't become disgusting by e
20:25 Never become disgusting by e
Dtr 12:15 may eat it as if they were e
15:22 them together as if they were e
28:55 of his children that he is e.
Jdg 19:8 the time e until late afternoon.
Rut 3:3 he's finished e and drinking.
1Sm 14:33 against the LORD by e meat
14:34 against the LORD by e meat
30:16 over the land, e, and drinking.
1Ki 1:25 They are e and drinking with
1:41 heard this as they finished e.
2Ki 4:40 As they were e the stew,

Job 1:13 sons and daughters were **e**
1:18 and your daughters were **e**
6:5 bray when it's ⌊**e**⌋ grass,
Psa 102:4 I have forgotten about **e**.
Pro 25:27 **E** too much honey is not good,
Ecc 9:7 Go, enjoy **e** your food,
Isa 29:8 people who dream that they're **e**
Dan 1:8 mind not to harm himself by **e**
1:13 us to the young men who are **e**
1:15 the young men who had been **e**
Amo 7:2 had finished **e** every plant
Mal 3:11 insects from **e** ⌊your crops⌋.
Mat 11:18 came neither **e** nor drinking,
11:19 of Man came **e** and drinking,
15:20 But **e** without washing one's
24:38 flood, people were **e**, drinking,
26:21 While they were **e**,
26:26 While they were **e**,
Mar 2:15 were followers of Jesus were **e**
2:16 who were Pharisees saw him **e**
14:18 While they were at the table **e**,
14:18 one who is **e** with me!"
14:22 While they were **e**,
16:14 apostles while they were **e**.
Luk 5:29 and others were **e** with them.
6:1 the husks, and **e** the grain.
7:33 neither **e** bread nor drinking
7:34 Man has come **e** and drinking,
7:36 house and was **e** at the table.
7:37 found out that Jesus was **e** at
14:15 One of those **e** with him heard
15:16 eaten what the pigs were **e**.
17:27 People were **e**, drinking,
17:28 People were **e**, drinking,
Jon 12:2 one of the people **e** with Jesus.
Act 15:20 from **e** the meat of strangled
15:20 and from **e** bloody meat.
15:29 from **e** bloody meat,
15:29 from **e** the meat of strangled
27:34 **E** will help you survive,
Rom 14:21 thing to do is to avoid **e** meat,
1Co 8:4 Now about **e** food that was
8:7 believe they are **e** food offered
8:10 **e** in the temple of a false god.
8:13 Therefore, if **e** food ⌊offered to
11:20 be **e** the Lord's Supper.
11:29 who eats and drinks is **e**
1Ti 4:3 and from **e** certain foods.
Rev 2:7 I will give the privilege of **e**

eats (31)

Exo 12:15 Whoever **e** anything with yeast
12:19 Whoever **e** anything with yeast
Lev 7:18 The person who **e** any of it
14:47 Whoever sleeps or **e** in the
17:14 Whoever **e** blood must be
Num 22:4 us the same way an ox **e** up
23:24 It doesn't lie down until it **e** its
Dtr 21:20 He **e** too much and is a drunk."
1Sm 14:24 "Cursed is anyone who **e** food
14:28 'Cursed is anyone who **e** food
Job 18:13 Death's firstborn son **e** away at
39:24 the horse **e** up the ground and
40:15 It **e** grass as cattle do.
Psa 106:20 the statue of a bull that **e** grass.
Pro 13:2 A person **e** well as a result of
13:25 A righteous person **e** to satisfy
30:20 She **e**, wipes her mouth,
Isa 9:20 another **e** and is never full.
9:20 Each person **e** the flesh from
Jer 31:30 Whoever **e** sour grapes will
50:7 who finds them **e** them.
Eze 18:11 He **e** at the illegal mountain
Luk 15:2 sinners and **e** with them."
Jon 6:50 so that whoever **e** it won't die.
6:51 Whoever **e** this bread will live
13:18 It says, 'The one who **e** my
Rom 14:17 of what a person **e** or drinks.
14:23 a person has doubts and still **e**,
1Co 11:21 Each of you **e** his own supper
11:27 Therefore, whoever **e** the bread
11:29 Anyone who **e** and drinks is

Ebal (8)

Gen 36:23 **E**, Shepho, and Onam.
Dtr 11:29 and the curse from Mount **E**.
27:4 up these stones on Mount **E**,
27:13 that will stand on Mount **E**
Jos 8:30 built an altar on Mount **E**
8:33 other half in front of Mount **E**.
1Ch 1:22 **E**, Abimael, Sheba,
1:40 **E**, Shephi, and Onam.

Ebed (6)

Jdg 9:26 Then Gaal (son of **E**) and his
9:28 Gaal (son of **E**) said,
9:30 what Gaal (son of **E**) had said,
9:31 Gaal (son of **E**) and his
9:35 Gaal (son of **E**) went out and
Ezr 8:6 from the family of Adin: **E**,

Ebed Melech (6)

Jer 38:7 the royal palace, **E** from Sudan,
38:8 **E** left the royal palace and
38:10 Then the king gave **E** from
38:11 So **E** took the men with him
38:12 **E** from Sudan said to Jeremiah,
39:16 "Say to **E** from Sudan,

Ebenezer (3)

1Sm 4:1 and camped near **E** while
5:1 brought it from **E** to Ashdod.
7:12 He named it **E** [Rock of Help]

Eber (16)

Gen 10:21 ancestor of all the sons of **E**.
10:24 and Shelah was the father of **E**.
10:25 Two sons were born to **E**.
11:14 he became the father of **E**.
11:15 After he became the father of **E**,
11:16 **E** was 34 years old when he
11:17 **E** lived 430 years and had
Num 24:24 will conquer Assyria and **E**.
1Ch 1:18 and Shelah was the father of **E**.
1:19 Two sons were born to **E**.
1:25 **E**, Peleg, Reu,
5:13 Jorai, Jacan, Zia, and **E**.
8:12 Elpaal's sons were **E**,
8:22 sons were Ishpan, **E**,
Neh 12:20 Sallai, Kallai; from Amok, **E**;
Luk 3:35 Peleg, son of **E**, son of Shelah,

Ebez (1)

Jos 19:20 Rabbith, Kishion, **E**,

Ebiasaph (3)

1Ch 6:23 Elkanah's son was **E**.
6:37 who was the son of **E**,
9:19 (son of Kore, grandson of **E**,

Ebiasaph's (1)

1Ch 6:23 Ebiasaph. **E** son was Assir.

ebony (1)

Eze 27:15 you ivory and **e** as payment.

Ecbatana (1)

Ezr 6:2 was found in the palace of **E**,

echo (1)

Isa 15:8 Cries for help **e** throughout the

echoes (3)

1Sm 4:5 that the earth rang with **e**.
Isa 15:8 Their wailing **e** as far as
15:8 Their wailing **e** as far as Beer

echoing (1)

Jer 25:31 The sound is **e** to the ends of

ecstatic (1)

Job 3:22 They are **e**, delighted to find

Eden (19)

Gen 2:8 God planted a garden in **E**,
2:10 A river flowed from **E** to water
2:15 and put him in the Garden of **E**
3:23 the man out of the Garden of **E**
3:24 east of the Garden of **E**.
4:16 Land of Wandering], east of **E**.
2Ki 19:12 and the people of **E** who were
2Ch 29:12 of Zimmah, and **E**, son of Joah.
31:15 **E**, Miniamin, Jeshua,
Isa 37:12 and the people of **E** who were
51:3 He will make its desert like **E**.
Eze 27:23 Haran, Canneh, **E**,
28:13 You were in **E**, God's garden.
31:9 the envy of all the trees in **E**,
31:16 Then all the trees in **E**,
31:18 No tree in **E** has ever been as
31:18 the earth with the trees of **E**.
36:35 become like the garden of **E**.
Joe 2:3 the land is like the garden of **E**.

Eder (4)

Jos 15:21 villages: Kabzeel, **E**, Jagur,
1Ch 8:15 sons were Zebadiah, Arad, **E**,
23:23 Mushi had three sons: Mahli, **E**,
24:30 Mahli, **E**, and Jerimoth (for

edge (38)

Gen 14:6 El Paran on the **e** of the desert.
Exo 13:20 on the **e** of the desert.
26:4 50 violet loops along the **e**
26:10 Make 50 loops along the **e** of
28:26 breastplate on the inside **e** next
28:32 center with a reinforced **e** (like
36:11 50 violet loops along the **e**
36:17 they made 50 loops along the **e**
39:19 breastplate on the inside **e** next
39:23 the robe had a finished **e** (like
Num 20:16 a city on the **e** of your territory.
33:6 on the **e** of the desert.
Dtr 2:36 From Aroer on the **e** of the
4:48 land went from Aroer on the **e**
22:8 put a railing around the **e** of the
Jos 3:15 carrying the ark came to the **e**
12:2 extended from Aroer on the **e**
13:9 extended from Aroer on the **e**
13:16 extended from Aroer on the **e**
15:21 On the farthest **e** of the Negev,
Jdg 7:11 went to the **e** of the camp.
7:17 When I come to the **e** of the
7:19 and his 100 men came to the **e**
Rut 3:7 so he went and lay at the **e** of
2Ki 7:5 When they came to the **e** of the
7:8 skin diseases came to the **e**
1Ch 5:9 lived eastward as far as the **e**
Ecc 10:10 blunt and the **e** isn't sharpened,
Isa 19:7 by the **e** of the Nile,
Jer 31:29 children's teeth are set on **e**.'
31:30 have his own teeth set on **e**.
Eze 18:2 children's teeth are set on **e**'?
40:17 along the **e** of the pavement.
43:13 All around the **e** of the altar
Mat 9:20 Jesus and touched the **e**
14:36 him to let them touch just the **e**
Mar 6:56 him to let them touch the **e**
Luk 8:44 touched the **e** of his clothes,

edged(7)

Jdg 3:16 Ehud made a two-**e** dagger for
Psa 149:6 and two-**e** swords in their hands
Pro 5:4 as sharp as a two-**e** sword.
Isa 41:15 with sharp, double-**e** teeth.
Heb 4:12 is sharper than any two-**e** sword
Rev 1:16 came a sharp, two-**e** sword.
2:12 holds the sharp two-**e** sword

edges (4)

Lev 19:27 never cut the **e** of your beard.
21:5 shaving the **e** of your beards,
1Ch 5:16 of Sharon to its extreme **e**.
Job 38:13 it could grab the earth by its **e**

Edom (99)

Gen 25:30 This is why he was called **E**.
32:3 Esau in Seir, the country of **E**.
36:1 **E**) and his descendants.
36:8 who was also known as **E**,
36:9 the father of the people of **E**
36:16 descended from Eliphaz in **E**.
36:17 descended from Reuel in **E**.
36:19 is, **E**), who were tribal leaders.
36:21 were the sons of Seir in **E**.
36:31 who ruled **E** before any king
36:32 Bela, son of Beor, ruled **E**.
36:43 the tribal leaders of **E** listed by

Gen 36:43 the father of the people of **E**.
Exo 15:15 The tribal leaders of **E** will be
Num 20:14 from Kadesh to the king of **E**.
20:23 near the border of **E**,
21:4 in order to get around **E**.
24:18 **E** will be conquered,
33:37 at Mount Hor on the border of **E**
34:3 of Zin along the border of **E**.
Jos 15:1 as far south as the territory of **E**
15:21 on the border of **E**,
Jdg 5:4 marched from the country of **E**,
11:17 messengers to the king of **E**.
11:17 But the king of **E** wouldn't
11:18 by-passing **E** and Moab.
1Sm 14:47 **E**, the kings of Zobah,
21:7 shepherds, he was from **E**.
22:9 Then Doeg from **E**,
22:18 Doeg from **E** turned and
22:22 Doeg from **E** was there that
2Sm 8:12 from **E**, Moab, Ammon,
8:14 He put troops everywhere in **E**,
1Ki 9:26 at Ezion Geber by Elath in **E**.
11:1 Moab, Ammon, **E**, and Sidon.
11:15 When David had conquered **E**,
11:15 and killed every male in **E**.
11:16 had destroyed every male in **E**.)
22:47 There was no king in **E**;
2Ki 3:8 road through the desert of **E**."
3:9 and the king of **E** took an
3:12 the king of **E** went to Elisha.
3:20 water flowed from **E** and filled
3:26 break through to the king of **E**.
8:20 During Jehoram's time **E**
8:22 So **E** rebelled against Judah's
14:10 You certainly defeated **E**,
16:6 of Elath and gave it back to **E**.
1Ch 1:43 who ruled **E** before any king
1:51 tribal leaders of **E** were Timna,
1:54 were the tribal leaders of **E**.
18:11 from other nations — from **E**,
18:13 He put troops in **E**,
2Ch 8:17 Ezion Geber and Elath in **E**.
20:2 side of the Dead Sea, from **E**.
21:8 During Jehoram's time **E**
21:10 So **E** rebelled against Judah's
21:10 At the same time **E** rebelled,
25:19 You say you defeated **E**,
Psa 60:8 I will throw my shoe over **E**.
60:9 Who will lead me to **E**?
83:6 the tents from **E** and Ishmael,
108:9 I will throw my shoe over **E**.
108:10 Who will lead me to **E**?
137:7 remember the people of **E**.
Isa 11:14 They will conquer **E** and Moab.
34:5 it will fall on **E** and on the
34:6 huge slaughter in the land of **E**.
34:10 **E** will lie in ruins for
63:1 is this coming from Bozrah in **E**
Jer 9:26 I will punish Egypt, Judah, **E**,
25:21 **E**, Moab, and the people of
27:3 messages to the kings of **E**,
40:11 who were in Moab, Ammon, **E**,
49:7 LORD of Armies says about **E**:
49:14 say, "Assemble, and attack **E**.
49:15 "**E**, I will make you the
49:17 "Then **E** will become
49:18 **E** will be like Sodom,
49:19 I will appoint over **E** whomever
49:20 the LORD is making against **E**
Lam 4:21 and be glad, people of **E**,
4:22 People of **E**, he will punish you
Eze 25:12 **E** took revenge on the nation of
25:13 I will use my power against **E**.
25:14 Israel to take revenge on **E**.
25:14 My people will deal with **E**
32:29 "**E** is there with its kings and
35:15 and so will all of **E**.
36:5 the nations and against all of **E**.
Dan 11:41 But **E**, Moab, and the leaders of
Joe 3:19 **E** will become a barren desert.
Amo 1:11 Because **E** has committed
9:12 capture the few survivors of **E**
Oba 1:1 Almighty LORD says about **E**:
1:1 Let's go to war against **E**."
1:2 "**E**, I will make you the
1:8 destroy the wise people in **E**
Oba 1:15 **E**, you will be treated as you

Edomite (3)
1Ki 11:14 raised up Hadad the **E** as
11:14 was from the **E** royal family.
11:17 He and some of his father's **E**

Edomites (18)
Num 20:18 But the **E** answered,
20:20 But the **E** said, "You may not
20:21 Since the **E** refused to let Israel
Dtr 23:7 consider the **E** disgusting.
2Sm 8:13 for himself by killing 18,000 **E**
8:14 and all the **E** were David's
2Ki 8:21 The **E** and their chariot
14:7 Amaziah killed 10,000 **E** in the
16:6 The **E** came to Elath and still
1Ch 18:12 son Abishai killed 18,000 **E**
2Ch 21:9 The **E** and their chariot
25:14 back from defeating the **E**,
28:17 The **E** had again invaded and
Eze 25:14 Then the **E** will know my
36:5 The **E** have taken possession
Amo 1:6 to hand them over to the **E**.
1:9 all the people over to the **E**.
1:11 The **E** pursued their relatives

Edom's (4)
2Ch 25:20 had sought help from **E** gods.
Isa 34:9 **E** streams will be turned to tar.
Jer 49:22 On that day **E** soldiers will be
Amo 2:1 Moabites have cremated **E** king

Edrei (8)
Num 21:33 out to fight the Israelites at **E**.
Dtr 1:4 ruled in Ashtaroth and in **E**.
3:1 his troops came to fight us at **E**.
3:10 Bashan as far as Salcah and **E**,
Jos 12:4 Ashtaroth and **E** was captured.
13:12 Og ruled in Ashtaroth and **E**.
13:31 of Gilead with Ashtaroth and **E**,
19:37 Kedesh, **E**, En Hazor,

educated (3)
1Ch 27:32 David's uncle Jonathan, an **e**
Jon 7:15 "How can this man be so **e**
Act 7:22 So Moses was **e** in all the

education (4)
Act 4:13 that Peter and John had no **e**
22:3 my **e** from Gamaliel here
22:3 My **e** was in the strict rules
26:24 Too much **e** is driving you

effect (10)
Dtr 8:18 It's still in **e** today.
Job 35:6 what **e** can you have on God?
Act 7:53 were put into **e** by angels.
Rom 7:2 law is no longer in **e** for her.
7:6 God has broken their **e** on us
Gal 3:15 to it once that will is put into **e**.
3:17 Abraham⌋ into **e** didn't cancel
3:19 was put into **e** through angels,
Heb 9:16 In order for a will to take **e**,
9:17 it goes into **e** only when

effective (2)
1Co 16:9 opportunity to do **e** work here,
Jas 5:16 who have God's approval are **e**.

effectively (2)
2Co 1:6 If we are comforted, we can **e**
2Th 2:7 But it cannot work **e** until the

effects (3)
Gen 41:55 in Egypt began to feel the **e**
1Sm 25:37 But in the morning, when the **e**
Gal 5:19 Now, the **e** of the corrupt nature

efficient (1)
Pro 22:29 Do you see a person who is **e**

effort (11)
Neh 5:16 Instead, I put my best **e** into the
Ecc 4:4 and skillful **e** come from rivalry.
Rom 9:16 on a person's desire or **e**,
Eph 6:18 Use every kind of **e** and make
Php 2:16 that my **e** was not wasted
1Th 2:17 have made every possible **e**
Heb 4:11 So we must make every **e** to
2Pe 1:5 Because of this, make every **e**
1:10 use more **e** to make God's
1:15 So I will make every **e** to see
3:14 make every **e** to have him find

efforts (13)
1Sm 25:26 getting a victory by your own **e**.
25:33 getting a victory by my own **e**.
Pro 16:3 Entrust your **e** to the LORD,
Rom 3:27 On the basis of our own **e**?
3:28 not because of his own **e**.
9:32 but they relied on their own **e**.
Gal 2:2 all my **e** have been wasted.
2:16 because of their own **e**
2:16 and not because of our own **e**.
2:16 because of their own **e**
3:2 receive the Spirit by your own **e**
3:5 among you through your own **e**
3:10 on all who rely on their own **e**

egg (3)
Job 6:6 any flavor in the white of an **e**?
Isa 59:5 When an **e** is crushed,
Luk 11:12 if your child asks you for an **e**,

eggs (7)
Dtr 22:6 a nest containing chicks or **e**,
Job 39:14 It lays its **e** on the ground and
Isa 10:14 as one gathers abandoned **e**.
34:15 there, lay **e**, and hatch them.
59:5 They hatch viper **e** and weave
59:5 Those who eat their **e** will die.
Jer 17:11 like a partridge that hatches **e**

Eglah (2)
2Sm 3:5 ⌊born⌋ to David's wife **E**.
1Ch 3:3 ⌊born⌋ to David's wife **E**.

Eglaim (1)
Isa 15:8 wailing echoes as far as **E**.

Eglath Shelishiyah (2)
Isa 15:5 people flee as far as Zoar at **E**.
Jer 48:34 from Zoar to Horonaim and **E**.

Eglon (16)
Jos 10:3 and King Debir of **E**:
10:5 and **E** combined their armies.
10:23 Jarmuth, Lachish, and **E**.
10:34 marched from Lachish to **E**,
10:36 and all Israel marched from **E**
10:37 no survivors, the same as at **E**.
12:12 the king of **E**, the king of
15:39 Lachish, Bozkath, **E**,
Jdg 3:12 So the LORD made King **E** of
3:13 **E** got the Ammonites and the
3:14 The Israelites served King **E** of
3:15 tax payment to King **E** of Moab.
3:17 the tax payment to King **E**.
3:17 (**E** was a very fat man.)
3:19 near Gilgal ⌊and returned to **E**⌋.
3:25 but **E** didn't open the doors.

Eglon's (3)
Jdg 3:21 and plunged it into **E** belly
3:22 **E** fat covered the blade
3:24 **E** advisers came in.

Egypt (606)
Gen 10:6 Cush, **E**, Put, and Canaan.
10:13 **E** was the ancestor of the
12:10 Abram went to **E** to stay awhile
12:11 When he was about to enter **E**,
12:14 When Abram arrived in **E**,
13:1 Abram left **E** with his wife and
13:10 the LORD's garden or like **E**.
15:18 is the land from the river of **E**
21:21 mother got him a wife from **E**.
25:18 to Shur, which is near **E**,
26:2 Isaac and said, "Don't go to **E**.
37:25 on their way to take them to **E**.
37:28 The Ishmaelites took him to **E**.

Gen	37:36	Meanwhile, in **E** the Midianites
	39:1	Joseph had been taken to **E**.
	40:1	their master, the king of **E**.
	40:5	for the king of **E** — had dreams
	41:8	magicians and wise men of **E**.
	41:19	such sickly cows in all of **E**!
	41:29	there will be plenty of food in **E**.
	41:30	there was plenty of food in **E**,
	41:33	man and put him in charge of **E**.
	41:36	of famine that will happen in **E**.
	41:41	"I now put you in charge of **E**."
	41:43	put Joseph in charge of **E**.
	41:44	no one anywhere in **E** will do
	41:45	Joseph traveled around **E**.
	41:46	of Pharaoh (the king of **E**).
	41:46	and traveled all around **E**.
	41:48	grown in **E** during those seven
	41:53	was plenty of food in **E** came
	41:54	Yet, there was food in **E**.
	41:55	When everyone in **E** began to
	41:56	the famine was severe in **E**.
	41:57	world came to Joseph in **E**
	42:1	out that grain was for sale in **E**,
	42:2	heard there's grain for sale in **E**.
	42:3	brothers went to buy grain in **E**.
	43:2	grain they had brought from **E**,
	43:15	They went to **E**, where they
	45:4	you sold into slavery in **E**!
	45:8	household, and ruler of **E**.
	45:9	"God has made me lord of **E**.
	45:11	I will provide for you in **E**,
	45:13	how greatly honored I am in **E**
	45:18	will give you the best land in **E**.
	45:19	'Take wagons with you from **E**
	45:20	of everything in **E** is yours.'"
	45:25	So they left **E** and came to their
	45:26	Yes, he is ruler of **E**."
	46:3	"Don't be afraid to go to **E**,
	46:4	I will go with you to **E**,
	46:6	and all his family arrived in **E**.
	46:8	descendants) who arrived in **E**.
	46:20	In **E**, Manasseh and Ephraim
	46:26	went with him to **E** was 66.
	46:27	two sons who were born in **E**.
	46:27	who went to **E** was 70.
	47:6	All of **E** is available to you.
	47:11	live in the best part of **E**,
	47:13	Neither **E** nor Canaan were
	47:14	money that could be found in **E**
	47:15	When the money in **E** and
	47:20	all the land in **E** for Pharaoh.
	47:21	All over **E** Joseph moved the
	47:26	the land in **E** which is still
	47:27	So the Israelites settled in **E** in
	47:28	Jacob lived in **E** 17 years,
	47:30	Take me out of **E**, and bury me
	48:5	who were born in **E** before I
	48:9	in **E**," Joseph answered his
	50:7	the leaders of **E** went with him.
	50:14	he went back to **E** along with
	50:22	his father's family stayed in **E**.
	50:26	and placed in a coffin in **E**.
Exo	1:1	Jacob) who came with him to **E**
	1:5	Joseph was already in **E**.
	1:8	began to rule in **E**.
	1:15	Then the king of **E** told the
	1:18	So the king of **E** called for the
	2:23	the king of **E** died.
	3:7	the misery of my people in **E**,
	3:10	my people Israel out of **E**."
	3:11	the people of Israel out of **E**?"
	3:12	you bring the people out of **E**,
	3:16	has been done to you in **E**.
	3:17	you away from your misery in **E**
	3:18	leaders must go to the king of **E**
	3:19	I know that the king of **E** will
	3:20	I will use my power to strike **E**.
	3:22	you will strip **E** of its wealth."
	4:18	go back to my own people in **E**.
	4:19	in Midian, "Go back to **E**,
	4:20	and started out for **E**.
	4:21	"When you get back to **E**,
	4:29	Moses and Aaron went ⌊to **E**⌋
	5:4	The king of **E** said to them,
	5:12	the people scattered all over **E**
	6:11	"Go tell Pharaoh (the king of **E**)
Exo	6:13	and Pharaoh (the king of **E**).
	6:13	to bring the Israelites out of **E**.
	6:26	"Bring the Israelites out of **E** in
	6:27	told Pharaoh (the king of **E**)
	6:27	to let the Israelites leave **E**.
	6:28	the LORD spoke to Moses in **E**.
	6:29	Tell Pharaoh (the king of **E**)
	7:3	signs and amazing things in **E**,
	7:4	my power to punish **E** severely,
	7:4	out of **E** in organized family
	7:5	when I use my power against **E**
	7:19	the waters of **E** — its rivers,
	7:19	will be blood everywhere in **E**,
	7:21	was blood everywhere in **E**.
	8:6	his staff over the waters of **E**.
	8:6	up and covered the land of **E**.
	8:16	All over **E** the dust will turn into
	8:17	in **E** turned into gnats.
	8:24	All over **E** the flies were ruining
	9:9	a fine dust throughout **E**.
	9:9	and animals throughout **E**."
	9:18	has ever happened in **E** since
	9:22	every plant in the fields of **E**."
	9:23	So the LORD made it hail on **E**.
	9:24	storm in all the land of **E** since
	9:25	All over **E** the hail knocked
	10:7	you realize that **E** is ruined?"
	10:12	"Stretch out your hand over **E**
	10:12	They will invade **E** and eat up
	10:13	held his staff over the land of **E**,
	10:14	They invaded all of **E** and
	10:15	any tree or plant anywhere in **E**.
	10:19	locust was left anywhere in **E**.
	10:21	it can be felt will come over **E**."
	10:22	and throughout **E** there was
	11:1	more plague on Pharaoh and **E**.
	11:5	firstborn son in **E** will die,
	11:6	be loud crying throughout **E**,
	11:7	between **E** and Israel.
	11:9	do more amazing things in **E**."
	12:1	said to Moses and Aaron in **E**,
	12:12	night I will go throughout **E**
	12:12	punish all the gods of **E**,
	12:13	or destroy you when I strike **E**.
	12:17	day that I brought you out of **E**
	12:23	The LORD will go throughout **E**
	12:27	the houses of the Israelites in **E**
	12:29	every firstborn male in **E** from
	12:30	was loud crying throughout **E**
	12:36	stripped **E** of its wealth.
	12:39	dough they had brought from **E**
	12:39	they'd been thrown out of **E**
	12:40	been living in **E** for 430 years.
	12:41	all the LORD's people left **E**
	12:42	watch to take them out of **E**.
	12:51	all the Israelites out of **E**
	13:3	day — the day when you left **E**,
	13:4	you are leaving **E**.
	13:8	did for us when we left **E**.'
	13:9	hand to bring you out of **E**,
	13:14	to bring us out of slavery in **E**.
	13:15	firstborn male in **E** — human
	13:16	hand to bring us out of **E**."
	13:17	their minds and go back to **E**."
	13:18	for battle when they left **E**.
	14:5	When Pharaoh (the king of **E**)
	14:7	as all the other chariots in **E**,
	14:8	(the king of **E**) so stubborn that
	14:8	who were boldly leaving **E**.
	14:11	there were no graves in **E**?
	14:11	done by bringing us out of **E**!
	14:12	Didn't we tell you in **E**,
	16:1	month after they had left **E**.
	16:3	the LORD had let us die in **E**!
	16:6	who brought you out of **E**.
	16:32	when I brought you out of **E**."
	17:3	"Why did you bring us out of **E**?
	18:1	had brought Israel out of **E**.
	19:1	after the Israelites left **E**,
	19:4	for yourselves what I did to **E**
	20:2	brought you out of slavery in **E**.
	22:21	you were foreigners living in **E**.
	23:9	you were foreigners living in **E**.
	23:15	that was when you left **E**.
	29:46	I brought them out of **E** so that I
	32:1	who led us out of **E**.
Exo	32:4	who brought you out of **E**."
	32:7	of **E** have ruined ⌊everything⌋.
	32:8	who brought you out of **E**.'"
	32:11	out of **E** using your great
	32:23	Moses who brought us out of **E**.
	33:1	brought out of **E** must leave this
	34:18	that month you came out of **E**.
	40:17	⌊after the Israelites had left **E**⌋.
Lev	11:45	I brought you out of **E** to be
	18:3	You used to live in **E**.
	19:34	you were foreigners living in **E**.
	19:36	God who brought you out of **E**.
	22:33	I brought you out of **E** to be
	23:43	when I brought them out of **E**.
	24:10	and whose father was from **E**,
	25:38	who brought you out of **E** to
	25:42	I brought them out of **E**.
	25:55	I brought them out of **E**.
	26:13	I brought you out of **E** so that
	26:45	I brought them out of **E** to be
Num	1:1	the second year after leaving **E**.
	3:13	killed every firstborn male in **E**,
	8:17	killed every firstborn male in **E**,
	9:1	year after the Israelites left **E**,
	11:5	all the free fish we ate in **E**
	11:18	We were better off in **E**!' So
	11:20	'Why did we ever leave **E**?'"
	13:22	seven years before Zoan in **E**.)
	14:2	we had died in **E** or this desert!
	14:3	better for us to go back to **E**?"
	14:4	a leader and go back to **E**."
	14:19	the time they left **E** until now."
	14:22	the miraculous signs I did in **E**
	15:41	who brought you out of **E** to be
	20:5	Why did you make us leave **E**
	20:15	Our ancestors went to **E**,
	20:16	and brought us out of **E**.
	21:5	"Why did you make us leave **E**
	22:5	has just come here from **E**.
	22:11	people have just come from **E**
	23:22	who brought them out of **E** has
	24:8	who brought them out of **E** has
	26:4	the Israelites who came from **E**:
	26:59	who was born in **E**.
	32:11	who came from **E**,
	33:1	set up camp after they left **E**
	33:38	after the Israelites had left **E**.
	34:5	toward the River of **E** so that
Dtr	1:3	year ⌊after they had left **E**⌋,
	1:27	why he brought us out of **E**.
	1:30	you saw him fight for you in **E**
	4:20	the LORD brought out of **E**,
	4:34	arm to do this for you in **E**.
	4:37	you out of **E** by his great
	4:45	Israelites after they had left **E**.
	4:46	defeated him after they left **E**.
	5:6	brought you out of slavery in **E**.
	5:15	that you were slaves in **E**
	6:12	brought you out of slavery in **E**.
	6:21	were Pharaoh's slaves in **E**,
	6:22	spectacular but terrible for **E**,
	7:8	under Pharaoh (the king of **E**).
	7:15	you experienced in **E**.
	7:18	did to Pharaoh and all of **E**.
	8:14	brought you out of slavery in **E**.
	9:7	day you left **E** until you came
	9:12	of **E** have ruined ⌊everything⌋.
	9:26	hand to bring them out of **E**.
	9:29	arm to bring them out ⌊of **E**⌋.
	10:19	you were foreigners living in **E**.
	10:22	your ancestors went to **E**,
	11:3	signs and deeds he did in **E**
	11:3	Egypt to Pharaoh (the king of **E**
	11:10	isn't like the land you left in **E**.
	13:5	who brought you out of **E** and
	13:10	brought you out of slavery in **E**.
	15:15	that you were slaves in **E**
	16:1	brought you out of **E** at night.
	16:3	of misery because you left **E**
	16:3	remember the day you left **E**.
	16:6	time you did it when you left **E**.
	16:12	that you were slaves in **E**,
	17:16	or make the people return to **E**
	20:1	who brought you out of **E**,
	23:4	and water on your trip from **E**.
	24:9	to Miriam on your trip from **E**.

Dtr 24:18 that you were slaves in **E**
24:22 that you were slaves in **E**.
25:17 did to you on your trip from **E**.
26:5 of them when they went to **E**
26:8 arm to bring us out of **E**.
28:60 diseases of **E** that you dreaded,
28:68 LORD will bring you back to **E**
29:2 the LORD did in **E** to Pharaoh,
29:16 You know how we lived in **E**
29:25 when he brought them out of **E**.
34:11 things in **E** to Pharaoh,
Jos 2:10 in front of you when you left **E**.
5:4 the desert after they left **E**.
5:5 The men who left **E** had been
5:6 their soldiers who left **E** died.
5:9 the disgrace of **E** from you."
9:9 him and everything he did in **E**.
13:3 the Shihor River, east of **E**,
15:4 It comes out at the River of **E**
15:47 villages as far as the River of **E**
24:4 Jacob and his sons went to **E**.
24:5 and I struck **E** with plagues.
24:6 I led your ancestors out of **E**,
24:7 for yourselves what I did to **E**.
24:14 of the Euphrates River and in **E**,
24:17 ancestors out of slavery in **E**.
24:32 of Israel had brought from **E**,
Jdg 2:1 He said, "I brought you out of **E**
2:12 God who brought them out of **E**.
6:8 I brought you out of **E**.
6:13 LORD brought us out of **E**?' But
11:13 the people of Israel left **E**,
11:16 the people of Israel left **E**,
19:30 Israel came out of **E** until today.
1Sm 2:27 under Pharaoh's control in **E**.
8:8 took them out of **E** — leaving
10:18 I brought Israel out of **E** and
12:6 brought your ancestors out of **E**
12:8 to **E** ⌊and were oppressed⌋,
12:8 Aaron to bring them out of **E**.
15:2 after the Israelites came from **E**.
15:6 when they came from **E**."
15:7 from Havilah to Shur, east of **E**.
27:8 from Telaim to Shur and **E**.)
2Sm 7:6 the day I took Israel out of **E**
7:23 whom you freed from **E** to be
1Ki 3:1 of Pharaoh (the king of **E**).
6:1 480 years after Israel left **E**.
8:9 to the Israelites after they left **E**.
8:16 my people Israel out of **E**,
8:21 he brought them out of **E**."
8:51 whom you brought out of **E**
8:53 brought our ancestors out of **E**."
8:65 of Hamath and the River of **E**
9:9 brought their ancestors out of **E**
9:16 (The king of **E** captured Gezer,
10:28 were imported from **E** and Kue.
10:29 chariot was imported from **E**
11:17 Edomite servants fled to **E**.
11:18 went to Pharaoh (the king of **E**).
11:21 When Hadad heard in **E** that
11:40 fled to King Shishak of **E**.
11:40 stayed in **E** until Solomon died.
12:2 (Nebat's son) was still in **E**,
12:2 he returned from **E**.
12:28 who brought you out of **E**."
14:25 of **E** attacked Jerusalem.
2Ki 17:4 messengers to King Dais of **E**
17:7 who brought them out of **E**
17:7 of Pharaoh (the king of **E**).
17:36 arm to bring you out of **E**.
18:21 When you trust **E**, If you lean on
18:21 Pharaoh (the king of **E**) is like
18:24 officers when you trust **E**
19:24 I'll dry up all the streams of **E**
21:15 ancestors left **E** until this day."
23:29 Necoh (the king of **E**) came
23:34 He took Jehoahaz away to **E**,
24:7 The king of **E** didn't leave his
24:7 the territory from the River of **E**
24:7 had belonged to the king of **E**.
25:26 the army commanders left for **E**
1Ch 1:8 Cush, **E**, Put, and Canaan.
1:11 **E** was the ancestor of the
13:5 from the Shihor River near **E**
17:5 day I brought Israel out ⌊of **E**⌋
1Ch 17:21 whom you freed from **E**.
2Ch 1:16 were imported from **E** and Kue.
1:17 imported each chariot from **E**
5:10 to the Israelites after they left **E**.
6:5 my people Israel out of **E**,
7:8 of Hamath and the River of **E**.
7:22 who brought them out of **E**.
9:28 imported for Solomon from **E**
10:2 (Nebat's son) was still in **E**,
10:2 he returned from **E**.
12:2 of **E** attacked Jerusalem.
12:3 and Sudanese from **E**.
12:9 King Shishak of **E** attacked
20:10 them when they came out of **E**.
26:8 fame spread to the border of **E**
35:20 King Neco of **E** came to fight a
36:3 The king of **E** removed him
36:4 The king of **E** made
36:4 took Jehoahaz away to **E**.
Neh 9:9 our ancestors suffered in **E**,
9:17 them back to slavery ⌊in **E**⌋.
9:18 who took you out of **E**.' They
Psa 68:31 will come from **E**.
78:12 miracles in the land of **E**,
78:43 his miraculous signs in **E**,
78:51 slaughtered every firstborn in **E**
80:8 You brought a vine from **E**.
81:5 Joseph rose to power over **E**.
81:10 one who brought you out of **E**.
87:4 LORD says,⌋ "I will add **E**
105:23 Then Israel came to **E**.
106:7 When our ancestors were in **E**,
106:21 did spectacular things in **E**,
114:1 When Israel left **E**,
135:8 killed every firstborn male in **E**.
135:9 the heart of **E** against Pharaoh
136:10 killed the firstborn males in **E**
Isa 7:18 branches of the Nile River in **E**
10:26 so he will lift it as he did in **E**.
11:11 Upper and Lower **E**,
11:16 for Israel when it came out of **E**.
19:1 is the divine revelation about **E**.
19:1 cloud and is coming to **E**.
19:12 Armies is planning against **E**.
19:15 can do anything for **E**.
19:18 five cities in **E** will have
19:19 will be in the middle of **E**,
19:20 the LORD of Armies is in **E**.
19:22 The LORD will strike **E** with a
19:23 will run from **E** to Assyria.
19:23 The Assyrians will come to **E**
19:24 along with **E** and Assyria.
19:25 them, saying, "My people **E**,
20:3 as an omen to **E** and Sudan.
20:4 and the old — captives from **E**
20:4 exposed in order to disgrace **E**.
20:5 hope and **E** was their beauty.
20:6 We ran ⌊to **E**⌋ for help to be
23:5 When the news reaches **E**,
27:12 River to the brook of **E**.
27:13 are banished to **E** will come
30:2 They go to **E** without asking
31:1 for those who go to **E** for help,
36:6 When you trust **E**, If you lean on
36:6 Pharaoh (the king of **E**) is like
36:9 officers when you trust **E**
37:25 I'll dry up all the streams of **E**
43:3 **E** is the ransom I exchanged
45:14 The products from **E**,
52:4 beginning my people went to **E**
Jer 2:6 who brought us from **E**?
2:18 gain anything by going to **E**
2:36 You will be put to shame by **E**
7:22 brought your ancestors out of **E**
7:25 your ancestors left **E** until now,
9:26 I will punish **E**, Judah, Edom,
11:4 when I brought them out of **E**,
11:7 when I brought them out of **E**,
16:14 the people of Israel out of **E**.
23:7 the people of Israel out of **E**.
24:8 and those who are living in **E**.
25:19 Pharaoh king of **E**,
26:21 about it and fled in fear to **E**.
26:22 Jehoiakim sent soldiers to **E**:
26:23 They brought Uriah from **E** and
31:32 hand and brought them out of **E**
Jer 32:20 signs and amazing things in **E**.
32:21 You brought your people from **E**
34:13 when I brought them from **E**,
37:5 army had come from **E**,
37:7 But it will go back to **E**,
41:17 Kimham on their way to **E**.
42:14 Then you say, 'We'll go to **E**,
42:15 you're determined to go to **E**,
42:16 fear will catch up with you in **E**.
42:16 you dread will follow you to **E**,
42:17 to go and live in **E** will die
42:18 out on you if you go to **E**.
42:19 are left in Judah not to go to **E**.
43:2 that we must not go to live in **E**.
43:5 who were left in Judah to **E**.
43:7 so they went to **E**.
43:11 He will defeat **E**. He will bring
43:12 Nebuchadnezzar will put on **E**
43:12 He will leave **E** peacefully.
43:13 will break the monuments in **E**
44:1 the Jews living in **E** at Migdol,
44:8 incense to other gods in **E**,
44:12 determined to go to live in **E**.
44:12 They will die in **E**.
44:13 I will punish those living in **E**
44:14 went to live in **E** will survive
44:15 in **E** answered Jeremiah.
44:24 people of Judah who are in **E**.
44:26 people of Judah who live in **E**.
44:26 anywhere in **E** will ever again
44:27 In **E** the people from Judah will
44:28 will return to Judah from **E**.
44:28 to live in **E** will know whose
44:30 Pharaoh Hophra, king of **E**,
46:2 This is the message about **E**,
46:2 of Pharaoh Neco, king of **E**.
46:8 **E** is like the rising Nile River,
46:8 **E** says, 'I will rise; I will cover
46:11 get medicine, dear people of **E**.
46:13 who will defeat **E**.
46:14 "Tell this in **E**; announce this
46:17 king of **E**, is a big windbag.
46:19 your bags, inhabitants of **E**,
46:20 "**E** is like a beautiful cow,
46:22 **E** will hiss like a snake as it
46:23 "since **E** can't be found.
46:24 The people of **E** will be put to
46:25 I will also punish Pharaoh, **E**,
Lam 5:6 We had to beg **E** and Assyria
Eze 17:15 sending his messengers to **E**
19:4 brought him with hooks to **E**.
20:5 myself known to them in **E**.
20:6 promised to bring them out of **E**
20:7 with the disgusting idols of **E**.
20:8 the disgusting idols of **E**.
20:8 unleash my anger on them in **E**.
20:9 bringing the Israelites out of **E**.
20:10 I brought the Israelites out of **E**
20:14 bring the Israelites out ⌊of **E**⌋.
20:22 bring the Israelites out ⌊of **E**⌋.
20:36 on trial in the desert of **E**,
23:3 They became prostitutes in **E**
23:8 that she started in **E**.
23:19 a prostitute in **E** when she was
23:21 did when she was young in **E**,
23:27 which you began in **E**.
23:27 or remember **E** anymore.
27:7 fine embroidered linen from **E**.
29:2 man, turn to Pharaoh, king of **E**,
29:2 against him and against all **E**.
29:3 you, Pharaoh, king of **E**.
29:6 Then all those living in **E** will
29:6 **E**, you have become like a
29:9 **E** will become a wasteland
29:10 I will turn **E** into a pile of rubble.
29:12 I will make **E** the most
29:16 Israel will never trust **E** again.
29:16 they turned to **E** ⌊for help⌋.
29:19 I'm going to give **E** to King
29:20 I have given him **E** as pay for
30:4 There will be war in **E** and
30:7 "**E** will become the most
30:8 because I will set fire to **E** and
30:9 will be in anguish when **E** is
30:10 of Babylon to bring an end to **E**.
30:11 draw their swords to attack **E**

Eze 30:13 will never rise again in **E**.
30:13 I will spread fear throughout **E**.
30:16 I will set fire to **E**. Sin will be in
30:18 Clouds will cover **E**,
30:19 I will bring punishment on **E**."
30:21 the arm of Pharaoh, king of **E**.
30:22 I'm against Pharaoh, king of **E**.
30:25 He will strike **E** with it.
31:2 man, say to Pharaoh, king of **E**,
32:2 song for Pharaoh, king of **E**.
32:12 They will shatter the pride of **E**
32:15 I will turn **E** into a wasteland.
32:16 will sing it as they mourn for **E**
32:18 cry for the many people of **E**.
32:20 Drag **E** and all its people away.
48:28 it will run along the Brook of **E**
Dan 9:15 brought your people out of **E**
11:8 of silver and gold back to **E**.
11:42 Even **E** will not escape.
Hos 2:15 did when she came out of **E**.
7:11 You call for **E** and run to
7:16 The people in **E** will ridicule
8:13 They will go back to **E**.
9:3 They will return to **E**,
9:6 **E** will capture them and
11:1 and I called my son out of **E**.
11:5 "They will not return to **E**.
11:11 trembling like birds from **E**
12:1 Assyria and take olive oil to **E**.
12:9 I brought you out of **E**.
12:13 the people of Israel out of **E**.
13:4 I brought you out of **E**.
Joe 3:19 **E** will become a wasteland.
Amo 2:10 I brought you out of **E**.
3:1 family that I brought out of **E**.
3:9 and in the palaces of **E**,
4:10 plagues on you as I did to **E**.
9:7 Didn't I bring Israel from **E**?
Mic 6:4 I brought you out of **E** and freed
7:12 Assyria and the cities of **E**,
7:12 from **E** to the Euphrates River,
7:15 like the time you came out of **E**.
Nah 3:9 Sudan and **E** were her endless
Hag 2:5 to you when you came out of **E**.
Zec 10:10 I will bring them back from **E**.
10:11 and the scepter of **E** will depart.
14:18 If the people of **E** won't go or
Mat 2:13 and his mother, and flee to **E**.
2:14 and left for **E** that night.
2:15 "I have called my son out of **E**."
2:19 in a dream to Joseph in **E**.
Act 2:10 Phrygia, Pamphylia, **E**,
7:9 and he was taken to **E**.
7:10 of Pharaoh (the king of **E**),
7:10 so that he became ruler of **E**
7:11 Then a famine throughout **E**
7:12 Jacob heard that **E** had food,
7:15 So Jacob went to **E**,
7:17 the number of our people in **E**
7:18 began to rule in **E**.
7:29 Moses quickly left **E** and lived
7:34 my people are mistreated in **E**.
7:34 So now I'm sending you to **E**.'
7:36 who led our ancestors out of **E**.
7:36 and worked miracles in **E**,
7:39 hearts they turned back to **E**.
7:40 who led us out of **E**.
13:17 they lived as foreigners in **E**.
13:17 arm to bring them out of **E**,
1Co 10:1 ⌊who left **E**⌋ were under
Heb 3:16 Moses led out of **E** rebelled.
8:9 hand and brought them out of **E**
11:22 about the Israelites leaving **E**
11:26 than having the treasures of **E**.
11:27 Faith led Moses to leave **E**
Jud 1:5 once saved his people from **E**.
Rev 11:8 of that city are Sodom and **E**.

Egyptian (39)

Gen 16:1 an **E** slave named Hagar.
16:3 Abram's wife Sarai took her **E**
21:9 by Hagar the **E** was laughing at
25:12 He was the son of Sarah's **E**
39:1 Potiphar, one of Pharaoh's **E**
39:2 in the house of his **E** master.
47:20 Every **E** sold his fields
Gen 50:11 **E** Funeral Ceremonies].
Exo 1:19 women are not like **E** women.
2:11 being beaten by an **E**.
2:12 he beat the **E** to death and hid
2:14 to kill me as you killed the **E**?"
2:19 They answered, "An **E**
3:22 should ask her **E** neighbor
7:11 These **E** magicians did the
7:22 But the **E** magicians did the
14:20 between the **E** camp and the
14:24 and threw the **E** camp into
Dtr 11:4 saw what he did to the **E** army,
1Sm 30:11 David's men found an **E** in the
30:13 "I'm an **E**, the slave of an
30:16 The **E** led him ⌊to them⌋.
2Sm 23:21 And he killed a handsome **E**.
23:21 The **E** had a spear in his hand.
1Ki 4:21 and as far as the **E** border.
2Ki 7:6 hired the Hittite and **E** kings
1Ch 2:34 had an **E** slave named Jarha.
11:23 He killed an eight-foot-tall **E**.
11:23 The **E** had a spear like a
2Ch 9:26 and as far as the **E** border.
Psa 106:11 Not one **E** survived.
Pro 7:16 with colored sheets of **E** linen.
Isa 11:15 dry up the gulf of the **E** Sea.
19:2 will turn one **E** against another.
Eze 29:14 I will bring back the **E** captives
Act 7:24 being treated unfairly by an **E**,
7:24 took revenge by killing the **E**.
7:28 as you killed the **E** yesterday?'
21:38 Aren't you the **E** who started a

Egyptian's (1)

Gen 39:5 LORD blessed the **E** household

Egyptians (105)

Gen 12:12 When the **E** see you,
12:14 the **E** saw how very beautiful
41:55 But Pharaoh said to all the **E**,
41:56 and sold grain to the **E**.
43:32 The **E** who were there with him
45:2 so loudly that the **E** heard him,
46:34 shepherds are disgusting to **E**."
47:15 all the **E** came to Joseph.
50:3 The **E** mourned for him 70
50:11 taken very seriously by the **E**."
Exo 1:11 So the **E** put slave drivers in
1:12 The **E** couldn't stand them
1:14 All the jobs the **E** gave them
3:8 them from the power of the **E**
3:9 how the **E** are oppressing them.
3:21 I will make the **E** kind to the
6:5 whom the **E** hold in slavery,
6:6 under the oppression of the **E**,
6:7 under the forced labor of the **E**.
7:5 The **E** will know that I am the
7:18 The **E** will not be able to drink
7:21 and it smelled so bad that the **E**
7:24 All the **E** dug along the Nile for
8:21 The homes of the **E** will be
8:26 our God are disgusting to **E**.
9:4 and the livestock of the **E**.
9:6 All the livestock of the **E** died,
9:11 had boils like all the other **E**.
10:2 exactly how I treated the **E**
10:6 officials and those of all the **E**.
11:2 and woman must ask the **E**
11:3 The LORD made the **E** kind to
11:3 officials and all the **E**.
11:4 I will go out among the **E**.
12:23 throughout Egypt to kill the **E**.
12:27 when he killed the **E**.'" Then
12:30 and all the ⌊other⌋ **E** got up
12:33 The **E** begged the people to
12:35 had told them and asked the **E**
12:36 The LORD made the **E**
14:4 and the **E** will know that I am
14:9 The **E** pursued the Israelites.
14:10 that the **E** were coming after
14:12 Let us go on serving the **E**?
14:12 better for us to serve the **E** than
14:13 You will never see these **E**
14:17 I am making the **E** so stubborn
14:18 The **E** will know that I am the
14:23 The **E** pursued them,
Exo 14:25 Then the **E** shouted,
14:26 water will flow back over the **E**,
14:27 The **E** tried to escape,
14:30 LORD saved Israel from the **E**,
14:30 and Israel saw the **E** lying
14:31 LORD had used against the **E**,
15:26 diseases I made the **E** suffer,
18:8 to Pharaoh and the **E** for Israel,
18:9 in rescuing them from the **E**.
18:10 He rescued you from the **E** and
18:10 people from the control of the **E**,
32:12 Don't let the **E** say,
Lev 18:3 Don't live the way the **E** do.
26:13 are no longer slaves of the **E**.
Num 14:13 "What if the **E** hear about it?
14:14 What if the **E** tell the people
20:15 The **E** mistreated us and our
33:3 left in full view of all the **E**.
33:4 The **E** were burying all their
Dtr 23:7 consider the **E** disgusting.
26:6 So the **E** treated us cruelly,
28:27 same boils that plagued the **E**.
Jos 24:6 The **E** with their chariots and
24:7 between you and the **E**.
Jdg 6:9 you from the power of the **E**
10:11 "When the **E**, the Amorites,
1Sm 4:8 are the gods who struck the **E**
6:6 you be as stubborn as the **E**
6:6 After he toyed with the **E**,
10:18 you from the power of the **E**
1Ki 4:30 and all the wisdom of the **E**.
Ezr 9:1 Moabites, **E**, and Amorites.
Psa 105:38 The **E** were terrified of Israel,
Isa 10:24 staff against you as the **E** did.
19:3 The **E** will lose courage.
19:4 I will hand over the **E** to a
19:13 of its tribes mislead the **E**.
19:14 So they lead the **E** astray like a
19:16 At that time **E** will act like
19:17 land of Judah will terrify the **E**.
19:21 make himself known to the **E**.
19:21 The **E** will know the LORD
19:23 to Egypt and the **E** to Assyria,
19:23 and the **E** will worship with the
23:5 the **E** will shudder over the
31:3 The **E** are humans,
Eze 16:26 your lustful neighbors, the **E**.
29:12 I will scatter the **E** among the
29:13 40 years I will gather the **E** from
30:4 Many **E** will fall dead.
30:23 I will scatter the **E** among the
30:26 I will scatter the **E** among the
32:20 "The **E** will lie among those
32:28 "You **E** will be crushed with
Act 7:22 in all the wisdom of the **E**
Heb 11:29 The **E** also tried this,

Egypt's (25)

Gen 41:34 take a fifth of **E** harvest during
45:23 carrying **E** best products
Exo 1:17 didn't obey the king of **E** orders.
Isa 19:1 **E** idols will tremble in his
19:1 **E** courage will fail.
19:6 **E** streams will be emptied and
19:10 **E** weavers will be crushed.
30:2 and look for refuge in **E** shadow
30:3 and the refuge in **E** shadow
30:7 **E** help is completely useless.
Jer 43:12 fire to the temples of **E** gods.
43:13 down the temples of **E** gods.'"
46:21 **E** hired soldiers are like
Eze 29:12 For 40 years **E** cities will lie in
30:4 will take away **E** wealth,
30:6 All **E** allies will die.
30:6 **E** strength will disappear.
30:7 and **E** cities will lie in ruins.
30:15 **E** fortress, and I will kill many
30:18 turn dark when I break **E** power
30:18 **E** strong army will be defeated.
Dan 11:43 treasures and all **E** treasuries.
Amo 8:8 and then sink like **E** river
9:5 the Nile and sinks like **E** river
Zec 14:19 be ⌊the punishment⌋ for **E** sin

Ehi (1)

Gen 46:21 **E**, Rosh, Muppim, Huppim,

Ehud (14)

Jdg 3:15 It was **E**, a left-handed man
3:15 (**E** was the son of Gera.)
3:16 **E** made a two-edged dagger for
3:18 When **E** had finished delivering
3:19 However, **E** turned around at
3:20 **E** came up to him as he sat
3:21 **E** reached with his left hand,
3:22 the blade because **E** didn't pull
3:23 **E** left the room. (He had closed
3:24 After **E** went out, They were
3:26 had been waiting, **E** escaped.
3:31 After **E** came Shamgar,
4:1 After **E** died, the people of
1Ch 7:10 **E**, Chenaanah, Zethan,

Ehud's (1)

1Ch 8:6 These were **E** sons, who were

eighth (35)

Exo 22:30 but on the **e** day you must give
Lev 9:1 On the **e** day Moses
14:10 "On the **e** day he must take
14:23 On the **e** day he will take them
15:14 On the **e** day he must take two
15:29 On the **e** day she must take
22:27 From the **e** day on it may be
23:36 On the **e** day there will be a
23:39 The first and the **e** days will be
25:22 You will plant ⌊again⌋ in the **e**
Num 6:10 On the **e** day he must bring two
7:54 On the **e** day the leader of the
29:35 "On the **e** day you must hold a
1Ki 6:38 In the month of Bul (the **e**
8:66 On the **e** day he dismissed the
12:32 the fifteenth day of the **e** month,
12:33 the fifteenth day of the **e** month,
2Ki 24:12 In the **e** year of his reign,
1Ch 12:12 The **e** was Johanan.
24:10 for Hakkoz, the **e** for Abijah,
25:15 The **e** chose Jeshaiah,
26:5 (the seventh), Peullethai (the **e**
27:11 was in charge of the **e** unit
27:11 eighth unit during the **e** month.
2Ch 7:9 On the **e** day there was an
29:17 On the **e** day they went into the
34:3 In the **e** year of his reign,
Neh 8:18 seven days, and on the **e** day,
10:32 the obligation to give an **e**
Eze 43:27 days are over, on the **e** day,
Zec 1:1 In the **e** month of Darius'
Act 7:8 circumcised him on the **e** day.
Php 3:5 was circumcised on the **e** day.
Rev 17:11 and is no longer is the **e** king.
21:20 the **e** beryl, the ninth topaz,

Eker (1)

1Ch 2:27 were Maaz, Jamin, and **E**.

Ekron (25)

Jos 13:3 as far as the border of **E**.
13:3 Ashkelon, Gath, and **E**,
15:11 goes on the north side of **E**
15:45 Judah also received **E** with its
15:46 with their villages between **E**
19:43 Elon, Timnah, **E**,
Jdg 1:18 and **E** with their territories.
1Sm 5:10 Gath sent the ark of God to **E**.
5:10 when the ark of God came to **E**,
5:10 the people of **E** cried out,
6:16 went back to **E** that same day.
6:17 Gaza, Ashkelon, Gath, and **E**.
7:14 The cities between **E** and Gath
17:52 as Gath and to the gates of **E**.
17:52 and all the way to Gath and **E**.
2Ki 1:2 So he sent messengers ⌊to **E**⌋.
1:2 ask Baalzebub, the god of **E**,
1:3 from Baalzebub, the god of **E**,
1:6 from Baalzebub, the god of **E**,
1:16 from Baalzebub, the god of **E**.
Jer 25:20 of Ashkelon, Gaza, and **E**,
Amo 1:8 I will turn my power against **E**.
Zep 2:4 and **E** will be torn out by the
Zec 9:5 also be in great pain, also **E**,
9:7 and **E** will be like a Jebusite.

Ela (1)

1Ki 4:18 Shimei, son of **E**, was in

Elah (18)

Gen 36:41 Oholibamah, **E**, Pinon,
1Sm 17:2 and camped in the **E** Valley.
17:19 are in the **E** Valley fighting the
21:9 you killed in the **E** Valley,
1Ki 16:6 His son **E** succeeded him as
16:8 **E**, son of Baasha, began to rule
16:9 **E** was getting drunk in Tirzah
16:10 Arza's house, attacked **E**,
16:10 Zimri succeeded **E** as king ⌊of
16:13 by Baasha and his son **E**.
16:14 Isn't everything else about **E** —
2Ki 15:30 Hoshea, son of **E**, son of
17:1 of Judah, Hoshea, son of **E**,
18:1 King Hoshea, son of **E**,
18:9 son of **E** of Israel) King
1Ch 1:52 Oholibamah, **E**, Pinon,
4:15 were Iru, **E**, and Naam.
9:8 Ibneiah (son of Jeroham), **E**

Elah's (2)

1Ki 16:9 **E** chariots, plotted against him.
1Ch 4:15 **E** son was Kenaz.

Elam (28)

Gen 10:22 Shem's descendants were **E**,
14:1 King Chedorlaomer of **E**,
14:9 King Chedorlaomer of **E**,
1Ch 1:17 descendants of Shem were **E**,
8:24 Hananiah, **E**, Anthothijah,
26:3 **E** (the fifth), Jehohanan (the
Ezr 2:7 of **E**: 1,254
2:31 of the other **E**: 1,254
4:9 Susa, (that is, those of **E**),
8:7 from the family of **E**:
10:2 one of the descendants of **E**,
10:26 From the descendants of **E**:
Neh 7:12 of **E**: 1,254
7:34 of the other **E**: 1,254
10:14 Pahath Moab, **E**, Zattu, Bani,
12:42 Malchiah, **E**, and Ezer.
Isa 11:11 Sudan, **E**, Babylonia, Hamath,
21:2 Go to war, **E**! Surround them,
22:6 **E** takes its quiver of arrows,
Jer 25:25 of Zimri, all the kings of **E**,
49:34 the prophet Jeremiah about **E**.
49:36 corners of heaven against **E**
49:37 I'll defeat the people of **E** in the
49:38 I'll set my throne in **E** and
49:39 I'll return the captives of **E**,
Eze 32:24 "**E** is there with all its soldiers,
32:25 A bed has been made for **E**
Dan 8:2 of Susa in the province of **E**.

Elamites (1)

Act 2:9 We're Parthians, Medes, and **E**.

Elam's (2)

Jer 49:35 to break the bows of **E** archers,
49:36 where **E** refugees won't go.

Elasah (2)

Ezr 10:22 Nethanel, Jozabad, and **E**
Jer 29:3 the letter with Shaphan's son **E**

Elath (7)

Dtr 2:8 goes through the plains to **E**
1Ki 9:26 at Ezion Geber by **E** in Edom.
2Ki 14:22 Azariah rebuilt **E** and returned
16:6 drove the Judeans out of **E**
16:6 The Edomites came to **E** and
2Ch 8:17 Ezion Geber and **E** in Edom.
26:2 Uzziah rebuilt **E** and returned it

El Berith (1)

Jgd 9:46 the basement of the temple of **E**.

El Bethel (1)

Gen 35:7 called that place **E** [God of the

elbow (1)

Job 31:22 let my arm be broken at the **e**.

Eldaah (2)

Gen 25:4 Epher, Hanoch, Abida, and **E**.
1Ch 1:33 Epher, Hanoch, Abida, and **E**.

Eldad (2)

Num 11:26 men, named **E** and Medad,
11:27 "**E** and Medad are prophesying

elderly (3)

Gen 43:27 told me about your **e** father.
Lev 19:32 "Show respect to the **e**,
2Sm 19:32 Barzillai was an **e** man,

Elead (1)

1Ch 7:21 Ephraim's sons Ezer and **E**

Eleadah (1)

1Ch 7:20 Tahath's son was **E**.

Eleadah's (1)

1Ch 7:20 **E** son was Tahath.

Elealeh (5)

Num 32:3 **E**, Sebam, Nebo, and Beon,
32:37 of Heshbon, **E**, Kiriathaim,
Isa 15:4 Heshbon and **E** also cry out.
16:9 with my tears, Heshbon and **E**.
Jer 48:34 from Heshbon to **E** and Jahaz.

Eleasah (4)

1Ch 2:39 Helez was the father of **E**.
2:40 **E** was the father of Sismai.
8:37 Raphah's son was **E**.
9:43 Rephaiah's son was **E**.

Eleasah's (2)

1Ch 8:37 Eleasah. **E** son was Azel.
9:43 Eleasah. **E** son was Azel.

Eleazar (71)

Exo 6:23 Nadab, Abihu, **E**, and Ithamar.
6:25 **E**, son of Aaron, married one of
28:1 Abihu, **E**, and Ithamar to you.
Lev 10:6 and his sons **E** and Ithamar:
10:12 surviving sons **E** and Ithamar,
10:16 angry with **E** and Ithamar,
Num 3:2 Abihu, **E**, and Ithamar.
3:4 So only **E** and Ithamar served
3:32 leader of the Levites was **E**,
4:16 "**E**, son of the priest Aaron,
16:37 "Tell **E**, son of the priest Aaron,
16:39 So the priest **E** took the bronze
19:3 Give it to the priest **E**.
19:4 The priest **E** will take some of
20:25 Bring Aaron and his son **E** up
20:26 and put them on his son **E**.
20:28 and put them on his son **E**.
20:28 Then Moses and **E** came down
25:7 Phinehas, son of **E** and
25:11 "Phinehas, son of **E** and
26:1 the LORD said to Moses and **E**,
26:3 So Moses and the priest **E**
26:60 Nadab, Abihu, **E**, and Ithamar.
26:63 Moses and the priest **E** added
27:2 him, the priest **E**, the leaders,
27:19 him stand in front of the priest **E**
27:21 stand in front of the priest **E**,
27:22 him stand in front of the priest **E**
31:6 son of the priest **E**.
31:12 to Moses, the priest **E**,
31:13 Moses, the priest **E**,
31:21 Then the priest **E** said to the
31:26 "You, the priest **E**,
31:29 and give them to the priest **E**
31:31 Moses and the priest **E** did as
31:41 LORD's taxes to the priest **E**,
31:51 Moses and the priest **E** took all
31:54 Moses and the priest **E** took
32:2 came to Moses, the priest **E**,
32:28 about them to the priest **E**,
34:17 the priest **E** and Joshua,
Dtr 10:6 and his son **E** succeeded him
Jos 14:1 The priest **E**, Joshua (son of
17:4 They came to the priest **E**,
19:51 The priest **E**, Joshua son of

Jos 21:1 of Levi came to the priest **E**,
22:13 son of the priest **E**,
22:31 son of the priest **E**,
22:32 Phinehas (son of the priest **E**)
24:33 Aaron's son **E** also died.
Jdg 20:28 (Phinehas, son of **E** and
1Sm 7:1 They gave Abinadab's son **E**
2Sm 23:9 Next in rank to him was **E**,
23:9 **E** was with David at Pas
23:10 The army returned to **E**,
1Ch 6:3 Nadab, Abihu, **E**, and Ithamar.
6:4 **E** was the father of Phinehas.
6:50 descendants: His son was **E**.
11:12 Next in rank to him was **E**,
11:13 **E** was with David at Pas
23:21 Mahli's sons were **E** and Kish.
23:22 **E** died without having any
24:1 and Abihu, **E** and Ithamar.
24:2 So **E** and Ithamar served as
24:6 One family was chosen for **E**,
24:28 **E** (who had no sons,
Ezr 8:33 the priest Uriah, as well as **E**,
10:25 **E**, Malchiah, and Benaiah
Neh 12:42 and Maaseiah, Shemaiah, **E**,
Mat 1:15 Eliud the father of **E**,
1:15 **E** the father of Matthan,

Eleazar's (7)

Num 3:32 It was **E** duty to supervise
1Ch 6:50 **E** son was Phinehas.
9:20 (Phinehas, **E** son, had been the
24:3 David, **E** descendant Zadok,
24:4 Since **E** descendants had more
24:4 **E** descendants had 16 family
24:5 **E** and Ithamar's descendants.

Eleazer (1)

Ezr 7:5 who was the son of **E**,

elected (1)

2Co 8:19 More than that, the churches **e**

elegance (1)

Sos 7:6 you are, my love, with your **e**.

elementary (2)

Heb 5:12 to teach you the **e** truths
6:1 over the **e** truths about Christ

Eleph (1)

Jos 18:28 Zela, **E**, Jebus (now called

elevate (1)

1Sm 17:25 to that man to marry and **e**

Elhanan (4)

2Sm 21:19 with the Philistines at Gob, **E**,
23:24 thirty leading men were **E** (son
1Ch 11:26 **E** (son of Dodo) from
20:5 **E**, son of Jair, killed Lahmi,

Eli (34)

1Sm 1:9 (The priest **E** was sitting on a
1:12 **E** was watching her mouth.
1:13 **E** thought she was drunk.
1:14 **E** asked her. "Get rid of your
1:17 **E** replied, "Go in peace,
1:25 bull and brought the child to **E**.
2:11 the LORD under the priest **E**.
2:20 **E** would bless Elkanah (and
2:22 Now, **E** was very old,
2:27 Then a man of God came to **E**
3:1 was serving the LORD under **E**.
3:2 One night **E** was lying down in
3:5 He ran to **E** and said,
3:5 "I didn't call you," **E** replied.
3:6 Samuel got up, went to **E**,
3:8 Samuel got up, went to **E**,
3:8 Then **E** realized that the LORD
3:9 "Go, lie down," **E** told Samuel.
3:12 that day I am going to do to **E**
3:15 afraid to tell **E** about the vision.
3:16 Then **E** called Samuel.
3:18 So Samuel told **E** everything.
3:18 **E** replied, "He is the LORD.
4:13 When he arrived, **E** was sitting
1Sm 4:14 Hearing the cry, **E** asked,
4:14 went quickly to tell **E** the news.
4:15 (**E** was 98 years old,
4:16 The man told **E**, "I'm the one
4:16 son?" **E** asked.
4:18 **E** fell from his chair backwards
14:3 and the grandson of **E**,
Mat 27:46 "**E**, Eli, lema sabachthani?"
27:46 "Eli, **E**, lema sabachthani?"
Luk 3:23 the son of Joseph, son of **E**,

Eliab (21)

Num 1:9 **E**, son of Helon, from the tribe
2:7 for the people of Zebulun is **E**,
7:24 of Zebulun, **E**, son of Helon,
7:29 These were the gifts from **E**,
10:16 **E**, son of Helon,
16:1 Dathan and Abiram (sons of **E**),
16:12 Dathan and Abiram, sons of **E**.
26:8 **E** was the son of Pallu,
26:9 and Abiram were the sons of **E**.
Dtr 11:6 and Abiram, the sons of **E**,
1Sm 16:6 he saw **E** and thought,
17:13 The firstborn was **E**,
17:28 **E**, David's oldest brother,
17:28 Then **E** became angry with
1Ch 2:13 the father of **E** (his firstborn),
6:27 Nahath's son was **E**.
12:9 Obadiah. The third was **E**.
15:18 Unni, **E**, Benaiah, Maaseiah,
15:20 Jehiel, Unni, **E**, Maaseiah,
16:5 **E**, Benaiah, Obed Edom,
2Ch 11:18 Abihail was the daughter of **E**,

Eliab's (1)

1Ch 6:27 **E** son was Jeroham.

Eliada (4)

2Sm 5:16 Elishama, **E**, and Eliphelet.
1Ki 11:23 son of **E**, as a rival to Solomon.
1Ch 3:8 Elishama, **E**, and Eliphelet
2Ch 17:17 man **E** (with 200,000 armed

Eliahba (1)

1Ch 11:33 Bahurim, **E** from Shaalbon,

Eliakim (15)

2Ki 18:18 called for King Hezekiah, **E**,
18:26 Then **E** (son of Hilkiah),
18:37 Then **E**, who was in charge of
19:2 Then he sent **E**, who was in
23:34 made Josiah's son **E** king
2Ch 36:4 Jehoahaz's brother **E** king
Neh 12:41 **E**, Maaseiah, Miniamin,
Isa 22:20 I will call my servant **E**,
36:3 **E**, who was in charge of the
36:11 Then **E**, Shebna, and Joah
36:22 Then **E**, who was in charge of
37:2 Then he sent **E**, who was in
Mat 1:13 Abiud the father of **E**,
1:13 **E** the father of Azor,
Luk 3:30 son of Jonam, son of **E**,

Eliakim's (2)

2Ki 23:34 Josiah and changed **E** name
2Ch 36:4 and changed **E** name

Eliam (2)

2Sm 11:3 daughter of **E** and wife of Uriah
23:34 **E** (son of Ahithophel) from Gilo,

Eliasaph (6)

Num 1:14 **E**, son of Deuel, from the tribe
2:14 for the people of Gad is **E**,
3:24 Gershonite households was **E**,
7:42 of Gad, **E**, son of Deuel,
7:47 These were the gifts from **E**,
10:20 **E**, son of Deuel,

Eliashib (16)

1Ch 3:24 **E**, Pelaiah, Akkub, Johanan,
24:12 the eleventh for **E**,
Ezr 10:6 room of Jehohanan, son of **E**.
10:24 **E** From the gatekeepers:
10:27 **E**, Mattaniah, Jeremoth, Zabad,
Ezr 10:36 Vaniah, Meremoth, **E**,
Neh 3:1 The chief priest **E** and his
3:2 were rebuilding next to **E**.
3:20 the house of the chief priest **E**.
12:10 Joiakim was the father of **E**.
12:10 **E** was the father of Joiada.
12:22 and the priests at the time of **E**,
12:23 of Johanan, grandson of **E**.
13:4 Even before this, the priest **E**,
13:7 the evil thing **E** had done by
13:28 the son of the chief priest **E**.)

Eliashib's (2)

Neh 3:21 from the door of **E** house
3:21 house to the end of **E** house

Eliathah (2)

1Ch 25:4 **E**, Giddalti, Romamti Ezer,
25:27 The twentieth chose **E**,

Elidad (1)

Num 34:21 **E**, son of Kislon, from the tribe

Eliehoenai (2)

1Ch 26:3 (the sixth), **E** (the seventh).
Ezr 8:4 Moab: **E**, son of Zerahiah,

Eliel (10)

1Ch 5:24 **E**, Azriel, Jeremiah, Hodaviah,
6:34 who was the son of **E**,
8:20 Elienai, Zillethai, **E**,
8:22 sons were Ishpan, Eber, **E**,
11:46 **E** the Mahavite, Jeribai and
11:47 **E**, Obed, and Jaasiel the
12:11 The seventh was **E**.
15:9 Hebron's descendants was **E**,
15:11 Shemaiah, **E**, and Amminadab.
2Ch 31:13 **E**, Ismachiah, Mahath,

Elienai (1)

1Ch 8:20 **E**, Zillethai, Eliel,

Eliezer (13)

Gen 15:2 **E** of Damascus will inherit my
Exo 18:4 The name of the other was **E**
1Ch 7:8 **E**, Elioenai, Omri, Jeremoth,
15:24 and **E** blew trumpets in front of
23:15 sons were Gershom and **E**.
23:17 **E** had no other sons,
27:16 for the tribe of Reuben: **E**,
2Ch 20:37 Then **E**, son of Dodavahu from
Ezr 8:16 Then I sent for **E**, Ariel,
10:18 **E**, Jarib, and Gedaliah,
10:23 Pethahiah, Judah, and **E**
10:31 of Harim: **E**, Isshiah, Malchiah,
Luk 3:29 son of Joshua, son of **E**,

Eliezer's (3)

1Ch 23:17 **E** only son was Rehabiah.
26:25 From his relatives on **E** side of
26:25 (**E** son was Rehabiah;

eligible (16)

Num 1:3 everyone in Israel who is **e**
1:20 old and **e** for military duty.
1:22 old and **e** for military duty.
1:24 old and **e** for military duty.
1:26 old and **e** for military duty.
1:28 old and **e** for military duty.
1:30 old and **e** for military duty.
1:32 old and **e** for military duty.
1:34 old and **e** for military duty.
1:36 old and **e** for military duty.
1:38 old and **e** for military duty.
1:40 old and **e** for military duty.
1:42 old and **e** for military duty.
1:45 years old and **e** for military duty
8:24 Men 25 years old or older are **e**
26:2 old and **e** for military duty."

Elihba (1)

2Sm 23:32 **E** from Shaalbon,

Elihoreph (1)

1Ki 4:3 **E** and Ahijah, the sons of

Elihu (12)

1Sm 1:1 son of Jeroham, grandson of **E**,
1Ch 12:20 Jozabad, **E**, and Zillethai.
26:7 as well as **E** and Semachiah.
27:18 for the tribe of Judah: **E**,
Job 32:2 Then **E**, son of Barachel,
32:3 **E** was also very angry with
32:4 **E** waited as they spoke to Job
32:5 When **E** saw that the three men
32:6 So **E**, son of Barachel,
34:1 **E** continued to speak ⌊to Job
35:1 **E** continued to speak ⌊to Job
36:1 **E** continued to speak ⌊to Job⌋,

Elijah (121)

1Ki 17:1 **E**, who was from Tishbe but
17:2 the LORD spoke his word to **E**:
17:5 **E** left and did what the word of
17:8 the LORD spoke his word to **E**:
17:13 Then **E** told her, "Don't be
17:15 She did what **E** had told her.
17:15 So she, **E**, and her family had
17:16 LORD had promised through **E**.
17:18 The woman asked **E**,
17:19 **E** took him from her arms,
17:21 Then **E** stretched himself over
17:23 **E** took the child, brought him
17:24 The woman said to **E**,
18:1 the LORD spoke his word to **E**:
18:2 So **E** went to present himself to
18:7 on the road when he met **E**.
18:7 "Is it you, my master **E**?"
18:8 "Yes," **E** answered him.
18:8 your master that **E** is here."
18:11 'Tell your master that **E** is here.'
18:14 tell my master that **E** is here.
18:15 **E** said, "I solemnly swear,
18:16 Ahab went to meet **E**.
18:17 When he saw **E**, Ahab said,
18:18 **E** answered, "I haven't troubled
18:21 **E** stood up in front of all the
18:22 So **E** told the people,
18:25 **E** told the prophets of Baal,
18:27 At noon **E** started to make fun
18:30 Then **E** said to all the people,
18:31 **E** took 12 stones, one for each
18:32 **E** built an altar in the LORD's
18:36 the prophet **E** stepped forward.
18:40 **E** told them, "Seize the
18:40 The people seized them, and **E**
18:41 Then **E** told Ahab,
18:42 **E** went to the top of Carmel and
18:43 Seven times **E** told him,
18:44 **E** said, "Go and tell Ahab,
18:46 The LORD's power was on **E**.
19:1 Jezebel everything **E** had done,
19:2 Jezebel sent a messenger to **E**.
19:3 **E** fled to save his life.
19:9 the LORD spoke his word to **E**.
19:9 "What are you doing here, **E**?"
19:13 When **E** heard it, he wrapped
19:13 "What are you doing here, **E**?"
19:19 **E** found Elisha, son of Shaphat.
19:19 **E** took off his coat and put it on
19:20 the oxen, ran after **E**, and said,
19:20 "Go back," **E** answered him.
19:21 he left to follow and assist **E**.
21:17 his word to **E** from Tishbe:
21:20 Ahab asked **E**, "So you've
21:20 **E** answered, "I found you.
21:23 ⌊through **E**⌋ about Jezebel:
21:28 his word to **E** from Tishbe:
2Ki 1:3 LORD said to **E** from Tishbe,
1:4 you will die there."' Then **E** left.
1:8 "That's **E** from Tishbe,"
1:9 army officer with 50 men to **E**.
1:9 When the officer found **E** sitting
1:9 a hill, he told **E**, "Man of God,
1:10 **E** answered the officer,
1:11 officer with 50 men to **E**.
1:12 **E** answered the officer,
1:13 the hill and knelt in front of **E**.
1:15 The angel of the LORD told **E**,
1:15 So **E** got up and went with him
1:16 **E** told the king, "This is what
2Ki 1:17 LORD had predicted through **E**.
2:1 the LORD was going to take **E**
2:1 **E** and Elisha left Gilgal.
2:2 **E** said to Elisha, "Please stay
2:4 **E** said, "Elisha, please stay
2:6 **E** said to Elisha, "Please stay
2:7 stood at a distance as **E**
2:8 **E** took his coat, rolled it up,
2:9 were crossing, **E** asked Elisha,
2:10 **E** said, "You have asked for
2:11 and **E** went to heaven in a
2:12 he couldn't see **E** anymore,
2:13 coat (which had fallen off **E**),
2:14 is the LORD God of **E**?"
9:36 his servant **E** from Tishbe.
10:10 he said through his servant **E**."
10:17 as the LORD had told **E**.
1Ch 8:27 Jaareshiah, **E**, and Zichri.
2Ch 21:12 came to him from the prophet **E**
Ezr 10:21 **E**, Shemaiah, Jehiel,
10:26 Jehiel, Abdi, Jeremoth, and **E**
Mal 4:5 the prophet **E** before that very
Mat 11:14 John is the **E** who was to
16:14 are John the Baptizer, others **E**,
17:3 Suddenly, Moses and **E**
17:4 one for Moses, and one for **E**."
17:10 say that **E** must come first?"
17:11 Jesus answered, "**E** is coming
17:12 Actually, I can guarantee that **E**
27:47 they said, "He's calling **E**."
27:49 Let's see if **E** comes to save
Mar 6:15 Others said, "He is **E**."
8:28 are John the Baptizer, others **E**,
9:4 Then **E** and Moses appeared to
9:5 one for Moses, and one for **E**."
9:11 say that **E** must come first?"
9:12 Jesus said to them, "**E** is
9:13 can guarantee that **E** has come.
15:35 "Listen! He's calling **E**."
15:36 The man said, "Let's see if **E**
Luk 1:17 the spirit and power that **E** had.
4:26 But God didn't send **E** to
9:8 said that **E** had appeared,
9:19 are John the Baptizer, others **E**,
9:30 Suddenly, both Moses and **E**
9:33 As Moses and **E** were leaving
9:33 one for Moses, and one for **E**."
Jon 1:21 asked him, "Well, are you **E**?"
1:25 Messiah or **E** or the prophet?"
Rom 11:2 Don't you know what **E** says in
Jas 5:17 **E** was human like us.

Elijah's (5)

1Ki 17:22 The LORD heard **E** request,
2Ki 2:13 Then he picked up **E** coat
2:15 "**E** spirit rests on Elisha!"
3:11 He used to be **E** assistant.
Luk 4:25 widows in Israel in **E** time.

Elika (1)

2Sm 23:25 from Harod, **E** from Harod,

Elim (6)

Exo 15:27 Next, they went to **E**,
16:1 of Israelites moved from **E**
16:1 which is between **E** and Sinai.
Num 33:9 from Marah and came to **E**.
33:9 **E** had 12 springs and 70 palm
33:10 They moved from **E** and set up

Elimelech (4)

Rut 1:2 The man's name was **E**,
1:3 Now, Naomi's husband **E** died,
4:3 that belonged to our relative **E**.
4:9 Naomi all that belonged to **E**

Elimelech's (2)

Rut 2:1 He was from **E** side of the
2:3 who was from **E** family

eliminated (4)

Isa 10:13 I've **e** the boundaries of nations.
Rom 3:27 Bragging has been **e**.
3:27 On what basis was it **e**?
3:27 it is **e** on the basis of faith.

Elioenai (6)

1Ch 3:23 Neariah's three sons were **E**,
4:36 **E**, Jaakobah, Jeshohaiah,
7:8 **E**, Omri, Jeremoth, Abijah,
Ezr 10:22 **E**, Maaseiah, Ishmael,
10:27 Zattu: **E**, Eliashib, Mattaniah,
Neh 12:41 Micaiah, **E**, Zechariah,

Elioenai's (1)

1Ch 3:24 **E** seven sons were Hodaviah,

Eliphal (1)

1Ch 11:35 the Hararite), **E** (son of Ur),

Eliphaz (14)

Gen 36:4 Adah gave birth to **E** for Esau,
36:10 **E**, son of Esau's wife Adah,
36:11 The sons of **E** were Teman,
36:12 a concubine of Esau's son **E**.
36:12 She gave birth to Amalek for **E**.
36:15 The sons of **E**, Esau's firstborn,
36:16 descended from **E** in Edom.
1Ch 1:35 Esau's sons were **E**,
Job 2:11 from his home — **E** of Teman,
4:1 Then **E** from Teman replied ⌊to
15:1 Then **E** from Teman replied ⌊to
22:1 Then **E** from Teman replied ⌊to
42:7 LORD said to **E** from Teman,
42:9 Then **E** of Teman,

Eliphaz's (1)

1Ch 1:36 **E** sons were Teman and Omar,

Eliphelehu (2)

1Ch 15:18 Mattithiah, **E**, and Mikneiah.
15:21 Mattithiah, **E**, Mikneiah,

Eliphelet (8)

2Sm 5:16 Elishama, Eliada, and **E**.
23:34 **E** (son of Ahasbai and
1Ch 3:6 Ibhar, Elishama, **E**,
3:8 and **E** (nine ⌊by other wives⌋).
8:39 and **E** (the third son).
14:7 Elishama, Beeliada, and **E**.
Ezr 8:13 from the family of Adonikam: **E**,
10:33 Zabad, **E**, Jeremai, Manasseh,

Eli's (9)

1Sm 1:3 **E** two sons, Hophni and
2:12 **E** sons, ⌊Hophni and
2:15 But ⌊in the case of **E** sons,⌋
2:17 The sin of **E** sons was a
3:14 oath concerning **E** family line:
3:14 sins that **E** family committed."
4:4 **E** two sons, Hophni and
4:11 Both of **E** sons, Hophni and
1Ki 2:27 at Shiloh about **E** family

Elisha (104)

Num 10:22 **E**, son of Ammihud, was in
1Ki 19:16 And anoint **E**, son of Shaphat,
19:17 Jehu's sword, **E** will kill him.
19:19 Elijah found **E**, son of Shaphat.
19:19 **E** was plowing behind 12 pairs
19:19 took off his coat and put it on **E**.
19:20 So **E** left the oxen,
19:21 **E** left him, took two oxen,
2Ki 2:1 Elijah and **E** left Gilgal.
2:2 Elijah said to **E**, "Please stay
2:2 **E** answered, "I solemnly
2:3 prophets at Bethel came to **E**.
2:4 Elijah said, "**E**, please stay
2:4 **E** answered, "I solemnly
2:5 were in Jericho approached **E**.
2:6 Elijah said to **E**, "Please stay
2:6 **E** answered, "I solemnly
2:7 as Elijah and **E** stood by
2:9 were crossing, Elijah asked **E**,
2:9 **E** answered, "Let me inherit a
2:12 When **E** saw this, he cried out,
2:14 and **E** crossed ⌊the river⌋.
2:15 "Elijah's spirit rests on **E**!"
2:16 **E** answered, "Don't send them
2:18 They returned to **E** in Jericho,
2:19 of the city ⌊of Jericho⌋ told **E**,

2Ki 2:20 **E** said, "Bring me a new jar,
2:22 is still pure, as **E** had said.
3:11 "**E**, the son of Shaphat, is here.
3:12 the king of Edom went to **E**.
3:13 **E** asked the king of Israel,
3:14 **E** answered, "I solemnly
3:15 LORD's power came over **E**.
4:1 of the prophets called to **E**,
4:2 **E** asked her, "What should I do
4:3 **E** said, "Borrow many empty
4:8 One day **E** was traveling
4:13 **E** said to Gehazi, "Ask her
4:14 **E** asked. Gehazi answered,
4:15 **E** said, "Call her." So Gehazi
4:16 **E** said, "At this time next
4:17 next year, as **E** had told her.
4:30 So **E** got up and followed her.
4:32 When **E** came to the house,
4:35 **E** got up, walked across the
4:36 **E** called Gehazi and said,
4:38 When **E** went back to Gilgal,
4:41 **E** said, "Bring some flour."
5:8 But when **E**, the man of God,
5:10 **E** sent a messenger to him.
5:15 stood in front of **E** and said,
5:16 **E** said, "I solemnly swear,
5:19 **E** told Naaman, "Go in peace."
5:19 After **E** had left him and gone
5:20 Gehazi, the servant of **E** (the
5:25 **E** asked him, "Where were
5:26 Then **E** said to him,
5:27 When he left **E**, Gehazi had a
6:1 of the prophets said to **E**,
6:2 **E** said, "Go ahead."
6:3 **E** answered, "I'll go."
6:6 When he showed **E** the place,
6:6 **E** cut off a piece of wood.
6:7 **E** said, "Pick it up."
6:10 **E** warned them so that they
6:12 **E**, the prophet in Israel,
6:16 **E** answered, "Don't be afraid.
6:17 Then **E** prayed, "LORD,
6:17 The mountain around **E** was
6:18 **E** prayed to the LORD,
6:18 blindness, as **E** had asked.
6:19 **E** told them, "This isn't the
6:20 into Samaria, **E** said, "LORD,
6:21 them, he asked **E**, "Master,
6:22 **E** answered, "Don't kill them.
6:31 strike me dead if the head of **E**,
6:32 **E** was sitting in his home with
6:32 **E** asked the leaders,
6:33 He said to **E**, "This severe
7:1 **E** answered, "Listen to the
7:2 **E** replied, "You will see it with
7:19 **E** answered, "You will see it
8:1 **E** had told the woman whose
8:4 the great things **E** has done."
8:5 telling the king how **E** brought
8:5 and this is her son whom **E**
8:7 **E** went to Damascus.
8:9 Hazael went to meet **E**.
8:9 He stood in front of **E** and said,
8:10 **E** replied, "Tell him that he will
8:12 **E** answered, "I know the evil
8:13 **E** answered, "The LORD has
8:14 Hazael left **E** and went to his
8:14 asked him what **E** had said.
9:1 The prophet **E** called one of the
13:14 **E** became fatally ill.
13:15 **E** told him, "Get a bow and
13:16 Then **E** told the king of Israel,
13:16 **E** laid his hands on the king's
13:17 **E** said, "Open the window that
13:17 "Shoot," **E** said, and the king
13:17 Then **E** said, "That is the arrow
13:18 Then **E** said, "Take the
13:20 **E** died and was buried.

Elishah (3)

Gen 10:4 were the people from **E**,
1Ch 1:7 were the people from **E**,
Eze 27:7 came from the coasts of **E**.

Elishama (16)

Num 1:10 **E**, son of Ammihud, from the
2:18 for the people of Ephraim is **E**,
7:48 Ephraim, **E**, son of Ammihud,
7:53 These were the gifts from **E**,
2Sm 5:16 **E**, Eliada, and Eliphelet.
2Ki 25:25 Nethaniah and grandson of **E**,
1Ch 2:41 Jekamiah was the father of **E**.
3:6 Ibhar, **E**, Eliphelet,
3:8 **E**, Eliada, and Eliphelet (nine
7:26 Ammihud's son was **E**.
14:7 **E**, Beeliada, and Eliphelet.
2Ch 17:8 and the priests **E** and Jehoram.
Jer 36:12 The scribe **E**, Delaiah (son of
36:20 in the side room of the scribe **E**,
36:21 the side room of the scribe **E**.
41:1 Nethaniah and grandson of **E**,

Elishama's (1)

1Ch 7:27 **E** son was Nun. Nun's son was

Elishaphat (1)

2Ch 23:1 of Adaiah, and **E**, son of Zichri.

Elisha's (7)

2Ki 4:32 dead boy was lying on **E** bed
5:9 at the entrance to **E** home
6:15 **E** servant asked, "Master,
6:32 ahead of him to **E** house.
13:21 put the man into **E** tomb.
13:21 the body touched **E** bones,
Luk 4:27 in Israel in the prophet **E** time.

Elisheba (1)

Exo 6:23 Aaron married **E**, daughter of

Elishua (2)

2Sm 5:15 Ibhar, **E**, Nepheg, Japhia,
1Ch 14:5 Ibhar, **E**, Elpelet,

elite (2)

2Sm 10:7 he sent Joab and all the **e**
1Ch 19:8 he sent Joab and all the **e**

Eliud (2)

Mat 1:14 Achim the father of **E**,
1:15 **E** the father of Eleazar,

Elizabeth (12)

Luk 1:5 Zechariah's wife **E** was a
1:6 Zechariah and **E** had God's
1:7 **E** couldn't become pregnant.
1:13 Your wife **E** will have a son,
1:24 Later, his wife **E** became
1:26 Six months after **E** had
1:36 "**E**, your relative, is six months
1:40 home and greeted **E**.
1:41 When **E** heard the greeting,
1:41 **E** was filled with the Holy
1:56 Mary stayed with **E** about three
1:57 When the time came for **E** to

Elizaphan (2)

Num 3:30 and households was **E**,
34:25 **E**, son of Parnach, the leader of

Elizaphan's (2)

1Ch 15:8 Leading **E** descendants was
2Ch 29:13 From **E** descendants were

Elizur (5)

Num 1:5 help you: **E**, son of Shedeur,
2:10 for the people of Reuben is **E**,
7:30 of Reuben, **E**, son of Shedeur,
7:35 These were the gifts from **E**,
10:18 **E**, son of Shedeur, was in

Elkanah (21)

Exo 6:24 were Assir, **E**, and Abiasaph.
1Sm 1:1 There was a man named **E**
1:2 **E** had two wives, one named
1:4 Whenever **E** offered a sacrifice,
1:8 Her husband **E** would ask her,
1:19 Early in the morning **E** and his
1:19 **E** made love to his wife
1:21 To keep his vow, the man **E**
1:23 her husband **E** told her.
2:11 Then **E** went home to Ramah.
1Sm 2:20 Eli would bless **E** (and his
1Ch 6:23 Assir's son was **E**.
6:26 Ahimoth's son was **E**.
6:27 Jeroham's son was **E**.
6:34 who was the son of **E**,
6:35 who was the son of **E**,
6:36 who was the son of **E**,
9:16 (son of Asa and grandson of **E**,
12:6 **E**, Isshiah, Azarel, Joezer,
15:23 Berechiah and **E** were
2Ch 28:7 in charge of the palace, and **E**,

Elkanah's (3)

1Ch 6:23 **E** son was Ebiasaph.
6:25 **E** sons were Amasai and
6:26 **E** son was Zophai.

Elkosh (1)

Nah 1:1 the vision of Nahum from **E**.

Ellasar (2)

Gen 14:1 of Shinar, King Arioch of **E**,
14:9 and King Arioch of **E** — four

Elmadam (1)

Luk 3:28 of Cosam, son of **E**, son of Er,

Elnaam (1)

1Ch 11:46 and Joshaviah (sons of **E**),

Elnathan (7)

2Ki 24:8 daughter of **E** from Jerusalem.
Ezr 8:16 **E**, Jarib, Elnathan, Nathan,
8:16 Jarib, **E**, Nathan, Zechariah,
8:16 Joiarib and **E** (who were wise).
Jer 26:22 **E** (son of Achbor) and other
36:12 Shemaiah), **E** (son of Achbor),
36:25 Even when **E**, Delaiah,

Eloi (2)

Mar 15:34 "**E**, Eloi, lema sabachthani?"
15:34 "Eloi, **E**, lema sabachthani?"

Elon (8)

Gen 26:34 daughter of **E** the Hittite.
36:2 daughter of **E** the Hittite;
46:14 were Sered, **E**, and Jahleel.
Num 26:26 family of Sered, the family of **E**,
Jos 19:43 **E**, Timnah, Ekron,
Jdg 12:11 After Ibzan, **E** from the tribe of
12:12 When **E** died, he was buried in
12:13 After **E**, Abdon, son of Hillel,

Elon Beth Hanan (1)

1Ki 4:9 Shaalbim, Beth Shemesh, and **E**

eloquent (1)

Act 18:24 He was an **e** speaker and

Elpaal (1)

1Ch 8:11 the parents of Abitub and **E**.

Elpaal's (2)

1Ch 8:12 **E** sons were Eber,
8:17 **E** sons were Zebadiah,

El Paran (1)

Gen 14:6 as far as **E** on the edge of the

Elpelet (1)

1Ch 14:5 Ibhar, Elishua, **E**,

Eltekeh (2)

Jos 19:44 **E**, Gibbethon, Baalath,
21:23 them four cities: **E**, Gibbethon,

Eltekon (1)

Jos 15:59 Maarath, Bethanoth, and **E**

Eltolad (2)

Jos 15:30 **E**, Chesil, Hormah,
19:4 **E**, Bethul, Hormah,

Elul (1)

Neh 6:15 day of the month of **E**.

Eluzai (1)
1Ch 12:5 E, Jerimoth, Bealiah,

Elymas (3)
Act 13:8 E, whose name means
13:9 the Holy Spirit. He stared at E
13:11 E couldn't see a thing.

Elzabad (2)
1Ch 12:12 Johanan. The ninth was E.
26:7 brothers Rephael, Obed, E,

Elzaphan (2)
Exo 6:22 were Mishael, E, and Sithri.
Lev 10:4 Moses called Mishael and E,

embalm (1)
Gen 50:2 in his service to e his father.

embalmed (2)
Gen 50:2 So the doctors e Israel.
50:26 His body was e and placed in

embalming (2)
Gen 37:25 for cosmetics, medicine, and e.
50:3 The e was completed in the

embankments (1)
Psa 48:13 Examine its e. Walk through its

embarrass (3)
1Co 11:22 church and e people who don't
2Co 9:4 This would e us for feeling so
9:4 as much as it would e you.

embarrassed (6)
2Ki 2:17 send the men⌋ until he was e.
8:11 at him until he became e.
Ezr 9:6 I am e to look at you.
Isa 1:29 wanted to worship and e by
24:23 The moon will be e.
Luk 14:9 E, you would have to take the

embarrassing (1)
Pro 23:33 and your mouth will say e

emblems (1)
Psa 74:4 set up their own e as symbols.

embrace (1)
Pro 4:8 bring you honor when you e it.

embroider (2)
Exo 35:35 They know how to e violet,
38:23 and he knew how to e violet,

embroidered (15)
Exo 26:36 linen yarn, e with violet, purple,
27:16 linen yarn, e with violet, purple,
28:39 should be e with colored yarn.
36:37 It was e with violet,
38:18 and bright red yarn e on ⌊fabric
39:29 The belt was e with violet,
Jdg 5:30 for Sisera, colorful, e clothes,
5:30 e cloth for the neck of the
Psa 45:13 Her dress is e with gold.
Eze 16:10 I put an e dress on you and fine
16:13 fine linen, silk, and e clothes.
16:18 You took off your e clothes and
26:16 and take off their e clothes.
27:7 out of fine e linen from Egypt.
27:24 clothes, purple robes, e cloth,

Emek Keziz (1)
Jos 18:21 families: Jericho, Beth Hoglah, E

emerald (6)
Exo 28:17 put red quartz, topaz, and e.
39:10 put red quartz, topaz, and e.
Sos 5:14 are disks of gold set with e.
Eze 28:13 sapphire, turquoise, and e.
Rev 4:3 throne which looked like an e.
21:19 the third agate, the fourth e,

emeralds (1)
Eze 27:16 They exchanged e,

Emim (1)
Gen 14:5 the E at Shaveh Kiriathaim,

emission (5)
Lev 15:16 "If a man has an e of semen,
15:18 woman and has an e of semen,
15:32 who has a discharge or an e
22:4 Any person who has an e of
Dtr 23:10 unclean from a nocturnal e,

Emites (2)
Dtr 2:10 The E used to live there.
2:11 but the Moabites called them E.

Emmaus (1)
Luk 24:13 going to a village called E.

emotions (8)
Gen 43:31 He was in control of his e
45:1 could no longer control his e
Job 15:12 Why have your e carried you
Psa 7:9 who examines thoughts and e.
Pro 29:11 A fool expresses all his e,
2Co 6:12 Your own e have cut you off
Php 3:19 Their own e are their god,
4:7 and e through Christ Jesus.

emperor (31)
Mat 22:17 to pay taxes to the e or not?"
22:21 give the e what belongs to the
22:21 emperor what belongs to the e,
Mar 12:14 to pay taxes to the e or not?
12:17 Jesus said to them, "Give the e
12:17 emperor what belongs to the e,
Luk 2:1 At that time the E Augustus
3:1 in the reign of the E Tiberius.
20:22 to pay taxes to the e or not?"
20:25 then give the e what belongs to
20:25 emperor what belongs to the e,
23:2 from paying taxes to the e,
Jon 19:12 you're not a friend of the e.
19:12 to be a king is defying the e."
19:15 "The e is the only king we
Act 11:28 while Claudius was e.
25:8 against the temple or the e."
25:11 I appeal my case to the e!"
25:12 appealed your case to the e,
25:12 so you'll go to the e!"
25:21 Majesty the E decide his case.
25:21 until I could send him to the e."
25:25 an appeal to His Majesty the E,
25:26 to write our e about him.
26:32 appealed his case to the e."
27:24 present your case to the e.
28:19 to appeal my case to the e.
Php 1:13 all the soldiers who guard the e
1Pe 2:13 Obey the e. He holds the
2:14 They are people the e has sent
2:17 Fear God. Honor the e.

emperor's (7)
Mat 22:21 They replied, "The e." Then
Mar 12:16 They told him, "The e."
Luk 20:24 They answered, "The e."
Act 17:7 the e decrees by saying that
25:10 "I am standing in the e court
27:1 he belonged to the e division
Php 4:22 in the e palace, greet you.

emphasize (1)
2Co 2:5 I don't want to e this too much

emphasized (1)
Jon 10:7 Jesus e, "I can guarantee this

empire (9)
2Ch 36:20 the Persian E began to rule.
Ezr 7:23 with the king's e and his sons?
Psa 103:22 in all the places of his e.
145:13 Your e endures throughout
Dan 11:3 He will rule a vast e and do as
11:4 The e will not be given to his
Dan 11:4 It will no longer be like his e,
11:5 than he is and rule a vast e.
Luk 2:1 a census of the Roman E.

emptied (3)
Gen 24:20 So she quickly e her jar into
Isa 19:6 Egypt's streams will be e and
Php 2:7 Instead, he e himself by taking

empty (38)
Gen 1:2 The earth was formless and e,
37:24 and put him into an e cistern.
41:27 The seven e heads of grain
Rut 1:21 LORD has brought me back e.
1Sm 6:3 don't send it away e,
20:18 be missed when your seat is e.
20:25 but David's place was e.
20:27 David's place was still e.
1Ki 17:14 the jar of flour will never be e
17:16 The jar of flour never became e,
2Ki 4:3 Elisha said, "Borrow many e
2Ch 24:11 the chief priest's officer would e
Job 3:7 Let that night be e.
11:3 Should your e talk silence
26:7 out his heavens over e space.
Psa 4:2 are you going to love what is e
69:25 be deserted and their tents e.
75:8 He will e it, ⌊and⌋ all the
Pro 13:25 of wicked people are always e.
14:4 the feeding trough is e,
Ecc 5:7 pointless actions, and e words,
Isa 5:9 "Many houses will become e.
5:18 along with lies and e promises,
19:5 and the river will be dry and e.
45:18 He did not create it to be e but
Jer 4:23 It's formless and e.
14:3 back with their containers e.
51:34 He has turned us into e jars.
Eze 6:10 I promised was not an e threat.
24:6 E the meat out of it piece by
24:11 Then set the e pot on the coals
36:4 and to the e ruins and
36:34 It will no longer remain e for
36:35 They were e and ruined,
36:36 crops in the land that was e.
Hab 3:17 even if the sheep pen is e and
Luk 24:24 went to the tomb and found it e,
1Jn 3:18 not through e words.

empty-handed (6)
Gen 31:42 have sent me away e by now.
Exo 3:21 you will not leave e.
Dtr 15:13 don't send them away e.
Rut 3:17 me not to come back to you e."
Job 22:9 You send widows away e,
Jer 50:9 who don't come back e.

empty-headed (1)
Job 11:12 But an e person will gain

emptying (2)
Gen 42:35 As they were e their sacks,
Hab 1:17 Will they keep on e their nets

enable (4)
1Ch 29:14 who are my people that you e
Psa 4:8 e me to live securely.
Eze 36:27 I will e you to live by my laws,
Jon 7:51 "Do Moses' Teachings e us to

enabled (4)
Jon 5:26 and he has e the Son to be the
Act 18:27 God's kindness e him to help
Heb 11:5 Faith e Enoch to be taken
11:11 Faith e Abraham to become a

Enaim (2)
Gen 38:14 sat down at the entrance to E,
38:21 was beside the road at E?"

Enam (1)
Jos 15:34 En Gannim, Tappuah, E,

Enan (5)
Num 1:15 Ahira, son of E, from the tribe of
2:29 of Naphtali is Ahira, son of E.

Num 7:78 of Naphtali, Ahira, son of **E**,
7:83 the gifts from Ahira, son of **E**.
10:27 Ahira, son of **E**,

enchant (1)
Sos 6:5 They **e** me! Your hair is like a

encircle (1)
Job 16:16 and dark shadows **e** my eyes,

encircled (2)
Psa 22:12 bulls from Bashan have **e** me.
22:16 A mob has **e** me. They have

enclosed (2)
Est 1:5 This banquet was held in the **e**
Sos 7:2 is a bundle of wheat **e** in lilies.

encourage (42)
Gen 23:8 **E** Ephron, son of Zohar,
Dtr 1:38 **E** him, because he will help
3:28 **E** and strengthen him,
2Sm 11:25 Say this to **e** him."
19:7 get up, go out, and **e** your men.
Job 16:5 I could **e** you with my mouth,
Psa 10:17 You **e** them. You pay close
64:5 They **e** one another in their evil
Isa 41:7 Craftsmen **e** goldsmiths.
41:7 Metalsmiths **e** blacksmiths
50:4 know how to **e** weary people.
Act 15:32 spoke a long time to **e** and
Rom 12:1 I **e** you to offer your bodies as
15:30 Brothers and sisters, I **e** you
1Co 1:10 Brothers and sisters, I **e** all of
4:16 So I **e** you to imitate me.
14:3 to **e** them, and to comfort them.
16:15 So I **e** you, brothers and
2Co 9:5 So I thought that I should **e** our
Eph 4:1 I, a prisoner in the Lord, **e** you
4:17 So I tell you and **e** you in the
6:22 doing and that he may **e** you.
Php 4:2 I **e** both Euodia and Syntyche
Col 4:8 and so that he may **e** you.
1Th 3:2 was to strengthen and **e** you
4:1 Lord Jesus we ask and **e** you
4:10 We **e** you as believers to excel
5:11 Therefore, **e** each other and
5:14 We **e** you, brothers and sisters,
2Th 2:17 may he **e** and strengthen you to
3:12 We order and **e** such people by
1Ti 2:1 I **e** you to make petitions,
6:2 Teach and **e** people to do
2Ti 4:2 warn people, and **e** them.
Tit 1:9 accurate teachings to **e** people
2:6 **E** young men to use good
2:15 **E** and correct them,
Heb 3:13 **E** each other every day while
10:24 consider how to **e** each other
10:25 Instead, we must continue to **e**
1Pe 5:12 I've written to **e** you and to
Jud 1:3 that I write to you and **e** you

encouraged (29)
Exo 32:21 do to you that you **e** them
1Sm 22:8 my son has **e** my servant David
2Ch 15:8 he was **e** and put away the
32:8 So the people were **e** by what
35:2 to their duties and **e** them
Ezr 7:28 I was **e** because the LORD my
Neh 2:18 So they **e** one another to begin
Ecc 8:11 people are **e** to commit crimes.
Jer 28:16 you have **e** rebellion against
29:32 because he has **e** rebellion
Eze 13:22 You **e** wicked people not to
Mal 3:15 Not only are evildoers **e**,
Act 11:23 So he **e** all the people to
14:22 disciples in these cities and **e**
16:40 believers, **e** them, and then left.
18:27 believers ⌊in Ephesus⌋ **e** him.
20:1 **e** them, said goodbye,
27:36 Everyone was **e** and had
28:15 he thanked God and felt **e**.
Rom 1:12 we may be **e** by each other's
1Co 14:31 everyone will learn and be **e**.
2Co 7:4 I'm **e** and feel very happy.
12:18 I **e** Titus to visit you,
Col 2:2 I work so that they may be **e**
1Th 2:3 When we **e** you, we didn't use
2:11 We comforted you and **e** you.
3:7 your faith has **e** us in all our
1Ti 1:3 I **e** you to stay in the city of
Heb 6:18 did this so that we would be **e**.

encouragement (11)
2Ch 32:6 He spoke these words of **e**:
Act 13:15 if you have any words of **e** for
15:31 with the **e** it brought them.
20:2 and spoke many words of **e**
Rom 12:8 devote yourself to giving **e**.
15:4 the endurance and **e** which
15:5 you this endurance and **e**,
2Co 13:11 Accept my **e**. Share the same
Php 2:1 do you have any **e**?
2Th 2:16 kindness gave us everlasting **e**
Phm 1:7 gives me a lot of joy and **e**.

encourages (3)
Act 4:36 means "a person who **e**."
1Co 10:23 but not everything **e** growth.
Gal 2:17 does that mean that Christ **e** us

encouraging (13)
2Ch 30:22 Hezekiah spoke **e** words to all
Pro 12:25 but an **e** word makes him
Luk 3:18 With many other **e** words,
Act 27:33 daybreak Paul was **e** everyone
27:34 So I'm **e** you to eat something.
Rom 12:8 If it is **e** others, devote yourself
1Co 8:10 Won't you be **e** that person to
Php 2:19 some **e** news about you.
1Ti 4:13 giving **e** messages,
Heb 12:5 You have forgotten the **e** words
13:22 listen patiently to my **e** words.
1Pe 2:11 I'm **e** you to keep away from
Rev 2:14 people of Israel by ⌊**e**⌋ them

end (249)
Gen 6:13 "I have decided to put an **e** to
8:3 At the **e** of 150 days the water
23:9 that he owns at the **e**
29:21 ⌊At the **e** of the seven years⌋
41:53 of food in Egypt came to an **e**.
Exo 23:16 of the Final Harvest at the **e**
25:19 one on each **e**. Form the angels
26:4 along the edge of the **e** sheet
26:10 along the edge of the **e** sheet
26:22 Make six frames for the far **e**,
26:23 of⌊ the corners at the far **e**
26:27 five for the frames on the far **e**
26:28 crossbar will run from one **e**
27:12 "The courtyard on the west **e**
27:13 On the east **e**, facing the rising
32:27 Go back and forth from one **e** of
34:16 Then your sons will **e** up
34:22 Harvest at the **e** of the season.
36:11 along the edge of the **e** sheet
36:17 along the edge of the **e** sheet
36:27 made six frames for the far **e**,
36:28 of⌊ the corners at the far **e**
36:33 so that it ran from one **e**
37:8 one on each **e**. He formed the
Num 14:35 They will meet their **e** in this
23:10 Let my **e** be like theirs."
24:20 but in the **e** it will be
34:3 border starts from the **e**
Dtr 4:32 Search from one **e** of heaven to
8:16 would go well for you in the **e**.
9:11 At the **e** of the 40 days and 40
13:7 from one **e** of the land to the
14:28 At the **e** of every third year
15:1 At the **e** of every seven years,
28:64 from one **e** of the earth to the
31:10 "At the **e** of every seventh year
Jos 13:1 near the **e** of his life.
13:1 near the **e** of your life,
13:27 extending to the **e** of the Sea of
15:2 border starts from the south **e**
15:5 border starts from the north **e**
15:8 to the west at the north **e**
18:16 in the north **e** of the valley of
18:19 of the Dead Sea at the south **e**
23:1 near the **e** of his life.
Jos 23:2 near the **e** of my life.
Jdg 11:39 At the **e** of those two months
1Sm 3:12 I said from beginning to **e**.
25:26 to harm you **e** up like Nabal.
2Sm 2:26 know this will **e** in bitterness?
14:26 At the **e** of every year,
2Ki 8:3 At the **e** of seven years,
10:21 filled it from one **e** to the other.
18:10 and captured it at the **e** of three
21:16 of innocent people from one **e**
2Ch 20:16 You will find them at the **e** of
21:19 as his life was coming to an **e**,
24:23 At the **e** of the year,
25:26 from beginning to **e**,
26:22 from beginning to **e**,
28:26 from beginning to **e** —
34:25 and will never come to an **e**.'"
Ezr 9:11 from one **e** to another.
Neh 3:21 to the **e** of Eliashib's house.
4:11 and bring the work to an **e**."
Est 7:7 that the king had a terrible **e**
Job 4:15 It made my hair stand on **e**.
16:3 speeches never **e**?
18:2 long before your words will **e**?
22:5 there no **e** to your wrongdoing?
28:3 ⌊Humans⌋ bring an **e** to
31:40 This is the **e** of Job's words.
Psa 1:6 way of wicked people will **e**.
7:9 wicked people come to an **e**,
19:6 It rises from one **e** of the
23:6 house for days without **e**.
39:4 about the **e** of my life.
40:14 Let all those who seek to **e** my
46:9 He puts an **e** to wars all over
49:10 stupid people meet the same **e**.
71:13 me come to a shameful **e**.
72:20 by David, son of Jesse, **e** here.
73:24 and in the **e** you will take me to
77:8 mercy come to an **e** forever?
78:33 He brought their days to an **e**
78:33 their years to an **e** in terror.
85:4 Put an **e** to your anger against
89:44 You put an **e** to his splendor
93:5 beautiful for days without **e**.
102:26 They will come to an **e**,
102:27 and your life will never **e**.
112:8 In the **e** he will look
115:8 Those who make idols **e** up
119:33 and I will obey them to the **e**.
135:18 Those who make idols **e** up
146:4 day their plans come to an **e**.
Pro 5:4 but in the **e** she is as bitter as
5:11 will groan when your **e** comes,
14:13 and joy can **e** in grief.
20:13 sleep or you will **e** up poor.
20:21 will never be blessed in the **e**.
25:8 What will you do in the **e** if
30:4 has set up the earth from one **e**
Ecc 3:11 beginning to the **e** ⌊of time⌋.
4:8 So there is no **e** to all the hard
4:16 There was no **e** to all those
7:2 is where everyone will **e** up.
7:8 The **e** of something is better
Isa 1:28 the LORD will come to an **e**.
2:7 and there is no **e** to their
2:7 there is no **e** to their chariots.
7:3 Jashub to meet Ahaz at the **e**
10:7 and put an **e** to many nations.
11:13 opponents will come to an **e**.
13:11 I will put an **e** to arrogant
14:4 the tyrant has come to an **e**!
14:4 his attacks have come to an **e**!"
16:4 people will come to an **e**.
16:4 The destruction will **e**.
16:10 because I have put an **e** to the
21:2 I will put an **e** to all the
23:15 At the **e** of the 70 years,
23:17 At the **e** of 70 years the LORD
29:20 to do wrong will come to an **e**:
41:4 and I will be there to the **e**.
46:10 the beginning I revealed the **e**.
47:7 in mind how they would **e**.
66:17 "They will come to an **e** at the
Jer 5:31 But what will you do in the **e**?"
12:12 destroys them from one **e**
14:15 bring an **e** to these prophets.

Jer 16:4 famines will bring them to an **e**.
17:11 In the **e**, he will be a godless
25:33 LORD will stretch from one **e**
27:8 until I have put an **e** to them by
44:12 be brought to an **e** by famines.
49:37 them until I put an **e** to them.
51:13 but your **e** has come.
51:64 The words of Jeremiah **e** here.
Lam 4:18 Our **e** was near. Our time was
4:18 time was up. Our **e** had come.
4:22 for your wickedness will **e**.
Eze 7:2 land of Israel: The **e** is coming!
7:2 The **e** is coming to the four
7:3 Now the **e** is coming for you.
7:6 The **e** is coming. The end is
7:6 The **e** is coming. It is stirring
16:41 I will put an **e** to your
22:4 You have brought an **e** to your
22:4 and you have come to the **e** of
22:15 put an **e** to your uncleanness.
26:18 Your **e** will terrify the islands in
27:36 You have come to a terrible **e**,
28:19 You have come to a terrible **e**,
30:10 Babylon to bring an **e** to Egypt.
30:13 the statues and put an **e**
39:14 At the **e** of seven months they
41:4 he measured the room at the **e**
41:12 At the far **e** of the open area,
42:12 was a doorway at the other **e**
Dan 1:18 At the **e** of the three-year
2:44 kingdoms and put an **e** to them.
4:34 At the **e** of the seven time
5:26 and will bring it to an **e**.
6:26 power lasts to the **e** ⌊of time⌋.
7:28 Here is the **e** of the matter.
8:17 the vision is about the **e** times."
8:19 because the **e** time has been
9:24 serve to bring an **e** to rebellion,
9:26 His **e** will come with a flood
9:26 come with a flood until the **e**
9:27 time periods⌋ come to an **e**.
11:27 because the **e** must wait until
11:35 them white until the **e** times.
11:40 "In the **e** times the southern
11:45 When he comes to his **e**,
12:4 seal the book until the **e** times.
12:8 how will these things **e**?"
12:9 and sealed until the **e** times.
12:13 But go on until the **e**.
12:13 inheritance at the **e** of time."
Hos 1:4 Then I will put an **e** to the
2:11 I will put an **e** to all her
11:6 and put an **e** to their plans.
Amo 8:10 and its **e** will be bitter.
Nah 1:8 He will put an **e** to Nineveh
1:9 who will bring Nineveh to an **e**.
2:9 There is no **e** to what is stored
3:3 There is no **e** to the corpses!
Zep 1:2 of the earth and put an **e** to it,"
1:3 "I will put an **e** to humans and
1:3 I will put an **e** to the birds in the
1:18 because he will put an **e**,
1:18 will put an end, a frightening **e**,
Mat 4:2 At the **e** of that time,
10:22 endures to the **e** will be saved.
12:45 In the **e** the condition of that
13:39 The harvest is the **e** of the
13:40 so it will be at the **e** of time.
13:49 will happen at the **e** of time.
20:8 and **e** with the first.'
24:3 will the world come to an **e**?
24:6 don't mean that the **e** has come.
24:8 the beginning pains ⌊of the **e**⌋.
24:13 endures to the **e** will be saved.
24:14 Then the **e** will come.
25:1 "When the **e** comes,
28:20 with you until the **e** of time."
Mar 3:26 That will be the **e** of him.
13:4 all this will come to an **e**?"
13:7 don't mean that the **e** has come.
13:8 the beginning pains ⌊of the **e**⌋.
13:13 endures to the **e** will be saved.
Luk 1:33 and his kingdom will never **e**."
9:12 Toward the **e** of the day,
11:26 In the **e** the condition of that
16:28 them so that they won't **e** up
17:24 that flashes from one **e**
21:9 but the **e** will not come
Jon 13:1 and he loved them to the **e**.
Rom 6:6 crucified with him to put an **e**
1Co 1:8 strength until the **e** so that no
6:13 but God will put an **e** to both of
13:8 Love never comes to an **e**.
15:24 Then the **e** will come.
2Co 5:4 Then ⌊eternal⌋ life will put an **e**
11:15 In the **e** they will get what they
Gal 3:3 way only to **e** up doing things
Eph 2:15 He brought an **e** to the
Php 3:19 In the **e** they will be destroyed.
2Th 2:8 will put an **e** to this man.
2Ti 4:6 My life is coming to an **e**,
Heb 1:11 They will come to an **e**,
1:12 and your life will never **e**.
2:10 to the **e** of his work through
3:14 original confidence until the **e**.
6:8 In the **e** it will be burned.
6:11 remain confident until the **e**.
6:16 they say and **e** all arguments.
9:26 But now, at the **e** of the ages,
1Pe 1:5 to be revealed at the **e** of time.
4:7 The **e** of everything is near.
4:17 what will be the **e** for those
1Jn 2:18 Children, it's the **e** of time.
2:18 how we know it's the **e** of time.
Rev 2:26 to do what I want until the **e**.
15:8 the seven angels came to an **e**.
21:6 the beginning and the **e**.
22:13 the beginning and the **e**.

endanger (1)

Lev 19:16 Never **e** your neighbor's life.

ended (17)

Gen 44:12 He began with the oldest and **e**
Rut 1:18 she **e** the conversation.
2:3 Now it happened that she **e** up
2:23 and the wheat harvest **e**.
2Sm 22:38 return until I had **e** their lives.
22:39 I **e** their lives by shattering
Psa 18:37 return until I had **e** their lives.
Isa 26:20 little while until his fury has **e**.
38:12 You **e** my life in one day.
38:13 You **e** my life in one day.
Jer 8:20 the summer has **e**,
Luk 22:45 When Jesus **e** his prayer,
Act 21:7 Our sea travel **e** when we
Rom 6:21 to do because it **e** in death.
Jas 5:11 You saw that the Lord **e** Job's
1Pe 2:8 this is how they **e** up.
Rev 20:5 not live until the 1,000 years **e**.

endless (16)

Neh 9:19 because of your **e** compassion,
9:27 because of your **e** compassion.
9:31 But your compassion is **e**.
Job 6:10 be happy despite my **e** pain,
15:2 person answer with **e** details
33:19 they are disciplined with **e**
Psa 119:20 My soul is overwhelmed with **e**
Dan 7:9 who has lived for **e** years,
7:13 who has lived for **e** years,
7:22 who has lived for **e** years,
Mic 6:7 of rams or with **e** streams
Nah 3:9 and Egypt were her **e** strength.
3:19 hasn't suffered from your **e**
Rom 9:2 I have deep sorrow and **e**
Col 2:18 gives **e** details of the visions
1Ti 1:4 with myths and **e** genealogies.

En Dor (1)

Jos 17:11 living in Dor, **E**, Taanach,

Endor (2)

1Sm 28:7 "There is a woman at **E** who
Psa 83:10 They were destroyed at **E**.

ends (75)

Exo 25:18 of hammered gold for the two **e**
28:25 Fasten the other **e** of the ropes
37:7 of hammered gold for the two **e**
39:18 They fastened the other **e** of
Num 34:4 It then goes past Zin and **e** at
34:5 of Egypt so that the border **e** at
34:8 of Hamath so that it **e** at Zedad.
34:9 to Ziphron and **e** at Hazar Enan.
34:12 the Jordan River so that it **e** at
Dtr 28:49 from the **e** of the earth.
33:17 nations including those at the **e**
Jos 15:4 of Egypt so that the border **e** at
15:7 Shemesh and **e** at En Rogel.
15:11 The border **e** at the
16:3 and **e** at the Mediterranean Sea.
16:7 and **e** at the Jordan River.
16:8 along the Kanah River and **e** at
17:9 which **e** at the Mediterranean
18:12 and **e** at the desert of Beth
18:14 and **e** at Kiriath Baal (now
18:19 slope of Beth Hoglah and **e** at
19:14 north to Hannathon and **e** at
19:22 and Beth Shemesh and **e** at the
19:29 then turns to Hosah and **e** at
19:33 and **e** at the Jordan River.
1Sm 2:10 The LORD judges the **e** of the
1Ki 8:8 were so long that their **e** could
2Ch 5:9 were so long that their **e** could
Job 28:24 because he can see to the **e** of
37:3 flashes to the **e** of the earth.
Psa 2:8 as your inheritance and the **e**
19:4 their message to the **e** of the
22:27 All the **e** of the earth will
48:10 your praise ⌊reaches⌋ to the **e**
59:13 that God rules Jacob to the **e**
61:2 From the **e** of the earth,
65:5 the hope of all the **e** of the earth
65:8 Those who live at the **e** of the
67:7 and may all the **e** of the earth
72:8 River to the **e** of the earth.
98:3 All the **e** of the earth have seen
119:112 offer a reward that never **e**.
135:7 the clouds rise from the **e**
Pro 11:23 of righteous people **e** only
11:23 of wicked people **e** only in fury.
14:12 but eventually it **e** in death.
16:25 but eventually it **e** in death.
18:18 Flipping a coin **e** quarrels and
21:5 in a hurry **e** up in poverty.
Ecc 10:13 and **e** up saying crazy
Isa 5:26 he signals those at the **e**
13:5 from the **e** of heaven.
24:16 From the **e** of the earth we hear
40:28 the Creator of the **e** of the earth,
41:5 The **e** of the earth tremble.
41:9 I have taken you from the **e** of
42:10 Sing his praise from the **e** of
43:6 from the **e** of the earth.
45:22 all who live at the **e** of the
48:20 Shout it out to the **e** of the earth.
52:10 All the **e** of the earth will see
62:11 LORD has announced to the **e**
Jer 10:13 makes clouds rise from the **e**
25:31 The sound is echoing to the **e**
48:47 The judgment against Moab **e**
50:41 will rise from the **e** of the earth.
51:16 makes clouds rise from the **e**
Eze 15:4 The fire burns up both its **e** and
Mic 5:4 will reach the **e** of the earth.
Zec 9:10 River to the **e** of the earth.
Mat 12:42 because she came from the **e**
Luk 11:31 because she came from the **e**
Act 1:8 and to the **e** of the earth."
Rom 1:17 This approval begins and **e**
10:18 words to the **e** of the earth."

endurance (19)

Luk 21:19 By your **e** you will save your
Rom 5:3 know that suffering creates **e**,
5:4 **e** creates character,
15:4 have confidence through the **e**
15:5 you this **e** and encouragement,
2Th 1:4 in God's churches about your **e**
3:5 show God's love and Christ's **e**.
1Ti 6:11 faith, love, **e**, and gentleness.
2Ti 3:10 patience, my love, and my **e**.
Tit 2:2 in faith, love, and **e**.
Heb 10:36 You need **e** so that after you
Jas 1:3 testing of your faith produces **e**.
5:11 You have heard about Job's **e**.
2Pe 1:6 to self-control add **e**;

2Pe 1:6 to e add godliness;
Rev 1:9 and e because of Jesus.
2:19 your love, faith, service, and e.
13:10 people need e and confidence.
14:12 their faith in Jesus, need e.

endure (34)

1Ch 17:24 Your name will e and be
Psa 61:6 e throughout every generation.
71:20 You have made me e many
72:17 May his name e forever.
89:29 I will make his dynasty e
104:31 the glory of the LORD e forever.
119:160 righteous regulations e forever.
Pro 18:14 person's spirit can e sickness,
19:21 the advice of the LORD will e.
Jer 10:10 The nations can't e his fury.
Lam 3:27 It is good for people to e
Joe 2:11 terrifying. Who can e it?
Amo 7:10 The country isn't able to e
Mic 7:9 So I will e his fury until he
Mal 3:2 But who will be able to e the
1Co 4:12 people persecute us, we e it.
10:13 also give you the ability to e
2Co 1:6 comfort you when you e
1:6 the same sufferings that we e.
1:8 it was beyond our ability to e.
Col 1:11 patiently e everything with joy.
2Ti 2:10 For that reason, I e everything
2:12 If we e, we will rule with him.
4:5 E suffering. Do the work of a
Heb 12:7 E your discipline. God corrects
13:13 to him outside the camp and e
Jas 1:4 E until your testing is over.
1:12 Blessed are those who e when
5:11 We consider those who e to be
1Pe 2:20 credit do you deserve if you e
2:20 But if you e suffering for doing
2:21 God called you to e suffering
Rev 3:10 obeyed my command to e,
6:17 and who is able to e it?"

endured (11)

Psa 69:7 for your sake I have e insults.
88:15 I have e your terrors,
132:1 and all the hardships he e.
2Co 6:4 We have e many things:
2Ti 3:11 I e those persecutions,
Heb 10:32 You e a lot of hardship and
12:2 so he e death on the cross and
12:3 who e opposition from sinners,
13:13 and endure the insults he e.
Rev 2:2 worked and how you have e.
2:3 You have e, suffered trouble

endures (52)

1Ch 16:34 because his mercy e forever.
16:41 "His mercy e forever."
2Ch 5:13 his mercy e forever."
7:3 his mercy e forever."
7:6 with "his mercy e forever"
20:21 because his mercy e forever!"
Ezr 3:11 mercy toward Israel e forever."
Psa 19:9 It e forever. The decisions of the
100:5 His mercy e forever.
100:5 e throughout every generation.
106:1 because his mercy e forever.
107:1 because his mercy e forever.
117:2 LORD's faithfulness e forever.
118:1 because his mercy e forever.
118:2 "His mercy e forever."
118:3 "His mercy e forever."
118:4 "His mercy e forever."
118:29 because his mercy e forever.
119:90 Your faithfulness e throughout
135:13 O LORD, your name e forever.
136:1 because his mercy e forever.
136:2 because his mercy e forever.
136:3 because his mercy e forever.
136:4 because his mercy e forever.
136:5 because his mercy e forever.
136:6 because his mercy e forever.
136:7 because his mercy e forever.
136:8 because his mercy e forever.
136:9 because his mercy e forever.
136:10 because his mercy e forever.
Psa 136:11 because his mercy e forever.
136:12 because his mercy e forever.
136:13 because his mercy e forever.
136:14 because his mercy e forever.
136:15 because his mercy e forever.
136:16 because his mercy e forever.
136:17 because his mercy e forever.
136:18 because his mercy e forever.
136:19 because his mercy e forever.
136:20 because his mercy e forever.
136:21 because his mercy e forever.
136:22 because his mercy e forever.
136:23 because his mercy e forever.
136:24 because his mercy e forever.
136:25 because his mercy e forever.
136:26 because his mercy e forever.
138:8 O LORD, your mercy e forever.
145:13 e throughout every generation.
Jer 33:11 because his mercy e forever.'
Mat 10:22 But the person who patiently e
24:13 But the person who e to the
Mar 13:13 But the person who e to the

enduring (4)

Neh 1:3 They are e serious troubles
Act 13:34 He said, 'I will give you the e
1Th 1:3 in our Lord Jesus Christ is e.
1Pe 2:19 person is aware of him while e

En Eglaim (1)

Eze 47:10 From En Gedi to E people will

enemies (308)

Gen 14:20 who has handed your e over to
49:8 will be on the neck of your e.
Exo 1:10 they will join our e,
15:6 O LORD, smashes your e.
23:22 I will be an enemy to your e
23:27 make all your e flee from you.
32:25 an object of ridicule to their e.
Lev 26:7 You will chase your e,
26:8 You will defeat your e,
26:16 because your e will eat them.
26:17 in defeat in front of your e.
26:32 so deserted that your e will
26:36 are left in the land of their e.
26:37 be able to stand up to their e.
26:38 land of their e will devour them.
26:39 away in the lands of their e
26:41 them into the lands of their e.
26:44 they are in the land of their e,
Num 10:9 and rescue you from your e.
10:35 Scatter your e! Make those who
14:42 You will be defeated by your e
23:11 brought you here to curse my e,
24:8 devour nations that are his e,
24:10 summoned you to curse my e,
25:17 "Treat the Midianites as your e,
25:18 because they treated you as e.
32:21 until the LORD forces out his e
Dtr 1:42 will be defeated by your e."'
6:19 see the LORD expel your e as
12:10 from all your e around you so
20:1 you go to war against your e,
20:3 going into battle against your e.
20:4 will fight for you against your e
21:10 When you go to war with your e
23:9 set up camp to fight your e,
23:14 you and hand your e over
25:19 from all your e around you
28:7 The LORD will defeat your e
28:25 will let your e defeat you.
28:31 flock will be given to your e,
28:48 So you will serve your e,
28:53 hardships your e will make you
28:55 hardships your e will make you
28:57 hardships your e will make you
28:68 yourselves as slaves to your e,
30:7 put all these curses on your e,
32:27 But I didn't want their e to make
32:31 Even our e will agree with this.
32:41 I will take revenge on my e
32:43 He will get even with his e and
33:7 Help them against their e."
33:22 they pounce ⌊on their e⌋."
33:27 He will force your e out of your
Dtr 33:29 Your e will come crawling to
Jos 5:13 you one of us or one of our e?"
7:12 themselves against their e.
7:12 They will run away from their e
7:13 against your e until you get
10:13 a nation got revenge on its e.
10:19 Chase your e! Cut off their rear
10:25 the e you're fighting against."
11:20 The LORD made their e
21:44 Not one of their e stood up to
21:44 handed all their e over to them.
22:8 from your e with your relatives."
23:1 with all their e around them.
Jdg 2:14 He also used their e around
2:14 longer stand up against their e.
2:18 them from their e as long as
5:31 May all your e die like that,
8:24 (Their e, the Ishmaelites,
8:34 from all the e around them.
1Sm 2:1 My mouth mocks my e.
4:3 us and save us from our e."
10:1 and save them from all their e.
12:10 But rescue us from our e now,
12:11 and rescued you from your e
14:24 I've gotten revenge on my e."
14:47 he fought against his e on
14:48 He rescued Israel from the e
18:25 on his e."' In this way Saul
20:15 will wipe each of David's e off
25:26 may your e and those who are
25:29 of your e like stones thrown
29:8 Why shouldn't I fight your e,
30:26 ⌊taken from⌋ the LORD's e."
2Sm 2:16 Gibeon is called the Field of E.
3:18 other e through my servant
5:20 LORD has overwhelmed my e
7:1 with all his e around him.
7:9 and I destroyed all your e in
7:11 give you peace with all your e.
18:19 has freed him from his e."
18:32 "May your e and all who turned
19:9 king rescued us from our e
19:22 You are my e today.
22:1 rescued him from all his e,
22:4 and I was saved from my e.
22:38 I chased my e and destroyed
22:41 You made my e turn their
22:49 He frees me from my e.
24:13 flee from your e as they pursue
1Ki 3:11 or the death of your e.
5:3 the LORD let him defeat his e.
8:37 E may blockade Israel's city
8:44 their e (wherever you may
8:48 land of their e where they are
2Ki 17:39 will rescue you from your e."'
21:14 under the control of their e,
21:14 property that their e capture.
1Ch 12:17 come to betray me to my e,
14:11 God has overwhelmed my e."
17:8 and I destroyed all your e in
17:10 I will crush all your e.
21:12 which your e will chase you
22:9 from all the e around him.
2Ch 6:28 E may blockade Israel's city
6:34 their e (wherever you may
20:27 had happened to⌋ their e.
20:29 waged war against Israel's e.
Ezr 4:1 When the e of Judah and
4:6 the e of Judah and Jerusalem
8:31 and he rescued us from our e
Neh 4:11 Our e said, "Before they know
4:12 were living near our e warned
4:12 times that our e would attack
4:14 "Don't be afraid of our e.
4:15 When our e heard that we
5:9 keep our e from ridiculing us?
6:1 and the rest of our e heard that I
6:16 When all our e heard about this,
9:27 handed them over to their e,
9:27 to rescue them from their e
9:28 You abandoned them to their e,
Est 8:13 to take revenge on their e.
9:1 On that very day, when the e of
9:5 the Jews attacked all their e,
9:16 free themselves from their e.
9:22 freed themselves from their e.

Psa 3:1 look how my e have increased!
3:7 You have slapped all my e in
6:7 They fail because of my e.
6:10 All my e will be put to shame
9:3 When my e retreat,
17:9 my deadly e who surround me.
18:3 and I was saved from my e.
18:37 I chased my e and caught up
18:40 You made my e turn their
18:48 He saves me from my e.
21:8 hand will discover all your e.
23:5 for me while my e watch.
25:2 not let my e triumph over me.
25:19 See how my e have increased
27:2 and e stumbled and fell.
27:6 above my e who surround me.
27:11 path because I have e who spy
30:1 not let my e rejoice over me.
31:15 Rescue me from my e,
35:19 Do not let my treacherous e
37:20 The LORD's e will vanish like
38:19 My mortal e are growing
41:2 place him at the mercy of his e.
41:5 My e say terrible things about
42:10 to my bones, my e taunt me.
44:5 you we can walk over our e.
44:7 But you saved us from our e.
45:5 in the heart of the king's e.
54:5 My e spy on me. Pay them back
54:7 My eyes will gloat over my e.
56:2 All day long my e spy on me.
56:5 All day long my e twist my
56:9 Then my e will retreat when I
57:6 ⌊My e⌋ spread out a net to
59:1 Rescue me from my e,
60:12 He will trample our e.
66:3 so great that your e will cringe
68:1 His e will be scattered.
68:21 of his e ⌊and destroy even⌋
68:23 may lick the blood of your e."
69:4 have no reason to be my e.
69:18 Set me free because of my e.
71:10 My e talk about me.
72:9 May his e lick the dust.
74:11 your pockets. Destroy your e!
78:53 while the sea covered their e.
78:66 He struck his e from behind
80:6 and our e made fun of us.
81:14 I would quickly defeat their e.
83:2 Look, your e are in an uproar.
89:10 arm you scattered your e.
89:23 I will crush his e in front of him
89:42 You held the right hand of his e
89:51 Your e insulted ⌊me⌋.
92:9 Now look at your e,
92:9 Now look at your e.
97:3 burns his e who surround him.
102:8 All day long my e insult me.
105:24 and stronger than their e.
106:42 Their e oppressed them and
107:2 from the power of their e
108:13 He will trample our e.
110:1 I make your e your footstool."
110:2 Rule your e who surround you.
112:8 will look triumphantly at his e.
119:98 make me wiser than my e,
119:139 because my e have forgotten
127:5 when he speaks with his e
132:18 I will clothe his e with shame,
136:24 us from the grasp of our e —
138:7 life against the anger of my e.
139:20 Your e misuse your name.
139:22 They have become my e.
142:3 ⌊My e⌋ have hidden a trap for
143:9 Rescue me from my e,
143:12 wipe out my e and destroy all
Pro 16:7 he makes even his e to be at
Isa 1:24 avenge myself against my e.
9:11 Israel and will stir up its e —
26:11 anger will destroy your e.
29:5 Your many e will be like fine
41:12 You will search for your e,
42:13 and overpowers his e.
49:25 I will fight your e, and I will
59:18 with wrath and punish his e.
62:8 "I will never again let your e

Isa 63:18 Our e have trampled on your
64:2 your name known to your e.
66:6 back his e as they deserve.
66:14 but he will condemn his e.
Jer 12:7 the people I love over to their e.
15:9 of their e," declares the LORD.
15:11 I will certainly make your e
15:14 I will make you serve your e in
17:4 I will make you serve your e in
19:7 with swords in front of their e
19:9 hardships that their e impose
20:5 of this city over to their e.
20:5 Their e will loot them,
21:7 and to their e who want
30:16 and all your e will be taken
34:20 I will hand them over to their e
34:21 over to their e who want
44:30 over to his e and to those who
46:10 he will take revenge on his e.
46:22 Its e will come with full force.
49:37 Elam in the presence of their e,
50:7 Their e say, 'We're not guilty.
50:33 All their e have captured them.
51:55 Waves of e will come roaring
Lam 1:2 betrayed it and become its e.
1:5 Its e have no worries.
1:7 fell into the power of their e
1:9 because my e have triumphed.'
1:10 The e laid their hands on all of
1:16 because my e have won."
1:21 "All my e have heard that I am
1:21 All my e have heard about my
1:21 Let my e be like me now.
2:7 of Zion's palaces over to its e.
2:7 The e made noise in the
2:16 All your e gawk at you.
2:17 He made your e gloat over you.
3:46 All our e gawk at us.
3:52 "Those who were my e for no
4:12 on earth could believe that e
5:5 ⌊Our e⌋ are breathing down our
Eze 16:27 you over to your greedy e,
25:15 to destroy their long-time e.
36:2 Your e said this about you,
36:3 Your e turned you into ruins
39:23 handed them over to their e.
39:27 from the countries of their e.
Dan 4:19 its meaning were about your e.
Amo 9:4 go into exile ahead of their e,
Mic 2:8 my people have turned into e.
4:10 will reclaim you from your e.
5:1 E will strike the judge of Israel
5:9 all your e will be destroyed.
7:6 People's e are the members of
7:8 Don't laugh at me, my e.
7:10 Then my e will see this,
Nah 1:2 takes revenge against his e
1:8 pursue his e with darkness.
2:2 although e have looted it and
3:13 are wide open to your e.
Zep 3:15 He has forced out your e.
Mat 5:44 But I tell you this: Love your e,
10:36 A person's e will be the
22:44 I put your e under your
Mar 12:36 I put your e under your
Luk 1:71 promised to save us from our e
6:27 who is listening: Love your e.
6:35 Rather, love your e,
19:27 Bring my e, who didn't want me
20:43 I make your e your footstool.'"
21:15 wisdom that none of your e will
23:12 They had been e before this.
Act 2:35 I put your e under your
Rom 5:10 God while we were still his e,
11:28 made the Jewish people e
Php 3:18 that many live as the e of the
1Th 2:15 They are e of the whole human
2Th 3:15 Yet, don't treat them like e,
Heb 1:13 I make your e your footstool."
10:13 he has been waiting for his e to
10:27 fire that will consume God's e.
Rev 11:5 mouths and burns up their e.
11:12 and their e watched them.

enemies' (9)

Gen 22:17 possession of their e cities
24:60 possession of their e cities.
Lev 26:34 and you are in your e land.
Dtr 20:14 You may enjoy your e goods
1Sm 14:30 of the e food, which they found
Psa 109:25 the victim of my e insults.
Jer 20:4 Their e swords will kill them,
50:16 because of the e swords
Luk 1:74 us from our e power so that we

enemy (117)

Exo 15:9 "The e said, 'I'll pursue them!
23:22 then I will be an e to your
Lev 26:25 fall under the control of your e.
Num 10:9 against an e who is oppressing
24:18 Seir, his e, will be conquered.
35:21 or if you beat your e to death
35:22 someone who wasn't your e.
35:23 was there, he wasn't your e,
Dtr 32:42 the heads of the e who vowed
Jos 7:8 after Israel ran away from its e?
10:10 The LORD threw the e into
Jdg 3:28 The LORD will hand your e
6:4 The e used to camp on the
6:35 went to meet the e in battle.
8:4 but they kept pursuing the e.
11:36 has punished your e Ammon."
16:23 Samson, our e, over to us."
16:24 said, "Our god gave our e,
1Sm 18:29 became David's constant e.
19:17 by sending my e away so that
24:4 'I'm going to hand your e over
24:19 When a person finds an e,
26:8 "Today God has turned your e
28:16 you and become your e?
29:4 to⌋ become our e during
2Sm 4:8 the son of your e Saul who
22:18 rescued me from my strong e
1Ki 8:33 "An e may defeat your people
8:46 over to an e who takes them
20:27 they went to meet the e.
21:20 "So you've found me, my e?"
2Ki 25:4 The e broke through the city
2Ch 6:24 "An e may defeat your people
6:36 over to an e who takes them
25:8 God will use the e to defeat
26:13 support the king against the e.
Ezr 8:22 to help us against an e attack
Est 3:10 it to Haman, the e of the Jews.
7:4 because the e is not worth
7:6 "Our vicious e is this wicked
8:1 of Haman, the e of the Jews,
9:10 son of Hammedatha and the e
9:24 the e of all the Jews,
Job 6:23 or 'Rescue me from an e,' or
13:24 me⌋ and consider me your e?
19:11 He considers me to be his e.
27:7 "Let my e be ⌊treated⌋ like
31:29 "If I enjoyed the ruin of my e or
33:10 He considers me his e.
Psa 7:5 then let the e chase me and
8:2 silence the e and the avenger.
9:6 The e is finished — in ruins
13:2 will my e triumph over me?
13:4 and my e will say,
18:17 rescued me from my strong e
31:8 not handed me over to the e.
41:11 and my e cannot shout in
42:9 while the e oppresses me?"
43:2 while the e oppresses me?
44:10 You make us retreat from the e.
44:16 of the e and the avenger.
55:3 because my e shouts at me
55:12 If an e had insulted me,
60:11 Give us help against the e
61:3 tower of strength against the e.
64:1 my life from a terrifying e.
74:3 The e has destroyed
74:10 will the e insult us?
74:10 Will the e despise you forever?
74:18 how the e insulted you,
89:22 No e will take him by surprise.
106:10 He rescued them from the e.
108:12 Give us help against the e
143:3 The e has pursued me.
Pro 24:17 not be happy when your e falls,
25:21 If your e is hungry,

Isa 63:10 turned against them as their e;
Jer 4:13 The e comes up like clouds.
6:25 The e has a sword.
18:17 scatter them in front of the e.
30:14 punished you as an e would.
31:16 return from the land of the e.
47:3 the rattling of e chariots,
48:15 The e will attack Moab and
48:40 The e will swoop down like
49:22 The e will swoop down like
51:14 fill you with many e armies.
51:32 The e has burned its marshes,
52:7 The e broke through the city
Lam 2:3 hand when they faced their e.
2:4 Like an e he bent his bow.
2:5 The Lord became an e.
2:22 My e has murdered the
4:18 ⌞The e⌟ kept tracking us down,
Eze 33:3 If he sees the e coming to
33:4 the warning and the e comes
33:6 watchman sees the e coming
33:6 the people and the e comes
35:5 always been an e of Israel.
Dan 11:10 they can overwhelm ⌞the e⌟
Hos 8:1 The e swoops down on the
8:3 The e will persecute them.
Amo 3:11 An e will surround your land,
Nah 3:11 fortress ⌞to escape⌟ from the e.
Zec 8:10 traveled was safe from the e.
10:5 like warriors who trample the e
Mat 5:43 your neighbor, and hate your e.'
13:25 his e planted weeds in the
13:28 "He told them, 'An e did this.'
13:39 The e who planted them is the
Luk 19:43 The time will come when e
Rom 12:20 But, "If your e is hungry,
1Co 15:25 put every e under his control.
15:26 The last e he will destroy is
Gal 4:16 it be that I have become your e
1Ti 5:14 and not give the e any chance
Jas 4:4 of this world is an e of God.

enemy's (5)

Exo 23:4 you come across your e ox
Pro 27:6 but an e kisses are too much to
Jer 46:16 and escape our e sword.
50:9 Its e arrows will be like skilled
Luk 10:19 and to destroy the e power.

energy (2)

Pro 31:17 a belt and goes to work with e.
Rom 12:11 Use your e to serve the Lord.

enforce (1)

Dan 6:7 make a statute and e a decree.

engaged (10)

Gen 19:14 out and spoke to the men e
Exo 22:16 seduces a virgin who is not e
Lev 19:20 with a female slave who is e
Dtr 20:7 If you are e to a woman but
22:23 with a virgin who is e
22:25 But if a man rapes an e girl out
22:28 man rapes a virgin who isn't e.
28:30 You will be e to a woman,
Sos 8:8 on the day she becomes e?
Jud 1:7 and e in homosexual activities.

En Gannim (3)

Jos 15:34 Zanoah, E, Tappuah, Enam,
19:21 Remeth, E, En Haddah, and
21:29 Jarmuth, and E

En Gedi (6)

Jos 15:62 Nibshan, Ir Hamelah, and E.
1Sa 23:29 stay in the fortified camps of E.
24:1 David is in the desert near E.
2Ch 20:2 Hazazon Tamar" (also called E).
Sos 1:14 in the vineyards of E.
Eze 47:10 From E to En Eglaim people

engrave (3)

Exo 28:9 Take two onyx stones, and e
28:11 E the names of the sons of
28:36 and e on it (as on a signet ring):

engraved (10)

Exo 28:21 each stone e (like a signet ring)
39:6 and e on them the names of the
39:14 each stone e (like a signet ring)
39:30 crown) out of pure gold and e
1Ki 7:29 and the cattle were e designs.
7:36 Hiram e angels, lions,
Job 19:24 I wish they were forever e on a
Isa 49:16 I have e you on the palms of
Jer 17:1 It is e with a diamond point on
2Ti 2:19 These words are e on it:

engraves (1)

Exo 28:11 the same way a jeweler e

engraving (2)

Job 13:27 You follow my trail by e marks
Zec 3:9 I am e an inscription on it,"

engravings (3)

1Ki 7:31 opening there w engravings.
2Ch 2:7 He should know how to make e
2:14 how to make all kinds of e

engulfed (1)

Isa 42:25 It e them in flames,

En Haddah (1)

Jos 19:21 Remeth, En Gannim, E, and

En Hakkore (1)

Jdg 15:19 he called the place E

En Harod (1)

Jdg 7:1 up early and camped above E

En Hazor (1)

Jos 19:37 Kedesh, Edrei, E,

enjoy (61)

Gen 18:12 will I e myself again?
45:18 Then you can e the best food
Lev 26:34 "Then the land will e its time
26:43 will e its time to honor the
Num 14:31 you rejected, and they will e it.
Dtr 12:7 and e everything you've worked
12:12 E yourselves in the presence
12:18 e everything you've worked
14:26 will eat and e yourselves there
16:11 E yourselves in the presence
16:11 E yourselves at the place the
16:14 E yourselves at the festival
16:15 You will e yourselves,
20:6 else will e the grapes.
20:14 You may e your enemies'
26:11 who live among you can e all
27:7 and e yourselves in the
28:30 but you won't e the grapes.
33:18 e yourselves when you go to
33:18 e yourselves when you stay at
33:23 "The people of Naphtali e the
Jdg 19:6 the night and e yourself?"
19:9 Stay here, and e yourself.
2Ki 14:10 E your fame, but stay home.
Neh 9:36 and ⌞e⌟ its good things.
Psa 17:14 from mortals who e their
25:13 He will e good things in life,
34:12 long enough to e good things?
37:11 and will e unlimited peace.
73:3 that wicked people e.
111:2 be studied by all who e them.
Pro 2:14 from those who e doing evil,
5:18 and e the girl you married when
7:18 Let's e making love,
23:24 who has a wise son will e him.
Ecc 2:1 with pleasure and e myself."
2:25 or e themselves without God?
3:12 be cheerful and e what is good
3:22 to do than to e their work
5:18 It is to eat and drink and to e
5:19 the power to e them,
6:2 give him the power to e any
8:15 and e themselves.
9:7 Go, e eating your food,
9:9 E life with your wife,
Ecc 11:8 they should e every one of
11:9 You young people should e
Isa 55:2 and e the best foods.
65:22 ones will e what they've done.
Jer 31:5 who plant them will e the fruit.
31:12 They will stream to it to e the
32:41 I will e blessing them.
Zec 8:17 Don't e false testimony.
Luk 12:19 eat, drink, and e yourself."'
Rom 1:13 What I want is to e some of the
Gal 5:1 has freed us so that we may e
1Ti 6:17 us with everything to e.
Heb 11:25 God's people rather than to e
12:11 We don't e being disciplined.
1Pe 3:10 a full life and e good days must
2Pe 2:13 They especially e deceiving

enjoyed (9)

Dtr 20:6 vineyard and not e the grapes,
Neh 9:25 They e the vast supply of good
9:35 in their own kingdom and e
Job 31:25 If I e being very rich because
31:29 "If I e the ruin of my enemy or
Mar 12:37 large crowd e listening to him.
Jon 5:35 For a time you e the pleasure
Rom 1:13 among you as I have also e
15:24 After I have e your company for

enjoying (5)

Jdg 16:25 Philistines were e themselves,
19:22 While they were e themselves,
Est 8:17 feasting and e a holiday.
Job 20:18 what he earned without e it.
Lam 3:17 has been kept from e peace.

enjoyment (2)

Exo 30:38 like it for his own e must
Ecc 8:15 So I recommend the e ⌞of life⌟.

enjoys (3)

Job 15:21 While he e peace,
Pro 12:14 One person e good things as a
Ecc 6:2 Instead, a stranger e them.

enlarged (1)

Amo 1:13 Ammonites e their territory

enlighten (1)

Job 33:30 away from the pit and to e them

enlist (1)

1Sm 14:52 Saul would e him in the army.

enlisted (1)

Act 12:20 They e the help of Blastus to

En Mishpat (1)

Gen 14:7 came to E (that is, Kadesh)

Enoch (14)

Gen 4:17 pregnant and gave birth to E.
4:17 and he named it E after his son.
4:18 To E was born Irad.
5:18 he became the father of E.
5:19 After he became the father of E,
5:21 When E was 65 years old,
5:22 E walked with God for 300
5:23 E lived a total of 365 years.
5:24 E walked with God;
1Ch 1:3 E, Methuselah, Lamech,
Luk 3:37 son of Methuselah, son of E,
Heb 11:5 Faith enabled E to be taken
11:5 states that before E was taken,
Jud 1:14 Furthermore, E, from the

enormous (1)

Est 1:4 He showed them the e wealth

Enos (1)

Luk 3:38 son of E, son of Seth, son of

Enosh (7)

Gen 4:26 and he named him E.
5:6 he became the father of E.
5:7 After he became the father of E,
5:9 When E was 90 years old,

Gen 5:10 **E** lived 815 years and had
5:11 **E** lived a total of 905 years;
1Ch 1:1 Adam, Seth, **E**,

enraged (1)

Neh 4:1 he became **e** and made fun of

En Rimmon (1)

Neh 11:29 in **E**, Zorah, Jarmuth,

En Rogel (4)

Jos 15:7 En Shemesh and ends at **E**.
18:16 city of Jebus, and down to **E**.
2Sa 17:17 Ahimaaz were waiting at **E**.
1Ki 1:9 at Zoheleth Rock near **E**.

enrolled (4)

1Ch 5:7 when they were **e** in the
2Ch 31:16 The way they were **e** in the
31:17 priests who were **e** by families
31:18 The priests and Levites were **e**

En Shemesh (2)

Jos 15:7 passes the Springs of **E** and
18:17 goes to **E** and from there to

enslave (1)

2Ch 28:10 Now you intend to **e** the men

ensure (1)

1Ch 23:28 to **e** that all the holy things

En Tappuah (1)

Jos 17:7 the people who live in **E**.

enter (131)

Gen 12:11 When he was about to **e** Egypt,
Exo 12:25 When you **e** the land that the
Num 14:30 But none of you will **e** it except
15:18 When you **e** the land where I'm
20:24 since he cannot **e** the land I'm
32:32 We will **e** Canaan as armed
34:2 When you **e** Canaan,
35:10 the Jordan River and **e** Canaan,
Dtr 1:8 **E**, and take possession of the
1:39 good and evil, will **e** that land.
2:37 So you didn't **e** the land along
4:1 you will live and be able to **e**
4:21 cross the Jordan River and **e**
6:1 Obey them after you **e** the land
6:18 and you will **e** and take
7:1 you to the land you're about to **e**
8:1 You will **e** and take
8:20 other nations as you **e** the land.
10:11 They will **e** and take
11:8 you will have the strength to **e**
11:10 The land you're about to **e** and
11:11 The land you're about to **e** is a
11:29 into the land you're about to **e**,
11:31 to cross the Jordan River to **e**
17:14 You will **e** the land that the
26:1 Soon you will **e** and take
27:2 cross the Jordan River and **e**
28:21 out of the land you're about to **e**
28:63 out of the land you're about to **e**
30:16 in the land that you're about to **e**
31:16 When these people **e** the land
32:52 but you may not **e** the land I'm
Jos 6:1 No one could **e** or leave.
Rut 1:22 They happened to **e**
2Ki 11:16 to the street where the horses **e**
2Ch 23:6 They may **e** because they are
23:19 unclean for any reason could **e**.
27:2 he didn't ⌊illegally⌋ **e** the
Neh 9:23 their parents to **e** and possess.
Est 4:2 could **e** it wearing sackcloth.)
4:11 have not been summoned to **e**
Psa 5:7 But I will **e** your house
45:15 They **e** the palace of the king.
95:11 'They will never **e** my place of
100:4 **E** his gates with a song of
106:24 They refused ⌊to **e**⌋ the
118:20 which righteous people will **e**.
Pro 23:10 marker or **e** fields that belong
Isa 13:2 Signal them with your hand to **e**
Jer 21:13 Who can **e** our places of
Lam 1:10 has seen the nations **e**
1:10 to **e** your congregation.'
Eze 13:9 They won't even **e** Israel.
20:38 You will never **e** Israel.
26:10 He will **e** as people enter a
26:10 as people **e** a conquered city.
37:5 I will cause breath to **e** you,
38:10 time ideas will **e** your head,
42:9 A person was able to **e** the
42:14 Once the priests **e** the holy
44:2 No one may **e** through it
44:3 He will **e** through the entrance
44:9 may not **e** my holy place.
44:16 They may **e** my holy place,
44:17 When they **e** the gateways to
44:21 they **e** the inner courtyard.
46:2 The prince must **e** from the
46:8 he must **e** through the entrance
46:8 He must **e** and leave the same
46:9 "The people will **e** the LORD's
46:10 When they **e**, he must enter.
46:10 When they enter, he must **e**.
Dan 11:7 **e** the stronghold of the
Joe 2:9 They **e** through windows like
Zec 5:4 and it will **e** the houses of
14:18 Egypt won't go or **e** Jerusalem,
Mat 5:20 you will never **e** the kingdom of
7:13 "**E** through the narrow gate
7:13 Many **e** through the wide gate.
7:21 will **e** the kingdom of heaven,
12:45 They **e** and take up permanent
18:3 you will never **e** the kingdom of
18:8 It is better for you to **e** life
18:9 It is better for you to **e** life with
19:17 If you want to **e** into life,
19:23 be hard for a rich person to **e**
19:24 than for a rich person to **e**
23:13 You don't **e** it yourselves,
23:13 others to **e** when they try.
Mar 1:45 no longer **e** any city openly.
5:12 into the pigs! Let us **e** them!"
9:25 of him and never **e** him again."
9:43 It is better for you to **e** life
9:45 It is better for you to **e** life lame
9:47 It is better for you to **e** the
10:15 child receives it will never **e** it."
10:23 it will be for rich people to **e**
10:24 how hard it is to **e** the kingdom
10:25 than for a rich person to **e**
11:2 As you **e** it, you will find a
Luk 8:32 Jesus to let them **e** those pigs.
11:26 They **e** and take up permanent
11:52 out those who wanted to **e**."
13:24 "Try hard to **e** through the
13:24 that many will try to **e**,
18:17 child receives it will never **e** it."
18:24 hard it is for rich people to **e**
18:25 than for a rich person to **e**
19:30 As you **e**, you will find a young
23:42 me when you **e** your kingdom."
24:26 things and **e** into his glory?"
Jon 3:5 No one can **e** the kingdom of
10:1 The person who doesn't **e** the
10:9 Those who **e** the sheep pen
Act 10:25 about to **e** Cornelius' house,
14:22 "We must suffer a lot to **e** the
16:7 of Mysia and tried to **e** Bithynia,
Heb 3:11 they would never **e** my place
3:18 swear would never **e** his place
3:19 So we see that they couldn't **e**
4:1 God's promise that we may **e**
4:1 you think you won't **e** his place
4:3 they would never **e** my place
4:5 'They will never **e** my place of
4:6 However, some people **e** that
4:6 the past did not **e** God's place
4:7 ancestors failed to **e** that place
4:11 every effort to **e** that place
Rev 15:8 No one could **e** the temple until
21:27 and no liars will ever **e** it.
21:27 the lamb's Book of Life will **e** it.

entered (60)

Gen 23:18 together with all who had **e**
41:46 was 30 years old when he **e**
Exo 24:18 Moses **e** the cloud as he went
Num 24:2 The Spirit of God **e** him,
Dtr 4:5 must obey them when you've **e**
23:20 you do once you've **e**
Jos 2:1 So they went to Jericho and **e**
2:2 "Some Israelites have **e** the
8:19 They **e** the city, captured it,
Jdg 18:15 So they stopped and **e** Micah's
18:18 When these men **e** Micah's
19:15 The Levite **e** Gibeah and sat
Rut 1:19 When they **e** Bethlehem,
2:3 She **e** a field and gathered the
1Sm 9:14 As they **e** it, Samuel was
14:26 When the troops **e** the woods,
22:8 me when my son **e** into
2Sm 10:2 servants **e** Ammonite territory,
1Ki 16:10 Zimri **e** Arza's house,
2Ki 9:31 When Jehu **e** the gateway,
1Ch 19:2 But when David's servants **e**
2Ch 23:15 So they arrested her as she **e**
29:15 from the LORD's word and **e**
29:16 The priests **e** the LORD's
Neh 2:15 **e** Valley Gate, and returned.
Psa 109:18 so cursing **e** his body like
Jer 7:31 It never **e** my mind.
9:21 windows and **e** our palaces.
19:5 It never **e** my mind.
32:23 They **e** and took possession of
32:35 It never **e** my mind.
Eze 2:2 he spoke to me, the Spirit **e** me,
3:24 Then the Spirit **e** me and stood
4:14 meat has ever **e** my mouth."
37:10 and the breath **e** them.
42:12 People **e** through that doorway.
44:2 God of Israel **e** through it.
46:9 through the same gate they **e**.
Dan 10:3 No meat or wine **e** my mouth.
Oba 1:11 Foreigners **e** his gates and
Jnh 3:4 Jonah **e** the city and walked for
Hab 3:16 A rotten feeling has **e** me.
Mat 2:11 When they **e** the house,
Luk 1:28 When the angel **e** her home,
1:40 She **e** Zechariah's home and
8:30 (Many demons had **e** him.)
22:3 Then Satan **e** Judas Iscariot,
Jon 13:27 piece of bread, Satan **e** him.
18:1 They **e** the garden that was
Act 9:17 left and **e** Judas' house.
10:27 As Peter talked, he **e** Cornelius'
17:10 they **e** the synagogue.
23:16 He **e** the barracks and told
24:6 He also **e** the temple courtyard
25:7 When Paul **e** the room,
25:23 next day Agrippa and Bernice **e**
25:23 important men of the city **e**
Heb 4:10 Those who **e** his place of rest
9:7 Once a year he **e** and brought
Rev 11:11 the breath of life from God **e**

entering (10)

Gen 23:10 so that everyone who was **e**
Num 32:7 might discourage them from **e**
32:9 the rest of the Israelites from **e**
33:51 the Jordan River and **e** Canaan.
Dtr 9:5 you're so honest that you're **e**
2Sm 15:37 as Absalom was **e** Jerusalem.
Eze 46:9 Those **e** through the north gate
46:9 Those **e** through the south gate
Heb 4:3 We who believe are **e** that
2Pe 1:11 be given the wealth of **e** into

enters (10)

Lev 16:17 meeting from the time Aaron **e**
Ecc 11:5 know how the breath of life **e**
Eze 26:10 walls when he **e** your gates.
44:5 attention to everyone who **e**
44:27 When he **e** the inner courtyard
46:8 When the prince **e**,
Luk 22:10 Follow him into the house he **e**.
Jon 10:2 But the one who **e** through the
1Co 9:25 Everyone who **e** an athletic
2Ti 2:5 Whoever **e** an athletic

entertain (3)

Jdg 16:25 "Call Samson in to **e** us."
16:27 who watched Samson **e** them.
Psa 137:3 us wanted us to **e** them.

enthroned (21)

1Sm 4:4 of Armies — who is e over
2Sm 6:2 who is e over the angels.)
2Ki 19:15 you are e over the angels.
1Ch 13:6 (The LORD is e over the
Psa 2:4 The one e in heaven laughs.
9:7 Yet, the LORD is e forever.
9:11 the LORD, who is e in Zion.
22:3 e on the praises of Israel.
29:10 The LORD sat e over the flood.
29:10 LORD sits e as king forever.
33:14 From the place where he sits e,
55:19 The one who has sat e from
61:7 May he sit e in the presence of
80:1 one who is e over the angels.
99:1 He is e over the angels.
123:1 the one who sits e in heaven.
132:14 Here I will sit e because I want
Pro 9:14 She is e on the high ground of
Isa 37:16 you are e over the angels.
40:22 God is e above the earth,
Lam 5:19 you, O LORD, sit e forever,

enthusiasm (1)

2Co 9:2 and your e has moved most of

enthusiastic (2)

Php 3:6 When it comes to being e,
Tit 2:14 who are e about doing good

entitled (1)

Pro 3:27 good from those who are e

entrance (196)

Gen 18:1 as he was sitting at the e
18:10 to be listening at the e
38:14 she sat down at the e to Enaim,
Exo 26:36 "For the e of the outer tent,
27:14 Each side ⌊of the e⌋ will be 22
27:16 "The e to the courtyard must
29:4 Aaron and his sons to the e
29:11 in the LORD's presence at the e
29:32 At the e to the tent of meeting,
29:42 in the LORD's presence at the e
32:26 he stood at the e to the camp
33:9 come down and stay at the e
33:10 of smoke standing at the e
33:10 touching the ground at the e
35:15 the screen for the e to the tent,
35:17 for the e to the courtyard,
36:37 out of fine linen yarn for the e
38:8 the women who served at the e
38:14 Each side of the e to the
38:18 The screen for the e to the
38:30 he made the bases for the e
38:31 the bases for the e to the
39:38 the screen for the e to the tent,
39:40 and screen for the e to the
40:5 the screen at the e to the tent.
40:6 burnt offerings in front of the e
40:8 screen at the e to the courtyard.
40:12 Aaron and his sons to the e
40:28 the screen at the e to the tent.
40:29 altar for burnt offerings at the e
40:33 and put up the screen at the e
Lev 1:3 Offer it at the e to the tent of
1:5 sides of the altar that is at the e
3:2 Then slaughter it at the e to the
4:4 the LORD's presence at the e
4:7 altar for burnt offerings at the e
4:18 altar for burnt offerings at the e
8:3 the whole congregation at the e
8:4 congregation gathered at the e
8:31 "Cook the meat at the e to the
8:33 You will not leave the e to the
8:35 You will stay at the e to the
10:7 You must not leave the e to the
12:6 bring them to the priest at the e
14:11 the LORD's presence at the e
14:23 priest for his cleansing at the e
15:14 the LORD's presence at the e
15:29 bring them to the priest at the e
16:7 the LORD's presence at the e
17:4 Bring the animal to the e of the
17:5 bring them to the priest at the e
Lev 17:6 the LORD's altar at the e
17:9 but do not bring them to the e of
19:21 offering to the LORD at the e
Num 3:25 the screen for the e to the tent
3:26 the screen for the e to the
4:25 the screen for the e to the tent
4:26 the screen for the e to the
6:10 pigeons to the priest at the e
6:13 They must come to the e of the
6:18 will shave their heads at the e
10:3 will meet with you at the e
11:10 every family crying at the e
12:5 of smoke and stood at the e
16:18 with Moses and Aaron at the e
16:19 Moses and Aaron — at the e
16:50 came back to Moses at the e
20:6 from the assembly to the e
25:6 while they were crying at the e
27:2 the whole community at the e
Dtr 22:21 they must take the girl to the e
31:15 of smoke at the e to the tent.
Jos 8:29 They threw it in the e of the
19:51 presence of the LORD at the e
20:4 There he will stand at the e to
Jdg 9:35 went out and stood at the e
9:40 were killed at the e of the city.
9:44 the city and captured its e.
9:52 against it and went near the e
18:16 Dan stood at the e to the city.
18:17 The priest stood at the e to the
2Sm 10:8 formed a battle line at the e
11:9 But Uriah slept at the e of the
11:23 we forced them back to the e
1Ki 6:3 The e hall in front of the main
6:8 The e to the first story was on
6:31 He made doors for the e to the
6:33 of olive wood for the temple's e.
7:6 hall was an e hall with pillars.
7:12 LORD's temple and the e hall.
7:19 in the e hall were lily-shaped.
7:21 the pillars in the temple's e hall.
14:27 them and put them by the e
17:10 As he came to the town's e,
19:13 and stood at the e of the cave.
22:10 on the threshing floor at the e
2Ki 5:9 at the e to Elisha's home.
7:3 skin diseases were at the e
10:8 "Put them in two piles at the e
12:9 The priests who guarded the e
16:18 He also removed the outer e for
23:8 down the worship site at the e
23:11 to the sun god at the e
1Ch 9:21 was the keeper at the e to the
19:9 formed a battle line at the e
26:17 there were four, two at each e.
28:11 Solomon the plans for the e hall
2Ch 3:4 The e hall in front of ⌊the main
4:22 the gold e to the temple,
8:12 he built in front of the e hall.
12:10 them and put them by the e
15:8 in front of the LORD's e hall.
18:9 on the threshing floor at the e
23:13 standing by the pillar at the e.
29:7 doors of the ⌊temple's⌋ e hall,
29:17 went into the LORD's e hall,
33:14 Spring in the valley to the e
Est 2:21 eunuchs who guarded the e,
5:1 inside the palace, facing the e.
5:2 Queen Esther standing in the e,
6:2 eunuchs who guarded the e,
Psa 74:5 Starting from its e,
84:10 I would rather stand in the e to
Pro 8:3 At the e ⌊wisdom⌋ sings its
Isa 24:10 The e to every house is barred
28:1 They are at the e to a fertile
28:4 They are at the e to a fertile
Jer 1:15 will set up their thrones at the e
19:2 valley of Ben Hinnom at the e
26:10 They sat at the e of New Gate
36:10 in the upper courtyard at the e
38:14 and brought him to the third e
43:9 the brick pavement at the e
48:28 their nests at the e of a cave.
Eze 8:3 to the e to the north gate of the
8:5 and there in the e to the north
8:7 Then he took me to the e of the
Eze 8:14 He brought me to the e of the
8:16 There at the e to the LORD's
8:16 between the e and the altar,
9:3 it had been, to the temple's e.
10:4 rose from the angels to the e
10:18 of the LORD left the temple's e
11:1 Twenty-five men were at the e
27:3 Tyre is the city at the e to the
40:6 its steps and measured the e
40:7 And the e to the gateway by
40:7 to the gateway by the e hall
40:8 He also measured the e hall of
40:9 The gateway's e hall faced the
40:11 measured the width of the e
40:14 He also measured the e hall.
40:14 In front of the e hall to the
40:15 inner part of the e hall was 87
40:16 The e hall also had windows
40:21 and its e hall were the same
40:22 up to it and led to its e hall.
40:24 recessed walls and its e hall.
40:25 The gateway and its e hall had
40:26 up to it and led to its e hall.
40:29 and e hall were the same size
40:29 The guardrooms and the e hall
40:30 There were e halls all around
40:31 The e halls faced the outer
40:33 and e halls were the same size
40:33 Its guardrooms and e hall had
40:34 Its e hall faced the outer
40:36 and e hall had windows all
40:38 that opened toward the e hall
40:39 In the e hall of the gateway
40:40 On each side of the e to the
40:40 and on the other side of the e
40:48 man brought me to the e hall
40:49 The e hall was 35 feet long
40:49 one on each side of the e hall.
41:2 The e was 17 ½ feet wide,
41:2 and on each side of the e the
41:3 The e was 10 ½ feet high and
41:25 hanging over the outer e hall.
41:26 on both sides of the e hall,
42:9 lower side rooms had an e
44:3 He will enter through the e hall
46:2 the outside through the e hall
46:2 He must worship at the e of the
46:8 he must enter through the e
47:1 water flowing from under the e
Joe 2:17 cry between the altar and the e
Mat 26:71 As he went to the e,
Mar 14:68 He went to the e. Then a rooster
16:3 the stone for us from the e
Luk 7:12 As he came near the e to the
11:52 You haven't gained e into
Jon 11:38 with a stone covering the e.
11:41 was moved away from the e
20:1 removed from the tomb's e.
Act 14:13 Zeus' temple was at the e to

entrances (8)

Exo 33:8 would rise and stand at the e
Num 16:27 out and were standing at the e
1Ch 9:19 serving as watchmen at the e
9:19 in charge of guarding the e
9:22 at the e totaled 212.
Pro 1:21 At the e to the city she speaks
Eze 41:11 in the side rooms were e into
43:11 its exits and e — its entire

entrust (6)

Psa 31:5 Into your hands I e my spirit.
37:5 E your ways to the LORD.
Pro 16:3 E your efforts to the LORD,
Luk 23:46 into your hands I e my spirit."
2Ti 2:2 E this message to faithful
1Pe 4:19 for them must e themselves

entrusted (23)

2Ki 12:15 require the men who were e
1Ch 9:31 was e with preparing the flat
16:7 For the first time David e
Sos 8:11 He e that vineyard to
Mat 25:14 He called his servants and e
Luk 12:48 who has been e with a lot.
Jon 5:22 He has e judgment entirely to

Act 14:23 with prayer and fasting they **e**
14:26 (In Antioch they had been **e** to
15:40 left after the believers **e** him
Rom 3:2 God **e** them with his word.
1Co 4:1 are **e** with God's mysteries.
9:17 doing what I've been **e** to do.
Gal 2:7 they saw that I had been **e** with
2:7 as Peter had been **e**
1Ti 1:11 I was **e** with that Good News.
6:20 News which has been **e** to you.
2Ti 1:12 is able to protect what he had **e**
1:14 News that has been **e** to you.
Tit 1:3 I was **e** with this word by the
1Pe 5:2 the flock God has **e** to you.
5:3 rulers over the people **e** to you,
Jud 1:3 for the Christian faith that was **e**

entrusting (1)

Act 20:32 "I am now **e** you to God and to

entrusts (1)

Psa 10:14 The victim **e** himself to you.

entryway (1)

Act 12:13 knocked on the door of the **e**,

envious (3)

Psa 73:3 because I was **e** of arrogant
106:16 men became **e** of Moses.
106:16 They also became **e** of Aaron,

envoy (1)

Pro 13:17 a dependable **e** brings healing.

envy (13)

Psa 37:1 Do not **e** those who do wicked
68:16 Why do you look with **e**,
73:21 my mind was seized ⌊with **e**⌋,
Pro 3:31 Do not **e** a violent person.
23:17 Do not **e** sinners in your heart.
24:1 Do not **e** evil people or wish
24:19 Do not **e** wicked people,
Eze 31:9 This tree was the **e** of all the
Mar 7:22 lust, **e**, cursing, arrogance,
Rom 1:29 They are filled with **e**,
Gal 5:21 **e**, drunkenness, wild partying,
5:26 and to provoke or **e** each other.
Php 1:15 of their jealousy and **e**.

Epaenetus (1)

Rom 16:5 Greet my dear friend **E**.

Epaphras (3)

Col 1:7 about this Good News from **E**,
4:12 **E**, a servant of Christ Jesus
Phm 1:23 **E**, who is a prisoner because

Epaphroditus (3)

Php 2:25 I feel that I must send **E** — my
2:29 you honor people like **E** highly.
4:18 Now that **E** has brought me

ephah (6)

Gen 25:4 The sons of Midian were **E**,
1Ch 1:33 The sons of Midian were **E**,
2:46 **E**, Caleb's concubine, was the
2:47 Geshan, Pelet, **E**, and Shaaph.
Isa 60:6 camels from Midian and **E**.
Eze 45:11 The **e** and the bath should hold

Ephai (1)

Jer 40:8 the sons of **E** from Netophah,

Epher (4)

Gen 25:4 **E**, Hanoch, Abida, and Eldaah.
1Ch 1:33 **E**, Hanoch, Abida, and Eldaah.
4:17 Jether, Mered, **E**, and Jalon.
5:24 **E**, Ishi, Eliel, Azriel, Jeremiah,

Ephes Dammim (1)

1Sa 17:1 between Socoh and Azekah at **E**

Ephesians (3)

Act 19:28 "Artemis of the **E** is great!"
19:34 "Artemis of the **E** is great!"
19:35 knows that this city of the **E** is

Ephesus (23)

Act 18:18 while longer, Paul left ⌊for **E**⌋.
18:19 and arrived in the city of **E**,
18:21 Paul took a boat from **E**
18:24 arrived in the city of **E**.
18:27 ⌊in **E**⌋ encouraged him.
19:1 provinces to get to the city of **E**.
19:1 He met some disciples in **E**
19:17 in the city of **E** heard about this.
19:23 broke out in the city of **E**.
19:26 that follows him not only in **E**
19:35 Then he said, "Citizens of **E**,
19:35 Everyone knows that **E** is the
20:16 Paul had decided to sail past **E**
20:17 messengers to the city of **E**
21:29 had seen Trophimus from **E**
1Co 15:32 fought with wild animals in **E**,
16:8 here in **E** until Pentecost.
Eph 1:1 with Christ in the city of **E**.
1Ti 1:3 you to stay in the city of **E**.
2Ti 1:18 possible to help me in **E**.
4:12 city of **E** as my representative.
Rev 1:11 **E**, Smyrna, Pergamum,
2:1 messenger of the church in **E**,

Ephlal (2)

1Ch 2:37 Zabad was the father of **E**.
2:37 **E** was the father of Obed.

ephod (50)

Exo 25:7 priest's⌋ **e** and his breastplate.
28:4 an **e** and the robe that is worn
28:6 "Make the **e** out of fine linen
28:8 belt that is attached to the **e** out
28:12 straps of the **e** as reminders
28:15 creatively as you make the **e**.
28:25 straps of the **e** ⌊so that
28:26 the inside edge next to the **e**.
28:27 straps on the front of the **e**.
28:27 just above the belt of the **e**.
28:28 by its rings to the rings of the **e**
28:28 it just above the belt of the **e**
28:31 that is worn with the **e** entirely
29:5 the **e** and the robe that is worn
35:9 priest's⌋ **e** and breastplate.
35:27 priest's⌋ **e** and breastplate.
39:2 They made the **e** out of fine
39:4 so that the **e** could be fastened.
39:5 belt that is attached to the **e** out
39:7 the shoulder straps of the **e** as
39:8 creatively as they made the **e**.
39:18 straps of the **e** ⌊so that
39:19 the inside edge next to the **e**.
39:20 straps on the front of the **e**.
39:20 just above the belt of the **e**.
39:21 by its rings to the rings of the **e**
39:21 just above the belt of the **e**
39:22 the robe that is worn with the **e**,
Lev 8:7 the robe that is worn with the **e**.
8:7 He fastened the **e** to it.
Num 34:23 Hanniel, son of **E**, the leader of
Jdg 17:5 He also made an **e** and
18:14 "Do you know that there's an **e**,
18:17 took the carved idol, the **e**,
18:18 idol, the **e**, the household idols,
18:20 He took the **e**, the household
1Sm 2:18 ⌊already⌋ wearing a linen **e**.
2:28 and to wear the **e** in my
14:3 was wearing the priestly **e**.
14:18 "Bring the priestly **e**," because
14:18 because Ahijah carried the **e** in
14:19 your hand ⌊from the **e**⌋."
21:9 in a cloth behind the priestly **e**.
22:18 wearing the linen priestly **e**.
23:6 brought a priestly **e** with him.
23:9 priest Abiathar, "Bring the **e**."
30:7 bring me the priestly **e**."
30:7 Abiathar brought David the **e**.
2Sm 6:14 Wearing a linen **e**,
1Ch 15:27 David also wore a linen **e**.

ephods (1)

Hos 3:4 and without **e** or family idols.

Ephphatha (1)

Mar 7:34 and said to the man, "**E**!"

Ephraim (175)

Gen 41:52 He named the second son **E**
46:20 In Egypt, Manasseh and **E**
48:1 and **E** ⌊to see Jacob⌋.
48:5 **E** and Manasseh will be mine
48:13 both of them, **E** on his right,
48:14 although **E** was the younger
48:20 'May God make you like **E** and
48:20 put **E** ahead of Manasseh.
Num 1:10 from the tribe of **E**;
1:10 (**E** and Manasseh are Joseph's
1:32 Joseph — those from **E** — listed
1:33 for the tribe of **E** was 40,500.
2:18 led by **E** will camp under
2:18 for the people of **E** is Elishama,
7:48 leader of the descendants of **E**,
13:8 from the tribe of **E**;
26:28 Manasseh and **E** were
26:35 The families descended from **E**
34:24 the leader of the tribe of **E**;
34:24 **E** are Joseph's descendants.)
Dtr 33:17 of thousands from the tribe of **E**
34:2 all of Naphtali, the territory of **E**
Jos 14:4 Manasseh and **E**, The Levites
16:4 sons, Manasseh and **E**,
16:5 the families descended from **E**.
16:8 to the families of the tribe of **E**
16:9 for **E** in Manasseh's territory.
16:10 So the Canaanites still live in **E**
17:8 of Manasseh, belongs to **E**.)
17:9 These cities belong to **E**,
17:10 ⌊of the river⌋ belongs to **E**,
17:15 of **E** are too confining
17:17 tribes of⌋ **E** and Manasseh,
19:50 Serah in the mountains of **E**.
20:7 in the mountains of **E**,
21:5 the families of the tribes of **E**
21:20 chosen by lot from the tribe of **E**
21:21 in the mountains of **E**,
24:30 in the mountains of **E** north
24:33 in the mountains of **E**.
Jdg 1:29 The tribe of **E** did not force out
2:9 This was in the mountains of **E**
3:27 the mountains of **E** ⌊to summon
4:5 Bethel in the mountains of **E**.
5:14 country came down from **E**.
5:14 came with its troops after **E**.
7:24 the whole mountain region of **E**
7:24 All the men of **E** were also
8:1 The men from **E** strongly
8:2 Aren't the grapes that **E** picked
10:1 Shamir in the mountains of **E**.
10:9 of Judah, Benjamin, and **E**.
12:1 The men of **E** were summoned
12:4 the men of Gilead and fought **E**.
12:4 The men of Gilead defeated **E**.
12:4 did this because⌋ **E** had said,
12:4 from **E** and Manasseh."
12:5 Jordan River leading back to **E**.
12:5 a fugitive from **E** said,
12:5 would ask, "Are you from **E**?"
12:6 At that time 42,000 men from **E**
12:15 in the territory of **E**,
17:1 from the mountain region of **E**.
17:8 house in the mountains of **E**
18:2 house in the mountains of **E**.
18:13 to the mountains of **E** as far as
19:1 area in the mountains of **E**.
19:16 from the mountain region of **E**
19:18 area in the mountains of **E**.
1Sm 1:1 Zophim in the mountains of **E**.
1:1 was Zuph from the tribe of **E**.
9:4 through the mountains of **E**
14:22 in the mountains of **E** heard that
2Sm 2:9 **E**, and Benjamin, that is,
13:23 at Baal Hazor near **E**.
18:6 to fight Israel in the forest of **E**.
20:21 A man from the mountains of **E**
1Ki 4:8 was in charge of the hills of **E**,
12:25 Shechem in the hills of **E**
2Ki 5:22 in the hills of **E** have arrived.
14:13 around Jerusalem from **E** Gate

1Ch 6:66 by lot from the tribe of **E**.
6:67 its pastureland in the hills of **E**,
7:22 Their father **E** mourned a long
7:23 She gave birth to a son, and **E**
9:3 Benjamin, **E**, and Manasseh:
27:10 from the descendants of **E**,
27:14 of the tribe of **E** from Pirathon,
27:20 for the tribe of **E**: Hoshea,
2Ch 13:4 in the mountains of **E**.
15:8 captured in the mountains of **E**.
15:9 who had come from **E**,
17:2 in the cities of **E** that his father
19:4 and the mountains of **E**.
25:7 He's not with these men from **E**.
25:10 that had come to him from **E**.
25:23 around Jerusalem from **E** Gate
28:7 Zichri, a fighting man from **E**,
28:12 of **E**) opposed those coming
30:1 the tribes of **E** and Manasseh.
30:10 territories of **E** and Manasseh,
30:18 Many people from **E**,
31:1 Benjamin, **E**, and Manasseh.
34:6 In the cities of Manasseh, **E**,
34:9 the tribes of Manasseh and **E**,
Neh 8:16 or in the open area at **E** Gate.
12:39 then past **E** Gate, over Old
Psa 60:7 **E** is the helmet on my head.
78:9 The men of **E**, turned ⌊and ran⌋
78:67 did not choose the tribe of **E**,
80:2 Appear in front of **E**,
108:8 **E** is the helmet on my head.
Isa 7:2 had made an alliance with **E**,
7:5 Aram, **E**, and Remaliah's son
7:8 **E** will be shattered within 65
7:9 The capital of **E** is Samaria,
7:17 any since **E** broke away from
9:9 All the people of **E** and the
9:21 Manasseh is against **E**.
9:21 **E** is against Manasseh.
11:13 **E** won't be jealous of Judah,
11:13 and Judah won't oppose **E**.
17:3 cities will disappear from **E**,
28:1 be for the arrogant drunks of **E**.
28:3 The arrogant drunks of **E** will
Jer 4:15 comes from the mountains of **E**.
31:6 the mountains of **E** will call out
31:9 and **E** will be my firstborn.
31:18 have certainly heard **E** mourn
31:20 Is **E** my dear son?
50:19 the mountains of **E** and Gilead.
Eze 37:16 and write on it, 'The stick of **E**,
48:5 **E** will have one part of the land
48:6 part of the land and border **E**
Hos 4:17 The people of **E** have chosen
5:3 I know **E**, and Israel isn't a
5:3 Now, **E**, you are acting like a
5:5 Israel and **E** stumble because
5:9 **E** will become a wasteland
5:11 **E** is oppressed — crushed by
5:12 I will destroy **E** as a moth
5:13 "When **E** saw that he was sick
5:13 **E** went to Assyria to ask the
5:14 I will be like a lion to **E** and
6:4 "What should I do with you, **E**?
6:10 **E** is acting like a prostitute,
7:8 "**E** mixes with other nations.
7:8 **E**, you are like a half-baked
7:11 **E**, you are like a silly,
8:9 The people of **E** sold
8:11 altars that the people of **E** build
9:3 The people of **E** won't stay in
9:8 are God's watchmen over **E**.
9:13 I have seen **E**, like Tyre,
9:13 But the people of **E** will bring
9:16 "The people of **E** are like sick
10:6 **E** will be disgraced.
10:11 "**E** is like a trained calf that
10:11 I will harness **E**. Judah must
11:3 taught the people of **E** to walk.
11:8 "How can I give you up, **E**?
11:9 I will not destroy **E** again.
11:12 "**E** surrounds me with lies.
12:1 The people of **E** try to catch the
12:8 The people of **E** say,
12:14 The people of **E** made the
13:1 When the tribe of **E** spoke,
Hos 13:1 The people of **E** were important
13:15 The people of **E** have become
14:8 "The people of **E** will have
Oba 1:19 of the lands of **E** and Samaria,
Zec 9:10 sure there are no chariots in **E**
9:13 my bow with **E** ⌊as its arrow⌋.
10:7 The people of **E** will be like
Jon 11:54 the desert, to a city called **E**,

Ephraim's (18)

Gen 48:14 **E** head, although Ephraim was
48:17 put his right hand on **E** head,
48:17 it from **E** head to Manasseh's.
50:23 his grandchildren, **E** children.
Num 2:24 troops in **E** camp is 108,100.
10:22 **E** descendants broke camp next.
26:37 the families of **E** descendants.
1Ch 7:20 **E** son was Shuthelah.
7:21 **E** sons Ezer and Elead were
7:28 homes of **E** descendants were
12:30 From **E** descendants there
Isa 11:13 **E** jealousy will vanish,
Jer 7:15 all of **E** descendants.
Eze 37:19 which is in **E** hand, and the
Hos 7:1 all I can see is **E** sin and
9:11 "**E** glory will fly away like a
9:15 "All **E** wickedness began in
13:12 "**E** wickedness is on record.

Ephrath (7)

Gen 35:16 still some distance from **E**,
35:19 buried on the way to **E** (that is,
48:7 still some distance from **E**.
48:7 there on the way to **E**" (that is,
1Sm 17:12 Jesse from the region of **E**
1Ch 2:19 Azubah died, Caleb married **E**.
2:50 the firstborn son of **E**,

Ephrathah (6)

Rut 1:2 They were descendants of **E**
4:11 your strength of character in **E**
1Ch 2:24 After Hezron died in Caleb **E**,
4:4 sons of Hur, the firstborn of **E**,
Psa 132:6 ark ⌊of the promise⌋ being in **E**.
Mic 5:2 You, Bethlehem **E**,

Ephrathite (1)

1Ki 11:26 Nebat and an **E** from Zeredah.

Ephron (11)

Gen 23:8 Encourage **E**, son of Zohar,
23:10 **E** was sitting among the
23:13 He spoke to **E** so that the
23:14 **E** answered Abraham,
23:16 So he weighed out for **E** the
25:9 of Machpelah in the field of **E**,
49:29 cave in the field of **E** the Hittite.
49:30 from **E** the Hittite to use as a
50:13 this tomb from **E** the Hittite.
Jos 15:9 it goes to the cities of Mount **E**
2Ch 13:19 and **E** and its villages.

Ephron's (2)

Gen 23:16 Abraham agreed to **E** terms.
23:17 So **E** field at Machpelah,

Epicurean (1)

Act 17:18 Some **E** and Stoic

epidemic (1)

2Ch 7:13 or send an **e** among my people.

epidemics (2)

Dtr 32:24 by pestilence and deadly **e**.
Psa 91:6 **e** that strike at noon.

epileptics (1)

Mat 4:24 They also brought **e**,

equal (14)

Gen 44:18 although you are **e** to Pharaoh.
Exo 22:17 pay an amount of money **e**
Lev 25:51 an amount **e** ⌊to those years⌋.
25:52 an amount **e** to those years.
Job 28:17 gold nor glass can **e** its value.
28:19 Ethiopia cannot **e** its value.
Psa 55:13 But it is you, my **e**,
Pro 3:15 and all your desires cannot **e** it.
8:11 Nothing you desire can **e** it.
Isa 40:25 Who is my **e**?" asks the Holy
46:5 compare me and make me **e**?
Eze 31:8 trees couldn't **e** its branches.
Jon 5:18 but also he made himself **e** to
Php 2:6 form of God and **e** with God,

equality (1)

Php 2:6 not take advantage of this **e**.

equip (1)

2Ti 3:17 They **e** God's servants so that

equipment (14)

Gen 27:3 Now take your hunting **e**,
Exo 39:40 the ropes and pegs — all the **e**
Num 1:50 including the **e** for the tent and
1:50 will carry the tent and all its **e**.
3:36 posts, sockets, and all the **e**.
4:26 and all the **e** used to set up the
4:32 must take care of all this **e**.
Dtr 23:13 pointed stick as part of your **e**.
1Sm 8:12 weapons and **e** for his chariots.
2Ki 7:15 littered with clothes and **e** that
Isa 10:28 They store their **e** at Michmash.
Dan 11:13 with a large army and a lot of **e**.
Zec 11:15 "Use the **e** of a foolish
Act 27:19 threw the ship's **e** overboard.

equipped (4)

1Ch 12:23 numbers of the men **e** for war.
12:24 there were 6,800 men **e** for war.
12:33 They were **e** for battle with
Eze 46:23 walls were **e** with fireplaces.

Er (11)

Gen 38:3 gave birth to a son named **E**.
38:6 a wife for his firstborn son **E**.
38:7 **E** angered the LORD.
46:12 The sons of Judah were **E**,
46:12 (**E** and Onan had died in
Num 26:19 **E** and Onan were sons of
1Ch 2:3 Judah's sons were **E**,
2:3 The LORD considered **E**,
2:3 so the LORD killed **E**.
4:21 Shelah, son of Judah, were **E**,
Luk 3:28 son of Elmadam, son of **E**,

era (3)

Mat 12:39 of an evil and unfaithful **e** look
1Ti 2:6 message is valid for every **e**.
Tit 1:3 this in every **e** by spreading his

Eran (1)

Num 26:36 Shuthelah were the family of **E**.

erase (5)

Exo 17:14 I will completely **e** any memory
Dtr 25:19 don't forget to **e** every memory
29:20 The LORD will **e** ⌊every
32:26 and **e** everyone's memory
Rev 3:5 I will never **e** their names from

erased (1)

Psa 69:28 Let their ⌊names⌋ be **e** from the

erasing (1)

Col 2:14 He did this by **e** the charges

Erastus (3)

Act 19:22 Timothy and **E**, to Macedonia,
Rom 16:23 **E**, the city treasurer,
2Ti 4:20 **E** stayed in the city of Corinth

Erech (2)

Gen 10:10 were Babylon, **E**, Accad,
Ezr 4:9 **E**, Babylon, Susa, (that is,

Eri (2)

Gen 46:16 Ezbon, **E**, Arodi, and Areli.
Num 26:16 family of Ozni, the family of **E**,

error (5)

Ecc 10:5 an **e** often made by rulers.

Dan 6:4 No **e** or fault could be found.
Jas 5:20 brings a sinner back from the **e**
2Pe 2:18 from those who live in **e**.
Jud 1:11 have rushed into Balaam's **e**

errors (3)

Dan 4:27 Stop committing the same **e**,
2Ti 3:16 for teaching, pointing out **e**,
4:2 Point out **e**, warn people,

Esarhaddon (3)

2Ki 19:37 His son **E** succeeded him as
Ezr 4:2 the time of King **E** of Assyria,
Isa 37:38 His son **E** succeeded him as

Esau (84)

Gen 25:25 so they named him **E** [Hairy].
25:27 **E** became an expert hunter,
25:28 of wild animals, he loved **E**.
25:29 was preparing a meal when **E**,
25:30 So **E** said to Jacob,
25:32 **E** said. "What good is my
25:33 So **E** swore an oath to him and
25:34 Then Jacob gave **E** a meal of
25:34 This is how **E** showed his
26:34 When **E** was 40 years old,
27:1 he called his older son **E** and
27:1 **E** answered, "Here I am."
27:5 was speaking to his son **E**.
27:5 When **E** went into the open
27:6 speaking to your brother **E**.
27:11 "My brother **E** is a hairy man,
27:19 father, "I'm **E**, your firstborn.
27:21 or not you really are my son **E**."
27:24 "Are you really my son **E**?"
27:30 left when his brother **E** came
27:32 firstborn son **E**," he answered.
27:34 When **E** heard these words
27:36 **E** said, "Isn't that why he's
27:37 Isaac answered **E**,
27:38 **E** asked, "Do you have only
27:38 And **E** sobbed loudly.
27:41 So **E** hated Jacob because of
27:41 **E** said to himself, "The time to
27:42 what her older son **E** had said,
27:42 Your brother **E** is comforting
28:5 was the mother of Jacob and **E**.
28:6 **E** learned that Isaac had
28:8 **E** realized that his father Isaac
32:3 of him to his brother **E** in Seir,
32:4 them to give this message to **E**,
32:6 "We went to your brother **E**.
32:8 "If **E** attacks the one camp,
32:11 save me from my brother **E**,
32:13 a gift for his brother **E** from
32:17 "When my brother **E** meets you
32:19 "Say the same thing to **E** when
33:1 Jacob saw **E** coming with 400
33:4 Then **E** ran to meet Jacob.
33:4 **E** hugged him, threw his arms
33:5 women and children, **E** asked,
33:8 Then **E** asked, "Why did you
33:9 **E** said, "I have enough.
33:11 So **E** took it because Jacob
33:12 Then **E** said, "Let's get ready to
33:15 **E** said, "Then let me leave
33:16 That day **E** started back to Seir.
35:1 fleeing from your brother **E**."
35:29 His sons **E** and Jacob buried
36:1 is the account of **E** (that is,
36:2 **E** chose his wives from the
36:4 gave birth to Eliphaz for **E**,
36:5 These were the sons of **E** who
36:6 **E** took his wives, his sons,
36:8 So **E**, who was also known as
36:9 This is the account of **E** and
36:14 Jeush, Jalam, and Korah for **E**.
36:19 the descendants of **E** (that is,
36:40 leaders descended from **E**,
36:43 **E** was the father of the people
Dtr 2:4 the descendants of **E**,
2:8 the descendants of **E**,
2:12 but the descendants of **E**
2:22 thing for the descendants of **E**,
2:22 the descendants of **E** came,
2:29 as the descendants of **E**,
Jos 24:4 To Isaac I gave Jacob and **E**.
24:4 I gave **E** the mountains in Seir
1Ch 1:34 Isaac's sons were **E** and Israel.
Jer 49:8 on the descendants of **E**.
49:10 will strip the descendants of **E**.
Oba 1:6 But you, **E**, will lose
1:18 But the descendants of **E** will
1:18 among the descendants of **E**."
Mal 1:2 "Wasn't **E** Jacob's brother?"
1:3 but **E** I hated. I turned his
1:4 descendants of **E** may say,
Rom 9:13 "I loved Jacob, but I hated **E**."
Heb 11:20 led Isaac to bless Jacob and **E**.
12:16 about earthly things as **E** was.

Esau's (25)

Gen 25:26 his hand holding on to **E** heel,
27:15 her older son **E** good clothes,
27:22 "but the hands are **E**."
27:23 hairy like his brother **E** hands.
36:10 the names of **E** sons: Eliphaz,
36:10 son of **E** wife Adah,
36:10 son of **E** wife Basemath.
36:12 a concubine of **E** son Eliphaz.
36:12 the grandsons of **E** wife Adah.
36:13 grandsons of **E** wife Basemath.
36:14 the sons of **E** wife Oholibamah,
36:15 leaders among **E** descendants:
36:15 **E** firstborn, were Teman,
36:17 descendants of **E** son Reuel:
36:17 grandsons of **E** wife Basemath.
36:18 of **E** wife Oholibamah:
36:18 from **E** wife Oholibamah,
Dtr 2:5 I've given **E** descendants the
2:22 **E** descendants claimed their land
2:22 **E** descendants are still there
1Ch 1:35 **E** sons were Eliphaz,
Oba 1:8 from **E** mountain," declares
1:9 Everyone on **E** mountain will
1:19 take possession of **E** mountain.
1:21 Mount Zion to rule **E** mountain.

escape (80)

Gen 7:7 the ship to **e** the floodwaters.
19:29 Lot was allowed to **e** from the
32:8 other camp will be able to **e**."
Exo 14:3 The desert is blocking their **e**.'
14:27 The Egyptians tried to **e**,
Num 35:6 You must allow murderers to **e**
Jos 20:9 kills someone may **e**
1Sm 19:12 and he ran away to **e**.
19:17 away so that he could **e**?"
27:1 to do is to make sure that I **e**
27:1 and I'll **e** from him."
2Sm 15:14 none of us will **e** from Absalom.
1Ki 18:40 Don't let any of them **e**."
2Ki 9:15 don't let anyone **e** from the city
10:24 I'm putting in your hands **e**,
19:30 of Judah who **e** will again take
19:31 and those who **e** will go out of
2Ch 12:7 while I will give them an **e**.
Job 11:20 Their **e** route will be closed.
15:30 "He won't **e** the darkness.
20:20 he desires to **e** ⌊his grasp⌋.
23:7 I would **e** my judgment forever.
Psa 33:17 cannot help someone **e**.
56:7 the wrong they do, can they **e**?
68:20 LORD is our **e** from death.
82:4 Help them **e** the power of
141:10 while I **e** unharmed.
142:4 **E** is impossible for me.
Pro 6:29 None who touch her will **e**
11:21 of righteous people will **e**.
17:5 distress will not **e** punishment.
19:5 One who tells lies will not **e**.
28:20 get rich will not **e** punishment.
Ecc 7:26 pleases God will **e** her,
Isa 20:6 of Assyria. How can we **e**?'"
37:31 of Judah who **e** will again take
37:32 and those who **e** will go out
46:2 They aren't able to **e** with
Jer 11:11 on them that they can't **e**.
21:9 You will **e** with your lives.
25:35 no **e** for the leaders of the flock.
32:4 of Judah will not **e** from
34:3 You will not **e** from him.
35:11 'Let's go to Jerusalem ⌊to **e**⌋
38:2 They will **e** with their lives.
38:18 and you will not **e** from them."
38:23 You will not **e** from them.
39:18 You will **e** with your life
42:17 No one will survive or **e** the
44:28 Those who **e** the wars will
45:5 I will let you **e** with your life.'"
46:6 The warriors can't **e**.
46:16 and **e** our enemy's sword.'
48:8 to every city, and no city will **e**.
50:29 Don't let anyone **e**.
Eze 6:8 Some people will **e** the battle
6:9 Then those who **e** will
7:16 Those who survive will **e** to
17:15 who does such things **e**?
Dan 8:4 and no one could **e** from its
11:41 will **e** from his power.
11:42 Even Egypt will not **e**.
Hos 9:6 Even if they **e** without being
Joe 2:32 Those who **e** will be on Mount
Amo 2:14 Runners will not be able to **e**.
2:15 runners will not be able to **e**.
9:1 None of them will be able to **e**.
Nah 3:11 fortress ⌊to **e**⌋ from the enemy.
Zec 2:7 **E**, you inhabitants of Babylon!
Mat 23:33 How can you **e** being
Luk 21:36 power to **e** everything that is
Act 27:30 The sailors tried to **e** from the
Rom 2:3 you will **e** God's judgment?
1Co 10:13 temptation as your way of **e**.
1Th 5:3 They won't be able to **e**.
Heb 2:3 So how will we **e** punishment
12:25 Your ancestors didn't **e** when
12:25 We certainly won't **e** if we turn
2Pe 2:20 and Savior Jesus Christ and **e**
Rev 9:6 but death will **e** them.

escaped (40)

Gen 14:13 Then a soldier who had **e**
Jos 8:22 None of them survived or **e**.
Jdg 3:26 they had been waiting, Ehud **e**.
3:26 the stone idols and **e** to Seirah.
3:29 Not one of them **e**.
1Sm 11:1 seven thousand men had **e**
19:18 David **e** and went to Samuel at
22:1 So David **e** from that place and
22:20 had one son who **e**.
23:13 "David has **e** from Keilah!"
30:17 No one **e** except 400 young
2Sm 1:3 "I **e** from the camp of Israel,"
4:6 and his brother Baanah **e**.
1Ki 20:20 King Benhadad of Aram **e** on a
2Ki 19:37 assassinated him and **e**
2Ch 16:7 king of Aram has **e** your grasp.
20:24 on the ground. No one had **e**.
30:6 to the few of you who **e** from
Job 1:15 only one who has **e** to tell you."
1:16 only one who has **e** to tell you."
1:17 only one who has **e** to tell you."
1:19 only one who has **e** to tell you."
19:20 and I have **e** only by the skin of
Psa 124:7 We **e** like a bird caught in a
124:7 The trap was broken, and we **e**.
Isa 37:38 assassinated him and **e** to the
Jer 41:15 Ishmael and eight of his men **e**
47:4 Philistine who might have **e**
51:50 You people who **e** from the
Lam 2:22 No one **e** or survived on the
Eze 6:12 who is left and has **e** will die
15:7 though they have **e** one fire,
Act 14:6 So they **e** to Lystra and Derbe,
16:27 Thinking the prisoners had **e**,
26:26 things has **e** his attention.
28:4 He may have **e** from the sea,
2Co 11:33 in the wall and **e** from him.
Heb 11:34 out raging fires, and **e** death.
2Pe 1:4 nature because you have **e**
2:18 have just **e** from those who

escapes (5)

Dtr 23:15 If a slave **e** from his master and
1Ki 19:17 If anyone **e** from Hazael's
19:17 And if anyone **e** from Jehu's
Pro 12:13 righteous person **e** from
Joe 2:3 a barren desert. Nothing **e** ⌊it!⌋

escaping (3)
1Sm 19:10 e from Saul that night.
Jer 48:19 who are e what is happening.
Act 27:42 from swimming away and e.

escort (2)
Ezr 8:22 to ask the king for an armed e
Act 16:37 Have them e us out!"

escorted (2)
Act 16:39 As the officials e Paul and
17:15 The men who e Paul took him

Esek (1)
Gen 26:20 named the well E [Argument],

Eshan (1)
Jos 15:52 their villages: Arab, Dumah, E,

Eshbaal (2)
1Ch 8:33 Malchishua, Abinadab, and E.
9:39 Malchishua, Abinadab, and E.

Eshban (2)
Gen 36:26 Hemdan, E, Ithran, and Cheran.
1Ch 1:41 Dishon's sons were Hamran, E,

Eshcol (6)
Gen 14:13 a brother of E and Aner.
14:24 But let my allies Aner, E,
Num 13:23 they came to the E Valley,
13:24 So they called that valley E
32:9 They went as far as the E
Dtr 1:24 they came to the E Valley,

Eshek's (1)
1Ch 8:39 His brother E sons were Ulam

Eshtaol (7)
Jos 15:33 villages: E, Zorah, Ashnah,
19:41 included Zorah, E, Ir Shemesh,
Jdg 13:25 between Zorah and E.
16:31 him between Zorah and E
18:2 men from Zorah and E.
18:8 their relatives in Zorah and E.
18:11 left Zorah and E armed for war.

Eshtaolites (1)
1Ch 2:53 came the Zorahites and E.

Eshtemoa (5)
Jos 21:14 Jattir, E,
1Sm 30:28 Aroer, Siphmoth, E,
1Ch 4:17 who first settled E.
4:19 and E of the Maacathites.
6:57 E with its pastureland,

Eshtemoh (1)
Jos 15:50 Anab, E, Anim,

Eshton (2)
1Ch 4:11 who was the father of E.
4:12 E was the first to settle Beth

Esli (1)
Luk 3:25 son of E, son of Naggai,

establish (21)
Exo 23:31 "I will e your borders from the
2Sm 3:10 and e David's throne over
7:12 I will e his kingdom.
7:13 and I will e the throne of his
1Ki 9:5 then I will e your royal dynasty
1Ch 17:11 I will e his kingdom.
17:12 and I will e his throne forever.
18:3 When David went to e his
22:10 I will e the throne of his
28:7 I will e his kingdom forever if
2Ch 7:18 then I will e your royal dynasty
Est 9:29 with full authority in order to e
9:31 He did this in order to e these
Isa 9:7 He will e David's throne and
26:12 you will e peace for us,
Jer 30:9 I will e him for you.
Eze 37:26 I will e them, make them
Dan 2:44 the God of heaven will e a
Heb 9:10 for the body until God would e
10:9 with sacrifices in order to e
11:28 Faith led Moses to e the

established (43)
Num 28:6 burnt offering which was e
1Sm 13:13 the LORD would have e your
2Sm 5:12 the LORD had e him as king
7:16 Your throne will be e forever.'"
7:26 will be e in your presence.
1Ki 2:12 and his power was firmly e.
2:24 the LORD who has e me lives,
2:45 be firmly e by the LORD."
2:46 as king was now firmly e.
1Ch 14:2 the LORD had e him as king
17:14 and his throne will be e
17:24 will be e in your presence.
2Ch 9:8 he has e them permanently and
12:1 When Rehoboam had e his
17:5 So the LORD e Jehoshaphat's
Est 9:21 He e the fourteenth and
9:27 the Jews e a tradition for
9:31 Jew and Queen Esther e them
9:31 as they had e for themselves
9:32 Esther's command had e these
Job 21:8 children firmly e with them,
Psa 78:5 He e written instructions for
99:4 You have e fairness.
119:5 may become firmly e so that
119:89 word is e in heaven forever.
Pro 3:19 he e the heavens.
8:28 when he e the skies above,
16:12 is e through righteousness.
24:3 With understanding it is e.
Isa 2:2 the LORD's house will be e as
44:7 when I e my people long
54:14 You will be e in righteousness.
Jer 30:20 Their community will be e in
Dan 2:44 But it will be e forever.
11:4 But as soon as he is e,
Mic 4:1 the LORD's house will be e as
Rom 13:1 exist if it hadn't been e by God.
13:2 opposes what God has e.
2Co 1:24 Certainly, you are firmly e in
Col 2:14 by the written laws God had e.
Heb 7:11 The people e the Levitical
7:12 different kind of priesthood is e,
1Pe 5:12 Remain firmly e in it!

establishes (6)
1Ki 7:21 and named it Jachin [He E].
2Ch 3:17 one on the right Jachin [He E]
Job 25:2 He e peace in his high places.
Isa 62:7 any rest until he e Jerusalem
Dan 2:21 He removes kings and e them.
2Co 1:21 God e us, together with you,

estate (1)
Ecc 2:21 Yet, he must turn over his e to

Esther (53)
Est 2:7 Hadassah, also known as E,
2:8 E also was taken to the king's
2:10 E did not reveal her nationality
2:11 quarters to find out how E was
2:15 (E was the daughter of Abihail,
2:15 Everyone who saw E liked her.
2:16 So E was taken to King
2:17 Now, the king loved E more
2:18 king held a great banquet for E.
2:20 E still had not revealed her
2:20 E always did whatever
2:22 about it and informed Queen E.
2:22 Then E told the king,
4:5 Then E called for Hathach,
4:8 was supposed to show it to E
4:9 So Hathach returned and told E
4:10 E spoke to Hathach and
4:12 told Mordecai what E said.
4:13 sent this answer back to E,
4:15 E sent this reply back to
4:17 just as E had commanded him.
5:1 On the third day E put on her
5:2 When the king saw Queen E
5:2 that was in his hand to E.
Est 5:2 E went up to him and touched
5:3 is troubling you, Queen E?
5:4 So E answered, "If it pleases
5:5 and do whatever E asks."
5:5 the dinner that E had prepared.
5:6 wine, the king asked E,
5:7 E answered, "My request?
5:12 Queen E allowed no one
6:14 to the dinner E had prepared.
7:1 to have dinner with Queen E.
7:2 wine, the king asked E,
7:2 is your request, Queen E?
7:3 Then Queen E answered,
7:5 interrupted Queen E and said,
7:6 E answered, "Our vicious
7:7 Haman stayed to beg Queen E
7:8 the couch where E was lying.
8:1 of the Jews, to Queen E.
8:1 king because E had told him
8:2 And E put Mordecai in charge
8:3 E spoke again to the king.
8:4 out his golden scepter to E,
8:4 and E got up and stood in front
8:7 King Xerxes said to Queen E
8:7 given Haman's property to E,
9:12 So the king said to Queen E,
9:13 E said, "If it pleases you,
9:29 Abihail's daughter Queen E
9:31 Mordecai the Jew and Queen E

Esther's (4)
Est 2:15 When E turn came to go to the
4:4 E servants and eunuchs came
4:12 So E servants told Mordecai
9:32 E command had established

estimate (1)
Lev 27:18 the priest will e its value based

Etam (5)
Jdg 15:8 to live in a cave in the cliff at E.
15:11 to the cave in the cliff at E.
1Ch 4:3 were the first settlers in E:
4:32 Their five cities were E,
2Ch 11:6 He rebuilt Bethlehem, E,

eternal (70)
Dtr 33:27 The e God is your shelter,
1Ki 10:9 Because of your God's e love
Psa 93:2 a long time ago. You are e.
133:3 promised the blessing of e life.
Pro 12:28 E death is not along its path.
Ecc 12:5 Mortals go to their e rest,
Isa 40:28 The e God, the LORD,
Jer 10:10 He is the living God and e king.
20:11 Their e shame will not be
23:40 I will bring e disgrace and
32:40 I will make an e promise to
Dan 4:3 His kingdom is an e kingdom.
7:14 His power is an e power that
7:27 Their kingdom is e.
Mat 19:16 deed should I do to gain e life?"
19:29 more and will inherit e life.
25:46 go away into e punishment,
25:46 approval will go into e life."
Mar 10:17 what should I do to inherit e
10:30 to come they will receive e life.
Luk 10:25 what must I do to inherit e life?"
16:9 you will be welcomed into an e
18:18 what must I do to inherit e life?"
18:30 this life and will receive e life
Jon 3:15 in him will have e life."
3:16 will not die but will have e life.
3:36 believes in the Son has e life,
4:14 spring that gushes up to e life."
4:36 He is gathering grain for e life.
5:24 who sent me will have e life.
5:39 you have the source of e life
5:40 to come to me to get e life.
6:27 for the food that lasts into e life.
6:40 believe in him to have e life.
6:47 Every believer has e life.
6:54 and drink my blood have e life,
6:68 Your words give e life.
10:28 and I give them e life.
12:50 what he commands is e life.

Jon 17:2 so that he can give **e** life
17:3 This is **e** life: to know you,
Act 11:18 think and act and have **e** life."
Rom 1:20 his **e** power and divine nature,
2Co 4:17 for us an **e** glory that is
5:1 It is an **e** house in heaven that
5:4 do want to put on the **e** house.
5:4 Then ⌊**e**⌋ life will put an end to
1Ti 1:17 belong forever to the **e** king,
2Ti 1:10 he has brought **e** life into full
Tit 1:2 on the confidence of **e** life.
1:2 promised this **e** life before the
Heb 5:9 he became the source of **e**
6:2 back to life, and **e** judgment.
9:14 Through the **e** Spirit he offered
11:35 so that they might gain **e** life.
11:40 we would gain **e** life with them.
12:23 and have gained **e** life.
13:20 the blood of an **e** promise.
1Pe 5:10 Christ Jesus to his **e** glory,
2Pe 1:11 of entering into the **e** kingdom
3:18 to him now and for that **e** day!
1Jn 1:2 to you about this **e** life that was
2:25 given us the promise of **e** life.
3:15 a murderer doesn't have **e** life.
5:11 God has given us **e** life,
5:13 will know that they have **e** life.
5:20 Christ is the real God and **e** life.
Jud 1:6 bound by **e** chains.
1:7 us of the punishment of **e** fire.
1:21 Jesus Christ to give you **e** life.

eternity (5)

Psa 25:6 They have existed from **e**.
41:13 God of Israel through all **e**!
Ecc 3:11 He has put a sense of **e** in
Eph 3:21 Christ Jesus for all time and **e**!
Jud 1:25 and for **e** glory, majesty, power,

Etham (4)

Exo 13:20 from Succoth and camped at **E**,
Num 33:6 Succoth and set up camp at **E**,
33:7 They moved from **E** and turned
33:8 three days in the Desert of **E**,

Ethan (7)

1Ki 4:31 than **E** the Ezrahite,
1Ch 2:6 Zerah's sons were Zimri, **E**,
6:42 who was the son of **E**,
6:44 On the left was **E**,
6:44 **E** was the son of Kishi,
15:17 son. they appointed **E**,
15:19 and **E** were appointed to play

Ethanim (1)

1Ki 8:2 ⌊of Booths⌋ in the month of **E**,

Ethan's (1)

1Ch 2:8 **E** son was Azariah.

Ethbaal (1)

1Ki 16:31 daughter of King **E** of Sidon.

Ether (2)

Jos 15:42 to Judah: Libnah, **E**, Ashan,
19:7 Ain, Rimmon, **E**, and Ashan.

ethical (1)

Job 8:6 if you are moral and **e**,

Ethiopia (3)

Job 28:19 Topaz from **E** cannot equal its
Eze 30:4 war in Egypt and anguish in **E**.
Act 8:27 of Queen Candace of **E**.

Ethiopian (1)

Act 8:27 An **E** man who had come to

Ethiopians (1)

Jer 13:23 Can **E** change the color of their

Eth Kazin (1)

Jos 19:13 Gath Hepher, **E**, and Rimmon,

Ethnan (1)

1Ch 4:7 were Zereth, Izohar, and **E**.

Ethni (1)

1Ch 6:41 who was the son of **E**,

Eubulus (1)

2Ti 4:21 **E**, Pudens, Linus, Claudia and

Eunice (1)

2Ti 1:5 Lois and your mother **E**.

eunuch (5)

2Ki 23:11 room of the **e** Nathan Melech.
Est 2:3 the care of the king's **e** Hegai,
2:14 care of the king's **e** Shaashgaz,
2:15 for what the king's **e** Hegai,
Act 8:27 The man was a **e**,

eunuchs (12)

2Ki 9:32 Then two or three **e** looked out
24:12 and **e** surrendered to the king of
24:15 the king's mother, wives, **e**,
Est 1:10 the seven **e** who served under
1:12 command that the **e** delivered
1:15 which the **e** delivered?"
2:21 two of the king's **e** who
4:4 Esther's servants and **e** came
4:5 one of the king's **e** appointed to
6:2 two of the king's **e** who
6:14 the king's **e** arrived and quickly
7:9 Harbona, one of the **e** present

Euodia (1)

Php 4:2 I encourage both **E** and

Euphrates (59)

Gen 2:14 The fourth river is the **E**.
15:18 Egypt to the great river, the **E**.
31:21 He crossed the **E** River and
Exo 23:31 the Sinai Desert to the **E** River.
Num 22:5 was at Pethor, on the **E** River,
Dtr 1:7 Lebanon as far as the **E** River.
11:24 from the **E** River to the
Jos 1:4 nearby Lebanon to the **E** River
24:2 lived on the other side of the **E**
24:3 the other side of the **E** River.
24:14 on the other side of the **E** River
24:15 on the other side of the **E**
2Sm 8:3 the territory⌋ along the **E** River,
10:16 from beyond the **E** River.
1Ki 4:21 the kingdoms from the **E** River
4:24 of the **E** River from Tiphsah
14:15 them beyond the **E** River
2Ki 23:29 king of Assyria at the **E** River.
24:7 River of Egypt to the **E** River.
1Ch 5:9 that extends to the **E** River,
18:3 the territory⌋ along the **E** River,
19:16 from beyond the **E** River.
2Ch 9:26 all the kings from the **E** River
35:20 at Carchemish at the **E** River.
Ezr 4:10 the lands west of the **E** River.)
4:11 the people west of the **E**:
4:16 province⌋ west of the **E** River.
4:17 to others west of the **E** River:
4:20 ⌊province⌋ west of the **E**.
5:3 province⌋ west of the **E** River,
5:6 province⌋ west of the **E** River,
6:6 the province⌋ west of the **E**,
6:8 the province⌋ west of the **E**.
6:13 province⌋ west of the **E** River,
7:21 province⌋ west of the **E** River
7:25 province⌋ west of the **E** River.
8:36 province⌋ west of the **E** River.
Neh 2:7 province⌋ west of the **E** River.
2:9 province⌋ west of the **E** River
3:7 province⌋ west of the **E** River.
Psa 72:8 from the **E** River to the ends of
80:11 Its shoots reached the **E** River.
Isa 7:20 from beyond the **E** River
8:7 floodwaters of the **E** River —
11:15 wave his hand over the **E** River
27:12 flowing stream of the **E** River
Jer 2:18 to drink water from the **E** River.
13:4 Go to the **E** River, and bury it
13:5 I went and buried it by the **E**,
13:6 LORD said to me, "Go to the **E**,
13:7 So I went back to the **E** and
Jer 46:2 along the **E** River during
46:6 fall in the north by the **E** River.
46:10 in the north by the **E** River.
51:63 it into the middle of the **E** River.
Mic 7:12 from Egypt to the **E** River,
Zec 9:10 to sea and from the ⌊**E**⌋ River
Rev 9:14 are held at the great **E** River."
16:12 his bowl on the great **E** River.

Eutychus (3)

Act 20:9 A young man named **E** was
20:9 **E** was gradually falling asleep.
20:11 Then **E** went upstairs again,

evaluate (4)

Ezr 7:14 advisers are sending you to **e**
1Co 2:14 must be spiritual to **e** them.
2:15 Spiritual people **e** everything
2Co 10:13 about things that no one can **e**?

evaluated (2)

2Co 10:15 done by others that can't be **e**?
1Ti 3:10 First, a person must be **e**.

evaluation (1)

1Co 2:15 but are subject to no one's **e**.

evaporates (1)

Pro 31:30 is deceptive, and beauty **e**,

Eve (4)

Gen 3:20 Adam named his wife **E** [Life]
4:1 Adam made love to his wife **E**.
2Co 11:3 snake deceived **E** by its tricks,
1Ti 2:13 Adam was formed first, then **E**.

evening (141)

Gen 1:5 There was **e**, then morning —
1:8 There was **e**, then morning — a
1:13 There was **e**, then morning — a
1:19 There was **e**, then morning — a
1:23 There was **e**, then morning — a
1:31 There was **e**, then morning —
3:8 In the cool of the **e**,
8:11 The dove came to him in the **e**,
19:1 to Sodom in the **e** as Lot was
24:11 It was **e**, when the women
24:63 Toward **e** Isaac went out into
29:23 In the **e** he took his daughter
30:16 coming in from the fields that **e**,
49:27 In the **e** he divides the plunder."
Exo 12:18 From the **e** of the fourteenth
12:18 day of the first month until the **e**
16:6 "In the **e** you will know that it
16:8 give you meat to eat in the **e**
16:13 That **e** quails came and
18:13 Moses from morning until **e**.
18:14 you from morning until **e**?"
27:21 presence from **e** until morning.
Lev 6:20 in the morning and half in the **e**.
11:24 bodies will be unclean until **e**.
11:25 He will be unclean until **e**.
11:27 bodies will be unclean until **e**.
11:28 and will be unclean until **e**.
11:31 bodies will be unclean until **e**.
11:32 and will be unclean until **e**.
11:39 body will be unclean until **e**.
11:40 and will be unclean until **e**.
11:40 and will be unclean until **e**.
14:46 up will be unclean until **e**.
15:5 They will be unclean until **e**.
15:6 They will be unclean until **e**.
15:7 They will be unclean until **e**.
15:8 He will be unclean until **e**.
15:10 They will be unclean until **e**.
15:11 He will be unclean until **e**.
15:16 He will be unclean until **e**.
15:17 It will be unclean until **e**.
15:18 They will be unclean until **e**.
15:19 her will be unclean until **e**.
15:21 They will be unclean until **e**.
15:22 They will be unclean until **e**.
15:23 it will be unclean until **e**.
15:27 They will be unclean until **e**.
17:15 They will be unclean until **e**.
22:6 will be unclean until **e**.

Lev 23:5 day of the first month, in the e,
23:32 yourselves starting on the e
23:32 From that e to the next,
24:3 presence from e until morning.
Num 9:15 From e until morning,
9:21 only from e until morning.
19:7 But he will be unclean until e.
19:8 He, too, will be unclean until e.
19:10 He will be unclean until e.
19:19 and in the e they will be clean.
19:21 water will be unclean until e.
19:22 it will be unclean until e."
Dtr 16:4 the meat you slaughter on the e
16:6 Do this in the e as the sun
23:11 Toward e he must wash,
28:67 you'll say, "If only it were e!"
28:67 And in the e you'll say,
Jos 5:10 the Passover on the e
7:6 They stayed there until e.
8:29 a pole and left him there until e.
10:26 bodies on five poles until e.
Jdg 19:9 said to him, "It's already e.
19:16 That e an old man came into
20:23 presence of the LORD until e.
20:26 and fasted that day until e.
21:2 in the presence of God until e.
Rut 2:17 grain in the field until e.
1Sm 14:24 eats food before the e comes
17:16 Each morning and e for 40
30:17 From dawn until e the next
2Sm 1:12 fasted until e because Saul,
11:2 Now, when e came,
11:13 But that e Uriah went to lie
1Ki 17:6 in the morning and in the e.
18:29 until the time for the e sacrifice.
22:35 He died that e. The blood from
2Ki 16:15 and the e grain offering,
1Ch 16:40 continually, morning and e,
23:30 to do the same thing in the e.
2Ch 2:4 offerings every morning and e,
13:11 every morning and every e.
13:11 gold lamp stand burn every e.
18:34 facing the Arameans until e.
31:3 the morning and e offerings,
35:14 offerings and the fat until that e.
Ezr 3:3 the LORD every morning and e.
9:4 I sat in shock until the e
9:5 At the e sacrifice I got up from
Est 2:14 She would go in the e and
Job 4:20 From morning to e,
7:4 But the e is long, and I'm
Psa 59:6 They return in the e.
59:14 They return in the e.
65:8 and e sunset sing joyfully.
90:6 In the e they wither and dry up.
92:2 and your faithfulness in the e
104:23 to do their tasks until e.
141:2 be accepted as an e sacrifice.
Pro 7:9 in the twilight, in the e,
Ecc 11:6 don't let your hands rest until e.
Isa 17:14 In the e there will be sudden
Jer 6:4 of e are growing longer.
Eze 12:4 In the e let them see you leave
12:7 In the e I dug a hole through the
24:18 and in the e my wife died.
33:22 The e before the refugee
46:2 gate must not be closed until e.
Dan 9:21 the time of the e sacrifice.
Hab 1:8 quicker than wolves in the e.
Zep 2:7 In the e they will lie down in
3:3 are ⌊like⌋ wolves in the e.
Zec 14:7 It will be light even in the e.
Mat 8:16 In the e the people brought him
14:15 In the e the disciples came to
14:23 When e came, he was there
16:2 He responded to them, "In the e
20:8 "When e came, the owner of
26:20 When e came, Jesus was at
27:57 In the e a rich man named
Mar 1:32 In the e, when the sun had set,
4:35 That e, Jesus said to his
6:47 When e came, the boat was in
11:19 (Every e Jesus and his
13:35 It could be in the e or at
14:17 When e came, Jesus arrived
15:42 It was Friday e, before the day

Jon 4:6 was about six o'clock in the e.
4:52 yesterday e at seven o'clock."
6:16 When e came, his disciples
20:19 That Sunday e, the disciples
Act 4:3 Since it was already e,
28:23 From morning until e,

evenings (2)

Dan 8:14 "For 2,300 e and mornings.
8:26 The vision about the ⌊2,300⌋ e

even-tempered (2)

Pro 16:32 Better to be e than to capture a
17:27 who has understanding is e.

events (13)

Jos 9:1 River heard about these e,
24:29 After these e, the LORD's
1Ki 12:15 LORD was directing these e
2Ch 10:15 LORD was directing these e
12:15 Aren't the e concerning
Est 1:1 the following e took place.
2:23 in his official record of daily e.
Ecc 9:11 But time and unpredictable e
Isa 41:22 Explain past e that your idols
41:22 Tell us about future e.
43:18 not dwell on e from long ago.
46:9 Remember the first e,
Gal 4:24 to use these historical e as

ever (195)

Gen 24:16 No man had e had sexual
Exo 5:23 E since I went to Pharaoh to
9:18 hailstorm that has e happened
10:10 you if I would e let you take
10:14 nor would there e be that many
10:28 Don't e let me see your face
11:6 never been or e will be again.
12:48 males may e eat
15:18 will rule as king forever and e."
33:16 How will anyone e know you're
Lev 17:12 foreigners should e eat blood.
18:26 any foreigner should e do any
21:18 defect may e come near ⌊the
Num 11:20 'Why did we e leave Egypt?'"
11:28 been Moses' assistant e since
22:30 Have I e done this to you
Dtr 1:35 of these evil people will e see
2:27 and won't e leave the road.
4:7 What great nation e had their
4:32 as this e happened before,
4:32 like it e been heard of?
4:33 Have any ⌊other⌋ people e
4:34 Or has any god e tried to come
5:26 Who has e heard the voice of
7:25 Don't e long for the silver and
13:11 Then no one among you will e
13:17 Don't e take any of the things
15:6 but no nation will e rule you.
17:6 but no one should e be
23:17 or woman should e become
28:64 you nor your ancestors e knew.
Jos 23:7 Don't e mention the names of
23:7 Don't e serve their gods or bow
23:9 Not one person has e been
23:14 God has given you has e failed
Jdg 11:25 Did he e have a case against
11:25 Or did he e fight against Israel?
16:17 no one has e cut the hair on my
16:17 If my hair is e shaved off,
21:1 "None of us will e let our
Rut 3:14 "I hope that no one will e know
1Sm 3:14 No offering or sacrifice will e
4:7 this has e happened before.
26:9 "No one has e attacked the
2Sm 7:7 did I e ask any of the judges of
7:11 e since I appointed judges to
1Ki 8:16 'E since I brought my people
2Ki 2:19 is as good as you will e find.
1Ch 17:6 did I e ask any of the judges of
17:10 e since I appointed judges to
29:10 our father forever and e.
29:25 king of Israel before him e had.
2Ch 6:5 'E since I brought my people
9:11 No one had e seen anything
32:13 of these other nations e able

Neh 13:1 Ammonite or Moabite should e
Job 4:7 Which innocent person ⌊e⌋
6:22 Did I e say, 'Give me a gift,'
16:18 Don't e let my cry ⌊for justice⌋
28:7 No hawk's eye has e seen it.
28:8 No proud beast has e walked
28:8 lion has e passed over it.
34:10 that God would e do evil
34:10 would e do wicked things.
38:12 "Have you e given orders to the
Psa 9:5 out their names forever and e.
10:16 LORD is king forever and e.
21:4 him a long life, forever and e.
25:3 No one who waits for you will e
45:6 throne, O God, is forever and e.
45:17 thanks to you forever and e.
48:14 God is our God forever and e.
49:7 No one can e buy back another
52:8 the mercy of God forever and e.
71:5 been my confidence e since
71:17 O God, you have taught me e
71:21 and make me greater than e.
77:7 Will he e accept me?
85:5 Will you e let go of your anger
88:15 E since I was young,
111:8 They last forever and e.
119:44 your teachings forever and e.
145:1 bless your name forever and e.
145:2 praise your name forever and e.
145:21 his holy name forever and e.
148:6 in their places forever and e.
Pro 2:19 Nor do they e reach the paths
Isa 34:10 No one will e travel through it.
47:12 You have practiced them e
47:15 with you e since you were
64:4 No one has e heard,
Jer 2:10 See if there has e been
2:11 any nation e exchanged gods?
3:4 been my companion e since
3:24 E since we were young,
3:25 E since we were young,
8:5 from me without e returning.
13:27 Will you e be clean?"
18:13 has e heard anything like
22:21 This is how you've been e
31:19 things I have done e since
31:37 would I e reject all of Israel's
32:30 E since they were young,
35:13 'Won't you e learn your lesson
44:26 in Egypt will e again call
48:11 "Moab has lived securely e
Lam 2:20 Have you e treated anyone like
4:12 or invaders would e get through
Eze 4:14 meat has e entered my mouth."
16:47 more corrupt than they e were.
16:51 things than they e did.
31:2 'Was there e anyone as great
31:14 will e stand that tall.
31:18 No tree in Eden has e been as
36:11 you better off than e before.
Dan 2:10 has e asked such a thing of
7:18 and keep it forever and e."
9:12 anything e happened like what
10:12 that you said e since
11:24 none of his predecessors e did.
12:3 like the stars forever and e.
Hos 10:9 Israel, you have sinned e since
Joe 1:2 Nothing like this has e
2:2 like this has e happened.
2:2 like this will e happen again.
Amo 3:3 Do two people e walk together
7:13 But don't ⌊e⌋ prophesy again in
Jnh 2:4 Will I e see your holy temple
Nah 2:9 a person could e want.
2:13 and no one will e hear the
Zec 10:8 numerous as they have e been.
Mat 5:17 "Don't e think that I came to set
6:31 "Don't e worry and say,
6:34 "So don't e worry about
11:11 Of all the people e born,
19:25 more than e when they heard
27:8 the Field of Blood e since.
Mar 2:25 "Haven't you e read what David
2:26 Haven't you e read how he
2:26 Haven't you e read how he also
10:26 his disciples more than e.

Mar 11:2 No one has e sat on it.
11:14 "No one will e eat fruit from you
Luk 7:28 that of all the people e born,
7:45 But e since I came in,
19:30 No one has e sat on it.
23:53 no one had e been buried.
Jon 1:18 No one has e seen God.
4:29 told me everything I've e done.
4:39 "He told me everything I've e
5:47 how will you e believe what I
7:46 "No human has e spoken like
8:58 Before Abraham was e born,
9:32 no one has e heard of anyone
14:26 that I have e told you.
19:8 he became more afraid than e.
Act 2:31 about that before it e happened.
5:14 More men and women than e
7:52 Was there e a prophet your
Rom 6:13 No part of your body should e
7:13 sin became more sinful than e.
8:38 that nothing can e separate
1Co 9:7 Does a soldier e serve in the
2Co 5:1 on earth is e taken down like
7:5 E since we arrived in the
8:22 more dedicated now than e
12:6 If I e wanted to brag,
Gal 6:14 I could e brag about anything
Eph 5:29 No one e hated his own body.
Php 1:14 boldly and fearlessly than e.
1Th 5:15 Make sure that no one e pays
Heb 1:8 throne, O God, is forever and e.
3:12 that none of you e develop a
7:13 No one from that tribe e served
1Pe 4:11 to Jesus Christ forever and e!
2Pe 1:21 No prophecy e originated from
3:4 E since our ancestors died,
1Jn 2:21 You know that no lie e comes
4:12 No one has e seen God.
Rev 1:5 Glory and power forever and e
4:9 one who lives forever and e,
4:10 one who lives forever and e.
5:13 and power forever and e."
7:12 be to our God forever and e!
7:16 heat will e overcome them.
10:6 one who lives forever and e,
11:15 will rule as king forever and e."
14:11 torture will go up forever and e.
15:7 who lives forever and e,
18:14 No one will e find them again.'
18:18 'Was there e a city as
19:3 goes up from her forever and e."
20:10 day and night forever and e.
21:27 and no liars will e enter it.
22:5 will rule as kings forever and e.

ever-flowing (2)

Psa 74:15 You dried up the e rivers.
Amo 5:24 righteousness like an e stream.

ever-increasing (1)

2Co 3:18 into his image with e glory.

everlasting (61)

Gen 9:16 I will see it and remember my e
17:7 to come as an e promise.
17:13 on your flesh, an e promise.
17:19 I will make an e promise to him
21:33 the LORD, the E God, there.
Num 18:19 It is an e promise of salt in the
Dtr 33:27 and his e arms support you.
1Ch 16:17 as an e promise to Israel,
16:36 of Israel from e to everlasting.
16:36 of Israel from everlasting to e.
Neh 9:5 From e to everlasting your
9:5 From everlasting to e your
Psa 90:2 are God from e to everlasting.
90:2 are God from everlasting to e.
103:17 But from e to everlasting,
103:17 But from everlasting to e,
105:10 as an e promise to Israel,
106:48 of Israel from e to everlasting.
106:48 of Israel from everlasting to e.
119:142 is an e righteousness,
139:24 Then lead me on the e path.
145:13 Your kingdom is an e kingdom.
Pro 8:23 I was appointed from e from the
Pro 10:25 person has an e foundation.
12:28 E life is on the way of
Isa 9:6 E Father, Prince of Peace.
24:5 and rejected the e promise.
26:4 the LORD alone, is an e rock.
35:10 E happiness will be on their
51:11 E happiness will be on their
54:8 on you with e kindness,"
55:3 I will make an e promise to you
55:13 name and an e sign that will
60:15 make you a source of e pride,
60:19 the LORD will be your e light.
60:20 The LORD will be your e light,
61:7 You will have e joy.
61:8 make an e promise to them.
63:12 to make an e name for himself?
63:16 name is our Defender From E.
Jer 31:3 "I love you with an e love.
Dan 2:20 "Praise God's name from e to
2:20 name from everlasting to e
9:24 to usher in e righteousness,
Mat 18:8 feet and be thrown into e fire.
25:41 Go into e fire that was prepared
Mar 3:29 He is guilty of an e sin."
Jon 12:25 world will guard them for e life.
Act 13:46 yourselves unworthy of e life,
13:48 prepared for e life believed.
Rom 2:7 He will give e life to those who
6:22 a holy life and, finally, in e life.
6:23 God freely gives is e life found
16:26 The e God ordered that what
Gal 6:8 you will harvest e life.
6:9 each of us will receive ⌊e life⌋
2Th 2:16 gave us e encouragement
1Ti 6:12 Take hold of e life to which
Tit 3:7 confidence that we have e life.
1Pe 1:23 but through God's e word that
Rev 14:6 with the e Good News

ever-present (1)

Psa 46:1 an e help in times of trouble.

everyday (2)

Rom 9:21 occasion or something for e
Gal 3:15 me use an example from e life.

Evi (2)

Num 31:8 the five kings of Midian — E,
Jos 13:21 him and Midian's leaders — E,

evicting (1)

Eze 45:9 Stop e my people,

evidence (11)

Exo 22:13 bring in the dead body as e.
Dtr 22:15 submit the e that their daughter
22:17 But here's the e!" Then the girl's
22:20 and no e that the girl was a
Jos 9:14 The men believed the e they
Psa 89:1 I will sing forever about the e of
89:49 Where is the e of your mercy,
Act 1:3 a lot of convincing e that
14:17 he has given e of his
1Co 12:7 The e of the Spirit's presence
Jas 5:3 will be used as e against you.

evident (1)

Jon 7:39 The Spirit was not yet e,

evil (510)

Gen 2:9 knowledge of good and e grew
2:17 of the knowledge of good and e
3:5 knowing good and e."
3:22 since he knows good and e.
6:5 The LORD saw how e humans
6:5 thoughts were nothing but e.
6:12 people on earth lived e lives.
8:21 hearts are set on nothing but e.
44:4 you paid me back with e when
44:5 What you have done is e!'"
48:16 who has rescued me from all e,
50:15 pay us back for all the e we did
50:17 to you was very e." So now,
50:20 you planned e against me,
Exo 32:22 know that these people are e.
Lev 19:26 "Never cast e spells,
Num 22:32 the trip you're taking is e.
22:34 If you still think this trip is e,
32:13 of those who had done e
Dtr 1:35 "Not one of these e people will
1:39 difference between good and e,
4:25 LORD your God considers e,
9:18 what the LORD considered e
13:5 You must get rid of this e.
17:2 what the LORD considers e.
17:5 or woman who did this e thing
17:7 You must get rid of this e.
17:12 must get rid of this e in Israel.
19:19 You must get rid of this e.
19:20 Never again will such an e
21:21 You must get rid of this e.
22:21 You must get rid of this e.
22:22 must get rid of this e in Israel.
22:24 You must get rid of this e.
24:7 You must get rid of this e.
28:20 disappear for the e you will do
31:18 of all the e they've done
31:29 by doing what he considers e."
Jos 23:15 bring about every e curse until
Jdg 2:11 what the LORD considered e.
2:19 They never gave up their e
3:7 what the LORD considered e.
3:12 what the LORD considered e.
3:12 what the LORD considered e.
4:1 what the LORD considered e.
6:1 what the LORD considered e.
9:23 Then God sent an e spirit to
9:56 paid back Abimelech for the e
9:57 men of Shechem for all their e.
10:6 what the LORD considered e.
13:1 what the LORD considered e.
19:23 Please don't do anything so e!
20:3 such an e thing could happen."
20:12 "How could such an e thing
20:13 of this kind of e in Israel."
20:34 realize their own e was about
20:41 that their e had overtaken them.
Rut 1:21 Almighty has done e to me?"
1Sm 12:19 We have added ⌊another⌋ e
12:20 "You did do all these e things.
12:25 if you go on doing what is e,
15:19 what the LORD considers e?"
16:14 and an e spirit from the LORD
16:15 Saul's officials told him, "An e
16:16 When the e spirit from God
16:23 and the e spirit left him.
18:10 The next day an e spirit from
19:9 Then an e spirit from the LORD
25:21 has paid me back with e when
25:28 May e never be found in you as
2Sm 3:39 as his e deeds deserve."
11:27 considered David's actions e.
12:9 by doing what I considered e?
1Ki 2:44 you know in your heart all the e
2:44 back for the e you have done.
3:9 difference between good and e.
11:6 what the LORD considered e.
13:33 didn't change his e ways,
14:9 You have done more e things
14:22 what the LORD considered e.
15:26 what the LORD considered e,
15:34 what the LORD considered e.
16:7 whichE the LORD considered e.
16:19 things the LORD considered e.
16:25 what the LORD considered e.
16:25 He did more e things than all
16:30 what the LORD considered e.
21:20 do what the LORD considers e.
21:21 So I am going to bring e on you.
21:25 what the LORD considered e.
21:29 I will not let any e happen to
21:29 I will bring e on it during his
22:8 good about me, only e."
22:18 good about me, only e?"
22:23 has spoken e about you."
22:52 what the LORD considered e.
2Ki 3:2 what the LORD considered e,
8:12 Elisha answered, "I know the e
8:18 what the LORD considered e.
8:27 what the LORD considered e,
13:2 what the LORD considered e.
13:11 what the LORD considered e

2Ki 14:24 what the LORD considered e.
15:9 what the LORD considered e,
15:18 what the LORD considered e.
15:24 what the LORD considered e.
15:28 what the LORD considered e.
17:2 what the LORD considered e,
17:11 They did e things and made
17:13 "Turn from your e ways,
17:17 black magic and cast e spells.
17:17 what the LORD considered e,
21:2 LORD considered e by copying
21:6 fortunetellers, cast e spells,
21:9 that they did more e things than
21:11 things more e than what the
21:15 have done what I consider e
21:20 what the LORD considered e,
23:32 what the LORD considered e,
23:37 what the LORD considered e,
24:9 what the LORD considered e,
24:19 what the LORD considered e,
1Ch 2:3 e, so the LORD killed Er.
4:10 me and free me from e so that
2Ch 7:14 and turn from their e ways,
12:14 He did e things because he
18:7 me is good; it's always e."
18:22 has spoken e about you."
20:9 'If e comes in the form of war,
20:35 who led him to do e.
21:6 what the LORD considered e.
22:4 what the LORD considered e,
29:6 LORD our God considered e.
33:2 LORD considered e by copying
33:6 fortunetellers, cast e spells,
33:9 that they did more e things than
33:22 what the LORD considered e,
36:5 LORD his God considered e.
36:9 what the LORD considered e.
36:12 LORD his God considered e
Ezr 9:13 of the e things we have
Neh 9:28 doing what you considered e.
13:7 the e thing Eliashib had
13:17 "What is this e thing you're
Est 8:3 mercy and to undo the e plot
8:6 to see my people suffer such e.
9:25 that the e plan Haman had
Job 1:1 and he stayed away from e.
1:8 and he stays away from e."
2:3 and he stays away from e.
15:35 trouble and give birth to e.
20:12 "Though e is sweet in his
28:28 away from e is understanding.'"
30:26 I waited for good, e came.
34:8 and associates with e people?
34:10 that God would ever do e
34:12 God will never do anything e,
34:26 In return for their e,
35:12 arrogance of ⌊those⌋ e people.
35:15 he isn't too concerned about e.
36:17 the judgment e people deserve.
36:18 bribe turn you ⌊to e ways⌋.
36:21 Don't turn to e, because you
36:21 chosen e instead of suffering.
42:11 and comforted him for all the e
Psa 5:4 E will never be your guest.
7:4 paid back my friend with e
7:9 Let the e within wicked people
7:14 how that person conceives e,
10:15 of the wicked and e person.
15:3 his tongue, do e to a friend,
21:11 and plan e against you,
26:10 E schemes are in their hands.
28:3 but have e in their hearts.
28:4 have done, for their e deeds.
34:13 Keep your tongue from saying e
34:14 Turn away from e,
34:16 confronts those who do e
34:21 E will kill wicked people,
35:12 back with e instead of good.
36:4 He does not reject e.
37:8 preoccupied. It only leads to e.
37:27 Avoid e, do good, and live
38:20 They pay me back with e
41:7 They think e things about me
49:5 slanderers surround me with e?
50:19 let your mouth say anything e.
51:4 done what you consider e.
Psa 52:1 brag about the e you've done,
52:3 You prefer e to good.
54:5 Pay them back with e.
55:15 because e lives in their homes
56:5 is an e plan against me.
64:5 one another in their e plans.
90:15 as we have experienced e.
97:10 who love the LORD hate e.
101:4 I will have nothing to do with e.
109:5 They reward me with e instead
109:6 ⌊I said,⌋ "Appoint the e one to
109:20 who say e things against me.
119:101 ⌊from walking⌋ on any e path
121:7 LORD guards you from every e.
139:24 See whether I am on an e path.
140:1 Rescue me from e people,
140:2 They plan e things in their
140:8 not let their e plans succeed,
140:11 Let e hunt down violent people
141:4 be persuaded to do anything e
141:5 is directed against e deeds.
Pro 1:16 because they rush to do e and
2:12 save you from the way of e,
2:14 from those who enjoy doing e,
2:14 joy in the deviousness of e.
3:7 and turn away from e.
4:14 Do not walk in the way of e
4:27 Walk away from e.
6:14 He devises e all the time with
6:24 to keep you from an e woman
8:13 To fear the LORD is to hate e.
8:13 pride, arrogance, e behavior,
10:23 when he carries out an e plan,
11:19 so whoever pursues e finds his
11:21 Certainly, an e person will not
11:27 but whoever looks for e finds it.
12:12 a trap for ⌊other⌋ e people,
12:13 An e person is trapped by his
12:20 the heart of those who plan e,
13:19 but turning from e is disgusting
14:16 and turns away from e,
14:17 a person who plots e is hated.
14:19 E people will bow to good
14:22 those who stray plan what is e,
15:3 They watch e people and good
15:26 The thoughts of e people are
15:28 pour out a flood of e things.
16:6 fear of the LORD, e is avoided.
16:17 people turns away from e.
16:30 lips has finished his e work.
17:11 A rebel looks for nothing but e.
17:13 Whoever pays back e for good
17:13 for good — e will never leave
20:8 sifts out every e with his eyes.
21:10 of a wicked person desires e
21:27 especially if they bring it with e
24:1 Do not envy e people or wish
24:8 Whoever plans to do e will be
24:20 because an e person has no
25:10 and his e report about you will
25:20 to one who has an e heart.
26:23 talk that covers up an e heart.
28:5 E people do not understand
28:10 people into e will fall into
29:6 To an e person sin is bait in a
Ecc 4:3 He hasn't seen the e that is
5:1 they are doing ⌊something⌋ e.
8:3 Don't take part in something e,
9:3 hearts of mortals are full of e.
Isa 1:13 I can't stand your e assemblies.
1:16 Get your e deeds out of my
1:16 out of my sight. Stop doing e.
5:20 be for those who call e good
5:20 who call evil good and good e,
7:5 have planned e against you,
7:15 to reject e and choose good.
7:16 the boy knows how to reject e
13:11 I will punish the world for its e
32:6 and their minds plan e in order
32:7 The tricks of scoundrels are e.
33:15 doesn't look for e things to do.
41:23 Yes, do something, good or e,
47:9 to you in spite of your e magic
47:11 But e will happen to you.
47:12 your spells and your e magic.
52:1 Godless and e people will no
Isa 55:7 Let e people abandon their
57:1 are spared when e comes.
59:4 trouble and give birth to e.
59:6 Their works are e.
59:7 Their feet run to do e.
59:7 Their plans are e. Ruin and
59:15 Those who turn away from e
65:12 You did what I consider e.
66:4 They did what I consider e.
Jer 2:19 should know and see how e
3:5 done all the e things that you
3:17 their own stubborn, e ways.
4:4 because of the e you do.
4:14 Jerusalem, wash the e from
4:14 Don't continue making e plans.
5:28 Their e deeds have no limits.
6:7 so Jerusalem keeps its e fresh.
7:12 because of the e done by my
7:24 and their stubborn, e ways.
7:30 what I consider e," declares
9:3 They go from one e thing to
11:8 their own stubborn, e ways.
11:10 They've gone back to the e
11:15 They rejoice when they do e."
11:17 This is because of the e things
12:14 say about all my e neighbors
16:12 e ways that keep you from
18:10 nation does what I consider e
18:11 Turn from your e ways,
18:12 go our own stubborn, e ways.'
18:20 should not be paid back with e.
21:12 of the e things you have
21:14 of the e things you have
23:2 you for the e you have done,"
23:10 The people are e, and they use
23:11 doing e," declares the LORD.
23:14 They support those who do e
23:22 turned back from their e ways
23:22 and the e they have done.
25:5 'Turn from your e ways and the
25:5 ways and the e you have done,
26:3 they'll turn from their e ways.
26:3 of the e they have done."
32:30 have done what I consider e.
32:32 me furious because they are e.
35:15 "Turn from your e ways,
36:7 they will turn from their e ways.
44:3 It is because their people did e,
51:24 for all the e things that they
51:56 am a God who punishes e.
52:2 what the LORD considered e,
Eze 6:9 will hate themselves for the e
6:11 people of Israel have done e
7:21 loot and to the most e people
7:24 I will send the most e nation,
11:2 these are the men who plan e
18:8 He refuses to do e things,
18:23 turn from their e ways and live.
18:24 right and he does e things.
18:26 doing right and does e things,
18:26 He will die because of the e
20:44 deal with you based on the e
28:15 until e was found in you.
33:13 he has done and he does e,
33:13 He will die because of the e
33:15 and does nothing e.
33:18 that he has done and does e,
36:31 Then you will remember your e
Dan 9:15 We have sinned and done e
11:27 kings will both plan to do e.
Hos 7:2 all the e things they've done.
7:12 I will punish you for all the e
7:15 Yet, they plan e against me.
10:13 wickedness and harvested e.
12:11 The people of Gilead are e.
Amo 5:13 because those times are so e.
5:14 Search for good instead of e so
5:15 Hate e and love good.
Mic 3:2 You hate good and love e.
3:4 you have done e things.
6:10 who use their money for e
7:3 hands are skilled in doing e.
Nah 1:11 a person who plans e against
3:4 charming mistress of e magic.
3:4 and people her e magic."
3:19 suffered from your endless e?

Hab 1:13 eyes are too pure to look at e.
Zec 1:4 Turn from your e ways and
1:4 evil ways and your e deeds.'
7:10 think of doing e to each other.
8:17 Don't even think of doing e to
Mal 2:17 "Everyone who does e is
Mat 5:11 and say all kinds of e things
5:37 than that comes from the e one.
5:39 But I tell you not to oppose an e
5:45 whether they are good or e.
6:13 rescue us from the e one.
6:23 But if your eye is e,
7:11 Even though you're e,
7:23 away from me, you e people.'
8:16 He forced the ⌊e⌋ spirits out of
9:4 "Why are you thinking e
10:1 authority to force e spirits out
12:34 How can you e people say
12:35 But e people do the evil things
12:35 But evil people do the e things
12:39 "The people of an e and
12:43 "When an e spirit comes out of
12:45 other spirits more e than itself.
12:45 will happen to the e people
13:19 The e one comes at once and
13:38 those who belong to the e one.
13:41 sin and everyone who does e.
13:49 the e people from people
13:50 will throw the e people into
15:19 **E** thoughts, murder, adultery,
16:4 "**E** and unfaithful people look
18:32 and said to him, 'You e servant!
21:41 will destroy those e people.
22:10 and all the e people they found.
22:18 Jesus recognized their e plan,
25:26 'You e and lazy servant!
Mar 1:23 was controlled by an e spirit.
1:26 The e spirit threw the man into
1:27 He gives orders to e spirits,
3:4 "Is it right to do good or to do e
3:11 Whenever people with e spirits
3:30 had said that he had an e spirit.
5:2 was controlled by an e spirit
5:8 Jesus said, "You e spirit,
5:13 The e spirits came out of the
6:7 and gave them authority over e
7:21 **E** thoughts, sexual sins,
7:25 had an e spirit heard about
9:25 he gave an order to the e spirit.
9:26 The e spirit screamed,
9:39 turn around and speak e of me.
Luk 3:19 Herod for all the e things
3:20 So Herod added one more e to
4:33 by a spirit, an e demon.
4:36 he gives orders to e spirits,
6:9 day of worship: to do good or e,
6:18 by e spirits were cured.
6:35 he is kind to unthankful and e
6:45 But e people do the evil that is
6:45 But evil people do the e that is
7:21 sicknesses, and e spirits.
8:2 They had been cured from e
8:29 Jesus ordered the e spirit to
8:29 (The e spirit had controlled the
9:42 Jesus ordered the e spirit to
10:20 However, don't be happy that e
11:13 Even though you're e,
11:24 "When an e spirit comes out of
11:26 other spirits more e than itself.
11:29 "The people living today are e.
11:34 But when your eye is e,
11:39 you are full of greed and e.
13:27 from me, all you e people.'
19:22 you've said, you e servant!
Jon 3:19 because their actions were e.
5:29 But those who have done e
7:7 that what everyone does is e.
17:15 to protect them from the e one.
Act 3:26 one of you from your e ways."
5:16 who were troubled by e spirits,
8:7 **E** spirits screamed as they
8:23 wrapped up in your e ways."
9:13 the many e things this man
16:16 She was possessed by an e
16:18 turned to the e spirit,
16:18 the e spirit left her.
Act 19:12 and e spirits would leave them.
19:13 to place and force e spirits out
19:13 Lord Jesus to force e spirits out
19:15 But the e spirit answered them,
19:16 by the e spirit attacked them.
23:5 'Don't speak e about a ruler of
Rom 2:9 for every person who does e,
3:8 Or can we say, "Let's do e so
7:19 Instead, I do the e that I don't
7:21 So I've discovered this truth: **E**
8:13 to put to death the e activities
12:9 Hate e. Hold on to what is good.
12:17 Don't pay people back with e
12:17 back with evil for the e they do
12:21 Don't let e conquer you,
12:21 but conquer e with good.
14:16 what you consider good is e.
16:19 is good and to avoid what is e.
1Co 10:6 that we won't desire what is e,
14:20 When it comes to e,
2Co 5:10 the good or e they have done
Gal 1:4 us from this present e world,
3:1 Who put you under an e spell?
Eph 5:16 because these are e days.
6:12 spiritual forces that control e
6:13 a stand during these e days.
6:16 the flaming arrows of the e one.
Php 3:2 of those who do e things.
Col 1:21 The e things you did showed
1Th 5:22 away from every kind of e.
2Th 3:2 from worthless and e people,
3:3 protect you against the e one.
1Ti 6:1 In this way no one will speak e
6:10 is the root of all kinds of e.
2Ti 3:13 But e people and phony
Tit 2:5 one can speak e of God's word.
Heb 5:14 difference between good and e.
Jas 1:13 God can't be tempted by e,
3:6 It is a world of e among the
3:8 It is an uncontrollable e filled
3:16 is disorder and every kind of e.
4:4 love for this ⌊e⌋ world is hatred
4:16 All such bragging is e.
1Pe 2:1 So get rid of every kind of e,
2:16 your freedom when you do e.
3:9 Don't pay people back with e
3:9 back with evil for the e they do
3:10 tongues from saying e things,
3:11 They must turn away from e
3:12 Lord confronts those who do e."
2Pe 2:16 But he was convicted for his e.
1Jn 2:13 won the victory over the e one.
2:14 won the victory over the e one.
2:17 the world and its e desires are
3:12 He was a child of the e one
3:12 the things Cain did were e
5:18 and the e one can't harm them.
5:19 under the control of the e one.
2Jn 1:11 shares the e things he's doing.
3Jn 1:11 Dear friend, never imitate e,
1:11 The person who does e has
Rev 16:13 Then I saw three e spirits like
17:4 and e things from her
18:2 is a prison for every e spirit,

evildoer (4)

2Sm 3:39 May the LORD repay this e as
Psa 37:7 with ⌊an e⌋ who succeeds
Pro 17:4 An e pays attention to wicked
Isa 9:17 one of them is a godless e,

evildoers (11)

Psa 26:5 I have hated the mob of e and
27:2 **E** closed in on me to tear me to
37:1 Do not be preoccupied with e.
37:9 **E** will be cut off ⌊from their
92:11 ⌊the cries⌋ of e attacking me.
94:16 will stand up for me against e?
119:115 Get away from me, you e,
Pro 24:19 Do not get overly upset with e.
Isa 1:4 They are descendants of e and
Mal 3:15 Not only are e encouraged,
4:1 All arrogant people and all e

Evil Merodach (2)

2Ki 25:27 King **E** of Babylon,
Jer 52:31 King **E** of Babylon,

evils (3)

Neh 13:18 that our God brought all these e
Psa 40:12 Countless e have surrounded
Mar 7:23 All these e come from within

ewes (1)

Psa 78:71 tending the e that had lambs

exact (9)

Gen 21:2 and at the e time God had
1Ki 13:11 Bethel that day and the e words
Est 1:4 for many days, 180 to be e.
4:7 He told him the e amount of
9:1 the e opposite happened:
Mat 2:16 This matched the e time he
Mar 13:33 You don't know the e time.
Heb 1:3 God's glory and the e likeness
10:1 They aren't an e likeness of

exactly (47)

Gen 34:12 I'll pay e what you tell me.
Exo 10:2 and grandchildren e how
10:8 "But e who will be going?"
12:41 After e 430 years all the
25:9 and all its furnishings e like
29:35 with Aaron and his sons e as
Lev 10:3 "This is e what the LORD said:
Num 8:4 It was made e like the one the
17:11 Moses did e what the LORD
Dtr 17:11 Do e what they tell you to do in
24:8 Be very careful to do e as the
Jos 14:7 to him e what I thought.
Jdg 7:17 edge of the camp, do e as I do.
Rut 3:6 and did e as her mother-in-law
1Sm 28:17 The LORD has done to you ⌊e⌋
2Sm 14:3 Joab told her e what to say.
14:19 He told me to say e what I said.
1Ki 1:30 I will do today e what I swore
16:26 He lived e like Jeroboam
2Ki 7:10 tents were left e as they were."
7:18 (It happened e as the man of
14:3 but not e what his ancestor
15:12 It happened e as the LORD had
16:11 Urijah built an altar e like the
1Ch 6:49 They did e what God's servant
Ezr 6:12 to be carried out e as ordered.
6:13 and their group did e what King
7:21 River to do e what Ezra
Ecc 5:16 They leave e as they came.
Isa 14:24 "It will happen e as I've
14:24 It will turn out e as I've planned.
Jer 35:18 and did e what he told you to
38:27 He told them e what the king
42:5 against us if we don't do e what
Eze 10:22 Their faces looked e like the
16:45 You are e like your sisters.
Dan 9:13 e as it was written in Moses'
Mat 2:7 found out from them e when
24:37 it will be e like the days of
Luk 2:23 They did e what was written in
Jon 5:19 Indeed, the Son does e what
8:26 So I tell the world e what he
14:31 and that I am doing e what
Act 7:44 Moses built this tent e as God
22:30 The officer wanted to find out e
Gal 4:29 That's e what's happening now.
1Jn 4:17 we are e like him ⌊with regard

exalted (1)

Gen 17:5 no longer be Abram [**E** Father],

examination (3)

Lev 13:36 the priest will make another e.
13:39 the priest will make an e.
14:48 priest comes and makes an e

examine (36)

Gen 37:32 You better e it to see whether
Lev 13:3 The priest will e the disease.
13:5 day the priest will e him again.
13:6 day the priest will e him again.
13:8 The priest will e him one more
13:10 The priest will e him.
13:13 the priest will e him.

Lev 13:15 The priest will e the raw flesh
13:17 The priest will e him again,
13:20 The priest will e it.
13:25 the priest will e it. If the hair on
13:27 day the priest will e him again.
13:30 the priest will e the disease.
13:32 the priest will e the disease.
13:34 seventh day the priest will e
13:43 The priest will e him.
13:50 The priest will e the mildew
13:51 On the seventh day he will e
13:55 The priest will e the area again
14:3 go outside the camp and e him.
14:36 will go inside to e the house.
14:37 He will e the mildew area on
14:39 will go back and e it again.
14:44 the priest will e it one more
1Ch 29:17 I know, my God, that you e
Job 7:18 and e him every moment?
Psa 11:4 They e Adam's descendants.
26:2 E me, O LORD, and test me.
37:10 Then you can carefully e
48:13 E its embankments.
139:23 E me, O God, and know my
Lam 3:40 closely at our ways and e them
Eze 21:21 and e animal livers.
Luk 16:2 Let me e your books.
2Co 13:5 E yourselves to see whether
Gal 6:4 Each of you must e your own

examined (6)

Lev 13:3 When the priest has e him,
Neh 2:13 Fountain and Dung Gate and e
2:15 valley that night and e the wall.
Job 28:27 He confirmed it and e it.
Psa 139:1 O LORD, you have e me,
Act 17:11 and every day they carefully e

examines (7)

Lev 13:21 But if the priest e the affected
13:26 But if the priest e it and the hair
13:31 But if the priest e the scabby
14:36 "Before the priest e the house,
Job 31:14 If he e me, how could I answer
Psa 7:9 who e thoughts and emotions.
Jer 20:12 of Armies e the righteous.

examining (1)

Job 34:24 into pieces without e them

example (60)

Num 5:21 may the LORD make you an e
Dtr 28:37 will send you will make an e
1Sm 8:3 didn't follow their father's e
8:5 sons aren't following your e.
1Ki 9:7 Israel will be an e and an
15:3 He followed the sinful e his
22:43 followed the e his father Asa
22:52 He followed the e of his father
2Ki 16:3 He followed the e of the kings
2Ch 7:20 I will make it an e and an
20:32 followed the e his father Asa
28:2 He followed the e of the kings
Neh 13:27 Should we follow your e,
Psa 71:7 I have become an e to many
Ecc 9:13 I also have seen this e of
Jer 24:9 will be a disgrace and an e.
Lam 2:13 "What e can I give you?
Eze 14:8 and I will make an e of him.
28:12 You were the perfect e,
Mat 15:4 For e, God said, 'Honor your
19:12 For e, some men are celibate
23:3 But don't follow their e,
Mar 7:4 For e, they must also wash
7:10 For e, Moses said, 'Honor your
Luk 10:37 "Go and imitate his e!"
Jon 13:15 I've given you an e that you
13:17 whenever you follow my e.
Act 20:35 I have given you an e that by
Rom 2:14 For e, whenever non-Jews
2:25 For e, circumcision is valuable
7:2 For e, a married woman is
7:7 For e, I wouldn't have known
9:9 For e, this is what the promise
9:15 For e, God said to Moses,
9:17 For e, Scripture says to
Rom 15:5 following the e of Christ Jesus.
1Co 8:10 For e, suppose someone with
10:11 to make them an e for others.
12:12 For e, the body is one unit and
14:8 For e, if the trumpet doesn't
16:16 to follow the e of people like
Gal 3:6 Abraham serves as an e.
3:15 let me use an e from everyday
Php 3:17 live by the e we have given
2Th 3:9 Rather, we wanted to set an e
1Ti 1:9 For e, a person must realize
1:16 This patience serves as an e
4:12 purity an e for other believers.
Tit 2:7 Always set an e by doing good
2:7 When you teach, be an e of
3:8 on setting an e by doing good
3:14 how to set an e by doing good
Heb 4:11 will be lost by following the e
9:9 The first part of the tent is an e
Jas 2:2 For e, two men come to your
5:10 follow the e of the prophets
1Pe 2:21 He left you an e so that you
2Pe 1:17 For e, we were eyewitnesses
2:6 He made those cities an e to
Jud 1:7 and the cities near them is an e

examples (7)

Jon 16:25 "I have used e to illustrate
16:25 is coming when I won't use e
16:29 in plain words and not using e.
1Co 10:6 These things have become e
Tit 2:3 but to be e of virtue.
Heb 12:1 by so many e of faith,
1Pe 5:3 but be e for the flock to follow.

excel (6)

Mat 13:12 and they will e in
Rom 12:10 E in showing respect for each
1Co 14:12 try to e in them so that you help
15:58 Always e in the work you do
1Th 4:1 we ask and encourage you to e
4:10 you as believers to e

Excellency (4)

Luk 1:3 an orderly account for Your E,
Act 23:26 sends greetings to Your E,
24:2 He said to Felix, "Your E,
26:25 "I'm not crazy, Your E Festus.

excellent (5)

Ezr 5:8 The builders are doing an e job
1Ti 3:1 he desires something e.
3:13 serve well gain an e reputation
4:6 and the e teachings which you
1Pe 2:9 to tell about the e qualities

exception (2)

Gen 17:13 is to be circumcised without e.
Jos 11:13 made an e and burned Hazor.

exceptional (1)

Php 2:9 has given him an e honor —

excesses (1)

1Pe 4:4 in the same e of wild living.

excessive (7)

Eze 18:8 for interest or make an e profit.
18:13 for interest and makes e profits.
18:17 interest or make e profits.
22:12 You collect interest and make e
22:13 of the e profits you have
22:27 people to make e profits.
2Co 12:7 especially because of the e

excessively (1)

1Ti 3:3 He must not drink e or be a

exchange (17)

Gen 23:16 at the current merchants' e rate.
47:16 and I'll give you food in e."
47:17 and he gave them food in e for
47:17 he supplied them with food in e
47:19 us and our land in e for food.
Lev 27:10 Don't e or substitute animals,
27:10 If you do e one animal for
Lev 27:33 to see if it is good or bad or e it.
27:33 But if you do e it, both the first
Num 35:31 accept a cash payment in e
Dtr 14:25 If so, e the tenth part of your
Ezr 3:7 Sidon and Tyre in e for cedar,
Sos 8:11 pounds of silver in e for its fruit.
Isa 43:4 I will e others for you.
Mic 3:11 Your leaders e justice for
Mat 16:26 will a person give in e for life?
Mar 8:37 a person give in e for life?

exchanged (17)

Gen 26:31 the next morning they e oaths.
Job 28:18 be e for it. Wisdom is more
Sos 8:7 If a man e all his family's
Isa 43:3 Egypt is the ransom I e for you.
Jer 2:11 Has any nation ever e gods?
2:11 Yet, my people have e their
Eze 16:8 I promised to love you, and I e
27:12 They e silver, iron, tin,
27:13 They e slaves and bronze
27:14 from Beth Togarmah e horses,
27:16 They e emeralds, purple cloth,
27:17 They e wheat from Minnith,
27:18 They e wine from Helbon and
27:19 They e wrought iron,
Rom 1:23 They e the glory of the
1:25 These people have e God's
1:26 Their women have e natural

exchanging (1)

Rut 4:7 back property and e goods:

excited (7)

Rut 1:19 whole town was e about them.
1Ki 1:45 celebrating, so the city is e.
Job 39:24 Anxious and e, the horse eats
Jer 50:11 "You are happy and e.
51:39 When they are e, I will prepare
Luk 24:32 "Weren't we e when he talked
Act 3:11 They were e, and everyone ran

excitement (1)

Isa 22:2 a town filled with noise and e.

exclaimed (1)

Gen 28:16 woke up from his sleep and e,

exclude (9)

Lev 17:10 I will condemn them and e
20:3 I will condemn them and e
20:5 I will e them from the people.
20:5 I will e from the people
20:6 I will e them from the people.
Isa 66:5 who hate you and e you for my
Eze 14:8 I will e him from my people.
Mal 2:12 May the LORD e anyone who
2:12 May he e them from Jacob's

excluded (30)

Gen 17:14 male must be e from his people
Exo 12:15 day must be e from Israel.
12:19 with yeast in it must be e from
30:33 must be e from the people."
30:38 must be e from his people."
31:14 day must be e from the people.
Lev 7:20 must be e from the people.
7:21 must be e from the people."
7:25 must be e from the people.
7:27 must be e from the people."
17:4 shed blood and must be e from
17:9 they must be e from the people.
17:14 must be e from the people.
18:29 must be e from the people.
19:8 must be e from the people.
20:17 They both must be publicly e
20:18 must be e from the people.
22:3 that person must be e from my
23:29 day will be e from the people.
Num 9:13 you must be e from the people.
12:14 wouldn't she be e from the
15:30 and must be e from the people.
15:31 He must be e completely.
19:13 person must be e from Israel,
19:20 that person must be e from the
Jdg 21:6 tribe has been e from Israel.

Ezr 10:8 all their property and be e from
Act 3:23 will be e from the people.'
Eph 2:12 You were e from citizenship in
4:18 They are e from the life that

excludes (1)

1Co 15:27 this clearly e God,

excrement (13)

Exo 29:14 and e outside the camp.
Lev 4:11 legs, internal organs, and e)
8:17 and e outside the camp,
16:27 The skin, meat, and e from the
Num 19:5 and e) will be burned while he
Dtr 23:13 you're done, cover up your e.
2Ki 18:27 will have to eat their own e
Isa 28:8 are covered with vomit and e.
36:12 will have to eat their own e
Eze 4:12 using human e for fuel."
4:15 manure in place of human e.
Mal 2:3 I'm going to spread e on your
2:3 the e from your festival

excuse (12)

Exo 5:21 given them an e to kill us."
Jdg 6:13 Gideon responded, "E me,
6:15 Gideon said to him, "E me,
Job 33:10 God is only looking for an e to
Ecc 5:6 God become angry at your e
Luk 14:18 I need to see it. Please e me.'
14:19 well they plow. Please e me.'
Jon 15:22 they have no e for their sin.
Rom 1:20 As a result, people have no e.
2:1 judge anyone, you have no e.
Gal 5:13 turn this freedom into an e
Jud 1:4 use God's kindness as an e

excused (2)

1Ki 15:22 in Judah and e no one.
Luk 14:18 "Everyone asked to be e.

execute (12)

Num 25:4 and e them in broad daylight in
Jdg 9:24 Abimelech e his brothers.
2Sm 21:6 We will e them in the LORD's
2Ki 14:6 But he didn't e their children.
2Ch 25:4 But he didn't e their children.
36:17 them and e their best young
Mat 26:59 against Jesus in order to e him.
27:1 the people decided to e Jesus.
Mar 14:55 against Jesus in order to e him.
Jon 18:31 "We're not allowed to e
Act 5:33 and wanted to e the apostles.
Rom 13:4 an avenger to e God's anger on

executed (26)

Jdg 9:5 There he e his 70 brothers,
9:18 You have e his 70 sons.
2Sm 1:15 David's young man e him
4:12 who e Rechab and Baanah,
21:9 who e them on the mountain in
21:13 of those who had been e.
1Ki 19:1 how he had e all the prophets.
19:10 and e your prophets.
19:14 and e your prophets.
2Ki 12:21 son of Shomer, e him.
14:5 he e the officials who had
25:21 The king of Babylon e them at
2Ch 21:4 and then e all his brothers
25:3 he e the officials who killed his
36:20 took those who weren't e
Ezr 9:7 over to foreign kings to be e.
Isa 13:15 Whoever is captured will be e.
Jer 26:23 The king e Uriah and threw his
52:27 The king of Babylon e them at
Luk 13:1 Pilate had e while they were
23:32 led away to be e with him.
Act 12:2 James, the brother of John, e.
12:19 gave orders to have them e.
13:28 asked Pilate to have him e.
22:4 into prison until they were e.
Heb 10:28 shown no mercy as he was e.

executing (2)

2Ch 22:8 When Jehu was e judgment on
Act 7:59 members were e Stephen,

execution (3)

Dtr 13:9 You must start the e.
17:7 The witnesses must start the e,
Mat 27:20 of Barabbas and the e of Jesus.

exempt (1)

Mat 17:26 the family members are e.

exercised (1)

1Ch 11:10 who e power with him in his

exert (1)

Job 28:9 "Humans e their power on the

exhaust (2)

Jer 51:58 People e themselves for
Hab 2:13 e themselves for nothing?

exhausted (24)

Gen 25:29 e, came in from outdoors.
25:30 to eat — that red stuff — I'm e."
Dtr 25:18 you when you were tired and e
Jdg 8:4 They were e when they
8:5 They're e, and I'm pursuing
8:15 'We shouldn't give your e men
1Sm 14:28 today."' Now, the army was e.
14:31 the troops were thoroughly e.
30:10 while 200 men who were too e
30:21 200 men who had been too e
2Sm 17:29 are hungry, e, and thirsty."
21:15 but David became e.
2Ch 28:15 They put everyone who was e
Job 7:4 and I'm e from tossing about
Psa 31:10 My life is e from sorrow,
68:9 it when your land was e.
69:3 I am e from crying for help.
Isa 3:26 Zion will sit on the ground, e.
Jer 48:45 "Those who flee will stand e in
Dan 8:27 was e and sick for days.
9:21 evening sacrifice. He was e.
Mat 15:32 or they may become e on their
Mar 8:3 they will become e on the road.
9:18 his teeth, and becomes e.

exhaustion (1)

Jdg 4:21 had fallen sound asleep from e,

exile (48)

2Sm 14:14 to keep a banished person in e.
15:19 an e from your homeland.
Ezr 2:2 men from the people in e:
2:36 These priests returned from e:
2:40 These Levites returned from e:
2:41 These singers returned from e:
2:42 gatekeepers returned from e:
2:43 servants returned from e:
2:55 servants returned from e:
3:8 who had come back from e
4:1 returned from e were building
6:16 returned from e celebrated at
6:19 from e celebrated the Passover.
6:20 who had returned from e,
6:21 who had returned from e
Neh 7:7 men from the people in e:
7:39 These priests returned from e:
7:43 These Levites returned from e:
7:44 These singers returned from e:
7:45 gatekeepers returned from e:
7:46 servants returned from e:
7:57 servants returned from e:
8:17 come back from e made booths
Est 2:6 who had gone into e along
Isa 5:13 "My people will go into e
Jer 48:46 sons will be taken away into e,
Lam 4:22 will not let you remain in e.
Eze 1:2 year of the e of King Jehoiakin,
12:3 as if you were going into e.
12:4 as if you were going into e.
12:4 like a captive going into e.
12:7 bags as if I were going into e.
12:11 will go into e and into captivity.
25:3 the nation of Judah went into e.
30:17 from these cities will go into e.
30:18 from its villages will go into e.
Amo 5:5 Gilgal will certainly go into e.
Amo 5:27 you into e beyond Damascus,
6:7 now be the first to go into e.
7:11 taken from its land into e."
7:17 taken from its land into e."
9:4 Even if they go into e ahead of
Mic 1:16 will be taken from you into e.
Zec 14:2 people in the city will go into e,
Mat 1:12 After the e to Babylon,
1:17 David until the e to Babylon,
1:17 from the e until the Messiah.
Act 7:43 I will send you into e beyond

exiled (6)

Ezr 7:26 orders should be promptly e,
Isa 49:21 I was e and rejected.
Lam 1:3 "Judah has been e after
Nah 3:10 went into captivity and was e.
Mat 1:11 the people were e to Babylon.
Rev 1:9 I was ⌊e⌋ on the island of

exiles (21)

Ezr 1:11 him when the e left Babylon
2:1 where the e had been taken
2:1 These e returned to Jerusalem
8:35 The e who had come back
8:36 The e delivered the king's
9:4 Since the former e had been
10:6 these former e had been so
10:7 all the former e must gather
10:8 from the community of former e
10:16 The former e did this.
Neh 7:6 where the e had been taken
Isa 20:4 from Egypt and e from Sudan.
45:13 and let my e go free without
Eze 1:1 while I was living among the e
3:11 Go to the e, to your people.
3:15 I went to Tel Abib, to the e who
11:24 me to the e in Babylonia.
11:25 I told the e everything the
Oba 1:20 E from Israel will take
1:20 E from Jerusalem who are in
Zec 6:10 an offering from the e Heldai,

exist (22)

1Sm 12:21 because they don't e.
Job 3:16 I would not e. I would be like
8:22 of the wicked will cease to e."
14:12 until the heavens cease to e.
Isa 41:12 to nothing and no longer e.
Jer 5:12 LORD and say, "He doesn't e!
Eze 26:21 and you will no longer e.
27:36 and you will never e again."'
28:19 and you will never e again."'
Hab 1:12 Didn't you e before time began,
Act 17:28 and e because of him.
23:8 that angels and spirits don't e.
Rom 4:15 But where laws don't e,
4:17 nations that don't even e.
7:23 still e throughout my body.
13:1 No government would e if it
13:1 The governments which e
1Co 8:4 gods in this world don't really e
11:11 women couldn't e without men
11:11 men couldn't e without women.
11:19 Factions have to e in order to
15:18 believers in Christ no longer e.

existed (15)

Job 10:19 it would be as if I had never e,
15:7 delivered before the hills ⌊e⌋?
Psa 25:6 They have e from eternity.
Dan 12:1 unlike any that has e from
Oba 1:16 like those who have never e.
Jon 1:1 beginning the Word already e.
1:15 me because he e before I did.'")
1:30 me because he e before I did.'
17:5 with you before the world e.
Col 1:17 He e before everything and
1Pe 1:20 long ago before the world e,
2Pe 3:5 heaven and earth e a long time
1Jn 1:1 The Word of life e from the
2:13 know Christ who has e from
2:14 who has e from the beginning.

existence (13)

Jon 1:3 came into e through him.

Jon 1:10 world came into e through him.
1:17 into e through Jesus Christ.
6:63 Your physical e doesn't
Act 14:17 he has given evidence of his e.
Rom 4:17 calls into e nations that don't
1Co 11:12 As a woman came into e from
11:12 so men come into e by women,
2Co 5:2 our present tent-like e we sigh,
5:4 will put an end to our mortal e.
5:17 way of living has come into e.
Heb 11:1 and convinces us of the e
Rev 4:11 Everything came into e and

exists (11)

Gen 8:22 As long as the earth e,
Jer 11:9 "Conspiracy e among the
Lam 3:29 Maybe a reason to hope e.
Zep 2:15 and no one else e but me"?
Jon 1:3 Not one thing that e was made
1Co 8:4 exist and that no god e except
Heb 2:10 through whom everything e.
4:9 and worship e for God's people.
11:6 to God must believe that God e
1Jn 2:8 It's a truth that e in Christ and in
4:18 No fear e where his love is.

exits (3)

Eze 42:11 They had the same e,
43:11 its e and entrances — its entire
48:30 These will be the e for the city:

expand (7)

Gen 9:27 May God e the territory of
Exo 34:24 and will e ⌊your country's⌋
Dtr 12:20 The LORD your God will e
19:8 The LORD your God may e
Pro 14:11 people will continue to e.
Isa 9:3 You will e the nation and
54:2 E the space of your tent.

expanded (2)

Isa 26:15 You have e the nation,
26:15 You have e the nation.

expanse (1)

Rev 20:9 they spread over the broad e

expect (19)

Isa 38:18 go down to the pit cannot e you
47:11 you suddenly. You won't e it.
64:3 things that we didn't e,
Dan 8:25 people when they don't e it.
Mat 24:44 return when you least e him.
Luk 6:34 to those from whom you e
12:40 return when you least e him."
Act 23:6 I'm on trial because I e that the
26:6 "I'm on trial now because I e
26:7 Our twelve tribes e this
26:7 against me because I e God
1Co 9:10 plows or threshes should e
9:12 If others have the right to e this
2Co 10:2 I e I will have to because some
Php 1:20 I eagerly e and hope that I will
Tit 2:13 At the same time we can e
Heb 11:1 Faith assures us of things we e
Jas 1:7 who has doubts shouldn't e
Jud 1:17 Lord Jesus Christ told you to e:

expected (14)

Gen 48:11 "I never e to see you again,
Exo 22:5 field was e to produce.
Jos 8:14 just where ⌊Joshua⌋ e.
1Ki 2:15 All Israel e me to be their king.
1Ch 15:16 They were e to play music on
Est 9:1 the enemies of the Jews e
Hag 1:9 "You e a lot, but you received a
Mat 20:10 they e to receive more.
Luk 12:48 A lot will be e from everyone
Jon 11:27 the one who was e to come
Act 3:5 He e to receive something from
26:20 Both groups were e to change
28:23 influential Jews ⌊than e⌋ went
2Co 8:5 They did more than we had e.

expecting (7)

Luk 6:35 and lend to them without e to
Luk 8:40 Everyone was e him.
Act 10:24 Cornelius was e them and had
12:11 the Jewish people are e
23:21 They are ready now and are e
25:18 him of the crimes I was e.
1Co 16:11 I'm e him to arrive with the

expects (2)

Dtr 23:21 The LORD your God e you to
Job 12:4 calls on God and e an answer.

expel (2)

Dtr 6:19 You will see the LORD e your
Jos 23:5 The LORD your God will e

expelled (1)

Lam 2:6 He e kings and priests

expels (1)

Dtr 9:4 When the LORD your God e

expense (4)

Psa 35:26 promote themselves at my e
38:16 promote themselves at my e."
Luk 7:5 our synagogue at his own e.'
1Co 9:7 serve in the army at his own e?

expenses (4)

Exo 21:19 time and for all his medical e.
30:16 and use it to pay the e of the
35:21 tent of meeting, to pay other e,
Act 21:24 and pay the e to shave their

expensive (15)

Gen 24:53 He also gave e presents to her
1Ki 5:17 e blocks of stone in order to
2Ch 21:3 and other e things,
32:23 to the LORD and e presents
Pro 21:17 Whoever loves wine and e
Ecc 7:1 name is better than e perfume,
Isa 3:24 sackcloth instead of e clothes.
23:18 plenty of food and e clothing.
Lam 4:5 Those who used to wear e
Dan 11:38 and other e things he will honor
Mat 26:7 with a bottle of very e perfume
Mar 14:3 She had a bottle of very e
Luk 16:19 a rich man who wore e clothes.
Jon 12:3 Mary took a bottle of very e
1Ti 2:9 or e clothes they wear.

experience (18)

Dtr 11:2 They didn't see or e any of
Jdg 2:10 They had no personal e with
1Sm 3:7 Samuel had no e with the
Job 32:7 and e should teach wisdom.'
Psa 60:3 made your people e hardships.
119:100 those with many years of e,
Ecc 1:16 I've had a lot of e with wisdom
2:12 ⌊my attention⌋ to e wisdom,
3:13 be able to eat and drink and e
Isa 30:6 lands where they e distress
38:15 my life because of my bitter e.
38:17 Now my bitter e turns into
51:20 They e the anger of the LORD,
Jer 5:12 We won't e war or famine.
Eze 34:29 They will no longer e hunger in
Rom 1:27 so they e among themselves
1Th 5:9 intention that we e his anger
Heb 5:13 who live on milk lack the e

experienced (25)

Num 31:16 The LORD's community e a
Dtr 1:13 are wise, intelligent, and e,
1:15 who were wise and e men
7:15 diseases you e in Egypt.
11:2 You saw and e his great power
Jdg 3:1 who had not e any war
20:44 There were 18,000 e men from
20:46 They were all e men.
2Sm 11:16 he knew the e warriors were.
17:8 Your father is an e soldier.
1Ki 9:27 ⌊who were⌋ e seamen
1Ch 12:33 there were 50,000 e soldiers.
12:36 were 40,000 e soldiers ready
2Ch 8:18 own servants and his e sailors
33:12 When he e this distress,
Psa 90:15 many years as we have e evil.
116:3 I e pain and agony.
Sos 3:8 in using swords, e in combat.
Lam 3:1 "I am the man who has e
1Co 3:10 As a skilled and e builder,
10:13 you have e which is unusual
2Co 1:8 about the suffering we e
Heb 2:18 Because Jesus e temptation
6:4 They e the heavenly gift and
6:5 They e the goodness of God's

experiences (1)

Psa 48:6 that a woman e during labor.

experiencing (5)

Gen 41:54 other countries were e famine.
Num 25:8 the Israelites were e stopped.
Psa 142:3 ⌊already⌋ know what I am e.
Ecc 6:6 without e anything good —
2Th 1:4 and suffering you are e.

experiment (1)

Ecc 2:1 "Now I want to e with pleasure

expert (8)

Gen 25:27 Esau became an e hunter,
Exo 31:5 He's an e in all trades.
35:33 He's an e in all trades.
Ezr 7:6 As a scribe, Ezra was an e in
Mat 22:35 an e in Moses' Teachings,
Luk 10:25 Then an e in Moses'
10:37 The e said, "The one who was
Act 5:34 He was a highly respected e in

experts (10)

Est 1:13 asked for advice from all the e
Isa 3:3 workers, and e in magic.
Jer 4:22 They are e in doing wrong,
Luk 5:17 some Pharisees and e in
7:30 But the Pharisees and the e in
11:45 One of the e in Moses'
11:46 horrible it will be for you e
11:52 horrible it will be for you e
14:3 asking the Pharisees and the e
1Ti 1:7 They want to be e in Moses'

explain (29)

Gen 44:16 "How else can we e it?
Psa 49:4 I will e my riddle with the
78:2 I will e what has been hidden
Ecc 8:1 Who knows how to e things?
9:1 and I e it in this way:
Isa 19:12 Let them e what the LORD of
28:9 will they e this message?
41:22 E past events that your idols
Jer 9:12 this so that they can e it?
Dan 2:9 Then I'll know that you can e
2:16 could e the dream's meaning.
2:18 be merciful and to e this secret
2:24 Take me to the king, and I'll e
2:25 captives from Judah who can e
8:16 e the vision to this man."
10:14 I have come to e to you what
Mat 13:36 "E what the illustration of the
15:15 "E this illustration to us."
Luk 24:27 and the Prophets to e
Act 11:4 Then Peter began to e to them
19:40 won't be able to e this mob."
Rom 11:33 impossible to e his decisions
15:8 Let me e. Christ became a
1Co 2:13 We e spiritual things to those
Gal 4:1 Let me e further. As long as an
5:16 Let me e further. Live your life
Eph 3:9 He allowed me to e the way
Heb 5:11 We have a lot to e about this.
1Pe 3:15 when anyone asks you to e it.

explained (15)

Exo 4:5 ⌊The LORD e,⌋ "This is to
1Sm 10:25 Samuel e the laws concerning
2Ch 22:9 They e, "Ahaziah is
Neh 8:7 and Pelaiah — e the Teachings
8:8 God's Teachings clearly and e
8:12 words that had been e to them.
Dan 2:15 Arioch e everything to Daniel.
8:26 and mornings that was e

Zec 1:10 among the myrtle trees e,
Mar 4:34 he e everything to them.
Act 10:8 Cornelius e everything to them
15:14 Simon has e how God first
17:3 He e and showed them that the
18:26 with them and e God's way
1Co 14:6 unless I e revelation,

explaining (3)

1Sm 6:2 and people skilled in e omens.
Act 28:23 Paul was e the kingdom of
Heb 5:11 attention, e it to you is hard.

explanation (1)

Dan 2:9 to make up a phony e

exploded (1)

Psa 124:3 when their anger e against us.

exploit (2)

1Th 4:6 of or e other believers that
2Pe 2:3 arguments to e you.

explore (13)

Num 13:2 "Send men to e Canaan,
13:16 men Moses sent to e the land.
13:17 Moses sent them to e Canaan,
14:36 So the men Moses sent to e
14:38 men who went to e the land,
Jos 14:7 Kadesh Barnea to e the land.
Jdg 18:2 throughout the land and e it.
18:2 "Go and e the land!"
2Sm 10:3 sent his men to e the city,
1Ch 19:3 Haven't his servants come to e,
Job 28:11 They e the sources of rivers so
Ecc 1:13 and e everything done under
7:25 my attention to study, to e,

explored (10)

Num 13:21 So the men e the land from the
13:32 about the land they had e.
13:32 They said, "The land we e is
14:6 of those who had e the land,
14:7 "The land we e is very good.
14:24 him to the land he already e.
14:34 For 40 days you e the land.
Dtr 1:24 to the Eshcol Valley, they e it.
Ecc 2:3 I e ways to make myself feel
2:3 I also e ways to do ⌊some⌋

explores (1)

Job 39:8 It e the mountains for its

exploring (1)

Num 13:25 came back from e the land.

export (2)

1Ki 10:29 price they obtained horses to e
2Ch 1:17 price they obtained horses to e

expose (9)

2Sm 6:20 mindless fool might e himself!"
Lam 2:14 They didn't e your guilt in order
4:22 He will e your sins."
Eze 13:14 level it and e its foundation.
Mic 1:6 a valley and e its foundations.
Hab 2:16 And e yourself as godless.
Zep 2:14 LORD will e the cedar beams.
Luk 2:34 He will be a sign that will e
Eph 5:11 e them for what they are.

exposed (11)

Neh 4:13 it was lowest and most e.
Job 33:21 not seen before, will be e.
Isa 20:4 Their buttocks will be e in
Jer 8:2 They will be spread out and e
36:30 corpse will be thrown out and e
Eze 16:36 You e yourself and uncovered
Mat 10:26 been covered that will not be e.
Luk 12:2 been covered that will not be e.
Jon 3:20 don't want their actions to be e.
Heb 4:13 Everything is uncovered and e
2Pe 3:10 have done on it will be e.

exposes (2)

Job 20:27 Heaven e his sin. Earth rises up
Eph 5:13 Light e the true character of

exposing (1)

2Sm 6:20 He was e himself before the

express (5)

Job 10:1 I will freely e my complaint.
Ecc 1:8 are more than anyone can e,
Luk 19:7 this began to e disapproval.
Jon 12:27 to know how to e my feelings.
Gal 5:13 your corrupt nature to e itself.

expressed (4)

Rom 8:26 that cannot be e in words.
2Co 12:4 things that can't be e in words,
1Pe 1:8 that can hardly be e in words
3:5 in God e their beauty

expresses (4)

Pro 8:7 My mouth e the truth,
29:11 A fool e all his emotions,
Gal 5:6 a faith that e itself through love.
1Pe 3:4 Beauty e itself in a gentle and

expressing (1)

Pro 18:2 but only in e his own opinion.

expression (4)

Job 9:27 I will change my e and smile,'
29:24 but the e on my face did not
Pro 15:2 give good e to knowledge,
Rev 15:1 are the final e of God's anger.

expressions (5)

Sos 1:2 Your e of love are better than
1:4 We will praise your e of love
4:10 beautiful are your e of love,
4:10 How much better are your e of
5:1 intoxicated with e of love!

extend (24)

Num 35:4 Levites will e 1,500 feet from
2Ki 20:10 "It's easy for the shadow to e
Psa 57:5 Let your glory e over the whole
57:11 Let your glory e over the whole
108:5 Let your glory e over the whole
110:2 The LORD will e your powerful
Isa 8:8 Its outspread wings will e over
Eze 45:7 his land will e to the
45:7 his land will e to the eastern
48:1 It will e from the road to
48:2 It will e from the eastern border
48:3 It will e from the eastern border
48:4 It will e from the eastern border
48:5 It will e from the eastern border
48:6 It will e from the eastern border
48:7 It will e from the eastern border
48:8 It will e from the eastern border
48:21 This land will e eastward from
48:21 and it will e westward to the
48:23 It will e from the eastern border
48:24 It will e from the eastern border
48:25 It will e from the eastern border
48:26 It will e from the eastern border
48:27 It will e from the eastern border

extended (17)

Gen 10:19 The border of the Canaanites e
10:30 The region where they lived e
Num 33:49 Their camp e from Beth
Jos 11:17 The land e from Mount Halak
12:2 His rule e from Aroer on the
12:7 ⌊Their lands e⌋ from Baal Gad
13:9 The border e from Aroer on the
13:16 Their territory e from Aroer on
13:26 It e from Heshbon to Ramath
13:30 territory e from Mahanaim
19:47 border of Dan e beyond them.
Jdg 1:36 The territory of the Amorites e
1Ki 6:3 It e 15 feet in front of the
6:27 The wings of the angels e so
Isa 13:22 Its days will not be e.
26:15 You have e all the land's
Eze 40:9 It e 14 feet from the temple.

extending (2)

Jos 13:27 e to the end of the Sea of
Mic 7:11 walls and e your borders is

extends (8)

Num 21:13 that e into Amorite territory.
34:7 "The northern border e from
34:10 "The eastern border e from
Jos 13:3 It e from the Shihor River,
15:1 Their territory e as far south as
17:7 Manasseh's border e from
1Sm 27:8 territory which e from Telaim
1Ch 5:9 as the edge of the desert that e

extensive (1)

2Ch 27:3 temple and did e building

extent (2)

2Ch 9:6 even told about half of the e
2Co 2:5 To some e — although I don't

exterminate (2)

Est 4:8 gave permission to e the Jews.
Dan 11:44 angry to destroy and e many.

exterminated (1)

2Ch 32:21 The LORD sent an angel who e

exterminating (1)

Psa 106:23 to prevent him from e them.

external (2)

2Co 11:28 Besides these e matters,
1Pe 3:3 let their beauty be something e.

extinguish (2)

2Sm 14:7 In this way they wish to e the
Sos 8:7 Raging water cannot e love,

extinguished (7)

2Sm 21:17 lamp of Israel must never be e."
2Ki 22:17 at this place will never be e.'"
2Ch 29:7 entrance hall, e the lamps,
Psa 118:12 but they were e like burning
Isa 34:10 They will not be e day or night,
43:17 They are e and snuffed out like
Jon 1:5 and the dark has never e it.

extortion (2)

Psa 62:10 Do not count on e ⌊to make
Isa 33:15 He rejects getting rich by e and

extra (2)

Mat 25:3 but they didn't take any e oil.
25:4 took along e oil for their lamps.

extraordinary (4)

2Ki 5:13 asked you to do some e act,
Dan 5:12 judgment, and an e spirit.
5:14 good judgment, and e wisdom.
6:3 because there was an e spirit

extravagant (1)

1Jn 2:16 and e lifestyles — comes from

extreme (12)

1Ch 5:16 of Sharon to its e edges.
Jer 13:9 and Jerusalem's e arrogance.
Mat 8:12 will cry and be in e pain there.
13:42 will cry and be in e pain there.
13:50 will cry and be in e pain there.
22:13 will cry and be in e pain there.'
24:51 will cry and be in e pain there.
25:30 will cry and be in e pain there.'
Luk 13:28 you will cry and be in e pain.
2Co 1:8 It was so e that it was beyond
8:2 along with their e poverty,
9:14 of the e kindness that God

extremes (1)

Ecc 7:18 will be able to avoid both e.

eye (66)

Exo 21:24 an e for an eye, a tooth for a
21:24 an eye for an e, a tooth for a

Exo 21:26 male or female slave in the **e**
21:26 to make up for the loss of the **e**.
Lev 24:20 a broken bone, an **e** for an eye,
24:20 a broken bone, an eye for an **e**,
26:16 You will suffer from **e** problems
Dtr 19:21 a life for a life, an **e** for an eye,
19:21 a life for a life, an eye for an **e**,
1Sm 11:1 poke out everyone's right **e**
11:1 whose right **e** King Nahash
11:2 I'll poke out everyone's right **e**
18:9 on Saul kept an **e** on David.
2Ki 9:30 She put on **e** shadow,
Ezr 5:5 were under God's watchful **e**.
Job 7:8 The **e** that watches over me
7:8 Your **e** will look for me,
13:1 "My **e** has certainly seen all of
28:7 No hawk's **e** has ever seen it.
Psa 17:8 as if I were the pupil in your **e**.
Pro 6:13 He winks his **e**, makes a
7:2 you protect the pupil of your **e**.
10:10 with his **e** causes heartache.
15:30 A twinkle in the **e** delights the
16:30 Whoever winks his **e** is
20:12 The ear that hears, the **e** that
30:17 The **e** that makes fun of a
31:27 She keeps a close **e** on the
Jer 4:30 Why do you wear **e** shadow?
32:4 in person and look him in the **e**.
Zec 2:8 you touches the apple of his **e**.
11:17 strike his arm and his right **e**.
11:17 His right **e** will be completely
Mat 5:29 "So if your right **e** causes you
5:38 'An **e** for an eye and a tooth for
5:38 'An eye for an **e** and a tooth for
6:22 "The **e** is the lamp of the body.
6:22 So if your **e** is unclouded,
6:23 But if your **e** is evil,
7:3 sawdust in another believer's **e**
7:3 wooden beam in your own **e**?
7:4 out of your **e**,' when you have
7:4 have a beam in your own **e**?
7:5 the beam from your own **e**.
7:5 from another believer's **e**.
18:9 If your **e** causes you to lose
18:9 you to enter life with one **e** than
19:24 for a camel to go through the **e**
Mar 9:47 If your **e** causes you to lose
9:47 of God with one **e** than
10:25 for a camel to go through the **e**
Luk 6:41 sawdust in another believer's **e**
6:41 wooden beam in your own **e**?
6:42 of your **e**,' when you don't see
6:42 see the beam in your own **e**?
6:42 the beam from your own **e**.
6:42 from another believer's **e**.
11:34 "Your **e** is the lamp of your
11:34 When your **e** is unclouded,
11:34 But when your **e** is evil,
18:25 for a camel to go through the **e**
1Co 2:9 Scripture says: "No **e** has seen,
12:16 an ear says, "I'm not an **e**,
12:17 If the whole body were an **e**,
12:21 An **e** can't say to a hand,
Rev 1:7 Every **e** will see him,

eyebrows (1)

Lev 14:9 his head, his beard, and his **e**,

eyelids (4)

Psa 77:4 (You keep my **e** open.)
132:4 shut my eyes, or close my **e**
Pro 6:4 your eyes rest or your **e** close.
Jer 9:18 Our **e** will flow with water.

eyes (266)

Gen 3:5 that when you eat it your **e** will
3:7 Then their **e** were opened,
21:19 God opened her **e**.
29:17 Leah had attractive **e**,
42:24 arrested right in front of their **e**.
46:4 close your **e** ⌊when you die⌋."
49:12 His **e** are darker than wine.
Num 14:14 seen you with their own **e**,
16:14 still pull the wool over our **e**?
20:8 Right before their **e**,
24:4 ⌊into a trance⌋ with his **e** open:
Num 24:16 ⌊into a trance⌋ with his **e** open:
33:55 will be like splinters in your **e**
Dtr 3:21 with your own **e** everything that
4:3 With your own **e** you saw what
4:9 have seen with your own **e**.
6:22 Right before our **e** the LORD
7:19 You saw with your own **e** the
10:21 you saw with your own **e**.
11:7 You saw with your own **e** all
28:32 You will watch with your own **e**
28:32 You will strain your **e** looking
29:2 You've seen with your own **e**
29:4 **e** that see, or ears that hear.
34:4 let you see it with your own **e**,
Jos 23:5 them right in front of your **e**
23:13 and thorns in your **e** until none
24:17 signs right before our **e**.
Jdg 16:21 They poked out his **e** and took
16:28 for at least one of my two **e**."
1Sm 2:33 my altar will have his **e** fail,
12:16 going to do right before your **e**.
14:27 put it to his mouth, his **e** lit up.
14:29 See how my **e** lit up when I
16:12 complexion, attractive **e**,
2Sm 6:20 exposing himself before the **e**
6:22 if I am humiliated in your **e**,
12:11 and before your own **e** I will
22:28 but your **e** bring down arrogant
1Ki 8:29 Night and day may your **e** be
8:52 "May your **e** always see my
9:3 My **e** and my heart will always
10:7 and saw it with my own **e**.
20:38 with a bandage over his **e**,
20:41 took the bandage off his **e**.
2Ki 4:34 his **e** on the boy's eyes,
4:34 his eyes on the boy's **e**,
4:35 seven times and opened his **e**.
6:17 please open his **e** so that he
6:17 LORD opened the servant's **e**
6:20 open the **e** of these men,
6:20 The LORD opened their **e** and
7:2 will see it with your own **e**,
7:19 will see it with your own **e**,
19:16 Open your **e**, LORD, and see.
22:20 and your **e** will not see any of
2Ch 6:20 Day and night may your **e** be
6:40 "Finally, my God, may your **e**
7:15 My **e** will be open,
7:16 My **e** and my heart will always
9:6 and saw it with my own **e**.
16:9 The LORD's **e** scan the whole
29:8 you can see with your own **e**.
34:28 and your **e** will not see any of
Ezr 3:12 temple with their own **e** began
9:8 Our God has made our **e** light
Neh 1:6 Open your **e**, and pay close
Job 3:10 or hide my **e** from trouble.
4:16 image was in front of my **e**.
7:7 will my **e** see anything good.
10:4 Do you actually have human **e**?
10:18 anyone had laid **e** on me.
15:12 Why do your **e** flash
16:16 dark shadows encircle my **e**,
16:20 My **e** drip ⌊with tears⌋ to God
17:2 My **e** are focused on their
17:7 Now my **e** are blurred from grief
18:3 considered stupid in your **e**?
19:27 I will see him with my own **e**,
20:9 **E** that saw him will see him no
21:20 His **e** should see his own ruin.
24:23 but his **e** are on their ways.
27:19 When he opens his **e**,
28:10 Their **e** see every precious
28:21 It is hidden from the **e** of every
29:11 ⌊Any⌋ **e** that saw me spoke
29:15 I was **e** for the blind person.
31:1 made an agreement with my **e**.
31:7 followed ⌊the desire of⌋ my **e**,
31:16 a widow's **e** stop ⌊looking
34:21 God's **e** are on a person's
36:7 He doesn't take his **e** off
39:29 and its **e** see it from far away.
40:24 Can anyone blind its **e** or
41:18 Its **e** are like the first rays of the
42:5 have seen you with my own **e**.
Psa 6:6 My **e** flood my bed every night.
Psa 6:7 My **e** blur from grief.
10:8 His **e** are on the lookout for
11:4 His **e** see. They examine
13:3 Light up my **e**, or else I will die
17:2 Let your **e** observe what is fair.
19:8 It makes the **e** shine.
25:15 My **e** are always on the LORD.
31:9 My **e**, my soul, and my body
32:8 you as my **e** watch over you.
33:18 The LORD's **e** are on those
34:15 The LORD's **e** are on righteous
35:21 Our own **e** have seen it."
38:10 the light of my **e** has left me.
54:7 My **e** will gloat over my
66:7 His **e** watch the nations.
69:3 My **e** are strained ⌊from⌋
73:7 Their **e** peer out from their fat
88:9 My **e** grow weak because of
91:8 only have to look with your **e**
92:11 My **e** gloat over those who spy
94:9 He formed **e**. Do you think he
101:3 wicked in front of my **e**.
101:6 My **e** will be watching the
115:5 They have **e**, but they cannot
116:8 You saved my **e** from tears
119:18 Uncover my **e** so that I may
119:37 Turn my **e** away from
119:82 My **e** have become strained
119:123 My **e** are strained from looking
119:136 Streams of tears flow from my **e**
119:148 My **e** are wide-open throughout
131:1 My **e** do not look down on
132:4 get into my bed, shut my **e**,
135:16 They have **e**, but they cannot
139:16 Your **e** saw me when I was
141:8 My **e** look to you, I have taken
145:15 The **e** of all creatures look to
Pro 4:25 Let your **e** look straight ahead
6:4 Don't let your **e** rest or your
6:17 arrogant **e**, a lying tongue,
6:25 not let her catch you with her **e**.
10:26 like smoke to the **e**,
15:3 The **e** of the LORD are
17:24 but the **e** of a fool ⌊are looking
20:8 sifts out every evil with his **e**.
20:13 Keep your **e** open,
22:12 The LORD's **e** watch over
23:26 Let your **e** find happiness in my
23:29 Who has bloodshot **e**?
23:33 Your **e** will see strange sights,
25:7 prince whom your **e** have seen.
27:20 a person's **e** are never satisfied.
28:11 person is wise in his own **e**,
Ecc 2:14 A wise person uses the **e** in
4:8 Their **e** are never satisfied with
11:7 and it is good for one's **e** to see
11:9 you and whatever your **e** see.
Sos 1:15 Your **e** are like doves!
4:1 Your **e** behind your veil are like
4:9 a single glance from your **e**,
5:12 His **e** are set like doves
6:5 Turn your **e** away from me.
7:4 Your **e** are like pools in
Isa 1:7 before your **e** by foreigners.
1:15 I will turn my **e** away from you.
2:11 The **e** of arrogant people will
5:15 And the **e** of arrogant people
6:10 Shut their **e**. Otherwise, they
6:10 they may see with their **e**,
11:3 He will not judge by what his **e**
13:16 to death right before their **e**.
17:7 and their **e** will look to the Holy
29:10 He will shut your **e**.
29:10 (Your **e** are the prophets.)
30:20 your teacher with your own **e**.
33:17 Your **e** will see how handsome
33:20 Your **e** will see Jerusalem as a
35:5 Then the **e** of the blind will be
37:17 Open your **e**, LORD, and see.
38:14 My **e** were tired from looking up
43:8 who are blind but still have **e**,
44:18 Their **e** are plastered shut,
52:8 will see it with their own **e**.
59:10 We grope like people without **e**.
65:16 They are hidden from my **e**.
Jer 5:3 LORD, your **e** look for the truth.

Jer 5:21 You have e, but you cannot
9:1 with⌋ water and my e were
9:18 Our e will run with tears.
13:17 I will cry bitterly, and my e will
14:17 "Say this to them: 'My e flow
20:4 you will see it with your own e.
22:17 "But your e and your mind are
34:3 of Babylon with your own e,
Lam 1:16 My e — my eyes flow with
1:16 My eyes — my e flow with
2:11 My e are worn out with tears.
2:18 Don't let your e rest.
3:48 tears run down from my e over
3:49 My e will keep flowing without
3:51 What I see with my e disturbs
4:17 "We are still straining our e,
5:17 This is why our e see less and
Eze 1:18 They were covered with e.
6:9 away from me, and by their e,
10:12 wheels were covered with e.
12:2 They have e, but they can't
23:40 for the men, painted their e,
40:4 "Son of man, look with your e,
Dan 7:8 This horn had e like human
7:8 horn had eyes like human e
7:20 That horn had e and a mouth
8:5 a prominent horn between its e.
8:21 horn between its e is its first
9:18 Open your e and look at our
10:6 His e were like flaming torches.
Joe 1:16 disappears right before our e.
Amo 9:4 I will keep my e on them so
9:8 have my e on this sinful
Hab 1:13 Your e are too pure to look at
Zep 3:20 before your e," says the LORD.
Zec 3:9 That one stone has seven e.
4:10 (These seven e of the LORD
9:2 (The e of humanity and of all
9:8 I have seen it with my own e.
14:12 Their e will rot in their sockets,
Mal 1:5 with your own e and say,
Mat 9:29 He touched their e and said,
13:15 They have shut their e so that
13:15 eyes so that their e never see.
13:16 "Blessed are your e because
18:9 one eye than to have two e
20:34 so he touched their e.
26:43 they couldn't keep their e open.
Mar 8:23 He spit into the man's e and
8:25 his hands on the man's e
9:47 one eye than to have two e
14:40 they couldn't keep their e open.
Luk 2:30 My e have seen your salvation,
24:31 Then their e were opened,
Jon 9:6 he smeared it on the man's e
9:11 smeared it on my e,
9:15 mixture of spit and dirt on my e.
12:40 so that their e don't see
Act 9:8 When he opened his e,
9:18 fish scales fell from Saul's e,
9:40 Tabitha opened her e,
20:19 often with tears in my e.
20:31 at times with tears in my e.
26:18 You will open their e and turn
28:27 They have shut their e so that
28:27 eyes so that their e never see.
Rom 11:8 Their e don't see, and their ears
1Co 4:13 have become garbage in the e
7:30 Those who have e filled with
2Co 2:4 In fact, I had tears in my e
Gal 4:15 you would have torn out your e
Php 3:18 now tell you with tears in my e,
1Pe 3:12 The Lord's e are on those who
2Pe 1:16 his majesty with our own e.
Rev 1:14 His e were like flames of fire.
2:18 whose e are like flames of fire
3:18 Buy ointment to put on your e
4:6 living creatures covered with e
4:8 and were covered with e,
5:6 had seven horns and seven e,
7:17 wipe every tear from their e."
19:12 His e are flames of fire.
21:4 wipe every tear from their e.

eyesight (12)

Gen 48:10 Israel's e was failing because
Num 24:3 of the man whose e is clear.
24:15 of the man whose e is clear.
Dtr 28:65 mind, failing e, and despair.
34:7 His e never became poor,
1Sm 3:2 His e had begun to fail so that
4:15 (Eli was 98 years old, and his e
1Ki 14:4 His e had failed because he
Job 11:20 But the wicked will lose their e.
17:5 have his children's e fail.)"
Jer 14:6 Their e fails because they
Mat 20:33 we want you to give us our e

eyewitness (2)

Jon 19:35 The one who saw this is an e.
21:24 This disciple was an e of

eyewitnesses (2)

Luk 1:2 from those who had been e
2Pe 1:17 For example, we were e when

Ezbai (1)

1Ch 11:37 from Carmel, Naari (son of E),

Ezbon (2)

Gen 46:16 Shuni, E, Eri, Arodi, and Areli.
1Ch 7:7 Bela's five sons were E,

Ezekiel (5)

Eze 1:3 spoke his word to the priest E,
1:3 of the LORD came over E.
12:27 'The vision that E sees won't
24:24 E is a sign to you.
29:21 again, and I will give you, E,

Ezem (3)

Jos 15:29 Baalah, Iim, E,
19:3 Hazar Shual, Balah, E,
1Ch 4:29 Bilhah, E, Tolad,

Ezer (9)

Gen 36:21 Dishon, E, and Dishan.
36:27 These were the sons of E:
36:30 Dishon, E, and Dishan.
1Ch 1:38 Anah, Dishon, E, and Dishan.
4:4 and E was the father of
7:21 Ephraim's sons E and Elead
12:9 E was the first of these
Neh 3:19Next to him E, Jeshua's son,
12:42 Malchiah, Elam, and E.

Ezer's (1)

1Ch 1:42 E sons were Bilhan,

Ezion Geber (7)

Num 33:35 set up camp at E.
33:36 moved from E and set up camp
Dtr 2:8 the plains to Elath and E
1Ki 9:26 at E by Elath in Edom.
22:48 the ships were wrecked at E.
2Ch 8:17 coast near E and Elath in Edom.
20:36 They made the ships in E.

Ezra (32)

Ezr 7:1 of Persia, E left Babylon.
7:1 E was the son of Seraiah,
7:6 As a scribe, E was an expert
7:6 The king gave E everything he
7:8 E arrived in Jerusalem.
7:10 E was determined to study the
7:11 that King Artaxerxes gave E
7:12 king of kings To: E the priest,
7:21 to do exactly what E the priest,
7:25 You, E, using your God's
7:27 ⌊I, E, said:⌋ Thanks be to the
10:1 While E was praying,
10:2 interrupted by saying to E,
10:3 as my lord ⌊E⌋ and the others
10:5 Then E got up and made the
10:6 Then E left the front of God's
10:6 E didn't eat any food or drink
10:10 E the priest stood up and said
10:16 E the priest chose men who
Neh 8:1 They told E the scribe to bring
8:2 Then E the priest brought the
8:4 E the scribe stood on a raised
8:5 E, standing higher than all the
Neh 8:6 E thanked the LORD,
8:9 E the priest and scribe,
8:13 met with E the scribe to study
8:18 E continued to read from the
12:1 Jeshua: Seraiah, Jeremiah, E,
12:13 from E, Meshullam;
12:26 the governor and of E
12:33 Azariah, E, Meshullam,
12:36 E the scribe led them.

Ezrah's (1)

1Ch 4:17 E sons were Jether,

Ezrahite (1)

1Ki 4:31 than Ethan the E, or Heman,

Ezri (1)

1Ch 27:26 in the fields: E, son of Chelub

F

fabric (8)

Exo 26:1 work an angel design into the f.
28:6 and bright red yarn into the f.
28:8 to the ephod out of the same f.
36:8 creatively worked into the f.
36:35 creatively worked into the f.
38:18 on ⌊f made from⌋ fine
39:5 to the ephod out of the same f.
Sos 3:10 its seat out of purple f.

face (220)

Gen 1:29 every plant with seeds on the f
6:7 So he said, "I will wipe off the f
7:4 I will wipe off the f of the earth
7:23 Every living creature on the f of
11:4 all over the f of the earth."
11:8 scattered them all over the f
11:9 them all over the f of the earth.
17:3 Abram bowed with his f
17:17 Abraham bowed with his f
18:2 with his f touching the ground.
19:1 with his f touching the ground.
23:7 with his f touching the ground.
24:26 with his f touching the ground.
30:40 of the sheep f any that were
32:30 that place Peniel [F of God],
32:30 "I have seen God f to face,
32:30 "I have seen God face to f,
33:3 seven times with his f touching
33:10 because I've seen your f as if I
33:10 as if I were seeing the f of God,
38:14 covered her f with a veil,
38:15 because she had covered her f.
43:31 Then he washed his f and
47:31 down in prayer with his f at
48:12 with his f touching the ground.
Exo 3:6 Moses hid his f because he
10:28 ever let me see your f again.
10:29 "You'll never see my f again."
18:7 Moses bowed with his f
25:20 They should f each other,
32:12 and wipe them off the f
33:16 people on the f of the earth."
33:20 But you can't see my f,
33:23 but my f must not be seen."
34:8 with his f touching the ground.
34:29 His f was shining from
34:30 Moses and saw his f shining,
34:33 he put a veil over his f.
34:35 see that Moses' f was shining.
Lev 21:18 who has a disfigured f,
Num 11:15 I can't f this trouble anymore."
12:8 I speak with him f to face,
12:8 I speak with him face to f,
12:14 her own father had spit in her f,
16:4 with his f touching the ground.
22:31 with his f touching the ground.
Dtr 5:4 The LORD spoke to you f to
5:4 spoke to you face to f from
6:15 you and will wipe you off the f
25:9 of his sandals and spit in his f.
34:10 the LORD dealt with f to face.

Dtr 34:10 the LORD dealt with face to **f**.
Jos 5:1 and had no courage left to **f**
5:14 Joshua bowed with his **f**
Jdg 6:22 of the LORD **f** to face."
6:22 of the LORD face to **f**."
1Sm 17:30 He turned to **f** another man and
17:49 he fell to the ground on his **f**.
20:15 enemies off the **f** of the earth.
20:41 three times with his **f** touching
24:8 with his **f** touching the ground.
25:23 with her **f** touching the ground.
25:41 She bowed down with her **f**
28:14 with his **f** touching the ground.
2Sm 1:2 with his **f** touching the ground.
2:22 brother Joab in the **f** again?"
9:6 down with his **f** touching
14:4 down with her **f** touching
14:7 remain on the **f** of the earth."
14:22 down with his **f** touching
14:33 down with his **f** touching
18:9 Absalom happened to come **f** to
18:9 happened to come face to **f**
18:21 down with his **f** touching
19:4 The king covered his **f** and
24:20 down with his **f** touching
1Ki 1:31 down with her **f** touching
13:34 and wiped off the **f** of the earth.
19:13 he wrapped his **f** in his coat,
21:4 turned his **f** ⌊from everyone⌋,
2Ki 4:29 Lay my staff on the boy's **f**."
4:31 and put the staff on the boy's **f**,
1Ch 21:21 down with his **f** touching
2Ch 20:12 We don't have the strength to **f**
20:17 Tomorrow go out to **f** them.
20:18 down with his **f** touching
30:9 He will not turn his **f** away from
Est 7:8 servants covered Haman's **f**.
Job 1:11 I bet he'll curse you to your **f**."
2:5 I bet he'll curse you to your **f**."
6:28 I won't lie to your **f**.
11:15 your **f** without being ashamed,
13:15 defend my behavior to his **f**.
13:16 no godless person could **f** him."
13:24 Why do you hide your **f** ⌊from
15:27 "His **f** is bloated with fat,
16:16 My **f** is red from crying,
17:6 Now they spit in my **f**.
21:31 Who will tell him to his **f** how
23:17 darkness that covers my **f**.
29:24 on my **f** did not change.
30:10 don't hesitate to spit in my **f**.
33:26 They will see God's **f** and
34:29 If he hides his **f**, who can see
37:12 round and round over the **f**
Psa 3:7 all my enemies in the **f**.
10:6 I'll never **f** any trouble."
10:11 He has hidden his **f**.
11:7 Decent people will see his **f**.
13:1 will you hide your **f** from me?
17:15 I will see your **f** when I am
22:24 He has not hidden his **f** from
24:6 who searches for the **f** of the
27:8 ⌊When you said,⌋ "Seek my **f**,"
27:8 I will seek your **f**."
27:9 Do not hide your **f** from me.
30:7 When you hid your **f**,
42:2 may I come to see God's **f**?
44:15 Shame covers my **f**
44:24 Why do you hide your **f**?
51:9 Hide your **f** from my sins,
69:7 Humiliation has covered my **f**.
69:17 so do not hide your **f** from me.
80:16 the threatening look on your **f**.
84:9 Look with favor on the **f** of your
88:14 do you hide your **f** from me?
102:2 Do not hide your **f** from me
104:29 You hide your **f**, and they are
104:30 You renew the **f** of the earth.
107:26 melted in ⌊the **f** of⌋ disaster.
119:87 almost wiped me off ⌊the **f** of⌋
143:7 Do not hide your **f** from me,
Pro 15:13 joyful heart makes a cheerful **f**,
27:19 As a **f** is reflected in water,
Ecc 6:8 have in knowing how to **f** life?
7:3 because, in spite of a sad **f**,
8:1 Wisdom makes one's **f** shine,

Isa 8:17 who hides his **f** from the
24:1 He will mar the **f** of the earth
25:8 wipe away tears from every **f**,
29:22 Jacob's **f** will no longer turn
50:6 I will not turn my **f** away from
50:7 I have set my **f** like a flint.
54:8 I hid my **f** from you for a
57:4 Whom are you making a **f** at?
59:2 made him hide his **f** so that
64:7 You have hidden your **f** from us.
Jer 18:17 show them my back, not my **f**."
28:16 going to remove you from the **f**
30:6 Why has every **f** turned pale?
33:5 I will hide my **f** from this city
34:3 and he will talk to you **f** to face.
34:3 and he will talk to you face to **f**.
Eze 1:10 each creature had the **f** of a
1:10 each one had the **f** of a lion.
1:10 each one had the **f** of a bull.
1:10 each one had the **f** of an eagle.
4:3 Turn your **f** toward the city as if
4:7 Turn your **f** toward the
7:22 I will turn my **f** away from the
10:14 The first was the **f** of an angel,
10:14 the second was the **f** of a
10:14 the third was the **f** of a lion,
10:14 the fourth was the **f** of an eagle.
12:6 Cover your **f** so that you won't
12:12 The prince will cover his **f** so
20:35 I will put you on trial **f** to face.
20:35 I will put you on trial face to **f**.
24:16 or let tears run down your **f**.
24:17 Don't cover your **f** or eat the
28:9 god when you **f** those who kill
39:23 So I hid my **f** from them and
39:24 and I hid my **f** from them.
39:29 no longer hide my **f** from them,
41:19 the **f** of a man, which was
41:19 on one side, and the **f** of a lion,
42:13 and southern side rooms that **f**
Dan 3:19 Abednego that his **f** turned red.
5:9 and his **f** turned pale.
10:6 His **f** looked like lightning.
10:8 My **f** turned deathly pale,
10:15 I bowed down with my **f**
Joe 2:6 Every **f** turns pale.
Amo 5:8 from the sea to pour it over the **f**
9:6 the sea and pours it over the **f**
9:8 I will wipe it off the **f** of the
Mic 3:4 He will hide his **f** from you at
Nah 2:10 Every **f** turns pale.
3:5 lift up your dress over your **f**.
Hab 1:9 Every **f** will be directed forward
Zep 1:2 I will gather everything on the **f**
1:3 remove all people from the **f**
Mat 6:17 When you fast, wash your **f**
17:2 His **f** became as bright as the
18:10 in heaven always see the **f**
22:20 "Whose **f** and name is this?"
26:39 he quickly bowed with his **f** to
26:67 Then they spit in his **f**,
Mar 12:16 "Whose **f** and name is this?"
14:65 They covered his **f** and hit him
Luk 5:12 he bowed with his **f** to the
9:29 appearance of his **f** changed,
20:24 Whose **f** and name is this?"
Jon 11:44 and his **f** was wrapped with a
18:22 Jesus slapped his **f** and said,
19:3 the Jews!" and slapped his **f**.
Act 6:15 and saw that his **f** looked like
6:15 face looked like an angel's **f**.
25:16 he must **f** his accusers and
27:10 "Men, we're going to **f** a
Rom 2:16 This happens as they **f** the day
1Co 15:31 I **f** death every day.
2Co 3:7 Israel couldn't look at Moses' **f**.
3:7 His **f** was shining with glory,
3:13 He kept covering his **f** with a
4:6 which shines from Christ's **f**.
Jas 1:23 who looks at his **f** in a mirror,
Rev 1:16 His **f** was like the sun when it
4:7 the third had a **f** like a human,
6:16 and hide us from the **f** of the
10:1 His **f** was like the sun,
22:4 and see his **f**. His name will be

faced (34)

Exo 37:9 They **f** each other,
Jos 8:33 They **f** the Levitical priests
2Sm 22:19 On the day when I **f** disaster,
1Ki 7:25 Three bulls **f** north,
7:25 three **f** west, three faced south,
7:25 three faced west, three **f** south,
7:25 faced south, and three **f** east.
2Ch 3:13 on their feet and **f** the main hall.
4:4 Three bulls **f** north,
4:4 three **f** west, three faced south,
4:4 three faced west, three **f** south,
4:4 faced south, and three **f** east.
Psa 18:18 On the day when I **f** disaster,
Lam 2:3 hand when they **f** their enemy.
Eze 10:11 they **f** without turning as
40:6 went to the gateway that **f** east.
40:9 entrance hall **f** the temple.
40:20 This was the gateway that **f**
40:24 I saw a gateway that **f** south.
40:31 The entrance halls **f** the outer
40:34 Its entrance hall **f** the outer
40:37 Its recessed walls **f** the outer
40:44 It **f** south. The other room was
40:44 of the south gateway. It **f** north.
42:2 The building that **f** north was
42:4 The doors of these side rooms **f**
42:8 The rooms that **f** the temple
42:10 They **f** the open area and the
43:17 The steps to the altar **f** east.
46:19 to the side rooms that **f** north.
47:1 (The temple **f** east.)
2Co 11:23 and have **f** death more often.
11:26 I've **f** dangers from raging rivers
11:26 I've **f** dangers in the city,

faces (69)

Gen 9:23 They turned their **f** away so
42:6 their **f** touching the ground.
43:26 their **f** touching the ground.
44:14 their **f** touching the ground.
Exo 4:31 their **f** touching the ground.
12:27 their **f** touching the ground.
33:10 they would all bow with their **f**
Lev 9:24 their **f** touching the ground.
Num 14:5 bowed with their **f** touching
16:22 they bowed with their **f**
16:45 their **f** touching the ground.
20:6 they bowed with their **f**
Jos 15:7 turns north to the region that **f**
17:7 which **f** Shechem.
18:14 the mountain that **f** Beth Horon,
Jdg 13:20 their **f** touching the ground.
1Ki 7:9 saws on their inner and outer **f**.
2Ki 2:15 their **f** touching the ground.
13:17 "Open the window that **f** east."
1Ch 21:16 their **f** touching the ground.
2Ch 7:3 they knelt down with their **f** on
24:17 of the king with their **f** touching
29:28 down with their **f** touching
Neh 8:6 and then bowed with their **f**
Est 3:2 to Haman with their **f** touching
Job 9:24 He covers the **f** of its judges.
24:15 as they cover their **f**.
40:13 and cover their **f** in the hidden
Psa 21:12 you aim your bow at their **f**.
34:5 Their **f** will never be covered
73:7 eyes peer out from their fat **f**,
83:16 Let their **f** blush with shame,
104:15 olive oil to make **f** shine,
Isa 3:9 The look on their **f** will be held
3:15 crush my people and grind the **f**
6:2 With two they covered their **f**,
13:8 Their **f** will be burning red.
49:23 front of you with their **f** touching
53:3 from whom people turn their **f**,
Jer 2:27 your backs, not your **f**, to me.
32:33 their backs, not their **f** to me.
51:51 Shame covers our **f**,
Lam 4:8 Their **f** are ⌊now⌋ blacker than
Eze 1:6 them had four **f** and four wings.
1:8 four of them had **f** and wings.
1:10 Their **f** looked like this:
1:11 That is what their **f** looked like.
7:18 All their **f** will be covered with

Eze 10:14 Each of the angels had four **f**.
10:21 Each had four **f** and four wings,
10:22 Their **f** looked exactly like the
10:22 looked exactly like the **f** that
11:1 (It's the gate that **f** east.)
24:22 Don't cover your **f** or eat the
27:35 Their **f** show their fear.
32:10 I swing my sword in their **f**.
40:45 "This room that **f** south is for
40:46 The room that **f** north is for the
41:18 and each angel had two **f**:
Mic 3:7 All of them will cover their **f**,
Mal 2:3 to spread excrement on your **f**,
Mat 6:16 They put on sad **f** to make it
Act 27:12 (Phoenix is a harbor that **f** the
1Co 14:25 bow with their **f** touching
2Co 3:18 Lord's glory with **f** that are not
11:20 you around, or slaps your **f**,
Rev 7:11 the throne with their **f** touching
9:7 Their **f** were like human faces.
9:7 Their faces were like human **f**.

facing (40)

Gen 43:33 The brothers were seated **f** him
48:13 on his right, **f** Israel's left,
48:13 on his left, **f** Israel's right,
Exo 14:2 set up their camp **f** Pi Hahiroth,
14:2 Set up your camp **f** north — by
14:9 the sea at Pi Hahiroth **f** north.
27:13 the east end, **f** the rising sun,
38:13 The east side, **f** the rising sun,
Lev 4:6 times in the LORD's presence **f**
4:17 LORD's presence **f** the canopy.
Num 2:2 around the tent of meeting, **f** it.
2:3 the east side, **f** the rising sun,
Dtr 11:30 who live on the plains **f** Gilgal,
Jos 18:18 to the north side of the slope **f**
Jdg 16:3 to the top of the hill **f** Hebron.
20:20 their battle line **f** Gibeah.
20:30 They formed their battle line **f**
1Sm 14:5 pillar on the north **f** Michmash,
14:5 the other stood south **f** Geba.
17:21 their battle lines **f** each other.
1Ki 7:4 were in three rows **f** each other
7:5 There were three doors **f** each
8:42 to pray **f** this temple,
20:29 They camped **f** one another for
22:35 in his chariot **f** the Arameans.
2Ch 6:32 they come to pray **f** this temple,
18:34 himself up in his chariot **f**
Est 5:1 **f** the king's throne room.
5:1 the palace, **f** the entrance.
Sos 7:4 a Lebanese tower **f** Damascus.
Eze 8:16 They were **f** east and
40:27 had a gateway **f** south.
41:15 the length of the building **f**
42:3 were corridors **f** corridors
Mat 27:61 were sitting there, **f** the tomb.
Mar 12:41 As Jesus sat **f** the temple
13:3 sitting on the Mount of Olives **f**
14:54 guards and warmed himself **f**
15:39 When the officer who stood **f**
Luk 22:56 servant saw him as he sat **f**

factions (3)

1Ki 16:21 of Israel was divided into two **f**.
1Co 11:19 **F** have to exist in order to
Gal 5:20 selfish ambition, conflict, **f**,

facts (5)

1Sm 23:23 come back to me with the **f**.
Act 21:34 The officer couldn't get any **f**
Rom 4:19 Through faith he regarded the **f**
2Co 10:7 Look at the plain **f**!
10:14 We're not overstating the **f**.

fade (6)

Dtr 4:9 Don't let them **f** from your
Psa 109:23 I **f** away like a lengthening
Isa 17:4 of Jacob's people will **f** away,
Zec 9:5 because its hope will **f**.
1Pe 1:4 or corrupted and can't **f** away.
5:4 of glory that will never **f** away.

faded (8)

Lev 13:6 If the diseased area has **f** and
13:21 the rest of the skin but has **f**,
13:26 the rest of the skin but has **f**,
13:28 area does not spread but has **f**,
Psa 9:6 Even the memory of them has **f**.
31:12 I have **f** from memory as if I
Ecc 9:5 the memory of them has **f**.
2Co 3:11 If that former ministry **f** away

fades (1)

Job 7:9 As a cloud **f** away and

fading (3)

2Co 3:7 even though that glory was **f**.
3:13 Israel to see the glory **f** away.
1Jn 2:8 The darkness is **f**,

fail (25)

Lev 5:15 "If any of you **f** to do your duty
Dtr 8:11 Don't **f** to obey his commands,
1Sm 2:33 my altar will have his eyes **f**,
3:2 His eyesight had begun to **f** so
20:13 father plans to harm you and I **f**
1Ki 2:4 you will never **f** to have an heir
8:25 You said, 'You will never **f** to
9:5 'You will never **f** to have an
2Ch 6:16 You said, 'You will never **f** to
7:18 'You will never **f** to have an
Est 9:27 that a person should never **f**
Job 17:5 his children's eyesight **f**.)"
Psa 6:7 They **f** because of my enemies.
112:6 He will never **f**. A righteous
Isa 13:7 and everyone's courage will **f**.
19:1 Egypt's courage will **f**.
32:10 the grape harvest will **f**
44:25 the signs of false prophets to **f**
51:6 my righteousness will never **f**.
Jer 33:17 David will never **f** to have a
33:18 Levitical priests will never **f**
Eze 47:12 they won't **f** to produce fruit.
Zep 3:5 He does not **f**. But those who
Luk 22:32 that your faith will not **f**.
Act 5:38 is of human origin, it will **f**.

failed (17)

Gen 24:27 The LORD hasn't **f** to be kind
41:9 remember a promise I **f** to keep.
Jos 23:14 God has given you has ever **f**
1Sm 4:15 and his eyesight had **f** so that
25:37 Nabal's heart **f**, and he could
1Ki 8:56 Moses has **f** to come true.
14:4 His eyesight had **f** because he
15:5 David never **f** to do anything
Ezr 9:1 have **f** to keep themselves
Psa 89:43 his sword out of his hand and **f**
Jer 51:30 Their strength has **f**.
Mat 25:45 Whatever you **f** to do for one of
25:45 you **f** to do for me.'
Rom 9:6 not as though God's word has **f**.
2Co 13:6 that we haven't **f** the test.
13:7 even if we seem to have **f**.
Heb 4:7 years after your ancestors **f**

failing (7)

Gen 48:10 Israel's eyesight was **f**
Lev 6:2 you sin against the LORD by **f**
Dtr 28:65 mind, **f** eyesight, and despair.
1Sm 12:23 to sin against the LORD by **f**
Isa 1:5 Your whole heart is **f**.
Rom 2:21 are you **f** to teach yourself?
2Co 13:5 it be that you're **f** the test?

fails (5)

Job 19:27 My heart **f** inside me!
Isa 44:12 and their strength **f**.
Jer 14:6 Their eyesight **f** because they
Hab 3:17 even if the olive tree **f** to
Mat 7:19 Any tree that **f** to produce good

failure (9)

Act 5:36 The whole movement was a **f**.
Rom 5:15 (God's gift and Adam's **f**.
5:15 as the result of one person's **f**,
5:16 **f** condemned everyone.
5:17 ruled because of one person's **f**.
5:18 was condemned through one **f**,
5:20 were added to increase the **f**.
11:11 By Israel's **f**, salvation has
11:12 Their **f** made people who are

failures (11)

2Ki 2:21 No more deaths or crop **f** will
Mat 6:14 "If you forgive the **f** of others,
6:15 Father will not forgive your **f**.
Mar 11:25 in heaven will forgive your **f**."
Rom 4:25 over to death because of our **f**
5:16 But, even after many **f**,
Eph 1:7 God forgives our **f** because of
2:1 because of your **f** and sins.
2:5 We were dead because of our **f**,
Col 2:13 once dead because of your **f**
2:13 Christ when he forgave all our **f**.

faint (11)

Pro 24:10 If you **f** in a crisis, you are
Isa 44:12 don't drink water, they will **f**.
57:10 strength, so you didn't **f**.
57:16 would grow **f** in my presence.
Jer 15:9 birth to seven sons will grow **f**
Lam 2:11 Little children and infants **f** in
2:12 as they **f** like wounded people
2:19 children who **f** from hunger at
Amo 8:13 and strong young men will **f**
Jnh 4:8 head so that he was about to **f**.
Luk 21:26 People will **f** as they fearfully

fainted (4)

Isa 51:20 Your children have **f**.
Eze 31:15 and all the trees in the field **f**
Dan 8:18 I **f** facedown on the ground,
10:9 I **f** facedown on the ground.

fair (72)

Gen 18:25 the whole earth do what is **f**?"
Dtr 4:8 great nation has such **f** laws
32:4 All his ways are **f**.
33:21 considers **f** and honorable."
2Sm 8:15 He did what was **f** and right for
24:24 buy it from you at a **f** price.
1Ki 21:2 I will pay you a **f** price for it."
1Ch 18:14 He did what was **f** and right for
Ezr 9:15 because you are **f**,
Neh 9:8 promise because you are **f**.
9:13 You gave them **f** rules,
9:33 But you were **f** about
Job 36:3 and prove that my Creator is **f**.
36:17 A **f** judgment will be upheld.
Psa 7:11 God is a **f** judge, a God who is
9:4 on your throne as a **f** judge.
17:2 your eyes observe what is **f**.
19:9 They are completely **f**.
37:30 His tongue speaks what is **f**.
58:1 rulers really give **f** verdicts?
94:15 of judges will again become **f**,
99:4 You have done what is **f** and
103:6 LORD does what is right and **f**
112:4 merciful, compassionate, and **f**.
119:75 that your regulations are **f**,
119:121 I have done what is **f** and right.
119:137 and your regulations are **f**.
119:138 **f** and completely dependable.
119:172 all your commandments are **f**.
145:17 The LORD is **f** in all his ways
Pro 2:9 and just and **f** — every good
8:8 Everything I say is **f**,
8:15 and rulers decree **f** laws.
8:16 so do nobles and all **f** judges.
12:5 of righteous people are **f**.
21:3 Doing what is right and **f** is
Isa 10:22 will be complete and **f**.
11:4 He will make **f** decisions for
45:19 I, the LORD, speak what is **f**
Jer 4:2 in an honest, **f**, and right way,
10:24 me, O LORD, but please be **f**.
22:15 and did what is **f** and right.
23:5 He will do what is **f** and right in
33:15 He will do what is **f** and right in
Lam 3:59 Give me a **f** verdict.
Eze 18:5 person does what is **f** and right.
18:19 has done what is **f** and right.
18:21 and does what is **f** and right.
18:25 nation of Israel, isn't my way **f**?
18:27 and does what is **f** and right,

Eze 18:29 Isn't my way f, nation of Israel?
33:14 and does what is f and right.
33:16 He has done what is f and right.
33:19 and does what is f and right,
45:9 and do what is f and right.
Hos 12:6 Be loyal and f, and always
Zec 8:16 Give correct and f verdicts for
Mar 6:20 Herod knew that John was a f
Luk 23:41 Our punishment is f.
Act 27:8 to a port called F Harbors.
Rom 2:5 reveal that his decisions are f.
3:5 do wrong shows that God is f,
Php 4:8 honorable, f, pure, acceptable,
Col 4:1 Masters, be just and f to your
2Ti 4:8 The Lord, who is a f judge,
Tit 1:8 good judgment, be f and moral,
Heb 6:10 God is f. He won't forget what
Rev 15:3 way you do them is f and true,
15:4 know about your f judgments."
16:5 of the water say, "You are f.
16:7 your judgments are true and f."
19:2 His judgments are true and f.

fairly (16)

Lev 19:15 Judge your neighbor f.
Dtr 1:16 Judge each case f,
16:18 They are to judge the people f.
Psa 9:8 He judges ⌊its⌋ people f.
58:1 judge Adam's descendants f?
75:2 the right time, I will judge f.
96:10 He will judge people f.
Pro 31:9 Speak out, judge f,
Jer 7:5 you really treat each other f.
11:20 O LORD of Armies, you judge f
21:12 Judge f every morning.
22:3 Judge f, and do what is right.
Eze 18:8 and he judges everyone f.
34:16 I will take care of my sheep f.
Act 8:33 he was not judged f.
1Pe 2:23 to the one who judges f.

fairness (4)

Psa 98:9 justice and its people with f.
99:4 You have established f.
Pro 1:3 and justice and f—
Isa 32:1 A king will rule with f,

faith (307)

Gen 15:6 and the LORD regarded that f to
1Sm 2:12 they had no f in the LORD.
23:16 David's ⌊f⌋ in the LORD.
Psa 116:10 I kept my f even when I said,
Hos 4:1 land: "There is no f, no love,
Mat 6:30 people who have so little f?
8:10 I haven't found f as great as
8:26 you cowards have so little f?"
9:2 When Jesus saw their f,
9:22 Your f has made you well."
11:6 Whoever doesn't lose his f in
13:21 he immediately falls ⌊from f⌋.
13:58 there because of their lack of f.
14:31 "You have so little f!
15:28 "Woman, you have strong f!
16:8 You have so little f!
17:20 "Because you have so little f.
17:20 If your f is the size of a mustard
18:6 causes one of them to lose f
18:7 it causes people to lose their f.
18:7 people to lose their f will arise.
18:7 causes someone to lose his f!
18:8 foot causes you to lose your f,
18:9 eye causes you to lose your f,
21:21 If you have f and do not doubt,
21:22 Have f that you will receive
24:10 Then many will lose f.
Mar 2:5 When Jesus saw their f,
4:17 they immediately fall ⌊from f⌋.
4:40 Don't you have any f yet?"
5:34 your f has made you well.
9:24 Help my lack of f."
9:42 causes one of them to lose f
9:43 hand causes you to lose your f,
9:45 foot causes you to lose your f,
9:47 eye causes you to lose your f,
10:52 your f has made you well."
11:22 said to them, "Have f in God!
Mar 11:24 That's why I tell you to have f
Luk 5:20 When Jesus saw their f,
7:9 that I haven't found f as great as
7:23 Whoever doesn't lose his f in
7:50 "Your f has saved you.
8:13 but when their f is tested,
8:25 "Where is your f?"
8:48 your f has made you well.
12:28 people who have so little f?
17:1 people to lose their f are certain
17:1 causes someone to lose his f!
17:2 of these little ones to lose his f.
17:5 to the Lord, "Give us more f."
17:6 The Lord said, "If you have f
17:19 Your f has made you well."
18:8 will he find f on earth?"
18:42 Your f has made you well."
22:32 that your f will not fail.
Jon 4:42 They told the woman, "Our f is
6:61 what I say make you lose f?
11:15 there so that you can grow in f.
16:1 so that you won't lose your f.
Act 5:12 The believers had a common f
6:5 who was a man full of f and the
6:7 of priests accepted the f.
9:35 and turned to the Lord in f.
11:24 was full of the Holy Spirit and f.
13:8 the meaning of the f so that
15:9 non-Jewish people through f as
16:5 were strengthened in the f
18:23 where he strengthened ⌊the f
24:24 him talk about f in Christ Jesus.
Rom 1:5 that is associated with f.
1:8 your f is spreading throughout
1:12 encouraged by each other's f.
1:17 ends with f as Scripture says,
1:17 approval will live because of f."
3:22 has God's approval through f
3:25 approval is given through f
3:27 is eliminated on the basis of f.
3:28 God's approval because of f,
3:30 people because of f
3:30 people through this same f.
3:31 Moses' Teachings by this f?
4:3 and that f was regarded by God
4:5 their f is regarded as God's
4:9 We say, "Abraham's f was
4:10 How was his f regarded as
4:11 Abraham's f was regarded as
4:11 circumcised, and their f, too,
4:12 in the footsteps of his f.
4:12 Our father Abraham had that f
4:13 through God's approval of his f.
4:14 then f is useless and the
4:16 the promise is based on f so
4:19 Through f he regarded the
4:20 God's promise out of a lack of f.
4:20 he became strong because of f
4:22 That is why his f was regarded
4:23 But the words "his f was
4:24 Our f will be regarded as God's
5:1 God's approval because of f,
9:30 an approval based on f.
9:32 They didn't rely on f to gain
10:4 who has f may receive God's
10:6 approval which is based on f,
10:8 message of f that we spread.
10:10 declaring your f you are saved.
10:17 So f comes from hearing the
12:6 say agrees with the Christian f.
14:1 people who are weak in f,
14:2 Other people with weak f
14:13 have doubts or lose their f.
14:23 because he didn't act in f.
14:23 that is not done in f is sin.
15:1 us who have a strong ⌊f⌋ must
15:1 of those whose ⌊f⌋ is not so
15:2 good things that will build his f.
15:13 peace through your f in him.
16:1 is our sister in the Christian f
16:17 f by teaching doctrine
16:23 our brother in the Christian f,
16:26 that is associated with f.
1Co 1:1 our brother in the Christian f.
2:5 so that your f would not be
3:1 were infants in your f in Christ.
1Co 3:5 who helped you come to f.
5:11 or sisters in the Christian f
5:12 are outside ⌊the Christian f⌋?
8:9 who is weak in f fall into sin.
8:11 a believer whose f is weak,
8:13 other believers to lose their f,
8:13 other believers lose their f.
9:22 became like a person weak in f
9:22 to win those who are weak in f.
12:9 Spirit gives ⌊courageous⌋ f.
13:2 I may even have enough f to
13:13 So these three things remain: f,
15:1 and on which your f is based.
15:14 meaning and your f also has no
15:17 your f is nonsense and sin still
15:58 off the foundation ⌊of your f⌋.
16:12 our brother in the Christian f:
16:13 Be firm in the Christian f.
2Co 1:24 control over your Christian f.
1:24 established in the Christian f.
4:13 We have that same spirit of f.
5:7 our lives are guided by f,
8:7 Indeed, the more your f,
10:15 that as your f grows,
13:5 you are still in the Christian f.
Gal 1:23 us is now spreading the f that
2:16 God's approval because of f
3:6 He believed God, and that f
3:7 f are Abraham's descendants.
3:8 non-Jewish people who have f.
3:9 with Abraham, the man of f.
3:11 approval will live because of f."
3:12 Laws have nothing to do with f,
3:14 the promised Spirit through f.
3:22 Therefore, a promise based on f
3:23 Moses' laws until this f came.
3:23 until this f which was about
3:24 God's approval because of f.
3:25 But now that this f has come,
5:5 f causes us to wait eagerly for
5:6 But what matters is a f that
Eph 1:15 I, too, have heard about your f
2:8 God saved you through f as an
3:12 confidence through f in Christ.
3:17 Christ will live in you through f.
4:5 There is one Lord, one f,
4:13 until all of us are united in our f
6:16 take the Christian f as your
6:23 peace and love along with f.
Php 1:25 to grow and be joyful in your f.
1:27 united in fighting for the f that
2:17 ⌊I offer to God⌋ for your f.
3:9 approval through f in Christ.
3:9 from God and is based on f
3:10 F knows the power that his
3:15 Whoever has a mature f should
Col 1:4 we have heard about your f
1:23 in f without being moved
2:5 and how firm your f in Christ is.
2:7 Be strengthened by the f that
2:8 rob you ⌊of this f⌋ through
2:12 to life with Christ through f
4:5 are outside ⌊the Christian f⌋.
1Th 1:3 forget that your f is active,
1:8 have heard about your f in God.
3:2 and encourage you in your f
3:5 to find out about your f.
3:6 news about your f and love.
3:7 So brothers and sisters, your f
3:10 you still need for your f.
5:8 We must put on f and love as a
2Th 1:3 your f is showing remarkable
1:4 about your endurance and f
1:11 do everything your f produces.
2:13 devotion and f in the truth.
3:2 not everyone shares our f.
1Ti 1:2 a genuine child in f.
1:4 which centers in f.
1:5 and from a sincere f.
1:14 his kindness he brought me to f
1:18 Use these prophecies in f and
1:19 Some have refused to let their f
1:19 and their f has been destroyed
2:7 not Jewish about f and truth.
2:15 they lead respectable lives in f,
3:9 the mystery of the Christian f.

1Ti 3:13 result of their **f** in Christ Jesus.
4:1 will desert the Christian **f**.
4:6 by the words of the Christian **f**
4:12 your speech, behavior, love, **f**,
5:8 he has denied the Christian **f**
5:12 by rejecting the Christian **f**,
5:12 the **f** they first accepted.
6:10 away from the Christian **f**
6:11 a godly life, **f**, love, endurance,
6:12 the good fight for the Christian **f**
6:20 use to oppose ⌊the Christian **f**⌋.
6:21 they have abandoned the **f**.
2Ti 1:5 of how sincere your **f** is.
1:5 That **f** first lived in your
1:13 With **f** and love for Christ
2:18 They are destroying the **f** of
2:22 Pursue **f**, love, and peace
3:8 and the **f** they teach is
3:10 my **f**, my patience, my love,
3:15 saved through **f** in Christ Jesus.
4:7 the race. I have kept the **f**.
Tit 1:1 lead God's chosen people to **f**
1:4 genuine child in the **f** we share.
1:13 continue to have **f** that is alive
2:2 and to be well-grounded in **f**,
Phm 1:6 As you share the **f** you have in
Heb 3:1 we make our declaration of **f**.
4:14 hold on to our declaration of **f**:
6:1 and the basics about **f** in God.
6:12 through **f** and patience.
10:22 a sincere heart and strong **f**.
10:23 firmly to our declaration of **f**.
10:38 approval will live because of **f**.
10:39 who have **f** and are saved.
11:1 **F** assures us of things we
11:2 ancestors because of their **f**.
11:3 **F** convinces us that God
11:4 **F** led Abel to offer God a better
11:4 Through his **f** Abel received
11:4 Through his **f** Abel still speaks,
11:5 **F** enabled Enoch to be taken
11:6 one can please God without **f**.
11:7 **F** led Noah to listen when God
11:7 Through **f** Noah condemned
11:7 approval that comes through **f**.
11:8 **F** led Abraham to obey when
11:9 **F** led Abraham to live as a
11:11 **F** enabled Abraham to become
11:13 All these people died having **f**.
11:17 **f** led him to offer his son Isaac.
11:20 **F** led Isaac to bless Jacob and
11:21 While Jacob was dying, **f** led
11:22 While Joseph was dying, **f** led
11:23 **F** led Moses' parents to hide
11:24 When Moses grew up, **f** led
11:27 **F** led Moses to leave Egypt
11:28 **F** led Moses to establish the
11:29 **F** caused the people to go
11:30 **F** caused the walls of Jericho
11:31 **F** led the prostitute Rahab to
11:33 Through **f** they conquered
11:39 people were known for their **f**,
12:1 by so many examples ⌊of **f**⌋,
12:2 the source and goal of our **f**.
13:7 turned out, and imitate their **f**.
Jas 1:3 of your **f** produces endurance.
2:1 practice your **f** in our glorious
2:5 in the world to become rich in **f**
2:14 do if someone claims to have **f**
2:14 Can this kind of **f** save him?
2:17 In the same way, **f** by itself is
2:18 person might say, "You have **f**,
2:18 Show me your **f** apart from the
2:18 I will show you my **f** by the
2:20 Do you have to be shown that **f**
2:22 You see that Abraham's **f** and
2:22 His **f** was shown to be genuine
2:23 and that **f** was regarded by God
2:26 In the same way **f** that does
5:15 (Prayers offered in **f** will save
1Pe 1:5 by God's power through **f**
1:7 is to test your **f** as fire tests
1:7 Your **f** is more precious than
1:9 that is the goal of your **f**.
1:21 So your **f** and confidence are in
2:17 brothers and sisters in the **f**.
1Pe 5:9 Be firm in the **f** and resist him,
2Pe 1:1 To those who have obtained a **f**
1:1 a **f** based on the approval that
1:5 effort to add integrity to your **f**;
1Jn 2:10 Nothing will destroy the **f** of
5:4 Our **f** is what wins the victory
3Jn 1:5 you are showing your **f** in
Jud 1:3 Christian **f** that was entrusted
1:20 use your most holy **f** to grow.
Rev 2:19 I know your love, **f**,
14:12 and keep their **f** in Jesus,

faithful (113)

Gen 17:9 come are to be **f** to my promise.
17:10 This is how you are to be **f** to
24:27 hasn't failed to be kind and **f**
47:29 you love me and are **f** to me.
Exo 19:5 you carefully obey me and are **f**
34:6 always **f** and ready to forgive.
Num 12:7 He is the most **f** person in my
Dtr 7:9 He is a **f** God, who keeps his
32:4 He is a **f** God, who does no
33:8 Urim belong to your **f** people.
33:9 obeyed your word and were **f**
1Sm 2:9 He safeguards the steps of his **f**
2:35 Then I will appoint a **f** priest to
2:35 I will give him **f** descendants,
26:23 person who is righteous and **f**.
2Sm 3:8 "Until now I've been **f** to your
20:19 are peaceful and **f** Israelites.
22:26 ⌊In dealing⌋ with **f** people you
22:26 with faithful people you are **f**,
1Ki 2:4 'If your descendants are **f** to me
8:25 Israel if your descendants are **f**
8:25 me as you have been **f** to me.'
9:4 "If you will be **f** to me as your
18:12 "I have been **f** to the LORD
2Ch 6:16 Israel if your descendants are **f**
6:16 me as you have been **f** to me.'
7:17 "If you will be **f** to me as your
31:18 priests and Levites had to be **f**
Neh 9:8 that his heart was **f** to you.
9:33 You have been **f**, but we have
Psa 12:1 **F** people have vanished from
18:25 ⌊In dealing⌋ with **f** people you
18:25 with faithful people you are **f**,
30:4 you **f** people who belong to
31:23 The LORD protects **f** people,
37:3 and practice being **f**.
51:10 and renew a **f** spirit within me.
78:8 Their spirits were not **f** to God.
78:10 They had not been **f** to God's
78:37 They were not **f** to his promise.
86:2 because I am **f** ⌊to you⌋.
86:15 always **f** and ready to forgive.
89:19 vision you said to your **f** ones:
89:37 be like a **f** witness in heaven."
98:3 forgotten to be merciful and **f**
101:6 My eyes will be watching the **f**
103:18 to those who are **f** to his
116:15 is the death of his **f** ones.
132:12 If your sons are **f** to my promise
143:1 you are **f** and righteous.
145:10 and your **f** ones will praise you.
145:17 is fair in all his ways and **f**
145:18 to every **f** person who prays to
146:6 The LORD remains **f** forever.
148:14 praiseworthy for his **f** ones,
Pro 14:22 are merciful and **f** plan what is
Isa 1:21 How the **f** town has become a
1:26 Righteous City, the **F** Town."
7:9 If you don't remain **f**,
26:2 the nation that remains **f**.
38:18 pit cannot expect you to be **f**.
49:7 The LORD is **f**. The Holy One of
Jer 6:9 Thoroughly pick through the **f**
42:5 "May the LORD be a true and **f**
50:20 I will forgive the **f** few whom I
Hos 2:19 I will be honest and **f** to you.
11:12 against the Holy One who is **f**.
Amo 5:15 pity on the **f** few of Joseph.
Mic 4:7 who are lame into a **f** people.
7:2 **F** people are gone from the
7:18 the rebellion of your **f** people.
7:20 You will be **f** to Jacob.
Zep 1:4 I will remove the **f** few of Baal
Zep 2:7 The coast will belong to the **f**
2:9 The **f** few of my people will
3:12 So with you I will leave a **f** few,
3:13 The **f** few in Israel will not do
Hag 1:12 and the **f** few who returned from
1:14 and the **f** few who returned from
2:2 and the **f** few who returned from
2:3 'Is there anyone among the **f**
Zec 8:8 be their God, who is **f** and just.
Mat 24:45 is the **f** and wise servant?
25:21 You're a good and **f** servant!
25:23 You're a good and **f** servant!
Luk 12:42 asked, "Who, then, is the **f**,
Act 14:22 the disciples to remain **f**.
Eph 1:1 To God's holy and **f** people
6:21 He is our dear brother and a **f**
Col 1:2 To God's holy and **f** people,
4:9 is from your city and is our **f**
1Th 5:24 The one who calls you is **f**,
2Th 3:3 But the Lord is **f** and will
2Ti 2:2 Entrust this message to **f**
2:13 we are unfaithful, he remains **f**
Tit 3:15 Greet our **f** friends.
Heb 2:17 could serve as a **f** chief priest
3:2 Jesus is **f** to God, in the same
3:2 way that Moses was **f** when
3:5 Moses was a **f** servant in
3:6 But Christ is a **f** son in charge
10:23 one who made the promise is **f**.
13:4 and wives should be **f**
Jas 1:1 To God's **f** people who have
1Pe 4:19 themselves to a **f** creator
5:12 whom I regard as a **f** brother.
1Jn 1:9 God is **f** and reliable.
Rev 2:10 Be **f** until death, and I will give
2:13 He was my **f** witness who was
3:14 the witness who is **f** and true,
17:14 and **f** are with him."
19:11 its rider is named **F** and True.
21:5 'These words are **f** and true.'"

faithfully (42)

Dtr 4:6 **F** obey these laws.
5:1 Learn them and **f** obey them.
6:25 If we **f** obey all these laws in
7:12 to these rules and **f** obey them,
11:13 If you **f** obey the commands
11:22 **F** obey all these commands I'm
12:1 laws and rules you must **f** obey
15:5 your God and **f** obey all these
17:19 and **f** obey everything found
19:9 He may do this because you **f**
26:16 You must **f** obey them with all
28:1 and **f** follow all his commands
28:13 if you **f** obey the commands of
28:15 LORD your God, and **f** follow all
28:58 You might not **f** obey every
29:9 **F** obey the terms of this
31:12 God and **f** obey every word
32:46 children to **f** obey every word
Jos 1:7 **f** doing everything in the
1:8 you will **f** do everything written
1Ki 14:8 He obeyed my commands and **f**
2Ki 17:37 **F** obey the laws, rules,
20:3 remember how I've lived **f** and
1Ch 17:23 "Now, LORD, **f** keep the
2Ch 31:12 they **f** brought in the
31:15 were to distribute the offerings **f**
32:1 Hezekiah had done so **f**,
34:12 The men did their work **f** under
Neh 1:5 you **f** keep your promise and
9:32 You **f** keep your promises.
Isa 16:5 He will rule **f**. He is from the
38:3 remember how I've lived **f** and
42:3 He will **f** bring about justice.
56:4 and **f** observe the conditions of
56:6 unholy and will **f** observe
61:8 I will **f** reward my people's
Jer 32:41 and soul I will **f** plant them
Eze 18:9 my rules and obeys my laws **f**.
Mat 5:20 approval and do it more **f** than
1Co 1:9 God **f** keeps his promises.
4:17 and he **f** does the Lord's work.
10:13 who **f** keeps his promises,

faithfulness (29)

Gen 32:10 the love and **f** you have shown
Jos 24:14 serve him with integrity and **f**.
1Ch 9:26 God's temple because of their **f**.
2Ch 19:9 the fear of the LORD and with **f**.
Psa 36:5 your **f** to the skies.
40:10 been outspoken about your **f**
71:22 Because of your **f**,
88:11 or about your **f** in Abaddon?
89:1 your **f** to every generation.
89:2 Your **f** stands firm in the
89:5 praise your miracles and your **f**
89:8 even your **f** surrounds you.
89:24 My **f** and mercy will be with
89:49 David on ⌊the basis of⌋ your **f**.
92:2 and your **f** in the evening
100:5 His **f** endures throughout every
115:1 because of your mercy and **f**.
117:2 The LORD's **f** endures forever.
119:30 I have chosen a life of **f**.
119:90 Your **f** endures throughout
Pro 16:6 By mercy and **f**, peace is made
Isa 11:5 **F** will be the belt around his
38:19 Fathers make your **f** known to
Lam 3:23 every morning. His **f** is great.
Hab 2:4 will live because of his **f**.
Mat 23:23 neglected justice, mercy, and **f**.
Rom 3:3 unfaithfulness cancel God's **f**?
Gal 5:22 kindness, goodness, **f**,
Phm 1:5 I hear about your **f** to the Lord

faithless (1)

Jos 22:16 'What is this **f** act you have

faithlessly (1)

Jos 22:20 Achan, son of Zerah, act **f**

falcons (2)

Lev 11:16 seagulls, all types of **f**,
Dtr 14:15 seagulls, all types of **f**,

fall (144)

Gen 2:21 LORD God caused him to **f** into
27:13 "Let any curse on you **f** on me,
Exo 9:22 and hail will **f** on people,
15:16 Terror and dread will **f** on them.
Lev 11:35 their dead bodies **f** is unclean.
11:37 If their dead bodies **f** on seed
11:38 and their dead bodies **f** on it,
26:25 on you and you will **f** under
26:36 They will run away and **f**,
Dtr 11:14 both in the **f** and in the spring.
28:40 the olives will **f** off the trees.
Jdg 15:18 But now I'll die from thirst and **f**
1Sm 14:45 a single hair of his head will **f**
18:25 planned to have David **f** into
26:12 The LORD had made them **f**
26:20 Don't let my blood **f** to the
2Sm 3:29 May the blame **f** on the head of
14:11 son's head will **f** to the ground."
17:12 We'll **f** on him as dew falls on
24:14 "Please let us **f** into the
24:14 let me **f** into human hands."
1Ki 1:52 not one hair on his head will **f**
2:33 for their blood will **f**
18:1 allow rain to **f** on the ground."
2Ki 6:6 of God asked, "Where did it **f**?"
1Ch 21:13 "Please let me **f** into the
21:13 let me **f** into human hands."
Job 13:11 the fear of him **f** upon you?
31:22 ⌊then⌋ let my shoulder **f** out of
33:15 when people **f** into a deep
37:6 to the snow, '**F** to the ground,'
Psa 4:8 I **f** asleep in peace the moment
10:10 They collapse, and they **f**
20:8 will sink to their knees and **f**,
35:8 Let them **f** into their own pit and
38:17 I am ready to **f**. I am continually
45:5 Nations **f** beneath you.
46:5 It cannot **f**. God will help it at
56:7 angrily make the nations **f**.
66:9 and has not allowed us to **f**.
73:18 and make them **f** into ruin.
78:28 He made the birds **f** in the
82:7 humans and **f** like any prince."
Psa 91:7 even though a thousand may **f**
118:13 pushed hard to make me **f**,
121:3 He will not let you **f**.
121:3 Your guardian will not **f** asleep.
140:10 Let burning coals **f** on them.
141:10 Let wicked people **f** into their
Pro 11:5 but wicked people **f** by their
11:14 A nation will **f** when there is no
11:28 Whoever trusts his riches will **f**,
16:18 arrogant attitude precedes a **f**.
20:4 person does not plow in the **f**.
22:14 by the LORD will **f** into it.
24:16 person may **f** seven times,
24:16 in a disaster wicked people **f**.
26:27 Whoever digs a pit will **f** into it.
28:10 into evil will **f** into his own
28:18 dishonestly will **f** all at once.
Ecc 10:8 Whoever digs a pit may **f** into it.
Isa 8:15 They will **f** and be broken.
10:4 among prisoners and to **f**
10:34 Lebanon will **f** in front of the
22:25 It will be cut off and will **f**,
24:18 news of a disaster will **f** into
24:20 It will **f** and not get up again.
28:13 is why they will **f** backwards.
30:13 with a bulging crack, ready to **f**.
30:13 All of a sudden it will **f**.
30:25 slaughter comes, towers will **f**.
31:3 one who receives help will **f**.
34:4 The stars will **f** like leaves
34:5 it will **f** on Edom and on the
40:20 set up idols that will not **f** over.
40:30 young men will stumble and **f**.
Jer 9:22 Dead bodies will **f** like manure
10:4 nails so that they won't **f** over.
14:2 Judah mourns; its gates **f** apart.
23:12 and they will **f** down in the
25:27 Drink, get drunk, vomit, **f** down,
46:6 They stumble and **f** in the north
46:12 and both will **f** together."
48:44 flees from a disaster will **f** into
50:15 Their towers will **f** and their
50:32 people will stumble and **f**,
51:4 Babylon's soldiers will **f** down
51:8 Babylon will suddenly **f** and be
51:39 They will **f** into a deep sleep
51:44 and its walls will **f**.
51:49 the earth, Babylon must **f**.
51:57 They will **f** into a deep sleep
Eze 6:7 and they will **f** among you.
7:19 gold caused them to **f** into sin.
13:11 paint that their wall will **f** down.
13:11 hailstones will **f** on it,
14:3 themselves to **f** into sin.
14:4 and allows himself to **f** into sin.
14:7 allowing himself to **f** into sin.
18:30 so that you will not **f** into sin.
26:11 pillars will **f** to the ground.
28:23 Your people will **f** dead.
29:5 You will **f** in an open field.
30:4 Many Egyptians will **f** dead.
30:22 the sword **f** from his hand.
30:25 but Pharaoh's arms will **f**.
35:8 Those killed in battle will **f** on
38:20 every wall will **f** to the ground.
44:12 and by making Israel **f** into sin.
Dan 7:20 made three of the horns **f** out.
11:11 a large army that will **f** into
11:19 will stumble, **f**, and disappear.
Hos 10:8 and to the hills, "**F** on us!"
Amo 3:14 cut off and will **f** to the ground.
8:14 Those who say this will **f** and
9:9 one pebble will **f** to the ground.
Nah 3:12 When shaken, the figs **f** into
Zep 1:3 the sins that make people **f**,
Hag 2:22 and the horses will **f** along with
Zec 14:17 then rain won't **f** on them.
14:18 then ⌊rain won't **f**⌋ on them.
Mat 5:45 He lets rain **f** on them whether
10:29 Not one of them will **f** to the
15:14 both will **f** into the same pit."
15:27 scraps that **f** from their masters'
24:29 the stars will **f** from the sky,
Mar 3:11 they would **f** down in front of
4:17 they immediately **f** ⌊from faith⌋.
13:25 the stars will **f** from the sky,
Luk 6:39 Won't both **f** into the same pit?
10:18 "I watched Satan **f** from heaven
23:30 say to the mountains, '**F** on us!'
Act 5:15 at least Peter's shadow might **f**
Rom 11:12 The **f** of the Jewish people
16:17 who make others **f** away ⌊from
1Co 8:9 who is weak in faith **f** into sin.
10:12 be careful that they don't **f**.
1Th 5:6 Therefore, we must not **f**
Heb 11:30 the walls of Jericho to **f** after
Jas 5:7 patiently for **f** and spring rains.
2Pe 1:10 you will never **f** away.
3:17 Then you won't **f** from your firm
Jud 1:24 guard you so that you don't **f**
Rev 6:16 mountains and rocks, "**F** on us,

fallen (45)

Lev 19:10 time or pick up **f** grapes.
Jdg 4:21 When Sisera had **f** sound
1Sm 5:3 saw that Dagon had **f** forward
5:4 Dagon had ⌊again⌋ **f** forward
2Sm 1:19 See how the mighty have **f**!
1:25 how the mighty have **f** in battle!
1:27 See how the mighty have **f**!
3:38 a great man, has **f** in Israel?
1Ki 17:7 no rain had **f** in the land.
2Ki 2:13 coat (which had **f** off Elijah),
Psa 36:12 the troublemakers who have **f**.
53:3 Everyone has **f** away.
69:9 who insult you have **f** on me.
94:17 quickly **f** silent ⌊in death⌋.
119:22 and contempt that have **f**
Pro 6:3 because you have **f** into your
Isa 3:8 has stumbled, and Judah has **f**,
9:10 "Bricks have **f**, but we will
14:8 "Since you have **f**,
14:12 How you have **f** from heaven,
21:9 Then he said, "Babylon has **f**!
21:9 It has **f**! All the idols they
29:4 When you have **f**, you will
59:14 Truth has **f** in the street,
Jer 13:18 crowns have **f** off your heads."
46:16 and now they have **f**.
Lam 5:16 The crown has **f** from our head.
Eze 31:13 the birds perched on the **f** tree,
Amo 5:2 The people of Israel have **f**,
9:11 day I will set up David's **f** tent.
Mic 7:8 Although I've **f**, I will get up.
Nah 3:18 have **f** into a deep sleep.
Zec 11:2 because the cedars have **f** and
11:2 your dense forest has **f** down.
Act 15:16 will set up David's **f** tent again.
Rom 3:23 they have **f** short of God's glory.
15:3 who insult you have **f** on me."
Gal 5:4 You have **f** out of God's favor.
Rev 2:5 Remember how far you have **f**.
9:1 I saw a star that had **f** to earth
14:8 followed him, and said, "**F**!
14:8 Babylon the Great has **f**!
17:10 Five of them have **f**,
18:2 out in a powerful voice, "**F**!
18:2 Babylon the Great has **f**!

falling (9)

Est 7:8 Haman was **f** on the couch
Psa 60:2 in it because it is **f** apart.
68:14 like snow **f** on Mount Zalmon."
Amo 4:7 I stopped the rain from **f** three
Luk 22:44 drops of blood **f** to the ground.
Act 20:9 was gradually **f** asleep.
1Ti 6:9 get rich keep **f** into temptation.
Heb 10:31 **F** into the hands of the living
Rev 11:6 order to keep rain from **f** during

fallow (2)

Dtr 14:5 deer, gazelles, **f** deer,
1Ki 4:23 **f** deer, and fattened birds.

falls (34)

Gen 49:17 so that its rider **f** off backwards.
Exo 9:19 die when the hail **f** on them."'
21:33 and a bull or a donkey **f** into it,
Lev 11:32 these creatures **f** on something,
11:33 "If any of these creatures **f** into
Num 24:4 and **f** ⌊into a trance⌋ with his
24:16 and **f** ⌊into a trance⌋ with his

Dtr 22:8 home if someone **f** off the roof.
2Sm 3:34 You fell as one **f** in front of
17:12 We'll fall on him as dew **f** on
Job 4:13 when deep sleep **f** on people,
14:18 As surely as a mountain **f** and
Psa 7:15 Then he **f** into the hole that he
37:24 When he **f**, he will not be
72:6 May he be like rain that **f** on
145:14 supports everyone who **f**.
Pro 24:17 be happy when your enemy **f**,
28:14 is hard-hearted **f** into disaster.
Ecc 4:10 If one **f**, the other can help his
4:10 who is ⌊all⌋ alone when he **f**.
11:3 If a tree **f** north or south,
Jer 8:4 LORD says: When someone **f**,
Eze 13:12 When the wall **f** down,
13:14 When the wall **f**, they will be
Mat 12:11 If it **f** into a pit on a day of
13:21 he immediately **f** ⌊from faith⌋.
17:15 Often he **f** into fire or water.
21:44 Anyone who **f** on this stone
21:44 If the stone **f** on anyone,
Luk 11:17 A house divided against itself **f**.
14:5 "If your son or your ox **f** into a
20:18 Everyone who **f** on that stone
20:18 If that stone **f** on anyone,
Heb 6:7 So rain often **f** on it,

false (100)

Exo 23:1 "Never spread **f** rumors.
23:1 people by giving **f** testimony.
Job 41:9 ⌊of defeating it⌋ is a **f** hope.
Psa 24:4 and does not long for what is **f**
27:12 **F** witnesses have risen
31:6 hate those who cling to **f** gods,
97:7 and brags about **f** gods will
135:5 is greater than all the **f** gods.
138:1 praise you in front of the **f** gods.
144:8 Their right hands take **f**
144:11 Their right hands take **f**
Pro 25:18 ⌊so⌋ is a person who gives **f**
Isa 44:20 I hold in my right hand a **f** god?
44:25 I cause the signs of **f** prophets
Jer 3:23 is the noise of **f** worship.
10:14 Their statues are **f** ⌊gods⌋.
13:25 forgotten me and trusted **f** gods.
23:16 They fill you with **f** hope.
50:36 A sword will kill the **f** prophets.
51:17 Their statues are **f** ⌊gods⌋.
Lam 2:14 They gave you **f** prophecies
Eze 7:20 detestable statues ⌊of **f** gods⌋.
12:24 There will no longer be any **f**
13:6 foolish prophets see **f** visions,
13:7 haven't you seen **f** visions and
13:8 Your predictions are **f**,
13:9 the prophets who see **f** visions
13:23 you will no longer see **f** visions
20:26 sons as gifts ⌊to their **f** gods⌋.
21:29 People see **f** visions about you
22:28 things by seeing **f** visions
Dan 11:21 the kingdom using **f** promises.
Amo 2:4 been led astray by **f** teachings,
Zec 8:17 Don't enjoy **f** testimony.
10:2 The fortunetellers see **f** visions.
10:2 They speak about **f** dreams.
13:2 I will also remove the ⌊**f**⌋
Mat 7:15 "Beware of **f** prophets.
19:18 Never give **f** testimony.
24:11 Many **f** prophets will appear
24:24 **F** christs and false prophets
24:24 False christs and **f** prophets
26:59 were searching for **f** testimony
26:60 came forward with **f** testimony.
Mar 10:19 Never give **f** testimony.
13:22 **F** christs and false prophets
13:22 False christs and **f** prophets
14:56 Many gave **f** testimony against
14:57 gave **f** testimony against him.
15:19 in front of him with **f** humility.
Luk 6:26 treated the **f** prophets.
18:20 Never give **f** testimony.
Act 7:41 They offered a sacrifice to that **f**
15:20 from things polluted by **f** gods,
15:29 from food sacrificed to **f** gods,
17:16 statues of **f** gods everywhere.
21:25 eat food sacrificed to **f** gods,
1Co 5:10 dishonest, or worship **f** gods.
5:11 sin, are greedy, worship **f** gods,
6:9 who worship **f** gods,
8:1 food offered to **f** gods:
8:4 food that was offered to **f** gods:
8:4 We know that the **f** gods in this
8:7 to worshiping **f** gods that they
8:7 eating food offered to a **f** god.
8:10 eating in the temple of a **f** god.
8:10 to eat food offered to a **f** god?
8:13 if eating food ⌊offered to **f**
10:7 So don't worship **f** gods as
10:14 the worship of **f** gods as you
10:19 made to a **f** god is anything,
10:19 or that a **f** god itself is
12:2 led to worship **f** gods you were
2Co 1:18 Our message to you isn't **f**;
1:19 told you about, was true not **f**.
6:16 God's temple contain **f** gods?
11:13 brag like this are **f** apostles.
11:26 who turned out to be **f** friends.
Gal 2:4 **F** Christians were brought in.
Col 2:18 Let no one who delights in ⌊**f**⌋
2:23 worship, ⌊**f**⌋ humility,
1Th 1:9 you turned away from **f** gods
1Ti 1:3 to stop teaching **f** doctrine
6:3 Whoever teaches **f** doctrine
6:20 of **f** knowledge that people
Tit 3:10 to teach **f** doctrine after you
1Pe 4:3 the forbidden worship of **f** gods.
2Pe 2:1 **F** prophets were among God's
2:1 as **f** teachers will be among
2:10 These **f** teachers are bold and
2:12 These **f** teachers insult what
2:13 These **f** teachers are stains
2:15 These **f** teachers have left the
2:17 These **f** teachers are dried-up
1Jn 4:1 because there are many **f**
5:21 guard yourselves from **f** gods.
Rev 16:13 the beast, and the **f** prophet.
19:20 The beast and the **f** prophet
19:20 By these miracles the **f** prophet
20:10 where the beast and the **f**

falsehood (1)

Isa 28:15 and **f** is our hiding place."

falsely (3)

Lev 6:5 it was that you swore **f** about.
Dtr 19:16 to accuse a person **f** of a crime.
Isa 32:6 They speak **f** about the LORD.

fame (12)

Dtr 26:19 He will give you praise, **f**,
Jos 6:27 and his **f** spread throughout the
1Ki 4:31 His **f** spread to all the nations
2Ki 14:10 Enjoy your **f**, but stay home.
1Ch 14:17 David's **f** spread through all
2Ch 25:19 enough to look for more **f**.
26:8 and his **f** spread to the border of
26:15 Uzziah's **f** spread far and wide
Isa 66:19 who have not heard of my **f**
Jer 13:11 be my people and bring **f**,
48:17 and everyone who knows its **f**.
Eze 16:15 and you used your **f** to become

familiar (7)

Exo 31:4 He's a master artist **f** with gold,
35:32 He's a master artist **f** with gold,
Job 24:17 because they are **f** with the
Psa 139:3 You are **f** with all my ways.
Isa 53:3 of sorrows, **f** with suffering.
Act 26:3 this since you are especially **f**
Rom 7:1 are **f** with Moses' Teachings.)

families (264)

Gen 10:5 had its own language and **f**.
10:18 Later the Canaanite **f** scattered.
10:20 were Ham's descendants by **f**
10:31 were Shem's descendants by **f**
10:32 These were the **f** of Noah's
42:19 grain back to your starving **f**.
42:33 food for your starving **f** and go.
45:18 Take your father and your **f**,
Exo 1:1 with him to Egypt with their **f**:
1:21 he gave them **f** of their own.
Exo 6:14 These were the heads of the **f**:
6:14 the **f** descended from Reuben.
6:15 the **f** descended from Simeon.
6:17 listed by their **f** were Libni
6:19 These were the **f** descended
6:24 the **f** descended from Korah.
6:25 households listed by their **f**.
12:21 lamb or a young goat for your **f**,
Lev 20:5 I will condemn them and their **f**.
25:45 you and from their **f** born
26:9 Your **f** will be large,
Num 1:2 of Israel by **f** and households.
1:20 The roster of **f** and households
1:22 The roster of **f** and households
1:24 The roster of **f** and households
1:26 The roster of **f** and households
1:28 The roster of **f** and households
1:30 The roster of **f** and households
1:32 The roster of **f** and households
1:34 The roster of **f** and households
1:36 The roster of **f** and households
1:38 The roster of **f** and households
1:40 The roster of **f** and households
1:42 The roster of **f** and households
3:15 Levites by households and **f**.
3:18 Their **f** were named after them.
3:19 Their **f** were named after them.
3:20 Their **f** were named after them.
3:20 the households of Levite **f**.
3:21 To Gershon belonged the **f**
3:21 the **f** descended from Gershon.
3:23 The **f** descended from Gershon
3:27 To Kohath belonged the **f**
3:27 the **f** descended from Kohath.
3:29 The **f** descended from Kohath
3:30 The leader of the Kohathite **f**
3:33 To Merari belonged the **f**
3:33 the **f** descended from Merari.
3:35 The leader of the Merarite **f** and
3:39 at the LORD's command, by **f**,
4:2 List them by **f** and households.
4:18 "Don't let the Kohathite **f** from
4:22 List them by households and **f**.
4:24 "This is what the Gershonite **f**
4:28 is the work of the Gershonite **f**
4:29 Merarites by **f** and households.
4:33 This is what the Merarite **f** will
4:34 by their **f** and households.
4:36 They were listed by **f**.
4:37 in the Kohathite **f** who served at
4:38 registered by **f** and households.
4:40 listed by **f** and households.
4:41 the Gershonite **f** who worked at
4:42 registered by **f** and households.
4:44 They were listed by **f**.
4:45 registered in the Merarite **f**.
4:46 listed by **f** and households.
16:32 their **f**, the followers of Korah,
26:7 These were the **f** of Reuben.
26:12 The **f** descended from Simeon
26:14 These were the **f** of Simeon.
26:15 The **f** descended from Gad
26:18 These were the **f** of Gad's
26:20 The **f** descended from Judah
26:22 These were the **f** of Judah.
26:23 The **f** descended from Issachar
26:25 These were the **f** of Issachar.
26:26 The **f** descended from Zebulun
26:27 These were the **f** of Zebulun.
26:28 The **f** descended from Joseph
26:34 These were the **f** of Manasseh.
26:35 The **f** descended from Ephraim
26:37 These were the **f** of Ephraim's
26:37 the **f** descended from Joseph.
26:38 The **f** descended from
26:41 These were the **f** descended
26:44 The **f** descended from Asher
26:47 These were the **f** of Asher's
26:48 The **f** descended from Naphtali
26:50 These were the **f** of Naphtali.
26:57 The **f** descended from Levi
26:58 These were the **f** of Levi:
27:1 belonged to the **f** of Manasseh,
31:26 and the heads of the **f** of the
32:16 and cities for our **f** here.
32:17 Meanwhile our **f** will live in

Num 32:24 Build cities for your **f** and stone
33:54 Divide the land among your **f**
33:54 Give more land to larger **f** and
36:1 whose **f** were descended from
36:1 (**f** of Joseph's descendants)
36:12 They married within the **f** of the
Dtr 11:6 them, their **f**, their tents,
12:7 you and your **f** will eat and
Jos 7:14 selects will come forward by **f**.
7:17 Then he had the **f** of Judah
13:15 to the tribe of Reuben for their **f**.
13:23 Reuben's inheritance for its **f**.
13:24 to the tribe of Gad for its **f**.
13:28 was Gad's inheritance for its **f**.
13:29 It was only for the **f** of that half
13:31 given to half the **f** of Machir,
15:1 The lot was drawn for the **f** of
15:12 Judah that belong to their **f**.
15:20 is the land inherited by the **f**
16:5 This is the territory for the **f**
16:8 given as an inheritance to the **f**
17:2 **f** descended from Manasseh,
17:2 son Manasseh listed by their **f**.
18:11 The lot was drawn for the **f** of
18:20 given to Benjamin for its **f**.
18:21 to the tribe of Benjamin for its **f**:
18:28 Benjamin's inheritance for its **f**.
19:1 second lot was drawn for the **f**
19:8 of the tribe of Simeon for its **f**.
19:10 The third lot was drawn for the **f**
19:16 the **f** descended from Zebulun.
19:17 the **f** descended from Issachar.
19:23 are the inheritance for the **f**
19:24 The fifth lot was drawn for the **f**
19:31 are the inheritance for the **f**
19:32 drawn for the **f** descended from
19:39 are the inheritance for the **f**
19:40 seventh lot was drawn for the **f**
19:48 are the inheritance for the **f**
19:51 and the leaders of the **f** divided
21:1 Then the leaders of the **f** of
21:1 and to the leaders of the **f** of the
21:4 These are the cities for the **f** of
21:5 received 10 cities from the **f**
21:6 received 13 cities from the **f**
21:7 12 cities for their **f** from
21:10 who were from the **f**
21:20 who were from the **f** of Kohath.
21:26 to the rest of the **f** of Kohath.
21:27 They gave the **f** of Gershon's
21:33 were given to Gershon's **f**.
21:34 To the **f** of Merari, who were
21:40 belonged to the **f** of Merari.
21:40 were the last of the **f** of Levi.
Jdg 12:9 people from outside their own **f**.
18:2 So all the **f** of Dan sent out five
18:19 or for a tribe in Israel and its **f**?"
21:17 must be allowed to have **f**.
1Sm 9:21 most insignificant of all the **f**
10:21 of Benjamin come forward by **f**,
23:23 him among all the **f** of Judah."
2Sm 2:3 his men and their **f** with him,
3:1 As the war between the royal **f**
3:6 During the war between the **f** of
15:22 his men and all the **f** who were
1Ki 8:1 the leaders of the Israelite **f**.
2Ki 10:13 We've come to greet the **f** of the
1Ch 2:53 the **f** of Kiriath Jearim,
2:55 and the **f** of scribes who lived
2:55 These **f** were the people of
4:2 were the **f** of the Zorathites.
4:8 the ancestor of the **f** of Aharhel,
4:21 **f** of the guild of linen workers at
4:38 by name were leaders in their **f**,
5:7 brothers according to their **f**,
5:12 Other **f** descended from Gad's
5:13 relatives by **f** were Michael,
5:15 was the head of their **f**.
5:24 the heads of Manasseh's **f**:
5:24 were famous heads of their **f**.
6:19 They are grouped by **f**:
6:60 a total of 13 cities for their **f**.
6:61 cities chosen by lot from the **f**
6:62 The **f** of Gershom's
6:63 The **f** of Merari's descendants
6:66 Some of the **f** of Kohath's
1Ch 6:70 with its pastureland for the **f**
6:71 with its pastureland from the **f**
7:2 were heads of the **f** of Tola.
7:3 All of them were heads (of **f**).
7:4 to their ancestry and **f**,
7:5 all of Issachar's **f**) were fighting
7:7 They were heads of **f** and
7:9 of their **f** and fighting men).
7:11 They headed **f** that produced
7:40 descendants — heads of their **f**,
8:6 who were heads of the **f** living
8:10 sons became heads of **f**.
8:13 the heads of the **f** who lived
8:28 These were the heads of **f**
8:28 They were the heads of **f**.
9:9 men were heads of their **f**.
9:13 of their **f** totaled 1,760 soldiers.
9:33 were the heads of the Levite **f**.
9:34 heads of the Levite **f** according
12:27 Jehoiada (leader of Aaron's **f**).
12:30 were famous among their **f**.
15:12 are the heads of the Levite **f**.
16:28 you **f** of the nations.
23:9 were the heads of Ladan's **f**.
23:24 grouped according to their **f**.
23:24 The heads of their **f** were
24:30 according to their **f**.
24:31 and the leaders of the **f** of the
24:31 The **f** of the oldest brother were
26:6 had sons who ruled their **f**
26:13 They drew lots by **f**,
26:21 were the heads of Ladan's **f**:
26:26 that King David, the heads of **f**,
26:31 Warriors from these **f** were
26:32 who were heads of **f**.
28:4 From the **f** of Judah he chose
29:6 Then the leaders of the **f**,
2Ch 1:2 and the heads of Israel's **f**.
5:2 the leaders of the Israelite **f**.
17:14 They are listed by **f**.
23:2 the leaders of the **f** of Israel,
25:5 and assigned them by **f**
31:17 priests who were enrolled by **f**
31:19 to all the males in the priestly **f**
Ezr 1:5 Then the heads of the **f** of
2:61 prove their **f** were Israelites:
2:68 of the heads of the **f** came
3:12 and the heads of the **f** who
4:2 and the heads of the **f**.
4:3 the heads of Israel's **f** told them,
8:1 These are the leaders of the **f**
8:29 and the leaders of Israel's **f**."
10:16 men who were heads of **f**.
Neh 4:13 people by their **f** behind
5:2 of them said, "We have large **f**!
7:70 Some of the heads of the **f**
7:71 Some of the heads of the **f**
8:13 second day the leaders of the **f**
10:34 of our **f** should bring wood
11:13 the heads of the **f**, totaled 242.
12:12 who were the leaders of their **f**:
Psa 22:27 All the **f** from all the nations
68:6 God places lonely people in **f**.
96:7 you **f** of the nations.
107:41 and makes their **f** like flocks.
Pro 12:7 but the **f** of righteous people
Jer 2:4 all the **f** in the nation of Israel.
23:34 I will punish them and their **f**.
25:9 so I'm going to send for all the **f**
25:9 I will bring the **f** from the north
31:1 be the God of all the **f** of Israel,
33:24 LORD has rejected the two **f**
Amo 3:2 Out of all the **f** on earth,
Mic 7:6 are the members of their own **f**.
Zec 12:14 All the **f** that are left will
14:17 If any of the **f** on the earth won't
Rom 1:31 don't show love to their own **f**
1Ti 3:12 their children and their **f** well.
5:3 Honor widows who have no **f**.
5:16 help widows who have no **f**.
2Ti 3:3 lack normal affection for their **f**.
Tit 1:11 whole **f** by teaching what

family (452)

Gen 7:1 into the ship with your whole **f**
12:3 Through you every **f** on earth
Gen 16:2 I can build a **f** through her."
18:19 his children and his **f** after him
19:32 preserve our **f** line through our
19:34 preserve our **f** line through our
24:7 home and the land of my **f**.
24:40 relatives and from my father's **f**.
28:14 your descendant every **f**
30:3 and I can build a **f** for myself
30:30 I do something for my own **f**?"
34:7 Israel's **f** by raping Jacob's
34:19 person in all his father's **f**.
34:30 my **f** and I will be wiped out."
35:2 So Jacob said to his **f** and
36:40 by **f**, place, and name: Timna,
41:51 and all about his father's **f**.
43:7 kept asking about us and our **f**:
45:11 Then you, your **f**, and all who
46:6 and all his **f** arrived in Egypt.
46:7 granddaughters — his entire **f**.
46:28 When Israel's **f** arrived in the
46:31 to his brothers and his father's **f**,
46:31 'My brothers and my father's **f**,
47:12 and all his father's **f** with food
50:22 Joseph and his father's **f**
Exo 2:1 A man from Levi's **f** married a
6:26 of Egypt in organized **f** groups."
7:4 out of Egypt in organized **f**
12:3 goat for his **f** — one animal
12:17 of Egypt in organized **f** groups.
12:41 left Egypt in organized **f** groups.
12:51 of Egypt in organized **f** groups.
Lev 16:6 the LORD for himself and his **f**.
16:10 the LORD for himself and his **f**.
16:11 the LORD for himself and his **f**.
25:10 to his property and to his **f**.
25:41 his children to go back to their **f**
25:47 foreigner or a member of his **f**.
27:22 was a part of your **f** property)
27:24 to whom it belongs as **f**
Num 1:18 genealogy by **f** and household.
1:44 each representing his own **f**,
1:52 Israelites will camp with each **f**
2:2 up their tents with each **f** under
2:34 with his own **f** and household.
11:10 people from every **f** crying at
18:1 and your **f** will be responsible
25:14 the leader of a **f** from Simeon.)
25:15 (Zur was the head of a **f** from
26:5 Reuben were the **f** of Hanoch,
26:5 family of Hanoch, the **f** of Pallu,
26:6 the **f** of Hezron, and the family
26:6 and the **f** of Carmi.
26:12 Simeon were the **f** of Nemuel,
26:12 of Nemuel, the **f** of Jamin,
26:12 family of Jamin, the **f** of Jakin,
26:13 the **f** of Zerah, and the family of
26:13 and the **f** of Shaul.
26:15 from Gad were the **f** of Zephon,
26:15 of Zephon, the **f** of Haggi,
26:15 family of Haggi, the **f** of Shuni,
26:16 the **f** of Ozni, the family of Eri,
26:16 the family of Ozni, the **f** of Eri,
26:17 the **f** of Arodi, and the family of
26:17 of Arodi, and the **f** of Areli.
26:20 Judah were the **f** of Shelah,
26:20 family of Shelah, the **f** of Perez,
26:20 and the **f** of Zerah.
26:21 of Perez were the **f**
26:21 of Hezron and the **f** of Hamul.
26:23 Issachar were the **f** of Tola,
26:23 family of Tola, the **f** of Puah,
26:24 the **f** of Jashub, and the family
26:24 and the **f** of Shimron.
26:26 Zebulun were the **f** of Sered,
26:26 family of Sered, the **f** of Elon,
26:26 and the **f** of Jahleel.
26:29 (from Manasseh) the **f** of
26:29 of Gilead) and the **f** of Gilead.
26:30 of Gilead were the **f** of Iezer,
26:30 family of Iezer, the **f** of Helek,
26:31 the **f** of Asriel, the family of
26:31 of Asriel, the **f** of Shechem,
26:32 the **f** of Shemida, and the
26:32 and the **f** of Hepher.
26:35 were the **f** of Shuthelah,
26:35 of Shuthelah, the **f** of Beker,

Num 26:35 and the f of Tahan.
26:36 of Shuthelah were the f of Eran.
26:38 Benjamin were the f of Bela,
26:38 family of Bela, the f of Ashbel,
26:38 of Ashbel, the f of Ahiram,
26:39 the f of Shupham, and the
26:39 and the f of Hupham.
26:40 Ard and Naaman) were the f
26:40 of Ard and the f of Naaman.
26:42 The f descended from Dan was
26:42 from Dan was the f of Shuham.
26:42 was the f descended from Dan.
26:43 total number of men in all the f
26:44 from Asher were the f of Imnah,
26:44 family of Imnah, the f of Ishvi,
26:44 and the f of Beriah.
26:45 descendants Beriah were the f
26:45 of Heber and the f of Malchiel.
26:48 Naphtali were the f of Jahzeel,
26:48 family of Jahzeel, the f of Guni,
26:49 the f of Jezer, and the family of
26:49 and the f of Shillem.
26:57 were listed as the f of Gershon,
26:57 of Gershon, the f of Kohath,
26:57 and the f of Merari.
26:58 families of Levi: the Libnite f,
26:58 Libnite family, the Hebronite f,
26:58 Hebronite family, the Mahlite f,
26:58 Mahlite family, the Mushite f,
26:58 and the Korahite f.
27:4 be allowed to die out in his f
27:10 on his father's side of the f.
27:11 to the nearest relative in his f,
32:28 and the f heads of the tribes of
33:54 given to each f by drawing lots.
36:6 but only within a f of their
36:8 may marry a man from any f
36:11 on their father's side of the f.
36:12 in the tribe of their father's f.
Dtr 6:22 Pharaoh, and his whole f.
14:26 Then you and your f will eat
15:16 he loves you and your f
15:20 Every year you and your f must
24:6 The f wouldn't be able to
25:5 must not marry outside the f.
25:9 to continue his brother's f line."
25:10 Then in Israel his f will be
25:10 his family will be called the F
26:11 God has given you and your f.
29:18 sure there is no man, woman, f,
Jos 2:12 to my father's f as I've been
2:18 your father's f into your house.
6:25 prostitute Rahab, her father's f,
7:14 Then the f the LORD selects
7:17 and the f of Zerah was
7:17 Then he had the f of Zerah
7:25 Achan and his f to death.
22:14 head of a f division in Israel.
24:15 my f and I will still serve the
Jdg 1:25 man and his whole f go free.
2:6 So each f went to take
4:17 of Hazor and Heber's f were
6:11 to Joash from Abiezer's f.
6:15 Look at my whole f.
6:15 important member of my f."
6:24 which belongs to Abiezer's f.
6:27 was too afraid of his father's f
6:34 Abiezer's f to follow him.
8:27 a trap for Gideon and his f.
8:32 city belonging to Abiezer's f.
8:35 And they were not kind to the f
9:1 on his mother's side of the f.
9:1 them and his mother's whole f.
9:16 Jerubbaal and his f well,
9:18 you have attacked my father's f.
9:19 toward Jerubbaal and his f,
13:2 Manoah was from the f of Dan.
14:11 When ⌞her f⌟ saw him,
14:15 burn you and your f to death.
16:31 and his father's whole f went
17:7 belongs to the f of Judah.)
17:12 his priest and a part of his f.
18:25 Then you and your f will lose
21:5 "Is there any f from Israel that
21:8 "Is there any f from Israel that
21:24 man went to his tribe and f.
Rut 2:1 from Elimelech's side of the f.
2:3 who was from Elimelech's f.
4:11 of whom built our f of Israel.
4:12 may your f become like the
4:12 become like the f of Perez,
4:18 the account of Perez and his f.
1Sm 1:19 Elkanah and his f got up
2:30 I certainly thought that your f
2:30 father's f would always live
2:31 no one will grow old in your f.
2:32 no one in your f will live to an
2:33 Any man in your f whom I do
3:12 to do to Eli and his f everything
3:14 an oath concerning Eli's f line:
3:14 the sins that Eli's f committed."
9:20 it be you and your father's f?"
9:21 My f is the most insignificant of
10:19 by your tribes and f groups."
10:21 the f of Matri was chosen.
17:25 the social status of his f."
18:2 didn't let him go back to his f.)
18:18 are my relatives or my father's f
20:15 never stop being kind to my f.
20:16 name is cut off from David's f,
22:1 rest of his f heard about it,
22:11 and his entire f who were the
22:15 me or anyone in my f for this.
22:16 you and your entire f are going
22:22 for all the lives of your f.
24:21 my name in my father's f."
27:3 Each one had his f,
2Sm 3:1 David's f became stronger and
3:1 and Saul's f became weaker
3:6 his position in Saul's royal f.
3:8 faithful to your father Saul's f,
3:10 the kingship from Saul's f
3:29 head of Joab and all of his f.
3:29 of Joab's f who have oozing
6:11 Obed Edom and his whole f.
6:20 David returned to bless his f,
9:1 "Is there anyone left in Saul's f
9:2 Now, Saul's f had a servant
9:3 there someone left in Saul's f
9:9 that belonged to Saul and his f.
9:10 your master's f will have food
14:7 Then the entire f turned against
14:9 Let my father's f be held
15:32 Hushai from Archi's f was there
16:2 donkeys are for the king's f
16:8 you spilled in the f of Saul,
16:16 Hushai from Archi's f came
17:5 is descended from Archi's f,
17:14 from Archi's f is better than
17:23 He gave instructions to his f.
19:17 the servant of Saul's f,
19:18 river to bring over the king's f
19:22 you sure we're from the same f,
19:28 killed anyone in my entire f,
19:41 bring Your Majesty and your f
21:1 "It's because of Saul and his f.
21:4 silver or gold from Saul's f,"
23:8 from Tahkemon's f was leader
24:17 me and against my father's f."
1Ki 2:27 spoken at Shiloh about Eli's f.
2:31 from me and my father's f.
2:33 may David, his descendants, f,
11:14 was from the Edomite royal f.
13:2 be a son born in David's f line.
13:34 the sin of Jeroboam's f so that
14:13 one of Jeroboam's f who will
15:29 everyone else in Jeroboam's f.
16:3 I will destroy Baasha and his f.
16:3 I will make his f like the family
16:3 I will make his family like the f
16:4 from Baasha's ⌞f⌟ who dies
16:4 anyone from his ⌞f⌟ who dies
16:7 against Baasha and his f
16:7 like ⌞the sin of⌟ Jeroboam's f.
16:7 destroyed Jeroboam's f.
16:11 he killed Baasha's entire f.
16:12 destroyed Baasha's entire f,
17:15 So she, Elijah, and her f had
18:18 You and your father's f have
21:22 I will make your f like the
21:22 will make your family like the f
21:29 any evil happen to his f while
2Ki 8:1 "Go away with your f.
8:2 She and her f went to live in
8:18 as Ahab's f had done,
8:27 followed the ways of Ahab's f.
8:27 as Ahab's f had done,
8:27 related to Ahab's f by marriage.
9:7 You will destroy the f of your
9:8 Ahab's entire f will die.
9:8 every male from Ahab's f,
9:9 I will make Ahab's f like the
9:9 make Ahab's family like the f
9:9 son) and like the f of Baasha,
10:3 Fight for your master's f."
10:10 spoken about Ahab's f will
10:17 Jehu killed the rest of Ahab's f,
10:30 I wanted done to Ahab's f.
11:1 to destroy the entire royal f.
17:21 Israel away from the f of David,
23:24 psychics, f idols, other idols,
1Ch 4:27 so their entire f didn't become
5:12 One f descended from Gad's
5:12 Another f descended from
6:33 was from Kohath's f line.
6:54 the f descended from Kohath.
9:19 f (Korah's descendants) were
12:28 from whose f came 22 officers.
12:29 them remained loyal to Saul's f.
13:14 home of Obed Edom with his f
13:14 LORD blessed Obed Edom's f
16:43 David went back to bless his f.
21:17 be against me and my father's f,
23:11 given an assignment as one f.
24:4 were f heads than Ithamar's
24:4 descendants had 16 f leaders
24:4 descendants had 8 f leaders.
24:6 and the f leaders of the priests
24:6 One f was chosen for Eleazar,
26:8 Edom's f included 62 men.
26:25 side of the f was Shelomith.
26:31 was researched f by family.
26:31 was researched family by f.
27:1 is a list of Israelite f heads,
27:17 of Kemuel for the f of Aaron:
28:4 Yet, from my entire f the LORD
28:4 of Judah he chose my father's f.
2Ch 11:22 as f head and prince among his
19:8 and f heads from Israel to
21:6 as Ahab's f had done,
21:7 didn't want to destroy David's f.
21:13 You, like Ahab's f,
21:13 your brothers, your father's f.
22:3 followed the ways of Ahab's f,
22:4 as Ahab's f had done.
22:4 to do what Ahab's f had done.
22:7 Jehu to destroy Ahab's f.)
22:8 judgment on Ahab's f,
22:9 "But no one in Ahaziah's f was
22:10 to destroy the entire royal f
26:12 The total number of f heads
31:10 Azariah from Zadok's f said,
35:4 Get yourselves ready with the f
35:5 representing the f divisions
35:5 be considered a part of each f.
35:12 according to their f divisions.
Ezr 2:36 (through the f of Jeshua) 973
2:59 father's f or their genealogy:
2:61 Gilead and took that ⌞f⌟ name).
2:62 searched for their ⌞f⌟ names
3:9 joined Henadad's f
8:2 from the f of Phinehas:
8:2 Gershom from the f of Ithamar:
8:3 from the f of David:
8:3 Shecaniah from the f of Parosh:
8:4 from the f of Pahath Moab:
8:5 from the f of Zattu:
8:6 from the f of Adin: Ebed, son of
8:7 from the f of Elam:
8:8 from the f of Shephatiah:
8:9 from the f of Joab: Obadiah,
8:10 from the f of Bani: Shelomith,
8:11 from the f of Bebai:
8:12 from the f of Azgad:
8:13 from the f of Adonikam:
8:14 from the f of Bigvai:
10:16 chose one from each f division.
Neh 1:6 as the sins that my father's f

Neh 7:39 (through the **f** of Jeshua):
7:61 father's **f** or their genealogy:
7:63 Gilead and took that ⌊**f**⌋ name).
7:64 searched for their ⌊**f**⌋ names
12:22 ⌊The names of⌋ the **f** heads of
12:23 ⌊The names of⌋ the **f** heads of
Est 2:10 nationality or her **f** background,
2:20 not revealed her **f** background
9:28 every age, **f**, province, and city.
Job 21:21 in his **f** after he's gone,
32:2 of Buz from the **f** of Ram,
Psa 41:5 will his **f** name disappear?"
109:13 be cut off and their **f** name
112:2 The **f** of a decent person will
114:1 when Jacob's **f** left people who
Pro 11:29 upon his **f** inherits ⌊only⌋ wind,
15:27 gain brings trouble to his **f**,
17:1 in peace than a **f** feast filled
18:24 friend can stick closer than **f**.
19:7 The entire **f** of a poor person
27:27 milk to feed you, to feed your **f**,
31:15 still dark and gives food to her **f**
31:21 She does not fear for her **f**
31:21 because her whole **f** has
31:27 eye on the conduct of her **f**,
Ecc 4:8 They have no children or other **f**
10:17 when the king is from a noble **f**
Isa 3:6 from his father's **f** and say,
3:7 make me a leader of our **f**."
7:2 When word reached David's **f**
7:17 and your ancestor's **f** a time
60:22 of them will become a **f**.
Jer 1:15 I am going to call every **f** and
3:14 every city and two from every **f**,
29:32 No one from his **f** will be left
35:2 "Go to the **f** of Rechab and talk
35:3 sons — the whole **f** of Rechab.
35:5 wine in front of the **f** of Rechab.
35:18 said to the **f** of Rechab,
41:1 a descendant of the royal **f** and
Eze 17:13 took someone from the royal **f**,
20:5 to the descendants of Jacob's **f**.
Dan 1:3 the royal **f**, and the nobility.
Hos 1:4 little while I will punish Jehu's **f**
3:4 and without ephods or **f** idols.
5:1 Open your ears, royal **f**!
Amo 3:1 against your whole **f** that I
Mic 2:2 They cheat a man and his **f**,
2:3 a disaster to punish your **f**.
Zec 12:7 so that the honor of David's **f**
12:8 and David's **f** will be like God,
12:10 and mercy on David's **f**
12:12 will mourn, each **f** by itself:
12:12 the **f** of David by itself,
12:12 the **f** of Nathan by itself,
12:13 the **f** of Levi by itself,
12:13 the **f** of Shimei by itself,
13:1 will be opened for David's **f**
Mat 10:12 you go into a house, greet the **f**.
10:13 If it is a **f** that listens to you,
10:25 they will certainly call the **f**
10:36 be the members of his own **f**.
17:25 Is it from their **f** members or
17:26 Then the **f** members are exempt
Mar 3:21 When his **f** heard about it,
5:19 "Go home to your **f**,
Luk 1:69 a mighty Savior for us in the **f**
8:39 "Go home to your **f**,
9:61 but first let me tell my **f**
10:5 greet the **f** right away with the
10:7 Stay with the **f** that accepts
12:52 From now on a **f** of five will be
14:12 your friends, **f**, other relatives,
19:9 "You and your **f** have been
Jon 4:53 his entire **f** became believers.
Act 4:6 the chief priest's **f** were present.
7:13 learned about Joseph's **f**.
7:46 place for the **f** of Jacob.
16:15 Lydia and her **f** were baptized,
16:31 you and your **f** will be saved."
16:33 **f** were baptized immediately.
16:34 He and his **f** were thrilled to be
18:8 and his whole **f** believed
Rom 12:10 to each other like a loving **f**.
16:10 belong to the **f** of Aristobulus.
16:11 belong to the **f** of Narcissus.
1Co 1:11 some people from Chloe's **f**
1:16 baptized Stephanas and his **f**.
16:15 You know that the **f** of
16:15 of Stephanas was the first **f**
16:15 This **f** has devoted itself to
Gal 6:10 especially for the **f** of believers.
Eph 2:19 people and members of God's **f**.
3:15 from whom all the **f** in heaven
1Ti 3:4 must manage his own **f** well.
3:5 how to manage his own **f**,
3:15 members of God's **f** must live.
3:15 God's **f** is the church of the
5:4 their own **f** by repaying their
5:5 A widow who has no **f** has
5:8 especially his immediate **f**,
2Ti 1:16 to the **f** of Onesiphorus.
4:19 and the **f** of Onesiphorus.
Heb 11:7 and built a ship to save his **f**.
12:8 you aren't part of the **f**.
1Pe 4:17 and it will begin with God's **f**.

family's (4)

Lev 16:17 his **f** sins, and the sins of the
Dtr 18:8 he gets from selling his **f** goods
24:6 Never let a **f** handmill for
Sos 8:7 man exchanged all his **f** wealth

famine (60)

Gen 12:10 There was a **f** in the land.
12:10 because the **f** was severe.
26:1 There was a **f** in the land in
41:27 Seven years of **f** are coming.
41:30 will come seven years of **f**.
41:30 and the **f** will ruin the land.
41:31 because the coming **f** will be
41:36 years of **f** that will happen
41:36 land will not be ruined by the **f**."
41:50 Before the years of **f** came,
41:54 Then the seven years of **f**
41:54 countries were experiencing **f**.
41:55 to feel the effects of the **f**,
41:56 When the **f** had spread all over
41:56 He did this because the **f** was
41:57 since the **f** was so severe all
42:5 there was also **f** in Canaan.
43:1 The **f** was severe in the land.
45:6 The **f** has been in the land for
45:11 will be five more years of **f**.
47:4 The **f** is so severe in Canaan
47:13 The **f** was so severe that there
47:13 crops because of the **f**.
47:20 because the **f** was so severe.
Rut 1:1 there was a **f** in the land.
2Sm 21:1 there was a **f** for three
24:13 "Should seven years of **f** come
1Ki 8:37 "There may be **f** in the land.
18:2 The **f** was particularly severe
2Ki 4:38 there was a **f** in the country.
6:33 "This severe **f** is from the
7:4 into the city, the **f** is also there,
8:1 LORD has decided to send a **f**
25:3 the **f** in the city became so
1Ch 21:12 either three years of **f**,
2Ch 6:28 "There may be **f** in the land.
20:9 form of war, flood, plague, or **f**,
Neh 5:3 some grain because of this **f**."
Job 5:20 "In **f** he will save you from
Psa 33:19 and keep them alive during a **f**.
37:19 Even in times of **f** they will be
105:16 He brought **f** to the land.
Isa 14:30 will put your root to death with **f**
51:19 Violence, destruction, **f**,
Jer 5:12 We won't experience war or **f**.
11:22 daughters will die because of **f**.
14:18 I see those sick because of **f**.
18:21 hand their children over to **f**.
21:7 survives the plague, war, and **f**.
21:9 will die in the war, **f**, or plague.
52:6 the **f** in the city became so
Eze 5:16 destructive arrows of **f** at you,
14:13 its food supply, send a **f** to it,
Amo 8:11 when I will send a **f** throughout
8:11 be an ordinary **f** or drought.
8:11 Instead, there will be a **f** of
Luk 4:25 and the **f** was severe
15:14 severe **f** spread throughout that
Act 7:11 Then a **f** throughout Egypt and
11:28 that a severe **f** would affect

famines (40)

Dtr 32:24 They will be starved by **f** and
Jer 14:12 with wars, **f**, and plagues."
14:13 'You won't see wars or **f**,
14:15 that there will be no wars or **f**
14:15 Wars and **f** will bring an end to
14:16 will be victims of **f** and wars.
15:2 are destined to die in **f** will die
15:2 to die in famines will die in **f**.
16:4 Wars and **f** will bring them to
24:10 I will send wars, **f**,
27:8 by wars, **f**, and plagues,
27:13 die in wars, **f**, and plagues?
29:17 them wars, **f**, and plagues.
29:18 I will chase them with wars, **f**,
32:24 Because of wars, **f**,
32:36 the city, 'Because of wars, **f**,
34:17 to die in wars, plagues, and **f**.
38:2 will die in wars, **f**, or plagues.
42:16 The **f** you dread will follow you
42:17 will die in wars, **f**, and plagues.
42:22 that you will die in wars, **f**,
44:12 or be brought to an end by **f**.
44:13 with wars, **f**, and plagues.
44:18 had nothing but wars and **f**."
44:27 in wars and **f** until everyone is
Eze 5:12 plagues and be devoured in **f**.
5:16 I will bring more and more **f**
5:17 I will send **f** and wild animals
6:11 So they will die in wars, **f**,
6:12 and has escaped will die in **f**.
7:15 and inside are plagues and **f**.
7:15 be devoured by **f** and plagues.
12:16 them from wars, **f**, and plagues.
14:21 I will send wars, **f**,
36:29 you will never again have **f**.
36:30 the nations because of **f**.
Mat 24:7 There will be **f** and
Mar 13:8 There will be earthquakes and **f**
Luk 21:11 will be terrible earthquakes, **f**,
Rev 6:8 people using wars, **f**, plagues,

famous (21)

Gen 6:4 These children were **f** long ago.
Exo 9:16 my name **f** throughout the earth
Jos 9:9 LORD your God has become **f**.
Rut 4:14 child's name will be **f** in Israel.
2Sm 5:12 Israel and made his kingship **f**
7:9 I will make your name **f** like the
23:18 He was as **f** as the three
23:22 He was as **f** as the three
1Ki 1:47 name more **f** than yours
1Ch 5:24 They were soldiers who were **f**
11:24 He was as **f** as the three
12:30 were **f** among their families.
14:2 that his kingdom was made **f**
22:5 magnificent, large, **f**, praised,
Jer 49:25 Why isn't that **f**, happy city
Eze 16:14 You became **f** in every nation
26:17 song for you: Tyre, you **f** city,
Dan 9:15 made yourself **f** even today.
Hos 14:7 They will be as **f** as the wines
Zep 3:19 I will make them praised and **f**
3:20 I will make you **f** and praised

fan (3)

Isa 54:16 I've created blacksmiths to **f**
Hos 7:4 have to **f** its flames when
2Ti 1:6 Now I'm reminding you to **f** that

fanatical (1)

Gal 1:14 I had become that **f** for the

fanfare (9)

Num 10:5 When they hear the trumpet **f**,
10:6 the trumpets sound a second **f**,
10:6 The **f** is the signal to break
10:7 will blow without sounding a **f**.
10:9 the trumpets will sound a **f**.
29:1 for ⌊the trumpets to sound⌋ a **f**.
31:6 and the trumpets for the **f**.
Mat 6:2 don't announce it with trumpet **f**
Act 25:23 the auditorium with a lot of **f**.

fang (2)

Job 20:16 A viper's **f** kills him.
Psa 140:3 as sharp as a snake's ⌊**f**⌋.

fangs (1)

Joe 1:6 They have **f** like grown lions.

fans (1)

Job 20:26 A fire that no one **f** will burn

far (256)

Gen 10:19 toward Gerar as **f** as Gaza
10:19 and Zeboiim as **f** as Lasha.
11:31 When they came as **f** as Haran,
13:3 from the Negev as **f** as Bethel,
13:10 in the direction of Zoar as **f** as
13:12 his tents as **f** as Sodom.
14:6 going as **f** as El Paran on the
19:19 I can't run as **f** as the hills.
21:16 Then she went about as **f**
44:4 They had not gone **f** from the
49:13 border will go as **f** as Sidon.
Exo 3:1 As he led the sheep to the **f**
7:16 So **f** you have not listened.
8:28 but don't go very **f**.
26:22 Make six frames for the **f** end,
26:23 of⌋ the corners at the **f** end
26:27 and five for the frames on the **f**
33:7 a tent and set it up **f** outside
36:27 made six frames for the **f** end,
36:28 of⌋ the corners at the **f** end
36:32 for the frames on the **f** side
Lev 5:19 you are certainly guilty as **f** as
13:12 from head to foot (so **f** as
Num 11:31 feet deep as **f** as you could
15:15 As **f** as the LORD is concerned,
16:3 "You've gone **f** enough!
16:7 You've gone **f** enough!"
32:9 They went as **f** as the Eshcol
Dtr 1:7 and into Lebanon as **f** as the
2:23 in villages as **f** away as Gaza.
2:36 in that valley as **f** as Gilead,
3:10 and all of Bashan as **f** as
3:14 whole territory of Argob as **f** as
4:49 side of the Jordan River as **f** as
12:21 name is too **f** away from you,
13:7 around you, who live near or **f**,
14:24 his name may be too **f** away.
14:24 a tenth of your income that **f**.
19:6 If the place is too **f** away,
20:15 that are **f** away which don't
28:49 you a nation from **f** away,
34:1 could see Gilead as **f** as Dan,
34:2 all the territory of Judah as **f** as
34:3 City of Palms) — as **f** as Zoar.
Jos 3:16 up like a dam as **f** away as
8:4 Don't go very **f** away from the
9:2 coast as **f** as Lebanon,
9:9 "We came from a country very **f**
9:22 'We live very **f** away from you,'
10:41 of Goshen as **f** as Gibeon.
11:8 The Israelites chased them as **f**
11:17 to Seir as **f** as Baal Gad
13:3 northward as **f** as the border of
13:4 to Sidon as **f** as Aphek,
13:11 all of Bashan as **f** as Salecah
13:25 half of Ammon as **f** as Aroer,
13:26 and from Mahanaim as **f** as the
15:1 Their territory extends as **f**
15:5 is the Dead Sea as **f** north as
15:47 their cities and villages as **f** as
19:8 cities as **f** as Baalath Beer
19:10 inheritance goes as **f** as Sarid.
19:28 and as **f** as Great Sidon.
Jdg 4:11 Heber went as **f** away as the
7:22 They fled as **f** as Beth Shittah,
7:22 and as **f** as the bank of the
7:24 Capture the watering holes as **f**
7:24 holes as **f** as Beth Barah
18:7 They were **f** from the people of
18:13 Ephraim as **f** as Micah's house.
18:28 their city was **f** from Sidon
19:10 He left and traveled as **f** as
1Sm 7:11 killed them as **f** as Beth Car.
17:52 and pursued the Philistines as **f**
1Sm 19:22 He went as **f** as the big cistern
2Sm 3:28 "As **f** as the LORD is
7:18 you have brought me this **f**?
22:24 I was innocent as **f** as he was
1Ki 4:21 of the Philistines and as **f** as
8:46 ⌊whether it is⌋ **f** or near.
12:30 The people went as **f** as Dan to
2Ki 7:15 They followed them as **f** as the
20:4 Isaiah hadn't gone as **f** as the
1Ch 4:33 around these cities as **f** as
5:8 lived in Aroer as **f** as Nebo
5:9 of them lived eastward as **f** as
5:11 Bashan as **f** ⌊east⌋ as Salcah.
7:28 and as **f** as Gaza and its
12:40 Also, their neighbors as **f** as
17:16 you have brought me this **f**?
2Ch 6:36 ⌊whether it is⌋ **f** or near.
9:26 of the Philistines and as **f** as
14:9 Zerah got as **f** as Mareshah.
14:13 pursued them as **f** as Gerar.
26:15 Uzziah's fame spread **f** and
30:10 Manasseh, as **f** as Zebulun.
34:6 and as **f** as Naphtali,
Ezr 3:13 The noise was heard from **f**
9:13 have punished us **f** less than
Neh 3:1 They rebuilt as **f** as the Tower
3:1 and then as **f** as the Tower of
3:8 Jerusalem as **f** as Broad Wall.
3:13 as **f** as Dung Gate.
3:15 by the King's Garden as **f** as
3:16 from the tombs of David as **f** as
3:26 repairs on the wall as **f** as
3:27 large projecting tower as **f** as
3:31 made repairs as **f** as the
3:31 Inspection Gate and as **f** as
12:38 as **f** as Broad Wall,
12:39 as **f** as Sheep Gate.
12:43 could be heard from **f** away.
Est 9:20 of King Xerxes, near and **f**.
Job 5:4 His children are **f** from help.
11:14 holding on to sin, put it **f** away,
19:13 "My brothers stay **f** away from
28:4 a mineshaft **f** from civilization,
36:3 I will get my knowledge from **f**
38:11 'You may come this **f** but no
39:25 and it smells the battle **f** away
39:29 and its eyes see it from **f** away.
Psa 18:23 I was innocent as **f** as he was
22:1 Why are you so **f** away from
22:1 so **f** away from the words of my
22:11 Do not be so **f** away from me.
22:19 Do not be so **f** away,
35:22 do not be so **f** away from me.
38:11 and my relatives stand **f** away
49:14 **f** away from their comfortable
55:7 Indeed, I would run **f** away.
73:27 those who are **f** from you will
88:8 You have taken my friends **f**
88:18 and friends **f** away from me.
101:4 I will keep **f** away from devious
103:12 As **f** as the east is from the
103:12 is from the west — that is how **f**
109:10 Let them seek help **f** from their
119:150 ⌊yet⌋ they are **f** away from your
119:155 Wicked people are **f** from being
139:2 You read my thoughts from **f**
Pro 4:24 Put deceptive speech **f** away
5:8 Stay **f** away from her.
15:29 The LORD is **f** from wicked
22:5 will stay **f** away from them.
22:15 will remove it **f** from him.
25:25 so is good news from **f** away.
27:10 is better than a relative **f** away.
30:8 Keep vanity and lies **f** away
31:10 is worth **f** more than jewels.
31:14 She brings her food from **f**
Isa 5:26 up a flag for the nations **f** away.
6:12 will send his people **f** away,
10:3 disaster comes from **f** away?
14:13 I'll sit on the mountain **f** away
15:4 Their voices are heard as **f**
15:5 Its people flee as **f** as Zoar at
15:8 wailing echoes as **f** as Eglaim.
15:8 echoes as **f** as Beer Elim.
16:8 ⌊once⌋ reached as **f** as Jazer
17:13 and they will run **f** away.
Isa 18:2 ⌊who are⌋ feared **f** and near,
18:7 ⌊who are⌋ feared **f** and near,
22:3 any of them could get **f** away.
22:18 He will throw you **f** away into
29:13 But their hearts are **f** from me,
30:27 is going to come from **f** away.
33:13 you people who are **f** away!
43:6 Bring my sons from **f** away and
46:12 who are **f** from being righteous.
46:13 near; it isn't **f** away.
49:1 you people **f** away.
49:12 They will come from **f** away.
54:14 You will be **f** from oppression,
54:14 You will be **f** from destruction,
57:9 sent your ambassadors **f** away
57:19 peace to those both **f** and near."
59:9 That is why justice is **f** from us,
59:11 for salvation, but it's **f** from us.
59:14 righteousness stands **f** away.
60:4 Your sons come from **f** away.
60:9 bring your children from **f** away.
Jer 2:5 they went so **f** away from me?
5:15 going to bring a nation from **f**
12:2 but their hearts are **f** from you.
23:23 am also a God who is **f** away,"
25:26 kings of the north, near and **f**,
27:10 to be taken **f** from your lands.
31:40 as **f** as the corner of Horse
43:7 They went as **f** as Tahpanhes.
48:24 the cities of Moab, **f** and near.
48:32 ⌊once⌋ spread as **f** as
48:32 and they reached as **f** as the
49:30 Run **f** away! Find a place to
Lam 1:16 Everyone is too **f** away from
Eze 6:12 will kill those who are **f** away.
8:6 things that will force me to go **f**
10:5 wings was heard as **f** as
11:15 'They are **f** away from the
11:16 Although I sent them **f** away
22:5 Those near and those **f** away
23:40 men to come from **f** away.
28:16 You traded **f** and wide.
38:6 of Togarmah from the **f** north.
38:15 from your place in the **f** north
39:2 I will bring you from the **f** north
41:12 At the **f** end of the open area,
43:9 of their kings **f** away from me.
44:10 "'Some Levites went **f** away
Dan 9:7 countries near and **f** — are still
Joe 2:20 the northern ⌊army⌋ **f** from you,
3:6 send them **f** away from their
3:8 a nation that is **f** away."
Amo 6:3 that a day of disaster is **f** away.
Oba 1:20 land as **f** as Zarephath.
Mic 4:3 many nations **f** and wide.
Hab 1:8 riders will come from **f** away.
Zec 6:15 Those who are **f** away will
14:5 mountains will go as **f** as Azel.
Mat 11:9 Let me tell you that he is **f** more
15:8 but their hearts are **f** from me.
Mar 7:6 but their hearts are **f** from me.
8:12 it will be **f** different than what
9:23 "As **f** as possibilities go,
12:34 "You're not too **f** from the
Luk 1:15 As **f** as the Lord is concerned,
7:6 He was not **f** from the house
7:26 Let me tell you that he is **f** more
14:32 the other king is still **f** away.
15:13 for a country **f** away from home.
Jon 6:9 But they won't go very **f** for so
16:24 So **f** you haven't asked for
21:8 They weren't **f** from the shore,
Act 2:39 and to everyone who is **f** away.
11:19 death went as **f** as Phoenicia,
13:6 the whole island as **f** as
17:27 In fact, he is never **f** from any
22:21 You'll go **f** away to people who
28:15 so they came as **f** as the cities
Rom 6:2 As **f** as sin is concerned,
1Co 10:14 get as **f** away from the worship
2Co 10:16 in the regions **f** beyond you.
11:23 but I'm a **f** better one.
Gal 1:14 You also heard how I was **f**
5:6 As **f** as our relationship to
Eph 1:21 He is **f** above all rulers,
2:13 who were once **f** away,

Eph 2:17 peace for you who were **f** away
3:19 which goes **f** beyond any
Php 1:23 That's by **f** the better choice.
3:8 It's **f** more than that!
3:16 by what we have learned so **f**.
2Ti 3:9 Certainly, they won't get very **f**.
Rev 2:5 Remember how **f** you have
18:10 they will stand **f** away and say,
18:15 these things will stand **f** away.
18:17 from the sea stood **f** away.

faraway (5)

Isa 46:11 for my plan from a **f** land.
Jer 30:10 to rescue you from a **f** place.
31:3 appeared to me in a **f** place
46:27 your descendants from a **f** land,
Zec 10:9 remember me even in **f** places.

farm (10)

Gen 2:5 there was no one to **f** the land.
2:15 him in the Garden of Eden to **f**
3:23 out of the Garden of Eden to **f**
4:12 When you **f** the ground,
1Sm 6:18 walled cities and **f** villages.
2Sm 9:10 and your servants should **f** the
1Ch 27:26 for the **f** workers in the fields:
Neh 10:37 from all our **f** communities.
Jer 27:11 People will **f** the land and live
Eze 48:19 all the tribes in Israel will **f** it.

farmed (2)

Jos 24:13 you a land that you hadn't **f**,
Jer 2:2 into a land that couldn't be **f**.

farmer (15)

Gen 4:2 a shepherd, and Cain was a **f**.
9:20 Noah, a **f**, was the first person
Isa 28:24 Does a **f** go on plowing every
Amo 6:12 Does a **f** plow the sea with
Zec 13:5 I'm a **f**. I've owned this land
Mat 13:3 A **f** went to plant seed.
13:18 the story about the **f** means.
Mar 4:3 A **f** went to plant seed.
4:14 "The **f** plants the word.
Luk 8:5 "A **f** went to plant his seeds.
22:31 me as a **f** separates wheat from
2Co 9:6 Remember this: The **f** who
9:6 But the **f** who plants because
9:10 God gives seed to the **f** and
2Ti 2:6 A hard-working **f** should have

farmers (11)

2Ch 26:10 He had **f** and vineyard workers
Psa 129:3 my back ⌊like **f** plow fields⌋.
Isa 55:10 so that it produces seed for **f**
Jer 14:4 The **f** are disappointed.
31:24 **F** and shepherds will also live
51:23 I will use you to crush **f** and
Joe 1:11 Be sad, you **f**! Cry loudly, you
Amo 1:1 one of the sheep **f** from Tekoa.
5:16 They will call on **f** to mourn
Heb 6:7 it produces useful crops for **f**.
Jas 5:7 See how **f** wait for their

farms (6)

2Ki 25:12 in the vineyards and on the **f**.
Jer 39:10 he gave them vineyards and **f**.
52:16 in the vineyards and on the **f**.
Mar 6:36 Send the people to the closest **f**
6:56 go into villages, cities, or **f**,
Luk 9:12 villages and **f** so that they

far-reaching (1)

Rev 13:2 and **f** authority to the beast.

farther (7)

Job 38:11 'You may come this far but no **f**.
Eze 42:6 were set **f** back than those
Hos 11:2 the **f** they went away.
Mat 26:39 After walking a little **f**,
Mar 1:19 As Jesus went on a little **f**,
14:35 After walking a little **f**,
Luk 24:28 acted as if he were going **f**.

farthest (2)

Jos 15:21 On the **f** edge of the Negev,
Jer 31:8 I will gather them from the **f**

fast (41)

2Sm 2:18 Asahel was as **f** on his feet as
12:23 But why should I **f** now that
1Ki 12:18 got on his chariot as **f** as
21:9 she wrote: "Announce a **f**.
21:12 They announced a **f** and had
1Ch 12:8 lions and were as **f** as gazelles
2Ch 10:18 got on his chariot as **f** as
20:3 a **f** throughout Judah.
Ezr 8:21 Then I announced a **f** there at
Neh 1:4 I continued to **f** and pray to the
Est 4:16 **F** for me: Do not eat or drink at
4:16 My servants and I will also **f**.
Ecc 9:11 race isn't ⌊won⌋ by **f** runners,
Isa 30:16 "We'll ride on **f** horses."
30:16 who chase you will also be **f**.
58:3 you see that on the days you **f**,
58:4 Don't you see that when you **f**,
58:4 The way you **f** today keeps
Jer 36:9 city in Judah to Jerusalem to **f**
Joe 1:14 Schedule a time to **f**!
2:15 Schedule a time to **f**.
Amo 2:15 **F** runners will not be able to
Jnh 3:5 They decided to **f**,
Hag 1:6 You spend money as **f** as you
Zec 7:3 "Should we mourn and **f** in the
8:19 The **f** in the fourth month,
8:19 the **f** in the fifth month,
8:19 the **f** in the seventh month,
8:19 and the **f** in the tenth month will
Mat 6:16 "When you **f**, stop looking sad
6:17 When you **f**, wash your face
9:14 do we and the Pharisees **f** often
9:15 from them. Then they will **f**.
Mar 2:18 and the Pharisees' disciples **f**,
2:19 "Can wedding guests **f** while
2:19 groom with them, they cannot **f**.
2:20 from them. Then they will **f**.
Luk 5:33 "John's disciples frequently **f**
5:34 force wedding guests to **f** while
5:35 At that time they will **f**."
18:12 I **f** twice a week, and I give you

fasted (15)

Jdg 20:26 of the LORD and **f** that day until
1Sm 7:6 of the LORD, and **f** that day.
31:13 Then they **f** seven days.
2Sm 1:12 They mourned, cried, and **f**
12:16 he **f** and lay on the ground all
12:21 You **f** and cried over the child
12:22 child was alive, I **f** and cried.
1Ki 21:27 He **f**, lay in sackcloth,
1Ch 10:12 Then they **f** seven days.
Ezr 8:23 So we **f** and asked our God for
Neh 9:1 month, they **f**, wore sackcloth,
Psa 69:10 I cried and **f**, but I was insulted
Isa 58:3 Why have we **f** if you are not
Dan 9:3 and **f** in sackcloth and ashes.
Zec 7:5 'When you **f** and mourned in

fasten (18)

Exo 25:12 and **f** them to its four feet,
25:26 and **f** them to the four corners,
28:12 and **f** them on the shoulder
28:14 and **f** these chains to the
28:17 **F** four rows of precious stones
28:24 Then **f** the two gold ropes to
28:25 **F** the other ends of the ropes to
28:26 Make two gold rings, and **f**
28:27 and **f** them to the bottom of the
28:37 **F** a violet cord to it,
29:6 and **f** the holy crown to it.
Pro 3:3 **F** them around your neck.
6:21 **F** them on your heart forever.
Isa 22:21 him in your linen robe and **f**
22:23 I will **f** him firmly in place like a
41:7 And they **f** things with nails so
Jer 10:4 and gold and **f** them ⌊together⌋
Eph 6:14 **F** truth around your waist like a

fastened (27)

Exo 28:7 corners so that it can be **f**.
28:28 should be **f** by its rings
37:13 cast four gold rings for it and **f**
39:4 so that the ephod could be **f**.
39:7 Then they **f** them on the
39:10 They **f** four rows of precious
39:17 They **f** the two gold ropes to
39:18 They **f** the other ends of the
39:19 They made two gold rings and **f**
39:20 ⌊more⌋ gold rings and **f** them
39:21 Then they **f** the breastplate by
39:25 out of pure gold and **f** them
39:31 They **f** a violet cord to it and
Lev 8:7 the linen robe on Aaron and **f**
8:7 He **f** the ephod to it.
8:9 He put the turban on him and **f**
8:13 **f** their belts around them,
Num 19:15 Every container without a lid **f**
Jdg 3:16 He **f** it to his right side under
15:4 Then he **f** a torch between their
1Sm 17:39 David **f** Saul's sword over his
31:10 the Asherahs — and **f** his corpse
1Ki 6:6 that this annex would not be **f**
1Ch 10:10 of their gods and **f** his head
Neh 4:18 each builder had his sword **f**
Isa 22:25 that day the peg which I firmly **f**
Eze 41:6 but these supports were not **f** to

fasteners (7)

Exo 26:6 Make 50 gold **f**. Use them to link
26:11 Make 50 bronze **f**, and put them
26:33 Hang the canopy from the **f** in
35:11 cover, along with the **f**, frames,
36:13 They also made 50 gold **f**.
36:18 They also made 50 bronze **f** to
39:33 the **f**, frames, crossbars, posts,

faster (5)

Psa 58:9 Let ⌊God⌋ sweep them away **f**
Jer 4:13 His horses are **f** than eagles.
Lam 4:19 hunting us were **f** than eagles
Hab 1:8 Their horses will be **f** than
Jon 20:4 but the other disciple ran **f** than

fastest (1)

Est 8:14 rode the king's **f** horses.

fasting (19)

Est 4:3 **f**, weeping, and wailing.
9:31 the practices of **f** with sadness.
Psa 35:13 I humbled myself with **f**.
109:24 way because I have been **f**.
Isa 58:5 Is this the kind of **f** I have
58:5 Is **f** just bowing your head like
58:5 Is this what you call **f**?
58:6 This is the kind of **f** I have
Jer 36:6 On a day of **f**, you must read
36:9 a time for **f** was called.
Joe 2:12 me with all your heart — with **f**,
Mat 6:16 to make it obvious that they're **f**.
6:18 Then your **f** won't be obvious.
Mar 2:18 and the Pharisees were **f**.
Luk 2:37 day and night by **f** and praying.
Act 13:2 were worshiping the Lord and **f**,
13:3 After **f** and praying,
14:23 and with prayer and **f** they
27:9 the day of **f** had already past.

fast-moving (1)

Isa 19:1 The LORD is riding on a **f**

fat (89)

Exo 23:18 The **f** sacrificed at my festivals
29:13 "Then take all the **f** that covers
29:13 two kidneys with the **f** on them,
29:22 this ⌊same⌋ ram take the **f**,
29:22 take the fat, the **f** from the tail,
29:22 the **f** that covers the internal
29:22 two kidneys with the **f** on them,
Lev 1:8 and the **f** on top of the wood
1:12 will lay the head and the **f**
3:3 your offering remove the **f**
3:4 and the two kidneys with the **f**
3:9 Then take the **f** from the
3:9 Remove all the **f** from the tail
3:9 the tail and the **f** that covers
3:10 the two kidneys with the **f**
3:14 Then bring the **f** that covers the
3:15 and the two kidneys with the **f**

Lev	3:16	All the **f** belongs to the LORD.
	3:17	Never eat any **f** or blood."
	4:8	He will remove all of the **f** from
	4:8	the **f** that covers the internal
	4:9	two kidneys with the **f** on them.
	4:19	He will remove all the **f** and
	4:26	He will burn all the **f** on the
	4:26	on the altar the same way the **f**
	4:31	He will remove all the **f** the
	4:35	He will remove all the **f** the
	4:35	all the fat the same way the **f**
	6:12	on the fire and burn the **f**
	7:3	He will offer all the **f**,
	7:3	all the fat, the **f** from the tail,
	7:3	the **f** covering the internal
	7:4	two kidneys with the **f** on them.
	7:23	Never eat any **f** from bulls,
	7:24	The **f** from an animal that dies
	7:25	Those who eat the **f** from an
	7:30	Bring the **f** with the breast.
	7:31	"The priest will burn the **f** on
	7:33	sons offer the blood and **f**
	8:16	Moses took all the **f** that was
	8:16	the two kidneys with their **f**,
	8:20	with the other pieces and the **f**.
	8:25	He took the **f**, the fat from the
	8:25	took the fat, the **f** from the tail,
	8:25	all the **f** on the internal organs,
	8:25	the two kidneys with their **f**,
	8:26	He put them on the **f** and the
	9:10	On the altar he burned the **f**,
	9:19	However, the **f** from the bull
	9:19	the bull and the ram (the **f** from
	9:19	tail, the layer of **f**, the kidneys,
	9:24	offering and the pieces of **f**
	10:15	and the **f** that is to be burned
	16:25	He will burn the **f** of the offering
	17:6	He will burn the **f** as a soothing
Num	18:17	and burn the **f** as an offering by
Dtr	31:20	they want and have become **f**,
	32:14	He gave them **f** from lambs,
	32:15	got **f** and disrespectful.
	32:15	(You got **f**! You were stuffed!
	32:38	ate the **f** from their sacrifices
Jdg	3:17	(Eglon was a very **f** man.)
	3:22	Eglon's **f** covered the blade
1Sm	2:15	before the people burned the **f**,
	2:16	"First let the **f** be burned,
	2:29	me by making yourselves **f**
	15:22	than sacrificing the **f** of rams.
2Sm	1:22	blood of those killed and the **f**
1Ki	8:64	and the **f** from the fellowship
2Ch	7:7	and the **f** because the bronze
	29:35	offerings in addition to the **f**
	35:14	and the **f** until that evening.
Neh	9:25	and were satisfied and grew **f**.
Job	15:27	"His face is bloated with **f**,
	15:27	and he is **f** around the waist.
Psa	73:7	eyes peer out from their **f** faces,
	109:24	become lean, without any **f**.
Isa	1:11	and enough **f** from your fattened
	10:27	because you have grown **f**.
	34:6	It is covered with **f**,
	34:6	with the **f** of rams' kidneys.
	34:7	dust will be covered with **f**.
Jer	5:28	They grow big and **f**.
Eze	34:16	those that are **f** and strong.
	34:20	disputes between the **f** sheep
	34:21	You **f** sheep push the skinny
	44:7	my temple when you offered **f**
	44:15	They may bring **f** and blood to
Zec	11:16	But he will eat the meat of the **f**

fatal (4)

Nah	3:19	Your wound is **f**. All who hear
Rev	13:3	looked like it had a **f** wound,
	13:3	but its **f** wound was healed.
	13:12	whose **f** wound was healed.

fatally (1)

2Ki	13:14	Elisha became **f** ill.

fate (4)

Job	12:5	He thinks it is the **f** of those
Isa	17:14	This will be the **f** of those who
Jer	13:25	This is your **f**, the destiny I
Jud	1:7	the same **f** that God's people

father (1010)

Gen	2:24	is why a man will leave his **f**
	4:18	Irad was the **f** of Mehujael.
	4:18	was the **f** of Methushael.
	4:18	was the **f** of Lamech.
	5:3	he became the **f** ⌞of a son⌟ in
	5:4	Adam became the **f** of Seth,
	5:6	he became the **f** of Enosh.
	5:7	After he became the **f** of Enosh,
	5:9	he became the **f** of Kenan.
	5:10	After he became the **f** of Kenan,
	5:12	he became the **f** of Mahalalel.
	5:13	he became the **f** of Mahalalel,
	5:15	he became the **f** of Jared.
	5:16	After he became the **f** of Jared,
	5:18	he became the **f** of Enoch.
	5:19	After he became the **f** of Enoch,
	5:21	he became the **f** of Methuselah.
	5:22	he became the **f** of Methuselah,
	5:25	he became the **f** of Lamech.
	5:26	he became the **f** of Lamech,
	5:28	he became the **f** of a son.
	5:30	Lamech became the **f** of Noah,
	5:32	he became the **f** of Shem,
	9:19	Ham was the **f** of Canaan.
	9:22	Ham, **f** of Canaan, saw his
	9:22	of Canaan, saw his **f** naked.
	9:23	they didn't see their **f** naked.
	10:8	Cush was the **f** of Nimrod,
	10:15	Canaan was the **f** of Sidon his
	10:24	was the **f** of Shelah,
	10:24	and Shelah was the **f** of Eber.
	10:26	Joktan was the **f** of Almodad,
	11:10	he became the **f** of Arpachshad.
	11:11	he became the **f** of Arpachshad,
	11:12	he became the **f** of Shelah.
	11:13	he became the **f** of Shelah,
	11:14	when he became the **f** of Eber.
	11:15	After he became the **f** of Eber,
	11:16	when he became the **f** of Peleg.
	11:17	After he became the **f** of Peleg,
	11:18	when he became the **f** of Reu.
	11:19	After he became the **f** of Reu,
	11:20	when he became the **f** of Serug.
	11:21	After he became the **f** of Serug,
	11:22	when he became the **f** of Nahor.
	11:23	After he became the **f** of Nahor,
	11:24	when he became the **f** of Terah.
	11:25	After he became the **f** of Terah,
	11:26	he became the **f** of Abram,
	11:27	Terah was the **f** of Abram,
	11:27	Haran was the **f** of Lot.
	11:28	While his **f** Terah was still
	11:29	(Haran was the **f** of Milcah and
	17:4	become the **f** of many nations.
	17:5	longer be Abram [Exalted **F**],
	17:5	but Abraham [**F** of Many]
	17:5	made you a **f** of many nations.
	17:20	He will be the **f** of 12 princes,
	19:31	the younger one, "Our **f** is old.
	19:32	Let's give our **f** wine to drink.
	19:32	our family line through our **f**."
	19:33	That night they gave their **f**
	19:33	one went to bed with her **f**.
	19:34	night I went to bed with my **f**.
	19:34	our family line through our **f**."
	19:35	That night they gave their **f**
	19:36	became pregnant by their **f**.
	22:7	Isaac spoke up and said, "**F**?"
	22:21	Kemuel (**f** of Aram),
	22:23	Bethuel is the **f** of Rebekah.
	25:3	Jokshan was the **f** of Sheba
	25:19	Abraham was the **f** of Isaac.
	26:3	that I swore to your **f** Abraham.
	26:15	during his **f** Abraham's lifetime.
	26:18	during his **f** Abraham's lifetime.
	26:18	that his **f** had given them.
	26:24	am the God of your **f** Abraham.
	27:6	"I've just heard your **f** speaking
	27:9	a good-tasting meal for your **f**,
	27:10	Then take it to your **f** to eat so
	27:12	My **f** will feel ⌞my skin⌟ and
	27:14	just the way his **f** liked it.
	27:18	He went to his **f** and said,
Gen	27:18	to his father and said, "**F**?"
	27:19	Jacob answered his **f**,
	27:22	So Jacob went over to his **f**.
	27:26	Then his **f** Isaac said to him,
	27:31	meal and brought it to his **f**.
	27:31	Then he said to his **f**,
	27:31	said to his father, "Please, **F**,
	27:32	his **f** Isaac asked him.
	27:34	heard these words from his **f**,
	27:34	and bitter cry and said to his **f**,
	27:34	to his father, "Bless me too, **F**!"
	27:38	you have only one blessing, **F**?
	27:38	Bless me too, **F**!" And Esau
	27:39	His **f** Isaac answered him,
	27:41	that his **f** had given him.
	27:41	time to mourn for my **f** is near.
	28:2	of Bethuel, your mother's **f**,
	28:7	that Jacob had obeyed his **f**
	28:8	Esau realized that his **f** Isaac
	29:12	she ran and told her **f**.
	31:1	that belonged to our **f**
	31:5	"I have seen that your **f** isn't as
	31:5	but the God of my **f** has been
	31:6	as hard as I could for your **f**.
	31:7	Your **f** has cheated me.
	31:16	took away from our **f** belongs
	31:18	back to his **f** Isaac in Canaan.
	31:29	Last night the God of your **f**
	31:35	Rachel said to her **f**,
	31:35	to her father, "Don't be angry, **F**,
	31:42	If the God of my **f**, the God of
	31:53	God of their **f**—judge between
	31:53	oath by the Fear of his **f** Isaac
	32:9	and God of my **f** Isaac!
	33:19	sons of Hamor, **f** of Shechem,
	34:4	Shechem said to his **f** Hamor,
	34:6	So Shechem's **f** Hamor came to
	34:11	Shechem said to Dinah's **f**
	34:13	gave Shechem and his **f** Hamor
	35:18	but his **f** named him Benjamin
	35:27	Jacob came home to his **f**
	36:9	He was the **f** of the people of
	36:24	that belonged to his **f** Zibeon.)
	36:43	Esau was the **f** of the people of
	37:1	where his **f** had lived.
	37:2	Joseph told his **f** about the bad
	37:4	saw that their **f** loved him more
	37:10	When he told his **f** and his
	37:10	his **f** criticized him by asking,
	37:11	but his **f** kept thinking about
	37:22	and bring him back to his **f**.
	37:32	long sleeves to their **f** and said,
	37:35	how Joseph's **f** cried over him.
	42:13	brother stayed with our **f**,
	42:29	When they came to their **f**
	42:32	sons of the same **f**.
	42:32	stayed with our **f** in Canaan.'
	42:35	When they and their **f** saw the
	42:36	Their **f** Jacob said to them,
	42:37	So Reuben said to his **f**,
	43:7	'Is your **f** still alive?
	43:8	Then Judah said to his **f** Israel,
	43:11	Then their **f** Israel said to them,
	43:23	Your God, the God of your **f**,
	43:27	told me about your elderly **f**.
	43:28	Our **f** is alive and well."
	44:17	can go back to your **f** in peace."
	44:19	'Do you have a **f** or a brother?'
	44:20	We answered, 'We have a **f**
	44:20	and his **f** loves him.'
	44:22	'The boy can't leave his **f**.
	44:22	boy leaves him, his **f** will die.'
	44:24	When we went back to our **f**,
	44:25	"Then our **f** said, 'Go back and
	44:27	"Then our **f** said to us,
	44:31	gray-haired old **f** to his grave.
	44:32	"I guaranteed my **f** that the boy
	44:32	blame me the rest of my life, **F**.'
	44:34	How could I go back to my **f** if
	45:3	Is my **f** still alive?"
	45:8	made me ⌞like⌟ a **f** to Pharaoh,
	45:9	"Hurry back to my **f**,
	45:13	Tell my **f** how greatly honored I
	45:13	Hurry and bring my **f** here!"
	45:18	Take your **f** and your families,
	45:19	Bring your **f**, and come back.

Gen 45:23 He sent his **f** ten male donkeys
45:25 to their **f** Jacob in Canaan.
45:27 Yet, when they told their **f**
46:1 to the God of his **f** Isaac.
46:3 the God of your **f**," he said.
46:5 Israel's sons put their **f** Jacob,
46:29 and went to meet his **f** Israel.
46:29 As soon as he saw his **f**,
47:1 "My **f** and my brothers have
47:5 "Your **f** and your brothers have
47:6 Have your **f** and your brothers
47:7 Then Joseph brought his **f**
47:11 Joseph had his **f** and his
47:12 Joseph also provided his **f**,
48:1 Joseph was told, "Your **f** is ill."
48:9 Joseph answered his **f**.
48:10 brought his sons close to his **f**,
48:15 and my **f** Isaac walked,
48:16 Abraham and my **f** Isaac.
48:17 When Joseph saw that his **f**
48:18 Then he said to his **f**,
48:18 his father, "That's not right, **F**!
48:19 His **f** refused and said,
49:2 Listen to your **f** Israel.
49:25 because of the God of your **f**
49:26 The blessings of your **f** are
49:28 of Israel and what their **f** said
50:1 Joseph threw himself on his **f**,
50:2 in his service to embalm his **f**.
50:5 'My **f** made me swear an oath.
50:5 let me go there and bury my **f**;
50:6 "Go and bury your **f**,
50:7 So Joseph left to bury his **f**.
50:14 After Joseph had buried his **f**,
50:14 there with him to bury his **f**.
50:16 "Before your **f** died,
Exo 2:18 they came back to their **f** Reuel,
20:12 "Honor your **f** and your mother,
21:15 "Whoever hits his **f** or mother
21:17 "Whoever curses his **f** or
22:17 If her **f** absolutely refuses to
40:15 as you anointed their **f**.
Lev 18:8 is related to you through your **f**.
18:11 with a daughter of your **f**
19:3 "Respect your mother and **f**.
20:9 "Whoever curses his **f** or
20:9 He has cursed his **f** or mother
21:2 **f**, son, daughter, or brother,
21:9 she dishonors her **f**.
21:11 even for his **f** or mother.
24:10 and whose **f** was from Egypt,
Num 3:4 the lifetime of their **f** Aaron.
6:7 Even if their own **f**,
12:14 "If her own **f** had spit in her
26:29 of Machir (Machir was the **f**
26:60 Aaron was the **f** of Nadab,
27:1 whose **f** was Manasseh,
27:3 "Our **f** died in the desert.
30:4 If her **f** says nothing to her
30:5 But if her **f** objects when he
30:5 oath⌋ because her **f** objected.
Dtr 5:16 "Honor your **f** and your mother
21:13 and mourn ⌊the loss of⌋ her **f**
21:16 When the day comes for the **f**
21:19 His **f** and mother must take him
22:15 The girl's **f** and mother must go
22:16 The girl's **f** will tell the leaders,
22:19 silver and give it to the girl's **f**.
22:29 give the girl's **f** 1 ¼ pounds
22:30 this would disgrace his **f**.
27:16 "Whoever curses his **f** or
27:20 He has disgraced his **f**."
32:6 Isn't he your **F** and Owner,
33:9 didn't know their **f** and mother.
Jos 2:13 that you'll protect my **f**,
2:18 Also, gather your **f**,
6:23 Rahab, her **f**, mother, brothers,
15:13 Arba was the **f** of Anak.
15:18 she persuaded him to ask her **f**
17:3 whose **f** was Manasseh,
21:11 Kiriath Arba (Arba was Anak's **f**
24:32 sons of Hamor, **f** of Shechem,
Jdg 1:14 she persuaded him to ask her **f**
8:32 tomb of his **f** Joash at Ophrah,
9:17 My **f** fought for you.
9:28 of Hamor, Shechem's **f**!
Jdg 9:56 evil he had done to his **f** when
11:1 Jephthah's **f** was named
11:2 get no inheritance from our **f**.
11:36 She said to him, "**F**,
11:37 Then she said to her **f**,
11:39 months she came back to her **f**.
14:2 and told his **f** and mother,
14:3 His **f** and mother asked him,
14:3 But Samson told his **f**,
14:4 His **f** and mother didn't know
14:5 Samson went with his **f** and
14:9 he came to his **f** and mother,
14:10 After his **f** went to see the
14:16 even told my **f** and mother,
15:1 But her **f** would not let him go
15:2 Her **f** said, "I thought you hated
15:6 wife and her **f** to death.
16:31 in the tomb of his **f** Manoah.
17:10 Be a **f** and a priest to me.
18:19 with us and be our **f** and priest.
19:3 Her **f** was thrilled to see him.
19:5 but the woman's **f** told his
19:6 The woman's **f** said to his
19:8 The woman's **f** said,
Rut 2:11 told me how you left your **f**
4:17 He became the **f** of Jesse,
4:17 who was the **f** of David.
4:18 Perez was the **f** of Hezron.
4:19 Hezron was the **f** of Ram.
4:19 Ram was the **f** of Amminadab.
4:20 was the **f** of Nahshon.
4:20 Nahshon was the **f** of Salmon.
4:21 Salmon was the **f** of Boaz.
4:21 Boaz was the **f** of Obed.
4:22 Obed was the **f** of Jesse.
4:22 Jesse was the **f** of David.
1Sm 1:1 whose **f** was Zuph from the
9:1 whose **f** was Aphiah,
9:3 to Saul's **f** Kish were lost,
9:5 or my **f** will stop worrying about
10:2 Your **f** no longer cares about
14:1 But Jonathan didn't tell his **f**
14:27 Jonathan hadn't heard that his **f**
14:28 "Your **f** forced the troops to take
14:29 Jonathan answered, "My **f** has
14:51 Kish (Saul's **f**) and Ner (Abner's
14:51 father) and Ner (Abner's **f**) were
19:2 "My **f** Saul is trying to kill you.
19:3 I'll go out and stand beside my **f**
19:3 I'll speak with my **f** about you.
19:4 well of David to his **f** Saul.
20:1 against your **f** that he's trying
20:2 My **f** does nothing without
20:2 Why should my **f** hide this from
20:3 "Your **f** certainly knows that
20:6 If your **f** really misses me,
20:8 bother taking me to your **f**?"
20:9 If I knew for sure that my **f** had
20:10 whether or not your **f** gives you
20:12 days how my **f** feels about you.
20:13 If my **f** plans to harm you and I
20:13 you as he used to be with my **f**.
20:32 Jonathan asked his **f**,
20:33 Then Jonathan knew his **f** was
20:34 been humiliated by his own **f**.
22:3 "Please let my **f** and mother
23:17 "my **f** Saul won't find you.
23:17 Even my **f** Saul knows this."
2Sm 3:8 faithful to your **f** Saul's family,
6:21 He chose me rather than your **f**
7:14 I will be his **F**, and he will be
9:7 for your **f** Jonathan's sake.
10:2 as his **f** Nahash showed me
10:3 think David is honoring your **f**
13:5 Act sick, and when your **f**
16:19 As I served your **f**,
16:21 have made your **f** despise you.
17:8 "You know your **f** and his men.
17:8 Your **f** is an experienced
17:10 all Israel knows that your **f** is
19:37 the grave of my **f** and mother.
21:14 in the tomb of Saul's **f** Kish.
1Ki 1:6 His **f** had never confronted him
2:12 sat on his **f** David's throne,
2:24 The LORD set me on my **f**
2:26 LORD ahead of my **f** David
1Ki 2:44 evil that you did to my **f** David.
3:3 and lived by his **f** David's rules.
3:6 shown great love to my **f** David,
3:7 me king in place of my **f** David.
3:14 commands as your **f** David did,
5:1 anointed king to succeed his **f**.
5:3 "You know that my **f** David
5:5 the LORD spoke to my **f** David:
6:12 made about you to your **f** David.
7:14 His **f**, a native of Tyre, was a
7:51 had belonged to his **f** David —
8:15 made a promise to my **f** David;
8:17 "My **f** David had his heart set
8:18 the LORD said to my **f** David,
8:20 have taken my **f** David's place,
8:24 your promise to my **f** David,
8:25 your promise to my **f** David,
8:26 you made to my **f** David,
9:4 to me as your **f** David was (with
9:5 I promised your **f** David when
11:4 God as his **f** David had been.
11:6 LORD as his **f** David had done.
11:12 because of your **f** David.
11:33 and decrees as his **f** David did.
12:4 "Your **f** made us carry a heavy
12:6 had served his **f** Solomon while
12:9 the burden my **f** put on them?"
12:11 If my **f** put a heavy burden on
12:11 If my **f** punished you with
12:14 He said, "If my **f** made your
12:14 If my **f** punished you with
13:11 When they told their **f**,
15:3 the sinful example his **f** had set
15:12 rid of the idols his **f** had made.
15:15 and the utensils he and his **f**
15:19 ⌊as⌋ there was between your **f**
15:19 between your father and my **f**.
15:26 evil, living as his **f** did,
19:20 "Please let me kiss my **f** and
20:34 "I will give back the towns my **f**
20:34 my father took from your **f**.
20:34 in Damascus as my **f** did
22:43 the example his **f** Asa had set
22:46 there from the time of his **f** Asa.
22:52 followed the example of his **f**
22:53 furious, as his **f** had done.
2Ki 3:2 but he didn't do what his **f** or
3:2 stone that his **f** had set up
4:18 later the boy went to his **f**,
4:19 ⌊Suddenly,⌋ he said to his **f**,
4:19 The **f** told his servant,
9:25 our chariots behind his **f** Ahab?
13:25 had taken from his **f** Jehoahaz.
14:3 his **f** Joash had done.
14:5 officials who had killed his **f**,
14:21 king in place of his **f** Amaziah.
15:3 as his **f** Amaziah had done.
15:34 as his **f** Azariah had done.
21:3 his **f** Hezekiah had destroyed.
21:20 as his **f** Manasseh had done.
21:21 He lived like his **f** in every way
21:21 the idols his **f** had worshiped.
23:30 made him king in place of his **f**.
23:34 king in place of his **f** Josiah
24:9 evil, as his **f** had done.
1Ch 1:10 Cush was the **f** of Nimrod,
1:13 Canaan was the **f** of Sidon his
1:18 was the **f** of Shelah,
1:18 and Shelah was the **f** of Eber.
1:20 Joktan was the **f** of Almodad,
1:34 Abraham was the **f** of Isaac.
2:10 Ram was the **f** of Amminadab.
2:10 was the **f** of Nahshon,
2:11 Nahshon was the **f** of Salma,
2:11 and Salma was the **f** of Boaz.
2:12 Boaz was the **f** of Obed,
2:12 and Obed was the **f** of Jesse.
2:13 Jesse was the **f** of Eliab (his
2:17 whose **f** was Jether,
2:20 Hur was the **f** of Uri,
2:20 and Uri was the **f** of Bezalel.
2:22 Segub was the **f** of Jair,
2:36 Attai was the **f** of Nathan.
2:36 Nathan was the **f** of Zabad.
2:37 Zabad was the **f** of Ephlal.
2:37 Ephlal was the **f** of Obed.

1Ch 2:38 Obed was the **f** of Jehu.
2:38 Jehu was the **f** of Azariah.
2:39 Azariah was the **f** of Helez.
2:39 Helez was the **f** of Eleasah.
2:40 Eleasah was the **f** of Sismai.
2:40 Sismai was the **f** of Shallum.
2:41 Shallum was the **f** of Jekamiah.
2:41 was the **f** of Elishama.
2:44 Shema was the **f** of Raham,
2:44 Rekem was the **f** of Shammai.
2:46 Haran was the **f** of Gazez.
4:2 was the **f** of Jahath.
4:2 Jahath was the **f** of Ahumai
4:4 Penuel was the **f** of Gedor,
4:4 and Ezer was the **f** of Hushah.
4:8 Koz was the **f** of Anub and
4:11 was the **f** of Mehir,
4:11 who was the **f** of Eshton.
4:12 He was the **f** of Paseah and
4:14 Meonothai was the **f** of Ophrah.
4:14 Seraiah was the **f** of Joab,
6:4 Eleazar was the **f** of Phinehas.
6:4 Phinehas was the **f** of Abishua.
6:5 Abishua was the **f** of Bukki.
6:5 Bukki was the **f** of Uzzi.
6:6 Uzzi was the **f** of Zerahiah.
6:6 Zerahiah was the **f** of Meraioth.
6:7 Meraioth was the **f** of Amariah.
6:7 Amariah was the **f** of Ahitub.
6:8 Ahitub was the **f** of Zadok.
6:8 Zadok was the **f** of Ahimaaz.
6:9 Ahimaaz was the **f** of Azariah.
6:9 Azariah was the **f** of Johanan.
6:10 Johanan was the **f** of Azariah.
6:11 Azariah was the **f** of Amariah.
6:11 Amariah was the **f** of Ahitub.
6:12 Ahitub was the **f** of Zadok.
6:12 Zadok was the **f** of Shallum.
6:13 Shallum was the **f** of Hilkiah.
6:13 Hilkiah was the **f** of Azariah.
6:14 Azariah was the **f** of Seraiah.
6:14 was the **f** of Jehozadak.
7:22 Their **f** Ephraim mourned
7:32 Heber was the **f** of Japhlet,
8:1 Benjamin was the **f** of Bela (his
8:7 He was the **f** of Uzza and
8:32 who was the **f** of Shimeah.
8:33 Ner was the **f** of Kish.
8:33 Kish was the **f** of Saul.
8:33 Saul was the **f** of Jonathan,
8:34 Meribbaal was the **f** of Micah.
8:36 Ahaz was the **f** of Jehoaddah.
8:36 was the **f** of Alemeth,
8:36 Zimri was the **f** of Moza.
8:37 Moza was the **f** of Binea.
9:4 (Imri's **f** was Bani.)
9:11 Zadok's **f** was Meraioth,
9:12 whose **f** was Meshillemith,
9:38 Mikloth was the **f** of Shimeam.
9:39 Ner was the **f** of Kish.
9:39 Kish was the **f** of Saul.
9:39 Saul was the **f** of Jonathan,
9:40 Meribbaal was the **f** of Micah.
9:42 Ahaz was the **f** of Jarah.
9:42 Jarah was the **f** of Alemeth,
9:42 Zimri was the **f** of Moza.
9:43 Moza was the **f** of Binea.
17:13 I will be his **F**, and he will be
19:2 his **f** Nahash showed me
19:3 think David is honoring your **f**
22:10 be my son, and I will be his **f**.
24:2 Abihu died before their **f** died,
25:3 were directed by their **f**,
26:10 His **f** appointed him head.
28:6 to be my son. I will be his **f**.
29:10 our **f** forever and ever.
29:23 as king in place of his **f** David.
2Ch 1:8 shown great love to my **f** David,
1:9 you made to my **f** David.
2:3 what you did for my **f** David.
2:7 men whom my **f** David provided
2:14 and his **f** is a native of Tyre.
2:14 of His Majesty David, your **f**.
2:17 as his **f** David had counted
3:1 LORD appeared to his **f** David.
5:1 had belonged to his **f** David —
2Ch 6:4 made a promise to my **f** David;
6:7 "My **f** David had his heart set
6:8 the LORD said to my **f** David,
6:10 I've taken my **f** David's place,
6:15 your promise to my **f** David,
6:16 your promise to my **f** David,
7:17 to me as your **f** David was,
7:18 in a promise to your **f** David,
8:14 As Solomon's **f** David had
10:4 "Your **f** made us carry a heavy
10:6 had served his **f** Solomon while
10:9 the burden my **f** put on them?"
10:11 If my **f** put a heavy burden on
10:11 If my **f** punished you with
10:14 He said, "If my **f** made your
10:14 If my **f** punished you with
15:18 and the utensils he and his **f**
16:3 ⌊as⌋ there was between your **f**
16:3 between your father and my **f**.
17:2 that his **f** Asa had captured.
20:14 whose **f** was Mattaniah,
20:32 the example his **f** Asa had set
21:3 Their **f** gave them many gifts:
21:12 the ways of your **f** Jehoshaphat
22:4 After his **f** died, they advised
24:22 how kind Zechariah's **f**,
25:3 the officials who killed his **f**,
26:1 king in place of his **f** Amaziah.
26:4 as his **f** Amaziah had done.
27:2 as his **f** Uzziah had done.
27:2 But unlike his **f**, he didn't
33:3 that his **f** Hezekiah had torn
33:22 as his **f** Manasseh had done.
33:22 his **f** Manasseh had made,
33:23 his **f** Manasseh had humbled
36:1 in Jerusalem in place of his **f**.
Neh 12:10 Jeshua was the **f** of Joiakim.
12:10 Joiakim was the **f** of Eliashib.
12:10 Eliashib was the **f** of Joiada.
12:11 Joiada was the **f** of Jonathan.
12:11 Jonathan was the **f** of Jaddua.
Est 2:7 When her **f** and mother died,
Job 15:10 They are older than your **f**.
17:14 'You are my **f**,' and to the worm,
29:16 I was **f** to the needy.
31:18 with me as though I were his **f**,
34:36 "My **F**, let Job be thoroughly
38:28 Does the rain have a **f**?
42:15 Their **f** gave them and their
Psa 2:7 Today I have become your **F**.
27:10 Even if my **f** and mother
45:16 will take the place of your **f**.
68:5 his holy dwelling place is the **f**
89:26 to me, 'You are my **F**, my God,
103:13 As a **f** has compassion for his
Pro 3:12 even as a **f** warns a son with
4:3 a boy ⌊learning⌋ from my **f**,
6:20 Obey the command of your **f**,
10:1 A wise son makes his **f** happy,
15:20 A wise son makes his **f** happy,
17:21 and the **f** of a godless fool has
17:25 son is a heartache to his **f**
19:13 A foolish son ruins his **f**,
19:26 A son who assaults his **f**
20:20 of the person who curses his **f**
23:22 Listen to your **f** since you are
23:24 A righteous person's **f** will
23:25 May your **f** and your mother be
28:7 with gluttons disgraces his **f**.
28:24 The one who robs his **f** or his
29:3 wisdom makes his **f** happy,
30:11 kind of person curses his **f**
30:17 The eye that makes fun of a **f**
Isa 9:6 Everlasting **F**, Prince of Peace.
22:21 and he will be like a **f** to those
45:10 for the one who says to his **f**,
63:16 You are our **F**. Even though
63:16 to us, O LORD, you are our **F**.
64:8 But now, LORD, you are our **F**.
Jer 2:27 You call wood your **f**.
3:4 You say, '**F**! You have been my
3:19 that you would call me **F**
20:15 who made my **f** very happy
20:15 that he had just become the **f**
22:11 who succeeded his **f** as king of
22:15 Your **f** ate and drank and did
Jer 31:9 I will be a **F** to Israel,
Lam 5:3 We are orphans without a **f**.
Eze 16:3 Your **f** was an Amorite,
16:45 and your **f** was an Amorite.
18:11 that his **f** never did.
18:14 all the sins that his **f** does.
18:18 But his **f** has oppressed others,
18:18 So the **f** will die because of his
18:20 and a **f** will not be punished for
44:25 if the dead person is his **f**,
Dan 11:7 from her roots to replace her **f**.
Amo 2:7 **F** and son sleep with the same
Mic 7:6 son treats his **f** with contempt.
Zec 13:3 his **f** and his mother,
13:3 Then his **f** and his mother,
Mal 1:6 A son honors his **f**,
1:6 So if I am a **f**, where is my
2:10 Don't all of us have the same **f**?
Mat 1:2 Abraham was the **f** of Isaac,
1:2 Isaac the **f** of Jacob,
1:2 Jacob the **f** of Judah and his
1:3 Judah and Tamar were the **f**
1:3 Perez was the **f** of Hezron,
1:3 Hezron the **f** of Ram,
1:4 Ram the **f** of Amminadab,
1:4 Amminadab the **f** of Nahshon,
1:4 Nahshon the **f** of Salmon.
1:5 Salmon and Rahab were the **f**
1:5 Boaz and Ruth were the **f** and
1:5 Obed was the **f** of Jesse,
1:6 Jesse the **f** of King David.
1:6 wife ⌊Bathsheba⌋ were the **f**
1:7 was the **f** of Rehoboam,
1:7 Rehoboam the **f** of Abijah,
1:7 Abijah the **f** of Asa,
1:8 Asa the **f** of Jehoshaphat,
1:8 Jehoshaphat the **f** of Joram,
1:8 Joram the **f** of Uzziah,
1:9 Uzziah the **f** of Jotham,
1:9 Jotham the **f** of Ahaz,
1:9 Ahaz the **f** of Hezekiah,
1:10 Hezekiah the **f** of Manasseh,
1:10 Manasseh the **f** of Amon,
1:10 Amon the **f** of Josiah.
1:11 Josiah was the **f** of Jechoniah
1:12 became the **f** of Shealtiel.
1:12 was the **f** of Zerubbabel,
1:13 Zerubbabel the **f** of Abiud,
1:13 Abiud the **f** of Eliakim,
1:13 Eliakim the **f** of Azor,
1:14 Azor the **f** of Zadok,
1:14 Zadok the **f** of Achim,
1:14 Achim the **f** of Eliud,
1:15 Eliud the **f** of Eleazar,
1:15 Eleazar the **f** of Matthan,
1:15 Matthan the **f** of Jacob.
1:16 Jacob was the **f** of Joseph,
2:22 succeeded his **f** Herod as king
4:21 They were in a boat with their **f**
4:22 and their **f** and followed Jesus.
5:16 do and praise your **F** in heaven.
5:45 children of your **F** in heaven.
5:48 you must be perfect as your **F**
6:1 If you do, your **F** in heaven will
6:4 Your **F** sees what you do in
6:6 Pray privately to your **F** who is
6:6 Your **F** sees what you do in
6:8 Your **F** knows what you need
6:9 should pray: Our **F** in heaven,
6:14 your heavenly **F** will also
6:15 your **F** will not forgive your
6:18 it will be obvious to your **F**
6:18 Your **F** sees what you do in
6:26 your heavenly **F** feeds them.
6:32 and your heavenly **F** certainly
7:11 So how much more will your **F**
7:21 what my **F** in heaven wants.
8:21 first let me go to bury my **f**."
10:20 The Spirit of your **F** will be
10:21 a **f** will hand over his child.
10:32 acknowledge in front of my **F**
10:33 But I will tell my **F** in heaven
10:35 to turn a man against his **f**,
10:37 "The person who loves his **f** or
11:25 **F**, Lord of heaven and earth,
11:26 Yes, **F**, this is what pleased

Mat 11:27 "My **F** has turned everything
11:27 Only the **F** knows the Son.
11:27 And no one knows the **F**
12:50 Whoever does what my **F** in
15:4 'Honor your **f** and your mother'
15:4 mother' and 'Whoever curses **f**
15:5 whoever tells his **f** or mother,
15:6 does not have to honor his **f**.
15:13 "Any plant that my heavenly **F**
16:17 but my **F** in heaven revealed it
18:10 always see the face of my **F**,
18:14 In the same way, your **F** in
18:19 my **F** in heaven will accept it.
18:35 That is what my **F** in heaven
19:5 why a man will leave his **f**
19:19 Honor your **f** and mother.
19:29 or sisters, **f**, mother, children,
20:23 My **F** has already prepared
21:30 "The **f** went to the other son
21:31 sons did what the **f** wanted?"
23:9 call anyone on earth your **f**,
23:9 because you have only one **F**,
24:36 Only the **F** knows.
25:34 my **F** has blessed you!
26:39 and prayed, "**F**, if it's possible,
26:42 a second time and prayed, "**F**,
26:53 think that I could call on my **F**
28:19 them in the name of the **F**,
Mar 1:20 and they left their **f** Zebedee
5:40 Then he took the child's **f**,
7:10 'Honor your **f** and your mother'
7:10 mother' and 'Whoever curses **f**
7:11 'If a person tells his **f** or mother
7:12 do anything for his **f** or mother.'
9:21 Jesus asked his **f**,
9:21 The **f** replied, "He has been
9:24 The child's **f** cried out at once,
10:7 why a man will leave his **f**
10:19 Honor your **f** and mother."
10:29 sisters, mother, **f**, children,
11:25 Then your **F** in heaven will
13:12 a **f** will hand over his child.
13:32 Only the **F** knows.
14:36 **F**! You can do anything. Take
15:21 He was the **f** of Alexander and
Luk 1:59 name him Zechariah after his **f**.
1:62 they motioned to the baby's **f**
1:67 His **f** Zechariah was filled with
2:33 Jesus' **f** and mother were
2:48 Your **f** and I have been worried
6:36 merciful as your **F** is merciful.
9:26 glory that he shares with the **F**
9:42 boy and gave him back to his **f**.
9:59 first let me go to bury my **f**."
10:21 Jesus said, "I praise you, **F**,
10:21 Yes, **F**, this is what pleased
10:22 "My **F** has turned everything
10:22 Only the **F** knows who the
10:22 And no one knows who the **F**
11:2 **F**, let your name be kept holy.
11:11 "If your child asks you, his **f**,
11:13 So how much more will your **F**
12:13 inheritance that our **f** left us."
12:30 but your **F** knows you need
12:32 Your **F** is pleased to give you
12:53 A **f** will be against his son and
12:53 his son and a son against his **f**.
15:12 The younger son said to his **f**,
15:12 son said to his father, '**F**,
15:12 So the **f** divided his property
15:18 I'll go at once to my **f**,
15:18 father, and I'll say to him, "**F**,
15:20 "So he went at once to his **f**.
15:20 his **f** saw him and felt sorry for
15:21 Then his son said to him, '**F**,
15:22 "The **f** said to his servants,
15:27 So your **f** has killed the
15:28 His **f** came out and begged him
15:29 But he answered his **f**,
15:31 "His **f** said to him, 'My child,
16:24 He yelled, '**F** Abraham!
16:27 responded, 'Then I ask you, **F**,
16:30 man replied, 'No, **F** Abraham!
18:20 Honor your **f** and your mother."
22:29 So as my **F** has given me a
22:42 "**F**, if it is your will, take this
Luk 23:34 Then Jesus said, "**F**,
23:46 cried out in a loud voice, "**F**,
24:49 you what my **F** promised.
Jon 1:14 It was the glory that the **F**
3:35 The **F** loves his Son and has
4:21 won't be worshiping the **F**
4:23 worshipers will worship the **F**
4:23 The **F** is looking for people like
4:53 Then the boy's **f** realized that it
5:17 "My **F** is working right now,
5:18 repeatedly that God was his **F**.
5:19 only what he sees the **F** doing.
5:19 does exactly what the **F** does.
5:20 The **F** loves the Son and
5:20 The **F** will show him even
5:21 In the same way that the **F**
5:22 "The **F** doesn't judge anyone.
5:23 the Son as they honor the **F**.
5:23 honor the **F** who sent him.
5:26 The **F** is the source of life,
5:30 As I listen ⌊to the **F**⌋,
5:36 The tasks that the **F** gave me
5:36 prove that the **F** has sent me.
5:37 The **F** who sent me testifies on
5:43 authority my **F** has given me,
5:45 you in the presence of the **F**.
6:27 After all, the **F** has placed his
6:32 but my **F** gives you the true
6:37 Everyone whom the **F** gives
6:40 My **F** wants all those who see
6:42 we know his **f** and mother?
6:44 me unless the **F** who sent me
6:45 learned from the **F** come to me.
6:46 that no one has seen the **F**.
6:46 is from God has seen the **F**.
6:57 The **F** who has life sent me,
6:57 and I live because of the **F**.
6:65 the **F** provides the way."
8:16 with the **F** who sent me.
8:18 so does the **F** who sent me."
8:19 "Where is your **f**?"
8:19 "You don't know me or my **F**.
8:19 you would also know my **F**."
8:27 talking to them about the **F**.)
8:28 I speak as the **F** taught me.
8:38 what you've heard from your **f**."
8:39 "Abraham is our **f**."
8:41 You're doing what your **f** does."
8:41 God is our only **F**."
8:42 "If God were your **F**,
8:44 You come from your **f**,
8:44 to do what your **f** wants you
8:44 He's a liar and the **f** of lies.
8:49 I honor my **F**, but you dishonor
8:53 you greater than our **f** Abraham,
8:54 My **F** is the one who gives me
8:56 Your **f** Abraham was pleased to
10:14 my sheep as the **F** knows me.
10:14 know me as I know the **F**.
10:17 The **F** loves me because I give
10:18 This is what my **F** ordered me
10:29 My **F**, who gave them to me,
10:29 can tear them away from my **F**.
10:30 The **F** and I are one."
10:32 things that come from the **F**.
10:37 not doing the things my **F** does,
10:38 and recognize that the **F** is
10:38 is in me and that I am in the **F**."
11:41 Jesus looked up and said, "**F**,
12:26 the **F** will honor them.
12:27 Should I say, '**F**, save me from
12:28 **F**, give glory to your name."
12:49 Instead, the **F** who sent me
12:50 Whatever I say is what the **F**
13:1 this world and go back to the **F**.
13:3 The **F** had put everything in
14:6 to the **F** except through me.
14:7 you will also know my **F**.
14:8 to Jesus, "Lord, show us the **F**,
14:9 has seen me has seen the **F**.
14:9 can you say, 'Show us the **F**'?
14:10 you believe that I am in the **F**
14:10 I am in the Father and the **F** is
14:10 The **F**, who lives in me,
14:11 when I say that I am in the **F**
14:11 in the Father and that the **F** is
Jon 14:12 because I am going to the **F**.
14:13 do anything you ask ⌊the **F**⌋
14:13 in my name so that the **F** will
14:16 I will ask the **F**, and he will
14:20 you will know that I am in my **F**
14:23 My **F** will love them,
14:24 comes from the **F** who sent me.
14:26 whom the **F** will send in my
14:28 be glad that I'm going to the **F**,
14:28 because the **F** is greater than I
14:31 world to know that I love the **F**
14:31 what the **F** has commanded me
15:1 and my **F** takes care of the
15:8 You give glory to my **F** when
15:9 same way the **F** has loved me.
15:15 that I've heard from my **F**.
15:16 and to ask the **F** in my name to
15:23 who hates me also hates my **F**.
15:24 and hated both me and my **F**.
15:26 to you from the **F** will come.
15:26 of Truth who comes from the **F**,
16:3 haven't known the **F** or me.
16:10 because I'm going to the **F** and
16:15 Everything the **F** says is also
16:17 and that he's going to the **F**."
16:23 If you ask the **F** for anything in
16:25 you about the **F** in plain words.
16:26 won't have to ask the **F** for you.
16:27 The **F** loves you because you
16:28 I left the **F** and came into the
16:28 world and go back to the **F**."
16:32 because the **F** is with me.
17:1 and said, "**F**, the time is here.
17:5 Now, **F**, give me glory in your
17:11 Holy **F**, keep them safe by the
17:13 ⌊**F**,⌋ I'm coming back to you.
17:21 **F**, are in me and I am in you.
17:24 "**F**, I want those you have
17:25 Righteous **F**, the world didn't
18:11 that my **F** has given me?"
20:17 I have not yet gone to the **F**.
20:17 'I am going to my **F** and your
20:17 going to my Father and your **F**,
20:21 As the **F** has sent me,
Act 1:4 for what the **F** had promised.
1:4 "I've told you what the **F**
1:7 that the **F** has determined by
2:33 Spirit as the **F** had promised,
7:4 After his **f** died, God made him
7:14 Joseph sent for his **f** Jacob
13:33 Today I have become your **F**.'
16:1 but his **f** was Greek.
16:3 that Timothy's **f** was Greek.
28:8 His **f** happened to be sick in
Rom 1:7 will and peace from God our **F**
4:11 Therefore, he is the **f** of every
4:12 He is also the **f** of those who
4:12 Our **f** Abraham had that faith
4:16 He is the **f** of all of us,
4:17 "I have made you a **f** of many
4:18 he became a **f** of many nations,
6:4 by the glorious power of the **F**,
8:15 "Abba! **F**!"
15:6 you will praise the God and **F**
1Co 1:3 will and peace from God our **F**
4:15 I became your **f** in the Christian
7:36 No **f** would want to do the
7:37 However, a **f** may have come
7:38 So it's fine for a **f** to give his
7:38 but the **f** who doesn't give his
8:6 "There is only one God, the **F**.
15:24 the kingdom to God the **F** as
2Co 1:2 will and peace from God our **F**
1:3 Praise the God and **F** of our
1:3 He is the **F** who is
6:18 says, "I will be your **F**,
11:31 The God and **F** of the Lord
Gal 1:1 and God the **F** who brought him
1:3 peace are yours from God the **F**
1:4 what our God and **F** wanted.
1:5 Glory belongs to our God and **F**
4:2 until the time set by his **f**.
4:6 "Abba! **F**!"
Eph 1:2 will and peace from God our **F**
1:3 Praise the God and **F** of our
1:17 I pray that the glorious **F**,

Eph 2:18 can go to the **F** in one Spirit.
3:14 I kneel in the presence of the **F**
4:6 one God and **F** of all,
5:20 Always thank God the **F** for
5:31 why a man will leave his **f**
6:2 "Honor your **f** and mother
6:23 May God the **F** and the Lord
Php 1:2 will and peace from God our **F**
2:11 Lord to the glory of God the **F**.
2:22 Like a **f** and son we worked
4:20 Glory belongs to our God and **F**
Col 1:2 from God our **F** are yours!
1:3 the **F** of our Lord Jesus Christ,
1:12 You will also thank the **F**,
3:17 to God the **F** through him.
1Th 1:1 united with God the **F**
1:3 the presence of our God and **F**,
2:11 the way a **f** treats his children.
3:11 We pray that God our **F** and the
3:13 of our God and **F** when our Lord
2Th 1:1 united with God our **F**
1:2 will and peace from God our **F**
2:16 God our **F** loved us and by his
1Ti 1:2 and peace from God the **F** and
5:1 talk to him as if he were your **f**.
2Ti 1:2 and peace from God the **F** and
Tit 1:4 will and peace from God the **F**
Phm 1:3 will and peace from God our **F**
1:10 his spiritual **f** here in prison.
Heb 1:3 one next to the **F** in heaven.
1:5 Today I have become your **F**."
1:5 of his angels, "I will be his **F**,
2:11 made holy have the same **F**.
5:5 Today I have become your **F**."
7:3 anything about Melchizedek's **f**,
7:4 even though Abraham was the **f**
11:11 Abraham to become a **f**,
12:7 God corrects you as a **f**
12:9 authority of God, the **f** of spirits,
Jas 1:17 from the **F** who made the sun,
1:17 The **F** doesn't change like the
1:27 according to God our **F**,
3:9 we praise our Lord and **F**.
1Pe 1:2 God the **F** knew you long ago
1:3 Praise the God and **F** of our
1:17 So if you call God your **F**,
2Pe 1:17 honor and glory from God the **F**
1Jn 1:2 was in the presence of the **F**
1:3 Our relationship is with the **F**
2:1 into the presence of the **F**.
2:14 because you know the **F**.
2:16 lifestyles — comes from the **F**.
2:22 The person who rejects the **F**
2:23 Son doesn't have the **F** either.
2:23 the Son also has the **F**.
2:24 live in the Son and in the **F**.
3:1 The **F** has given us his love.
4:14 the fact that the **F** sent his Son
5:1 Everyone who loves the **F** also
2Jn 1:3 They come from God the **F**
1:4 as the **F** has commanded us.
1:9 has both the **F** and the Son.
Jud 1:1 who are loved by God the **F**,
Rev 1:6 priests for God his **F**.
2:26 received authority from my **F**.
3:5 of my **F** and his angels.
3:21 down with my **F** on his throne.

fathered (9)

Dtr 32:18 (You ignored the rock who **f**
2Sm 5:13 and he **f** more sons and
1Ch 2:25 of Hezron) **f** Ram (his firstborn)
14:3 in Jerusalem and **f** more sons
2Ch 11:21 He **f** 28 sons and 60 daughters.)
13:21 He married 14 wives and **f** 22
Isa 49:21 "Who has **f** these ⌊children⌋ for
Dan 11:6 and the one who **f** and
Act 7:29 In Midian he **f** two sons.

father-in-law (23)

Gen 38:13 Tamar was told that her **f** was
38:25 she sent a message to her **f**,
Exo 3:1 of the sheep of his **f** Jethro,
4:18 went back to his **f** Jethro.
18:1 Moses' **f** Jethro, the priest of
18:2 his **f** Jethro had taken her in,
Exo 18:5 Moses' **f** Jethro brought Moses'
18:7 Moses went out to meet his **f**.
18:8 Moses told his **f** everything the
18:12 Then Jethro, Moses' **f**,
18:12 Moses' **f** in God's presence.
18:14 When Moses' **f** saw everything
18:15 Moses answered his **f**,
18:17 Moses' **f** replied, "What you're
18:24 Moses listened to his **f** and did
18:27 Moses sent his **f** on his way.
Jdg 1:16 The descendants of Moses' **f**,
4:11 of Hobab, Moses' **f**).
19:7 his **f** urged him to stay another
19:9 But his **f** said to him,
1Sm 4:19 had been captured and her **f**
4:21 captured and because her **f**
Jon 18:13 to Annas, the **f** of Caiaphas.

fatherless (3)

Psa 68:5 place is the father of the **f**
109:9 "Let his children become **f** and
109:12 show any pity to his **f** children.

father's (154)

Gen 9:23 and covered their **f** naked body.
12:1 your relatives, and your **f** home.
20:12 is my sister — my **f** daughter
20:13 God had me leave my **f** home
24:7 took me from my **f** home
24:23 there is room in your **f** house
24:38 Instead, go to my **f** home and to
24:40 relatives and from my **f** family
26:15 his **f** servants had dug during
28:21 return safely to my **f** home, then
29:9 Rachel arrived with her **f** sheep,
29:12 that he was her **f** nephew
31:9 taken away your **f** livestock
31:14 anything left in our **f** household
31:19 Rachel stole her **f** idols
31:30 you have left for your **f** home
34:19 person in all his **f** family
35:22 with his **f** concubine Bilhah,
37:2 Bilhah and Zilpah, his **f** wives.
37:12 of their **f** flocks at Shechem.
38:11 "Return to your **f** home.
38:11 went to live in her **f** home
41:51 and all about his **f** family
44:30 "Our **f** life is wrapped up with
44:34 bear to see my **f** misery!
45:23 and food for his **f** trip
46:31 and his **f** family, "I'm going
46:31 'My brothers and my **f** family,
47:12 and all his **f** family with food
48:12 Joseph took them off his **f** lap
48:17 So he took his **f** hand in order
49:4 you climbed into your **f** bed.
49:8 Your **f** sons will bow down to
50:8 and his **f** household also went
50:10 days to mourn his **f** death
50:15 what their **f** death could mean.
50:17 your **f** God." Joseph cried when
50:22 Joseph and his **f** family stayed
Exo 2:16 troughs to water their **f** sheep
6:20 married his **f** sister Jochebed.
15:2 my **f** God, and I will honor him.
18:4 "My **f** God was my helper.
Lev 16:32 priest in his **f** place will pay
18:9 whether she is your **f** daughter
18:12 intercourse with your **f** sister.
18:14 with the wife of your **f** brother.
20:11 with his **f** wife has violated his
20:11 has violated his **f** marriage.
20:11 Both he and his **f** wife must be
20:17 his **f** daughter or his mother's
20:19 mother's sister or your **f** sister.
22:13 live in her **f** home, she may eat
22:13 she may eat her **f** food.
Num 27:4 Why should our **f** name be
27:4 property among our **f** relatives.
27:7 own among their **f** relatives.
27:7 Turn their **f** property over to
27:10 to his uncles on his **f** side
30:3 who still lives in her **f** house,
36:11 their cousins on their **f** side
36:12 in the tribe of their **f** family
Dtr 22:21 to the entrance of her **f** house.
Dtr 22:21 was still living in her **f** house.
22:30 must never marry his **f** wife
27:20 intercourse with his **f** wife will
27:22 his **f** daughter, or his mother's
Jos 2:12 kind to my **f** family as I've been
2:18 and all your **f** family into your
6:25 her **f** family, and everything she
17:4 among their **f** relatives as
Jdg 6:25 "Take a bull from your **f** herd, a
6:25 Tear down your **f** altar
6:27 He was too afraid of his **f** family
9:5 Then he went to his **f** home in
9:18 you have attacked my **f** family.
9:18 is the son of my **f** slave girl,
11:7 throw me out of my **f** house?
14:19 and he went to his **f** house
16:31 and his **f** whole family went
19:2 left him and went to her **f** home,
19:3 her husband into her **f** house.
1Sm 2:25 listen to their **f** warning —
2:30 your **f** family would always live
2:31 of your **f** house so that no
8:3 didn't follow their **f** example
9:20 it be you and your **f** family?
17:15 where he tended his **f** flock
17:34 am a shepherd for my **f** sheep.
18:18 are my relatives or my **f** family
24:21 my name in my **f** family.
2Sm 2:32 and buried him in his **f** tomb
3:7 sex with my **f** concubine?
6:21 or anyone in your **f** house,
10:2 Hanun after his **f** ⌊death⌋.
14:9 Let my **f** family be held
15:34 I was your **f** servant in the past,
16:21 "Sleep with your **f** concubines
16:22 he slept with his **f** concubines
17:23 and was buried in his **f** tomb
24:17 me and against my **f** family.
1Ki 2:26 you shared all my **f** sufferings.
2:31 from me and my **f** family
2:32 this without my **f** knowledge
11:17 He and some of his **f** Edomite
12:10 heavier than my **f** whole body.
18:18 You and your **f** family have
2Ki 3:13 Go to your **f** prophets or your
1Ch 5:1 he dishonored his **f** bed.
19:2 Hanun after his **f** ⌊death⌋.
21:17 be against me and my **f** family,
28:4 of Judah he chose my **f** family.
28:4 From among my **f** sons he was
28:9 learn to know your **f** God.
2Ch 10:10 heavier than my **f** whole body.
21:4 had taken over his **f** kingdom,
21:13 your brothers, your **f** family.
Ezr 2:59 on the basis of their **f** family
Neh 1:6 as the sins that my **f** family
7:61 on the basis of their **f** family
Psa 45:10 and forget your **f** house
Pro 1:8 listen to your **f** discipline, and
4:1 listen to ⌊your⌋ **f** discipline,
13:1 son listens to his **f** discipline,
15:5 fool despises his **f** discipline,
27:10 your friend or your **f** friend.
Isa 3:6 of his relatives from his **f** family
22:23 of honor for his **f** household
22:24 his **f** household, descendants
Jer 12:6 of your **f** household betray you.
Eze 18:17 He won't die for his **f** sins.
18:19 the son punished for his **f** sin?'
18:20 not be punished for his **f** sins,
22:10 have sex with their **f** wives.
22:11 their sisters, their **f** daughters
Mat 10:29 without your **F** permission
13:43 like the sun in their **F** kingdom.
16:27 with his angels in his **F** glory.
26:29 with you in my **F** kingdom.
Mar 8:38 the holy angels in his **F** glory.
Luk 2:49 that I had to be in my **F** house?
15:17 'How many of my **f** hired men
16:27 Lazarus back to my **f** home
Jon 1:18 to the **F** heart, has made him
2:16 my **F** house a marketplace!"
5:38 the **F** message within you,
8:38 I have seen in my **F** presence.
10:25 that I do in my **F** name testify
14:2 My **F** house has many rooms.

Jon 14:21 love me will have my **F** love,
15:10 obeyed my **F** commandments,
1Co 5:1 is actually married to his **f** wife
1Jn 2:15 don't have the **F** love in them.
2Jn 1:3 in truth and love is the **F** Son
Rev 14:1 name and his **F** name written

fathers (32)

Gen 48:21 you back to the land of your **f**.
Num 30:16 and for **f** with young daughters
Dtr 32:7 Ask your **f** to remind you,
Jdg 21:22 When their **f** or brothers come
1Ch 25:6 the direction of their **f** Asaph,
2Ch 29:9 Our **f** were killed in battle,
Job 30:1 I didn't think their **f** were fit to
Psa 78:51 Ham when their **f** were young.
105:36 land when their **f** were young.
Pro 19:14 and wealth are inherited from **f**,
Isa 38:19 **F** make your faithfulness
49:23 Then kings will be your foster **f**,
Jer 7:18 gather wood, **f** light fires,
16:3 and **f** who have children
16:7 have lost their **f** or mothers.
31:29 '**F** have eaten sour grapes,
47:3 **F** who lack courage abandon
Eze 18:2 '**F** have eaten sour grapes,
18:4 **F** and their children belong to
22:7 in you hate their **f** and mothers.
Luk 14:26 are not ready to abandon their **f**,
Act 7:2 "Brothers and **f**, listen to me.
22:1 "Brothers and **f**, listen as I now
1Co 4:15 don't have many ⌊spiritual⌋ **f**.
Eph 6:4 **F**, don't make your children
Col 3:21 **F**, don't make your children
1Ti 1:9 for those who kill their **f**,
Heb 12:7 are disciplined by their **f**.
12:9 On earth we have **f** who
12:10 For a short time our **f**
1Jn 2:13 I'm writing to you, **f**,
2:14 I've written to you, **f**,

fattened (16)

1Sm 15:9 cows, the **f** animals, the lambs,
28:24 butchered a **f** calf that she
2Sm 6:13 David sacrificed a bull and a **f**
1Ki 1:9 and **f** calves at Zoheleth Rock
1:19 has sacrificed many **f** calves,
1:25 bulls, **f** calves, and sheep.
4:23 10 **f** cows, 20 cows from the
4:23 fallow deer, and **f** birds.
Psa 66:15 I will offer you a sacrifice of **f**
Isa 1:11 enough fat from your **f** calves.
Jer 46:21 hired soldiers are like **f** calves.
Mat 22:4 My bulls and **f** calves have
Luk 15:23 Bring the **f** calf, kill it, and let's
15:27 So your father has killed the **f**
15:30 you killed the **f** calf for him.'
Jas 5:5 You have **f** yourselves for the

fault (11)

Gen 16:5 And it's your **f**! I know that I
Exo 5:16 but your men are at **f**."
Job 40:2 "Will the person who finds **f**
Dan 6:4 No error or **f** could be found.
Rom 9:19 God still find **f** with anyone?
2Co 6:3 people any opportunity to find **f**
8:20 We don't want anyone to find **f**
Col 1:22 without sin, **f**, or blame.
Jas 1:5 and doesn't find **f** with them.
Jud 1:16 These people complain, find **f**,
1:24 his glorious presence without **f**.

faultless (1)

Job 15:14 should a mortal be considered **f**

faults (4)

Psa 19:12 Forgive my hidden **f**.
2Co 5:19 hold people's **f** against them,
Eph 5:27 or wrinkle — holy and without **f**.
Php 2:15 any **f** among people who

favor (79)

Gen 20:13 'Do me a **f**: Wherever we go,
30:6 "Now God has judged in my **f**.
32:5 news⌋ in order to win your **f**."'
33:8 He answered, "To win your **f**,
Gen 33:15 "I only want to win your **f**.
34:11 and her brothers, "Do me this **f**.
40:14 and please do me a **f**.
Num 6:26 LORD will look on you with **f**
Dtr 33:16 bless their land with the **f**
33:23 of Naphtali enjoy the LORD's **f**
Jdg 8:24 said to them, "Do me a **f**.
11:37 said to her father, "Do me a **f**.
1Sm 2:26 to grow and gained the **f**
13:12 I haven't sought the LORD's **f**.' I
29:4 to try to regain his master's **f**?
Est 5:2 in the entrance, she won his **f**.
5:8 If I have found **f** with you,
7:3 "If I have found **f** with you,
8:5 and if I have found **f** with you,
Job 10:3 work of your hands while you **f**
11:19 people will try to gain your **f**.
13:8 Will you **f** him ⌊as⌋ if you were
13:10 you if you secretly **f** ⌊him⌋?
Psa 5:12 you surround them with your **f**.
20:3 grain offerings and look with **f**
30:5 His **f** lasts a lifetime.
30:7 O LORD, by your **f** you have
45:12 want to win your **f** with a gift.
51:18 **F** Zion with your goodness.
84:9 Look with **f** on the face of your
84:11 The LORD grants **f** and honor.
89:17 By your **f** you give us victory.
102:13 it is time to grant a **f** to it.
106:4 when you show **f** to your
119:58 my heart I want to win your **f**.
Pro 3:4 Then you will find **f** and much
8:35 and obtains **f** from the LORD.
12:2 A good person obtains **f** from
13:15 Good sense brings **f**,
16:15 and his **f** is like a cloud
18:22 has obtained **f** from the LORD.
19:12 but his **f** is like dew on the
Isa 49:8 In the time of **f** I will answer
60:10 but in my **f** I have compassion
Jer 26:19 LORD and sought the LORD's **f**.
31:2 survived the wars have found **f**
Dan 7:22 came and judged in **f** of the
9:13 we never tried to gain your **f** by
11:30 and **f** those who abandon the
Zec 11:7 staffs and named one **F**
11:10 Then I took my staff called **F**
Mat 20:20 in front of him to ask him for a **f**.
22:16 You don't **f** individuals because
Mar 10:35 we want you to do us a **f**."
12:14 You don't **f** individuals because
Luk 1:30 You have found **f** with God.
2:40 and God's **f** was with him.
2:52 He gained **f** from God and
4:19 the year of the Lord's **f**."
14:12 they will return the **f**.
Act 6:8 filled with God's **f** and power.
7:10 God gave Joseph divine **f** and
7:46 who won God's **f**. David asked
24:27 wanted to do the Jews a **f**.
25:3 Festus to do them the **f** of
25:9 wanted to do the Jews a **f**.
25:11 hand me over to them as a **f**.
25:16 can't be sentenced as a **f**.
Rom 5:2 God and stand in his **f**.
6:14 by laws, but by God's **f**.
6:15 but are controlled by God's **f**?
2Co 1:11 people will thank God for the **f**
Gal 5:4 You have fallen out of God's **f**.
Eph 4:7 God's **f** has been given to each
6:24 His **f** is with everyone who has
Php 1:7 Together we share God's **f**,
Phm 1:14 I want you to do this **f** for me
Jas 2:9 If you **f** one person over
Rev 2:6 But you have this in your **f** —

favorably (8)

2Sm 15:25 If the LORD looks **f** on me,
Psa 26:1 Judge me **f**, O LORD,
Lam 4:16 will no longer look **f** on them.
Dan 9:17 look **f** on your holy place,
Luk 1:48 he has looked **f** on me,
Jon 3:26 you spoke so **f** about when
5:36 something that testifies more **f**
Act 13:22 God spoke **f** about David.

favored (4)

2Sm 13:21 He **f** Amnon because he was
Est 2:17 other women and **f** her over all
Psa 85:1 You **f** your land, O LORD.
Luk 1:28 "You are **f** by the Lord!

favoring (1)

Jas 2:1 Christ by not **f** one person over

favorite (1)

Dtr 33:24 May they be the Israelites' **f**

favorites (9)

Dtr 10:17 He never plays **f** and never
Luk 20:21 Besides, you don't play **f**.
Act 10:34 that God doesn't play **f**.
Rom 2:11 God does not play **f**.
Gal 2:6 since God doesn't play **f**.)
Eph 6:9 and he doesn't play **f**.
Col 3:25 God does not play **f**.
1Ti 5:21 I've told you. Never play **f**.
1Pe 1:17 and he doesn't play **f**.

favors (7)

Exo 23:3 Never give special **f** to poor
Lev 19:15 Never give special **f** to poor
2Sm 20:11 "Anyone who **f** Joab and is on
Job 34:19 mighty does not grant special **f**
Ecc 10:12 A wise person's words win **f**,
Eze 16:34 No one goes after you for **f**.
1Pe 5:5 the arrogant but **f** the humble.

fawns (3)

Gen 49:21 doe set free that has beautiful **f**.
Sos 4:5 Your breasts are like two **f**,
7:3 Your breasts are like two **f**,

fear (211)

Gen 9:2 and all the birds will **f** you
22:12 Now I know that you **f** God,
31:42 of Abraham and the **F** of Isaac,
31:53 Jacob swore this oath by the **F**
42:18 and you will live. I, too, **f** God.
Exo 9:30 still don't **f** the LORD God."
18:21 all the people, men who **f** God,
19:16 in the camp shook with **f**.
20:18 So they shook with **f** and stood
Lev 19:14 Instead, **f** your God.
25:17 **F** your God, because I am the
25:36 **F** your God by respecting other
25:43 them harshly. **F** your God.
Dtr 4:10 Then they will learn to **f** me as
5:29 If only they would **f** me and
6:2 and your grandchildren must **f**
6:13 You must **f** the LORD your God,
6:24 all these laws and to **f** him.
8:6 his directions, and **f** him.
10:12 He wants you to **f** him,
10:20 **F** the LORD your God,
13:4 **f** him, obey his commands,
14:23 Then you will learn to **f** the
17:19 He will learn to **f** the LORD his
28:58 You might not **f** this glorious
31:12 Have them listen and learn to **f**
31:13 must hear them and learn to **f**
Jos 4:24 power and that you would **f**
24:14 "**F** the LORD, and serve him
Jdg 6:10 You must never **f** the gods of
1Sm 5:11 There was a **f** of death
12:14 If you **f** the LORD, serve him,
12:24 **F** the LORD, and serve him
13:7 followed him trembled ⌊in⌋ **f**.
14:15 party also trembled ⌊in⌋ **f**.
16:4 of the city, trembling with **f**,
17:11 they were gripped with **f**.
2Sm 23:3 justice rules with the **f** of God.
1Ki 8:40 our ancestors, they will **f** you.
8:43 your name and **f** you like your
2Ki 17:34 They don't **f** the LORD or live
1Ch 14:17 made all the nations **f** him.
2Ch 6:31 they will **f** you and follow you.
6:33 your name and **f** you like your
17:10 **F** of the LORD came to all the
19:7 May you have the **f** of the
19:9 wholeheartedly — with the **f**

2Ch 20:29 The f of the LORD came over
26:5 who taught him to f God.
Neh 5:9 Shouldn't you live in the f of our
Job 1:9 given Job a reason to f God?
3:25 What I f most overtakes me.
4:6 Doesn't your f of God give you
4:14 f and trembling came over me,
6:14 abandons the f of the Almighty.
13:11 Doesn't the f of him fall upon
15:4 Yes, you destroy the f ⌊of
19:29 F death, because ⌊your anger⌋
21:9 Their homes are free from f,
22:4 of law because you f him?
22:10 and great f suddenly grips you.
28:28 'The f of the Lord is wisdom!
37:24 is why people should f him.
39:22 It laughs at f, is afraid of
Psa 2:11 Serve the LORD with f,
15:4 honors those who f the LORD.
19:9 The f of the LORD is pure.
22:23 All who f the LORD,
22:25 of those who f the LORD.
23:4 you are with me, I f no harm.
25:14 The LORD advises those who f
27:1 Who is there to f? The LORD is
31:19 reserve it for those who f you.
33:8 Let all the earth f the LORD.
33:18 eyes are on those who f him,
34:7 camps around those who f him,
34:9 F the LORD, you holy people
34:9 Those who f him are never in
34:11 teach you the f of the LORD.
47:2 We must f the LORD,
48:5 were terrified and ran away in f.
52:6 see ⌊this⌋ and be struck with f.
55:5 F and trembling have
55:19 They never f God.
60:4 flag for those who f you so that
61:5 to those who f your name.
64:4 them suddenly, without any f.
66:16 Come and listen, all who f God,
72:5 May they f you as long as the
78:53 They had no f while the sea
85:9 is near those who f him,
91:5 You do not need to f terrors of
102:15 The nations will f the LORD's
102:15 of the earth will f your glory.
103:11 is toward those who f him.
103:13 for those who f him.
103:17 mercy is on those who f him.
111:5 food for those who f him.
111:10 The f of the LORD is the
115:11 If you f the LORD, trust the
115:13 bless those who f the LORD,
118:4 Those who f the LORD should
119:38 to me so that I can f you.
119:74 Those who f you will see me
119:79 Let those who f you turn to me
119:120 My body shudders in f of you,
128:1 Blessed are all who f the
135:20 You people who f the LORD,
145:19 the needs of those who f him.
147:11 pleased with those who f him,
Pro 1:7 The f of the LORD is the
1:29 not choose the f of the LORD.
2:5 then you will understand the f
3:7 F the LORD, and turn away
8:13 To f the LORD is to hate evil.
9:10 The f of the LORD is the
10:27 The f of the LORD lengthens
14:26 In the f of the LORD there is
14:27 The f of the LORD is a fountain
15:16 Better to have a little with the f
15:33 The f of the LORD is discipline
16:6 By the f of the LORD,
19:23 The f of the LORD leads to life,
22:4 On the heels of humility (the f
23:17 continue to f the LORD.
24:21 F the LORD, my son. Fear the
24:21 F the king as well.
29:25 A person's f sets a trap ⌊for
31:21 She does not f for her family
31:30 ⌊but⌋ a woman who has the f
Ecc 3:14 this so that people will f him.
5:7 you should still f God.
8:12 go well for those who f God,
2Ki 8:12 because they f him.
8:13 because they don't f God.
12:13 this is the conclusion: F God,
Isa 8:12 Don't f what they fear.
8:12 Don't fear what they f.
8:13 He is the one you should f and
11:2 knowledge and f of the LORD.
11:3 He will gladly bear the f of the
25:3 by the world's tyrants will f you.
33:6 The f of the LORD is ⌊your⌋
40:9 Raise your voice without f.
51:13 should you live in constant f
57:11 Whom did you dread and f so
57:11 Is that why you don't f me?
59:19 The people of the west will f
59:19 in the east will f his glory.
63:17 that we are unable to f you?
66:4 and bring on them what they f.
Jer 2:19 your God and do not f me,"
5:22 Don't you f me?" asks the
5:24 'We should f the LORD our
22:25 those you f— King
26:21 about it and fled in f to Egypt.
30:5 "We hear cries of f,
32:39 so that they will f me as long
32:40 I will make them f me so that
36:24 his attendants didn't show any f
36:24 clothes in f when they heard
39:17 be handed over to those you f.
42:11 of Babylon, whom you now f.
42:16 Then the wars you f will catch
49:23 They melt in f. They are
50:38 that will go crazy with f.
Eze 26:15 shake with f when they hear
27:35 Their faces show their f.
30:13 I will spread f throughout Egypt
31:16 I made the nations tremble in f
32:10 all of them will tremble in f for
Hos 10:3 because we didn't f the LORD.
10:5 Those who live in Samaria f
Mic 6:9 (The f of your name is wisdom.)
7:17 away from your presence in f,
Hab 3:2 LORD, I f your work.
Zep 3:7 ⌊to my people⌋, 'You will f me.
3:15 You will never f disaster again.
Mal 3:5 None of them f me,"
4:2 for you people who f my name.
Mat 10:28 Instead, f the one who can
28:8 away from the tomb with f
Mar 4:41 They were overcome with f
5:33 The woman trembled with f.
Luk 1:12 troubled and overcome with f.
1:50 For those who f him,
1:74 we could serve him without f
7:16 Everyone was struck with f
18:2 was a judge who didn't f God
18:4 Although I don't f God or
23:40 "Don't you f God at all?
Act 2:43 A feeling of f came over
9:31 as people lived in the f
Rom 8:15 that leads you into f again.
2Co 5:11 what it means to f the Lord,
7:1 live a holy life in the f of God.
7:15 him with f and trembling.
Php 2:12 salvation with f and trembling.
Heb 12:28 we must serve God with f and
Jas 2:19 and they tremble with f.
1Pe 1:17 residents on earth in f.
2:17 F God. Honor the emperor.
1Jn 4:18 No f exists where his love is.
4:18 Rather, perfect love gets rid of f,
4:18 f involves punishment.
4:18 The person who lives in f
Rev 11:11 Great f fell on those who
11:18 and those who f your name,
14:7 "F God and give him glory,
15:4 Lord, who won't f and praise
19:5 all who serve and f him,

feared (21)

Exo 1:17 However, the midwives f God
1:21 Because the midwives f God,
14:31 they f the LORD and believed
Jos 9:24 We deceived you because we f
1Sm 12:18 and rain so that all the people f
2Ki 4:1 You know how he f the LORD.
1Ch 16:25 He should be f more than all
Neh 5:15 didn't do that, because I f God.
7:2 and he f God more than most
Job 1:1 He was decent, he f God,
Psa 76:7 You alone must be f!
76:11 gifts to the one who must be f.
96:4 He should be f more than all
130:4 so that you can be f.
Isa 18:2 a people ⌊who are⌋ f far and
18:7 a people ⌊who are⌋ f far and
Jer 26:19 Hezekiah f the LORD and
44:10 You haven't f me or lived your
Hag 1:12 the people f the LORD.
Mal 3:16 Then those who f the LORD
3:16 to be a reminder to those who f

fearful (3)

Psa 76:8 The earth was f and silent
99:3 to your great and f name.
Pro 28:14 one who is always f ⌊of sin⌋,

fearfully (2)

Eze 4:16 and f drink rationed water.
Luk 21:26 People will faint as they f wait

fearing (4)

Gen 20:11 because there are no G-f people
Psa 86:11 Focus my heart on f you.
Act 27:17 F that they would hit the large
27:29 F we might hit rocks,

fearless (1)

Job 41:33 compare to it. It was made f.

fearlessly (1)

Php 1:14 more boldly and f than ever.

fears (14)

Job 1:8 He is decent, he f God,
2:3 He is decent, he f God,
Psa 25:12 is this person that f the LORD?
34:4 and rescued me from all my f.
90:11 A person f you more when he
112:1 Blessed is the person who f
119:63 I am a friend to everyone who f
128:4 bless the person who f him.
Pro 13:13 but the one who f ⌊God's⌋
14:2 Whoever lives right f the LORD,
Ecc 7:18 because the one who f God
Isa 50:10 Who among you f the LORD
Jer 10:7 Everyone f you, O King of the
2Co 7:5 and inwardly we have f.

fearsome (1)

Hab 1:7 They will be terrifying and f.

feast (17)

Gen 21:8 Abraham held a big f.
29:22 place and gave a wedding f.
Exo 32:6 Afterward, they sat down to a f,
1Sm 9:24 When I invited people to the f,
2Sm 3:20 and David had a f for Abner and
13:24 are invited ⌊to f⌋ with me."
1Ki 1:19 of the army ⌊to his f⌋.
1:25 the priest Abiathar ⌊to his f⌋.
2Ki 6:23 king prepared a great f for them
Job 24:20 Worms f on them. No one
Pro 15:15 cheerful heart has a continual f.
17:1 than a family f filled with strife.
Isa 25:6 will prepare for all people a f
Jer 51:39 I will prepare a f for them and
Eze 39:17 It will be a huge f on the
Luk 15:23 and let's celebrate with a f.
1Co 10:7 "The people sat down to a f

feasting (5)

Est 8:17 f and enjoying a holiday.
9:17 it a day of f and celebration.
9:18 it a day of f and celebration.
9:19 a holiday for f and celebration.
9:22 these days are to be days for f

feasts (1)

Isa 5:12 At their f there are lyres and

feathers (7)

Dtr 32:11 and carries them on its **f**,
Job 39:13 or do its wings lack **f**?
Psa 68:13 its **f** with yellow gold.
91:4 He will cover you with his **f**,
Eze 17:3 wings with long, colorful **f**.
17:7 with large wings and many **f**.
Dan 4:33 hair grew as long as eagles' **f**

features (2)

Gen 29:17 beautiful figure and beautiful **f**.
Jas 1:24 studies his **f**, goes away,

feces (2)

Job 20:7 will certainly rot like his own **f**.
Pro 30:12 is not washed from his own **f**.

fed (11)

Dtr 8:3 from hunger and then **f** you
8:16 He was the one who **f** you in
32:13 heights of the earth and **f** them
Jdg 19:21 to his house and **f** the donkeys.
Neh 5:17 I **f** 1 50 Jewish leaders and
Eze 19:2 the lions. She **f** many cubs.
Dan 4:12 It **f** every living creature.
Hos 11:4 I bent down and **f** them.
13:6 When I **f** you, you were full.
Hab 1:16 and well **f** because of them.
Luk 1:53 He **f** hungry people with good

fee (1)

Exo 22:15 the rental **f** covers the loss.

feed (53)

Gen 24:25 We have plenty of straw and **f**
24:32 and given straw and **f**.
42:27 his sack to **f** his donkey.
43:24 feet and **f** for their donkeys.
2Sm 13:5 my sister Tamar come to **f** me.
13:5 and she can **f** me.'"
13:6 and she can **f** me."
13:10 bedroom so that you can **f** me."
1Ki 17:4 and I've commanded ravens to **f**
17:9 a widow there to **f** you."
22:27 and **f** him nothing but bread and
2Ch 18:26 and **f** him nothing but bread and
Job 24:6 in the field ⌊to **f** themselves⌋.
39:30 Its young ones **f** on blood.
Psa 81:16 But I would **f** Israel with the
Pro 10:21 of a righteous person **f** many,
15:14 mouths of fools **f** on stupidity.
27:27 be enough goat milk to **f** you,
27:27 to feed you, to **f** your family,
30:8 **F** me ⌊only⌋ the food I need,
Isa 1:3 where their masters **f** them.
18:6 The birds of prey will **f** on them
18:6 the wild animals on earth will **f**
27:10 They will **f** on the branches.
58:10 own food to ⌊**f**⌋ those who are
58:14 I will **f** you with the inheritance
65:25 and lambs will **f** together,
Jer 3:15 They will be shepherds who **f**
9:15 I am going to **f** these people
Eze 15:6 forest to be used to **f** the fire,
29:5 I will **f** you to wild animals and
32:4 all over the earth will **f** on you.
34:14 I will **f** them in good pasture,
34:14 and they will **f** on the best
34:18 Isn't it enough for you to **f** on
Dan 4:12 enough to **f** everyone.
4:21 enough to **f** everyone.
Hos 4:8 They **f** on the sins of my
4:16 How can the LORD **f** them like
9:2 be enough grain to **f** people.
Mic 3:5 against those who don't **f** them.
7:14 Let them **f** in Bashan and
Nah 2:12 its prey to pieces to **f** its cubs.
Hab 2:13 that people grow tired only to **f**
Mat 15:33 we get enough bread to **f** such
25:37 we see you hungry and **f** you
Mar 6:37 wages on bread to **f** them?"
8:4 enough bread to **f** these people
Luk 15:15 country and was sent to **f** pigs
Jon 6:57 So those who **f** on me will live
21:15 Jesus told him, "**F** my lambs."
Jon 21:17 Jesus told him, "**F** my sheep.
Rom 12:20 "If your enemy is hungry, **f** him.

feeding (7)

1Sm 7:9 took a lamb, one still **f** on milk,
Job 39:9 at night beside your **f** trough?
Pro 14:4 the **f** trough is empty,
Nah 2:11 that **f** place for young lions?
Mat 8:30 of pigs was **f** in the distance.
Mar 5:11 A large herd of pigs was **f** on a
Luk 8:32 A large herd of pigs was **f** on a

feeds (4)

Isa 1:3 don't understand ⌊who **f** them⌋.
Mat 6:26 your heavenly Father **f** them.
Luk 12:24 Yet, God **f** them. You are worth
Eph 5:29 he **f** and takes care of it,

feel (74)

Gen 27:12 My father will **f** ⌊my skin⌋ and
27:21 here so that I can **f** your skin,
41:55 everyone in Egypt began to **f**
Dtr 13:8 Don't **f** sorry for them or protect
28:66 You will never **f** sure of your
1Sm 16:16 and you'll **f** better."
20:12 If he does **f** kindly toward you,
2Sm 13:28 "When Amnon begins to **f** good
19:5 made all your men **f** ashamed,"
Job 10:1 I will speak as bitterly as I **f**.
11:18 You will **f** confident because
24:22 will never **f** secure about life.
24:23 ⌊God⌋ may let them **f**
Psa 22:9 the one who made me **f** safe at
77:10 Then I said, "It makes me **f**
109:22 I can **f** the pain in my heart.
115:7 have hands, but they cannot **f**.
119:6 Then I will never **f** ashamed
119:46 of kings and not **f** ashamed.
Pro 23:35 "They strike me, but I **f** no pain.
24:17 and do not **f** glad when he
25:22 you will make him **f** guilty
30:9 or I may **f** satisfied and deny
Ecc 2:3 myself **f** better by drinking
Isa 47:10 You **f** safe in your wickedness
51:19 Who will **f** sorry for you?
Jer 2:26 nation of Israel will **f** ashamed.
2:26 and prophets will also **f**
5:3 these people, but they don't **f** it.
7:14 the place where you **f** so safe.
10:18 for them so that they will **f** it.
15:1 I would not **f** sorry for these
Lam 1:22 I groan so much and I **f** so sick
5:17 This is why we **f** sick.
Eze 5:11 for you or **f** sorry for you.
7:4 compassion for you or **f** sorry
7:9 not have compassion or **f** sorry.
8:18 compassion for them or **f** sorry
9:5 compassion, and don't **f** sorry.
9:10 not have compassion or **f** sorry.
Dan 11:24 When people **f** secure,
Amo 6:1 for those who **f** secure on the
Jnh 4:10 Yet, you **f** sorry for this plant.
4:11 Shouldn't I **f** sorry for this
Nah 3:7 Who will **f** sorry for her?'
Mat 15:32 "I **f** sorry for the people.
26:37 beginning to **f** deep anguish.
26:38 "My anguish is so great that I **f**
Mar 8:2 "I **f** sorry for the people.
14:33 to **f** distressed and anguished.
14:34 "My anguish is so great that I **f**
Luk 1:43 I **f** blessed that the mother of
Jon 3:29 This is the joy that I **f**.
16:20 You will **f** pain, but your pain
Act 13:15 for the people, **f** free to speak."
Rom 11:20 Don't **f** arrogant, but be afraid.
12:20 him **f** guilty and ashamed."
14:22 knows is right shouldn't **f** guilty.
1Co 4:14 this to make you **f** ashamed
8:7 So they **f** guilty because their
12:25 that all of its parts should **f**
2Co 1:9 In fact, we still **f** as if we're
5:4 We **f** distressed because we
7:4 encouraged and **f** very happy.
9:7 sorry that you gave or **f** forced
Gal 4:27 shouting, those who **f** no pains
Php 2:25 I **f** that I must send
Php 2:28 him again and I will **f** relieved.
2Th 3:14 so that they will **f** ashamed.
Heb 12:18 to something that you can **f**,
1Pe 3:16 will **f** ashamed that they
4:12 Don't **f** as though something
4:16 a Christian, don't **f** ashamed,
Jud 1:12 with you and don't **f** ashamed.

feeling (13)

1Sm 23:21 bless you for **f** sorry for me!
Est 5:9 he was happy and **f** good.
Psa 17:10 They have shut out all **f**.
Eze 3:14 I went away **f** bitter and angry.
7:24 who are strong from **f** proud,
Dan 11:21 when people are **f** secure,
Hab 3:16 A rotten **f** has entered me.
Mal 3:14 or if we walk around **f** sorry
Mat 26:22 **F** deeply hurt, they asked him
Mar 14:19 **F** hurt, they asked him one by
Act 2:43 A **f** of fear came over everyone
2Co 9:4 This would embarrass us for **f**
Phm 1:14 own free will without **f** forced

feelings (2)

Jon 12:27 to know how to express my **f**.
2Co 7:15 His deepest **f** go out to you

feels (6)

1Sm 20:12 how my father **f** about you.
Job 14:22 He **f** only his body's pain.
21:23 prime and **f** altogether happy
Pro 21:26 All day long he **f** greedy,
31:6 wine to one who **f** resentful.
Jer 2:26 "As a thief **f** ashamed when

fees (4)

Ezr 4:13 taxes, **f**, and tolls. Ultimately,
4:20 Taxes, **f**, and tolls were paid to
7:24 God pay any taxes, **f**, or tolls.
Mat 17:25 of the world collect **f** or taxes?

feet (441)

Gen 6:15 the ship is to be 450 **f** long,
6:15 75 **f** wide, and 45 feet high.
6:15 75 feet wide, and 45 **f** high.
7:20 23 **f** above the mountaintops.
18:4 After you wash your **f**,
19:2 ⌊You can⌋ wash your **f** there.
24:32 and his men to wash their **f**.
43:24 gave them water to wash their **f**
49:10 his **f** until Shiloh comes
49:33 he pulled his **f** into his bed.
Exo 4:25 and touched Moses' **f** ⌊with it⌋.
12:11 your sandals on your **f**,
24:10 Under his **f** was something like
25:12 and fasten them to its four **f**,
26:2 Each sheet will be 42 **f** long
26:2 42 feet long and 6 **f** wide — all
26:8 the 11 sheets will be 45 **f** long
26:8 be 45 feet long and 6 **f** wide.
26:16 Each frame is to be 15 **f** long
27:1 It should be 7 ½ **f** square,
27:1 feet square, and 4 ½ **f** high.
27:9 courtyard should be 150 **f** long
27:11 should be the same: 150 **f** long,
27:12 west end should be 75 **f** wide
27:13 should also be 75 **f** wide.
27:14 entrance⌋ will be 22 ½ **f** wide
27:18 courtyard should be 150 **f** long,
27:18 75 **f** wide, and 7 ½ feet high,
27:18 75 feet wide, and 7 ½ **f** high.
29:20 on the big toes of their right **f**.
30:19 it for washing their hands and **f**.
30:21 their hands and **f** so that they
36:9 Each sheet was 42 **f** long and
36:9 42 feet long and 6 **f** wide — all
36:15 Each of the 11 sheets was 45 **f**
36:15 was 45 feet long and 6 **f** wide.
36:21 Each frame was 15 **f** long and
37:3 cast four gold rings for its four **f**,
38:1 of acacia wood 7 ½ **f** square
38:1 ½ feet square and 4 ½ **f** high.
38:9 of the courtyard was 150 **f** long
38:11 The north side was also 150 **f**
38:12 The west side was 75 **f** long
38:13 rising sun, was 75 **f** ⌊wide⌋.

Exo 38:14 the courtyard was 22 ½ **f** wide
38:18 It was 30 **f** long and 7 ½ feet
38:18 30 feet long and 7 ½ **f** high,
40:31 to wash their hands and **f**.
Lev 8:24 on the big toes of their right **f**.
Num 11:31 ground about three **f** deep as far
35:4 Levites will extend 1,500 **f** from
35:5 the city measure off 3,000 **f**
35:5 3,000 **f** on the south side,
35:5 3,000 **f** on the west side,
35:5 and 3,000 **f** on the north side,
Dtr 1:36 give the land that he set his **f**
3:11 and was more than 13 **f** long
3:11 than 13 feet long and 6 **f** wide.
8:4 and your **f** didn't swell these
22:4 help him get it back on its **f**.
28:35 body from the soles of your **f**
33:3 They bow at your **f** to receive
33:24 and wash their **f** in olive oil.
Jos 4:3 where the priests' **f** stood firmly.
4:18 When their **f** stepped onto dry
10:24 "Come forward and put your **f**
14:9 'The land your **f** walked on will
Jdg 5:27 He lay between her **f**!
5:27 He fell between her **f**.
Rut 2:7 on her **f** from daybreak until
3:4 Then uncover his **f**,
3:7 uncovered his **f**, and lay down.
3:8 to see a woman lying at his **f**.
3:14 Ruth lay at his **f** until morning.
1Sm 17:4 from Gath. He was ten **f** tall.
25:24 After she bowed at his **f**,
25:41 "I am ready to wash the **f** of my
2Sm 2:18 Asahel was as fast on his **f** as
3:34 Your **f** were not chained.
4:12 cut off their hands and **f**,
11:8 "and wash your **f**."
19:24 He had not tended to his **f**,
22:10 with a dark cloud under his **f**.
22:34 He makes my **f** like those of a
22:37 on so that my **f** do not slip.
22:39 They fell under my **f**.
22:40 my opponents bow at my **f**.
1Ki 2:5 waist and the shoes on his **f**.
6:2 for the LORD was 90 **f** long,
6:2 30 **f** wide, and 45 feet high.
6:2 30 feet wide, and 45 **f** high.
6:3 It extended 15 **f** in front of the
6:6 of the annex was 7 ½ **f** wide,
6:6 the second story was 9 **f** wide,
6:6 third story was 10 ½ **f** wide.
6:10 annex 7 ½ **f** high alongside
6:20 The inner room was 30 **f** long,
6:20 30 **f** wide, and 30 feet high.
6:20 30 feet wide, and 30 **f** high.
6:24 of the angels was 7 ½ **f** long.
6:24 to the tip of the other was 15 **f**.
6:26 Each was 15 **f** high.
7:2 It was 150 **f** long, 75 feet wide,
7:2 It was 150 feet long, 75 **f** wide,
7:2 75 feet wide, and 45 **f** high.
7:6 the Hall of Pillars 75 **f** long
7:6 75 feet long and 45 **f** wide.
7:10 stones (some 12 **f** long,
7:10 12 feet long, others 15 **f** long).
7:15 Each was 27 **f** high and 18 feet
7:15 high and 18 **f** in circumference.
7:16 Each capital was 7 ½ **f** high.
7:19 ⌊Each⌋ was six **f** high.
7:23 It was 15 **f** in diameter.
7:23 It was round, 7 ½ **f** high,
7:23 had a circumference of 45 **f**.
7:27 Each stand was 6 **f** square and
7:27 6 feet square and 4 ½ **f** high.
7:31 and was **t** feet ⌊wide⌋.
7:32 Each wheel was two **f** high.
7:38 Every basin was six **f** ⌊wide⌋.
2Ki 4:27 she took hold of his **f**.
4:37 immediately bowed at his **f**.
9:35 except her skull, **f**, and hands.
19:24 with the trampling of my **f**."
21:8 make Israel's **f** wander from
25:17 One pillar was 27 **f** high and
25:17 on it that was 4 ½ **f** high.
1Ch 28:2 would be a stool for our God's **f**,
2Ch 3:3 It was 90 **f** long and 35 feet
2Ch 3:3 was 90 feet long and 35 **f** wide.
3:4 room⌋ was 30 **f** wide (the same
3:4 of the temple) and 30 **f** high.
3:8 the temple was wide, 30 **f** long.
3:8 It was also 30 **f** wide.
3:11 of the angels' wings was 30 **f**.
3:11 of the angels was 7 ½ **f** long
3:11 Its other wing was 7 ½ **f** long
3:12 of the angels was 7 ½ **f** long
3:12 Its other wing was 7 ½ **f** long
3:12 combined wingspan was 30 **f**.
3:13 They stood on their **f** and faced
3:15 They were 53 **f** long,
3:15 each pillar was 7 ½ **f** ⌊high⌋.
4:1 made a bronze altar 30 **f** long,
4:1 30 **f** wide, and 15 feet high.
4:1 30 feet wide, and 15 **f** high.
4:2 It was 15 **f** in diameter.
4:2 It was round, 7 ½ **f** high,
4:2 had a circumference of 45 **f**.
6:13 a bronze platform 7 ½ **f** long,
6:13 7 ½ feet long, 7 ½ **f** wide,
6:13 ½ feet wide, and 4 ½ **f** high.
Ezr 6:3 It should be 90 **f** high and 90
6:3 be 90 feet high and 90 **f** wide
Neh 3:13 and they repaired 1,500 **f** of the
9:21 and their **f** didn't swell.
Est 5:14 "Have a pole set up, 75 **f** high,
8:3 She fell down at his **f** crying
Job 2:7 boils from the soles of his **f**
13:27 You put my **f** in shackles.
13:27 marks on the soles of my **f**.
18:8 His own **f** get him tangled in a
29:15 I was **f** for the lame person.
30:12 They trip my **f** and then prepare
31:5 with lies or my **f** have run after
33:11 He puts my **f** in the stocks and
Psa 9:15 Their **f** are caught in the net
17:5 My **f** have not slipped.
18:9 with a dark cloud under his **f**.
18:33 He makes my **f** like those of a
18:36 on so that my **f** do not slip.
18:38 They fell under my **f**.
18:39 my opponents bow at my **f**.
22:16 have pierced my hands and **f**.
25:15 He removes my **f** from traps.
26:12 My **f** stand on level ground.
31:8 You have set my **f** in a place
36:11 Do not let the **f** of arrogant
37:31 in his heart. His **f** do not slip.
40:2 He set my **f** on a rock and
44:18 Our **f** never left your path.
47:3 and ⌊puts⌋ nations under our **f**.
56:13 You have kept my **f** from
58:10 They will wash their **f** in the
68:23 may bathe your **f** in blood and
73:2 But my **f** had almost stumbled.
94:18 I said, "My **f** are slipping,"
105:18 They hurt his **f** with shackles,
115:7 They have **f**, but they cannot
116:8 ⌊and⌋ my **f** from stumbling.
119:59 and I have directed my **f** back
119:101 I have kept my **f** ⌊from
119:105 Your word is a lamp for my **f**
122:2 Our **f** are standing inside your
Pro 5:5 Her **f** descend to death.
6:18 **f** that are quick to do wrong,
6:28 coals without burning his **f**?
7:11 Her **f** will not stay at home.
26:6 a message cuts off his own **f**
Sos 5:3 I have washed my **f**!
7:1 How beautiful are your **f** in their
Isa 1:6 From the bottom of your **f** to the
3:16 the ankle bracelets on their **f**."
6:2 with two they covered their **f**,
26:6 **F** trample it, the feet of the
26:6 the **f** of the oppressed,
37:25 with the trampling of my **f**."
41:3 a path his **f** have never traveled
49:23 They will lick the dust at your **f**.
52:7 on the mountains are the **f**
59:7 Their **f** run to do evil.
60:13 the place where my **f** rest.
60:14 despise you will bow at your **f**.
Jer 2:25 Don't run until your **f** are bare
13:16 before your **f** stumble on the
Jer 14:10 They don't keep their **f** where
18:22 me and hid snares for my **f**.
38:22 Your **f** are stuck in the mud,
52:21 One pillar was 27 **f** high and 18
52:21 high and 18 **f** in circumference.
52:22 that was on it was 7 ½ **f** high
Lam 1:13 He spread a net for my **f**.
Eze 1:7 Their legs were straight, their **f**
2:2 entered me, stood me on my **f**,
3:24 me and stood me on my **f**.
6:11 stomp your **f**, and say, "Oh no!"
16:10 fine leather sandals on your **f**.
24:23 and your sandals on your **f**.
25:6 your hands and stomped your **f**.
32:2 stir up the water with your **f**.
32:13 The **f** of humans and the hoofs
34:18 rest of the pasture with your **f**?
34:18 rest of the water with your **f**?
34:19 Must my sheep eat what your **f**
34:19 what your **f** have muddied?
37:10 to life and stood on their **f**.
40:5 stick that was 10 ½ **f** long.
40:5 It was 10 ½ **f** thick and 10 ½
40:5 ½ feet thick and 10 ½ **f** high.
40:6 It was 10 ½ **f** wide.
40:7 Each guardroom was 10 ½ **f**
40:7 ½ feet long and 10 ½ **f** wide.
40:7 the guardrooms was 9 **f** thick.
40:7 the temple was 10 ½ **f** wide.
40:9 It extended 14 **f** from the
40:9 walls were 3 ½ **f** thick.
40:11 It was 17 ½ **f** wide,
40:11 and the gateway was 23 **f** long.
40:12 The guardrooms were 10 ½ **f**
40:13 It was 44 **f** wide from one door
40:14 It was 35 **f** wide. In front of the
40:15 the entrance hall was 87 ½ **f**.
40:19 It was 175 **f** from east to north.
40:21 The gateway was 87 ½ **f** long
40:21 87 ½ feet long and 44 **f** wide.
40:23 to the other gate. It was 175 **f**.
40:25 It was 87 ½ **f** long and 44 feet
40:25 It was 87 ½ feet long and 44 **f**
40:27 gateway. It was 175 **f**.
40:29 The gateway was 87 ½ **f** long
40:29 87 ½ feet long and 44 **f** wide.
40:30 They were all 44 **f** long and 9
40:30 all 44 feet long and 9 **f** wide.
40:33 The gateway was 87 ½ **f** long
40:33 87 ½ feet long and 44 **f** wide.
40:36 The gateway was 87 ½ **f** long
40:36 87 ½ feet long and 44 **f** wide.
40:42 They were 3 **f** long,
40:42 They were 3 feet long, 3 **f** wide,
40:47 It was a perfect square — 175 **f**
40:47 175 feet long and 175 **f** wide.
40:48 They were 9 **f** on each side.
40:48 gateway was 24 ½ **f** wide,
40:48 on each side were 5 **f** wide.
40:49 The entrance hall was 35 **f**
40:49 was 35 feet long and 21 **f** wide.
41:1 They were 10 ½ **f** wide on
41:2 entrance was 17 ½ **f** wide,
41:2 the walls were 9 **f** wide.
41:2 It was 70 **f** long and 35 feet
41:2 It was 70 feet long and 35 **f**
41:3 It was 3 ½ **f** thick.
41:3 The entrance was 10 ½ **f** high
41:3 10 ½ feet high and 12 **f** wide.
41:4 It was 35 **f** long and 35 feet
41:4 was 35 feet long and 35 **f** wide.
41:5 It was 10 ½ **f** wide.
41:5 around the temple was 7 **f**.
41:8 of the measuring rod, 10 ½ **f**.
41:9 of the side rooms was 9 **f** thick.
41:10 It was 35 **f** wide and went all
41:11 the open area was 9 **f** wide all
41:12 was a building 122 ½ **f** wide.
41:12 The wall of the building was 9 **f**
41:12 and it was 157 ½ **f** long.
41:13 It was 175 **f** long. This included
41:13 All together it was 175 **f** long.
41:14 was also 175 **f** wide.
41:15 It was 175 **f** long. The holy
41:22 5 **f** high and 3 ½ feet wide.
41:22 5 feet high and 3 ½ **f** wide.

Eze 42:2 that faced north was 175 **f** long
42:2 175 feet long and 87 ½ **f** wide.
42:3 an area that was 35 **f** wide,
42:4 17 ½ **f** wide and 175 feet long.
42:4 17 ½ feet wide and 175 **f** long.
42:7 the side rooms for 87 ½ **f**.
42:8 courtyard was 87 ½ **f** long.
42:8 the temple were 175 **f** long.
42:16 It was 875 **f** long according to
42:17 It was 875 **f** long according to
42:18 It was 875 **f** long according to
42:19 It was 875 **f** long according to
42:20 The wall was 875 **f** long and
42:20 875 feet long and 875 **f** wide.
43:7 and the place where my **f** rest.
43:14 lower ledge it was 3 ½ **f** high,
43:14 the upper ledge it was 7 **f** high
43:15 were burned was 7 **f** high.
43:16 21 **f** wide and 21 feet long.
43:16 21 feet wide and 21 **f** long.
43:17 It was 24 ½ **f** long and 24 ½
43:17 ½ feet long and 24 ½ **f** wide.
45:1 Set aside an area 43,750 **f** long
45:1 feet long and 35,000 **f** wide
45:2 An area of 875 **f** square will be
45:2 an open area 87 ½ **f** wide.
45:3 Measure off an area 43,750 **f**
45:3 feet long and 17,500 **f** wide.
45:5 An area 43,750 **f** long and
45:5 and 17,500 **f** wide will belong
45:6 designate an area 8,750 **f** wide
45:6 feet wide and 43,750 **f** long as
46:22 of the courtyard were 60 **f** long
46:22 60 feet long and 45 **f** wide.
48:8 It will be 43,750 **f** wide,
48:9 the LORD will be 43,750 **f** long
48:9 feet long and 17,500 **f** wide.
48:10 side it will be 43,750 **f** long.
48:10 side it will be 17,500 **f** wide.
48:10 side it will be 17,500 **f** wide.
48:10 side it will be 43,750 **f** long.
48:13 It will be 43,750 **f** long and
48:13 feet long and 17,500 **f** wide.
48:15 A strip of land, 8,750 **f** wide by
48:15 feet wide by 43,750 **f** long,
48:16 side it will be 7,875 **f** long.
48:16 side it will be 7,875 **f** long.
48:16 side it will be 7,875 **f** wide.
48:16 side it will be 7,875 **f** wide.
48:17 pastureland will be 4,375 **f**
48:17 4,375 **f** on the south,
48:17 4,375 **f** on the east,
48:17 and 4,375 **f** on the west.
48:18 This land will be 17,500 **f** on
48:18 on its east side and 17,500 **f**
48:20 The whole area will be 43,750 **f**
48:30 The north side will be 7,875 **f**
48:32 east side will be 7,875 **f** long.
48:33 south side will be 7,875 **f** long.
48:34 west side will be 7,875 **f** long.
48:35 will measure about 31,500 **f** all
Dan 2:33 Its **f** were made partly of iron
2:34 **f** and smashed them.
2:41 You also saw the **f** and toes.
3:1 made a gold statue 90 **f** high
3:1 90 feet high and 9 **f** wide.
3:24 He sprang to his **f**.
7:4 It was made to stand on two **f**
Nah 1:3 clouds are the dust from his **f**.
1:15 on the mountains are the **f**
Hab 3:19 He makes my **f** like those of a
Zec 5:2 "It's 30 **f** long and 15 feet wide."
5:2 "It's 30 feet long and 15 **f** wide."
14:4 On that day his **f** will stand on
14:12 they are standing on their **f**.
Mal 4:3 under the soles of your **f**," says
Mat 10:14 and shake its dust off your **f**.
15:30 They laid them at his **f**,
18:8 than to have two hands or two **f**
18:26 fell at his master's **f** and said,
18:29 that other servant fell at his **f**
22:13 'Tie his hands and **f**,
28:9 and took hold of his **f**.
Mar 5:4 and broke the chains from his **f**.
6:11 shake the dust from your **f** as
9:45 life lame than to have two **f**
Luk 7:38 and knelt at his **f**. She was
7:38 was crying and washed his **f**
7:38 Then she dried his **f** with her
7:44 You didn't wash my **f**.
7:44 But she has washed my **f** with
7:45 has not stopped kissing my **f**.
7:46 has poured perfume on my **f**.
8:35 he was sitting at Jesus' **f**.
9:5 and shake its dust off your **f** as
10:11 your city's dust from our **f**
10:39 Mary sat at the Lord's **f** and
15:22 his finger and sandals on his **f**.
17:16 He quickly bowed at Jesus' **f**
24:39 Look at my hands and **f**,
24:40 showed them his hands and **f**.
Jon 11:2 on the Lord and wiped his **f**
11:32 she knelt at his **f** and said,
11:44 wound around his **f** and hands,
12:3 nard and poured it on Jesus' **f**.
12:3 Then she dried his **f** with her
13:5 began to wash the disciples' **f**
13:6 are you going to wash my **f**?"
13:8 "You will never wash my **f**."
13:9 don't wash only my **f**.
13:10 to have only their **f** washed.
13:12 After Jesus had washed their **f**
13:14 have washed your **f**,
13:14 you must wash each other's **f**.
20:12 was where his **f** had been.
Act 3:7 Immediately, the man's **f** and
3:8 Springing to his **f**, he stood up
7:5 not even a place to rest his **f**.
13:51 shook the dust off their **f**
16:24 with their **f** in leg irons.
21:11 Paul's belt and tied his own **f**
27:28 It sank 120 **f**. They waited a
27:28 This time the line sank 90 **f**.
Rom 10:15 "How beautiful are the **f** of the
16:20 crush Satan under your **f**.
1Co 12:21 the head can't say to the **f**,
Jas 2:3 or "Sit on the floor at my **f**."
Rev 1:13 a robe that reached his **f**.
1:15 His **f** were like glowing bronze
1:17 I fell down at his **f** like a dead
2:18 and whose **f** are like glowing
3:9 come and bow at your **f**
10:1 and his **f** were like columns of
11:11 and they stood on their **f**.
12:1 who had the moon under her **f**
13:2 Its **f** were like bear's feet.
13:2 Its feet were like bear's **f**.
19:10 I bowed at his **f** to worship him.
22:8 I bowed to worship at the **f** of

Felix (11)

Act 23:24 take him safely to Governor **F**."
23:26 Your Excellency, Governor **F**:
24:2 He said to **F**, through your wise
24:22 **F** knew the way ⌊of Christ⌋
24:23 **F** ordered the sergeant to guard
24:24 Some days later **F** arrived with
24:25 **F** became afraid and said,
24:26 At the same time, **F** was
24:26 For that reason, **F** would send
24:27 (Since **F** wanted to do the
25:14 "**F** left a man here in prison.

Felix's (1)

Act 24:27 Porcius Festus took **F** place.

fell (83)

Gen 14:10 they **f** because of the tar pits,
41:5 He **f** asleep again and had a
Num 11:9 When dew **f** on the camp at
11:9 camp at night, manna **f** with it.)
Jos 2:8 Before the spies **f** asleep,
Jdg 5:27 He **f**. He lay between her feet!
5:27 He **f** between her feet.
5:27 Where he sank, he **f** dead.
7:13 turned upside down, and **f** flat."
16:4 After ⌊leaving Gaza⌋, he **f** in
16:30 and the building **f** on the rulers
1Sm 4:18 Eli **f** from his chair backwards
17:49 and he **f** to the ground on his
18:20 Saul's daughter Michal **f** in love
28:20 Saul **f** flat on the ground.
1Sm 31:4 Saul took the sword and **f** on it.
31:5 he also **f** on his sword and died
2Sm 2:16 and they **f** down together.
2:23 He **f** down there and died on
2:23 to the place where Asahel **f**
3:34 You **f** as one falls in front of
4:4 and he **f** ⌊from her arms⌋ and
11:17 **f** and died — including Uriah
13:1 After this, David's son Amnon **f**
22:39 They **f** under my feet.
1Ki 18:38 So a fire from the LORD **f** down
20:30 the city where the wall **f** on
2Ki 1:2 King Ahaziah **f** through
6:5 the ax head **f** into the water.
1Ch 10:4 Saul took the sword and **f** on it.
10:5 he also **f** on the sword and
2Ch 21:19 his intestines **f** out because of
Est 8:3 She **f** down at his feet crying
Job 1:16 "A fire from God **f** from heaven
1:19 It **f** on the young people,
1:20 Then he **f** to the ground and
29:22 my words **f** gently on them.
Psa 18:38 They **f** under my feet.
27:2 and enemies stumbled and **f**.
57:6 but then they **f** into it.
107:12 They **f** down, but no one was
Ecc 2:20 Then I **f** into despair over
11:3 the tree will remain where it **f**.
Lam 1:7 when its people **f** into the
Eze 23:7 those with whom she **f** in love.
23:16 She **f** in love with them at first
31:12 Its branches **f** on the
31:12 Its broken branches **f** in every
Dan 3:23 and Abednego — **f** into the
Mat 17:6 they heard this and **f** facedown
18:26 Then the servant **f** at his
18:29 "Then that other servant **f** at his
25:5 became drowsy and **f** asleep.
Mar 1:40 The man **f** to his knees and
9:20 He **f** on the ground,
14:35 After walking a little farther, he **f**
Luk 8:23 sailing along, Jesus **f** asleep.
8:28 he shouted, **f** in front of him,
13:4 the tower at Siloam **f** on them?
16:21 eaten any scraps that **f** from
Jon 18:6 away and **f** to the ground.
Act 1:18 of land where he **f** headfirst
9:4 He **f** to the ground and heard a
9:18 something like fish scales **f**
10:10 prepared, he **f** into a trance.
11:5 the city of Joppa when I **f** into
12:7 the chains **f** from Peter's hands.
19:35 statue that **f** down from Zeus.
20:9 overcome by sleep, he **f** from
22:7 I **f** to the ground and heard a
22:17 courtyard, I **f** into a trance
26:14 All of us **f** to the ground,
Rom 11:22 He is severe to those who **f**,
2Ti 4:10 He **f** in love with this present
Jas 5:17 no rain **f** on the ground for
Rev 1:17 When I saw him, I **f** down at
6:13 The stars **f** from the sky to the
8:10 star flaming like a torch **f** from
8:10 It **f** on one-third of the rivers and
11:11 Great fear **f** on those who
16:19 and the cities of the nations **f**.
16:21 Large, heavy hailstones **f** from
18:3 All the nations **f** because of the

fellowship (83)

Exo 20:24 offerings and your **f** offerings,
24:5 burnt offerings and **f** offerings
29:28 the LORD from the **f** offerings.
32:6 and brought **f** offerings.
Lev 3:1 "If your sacrifice is a **f** offering
3:6 "If your sacrifice is a **f** offering
3:9 Then take the fat from the **f**
3:11 Then the priest will burn the **f**
4:10 the bull used for the **f** offering.
4:26 fat of the **f** offering is burned.
4:31 is removed from the **f** offering.
4:35 is removed from the **f** offerings.
6:12 burn the fat of the **f** offering.
7:11 for the **f** offering that you
7:13 your **f** offering of thanksgiving.
7:14 the blood of the **f** offering.

Lev 7:15 "The meat from your **f** offering
7:18 meat from the **f** offering is eaten
7:20 LORD's **f** offering while unclean
7:21 eat the LORD's **f** offering must
7:29 LORD a **f** offering must bring
7:33 blood and fat of the **f** offering,
7:34 From the **f** offerings of the
7:37 offering, and the **f** offering.
9:4 a bull and a ram as a **f** offering,
9:18 ram for the people's **f** offering.
9:22 burnt offering, and the **f** offering
10:14 your part of the **f** offerings from
17:5 sacrifice them as **f** offerings
19:5 "When you bring a **f** offering to
22:21 may bring the LORD a **f** offering
23:19 lambs as a **f** offering.
Num 6:14 and a ram as a **f** offering.
6:17 He will sacrifice the ram as a **f**
6:18 and put it on the fire under the **f**
7:17 male lambs as a **f** offering.
7:23 male lambs as a **f** offering.
7:29 male lambs as a **f** offering.
7:35 male lambs as a **f** offering.
7:41 male lambs as a **f** offering.
7:47 male lambs as a **f** offering.
7:53 male lambs as a **f** offering.
7:59 male lambs as a **f** offering.
7:65 male lambs as a **f** offering.
7:71 male lambs as a **f** offering.
7:77 male lambs as a **f** offering.
7:83 male lambs as a **f** offering.
7:88 animals for **f** offerings was 24
10:10 burnt offerings and **f** offerings.
15:8 to keep a vow or as a **f** offering.
29:39 and your **f** offerings."
Dtr 27:7 Sacrifice **f** offerings,
Jos 8:31 LORD and sacrificed **f** offerings
22:23 grain offerings, or **f** offerings,
22:27 sacrifices, and **f** offerings.'
Jdg 20:26 burnt offerings and **f** offerings
21:4 burnt offerings and **f** offerings.
1Sm 10:8 offerings and make **f** offerings.
11:15 There they sacrificed **f**
13:9 offering and the **f** offerings."
2Sm 6:17 burnt offerings and **f** offerings
6:18 offerings and the **f** offerings,
24:25 burnt offerings and **f** offerings.
1Ki 3:15 burnt offerings and **f** offerings
8:63 120,000 sheep as **f** offerings
8:64 and the fat from the **f** offerings
9:25 burnt offerings and **f** offerings
2Ki 16:13 and sprinkled the blood of his **f**
1Ch 16:1 burnt offerings and **f** offerings
16:2 burnt offerings and **f** offerings,
21:26 burnt offerings and **f** offerings.
2Ch 29:35 to the fat of the **f** offerings
30:22 sacrificed **f** offerings,
31:2 sacrificing **f** offerings,
33:16 altar and sacrificed **f** offerings
Eze 43:27 burnt offerings and **f** offerings
45:15 and **f** offerings to make peace
45:17 and **f** offerings to make peace
46:2 burnt offerings and **f** offerings.
46:12 either a burnt offering or a **f**
46:12 offerings and **f** offerings as
Amo 5:22 I won't even look at the **f**
Act 2:42 to **f**, to the breaking of bread,

felt (37)

Gen 27:22 Isaac **f** ⌊his skin⌋.
34:7 The men **f** outraged and very
Exo 2:6 and she **f** sorry for him.
10:21 that it can be **f** will come over
17:12 Moses' hands **f** heavy.
Num 13:33 We **f** as small as grasshoppers,
Jdg 16:29 Samson **f** the two middle
21:6 The people of Israel **f** sorry for
21:15 The congregation **f** sorry for
1Sm 13:12 I **f** pressured into sacrificing the
16:23 ⌊from his terror⌋ and **f** better,
22:8 No one **f** sorry for me and
2Sm 13:15 than the lust he had **f** for her.
18:11 Then I would have **f** obligated
18:12 "Even if I **f** the weight of 25
Neh 9:28 As soon as they **f** some relief,
Eze 16:5 No one who saw you **f** sorry
25:6 You rejoiced and **f** contempt for
Mat 9:36 he **f** sorry for them.
14:14 He **f** sorry for them and cured
18:27 "The master **f** sorry for his
18:31 had happened and **f** very sad.
20:34 Jesus **f** sorry for them,
Mar 1:41 Jesus **f** sorry for him,
5:29 She **f** cured from her illness.
5:30 At that moment Jesus **f** power
6:34 he saw a large crowd and **f**
Luk 1:41 she **f** the baby kick.
1:44 I **f** the baby jump for joy.
7:13 Lord saw her, he **f** sorry for her.
10:33 he **f** sorry for the man,
13:17 who opposed him **f** ashamed.
15:20 his father saw him and **f** sorry
Jon 21:17 Peter **f** sad because Jesus had
Act 28:15 thanked God and **f** encouraged.
2Co 13:3 makes his power **f** among you.
1Th 2:8 We **f** so strongly about you that

female (81)

Gen 1:27 He created them male and **f**.
5:2 He created them male and **f**.
6:19 They must be male and **f**.
7:2 of clean animal (a male and a **f**
7:2 animal (a male and a **f**).
7:3 kind of bird (a male and a **f**
7:9 the ship in pairs (a male and **f**
7:16 A male and a **f** of every animal
12:16 male and **f** slaves,
15:9 a three-year-old **f** goat,
20:14 and male and **f** slaves and
20:17 and his **f** slaves so that they
21:28 set apart seven **f** lambs from
21:29 these seven **f** lambs you have
24:35 male and **f** slaves,
30:35 all the speckled and spotted **f**
30:43 male and **f** slaves,
32:5 and male and **f** slaves.
32:14 200 **f** goats and 20 male goats,
32:14 200 **f** sheep and 20 male
32:15 30 **f** camels with their young,
32:15 20 **f** donkeys and 10 male
45:23 ten **f** donkeys carrying grain,
Exo 11:5 to the firstborn children of **f**
20:10 your male and **f** slaves,
20:17 his male or **f** slave,
21:20 owner hits his male or **f** slave
21:26 owner hits his male or **f** slave
21:27 the tooth of his male or **f** slave,
21:32 the bull gores a male or **f** slave,
Lev 3:1 it must be a male or **f** animal
3:6 you must bring a male or **f**
4:28 he must bring a **f** goat that has
4:32 he must bring a **f** that has no
5:6 It must be a **f** sheep or goat as
14:10 a one-year-old **f** lamb that has
19:20 with a **f** slave who is
25:6 your male and **f** slaves,
25:44 may have male and **f** slaves,
Num 6:14 a one-year-old **f** lamb as an
15:27 a one-year-old **f** goat must be
Dtr 5:14 your male and **f** slaves,
5:14 In this way your male and **f**
5:21 his male or **f** slave,
12:12 male and **f** slaves,
12:18 male and **f** slaves,
15:17 Do the same to a **f** slave ⌊if
16:11 male and **f** slaves,
16:14 male and **f** slaves,
Jdg 21:11 Claim every **f** who has gone to
1Sm 8:16 take your male and **f** slaves,
25:42 of her **f** servants following her.
2Sm 12:3 had only one little **f** lamb that
2Ch 15:13 male or **f**) who refused to
35:25 All the male and **f** singers still
Ezr 2:65 In addition to the male and **f**
2:65 they also had 200 male and **f**
Neh 6:14 Also, remember the **f** prophet
7:67 In addition to the male and **f**
7:67 they also had 245 male and **f**
Est 2:9 and seven suitable **f** servants
Job 19:15 My **f** slaves consider me to be
31:13 rights of my servants, male or **f**,
Psa 86:16 I am the son of your **f** servant.
116:16 the son of your **f** servant.
Pro 31:15 portions of food to her **f** slaves.
Ecc 2:7 I bought male and **f** slaves.
2:8 myself with male and **f** singers
Isa 14:2 nations as male and **f** slaves
24:2 **f** slaves and masters,
Jer 34:9 slaves, both male and **f**.
34:10 to free their male and **f** slaves
34:16 the male and **f** slaves that you
34:16 your male and **f** slaves again.
Mat 19:4 male and **f** in the beginning
26:69 A **f** servant came to him and
26:71 another **f** servant saw him.
Mar 10:6 But God made them male and **f**
14:66 One of the chief priest's **f**
Luk 22:56 A **f** servant saw him as he sat
Act 16:16 a **f** servant met us.

females (1)

Gal 3:28 nor free people, males nor **f**.

fence (3)

Job 1:10 put a protective **f** around him,
Psa 62:3 a leaning wall or a sagging **f**?
Pro 24:31 and its stone **f** was torn down.

fenced (1)

Job 3:23 to those whom God has **f** in?

fenced-off (1)

Zep 2:6 and **f** places for sheep.

fences (5)

Num 32:16 "Allow us to build stone **f** for
32:24 for your families and stone **f**
32:36 built stone **f** for their flocks.
Psa 80:12 the stone **f** around this vine?
Nah 3:17 that settle on the **f** when

ferocious (6)

Num 23:24 like a lioness and is as **f** as
Job 4:10 the growl of the **f** lion ⌊is loud⌋,
10:16 **f** lion you hunt me down.
28:8 No **f** lion has ever passed over
Psa 22:13 their mouths to attack me like **f**,
Pro 26:13 "There's a **f** lion out on the road!

fertile (33)

Gen 1:22 said, "Be **f**, increase in number,
1:28 said, "Be **f**, increase in number,
8:17 Be **f**, increase in number,
9:1 "Be **f**, increase in number,
9:7 Be **f**, and increase in number.
17:20 I will bless him, make him **f**,
27:28 **f** fields on the earth,
27:39 you live will lack the **f** fields
28:3 bless you, make you **f**,
35:11 Be **f**, and increase in number.
48:4 said to me, 'I will make you **f**
2Ki 19:23 borders and its most **f** forests.
2Ch 26:10 the mountains and the **f** fields
Neh 9:35 **f** land which was set in front of
Job 21:10 Their bulls are **f** when they
Psa 107:34 and **f** ground into a layer of salt
Isa 5:1 had a vineyard on a **f** hill.
22:7 Then your **f** valleys will be
28:1 They are at the entrance to a **f**
28:4 are at the entrance to a **f** valley.
29:17 will be turned into a **f** field
29:17 a fertile field and the **f** field will
32:15 will be turned into a **f** field,
32:15 and the **f** field will be
32:16 will be at home in the **f** field.
37:24 heights and its most **f** forests.
Jer 2:7 I brought them into a **f** land to
3:16 In those days you will be **f**,
4:26 I see that the **f** land has
23:3 and they will be **f** and increase
49:4 your valleys, your **f** valleys,
Eze 17:5 planted the seedling in **f** soil.
Mic 7:14 in the woods, in **f** pastures.

fertilize (2)

Psa 83:10 became manure to **f** the ground.
Luk 13:8 I'll dig around it and **f** it.

fester (1)

Psa 38:5 They **f** because of my stupidity.

festival (121)

Exo 5:1 to celebrate a **f** in my honor."
10:9 For us it's a pilgrimage **f** in the
12:14 this day as a pilgrimage **f**
12:17 You must celebrate the **F** of
13:6 day will be a pilgrimage **f**
13:9 This ⌊**f**⌋ will be ⌊like⌋ a mark
13:16 So this ⌊**f**⌋ will be ⌊like⌋ a
23:14 a pilgrimage **f** in my honor.
23:15 "Celebrate the **F** of
23:16 "Celebrate the **F** of the Harvest
23:16 "Celebrate the **F** of the Final
32:5 "Tomorrow there will be a **f** in
34:18 "You must celebrate the **F** of
34:22 "You must celebrate the **F** of
34:22 and the **F** of the Final Harvest
34:25 at the Passover **F** should
Lev 16:31 important worship **f** there is
23:6 same month is the LORD's **F**
23:24 month hold a worship **f**.
23:34 of this seventh month is the **F**
23:36 This is the last **f** of the year.
23:39 celebrate the LORD's **f** for
23:41 It is the LORD's **f**. Celebrate it
23:41 Celebrate this **f** in the seventh
25:4 the seventh year will be a **f**
25:5 year will be a **f** for the land.
Num 10:10 Also, on your **f** days and on the
15:3 or as one of your **f** offerings.
28:17 same month is a pilgrimage **f**.
28:26 "During the **F** of Weeks,
29:12 Instead, celebrate a **f** to the
Dtr 16:3 eat unleavened bread at this **f**.
16:10 Then celebrate the **F** of Weeks
16:13 celebrate the **F** of Booths for
16:14 Enjoy yourselves at the **f** along
16:15 will celebrate this **f** dedicated
16:16 at the **F** of Unleavened Bread,
16:16 Bread, the **F** of Weeks,
16:16 and the **F** of Booths.
31:10 during the **F** of Booths,
Jdg 21:19 "Every year the LORD's **f** is
1Sm 20:5 "Tomorrow is the New Moon **F**,
20:18 Moon **F**," Jonathan told him,
20:24 When the New Moon **F** came,
20:24 King Saul sat down to eat the **f**
1Ki 8:2 Solomon at the **F** ⌊of Booths⌋
8:65 celebrated the **F** ⌊of Booths⌋.
12:32 Jeroboam appointed a **f** on the
12:32 just like the **f** in Judah.
12:33 ⌊the **f**⌋ he had invented for the
2Ki 4:23 It isn't a New Moon **F** or a day
2Ch 5:3 the king at the **F** ⌊of Booths⌋
7:8 celebrated the **F** ⌊of Booths⌋.
7:9 days and celebrated the **f**
8:13 the three annual festivals (the **F**
8:13 Bread, the **F** of Weeks,
8:13 and the **F** of Booths) as Moses
30:13 in Jerusalem to celebrate the **F**
30:21 in Jerusalem celebrated the **F**
30:22 They ate the **f** meals for seven
30:23 decided to celebrate the **f**
35:17 They also celebrated the **F** of
Ezr 3:4 celebrated the **F** of Booths.
3:5 offerings for the New Moon **F**
6:22 days they celebrated the **F**
Neh 8:14 should live in booths during a **f**
8:18 from the first day of the **f** to the
8:18 The people celebrated the **f** for
8:18 they had a closing **f** assembly
Psa 42:4 of people celebrated a **f**.
55:14 God's house with the **f** crowds.
68:24 Your **f** processions,
81:3 of the full moon, on our **f** days.
118:27 March in a **f** procession with
Isa 30:29 the song you sing on a **f** night.
Lam 2:7 as though it were a **f** day.
2:22 though they were invited to a **f**.
Eze 45:21 a **f** lasting seven days when
45:23 during the seven days of the **f**,
45:25 at the **F** of Booths,
46:1 be opened on the New Moon **F**.
46:11 "'On **f** days and at appointed
Hos 9:5 do on the day of an appointed **f**
9:5 or on the LORD's **f** days?
Amo 8:5 "When will the New Moon **F**
Zec 14:16 to celebrate the **F** of Booths.
14:18 to celebrate the **F** of Booths.
14:19 go to celebrate the **F** of Booths.
Mal 2:3 from your **f** sacrifices.
Mat 26:5 shouldn't arrest him during the **f**
26:17 On the first day of the **F** of
27:15 At every Passover **f** the
Mar 14:1 before the Passover and the **F**
14:2 shouldn't arrest him during the **f**
14:12 on the first day of the **F**
15:6 At every Passover **f**,
Luk 2:41 to Jerusalem for the Passover **f**.
2:43 When the **f** was over,
22:1 The **F** of Unleavened Bread,
22:7 The day came during the **F** of
Jon 2:23 in Jerusalem at the Passover **f**,
4:45 had done at the **f** in Jerusalem,
4:45 had attended the **f**.
5:1 to Jerusalem for a Jewish **f**.
6:4 Jewish Passover **f** was near.
7:2 The time for the Jewish **F** of
7:8 Go to the **f**. I'm not going to this
7:8 I'm not going to this **f** right now.
7:10 his brothers had gone to the **f**,
7:11 for Jesus in the crowd at the **f**.
7:14 When the **f** was half over,
7:37 and most important day of the **f**,
10:22 The **F** of the Dedication of the
11:56 he'll avoid coming to the **f**?"
12:12 the Passover **f** heard that Jesus
12:20 worship during the Passover **f**.
13:1 Before the Passover **f**,
13:29 buy what they needed for the **f**
19:14 on the Friday of the Passover **f**.
Act 20:6 After the **F** of Unleavened
1Co 5:8 So we must not celebrate our **f**

festivals (48)

Gen 1:14 signs and will mark religious **f**,
Exo 23:18 The fat sacrificed at my **f**
34:24 times a year to the LORD's **f**.
Lev 23:2 These are the appointed **f** with
23:4 are the LORD's appointed **f**
23:37 are the LORD's appointed **f**.
23:39 eighth days will be worship **f**.
23:44 about the LORD's appointed **f**.
Num 29:39 bring to the LORD at your **f**.
1Ch 23:31 worship days, at New Moon **F**,
23:31 and on appointed annual **f**.
2Ch 2:4 worship days, New Moon **F**,
2:4 and during the annual **f**
2:4 (⌊These **f**⌋ are always to be
8:13 on the New Moon **F**,
8:13 and on the three annual **f** (the
31:3 days, the New Moon **F**,
31:3 Festivals, and the annual **f**,
Ezr 3:5 Festival and all the other holy **f**
Neh 10:33 and on the New Moon **F**,
10:33 and at the appointed annual **f**,
Isa 1:13 so are your New Moon **F**,
1:14 I hate your New Moon **F** and
1:14 Festivals and your appointed **f**.
29:1 Let your annual **f** go on.
33:20 Look at Zion, the city of our **f**.
Lam 1:4 No one comes to the annual **f**.
2:6 and destroyed his own **f**.
2:6 wiped out the memory of **f**
Eze 36:38 during the appointed **f**.
44:24 and my regulations at all my **f**.
45:17 wine offerings at the annual **f**,
45:17 festivals, the New Moon **F**,
45:17 and all the other appointed **f** of
46:3 worship and on New Moon **F**.
46:9 at the time of the appointed **f**.
46:11 days and at appointed **f**,
Hos 2:11 her celebrations: her annual **f**,
2:11 festivals, her New Moon **F**,
2:11 days — all her appointed **f**.
5:7 Now their New Moon ⌊**F**⌋ will
12:9 you did during your appointed **f**.
Amo 5:21 I hate your **f**; I despise them.
8:10 I will turn your **f** into funerals
Nah 1:15 Celebrate your **f**, Judah!
Zep 3:18 are troubled because of the **f**.
Zec 8:19 occasions as well as happy **f**
Col 2:16 holy days, New Moon **F**,

festivities (1)

Gen 29:27 Finish the week of wedding **f**

Festus (18)

Act 25:1 Three days after **F** took over
25:2 informed **F** about their charges
25:3 **F** to do them the favor of
25:4 **F** replied that he would be
25:6 **F** stayed in Jerusalem for eight
25:6 The next day **F** took his place
25:9 But **F** wanted to do the Jews a
25:12 **F** discussed the appeal with
25:13 city of Caesarea to welcome **F**.
25:14 **F** told the king about Paul's
25:14 **F** said, "Felix left a man here
25:22 Agrippa told **F**, "I would like to
25:22 **F** replied, "You'll hear him
25:23 **F** gave the order, and Paul was
25:24 Then **F** said, "King Agrippa
26:24 **F** shouted, "Paul, you're crazy!
26:25 Your Excellency **F**.
26:32 Agrippa told **F**, "This man

fetus (2)

Psa 139:16 saw me when I was only a **f**.
1Co 15:8 I'm like an aborted **f** ⌊who was

fever (11)

Lev 26:16 you with disease and **f**.
Dtr 28:22 disease, **f**, and inflammation;
Job 30:30 My body burns with **f**.
Mat 8:14 mother-in-law in bed with a **f**.
8:15 and the **f** went away.
Mar 1:30 was in bed with a **f**.
1:31 The **f** went away, and she
Luk 4:38 was sick with a high **f**.
4:39 ordered the **f** to leave,
Jon 4:52 His servants told him, "The **f**
Act 28:8 suffering from **f** and dysentery.

field (185)

Gen 23:9 that he owns at the end of his **f**.
23:11 I'm giving you the **f** together
23:13 I will pay you the price of the **f**.
23:17 So Ephron's **f** at Machpelah,
23:18 His property included the **f** with
23:18 inside the boundaries of the **f**.
23:19 the cave in the **f** of Machpelah,
23:20 So the **f** and its cave were sold
24:63 went out into the **f** to meditate.
24:65 over there coming through the **f**
25:9 of Machpelah in the **f** of Ephron,
25:10 This was the **f** that Abraham
29:2 He looked around, and out in a **f**
37:7 grain into bundles out in the **f**,
49:29 ancestors in the cave in the **f**
49:30 that is in the **f** of Machpelah,
49:32 The **f** and the cave in it were
50:13 the cave in the **f** of Machpelah,
Exo 22:5 lets his livestock graze in a **f**
22:5 and graze in another person's **f**,
22:5 the damaged **f** was expected
22:5 if he lets them ruin the whole **f**
22:5 must make up from his own **f**
22:5 best from his **f** and vineyard.
22:6 or standing grain or ruins a **f**,
Lev 19:19 two kinds of crops in your **f**.
25:12 eat what the **f** itself produces.
25:34 But a **f** that belongs to their
26:4 and the trees in the **f** will
27:16 "If a person gives part of a **f** to
27:17 If you give your **f** in the jubilee
27:18 But if you give the **f** after the
27:21 When the **f** is released in the
27:21 it will be holy like a **f** claimed
27:22 You may give a **f** you bought
27:24 In the jubilee year the **f** will go
27:28 or a **f** that belongs to you —
Num 22:4 an ox eats up the grass in a **f**."
22:23 turned off the road into a **f**.

Num 23:14 So he took him to the **F** of
Dtr 5:21 his **f**, his male or female slave,
20:19 because the trees of the **f** are
21:1 find a murder victim lying in a **f**
23:25 go into your neighbor's grain **f**,
24:19 harvesting wheat in your **f**.
Jos 15:18 him to ask her father for a **f**.
Jdg 1:14 him to ask her father for a **f**.
Rut 2:2 "Please let me go to the **f** of
2:3 She entered a **f** and gathered
2:3 in the part of the **f** that belonged
2:8 Don't go in any other **f** to gather
2:9 the young women in that **f**.
2:17 grain in the **f** until evening.
2:22 If you go to someone else's **f**,
4:3 is selling the **f** that belonged to
4:5 you buy the **f** from Naomi,
1Sm 4:2 about 4,000 soldiers in the **f**.
6:14 The cart came into the **f** of
6:18 It is still there today in the **f** of
11:5 from the **f** behind some oxen.
14:15 panic among the army in the **f**
19:3 father in the **f** where you'll be.
2Sm 2:16 is called the **F** of Enemies.
11:11 mercenaries are living in the **f**.
11:23 and came to attack us in the **f**.
14:6 sons who quarreled in the **f**,
14:30 Joab's **f** is next to mine.
14:30 have set ⌊your⌋ **f** on fire."
14:31 your servants set my **f** on fire?"
20:12 Amasa from the road to the **f**
23:11 where there was a **f** of ripe
23:12 he stood in the middle of the **f**
2Ki 3:25 rocks on every good **f** until
4:39 One of them went into the **f** to
9:21 They found him in the **f** that
9:25 and throw him into the **f** that
9:26 pay you back in this **f**,' declares
9:26 him and throw him into the **f** as
18:17 and his **f** commander with a
18:17 the road to the Laundryman's **F**.
18:18 went out to the **f** commander.
18:26 Joah said to the **f** commander,
18:27 But the **f** commander asked
18:28 Then the **f** commander stood
18:37 from the **f** commander.
19:4 the words of the **f** commander.
19:8 The **f** commander returned and
19:26 They will be like plants in the **f**,
23:4 Jerusalem in an open **f** near
1Ch 11:13 There was a **f** of ripe barley.
11:14 they stood in the middle of the **f**
2Ch 26:23 in a **f** containing tombs that
Job 5:23 with the stones in the **f**,
24:6 in the **f** ⌊to feed themselves⌋.
Psa 103:15 blossoms like a flower in the **f**.
Pro 24:27 ready for yourself in the **f**.
24:30 I passed by a lazy person's **f**,
27:26 the male goats will buy a **f**.
31:16 "She picks out a **f** and buys it.
Ecc 11:6 You don't know whether this **f**
11:6 whether this field or that **f** will
Sos 2:7 the does in the **f** that you will
3:5 gazelles or by the does in the **f**,
7:11 Let's go into the **f**. Let's spend
Isa 1:8 like a shack in a cucumber **f**,
5:8 house and buy **f** after field until
5:8 field after **f** until there's nothing
7:3 the road to the Laundryman's **F**.
29:17 will be turned into a fertile **f**
29:17 fertile field and the fertile **f** will
32:15 will be turned into a fertile **f**,
32:15 and the fertile **f** will be
32:16 will be at home in the fertile **f**.
36:2 Assyria sent his **f** commander
36:2 on the road to Laundryman's **F**.
36:3 went out to the **f** commander.
36:11 Joah said to the **f** commander,
36:12 But the **f** commander asked,
36:13 Then the **f** commander stood
36:22 from the **f** commander.
37:4 the words of the **f** commander.
37:8 The **f** commander returned and
37:27 They will be like plants in the **f**,
40:6 beauty is like a flower in the **f**.
56:9 All you animals in the **f**,

Jer 4:17 them like men guarding a **f**,
6:25 Don't go into the **f** or walk on
9:22 will fall like manure on the **f**.
12:4 in every **f** remain dried up?
12:9 gather all the animals in the **f**,
14:18 If I go to the **f**, I see those killed
26:18 Zion will be plowed like a **f**,
32:7 "Buy my **f** that is in Anathoth,
32:8 to me, 'Please buy my **f** that is
32:9 "So I bought the **f** in Anathoth
32:9 The **f** cost seven ounces of
32:25 told me to buy a **f** with money
40:7 who were in the **f** heard that
Eze 7:15 Whoever is in a **f** will die in
16:5 you were thrown into an open **f**.
16:7 you grow like a plant in the **f**.
17:24 Then all the trees in the **f** will
29:5 You will fall in an open **f**.
31:5 than all the other trees in the **f**.
31:15 and all the trees in the **f** fainted
32:4 and toss you into an open **f**.
33:27 Whoever is in the open **f** will
34:27 Then the trees in the **f** will
39:5 You will die in the open **f**
39:10 not need to get wood from the **f**
Dan 4:15 chain in the grass in the **f**.
4:23 chain in the grass in the **f**.
Hos 8:7 A **f** of grain that doesn't ripen
10:4 weeds in the furrows of a **f**.
12:11 of rubble beside a plowed **f**.
Joe 1:11 harvest is destroyed in the **f**.
Amo 4:7 One **f** had rain. Another field
4:7 Another **f** had none and dried
Mic 3:12 Zion will be plowed like a **f**,
Zec 10:1 showers for the plants in the **f**.
Mat 6:28 how the flowers grow in the **f**.
6:30 God clothes the grass in the **f**.
13:24 who planted good seed in his **f**.
13:25 in the wheat **f** and went away.
13:27 you plant good seed in your **f**?
13:31 that someone planted in a **f**.
13:36 of the weeds in the **f** means."
13:38 The **f** is the world.
13:44 is like a treasure buried in a **f**.
13:44 he had, and bought that **f**.
24:18 Those who are in the **f** should
24:40 men will be working in the **f**.
27:7 to use it to buy a potter's **f**
27:8 That's why that **f** has been
27:8 that field has been called the **F**
27:10 the coins to buy a potter's **f**,
Mar 13:16 Those who are in the **f** should
Luk 12:28 God clothes the grass in the **f**.
14:18 first said to him, 'I bought a **f**,
15:25 "His older son was in the **f**.
17:7 when he comes from the **f**,
17:31 are in the **f** shouldn't turn back.
Act 1:19 which means '**F** of Blood' in
1Co 3:9 You are God's **f**. You are God's
1Pe 1:24 beauty is like a flower of the **f**.

field's (1)

Lev 27:23 must figure out the **f** value until

fields (119)

Gen 4:8 Later, when they were in the **f**,
27:28 fertile **f** on the earth,
27:39 you live will lack the fertile **f**
30:14 Reuben went out into the **f**
30:16 in from the **f** that evening,
34:28 was in the city or out in the **f**.
39:5 in his house and in his **f**.
41:48 put the food from the **f** around it.
47:20 Every Egyptian sold his **f**
47:24 yours to use as seed for your **f**
Exo 1:14 and every kind of work in the **f**.
8:13 in the yards, and in the **f**.
9:22 every plant in the **f** of Egypt."
9:25 and every plant in the **f** and
9:25 destroyed every tree in the **f**.
10:5 every tree still standing in the **f**.
23:10 in your **f** and harvest them,
23:16 whatever you plant in your **f**.
23:16 harvest your crops from the **f**.
Lev 17:5 have been making in the open **f**
19:9 the grain in the corners of your **f**

Lev 23:22 the grain in the corners of your **f**
25:3 you may plant crops in your **f**,
25:4 Don't plant crops in your **f** or
25:31 regarded as belonging to the **f**
Num 16:14 and honey or given us any **f**
20:17 any of your **f** or vineyards,
21:22 won't go through any of your **f**
28:26 produce harvested from your **f**.
Dtr 11:15 I will provide grass in the **f** for
14:22 whatever you plant in your **f**.
26:2 produce harvested from the **f**
26:10 from the **f** you gave me,
28:38 will plant many crops in your **f**,
28:42 trees and the crops in your **f**.
28:51 your **f** until you're destroyed.
32:13 them with the produce of the **f**.
32:32 and from the **f** of Gomorrah.
Jos 8:24 all the inhabitants of Ai in the **f**
21:12 But they gave its **f** and villages
Jdg 9:32 in the **f** ⌊around Shechem⌋.
9:42 ⌊of Shechem⌋ went into the **f**.
9:43 and set an ambush in the **f**.
9:44 in the **f** and attacked them.
13:9 she was sitting out in the **f**.
15:5 foxes in the Philistines' grain **f**.
15:5 it was stacked or in the **f**.
19:16 the city from his work in the **f**.
Rut 2:22 that you go out to the **f** with his
1Sm 8:14 He will take the best of your **f**,
22:7 one of you **f** and vineyards?
25:15 them when we were in the **f**.
2Ki 9:37 in the **f** surrounding Jezreel so
1Ch 6:56 but the **f** belonging to the city
16:32 Let the **f** and everything in them
27:25 of Adiel for the goods in the **f**,
27:26 for the farm workers in the **f**:
2Ch 26:10 the mountains and the fertile **f**
31:5 and every crop from the **f**.
Neh 5:3 "We've had to mortgage our **f**,
5:4 taxes on our **f** and vineyards.
5:5 do anything else when our **f**
5:11 You must return their **f**,
10:31 we won't plant the **f** or collect
10:37 of the produce from our **f**,
11:25 lived in villages that had **f**.
11:30 in Lachish and its **f**,
12:44 and Levites from the **f** around
13:10 had left for their own **f**.
Job 5:10 earth and sends water to the **f**.
Psa 50:11 that moves in the **f** is mine.
65:10 You drench plowed **f** ⌊with
78:12 land of Egypt, in the **f** of Zoan.
78:43 his wonders in the **f** of Zoan.
96:12 Let the **f** and everything in them
105:35 devoured the crops in the **f**.
107:37 They plant in **f** and vineyards
129:3 my back ⌊like farmers plow **f**⌋.
144:13 tens of thousands in our **f**.
Pro 8:26 he had not yet made land or **f**
23:10 marker or enter **f** that belong
Ecc 5:9 for a country with cultivated **f**.
Isa 1:7 Your **f** are destroyed right
1:7 Your **f** are devastated and
16:8 The **f** of Heshbon and the
19:7 and all the **f** planted beside the
32:10 will be brought in ⌊from the **f**⌋.
32:12 breasts as you mourn for the **f**,
61:5 will work your **f** and vineyards.
Jer 4:3 Plow your unplowed **f**,
6:12 Their households, their **f**,
8:10 wives to other men and their **f**
13:27 on the hills and in the **f**.
14:5 Even deer in the **f** give birth
32:15 **f**, and vineyards in this land.'
32:43 once again buy **f** in this land.
32:44 They will buy **f** for money,
35:7 or plant any **f** or vineyards.
48:33 the orchards and **f** of Moab.
Lam 4:9 there is nothing in the **f** to eat.
Eze 36:30 crops grow in the **f** so that you
Hos 5:7 will devour them and their **f**.
Joe 1:10 Israel's **f** are ruined,
Mic 2:2 They desire ⌊other people's⌋ **f**,
2:4 our **f** among our captors."
4:10 the city, live in the open **f**,
Hab 3:17 produce and the **f** yield no food,

Mal 3:11 The vines in your **f** will not
Mat 19:29 or **f** because of my name will
22:5 went to work in their own **f**,
Mar 10:29 or **f** because of me and the
10:30 sisters, mothers, children and **f**,
11:8 cut leafy branches in the **f**
Luk 2:8 were in the **f** near Bethlehem.
15:15 was sent to feed pigs in the **f**.
17:7 has a servant who is plowing **f**
21:21 Those of you in the **f** shouldn't
Jon 4:35 and see that the **f** are ready
Jas 5:4 your **f** shout to God

fierce (24)

Gen 49:7 be cursed because it's so **f**.
Dtr 29:23 cities the LORD destroyed in **f**
29:28 In his **f** anger and fury the
Jdg 20:34 The battle was **f**. But
2Sm 2:17 **F** fighting broke out that day,
17:8 They are warriors as **f** as a
1Ki 19:11 a **f** wind tore mountains and
2Ki 22:13 The LORD's **f** anger is directed
2Ch 34:21 The LORD's **f** anger has been
Psa 59:3 **F** men attack me, O LORD,
Isa 7:4 heart because of the **f** anger
13:9 cruel day with fury and **f** anger.
27:1 day the LORD will use his **f**
27:8 He removed it with a **f** blast
Lam 1:12 suffer on the day of his **f** anger.
2:6 priests because of his **f** anger.
Eze 5:15 my anger, fury, and **f** revenge,
25:17 I will take **f** revenge on them
Hab 1:6 that **f** and reckless nation.
Act 15:2 Paul and Barnabas had a **f**
20:29 I know that **f** wolves will come
Rev 12:12 down to them with **f** anger,
16:19 cup of wine from his **f** anger.
19:15 the winepress of the **f** anger

fierce-looking (1)

Dtr 28:50 Its people will be **f**.

fiercely (3)

Lev 26:28 I will **f** resist you. I will
Jer 6:29 of the blast furnace blow **f**
Zec 8:2 I am **f** possessive of it.

fiery (29)

2Ki 2:11 a **f** chariot with fiery horses
2:11 a fiery chariot with **f** horses
6:17 full of **f** horses and chariots.
Psa 78:14 day and by a **f** light throughout
105:19 him through **f** trials until his
Isa 14:29 will be a flying, **f** serpent.
Eze 21:31 breathe on you with my **f** anger.
22:20 to melt them with a **f** blast.
22:21 breathe on you with my **f** anger,
22:31 and with my **f** anger I will
28:14 You walked among **f** stones.
28:16 you out from the **f** stones.
36:5 In my **f** anger I have spoken
38:19 In my **f** anger I tell you this.
Dan 7:9 His throne was **f** flames,
Nah 2:3 on his chariots flashes **f** red,
Zep 1:18 be consumed by his **f** anger,
3:8 will be consumed by my **f** fury.
1Pe 4:12 don't be surprised by the **f**
Rev 6:4 It was **f** red. Its rider was given
9:17 breastplates that were **f** red,
12:3 a huge **f** red serpent with seven
14:10 Then he will be tortured by **f**
19:20 thrown alive into the **f** lake
20:10 was thrown into the **f** lake of
20:14 hell were thrown into the **f** lake.
20:14 (The **f** lake is the second
20:15 Life were thrown into the **f** lake.
21:8 find themselves in the **f** lake

fifteenth (18)

Exo 16:1 This was on the **f** day of the
Lev 23:6 The **f** day of this same month
23:34 "Tell the Israelites: The **f** day
23:39 "However, on the **f** day of the
Num 28:17 The **f** of this same month is a
29:12 "On the **f** day of the seventh
33:3 from Rameses on the **f** day
1Ki 12:32 a festival on the **f** day
12:33 to burn an offering on the **f** day
2Ki 14:23 was in his **f** year as king
1Ch 24:14 the **f** for Bilgah, the sixteenth
25:22 The **f** chose Jeremoth,
2Ch 15:10 In the third month of the **f** year
Est 9:18 They rested on the **f** and made
9:21 the fourteenth and **f** days
Eze 32:17 On the **f** day of the month in the
45:25 On the **f** day of the seventh
Luk 3:1 It was the **f** year in the reign of

fifth (45)

Gen 1:23 then morning — a **f** day.
24:22 a gold nose ring weighing a **f**
30:17 birth to her **f** son for Jacob.
41:34 over the land to take a **f**
Lev 19:25 In the **f** year you may eat the
Num 7:36 On the **f** day the leader of the
29:26 "On the **f** day bring 9 bulls,
33:38 on the first day of the **f** month
Jos 19:24 The **f** lot was drawn for the
Jdg 19:8 On the morning of the **f** day,
2Sm 3:4 The **f** was Shephatiah,
1Ki 14:25 In the **f** year of Rehoboam's
2Ki 8:16 Joram (Ahab's son) was in his **f**
25:8 On the seventh day of the **f**
1Ch 2:14 Raddai (his **f** son),
3:3 The **f** was Shephatiah,
8:2 and Rapha (his **f** son).
12:10 The **f** was Jeremiah.
24:9 the **f** for Malchiah, the sixth for
25:12 The **f** chose Nethaniah,
26:3 Elam (the **f**), Jehohanan (the
26:4 (the fourth), Nethanel (the **f**),
27:8 was commander of the **f** unit
27:8 the fifth unit during the **f** month.
2Ch 12:2 In the **f** year of Rehoboam's
Ezr 7:8 that same year in the **f** month,
7:9 on the first day of the **f** month,
Neh 6:5 me the same message a **f** time,
Jer 1:3 into captivity in the **f** month
28:1 in the **f** month of his fourth year
36:9 In the ninth month of the **f** year
52:12 On the tenth day of the **f** month
Eze 1:1 On the **f** day of the fourth month
1:2 On the **f** day of the month,
1:2 during the **f** year of the exile of
8:1 On the **f** day of the sixth month
20:1 On the tenth day of the **f** month
33:21 On the **f** day of the tenth month
Zec 7:3 and fast in the **f** month as we
7:5 you fasted and mourned in the **f**
8:19 the fast in the **f** month,
Rev 6:9 the lamb opened the **f** seal,
9:1 When the **f** angel blew his
16:10 The **f** angel poured his bowl on
21:20 the **f** onyx, the sixth red quartz,

fifties (1)

Mar 6:40 in groups of hundreds and **f**.

fiftieth (4)

Lev 25:10 Set apart the **f** year as holy,
25:11 That **f** year will be your jubilee
2Ki 15:23 In Azariah's **f** year as king of
Act 2:1 the **f** day after Passover,

fig (48)

Gen 3:7 They sewed **f** leaves together
Dtr 8:8 **f** trees, and pomegranates.
Jdg 9:10 Then the trees said to the **f** tree,
9:11 But the **f** tree responded,
1Sm 25:18 and 200 **f** cakes and loaded
30:12 They gave him a slice of **f**
1Ki 4:25 under his own vine and **f** tree.
10:27 cedars as plentiful as **f** trees
2Ki 18:31 his own grapevine and **f** tree
20:7 Isaiah said, "Get a **f** cake,
1Ch 12:40 **f** cakes, raisins, wine, olive oil,
27:28 for the olive and **f** trees in the
2Ch 1:15 cedars as plentiful as **f** trees
9:27 cedars as plentiful as **f** trees
Psa 78:47 hail and their **f** trees with frost.
105:33 He struck their grapevines and **f**
Pro 27:18 Whoever takes care of a **f** tree
Isa 9:10 **F** trees have been cut down,
34:4 like green figs from a **f** tree.
36:16 his own grapevine and **f** tree
38:21 Isaiah said, "Take a **f** cake,
Jer 5:17 grapevines and your **f** trees.
Hos 2:12 her grapevines and **f** trees.
Joe 1:7 They ruined my **f** trees.
1:12 The **f** trees are withered.
Amo 4:9 **f** trees, and olive trees.
Mic 4:4 grapevines and their **f** trees,
Nah 3:12 All your defenses will be like **f**
Hab 3:17 Even if the **f** tree does not
Hag 2:19 The vine, the **f** tree,
Zec 3:10 sit under your vine and **f** tree."
Mat 21:19 When he saw a **f** tree by the
21:19 At once the **f** tree dried up.
21:20 They asked, "How did the **f**
21:21 to do what I did to the **f** tree.
24:32 from the story of the **f** tree.
Mar 11:13 In the distance he saw a **f** tree
11:20 they saw that the **f** tree had
11:21 The **f** tree you cursed has dried
13:28 from the story of the **f** tree.
Luk 13:6 "A man had a **f** tree growing in
13:7 to look for figs on this **f** tree
19:4 ran ahead and climbed a **f** tree
21:29 "Look at the **f** tree or any other
Jon 1:48 "I saw you under the **f** tree
1:50 that I saw you under the **f** tree.
Jas 3:12 can a **f** tree produce olives?
Rev 6:13 figs dropping from a **f** tree when

fight (175)

Gen 16:12 He will **f** with everyone,
16:12 and everyone will **f** with him.
Exo 1:10 join our enemies, **f** against us,
2:13 the one who started the **f**,
13:17 see that they have to **f** a war,
17:9 Then **f** the Amalekites.
21:22 you must do whenever men **f**
Num 21:33 and all his troops came out to **f**
22:11 Maybe I'll be able to **f** them and
32:21 and **f** until the LORD forces out
33:55 They will constantly **f** with you
Dtr 1:30 will **f** for you as you saw him
1:30 fight for you as you saw him **f**
1:41 We'll go and **f**, as the LORD our
1:42 me, "Tell them, 'Don't go and **f**,
2:5 Don't start a **f** with them,
2:19 them or start a **f** with them.
2:24 **F** him, and take possession of
3:1 his troops came to **f** us at Edrei.
3:22 your God himself will **f** for you."
20:4 He will **f** for you against your
23:9 set up camp to **f** your enemies,
25:11 If she tries to stop the **f** by
29:7 Og of Bashan came out to **f** us,
32:42 of the enemy who vowed to **f**.
Jos 9:2 they joined together to **f** Joshua
11:5 of Merom in order to **f** Israel.
Jdg 1:1 "Who will go first to **f** the
1:3 and together we will **f** the
1:9 the men of Judah went to **f** the
1:10 Then they went to **f** the
1:11 there Judah's troops went to **f**
1:17 The tribe of Judah went to **f**
4:10 Ten thousand men went to **f**
4:12 had come to **f** at Mount Tabor.
5:2 Men in Israel vowed to **f**,
7:22 Midian to **f** among themselves.
8:1 us to go **f** Midian with you."
9:38 Now go out and **f** him."
9:39 of Shechem out to **f** Abimelech.
9:52 He began to **f** against it and
10:9 crossed the Jordan River to **f**
10:17 of Ammon were summoned to **f**,
10:18 "Whoever starts the **f** against
11:9 "If you take me back to **f**
11:25 Or did he ever **f** against Israel?
11:32 went to **f** against Ammon.
12:1 Ephraim were summoned to **f**.
12:1 "Why did you **f** against Ammon
12:3 I risked my life and went to **f**
12:3 come to **f** against me today?"
15:10 "Why did you come to **f** us?"
20:18 will go first to **f** Benjamin?"

Jdg 20:23 LORD answered, "Go **f** them!"
20:30 day the men of Israel went to **f**
1Sm 4:1 Israel went to **f** against the
4:9 Act like men and **f**."
7:10 came to **f** against Israel.
8:20 out ⌊to war⌋, and **f** our battles."
13:5 assembled to **f** against Israel.
17:2 a battle line to **f** the Philistines.
17:8 and let him come down to ⌊**f**⌋
17:9 If he can **f** me and kill me,
17:10 so that we can **f** each other."
17:32 I will go and **f** this Philistine."
17:33 "You can't **f** this Philistine.
18:17 to be a warrior for me and **f**
18:30 still went out ⌊to **f** Israel⌋.
18:30 whenever they went out ⌊to **f**⌋,
19:8 David went to **f** the Philistines.
23:28 and went to **f** the Philistines.
28:1 their army to **f** against Israel.
29:8 Why shouldn't I **f** your enemies,
2Sm 2:28 didn't chase or **f** Israel anymore.
10:13 advanced to **f** the Arameans,
11:20 you go so close to the city to **f**?
18:6 out to the country to **f** Israel
21:15 men went to **f** the Philistines,
1Ki 12:21 to **f** against the people of Israel
20:1 Samaria and **f** against it.
20:18 out to make peace or to **f**."
20:23 if we **f** them on the plain,
20:25 Then, if we **f** them on the plain,
20:26 and went to Aphek to **f** Israel.
20:39 "I went to **f** in the battle.
22:4 "Will you go with me to **f** at
22:31 He said, "Don't **f** anyone
22:32 So they turned to **f** him.
2Ki 3:7 Will you **f** Moab with me?"
3:21 the kings had come to **f** them.
3:21 to bear arms were called to **f**.
5:7 he's trying to pick a **f** with me."
8:28 Joram to **f** against King Hazael
10:3 **F** for your master's family."
16:5 Ahaz but couldn't get him to **f**.
19:9 of Sudan was coming to **f** him.
24:16 and all the men who could **f** in
1Ch 12:8 able to **f** with shields and
12:21 They helped David **f** raiding
12:37 120,000 soldiers ready to **f**
14:15 then go out and **f** because God
19:14 advanced to **f** the Arameans,
2Ch 11:1 to **f** against Israel and return the
13:12 to call ⌊the army⌋ to **f** you.
14:11 so that they can **f** against
14:13 army couldn't **f** again.
16:9 you will have to **f** wars."
18:30 He said, "Don't **f** anyone
18:31 him in order to **f** him.
20:17 You won't **f** this battle.
22:5 Israel to **f** against King Hazael
32:8 to help us and **f** our battles."
35:20 King Neco of Egypt came to **f** a
35:21 I've come to **f** those who are at
35:22 and he went to **f** in the valley of
Neh 4:14 **F** for your brothers,
4:20 Our God will **f** for us!"
Psa 35:1 **F** against those who fight
35:1 those who **f** against me.
74:22 **F** for your own cause!
109:3 They **f** against me for no
144:1 who trained my hands to **f** and
Pro 15:18 A hothead stirs up a **f**,
20:3 any stubborn fool can start a **f**.
28:25 A greedy person stirs up a **f**,
29:22 An angry person stirs up a **f**,
30:33 stirring up anger produces a **f**.
Isa 2:4 Nations will never **f** against
19:2 They will **f** — brother against
20:1 to **f** against Ashdod,
27:4 I would **f** them in battle and set
29:8 that **f** against Mount Zion.
30:32 He will **f** them in battle,
31:4 of shepherds is called to **f** it.
31:4 LORD of Armies will come to **f**
37:9 of Sudan was coming to **f** him.
49:25 I will **f** your enemies,
58:4 you quarrel and **f** and beat your
Jer 1:19 They will **f** you, but they will
Jer 15:20 They will **f** you, but they will
21:4 are using these weapons to **f**
21:5 I will **f** you in anger,
32:5 When you **f** the Babylonians,
41:12 men and went to **f** Ishmael.
51:46 Rumors that one ruler will **f**
Eze 29:18 his army **f** hard against Tyre.
Dan 10:20 Now I will return to **f** the
10:21 No one will support me when I **f**
11:7 northern king, **f** against them,
11:11 He will go to **f** the northern
11:28 He will be determined to **f**
Mic 4:3 Nations will never **f** against
Zec 10:5 They will **f** because the LORD
12:3 ⌊to **f**⌋ against Jerusalem."
14:3 out and **f** against those nations
14:14 Judah will also **f** in Jerusalem.
Mat 24:7 Nation will **f** against nation and
Mar 13:8 Nation will **f** against nation and
Luk 14:31 his 10,000 soldiers **f** against
21:10 "Nation will **f** against nation
22:49 we use our swords to **f**?"
Jon 18:36 my followers would **f** to keep
2Co 10:3 but we don't **f** like humans.
10:4 The weapons we use in our **f**
1Ti 1:18 conscience to **f** this noble war.
6:12 **F** the good fight for the
6:12 Fight the good **f** for the
2Ti 4:7 I have fought the good **f**.
Jas 4:1 desires that **f** to control you?
4:2 You quarrel and **f**. You don't
Jud 1:3 you to continue your **f**
Rev 11:7 the bottomless pit will **f** them,
12:7 Michael and his angels had to **f**
12:17 So it went away to **f** with her
13:4 Who can **f** a war with it?"

fighters (1)

1Ch 5:18 They were skilled **f** who could

fighting (69)

Exo 2:13 he saw two Hebrew men **f**.
14:14 The LORD is **f** for you!
14:25 The LORD is **f** for Israel!
Dtr 25:11 must do when two men are **f**
Jos 10:25 the enemies you're **f** against."
11:20 to continue **f** against Israel so
23:10 LORD your God was **f** for you,
24:12 of your battle skills or **f** ability.
Jdg 3:29 thousand of Moab's best **f** men.
1Sm 14:52 or any skilled **f** man came
17:19 Elah Valley **f** the Philistines."
18:5 put him in charge of the **f** men.
23:1 are **f** against Keilah?
24:1 back from ⌊**f**⌋ the Philistines,
25:28 because you are **f** the LORD's
31:1 were **f** against Israel,
31:3 The heaviest **f** was against
31:12 all the **f** men marched all night
2Sm 2:17 Fierce **f** broke out that day,
8:10 David and congratulate him for **f**
11:15 line where the **f** is heaviest.
18:8 The **f** spread over the whole
18:16 the ram's horn to stop their ⌊**f**⌋,
21:19 When more **f** broke out with the
23:8 are the names of David's **f** men:
23:9 another one of the three **f** men.
23:16 So the three **f** men burst into
23:17 which the three **f** men did.
23:22 as famous as the three **f** men.
1Ki 1:8 and David's ⌊thirty⌋ **f** men did
1:10 Nathan, Benaiah, the **f** men,
2Ki 3:23 The kings have been **f** one
6:8 of Aram was **f** against Israel,
6:14 chariots and a large **f** unit there.
9:15 received while **f** King Hazael
19:8 of Assyria **f** against Libnah.
1Ch 5:20 and received help while **f** them.
7:5 all of Issachar's families) were **f**
7:7 heads of families and **f** men.
7:9 of their families and **f** men).
7:11 17,200 **f** men who could
10:3 The heaviest **f** was against
10:12 all the **f** men came and took
11:10 commanders of David's **f** men,
11:11 The first of David's **f** men was
1Ch 11:12 another one of the three **f** men.
11:19 which the three **f** men did.
11:24 as famous as the three **f** men.
11:26 The distinguished **f** men were
12:4 Gibeon (one of the thirty **f** men
18:10 David and congratulate him for **f**
20:5 When more **f** broke out with the
27:6 was one of the thirty **f** men
28:1 the soldiers, and the **f** men.
2Ch 14:8 All of these men were good **f**
17:14 Adnah (with 300,000 **f** men),
17:16 the LORD (with 200,000 **f** men).
17:17 From Benjamin there was the **f**
28:7 Zichri, a **f** man from Ephraim,
Psa 55:18 many ⌊soldiers **f**⌋ against me.
56:2 are so many **f** against me.
Isa 37:8 of Assyria **f** against Libnah.
Jer 47:6 how long will you keep on **f**?
51:30 of Babylon have stopped **f**.
Nah 2:5 He remembers his best **f** men.
3:18 Your best **f** men are at rest.
Act 5:39 that you're **f** against God."
7:26 Moses saw two Israelites **f**,
Php 1:27 united in **f** for the faith that the

fights (4)

Psa 140:2 They start **f** every day.
Zec 14:3 as he does when he **f** a battle.
Tit 3:9 and **f** about Moses' Teachings.
Jas 4:1 What causes **f** and quarrels

figs (34)

Num 13:23 some pomegranates and **f**.
20:5 Even **f**, grapes, And there's no
Neh 13:15 **f**, and every other kind of load.
Sos 2:13 The green **f** ripen. The
Isa 28:4 They will be like **f** that ripened
34:4 like green **f** from a fig tree.
Jer 8:13 There are no **f** on the tree,
24:1 me two baskets of **f** set
24:2 One basket had very good **f**,
24:2 like **f** that ripen first.
24:2 other basket had very bad **f**.
24:2 These **f** were so bad that they
24:3 I answered, "**F**. Figs that are
24:3 **F** that are very good.
24:3 I also see **f** that are very bad,
24:5 are like these good **f**.
24:8 says about the bad **f** that are so
24:8 LORD says, 'Like these bad **f**,
29:17 people are like rotten **f** to me,
29:17 **f** that are so bad that they can't
Hos 9:10 it was like seeing the first **f** of
Joe 2:22 are plenty of **f** and grapes.
Amo 7:14 am a rancher and a grower of **f**.
Mic 7:1 eat or any ripened **f** that I crave.
Nah 3:12 like fig trees with the earliest **f**.
3:12 When shaken, the **f** fall into the
Mat 7:16 thornbushes or **f** from thistles,
Mar 11:13 see if he could find any **f** on it.
11:13 it wasn't the season for **f**.
Luk 6:44 You don't pick **f** from thorny
13:7 years I've come to look for **f**
13:9 Maybe next year it'll have **f**.
Jas 3:12 Can a grapevine produce **f**?
Rev 6:13 to the earth like **f** dropping from

figurative (1)

Heb 11:19 from the dead in a **f** sense.

figure (11)

Gen 29:17 **f** and beautiful features.
Lev 27:23 The priest must **f** out the field's
Est 2:7 young woman had a beautiful **f**
Sos 2:14 let me see your **f** and hear your
2:14 and your **f** is lovely."
7:7 your **f** is like a palm tree,
Eze 1:26 On the throne was a **f** that
Luk 1:29 said and tried to **f** out what this
14:28 You would first sit down and **f**
Jon 16:19 "Are you trying to **f** out among
Rev 13:18 person who has insight **f** out

figures (4)

Lev 26:1 Never cut **f** in stone to worship
2Sm 24:9 Joab reported the census **f** to

1Ch 21:5 reported the census **f** to David:
Eze 23:14 They were **f** of Babylonian

figurines (1)

2Ch 4:3 two rows of **f** shaped like bulls

filed (1)

Mic 6:2 The LORD has **f** a lawsuit

filigree (13)

1Ki 7:17 He also made seven rows of **f**
7:18 ⌊of decorations⌋ around the **f**
7:20 bowl-shaped parts around the **f**
7:41 and 2 sets of **f** to cover the 2
7:42 for the 2 sets of **f** (2 rows
7:42 of pomegranates for each **f**
2Ki 25:17 The **f** and the pomegranates
25:17 pillar and its **f** were the same.
2Ch 4:12 and 2 sets of **f** to cover the 2
4:13 for the 2 sets of **f** (2 rows
4:13 of pomegranates for each **f**
Jer 52:22 it was 7 ½ feet high with a **f**
52:23 on the surrounding **f** was 100.

fill (63)

Gen 1:22 increase in number, **f** the sea,
1:28 **f** the earth, and be its master.
9:1 in number, and **f** the earth.
42:25 Joseph gave orders to **f** their
44:1 "**F** the men's sacks with as
Exo 10:6 They will **f** your houses and
30:18 and **f** it with water.
Lev 26:36 I will **f** with despair those who
1Sm 16:1 **F** a flask with olive oil and go.
1Ki 18:34 He said, "**F** four jars with water.
Job 8:21 He will **f** your mouth with
15:2 details and **f** his stomach
20:23 Let that misery **f** his belly.
41:7 Can you **f** its hide with
Psa 16:3 noble ones who **f** me with joy.
17:14 You **f** their bellies with your
81:10 your mouth wide, and I will **f** it.
104:13 You **f** the earth with the fruits of
104:16 which he planted, drink their **f**.
110:6 on the nations and **f** them
119:161 but it is only your words that **f**
129:7 It will never **f** the barns of those
Pro 1:13 We'll **f** our homes with stolen
7:18 Come, let's drink our **f** of love
8:21 me and to **f** their treasuries.
Ecc 10:6 are left to **f** lower positions.
Isa 27:6 and **f** the whole world with fruit.
33:5 He will **f** Zion with justice and
56:12 and we'll **f** ourselves with
Jer 23:16 They **f** you with false hope.
23:24 "I **f** heaven and earth!"
51:11 the arrows; **f** the quivers.
51:14 "I will certainly **f** you with
Lam 3:30 them and take their **f** of insults.
Eze 3:3 and **f** your stomach with it."
7:19 hunger or **f** their stomachs.
8:17 Yet, they also **f** the land with
9:7 **F** its courtyards with dead
10:2 and **f** your hands with burning
24:4 **F** the pot with the meatiest
30:11 swords to attack Egypt and **f**
32:5 your flesh on the hills and **f**
35:8 I will **f** your mountains with
43:5 the LORD's glory **f** the temple.
44:4 I saw the LORD's glory **f** the
Amo 4:10 from your camps **f** your noses.
Nah 2:12 It used to **f** its caves with torn
Zep 1:9 all who **f** their master's house
Hag 2:7 Then I will **f** this house with
Mar 8:19 how many baskets did you **f**
8:20 many large baskets did you **f**
Luk 2:10 that will **f** everyone with joy.
Jon 2:7 "**F** the jars with water."
Act 5:3 why did you let Satan **f** you
Rom 15:13 May God, the source of hope, **f**
2Co 8:14 their surplus may **f** your need.
Php 1:11 Jesus Christ will **f** your lives
2:2 Then **f** me with joy by having
4:19 My God will richly **f** your every
Col 1:9 We ask ⌊God⌋ to **f** you with
1Pe 1:2 will and peace **f** your lives!
2Pe 1:2 May good will and peace **f** your
Jud 1:2 and love **f** your lives!

filled (232)

Gen 21:19 She **f** the container with water
24:16 **f** her jar, and came back.
26:15 So the Philistines **f** in all the
26:18 The Philistines had **f** them in
28:17 **F** with awe, he said,
42:25 After their bags were **f**,
Exo 1:7 that the land was **f** with them.
2:16 They drew water and **f** the
8:21 Egyptians will be **f** with flies,
31:3 I have **f** Bezalel with the Spirit
35:31 The LORD has **f** Bezalel with
40:34 the glory of the LORD **f** the tent.
40:35 the glory of the LORD **f** the tent.
Lev 19:29 will turn to prostitution and be **f**
Num 7:13 Each dish was **f** with flour
7:14 4 ounces, **f** with incense;
7:19 Each dish was **f** with flour
7:20 4 ounces, **f** with incense;
7:25 Each dish was **f** with flour
7:26 4 ounces, **f** with incense;
7:31 Each dish was **f** with flour
7:32 4 ounces, **f** with incense;
7:37 Each dish was **f** with flour
7:38 4 ounces, **f** with incense;
7:43 Each dish was **f** with flour
7:44 4 ounces, **f** with incense;
7:49 Each dish was **f** with flour
7:50 4 ounces, **f** with incense;
7:55 Each dish was **f** with flour
7:56 4 ounces, **f** with incense;
7:61 Each dish was **f** with flour
7:62 4 ounces, **f** with incense;
7:67 Each dish was **f** with flour
7:68 4 ounces, **f** with incense;
7:73 Each dish was **f** with flour
7:74 4 ounces, **f** with incense;
7:79 Each dish was **f** with flour
7:80 4 ounces, **f** with incense;
7:86 The 12 gold dishes **f** with
22:18 if Balak gave me his palace **f**
24:13 would give me his palace **f**
Dtr 6:11 Your houses will be **f** with all
33:23 the LORD's favor and are **f**
34:9 was **f** with the Spirit of wisdom,
Jos 9:13 wineskins when we **f** them.
Jdg 16:27 The building was **f** with people.
1Ki 8:10 a cloud **f** the LORD's temple.
8:11 The LORD's glory **f** his temple.
18:35 the trench was **f** with water.
20:27 Arameans who **f** the country,
2Ki 3:17 this valley will be **f** with water.
3:20 Edom and **f** the countryside.
4:39 He **f** his clothes with wild
10:21 into the temple of Baal and **f**
19:3 Today is a day **f** with misery,
23:14 and **f** their places with human
2Ch 5:13 temple was **f** with a cloud.
5:14 LORD's glory **f** God's temple.
7:1 the LORD's glory **f** the temple.
7:2 glory had **f** the LORD's temple.
30:26 of Jerusalem was **f** with joy.
Ezr 9:11 disgusting practices that have **f**
Neh 4:7 that the gaps were being **f** in,
9:25 took possession of houses **f**
Job 3:15 who **f** their homes with silver.
7:3 inherited nights **f** with misery.
10:15 I am **f** with disgrace while I
22:18 Yet, he **f** their homes with good
23:16 Almighty has **f** me with terror.
31:31 'We wish we had never **f** ⌊our
Psa 11:6 a cup **f** with scorching wind.
38:7 My insides are **f** with burning
48:10 hand is **f** with righteousness.
65:4 We will be **f** with good food
65:9 river of God is **f** with water.)
71:8 My mouth is **f** with your praise,
72:19 May the whole earth be **f** with
73:21 When my heart was **f** with
74:20 of the land is **f** with violence.
80:9 that it took root and **f** the land.
88:3 My soul is **f** with troubles,
104:24 earth is **f** with your creatures.
Psa 104:28 and they are **f** with blessings.
105:40 and he brought them quail and **f**
107:9 He **f** those who were hungry
114:8 He turns a rock into a pool **f**
119:80 Let my heart be **f** with integrity
119:158 and I am **f** with disgust.
126:2 Then our mouths were **f** with
127:5 Blessed is the man who has **f**
144:13 May our barns be **f** with all
Pro 8:24 there were springs **f** with water.
17:1 than a family feast **f** with strife.
20:17 his mouth will be **f** with gravel.
24:4 With knowledge its rooms are **f**
26:24 Whoever is **f** with hate
30:22 fool when he is **f** with food,
Ecc 2:23 Their entire life is **f** with pain,
Sos 7:2 May it always be **f** with spiced
Isa 2:6 because they are **f** with
2:7 Their land is **f** with silver and
2:7 Their land is **f** with horses,
2:8 Their land is **f** with idols,
3:14 Your houses are **f** with goods
6:1 bottom of his robe **f** the temple.
6:3 whole earth is **f** with his glory."
6:4 and the temple **f** with smoke.
7:24 the whole land will be **f**
7:25 because they will be **f**
11:9 The world will be **f** with the
22:2 You are a city **f** with shouting,
22:2 a town **f** with noise and
22:7 valleys will be **f** with chariots,
29:2 and the city will be **f** with
30:27 His lips are **f** with fury.
37:3 Today is a day **f** with misery,
51:17 That cup was **f** with his anger.
Jer 5:27 Like cages **f** with birds,
5:27 their houses are **f** with deceit.
6:11 I am **f** with the anger of the
9:1 "I wish that my head were ⌊**f**
13:12 bottle will be **f** with wine.'
13:12 every bottle will be **f** with wine.'
15:17 You **f** me with outrage.
16:18 They have **f** my property with
19:4 They have **f** this place with the
23:10 The land is **f** with adulterers.
25:15 Take from my hand this cup **f**
29:11 to give you a future **f** with hope.
31:14 My people will be **f** with my
31:17 Your future is **f** with hope,
31:25 everyone who is **f** with sorrow."
31:40 The whole valley, **f** with its
33:5 Now their houses are **f** with the
35:5 Then I set cups and pitchers **f**
41:9 **f** it with the bodies.
50:2 Marduk will be **f** with terror.
50:2 Its idols will be **f** with terror.'
51:34 He has **f** his belly with our
Lam 3:15 He has **f** me with bitterness.
Eze 7:23 The land is **f** with murder,
7:23 and the city is **f** with violence.
9:9 The land is **f** with murder,
9:9 the city is **f** with wrongdoing.
10:3 A cloud **f** the inner courtyard.
10:4 the cloud **f** the temple,
10:4 LORD's glory **f** the courtyard.
11:6 this city and have **f** its streets
22:5 you will be **f** with confusion.
23:33 of your sister Samaria will be **f**
27:25 You were like a ship **f** with
27:33 You **f** many people with your
32:6 Ravines will be **f** with your
36:38 Their ruined cities will be **f**
37:1 The valley was **f** with bones.
38:18 I will be **f** with burning anger,
39:20 At my table you will be **f** with
Dan 2:35 which **f** the whole world.
3:19 Nebuchadnezzar was so **f** with
Hos 6:8 is a city **f** with troublemakers.
Joe 2:24 floors will be **f** with grain.
Mic 3:8 But I am **f** with the power of the
6:11 bags **f** with inaccurate weights.
Hab 2:14 But the earth will be **f** with the
2:16 You are **f** with disgrace rather
Zec 8:5 The city will be **f** with boys
9:15 They will be **f** like a sacrificial
Mat 9:8 they were **f** with awe and

Mat 14:20 they **f** twelve baskets.
15:37 and **f** seven large baskets.
16:9 and how many baskets you **f**?
16:10 how many large baskets you **f**?
22:10 hall was **f** with guests.
Mar 6:43 they **f** twelve baskets with
8:8 and **f** seven large baskets.
Luk 1:15 He will be **f** with the Holy Spirit
1:41 Elizabeth was **f** with the Holy
1:65 neighbors were **f** with awe.
1:67 His father Zechariah was **f** with
2:9 The glory of the Lord **f** the area
2:40 He was **f** with wisdom,
3:5 Every valley will be **f**.
4:1 Jesus was **f** with the Holy
5:7 Their partners came and **f** both
5:26 They were **f** with awe and said,
9:17 they **f** twelve baskets.
10:21 In that hour the Holy Spirit **f**
16:25 that you had a life **f** with good
16:25 Lazarus' life was **f** with misery.
Jon 2:7 The servers **f** the jars to the
6:13 of bread and **f** twelve baskets.
8:12 follows me will have a life **f**
12:3 of the perfume **f** the house.
16:6 you're **f** with sadness.
19:29 A jar **f** with vinegar was there.
21:11 Though the net was **f** with 153
Act 2:2 wind came from the sky and **f**
2:4 All the believers were **f** with
4:8 Then Peter, because he was **f**
4:31 All of them were **f** with the Holy
5:28 Yet, you've **f** Jerusalem with
6:8 Stephen was a man **f** with
9:17 you to see again and to be **f**
12:7 and his cell was **f** with light.
13:9 was **f** with the Holy Spirit.
19:17 All of them were **f** with awe for
Rom 1:29 Their lives are **f** with of all
1:29 They are **f** with envy,
15:14 are **f** with goodness.
1Co 7:30 Those who have eyes **f** with
Eph 2:10 us in Christ Jesus to live lives **f**
3:19 may be completely **f** with God.
5:8 but now the Lord has **f** you with
5:18 Instead, be **f** with the Spirit
Php 2:17 Yet, I am **f** with joy,
2:18 reason you also should be **f**
4:10 The Lord has **f** me with joy
4:18 you have **f** my needs.
2Ti 1:4 that I can be **f** with happiness.
Tit 2:12 us to avoid ungodly lives **f**
Heb 9:4 were the gold jar **f** with manna,
Jas 3:8 evil **f** with deadly poison.
3:14 if you are bitterly jealous and **f**
3:17 **f** with mercy and good deeds,
1Jn 1:4 can be completely **f** with joy.
2Jn 1:12 will be completely **f** with joy.
Rev 7:17 He will lead them to springs **f**
8:5 **f** it with fire from the altar,
15:8 The temple was **f** with smoke
17:4 she was holding a gold cup **f**
21:6 give a drink from the fountain **f**
22:1 The angel showed me a river **f**

filling (1)

Mar 4:37 boat so that it was quickly **f** up.

fills (18)

Num 14:21 and as the glory of the LORD **f**
Job 9:18 He **f** me with bitterness.
27:3 and God's breath **f** my nostrils,
36:32 He **f** his hands with lightning
Psa 33:5 His mercy **f** the earth.
103:5 the one who **f** your life with
119:64 mercy, O LORD, **f** the earth.
145:19 He **f** the needs of those who
Sos 1:12 my perfume **f** the air with its
Jer 46:12 your cry **f** the earth.
50:22 and great destruction **f** the land.
Hab 3:3 His praise **f** the earth.
Act 14:17 He **f** you with food and your
2Co 2:14 It's like a fragrance that **f** the air.
8:14 your surplus **f** their need so that
Eph 1:23 him as he **f** everything
4:10 so that he **f** everything.

Col 2:18 whose sinful mind **f** him with

filth (7)

Lev 1:16 Remove the gizzard with its **f**
Isa 4:4 The Lord will wash away the **f**
Lam 1:9 Jerusalem's own **f** ⌊covers⌋ its
Eze 24:13 clean yourself from your **f**.
Nah 3:6 I will throw **f** on you.
2Pe 2:20 Christ and escape the world's **f**.
2:20 But if they get involved in this **f**

filthy (8)

Psa 106:39 They became **f** because of
Lam 1:8 that it has become a **f** thing.
1:17 become a **f** thing among them.
Eze 24:13 tried to clean you of your **f** lust,
Zec 3:3 Joshua was wearing **f** clothes
3:4 "Remove Joshua's **f** clothes.
Rev 22:11 and let **f** people continue to be
22:11 filthy people continue to be **f**.

final (10)

Exo 23:16 "Celebrate the Festival of the **F**
34:22 and the Festival of the **F**
Dtr 21:5 Their decision is **f** in all cases
2Ki 20:1 Give **f** instructions to your
Psa 49:13 This is the **f** outcome for fools
Isa 38:1 Give **f** instructions to your
Eze 21:25 your **f** punishment has come.
21:29 time of **f** punishment has come.
35:5 during their **f** punishment.
Rev 15:1 which are the **f** expression

finances (1)

2Ch 8:15 including the ⌊temple's⌋ **f**.

financial (2)

Luk 8:3 They provided **f** support for
2Co 11:9 I kept myself from being a **f**

find (314)

Gen 8:9 The dove couldn't **f** a place to
18:6 hurried into the tent to **f** Sarah.
18:26 The LORD said, "If I **f** 50
18:28 will not destroy it if I **f** 45 there."
18:30 He answered, "If I **f** 30 there,
19:11 gave up trying to **f** the door.
27:20 "How did you **f** it so quickly,
27:21 ⌊to **f** out⌋ whether or not you
31:32 If you **f** your gods, the one who
31:35 he didn't **f** the idols.
31:37 did you **f** anything from your
32:19 thing to Esau when you **f** him.
38:20 but his friend couldn't **f** her.
38:22 and said, "I couldn't **f** her.
38:23 but you couldn't **f** her."
41:38 "Can we **f** anyone like this — a
42:9 "And you've come to **f** out
42:12 You've come to **f** out where our
44:15 a man like me can **f** things out
Exo 5:11 straw wherever you can **f** it,
16:25 You won't **f** anything on the
16:26 of worship, you won't **f** any."
16:27 but they didn't **f** any.
18:15 come to me to **f** out God's will.
22:8 brought to God to **f** out whether
Lev 6:3 If you **f** something that
10:16 Moses tried to **f** out what had
Num 9:8 "Wait here until I **f** out what the
10:33 of three days' journey to **f** them
22:19 and I'll **f** out what else the
Dtr 1:33 who went ahead of you to **f**
4:29 you will **f** him whenever you
13:3 is testing you to **f** out if you
21:1 is what you must do if you **f**
22:3 Do the same if you **f** a donkey,
22:6 Whenever you're traveling and **f**
28:65 nations you will **f** no peace,
32:20 from them and **f** out what will
Jos 2:16 are pursuing you will not **f** you.
7:21 You will **f** them buried inside
Jdg 3:4 to **f** out if they would obey the
6:17 "If you **f** me acceptable,
16:5 and **f** out what makes him so
16:5 **F** out how we can overpower
17:8 wherever he could **f** ⌊a place⌋.

Jdg 17:9 wherever I can **f** ⌊a place⌋."
18:5 They said to him, "Please **f** out
18:8 asked them, "What did you **f**?"
Rut 1:9 you so that you may **f** security
1Sm 9:4 but ⌊still⌋ didn't **f** them.
9:8 tell us where to **f** the donkeys."
9:13 you can **f** him before he goes to
9:13 should be able to **f** him now."
10:2 "What can I do ⌊to **f**⌋ my son?'"
10:3 There you will **f** three men on
10:14 and when we couldn't **f** them,
10:21 for him but couldn't **f** him.
14:38 **F** out what sin was committed
16:17 Saul told his officials, "Please **f**
17:56 The king said, "**F** out whose
19:3 If I **f** out anything, I'll tell you."
20:12 "I'll **f** out in the next two or
20:21 boy and say, 'Go, **f** the arrows.'
20:36 "please **f** the arrows I shoot."
21:3 of bread or whatever you can **f**."
23:17 "my father Saul won't **f** you.
28:7 Saul told his officers, "**F** me a
2Sm 3:25 to **f** out about your movements
17:12 attack him wherever we **f** him.
17:20 for them but did not **f** them.
20:6 or he will **f** some fortified cities
1Ki 18:5 If we can **f** grass, then we can
18:12 but he won't be able to **f** you.
22:5 **f** out what the word of the
22:25 Micaiah answered, "You will **f**
2Ki 2:19 is as good as you will ever **f**.
5:8 come to me and **f** out that there
6:13 "**F** out where he is.
7:14 them to **f** out what happened.
9:35 they couldn't **f** any of her body
1Ch 4:39 to **f** pasture for their flocks.
2Ch 15:4 for him, he let them **f** him.
15:15 and he let them **f** him.
16:9 world to **f** those whose hearts
18:4 **f** out what the word of the
18:24 Micaiah answered, "You will **f**
20:16 You will **f** them at the end of
30:9 will **f** compassion from those
32:4 of Assyria **f** plenty of water?"
32:31 God did this to test him, to **f** out
Ezr 4:15 You will **f** in those official
7:16 any silver and gold that you **f**
8:15 but I didn't **f** any Levites.
Neh 9:29 he will **f** life in them.
Est 2:11 quarters to **f** out how Esther
4:5 to Mordecai and **f** out what was
Job 3:19 There ⌊you **f**⌋ both the
3:20 life to those who **f** it so bitter,
3:22 delighted to **f** the grave.
4:7 **F** me a decent person who has
5:24 house and **f** nothing missing.
5:25 "You will **f** that your children
8:8 **F** out what their ancestors had
9:14 How can I **f** the right words ⌊to
9:31 clothes would **f** me disgusting.
11:7 able to **f** the Almighty's limits?
17:10 I won't **f** one wise man among
23:3 I knew where I could **f** God!
23:8 If I go west, I can't **f** him.
23:10 ⌊I can't **f** him⌋ because he
24:8 because they can't **f** shelter.
32:11 you could **f** the right words.
Psa 9:2 I will **f** joy and be glad about
9:14 in the gates of Zion and **f** joy
10:15 until you **f** no more.
17:7 O Savior of those who **f** refuge
21:8 Your powerful hand will **f** all
22:2 also at night, but I **f** no rest.
32:11 Be glad and **f** joy in the LORD,
33:21 In him our hearts **f** joy.
35:9 My soul will **f** joy in the LORD
44:21 wouldn't God **f** out,
55:6 I would fly away and **f** rest.
55:8 I would hurry to **f** shelter from
59:15 They wander around to **f**
63:11 But the king will **f** joy in God.
64:10 Righteous people will **f** joy in
68:30 the people who **f** joy in war.
84:3 Even sparrows **f** a home,
84:3 and swallows **f** a nest for
84:5 Blessed are those who **f**

Psa	85:6	your people may **f** joy in you?
	89:16	They **f** joy in your name all day
	91:4	his wings you will **f** refuge.
	92:4	You made me **f** joy in what you
	97:12	**F** joy in the LORD,
	104:31	May the LORD **f** joy in what he
	104:34	I will **f** joy in the LORD.
	106:5	**f** joy in our people's happiness,
	106:46	He let them **f** compassion from
	119:14	I **f** joy in the way ⌞shown by⌟
	119:14	instructions more than I **f** joy
	119:162	I **f** joy in your promise like
	121:1	Where can I **f** help?
	132:5	until I **f** a place for the LORD,
	149:2	Let Israel **f** joy in their creator.
Pro	1:13	We'll **f** all kinds of valuable
	1:22	How long will you mockers **f**
	1:28	but they will not **f** me,
	2:5	fear of the LORD and you will **f**
	2:14	from those who **f** joy in the
	3:4	Then you will **f** favor and much
	4:22	are life to those who **f** them
	6:33	An adulterous man will **f**
	8:17	looking for me will **f** me.
	18:2	A fool does not **f** joy in
	20:6	but who can **f** someone who is
	21:21	and mercy will **f** life,
	23:26	Let your eyes **f** happiness in
	24:14	If you **f** it, then there is a future,
	25:16	When you **f** honey,
	31:10	"Who can **f** a wife with a strong
Ecc	2:24	and **f** satisfaction in their work.
	7:24	Who can **f** out what it is?
	7:26	I **f** that a woman whose
	7:27	one thing to another in order to **f**
	7:28	all these I didn't **f** one woman.
	8:17	he will not **f** ⌞its meaning⌟.
	11:1	because you will **f** it again after
	12:10	The spokesman tried to **f** just
Sos	3:1	I looked for him but did not **f**
	3:2	I looked for him but did not **f**
	5:6	for him, but I did not **f** him.
	5:8	swear to me that if you **f** my
Isa	8:6	water of Shiloah and **f** joy
	13:3	They **f** joy in my triumphs.
	13:12	I will make people harder to **f**
	14:32	people will **f** refuge in it.
	23:12	Even there you will **f** no rest.
	29:8	wake up to **f** they're hungry.
	29:8	wake up to **f** they're lightheaded
	29:19	Humble people again will **f** joy
	29:19	The poorest of people will **f** joy
	34:14	owls will rest there and **f**
	41:12	but you will not **f** them.
	41:16	But you will **f** joy in the LORD
	49:9	and they will **f** pastures on
	50:9	Who will **f** me guilty?
	52:5	So what do I **f** here?
	58:14	then you will **f** joy in the LORD.
	61:10	I will **f** joy in the LORD.
Jer	2:5	What did your ancestors **f**
	2:24	They will **f** you during your
	5:1	See if you can **f** anyone who
	6:16	Live that way, and **f** a resting
	12:6	also formed a mob to **f** you.
	14:3	but they don't **f** any water.
	29:6	**F** wives for your sons,
	29:13	you look for me, you will **f** me.
	29:14	I will let you **f** me, declares the
	31:2	Israel went to **f** its rest.
	38:25	The officials may **f** out that I've
	45:3	groaning. I can't **f** any rest.'
	49:10	I will **f** their hiding places.
	49:30	**F** a place to hide, declares the
	50:20	but they will **f** none.
	51:26	People won't **f** any stones in
	51:26	They won't **f** any stones in you
Lam	1:3	the nations; they **f** no rest.
	1:6	deer that couldn't **f** any pasture.
	2:9	Its prophets can **f** no visions
	3:21	"The reason I can ⌞still⌟ **f** hope
	3:24	That is why I **f** hope in him.'
	4:17	trying in vain to **f** help.
Eze	3:1	"Son of man, eat what you **f**.
	17:23	kind of bird will nest in it and **f**
	22:30	But I couldn't **f** anyone.
Dan	2:13	and some men were sent to **f**
	6:4	and satraps tried to **f** something
	6:4	But they couldn't **f** anything
	6:5	These men said, "We won't **f**
	6:5	unless we **f** it in his religious
Hos	2:7	but she won't **f** them.
	5:6	but they can't **f** him.
	12:8	no one will **f** us guilty of any
Joe	2:23	People of Zion, be glad and **f**
Amo	2:14	Strong men will **f** that their
	8:12	the LORD. But they won't **f** it.
Jnh	1:7	"Let's throw dice to **f** out who is
Nah	3:7	Where can I **f** anyone to
Hab	3:18	I will truly **f** joy in God,
Zep	2:3	Maybe you will **f** shelter on the
Zec	10:7	Their hearts will **f** joy in the
Mat	2:4	and tried to **f** out from them
	7:7	Search, and you will **f**.
	7:8	The one who searches will **f**,
	7:14	a few people **f** the narrow gate.
	11:29	you will **f** rest for yourselves
	12:43	But it doesn't **f** any.
	16:25	their lives for me will **f** them.
	17:27	and you will **f** a coin.
	21:2	You will **f** a donkey tied there
	22:9	everyone you **f** to the wedding.'
	25:9	**F** someone to sell you some
	26:60	But they did not **f** any,
Mar	11:2	As you enter it, you will **f** a
	11:13	He went to see if he could **f**
	13:36	suddenly and **f** you asleep.
	14:55	But they couldn't **f** any.
Luk	2:12	You will **f** an infant wrapped in
	2:45	When they didn't **f** him,
	5:19	But they could not **f** a way to
	6:7	of worship so that they could **f**
	9:12	so that they can **f** some food
	11:9	Search, and you will **f**.
	11:10	The one who searches will **f**,
	11:24	But it doesn't **f** any.
	13:6	fruit on the tree but didn't **f** any.
	18:8	will he **f** faith on earth?"
	18:36	he tried to **f** out what was
	19:30	As you enter, you will **f** a
	19:48	But they could not **f** a way to
	22:37	must **f** its fulfillment in me.
	23:4	"I can't **f** this man guilty of any
	24:3	they did not **f** the body of the
	24:23	and didn't **f** his body.
Jon	7:34	but you won't **f** me.
	7:35	to go so that we won't **f** him?
	7:36	but you won't **f** me,'
	8:6	They wanted to **f** a reason to
	10:9	out of the sheep pen and **f** food.
	18:38	"I don't **f** this man guilty of
	19:4	that I don't **f** this man guilty
	19:6	I don't **f** this man guilty of
Act	4:21	the authorities couldn't **f** any
	5:22	they didn't **f** the apostles.
	7:11	ancestors couldn't **f** any food.
	11:11	sent from Caesarea to **f** me.
	12:19	for Peter but couldn't **f** him.
	13:11	He tried to **f** people to lead him.
	13:28	Although they couldn't **f** any
	17:6	When they didn't **f** Paul and
	17:27	reach for him, and **f** him.
	22:24	The officer wanted to **f** out why
	22:30	The officer wanted to **f** out
	23:9	They said, "We don't **f** anything
	24:8	you'll be able to **f** out from him
	24:25	When I **f** time, I'll send for you
	25:27	I **f** it ridiculous to send a
Rom	9:19	"Why does God still **f** fault with
	9:33	rock that people **f** offensive.
1Co	9:6	except to **f** work to support
2Co	2:13	because I couldn't **f** Titus,
	6:3	people any opportunity to **f** fault
	8:20	We don't want anyone to **f** fault
	8:22	We **f** that he is much more
	9:4	they might **f** out that you're not
	12:20	I'm afraid that I may come and **f**
	12:20	and that you may **f** me different
Gal	2:4	They hoped to **f** a way to
Php	1:23	I **f** it hard to choose between
1Th	3:5	I sent ⌞Timothy⌟ to **f** out about
2Ti	2:1	My child, **f** your source of
Heb	4:16	receive mercy and **f** kindness,
	11:5	No one could **f** him,
Jas	1:5	and doesn't **f** fault with them.
1Pe	1:11	So they tried to **f** out what time
	2:8	rock that people **f** offensive."
2Pe	3:14	make every effort to have him **f**
2Jn	1:4	I was very happy to **f** some of
Jud	1:16	These people complain, **f** fault,
Rev	9:6	look for death and never **f** it.
	18:14	No one will ever **f** them again.'
	21:8	and all liars will **f** themselves

finding (12)

Exo	15:22	in the desert without **f** water.
Jdg	5:30	"They're really **f** and dividing
1Sm	9:4	Shalisha without **f** the donkeys.
2Ki	2:17	for three days without **f** him.
Job	10:17	You keep **f** new witnesses
Psa	107:4	road without **f** an inhabited city.
Pro	14:6	for wisdom without **f** it,
Hos	9:10	it was like **f** grapes in the
Jon	7:51	a person without **f** out what that
Act	11:26	After **f** Saul, Barnabas brought
Rom	5:7	**F** someone who would die for
1Th	4:4	Each of you should know that **f**

finds (39)

Gen	4:14	Now anyone who **f** me will kill
Num	35:27	avenge the death **f** you outside
1Sm	2:1	"My heart **f** joy in the LORD.
	24:19	When a person **f** an enemy,
Job	39:21	It paws in strength and **f** joy in
	40:2	"Will the person who **f** fault
Psa	13:5	My heart **f** joy in your salvation.
	21:1	The king **f** joy in your strength,
	119:162	who **f** a priceless treasure.
	147:10	He **f** no joy in strong horses,
Pro	3:13	Blessed is the one who **f**
	8:35	Whoever **f** me finds life and
	8:35	Whoever finds me **f** life and
	11:19	pursues evil **f** his own death.
	11:27	but whoever looks for evil **f** it.
	14:33	Wisdom **f** rest in the heart of an
	17:20	mind never **f** happiness,
	18:22	Whoever **f** a wife finds
	18:22	Whoever finds a wife **f**
	19:8	**f** something good.
	20:4	in the harvest but **f** nothing.
Ecc	6:5	the baby **f** more rest than the
Isa	10:14	of nations as one **f** a nest.
	65:8	When someone **f** juice for new
Jer	50:7	Everyone who **f** them eats
Mat	12:44	it **f** the house unoccupied,
	18:13	guarantee this truth: If he **f** it,
	24:46	if his master **f** him doing this
Luk	1:47	My spirit **f** its joy in God,
	11:25	When it comes, it **f** the house
	12:37	the master **f** awake when
	12:38	morning and **f** them awake.
	12:43	if his master **f** him doing this
	15:4	for the lost sheep until he **f** it?
	15:5	When he **f** it, he's happy.
	15:8	the coin carefully until she **f** it?
	15:9	When she **f** it, she calls her
	22:16	it again until it **f** its fulfillment
2Ti	1:18	Onesiphorus **f** mercy when that

fine (110)

Gen	18:5	They answered, "That's **f**.
	29:6	"He's **f**," they answered.
	41:42	dressed in robes of **f** linen
Exo	9:9	They will become a **f** dust
	21:22	offender must pay whatever **f**
	25:4	red yarn, **f** linen, goats' hair,
	25:5	rams' skins dyed red, **f** leather,
	26:1	sheets made from **f** linen yarn.
	26:14	Over that put a cover made of **f**
	26:31	angel design into **f** linen yarn.
	26:36	a screen out of **f** linen yarn,
	27:9	made out of **f** linen yarn,
	27:16	screen made from **f** linen yarn,
	27:18	with ⌞curtains⌟ made of **f** linen
	28:5	and bright red yarn, and **f** linen.
	28:6	the ephod out of **f** linen yarn.
	28:15	red yarn and out of **f** linen yarn.
	28:39	woven inner robe of **f** linen.

Exo 28:39 Make the turban of **f** linen,
30:36 some of it into a **f** powder,
35:6 red yarn, **f** linen, goats' hair,
35:7 rams' skins dyed red, **f** leather,
35:23 red yarn, **f** linen, goats' hair,
35:23 or **f** leather brought them.
35:25 and bright red yarn, and **f** linen,
35:35 and bright red yarn on **f** linen.
36:8 sheets made from **f** linen yarn
36:19 put a cover made of **f** leather.
36:35 bright red yarn and **f** linen yarn.
36:37 They made a screen out of **f**
38:9 made out of **f** linen yarn,
38:16 were made out of **f** linen yarn.
38:18 ⌊fabric made from⌋ **f** linen yarn.
38:23 and bright red yarn on **f** linen.
39:2 They made the ephod out of **f**
39:3 and throughout the **f** linen.
39:8 and of **f** linen yarn.
39:24 and bright red yarn, and **f** yarn.
39:27 They wove inner robes out of **f**
39:28 beautiful turbans out of **f** linen.
39:28 and belt out of **f** linen yarn.
39:34 the cover made of **f** leather,
Lev 19:20 He will only pay a **f** because
Num 4:6 will put a covering of **f** leather.
4:8 will cover all this with **f** leather.
4:10 under a covering of **f** leather
4:11 cover the cloth with **f** leather.
4:12 cover that with **f** leather,
4:14 They will spread a covering of **f**
4:25 the outer cover of **f** leather that
Dtr 9:21 until it was as **f** as powder.
22:19 They will **f** him 2 ½ pounds of
Jos 7:21 I saw a **f** robe from Babylonia,
1Sm 19:4 some very **f** things for you:
2Sm 20:21 "That's **f**," the woman told
22:43 I beat them into a powder as **f**
1Ki 10:18 and covered it with **f** gold.
10:21 Forest of Lebanon were **f** gold.
18:24 people answered, "That's **f**."
2Ki 4:26 "Everyone's **f**," she answered.
20:13 **f** olive oil, his entire armory,
1Ch 15:27 was dressed in a **f** linen robe,
2Ch 3:5 overlaid it with **f** gold,
3:8 it with 45,000 pounds of **f** gold.
5:12 were dressed in **f** linen
9:20 Forest of Lebanon were **f** gold.
Ezr 8:27 and two utensils of **f** polished
Est 1:6 of white and purple **f** linen.
8:15 a purple outer robe of **f** linen.
Job 31:24 in gold or said to **f** gold,
Psa 18:42 I beat them into a powder as **f**
21:3 things and set a crown of **f** gold
133:2 It is like **f**, scented oil on the
Pro 3:14 Its yield is better than **f** gold.
8:10 and my knowledge rather than **f**
8:19 What I yield is better than **f**
25:12 gold ring and a **f** gold ornament,
Isa 3:18 will take away their **f** things:
3:22 **f** robes, coats, shawls, purses,
29:5 enemies will be like **f** dust.
39:2 **f** olive oil, his entire armory,
40:15 of the islands is like **f** dust.
Jer 25:34 and you will break like **f**
Lam 4:1 The **f** gold has changed!
4:2 are worth their weight in **f** gold,
Eze 16:10 on you and **f** leather sandals
16:10 I dressed you in **f** linen and
16:13 You were dressed in **f** linen,
23:41 They sat on their **f** couches
27:7 Your sails were made out of **f**
28:7 swords against your **f** wisdom
31:3 with **f** branches that shaded
Dan 2:32 this statue was made of **f** gold.
Zec 3:4 and I will dress you in **f**
Mat 5:26 you pay every penny of your **f**.
11:8 A man dressed in **f** clothes?
11:8 Those who wear **f** clothes are
13:45 who was searching for **f** pearls.
16:2 say that the weather will be **f**
Luk 7:25 A man dressed in **f** clothes?
12:59 you pay every penny of your **f**."
21:5 that it was built with **f** stones
1Co 7:37 want to get married, that's **f**.
7:38 So it's **f** for a father to give his
Jas 2:2 gold rings and **f** clothes;
2:3 to the man wearing **f** clothes
2:19 That's **f**! The demons also
Rev 18:12 **f** linen, purple cloth, silk,
18:16 city which was wearing **f** linen,
19:8 This **f** linen represents the

fined (3)

1Ki 20:39 your own life or be **f** 75 pounds
2Ki 23:33 his reign in Jerusalem and **f**
2Ch 36:3 from office in Jerusalem and **f**

fines (1)

Amo 2:8 wine that they bought with **f**.

finest (16)

Exo 29:2 Use the **f** wheat flour,
30:23 "Take the **f** spices:
Dtr 33:15 the **f** fruits from the oldest
2Ki 19:23 cedars and its **f** cypresses.
Psa 19:10 than gold, even the **f** gold.
81:16 feed Israel with the **f** wheat
147:14 your ⌊hunger⌋ with the **f** wheat.
Sos 5:11 His head is the **f** gold.
Isa 25:6 with the best foods and the **f**
37:24 cedars and its **f** cypresses.
Jer 22:7 They will cut down your **f**
48:15 Its **f** young men will be
Eze 27:22 They traded the **f** spices,
34:3 and butcher the **f** sheep.
Joe 3:5 You brought my **f** treasures to
Amo 6:6 They rub the **f** oils all over

finger (25)

Gen 41:42 ring and put it on Joseph's **f**.
Exo 29:12 horns of the altar with your **f**.
Lev 4:6 The priest will dip his **f** in it
4:17 The priest will dip his **f** in
4:25 of the offering for sin with his **f**
4:30 some of the blood with his **f**
4:34 the offering for sin with his **f**
8:15 of the altar all around with his **f**
9:9 He dipped his **f** in the blood
14:16 He will dip his right **f** in the oil
14:16 and with his **f** sprinkle some of
14:27 With his right **f** he will sprinkle
16:14 blood and sprinkle it with his **f**
16:14 blood with his **f** seven times
16:19 With his **f** he will sprinkle
Num 19:4 some of the blood with his **f**
1Ki 12:10 'My little **f** is heavier than my
2Ch 10:10 'My little **f** is heavier than my
Isa 58:9 Don't point your **f** and say
Mat 23:4 willing to lift a **f** to move them.
Luk 11:46 But you won't lift a **f** to carry
15:22 Put a ring on his **f** and sandals
16:24 Lazarus to dip the tip of his **f**
Jon 8:6 bent down and used his **f**
20:27 to Thomas, "Put your **f** here,

fingers (16)

2Sm 21:20 had a total of 24 **f** and toes:
21:20 six **f** on each hand and six
1Ch 20:6 tall man who had 24 **f** and toes:
20:6 six **f** on each hand and six
Psa 8:3 the creation of your **f**,
144:1 to fight and my **f** to do battle,
Pro 6:13 ⌊and⌋ points with his **f**.
7:3 Tie them on your **f**.
31:19 and her **f** hold a spindle.
Sos 5:5 and my **f** were drenched with
Isa 2:8 and what their **f** have molded.
17:8 altars which their **f** molded.
59:3 and your **f** are stained with sin.
Dan 5:5 Suddenly, the **f** of a person's
Mar 7:33 He put his **f** into the man's ears,
Jon 20:25 put my **f** into them,

finish (32)

Gen 29:27 **F** the week of wedding
Exo 5:13 They said, "**F** the same
5:14 "You didn't **f** all the bricks you
Num 6:21 and **f** whatever they vowed
19:19 person will **f** taking away their
Dtr 20:9 When the officers **f** speaking to
2Sm 11:19 "When you **f** telling the king
2Sm 21:5 the man who wanted to **f** us off.
1Ki 7:1 years to **f** building his palace.
1Ch 27:24 to count them but didn't **f**.
Ezr 5:3 this temple and **f** its walls?"
5:9 this temple and **f** its walls?"
Neh 4:2 Can they **f** it in a day?
6:9 give up and not **f** the work.
6:15 The wall took 52 days to **f**.
Jer 20:18 I will **f** my days in shame.
51:63 When you **f** reading this scroll,
Eze 4:6 When you **f** this, you will lie
43:23 When you **f** removing sin,
Zec 4:9 and his hands will **f** it.
Mat 23:32 **f** what your ancestors started!
Luk 13:32 I will **f** my work on the third
14:28 you have enough money to **f** it.
14:29 and can't **f** the building,
14:30 to build but couldn't **f** the job.'
Jon 4:34 me wants me to do and to **f**
Act 20:24 I want to **f** the race I'm running.
Rom 13:8 one debt you can never **f**
2Co 8:6 This led us to urge Titus to **f**
8:11 So **f** what you began to do.
2Ti 4:17 so that I could **f** spreading
Rev 11:7 the witnesses **f** their testimony,

finished (111)

Gen 2:1 and everything in them were **f**.
2:2 By the seventh day God had **f**
17:22 When God **f** speaking with
18:33 When the LORD **f** speaking to
24:15 Before he had **f** praying,
24:19 When she had **f** giving him a
24:22 the camels had **f** drinking,
24:45 "Before I had **f** praying,
27:30 Isaac **f** blessing Jacob.
29:28 He **f** the week with Leah.
38:12 When Judah had **f** mourning,
43:2 When they **f** eating the grain
49:33 When Jacob **f** giving these
Exo 31:18 The LORD **f** speaking to
34:33 When Moses **f** speaking to
39:23 of the robe had a **f** edge (like
40:33 Finally, Moses **f** the work.
Lev 19:9 gather what is left after you're **f**.
23:22 gather what is left after you're **f**.
Num 4:15 and his sons have **f** covering
7:1 When Moses **f** setting up the
16:31 As soon as he had **f** saying all
Dtr 31:24 Finally, Moses **f** writing all the
32:45 When Moses had **f** reciting all
Jos 4:1 The whole nation **f** crossing
8:24 Israel had **f** killing all the
19:51 So they **f** dividing the land.
Jdg 3:18 When Ehud had **f** delivering the
15:17 When he **f** saying this,
Rut 2:21 until they have **f** the harvest.'"
3:3 until he's **f** eating and drinking.
1Sm 10:13 when he had **f** prophesying,
13:10 As he **f** sacrificing the burnt
14:13 was behind him, **f** killing them.
18:1 David **f** talking to Saul.
24:16 When David **f** saying this,
2Sm 6:18 When David had **f** sacrificing
13:36 When he **f** speaking,
1Ki 1:41 heard this as they **f** eating.
3:1 until he **f** building his own
6:7 with stone blocks that were **f** at
6:9 When he had **f** building the
6:14 When Solomon had **f** building
6:36 with three courses of **f** stones
6:36 and a course of **f** cedar beams.
6:38 the temple was **f** according to
7:22 He **f** the work on the pillars.
7:40 So Hiram **f** all the work for King
7:51 on the LORD's temple was **f**.
8:54 When Solomon **f** praying this
9:1 Solomon **f** building the LORD's
9:11 ⌊When King Solomon had **f**,⌋
9:25 And he **f** the temple.
2Ki 16:11 He **f** it before Ahaz returned
1Ch 16:2 When David had **f** sacrificing
28:20 work on the LORD's temple is **f**.
2Ch 4:11 So Huram **f** the work for King
5:1 on the LORD's temple was **f**.
7:1 When Solomon **f** praying,

2Ch 7:11 Solomon **f** the LORD's temple
8:16 LORD's temple was ⌞now⌟ **f**.
20:23 After they had **f** off the people
24:14 When they **f**, they brought the
29:17 They **f** on the sixteenth day of
29:28 until the burnt offering was **f**.
29:29 When the burnt offerings were **f**
31:7 in the seventh month they **f**.
Ezr 4:13 is rebuilt and its walls are **f**,
4:16 is rebuilt and its walls are **f**,
5:16 until now, but it still isn't **f**."
6:14 They **f** building as the God of
6:15 This temple was **f** on the third
10:17 they had **f** dealing with all the
Neh 6:15 The wall was **f** on the
Job 1:5 When they **f** having their
Psa 9:6 The enemy is **f** — in ruins
22:31 righteousness — that he has **f** it.
Pro 16:30 his lips has **f** his evil work.
Isa 10:12 When the Lord has **f** all his
29:20 Mockers will be **f**. All who look
33:1 When you've **f** destroying,
33:1 When you've **f** being a traitor,
Jer 26:8 But as soon as Jeremiah **f**
43:1 So Jeremiah **f** telling all the
Lam 3:54 my head. I thought I was **f**.
Eze 4:8 have **f** attacking ⌞Jerusalem⌟.
42:15 When the man had **f** measuring
Dan 8:23 when rebellions are **f**,
12:7 then all these things will be **f**."
Amo 7:2 When the locusts had **f** eating
Mat 7:28 When Jesus **f** this speech,
11:1 After Jesus **f** giving his twelve
13:53 Jesus had **f** these illustrations,
19:1 When Jesus **f** speaking,
26:1 When Jesus **f** saying all these
27:31 After the soldiers **f** making fun
Mar 15:20 After the soldiers **f** making fun
Luk 4:13 After the devil had **f** tempting
5:4 When he **f** speaking,
7:1 When Jesus had **f** everything
Jon 18:1 After Jesus **f** his prayer,
19:28 that everything had now been **f**,
19:30 the vinegar, he said, "It is **f**!"
Act 4:31 the apostles had **f** praying,
13:29 When they had **f** doing
14:26 for the work they had now **f**.)
15:13 After they **f** speaking,
20:36 When Paul had **f** speaking,
Rom 15:19 I have **f** spreading the Good
Heb 4:3 though he had **f** his work when
5:9 After he had **f** his work,

finishes (1)

Lev 16:20 "When he **f** making peace with

finishing (3)

Ezr 4:12 They are close to **f** the walls.
Jon 17:4 I have given you glory by **f**
Act 13:25 When John was **f** his work,

fins (5)

Lev 11:9 streams that has **f** and scales.
11:10 have no **f** or scales disgusting.
11:12 creature in the water without **f**
Dtr 14:9 creature that has **f** and scales.
14:10 that doesn't have **f** and scales.

fir (4)

Psa 104:17 Storks makes their homes in **f**
Isa 41:19 I will place cedar, **f**,
44:14 Then they choose **f** trees or
60:13 glory will come to you: Cedar, **f**,

fire (398)

Gen 19:24 burning sulfur and **f** rain out
Exo 3:2 there as flames of **f** coming out
3:2 although the bush was on **f**,
12:8 It must be roasted over a **f** and
12:9 roast the whole animal over a **f**.
13:21 ahead of them in a column of **f**
13:22 The column of **f** was always
14:24 down from the column of **f**
19:18 had come down on it in **f**.
22:6 "Whenever a **f** starts and
22:6 the person who started the **f**
Exo 24:17 the LORD looked like a raging **f**
29:18 an offering by **f** to the LORD.
29:25 an offering by **f** to the LORD.
29:41 an offering by **f** to the LORD.
30:20 an offering by **f** to the LORD,
32:24 I threw it into the **f**,
35:3 Never light a **f** in any of your
40:38 and there was **f** in the smoke at
Lev 1:7 of the priest Aaron will start a **f**
1:7 altar and lay the wood on the **f**.
1:9 a burnt offering, an offering by **f**
1:13 a burnt offering, an offering by **f**
1:17 a burnt offering, an offering by **f**
2:2 It is an offering by **f**,
2:3 from the LORD's offering by **f**.
2:9 It is an offering by **f**,
2:10 from the LORD's offering by **f**.
2:14 roast the cracked grain over **f**.
2:16 is an offering by **f** to the LORD."
3:4 fat on them and offer them by **f**
3:5 It is an offering by **f**,
3:9 offering and offer it by **f**
3:11 an offering by **f** to the LORD.
3:15 fat on them as an offering by **f**
3:16 an offering by **f** to the LORD.
4:12 will burn it there on a wood **f**.
4:35 the altar with the offering by **f**
5:12 on top of the offering by **f**
6:9 while the altar **f** is kept burning.
6:10 altar from the **f** that consumed
6:12 The **f** must always be burning
6:12 lay the burnt offering on the **f**
6:13 The **f** must always be burning
6:17 from the offerings by **f** made
6:18 come regarding the offering by **f**
7:5 guilt offering by **f** to the LORD.
7:25 which they sacrificed by **f**
7:30 Bring the sacrifices by **f** made
7:35 from the sacrifices by **f** made
8:21 an offering by **f** to the LORD.
8:28 offerings, offerings by **f**,
9:24 **F** came out from the LORD's
10:1 they offered this unauthorized **f**.
10:2 A **f** flashed from the LORD and
10:6 Israelites may cry over the **f**
10:12 left over from the offering by **f**
10:13 it is the part of the offering by **f**
16:13 he will put the incense on the **f**
21:6 you bring sacrifices by **f**
21:21 must never bring sacrifices by **f**
22:22 in a sacrifice by **f** on the altar.
22:27 as a sacrifice by **f** to the LORD.
23:8 Bring the LORD a sacrifice by **f**
23:13 This will be a sacrifice by **f**
23:18 They will be a sacrifice by **f**,
23:25 a sacrifice by **f** to the LORD."
23:27 bring the LORD a sacrifice by **f**.
23:36 days bring a sacrifice by **f**
23:36 Bring the LORD a sacrifice by **f**.
23:37 for bringing sacrifices by **f**
24:7 an offering by **f** to the LORD.
24:9 from the LORD's offering by **f**.
Num 3:4 they offered unauthorized **f**
6:18 and put it on the **f** under the
9:15 over the tent glowed like **f**.
9:16 covering the tent glowed like **f**.
11:1 and **f** from the LORD began to
11:2 and the **f** died down.
11:3 place was called Taberah [F]
11:3 Taberah [Fire] because **f** from
14:14 and in a column of **f** by night.
15:3 you may bring offerings by **f** to
15:10 It is an offering by **f**,
15:13 they bring an offering by **f**,
15:14 If they bring an offering by **f**,
15:25 an offering by **f** and an offering
16:35 **F** came from the LORD and
16:37 the incense burners out of the **f**
18:17 burn the fat as an offering by **f**,
21:28 **F** came out of Heshbon,
26:10 died when the **f** consumed
26:61 they offered unauthorized **f**
28:2 They are offerings by **f**,
28:3 These are the offerings by **f**
28:6 an offering by **f** to the LORD.
28:8 This is an offering by **f**,
Num 28:13 an offering by **f** to the LORD.
28:19 bring the LORD an offering by **f**,
28:24 They are offerings by **f**,
29:6 an offering by **f** to the LORD.
29:13 a burnt offering, an offering by **f**
29:36 a burnt offering, an offering by **f**
31:23 burn — must be put through **f**
Dtr 1:33 He appeared in a column of **f** at
4:11 which was on **f** with flames
4:12 LORD spoke to you from the **f**.
4:15 you from the **f** at Mount Horeb.
4:24 LORD your God is a raging **f**,
4:33 God speak from a **f** and lived?
4:36 you his great **f** on earth,
4:36 him speak from the column of **f**.
5:4 face from the **f** on the mountain.
5:5 you were afraid of the **f**
5:22 in a loud voice from the **f**,
5:23 the mountain blazing with **f**,
5:24 his voice come from the **f**.
5:25 This great **f** will consume us!
5:26 the living God speak from a **f**,
9:3 ahead of you like a raging **f**.
9:10 LORD spoke to you from the **f**
9:15 while it was still burning with **f**.
10:4 these words to you from the **f**
18:16 God or see this raging **f** again.
32:22 My anger has started a **f** that
32:22 of the mountains on **f**.
33:2 right was a raging **f** for them.
Jos 8:8 captured the city, set it on **f**.
8:19 and quickly set it on **f**.
Jdg 1:8 there and set the city on **f**.
6:21 **F** flared up from the rock and
9:15 But if not, **f** will come out of the
9:20 But if that's not the case, let **f**
9:20 Also let **f** come out of citizens
9:49 of the basement and set it on **f**
15:5 He set the torches on **f** and
15:5 So he set **f** to all their grain,
15:5 olive orchards also caught on **f**.
15:14 like strings burned in a **f**,
16:9 thread snaps when it touches **f**.
2Sm 14:30 Go and set it on **f**."
14:30 Absalom's servants set it on **f**.
14:30 have set ⌞your⌟ field on **f**."
14:31 servants set my field on **f**?"
22:9 and a raging **f** came out of his
23:7 **F** will burn them up completely
1Ki 18:23 on the wood, but not set it on **f**.
18:24 The god who answers by **f** is
18:25 but don't set the wood on **f**."
18:38 So a **f** from the LORD fell down
18:38 The **f** even dried up the water
19:12 the earthquake there was a **f**.
19:12 But the LORD wasn't in the **f**.
19:12 And after the **f** there was a
2Ki 1:10 **f** will come from heaven and
1:10 Then **f** came from heaven and
1:12 **f** will come from heaven and
1:12 Then God's **f** came from
1:14 **F** has come from heaven and
4:38 "Put a large pot on the **f**,
8:12 will set their fortresses on **f**,
1Ch 21:26 by ⌞sending⌟ **f** from heaven
2Ch 7:1 **f** came down from heaven and
7:3 Israelites saw the **f** come down
Neh 1:3 have been destroyed by **f**."
9:12 the night by a column of **f**
9:19 The column of **f** didn't leave
Job 1:16 "A **f** from God fell from heaven
5:7 as sparks fly up ⌞from a **f**⌟.
15:34 and **f** burns up the tents of
18:5 flame of his **f** stops glowing.
18:15 **F** lives in his tent.
20:26 A **f** that no one fans will burn
22:20 and a **f** has burned up what
28:5 as if ⌞it were burned⌟ by **f**.
31:12 It would be a **f** that burns even
41:19 Sparks of **f** fly from it.
41:21 Its breath sets coals on **f**,
Psa 11:6 He rains down **f** and burning
18:8 and a raging **f** came out of his
21:9 **F** will devour them.
39:3 My heart burned like a **f** flaring
50:3 A devouring **f** is in front of him

Psa 66:12 We went through **f** and water,
68:2 presence like wax next to a **f**.
78:21 His **f** burned against Jacob and
78:63 **F** consumed his best young
79:5 fury continue to burn like **f**?
83:15 the way **f** burns a forest and
83:15 and flames set mountains on **f**.
89:46 anger continue to burn like **f**?
97:3 **F** spreads ahead of him.
104:4 and your servants flames of **f**.
105:39 as a protective covering and a **f**
106:18 A **f** broke out among their
Pro 6:27 Can a man carry **f** in his lap
16:27 his speech is like a burning **f**.
17:3 hearts ⌊by **f**⌋ is the LORD.
26:20 Without wood a **f** goes out,
26:21 burning coals and wood fuels **f**,
30:16 a **f** that does not say,
Sos 8:6 Love's flames are flames of **f**,
Isa 1:31 will become tinder for a **f**,
1:31 will be no one to put out the **f**.
4:5 and a glowing flame of **f** during
9:5 will be burned as fuel in the **f**.
9:18 Surely wickedness burns like **f**.
9:18 underbrush in the forest on **f**,
9:19 the people are like fuel for the **f**.
10:16 into a raging **f** under his power.
10:17 Its Holy One will become a **f**.
27:4 battle and set all of them on **f**.
27:11 come and build a **f** with them.
29:6 rainstorms, and **f** storms.
30:30 with **f** storms, windstorms,
30:33 of burning sulfur, setting it on **f**.
31:9 His **f** is in Zion and his furnace
33:11 Your breath will be a **f** which
33:12 set on **f** like dry thornbushes.
33:14 live through a **f** that destroys?
33:14 through a **f** that burns forever?
43:2 When you walk through **f**,
44:16 of the wood they burn in the **f**.
44:16 We can see the **f**!"
44:19 burned half of the wood in the **f**.
47:14 **F** burns them. They can't rescue
47:14 to keep them warm and no **f**
64:2 Be like the **f** that kindles
65:5 like a smoldering **f** all day long.
66:15 The LORD will come with **f**
66:15 punish them with flames of **f**.
66:16 The LORD will judge with **f**,
66:24 The **f** that burns them will not
Jer 4:4 my fury will flare up like a **f**,
5:14 words in your mouth like a **f**.
6:29 to make the **f** melt away
9:7 I will now refine them with **f**
11:16 He will set **f** to you with a
15:14 my anger has started a **f**.
17:4 you have stirred up the **f**
17:27 I will set its gates on **f**.
17:27 The **f** will burn down the
20:9 me like a burning **f** shut up
21:12 will break out and burn like **f**.
21:14 "I will start a **f** in your forests,
22:7 trees and throw them on a **f**.
23:29 "Isn't my word like **f** or like a
32:29 will break in, set this city on **f**,
36:22 in front of the **f** in the fireplace.
36:23 knife and throw them into the **f**
43:12 He will set **f** to the temples of
48:45 A **f** will come out of Heshbon
49:27 "I will set **f** to the walls of
50:32 I will light a **f** in their cities that
51:30 Their buildings are set on **f**.
51:58 its high gates will be set on **f**.
51:58 out only to have a **f**.
Lam 1:13 He sent **f** from above.
2:3 He burned like a raging **f** in
2:4 He poured out his fury like **f** on
4:11 He started a **f** in Zion that even
Eze 1:13 **F** moved back and forth
1:13 The **f** was bright, and lightning
1:13 and lightning came out of the **f**.
1:27 bronze with **f** all around it.
1:27 waist down, he looked like **f**.
5:2 burn one-third of your hair in a **f**
5:4 and throw them in a **f** and burn
5:4 From there a **f** will spread
Eze 8:2 down its body looked like **f**.
10:7 into the **f** that was between
15:4 is only thrown into the **f** as fuel.
15:4 The **f** burns up both its ends
15:5 anything after the **f** has burned
15:6 forest to be used to feed the **f**,
15:7 they have escaped one **f**,
15:7 another **f** will burn them.
19:14 **F** has spread from the vine's
19:14 **F** has destroyed its fruit.
20:47 I am about to set **f** to you to
20:47 The blazing **f** will not be put
20:48 that I, the LORD, started the **f**.
21:32 You will be fuel for the **f**.
24:3 Put the pot on the **f**;
24:10 Pile it high, and light the **f**.
24:12 Even the **f** can't take away its
28:18 So I set **f** to you to burn you up.
30:8 because I will set **f** to Egypt
30:14 destroy Pathros, set **f** to Zoan,
30:16 I will set **f** to Egypt.
38:22 rainstorms, large hailstones, **f**,
39:6 I will send **f** on Magog and on
39:9 They will set **f** to weapons and
Dan 3:22 killed by the flames from the **f**.
3:24 we throw three men into the **f**?"
3:25 walking in the middle of the **f**,
3:26 Abednego came out of the **f**.
3:27 They saw that the **f** had not
7:9 and its wheels were burning **f**.
7:10 A river of **f** flowed.
7:11 and put into a raging **f**.
Hos 7:6 morning it burns like a raging **f**.
7:7 their judges ⌊like a **f**⌋.
8:14 I will send a **f** on their cities
Joe 1:19 **F** has burned up the open
1:20 **F** has burned up the open
2:3 In front of this army a **f** burns.
2:5 like crackling **f** burning up
2:30 blood, **f**, and clouds of smoke.
Amo 1:4 I will send a **f** on the house of
1:7 I will send a **f** on the walls of
1:10 I will send a **f** on the walls of
1:12 I will send a **f** on Teman and
1:14 I will set **f** to the walls of
2:2 I will send a **f** on Moab and
2:5 I will send a **f** on Judah and
4:11 a burning log snatched from a **f**.
5:6 he will spread like a **f** through
7:4 was calling for judgment by **f**.
7:4 The **f** dried up the ocean and
Oba 1:18 of Jacob will be like a **f**.
Mic 1:4 under him like wax near a **f**.
Nah 1:6 He pours out his rage like **f** and
3:13 **F** has destroyed the bars of
3:15 **F** will consume you there.
Zec 2:5 I will be a wall of **f** around it,
3:2 burning log snatched from a **f**?"
11:1 so that **f** will be able to burn
12:6 the leaders of Judah like a **f**
13:9 ⌊of the people⌋ through the **f**.
Mal 3:2 He is like a purifying **f** and like
Mat 3:10 cut down and thrown into a **f**.
3:11 you with the Holy Spirit and **f**.
3:12 but he will burn the husks in a **f**
7:19 is cut down and thrown into a **f**.
17:15 Often he falls into **f** or water.
18:8 be thrown into everlasting **f**.
25:41 Go into everlasting **f** that was
Mar 9:22 has often thrown him into **f**
9:43 to the **f** that cannot be put out.
9:48 and the **f** is never put out.
9:49 Everyone will be salted with **f**.
14:54 himself facing the glow of a **f**.
Luk 3:9 cut down and thrown into a **f**."
3:16 you with the Holy Spirit and **f**.
3:17 but he will burn the husks in a **f**
9:54 do you want us to call down **f**
12:49 "I have come to throw **f** on the
16:24 I am suffering in this **f**.'
17:29 **f** and sulfur rained from the sky
22:55 Some men had lit a **f** in the
22:56 he sat facing the glow of the **f**.
Jon 15:6 thrown into a **f**, and burned.
18:18 around a **f** they had built
18:25 and warm himself by the **f**.
Jon 21:9 they saw a **f** with a fish lying
Act 2:3 Tongues that looked like **f**
2:19 blood, **f**, and clouds of smoke.
28:2 They made a **f** and welcomed
28:3 brushwood and put it on the **f**.
28:5 into the **f** and wasn't harmed.
1Co 3:13 visible because **f** will reveal it.
3:13 That **f** will determine what kind
3:15 it will be like going through a **f**.
1Th 5:19 Don't put out the Spirit's **f**.
2Th 1:7 mighty angels in a blazing **f**.
Heb 1:7 his servants flames of **f**."
10:27 a raging **f** that will consume
12:18 feel, to a blazing **f**, to darkness,
12:29 our God is a destructive **f**.
Jas 3:5 A large forest can be set on **f**
3:6 The tongue sets our lives on **f**,
3:6 and is itself set on **f** from hell.
5:3 Like **f**, it will destroy your body.
1Pe 1:7 faith as **f** tests how genuine
2Pe 3:12 heaven will be on **f** and will be
Jud 1:7 of the punishment of eternal **f**.
1:23 them from the **f** ⌊of hell⌋.
Rev 1:14 His eyes were like flames of **f**.
2:18 whose eyes are like flames of **f**
3:18 Buy gold purified in **f** from me
8:5 filled it with **f** from the altar,
8:7 hail and **f** were mixed with
8:8 burning with **f** was thrown into
9:17 **F**, smoke, and sulfur came out
9:18 These three plagues — the **f**,
10:1 his feet were like columns of **f**.
11:5 If anyone wants to hurt them, **f**
13:13 It even makes **f** come down
14:18 the altar with authority over **f**.
15:2 a sea of glass mixed with **f**.
16:8 allowed to burn people with **f**.
17:16 her flesh and burn her up in a **f**.
18:8 She will be burned up in a **f**,
18:9 smoke rise from her raging **f**.
18:18 smoke rise from her raging **f**,
19:12 His eyes are flames of **f**.
20:9 **F** came from heaven and

fireplace (3)

Isa 30:14 to carry live coals from a **f**
Jer 36:22 sitting in front of the fire in the **f**.
36:23 throw them into the fire in the **f**.

fireplaces (1)

Eze 46:23 walls were equipped with **f**.

fires (9)

2Ki 19:18 gods from these countries into **f**
Isa 37:19 gods from these countries into **f**
44:15 They start **f** and bake bread.
50:11 But all of you light **f** and arm
Jer 7:18 gather wood, fathers light **f**,
34:5 People will burn ⌊funeral⌋ **f** for
Eze 39:10 They will make **f** with the
Mal 1:10 so that you could not light **f**
Heb 11:34 put out raging **f**, and escaped

firewood (3)

2Sm 24:22 and oxen yokes for **f**."
1Ki 19:21 using the oxen's yoke ⌊for **f**⌋.
1Ch 21:23 burnt offering, threshers for **f**,

firm (23)

2Ki 14:5 As soon as he had a **f** control
1Ch 16:30 "The earth stands **f**;
2Ch 25:3 As soon as he had **f** control
Job 37:18 him and make them as **f** as
Psa 20:8 but we will rise and stand **f**.
30:7 made my mountain stand **f**.
33:11 LORD's plan stands **f** forever.
33:11 stand **f** in every generation.
48:8 makes Zion stand **f** forever.
89:2 stands **f** in the heavens."
89:37 his throne will stand **f** forever.
96:10 The earth stands **f**;
125:1 It remains **f** forever.
Pro 3:18 of life for those who take **f** hold
12:3 A person cannot stand **f** on a
Isa 32:8 act honorably and stand **f**
1Co 16:13 Be **f** in the Christian faith.

Gal 5:1 be **f** ⌊in this freedom⌋.
Php 4:1 relationship with the Lord **f**!
Col 2:5 you are and how **f** your faith
1Th 3:8 relationship with the Lord **f**.
1Pe 5:9 Be **f** in the faith and resist him,
2Pe 3:17 Then you won't fall from your **f**

firmly (21)

Jos 3:17 of the LORD's promise stood **f**
4:3 where the priests' feet stood **f**.
1Ki 2:12 and his power was **f**
2:45 will always be **f** established by
2:46 as king was now **f** established.
Job 21:8 They see their children **f**
Psa 17:5 my steps have remained **f** in
24:2 seas and set it **f** on the rivers.
119:5 become **f** established so that
Pro 22:15 Foolishness is **f** attached to a
Ecc 12:11 nails that have been driven in **f**.
Isa 22:23 I will fasten him **f** in place like
22:25 "On that day the peg which I **f**
Hos 14:5 They will be **f** rooted like
1Co 10:12 think they are standing **f** should
2Co 1:24 Certainly, you are **f** established
Php 1:27 I'll hear that you are **f** united in
2:16 as you hold **f** to the word of life.
2Th 2:15 Then, brothers and sisters, **f**
Heb 10:23 We must continue to hold **f** to
1Pe 5:12 Remain **f** established in it!

firmness (1)

Dan 2:41 which has some of the **f** of iron.

first (451)

Gen 1:5 then morning — the **f** day.
2:11 The name of the **f** river is
4:20 He was the **f** person to live in
4:21 He was the **f** person to play the
8:5 On the **f** day of the tenth month,
8:13 By the **f** day of the first month
8:13 By the first day of the **f** month
8:13 Noah's six hundred and **f** year,
9:20 Noah, a farmer, was the **f**
10:8 the **f** mighty warrior on the
10:10 The **f** ⌊cities⌋ in his kingdom
13:4 where he had **f** made an altar.
25:25 The **f** one born was red.
25:31 Jacob responded, "**F**,
25:33 "**F**, swear an oath," Jacob said.
32:17 He commanded the **f** servant,
38:17 She said, "**F** give me
38:28 "This one came out **f**."
41:3 They stood behind the **f** seven
43:18 back into our sacks the **f** time.
49:3 the very **f** son I had,
49:3 **f** in majesty and first in power.
49:3 first in majesty and **f** in power.
49:4 You will no longer be **f**
Exo 4:8 to the **f** miraculous sign,
10:6 the time they **f** came here until
12:2 "This month will be the very **f**
12:15 On the very **f** day you must
12:15 in it from the **f** day through
12:16 a holy assembly on the **f** day
12:18 day of the **f** month until
12:48 **F**, every male in the household
21:10 he must not deprive the **f** wife
23:16 the **f** produce harvested from
23:19 of the **f** produce harvested from
28:17 In the **f** row put red quartz,
29:40 With the **f** lamb make an
34:1 stone tablets like the **f** ones,
34:1 were on the **f** tablets which you
34:4 stone tablets like the **f** ones.
34:19 "Every **f** male offspring is mine,
34:22 with the **f** grain from your
34:26 "You must bring the **f** and best
39:10 In the **f** row they put red quartz,
40:2 tent of meeting) on the **f** day
40:2 on the first day of the **f** month
40:17 So the tent was set up on the **f**
40:17 on the first day of the **f** month
Lev 1:15 **F**, he will drain the blood
2:12 as offerings of your **f** products.
2:14 from the **f** grain you harvest,
4:21 same way he burned the **f** bull.

Lev 5:8 sacrifice the offering for sin **f**.
9:21 However, he **f** took the breasts
15:11 without **f** rinsing his hands,
19:23 the fruit for ⌊the **f**⌋ three years.
23:5 fourteenth day of the **f** month,
23:7 On the **f** day there will be a
23:10 of the **f** grain you harvest.
23:17 They are the **f** harvested grain
23:20 of the **f** harvested grain as
23:24 "Tell the Israelites: On the **f**
23:35 On the **f** day there will be a
23:39 The **f** and the eighth days will
23:40 On the **f** day take the best
27:26 LORD because it was born **f**.
27:33 both the **f** animal and its
Num 1:1 It was the **f** day of the second
1:18 whole community on the **f** day
2:9 They will be the **f** group to
4:5 **F** they will cover the ark with
6:12 The **f** time period won't count.
7:12 gifts on the **f** day was Nahshon,
9:1 In the **f** month of the second
9:5 day of the **f** month at dusk
10:5 the east side will break camp **f**.
10:10 festival days and on the **f** day
10:13 This was the **f** time they
10:14 descendants broke camp **f**.
18:12 "I am also giving you the **f** of
18:13 The **f** of all produce harvested
20:1 In the **f** month the whole
24:20 "Amalek was **f** among the
28:11 "On the **f** of every month bring
28:16 "The fourteenth day of the **f**
28:18 On the **f** day there will be a
28:26 the **f** produce harvested from
29:1 "On the **f** day of the seventh
33:3 the fifteenth day of the **f** month,
33:38 He died there on the **f** day of
Dtr 1:3 On the **f** day of the eleventh
10:1 stone tablets like the **f** ones,
10:2 that were on the **f** tablets,
10:3 stone tablets like the **f** ones.
10:10 40 nights as I did the **f** time.
16:4 on the evening of the **f** day.
18:4 them the **f** produce harvested:
18:4 and the **f** wool you shear from
21:17 That son is the very **f** son he
24:4 her **f** husband is not allowed to
25:6 Then the **f** son she has will
26:2 take some of the **f** produce
26:10 So now I've brought the **f**
Jos 4:19 On the tenth day of the **f** month,
8:5 attack us as they did the **f** time,
8:6 from us just like the **f** time.'
21:10 Their lot was the **f** one drawn.
Jdg 1:1 "Who will go **f** to fight the
1:2 "Judah's troops will go **f**.
20:18 asked God, "Who will go **f**
20:18 answered, "Judah will go **f**."
20:22 they had formed it on the **f** day.
20:39 just like in the **f** battle."
Rut 3:10 or poor — is better than the **f**.
1Sm 2:16 "**F** let the fat be burned,
14:14 In their **f** slaughter Jonathan
14:35 it was the **f** time he had built an
14:36 "Let's consult God **f**."
22:15 Is this the **f** time I have prayed
2Sm 3:2 His **f** son was Amnon,
18:27 "It seems to me that the **f** one
19:20 Today I've come as the **f** of all
19:43 Weren't we the **f** to suggest
1Ki 3:22 The **f** woman kept on saying,
3:27 the living child to the **f** woman.
6:8 The entrance to the **f** story was
17:13 But **f** make a small loaf and
18:25 Prepare yours **f**, because there
20:9 messengers told me the **f** time,
20:17 district governors went out **f**.
22:5 said to the king of Israel, "But **f**,
2Ki 1:14 and burned up the **f** two officers
4:42 from the **f** harvested grain,
17:25 When they **f** came to live there,
25:27 in the **f** year of his reign,
1Ch 1:10 the **f** mighty warrior on the
2:21 the man who **f** settled Gilead.
2:23 the man who **f** settled Gilead.

1Ch 2:24 who **f** settled Tekoa.
2:42 who **f** settled Ziph,
2:42 who **f** settled Hebron.
2:44 who **f** settled Jorkeam.
2:45 who **f** settled Beth Zur.
2:49 who **f** settled Madmannah,
2:49 who **f** settled Machbenah and
2:50 who **f** settled Kiriath Jearim,
2:51 who **f** settled Bethlehem,
2:51 who **f** settled Beth Gadar.
2:52 who **f** settled Kiriath Jearim,
2:54 ⌊who **f** settled⌋ Bethlehem,
2:54 ⌊who **f** settled⌋ Beth Joab,
2:55 They **f** settled Beth Rechab.
3:1 His **f** son was Amnon,
4:3 These were the **f** settlers in
4:4 who **f** settled Bethlehem.
4:5 Ashhur, who **f** settled Tekoa,
4:12 Eshton was the **f** to settle Beth
4:12 who **f** settled the city of
4:14 who **f** settled the valley of
4:17 who **f** settled Eshtemoa.
4:18 who **f** settled Gedor,
4:18 who **f** settled Soco,
4:18 who **f** settled Zanoah.
4:19 **f** settled Keilah of the Garmites
4:21 who **f** settled Lecah,
4:21 who **f** settled Mareshah,
5:7 as follows: The **f** was Jeiel,
5:12 from Gad's **f** son Joel.
6:54 The ⌊**f**⌋ lot was drawn for the
7:14 was the **f** to settle Gilead.
7:31 who **f** settled Birzaith.
8:29 Jeiel, who **f** settled Gibeon,
9:2 The **f** to settle again on their
9:35 Jeiel, who **f** settled Gibeon,
11:6 "Whoever is the **f** to kill a
11:6 Zeruiah's son Joab was the **f** to
11:11 The **f** of David's fighting men
12:9 Ezer was the **f** of these
12:15 In the **f** month of the year,
15:13 you weren't there the **f** time,
16:7 For the **f** time David entrusted
23:8 Jehiel was the **f**, then Zetham,
23:11 Jahath was the **f**, and Ziza
23:19 Hebron's **f** son was Jeriah;
23:20 Uzziel's **f** son was Micah;
24:7 The **f** lot drawn was for
25:9 The **f** lot drawn chose Joseph,
27:2 was in charge of the **f** unit,
27:2 the one during the **f** month.
27:3 army's officers for the **f** month.
29:29 about King David from **f**
2Ch 3:12 and touched the wing of the **f**.
9:29 rest of Solomon's acts from **f**
12:15 concerning Rehoboam from **f**
16:11 Everything about Asa from **f** to
18:4 said to the king of Israel, "But **f**,
20:34 else about Jehoshaphat from **f**
29:3 In the **f** month of his first year
29:3 In the first month of his **f** year
29:17 They started on the **f** day of the
29:17 on the first day of the **f** month.
29:17 sixteenth day of the **f** month.
31:5 plenty of offerings from the **f**
35:1 fourteenth day of the **f** month.
35:27 and his acts from **f** to last — are
36:22 true in Cyrus' **f** year as king
Ezr 1:1 true in Cyrus' **f** year as king
3:6 to the LORD on the **f** day
3:12 to have seen the **f** temple
5:13 "However, in the **f** year of the
6:3 Cyrus' **f** year as king From:
6:19 fourteenth day of the **f** month,
7:5 who was the son of Aaron (the **f**
7:9 He had left Babylon on the **f**
7:9 on the first day of the **f** month,
7:9 and on the **f** day of the fifth
8:31 the twelfth day of the **f** month
10:16 They sat down on the **f** day of
10:17 By the **f** day of the first month,
10:17 By the first day of the **f** month,
Neh 7:5 who came back the **f** time.
8:2 This took place on the **f** day of
8:18 Day by day, from the **f** day of
10:35 bring the **f** produce harvested

Neh 10:35 and the **f** fruit from every
12:44 the **f** produce harvested,
13:31 and for bringing the **f** produce
Est 3:7 Nisan, the **f** month, until Adar,
3:12 On the thirteenth day of the **f**
Job 3:9 Let it not see the **f** light of dawn
15:7 "Were you the **f** human to be
40:19 Behemoth is the **f** of God's
41:18 Its eyes are like the **f** rays of
42:14 the **f** ⌊daughter⌋ Jemimah,
Psa 105:36 the **f** ones born in the land
Pro 3:9 with your wealth and with the **f**
8:23 from everlasting from the **f**,
8:26 made land or fields or the **f** dust
18:17 The **f** to state his case seems
Isa 41:4 I, the LORD, was there **f**,
41:27 I was the **f** to tell Zion,
43:13 "From the ⌊**f**⌋ day I was the
43:27 Your **f** ancestor sinned,
44:6 I am the **f** and the last,
46:9 Remember the **f** events,
48:12 I am the **f** and the last.
60:9 ships from Tarshish are the **f**
65:7 so I will be the **f** to pay them
Jer 3:1 her **f** husband shouldn't go
4:31 as she gives birth to her **f** child.
7:12 where I **f** made a dwelling
16:18 **F**, I will have them pay twice
24:2 like figs that ripen **f**.
25:1 (This was the **f** year that
50:17 The **f** to devour them was the
52:31 in the **f** year of his reign,
Eze 10:14 The **f** was the face of an angel,
17:9 Won't the **f** eagle uproot it and
23:16 She fell in love with them at **f**
26:1 On the **f** day of the month in the
29:17 On the **f** day of the first month
29:17 On the first day of the **f** month
30:20 On the seventh day of the **f**
31:1 On the **f** day of the third month
32:1 On the **f** day of the twelfth
41:7 A stairway went from the **f**
42:5 narrower than those on the **f**
42:6 on the **f** and second stories.
44:30 best of all the **f** ripened fruits.
45:18 On the **f** day of the first month,
45:18 On the first day of the **f** month,
45:21 fourteenth day of the **f** month,
46:6 On the **f** day of the month,
Dan 1:21 the royal palace until the **f** year
7:1 In Belshazzar's **f** year as king
7:4 The **f** animal was like a lion,
8:21 between its eyes is its **f** king.
8:22 be as strong as the **f** king was.
9:2 In the **f** year of his reign,
9:21 I had seen in the **f** vision,
10:4 day of the **f** month,
10:12 since the **f** day you decided
11:1 During Darius the Mede's **f** year
11:13 an army larger than the **f** one.
11:29 time will be different from the **f**.
Hos 1:2 When the LORD **f** spoke to
2:7 'I'll go back to my **f** husband.
9:10 it was like seeing the **f** figs of
Amo 3:3 together without meeting **f**?
3:7 he ⌊**f**⌋ reveals his secret
6:7 is why they will now be the **f**
Jnh 4:2 to run to Tarshish in the **f** place.
Mic 1:13 You were the **f** to lead the
Nah 2:8 pool of water from its **f** day on.
Hag 1:1 On the **f** day of the sixth month
Zec 6:2 The **f** chariot had red horses.
12:7 will save Judah's tents **f** so that
14:10 Gate to the place of **F** Gate,
Mat 5:24 **F** go away and make peace
6:24 He will hate the **f** master and
6:24 or he will be devoted to the **f**
6:33 But **f**, be concerned about his
7:5 **F** remove the beam from your
8:21 **f** let me go to bury my father."
10:2 apostles: **f** and foremost,
12:29 **F** he must tie up the strong
13:30 workers to gather the weeds **f**
17:10 say that Elijah must come **f**?"
17:27 Take the **f** fish that you catch.
19:30 many who are **f** will be last,
Mat 19:30 many who are last will be **f**.
20:8 and end with the **f**.'
20:10 who had been hired **f** came,
20:16 "In this way the last will be **f**,
20:16 and the **f** will be last."
21:28 He went to the **f** and said,
21:31 "The **f**," they answered.
22:25 The **f** married and died.
23:26 **F** clean the inside of the cups
26:17 On the **f** day of the Festival of
27:64 will be worse than the **f**."
Mar 1:30 The **f** thing they did was to tell
3:27 **F** he must tie up the strong
4:28 **F** the green blade appears,
7:4 eat unless they have washed **f**.
7:27 Jesus said to her, "**F**,
9:11 say that Elijah must come **f**?"
9:12 "Elijah is coming **f** and will put
10:31 But many who are **f** will be last,
10:31 and the last will be **f**."
12:20 The **f** got married and died
13:10 But **f**, the Good News must be
14:12 was customary on the **f** day
16:9 he appeared **f** to Mary from
Luk 2:2 This was the **f** census taken
6:42 **F** remove the beam from your
9:59 **f** let me go to bury my father."
9:61 but **f** let me tell my family
13:30 Some who are last will be **f**,
13:30 some who are **f** will be last."
14:18 The **f** said to him, 'I bought a
14:28 You would **f** sit down and
14:31 He would **f** sit down and think
16:5 He said to the **f**, 'How much do
16:13 He will hate the **f** master and
16:13 or he will be devoted to the **f**
17:25 But **f** he must suffer a lot and
19:16 "The **f** servant said,
20:29 The **f** got married and died
21:9 These things must happen **f**,
Jon 2:10 serves the best wine **f**.
7:51 without **f** hearing that person's
8:7 who is sinless should be the **f**
10:40 where John **f** baptized people.
12:16 At **f** Jesus' disciples didn't
16:4 I didn't tell you this at **f**,
18:13 and took him **f** to Annas,
19:32 broke the legs of the **f** man
19:39 Nicodemus, the one who had **f**
20:4 Peter and came to the tomb **f**.
20:8 who arrived at the tomb **f**,
Act 1:1 In my **f** book, Theophilus,
3:26 life and has sent him to you **f**.
7:12 That was their **f** trip.
11:26 called Christians for the **f** time
12:10 They passed the **f** and second
13:46 speak the word of God to you **f**.
15:14 how God **f** showed his concern
20:18 my time with you from the **f** day
21:16 and was one of the **f** disciples.
26:20 I spread the message that I **f**
26:23 would suffer and be the **f**
27:43 overboard **f** and swim ashore.
Rom 1:8 **F**, I thank my God through
1:16 Jews **f** and Greeks as well.
2:9 for Jews **f** and Greeks as well.
2:10 for Jews **f** and Greeks as well.
3:2 **F** of all, God entrusted them
8:23 who have the Spirit as the **f**
10:19 Moses was the **f** to say,
11:16 If the **f** handful of dough is holy,
13:11 when we **f** became believers.
16:5 He was the **f** person in the
1Co 11:18 In the **f** place, I hear that when
12:28 God has appointed **f** apostles,
14:30 the **f** speaker should be silent.
15:20 He is the very **f** person of those
15:23 Christ is the **f**, then at his
15:36 come to life unless it dies **f**.
15:45 says: "The **f** man, Adam,
15:46 The spiritual does not come **f**,
15:47 The **f** man was made from the
16:15 of Stephanas was the **f** family
2Co 8:5 **F**, they gave themselves to the
10:14 The fact is that we were the **f**
Gal 4:13 You know that the **f** time I
Php 1:5 from the **f** day ⌊you believed⌋
Col 1:6 you from the **f** day you heard
1:18 He is the beginning, the **f** to
1:18 have **f** place in everything.
1Th 4:16 **F**, the dead who believed in
2Th 2:3 unless⌋ a revolt takes place **f**,
1Ti 2:1 **F** of all, I encourage you to
2:13 After all, Adam was formed **f**,
3:10 **F**, a person must be evaluated.
5:4 of a widow must **f** learn
5:12 the faith they **f** accepted.
2Ti 1:5 That faith **f** lived in your
2:6 farmer should have the **f** share
4:16 At my **f** hearing no one stood
Heb 2:3 **F**, the Lord told this saving
7:2 In the **f** place, He is also called
7:27 **F** they brought sacrifices for
8:7 been wrong with the **f** promise,
8:13 the **f** promise was outdated.
9:1 The **f** promise had rules for the
9:2 The **f** part of this tent was
9:6 always went into the **f** part
9:9 The **f** part of the tent is an
9:15 committed under the **f** promise.
9:18 That is why even the **f** promise
10:8 In this passage Christ **f** said,
10:32 when you **f** learned the truth.
Jas 3:17 that comes from above is **f**
2Pe 1:20 **F**, you must understand this:
3:3 **F**, you must understand this:
1Jn 4:19 love because God loved us **f**.
Rev 1:5 the **f** to come back to life,
1:17 I am the **f** and the last,
2:4 The love you had at **f** is gone.
2:5 and do what you did at **f**.
2:8 The **f** and the last,
2:19 greater than what you did at **f**.
4:1 I heard the **f** voice like a
4:7 The **f** living creature was like a
6:1 as the lamb opened the **f**
8:7 When the **f** angel blew his
9:12 The **f** catastrophe is over.
13:12 all the authority of the **f** beast
13:12 living on it worship the **f** beast,
13:14 to do in front of the ⌊**f**⌋ beast.
13:15 into the statue of the ⌊**f**⌋ beast.
13:15 Then the statue of the ⌊**f**⌋
14:4 humanity as the **f** ones offered
16:2 The **f** angel poured his bowl
20:5 This is the **f** time that people
20:6 included the **f** time that people
21:1 because the **f** heaven and earth
21:4 the **f** things have disappeared."
21:19 The **f** foundation was gray
22:13 A and the Z, the **f** and the last,

firstborn (137)

Gen 4:4 parts of the **f** animals from his
10:15 was the father of Sidon his **f**,
22:21 Uz (the **f**), Buz (his brother),
25:13 Nebaioth (Ishmael's **f**),
25:31 sell me your rights as **f**."
25:33 and sold him his rights as **f**.
25:34 his contempt for his rights as **f**.
27:19 his father, "I'm Esau, your **f**.
27:32 "I'm your **f** son Esau,"
27:36 He took my rights as **f**,
35:23 of Leah were Jacob's **f** Reuben,
36:15 Esau's **f**, were Teman, Omar,
38:6 chose a wife for his **f** son Er.
41:51 Joseph named his **f** son
46:8 Reuben was Jacob's **f**.
48:18 This is the **f**. Put your right hand
49:3 "Reuben, you are my **f**,
Exo 4:22 LORD says: Israel is my **f** son.
4:23 So now I'm going to kill your **f**
6:14 Israel's **f**, were Hanoch, Pallu,
11:5 Every **f** son in Egypt will die,
11:5 from the **f** of Pharaoh who rules
11:5 to the **f** children of female
11:5 every **f** domestic animal.
12:12 Egypt and kill every **f** male,
12:29 the LORD killed every **f** male
12:29 male in Egypt from the **f** son
12:29 who ruled the land to the **f** son
12:29 and also every **f** animal.

Exo 13:2 "Set apart every **f** male for me.
13:2 Every **f** male offspring among
13:12 sacrifice every **f** male offspring
13:12 The **f** male offspring of each of
13:13 to buy any **f** donkey back from
13:13 You must also buy every **f** son
13:15 the LORD killed every **f** male in
13:15 why we sacrifice every **f** male
13:15 and buy every **f** son back from
22:29 "You must give me your **f** son.
34:19 even the **f** males of all your
34:20 goat to buy back the **f** donkey.
34:20 You must buy back every **f** of
Lev 27:26 "A **f** animal already belongs to
Num 1:20 of Reuben, Israel's **f** son,
3:2 Aaron's sons are Nadab (the **f**),
3:12 every **f** male offspring among
3:13 because every **f** is mine.
3:13 The day I killed every **f** male in
3:13 apart as holy every **f** in Israel,
3:40 "Register every **f** male of the
3:41 substitutes for all **f** Israelites.
3:41 be substitutes for all **f** animals
3:42 So Moses registered all the **f**
3:43 The total of all the **f** males at
3:45 for all the **f** Israelites
3:46 There are 273 more **f** male
3:50 for the **f** Israelites weighed 34
8:16 for every **f** male offspring
8:17 Every **f** in Israel, is mine. The
8:17 The day I killed every **f** male in
8:18 as substitutes for all the **f** sons
18:15 Every **f** male, human or animal,
18:15 But you must buy back every **f**
18:15 firstborn son and the **f** male
18:17 must never buy back a **f** ox,
26:5 Reuben was Israel's **f**.
33:4 were burying all their **f** sons,
Dtr 12:6 and the **f** of your cattle,
12:17 the **f** of your cattle,
14:23 and eat the **f** of your cattle,
15:19 You must dedicate every **f**
15:19 Never use a **f** ox for work,
15:19 and never shear a **f** sheep.
21:15 and the **f** son might belong to
21:16 loves as if that son were the **f**.
21:16 disregard for the real **f** (the son
21:17 wife he doesn't love as the **f**.
21:17 The rights of the **f** son are his.
33:17 will be as majestic as a **f** bull.
Jos 6:26 It will cost him his **f** son to lay
17:1 Manasseh was Joseph's **f**.
17:1 Machir, Manasseh's **f**,
Jdg 8:20 Then he told Jether, his **f** son,
1Sm 8:2 The name of his **f** son was
14:49 were Merab (the **f** daughter)
17:13 The **f** was Eliab, the second
2Sm 13:21 because he was his **f** son.
1Ki 16:34 foundation cost him his **f** son,
2Ki 3:27 Then he took his **f** son,
1Ch 1:13 was the father of Sidon his **f**,
1:29 Ishmael's **f** was Nebaioth,
2:3 considered Er, Judah's **f**, evil,
2:13 was the father of Eliab (his **f**),
2:25 Jerahmeel (the **f** son of Hezron)
2:25 of Hezron) fathered Ram (his **f**),
2:27 The sons of Ram (the **f** son of
2:42 brother) were his **f** son Mesha,
2:50 the **f** son of Ephrath,
3:15 Josiah's **f** son was Johanan,
4:4 the **f** of Ephrathah,
5:1 the sons of Reuben, Israel's **f**.
5:1 (Although he was the **f**,
5:1 his rights as **f** were given to his
5:1 in the genealogy as the **f** son.
5:2 received the rights as **f**.)
5:3 The sons of Reuben, Israel's **f**,
6:28 who was his **f**, and Abijah,
8:1 was the father of Bela (his **f**),
8:30 His **f** son was Abdon,
8:39 Eshek's sons were Ulam (the **f**),
9:5 Asaiah (the **f**) and his sons.
9:31 the **f** son of Shallum,
9:36 His **f** son was Abdon,
26:2 sons were Zechariah (the **f**),
26:4 Edom's sons Shemaiah (the **f**),
1Ch 26:10 although he was not the **f**.
2Ch 21:3 to Jehoram, who was the **f**.
Neh 10:36 decide who should bring the **f**
Job 18:13 Death's **f** son eats away at the
Psa 78:51 slaughtered every **f** in Egypt,
89:27 Yes, I will make him the **f**.
105:36 He killed all the **f** sons,
135:8 He is the one who killed every **f**
136:10 the one who killed the **f** males
Jer 31:9 and Ephraim will be my **f**.
Eze 20:26 all their **f** sons as gifts
Mic 6:7 Should I give him my **f** child
Zec 12:10 for him as one cries for a **f** son.
Luk 2:7 She gave birth to her **f** son.
2:23 "Every **f** boy is to be set apart
Rom 8:29 is the **f** among many children.
Col 1:15 the **f** of all creation.
Heb 1:6 about to send his **f** Son into
11:28 angel would not kill the **f** sons.
12:16 He sold his rights as the **f** son
12:17 the blessing that the **f** son was
12:23 and to the assembly of God's **f**

fish (69)

Gen 1:26 Let them rule the **f** in the sea,
1:28 Rule the **f** in the sea,
9:2 on the ground and all the **f**
Exo 7:18 The **f** in the Nile will die,
7:21 The **f** in the Nile died,
Num 11:5 Remember all the free **f** we ate
11:22 they have enough if all the **f**
Dtr 4:18 or any **f** in the water.
1Ki 4:33 animals, birds, reptiles, and **f**.
2Ch 33:14 to the entrance of **F** Gate.
Neh 3:3 of Hassenaah rebuilt **F** Gate.
12:39 over Old Gate and **F** Gate,
13:16 in Jerusalem were bringing in **f**
Job 12:8 Even the **f** will relate ⌊the
Psa 8:8 the birds, the **f**,
105:29 blood and caused their **f** to die.
Ecc 9:12 Like **f** that are caught in a cruel
Isa 50:2 Their **f** stink because there is
Eze 29:4 in your jaws and make the **f**
29:4 out of your river with all the **f**
29:5 you and all the **f** from the Nile.
38:20 **F**, birds, wild animals,
47:9 will be many **f** and animals.
47:10 As many kinds of **f** will be
Hos 4:3 animals, birds, and **f** are dying.
Jnh 1:17 The LORD sent a big **f** to
1:17 Jonah was inside the **f** for three
2:1 From inside the **f** Jonah prayed
2:10 Then the LORD spoke to the **f**,
Hab 1:14 You make all people like the **f**
Zep 1:3 in the sky, the **f** in the sea,
1:10 loud cry will come from **F** Gate,
Mat 4:19 to catch people instead of **f**."
7:10 Or if your child asks for a **f**,
12:40 was in the belly of a huge **f**
13:47 It gathered all kinds of **f**.
13:48 the good **f** into containers,
14:17 five loaves of bread and two **f**."
14:19 the five loaves and the two **f**,
15:34 and a few small **f**."
15:36 took the seven loaves and the **f**
15:36 the bread and **f** to the people.
17:27 Take the first **f** that you catch.
Mar 1:17 to catch people instead of **f**."
6:38 loaves of bread and two **f**."
6:41 the five loaves and the two **f**,
6:41 pieces of the two **f** to everyone.
6:43 baskets with bread and **f**.
8:7 They also had a few small **f**.
8:7 and said that the **f** should also
Luk 5:4 your nets to catch some **f**."
5:6 large number of **f** that their nets
5:9 number of **f** they had caught.
5:10 will catch people instead of **f**."
9:13 five loaves of bread and two **f**.
9:16 the five loaves and the two **f**,
11:11 asks you, his father, for a **f**,
24:42 gave him a piece of broiled **f**.
Jon 6:9 bread and two small **f** is here.
6:11 did the same thing with the **f**.
21:5 haven't you caught any **f**?"
21:6 because so many **f** were in it.
Jon 21:8 and dragged the net full of **f**.
21:9 they saw a fire with a **f** lying on
21:10 of the **f** you've just caught."
21:11 net was filled with 153 large **f**,
21:13 and did the same with the **f**.
Act 9:18 Immediately, something like **f**
1Co 15:39 and **f** have still another.

fishermen (5)

Isa 19:8 **F** will cry. All who cast their
Jer 16:16 "I'm going to send for many **f**,"
Mat 4:18 the sea because they were **f**.
Mar 1:16 the sea because they were **f**.
Luk 5:2 The **f** had stepped out of them

fishhook (1)

Job 41:1 out ⌊of the water⌋ with a **f**

fishhooks (2)

Amo 4:2 and the rest of you on **f**.
Hab 1:15 pull them all up with **f**,

fishing (7)

Job 41:7 or its head with **f** spears?
Eze 26:5 people spread their **f** nets.
26:14 a place to spread **f** nets.
47:10 sea with their **f** nets spread out.
Mat 4:21 preparing their nets to go **f**.
Mar 1:19 preparing their nets ⌊to go **f**⌋.
Jon 21:3 said to the others, "I'm going **f**."

fist (7)

Exo 21:18 other with a rock or with his **f**
Job 31:21 If I have shaken my **f** at an
Isa 10:32 They shake their **f** at the
19:16 Armies will shake his **f** at them.
Lam 2:15 the road shakes a **f** at you.
Eze 4:7 Shake your **f** and prophesy
Zec 2:9 I'm going to shake my **f** at the

fists (3)

Isa 30:32 them in battle, swinging his **f**.
Mat 26:67 hit him with their **f**,
Mar 14:65 his face and hit him with their **f**.

fit (14)

Gen 49:20 provide delicacies **f** for a king.
Num 5:14 "A husband may have a **f** of
5:30 to do when a husband has a **f**
Jos 14:11 I'm still as **f** to go to war now
Job 30:1 I didn't think their fathers were **f**
Pro 17:7 does lying **f** a noble person!
19:10 Luxury does not **f** a fool,
Dan 3:13 Then, in a **f** of rage and anger,
Nah 1:12 of Nineveh are physically **f**
Mat 23:15 make that person twice as **f**
Luk 9:62 to plow and looks back is not **f**
1Co 15:9 I'm not even **f** to be called an
Eph 2:21 parts of the building **f** together
4:16 He makes the whole body **f**

fitting (1)

Pro 17:7 Refined speech is not **f** for a

fittings (2)

1Ch 22:3 quantity of iron for nails and **f**
2Ch 34:11 stones and wood for the **f**

fixed (4)

Num 18:16 buy them back at the **f** price
1Ki 10:28 them from Kue for a **f** price.
2Ki 9:30 put on eye shadow, **f** her hair,
2Ch 1:16 them from Kue for a **f** price.

flag (24)

Num 1:52 in its own area under its own **f**.
2:2 under the **f** that symbolizes its
2:3 Judah will camp under their **f**.
2:10 Reuben will camp under their **f**.
2:17 in place under his own **f**.
2:18 Ephraim will camp under their **f**.
2:25 by Dan will camp under their **f**.
2:31 will travel under their own **f**."
10:14 With their **f** in front,
10:18 With their **f** in front,
10:22 With their **f** in front,

Num 10:25 camp last with their **f** in front.
Psa 60:4 Yet, you have raised a **f** for
Isa 5:26 The LORD raises up a **f** for the
18:3 Look when someone raises a **f**
31:9 at the sight of the battle **f**.
49:22 I will raise my **f** for the people.
62:10 Raise a **f** for the people!
Jer 4:6 Raise the **f** to signal people to
4:21 How long must I see the battle **f**
6:1 Raise the **f** over Beth
50:2 Raise a **f**, and announce it.
51:12 Raise your battle **f** in front of
51:27 Raise your battle **f** throughout

flagpole (1)

Isa 30:17 you will be left alone like a **f**

flags (3)

Num 2:34 They set up camp under their **f**,
Psa 20:5 We will wave our **f** in the name
Eze 27:7 They were like your **f**.

flakes (1)

Exo 16:14 with a thin layer of **f** like frost

flaky (2)

Exo 4:6 It looked as **f** as snow.
2Ki 5:27 made his skin as **f** as snow.

flame (13)

Jdg 13:20 As the **f** went up toward
13:20 of the LORD went up in the **f**.
Job 15:30 A **f** will shrivel his branches.
18:5 The **f** of his fire stops glowing.
41:21 and a **f** pours from its mouth.
Isa 4:5 during the day and a glowing **f**
10:16 A **f** will be turned into a raging
10:17 Israel's light will become a **f**.
30:27 His tongue is like a devouring **f**.
Jer 48:45 of Heshbon and a **f** from Sihon.
Oba 1:18 of Joseph will be like a **f**.
Jas 3:5 can be set on fire by a little **f**.
3:6 The tongue is that kind of **f**.

flames (31)

Exo 3:2 appeared to him there as **f**
Num 21:28 **f** from Sihon's city.
Dtr 4:11 which was on fire with **f**
Job 41:19 **F** shoot from its mouth.
Psa 2:12 his anger will burst into **f**.
83:15 the way fire burns a forest and **f**
104:4 and your servants **f** of fire.
106:18 **F** burned up wicked people.
Sos 8:6 Love's **f** are flames of fire,
8:6 Love's flames are **f** of fire,
8:6 **f** that come from the LORD.
Isa 5:24 As **f** burn up straw and dry
5:24 and dry grass shrivels in **f**,
42:25 It engulfed them in **f**,
43:2 and the **f** will not harm you.
47:14 rescue themselves from the **f**.
54:16 to fan the coals into **f**
66:15 and punish them with **f** of fire.
Dan 3:22 killed by the **f** from the fire.
7:9 His throne was fiery **f**,
11:33 be defeated by swords and **f**.
Hos 7:4 doesn't have to fan its **f** when
Joe 1:19 **F** have burned up all the trees
2:3 Behind it **f** are blazing.
Hab 2:13 grow tired only to feed the **f**
Act 7:30 appeared to him in the **f**
2Ti 1:6 you to fan that gift into **f**.
Heb 1:7 makes his servants **f** of fire."
Rev 1:14 His eyes were like **f** of fire.
2:18 whose eyes are like **f** of fire
19:12 His eyes are **f** of fire.

flaming (10)

Gen 3:24 God placed angels and a **f**
15:17 and a **f** torch passed between
Psa 7:13 and turns them into **f** arrows.
76:3 There he destroyed **f** arrows,
Pro 26:18 madman who shoots **f** arrows,
Isa 50:11 arm yourselves with **f** torches.
Dan 10:6 His eyes were like **f** torches.
Eph 6:16 With it you can put out all the **f**
Rev 4:5 Seven **f** torches were burning
8:10 a huge star **f** like a torch fell

flap (1)

Job 39:13 "Does the ostrich **f** its wings in

flapped (1)

Isa 10:14 Not one of them **f** a wing,

flare (1)

Jer 4:4 my fury will **f** up like a fire.

flared (5)

Jdg 6:21 Fire **f** up from the rock and
2Sm 22:9 Glowing coals **f** up from it.
Psa 18:8 Glowing coals **f** up from it.
78:21 and his anger **f** up at Israel
78:31 the anger of God **f** up against

flaring (1)

Psa 39:3 My heart burned like a fire **f** up

flash (9)

Job 15:12 Why do your eyes **f**
20:28 a **f** flood on the day of his
37:15 the lightning **f** from his clouds?
41:18 it gives out a **f** of light.
Jer 10:13 He makes lightning **f** with the
Eze 21:10 and polished to **f** like lightning.
21:15 It's ready to **f** like lightning.
21:28 to destroy and **f** like lightning.
Nah 3:3 Swords **f**! Spears glitter! Many

flashed (7)

Exo 9:24 and lightning **f** while it hailed.
Lev 10:2 A fire **f** from the LORD and
2Sm 22:15 He **f** streaks of lightning and
Psa 18:14 He **f** streaks of lightning and
77:17 your arrows **f** in every direction.
Act 9:3 heaven suddenly **f** around him.
22:6 heaven suddenly **f** around me.

flashes (9)

Job 36:30 Look, he scatters his **f** of
37:3 He **f** his lightning everywhere
37:3 His light **f** to the ends of the
38:35 Can you send lightning **f** so
Psa 29:7 strikes with **f** of lightning.
97:4 His **f** of lightning light up the
Nah 2:3 metal on his chariots **f** fiery red,
Mat 24:27 just as lightning **f** from east
Luk 17:24 lightning that **f** from one end

flashing (3)

Dtr 32:41 I will sharpen my **f** sword and
Job 39:23 with the **f** spear and javelin.
Eze 1:4 with **f** lightning surrounded by

flask (5)

1Sm 10:1 Samuel took a **f** of olive oil,
16:1 Fill a **f** with olive oil and go.
16:13 Samuel took the **f** of olive oil
2Ki 9:1 Take this **f** of olive oil,
9:3 Take the **f** of oil, pour it on his

flat (5)

Exo 12:39 they baked round, **f** bread.
Jdg 7:13 turned upside down, and fell **f**."
1Sm 28:20 Saul fell **f** on the ground.
2Sm 13:8 made **f** bread in front of him,
1Ch 9:31 with preparing the **f** bread.

flats (1)

Job 39:6 in and the salt **f** as its dwelling

flatten (1)

Amo 6:11 big houses and **f** little houses.

flattened (1)

Isa 32:19 The forest will be **f** because of

flatter (4)

Job 32:21 toward anyone or **f** anyone.
32:22 I don't know how to **f**.
Psa 5:9 They **f** with their tongues.
Jud 1:16 and **f** people in order to take

flattered (1)

Psa 78:36 They **f** him with their mouths

flattering (5)

Psa 12:2 They speak with **f** lips.
12:3 May the LORD cut off every **f**
Pro 26:28 and a **f** mouth causes ruin.
Eze 12:24 false visions or **f** fortunetelling
Rom 16:18 By their smooth talk and **f**

flatters (3)

Psa 36:2 He **f** himself and does not hate
Pro 28:23 the one who **f** with his tongue.
29:5 A person who **f** his neighbor is

flattery (2)

Dan 11:32 With **f** he will corrupt those
1Th 2:5 As you know, we never used **f**

flavor (4)

Job 6:6 or is there any **f** in the white of
Jer 48:11 That is why its **f** has remained
Mar 9:50 how will you restore its **f**?
Luk 14:34 how will you restore its **f**?

flaws (3)

Mat 9:13 think they don't have any **f**."
Mar 2:17 think they don't have any **f**."
Luk 5:32 think they don't have any **f**."

flax (3)

Exo 9:31 (The **f** and the barley were
9:31 heads and the **f** was in bloom.
Jos 2:6 them with the **f** which she had

flea (2)

1Sm 24:14 A dead dog? One **f**?
26:20 for one **f** like someone hunting

fled (91)

Gen 14:10 of Sodom and Gomorrah **f**,
14:10 but the other kings **f** to the hills.
Exo 2:15 But Moses **f** from Pharaoh and
14:5 was told that the people had **f**,
Num 35:25 to the city of refuge you **f** to.
35:26 the city of refuge you **f** to.
35:32 accused murderer who has **f**
Jos 7:4 they **f** from the men of Ai.
10:11 As they **f** from the Israelites
Jdg 1:6 Adoni Bezek **f**. Judah's troops
4:15 from his chariot and **f** on foot.
4:17 Meanwhile, Sisera **f** on foot
7:21 screaming as they **f**.
7:22 They **f** as far as Beth Shittah,
8:12 Zebah and Zalmunna **f** as
9:51 and leaders of the town **f** to it.
11:3 Jephthah **f** from his brothers.
20:45 The others turned and **f** into the
20:47 But 600 men turned and **f** into
1Sm 4:10 Every Israelite soldier **f** to
4:16 I **f** from the front line today."
4:17 "Israel **f** from the Philistines,"
17:24 they **f** from him because they
17:51 hero had been killed, they **f**.
19:8 decisively that they **f** from him.
19:10 David **f**, escaping from Saul
20:1 David **f** from the pastures at
22:1 escaped from that place and **f**
22:20 was Abiathar. He **f** to David.
23:6 Ahimelech's son Abiathar **f**
27:4 told that David had **f** to Gath,
31:1 the men of Israel **f** from the
31:7 saw that the men of Israel had **f**
2Sm 1:4 "The army **f** from the battle,
4:3 of Beeroth had **f** to Gittaim.
4:4 him up and **f** to Gittaim.
10:13 and the Arameans **f**.
10:14 saw that the Arameans had **f**,
10:14 the Ammonites **f** from Abishai
10:18 The Arameans **f** from Israel,
13:29 up, mounted their mules, and **f**.
13:34 Absalom has **f**." When the
13:37 **f** to Geshur's King Talmai,
13:38 Absalom, having **f** to Geshur,
18:17 Meanwhile, all Israel **f** and

2Sm 19:3 city as if they had f from battle
19:8 Meanwhile, Israel had f and
19:9 but now he has f from Absalom
23:11 the troops f from the Philistines,
1Ki 2:28 So Joab f to the LORD's tent
2:29 Solomon heard that Joab had f
2:39 two of Shimei's slaves f to
11:17 Edomite servants f to Egypt.
11:23 Rezon f from his master,
11:40 but Jeroboam f to King Shishak
12:2 where he had f from King
12:18 as he could and f to Jerusalem.
19:3 Elijah f to save his life.
20:20 The Arameans f, and Israel
20:30 The survivors f to Aphek,
20:30 Benhadad had also f.
2Ki 3:24 and they f from the Israelites.
7:7 So at dusk they f. They
8:21 and his troops f home.
9:27 he f on the road leading to Beth
14:12 the Judeans f to their homes.
14:19 so he f to Lachish.
1Ch 10:1 the men of Israel f from the
10:7 saw that ⌊their army⌋ had f
11:13 the troops f from the Philistines,
19:14 and the Arameans f.
19:15 saw that the Arameans had f,
19:15 f from Joab's brother Abishai
19:18 The Arameans f from Israel,
2Ch 10:2 where he had f from King
10:18 as he could and f to Jerusalem.
13:16 The Israelites f from Judah's
14:12 The Sudanese army f.
25:22 the Judeans f to their homes.
25:27 Amaziah f to Lachish,
Psa 104:7 and f because of your threat.
Isa 22:3 All your leaders f together and
Jer 9:10 Birds and cattle have f.
26:21 But Uriah heard about it and f in
39:4 the soldiers saw them, they f.
41:15 from Johanan and f to Ammon.
52:7 and all Judah's soldiers f.
Lam 4:15 When they f and wandered
Hos 12:12 Jacob f to the country of Syria.
Rev 12:6 Then the woman f into the
20:11 The earth and the sky f from

flee (50)

Gen 19:20 a city near enough to f to,
Exo 21:13 the killer should f to a place I
23:27 all your enemies f from you.
Num 35:15 person may f to these cities.
Dtr 4:42 they had never hated could f
32:30 people make ten thousand f?
Jdg 20:32 "Let's f in order to lead them
2Sm 15:14 "Let's f immediately,
17:2 All the people with him will f,
18:3 "If we f, they won't care about
24:13 which you f from your enemies
2Ki 9:23 his chariot around and tried to f,
9:27 Ahaziah continued to f until he
Job 39:18 its rider when it gets up to f.
Psa 11:1 "F to your mountain like a bird?
21:12 They turn their backs ⌊and f⌋
68:1 who hate him will f from him.
68:12 "The kings of the armies f;
Sos 2:17 breeze and the shadows f,
4:6 cool breeze and the shadows f,
Isa 10:29 the people in Saul's Gibeah f.
10:31 The people in Madmenah f;
13:14 return to his own people and f
15:5 Its people f as far as Zoar at
21:15 They f from swords,
30:16 said, "No, we'll f on horses."
30:16 So you f. You've added, "We'll
30:17 One thousand people will f
30:17 and you will f when five
31:8 They will f from battle,
33:3 People f from the noise of
48:20 f from the Babylonians!
Jer 4:29 All the people in the city will f
25:35 no place for the shepherds to f,
46:5 They f without looking back.
46:6 "The infantry can't f.
48:45 "Those who f will stand
49:24 They turn to f, but panic grips
Jer 50:16 turn to his own people and f
Zec 2:6 F from the land of the north,
14:5 Then you will f to the valley of
14:5 You will f as you did from the
Mat 2:13 and his mother, and f to Egypt.
3:7 Who showed you how to f from
10:23 you in one city, f to another.
24:16 should f to the mountains.
24:20 or a day of worship when you f.
Mar 13:14 should f to the mountains.
Luk 3:7 Who showed you how to f from
21:21 those of you in Judea should f

fleeing (9)

Gen 35:1 you were f from your brother
35:7 when he was f from his brother.
1Sm 14:22 that the Philistines were f,
21:10 He was ⌊still⌋ f from Saul
22:17 "When they knew David was f,
1Ki 2:7 They helped me when I was f
Job 26:13 With his hand he stabbed the f
Jer 48:19 Ask those who are f and those
Nah 2:8 But now its people are f.

flees (6)

Job 20:24 If that person f from an iron
27:22 He f from its power.
Pro 28:1 A wicked person f when no
Isa 24:18 Whoever f from news of a
Jer 48:44 "Whoever f from a disaster will
Amo 5:19 It is like a person who f from a

fleet (6)

1Ki 9:26 King Solomon also built a f
9:27 experienced seamen with the f.
10:11 Hiram's f that brought gold
10:22 The king had a f headed for
10:22 for Tarshish with Hiram's f.
10:22 the Tarshish f would bring gold,

fleeting (5)

1Ch 29:15 Our days are as f as shadows
Job 8:9 Our days on earth are only a f
14:2 He is like a f shadow;
Psa 144:4 Their life span is like a f
Pro 23:5 Will you catch only a f glimpse

flesh (66)

Gen 2:21 closed up the f at that place.
2:23 is now bone of my bones and f
2:23 of my bones and flesh of my f.
2:24 and they will become one f.
6:3 because they are f and blood.
17:13 will be a sign on your f,
29:14 "You are my own f and blood."
37:27 our own f and blood."
40:19 will eat the f from your bones."
Lev 13:10 and if there is raw f in the sore,
13:14 But if raw f appears,
13:15 priest will examine the raw f
13:15 The raw f is unclean.
13:16 But if the raw f turns white
13:24 a burn on his skin and the raw f
Dtr 28:53 you will eat the f of your own
28:55 give none of them any of the f
Jdg 9:2 I'm your own f and blood.'"
2Sm 5:1 "We are your own f and blood,"
16:11 my own f and blood,
19:12 my own f and blood.
19:13 'Aren't you my f and blood?
1Ch 11:1 "We are your own f and blood,"
Neh 5:5 We have the same f and blood
Job 2:5 and strike his f and bones.
10:11 you dress me in skin and f
19:22 you never satisfied with my f?
19:26 I will see God in my own f.
33:21 Their f becomes so thin that it
33:25 Then their f will become softer
41:23 The folds of its f stick to each
Psa 56:4 What can mere f ⌊and blood⌋
78:39 that they were only f and blood,
79:2 They have given the f of your
Pro 5:11 your body and f are consumed.
Isa 9:20 Each person eats the f from his
31:3 Their horses are f and blood,
49:26 your oppressors eat their own f,
Jer 17:5 who makes f and blood his
19:9 I will make the people eat the f
19:9 They will eat each other's f
Lam 3:4 He has made my f and my skin
Eze 32:5 I will scatter your f on the hills
Mic 3:2 people and the f off their bones.
3:3 You eat my people's f.
Nah 2:12 and its dens with torn f.
Zec 14:12 Their f will rot while they are
Mal 2:15 Your f and spirit belong to him.
Luk 24:39 Ghosts don't have f and bones,
Jon 3:6 F and blood give birth to flesh
3:6 blood give birth to f and blood,
6:51 bring life to the world is my f."
6:52 this man give us his f to eat?"
6:53 If you don't eat the f of the Son
6:54 Those who eat my f and drink
6:55 My f is true food, and my blood
6:56 Those who eat my f and drink
1Co 15:39 Not all f is the same.
15:39 Humans have one kind of f,
15:50 F and blood cannot inherit the
Heb 2:14 daughters have f and blood,
2:14 Jesus took on f and blood to be
2Jn 1:7 Christ came in f and blood.
Rev 17:16 They will eat her f and burn her
19:18 Eat the f of kings, generals,
19:21 gorged themselves on the f

flew (5)

2Sm 22:11 on one of the angels as he f,
Psa 18:10 on one of the angels as he f,
Isa 6:2 and with two they f.
6:6 Then one of the angels f to me.
Act 16:26 the doors immediately f open,

flies (15)

Exo 8:21 I will send swarms of f on you,
8:21 Egyptians will be filled with f,
8:22 There won't be any f there.
8:24 Dense swarms of f came into
8:24 the f were ruining everything.
8:29 Tomorrow the swarms of f will
8:31 The swarms of f left Pharaoh,
Dtr 4:17 any creature with wings that f,
19:5 the head f off the handle,
Job 39:27 your order that the eagle f high
Psa 78:45 He sent a swarm of f that bit
105:31 He spoke, and swarms of f and
Ecc 10:1 Dead f will make a bottle of
Isa 7:18 will whistle for the f that are at
51:6 who live there will die like f.

flimsy (1)

Eze 13:10 When someone builds a f wall,

flint (7)

Exo 4:25 Then Zipporah took a f knife,
Jos 5:2 to Joshua, "Make f knives,
5:3 So Joshua made f knives and
Psa 114:8 filled with water and turns f into
Isa 5:28 horses' hoofs are as hard as f.
50:7 I have set my face like a f.
Zec 7:12 hearts as hard as f so that they

flinty (1)

Job 28:9 exert their power on the f rocks

flipping (1)

Pro 18:18 F a coin ends quarrels and

float (1)

2Ki 6:6 place and made the ax head f.

floated (1)

Gen 7:18 the ship f on top of the water.

flock (61)

Gen 4:4 the firstborn animals from his f.
21:28 seven female lambs from the f.
27:9 Go to the f, and get me two
30:40 separated the rams from the f
31:39 I never brought you any of the f
31:39 any of the f was stolen during
38:17 goat from the f," he answered.
Lev 5:18 that has no defects from the f

Dtr 16:2 Slaughter an animal from your **f**
28:31 Your **f** will be given to your
1Sm 17:15 where he tended his father's **f**.
17:34 carried off a sheep from the **f**,
Ezr 10:19 sacrificed a ram from their **f** as
Job 21:11 out ⌊to play⌋ like a **f** of lambs,
30:1 fit to sit with the dogs of my **f**.
Psa 68:10 Your **f** settled there.
78:52 like a **f** through the wilderness.
79:13 the **f** in your pasture,
95:7 the **f** that he leads.
Pro 27:23 aware of the condition of your **f**,
Sos 1:7 where do you graze your **f**?
1:7 Where does your **f** lie down at
2:16 grazes his **f** among the lilies.
4:1 Your hair is like a **f** of goats
4:2 Your teeth are like a **f** of sheep
6:2 to graze his **f** in the gardens
6:3 grazes his **f** among the lilies.
6:5 Your hair is like a **f** of goats
6:6 Your teeth are like a **f** of sheep,
Isa 40:11 shepherd he takes care of his **f**.
63:11 with the shepherds of his **f**?
Jer 6:3 of them will tend his own **f**.
13:17 tears because the LORD's **f** will
13:20 Where is the **f** that was given
23:3 remaining part of my **f** from all
25:34 you leaders of the **f**.
25:35 escape for the leaders of the **f**.
25:36 leaders of the **f** are mourning
31:10 a shepherd watches over his **f**.'
49:20 away the little ones of the **f**.
50:8 the male goats that lead the **f**.
50:45 away the little ones of the **f**.
Eze 34:12 As a shepherd looks after his **f**
43:25 and a ram from the **f** as an
Amo 7:15 me away from herding the **f**
Mic 2:12 like a **f** in its pasture.
4:8 watchtower of the **f**,
5:4 become the shepherd of his **f**.
Zec 9:16 God will rescue them as the **f**
10:3 of Armies takes care of his **f**,
Mat 26:31 sheep in the **f** will be scattered.'
Luk 2:8 their **f** during the night.
2:20 shepherds returned to their **f**,
12:32 Don't be afraid, little **f**.
Jon 10:12 sheep away and scatters the **f**.
10:16 be one **f** with one shepherd.
Act 20:28 to yourselves and to the entire **f**
20:29 and they won't spare the **f**.
1Co 9:7 Does anyone take care of a **f**
1Pe 5:2 Be shepherds over the **f** God
5:3 be examples for the **f** to follow.

flocks (81)

Gen 26:14 Because he owned so many **f**,
29:2 Three **f** of sheep were lying
29:2 because the **f** were watered
29:3 When all the **f** were gathered
29:8 can't until all the **f** are gathered.
30:31 of and watching your **f** again.
30:32 Let me go through all of your **f**
30:36 care of the rest of Laban's **f**.
30:38 troughs directly in front of the **f**,
30:38 places where the **f** came
30:40 striped or black in Laban's **f**.
30:40 did not add them to Laban's **f**.
30:41 Whenever the stronger of the **f**
30:42 But when the **f** in heat were
30:43 He had large **f**, male and
31:4 open country where his **f** were.
31:8 all the **f** gave birth to speckled
31:8 all the **f** gave birth to striped
31:38 never ate any rams from your **f**.
31:41 and 6 years for your **f**,
31:43 my grandchildren, and my **f**.
33:13 that I have to take care of the **f**
33:13 even one day, all the **f** will die.
37:2 He took care of the **f** with the
37:12 of their father's **f** at Shechem.
37:13 taking care of the **f** at Shechem.
37:14 brothers and the **f** are doing,
37:16 they're taking care of their **f**."
45:10 as well as your **f**, your herds,
46:32 They've brought their **f** and
47:1 arrived from Canaan with their **f**
Gen 47:4 that there's no pasture for our **f**.
50:8 (Only their children, their **f**,
Exo 10:9 our **f** and herds with us.
10:24 but your **f** and herds must stay
12:32 Take your **f** and herds,
34:3 Even the **f** and herds may not
Num 11:22 they have enough if all the **f**
32:24 and stone fences for your **f**,
32:36 built stone fences for their **f**.
35:3 for their cattle, the **f** they own,
Dtr 7:13 and your **f** with lambs and kids.
8:13 Your herds and **f**, silver and
12:21 animal from the herds or **f** that
15:14 provisions — sheep from your **f**,
15:19 male from your herds and **f**
28:4 and your **f** will have lambs and
28:18 and your **f** will have few lambs
28:51 no lambs or kids from your **f**.
1Sm 8:17 He will take a tenth of your **f**.
1Ch 4:39 to find pasture for their **f**.
4:41 order to have pasture for their **f**.
27:31 for the **f**: Jaziz from Hagar
2Ch 17:11 The Arabs also brought him **f**:
32:28 all his cattle and stalls for his **f**.
Neh 10:36 and our **f** to the priests serving
Job 1:16 burned your **f** and servants.
24:2 They steal **f** and tend them as
Psa 65:13 pastures are covered with **f**.
107:41 and makes their families like **f**.
Ecc 2:7 I owned more herds and **f** than
Sos 1:7 the **f** of your companions.
1:8 follow the tracks of the **f**,
Isa 13:20 won't let their **f** rest there.
32:14 donkeys and pastures for **f**
60:7 All of the **f** from Kedar will
61:5 become shepherds for your **f**,
65:10 Plain will be a pasture for **f**.
Jer 3:24 worked for, their **f** and herds,
5:17 They will devour your **f** and
6:3 With their **f**, shepherds will
10:21 and all their **f** will be scattered.
33:12 shepherds can rest their **f**.
49:29 Their tents and their **f** will be
51:23 to crush shepherds and their **f**.
Eze 36:38 will be filled with **f** of people.
Joe 1:18 Even **f** of sheep are suffering.
Amo 6:4 and eat lambs from their **f**
Mic 5:8 a young lion among **f** of sheep.
Zep 2:14 **F** will lie down in it along with
Mal 1:14 animals in their **f** that they vow

flood (39)

Gen 6:17 I'm about to send a **f** on the
7:3 life all over the earth after the **f**.
7:6 600 years old when the **f** came
7:10 Seven days later the **f** came on
7:17 The **f** continued for 40 days on
9:11 Never again will there be a **f**
9:15 again will water become a **f**
9:28 Noah lived 350 years after the **f**.
10:1 Japheth had children after the **f**.
10:32 spread over the earth after the **f**.
11:10 Two years after the **f** when
49:4 you were out of control like a **f**
Jos 4:18 returned to its seasonal **f** level.
2Sm 5:20 of me like an overwhelming **f**."
1Ch 14:11 power like an overwhelming **f**,
2Ch 20:9 of war, **f**, plague, or famine,
Job 6:15 the seasonal riverbeds that **f**.
11:2 answer this **f** of words?
12:15 releases them, they **f** the earth.
20:28 A **f** will sweep away his house,
20:28 a flash **f** on the day of his
22:11 you and you cannot see and a **f**
27:20 Terrors overtake him like a **f**.
38:34 call to the clouds and have a **f**
Psa 6:6 My eyes **f** my bed every night.
29:10 LORD sat enthroned over the **f**.
69:2 A **f** is sweeping me away.
Pro 15:2 of fools pour out a **f** of stupidity.
15:28 pour out a **f** of evil things.
Isa 28:2 an overwhelming **f**.
30:33 LORD's breath will be like a **f**
Dan 9:26 His end will come with a **f** until
Nah 1:8 to Nineveh with a devastating **f**.
Mal 3:10 you and **f** you with blessings.
Mat 24:38 In the days before the **f**,
24:39 was happening until the **f** came
Luk 6:48 When a **f** came, But the house
17:27 Then the **f** destroyed all of
2Pe 2:5 He brought the **f** on the world of

flooded (1)

2Pe 3:6 Water also **f** and destroyed that

floodgate (1)

Pro 17:14 a quarrel is ⌊like⌋ opening a **f**,

floodgates (1)

Isa 24:18 The **f** in the sky will be opened,

flooding (2)

1Ch 12:15 River when it was **f** its banks.
Job 38:25 "Who made a channel for the **f**

floods (3)

Job 14:19 **f** wash away soil from the land,
Mat 7:25 Rain poured, and **f** came.
7:27 Rain poured, and **f** came.

floodwater (1)

Psa 32:6 Then raging **f** will not reach

floodwaters (12)

Gen 7:7 into the ship to escape the **f**.
7:24 The **f** were on the earth for 150
9:11 again will all life be killed by **f**.
Psa 69:15 Do not let **f** sweep me away.
124:4 Then the **f** would have swept
Isa 8:7 them the raging and powerful **f**
28:17 and **f** will wash away your
54:9 "To me this is like Noah's **f**,
54:9 that Noah's **f** would never cover
Hab 3:10 **F** pass by. The deep ocean
Luk 6:48 When a flood came, the **f**
6:49 The **f** pushed against it,

floor (46)

Gen 50:10 came to the threshing **f** of Atad,
50:11 at the threshing **f** of Atad,
Num 5:17 and put some dust from the **f**
15:20 you make from the threshing **f**.
18:27 to be grain from the threshing **f**
18:30 the threshing **f** or winepress.
Dtr 15:14 grain from your threshing **f**,
16:13 the grain from your threshing **f**
Jdg 3:25 to see their ruler lying on the **f**,
6:37 some wool on the threshing **f**.
Rut 3:2 on the threshing **f** tonight.
3:3 and go down to the threshing **f**.
3:6 Ruth went to the threshing **f**
3:14 came to the threshing **f**."
2Sm 6:6 came to Nacon's threshing **f**,
22:16 Then the ocean **f** could be
24:16 LORD was at the threshing **f**
24:18 the Jebusite's threshing **f**."
24:21 "To buy the threshing **f** from
24:24 So David bought the threshing **f**
1Ki 6:15 with wood from **f** to ceiling.
6:15 He covered the **f** of the temple
6:16 with cedar boards from the **f**
6:30 He covered the **f** of the inner
7:7 with cedar from **f** to ceiling.
22:10 They were on the threshing **f** at
2Ki 6:27 threshing **f** or the winepress."
1Ch 13:9 came to Chidon's threshing **f**,
21:15 was standing by the threshing **f**
21:18 the Jebusite's threshing **f**.
21:21 So he left the threshing **f** and
21:22 the land this threshing **f** is on.
21:28 answered him at the threshing **f**
2Ch 3:1 the site on the threshing **f**
18:9 sitting on the threshing **f** at
Job 39:12 and take it to your threshing **f**?
Psa 18:15 Then the ocean **f** could be
Jer 51:33 Babylon are like a threshing **f** at
Eze 41:16 from the **f** up to the windows,
41:20 carved on the walls from the **f**
Dan 2:35 on a threshing **f** in summer.
Hos 9:1 sold sex on every threshing **f**.
Mic 4:12 like cut grain on the threshing **f**.
Mat 3:12 he will clean up his threshing **f**.

Luk 3:17 to clean up his threshing **f**.
Jas 2:3 or "Sit on the **f** at my feet."

floors (3)

1Sm 23:1 are robbing the threshing **f**."
Hos 13:3 blown away from threshing **f**.
Joe 2:24 The threshing **f** will be filled

flour (74)

Gen 18:6 "get three measures of **f**,
Exo 29:2 Use the finest wheat **f**,
29:40 offering of eight cups of **f** mixed
Lev 2:1 your offering must be **f**.
2:2 Take from this a handful of **f**
2:4 bread made of **f** mixed
2:5 bread made of **f** mixed
2:7 will be made of **f** with olive oil.
2:16 The priest will burn the **f**,
5:11 then bring eight cups of **f** as an
6:15 will remove a handful of **f** from
6:20 he is anointed — eight cups of **f**.
7:12 and loaves made from **f** mixed
14:10 also take eight cups of **f** mixed
14:21 He will take only eight cups of **f**
23:13 offering of four quarts of **f**
23:17 Bake them with four quarts of **f**.
24:5 "Also take **f** and bake twelve
24:5 ring will contain four quarts of **f**.
Num 5:15 with eight cups of barley **f** as
5:15 must not pour olive oil on the **f**
7:13 Each dish was filled with **f**
7:19 Each dish was filled with **f**
7:25 Each dish was filled with **f**
7:31 Each dish was filled with **f**
7:37 Each dish was filled with **f**
7:43 Each dish was filled with **f**
7:49 Each dish was filled with **f**
7:55 Each dish was filled with **f**
7:61 Each dish was filled with **f**
7:67 Each dish was filled with **f**
7:73 Each dish was filled with **f**
7:79 Each dish was filled with **f**
8:8 and the grain offering of **f** mixed
15:4 offering of eight cups of **f** mixed
15:6 offering of 16 cups of **f** mixed
15:9 offering of 24 cups of **f** mixed
28:5 offering of eight cups of **f** mixed
28:9 a grain offering of 16 cups of **f**
28:12 offering of 24 cups of **f** mixed
28:12 offering of 16 cups of **f** mixed
28:13 offering of 8 cups of **f** mixed
28:20 bring grain offerings of **f** mixed
28:28 bring grain offerings of **f** mixed
29:3 bring grain offerings of **f** mixed
29:9 bring grain offerings of **f** mixed
29:14 bring grain offerings of **f** mixed
Dtr 24:6 family's handmill for grinding **f**
Jdg 6:19 bread made with 18 quarts of **f**.
1Sm 1:24 bull, half a bushel of **f**,
28:24 She took **f**, kneaded it,
2Sm 4:6 they were going to get some **f**.
17:28 **f**, roasted grain, beans, lentils,
1Ki 4:22 one day was 180 bushels of **f**,
4:22 360 bushels of coarse **f**,
17:12 I have one handful of **f** in a jar
17:14 the jar of **f** will never be empty
17:16 The jar of **f** never became
2Ki 4:41 Elisha said, "Bring some **f**."
7:1 24 cups of the best **f** will sell
7:16 Then 24 cups of the best **f** sold
7:18 cups of the best **f** will sell
1Ch 9:29 the **f**, wine, olive oil, incense,
12:40 There was plenty of **f**,
23:29 the **f** for the grain offerings,
Neh 10:37 bring the best of our coarse **f**,
Isa 28:28 Grain is ground into **f**,
47:2 Take millstones and grind **f**.
Eze 16:13 Your food was **f**, honey,
16:19 You gave **f**, olive oil,
46:14 of olive oil to moisten the **f**.
Mat 13:33 into a large amount of **f** until
Luk 13:21 into a large amount of **f** until
Rev 18:13 **f**, wheat, cattle, sheep, horses,

flourish (4)

Psa 72:16 May those from the city **f** like
92:12 Righteous people **f** like palm
Pro 11:28 but righteous people will **f** like
Isa 66:14 and you will **f** like new grass.

flourished (1)

Eze 7:10 blossomed. Arrogance has **f**.

flow (32)

Exo 14:26 that the water will **f** back over
15:19 of the sea **f** back over them.
Lev 12:7 be clean from her **f** of blood.
Num 24:7 Water will **f** from their buckets,
Jos 24:7 He made the sea **f** back and
Neh 9:15 hunger and made water **f** from
Psa 78:16 He made the water **f** like rivers.
119:136 Streams of tears **f** from my
147:18 wind blow ⌊and⌋ water **f**.
Pro 5:16 Why should water **f** out of your
5:16 your streams **f** into the streets?
Ecc 1:7 All streams **f** into the sea,
Sos 4:16 Let its spices **f** from it.
Isa 41:18 I will make rivers **f** on bare
41:18 make springs **f** through valleys.
48:21 He made water **f** from a rock for
Jer 9:18 Our eyelids will **f** with water.
13:17 and my eyes will **f** with tears
14:17 "Say this to them: 'My eyes **f**
46:7 like streams that **f** swiftly?
Lam 1:16 eyes — my eyes **f** with tears.
Eze 28:23 against you and make blood **f**
32:14 and make its streams **f** like oil,
Joe 3:18 Milk will **f** on the hills.
3:18 Water will **f** in all the brooks of
3:18 A spring will **f** from the LORD's
Amo 5:24 But let justice **f** like a river and
9:13 the mountains and **f** from all
Zec 14:8 On that day living water will **f**
Jon 7:38 'Streams of living water will **f**
1Ti 1:5 this order is for love to **f** from
Jas 3:11 Do clean and polluted water **f**

flowed (14)

Gen 2:10 A river **f** from Eden to water the
Exo 14:28 The water **f** back and covered
Dtr 9:21 river that **f** down the mountain.
1Ki 18:28 and spears until their blood **f**.
18:35 The water **f** around the altar,
22:35 The blood from the wound had **f**
2Ki 3:20 water **f** from Edom and filled
2Ch 32:4 and the brook that **f** through
Job 11:16 water that has **f** downstream.
Psa 105:41 and water gushed and **f** like a
Lam 3:54 Water **f** over my head.
Eze 31:4 Rivers **f** around the place
Dan 7:10 A river of fire **f**. It came from him
Rev 14:20 Blood **f** out of the winepress as

flower (14)

Exo 25:31 as well as the **f** cups,
25:33 have three **f** cups shaped like
25:34 to have four **f** cups shaped like
37:17 as well as the **f** cups,
37:19 had three **f** cups shaped like
37:20 The lamp stand itself had four **f**
Job 14:2 He comes up like a **f**;
Psa 103:15 It blossoms like a **f** in the field.
103:16 the wind blows over the **f**,
Isa 28:1 beauty is ⌊like⌋ a withered **f**.
28:4 beauty is ⌊like⌋ a withered **f**.
40:6 beauty is like a **f** in the field.
1Pe 1:24 and all their beauty is like a **f** of
1:24 dries up and the **f** drops off,

flowers (20)

1Ki 6:18 Gourds and **f** were carved into
6:29 and **f** into the walls all around
6:32 and **f** into them and covered
6:35 angels, palm trees, and **f**.
7:49 room), **f**, lamps, gold tongs,
2Ch 4:21 **f**, lamps, pure gold tongs,
Psa 92:7 blossom ⌊like⌋ **f**,
Sos 1:14 beloved is a bouquet of henna **f**
4:13 best fruits, henna **f** and nard,
7:11 the night among the henna **f**.
Isa 40:7 Grass dries up, and **f** wither
40:8 Grass dries up, and **f** wither,
Hos 14:5 They will blossom like **f**.
Nah 1:4 The **f** of Lebanon wither.
Mat 6:28 Notice how the **f** grow in the
6:29 dressed like one of these **f**.
Luk 12:27 Consider how the **f** grow.
12:27 dressed like one of these **f**.
Jas 1:10 Rich people will wither like **f**.
1:11 The **f** drop off, and the beauty

flower-shaped (2)

Exo 28:36 "Make a **f** medallion out of pure
39:30 They made the **f** medallion (the

flowery (1)

Act 14:13 with **f** wreaths around their

flowing (50)

Exo 3:8 It is a land **f** with milk and
3:17 a land **f** with milk and honey.'"
13:5 he brings you into that land **f**
33:3 Go to that land **f** with milk and
Lev 20:24 It is a land **f** with milk and
Num 13:27 It really is a land **f** with milk
14:8 This is a land **f** with milk and
16:13 you brought us out of a land **f**
16:14 haven't brought us into a land **f**
Dtr 6:3 will increase in a land **f**
8:7 underground streams **f** through
11:9 their descendants — a land **f**
26:9 place and gave us this land **f**
26:15 people Israel and the land **f**
27:3 ancestors is giving you a land **f**
31:20 a land **f** with milk and honey.
Jos 3:13 Then the water **f** from upstream
3:16 water stopped **f** from upstream.
3:16 The water **f** down toward the
4:7 the river stopped **f**.
5:6 not let them see this land **f**
1Sm 14:26 the woods, the honey was **f**.
2Ki 4:6 So the olive oil stopped **f**.
2Ch 32:3 to stop the water from **f** out
32:30 stopped the water from **f** from
Job 39:19 dress its neck with a **f** mane?
Psa 42:1 As a deer longs for **f** streams,
74:14 You dried up the ever-**f** rivers.
114:8 flint into a spring **f** with water.
Ecc 1:7 in order to ⌊start⌋ **f** again.
Sos 4:15 of living water **f** from Lebanon.
7:5 Your **f** locks could hold a king
Isa 8:6 have rejected the gently **f** water
27:12 his threshing from the **f** stream
58:11 whose water does not stop **f**.
Jer 11:5 and give them a land **f**
32:22 the land **f** with milk and honey.
48:33 I will stop the wine **f** from the
Lam 3:49 My eyes will keep **f** without
Eze 20:6 a land **f** with milk and honey.
20:15 a land **f** with milk and honey.
23:15 their waists and **f** turbans
31:15 many water sources stopped **f**.
32:6 the earth with your **f** blood all
47:1 I saw water **f** from under the
47:1 The water was **f** under the
47:2 The water was **f** down the
Amo 5:24 righteousness like an ever-**f**
Luk 4:22 gracious words **f** from his lips.
Rev 22:1 It was **f** from the throne of God

flown (1)

Jer 4:25 and every bird has **f** away.

flows (11)

Gen 2:14 This is the one that **f** east of
Ezr 8:15 by the river that **f** to Ahava,
Job 40:23 Though the river **f** powerfully
Psa 104:10 It **f** between the mountains.
Pro 4:23 the source of your life **f** from it.
24:13 Honey that **f** from the
Eze 47:8 "This water **f** through the land
47:8 When the water **f** into the Dead
47:9 Wherever the river **f**,
47:9 Wherever the river **f**,
47:12 fruit because this water **f** from

fluid (1)

Luk 14:2 was swollen with **f** was there.

flute (9)

Gen 4:21 to play the harp and the **f**.
1Sm 10:5 a tambourine, a **f**, and a lyre.
Job 21:12 happy with the music of the **f**.
30:31 and my **f** for loud weeping.
Isa 30:29 like someone going out with a **f**
Jer 48:36 is why I moan for Moab like a **f**.
48:36 I sound like a **f** for the people of
Mat 9:23 He saw **f** players and a noisy
1Co 14:7 Musical instruments like the **f**

flutes (8)

Jdg 5:16 the shepherds playing their **f**?
1Ki 1:40 people followed him, blew **f**,
Psa 150:4 with stringed instruments and **f**.
Isa 5:12 tambourines and **f**,
Dan 3:5 of rams' horns, **f**, lyres, harps,
3:7 of rams' horns, **f**, lyres, harps,
3:10 of rams' horns, **f**, lyres, harps,
3:15 the rams' horns, **f**, lyres, harps,

flutists (1)

Rev 18:22 sound of harpists, musicians, **f**,

fluttering (3)

Job 13:25 Are you trying to make a **f** leaf
Pro 26:2 Like a **f** sparrow, like a darting
Isa 16:2 daughters are like **f** birds,

fly (18)

Gen 1:20 and let birds **f** through the sky
Exo 8:31 Not one **f** was left.
Lev 14:7 Then he will let the living bird **f**
14:53 Then he will let the living bird **f**
Job 5:7 as surely as sparks **f** up ⌊from
20:8 He will **f** away like a dream
39:26 make a bird of prey **f**
41:19 Sparks of fire **f** from it.
Psa 55:6 like a dove — I would **f** away
90:10 are soon gone, and we **f** away.
91:5 arrows that **f** during the day,
Isa 60:8 "Who are these people that **f**
Dan 4:14 the birds **f** from its branches.
Hos 9:11 "Ephraim's glory will **f** away
Oba 1:4 Even though you **f** high like an
Nah 3:16 that attack and then **f** away.
Hab 1:8 They will **f** like an eagle that
Rev 12:14 eagle in order to **f** away from

flying (11)

Gen 1:21 water and every type of **f** bird.
8:7 It kept **f** back and forth until the
Dtr 14:20 ⌊other kind of⌋ **f** creature that is
Pro 23:5 like an eagle **f** into the sky.
Isa 14:29 and his descendant will be a **f**,
Zec 5:1 I looked up again and saw a **f**
5:2 "I see a **f** scroll," I answered.
Rev 4:7 and the fourth was like a **f**
8:13 I saw an eagle **f** overhead,
14:6 I saw another angel **f** overhead
19:17 to all the birds **f** overhead,

foam (1)

Jud 1:13 Their shame is like the **f** on the

foamed (1)

Mar 9:20 and **f** at the mouth.

foaming (2)

Psa 75:8 (Its **f** wine is thoroughly mixed
93:4 mightier than the **f** waves of the

foams (3)

Psa 46:3 Water roars and **f**, Selah
Mar 9:18 Then he **f** at the mouth,
Luk 9:39 and **f** at the mouth.

focus (5)

Psa 86:11 **F** my heart on fearing you.
Rom 12:17 **F** your thoughts on those
Col 3:1 **f** on the things that are above —
1Ti 4:16 **F** on your life and your
Heb 12:2 We must **f** on Jesus,

focused (5)

Job 17:2 eyes are **f** on their opposition.
Psa 17:11 They have **f** their attention on
Pro 4:25 ahead and your sight be **f**
Eph 1:12 we who had already **f** our hope
2Pe 2:14 Their minds are **f** on their greed.

fodder (1)

Jdg 19:19 We have straw and **f** for our

foes (3)

Psa 81:14 turn my power against their **f**.
Isa 29:5 Your many **f** will be like husks
Nah 1:2 holds a grudge against his **f**.

fog (4)

Psa 148:8 lightning and hail, snow and **f**,
Pro 25:14 ⌊Like⌋ a dense **f** or a dust
Hos 6:4 Your love is like **f** in the
13:3 That is why they will be like **f**

fold (2)

Exo 26:9 **F** the sixth sheet in half ⌊to
28:16 **F** it in half so that it's 9 inches

folded (1)

Exo 39:9 It was **f** in half and was 9

folding (1)

1Ki 6:34 Each of the doors had two **f**

folds (4)

Job 38:14 stand out like ⌊**f** in⌋ clothing.
41:23 The **f** of its flesh stick to each
Ecc 4:5 A fool **f** his hands and wastes
Hag 2:12 for a holy purpose and he **f**

follow (237)

Exo 11:8 and all the people who **f** you,
12:24 "You must **f** these instructions.
13:10 you must **f** these rules every
14:17 that they will **f** the Israelites.
16:4 not they will **f** my instructions.
23:2 Never **f** a crowd in doing wrong.
23:24 their gods or **f** their practices.
Lev 18:4 **F** my rules, and live by my
18:30 So you must **f** my instructions.
20:23 Never **f** the practices of the
25:18 and carefully **f** my rules.
26:33 War will **f** you. Your country will
Num 9:3 **F** all the rules and regulations
9:12 You must **f** all the rules for the
9:14 They must **f** these same rules
14:25 and **f** the road that goes to the
32:11 didn't wholeheartedly **f** me.'
Dtr 1:40 and **f** the road that goes to the
5:33 **F** all the directions the LORD
8:6 **F** his directions, and fear him.
8:19 your God and **f** other gods,
10:12 **f** all his directions,
11:22 **f** all his directions,
12:30 tempted to **f** their customs.
17:10 **F** all their instructions carefully,
19:9 God and **f** his directions as
26:17 that you will **f** his directions,
27:10 Obey the LORD your God and **f**
28:1 and faithfully **f** all his
28:9 your God and **f** his directions.
28:15 and faithfully **f** all his
28:45 your God or **f** his commands
30:8 LORD and **f** all his commands
30:10 obey him and **f** his commands
30:16 your God, **f** his directions,
Jos 3:3 break camp and **f** them.
22:5 Carefully **f** the commands and
22:5 your God, **f** his directions,
23:16 your God and **f** other gods,
Jdg 2:22 or not they will carefully **f**
3:28 He told them, "**F** me!
6:34 Abiezer's family to **f** him.
6:35 to summon the people to **f** him.
6:35 were also summoned to **f** him,
9:3 They were persuaded to **f**
9:4 and reckless men to **f** him.
Rut 2:9 and **f** the young women in that
1Sm 8:3 The sons didn't **f** their father's
11:7 of anyone who doesn't **f** Saul
12:14 then you and your king will **f**
12:21 Don't turn away to **f** other gods.
13:13 "You didn't **f** the command of
13:14 because you didn't **f** the
14:12 "**F** me up ⌊to the military post⌋
15:22 To **f** instructions is better than
25:19 her young men, "and I'll **f** you."
2Sm 20:2 of Israel left David to **f** Sheba,
20:11 on David's side should **f** Joab."
1Ki 1:35 **F** him ⌊back⌋ here when he
3:14 And if you **f** me and obey my
6:12 live by my laws, **f** my rules,
8:58 Then we will **f** him and keep
9:6 and **f** and serve other gods and
11:2 tempt you to **f** their gods."
11:4 tempted him to **f** other gods.
11:6 He did not wholeheartedly **f** the
11:10 told him⌋ not to **f** other gods.
11:38 all I command you, **f** my ways,
18:21 If the LORD is God, **f** him;
18:21 him; if Baal is God, **f** him."
19:20 Then I will **f** you." "Go back,"
19:21 he left to **f** and assist Elijah.
2Ki 6:19 **F** me, and I will lead you to the
7:14 and the king sent them to **f** the
9:18 **F** me." So the watchman
9:19 that matter to you? **F** me."
23:3 to the LORD that he would **f**
1Ch 22:12 to take charge of Israel and to **f**
23:32 They were appointed to **f** the
2Ch 2:14 of engravings and **f** any set
6:31 they will fear you and **f** you.
7:19 and **f** and serve other gods and
14:4 ancestors and **f** his teachings
23:6 **f** the LORD's regulations.
34:31 to the LORD that he would **f**
Ezr 7:26 Whoever will not strictly **f** your
Neh 8:1 had commanded Israel ⌊to **f**⌋.
10:29 oath to **f** God's teachings given
10:29 also bound themselves to **f** all
13:27 Should we **f** your example,
Job 13:27 You **f** my trail by engraving
22:3 he gain anything when you **f**
Psa 1:1 is the person who does not **f**
37:34 for the LORD, and **f** his path,
40:4 people or those who **f** lies.
45:14 Her bridesmaids **f** her.
49:17 His greatness cannot **f** him.
78:10 They refused to **f** his teachings.
81:12 ways and **f** their own advice.
81:13 If only Israel would **f** me!
103:18 to **f** his guiding principles.
105:45 his laws and **f** his teachings.
119:1 those who **f** the teachings of
119:3 They **f** his directions.
119:34 so that I can **f** your teachings.
119:44 I will **f** your teachings forever
119:55 and I **f** your teachings.
119:106 an oath to **f** your regulations,
119:128 I **f** the straight paths of your
119:136 others do not **f** your teachings.
119:173 ⌊to **f**⌋ your guiding principles.
Pro 1:15 do not **f** them in their way.
7:2 **F** my teachings just as you
8:32 are those who **f** my ways.
28:4 but those who **f** ⌊God's⌋
29:18 those who **f** ⌊God's⌋ teachings.
Ecc 11:9 **F** wherever your heart leads
Sos 1:8 **f** the tracks of the flocks,
Isa 8:11 He warned me not to **f** the
26:8 ⌊as we **f**⌋ the path of your
30:21 **F** it, whether it turns to the right
45:14 They will **f** you. They will come
Jer 2:25 You love foreign gods and **f**
3:17 They will no longer **f** their own
7:6 And suppose you do not **f** other
9:13 and they didn't **f** them.
13:10 stubborn ways and **f** other gods
25:6 Don't **f** other gods to serve and
26:4 and don't **f** my teachings that
32:23 obey you or to **f** your teachings.
35:15 and don't **f** other gods in order
42:16 The famines you dread will **f**

Jer 51:31 Messengers **f** messengers.
Eze 7:26 One rumor will **f** another.
9:5 "**F** him throughout the city and
13:3 They **f** their own ideas,
16:47 You didn't **f** their ways.
20:19 Obey my rules and **f** them.
20:21 didn't obey my rules and **f** them.
20:24 They didn't **f** my rules,
20:25 I also allowed them to **f** laws
43:11 its design and **f** all its rules.
44:10 wandered off to **f** their idols.
Hos 11:10 "My people will **f** me when I
Hab 3:5 Plagues **f** after him.
Zec 3:7 ways and **f** my requirements,
Mat 4:19 said to them, "Come, **f** me!
8:19 I'll **f** you wherever you go."
8:22 But Jesus told him, "**F** me,
9:9 Jesus said to him, "**F** me!"
10:38 cross and **f** me doesn't deserve
16:24 pick up their crosses, and **f** me.
19:21 in heaven. Then **f** me!"
19:27 given up everything to **f** you.
23:3 But don't **f** their example,
Mar 1:17 said to them, "Come, **f** me!
2:14 Jesus said to him, "**F** me!"
7:3 They **f** the traditions of their
7:4 They have been taught to **f**
7:5 "Why don't your disciples **f** the
7:8 of God to **f** human traditions."
8:34 "Those who want to **f** me must
8:34 pick up their crosses, and **f** me.
10:21 in heaven. Then **f** me!"
10:28 "We've given up everything to **f**
14:13 carrying a jug of water. **F** him.
Luk 5:27 Jesus said to him, "**F** me!"
9:23 crosses every day, and **f** me.
9:57 "I'll **f** you wherever you go."
9:59 He told another man, "**F** me!"
9:61 Another said, "I'll **f** you,
14:27 their crosses and **f** me cannot
18:22 in heaven. Then **f** me!"
18:28 "We've left everything to **f** you."
19:14 They sent representatives to **f**
21:8 'The time is near.' Don't **f** them!
22:10 **F** him into the house he enters.
Jon 1:43 Philip and told him, "**F** me!"
7:17 Those who want to **f** the will of
7:23 worship to **f** Moses' Teachings,
9:16 from God because he doesn't **f**
10:4 The sheep **f** him because they
10:5 They won't **f** a stranger.
10:27 who they are. They **f** me,
12:26 who serve me must **f** me.
12:47 my words and doesn't **f** them,
13:15 an example that you should **f**.
13:17 whenever you **f** my example.
13:36 "You can't **f** me now to the
13:36 However, you will **f** me later."
13:37 why can't I **f** you now?
21:19 this, Jesus told Peter, "**F** me!"
21:22 does that concern you? **F** me!"
Act 12:8 "Put your coat on, and **f** me."
15:5 ordered to **f** Moses' Teachings."
16:17 She used to **f** Paul and shout,
21:21 children or **f** Jewish customs.
21:23 So **f** our advice. We have four
21:24 carefully **f** Moses' Teachings.
27:44 Then he ordered the rest to **f** on
Rom 2:8 truth and who **f** what is wrong.
2:25 valuable if you **f** Moses' laws.
2:25 If you don't **f** those laws,
1Co 1:12 "I **f** Paul," or "I follow Apollos,"
1:12 "I follow Paul," or "I **f** Apollos,"
1:12 Apollos," or "I **f** Cephas,"
1:12 follow Cephas," or "I **f** Christ."
3:4 "I **f** Paul" and others say,
3:4 and others say, "I **f** Apollos,"
16:16 to **f** the example of people like
Gal 1:6 to **f** a different kind of good
5:16 Then you will never **f** through
6:2 you will **f** Christ's teachings.
6:13 did this to **f** Jewish laws.
2Th 3:6 a disciplined life and doesn't **f**
3:9 to set an example for you to **f**.
1Ti 4:1 They will **f** spirits that deceive,
5:15 already turned away to **f** Satan.
1Ti 5:21 when you **f** what I've told
5:24 The sins of others **f** them there.
2Ti 4:3 Instead, they will **f** their own
Heb 13:9 rules that don't help those who **f**
Jas 5:10 Brothers and sisters, **f** the
1Pe 1:11 and the glory that would **f**.
2:21 you could **f** in his footsteps.
5:3 be examples for the flock to **f**.
2Pe 2:2 Many people will **f** them in their
2:10 those who **f** their corrupt nature
2:15 path and wandered off to **f**
3:3 In the last days people who **f**
Jud 1:16 **f** their own desires,
1:18 They will **f** their own ungodly
Rev 2:14 who **f** what Balaam taught
2:15 You also have some who **f**
14:4 They **f** the lamb wherever he
19:14 **f** him on white horses.
22:9 and those who **f** the words in

followed (168)

Gen 24:61 on camels, they **f** the man.
32:19 all the others who **f** the herds.
Exo 14:23 and cavalry **f** them into the sea.
14:28 the cavalry that had **f** Israel into
15:20 with tambourines, **f** her.
39:1 They **f** the LORD's instructions
39:5 They **f** the LORD's instructions
39:7 They **f** the LORD's instructions
39:21 They **f** the LORD's instructions
39:26 They **f** the LORD's instructions
39:29 They **f** the LORD's instructions
39:31 They **f** the LORD's instructions
39:32 The Israelites **f** all the LORD's
39:43 work and saw that they had **f**
40:19 **f** the LORD's instructions.
40:21 **f** the LORD's instructions.
40:29 **f** the LORD's instructions.
40:32 **f** the LORD's instructions.
Num 14:24 and has wholeheartedly **f** me,
16:25 and the leaders of Israel **f** him.
21:33 Then they turned and **f** the road
31:16 they were the ones who **f**
32:12 wholeheartedly **f** the LORD.
Dtr 1:36 he wholeheartedly **f** the LORD."
3:1 Next we turned and **f** the road
Jos 6:8 of the LORD's promise **f** them.
6:9 The rear guard **f** the ark while
6:13 and the rear guard **f** the LORD's
Jdg 2:12 They **f** the other gods of the
2:19 They **f**, served, and worshiped
3:28 They **f** him and captured the
9:49 brushwood and **f** Abimelech.
13:11 Manoah immediately **f** his wife.
1Sm 6:12 The rulers of the Philistines **f**
13:7 and all the people who **f** him
13:15 The rest of the people **f** Saul to
14:13 and his armorbearer **f** him.
15:31 Then Samuel turned and **f** Saul,
2Sm 2:10 but the tribe of Judah **f** David.
3:31 King David **f** the open casket.
7:8 where you **f** sheep so that
15:16 and his whole household **f** him
15:18 and all 600 men who had **f** him
17:23 that his advice hadn't been **f**,
20:13 everyone **f** Joab and pursued
20:14 gathered together and **f** him
1Ki 1:40 All the people **f** him,
11:5 Solomon **f** Astarte (the goddess
11:33 He has not **f** my ways.
14:8 and faithfully **f** me by doing
15:3 He **f** the sinful example his
16:21 Half of the army **f** Tibni,
16:21 The ⌊other⌋ half **f** Omri.
16:22 But the half which **f** Omri was
16:22 than the half which **f** Tibni,
20:19 and the troops **f** them.
20:25 He took their advice and **f** it.
22:43 Jehoshaphat carefully **f** the
22:52 He **f** the example of his father
2Ki 4:30 So Elisha got up and **f** her.
7:15 They **f** them as far as the
8:18 He **f** the ways of the kings of
8:27 Ahaziah **f** the ways of Ahab's
16:3 He **f** the example of the kings
17:22 The Israelites **f** all the sins
1Ch 17:7 where you **f** sheep so that
2Ch 11:16 seek the LORD God of Israel **f**
20:32 Jehoshaphat carefully **f** the
21:6 He **f** the ways of the kings of
21:12 You haven't **f** the ways of your
21:13 Instead, you have **f** the ways of
22:3 Ahaziah also **f** the ways of
22:5 Ahaziah **f** their advice and
28:2 He **f** the example of the kings
36:14 increasingly unfaithful and **f** all
Ezr 3:2 They ⌊**f** the directions⌋ written
Neh 12:32 of the leaders of Judah **f** them.
12:34 and Jeremiah also **f**.
12:36 these relatives of Zechariah **f**:
12:38 I **f** them with the other half of
Est 1:8 The drinking **f** this rule:
Job 23:11 I have **f** his footsteps closely.
31:7 or my heart has **f** ⌊the desire
37:4 It is **f** by the roar of his voice.
Psa 119:4 principles be carefully **f**.
119:168 I have **f** your guiding principles
Isa 65:2 They **f** their own plans.
Jer 2:2 I remember how you **f** me into
2:5 They **f** worthless idols and
2:8 Baal and **f** statues that couldn't
2:23 and haven't **f** other gods —
7:24 They **f** their own plans and
9:14 They **f** their own stubborn
11:8 They **f** their own stubborn,
16:11 They **f** other gods,
35:18 **f** all his instructions,
Eze 11:12 You have **f** the standards set
18:19 He obeyed my rules and **f** them.
46:14 These rules are to be **f** always.
Amo 2:4 same ones their ancestors **f**.
7:1 It was the harvest that **f** the
Mic 6:16 and you have **f** their advice.
Mal 2:9 you have not **f** my ways.
3:7 my laws and have not **f** them.
Mat 4:20 left their nets and **f** him.
4:22 and their father and **f** Jesus.
4:25 Large crowds **f** him.
8:1 large crowds **f** him.
9:9 So Matthew got up and **f** him.
9:19 disciples got up and **f** the man.
9:27 two blind men **f** him.
9:28 and the blind men **f** him.
12:15 Many people **f** him,
14:13 heard about this and **f** him
19:2 Large crowds **f** him,
20:29 a large crowd **f** Jesus.
20:34 at once, and they **f** him.
21:9 and that **f** him was shouting,
26:58 Peter **f** at a distance until he
27:55 They had **f** Jesus from Galilee
Mar 1:18 left their nets and **f** him.
1:20 men in the boat and **f** Jesus.
2:14 So Levi got up and **f** him.
3:8 around Tyre and Sidon **f** him.
5:24 A huge crowd **f** Jesus and
6:1 His disciples **f** him.
10:32 The others who **f** were afraid.
10:52 and he **f** Jesus on the road.
11:9 those who **f** him were shouting,
14:54 Peter **f** him at a distance and
15:41 They had **f** him and supported
Luk 1:3 I, too, have **f** everything closely
1:6 They **f** all the Lord's commands
5:11 left everything, and **f** Jesus.
5:28 up, left everything, and **f** him.
9:11 found out about this and **f** him.
18:43 He **f** Jesus and praised God.
22:39 His disciples **f** him.
22:54 Peter **f** at a distance.
23:27 A large crowd **f** Jesus.
23:49 including the women who had **f**
23:55 **f** closely behind Joseph.
Jon 1:37 John say this, they **f** Jesus.
1:40 who heard John and **f** Jesus.
4:38 and you have **f** them in their
6:2 A large crowd **f** him because
6:66 had led before they **f** Jesus.
11:31 So they **f** her. They thought that
18:15 and another disciple **f** Jesus.
Act 3:24 who **f** him spoke about
9:2 arrest any man or woman who **f**

Act 12:9 Peter **f** the angel out of the cell.
13:43 and converts to Judaism **f** Paul
16:24 So the jailer **f** these orders and
22:4 I persecuted people who **f** the
22:12 who **f** Moses' Teachings.
26:5 that I **f** the strictest party of our
27:21 you should have **f** my advice
Rom 5:16 The verdict which **f** one
Gal 1:13 the way I once lived when I **f**
Eph 2:2 You **f** the ways of this present
2:3 and **f** the desires of our corrupt
1Ti 4:6 which you have **f** closely.
Jud 1:11 They have **f** the path of Cain.
Rev 6:8 Hell **f** him. They were given
13:3 were amazed and **f** the beast.
14:8 one, **f** him, and said, "Fallen!
14:9 angel, a third one, **f** them,

follower (3)

Mat 23:15 and sea to recruit a single **f**,
Act 24:14 But I'll admit to you that I'm a **f**
2Co 12:2 I know a **f** of Christ who was

followers (32)

Num 16:5 he said to Korah and all his **f**,
16:6 Korah, you and all your **f** must
16:11 So you and all your **f** have
16:16 "Tomorrow you and all your **f**
16:19 gathered all his **f** — those who
16:32 their families, the **f** of Korah,
16:40 will die like Korah and his **f**.
26:9 They joined Korah's **f** when
26:10 They and their **f** died when the
27:3 He was not a part of Korah's **f**
Psa 49:13 and their **f** who are delighted
106:17 It buried Abiram's **f**.
106:18 A fire broke out among their **f**.
Isa 19:15 No one — leaders or **f**,
Dan 11:24 loot and wealth to his **f**.
Mat 10:42 gives any of my humble **f**
12:27 who helps your **f** force them
19:28 in the world to come, you, my **f**,
22:16 to him along with Herod's **f**.
23:8 one teacher, and you are all **f**.
28:10 Go, tell my **f** to go to Galilee.
Mar 2:15 and sinners who were **f**
3:6 and with Herod's **f** they
4:10 When he was alone with his **f**
12:13 and some of Herod's **f** to Jesus.
Luk 11:19 who helps your **f** force them
Jon 18:36 my **f** would fight to keep me
21:23 die spread among Jesus' **f**.
Act 5:36 and all his **f** were scattered.
5:37 and all his **f** were scattered.
11:21 Lord's power was with his **f**,
12:24 to spread and win many **f**.

following (106)

Gen 22:24 had the **f** children: Tebah,
Exo 36:6 the **f** message announced all
39:42 had done all the work **f**
40:23 **f** the LORD's instructions.
40:25 **f** the LORD's instructions.
40:27 **f** the LORD's instructions.
Lev 5:10 Then, **f** the proper procedures,
9:16 **F** the proper procedures,
11:29 "The **f** swarming creatures that
23:4 "The **f** are the LORD's
Num 10:13 **f** the command that the LORD
16:40 **f** the command that the LORD
21:4 **f** the road that goes to the Red
Dtr 2:1 We went back into the desert, **f**
2:26 with the **f** offer of peace:
13:5 trying to lead you away from **f**
27:4 **f** the command I'm giving you
Jos 21:3 were given the **f** cities
21:13 So they gave the **f** cities with
22:16 you have turned away from **f**
22:18 turned away from **f** the LORD!
22:23 the intention of no longer **f** him,
22:29 or to turn back today from **f**
Rut 1:16 make me turn back from **f** you.
1Sm 8:5 sons aren't **f** your example.
9:15 the LORD had revealed the **f**
11:7 of Israel with the **f** message:
15:24 "I have sinned by not **f** the
1Sm 25:42 of her female servants **f** her.
2Sm 2:22 "Stop **f** me," he said.
3:17 Meanwhile, Abner sent the **f**
1Ki 18:18 the LORD's commands and **f**
20:10 Then Benhadad sent Ahab the **f**
2Ki 6:32 because the king will be **f** him."
17:34 they are still **f** their customs,
1Ch 1:32 gave birth to the **f** sons:
8:9 his wife Hodesh had the **f** sons:
24:20 ⌞The **f** men were leaders⌟ for
24:26 The **f** men were leaders from
26:1 The **f** were the divisions of the
27:16 The **f** officers were in charge of
2Ch 11:19 gave birth to the **f** sons:
13:11 We're **f** the instructions the
17:14 The **f** is a breakdown of these
21:2 He had the **f** brothers,
34:33 they didn't stop **f** the LORD
35:26 to God by **f** what is written
Ezr 2:59 The **f** people came from Tel
3:4 **F** the written directions,
3:8 of the second year **f** their return
5:7 They sent him the **f** report:
5:9 their leaders the **f** question:
6:18 of God in Jerusalem by **f**
10:18 the **f** were married to foreign
Neh 7:5 I found the **f** written in it:
7:61 The **f** people came from Tel
7:70 The governor contributed the **f**
9:29 by not **f** your regulations.
10:1 The **f** people sealed the
10:36 **F** the directions in the
13:13 I appointed the **f** men to be in
Est 1:1 In the days of Xerxes the **f**
Job 22:15 "Are you **f** the old path that
34:27 they turned away from **f** him
Psa 19:11 There is a great reward in **f**
60:6 God has promised the **f** through
108:7 God has promised the **f** through
Pro 6:3 Do the **f** things, my son, so that
Jer 11:10 They are **f** other gods and
16:12 All of you are **f** your own
Eze 11:21 minds are set on **f** detestable
16:44 speak the **f** saying against you:
Zep 1:6 who have turned away from **f**
Zec 6:6 the white horses are **f** them.
Mat 8:10 said to those who were **f** him,
10:5 out with the **f** instructions:
Mar 14:51 young man was **f** Jesus.
Luk 7:9 He turned to the crowd **f** him
17:9 thank the servant for **f** orders.
Jon 1:38 around and saw them **f** him.
12:19 The whole world is **f** him!"
21:20 That disciple was **f** them.
Act 10:24 The **f** day they arrived in
11:19 out **f** Stephen's death went
13:47 The Lord gave us the **f** order:
20:15 On the **f** day we approached
20:30 to lure disciples into **f** them.
23:25 governor with the **f** message:
Rom 2:27 condemn you for not **f** them.
3:20 by **f** Moses' Teachings.
4:12 are circumcised but also are **f**
10:5 God's approval by **f** his laws.
15:5 in harmony with each other by **f**
1Co 11:2 about me and for carefully **f**
11:17 as I instruct you in the **f** matter:
2Co 4:13 The **f** is written, "I believed;
Gal 1:14 other Jews in my age group in **f**
2:14 that they were not properly **f**
3:18 the inheritance by **f** those laws,
Col 2:8 doing things rather than **f** Christ
Heb 4:11 Then no one will be lost by **f**
7:17 Scriptures say the **f** about him:
8:4 ⌞other⌟ priests offer gifts by **f**
13:9 come from **f** rules about food,
Jas 4:11 you are no longer **f** them.
Jud 1:4 in writing for the **f** reason:

follows (19)

1Ki 20:10 to each soldier who **f** me."
2Ki 11:15 sword to kill anyone who **f** her."
1Ch 5:7 were as **f**: The first was Jeiel,
24:1 Aaron's descendants were as **f**:
2Ch 23:14 sword to kill anyone who **f** her."
Neh 9:29 If anyone **f** them, he will find
Est 2:12 treatment was spent as **f**:
Job 21:33 Everyone **f** him. Countless
Psa 111:10 **f** ⌞God's guiding principles⌟.
119:63 who **f** your guiding principles.
Pro 7:22 He immediately **f** her like a
28:7 Whoever **f** ⌞God's⌟ teachings
Jer 4:20 One disaster **f** another.
9:6 Oppression **f** oppression.
9:6 Deceit **f** deceit. They refuse to
Jon 8:12 Whoever **f** me will have a life
Act 19:26 large crowd that **f** him not only
Col 2:8 Such a person **f** human
Rev 22:7 Blessed is the one who **f** the

fond (5)

Gen 34:3 He became very **f** of Jacob's
1Sm 16:22 because I have grown **f** of him."
18:22 and all his officers are **f** of you.
19:1 Jonathan was very **f** of David,
1Th 3:6 you always have **f** memories

fondle (1)

Pro 5:20 an adulterous woman and **f**

fondled (2)

Eze 23:3 There men **f** and caressed their
23:21 caressed and **f** her breasts.

fondly (1)

Jer 31:20 I still think **f** of him.

food (378)

Gen 1:29 This will be your **f**.
1:30 have given all green plants as **f**
3:17 will eat ⌞**f** that comes⌟ from
3:19 you will produce **f** to eat until
6:21 Take every kind of **f** that can
6:21 It will be **f** for you and the
9:3 lives and moves will be your **f**.
9:3 I gave you green plants as **f**;
14:11 as well as all their **f**,
24:33 When the **f** was put in front of
28:20 me on my trip and give me **f**
39:6 anything except the **f** he ate.
41:29 will be plenty of **f** in Egypt.
41:30 there was plenty of **f** in Egypt,
41:31 that there once was plenty of **f**
41:35 Have them collect all the **f**
41:35 to be kept for **f** in the cities.
41:36 This **f** will be a reserve supply
41:48 Joseph collected all the **f**
41:48 seven years and put this **f**
41:48 In each city he put the **f** from
41:53 when there was plenty of **f**
41:54 Yet, there was **f** in Egypt.
41:55 people cried to Pharaoh for **f**.
42:7 to buy **f**," they answered.
42:10 "We've come to buy **f**.
42:33 Take **f** for your starving
43:2 back and buy us a little more **f**."
43:4 we'll go and buy **f** for you.
43:20 came here to buy **f** once before.
43:22 brought more money to buy **f**.
43:31 when he said, "Serve the **f**."
43:34 Joseph had portions of **f**
44:1 with as much **f** as they can
44:25 back and buy us a little more **f**.'
45:18 can enjoy the best **f** in the land.'
45:23 and **f** for his father's trip.
47:12 and all his father's family with **f**
47:13 that there was no **f** anywhere.
47:15 "Give us **f**," they said.
47:16 and I'll give you **f** in exchange."
47:17 and he gave them **f** in
47:17 year he supplied them with **f**
47:19 and our land in exchange for **f**.
47:24 and as **f** for your households."
49:20 "Asher's **f** will be rich.
Exo 12:39 no time to prepare **f** for the trip.
16:3 and ate all the **f** we wanted!
16:4 "I'm going to send you **f** from
16:8 evening and all the **f** you want
16:12 you will eat all the **f** you want.
16:15 Moses said to them, "It's the **f**
16:21 as much **f** as they could
16:22 they gathered twice as much **f**,

Exo 16:26 You can gather **f** on six days,
16:27 people went out to gather **f**,
16:29 why he gives you enough **f**
16:31 Israelites called the **f** manna.
16:32 This way they will see the **f**
21:10 not deprive the first wife of **f**,
23:11 your people will have **f** to eat,
23:25 he will bless your **f** and water.
34:28 40 nights without **f** or water.
Lev 3:11 It is **f**, an offering by fire to the
3:16 It is **f**, an offering by fire to the
11:34 that pottery⌋ touches any **f**,
11:34 any food, the **f** is unclean.
21:6 It is the **f** of your God.
21:8 Be holy because you offer the **f**
21:17 he must never bring **f** to offer to
21:21 He must never bring **f** to offer to
21:22 He may eat the **f** of his God —
22:7 because they are his **f**.
22:11 may eat the priest's **f**.
22:12 she must never eat the **f** taken
22:13 she may eat her father's **f**.
22:25 from a foreigner as a **f** offering
25:37 or on the **f** you give them.
26:10 You will clear out old **f**
26:26 I will destroy your **f** supply.
26:26 only one oven to prepare your **f**.
Num 11:4 craving for ⌊other kinds of⌋ **f**.
15:19 and eat any of the **f** from the
21:5 we can't stand this awful **f**!"
28:2 They are my **f**. They are
28:24 They are **f**. They are offerings
Dtr 2:6 them in silver for the **f** you eat
2:28 We'll pay you in silver for the **f**
8:9 land will have enough **f** for you,
9:9 40 nights without **f** or water.
9:18 I went without **f** and water for
10:18 and gives them **f** and clothes.
18:8 he'll get the same amount of **f**
23:4 they didn't greet you with **f**
23:19 any interest on money, **f**,
24:6 wouldn't be able to prepare **f**
28:26 Your dead bodies will be **f** for
Jdg 1:7 to pick up **f** under my table.
8:5 "Please give me some **f** for the
8:6 "We shouldn't give your army **f**.
8:15 men **f** before you've captured
13:4 or liquor or eat any unclean **f**.
13:7 or liquor or eat any unclean **f**
13:14 or eat any unclean **f**.
13:16 I will not eat any of your **f**.
Rut 1:6 his people and give them **f**.
1Sm 9:7 we bring the man since the **f**
14:24 "Cursed is anyone who eats **f**
14:24 none of his troops tasted any **f**.
14:28 who eats **f** today.'" Now,
14:30 eaten some of the enemies' **f**,
17:20 He took ⌊the **f**⌋ and went,
22:10 LORD for David and gave him **f**
30:11 They gave him **f** to eat and
30:12 (He hadn't eaten any **f** or drunk
2Sm 3:29 and who never have any **f**."
3:35 tried to get David to eat some **f**.
3:35 strike me dead if I taste any **f**
9:10 family will have **f** to eat.
12:3 She would eat his **f** and drink
12:20 he went home and asked for **f**.
12:20 They placed **f** in front of him,
13:7 "and prepare some **f** for him."
13:10 Amnon told Tamar, "Bring the **f**
17:28 brought ⌊supplies⌋ and **f** for
19:32 he had provided the king with **f**
19:42 Did we eat the king's **f**,
1Ki 4:7 They were to provide **f** for the
4:7 Each one had to supply **f** for
4:22 Solomon's **f** supply for one day
4:27 of the governors provided **f**
5:9 by providing **f** for my palace."
10:5 the **f** on his table, his officers'
11:18 home, a **f** allowance, and land.
17:15 and her family had **f** for a long
19:8 Strengthened by that **f**,
2Ki 4:40 They dished out the **f** for the
6:22 Give them **f** and water.
25:3 the common people had no **f**.
25:30 him a daily **f** allowance as long

1Ch 12:40 Naphtali brought **f** on donkeys,
2Ch 9:4 the **f** on his table, his officers'
11:11 army officers with reserves of **f**,
17:13 He had large supplies of **f** in
Ezr 2:63 eat any of the most holy **f** until
3:7 Then they gave **f**, drink,
10:6 Ezra didn't eat any **f** or drink
Neh 5:14 I never ate any **f** that was paid
5:14 by the governor's **f** allowance.
5:15 people by taking from them **f**
5:18 from the governor's **f** allowance,
7:65 eat any of the most holy **f** until
13:2 the Israelites with **f** and water.
13:15 about selling **f** on that day.
Est 2:9 a daily supply of **f**,
9:19 send gifts of **f** to one another.
9:22 and for sending gifts of **f**
Job 3:24 "When my **f** is in front of me,
6:6 Is tasteless **f** eaten without
12:11 sounds and the tongue taste **f**?
15:23 wanders around for **f** and asks,
20:14 the **f** in his belly turns sour.
22:7 and you take **f** away from
24:5 to do their work, looking for **f**.
24:5 provide **f** for their children.
24:6 They harvest animal **f** in the
27:14 won't have enough **f**.
28:5 "Above the ground **f** grows,
28:5 but beneath it the **f** decays as if
30:4 of the broom plant are their **f**.
31:17 or have eaten my **f** alone
31:31 ⌊our stomachs⌋ with his **f**' ...
33:20 that their whole being hates **f**
34:3 words like the tongue tastes **f**.
36:31 give them more than enough **f**.
38:41 "Who provides **f** for the crow
38:41 wander around in need of **f**?
39:29 From there it seeks **f**,
40:20 The hills bring it **f**,
Psa 14:4 as if they were devouring **f**,
37:25 his descendants begging for **f**.
42:3 My tears are my **f** day and
53:4 as if they were devouring **f**,
63:10 will be left as **f** for jackals.
65:4 We will be filled with good **f**
69:21 They poisoned my **f**,
74:14 the creatures of the desert for **f**.
78:18 demanding the **f** they craved.
78:25 and God sent them plenty of **f**.
78:30 While the **f** was still in their
79:2 your servants to the birds for **f**.
80:5 You made them eat tears as **f**.
104:14 in order to get **f** from the ground
104:21 prey and seek their **f** from God.
104:27 to you to give them their **f** at
105:16 He took away their **f** supply.
106:14 an unreasonable desire ⌊for **f**⌋
107:9 who were hungry with good **f**.
107:18 All **f** was disgusting to them,
111:5 He provides **f** for those who
127:2 to work hard for the **f** you eat by
127:2 The LORD gives ⌊**f**⌋ to those
132:15 satisfy its needy people with **f**.
136:25 He gives **f** to every living
145:15 and you give them their **f** at the
146:7 He gives **f** to those who are
147:9 He is the one who gives **f** to
Pro 4:17 They eat **f** obtained through
6:8 it stores its **f** supply.
6:8 At harvest time it gathers its **f**.
9:17 and **f** eaten in secret is tasty."
13:4 A lazy person craves **f** and
13:23 able to plow, there is much **f**,
19:24 person puts his fork in his **f**.
20:17 **F** gained dishonestly tastes
21:17 expensive **f** will not become
22:9 has shared his **f** with the poor.
23:3 this is **f** that deceives you.
23:6 Do not eat the **f** of one who is
25:21 give him some **f** to eat,
26:15 person puts his fork in his **f**.
27:7 even bitter **f** tastes sweet.
28:3 a driving rain that leaves no **f**.
30:8 Feed me ⌊only⌋ the **f** I need,
30:22 fool when he is filled with **f**,
30:25 yet they store their **f** in summer.

Pro 31:14 She brings her **f** from far away.
31:15 while it is still dark and gives **f**
31:15 to her family and portions of **f**
Ecc 9:7 Go, enjoy eating your **f**,
9:11 people don't necessarily have **f**.
Isa 3:1 entire supply of **f** and water.
3:7 I don't have any **f** or a coat in
4:1 "We'll eat our own **f** and
9:20 On the right, one gobbles up **f**
19:21 with sacrifices and **f** offerings.
21:14 Bring **f** to the fugitives.
23:18 of **f** and expensive clothing.
30:23 and the **f** that the ground
30:24 eat a mixture of **f** that has been
33:16 He will have plenty of **f** and a
51:14 They will not go without **f**.
55:10 produces seed for farmers and **f**
58:7 Share your **f** with the hungry,
58:10 If you give some of your own **f**
65:25 and dust will be **f** for snakes.
Jer 5:17 devour your harvest and your **f**.
7:33 of these people will become **f**
14:12 Even if they go without **f**,
16:4 Their bodies will be **f** for birds
16:7 No one will offer **f** to comfort
19:7 I will give their bodies as **f** to
31:14 satisfy the priests with rich **f**.
34:20 and their corpses will be **f** for
40:5 guard gave Jeremiah some **f**
52:6 the common people had no **f**.
52:34 him a daily **f** allowance as long
Lam 1:11 They trade their treasures for **f**
1:19 looking for **f** to keep
4:10 The children were used for **f** by
5:6 to beg Egypt and Assyria for **f**.
5:9 To get our **f**, we have to risk
Eze 4:10 The **f** that you eat should be
4:10 Eat eight ounces of **f** every day
4:17 of the lack of **f** and water.
5:16 and I will cut off your **f** supply.
12:18 shake as you eat your **f**.
12:19 be worried as they eat their **f**
14:13 cut off its **f** supply,
16:13 Your **f** was flour, honey,
16:19 and honey — all the **f** that I gave
16:20 sacrificed them as **f** to idols.
16:49 proud that they had plenty of **f**
18:7 He gives **f** to people who are
18:16 He gives **f** to people who are
22:9 People who live in you eat **f**
24:17 or eat the **f** that mourners eat."
24:22 or eat the **f** that mourners eat.
33:27 in the open field will become **f**
34:5 they became **f** for every wild
34:8 My sheep have become **f** for
34:10 sheep will no longer be their **f**.
39:4 I will let you become **f** for every
44:3 prince may sit there and eat **f**
47:12 The fruit will be good **f**,
48:18 It will be used to provide **f** for
Dan 1:5 of the king's rich **f** and wine.
1:8 by eating the king's rich **f**
1:13 who are eating the king's rich **f**.
1:15 been eating the king's rich **f**.
1:16 took away the king's rich **f**
6:18 the night without **f** or company.
9:27 the sacrifices and **f** offerings.
10:3 I didn't eat any good-tasting **f**.
11:26 People who eat the king's rich **f**
Hos 2:5 They will give me **f** and water,
9:3 will eat unclean **f** in Assyria.
9:4 be like the **f** that mourners eat.
9:4 All who eat this **f** will be
9:4 Their **f** will only satisfy their
Joe 1:16 **F** disappears right before our
Amo 4:6 I left you with no **f** in your entire
Oba 1:7 Those who eat **f** with you will
Hab 3:17 and the fields yield no **f**,
Hag 2:12 touch bread, boiled **f**, wine, oil,
2:12 food, wine, oil, or any kind of **f**,
2:12 does that make the **f** holy?"
Mal 1:7 "You offer contaminated **f** on
1:12 and that its **f** may be despised.
3:10 so that there may be **f**
Mat 6:25 Isn't life more than **f** and the
14:15 to buy **f** for themselves."

Mat 14:19 up to heaven and blessed the **f**.
15:26 not right to take the children's **f**
24:45 the other servants their **f** at
Mar 6:8 They were not to take any **f**,
6:41 up to heaven and blessed the **f**.
7:27 not right to take the children's **f**
Luk 1:53 fed hungry people with good **f**.
3:11 Whoever has **f** should share it
9:3 traveling bag, any **f**, money,
9:12 so that they can find some **f**
9:13 Unless we go to buy **f** for all
9:16 to heaven, and blessed the **f**.
12:23 Life is more than **f**,
12:42 other servants their share of **f** at
14:24 will taste any **f** at my banquet.'"
15:16 country would give him any **f**,
15:17 men have more **f** than they can
Jon 4:8 into the city to buy some **f**.)
4:32 Jesus told them, "I have **f** to
4:34 Jesus told them, "My **f** is to do
6:27 Don't work for **f** that spoils.
6:27 Instead, work for the **f** that lasts
6:27 This is the **f** the Son of Man
6:55 My flesh is true **f**, and my blood
10:9 out of the sheep pen and find **f**.
Act 2:46 homes and shared their **f**.
6:1 neglected every day when **f**
6:2 word in order to distribute **f**.
7:11 ancestors couldn't find any **f**.
7:12 Jacob heard that Egypt had **f**,
10:10 While the **f** was being prepared,
12:20 on Herod for their **f** supply.
14:17 He fills you with **f** and your
15:29 by keeping away from **f**
21:25 they should not eat **f** sacrificed
23:14 taste any **f** before we've killed
Rom 14:2 that they can eat all kinds of **f**.
14:14 that no **f** is unacceptable
14:20 All **f** is acceptable,
1Co 3:2 I didn't give you solid **f**
6:13 **F** is for the stomach,
6:13 and the stomach is for **f**,
8:1 Now, concerning **f** offered to
8:4 Now about eating **f** that was
8:7 believe they are eating **f** offered
8:8 **F** will not affect our
8:8 no worse off if we eat ⌊that **f**⌋
8:10 that person to eat **f** offered
8:13 Therefore, if eating **f** ⌊offered to
8:13 I will never eat that kind of **f** so
9:13 at the temple get their **f** from
10:3 of them ate the same spiritual **f**,
10:30 thanks to God for the **f** I eat,
2Co 6:5 sleepless nights, and lack of **f**.
9:10 gives seed to the farmer and **f**
11:27 and gone without **f** and without
2Th 3:8 We didn't eat anyone's **f**
1Ti 4:3 God created **f** to be received
6:8 long as we have **f** and clothes,
Heb 5:12 You need milk, not solid **f**.
5:14 solid **f** is for mature people,
9:10 sacrifices were meant to be **f**,
13:9 from following rules about **f**,
Jas 2:15 needs clothes or **f**
Rev 2:14 them to eat **f** sacrificed
2:20 and to eat **f** sacrificed to idols.

foods (13)

Neh 8:10 eat rich **f**, drink sweet drinks,
Job 36:16 table was covered with rich **f**.
Psa 36:8 are refreshed with the rich **f**
63:5 my soul with the richest **f**.
Isa 25:6 people a feast with the best **f**,
25:6 with the best **f** and the finest
55:2 and enjoy the best **f**.
65:4 pots made broth from unclean **f**.
Mar 7:19 Jesus declared all **f**
Rom 14:3 People who eat all **f** should not
14:3 criticize people who eat all **f**,
14:6 When people eat all kinds of **f**,
1Ti 4:3 and from eating certain **f**.

fool (81)

Gen 39:14 this Hebrew here to **f** around
39:17 in and tried to **f** around with me.
Num 22:29 "You've made a **f** of me!
Dtr 32:15 rock of their salvation like a **f**.
1Sm 25:25 His name is Nabal [Godless **F**],
26:21 I've acted like a **f** and made a
2Sm 3:33 Abner die like a godless **f**?
6:20 **f** might expose himself!"
Job 2:10 "You're talking like a godless **f**.
5:2 anger kills a stubborn **f**,
5:3 seen a stubborn **f** take root,
5:5 What a stubborn **f** gathers,
Psa 92:6 and a **f** cannot understand
Pro 10:14 of a stubborn **f** invites ruin.
10:18 Whoever spreads slander is a **f**.
10:23 Like the laughter of a **f** when he
11:29 and that stubborn **f** becomes a
12:15 A stubborn **f** considers his own
12:16 When a stubborn **f** is irritated,
13:16 but a **f** displays stupidity.
14:7 Stay away from a **f**,
14:16 but a **f** is careless and
15:5 A stubborn **f** despises his
17:7 is not fitting for a godless **f**.
17:10 a hundred lashes impress a **f**.
17:12 cubs than a **f** ⌊carried away⌋
17:16 Why should a **f** have money in
17:21 The parent of a **f** has grief,
17:21 father of a godless **f** has no joy.
17:24 but the eyes of a **f** ⌊are looking
17:28 Even a stubborn **f** is thought to
18:2 A **f** does not find joy in
18:6 a **f** gets into an argument,
19:1 talks dishonestly and is a **f**.
19:10 Luxury does not fit a **f**,
20:3 any stubborn **f** can start a fight.
21:20 but a **f** devours them.
23:9 Do not talk directly to a **f**,
24:7 the grasp of a stubborn **f**.
26:1 so honor is not right for a **f**.
26:4 Do not answer a **f** with his own
26:5 Answer a **f** with his own
26:6 Whoever uses a **f** to send a
26:8 so is giving honor to a **f**.
26:11 ⌊so⌋ a **f** repeats his stupidity.
26:12 more hope for a **f** than for him.
27:3 by a stubborn **f** is heavier than
27:22 If you crush a stubborn **f** in a
28:26 trusts his own heart is a **f**.
29:9 goes to court with a stubborn **f**,
29:11 A **f** expresses all his emotions,
29:20 more hope for a **f** than for him.
30:22 a godless **f** when he is filled
30:32 If you are such a godless **f** as
Ecc 2:14 but a **f** walks in the dark.
2:15 that waits for the **f** waits
2:16 the wise person nor the **f** will
2:16 wise person and the **f** will die.
4:5 A **f** folds his hands and wastes
6:8 a wise person have over a **f**?
7:6 The laughter of a **f** is like the
7:7 can turn a wise person into a **f**,
7:17 be too wicked, and don't be a **f**.
10:2 The heart of a **f** leads the
10:3 Even when a **f** goes walking,
10:3 everyone else that he's a **f**.
10:13 A **f** starts out by talking
Jer 17:11 he will be a godless **f**."
Nah 3:6 I will make you look like a **f**.
Mat 5:22 another believer a **f** will answer
Luk 12:20 "But God said to him, 'You **f**!
Act 17:18 "What is this babbling **f** trying
1Co 15:36 You **f**! The seed you plant
2Co 11:16 no one should think that I'm a **f**.
11:16 then take me for a **f** so that I
11:21 I, like a **f**, can also brag about.
12:6 to brag, I wouldn't be a **f**.
12:11 I have become a **f**.
Gal 6:7 You can never make a **f** out of
Jas 1:22 or you will **f** yourselves.
2:20 You **f**! Do you have to be shown

fooled (1)

Jas 1:16 brothers and sisters, don't be **f**.

fooling (2)

Gal 6:3 you're only **f** yourself.
Jas 1:26 his tongue, he is **f** himself.

foolish (40)

Gen 31:28 You've done a **f** thing.
Num 12:11 us for this **f** sin we committed.
Dtr 32:6 you **f** and silly people?
Jdg 11:35 I made a **f** promise to the
1Sm 13:13 "You did a **f** thing,"
25:25 [Godless Fool], and he's **f**.
2Sm 15:31 make Ahithophel's advice **f**."
Psa 49:10 that **f** and stupid people meet
Pro 10:1 but a **f** son brings grief to his
12:23 but **f** minds preach stupidity.
15:7 but a **f** attitude does not.
15:20 but a **f** child despises its
17:25 A **f** son is a heartache to his
19:13 A **f** son ruins his father,
24:9 **F** scheming is sinful,
Ecc 2:3 ways to do ⌊some⌋ **f** things.
2:19 that person will be wise or **f**?
4:13 **f** king who won't take advice
10:6 **F** people are often given high
Isa 28:14 you **f** talkers who rule the
Jer 5:4 "These are poor, **f** people.
10:21 The shepherds are **f**.
Eze 13:3 it will be for the **f** prophets.
13:6 These **f** prophets see false
Hos 4:14 These **f** people will be
Zec 11:15 of a **f** shepherd again.
11:17 "How horrible it will be for the **f**
Mat 7:26 will be like a **f** person who built
25:2 Five of them were **f**,
25:3 The **f** bridesmaids took their
25:8 "The **f** ones said to the wise
Luk 24:25 said to them, "How **f** you are!
Act 19:36 be quiet and not do anything **f**.
2Co 10:12 they show how **f** they are.
Eph 5:4 not right that dirty stories, **f** talk
5:15 Don't live like **f** people but like
5:17 So don't be **f**, but understand
2Ti 2:23 Don't have anything to do with **f**
Tit 3:9 Avoid **f** controversies,
1Pe 2:15 ignorance of **f** people by doing

foolishly (8)

2Sm 24:10 because I have acted very **f**."
1Ch 21:8 because I have acted very **f**."
2Ch 16:9 You acted **f** in this matter.
Psa 12:2 All people speak **f**.
41:6 comes to visit me, he speaks **f**.
Pro 10:8 but the one who talks **f** will be
10:10 The one who talks **f** will be
Isa 19:13 leaders of Zoan are acting **f**.

foolishness (12)

Pro 22:15 **F** is firmly attached to a child's
Ecc 2:12 wisdom, madness, and **f**.
2:13 advantage over **f** as light has
7:25 is stupid and **f** is madness.
10:1 A little **f** outweighs wisdom
10:13 A fool starts out by talking **f**
Isa 9:17 and every mouth speaks **f**.
32:6 Godless fools speak **f**,
44:25 and turn their knowledge into **f**.
Mar 7:22 and **f** come from within a
2Co 11:1 to put up with a little **f** from me.
11:17 I say as I start bragging is **f**.

foolproof (1)

Psa 64:6 have perfected a **f** scheme!"

fool's (3)

Pro 14:3 Because of a stubborn **f** words
18:7 A **f** mouth is his ruin.
Ecc 10:12 but a **f** lips are self-destructive.

fools (53)

Dtr 32:21 and a nation of godless **f**
2Sm 13:13 one of the godless **f** in Israel!
Job 12:17 and makes **f** out of judges.
30:8 Godless **f** and worthless
42:8 not to treat you as godless **f**.
Psa 14:1 Godless **f** say in their hearts,
39:8 me in front of godless **f**.
49:13 This is the final outcome for **f**
53:1 Godless **f** say in their hearts,
74:18 godless **f** despised your name.

Psa 74:22 Remember how godless **f**
94:8 will you become wise, you **f**?
107:17 **F** suffered because of their
Pro 1:7 Stubborn **f** despise wisdom
1:22 will you **f** hate knowledge?
1:32 **F** destroy themselves because
3:35 but **f** will bear disgrace.
8:5 You **f**, get a heart that has
10:21 but stubborn **f** die because they
13:19 from evil is disgusting to **f**.
13:20 associates with **f** will suffer.
14:8 stupidity of **f** misleads them.
14:9 Stubborn **f** make fun of guilt,
14:24 The stupidity of **f** is just that —
14:33 Even **f** recognize this.
15:2 but the mouths of **f** pour out a
15:14 mouths of **f** feed on stupidity.
16:22 but stubborn **f** punish
19:29 and beatings for the backs of **f**.
26:3 and a rod is for the backs of **f**.
26:7 is a proverb in the mouths of **f**.
26:9 is a proverb in the mouths of **f**.
26:10 so is one who hires **f** or drifters.
Ecc 5:1 to bring the sacrifices **f** bring.
5:1 **F** are unaware that they are
5:4 it because God doesn't like **f**.
7:4 of **f** think about banquets.
7:5 you than to **f** who sing your
7:9 because anger is typical of **f**.
9:17 than shouting from a ruler of **f**.
10:15 **F** wear themselves out with
Isa 19:11 of Zoan are nothing but **f**.
32:5 Godless **f** will no longer be
32:6 Godless **f** speak foolishness,
35:8 Godless **f** won't wander ⌊onto
44:25 fail and make **f** of fortunetellers.
Jer 4:22 "My people are **f**. They don't
50:36 They will become **f**.
Hos 9:7 ⌊They think that⌋ prophets are **f**
Mat 23:17 You blind **f**! What is more
Luk 11:40 You **f**! Didn't the one who made
Rom 1:22 to be wise, they became **f**.
2Co 11:19 so you'll gladly put up with **f**.

foot (70)

Exo 12:37 six hundred thousand men on **f**,
19:17 stood at the **f** of the mountain.
21:24 a hand for a hand, a **f** for a foot,
21:24 a hand for a hand, a foot for a **f**,
24:4 morning he built an altar at the **f**
32:19 them at the **f** of the mountain.
Lev 8:23 and on the big toe of his right **f**.
13:12 person from head to **f** (so far as
14:14 and on the big toe of the right **f**
14:17 and on the big toe of the right **f**
14:25 and on the big toe of the right **f**
14:28 and on the big toe of the right **f**
21:19 or a crippled hand or **f**,
Num 11:21 "Here I am with 600,000 **f**
20:19 We want to pass through on **f**.
22:25 and pinned Balaam's **f** against
Dtr 4:11 So you came and stood at the **f**
4:49 as far as the Dead Sea at the **f**
11:24 every place on which you set **f**.
19:21 for a hand, and a **f** for a foot.
19:21 for a hand, and a foot for a **f**.
32:35 In due time their **f** will slip,
Jos 1:3 every place on which you set **f**,
3:15 of the Jordan River and set **f**
11:3 and the Hivites at the **f** of
11:17 in the Lebanon Valley at the **f**
12:3 from Beth Jeshimoth to the **f**
13:5 eastward from Baal Gad at the **f**
18:16 the border descends to the **f**
Jdg 4:15 from his chariot and fled on **f**.
4:17 Meanwhile, Sisera fled on **f**
20:2 400,000 **f** soldiers with swords.
1Sm 4:10 30,000 Israelite **f** soldiers died.
15:4 200,000 **f** soldiers and 10,000
2Sm 8:4 and 20,000 **f** soldiers from him.
10:6 and Zobah (20,000 **f** soldiers),
15:16 The king left on **f**, and his
15:17 were leaving the city on **f**,
21:20 hand and six toes on each **f**.
1Ki 14:12 The moment you set **f** in the
15:23 he had a **f** disease.
1Ki 20:29 100,000 Aramean **f** soldiers
2Ki 13:7 and 10,000 **f** soldiers because
1Ch 18:4 and 20,000 **f** soldiers from him.
19:18 drivers and 40,000 **f** soldiers.
20:6 hand and six toes on each **f**.
2Ch 16:12 Asa got a **f** disease that
Job 28:4 where no one has set **f**.
39:15 It forgets that a **f** may crush
Psa 38:16 When my **f** slips, do not let
66:6 They crossed the river on **f**.
91:12 never hit your **f** against a rock.
Pro 1:15 Do not even set **f** on their path,
3:23 and you will not hurt your **f**.
3:26 keep your **f** from getting caught.
6:13 makes a signal with his **f**,
25:17 Do not set **f** in your neighbor's
25:19 a broken tooth and a lame **f**,
Ecc 10:7 people going on **f** like slaves.
Jer 12:5 have raced against others on **f**,
Jnh 2:6 I sank to the **f** of the mountains.
Mat 4:6 never hit your **f** against a rock.'"
14:13 him on **f** from the cities.
18:8 "If your hand or your **f** causes
Mar 5:4 often been chained hand and **f**.
9:45 If your **f** causes you to lose
Luk 4:11 never hit your **f** against a rock.'"
8:29 He was chained hand and **f**.
1Co 12:15 Suppose a **f** says,
Rev 10:2 He set his right **f** on the sea

foothills (19)

Dtr 1:7 in the **f**, in the Negev,
Jos 9:2 kings in the mountains, the **f**,
10:40 Negev, the **f**, and the slopes.
11:2 south of Chinneroth, the **f**,
11:16 of Goshen, the **f**, the plains,
11:16 the mountains and **f** of Israel.
12:8 It included the mountains, **f**,
15:33 In the **f** they gave Judah 14
Jdg 1:9 the Negev, and the **f**.
1Ki 10:27 as plentiful as fig trees in the **f**.
1Ch 27:28 the olive and fig trees in the **f**:
2Ch 1:15 as plentiful as fig trees in the **f**.
9:27 as plentiful as fig trees in the **f**.
26:10 he had a lot of herds in the **f**
28:18 The Philistines had raided the **f**
Jer 17:26 from the **f**, from the mountains,
33:13 in the **f**, in the Negev,
Oba 1:19 People from the **f** will take
Zec 7:7 and the **f** were still inhabited?'"

footing (2)

2Sm 22:34 gives me sure **f** on high places.
Psa 18:33 gives me sure **f** on high places.

footings (1)

Job 38:6 On what were its **f** sunk?

footprints (2)

Psa 77:19 but your **f** could not be seen.
Hos 6:8 It is stained with bloody **f**.

footsteps (5)

1Ki 14:6 Ahijah heard her **f** when she
Job 23:11 I have followed his **f** closely.
Isa 26:6 the oppressed, the **f** of the poor.
Rom 4:12 but also are following in the **f**
1Pe 2:21 that you could follow in his **f**.

footstool (11)

2Ch 9:18 which had a gold **f** attached to
Psa 99:5 Bow down at his **f**.
110:1 I make your enemies your **f**."
132:7 Let's worship at his **f**.
Isa 66:1 The earth is my **f**. Where can
Lam 2:1 didn't ⌊even⌋ remember his **f**
Mat 5:35 or by the earth, which is his **f**,
Luk 20:43 I make your enemies your **f**.'"
Act 7:49 The earth is my **f**. What kind of
Heb 1:13 I make your enemies your **f**."
10:13 his enemies to be made his **f**.

forbid (1)

Mat 16:22 He said, "Heaven **f**,

forbidden (12)

Lev 4:2 even one thing that is **f** by any
4:13 even one thing that is **f** by any
4:22 even one thing that is **f** by any
4:27 wrong — even one thing **f** by
5:17 even one thing **f** by any
Dtr 2:37 But the LORD our God had **f**
4:23 the LORD your God has **f**.
17:3 army of heaven. I have **f** this.
1Ki 21:3 "The LORD has **f** me to give
Ezr 7:24 are notifying you that you are **f**
Lam 1:10 are the same people you have **f**
1Pe 4:3 and took part in the **f** worship of

force (113)

Gen 31:31 daughters away from me by **f**.
47:26 Egypt which is still in **f** today:
Exo 11:1 he will be certain to **f** all of you
19:21 not to **f** their way through
19:24 must not **f** their way through
23:28 ahead of you to **f** the Hivites,
23:29 I will not **f** them out of your way
23:30 Little by little I will **f** them out of
23:31 and you will **f** them out of your
33:2 and I will **f** out the Canaanites,
34:11 Then I will **f** the Amorites,
34:24 I will **f** nations out of your way
Num 22:6 to defeat them and **f** them out
22:11 to fight them and **f** them out.'"
33:52 As you advance, **f** out all the
33:55 "But if you do not **f** out those
Dtr 4:27 the LORD will **f** you to live.
7:1 He will **f** many nations out of
7:17 How can we **f** them out?"
7:22 Little by little he will **f** these
11:23 Then the LORD will **f** all these
12:29 you're going and **f** them out
19:1 You will **f** them out and live in
33:27 He will **f** your enemies out of
Jos 3:10 will certainly **f** the Canaanites,
13:6 I will **f** out of the way of the
13:13 But the Israelites did not **f** out
14:12 is with me, I can **f** them out,
15:63 Judah was not able to **f** out the
16:10 However, they did not **f** out the
17:13 since they didn't **f** all of them
17:18 But you must **f** out the
23:5 of your eyes and **f** them out
23:13 never again **f** these people out
24:12 I sent hornets ahead of you to **f**
Jdg 1:19 But they could not **f** out the
1:21 The men of Benjamin did not **f**
1:27 the tribe of Manasseh did not **f**
1:28 But they did not **f** all of them
1:29 The tribe of Ephraim did not **f**
1:30 The tribe of Zebulun did not **f**
1:31 The tribe of Asher did not **f** out
1:32 they did not **f** them out.
1:33 The tribe of Naphtali did not **f**
2:3 this to say, 'I will not **f** them out
2:21 I will no longer **f** out the nations
18:7 to take away their property by **f**.
Rut 1:16 "Don't **f** me to leave you.
1Sm 2:16 it to me now, or I'll take it by **f**."
2Ch 20:7 Didn't you, our God, **f** those
20:11 paying us back by coming to **f**
26:13 They were a powerful **f** that
Neh 5:5 Yet, we have to **f** our sons and
Est 8:11 and to destroy every armed **f** of
Job 20:19 He has taken by **f** a house that
20:22 with all his wealth the full **f**
24:4 They **f** needy people off the
28:25 When he gave the wind its **f**
Psa 51:11 Do not **f** me away from your
62:4 They plan to **f** him out of his
129:5 hate Zion. **F** them to retreat.
Jer 7:15 I will **f** you out of my sight as I
46:22 enemies will come with full **f**.
Eze 8:6 things that will **f** me to go far
11:7 I will **f** you out of the city.
11:9 I will **f** you out of the city.
12:15 nations and **f** them into other
20:23 nations and **f** them into other
22:15 the nations and **f** you into other
29:12 nations and **f** them into other

Ezr 10:11 land and from your **f** wives."
10:14 everyone who has married a **f**
10:17 men who had married **f** women.
10:18 were married to **f** women:
10:44 men had married **f** women.
Neh 13:30 from everything that was **f**.
Job 21:16 (The plan of the wicked is **f** to
22:18 (The plan of the wicked is **f** to
Psa 39:12 for I am a **f** resident with you,
81:9 Never worship a **f** god.
114:1 who spoke a **f** language,
137:4 the LORD's song in a **f** land?
Isa 28:11 by speaking in a **f** language.
33:19 with a **f** language that you can't
43:12 There was no **f** ⌊god⌋ among
Jer 2:25 You love **f** gods and follow
5:19 me and served **f** gods
8:19 their idols, with their **f** gods.
25:20 and all the **f** people living
25:24 and all the kings of the **f**
Eze 47:22 It will also be for the **f**
47:23 **F** residents will receive their
Dan 11:39 With the help of a **f** god,
Hos 8:12 these things strange and **f**.
Zep 1:8 and all who dress in **f** clothing.
Mal 2:11 woman who worships a **f** god.
Act 17:18 to be speaking about **f** gods."
1Co 14:21 "Through people who speak **f**
Eph 2:12 in his⌋ promise were **f** to you.

foreigner (35)

Gen 17:12 from a **f** who's not related
17:27 or bought with money from a **f**,
Exo 2:22 named him Gershom [**F**],
2:22 "I was a **f** living in another
12:43 "No **f** may eat the Passover
12:45 "No **f** visiting you may eat it.
18:3 son was named Gershom [**F**],
18:3 "I was a **f** living in another
Lev 18:26 Neither you nor any **f** should
19:33 "Never mistreat a **f** living in
22:25 animal received from a **f** as
24:22 difference whether you are a **f**
25:47 "Someone who is a **f** without a
25:47 may sell himself to that **f**
Num 15:30 or **f** who deliberately does
Dtr 15:3 You may demand that a **f** pay,
17:15 Never let a **f** be king,
23:20 You may charge a **f** interest,
Rut 2:10 attention to me? I'm only a **f**."
2Sm 15:19 You are a **f**, an exile from your
Job 19:15 I am like a **f** to them.
Psa 69:8 a **f** to my mother's sons.
105:23 Jacob lived as a **f** in the land of
119:19 I am a **f** in this world.
119:54 this place where I am only a **f**.
120:5 How horrible it is to live as a **f**
Pro 20:16 makes a loan on behalf of a **f**.
27:13 makes a loan in behalf of a **f**.
Eze 14:7 Suppose an Israelite or a **f** who
44:9 Any godless **f** who lives
Luk 17:18 Only this **f** came back to praise
Act 7:29 and lived in Midian as a **f**.
1Co 14:11 I will be a **f** to the person who
14:11 that person will be a **f** to me.
Heb 11:9 Faith led Abraham to live as a **f**

foreigners (130)

Gen 31:15 Doesn't he think of us as **f**?
Exo 6:4 the land where they lived as **f**.
12:48 "**F** may want to celebrate the
12:49 Israelites as well as **f**."
20:10 and the **f** living in your city
21:8 He has no right to sell her to **f**,
22:21 "Never mistreat or oppress **f**,
22:21 you were **f** living in Egypt.
23:9 "Never oppress **f**. You know
23:9 You know what it's like to be **f**
23:9 you were **f** living in Egypt.
23:12 your household and **f** will also
Lev 16:29 and **f** must humble themselves.
17:8 "Tell them: If Israelites or **f**
17:10 "If Israelites or **f** eat any blood,
17:12 Neither you nor **f** should ever
17:13 "If Israelites or **f** hunt any
17:15 "Native Israelites or **f** who eat
Lev 19:10 them for poor people and **f**.
19:34 **F** living among you will be like
19:34 because you were **f** living in
20:2 If Israelites or **f** living among
22:18 Israelites or **f** may bring burnt
23:22 Leave it for poor people and **f**.
24:16 whether they are Israelites or **f**.
25:6 hired workers, **f** among you,
25:45 from the **f** living among you
Num 9:14 "**F** living with you may want to
9:14 to **f** and native-born Israelites."
11:4 Some **f** among the Israelites
15:14 "Suppose **f** are visiting you or
15:15 for you and **f** who are living
15:15 you and **f** are the same.
15:16 you as well as **f** who are living
15:26 including **f** who are living
19:10 Israelites and for the **f** who live
35:15 **f**, and strangers among you.
Dtr 5:14 your animals — even the **f** living
10:18 He loves **f** and gives them food
10:19 So you should love **f**,
10:19 you were **f** living in Egypt.
14:21 You may give it to the **f** who
14:21 You may also sell it to **f** who
14:29 **F**, orphans, and widows who
16:11 in your cities, the **f**, orphans,
16:14 slaves, the Levites, **f**, orphans,
23:7 You once were **f** living in their
24:14 whether they are Israelites or **f**
24:17 Never deprive **f** and orphans of
24:19 Leave it there for **f**,
24:20 Leave some for **f**, orphans,
24:21 Leave some for **f**, orphans,
26:5 went to Egypt and lived as **f**.
26:11 Then you, the Levites, and the **f**
26:12 to the Levites, **f**, orphans,
26:13 I distributed it to the Levites, **f**,
27:19 "Whoever deprives **f**,
28:43 living for the⌋ **f** who live among
29:11 and the **f** who cut wood and
29:22 children and **f** who come from
31:12 as well as the **f** who live in
31:16 are living among the **f** there,
Jos 8:33 whether **f** or native Israelites,
8:35 and **f** living among them.
20:9 including the **f** living among
Jdg 19:12 "We'll never go into a city of **f**.
2Sm 22:45 **F** will cringe in front of me.
22:46 **F** will lose heart, although they
1Ch 16:19 a small group of **f** living in that
22:2 David ordered the **f** living in
29:15 **f** without permanent homes.
2Ch 2:17 counted all the men who were **f**
2:17 Solomon counted 153,600 **f**.
15:9 and the **f** who had come
30:25 the **f** who came from Israel,
Neh 9:2 themselves from all **f**.
Psa 18:44 **F** will cringe in front of me.
18:45 **F** will lose heart, and they will
94:6 They kill widows and **f**,
105:12 a small group of **f** living in that
146:9 The LORD protects **f**.
Isa 1:7 right before your eyes by **f**.
1:7 devastated and taken over by **f**.
2:6 and they make deals with **f**.
5:17 and **f** will eat among the ruins
9:1 River, to Galilee, where **f** live.
14:1 **F** will join them and unite with
25:5 You calm the uproar of **f**.
52:4 went to Egypt to live there as **f**.
56:3 **F** who have joined the LORD
56:6 And ⌊I will remember⌋ the **f**
60:10 "**F** will rebuild your walls,
61:5 **F** will come forward and
61:5 and children of **f** will work your
62:8 nor will **f** drink the new wine
Jer 5:19 So you will serve **f** in a land
7:6 Suppose you do not oppress **f**,
22:3 Don't mistreat **f**, orphans,
30:8 **F** will no longer make you
50:37 and all the **f** within their ranks.
51:51 because **f** have gone into the
Lam 5:2 have been turned over to **f**.
Eze 7:21 I will hand their jewels over to **f**
7:21 These **f** will dishonor the
Eze 7:22 and **f** will dishonor my
11:9 I will hand you over to **f**,
22:7 They oppress **f** in you.
22:29 They oppress **f** for no reason.
28:7 am going to bring **f** against you,
28:7 the most ruthless **f** among the
28:10 You will die at the hands of **f**
30:12 I will have **f** destroy the land
31:12 **F** from the most ruthless nation
44:7 You brought godless **f** into my
44:8 You put **f** in charge of my
Hos 7:9 **F** are using up your strength,
8:7 produce grain, **f** would eat it all.
Joe 3:17 **F** will never invade it again.
Oba 1:11 **F** entered his gates and threw
Zec 7:10 orphans, **f**, and poor people.
Mal 3:5 against those who deprive **f**
Mat 4:15 River, Galilee, where **f** live!
20:19 and hand him over to **f**.
Mar 10:33 to death and hand him over to **f**.
Luk 18:32 He will be handed over to **f**.
Act 7:6 descendants would be **f** living
13:17 while they lived as **f** in Egypt.
1Co 14:21 and through the mouths of **f**
Eph 2:19 That is why you are no longer **f**
1Pe 2:11 Dear friends, since you are **f**

foreigners' (3)

Psa 144:7 raging waters and from **f** hands
144:11 and rescue me from **f** hands.
Isa 25:2 and **f** palaces into cities that

foreman (2)

Exo 5:10 The slave drivers and **f** went
1Sm 21:7 A **f** for Saul's shepherds,

foremen (14)

Exo 5:6 to the slave drivers and **f**:
5:14 drivers had placed Israelite **f**
5:14 drivers beat the **f** and said,
5:15 Then the Israelite **f** complained
5:19 The Israelite **f** realized they
1Ki 5:16 and 3,300 **f** who were in charge
9:23 550 **f** for the people who did the
2Ki 22:5 Give ⌊some of⌋ it to the **f** who
2Ch 2:2 in the mountains, and 3,600 **f**.
2:18 them supervise the work as **f**.
8:10 250 **f** for the people who did the
24:12 to the **f** who were working
34:10 They gave the money to the **f**
34:10 These **f** gave it to the workmen

foremen's (1)

2Ch 24:13 under the **f** guidance.

foremost (3)

Mat 10:2 the twelve apostles: first and **f**,
1Ti 1:15 and I am the **f** sinner.
1:16 could use me, the **f** sinner,

foresee (2)

Pro 22:3 Sensible people **f** trouble and
27:12 Sensible people **f** trouble and

foresight (5)

Pro 1:4 to give knowledge and **f** to the
2:11 **F** will protect you.
3:21 Use priceless wisdom and **f**.
5:2 so that you may act with **f** and
8:12 and I acquire knowledge and **f**.

foreskin (1)

Exo 4:25 a flint knife, cut off her son's **f**,

foreskins (4)

1Sm 18:25 except 100 Philistine **f** so that
18:27 David brought the **f**,
2Sm 3:14 of 100 Philistine **f** for her."
Jer 4:4 and get rid of the **f** of your

forest (47)

Jos 17:15 so many of you, go into the **f**!
17:18 It is a **f**, so you will have to
1Sm 22:5 David went to the **f** of Hereth.
2Sm 18:6 fight Israel in the **f** of Ephraim.
18:17 him into a huge pit in the **f**,

1Ki 7:2 hall ⌊named⌋ the **F** of Lebanon.
10:17 he called⌋ the **F** of Lebanon.
10:21 hall ⌊which he called⌋ the **F**
1Ch 16:33 Then the trees in the **f** will sing
2Ch 9:16 hall ⌊named⌋ the **F** of Lebanon.
9:20 for the hall ⌊named⌋ the **F**
Neh 2:8 supervisor of Your Majesty's **f**.
Psa 50:10 Every creature in the **f**,
74:5 away like a woodcutter in a **f**.
80:13 Wild boars from the **f** graze on
83:15 the way fire burns a **f** and
96:12 trees in the **f** will sing joyfully
104:20 wild animals in the **f** come out.
Pro 27:9 of a friend is a fragrant **f**.
Ecc 2:6 to water the **f** of growing trees.
Sos 2:3 tree among the trees in the **f**,
Isa 7:2 the trees of the **f** are shaken by
9:18 the underbrush in the **f** on fire,
10:18 The majestic **f** and the orchard
10:19 The trees that remain in the **f**
10:34 down the underbrush of the **f**
21:13 the night in the **f** of Arabia.
22:8 weapons in the House of the **F**.
29:17 field will be considered a **f**.
32:15 field will be considered a **f**.
32:19 The **f** will be flattened because
44:14 strong among the trees in the **f**.
56:9 all you animals in the **f**,
Jer 5:6 That is why a lion from the **f**
10:3 cut down trees from the **f**.
12:8 turned on me like a lion in the **f**.
46:23 They will cut down the **f**,"
Eze 15:2 the wood from a tree in the **f**?
15:6 from among the trees in the **f**
20:46 against the **f** in the Negev.
20:47 Tell the **f** in the Negev,
31:3 fine branches that shaded the **f**.
Hos 2:12 I will turn her vineyards into a **f**,
Amo 3:4 Does a lion roar in the **f** if it has
Mic 5:8 a lion among animals in the **f**,
Zec 11:2 your dense **f** has fallen down.
Jas 3:5 A large **f** can be set on fire by a

forests (5)

2Ki 19:23 borders and its most fertile **f**.
Psa 29:9 strips ⌊the trees of⌋ the **f** bare.
Isa 37:24 heights and its most fertile **f**.
44:23 you **f** and every tree in them.
Jer 21:14 "'I will start a fire in your **f**,

foretell (1)

Isa 47:13 who **f** the future month by

foretold (1)

Isa 43:9 Who among them could have **f**

forever (306)

Gen 3:22 Then he would live **f**."
6:3 will not struggle with humans **f**,
Exo 3:15 This is my name **f**.
15:18 will rule as king **f** and ever."
Num 14:18 patient, **f** loving ....
Dtr 5:29 for them and their children **f**.
11:4 So the LORD destroyed them **f**.
18:5 in the name of the LORD **f**.
28:46 you and your descendants **f**.
29:29 to us and to our children **f**.
32:40 As surely as I live **f**,
1Sm 20:23 between you and me **f**."
20:42 descendants **f**.'" So David left,
2Sm 2:26 "Should this slaughter go on **f**?
3:28 my kingdom and I are **f**
7:13 the throne of his kingdom **f**.
7:16 will remain in my presence **f**.
7:16 throne will be established **f**.'"
7:24 of Israel to be your people **f**.
7:25 made to me and my house **f**.
7:26 Your name will be respected **f**
7:29 continue in your presence **f**.
7:29 my house will be blessed **f**."
22:51 and to his descendant **f**.
1Ki 1:31 Majesty, King David, live **f**!"
2:33 on Joab and his descendants **f**.
9:3 name may be placed there **f**.
9:5 royal dynasty over Israel **f** as
2Ki 21:7 I will put my name here **f**.
1Ch 15:2 carry his ark and to serve him **f**.
16:15 Remember his promise **f**,
16:34 because his mercy endures **f**.
16:41 "His mercy endures **f**."
17:12 and I will establish his throne **f**.
17:14 place him in my royal house **f**,
17:14 throne will be established **f**.'"
17:22 of Israel to be your people **f**.
17:23 made to me and my house **f**.
17:24 **f** when ⌊people⌋ say,
17:27 continue in your presence **f**.
17:27 It will be blessed **f**."
23:13 Aaron and his sons were **f**
23:25 He will now live in Jerusalem **f**.
28:7 I will establish his kingdom **f** if
29:10 our father **f** and ever.
2Ch 5:13 his mercy endures **f**."
7:3 his mercy endures **f**."
7:6 with "his mercy endures **f**"
7:16 name may be placed there **f**.
13:5 to David and his descendants **f**
20:21 because his mercy endures **f**!"
30:8 holy place that he made holy **f**.
33:4 name will be in Jerusalem **f**."
33:7 I will put my name here **f**.
Ezr 3:11 mercy toward Israel endures **f**."
Neh 2:3 "May the king live **f**!"
Job 4:20 They will disappear **f** without
7:16 I do not want to live **f**.
14:20 You overpower him **f**,
19:24 I wish they were **f** engraved on
23:7 I would escape my judgment **f**.
36:7 with kings to honor them **f**.
Psa 5:11 Let them sing with joy **f**.
9:5 out their names **f** and ever.
9:6 enemy is finished — in ruins **f**.
9:7 Yet, the LORD is enthroned **f**.
9:18 of oppressed people be lost **f**.
10:16 The LORD is king **f** and ever.
12:7 one safe from those people **f**.
13:1 Will you forget me **f**?
16:11 Pleasures are by your side **f**.
18:50 and to his descendant **f**.
19:9 It endures **f**. The decisions of
21:4 gave him a long life, **f** and ever.
21:6 you made him a blessing **f**.
22:26 will praise him. May you live **f**.
28:9 shepherd, and carry them **f**.
29:10 LORD sits enthroned as king **f**.
30:12 I will give thanks to you **f**.
33:11 The LORD's plan stands firm **f**.
37:18 Their inheritance will last **f**.
37:27 Avoid evil, do good, and live **f**.
37:28 They will be kept safe **f**,
41:12 you set me in your presence **f**.
44:8 We give thanks to you **f**.
44:23 Awake! Do not reject us **f**!
45:2 is why God has blessed you **f**.
45:6 throne, O God, is **f** and ever.
45:17 give thanks to you **f** and ever.
48:8 God makes Zion stand firm **f**.
48:14 God is our God **f** and ever.
49:9 in order to live **f** and never see
52:5 But God will ruin you **f**.
52:8 the mercy of God **f** and ever.
52:9 I will give thanks to you **f** for
61:4 like to be a guest in your tent **f**
61:7 in the presence of God **f**.
61:8 music to praise your name **f**,
66:7 He rules **f** with his might.
68:16 the LORD will live there **f**.
72:17 May his name endure **f**.
72:19 be to his glorious name **f**.
73:26 of my life and my inheritance **f**.
74:1 have you rejected us **f**?
74:10 Will the enemy despise you **f**?
74:19 life of your oppressed people **f**.
75:9 speak ⌊about your miracles⌋ **f**.
77:8 his mercy come to an end **f**?
78:66 behind and disgraced them **f**.
79:5 Will you remain angry **f**?
79:13 will give thanks to you **f**.
81:15 ⌊for punishment⌋ would last **f**.
83:17 be put to shame and terrified **f**.
85:5 Will you be angry with us **f**?
86:12 my God. I will honor you **f**
Psa 89:1 I will sing **f** about the evidence
89:2 I said, "Your mercy will last **f**.
89:4 make your dynasty continue **f**.
89:28 My mercy will stay with him **f**.
89:29 will make his dynasty endure **f**
89:36 His dynasty will last **f**.
89:37 his throne will stand firm **f**.
89:46 Will you hide yourself **f**?
89:52 Thank the LORD **f**.
92:7 only to be destroyed **f**.
92:8 are highly honored **f**.
100:5 His mercy endures **f**.
102:12 But you, O LORD, remain **f**.
103:9 wrong or be angry ⌊with us⌋ **f**.
104:31 the glory of the LORD endure **f**.
106:1 because his mercy endures **f**.
106:31 was considered righteous **f**,
107:1 because his mercy endures **f**.
110:4 "You are a priest **f**,
111:3 His righteousness continues **f**.
111:8 They last **f** and ever.
111:9 his promise should continue **f**.
111:10 His praise continues **f**.
112:3 His righteousness continues **f**.
112:9 His righteousness continues **f**.
113:2 name of the LORD now and **f**.
115:18 will thank the LORD now and **f**.
117:2 LORD's faithfulness endures **f**.
118:1 because his mercy endures **f**.
118:2 "His mercy endures **f**."
118:3 "His mercy endures **f**."
118:4 "His mercy endures **f**."
118:29 because his mercy endures **f**.
119:44 your teachings **f** and ever.
119:89 is established in heaven **f**.
119:111 written instructions are mine **f**.
119:152 that you made them to last **f**.
119:160 righteous regulations endure **f**.
121:8 you come and go, now and **f**.
125:1 be shaken. It remains firm **f**.
125:2 his people now and **f**.
131:3 hope in the LORD now and **f**.
132:12 will also sit on your throne **f**."
132:14 will be my resting place **f**.
135:13 O LORD, your name endures **f**.
136:1 because his mercy endures **f**.
136:2 because his mercy endures **f**.
136:3 because his mercy endures **f**.
136:4 because his mercy endures **f**.
136:5 because his mercy endures **f**.
136:6 because his mercy endures **f**.
136:7 because his mercy endures **f**.
136:8 because his mercy endures **f**.
136:9 because his mercy endures **f**.
136:10 because his mercy endures **f**.
136:11 because his mercy endures **f**.
136:12 because his mercy endures **f**.
136:13 because his mercy endures **f**.
136:14 because his mercy endures **f**.
136:15 because his mercy endures **f**.
136:16 because his mercy endures **f**.
136:17 because his mercy endures **f**.
136:18 because his mercy endures **f**.
136:19 because his mercy endures **f**.
136:20 because his mercy endures **f**.
136:21 because his mercy endures **f**.
136:22 because his mercy endures **f**.
136:23 because his mercy endures **f**.
136:24 because his mercy endures **f**.
136:25 because his mercy endures **f**.
136:26 because his mercy endures **f**.
138:8 O LORD, your mercy endures **f**.
145:1 bless your name **f** and ever.
145:2 praise your name **f** and ever.
145:21 his holy name **f** and ever.
146:6 The LORD remains faithful **f**.
146:10 The LORD rules as king **f**.
148:6 them in their places **f** and ever.
Pro 6:21 Fasten them on your heart **f**.
12:19 The word of truth lasts **f**,
27:24 Wealth is not **f**. Nor does a
Ecc 1:4 but the earth lasts **f**.
3:14 whatever God does will last **f**.
Isa 9:7 and righteousness now and **f**.
25:8 He will swallow up death **f**.
32:17 peace, calm, and safety **f**.

Isa 33:14 live through a fire that burns **f**?
40:8 the word of our God will last **f**."
45:17 has been saved by the LORD **f**.
51:6 But my salvation will last **f**,
51:8 my righteousness will last **f**,
57:15 The High and Lofty One lives **f**,
57:16 I will not accuse you **f**.
57:16 I will not be angry with you **f**.
64:9 Don't remember our sin **f**.
65:18 Be glad, and rejoice **f** in what
Jer 3:5 He won't hold a grudge **f**.
17:4 fire of my anger. It will burn **f**.
18:16 something to be hissed at **f**.
33:11 because his mercy endures **f**.' I
Lam 3:31 will not reject ⌊such⌋ people **f**.
5:19 you, O LORD, sit enthroned **f**,
Eze 16:60 it a promise that will last **f**.
37:26 This promise will last **f**.
43:7 will live among the Israelites **f**.
43:9 Then I will live among them **f**.
Dan 2:4 "Your Majesty, may you live **f**!
2:44 But it will be established **f**.
3:9 "Your Majesty, may you live **f**!
4:34 honored the one who lives **f**,
4:34 because his power lasts **f** and
5:10 "Your Majesty, may you live **f**!
6:6 "May King Darius live **f**!
6:21 "Your Majesty, may you live **f**!
6:26 the living God who continues **f**.
7:18 and keep it **f** and ever."
12:2 Some will wake up to live **f**,
12:2 to be ashamed and disgraced **f**.
12:3 shine like the stars **f** and ever.
12:7 an oath by the one who lives **f**.
Hos 2:19 I will make you my wife **f**.
Oba 1:10 You will be destroyed **f**.
Jnh 2:6 where bars held me **f**.
Mic 2:9 glory away from their children **f**
4:5 name of the LORD our God **f**.
4:7 them on Mount Zion now and **f**.
7:18 You will not be angry **f**,
Zep 2:9 of weeds, salt pits, and ruins **f**.
Luk 1:33 will be king of Jacob's people **f**,
1:54 to help his servant Israel **f**.
Jon 6:51 eats this bread will live **f**.
6:58 who eat this bread will live **f**."
8:35 slave doesn't live in the home **f**,
12:34 the Messiah will remain here **f**.
14:16 helper who will be with you **f**.
Rom 1:25 the Creator, who is blessed **f**.
5:21 This results in our living **f**
9:5 God over everything, **f** blessed.
11:10 carry back-breaking burdens **f**."
11:36 Glory belongs to him **f**!
16:27 to him through Jesus Christ **f**!
1Co 15:52 changed so that they can live **f**.
15:53 into a body that will live **f**.
15:54 into a body that will live **f**,
2Co 4:18 things that can't be seen last **f**.
9:9 His righteousness continues **f**."
11:31 Lord Jesus, who is praised **f**,
Gal 1:5 to our God and Father **f**!
Php 4:20 to our God and Father **f**!
2Th 1:9 penalty by being destroyed **f**,
1Ti 1:16 would believe in him and live **f**.
1:17 Worship and glory belong **f** to
6:16 and power belong to him **f**!
2Ti 2:10 Jesus with glory that lasts **f**.
4:18 Glory belongs to him **f**!
Phm 1:15 you could have him back **f**—
Heb 1:8 throne, O God, is **f** and ever.
1:11 to an end, but you will live **f**.
5:6 "You are a priest **f**,
6:20 has become the chief priest **f**
7:3 continues to be a priest **f**.
7:17 "You are a priest **f**,
7:21 You are a priest **f**."
7:24 But Jesus lives **f**, so he serves
7:24 so he serves as a priest **f**.
7:28 designated the Son who **f**
9:12 once and for all to free us **f**.
9:15 an inheritance that will last **f**.
10:12 and this sacrifice lasts **f**.
10:14 of setting them apart for God **f**.
13:8 same yesterday, today, and **f**.
13:21 Glory belongs to Jesus Christ **f**.
1Pe 1:25 but the word of the Lord lasts **f**."
4:11 to Jesus Christ **f** and ever!
5:11 Power belongs to him **f**.
1Jn 2:17 does what God wants lives **f**.
2Jn 1:2 in us and will be with us **f**.
Jud 1:13 gloomy darkness is kept **f**.
Rev 1:5 Glory and power **f** and ever
1:18 but now I am alive **f**.
4:9 to the one who lives **f** and ever,
4:10 the one who lives **f** and ever.
5:13 and power **f** and ever."
7:12 be to our God **f** and ever!
10:6 the one who lives **f** and ever,
11:15 he will rule as king **f** and ever."
14:11 torture will go up **f** and ever.
15:7 who lives **f** and ever,
19:3 goes up from her **f** and ever."
20:10 day and night **f** and ever.
22:5 will rule as kings **f** and ever.

forfeiting (1)

Hab 2:10 people and **f** your own life.

forfeits (1)

Pro 20:2 makes him angry **f** his life.

forgave (4)

Psa 32:5 Then you **f** all my sins.
78:38 He **f** their sin. He did not
Col 2:13 Christ when he **f** all our failures.
3:13 Forgive as the Lord **f** you.

forges (1)

Pro 15:21 understanding **f** straight ahead.

forget (66)

Gen 20:16 He said to Sarah, "Don't **f**,
41:30 People will **f** that there was
41:51 Manasseh [He Helps Me **F**],
41:51 because God helped him **f** all
Dtr 4:9 closely so that you don't **f**
4:10 Never **f** the day you stood in
4:23 Be careful that you don't **f** the
4:31 or **f** the promise to your
4:39 Remember today, and never **f**
6:12 that you don't **f** the LORD,
8:11 Be careful that you don't **f** the
8:14 don't become arrogant and **f**
8:19 I warn you today that if you **f**
9:7 Never **f** how you made the
12:19 Don't **f** to take care of the
14:27 Never **f** to take care of the
24:19 If you **f** to bring in one of the
25:19 don't **f** to erase every memory
26:13 and I didn't **f** to do what you
2Ki 17:38 Never **f** the promise I made to
Job 8:13 thing happens to all who **f** God.
9:27 'I will **f** my complaining;
11:16 ⌊Then⌋ you will **f** your misery
Psa 9:17 all the nations who **f** God,
10:12 Do not **f** oppressed people!
13:1 Will you **f** me forever?
44:24 Why do you **f** our suffering and
45:10 **F** your people, and forget your
45:10 and **f** your father's house.
50:22 you people who **f** God.
59:11 Otherwise, my people may **f**.
74:19 Do not **f** the life of your
74:23 Do not **f** the shouting of your
74:23 Do not **f** the uproar made by
103:2 and never **f** all the good he has
119:16 I never **f** your word.
119:61 I never **f** your teachings.
119:93 I will never **f** your guiding
119:109 but I never **f** your teachings.
119:141 never **f** your guiding principles.
137:5 If I **f** you, Jerusalem, let my
137:5 let my right hand **f** ⌊how to play
Pro 3:1 My son, do not **f** my teachings,
4:5 Do not **f**. Do not turn away from
31:5 Otherwise, they drink and **f**
Isa 43:18 **F** what happened in the past,
44:21 Israel, I will not **f** you.
49:15 Can a woman **f** her nursing
49:15 Although mothers may **f**,
49:15 may forget, I will not **f** you.
Isa 54:4 You'll **f** the shame you've had
Jer 2:32 A young woman can't **f** her
20:9 I think to myself, "I can **f** the
23:27 to make my people **f** my name,
23:39 I will certainly **f** you.
Eze 39:26 they will **f** their shame and all
Hos 4:6 so I will **f** your children.
Amo 8:7 "I will never **f** anything that
Luk 12:6 God doesn't **f** any of them.
Rom 13:14 and **f** about satisfying the
1Th 1:3 we never **f** that your faith is
1:4 Brothers and sisters, we never **f**
Heb 6:10 He won't **f** what you've done or
13:2 Don't **f** to show hospitality to
13:16 Don't **f** to do good things for
Jas 1:25 that don't merely listen and **f**;

forgets (6)

Job 11:6 know that God **f** your sin.
24:20 The womb **f** them.
39:15 It **f** that a foot may crush them
Pro 2:17 and **f** her marriage vows to her
31:7 Such a person drinks and **f** his
Jas 1:24 and immediately **f** what he

forgive (92)

Gen 50:17 "I'm begging you to **f** the crime
50:17 please **f** our crime,
Exo 10:17 Please **f** my sin one more time.
23:21 he will not **f** your disobedience.
32:32 But will you **f** their sin?
34:6 always faithful and ready to **f**.
34:9 **f** our sin and the wrong we
Num 14:19 please **f** these people's sins,
14:20 The LORD said, "I **f** them,
Dtr 29:20 be willing to **f** that person,
Jos 24:19 He will not **f** your rebellious
1Sm 15:25 Now please **f** my sin and come
25:28 Please **f** my offense.
2Sm 14:14 But doesn't God **f** a person?
24:10 LORD, please **f** me because I
1Ki 8:30 where you live. Hear and **f**.
8:34 **f** the sins of your people Israel,
8:36 **F** the sins of your servants,
8:39 **F** ⌊them⌋, and take action.
8:50 **F** your people, who have
8:50 ⌊**F**⌋ all their wrongs when they
2Ki 5:18 May the LORD **f** me when my
5:18 When I do this, may the LORD **f**
24:4 and the LORD refused to **f** him.
1Ch 21:8 **F** me because I have acted
2Ch 6:21 where you live. Hear and **f**.
6:25 **f** the sins of your people Israel,
6:27 **F** the sins of your servants,
6:30 **F** ⌊them⌋, and give each
6:39 **F** your people, who have
7:14 from heaven, **f** their sins,
30:18 "May the good LORD **f**
Neh 9:17 and always ready to **f**.
Job 7:21 Why don't you **f** my
Psa 19:12 **F** my hidden faults.
25:18 and suffering, and **f** all my sins.
79:9 Rescue us, and **f** our sins for
86:15 always faithful and ready to **f**.
103:8 and always ready to **f**.
145:8 and always ready to **f**.
Isa 2:9 will be humbled. Do not **f** them.
55:7 because he will freely **f** them.
Jer 3:22 and I will **f** you for being
5:1 Then I will **f** Jerusalem.
5:7 "Why should I **f** you?
18:23 Don't **f** their crimes.
31:34 "because I will **f** their
33:8 I will **f** them for all the sins that
36:3 Then I will **f** their wickedness
50:20 I will **f** the faithful few whom I
Eze 16:63 of your disgrace when I **f** you
37:23 I will **f** them for all the times
Dan 9:19 **F** us, Lord. Pay attention,
9:24 to stop sin, to **f** wrongs,
Hos 1:6 I will no longer **f** them.
14:2 things to him: "**F** all our sins,
Joe 2:13 and always ready to **f** and to
Amo 7:2 "Almighty LORD, please **f** us!
Jnh 4:2 and always ready to **f** and to
Mic 7:18 You **f** sin and overlook the

Mat 6:12 F us as we forgive others.
6:12 Forgive us as we f others.
6:14 "If you f the failures of others,
6:14 your heavenly Father will also f
6:15 But if you don't f others,
6:15 Father will not f your failures.
9:6 has authority on earth to f sins."
18:21 how often do I have to f a
18:35 not sincerely f other believers."
Mar 2:7 Who besides God can f sins?"
2:10 has authority on earth to f sins."
11:25 Whenever you pray, f anything
11:25 in heaven will f your failures."
Luk 4:18 to f those who have been
5:21 Who besides God can f sins?"
5:24 has authority on earth to f sins."
6:37 F, and you will be forgiven.
11:4 F us as we forgive everyone
11:4 us as we f everyone else.
17:3 way he thinks and acts, f him.
17:4 says that he is sorry, f him."
23:34 Jesus said, "Father, f them.
Jon 20:23 Whenever you f sins,
20:23 Whenever you don't f them,
Act 5:31 and act, and to f their sins.
8:22 and ask the Lord if he will f
2Co 2:7 So now f and comfort him.
2:10 If you f someone, so do I.
12:13 F me for this wrong!
Col 3:13 Put up with each other, and f
3:13 F as the Lord forgave you.
Heb 8:12 because I will f their

forgiven (52)

Lev 4:20 the people, and they will be f.
4:26 and the leader will be f.
4:31 and that person will be f.
4:35 and that person will be f."
5:13 did wrong, and you will be f.
5:16 did wrong, and you will be f.
5:18 you did), and you will be f.
6:7 Then you will be f for whatever
19:22 The man will be f for this sin.
Num 15:25 Then they will be f because
15:26 community of Israel will be f,
15:28 and that person will be f.
Psa 32:1 whose disobedience is f
Isa 6:7 and your sin has been f."
22:14 this wrong will not be f even
33:24 sins of its inhabitants will be f.
Lam 3:42 rebellious. You haven't f us.
Mat 9:2 friend! Your sins are f."
9:5 'Your sins are f,' or to say,
12:31 guarantee that people will be f
12:31 cursing the Spirit will not be f.
12:32 the Son of Man will be f.
12:32 the Holy Spirit will not be f
26:28 many people so that sins are f.
Mar 2:5 man, "Friend, your sins are f."
2:9 'Your sins are f,' or to say,
3:28 People will be f for any sin or
3:29 the Holy Spirit will never be f.
4:12 return to me and are never f.'"
Luk 5:20 he said, "Sir, your sins are f."
5:23 'Your sins are f,' or to say,
6:37 Forgive, and you will be f.
7:47 that her many sins have been f.
7:48 "Your sins have been f."
12:10 the Son of Man will be f.
12:10 the Holy Spirit will not be f.
24:47 act so that their sins will be f.
Jon 20:23 you forgive sins, they are f.
20:23 forgive them, they are not f."
Act 2:38 so that your sins will be f.
13:38 Jesus your sins can be f.
Rom 4:7 those whose disobedience is f
2Co 2:7 that if he's not f and comforted.
2:10 Indeed, what I have f,
2:10 if I have f anything,
Eph 4:32 God has f you through Christ.
Col 1:14 means that our sins are f.
Heb 9:22 blood is shed, no sins can be f.
10:18 When sins are f, there is no
Jas 5:15 you have sinned, you will be f.
5:20 and many sins will be f.
1Jn 2:12 your sins are f through Christ.

forgiveness (10)

Psa 130:4 But with you there is f so that
130:7 with him there is unlimited f.
Pro 14:9 there is f among decent people.
Mar 1:4 of repentance for the f of sins.
Luk 1:77 through the f of their sins.
3:3 of repentance for the f of sins.
4:18 He has sent me to announce f
7:47 little f loves very little."
Act 10:43 the one named Jesus receive f
26:18 Then they will receive f for

forgives (7)

Num 14:18 He f wrongdoing and
Psa 65:3 one who f our rebellious acts.
103:3 He is the one who f all your
Pro 17:9 Whoever f an offense seeks
Luk 7:49 "Who is this man who even f
Eph 1:7 God f our failures because of
1Jn 1:9 If we confess our sins, he f

forgiving (7)

Exo 34:7 f wrongdoing, disobedience,
Num 14:19 as you have been f them from
Neh 9:17 But you are a f God,
Psa 86:5 You, O Lord, are good and f,
99:8 them that you are a f God
Dan 9:9 are compassionate and f,
Eph 4:32 f each other as God has

forgot (13)

Gen 40:23 He f all about him.
Dtr 32:18 the rock who fathered you and f
Jdg 3:7 They f the LORD their God and
1Sm 12:9 But they f the LORD their God.
Neh 9:17 They f the miracles you
Psa 44:17 to us, we never f you.
44:20 If we f the name of our God or
78:11 They f what he had done — the
106:13 They quickly f what he did.
106:21 They f God, their savior,
Jer 23:27 as their ancestors f my name
Hos 2:13 She f me," declares the LORD.
13:6 That is why you f me.

forgotten (45)

Gen 27:45 gone and he has f what you did
Dtr 31:21 because it will never be f by
Est 9:28 these days must never be f by
Job 19:14 My house guests have f me.
Psa 9:12 He has never f their cries.
9:18 people will not always be f.
10:11 He says to himself, "God has f.
42:9 "Why have you f me?
77:9 Has God f to be merciful?
88:12 the place where f people live?
98:3 He has not f to be merciful and
102:4 because I have f about eating.
119:83 I have not f your laws.
119:139 my enemies have f your words.
119:153 I have never f your teachings.
119:176 never f your commandments.
Ecc 2:16 since both will be f in the days
Isa 17:10 You have f the God of your
23:15 Tyre will be f for 70 years,
23:16 in the city, you f prostitute.
49:14 My Lord has f me."
51:13 Why have you f the LORD,
56:5 name that will not be f.
65:11 LORD and f my holy mountain.
65:16 Past troubles are f.
Jer 2:32 Yet, my people have f me for
3:21 become crooked and have f
13:25 "You have f me and trusted
18:15 But my people have f me.
20:11 eternal shame will not be f.
23:40 on you. It will never be f."
30:14 All your lovers have f you,
44:9 Have you f the wicked things
50:5 with the LORD. It will not be f.
50:6 They have f their resting place.
Lam 3:17 I have f what happiness is.
5:20 Why have you completely f us?
Eze 22:12 You have f me, declares the
23:35 You have f me and turned your
Hos 4:6 You have f the teachings of
8:14 and they have f their Maker.
Mat 16:5 The disciples had f to take any
Mar 8:14 The disciples had f to take any
Heb 12:5 You have f the encouraging
2Pe 1:9 you're shortsighted and have f

fork (6)

1Sm 2:13 a three-pronged f in his hand.
2:14 Whatever the f brought up
Pro 19:24 A lazy person puts his f in his
26:15 A lazy person puts his f in his
Eze 21:19 start to f toward the cities.
21:21 where there is a f in the road.

forks (6)

Exo 27:3 bowls, f, and incense burners.
38:3 bowls, f, and incense burners.
Num 4:14 These are the trays, f,
1Ch 28:17 the pure gold for the f,
2Ch 4:16 and three-pronged f.
Isa 30:24 winnowed with f and shovels.

form (27)

Gen 9:14 Whenever I f clouds over the
Exo 25:19 F the angels and the throne of
26:7 11 sheets of goats' hair to f
36:14 11 sheets of goats' hair to f
Num 12:8 He even sees the f of the
Jdg 19:30 F a plan, and speak out!"
1Sm 17:8 "Why do you f a battle line?
28:14 "In what f?" he asked her. She
2Ch 3:5 ⌊designs in the f of⌋ palm trees
20:9 'If evil comes in the f of war,
Job 31:15 Didn't the same God f us in the
41:12 its strength, or its graceful f.
Psa 83:5 They f an alliance against you:
Sos 5:15 His f is like Lebanon,
Isa 53:2 He had no f or majesty that
Eze 37:10 There were enough of them to f
37:22 I will f them into one nation in
Luk 3:22 Spirit came down to him in the f
Jon 5:37 and you have never seen his f.
Rom 8:29 them to have the same f as
1Co 7:31 its present f is passing away.
12:12 As all the parts f one body,
15:37 It doesn't have the f that the
15:38 God gives the plant the f he
15:38 of seed grows into its own f.
Php 2:6 Although he was in the f of
2:7 himself by taking on the f

formal (3)

Dtr 21:7 must make this f statement:
25:9 must make this f statement:
26:5 You will make this f statement

formation (3)

Num 32:17 ⌊to march⌋ in battle f ahead
Jos 1:14 must march in battle f ahead
4:12 They marched across in battle f

formed (49)

Gen 2:7 Then the LORD God f the man
2:8 he put the man whom he had f.
2:19 The LORD God had f all the
2:22 Then the LORD God f a
3:23 from which the man had been f.
Exo 9:31 because the barley had f heads
37:8 He f the angels and the throne
Dtr 32:6 who made you and f you?
Jos 14:4 and Ephraim, f two tribes.
Jdg 20:20 The Israelites f their battle line
20:22 They f their battle line where
20:22 battle line where they had f
20:30 They f their battle line facing
20:33 They f their battle line at Baal
1Sm 17:2 They f a battle line to fight the
17:21 Israel and the Philistines f their
2Sm 10:8 The Ammonites f a battle line
10:17 The Arameans f a battle line
1Ki 7:31 The opening was r,
1Ch 19:9 The Ammonites f a battle line
19:17 David f a battle line against the
2Ch 30:13 They f a large assembly.
Job 1:17 "The Chaldeans f three

Job 10:8 "Your hands **f** me and made
33:6 was **f** from a piece of clay.
Psa 33:15 The one who **f** their hearts
94:9 He **f** eyes. Do you think he can't
95:5 and his hands **f** the dry land.
Isa 22:11 see the one who **f** it long ago.
43:1 created Jacob and **f** Israel.
43:7 whom I **f** and made.
43:10 No god was **f** before me,
43:21 I have **f** these people for
44:2 **f** you in the womb,
44:21 I **f** you; you are my servant.
44:24 He **f** you in the womb.
45:18 God **f** the earth and made it.
45:18 not create it to be empty but **f**
49:5 The LORD **f** me in the womb to
Jer 1:5 "Before I **f** you in the womb,
12:6 They have also **f** a mob to find
33:2 "I made ⌊the earth⌋, **f** it,
Hab 2:18 The one who **f** it trusts himself
Mat 13:26 wheat came up and **f** kernels,
Act 17:5 the public square, **f** a mob,
21:30 city was in chaos, and a mob **f**.
23:12 the Jews **f** a conspiracy.
Gal 4:19 again until Christ is **f** in you.
1Ti 2:13 After all, Adam was **f** first,

former (17)

Num 21:26 He had fought the **f** king of
1Sm 19:7 So David was returned to his **f**
1Ki 12:27 the **f** master of these people,
16:24 named the city after its **f** owner,
2Ki 14:5 had killed his father, the **f** king.
2Ch 25:3 who killed his father, the **f** king.
Ezr 2:68 God's temple on its ⌊**f**⌋ site.
9:4 Since the **f** exiles had been
10:6 these **f** exiles had been
10:7 that all the **f** exiles must gather
10:8 from the community of **f** exiles.
10:16 The **f** exiles did this.
Mic 4:8 your **f** government will come
Hag 2:3 saw this house in its **f** glory?
2:9 will be more glorious than the **f**,
2Co 3:11 If that **f** ministry faded away
Heb 7:18 The **f** requirements are rejected

forming (2)

Zec 14:4 **f** a very large valley from east
2Co 6:14 Stop **f** inappropriate

formless (2)

Gen 1:2 The earth was **f** and empty,
Jer 4:23 It's **f** and empty. I see the sky.

forms (4)

Psa 49:14 Their **f** will decay in the grave,
Isa 44:13 carve them into **f** of people,
Amo 4:13 God **f** the mountains and
Zec 12:1 and **f** the spirit in a person —

formula (2)

Exo 30:32 any perfumed oil using this **f**.
30:37 for yourselves using this **f**.

fortifications (5)

2Sm 22:46 they are armed in their **f**.
Psa 18:45 when they come out of their **f**.
Isa 23:11 that Canaan's **f** be destroyed.
26:1 Its walls and **f** provide safety.
Dan 11:24 invent new ways of attacking **f**.

fortified (71)

Num 21:24 of the Ammon because it was **f**.
Dtr 3:5 All of these cities were **f** with
28:52 **f** walls in which you trust come
Jos 10:20 got back into the **f** cities.
14:12 that they have large, **f** cities.
19:29 Ramah and goes on to the **f** city
19:35 The **f** cities were Ziddim,
Jdg 6:26 your God on top of this **f** place.
1Sm 22:4 David was living in his **f** camp.
22:5 "Don't live in your **f** camp,"
23:14 David lived in **f** camps in the
23:14 and he lived in **f** camps in the
23:19 "David is hiding with us in **f**
23:29 went to stay in the **f** camps
1Sm 24:22 his men went to their **f** camp.
2Sm 20:6 or he will find some **f** cities and
23:14 While David was in the **f** camp,
24:7 They went to the **f** city of Tyre
1Ki 15:17 invaded Judah and **f** Ramah
15:23 and the cities he **f** — written in
16:24 He **f** the hill and built the city of
22:39 and all the cities he **f** — written
2Ki 10:2 horses, **f** cities, and weapons.
17:9 to the ⌊largest⌋ **f** city.
18:8 to the ⌊largest⌋ **f** city all
18:13 Assyria attacked all the **f** cities
19:25 you will turn **f** cities into piles
1Ch 11:16 While David was in the **f** camp,
12:8 Gad to join David at the **f** camp
12:16 came to David at the **f** camp.
2Ch 8:5 Horon into cities **f** with walls,
11:5 and built **f** cities in Judah.
11:10 These were **f** cities in Judah
11:23 and Benjamin, in every **f** city.
12:4 He captured the **f** cities in
14:6 He built **f** cities in Judah
16:1 invaded Judah and **f** Ramah
17:2 He put troops in all the **f** cities
17:19 in the **f** cities throughout Judah.
19:5 in each **f** city of Judah.
21:3 along with **f** cities in Judah.
32:1 camp ⌊to attack⌋ the **f** cities.
33:14 in every **f** city in Judah.
Neh 9:25 The Israelites captured **f** cities
Psa 60:9 will bring me into the **f** city?
89:40 have laid his **f** cities in ruins.
108:10 will bring me into the **f** city?
Isa 2:15 high tower and every **f** wall,
17:3 **F** cities will disappear from
17:9 When that day comes, the **f**
25:2 **f** cities into piles of rubble,
25:12 bring down Moab's high **f** walls,
27:10 The **f** city is isolated.
36:1 Assyria attacked all the **f** cities
37:26 you will turn **f** cities into piles
Jer 1:18 I have made you like a **f** city,
4:5 Let's go into the **f** cities."
5:17 destroy the **f** cities you trust.
8:14 Let's go into the **f** cities and die
30:18 and **f** palaces will be built in
34:7 These were the only **f** cities of
48:41 and the **f** places will be
51:30 They stay in their **f** cities.
Lam 2:2 He tore down the **f** cities of
Eze 21:20 and the **f** city of Jerusalem.
33:27 Whoever is in **f** places and
36:35 but now they are **f** and have
Dan 11:15 and capture a **f** city.
Hos 8:14 Judah have built many **f** cities.
Hab 1:10 They will laugh at every **f** city
Zep 1:16 battle cries against the **f** cities

fortify (6)

1Ki 15:22 been using those to **f** the city.
15:22 used the materials to **f** Geba
2Ch 16:6 been using those to **f** the city.
16:6 Asa used the materials to **f**
Isa 22:10 houses in order to **f** the walls.
Jer 51:53 They might **f** their strongholds.

fortifying (2)

1Ki 15:21 he stopped **f** Ramah and lived
2Ch 16:5 he stopped **f** Ramah and

fortress (47)

2Sm 5:7 But David captured the **f** Zion
5:9 David lived in the **f** and called
5:17 heard about it and went to the **f**.
12:26 Rabbah and captured its royal **f**.
12:27 the **f** guarding its water
22:2 rock and my **f** and my Savior,
2Ki 15:25 and Arieh in the **f** of the royal
1Ch 11:5 But David captured the **f** Zion
11:7 David lived in the **f**,
Neh 1:1 while I was in the **f** at Susa,
2:8 wood for the gates of the **f** near
7:2 the commander of the **f**,
Est 1:2 the royal throne in the **f** of Susa,
1:5 for all people in the **f** of Susa,
2:3 and bring them to the **f** of Susa,
Est 2:5 In the **f** of Susa there was a
2:8 and brought to the **f** of Susa.
3:15 also issued at the **f** of Susa.
8:14 issued also in the **f** of Susa.
9:6 In the **f** of Susa the Jews killed
9:11 number of those killed in the **f**
9:12 "In the **f** of Susa the Jews have
Job 39:28 Its **f** is on a jagged peak.
Psa 8:2 you have built a **f** against your
18:2 The LORD is my rock and my **f**
27:1 The LORD is my life's **f**.
28:8 strength of his people and a **f**
31:2 a strong **f** to save me.
31:3 you are my rock and my **f**.
37:39 He is their **f** in times of trouble.
43:2 You are my **f**, O God!
52:7 who refused to make God his **f**!
71:3 you are my rock and my **f**.
91:2 "⌊You are⌋ my refuge and my **f**,
144:2 my merciful one, my **f**,
Pro 10:29 The way of the LORD is a **f** for
Isa 23:14 your **f** will be destroyed.
33:16 His stronghold will be a **f** made
Jer 16:19 LORD is my strength and my **f**,
Eze 30:15 out my fury on Sin, Egypt's **f**,
Dan 8:2 my vision I saw myself in the **f**
11:31 dishonor the holy place (the **f**),
Nah 1:7 ⌊He is⌋ a **f** in the day of trouble.
2:1 Guard your **f**! Keep a lookout on
3:11 Even you will look for a **f** ⌊to
Zec 9:3 Tyre built itself a **f**.
9:12 Return to your **f**, you captives

fortresses (12)

2Ki 8:12 You will set their **f** on fire,
2Ch 17:12 He built **f** and cities where
Isa 32:14 **F** and watchtowers will
34:13 Its **f** have nettles and thistles.
Jer 48:18 They will destroy your **f**.
Eze 19:7 He destroyed **f** and turned
Dan 11:19 He will turn back toward the **f**
11:38 he will honor the god of **f**.
11:39 he will deal with strong **f**.
Hos 10:14 All your **f** will be destroyed like
Amo 5:9 strongholds and ruins **f**.
Mic 5:11 land and tear down all your **f**.

forts (1)

2Ch 27:4 and he built **f** and towers in the

fortunate (1)

Act 26:2 "King Agrippa, I think I'm **f**

Fortunatus (1)

1Co 16:17 I am glad that Stephanas, **F**,

fortune (3)

Isa 65:11 a table for the god of good **f**
Eze 16:53 restore your **f** along with theirs.
Hos 12:8 We've made a **f**. With all this

fortunes (15)

Dtr 30:3 he will restore your **f**.
2Ch 1:11 You didn't ask for riches, **f**,
1:12 I will also give you riches, **f**,
Psa 14:7 When the LORD restores the **f**
53:6 When God restores the **f** of his
85:1 You restored the **f** of Jacob.
126:1 the LORD restored the **f** of Zion,
126:4 Restore our **f**, O LORD, as you
Jer 33:11 I will restore the **f** of the land to
33:26 restore their **f** and love them."
Eze 16:53 "I will restore the **f** of Sodom
Zep 2:7 of them and will restore their **f**.
3:20 I restore your **f** right before
Act 16:16 by an evil spirit that told **f**.
16:16 for her owners by telling **f**.

fortuneteller (4)

Dtr 18:10 be a **f**, witch, or sorcerer,
Jer 39:3 quartermaster and the chief **f**),
39:13 quartermaster and the chief **f**),
Dan 2:27 or **f** can tell the king this secret.

fortunetellers (15)

Lev 19:26 and never consult **f**.

Dtr 18:14 you are forcing out listen to **f**
2Ki 21:6 consulted **f**, cast evil spells,
2Ch 33:6 consulted **f**, cast evil spells,
Isa 2:6 They are **f** like the Philistines,
3:2 and prophets, **f** and statesmen,
8:19 from the mediums and the **f**,
19:3 idols, ghosts, mediums, and **f**.
44:25 to fail and make fools of **f**.
Jer 27:9 interpreters of dreams, **f**,
Dan 4:7 astrologers, and **f** came to me.
5:7 and **f** to be brought to him.
5:11 psychics, astrologers, and **f**.
Mic 5:12 and you will have no more **f**.
Zec 10:2 The **f** see false visions.

Fortunetellers' (1)

Jdg 9:37 along the road by the **F** Tree.

fortunetelling (1)

Eze 12:24 or flattering **f** to the people.

foster (1)

Isa 49:23 kings will be your **f** fathers,

fought (53)

Gen 14:9 They **f** against King
25:18 They all **f** with each other.
Exo 17:8 **f** Israel at Rephidim.
17:10 told him and **f** the Amalekites,
32:29 today because each of you **f**
Num 21:1 he **f** them and took some of
21:23 they **f** against Israel.
21:26 He had **f** the former king of
Jos 10:14 because the LORD **f** for Israel.
10:42 LORD God of Israel **f** for Israel.
23:3 The LORD your God **f** for you!
24:8 They **f** you. However, I handed
24:9 of King Zippor of Moab, **f** Israel.
24:11 and Jebusites **f** you.
Jdg 1:5 They **f** him and defeated the
5:19 Kings came and **f**.
5:19 Then the kings of Canaan **f**.
5:19 They **f** at Taanach by the
5:20 The stars **f** from heaven.
5:20 They **f** against Sisera from their
9:17 My father **f** for you.
12:4 men of Gilead and **f** Ephraim.
1Sm 4:10 The Philistines **f** and defeated
12:9 them **f** against your ancestors.
14:47 he **f** against his enemies on
23:5 to Keilah, **f** the Philistines,
2Sm 10:17 David's ⌊troops⌋ and **f** him.
11:17 of the city came out and **f** Joab.
12:26 Meanwhile, Joab **f** against the
12:27 "I **f** against Rabbah and
12:29 He **f** against the city and
1Ki 22:45 and ⌊the wars⌋ he **f** — written
2Ki 8:29 when he **f** against King Hazael
12:17 Hazael of Aram **f** against Gath
13:12 his heroic acts when he **f**
14:15 his heroic acts when he **f**
14:28 his heroic acts when he **f**,
1Ch 5:10 In Saul's day they **f** a war
10:1 the Philistines **f** against Israel,
12:34 With them were 37,000 who **f**
19:17 the Arameans, and they **f** him.
22:8 caused a lot of bloodshed and **f**
28:3 You have **f** wars and caused
2Ch 21:17 They **f** against Judah,
22:6 when he **f** against King Hazael
27:5 He **f** with the king of the
Isa 63:10 their enemy; he **f** against them.
Eze 29:18 no reward for their hard-**f** battle
Jer 33:5 of Israel **f** the Babylonians.
1Co 15:32 If I have **f** with wild animals in
Php 4:3 They **f** beside me to spread the
2Ti 4:7 I have **f** the good fight.
Rev 12:7 The serpent and its angels **f**.

foul (1)

Joe 2:20 A **f** odor will rise from the dead

foul-smelling (1)

Job 31:40 and **f** weeds instead of barley."

found (316)

Gen 2:12 Bdellium and onyx are also ⌊**f**⌋
2:20 But the man **f** no helper who
9:24 When Noah sobered up, he **f**
11:2 they **f** a plain in Shinar
16:7 The Messenger of the LORD **f**
18:29 "What if 40 are **f** there?"
18:30 "What if 30 are **f** there?"
18:31 "What if 20 are **f** there?"
18:32 "What if 10 are **f** there?"
26:19 valley and **f** a spring-fed well.
26:32 said to him, "We've **f** water."
30:14 fields and **f** some mandrakes.
31:33 But he **f** nothing. He came out of
31:34 the whole tent but **f** nothing.
36:24 (Anah **f** the hot springs in the
37:15 a man **f** him wandering around
37:17 brothers and **f** them at Dothan.
37:32 their father and said, "We **f** this.
42:1 When Jacob **f** out that grain
42:35 each man **f** his bag of money in
43:21 and each man **f** all of his
43:32 because they **f** it offensive to
44:8 We brought the money we **f** in
44:12 cup was **f** in Benjamin's sack.
47:14 all the money that could be **f**
Exo 5:20 As they left Pharaoh, they **f**
9:7 Pharaoh **f** out that not one of
22:4 But if the stolen animal is **f**
Lev 6:4 the lost item you **f**,
Num 15:32 they **f** a man gathering wood on
15:33 Those who **f** him gathering
17:8 He **f** that Aaron's staff for the
23:6 So he went back to Balak and **f**
23:17 He came to Balak and **f** him
31:50 that each of us **f** — arm bands,
Dtr 17:19 and faithfully obey everything **f**
19:18 If it is **f** that the witness lied
22:14 I **f** out she wasn't a virgin."
22:17 He says he **f** out that my
22:20 the girl was a virgin can be **f**,
22:27 The man **f** the girl out in the
24:1 (He divorced her because he **f**
32:10 He **f** his people in a desert land,
Jos 2:22 the road but had not **f** them.
10:17 "The five kings have been **f**.
Jdg 15:15 Samson **f** the jawbone from a
16:9 So no one **f** out why he was so
20:48 all the people and cattle they **f**
21:12 they **f** 400 unmarried women
21:14 the congregation had not **f**
1Sm 4:6 The Philistines **f** out that the
9:20 ago because they've been **f**.
10:2 They'll tell you, 'We've **f** the
10:16 had been **f**," Saul answered his
12:5 today that you've **f** nothing
13:19 No blacksmith could be **f** in the
13:22 or spear could be **f** among all
14:17 They looked and **f** that
14:20 They **f** Philistine soldiers
14:30 which they **f** today.
22:6 David and his men had been **f**.
25:15 and we **f** that nothing was
25:28 May evil never be **f** in you as
29:3 I've **f** nothing wrong with him
29:6 because I've never **f** anything
30:6 But David **f** strength in the
30:11 David's men **f** an Egyptian in
31:8 they **f** Saul and his three sons
2Sm 7:27 That is why I have **f** the
17:13 even a pebble will be **f** there."
1Ki 1:3 They **f** Abishag from Shunem
13:14 of God and **f** him sitting under
13:24 A lion **f** him ⌊as he traveled⌋
13:28 He **f** the body of the man
13:28 He also **f** the donkey and the
14:13 God of Israel **f** anything good.
18:10 an oath that they hadn't **f** you.
19:19 Elijah **f** Elisha, son of Shaphat.
20:36 a lion **f** him and killed him.
20:37 the disciple **f** another man.
21:20 "So you've **f** me, my enemy?"
21:20 Elijah answered, "I **f** you.
2Ki 1:9 When the officer **f** Elijah sitting
4:39 field to gather vegetables and **f**
2Ki 7:8 and clothes they **f** in that tent.
9:21 They **f** him in the field that
10:13 he **f** some relatives of King
12:18 and all the gold that could be **f**
14:14 and all the utensils he **f** in the
16:8 took the silver and gold he **f**
17:4 The king of Assyria **f** Hoshea
18:15 him all the silver that could be **f**
19:8 field commander returned and **f**
22:8 "I have **f** the book of Moses'
22:13 in this book that has been **f**.
23:2 in the Book of the Promise **f**
23:24 the book that the priest Hilkiah **f**
25:19 access to the king whom he **f**
25:19 people whom he **f** in the city.
1Ch 4:40 They **f** pasture that was rich
10:8 they **f** Saul and his sons lying
17:25 That is why I have **f** ⌊the
20:2 (The crown was **f** to weigh 75
26:31 these families were **f** at Jazer
2Ch 20:25 they **f** among them a lot of
20:25 They **f** more than they could
21:17 away everything that could be **f**
22:8 he **f** Judah's leaders (Ahaziah's
25:5 at least 20 years old and **f** that
25:24 and all the utensils he **f** in the
29:16 every unclean thing that they **f**
34:14 the priest Hilkiah **f** the book of
34:15 "I have **f** the book of the
34:21 words in this book that was **f**.
34:30 in the Book of the Promise **f**
34:32 He also made all those **f** in
34:33 He made all people **f** in Israel
35:18 people of Israel who could be **f**,
Ezr 2:62 their names couldn't be **f** there.
6:2 A scroll was **f** in the palace of
Neh 7:5 I **f** the book with the genealogy
7:5 I **f** the following written in it:
7:64 their names couldn't be **f** there.
8:14 They **f** written in the Teachings
9:8 You **f** that his heart was faithful
Est 2:22 But Mordecai **f** out about it and
2:23 report was investigated and **f**
4:1 When Mordecai **f** out about
5:8 If I have **f** favor with you,
7:3 "If I have **f** favor with you,
8:5 and if I have **f** favor with you,
Job 6:4 Almighty ⌊have **f** their target⌋
9:29 I've already been **f** guilty.
19:28 root of the problem is **f** in him.'
20:8 away like a dream and not be **f**.
28:12 "Where can wisdom be **f**?
28:13 It cannot be **f** in this world of
31:25 hand had **f** great ⌊wealth⌋ ....
32:3 because they had **f** no answer.
32:13 So don't say, 'We've **f** wisdom.
33:24 I have **f** a ransom.'
39:30 It is **f** wherever there are dead
42:15 could be **f** women who were
Psa 17:3 but you **f** nothing wrong.
26:4 will not be **f** among hypocrites.
32:6 pray to you when you may be **f**.
37:36 but he could not be **f**.
69:20 to comfort me, but I **f** no one.
69:27 Do not let them be **f** innocent.
89:20 I **f** my servant David.
109:7 stands trial, let him be **f** guilty.
119:52 and I **f** comfort ⌊in them⌋.
119:143 and hardship have **f** me,
132:6 We have **f** it in Jaar.
Pro 7:15 I looked for you, and I've **f** you.
8:31 **f** joy in his inhabited world,
10:9 lives dishonestly will be **f** out.
10:13 Wisdom is **f** on the lips of a
16:31 Silver hair is a beautiful crown **f**
22:26 Do not be ⌊**f**⌋ among those
30:6 and you will be **f** to be a liar.
30:10 and you will be **f** guilty."
30:28 can even be **f** in royal palaces.
Ecc 2:10 since I **f** pleasure in my work.
3:16 where justice should be **f**.
3:16 righteousness should be **f**.
7:27 "This is what I've **f**:
7:28 but have not **f** any.
7:28 I **f** one man out of a thousand
7:29 I have **f** only this: God made

Ecc 9:15 wise person was **f** in that town.
12:1 "I have **f** no pleasure in them."
Sos 3:3 their rounds in the city **f** me.
3:4 I had just left them when I **f** the
5:7 their rounds in the city **f** me.
8:10 me to be one who has **f** peace.
Isa 10:14 I've **f** the riches of nations as
13:15 Whoever is **f** will be stabbed to
22:3 All those who were **f** were
35:9 They won't be **f** there.
37:8 field commander returned and **f**
45:24 and strength are **f**
51:3 Joy and gladness will be **f** in it,
55:6 the LORD while he may be **f**.
57:10 You've **f** renewed strength,
65:1 I was **f** by those who weren't
Jer 3:17 of the LORD will be **f** there.
5:26 "Wicked people are **f** among
15:16 Your words were **f**,
23:11 Even in my temple I've **f** them
31:2 survived the wars have **f** favor
40:1 Nebuzaradan **f** Jeremiah in
41:3 soldiers that he **f** there.
46:23 "since Egypt can't be **f**.
50:20 Judah's sins, but none will be **f**.
50:24 You will be **f** and captured
52:25 access to the king whom he **f**
52:25 people whom he **f** in the city.
Lam 3:47 Panic and pitfalls have **f** us,
Eze 16:37 with whom you **f** pleasure.
28:15 until evil was **f** in you.
Dan 1:19 The king talked to them and **f**
1:20 he **f** that they knew ten times
2:25 He told the king, "I've **f** one of
2:35 not a trace of them could be **f**.
4:12 Wild animals **f** shade under it.
5:11 he was **f** to have insight,
5:12 renamed Belteshazzar) was **f**
5:27 been weighed on a scale and **f**
6:4 No error or fault could be **f**.
6:11 as a group and **f** Daniel praying
Hos 9:10 LORD said,⌋ "When I **f** Israel,
12:4 Jacob **f** him at Bethel,
Jnh 1:3 He went to Joppa and **f** a ship
Mic 1:13 acts of Israel are **f** in you.
Zec 8:23 from every language **f** among
Mal 2:6 Nothing unjust was **f** on his
Mat 2:7 wise men and **f** out from them
2:8 When you have **f** him,
8:10 I haven't **f** faith as great as this
13:46 When he **f** a valuable pearl,
18:28 he **f** a servant who owed him
18:28 He grabbed the servant he **f**
20:6 he went out and **f** some others
21:19 he went up to the tree and **f**
22:10 and all the evil people they **f**.
26:40 the disciples, he **f** them asleep.
26:43 He **f** them asleep again
27:32 On the way they **f** a man
Mar 1:37 When they **f** him, they told him,
6:38 When they **f** out, they told him,
7:30 The woman went home and **f**
11:4 The disciples **f** the young
11:13 When he came to it, he **f**
14:16 They went into the city and **f**
14:37 went back and **f** them asleep.
14:40 He **f** them asleep because they
Luk 1:30 You have **f** favor with God.
2:16 They went quickly and **f** Mary
2:46 Three days later, they **f** him in
4:17 He opened it and **f** the place
7:9 "I can guarantee that I haven't **f**
7:10 they **f** the servant healthy
7:37 life in that city **f** out that Jesus
8:35 They came to Jesus and **f** the
9:11 But the crowds **f** out about this
13:7 on this fig tree but haven't **f** any.
15:6 I've **f** my lost sheep!'
15:9 I've **f** the coin that I lost.'
15:24 was lost but has been **f**.' Then
15:32 He was lost but has been **f**.'"
19:32 The men Jesus sent **f** it as he
22:13 They **f** everything as Jesus
22:45 He **f** them asleep and
23:2 "We **f** that he stirs up trouble
23:7 When Pilate **f** out that he was,
Luk 23:14 and haven't **f** this man guilty
23:22 I haven't **f** this man deserving
24:2 They **f** that the stone had been
24:24 went to the tomb and **f** it empty,
24:33 They **f** the eleven apostles and
Jon 1:41 Andrew at once **f** his brother
1:41 "We have **f** the Messiah"
1:43 He **f** Philip and told him,
1:45 Philip **f** Nathanael and told him,
1:45 "We have **f** the man whom
2:14 He **f** those who were selling
2:14 **f** moneychangers sitting there.
6:25 When they **f** him on the other
9:35 So when Jesus **f** the man,
11:17 When Jesus arrived, he **f** that
12:9 A large crowd of Jews **f** out
Act 4:13 After they **f** out that Peter and
5:10 they **f** Sapphira dead.
5:23 "We **f** the prison securely
5:23 we **f** no one inside."
8:40 Philip **f** himself in the city of
9:30 As soon as the disciples **f** out
9:33 In Lydda Peter **f** a man named
10:17 the men sent by Cornelius **f**
10:27 house and **f** that many people
13:22 He said, 'I have **f** that David,
14:5 Paul and Barnabas **f** out that
17:13 in Thessalonica **f** out that Paul
19:19 books and **f** that they were
20:3 he **f** out that the Jews were
21:2 In Patara, we **f** a ship that was
21:4 After we **f** them, we stayed
22:29 was afraid when he **f** out that
23:27 When I **f** out that he was a
23:29 and **f** their accusations had to
23:34 When he **f** out that Paul was
24:5 We have **f** this man to be a
24:12 No one **f** me having a
24:18 My accusers **f** me in the temple
27:6 In Myra the officer **f** a ship from
28:1 we **f** out that the island was
Rom 2:15 show that some requirements **f**
6:23 freely gives is everlasting life **f**
7:10 I **f** that the commandment
10:20 Isaiah said very boldly, "I was **f**
2Co 8:22 tested in many ways and **f**
Eph 2:15 commandments and demands **f**
2Ti 1:17 he searched hard for me and **f**
3:14 in what you have learned and **f**
Heb 8:8 But God **f** something wrong
11:15 they could have **f** a way to go
11:34 They **f** strength when they
1Jn 5:11 and this life is **f** in his Son.
Rev 3:2 I have **f** that what you are doing
5:4 no one was **f** who deserved
18:21 It will never be **f** again.
18:22 craftsman will never be **f**
18:24 murdered on earth was **f** in it."
20:11 but no place was **f** for them.
20:15 Those whose names were not **f**

foundation (59)

Jos 6:26 his firstborn son to lay the **f**.
1Ki 5:17 of stone in order to provide a **f**
6:37 the **f** of the LORD's temple was
7:9 From the **f** to the roof,
7:10 The **f** was made with large,
7:11 Above ⌊the **f**⌋ were cedar
16:34 Laying the **f** cost him his
2Ch 3:3 This is how Solomon laid the **f**
8:16 carried out from the day the **f**
23:5 another third must be at **F** Gate.
Ezr 3:6 even though the **f** of the
3:10 The builders laid the **f** of the
3:11 because the **f** for the house of
3:12 to sob when they saw the **f**
5:16 Then Sheshbazzar laid the **f** of
6:3 Its **f** should be laid.
6:7 God's temple on its ⌊original⌋ **f**.
Job 4:19 in clay houses that have their **f**
22:16 A river washes their **f** away.
38:4 were you when I laid the **f**
Psa 24:2 He laid its **f** on the seas and
73:26 but God remains the **f** of my life
102:25 Long ago you laid the **f** of the
137:7 Tear it down to its **f**."
Pro 3:19 By Wisdom the LORD laid the **f**
10:25 person has an everlasting **f**.
12:3 firm on a **f** of wickedness,
Isa 14:32 the LORD has laid Zion's **f**,
28:16 precious cornerstone, a solid **f**.
33:6 He will be the **f** of your future.
44:28 "Your **f** will be laid."
48:13 My hand laid the **f** of the earth.
Jer 51:26 any stones in you to use for a **f**.
Eze 13:14 I will level it and expose its **f**.
41:8 This base was the **f** for the
Amo 9:6 up to heaven and sets their **f**
Hag 2:18 from the day when the **f** of the
Zec 4:9 hands have laid the **f**
8:9 prophets who spoke when the **f**
12:1 laid the **f** of the earth,
Mat 7:25 because its **f** was on rock.
Luk 6:48 down to bedrock to lay the **f**
6:48 away because it had a good **f**.
6:49 on the ground without any **f**.
14:29 Otherwise, if you lay a **f** and
Rom 15:20 I didn't want to build on a **f**
1Co 3:10 to lay the **f** ⌊for that building⌋.
3:11 no one can lay any other **f** than
3:11 and that **f** is Jesus Christ.
3:12 may build on this **f** with gold,
15:58 you off the **f** ⌊of your faith⌋.
Eph 2:20 You are built on the **f** of the
3:17 and on which you have your **f**.
Col 1:23 being moved from the solid **f**
1Ti 3:15 the pillar and **f** of the truth.
6:19 themselves which is a good **f**
2Ti 2:19 God's ⌊people⌋ have a solid **f**.
Heb 1:10 in the beginning you laid the **f**
Rev 21:19 The first **f** was gray quartz,

foundations (30)

Dtr 32:22 earth and its crops and set the **f**
2Sm 22:8 Even the **f** of the heavens
22:16 The **f** of the earth were laid
Ezr 4:12 The **f** are already in place.
Psa 11:3 When the **f** ⌊of life⌋ are
18:7 Even the **f** of the mountains
18:15 The **f** of the earth were laid
75:3 I will make its **f** as solid as
82:5 all the **f** of the earth shake.
89:14 and justice are the **f**
97:2 justice are the **f** of his throne.
104:5 You set the earth on its **f** so
Pro 8:29 he traced the **f** of the earth,
Isa 6:4 Their voices shook the **f** of the
24:18 and the **f** of the earth will
40:21 understand the **f** of the earth?
51:13 out the heavens and laid the **f**
51:16 laid the **f** of the earth,
54:11 will reset your **f** with sapphires.
58:12 ancient ruins and restore the **f**
Jer 31:37 could be measured or the **f**
Lam 4:11 in Zion that even burned its **f**.
Eze 30:4 and its **f** will be torn down.
Amo 9:1 the pillars so that the **f** shake.
Mic 1:6 into a valley and expose its **f**.
6:2 Listen, you strong **f** of the earth.
Act 16:26 violent earthquake shook the **f**
Heb 11:10 the city with permanent **f**.
Rev 21:14 The wall of the city had 12 **f**.
21:19 The **f** of the city wall were

founded (2)

Psa 87:1 ⌊The city⌋ the LORD has **f**
Isa 23:7 Is this your bustling city **f** in the

foundries (2)

1Ki 7:46 The king cast them in **f** in the
2Ch 4:17 The king cast them in **f** in the

founds (1)

Hab 2:12 builds a city by slaughter and **f**

fountain (16)

Neh 2:13 Gate that night toward Snake **F**
2:14 Passing through **F** Gate,
3:15 of Mizpah, repaired **F** Gate.
12:37 At **F** Gate they went straight up
Psa 36:9 Indeed, the **f** of life is with you.
Pro 5:18 Let your own **f** be blessed,

Pro 10:11 a righteous person is a **f** of life,
13:14 of a wise person are a **f**
14:27 The fear of the LORD is a **f** of
16:22 Understanding is a **f** of life to
18:4 The **f** of wisdom is an
Jer 2:13 the **f** of life-giving water.
9:1 water and my eyes were a **f**
17:13 the **f** of life-giving water.
Zec 13:1 "On that day a **f** will be opened
Rev 21:6 I will give a drink from the **f**

fourteenth (24)

Gen 14:5 In the **f** year Chedorlaomer and
Exo 12:6 Take care of it until the **f** ⌊day⌋
12:18 From the evening of the **f** day
Lev 23:5 "The **f** day of the first month,
Num 9:3 You must celebrate it on the **f**
9:5 and they celebrated it on the **f**
9:11 You will celebrate it on the **f**
28:16 "The **f** day of the first month is
Jos 5:10 on the evening of the **f** day
2Ki 18:13 In Hezekiah's **f** year as king,
1Ch 24:13 the **f** for Jeshebeab,
25:21 The **f** chose Mattithiah,
2Ch 30:15 the Passover lamb on the **f** day
35:1 was slaughtered on the **f** day
Ezr 6:19 On the **f** day of the first month,
Est 9:15 also assembled on the **f** day
9:17 On the **f** they rested and made
9:18 on the thirteenth and **f**.
9:19 unwalled towns make the **f** day
9:21 He established the **f** and
Isa 36:1 In Hezekiah's **f** year as king,
Eze 45:21 "'On the **f** day of the first month,
Act 27:27 On the **f** night we were still
27:33 "This is the **f** day you have

fourth (75)

Gen 1:19 then morning — a **f** day.
2:14 The **f** river is the Euphrates.
15:16 In the **f** generation your
Exo 20:5 to the third and **f** generation
28:20 In the **f** row put beryl,
34:7 to the third and **f** generation."
39:13 In the **f** row they put beryl,
Lev 19:24 In the **f** year all the fruit will be
Num 7:30 On the **f** day the leader of the
14:18 to the third and **f** generation ....'
29:23 "On the **f** day bring 10 bulls,
Dtr 5:9 to the third and **f** generation
Jos 19:17 The **f** lot was drawn for the
Jdg 14:15 On the **f** day they said to
19:5 On the **f** day they got up early
2Sm 3:4 The **f** was Adonijah,
1Ki 6:1 (the second month) of the **f** year
6:37 In the month of Ziv of the **f** year
22:41 Judah in Ahab's **f** year as king
2Ki 18:9 In Hezekiah's **f** year as king
25:3 On the ninth day of the **f** month,
1Ch 2:14 Nethanel (his **f** son),
3:2 The **f** was Adonijah,
3:15 and the **f** was Shallum.
8:2 Nohah (his **f** son), and Rapha
12:10 The **f** was Mishmannah.
23:19 his **f** was Jekameam.
24:8 third for Harim, the **f** for Seorim
24:23 **f** ⌊of Hebron's descendants⌋),
25:11 The **f** chose Izri, his sons,
26:2 (the third), Jathniel (the **f**),
26:4 Joah (the third), Sachar (the **f**),
26:11 and Zechariah (the **f**).
27:7 was in charge of the **f** unit
27:7 fourth unit during the **f** month,
2Ch 3:2 the second month of the **f** year
20:26 On the **f** day they gathered in
Ezr 8:33 On the **f** day we weighed the
Neh 9:3 and for another **f** ⌊of the day⌋,
Jer 25:1 was in his **f** year as king.
28:1 in the fifth month of his **f** year
36:1 In the **f** year of the reign of
39:2 On the ninth day of the **f** month
45:1 the **f** year that Jehoiakim,
46:2 the **f** year that Jehoiakim,
51:59 Zedekiah of Judah in the **f** year
52:6 On the ninth day of the **f** month,
Eze 1:1 On the fifth day of the **f** month
Eze 10:14 and the **f** was the face of an
Dan 2:40 There will also be a **f** kingdom.
2:40 As iron crushes things, this **f**
3:25 The **f** one looks like a son of
7:7 After this, I saw a **f** animal in
7:19 the truth about the **f** animal,
7:23 He said, "The **f** animal will be
7:23 "The fourth animal will be the **f**
11:2 Then there will be a **f**,
Amo 1:3 and now a **f** crime,
1:6 and now a **f** crime,
1:9 and now a **f** crime,
1:11 and now a **f** crime,
1:13 and now a **f** crime,
2:1 and now a **f** crime,
2:4 and now a **f** crime,
2:6 and now a **f** crime,
Zec 6:3 And the **f** had strong,
7:1 On the **f** day of the ninth month
7:1 in Darius' **f** year as king,
8:19 The fast in the **f** month,
Rev 4:7 and the **f** was like a flying
6:7 the lamb opened the **f** seal,
6:7 I heard the voice of the **f** living
8:12 When the **f** angel blew his
16:8 The **f** angel poured his bowl on
21:19 the third agate, the **f** emerald,

fox (2)

Neh 4:3 "Even a **f** would make their
Luk 13:32 Jesus said to them, "Tell that **f**

foxes (8)

Jdg 15:4 So Samson caught 300 **f**.
15:5 on fire and released the **f**
Sos 2:15 Catch the **f** for us, the little
2:15 the little **f** that ruin vineyards.
Lam 5:18 **F** roam around on Mount Zion,
Eze 13:4 Israel, your prophets are like **f**
Mat 8:20 Jesus told him, "**F** have holes,
Luk 9:58 Jesus told him, "**F** have holes,

fragrance (12)

Sos 1:3 better than the **f** of cologne.
1:12 perfume fills the air with its **f**.
2:13 bloom and give off a **f**.
4:10 of love than wine and the **f**
4:11 The **f** of your clothing is like
4:11 is like the **f** of Lebanon.
7:8 May the **f** of your breath be like
7:13 The mandrakes give off a **f**,
Jon 12:3 The **f** of the perfume filled the
2Co 2:14 It's like a **f** that fills the air.
2:16 some people we are a deadly **f**,
2:16 to others we are a life-giving **f**.

fragrant (9)

Exo 30:23 6 ¼ pounds of **f** cinnamon;
30:23 6 ¼ pounds of **f** cane;
30:25 into a holy oil, a **f** mixture,
30:34 "Take one part **f** spices (two
30:35 perfumer make it into **f** incense,
Psa 45:8 your robes are ⌊**f**⌋ with myrrh,
Pro 27:9 of a friend is a **f** forest.
Eze 16:19 them sweet and **f** sacrifices.
Hos 14:6 They will be **f** like cedars from

frail (2)

Gen 33:13 you know that the children are **f**
Job 16:8 My **f** body rises up and testifies

frame (12)

Exo 26:16 Each **f** is to be 15 feet long and
26:19 sockets at the bottom of each **f**
26:21 two at the bottom of each **f**.
26:25 two at the bottom of each **f**.
36:21 Each **f** was 15 feet long and 27
36:24 sockets at the bottom of each **f**
36:26 two at the bottom of each **f**.
36:30 two at the bottom of each **f**.
Num 4:10 put them on a **f** to carry them.
4:12 put them on a **f** to carry them.
1Ki 6:14 building the temple's ⌊**f**⌋,
7:31 in the center to the **c** frame

frames (30)

Exo 26:17 Make all the **f** for the inner tent
26:18 Make 20 **f** for the south side of
26:19 at the bottom of the 20 **f**,
26:20 of the inner tent ⌊make⌋ 20 **f**
26:22 Make six **f** for the far end,
26:23 Make two **f** for ⌊each of⌋ the
26:24 Both corner **f** will be made this
26:25 There will be eight **f** with 16
26:26 five for the **f** on one side of the
26:27 and five for the **f** on the far end
26:28 to the other, halfway up the **f**.
26:29 Cover the **f** with gold,
35:11 fasteners, **f**, crossbars, posts,
36:22 They made all the **f** for the
36:23 They made 20 **f** for the south
36:24 at the bottom of the 20 **f**,
36:25 the inner tent ⌊they made⌋ 20 **f**
36:27 They made six **f** for the far end,
36:28 They made two **f** for ⌊each of⌋
36:29 Both corner **f** were made this
36:30 There were eight **f** with 16
36:31 Five were for the **f** on one side
36:32 and five were for the **f** on the
36:33 to the other, halfway up the **f**.
36:34 They covered the **f** with gold
39:33 **f**, crossbars, posts, sockets,
40:18 sockets in place, put up the **f**,
1Ki 7:28 They had side panels set in **f**.
7:29 the panels set in **f** were lions,
7:29 These were also on the **f**.

framework (4)

Exo 26:15 "Make a **f** out of acacia wood
36:20 They made a **f** out of acacia
Num 3:36 to be in charge of the **f**
4:31 They will carry the **f** for the

frankincense (4)

Exo 30:34 mix them with one part pure **f**.
Num 5:15 oil on the flour or put **f** on it,
Mat 2:11 him gifts of gold, **f**, and myrrh.
Rev 18:13 **f**, wine, olive oil, flour, wheat,

fraud (1)

Psa 55:11 Oppression and **f** never leave

frauds (1)

Mic 2:11 Liars and **f** may go around and

free (172)

Gen 2:16 He said, "You are **f** to eat from
16:12 He will be as **f** and wild as an
24:8 then you'll be **f** from this oath
24:41 Then you will be **f** from your
24:41 You will also be **f** of your oath
44:10 and the rest of you can go **f**."
49:21 "Naphtali is a doe set **f** that has
Exo 6:6 and I will **f** you from slavery.
21:2 year he may leave as a **f** man,
21:5 I don't want to leave as a **f**
21:7 she will not go **f** the way male
21:11 three things, she can go **f**,
21:26 he must let the slave go **f** to
21:27 he must let the slave go **f** to
21:28 owner is **f** from any liability.
Lev 26:13 made you live as a **f** people.
Num 11:5 Remember all the **f** fish we ate
30:5 The LORD will **f** her ⌊from this
30:8 The LORD will **f** her ⌊from this
30:12 and the LORD will **f** her ⌊from
Dtr 15:12 year you must let them go **f**.
15:18 you have to let your slave go **f**,
24:5 will be **f** from military duty
24:5 For one year he is **f** to stay at
32:36 neither slaves nor **f** people.
Jos 2:17 The men told her, "We will be **f**
2:19 We will be **f** from that
2:20 we will be **f** from the oath
Jdg 1:25 man and his whole family go **f**.
16:20 as usual and shake myself **f**."
1Sm 24:15 matter and set me **f** from you."
26:9 king and remained **f** of guilt.
2Sm 7:23 on earth that God came to **f**
22:33 His perfect way sets me **f**.

2Ki 14:26 No slave or **f** person could help
1Ch 4:10 be with me and **f** me from evil
9:33 and were **f** from other duties
17:21 on earth that God came to **f**
Est 9:16 and **f** themselves from their
Job 3:19 the slave is **f** from his master.
10:14 you watch me and will not **f** me
21:9 Their homes are **f** from fear,
33:24 '**F** them from going into the pit.
39:5 lets the wild donkey go **f**?
Psa 17:1 comes⌋ from lips **f** from deceit.
19:13 and I will be **f** from any great
44:2 but you set our ancestors **f**.
69:18 Set me **f** because of my
71:2 Rescue me and **f** me because
71:4 My God, **f** me from the hands of
89:48 Who can set himself **f** from the
102:20 and set **f** those who were
105:20 The ruler of nations set him **f**.
118:5 me ⌊and⌋ set me **f** ⌊from all
146:7 The LORD sets prisoners **f**.
Pro 1:33 without worry and will be **f** from
6:3 so that you may **f** yourself,
6:5 **F** yourself like a gazelle from
Isa 45:13 go **f** without any payment
51:14 Chained prisoners will be set **f**.
52:2 **F** yourself from the chains
55:1 You don't have to pay; its **f**!
58:6 let the oppressed go **f**,
61:1 that captives will be set **f**
Jer 2:31 my people say that they are **f**
15:21 wicked people and **f** you from
31:11 The LORD will **f** the
34:8 promised to **f** their slaves.
34:9 Everyone was supposed to **f**
34:10 and promised to **f** their male
34:10 So they set them **f**.
34:14 of you must **f** any Hebrews who
34:14 you must set them **f**.' But
34:15 You agreed to **f** your neighbors,
34:16 slaves that you had set **f**
34:17 Now I am going to **f** you,"
34:17 "I will **f** you to die in wars,
37:4 Jeremiah was still **f** to come
Eze 13:20 tear them from your arms and **f**
Hos 13:14 "I want to **f** them from the
Zec 3:7 Then I will give you **f** access
9:11 I will set your captives **f** from
Mat 16:19 And whatever you set **f**,
16:19 you set free, God will set **f**."
18:18 And whatever you set **f**,
18:18 you set free, God will set **f**.
27:15 would **f** one prisoner whom
27:17 do you want me to **f** for you?
27:17 Do you want me to **f** Barabbas
27:21 do you want me to **f** for you?"
Mar 15:6 Pilate would **f** one prisoner
15:9 "Do you want me to **f** the king
15:11 so that Pilate would **f** Barabbas
Luk 1:68 of his people and to set them **f**.
2:38 for Jerusalem to be set **f**.
7:40 "Teacher, you're **f** to speak."
13:12 you are **f** from your disability."
13:15 Don't each of you **f** your ox or
13:16 Isn't it right to **f** her on the day
21:28 The time when you will be set **f**
23:16 to have him whipped and set **f**."
23:18 **F** Barabbas for us."
23:20 Pilate wanted to **f** Jesus,
23:22 to have him whipped and set **f**."
24:21 the one who would **f** Israel.
Jon 8:32 and the truth will set you **f**."
8:33 you say that we will be set **f**?"
8:36 So if the Son sets you **f**,
8:36 you will be absolutely **f**.
10:18 I give my life of my own **f** will.
11:44 Jesus told them, "**F** Lazarus,
18:39 that I should **f** one person
18:39 Would you like me to **f** the king
18:40 again, "Don't **f** this man!
18:40 **F** Barabbas!" (Barabbas was a
19:10 that I have the authority to **f** you
19:12 he wanted to **f** him.
19:12 shouted, "If you **f** this man,
Act 3:13 had decided to let him go **f**.
7:35 This is the one God sent to **f**
13:15 for the people, feel **f** to speak."
26:1 "You're **f** to speak for yourself."
26:32 man could have been set **f** if
27:40 They cut the anchors **f** and left
Rom 3:24 paid to set us **f** ⌊from sin⌋.
6:20 you were **f** from doing what
7:3 she is **f** from this law,
8:2 have set you **f** from the
8:21 that it would also be set **f** from
1Co 7:21 have a chance to become **f**,
7:22 you are the Lord's **f** person.
7:22 In the same way, if you were **f**
7:39 If her husband dies, she is **f** to
9:1 you agree that I'm a **f** man?
9:18 the Good News **f** of charge.
9:19 Although I'm **f** from all people,
12:13 are Jewish or Greek, slave or **f**,
2Co 8:3 I assure you that by their own **f**
8:17 to visit you by his own **f** will.
11:7 you the Good News of God **f**
Gal 1:4 In order to **f** us from this present
3:13 Christ paid the price to **f** us
3:28 slaves nor **f** people,
4:22 and the other by a **f** woman.
4:23 but the son of the **f** woman was
4:26 Jerusalem that is above is **f**,
4:30 with the son of the **f** woman."
4:31 woman but of the **f** woman.
5:13 You were indeed called to be **f**,
Eph 1:7 we are set **f** from our sins.
1:14 this guarantee until we are set **f**
4:30 the day you will be set **f** ⌊from
6:8 whether we're slaves or **f**
Php 1:19 I know that I will be set **f**
Col 1:14 His Son paid the price to **f** us,
3:11 person, slave, or **f** person.
1Ti 2:6 all people to **f** them from their
2Ti 2:26 and God will **f** them from
Tit 2:14 for us to set us **f** from every sin
Phm 1:14 your own **f** will without feeling
Heb 2:15 In this way he would **f** those
9:12 once and for all to **f** us forever.
9:15 the price to set people **f** from
10:2 would have been **f** from sin.
10:22 sprinkled ⌊with his blood⌋ to **f**
Jas 1:25 teachings that make people **f**
1Pe 1:18 Realize that you weren't set **f**
2:16 Live as **f** people, but don't hide
Rev 6:15 and all the slaves and **f** people
13:16 **f** people and slaves — to be
19:18 and all **f** people and slaves,
20:3 After that it must be set **f** for a

freed (40)

Lev 25:10 Every slave will be **f** in order to
25:13 year every slave will be **f**
Dtr 7:8 He **f** you from slavery under
13:5 of Egypt and **f** you from slavery.
15:15 and the LORD your God **f** you.
21:8 your people Israel, whom you **f**.
24:18 your God **f** you from slavery.
1Sm 14:41 the people were **f** ⌊from guilt⌋.
2Sm 7:23 whom you **f** from Egypt to be
18:19 the LORD has **f** him from his
18:31 "Today the LORD has **f** you
2Ki 13:5 and they were **f** from Aram's
25:27 **f** King Jehoiakin of Judah from
1Ch 17:21 whom you **f** from Egypt.
Est 9:22 Jews **f** themselves from their
Job 12:14 that person cannot be **f**.
33:28 The messenger has **f** my soul
Psa 4:1 You have **f** me from my
78:42 the day he **f** them from their
81:6 hands were **f** from the basket.
116:16 You have **f** me from my chains.
Isa 49:24 prisoners be **f** from conquerors?
49:25 Prisoners will be **f** from mighty
Jer 34:11 the men and women they had **f**
34:17 You haven't **f** your relatives and
52:31 **f** King Jehoiakin of Judah and
Mic 6:4 I brought you out of Egypt and **f**
Mat 18:27 **f** him, and canceled his debt.
27:26 Then Pilate **f** Barabbas for the
Mar 15:15 so he **f** Barabbas for them.
Luk 23:25 He **f** Barabbas, who had been
Rom 6:7 has died has been **f** from sin.
6:18 **F** from sin, you were made
6:22 Now you have been **f** from sin
Gal 5:1 Christ has **f** us so that we may
Heb 13:23 our brother, has been **f**.
1Pe 1:19 Rather, the payment that **f** you
2:24 cross so that **f** from our sins,
Rev 1:5 the one who loves us and has **f**
20:7 Satan will be **f** from his prison.

Freedmen's (1)

Act 6:9 called **F** Synagogue

freedom (26)

Gen 27:40 eventually you will gain your **f**
Exo 21:2 without paying for his **f**.
21:11 paying any money for her **f**.
Lev 19:20 and if her **f** was never bought
25:49 he could buy his own **f**.
25:54 If he cannot buy his **f** in these
Eze 46:17 servant only until the year of **f**.
Act 7:25 going to use him to give them **f**.
24:23 Paul but to let him have some **f**
Rom 8:21 order to share the glorious **f** that
1Co 8:9 using your **f** you don't somehow
10:29 Why should my **f** be judged by
2Co 3:17 the Lord's Spirit is, there is **f**.
Gal 2:4 about the **f** Christ Jesus gives
4:5 God sent him to pay for the **f** of
5:1 we may enjoy the benefits of **f**.
5:1 Therefore, be firm ⌊in this **f**⌋,
5:13 Don't turn this **f** into an excuse
Jas 2:12 be judged by laws that bring **f**.
1Pe 2:16 but don't hide behind your **f**
2:16 use your **f** to serve God.
2Pe 2:2 follow them in their sexual **f**
2:7 principles and lived in sexual **f**.
2:18 especially to sexual **f**.
2:19 They promise these people **f**,
Jud 1:4 as an excuse for sexual **f**

freeing (1)

Rom 8:23 the **f** of our bodies ⌊from sin⌋.

freely (24)

Gen 34:10 move about **f** in this area,
34:21 in our land and move about **f**
42:34 move about **f** in this country.'"
Exo 25:2 each person **f** gives.
Dtr 15:8 and **f** lend them as much as
23:23 You **f** chose to make your vow
Ezr 1:6 everything that was **f** offered.
Job 10:1 I will **f** express my complaint.
Psa 31:8 in a place where I can move **f**.
37:26 always generous and lends **f**.
112:9 He gives **f** to poor people.
119:45 I will walk around **f** because I
Pro 11:24 One person spends **f** and yet
Isa 32:20 let oxen and donkeys roam **f**.
55:7 because he will **f** forgive them.
Hos 14:4 I will love them **f**. I will no
Mar 1:45 the man left, he began to talk **f**.
Rom 3:24 They receive God's approval **f**
6:23 but the gift that God **f** gives is
1Co 2:12 which God has **f** given us.
2Co 9:9 "The righteous person gives **f**
Gal 3:18 However, God **f** gave the
Eph 1:5 He **f** chose to do this
3:7 through God's kindness **f** given

freeman (3)

1Ki 14:10 whether slave or **f** in Israel.
21:21 whether slave or **f** in Israel.
2Ki 9:8 whether slave or **f** in Israel.

frees (1)

2Sm 22:49 He **f** me from my enemies.

freewill (20)

Exo 35:29 to the LORD as a **f** offering.
36:3 him **f** offerings every morning.
Lev 7:16 you vowed or a **f** offering,
22:18 they vowed or as **f** offerings.
22:21 to fulfill a vow or for a **f** offering.
22:23 in growth as a **f** offering.
23:38 and your **f** offerings to the
Num 15:3 to fulfill a vow, as a **f** offering,

Num 29:39 to the LORD, your **f** offerings,
Dtr 12:6 vow to bring, your **f** offerings,
12:17 vow to bring; your **f** offerings;
16:10 Bring a **f** offering in proportion
2Ch 31:14 care of the **f** offerings made
Ezr 1:4 and **f** offerings to be used in
2:68 they contributed **f** offerings to
3:5 and all the **f** offerings brought to
8:28 The silver and gold are **f**
Psa 54:6 to you along with a **f** offering.
Eze 46:12 prepares a **f** burnt offering,
Amo 4:5 boast about your **f** offerings.

freeze (1)

Job 37:10 and the seas **f** over.

freezes (1)

Job 38:30 and the surface of the ocean **f**

freezing (1)

Zec 14:6 will be neither heat nor **f** cold.

freight (1)

Num 7:3 six **f** wagons and twelve oxen,

frequent (1)

Num 17:5 In this way I will silence the **f**

fresh (33)

Gen 27:28 and plenty of **f** grain and new
27:37 I've provided **f** grain and new
Lev 14:5 a clay bowl containing **f** water.
14:6 that was killed over the **f** water.
14:50 a clay bowl containing **f** water.
14:51 them in the **f** water containing
14:52 the **f** water, the living bird,
15:13 clothes and his body in **f** water.
23:14 or **f** grain until this same day,
Num 6:3 never eat **f** grapes or raisins.
18:12 of the new wine and **f** grain.
19:17 Then pour **f** water on them.
2Ki 4:42 and **f** grain to the man of God.
19:26 like **f**, green grass on the roofs,
2Ch 31:5 new wine, **f** olive oil, honey,
32:28 grain, new wine, and **f** olive oil,
Job 8:12 Even if they were **f** and not cut,
29:20 power will be **f** ⌊every day⌋,
Psa 92:14 They are always healthy and **f**.
Pro 3:10 vats will overflow with **f** wine.
Isa 1:6 bruises, sores, and **f** wounds.
37:27 like **f**, green grass on the roofs,
Jer 6:7 As a well keeps its water **f**,
6:7 so Jerusalem keeps its evil **f**.
31:12 **f** grain, new wine, and olive oil,
Eze 47:8 salt water there with **f** water.
47:9 the water in the Dead Sea **f**.
47:11 and marshes won't become **f**.
47:12 Each month they will produce **f**
Mat 9:17 pour new wine into **f** skins,
Mar 2:22 new wine is to be poured into **f**
Luk 5:38 new wine is to be poured into **f**
Jas 3:12 salt water can't produce **f** water.

fresh-cut (1)

Gen 30:37 Then Jacob took **f** branches of

freshen (1)

Rut 3:3 **F** up, put on some perfume,

freshly (3)

Gen 8:11 and in its beak was a **f**
Psa 72:6 rain that falls on ⌊**f**⌋ cut grass,
Zec 12:6 torch among **f** cut straw.

Friday (4)

Mar 15:42 It was **F** evening, before the
Luk 23:54 It was **F**, and the day of
Jon 19:14 o'clock in the morning on the **F**
19:31 Since it was **F** and the next

friend (77)

Gen 26:26 Abimelech, his **f** Ahuzzath,
38:12 he and his **f** Hirah from Adullam
38:20 Judah sent his **f** Hirah to
38:20 but his **f** couldn't find her.
Exo 33:11 as a man speaks to his **f**.
Dtr 13:6 or your best **f** may secretly
Jdg 7:13 a man telling his **f** a dream.
7:14 His **f** replied, "That can only be
Rut 4:1 come over here and sit, my **f**."
1Sm 18:1 became David's closest **f**.
2Sm 13:3 Amnon had a **f** by the name of
15:37 So Hushai, David's **f**,
16:16 When David's **f** Hushai from
16:17 how loyal you are to your **f**?"
16:18 I will be his ⌊**f**⌋ and stay with
1Ki 5:1 had always been David's **f**.
20:35 of the prophets spoke to a **f** as
20:36 When the **f** left, a lion found
1Ch 27:33 of Archi, was the king's **f**.
2Ch 20:7 descendants of your **f** Abraham
Job 6:14 "A **f** should treat a troubled
6:27 Would you buy and sell your **f**?
16:21 Son of Man will plead for his **f**!"
Psa 7:4 if I have paid back my **f** with
15:3 with his tongue, do evil to a **f**,
35:14 as if I were mourning for my **f**
41:9 Even my closest **f** whom I
55:13 my best **f**, one I knew so well!
55:20 ⌊My best **f**⌋ has betrayed his
88:18 Darkness is my only **f**!
119:63 I am a **f** to everyone who fears
Pro 2:17 the closest **f** of her youth,
17:17 A **f** always loves, and a brother
17:18 a loan in the presence of his **f**.
18:24 but a loving **f** can stick closer
19:4 person is separated from his **f**.
19:6 and everyone is a **f** to a person
22:11 graciously has a king as his **f**.
22:24 Do not be a **f** of one who has a
27:6 Wounds made by a **f** are
27:9 but the sweetness of a **f** is a
27:10 Do not abandon your **f** or your
27:10 your friend or your father's **f**.
27:14 Whoever blesses his **f** early in
Ecc 4:10 the other can help his **f** get up.
Sos 5:16 is my beloved, and this is my **f**,
Isa 41:8 of Abraham, my dear **f**.
Zec 13:7 against the man who is my **f**,"
Mat 9:2 said to the man, "Cheer up, **f**!
11:19 He's a glutton and a drunk, a **f**
20:13 '**F**, I'm not treating you unfairly.
22:12 He said to him, '**F**,
26:50 Jesus said to him, "**F**,
Mar 2:5 "**F**, your sins are forgiven."
Luk 6:42 you say to another believer, '**F**,
7:34 He's a glutton and a drunk, a **f**
11:5 "Suppose one of you has a **f**.
11:5 to him at midnight and say, '**F**,
11:6 A **f** of mine on a trip has
11:7 Your **f** might answer you from
11:8 you need because he is your **f**
14:10 comes, he will tell you, '**F**,
Jon 11:3 your close **f** is sick."
11:11 "Our **f** Lazarus is sleeping,
19:12 you're not a **f** of the emperor.
Act 13:1 Manaen (a close **f** of Herod
Rom 16:5 Greet my dear **f** Epaenetus.
16:8 Greet Ampliatus my dear **f** in
16:9 and my dear **f** Stachys.
2Co 12:18 and I sent my **f** with him.
Col 4:14 My dear **f** Luke, the physician,
Jas 2:23 Abraham was called God's **f**.
4:4 Whoever wants to be a **f** of this
3Jn 1:1 To my dear **f** Gaius,
1:2 Dear **f**, I know that you are
1:5 Dear **f**, you are showing your
1:11 Dear **f**, never imitate evil,

friendly (8)

Gen 31:2 that Laban did not appear as **f**
31:5 seen that your father isn't as **f**
34:21 "These people are **f** toward us,
37:4 speak to him on **f** terms.
1Ki 2:13 "Is this a **f** visit?" she asked.
Act 15:33 to Jerusalem with **f** greetings
24:26 have **f** conversations with him.
Rom 12:16 but be **f** to humble people.

friend's (1)

Zec 13:6 'I was hurt at my **f** house.

friends (120)

Gen 19:7 "Please, my **f**, don't be so
29:4 "My **f**, where are you from?"
Exo 32:27 relatives, **f**, and neighbors."
Jdg 11:37 Give me two months for my **f**
11:38 She and her **f** went to the
14:11 they chose 30 of their **f** to be
14:16 You gave my **f** a riddle and
14:17 Then she told her **f** the answer
19:23 He told them, "No, my **f**!
1Sm 30:26 he sent part of the loot to his **f**,
2Sm 3:8 to his relatives and **f**,
1Ki 16:11 of Baasha's male relatives or **f**.
2Ki 10:11 powerful men, **f**, and priests.
1Ch 12:17 come to help me as **f** would,
Est 5:10 He went home and sent for his **f**
5:14 wife Zeresh and all his **f** said
6:13 to all his **f** everything that had
Job 2:11 When Job's three **f** heard about
6:1 Then Job replied ⌊to his **f**⌋,
9:1 Then Job replied ⌊to his **f**⌋,
12:1 Then Job replied ⌊to his **f**⌋,
16:1 Then Job replied ⌊to his **f**⌋,
17:5 (Whoever turns in **f** to get their
19:1 Then Job replied ⌊to his **f**⌋,
19:13 My **f** are complete strangers to
19:14 My relatives and my closest **f**
19:19 All my closest **f** are disgusted
19:21 "Have pity on me, my **f**!
21:1 Then Job replied ⌊to his **f**⌋,
23:1 Then Job replied ⌊to his **f**⌋,
26:1 Then Job replied ⌊to his **f**⌋,
32:3 very angry with Job's three **f**
32:15 "Job's **f** have been
34:1 to speak ⌊to Job and his **f**⌋,
35:1 to speak ⌊to Job and his **f**⌋,
35:4 I will answer you and your **f**.
42:7 angry with you and your two **f**
42:10 After Job prayed for his **f**,
Psa 31:11 someone dreaded by my **f**,
38:11 My loved ones and my **f** keep
50:18 you want to make **f** with him.
55:20 best friend⌋ has betrayed his **f**.
69:22 a trap and a snare for their **f**.
88:8 You have taken my **f** far away
88:18 loved ones and **f** far away from
119:24 They are my best **f**.
122:8 the sake of my relatives and **f**,
Pro 16:28 separates the closest of **f**.
17:9 separates the closest of **f**.
18:24 **F** can destroy one another,
19:4 Wealth adds many **f**,
19:7 How much more do his **f** keep
Sos 5:1 Eat, my **f**! Drink and become
8:13 while your **f** are listening to
Isa 1:23 rulers are rebels, **f** with thieves.
Jer 6:21 Neighbors and their **f** will die.
13:21 were your **f** your new masters?
20:4 terrify yourself and all your **f**.
20:6 there together with all your **f**
20:10 All my closest **f** are waiting to
38:22 'Your trusted **f** have misled you
38:22 and your **f** have deserted you.'
Lam 1:2 All of Jerusalem's **f** have
Dan 2:13 Daniel and his **f** and kill them.
2:17 home and told his **f** Hananiah,
Mic 7:5 have confidence in ⌊your⌋ **f**.
Zec 3:8 Chief Priest Joshua and your **f**
Mat 5:47 if you welcome only your **f**?
Mar 1:36 and his **f** searched for him.
16:10 She went and told his **f**,
Luk 1:61 Their **f** said to her,
2:44 him among their relatives and **f**.
4:40 everyone who had **f** suffering
7:6 house when the officer sent **f**
12:4 "My **f**, I can guarantee that you
14:12 don't invite only your **f**,
15:6 Then he calls his **f** and
15:9 she calls her **f** and neighbors
15:29 goat for a celebration with my **f**.
16:9 use it to make **f** for yourselves.
21:16 and **f** will betray you and kill
22:25 call themselves **f** of the people.
23:12 and Pilate became **f** that day.
23:49 All his **f**, including the women

Jon 15:13 is to give your life for your f.
15:14 You are my f if you obey my
15:15 But I've called you f because
21:5 Jesus asked them, "F,
Act 10:24 relatives and close f together.
19:31 were Paul's f sent messengers
24:23 and to let his f take care
27:3 and allowed him to visit his f
Rom 12:19 Don't take revenge, dear f.
1Co 10:14 Therefore, my dear f,
2Co 7:1 have these promises, dear f,
11:9 My f from the province of
11:26 who turned out to be false f.
12:19 Everything we do, dear f,
Php 2:12 My dear f, you have always
4:1 Therefore, dear f, keep your
Tit 3:15 Greet our faithful f.
Heb 6:9 Dear f, even though we say
11:31 to welcome the spies as f.
1Pe 2:11 Dear f, since you are foreigners
4:12 Dear f, don't be surprised by the
2Pe 3:1 Dear f, this is the second letter
3:8 Dear f, don't ignore this fact:
3:14 Therefore, dear f, with this to
3:17 Dear f, you already know these
1Jn 2:7 Dear f, it's not as though I'm
3:2 Dear f, now we are God's
3:21 Dear f, if our conscience
4:1 Dear f, don't believe all people
4:7 Dear f, we must love each
4:11 Dear f, if this is the way God
3Jn 1:15 Your f here send you their
1:15 Greet each of our f by name.
Jud 1:3 Dear f, I had intended to write
1:17 Dear f, remember what the
1:20 Dear f, use your most holy faith

friendship (1)

Dtr 23:6 Never offer them peace or f as

frighten (14)

1Ch 17:9 The wicked will no longer f
2Ch 32:18 They tried to f and terrify the
Job 7:14 then you f me with dreams and
11:19 lie down with no one to f you,
13:21 Don't let your terror f me.
Jer 7:33 will be there to f them away.
30:10 and no one will f them.
Eze 2:6 let the things they say f you.
34:28 and no one will f them.
39:26 land where no one will f them,
Dan 4:19 dream and its meaning f you."
5:10 Don't let your thoughts f you,
11:44 east and the north will f him.
2Co 10:9 to think that I'm trying to f you

frightened (30)

Gen 42:35 the bags of money, they were f.
43:18 The men were f, because they
Jdg 7:3 'Whoever is scared or f should
1Sm 4:7 Then they were f and said,
28:20 He was f by Samuel's words.
2Sm 14:15 because the people have f me.
1Ki 1:49 Adonijah's guests were f,
19:3 F, Elijah fled to save his life.
1Ch 21:30 God because he was f by
2Ch 20:3 F, Jehoshaphat decided to ask
20:15 Don't be f or terrified by this
20:17 Don't be f or terrified.
32:7 Don't be f or terrified
Isa 14:31 Be f, all you Philistines!
31:4 It isn't f by their voices or
31:9 and their officers will be f at
44:11 will be f and ashamed together.
Jer 10:2 Don't be f by the signs in the
10:2 the nations are f by them.
49:16 You have f other people.
Dan 4:5 I had while I was asleep f me.
4:19 What he was thinking f him.
5:6 and his thoughts f him.
7:15 and my visions f me.
Mar 5:15 The people were f.
Luk 8:25 F and amazed, they asked
8:35 The people were f.
9:34 They were f as they went into
Rev 18:10 F by her torture, they will stand
Rev 18:15 "F by her torture, the merchants

frightening (6)

Jdg 13:6 He had a very f appearance
Eze 1:18 of the wheels were large and f.
Zep 1:14 The f day of the LORD is near.
1:18 he will put an end, a f end,
Rev 6:17 because the f day of their anger
16:14 them for the war on the f day

frogs (15)

Exo 8:2 I will bring a plague of f on your
8:3 Nile River will swarm with f.
8:4 The f will jump on you,
8:5 This will bring f onto the land.'"
8:6 The f came up and covered the
8:7 and brought f onto the land.
8:8 will take the f away from me
8:9 Then the f will leave you and
8:11 The f will leave you,
8:11 The only f left will be those in
8:12 prayed to the LORD about the f
8:13 The f died in the houses,
Psa 78:45 bit them and f that ruined them.
105:30 made their land swarm with f,
Rev 16:13 three evil spirits like f come out

frost (4)

Exo 16:14 of flakes like f on the ground.
Job 38:29 given birth to the f in the air?
Psa 78:47 hail and their fig trees with f.
147:16 wool and scatters f like ashes.

frown (1)

Jer 3:12 I will no longer f on you

fruit (121)

Gen 1:11 and f trees bearing fruit with
1:11 fruit trees bearing f with seeds,
1:12 and trees bearing f with seeds,
1:29 tree that has f with seeds.
2:9 and their f was good to eat.
3:1 'You must never eat the f of
3:2 "We're allowed to eat the f from
3:6 the tree had f that was good
3:6 So she took some of the f and
3:11 Did you eat f from the tree I
3:12 gave me some f from the tree,
3:17 to your wife and ate f from
3:17 'You must never eat its f.' The
3:22 reach out and take the f from
Exo 10:15 ate all the plants and all the f
Lev 19:23 and plant all kinds of f trees,
19:23 you must not eat the f for ⌊the
19:24 In the fourth year all the f will
19:25 the fifth year you may eat the f.
26:4 in the field will produce their f.
26:20 and the trees will produce no f.
27:30 the land, whether grain or f,
Num 13:20 best to bring back some f from
13:26 them the f from the land.
13:27 Here's some of its f.
Dtr 1:25 took some of the region's f
20:19 Don't harm any of its f trees
20:19 You can eat the f. Never cut
20:20 that you know are not f trees.
Jdg 9:11 sweet f in order to rule the
2Sm 16:1 100 pieces of ripened f,
16:2 "The bread and the ripe f are for
Neh 9:25 and plenty of f trees.
10:35 and the first f from every tree
10:37 f from every tree, new wine,
Psa 1:3 streams — a tree that produces f
72:16 its f like ⌊the treetops of⌋
80:12 who pass by are picking its f.
92:14 they are old, they still bear f.
148:9 f trees and all cedar trees,
Pro 1:31 They will eat the f of their
11:30 The f of a righteous person is a
12:12 righteous people produce ⌊f⌋.
27:18 care of a fig tree can eat its f,
Ecc 2:5 every kind of f tree in them.
12:5 the caper bush has ⌊no⌋ f.
Sos 2:3 His f tastes sweet to me.
4:16 let him eat his own precious f.
Sos 7:8 palm tree and take hold of its f."
8:11 of silver in exchange for its f.
8:12 to those who take care of its f.
Isa 3:10 will taste the f of their labor.
4:2 The f of the land will be the
11:1 branch from its roots will bear f.
27:6 and fill the whole world with f.
32:10 harvest will fail and no f will
65:21 vineyards and eat f from them.
Jer 2:7 into a fertile land to eat its f
11:16 olive tree that has beautiful f
11:19 "Let's destroy the tree with its f.
12:2 They grow, and they produce f.
17:8 It will not stop producing f.
31:5 who plant them will enjoy the f.
40:10 Gather grapes, summer f,
40:12 of grapes and summer f.
Eze 17:8 it could grow branches, bear f,
17:9 eagle uproot it and tear off its f?
17:23 grow branches and produce f.
19:10 It had a lot of f and many
19:12 The east wind dried up its f.
19:14 Fire has destroyed its f.
34:27 trees in the field will produce f,
36:8 will grow branches and bear f
36:30 I will make f grow on the trees
47:12 All kinds of f trees will grow on
47:12 and they won't fail to produce f.
47:12 month they will produce fresh f
47:12 The f will be good food,
Dan 4:12 beautiful leaves and plenty of f,
4:14 Scatter its f! Make the animals
4:21 beautiful leaves and plenty of f,
Hos 9:16 They have no f. Even if they
10:1 vines that used to produce f.
10:1 The more f they produced,
10:12 and harvest the f that your
10:13 You have eaten the f that your
14:8 Their f comes from me."
Joe 2:22 The trees have produced their f.
Amo 2:9 I destroyed their f above the
8:1 a basket of ripe summer f.
8:2 of ripe summer f," I answered.
9:14 plant gardens and eat their f.
Mic 7:1 like those gathering summer f,
Mat 3:10 that doesn't produce good f will
7:17 good tree produces good f,
7:17 but a rotten tree produces bad f.
7:18 good tree cannot produce bad f,
7:18 tree cannot produce good f.
7:19 to produce good f is cut down
12:33 and then its f will be good.
12:33 and then its f will be rotten.
12:33 can recognize a tree by its f.
21:19 He said to the tree, "May f
Mar 11:14 "No one will ever eat f from you
Luk 3:9 that doesn't produce good f will
6:43 tree doesn't produce rotten f,
6:43 tree doesn't produce good f.
6:44 Each tree is known by its f.
13:6 He went to look for f on the tree
Jon 15:2 branches that doesn't produce f.
15:2 branch that does produce f
15:2 fruit to make it produce more f.
15:4 cannot produce any f by itself.
15:4 you cannot produce f unless
15:5 in them will produce a lot of f.
15:8 when you produce a lot of f
15:16 to produce f that will last,
Jud 1:12 uprooted trees without any f.
Rev 18:14 'The f you craved is gone.
22:2 It produced 12 kinds of f.
22:2 Each month had its own f.

fruitful (3)

Gen 49:22 "Joseph is a f tree,
49:22 a f tree by a spring,
Psa 128:3 Your wife will be like a f vine

fruits (8)

Lev 23:40 On the first day take the best f,
Dtr 33:15 the finest f from the oldest
Psa 104:13 earth with the f of your labors.
Sos 4:13 pomegranates and the best f,
7:13 door are all kinds of precious f.
Isa 16:9 shouts of joy for your ripened f

Jer 48:32 your ripened **f** and your grapes.
Eze 44:30 the best of all the first ripened **f**.

frustrated (1)

2Co 4:8 We're **f**, but we don't give up.

frustrates (1)

Psa 33:10 He **f** the schemes of the people

frustration (4)

Dtr 28:20 and **f** in everything you do until
Ecc 5:17 in constant **f**, sickness,
Rom 8:20 Creation was subjected to **f** but
8:20 The one who subjected it to **f**

frying (4)

Lev 2:5 offering is prepared in a **f** pan,
6:21 Prepare it in a **f** pan with olive
7:9 prepared in a skillet or a **f** pan,
1Ch 23:29 and the bread made in **f** pans.

fuel (6)

Isa 9:5 will be burned as **f** in the fire.
9:19 and the people are like **f** for the
44:15 These trees become ⌊**f**⌋ for
Eze 4:12 using human excrement for **f**."
15:4 is only thrown into the fire as **f**.
21:32 You will be **f** for the fire.

fuels (3)

Pro 26:21 ⌊As⌋ charcoal **f** burning coals
26:21 burning coals and wood **f** fire,
26:21 quarrelsome person **f** a dispute.

fugitive (5)

Gen 4:12 You will be a **f**, a wanderer on
4:14 hide from you and become a **f**,
Jdg 12:5 Whenever a **f** from Ephraim
12:6 If the **f** would say sibboleth,
Pro 28:17 guilt of murder will be a **f** down

fugitives (6)

Jdg 12:4 are nothing but **f** from Ephraim
Isa 15:9 A lion will attack the **f** from
16:3 Hide the **f**. Don't betray the
16:4 Let the **f** from Moab stay with
21:14 Bring food to the **f**.
Jer 50:28 **F** and refugees from Babylon

fulfill (9)

Lev 22:21 LORD a fellowship offering to **f**
Num 6:21 They must **f** the requirements
15:3 They may be offered to **f** a vow,
1Ki 2:3 **F** your duty to the LORD your
6:12 I will **f** the promise I made
Psa 20:5 LORD will **f** all your requests.
22:25 I will **f** my vows in the
Luk 9:31 he was about to **f** in Jerusalem.
1Th 2:17 possible effort to **f** our desire

fulfilled (13)

Num 32:22 You will have **f** your military
1Ki 2:27 as the LORD's priest and **f**
2Ki 10:10 about Ahab's family will be **f**.
23:16 This **f** the word of the LORD
2Ch 36:21 through Jeremiah would be **f**.
Pro 13:12 but a **f** longing is a tree of life.
13:19 A **f** desire is sweet to the soul,
Mat 26:54 are the Scriptures to be **f** that
Act 13:27 condemned Jesus and **f** what
13:33 God has **f** the promise for us,
Rom 11:27 My promise to them will be **f**
13:8 has **f** Moses' Teachings.
15:8 As a result, he **f** God's promise

fulfilling (1)

Jon 12:16 taken part in **f** the prophecies.

fulfillment (4)

Psa 119:123 me and from looking for the **f**
Luk 22:16 eat it again until it finds its **f**
22:37 must find its **f** in me.
Rom 10:4 Christ is the **f** of Moses'

fulfills (2)

Isa 44:26 the word of his servant and **f**
Rom 13:10 love **f** Moses' Teachings.

full (127)

Gen 6:11 in God's sight and **f** of violence.
6:13 people because the earth is **f**
14:10 The valley of Siddim was **f** of
23:9 He should sell it to me for its **f**
25:8 After a long and **f** life,
41:1 After two **f** years Pharaoh had a
41:7 of grain swallowed the seven **f**,
41:22 **f** heads of grain growing on a
Exo 16:20 and it was **f** of worms and
Lev 6:5 Pay it back in **f** plus one-fifth
16:12 He will take an incense burner **f**
23:15 "Count seven **f** weeks from the
27:13 you must pay its **f** value plus
27:15 you must pay its **f** value plus
27:17 it will have its **f** value.
27:19 you must pay its **f** value plus
27:27 The payment will be its **f** value
Num 5:7 pay in **f** for what you did wrong,
21:30 shot the Amorites **f** of arrows.
33:3 The Israelites boldly left in **f**
Dtr 23:24 grapes as you like until you're **f**.
Jdg 6:38 He squeezed out a bowl **f** of
Rut 1:21 I went away **f**, but the LORD
1Sm 1:24 of flour, and a **f** wineskin.
10:3 and one will be carrying a ⌊**f**⌋
16:20 bushels of bread, a **f** wineskin,
25:18 loaves of bread, 2 **f** wineskins,
2Sm 14:28 two **f** years without seeing
16:1 ripened fruit, and a **f** wineskin.
2Ki 3:16 Make this valley **f** of ditches.
4:4 When one is **f**, set it aside."
4:6 When the containers were **f**,
6:17 mountain around Elisha was **f**
1Ch 21:22 Sell it to me for the **f** price.
21:24 on buying it for the **f** price.
29:28 His long life was **f** of wealth
2Ch 16:14 They laid him on a bed **f** of
24:10 it into the box until it was **f**.
Ezr 6:8 **F** payment should be made to
Est 9:29 the Jew wrote with **f** authority
Job 14:1 is short-lived and is **f** of trouble.
20:11 once **f** of youthful vigor,
20:22 ⌊Even⌋ with all his wealth the **f**
21:24 His stomach is **f** of milk,
32:18 I'm **f** of words. The Spirit within
Psa 10:7 His mouth is **f** of cursing,
22:26 people will eat until they are **f**.
26:10 Their right hands are **f** of bribes
31:23 but he pays back in **f** those
34:12 Which of you wants a **f** life?
59:15 If they are not **f** enough,
81:3 on the day of the **f** moon,
86:5 **f** of mercy toward everyone
112:7 **f** of confidence in the LORD.
Pro 3:10 Then your barns will be **f**,
27:7 One who is **f** despises honey,
Ecc 1:6 It blows in a **f** circle.
1:7 but the sea is never **f**.
5:12 But the **f** stomachs that rich
9:3 hearts of mortals are **f** of evil.
11:3 If the clouds are **f** of rain,
Isa 1:21 She was **f** of justice,
9:20 another eats and is never **f**.
13:21 Their homes will be **f** of owls.
21:3 why my body is **f** of trembling.
44:16 they can eat until they are **f**.
56:11 They are never **f**. They are the
65:6 I will repay you in **f**.
65:7 the first to pay them back in **f**.
65:11 good fortune and offered cups **f**
66:11 heart's delight at her **f** breasts.
Jer 46:10 will drink their blood until it's **f**.
46:22 enemies will come with **f** force.
50:19 They will eat until they are **f** on
Eze 23:12 and commanders in **f** dress.
28:12 **f** of wisdom and perfect in
39:19 eat the best meat until you are **f**
41:8 It measured the **f** length of the
Hos 4:10 but they'll never be **f**.
13:6 When I fed you, you were **f**.
13:6 When you were **f**, you became
Joe 2:26 plenty to eat, and you will be **f**.
3:13 The winepress is **f**.
Mic 6:14 You will eat, but you won't be **f**.
Nah 1:2 takes revenge and is **f** of anger.
3:1 It is completely **f** of lies and
Hag 1:6 You eat, but you're never **f**.
Mat 6:22 whole body will be **f** of light.
6:23 body will be **f** of darkness.
7:14 that lead to life are **f** of trouble.
13:48 When it was **f**, they pulled it to
23:25 But inside they are **f** of greed
23:27 on the outside but inside are **f**
23:28 but inside you are **f** of
Mar 4:28 then the head **f** of grain.
Luk 11:34 your whole body is **f** of light.
11:34 your body is **f** of darkness.
11:36 If your whole body is **f** of light
11:39 But inside you are **f** of greed
14:23 to my house. I want it to be **f**.
Jon 1:14 a glory **f** of kindness and truth.
6:12 When the people were **f**,
9:34 "You were born **f** of sin.
16:13 will guide you into the **f** truth.
21:8 and dragged the net **f** of fish.
Act 6:5 who was a man **f** of faith and
7:55 But Stephen was **f** of the Holy
11:24 and he was **f** of the Holy Spirit
13:10 and said, "You are **f** of dirty
13:52 ⌊in Antioch⌋ continued to be **f**
28:30 a place to live for two **f** years
Rom 2:20 because you have the **f** content
3:14 Their mouths are **f** of curses
15:29 bring the **f** blessing of Christ.
Php 4:12 secret of how to live when I'm **f**
4:18 You have paid me in **f**,
2Ti 1:10 brought eternal life into **f** view.
Tit 2:15 using your **f** authority.
1Pe 3:10 "People who want to live a **f**
4:13 Then you will also be **f** of joy
1Jn 2:1 who has God's **f** approval.
2Jn 1:8 but that you receive your **f**
Jud 1:24 fall and so that you can be **f**
Rev 5:8 and a gold bowl **f** of incense,
6:12 The **f** moon turned as red as
15:7 gave seven gold bowls **f**
21:9 who had the seven bowls **f**

full-grown (1)

Psa 144:12 May our sons be like **f**,

fun (46)

Jdg 16:10 you're making **f** of me by telling
16:13 "You're still making **f** of me by
16:15 You've made **f** of me three
1Sm 31:4 and make **f** of me."
1Ki 18:27 Elijah started to make **f** of them.
1Ch 10:4 will come and make **f** of me."
2Ch 36:16 and made **f** of his prophets until
Neh 2:19 they made **f** of us and ridiculed
4:1 and made **f** of the Jews.
Job 9:23 he makes **f** of the despair of
11:3 others so that you can make **f**
19:18 If I stand up, they make **f** of me.
22:19 and the innocent made **f** of
30:9 "And now they make **f** of me
Psa 2:4 The Lord makes **f** of them.
22:7 All who see me make **f** of me.
59:8 You make **f** of all the nations.
80:6 and our enemies made **f** of us.
Pro 1:11 ambush innocent people for **f**.
1:26 I will make **f** of you when panic
14:9 Stubborn fools make **f** of guilt,
15:21 Stupidity is **f** to the one without
17:5 Whoever makes **f** of a poor
30:17 The eye that makes **f** of a
Isa 3:5 The young will make **f** of the
3:5 will make **f** of their superiors.
57:4 Whom are you making **f** of?
Jer 15:17 those who laugh and have **f**.
20:7 I've been made **f** of all day long.
Lam 3:14 All day long ⌊they make **f** of
3:63 they make **f** of me in their
Mic 2:4 people will make **f** of you.
Hab 1:10 They will make **f** of kings and
Mat 20:19 They will make **f** of him,
27:29 knelt in front of him and made **f**
27:31 finished making **f** of Jesus,
27:41 scribes and the leaders made **f**

Mar	10:34	They will make **f** of him,
	15:20	finished making **f** of Jesus,
	15:31	priests and the scribes made **f**
Luk	14:29	watches will make **f** of you.
	18:32	They will make **f** of him,
	22:63	were guarding Jesus made **f**
	23:11	contempt and made **f** of him.
	23:36	soldiers also made **f** of him.
Heb	11:36	Some were made **f** of and

funeral (28)

Gen	50:11	there saw the **f** ceremonies at
	50:11	"These **f** ceremonies are taken
	50:11	Egyptian **F** Ceremonies].
2Sm	3:33	The king sang a **f** song for
2Ch	35:25	Jeremiah sang a **f** song about
	35:25	still sing **f** songs about Josiah
	35:25	in ⌊the Book of⌋ the **F** Songs.
Ecc	7:2	It is better to go to a **f** than to a
Jer	9:10	I will sing a **f** song for the
	9:20	Teach your neighbors **f** songs.
	34:5	People will burn ⌊**f**⌋ fires for
Eze	2:10	There were **f** songs,
	19:1	Sing a **f** song for the princes of
	19:14	This is a **f** song. It is to be used
	19:14	It is to be used as a **f** song.
	26:17	Then they will sing this **f** song
	27:2	sing a **f** song about Tyre.
	27:32	They sang a **f** song for you
	28:12	"Son of man, sing a **f** song for
	32:2	sing a **f** song for Pharaoh,
	32:16	"This is a **f** song. The people
Amo	5:1	Listen to this message, this **f**
	8:10	and all your songs into **f** songs.
	8:10	make that day seem like a **f**
Mat	11:17	We sang a **f** song,
Luk	7:12	he met a **f** procession.
	7:32	We sang a **f** song,
	23:27	cried and sang **f** songs for him.

funerals (3)

Ecc	7:4	of wise people think about **f**,
Jer	9:17	Call for the women who cry at **f**.
Amo	8:10	I will turn your festivals into **f**

fungus (1)

Lev	14:54	for any kind of mildew or **f**

funguses (2)

1Ki	8:37	Plant diseases, heat waves, **f**,
2Ch	6:28	Plant diseases, heat waves, **f**,

furious (59)

Dtr	4:25	considers evil, making him **f**,
	9:18	evil and made him **f**.
	31:29	the LORD **f** by doing what
	32:16	They made him **f** because they
	32:21	They made him **f** because they
1Ki	14:9	You made me **f** and turned your
	14:15	Asherah and made the LORD **f**.
	15:30	made the LORD God of Israel **f**.
	16:2	and their sins make me **f**.
	16:7	which made the LORD **f**,
	16:7	The LORD was also **f** because
	16:13	made the LORD God of Israel **f**
	16:26	made the LORD God of Israel **f**.
	16:33	LORD God of Israel **f** than all
	21:22	because you made me **f**.
	22:53	made the LORD God of Israel **f**,
2Ki	17:11	things and made the LORD **f**.
	17:17	and they made him **f**.
	21:6	things that made the LORD **f**.
	21:15	have been making me **f** from
	22:17	gods in order to make me **f**.
	23:19	places to make the LORD **f**.
	23:26	all these things to make him **f**.
2Ch	16:10	Asa was **f** at the seer.
	25:10	But they became **f** with Judah
	33:6	things that made the LORD **f**.
	34:25	gods in order to make me **f**.
Neh	4:7	being filled in, they became **f**.
	5:6	I became **f** when I heard their
	13:8	I was **f**. So I threw all of
Est	5:9	Haman was **f** with Mordecai.
	7:7	The king was **f** as he got up
Psa	78:21	LORD heard this, he became **f**.
Psa	78:58	They made him **f** because they
	78:59	When God heard, he became **f**.
	78:62	He was **f** with those who
Pro	14:35	but he is **f** with one who acts
Isa	8:21	they are hungry, they will be **f**.
	30:30	with **f** anger, with fire storms,
	34:2	He is **f** with all their armies.
Jer	7:18	gods in order to make me **f**.
	8:19	They make me **f** with their
	11:17	They have made him **f** by
	25:6	Don't make me **f** about the idols
	25:7	You have made me **f** about the
	32:29	who made me **f** by going up
	32:30	made me **f** by what they've
	32:31	made me so angry and **f** from
	32:32	and Judah have made me **f**
Dan	2:12	the king so angry and **f** that
Hos	13:11	I took him away when I was **f**.
Hab	3:8	if you are **f** with the sea,
Mat	2:16	had tricked him, he became **f**.
Luk	4:28	became **f** when they heard
	6:11	scribes and Pharisees were **f**
Act	5:33	they became **f** and wanted to
	7:54	they became noticeably **f**.
	19:28	they became **f** and began
	26:11	In my **f** rage against them,

furiously (1)

Dan	8:6	the gate. It **f** ran at the ram.

furnace (24)

Gen	19:28	land like the thick smoke of a **f**.
Psa	12:6	like silver refined in a **f** and
	21:9	them ⌊burn⌋ like a blazing **f**.
Isa	31:9	Zion and his **f** is in Jerusalem.
	48:10	tested you in the **f** of suffering.
Jer	6:29	The bellows of the blast **f** blow
Eze	22:18	and lead in a smelting **f**.
	22:20	and tin together in a smelting **f**
	22:22	like silver that is melted in a **f**.
Dan	3:6	be thrown into a blazing **f**."
	3:11	will be thrown into a blazing **f**.
	3:15	be thrown into a blazing **f**.
	3:17	can save us from a blazing **f**
	3:19	He ordered that the **f** should be
	3:20	be thrown into the blazing **f**.
	3:21	were thrown into the blazing **f**.
	3:22	and the **f** was so extremely
	3:23	fell into the blazing **f**.
	3:26	door of the blazing **f** and said,
Mal	4:1	It will burn like a **f**.
Mat	13:42	will throw them into a blazing **f**.
	13:50	the evil people into a blazing **f**.
Rev	1:15	glowing bronze refined in a **f**.
	9:2	like the smoke from a large **f**.

furnished (2)

Mar	14:15	The room will be completely **f**.
Luk	22:12	and show you a large **f** room.

furnishings (11)

Exo	25:9	Make the tent and all its **f**
	31:7	and all the ⌊other⌋ **f** for the tent,
	39:33	the outer tent and all its **f**,
	40:9	you will dedicate it and all its **f**.
Num	3:8	They will take care of all the **f**
	7:1	it and dedicated it and all the **f**.
	18:3	not come near the altar or the **f**
	19:18	and sprinkle the tent, all the **f**,
1Ki	7:48	Solomon made all the **f** for the
2Ki	24:13	off all the **f** that King Solomon
2Ch	4:19	Solomon made all the **f** for

furrow (1)

Job	39:10	Can you guide a wild ox in a **f**,

furrows (4)

Job	31:38	and its **f** have wept ....
Psa	129:3	made long slashes ⌊like **f**⌋."
Isa	28:24	soil and make **f** in the ground?
Hos	10:4	weeds in the **f** of a field.

further (9)

1Sm	24:3	and his men were sitting **f** back
Job	32:5	three men had no **f** responses,
Eze	23:14	carried her prostitution even **f**.
Act	4:17	any **f** among the people."
	11:18	they had no **f** objections.
	27:7	the wind would not let us go **f**.
2Co	9:1	I don't need to write anything **f**
Gal	4:1	Let me explain **f**. As long as an
	5:16	Let me explain **f**. Live your life

fury (90)

Gen	49:7	May their **f** be cursed because
Num	25:11	turned my **f** away from the
Dtr	9:19	of the LORD's anger and **f**.
	29:28	In his fierce anger and **f** the
Psa	7:6	Stand up against the **f** of my
	78:38	He did not display all of his **f**.
	78:49	**f**, and hostility against them.
	79:5	Will your **f** continue to burn like
	79:6	Pour your **f** on the nations that
	85:3	You laid aside all your **f**.
	90:9	slip away because of your **f**.
	90:11	he better understands your **f**.
Pro	6:34	jealousy arouses a husband's **f**.
	11:4	are of no help on the day of **f**,
	11:23	wicked people ends only in **f**.
	21:14	a secret bribe calms great **f**.
	22:8	of his own **f** will be destroyed.
	27:4	and **f** is overwhelming,
Isa	9:19	The land is scorched by the **f**
	10:5	My **f** is the staff in the
	10:6	In my **f** I order them against the
	10:25	Very soon I will unleash my **f**,
	13:5	with the weapons of his **f**
	13:9	It will be a cruel day with **f** and
	14:6	They struck the people with **f**,
	26:20	while until his **f** has ended.
	30:27	His lips are filled with **f**.
	51:13	you live in constant fear of the **f**
	51:13	Where is the **f** of those who
	51:20	of the LORD, the **f** of your God.
	51:22	the bowl, the cup of my **f**.
	59:17	wraps himself with **f** as a coat.
Jer	4:4	my **f** will flare up like a fire.
	7:20	My anger and **f** will be poured
	7:20	My anger and **f** will burn and
	10:10	The nations can't endure his **f**.
	10:25	Pour out your **f** on the nations
	21:5	I will fight you in anger, **f**,
	21:12	Otherwise, my **f** will break out
	25:15	cup filled with the wine of my **f**,
	25:38	because of the **f** of his anger.
	32:37	anger, **f**, and terrifying wrath.
	33:5	I killed in my anger and my **f**.
	36:7	with his terrifying anger and **f**."
	42:18	As my anger and my **f** were
	42:18	so my **f** will be poured out on
	44:6	That is why my **f** and anger
	50:25	bring out the weapons of his **f**,
Lam	2:2	fortified cities of Judah in his **f**.
	2:4	He poured out his **f** like fire on
	3:1	under the rod of God's **f**.
	4:11	The LORD's **f** has
	4:21	The cup ⌊of the LORD's **f**⌋ will
Eze	5:13	I will use my **f** against you,
	5:13	When my **f** is unleashed
	5:15	my anger, **f**, and fierce revenge,
	7:8	Soon I will pour out my **f** on
	7:12	because ⌊my⌋ **f** will be against
	7:14	because my **f** is against their
	13:13	In my **f** I'll cause a storm to
	13:15	I will unleash my **f** on the wall
	14:19	that country or pour out my **f**
	16:38	in my **f** and burning anger.
	16:42	will rest from my **f** against you,
	20:8	So I was going to pour out my **f**
	20:13	So I was going to pour out my **f**
	20:21	So I was going to pour out my **f**
	20:33	and I will pour out my **f**.
	20:34	I will pour out my **f**.
	21:17	my hands and rest from my **f**.
	21:31	I will pour out my **f** on you and
	22:20	in my anger and **f** I will gather
	22:22	have poured out my **f** on you."
	24:8	In order to stir up my **f** so that I
	24:13	until I unleash my **f** on you.
	25:14	based on my anger and my **f**.
	25:17	them and punish them with **f**.
	30:15	I will pour out my **f** on Sin,

Eze 36:6 am speaking in my anger and **f**
36:18 So I poured out my **f** on them
Dan 9:16 turn your anger and **f** away from
Hos 5:10 I will pour my **f** on them like
Amo 1:11 They refused to control their **f**.
Mic 7:9 So I will endure his **f** until he
Hab 3:12 march through the earth with **f**.
Zep 1:15 will be a day of overflowing **f**,
1:18 of the LORD's overflowing **f**.
3:8 will be consumed by my fiery **f**.
Rom 2:8 anger and **f** on those who,
Rev 14:10 will drink the wine of God's **f**,

fuss (1)

Luk 10:41 You worry and **f** about a lot of

future (61)

Gen 44:5 that he uses for telling the **f**?
44:15 out because he knows the **f**?"
Exo 12:17 law for **f** generations:
12:42 (All Israelites in **f** generations
13:14 "In the **f** when your children
Lev 17:7 people and for **f** generations.
21:17 (now or in **f** generations) has
22:3 "Tell them: In **f** generations if
Num 15:14 among you in **f** generations.
15:15 law for **f** generations.
18:23 law for **f** generations.
35:29 "These will be the rules for **f**
Dtr 6:20 In the **f** your children will ask
Jos 4:6 In the **f** your children will ask,
4:21 "In the **f** when children ask
22:24 We thought sometime in the **f**
22:28 or to our descendants in the **f**,
2Sm 7:19 also spoken about the distant **f**
1Ch 17:17 spoken about the distant **f**
Job 8:7 prosperity you'll have in the **f**.
Psa 31:15 My **f** is in your hands.
37:37 the peacemaker has a **f**.
37:38 The **f** of wicked people will be
102:18 This will be written down for a **f**
Pro 23:18 There is indeed a **f**,
24:14 If you find it, then there is a **f**,
24:20 an evil person has no **f**,
28:23 highly regarded in the **f** than
31:25 and she smiles at the **f**.
Ecc 1:11 Even in the **f**, nothing will be
3:15 the **f**⌋ has already happened
6:12 about their **f** under the sun?
7:14 mortals cannot predict their **f**.
8:7 don't know what the **f** will bring.
10:14 knows what the **f** will bring,
Isa 9:1 But in the **f** he will bring glory
30:8 that it will be there in the **f** as
30:10 'Don't see ⌊the **f**⌋.' They
33:6 will be the foundation of your **f**.
41:22 Tell us about **f** events.
42:23 attention and listen in the **f**?
47:13 who foretell the **f** month by
Jer 29:11 to give you a **f** filled with hope.
31:17 Your **f** is filled with hope,
Lam 1:9 It gave no thought to its **f**.
Eze 12:27 will happen in the distant **f**.'
Dan 2:29 would happen in the **f** came
2:45 you what will happen in the **f**,
8:26 will happen in the distant **f**."
Mic 3:11 prophets tell the **f** for money.
5:2 Yet, from you Israel's **f** ruler will
Luk 1:66 "What does the **f** hold for this
Rom 8:38 the present or anything in the **f**,
1Co 3:22 present or **f** things,
2Co 1:10 and he will rescue us in the **f**.
1Ti 6:19 is a good foundation for the **f**.
Heb 3:5 what God would say in the **f**.
10:1 of the good things in the **f**.
11:7 about the things in the **f** that
11:13 in the distant **f** and rejoiced.
13:14 city that we will have in the **f**.

G

Gaal (11)

Jdg 9:26 Then **G** (son of Ebed) and his
9:28 **G** (son of Ebed) said,
9:30 heard what **G** (son of Ebed)
9:31 **G** (son of Ebed) and his
9:33 When **G** and his men come out
9:35 **G** (son of Ebed) went out and
9:36 When **G** saw the troops,
9:37 **G** spoke again, "No, there are
9:39 Then **G** led citizens of
9:40 Abimelech chased **G** so that
9:41 Zebul threw **G** and his brothers

Gaash (4)

Jos 24:30 of Ephraim north of Mount **G**.
Jdg 2:9 of Ephraim north of Mount **G**.
2Sm 23:30 Hiddai from the **G** ravines,
1Ch 11:32 Hurai from the **G** ravines,

Gabbai (1)

Neh 11:8 and after him, **G** ⌊and⌋ Sallai.

Gabbatha (1)

Jon 19:13 (In Hebrew it is called **G**.)

Gabriel (5)

Dan 8:16 in Ulai ⌊Gate⌋ call loudly, "**G**,
8:17 **G** came up beside me,
9:21 I was praying, the man **G**,
Luk 1:19 angel answered him, "I'm **G**!
1:26 sent the angel **G** to Nazareth,

Gad (85)

Gen 30:11 So she called him **G** [Luck].
35:26 Zilpah were **G** and Asher.
46:16 The sons of **G** were Ziphion,
49:19 "**G** will be attacked by a band
Exo 1:4 Dan and Naphtali; **G** and Asher.
Num 1:14 from the tribe of **G**;
1:24 for the descendants of **G** listed
1:25 for the tribe of **G** was 45,650.
2:14 "Then ⌊will be⌋ the tribe of **G**.
2:14 for the people of **G** is Eliasaph,
7:42 leader of the descendants of **G**,
10:20 commanded the army of **G**.
13:15 from the tribe of **G**.
26:15 The families descended from **G**
32:1 The tribes of Reuben and **G**
32:6 the tribes of **G** and Reuben,
32:16 Then the tribes of **G** and
32:25 Then the tribes of **G** and
32:29 "If the tribes of **G** and Reuben
32:31 The tribes of **G** and Reuben
32:33 So Moses gave the tribes of **G**,
32:34 The tribe of **G** rebuilt the cities
34:14 from the tribes of Reuben, **G**,
Dtr 3:12 the tribes of Reuben and **G**
3:16 tribes of Reuben and **G** some
3:18 the tribes of Reuben and **G**
4:43 in Gilead for the tribe of **G**,
27:13 **G**, Asher, Zebulun, Dan,
29:8 it to the tribes of Reuben, **G**,
33:20 About the tribe of **G** he said,
33:20 the people of **G** more land.
Jos 1:12 to the tribes of Reuben and **G**
4:12 The men of Reuben, **G**,
12:6 to the tribes of Reuben and **G**
13:8 The tribes of Reuben and **G**
13:24 to the tribe of **G** for its families.
18:7 The tribes of **G** and Reuben
20:8 in Gilead from the tribe of **G**,
21:7 of Reuben, **G**, and Zebulun.
21:38 The tribe of **G** also gave them
22:1 the tribes of Reuben and **G**
22:9 So the tribes of Reuben and **G**
22:10 Reuben, **G**, and half of the tribe
22:11 Reuben, **G**, and half of the tribe
22:13 to the tribes of Reuben and **G**
22:21 the tribes of Reuben and **G**
22:25 descendants of Reuben and **G**.
22:30 **G**, and Manasseh said,
22:31 of Reuben, **G**, and Manasseh,
22:32 returned from Reuben and **G**
22:33 to war against Reuben and **G**
22:34 The tribes of Reuben and **G**
1Sm 11:1 the tribes of **G** and Reuben.
13:7 the territory of **G** and Gilead.
22:5 the prophet **G** told David.
2Sm 23:36 Bani from the tribe of **G**,
24:5 they went to **G** and to Jazer.
24:11 his word to the prophet **G**,
24:13 When **G** came to David,
24:14 situation," David told **G**.
24:18 That day **G** came to David and
24:19 David went as **G** had told him
2Ki 10:33 (the territory belonging to **G**,
1Ch 2:2 Naphtali, **G**, and Asher.
5:18 descendants of Reuben, **G**,
5:22 Reuben, **G**, and half of the tribe
5:25 But **G**, Reuben, and half of the
5:26 of Assyria) to take Reuben, **G**,
6:63 of Reuben, **G**, and Zebulun.
6:80 From the tribe of **G**,
12:8 Some men left **G** to join David
12:14 These descendants of **G** were
12:37 Jordan River, from Reuben, **G**,
21:9 The LORD spoke to **G**,
21:11 When **G** came to David,
21:13 situation," David told **G**.
21:18 The LORD's Messenger told **G**
21:19 David went as **G** had told him
26:32 for the tribes of Reuben, **G**,
29:29 Nathan, and the seer **G**.
2Ch 29:25 as David, the king's seer **G**,
Eze 48:27 **G** will have one part of the land
48:28 The southern border of **G** will
48:34 the west side will be **G** Gate,
Rev 7:5 12,000 from the tribe of **G**,

Gadarenes (1)

Mat 8:28 arrived in the territory of the **G**

Gaddi (1)

Num 13:11 **G**, son of Susi, from the tribe of

Gaddiel (1)

Num 13:10 **G**, son of Sodi, from the tribe of

Gadi (2)

2Ki 15:14 Then Menahem, son of **G**,
15:17 of Judah, Menahem, son of **G**,

Gad's (8)

Num 26:18 the families of **G** descendants.
Jos 13:28 This was **G** inheritance for its
1Ch 5:11 **G** descendants lived next to
5:12 from **G** first son Joel.
5:12 from **G** second son Shapham.
5:12 descended from **G** sons Janai
Jer 49:1 inheritance of **G** descendants?
49:1 people live in **G** cities

Gaham (1)

Gen 22:24 **G**, Tahash, and Maacah."

Gahar (2)

Ezr 2:47 Giddel, **G**, Reaiah,
Neh 7:49 Hanan, Giddel, **G**,

gain (49)

Gen 27:40 But eventually you will **g** your
37:26 "What will we **g** by killing our
2Ki 15:19 of silver to **g** his support
Job 10:3 What do you **g** by mistreating
11:12 will **g** understanding when
11:19 people will try to **g** your favor.
21:15 What do we **g** if we pray to
22:3 Does he **g** anything when you
35:3 'What would I **g** by sinning?'
Psa 9:19 Do not let mortals **g** any power.
19:13 Do not let anyone **g** control
44:3 They did not **g** victory with
62:10 Do not hope to **g** anything
119:104 From your guiding principles I **g**
Pro 1:5 person will **g** direction —
1:19 who is greedy for unjust **g**.
4:1 and pay attention in order to **g**
11:16 but ruthless men **g** riches.
12:24 Hard-working hands **g** control,
13:10 but those who take advice **g**
15:27 Whoever is greedy for unjust **g**
16:16 How much better it is to **g**
19:25 and he will **g** more knowledge.
28:16 hate unjust **g** will live longer.

Ecc 1:3 What do people **g** from all their
3:9 What do working people **g** from
5:11 What do owners **g** from all
5:16 What advantage do they **g** from
6:11 do mortals **g** from this?
Isa 29:24 in spirit will **g** understanding,
41:1 Let the people **g** new strength.
56:11 Each one seeks his own **g**.
Jer 2:18 You won't **g** anything by going
2:18 You won't **g** anything by going
Dan 8:10 It continued to **g** power until it
9:13 we never tried to **g** your favor
Mal 3:14 What do we **g** if we meet his
Mat 19:16 should I do to **g** eternal life?"
Rom 6:21 What did you **g** by doing those
9:30 trying to **g** God's approval won
9:31 The people of Israel tried to **g**
9:32 on faith to **g** God's approval,
1Co 6:12 but I won't allow anything to **g**
Gal 3:18 If we have to **g** the inheritance
Php 3:8 I threw it all away in order to **g**
1Ti 3:13 deacons who serve well **g**
Tit 3:5 we had done to **g** his approval.
Heb 11:35 so that they might **g** eternal life.
11:40 so that we would **g** eternal life

gained (22)

Gen 31:1 father and has **g** all his wealth
1Sm 2:26 continued to grow and **g**
18:30 So David **g** a good reputation.
Est 4:14 you may have **g** your royal
Psa 44:12 and at that price you have **g**
98:1 holy arm have **g** victory for him.
Pro 3:14 The profit (**g**) from (wisdom)
3:14 than the profit (**g**) from silver.
10:2 Treasures **g** dishonestly profit
13:11 Wealth (**g**) through injustice
14:23 there is always something **g**,
16:8 Better a few (possessions) **g**
16:8 than many **g** through injustice.
20:17 Food **g** dishonestly tastes
Ecc 2:11 I **g** nothing (from any of my
Jer 12:13 but they **g** nothing by it.
48:36 wealth they **g** has disappeared.
Dan 8:9 It **g** power over the south,
Luk 2:52 He **g** favor from God and
11:52 You haven't **g** entrance into
1Co 15:32 what have I **g** according to the
Heb 12:23 and have **g** eternal life.

gaining (3)

Pro 16:16 and the **g** of understanding
Act 19:20 was spreading and **g** strength.
Heb 13:9 **G** inner strength from God's

gains (4)

Pro 15:32 to warning **g** understanding.
19:8 A person who **g** sense loves
21:11 is instructed, he **g** knowledge.
29:23 but a humble spirit **g** honor.

Gaius (5)

Act 19:29 grabbed **G** and Aristarchus,
20:4 **G** from Derbe, Timothy,
Rom 16:23 **G** greets you. He is host to me
1Co 1:14 of you except Crispus and **G**
3Jn 1:1 To my dear friend **G**,

Galal (3)

1Ch 9:15 Bakbakkar, Heresh, **G**,
9:16 of Shemaiah, grandson of **G**,
Neh 11:17 who was the son of **G**,

Galatia (7)

Act 16:6 the regions of Phrygia and **G**
18:23 the regions of **G** and Phrygia,
1Co 16:1 as I directed the churches in **G**.
Gal 1:2 To the churches in **G**.
3:1 You stupid people of **G**!
2Ti 4:10 went to the province of **G**,
1Pe 1:1 Pontus, **G**, Cappadocia, Asia,

Galeed (2)

Gen 31:47 but Jacob called it **G**.
31:48 This is why it was named **G**

Galilean (3)

Mat 26:69 were with Jesus the **G**."
Mar 14:70 one of them. You're a **G**!"
Luk 22:59 man was with him. He's a **G**!"

Galileans (2)

Luk 13:1 about some **G** whom Pilate had
Act 2:7 men who are speaking are **G**.

Galilee (89)

Num 34:11 eastern slope of the Sea of **G**.
Dtr 3:17 from the Sea of **G** to the Sea of
Jos 12:3 plains from the Sea of **G**
13:27 to the end of the Sea of **G**.
20:7 Kedesh in **G** in the mountains
21:32 Kedesh in **G** (a city of refuge
1Ki 9:11 Hiram of Tyre 20 cities in **G**.
2Ki 15:29 Kedesh, Hazor, Gilead, **G**,
1Ch 6:76 they received Kedesh in **G**
Isa 9:1 to **G**, where foreigners live.
Mat 2:22 in a dream, he left for **G**
3:13 He came from **G** to the Jordan
4:12 he went back to **G**.
4:13 on the shores of the Sea of **G**.
4:15 River, **G**, where foreigners live!
4:18 walking along the Sea of **G**,
4:23 Jesus went all over **G**.
4:25 They came from **G**,
8:18 the other side of the Sea of **G**.
8:28 other side (of the Sea of **G**),
13:1 and sat down by the Sea of **G**.
14:1 At that time Herod, ruler of **G**,
15:29 and went along the Sea of **G**.
16:5 the other side of the Sea of **G**.
17:22 were traveling together in **G**,
19:1 he left **G** and traveled along the
21:11 Jesus from Nazareth in **G**."
26:32 I will go to **G** ahead of you."
27:55 had followed Jesus from **G**
28:7 going ahead of them into **G**.
28:10 tell my followers to go to **G**.
28:16 in **G** where Jesus had
Mar 1:9 Jesus came from Nazareth in **G**
1:14 Jesus went to **G** and told
1:16 was going along the Sea of **G**,
1:28 the surrounding region of **G**.
1:39 in the synagogues all over **G**,
3:7 his disciples for the Sea of **G**.
3:7 A large crowd from **G**,
4:1 to teach again by the Sea of **G**.
5:1 the other side of the Sea of **G**.
5:21 to the other side of the Sea of **G**
6:21 the most important people of **G**.
7:31 the Ten Cities to the Sea of **G**.
8:13 the other side of the Sea of **G**.
9:30 and were passing through **G**.
14:28 I will go to **G** ahead of you."
15:41 him while he was in **G**.
16:7 he's going ahead of them to **G**.
Luk 1:26 to Nazareth, a city in **G**.
2:4 went from Nazareth, a city in **G**,
2:39 hometown of Nazareth in **G**.
3:1 Herod ruled **G**, and his brother
4:14 Jesus returned to **G**.
4:31 went to Capernaum, a city in **G**,
5:1 was standing by the Sea of **G**.
5:17 come from every village in **G**
8:26 the Gerasenes across from **G**.
13:2 than other people from **G**?
17:11 border between Samaria and **G**
23:5 He started in **G** and has come
23:6 asked if the man was from **G**.
23:7 Herod ruled **G** and was in
23:49 who had followed him from **G**,
23:55 from **G** followed closely behind
24:6 you while he was still in **G**.
Jon 1:43 day Jesus wanted to go to **G**.
2:1 place in the city of Cana in **G**.
2:11 Cana in **G** was the place
4:3 and went back to **G**.
4:43 in Samaria, Jesus left for **G**.
4:45 But when Jesus arrived in **G**,
4:45 the people of **G** welcomed him.
4:46 to the city of Cana in **G**,
4:47 had returned from Judea to **G**.
Jon 4:54 come back from Judea to **G**.
6:1 other side of the Sea of **G** (or
7:1 later traveled throughout **G**.
7:9 Jesus stayed in **G**.
7:41 can the Messiah come from **G**?
7:52 this because you're from **G**?
7:52 that no prophet comes from **G**."
12:21 (who was from Bethsaida in **G**)
21:2 Nathanael from Cana in **G**,
Act 1:11 "Why are you men from **G**
5:37 Judas from **G** appeared and led
9:31 **G**, and Samaria had peace.
10:37 Everything began in **G** after
13:31 with him to Jerusalem from **G**.

gall (1)

Mat 27:34 mixed with a drug called **g**.

gallbladder (1)

Job 20:25 point comes out of his **g**.

Gallim (2)

1Sm 25:44 Laish's son, who was from **G**.
Isa 10:30 Cry aloud, you people in **G**!

Gallio (4)

Act 18:12 While **G** was governor of
18:14 about to answer when **G** said
18:16 So **G** had them forced out of
18:17 But **G** couldn't have cared less.

gallon (4)

Eze 45:24 He must also give one **g** of
46:5 One **g** of olive oil must be
46:7 One **g** of olive oil must be
46:11 One **g** of olive oil must be

gallons (11)

1Ki 5:11 of wheat and 120,000 **g**
7:26 a lily's bud. It held 12,000 **g**.
7:38 Each basin held 240 **g**.
2Ch 2:10 200,000 **g** of wine,
2:10 and 200,000 **g** of olive oil."
4:5 a lily's bud. It held 18,000 **g**.
Ezr 7:22 of wheat, 600 **g** of wine,
7:22 of wine, 600 **g** of olive oil,
Isa 5:10 will produce only six **g** of wine,
Luk 16:6 'Eight hundred **g** of olive oil.'
Jon 2:6 Each jar held 18 to 27 **g**.

gallop (2)

Nah 3:2 Horses **g**! Chariots bounce
Hab 1:8 riders will **g** along proudly.

galloped (1)

Jdg 5:22 mighty war horses **g** on and on.

galloping (1)

Jer 47:3 hear the sound of **g** war horses,

Gamaliel (7)

Num 1:10 Ephraim; **G**, son of Pedahzur,
2:20 the people of Manasseh is **G**,
7:54 **G**, son of Pedahzur,
7:59 These were the gifts from **G**,
10:23 **G**, son of Pedahzur,
Act 5:34 a Pharisee named **G** stood up.
22:3 my education from **G** here

game (5)

Gen 27:3 and hunt some wild **g** for me.
27:5 for some wild **g** to bring back,
27:7 said, 'Bring me some wild **g**,
27:25 "Bring me some of the **g**,
27:33 "Who hunted **g** and brought it to

Gammad (1)

Eze 27:11 People from **G** guarded your

Gamul (1)

1Ch 24:17 the twenty-second for **G**,

gang (1)

Hab 3:14 You pierce the leader of his **g**

gangs (2)

Jer 6:11 in the street and on the **g**
Hos 6:9 The priests are like **g** of

gaped (1)

Job 16:10 People **g** at me with wide-open

gaps (4)

Neh 4:7 and that the **g** were being filled
6:1 wall and that no **g** had been left
Eze 13:5 They haven't repaired the **g** in
22:30 or stand in front of me by the **g**

garbage (6)

Psa 113:7 He lifts the needy from a **g**
Isa 5:25 and dead bodies lie like **g** in
Lam 4:5 now pick through piles of **g**.
Eze 7:19 and gold into the streets like **g**.
Amo 4:3 will be thrown into a **g** dump.
1Co 4:13 Right now we have become **g**

garden (63)

Gen 2:8 LORD God planted a **g** in Eden,
2:9 evil grew in the middle of the **g**.
2:10 from Eden to water the **g**.
2:10 Outside the **g** it divided into
2:15 the man and put him in the **G**
2:16 to eat from any tree in the **g**.
3:1 the fruit of any tree in the **g**?"
3:2 the fruit from any tree in the **g**
3:3 the tree in the middle of the **g**.
3:8 God walking around in the **g**.
3:8 God among the trees in the **g**.
3:10 "I heard you in the **g**.
3:23 God sent the man out of the **G**
3:24 east of the **G** of Eden.
13:10 well-watered like the LORD's **g**
Dtr 11:10 to water it like a vegetable **g**.
1Ki 21:2 It will become my vegetable **g**
2Ki 21:18 He was buried in the **g** of his
21:18 own palace, in the **g** of Uzza.
21:26 in his tomb in the **g** of Uzza.
25:4 two walls beside the king's **g**.
Neh 3:15 by the King's **G** as far as
Est 1:5 was held in the enclosed **g**
1:6 The **g** had white and violet
7:7 and went into the palace **g**.
7:8 king returned from the palace **g**
Job 8:16 The shoots spread over his **g**.
Sos 4:12 my sister is a **g** that is locked,
4:12 is locked, a **g** that is locked,
4:16 Blow on my **g**! Let its spices
4:16 Let my beloved come to his **g**,
5:1 I will come to my **g**.
5:13 cheeks are like a **g** of spices,
5:13 a **g** that produces scented
6:2 My beloved went to his **g**,
Isa 1:29 by the **g** that you have
1:30 and like a **g** without water.
5:7 the people of Judah are the **g**
51:3 make its wilderness like the **g**
58:11 will become like a watered **g**
61:11 crops and like a **g** that makes
66:17 themselves for their **g** rituals.
66:17 They go into the **g** and devour
Jer 39:4 by way of the king's **g** through
52:7 two walls beside the king's **g**.
Lam 2:6 his own booth as if it were a **g**
Eze 17:7 turned away from the **g** where
17:10 It will certainly wither in the **g**
28:13 You were in Eden, God's **g**.
31:8 The cedar trees in God's **g**
31:8 All the trees in God's **g** couldn't
31:9 the trees in Eden, in God's **g**.
36:35 has become like the **g** of Eden.
Joe 2:3 it the land is like the **g** of Eden.
Mat 13:32 it is taller than the **g** plants.
Mar 4:32 taller than all the **g** plants.
Luk 11:42 mint, spices, and every **g** herb.
13:19 that someone planted in a **g**.
Jon 18:1 entered the **g** that was there.
18:3 Pharisees and went to the **g**.
18:26 I see you with Jesus in the **g**?"
19:41 A **g** was located in the place
19:41 In that **g** was a new tomb in

gardener (3)

Luk 13:7 He said to the **g**, 'For the last
13:8 "The **g** replied, 'Sir, let it stand
Jon 20:15 Mary thought it was the **g**

gardens (12)

Num 24:6 out like rivers, like **g** by a river,
Ecc 2:5 I made **g** and parks for myself.
Sos 4:15 ⌊You are⌋ a spring for **g**,
6:2 flock in the **g** and gather lilies.
8:13 Young woman living in the **g**,
Isa 65:3 They offered sacrifices in **g**
Jer 10:5 like scarecrows in cucumber **g**.
29:5 Plant **g**, and eat what they
29:28 Plant **g**, and eat what they
31:12 will be like well-watered **g**,
Amo 4:9 repeatedly devoured your **g**,
9:14 They will plant **g** and eat their

Gareb (3)

2Sm 23:38 **G** (descendant of Ithra),
1Ch 11:40 **G** (descendant of Ithra),
Jer 31:39 there straight to the Hill of **G**,

garland (2)

Pro 1:9 and teachings are a graceful **g**
4:9 It will give you a graceful **g** for

garlic (1)

Num 11:5 leeks, onions, and **g** we had?

garment (9)

Rut 3:9 Spread the corner of your **g**
1Sm 19:13 and covered the idols with a **g**.
1Ki 11:30 Ahijah took his new **g** and tore
2Ki 2:12 he grabbed his own **g** and tore
Pro 20:16 Hold on to the **g** of one who
27:13 Hold on to the **g** of one who
30:4 Who has wrapped water in a **g**?
Isa 9:5 of battle and every **g** rolled
50:9 They will all wear out like a **g**.

garments (3)

Gen 49:11 his **g** in the blood of grapes.
Pro 31:24 "She makes linen **g** and sells
Isa 63:2 red and your **g** like those who

Garmites (1)

1Ch 4:19 first settled Keilah of the **G** and

gashes (1)

Jer 48:37 There are **g** on every hand and

gasp (2)

1Ki 9:8 They will **g** and ask,
Isa 42:14 I will cry out. I will **g** and pant.

gasping (1)

Jer 4:31 My people Zion are **g** for breath.

Gatam (3)

Gen 36:11 Omar, Zepho, **G**, and Kenaz.
36:16 Korah, **G**, and Amalek.
1Ch 1:36 and Omar, Zephi and **G**,

gate (199)

Gen 23:10 the city **g** could hear him.
23:18 had entered the city **g** were
34:20 Shechem went to their city **g**
34:24 come out to the city **g** agreed
34:24 all circumcised at the city **g**.
Dtr 21:19 leaders of the city at the city **g**.
22:15 must go to the city **g** where
22:24 take them to the **g** of the city
25:7 leaders of the city at the city **g**.
Jos 2:5 When it was dark and the **g**
2:7 men had left, the **g** was closed.
7:5 chasing them from the city **g** to
Jdg 16:2 waited all night at the city **g**
16:3 and bar of the city **g** and pulled
Rut 4:1 Boaz went to the city **g** and sat
4:11 the people who were at the **g**,
1Sm 2:22 the women who served at the **g**
4:18 chair backwards toward the **g**.
21:13 on the doors of the city **g**
23:7 a city which has ⌊a **g** with⌋
2Sm 10:8 at the entrance of the ⌊city⌋ **g**,
11:23 to the entrance of the city **g**.
15:2 the road leading to the city **g**.
18:4 So the king stood by the **g**
18:24 along the roof of the **g** by
18:33 the room above the **g** and cried.
23:15 at the city **g** of Bethlehem."
1Ki 22:10 entrance to the **g** of Samaria.
2Ki 7:3 at the entrance of the city **g**.
7:17 to lean to be in charge of the **g**.
11:6 Another third must be at Sur **G**.
11:6 third must be at the **g** behind
11:19 that goes through Guards' **G**
14:13 from Ephraim **G** to Corner Gate
14:13 from Ephraim Gate to Corner **G**
15:35 Jotham built the Upper **G** of the
23:8 entrance of the **G** of Joshua,
23:8 the **g** named after the mayor of
23:8 going through the city **g**.)
25:4 on the road of the **g** between
1Ch 9:18 were stationed at the king's **g**
11:17 at the city **g** of Bethlehem."
16:42 sons were stationed at the **g**.
26:13 and oldest alike, for every **g**.
26:16 side with Shallecheth **G** at
2Ch 8:14 of doorkeepers at every **g**
18:9 entrance to the **g** of Samaria.
23:5 third must be at Foundation **G**.
23:15 her as she entered Horse **G**
23:20 They went through Upper **G** to
24:8 box and placed it outside the **g**
25:23 from Ephraim **G** to Corner Gate
25:23 from Ephraim Gate to Corner **G**
26:9 Wall, Valley **G**, and the Angle,
27:3 Jotham built the Upper **G** of the
31:14 was the gatekeeper at East **G**
32:6 in the square by the city **g**.
33:14 to the entrance of Fish **G**.
35:15 were stationed at each **g**.
Neh 2:13 I went through Valley **G** that
2:13 Snake Fountain and Dung **G**
2:14 Passing through Fountain **G**,
2:15 entered Valley **G**, and returned.
3:1 started by rebuilding Sheep **G**.
3:3 of Hassenaah rebuilt Fish **G**.
3:6 made repairs on Old **G**.
3:13 of Zanoah repaired Valley **G**.
3:13 of the wall, as far as Dung **G**.
3:14 Dung **G** itself was repaired by
3:15 repaired Fountain **G**.
3:26 across from Water **G** toward
3:28 Above Horse **G** the priests
3:29 the guard at East **G**,
3:31 across from Inspection **G**
3:32 at the corner and Sheep **G**.
8:1 courtyard in front of Water **G**.
8:3 the courtyard in front of Water **G**
8:16 in the open area by Water **G**,
8:16 in the open area at Ephraim **G**.
12:31 the right on the wall to Dung **G**.
12:37 At Fountain **G** they went
12:37 reaches Water **G** on the east.
12:39 then past Ephraim **G**,
12:39 over Old **G** and Fish Gate,
12:39 over Old Gate and Fish **G**,
12:39 as far as Sheep **G**.
12:39 choir stopped at Guard's **G**.
Est 2:19 was sitting at the king's **g**.
2:21 was sitting at the king's **g**,
3:2 advisers were at the king's **g**,
3:3 at the king's **g** asked Mordecai,
4:2 went right up to the king's **g**.
4:6 square in front of the king's **g**.
5:9 saw Mordecai at the king's **g**,
5:13 the Jew sitting at the king's **g**."
6:10 Jew who sits at the king's **g**.
6:12 returned to the king's **g**,
Job 5:4 They are crushed at the city **g**,
29:7 When I went through the city **g**
Psa 69:12 Those who sit at the **g** gossip
118:20 This is the **g** of the LORD
127:5 with his enemies in the city **g**.
Pro 17:19 city **g** high invites destruction.
18:19 disputes are like the locked **g**
22:22 oppressed person at the city **g**,

Pro 24:7 At the city **g** he does not open
Sos 7:4 pools by the **g** of Bath Rabbim.
Isa 14:31 Cry loudly in the **g**!
22:7 stand ready in front of the **g**.
24:12 Its **g** is battered to pieces.
Jer 7:2 "Stand at the **g** of the LORD's
17:19 Stand at People's **G**,
17:19 stand at every **g** in Jerusalem.
19:2 at the entrance to Potsherd **G**.
20:2 at Upper Benjamin **G** that was
26:10 sat at the entrance of New **G**
31:38 Tower of Hananel to Corner **G**.
31:40 as far as the corner of Horse **G**
36:10 at the entrance of New **G**
37:13 when he came to Benjamin **G**,
38:7 to be sitting at Benjamin **G**.
38:8 to the king at Benjamin **G**.
39:3 came in and sat in Middle **G**:
39:4 garden through the **g** between
52:7 at night through the **g** between
Lam 5:14 stopped meeting at the city **g**,
Eze 8:3 to the entrance to the north **g** of
8:5 entrance to the north **g** beside
8:14 to the entrance of the north **g**
9:2 came from the upper north **g**.
10:19 stood at the door to the east **g**
11:1 me and took me to the east **g**
11:1 (It's the **g** that faces east.)
11:1 were at the entrance of the **g**.
40:23 opposite the north **g** just like
40:23 the distance from one **g**
40:23 from one gate to the other **g**.
42:15 led me out through the east **g**.
43:1 the man took me to the east **g**.
43:4 the temple through the east **g**.
44:1 me back to the outer east **g**
44:1 and the **g** was shut.
44:2 The LORD said to me, "This **g**
44:4 brought me through the north **g**
46:1 The east **g** of the inner
46:2 The **g** must not be closed until
46:9 entering through the north **g**
46:9 must leave through the south **g**.
46:9 the south **g** must leave through
46:9 must leave through the north **g**.
46:9 the same **g** they entered.
46:9 leave through the opposite **g**.
46:12 the east **g** must be opened for
46:12 the **g** must be shut after him.
47:2 he led me through the north **g**
47:2 and around to the outer east **g**.
47:2 down the south side of the **g**.
48:31 north side will be Reuben **G**,
48:31 Gate, Judah **G**, and Levi Gate.
48:31 Gate, Judah Gate, and Levi **G**.
48:32 the east side will be Joseph **G**,
48:32 Benjamin **G**, and Dan Gate.
48:32 Benjamin Gate, and Dan **G**.
48:33 south side will be Simeon **G**,
48:33 Issachar **G**, and Zebulun Gate.
48:33 Issachar Gate, and Zebulun **G**.
48:34 the west side will be Gad **G**,
48:34 Asher **G**, and Naphtali Gate.
48:34 Asher Gate, and Naphtali **G**.
Dan 8:2 vision I saw myself at Ulai **G**.
8:3 ram standing beside the **g**.
8:6 seen standing beside the **g**.
8:16 a man in Ulai ⌊**G**⌋ call loudly,
Mic 2:13 go through the **g**, and leave.
Zep 1:10 loud cry will come from Fish **G**,
Zec 14:10 from Benjamin **G** to the place
14:10 Gate to the place of First **G**,
14:10 place of First Gate, Corner **G**,
Mat 7:13 "Enter through the narrow **g**
7:13 the narrow gate because the **g**
7:13 Many enter through the wide **g**.
7:14 But the narrow **g** and the road
7:14 a few people find the narrow **g**.
Luk 16:20 was regularly brought to the **g**
Jon 5:2 Near Sheep **G** in Jerusalem
10:1 the sheep pen through the **g**
10:2 through the **g** is the shepherd.
10:3 gatekeeper opens the **g** for him,
10:7 I am the **g** for the sheep.
10:9 I am the **g**. Those who enter the
18:16 was standing outside the **g**.
Act 3:2 would put the lame man at a **g**
3:2 The **g** was called Beautiful
3:2 gate was called Beautiful **G**.
3:10 beg at the temple's Beautiful **G**.
10:17 house and went to the **g**.
12:10 came to the iron **g** that led into
12:10 This **g** opened by itself for
Rev 21:21 Each **g** was made of one pearl.

gatekeeper (5)

2Ch 31:14 was the **g** at East Gate and
Ezr 7:24 Levite, singer, **g**, servant,
Jon 10:3 The **g** opens the gate for him,
18:16 to the woman who was the **g**
18:17 The **g** asked Peter,

gatekeepers (34)

2Ki 7:10 So they called the city **g** and
7:11 The **g** announced the news to
1Ch 9:17 The **g** were Shallum,
9:18 They were the **g** for the Levite
9:20 the official in charge of the **g**,
9:22 The men chosen to be **g** at the
9:23 were assigned to be **g**
9:24 The **g** were on the four sides
9:26 The four chief Levite **g** were in
15:18 and Jeiel were appointed **g**.
15:23 and Elkanah were **g** for the ark.
16:38 son) and Hosah were to be **g**.
23:5 4,000 were appointed to be **g**,
26:1 were the divisions of the **g**:
26:12 These divisions of **g** through
26:19 of the **g** among Korah's
2Ch 23:19 Jehoiada appointed **g** for the
34:13 as scribes, officials, or **g**.
35:15 The **g** were stationed at each
Ezr 2:42 These **g** returned from exile:
2:70 the people, the singers, the **g**,
7:7 priests, Levites, singers, **g**,
10:24 Eliashib From the **g**:
Neh 7:1 The **g**, the singers, and the
7:3 While the ⌊**g**⌋ are still standing
7:45 These **g** returned from exile:
7:73 The priests, Levites, the **g**,
10:28 **g**, singers, temple servants,
10:39 the priests who serve and the **g**
11:19 These were the **g**:
12:25 and Akkub were **g** standing
12:45 The singers and the **g** did what
12:47 of the singers and the **g**.
13:5 to the Levites, singers, and **g**.

gatekeepers' (1)

1Ch 9:25 serve under the **g** supervision

gates (114)

Dtr 3:5 high walls and double-door **g**
3:5 gates with bars across the **g**.
6:9 of your houses and on your **g**.
11:20 of your houses and on your **g**.
17:5 who did this evil thing to the **g**
20:11 it and open ⌊their **g**⌋ to you,
33:25 the locks and bolts of your **g**
Jdg 5:8 war broke out inside the city **g**.
5:11 people went down to the city **g**.
1Sm 17:52 as Gath and to the **g** of Ekron.
2Sm 18:24 sitting between the two **g** while
1Ki 4:13 and bronze bars across their **g**.
8:37 may blockade Israel's city **g**.
2Ki 15:16 the city didn't open its **g** for him,
1Ch 22:3 fittings on the doors of the **g**.
2Ch 6:28 may blockade Israel's city **g**.
8:5 walls, double-door **g**, and bars.
23:4 of worship, must guard the **g**.
23:19 appointed gatekeepers for the **g**
31:2 or praising within the **g** of the
Neh 1:3 and its **g** have been destroyed
2:3 and its **g** are burned down?"
2:8 him to give me wood for the **g**
2:13 where its **g** had been burned.
2:17 and its **g** are burned down.
6:1 hung the doors in the city **g**).
7:3 I told them, "The **g** of
11:19 who guarded the **g** totaled 172.
12:25 at the storehouses by the **g**.
12:30 the people, the **g**, and the wall.
Neh 13:19 when the **g** of Jerusalem were
13:19 some of my men by the **g**
13:22 themselves and guard the **g**
Job 17:16 hope go down with me to the **g**
38:8 "Who shut the sea behind **g**
38:10 for it and put up bars and **g**,
Psa 9:13 me away from the **g** of death
9:14 praises one by one in the **g**
24:7 Lift your heads, you **g**.
24:9 Lift your heads, you **g**.
100:4 Enter his **g** with a song of
107:16 He shattered bronze **g** and cut
107:18 and they came near death's **g**.
118:19 Open the **g** of righteousness for
122:2 feet are standing inside your **g**,
147:13 the bars across your **g** strong.
Pro 8:3 near the **g** to the city.
14:19 people will bow at the **g**
31:23 is known at the city **g** when
31:31 praise her at the city **g**."
Isa 3:26 The **g** of Zion will cry and
13:2 your hand to enter Nobles' **G**.
26:2 Open the **g**, and let the
28:6 who defend the city **g** in battle.
38:10 life I would go down to the **g**
45:1 of him so that the **g** would not
54:12 your **g** with sparkling stones,
60:11 Your **g** will always be open.
60:18 Salvation and your **g** Praise.
62:10 Go through the **g**! Prepare a way
Jer 1:15 the entrance of Jerusalem's **g**.
7:2 Judah who go through these **g**
14:2 Judah mourns; its **g** fall apart.
15:7 winnowing shovel at the city **g**.
17:20 and go through these **g**.
17:21 it through the **g** of Jerusalem.
17:24 not bring anything through the **g**
17:25 throne will come through the **g**
17:27 carrying anything through the **g**
17:27 I will set its **g** on fire.
22:2 people who come into these **g**,
22:4 throne will ride through the **g**
22:19 outside the **g** of Jerusalem.
49:31 It is a nation with no **g** or bars.
51:30 bars across their **g** are broken.
51:58 and its high **g** will be set on
Lam 1:4 passes through any of its **g**.
2:9 "⌊Zion's⌋ **g** have sunk into the
2:9 the bars across its ⌊**g**⌋.
4:12 get through the **g** of Jerusalem.
Eze 21:15 people at all their **g** so that their
21:22 rams against the city **g**,
26:10 walls when he enters your **g**.
38:11 live without walls, locks, or **g**.
44:11 They could have guarded the **g**
48:31 The **g** of the city will be named
48:31 The three **g** on the north side
48:32 The three **g** on the east side
48:33 The three **g** on the south side
48:34 The three **g** on the west side
Hos 11:6 demolish their city **g**,
Amo 1:5 bars ⌊on the **g**⌋ of Damascus.
Oba 1:11 Foreigners entered his **g** and
1:13 Don't march through the **g** of
Mic 1:9 It will reach the **g** of my people
1:12 come on the **g** of Jerusalem.
Nah 2:6 The **g** of the rivers are opened,
3:13 The **g** of your country are wide
3:13 destroyed the bars of your **g**.
Mat 16:18 And the **g** of hell will not
Act 9:24 They were watching the city **g**
14:13 their necks to the temple **g**.
Heb 13:12 outside the **g** of Jerusalem.
Rev 21:12 high wall with 12 **g**.
21:12 Twelve angels were at the **g**.
21:12 of Israel were written on the **g**.
21:13 There were three **g** on the east,
21:13 three **g** on the north,
21:13 three **g** on the south,
21:13 and three **g** on the west.
21:15 the city, its **g**, and its wall.
21:21 The 12 **g** were 12 pearls.
21:25 Its **g** will be open all day.
22:14 go through the **g** into the city.

gateway (65)

Gen 19:1 as Lot was sitting in the **g**.
28:17 of God and the **g** to heaven!"
1Sm 9:18 Samuel inside the **g** and said,
2Sm 3:27 Joab took him aside in the **g**
19:8 The king sat in the **g**.
19:8 "The king is sitting in the **g**,"
2Ki 7:1 of silver in the **g** to Samaria.
7:17 trampled him to death in the **g**,
7:18 tomorrow in the **g** to Samaria."
7:20 trampled him to death in the **g**.
9:31 When Jehu entered the **g**,
10:8 entrance to the **g** until morning
1Ch 26:16 Gate at the **g** that goes
26:18 there were four Levites at the **g**
Eze 26:2 'The city that was the **g** for the
40:3 and he stood in a **g**.
40:6 Then the man went to the **g**
40:6 measured the entrance to the **g**.
40:7 And the entrance to the **g** by
40:8 the entrance hall of the **g**.
40:10 on each side of the eastern **g**.
40:11 width of the entrance to the **g**.
40:11 and the **g** was 23 feet long.
40:13 He measured the **g** from the top
40:14 the entrance hall to the **g** was
40:15 The total length of the **g** from
40:16 the **g** had small windows
40:19 from the inside of the lower **g**
40:20 the length and width of the **g**.
40:20 This was the **g** that faced north.
40:21 size as those in the east **g**.
40:21 The **g** was 87 ½ feet long and
40:22 size as those in the east **g**.
40:23 The inner courtyard had a **g**
40:23 north gate just like the east **g**.
40:24 and I saw a **g** that faced south.
40:25 The **g** and its entrance hall had
40:27 courtyard had a **g** facing south.
40:27 the distance from the **g**
40:27 the south side to its opposite **g**.
40:28 courtyard through the south **g**.
40:28 He measured the south **g**.
40:29 The **g** was 87 ½ feet long and
40:31 eight steps led up to each **g**.
40:32 He measured the **g**.
40:33 The **g** was 87 ½ feet long and
40:34 and eight steps led up to the **g**.
40:35 man brought me to the north **g**.
40:36 The **g** was 87 ½ feet long and
40:37 and eight steps led up to the **g**.
40:38 the entrance hall of the **g**.
40:39 In the entrance hall of the **g**
40:40 to the north **g** there were two
40:40 hall of the **g** there were two
40:41 tables on each side of the **g**,
40:44 was at the side of the north **g**.
40:44 was at the side of the south **g**.
40:48 The **g** was 24 ½ feet wide,
44:3 the entrance hall of the **g**
46:2 the entrance hall of the **g**.
46:2 stand by the doorposts of the **g**.
46:2 worship at the entrance of the **g**
46:3 worship at the door of the **g**
46:8 the entrance hall of the **g**.
46:19 through a passage beside the **g**

gateway's (1)

Eze 40:9 The **g** entrance hall faced the

gateways (12)

2Ch 9:11 sandalwood the king made **g**
Job 38:17 Have the **g** to death been
38:17 seen the **g** to total darkness?
Eze 40:18 courtyard ran alongside the **g**.
40:24 size as those of the other **g**.
40:25 like the windows in the other **g**.
40:29 the same size as the other **g**.
40:33 size as those of the other **g**.
40:44 Outside the **g** to the inner
44:17 When they enter the **g** to the
44:17 them while they serve in the **g**
45:19 and on the doorposts of the **g** of

Gath (42)

Jos 11:22 left in Gaza, **G**, and Ashdod.
13:3 Ashkelon, **G**, and Ekron,
1Sm 5:8 of Israel must be taken to **G**,"
5:10 So the people of **G** sent the ark
6:17 Gaza, Ashkelon, **G**, and Ekron.
7:14 between Ekron and **G** which
17:4 His name was Goliath from **G**.
17:23 champion, Goliath from **G**,
17:52 the Philistines as far as **G**
17:52 and all the way to **G** and Ekron.
21:10 he came to King Achish of **G**.
21:12 terrified of King Achish of **G**.
27:2 600 men to King Achish of **G**,
27:3 men stayed with Achish in **G**.
27:4 told that David had fled to **G**,
27:11 man or woman back to **G** alive.
2Sm 1:20 Don't tell the news in **G**.
6:10 Obed Edom, who was from **G**.
6:11 the home of Obed Edom from **G**
15:18 him from **G** were marching past
15:19 The king asked Ittai from **G**,
15:22 So Ittai from **G** marched on
18:2 the last third under Ittai from **G**.
21:19 killed Goliath of **G**.
21:20 In another battle at **G**,
21:22 of Haraphah from **G**,
1Ki 2:39 told that his slaves were in **G**,
2:40 and went to Achish in **G**
2:40 Shimei went to **G** and got his
2:41 from Jerusalem to **G** and back,
2Ki 12:17 of Aram fought against **G**
1Ch 7:21 the men of **G** when they came
8:13 out the people living in **G**.
13:13 Obed Edom, who was from **G**.
18:1 He took **G** and its surrounding
20:5 the brother of Goliath from **G**.
20:6 In another battle at **G**,
20:8 of Haraphah from **G**,
2Ch 11:8 **G**, Mareshah, Ziph,
26:6 He tore down the walls of **G**,
Amo 6:2 Then go to **G**, the city of the
Mic 1:10 Don't report it in **G**.

gather (162)

Gen 29:7 isn't time yet to **g** the livestock.
31:46 his relatives, "**G** some stones."
49:2 "**G** around and listen,
Exo 5:7 Let them **g** their own straw,
5:12 Egypt to **g** stubble for straw.
16:4 go out and **g** only what they
16:5 much as they **g** on other days."
16:16 Each of you should **g** as much
16:26 You can **g** food on six days,
16:27 people went out to **g** food,
Lev 8:3 **G** the whole congregation at
19:9 of your fields or **g** what is left
23:22 of your fields or **g** what is left
25:3 and **g** what they produce.
26:25 When you **g** in your cities,
Num 10:7 But when you **g** the assembly,
11:8 would go around and **g** it,
20:8 brother Aaron **g** the community
21:16 said to Moses, "**G** the people,
Dtr 1:22 of us to **g** information about
11:14 Then you will **g** your own grain,
13:16 **G** their goods into the middle of
28:39 drink any wine or **g** any grapes,
30:3 on you and **g** you from all
30:4 the LORD your God will **g** you
Jos 2:2 They came to **g** information
2:3 They came here to **g**
2:18 Also, **g** your father,
Jdg 4:6 '**G** troops on Mount Tabor.
11:29 in Gilead ⌊to **g** an army⌋.
Rut 2:2 There I will **g** the grain left
2:7 'Please let me **g** grain.
2:7 I will only **g** among the bundles
2:8 go in any other field to **g** grain,
2:15 When she got up to **g** grain,
2:15 "Let her **g** grain even among
2:16 and leave it for her to **g**.
2:19 "Where did you **g** grain today?
1Sm 7:5 Then Samuel said, "**G** all the
2Sm 3:21 "I must go now so that I can **g**
2Sm 12:28 **G** the rest of the troops,
17:11 So my advice is to **g** all Israel's
1Ki 18:19 Order all Israel to **g** around me
2Ki 4:39 into the field to **g** vegetables
1Ch 16:35 **G** us and save us from the
22:2 foreigners living in Israel to **g**.
Ezr 8:15 I had this group **g** by the river
10:7 exiles must **g** in Jerusalem.
Neh 7:5 head that I should **g** the nobles,
Est 2:3 of your kingdom to **g** all
Psa 1:5 where righteous people **g**.
2:1 Why do the nations **g** together?
7:7 of people **g** around you.
47:9 from the nations **g** together as
50:5 "**G** around me, my godly
102:22 when nations and kingdoms **g**
104:22 When the sun rises, they **g** and
104:28 give it to them, and they **g** it up.
106:47 and **g** us from the nations so
129:7 arms of those who **g** bundles.
Pro 21:6 Those who **g** wealth by lying
Ecc 3:5 stones and a time to **g** them,
Sos 5:1 I will **g** my myrrh with my
6:2 in the gardens and **g** lilies.
Isa 11:10 for the people ⌊to **g** around⌋.
11:12 for the nations ⌊to **g** around⌋.
11:12 He will **g** the outcasts of Israel
13:14 sheep with no one to **g** them.
34:15 They will **g** their young in the
34:15 Vultures also will **g** there,
34:16 his Spirit will **g** them together.
43:5 from the east and **g** you from
48:14 **G** together, all of you,
49:5 Jacob back to him and **g** Israel
56:8 "I will **g** still others besides
60:7 of the flocks from Kedar will **g**
62:9 Those who **g** grapes will drink
66:18 I am coming to **g** the nations of
Jer 3:17 All nations will **g** in Jerusalem
4:5 loudly and say, "**G** together!
7:18 Children **g** wood, fathers light
12:9 **g** all the animals in the field,
23:3 "Then I will **g** the remaining
29:14 I will **g** you from all the nations
31:8 I will **g** them from the farthest
31:10 the people of Israel will **g** them
32:37 I am going to **g** the people from
40:10 **G** grapes, summer fruit,
49:5 No one will **g** the refugees.
Eze 11:17 the nations and **g** them from
16:37 That is why I will **g** all your
16:37 you and hate you **g** around.
20:34 from the nations and **g** you from
20:41 from the nations and **g** you from
22:19 I'm going to **g** you in Jerusalem.
22:20 People **g** silver, copper, iron,
22:20 in my anger and fury I will **g**
22:21 Yes, I will **g** you, breathe on
28:25 When I **g** the people of Israel
29:13 After 40 years I will **g** the
32:3 When many nations **g** together,
34:13 **g** them from the countries,
36:24 nations and **g** you from every
37:21 I will **g** them from everywhere
39:27 other nations and **g** them from
Hos 8:10 the nations, I will **g** them now.
10:10 Armies will **g** to attack them.
Joe 1:14 **G** the leaders and everyone
2:16 **G** the people. Prepare them for
2:16 **G** the children, even the
3:2 I will **g** all the nations.
3:11 and **g** there, all you nations.
Amo 3:9 "**G** together on the mountains
Mic 2:12 I will surely **g** all of you,
2:12 I will **g** them together like
4:6 "I will **g** those who are lame.
4:11 many nations **g** against you.
5:1 Now, **g** your troops,
Nah 3:18 and there is no one to **g** them.
Hab 1:9 They will **g** prisoners like sand.
1:15 and **g** them in dragnets.
Zep 1:2 "I will **g** everything on the face
2:1 **G** yourselves together!
2:1 together! Yes, **g** together,
3:8 I have decided to **g** nations,
3:18 "I will **g** those among you who

Zep 3:19 I will **g** those who have been
3:20 that time I will **g** you together.
Zec 10:8 them with a whistle and **g** them
10:10 I will **g** them from Assyria.
12:3 world will **g** to fight against
14:2 I will **g** all the nations to
Mat 3:12 He will **g** his wheat into a barn,
6:26 or **g** the harvest into barns.
12:30 doesn't **g** with me scatters.
13:30 I will tell the workers to **g** the
13:41 They will **g** everything in his
23:37 How often I wanted to **g** your
24:28 Vultures will **g** wherever there
24:31 they will **g** those whom God
25:24 and **g** where you haven't
25:26 I haven't planted and **g** where
Mar 13:27 they will **g** those whom God
Luk 3:17 He will **g** the wheat into his
11:23 doesn't **g** with me scatters.
13:34 How often I wanted to **g** your
17:37 "Vultures will **g** wherever there
Jon 6:12 "**G** the leftover pieces so that
18:20 where all the Jews **g**.
Act 5:16 around Jerusalem would **g**.
1Co 11:17 following matter: When you **g**,
11:18 I hear that when you **g** as a
11:20 When you **g** in the same place,
11:33 when you **g** to eat,
14:26 When you **g**, each person has
Jas 5:4 cries of those who **g** the crops.
Rev 14:15 your sickle, and **g** the harvest.
14:15 The time has come to **g** it,
14:18 and **g** the bunches of grapes
16:14 of the whole world and **g** them
19:17 **G** for the great banquet of God.
20:8 and **g** them for war.

gathered (161)

Gen 29:3 all the flocks were **g** there,
29:8 can't until all the flocks are **g**.
32:22 he got up and **g** his two wives,
37:7 bundles **g** around my bundle
48:2 Israel **g** his strength and sat up
Exo 16:17 Some **g** more, some less.
16:18 Those who had **g** more didn't
16:18 Those who had **g** less didn't
16:18 They **g** as much as they could
16:21 Each morning they **g** as much
16:22 But on the sixth day they **g**
32:1 they **g** around Aaron.
32:26 all the Levites **g** around him.
Lev 8:4 and the congregation **g** at the
23:39 when you have **g** what the land
Num 11:24 He **g** 70 of the leaders of the
11:32 went out and **g** the quails.
11:32 No one **g** less than 60 bushels.
16:19 When Korah had **g** all his
21:23 Sihon **g** all his troops and
Dtr 16:13 After you have **g** the grain from
Jos 18:1 of Israel **g** at Shiloh
22:12 of Israel **g** at Shiloh.
24:1 Joshua **g** all the tribes of Israel
Jdg 9:47 was told that they had **g** there,
10:17 The people of Israel also **g**
11:3 Worthless men **g** around
12:4 Then Jephthah **g** all the men of
16:23 Now, the Philistine rulers **g**
Rut 2:3 She entered a field and **g** the
2:17 So Ruth **g** grain in the field until
2:18 saw what she had **g**.
2:23 She **g** grain until both the
1Sm 7:6 So the Israelites **g** together at
7:7 the Israelites had **g** at Mizpah,
8:4 Then all the leaders of Israel **g**
17:47 Then everyone **g** here will
20:38 Jonathan's young servant **g** the
25:1 Samuel died, and all Israel **g** to
28:1 the Philistines had **g** their army
2Sm 2:30 When he had **g** all the troops,
12:29 So David **g** all the troops and
14:14 on the ground and can't be **g** up.
20:14 All the Berites were **g** together
21:13 his men **g** the bones of those
23:9 when the Philistines **g** there
23:11 The Philistines had **g** at Lehi,
1Ki 8:2 All the people of Israel **g**
1Ki 11:24 Rezon **g** men and became the
12:21 he **g** all the people of Judah
20:1 King Benhadad of Aram **g**
1Ch 11:1 All Israel **g** around David at
11:13 when the Philistines **g** there
13:5 So David **g** all Israel from the
19:7 The Ammonites **g** for the battle
23:2 He **g** all the officials of Israel
29:2 With all my might I **g** the
29:3 addition to everything else I **g**
29:16 all this wealth that we **g** to
2Ch 5:3 All the men of Israel **g** around
11:1 he **g** the people of Judah and
12:5 the leaders of Judah who had **g**
13:7 men **g** around him.
15:9 Then Asa **g** all the people from
15:10 they **g** in Jerusalem.
20:4 The people of Judah **g** to seek
20:26 On the fourth day they **g** in the
23:2 They went around Judah, **g** the
24:5 He **g** the priests and the
29:15 These men **g** their relatives
29:20 in the morning Hezekiah **g**
30:3 people hadn't **g** in Jerusalem.
30:13 Many people **g** in Jerusalem to
32:4 A large crowd **g** as they
32:6 over the troops and **g**
Ezr 3:1 the people **g** together in
7:28 So I **g** leaders in Israel to go
9:4 everyone who **g** around me
10:1 and children **g** around him.
10:9 Benjamin **g** within three days
Neh 5:16 All my men **g** here for work.
8:1 all the people **g** together in the
Est 2:8 many young women were **g**
2:19 When the virgins were **g** a
Job 4:8 misery, they **g** its harvest.
Psa 35:15 they rejoiced and **g** together.
35:15 They **g** together against me.
48:4 The kings have **g**.
107:3 and **g** from other countries,
107:32 the people are **g** for worship.
Pro 27:25 vegetables are **g** on the hills.
30:4 Who has **g** the wind in the
Ecc 2:8 I also **g** silver and gold for
2:8 I **g** the treasures of kings and
Isa 10:14 I've **g** the whole world as one
24:22 They'll be **g** like prisoners in a
27:12 you will be **g** one by one.
33:4 You nations, your loot is **g** as
41:5 They have come near and **g**
43:9 All nations have **g** together,
56:8 those I have already **g**."
Jer 8:2 bones will not be **g** or buried,
8:13 "'I would have **g** their harvest,'"
9:22 that has been cut but not **g**.
40:12 They **g** a large harvest of
40:15 All the Jews who have **g**
Eze 38:8 Its people have been **g** from
38:12 the people who were **g** from
Dan 3:27 and advisers **g** around the three
6:15 Then Daniel's accusers **g** in
Hos 1:11 and Israel will be **g** together.
Mat 13:2 The crowd that **g** around him
13:40 as weeds are **g** and burned,
13:47 It **g** all kinds of fish.
13:48 **g** the good fish into containers,
22:34 Sadducees, they **g** together.
22:41 the Pharisees were still **g**,
25:32 people of every nation will be **g**
26:3 and the leaders of the people **g**
26:57 and the leaders had **g** together.
27:17 So when the people **g**,
27:27 Jesus into the palace and **g**
27:62 and Pharisees **g** together
28:12 The chief priests **g** together
Mar 1:33 whole city had **g** at his door.
2:2 Many people had **g**.
3:20 Another crowd **g** so that Jesus
4:1 very large crowd **g** around him,
5:21 A large crowd **g** around him by
6:30 The apostles **g** around Jesus.
7:1 Jerusalem **g** around Jesus.
10:1 Crowds **g** around him again,
14:53 and scribes had **g** together.
Luk 5:15 Large crowds **g** to hear him and
Luk 8:4 When a large crowd had **g** and
12:1 thousands of people had **g**.
15:13 the younger son **g** his
22:66 and the scribes, **g** together.
23:48 Crowds had **g** to see the sight.
24:33 who were with them **g** together.
Jon 6:13 The disciples **g** the leftover
15:6 Branches like this are **g**,
18:2 and his disciples often **g** there.
Act 1:15 120 disciples had **g** together,
2:6 They **g** when they heard the
10:27 found that many people had **g**.
12:12 Many people had **g** at her home
13:44 almost the whole city **g** to hear
14:20 the disciples **g** around him,
15:30 They **g** the congregation
16:13 Jewish people **g** for prayer.
16:13 to the women who had **g** there.
19:19 in the occult **g** their books
28:3 Paul **g** a bundle of brushwood
1Co 5:4 When you have **g** together,
2Co 8:15 "Those who had **g** a lot didn't
8:15 and those who **g** a little didn't
Heb 12:22 of angels joyfully **g** together
Rev 14:19 his sickle on the earth and **g**
16:16 The spirits **g** the kings at the
19:19 and their armies **g** to wage war

gathering (21)

Lev 26:5 time will last until grape **g**,
26:5 and grape **g** will last until
Num 15:32 they found a man **g** wood on
15:33 Those who found him **g** wood
1Ki 17:10 a widow was **g** wood.
17:12 I'm **g** wood. I'm going to prepare
Psa 35:18 give you thanks in a large **g**.
Ecc 2:26 he gives the job of **g** and
Isa 13:4 and nations **g** together.
17:5 It will be like **g** grain in the
49:18 All of your children are **g**
Jer 7:11 name has become a **g** place
Mic 7:1 I am like those **g** summer fruit,
Mat 21:13 it into a **g** place for thieves!"
Mar 11:17 it into a **g** place for thieves."
Luk 11:29 the people were **g** around him,
19:46 it into a **g** place for thieves."
Jon 4:36 He is **g** grain for eternal life.
1Co 11:34 have a **g** that brings judgment
2Th 2:1 coming and our **g** to meet him.
Heb 10:25 We should not stop **g** together

gathers (13)

Job 5:5 What a stubborn fool **g**,
Psa 33:7 He **g** the water in the sea like a
147:2 He is the one who **g** the
Pro 6:8 At harvest time it **g** its food.
10:5 Whoever **g** in the summer is a
13:11 but whoever **g** little by little has
Isa 10:14 as one **g** abandoned eggs.
40:11 He **g** the lambs in his arms.
56:8 The Almighty LORD, who **g** the
Hab 2:5 He **g** all the nations to himself.
Mat 23:37 way a hen **g** her chicks under
Luk 13:34 way a hen **g** her chicks under
1Co 14:23 the whole congregation **g**

Gath Hepher (2)

Jos 19:13 there it goes directly east to **G**,
2Ki 14:25 the prophet from **G** and the son

Gath Rimmon (4)

Jos 19:45 Jehud, Bene Berak, **G**,
21:24 Aijalon, and **G**.
21:25 pasturelands: Taanach and **G**.
1Ch 6:69 and **G** with its pastureland.

Gath's (1)

1Ki 2:39 slaves fled to **G** King Achish,

gave (769)

Gen 3:6 She also **g** some to her
3:12 woman, the one you **g** me,
3:12 **g** me some fruit from the tree,
4:1 She became pregnant and **g**
4:2 Then she **g** birth to another
4:15 The LORD **g** Cain a sign so

Gen 4:17 She became pregnant and **g**
4:20 Adah **g** birth to Jabal.
4:25 She **g** birth to a son and named
9:3 I **g** you green plants as food;
12:20 Pharaoh **g** his men orders
14:20 Then Abram **g** him a tenth of
16:3 Egyptian slave Hagar and **g** her
16:5 I know that I **g** my slave to you,
16:15 Hagar **g** birth to Abram's son.
16:16 when Hagar **g** birth to Ishmael.
18:7 He **g** it to his servant,
19:11 with blindness so that they **g**
19:33 That night they **g** their father
19:35 That night they **g** their father
19:37 The older one **g** birth to a son
19:38 The younger daughter also **g**
20:14 and female slaves and **g** them
20:14 He also **g** his wife Sarah back
21:2 she **g** birth to a son for
21:14 a container of water and **g** them
21:14 He also **g** her the boy and sent
21:19 the container with water and **g**
21:27 sheep and cattle and **g** them
22:6 for the burnt offering and **g**
24:18 to her hand and **g** him a drink.
24:36 My master's wife Sarah **g** him a
24:53 jewelry and clothes and **g** them
24:53 He also **g** expensive presents
24:60 They **g** Rebekah a blessing:
25:2 Keturah **g** birth to these sons of
25:34 Then Jacob **g** Esau a meal of
26:5 and instructions I **g** him."
26:18 He **g** them the same names
27:17 Then she **g** her son Jacob the
27:27 He went over and **g** him a kiss.
28:4 land that God **g** to Abraham."
29:22 place and **g** a wedding feast.
29:28 Then Laban **g** his daughter
29:32 Leah became pregnant and **g**
29:33 pregnant again and **g** birth
29:34 pregnant again and **g** birth
29:35 pregnant again and **g** birth
30:4 So she **g** him her slave Bilhah
30:5 and she **g** birth to a son for
30:7 pregnant again and **g** birth
30:9 she took her slave Zilpah and **g**
30:10 Leah's slave Zilpah **g** birth to a
30:12 Leah's slave Zilpah **g** birth to
30:17 She became pregnant and **g**
30:18 reward because I **g** my slave
30:19 pregnant again and **g** birth
30:21 Later she **g** birth to a daughter
30:23 So she became pregnant and **g**
30:25 After Rachel **g** birth to Joseph,
30:39 Then they **g** birth to young that
31:8 all the flocks **g** birth to
31:8 all the flocks **g** birth to striped
34:13 Then Jacob's sons **g** Shechem
35:4 So they **g** Jacob all the foreign
35:12 I will give you the land that I **g**
36:4 Adah **g** birth to Eliphaz for
36:4 and Basemath **g** birth to Reuel.
36:5 Oholibamah **g** birth to Jeush,
36:12 She **g** birth to Amalek for
36:14 She **g** birth to Jeush,
38:3 She became pregnant and **g**
38:4 pregnant again and **g** birth
38:5 pregnant again and **g** birth
38:18 So he **g** them to her.
38:23 "Let her keep what I **g** her,
39:21 love and **g** him protection.
40:20 Of all his servants he **g** special
41:45 and **g** him Asenath as
41:49 that he finally **g** up keeping any
41:52 because God **g** him children in
42:25 Joseph **g** orders to fill their
42:25 his sack and **g** them supplies
43:3 Judah said to him, "The man **g**
43:24 He **g** them water to wash their
43:26 they **g** him the gifts they had
44:27 wife (Rachel) **g** me two sons.
45:21 Joseph **g** them wagons and
45:22 He **g** each of them a change of
45:22 but he **g** Benjamin three
46:15 of the sons Leah **g**
46:18 whom Laban **g** to his daughter
Gen 46:18 She **g** birth to these children for
46:25 whom Laban **g** to his daughter
46:25 She **g** birth to these sons for
47:11 He **g** them property there.
47:17 and he **g** them food in
49:28 said to them when he **g** each
49:29 Then he **g** them these
Exo 1:14 All the jobs the Egyptians **g**
1:21 he **g** them families of their own.
2:21 So Reuel **g** his daughter
2:22 She **g** birth to a son.
4:11 "Who **g** humans their mouths?
5:6 That same day Pharaoh **g**
6:20 She **g** birth to Aaron and
6:23 She **g** birth to Nadab,
6:25 She **g** birth to Phinehas.
12:36 and they **g** them what they
16:32 will see the food that I **g** you
31:18 Then he **g** him the two tablets
32:24 They **g** it to me. I threw it into
32:29 God **g** you a blessing today
36:6 So Moses **g** instructions to
Lev 7:38 On Mount Sinai the LORD **g**
9:12 Aaron's sons **g** him the blood,
9:13 They also **g** him the burnt
9:18 Aaron's sons **g** him the blood,
10:11 that I **g** them through Moses."
20:3 They **g** one of their children to
26:46 instructions that the LORD **g**
27:34 commands the LORD **g** Moses
Num 3:51 the LORD said and **g** Aaron
7:6 and the oxen and **g** them
7:7 He **g** two wagons and four
7:8 He **g** four wagons and eight
7:9 But Moses **g** none of these
13:16 But Moses **g** Hoshea,
13:26 They **g** their report and showed
15:22 commands the LORD **g** Moses.
15:23 the LORD **g** the commands.)
17:6 Their leaders **g** him 12 staffs,
22:18 "Even if Balak **g** me his palace
26:59 She **g** birth to Amram's children
27:23 and **g** him his instructions
30:16 These are the laws the LORD **g**
31:41 Moses **g** the LORD's taxes to
31:47 Then he **g** all this to the
32:28 So Moses **g** orders about them
32:33 So Moses **g** the tribes of Gad,
32:38 These are the names they **g**
32:40 So Moses **g** Gilead to the
36:5 So Moses **g** the Israelites a
36:13 and rules the LORD **g**
Dtr 1:1 This is the speech Moses **g** in
1:16 Also at that time I **g** these
2:12 the land that the LORD **g** them.
2:33 The LORD our God **g** Sihon to
2:36 The LORD our God **g** us all of
3:12 I **g** the tribes of Reuben and
3:13 I **g** the rest of Gilead and all of
3:15 I **g** Gilead to Machir.
3:16 I **g** the tribes of Reuben and
3:18 I **g** the tribes of Reuben and
3:19 here in the cities that I **g** you.
3:20 go back to the land I **g** you."
3:21 I also **g** Joshua this command:
4:45 and rules Moses **g** the
4:46 He **g** these to the people when
5:22 stone tablets and **g** them to me.
9:10 Then the LORD **g** me the two
9:11 the LORD **g** me the two stone
10:4 Then the LORD **g** them to me.
13:5 the LORD your God **g** you.
22:16 "I **g** my daughter in marriage to
26:9 brought us to this place and **g**
26:10 from the fields you **g** me,
27:11 That same day Moses **g** the
29:1 the LORD **g** them at Mount
29:8 We took their land and **g** it to
31:9 these teachings and **g** them
31:23 The LORD **g** this command to
31:25 He **g** this command to the
32:8 When the Most High **g** nations
32:13 He **g** them honey from rocks
32:14 He **g** them fat from lambs,
32:18 forgot the God who **g** you life.)
32:30 and the LORD **g** them no help.
Dtr 33:4 Moses **g** us these teachings.
Jos 1:14 the land that Moses **g** you east
1:15 LORD's servant Moses **g** you."
6:23 They **g** them a place outside
8:29 Joshua **g** the order to take his
10:27 Joshua **g** the order to take them
11:23 He **g** it to Israel as a
12:6 Then he **g** their land as a
12:7 Joshua **g** it as a possession to
13:15 Moses **g** some land as an
13:24 Moses **g** some land as an
13:29 Moses **g** some land as an
14:4 Joseph's descendants **g** the
14:13 and **g** him Hebron as his
15:13 Joshua **g** Caleb, son of
15:17 So Caleb **g** him his daughter
15:19 So Caleb **g** her the upper and
15:21 they **g** the tribe of Judah 29
15:33 In the foothills they **g** Judah 14
15:37 They also **g** Judah 16 other
15:48 In the mountains they **g** Judah
15:52 They also **g** Judah nine other
17:4 So they **g** them an inheritance
18:7 LORD's servant Moses **g** them
19:49 the people of Israel also **g** land
19:50 They **g** him the city he asked
21:8 The Israelites **g** these cities
21:10 that they **g** Aaron's
21:11 They **g** them Kiriath Arba (Arba
21:12 But they **g** its fields and
21:13 So they **g** the following cities
21:17 The tribe of Benjamin also **g**
21:23 The tribe of Dan **g** them four
21:25 Half of the tribe of Manasseh **g**
21:27 They **g** the families of
21:34 the tribe of Zebulun **g** four
21:36 The tribe of Reuben also **g**
21:38 The tribe of Gad also **g** them
21:43 So the LORD **g** Israel the
22:4 servant Moses **g** you east
22:5 LORD's servant Moses **g** you.
22:32 Canaan and **g** them the report.
22:34 tribes of Reuben and Gad **g**
23:1 the LORD **g** the Israelites
24:3 and **g** him many descendants.
24:3 I also **g** him Isaac.
24:4 To Isaac I **g** Jacob and Esau.
24:4 I **g** Esau the mountains in Seir
24:13 So I **g** you a land that you
Jdg 1:13 So Caleb **g** him his daughter
1:15 So Caleb **g** her the upper and
2:19 They never **g** up their evil
2:20 the promise I **g** their ancestors
4:19 But instead she **g** him milk to
5:25 She **g** him milk. She offered him
5:29 Her wisest servants **g** her an
6:9 of your way. I **g** you their land.
6:34 Spirit **g** Gideon strength.
7:16 He **g** them each rams' horns
8:8 But they **g** him the same reply
8:8 reply that the men of Succoth **g**.
8:31 at Shechem also **g** birth
9:4 So they **g** him 70 pieces of
11:2 Gilead's wife also **g** birth to
14:9 he **g** them some of the honey to
14:16 You **g** my friends a riddle and
14:19 He took their clothes and **g**
15:2 So I **g** her to your best man.
15:6 took Samson's wife and **g** her
16:24 "Our god **g** our enemy,
17:3 So Micah **g** the 1,100 pieces of
17:4 200 pieces of the silver and **g**
Rut 1:12 And even if I **g** birth to sons,
2:18 from lunch and **g** it to Naomi.
3:17 She said, "He **g** me these six
4:12 the son whom Tamar **g** birth to
4:13 and the LORD **g** her the ability
4:13 So she **g** birth to a son.
4:17 So they **g** him the name Obed.
1Sm 1:20 Hannah became pregnant and **g**
2:28 And I **g** your ancestors the right
4:19 labor prematurely and **g** birth
7:1 They **g** Abinadab's son Eleazar
9:23 the sacrificial meat that I **g** you
17:30 and the other soldiers **g** him the
18:4 off the coat he had on and **g**

1Sm 18:27 Then Saul **g** him his daughter
19:5 and the LORD **g** all Israel a
20:40 Then Jonathan **g** his weapons
21:6 So the priest **g** him holy
22:10 LORD for David and **g** him food
22:13 You **g** him bread and a sword
23:13 So he **g** up the campaign.
23:28 Saul **g** up pursuing David and
27:6 immediately **g** him Ziklag.
30:11 They **g** him food to eat and
30:12 They **g** him a slice of fig cake
2Sm 4:12 So David **g** an order to his
7:1 the LORD **g** him peace with all
8:6 the LORD **g** him victories.
8:14 the LORD **g** him victories.
11:27 Then she **g** birth to a son.
12:8 I **g** you your master Saul's
12:8 I **g** you the house of Israel and
12:24 and she later **g** birth to a son.
13:28 Then Absalom **g** an order to his
17:23 He **g** instructions to his family.
18:12 heard the order the king **g** you,
21:8 Rizpah (Aiah's daughter) **g** birth
21:8 Merab (Saul's daughter) **g** birth
24:23 All this Araunah **g** to the king
1Ki 1:5 His mother **g** birth to him after
2:15 because the LORD **g** it to him.
2:24 father David's throne and **g** me
2:25 King Solomon **g** this task to
2:43 obey the command I **g** you?
2:46 Then the king **g** orders to
3:17 I **g** birth ⌊to a son⌋ while she
3:18 this woman also **g** birth ⌊to
4:29 God **g** Solomon wisdom —
5:10 So Hiram **g** Solomon all the
5:11 Solomon **g** Hiram 120,000
5:12 The LORD **g** Solomon wisdom
8:34 that you **g** to their ancestors.
8:36 which you **g** to your people as
8:40 they live in the land that you **g**
8:48 land that you **g** their ancestors,
9:6 and laws that I **g** to you,
9:7 Israel out of the land I **g** them.
9:11 he **g** King Hiram of Tyre 20
9:12 see the cities Solomon **g** him.
9:16 Then he **g** it to his daughter,
10:10 She **g** the king 9,000 pounds of
10:10 of Sheba **g** King Solomon.
10:13 King Solomon **g** the queen of
10:24 wisdom that God **g** Solomon.
11:18 Pharaoh **g** Hadad a home,
11:19 So he **g** Hadad his
12:8 advice the older leaders **g** him.
12:13 advice the older leaders **g** him.
13:3 man of God ⌊also⌋ **g** ⌊them⌋
13:8 "Even if you **g** me half of your
13:21 that the LORD your God **g** you.
13:26 The LORD **g** him to the lion.
14:8 away from David's heirs and **g**
14:15 which he **g** their ancestors.
17:23 and **g** him to his mother.
18:26 They took the bull he **g** them,
19:21 He **g** the meat to the people to
2Ki 5:23 He **g** them to a couple of his
10:15 When he **g** Jehu his hand,
11:10 He **g** the commanders the
11:12 **g** him the crown and the
13:2 He never **g** up committing
13:5 So the LORD **g** the Israelites
13:11 evil and never **g** up committing
14:7 He **g** it the name Joktheel,
15:19 So Menahem **g** Pul 75,000
15:20 Each **g** 20 ounces of silver for
16:6 the Judeans out of Elath and **g**
16:15 King Ahaz **g** this command to
17:27 of Assyria **g** this command:
17:34 or commands that the LORD **g**
18:15 Hezekiah **g** him all the silver
18:16 He **g** the gold to the king of
21:8 wander from the land that I **g**
21:8 that my servant Moses **g** them."
22:8 Hilkiah **g** the book to Shaphan,
22:12 Then the king **g** an order to the
23:35 Jehoiakim **g** Pharaoh the silver
25:28 He treated him well and **g** him
25:30 The king of Babylon **g** him a

1Ch 1:32 **g** birth to the following sons:
2:4 **g** birth to Judah's sons Perez
2:19 Ephrath. She **g** birth to Hur.
2:21 She **g** birth to Segub.
2:24 Hezron's wife Abijah **g** birth to
2:29 She **g** birth to Ahban and Molid.
2:35 She **g** birth to Attai.
4:6 Naarah **g** birth to Ahuzzam,
4:10 God **g** him what he prayed for.
4:17 His wife **g** birth to Miriam,
6:64 So the Israelites **g** the Levites
6:65 They **g** ⌊them⌋ the cities
7:18 Bedan's sister Hammolecheth **g**
7:23 She **g** birth to a son,
12:18 Then the Spirit **g** Amasai,
16:40 Teachings that he **g** Israel.
18:6 the LORD **g** him victories.
18:13 the LORD **g** him victories.
21:25 So David **g** Ornan 15 pounds of
25:5 So God **g** Heman 14 sons and
28:11 Then David **g** his son Solomon
28:12 He **g** him plans for the
28:18 He also **g** Solomon the plans
29:6 of the king's work **g** generously.
29:7 They **g** 375,186 pounds of gold,
29:8 to have precious stones **g** them
29:9 the leaders **g** so generously
29:25 The people of Israel **g** him
2Ch 2:1 Solomon **g** orders to begin
6:25 back to the land that you **g**
6:27 which you **g** to your people as
6:31 they live in the land that you **g**
6:38 land that you **g** their ancestors,
7:19 and laws that I **g** you,
7:20 Israel from the land I **g** them.
8:2 rebuilt the cities Huram **g** him,
9:9 She **g** the king 9,000 pounds of
9:9 of Sheba **g** King Solomon.
9:12 King Solomon **g** the queen of
9:23 wisdom that God **g** Solomon.
10:8 advice the older leaders **g** him.
11:19 Mahalath **g** birth to the
11:20 She **g** birth to Abijah,
11:23 He **g** them allowances and
13:5 that the LORD God of Israel **g**
13:11 the LORD our God **g** us,
14:6 years because the LORD **g** him
17:5 All the people of Judah **g** gifts
20:11 of your land that you **g** to us.
20:27 The LORD **g** them a reason to
21:3 Their father **g** them many gifts:
21:3 But Jehoshaphat **g** the
22:3 because his mother **g** him
23:9 Jehoiada **g** the commanders
23:11 **g** him the crown and the
24:20 God's Spirit **g** Zechariah,
25:9 the 7,500 pounds of silver I **g**
26:5 the LORD **g** him success.
27:5 That year the Ammonites **g**
27:5 The Ammonites **g** him the
28:15 prisoners and **g** clothes from
28:15 for them, **g** them sandals,
28:15 **g** them something to eat and
28:21 and he **g** them to the king of
30:12 the king and the leaders **g** from
32:22 The LORD **g** them peace with
32:24 who answered him and **g** him a
33:8 ⌊I **g**⌋ through Moses."
34:9 chief priest Hilkiah and **g** him
34:10 They **g** the money to the
34:10 These foremen **g** it to the
34:15 Hilkiah **g** the book to Shaphan.
34:17 in the LORD's temple and **g**
34:20 Then the king **g** an order to
35:8 His officials also voluntarily **g**
35:8 **g** the priests 2,600 sheep and
35:9 **g** the Levites 5,000 sheep and
Ezr 3:7 So they **g** money to the
3:7 Then they **g** food, drink,
3:11 As they praised and **g** thanks
4:19 I **g** the order, and a search was
5:3 "Who **g** you permission to
5:9 "Who **g** you permission to
5:13 Cyrus **g** permission for God's
5:14 Cyrus **g** them to a man named
5:17 King Cyrus **g** permission

Ezr 6:1 Then King Darius **g** the order to
7:6 The king **g** Ezra everything he
7:11 that King Artaxerxes **g** Ezra
8:36 These officials then **g** their
9:11 The commandments you **g** us
Neh 1:7 or regulations that you **g** us
2:1 up the cup of wine and **g**
2:6 When I **g** him a specific date,
2:9 the Euphrates River and **g** them
9:7 Ur of the Chaldeans and **g** him
9:13 You **g** them fair rules,
9:14 You **g** them commandments,
9:15 You **g** them bread from heaven
9:19 but it **g** them light to see the
9:20 You **g** them your good Spirit to
9:20 You **g** them water to quench
9:22 You **g** kingdoms and nations to
9:25 of good things you **g** them.
9:27 You **g** them saviors to rescue
9:29 But they **g** you the cold
9:34 the warnings that you **g** them.
9:35 good things that you **g** them
9:36 In the land you **g** our ancestors,
Est 3:1 He **g** Haman a position higher
3:10 removed his signet ring and **g**
4:8 He also **g** him a copy of the
4:8 The decree **g** permission to
8:1 that same day King Xerxes **g**
8:2 and **g** it to Mordecai.
Job 4:4 you **g** them strength.
10:12 You **g** me life and mercy.
28:25 When he **g** the wind its force
38:28 Who **g** birth to the dewdrops?
38:36 in the heart or **g** understanding
39:6 I **g** it the desert to live in and
42:10 prosperity and **g** him twice as
42:11 Each one **g** him some money
42:15 Their father **g** them and their
Psa 21:2 You **g** him his heart's desire.
21:4 You **g** him a long life,
33:9 He **g** the order, and there it
69:21 they **g** me vinegar to drink.
71:3 You **g** the order to save me!
74:14 heads of Leviathan and **g** them
78:5 He **g** his teachings to Israel.
78:15 He **g** them plenty to drink,
78:24 to eat and **g** them grain from
78:29 He **g** them what they wanted,
78:46 He **g** their crops to
78:55 out of their way and **g** them
90:2 before you **g** birth to the earth
99:7 and the laws that he **g** them.
105:32 He **g** them hail and lightning
105:44 He **g** them the lands of ⌊other⌋
106:7 they **g** no thought to your
106:15 He **g** them what they asked for.
106:15 He ⌊also⌋ **g** them a
107:9 He **g** plenty to drink to those
119:49 the word ⌊you **g**⌋ me.
119:49 Through it you **g** me hope.
119:50 Your promise **g** me a new life.
119:93 because you **g** me a new life
135:12 He **g** their land as an
136:21 He **g** their land as an
137:8 the same treatment you **g** us.
Pro 23:25 May she who **g** birth to you
31:2 What, son to whom I **g** birth?
Ecc 12:7 life goes back to God who **g** it.
Sos 6:9 She is pure to the one who **g**
8:5 There she went into labor and **g**
Isa 8:3 She became pregnant and **g**
23:13 Assyria **g** this land to the
40:14 Who **g** him understanding?
41:27 I **g** Jerusalem a messenger
42:5 He **g** life to the people who are
42:24 Who **g** Jacob away as loot and
51:2 and **g** him many descendants.
51:18 all the children she **g** birth to,
54:1 women who never **g** birth
66:8 she also **g** birth to her children.
Jer 3:8 and that I **g** Israel her divorce
3:18 land that I **g** their ancestors as
7:7 in the land that I **g** permanently
7:14 This is the place I **g** to you and
12:14 that I **g** my people Israel:
16:15 the land that I **g** their ancestors.

Jer 17:4 the inheritance that I **g** you.
20:14 the day that my mother **g** birth
23:39 and out of the city that I **g** you
24:10 disappear from the land that I **g**
25:5 that the LORD permanently **g**
30:3 the land that I **g** their ancestors,
32:9 my cousin Hanamel and **g** him
32:12 I **g** the copies of the deeds to
32:13 Then I **g** Baruch these orders:
32:22 You **g** them the land that you
35:6 Rechab's son, **g** us this order:
35:15 will live in the land that I **g** you
36:32 took another scroll and **g**
37:21 King Zedekiah **g** the command
37:21 He **g** him a loaf of bread every
38:10 Then the king **g** Ebed Melech
38:16 "The LORD **g** us life.
39:10 At that time he **g** them
39:11 of Babylon **g** Nebuzaradan
40:5 The captain of the guard **g**
44:10 decrees that I **g** your ancestors.
50:12 The woman who **g** birth to you
51:59 prophet Jeremiah **g** to Seraiah,
52:32 He treated him well and **g** him
52:34 The king of Babylon **g** him a
Lam 1:9 It **g** no thought to its future.
2:14 They **g** you false prophecies
3:37 It was the Lord who **g** the order.
Eze 3:2 and he **g** me the scroll to eat.
16:11 I **g** you jewelry. I put bracelets
16:14 because I **g** you my glory,
16:19 You **g** flour, olive oil,
16:19 and honey — all the food that I **g**
16:36 body when you **g** yourself
20:11 I **g** them my laws and made my
20:12 I also **g** them certain days to
23:4 I married them, and they **g** birth
23:37 the children they **g** birth
28:25 the land I **g** to my servant
31:6 All the wild animals **g** birth to
36:28 the land that I **g** your ancestors.
37:25 land that I **g** my servant Jacob,
44:16 and take care of everything I **g**
Dan 1:7 The chief-of-staff **g** them
1:7 To Daniel he **g** the name
1:7 To Hananiah he **g** the name
1:7 To Mishael he **g** the name
1:7 he **g** the name Abednego.
1:16 wine and **g** them vegetables.
1:17 God **g** these four men
2:12 so angry and furious that he **g**
2:23 You **g** me wisdom and power.
2:48 and **g** him many wonderful
3:10 Your Majesty, you **g** an order
5:18 the Most High God **g** your
5:19 because God **g** him power.
6:16 So the king **g** the order,
9:10 or lived by the teachings you **g**
Hos 2:8 believe that I **g** her grain,
2:8 I **g** her plenty of silver and gold,
2:9 wool and the linen that I **g** her
12:10 I spoke to the prophets and **g**
13:11 I **g** you a king when I was
Amo 9:15 from the land that I **g** them,
Zec 11:13 I **g** the pieces of silver to the
13:3 who **g** birth to him,
13:3 who **g** birth to him,
Mal 2:5 I **g** them to him so that he
4:4 rules and regulations that I **g**
Mat 1:25 with her before she **g** birth
3:15 Then John **g** in to him.
8:26 Then he got up, **g** an order to
10:1 disciples and **g** them authority
14:19 **g** them to the disciples,
14:19 and they **g** them to the people.
15:36 and the fish and **g** thanks
15:36 Then he broke the bread and **g**
15:36 and they **g** the bread and fish to
19:29 And everyone who **g** up homes,
20:14 last worker as much as I **g** you.
25:15 He **g** one man ten thousand
25:20 you **g** me ten thousand dollars.
25:22 you **g** me four thousand dollars.
25:35 and you **g** me something to eat.
25:35 I was thirsty, and you **g** me
25:36 I needed clothes, and you **g** me
Mat 25:42 and you **g** me nothing to eat.
25:42 and you **g** me nothing to drink.
26:26 **g** it to his disciples,
26:27 He **g** it to them and said,
27:34 They **g** him a drink of wine
27:50 once again and **g** up his life.
28:12 They **g** the soldiers a large
Mar 2:26 ever read how he also **g** some
3:12 He **g** them orders not to tell
6:2 Who **g** him this kind of wisdom
6:7 and **g** them authority over evil
6:21 Herod **g** a dinner for his top
6:28 the head on a platter and **g**
6:28 and the girl **g** it to her mother.
6:41 He also **g** pieces of the two
8:6 He took the seven loaves and **g**
8:6 Then he broke the bread and **g**
9:25 he **g** an order to the evil spirit.
10:29 Anyone who **g** up his home,
14:22 He broke the bread, **g** it to them,
14:23 and **g** the cup to them.
14:56 Many **g** false testimony against
14:57 Then some men stood up and **g**
15:39 saw how he **g** up his spirit,
16:19 where God **g** him the highest
Luk 1:57 she **g** birth to a son.
2:7 She **g** birth to her firstborn son.
4:17 The attendant **g** him the book
4:20 **g** it back to the attendant,
6:4 and **g** some of it to the men
6:39 Jesus also **g** them this
7:15 and Jesus **g** him back to his
9:1 together and **g** them power
9:42 He cured the boy and **g** him
10:35 out two silver coins and **g** them
11:27 is the mother who **g** birth
14:16 Jesus said to him, "A man **g** a
18:29 Anyone who **g** up his home,
19:13 servants and **g** them ten coins.
19:15 servants to whom I **g** money.
19:16 the coin you **g** me has earned
19:18 'The coin you **g** me,
20:7 they didn't know who **g** John
22:19 He broke the bread, **g** it to them,
22:43 to him and **g** him strength.
24:30 the bread and **g** it to them.
24:42 They **g** him a piece of broiled
Jon 1:12 However, he **g** the right to
3:16 He **g** his only Son so that
4:12 He **g** us this well. He and his
5:35 John was a lamp that **g** off
5:36 The tasks that the Father **g** me
6:11 took the loaves, **g** thanks,
6:23 bread after the Lord **g** thanks.
6:31 Scripture says, 'He **g** them
6:39 to lose any of those he **g** me.
7:22 Moses **g** you the teaching
9:14 mixed the spit and dirt and **g**
9:17 the man who **g** you sight?"
9:21 how he got his sight or who **g**
9:24 We know that this man who **g**
9:30 Yet, he **g** me sight.
10:29 My Father, who **g** them to me,
10:35 to whom he **g** the Scriptures),
11:37 "Couldn't this man who **g** a
13:26 Jesus dipped the bread and **g**
17:2 life to all those you **g** to him.
17:4 the work you **g** me to do.
17:6 known to the people you **g** me.
17:6 and you **g** them to me.
17:7 you **g** me comes from
17:8 because I **g** them the message
17:8 the message that you **g** me.
17:9 world but for those you **g** me,
17:11 the name that you **g** me,
17:12 the name that you **g** me.
17:22 them the glory that you **g** me.
17:24 which you **g** me because you
18:9 "I lost none of those you **g** me."
19:38 Pilate **g** him permission to
21:13 took the bread, **g** it to them,
Act 1:2 he **g** instructions through the
2:4 languages as the Spirit **g** them
2:22 amazing things, and **g** signs.
5:28 He said, "We **g** you strict
6:14 the customs that Moses **g** us."
Act 7:8 "God **g** Abraham circumcision
7:10 God **g** Joseph divine favor and
9:36 helped people and **g** things
10:2 Cornelius **g** many gifts to poor
11:17 When they believed, God **g**
11:17 them the same gift that he **g**
12:19 the guards and **g** orders
13:19 in Canaan and **g** their land
13:20 "After that he **g** his people
13:21 so God **g** them Saul,
13:47 The Lord **g** us the following
15:8 them the Holy Spirit as he **g**
16:34 home and **g** them something
21:40 The officer **g** Paul permission
22:5 In fact, they even **g** me letters
23:35 Then the governor **g** orders to
25:23 Festus **g** the order,
Rom 8:30 and he **g** glory to those whom
11:35 Who **g** the Lord something
12:6 God in his kindness **g** each of
15:15 this because God **g** me the gift
1Co 3:2 I **g** you milk to drink.
3:5 did what the Lord **g** him to do.
3:10 I used the gift that God **g** me to
7:17 that the Lord **g** him when God
12:13 God **g** all of us one Spirit to
2Co 2:12 the Lord **g** me an opportunity to
8:5 First, they **g** themselves to the
9:7 shouldn't be sorry that you **g**
10:8 authority which the Lord **g** us,
10:8 The Lord **g** us this authority to
13:10 the authority that the Lord **g** me
13:10 The Lord **g** us this authority to
Gal 1:8 Good News we **g** you should
3:18 However, God freely **g** the
4:4 A woman **g** birth to him,
Eph 1:20 him back to life and **g** him
3:2 you have heard how God **g** me
4:7 out to us by Christ who **g** it.
4:8 us and **g** gifts to people."
4:11 He also **g** apostles,
5:2 He **g** his life for us as an
5:25 loved the church and **g** his life
Php 4:15 You **g** me what I needed,
4:15 and you received what I **g** you.
Col 1:25 of the church when God **g** me
1Th 2:2 But our God **g** us the courage
4:2 You know what orders we **g**
2Th 1:10 the testimony we **g** you.
2:16 loved us and by his kindness **g**
3:10 we **g** you the order:
1Ti 1:14 he brought me to faith and **g** me
6:13 who **g** a good testimony in front
2Ti 4:17 the Lord stood by me and **g** me
Tit 2:14 He **g** himself for us to set us
Heb 7:2 Abraham **g** Melchizedek a
7:4 Abraham **g** him a tenth of what
7:9 when Abraham **g** Melchizedek
7:9 Levi **g**, although later his
8:4 the instructions that Moses **g**.
10:29 he insults the Spirit that God **g**
1Pe 1:21 back to life and **g** him glory.
2Pe 3:15 using the wisdom God **g** him.
1Jn 3:16 we realize that Christ **g** his life
Rev 1:1 God **g** it to him to show his
2:21 I **g** her time to turn to me and
11:13 They **g** glory to the God of
12:5 She **g** birth to a son,
13:2 The serpent **g** its power,
15:7 creatures **g** seven gold bowls
18:6 her twice as much as she **g**.
18:7 She **g** herself glory and luxury.
20:13 The sea **g** up its dead.
20:13 Death and hell **g** up their dead.
21:23 the glory of God **g** it light.

gawk (2)

Lam 2:16 All your enemies **g** at you.
3:46 All our enemies **g** at us.

Gaza (26)

Gen 10:19 Sidon toward Gerar as far as **G**
Dtr 2:23 in villages as far away as **G**.
Jos 10:41 from Kadesh Barnea to **G**
11:22 Some of them were left in **G**,
13:3 are five Philistine rulers over **G**,

Dtr 29:22 Then the next g of your
Jdg 2:10 That whole g had joined their
2:10 So another g grew up after
1Ch 17:17 you've shown me the g of the
Psa 22:30 a g that will be told about the
33:11 thoughts stand firm in every g.
45:17 throughout every g.
48:13 Then you can tell the next g,
49:11 places throughout every g.
49:19 he must join the g of his
61:6 endure throughout every g.
72:5 ⌊shine⌋ — throughout every g.
77:8 canceled throughout every g?
78:4 We will tell the next g about
78:6 so that the next g would know
78:8 a stubborn and rebellious g.
79:13 praise you throughout every g.
89:1 your faithfulness to every g.
89:4 last throughout every g.'" Selah
90:1 our refuge throughout every g.
100:5 endures throughout every g.
102:12 throughout every g.
102:18 down for a future g so that
102:24 on⌋ throughout every g.
106:31 throughout every g.
109:13 be wiped out by the next g.
119:90 endures throughout every g.
135:13 throughout every g.
145:4 One g will praise your deeds to
145:4 Each g will talk about your
145:13 endures throughout every g.
146:10 God rules throughout every g.
Pro 27:24 last from one g to the next.
Isa 51:8 will last throughout every g.
Jer 2:31 of the LORD, people of this g.
7:29 abandoned the people of this g.
Lam 5:19 continues throughout every g.
Dan 4:3 lasts from one g to the next.
4:34 lasts from one g to the next.
Mat 17:17 "You unbelieving and corrupt g!
24:34 This g will not disappear until
Mar 8:38 in this unfaithful and sinful g,
9:19 "You unbelieving g!
13:30 This g will not disappear until
Luk 1:50 mercy lasts throughout every g.
9:41 "You unbelieving and corrupt g!
21:32 This g will not disappear until
Act 2:40 yourselves from this corrupt g."
8:33 Who from his g will talk about
Jud 1:14 from the seventh g after Adam,

generations (68)

Gen 9:12 that is with you for g to come.
17:7 you and your descendants for g
17:9 and your descendants in g
17:12 For g to come every male child
Exo 12:14 a permanent law for g to come:
12:17 is a permanent law for future g:
12:42 (All Israelites in future g must
20:6 I show mercy to thousands of g
27:21 the Israelites for g to come."
29:42 "For g to come this will be the
30:8 For g to come an incense
30:10 Once a year — for g to come —
30:21 his descendants for g to come."
30:31 the Israelites, 'For g to come,
31:13 sign between me and you for g
31:16 celebrating it for g to come as a
34:7 his love to thousands of g,
40:15 for them for g to come."
Lev 3:17 This is a permanent law for g
6:18 It is a permanent law for g to
7:34 a permanent law for g to come.
7:36 a permanent law for g to come."
10:9 a permanent law for g to come.
17:7 for the people and for future g.
21:17 (now or in future g) has
22:3 "Tell them: In future g if any of
23:14 It is a permanent law for g to
23:21 It is a permanent law for g to
23:31 It is a permanent law for g to
23:41 a permanent law for g to come.
23:43 so that g to come may learn
24:3 a permanent law for g to come.
25:30 to the buyer for g to come.
Num 15:14 or living among you in future g.
Num 15:15 is a permanent law for future g.
15:21 For g to come, you must give
15:23 Moses holds as true for g
15:38 For g to come they must wear
18:23 is a permanent law for future g.
35:29 for future g wherever you live.
Dtr 5:10 I show mercy to thousands of g
7:9 is merciful to thousands of g
23:2 of the LORD for ten g.
23:3 of the LORD for ten g.
32:7 Think about all the past g.
Jos 22:27 between us for g to come.
2Ki 10:30 That is why four g of your
15:12 "Four g of your descendants
1Ch 16:15 commanded for a thousand g,
Est 9:28 be forgotten by the g to come.
Job 8:8 "Ask the people of past g.
Psa 85:5 of your anger in the g to come?
105:8 commanded for a thousand g,
Ecc 1:4 G come, and generations go,
1:4 Generations come, and g go,
Isa 13:20 and no one will live in it for g.
34:10 Edom will lie in ruins for g.
34:17 and live there for g.
51:9 long past, as in g long ago.
58:12 the foundations of past g.
60:15 everlasting pride, a joy for all g.
61:4 the places destroyed g ago.
Jer 32:18 show mercy to thousands of g.
50:39 be inhabited or lived in for g.
Mat 1:17 So there were 14 g from
1:17 14 g from David until the exile
1:17 14 g from the exile until the
Act 15:21 been spread to every city for g.

generosity (7)

1Ki 10:13 had given her out of his royal g.
Est 1:7 of royal wine out of his royal g.
2:18 out gifts from his royal g.
Mat 20:15 resent my g towards others?'
2Co 9:11 Your g will produce
9:13 of Christ and because of your g
Eph 2:7 Christ Jesus out of his g

generous (17)

Exo 12:36 LORD made the Egyptians g
Dtr 15:8 Be g to these poor people,
15:11 why I command you to be g
15:14 Be as g to them as the LORD
Psa 37:21 person is g and giving.
37:26 He is always g and lends
112:5 well for the person who is g
Pro 11:25 A g person will be made rich,
19:6 win the kindness of a g person,
22:9 Whoever is g will be blessed
Rom 12:8 If it is sharing, be g.
2Co 8:2 has made them even more g.
8:20 we are administering this g gift.
9:11 so that you can always be g.
1Ti 6:18 things, to be g, and to share.
Tit 3:6 God poured a g amount of the
Jas 1:5 God is g to everyone and

generously (5)

Dtr 15:14 G give them provisions —
1Ch 29:6 of the king's work gave g.
29:9 that the leaders gave so g
29:14 you enable us to give so g?
Pro 1:23 I will g pour out my spirit for

genitals (2)

Dtr 25:11 by grabbing the other man's g,
Eze 23:20 whose g were like those of

Gennesaret (2)

Mat 14:34 the sea and landed at G.
Mar 6:53 came to shore at G,

gentle (17)

Dtr 32:2 like g rain on grass,
Pro 15:1 A g answer turns away rage,
Mat 5:5 Blessed are those who are g.
11:29 because I am g and humble.
21:5 He's g, riding on a donkey, on a
Act 27:13 When a g breeze began to
1Co 4:21 show you love and a g spirit?
Gal 6:1 Do it in a g way. At the same
Eph 4:2 Be humble and g in every way.
Col 3:12 kind, humble, g, and patient.
1Th 2:7 Instead, we were g when we
1Ti 3:3 person, but he must be g.
2Ti 2:25 He must be g in correcting
Tit 3:2 but they should be g and show
Heb 5:2 The chief priest can be g with
Jas 3:17 Then it is peaceful, g,
1Pe 3:4 Beauty expresses itself in a g

gentlemen (3)

Gen 19:2 He said, "Please, g,
Num 32:4 G, we have livestock.
Isa 32:5 scoundrels be considered g.

gentleness (5)

Psa 18:35 Your g makes me great.
2Co 10:1 my appeal to you with the g
Gal 5:23 g, and self-control. There are
1Ti 6:11 faith, love, endurance, and g.
1Pe 3:15 defense with g and respect.

gently (8)

Gen 33:14 I will slowly and g guide the
2Sm 18:5 the young man Absalom g
1Ki 12:7 humble yourself, and speak g,
2Ch 10:7 them by speaking g to them,
Job 15:11 even when g spoken to you?
29:22 my words fell g on them.
Isa 8:6 rejected the g flowing water
40:11 He g helps the sheep and their

Genubath (2)

1Ki 11:20 sister had a son ⌊named⌋ G.
11:20 and G lived in the palace

genuine (9)

1Co 11:19 who the g believers among you
2Co 8:8 but I'm testing how g your love
9:13 honor God through this g act
Php 2:20 He takes a g interest in your
1Ti 1:2 To Timothy, a g child in faith.
Tit 1:4 a g child in the faith we share.
Jas 2:22 His faith was shown to be g by
1Pe 1:7 faith as fire tests how g gold is.
5:12 that this is God's g good will.

Gera (8)

Gen 46:21 Ashbel, G, Naaman, Ehi, Rosh,
Jdg 3:15 (Ehud was the son of G.)
2Sm 16:5 name was Shimei, son of G.
1Ki 2:8 "Shimei, son of G from
1Ch 8:3 Bela's sons were Addar, G,
8:5 G, Shephuphan, and Huram.
8:7 Naaman, Ahijah, and G.
8:7 G led the rest of them away as

gerahs (1)

Eze 45:12 One shekel must weigh 20 g.

Gerar (10)

Gen 10:19 from Sidon toward G as far as
20:1 While he was living in G,
20:2 So King Abimelech of G sent
26:1 of the Philistines in G.
26:6 So Isaac lived in G.
26:17 He set up his tents in the G
26:20 The herders from G quarreled
26:26 came from G to see Isaac.
2Ch 14:13 pursued them as far as G.
14:14 attacked all the cities around G

Gera's (2)

2Sm 19:16 Shimei, G son from the tribe of
19:18 Shimei, G son, bowed down in

Gerasenes (3)

Mar 5:1 arrived in the territory of the G
Luk 8:26 of the G across from Galilee.
8:37 region of the G asked Jesus

Gerizim (4)

Dtr 11:29 the blessing from Mount G
27:12 that will stand on Mount G
Jos 8:33 people were in front of Mount G

Jdg 9:7 to a high spot on Mount G.

Gershom (8)

Exo 2:22 named him G [Foreigner],
18:3 son was named G [Foreigner],
Jdg 18:30 Jonathan (son of G and
1Ch 6:16 Levi's sons were G,
6:43 who was the son of G,
23:15 sons were G and Eliezer.
26:24 a descendant of Moses' son G.
Ezr 8:2 G from the family of Ithamar:

Gershom's (6)

1Ch 6:17 are the names of G sons: Libni
6:20 G son was Libni. Libni's son
6:62 The families of G descendants
6:71 G descendants received Golan
15:7 Leading G descendants was
23:16 G only son was Shebuel.

Gershon (13)

Gen 46:11 The sons of Levi were G,
Exo 6:16 order: G, Kohath, and Merari.
6:17 The sons of G listed by their
Num 3:17 G, Kohath, and Merari were the
3:18 and Shimei were the sons of G.
3:21 To G belonged the families
3:21 the families descended from G.
3:23 The families descended from G
26:57 were listed as the family of G,
1Ch 6:1 Levi's sons were G,
23:6 on which of Levi's sons (G,
26:21 who was descended from G.
26:21 the descendant of G,

Gershonite (4)

Num 3:24 The leader of the G
4:24 "This is what the G families
4:28 This is the work of the G
4:41 in the G families who worked

Gershonites (7)

Num 3:25 At the tent of meeting the G
4:22 "Also take a census of the G.
4:26 The G will do everything that
4:38 The G were registered by
4:41 Moses and registered the G.
7:7 wagons and four oxen to the G
10:17 and the G and Merarites,

Gershon's (6)

Jos 21:6 G descendants received 13
21:27 of G descendants, who were
21:33 were given to G families
1Ch 23:7 Shimei were G descendants
29:8 G descendant, for the treasury
2Ch 29:12 From G descendants were

Geruth Kimham (1)

Jer 41:17 stayed near Bethlehem at G

Geshan (1)

1Ch 2:47 G, Pelet, Ephah, and Shaaph.

Geshem (4)

Neh 2:19 and G the Arab heard about
6:1 Sanballat, Tobiah, G the Arab,
6:2 Then Sanballat and G sent this
6:6 and G has confirmed it,

Geshur (11)

Jos 12:5 to the border of G and Maacath,
13:2 belong to the Philistines and G.
13:11 the people of G and Maacath,
13:13 the people of G and Maacath.
2Sm 3:3 of King Talmai) from G.
13:38 Absalom, having fled to G,
14:23 So Joab went to G and brought
14:32 him why I had to come from G.
15:8 while I was living at G in Aram.
1Ch 2:23 G and Aram captured Havvoth
3:2 of King Talmai) from G.

Geshurites (2)

Dtr 3:14 as far as the border of the G
1Sm 27:8 and his men went to raid the G,

Geshur's (1)

2Sm 13:37 fled to G King Talmai,

gesture (1)

Zep 2:15 hiss and make an obscene g.

Gether (2)

Gen 10:23 were Uz, Hul, G, and Mash.
1Ch 1:17 Uz, Hul, G, and Meshech.

Gethsemane (2)

Mat 26:36 disciples to a place called G.
Mar 14:32 they came to a place called G.

Geuel (1)

Num 13:15 G, son of Machi, from the tribe

Gezer (15)

Jos 10:33 At that time King Horam of G
12:12 the king of Eglon, the king of G,
16:3 and Lower Beth Horon, on to G,
16:10 the Canaanites who lived in G.
21:21 the mountains of Ephraim, G,
Jdg 1:29 the Canaanites who lived in G.
1:29 to live with them in G.
2Sm 5:25 the Philistines from Geba to G.
1Ki 9:15 of Hazor, Megiddo, and G.
9:16 (The king of Egypt captured G,
9:17 So Solomon rebuilt G,
1Ch 6:67 G with its pastureland,
7:28 G with its villages to the west,
14:16 army from Gibeon to G.
20:4 out with the Philistines at G.

ghost (4)

Isa 29:4 of the ground like that of a g.
Mat 14:26 They said, "It's a g!"
Mar 6:49 the sea, they thought, "It's a g!"
Luk 24:37 thought they were seeing a g.

ghosts (4)

Dtr 18:11 ask g or spirits for help,
Isa 14:9 It wakes up the g of the dead,
19:3 They will turn to idols, g,
Luk 24:39 G don't have flesh and bones,

Giah (1)

2Sm 2:24 opposite G on the road from

Gibbar (1)

Ezr 2:20 of G: 95

Gibbethon (5)

Jos 19:44 Eltekeh, G, Baalath,
21:23 them four cities: Eltekeh, G,
1Ki 15:27 city of G while Nadab
16:15 near the Philistine city of G.
16:17 him left G and attacked Tirzah.

Gibea (1)

1Ch 2:49 first settled Machbenah and G.

Gibeah (47)

Jos 15:57 Kain, G, and Timnah.
Jdg 19:12 Israelites. We'll go on to G."
19:13 the night either at G or Ramah."
19:14 by the time they arrived at G.
19:14 (G belonged to the tribe of
19:15 The Levite entered G and sat
19:16 of Ephraim but lived in G.
20:4 "My concubine and I went to G
20:5 The citizens of G came to
20:6 citizens of G did this perverted
20:9 This is what we'll do to G.
20:10 When the troops go to G in the
20:10 can punish the citizens of G
20:13 over those worthless men in G.
20:14 towns and assembled at G
20:19 the morning and camped at G.
20:20 their battle line facing G.
20:21 of Benjamin came out from G.
20:25 Benjamin went out from G to
20:29 troops in ambush around G.
20:30 battle line facing G as they did
20:31 on the roads to Bethel and G.
Jdg 20:33 their position to the west of G.
20:34 of Israel's best men attacked G.
20:36 waiting in ambush near G.
20:37 quickly charged toward G.
20:43 They overtook them east of G.
1Sm 10:26 Saul also went home to G.
11:4 came to Saul's town, G.
13:2 Jonathan at G in Benjamin.
13:15 from Gilgal to G in Benjamin,
14:2 on the outskirts of G under
14:16 Saul's watchmen at G in
15:34 Saul went to his home at G.
22:6 Saul was staying in G under
23:19 men of Ziph went to Saul in G.
26:1 of Ziph came to Saul at G.
2Sm 21:6 presence at Saul's town G."
23:29 of Ribai) from G in Benjamin,
1Ch 11:31 of Ribai) from G in Benjamin,
12:3 the sons of Shemaah from G),
2Ch 13:2 daughter of Uriel from G.
Isa 10:29 the people in Saul's G flee.
Hos 5:8 "Blow the ram's horn in G.
9:9 as they once did at G.
10:9 ever since the incident at G.
10:9 the wicked people in G.

Gibeah's (1)

Jdg 20:15 along with 700 of G best men.

Gibeath (1)

Jos 18:28 Jerusalem), G, and Kiriath.

Gibeon (42)

Jos 9:3 When the people living in G
9:17 They came to the cities of G,
9:22 for the people of G and asked,
10:1 people of G had made peace
10:2 terribly afraid because G was
10:4 "Come, help me destroy G
10:5 They marched to G,
10:6 The men of G sent this
10:10 defeated them decisively at G.
10:12 stand still over G, and moon,
10:41 country of Goshen as far as G.
11:19 the people of Israel except G,
18:25 villages: G, Ramah, Beeroth,
21:17 gave them four cities: G, Geba,
2Sm 2:12 went from Mahanaim to G.
2:13 groups met at the pool of G.
2:16 Therefore, that place in G is
2:24 the road from G to the desert.
3:30 Asahel in the battle at G.)
20:8 were at the large rock in G,
21:1 they killed the people of G."
1Ki 3:4 King Solomon went to G to
3:5 In G the LORD appeared to
9:2 he had appeared to him in G.
1Ch 8:29 Jeiel, who first settled G,
8:29 first settled Gibeon, lived in G,
9:35 Jeiel, who first settled G,
9:35 first settled Gibeon, lived in G,
12:4 Ishmaiah from G (one of the
14:16 army from G to Gezer.
16:39 at the place of worship in G.
21:29 were at the worship site at G.
2Ch 1:3 to the place of worship in G
1:13 of worship in G to Jerusalem.
Neh 3:7 Next to them Melatiah from G
3:7 with men from G and Mizpah,
7:25 of G: 95
Isa 28:21 wake up as he did in G Valley.
Jer 28:1 son of Azzur, from G,
41:12 with him at the large pool in G.
41:16 and commanders from G.
41:17 When they left G, they stayed

Gibeonites (4)

2Sm 21:2 (The G were not a part of Israel
21:2 The king called the G
21:4 the G answered him.
21:9 handed them over to the G,

Giddalti (2)

1Ch 25:4 Eliathah, G, Romamti Ezer,
25:29 The twenty-second chose G,

Giddel (4)

Ezr 2:47 G, Gahar, Reaiah,
2:56 Jaalah, Darkon, G,
Neh 7:49 Hanan, G, Gahar,
7:58 Jaala, Darkon, G,

Gideon (61)

Jdg 6:11 Joash's son G was beating out
6:12 LORD appeared to G and said,
6:13 G responded, "Excuse me, sir!
6:15 G said to him, "Excuse me,
6:17 G said to him, "If you find me
6:19 Then G went into ⌊his house⌋
6:20 the broth over them." G did so.
6:22 That's when G realized that
6:24 So G built an altar there to the
6:25 night the LORD said to G,
6:27 G took ten of his servants and
6:29 "G, son of Joash, did this."
6:32 So that day they nicknamed G
6:34 LORD's Spirit gave G strength.
6:34 So G blew the ram's horn to
6:36 Then G said to God,
6:38 The next morning G got up
6:39 Then G said to God,
6:40 God did what G asked.
7:1 Jerubbaal (that is, G) and all
7:2 The LORD said to G,
7:4 The LORD said to G,
7:5 So G took the men down to the
7:7 Then the LORD said to G,
7:8 So G sent the other men of
7:9 That night the LORD said to G,
7:11 So G and his servant Purah
7:13 When G got there,
7:14 can only be the sword of G,
7:15 When G heard the dream and
7:16 G divided the 300 men into
7:18 'For the LORD and for G!'"
7:19 G and his 100 men came to the
7:20 sword for the LORD and for G!"
7:24 G also sent messengers to the
7:25 heads of Oreb and Zeeb to G
8:2 G replied, "I haven't done
8:3 When they heard what G said,
8:4 G and his 300 men headed
8:5 So G said to the men of
8:7 G responded, "Alright, then.
8:8 Then G went to Penuel and
8:11 So G went up Tent Dwellers
8:12 fled as G pursued them.
8:13 G, son of Joash, returned from
8:15 G went to the men of Succoth
8:16 So G took the leaders of the
8:19 G replied, "They were my
8:21 So G got up and killed them.
8:22 The men of Israel said to G,
8:23 G replied, "I will not rule you
8:24 Then G said to them,
8:26 The gold earrings G had asked
8:27 Then G used the gold to make
8:27 a trap for G and his family.
8:30 G had 70 sons because he had
8:32 G, son of Joash, died at a very
8:33 As soon as G died,
8:35 G) despite all the good he had
9:1 son of Jerubbaal [G],
Heb 11:32 time to tell you about G,

Gideoni (5)

Num 1:11 Abidan, son of G, from the tribe
2:22 Benjamin is Abidan, son of G.
7:60 of Benjamin, Abidan, son of G,
7:65 the gifts from Abidan, son of G.
10:24 Abidan, son of G,

Gideon's (2)

Jdg 8:1 strongly protested G actions.
8:28 peace for 40 years during G life

Gidom (1)

Jdg 20:45 2,000 and killed them near G.

gift (87)

Gen 32:13 Then he prepared a g for his
32:18 This is a g sent to you.
32:20 him this g that I'm sending
32:21 So Jacob sent the g ahead of
33:10 please take the g I'm giving
34:12 must pay for the bride and the g
43:11 then take the man a g.
Lev 7:29 sacrifice as a g to the LORD.
Num 7:11 different leader will bring his g
18:6 They are a g given to the
18:7 This is my g to you:
Dtr 16:17 Each man must bring a g in
33:13 the best g heaven can send,
33:14 the best g the sun can give,
Jdg 6:18 I want to bring my g and set it
1Sm 25:27 Here is a g I am bringing to you.
30:26 He said, "Here is a g for you
1Ki 13:7 and I will give you a g."
Job 6:22 Did I ever say, 'Give me a g,' or
Psa 45:12 want to win your favor with a g.
Pro 18:16 A g opens doors for the one
21:14 A g ⌊given⌋ in secret calms
25:14 who brags about a g that
Ecc 3:13 It is a g from God to be able to
5:19 It is a g from God when God
Eze 44:30 The best of every g from all
46:16 his sons a g from his property.
46:16 The g will belong to his
46:17 offers a g from his property
46:17 The g will belong to the
46:17 Then the g will go back to the
48:8 you set aside as a special g
48:20 give this land as a special g
Mat 5:23 "So if you are offering your g at
5:24 leave your g at the altar.
5:24 come back and offer your g.
19:11 Only those who have that g
23:18 But to swear an oath by the g
23:19 What is more important, the g
23:19 the altar that makes the g holy?
Luk 11:41 Give what is inside as a g to
Jon 1:16 Each of us has received one g
4:10 "If you only knew what God's g
Act 2:38 receive the Holy Spirit as a g.
8:20 thought you could buy God's g.
10:45 Peter were amazed that the g
11:17 God gave them the same g
Rom 4:4 their pay is not regarded as a g
4:16 on faith so that it can be a g.
5:15 comparison between ⌊God's⌋ g
5:15 and the g given through
5:16 comparison between ⌊God's⌋ g
5:16 the g brought God's approval.
5:17 overflowing kindness and the g
6:23 but the g that God freely gives
12:6 If your g is speaking God's
12:7 If your g is serving,
15:15 because God gave me the g
1Co 1:7 Therefore, you don't lack any g
3:10 I used the g that God gave me
4:7 bragging as if it weren't a g?
7:7 has a special g from God,
12:6 every g in every person.
12:28 who have the g of healing,
13:2 I may have the g to speak what
13:8 There is the g of speaking
13:8 There is the g of speaking in
13:8 There is the g of knowledge,
14:1 but especially the g of
14:22 So the g of speaking in other
14:22 The g of speaking what God
16:3 You can send your g to
2Co 8:19 travel with us and bring this g
8:20 administering this generous g.
9:5 for this g that you had
9:15 I thank God for his g that words
Gal 2:9 had given me this special g.
Eph 2:8 Being saved is a g from God.
3:16 I'm asking God to give you a g
Php 4:17 It's not that I'm looking for a g.
1Ti 4:14 Don't neglect the g which you
2Ti 1:6 You received a g from God
1:6 you to fan that g into flames.
Heb 6:4 experienced the heavenly g
Jas 1:17 perfect g comes from above,
1Pe 4:10 must use the g that God has
Rev 22:17 the water of life take it as a g.

gifted (2)

Pro 14:18 people are g with stupidity,
1Co 14:37 g must acknowledge that

gifts (121)

Gen 25:6 Abraham had given g to the
43:15 The men took the g,
43:25 They got their g ready for
43:26 they gave him the g they had
Exo 28:38 whatever their g may be.
35:21 The g were used to construct
35:22 They took these g of gold and
36:6 the people stopped bringing g.
Lev 23:38 worship, your g, all your vows,
Num 7:3 They brought these g to the
7:5 "Accept these g from them to
7:5 need these g for their work."
7:9 Moses gave none of these g
7:10 They presented their g in front
7:12 The one who brought his g on
7:17 were the g from Nahshon,
7:18 tribe of Issachar, brought his g.
7:23 were the g from Nethanel,
7:25 brought his g: a silver plate that
7:29 These were the g from Eliab,
7:31 brought his g: a silver plate that
7:35 These were the g from Elizur,
7:37 brought his g: a silver plate that
7:41 were the g from Shelumiel,
7:43 brought his g: a silver plate that
7:47 were the g from Eliasaph,
7:49 brought his g: a silver plate that
7:53 were the g from Elishama,
7:55 brought his g: a silver plate that
7:59 were the g from Gamaliel,
7:61 brought his g: a silver plate that
7:65 These were the g from Abidan,
7:67 brought his g: a silver plate that
7:71 These were the g from Ahiezer,
7:73 brought his g: a silver plate that
7:77 These were the g from Pagiel,
7:79 brought his g: a silver plate that
7:83 These were the g from Ahira,
7:84 These were the g from the
7:88 These were the g for the
18:8 descendants all the holy g from
18:11 that come as g taken from
18:29 Out of all the g you receive,
31:50 So we have brought as g to the
Dtr 23:18 Never bring g or money earned
2Sm 19:42 or did he give us any g?"
1Ki 10:25 who came brought him g:
2Ki 12:18 all the g his ancestors Kings
1Ch 26:20 of the g dedicated to God.
26:26 treasuries of the g dedicated
28:12 and the g dedicated to God.)
2Ch 9:24 who came brought him g:
17:5 Judah gave g to Jehoshaphat,
17:11 of the Philistines brought g
21:3 Their father gave them many g:
31:12 and the g dedicated to God.
31:14 the holy g dedicated to God.
32:23 went to Jerusalem to bring g
Ezr 1:6 and valuable g besides
7:16 you take the g contributed by
7:16 willingly contributed these g
Neh 10:33 for the holy g and offerings for
12:44 the g designated by Moses'
12:47 all the Israelites were giving g
12:47 They set aside holy g for ⌊the
12:47 the Levites set aside holy g
Est 2:18 and he handed out g from his
9:19 They also send g of food to
9:22 celebrating and for sending g
9:22 especially g to the poor.
Psa 68:18 You received g from people,
68:29 Kings will bring you g because
72:10 from Sheba and Seba bring g.
76:11 everyone around him bring g
Pro 19:6 friend to a person who gives g.
Isa 1:23 all love bribes and run after g.
18:7 At that time g will be brought to
Eze 16:33 But you give g to all your
20:26 sons as g ⌊to their false
20:39 my holy name with your g

Eze 20:40 for your offerings, your best g,
20:40 and all your holy g.
Dan 2:6 I will give you g, awards,
2:46 He ordered that g and offerings
2:48 gave him many wonderful g.
5:17 told the king, "Keep your g.
5:17 Give your g and awards to
Hos 2:12 She said that they were g from
Mic 1:14 is why you will give farewell g
7:3 Officials ask for g.
Mat 2:11 and offered him g of gold,
7:11 you know how to give good g
Luk 11:13 you know how to give good g
21:1 dropping their g into the temple
21:5 and decorated with beautiful g.
Act 10:2 Cornelius gave many g to poor
10:4 of your prayers and your g
10:31 remembered your g to the poor.
20:35 'Giving g is more satisfying
24:17 to my people and brought g
Rom 8:23 the Spirit as the first of God's g,
11:29 his mind when he gives g
12:6 gave each of us different g.
1Co 7:7 and these g vary from person to
12:1 concerning spiritual g.
12:4 There are different spiritual g,
12:30 or have g of healing?
12:31 You ⌊only⌋ want the better g,
14:1 and desire spiritual g,
14:12 you're eager to have spiritual g,
Eph 4:8 us and gave g to people."
4:11 teachers as g ⌊to his church⌋.
Php 4:18 has brought me your g,
4:18 Your g are a soothing aroma,
Heb 2:4 and with other g from the Holy
5:1 to offer g and sacrifices for sin.
8:3 to offer g and sacrifices.
8:4 On earth ⌊other⌋ priests offer g
9:9 The g and sacrifices that were
9:10 These g and sacrifices were
Rev 11:10 They will celebrate and send g

Gihon (6)

Gen 2:13 name of the second river is G.
1Ki 1:33 and take him to G.
1:38 mule and brought him to G.
1:45 have anointed him king at G.
2Ch 32:30 from the upper outlet of G.
33:14 of David from west of G Spring

Gilalai (1)

Neh 12:36 G, Maai, Nethanel, Judah,

Gilboa (8)

1Sm 28:4 and they camped at G.
31:1 killed in battle on Mount G.
31:8 three sons lying on Mount G.
2Sm 1:6 "I happened to be on Mount G.
1:21 You mountains in G,
21:12 the day they killed Saul at G.
1Ch 10:1 killed in battle on Mount G.
10:8 and his sons lying on Mount G.

Gilead (120)

Gen 31:21 toward the mountains of G.
31:23 with him in the mountains of G.
31:25 tents in the mountains of G.
37:25 of Ishmaelites coming from G.
Num 26:29 (Machir was the father of G)
26:29 of Gilead) and the family of G.
26:30 The descendants of G were
27:1 son of Hepher, grandson of G,
32:1 regions of Jazer and G were
32:26 will stay here in the cities of G.
32:29 give them G as their own
32:39 went to G, captured it,
32:40 So Moses gave G to the
32:41 captured the settlements in G.
36:1 were descended from G,
Dtr 2:36 city in that valley as far as G,
3:10 cities of the plateau, all of G,
3:12 region of G with its cities.
3:13 I gave the rest of G and all of
3:15 I gave G to Machir.
3:16 and Gad some of G from
4:43 Ramoth in G for the tribe of
Dtr 34:1 He could see G as far as Dan,
Jos 12:2 of the valley and half of G.
12:5 and half of G to the border of
13:11 It also included G,
13:25 Jazer, all the cities of G,
13:31 It also included half of G with
17:1 of the people living in G,
17:1 had received G and Bashan
17:3 son of Hepher, grandson of G,
17:5 besides the land of G and
17:6 while G belonged to
20:8 Ramoth in G from the tribe of
21:38 Ramoth in G (a city of refuge
22:9 They returned to G.
22:13 of the tribe of Manasseh in G.
22:15 leaders said to the people of G,
22:32 from Reuben and Gad in G
Jdg 5:17 G remained east of the Jordan
7:3 should leave Mount G
10:3 Jair from G became a judge.
10:4 They are in the region of G.
10:8 in the land of the Amorites in G.
10:17 and they camped at G.
10:18 The leaders of the people of G
10:18 rule everyone who lives in G."
11:1 a soldier from the region of G.
11:1 father was named G.
11:8 of everyone who lives in G."
11:29 Jephthah went through G,
11:29 and Mizpah in G ⌊to gather an
11:40 of Jephthah, the man from G.
12:4 gathered all the men of G
12:4 men of G defeated Ephraim.
12:4 "You people from G are nothing
12:5 The men of G captured the
12:5 the men of G would ask,
12:7 Then Jephthah of G died and
12:7 buried in one of the cities of G.
20:1 to Beersheba and from G came
1Sm 13:7 into the territory of Gad and G.
2Sm 2:9 Abner made him king of G,
17:26 camped in the region of G.
17:27 and Barzillai from Rogelim in G
19:31 Barzillai, the man from G,
24:6 They went to G and to Tahtim
1Ki 2:7 to the sons of Barzillai from G.
4:13 descendant of Manasseh, in G.
4:19 was in charge of G,
17:1 Tishbe but had settled in G,
22:3 "Do you know that Ramoth in G
22:4 me to fight at Ramoth in G?"
22:6 against Ramoth in G or not?"
22:12 "Attack Ramoth in G,
22:15 against Ramoth in G or not?"
22:20 killed at Ramoth in G?' Some
22:29 of Judah went to Ramoth in G.
2Ki 10:33 the entire region of G (the
10:33 Arnon River, to G and Bashan.
15:25 With 50 men from G,
15:29 Kedesh, Hazor, G, Galilee,
1Ch 2:21 the man who first settled G.
2:22 who had 23 towns in G.
2:23 the man who first settled G.
5:9 had so much livestock in G.
5:10 the entire region east of G.
5:14 and great-grandson of G.
5:14 G was the son of Michael,
5:16 They lived in G, in Bashan
6:80 they received Ramoth in G
7:14 Machir was the first to settle G.
7:17 These were the people of G,
26:31 were found at Jazer in G.
27:21 for the half of Manasseh in G:
2Ch 18:2 to attack Ramoth in G with him.
18:3 go with me to Ramoth in G?"
18:5 against Ramoth in G or not?"
18:11 "Attack Ramoth in G,
18:14 against Ramoth in G or not?"
18:19 killed at Ramoth in G?' Some
18:28 of Judah went to Ramoth in G.
Ezr 2:61 daughters of Barzillai from G
Neh 7:63 daughters of Barzillai from G
Psa 60:7 G is mine. Manasseh is mine.
108:8 G is mine. Manasseh is mine.
Sos 4:1 goats moving down Mount G.
6:5 of goats moving down from G.
Jer 8:22 Isn't there medicine in G?
22:6 This palace is like G to me,
46:11 Go to G, and get medicine,
50:19 mountains of Ephraim and G.
Eze 47:18 serve as the border between G
Hos 6:8 G is a city filled with
12:11 The people of G are evil.
Amo 1:3 crushed ⌊the people of⌋ G
1:13 open pregnant women in G.
Oba 1:19 will take possession of G.
Mic 7:14 in Bashan and G like before.
Zec 10:10 I will bring them to G and to

Gilead Jephthah (1)

Jdg 11:29 From Mizpah in G went to

Gilead's (5)

Jdg 11:2 G wife also gave birth to sons.
11:5 G leaders went to get Jephthah
11:7 to G leaders, "Don't you hate
11:8 G leaders answered Jephthah,
11:10 G leaders said to Jephthah,

Gilgal (40)

Dtr 11:30 live on the plains facing G,
Jos 4:19 They made their camp at G,
4:20 At G Joshua set up the 12
5:9 So Joshua named the place G,
5:10 people of Israel camped at G
9:6 to Joshua in the camp at G.
10:6 to Joshua at the camp in G:
10:7 best warriors, set out from G.
10:9 marched all night from G
10:15 returned to the camp at G.
10:43 returned to the camp at G.
12:23 the king of Goiim in G,
14:6 of Judah came to Joshua at G.
Jdg 2:1 LORD went from G to Bochim.
3:19 idols near G ⌊and returned
1Sm 7:16 he went around to Bethel, G,
10:8 Go ahead of me to G.
11:14 let's go to G and there
11:15 Then all the troops went to G,
13:4 troops rallied behind Saul at G.
13:7 But Saul remained in G,
13:8 But Samuel had not come to G,
13:12 will come against me at G,
13:15 Samuel left G. The rest of the
13:15 They went from G to Gibeah in
15:12 he left there and went to G."
15:21 to the LORD your God in G."
15:33 the presence of the LORD at G.
2Sm 19:15 the people of Judah came to G
19:40 The king crossed the river to G,
20:1 Benjamin happened to be at G.
2Ki 2:1 Elijah and Elisha left G.
4:38 When Elisha went back to G,
Hos 4:15 Don't go to G. Don't go to Beth
9:15 wickedness began in G;
12:11 They sacrifice bulls in G.
Amo 4:4 Go to G and sin even more.
5:5 Don't go to G. Don't travel to
5:5 G will certainly go into exile.
Mic 6:5 from Shittim to G so that you

Gilo (1)

2Sm 23:34 (son of Ahithophel) from G,

Giloh (2)

Jos 15:51 Goshen, Holon, and G.
2Sm 15:12 to come from his home in G.

Gimzo (1)

2Ch 28:18 and G and its villages.

Ginath (1)

1Ki 16:21 army followed Tibni, son of G,

Ginath's (1)

1Ki 16:22 which followed Tibni, G son.

Ginnethoi (1)

Neh 12:4 Iddo, G, Abijah,

Ginnethon (2)

Neh 10:6 Daniel, G, Baruch,

Neh 12:16 from Iddo, Zechariah; from G,

Girgashites (7)

Gen 10:16 Jebusites, the Amorites, the G,
15:21 the G, and the Jebusites."
Dtr 7:1 G, Amorites, Canaanites,
Jos 3:10 Perizzites, G, Amorites,
24:11 Canaanites, Hittites, G, Hivites,
1Ch 1:14 Jebusites, the Amorites, the G,
Neh 9:8 and G to his descendants.

girl (43)

Gen 24:14 I will ask a g, 'May I please
24:16 The g was a very attractive
24:28 The g ran and told her mother's
24:55 "Let the g stay with us ten
24:57 "We'll call the g and ask her."
34:3 He loved the g and spoke
34:4 "Get me this g for my wife."
34:12 Give me the g as my wife."
Exo 1:16 If it's a boy, kill it, but if it's a g,
1:22 but to let every g live.
2:5 and sent her slave g to get it.
2:8 So the g brought the baby's
Lev 12:5 a woman gives birth to a g,
12:7 who gives birth to a boy or a g.
27:5 and for a g give 4 ounces.
27:6 and for a g give about one
Num 30:3 "A young g, who still lives in
31:18 But save for yourselves every g
Dtr 22:20 and no evidence that the g was
22:21 they must take the g to the
22:24 The g must die because she
22:25 a man rapes an engaged g out
22:26 Don't do anything to the g.
22:27 The man found the g out in the
Jdg 5:30 A g or two for each soldier,
9:18 the son of my father's slave g,
2Sm 17:17 so a servant g was to go and
2Ki 5:2 back a little g from Israel.
5:3 The g told her mistress,
5:4 him what the g from Israel had
Pro 5:18 and enjoy the g you married
Eze 23:4 "The older g was named
23:4 and the younger g was named
Mat 9:24 The g is not dead.
9:25 and the g came back to life.
14:11 on a platter and given to the g,
Mar 5:41 which means, "Little g,
5:42 The g got up at once and
5:43 the little g something to eat.
6:22 The king told the g,
6:25 So the g hurried back to the
6:28 on a platter and gave it to the g,
6:28 and the g gave it to her mother.

girl's (5)

Dtr 22:15 The g father and mother must
22:16 The g father will tell the
22:17 Then the g parents must
22:19 silver and give it to the g father.
22:29 give the g father 1 ¼ pounds

girls (15)

Gen 24:13 and the g of the city are coming
Jdg 11:40 for four days every year the g
1Sm 9:11 they met g coming out to get
9:11 They asked the g,
9:12 The g answered, "He's there
2Sm 6:20 before the eyes of the slave g
6:21 in front of the slave g but⌋
6:22 slave g you speak about."
2Ch 28:8 and g from their relatives ⌊the
Job 41:5 or keep it on a leash for your g?
Pro 9:3 She has sent out her servant g.
27:27 and to keep your servant g
Lam 5:11 so are the g in the cities of
Joe 3:3 They sold g so that they could
Zec 8:5 filled with boys and g playing

Girzites (1)

1Sm 27:8 the G, and the Amalekites.

Gishpa (1)

Neh 11:21 Mount Ophel with Ziha and G

Gittaim (3)

2Sm 4:3 people of Beeroth had fled to G.
4:4 picked him up and fled ⌊to G⌋.
Neh 11:33 Hazor, Ramah, G,

give (1074)

Gen 1:17 God put them in the sky to g
3:16 and your labor when you g birth
9:3 I now g you everything else.
12:7 "I'm going to g this land to your
13:15 I will g all the land you see to
13:16 I will also g you as many
13:17 land because I will g it to you."
14:21 "G me the people,
15:2 what will you g me?
15:7 Chaldeans to g you this land
15:18 He said, "I will g this land to
16:10 "I will g you many
16:11 and you will g birth to a son.
17:2 I will g you my promise,
17:2 and I will g you very many
17:6 I will g you many descendants.
17:16 bless her, and I will also g you
17:19 Your wife Sarah will g you a
17:21 Sarah will g birth to him at this
19:32 Let's g our father wine to drink.
19:34 Let's g him wine to drink again
20:7 G the man's wife back to him
20:7 But if you don't g her back,
22:12 because you did not refuse to g
22:16 not refused to g me your son,
24:7 'I will g this land to your
24:17 "Please g me a drink of water."
24:43 "Please g me a drink of water."
25:24 When the time came for her to g
26:3 I will g all these lands to you
26:4 in the sky and g all these lands
27:26 "Come here and g me a kiss,
27:28 May God g you dew from the
28:4 May he g to you and your
28:13 I will g the land on which you
28:20 me on my trip and g me food
28:22 and I will surely g you a tenth
28:22 a tenth of everything you g me."
29:19 "It's better that I g her to you
29:21 "The time is up; g me my wife!
29:26 "It's not our custom to g the
29:27 Then we will g you the other
30:1 "G me children, or I'll die!"
30:14 Rachel said to Leah, "Please g
30:24 Joseph [May He G Another]
30:24 the LORD g me another son."
30:26 G me my wives and my
30:31 "What should I g you?"
30:31 "Don't g me anything,"
32:4 He commanded them to g this
34:9 g your daughters to us,
34:11 I'll g you whatever you ask.
34:12 and the gift I must g her as high
34:12 G me the girl as my wife."
34:14 We can't g our sister to a man
34:15 We will g our consent to you
34:16 Then we'll g our daughters to
35:12 I will g you the land that I gave
35:12 I will also g this land to your
38:17 She said, "First g me
38:18 "What should I g you as a
38:27 time came for Tamar to g birth,
41:16 but God can g Pharaoh the
42:34 I'll g your brother back to you,
45:18 I will g you the best land in
45:19 "G them this order:
47:15 "G us food," they said. "Do you
47:16 g me your livestock,
47:16 and I'll g you food in
47:19 But g us seed so that we won't
47:24 Every time you harvest, g
48:4 I will g this land to your
50:24 with an oath to g to Abraham,
Exo 5:7 "Don't g the people any more
6:4 a promise to g them Canaan,
6:8 swore to g to Abraham,
6:8 I will g it to you as your own
7:9 "When Pharaoh says to you, 'G
12:25 that the LORD will g you as
Exo 13:5 ancestors that he would g you
13:21 column of fire to g them light so
16:8 "The LORD will g you meat to
17:2 "G us water to drink!"
18:19 and I'll g you some advice.
21:11 If he doesn't g her these three
22:17 absolutely refuses to g her
22:26 g it back to him by sunset.
22:29 "You must g me your firstborn
22:30 day you must g them to me.
23:3 Never g special favors to poor
24:12 Stay there, and I will g you the
25:2 choose something to g me as
25:16 my promise which I will g you.
25:21 my promise which I will g you,
25:22 meet with you and g you all my
28:2 brother Aaron to g him dignity
28:40 These clothes will g them
29:28 that the Israelites g this portion
30:13 he must g one-fifth of an ounce
30:14 old must g this contribution
30:15 The rich must not g more than
30:15 and the poor must not g less.
30:16 Take the money the Israelites g
32:13 I will g to your descendants all
33:1 'I will g it to your descendants.'
33:14 and I will g you peace."
35:5 something of your own to g as
35:24 Those who could g silver or
36:6 more to g as their special
Lev 5:16 G it to the priest. So the priest
6:5 G it back to its owner on the
7:32 You will also g the priest the
7:36 commanded the Israelites to g
14:34 that I am going to g to you,
15:14 He will g these birds to the
18:21 Never g your children as
19:15 Never g special favors to poor
20:2 living among you g one
20:4 those who g their children
20:24 I will g it to you as your own.
22:14 must g another holy offering
22:22 Never g the LORD any of these
23:10 to the land I am going to g you
25:19 The land will g you its
25:21 I will g you my blessing in the
25:37 or on the food you g them.
25:38 out of Egypt to g you Canaan
26:4 "I will g you rain at the right
27:2 you makes a special vow ⌊to g
27:2 you may g money instead of
27:3 The amount you must g for a
27:4 If it is a woman, g 12 ounces.
27:5 g 8 ounces and for a girl give 4
27:5 and for a girl g 4 ounces.
27:6 g 2 ounces of silver and for a
27:6 for a girl g about one ounce.
27:7 For a man 60 years or over, g 6
27:7 and for a woman g 4 ounces.
27:9 "If ⌊the vow⌋ is to g the kind of
27:14 "If you g your house to the
27:17 If you g your field in the jubilee
27:18 But if you g the field after the
27:22 You may g a field you bought
Num 3:9 G the Levites to Aaron and his
3:48 G the silver to Aaron and his
5:7 and g it to the person who was
6:26 with favor and g you peace.'
7:2 came to g their offerings.
7:5 G them to the Levites to use
8:19 will be the only Israelites I g
10:29 the LORD promised to g us.
11:12 Did I g birth to them?
11:13 They keep crying for me to g
11:18 So I will g them meat.
11:21 Yet, you say, 'I will g them
14:8 bring us into this land and g
14:30 an oath to g you this land
15:4 brings the offering must also g
15:5 also g an offering of one quart
15:6 "With a ram, g a grain offering
15:10 Also g an offering of two quarts
15:19 g some of it as a contribution to
15:21 you must g one part of your
15:29 You must g the same
18:12 the produce they g the LORD:

Num	18:24	Instead, I will **g** the Levites
	18:28	You will **g** the LORD's
	19:3	**G** it to the priest Eleazar.
	20:8	tell the rock to **g** up its water.
	20:8	In this way you will **g** the
	21:16	and I will **g** them water."
	23:5	and **g** him my message."
	23:16	and **g** him my message."
	24:13	'Even if Balak would **g** me his
	24:14	I'll **g** you some advice.
	26:54	**G** more land to larger tribes and
	27:4	**G** us property among our
	27:7	You must **g** them property of
	27:9	**g** his property to his brothers.
	27:10	If he has no brothers, **g** his
	27:11	If he has no uncles, **g** his
	27:12	the land I will **g** the Israelites.
	27:19	and **g** him his instructions in
	27:20	**G** him some of your authority
	28:2	"**G** this command to the
	29:39	for anything you vowed to **g**
	31:29	and **g** them to the priest
	31:30	**G** them to the Levites who are
	32:5	Please **g** us this land as our
	32:29	**g** them Gilead as their own
	33:53	because I will **g** it to you for
	33:54	**G** more land to larger families
	34:2	"**G** the Israelites these
	35:2	"Tell the Israelites to **g** the
	35:2	They must also **g** the Levites
	35:4	around the cities that you **g**
	35:6	"Six of the cities you **g** the
	35:6	In addition, you must also **g** the
	35:7	So you will **g** a total of 48
	35:8	The cities you **g** the Levites
	36:2	the LORD commanded you to **g**
	36:2	also commanded you to **g**
Dtr	1:8	the land the LORD swore to **g**
	1:35	I swore to **g** to your ancestors,
	1:36	He will see it, and I will **g** the
	1:39	I will **g** it to them, and they will
	2:4	**G** the people these
	2:31	"I have begun to **g** you Sihon
	3:28	**G** instructions to Joshua.
	4:2	LORD your God that I **g** you.
	4:38	bring you into their land and **g**
	5:31	I will **g** you all the commands,
	6:6	these words that I **g** you today.
	6:10	bring you into the land and **g**
	6:23	of there to bring us here and **g**
	7:13	the land the LORD will **g** you,
	8:1	every command I **g** you today.
	10:11	of the land I will **g** them,
	11:9	swore to **g** your ancestors
	11:21	land that the LORD swore to **g**
	11:24	I will **g** you every place on
	12:10	He will **g** you peace from all
	14:21	You may **g** it to the foreigners
	15:9	Israelites and **g** them nothing.
	15:10	Be sure to **g** to them without
	15:14	Generously **g** them provisions
	17:9	and they will **g** you their verdict
	18:4	Also, **g** them the first produce
	18:16	the LORD your God to **g** you
	19:8	He may **g** you the whole land
	19:8	land he promised to **g** them.
	20:4	enemies and **g** you victory."
	21:16	for the father to **g** his sons their
	21:17	He must **g** that son a double
	22:2	looking for it. Then **g** it back.
	22:9	Otherwise, you will have to **g**
	22:19	2 ½ pounds of silver and **g**
	22:29	intercourse with her must **g**
	23:18	as an offering you vowed to **g**.
	26:19	He will **g** you praise,
	28:11	The LORD will **g** you plenty of
	28:11	the land the LORD will **g** you,
	28:55	He will **g** none of them any of
	28:65	There the LORD will **g** you an
	29:1	LORD commanded Moses to **g**
	30:9	The LORD your God will **g** you
	30:20	land that the LORD swore to **g**
	31:7	land that the LORD will **g** them,
	31:14	and I will **g** him his
	31:20	into the land that I swore to **g**
	31:21	the land that I swore to **g** them."
Dtr	31:23	the land that I swore to **g** them,
	32:3	**G** our God the greatness he
	33:10	and **g** Israel your teachings.
	33:14	the best gift the sun can **g**,
	34:4	I said I would **g** it to their
Jos	1:2	the land that I am going to **g**
	1:3	I will **g** you every place on
	1:6	I swore to **g** their ancestors.
	1:11	your God is going to **g** you.'"
	1:13	'The LORD your God will **g**
	1:15	your God is going to **g** them.
	2:9	"I know the LORD will **g** you
	2:12	Also **g** me some proof
	5:6	had sworn to **g** our ancestors.
	7:19	Joshua said to Achan, "Son, **g**
	9:24	his servant Moses to **g** you
	11:6	because I am going to **g** them
	13:14	Moses did not **g** any land as an
	13:33	Moses did not **g** any land as an
	14:3	He did not **g** any land as an
	14:12	Now **g** me this mountain region
	15:16	Caleb said, "I will **g** my
	15:19	"**G** me a blessing.
	15:19	also **g** me some springs."
	17:4	LORD commanded Moses to **g**
	17:14	"Why did you **g** us only one
	20:4	him into their city and **g** him
	21:20	lot from the tribe of Ephraim to **g**
	21:43	had sworn to **g** their ancestors.
Jdg	1:12	Caleb said, "I will **g** my
	1:15	"**G** me a blessing.
	1:15	also **g** me some springs."
	2:1	into the land that I swore to **g**
	4:19	Sisera said to her, "Please **g**
	6:17	**g** me a sign that it is really you
	8:5	"Please **g** me some food for the
	8:6	"We shouldn't **g** your army food.
	8:15	'We shouldn't **g** your
	8:24	Each of you **g** me the earrings
	8:25	we'll **g** them to you."
	11:13	Now **g** it back peacefully."
	11:37	**G** me two months for my
	14:12	I'll **g** you 30 linen shirts and 30
	14:13	you will **g** me the same things."
	16:5	Each of us will **g** you 1,100
	16:28	God, **g** me strength just one
	17:10	I'll **g** you ten pieces of silver a
	20:7	**G** me your advice right now!"
	21:18	However, we can't **g** them any
	21:22	because you didn't **g** them
Rut	1:6	his people and **g** them food.
	2:15	Don't **g** her any problems.
	2:16	Don't **g** her a hard time about it
	4:7	would take off his sandal and **g**
	4:12	the LORD will **g** you from this
	4:14	today to **g** you someone who
1Sm	1:4	he would **g** portions of it to his
	1:5	He would also **g** one portion to
	1:11	remember me, and **g** me a boy,
	1:11	then I will **g** him to you for as
	2:15	"**G** the meat to the priest to
	2:16	say to him, "**G** it to me now,
	2:20	"May the LORD **g** you children
	2:35	I will **g** him faithful
	6:4	guilt offering should we **g** him?"
	6:5	and **g** glory to the God of Israel.
	8:14	and olive orchards and **g** them
	8:15	of your grain and wine and **g**
	8:22	and **g** them a king."
	9:8	I'll **g** it to the man of God.
	10:4	They will greet you and **g** you
	11:3	"**G** us seven days so that we
	12:3	⌞If so,⌟ I will **g** it all back."
	17:25	He will **g** his daughter to that
	17:44	"and I'll **g** your body to the
	17:46	And this day I will **g** the dead
	18:17	I will **g** her to you as your wife
	18:19	But when the time came to **g**
	18:21	thought, "I'll **g** her to David.
	21:3	**G** me five loaves of bread or
	22:7	Will Jesse's son **g** every one of
	25:8	Please **g** us and your son
	25:11	for my shearers and **g** them
	25:28	The LORD will certainly **g** you,
	27:1	Then Saul will **g** up looking all
2Sm	3:14	"**G** me my wife Michal.
2Sm	7:11	So I will **g** you peace with all
	9:7	I will **g** back to you all the land
	12:11	take your wives and **g** them
	13:25	he did **g** Absalom his blessing.
	14:7	They said, '**G** us the man who
	16:3	of Israel will **g** me back my
	18:5	All the troops heard him **g** all
	18:11	obligated to **g** you four ounces
	19:36	Why should you **g** me such a
	19:42	or did he **g** us any gifts?"
	20:21	**G** him to me, and I'll withdraw
	21:3	What should I **g** you to make
	21:5	They answered the king, "**G**
	21:6	"I will **g** them ⌞to you.⌟"
	22:50	That is why I will **g** thanks to
	24:13	decide what answer I should **g**
1Ki	1:12	Bathsheba, let me **g** you some
	2:17	"Please ask King Solomon to **g**
	3:5	He said, "What can I **g** you?"
	3:9	**G** me a heart that listens so
	3:14	then I will also **g** you a long
	3:25	**G** half to the one and half to the
	3:26	**g** her the living child.
	3:27	The king replied, "**G** the living
	8:39	**G** each person the proper reply.
	8:59	Then he will **g** me and his
	11:11	I will **g** it to one of your
	11:13	I will **g** your son one tribe for
	11:31	hands and **g** ten tribes
	11:35	his son and **g** you ten tribes.
	11:36	I will **g** his son one tribe so that
	11:38	And I will **g** you Israel.
	13:3	sign that the LORD will **g** you:
	13:7	and I will **g** you a gift."
	14:6	I've been told to **g** you some
	17:19	said to her, "**G** me your son."
	18:23	**G** us two bulls. Let the prophets
	20:5	are mine. **G** ⌞them to me⌟.
	20:10	dust left from Samaria to **g**
	20:34	Benhadad told him, "I will **g**
	21:2	"**G** me your vineyard.
	21:2	I will **g** you a better vineyard
	21:3	has forbidden me to **g** you what
	21:4	said,⌟ "I will not **g** you what
	21:6	I'll **g** you another vineyard for it.'
	21:6	'I won't **g** you my vineyard.'"
	21:7	I'll **g** you the vineyard
2Ki	3:3	But he would not **g** up the sins
	4:42	"**G** it to the people to eat."
	4:43	"**G** it to the people to eat,"
	5:17	please have someone **g** me as
	5:22	Please **g** them 75 pounds of
	5:23	"Please let me **g** you 150
	6:22	**G** them food and water.
	6:27	I can't **g** you something from
	6:28	told me, '**G** up your son.
	6:29	day I told her, '**G** up your son.
	7:4	If they **g** us something to keep
	8:19	that he would always **g** him
	10:15	"If you are, **g** me your hand."
	12:11	Then they would **g** the money
	12:15	for the workers to **g** an account,
	18:14	whatever penalty you **g** me."
	18:20	You **g** useless advice about
	18:23	I'll **g** you 2,000 horses if you
	18:31	Come out and **g** yourselves up
	19:3	woman who is about to **g** birth
	20:1	**G** final instructions to your
	20:6	I'll **g** you 15 more years to live.
	22:5	**G** ⌞some of⌟ it to the foremen
	22:5	They should **g** it to the
	22:7	for the money you **g** them."
	23:35	the people of the land and **g**
1Ch	4:10	"Please bless me and **g** me
	16:8	"**G** thanks to the LORD.
	16:18	by saying, 'I will **g** you Canaan.
	16:28	"**G** to the LORD, you families
	16:28	**G** to the LORD glory and
	16:29	**G** to the LORD the glory his
	16:34	"**G** thanks to the LORD
	16:35	so that we may **g** thanks
	16:41	to **g** thanks to the LORD ⌞by
	21:12	Decide what answer I should **g**
	21:23	I'll **g** you oxen for the burnt
	21:23	I'll **g** you everything."
	22:9	I will **g** him peace from all the

1Ch 22:9 and in his time I will **g** Israel
22:12 The LORD will **g** you insight
22:13 Moses to **g** to Israel.
23:13 and always **g** the blessing in
23:30 appointed to stand to **g** thanks
29:14 enable us to **g** so generously?
29:14 We **g** you only what has come
2Ch 1:7 He said, "What can I **g** you?"
1:10 **G** me wisdom and knowledge
1:12 I will also **g** you riches,
2:10 I will **g** your lumberjacks
6:30 Forgive ⌊them⌋, and **g** each
12:7 In a little while I will **g** them an
20:7 Didn't you **g** this country to the
21:7 that he would always **g** him
24:6 Israel to **g** contributions
24:12 The king and Jehoiada would **g**
25:9 "The LORD can **g** you much
31:4 people living in Jerusalem to **g**
31:19 Men were appointed to **g** a
35:12 the burnt offerings to **g** them
Ezr 4:21 being rebuilt until I **g** the order.
7:22 ⌊You may **g** him⌋ up to 7,500
9:8 survivors from Babylon and to **g**
9:9 He did this to **g** us an
9:9 and restore its ruins and to **g**
9:12 and be able to **g** this land as a
Neh 1:11 Please **g** me success today
2:8 In the letter order him to **g** me
2:10 that someone had come to **g**
2:20 of heaven will **g** us success,"
4:2 and **g** them new strength?"
6:9 They thought we would **g** up
6:13 Then they could **g** me a bad
9:6 You **g** life to them all,
9:8 You made a promise to him to **g**
9:12 a column of fire to **g** them light
9:15 you swore you would **g** them.
10:32 ourselves the obligation to **g**
12:31 two large choirs to **g** thanks
Est 1:19 you should **g** her royal position
6:9 **G** the robe and the horse to one
Job 2:4 Certainly, a man will **g**
3:20 "Why **g** light to one in misery
3:23 Why **g** light to those whose
4:6 Doesn't your fear of God **g** you
4:6 lifetime of integrity **g** you hope?
6:8 that God would **g** me what I'm
6:22 Did I ever say, 'G me a gift,'
7:13 'My couch may **g** me comfort.
8:20 reject a person of integrity or **g**
15:35 They conceive trouble and **g**
20:10 will have to **g** back his wealth.
20:18 He will **g** back what he earned
21:10 Their cows **g** birth to calves
21:17 How often does an angry God **g**
22:7 You don't even **g** a tired person
27:5 I will never **g** up my claim of
32:17 "I'll **g** my answer. I'll tell you
34:11 and will **g** each person what
35:7 what can you **g** him,
36:31 people and to **g** them more than
39:1 the mountain goats **g** birth?
39:2 the time when they'll **g** birth?
39:3 They kneel down to **g** birth and
39:17 did not **g** it any understanding.
39:19 "Can you **g** strength to a horse
Psa 2:8 Ask me, and I will **g** you the
7:17 I will **g** thanks to the LORD for
9:1 I will **g** ⌊you⌋ thanks,
18:49 That is why I will **g** thanks to
20:4 He will **g** you your heart's
20:6 that the LORD will **g** victory
20:9 **G** victory to the king,
23:4 and your staff **g** me courage.
28:4 and **g** them what they deserve.
28:7 I **g** thanks to him with my song.
29:1 **G** to the LORD, you heavenly
29:1 **G** to the LORD glory and
29:2 **G** to the LORD the glory his
29:11 The LORD will **g** power to his
30:9 Will the dust ⌊of my body⌋ **g**
30:12 I will **g** thanks to you forever.
33:2 **G** thanks with a lyre to the
35:18 I will **g** you thanks in a large
37:4 and he will **g** you the desires of
Psa 43:4 and I will **g** thanks to you on
44:8 We **g** thanks to you forever.
45:17 That is why the nations will **g**
49:8 He must always **g** up
52:9 I will **g** thanks to you forever
54:6 I will **g** thanks to your good
57:9 I want to **g** thanks to you
58:1 you rulers really **g** fair verdicts?
60:11 **G** us help against the enemy
67:3 Let everyone **g** thanks to you,
67:3 Let everyone **g** thanks to you.
67:5 Let the people **g** thanks to you,
67:5 all the people **g** thanks to you.
71:22 even I will **g** thanks to you as I
72:1 O God, **g** the king your justice
75:1 We **g** thanks to you,
75:1 to you, O God; we **g** thanks.
78:20 But can he also **g** us bread or
79:13 will **g** thanks to you forever.
80:18 **G** us life again, and we will
85:12 The LORD will certainly **g** us
86:4 **G** me joy, O Lord, because I lift
86:12 I will **g** thanks to you with all
86:16 **G** me your strength because I
88:10 of the dead rise and **g** thanks
89:17 By your favor you **g** us victory.
89:21 arm will also **g** him strength.
92:1 It is good to **g** thanks to the
94:2 **G** arrogant people what they
94:13 You **g** him peace and quiet
96:7 **G** to the LORD, you families of
96:7 **G** to the LORD glory and
96:8 **G** to the LORD the glory he
97:12 **G** thanks to him as you
99:3 Let them **g** thanks to your great
100:4 **G** thanks to him; praise his
104:27 All of them look to you to **g**
104:28 You **g** it to them, and they
105:1 **G** thanks to the LORD.
105:11 by saying, "I will **g** you the
106:1 **G** thanks to the LORD because
106:47 so that we may **g** thanks
107:1 **G** thanks to the LORD because
107:8 Let them **g** thanks to the LORD
107:15 Let them **g** thanks to the LORD
107:21 Let them **g** thanks to the LORD
107:31 Let them **g** thanks to the LORD
108:3 I want to **g** thanks to you
108:12 **G** us help against the enemy
109:24 My knees **g** way because I
109:30 With my mouth I will **g** many
111:1 I will **g** thanks to the LORD
115:1 Don't **g** glory to us,
115:1 Don't **g** glory to us.
115:1 Instead, **g** glory to your name
118:1 **G** thanks to the LORD because
118:19 I will go through them ⌊and⌋ **g**
118:21 I **g** thanks to you, because you
118:25 you, O LORD, **g** us success!
118:28 and I **g** thanks to you.
118:29 **G** thanks to the LORD because
119:7 I will **g** thanks to you as I learn
119:25 **G** me a new life as you
119:37 **G** me a new life in your ways.
119:40 **G** me a new life in your
119:62 At midnight I wake up to **g**
119:88 **G** me a new life through your
119:107 **G** me a new life, O LORD,
119:108 the praise I gladly **g** you,
119:149 O LORD, **g** me a new life
119:154 **G** me a new life as you
119:156 **G** me a new life guided by your
119:159 your mercy, **g** me a new life.
120:3 what can the LORD **g** you?
120:4 He will **g** you a warrior's
122:4 it is a law in Israel to **g** thanks
136:1 **G** thanks to the LORD because
136:2 **G** thanks to the God of gods
136:3 **G** thanks to the Lord of lords
136:4 **G** thanks to the only one who
136:10 **G** thanks to the one who killed
136:13 **G** thanks to one who divided
136:16 **G** thanks to the one who led
136:17 **G** thanks to the one who
136:26 **G** thanks to the God of heaven
138:1 I will **g** thanks to you with all
Psa 138:2 I will **g** thanks to your name
138:4 All the kings of the earth will **g**
139:14 I will **g** thanks to you because I
140:8 O LORD, do not **g** wicked
140:13 Indeed, righteous people will **g**
142:7 prison so that I may **g** thanks
144:13 May our sheep **g** birth to
145:10 you have made will **g** thanks
145:15 and you **g** them their food at the
Pro 1:4 to **g** insight to gullible people,
1:4 to **g** knowledge and foresight to
3:28 I'll **g** you something then."
4:9 It will **g** you a graceful garland
6:31 He must **g** up all the
7:4 **G** the name "my relative" to
7:21 she makes him **g** in.
8:21 to **g** an inheritance to those
9:9 **G** ⌊advice⌋ to a wise person,
15:2 The tongues of wise people **g**
22:17 mind on the knowledge I **g** you.
22:21 words of truth so that you can **g**
23:26 My son, **g** me your heart.
25:14 about a gift that he does not **g**.
25:21 **g** him some food to eat,
25:21 **g** him some water to drink.
26:16 who **g** a sensible answer.
29:17 Correct your son, and he will **g**
30:8 Don't **g** me either poverty or
30:9 become poor and steal and **g**
30:15 leech has two daughters — "G!"
30:15 and "G!" Three things are never
31:3 Don't **g** your strength to women
31:6 **G** liquor to a person who is
Ecc 5:14 but now they have nothing to **g**
5:20 These people won't **g** much
6:2 Yet, God doesn't **g** him the
11:9 that God will make you **g**
Sos 2:13 The grapevines bloom and **g**
7:12 There I will **g** you my love.
7:13 The mandrakes **g** off a
8:2 I would **g** you some spiced
Isa 1:26 I will **g** you judges like you had
7:14 So the Lord himself will **g** you
7:14 become pregnant and **g** birth
8:10 **G** orders, but they won't be
14:3 the LORD will **g** you relief from
16:3 **G** us advice. Make a decision.
22:21 I will **g** him your authority,
26:17 women ready to **g** birth.
26:18 with labor pains only to **g** birth
28:6 He will **g** a spirit of justice to
28:6 He will **g** strength to those who
29:11 You **g** this book to someone
29:12 Then you **g** the book to
30:5 That nation can't **g** aid or help
30:20 The Lord may **g** you troubles
30:23 The Lord will **g** you rain for the
33:11 You will **g** birth to straw.
36:5 You **g** useless advice about
36:8 I'll **g** you 2,000 horses if you
36:16 and **g** yourselves up to me!
37:3 woman who is about to **g** birth
38:1 **G** final instructions to your
38:5 I'm going to **g** you 15 more
38:16 You **g** me health and keep me
41:28 will they **g** an answer?
42:7 You will **g** sight to the blind,
42:8 I will not **g** my glory to anyone
42:12 Let them **g** glory to the LORD
42:22 with no one to say, "G it back."
43:6 "G them up," and to the south,
45:3 I will **g** you treasures from dark
45:11 Are you going to **g** me orders
48:11 I will not **g** my glory to anyone
50:1 Did I **g** her any to get rid of her?
53:12 So I will **g** him a share among
56:5 I will **g** them something better
56:5 I will **g** them a monument and
56:5 I will **g** them a permanent name
57:18 I'll guide them and **g** them rest.
58:10 If you **g** some of your own food
59:4 trouble and **g** birth to evil.
60:19 of the moon **g** you light,
61:3 to **g** them crowns instead of
62:6 do not **g** yourselves any rest,
62:7 and do not **g** him any rest until

Isa 65:23 They will never again **g** birth to
Jer 3:15 I will **g** you shepherds after my
3:19 you like children and **g** you
6:10 Whom can I **g** a warning to?
8:10 That is why I will **g** their wives
9:15 bitterness and **g** them poison
11:5 to your ancestors and **g** them
13:12 "**G** this message to them,
14:5 Even deer in the fields **g** birth
14:13 will **g** you lasting peace in this
14:22 the skies can't **g** showers.
15:10 Why did my mother **g** birth to
15:13 I will **g** away your wealth and
16:7 No one will **g** a consoling drink
18:2 I will **g** you my message."
19:7 I will **g** their bodies as food to
21:8 I am going to **g** you the choice
23:15 I will **g** them wormwood to eat
24:7 I will **g** them the desire to know
27:4 **G** them an order for their
27:5 I **g** it to anyone I please.
29:11 plans to **g** you a future filled
30:6 Can a man **g** birth to a child?
31:13 I will **g** them joy in place of
31:25 I will **g** those who are weary
32:22 an oath to **g** their ancestors,
32:39 I will **g** them the same attitude
33:6 and I will **g** them peace and
33:9 that I will **g** to Jerusalem.
33:11 '**G** thanks to the LORD of
34:22 I am going to **g** a command,"
38:15 If I **g** you advice, you won't
44:29 I will **g** you this sign,'
Lam 1:16 No one can **g** me the comfort I
2:13 "What example can I **g** you?
3:59 **G** me a fair verdict.
5:21 **G** us back the life we had long
Eze 7:27 and princes will **g** up hope.
7:27 I will **g** them what they
11:2 who plan evil and **g** bad advice
11:17 I will **g** them the land of Israel.
11:19 I will **g** them a single purpose
11:19 and **g** them obedient hearts.
14:4 will **g** that Israelite an answer,
14:7 will **g** him an answer.
16:33 But you **g** gifts to all your
16:38 I will **g** you the death penalty in
16:59 I will **g** you what you deserve.
16:61 I will **g** them to you as
17:2 **G** this illustration to the nation
20:15 that I had promised to **g** them.
20:28 land that I promised to **g** them.
20:42 I promised to **g** your ancestors.
21:22 rams there, **g** the order to kill,
21:27 Then I will **g** it to him.
29:19 I'm going to **g** Egypt to King
29:21 and I will **g** you, Ezekiel,
34:29 I will **g** them a place that is
36:26 I will **g** you a new heart and put
36:26 and **g** you obedient hearts.
39:11 "'When that day comes, I will **g**
43:19 **G** a young bull to the priests as
44:28 Don't **g** them any possessions
45:8 They will **g** land to each tribe
45:13 is the contribution you must **g**
45:14 You must **g** one percent of your
45:16 All the common people must **g**
45:24 He must also **g** as a grain
45:24 He must also **g** one gallon of
46:18 He must not force them to **g** up
46:18 He must **g** his own property as
47:14 hand and swore that I would **g**
48:20 You must **g** this land as a
Dan 1:12 **G** us only vegetables to eat
2:6 I will **g** you gifts, awards,
2:9 a phony explanation to **g** me,
2:16 the king to **g** him some time
4:16 and **g** it the mind of an animal.
4:37 and **g** glory to the King of
5:17 **G** your gifts and awards to
9:22 I have come to **g** you insight.
9:23 I have come to **g** you the reply
11:17 He will **g** the southern king his
11:39 He will **g** high honors to those
Hos 2:5 They will **g** me food and water,
2:15 I will **g** her vineyards there.
Hos 6:6 not to **g** me burnt offerings.
9:14 **g** them what they deserve.
11:8 "How can I **g** you up,
13:10 '**G** us kings and officials!'
Joe 2:14 Then you could **g** grain
Amo 6:11 The LORD is going to **g** the
9:9 I'm going to **g** the order.
Jnh 4:6 beside Jonah to **g** him shade
Mic 1:14 That is why you will **g** farewell
6:7 Should I **g** him my firstborn
6:7 Should I **g** him my young child
Zep 3:9 "Then I will **g** all people pure
Hag 2:9 And in this place I will **g** ⌊them
Zec 3:7 Then I will **g** you free access
8:12 I will **g** the few remaining
8:16 **G** correct and fair verdicts for
10:2 They **g** useless comfort.
11:13 "**G** it to the potter."
Mal 1:14 flocks that they vow to **g** ⌊as
2:2 I'll curse the blessings you **g**.
Mat 1:21 She will **g** birth to a son,
1:23 become pregnant and **g** birth
4:9 The devil said to him, "I will **g**
5:31 divorces his wife must **g** her
5:33 but **g** to the Lord what you
5:33 you swore in an oath to **g** him.'
5:42 **G** to everyone who asks you
6:2 So when you **g** to the poor,
6:3 When you **g** to the poor,
6:4 **G** your contributions privately.
6:11 **G** us our daily bread today.
7:6 "Don't **g** what is holy to dogs or
7:9 any of you **g** him a stone?
7:10 would you **g** him a snake?
7:11 you know how to **g** good gifts
7:11 Father in heaven **g** good things
8:8 But just **g** a command,
10:8 **G** these things without
11:28 and I will **g** you rest.
12:36 day people will have to **g**
14:7 he swore he would **g** her
14:8 "**G** me the head of John the
14:16 You **g** them something to eat."
16:19 I will **g** you the keys of the
16:26 Or what will a person **g** in
17:27 **G** that coin to them for you and
19:7 did Moses order a man to **g** his
19:18 Never **g** false testimony.
19:21 **G** the money to the poor,
20:4 and I'll **g** you whatever is right.'
20:8 and **g** them their wages.
20:14 I want to **g** this last worker as
20:28 He came to serve and to **g** his
20:33 we want you to **g** us our
21:41 who will **g** him his share
22:21 **g** the emperor what belongs to
22:21 and **g** God what belongs to
23:23 You **g** ⌊God⌋ one-tenth of your
24:29 the moon will not **g** light,
25:8 '**G** us some of your oil.
25:28 **G** it to the one who has the ten
25:37 thirsty and **g** you something
25:38 of clothes and **g** you something
25:43 and you didn't **g** me anything to
27:64 Therefore, **g** the order to make
Mar 3:4 to **g** a person back his health or
4:24 measure ⌊of attention⌋ you **g**.
5:43 He also told them to **g** the little
6:22 and I'll **g** it to you."
6:23 "I'll **g** you anything you ask for,
6:25 She said, "I want you to **g** me
6:37 "You **g** them something to eat."
6:41 them to the disciples to **g**
8:37 Or what should a person **g** in
10:3 "What command did Moses **g**
10:4 "Moses allowed a man to **g** his
10:19 Never **g** false testimony.
10:21 **G** the money to the poor,
10:45 He came to serve and to **g** his
12:9 and destroy the workers and **g**
12:17 Jesus said to them, "**G** the
12:17 and **g** God what belongs to
13:24 the moon will not **g** light,
14:11 and promised to **g** him money.
15:23 They tried to **g** him wine mixed
Luk 1:31 pregnant, **g** birth to a son,
Luk 1:32 The Lord God will **g** him the
1:79 He will **g** light to those who
4:6 The devil said to him, "I will **g**
4:6 and I **g** it to anyone I please.
6:9 to **g** a person his health or to
6:30 **G** to everyone who asks you
6:38 **G**, and you will receive.
7:7 But just **g** a command,
7:45 You didn't **g** me a kiss.
8:55 He ordered her parents to **g** her
9:13 "You **g** them something to eat."
9:16 the disciples to **g** to the crowd.
11:3 **G** us our bread day by day.
11:7 I can't get up to **g** you anything.'
11:8 to get up to **g** you anything,
11:8 he will get up and **g** you
11:11 would you **g** him a snake
11:12 would you **g** him a scorpion?
11:13 you know how to **g** good gifts
11:13 will your Father in heaven **g**
11:41 **G** what is inside as a gift to the
11:42 You **g** ⌊God⌋ one-tenth of your
12:13 tell my brother to **g** me my
12:32 pleased to **g** you the kingdom.
12:33 and **g** the money to the poor.
13:15 then take it out of its stall to **g**
14:9 '**G** this person your place.'
14:13 Instead, when you **g** a banquet,
14:33 unless you **g** up everything.
15:12 **g** me my share of the property.'
15:16 No one in the country would **g**
16:12 who will **g** you your own?
17:5 to the Lord, "**G** us more faith."
18:1 all the time and never **g** up.
18:3 him and saying, '**G** me justice.'
18:5 I'll have to **g** her justice.
18:7 Won't God **g** his chosen people
18:8 I can guarantee that he will **g**
18:12 I fast twice a week, and I **g**
18:20 Never **g** false testimony.
19:8 I'll **g** half of my property to the
19:24 and **g** it to the man who has
20:16 destroy those workers and **g**
20:25 He said to them, "Well, then **g**
20:25 and **g** God what belongs to
21:15 I will **g** you words and wisdom
22:5 agreed to **g** him some money.
23:24 Pilate decided to **g** in to their
23:29 who couldn't **g** birth,
Jon 3:6 Flesh and blood **g** birth to flesh
4:7 "**G** me a drink of water."
4:14 that I will **g** them will never
4:14 In fact, the water I will **g** them
4:15 Jesus, "Sir, **g** me this water!
6:27 food the Son of Man will **g** you.
6:32 Moses didn't **g** you bread from
6:34 **g** us this bread all the time."
6:51 The bread I will **g** to bring life
6:52 said, "How can this man **g**
6:68 Your words **g** eternal life.
7:19 Didn't Moses **g** you his
9:24 They told him, "**G** glory to God.
9:26 How did he **g** you sight?"
10:15 So I **g** my life for my sheep.
10:17 loves me because I **g** my life
10:18 I **g** my life of my own free will.
10:18 I have the authority to **g** my life,
10:21 Can a demon **g** sight to the
10:28 and I **g** them eternal life.
11:22 God will **g** you whatever you
12:28 Father, **g** glory to your name."
12:28 and I will **g** it glory again."
13:26 "He's the one to whom I will **g**
13:29 the festival or to **g** something
13:37 I'll **g** my life for you."
13:38 "Will you **g** your life for me?
14:16 and he will **g** you another
14:27 I don't **g** you the kind of peace
15:8 You **g** glory to my Father when
15:13 you can show is to **g** your life
15:16 name to **g** you whatever you
16:14 He will **g** me glory,
16:21 when her time to **g** birth comes.
16:23 in my name, he will **g** it to you.
17:1 **G** your Son glory so that your
17:1 that your Son can **g** you glory.

Jon 17:2 so that he can **g** eternal life
17:5 Now, Father, **g** me glory in your
Act 2:19 miracles in the sky and **g** signs
2:33 God used his power to **g** Jesus
3:6 but I'll **g** you what I do have.
5:31 God used his power to **g** Jesus
6:2 "It's not right for us to **g** up
7:5 "Yet, God didn't **g** Abraham
7:5 But God promised to **g** this
7:25 to use him to **g** them freedom.
7:38 life-giving messages to **g** to us,
8:19 and said, "**G** me this power so
11:14 He will **g** you a message that
13:34 He said, 'I will **g** you the
20:32 help you grow and can **g** you
24:26 Paul would **g** him some money.
Rom 2:7 He will **g** everlasting life to
8:32 So he will also **g** us everything
12:20 If he is thirsty, **g** him a drink.
14:6 since they **g** thanks to God.
14:6 and they, too, **g** thanks to God.
14:12 All of us will have to **g** an
15:4 which the Scriptures **g** us.
15:9 "That is why I will **g** thanks to
15:12 and he will **g** the nations hope."
16:2 **G** her a Christian welcome that
1Co 1:8 He will continue to **g** you
3:2 I didn't **g** you solid food
3:18 you should **g** up that wisdom in
7:25 I'll **g** you my opinion.
7:38 So it's fine for a father to **g** his
7:38 but the father who doesn't **g** his
10:13 he will also **g** you the ability to
10:30 If I **g** thanks to God for the food
11:34 I will **g** directions concerning
12:11 God wants to **g** to each person.
12:23 the ones we **g** special honor.
13:3 I may even **g** away all that I
13:3 that I have and **g** up my body
15:56 standards **g** sin its power.
16:3 When I come, I will **g** letters of
16:6 Then you can **g** me your
16:11 Without quarreling, **g** him your
2Co 4:8 frustrated, but we don't **g** up.
6:3 We don't **g** people any
8:12 if they **g** what they are
8:12 give what they are able to **g**.
8:24 So **g** these men a
9:5 you had already promised to **g**.
9:7 Each of you should **g** whatever
9:7 you gave or feel forced to **g**,
9:8 Besides, God will **g** you his
9:10 God will also **g** you seed and
10:15 you will think enough of us to **g**
12:15 I'll even **g** myself for you.
Gal 2:5 But we did not **g** in to them for
3:8 that God would **g** his approval
3:21 If those laws could **g** us life,
4:27 who cannot **g** birth to any
6:9 proper time, if we don't **g** up.
Eph 1:12 praise him and **g** him glory.
1:17 would **g** you a spirit of wisdom
3:16 I'm asking God to **g** you a gift
3:16 I pray that he would **g** you inner
4:27 Don't **g** the devil any
4:29 that you can **g** help wherever
4:30 Don't **g** God's Holy Spirit any
5:4 Instead, **g** thanks ⌊to God⌋.
6:19 Also pray that God will **g** me
6:23 Lord Jesus Christ **g** our brothers
Php 1:26 I want to **g** you even more
2:29 **G** him a joyful Christian
2:30 for the help you couldn't **g** me.
Col 3:24 that your real master will **g** you
4:3 Pray that God will **g** us an
1Th 3:9 enough for all the joy you **g**
5:18 Whatever happens, **g** thanks,
2Th 1:6 Certainly, it is right for God to **g**
1:7 It is also right for God to **g** all of
3:16 May the Lord of peace **g** you
1Ti 5:14 and not **g** the enemy any
5:17 **G** double honor to spiritual
6:1 All slaves who believe must **g**
2Ti 1:7 God didn't **g** us a cowardly
2:19 Lord must **g** up doing wrong."
3:15 They have the power to **g** you
2Ti 4:8 will **g** me that prize on that day.
4:8 He will **g** it not only to me but
4:19 **G** my greetings to Prisca and
Tit 3:13 **G** Zenas the lawyer and
Phm 1:20 **G** me some comfort because of
1:22 God will **g** me back to you.
Heb 6:14 "I will certainly bless you and **g**
9:9 were brought there could not **g**
11:22 and **g** them instructions about
11:27 Moses didn't **g** up but
11:40 God planned to **g** us something
12:1 ahead of us and never **g** up.
12:3 don't become tired and **g** up.
12:5 Don't **g** up when he corrects
Jas 1:5 and he will **g** it to you.
1:18 God decided to **g** us life
2:3 Suppose you **g** special
4:10 Then he will **g** you a high
5:8 Don't **g** up hope. The Lord will
1Pe 4:5 They will **g** an account to the
2Pe 2:20 in this filth again and **g**
1Jn 2:7 as though I'm writing to **g** you
2:8 I'm writing to **g** you a new
3:16 That means we must **g** our
5:16 God would **g** that person life.
2Jn 1:5 as though I'm writing to **g** you
Jud 1:21 Christ to **g** you eternal life.
Rev 2:7 I will **g** the privilege of eating
2:10 and I will **g** you the crown of
2:17 I will **g** some of the hidden
2:17 I will also **g** each person a
2:26 I will **g** authority over the
2:28 I will also **g** them the morning
4:9 Whenever the living creatures **g**
10:9 angel and asked him to **g** me
11:17 and said, "We **g** thanks to you,
12:4 was going to **g** birth so that
12:11 that they refused to **g** it up.
14:7 "Fear God and **g** him glory,
16:9 think and act and **g** him glory.
16:19 God remembered to **g** Babylon
17:13 They have one purpose — to **g**
17:17 So they will **g** their kingdom to
18:6 **G** her twice as much as she
18:7 Now **g** her just as much torture
19:7 Let us rejoice, be happy, and **g**
21:6 I will **g** a drink from the
21:23 need any sun or moon to **g**
22:16 have sent my angel to **g** this

given (448)

Gen 1:29 God said, "I have **g** you every
1:30 I have **g** all green plants as
4:25 "God has **g** me another child in
12:16 and he was **g** sheep,
15:3 You have **g** me no children,
20:16 I've **g** your brother 25 pounds of
21:7 Yet, I have **g** him a son in his
22:20 "Milcah has **g** birth to these
24:32 were unloaded and **g** straw
24:35 The LORD has **g** him sheep
24:36 and my master has **g** that son
25:6 Abraham had **g** gifts to the
26:18 that his father had **g** them.
27:41 that his father had **g** him.
29:24 (Laban had **g** his slave Zilpah
29:29 (Laban had **g** his slave Bilhah
29:33 and he also has **g** me this son."
29:34 because I've **g** him three sons."
30:6 heard my prayer and has **g** me
30:18 Leah said, "God has **g** me my
30:20 I have **g** him six sons."
31:9 and has **g** them to me.
33:5 God has graciously **g** me,
33:11 to me and has **g** me all that
38:14 and she hadn't been **g** to him in
38:26 because I haven't **g** her my son
40:16 that the meaning Joseph had **g**
43:23 must have **g** you treasure in
48:9 whom God has **g** me here in
Exo 4:21 things that I have **g** you
5:16 We're **g** no straw, and yet we're
5:18 You won't be **g** any straw,
5:21 You have **g** them an excuse to
16:15 the LORD has **g** you to eat.
16:29 Remember: The LORD has **g**
Exo 28:3 to whom I have **g** this ability —
30:15 This contribution is **g** to make
31:6 I have **g** every craftsman the
35:34 Also, the LORD has **g** Bezalel
36:1 to whom the LORD has **g**
36:2 the LORD had **g** these skills
38:8 out of the bronze mirrors **g** by
Lev 6:17 I have **g** it to them as their
7:34 I have **g** them to the priest
7:35 It was **g** to them on the day
10:14 and the thigh that was **g** as
10:15 They will bring the thigh **g** as a
10:17 It is very holy and was **g** to you
17:11 I have **g** this blood to you to
19:20 was never bought or **g** to her,
27:27 it must be sold at the value **g** it.
Num 3:9 be the only Israelites **g** to them.
5:8 what you did wrong must be **g**
5:10 but whatever is **g** to the priest
6:20 and the thigh that is **g**.
8:16 be the only Israelites **g** to me.
9:23 LORD had **g** through Moses.
10:13 LORD had **g** through Moses.
16:14 with milk and honey or **g**
16:40 LORD had **g** through Moses.
18:6 They are a gift **g** to the LORD
18:8 of all the contributions **g** to me.
18:32 the holy offerings **g** by
26:62 because they were **g** no land of
32:7 the land the LORD has **g** them.
32:9 land that the LORD had **g** them.
33:54 The land must be **g** to each
34:2 the land that will be **g** to you
34:13 that this land will be **g**
35:8 Israelites must be **g** based
35:31 murderer who has been **g**
Dtr 2:5 I've **g** Esau's descendants the
2:9 I have **g** it to the descendants
2:19 of the land that I have already **g**
3:18 "The LORD your God has **g**
4:19 The LORD your God has **g**
5:33 the LORD your God has **g** you.
6:17 and laws he has **g** you.
8:10 for the good land he has **g** you.
12:21 that the LORD has **g** you.
16:10 the LORD your God has **g** you.
16:17 the LORD your God has **g** him.
20:14 the LORD your God has **g** you.
25:3 Forty lashes may be **g**,
25:3 If an Israelite were **g** more than
26:11 the LORD your God has **g** you
26:15 and honey that you have **g** us,
28:31 Your flock will be **g** to your
28:32 your sons and daughters are **g**
28:53 the LORD your God has **g** you.
29:4 this day the LORD hasn't **g** you
32:46 warnings I've **g** you today.
Jos 2:24 "The LORD has **g** us the whole
6:8 After Joshua had **g** orders to
6:16 the LORD has **g** you the city!
13:8 Moses had already **g** it to them.
13:31 They were **g** to half the
14:3 Moses had **g** the two-and-a-half
14:4 The Levites were not **g** a share
15:19 Since you've **g** me some dry
15:42 their villages were **g** to Judah:
15:59 villages that were **g** to Judah.
15:60 villages ⌊were **g** to Judah⌋.
15:61 In the desert Judah was **g** six
16:8 This is the land **g** as an
17:2 The land was **g** to the rest of
17:6 Manasseh's daughters were **g**
18:3 of your ancestors has **g** you?
18:20 surrounding the inheritance **g**
19:16 villages are the inheritance **g**
21:3 Levi's descendants were **g** the
21:19 cities with pasturelands were **g**
21:26 cities with pasturelands were **g**
21:28 with pasturelands were also **g**
21:30 cities with pasturelands were **g**
21:32 cities with pasturelands were **g**
21:33 were **g** to Gershon's families.
21:45 promise that the LORD had **g**
22:4 has **g** your relatives peace,
22:7 Moses had **g** land in Bashan
22:7 and Joshua had **g** the other half

Jos 23:4 I have **g** you the territory of the
23:13 the LORD your God has **g** you.
23:14 your God has **g** you has ever
23:15 good land that he has **g** you.
23:16 the good land he has **g** you."
24:33 on the hill that had been **g**
Jdg 1:3 with us into the territory **g**
1:15 Since you've **g** me some dry
1:20 Hebron was **g** to Caleb,
3:4 had **g** their ancestors through
4:6 "The LORD God of Israel has **g**
14:20 Samson's wife was **g** to his
15:18 "You have **g** me this great
21:14 These men were **g** the women
Rut 4:15 because she has **g** birth."
1Sm 2:20 of the one which she has **g**
4:20 You've **g** birth to a son."
15:28 He has **g** it to your neighbor
21:2 and about the orders I've **g** you.
25:27 May it be **g** to the young men
25:31 the LORD has **g** you success,
25:44 Saul had **g** his daughter Michal,
28:17 out of your hands and **g**
30:22 they shouldn't be **g** any of the
30:23 which the LORD has **g** us.
2Sm 4:8 "Today the LORD has **g** Your
9:9 "I have **g** your master's
12:8 I would have **g** you even more.
12:15 that Uriah's wife had **g** birth
13:28 I've **g** you the order,
14:16 son from ⌊our⌋ God-**g** inheritance
19:13 unless you are **g** Joab's place
20:5 to do it than David had **g** him.
22:36 You have **g** me the shield of
1Ki 2:21 "Let Abishag from Shunem be **g**
2:22 from Shunem be **g** to Adonijah?
5:7 He has **g** David a wise son to
8:56 He has **g** his people Israel rest,
8:66 LORD had **g** his servant David
9:13 kind of cities have you **g** me,
10:13 besides what he had **g** her out
11:10 God had **g** him commands
18:29 no attention **g** to them.
20:27 organized and **g** provisions,
22:31 The king of Aram had **g** orders
2Ki 5:1 The LORD had **g** Aram a
12:14 Instead, the money was **g** to
17:15 the warnings he had **g** them.
18:6 LORD had **g** through Moses,
22:9 in the temple and have **g**
22:10 "The priest Hilkiah has **g** me a
1Ch 5:1 his rights as firstborn were **g** to
6:55 They were **g** Hebron in the
6:56 its villages were **g** to Caleb,
6:57 Aaron's descendants were **g**
6:62 were **g** 13 cities chosen
6:63 were **g** 12 cities chosen
6:67 They were **g** these cities of
6:70 they were **g** Aner with its
17:18 light of the honor ⌊you have **g**⌋
22:18 Hasn't he **g** you peace with all
23:11 so they were **g** an assignment
23:25 "The LORD God of Israel has **g**
25:5 They were **g** to him to make
28:5 LORD has **g** me many sons)
2Ch 1:12 knowledge will be **g** to you.
2:12 the earth and has **g** King David
2:14 of plans that will be **g** to him.
7:10 the LORD had **g** David,
18:30 The king of Aram had **g** orders
26:18 who have been **g** the holy task
32:29 God had **g** him a lot of property.
34:18 "The priest Hilkiah has **g** me a
36:23 God of heaven has **g** me all
Ezr 1:2 God of heaven has **g** me all
7:6 the LORD God of Israel had **g**.
7:19 The utensils that have been **g**
9:8 our eyes light up and has **g**
10:44 women had **g** birth to children.
Neh 8:14 Teachings that the LORD had **g**
10:29 God's teachings **g** by Moses,
12:43 God had **g** them reason
13:10 had not been **g** their portions.
Est 2:13 the king's palace was **g** to her.
8:7 "I have **g** Haman's property to
8:11 that the king had **g** permission

Job 1:9 "Haven't you **g** Job a reason to
1:21 The LORD has **g**, and the
7:3 Likewise, I have been **g**
15:19 (The land was **g** to them alone,
36:17 But you are **g** the judgment evil
38:12 "Have you ever **g** orders to the
38:29 and who has **g** birth to the frost
Psa 18:35 You have **g** me the shield of
60:3 You have **g** us wine that
61:5 You have **g** me the inheritance
72:15 gold from Sheba be **g** to him.
79:2 They have **g** the dead bodies
79:2 They have **g** the flesh of your
107:11 had despised the advice **g** by
115:16 but he has **g** the earth to the
118:27 and he has **g** us light.
148:14 He has **g** his people a strong
Pro 1:1 who was king of Israel, ⌊**g**⌋
21:14 A gift ⌊**g**⌋ in secret calms
27:21 tested⌋ by the praise **g** to him.
Ecc 8:10 Then I saw wicked people **g**
8:15 which God has **g** them under
9:9 God has **g** you your pointless
10:6 are often **g** high positions,
Isa 8:18 that the LORD has **g** me.
9:6 A son will be **g** to us.
23:4 never been in labor or **g** birth.
45:4 I have **g** you a title of honor,
48:1 You are **g** the name of Israel.
57:6 You have **g** them wine
62:2 You will be **g** a new name that
63:14 they were **g** rest by the LORD's
Jer 3:13 You have **g** yourself to
8:13 What I have **g** them will be
8:14 He has **g** us poison to drink
13:20 Where is the flock that was **g**
23:6 is the name that he will be **g**:
29:15 the LORD has **g** you prophets
32:16 "After I had **g** the copies to
Lam 1:17 The LORD has **g** this order
Eze 11:15 This land has been **g** to us as
16:17 silver jewelry that I had **g** you
29:20 I have **g** him Egypt as pay for
33:24 and he was **g** the land.
33:24 the land has been **g** to us.'
33:25 Should the land be **g** to you?
33:26 Should the land be **g** to you?'
45:5 It will be **g** to them so that they
47:22 among you and have **g** birth
Dan 2:37 The God of heaven has **g** you
2:37 He has **g** you power,
2:38 He has **g** you control over
2:46 and offerings be **g** to Daniel.
4:36 and glory were also **g** back
4:36 I was **g** back my kingdom and
5:28 kingdom will be divided and **g**
7:4 and was **g** a human mind.
7:6 It was **g** power to rule.
7:14 He was **g** power, honor, and a
7:27 will be **g** to the holy people of
8:12 In its rebelliousness it was **g**
9:25 from the time the command is **g**
10:1 he was **g** insight during
11:4 The empire will not be **g** to his
11:4 be uprooted and **g** to others.
11:6 protected her will be **g** away.
11:21 He will not be **g** royal splendor.
Joe 2:23 The LORD has **g** you the
Oba 1:15 will get back what you have **g**.
Jnh 3:2 the message I have **g** you."
Nah 1:14 The LORD has **g** this
Mal 2:10 the promise **g** to our ancestors?
Mat 10:19 you will be **g** what to say.
13:11 of heaven has been **g** to you.
13:11 it has not been **g** to the crowd.
13:12 will be **g** ⌊more knowledge⌋,
14:11 was brought on a platter and **g**
15:5 'I have **g** to God whatever
16:4 But the only sign they will be **g**
19:27 we've **g** up everything to follow
21:43 be taken away from you and **g**
25:15 Each was **g** money based on
25:29 all who have, more will be **g**,
26:9 could have been **g** to the poor."
26:48 the traitor had **g** them a signal.
27:58 ordered that it be **g** to him.

Mat 28:18 and on earth has been **g** to me.
Mar 4:11 of God has been **g** ⌊directly⌋
4:11 on the outside, it is **g** in stories:
4:25 will be **g** ⌊more knowledge⌋.
8:12 If these people are **g** a sign,
10:28 Then Peter spoke up, "We've **g**
12:43 This poor widow has **g** more
12:44 All of them have **g** what they
12:44 But she, in her poverty, has **g**
13:11 Instead, say whatever is **g** to
14:5 the money could have been **g**
14:44 the traitor had **g** them a signal.
Luk 2:21 the angel had **g** him before his
4:6 All of it has been **g** to me,
8:10 of God has been **g** ⌊directly⌋
8:10 But it is **g** to others in stories.
8:18 will be **g** ⌊more knowledge⌋.
10:19 I have **g** you the authority to
12:48 everyone who has been **g** a lot.
15:29 Yet, you've never **g** me so
19:26 has something will be **g** more.
19:28 Jesus had **g** this illustration,
21:3 This poor widow has **g** more
21:4 All of these people have **g**
21:4 But she, in her poverty, has **g**
22:19 which is **g** up for you.
22:29 So as my Father has **g** me a
Jon 1:17 were **g** through Moses,
3:27 anything unless it has been **g**
4:5 piece of land that Jacob had **g**
4:10 would have **g** you living water."
4:34 to finish the work he has **g** me.
5:27 "He has also **g** the Son
5:43 authority my Father has **g** me,
9:18 blind and had been **g** sight.
9:39 Blind people will be **g** sight,
11:57 had **g** orders that whoever
12:5 and the money **g** to the poor?"
12:28 heaven said, "I have **g** it glory,
13:15 I've **g** you an example that you
14:13 that the Father will be **g** glory
17:2 After all, you've **g** him authority
17:4 On earth I have **g** you glory by
17:10 I have been **g** glory by the
17:10 by the people you have **g** me.
17:14 I have **g** them your message.
17:22 I have **g** them the glory that you
17:24 I want those you have **g** to me
18:11 that my Father has **g** me?"
19:11 over me if it hadn't been **g**
Act 1:17 been one of us and had been **g**
2:23 who was **g** over ⌊to death⌋ by
3:14 You asked to have a murderer **g**
5:32 whom God has **g** to those who
6:10 that the Spirit had **g** him.
7:56 authority that God has **g** him!"
8:18 saw that the Spirit was **g**
14:17 Yet, by doing good, he has **g**
14:27 especially that he had **g**
17:26 He has **g** them the seasons of
17:31 God has **g** proof to everyone
20:35 I have **g** you an example that
23:1 with God has always **g** me
Rom 1:27 Likewise, their men have **g** up
3:25 approval is **g** through faith
5:5 who has been **g** to us.
5:9 Since Christ's blood has now **g**
5:15 kindness and the gift **g** through
6:17 teachings which you were **g**.
11:8 "To this day God has **g** them a
12:3 based on what God has **g** each
13:6 do the work he has **g** them.
14:14 The Lord Jesus has **g** me the
1Co 2:12 which God has freely **g** us.
4:7 you have that wasn't **g** to you?
4:7 If you were **g** what you have,
4:10 We have **g** up our wisdom for
11:15 Her hair is **g** to her in place of a
11:24 which is **g** for you.
12:7 of the Spirit's presence is **g**
12:24 together and **g** special honor
15:8 aborted fetus ⌊who was **g** life⌋.
15:31 Christ Jesus our Lord has **g** me:
2Co 1:12 We have lived with a God-**g**
1:22 ownership⌋ on us and has **g**
4:1 since God has **g** us this

2Co 4:6 out of darkness has **g** us light.
5:5 prepared us for this and has **g**
5:18 and has **g** us this ministry of
5:19 and he has **g** us this message
8:3 will they have **g** all they could,
10:13 brag about what God has **g**
Gal 2:9 that God had **g** me this special
3:17 The laws ⌊**g** to Moses⌋ 430
3:19 of the laws **g** to Moses?
3:19 the promise was **g** came.
3:21 that the laws **g** to Moses
3:22 faith in Jesus Christ could be **g**
4:15 your eyes and **g** them to me.
Eph 1:6 so that the kindness he had **g**
1:6 would be praised and **g** glory.
2:6 with Christ Jesus and has **g**
3:7 through God's kindness freely **g**
4:7 God's favor has been **g** to each
Php 1:14 the Lord has **g** most of our
1:29 God has **g** you the privilege not
2:9 This is why God has **g** him an
3:17 by the example we have **g** you.
Col 1:8 love that the Spirit has **g** you.
2:19 through support and unity **g** by
1Ti 1:12 with the strength he has **g** me.
Tit 1:14 or commands **g** by people who
3:7 God in his kindness has **g** us
Heb 1:4 the angels since he has been **g**
2:13 and daughters God has **g** me."
4:8 If Joshua had **g** the people rest,
5:5 the glory was **g** to him by God,
6:18 confidence we have been **g**.
8:6 Jesus has been **g** a priestly
12:20 obey the command that was **g**,
1Pe 1:3 God has **g** us a new birth
4:10 use the gift that God has **g** you
2Pe 1:3 God's divine power has **g** us
1:3 This power was **g** to us
1:4 his glory and integrity he has **g**
1:11 Then you will also be **g** the
1:21 Instead, it was **g** by the Holy
1Jn 2:25 Christ has **g** us the promise of
3:1 The Father has **g** us his love.
3:24 because he has **g** us the Spirit.
4:13 because he has **g** us his Spirit.
4:21 Christ has **g** us this
5:9 that he has **g** about his Son.
5:10 that God has **g** about his Son.
5:11 God has **g** us eternal life,
5:20 of God has come and has **g**
Rev 6:2 He was **g** a crown and rode off
6:4 Its rider was **g** the power to
6:4 So he was **g** a large sword.
6:8 They were **g** power over
6:9 they had **g** about him.
6:11 Each of the souls was **g** a
8:2 they were **g** seven trumpets.
8:3 He was **g** a lot of incense to
9:1 The star was **g** the key to the
9:3 and they were **g** power like the
11:1 Then I was **g** a stick like a
11:2 because it is **g** to the nations,
12:13 the woman who had **g** birth
12:14 The woman was **g** the two
13:4 because it had **g** authority
13:5 It was **g** authority to act for 42
13:7 It was also **g** authority over
16:6 You have **g** them blood to drink
19:8 She has been **g** the privilege of

giver (1)

2Co 9:7 since God loves a cheerful **g**.

gives (165)

Gen 49:25 because of the Almighty who **g**
Exo 4:11 Who **g** them sight or makes
13:11 land of the Canaanites and **g**
16:29 That's why he **g** you enough
21:4 If his master **g** him a wife and
21:4 him a wife and she **g** birth
21:22 so that she **g** birth prematurely.
22:7 someone **g** his neighbor silver
22:10 someone **g** his neighbor
25:2 each person freely **g**.
Lev 12:2 When a woman **g** birth to a boy,
12:5 "When a woman **g** birth to a
Lev 12:7 for the woman who **g** birth
27:16 "If a person **g** part of a field to
Num 10:32 good things the LORD **g** us."
16:22 you are the God who **g** the
27:16 "LORD, you are the God who **g**
Dtr 7:2 When the LORD your God **g**
10:18 He loves foreigners and **g** them
24:1 of divorce, **g** it to his wife,
25:19 So when the LORD your God **g**
28:57 and the children she **g** birth to.
33:20 "Blessed is the one who **g** the
Jos 2:14 when the LORD **g** us this land."
Jdg 11:9 and the LORD **g** them
21:18 an oath that whoever **g** wives
1Sm 2:5 who was childless **g** birth
2:6 "The LORD kills, and he **g** life.
2:10 He **g** strength to his King and
20:10 whether or not your father **g** you
2Sm 22:34 of a deer and **g** me sure footing
22:48 God **g** me vengeance!
22:51 He **g** great victories to his king.
Job 2:10 accept the good that God **g** us.
5:10 He **g** rain to the earth and
20:3 understanding **g** me answers.
20:29 This is the reward God **g** to the
32:8 that **g** them understanding.
33:4 breath of the Almighty **g** me life.
41:18 it **g** out a flash of light.
Psa 7:14 with harm, and **g** birth to lies.
18:33 of a deer and **g** me sure footing
18:47 God **g** me vengeance!
18:50 He **g** great victories to his king.
68:11 The Lord **g** instructions.
68:35 He **g** strength and power to his
112:9 He **g** freely to poor people.
127:2 The LORD **g** ⌊food⌋ to those
136:25 He **g** food to every living
144:10 You are the one who **g** victory
146:7 He **g** food to those who are
146:8 The LORD **g** sight to blind
146:9 The LORD **g** relief to orphans
147:4 He **g** each one a name.
147:6 The LORD **g** relief to those
147:9 He is the one who **g** food to
Pro 2:6 The LORD **g** wisdom.
11:13 gossips **g** away secrets,
16:20 Whoever **g** attention to the
17:8 a jewel to the one who **g** it.
18:13 Whoever **g** an answer before
18:16 opens doors for the one who **g**
19:6 a friend to a person who **g** gifts.
21:26 but a righteous person **g** and
25:18 ⌊So⌋ is a person who **g** false
25:26 is a righteous person who **g**
28:27 Whoever **g** to the poor lacks
29:13 The LORD **g** both of them sight.
31:15 while it is still dark and **g** food
Ecc 2:26 God **g** wisdom, knowledge,
2:26 he **g** the job of gathering and
5:18 during the brief lives God **g** us.
5:19 God **g** some people wealth
6:2 God **g** one person riches,
7:12 of wisdom is that it **g** life
Isa 19:11 counselors **g** stupid advice.
31:3 the one who **g** help will
40:29 He **g** strength to those who
41:2 to whom the LORD **g** victory
42:13 He shouts, **g** the battle cry,
66:7 goes into labor, she **g** birth.
Jer 4:31 cry with anguish as she **g** birth
15:9 A mother who **g** birth to seven
Eze 18:7 He returns what a borrower **g**
18:7 He **g** food to people who are
18:7 and he **g** clothes to those who
18:16 He **g** food to people who are
18:16 and he **g** clothes to those who
24:21 my holy place **g** you strength.
Dan 2:21 He **g** wisdom to those who are
4:17 He **g** them to whomever he
4:25 kingdoms and that he **g** them
4:32 kingdoms and that he **g** them
Mic 2:4 The LORD **g** our people's
Zec 10:1 He **g** everyone rain showers for
Mat 9:38 So ask the Lord who **g** this
10:42 Whoever **g** any of my humble
21:23 They asked, "What **g** you the
Mat 26:73 Your accent **g** you away!"
Mar 1:27 He **g** orders to evil spirits,
9:41 Whoever **g** you a cup of water
11:28 They asked him, "What **g** you
Luk 3:6 see the salvation that God **g**.'"
4:36 With authority and power he **g**
8:25 He **g** orders to the wind and the
10:2 So ask the Lord who **g** this
20:2 what **g** you the right to do these
Jon 3:6 but the Spirit **g** birth to things
3:34 After all, God **g** him the Spirit
5:21 back the dead and **g** them life,
5:21 the Son **g** life to anyone he
6:32 but my Father **g** you the true
6:33 comes from heaven and **g** life
6:37 Everyone whom the Father **g**
8:54 is the one who **g** me glory,
10:11 The good shepherd **g** his life
14:27 kind of peace that the world **g**.
Act 7:55 position of authority that God **g**.
14:17 He **g** you rain from heaven and
17:25 He **g** everyone life,
Rom 4:17 presence of the God who **g** life
6:11 the power Christ Jesus **g** you.
6:23 but the gift that God freely **g** is
8:2 who **g** life through Christ Jesus,
8:37 The one who loves us **g** us an
10:12 who **g** his riches to everyone
11:29 his mind when he **g** gifts
14:17 as the joy that the Holy Spirit **g**.
15:5 May God, who **g** you this
15:17 So Christ Jesus **g** me the right
1Co 12:4 but the same Spirit **g** them.
12:8 The Spirit **g** one person the
12:8 The same Spirit **g** another
12:9 Spirit **g** ⌊courageous⌋ faith.
12:9 person the same Spirit **g**
13:7 never stops hoping, never **g** up.
15:38 God **g** the plant the form he
15:56 Sin **g** death its sting,
15:57 Thank God that he **g** us the
2Co 1:3 and the God who **g** comfort.
3:4 Christ **g** us confidence about
9:9 "The righteous person **g** freely
9:10 God **g** seed to the farmer and
Gal 2:4 the freedom Christ Jesus **g** us.
5:10 The Lord **g** me confidence that
Eph 4:3 the unity that the Spirit **g**.
6:15 the Good News that **g** peace.
Php 2:24 But the Lord **g** me confidence
3:10 that his coming back to life **g**
4:9 Then the God who **g** this
Col 2:18 **g** endless details of the visions
1Th 1:6 of joy that the Holy Spirit **g**.
4:8 who **g** you his Holy Spirit.
5:23 May the God who **g** peace
2Th 3:4 The Lord **g** us confidence that
1Ti 3:16 The mystery that **g** us our
6:13 who **g** life to everything,
Tit 3:5 in which the Holy Spirit **g**
Phm 1:7 Your love ⌊for God's people⌋ **g**
Heb 7:19 we have something else that **g**
Jas 1:15 becomes pregnant and **g** birth
1:15 sin grows up, it **g** birth to death.
1Pe 1:7 the test, it **g** praise, glory,
3:22 the highest position that God **g**.
2Pe 2:19 a slave to whatever he **g** in to.

giving (163)

Gen 9:12 the sign of the promise I am **g**
17:8 I am also **g** this land where you
23:11 I'm **g** you the field together with
23:11 people are witnesses that I'm **g**
24:19 When she had finished **g** him a
32:20 "I'll make peace with him by **g**
33:10 please take the gift I'm **g** you,
38:9 ground to avoid **g** his brother
38:28 When she was **g** birth,
48:22 I'm **g** you one more mountain
49:33 When Jacob finished **g** these
Exo 5:10 I'm no longer **g** you straw.
20:12 the LORD your God is **g** you.
23:1 people by **g** false testimony.
Lev 25:2 come into the land I'm **g** you,
Num 13:2 which I'm **g** to the Israelites.
15:2 settled in the land I'm **g** you,

Num 18:8 I am **g** you and your
18:11 I am **g** these to you,
18:12 "I am also **g** you the first of the
18:19 I am **g** you, your sons, and your
18:21 "I am **g** the Levites one-tenth of
18:26 income which I'm **g** you as your
20:12 into the land I'm **g** them."
20:24 the land I'm **g** the Israelites.
26:54 from the census, in **g** land
Dtr 1:8 I'm **g** you this land.
1:20 which the LORD our God is **g**
1:21 The LORD your God is **g** you
1:25 LORD our God is **g** us is good."
2:5 because I'm not **g** you any of
2:9 I'm not **g** you any of Ar as your
2:19 I'm not **g** you any of the land
2:29 the LORD our God is **g** us."
3:20 the LORD your God is **g** them
4:1 God of your ancestors is **g** you.
4:8 teachings I am **g** you today?
4:21 good land he is **g** you as your
4:40 which I'm **g** you today.
4:40 The LORD your God is **g** you
5:16 the LORD your God is **g** you.
5:31 which I'm **g** them to possess."
6:2 and commands that I'm **g** you,
7:11 and rules I'm **g** you today.
8:11 and laws that I'm **g** you today.
9:6 your God is **g** you this good
9:23 of the land I'm **g** you."
10:13 and laws that I'm **g** you today
11:8 the commands I'm **g** you today.
11:13 commands that I'm **g** you today,
11:17 good land the LORD is **g** you.
11:22 all these commands I'm **g** you.
11:26 Today I'm **g** you the choice of a
11:27 your God that I'm **g** you today.
11:31 the LORD your God is **g** you.
11:32 laws and rules I'm **g** you today.
12:1 your ancestors is **g** you as your
12:9 the LORD your God is **g** you.
12:10 your God is **g** you as your
12:28 all these instructions I'm **g** you.
13:12 the LORD your God is **g** you
13:18 commands that I'm **g** you today,
15:4 in the land he is **g** you as your
15:5 commands I'm **g** you today.
15:7 the LORD your God is **g** you.
15:15 That's why I'm **g** you this
16:5 the LORD your God is **g** you.
16:18 the LORD your God is **g** you.
16:20 the LORD your God is **g** you.
17:2 the LORD your God is **g** you,
17:14 the LORD your God is **g** you.
18:9 the LORD your God is **g** you,
19:1 in the land that he's **g** you.
19:2 the LORD your God is **g** you.
19:3 your God is **g** you into three
19:9 commands I am now **g** you —
19:10 the LORD your God is **g** you,
19:14 the LORD your God is **g** you.
20:16 your God is **g** you as your
21:1 the LORD your God is **g** you.
21:23 your God is **g** you must never
24:4 your God is **g** you as your
25:15 the LORD your God is **g** you.
25:19 land that he is **g** you as your
26:1 your God is **g** you as your
26:2 the LORD your God is **g** you,
26:3 the land that the LORD is **g** us,
27:1 command I'm **g** you today.
27:2 the LORD your God is **g** you,
27:3 God of your ancestors is **g** you
27:4 the command I'm **g** you today.
27:10 laws which I'm **g** you today."
28:1 commands that I'm **g** you today.
28:8 you in the land that he is **g** you.
28:13 your God that I am **g** you today.
28:15 and laws that I am **g** you today.
28:45 and laws, which I'm **g** you.
28:52 the LORD your God is **g** you.
29:12 LORD your God is **g** you today.
30:8 commands that I'm **g** you today.
30:11 This command I'm **g** you today
32:49 at the land of Canaan that I'm **g**
32:52 the land I'm **g** the Israelites."
Jdg 17:3 So now I'm **g** the silver back to
1Sm 1:28 I am **g** him to the LORD.
6:8 objects which you're **g** him as
23:4 I'm **g** you the power to defeat
2Sm 16:8 The LORD is **g** the kingship to
1Ki 2:22 That would be the same as **g**
3:6 him your great love by **g** him
3:12 I'm **g** you a wise and
3:13 I'm also **g** you what you haven't
1Ch 29:3 of gold and silver that I'm **g**
2Ch 31:2 offerings, serving, **g** thanks,
Neh 12:47 all the Israelites were **g** gifts for
Job 34:36 for **g** answers like wicked
39:3 Then the pain of **g** birth is over.
Psa 30:4 Remember his holiness by **g**
37:21 person is generous and **g**.
37:34 and he will honor you by **g** you
85:7 by **g** us your salvation.
111:6 works to his people by **g** them
Pro 22:16 the poor for profit or **g**
24:26 **G** a straight answer is like a
26:8 so is **g** honor to a fool.
Isa 13:8 They'll writhe like a woman **g**
Jer 6:24 and pain like a woman **g** birth
22:23 pain like a woman **g** birth to a
30:6 in pain like a woman **g** birth
Eze 2:8 and eat what I am **g** to you."
3:3 eat this scroll I'm **g** you,
14:9 is tricked into **g** a prophecy,
Hos 4:12 They commit adultery by **g**
Mal 2:2 if you won't consider **g** honor
Mat 9:8 God for **g** such authority
11:1 After Jesus finished **g** his
24:45 put that person in charge of **g**
Mar 6:41 loaves apart and kept **g** them
Luk 7:21 Also, he was **g** back sight to
9:16 loaves apart and kept **g** them
12:42 master will put in charge of **g**
22:29 me a kingdom, I'm **g** it to you.
Jon 9:32 ever heard of anyone **g** sight
13:34 "I'm **g** you a new
14:27 I'm **g** you my peace.
Act 12:23 Lord killed Herod for not **g** glory
15:8 who aren't Jewish by **g** them
20:35 '**G** gifts is more satisfying than
Rom 4:20 Instead, **g** honor to God for the
12:8 yourself to **g** encouragement.
1Co 12:11 things by **g** what God wants
2Co 5:12 but we are **g** you an opportunity
8:10 I'm **g** you my opinion because
Eph 1:8 poured out his kindness by **g**
Php 4:6 and requests while **g** thanks.
Col 1:27 **g** you the hope of glory.
3:17 **g** thanks to God the Father
1Ti 1:5 My goal in **g** you this order is
1:18 Timothy, my child, I'm **g** you
4:13 **g** encouraging messages,
Heb 7:9 Levi was **g** a tenth of
1Jn 2:7 Rather, I'm **g** you an old
Rev 12:2 pains and the agony of **g** birth.

Gizon (1)

1Ch 11:34 Bene Hashem from **G**,

gizzard (1)

Lev 1:16 Remove the **g** with its filth and

glad (58)

Exo 4:14 he will be very **g** to see you.
Dtr 28:63 the LORD was more than **g**
28:63 the LORD will be more than **g**
2Sm 1:20 of the Philistines will be **g**,
1Ki 5:7 Hiram was very **g** to hear what
1Ch 16:31 rejoice and the earth be **g**.
Job 22:19 righteous saw it and were **g**,
Psa 9:2 find joy and be **g** about you.
14:7 will rejoice. Israel will be **g**.
16:9 That is why my heart is **g** and
21:6 You made him **g** with the joy of
31:7 I will rejoice and be **g** because
32:11 Be **g** and find joy in the LORD,
40:16 who seek you rejoice and be **g**
48:11 Let Mount Zion be **g** and the
53:6 will rejoice. Israel will be **g**.
67:4 Let the nations be **g** and sing
70:4 who seek you rejoice and be **g**
Psa 96:11 rejoice and the earth be **g**.
105:38 so they were **g** when Israel left.
107:30 The sailors were **g** that the
118:24 Let's rejoice and be **g** today!
122:1 I was **g** when they said to me,
Pro 11:10 people prosper, a city is **g**.
23:25 father and your mother be **g**.
24:17 not feel **g** when he stumbles.
27:9 and incense make the heart **g**,
27:11 and make my heart **g** so that I
29:6 runs away from it and is **g**.
Isa 25:9 Let us rejoice and be **g**
35:1 and the dry land will be **g**,
35:10 They will be **g** and joyful.
51:11 They will be **g** and joyful.
65:13 My servants will be **g**,
65:18 Be **g**, and rejoice forever in
65:19 and be **g** about my people.
66:10 mourn for her, be **g** with her.
Jer 41:13 were with him, they were **g**.
Lam 4:21 "Rejoice and be **g**,
Eze 25:3 You were **g** when my holy
35:14 The whole earth will be **g**
Joe 2:21 Be **g** and rejoice. The LORD
2:23 People of Zion, be **g** and find
Zec 8:19 joyful and **g** occasions as well
10:7 Their hearts will be **g** as if they
10:7 Their sons will see it and be **g**.
Mat 5:12 Rejoice and be **g** because you
Luk 1:14 and many people will be **g** that
19:6 came down and was **g**
Jon 11:15 but I'm **g** that I wasn't there so
14:28 you would be **g** that I'm going
20:20 The disciples were **g** to see
Act 2:26 That is why my heart is **g** and
1Co 16:17 I am **g** that Stephanas,
2Co 6:10 sad although we're always **g**,
12:15 I will be very **g** to spend
13:9 We're **g** when we are weak and
Rev 12:12 Be **g** for this reason,

gladly (4)

Psa 119:108 accept the praise I **g** give you,
Isa 11:3 He will **g** bear the fear of the
64:5 You greeted the one who **g**
2Co 11:19 so you'll **g** put up with fools.

gladness (4)

Psa 51:8 me hear sounds of joy and **g**.
Isa 51:3 Joy and **g** will be found in it,
65:14 will sing because of the **g**
Jer 48:33 Joy and **g** have disappeared

glance (2)

Sos 4:9 with a single **g** from your eyes,
Hab 3:6 He casts a **g** and startles the

glances (1)

Isa 3:16 making seductive **g**,

glass (7)

Job 28:17 Neither gold nor **g** can equal its
Pro 23:30 Those who drink **g** after glass
23:30 Those who drink glass after **g**
Rev 4:6 like a sea of **g** as clear as
15:2 looked like a sea of **g** mixed
21:18 of pure gold, as clear as **g**.
21:21 of pure gold, as clear as **g**.

glassy (1)

Rev 15:2 were standing on the **g** sea.

glides (1)

Sos 7:9 to my beloved and **g** over

glimpse (1)

Pro 23:5 Will you catch only a fleeting **g**

glimpses (1)

Job 26:14 "These are only **g** of what he

glitter (1)

Nah 3:3 Spears **g**! Many are killed! Dead

glittered (1)

Eze 1:7 they **g** like polished bronze.

glittering (1)

Job 20:25 The **g** point comes out of his

gloat (14)

Psa 22:17 People stare. They **g** over me.
35:19 enemies **g** over me.
35:24 Do not let them **g** over me
35:26 Let those who **g** over my
38:16 "Do not let them **g** over me.
54:7 eyes will **g** over my enemies.
59:10 He will let me **g** over those
92:11 My eyes **g** over those who spy
Lam 2:17 made your enemies **g** over you.
Oba 1:12 Don't **g** over your relative's
1:13 strikes or **g** over their misery
Mic 4:11 dishonor Zion and **g** over it."
Rev 11:10 Those living on earth will **g**
18:20 "**G** over it, heaven,

gloom (11)

Job 3:5 hang over it. Let the **g** terrify it.
10:21 to a land of darkness and **g**,
12:22 and brings **g** into the light.
Isa 8:22 and see only distress and **g**.
9:1 But there will be no more **g** for
29:18 see out of their **g** and darkness.
59:9 brightness, but we walk in **g**.
Joe 2:2 It is a day of darkness and **g**,
Zep 1:15 a day of darkness and **g**,
Heb 12:18 to darkness, to **g**, to a storm,
Jas 4:9 mourning and your joy into **g**.

gloomy (7)

Dtr 4:11 It was dark, cloudy, and **g**.
5:22 and the **g** darkness.
Job 28:3 and search to the limit of the **g**,
Eze 30:3 It will be a **g** day, a time of
34:12 a cloudy and **g** day from every
2Pe 2:17 **G** darkness has been kept for
Jud 1:13 for whom **g** darkness is kept

glorified (10)

2Sm 22:47 the rock of my salvation, be **g**.
Luk 2:20 they **g** and praised God for
Jon 7:39 be after Jesus had been **g**.
12:16 However, when Jesus was **g**,
12:23 for the Son of Man to be **g**.
13:31 "The Son of Man is now **g**,
13:31 and because of him God is **g**.
13:32 If God is **g** because of the Son
Act 3:13 and Jacob has **g** his servant
Php 3:21 and make them like his **g** body.

glorify (4)

Psa 22:23 descendants of Jacob, **g** him!
107:32 Let them **g** him when the
Jon 13:32 God will **g** the Son of Man
13:32 and he will **g** the Son of Man at

glorious (40)

Exo 15:1 He has won a **g** victory.
15:11 You are **g** because of your
15:21 He has won a **g** victory.
Dtr 5:24 us see how great and **g** he is.
28:58 You might not fear this **g** and
1Sm 2:8 to make them inherit a **g** throne.
Neh 9:5 your **g** name is praised
Psa 45:13 The daughter of the king is **g**
66:2 Make his praise **g**.
72:19 be to his **g** name forever.
87:3 **G** things are said about you,
90:16 Let our children see your **g**
106:20 They traded their **g** God for the
111:3 His work is **g** and majestic.
145:5 I will think about the **g** honor of
145:12 mighty deeds and the **g** honor
Isa 11:10 His resting place will be **g**.
24:23 He will be **g** in the presence of
28:1 Their **g** beauty is ⌊like⌋ a
28:4 Their **g** beauty is ⌊like⌋ a
28:5 of Armies will be like a **g** crown
42:21 teachings and makes them **g**.
Jer 14:21 Don't dishonor your **g** throne.
17:12 Our holy place is a **g** throne,
Dan 4:30 power and for my **g** honor."
Hag 2:9 This new house will be more **g**
Mat 19:28 Son of Man sits on his **g** throne
25:31 he will sit on his **g** throne.
Rom 6:4 death to life by the **g** power
8:21 to share the **g** freedom that
2Co 3:11 remains continue to be **g**?
Eph 1:17 I pray that the **g** Father,
1:18 and the **g** wealth that God's
5:27 it to himself as a **g** church,
Php 4:19 need in a **g** way through Christ
Col 1:11 strengthen you by his **g** might
1:27 the world to know the **g** riches
2Th 1:9 presence and from his **g** power.
Jas 2:1 practice your faith in our **g** Lord
Jud 1:24 in his **g** presence without fault.

glory (301)

Exo 15:6 wins **g** because it is strong.
16:7 the morning you will see the **g**
16:10 Suddenly, they saw the **g** of
24:16 The **g** of the LORD settled on
24:17 To the Israelites, the **g** of the
29:43 and my **g** will make this place
33:18 "Please let me see your **g**."
33:22 When my **g** passes by,
40:34 and the **g** of the LORD filled the
40:35 smoke settled on it and the **g**
Lev 9:6 you may see the LORD's **g**."
9:23 Then the LORD's **g** appeared to
10:3 I will show my **g** to all the
Num 14:10 they all saw the **g** of the LORD
14:21 But as I live and as the **g** of the
14:22 of the people who saw my **g**
16:19 the **g** of the LORD appeared to
16:42 and the **g** of the LORD
20:6 and the **g** of the LORD
Dtr 10:21 He is your **g**. He is your God,
1Sm 4:21 called the boy Ichabod [No **G**],
4:21 "Israel's **g** is gone,"
4:22 "Israel's **g** is gone because the
6:5 and give **g** to the God of Israel.
15:29 In addition, the **G** of Israel does
2Sm 1:19 "Your **g**, Israel, lies dead on
1Ki 8:11 The LORD's **g** filled his temple.
1Ch 16:24 Tell people about his **g**.
16:28 Give to the LORD **g** and power.
16:29 Give to the LORD the **g** his
16:35 and make your praise our **g**.'
29:11 Greatness, power, splendor, **g**,
2Ch 5:14 LORD's **g** filled God's temple.
7:1 the LORD's **g** filled the temple.
7:2 the LORD's **g** had filled
7:3 come down and the LORD's **g**
Job 40:10 yourself in splendor and **g**.
Psa 3:3 You are my **g**. You hold my
8:1 Your **g** is sung above the
8:5 crowned him with **g** and honor.
19:1 heavens declare the **g** of God,
21:5 of your victory his **g** is great.
24:7 that the king of **g** may come in.
24:8 Who is this king of **g**?
24:9 that the king of **g** may come in.
24:10 Who, then, is this king of **g**?
24:10 of Armies is the king of **g**!
26:8 the place where your **g** dwells.
29:1 Give to the LORD **g** and power.
29:2 Give to the LORD the **g** his
29:3 The God of **g** thunders.
29:9 in his temple is saying, "**G**!"
57:5 Let your **g** extend over the
57:11 Let your **g** extend over the
62:7 My salvation and my **g** depend
63:2 to see your power and your **g**.
66:2 Make music to praise the **g** of
71:8 with your **g** all day long.
72:19 whole earth be filled with his **g**.
73:24 the end you will take me to **g**.
78:61 captive and handed his **g** over
79:9 for the **g** of your name.
85:9 and ⌊his⌋ **g** will remain in our
89:17 because you are the **g** of their
96:3 Tell people about his **g**.
96:7 Give to the LORD **g** and power.
96:8 to the LORD the **g** he deserves.
97:6 people of the world see his **g**.
102:15 of the earth will fear your **g**.
Psa 102:16 he will appear in his **g**.
104:31 May the **g** of the LORD endure
106:47 and make your praise our **g**.
108:5 Let your **g** extend over the
113:4 His **g** is above the heavens.
115:1 Don't give **g** to us, O LORD.
115:1 Don't give **g** to us. Instead, give
115:1 Instead, give **g** to your name
145:11 Everyone will talk about the **g**
148:13 His **g** is above heaven and
149:5 Let godly people triumph in **g**.
Pro 17:6 are the **g** of their children.
20:29 While the **g** of young men is
25:2 It is the **g** of God to hide things
25:2 of God to hide things but the **g**
28:12 people triumph, there is great **g**,
Isa 4:5 His **g** will cover everything.
6:3 whole earth is filled with his **g**."
9:1 But in the future he will bring **g**
35:2 It will have the **g** of Lebanon,
35:2 Everyone will see the **g** of the
40:5 Then the LORD's **g** will be
42:8 I will not give my **g** to anyone
42:12 Let them give **g** to the LORD
43:7 whom I created for my **g**,
44:23 He will display his **g** in Israel.
46:13 Zion and bring my **g** to Israel.
48:11 not give my **g** to anyone else.
49:3 will display my **g** through you."
58:8 and the **g** of the LORD will
59:19 in the east will fear his **g**.
60:1 Your light has come, and the **g**
60:2 and his **g** appears over you.
60:13 "Lebanon's **g** will come to you:
60:19 Your God will be your **g**.
61:3 so that he might display his **g**.
62:2 All kings will see your **g**.
66:5 "Let the LORD show his **g**;
66:18 They will come and see my **g**.
66:19 heard of my fame or seen my **g**.
66:19 about my **g** among the nations.
Jer 2:11 people have exchanged their **G**
Eze 1:28 It was like the LORD's **g**.
3:12 "Blessed is the LORD's **g**,
3:23 The LORD's **g** was standing
3:23 was standing there like the **g**
8:4 There I saw the **g** of Israel's
9:3 Then the **g** of the God of Israel
10:4 The LORD's **g** rose from the
10:4 LORD's **g** filled the courtyard.
10:18 Then the **g** of the LORD left the
10:19 and the **g** of the God of Israel
11:22 The **g** of the God of Israel was
11:23 The LORD's **g** left the middle of
16:14 because I gave you my **g**,
43:2 I saw the **g** of the God of Israel
43:2 was shining because of his **g**.
43:4 The LORD's **g** came into the
43:5 the LORD's **g** fill the temple.
44:4 I saw the LORD's **g** fill the
Dan 4:36 My royal honor and **g** were also
4:37 and give **g** to the King of
5:18 a kingdom, might, honor, and **g**.
Hos 4:7 So I will turn their **g** into shame.
9:11 "Ephraim's **g** will fly away like
10:5 cry loudly because its **g** will
Mic 1:15 The **g** of Israel will come to
2:9 and take my **g** away from their
Nah 2:2 Jacob's **g** like Israel's glory,
2:2 Jacob's glory like Israel's **g**,
Hab 2:14 knowledge of the LORD's **g** like
2:16 with disgrace rather than **g**.
2:16 and disgrace will cover your **g**.
Hag 2:3 saw this house in its former **g**?
2:7 I will fill this house with **g**,
Zec 2:5 I will be the **g** within it.'
2:8 the **G** sent me to the nations
Mat 4:8 in the world and their **g**.
16:27 his angels in his Father's **g**.
24:30 the sky with power and great **g**.
25:31 the Son of Man comes in his **g**
Mar 8:38 holy angels in his Father's **g**."
10:37 the other at your left in your **g**."
13:26 clouds with great power and **g**.
Luk 2:9 The **g** of the Lord filled the area
2:14 "**G** to God in the highest

Luk 2:32 to the nations and bring **g**
4:6 give you all the power and **g**
9:26 when he comes in the **g** that
9:31 They appeared in heavenly **g**
9:32 they saw Jesus' **g** and the two
19:38 and **g** in the highest heaven."
21:27 a cloud with power and great **g**.
24:26 things and enter into his **g**?"
Jon 1:14 We saw his **g**. It was the glory
1:14 It was the **g** that the Father
1:14 a **g** full of kindness and truth.
2:11 He made his **g** public there,
7:18 are looking for their own **g**.
7:18 the man who wants to bring **g**
8:50 I don't want my own **g**.
8:54 "If I bring **g** to myself,
8:54 to myself, my **g** is nothing.
8:54 is the one who gives me **g**,
9:24 They told him, "Give **g** to God.
11:4 this sickness will bring **g** to
11:4 God will receive **g** through it."
11:40 you would see God's **g**?"
12:28 Father, give **g** to your name."
12:28 heaven said, "I have given it **g**,
12:28 and I will give it **g** again."
12:41 because he had seen Jesus' **g**
14:13 that the Father will be given **g**
15:8 You give **g** to my Father when
16:14 He will give me **g**,
17:1 Give your Son **g** so that your
17:1 that your Son can give you **g**.
17:4 On earth I have given you **g** by
17:5 Now, Father, give me **g** in your
17:5 in your presence with the **g**
17:10 I have been given **g** by the
17:22 I have given them the **g** that
17:24 I want them to see my **g**,
21:19 Peter would bring **g** to God.
Act 7:2 The God who reveals his **g**
7:55 into heaven, saw God's **g**,
12:23 Herod for not giving **g** to God.
19:27 will be robbed of her **g**."
Rom 1:23 They exchanged the **g** of the
2:7 life to those who search for **g**,
2:10 But there will be **g**,
3:7 If my lie increases the **g** that
3:23 have fallen short of God's **g**.
5:2 we will receive **g** from God.
8:17 suffering in order to share his **g**,
8:18 to the **g** that will soon
8:30 and he gave **g** to those whom
9:4 They have the Lord's **g**,
9:23 also reveal the riches of his **g**
9:23 he had already prepared for **g**?
11:36 **G** belongs to him forever!
15:7 He did this to bring **g** to God.
16:27 **G** belongs to him through
1Co 2:7 had planned for our **g** before
2:8 have crucified the Lord of **g**.
6:20 So bring **g** to God in the way
10:31 do everything to the **g** of God.
11:7 He is God's image and **g**.
11:7 woman, however, is man's **g**.
2Co 3:7 Yet, it came with such **g** that
3:7 His face was shining with **g**,
3:7 even though that **g** was fading.
3:8 the Spirit have even more **g**?
3:9 that brings punishment has **g**,
3:9 has an overwhelming **g**.
3:10 brings punishment lost its **g**
3:10 glory because of the superior **g**
3:11 faded away despite its **g**,
3:13 Israel to see the **g** fading away.
3:18 As all of us reflect the Lord's **g**
3:18 image with ever-increasing **g**.
4:4 Good News about Christ's **g**.
4:6 God's **g** which shines from
4:15 thanksgiving to the **g** of God.
4:17 us an eternal **g** that is greater
8:19 it in a way that brings **g**
8:23 churches and bring **g** to Christ.
Gal 1:5 **G** belongs to our God and
Eph 1:6 would be praised and given **g**.
1:12 praise him and give him **g**.
1:14 receives praise and **g** for this.
3:13 In fact, my troubles bring you **g**.
Eph 3:16 a gift from the wealth of his **g**.
3:20 **G** belongs to God,
3:21 **G** belongs to God in the church
Php 1:11 Your lives will then bring **g** and
2:11 Jesus Christ is Lord to the **g**
4:20 **G** belongs to our God and
Col 1:27 giving you the hope of **g**.
3:4 will appear with him in **g**.
1Th 2:12 you into his kingdom and **g**.
2:20 You are our **g** and joy!
2Th 2:14 so that you would obtain the **g**
1Ti 1:11 Good News that contains the **g**
1:17 Worship and **g** belong forever
3:16 and was taken to heaven in **g**.
2Ti 2:10 Jesus with **g** that lasts forever.
4:18 **G** belongs to him forever!
Tit 2:13 for — the appearance of the **g**
Heb 1:3 Son is the reflection of God's **g**
2:7 crowned him with **g** and honor.
2:9 but we see him crowned with **g**
2:10 many sons and daughters to **g**,
5:5 So Christ did not take the **g** of
5:5 the **g** was given to him by God,
9:5 angels of **g** ⌊with their wings⌋
13:21 **G** belongs to Jesus Christ
1Pe 1:7 praise, **g**, and honor to God.
1:11 and the **g** that would follow.
1:21 back to life and gave him **g**.
4:11 **g** through Jesus Christ.
4:11 **G** and power belong to Jesus
4:13 he appears again in his **g**.
4:14 because the Spirit of **g** —
5:1 and will share in the **g** that will
5:4 you will receive the crown of **g**
5:10 Christ Jesus to his eternal **g**,
2Pe 1:3 us by his own **g** and integrity.
1:4 Through his **g** and integrity he
1:17 received honor and **g** from God
2:10 afraid to insult the ⌊Lord's⌋ **g**.
3:18 **G** belongs to him now and for
Jud 1:8 authority, and insult his **g**.
1:25 and for eternity **g**, majesty,
Rev 1:5 **G** and power forever and ever
4:9 the living creatures give **g**,
4:11 you deserve to receive **g**,
5:12 strength, honor, **g**, and praise."
5:13 **g**, and power forever and ever."
7:12 Praise, **g**, wisdom, thanks,
11:13 They gave **g** to the God of
14:7 "Fear God and give him **g**,
15:8 filled with smoke from the **g**
16:9 think and act and give him **g**.
18:1 and his **g** lit up the earth.
18:7 She gave herself **g** and luxury.
19:1 Salvation, **g**, and power belong
19:7 and give him **g** because it's
21:11 It had the **g** of God.
21:23 to give it light because the **g**
21:24 earth will bring their **g** into it.
21:26 They will bring the **g** and

glory's (1)

Isa 48:9 For my **g** sake I'll hold my

glow (2)

Mar 14:54 himself facing the **g** of a fire.
Luk 22:56 saw him as he sat facing the **g**

glowed (3)

Num 9:15 smoke over the tent **g** like fire.
9:16 The smoke always **g** this way.
9:16 covering the tent **g** like fire.

glowing (10)

2Sm 22:9 **G** coals flared up from it.
Job 18:5 The flame of his fire stops **g**.
Psa 18:8 **G** coals flared up from it.
Isa 4:5 during the day and a **g** flame
47:14 There are no **g** coals to keep
Eze 1:4 lightning looked like **g** metal.
1:27 He looked like **g** bronze with
8:2 up its body looked like **g** metal.
Rev 1:15 His feet were like **g** bronze
2:18 whose feet are like **g** bronze,

glows (1)

Eze 24:11 that it gets hot and its copper **g**.

glutton (3)

Pro 23:21 because both a drunk and a **g**
Mat 11:19 He's a **g** and a drunk,
Luk 7:34 He's a **g** and a drunk,

gluttons (2)

Pro 28:7 with **g** disgraces his father.
Tit 1:12 savage animals, and lazy **g**."

gnats (7)

Exo 8:16 Egypt the dust will turn into **g**.'"
8:17 It turned into **g** that bit people
8:17 in Egypt turned into **g**.
8:18 to produce **g** using their magic
8:18 The **g** bit people and animals.
Psa 105:31 and swarms of flies and **g**
Mat 23:24 You strain **g** ⌊out of your wine⌋,

gnaw (3)

Job 30:3 they **g** at the dry and barren
Jer 50:17 The last to **g** at their bones
Zep 3:3 They leave nothing to **g** on for

gnawed (1)

Rev 16:10 People **g** on their tongues in

go (1405)

Gen 6:18 sons' wives will **g** into the ship.
7:1 The LORD said to Noah, "**G**
7:9 came to Noah to **g** into the ship
7:15 came to Noah to **g** into the ship.
8:1 and the water started to **g**
11:7 Let us **g** down there and mix
11:31 the Chaldeans to **g** to Canaan.
12:1 **G** to the land that I will show
12:19 your wife! Take her and **g**! "
13:9 If you **g** to the left, I'll go to the
13:9 go to the left, I'll **g** to the right,
13:9 and if you **g** to the right,
13:9 go to the right, I'll **g** to the left."
13:17 **G**! Walk back and forth across
16:9 "**G** back to your owner,
18:21 I must **g** down and see
19:32 Then we'll **g** to bed with him so
19:34 Then you **g** to bed with him so
20:13 'Do me a favor: Wherever we **g**,
22:2 you love, and **g** to Moriah.
22:5 the boy and I **g** over there.
24:4 Instead, you will **g** to the land
24:11 when the women would **g** out
24:38 Instead, **g** to my father's home
24:41 to do this when you **g** to them.'
24:51 Take her and **g**! She will
24:54 "Let me **g** back to my master."
24:55 After that she may **g**."
24:56 Let me **g** back to my master."
24:58 "Will you **g** with this man?"
24:58 She said, "Yes, I'll **g**."
24:59 sister Rebekah and her nurse **g**
25:23 Two nations will **g** their
26:2 and said, "Don't **g** to Egypt.
26:16 to Isaac, "**G** away from us!
26:29 to you and let you **g** in peace.
27:3 and **g** out into the open country
27:9 **G** to the flock, and get me two
27:13 Just obey me and **g**!
28:2 **G** to Paddan Aram.
28:2 **G** to the home of Bethuel,
28:15 over you wherever you **g**.
30:15 Jacob can **g** to bed with you
30:25 "Let me **g** home to my own
30:26 I've worked, and let me **g**.
30:31 then I'll **g** back to taking care of
30:32 Let me **g** through all of your
31:3 "**G** back to the land of your
31:13 Now leave this land, and **g**
31:52 witnesses that I will not **g** past
31:52 and that you will not **g** past the
32:9 LORD, you said to me, '**G** back
32:16 his servants, "**G** ahead of me,
32:26 Then the man said, "Let me **g**;
32:26 "I won't let you **g** until you

Gen 33:12 "Let's get ready to **g**,
33:12 and I'll **g** with you."
33:14 **G** ahead of me, sir. I will
34:17 we'll take our daughter and **g**."
35:1 "**G** to Bethel and live there.
35:3 Then let's **g** to Bethel.
37:13 Joseph responded, "I'll **g**."
37:17 I heard them say, 'Let's **g** to
38:8 Then Judah said to Onan, "**G**
39:10 he refused to **g** to bed with her
39:14 He came in and tried to **g** to
40:14 Remember me when things **g**
41:55 the Egyptians, "**G** to Joseph!
42:2 **G** there and buy some for us so
42:19 The rest of you will **g** and take
42:33 for your starving families and **g**.
42:38 "My son will not **g** with you.
43:2 "**G** back and buy us a little
43:4 If you let our brother **g** with us,
43:4 we'll **g** and buy food for you.
43:5 If you won't let him **g**,
43:5 won't let him go, we won't **g**.
43:13 and **g** back to the man.
44:4 "**G** after those men at once,
44:10 and the rest of you can **g** free."
44:17 The rest of you can **g** back to
44:25 "Then our father said, '**G** back
44:26 answered, 'We can't **g** back.
44:26 We can only **g** back if our
44:33 and let the boy **g** back with his
44:34 How could I **g** back to my
45:17 and **g** back to Canaan.
45:28 I will **g** and see him before I
46:3 "Don't be afraid to **g** to Egypt,
46:4 I will **g** with you to Egypt,
49:13 His border will **g** as far as
50:5 Please let me **g** there and bury
50:6 "**G** and bury your father,
Exo 2:7 "Should I **g** and get one of the
2:20 **G**, invite him to supper."
3:3 I must **g** over there and see this
3:10 Now, **g**! I am sending you to
3:11 "Who am I that I should **g** to
3:13 "Suppose I **g** to the people of
3:16 "**G**, assemble the leaders of
3:18 you and the leaders must **g**
3:19 king of Egypt will not let you **g**,
3:20 I will do there, he will let you **g**.
4:12 Now **g**, and I will help you
4:18 "Please let me **g** back to my
4:18 said to Moses, "You may **g**."
4:19 in Midian, "**G** back to Egypt,
4:21 that he will not let the people **g**.
4:23 I told you to let my son **g** so
4:23 But you refused to let him **g**.
5:1 Let my people **g** into the desert
5:2 I obey him and let Israel **g**?
5:2 and I won't let Israel **g**."
5:3 If we don't **g**, he may kill us
5:8 'Let us **g** offer sacrifices to our
5:17 'Let us **g** offer sacrifices to the
6:1 and he will let my people **g**.
6:11 "**G** tell Pharaoh (the king of
7:14 He refuses to let my people **g**.
7:16 "Let my people **g** to worship
8:1 "**G** to Pharaoh, and tell him,
8:1 Let my people **g** to worship me.
8:2 If you refuse to let them **g**,
8:8 Then I will let your people **g** to
8:20 Let my people **g** to worship me.
8:21 If you will not let my people **g**,
8:25 Moses and Aaron and said, "**G**,
8:28 Pharaoh said, "I will let you **g**,
8:28 but don't **g** very far.
8:29 of flies will **g** away from you,
8:29 us by not letting the people **g**
8:32 and did not let the people **g**.
9:1 "**G** to Pharaoh, and tell him,
9:1 Let my people **g** to worship me.
9:2 If you refuse to let them **g** and
9:7 and would not let the people **g**.
9:13 **g** to Pharaoh and say to him,
9:13 Let my people **g** to worship me.
9:28 I'll let you **g**; you don't have to
9:35 would not let the Israelites **g**,
10:1 said to Moses, "**G** to Pharaoh.

Exo 10:3 Let my people **g** to worship me.
10:4 If you refuse to let my people **g**,
10:7 Let the Israelite men **g** to
10:8 "**G**, worship the LORD your
10:11 Only the men may **g** to
10:20 he did not let the Israelites **g**.
10:24 said, "**G**, worship the LORD!
10:24 and children may **g** with you,
10:26 our livestock must **g** with us.
10:27 so he refused to let them **g**.
11:1 After that he will let you **g**.
11:4 About midnight I will **g** out
12:12 "On that same night I will **g**
12:23 The LORD will **g** throughout
12:31 **G**, worship the LORD as you
12:32 Just **g**! And bless me, too!"
12:37 left Rameses to **g** to Succoth.
13:15 was too stubborn to let us **g**,
13:17 When Pharaoh let the people **g**,
13:17 minds and **g** back to Egypt."
14:2 "Tell the Israelites to **g** back
14:5 because we've let Israel **g**."
14:12 Let us **g** on serving the
14:16 Then the Israelites will **g**
16:4 Each day the people should **g**
17:5 and **g** to where the people can
18:23 so that they can **g** home."
19:10 to Moses, "**G** to the people,
19:12 and tell them not to **g** up the
19:13 The people may **g** up the
19:21 The LORD said to him, "**G**
19:24 LORD said to him, "**G** down,
20:26 Never use stairs to **g** up to my
21:7 she will not **g** free the way
21:11 three things, she can **g** free,
21:26 he must let the slave **g** free to
21:27 he must let the slave **g** free to
23:23 "My Messenger will **g** ahead of
27:20 so that the lamps won't **g** out.
28:43 wear them when they **g** into
30:20 Before they **g** into the tent of
32:7 "**G** back down there.
32:27 **G** back and forth from one end
32:30 Now I will **g** up the mountain to
32:34 Now, **g**! Lead the people to the
32:34 My Messenger will **g** ahead of
33:1 **G** to the land I promised to
33:3 **G** to that land flowing with milk
33:7 LORD's will used to **g** outside
33:14 presence will **g** ⌊with you,⌋
33:16 and me unless you **g** with us?
34:7 lets the guilty **g** unpunished,
34:9 said, "Lord, please **g** with us!
40:35 Moses couldn't **g** into the tent
Lev 6:12 It must never **g** out.
6:13 It must never **g** out.
10:9 wine or liquor when you **g** into
12:4 touch anything holy or **g** into
13:16 he must **g** to the priest.
14:3 The priest will **g** outside the
14:8 After that he may **g** into the
14:36 Then the priest will **g** inside to
14:38 the priest will **g** out to the door
14:39 day the priest will **g** back
16:2 Aaron that he cannot **g** into
16:15 **g** up to the canopy,
16:18 Then he will **g** out to the altar
16:23 "Then Aaron will **g** to the tent
16:23 clothes he had put on to **g** into
21:11 He must never **g** near any dead
24:2 so that the lamps won't **g** out.
25:41 him and his children to **g** back
26:17 you so that you will **g** down
26:26 will eat and **g** away hungry.
27:24 year the field will **g** back
Num 4:5 Aaron and his sons will **g** in
4:19 Aaron and his sons will **g** into
4:20 But the Kohathites must not **g**
5:22 bring a curse **g** into your body
5:24 This water will **g** into her
5:27 bring the curse will **g** into her
6:6 they must never **g** near a dead
10:9 "When you **g** to war in your
10:30 answered, "No, I won't **g**.
10:30 I want to **g** back to my own
11:8 The people would **g** around

Num 13:17 "**G** through the Negev and then
13:30 Caleb said, "Let's **g** now and
14:3 for us to **g** back to Egypt?"
14:4 a leader and **g** back to Egypt."
14:14 and that you **g** ahead of them in
14:18 lets the guilty **g** unpunished,
14:25 **g** back into the desert,
14:40 Now we'll **g** to the place the
14:42 Don't **g**! You will be defeated by
15:39 want and **g** after whatever you
16:30 and they **g** down alive to their
16:46 and **g** quickly into the
19:7 he may **g** into the camp.
20:17 Please let us **g** through your
20:17 We won't **g** through any of your
20:21 Israel **g** through their territory,
20:27 community saw them **g** up
21:15 of the valleys that **g** down
21:22 "Let us **g** through your country.
21:22 We won't **g** through any of your
22:12 "Don't **g** with them!
22:13 "**G** back to your own country,
22:13 refused to let me **g** with you."
22:20 to summon you, **g** with them,
22:34 this trip is evil, I'll **g** back."
22:35 to Balaam, "**G** with the men,
23:5 told Balaam, "**G** back to Balak,
23:16 and told him, "**G** back to Balak,
24:11 **G** home! I said I'd reward you
27:12 The LORD said to Moses, "**G**
27:21 of Israel will **g** into battle.
28:10 wine offerings that **g** with them.
31:3 of your men must get ready to **g**
32:6 rest of the Israelites **g** to war?
32:27 ready for battle and **g** with you,
32:30 ready for battle and **g** with you,
35:26 "But don't **g** outside the city of
35:28 They may **g** back to their own
35:32 of refuge must never **g** back
Dtr 1:2 (It takes 11 days to **g** from
1:7 **G** to the mountain region of the
1:7 and **g** to everyone living on the
1:21 **G** ahead! Take possession of it,
1:26 your God and refused to **g**.
1:37 "You won't **g** there either.
1:38 son of Nun, will **g** there.
1:40 **g** back into the desert,
1:41 We'll **g** and fight, as the LORD
1:42 "Tell them, 'Don't **g** and fight,
2:3 long enough. Now **g** north.
2:27 we'll **g** straight through and
2:28 Please let us **g** through,
2:31 **G** ahead! Take possession of
2:37 you to **g** anywhere near
3:20 Your soldiers will **g** with the
3:20 After that each of you may **g**
3:25 Please let me **g** over and see
3:27 **G** to the top of Mount Pisgah,
4:22 but you're going to **g** across
4:40 Then things will **g** well for you
5:5 afraid of the fire and didn't **g** up
5:16 and things will **g** well for you in
5:27 ⌊Moses,⌋ **g** and listen to
5:29 Then things would **g** well for
5:30 "Tell the people to **g** back to
5:33 life will **g** well for you,
6:3 Then things will **g** well for you
6:18 Then things will **g** well for you,
8:16 this so that things would **g** well
9:23 "**G** and take possession of the
11:25 wherever you **g** in this land.
12:5 **G** there and worship him.
12:25 things will **g** well for you and
12:26 and **g** to the place the LORD
12:28 Then things will always **g** well
13:6 "Let's **g** worship other gods."
14:25 Take the silver with you, and **g**
15:12 year you must let them **g** free.
15:13 But when you let them **g**,
15:18 have to let your slave **g** free,
16:7 In the morning you may **g** back
17:9 **G** to the Levitical priests and
17:16 will never **g** back there again."
19:5 Suppose two people **g** into the
19:13 things will **g** well for Israel.
20:1 When you **g** to war against

Dtr 20:5 dedicated it, you may **g** home.
20:6 the grapes, you may **g** home.
20:7 married her, you may **g** home.
20:8 your courage, you may **g** home.
21:2 your leaders and judges must **g**
21:10 When you **g** to war with your
21:14 let her **g** wherever she wants.
22:7 make sure you let the mother **g**.
22:7 Then things will **g** well for you,
22:15 girl's father and mother must **g**
23:10 he must **g** outside the camp
23:12 you can **g** ⌊to relieve yourself⌋.
23:13 When you **g** outside to squat,
23:24 If you **g** into your neighbor's
23:25 If you **g** into your neighbor's
24:10 don't **g** into his house to take a
24:19 don't **g** back to get it.
25:7 she must **g** to the leaders of the
25:9 his brother's widow must **g** up
26:2 Then **g** to the place where the
26:3 **G** to the priest who is serving
28:6 come and blessed when you **g**.
28:19 come and cursed when you **g**.
28:27 and itching that won't **g** away.
29:19 "I'll be safe even if I **g** my own
30:12 "Who will **g** to heaven to get
31:7 You will **g** with these people
32:49 "**G** into the Abarim Mountains,
33:18 yourselves when you **g** to war,
34:4 but you may not **g** there."
Jos 1:7 will succeed wherever you **g**.
1:9 is with you wherever you **g**.'"
1:11 "**G** through the camp.
1:15 After that, you may **g** back and
1:16 us and **g** wherever you send
2:1 He told them, "**G**, look at that
2:16 She told them, "**G** to the
2:16 Then you can **g** on your way."
2:21 So she let them **g** and tied the
3:4 you will know which way to **g**
3:6 and **g** ahead of the people."
4:5 He said to them, "**G** to the
6:19 They must **g** into the LORD's
6:22 "**G** to the prostitute's house.
7:2 He said to them, "**G**,
8:4 Don't **g** very far away from the
8:20 They had no place to **g**,
9:11 for the trip, and **g** meet them.
14:11 I'm still as fit to **g** to war now
17:15 many of you, **g** into the forest!
18:8 As the men got ready to **g**,
18:8 He said, "**G** survey the land.
20:6 Then he may **g** back to his
23:12 "But if you turn away and **g**
Jdg 1:1 "Who will **g** first to fight the
1:2 "Judah's troops will **g** first.
1:3 Then we'll **g** with you into your
1:25 and his whole family **g** free.
4:8 to her, "If you **g** with me, I'll go.
4:8 to her, "If you go with me, I'll **g**.
4:8 But if you don't **g** with me,
4:8 you don't go with me, I won't **g**."
4:9 "Certainly, I'll **g** with you.
4:14 The LORD will **g** ahead of
7:3 Gilead and **g** back home.'" So
7:4 'This one will **g** with you,'
7:4 he must **g** with you.
7:4 'This one won't **g** with you,'
7:4 go with you,' he must not **g**."
7:7 All the other men should **g**
7:9 **G** into the camp! I will hand it
7:10 But if you're afraid to **g**,
7:11 you will have the courage to **g**
7:24 "**G** into battle against Midian.
8:1 You didn't invite us to **g** fight
9:38 Now **g** out and fight him."
11:8 now is that we want you to **g**
11:17 They said, 'Please let us **g**
11:19 'Please let us **g** through your
11:20 let them **g** through his territory.
11:38 "**G**!" he said, and he sent her off
11:40 the girls in Israel would **g** out
12:1 inviting us to **g** with you?
15:1 father would not let him **g** in.
18:2 "**G** and explore the land!"
18:6 priest told them, "**G** in peace.
Jdg 18:9 **G** at once and take the land.
19:5 strength and then you can **g**."
19:9 can start out early to **g** home."
19:11 "Let's **g** spend the night in
19:12 "We'll never **g** into a city of
19:12 We'll **g** on to Gibeah."
19:13 "Let's **g** someplace else.
19:25 They let her **g** when the sun
19:28 Let's **g**!" But she did not answer.
20:8 "None of us will **g** to his tent or
20:10 When the troops **g** to Gibeah in
20:14 and assembled at Gibeah to **g**
20:18 They asked God, "Who will **g**
20:18 "Judah will **g** first."
20:23 answered, "**G** fight them!"
20:28 The LORD answered, "**G**!
21:10 They ordered them, "**G** and kill
21:21 Then **g** back to the territory of
Rut 1:8 two daughters-in-law, "**G** back!
1:8 Each of you should **g** back to
1:11 But Naomi said, "**G** back,
1:11 Why should you **g** with me?
1:12 **G** back, my daughters. Go,
1:12 **G**, because I am too old to get
1:15 **G** back with your sister-in-law."
1:16 Wherever you **g**, I will go,
1:16 Wherever you go, I will **g**,
1:18 was determined to **g** with her,
2:2 "Please let me **g** to the field of
2:2 Naomi told her, "**G**,
2:8 Don't **g** in any other field to
2:9 When you're thirsty, **g** to the
2:22 that you **g** out to the fields with
2:22 If you **g** to someone else's field,
3:3 and **g** down to the threshing
3:10 that you didn't **g** after
3:16 "How did things **g**,
1Sm 1:3 Every year this man would **g**
1:17 Eli replied, "**G** in peace,
1:22 But Hannah didn't **g**.
2:6 He makes ⌊people⌋ **g** down to
2:20 Then they would **g** home.
3:5 "**G** back to bed." So Samuel
3:6 responded. "**G** back to bed."
3:9 "**G**, lie down," Eli told Samuel.
3:19 any of his words **g** unfulfilled.
5:11 "Let it **g** back to its own place
6:20 And to which people will he **g**
8:22 "**G** ⌊back⌋ to your own cities."
9:3 and **g** look for the donkeys."
9:5 was with him, "Let's **g** back,
9:6 Let's **g** there. Maybe he'll tell us
9:6 us which way we should **g**."
9:7 "If we **g**," Saul asked his
9:9 let's **g** to the seer,"
9:10 Come on, let's **g**." They went to
9:13 As you **g** into the city,
9:13 **G**. You should be able to find
9:19 **G** ahead of me to the worship
9:19 In the morning I'll let you **g** after
9:27 "Have the servant **g** ahead of
10:8 **G** ahead of me to Gilgal.
10:14 "Where did you **g**?"
11:14 let's **g** to Gilgal and there
12:23 I will **g** on teaching you the
12:25 But if you **g** on doing what is
13:20 Everyone in Israel had to **g** to
14:1 "Let's **g** to the Philistine
14:6 "Let's **g** to the military post of
14:7 **G** ahead! I agree with you."
14:9 we are and not **g** up to them.
14:10 'Come up here,' then we'll **g** up,
15:3 Now **g** and attack Amalek.
15:26 Samuel told Saul, "I will not **g**
16:1 Fill a flask with olive oil and **g**.
16:2 "How can I **g**?" Samuel asked.
16:12 The LORD said, "**G** ahead,
17:32 I will **g** and fight this
17:37 "**G**," Saul told David,
18:2 and didn't let him **g** back
19:2 **G** into hiding, and stay out of
19:3 I'll **g** out and stand beside my
19:17 "He told me, 'Let me **g**!
20:5 But let me **g** and hide in the
20:11 "Let's **g** out into the country."
20:19 So **g** to the place where you
1Sm 20:21 say, '**G**, find the arrows.' Now,
20:22 arrows are next to you,' then **g**,
20:28 me ⌊to let him **g**⌋ to Bethlehem.
20:29 said to me 'Please let me **g**.
20:29 please let me **g** to see my
20:42 "**G** in peace!" Jonathan told
21:5 us as usual when we **g** ⌊on
22:5 "**G** to the land of Judah."
23:2 "Should I **g** and attack these
23:2 "**G**," the LORD told David,
23:3 do you think we'll be⌋ if we **g**
23:4 He said, "**G** to Keilah.
23:8 together all the troops to **g**
23:13 went wherever they could **g**.
23:23 Then I'll **g** with you,
25:5 "**G** to Carmel, visit Nabal,
25:19 "**G** on ahead," she told her
25:35 "**G** home in peace.
26:6 "Who will **g** with me to Saul in
26:6 answered, "I'll **g** with you."
26:10 or he'll **g** into battle and be
26:11 that jar of water, and let's **g**."
26:19 '**G** and serve other gods,'
28:7 Then I'll **g** to her and ask for her
29:4 He shouldn't **g** with us into
29:9 'He shouldn't **g** into battle with
29:10 and **g** to the place I have
30:21 had been too exhausted to **g**
30:22 "Since they didn't **g** with us,
30:24 the share of those who **g** into
2Sm 2:1 "Should I **g** to one of the cities
2:1 "**G**," the LORD answered him.
2:1 "Where should I **g**?"
2:26 this slaughter **g** on forever?
3:16 "**G** home," Abner told him.
3:21 Abner told David, "I must **g**
11:1 the time when kings **g** out to
11:8 "**G** home," David said to Uriah,
11:9 mercenaries. He didn't **g** home.
11:10 "Uriah didn't **g** home,"
11:10 Why didn't you **g** home?"
11:11 Should I then **g** to my house to
11:11 house to eat and drink and **g**
11:13 mercenaries. He didn't **g** home.
11:20 'Why did you **g** so close to the
11:21 Why did you **g** so close to the
12:11 He will **g** to bed with your
12:23 ⌊Someday⌋ I'll **g** to him,
13:7 "Please **g** to your brother
13:13 Where could I **g** in my
13:25 "If we all **g**, we'll be a burden to
13:25 David did not want to **g**,
13:26 Absalom said, "If you won't **g**,
13:26 my brother Amnon **g** with us."
13:26 "Why should he **g** with you?"
13:27 of the king's sons **g** with him.
14:3 **G** to the king, and tell him this
14:8 "**G** home," the king told the
14:30 **G** and set it on fire."
15:7 "Let me **g** to Hebron and keep
15:9 "**G** in peace," the king told him.
15:19 "Why should you **g** with us?
15:19 **G** back, and stay with King
15:20 **G** back, and take your
15:22 "**G** ahead and keep marching."
15:27 "**G** back to the city peacefully,
15:33 told him, "If you **g** with me,
15:34 But if you **g** back to the city
16:9 Let me **g** over there and tear off
16:17 "Why didn't you **g** with him?"
17:1 leave tonight to **g** after David.
17:17 so a servant girl was to **g** and
17:17 and they were to **g** and tell
18:21 said to a man from Sudan, "**G**,
19:7 Now, get up, **g** out,
19:7 the LORD that if you don't **g** out,
19:25 "Why didn't you **g** with me,
19:26 ride on it and **g** with the king.'
19:34 I shouldn't **g** with Your Majesty
19:37 Please let me **g** back so that I
19:37 Let him **g** across with you.
19:38 "Chimham will **g** across with
20:6 Take my men and **g** after him,
21:17 "You'll never **g** into battle with
24:1 He said, "**G**, count Israel and
24:2 "**G** throughout the tribes of

2Sm 24:12 "**G** and tell David, 'This is
24:18 to David and said to him, "**G**,
1Ki 1:13 **G** to King David and ask him,
1:53 "**G** home," Solomon told him.
2:3 you do wherever you may **g**.
2:6 old man **g** to his grave
2:9 don't let him **g** unpunished.
2:26 "**G** to your land in Anathoth.
2:36 ⌊the city⌋ to **g** anywhere else.
2:42 left ⌊the city⌋ to **g** anywhere,
5:9 them into rafts to **g** by sea
8:44 "When your people **g** to war
11:21 "Let me **g** to my own country."
11:22 makes you eager to **g** home?"
12:24 Everyone, **g** home.
12:27 will regain popularity if they **g**
13:8 I would never **g** with you to eat
13:9 me not to eat or drink or **g** back
13:10 another road and didn't **g** back
13:16 "I'm not allowed to **g** back with
13:17 to eat or drink there or **g** back
14:2 told his wife, "**G** to Shiloh,
14:3 honey with you, and **g** to him.
14:12 "Get up, and **g** home.
17:9 "Get up, **g** to Zarephath (which
17:13 **G** home, and do as you've said.
18:5 Ahab told Obadiah, "Let's **g**
18:43 "Please **g** back to ⌊Mount
18:43 Elijah told him, "**G** back."
18:44 Elijah said, "**G** and tell Ahab,
18:45 his chariot to **g** back to Jezreel.
19:11 God said, "**G** out and stand in
19:15 The LORD told him, "**G** back to
19:20 "**G** back," Elijah answered him.
20:31 and **g** to the king of Israel.
20:34 into a treaty, I will let you **g**."
20:34 with Benhadad and let him **g**.
20:42 You let the man **g**.
21:18 "**G**, meet King Ahab of Israel,
22:4 "Will you **g** with me to fight at
22:6 He asked them, "Should I **g** to
22:6 "**G**," they said. "The Lord will
22:15 should we **g** to war against
22:17 Let each one **g** home in peace."
22:22 "The Spirit answered, 'I will **g**
22:22 in deceiving him. **G** and do it.'
22:25 find out on the day you **g** into
22:30 myself and **g** into battle,
22:48 made Tarshish-style ships to **g**
22:48 But they didn't **g** because the
22:49 "Let my servants **g** with your
2Ki 1:2 "**G** ask Baalzebub,
1:6 "**G** back to the king who sent
1:15 LORD told Elijah, "**G** with him.
2:16 Please let them **g** and search
2:18 "Didn't I tell you not to **g**?"
2:23 They said, "**G** away,
2:23 baldy! **G** away!"
3:7 Jehoshaphat answered, "I'll **g**.
3:13 **G** to your father's prophets or
4:22 I will **g** quickly to the man of
4:29 staff in your hand, and **g**.
5:5 king of Aram said, "You may **g**.
5:19 told Naaman, "**G** in peace."
5:20 **g** without accepting what
5:25 "I didn't **g** anywhere,"
6:2 Let's **g** to the Jordan River.
6:2 Elisha said, "**G** ahead."
6:3 Elisha answered, "I'll **g**."
6:9 "Be careful not to **g** by that
6:22 Then let them **g** back to their
7:4 If we **g** into the city,
7:4 So let's **g** to the Aramean camp.
7:5 So they started out at dusk to **g**
8:1 "**G** away with your family.
9:1 and **g** to Ramoth Gilead.
9:2 **G** inside, and have him get up
11:7 who ⌊normally⌋ **g** off duty
11:9 who were about to **g** off duty
17:27 Let him **g** back to teach them
18:14 **G** away, and leave me alone.
19:27 when you **g** out and come in,
19:28 I will make you **g** back the way
19:31 Those few people will **g** out
19:31 and those who escape will **g**
19:33 He will **g** back the way he
2Ki 20:5 "**G** back and say to Hezekiah,
20:5 day after tomorrow you will **g**
20:8 will heal me and that I'll **g**
20:9 Do you want the shadow to **g**
20:11 Ahaz's stairway **g** back up ten
22:4 "**G** to the chief priest Hilkiah.
1Ch 5:18 soldiers ready to **g** to war.
7:11 men who could **g** to war.
11:6 the first to **g** ⌊into Jerusalem⌋,
14:14 "Don't **g** after them.
14:15 then **g** out and fight because
17:11 the time comes for you to **g**
20:1 the time when kings **g** out to
21:2 the leaders of the people, "**G**,
21:10 "**G** and tell David, 'This is
21:18 told Gad to tell David to **g**
21:30 However, David couldn't **g**
2Ch 6:34 "When your people **g** to war
7:2 The priests couldn't **g** into the
11:4 Everyone, **g** home.
14:11 In your name we **g** against this
15:5 could come and **g** in peace,
18:3 "Will you **g** with me to Ramoth
18:5 He asked them, "Should we **g**
18:5 "**G**," they said. "God will hand
18:14 should we **g** to war against
18:16 each one **g** home in peace."'
18:21 "The Spirit answered, 'I will **g**
18:21 in deceiving him. **G** and do it.'
18:23 "Which way did the Spirit **g**
18:24 find out on the day you **g** into
18:29 myself and **g** into battle,
20:16 Tomorrow **g** into battle against
20:17 Tomorrow **g** out to face them.
20:36 making ships to **g** to Tarshish.
20:37 and couldn't **g** to Tarshish.
23:8 who were about to **g** off duty.
24:5 "**G** to the cities of Judah,
25:7 army must not **g** with you,
25:8 If you **g** into battle with them,
25:13 back so that they couldn't **g**
26:11 They were ready to **g** to war in
33:14 He made the wall **g** around the
36:23 are his people. You may **g**.
Ezr 1:3 You may **g** to Jerusalem
1:11 left Babylon to **g** to Jerusalem.
7:13 in my kingdom and want to **g**
7:13 with you to Jerusalem may **g**.
7:28 leaders in Israel to **g** with me.
8:31 first month to **g** to Jerusalem.
Neh 2:5 my request, let me **g** to Judah,
2:6 he was willing to let me **g**.
6:11 Would a man like me **g** into the
6:11 to save his life? I won't **g**."
8:10 Then he told them, "**G**,
8:15 "**G** to the mountains,
9:12 to see the way they should **g**.
9:19 to see the way they should **g**.
9:37 products ⌊from our land⌋ **g**
Est 2:12 young woman had her turn to **g**
2:13 the young woman would **g** to
2:14 She would **g** in the evening
2:15 When Esther's turn came to **g**
4:5 She commanded him to **g** to
4:8 to inform and command her to **g**
4:16 After that, I will **g** to the king,
5:14 Then **g** with the king to the
Job 1:4 His sons used to **g** to each
2:11 They had agreed they would **g**
6:11 ⌊left⌋ that I can **g** on hoping?
6:18 They **g** into a wasteland and
7:6 My days **g** swifter than a
9:25 "My days **g** by more quickly
10:21 before I **g** away to a land of
13:9 Will it **g** well when he
14:5 then he cannot **g** past it.
14:14 will he **g** on living?
16:6 how much of it will **g** away?
17:16 Will hope **g** down with me to
19:8 my path so that I can't **g** on.
20:13 he savors it and won't let **g**
21:3 you may **g** on mocking.
21:7 do the wicked **g** on living,
21:13 and they **g** peacefully to the
23:3 I would **g** where he lives.
23:8 However, if I **g** east,
Job 23:8 If I **g** west, I can't find him.
23:9 If I **g** northward, where he is at
24:4 of the country **g** into hiding.
24:5 poor people **g** out to do their
24:10 why⌋ the poor **g** around naked.
27:6 righteousness and won't let **g**.
27:19 He may **g** to bed rich,
31:34 quiet and didn't **g** outside ....
33:25 They will **g** back to the days of
36:23 him which way he should **g**?
37:8 Animals **g** into their dens and
38:35 flashes so that they may **g**
39:5 lets the wild donkey **g** free?
42:8 **G** to my servant Job,
Psa 22:29 All those who **g** down to the
24:3 Who may **g** up the LORD's
28:1 be like those who **g** into the pit.
30:9 blood is shed, if I **g** into the pit?
32:8 you the way that you should **g**.
34:10 Young lions **g** hungry and may
36:4 on his bed and chooses to **g**
37:8 Let **g** of anger, and leave rage
39:13 smile again before I **g** away
43:4 Then let me **g** to the altar of
44:9 You do not even **g** along with
46:10 Let **g** ⌊of your concerns⌋!
48:12 **G** around it. Count its towers.
55:10 Day and night they **g** around on
55:15 Let them **g** into the grave while
58:3 From their birth liars **g** astray.
63:9 try to destroy my life will **g** into
71:3 a place where I may always **g**.
81:12 So I let them **g** their own
84:7 Their strength grows as they **g**
85:5 Will you ever let **g** of your
85:8 But they must not **g** back to
85:13 Righteousness will **g** ahead of
88:4 with those who **g** into
89:48 Can a mortal **g** on living and
102:26 but you will still **g** on.
102:28 children of your servants will **g**
104:23 Then people **g** to do their work,
115:17 nor do those who **g** into the
118:19 I will **g** through them ⌊and⌋
121:8 guards you as you come and **g**.
122:1 "Let's **g** to the house of the
122:4 All of the LORD's tribes **g** to
122:8 "May it **g** well for you!"
128:2 May things **g** well for you!
132:7 Let's **g** to his dwelling place.
138:8 Do not let **g** of what your hands
139:7 Where can I **g** ⌊to get away⌋
139:8 If I **g** up to heaven,
143:7 be like those who **g** into the pit.
143:8 know the way that I should **g**.
Pro 1:10 lure you, do not **g** along.
1:12 good health who **g** into the pit.
1:18 They **g** into hiding only to lose
3:23 Then you will **g** safely on your
3:28 tell your neighbor, "**G** away!
5:8 Do not even **g** near her door.
11:21 person will not **g** unpunished,
15:12 He will not **g** to wise people.
15:22 Without advice plans **g** wrong,
16:5 ⌊such a person⌋ will not **g**
18:8 and they **g** down into a
19:5 witness will not **g** unpunished.
19:9 witness will not **g** unpunished.
19:15 and an idle person will **g**
22:3 but gullible people **g** ahead
22:6 a child in the way he should **g**,
25:8 not be in a hurry to **g** to court.
26:22 and they **g** down into a
27:10 Do not **g** to a relative's home
27:12 people **g** ahead ⌊and⌋ suffer.
Ecc 1:4 and generations **g**,
5:1 Watch your step when you **g** to
5:1 It is better to **g** there and listen
6:6 anything good — don't we all **g**
6:9 in front of you than to **g** looking
7:2 It is better to **g** to a funeral than
7:15 Wicked people **g** on living in
7:18 hold on to the one and not let **g**
8:10 They used to **g** in and out of
8:12 with certainty that it will **g** well
8:13 But it will not **g** well for the

Ecc 9:7 **G**, enjoy eating your food,
9:8 and never **g** without lotion on
12:5 Mortals **g** to their eternal rest,
12:5 and mourners **g** out in the
Sos 3:4 and would not let him **g** until
4:6 I will **g** to the mountain of myrrh
6:1 Where did your beloved **g**,
7:11 Let's **g** into the field.
7:12 Let's **g** to the vineyards early.
8:12 and 5 pounds **g** to those who
Isa 2:3 "Let's **g** to the mountain of the
2:3 The teachings will **g** out from
2:3 will **g** out from Jerusalem.
2:10 **G** in among the rocks and hide
2:19 People will **g** into caves in the
2:21 They will **g** into caves in the
3:12 don't know which way to **g**."
5:13 "My people will **g** into exile
5:14 people will **g** down into it.
5:14 and joyous will **g** down into it.
6:8 Who will **g** for us?"
6:9 "**G** and tell these people,
7:3 "**G** out with your son Shear
7:25 you will no longer be able to **g**
8:7 its channels and **g** over all its
8:20 They should **g** to the teachings
8:22 They will **g** in anguish and be
10:29 They **g** through the mountain
14:13 You thought, "I'll **g** up to
14:14 I'll **g** above the top of the
14:17 who didn't let his prisoners **g**
14:19 You **g** down to the stones of
15:2 The people of Dibon **g** to the
15:5 They **g** up the mountain road to
18:2 **G**, swift messengers, to a tall
21:2 **G** to war, Elam! Surround them,
22:1 Why do all of you **g** up on the
22:15 of Armies says: **G** to Shebna,
23:16 **G** around in the city,
23:17 Then she will **g** back to
26:20 My people, **g** to your rooms,
28:24 Does a farmer **g** on plowing
29:1 Let year after year **g** by.
29:1 Let your annual festivals **g** on.
29:7 from all the nations will **g**
29:7 They will **g** to war against it,
30:2 They **g** to Egypt without asking
31:1 it will be for those who **g**
32:6 They let people **g** hungry and
34:10 and smoke will always **g** up
35:9 Wild animals won't **g** on it.
37:28 when you **g** out and come in,
37:29 I will make you **g** back the way
37:32 Those few people will **g** out
37:32 and those who escape will **g**
37:34 He will **g** back the way he
38:5 "**G** and say to Hezekiah,
38:22 "What is the sign that I'll **g** to
38:8 I'm going to make the shadow **g**
38:10 prime of my life I would **g** down
38:18 Those who **g** down to the pit
40:9 **G** up a high mountain,
43:2 When you **g** through the sea,
43:2 When you **g** through rivers,
45:2 I will **g** ahead of you,
45:10 Why did you **g** through labor
45:13 let my exiles **g** free without any
45:16 **g** away completely disgraced.
46:2 They **g** away into captivity.
47:1 **G**, sit in the dirt, virgin princess
47:5 **G** into the dark, and sit in
47:15 They will **g** their own ways,
48:17 I lead you where you should **g**.
51:4 My teachings will **g** out from
51:14 They will not **g** without food.
52:12 You will not **g** away in a hurry,
52:12 nor will you **g** away quickly.
52:12 The LORD will **g** ahead of you.
53:6 Each one of us has turned to **g**
55:10 They do not **g** back again until
55:12 You will **g** out with joy and be
56:11 All of them have turned to **g**
58:6 let the oppressed **g** free,
58:8 Your righteousness will **g**
60:20 Your sun will no longer **g** down,
62:10 **G** through! Go through the
Isa 62:10 **G** through the gates!
65:2 They chose to **g** the wrong
66:17 They **g** into the garden and
66:24 Then they will **g** out and look
66:24 that burns them will not **g** out.
Jer 1:7 You will **g** wherever I send you.
2:2 "**G** and announce to Jerusalem,
2:10 **G** over to the coasts of Cyprus,
3:1 her first husband shouldn't **g**
3:12 **G** and proclaim these things to
4:5 Let's **g** into the fortified cities."
4:6 to signal people to **g** to Zion.
4:10 that everything would **g** well
4:29 They will **g** off into the thickets
5:5 Let me **g** to important people
5:10 "**G** among Jerusalem's rows of
6:25 Don't **g** into the field or walk on
6:28 They **g** around slandering.
6:29 It is useless to **g** on refining
7:2 all you people of Judah who **g**
7:12 "'But **g** to my place that was at
7:23 that things will **g** well for you.'
8:6 They **g** their own ways like
8:14 Let's **g** into the fortified cities
9:2 people and **g** away from them.
9:3 They **g** from one evil thing to
12:9 **G**, gather all the animals in the
13:4 **G** to the Euphrates River,
13:6 "**G** to the Euphrates,
13:10 They **g** their own stubborn
14:3 They **g** to the cisterns,
14:12 Even if they **g** without food,
14:18 If I **g** to the field, I see those
14:18 If I **g** to the city, I see those
15:1 away from me, and let them **g**.
15:2 ask you where they should **g**,
16:5 Don't **g** into a house where
16:5 Don't **g** to mourn or to grieve for
16:8 "Don't even **g** into a home
17:19 where the kings of Judah **g** in
17:20 and **g** through these gates.
18:2 "**G** to the potter's house.
18:12 We'll **g** our own stubborn,
18:15 They **g** on side roads and not
19:1 This is what the LORD says: **G**
19:2 **G** to the valley of Ben Hinnom
20:6 your house will **g** into captivity.
20:6 You will **g** to Babylon,
21:9 Those of you who **g** out and
22:1 This is what the LORD says: **G**
22:20 "**G** to Lebanon and cry!
22:22 your lovers will **g** into captivity.
23:17 'Everything will **g** well for
23:32 them or command them to **g**.
25:16 they will stagger and **g** insane
25:29 you think you'll **g** unpunished?
25:29 You will not **g** unpunished!
30:11 let you **g** entirely unpunished.
31:4 and you will **g** dancing with
31:6 Let's **g** to Zion, to the LORD our
34:2 **G** to King Zedekiah of Judah,
34:3 Then you will **g** to Babylon.
35:2 "**G** to the family of Rechab and
35:11 'Let's **g** to Jerusalem to
36:5 "I'm no longer allowed to **g** to
37:4 still free to come and **g** among
37:7 But it will **g** back to Egypt,
37:12 to leave Jerusalem and **g**
38:20 Then everything will **g** well for
40:1 let him **g** at Ramah.
40:4 **G** wherever you want.
40:5 then **g** back to Gedaliah,
40:5 or **g** anywhere you want."
40:5 and a present and let him **g**.
42:3 God tell us where we should **g**
42:6 everything will **g** well for us."
42:14 you say, 'We'll **g** to Egypt,
42:15 you're determined to **g** to Egypt,
42:15 and you **g** and live there.
42:17 all the people who decide to **g**
42:18 out on you if you **g** to Egypt.
42:19 left in Judah not to **g** to Egypt.
42:22 where you want to **g** and live."
43:2 to tell us that we must not **g**
44:12 who were determined to **g**
44:25 "So **g** ahead. Keep your vows,
Jer 45:5 But wherever you **g** I will let
46:9 **G** into battle, you horsemen.
46:11 **G** to Gilead, and get medicine,
46:16 Let's **g** back to our people,
46:28 let you **g** entirely unpunished."
47:6 **G** back into your scabbard.
48:5 People **g** up the pass of Luhith,
48:5 crying bitterly as they **g**.
48:7 Chemosh will **g** into captivity
49:12 why should you **g** unpunished?
49:12 You won't **g** unpunished.
49:36 where Elam's refugees won't **g**.
50:4 will cry as they **g** together
50:5 They will **g** there to make a
50:6 They **g** from mountains to hills.
50:27 Let them **g** to be slaughtered.
50:33 They refuse to let them **g**.
50:38 that will **g** crazy with fear.
51:9 Let's abandon it and **g** to our
51:53 The people of Babylon might **g**
Lam 1:5 Its children **g** ahead of their
1:13 He made it **g** deep into my
4:18 so we couldn't even **g** out into
Eze 1:12 their spirit wanted to **g**,
1:20 their spirit wanted to **g**,
3:4 **g** to the people of Israel,
3:11 **G** to the exiles, to your people.
3:22 "Get up, and **g** to the plain.
3:24 He said, "**G** into your home,
3:25 so that you can't **g** outside.
5:2 will draw a sword and **g** after it.
7:14 But no one will **g** into battle,
7:22 Robbers will **g** in and dishonor
8:6 things that will force me to **g**
8:9 He said to me, "**G** in,
9:4 "**G** throughout the city of
10:2 "**G** between the wheels under
12:11 You will **g** into exile and into
12:12 holes in the wall to **g** through.
12:16 Wherever they **g** among the
12:22 you have in Israel: 'Days **g** by,
14:17 'I will let a war **g** throughout
17:15 He can't break a treaty and **g**
17:18 and he can't **g** unpunished.
21:22 will indicate that he should **g**
26:20 ruins with those who **g** down
30:17 these cities will **g** into exile.
30:18 its villages will **g** into exile.
31:14 Every tree is going to die and **g**
32:19 **G** down and join the godless
33:30 'Let's **g** and hear the word that
39:9 in the cities of Israel will **g** out.
39:14 "People will be chosen to **g**
39:15 Whenever they **g** through the
42:14 they must not **g** out of the holy
42:14 Then they can **g** into the area
44:19 When they **g** out among the
44:30 all your contributions must **g**
44:30 The best of your dough must **g**
46:17 Then the gift will **g** back to the
Dan 10:20 When I **g**, the commander of
11:6 southern king's daughter will **g**
11:11 He will **g** to fight the northern
11:20 He will have a cruel official **g**
12:9 He replied, "**G**, Daniel.
12:13 But **g** on until the end.
Hos 2:7 'I'll **g** back to my first husband.
4:14 The men **g** to prostitutes and
4:15 Don't **g** to Gilgal. Don't go to
4:15 Don't **g** to Beth Aven.
5:6 They **g** with their sheep and
5:15 I will **g** back to my place until
7:12 When you **g**, I will spread my
8:13 They will **g** back to Egypt.
9:2 be enough wine to **g** around.
Amo 1:5 The people of Aram will **g** into
1:15 Their king will **g** into captivity
4:4 **G** to Bethel and sin.
4:4 **G** to Gilgal and sin even more.
5:5 Don't **g** to Gilgal. Don't travel to
5:5 will certainly **g** into exile.
6:2 **G** to Calneh and look.
6:2 **G** from there to the great city of
6:2 Then **g** to Gath, the city of the
6:7 now be the first to **g** into exile.
8:9 I will make the sun **g** down at

Amo 9:2 Even if they **g** up to heaven,
9:4 Even if they **g** into exile ahead
Oba 1:1 Let's **g** to war against Edom."
Jnh 1:3 He wanted to **g** to Tarshish to
Mic 2:10 Get up, and **g** away!
2:11 Liars and frauds may **g** around
2:13 **g** through the gate,
4:2 "Let's **g** to the mountain of the
4:2 The teachings will **g** out from
4:2 will **g** out from Jerusalem.
4:10 open fields, and **g** to Babylon.
5:2 His origins **g** back to the
Nah 1:3 let the guilty **g** unpunished.
Hab 2:6 How long will this **g** on?'
3:5 Diseases **g** ahead of him.
3:13 You **g** out to save your people,
Hag 1:8 "**G** to the mountains,
Zec 5:3 "This is a curse that will **g** out
6:7 He said, "**G**, patrol the earth!"
6:10 This same day **g** to the house
8:23 They will say, "Let us **g** with
9:8 against those who come and **g**.
9:14 and his arrow will **g** out like
11:5 kill them and **g** unpunished.
14:2 in the city will **g** into exile,
14:3 Then the LORD will **g** out and
14:5 the mountains will **g** as far as
14:17 the families on the earth won't **g**
14:18 If the people of Egypt won't **g** or
14:19 of all the nations that won't **g**
Mal 4:2 You will **g** out and leap like
Mat 2:8 "**G** and search carefully for the
2:8 report to me so that I may **g**
2:12 them in a dream not to **g** back
2:20 and his mother, and **g** to Israel.
2:22 Joseph was afraid to **g** there.
4:10 Jesus said to him, "**G** away,
4:21 preparing their nets to **g** fishing.
5:24 First **g** away and make peace
5:30 than to have all of it **g** into hell.
5:41 forces you to **g** one mile,
5:41 **g** two miles with him.
6:6 When you pray, **g** to your room
8:9 I tell one of them, '**G**!' and
8:13 Jesus told the officer, "**G**!
8:19 I'll follow you wherever you **g**."
8:21 first let me **g** to bury my father."
8:32 Jesus said to them, "**G**!"
9:6 up your stretcher, and **g** home."
10:5 "Don't **g** among people who are
10:6 Instead, **g** to the lost sheep of
10:7 As you **g**, spread this
10:11 "When you **g** into a city or
10:12 When you **g** into a house,
11:4 John's disciples, "**G** back,
11:7 "What did you **g** into the desert
11:8 Really, what did you **g** to see?
11:9 "Really, what did you **g** to see?
11:23 No, you will **g** down to hell!
12:29 How can anyone **g** into a
12:29 Then he can **g** through his
12:44 'I'll **g** back to the home I left.'
13:49 The angels will **g** out and
14:16 "They don't need to **g** away.
16:21 that he had to **g** to Jerusalem.
17:27 **g** to the sea and throw in a
18:15 does something wrong, **g**,
19:24 easier for a camel to **g** through
20:14 Take your money and **g**!
21:2 He said to them, "**G** into the
21:28 **g** to work in the vineyard today.'
21:30 'I will, sir,' but he didn't **g**.
22:9 **G** where the roads leave the
23:32 **G** ahead, finish what your
24:26 don't **g** out ⌊looking for him⌋.
25:9 **G**! Find someone to sell you
25:41 **G** into everlasting fire that was
25:46 "These people will **g** away into
25:46 approval will **g** into eternal life."
26:18 "**G** to a certain man in the city,
26:32 I will **g** to Galilee ahead of
26:36 "Stay here while I **g** over there
26:46 Let's **g**! The one who is
27:65 **G** and make the tomb as
28:7 Then **g** quickly, and tell his
28:10 **G**, tell my followers to go to
Mat 28:10 my followers to **g** to Galilee.
28:16 Jesus had told them to **g**.
28:19 So wherever you **g**,
Mar 1:19 their nets ⌊to **g** fishing⌋.
1:38 "Let's **g** somewhere else,
2:11 pick up your cot, and **g** home!"
3:27 "No one can **g** into a strong
3:27 Then he can **g** through the
5:19 "**G** home to your family,
5:34 **G** in peace! Be cured from your
5:37 Jesus allowed no one to **g** with
5:40 he made all of them **g** outside.
6:10 "Whenever you **g** into a home,
6:31 So he said to them, "Let's **g** to
6:37 They said to him, "Should we **g**
6:38 **G** and see." When they found
6:56 he would **g** into villages,
7:19 It doesn't **g** into his thoughts
7:29 you have said this, **g**!
8:26 "Don't **g** into the village."
9:23 "As far as possibilities **g**,
9:43 have two hands and **g** to hell,
10:25 It is easier for a camel to **g**
10:52 Jesus told him, "**G**,
11:2 He said to them, "**G** into the
11:6 So the men let them **g**.
14:13 and told them, "**G** into the city.
14:28 I will **g** to Galilee ahead of
14:42 Let's **g**! The one who is
16:1 spices to **g** and anoint Jesus.
16:7 **G** and tell his disciples and
16:15 "**G** everywhere in the world,
Luk 1:9 by priestly custom to **g** into
1:17 He will **g** ahead of the Lord
1:24 pregnant and didn't **g** out
1:76 You will **g** ahead of the Lord to
2:15 "Let's **g** to Bethlehem and see
2:41 year Jesus' parents would **g**
5:16 But he would **g** away to places
5:24 up your stretcher, and **g** home."
7:8 I tell one of them, '**G**!' and
7:22 John's disciples, "**G** back,
7:24 "What did you **g** into the desert
7:25 Really, what did you **g** to see?
7:26 Really, what did you **g** to see?
7:50 has saved you. **G** in peace!"
8:29 force him to **g** into the desert.)
8:31 not to order them to **g** into
8:38 "Let me **g** with you."
8:39 "**G** home to your family,
8:48 made you well. **G** in peace!"
8:51 He allowed no one to **g** with
9:4 When you **g** into a home,
9:13 Unless we **g** to buy food for all
9:51 determined to **g** to Jerusalem.
9:57 "I'll follow you wherever you **g**."
9:59 first let me **g** to bury my father."
9:60 You must **g** everywhere and
10:1 70 other disciples to **g** ahead
10:1 and place that he intended to **g**.
10:3 **G**! I'm sending you out like
10:5 Whenever you **g** into a house,
10:8 Whenever you **g** into a city and
10:10 "But whenever you **g** into a city
10:15 No, you will **g** to hell!
10:37 "**G** and imitate his example!"
11:5 Suppose you **g** to him at
11:24 'I'll **g** back to the home I left.'
12:50 I have a baptism to **g** through,
13:31 and **g** somewhere else!
14:23 '**G** to the roads and paths!
15:18 I'll **g** at once to my father,
15:28 angry and wouldn't **g** into
17:19 the man, "Get up, and **g** home!
18:25 it is easier for a camel to **g**
19:30 He said to them, "**G** into the
21:21 shouldn't **g** back into them.
21:37 But at night he would **g** to the
22:8 and John and told them, "**G**,
22:10 He told them, "**G** into the city,
22:33 I'm ready to **g** to prison with
23:36 They would **g** up to him,
Jon 1:43 Jesus wanted to **g** to Galilee.
3:4 He can't **g** back inside his
4:4 had to **g** through Samaria.
4:16 "**G** to your husband,
Jon 4:47 to Jesus and asked him to **g**
4:50 Jesus told him, "**G** home.
6:9 But they won't **g** very far for so
6:62 see the Son of Man **g** where
6:66 many of his disciples **g** back
6:68 to what person could we **g**?
7:3 and **g** to Judea so that your
7:6 is not the right time for me to **g**.
7:8 **G** to the festival. I'm not going to
7:8 is not the right time for me to **g**."
7:10 didn't **g** publicly but secretly.
7:33 Then I'll **g** to the one who sent
7:34 You can't **g** where I'm going."
7:35 this man intend to **g** so that we
7:36 'You can't **g** where I'm going'?"
8:10 "Where did they **g**?
8:11 **G**! From now on don't sin."
8:21 You can't **g** where I'm going."
8:22 'You can't **g** where I'm going'?"
9:11 '**G** to Siloam, and wash it off.'
10:9 They will **g** in and out of the
11:7 "Let's **g** back to Judea."
11:8 really want to **g** back there?"
11:15 Let's **g** to Lazarus."
11:16 "Let's **g** so that we,
11:44 "Free Lazarus, and let him **g**."
13:1 to leave this world and **g** back
13:33 but you can't **g** where I'm going.
14:3 If I **g** to prepare a place for you,
14:23 and we will **g** to them and
15:16 I have appointed you to **g**,
16:7 If I don't **g** away, the helper
16:7 But if I **g**, I will send him to
16:28 to leave the world and **g** back
16:32 Each of you will **g** your own
18:8 let these other men **g**."
18:28 The Jews wouldn't **g** into the
20:5 lying there but didn't **g** inside.
20:17 But **g** to my brothers and
21:18 you would get ready to **g** where
21:18 you where you don't want to **g**."
Act 1:11 that you saw him **g** to heaven."
1:25 abandoned his position to **g**
2:34 David didn't **g** up to heaven,
3:3 and John were about to **g** into
3:11 The man wouldn't let **g** of Peter
3:13 had decided to let him **g** free.
4:21 even more and then let them **g**.
5:40 named Jesus, and let them **g**.
7:3 **G** to the land that I will show
8:29 "**G** to that carriage,
9:6 **G** into the city, and you'll be
9:11 **G** to Judas' house on Straight
9:15 The Lord told Ananias, "**G**!
10:20 Get up, and **g** downstairs.
10:20 Don't hesitate to **g** with these
11:12 The Spirit told me to **g** with
11:25 Then Barnabas left Antioch to **g**
12:8 and get ready to **g**!"
15:36 "Let's **g** back to every city
16:3 wanted Timothy to **g** with him.
16:10 for a way to **g** to Macedonia.
17:9 post bond, they let them **g**.
19:8 For three months Paul would **g**
19:21 Paul decided to **g** to Jerusalem
19:30 Paul wanted to **g** into the
20:3 to **g** back through Macedonia.
20:22 "I am determined to **g** to
21:4 tell Paul not to **g** to Jerusalem.
21:12 Paul not to **g** to Jerusalem.
21:15 we got ready to **g** to Jerusalem.
21:24 Take these men, **g** through the
22:10 **G** into the city of Damascus,
22:21 "But the Lord told me, '**G**!
22:21 You'll **g** far away to people who
23:15 You and the council must **g** to
23:23 Have them ready to **g** to
24:25 You can **g**. When I find time, I'll
25:9 "Are you willing to **g** to
25:12 so you'll **g** to the emperor!"
25:20 asked Paul if he would like to **g**
27:7 wind would not let us **g** further.
28:3 Paul's hand and wouldn't let **g**.
28:18 me and wanted to let me **g**
28:26 '**G** to these people and say,
Rom 3:16 and suffering wherever they **g**.

Rom 10:6 "Don't ask yourself who will **g**
10:7 "Don't ask who will **g** down
1Co 4:6 from us not to **g** beyond what is
6:1 how dare you **g** to court to
7:15 partners leave, let them **g**.
10:27 and you wish to **g**,
16:4 think it's worthwhile for me to **g**
16:4 they can **g** with me.
16:5 After I **g** through the province of
16:6 wherever I decide to **g**.
2Co 1:8 if we could **g** on living.
1:16 My plans had been to **g** from
2:14 Wherever we **g**, God uses us
2:17 At least we don't **g** around
6:9 as you see, we **g** on living.
7:15 His deepest feelings **g** out to
11:12 But I'll **g** on doing what I'm
12:1 I'll **g** on to visions and
Gal 1:17 I didn't even **g** to Jerusalem to
Eph 2:18 and non-Jewish people can **g**
3:12 We can **g** to God with bold
4:26 Don't **g** to bed angry.
6:3 that everything may **g** well for
1Th 3:8 Now we can **g** on living as
4:15 will not **g** ⌊into his kingdom⌋
2Th 3:11 You're not working, so you **g**
1Ti 5:13 they learn to **g** around from
2Ti 3:6 Some of these men **g** into
3:13 preachers will **g** from bad
Heb 4:16 So we can **g** confidently to the
9:24 Christ didn't **g** into a holy place
9:24 He didn't **g** into a model of the
9:25 However, Christ didn't **g** into
10:19 we can now confidently **g** into
10:20 living way for us to **g** through
10:26 If we **g** on sinning after we
11:8 obey when God called him to **g**
11:15 have found a way to **g** back.
11:29 Faith caused the people to **g**
13:13 So we must **g** to him outside
Jas 3:4 wherever they want them to **g**.
4:13 "Today or tomorrow we will **g**
1Jn 3:6 Those who live in Christ don't **g**
3:6 Those who **g** on sinning
5:18 from God don't **g** on sinning.
3Jn 1:8 must support believers who **g**
Rev 2:10 Your suffering will **g** on for ten
6:1 with a voice like thunder, "**G**!"
6:3 living creature say, "**G**!"
6:5 third living creature say, "**G**!"
6:7 fourth living creature say, "**G**!"
13:10 he must **g** to prison.
14:11 their torture will **g** up forever
16:14 These spirits **g** to the kings of
16:15 He will not have to **g** naked
17:8 from the bottomless pit and **g**
17:14 They will **g** to war against the
20:8 He will **g** out to deceive Gog
22:11 God's approval **g** without it,
22:14 tree of life and may **g** through

Goah (1)

Jer 31:39 and then it will turn to **G**.

goal (17)

Job 6:11 What **g** do I have that I would
Psa 146:9 people from reaching their **g**.
Hab 2:3 It hurries toward its **g**.
Rom 9:31 but they did not reach their **g**.
15:6 Then, having the same **g**,
15:20 My **g** was to spread the Good
1Co 3:8 who waters have the same **g**,
9:26 but not without a clear **g** ahead
2Co 5:9 our **g** is to be pleasing to him.
Eph 1:10 all of history to its **g** in Christ.
Php 3:12 that I've already reached the **g**
3:14 I run straight toward the **g** to
1Th 4:11 make it your **g** to live quietly,
1Ti 1:5 My **g** in giving you this order is
Heb 12:2 the source and **g** of our faith.
1Pe 1:9 that is the **g** of your faith.
1Jn 4:17 love has reached its **g** in us.

goat (90)

Gen 15:9 a three-year-old female **g**,
30:32 every spotted or speckled **g**.
30:33 Any **g** I have that isn't speckled
37:31 took Joseph's robe, killed a **g**,
38:17 "I'll send you a young **g** from
38:20 to deliver the young **g** so that
38:23 I did send her this young **g**,
Exo 12:3 must take a lamb or a young **g**
12:5 choose a lamb or a young **g**.
12:21 "Pick out a lamb or a young **g**
13:13 It will cost you a sheep or a **g**
23:19 "Never cook a young **g** in its
34:20 It will cost you a sheep or a **g**
34:26 "Never cook a young **g** in its
Lev 1:10 "If your offering is a sheep or **g**,
3:12 "If your offering is a **g**,
4:23 he must bring a male **g** that has
4:28 he must bring a female **g** that
5:6 It must be a female sheep or **g**
9:3 'Take a male **g** as an offering
9:15 He took the male **g** for the
10:16 the male **g** that was supposed
16:9 Aaron must sacrifice the **g**
16:10 But he must bring the **g** chosen
16:15 Aaron will slaughter the **g** for
16:20 he will bring the living **g**
16:21 to release the **g** in the desert.
16:22 The **g** will take all their sins
16:22 release the **g** in the desert.
16:26 "The man who released the **g**
16:27 He must take the bull and the **g**
17:3 or **g** inside or outside the camp
17:7 must stop sacrificing to **g** idols
22:27 a calf, a lamb, or a **g** is born,
23:19 Also sacrifice one male **g** as
Num 7:16 a male **g** as an offering for sin;
7:22 a male **g** as an offering for sin;
7:28 a male **g** as an offering for sin;
7:34 a male **g** as an offering for sin;
7:40 a male **g** as an offering for sin;
7:46 a male **g** as an offering for sin;
7:52 a male **g** as an offering for sin;
7:58 a male **g** as an offering for sin;
7:64 a male **g** as an offering for sin;
7:70 a male **g** as an offering for sin;
7:76 a male **g** as an offering for sin;
7:82 a male **g** as an offering for sin;
15:5 With each sheep or **g** for the
15:11 and each sheep or **g**.
15:24 and a male **g** as an offering for
15:27 a one-year-old female **g** must
18:17 back a firstborn ox, sheep, or **g**.
28:15 one male **g** must be offered to
28:22 Also bring one male **g** as an
28:30 Also bring one male **g** to make
29:5 Also bring one male **g** as an
29:11 Also bring one male **g** as an
29:16 Also bring one male **g** as an
29:19 Also bring one male **g** as an
29:22 Also bring one male **g** as an
29:25 Also bring one male **g** as an
29:28 Also bring one male **g** as an
29:31 Also bring one male **g** as an
29:34 Also bring one male **g** as an
29:38 Also bring one male **g** as an
Dtr 14:21 Never cook a young **g** in its
18:3 or a **g**: the shoulder, jaws,
Jdg 6:19 house⌋ and prepared a young **g**
13:15 while we prepare a young **g**
13:19 So Manoah took a young **g** and
14:6 apart as if it were a young **g**.
15:1 He took a young **g** along for her.
1Sm 16:20 and a young **g** and sent them
2Ch 11:15 illegal worship sites and the **g**
Ezr 6:17 one **g** for each of the tribes of
Psa 50:9 a single male **g** from your pens.
Pro 27:27 There will be enough **g** milk to
30:31 a strutting rooster, a male **g**,
Eze 43:22 day bring a male **g** that has no
43:25 days you must sacrifice a **g**,
45:23 and one male **g** as an offering
Dan 8:5 I saw a male **g** coming from the
8:5 This **g** had a prominent horn
8:6 The **g** was coming toward the
8:7 The **g** was extremely angry
8:7 to stand up against the **g**.
8:8 The male **g** became very
8:8 when the **g** became powerful,
Dan 8:21 The hairy male **g** is the
Luk 15:29 given me so much as a little **g**

goat-hair (2)

1Sm 19:13 put a **g** blanket at its head,
19:16 idols with the **g** blanket at its

goat's (4)

Lev 4:24 place his hand on the **g** head
16:18 bull and some of the **g** blood
16:21 will transfer them to the **g** head.
Dan 8:7 the ram from the **g** power

goats (97)

Gen 27:9 and get me two good young **g**.
27:13 Get me ⌊the young **g**.⌋"
27:16 put the skins from the young **g**
30:35 the striped and spotted male **g**,
30:35 spotted female **g** (every one
31:10 the male **g** which were mating
31:12 all the male **g** which are mating
31:38 sheep and **g** never miscarried,
32:5 and donkeys, sheep and **g**,
32:7 the sheep and **g**, the cattle,
32:14 200 female **g** and 20 male
32:14 female goats and 20 male **g**,
34:28 They took the sheep and **g**,
47:17 sheep, **g**, cattle, and donkeys.
Exo 9:3 camels, cattle, sheep, and **g**.
12:38 of sheep, **g**, and cattle.
20:24 your sheep, **g**, and cattle on it.
34:19 whether cattle, sheep, or **g**.
Lev 1:2 from your cattle, sheep, or **g**.
7:23 any fat from bulls, sheep, or **g**.
16:5 He will take two male **g** from
16:7 He must take the two male **g**
16:8 must throw lots for the two **g**.
22:19 or **g** in order to be accepted.
22:21 it is from the cattle, sheep, or **g**,
Num 7:17 bulls, five rams, five male **g**,
7:23 bulls, five rams, five male **g**,
7:29 bulls, five rams, five male **g**,
7:35 bulls, five rams, five male **g**,
7:41 bulls, five rams, five male **g**,
7:47 bulls, five rams, five male **g**,
7:53 bulls, five rams, five male **g**,
7:59 bulls, five rams, five male **g**,
7:65 bulls, five rams, five male **g**,
7:71 bulls, five rams, five male **g**,
7:77 bulls, five rams, five male **g**,
7:83 bulls, five rams, five male **g**,
7:87 Twelve male **g** were used as
7:88 24 bulls, 60 rams, 60 male **g**,
15:3 They may be cattle, sheep, or **g**
22:40 sacrificed cattle, sheep, and **g**,
31:28 cattle, donkeys, sheep, and **g**.
31:30 cattle, donkeys, sheep, **g**,
31:32 675,000 sheep and **g**,
31:36 sheep and **g** they received,
31:43 received 337,500 sheep and **g**,
Dtr 12:6 of your cattle, sheep, and **g**.
12:17 of your cattle, sheep, or **g**;
14:4 you may eat: oxen, sheep, **g**,
14:5 deer, wild **g**, mountain goats,
14:5 goats, mountain **g**, antelope,
14:23 and **g** in the presence of the
14:26 want: cattle, sheep, **g**, wine,
32:14 drank milk from sheep and **g**.
32:14 male **g**, and the best wheat.
1Sm 10:3 will be carrying three young **g**,
24:2 on the Rocks of the Wild **G**.
25:2 had 3,000 sheep and 1,000 **g**.
1Ki 20:27 seemed like two newborn **g**.
1Ch 5:21 250,000 sheep and **g**,
2Ch 17:11 7,700 rams and 7,700 male **g**.
29:21 and seven male **g** as an
29:23 Then they brought the male **g**
29:24 The priests slaughtered the **g**
35:7 with 33,000 sheep and **g**
35:8 the priests 2,600 sheep and **g**
35:9 the Levites 5,000 sheep and **g**
Ezr 6:17 They sacrificed 12 male **g** as
8:35 and 12 male **g** for an offering for
Job 1:3 He owned 7,000 sheep and **g**,
39:1 the mountain **g** give birth?
42:12 He had 14,000 sheep and **g**,

Psa 50:13 of bulls or drink the blood of g?
66:15 I will offer cattle and g.
104:18 high mountains are for wild g.
Pro 27:26 and the money from the male g
Sos 1:8 and graze your young g near
4:1 Your hair is like a flock of g
6:5 Your hair is like a flock of g
Isa 1:11 of bulls, lambs, or male g.
11:6 Leopards will lie down with g.
13:21 and wild g will skip about.
34:6 with the blood of lambs and g,
34:14 Male g will call to their mates.
Jer 50:8 Be like the male g that lead the
51:40 like lambs, rams, and male g.
Eze 27:21 lambs, rams, and male g.
34:17 between rams and male g.
39:18 be killed like rams, lambs, g,
Zec 10:3 I will punish the male g.
Mat 25:32 separates the sheep from the g.
25:33 on his right but the g on his left.
Heb 9:12 not the blood of g and bulls,
9:13 The blood of g and bulls and
9:19 blood of calves and g together
10:4 (The blood of bulls and g
11:37 wore the skins of sheep and g.

goats' (7)

Exo 25:4 red yarn, fine linen, g hair,
26:7 "Make 11 sheets of g hair to
35:6 red yarn, fine linen, g hair,
35:23 g hair, rams' skins dyed red,
35:26 had the skill spun the g hair
36:14 They made 11 sheets of g hair
Num 31:20 of leather, g hair, or wood."

Gob (2)

2Sm 21:18 battle with the Philistines at G.
21:19 out with the Philistines at G,

gobbles (1)

Isa 9:20 On the right, one g up food and

God; god (4119)

Gen 1:1 G created heaven and earth.
1:2 The Spirit of G was hovering
1:3 Then G said, "Let there be
1:4 G saw the light was good.
1:4 So G separated the light from
1:5 G named the light day,
1:6 Then G said, "Let there be a
1:7 So G made the horizon and
1:8 G named ⌞what was above⌟
1:9 Then G said, "Let the water
1:10 G named the dry land earth.
1:10 G saw that it was good.
1:11 Then G said, "Let the earth
1:12 G saw that they were good.
1:14 Then G said, "Let there be
1:16 G made the two bright lights:
1:17 G put them in the sky to give
1:18 G saw that it was good.
1:20 Then G said, "Let the water
1:21 So G created the large sea
1:21 G saw that they were good.
1:22 G blessed them and said,
1:24 Then G said, "Let the earth
1:25 G made every type of wild
1:25 G saw that they were good.
1:26 Then G said, "Let us make
1:27 So G created humans in his
1:27 In the image of G he created
1:28 G blessed them and said,
1:29 G said, "I have given you
1:31 And G saw everything that he
2:2 By the seventh day G had
2:3 Then G blessed the seventh
2:4 at the time when the LORD G
2:5 the LORD G hadn't sent rain
2:7 Then the LORD G formed the
2:8 The LORD G planted a garden
2:9 The LORD G made all the
2:15 Then the LORD G took the
2:16 The LORD G commanded the
2:18 Then the LORD G said,
2:19 The LORD G had formed all
2:21 So the LORD G caused him to
Gen 2:21 the LORD G took out one of the
2:22 Then the LORD G formed a
3:1 the LORD G had made.
3:1 the woman, "Did G really say,
3:3 G said, 'You must never eat it
3:5 "G knows that when you eat it
3:5 You'll be like G, knowing good
3:8 the LORD G walking around
3:8 So they hid from the LORD G
3:9 The LORD G called to the man
3:11 G asked, "Who told you that
3:13 Then the LORD G asked the
3:14 So the LORD G said to the
3:21 The LORD G made clothes
3:22 Then the LORD G said,
3:23 So the LORD G sent the man
3:24 After he sent the man out, G
4:25 "G has given me another child
5:1 When G created humans,
5:1 them in the likeness of G.
5:22 Enoch walked with G for 300
5:24 Enoch walked with G;
5:24 was gone because G took him.
6:2 The sons of G saw that the
6:4 when the sons of G slept with
6:9 He walked with G.
6:12 G saw the world and how
6:13 G said to Noah, "I have
6:22 that G had commanded him.
7:9 as G had commanded Noah.
7:16 in as G had commanded Noah.
8:1 G remembered Noah and all
8:1 So G made a wind blow over
8:15 Then G spoke to Noah,
9:1 G blessed Noah and his sons
9:6 because in the image of G,
9:6 of God, G made humans.
9:8 G also said to Noah and his
9:12 G said, "This is the sign of the
9:17 So G said to Noah,
9:26 the LORD, the G of Shem!
9:27 May G expand the territory of
14:18 was a priest of G Most High.
14:19 is Abram by G Most High,
14:20 Blessed is G Most High,
14:22 to the LORD G Most High,
15:13 G said to Abram, "You can
16:11 name him Ishmael [G Hears],
16:13 "You Are the G Who Watches
17:1 to Abram, "I am G Almighty.
17:3 and again G spoke to him,
17:7 I will be your G and the God of
17:7 and the G of your descendants.
17:8 And I will be your G."
17:9 G also said to Abraham,
17:15 G said to Abraham,
17:18 Then Abraham said to G,
17:19 G replied, "No! Your wife Sarah
17:22 When G finished speaking
17:23 as G had told him.
19:29 When G destroyed the cities
20:3 G came to Abimelech in a
20:6 G said to him in the dream.
20:13 When G had me leave my
20:17 Abraham prayed to G,
20:17 and G healed Abimelech,
21:2 the exact time G had promised,
21:4 Abraham circumcised him as G
21:6 "G has brought me laughter,
21:12 But G said to Abraham,
21:17 G heard the boy crying,
21:17 and the Messenger of G called
21:17 G has heard the boy crying
21:19 G opened her eyes.
21:20 G was with the boy as he grew
21:22 "G is with you in everything
21:23 here in front of G that you will
21:33 the Everlasting G,
22:1 Later G tested Abraham and
22:2 G said, "Take your son,
22:3 he set out for the place that G
22:8 Abraham answered, "G will
22:9 to the place that G had told him
22:12 Now I know that you fear G,
24:3 you to swear by the LORD G
24:7 "The LORD G of heaven took
Gen 24:7 "G will send his angel ahead
24:12 G of my master Abraham,
24:27 the G of my master Abraham.
24:42 'LORD G of my master
24:48 the G of my master Abraham.
25:11 G blessed his son Isaac,
26:24 "I am the G of your father
27:20 "The LORD your G brought it to
27:28 May G give you dew from the
28:3 May G Almighty bless you,
28:4 land that G gave to Abraham."
28:12 He saw the angels of G going
28:13 the G of your grandfather
28:13 Abraham and the G of Isaac.
28:17 Certainly, this is the house of G
28:19 that place Bethel [House of G].
28:20 Then Jacob made a vow: "If G
28:21 then the LORD will be my G.
28:22 marker will be the house of G,
30:2 "Can I take the place of G,
30:6 Rachel said, "Now G has
30:17 G answered Leah's prayer.
30:18 Leah said, "G has given me
30:20 Leah said, "G has presented
30:22 Then G remembered Rachel.
30:22 G answered her prayer and
30:23 Then she said, "G has taken
31:5 but the G of my father has been
31:7 But G hasn't let him harm me.
31:9 So G has taken away your
31:11 the Messenger of G called
31:13 I am the G who appeared to
31:16 Certainly, all the wealth that G
31:16 do whatever G has told you."
31:24 G came to Laban the Aramean
31:29 Last night the G of your father
31:42 If the G of my father,
31:42 If the God of my father, the G of
31:42 G has seen my misery and
31:50 remember that G stands as a
31:53 May the G of Abraham and
31:53 of Abraham and Nahor — the G
32:9 Then Jacob prayed, "G of my
32:9 my grandfather Abraham and G
32:28 Israel [He Struggles With G],
32:28 you have struggled with G
32:30 that place Peniel [Face of G],
32:30 "I have seen G face to face,
32:32 hip socket because G touched
33:5 "The children G has graciously
33:10 if I were seeing the face of G,
33:11 because G has been gracious
33:20 an altar there and named it G Is
33:20 named it God Is the G of Israel.
35:1 Then G said to Jacob,
35:1 I am the G who appeared to
35:3 I will make an altar there to G,
35:5 As they moved on, G made the
35:7 called that place El Bethel [G
35:7 Bethel [God of the House of G].
35:7 That's where G had revealed
35:9 Then G appeared once more to
35:10 G said to him, "Your name is
35:11 G also said to him,
35:11 said to him, "I am G Almighty.
35:13 Then G went up from him at
35:14 to mark the place where G had
35:15 the place where G had spoken
35:15 with him Bethel [House of G].
39:9 thing and sin against G?"
40:8 "Isn't G the only one who can
41:16 but G can give Pharaoh the
41:25 G has told Pharaoh what he's
41:28 G has shown Pharaoh what
41:32 been definitely decided by G,
41:39 "Because G has let you know
41:51 because G helped him forget
41:52 because G gave him children
42:18 and you will live. I, too, fear G.
42:28 "What has G done to us?"
43:14 May G Almighty make him
43:23 Your G, the God of your father,
43:23 Your God, the G of your father,
43:29 "G be gracious to you,
44:16 G has uncovered our guilt.
45:5 G sent me ahead of you to

Gen 45:7 **G** sent me ahead of you to
45:8 you who sent me here, but **G**.
45:9 "**G** has made me lord of Egypt.
46:1 he offered sacrifices to the **G** of
46:2 **G** spoke to Israel in a vision
46:3 "I am **G**, the God of your
46:3 am God, the **G** of your father,"
48:3 Jacob said to Joseph, "**G**
48:9 "They are my sons, whom **G**
48:11 and now **G** has even let me
48:15 blessed Joseph, "May **G**,
48:15 father Isaac walked, may **G**,
48:20 'May **G** make you like Ephraim
48:21 but **G** will be with you.
49:25 because of the **G** of your father
50:17 are servants of your father's **G**."
50:20 **G** planned good to come out of
50:24 **G** will definitely take care of
50:25 He said, "**G** will definitely take
Exo 1:17 the midwives feared **G** and
1:20 **G** was good to the midwives.
1:21 the midwives feared **G**,
2:23 cries for help went up to **G**.
2:24 **G** heard their groaning,
2:25 **G** saw the Israelites ⌊being
3:1 the mountain of **G**.
3:4 **G** called to him from the bush,
3:5 **G** said, "Don't come any
3:6 I am the **G** of your ancestors,
3:6 the **G** of Abraham,
3:6 he was afraid to look at **G**.
3:11 But Moses said to **G**,
3:12 **G** answered, "I will be with
3:12 worship **G** on this mountain."
3:13 Then Moses replied to **G**,
3:13 'The **G** of your ancestors has
3:14 **G** answered Moses,
3:15 Again **G** said to Moses,
3:15 The LORD **G** of your ancestors,
3:15 the **G** of Abraham,
3:16 Say to them, 'The LORD **G** of
3:16 the **G** of Abraham,
3:18 'The LORD **G** of the Hebrews
3:18 sacrifices to the LORD our **G**.'
4:5 the people that the LORD **G**
4:5 the **G** of Abraham,
4:16 and you will be like **G**.
4:20 him the staff **G** had told him
4:27 Moses at the mountain of **G**,
5:1 "This is what the LORD **G** of
5:3 They replied, "The **G** of the
5:3 sacrifices to the LORD our **G**.
5:8 us go offer sacrifices to our **G**.'
6:2 **G** spoke to Moses,
6:3 and Jacob as **G** Almighty,
6:7 and I will be your **G**.
6:7 that I am the LORD your **G**,
7:1 have made you a **g** to Pharaoh,
7:9 'Give me a sign to prove that **G**
7:16 Say to him, 'The LORD **G** of
8:10 is no one like the LORD our **G**.
8:19 "This is the hand of **G**!"
8:25 sacrifice to your **G** here in this
8:26 the LORD our **G** are disgusting
8:27 sacrifices to the LORD our **G**,
8:28 sacrifices to the LORD your **G**
9:1 'This is what the LORD **G** of
9:13 'This is what the LORD **G** of
9:30 still don't fear the LORD **G**."
10:3 "This is what the LORD **G** of
10:7 to worship the LORD their **G**.
10:8 worship the LORD your **G**," he
10:16 LORD your **G** and against you.
10:17 Pray to the LORD your **G** to
10:25 to make to the LORD our **G**.
10:26 for worshiping the LORD our **G**,
13:17 **G** didn't lead them on the road
13:17 **G** said, "If they see that they
13:18 So **G** led the people around the
13:19 Joseph had said, "**G** will
14:19 The Messenger of **G**,
15:2 This is my **G**, and I will praise
15:2 I will praise him, my father's **G**,
15:26 carefully to the LORD your **G**
16:12 that I am the LORD your **G**.'"
17:9 in my hand the staff **G** told me
Exo 18:1 heard about everything **G** had
18:4 the other was Eliezer [My **G** Is
18:4 "My father's **G** was my helper.
18:5 near the mountain of **G**.
18:12 and other sacrifices to **G**.
18:19 May **G** be with you!
18:19 the people's representative to **G**
18:21 all the people, men who fear **G**,
18:23 If **G** commands you,
19:3 went up the mountain to **G**,
19:17 out of the camp to meet with **G**,
19:19 the voice of **G** answered him.
20:1 Then **G** spoke all these words:
20:2 "I am the LORD your **G**,
20:3 "Never have any other **g**.
20:5 because I, the LORD your **G**,
20:5 am a **G** who does not tolerate
20:7 of the LORD your **G** carelessly.
20:10 dedicated to the LORD your **G**.
20:12 the LORD your **G** is giving you.
20:19 But don't let **G** speak to us,
20:20 **G** has come only to test you,
20:21 to the dark cloud where **G** was.
21:6 his master must bring him to **G**.
21:13 but **G** let it happen,
22:8 the house must be brought to **G**
22:9 must bring their case to **G**.
22:9 The one whom **G** declares
22:20 "Whoever sacrifices to any **g**
22:28 "Never show disrespect for **G**
23:19 the house of the LORD your **G**.
23:25 must serve the LORD your **G**,
24:10 They saw the **G** of Israel.
24:11 **G** didn't harm these leaders of
24:11 So they saw **G**, and then they
24:13 went up on the mountain of **G**.
29:45 the Israelites and be their **G**.
29:46 that I am the LORD their **G**.
29:46 I am the LORD their **G**."
31:3 Bezalel with the Spirit of **G**,
31:18 stone tablets inscribed by **G**
32:11 pleaded with the LORD his **G**.
32:16 The tablets were the work of **G**,
32:27 "This is what the LORD **G** of
32:29 **G** gave you a blessing today
34:6 compassionate and merciful **G**,
34:14 (Never worship any other **g**,
34:14 because the LORD is a **G** who
34:23 the LORD **G** of Israel.
34:26 the house of the LORD your **G**.
35:31 Bezalel with the Spirit of **G**,
Lev 4:22 of the LORD his **G** —
7:18 It is repulsive to **G**.
11:44 I am the LORD your **G**.
11:45 you out of Egypt to be your **G**.
18:2 I am the LORD your **G**.
18:4 I am the LORD your **G**.
18:21 to the **g** Molech ⌊by burning
18:21 the name of your **G**.
18:30 I am the LORD your **G**."
19:2 I, the LORD your **G**, am holy.
19:3 I am the LORD your **G**.
19:4 I am the LORD your **G**.
19:10 I am the LORD your **G**.
19:12 dishonors the name of your **G**.
19:14 Instead, fear your **G**.
19:25 I am the LORD your **G**.
19:31 I am the LORD your **G**.
19:32 you show respect for your **G**.
19:34 I am the LORD your **G**.
19:36 I am the LORD your **G** who
20:2 a sacrifice to ⌊the **g**⌋ Molech,
20:7 I am the LORD your **G**.
20:24 I am the LORD your **G** who
21:6 dishonor the name of your **G**.
21:6 It is the food of your **G**.
21:8 you offer the food of your **G**.
21:12 not leave the holy tent of his **G**.
21:12 with the anointing oil of his **G**.
21:17 never bring food to offer to **G**.
21:21 never bring food to offer to **G**.
21:22 He may eat the food of his **G** —
22:25 as a food offering for your **G**.
22:33 you out of Egypt to be your **G**.
23:14 you bring the offering to your **G**
23:22 I am the LORD your **G**."
Lev 23:28 peace with the LORD your **G**.
23:40 LORD your **G** for seven days.
23:43 I am the LORD your **G**."
24:15 Those who treat their **G** with
24:22 I am the LORD your **G**."
25:17 Fear your **G**, because I am the
25:17 I am the LORD your **G**.
25:36 Fear your **G** by respecting
25:38 I am the LORD your **G**,
25:38 you Canaan and to be your **G**.
25:43 them harshly. Fear your **G**.
25:55 I am the LORD your **G**."
26:1 I am the LORD your **G**.
26:12 live among you and be your **G**,
26:13 I am the LORD your **G**.
26:44 I am the LORD their **G**.
26:45 be their **G** while nations looked
Num 6:7 Nazarites show their vow to **G**
10:9 Then the LORD your **G** will
10:10 I am the LORD your **G**."
12:13 LORD, "Please, **G**, heal her!"
15:40 and you will be holy to your **G**.
15:41 I am the LORD your **G**,
15:41 you out of Egypt to be your **G**.
15:41 I am the LORD your **G**."
16:9 Isn't it enough for you that the **G**
16:22 the ground and said, "O **G**,
16:22 you are the **G** who gives the
21:5 and criticized **G** and Moses.
21:29 you people of the **g** Chemosh.
22:9 **G** came to Balaam and asked,
22:12 But **G** said to Balaam,
22:18 LORD my **G** no matter whether
22:20 That night **G** came to Balaam
22:22 **G** became angry that he was
22:38 I can only say what **G** tells me
23:4 **G** came to him, and Balaam
23:8 How can I curse those whom **G**
23:15 while I meet with **G** over there."
23:19 **G** is not like people.
23:21 The LORD their **G** is with them,
23:22 The **G** who brought them out of
23:23 'See what **G** has done!'
23:27 Maybe **G** wants you to curse
24:2 The Spirit of **G** entered him,
24:4 one who hears the words of **G**,
24:8 The **G** who brought them out of
24:16 one who hears the words of **G**,
24:23 Who will live when **G** decides
25:3 joined in worshiping the **g** Baal
25:5 worshiping the **g** Baal of Peor."
25:13 because he stood up for his **G**
27:16 "LORD, you are the **G** who
Dtr 1:6 Horeb the LORD our **G** said
1:10 The LORD your **G** has made
1:11 May the LORD **G** of your
1:17 your decisions come from **G**.
1:19 LORD our **G** had commanded.
1:20 the LORD our **G** is giving us.
1:21 The LORD your **G** is giving
1:21 as the LORD **G** of your
1:25 "The land that the LORD our **G**
1:26 command of the LORD your **G**
1:30 The LORD your **G**,
1:31 the LORD your **G** carried you,
1:32 didn't trust the LORD your **G**,
1:41 as the LORD our **G**
2:7 The LORD your **G** has blessed
2:7 the LORD your **G** has been
2:29 the LORD our **G** is giving us."
2:30 The LORD your **G** made him
2:33 The LORD our **G** gave Sihon to
2:34 them for **G** by destroying men,
2:36 The LORD our **G** gave us all of
2:37 But the LORD our **G** had
3:3 So the LORD our **G** also
3:6 We claimed them all for **G**,
3:18 "The LORD your **G** has given
3:20 LORD your **G** is giving them
3:21 that the LORD your **G** has done
3:22 because the LORD your **G**
3:24 What kind of **g** is there in
4:1 of the land that the LORD **G**
4:2 of the LORD your **G** that
4:3 The LORD your **G** destroyed
4:3 worshiped the **g** Baal while you

Dtr 4:4 were loyal to the LORD your G
4:5 LORD my G commanded me.
4:7 as the LORD our G is near
4:10 LORD your G at Mount Horeb.
4:19 The LORD your G has given
4:21 So the LORD your G took an
4:23 that the LORD your G made
4:23 LORD your G has forbidden.
4:24 The LORD your G is a raging
4:24 a G who does not tolerate
4:25 LORD your G considers evil,
4:29 the LORD your G when you are
4:30 LORD your G and obey him.
4:31 The LORD your G is a merciful
4:31 your God is a merciful G.
4:32 Start from the very day G
4:33 ever heard G speak from
4:34 Or has any g ever tried to come
4:34 The LORD your G used his
4:35 know that the LORD is G.
4:35 There is no other g.
4:39 never forget that the LORD is G
4:39 There is no other g.
4:40 The LORD your G is giving
5:2 The LORD our G made a
5:6 "I am the LORD your G,
5:9 because I, the LORD your G,
5:9 am a G who does not tolerate
5:11 of the LORD your G carelessly.
5:12 your G has commanded you.
5:14 dedicated to the LORD your G.
5:15 LORD your G used his mighty
5:15 This is why the LORD your G
5:16 your G has commanded you.
5:16 the LORD your G is giving you.
5:24 You said, "The LORD our G
5:24 live even if G speaks to them.
5:25 the voice of the LORD our G,
5:26 of the living G speak from
5:27 that the LORD our G says.
5:27 the LORD our G tells you.
5:32 your G has commanded you.
5:33 LORD your G has given you.
6:1 and rules the LORD your G
6:2 must fear the LORD your G.
6:3 as the LORD G of your
6:4 The LORD is our G.
6:4 The LORD is the only G.
6:5 Love the LORD your G with all
6:10 The LORD your G will bring
6:13 must fear the LORD your G,
6:15 If you do, the LORD your G
6:15 because the LORD your G,
6:15 is a G who does not tolerate
6:16 Never test the LORD your G as
6:17 commands of the LORD your G
6:20 our G commanded you mean
6:24 The LORD our G commanded
6:25 presence of the LORD our G,
7:1 The LORD your G will bring
7:2 When the LORD your G gives
7:6 belong to the LORD your G.
7:9 the LORD your G is ⌊the only⌋
7:9 your God is ⌊the only⌋ G.
7:9 He is a faithful G, who keeps
7:12 the LORD your G will keep his
7:16 the LORD your G hands over
7:18 what the LORD your G did
7:20 The LORD your G will spread
7:21 because the LORD your G is
7:21 is a great and awe-inspiring G.
7:23 The LORD your G will hand
7:25 disgusting to the LORD your G.
8:2 years the LORD your G led you
8:5 The LORD your G was
8:6 of the LORD your G.
8:7 The LORD your G is bringing
8:10 thank the LORD your G for the
8:11 don't forget the LORD your G.
8:14 and forget the LORD your G,
8:18 But remember the LORD your G
8:19 if you forget the LORD your G
8:20 don't obey the LORD your G.
9:3 today that the LORD your G is
9:4 When the LORD your G expels
9:5 LORD your G is forcing them

Dtr 9:6 the LORD your G is giving you
9:7 made the LORD your G angry
9:10 tablets inscribed by G himself.
9:16 against the LORD your G.
9:23 the word of the LORD your G.
10:9 The LORD your G is their only
10:12 what does the LORD your G
10:14 belong to the LORD your G.
10:17 The LORD your G is God of
10:17 The LORD your God is G of
10:17 and awe-inspiring G.
10:20 Fear the LORD your G,
10:21 He is your G, who did for you
10:22 Now the LORD your G has
11:1 Love the LORD your G,
11:2 learned from the LORD your G.
11:12 the LORD your G cares about.
11:13 love the LORD your G,
11:22 Love the LORD your G,
11:25 As the LORD your G promised,
11:27 the LORD your G that I'm giving
11:28 of the LORD your G,
11:29 When the LORD your G brings
11:31 the LORD your G is giving you.
12:1 in the land that the LORD G
12:4 worship the LORD your G
12:5 The LORD your G will choose
12:7 presence of the LORD your G,
12:7 LORD your G has blessed you.
12:9 the LORD your G is giving you.
12:10 the LORD your G is giving you
12:11 Then the LORD your G will
12:12 of the LORD your G along
12:15 LORD your G has blessed you
12:18 of the LORD your G at
12:18 your G enjoy everything you've
12:20 The LORD your G will expand
12:21 If the place the LORD your G
12:27 the altar of the LORD your G.
12:27 the altar of the LORD your G,
12:28 LORD your G considers good
12:29 The LORD your G will destroy
12:31 worship the LORD your G
13:3 The LORD your G is testing
13:4 Worship the LORD your G,
13:5 against the LORD your G,
13:5 the LORD your G gave you.
13:10 away from the LORD your G,
13:12 the LORD your G is giving you
13:13 your G by worthless people.
13:15 they are claimed by G.
13:16 offering to the LORD your G.
13:18 The LORD your G will do this
14:1 children of the LORD your G.
14:2 are holy to the LORD your G.
14:21 are holy to the LORD your G.
14:23 presence of the LORD your G
14:23 the LORD your G as long as
14:24 But the place the LORD your G
14:25 the LORD your G will choose.
14:26 presence of the LORD your G.
14:29 Then the LORD your G will
15:4 because the LORD your G will
15:5 carefully to the LORD your G
15:6 The LORD your G will bless
15:7 the LORD your G is giving you.
15:10 the LORD your G will bless
15:14 as the LORD your G has been
15:15 the LORD your G freed you.
15:18 Besides, the LORD your G will
15:19 and flocks to the LORD your G.
15:20 presence of the LORD your G
15:21 sacrifice it to the LORD your G.
16:1 Honor the LORD your G by
16:1 LORD your G brought you out
16:2 sacrifice to the LORD your G.
16:5 the LORD your G is giving you.
16:6 the LORD your G will choose
16:7 the LORD your G will choose.
16:8 dedicated to the LORD your G.
16:10 of Weeks to the LORD your G.
16:10 LORD your G has given you.
16:11 of the LORD your G along
16:11 the LORD your G will choose
16:15 dedicated to the LORD your G
16:15 because the LORD your G will

Dtr 16:16 of the LORD your G at
16:17 LORD your G has given him.
16:18 the LORD your G is giving you.
16:20 the LORD your G is giving you.
16:21 the altar for the LORD your G,
16:22 things the LORD your G hates.
17:1 a sacrifice to the LORD your G.
17:2 the LORD your G is giving you,
17:8 the LORD your G will choose.
17:12 (who serves the LORD your G)
17:14 the LORD your G is giving you.
17:15 the LORD your G will choose.
17:17 or he will turn away ⌊from G⌋.
17:19 learn to fear the LORD his G
18:5 the LORD your G has chosen
18:7 of the LORD his G like all
18:9 the LORD your G is giving you,
18:12 The LORD your G is forcing
18:13 with the LORD your G.
18:14 But the LORD your G won't let
18:15 The LORD your G will send
18:16 you asked the LORD your G
18:16 the voice of the LORD our G
19:1 The LORD your G will destroy
19:2 the LORD your G is giving you.
19:3 the LORD your G is giving you
19:8 The LORD your G may expand
19:9 you — to love the LORD your G
19:10 the LORD your G is giving you,
19:14 the LORD your G is giving you.
20:1 because the LORD your G,
20:4 The LORD your G is going
20:13 When the LORD your G hands
20:14 LORD your G has given you.
20:16 the LORD your G is giving you
20:17 your G has commanded you.
20:18 sin against the LORD your G.
21:1 the LORD your G is giving you.
21:5 The LORD your G has chosen
21:10 LORD your G hands them over
21:23 hung on a pole is cursed by G.
21:23 The land that the LORD your G
22:5 disgusting to the LORD your G.
23:5 But the LORD your G refused
23:5 the LORD your G loves you.
23:14 The LORD your G moves
23:18 house of the LORD your G as
23:18 disgusting to the LORD your G.
23:20 Then the LORD your G will
23:21 a vow to the LORD your G,
23:21 The LORD your G expects you
23:23 your vow to the LORD your G.
24:4 the LORD your G is giving you
24:9 what the LORD your G did
24:13 presence of the LORD your G.
24:18 LORD your G freed you from
24:19 Then the LORD your G will
25:15 the LORD your G is giving you.
25:18 They weren't afraid of G.
25:19 So when the LORD your G
26:1 the LORD your G is giving you
26:2 the LORD your G is giving you,
26:2 the LORD your G will choose
26:3 today to the LORD your G that
26:4 of the altar of the LORD your G.
26:5 presence of the LORD your G:
26:7 We cried out to the LORD G of
26:10 presence of the LORD your G
26:11 LORD your G has given you
26:13 say to the LORD your G,
26:14 I have obeyed the LORD my G.
26:16 Today the LORD your G is
26:17 that the LORD is your G
26:19 holy to the LORD your G,
27:2 the LORD your G is giving you,
27:3 The LORD G of your ancestors
27:5 dedicated to the LORD your G.
27:6 the altar of the LORD your G.
27:6 on it to the LORD your G.
27:7 presence of the LORD your G.
27:9 the people of the LORD your G.
27:10 Obey the LORD your G and
28:1 obey the LORD your G,
28:1 If you do, the LORD your G
28:2 you obey the LORD your G:
28:8 The LORD your G will bless

Dtr 28:9 commands of the LORD your G
28:13 of the LORD your G that
28:15 Obey the LORD your G,
28:45 didn't obey the LORD your G
28:47 didn't serve the LORD your G
28:52 the LORD your G is giving you.
28:53 LORD your G has given you.
28:58 name: the LORD your G.
28:62 didn't obey the LORD your G.
29:6 that I am the LORD your G.
29:10 presence of the LORD your G.
29:12 the LORD your G is giving you
29:13 people and that he is your G.
29:15 presence of the LORD our G
29:18 who turns from the LORD our G
29:25 the promise of the LORD G
29:29 belong to the LORD our G.
30:1 LORD your G will scatter you.
30:2 return to the LORD your G
30:4 the LORD your G will gather
30:5 The LORD your G will bring
30:6 The LORD your G will
30:6 You will love the LORD your G
30:7 Then the LORD your G will put
30:9 The LORD your G will give
30:10 and return to the LORD your G
30:16 Love the LORD your G,
30:16 and the LORD your G will
30:20 Love the LORD your G,
31:3 The LORD your G is the one
31:6 The LORD your G is the one
31:11 of the LORD your G at
31:12 learn to fear the LORD your G
31:13 the LORD your G as long as
31:17 because our G isn't with us?'
31:26 promise of the LORD your G,
32:3 Give our G the greatness he
32:4 He is a faithful G, who does no
32:12 No foreign g was with him.
32:15 They abandoned the G who
32:17 to demons that are not G,
32:18 and forgot the G who gave you
32:39 See, I am the only G.
33:1 Moses, the man of G,
33:26 "There's no one like your G,
33:27 The eternal G is your shelter,
Jos 1:9 because the LORD your G is
1:11 land the LORD your G is going
1:13 Moses said, 'The LORD your G
1:15 land the LORD your G is going
1:17 May the LORD your G be with
2:11 The LORD your G is the God
2:11 The LORD your God is the G
3:3 promise of the LORD your G
3:9 the words of the LORD your G."
3:10 that the living G is among you
4:5 of the ark of the LORD your G.
4:23 The LORD your G dried up the
4:24 the LORD your G every day
7:13 This is what the LORD G of
7:19 praise to the LORD G of Israel!
7:20 against the LORD G of Israel.
8:7 The LORD your G will hand it
8:30 Ebal to the LORD G of Israel.
9:9 your G has become famous.
9:18 them to the LORD G of Israel.
9:19 them to the LORD G of Israel,
9:23 carriers for the house of my G."
9:24 your G commanded his servant
10:19 because the LORD your G has
10:40 as the LORD G of Israel had
10:42 because the LORD G
13:14 offered to the LORD G
13:33 The LORD G of Israel is what
14:6 said to Moses, the man of G,
14:8 loyal to the LORD my G.
14:9 loyal to the LORD my G.'
14:14 loyal to the LORD G of Israel.
18:3 the land which the LORD G
18:6 presence of the LORD our G.
22:3 of the LORD your G.
22:4 "Now the LORD your G has
22:5 Love the LORD your G,
22:16 against the G of Israel?'
22:19 to the altar of the LORD our G.
22:22 LORD is ⌊the only true⌋ G!

Jos 22:22 The LORD is ⌊the only true⌋ G!
22:24 with the LORD G of Israel?
22:29 altar of the LORD our G that is
22:33 So they praised G and didn't
22:34 LORD Is ⌊the Only True⌋ G.
23:3 the LORD your G did
23:3 LORD your G fought for you!
23:5 The LORD your G will expel
23:5 as the LORD your G told you.
23:8 be loyal to the LORD your G,
23:10 the LORD your G was fighting
23:11 to love the LORD your G.
23:13 LORD your G will never again
23:13 LORD your G has given you.
23:14 LORD your G has given you
23:15 your G has promised you
23:16 on you by the LORD your G
24:1 presented themselves to G.
24:2 "This is what the LORD G of
24:17 The LORD our G brought us
24:18 because he is our G."
24:19 "Since the LORD is a holy G,
24:19 He is a G who does not
24:23 over to the LORD G of Israel."
24:24 the LORD our G and obey him."
24:27 You cannot deceive your G."
Jdg 1:7 G has paid me back for what I
2:12 abandoned the LORD G
2:12 the G who brought them out of
2:13 the LORD to serve the g Baal
3:7 They forgot the LORD their G
3:20 a message from G for you."
4:6 She told him, "The LORD G of
4:23 So on that day, G used the
5:3 music to the LORD G of Israel.
5:5 of the LORD G of Sinai,
5:5 of the LORD G of Israel.
6:8 "This is what the LORD G of
6:10 'I am the LORD your G.
6:22 So he said, "LORD G!
6:25 altar dedicated to the g Baal
6:26 an altar to the LORD your G
6:31 If he's a g, let him defend
6:36 Then Gideon said to G,
6:39 Then Gideon said to G,
6:40 G did what Gideon asked.
7:14 G is going to hand Midian and
8:3 G handed Oreb and Zeeb,
8:33 They made Baal Berith their g.
8:34 remember the LORD their G,
9:7 so that G might listen to you.
9:23 Then G sent an evil spirit to
9:24 G did this so that the bloody
9:56 So G paid back Abimelech for
9:57 G also paid back the men of
10:10 We have abandoned our G and
11:21 But the LORD G of Israel
11:23 "The LORD G of Israel forced
11:24 of what your g Chemosh took
11:24 the LORD our G took for us?
13:5 dedicated to G from birth.
13:6 "A man of G came to me.
13:6 like the Messenger of G.
13:7 a Nazirite dedicated to G from
13:8 let the man of G you sent come
13:9 G did what Manoah asked.
13:9 The Messenger of G came
13:22 die because we have seen G."
15:19 So G split open the hollow
16:17 I was dedicated to G before I
16:23 great sacrifice to their g Dagon
16:23 "Our g handed Samson,
16:24 they praised their g.
16:24 "Our g gave our enemy,
16:28 G, give me strength just one
18:5 "Please find out from G if our
18:10 G will hand it over to you.
18:31 the house of G was at Shiloh.
20:18 They asked G, "Who will go
21:2 presence of G until evening.
21:3 "LORD G of Israel,
Rut 1:16 and your G will be my God.
1:16 and your God will be my G.
2:12 from the LORD G of Israel,
1Sm 1:17 and may the G of Israel grant
1:20 named him Samuel [G Hears],

1Sm 2:2 There is no Rock like our G.
2:3 the LORD is a G of knowledge,
2:25 G will take care of him.
2:27 Then a man of G came to Eli
2:30 the LORD G of Israel declares:
3:3 where the ark of G was kept.
3:13 that they were cursing G—
3:17 May G strike you dead if you
4:7 "A g has come into ⌊their⌋
4:11 The ark of G was captured.
4:13 was worried about the ark of G.
4:17 ark of G has been captured."
4:18 mentioned the ark of G,
4:19 the ark of G had been captured
4:21 because the ark of G had been
4:22 ark of G has been captured,"
5:1 had captured the ark of G,
5:7 "The ark of the G of Israel must
5:7 because their G is dealing
5:7 with us and our g Dagon."
5:8 with the ark of the G of Israel?"
5:8 "The ark of the G of Israel must
5:8 the ark of the G of Israel there.
5:10 Gath sent the ark of G to Ekron.
5:10 But when the ark of G came to
5:10 "They brought the ark of the G
5:11 "Send the ark of the G of Israel
5:11 where G dealt ⌊with them⌋.
6:3 the ark of the G of Israel,
6:5 give glory to the G of Israel.
6:19 G struck down some of the
6:20 before the LORD, this holy G?
7:8 to the LORD our G for us!
9:6 "There's a man of G in this city,
9:7 we can bring the man of G.
9:8 I'll give it to the man of G.
9:9 went to ask G ⌊a question⌋,
9:10 city where the man of G was.
10:3 way to worship G at Bethel:
10:5 you will come to the hill of G,
10:7 because G is with you.
10:9 G changed Saul's attitude.
10:18 "This is what the LORD G of
10:19 now you have rejected your G,
10:26 whose hearts G had touched.
12:9 they forgot the LORD their G.
12:12 LORD your G was your king.
12:14 will follow the LORD your G.
12:19 "Pray to the LORD your G for
13:13 command of the LORD your G.
14:15 there was a panic sent from G.
14:36 "Let's consult G first."
14:37 Then Saul asked G,
14:41 to the LORD, "O G of Israel,
14:41 Jonathan's, LORD G of Israel,
14:44 Saul said, "May G do worse
15:3 have for G by destroying it.
15:8 for G by destroying them.
15:9 them for G by destroying them.
15:9 did claim for G and destroy.
15:15 sacrifice to the LORD your G.
15:15 claimed for G and destroyed."
15:20 claimed the Amalekites for G.
15:21 and cows were claimed for G—
15:21 to the LORD your G in Gilgal."
15:30 me worship the LORD your G."
16:7 G does not see as humans
16:15 spirit from G is tormenting you.
16:16 When the evil spirit from G
17:26 the army of the living G?"
17:36 the army of the living G."
17:45 the G of the army of Israel,
17:46 will know that Israel has a G.
18:10 evil spirit from G seized Saul.
20:12 "As the LORD G of Israel ⌊is
22:3 until I know what G is going
22:13 and a sword and prayed to G
22:15 I have prayed to G for him?
23:7 "G has delivered him into my
23:10 "LORD G of Israel,
23:11 LORD G of Israel, please tell
23:14 but G didn't let him capture
25:22 May G punish me if I leave
25:29 comes from the LORD your G.
25:32 be the LORD G of Israel,
25:34 as the LORD G of Israel,

1Sm 26:8 "Today **G** has turned your
28:13 "I see a **g** rising from the
28:15 and **G** has turned against me
30:6 strength in the LORD his **G**.)
30:15 "Take an oath in front of **G** that
2Sm 2:27 "I solemnly swear, as **G** lives,
3:9 May **G** strike me dead unless I
3:35 "May **G** strike me dead if I
5:10 powerful because the LORD **G**
6:6 for the ark of **G** and grabbed it.
6:7 so **G** killed him there for his
6:7 He died beside the ark of **G**.
6:12 owns because of the ark of **G**."
6:12 the ark of **G** from Obed Edom's
7:2 while the ark of **G** remains in
7:22 is why you are great, LORD **G**.
7:22 there is no other **g** except you,
7:23 nation on earth that **G** came
7:24 you, LORD, became their **G**.
7:25 "Now, LORD **G**, keep the
7:26 of Armies is **G** over Israel.'
7:27 LORD of Armies, **G** of Israel,
7:28 "Almighty LORD, you are **G**,
10:12 and for the cities of our **G**,
12:7 "This is what the LORD **G** of
12:16 David pleaded with **G** for the
14:11 pray to the LORD your **G**
14:14 But doesn't **G** forgive a person?
14:17 the LORD your **G** be with you!"
15:24 They set down the ark of **G**
15:29 Abiathar took the ark of **G** back
15:32 where people worshiped **G**,
16:23 like getting an answer from **G**.
18:28 the LORD your **G** be praised.
19:13 May **G** strike me dead unless
21:14 After that, **G** answered the
22:3 my **G**, my rock in whom I take
22:7 I called to my **G** for help.
22:22 turned away from my **G**,
22:30 With my **G** I can break through
22:32 Who is **G** but the LORD?
22:32 Who is a rock other than our **G**?
22:33 **G** arms me with strength.
22:47 May **G**, the rock of my
22:48 **G** gives me vengeance!
23:1 by the man whom **G** raised up,
23:1 whom the **G** of Jacob anointed,
23:3 The **G** of Israel spoke to them.
23:3 justice rules with the fear of **G**.
23:5 "Truly, **G** considers my house
24:3 "May the LORD your **G**
24:23 the LORD your **G** accept you."
24:24 I won't offer the LORD my **G**
1Ki 1:17 an oath to the LORD your **G**.
1:30 to you by the LORD **G** of Israel.
1:36 LORD your **G** says so too.
1:47 'May your **G** make Solomon's
1:48 and said, 'Praise the LORD **G**
2:3 your duty to the LORD your **G**.
2:23 "May **G** strike me dead if
3:7 "LORD my **G**, although I'm
3:11 **G** replied, "You've asked for
3:28 he possessed wisdom from **G**
4:29 **G** gave Solomon wisdom —
5:3 name of the LORD our **G** until
5:4 But the LORD my **G** has
5:5 the name of the LORD my **G** as
8:15 be to the LORD **G** of Israel.
8:17 name of the LORD **G** of Israel.
8:20 name of the LORD **G** of Israel.
8:23 and said, "LORD **G** of Israel,
8:23 there is no **g** like you in heaven
8:25 "Now, LORD **G** of Israel,
8:26 "So now, **G** of Israel,
8:27 "Does **G** really live on earth?
8:28 Nevertheless, my LORD **G**,
8:53 After all, you, LORD **G**,
8:57 May the LORD our **G** be with
8:59 be near the LORD our **G** day
8:60 will know that the LORD is **G**
8:60 God and there is no other ⌊**g**⌋.
8:61 committed to the LORD our **G**.
8:65 LORD our **G** for seven days.
9:9 abandoned the LORD their **G**,
9:20 them for **G** by destroying them.
10:9 Thank the LORD your **G**,
1Ki 10:24 wisdom that **G** gave Solomon.
11:4 to the LORD his **G** as his father
11:9 from the LORD **G** of Israel,
11:10 **G** had given him commands
11:23 **G** also raised up Rezon,
11:31 this is what the LORD **G**
11:33 Chemosh (the **g** of Moab),
11:33 and Milcom (the **g** of Ammon).
12:22 But **G** spoke his word to
12:22 to Shemaiah, the man of **G**.
13:1 A man of **G** from Judah had
13:3 That day the man of **G** ⌊also⌋
13:4 the man of **G** condemning
13:4 the man of **G** was paralyzed so
13:5 sign the man of **G** performed at
13:6 the king asked the man of **G**,
13:6 an appeal to the LORD your **G**,
13:6 So the man of **G** made an
13:7 The king told the man of **G**,
13:8 The man of **G** told the king,
13:10 So the man of **G** left on another
13:11 everything the man of **G** did
13:12 the man of **G** from Judah had
13:14 He went after the man of **G** and
13:14 "Are you the man of **G** who
13:16 The man of **G** said,
13:19 The man of **G** went back with
13:20 had brought back the man of **G**.
13:21 also called to the man of **G**.
13:21 the LORD your **G** gave you.
13:24 The man of **G** left.
13:26 brought the man of **G** back from
13:26 "It's the man of **G** who rebelled
13:29 up the body of the man of **G**,
13:30 laid the body of the man of **G**
13:31 he had buried the man of **G**,
13:31 the man of **G** was buried.
14:7 'This is what the LORD **G** of
14:13 house in whom the LORD **G**
15:3 LORD his **G** as his ancestor
15:4 the LORD his **G** made Abijam
15:30 the LORD **G** of Israel furious.
16:13 and made the LORD **G** of Israel
16:26 the LORD **G** of Israel furious.
16:33 did more to make the LORD **G**
17:1 as the LORD **G** of Israel whom
17:12 as the LORD your **G** lives,
17:14 This is what the LORD **G** of
17:18 I have in common, man of **G**?
17:20 to the LORD, "LORD my **G**,
17:21 to the LORD, "LORD my **G**,
17:24 that you are a man of **G**
18:10 as the LORD your **G** lives,
18:21 If the LORD is **G**, follow him;
18:21 him; if Baal is **G**, follow him."
18:24 The **g** who answers by fire is
18:24 answers by fire is the real **G**."
18:25 Call on the name of your **g**,
18:27 "Shout louder, since he is a **g**.
18:36 He said, "LORD **G** of Abraham,
18:36 known today that you are **G**
18:37 are **G** and that you are winning
18:39 "The LORD is **G**!"
18:39 "The LORD is **G**!"
19:8 the mountain of **G**.
19:10 "LORD **G** of Armies,
19:11 **G** said, "Go out and stand in
19:14 "LORD **G** of Armies,
20:23 "Their **g** is a god of the hills.
20:23 "Their god is a **g** of the hills.
20:28 The man of **G** came again.
20:28 said that the LORD is a **g**
20:28 is a god of the hills but not a **g**
20:42 He was claimed by **G** and
21:10 and accuse him of cursing **G**
21:13 accused Naboth of cursing **G**
22:53 and made the LORD **G** of Israel
2Ki 1:2 ask Baalzebub, the **g** of Ekron,
1:3 from Baalzebub, the **g** of Ekron,
1:3 think⌋ there is no **G** in Israel?
1:6 from Baalzebub, the **g** of Ekron,
1:6 think⌋ there is no **G** in Israel?
1:9 "Man of **G**, the king says,
1:10 the officer, "If I'm a man of **G**,
1:11 The officer said, "Man of **G**,
1:12 the officer, "If I'm a man of **G**,
2Ki 1:13 officer begged him, "Man of **G**,
1:16 from Baalzebub, the **g** of Ekron.
1:16 ⌊you think⌋ there is no **G**
2:14 is the LORD **G** of Elijah?"
4:7 went and told the man of **G**.
4:9 "I know he's a holy man of **G**.
4:16 You're a man of **G**."
4:21 him on the bed of the man of **G**,
4:22 will go quickly to the man of **G**
4:25 So she came to the man of **G**
4:27 she came to the man of **G** at
4:27 But the man of **G** said,
4:29 The man of **G** told Gehazi,
4:31 back to meet the man of **G**.
4:40 death in the pot, man of **G**!"
4:42 and fresh grain to the man of **G**.
4:42 The man of **G** said,
4:43 the man of **G** said.
5:7 He asked, "Am I **G**?
5:8 But when Elisha, the man of **G**,
5:11 the name of the LORD his **G**,
5:14 as the man of **G** had instructed
5:15 men returned to the man of **G**.
5:15 "Now I know that there's no **g**
5:15 except the **G** of Israel.
5:20 of Elisha (the man of **G**),
6:6 The man of **G** asked,
6:9 So the man of **G** would send a
6:10 the man of **G** told him about.
6:15 servant of the man of **G** got up
6:31 He said, "May **G** strike me
7:2 answered the man of **G**,
7:17 as the man of **G** had predicted
7:18 exactly as the man of **G** told
7:19 answered the man of **G**,
8:2 did what the man of **G** told her.
8:4 the servant of the man of **G**.
8:7 "The man of **G** has come here."
8:8 and meet the man of **G**.
8:11 the man of **G** began to cry.
9:6 "This is what the LORD **G** of
10:31 of the LORD **G** of Israel.
13:19 Then the man of **G** became
14:25 the Dead Sea as the LORD **G**
16:2 LORD his **G** considered right,
17:7 against the LORD their **G**,
17:9 LORD their **G** that weren't right:
17:14 to trust the LORD their **G**.
17:16 of the LORD their **G**:
17:19 commands of the LORD their **G**
17:26 don't know the customs of the **g**
17:26 of the **g** of this country."
17:27 of the **g** of that country."
17:39 worship the LORD your **G**,
18:5 trusted the LORD **G** of Israel.
18:12 to obey the LORD their **G**
18:22 trusting the LORD our **G**."
18:22 He's the **g** whose places of
19:4 The LORD your **G** may have
19:4 sent him to defy the living **G**.
19:4 The LORD your **G** may punish
19:4 that the LORD your **G** heard.
19:10 'Don't let the **g** whom you trust
19:15 "LORD of Armies, **G** of Israel,
19:15 You alone are **G** of all the
19:16 sent to defy the living **G**.
19:19 Now, LORD our **G**,
19:19 you alone are the LORD **G**."
19:20 "This is what the LORD **G** of
19:37 in the temple of his **g** Nisroch,
20:5 'This is what the LORD **G** of
21:12 the LORD **G** of Israel,
21:22 He abandoned the LORD **G** of
22:15 "This is what the LORD **G** of
22:18 'This is what the LORD **G** of
23:5 Baal, the sun **g**, the moon god,
23:5 god, the moon **g**, the zodiac,
23:10 burning them to the **g** Molech.
23:11 had dedicated to the sun **g** at
23:11 the chariots of the sun **g**,
23:13 (the disgusting **g** of Moab),
23:13 disgusting **g** of the Ammonites).
23:16 announced by the man of **G**.
23:17 "It's the tomb of the man of **G**
23:21 for the LORD their **G** as
1Ch 2:7 goods that were claimed by **G**.

1Ch 4:10 Jabez prayed to the **G** of Israel,
4:10 **G** gave him what he prayed for.
4:41 claimed the Meunites for **G**
5:20 They had called out to **G**
5:25 were unfaithful to the **G**
5:25 **G** had destroyed these people
5:26 Then the **G** of Israel led King
6:48 in the tent, the house of **G**.
6:49 to make Israel acceptable to **G**.
11:2 The LORD your **G** has said to
11:19 that I would do this, **G**.
12:17 may the **G** of our ancestors see
12:18 because your **G** is helping
13:2 LORD our **G** has consented,
13:12 David was afraid of **G** that day.
14:10 David asked **G**, "Should I
14:11 **G** has overwhelmed my
14:14 Once more David asked **G**.
14:14 **G** answered him, "Don't go
14:15 because **G** has gone ahead
14:16 David did as **G** ordered him,
15:12 bring the ark of the LORD **G**
15:13 the LORD our **G** struck us.
15:14 the ark of the LORD **G** of Israel.
15:26 Because **G** helped the Levites
16:4 praise to the LORD **G** of Israel.
16:14 "He is the LORD our **G**.
16:35 'Rescue us, O **G** our Savior.
16:36 Thanks be to the LORD **G** of
17:2 because **G** is with you."
17:3 But that same night **G** spoke
17:16 am I, LORD **G**," he asked,
17:17 consider to be a small act, **G**.
17:17 LORD **G**, you've shown me the
17:20 there is no other **g** except you,
17:21 nation on earth that **G** came
17:22 you, LORD, became their **G**.
17:24 the **G** of Israel, is Israel's God.'
17:24 of Israel, is Israel's **G**.' And
17:25 You, my **G**, have revealed
17:26 "Almighty LORD, you are **G**.
19:13 and for the cities of our **G**,
21:7 **G** considered the census to be
21:8 David said to **G**, "I have
21:15 **G** also sent a Messenger to
21:17 David said to **G**, "I'm the one
21:17 LORD my **G**, let your
21:30 couldn't go there to consult **G**
22:6 for the LORD **G** of Israel.
22:7 the name of the LORD, my **G**.
22:11 temple of the LORD your **G** as
22:12 Teachings of the LORD your **G**.
22:18 the LORD your **G** with you?
22:19 to serving the LORD your **G**.
22:19 of the LORD **G** so that you
23:5 David had made for praising **G**.
23:13 the most holy things (to **G**),
23:14 sons of Moses, the man of **G**,
23:25 David had said, "The LORD **G**
24:5 for **G** among both Eleazar's
24:19 as the LORD **G** of Israel had
25:5 as **G** had promised.
25:5 So **G** gave Heman 14 sons and
26:5 **G** had blessed Obed Edom.
26:20 of the gifts dedicated to **G**.
26:26 dedicated to **G** that King David,
26:32 in every matter involving **G**
27:24 **G** was angry with Israel
28:3 But **G** told me, 'You must not
28:4 my entire family the LORD **G**
28:8 and as our **G** listens
28:8 LORD your **G** has commanded.
28:9 learn to know your father's **G**.
28:12 and the gifts dedicated to **G**.)
28:20 The LORD **G**, my God, will be
28:20 The LORD God, my **G**,
29:1 the one whom **G** has chosen,
29:1 a person but for the LORD **G**.
29:2 for the temple of my **G**:
29:3 I delight in the temple of my **G**.
29:10 be praised, LORD **G** of Israel,
29:13 "Our **G**, we thank you and
29:16 "LORD, our **G**, all this wealth
29:17 I know, my **G**, that you
29:18 LORD **G** of our ancestors
29:20 "Praise the LORD your **G**!"

1Ch 29:20 assembly praised the LORD **G**
2Ch 1:1 The LORD his **G** was with him
1:7 That night **G** appeared to
1:8 Solomon responded to **G**,
1:9 Now, LORD **G**, you've kept the
1:11 **G** replied to Solomon,
2:4 the name of the LORD my **G**.
2:4 appointed by the LORD our **G**.
2:5 because our **G** is greater than
2:12 "May the LORD **G** of Israel be
5:11 holy to **G** without regard
6:4 be to the LORD **G** of Israel.
6:7 name of the LORD **G** of Israel.
6:10 name of the LORD **G** of Israel.
6:14 He said, "LORD **G** of Israel,
6:14 there is no **g** like you in heaven
6:16 "Now, LORD **G** of Israel,
6:17 "So now, LORD **G** of Israel,
6:18 "Does **G** really live on earth
6:19 Nevertheless, my LORD **G**,
6:40 "Finally, my **G**, may your eyes
6:41 LORD **G** — you and the ark of
6:41 Clothe your priests, LORD **G**,
6:42 LORD **G**, do not reject your
7:22 'They abandoned the LORD **G**
8:14 the man of **G**, had commanded.
9:8 Thank the LORD your **G**,
9:8 on behalf of the LORD your **G**.
9:23 wisdom that **G** gave Solomon.
11:2 But **G** spoke his word to
11:2 to Shemaiah, the man of **G**.
11:16 to seek the LORD **G**
11:16 the LORD **G** of their ancestors.
13:5 you know that the LORD **G**
13:10 "However, the LORD is our **G**.
13:11 the LORD our **G** gave us,
13:12 **G** is with us as our leader.
13:12 wage war against the LORD **G**
13:15 When they shouted, **G**
13:16 and **G** handed them over to
13:18 the LORD **G** of their ancestors.
14:2 Asa did what the LORD his **G**
14:4 lives to serving the LORD **G**
14:7 to serving the LORD our **G**.
14:11 Asa called on the LORD his **G**.
14:11 Help us, LORD our **G**,
14:11 You are the LORD our **G**.
15:3 Israel was without the true **G**,
15:4 turned to the LORD **G** of Israel.
15:6 **G** had tormented them with
15:9 when they saw that Asa's **G**,
15:12 lives to serving the LORD **G**
15:13 their lives to the LORD **G**
16:7 depend on the LORD your **G**,
17:4 his life to his ancestor's **G**
18:5 "**G** will hand over Ramoth to
18:13 whatever my **G** says to me."
18:31 **G** drew them away from him,
19:3 your life to serving **G**."
19:4 the LORD **G** of their ancestors.
19:7 The LORD our **G** is never
20:6 "LORD **G** of our ancestors,
20:6 aren't you the **G** in heaven?
20:7 Didn't you, our **G**, force those
20:12 You're our **G**. Won't you judge
20:19 stood up to praise the LORD **G**
20:20 Trust the LORD your **G**,
20:30 since his **G** surrounded him
20:33 set on the **G** of their ancestors.
21:10 the LORD **G** of his ancestors.
21:12 "This is what the LORD **G** of
22:7 **G** brought about Ahaziah's
24:5 temple of your **G** every year.
24:16 in Israel for **G** and the temple.
24:18 the temple of the LORD **G**
24:20 "This is what **G** says:
24:24 had abandoned the LORD **G**
25:7 But a man of **G** came to him
25:8 **G** will use the enemy to defeat
25:8 because **G** has the power to
25:9 Amaziah asked the man of **G**,
25:9 The man of **G** answered,
25:16 He said, "I know that **G** has
25:20 (**G** made this happen because
26:5 dedicated his life to serving **G**
26:5 who taught him to fear **G**.

2Ch 26:7 **G** helped him when he
26:16 unfaithful to the LORD his **G**.
26:18 The LORD **G** will not honor
27:6 as the LORD his **G** wanted.
28:5 So the LORD his **G** handed
28:6 the LORD **G** of their ancestors.
28:9 He said to them, "The LORD **G**
28:10 against the LORD your **G**?
28:25 So he made the LORD **G** of his
29:5 the temple of the LORD **G**
29:6 LORD our **G** considered evil.
29:7 holy place to the **G** of Israel.
29:10 make a pledge to the LORD **G**
29:36 because of what **G** had done
30:1 of the LORD **G** of Israel.
30:5 of the LORD **G** of Israel.
30:6 to the LORD **G** of Abraham,
30:7 were unfaithful to the LORD **G**
30:8 Serve the LORD your **G**,
30:9 The LORD your **G** is merciful
30:12 Also, **G** guided the people of
30:16 (Moses was a man of **G**.)
30:19 their lives to serving **G**.
30:19 May the LORD **G** of their
30:22 the LORD **G** of their ancestors.
31:6 dedicated to the LORD their **G**.
31:12 and the gifts dedicated to **G**.
31:14 freewill offerings made to **G**.
31:14 the holy gifts dedicated to **G**.
31:20 and true to the LORD his **G**.
31:21 dedicated his life to serving **G**.
32:8 but the LORD our **G** is on our
32:11 'The LORD our **G** will rescue
32:14 Is your **G** able to rescue you
32:15 No **g** of any nation or kingdom
32:15 Certainly, your **G** will not
32:16 said more against the LORD **G**
32:17 cursing the LORD **G** of Israel.
32:17 Hezekiah's **G** cannot rescue
32:19 They spoke about the **G** of
32:21 went into the temple of his **g**,
32:29 **G** had given him a lot of
32:31 in the land, **G** left him.
32:31 **G** did this to test him,
32:32 including his devotion to **G**,
33:7 where **G** had said to David and
33:12 he begged the LORD his **G** to
33:12 front of the **G** of his ancestors.
33:13 knew that the LORD is **G**.
33:16 to serve the LORD **G** of Israel.
33:17 only to the LORD their **G**.
33:18 including his prayer to his **G**
33:18 him in the name of the LORD **G**
33:19 His prayer and how **G**
34:3 his life to serving the **G**
34:8 the temple of the LORD his **G**.
34:23 "This is what the LORD **G** of
34:26 'This is what the LORD **G** of
34:27 in front of **G** when you heard
34:32 according to the promise of **G**,
34:32 the **G** of their ancestors.
34:33 Israel serve the LORD their **G**.
34:33 the LORD **G** of their ancestors.
35:3 Serve the LORD your **G** and
35:21 **G** told me to hurry.
35:21 **G** is with me, so stop now or
35:22 which came from **G**,
35:26 to **G** by following what
36:5 LORD his **G** considered evil.
36:12 He did what the LORD his **G**
36:13 back to the LORD **G** of Israel.
36:15 The LORD **G** of their ancestors
36:17 **G** handed all of them over to
36:23 The LORD **G** of heaven has
36:23 May the LORD **G** be with all of
Ezr 1:2 The LORD **G** of heaven has
1:3 May **G** be with all of you who
1:3 for the LORD **G** of Israel.
1:3 He is the **G** who is in
1:5 and the Levites — everyone **G**
1:7 in the temple of his own **g**.
3:2 built an altar for the **G** of Israel.
3:2 (Moses was a man of **G**).
4:1 for the LORD **G** of Israel,
4:2 the same **G** you worship.
4:3 a temple for our **G** together.

Ezr 4:3 alone for the LORD **G** of Israel,
5:1 in the name of Israel's **G**,
5:8 to the temple of the great **G**.
5:11 "We are the servants of the **G**
5:12 our ancestors made the **G**
5:17 permission for the temple of **G**
6:9 for burnt offerings to the **G**
6:10 sacrifices that please the **G**
6:12 May the **G** whose name is
6:12 temple of the **G** in Jerusalem.
6:14 They finished building as the **G**
6:18 ⌊to lead⌋ the worship of **G**
6:21 worship the LORD **G** of Israel.
6:22 their work on the temple of **G**,
6:22 temple of God, the **G** of Israel.
7:6 which the LORD **G** of Israel
7:6 LORD his **G** was guiding him.
7:9 since his **G** was good to him.
7:12 Teachings of the **G** of Heaven:
7:15 contributed to the **G** of Israel,
7:15 the **G** whose temple is in
7:16 temple of their **G** in Jerusalem.
7:17 temple of your **G** in Jerusalem.
7:18 conform to the will of your **G**.
7:19 to the **G** of Jerusalem.
7:21 Teachings of the **G** of Heaven,
7:23 Whatever the **G** of heaven has
7:23 the temple of the **G** of heaven.
7:23 Why should **G** become angry
7:24 temple of this **G** pay any taxes,
7:27 Thanks be to the LORD **G** of
7:28 LORD my **G** was guiding me.
8:18 **G** was guiding us,
8:21 in the presence of our **G**
8:22 "Our **G** works things out for the
8:23 So we fasted and asked our **G**
8:28 the LORD **G** of your ancestors.
8:30 temple of our **G** in Jerusalem.
8:31 **G** was guiding us,
8:35 offerings to the **G** of Israel:
8:36 the people and the temple of **G**.
9:4 at the words of the **G** of Israel.
9:5 to the LORD my **G** in prayer,
9:6 said, "I am ashamed, my **G**.
9:8 the LORD our **G** has been kind
9:8 Our **G** has made our eyes light
9:9 We are slaves, but our **G** hasn't
9:10 "And now, our **G**, what can we
9:13 overwhelming guilt, you, our **G**,
9:15 LORD **G** of Israel, because you
10:2 to our **G** by marrying foreign
10:3 now make a promise to our **G**
10:3 of our **G** have advised
10:11 Confess to the LORD **G** of your
Neh 1:4 and pray to the **G** of heaven.
1:5 I said, "LORD **G** of heaven,
1:5 great and awe-inspiring **G**,
2:4 So I prayed to the **G** of heaven,
2:8 because **G** was guiding me.)
2:12 what my **G** had inspired me
2:18 Then I told them that my **G** had
2:20 "The **G** of heaven will give us
4:4 ⌊Nehemiah prayed,⌋ "Our **G**,
4:9 But we prayed to our **G** and set
4:15 and that **G** had prevented their
4:20 Our **G** will fight for us!"
5:9 you live in the fear of our **G**
5:13 may **G** brush off from home and
5:15 because I feared **G**.
5:19 Remember me, my **G**.
6:9 But **G** made me strong.
6:10 "Let's meet in the house of **G**,
6:12 Then I realized that **G** hadn't
6:14 ⌊Nehemiah prayed,⌋ "My **G**,
6:16 work with the help of our **G**.
7:2 and he feared **G** more than
7:5 Then my **G** put the idea into
8:6 thanked the LORD, the great **G**.
8:9 holy day for the LORD your **G**.
9:3 of the LORD their **G** was read,
9:3 worshiped the LORD their **G**.
9:4 loudly to the LORD their **G**.
9:5 and thank the LORD your **G**:
9:7 You are the LORD, the **G** who
9:17 But you are a forgiving **G**,
9:18 This is your **g** who took you
Neh 9:31 merciful and compassionate **G**.
9:32 And now, our **G**, you are the
9:32 and awe-inspiring **G**.
10:33 make peace with **G** for Israel,
10:33 work in the temple of our **G**.
10:34 LORD our **G** at appointed times
12:24 the man of **G**, had ordered.
12:36 of David, the man of **G**.
12:43 because **G** had given them
12:45 doing what their **G** required,
12:46 hymns of thanksgiving to **G**.
13:2 But our **G** turned the curse into
13:14 me for what I have done, my **G**,
13:18 with the results that our **G**
13:22 for this, my **G**, and spare me,
13:25 I made them swear by **G**:
13:26 **G** loved him, and God made
13:26 God loved him, and **G** made
13:27 a serious crime against our **G**,
13:29 "Remember them, my **G**,
13:31 me, my **G**, for my benefit."
Job 1:1 He was decent, he feared **G**,
1:5 may have sinned and cursed **G**
1:6 One day when the sons of **G**
1:8 He is decent, he fears **G**,
1:9 given Job a reason to fear **G**?
1:16 "A fire from **G** fell from heaven
1:22 this Job did not sin or blame **G**
2:1 One day when the sons of **G**
2:3 He is decent, he fears **G**,
2:9 principles? Curse **G** and die!"
2:10 the good that **G** gives us.
3:4 Let **G** above not ⌊even⌋ care
3:23 those whom **G** has fenced in?
4:6 Doesn't your fear of **G** give you
4:9 **G** destroys them with his
4:17 mortal be righteous to **G**?
4:18 "You see, **G** doesn't trust his
5:17 is the person whom **G** corrects.
5:18 **G** injures, but he bandages.
6:8 that **G** would give me
6:9 that **G** would ⌊finally⌋ be
8:3 Does **G** distort justice,
8:5 If you search for **G** and plead
8:13 happens to all who forget **G**.
8:20 "Certainly, **G** does not reject a
9:2 be declared righteous to **G**?
9:3 If he wished to debate with **G**,
9:4 "**G** is wise in heart and mighty
9:13 **G** does not hold back his
9:14 can I possibly answer **G**?
9:32 like me cannot answer **G**,
9:34 **G** should take his rod away
10:2 I will say to **G**, 'Don't condemn
11:5 I only wish **G** would speak and
11:6 know that **G** forgets your sin.
11:10 If **G** comes along and
12:4 I am one who calls on **G** and
12:6 for those who provoke **G**,
12:6 those whose **g** is their power.
12:13 **G** has wisdom and strength.
12:16 "**G** has power and priceless
13:3 to argue my case in front of **G**.
13:7 "Will you talk wickedly for **G**
13:15 If **G** would kill me,
15:4 you destroy the fear ⌊of **G**⌋
15:4 and diminish devotion to **G**.
15:13 when you turn against **G** and
15:15 If **G** doesn't trust his holy ones,
15:25 out his hand against **G**
16:7 "But now, **G** has worn me out.
16:7 You, ⌊**G**,⌋ have destroyed
16:11 **G** handed me over to unjust
16:20 My eyes drip ⌊with tears⌋ to **G**
16:21 plead for a human in front of **G**.
18:21 to those who do not know **G**."
19:6 then I want you to know that **G**
19:8 "**G** has blocked my path so
19:22 do you pursue me as **G** does?
19:26 I will see **G** in my own flesh.
20:15 **G** forces them out of his
20:23 ⌊**G**⌋ throws his burning anger
20:29 This is the reward **G** gives to
20:29 the inheritance **G** has
21:9 and **G** doesn't use his rod on
21:14 But they say to **G**,
Job 21:17 an angry **G** give them pain?
21:19 "⌊You say,⌋ '**G** saves a
21:19 **G** should pay back that person
21:22 anyone teach **G** knowledge?
22:2 be of any use to **G** when even
22:4 Does **G** correct you and bring
22:12 "Isn't **G** high above in the
22:13 You ask, 'What does **G** know?
22:17 They told **G**, 'Leave us alone!
22:21 harmony and at peace with **G**.
22:26 Almighty and look up toward **G**.
23:3 I knew where I could find **G**!
23:13 "But **G** is one of a kind.
23:16 **G** has discouraged me.
24:12 but **G** pays no attention to their
24:22 ⌊**G**⌋ will drag away ⌊these⌋
24:23 ⌊**G**⌋ may let them feel
25:2 and terror belong to **G**.
25:4 a person be righteous to **G**?
27:2 "I swear an oath by **G**,
27:8 when **G** takes away his life?
27:9 Will **G** hear his cry when
27:10 Can he call on **G** at all times?
27:13 This is what **G** has waiting for
28:23 "**G** understands the way to it.
29:2 when **G** watched over me,
29:4 when **G** was an adviser in my
30:11 Because **G** has untied my cord
30:17 At night **G** pierces my bones.
30:24 "But **G** doesn't stretch out his
31:2 What would **G** above do ⌊to
31:6 ⌊then⌋ let **G** weigh me on
31:14 what could I do if **G** rises up?
31:15 Didn't the same **G** form us in
31:23 "A disaster from **G** terrifies me.
31:28 and I would have denied **G**
32:2 he was more righteous than **G**.
32:3 it look as if **G** were wrong.
32:13 Let **G**, not humans, defeat him.'
33:6 I stand in front of **G** as you do.
33:9 rebellious acts ⌊against **G**⌋.
33:10 **G** is only looking for an
33:12 **G** is greater than any mortal.
33:14 "**G** speaks in one way,
33:26 They will pray to **G**,
33:29 Truly, **G** does all this two or
34:5 but **G** has taken away my
34:9 do any good to try to please **G**.'
34:10 It is unthinkable that **G** would
34:11 **G** will repay humanity for what
34:12 **G** will never do anything evil,
34:31 such a person says to **G**,
34:33 Should **G** reward you on your
34:37 his words against **G**."
35:6 effect can you have on **G**?
35:10 But no one asks, 'Where is **G**,
35:13 "Surely, **G** doesn't listen to idle
36:5 "Certainly, **G** is mighty.
36:22 "**G** does great things by his
36:26 "Certainly, **G** is so great that he
37:15 Do you know how **G** controls
37:22 terrifying majesty is around **G**.
38:7 the sons of **G** shouted for joy?
38:41 when its young ones cry to **G**
39:17 because **G** has deprived it of
40:2 argues with **G** answer him?"
Psa 3:2 "Even with **G** ⌊on his side⌋,
3:7 Save me, O my **G**!
4:1 O **G** of my righteousness.
5:2 my king and my **G**,
5:4 You are not a **G** who takes
5:10 Condemn them, O **G**.
7:1 O LORD my **G**, I have taken
7:3 O LORD my **G**, if I have done
7:6 Wake up, my **G**. You have
7:9 O righteous **G** who examines
7:10 My shield is **G** above,
7:11 **G** is a fair judge, a God who is
7:11 God is a fair judge, a **G** who is
7:12 **G** sharpens his sword.
9:17 all the nations who forget **G**,
10:4 ⌊and says⌋, "**G** doesn't care."
10:4 ⌊concludes⌋, "There is no **G**."
10:11 to himself, "**G** has forgotten.
10:12 Lift your hand, O **G**.
10:13 the wicked person despise **G**?

Psa 10:13 to himself, "**G** doesn't care"?
13:3 Answer me, O LORD my **G**!
14:1 in their hearts, "There is no **G**."
14:2 who seeks help from **G**.
14:5 panic-stricken because **G** is
15:4 despises those rejected by **G**
16:1 Protect me, O **G**, because I
17:6 because you answer me, O **G**.
18:2 fortress and my Savior, my **G**,
18:6 I cried to my **G** for help.
18:21 turned away from my **G**,
18:28 My **G** turns my darkness into
18:29 With my **G** I can break through
18:31 Who is **G** but the LORD?
18:31 Who is a rock except our **G**?
18:32 **G** arms me with strength and
18:46 May **G** my Savior be honored.
18:47 **G** gives me vengeance!
19:1 heavens declare the glory of **G**,
20:1 The name of the **G** of Jacob
20:5 our flags in the name of our **G**.
20:7 in the name of the LORD our **G**.
22:1 My **G**, my God, why have you
22:1 My God, my **G**, why have you
22:2 My **G**, I cry out by day, but you
22:8 Let **G** rescue him since he is
22:10 womb you have been my **G**.
24:5 and righteousness from **G**,
24:6 for the face of the **G** of Jacob.
25:2 I trust you, O my **G**.
25:5 teach me because you are **G**,
25:22 Rescue Israel, O **G**,
27:9 Do not abandon me, O **G**,
29:3 The **G** of glory thunders.
30:2 O LORD my **G**, I cried out to
30:12 O LORD my **G**, I will give
31:5 me, O LORD, **G** of truth.
31:14 I said, "You are my **G**."
33:12 Blessed is the nation whose **G**
35:23 O my **G** and my Lord.
35:24 righteousness, O LORD my **G**.
36:1 He is not terrified of **G**.
36:6 is like the mountains of **G**,
36:7 mercy is so precious, O **G**,
37:31 The teachings of his **G** are in
38:15 You will answer, O Lord, my **G**.
38:21 O my **G**, do not be so distant
40:3 a song of praise to our **G**.
40:5 things, O LORD my **G**.
40:8 to do your will, O my **G**."
40:17 O my **G**, do not delay!
41:13 Thank the LORD **G** of Israel
42:1 so my soul longs for you, O **G**.
42:2 My soul thirsts for **G**,
42:2 thirsts for God, for the living **G**.
42:3 "Where is your **G**?"
42:5 Put your hope in **G**,
42:5 He is my savior and my **G**.
42:8 a prayer to the **G** of my life.
42:9 I will ask **G**, my rock,
42:10 "Where is your **G**?"
42:11 Put your hope in **G**,
42:11 He is my savior and my **G**.
43:1 Judge me, O **G**, and plead my
43:2 You are my fortress, O **G**!
43:4 Then let me go to the altar of **G**,
43:4 to **G** my ⌊highest⌋ joy,
43:4 you on the lyre, O **G**, my God.
43:4 you on the lyre, O God, my **G**.
43:5 Put your hope in **G**,
43:5 He is my savior and my **G**.
44:1 O **G**, we have heard it with our
44:4 You alone are my king, O **G**.
44:8 All day long we praise our **G**.
44:20 If we forgot the name of our **G**
44:20 our hands to pray to another **g**,
44:21 wouldn't **G** find out,
45:2 That is why **G** has blessed
45:6 Your throne, O **G**, is forever
45:7 That is why **G**, your God,
45:7 That is why God, your **G**,
46:1 **G** is our refuge and strength,
46:4 bring joy to the city of **G**,
46:5 **G** is in that city. It cannot fall.
46:5 **G** will help it at the break of
46:7 The **G** of Jacob is our

Psa 46:10 you will know that I am **G**.
46:11 The **G** of Jacob is our
47:1 Shout to **G** with a loud,
47:5 **G** has gone up with a joyful
47:6 Make music to praise **G**.
47:7 **G** is the king of the whole
47:8 **G** rules the nations.
47:9 the people of the **G** of Abraham.
47:9 rulers of the earth belong to **G**.
48:1 mountain is in the city of our **G**.
48:3 **G** is in its palaces.
48:8 in the city of our **G**.
48:8 **G** makes Zion stand firm
48:9 reflect on your mercy, O **G**.
48:10 Like your name, O **G**,
48:14 "This **G** is our God forever and
48:14 "This God is our **G** forever and
49:7 back another person or pay **G**
49:15 But **G** will buy me back from
50:1 The LORD, the only true **G**,
50:2 **G** shines from Zion,
50:3 Our **G** will come and will not
50:6 righteousness because **G** is
50:7 against you: I am **G**, your God!
50:7 against you: I am God, your **G**!
50:14 Bring ⌊your⌋ thanks to **G** as a
50:16 But **G** says to wicked people,
50:22 you people who forget **G**.
50:23 salvation that comes from **G**."
51:1 Have pity on me, O **G**,
51:10 a clean heart in me, O **G**,
51:14 guilt of murder, O **G**, my savior.
51:17 The sacrifice pleasing to **G** is
51:17 O **G**, you do not despise a
52:1 The mercy of **G** lasts all day
52:5 But **G** will ruin you forever.
52:7 refused to make **G** his fortress!
52:8 mercy of **G** forever and ever.
53:1 in their hearts, "There is no **G**."
53:2 **G** looks down from heaven on
53:2 who seeks help from **G**.
53:4 that they do not call on **G**?
53:5 because **G** has scattered the
53:5 After all, **G** has rejected them.
53:6 When **G** restores the fortunes
54:1 O **G**, save me by your name,
54:2 O **G**, hear my prayer, and open
54:3 They do not think about **G**.
54:4 **G** is my helper! The Lord is the
55:1 your ears to my prayer, O **G**.
55:16 But I call on **G**, and the LORD
55:19 **G** will listen. The one who has
55:19 They never fear **G**.
55:23 But you, O **G**, will throw
56:1 Have pity on me, O **G**,
56:4 I praise the word of **G**.
56:4 I trust **G**. I am not afraid. What
56:7 O **G**, angrily make the nations
56:9 This I know: **G** is on my side.
56:10 I praise the word of **G**.
56:11 I trust **G**. I am not afraid. What
56:12 by my vows to you, O **G**.
57:1 Have pity on me, O **G**.
57:2 I call to **G** Most High,
57:2 to the **G** who does everything
57:3 Selah **G** sends his mercy and
57:5 above the heavens, O **G**.
57:7 My heart is confident, O **G**.
57:11 above the heavens, O **G**.
58:3 people are strangers ⌊to **G**⌋.
58:6 O **G**, knock the teeth out of
58:9 Let ⌊**G**⌋ sweep them away
58:10 they see ⌊**G**⌋ take revenge.
58:11 There is a **G** who judges on
59:1 me from my enemies, O my **G**.
59:5 O LORD **G** of Armies,
59:5 God of Armies, **G** of Israel,
59:9 **G** is my stronghold,
59:9 my stronghold, my merciful **G**!
59:10 **G** will come to meet me.
59:13 Then they will know that **G**
59:17 **G** is my stronghold,
59:17 my stronghold, my merciful **G**!
60:1 O **G**, you have rejected us.
60:6 **G** has promised the following
60:10 Isn't it you, O **G**, who rejected

Psa 60:10 Isn't it you, O **G**, who refused
60:12 With **G** we will display great
61:1 Listen to my cry for help, O **G**.
61:5 O **G**, you have heard my vows.
61:7 in the presence of **G** forever.
62:1 soul waits calmly for **G** alone.
62:5 Wait calmly for **G** alone,
62:7 and my glory depend on **G**.
62:7 **G** is the rock of my strength,
62:8 **G** is our refuge. Selah
62:11 **G** has spoken once.
62:11 "Power belongs to **G**.
63:1 O **G**, you are my God.
63:1 O God, you are my **G**.
63:11 But the king will find joy in **G**.
63:11 takes an oath by **G** will brag,
64:1 Hear my voice, O **G**,
64:7 But **G** will shoot them with an
64:9 "This is an act of **G**!"
65:1 with silence in Zion, O **G**,
65:5 righteousness, O **G**, our savior,
65:9 (The river of **G** is filled with
66:1 Shout happily to **G**,
66:3 Say to **G**, "How awe-inspiring
66:5 Come and see what **G** has
66:8 Thank our **G**, you nations.
66:10 You have tested us, O **G**.
66:16 and listen, all who fear **G**,
66:19 But **G** has heard me.
66:20 Thanks be to **G**, who has not
67:1 May **G** have pity on us and
67:3 give thanks to you, O **G**.
67:5 give thanks to you, O **G**.
67:6 May **G**, our God, bless us.
67:6 May God, our **G**, bless us.
67:7 May **G** bless us, and may all
68:1 **G** will arise. His enemies will
68:4 Sing to **G**; make music to
68:5 The **G** who is in his holy
68:6 **G** places lonely people in
68:7 O **G**, when you went in front of
68:8 the presence of the **G** of Sinai,
68:8 the presence of the **G** of Israel.
68:9 land with plenty of rain, O **G**.
68:10 Out of your goodness, O **G**,
68:15 of Bashan is the mountain of **G**.
68:16 at the mountain where **G** has
68:17 The chariots of **G** are twenty
68:17 ⌊The **G** of⌋ Sinai is in his holy
68:18 the LORD **G** may live there.
68:19 **G** is our salvation.
68:20 Our **G** is the God of victories.
68:20 Our God is the **G** of victories.
68:21 Certainly, **G** will crush the
68:24 Your festival processions, O **G**,
68:24 are the processions for my **G**,
68:26 Thank **G**, the Lord, the source
68:28 Your **G** has decided you will
68:28 Display your strength, O **G**,
68:31 out its hands to **G** ⌊in prayer⌋.
68:32 of the world, sing to **G**.
68:33 **G** rides through the ancient
68:34 Acknowledge the power of **G**.
68:35 **G**, the God of Israel,
68:35 God, the **G** of Israel,
68:35 to his people. Thanks be to **G**!
69:1 Save me, O **G**! The water is
69:3 ⌊from⌋ looking for my **G**.
69:5 O **G**, you know my stupidity,
69:6 because of me, O **G** of Israel.
69:13 O **G**, out of the greatness of
69:29 saving power protect me, O **G**.
69:30 I want to praise the name of **G**
69:32 hearts of those who look to **G**
69:35 When **G** saves Zion,
70:1 quickly to rescue me, O **G**!
70:4 continually say, "**G** is great!"
70:5 O **G**, come to me quickly.
71:4 My **G**, free me from the hands
71:11 "**G** has abandoned him.
71:12 O **G**, do not be so distant from
71:12 O my **G**, come quickly to help
71:17 O **G**, you have taught me ever
71:18 gray, do not abandon me, O **G**.
71:19 reaches to the heavens, O **G**.
71:19 O **G**, who is like you?

Psa 71:22 of your faithfulness, O my **G**,
72:1 O **G**, give the king your justice
72:18 Thank the LORD **G**,
72:18 the LORD God, the **G** of Israel,
73:1 **G** is truly good to Israel,
73:11 "What does **G** know?"
73:26 but **G** remains the foundation of
73:28 Being united with **G** is my
74:1 Why, O **G**, have you rejected
74:8 meeting place of **G** in the land.
74:10 How long, O **G**, will the enemy
74:12 And yet, from long ago **G** has
74:22 Arise, O **G**! Fight for your own
75:1 We give thanks to you, O **G**;
75:7 **G** alone is the judge.
75:9 music to praise the **G** of Jacob.
76:1 **G** is known in Judah.
76:6 stern warning, O **G** of Jacob,
76:9 when you rose to judge, O **G**,
76:11 vows to the LORD your **G**,
77:1 Loudly, I cried to **G**.
77:1 Loudly, I cried to **G** so that he
77:3 I sigh as I remember **G**.
77:9 Has **G** forgotten to be merciful?
77:13 O **G**, your ways are holy!
77:13 What **g** is as great as our God?
77:13 What god is as great as our **G**?
77:14 You are the **G** who performs
77:16 The water saw you, O **G**.
78:7 to trust **G**, to remember what he
78:8 spirits were not faithful to **G**.
78:18 They deliberately tested **G** by
78:19 spoke against **G** by saying,
78:19 "Can **G** prepare a banquet in
78:22 because they did not believe **G**
78:25 and **G** sent them plenty of food.
78:31 the anger of **G** flared up against
78:34 sins and eagerly looked for **G**.
78:35 They remembered that **G** was
78:41 Again and again they tested **G**,
78:56 They tested **G** Most High and
78:59 When **G** heard, he became
79:1 O **G**, the nations have invaded
79:9 Help us, O **G**, our savior,
79:10 "Where is their **G**?"
80:3 O **G**, restore us and smile on
80:4 O LORD **G**, commander of
80:7 O **G**, commander of armies,
80:14 O **G**, commander of armies,
80:19 O LORD **G**, commander of
81:1 Sing joyfully to **G**,
81:1 happily to the **G** of Jacob.
81:4 decision from the **G** of Jacob.
81:5 These are the instructions **G**
81:9 keep any strange **g** among you.
81:9 Never worship a foreign **g**.
81:10 I am the LORD your **G**,
82:1 **G** takes his place in his own
82:8 Arise, O **G**! Judge the earth,
83:1 O **G**, do not remain silent.
83:1 Do not keep quiet, O **G**.
83:13 O my **G**, blow them away like
83:18 You alone are the Most High **G**
84:2 shouts for joy to the living **G**.
84:3 my king and my **G**.
84:7 appears in front of **G** in Zion.
84:8 O LORD **G**, commander of
84:8 Open your ears, O **G** of Jacob.
84:9 Look at our shield, O **G**.
84:11 The LORD **G** is a sun and
85:4 Restore us, O **G**, our savior.
85:8 I want to hear what **G** the
86:2 who trusts you. You are my **G**.
86:8 No **g** is like you, O Lord.
86:10 of miracles. You alone are **G**.
86:12 with all my heart, O Lord my **G**.
86:14 O **G**, arrogant people attack
86:15 compassionate and merciful **G**.
87:3 are said about you, O city of **G**!
88:1 O LORD **G**, my savior, I cry out
89:7 **G** is terrifying in the council of
89:8 O LORD **G** of Armies,
89:26 me, 'You are my Father, my **G**,
90:2 and the world, you were **G**.
90:2 You are **G** from everlasting to
90:17 the kindness of the Lord our **G**

Psa 91:2 my **G** in whom I trust."
94:1 O LORD, **G** of vengeance,
94:1 O **G** of vengeance,
94:7 The **G** of Jacob doesn't even
94:9 **G** created ears. Do you think he
94:22 My **G** has become my rock of
94:23 LORD our **G** will destroy them.
95:3 The LORD is a great **G** and a
95:7 because he is our **G** and we
98:3 seen how our **G** saves ⌊them⌋.
99:5 Highly honor the LORD our **G**.
99:8 O LORD, our **G**, you answered
99:8 them that you are a forgiving **G**
99:8 you are a **G** who punishes their
99:9 Highly honor the LORD our **G**.
99:9 The LORD our **G** is holy!
100:3 that the LORD alone is **G**.
102:24 I said, "My **G**, don't take me
104:1 O LORD my **G**, you are very
104:21 and seek their food from **G**.
104:33 to praise my **G** as long as
105:7 He is the LORD our **G**.
106:14 In the desert they tested **G**.
106:20 They traded their glorious **G** for
106:21 They forgot **G**, their savior,
106:23 **G** said he was going to destroy
106:28 They joined in worshiping the **g**
106:29 They infuriated **G** by what they
106:30 Phinehas stood between **G**
106:32 They made **G** angry by the
106:47 Rescue us, O LORD our **G**,
106:48 Thanks be to the LORD **G** of
108:1 My heart is confident, O **G**.
108:5 above the heavens, O **G**.
108:7 **G** has promised the following
108:11 Isn't it you, O **G**, who rejected
108:11 Isn't it you, O **G**, who refused
108:13 With **G** we will display great
109:1 O **G**, whom I praise, do not
109:26 Help me, O LORD my **G**.
113:5 Who is like the LORD our **G**?
114:7 the presence of the **G** of Jacob.
115:2 "Where is their **G**?"
115:3 Our **G** is in heaven.
116:5 Our **G** is compassionate.
118:27 The LORD is **G**, and he has
118:28 You are my **G**, and I give
118:28 My **G**, I honor you highly.
119:115 the commandments of my **G**.
119:116 Help me **G**, as you promised,
122:9 the house of the LORD our **G**,
123:2 on the LORD our **G** until
135:2 of the house of our **G**.
136:2 Give thanks to the **G** of gods
136:26 Give thanks to the **G** of heaven
139:17 thoughts concerning me, O **G**!
139:19 would kill wicked people, O **G**,
139:23 Examine me, O **G**,
140:6 to the LORD, "You are my **G**."
143:10 because you are my **G**.
144:9 O **G**, I will sing a new song to
144:15 people whose **G** is the LORD!
145:1 I will highly praise you, my **G**,
146:2 to praise my **G** as long as
146:5 help from the **G** of Jacob.
146:5 rests on the LORD their **G**,
146:10 Zion, your **G** rules throughout
147:1 good to sing psalms to our **G**.
147:7 music to our **G** with a lyre.
147:12 Praise your **G**, Zion!
149:6 Let the high praises of **G** be in
150:1 Praise **G** in his holy place.
Pro 2:5 will find the knowledge of **G**.
2:17 her marriage vows to her **G**.
3:4 in the sight of **G** and humanity.
14:14 A heart that turns ⌊from **G**⌋
25:2 It is the glory of **G** to hide
29:2 the people ⌊of **G**⌋ rejoice,
30:1 declaration: "I'm weary, O **G**.
30:1 I'm weary and worn out, O **G**.
30:5 "Every word of **G** has proven to
30:9 name of my **G** a bad reputation.
Ecc 1:13 burden that **G** has placed
2:24 this comes from the hand of **G**.
2:25 enjoy themselves without **G**?
2:26 **G** gives wisdom, knowledge,

Ecc 2:26 to the person who pleases **G**.
3:10 a burden that **G** has placed
3:11 It is beautiful how **G** has done
3:11 mortals still can't grasp what **G**
3:13 It is a gift from **G** to be able to
3:14 I realize that whatever **G** does
3:14 **G** does this so that people will
3:15 **G** will call the past to account.
3:17 I thought to myself, "**G** will
3:18 I thought to myself, "**G** is going
5:1 when you go to the house of **G**.
5:2 to speak in the presence of **G**.
5:2 Since **G** is in heaven and you
5:4 you make a promise to **G**,
5:4 it because **G** doesn't like fools.
5:6 Why should **G** become angry
5:7 you should still fear **G**.
5:18 the brief lives **G** gives us.
5:19 It is a gift from **G** when God
5:19 It is a gift from God when **G**
5:20 **G** keeps them occupied
6:2 **G** gives one person riches,
6:2 Yet, **G** doesn't give him the
7:13 Consider what **G** has done!
7:13 straighten what **G** has bent?
7:14 **G** has made the one time as
7:18 because the one who fears **G**
7:26 Whoever pleases **G** will
7:29 **G** made people decent,
8:12 go well for those who fear **G**,
8:13 because they don't fear **G**.
8:15 lives which **G** has given them
8:17 everything that **G** has done.
9:7 because **G** has already
9:9 **G** has given you your pointless
11:5 also don't understand how **G**,
11:9 But realize that **G** will make
12:7 goes back to **G** who gave it.
12:13 this is the conclusion: Fear **G**,
12:14 **G** will certainly judge
Isa 1:10 to the teachings from our **G**,
2:3 to the house of the **G** of Jacob.
5:16 The holy **G** will show himself
5:19 They say, "Let **G** hurry and
7:11 "Ask the LORD your **G** for a
7:13 also try the patience of my **G**?
7:14 him Immanuel [**G** Is With Us].
8:10 because **G** is with us!
8:19 Shouldn't people ask their **G**
8:21 cursing their king and **G**.
9:1 **G** humbled the lands of
9:6 Mighty **G**, Everlasting Father,
10:21 will return to the mighty **G**.
12:2 **G** is my Savior. I am confident
13:19 when **G** destroyed them.
17:6 declares the LORD **G** of Israel.
17:10 You have forgotten the **G** of
21:10 of Armies, the **G** of Israel.
21:17 The LORD **G** of Israel has
24:15 Honor the name of the LORD **G**
25:1 O LORD, you are my **G**.
25:9 will say, "This is our **G**;
26:13 O LORD, our **G**, you are not the
28:26 **G** will guide him in judgment,
28:26 and his **G** will teach him.
29:23 stand in terror of the **G** of Israel.
30:18 The LORD is a **G** of justice.
35:2 the majesty of our **G**.
35:4 Your **G** will come with
36:7 trusting the LORD our **G**."
36:7 He's the **g** whose places of
37:4 The LORD your **G** may have
37:4 sent him to defy the living **G**.
37:4 The LORD your **G** may punish
37:4 that the LORD your **G** heard.
37:10 'Don't let the **g** whom you trust
37:16 "LORD of Armies, **G** of Israel,
37:16 You alone are **G** of the
37:17 sent to defy the living **G**.
37:20 Now, LORD our **G**,
37:21 "This is what the LORD **G** of
37:38 in the temple of his **g** Nisroch,
38:5 'This is what the LORD **G** of
40:1 Comfort them!" says your **G**.
40:3 in the wilderness for our **G**.
40:8 word of our **G** will last forever."

Isa 40:9 of Judah: "Here is your **G**!"
40:18 can you compare **G**?
40:22 **G** is enthroned above the earth,
40:27 rights are ignored by my **G**"?
40:28 The eternal **G**, the LORD,
41:10 be intimidated; I am your **G**.
41:13 I, the LORD your **G**,
41:17 I, the **G** of Israel, will not
42:5 The LORD **G** created the
42:5 This is what the LORD **G** says:
43:3 I am the LORD your **G**,
43:10 No **g** was formed before me,
43:12 was no foreign **g** among you.
43:12 I am **G**," declares the LORD.
44:6 and there is no **G** except me.
44:8 Is there any **G** except me?
44:20 hold in my right hand a false **g**?
45:3 the LORD **G** of Israel,
45:5 is no other **G** besides me.
45:6 that there is no **G** except me.
45:14 "Certainly **G** is with you alone,
45:14 and there is no other **G**."
45:15 Certainly, you are a **G** who has
45:15 You are the **G** of Israel,
45:18 **G** formed the earth and made it.
45:21 There is no other **G** except me.
45:21 There is no other righteous **G**
45:22 of the earth, because I am **G**,
46:1 The **g** Bel bows down;
46:1 the **g** Nebo stoops low.
46:6 He makes it into a **g**.
46:9 first events, because I am **G**,
46:9 I am **G**, and there's no one like
48:1 acknowledge the **G** of Israel,
48:2 You depend on the **G** of Israel.
48:17 I am the LORD your **G**.
49:4 and my reward is with my **G**."
49:5 and my **G** has become my
50:10 and depend upon their **G**.
51:15 I am the LORD your **G** who
51:20 of the LORD, the fury of your **G**.
51:22 The LORD your **G** defends his
52:7 Zion that its **G** rules as king.
52:10 will see the salvation of our **G**.
52:12 The **G** of Israel will guard you
53:4 but we thought that **G** had
54:5 He is called the **G** of the whole
54:6 was rejected," says your **G**.
55:5 because of the LORD your **G**,
55:7 Let them return to our **G**,
57:21 for the wicked," says my **G**.
58:2 They want **G** to be near them.
59:2 separated you from your **G**,
59:13 have turned away from our **G**.
60:9 the name of the LORD your **G**,
60:19 Your **G** will be your glory.
61:6 be called the servants of our **G**.
61:10 I will delight in my **G**.
62:3 crown in the hand of your **G**.
62:5 so your **G** will rejoice over you.
64:4 has seen any **g** except you.
65:11 have prepared a table for the **g**
65:13 This is what the LORD **G** says:
65:16 be blessed by the **G** of Truth.
65:16 will swear by the **G** of Truth.
66:9 have children?" asks your **G**.
Jer 2:17 the LORD your **G** when
2:19 you abandon the LORD your **G**
2:35 **G** will turn his anger from me,
3:13 against the LORD your **G**.
3:21 forgotten the LORD their **G**.
3:22 you are the LORD our **G**.
3:23 the LORD our **G** will rescue us.
3:25 against the LORD our **G**.
3:25 obeyed the LORD our **G**.
5:4 the justice that **G** demands.
5:5 the justice that **G** demands."
5:14 This is what the LORD **G** of
5:19 "Why has the LORD our **G**
5:24 should fear the LORD our **G**.
7:3 Armies, the **G** of Israel, says:
7:21 Armies, the **G** of Israel, says:
7:23 and I will be your **G**,
7:28 did not obey the LORD their **G**.
8:14 The LORD our **G** has
9:15 Armies, the **G** of Israel, says:

Jer 10:10 But the LORD is the only **G**.
10:10 He is the living **G** and eternal
10:16 Jacob's **G** isn't like them.
11:3 LORD, the **G** of Israel, says:
11:4 and I will be your **G**.
12:4 They think that **G** doesn't know
13:12 'This is what the LORD **G** of
13:16 Honor the LORD your **G** before
13:21 What will you say when **G**
14:22 But you can, O LORD our **G**.
15:16 O LORD **G** of Armies.
16:9 Armies, the **G** of Israel, says:
16:10 against the LORD our **G**?'
19:3 Armies, the **G** of Israel, says:
19:15 Armies, the **G** of Israel, says:
21:4 'This is what the LORD **G** of
22:9 promise of the LORD their **G**.
23:2 the LORD **G** of Israel,
23:23 "I am a **G** who is near.
23:23 I am also a **G** who is far away,"
23:36 twist the words of the living **G**,
23:36 the LORD of Armies, our **G**.
24:5 "This is what the LORD **G** of
24:7 and I will be their **G**,
25:15 This is what the LORD **G** of
25:27 the **G** of Israel, says: Drink,
26:13 and listen to the LORD your **G**.
26:16 the name of the LORD our **G**."
27:4 Armies, the **G** of Israel, says:
27:21 of Armies, the **G** of Israel,
28:2 Armies, the **G** of Israel, says:
28:14 Armies, the **G** of Israel, says:
29:4 of Armies, the **G** of Israel,
29:8 Armies, the **G** of Israel, says:
29:21 of Armies, the **G** of Israel,
29:25 Armies, the **G** of Israel, says:
30:2 "This is what the LORD **G** of
30:9 will serve the LORD your **G**
30:22 and I will be your **G**.
31:1 "I will be the **G** of all the
31:6 to the LORD our **G**.'"
31:18 you are the LORD my **G**.
31:23 Armies, the **G** of Israel, says:
31:33 I will be their **G**, and they will
32:14 Armies, the **G** of Israel, says:
32:15 Armies, the **G** of Israel, says:
32:18 You, **G**, are great and mighty.
32:27 "I am the LORD **G** of all
32:36 the LORD **G** of Israel says:
32:38 and I will be their **G**.
33:4 This is what the LORD **G** of
34:2 "This is what the LORD **G** of
34:13 "This is what the LORD **G** of
35:4 Igdaliah's son, the man of **G**.)
35:13 Armies, the **G** of Israel, says:
35:17 is what the LORD **G** of Armies,
35:17 Armies, the **G** of Israel, says:
35:18 Armies, the **G** of Israel, says:
35:19 Armies, the **G** of Israel, says:
37:3 pray to the LORD our **G** for us."
37:7 "This is what the LORD **G** of
38:17 is what the LORD **G** of Armies,
38:17 Armies, the **G** of Israel, says:
39:16 Armies, the **G** of Israel, says:
40:2 "The LORD your **G** threatened
42:2 and pray to the LORD your **G**
42:3 Let the LORD your **G** tell us
42:4 I will pray to the LORD your **G**
42:5 what the LORD your **G** tells
42:6 We will obey the LORD our **G**
42:6 we will obey the LORD our **G**
42:9 the LORD **G** of Israel says:
42:13 you disobey the LORD your **G**.
42:15 Armies, the **G** of Israel, says:
42:18 Armies, the **G** of Israel, says:
42:20 to the LORD your **G** and said,
42:20 'Pray to the LORD our **G** for us,
42:20 that the LORD our **G** says,
42:21 the LORD your **G** sent me
43:1 from the LORD their **G**.
43:1 the LORD their **G** sent him
43:2 The LORD our **G** didn't send
43:10 Armies, the **G** of Israel, says:
44:2 Armies, the **G** of Israel, says:
44:7 is what the LORD **G** of Armies,
44:7 Armies, the **G** of Israel, says:

Jer 44:11 Armies, the **G** of Israel, says:
44:25 Armies, the **G** of Israel, says:
45:2 "This is what the LORD **G** of
46:25 Armies, the **G** of Israel, says,
46:25 who is the **g** of Thebes.
48:1 of Armies, the **G** of Israel,
49:1 Why, then, has the **g** Milcom
50:4 to seek the LORD their **G**.
50:18 Armies, the **G** of Israel, says:
50:28 vengeance of the LORD our **G**,
50:40 when I, **G**, destroyed them.
51:5 been abandoned by their **G**,
51:9 **G** has judged Babylon.
51:10 the LORD our **G** has done.
51:19 Jacob's **G** isn't like them.
51:33 Armies, the **G** of Israel, says:
51:56 am a **G** who punishes evil.
Lam 3:2 **G** has driven me away and
3:35 presence of the Most High **G**,
3:38 the mouth of the Most High **G**.
3:41 and hands to **G** in heaven.
Eze 1:1 and I saw visions from **G**.
8:3 In these visions from **G**,
8:4 I saw the glory of Israel's **G** as
8:5 **G** said to me, "Son of man,
8:12 **G** asked me, "Son of man,
8:12 is in the room where his **g** is,
8:14 and crying for the **g** Tammuz.
9:3 Then the glory of the **G** of
10:5 Almighty **G** when he speaks.
10:19 and the glory of the **G** of Israel
10:20 that I saw under the **G**
11:20 and I will be their **G**.
11:22 The glory of the **G** of Israel
14:11 and I will be their **G**.
20:5 "I am the LORD your **G**."
20:7 I am the LORD your **G**."
20:19 I am the LORD your **G**.
20:20 that I am the LORD your **G**."
28:2 arrogance you say, "I'm a **g**.
28:2 you're only human and not a **g**,
28:2 although you think you are a **g**.
28:6 You think you are wise like **G**.
28:9 that you are a **g** when you face
28:9 You will be a human, not a **g**,
28:26 that I am the LORD their **G**.'"
34:24 I, the LORD, will be their **G**,
34:30 know that I, the LORD their **G**,
34:31 are mortal, and I am your **G**,
36:28 and I will be your **G**.
37:23 and I will be their **G**.
37:27 I will be their **G**, and they will
39:22 that I am the LORD their **G**.
39:28 that I am the LORD their **G**.
40:2 In visions, **G** brought me to
43:2 I saw the glory of the **G** of
44:2 through it because the LORD **G**
Dan 1:2 utensils to the temple of his **g**
1:9 **G** made the chief-of-staff kind
1:17 **G** gave these four men
2:18 He told them to ask the **G** of
2:19 Daniel praised the **G** of heaven.
2:23 **G** of my ancestors,
2:28 But there is a **G** in heaven who
2:37 The **G** of heaven has given
2:44 the **G** of heaven will establish
2:45 The great **G** has told you what
2:47 "Your **G** is truly the greatest of
3:15 What **g** can save you from my
3:17 If our **G**, whom we honor,
3:26 of the Most High **G** — come out
3:28 "Praise the **G** of Shadrach,
3:28 worship any **g** except their own
3:28 any god except their own **G**.
3:29 about the **G** of Shadrach,
3:29 No other **g** can rescue like
4:2 the Most High **G** did for me.
4:8 Belteshazzar after my **g** Bel.)
5:18 "Your Majesty, the Most High **G**
5:19 because **G** gave him power.
5:21 Most High **G** has power over
5:21 **G** puts whomever he wishes in
5:23 You didn't honor **G**,
5:26 Numbered — **G** has numbered
6:7 asks for anything from any **g**
6:10 his knees and prayed to his **G**.

Dan 6:10 always praised G this way.
6:11 praying and pleading to his G.
6:12 asks for anything from any g
6:16 king told Daniel, "May your G,
6:20 servant of the living G!
6:20 Was G, whom you always
6:22 My G sent his angel and shut
6:23 because he trusted his G.
6:26 with terror in front of Daniel's G
6:26 the living G who continues
7:25 speak against the Most High G,
8:14 will be made acceptable to G."
9:3 So I turned to the Lord G and
9:4 I prayed to the LORD my G.
9:4 deserve respect as the only G.
9:9 "But you, Lord our G,
9:13 LORD our G, we never tried to
9:14 LORD our G, you are righteous
9:15 "Lord our G, you brought your
9:17 "Our G, listen to my prayer and
9:18 your ears and listen, my G.
9:19 Do this for your sake, my G,
9:20 in front of the LORD my G.
10:12 G has heard everything that
10:12 in front of your G so that you
11:32 people who know their G will
11:36 honor himself above every g.
11:36 things against the G of Gods.
11:37 will have no interest in any g,
11:38 will honor the g of fortresses.
11:38 honor a g his ancestors never
11:39 With the help of a foreign g,
Hos 1:7 I am the LORD their G.
1:9 and I am no longer your G.
1:10 are the children of the living G.'
2:23 they will say, 'You are our G!'"
3:5 and look to the LORD their G
4:1 no knowledge of G in the land.
4:6 the teachings of your G,
5:4 them from returning to their G.
7:10 don't turn to the LORD your G
8:2 acknowledge you as our G.'
8:6 It is not a g. It will be smashed
9:1 have been unfaithful to your G.
9:8 hostile in the temple of their G.
9:9 G will remember their
9:17 My G will reject them because
10:2 G will tear down their altars
11:9 I am G, not a human. I am the
11:12 Judah rebels against G,
12:3 he struggled with G.
12:5 The LORD is the G of Armies.
12:6 Return to your G. Be loyal and
12:6 wait with hope for your G.
12:9 I am the LORD your G.
13:4 "I am the LORD your G.
13:4 have known no g besides me.
13:16 they rebelled against their G.
14:1 return to the LORD your G.
Joe 1:13 you servants of my G.
1:14 the temple of the LORD your G,
2:13 Return to the LORD your G.
2:14 offerings to the LORD your G.
2:17 'Where is their G?'"
2:23 find joy in the LORD your G.
2:26 the name of the LORD your G,
2:27 I am the LORD your G,
3:17 that I am the LORD your G.
Amo 3:13 LORD, the G of Armies.
4:12 Prepare to meet your G.
4:13 G forms the mountains and
4:13 name is the LORD G of Armies.
5:8 G made the ⌊constellations⌋
5:14 Then the LORD G of Armies
5:15 Maybe the LORD G of Armies
5:16 the Almighty G of Armies,
5:26 of ⌊the g⌋ Sikkuth as your
5:27 name is the G of Armies.
6:8 The LORD G of Armies
6:14 declares the LORD G of the
8:14 as your g lives ...."
9:15 says the LORD your G.
Jnh 1:6 Get up, and pray to your G.
1:9 the LORD, the G of heaven.
1:9 He is the G who made the sea
2:1 prayed to the LORD his G.
Jnh 2:6 from the pit, O LORD, my G.
3:5 people of Nineveh believed G.
3:8 Cry loudly to G for help.
3:9 G may reconsider his plans
3:10 G saw what they did.
3:10 So G reconsidered his threat to
4:2 merciful and compassionate G,
4:6 The LORD G made a plant
4:7 At dawn the next day, G sent a
4:8 G made a hot east wind blow.
4:9 Then G asked Jonah,
Mic 3:7 because G won't answer them.
4:2 to the house of the G of Jacob.
4:5 of the LORD our G forever.
5:4 name of the LORD his G.
6:6 in front of the G of heaven?
6:8 and to live humbly with your G.
7:7 I will wait for G to save me.
7:7 I will wait for my G to listen to
7:10 "Where is the LORD your G?"
7:17 in fear, O LORD our G.
7:18 Who is a G like you?
Nah 1:2 G is jealous. The LORD takes
Hab 1:11 their own strength is their g.
1:12 O LORD, my G, my Holy One?
3:3 G comes from Teman.
3:18 I will truly find joy in G,
Zep 1:5 loyalty to the g Milcom.
2:7 The LORD their G will take
2:9 of Armies, the G of Israel,
3:2 It does not draw close to its G.
3:17 The LORD your G is with you.
Hag 1:12 obeyed the LORD their G.
1:12 the LORD their G had sent him
1:14 of the LORD of Armies, their G.
Zec 6:15 the LORD your G completely.'"
8:8 and I will be their G,
8:23 have heard that G is with you."
9:7 them will be left for our G like
9:16 On that day the LORD their G
10:6 I am the LORD their G,
11:4 is what the LORD my G says:
12:5 of the LORD of Armies, their G.'
12:8 David's family will be like G,
13:9 'The LORD is our G.'"
14:5 The LORD my G will come,
Mal 1:9 "Now try asking G to be kind to
2:10 Hasn't the same G created us?
2:11 who worships a foreign g.
2:15 Didn't ⌊G⌋ make you one?
2:15 And what does the same ⌊G⌋
2:16 says the LORD G of Israel.
2:17 or "Where is the G of justice?"
3:8 "Can a person cheat G?
3:14 'It's pointless to serve G.
3:15 they even test G and get away
3:18 between the one who serves G
Mat 1:23 which means "G is with us."
2:12 G warned them in a dream not
3:2 "Turn to G and change the way
3:8 that prove you have turned to G
3:9 I can guarantee that G can
3:15 to do everything that G requires
3:16 and he saw the Spirit of G
4:3 "If you are the Son of G,
4:4 on every word that G speaks.'"
4:6 "If you are the Son of G,
4:7 'Never tempt the Lord your G.'"
4:10 'Worship the Lord your G and
4:17 "Turn to G and change the way
5:8 are pure. They will see G.
5:10 for doing what G approves of.
6:24 cannot serve G and wealth.
6:30 That's the way G clothes the
8:29 bothering us now, Son of G?
9:3 "He's dishonoring G."
9:8 filled with awe and praised G
12:4 he went into the house of G
12:28 then the kingdom of G has
12:41 because they turned to G and
14:33 "You are truly the Son of G."
15:3 break the commandment of G
15:4 For example, G said,
15:5 'I have given to G whatever
15:31 So they praised the G of Israel.
15:36 the fish and gave thanks to G.
Mat 16:16 the Son of the living G!"
16:19 you imprison, G will imprison.
16:19 you set free, G will set free."
16:23 You aren't thinking the way G
18:18 you imprison, G will imprison.
18:18 you set free, G will set free.
19:6 what G has joined together."
19:14 are part of the kingdom of G."
19:24 to enter the kingdom of G."
19:26 everything is possible for G."
21:31 the kingdom of G ahead of you.
21:32 you the way that G wants you
21:43 that the kingdom of G will
21:43 will produce what G wants.
22:16 the truth about the way of G.
22:21 and give G what belongs to
22:21 give God what belongs to G."
22:31 Haven't you read what G told
22:32 'I am the G of Abraham,
22:32 He's not the G of the dead but
22:37 "'Love the Lord your G with all
23:23 You give ⌊G⌋ one-tenth of your
24:22 If G does not reduce the
24:22 of those whom G has chosen.
24:24 those whom G has chosen.
24:31 those whom G has chosen.
25:41 G has cursed you!
26:63 an oath in front of the living G
26:63 the Messiah, the Son of G?"
26:65 "He has dishonored G!
26:65 just heard him dishonor G!
27:40 If you're the Son of G,
27:43 He trusted G. Let God rescue
27:43 Let G rescue him now if he
27:43 'I am the Son of G.'"
27:46 which means, "My G,
27:46 which means, "My God, my G,
27:54 this was the Son of G!"
Mar 1:1 Jesus Christ, the Son of G.
1:14 people the Good News of G.
1:15 and the kingdom of G is near.
1:24 you are — the Holy One of G!"
2:7 He's dishonoring G.
2:7 besides G can forgive sins?"
2:12 was amazed and praised G,
2:26 house of G when Abiathar was
3:11 "You are the Son of G!"
3:35 Whoever does what G wants
4:11 kingdom of G has been given
4:26 Jesus said, "The kingdom of G
4:30 what the kingdom of G is like?
5:7 Son of the Most High G?
5:7 Swear to G that you won't
6:12 that they should turn to G
7:8 the commandments of G
7:9 the commandments of G
7:11 (that is, an offering to G),
8:6 loaves and gave thanks to G.
8:33 You aren't thinking the way G
9:1 of G arrive with power."
9:47 you to enter the kingdom of G
10:6 But G made them male and
10:9 what G has joined together."
10:14 are part of the kingdom of G.
10:15 receive the kingdom of G as
10:18 No one is good except G
10:23 to enter the kingdom of G!"
10:24 it is to enter the kingdom of G!
10:25 to enter the kingdom of G."
10:27 but it's not impossible for G to
10:27 Everything is possible for G."
11:22 said to them, "Have faith in G!
12:14 teach the way of G truthfully.
12:17 and give G what belongs to
12:17 give God what belongs to G."
12:26 about the bush, where G said,
12:26 'I am the G of Abraham,
12:27 He's not the G of the dead but
12:29 the Lord our G is the only Lord.
12:30 So love the Lord your G with
12:32 truth that there is only one G
12:34 too far from the kingdom of G."
13:20 of those whom G has chosen.
13:22 those whom G has chosen.
13:27 those whom G has chosen.
14:25 new wine in the kingdom of G."

Mar 14:64 You've heard him dishonor **G**!
15:34 which means, "My **G**,
15:34 which means, "My God, my **G**,
15:39 this man was the Son of **G**!"
15:43 waiting for the kingdom of **G**.
16:19 where **G** gave him the highest
Luk 1:13 **G** has heard your prayer.
1:16 Israel back to the Lord their **G**.
1:19 **G** sent me to tell you this good
1:26 **G** sent the angel Gabriel to
1:30 You have found favor with **G**.
1:32 The Lord **G** will give him the
1:35 you will be called the Son of **G**.
1:37 nothing is impossible for **G**."
1:47 My spirit finds its joy in **G**,
1:64 and he began to praise **G**.
1:68 "Praise the Lord **G** of Israel!
1:78 above because our **G** is loving
2:13 were praising **G** by saying,
2:14 "Glory to **G** in the highest
2:20 they glorified and praised **G** for
2:28 arms and praised **G** by saying,
2:38 Joseph and began to thank **G**.
2:52 favor from **G** and people.
3:2 were chief priests that **G** spoke
3:6 the salvation that **G** gives.'"
3:8 prove that you have turned to **G**
3:8 I guarantee that **G** can raise up
3:38 of Seth, son of Adam, son of **G**.
4:3 "If you are the Son of **G**,
4:8 'Worship the Lord your **G** and
4:9 "If you are the Son of **G**,
4:12 'Never tempt the Lord your **G**.'"
4:26 But **G** didn't send Elijah to
4:27 But **G** cured no one except
4:34 you are — the Holy One of **G**!"
4:41 "You are the Son of **G**!"
4:43 News about the kingdom of **G**
5:21 He's dishonoring **G**!
5:21 besides **G** can forgive sins?"
5:25 Praising **G**, he went home.
5:26 was amazed and praised **G**.
6:4 he went into the house of **G**,
6:12 the whole night in prayer to **G**.
6:20 The kingdom of **G** is theirs.
6:35 the children of the Most High **G**
7:16 struck with fear and praised **G**.
7:16 and "**G** has taken care of his
7:28 kingdom of **G** is greater than
7:29 They admitted that **G** was right
8:10 kingdom of **G** has been given
8:28 Son of the Most High **G**?
8:39 and tell them how much **G** has
9:2 about the kingdom of **G**
9:11 them about the kingdom of **G**,
9:20 whom **G** has sent."
9:27 they see the kingdom of **G**."
9:60 tell about the kingdom of **G**."
9:62 is not fit for the kingdom of **G**."
10:9 'The kingdom of **G** is near you!'
10:11 the kingdom of **G** is near you!'
10:27 "'Love the Lord your **G** with all
11:20 then the kingdom of **G** has
11:32 the men of Nineveh turned to **G**
11:42 You give **G** one-tenth of your
11:42 justice and the love of **G**.
11:49 why the Wisdom of **G** said,
12:6 **G** doesn't forget any of them.
12:20 "But **G** said to him,
12:21 and his riches don't serve **G**."
12:24 Yet, **G** feeds them.
12:28 That's the way **G** clothes the
13:3 But if you don't turn to **G** and
13:5 But if you don't turn to **G** and
13:13 up straight and praised **G**.
13:18 is the kingdom of **G** like?
13:20 I compare the kingdom of **G** to?
13:28 They'll be in the kingdom of **G**,
13:29 will eat in the kingdom of **G**.
14:15 the kingdom of **G** is blessed."
15:7 over one person who turns to **G**
15:7 who already have turned to **G**
15:10 one person who turns to **G**
16:13 cannot serve **G** and wealth."
16:15 But **G** knows what's in your
16:15 to humans is disgusting to **G**.
Luk 16:16 News about the kingdom of **G**,
16:30 they will turn to **G** and change
17:15 he turned back and praised **G**
17:18 came back to praise **G**."
17:20 the kingdom of **G** would come.
17:20 coming of the kingdom of **G**.
17:21 kingdom of **G** is within you."
18:2 didn't fear **G** or respect people.
18:4 I don't fear **G** or respect people,
18:7 Won't **G** give his chosen
18:9 who were sure that **G** approved
18:11 stood up and prayed, '**G**,
18:13 '**G**, be merciful to me, a sinner!'
18:16 are part of the kingdom of **G**.
18:17 receive the kingdom of **G** as
18:19 No one is good except **G**.
18:24 to enter the kingdom of **G**!
18:25 to enter the kingdom of **G**."
18:27 to do are possible for **G** to do."
18:29 because of the kingdom of **G**
18:43 followed Jesus and praised **G**.
18:43 this, and they, too, praised **G**.
19:11 of **G** would appear suddenly.
19:37 of disciples began to praise **G**
19:44 the time when **G** came
20:21 Rather, you teach the way of **G**
20:25 and give **G** what belongs to
20:25 give God what belongs to **G**."
20:37 the Lord is the **G** of Abraham,
20:38 He's not the **G** of the dead but
21:31 that the kingdom of **G** is near.
22:16 fulfillment in the kingdom of **G**."
22:18 until the kingdom of **G** comes."
22:70 "So you're the Son of **G**?"
23:35 Messiah that **G** has chosen,
23:40 "Don't you fear **G** at all?
23:47 he praised **G** and said,
23:51 waiting for the kingdom of **G**.
24:19 did and said in the sight of **G**
24:47 people must be told to turn to **G**
24:53 where they praised **G**.
Jon 1:1 The Word was with **G**,
1:1 and the Word was **G**.
1:2 with **G** in the beginning.
1:6 **G** sent a man named John to
1:13 Their birth was from **G**.
1:18 No one has ever seen **G**.
1:29 This is the Lamb of **G** who
1:33 But **G**, who sent me to baptize
1:34 that this is the Son of **G**."
1:36 This is the Lamb of **G**."
1:49 you are the Son of **G**!
3:2 we know that **G** has sent you
3:2 perform unless **G** is with him."
3:3 of **G** without being born
3:5 of **G** without being born
3:16 **G** loved the world this way:
3:17 **G** sent his Son into the world,
3:21 the things they do for **G** may
3:33 have affirmed that **G** is truthful.
3:34 The man whom **G** has sent
3:34 After all, **G** gives him the Spirit
4:24 **G** is a spirit. Those who
5:18 made himself equal to **G** when
5:18 that **G** was his Father.
5:25 hear the voice of the Son of **G**
5:42 You don't have any love for **G**.
5:44 that comes from the only **G**?
6:28 "What does **G** want us to do?"
6:29 Jesus replied to them, "**G**
6:45 '**G** will teach everyone.'
6:46 Only the one who is from **G**
6:69 you are the Holy One of **G**."
7:17 follow the will of **G** will know if
7:17 know if what I teach is from **G**
8:40 the truth that I heard from **G**.
8:41 **G** is our only Father."
8:42 "If **G** were your Father,
8:42 and I came from **G**.
8:42 Instead, **G** sent me.
8:47 The person who belongs to **G**
8:47 God understands what **G** says.
8:47 you don't belong to **G**."
8:54 and you say that he is your **G**.
9:3 he was born blind so that **G**
9:16 man who did this is not from **G**
Jon 9:24 told him, "Give glory to **G**.
9:29 We know that **G** spoke to
9:31 We know that **G** doesn't listen
9:33 If this man were not from **G**,
10:33 but for dishonoring **G**.
10:33 You claim to be **G**,
10:35 So if **G** calls people gods (and
10:36 you say that I'm dishonoring **G**
10:36 'I'm the Son of **G**'?
10:36 **G** set me apart for this holy
11:4 will bring glory to **G** so that
11:4 the Son of **G** will receive glory
11:22 But even now I know that **G**
11:27 are the Messiah, the Son of **G**,
12:40 "**G** blinded them and made
12:43 about what **G** thought of them.
13:3 knew that he had come from **G**
13:3 God and was going back to **G**.
13:31 because of him **G** is glorified.
13:32 If **G** is glorified because of the
13:32 **G** will glorify the Son of Man
14:1 Believe in **G**, and believe in
16:2 think that they are serving **G**.
16:8 the world that **G** judges it.
16:11 the world that **G** judges it,
16:27 believed that I came from **G**.
16:30 that you have come from **G**."
17:3 to know you, the only true **G**,
19:7 he claimed to be the Son of **G**."
20:17 to my **G** and your God.'"
20:17 to my God and your **G**.'"
20:28 "My Lord and my **G**!"
20:31 is the Messiah, the Son of **G**,
21:19 Peter would bring glory to **G**.
Act 1:3 them about the kingdom of **G**.
2:11 the miracles that **G** has done."
2:17 'In the last days, **G** says,
2:17 speak what **G** has revealed.
2:18 speak what **G** has revealed.
2:22 was a man whom **G** brought
2:22 this man **G** worked miracles,
2:23 a plan that **G** had determined
2:24 But **G** raised him from death to
2:30 and knew that **G** had promised
2:32 "**G** brought this man Jesus
2:33 **G** used his power to give
2:36 a doubt that **G** made Jesus,
2:38 "All of you must turn to **G** and
2:39 who worships the Lord our **G**."
2:47 they praised **G** and had the
3:8 jumping, and praising **G**.
3:9 him walking and praising **G**.
3:13 The **G** of our ancestors
3:15 But **G** brought him back to life,
3:18 But in this way **G** made the
3:18 **G** had predicted these
3:19 and turn to **G** to have your
3:21 as **G** promised through his
3:22 "Moses said, 'The Lord your **G**
3:25 of the promise that **G** made
3:26 **G** has brought his servant back
3:26 **G** did this to bless you by
4:10 but **G** has brought him back to
4:19 whether **G** wants people
4:21 all the people were praising **G**
4:24 united and loudly prayed to **G**,
4:31 to speak the word of **G** boldly.
5:4 didn't lie to people but to **G**!"
5:29 obey **G** rather than people.
5:30 But the **G** of our ancestors
5:31 **G** used his power to give
5:32 whom **G** has given to those
5:39 However, if it's from **G**,
5:39 that you're fighting against **G**."
6:7 The word of **G** continued to
6:11 him slander Moses and **G**."
7:2 The **G** who reveals his glory
7:3 **G** told him, 'Leave your land
7:4 After his father died, **G** made
7:5 "Yet, **G** didn't give Abraham
7:5 But **G** promised to give this
7:6 **G** told Abraham that his
7:7 **G** also told him, "I will punish
7:8 "**G** gave Abraham circumcision
7:9 But **G** was with Joseph
7:10 **G** gave Joseph divine favor

Act	7:17	"When the time that **G** had
	7:25	understand that **G** was going
	7:32	'I am the **G** of your ancestors —
	7:32	ancestors — the **G** of Abraham,
	7:35	This is the one **G** sent to free
	7:37	'**G** will send you a prophet,
	7:41	a sacrifice to that false **g**
	7:42	"So **G** turned away from them
	7:43	the star of the **g** Rephan,
	7:44	tent exactly as **G** had told him.
	7:45	the nations that **G** forced out
	7:47	one who built a house for **G**.
	7:55	of authority that **G** gives.
	7:56	authority that **G** has given him!"
	8:10	"This man is the power of **G**,
	8:12	News about the kingdom of **G**
	8:14	had accepted the word of **G**,
	8:21	in this because **G** can see how
	9:20	that Jesus was the Son of **G**.
	10:2	were devout and respected **G**.
	10:2	and always prayed to **G**.
	10:3	He clearly saw an angel from **G**
	10:4	The angel answered him, "**G** is
	10:15	which **G** has made clean
	10:22	approval and who respects **G**.
	10:28	But **G** has shown me that I
	10:31	He said to me, 'Cornelius, **G**
	10:33	here now in the presence of **G**
	10:34	that **G** doesn't play favorites.
	10:35	Rather, whoever respects **G**
	10:36	**G** sent his word to the people
	10:38	You know that **G** anointed
	10:38	because **G** was with him.
	10:40	but **G** brought him back to life
	10:40	**G** didn't show him
	10:42	'**G** has appointed Jesus to
	10:46	languages and praising **G**.
	11:9	which **G** has made clean
	11:17	When they believed, **G** gave
	11:17	who was I to interfere with **G**?
	11:18	They praised **G** by saying,
	11:18	"Then **G** has also led people
	11:23	he was pleased to see what **G**
	12:5	praying very hard to **G** for him.
	12:22	"The voice of a **g** and not of a
	12:23	Herod for not giving glory to **G**.
	13:7	wanted to hear the word of **G**.
	13:17	The **G** of the people of Israel
	13:21	so **G** gave them Saul,
	13:22	**G** removed Saul and made
	13:22	**G** spoke favorably about David.
	13:23	"**G** had the Savior,
	13:26	that **G** saves people was
	13:30	But **G** brought him back to life,
	13:32	What **G** promised our
	13:33	**G** has fulfilled the promise for
	13:34	"**G** stated that he brought
	13:37	However, the man **G** brought
	13:46	had to speak the word of **G**
	14:13	The priest of the **g** Zeus
	14:15	worthless gods to the living **G**.
	14:15	The living **G** made the sky,
	14:16	In the past **G** allowed all
	14:22	a lot to enter the kingdom of **G**."
	14:27	They reported everything **G**
	15:3	people were turning to **G**.
	15:4	that **G** had done through
	15:7	**G** chose me so that people
	15:8	**G**, who knows everyone's
	15:9	**G** doesn't discriminate
	15:10	So why are you testing **G**?
	15:12	things that **G** had done through
	15:14	Simon has explained how **G**
	15:19	people who are turning to **G**.
	16:10	We concluded that **G** had
	16:17	servants of the Most High **G**.
	16:25	singing hymns of praise to **G**.
	16:34	thrilled to be believers in **G**.
	17:23	'To an unknown **g**.' I'm
	17:23	the unknown **g** you worship.
	17:24	The **G** who made the universe
	17:27	so that they would look for **G**,
	17:30	"**G** overlooked the times when
	17:31	**G** has given proof to everyone
	18:5	time to teaching the word of **G**.
	18:11	taught the word of **G** to them.
Act	18:13	people to worship **G**
	18:21	"I'll come back to visit you if **G**
	19:6	to speak what **G** had revealed.
	19:8	them about the kingdom of **G**.
	19:11	**G** worked unusual miracles
	20:25	kingdom ⌊of **G**⌋ will see me
	20:27	telling you the whole plan of **G**.
	20:32	"I am now entrusting you to **G**
	21:9	to speak what **G** had revealed.
	21:19	Paul related everything **G** had
	21:20	everything, they praised **G**.
	21:23	who have made a vow to **G**.
	22:3	I was as devoted to **G** as all of
	22:14	"Ananias said, 'The **G** of our
	23:1	my relationship with **G** has
	23:3	"**G** will strike you,
	23:12	They asked **G** to curse them if
	23:14	"We've asked **G** to curse us if
	23:21	They have asked **G** to curse
	24:14	that I serve our ancestors' **G**
	24:16	in the sight of **G** and people.
	24:17	the poor and offerings ⌊for **G**⌋.
	26:6	trial now because I expect **G**
	26:7	against me because I expect **G**
	26:8	believe that **G** can bring dead
	26:14	⌊a mortal like⌋ you to resist **G**.'
	26:20	and acted and to turn to **G**.
	26:22	"**G** has been helping me to this
	26:29	Paul replied, "I wish to **G** that
	27:23	because an angel from the **G**
	27:24	**G** has granted safety to
	27:25	I trust **G** that everything will
	27:35	thanked **G** in front of everyone,
	28:6	minds and said he was a **g**.
	28:15	he thanked **G** and felt
	28:23	the kingdom of **G** to them.
	28:28	"You need to know that **G** has
Rom	1:1	to spread the Good News of **G**.
	1:2	(**G** had already promised this
	1:4	he was declared the Son of **G**.
	1:7	To everyone in Rome whom **G**
	1:7	Good will and peace from **G**
	1:8	First, I thank my **G** through
	1:9	I serve **G** by spreading the
	1:9	**G** is my witness that I always
	1:10	I ask that somehow **G** will now
	1:19	What can be known about **G** is
	1:21	They knew **G** but did not
	1:21	and thank him for being **G**.
	1:23	the glory of the immortal **G**
	1:24	For this reason **G** allowed their
	1:26	For this reason **G** allowed their
	1:28	worthless to acknowledge **G**,
	1:28	**G** allowed their own immoral
	1:30	slanderers, haters of **G**,
	2:4	Do you have contempt for **G**,
	2:5	anger that **G** will have against
	2:5	day when **G** vents his anger.
	2:5	At that time **G** will reveal that
	2:11	**G** does not play favorites.
	2:12	having laws from **G** will still
	2:12	And whoever has laws from **G**
	2:13	laws from **G** don't have God's
	2:14	have laws from **G** do by nature
	2:14	don't have any laws from **G**.
	2:16	as they face the day when **G**,
	2:17	brag about your **G**,
	2:23	are you dishonoring **G** by
	2:29	praise will come from **G**,
	3:2	First of all, **G** entrusted them
	3:4	**G** is honest, and everyone else
	3:5	do wrong shows that **G** is fair,
	3:5	Is **G** unfair when he vents his
	3:6	Otherwise, how would **G** be
	3:7	that **G** receives by showing
	3:7	by showing that **G** is truthful,
	3:11	No one searches for **G**.
	3:18	They are not terrified of **G**."
	3:19	under the judgment of **G**.
	3:25	**G** showed that Christ is the
	3:25	In his patience **G** waited to
	3:26	shows that he is a **G** of justice,
	3:26	a **G** who approves of people
	3:29	Is **G** only the God of the Jews?
	3:29	Is God only the **G** of the Jews?
	3:29	Isn't he also the **G** of people
Rom	3:30	since it is the same **G** who
	4:2	he could not brag to **G** about it.
	4:3	"Abraham believed **G**,
	4:3	that faith was regarded by **G**
	4:5	don't work but believe **G**,
	4:6	**G** approves of a person without
	4:17	of the **G** who gives life
	4:20	Instead, giving honor to **G** ⌊for
	4:21	confident that **G** would do what
	5:1	we have peace with **G**
	5:2	Christ we can approach **G**
	5:2	we will receive glory from **G**.
	5:10	with **G** while we were
	5:11	us continue to brag about **G**.
	5:11	restored relationship with **G**.
	6:10	and he lives for **G**.
	6:11	to sin's power but living for **G**
	6:13	Instead, offer yourselves to **G**
	6:13	all the parts of your body to **G**.
	6:13	everything that **G** approves of.
	6:17	But I thank **G** that you have
	6:18	who do what **G** approves of.
	6:19	that do what **G** approves of.
	6:20	from doing what **G** approves of.
	6:23	but the gift that **G** freely gives
	7:4	we can do what **G** wants.
	7:6	**G** has broken their effect on us
	7:25	I thank **G** that our Lord Jesus
	8:3	But **G** sent his Son to have a
	8:3	That way **G** condemned sin in
	8:7	has a hostile attitude toward **G**.
	8:8	corrupt nature can't please **G**.
	8:19	is eagerly waiting for **G**
	8:21	that the children of **G** will have.
	8:27	the way **G** wants him to.
	8:28	who love **G** — those whom
	8:31	If **G** is for us, who can be
	8:32	**G** didn't spare his own Son but
	8:33	those whom **G** has chosen?
	8:33	**G** has approved of them.
	9:5	Messiah is **G** over everything,
	9:14	can we say — that **G** is unfair?
	9:15	For example, **G** said to Moses,
	9:18	Therefore, if **G** wants to be
	9:19	You may ask me, "Why does **G**
	9:19	whatever **G** wants to do?"
	9:20	are to talk back to **G** like that?
	9:22	If **G** wants to demonstrate his
	9:23	Can't **G** also reveal the riches
	9:24	This is what **G** did for us
	9:25	As **G** says in Hosea:
	9:26	called children of the living **G**."
	10:1	heart's desire and prayer to **G**
	10:2	they are deeply devoted to **G**,
	10:9	and believe that **G** brought him
	11:1	So I ask, "Has **G** rejected his
	11:2	**G** has not rejected his people
	11:2	complains to **G** about Israel?
	11:4	**G** said, "I've kept 7,000 people
	11:5	there are now a few left that **G**
	11:7	However, those whom **G** has
	11:8	"To this day **G** has given them
	11:15	has been brought back to **G**,
	11:21	If **G** didn't spare the natural
	11:22	kind and how severe **G** can be.
	11:23	because **G** is able to do that.
	11:29	**G** never changes his mind
	11:30	In the past, you disobeyed **G**.
	11:30	But now **G** has been merciful
	11:31	also disobeyed so that **G** may
	11:32	**G** has placed all people into
	12:1	dedicated to **G** and pleasing to
	12:2	what **G** really wants —
	12:3	Because of the kindness that **G**
	12:3	on what **G** has given each
	12:6	**G** in his kindness gave each of
	13:1	it hadn't been established by **G**.
	13:1	have been put in place by **G**.
	13:2	what **G** has established.
	14:3	because **G** has accepted those
	14:6	since they give thanks to **G**.
	14:6	and they, too, give thanks to **G**.
	14:10	stand in front of **G** to be judged.
	14:11	and everyone will praise **G**."
	14:12	an account of ourselves to **G**.
	14:18	this in mind is pleasing to **G**

Rom 14:22 it between yourself and **G**.
15:5 May **G**, who gives you this
15:6 you will praise the **G** and
15:7 He did this to bring glory to **G**.
15:9 who are not Jewish praise **G**
15:13 May **G**, the sourcce of hope,
15:15 I'm doing this because **G** gave
15:16 spreading the Good News of **G**.
15:16 might bring the nations to **G** as
15:17 brag about what I'm doing for **G**
15:30 my struggle. Pray to **G** for me
15:32 Also pray that by the will of **G** I
15:33 May the **G** of peace be with
16:20 The **G** of peace will quickly
16:25 **G** can strengthen you by the
16:26 The everlasting **G** ordered that
16:27 **G** alone is wise. Glory belongs
1Co 1:1 of Christ Jesus by the will of **G**,
1:3 Good will and peace from **G**
1:4 I always thank **G** for you
1:9 **G** faithfully keeps his
1:14 I thank **G** that I didn't baptize
1:20 Hasn't **G** turned the wisdom of
1:21 was unable to recognize **G**
1:21 So **G** decided to use the
1:26 you were when **G** called you
1:27 But **G** chose what the world
1:27 **G** chose what the world
1:28 **G** chose what the world
1:30 Christ Jesus because of **G**.
1:30 our wisdom sent from **G**,
2:7 which **G** had planned for our
2:9 the things that **G** has prepared
2:10 **G** has revealed those things to
2:10 the deep things of **G**.
2:11 about **G** except God's Spirit.
2:12 who comes from **G** so that we
2:12 which **G** has freely given
3:6 but **G** made it grow.
3:7 ⌊only⌋ **G** makes it grow.
3:10 I used the gift that **G** gave me
3:17 **G** will destroy him because
3:19 That's why Scripture says, "**G**
3:23 and Christ belongs to **G**.
4:5 will receive praise from **G**.
4:9 As I see it, **G** has placed us
5:13 **G** will judge those who are
6:9 won't inherit the kingdom of **G**?
6:10 not inherit the kingdom of **G**.
6:11 Christ and in the Spirit of our **G**.
6:13 but **G** will put an end to both of
6:14 **G** raised the Lord, and by his
6:14 and by his power **G** will also
6:16 **G** says, "The two will be one."
6:19 whom you received from **G**,
6:20 So bring glory to **G** in the way
7:7 has a special gift from **G**,
7:14 would be unacceptable ⌊to **G**⌋,
7:15 **G** has called you to live in
7:17 gave him when **G** called him.
7:19 **G** commands is everything.
7:24 were in when **G** called you.
7:24 **G** is with you in those
8:3 But if they love **G**,
8:3 they are known by **G**.
8:4 and that no **g** exists except
8:4 god exists except the one **G**.
8:6 for us, "There is only one **G**,
8:7 eating food offered to a false **g**.
8:8 affect our relationship with **G**.
8:10 in the temple of a false **g**.
8:10 to eat food offered to a false **g**?
10:5 Yet, **G** was not pleased with
10:13 **G**, who faithfully keeps his
10:19 made to a false **g** is anything,
10:19 that a false **g** itself is anything?
10:20 made to demons and not to **G**.
10:28 "This was sacrificed to a **g**,"
10:30 If I give thanks to **G** for the food
10:31 do everything to the glory of **G**.
11:3 and **G** has authority over Christ.
11:4 what **G** has revealed dishonors
11:5 or speaks what **G** has revealed
11:12 but everything comes from **G**.
11:13 proper for a woman to pray to **G**
11:16 do any of the churches of **G**.

1Co 12:6 but the same **G** produces every
12:10 speak what **G** has revealed.
12:11 things by giving what **G** wants
12:13 **G** gave all of us one Spirit to
12:18 So **G** put each and every part
12:24 **G** has put the body together
12:28 In the church **G** has appointed
13:2 to speak what **G** has revealed,
13:8 speaking what **G** has revealed,
13:9 speak what **G** has revealed is
13:12 as **G** has complete knowledge
14:1 speaking what **G** has revealed.
14:2 speak to people but to **G**.
14:3 speaks what **G** has revealed,
14:4 speaks what **G** has revealed,
14:5 speak what **G** has revealed.
14:5 speaks what **G** has revealed is
14:16 Otherwise, if you praise **G** only
14:18 I thank **G** that I speak in other
14:22 The gift of speaking what **G**
14:24 speak what **G** has revealed.
14:25 the ground, worship **G**,
14:25 and confess that **G** is truly
14:28 speak to themselves and to **G**.
14:29 speak what **G** has revealed.
14:30 If **G** reveals something to
14:31 speaking what **G** has revealed.
14:32 People who speak what **G** has
14:33 **G** is not a God of disorder but a
14:33 God is not a **G** of disorder but
14:33 of disorder but a **G** of peace.
14:37 thinks that he speaks for **G**
14:39 to speak what **G** has revealed,
15:15 witnesses who lied about **G**
15:15 then **G** didn't bring Christ back
15:24 hand over the kingdom to **G**
15:25 Christ must rule until **G** has put
15:27 Clearly, **G** has put everything
15:27 When **G** says that everything
15:27 this clearly excludes **G**,
15:27 since **G** has put everything
15:28 But when **G** puts everything
15:28 since **G** had put everything
15:28 Then **G** will be in control of
15:34 don't know anything about **G**.
15:38 **G** gives the plant the form he
15:50 inherit the kingdom of **G**.
15:57 Thank **G** that he gives us the
2Co 1:1 of Christ Jesus by the will of **G**,
1:2 Good will and peace from **G**
1:3 Praise the **G** and Father of our
1:3 and the **G** who gives comfort.
1:4 we have received from **G**.
1:9 ourselves and learn to trust **G**,
1:11 Then many people will thank **G**
1:18 You can depend on **G**.
1:20 people also honor **G** by saying,
1:21 **G** establishes us, together with
1:23 I appeal to **G** as a witness on
2:14 But I thank **G**, who always
2:14 Wherever we go, **G** uses us to
2:15 To **G** we are the aroma of
2:17 word of **G** like many others.
2:17 message that comes from **G**.
3:3 with the Spirit of the living **G**,
3:5 Rather, **G** makes us qualified.
4:1 since **G** has given us this
4:2 As **G** watches, we clearly
4:4 The **g** of this world has blinded
4:6 the same **G** who said that
4:7 of this treasure belongs to **G**
4:14 us to **G** together with you.
4:15 thanksgiving to the glory of **G**.
5:1 we still have a building from **G**.
5:5 **G** has prepared us for this and
5:11 **G** already knows what we are,
5:13 if we were crazy, it was for **G**.
5:18 **G** has done all this.
5:19 In other words, **G** was using
5:20 and through us **G** is calling
5:20 to become reunited with **G**.
5:21 **G** had Christ, who was
6:2 **G** says, "At the right time I
6:16 are the temple of the living **G**.
6:16 As **G** said, "I will live and walk
6:16 I will be their **G**, and they will

2Co 7:1 live a holy life in the fear of **G**.
7:6 Yet **G**, who comforts those
8:1 we want you to know how **G**
8:12 **G** doesn't ask for what they
8:16 I thank **G** for making Titus as
9:7 since **G** loves a cheerful giver.
9:8 Besides, **G** will give you his
9:10 **G** gives seed to the farmer and
9:10 **G** will also give you seed and
9:11 **G** will make you rich enough
9:11 to **G** because of us.
9:12 prayers of thanksgiving to **G**.
9:13 You will honor **G** through this
9:14 that **G** has shown you.
9:15 I thank **G** for his gift that words
10:4 are powerful weapons from **G**.
10:5 oppose the knowledge of **G**.
10:13 we will only brag about what **G**
11:2 I'm as protective of you as **G** is.
11:7 you the Good News of **G** free
11:11 **G** knows that I do love you.
11:31 The **G** and Father of the Lord
12:2 or spiritually. Only **G** knows.
12:4 or spiritually. Only **G** knows.
12:21 my **G** may humble me.
13:7 We pray to **G** that you won't do
13:11 The **G** of love and peace will
Gal 1:1 but by Jesus Christ and **G**
1:3 and peace are yours from **G**
1:4 what our **G** and Father wanted.
1:5 Glory belongs to our **G** and
1:10 the approval of people or **G**?
1:15 But **G**, who appointed me
1:20 (**G** is my witness that what I'm
1:24 So they praised **G** for what had
2:2 to a revelation ⌊from **G**⌋.
2:6 since **G** doesn't play favorites.)
2:9 that **G** had given me
2:19 I live in a relationship with **G**.
3:5 Does **G** supply you with the
3:6 He believed **G**, and that faith
3:6 that faith was regarded by **G**
3:8 of time that **G** would give his
3:17 years after **G** had already put
3:18 However, **G** freely gave the
3:20 and **G** has acted on his own.
3:29 and heirs, as **G** promised.
4:4 right time came, **G** sent his Son
4:5 **G** sent him to pay for the
4:6 **G** has sent the Spirit of his Son
4:7 **G** has also made you heirs.
4:8 When you didn't know **G**,
4:9 But now you know **G**,
4:9 God, or rather, **G** knows you.
5:21 not inherit the kingdom of **G**.
6:7 can never make a fool out of **G**.
6:16 They are the Israel of **G**.
Eph 1:2 Good will and peace from **G**
1:3 Praise the **G** and Father of our
1:3 Through Christ, **G** has blessed
1:7 **G** forgives our failures because
1:11 **G** also decided ahead of time
1:14 **G** receives praise and glory for
1:16 I never stop thanking **G** for you.
1:17 the **G** of our Lord Jesus Christ,
1:22 **G** has put everything under the
2:2 people who refuse to obey **G**.
2:4 But **G** is rich in mercy because
2:6 **G** has brought us back to life
2:8 **G** saved you through faith as
2:8 Being saved is a gift from **G**.
2:10 **G** has made us what we are.
2:12 and the pledges ⌊**G** made in
2:12 were in the world without **G**.
2:16 He also brought them back to **G**
2:22 into a place where **G** lives.
3:2 you have heard how **G** gave
3:6 the same promise that **G** made
3:8 Yet, **G** showed me his
3:9 **G**, who created all things,
3:12 We can go to **G** with bold
3:16 I'm asking **G** to give you a gift
3:19 be completely filled with **G**.
3:20 Glory belongs to **G**,
3:21 Glory belongs to **G** in the
4:1 proves that **G** has called you.

Eph 4:6 one **G** and Father of all,
4:18 from the life that **G** approves
4:24 person created to be like **G**,
4:32 forgiving each other as **G** has
5:1 Imitate **G**, since you are the
5:2 a soothing aroma to **G**.
5:4 Instead, give thanks ⌊to **G**⌋.
5:5 the kingdom of Christ and of **G**.
5:20 Always thank **G** the Father for
6:6 to do what **G** wants them
6:11 all the armor that **G** supplies.
6:13 all the armor that **G** supplies.
6:17 helmet and the word of **G** as
6:19 Also pray that **G** will give me
6:23 May **G** the Father and the Lord
Php 1:2 Good will and peace from **G**
1:3 I thank my **G** for all the
1:6 I'm convinced that **G**,
1:8 **G** is my witness that,
1:11 bring glory and praise to **G**.
1:16 of love know that **G** has put me
1:29 **G** has given you the privilege
2:6 he was in the form of **G**
2:6 form of God and equal with **G**,
2:9 This is why **G** has given him
2:11 to the glory of **G** the Father.
2:13 It is **G** who produces in you the
2:17 and service ⌊I offer to **G**⌋
2:27 But **G** had mercy not only on
3:3 circumcised people ⌊of **G**⌋
3:9 the approval that comes from **G**
3:15 **G** will show you how to think.
3:19 Their own emotions are their **g**,
4:6 But in every situation let **G**
4:9 Then the **G** who gives this
4:18 a sacrifice that **G** accepts and
4:19 My **G** will richly fill your every
4:20 Glory belongs to our **G** and
Col 1:2 Good will and peace from **G**
1:3 We always thank **G**,
1:4 We thank **G** because we have
1:9 We ask ⌊**G**⌋ to fill you with the
1:10 by this knowledge about **G**.
1:13 **G** has rescued us from the
1:15 is the image of the invisible **G**,
1:19 **G** was pleased to have all of
1:20 **G** was also pleased to bring
1:21 you were separated from **G**.
1:22 brought you back to **G** by dying
1:25 of the church when **G** gave me
1:26 In the past **G** hid this mystery,
1:27 **G** wanted his people
2:2 He is the mystery of **G**.
2:3 **G** has hidden all the treasures
2:9 All of **G** lives in Christ's body,
2:10 and **G** has made you complete
2:12 through faith in the power of **G**,
2:13 But **G** made you alive with
2:14 laws **G** had established.
2:19 whole body grow as **G** wants
3:3 life is hidden with Christ in **G**.
3:12 As holy people whom **G** has
3:15 **G** has called you into this
3:16 Sing to **G** in your hearts.
3:17 giving thanks to **G** the Father
3:25 **G** does not play favorites.
4:3 Pray that **G** will give us an
4:12 of everything that **G** wants.
1Th 1:1 at Thessalonica united with **G**
1:2 We always thank **G** for all of
1:3 presence of our **G** and Father,
1:4 we know that **G** loves you
1:8 heard about your faith in **G**.
1:9 gods to serve the real, living **G**
2:2 But our **G** gave us the courage
2:4 **G** trusts us to do this because
2:4 don't try to please people but **G**,
2:5 money. **G** is our witness!
2:8 not only the Good News of **G**
2:9 Good News of **G** without being
2:10 You and **G** are witnesses of
2:12 belong to the **G** who calls you
2:13 why we never stop thanking **G**:
2:13 it really is — the word of **G**.
2:14 were like the churches of **G** in
2:15 They are displeasing to **G**.
1Th 3:2 He serves **G** by spreading the
3:9 We can never thank **G** enough
3:11 We pray that **G** our Father and
3:13 in the presence of our **G**
4:5 of people who don't know **G**.
4:7 **G** didn't call us to be sexually
4:8 human authority but **G**,
4:9 **G** has taught you to love each
4:14 **G** will bring back those who
4:16 with the trumpet ⌊call⌋ of **G**.
5:20 despise what **G** has revealed.
5:23 May the **G** who gives peace
2Th 1:1 united with **G** our Father
1:2 Good will and peace from **G**
1:3 have to thank **G** for you,
1:6 Certainly, it is right for **G** to
1:7 It is also right for **G** to give all
1:8 who refuse to acknowledge **G**
1:11 we always pray that our **G** will
1:12 Jesus Christ, our **G** and Lord,
2:4 He opposes every so-called **g**
2:4 temple and claiming to be **G**.
2:10 He will use everything that **G**
2:11 That's why **G** will send them a
2:12 with what **G** disapproves of,
2:13 have to thank **G** for you,
2:13 the Lord and we thank **G** that
2:16 **G** our Father loved us and by
1Ti 1:1 the command of **G** our Savior
1:2 and peace from **G** the Father
1:11 the glory of the blessed **G**.
1:17 immortal, invisible, and only **G**.
1:20 teach them not to dishonor **G**.
2:3 good and pleases **G** our Savior.
2:5 There is one **G**. There is also
2:5 also one mediator between **G**
2:10 claim to have reverence for **G**.
3:15 is the church of the living **G**,
3:16 for **G** is acknowledged
4:3 **G** created food to be received
4:4 Everything **G** created is good.
4:5 The word of **G** and prayer set it
4:10 our confidence in the living **G**.
5:5 her confidence in **G** by praying
5:17 at teaching the word ⌊of **G**⌋.
5:21 call on you in the sight of **G**,
6:11 But you, man of **G**,
6:11 Pursue what **G** approves of:
6:13 In the sight of **G**, who gives life
6:15 At the right time **G** will make
6:15 **G** is the blessed and only ruler.
6:17 in **G** who richly provides
2Ti 1:2 and peace from **G** the Father
1:3 night and day when I thank **G**,
1:6 You received a gift from **G**
1:7 **G** didn't give us a cowardly
1:9 **G** saved us and called us to be
1:9 Before the world began, **G**
2:14 and warn them in the sight of **G**
2:15 best to present yourself to **G** as
2:25 Maybe **G** will allow them to
2:26 senses and **G** will free them
3:4 love pleasure rather than **G**.
3:16 passage is inspired by **G**.
4:1 on you in the presence of **G**
4:6 poured out as a sacrifice to **G**.
Tit 1:1 From Paul, a servant of **G** and
1:2 **G**, who never lies,
1:3 **G** has revealed this in every
1:3 the command of **G** our Savior.
1:4 Good will and peace from **G**
1:7 is a supervisor appointed by **G**,
1:16 They claim to know **G**,
2:3 shows they are dedicated to **G**.
2:10 teachings about **G** our Savior
2:13 glory of our great **G** and Savior,
3:4 However, when **G** our Savior
3:6 **G** poured a generous amount of
3:7 As a result, **G** in his kindness
3:8 believe in **G** can concentrate
Phm 1:3 Good will and peace from **G**
1:4 I always thank my **G** when I
1:22 **G** will give me back to you.
Heb 1:1 In the past **G** spoke to our
1:2 **G** made his Son responsible
1:2 whom **G** made the universe.
Heb 1:5 **G** never said to any of his
1:5 And **G** never said to any of his
1:6 When **G** was about to send his
1:7 **G** said about the angels,
1:8 But **G** said about his Son,
1:8 O **G**, is forever and ever.
1:9 That is why **G**, your God,
1:9 That is why God, your **G**,
1:10 **G** also said, "Lord, in the
1:13 But **G** never said to any of the
2:3 the message that **G** saved us?
2:4 **G** verified what they said
2:8 When **G** put everything under
2:10 **G** is the one for whom and
2:10 Therefore, while **G** was
2:13 daughters **G** has given me."
2:17 peace with **G** for their sins.
3:2 Jesus is faithful to **G**,
3:4 the builder of everything is **G**.
3:5 He told ⌊the people⌋ what **G**
3:7 "If you hear **G** speak today,
3:12 turns away from the living **G**.
3:15 "If you hear **G** speak today,
3:16 Who heard **G** and rebelled?
3:17 With whom was **G** angry for 40
3:18 Who did **G** swear would never
4:3 As **G** said, "So I angrily took a
4:3 **G** said this even though he had
4:4 Somewhere in Scripture **G** has
4:4 "On the seventh day **G** rested
4:5 **G** also said in the same
4:6 because they did not obey **G**.
4:7 So **G** set another day.
4:7 place of rest⌋ **G** spoke about
4:7 "If you hear **G** speak today,
4:8 **G** would not have spoken
4:10 their work as **G** did from his.
4:13 No creature can hide from **G**.
4:14 person is Jesus, the Son of **G**.
5:1 to represent them in front of **G**,
5:4 **G** calls him as he called Aaron.
5:5 glory was given to him by **G**,
5:6 place in Scripture, **G** said,
5:7 Jesus prayed to **G**,
5:7 because of his devotion to **G**.
5:8 Jesus was the Son ⌊of **G**⌋,
5:10 **G** appointed him chief priest in
6:1 and the basics about faith in **G**.
6:3 If **G** permits, we will do this.
6:6 crucifying the Son of **G** again
6:6 be led a second time to **G**.
6:7 **G** blesses the earth.
6:10 **G** is fair. He won't forget what
6:13 **G** made a promise to Abraham.
6:15 So Abraham received what **G**
6:17 **G** wouldn't change his plan.
6:18 **G** did this so that we would be
6:18 **G** cannot lie when he takes an
7:1 and priest of the Most High **G**.
7:3 Like the Son of **G**,
7:19 everything that **G** required.
7:19 and allows us to approach **G**.
7:21 became a priest when **G** took
7:21 **G** said about him, "The Lord
7:25 who come to **G** through him.
7:28 everything that **G** required.
8:5 make the tent, **G** warned him,
8:6 promise from **G** that is based
8:8 But **G** found something wrong
8:10 I will be their **G**, and they will
8:13 **G** made this new promise and
9:10 body until **G** would establish
9:14 Spirit he offered himself to **G**
9:14 Now we can serve the living **G**.
9:15 Christ offered himself to **G**,
9:15 to bring a new promise from **G**.
9:20 seals the promise **G** has made
10:7 to do what you want, my **G**.'"
10:9 the obedience that **G** wants.
10:10 Christ did what **G** wanted him
10:14 setting them apart for **G** forever.
10:29 for the Son of **G** deserves?
10:29 and he insults the Spirit that **G**
10:30 We know the **G** who said,
10:30 **G** also said, "The Lord will
10:31 into the hands of the living **G** is

Heb 10:36 have done what G wants you
11:2 G accepted our ancestors
11:3 Faith convinces us that G
11:4 Faith led Abel to offer G a
11:4 since G accepted his
11:5 because G had taken him.
11:5 G was pleased with him.
11:6 one can please G without faith.
11:6 Whoever goes to G must
11:6 God must believe that G exists
11:7 when G warned him about
11:7 He obeyed G and built a ship
11:8 to obey when G called him
11:9 that G had promised him.
11:9 the same promise from G.
11:10 for the city that G had designed
11:11 Abraham trusted that G would
11:13 that G had promised them,
11:16 That is why G is not ashamed
11:16 ashamed to be called their G.
11:17 When G tested Abraham,
11:17 received the promises from G,
11:18 G had said to him,
11:19 Abraham believed that G could
11:21 of his staff and worshiped G.
11:27 actually see the invisible G.
11:31 those who refused to obey G.
11:33 did what G approved,
11:33 received what G had promised.
11:39 received what G had promised.
11:40 G planned to give us
12:2 the one next to the throne of G.
12:5 words that G speaks
12:7 G corrects you as a father
12:9 under the authority of G,
12:10 Yet, G disciplines us for our
12:15 from G so that bitterness
12:22 to the city of the living G,
12:23 have come to a judge (the G
12:24 brings the new promise from G,
12:25 to listen when G speaks.
12:25 they refused to listen to G,
12:25 escape if we turn away from G,
12:26 When G spoke to your
12:27 clearly that G will change what
12:28 we must serve G with fear and
12:29 our G is a destructive fire.
13:4 G will judge those who commit
13:5 you have because G has said,
13:15 we should always bring G
13:16 of sacrifices that please G.
13:20 The G of peace brought the
13:21 May this G of peace prepare
Jas 1:1 From James, a servant of G
1:5 you should ask G,
1:5 G is generous to everyone and
1:12 of life that G has promised
1:13 he shouldn't say that G is
1:13 G can't be tempted by evil,
1:13 and G doesn't tempt anyone.
1:18 G decided to give us life
1:20 doesn't do what G approves of.
1:21 Humbly accept the word that G
1:27 according to G our Father,
2:5 Didn't G choose poor people in
2:16 that person, "G be with you!
2:19 You believe that there is one G.
2:23 It says, "Abraham believed G,
2:23 that faith was regarded by G
4:4 world is hatred toward G?
4:4 of this world is an enemy of G.
4:6 But G shows us even more
4:6 "G opposes arrogant people,
4:8 Come close to G, and he will
5:4 shout ⌊to G⌋ against you.
1Pe 1:2 G the Father knew you long
1:3 Praise the G and Father of our
1:3 G has given us a new birth
1:7 praise, glory, and honor to G.
1:12 G revealed to the prophets that
1:14 you are children who obey G,
1:15 But because the G who called
1:17 So if you call G your Father,
1:17 He is the G who judges all
1:21 Through him you believe in G
1:21 faith and confidence are in G.

1Pe 2:4 was chosen as precious by G.
2:5 that G accepts through Jesus
2:9 people who belong to G.
2:9 the excellent qualities of G,
2:12 they will praise G on the day
2:15 G wants you to silence the
2:16 use your freedom to serve G.
2:17 Fear G. Honor the emperor.
2:19 G is pleased if a person is
2:20 G is pleased with you.
2:21 G called you to endure
3:4 which G considers precious.
3:5 in G expressed their beauty
3:14 for doing what G approves,
3:15 ⌊in G⌋ when anyone asks
3:18 so that he could bring you to G.
3:20 when G waited patiently while
3:21 baptism is a request to G for a
3:22 highest position that G gives.
4:2 you will be guided by what G
4:6 earthly lives and live like G
4:10 the gift that G has given you
4:11 the strength G supplies so that
4:11 way G receives glory through
4:14 the Spirit of G — is resting
4:16 but praise G for being called
4:17 to obey the Good News of G?
5:2 Be shepherds over the flock G
5:2 Watch over it as G does:
5:5 because G opposes the
5:7 Turn all your anxiety over to G
5:10 G, who shows you his
5:13 in Babylon, chosen by G,
2Pe 1:1 comes from our G and Savior,
1:2 about Jesus, our G and Lord!
1:17 honor and glory from G
1:17 majestic G spoke these words
2:4 G didn't spare angels who
2:5 G didn't spare the ancient
2:6 G condemned the cities of
2:7 Yet, G rescued Lot,
2:21 the way of life that G approves
2:21 on the holy life G told them
3:12 look forward to the day of G
3:13 But we look forward to what G
3:15 using the wisdom G gave him.
1Jn 1:5 are reporting to you: G is light,
1:6 have a relationship with G"
1:7 light in the same way that G is
1:9 G is faithful and reliable.
1:10 we turn G into a liar and his
2:17 what G wants lives forever.
2:29 who does what G approves
2:29 of has been born from G.
3:4 sinful lives are disobeying G.
3:7 Whoever does what G
3:8 The reason that the Son of G
3:9 born from G don't live sinful
3:9 What G has said lives in them,
3:9 They have been born from G.
3:20 we will be reassured that G is
3:21 we can boldly look to G
3:24 commandments live in G,
3:24 and G lives in them.
4:1 the spirit they have is from G,
4:2 has the Spirit that is from G.
4:3 has a spirit that isn't from G.
4:4 Dear children, you belong to G.
4:6 We belong to G. The person
4:6 The person who knows G
4:6 Whoever doesn't belong to G
4:7 because love comes from G.
4:7 born from G and knows God.
4:7 born from God and knows G.
4:8 doesn't love doesn't know G,
4:8 because G is love.
4:9 G has shown us his love by
4:10 not that we have loved G,
4:11 if this is the way G loved us,
4:12 No one has ever seen G.
4:12 love each other, G lives in us,
4:15 G lives in those who declare
4:15 that Jesus is the Son of G,
4:15 and they live in G.
4:16 and believed that G loves us.
4:16 G is love. Those who live in

1Jn 4:16 live in God's love live in G,
4:16 and G lives in them.
4:19 love because G loved us first.
4:20 Whoever says, "I love G," but
4:20 they have seen, can't love G,
4:21 The person who loves G must
5:1 Messiah has been born from G.
5:2 we love G by obeying his
5:3 To love G means that we obey
5:4 has been born from G has won
5:5 that Jesus is the Son of G?
5:6 This Son of G is Jesus Christ,
5:10 believe in the Son of G have
5:10 the testimony of G in them.
5:10 Those who don't believe G
5:10 God have made G a liar.
5:10 that G has given about
5:11 G has given us eternal life,
5:12 the Son of G doesn't have this
5:13 in the Son of G so that they
5:14 We are confident that G listens
5:16 you should pray that G would
5:18 have been born from G don't go
5:18 the Son of G protects them,
5:19 We know that we are from G,
5:20 We know that the Son of G
5:20 so that we know the real G.
5:20 is the real G and eternal life.
2Jn 1:3 They come from G the Father
1:9 Christ taught doesn't have G.
3Jn 1:6 that proves you belong to G.
1:11 who does good is from G.
1:11 does evil has never seen G.
Jud 1:1 who are loved by G the Father,
1:4 to whom G means nothing.
1:18 who ridicule ⌊G⌋ will appear.
1:24 G can guard you so that you
1:25 authority belong to the only G,
Rev 1:1 G gave it to him to show his
1:6 priests for G his Father.
1:8 A and the Z," says the Lord G,
2:7 stands in the paradise of G,
2:18 Thyatira, write: The Son of G,
3:2 completed in the sight of my G.
3:12 a pillar in the temple of my G.
3:12 on them the name of my G,
3:12 the name of the city of my G
3:12 out of heaven from my G),
4:5 are the seven spirits of G.
4:8 holy is the Lord G Almighty,
4:11 "Our Lord and G, you deserve
5:6 seven spirits of G sent all over
5:10 kingdom and priests for our G.
7:2 with the seal of the living G.
7:3 of the servants of our G."
7:10 "Salvation belongs to our G,
7:11 the ground, worshiped G,
7:12 and strength be to our G
7:15 are in front of the throne of G.
7:17 and G will wipe every tear from
8:4 the angel's hand to G along
9:4 seal of G on their foreheads.
9:13 of the gold altar in front of G.
10:7 the mystery of G will be
10:11 "Again you must speak what G
11:1 and measure the temple of G
11:3 to speak what G has revealed.
11:6 speak what G has revealed.
11:11 the breath of life from G entered
11:13 gave glory to the G of heaven.
11:16 bowed, worshiped G,
11:17 to you, Lord G Almighty,
12:5 snatched away and taken to G
12:6 where G had prepared
12:10 power, kingdom of our G,
12:10 night in the presence of our G,
13:6 It opened its mouth to insult G,
14:4 as the first ones offered to G
14:7 "Fear G and give him glory,
15:3 and amazing, Lord G Almighty.
15:7 bowls full of the anger of G,
15:8 with smoke from the glory of G
16:7 answer, "Yes, Lord G Almighty,
16:9 They cursed the name of G,
16:11 and cursed the G of heaven for
16:14 frightening day of G Almighty.

Rev	16:19	**G** remembered to give Babylon
	16:21	The people cursed **G** because
	17:17	**G** has made them do what he
	18:5	and **G** has remembered her
	18:8	because the Lord **G**,
	18:20	**G** has condemned it for you."
	19:1	and power belong to our **G**.
	19:4	bowed and worshiped **G**,
	19:5	It said, "Praise our **G**,
	19:6	The Lord our **G**, the Almighty,
	19:9	are the true words of **G**."
	19:10	Worship **G**, because the
	19:13	and his name is the Word of **G**.
	19:15	the fierce anger of **G** Almighty.
	19:17	for the great banquet of **G**.
	20:4	and because of the word of **G**.
	20:6	to be priests of **G** and Christ.
	21:2	coming down from **G** out of
	21:3	"**G** lives with humans!
	21:3	**G** will make his home with
	21:3	**G** himself will be with them
	21:3	be with them and be their **G**.
	21:7	I will be their **G**, and they will
	21:10	down from **G** out of heaven.
	21:11	It had the glory of **G**.
	21:22	because the Lord **G** Almighty
	21:23	because the glory of **G** gave
	22:1	the throne of **G** and the lamb.
	22:3	The throne of **G** and the lamb
	22:5	because the Lord **G** will shine
	22:6	The Lord **G** of the spirits of the
	22:9	in this book. Worship **G**!"
	22:18	**G** will strike him with the
	22:19	**G** will take away his portion of

goddess (33)

Exo	34:13	dedicated to the **g** Asherah.
Dtr	7:5	dedicated to the **g** Asherah,
	12:3	dedicated to the **g** Asherah,
	16:21	tree dedicated to the **g** Asherah.
Jdg	2:13	the god Baal and the **g** Astarte.
	6:25	to the **g** Asherah that is
1Sm	7:3	the statues of the **g** Astarte.
1Ki	11:5	followed Astarte (the **g**
	11:33	and worshiped Astarte (the **g**
	14:15	poles to the **g** Asherah
	15:13	of the repulsive **g** Asherah.
	16:33	dedicated to the **g** Asherah.
2Ki	13:6	the pole dedicated to the **g**
	17:10	dedicated to the **g** Asherah
	17:16	dedicated to the **g** Asherah.
	18:4	dedicated to the **g** Asherah.
	21:3	to the **g** Asherah as King
	23:6	dedicated to the **g** Asherah from
	23:13	for Astarte (the disgusting **g**
2Ch	14:3	dedicated to the **g** Asherah.
	15:16	of the repulsive **g** Asherah.
	17:6	to the **g** Asherah in Judah.
	24:18	dedicated to the **g** Asherah.
	31:1	dedicated to the **g** Asherah,
	33:3	to the **g** Asherah as King
	33:19	dedicated to the **g** Asherah.
	34:3	dedicated to the **g** Asherah,
Isa	27:9	dedicated to the **g** Asherah
	65:11	spiced wine to the **g** of destiny.
Jer	17:2	to the **g** Asherah beside large
Mic	5:14	dedicated to the **g** Asherah.
Act	19:27	the great **g** Artemis is nothing.
	19:37	don't rob temples or insult our **g**

goddesses (4)

Jdg	3:7	and served other gods and **g**—
	10:6	to serve other gods and **g**—
1Sm	12:10	and served other gods and **g**—
	31:10	armor in the temple of their **g**—

God-fearing (1)

Gen	20:11	because there are no **G** people

God-given (2)

2Sm	14:16	son from ⌊our⌋ **G** inheritance.'
2Co	1:12	We have lived with a **G**

godless (67)

Gen	34:7	such a **g** act against Israel's
Dtr	22:21	has committed such a **g** act
	32:21	jealous and a nation of **g** fools
Jos	7:15	and done a **g** thing in Israel.'"
Jdg	14:3	from those **g** Philistines?"
	15:18	fall into the power of **g** men."
	19:23	Don't do such a **g** thing!
	19:24	Just don't do such a **g** thing to
	20:6	perverted and **g** thing in Israel.
	20:10	Gibeah for the **g** thing they did
1Sm	25:25	His name is Nabal [**G** Fool],
	31:4	or these **g** men will come,
2Sm	1:20	of **g** men will celebrate.
	3:33	Should Abner die like a **g** fool?
	13:12	Don't do this **g** act!
	13:13	considered one of the **g** fools
1Ch	10:4	Stab me, or these **g** men will
Job	2:10	"You're talking like a **g** fool.
	8:13	The hope of the **g** dies.
	13:16	no **g** person could face
	15:34	because a mob of **g** people
	17:8	the innocent against **g** people.
	20:5	and the joy of the **g** person
	20:16	The **g** person sucks the poison
	20:23	burning anger at the **g** person
	20:25	"Terrors come quickly to the **g**
	27:8	After all, what hope does the **g**
	30:8	**G** fools and worthless people
	34:30	⌊He does this⌋ so that **g**
	36:13	But those who have **g** hearts
	42:8	not to treat you as **g** fools.
Psa	14:1	**G** fools say in their hearts,
	39:8	Do not disgrace me in front of **g**
	53:1	**G** fools say in their hearts,
	74:18	nation of **g** fools despised your
	74:22	Remember how **g** fools insult
Pro	11:9	With his talk a **g** person can
	17:7	speech is not fitting for a **g** fool.
	17:21	and the father of a **g** fool has no
	30:22	a **g** fool when he is filled with
	30:32	If you are such a **g** fool as to
Isa	9:17	one of them is a **g** evildoer,
	10:6	I send them against a **g** nation.
	32:5	**G** fools will no longer be called
	32:6	**G** fools speak foolishness,
	35:8	**G** fools won't wander ⌊onto it⌋.
	52:1	**G** and evil people will no
Jer	5:7	They took **g** oaths.
	17:11	In the end, he will be a **g** fool."
	23:11	The prophets and priests are **g**.
Eze	28:10	of foreigners like a **g** person.
	31:18	You will lie among the **g**
	32:19	Go down and join the **g** people.'
	32:21	and you now lie with the **g**
	32:24	below the earth as **g** people.
	32:25	The soldiers were **g** people.
	32:26	soldiers were all **g** people.
	32:27	They don't lie with the **g**
	32:28	be crushed with the **g** people,
	32:29	They lie there with the **g**
	32:30	They were **g** people.
	32:32	among the **g** people who were
	44:7	You brought **g** foreigners into
	44:9	Any **g** foreigner who lives
Hab	2:16	And expose yourself as **g**.
1Ti	4:7	to do with **g** myths that old
1Pe	4:18	what will happen to the **g**

godlessness (2)

Jer	23:15	spread **g** throughout the land.
Rom	11:26	He will remove **g** from Jacob.

godliness (3)

2Pe	1:3	we need for life and for **g**.
	1:6	to endurance add **g**;
	1:7	to **g** add Christian affection;

godly (38)

2Ch	6:41	Let your **g** ones rejoice in what
Psa	4:3	the LORD singles out **g** people
	12:1	No **g** person is left.
	31:23	Love the LORD, all you **g** ones!
	32:6	For this reason let all **g** people
	37:28	he will not abandon his **g** ones.
	50:5	"Gather around me, my **g**
	52:9	the presence of your **g** people,
	79:2	given the flesh of your **g** ones
	85:8	to his people, to his **g** ones.
	97:10	lives of his **g** ones will rescue
	132:9	Let your **g** ones sing with joy.
	132:16	Then its **g** ones will sing
	149:1	in the assembly of **g** people.
	149:5	Let **g** people triumph in glory.
	149:9	that belongs to all his **g** ones.
Pro	2:8	over the way of his **g** ones.
Mal	2:15	look for but **g** descendants?
Act	3:12	by our own power or **g** life?
Rom	5:7	would die for a **g** person is rare.
2Co	7:9	were distressed in a **g** way,
	7:10	In fact, to be distressed in a **g**
	7:11	became distressed in a **g** way,
1Ti	2:2	lived in a **g** and reverent way.
	4:7	train yourself to live a **g** life.
	4:8	but **g** living helps in every way.
	4:8	**G** living has the promise of life
	4:10	and struggle to live a **g** life,
	6:3	Jesus Christ and **g** teachings
	6:5	They think that a **g** life is a
	6:6	A **g** life brings huge profits to
	6:11	a **g** life, faith, love, endurance,
2Ti	3:5	will appear to have a **g** life,
	3:12	Those who try to live a **g** life
Tit	1:1	of the truth that leads to a **g** life.
	2:12	and **g** lives in this present
2Pe	2:9	he knows how to rescue **g**
	3:11	of holy and **g** lives you must

God-pleasing (2)

Neh	2:18	another to begin this **G** work.
1Th	4:1	in living a **G** life even more

God's (788)

Gen	6:9	Noah had **G** approval and was
	6:11	world was corrupt in **G** sight
	32:1	**G** angels met him.
	32:2	"This is **G** camp!" He named
	41:38	man who has **G** Spirit in him?"
	50:19	I can't take **G** place
Exo	9:28	We've had enough of **G** thunder
	16:34	front of the words of **G** promise
	18:12	father-in-law in **G** presence
	18:15	come to me to find out **G** will
	18:16	them **G** laws and instructions."
	32:15	the two tablets with **G** words.
	32:16	and the writing was **G** writing
	34:29	the two tablets with **G** words
	38:21	tent of the words of **G** promise).
	39:35	the words of **G** promise
	40:20	He took the words of **G** promise
Lev	2:13	The salt of **G** promise must
	16:13	the words of **G** promise, so that
	21:6	"Be **G** holy men, and don't
	21:7	a priest is **G** holy man.
Num	1:50	the tent of **G** words, including
	1:53	all around the tent of **G** words.
	1:53	charge of the tent of **G** words.
	4:5	the words of **G** promise.
	7:89	of **G** promise, from between
	9:15	of **G** promise was set up,
	10:10	reminder for you in **G** presence.
	10:11	tent of the words of **G** promise
	17:7	tent of the words of **G** promise
Dtr	1:5	began to review **G** teachings.
	17:13	will never defy ⌊**G** law⌋ again.
Jos	24:26	in the Book of **G** Teachings.
Jdg	20:2	the congregation of **G** people.
	20:27	ark of **G** promise was at Bethel.
1Sm	3:3	The lamp in **G** temple hadn't
	4:4	came along with **G** ark
	9:27	and I will tell you **G** word.
	10:10	and **G** Spirit came over him.
	11:6	**G** Spirit came over him,
	14:45	done this with **G** help today."
	16:23	Whenever **G** spirit came to
	19:20	**G** Spirit came over Saul's
	19:23	**G** Spirit came over him too.
	29:9	as good as **G** Messenger.
2Sm	6:2	to bring **G** ark ⌊to Jerusalem⌋.
	6:3	David and his men put **G** ark
	9:3	**G** kindness?" "Jonathan has
	14:13	against **G** people?" she said.
	14:17	You are like **G** Messenger,
	14:20	**G** Messenger, who knows
	15:24	carrying the ark of **G** promise.

2Sm 15:25 "Take G ark back to the city.
19:27 you are like G Messenger.
22:31 G way is perfect! The promise
1Ki 10:9 Because of your G eternal love
11:10 did not obey G command
2Ki 1:12 Then G fire came from heaven
1Ch 5:22 battle because this was G war.
6:49 G servant Moses had
9:11 official in charge of G temple)
9:13 They served in G temple and
9:26 and treasures in G temple
9:27 stationed around G temple
12:22 an army as large as G army
13:3 our G ark, which we ignored
13:5 bring G ark from Kiriath Jearim.
13:6 to bring G ark ⌊to Jerusalem⌋.
13:7 David and his men put G ark
13:8 were celebrating in G presence
13:10 He died in G presence
13:12 "How can I bring G ark to my
13:13 So he didn't bring G ark to his
13:14 G ark stayed at the home of
15:1 he prepared a place for G ark
15:2 only the Levites carry G ark
15:15 The Levites carried G ark on
15:24 blew trumpets in front of G ark.
16:1 offerings in G presence
16:6 in front of the ark of G promise
22:1 the LORD G temple will be.
22:2 to cut stones to build G temple
22:19 and G holy utensils into
23:28 and to serve in G temple
25:6 for worship in G temple under
26:20 of the treasuries in G temple
28:2 would be a stool for our G feet,
28:12 as treasuries for G temple
28:21 type of worship in G temple.
29:3 that I'm giving to my G temple
29:7 of iron for the work on G temple
2Ch 1:3 in Gibeon because G tent
1:4 G ark from Kiriath Jearim
3:3 foundation to build G temple.
4:11 for King Solomon in G temple:
4:19 all the furnishings for G temple:
5:1 in the storerooms of G temple
5:14 LORD's glory filled G temple
7:5 the people dedicated G temple
9:8 Because of your G love for the
15:1 G Spirit came to Azariah,
15:18 He brought into G temple the
17:4 and lived by G commands.
20:15 The battle isn't yours. It's G.
22:12 He was hidden in G temple for
23:3 with the king in G temple.
23:9 but were now in G temple
24:6 the words of G promise.
24:7 had broken into G temple
24:13 They restored G temple to its
24:18 brought G anger upon Judah
24:20 G Spirit gave Zechariah,
24:27 and the rebuilding of G temple
25:24 utensils he found in G temple
28:24 in G temple, cut them up,
30:27 prayers went to G holy place
31:13 of G temple, appointed Jehiel,
31:21 did for the worship in G temple,
33:7 Then he set it up in G temple,
34:9 had been brought to G temple,
35:8 the men in charge of G temple,
36:13 of allegiance to him in G name.
36:16 G messengers, despised his
36:18 of the utensils from G temple,
36:19 They burned G temple, tore
Ezr 1:4 used in G temple in Jerusalem.
2:68 to help rebuild G temple
3:8 return to ⌊the site⌋ of G house
3:9 those working on G house
4:24 Then the work on G temple in
5:2 began to rebuild G temple in
5:2 G prophets were with them and
5:5 were under G watchful eye.
5:13 gave permission for G temple
5:14 that belonged to G temple.
5:14 had taken them out of G temple
5:15 Rebuild G temple on its
5:16 laid the foundation of G temple
Ezr 6:3 G temple in Jerusalem.
6:5 that belonged to G temple.
6:5 had taken them out of G temple
6:5 put each one in G temple
6:7 with the work on G temple.
6:7 of Judah rebuild G temple
6:8 leaders rebuild G temple:
6:16 at the dedication of G temple
6:17 At the dedication of G temple,
7:14 G Teachings, which you hold
7:19 used in your G temple must all
7:20 must provide for your G temple
7:25 using your G wisdom — the
7:25 who know your G Teachings
7:26 follow your G Teachings
8:17 who can serve in our G temple
8:25 contributed for our G temple
8:33 the utensils in our G temple.
9:9 to rebuild our G temple
10:1 down in front of G temple,
10:6 Ezra left the front of G temple
10:9 in the courtyard of G temple.
10:14 our G burning anger has turned
Neh 8:8 Book of G Teachings clearly
8:9 to the reading of G Teachings
8:13 the words of G Teachings
8:16 in the courtyards of G temple,
8:18 from the Book of G Teachings.
10:28 for the sake of G Teachings.
10:29 G teachings given by Moses,
10:29 given by Moses, G servant.
10:32 for worship in our G temple:
10:34 bring wood to our G temple
10:36 priests serving in our G temple
10:38 tenths to our G temple, into
10:39 We won't neglect our G temple
11:11 was the supervisor of G temple
11:16 of the work outside G temple
11:22 charge of worship in G temple
12:40 stood in G temple, as did
12:41 stood in G temple: Eliakim,
13:1 be admitted into G assembly
13:4 the storerooms of our G temple,
13:7 Tobiah with a room in G temple
13:9 the utensils from G temple,
13:11 "Why is G temple being
Job 5:8 "But I would seek G help and
6:4 G terrors line up in battle
11:7 you discover G hidden secrets,
11:8 ⌊G wisdom is⌋ higher than
13:8 arguing in court on G behalf
15:8 Did you listen in on G council
15:11 Isn't G comfort enough for you,
16:9 "G anger tore me ⌊apart⌋ and
19:21 because G hand has struck me
21:30 On the day of ⌊G⌋ anger he is
26:6 Sheol is naked in G presence,
27:3 and G breath fills my nostrils,
27:11 will teach you about G power.
33:4 "G Spirit has made me.
33:26 They will see G face and
34:21 G eyes are on a person's ways.
35:2 'My case is more just than G,'
36:2 is more to be said in G defense
37:2 Listen to the roar of G voice, to
37:5 G voice thunders in miraculous
37:10 G breath produces ice,
37:14 Stop and consider G miracles
40:9 Do you have power like G?
40:19 is the first of G conquests.
Psa 18:30 G way is perfect! The promise
42:2 may I come to see G face
42:4 it in a procession to G house.
46:6 at the sound of ⌊G⌋ voice
52:8 a large olive tree in G house.
55:14 and walk into G house
68:2 in G presence like wax next
68:3 them celebrate in G presence.
73:10 That is why G people turn to
73:15 would have betrayed G people
73:17 Only when I came into G holy
78:10 not been faithful to G promise.
83:12 G pasturelands for ourselves."
84:10 to my G house than live inside
92:13 blossom in our G courtyards
107:11 had rebelled against G words
Psa 111:10 follows ⌊G guiding principles⌋.
Pro 13:13 Whoever despises ⌊G⌋ words
13:13 who fears ⌊G⌋ commands will
14:14 is satisfied with G ways
28:4 G teachings praise wicked
28:4 G teachings oppose wicked
28:7 follows ⌊G⌋ teachings is
28:9 to ⌊G⌋ teachings is disgusting.
29:18 who follow ⌊G⌋ teachings
Ecc 8:2 oath you took in G presence
9:1 are in G hands. No one knows
Isa 14:13 up my throne above G stars.
19:24 one-third ⌊of G people⌋, along
58:2 G judgment ⌊on them⌋.
61:2 the day of our G vengeance,
Lam 1:14 tied together by G own hands.
3:1 suffering under the rod of G
Eze 8:3 up ⌊G⌋ anger was located.
8:5 the idol that stirs up ⌊G⌋ anger
11:24 In this vision from G Spirit, the
28:2 I sit on G throne in the sea."
28:13 You were in Eden, G garden.
28:14 You were on G holy mountain.
28:16 you down from G mountain
31:8 The cedar trees in G garden
31:8 All the trees in G garden
31:9 the trees in Eden, in G garden
Dan 1:2 utensils from G temple over
2:20 He said, "Praise G name from
5:3 had been taken from G temple
8:19 ⌊the time of G⌋ anger, because
9:20 about my G holy mountain
11:36 He will succeed until G anger
Hos 9:8 Prophets are G watchmen over
14:7 will live again in G shadow.
Joe 1:13 withheld from your G temple
1:16 disappear from our G temple
Hab 2:15 of G rage, making him drunk
Mat 3:7 to flee from G coming anger?
5:6 and thirst for G approval.
5:9 They will be called G children
5:20 live a life that has G approval
5:34 which is G throne,
12:28 with the help of G Spirit, then
13:17 and many of G people longed
13:43 have G approval will shine like
13:49 people who have G approval
15:6 the authority of G word
22:29 know the Scriptures or G power
23:22 heaven is to swear by G throne
23:28 though you have G approval,
23:29 of those who had G approval
25:37 who have G approval will reply
25:46 but those with G approval will
26:61 'I can tear down G temple and
27:40 going to tear down G temple
Mar 2:2 speaking ⌊G⌋ word to them.
4:33 Jesus spoke ⌊G⌋ word to them
7:13 the authority of G word.
12:24 the Scriptures or G power
13:19 of G creation until now,
15:29 going to tear down G temple
Luk 1:2 and servants of G word from
1:6 and Elizabeth had G approval.
1:8 As he served in G presence,
1:17 of those who have G approval.
1:19 I stand in G presence.
2:40 and G favor was with him.
3:7 to flee from G coming anger?
5:1 him as they listened to G word
7:30 Teachings rejected G plan
8:1 Good News about G kingdom.
8:11 The seed is G word
8:21 and do what G word says."
9:43 to see G wonderful power.
11:20 with the help of G power, then
11:28 who hear and obey G word.
12:8 of G angels every person who
12:9 But G angels will be told that I
14:14 have G approval come back
15:10 that G angels are happy about
18:14 went home with G approval,
20:36 They are G children who have
20:38 In G sight all people are living."
23:50 good man who had G approval.
Jon 1:12 the right to become G children

Jon 1:18 **G** only Son, the one who is
1:51 open and **G** angels going up
3:18 don't believe in **G** only Son.
3:34 has sent speaks **G** message.
3:36 he will see **G** constant anger."
4:10 "If you only knew what **G** gift
6:33 **G** bread is the man who
11:40 you would see **G** glory?
11:52 **G** scattered children together
16:8 the world what has **G** approval,
16:10 the world what has **G** approval,
Act 4:33 ⌊**G**⌋ abundant good will was
6:2 right for us to give up **G** word
6:8 was a man filled with **G** favor
7:44 had the tent of **G** promise.
7:46 who won **G** favor. David asked
7:52 with **G** approval would come.
7:55 saw **G** glory, and Jesus in the
8:20 thought you could buy **G** gift
9:32 going around to all of **G** people,
10:22 a man who has **G** approval
11:1 Jewish had accepted **G** word
11:19 They spoke **G** word only to
12:24 But **G** word continued to
13:5 they began to spread **G** word in
13:10 everything that has **G** approval.
13:36 After doing **G** will by serving
13:38 **G** approval through Moses'
13:39 in Jesus receives **G** approval
13:43 continue trusting **G** good will.
14:26 had been entrusted to **G** care
17:11 willing to receive **G** message,
17:13 was also spreading **G** word
17:28 'We are **G** children.
17:29 So if we are **G** children, we
18:26 them and explained **G** way
18:27 **G** kindness enabled him to
20:24 the Good News of **G** kindness
20:28 shepherds for **G** church which
20:32 shared by all of **G** holy people.
22:14 the one who has **G** approval,
23:4 "You're insulting **G** chief
24:15 that people with **G** approval
24:25 of **G** approval, self-control,
26:18 and from Satan's control to **G**.
26:18 among **G** people who are made
28:31 the message about **G** kingdom
Rom 1:5 we have received **G** kindness
1:16 It is **G** power to save everyone
1:17 **G** approval is revealed in this
1:17 who has **G** approval will live
1:18 **G** anger is revealed from
1:20 **G** invisible qualities,
1:25 people have exchanged **G** truth
1:32 **G** judgment that those who
2:2 We know that **G** judgment is
2:3 you will escape **G** judgment
2:4 it is **G** kindness that is trying
2:13 God don't have **G** approval.
2:13 demand will have **G** approval
2:24 As Scripture says, "**G** name is
3:3 cancel **G** faithfulness
3:10 one person has **G** approval
3:20 **G** approval by following Moses'
3:21 the way to receive **G** approval
3:22 has **G** approval through faith
3:23 have fallen short of **G** glory
3:24 They receive **G** approval freely
3:25 **G** approval is given through
3:28 that a person has **G** approval
4:2 If Abraham had **G** approval
4:5 faith is regarded as **G** approval
4:9 regarded as **G** approval of him."
4:10 faith regarded as **G** approval?
4:11 regarded as **G** approval while
4:11 as **G** approval of them.
4:13 it was through **G** approval of
4:20 He didn't doubt **G** promise out
4:22 regarded as **G** approval of him.
4:23 was regarded as **G** approval
4:24 will be regarded as **G** approval
4:25 we could receive **G** approval
5:1 Now that we have **G** approval
5:5 because **G** love has been
5:8 demonstrates **G** love for us.
5:9 us **G** approval, we are even
Rom 5:9 will save us from **G** anger
5:15 comparison between ⌊**G**⌋ gift
5:15 certainly true that **G** kindness
5:16 comparison between ⌊**G**⌋ gift
5:16 the gift brought **G** approval
5:17 **G** overflowing kindness
5:18 **G** life-giving approval through
5:19 will receive **G** approval
5:20 **G** kindness increased even
5:21 **G** kindness would rule by
6:1 that **G** kindness will increase?
6:14 by laws, but by **G** favor
6:15 but are controlled by **G** favor?
6:16 master leads to **G** approval
6:22 and have become **G** slaves.
7:14 I know that **G** standards are
7:16 that **G** standards are good.
7:21 what **G** standards say is good.
7:22 I take pleasure in **G** standards
7:25 I am obedient to **G** standards
8:3 do what **G** standards demand
8:4 are able to meet **G** standards
8:7 the authority of **G** standards
8:9 But if **G** Spirit lives in you,
8:10 because you have **G** approval
8:14 all who are guided by **G** Spirit
8:14 by God's Spirit are **G** children
8:15 of **G** adopted children by which
8:16 our spirit that we are **G** children
8:17 we are also **G** heirs.
8:23 of **G** gifts, also groan inwardly.
8:27 Spirit intercedes for **G** people
8:38 from **G** love which Christ Jesus
9:4 **G** adopted children.
9:6 Now it is not as though **G** word
9:8 are not necessarily **G** children.
9:11 so that **G** plan would remain
9:12 a choice based on **G** call and
9:16 Therefore, **G** choice does not
9:16 desire or effort, but on **G** mercy
9:30 **G** approval won his approval,
9:31 **G** approval by obeying Moses'
9:32 rely on faith to gain **G** approval,
10:3 ⌊how to receive⌋ **G** approval.
10:3 they have not accepted **G** way
10:4 faith may receive **G** approval
10:5 **G** approval by following his
10:6 **G** approval which is based
10:10 you receive **G** approval,
11:4 But what was **G** reply?
11:6 **G** kindness, they weren't chosen
11:6 Otherwise, **G** kindness
11:25 **G** non-Jewish people are
11:28 But by **G** choice they are loved
11:33 **G** riches, wisdom,
12:1 because of **G** compassion
12:6 If your gift is speaking **G** word,
12:13 have with **G** people who are
12:19 let **G** anger take care of it.
13:4 The government is **G** servant
13:4 It is **G** servant, an avenger to
13:4 an avenger to execute **G** anger
13:5 you're afraid of **G** anger
13:6 are **G** servants while they do
14:17 **G** kingdom does not consist of
14:17 Rather, **G** kingdom consists of
14:17 consists of **G** approval
14:20 Don't ruin **G** work because of
15:8 people to reveal **G** truth.
15:8 he fulfilled **G** promise to the
15:19 and by the power of **G** Spirit, I
15:31 Pray that **G** people in
16:2 shows you are **G** holy people.
16:15 and all **G** people who are with
1Co 1:2 To **G** church that was made
1:2 and called to be **G** holy people
1:4 has shown you **G** good will.
1:18 but it is **G** power to us who are
1:24 **G** power and God's wisdom.
1:24 God's power and **G** wisdom
1:25 **G** nonsense is wiser than
1:25 and **G** weakness is stronger
1:29 no one can brag in **G** presence
2:1 I didn't speak about **G** mystery
2:5 human wisdom but on **G** power
2:7 the mystery of **G** wisdom.
1Co 2:11 about God except **G** Spirit
2:14 the teachings of **G** Spirit.
3:9 We are **G** coworkers.
3:9 You are **G** field. You are God's
3:9 You are **G** building
3:16 know that you are **G** temple
3:16 temple and that **G** Spirit lives
3:17 If anyone destroys **G** temple,
3:17 him because **G** temple is holy.
3:19 world is nonsense in **G** sight.
4:1 are entrusted with **G** mysteries
4:4 mean I have **G** approval.
4:20 **G** kingdom is not just talk,
6:1 it in front of **G** holy people?
6:2 Don't you know that **G** people
6:11 you have received **G** approval
7:40 I think that I, too, have **G** Spirit
9:9 **G** concern isn't for oxen.
9:21 though I have **G** teachings.
10:32 or members of **G** church
11:7 He is **G** image and glory.
11:22 Do you despise **G** church and
12:3 one speaking by **G** Spirit says,
12:25 **G** purpose was that the body
14:21 **G** word says, "Through people
14:33 As in all the churches of **G** holy
14:36 Did **G** word originate with you?
15:9 because I persecuted **G** church
15:10 But **G** kindness made me what
15:10 but **G** kindness was with me.
15:28 **G** authority, since God had
15:56 and **G** standards give sin its
16:1 for **G** people ⌊in Jerusalem⌋:
16:15 itself to serving **G** people.
2Co 1:1 To **G** church in the city of
1:1 all **G** holy people everywhere
1:12 have lived but by **G** kindness
1:19 **G** Son, Jesus Christ,
1:20 Certainly, Christ made **G** many
2:17 and in **G** presence, we speak
3:4 about you in **G** presence
3:9 that brings **G** approval has
4:2 and we don't distort **G** word.
4:4 It is Christ who is **G** image
4:6 **G** glory which shines from
4:15 as **G** kindness overflows in the
5:21 **G** approval through him.
6:1 Since we are **G** coworkers, we
6:1 urge you not to let **G** kindness
6:2 now is **G** acceptable time!
6:4 that we are **G** servants.
6:7 and the presence of **G** power.
6:7 that we are **G** servants
6:16 Can **G** temple contain false
7:12 your devotion to us in **G** sight
8:4 in the ministry of **G** kindness
8:5 since this was **G** will
8:6 work of **G** kindness among you
8:7 in this work of **G** kindness
8:19 bring this gift of **G** kindness.
9:6 **G** blessings will receive
9:6 of **G** blessings in return.
9:12 for the needs of **G** people,
11:15 servants who have **G** approval.
12:19 as Christ's people in **G** sight.
13:4 but by **G** power he lives.
13:4 but by **G** power we will live for
13:12 All of **G** holy people greet you.
13:13 **G** love, and the Holy Spirit's
Gal 1:13 I violently persecuted **G** church
2:16 people don't receive **G** approval
2:16 in order to receive **G** approval
2:16 won't receive **G** approval
2:17 are searching for **G** approval
2:20 in **G** Son, who loved me
2:21 I don't reject **G** kindness.
2:21 If we receive **G** approval by
3:11 No one receives **G** approval by
3:11 who has **G** approval will live
3:13 that **G** laws bring by becoming
3:21 Moses contradict **G** promises?
3:21 we would receive **G** approval
3:24 we could receive **G** approval
3:26 You are all **G** children by
4:4 under the control of **G** laws
4:6 Because you are **G** children,

Gal 4:7 longer slaves but **G** children.
4:7 Since you are **G** children, God
4:14 me as if I were **G** messenger
5:4 earn **G** approval by obeying his
5:4 You have fallen out of **G** favor
5:5 that comes with **G** approval
5:10 suffer **G** judgment regardless
6:6 taught **G** word should share all
Eph 1:1 of Christ Jesus by **G** will.
1:1 To **G** holy and faithful people
1:15 your love for all of **G** people.
1:18 that **G** people will inherit.
2:3 we deserved **G** anger just like
2:5 (It is **G** kindness that saved
2:19 citizens together with **G** people
2:19 and members of **G** family
3:7 **G** kindness freely given
3:8 I am the least of all **G** people.
3:11 This was **G** plan for all of
3:18 This way, with all of **G** people
4:7 **G** favor has been given to each
4:12 purpose is to prepare **G** people,
4:13 about **G** Son, until we become
4:30 Don't give **G** Holy Spirit any
5:3 behavior for **G** holy people.
5:6 like these that **G** anger comes
5:9 that has **G** approval, and that is
6:14 Put on **G** approval as your
6:18 of request for all of **G** people
Php 1:1 To **G** people in the city of
1:7 Together we share **G** favor,
1:11 that **G** approval produces.
1:14 to speak **G** word more boldly
1:28 This is **G** way of showing
2:15 You will be **G** children without
3:3 because we serve **G** Spirit
3:6 **G** approval by keeping Jewish
3:9 **G** approval by obeying his
3:9 I have **G** approval through faith
3:14 that **G** heavenly call offers
4:7 Then **G** peace, which goes
4:22 All **G** people here,
Col 1:1 of Christ Jesus by **G** will,
1:2 To **G** holy and faithful people,
1:4 your love for all of **G** people
1:6 what **G** kindness truly means.
1:12 which is what **G** people inherit.
1:22 into **G** presence without sin,
3:6 these sins that **G** anger comes
3:16 about ⌊**G**⌋ kindness.
4:11 with me for **G** kingdom.
4:18 **G** good will be with you.
1Th 1:6 you welcomed **G** word with the
1:10 us from ⌊**G**⌋ coming anger.
2:13 When you received **G** word
2:16 they are receiving ⌊**G**⌋ anger
3:9 us as we rejoice in **G** presence
3:13 comes with all **G** holy people.
4:3 It is **G** will that you keep away
5:9 It was not **G** intention that we
5:18 because it is **G** will in Christ
2Th 1:4 **G** churches about your
1:5 proves that **G** judgment is right
2:4 sitting in **G** temple and
3:5 your lives as you show **G** love
1Ti 1:4 **G** plan, which centers
1:9 people who have **G** approval.
3:5 can he take care of **G** church?
3:15 members of **G** family must live.
3:15 **G** family is the church of the
5:4 This is pleasing in **G** sight
6:1 one will speak evil of **G** name
6:21 **G** good will be with all of you.
2Ti 1:1 of Christ Jesus by **G** will —
1:8 Instead, by **G** power, join me in
1:9 would show us **G** kindness
2:9 **G** word is not imprisoned.
2:19 In spite of all that, **G** ⌊people⌋
2:22 Pursue what has **G** approval.
3:16 for a life that has **G** approval
3:17 They equip **G** servants so that
4:8 **G** approval is now waiting
Tit 1:1 I was sent to lead **G** chosen
2:5 one can speak evil of **G** word
2:11 After all, **G** saving kindness
3:15 ⌊**G**⌋ good will be with all of

Phm 1:5 your love for all of **G** people
1:7 Your love ⌊for **G** people⌋ gives
1:7 have comforted **G** people
Heb 1:3 Son is the reflection of **G** glory
1:3 the exact likeness of **G** being.
1:6 "All of **G** angels must worship
2:9 Through **G** kindness he died
2:17 chief priest in **G** presence
3:2 when he served in **G** house
3:5 faithful servant in **G** household.
3:6 son in charge of **G** household.
4:1 **G** promise that we may enter
4:6 the past did not enter **G** place
4:9 worship exists for **G** people
4:12 **G** word is living and active.
4:12 **G** word judges a person's
4:16 to the throne of **G** kindness
5:12 elementary truths of **G** word.
6:4 Some people once had **G** light.
6:5 the goodness of **G** word
7:6 who had **G** promises
7:28 But **G** promise, which came
9:24 to appear in **G** presence
10:21 priest in charge of **G** house
10:27 that will consume **G** enemies
10:38 who has **G** approval will live
11:4 **G** approval, since God accepted
11:7 **G** approval that comes through
11:25 suffer with **G** people rather than
12:23 **G** firstborn children (whose
12:23 of people who have **G** approval
13:7 who have spoken **G** word
13:9 from **G** kindness is good
13:24 leaders and all **G** holy people.
13:25 May **G** good will be with all of
Jas 1:1 To **G** faithful people who have
1:22 Do what **G** word says.
1:23 If someone listens to **G** word
1:25 **G** perfect teachings that make
1:25 do what **G** teachings say.
2:10 If someone obeys all of **G** laws
2:11 a person who disobeys **G** laws
2:21 Abraham receive **G** approval as
2:23 Abraham was called **G** friend
2:24 a person receives **G** approval
2:25 She received **G** approval
3:9 were created in **G** likeness
3:18 A harvest that has **G** approval
4:7 yourselves under **G** authority.
4:11 slander and judge **G** teachings.
4:11 If you judge **G** teachings, you
5:6 **G** approval, even though they
5:16 have **G** approval are effective.
1Pe 1:1 To **G** chosen people who are
1:5 by **G** power through faith
1:10 **G** kindness that would come
1:13 what **G** kindness will bring you
1:23 but through **G** everlasting word
2:2 Desire **G** pure word as
2:10 Once you were not **G** people,
2:24 live a life that has **G** approval.
3:1 may not obey **G** word.
3:7 **G** life-giving kindness so that
3:17 After all, if it is **G** will, it's better
4:11 speaks must speak **G** words.
4:17 and it will begin with **G** family.
4:18 the person who has **G** approval
4:19 suffer because that is **G** will
5:6 Be humbled by **G** power so
5:12 this is **G** genuine good will.
2Pe 1:3 **G** divine power has given us
1:10 more effort to make **G** calling
1:21 spoke under **G** direction
2:1 were among **G** people ⌊in
2:5 kind of life that has **G** approval
2:8 a man who had **G** approval,
3:3 will ridicule ⌊**G** promise⌋
3:5 Because of **G** word, heaven
3:7 By **G** word, the present heaven
3:13 that has **G** approval lives.
1Jn 2:1 who has **G** full approval.
2:5 in whom **G** love is perfected.
2:14 are strong and **G** word lives
2:29 has **G** approval, you also know
3:1 actually called **G** dear children.
3:2 now we are **G** children.

1Jn 3:7 of has **G** approval as Christ has
3:7 as Christ has **G** approval
3:10 This is the way **G** children are
3:10 other believers isn't **G** child
3:12 his brother did had **G** approval
3:17 How can **G** love be in that
4:2 **G** Spirit: Every person who
4:16 Those who live in **G** love live
4:17 **G** love has reached its goal in
5:2 love **G** children when we love
5:9 **G** testimony is greater because
Jud 1:3 to **G** holy people once
1:4 They use **G** kindness as an
1:7 the same fate that **G** people
1:21 Remain in **G** love as you look
Rev 1:2 **G** word and the testimony
1:9 of Patmos because of **G** word
3:1 The one who has **G** seven
3:14 the source of **G** creation, says:
5:8 the prayers of the **G** holy
5:9 with your blood to be **G** own.
6:9 slaughtered because of **G** word
8:2 who stand in **G** presence,
8:3 the prayers of all of **G** people
8:4 with the prayers of **G** people
11:16 **G** presence, immediately bowed,
11:19 **G** temple in heaven was
12:17 ones who keep **G** commands
13:7 war against **G** holy people
13:10 In this situation **G** holy people
14:10 will drink the wine of **G** fury,
14:10 into the cup of **G** anger.
14:12 In this situation **G** holy people,
14:19 into the winepress of **G** anger
15:1 the final expression of **G** anger
15:2 They were holding **G** harps
15:3 the song of **G** servant Moses
15:5 words of **G** promise was open
16:1 seven bowls of **G** anger over
16:6 out the blood of **G** people
17:6 with the blood of **G** holy people
17:17 until **G** words are carried out.
18:20 **G** people, apostles,
18:24 **G** people, and everyone who
19:8 that **G** holy people do that
20:9 the camp of **G** holy people
22:11 have **G** approval go without it,
22:11 Let those who have **G** approval

gods (331)

Gen 31:30 But why did you steal my **g**?"
31:32 If you find your **g**, the one who
31:32 that Rachel had stolen the **g**.)
35:2 "Get rid of the foreign **g** which
35:4 all the foreign **g** that they had
Exo 12:12 punish all the **g** of Egypt,
15:11 "Who is like you among the **g**,
18:11 is greater than all other **g**."
20:23 Never make any **g** of silver or
23:13 mention the names of other **g**
23:24 Never worship or serve their **g**
23:24 you must destroy their **g** and
23:32 a treaty with them and their **g**.
23:33 trap you into serving their **g**."
32:1 Make **g** who will lead us."
32:4 here are your **g** who brought
32:8 here are your **g** who brought
32:23 Make **g** for us. They will lead us
32:31 They made **g** out of gold for
34:15 When they chase after their **g**
34:16 after their **g** as though they
Lev 19:4 "Don't turn to worthless **g** or
19:4 make any **g** for yourselves.
Num 25:2 the sacrifices offered to their **g**.
25:2 and worshiped these **g**.
33:4 act of judgment on their **g**.
Dtr 4:7 nation ever had their **g** as near
4:28 and stone **g** made by human
4:28 These **g** can't see,
5:7 "Never have any other **g**.
6:14 Never worship any of the **g**
7:4 from me to worship other **g**.
7:16 and never worship their **g**,
8:19 your God and follow other **g**,
10:17 LORD your God is God of **g**
11:16 turn away and worship other **g**

Dtr 11:28 other g you never knew.
12:2 worship their g in these places.
12:3 of their g from those places.
12:4 in the way they worship their g.
12:30 even ask about their g and say,
12:30 these people worship their g?
12:31 in the way they worship their g,
12:31 they do for their g is disgusting
12:31 as sacrifices to their g.
13:2 worship and serve other g."
13:2 (Those g may be gods you've
13:2 (Those gods may be g you've
13:6 "Let's go worship other g."
13:6 (Those g may be gods that you
13:6 (Those gods may be g that you
13:7 They may be the g of the
13:13 "Let's worship other g."
13:13 (Those g may be gods you've
13:13 (Those gods may be g you've
17:3 and bowing down to other g,
18:20 the name of other g must die."
20:18 things they do for their g,
28:14 worship other g or serve them.
28:36 There you will worship g made
28:64 There you will serve g made of
29:17 You saw their disgusting g and
29:18 LORD our God to worship the g
29:26 They worshiped other g and
29:26 These were g they never heard
29:26 g the LORD didn't permit them
30:17 to other g and worship them.
31:16 they will chase after foreign g
31:18 done in turning to other g.
31:20 they will turn to other g and
32:16 they worshiped foreign g
32:17 to g they never heard of.
32:17 These were new g,
32:17 g your ancestors never
32:21 they worshiped foreign g
32:37 "Where are their g?
32:38 Where are the g who ate the fat
Jos 23:7 mention the names of their g
23:7 Don't ever serve their g or bow
23:16 your God and follow other g,
24:2 River and served other g.
24:14 Get rid of the g your ancestors
24:15 Even if you choose the g your
24:15 side of the Euphrates or the g
24:16 the LORD to serve other g.
24:20 the LORD and serve foreign g,
24:23 "Get rid of the foreign g that are
Jdg 2:3 and their g will become a trap
2:11 to serve other g — the Baals.
2:12 They followed the other g of
2:12 They worshiped these g,
2:17 after other g as though they
2:19 and worshiped other g.
3:6 Israel also served their g.
3:7 their God and served other g
5:8 When the people chose new g,
6:10 You must never fear the g of
8:33 of Israel chased after other g —
9:9 use to honor g and humans,
9:13 which makes g and humans
9:27 praise in the temple of their g.
10:6 They began to serve other g
10:6 Astartes — and the g of Aram,
10:6 and the g of the Philistines.
10:10 served other g — the Baals."
10:13 me and served other g.
10:14 out for help to the g you chose.
10:16 got rid of the foreign g they had
18:24 "You've taken away the g I
Rut 1:15 back to her people and to her g.
1Sm 4:8 the power of these mighty g?
4:8 These are the g who struck the
6:5 you, your g, and your country.
7:3 rid of the foreign g you have,
8:8 leaving me and serving other g.
12:10 the LORD and served other g
12:21 turn away to follow other g.
17:43 called on his g to curse David.
26:19 and serve other g,' they tell me.
2Sm 7:23 You forced nations and their g
1Ki 9:6 other g and worship them,
9:9 They adopted other g,
1Ki 11:2 tempt you to follow their g."
11:4 tempted him to follow other g.
11:8 and sacrificed to their g.
11:10 told him not to follow other g.
12:28 Israel, here are your g who
14:9 You made other g,
18:18 following the various Baal g.
18:24 call on the name of your g,
19:2 She said, "May the g strike me
20:10 "May the g strike me dead if
2Ki 5:17 or sacrifice to any other g.
17:7 They worshiped other g
17:29 continued to make its own g.
17:31 the g of Sepharvaim.
17:33 served their own g according
17:35 "Never worship other g,
17:37 'Never worship other g.
17:38 Never worship other g.
18:33 Did any of the g of the nations
18:34 Where are the g of Hamath and
18:34 Where are the g of Sepharvaim,
18:35 Did the g of those countries
19:12 Did the g of the nations which
19:18 They have thrown the g from
19:18 these g aren't real gods.
19:18 these gods aren't real g.
22:17 me and sacrificed to other g
23:24 and disgusting g that could be
1Ch 5:25 They chased after the g of the
10:10 armor in the temple of their g
14:12 Philistines left their g there,
14:12 ordered that the g be burned.
16:25 feared more than all ⌊other⌋ g
16:26 because all the g of the nations
17:21 the nations and their g out
2Ch 2:5 God is greater than all other g.
7:19 other g and worship them,
7:22 They adopted other g,
13:8 Jeroboam made to be your g.
13:9 as a priest of nonexistent g.
14:3 got rid of the altars of foreign g,
17:3 to serving other g — the Baals.
21:11 chase after foreign g as if they
21:13 chase after foreign g as if they
24:7 worship ⌊other⌋ g — the Baals.)
25:14 he brought the g of the people
25:14 set them up as his g,
25:15 your life to serving the g
25:15 Those g couldn't save their
25:20 sought help from Edom's g.)
28:2 worshiping other g — the Baals.
28:23 to the g of Damascus,
28:23 the g who had defeated him.
28:23 He thought, "The g of the kings
28:25 worship to sacrifice to other g.
32:13 Were any of the g of these
32:14 Were the g of these nations
32:17 These letters said, "As the g of
32:19 one of the g made by human
33:3 up altars dedicated to other g —
33:15 got rid of the foreign g
34:4 of the various Baal g torn down.
34:25 me and sacrificed to other g
Psa 16:4 other g multiply their sorrows.
31:6 hate those who cling to false g,
82:1 judgment among the g:
82:6 I said, "You are g. You are all
95:3 and a great king above all g.
96:4 feared more than all ⌊other⌋ g
96:5 because all the g of the nations
97:7 and brags about false g will
97:7 All the g will bow to him.
97:9 You are above all the g.
135:5 is greater than all the false g.
136:2 Give thanks to the God of g
138:1 you in front of the false g.
Isa 1:29 you have chosen for your g.
14:13 north where the g assemble.
31:3 Egyptians are humans, not g.
36:18 Did any of the g of the nations
36:19 Where are the g of Hamath and
36:19 are the g of Sepharvaim?
36:20 Did the g of these countries
37:12 Did the g of the nations which
37:19 They have thrown the g from
37:19 these g aren't real gods.
Isa 37:19 these gods aren't real g.
41:23 we may know that you are g.
42:17 "You are our g" will be turned
44:10 Nothing comes from making g
44:11 Everyone associated with the g
44:15 They also make g from these
44:17 of the wood they make into g,
44:17 because you are our g."
45:20 and pray to g that cannot save
46:1 The g that you carry are
46:2 These g stoop low and bow
48:5 "My g have done these things.
Jer 1:16 burned incense to other g,
2:11 any nation ever exchanged g?
2:11 (Their g aren't really gods.)
2:11 (Their gods aren't really g.)
2:23 and haven't followed other g —
2:25 love foreign g and follow them.
2:28 Where are the g that you made
2:28 You have as many g as you
5:19 me and served foreign g
7:6 not follow other g that lead you
7:9 and run after other g that you do
7:18 out wine offerings to other g
8:19 with their foreign g.
9:14 stubborn ways and other g —
10:11 Tell them this: These g will
10:14 Their statues are false ⌊g⌋.
11:10 They are following other g and
11:12 in Jerusalem will cry to the g
11:12 But these g will never rescue
11:13 Judah, you have as many g as
13:10 ways and follow other g
13:25 me and trusted false g.
14:22 The worthless g of the nations
16:11 They followed other g,
16:13 There you will serve other g
16:19 worthless and unprofitable g."
16:20 can't make g for themselves.
16:20 They aren't really g.
19:4 to other g that they hadn't
19:13 out wine offerings to other g."
22:9 other g and served them."'
25:6 Don't follow other g to serve
32:29 out wine offerings to other g.
35:15 and don't follow other g in order
43:12 fire to the temples of Egypt's g.
43:12 and take their g captive.
43:13 the temples of Egypt's g."'
44:3 serve other g that neither you
44:5 as an offering to other g.
44:8 incense to other g in Egypt,
44:15 burning incense to other g,
44:23 incense as offerings to other g,
46:25 Pharaoh, Egypt, its g, its kings,
48:35 to their g," declares the LORD.
51:17 Their statues are false ⌊g⌋.
Eze 7:20 detestable statues ⌊of false g⌋.
20:26 sons as gifts ⌊to their false g⌋.
21:21 ask his household g for help,
Dan 2:11 you dreamed except the g,
2:47 God is truly the greatest of g,
3:12 They don't honor your g or
3:14 it true that you don't honor my g
3:18 we'll never honor your g or
3:25 one looks like a son of the g."
4:8 The spirit of the holy g is in
4:9 I know the spirit of the holy g is
4:18 spirit of the holy g is in you."
5:4 wine and praised their g made
5:11 who has the spirit of the holy g.
5:11 like the wisdom of the g.
5:14 that you have the spirit of the g
5:23 You praised your g made of
5:23 These g can't see,
11:8 take the metal statues of their g
11:36 things against the God of G.
11:37 He will have no interest in the g
Hos 2:13 as an offering to other g —
2:17 names of other g called Baal.
3:1 they have turned to other g
4:12 giving themselves to other g.
10:1 they set up ⌊to honor other g⌋.
11:2 They sacrificed to other g — the
14:3 our hands have made are our g.
Amo 2:8 In the temples of their g,

Amo 5:26 the **g** you made for yourselves.
Jnh 1:5 they cried to their **g** for help.
Mic 4:5 live by the names of their **g**,
Nah 1:14 idols from the temple of your **g**.
Zep 2:11 because he will make all the **g**
Jon 10:34 say, 'I said, "You are **g**"'?
10:35 So if God calls people **g** (and
Act 7:40 So make **g** who will lead us.'
14:11 "The **g** have come to us,
14:15 away from these worthless **g**
15:20 from things polluted by false **g**,
15:29 from food sacrificed to false **g**,
17:16 statues of false **g** everywhere.
17:18 to be speaking about foreign **g**."
19:26 He tells people that **g** made by
19:26 made by humans are not **g**.
21:25 eat food sacrificed to false **g**,
28:11 The ship had the **g** Castor and
1Co 5:10 or worship false **g**.
5:11 are greedy, worship false **g**,
6:9 who worship false **g**,
8:1 food offered to false **g**:
8:4 food that was offered to false **g**:
8:4 We know that the false **g** in
8:5 People may say that there are **g**
8:5 heaven and on earth — many **g**
8:7 false **g** that they believe
8:13 false **g** causes other believers
10:7 So don't worship false **g** as
10:14 worship of false **g** as you can.
12:2 false **g** you were worshiping
12:2 worshiping **g** who couldn't even
2Co 6:16 God's temple contain false **g**?
Gal 4:8 which are really not **g** at all.
1Th 1:9 you turned away from false **g**
1Pe 4:3 forbidden worship of false **g**.
1Jn 5:21 guard yourselves from false **g**.

goes (141)

Exo 28:29 "Whenever Aaron **g** into the
28:35 when he comes into and **g** out
29:30 as priest — the one who **g** into
Lev 11:42 creature with many legs that **g**
14:46 Whoever **g** into the house any
16:2 If he **g** up to the canopy and
Num 4:25 of fine leather that **g** over it,
14:25 and follow the road that **g** to the
19:14 Everyone who **g** into the tent
21:4 following the road that **g** to the
21:33 the road that **g** to Bashan.
28:9 the wine offering that **g** with it.
28:14 The wine offering that **g** with
28:24 the wine offering that **g** with it.
34:4 It then **g** past Zin and ends at
34:4 From there it **g** to Hazar Addar
34:9 From there the border **g** to
34:11 From Shepham the border **g**
34:12 Then the border **g** along the
Dtr 1:40 and follow the road that **g** to the
2:1 following the road that **g** to the
2:8 We turned off the road that **g**
2:8 and took the road that **g** through
3:1 the road that **g** to Bashan.
11:30 beyond the road that **g** west,
16:6 the evening as the sun **g** down.
Jos 3:11 of the whole earth as it **g** ahead
10:10 them along the road that **g**
12:3 the road that **g** south from Beth
15:3 and **g** south of the Akrabbim
15:3 It then passes Zin and **g** up
15:3 From there it **g** to Hezron,
15:6 and **g** up to Beth Hoglah.
15:6 north to Beth Arabah and **g** up
15:7 the border **g** up to Debir and
15:8 It then **g** to the top of the
15:9 mountain the border **g** around
15:9 From there it **g** to the cities of
15:10 Then it **g** down to Beth
15:11 From there the border **g** on the
16:1 of Joseph's territory **g** from
16:1 through the desert that **g** up
16:2 From Bethel the border **g** to Luz
16:6 From there the border **g** west,
16:8 At Tappuah the border **g** west
17:7 Then the border **g** south toward
18:12 **g** up the slope north of Jericho,
Jos 18:13 From there the border **g** to the
18:13 Then the border **g** down to
18:14 The border turns and **g** around
18:15 Kiriath Jearim and **g** west,
18:17 Then it turns north and **g** to En
19:10 The border of their inheritance **g**
19:13 From there it **g** directly east to
19:27 of Iphtah El in the north and **g**
19:27 there it **g** northward to Cabul,
19:29 Then it turns at Ramah and **g**
Jdg 5:9 My heart **g** out to Israel's
1Sm 6:9 but then watch where it **g**.
6:9 If it **g** up the road to its own
9:13 you can find him before he **g** to
23:22 and watch where he **g**.
2Sm 3:35 else before the sun **g** down."
1Ki 20:11 answered, "The saying **g**,
2Ki 5:18 forgive me when my master **g**
11:8 with the king wherever he **g**."
11:19 that **g** through Guards' Gate
12:20 on the road that **g** down to Silla.
18:21 your hand and **g** through it.
1Ch 26:16 Gate at the gateway that **g**
2Ch 23:7 with the king wherever he **g**."
Job 7:9 so a person **g** into the grave
9:11 He **g** past me, and I don't even
24:18 road that **g** to their vineyards.
Psa 112:5 All **g** well for the person who is
126:6 The person who **g** out weeping,
Pro 20:14 Then, as he **g** away,
20:19 Whoever **g** around as a gossip
23:31 because it **g** down smoothly.
26:11 As a dog **g** back to its vomit,
26:20 Without wood a fire **g** out,
29:9 When a wise person **g** to court
31:17 on strength like a belt and **g**
Ecc 1:7 The water **g** back to the place
3:20 All (life) **g** to the same place.
3:20 and all of it **g** back to the
3:21 a human spirit **g** upward
3:21 an animal spirit **g** downward
6:4 a pointless birth and **g** out into
6:7 so hard for **g** into their mouths,
10:3 Even when a fool **g** walking,
12:7 Then the dust (of mortals) **g**
12:7 and the breath of life **g** back to
Sos 7:9 that **g** down smoothly to my
Isa 36:6 your hand and **g** through it.
66:7 Before a woman **g** into labor,
Jer 9:4 neighbor **g** around slandering.
14:2 Their cry **g** up from Jerusalem.
19:8 Everyone who **g** by it will be
50:5 They will ask which road **g** to
Eze 14:4 Suppose he **g** to a prophet (to
14:7 If he **g** to a prophet to ask for
16:34 No one **g** after you for favors.
35:7 who comes or **g** from there.
Amo 5:19 It is like a person who **g** home
Mat 8:9 and he **g**, and another, 'Come!'
12:43 it **g** through dry places looking
12:45 Then it **g** and brings along
15:11 What **g** into a person's mouth
15:17 Don't you know that whatever **g**
15:17 goes into the mouth **g** into
15:18 But whatever **g** out of the
Mar 7:15 Nothing that **g** into a person
7:18 Don't you know that whatever **g**
14:14 When he **g** into a house,
Luk 7:8 and he **g**, and another, 'Come!'
8:14 but as life **g** on the worries,
9:39 **g** into convulsions,
9:39 a struggle, the spirit **g** away,
11:24 it **g** through dry places looking
11:26 Then the spirit **g** and brings
15:6 **g** home. Then he calls his
Jon 14:6 No one **g** to the Father except
Act 8:26 and take the desert road that **g**
1Co 6:6 Instead, one believer **g** to court
9:25 contest **g** into strict training.
11:21 So one person **g** hungry and
2Co 13:2 That **g** for all those who
Eph 3:19 which **g** far beyond any
Php 4:7 Then God's peace, which **g**
Tit 2:1 live the kind of life that **g** along
Heb 6:19 This confidence **g** into the
9:17 because it **g** into effect only
Heb 11:6 Whoever **g** to God must
Jas 1:24 studies his features, **g** away,
2Pe 2:22 "A dog **g** back to its vomit,"
2:22 that has been washed **g** back
Rev 14:4 follow the lamb wherever he **g**.
14:13 they have done **g** with them."
17:11 kings and **g** to its destruction.
19:3 The smoke **g** up from her

Gog (12)

1Ch 5:4 Shemaiah's son was **G**.
Eze 38:2 "Son of man, turn to **G** from the
38:3 says: I am against you, **G**,
38:14 Tell **G**, 'This is what the
38:18 On the day that **G** attacks the
38:21 I will declare war against **G** on
38:22 I will punish **G** with plagues
39:1 prophesy against **G**.
39:1 says: I am against you, **G**,
39:11 I will give **G** a burial place in
39:11 **G** and his whole army will be
Rev 20:8 out to deceive **G** and Magog,

Gog's (3)

1Ch 5:4 **G** son was Shimei.
Eze 39:11 be called the valley of **G** troops
39:15 bone in the valley of **G** troops

Goiim (3)

Gen 14:1 and King Tidal of **G** —
14:9 of Elam, King Tidal of **G**,
Jos 12:23 the king of **G** in Gilgal,

going (518)

Gen 6:13 Now I'm **g** to destroy them
9:9 "I am **g** to make my promise to
12:7 "I'm **g** to give this land to your
14:6 **g** as far as El Paran on the
15:2 Since I'm **g** to die without
16:8 and where are you **g**?"
18:17 "I shouldn't hide what I am **g** to
18:18 After all, Abraham is **g** to
18:23 "Are you really **g** to sweep
18:24 Are you really **g** to sweep them
19:9 We're **g** to treat you worse than
19:13 because we're **g** to destroy this
19:14 because the LORD is **g** to
20:3 "You're **g** to die because of the
21:18 because I'm **g** to make him into
24:49 Tell me whether or not you're **g**
27:1 Isaac was old and **g** blind,
27:2 I don't know when I'm **g** to die.
28:12 He saw the angels of God **g** up
30:15 Are you also **g** to take my son's
32:17 and where are you **g**,
37:8 "Are you **g** to be our king or rule
37:13 I'm **g** to send you to them."
37:30 What am I **g** to do?"
41:25 told Pharaoh what he's **g** to do.
41:28 Pharaoh what he's **g** to do.
42:5 left with the others who were **g**
42:36 "You're **g** to make me lose all
43:8 Let's get **g** so that we won't
43:16 because they are **g** to eat with
43:18 They're **g** to attack us,
43:25 heard they were **g** to eat there.
46:31 "I'm **g** to Pharaoh to tell him,
Exo 2:14 Are you **g** to kill me as you
4:23 So now I'm **g** to kill your
7:17 I'm **g** to strike the Nile,
8:20 in Pharaoh's way when he's **g**
10:8 "But exactly who will be **g**?"
16:4 LORD said to Moses, "I'm **g**
23:20 "I'm **g** to send a Messenger in
32:10 I'm so angry with them I am **g**
33:15 presence is not **g** (with us),
34:12 live in the land where you're **g**.
Lev 14:34 you come to Canaan that I am **g**
23:10 you come to the land I am **g**
Num 6:7 unclean by **g** near them.
10:29 "We are **g** to the place the
11:15 If this is how you're **g** to treat
17:12 "Now we're **g** to die!
17:13 Are we all **g** to die?"
22:22 became angry that he was **g**.
24:14 Even though I'm **g** back to my

Num 32:6 "Are you **g** to stay here while
Dtr 1:28 Where are we **g** anyway?
1:30 who is **g** ahead of you,
2:4 'You're **g** to pass through the
2:18 "Today you are **g** to pass by
2:24 I'm **g** to hand King Sihon of
2:29 We'll keep **g** until we cross the
3:21 Jordan River⌋ where you're **g**.
4:22 I'm **g** to die in this land and not
4:22 but you're **g** to go across and
4:26 disappear from the land you're **g**
5:33 land that you are **g** to possess.
8:20 The LORD is **g** to destroy other
9:3 God is the one who is **g** ahead
12:29 the nations where you're **g**
20:3 today you're **g** into battle
20:4 LORD your God is **g** with you.
30:18 time in the land that you're **g**
31:6 is the one who is **g** with you.
31:8 The LORD is the one who is **g**
31:13 live in the land that you are **g**
31:16 "Soon you are **g** to lie down in
32:47 time in the land that you are **g**
32:50 this mountain where you're **g**,
Jos 1:2 River into the land that I am **g**
1:11 your God is **g** to give you.'"
1:15 land the LORD your God is **g**
8:20 they could see the city **g** up in
8:21 the city and that it was **g** up
11:6 afraid of them because I am **g**
18:3 "How long are you **g** to waste
22:33 and didn't talk anymore about **g**
Jdg 4:9 for the way you're **g** about this,
6:31 "You're not **g** to defend Baal,
7:14 God is **g** to hand Midian and
12:1 Now we're **g** to burn your house
13:5 You're **g** to become pregnant
13:7 He told me, 'You're **g** to
15:1 He said, "I'm **g** to sleep with
15:3 even though I'm **g** to do
15:7 "If that's how you're **g** to act,
17:9 I'm **g** to live wherever I can find
19:17 And where are you **g**?"
19:18 Now I'm **g** to the LORD's house,
20:40 the whole city **g** up in smoke.
21:19 east of the highway **g** from
Rut 1:10 They said to her, "We are **g**
1Sm 1:14 "How long are you **g** to stay
2:34 What is **g** to happen to your
3:11 "I am **g** to do something in
3:12 On that day I am **g** to do to Eli
9:11 As they were **g** up the hill to
9:27 As they were **g** toward the city
10:3 Keep **g** until you come to the
12:16 this great thing the LORD is **g**
14:1 tell his father ⌊he was **g**⌋.
16:1 "How long are you **g** to mourn
17:20 camp as the army was **g** out
17:55 As Saul watched David **g** out
20:2 You're not **g** to die!
20:39 had no idea what was **g** on,
22:3 you until I know what God is **g**
22:16 your entire family are **g** to die."
23:7 He has trapped himself by **g**
23:10 actually heard that Saul is **g**
23:26 and Saul and his men were **g**
24:4 'I'm **g** to hand your enemy over
28:1 that you and your men will be **g**
29:4 Is this man **g** to try to regain his
30:24 Besides, who is **g** to pay
2Sm 4:6 house as though they were **g**
11:7 were and how the war was **g**.
14:7 We're **g** to destroy the one who
14:14 We are all **g** to die;
14:18 to answer the question I'm **g**
15:20 I don't even know where I'm **g**?
18:2 "I am **g** ⌊into battle⌋ with you,"
18:3 "You're not **g** ⌊with us⌋,"
19:18 in front of the king as he was **g**
1Ki 2:44 The LORD is **g** to pay you
3:12 So I'm **g** to do what you've
11:31 I am **g** to tear the kingdom out
15:17 Ramah to keep anyone from **g**
17:11 As she was **g** to get it,
17:12 I'm **g** to prepare something for
20:6 At this time tomorrow I'm **g** to

1Ki 21:21 So I am **g** to bring evil on you.
2Ki 2:1 When the LORD was **g** to take
2:3 you know that the LORD is **g**
2:5 you know that the LORD is **g**
4:23 "Why are you **g** to him today?
8:10 me that he is actually **g** to die."
14:27 LORD had said he was not **g**
19:7 I'm **g** to put a spirit in him so
20:5 Now I'm **g** to heal you.
20:17 'The days are **g** to come when
21:12 I'm **g** to bring such a disaster
22:16 I'm **g** to bring disaster on this
22:20 That is why I'm **g** to bring you
22:20 I'm **g** to bring you to your grave
22:20 not see any of the disaster I'm **g**
23:8 to the left of anyone **g** through
2Ch 9:21 The king had ships **g** to
16:1 Ramah to keep anyone from **g**
34:24 I'm **g** to bring disaster on this
34:28 That is why I'm **g** to bring you
34:28 I'm **g** to bring you to your grave
34:28 not see any of the disaster I'm **g**
Ezr 9:11 'The land you are **g** to take
Neh 2:19 Are you **g** to rebel against the
2:20 his servants, are **g** to rebuild.
3:15 as far as the stairs **g** down from
4:2 Are they **g** to offer sacrifices?
5:2 need some grain ⌊if we are **g**⌋
9:32 been **g** through as unimportant.
12:27 the wall of Jerusalem was **g**
Est 4:5 out what was **g** on and why.
7:8 The king thought, "Is he even **g**
Job 9:12 Who is **g** to ask him,
31:19 or a poor person **g** naked ....
33:24 'Free them from **g** into the pit.
33:28 has freed my soul from **g** into
Psa 4:2 how long are you **g** to insult my
4:2 How long are you **g** to love
82:2 "How long are you **g** to judge
82:2 How long are you **g** to side
106:23 God said he was **g** to destroy
127:2 eat by getting up early and **g**
Pro 23:19 and keep your mind **g** in the
23:35 I'm **g** to look for another drink."
Ecc 3:15 Whatever is **g** to happen ⌊in
3:18 I thought to myself, "God is **g**
8:16 earth (even **g** without sleep day
9:10 in the grave where you're **g**.
10:7 horses and influential people **g**
Isa 3:1 is **g** to take from Jerusalem and
8:7 That is why the Lord is **g** to
13:9 day of the LORD is **g** to come.
13:17 I'm **g** to stir up the Medes
22:13 tomorrow we're **g** to die."
24:1 The LORD is **g** to turn the earth
26:21 The LORD is **g** to come out
28:16 I am **g** to lay a rock in Zion,
29:14 That is why I am **g** to do
30:27 The name of the LORD is **g** to
30:29 be happy like someone **g** out
37:7 I'm **g** to put a spirit in him so
38:5 I'm **g** to give you 15 more years
38:8 I'm **g** to make the shadow go
38:20 The LORD is **g** to rescue me,
39:6 'The days are **g** to come when
41:15 "I am **g** to make you into a new
41:22 can tell us what's **g** to happen.
41:23 Tell us what's **g** to happen so
43:19 I am **g** to do something new.
43:25 I alone am the one who is **g** to
45:11 Ask me about what is **g** to
45:11 Are you **g** to give me orders
58:13 if you honor it by not **g** your
58:13 by not **g** out when you want,
63:1 **g** forward with great strength?
63:14 Like animals **g** down into a
65:18 and rejoice forever in what I'm **g**
65:18 because I'm **g** to create
Jer 1:15 I am **g** to call every family and
2:18 You won't gain anything by **g** to
2:18 You won't gain anything by **g** to
4:30 You are **g** to be destroyed!
4:30 What are you **g** to do?
5:14 I'm **g** to put my words in your
5:15 Nation of Israel, I'm **g** to bring a
6:19 I'm **g** to bring disaster on these

Jer 6:21 I'm **g** to lay stumbling blocks in
6:22 An army is **g** to come from the
8:17 "I am **g** to send snakes among
9:15 I am **g** to feed these people
10:18 I am **g** to throw out those who
11:11 I'm **g** to bring a disaster on
11:22 I'm **g** to punish them.
12:14 I am **g** to uproot those
13:13 I'm **g** to make everyone who
16:9 I'm **g** to put a stop to the
16:16 "I'm **g** to send for many
18:11 I'm **g** to prepare a disaster and
19:3 I'm **g** to bring such a disaster
19:15 I'm **g** to bring on this city and
20:4 I'm **g** to make you terrify
21:4 I'm **g** to take your weapons
21:8 I am **g** to give you the choice of
25:9 so I'm **g** to send for all the
25:9 I'm **g** to destroy them and turn
25:16 wars that I'm **g** to send them.
25:27 the wars that I'm **g** to send you.'
25:29 I am **g** to bring disaster on the
28:16 I'm **g** to remove you from the
29:17 I'm **g** to send them wars,
29:21 I'm **g** to hand them over to King
29:32 not see the blessings that I'm **g**
30:10 I'm **g** to rescue you from a
30:10 I'm **g** to rescue your
30:18 I'm **g** to bring the captives back
32:3 I'm **g** to hand this city over to
32:7 is **g** to come to you and say,
32:28 I'm **g** to hand this city over to
32:29 who made me furious by **g** up
32:37 I am **g** to gather the people from
34:2 I'm **g** to hand this city over to
34:17 Now I am **g** to free you,"
34:22 I am **g** to give a command,"
35:17 I am **g** to bring on Judah and on
38:14 "I'm **g** to ask you a question,"
39:16 I'm **g** to carry out my threat
40:10 I'm **g** to live in Mizpah and
43:10 I'm **g** to send for my servant
44:11 I'm **g** to bring disaster on you
44:27 I am **g** to watch over them.
44:27 I am **g** to watch over them to
44:30 I'm **g** to hand Pharaoh Hophra,
45:5 because I'm **g** to bring disaster
46:25 "I'm **g** to punish Amon,
46:27 I'm **g** to rescue you and your
49:5 I am **g** to bring terror on you
49:35 I'm **g** to break the bows of
50:9 I am **g** to stir up an alliance of
50:18 I am **g** to punish the king of
50:41 "People are **g** to come from the
51:36 I am **g** to take up your cause
Eze 4:3 toward the city as if you were **g**
4:16 I am **g** to cut off the bread
6:3 I am **g** to attack you with a
9:1 those who are **g** to punish this
11:5 what's **g** through your mind.
12:3 as if you were **g** into exile.
12:4 as if you were **g** into exile.
12:4 like a captive **g** into exile.
12:7 bags as if I were **g** into exile.
20:8 So I was **g** to pour out my fury
20:13 So I was **g** to pour out my fury
20:21 So I was **g** to pour out my fury
20:29 worship site you're **g** to?'" (So
21:4 I'm **g** to kill the righteous
21:26 Things are **g** to change.
22:19 That is why I'm **g** to gather you
23:22 I'm **g** to stir up your lovers
23:28 I'm **g** to hand you over to those
24:16 with one blow I'm **g** to take
24:21 I'm **g** to dishonor my holy place.
25:4 That is why I'm **g** to hand you
25:9 That is why I'm **g** to open up
25:16 I'm **g** to use my power against
26:7 From the north I'm **g** to bring
28:7 That is why I am **g** to bring
29:8 I am **g** to attack you with a
29:19 I'm **g** to give Egypt to King
31:14 Every tree is **g** to die and go
40:4 attention to everything I'm **g**
44:5 and listen to everything I'm **g** to
44:25 himself unclean by **g** near

Dan 2:28 Nebuchadnezzar what is **g**
2:29 told you what is **g** to happen.
Hos 2:14 "That is why I'm **g** to win her
Joe 1:8 for the man she was **g** to marry.
2:19 "I am **g** to send grain,
3:7 I am **g** to make them leave the
Amo 2:13 I am **g** to crush you as an
3:2 That is why I am **g** to punish
4:2 the time is **g** to come when you
6:11 The LORD is **g** to give the
6:14 I am **g** to lead a nation to attack
7:8 Then the Lord said, "I'm **g** to
8:11 The days are **g** to come,
9:9 I'm **g** to give the order.
9:13 The days are **g** to come,
Jnh 1:3 the LORD by **g** to Tarshish.
1:3 and found a ship **g** to Tarshish.
Mic 1:3 The LORD is **g** to come from
1:3 He is **g** to come down and step
Hab 1:5 I am **g** to do something in your
1:6 I am **g** to send the Babylonians,
2:7 rise up and those who are **g**
Hag 2:6 I am **g** to shake the sky and the
2:21 'I am **g** to shake the heavens
Zec 1:21 "What are they **g** to do?"
2:2 asked him, "Where are you **g**?"
2:2 He answered, "I am **g** to
2:9 I'm **g** to shake my fist at the
2:10 I'm **g** to come and live among
3:8 I'm **g** to bring my servant,
5:11 He answered me, "They are **g**
6:1 chariots **g** out from between
6:5 They are **g** out after standing in
6:6 the black horses is **g** toward
6:6 ones are **g** toward the south."
8:7 I am **g** to save my people from
8:20 from many cities are **g** to come.
8:21 "Let's make a habit of **g** to ask
8:21 LORD of Armies. I'm also **g**."
11:6 I am **g** to hand the people over
12:2 "I'm **g** to make Jerusalem like a
14:1 A day is **g** to come for the
Mal 2:3 "I'm **g** to punish your
2:3 I'm **g** to spread excrement on
3:1 "I'm **g** to send my messenger,
4:5 "I'm **g** to send you the prophet
Mat 6:31 'What are we **g** to eat?'
6:31 or 'What are we **g** to drink?'
6:31 or 'What are we **g** to wear?'
8:25 Save us! We're **g** to die!"
8:31 "If you're **g** to force us out,
14:24 it was **g** against the wind.
17:12 In the same way they're **g** to
20:18 "We're **g** to Jerusalem.
20:22 the cup that I'm **g** to drink?"
20:26 But that's not the way it's **g** to
21:31 and prostitutes are **g** into
25:8 Our lamps are **g** out.'
25:14 of heaven is like a man **g**
26:10 Jesus knew what was **g** on,
26:21 One of you is **g** to betray me."
26:24 The Son of Man is **g** to die as
27:40 and said, "You were **g** to tear
28:7 He's **g** ahead of them into
Mar 1:16 As he was **g** along the Sea of
2:23 worship Jesus was **g** through
4:38 you care that we're **g** to die?"
6:31 people were coming and **g**,
6:48 because they were **g** against
10:32 ⌊that he was **g** to Jerusalem⌋.
10:32 began to tell them what was **g**
10:33 "We're **g** to Jerusalem.
10:38 drink the cup that I'm **g** to drink
10:38 baptism that I'm **g** to receive?"
10:39 drink the cup that I'm **g** to drink.
10:39 baptism that I'm **g** to receive.
10:43 But that's not the way it's **g** to
13:1 As Jesus was **g** out of the
14:18 One of you is **g** to betray me,
14:21 The Son of Man is **g** to die as
15:29 You were **g** to tear down God's
16:2 On Sunday they were **g** to the
16:7 and Peter that he's **g** ahead
Luk 1:59 They were **g** to name him
8:24 We're **g** to die!" Then he got up
12:54 'There's **g** to be a rainstorm,'
Luk 12:55 you say, 'It's **g** to be hot,'
13:23 are only a few people **g** to be
14:31 "Or suppose a king is **g** to war
18:31 "We're **g** to Jerusalem.
18:36 When he heard the crowd **g** by,
19:14 say ⌊to the person who was **g**
22:22 The Son of Man is **g** to die the
22:26 But you're not **g** to be that way!
22:49 saw what was **g** to happen.
23:16 So I'm **g** to have him whipped
23:22 So I'm **g** to have him whipped
24:13 two of Jesus' disciples were **g**
24:28 the village where they were **g**,
24:28 Jesus acted as if he were **g**
Jon 1:51 open and God's angels **g** up
2:20 Do you really think you're **g** to
3:8 comes from or where it's **g**.
3:26 and everyone is **g** to him!"
4:11 So where are you **g** to get this
6:21 the shore where they were **g**.
6:30 "What miracle are you **g** to
6:30 What are you **g** to do?
7:8 I'm not **g** to this festival right
7:34 You can't go where I'm **g**."
7:36 and 'You can't go where I'm **g**'?"
8:14 I came from and where I'm **g**.
8:14 I came from or where I'm **g**.
8:21 He said, "I'm **g** away,
8:21 You can't go where I'm **g**."
8:22 "Is he **g** to kill himself?
8:22 'You can't go where I'm **g**'?"
10:13 is concerned about what he's **g**
10:33 "We're **g** to stone you to death,
11:11 and I'm **g** to Bethany to wake
11:31 They thought that she was **g** to
12:4 who was **g** to betray him,
12:33 indicated how he was **g** to die.
12:35 don't know where they're **g**.
13:3 God and was **g** back to God.
13:6 are you **g** to wash my feet?"
13:11 (Jesus knew who was **g** to
13:21 One of you is **g** to betray me!"
13:33 but you can't go where I'm **g**.
13:36 where are you **g**?"
13:36 now to the place where I'm **g**.
14:2 would I have told you that I'm **g**
14:4 way to the place where I am **g**."
14:5 we don't know where you're **g**.
14:12 because I am **g** to the Father.
14:22 has happened that you are **g**
14:28 heard me tell you, 'I'm **g** away,
14:28 you would be glad that I'm **g** to
16:5 "Now I'm **g** to the one who sent
16:5 of you asks me where I'm **g**.
16:7 good for you that I'm **g** away.
16:10 because I'm **g** to the Father and
16:17 and that he's **g** to the Father."
16:28 Again, ⌊as I've said,⌋ I'm **g** to
18:4 knew everything that was **g**
19:10 "Aren't you **g** to answer me?
20:17 'I am **g** to my Father and your
21:3 to the others, "I'm **g** fishing."
21:3 "We're **g** with you."
21:20 who is **g** to betray you?"
Act 1:6 is this the time when you're **g**
3:1 Peter and John were **g** to the
3:2 people **g** into the courtyard.
7:25 understand that God was **g**
7:49 What kind of house are you **g**
8:36 As they were **g** along the road,
9:32 When Peter was **g** around to all
12:6 The night before Herod was **g**
12:20 They were **g** to meet with
13:41 I am **g** to do something in your
13:46 we are now **g** to turn to people
15:3 As they were **g** through
16:16 One day when we were **g** to
16:37 Now are they **g** to throw us out
16:37 There's no way they're **g** to get
17:23 As I was **g** through your city
17:31 He has set a day when he is **g**
18:6 From now on I'm **g** to people
19:31 not to risk **g** into the theater.
20:3 When Paul was **g** to board a
20:13 we were **g** to pick up Paul.
21:2 a ship that was **g** to Phoenicia,
Act 22:5 I was **g** there to tie up believers
22:29 the soldiers who were **g** to
23:20 They're **g** to make it look as
23:27 seized this man and were **g**
27:2 The ship was **g** to stop at ports
27:10 "Men, we're **g** to face a
27:30 sea and pretended they were **g**
28:10 and when we were **g** to set
Rom 8:13 corrupt nature, you are **g** to die.
15:25 Right now I'm **g** to Jerusalem to
1Co 3:15 it will be like **g** through a fire.
5:1 aware that there is sexual sin **g**
6:2 So if you're **g** to judge the
15:32 tomorrow we're **g** to die!"
16:5 (I will be **g** through Macedonia
2Co 12:6 But I'm **g** to spare you so that
Gal 4:24 I'm **g** to use these historical
Php 2:23 soon as I see how things are **g**
1Th 3:4 ahead of time that we were **g**
1Ti 1:3 When I was **g** to the province
5:24 **g** ahead of them to judgment.
2Ti 4:1 who is **g** to judge those who
Heb 1:14 who are **g** to receive salvation.
6:1 we should stop **g** over the
11:8 knowing where he was **g**.
Jas 2:12 and act as people who are **g**
1Pe 5:9 the world are **g** through
2Pe 2:6 to ungodly people of what is **g**
1Jn 2:11 don't know where they're **g**,
Rev 1:19 and what is **g** to happen after
2:10 of what you are **g** to suffer.
2:10 The devil is **g** to throw some of
2:22 I'm **g** to throw her into a
3:16 I'm **g** to spit you out of my
10:4 I was **g** to write it down.
12:4 front of the woman who was **g**

Golan (4)

Dtr 4:43 and **G** in Bashan for the tribe of
Jos 20:8 and **G** in Bashan from the tribe
21:27 **G** in Bashan (a city of refuge
1Ch 6:71 descendants received **G**

gold (475)

Gen 2:11 Havilah, where there is **g**.
2:12 (The **g** of that land is pure.
13:2 he had livestock, silver, and **g**.
24:22 the man took out a **g** nose ring
24:22 two **g** bracelets weighing four
24:35 sheep and cattle, silver and **g**,
24:53 The servant took out **g** and
41:42 and put a **g** chain around his
44:8 silver or **g** from your master's
Exo 3:22 home for silver and **g** jewelry
11:2 for silver and **g** jewelry."
12:35 and asked the Egyptians for **g**
20:23 of silver or **g** for yourselves.
25:3 them: **g**, silver, and bronze,
25:11 Cover it with pure **g** inside and
25:11 and put a **g** molding around it.
25:12 Cast four **g** rings for it,
25:13 and cover them with **g**.
25:17 ark out of pure **g** 45 inches long
25:18 two angels out of hammered **g**
25:19 of mercy out of one piece of **g**.
25:24 Cover it with pure **g**,
25:24 and put a **g** molding around it.
25:25 and put a **g** molding around the
25:26 Make four **g** rings for it,
25:28 cover them with **g**,
25:29 for the table out of pure **g**,
25:31 a lamp stand out of pure **g**.
25:31 out of one piece of **g**.
25:36 of the same piece of pure **g** as
25:38 must be made of pure **g**.
25:39 Use 75 pounds of pure **g** to
26:6 Make 50 **g** fasteners.
26:29 Cover the frames with **g**,
26:29 make **g** rings to hold the
26:29 and cover the crossbars with **g**.
26:32 Use **g** hooks to hang it on four
26:32 of acacia wood covered with **g**,
26:37 screen and cover them with **g**.
26:37 Make **g** hooks for this screen.
28:5 They must use **g**, violet,
28:6 Creatively work **g**,

Exo 28:11 Mount them in **g** settings,
28:13 Make **g** settings
28:14 and two chains of pure **g**,
28:15 Make it out of **g**, violet, purple,
28:20 Mount them in **g** settings.
28:22 make chains out of pure **g**,
28:23 Make two **g** rings for the
28:24 Then fasten the two **g** ropes to
28:26 Make two **g** rings, and fasten
28:27 Make two ⌊more⌋ **g** rings,
28:33 and bright red yarn with **g** bells
28:34 a **g** bell alternating with a
28:36 medallion out of pure **g**,
30:3 Cover all of it with pure **g** — the
30:3 Put a **g** molding around it.
30:4 Make two **g** rings, and put them
30:5 and cover them with **g**.
31:4 a master artist familiar with **g**,
31:8 the pure ⌊**g**⌋ lamp stand and all
32:2 and daughters take off the **g**
32:3 So all the people took off their **g**
32:4 After he had worked on the **g**
32:24 So I told them to take off any **g**
32:31 gods out of **g** for themselves.
35:5 LORD: **g**, silver, and bronze,
35:22 brought all kinds of **g** jewelry:
35:22 They took these gifts of **g** and
35:32 a master artist familiar with **g**,
36:13 They also made 50 **g** fasteners.
36:34 They covered the frames with **g**
36:34 with gold and made **g** rings
36:34 covered the crossbars with **g**.
36:36 for it and covered them with **g**.
36:36 They made **g** hooks for the
36:38 the posts and the bands with **g**,
37:2 He covered it with pure **g**
37:2 and put a **g** molding around it.
37:3 He cast four **g** rings for its four
37:4 wood and covered them with **g**.
37:6 out of pure **g** 45 inches long
37:7 two angels out of hammered **g**
37:8 mercy out of one piece ⌊of **g**⌋.
37:11 He covered it with pure **g** and
37:11 and put a **g** molding around it.
37:12 it and put a **g** molding around
37:13 He cast four **g** rings for it and
37:15 wood and were covered with **g**.
37:16 them were made out of pure **g**.
37:17 the lamp stand out of pure **g**.
37:17 out of one piece ⌊of **g**⌋.
37:22 of the same piece of pure **g** as
37:23 incense burners out of pure **g**.
37:24 out of 75 pounds of pure **g**.
37:26 He covered all of it with pure **g**
37:26 he put a **g** molding around it.
37:27 He made two **g** rings and put
37:28 wood and covered them with **g**.
38:24 The total amount of **g** from the
39:2 out of fine linen yarn and **g**,
39:3 They hammered the **g** into thin
39:3 They twisted the **g** into threads,
39:6 the onyx stones in **g** settings,
39:8 It was made out of **g**,
39:13 The stones were mounted in **g**
39:15 they made chains out of pure **g**,
39:16 They made two **g** settings and
39:16 gold settings and two **g** rings
39:17 They fastened the two **g** ropes
39:19 They made two **g** rings and
39:20 They made two ⌊more⌋ **g** rings
39:25 They made bells out of pure **g**
39:26 A **g** bell alternated with a
39:30 (the holy crown) out of pure **g**
39:37 the pure ⌊**g**⌋ lamp stand with
39:38 the **g** altar, the anointing oil,
40:5 Put the **g** altar for incense in
40:26 Moses put the **g** altar in the tent
Lev 8:9 the **g** medallion (the holy
24:4 on the pure **g** lamp stand lit
24:6 of six each on the **g** table
Num 4:11 a violet cloth over the **g** altar
7:14 He also brought a **g** dish that
7:20 He also brought a **g** dish that
7:26 He also brought a **g** dish that
7:32 He also brought a **g** dish that
7:38 He also brought a **g** dish that
Num 7:44 He also brought a **g** dish that
7:50 He also brought a **g** dish that
7:56 He also brought a **g** dish that
7:62 He also brought a **g** dish that
7:68 He also brought a **g** dish that
7:74 He also brought a **g** dish that
7:80 He also brought a **g** dish that
7:84 silver bowls, and 12 **g** dishes.
7:86 The 12 **g** dishes filled with
7:86 Together all the **g** dishes
8:4 was hammered out of **g**.
22:18 palace filled with silver and **g**,
24:13 palace filled with silver and **g**,
31:22 Any **g**, silver, bronze, iron, tin,
31:50 LORD the **g** jewelry that each
31:51 **g** articles from them.
31:52 All the **g** contributed to the
31:54 priest Eleazar took the **g** from
Dtr 7:25 ever long for the silver and **g**
8:13 herds and flocks, silver and **g**,
17:17 never own a lot of **g** and silver.
29:17 of wood, stone, silver, and **g**.
Jos 6:19 All the silver and **g** and
6:24 But they put the silver and **g**
7:21 and a bar of **g** weighing about
7:24 the silver, the robe, the bar of **g**,
22:8 silver, **g**, bronze, iron,
Jdg 8:24 Ishmaelites, wore **g** earrings.)
8:26 The **g** earrings Gideon had
8:27 Then Gideon used the **g** to
1Sm 6:4 The priests answered, "Five **g**
6:4 "Five gold tumors and five **g**
6:8 Put the **g** objects which you're
6:11 the box containing the **g** mice
6:15 which contained the **g** objects
6:17 The **g** hemorrhoids which the
6:18 And the number of **g** mice was
2Sm 1:24 who put **g** jewelry on your
8:7 David took the **g** shields that
8:10 Joram brought articles of **g**,
8:11 along with the silver and **g** he
12:30 He took the **g** crown from the
21:4 "We do not want silver or **g**
1Ki 6:20 and the cedar altar with pure **g**.
6:21 of the temple with pure **g**.
6:21 which was covered with **g**.
6:22 inside of the temple with **g**.
6:22 altar in the inner room with **g**.
6:28 He covered the angels with **g**.
6:30 rooms of the temple with **g**.
6:32 them and covered them with **g**.
6:32 The **g** was hammered onto the
6:35 He evenly covered them with **g**.
7:48 the LORD's temple: the **g** altar,
7:48 the **g** table on which the bread
7:49 lamp stands of pure **g** (five on
7:49 room), flowers, lamps, **g** tongs,
7:50 incense burners of pure **g**,
7:50 the **g** sockets for the doors of
7:51 his father David — the silver, **g**,
9:11 lumber and **g** as he wanted.)
9:14 the king 9,000 pounds of **g**.
9:28 got 31,500 pounds of **g**,
10:2 a very large quantity of **g**,
10:10 the king 9,000 pounds of **g**,
10:11 Hiram's fleet that brought **g**
10:14 The **g** that came to Solomon in
10:15 not counting ⌊the **g**⌋ which
10:16 large shields of hammered **g**,
10:16 15 pounds of **g** on each shield.
10:17 small shields of hammered **g**,
10:17 using four pounds of **g** on each
10:18 and covered it with fine **g**.
10:21 King Solomon's cups were **g**,
10:21 Forest of Lebanon were fine **g**.
10:22 Tarshish fleet would bring **g**,
10:25 articles of silver and **g**,
14:26 He took all the **g** shields
15:15 LORD's temple the silver, the **g**,
15:18 all the silver and **g** that was left
15:19 you a present of silver and **g**.
20:3 Your silver and **g** are mine.
20:5 to you: 'Your silver, **g**, wives,
20:7 and **g**, I didn't refuse him."
22:48 ships to go to Ophir for **g**.
2Ki 5:5 of silver, 150 pounds of **g**,
2Ki 7:8 and carried off the silver, **g**,
12:13 or any other **g** and silver
12:18 and all the **g** that could be
14:14 He took all the **g**, silver, and all
16:8 Ahaz took the silver and **g** he
18:14 of silver and 2,250 pounds of **g**.
18:16 Hezekiah stripped ⌊the **g**⌋ off
18:16 had them covered ⌊with **g**.⌋)
18:16 He gave the **g** to the king of
20:13 silver, **g**, balsam, fine olive oil,
23:33 of silver and 75 pounds of **g**.
23:35 Pharaoh the silver and the **g**.
23:35 could get the silver and **g** from
24:13 Nebuchadnezzar stripped the **g**
25:15 that were made of **g** or silver.
1Ch 18:7 David took the **g** shields that
18:11 dedicated all the articles of **g**,
18:11 along with the silver and **g** he
20:2 He took the **g** crown from the
21:25 15 pounds of **g** for that place.
22:14 are 7,500,000 pounds of **g**,
22:16 The **g**, silver, bronze, and iron
28:14 specified the weight of **g**
28:15 the weight of the **g** lamp stands
28:15 and their **g** lamps (⌊that is,⌋
28:15 the weight of **g** for each lamp
28:16 the weight of **g** for each table
28:17 the pure **g** for the forks,
28:17 the weight of each **g** bowl,
28:18 and the refined **g** for the altar of
28:18 the **g** angels with their wings
29:2 of my God: **g** for gold objects,
29:2 of my God: gold for **g** objects,
29:3 I have a personal treasury of **g**
29:4 There are 225,000 pounds of **g**
29:5 to make **g** objects,
29:7 gave 375,186 pounds of **g**,
2Ch 1:15 The king made silver and **g** as
2:7 has the skill to work with **g**,
2:14 knows how to work with **g**,
3:4 its inside walls with pure **g**.
3:5 overlaid it with fine **g**,
3:6 it and used **g** from Parvaim.
3:7 and the doors with **g**,
3:8 it with 45,000 pounds of fine **g**.
3:9 The **g** nails weighed 20
3:9 the upper rooms with **g**.
3:10 and covered them with **g**.
4:7 Huram made ten **g** lamp stands
4:8 And he made 100 **g** bowls.
4:19 for God's temple: the **g** altar,
4:19 the **g** tables on which the bread
4:20 and lamps of pure **g** (to burn as
4:21 flowers, lamps, pure **g** tongs,
4:22 incense burners of pure **g**,
4:22 the **g** entrance to the temple,
4:22 the **g** doors of the inner ⌊room⌋
4:22 and the **g** doors of the temple.
5:1 his father David — the silver, **g**,
8:18 got 33,750 pounds of **g**,
9:1 a large quantity of **g**,
9:9 the king 9,000 pounds of **g**,
9:10 who brought **g** from Ophir also
9:13 The **g** that came to Solomon in
9:14 not counting ⌊the **g**⌋ which the
9:14 of the land also brought **g**
9:15 large shields of hammered **g**,
9:15 15 pounds of **g** on each shield.
9:16 small shields of hammered **g**,
9:16 using 7 ½ pounds of **g** on
9:17 and covered it with pure **g**.
9:18 which had a **g** footstool
9:20 King Solomon's cups were **g**,
9:20 Forest of Lebanon were fine **g**.
9:21 Tarshish ships would bring **g**,
9:24 articles of silver and **g**,
12:9 He took the **g** shields Solomon
13:8 and you have the **g** calves that
13:11 The lamps on the **g** lamp stand
15:18 God's temple the silver, the **g**,
16:2 all the silver and **g** that was left
16:3 I'm sending you silver and **g**.
21:3 **g**, and other expensive things,
24:14 They made dishes and **g** and
25:24 He took all the **g**,
32:27 **g**, precious stones, spices,

2Ch 36:3 of silver and 75 pounds of g.
Ezr 1:4 silver, g, supplies, livestock,
1:6 articles made from silver and g,
1:9 This is the inventory: g dishes:
1:10 g bowls: 30 other silver bowls:
1:11 The g and silver utensils
2:69 1,030 pounds of g,
5:14 out of a temple in Babylon the g
6:5 out of a temple in Babylon the g
7:15 you must take the silver and g
7:16 Take any silver and g that you
7:18 with the rest of the silver and g.
8:25 silver, the g, and the utensils.
8:26 7,500 pounds of g,
8:27 20 g bowls weighing 18
8:27 that were as precious as g.
8:28 The silver and g are freewill
8:30 silver, the g, and the utensils.
8:33 we weighed the silver, the g,
Neh 7:70 nearly 18 pounds of g,
7:71 337 pounds of g and 3,215
7:72 contributed 337 pounds of g,
Est 1:6 G and silver couches were on
8:15 white robe, a large g crown,
Job 3:15 be with princes who had g,
22:24 and lay your g down in the
22:24 and put your g from Ophir
22:25 Almighty will become your g
23:10 I'll come out as pure as g.
28:1 and a place where g is refined.
28:6 Its dust contains g.
28:15 cannot obtain it with solid g
28:16 It can't be bought with the g
28:17 Neither g nor glass can equal
28:17 Nor can g ornaments,
28:19 for ⌊any amount of⌋ pure g.
31:24 "If I put my confidence in g or
31:24 in gold or said to fine g,
42:11 him some money and a g ring.
Psa 19:10 They are more desirable than g,
19:10 than gold, even the finest g.
21:3 a crown of fine g on his head.
45:9 hand and wears g from Ophir.
45:13 dress is embroidered with g.
68:13 its feathers with yellow g.
72:15 May the g from Sheba be given
105:37 Israel out with silver and g,
115:4 idols are made of silver and g.
119:72 than thousands in g or silver.
119:127 commandments more than g,
119:127 than gold, more than pure g.
135:15 are made of silver and g.
Pro 3:14 Its yield is better than fine g.
8:10 knowledge rather than fine g,
8:19 What I produce is better than g,
8:19 is better than gold, pure g.
11:22 ⌊Like⌋ a g ring in a pig's snout,
16:16 it is to gain wisdom than g,
17:3 silver and the smelter for g,
20:15 There are g and plenty of
22:1 is better than silver or g.
25:12 ⌊Like⌋ a g ring and a fine gold
25:12 gold ring and a fine g ornament,
27:21 silver and the smelter for g,
Ecc 2:8 silver and g for myself.
Sos 1:11 We will make g ornaments
3:10 out of silver, its top out of g,
5:11 His head is the finest g.
5:14 His hands are disks of g set
5:15 marble set on bases of pure g.
Isa 2:7 land is filled with silver and g,
2:20 the silver and g idols that they
13:12 harder to find than pure g
13:12 more rare than g from Ophir.
13:17 silver and aren't happy with g.
31:7 the silver and g idols that your
39:2 silver, g, balsam, fine olive oil,
40:19 Goldsmiths cover them with g.
46:6 People pour g out of their bags
60:6 They will bring g and incense.
60:9 Their silver and their g comes
60:17 I will bring g instead of bronze.
Jer 4:30 in red and put on g jewelry?
10:4 decorate them with silver and g
10:9 Tarshish and g from Uphaz.
52:19 that were made of g or silver.
Lam 4:1 "Look how the g has become
4:1 The fine g has changed!
4:2 are worth their weight in fine g,
Eze 7:19 will throw their silver and g into
7:19 Their silver and g won't be able
7:19 Their silver and g caused them
16:13 So you wore g and silver
16:17 You took your beautiful g and
27:22 and g for your merchandise.
28:4 You saved g and silver in your
28:13 were made of g when you were
38:13 large amounts of silver and g
Dan 2:32 this statue was made of fine g.
2:35 and g were smashed.
2:38 You are the head of g.
2:45 iron, bronze, clay, silver, and g.
3:1 made a g statue 90 feet
3:5 bow down and worship the g
3:7 g statue King Nebuchadnezzar
3:10 down and worship the g statue.
3:14 or worship the g statue that
3:15 down and worship the g statue
3:18 or worship the g statue that you
5:2 Belshazzar ordered that the g
5:3 So the servants brought the g
5:4 praised their gods made of g,
5:7 wear a g chain on his neck,
5:16 wear a g chain on your neck,
5:23 g, bronze, iron, wood, or stone.
5:29 in purple and wear a g chain
10:5 and he had a belt made of g
11:8 utensils of silver and g back
11:38 With g, silver, precious stones,
11:43 He will control g and silver
Hos 2:8 gave her plenty of silver and g,
8:4 with their own silver and g.
Joe 3:5 You took my silver and my g.
Nah 2:9 Steal the g! There is no end to
Hab 2:19 It's covered with g and silver,
Zep 1:18 Their silver and their g will not
Hag 2:8 is mine, and the g is mine,
Zec 4:2 I answered, "I see a solid g
4:12 pipes that are pouring out g?"
6:11 Take the silver and g,
9:3 It piled up silver like dust and g
13:9 I will test them as g is tested.
14:14 a very large amount of g,
Mal 3:3 refine them like g and silver.
Mat 2:11 and offered him gifts of g,
10:9 "Don't take any g, silver,
23:16 But to swear an oath by the g
23:17 What is more important, the g
23:17 temple that made the g holy?
Act 17:29 is like an image made from g,
20:33 anyone's silver, g, or clothes.
1Co 3:12 build on this foundation with g,
1Ti 2:9 hair styles or the g jewelry,
2Ti 2:20 objects made of g and silver,
Heb 9:4 It contained the g incense
9:4 completely covered with g.
9:4 In the ark were the g jar filled
Jas 2:2 One man is wearing g rings
5:3 Your g and silver are corroded,
1Pe 1:7 as fire tests how genuine g is.
1:7 faith is more precious than g,
1:18 of silver or g which can
3:3 g jewelry, or clothes.
Rev 1:12 I saw seven g lamp stands.
1:13 He wore a g belt around his
1:20 and the seven g lamp stands is
2:1 the seven g lamp stands,
3:18 I advise you: Buy g purified in
4:4 They had g crowns on their
5:8 Each held a harp and a g bowl
8:3 Another angel came with a g
8:3 of incense to offer on the g altar
9:7 have crowns that looked like g
9:13 the four horns of the g altar
9:20 demons and idols made of g,
14:14 He had a g crown on his head
15:6 shining linen with g belts
15:7 gave seven g bowls full
17:4 g jewelry, gems, and pearls.
17:4 she was holding a g cup filled
18:12 No one buys their cargo of g,
18:16 g jewelry, gems, and pearls.
Rev 21:15 to me had a g measuring stick
21:18 The city was made of pure g,
21:21 of the city was made of pure g,

gold-covered (1)

Isa 30:22 idols and your g statues.

golden (13)

1Ki 6:21 He put g chains across the
12:28 the king made two g calves.
2Ki 10:29 of⌋ the g calves that were
Est 1:7 People drank from g cups.
4:11 Only if the king holds out the g
5:2 So the king held out the g
8:4 The king held out his g scepter
Job 37:22 A g light comes from the north.
Pro 1:9 and a ⌊g⌋ chain around your
25:11 ⌊Like⌋ g apples in silver
Ecc 12:6 the g bowl is broken,
Jer 51:7 Babylon was a g cup in the
Zec 4:12 next to the two g pipes that are

goldsmith (2)

Neh 3:8 son, a g, made repairs.
Isa 46:6 They hire a g. He makes it into

goldsmiths (5)

Neh 3:31 him Malchiah, one of the g,
3:32 The g and merchants made
Isa 40:19 G cover them with gold.
41:7 Craftsmen encourage g.
Jer 10:9 Craftsmen and g shape these

Golgotha (3)

Mat 27:33 They came to a place called G
Mar 15:22 They took Jesus to G (which
Jon 19:17 Hebrew this place is called G.)

Goliath (10)

1Sm 17:4 His name was G from Gath.
17:8 G stood and called to the
17:23 champion, G from Gath,
17:24 all the men of Israel saw G,
17:27 who kills G would be treated.
19:5 life and killed the Philistine G,
21:9 "The sword of G the Philistine,
22:10 the sword of G the Philistine."
2Sm 21:19 Bethlehem, killed G of Gath.
1Ch 20:5 the brother of G from Gath.

Goliath's (4)

1Sm 17:49 stone sank into G forehead,
17:51 He took G sword, pulled it out
17:54 but he kept G armor in his tent.
2Sm 21:19 (The shaft of G spear was like

Gomer (6)

Gen 10:2 Japheth's descendants were G,
1Ch 1:5 Japheth's descendants were G,
Eze 38:6 G will come with all its troops
Hos 1:3 So Hosea married G,
1:6 G became pregnant again and
1:8 After G had weaned Lo

Gomer's (2)

Gen 10:3 G descendants were
1Ch 1:6 G descendants were

Gomorrah (24)

Gen 10:19 then toward Sodom, G, Admah,
13:10 destroyed Sodom and G.)
14:2 of Sodom, King Birsha of G,
14:8 Then the kings of Sodom, G,
14:10 the kings of Sodom and G fled,
14:11 possessions of Sodom and G,
18:20 "Sodom and G have many
19:24 out of heaven on Sodom and G.
19:28 he looked toward Sodom and G
Dtr 29:23 G, Admah, and Zeboiim,
32:32 Sodom and from the fields of G.
Isa 1:9 have been like Sodom and G.
1:10 from our God, you people of G!
13:19 will be like Sodom and G
Jer 23:14 live in Jerusalem are like G."
49:18 Edom will be like Sodom, G,
50:40 Babylon will be like Sodom, G,

Amo 4:11 as I destroyed Sodom and **G**.
Zep 2:9 Ammon will become like **G**:
Mat 10:15 be better for Sodom and **G** than
Rom 9:29 have been like Sodom and **G**."
2Pe 2:6 the cities of Sodom and **G**
2:8 the people of Sodom and **G**.
Jud 1:7 happened to Sodom and **G**

gone (164)

Gen 5:24 then he was **g** because God
8:8 to see if the water was **g** from
8:11 the water was **g** from the earth.
15:17 The sun had **g** down,
19:4 Before they had **g** to bed,
21:15 water in the container was **g**,
26:10 the people might have easily **g**
27:45 When your brother's anger is **g**
28:11 because the sun had **g** down.
35:3 been with me wherever I've **g**."
37:12 His brothers had **g** to take care
39:13 she realized that he had **g**
44:4 They had not **g** far from the city
44:28 One is **g**, and I said, "He must
47:15 in Egypt and Canaan was **g**,
47:18 "you know that our money is **g**,
50:14 and everyone who had **g** there
Exo 14:29 Meanwhile, the Israelites had **g**
15:19 However, the Israelites had **g**
16:14 When the dew was **g**,
34:24 land while you're **g** three times
Lev 14:48 house clean. The mildew is **g**.
Num 11:26 the other leaders but hadn't **g**
13:31 But the men who had **g** with
16:3 "You've **g** far enough!
16:7 You've **g** far enough!"
23:3 your burnt offering while I'm **g**.
31:17 Midianite woman who has **g**
31:18 every girl who has never **g**
31:21 soldiers who had **g** into battle,
31:35 women who had never **g**
32:13 in the LORD's presence was **g**.
36:4 our ancestors' tribe will be **g**."
Dtr 32:36 he sees that their strength is **g**
Jos 3:4 have not **g** this way before."
10:24 officers who had **g** with him,
Jdg 18:14 Then the five men who had **g**
18:17 The five men who had **g** to spy
18:22 When they had already **g** some
19:18 I had **g** to Bethlehem in Judah.
21:11 Claim every female who has **g**
21:12 women who had never **g**
Rut 1:15 your sister-in-law has **g** back to
1Sm 3:3 God's temple hadn't **g** out yet,
4:21 "Israel's glory is **g**," because
4:22 "Israel's glory is **g** because the
9:7 the food in our sacks is **g**?
11:1 from the Ammonites and **g**
13:23 Now, Philistine troops had **g**
30:2 other prisoners⌋ and **g** away.
30:22 and worthless man who had **g**
2Sm 5:24 the LORD has **g** ahead
6:13 of the LORD had **g** six steps,
16:1 When David had **g** over the top
1Ki 2:41 Shimei had **g** from Jerusalem
12:1 because all Israel had **g**
14:10 burn like manure until it is **g**.
2Ki 4:13 since she has **g** to a lot of
5:19 left him and **g** some distance,
20:4 Isaiah hadn't **g** as far as the
20:11 the shadow that had **g** down
23:9 worship sites had never **g**
1Ch 14:15 fight because God has **g** ahead
17:5 but I've **g** from tent site to tent
2Ch 10:1 because all Israel had **g**
Neh 2:6 "How long will you be **g**,
2:16 didn't know where I had **g**
Est 2:6 who had **g** into exile along
Job 7:8 will look for me, but I'll be **g**.
7:21 will search for me, but I'll be **g**!"
19:10 down on every side until I'm **g**.
21:21 in his family after he's **g**,
24:24 a little while, but then they're **g**.
27:21 carries him away, and he's **g**.
30:2 Their strength is **g**.
38:16 Have you **g** to the springs in
Psa 19:4 ⌊Yet,⌋ their sound has **g** out
Psa 30:3 those who had **g** into the pit.
47:5 God has **g** up with a joyful
47:5 The LORD has **g** up with the
90:10 Indeed, they are soon **g**,
Pro 7:19 He has **g** on a long trip.
19:7 them with words, they are **g**.
20:7 are his children after he is **g**.
23:5 of wealth before it is **g**?
30:4 "Who has **g** up to heaven and
Sos 2:11 The rain is over and **g**.
5:6 He was **g**! I almost died when
Isa 15:4 Their courage is **g**.
16:4 who tramples others will be **g**.
17:14 Before morning they will be **g**.
18:5 when blossoms are **g** and
20:3 "My servant Isaiah has **g**
21:16 All of Kedar's honor will be **g** in
23:13 These people will be **g**.
29:20 Tyrants will be **g**. Mockers will
38:8 up the ten steps it had **g** down.
45:23 A word has **g** out from my
49:19 devoured you will be long **g**.
57:7 You've **g** to offer sacrifices
Jer 4:23 I see the sky. Its lights are **g**.
8:2 **g** after, sought, and worshiped.
9:10 cattle have fled. They are **g**.
11:10 They've **g** back to the evil
37:21 all the bread in the city was **g**.
44:27 famines until everyone is **g**.
48:11 They haven't **g** into captivity.
51:7 That is why the nations have **g**
51:51 because foreigners have **g** into
Lam 1:18 men have **g** into captivity.
5:7 Now they are **g**, ⌊but⌋ we have
Eze 11:16 the countries where they've **g**.'
13:15 will say to you, "The wall is **g**,
13:16 prophesied to Jerusalem are **g**.
13:16 when it wasn't alright, are **g**,
31:14 who have died and **g** down
31:16 to join those who had **g** down
31:17 They had **g** down with the tree
32:18 with those who have **g** down
32:24 with those who have **g** down
32:25 with those who have **g** down
32:29 with those who have **g** down
36:22 nations wherever you have **g**.
37:21 of the nations where they've **g**.
Jnh 1:5 Now, Jonah had **g** below deck
Mic 7:2 Faithful people are **g** from the
Nah 3:17 No one knows where they've **g**.
Zec 14:12 from the nations that have **g**
Mat 10:23 Before you have **g** through
Mar 5:30 Jesus felt power had **g** out
7:17 had left the people and **g** home,
7:30 and the demon was **g**.
Luk 8:2 seven demons had **g** out;
8:35 whom the demons had **g** out.
8:38 demons had **g** out begged him,
8:46 I know power has **g** out of me."
11:14 When the demon had **g** out,
Jon 2:3 When the wine was **g**,
3:13 No one has **g** to heaven except
4:8 (His disciples had **g** into the
6:22 had **g** away without him.
7:10 But after his brothers had **g** to
7:15 when he hasn't **g** to school?"
13:31 When Judas was **g**,
20:17 I have not yet **g** to the Father.
Act 13:5 John Mark had **g** along to help
14:24 they had **g** through Pisidia,
15:38 in Pamphylia and had not **g**
16:19 hope of making money was **g**,
24:18 things after I had **g** through
Rom 10:18 the messengers has **g** out into
1Co 2:6 in power today and **g** tomorrow.
2Co 11:27 I've often **g** without sleep,
11:27 and **g** without food and without
Eph 4:9 except that he also had **g** down
4:10 The one who had **g** down also
Phm 1:15 Maybe Onesimus was **g** for a
Heb 4:14 chief priest who has **g** through
Jas 1:11 and the beauty is **g**.
1Pe 3:22 Christ has **g** to heaven where
2Jn 1:7 who deceive others have **g** into
Rev 2:4 The love you had at first is **g**.
18:14 'The fruit you craved is **g**.
Rev 21:1 and the sea was **g**.

gong (1)

1Co 13:1 I am a loud **g** or a clashing

good (630)

Gen 1:4 God saw the light was **g**.
1:10 God saw that it was **g**.
1:12 God saw that they were **g**.
1:18 God saw that it was **g**.
1:21 God saw that they were **g**.
1:25 God saw that they were **g**.
1:31 made and that it was very **g**.
2:9 and their fruit was **g** to eat.
2:9 the tree of the knowledge of **g**
2:17 the tree of the knowledge of **g**
2:18 "It is not **g** for the man to be
3:5 knowing **g** and evil."
3:6 tree had fruit that was **g** to eat,
3:22 since he knows **g** and evil.
19:19 Even though you've been so **g**
25:32 "What **g** is my inheritance to
26:29 We have done only **g** to you
27:9 and get me two **g** young goats.
27:15 her older son Esau's **g** clothes,
34:18 Their proposal seemed **g** to
39:21 also put Joseph on **g** terms
40:16 to the cupbearer's dream was **g**.
41:5 Seven **g**, healthy heads of
41:22 second dream I saw seven **g**,
41:24 swallowed the seven **g** heads.
41:26 The seven **g** cows are seven
41:26 and the seven **g** heads of grain
41:34 during the seven **g** years.
41:35 the food during these **g** years
41:47 During the seven **g** years the
44:4 with evil when I was **g** to you?
49:15 sees that his resting place is **g**
50:20 God planned **g** to come out of
Exo 1:20 God was **g** to the midwives.
3:8 them from that land to a **g** land
4:10 I'm not a **g** speaker.
4:10 I've never been a **g** speaker,
10:10 I know you're up to no **g**!
18:9 ⌊to hear⌋ about all the **g** things
18:17 "What you're doing is not **g**.
Lev 27:10 a **g** one for a bad one or a bad
27:10 one or a bad one for a **g** one.
27:33 must not look to see if it is **g**
Num 10:29 We will be **g** to you,
10:29 promised **g** things to Israel."
10:32 we will share with you all the **g**
13:19 the land they live in **g** or bad?
14:7 land we explored is very **g**.
24:13 command no matter how **g**
32:1 were a **g** place for livestock.
32:4 is a **g** place for livestock.
Dtr 1:14 You agreed that this was a **g**
1:23 It seemed like a **g** idea to me.
1:25 our God is giving us is **g**."
1:35 will ever see the **g** land that
1:39 difference between **g** and evil,
4:21 River and enter the **g** land
4:22 take possession of that **g** land.
5:28 Everything they said was **g**.
6:18 LORD considers right and **g**.
6:18 of that **g** land which
6:24 These laws are for our own **g**
8:7 is bringing you into a **g** land.
8:10 LORD your God for the **g** land
9:6 God is giving you this **g** land
10:13 you today for your own **g**.
11:17 disappear from this **g** land
12:28 your God considers **g** and right.
18:17 "What they've said is **g**.
26:11 enjoy all the **g** things which
32:28 people have lost their **g** sense.
Jos 9:25 what you think is **g** and right."
21:45 Every single **g** promise that the
23:13 of you are left in this **g** land that
23:15 "Every **g** word the LORD your
23:15 you from this **g** land that
23:16 disappear from the **g** land
24:20 he has been so **g** to you."
Jdg 8:35 Gideon) despite all the **g** he
9:11 'Should I stop producing my **g**,

Jdg	17:13	that the LORD will be **g** to me.
	18:9	It's very **g**! "Don't just sit there!
Rut	2:22	"It's a **g** idea, my daughter,
	3:1	home that would be **g** for you?
	3:13	to take care of you, that is **g**.
1Sm	2:24	of the LORD spreading isn't **g**!
	2:32	In spite of the **g** that I do for
	9:10	his servant, "That's a **g** idea!
	12:23	you the way that is **g** and right.
	17:42	When the Philistine got a **g**
	17:42	complexion and **g** looks.
	18:30	So David gained a **g** reputation.
	20:7	If he says, '**G**!' then
	24:18	Today you have proved how **g**
	25:15	Those men were very **g** to us.
	25:21	with evil when I was **g** to him.
	25:30	When the LORD does all the **g**
	25:31	spilled blood for no **g** reason
	25:33	May your **g** judgment be
	25:36	He was in a **g** mood and very
	26:16	What you've done isn't **g**.
	29:6	campaigning with me a **g** thing,
	29:9	as **g** as God's Messenger.
	31:9	to tell the people this **g** news
2Sm	2:6	I, too, will be **g** to you because
	3:13	"**G**!" David answered. "I'll make
	4:10	he was bringing **g** news.
	7:28	You promised me this **g** thing.
	13:28	"When Amnon begins to feel **g**
	14:25	praised for his **g** looks as much
	15:3	"Your case is **g** and proper,
	16:4	to remain in your **g** graces,
	17:7	advice is no **g**," Hushai said
	17:14	Ahithophel's **g** advice
	18:19	bring the king the **g** news that
	18:20	the man carrying **g** news today.
	18:25	"he has **g** news to tell."
	18:26	"This one is also bringing **g**
	18:27	"He's a **g** man," the king said.
	18:27	"He must be coming with **g**
	18:31	"**G** news for Your Majesty!"
1Ki	1:42	so you must be bringing **g**
	3:9	difference between **g** and evil.
	3:21	I took a **g** look at him and
	8:18	your intentions were **g**.
	8:56	None of the **g** promises he
	9:13	region of Cabul [**G** for Nothing
	14:13	God of Israel found anything **g**.
	14:15	He will uproot Israel from this **g**
	20:33	The men, watching for a **g** sign,
	22:8	prophesy anything **g** about me,
	22:13	the king the same **g** message.
	22:13	Say something **g**."
	22:18	prophesy anything **g** about me,
2Ki	2:19	"This city's location is as **g** as
	3:19	You will cut down every **g** tree,
	3:19	to ruin every **g** piece of land."
	3:25	rocks on every **g** field until
	3:25	well and cut down every **g** tree.
	5:1	This man was a **g** soldier,
	7:9	This is a day of **g** news,
	20:19	that you have spoken is **g**."
1Ch	4:40	pasture that was rich and **g**.
	10:9	and the people this **g** news.
	16:34	to the LORD because he is **g**,
	17:26	You promised me this **g** thing.
	28:8	be able to possess this **g** land
2Ch	5:13	in praise to the LORD: "He is **g**;
	6:8	your intentions were **g**.
	6:41	godly ones rejoice in what is **g**.
	7:3	LORD, ⌊by saying,⌋ "He is **g**;
	10:7	They told him, "If you are **g** to
	14:2	his God considered **g** and right.
	14:8	these men were **g** fighting men.
	18:7	he prophesies about me is **g**;
	18:12	the king the same **g** message.
	18:12	Say something **g**."
	18:17	anything **g** about me?"
	19:3	you've done some **g** things:
	24:16	with the kings because of the **g**
	30:18	"May the **g** LORD forgive
	31:20	He did what was **g** and right
Ezr	3:11	sang antiphonally: "He is **g**;
	7:9	since his God was **g** to him.
	8:22	God works things out for the **g**
	9:12	be able to eat the **g** things the
Neh	9:13	**g** laws and commandments.
	9:20	You gave them your **g** Spirit to
	9:25	filled with all sorts of **g** things,
	9:25	supply of **g** things you gave
	9:35	the many **g** things that you
	9:36	and ⌊enjoy⌋ its **g** things.
	13:14	and don't wipe out the **g** things
Est	5:9	he was happy and feeling **g**.
	5:14	king to the dinner in **g** spirits."
	10:3	since he provided for the **g** of
Job	2:10	We accept the **g** that God
	7:7	will my eyes see anything **g**.
	9:25	They don't see anything **g**.
	11:2	Should a **g** public speaker be
	12:20	and takes away the **g** judgment
	22:18	Yet, he filled their homes with **g**
	30:26	When I waited for **g**,
	33:27	and it did me no **g**.
	34:4	ourselves as to what is **g**,
	34:9	He says, 'It doesn't do any **g** to
	35:16	Job opens his mouth for no **g**
	37:13	or for ⌊the **g** of⌋ his earth,
Psa	4:6	can show us anything **g**?"
	13:6	because he has been **g** to me.
	14:1	There is no one who does **g**
	14:3	one person, does **g** things.
	16:2	Without you, I have nothing **g**."
	21:3	with the blessings of **g** things
	25:8	The LORD is **g** and decent.
	25:13	He will enjoy **g** things in life,
	34:8	and see that the LORD is **g**.
	34:10	have all the **g** things they need.
	34:12	long enough to enjoy **g** things?
	34:14	Turn away from evil, and do **g**.
	35:12	me back with evil instead of **g**.
	36:3	doing what is wise and **g**.
	37:3	the LORD, and do **g** things.
	37:27	Avoid evil, do **g**, and live
	38:20	me back with evil instead of **g**,
	38:20	because I try to do what is **g**.
	39:2	although it did me no **g**.
	40:9	I will announce the **g** news of
	45:1	is overflowing with **g** news.
	52:3	You prefer evil to **g**.
	52:9	I will wait with hope in your **g**
	53:1	There is no one who does **g**
	53:3	one person, does **g** things.
	54:6	give thanks to your **g** name,
	65:4	We will be filled with **g** food
	68:11	who announce the **g** news are
	69:16	because your mercy is **g**.
	73:1	God is truly **g** to Israel,
	73:28	with God is my highest **g**.
	85:12	will certainly give us what is **g**,
	86:5	O Lord, are **g** and forgiving,
	90:10	or even 80 if we are in **g** health.
	92:1	It is **g** to give thanks to the
	92:2	It is **g** to announce your mercy
	100:5	The LORD is **g**. His mercy
	103:2	forget all the **g** he has done:
	106:1	to the LORD because he is **g**,
	107:1	to the LORD because he is **g**,
	107:9	who were hungry with **g** food.
	109:5	me with evil instead of **g**
	111:10	**G** sense is shown by everyone
	116:7	the LORD has been **g** to you.
	116:12	the LORD for all the **g** that
	118:1	to the LORD because he is **g**,
	118:29	to the LORD because he is **g**,
	119:39	because your regulations are **g**.
	119:66	Teach me ⌊to use⌋ **g** judgment
	119:68	You are **g**, and you do good
	119:68	and you do **g** things.
	119:71	It was **g** that I had to suffer in
	122:9	I will seek what is **g** for you.
	125:4	Do **g**, O LORD, to those who
	125:4	to those who are **g**,
	133:1	See how **g** and pleasant it is
	135:3	the LORD because he is **g**.
	136:1	to the LORD because he is **g**,
	142:7	me because you are **g** to me.
	143:10	May your **g** Spirit lead me on
	145:9	The LORD is **g** to everyone
	147:1	It is **g** to sing psalms to our
Pro	1:12	like those in **g** health who go
	1:17	It does no **g** to spread a net
Pro	2:9	fair — every **g** course ⌊in life⌋.
	2:20	So walk in the way of **g** people
	3:2	long life, **g** years, and peace.
	3:27	Do not hold back anything **g**
	3:28	When you have the **g** thing
	11:22	woman who lacks **g** taste.
	11:23	people ends only in **g**,
	11:27	Whoever eagerly seeks **g**
	12:2	A **g** person obtains favor from
	12:14	One person enjoys **g** things as
	13:15	**G** sense brings favor,
	13:21	people are rewarded with **g**.
	13:22	**G** people leave an inheritance
	14:14	but a **g** person is satisfied with
	14:19	people will bow to **g** people.
	14:22	and faithful plan what is **g**?
	15:2	wise people give **g** expression
	15:3	They watch evil people and **g**
	15:5	a warning shows **g** sense.
	15:23	and a timely word — oh, how **g**!
	15:30	**G** news refreshes the body.
	16:29	him on a path that is not **g**.
	17:13	Whoever pays back evil for **g** —
	17:18	A person without **g** sense
	17:22	A joyful heart is **g** medicine,
	17:26	an innocent person is not **g**.
	18:5	It is not **g** to be partial toward a
	18:22	finds a wife finds something **g**
	19:2	without knowledge is no **g**.
	19:8	finds something **g**.
	19:11	A person with **g** sense is
	19:17	and he will repay him for his **g**
	20:23	and dishonest scales are no **g**.
	22:1	A **g** name is more desirable
	24:13	honey, my son, because it is **g**.
	24:23	partiality as a judge is not **g**.
	25:25	so is **g** news from far away.
	25:27	Eating too much honey is not **g**,
	28:10	people will inherit **g** things.
	28:21	Showing partiality is not **g**,
	31:11	he does not lack anything **g**.
	31:18	that she is making a **g** profit.
Ecc	2:3	determine whether this was **g**
	3:12	enjoy what is **g** in their lives.
	3:13	the **g** that comes from
	4:8	themselves of **g** things.
	4:9	they have a **g** reward
	5:18	seen what is **g** and beautiful:
	5:18	eat and drink and to enjoy the **g**
	6:3	satisfied with **g** things ⌊while
	6:6	anything **g** — don't we
	6:12	Who knows what may be **g** for
	7:1	A **g** name is better than
	7:11	Wisdom is as **g** as an
	7:14	When times are **g**,
	7:18	It's **g** to hold on to the one and
	7:20	does what is **g** and never sins.
	9:2	wicked, or **g**, clean or unclean,
	9:2	**G** people are treated like
	9:18	can destroy much that is **g**.
	11:7	Light is sweet, and it is **g** for
	12:14	whether it is **g** or bad.
Isa	1:17	Learn to do **g**. Seek justice.
	5:2	for it to produce **g** grapes,
	5:4	for it to produce **g** grapes,
	5:20	will be for those who call evil **g**
	5:20	who call evil good and **g** evil,
	7:15	to reject evil and choose **g**.
	7:16	to reject evil and choose **g**,
	39:8	that you have spoken is **g**."
	40:9	Tell the **g** news! Call out with a
	40:9	Tell the **g** news! Raise your
	41:7	say that their soldering is **g**.
	41:23	Yes, do something, **g** or evil,
	41:27	a messenger with the **g** news.
	52:7	who announces the **g** news,
	52:7	He brings the **g** news,
	55:2	carefully to me: Eat what is **g**,
	61:1	anointed me to deliver **g** news
	63:7	He has done many **g** things for
	65:11	a table for the god of **g** fortune
Jer	4:22	they don't know how to do **g**."
	5:25	Your sins have kept **g** things
	6:20	from Sheba is no **g** to me.
	6:20	a distant land is no **g** to me.
	8:15	but nothing **g** has happened.

Jer	10:5	They can't do you any **g** either.
	12:6	they say **g** things about you.
	13:7	It was **g** for nothing.
	13:23	Can you do **g** when you're
	14:11	pray for the **g** of these people.
	14:19	but no **g** comes from it.
	15:11	rescue you for a **g** reason.
	17:6	see when something **g** comes.
	18:10	my plans about the **g** that
	18:11	change your lives, and do **g**.'
	18:20	**G** should not be paid back with
	21:10	harm this city, not to do **g** to it,
	24:2	One basket had very **g** figs,
	24:3	Figs that are very **g**.
	24:5	are like these **g** figs.
	24:6	over them for their own **g**,
	26:14	you think is **g** and right.
	29:7	Work for the **g** of the city where
	32:39	This will be for their own **g** and
	32:39	and for the **g** of their children.
	33:11	Armies because the LORD is **g**,
	42:6	whether it's **g** or bad.
Lam	2:14	They painted a **g** picture of you.
	3:25	The LORD is **g** to those who
	3:26	"It is **g** to continue to hope and
	3:27	It is **g** for people to endure
	3:38	Both **g** and bad come from the
Eze	15:2	"Son of man, what **g** is the
	17:8	It was planted in **g** soil beside
	20:25	to follow laws that were no **g**
	27:10	victories made you look **g**.
	34:14	I will feed them in **g** pasture,
	34:14	They will rest on the **g** land
	34:18	you to feed on the **g** pasture?
	34:29	that is known for its **g** crops.
	47:12	The fruit will be **g** food,
Dan	5:11	to have insight, **g** judgment,
	5:14	you have insight, **g** judgment,
	6:1	Darius decided it would be **g** to
Hos	4:13	these trees provide **g** shade.
	8:3	they have rejected what is **g**.
Amo	5:14	Search for **g** instead of evil so
	5:15	Hate evil and love **g**.
Mic	1:12	Wait anxiously for **g**,
	2:7	Are his words **g** for those who
	3:2	You hate **g** and love evil.
	6:8	LORD has told you what is **g**.
Nah	1:7	The LORD is **g**. He is a
	1:15	who announces the **g** news:
Zep	1:12	won't do anything — **g** or bad.
Zec	8:15	but this time to do **g** to
Mal	2:17	does evil is considered **g** by
Mat	3:10	Any tree that doesn't produce **g**
	5:13	It is no longer **g** for anything
	5:16	Then they will see the **g** that
	5:45	whether they are **g** or evil.
	6:1	"Be careful not to do your **g**
	7:11	you know how to give **g** gifts to
	7:11	Father in heaven give **g** things
	7:17	In the same way every **g** tree
	7:17	good tree produces **g** fruit,
	7:18	A **g** tree cannot produce bad
	7:18	tree cannot produce **g** fruit.
	7:19	Any tree that fails to produce **g**
	12:12	So it is right to do **g** on the day
	12:33	"Make a tree **g**, and then its
	12:33	and then its fruit will be **g**.
	12:34	evil people say anything **g**?
	12:35	**G** people do the good things
	12:35	Good people do the **g** things
	13:8	were planted on **g** ground
	13:23	But the seed planted on **g**
	13:24	like a man who planted **g** seed
	13:27	didn't you plant **g** seed in your
	13:37	"The one who plants the **g**
	13:38	The **g** seeds are those who
	13:48	gathered the **g** fish into
	16:26	What **g** will it do for people to
	17:4	it's **g** that we're here.
	19:16	what **g** deed should I do to gain
	19:17	you ask me about what is **g**?
	19:17	There is only one who is **g**.
	22:10	and brought in all the **g** people
	25:21	"His master replied, '**G** job!
	25:21	You're a **g** and faithful servant!
	25:23	"His master replied, '**G** job!
Mat	25:23	You're a **g** and faithful servant!
Mar	3:4	"Is it right to do **g** or to do evil
	4:8	were planted on **g** ground,
	4:20	like seeds planted on **g** ground.
	8:36	What **g** does it do for people to
	9:5	it's **g** that we're here.
	9:50	Salt is **g**. But if salt loses its
	10:17	He asked Jesus, "**G** Teacher,
	10:18	"Why do you call me **g**?
	10:18	No one is **g** except God alone.
	12:40	to make themselves look **g**.
Luk	1:3	So I thought it would be a **g**
	1:19	God sent me to tell you this **g**
	1:53	fed hungry people with **g** food.
	2:10	I have **g** news for you,
	3:9	Any tree that doesn't produce **g**
	6:9	day of worship: to do **g** or evil,
	6:43	"A **g** tree doesn't produce rotten
	6:43	tree doesn't produce **g** fruit.
	6:45	**G** people do the good that is in
	6:45	Good people do the **g** that is in
	6:48	because it had a **g** foundation.
	8:8	were planted on **g** ground.
	8:14	they don't produce anything **g**.
	8:15	planted on **g** ground are people
	8:15	But they keep it in their **g** and
	8:15	what is **g** despite what life
	9:25	What **g** does it do for people to
	9:33	it's **g** that we're here.
	11:13	you know how to give **g** gifts to
	12:16	had land that produced **g** crops.
	12:19	"You've stored up a lot of **g**
	13:7	Why should it use up **g** soil?'
	14:34	"Salt is **g**. But if salt loses its
	14:35	It's not any **g** for the ground or
	16:25	had a life filled with **g** times,
	18:18	asked Jesus, "**G** Teacher,
	18:19	"Why do you call me **g**?
	18:19	No one is **g** except God.
	19:17	"The king said to him, '**G** job!
	19:17	You're a **g** servant.
	20:47	to make themselves look **g**.
	23:50	There was a **g** man who had
	24:41	because this seemed too **g**
Jon	1:46	"Can anything **g** come from
	7:12	people said, "He's a **g** man,"
	10:11	"I am the **g** shepherd.
	10:11	The **g** shepherd gives his life
	10:14	"I am the **g** shepherd.
	10:32	"I've shown you many **g** things
	10:32	For which of these **g** things do
	10:33	not for any **g** things you've
	16:7	It's **g** for you that I'm going
Act	4:9	us about the **g** we did
	10:38	everywhere and did **g** things,
	13:25	I'm not even **g** enough to untie
	13:28	they couldn't find any **g** reason
	14:17	Yet, by doing **g**, he has given
	19:9	and had nothing **g** to say in
	19:25	you know that we're earning a **g**
	27:12	Since the harbor was not a **g**
Rom	2:7	persisting in doing what is **g**.
	2:10	person who does what is **g**,
	3:8	"Let's do evil so that **g**
	3:12	No one does anything **g**,
	4:19	His body was already as **g** as
	5:7	courage to die for a **g** person.
	7:12	is holy, right, and **g**.
	7:13	Now, did something **g** cause
	7:16	that God's standards are **g**.
	7:18	I know that nothing **g** lives in
	7:18	nothing **g** lives in my corrupt
	7:19	I don't do the **g** I want to do.
	7:21	what God's standards say is **g**.
	8:28	things work together for the **g**
	9:11	or had done anything **g** or bad,
	12:2	God really wants — what is **g**,
	12:3	you to use **g** judgment based
	12:9	Hold on to what is **g**.
	12:21	but conquer evil with **g**.
	13:4	servant working for your **g**.
	14:16	what you consider **g** is evil.
	14:19	and which are **g** for each other.
	15:2	and the **g** things that will
	16:19	I want you to do what is **g** and
1Co	5:6	It's not **g** for you to brag.
1Co	7:1	It's **g** for men not to get married.
	7:8	It is **g** for you to stay single like
	7:26	present crisis I believe it is **g**
	10:33	think about what would be **g**
	10:33	me but about what would be **g**
	11:17	it results in more harm than **g**.
	12:7	for the common **g** of everyone.
	14:6	it wouldn't do you any **g** if I
	14:17	of thanksgiving may be very **g**,
1Co	5:10	what they deserve for the **g**
	9:8	you can do more and more **g**
	11:4	When someone tells you **g**
	11:6	though I'm not **g** with words,
	12:1	although it doesn't do any **g**.
Gal	1:6	to follow a different kind of **g**
	1:7	are calling **g** news is not
	1:7	is not really **g** news at all.
	1:8	Whoever tells you **g** news that
	1:9	If anyone tells you **g** news that
	4:17	but not in a **g** way.
	4:18	(Devotion to a **g** cause is
	4:18	to a good cause is always **g**,
	6:6	word should share all **g** things
	6:10	to do what is **g** for everyone,
Eph	1:22	for the **g** of the church.
	2:10	lives filled with **g** works that
	4:28	They should do something **g**
	4:29	Instead, speak only what is **g**
	5:9	produces everything that is **g**,
	5:19	spiritual songs for your own **g**.
	6:8	all of us for whatever **g** we do,
Php	1:6	who began this **g** work in you,
Col	1:10	every kind of **g** work by this
	2:4	arguments that merely sound **g**.
1Th	1:5	you and the **g** things we did
	5:15	always try to do what is **g** for
	5:21	Hold on to what is **g**.
2Th	1:11	you accomplish every **g** desire
	2:16	encouragement and **g** hope.
	2:17	do and say everything that is **g**.
1Ti	1:8	Teachings are **g** if they are
	2:3	This is **g** and pleases God our
	3:2	must have a **g** reputation.
	3:2	wife, be sober, use **g** judgment,
	3:8	must also be of **g** character.
	3:10	Then, if he has a **g** reputation,
	3:11	must also be of **g** character.
	4:4	Everything God created is **g**.
	4:6	You are a **g** servant of Christ
	5:7	will have **g** reputations.
	5:10	People should tell about the **g**
	5:10	or always doing **g** things.
	5:25	In the same way, the **g** things
	6:12	Fight the **g** fight for the
	6:12	which you made a **g** testimony
	6:13	who gave a **g** testimony in front
	6:18	Tell them to do **g**, to do a lot of
	6:18	to do a lot of **g** things,
	6:19	which is a **g** foundation
2Ti	1:7	of power, love, and **g** judgment.
	2:3	Join me in suffering like a **g**
	2:14	Quarreling doesn't do any **g** but
	2:21	prepared to do **g** things.
	2:24	He must be a **g** teacher.
	3:3	and have no love for what is **g**.
	3:17	prepared to do **g** things.
	4:7	I have fought the **g** fight.
Tit	1:6	A spiritual leader must have a **g**
	1:7	he must have a **g** reputation.
	1:8	be hospitable, love what is **g**,
	1:8	what is good, use **g** judgment,
	1:16	and unfit to do anything **g**.
	2:2	them to be men of **g** character,
	2:2	to use **g** judgment,
	2:5	to use **g** judgment,
	2:6	Encourage young men to use **g**
	2:7	an example by doing **g** things.
	2:10	to show their masters how **g**
	2:14	about doing **g** things.
	3:1	with every **g** thing they do.
	3:8	an example by doing **g** things.
	3:8	This is **g** and helps other
	3:14	by doing **g** things when urgent
Heb	5:14	difference between **g** and evil.
	9:11	priest of the **g** things that are
	10:1	only a shadow of the **g** things

Heb 10:24 show love and to do **g** things.
11:12 Abraham was as **g** as dead.
11:38 didn't deserve these **g** people.
12:10 us for our own **g** so that we
13:9 from God's kindness is **g** for us.
13:16 Don't forget to do **g** things for
13:21 prepare you to do every **g** thing
Jas 1:17 Every **g** present and every
2:7 Don't they curse the **g** name ⌊of
2:14 My brothers and sisters, what **g**
2:14 but doesn't do any **g** things?
2:16 what **g** does it do?
2:17 cause you to do any **g** things.
2:18 have faith, but I do **g** things."
2:18 apart from the **g** things you do.
2:18 my faith by the **g** things I do.
3:17 filled with mercy and **g** deeds,
1:20 but for your **g** he became
2:3 have tasted that the Lord is **g**!
2:12 are watching you do **g** things,
2:18 owners who are **g** and kind,
2:20 suffering for doing something **g**
3:6 make you afraid to do **g**.
3:10 and enjoy **g** days must keep
3:11 turn away from evil and do **g**.
3:13 are devoted to doing what is **g**?
3:16 Then those who treat the **g**
3:17 it's better to suffer for doing **g**
4:10 Each of you as a **g** manager
4:19 and continue to do what is **g**.
3Jn 1:11 never imitate evil, but imitate **g**.
1:11 The person who does **g** is from
1:12 says **g** things about Demetrius.
1:12 We also say **g** things about

goodbye (10)

Rut 1:9 When she kissed them **g**,
1:14 kissed her mother-in-law **g**,
1Ki 19:20 kiss my father and mother **g**.
2Ki 4:23 But she said **g** to him.
Mar 6:46 After saying **g** to them,
Luk 9:61 but first let me tell my family **g**."
Act 20:1 said **g**, and left for Macedonia.
21:6 and said **g** to each other.
2Co 2:13 So I said **g** to the people in
13:11 and sisters, I must say **g**.

good-for-nothing (10)

1Sm 1:16 Don't take me to be a **g** woman.
2:12 and Phinehas,⌋ were **g** priests;
10:27 some **g** people asked,
2Sm 20:1 A **g** man by the name of Sheba,
1Ki 21:10 Have two **g** men sit opposite
21:13 The two **g** men came in and
2Ch 13:7 **g** men gathered around him.
Job 34:18 to a king, 'You **g** scoundrel!'
Pro 6:12 A **g** scoundrel is a person who
Jer 13:10 They are like this **g** belt.

good-looking (1)

Dan 1:4 men who were healthy, **g**,

goodness (13)

Exo 33:19 "I will let all my **g** pass in front
Psa 23:6 Certainly, **g** and mercy will
25:7 with your mercy and your **g**.
27:13 I believe that I will see the **g** of
51:18 Favor Zion with your **g**.
65:11 You crown the year with your **g**,
68:10 Out of your **g**, O God,
86:17 Grant me some proof of your **g**
109:21 deal with me out of the **g** of
145:7 they remember of your great **g**,
Rom 15:14 that you, too, are filled with **g**.
Gal 5:22 kindness, **g**, faithfulness,
Heb 6:5 They experienced the **g** of

Good News (148)

Mat 4:23 and spread the **G**
9:35 and spread the **G**
11:5 and poor people hear the **G**
24:14 "This **G** about the
26:13 Wherever this **G** is
Mar 1:1 This is the beginning of the **G**
1:14 told people the **G** of God.
1:15 and believe the **G**."
Mar 1:38 I have to spread ⌊the **G**⌋
1:39 So he went to spread ⌊the **G**
3:14 him to spread ⌊the **G**⌋.
8:35 and for the **G** will save
10:29 because of me and the **G**
13:10 But first, the **G** must be
14:9 Wherever the **G** is
16:15 and tell everyone the **G**.
16:20 ⌊the **G**⌋ everywhere.
Luk 3:18 he told the **G** to the
4:18 anointed me to tell the **G**
4:43 "I have to tell the **G**
7:22 and poor people hear the **G**
8:1 He spread the **G** about
9:6 to village, told the **G**,
16:16 people have been telling the **G**
20:1 and telling them the **G**.
Act 5:42 telling the **G** that Jesus
8:12 when Philip spread the **G**
8:25 they spread the **G** in
8:35 the **G** about Jesus.
8:40 and spread the **G** until
10:36 and brought them the **G**
11:20 They started to spread the **G**
13:32 We are telling you the **G**:
14:7 They spread the **G** there.
14:15 We're spreading the **G** to
14:21 They spread the **G** in
15:7 hear the **G** and believe.
15:35 word and spread the **G**.
16:10 Macedonia about the **G**.
17:18 telling the **G** about Jesus
20:24 of testifying to the **G**
Rom 1:1 to spread the **G** of God.
1:2 this **G** through his
1:3 This **G** is about his Son,
1:9 I serve God by spreading the **G**
1:15 live in Rome the **G** also.
1:16 not ashamed of the **G**.
1:17 is revealed in this **G**.
2:16 He will use the **G** that I
10:14 if no one tells ⌊the **G**⌋?
10:15 How can people tell the **G**
10:15 who announce the **G**."
10:16 has believed the **G**.
11:28 The **G** made the Jewish
15:16 priest by spreading the **G**
15:19 I have finished spreading the **G**
15:20 My goal was to spread the **G**
16:25 strengthen you by the **G**
1Co 1:17 sent me to spread the **G**.
1:21 of the **G** we speak
4:15 you the **G** about Christ
9:12 order not to hinder the **G**
9:14 spread the **G** should earn
9:14 their living from the **G**.
9:16 If I spread the **G**,
9:16 if I don't spread the **G**!
9:17 I spread the **G** willingly,
9:17 spread the **G** unwillingly,
9:18 It is to spread the **G** free
9:18 those who spread the **G**.
9:23 this for the sake of the **G**
9:27 spread the **G** to others.
15:1 I'm making known to you the **G**
15:2 you are saved by this **G**
2Co 2:12 the **G** about Christ.
4:3 So if the **G** that we tell
4:4 they don't see the light of the **G**
4:7 the treasure of the **G**
8:18 the way he tells the **G**.
9:13 to spread the **G**
10:14 with the **G** about Christ.
10:16 spreading the **G** in the
11:4 from the **G** you already
11:7 by telling you the **G**
Gal 1:7 the **G** about Christ.
1:8 from the **G** we gave
1:9 from the **G** you received,
1:11 that the **G** I have spread
1:16 that his Son is the **G**.
2:2 the **G** among people
2:5 so that the truth of the **G**
2:7 with telling the **G**
2:14 the truth of the **G**.
3:8 So Scripture announced the **G**
Gal 4:13 time I brought you the **G**
4:17 the **G**⌋ are devoted
Eph 1:13 the **G** that he has saved
2:17 He came with the **G** of
3:6 This mystery is the **G**
3:7 I became a servant of this **G**
3:8 me to spread the **G**
6:15 spread the **G** that gives
6:19 the mystery of the **G**.
6:20 about this **G** as boldly
Php 1:5 with you in the **G** from
1:7 the truth of the **G**.
1:12 helped to spread the **G**.
1:16 me here to defend the **G**.
1:27 the **G** about Christ.
1:27 faith that the **G** brings.
2:22 together to spread the **G**.
4:3 me to spread the **G** along
4:15 to spread the **G**,
Col 1:5 hope in the **G** which is
1:6 This **G** is present with
1:7 You learned about this **G**
1:23 hope that the **G** contains.
1:23 You've heard this **G** of
1Th 1:5 We know this because the **G**
2:2 courage to tell you his **G**
2:4 always spreading the **G**.
2:8 with you not only the **G**
2:9 we could bring you the **G**
3:2 the **G** about Christ.
3:6 told us the **g** news about your
2Th 1:8 to the **G** about our
2:14 you by the **G** which we
1Ti 1:11 with the **G** that contains
1:11 I was entrusted with that **G**.
2:7 to spread this **G**
6:20 Timothy, guard the **G**
2Ti 1:8 for the sake of the **G**.
1:10 and through the **G** he
1:11 and to spread this **G**.
1:14 protect the **G** that has
2:8 This is the **G** that I tell
2:9 for spreading this **G**.
2:25 those who oppose the **G**.
4:17 finish spreading the **G**
Phm 1:13 for spreading the **G**.
Heb 4:2 We have heard the same **G**
4:6 Those who heard the **G**
1Pe 1:12 spread the **G** among you.
1:25 This word is the **G** that
4:6 After all, the **G** was told
4:17 to obey the **G** of God?
Rev 10:7 as he had made this **G**
14:6 with the everlasting **G**

goods (51)

Gen 40:16 baskets of white baked **g** were
40:17 kinds of baked **g** for Pharaoh,
Dtr 2:35 taking the cattle and **g**.
3:7 taking all of the cattle and **g**.
13:16 Gather their **g** into the middle of
13:16 burn their city and all their **g** as
18:8 gets from selling his family's **g**.
20:14 including all its **g**, as your loot.
20:14 You may enjoy your enemies' **g**
Jos 7:11 and put it among their own **g**.
Rut 4:7 property and exchanging **g**:
1Sm 17:53 they looted all the **g** in the
2Sm 3:22 home from a raid with a lot of **g**.
8:12 and from the **g** taken from
12:30 took a lot of **g** from the city.
2Ki 3:23 Moabites, let's take their **g**!"
8:9 all kinds of **g** from Damascus.
8:9 He had loaded the **g** on 40
1Ch 2:7 by taking **g** that were claimed
20:2 took a lot of **g** from the city.
27:25 son of Adiel for the **g** in the
2Ch 14:13 army captured a lot of **g**.
20:25 found among them a lot of **g**,
25:13 people and took a lot of **g**.
28:8 They also took a lot of **g** from
Ezr 7:26 have his **g** confiscated,
8:21 our little ones, and for all our **g**.
Neh 13:8 all of Tobiah's household **g** out
13:16 in fish and all kinds of **g**.
13:20 who sell all kinds of **g** spent

Est 8:11 and to seize their **g**.
Job 22:6 take your brothers' **g** as security
Psa 68:12 at home will divide the **g**.
Pro 1:13 fill our homes with stolen **g**.
16:19 stolen **g** with arrogant people.
Ecc 5:11 As the number of **g** increase,
5:11 **g** except ⌊the opportunity⌋
Isa 3:14 Your houses are filled with **g**
Eze 26:12 and take your **g** as prizes.
27:13 and bronze items for your **g**.
27:15 from Dedan traded **g** with you.
27:17 baked **g**, honey, olive oil,
27:17 and balsam for your **g**.
27:19 and sugar cane for your **g**.
27:25 from Tarshish carried your **g**.
27:27 and the **g** you sell,
27:33 your great wealth and your **g**.
27:34 Your **g** and your whole crew
Nah 3:1 and stolen **g** — never without
Luk 12:18 all my grain and **g** in them.
1Co 9:11 the harvest from your earthly **g**

good-sounding (1)

2Pe 2:3 In their greed they will use **g**

good-tasting (7)

Gen 27:4 Prepare a **g** meal for me,
27:7 and prepare a **g** meal for me to
27:9 I'll prepare them as a **g** meal for
27:14 She prepared a **g** meal,
27:17 gave her son Jacob the **g** meal
27:31 He, too, prepared a **g** meal and
Dan 10:3 I didn't eat any **g** food.

good will (45)

Pro 10:32 person announce **g**,
11:27 seeks good searches for **g**,
Isa 61:2 the year of the LORD's **g**
Luk 2:14 to those who have his **g**!"
Jon 5:29 Those who have done **g**
Act 2:47 they praised God and had the **g**
4:33 ⌊God's⌋ abundant **g** was
13:43 continue trusting God's **g**.
14:3 about his **g** by having
Rom 1:7 **G** and peace from God our
16:20 May the **g** of our Lord
1Co 1:3 **G** and peace from God our
1:4 has shown you God's **g**.
16:23 May the **g** of the Lord
2Co 1:2 **G** and peace from God our
13:13 the Lord Jesus Christ's **g**,
Gal 1:3 **G** and peace are yours
6:18 May the **g** of our Lord
Eph 1:2 **G** and peace from God our
Php 1:2 **G** and peace from God our
1:15 him because of their **g**.
4:23 May the **g** of our Lord
Col 1:2 **G** and peace from God our
4:18 God's **g** be with you.
1Th 1:1 **G** and peace are yours!
5:28 The **g** of our Lord Jesus
2Th 1:2 **G** and peace from God our
1:12 Then, because of the **g** of
3:18 The **g** of our Lord Jesus
1Ti 1:2 **G**, mercy, and peace from
6:21 God's **g** be with all of you.
2Ti 1:2 **G**, mercy, and peace from
4:22 His **g** be with all of you.
Tit 1:4 **G** and peace from God the
3:15 ⌊God's⌋ **g** be with all of
Phm 1:3 **G** and peace from God our
1:25 The **g** of our Lord Jesus
Heb 13:25 May God's **g** be with all of
1Pe 1:2 May **g** and peace fill your
5:12 this is God's genuine **g**.
2Pe 1:2 May **g** and peace fill your
3:18 But grow in the **g** and
2Jn 1:3 **G**, mercy, and peace will
Rev 1:4 **G** and peace to you from
22:21 The **g** of the Lord Jesus be

gores (3)

Exo 21:28 "Whenever a bull **g** a man or a
21:31 If the bull **g** someone's son or
21:32 If the bull **g** a male or female

gorged (2)

Dtr 32:15 You were **g**!) They abandoned
Rev 19:21 All the birds **g** themselves on

goring (2)

Exo 21:29 the bull has had the habit of **g**,
21:36 that the bull had the habit of **g**,

Goshen (14)

Gen 45:10 Live in the land of **G**,
46:28 Joseph to get directions to **G**.
46:28 arrived in the region of **G**,
46:34 you may live in the region of **G**,
47:1 Now they are in **G**."
47:4 So please let us live in **G**."
47:6 Let them live in **G**.
47:27 in Egypt in the region of **G**.
50:8 and their cattle were left in **G**.)
Exo 8:22 treat the region of **G** differently.
9:26 didn't hail was the region of **G**,
Jos 10:41 all the country of **G** as far as
11:16 all the land of **G**, the foothills,
15:51 **G**, Holon, and Giloh.

gossip (11)

Lev 19:16 Never **g**. Never endanger your
Psa 41:6 His heart collects **g**.
69:12 who sit at the gate **g** about me,
Pro 16:28 A **g** separates the closest of
18:8 The words of a **g** are
20:19 around as a **g** tells secrets.
26:20 and without **g** a quarrel dies
26:22 The words of a **g** are
Eze 36:3 began to talk and **g** about you.
2Co 12:20 ambition, slander, **g**, arrogance,
1Ti 5:13 Not only this, but they also **g**

gossiped (1)

Eze 23:10 Women **g** about how she was

gossips (4)

Pro 11:13 Whoever **g** gives away secrets,
Rom 1:29 and viciousness. They are **g**,
1Ti 3:11 They must not be **g**,
Tit 2:3 Tell them not to be **g** or

gotten (3)

Gen 4:1 She said, "I have **g** the man
1Sm 14:24 and before I've **g** revenge
Col 3:9 You've **g** rid of the person you

gourds (3)

1Ki 6:18 **G** and flowers were carved into
7:24 were two rows of **g** all around
2Ki 4:39 filled his clothes with wild **g**.

govern (14)

1Sm 9:17 This man will **g** my people."
2Ki 25:22 to **g** the remaining people in the
Job 34:17 hates justice be allowed to **g**?
Psa 125:3 ruler will not be allowed to **g**
Isa 3:4 Children will **g** them."
Jer 40:5 king of Babylon appointed to **g**
40:7 to **g** the country and some of
40:11 of Shaphan, to **g** them.
41:2 had appointed to **g** the land.
41:18 had appointed to **g** the land.
Dan 2:49 and Abednego to **g** the
3:12 Jews whom you appointed to **g**
Zec 3:7 you will **g** my temple and
Eph 6:12 the powers who **g** this world of

governed (5)

1Ki 9:19 or the entire territory that he **g**.
2Ki 15:5 of the palace and **g** the country.
23:22 time of the judges who **g** Israel
2Ch 8:6 or the entire territory that he **g**.
26:21 royal palace and **g** the country.

government (14)

Isa 9:6 The **g** will rest on his
9:7 His **g** and peace will have
Mic 4:8 your former **g** will come back to
Luk 23:14 turns the people against the **g**.
Jon 4:46 A **g** official was in Cana.
Rom 13:1 Every person should obey the **g**
13:1 No **g** would exist if it hadn't
13:2 the **g** opposes what God
13:3 don't have to be afraid of the **g**.
13:3 without being afraid of the **g**?
13:4 The **g** is God's servant working
13:4 The **g** has the right to carry out
13:6 People in the **g** are God's
Tit 3:1 the authority of **g** officials.

governments (2)

Rom 13:1 The **g** which exist have been
1Pe 2:13 under the authority of human **g**

governor (53)

Gen 42:6 As **g** of the country,
42:30 "The **g** of that land spoke
42:33 "Then the **g** of that land said to
1Ki 4:19 was only one **g** in that territory.)
22:26 the **g** of the city, and to Joash,
2Ch 18:25 the **g** of the city, and to Joash,
Ezr 2:63 The **g** told them not to eat any
5:3 At the same time, **G** Tattenai
5:6 Here is a copy of the letter **G**
5:14 whom he had made **g**.
6:6 **G** Tattenai ⌊from the province⌋
6:7 Let the **g** of the Jews and the
6:13 Then **G** Tattenai ⌊from the
Neh 3:7 the authority of the **g** ⌊from
5:14 During the 12 years that I was **g**
7:65 The **g** told them not to eat any
7:70 The **g** contributed the following
8:9 Then Nehemiah the **g**,
10:1 **G** Nehemiah (son of Hacaliah),
12:26 in the days of Nehemiah the **g**
Isa 60:17 I will appoint peace as your **g**
Dan 2:48 made Daniel **g**
Hag 1:1 the son of Shealtiel and was **g**
1:14 Shealtiel and was **g** of Judah),
2:2 of Shealtiel and is **g** of Judah),
2:21 to Zerubbabel (**g** of Judah),
Mal 1:8 Try offering it to your **g**.
Mat 27:2 him over to Pilate, the **g**.
27:11 Jesus stood in front of the **g**,
27:11 The **g** asked him, "Are you the
27:14 so the **g** was very surprised.
27:15 festival the **g** would free one
27:21 The **g** asked them,
28:14 "If the **g** hears about it,
Luk 2:2 while Quirinius was **g** of Syria.
3:1 Pontius Pilate was **g** of Judea.
20:20 could hand him over to the **g**.
Act 13:7 who was the **g** of the island.
13:7 The **g** sent for Barnabas and
13:8 so that the **g** wouldn't believe.
13:12 When the **g** saw what had
18:12 While Gallio was **g** of Greece,
23:24 and take him safely to **G**
23:25 officer wrote a letter to the **g**
23:26 to Your Excellency, **G** Felix:
23:33 they delivered the letter to the **g**
23:34 After the **g** had read the letter,
23:35 Then the **g** gave orders to keep
24:1 They reported to the **g** their
24:10 The **g** motioned for Paul to
26:30 The king, the **g**, Bernice,
28:7 who was the **g** of the island,
2Co 11:32 The **g** under King Aretas put

governor's (5)

Neh 5:14 for by the **g** food allowance.
5:18 from the **g** food allowance,
Mat 27:27 Then the **g** soldiers took Jesus
Jon 18:28 house to the **g** palace.
Act 18:17 Then all ⌊the **g** officers⌋ took

governors (34)

1Ki 4:5 was in charge of the district **g**.
4:7 Solomon appointed 12 district **g**
4:27 Each of the **g** provided food for
4:27 The **g** saw to it that nothing
10:15 and the **g** of the country.
20:14 young officers of the district **g**."
20:15 young officers of the district **g**.
20:17 of the district **g** went out first.
20:19 officers of the district **g** led

1Ki 20:24 and substitute **g** for them.
2Ch 9:14 All the Arab kings and **g** of the
23:20 the nobles, the people's **g**,
23:20 The nobles, the **g** of the people,
Ezr 8:36 to the king's satraps and **g** in
Neh 2:7 letters addressed to the **g** of
2:9 I went to the **g** of the
5:15 Those who were **g** before me
Est 3:12 the **g** of every province,
8:9 the Jews and to the satraps, **g**,
9:3 provinces, the satraps, the **g**,
Jer 51:23 you to crush **g** and officials.
51:28 their **g**, all their deputies,
51:57 along with their **g**, officers,
Eze 23:6 They were **g** and commanders
23:12 They were **g** and commanders
23:23 **g** and commanders,
Dan 3:2 **g**, mayors, military advisers,
3:3 Then the satraps, **g**,
3:27 The king's satraps, **g**,
6:7 All the officials, **g**,
Mat 10:18 even be brought in front of **g**
Mar 13:9 You will stand in front of **g** and
Luk 21:12 drag you in front of kings and **g**
1Pe 2:14 Also obey **g**. They are people

governors' (1)

Neh 5:15 Even the **g** servants took

gown (3)

2Sm 13:18 was wearing a long-sleeved **g**.
13:19 tore the long-sleeved **g** she had
Psa 45:14 Wearing a colorful **g**,

Gozan (5)

2Ki 17:6 along the Habor River in **G**,
18:11 along the Habor River in **G**,
19:12 ancestors destroyed rescue **G**,
1Ch 5:26 Habor, Hara, and the **G** River.
Isa 37:12 ancestors destroyed rescue **G**,

grab (12)

Exo 4:4 "Reach out and **g** the snake by
Jdg 12:6 they would **g** him and kill him
1Ch 13:9 Uzzah reached out to **g** the ark.
Job 38:13 so that it could **g** the earth by
Psa 52:5 He will **g** you and drag you out
71:11 Pursue him and **g** him because
Isa 3:6 A person will **g** of one of his
4:1 seven women will **g** one man
22:17 throw you out. He will **g** you.
Eze 39:10 and they will **g** things back
Nah 3:14 the clay! **G** the brick mold!
Zec 14:13 One person will **g** the hand of

grabbed (28)

Gen 19:16 the men **g** him, his wife,
39:12 She **g** him by his clothes and
Exo 4:4 He reached out and **g** it,
Jdg 16:21 The Philistines **g** him.
19:25 So the Levite **g** his concubine
1Sm 15:27 Saul **g** the hem of his robe,
2Sm 1:11 Then David **g** his own clothes
2:16 Each one **g** his opponent by
6:6 out for the ark of God and **g** it.
13:11 to him to eat, he **g** her and said,
13:14 He **g** his sister and raped her.
23:21 **g** the spear from him,
2Ki 2:12 he **g** his own garment and tore
1Ch 11:23 **g** the spear away from him,
Job 16:12 He **g** me by the back of the
Jer 26:8 and all the people **g** him and
Eze 8:3 looked like a hand and **g** me by
29:7 When Israel **g** you,
39:10 from those who **g** their things,
Mat 18:28 He **g** the servant he found and
21:39 So they **g** him, threw him out of
22:6 The rest **g** the king's servants,
Luk 23:26 they **g** a man named Simon,
Act 16:19 they **g** Paul and Silas and
19:29 They **g** Gaius and Aristarchus,
21:27 up the whole crowd and **g** Paul.
21:30 The mob **g** Paul and dragged
21:33 the officer went to Paul, **g** him,

grabbing (2)

Dtr 25:11 If she tries to stop the fight by **g**
Pro 26:17 Like **g** a dog by the ears,

grabs (3)

Job 30:18 great strength he **g** my clothes.
Psa 137:9 Blessed is the one who **g** your
Pro 7:13 She **g** him and kisses him and

grace (2)

Psa 45:2 **G** is poured on your lips.
Pro 3:22 and they will **g** your neck.

graceful (4)

Job 41:12 limbs, its strength, or its **g** form.
Pro 1:9 and teachings are a **g** garland
4:9 It will give you a **g** garland for
5:19 a loving doe and a **g** deer.

graces (1)

2Sm 16:4 hope to remain in your good **g**,

gracious (6)

Gen 33:11 because God has been **g** to me
43:29 "God be **g** to you, my son,"
2Sm 12:22 The LORD may be **g** to me and
Pro 3:34 he is **g** to humble people.
11:16 A **g** woman wins respect,
Luk 4:22 hear the **g** words flowing from

graciously (3)

Gen 33:5 children God has **g** given me,
Psa 119:29 **G** provide me with your
Pro 22:11 and whoever speaks **g** has

grafted (5)

Rom 11:17 have been **g** in their place.
11:19 that I could be **g** onto the tree."
11:23 they will be **g** onto the tree
11:24 you have been **g** onto a
11:24 natural branches to be **g** onto

grain (310)

Gen 27:28 plenty of fresh **g** and new wine.
27:37 I've provided fresh **g** and new
37:7 We were tying **g** into bundles
41:5 Seven good, healthy heads of **g**
41:6 Seven other heads of **g**,
41:7 The thin heads of **g** swallowed
41:22 full heads of **g** growing on a
41:23 Seven other heads of **g**,
41:24 The thin heads of **g** swallowed
41:26 and the seven good heads of **g**
41:27 The seven empty heads of **g**
41:35 up **g** under Pharaoh's control,
41:49 Joseph stored up **g** in huge
41:56 all the storehouses and sold **g**
41:57 to Joseph in Egypt to buy **g**,
42:1 When Jacob found out that **g**
42:2 I've heard there's **g** for sale in
42:3 brothers went to buy **g** in Egypt.
42:5 who were going to buy **g**,
42:6 was selling **g** to everyone.
42:19 of you will go and take **g** back
42:25 orders to fill their bags with **g**.
42:26 they loaded their **g** on their
43:2 When they finished eating the **g**
44:2 along with the money for his **g**."
45:23 ten female donkeys carrying **g**,
47:14 for the **g** people bought.
Exo 9:32 Neither the wheat nor the wild **g**
22:6 burns up stacked or standing **g**
29:41 and with it make the same **g**
30:9 burnt offerings or **g** offerings.
34:22 with the first **g** from your wheat
40:29 burnt offerings and **g** offerings
Lev 2:1 if any of you bring a **g** offering
2:3 The rest of the **g** offering will
2:4 "If you bring a **g** offering which
2:5 If your **g** offering is prepared in
2:6 oil over it. It is a **g** offering.
2:7 If your **g** offering is prepared in
2:8 "Bring the LORD the **g** offering
2:9 remove part of the **g** offering
2:10 The rest of the **g** offering
Lev 2:11 "Every **g** offering that you bring
2:13 salt on each of your **g** offerings.
2:13 be left out of your **g** offerings.
2:14 "If you bring a **g** offering to the
2:14 from the first **g** you harvest,
2:14 roast the cracked **g** over fire.
2:15 incense on it. It is a **g** offering.
5:13 to the priest like the **g** offering."
6:14 instructions for the **g** offering.
6:15 of flour from the **g** offering,
6:21 Offer baked pieces of the **g**
6:23 Every **g** offering made by a
7:9 Every **g** offering, belongs to the
7:10 Every **g** offering, will be shared
7:37 the burnt offering, the **g** offering
9:4 and a **g** offering mixed with
9:17 He also brought the **g** offering.
9:17 He took a handful of **g** and
10:12 "Take the **g** offering left over
14:10 olive oil for a **g** offering along
14:20 burnt offering and the **g** offering
14:21 with olive oil as a **g** offering,
14:31 together with the **g** offering.
19:9 "When you harvest the **g** in
19:9 don't harvest the **g** in the
23:10 to give you and you harvest **g**,
23:10 of the first **g** you harvest.
23:13 Bring a **g** offering of four quarts
23:14 Don't eat bread, roasted **g**,
23:14 or fresh **g** until this same day,
23:15 you bring the bundle of **g** as
23:16 Then bring a new **g** offering to
23:17 first harvested **g** for the LORD.
23:18 these offerings also bring **g**
23:20 bread of the first harvested **g** as
23:22 "When you harvest the **g** in
23:22 don't harvest the **g** in the
23:37 burnt offerings, **g** offerings,
27:30 from the land, whether **g** or fruit
Num 4:16 the daily **g** offering,
5:15 since it is a **g** offering brought
5:18 the **g** offering brought because
5:25 The priest will take the **g**
5:26 a handful of the **g** offering as
6:15 along with other **g** offerings and
6:17 and make the **g** offerings and
7:13 with olive oil as a **g** offering.
7:19 with olive oil as a **g** offering.
7:25 with olive oil as a **g** offering.
7:31 with olive oil as a **g** offering.
7:37 with olive oil as a **g** offering.
7:43 with olive oil as a **g** offering.
7:49 with olive oil as a **g** offering.
7:55 with olive oil as a **g** offering.
7:61 with olive oil as a **g** offering.
7:67 with olive oil as a **g** offering.
7:73 with olive oil as a **g** offering.
7:79 with olive oil as a **g** offering.
7:87 along with their **g** offerings.
8:8 a young bull and the **g** offering
15:4 also give the LORD a **g** offering
15:6 "With a ram, give a **g** offering of
15:9 Offer with the young bull a **g**
15:24 along with the proper **g** and
18:9 It may come from a **g** offering,
18:12 of the new wine and fresh **g**.
18:27 will be considered to be **g** from
28:5 of them, also bring a **g** offering
28:8 along with the same **g** offering
28:9 a **g** offering of 16 cups of flour
28:12 With each bull there will be a **g**
28:12 with each ram a **g** offering of 16
28:13 one-year-old lamb a **g** offering
28:20 Along with them bring **g**
28:26 the LORD your new **g** offering,
28:28 Along with them bring **g**
28:31 offerings and their **g** offerings."
29:3 Along with them bring **g**
29:6 burnt offering with its **g** offering
29:6 with their proper **g** offerings
29:9 Along with them bring **g**
29:11 offerings with their **g** offerings
29:14 Along with them bring **g**
29:16 offerings with their **g** offerings
29:18 the proper amount of **g** offerings
29:19 offerings with their **g** offerings

Num 29:21 the proper amount of **g** offerings
29:22 offerings with their **g** offerings
29:24 the proper amount of **g** offerings
29:25 offerings with their **g** offerings
29:27 the proper amount of **g** offerings
29:28 offerings with their **g** offerings
29:30 the proper amount of **g** offerings
29:31 offerings with their **g** offerings
29:33 the proper amount of **g** offerings
29:34 offerings with their **g** offerings
29:37 the proper amount of **g** offerings
29:38 offerings with their **g** offerings
29:39 burnt offerings, your **g** offerings
Dtr 7:13 **g**, new wine, and olive oil.
11:14 you will gather your own **g**,
12:17 one-tenth of your **g**,
14:23 Eat the tenth of your **g**,
15:14 **g** from your threshing floor,
16:9 the time you start harvesting **g**.
16:13 After you have gathered the **g**
18:4 **g**, new wine, olive oil,
23:25 go into your neighbor's **g** field,
23:25 you may pick **g** by hand.
23:25 sickle to cut your neighbor's **g**.
25:4 an ox when it's threshing **g**.
28:5 The **g** you harvest and the
28:17 The **g** you harvest and the
28:51 They'll leave you no **g**,
33:28 be left alone in a land of **g**
Jos 5:11 bread and roasted **g**.
22:23 burnt offerings, **g** offerings,
22:29 for burnt offerings, **g** offerings,
Jdg 13:19 a young goat and a **g** offering
13:23 our burnt offering and **g** offering
15:5 in the Philistines' **g** fields.
15:5 So he set fire to all their **g**,
16:21 chains and made him grind **g**
Rut 2:2 There I will gather the **g** left
2:3 gathered the **g** left behind by
2:7 'Please let me gather **g**.
2:8 go in any other field to gather **g**,
2:14 he handed her some roasted **g**.
2:15 When she got up to gather **g**,
2:15 "Let her gather **g** even among
2:16 Even pull some **g** out of the
2:17 So Ruth gathered **g** in the field
2:17 Then she separated the **g** from
2:19 "Where did you gather **g** today?
2:23 She gathered **g** until both the
3:7 lay at the edge of a pile of **g**.
1Sm 2:29 sacrifices and **g** offerings that
8:15 He will take a tenth of your **g**
17:17 this half-bushel of roasted **g**
25:18 a bushel of roasted **g**,
2Sm 17:19 and scattered some **g** over it
17:28 flour, roasted **g**, beans, lentils,
1Ki 8:64 the burnt offerings, **g** offerings,
18:32 12 quarts of **g** around the altar.
2Ki 3:20 At the time of the **g** offering,
4:42 made from the first harvested **g**,
4:42 and fresh **g** to the man of God.
16:13 his burnt offering and **g** offering
16:15 and the evening **g** offering,
16:15 burnt offerings and **g** offerings,
16:15 the burnt offerings, **g** offerings,
18:32 It's a country with **g** and new
1Ch 21:23 and wheat for the **g** offering.
23:29 the flour for the **g** offerings,
2Ch 7:7 the burnt offerings, **g** offerings,
31:5 **g**, new wine, fresh olive oil,
32:28 to store his harvests of **g**,
Ezr 7:17 to buy bulls, rams, lambs, **g**,
Neh 5:2 We need some **g** if we are
5:3 homes in order to get some **g**
5:10 and I are lending money and **g**
5:11 on the money, **g**, new wine,
10:31 the land bring merchandise or **g**
10:33 and for the daily **g** offerings and
10:39 their contributions of **g**,
13:5 been used to store **g** offerings,
13:5 a tenth of all the **g** harvested,
13:12 a tenth of all the **g** harvested,
Job 24:10 yet they carry bundles of **g**.
24:24 They wither like heads of **g**.
39:12 rely on it to bring your **g** back
Psa 4:7 in my heart than when their **g**
20:3 He will remember all your **g**
65:9 You provide **g** for them.
65:13 valleys are carpeted with **g**.
72:16 May there be plenty of **g** in the
78:24 and gave them **g** from heaven.
126:6 carrying his bundles of **g**.
Pro 11:26 curse the one who hoards **g**,
27:22 with a pestle along with **g**,
Isa 1:13 any more worthless **g** offerings.
5:10 produce only four quarts of **g**."
17:5 like harvesting bundles of **g** by
17:5 It will be like gathering **g** in the
23:3 The **g** of Shihor is on the
28:28 **G** is ground into flour,
36:17 It's a country with **g** and new
43:23 you by requiring **g** offerings
57:6 and sacrificed **g** offerings
62:8 let your enemies eat your **g**,
62:9 Those who harvest **g** will eat it
66:3 Whoever offers a **g** sacrifice is
66:20 every nation like a **g** offering
66:20 who bring their **g** offerings
Jer 9:22 They will be like **g** that has
14:12 burnt offerings and **g** offerings,
17:26 **g** offerings, and incense.
23:28 What does **g** have to do with
31:12 blessings: fresh **g**, new wine,
33:18 to burn **g** offerings,
41:5 They brought **g** offerings and
50:26 up their corpses like piles of **g**,
Eze 36:29 I will make the **g** grow so that
42:13 offerings there: the **g** offerings,
44:29 They will eat **g** offerings,
45:15 sacrifice them with **g** offerings,
45:17 burnt offerings, **g** offerings,
45:17 sin, **g** offerings, burnt offerings,
45:24 He must also give as a **g**
45:24 oil for every half-bushel of **g**.
45:25 **g** offerings, and olive oil.
46:5 The **g** offering that is to be
46:5 and the **g** offering that is to be
46:5 with each half-bushel of **g**.
46:7 must include a half-bushel of **g**,
46:7 with each half-bushel of **g**.
46:11 a **g** offering of a half-bushel
46:11 with each half-bushel of **g**.
46:14 Also, prepare a **g** offering with
46:14 three-and-a-third quarts of **g**
46:14 It will be a **g** offering dedicated
46:15 Prepare the lamb, the **g** offering
46:20 must bake **g** offerings so that
Hos 2:8 believe that I gave her **g**,
2:9 I will take back my **g** when
2:22 and the earth will produce **g**,
7:14 their bodies while praying for **g**
8:7 A field of **g** that doesn't ripen
8:7 ripen will never produce any **g**.
8:7 Even if it did produce **g**,
9:2 There won't be enough **g** to
10:11 calf that loves to thresh **g**.
14:7 They will grow like **g**.
Joe 1:9 **G** offerings and wine offerings
1:10 The **g** has been destroyed.
1:13 **G** offerings and wine offerings
1:17 The **g** has dried up.
2:14 Then you could give **g**
2:19 "I am going to send **g**,
2:24 floors will be filled with **g**.
3:13 Cut them down like **g**.
Amo 5:22 burnt offerings and **g** offerings,
5:25 me sacrifices and **g** offerings
8:5 so that we can sell more **g**?
Mic 4:12 bring them together like cut **g**
Hag 1:11 and on the **g**, the new wine,
2:16 came to a pile of **g** to get
Zec 9:17 Young men will prosper on **g**,
Mat 12:1 to pick the heads of **g** to eat.
13:8 good ground and produced **g**.
13:30 When the **g** is cut,
Mar 2:23 began to pick the heads of **g**.
4:28 ground produces **g** by itself.
4:28 then the head full of **g**.
4:29 As soon as the **g** is ready,
Luk 6:1 were picking the heads of **g**,
6:1 the husks, and eating the **g**.
12:18 so that I can store all my **g**
17:35 will be grinding **g** together.
19:21 harvest **g** you haven't planted.'
19:22 and harvest **g** I haven't planted.
Jon 4:36 He is gathering **g** for eternal life.
4:36 So the person who plants the **g**
12:24 A single **g** of wheat doesn't
12:24 it will produce a lot of **g**.
Act 7:42 me sacrifices and **g** offerings
1Co 9:9 an ox when it is threshing **g**."
1Ti 5:18 an ox when it is threshing **g**."

grainfields (4)

Jer 35:9 vineyards, pastures, or **g**.
Mat 12:1 Jesus walked through the **g**.
Mar 2:23 Jesus was going through the **g**.
Luk 6:1 was walking through some **g**.

grains (12)

Gen 22:17 the stars in the sky and the **g**
32:12 will be as many as the **g**
Jos 11:4 were as numerous as the **g**
Jdg 7:12 were as numerous as the **g**
Psa 139:18 them than there are **g** of sand.
Isa 10:22 be as numerous as the **g**
48:19 children would be like its **g**.
Jer 15:8 be more numerous than the **g**
Hos 1:10 become as numerous as the **g**
Rom 9:27 Israel are as numerous as the **g**
Heb 11:12 sky and as countless as the **g**
Rev 20:8 will be as numerous as the **g**

grand (10)

Gen 46:27 The **g** total of people in Jacob's
Num 1:45 The **g** total of men who were at
2:9 "The **g** total of all the troops in
2:16 "The **g** total of all the troops in
2:24 "The **g** total of all the troops in
2:31 "The **g** total of all the men in
2:32 The **g** total of all the troops in
3:39 The **g** total of Levites that
4:46 The **g** total of all the Levites
Dan 10:8 So I was left alone to see this **g**

grandchildren (21)

Gen 31:28 didn't even let me kiss my **g**
31:43 my **g**, and my flocks.
31:55 morning Laban kissed his **g**
45:10 with your children and your **g**,
50:23 He saw his **g**, Even the children
Exo 10:2 children and **g** exactly how
34:7 punishing children and **g** for
Dtr 4:9 them to your children and **g**.
4:25 when you have children and **g**
6:2 and your **g** must fear the LORD
23:8 Their **g** may join the assembly
2Ki 17:41 So did their children and their **g**.
Job 42:16 He saw his children, **g**,
Psa 103:17 belongs to their children and **g**,
Pro 13:22 leave an inheritance to their **g**,
17:6 **G** are the crown of
Isa 59:21 and your **g** permanently,"
Jer 2:9 charges against your **g**.
Eze 37:25 They, their children, and their **g**
Joe 1:3 Have your **g** tell their children.
1Ti 5:4 The children or **g** of a widow

granddaughter (10)

Gen 36:2 daughter of Anah and **g** of
36:14 of Anah and **g** of Zibeon.
36:39 of Matred and **g** of Mezahab.
Lev 18:10 sexual intercourse with your **g**,
18:17 daughter or a woman and her **g**.
2Ki 8:26 the **g** of King Omri of Israel.
1Ch 1:50 of Matred and **g** of Mezahab.
2Ch 11:20 married Maacah, Absalom's **g**.
11:21 loved Maacah, Absalom's **g**,
22:2 was Athaliah, the **g** of Omri.

granddaughters (1)

Gen 46:7 and his **g** — his entire family.

grandfather (10)

Gen 28:13 the God of your **g** Abraham and
32:9 "God of my **g** Abraham and
48:15 in whose presence my **g**
48:16 by the names of my **g** Abraham

2Sm 9:7 you all the land of your **g** Saul,
Dan 5:2 **g** Nebuchadnezzar had taken
5:11 In the days of your **g**,
5:11 Your **g**, King Nebuchadnezzar,
5:13 that my **g** brought from Judah?
5:18 the Most High God gave your **g**

grandfather's (1)

2Sm 16:3 give me back my **g** kingdom.'"

grandmother (4)

1Ki 15:10 His **g** was named Maacah,
15:13 He also removed his **g** Maacah
2Ch 15:16 King Asa also removed his **g**
2Ti 1:5 That faith first lived in your **g**

grandparents (1)

Pro 17:6 are the crown of **g**,

grandson (96)

Gen 11:31 his **g** Lot (son of Haran),
29:5 you know Laban, Nahor's **g**?"
Exo 31:2 son of Uri and **g** of Hur,
35:30 son of Uri and **g** of Hur,
38:22 son of Uri and **g** of Hur,
Num 25:7 Phinehas, son of Eleazar and **g**
25:11 son of Eleazar and **g**
27:1 son of Hepher, **g** of Gilead,
36:1 of Machir and **g** of Manasseh,
Jos 7:1 son of Carmi, **g** of Zabdi,
7:18 the son of Carmi, **g** of Zabdi,
14:6 of Jephunneh and **g** of Kenaz,
14:14 of Jephunneh and **g** of Kenaz,
17:3 son of Hepher, **g** of Gilead,
Jdg 8:22 and then your **g**, must rule us.
10:1 who was the son of Puah and **g**
18:30 (son of Gershom and **g**
20:28 son of Eleazar and **g** of Aaron,
1Sm 1:1 the son of Jeroham, **g** of Elihu,
9:1 was a son of Abiel, **g** of Zeror,
14:3 of Phinehas and the **g** of Eli,
2Sm 9:6 (son of Jonathan and **g**
9:9 "I have given your master's **g**
9:10 However, your master's **g**
16:3 is your master Saul's **g**?"
19:24 Mephibosheth, Saul's **g**,
21:7 Jonathan's son and Saul's **g**,
23:9 the son of Dodo and **g** of Aho.
23:34 Eliphelet (son of Ahasbai and **g**
1Ki 15:18 of Tabrimmon and **g** of Hezion.
2Ki 9:2 Jehoshaphat and **g** of Nimshi.
9:14 Jehoshaphat and **g** of Nimshi,
9:20 lunatic, like Jehu, **g** of Nimshi."
14:8 son of Jehoahaz and **g** of Jehu
14:13 son of Joash and **g** of Ahaziah
22:3 of Azaliah and **g** of Meshullam,
22:14 son of Tikvah and **g** of Harhas.
25:22 of Ahikam and **g** of Shaphan,
25:25 Nethaniah and **g** of Elishama,
1Ch 4:35 (son of Joshibiah, **g** of Seraiah,
4:37 Ziza (son of Shiphi, **g** of Allon,
5:8 Bela (son of Azaz, **g** of Shema,
5:14 the son of Huri, **g** of Jaroah,
5:14 son of Michael, **g** of Jeshishai,
5:15 son of Abdiel and **g** of Guni,
9:4 the son of Ammihud, **g** of Omri,
9:7 of Meshullam, **g** of Hodaviah,
9:8 (son of Uzzi and **g** of Michri),
9:8 (son of Shephatiah, **g** of Reuel,
9:11 son of Hilkiah, **g** of Meshullam,
9:12 (son of Jeroham, **g** of Pashhur,
9:12 (son of Adiel, **g** of Jahzerah,
9:14 (son of Hasshub, **g** of Azrikam,
9:15 (son of Mica, **g** of Zichri,
9:16 (son of Shemaiah, **g** of Galal,
9:16 (son of Asa and **g** of Elkanah,
9:19 (son of Kore, **g** of Ebiasaph,
11:12 the son of Dodo and **g** of Aho.
26:25 his **g** was Jeshaiah;
26:25 his **g** was Shelomith.)
2Ch 1:5 son of Uri and **g** of Hur,
20:14 son of Zechariah, **g** of Benaiah,
22:7 to meet Jehu, **g** of Nimshi.
22:9 "Ahaziah is Jehoshaphat's **g**.
25:17 son of Jehoahaz and **g** of Jehu
25:23 son of Joash and **g** of Ahaziah
2Ch 34:22 of Tokhath and **g** of Hasrah.
Ezr 5:1 and Zechariah, **g** of Iddo,
6:14 and Zechariah, the **g** of Iddo.
Neh 3:4 son of Uriah and **g** of Hakkoz,
3:4 and **g** of Meshezabel,
3:21 son of Uriah and **g** of Hakkoz,
3:23 of Maaseiah and **g** of Ananiah,
6:10 of Delaiah and **g** of Mehetabel.
12:23 time of Johanan, **g** of Eliashib.
12:26 son of Jeshua, **g** of Jozadak,
13:13 son of Zaccur and **g** of
Est 2:5 the son of Jair, the **g** of Shimei,
Isa 7:1 son of Jotham and **g** of Uzziah,
Jer 27:7 and his **g** until Babylon is
32:12 of Neriah and **g** of Mahseiah.
35:3 and the **g** of Habazziniah,
36:11 and the **g** of Shaphan,
36:14 the **g** of Shelemiah,
37:13 Shelemiah and **g** of Hananiah,
39:14 of Ahikam and **g** of Shaphan,
40:5 of Ahikam and **g** of Shaphan,
40:9 of Ahikam and **g** of Shaphan,
40:11 of Ahikam and **g** of Shaphan,
41:1 Nethaniah and **g** of Elishama,
41:2 of Ahikam and **g** of Shaphan.
43:6 of Ahikam and **g** of Shaphan,
51:59 of Neriah and **g** of Mahseiah,
Zep 1:1 son of Cushi, the **g** of Gedaliah,
Zec 1:1 of Berechiah and the **g** of Iddo.
1:7 of Berechiah and the **g** of Iddo.

grandsons (8)

Gen 36:12 These were the **g** of Esau's
36:13 These were the **g** of Esau's
36:16 They were the **g** of Adah.
36:17 They were the **g** of Esau's wife
46:7 He had brought his sons, his **g**,
Jdg 12:14 He had 40 sons and 30 **g** who
1Ch 7:13 They were Bilhah's **g**.
8:40 They had many sons and **g**,

grant (12)

Gen 19:21 I will **g** you this request too.
1Sm 1:17 God of Israel **g** your request."
Neh 2:5 you are willing to **g** my request,
2:7 In the letters tell them to **g** me
Est 5:8 may you ⌊then⌋ **g** my request
Job 34:19 does not **g** special favors
Psa 72:4 May he **g** justice to the people
86:17 **G** me some proof of your
102:13 because it is time to **g** a favor
Mat 20:23 don't have the authority to **g** you
Mar 10:40 don't have the authority to **g** you
2Ti 1:18 May the Lord **g** that

granted (11)

1Sm 1:27 and the LORD **g** my request.
25:35 said and **g** your request."
Est 5:3 it will be **g** to you."
5:6 It will be **g** to you. What would
5:6 of the kingdom, it will be **g**."
7:2 It will be **g** to you. And what
7:2 of the kingdom, it will be **g**."
9:12 It will be **g** to you. And what
9:12 you like? It, too, will be **g**."
Mat 14:9 he ordered that her wish be **g**.
Act 27:24 God has **g** safety to everyone

granting (1)

Est 9:30 official documents **g** peace

grants (4)

1Sm 2:7 causes poverty and **g** wealth.
Job 36:6 He **g** justice to those who are
Psa 84:11 The LORD **g** favor and honor.
Pro 10:24 but ⌊the LORD⌋ **g** the desire of

grape (8)

Lev 26:5 time will last until **g** gathering,
26:5 and **g** gathering will last until
Num 6:3 or any kind of **g** juice,
6:4 not even **g** seeds or skins.
Sos 7:12 if the **g** blossoms have opened,
Isa 24:13 what's left after the **g** harvest.
32:10 because the **g** harvest will fail
Joe 1:11 Cry loudly, you **g** growers!

grapes (73)

Gen 40:10 Then its clusters ripened into **g**.
40:11 so I took the **g** and squeezed
49:11 his garments in the blood of **g**.
Lev 19:10 second time or pick up fallen **g**.
25:5 or harvest **g** from your vines.
25:11 grows by itself or pick **g** from
Num 6:3 never eat fresh **g** or raisins.
13:20 (It was the season when **g**
13:23 with only one bunch of **g** on it.
13:24 that valley Eshcol [Bunch of G]
13:24 because of the bunch of **g**
20:5 Even figs, **g**, And there's no
Dtr 20:6 vineyard and not enjoyed the **g**,
20:6 someone else will enjoy the **g**.
22:9 and the **g** from the vineyard.
23:24 you may eat as many **g** as you
24:21 When you pick the **g** in your
28:30 but you won't enjoy the **g**.
28:39 drink any wine or gather any **g**,
32:14 drank the blood-red wine of **g**.
32:32 Their **g** are poisonous,
Jdg 8:2 Aren't the **g** that Ephraim
8:2 the harvest better than all the **g**
9:27 the country and harvested **g**
Neh 13:15 people in Judah stomping **g**
13:15 in loads of wine, **g**, figs,
Job 15:33 He will drop his unripened **g**
24:6 They pick the leftover **g** in the
24:11 They stomp on **g** in wine vats,
Isa 5:2 waited for it to produce good **g**,
5:2 it produced only sour, wild **g**.
5:4 waited for it to produce good **g**,
5:4 it produce only sour, wild **g**?
16:8 the nations have cut off their **g**.
16:10 No one stomps on **g** in the
18:5 when blossoms are gone and **g**
32:12 for the vines bearing **g**.
62:9 Those who gather **g** will drink
63:2 who trample **g** in a winepress?
65:8 for new wine in a cluster of **g**,
Jer 6:9 Like someone picking **g**,
8:13 "'but there are no **g** on the vine.
25:30 shouts like those who stomp **g**.
31:29 'Fathers have eaten sour **g**,
31:30 Whoever eats sour **g** will have
40:10 Gather **g**, summer fruit,
40:12 harvest of **g** and summer fruit.
48:32 your ripened fruits and your **g**.
48:33 No one will stomp on **g** with
49:9 If people come to pick your **g**,
49:9 they leave a few **g** behind?
Eze 18:2 'Fathers have eaten sour **g**,
Hos 9:10 it was like finding **g** in the
Joe 2:22 There are plenty of figs and **g**.
3:13 them as you would stomp on **g**.
Amo 9:13 and the one who stomps on **g**
Oba 1:5 If people come to pick your **g**,
1:5 won't they leave a few **g**
Mic 7:1 like those picking **g**.
7:1 But there aren't any **g** to eat or
Hab 3:17 bloom and the vines have no **g**,
Zec 8:12 Vines will produce their **g**.
Mal 3:11 lose their unripened **g**," says
Mat 7:16 "People don't pick **g** from
21:34 "When the **g** were getting ripe,
Mar 12:2 of the **g** from the vineyard.
Luk 6:44 plants or **g** from a thornbush.
20:10 from them a share of the **g** from
1Co 9:7 a vineyard and not eat the **g**?
Rev 14:18 and gather the bunches of **g**
14:18 because those **g** are ripe."
14:19 earth and gathered the **g** from
14:20 The **g** were trampled in the

grapevine (13)

Gen 40:9 He said "In my dream a **g** with
49:11 He will tie his donkey to a **g**,
Num 6:4 anything that comes from a **g**,
Jdg 9:12 Then the trees said to the **g**,
9:13 But the **g** responded,
2Ki 18:31 will eat from his own **g**
Sos 6:11 to see if the **g** had budded and
Isa 34:4 will fall like leaves from a **g**,
36:16 will eat from his own **g**

Jer 2:21 I planted you like a choice **g**
6:9 someone picks through a **g**.
Eze 19:10 Your mother was like a **g** that
Jas 3:12 Can a **g** produce figs?

grapevines (17)

Dtr 8:8 **g**, fig trees, and pomegranates.
32:32 Their **g** come from the
Jdg 13:14 anything that comes from the **g**,
Psa 105:33 He struck their **g** and fig trees
Sos 2:13 The **g** bloom and give off a
Isa 16:8 The **g** ⌊once⌋ reached as far
16:9 I will cry for the **g** of Sibmah as
17:10 have set out the imported **g**.
24:7 and **g** waste away.
Jer 5:10 among Jerusalem's rows of **g**
5:17 They will devour your **g** and
48:32 I will cry for you, **g** of Sibmah.
Hos 2:12 I will destroy her **g** and fig
14:7 They will blossom like **g**.
Joe 1:7 They destroyed my **g**.
1:12 The **g** are dried up.
Mic 4:4 They will sit under their **g** and

grasp (13)

2Ch 16:7 of Aram has escaped your **g**.
Job 20:20 he desires to escape ⌊his **g**⌋.
Psa 71:4 from the **g** of one who is cruel
136:24 He snatched us from the **g** of
139:6 knowledge is beyond my **g**.
Pro 1:2 to **g** wisdom and discipline,
13:14 away from the **g** of death.
14:27 away from the **g** of death.
17:16 have a mind to **g** anything?
24:7 of wisdom are beyond the **g**
Ecc 3:11 Yet, mortals still can't **g** what
8:17 No one is able to **g** the work
8:17 he is not able to **g** it.

grass (57)

Num 22:4 same way an ox eats up the **g**
Dtr 11:15 I will provide **g** in the fields for
32:2 like gentle rain on **g**,
2Sm 23:4 The rain makes the **g** grow
1Ki 18:5 If we can find **g**, then we can
2Ki 19:26 green **g** on the roofs,
Job 5:25 are like the **g** of the earth.
6:5 bray when it's ⌊eating⌋ **g**,
8:12 would wither quicker than **g**.
38:27 order to make it sprout with **g**?
40:15 It eats **g** as cattle do.
Psa 37:2 They will quickly dry up like **g**
72:6 that falls on ⌊freshly⌋ cut **g**,
72:16 like the **g** on the ground.
90:5 again in the morning like cut **g**.
92:7 wicked people sprout like **g**
102:4 down and withered like **g**
102:11 and I wither away like **g**.
103:15 life is as short-lived as **g**.
104:14 You make **g** grow for cattle and
106:20 the statue of a bull that eats **g**.
129:6 Make them be like **g** on a roof,
129:6 like **g** that dries up before it
147:8 He makes **g** grow on the
Pro 19:12 his favor is like dew on the **g**.
27:25 ⌊When⌋ **g** is cut short,
Isa 5:24 up straw and dry **g** shrivels
15:6 The **g** dries up, the vegetation
35:7 **G** will become cattails and
37:27 green **g** on the roofs,
40:6 "Call out: All people are like **g**,
40:7 **G** dries up, and flowers wither
40:7 Yes, people are like **g**.
40:8 **G** dries up, and flowers wither,
44:4 They will spring up with the **g**
51:12 die, of humans, who are like **g**?
66:14 you will flourish like new **g**.
Jer 14:5 young because there's no **g**.
50:11 around like calves on the **g**
Dan 4:15 iron and bronze chain in the **g**
4:23 iron and bronze chain in the **g**
4:25 You will eat **g** like cattle.
4:32 You will eat **g** like cattle.
4:33 people and ate **g** like cattle.
5:21 wild donkeys, ate **g** like cattle,
Mic 5:7 like showers on the **g**.
Mat 6:30 the way God clothes the **g**
11:7 Tall **g** swaying in the wind?
14:19 the people to sit down on the **g**.
Mar 6:39 down in groups on the green **g**.
Luk 7:24 Tall **g** swaying in the wind?
12:28 the way God clothes the **g**
Jon 6:10 The people had plenty of **g** to
1Pe 1:24 "All people are like **g**,
1:24 The **g** dries up and the flower
Rev 8:7 all the green **g** was burned up.
9:4 were told not to harm any **g**,

grasshopper (3)

Lev 11:22 of locust, cricket, katydid, or **g**.
Psa 109:23 I have been shaken off like a **g**.
Ecc 12:5 the **g** drags itself along,

grasshoppers (10)

Num 13:33 We felt as small as **g**,
1Ki 8:37 or **g** may destroy crops.
2Ch 6:28 or **g** may destroy crops.
7:13 or command **g** to devour the
Psa 78:46 He gave their crops to **g** and
105:34 and countless locusts and **g**
Isa 33:4 your loot is gathered as **g**
40:22 those who live on it are like **g**.
Joe 1:4 adult locusts leave, **g** will eat.
2:25 the adult locusts, the **g**,

grate (8)

Exo 27:4 "Make a **g** for it out of bronze
27:4 of⌋ the four corners of the **g**.
27:5 Put the **g** under the ledge of the
35:16 offerings with its bronze **g**,
38:4 He made a **g** for the altar out of
38:5 four corners of the bronze **g**).
38:30 bronze altar with its bronze **g**
39:39 bronze altar with its bronze **g**,

gratification (1)

1Jn 2:16 the world offers — physical **g**,

gratitude (1)

2Ti 3:2 curse their parents, show no **g**,

grave (63)

Gen 35:20 a stone as a marker for her **g**.
35:20 marker is at Rachel's **g** today.
42:38 gray-haired old man to his **g**!"
44:29 gray-haired old man to his **g**.'
44:31 gray-haired old father to his **g**.
Num 19:16 a human bone or a **g** will
19:18 touched a human bone or a **g**
Dtr 34:6 no one knows where his **g** is.
1Sm 2:6 ⌊people⌋ go down to the **g**,
10:2 two men will be at Rachel's **g**
2Sm 3:32 king cried loudly at Abner's **g**,
19:37 I can die in my city near the **g**
22:6 The ropes of the **g** had
1Ki 2:6 old man go to his **g** peacefully.
2:9 into his **g** by slaughtering him."
2Ki 22:20 to bring you to your **g** in peace,
2Ch 34:28 to bring you to your **g** in peace,
Job 3:22 delighted to find the **g**.
5:26 "You will come to your **g** at a
7:9 so a person goes into the **g**
17:13 If I look for the **g** as my home
17:16 with me to the gates of the **g**?
21:13 and they go peacefully to the **g**.
21:32 and his **g** is guarded.
24:19 so the **g** steals people who sin.
Psa 6:5 In the **g**, who praises you?
9:17 will return to the **g**.
16:10 not abandon my soul to the **g**
18:5 The ropes of the **g** had
30:3 you brought me up from the **g**.
31:17 Let them be silent in the **g**.
49:14 Their forms will decay in the **g**,
55:15 Let them go into the **g** while
88:3 my life comes closer to the **g**.
89:48 free from the power of the **g**?
107:20 He rescued them from the **g**.
115:17 go into the silence ⌊of the **g**⌋.
116:3 The horrors of the **g** took hold
141:7 planted at the mouth of the **g**.
Pro 1:12 swallow them alive like the **g**,
Pro 28:17 will be a fugitive down to his **g**.
30:16 the **g**, a barren womb, a land
Ecc 9:10 in the **g** where you're going.
Sos 8:6 is as unyielding as the **g**.
Isa 28:15 and an agreement with the **g**.
28:18 Your agreement with the **g** will
Jer 20:17 mother would have been my **g**,
Eze 26:20 those who descend to the **g**
26:20 those who go down to the **g**.
31:15 the tree went down to the **g**,
31:16 I brought the tree down to the **g**
31:17 down with the tree in the **g**
32:21 will say to Pharaoh from the **g**,
32:23 army lies around its **g**.
32:27 died and went down to the **g**
39:15 until the **g** diggers have buried
Hos 13:14 them from the power of the **g**.
13:14 **G**, I want to destroy you.
Jnh 2:2 the depths of my ⌊watery⌋ **g**
Nah 1:14 I will prepare your **g** because
Hab 2:5 has a large appetite like the **g**.
Act 2:27 not abandon my soul to the **g**
2:31 wouldn't be left in the **g**

gravel (2)

Pro 20:17 his mouth will be filled with **g**.
Lam 3:16 He has ground my teeth with **g**.

grave's (1)

Isa 5:14 why the **g** appetite increases.

graves (22)

Exo 14:11 there were no **g** in Egypt?
Num 11:34 called Kibroth Hattaavah [**G**
16:30 alive to their **g** — then you'll
16:33 They went down alive to their **g**
Psa 5:9 Their throats are open **g**.
49:11 their **g** have become their
88:5 have been killed and lie in **g**,
109:16 brokenhearted people to their **g**
Isa 65:4 They sat among the **g** and
Jer 5:16 arrow quivers are like open **g**.
8:1 will be taken out of their **g**.
Eze 32:22 and the **g** of its soldiers are all
32:23 Their **g** are in the deepest parts
32:24 and the **g** of its soldiers are all
32:25 The **g** of its soldiers are all
32:26 and the **g** of their soldiers are
37:12 I will open your **g** and take you
37:13 because I will open your **g** and
37:13 and bring you out of your **g**.
Mat 23:27 You are like whitewashed **g**
Luk 11:44 You are like unmarked **g**.
Rom 3:13 Their throats are open **g**.

gray (10)

Exo 28:20 put beryl, onyx, and **g** quartz.
39:13 put beryl, onyx, and **g** quartz.
1Sm 12:2 I am old and **g**, but my sons are
Psa 71:18 Even when I am old and **g**,
Isa 46:4 Even when your hair turns **g**,
Eze 28:13 **g** quartz, sapphire, turquoise,
Rev 4:3 there looked like **g** quartz
21:11 a valuable gem, like **g** quartz,
21:18 Its wall was made of **g** quartz.
21:19 first foundation was **g** quartz,

gray-haired (8)

Gen 42:38 the grief would drive this **g** old
44:29 you'll drive this **g** old man to
44:31 The grief would drive our **g** old
Dtr 32:25 as nursing babies and **g** men.
1Ki 2:6 Don't let that **g**, old man go to
2:9 what to do to him: Put that **g**,
Job 15:10 Both the old and the **g** are
Hos 7:9 You have become a **g**,

graze (19)

Gen 29:7 the sheep. Then let them **g**."
41:2 began to **g** among the reeds.
41:18 began to **g** among the reeds.
Exo 22:5 someone lets his livestock **g**
22:5 and they stray and **g** in another
34:3 the flocks and herds may not **g**
2Ch 14:15 who were letting their cattle **g**
Psa 80:13 boars from the forest **g** on it.

Sos 1:7 where do you **g** your flock?
1:8 and **g** your young goats near
6:2 to **g** his flock in the gardens
Isa 5:17 Then lambs will **g** as if they
27:10 Calves will **g** there.
30:23 cattle will **g** in large pastures.
49:9 They will **g** along every path,
Eze 34:14 and they will **g** on the
34:14 on the good land where they **g**,
Zep 2:7 There they will **g** their sheep.
3:13 They will **g** their sheep and lie

grazes (2)

Sos 2:16 He is the one who **g** his flock
6:3 He is the one who **g** his flock

grazing (5)

Exo 22:5 ruin the whole field with their **g**,
1Ch 27:29 for the herds **g** in Sharon:
Job 1:14 the donkeys were **g** nearby,
Sos 4:5 gazelles **g** among the lilies.
Luk 15:4 he leave the 99 sheep **g**

greater (55)

Gen 39:9 No one in this house is **g** than I.
49:26 of your father are **g** than
Exo 18:11 Now I know that the LORD is **g**
Num 24:7 Their king will be **g** than Agag,
Dtr 4:38 He forced nations **g** and
2Sm 13:15 His hatred for her was **g** than
13:16 sending me away is a **g** wrong
19:43 in the king and a **g** claim
1Ki 1:37 May Solomon be an even **g**
1:47 and his reign **g** than your reign.'
4:30 Solomon's wisdom was **g** than
10:23 King Solomon was **g** than all
2Ch 2:5 our God is **g** than all other
9:22 King Solomon was **g** than all
32:7 Someone **g** is on our side.
Job 33:12 God is **g** than any mortal.
Psa 71:21 You comfort me and make me **g**
89:7 He is **g** and more awe-inspiring
135:5 that our Lord is **g** than all the
138:2 your promise **g** than everything.
Pro 3:14 from ⌊wisdom⌋ is **g** than
Ecc 1:18 The **g** ⌊your⌋ knowledge,
1:18 knowledge, the **g** ⌊your⌋ pain.
Isa 10:15 Can a saw make itself **g** than
Dan 5:23 But you made yourself **g** than
11:37 himself **g** than anyone else.
Zep 2:10 made themselves **g** than them.
Zec 12:7 in Jerusalem will not be **g** than
Mat 11:11 no one is **g** than John the
11:11 of heaven is **g** than John.
12:6 that something **g** than
12:41 someone **g** than Jonah is here!
12:42 But look, someone **g** than
Mar 12:31 commandment is **g** than these."
Luk 7:28 no one is **g** than John.
7:28 kingdom of God is **g** than John.
11:31 But look, someone **g** than
11:32 someone **g** than Jonah is here!
Jon 1:50 will see **g** things than that."
5:20 will show him even **g** things
8:53 Are you **g** than our father
10:29 is **g** than everyone else,
14:12 They will do even **g** things
14:28 the Father is **g** than I am.
15:20 'A servant isn't **g** than his
19:11 over to you is guilty of a **g** sin."
2Co 4:17 glory that is **g** than anything we
Heb 1:4 The Son has become **g** than
6:13 Since he had no one **g** on
6:16 someone **g** than themselves.
7:19 else that gives us **g** confidence
1Jn 3:20 God is **g** than our conscience
4:4 the one who is in you is **g** than
5:9 God's testimony is **g** because
Rev 2:19 doing now is **g** than what you

greatest (18)

Jos 14:15 Arba was the **g** man among the
2Sm 7:9 names of the **g** people on earth.
1Ch 17:8 names of the **g** people on earth.
Eze 26:7 He is the **g** king. He will bring
Dan 2:37 you are the **g** king.
Dan 2:47 God is truly the **g** of gods,
Mat 18:1 "Who is **g** in the kingdom of
18:4 like this little child is the **g**
22:36 is the **g** in Moses' Teachings?"
22:38 This is the **g** and most
23:11 The person who is **g** among
Mar 9:34 argued about who was the **g**.
Luk 9:46 about who would be the **g**.
9:48 all of you is the one who is **g**."
22:24 should be considered the **g**.
22:26 Rather, the **g** among you must
22:27 Who's the **g**, the person who
Jon 15:13 The **g** love you can show is to

great-grandchildren (1)

Job 42:16 children, grandchildren, and **g**.

great-grandson (25)

Jos 7:1 grandson of Zabdi, **g** of Zerah,
7:18 of Zabdi, and **g** of Zerah.
17:3 of Gilead, and **g** of Machir,
1Sm 1:1 grandson of Elihu, **g** of Tohu,
9:1 and **g** of Becorath,
1Ch 4:35 of Seraiah, and **g** of Asiel),
4:37 grandson of Allon, **g** of Jedaiah,
5:8 of Shema, and **g** of Joel).
5:14 of Jaroah, and **g** of Gilead.
5:14 of Jeshishai, **g** of Jahdo,
9:4 grandson of Omri, and **g** of Imri.
9:7 and **g** of Hassenuah),
9:8 of Reuel, and **g** of Ibniah),
9:11 of Meshullam, and **g** of Zadok.
9:12 and **g** of Malchiah) and Maasai
9:12 and **g** of Meshullam,
9:14 and **g** of Hashabiah),
9:15 of Zichri, and **g** of Asaph),
9:16 and **g** of Jeduthun),
9:19 **g** of Korah) and the members of
26:25 Jeshaiah; his **g** was Joram.
2Ch 20:14 grandson of Benaiah, **g** of Jeiel,
Est 2:5 of Shimei, and the **g** of Kish.
Jer 36:14 and the **g** of Cushi,
Zep 1:1 and the **g** of Amariah,

great-great-grandson (1)

1Ch 5:14 of Jahdo, and **g** of Buz.

greatness (23)

Dtr 32:3 our God the **g** he deserves!
1Ch 29:11 **G**, power, splendor, glory,
Est 1:4 and the costly splendor of his **g**
10:2 account of the **g** of Mordecai,
Psa 34:3 Praise the LORD's **g** with me.
49:16 when the **g** of his house
49:17 His **g** cannot follow him.
69:13 out of the **g** of your mercy,
69:30 I want to praise its **g** with a
145:3 His **g** is unsearchable.
145:6 and I will tell about your **g**.
150:2 Praise him for his immense **g**.
Isa 40:26 Because of the **g** of his might
42:21 He praises the **g** of his
Eze 28:7 wisdom and dishonor your **g**.
28:17 wisdom because of your **g**.
28:22 I will show my **g** through you.
38:23 I will show my **g** and my
39:21 "I will show my **g** among the
Dan 7:27 along with the power and **g** of
Mic 5:4 safety because his **g** will reach
Luk 1:46 "My soul praises the Lord's **g**!
Eph 1:19 will also know the unlimited **g**

Greece (18)

Eze 27:13 People from **G**, Tubal,
Dan 8:21 male goat is the kingdom of **G**,
10:20 the commander of **G** will come.
11:2 against the kingdom of **G**.
Zec 9:13 Zion, against your people, **G**,
Act 18:12 Gallio was governor of **G**,
18:27 Apollos wanted to travel to **G**,
18:27 wrote to the disciples in **G**
18:27 When he arrived in **G**,
19:21 through Macedonia and **G**.
20:2 Then he went to **G**
Rom 15:26 in Macedonia and **G** owe
1Co 16:15 to be won ⌊for Christ⌋ in **G**.
2Co 1:1 holy people everywhere in **G**.
9:2 I tell them, "The people of **G**
11:10 not be silenced anywhere in **G**.
1Th 1:7 province of Macedonia and **G**.
1:8 province of Macedonia and **G**

greed (16)

Psa 52:7 became strong through his **g**."
Pro 1:19 **G** takes away his life.
11:6 are trapped by their own **g**.
Isa 57:17 angry because of their sinful **g**,
Mat 23:25 of **g** and uncontrolled desires.
Mar 7:22 adultery, **g**, wickedness,
Luk 11:39 inside you are full of **g** and evil.
12:15 from every kind of **g**.
Rom 1:29 sins, wickedness, and **g**.
Eph 5:3 or **g** even be mentioned among
5:5 or **g** (which means worshiping
Col 3:5 and **g** (which is the same thing
1Pe 5:2 Don't do it out of **g**,
2Pe 2:3 In their **g** they will use
2:14 minds are focused on their **g**.
1Jn 2:16 physical gratification, **g**,

greedily (2)

Pro 18:8 of a gossip are swallowed **g**,
26:22 of a gossip are swallowed **g**,

greedy (8)

Pro 1:19 happens to everyone who is **g**
15:27 Whoever is **g** for unjust gain
21:26 All day long he feels **g**,
28:25 A **g** person stirs up a fight,
Eze 16:27 you over to your **g** enemies,
1Co 5:10 sins, are **g**, are dishonest,
5:11 sin, are **g**, worship false gods,
6:10 those who are **g** or drunk,

Greek (12)

Mar 7:26 The woman happened to be **G**,
Jon 19:20 in Hebrew, Latin, and **G**.
Act 9:36 Her **G** name was Dorcas.
16:1 but his father was **G**.
16:3 that Timothy's father was **G**.
17:12 prominent **G** men and women.
21:37 "Can you speak **G**?
1Co 10:32 whether they are Jewish, **G**,
12:13 Whether we are Jewish or **G**,
Gal 2:3 and although he is **G**,
Col 3:11 there is no **G** or Jew,
Rev 9:11 and in **G** he is called Apollyon.

Greeks (22)

Eze 27:19 "'Danites and **G** from Uzal
Joe 3:6 Judah and Jerusalem to the **G**.
Jon 7:35 who are scattered among the **G**
7:35 and that he'll teach the **G**?
12:20 Some **G** were among those
Act 11:20 about the Lord Jesus to **G**.
14:1 crowd of Jews and **G** believed.
17:4 especially a large group of **G**
18:4 and **G** who had converted
19:10 all the Jews and **G** who lived
19:17 All the Jews and **G** living in
20:21 I warned Jews and **G** to
21:28 He has even brought **G** into the
Rom 1:16 Jews first and **G** as well.
2:9 for Jews first and **G** as well.
2:10 for Jews first and **G** as well.
3:9 everyone (both Jews and **G**)
10:12 between Jews and **G**.
15:27 These Macedonians and **G**
1Co 1:22 and **G** look for wisdom,
1:24 But to those Jews and **G** who
Gal 3:28 There are neither Jews nor **G**,

Greek-speaking (3)

Act 6:1 **G** Jews complained about the
6:1 The **G** Jews claimed that the
9:29 and argued with **G** Jews,

green (27)

Gen 1:30 I have given all **g** plants as
9:3 I gave you **g** plants as food;
Exo 10:15 Nothing **g** was left on any tree
Lev 13:47 about clothing — if there is a **g**

Lev 14:37 If it is **g** and red in sunken
Dtr 32:2 like showers on **g** plants.
2Ki 19:26 **g** grass on the roofs,
Job 15:32 his branch will not become **g**.
39:8 and looks for anything **g**.
Psa 23:2 me lie down in **g** pastures.
37:2 and wither away like **g** plants.
Pro 11:28 will flourish like a **g** leaf.
Sos 2:13 The **g** figs ripen. The
Isa 15:6 and nothing **g** is left.
34:4 like **g** figs from a fig tree.
37:27 **g** grass on the roofs,
Jer 14:6 because they have no **g** plants.
17:8 Its leaves will turn **g**.
Eze 17:24 I dry up **g** trees, and I make dry
20:47 you to destroy all your **g** trees
Joe 2:22 the wilderness have turned **g**.
Mar 4:28 First the **g** blade appears,
6:39 down in groups on the **g** grass.
Luk 23:31 If people do this to a **g** tree,
Rev 8:7 and all the **g** grass was burned
9:4 **g** plant, or tree on the earth.
21:20 ninth topaz, the tenth **g** quartz,

greet (50)

Gen 31:35 but I can't get up to **g** you;
Dtr 23:4 join because they didn't **g** you
1Sm 10:4 They will **g** you and give you
13:10 and Saul went to **g** him.
25:5 visit Nabal, and **g** him for me.
25:14 from the desert to **g** our master,
2Sm 8:10 he sent his son Joram to **g**
2Ki 4:29 don't stop to **g** him.
10:13 We've come to **g** the families of
1Ch 18:10 he sent his son Hadoram to **g**
Isa 14:10 All of them will **g** you,
Mat 10:12 go into a house, **g** the family.
Mar 15:18 Then they began to **g** him,
Luk 10:4 and don't stop to **g** anyone on
10:5 **g** the family right away with the
Rom 16:3 **G** Prisca and Aquila,
16:5 Also **g** the church that meets in
16:5 **G** my dear friend Epaenetus.
16:6 **G** Mary, who has worked very
16:7 **G** Andronicus and Junias,
16:8 **G** Ampliatus my dear friend in
16:9 **G** Urbanus our coworker in the
16:10 **G** Apelles, a true Christian.
16:10 **G** those who belong to the
16:11 **G** Herodion, who is Jewish by
16:11 **G** those Christians who belong
16:12 **G** Tryphaena and Tryphosa,
16:12 **G** dear Persis, who has
16:13 **G** Rufus, that outstanding
16:14 **G** Asyncritus, Phlegon,
16:15 **G** Philologus and Julia,
16:16 **G** each other with a holy kiss.
16:16 All the churches of Christ **g**
1Co 16:19 in the province of Asia **g** you.
16:20 and sisters ⌊here⌋ **g** you.
16:20 **G** each other with a holy kiss.
2Co 13:12 **G** one another with a holy kiss.
13:12 All of God's holy people **g** you.
Php 4:21 **G** everyone who believes in
4:22 in the emperor's palace, **g** you.
Col 4:14 and Demas **g** you.
4:15 **G** our brothers and sisters in
1Th 5:26 **G** all the brothers and sisters
Tit 3:15 **G** our faithful friends.
Heb 13:24 **G** all your leaders and all
13:24 are with us from Italy **g** you.
1Pe 5:14 **G** each other with a kiss of
2Jn 1:10 into your home or even **g** him.
1:13 of your chosen sister **g** you.
3Jn 1:15 **G** each of our friends by name.

greeted (16)

Jdg 18:15 house and **g** the young Levite.
1Sm 16:4 with fear, **g** him and said,
17:22 and **g** his brothers.
30:21 the men, he **g** them.
2Sm 18:28 came up to the king, **g** him,
2Ki 10:15 Jehu **g** him and asked,
Isa 64:5 You **g** the one who gladly does
Mat 23:7 They love to be **g** in the
28:9 Jesus met them and **g** them.
Mar 12:38 to be **g** in the marketplaces,
Luk 1:28 her home, he **g** her and said,
1:40 home and **g** Elizabeth.
11:43 to be **g** in the marketplaces.
20:46 in long robes and love to be **g**
Act 18:22 ⌊to Jerusalem⌋, **g** the church,
21:7 We **g** the believers in

greeting (11)

Mat 10:13 allow your **g** to stand.
10:13 not receptive, take back your **g**.
Luk 1:29 to figure out what this **g** meant.
1:41 When Elizabeth heard the **g**,
1:44 As soon as I heard your **g**,
10:6 your **g** will be accepted.
10:6 your **g** will be rejected.
Act 21:19 After **g** them, Paul related
1Co 16:21 I, Paul, am writing this **g** with
Col 4:18 I, Paul, am writing this **g** with
2Th 3:17 I, Paul, am writing this **g** with

greetings (14)

1Sm 16:5 "**G**," he replied, "I have come
Act 15:33 to Jerusalem with friendly **g**
23:26 Claudius Lysias sends **g** to
Rom 16:22 send you Christian **g**.
1Co 16:19 send their warmest Christian **g**.
Php 4:21 who are with me send **g** to you.
Col 4:10 is a prisoner like me, sends **g**.
2Ti 4:19 Give my **g** to Prisca and Aquila
4:21 and sisters send you **g**.
Tit 3:15 Everyone with me sends you **g**.
Phm 1:24 and Luke send you **g**.
Jas 1:1 who have been scattered. **G**.
1Pe 5:13 and my son Mark send you **g**.
3Jn 1:15 friends here send you their **g**.

greets (8)

2Ki 4:29 If he **g** you, don't stop to
Rom 16:21 Timothy my coworker **g** you;
16:23 Gaius **g** you. He is host to me
16:23 the city treasurer, **g** you.
16:23 in the Christian faith, **g** you.
Col 4:11 called Justus, also **g** you.
4:12 Jesus from your city, **g** you.
2Jn 1:11 Whoever **g** him shares the evil

grew (55)

Gen 2:9 knowledge of good and evil **g**
19:25 and whatever **g** on the ground.
21:8 The child **g** and was weaned.
21:20 was with the boy as he **g** up.
25:27 They **g** up. Esau became an
Exo 2:11 the course of time Moses **g** up.
19:19 As the sound of the horn **g**
Jos 5:12 eat the crops that **g** in Canaan.
Jdg 2:10 So another generation **g** up
11:2 When his wife's sons **g** up,
13:24 The boy **g** up, and the LORD
Rut 1:13 would you wait until they **g** up
1Sm 2:21 Meanwhile, the boy Samuel **g**
3:19 Samuel **g** up. The LORD was
14:19 in the Philistine camp **g** worse
2Sm 12:3 He raised her, and she **g** up in
15:12 the conspiracy **g** stronger,
1Ki 18:45 Gradually, the sky **g** darker
2Ch 27:6 Jotham **g** powerful because he
Neh 9:25 and were satisfied and **g** fat.
Job 31:18 (From my youth the orphan **g**
Psa 39:2 in thought, my pain **g** worse.
Ecc 2:9 So I **g** richer than anyone in
Isa 53:2 He **g** up in his presence like a
55:13 will grow where thornbushes **g**.
55:13 trees will grow where briars **g**.
Eze 16:7 You **g** up, matured,
16:7 developed, and your hair **g**.
17:6 The plant sprouted and **g** into a
17:6 but its roots **g** downward.
19:11 It **g** to be tall with many
31:5 That is why it **g** taller than all
31:10 The tree **g** very tall,
41:7 The side rooms **g** wider all the
41:7 The structure **g** wider as it
Dan 4:11 The tree **g**, and it became
4:22 You **g** and became strong and
4:33 wet until his hair **g** as long as
4:33 and his nails **g** as long as
8:8 In its place **g** four horns.
Jnh 4:10 "This plant **g** up overnight
Mat 13:7 and the thornbushes **g** up and
Mar 4:7 The thornbushes **g** up and
Luk 1:80 The child John **g** and became
2:40 The child **g** and became strong.
2:52 Jesus **g** in wisdom and
8:7 The thornbushes **g** up with
13:19 It **g** and became a tree,
Act 4:4 who believed **g** to about 5,000.
6:1 as the number of disciples **g**,
6:7 in Jerusalem **g** very large.
9:22 Saul **g** more powerful,
16:5 strengthened in the faith and **g**
Heb 11:24 When Moses **g** up,
Rev 18:19 who had a ship at sea **g** rich

grief (43)

Gen 26:35 Isaac and Rebekah a lot of **g**.
37:29 he tore his clothes in **g**.
37:34 Then, to show his **g**,
42:38 the **g** would drive this
44:13 they tore their clothes in **g**.
44:31 The **g** would drive our
Jos 7:6 of Israel tore their clothes in **g**.
Jdg 11:35 tore his clothes in **g** and said,
2Sm 1:11 clothes and tore them ⌊in **g**⌋.
13:31 clothes torn ⌊to show their **g**⌋.
14:30 came to him ⌊in **g**⌋ and said,
2Ki 2:12 tore it in two ⌊to show his **g**⌋.
18:37 with their clothes torn in **g**.
19:1 he tore his clothes in **g**,
Est 9:22 In that month their **g** turned to
Job 1:20 tore his robe ⌊in **g**⌋,
2:12 tore his own clothes ⌊in **g**⌋.
6:2 "If only my **g** could be weighed,
17:7 my eyes are blurred from **g**.
Psa 6:7 My eyes blur from **g**.
10:14 taken note of trouble and **g**
31:9 my body waste away from **g**.
78:40 caused him **g** in the desert!
Pro 10:1 son brings **g** to his mother.
14:13 and joy can end in **g**.
17:21 The parent of a fool has **g**,
17:25 father and bitter **g** to his mother.
Isa 17:11 a day of **g** and incurable pain.
25:7 the veil of **g** covering all people
35:10 They will have no sorrow or **g**.
36:22 with their clothes torn in **g**.
37:1 he tore his clothes in **g**,
51:11 They will have no sorrow or **g**.
54:6 who was abandoned and in **g**,
61:3 of joy instead of ⌊tears of⌋ **g**,
Jer 20:18 All I've seen is trouble and **g**.
31:15 the sound of crying in bitter **g**.
45:3 The LORD has added **g** to my
Lam 3:33 bring suffering or **g** to anyone,
Eze 13:22 I hadn't brought them any **g**.
Mat 2:18 the sound of crying in bitter **g**.
1Ti 6:10 caused themselves a lot of **g**.
Rev 21:4 There won't be any **g**,

grieve (11)

Job 30:25 Didn't my soul **g** for the poor?
Isa 3:26 gates of Zion will cry and **g**,
16:7 Mourn and **g** over the raisin
61:2 to comfort all those who **g**.
61:3 for all those who **g** in Zion,
Jer 16:5 go to mourn or to **g** for them.
Eze 21:12 So beat your breast, and **g**.
24:17 Don't **g** for the person who dies.
24:23 Don't **g** or cry! You will waste
2Co 12:21 I may have to **g** over many who
1Th 4:13 We don't want you to **g** like

grieved (1)

Eze 31:15 field fainted as they **g** over it.

grieves (2)

1Sm 2:5 of many children **g** all alone.
Isa 33:9 The country **g** and wastes

grieving (4)

2Sm 19:2 that the king was **g** for his son.
Isa 29:2 with people **g** and mourning.

Jer 16:5 a house where people are **g**.
Mar 16:10 who were **g** and crying.

grim (1)

Ecc 8:1 and it changes one's **g** look.

grind (6)

Exo 30:36 **G** some of it into a fine powder,
Num 11:8 then **g** it in a handmill or crush
Jdg 16:21 chains and made him **g** grain
Job 31:10 ⌊then⌋ let my wife **g** for another
Isa 3:15 can you crush my people and **g**
47:2 Take millstones and **g** flour.

grinding (5)

Dtr 9:21 I crushed it, **g** it thoroughly
24:6 a family's handmill for **g** flour —
Ecc 12:3 the women at the mill stop **g**
Isa 28:28 but the **g** eventually stops.
Luk 17:35 women will be **g** grain together.

grinds (1)

Mar 9:18 foams at the mouth, **g** his teeth,

grip (5)

Exo 10:7 will this man hold us in his **g**?
Pro 4:13 Do not relax your **g** on it.
Jer 13:21 Won't pain **g** you like a woman
49:24 Anguish and pain **g** them like a
50:43 Anguish will **g** him as pain

gripped (2)

1Sm 17:11 they were **g** with fear.
Jer 6:24 We are **g** by anguish and pain

grips (6)

Job 22:10 and great fear suddenly **g** you.
Isa 21:3 Pain **g** me like the pain of
Jer 8:21 I mourn; terror **g** me.
49:24 turn to flee, but panic **g** them.
50:43 Anguish will grip him as pain **g**
Mic 4:9 Pain **g** you like a woman in

grit (2)

Psa 35:16 they **g** their teeth at me.
Lam 2:16 They hiss and **g** their teeth.

grits (2)

Psa 37:12 righteous one and **g** his teeth at
112:10 He angrily **g** his teeth and

gritted (1)

Job 16:9 He **g** his teeth at me.

groan (18)

Job 24:12 Those dying in the city **g**.
Psa 12:5 are robbed and needy people **g**,
55:17 and night I complain and **g**,
Pro 5:11 Then you will **g** when your end
Isa 24:7 All happy people **g**.
Jer 22:23 But you will **g** when pain
Lam 1:22 I **g** so much and feel so sick at
Eze 9:4 those who sigh and **g** about all
21:6 "So, son of man, **g** with a
24:17 **G** silently. Don't grieve for the
24:23 your guilt and **g** to one another.
26:15 They will **g** when your people
30:24 Pharaoh will **g** like a person
Joe 1:18 The animals **g**. Herds of cattle
Mic 4:10 writhe in pain and **g** like a
Mal 2:13 You moan and **g** because he
Rom 8:23 of God's gifts, also **g** inwardly.
8:23 We **g** as we eagerly wait for

groaned (1)

Exo 2:23 The Israelites still **g** because

groaning (17)

Exo 2:24 God heard their **g**, and he
6:5 Now I have heard the **g** of the
Jdg 2:18 The LORD was moved by the **g**
Job 3:24 I pour out my **g** like water.
Psa 6:6 I am worn out from my **g**.
22:1 away from the words of my **g**?
31:10 from sorrow, my years from **g**.
32:3 because of my **g** all day long.
38:9 and my **g** has not been hidden
Isa 21:2 I will put an end to all the **g**.
Jer 45:3 I'm worn out from **g**.
Lam 1:4 Its priests are **g**. Its young
1:11 All the people are **g** as they
1:21 have heard that I am **g**.
Eze 21:7 they ask you why you are **g**,
Act 7:34 I've heard their **g** and have
Rom 8:22 that all creation has been **g**

groans (7)

Psa 79:11 Let the **g** of prisoners come into
102:5 bones because of my loud **g**.
102:20 He heard the **g** of the prisoners
Pro 29:2 person rules, everybody **g**.
Lam 1:8 Jerusalem **g** and turns away.
Rom 8:23 However, not only creation **g**.
8:26 along with our **g** that cannot

groom (14)

Mat 9:15 be sad while the **g** is still
9:15 The time will come when the **g**
25:1 lamps and went to meet the **g**.
25:5 Since the **g** was late,
25:6 shouted, 'The **g** is here!
25:10 were buying oil, the **g** arrived.
Mar 2:19 guests fast while the **g** is still
2:19 as they have the **g** with them,
2:20 time will come when the **g** will
Luk 5:34 to fast while the **g** is still
5:35 The time will come when the **g**
Jon 2:9 person in charge called the **g**
3:29 "The **g** is the person to whom
3:29 overjoyed when the **g** speaks.

grooms (6)

Jer 7:34 and the sounds of brides and **g**,
16:9 and the sounds of brides and **g**
25:10 the sounds of brides and **g**,
33:11 and the sounds of brides and **g**.
Joe 2:16 **G** leave their rooms.
Rev 18:23 Voices of brides and **g** will

grope (6)

Dtr 28:29 You will **g** in broad daylight as
28:29 daylight as blind people **g**
Job 5:14 they meet darkness and **g**
12:25 They **g** in the dark with no light,
Isa 59:10 We **g** like blind men along a
59:10 We **g** like people without eyes.

ground (350)

Gen 1:25 of creature that crawls on the **g**.
2:6 the entire surface of the **g**.
2:9 all the trees grow out of the **g**.
2:19 and all the birds out of the **g**.
3:17 The **g** is cursed because of
3:18 The **g** will grow thorns and
3:19 to eat until you return to the **g**,
3:23 Eden to farm the **g** from which
4:10 is crying out to me from the **g**.
4:11 now you are cursed from the **g**,
4:12 When you farm the **g**,
5:29 the LORD has cursed the **g**."
6:20 that crawls on the **g** will come
7:8 creatures that crawl on the **g**
7:17 so that it rose high above the **g**.
8:8 gone from the surface of the **g**.
8:13 and saw the surface of the **g**.
8:21 "I will never again curse the **g**
9:2 creature that crawls on the **g**
17:3 with his face touching the **g**,
17:17 with his face touching the **g**.
18:2 with his face touching the **g**.
19:1 with his face touching the **g**.
19:25 and whatever grew on the **g**.
23:7 with his face touching the **g**.
24:26 with his face touching the **g**.
33:3 with his face touching the **g** as
38:9 he wasted his semen on the **g**
42:6 with their faces touching the **g**.
43:26 with their faces touching the **g**.
44:11 his sack to the **g** and opened it.
44:14 with their faces touching the **g**.
47:19 death and the **g** won't become
48:12 with his face touching the **g**.
49:25 the deep springs below the **g**,
Exo 3:5 you are standing is holy **g**.
4:3 "Throw it on the **g**."
4:3 When Moses threw it on the **g**,
4:9 Nile River and pour it on the **g**.
4:9 will turn into blood on the **g**."
4:31 with their faces touching the **g**.
8:16 and strike the dust on the **g**.
8:17 and struck the dust on the **g**.
8:17 All the dust on the **g**
8:21 and even the **g** outside will be
9:33 came pouring down on the **g**.
10:5 the land so that the **g** can't
10:15 They covered all the **g** until it
12:27 with their faces touching the **g**.
14:16 go through the sea on dry **g**.
14:21 and turned the sea into dry **g**.
14:22 the middle of the sea on dry **g**.
14:29 through the sea on dry **g** while
15:19 gone through the sea on dry **g**.
16:14 When the dew was gone, the **g**
16:14 of flakes like frost on the **g**.
16:25 find anything on the **g** today.
18:7 with his face touching the **g**
32:20 burned it, **g** it into powder,
33:10 their faces touching the **g** at
34:8 with his face touching the **g**.
Lev 9:24 with their faces touching the **g**.
11:20 that walks across the **g** like
11:21 use their legs to hop on the **g**.
11:23 that walks across the **g** like
11:29 that move on the **g** are unclean
11:31 creatures that move on the **g**.
11:41 swarms on the **g** is disgusting
11:42 on its belly or on the **g** like
11:42 creature that swarms on the **g**.
11:43 anything that swarms on the **g**.
11:44 that swarms or crawls on the **g**.
11:46 creature that swarms on the **g**.
16:12 and two handfuls of finely **g**,
20:25 anything that crawls on the **g**.
27:16 **G** planted with 2 quarts of
Num 11:31 There were quails on the **g**
14:5 with their faces touching the **g**
16:4 with his face touching the **g**.
16:22 faces touching the **g** and said,
16:30 totally new — if the **g** opens up,
16:31 the **g** under them split,
16:33 The **g** covered them,
16:34 They thought the **g** would
16:45 with their faces touching the **g**.
20:6 with their faces touching the **g**,
22:31 with his face touching the **g**.
26:10 The **g** opened up and
Dtr 4:18 creature that crawls on the **g**,
11:6 the Israelites the **g** opened up
11:17 Then the **g** won't grow any
12:16 Pour it on the **g** like water.
12:24 Pour it on the **g** like water.
15:23 Pour it on the **g** like water.
28:23 and the **g** below will be as hard
29:19 away well-watered **g** along
29:19 ground along with dry **g**."
32:24 animals that crawl on the **g**.
33:13 and deep springs below the **g**.
Jos 3:17 promise stood firmly on dry **g**
3:17 the Jordan River on dry **g**.
4:22 the Jordan River on dry **g**.
5:14 touching the **g** and worshiped.
7:6 and bowed down to the **g**
7:10 are you doing bowing on the **g**?
17:15 Clear **g** for yourselves there in
24:32 the plot of **g** Jacob had bought
Jdg 4:21 through his temples into the **g**.
6:37 the wool while all the **g** is dry,
6:39 dry while all the **g** is covered
6:40 The wool was dry, but all the **g**
13:20 with their faces touching the **g**.
20:36 Benjamin to take back some **g**.
Rut 2:10 bowed down to the **g**
1Sm 5:3 had fallen forward on the **g**
5:4 ⌊again⌋ fallen forward on the **g**
8:12 to plow his **g** and harvest his
14:25 and there was honey on the **g**.
14:32 and butchered them on the **g**.
14:45 of his head will fall to the **g**,

1Sm 17:49 and he fell to the **g** on his face.
20:41 with his face touching the **g**.
24:8 with his face touching the **g**.
25:23 with her face touching the **g**.
25:41 with her face touching the **g**.
26:7 stuck in the **g** near his head.
26:8 Please let me nail him to the **g**
26:20 Don't let my blood fall to the **g**,
28:13 the **g**," the woman answered.
28:14 with his face touching the **g**.
28:20 Saul fell flat on the **g**.
28:23 So he got up from the **g** and sat
2Sm 1:2 with his face touching the **g**.
8:2 the Moabites lie down on the **g**,
9:6 with his face touching the **g**.
12:16 and lay on the **g** all night.
12:17 him to raise him up from the **g**,
12:20 So David got up from the **g**,
13:31 and lay down on the **g**.
14:4 with her face touching the **g**.
14:11 son's head will fall to the **g**."
14:14 water that is poured on the **g**
14:22 with his face touching the **g**,
14:33 with his face touching the **g**.
17:12 on him as dew falls on the **g**.
18:11 didn't you strike him to the **g**?
18:21 with his face touching the **g**
20:10 intestines poured out on the **g**.
22:43 as fine as the dust on the **g**.
24:20 with his face touching the **g**
1Ki 1:31 with her face touching the **g**
1:40 that their voices shook the **g**.
1:52 on his head will fall to the **g**.
13:3 it will be poured ⌊on the **g**⌋."
13:5 altar were poured ⌊on the **g**⌋.
18:1 I will allow rain to fall on the **g**."
18:7 bowed down to the **g**.
18:39 bowed down to the **g**.
18:42 bowed down on the **g** to pray.
2Ki 2:8 crossed ⌊the river⌋ on dry **g**.
2:15 with their faces touching the **g**.
9:37 will be like manure on the **g**
23:6 the Kidron Valley, **g** it to dust,
1Ch 21:16 with their faces touching the **g**.
21:21 with his face touching the **g**
29:15 fleeting as shadows on the **g**.
2Ch 1:9 as specks of dust on the **g**.
2:10 120,000 bushels of **g** wheat,
20:18 with his face touching the **g**.
20:24 Corpses were lying on the **g**.
24:17 with their faces touching the **g**.
29:28 with their faces touching the **g**,
34:4 He **g** them into powder and
Neh 8:6 bowed with their faces to the **g**
9:11 walk through the sea on dry **g**.
Est 3:2 with their faces touching the **g**,
Job 1:20 he fell to the **g** and worshiped.
2:13 Then they sat down on the **g**
5:6 doesn't sprout from the **g**.
8:18 ⌊the **g**⌋ denies it ⌊and says⌋,
8:19 others sprout from the same **g**
14:8 If its roots grow old in the **g**
16:13 and spills my blood on the **g**.
18:10 rope is hidden on the **g** for him.
28:2 Iron is taken from the **g**,
28:5 "Above the **g** food grows,
30:3 and barren **g** during the night.
30:6 dry riverbeds, in holes in the **g**,
37:6 'Fall to the **g**,' and to the
39:14 It lays its eggs on the **g** and
39:24 the horse eats up the **g** and
Psa 7:5 him trample my life into the **g**.
17:11 on throwing me to the **g**.
26:12 My feet stand on level **g**.
44:25 Our bodies cling to the **g**.
65:9 Indeed, you even prepare the **g**.
72:16 flourish like the grass on the **g**.
74:7 burned your holy place to the **g**.
80:9 You cleared the **g** for it so that
83:10 manure to fertilize the **g**.
85:11 Truth sprouts from the **g**,
89:44 and hurled his throne to the **g**.
104:14 in order to get food from the **g**.
106:17 The **g** split open and
107:33 springs into thirsty **g**,
107:34 and fertile **g** into a layer of salt
Psa 107:35 lakes and dry **g** into springs.
141:7 plows and breaks up the **g**,
143:3 He has **g** my life into the dirt.
143:10 good Spirit lead me on level **g**.
146:4 they return to the **g**.
147:6 wicked people down to the **g**.
147:8 He provides rain for the **g**.
Pro 8:2 takes its stand on high **g**,
9:14 on the high **g** of the city
24:31 The **g** was covered with
Ecc 3:20 All ⌊life⌋ comes from the **g**,
3:20 and all of it goes back to the **g**.
12:7 mortals⌋ goes back to the **g** as
Sos 1:16 The leaf-scattered **g** will be our
Isa 2:19 rocks and into holes in the **g**
3:15 faces of the poor ⌊into the **g**⌋?"
3:26 and Zion will sit on the **g**,
14:12 have been cut down to the **g**,
21:9 worship lie shattered on the **g**."
25:12 them into the dust on the **g**.
26:5 He levels it to the **g** and throws
28:2 He will throw them to the **g**
28:24 soil and make furrows in the **g**?
28:28 Grain is **g** into flour,
29:4 will speak as you lie on the **g**.
29:4 will come out of the **g** like that
30:23 the seed that you plant in the **g**,
30:23 and the food that the **g** provides
32:2 be like streams on parched **g**
35:7 and dry **g** will have springs.
40:24 have hardly taken root in the **g**.
44:3 I will pour water on thirsty **g**
47:1 Sit on the **g**, not on a throne,
49:23 with their faces touching the **g**.
51:23 you made your back like the **g**
53:2 like a root out of dry **g**.
61:11 Like the **g** that brings forth its
63:6 poured their blood on the **g**."
64:11 has been burned to the **g**.
Jer 8:2 will become manure on the **g**.
14:2 Judah sit in mourning on the **g**.
14:4 The **g** is cracked because
16:4 will be like manure on the **g**.
25:33 become like manure on the **g**.
26:23 threw his body into the burial **g**
46:21 They won't stand their **g**.
48:18 of honor and sit on the dry **g**.
Lam 2:2 down to the **g** in dishonor.
2:9 gates have sunk into the **g**.
2:10 people sit silently on the **g**.
2:10 bow their heads to the **g**.
2:11 My heart is poured out on the **g**
2:21 Young and old lie on the **g** in
3:16 He has **g** my teeth with gravel.
Eze 1:15 I saw a wheel on the **g** beside
10:16 their wings to rise from the **g**,
10:19 their wings and rose from the **g**.
17:6 low vine that spread over the **g**.
19:12 uprooted and thrown to the **g**.
24:7 It wasn't poured on the **g** where
26:11 strong pillars will fall to the **g**.
26:16 they will sit on the **g**.
28:17 So I threw you to the **g** and left
28:18 I turned you into ashes on the **g**
32:4 I will throw you on the **g** and
38:20 everything that crawls on the **g**,
38:20 and every wall will fall to the **g**.
39:14 soldiers that are still on the **g**.
43:14 From the base on the **g** to the
Dan 2:46 bowed down on the **g**
4:15 the stump and its roots in the **g**.
4:15 on the **g** with the animals.
4:23 the stump and its roots in the **g**.
4:23 its share of the plants on the **g**
7:4 off and it was lifted off the **g**.
8:7 down on the **g** and trampled.
8:10 on the **g** and trampled them.
8:12 It threw truth on the **g**.
8:18 I fainted facedown on the **g**,
10:9 I fainted facedown on the **g**.
10:15 touching the **g** and was silent.
12:2 Many sleeping in the **g** will
Hos 2:18 the animals that crawl on the **g**.
6:3 spring rains that water the **g**.
10:11 Jacob must break up the **g**.
10:12 "Break new **g**. Plant
Joe 1:10 and the **g** is dried up.
Amo 2:9 destroyed their fruit above the **g**
2:15 Archers will not stand their **g**.
3:5 in a trap on the **g** if there's no
3:5 Does a trap spring up from the **g**
3:14 be cut off and will fall to the **g**.
5:7 throw righteousness on the **g**.
9:9 Not one pebble will fall to the **g**.
Mic 7:17 animals that crawl on the **g**.
Hag 1:11 and whatever the **g** produces,
Mat 10:29 Not one of them will fall to the **g**
13:5 seeds were planted on rocky **g**,
13:8 seeds were planted on good **g**
13:20 The seed planted on rocky **g**
13:23 But the seed planted on good **g**
15:35 the crowd to sit down on the **g**.
17:6 this and fell facedown on the **g**.
25:18 dug a hole in the **g**,
25:25 two thousand dollars in the **g**.
26:39 his face to the **g** and prayed,
Mar 4:5 seeds were planted on rocky **g**,
4:8 seeds were planted on good **g**,
4:16 that were planted on rocky **g**.
4:20 like seeds planted on good **g**.
4:26 who scatters seeds on the **g**.
4:28 The **g** produces grain by itself.
4:31 mustard seed planted in the **g**.
8:6 the crowd to sit down on the **g**.
9:18 it throws him to the **g**.
9:20 He fell on the **g**, rolled around,
14:35 he fell to the **g** and prayed that
Luk 5:12 bowed with his face to the **g**.
6:49 the **g** without any foundation.
8:8 Others were planted on good **g**.
8:15 on good **g** are people who
9:42 knocked the boy to the **g**
14:35 It's not any good for the **g** or for
19:44 They will level you to the **g**
22:44 drops of blood falling to the **g**.
24:5 terrified and bowed to the **g**.
Jon 8:6 his finger to write on the **g**.
8:8 and continued writing on the **g**.
9:6 he spit on the **g** and mixed the
12:24 it is planted in the **g** and dies.
18:6 backed away and fell to the **g**.
Act 7:33 where you're standing is holy **g**.
9:4 He fell to the **g** and heard a
9:8 Saul was helped up from the **g**.
10:11 by its four corners to the **g**.
22:7 I fell to the **g** and heard a voice
26:14 All of us fell to the **g**.
1Co 14:25 with their faces touching the **g**,
Eph 3:17 may be the **g** into which you
6:13 will be able to stand your **g**.
Heb 11:38 in caves and holes in the **g**.
Jas 5:17 the **g** for three-and-a-half years.
5:18 and the **g** produced crops.
Rev 7:11 with their faces touching the **g**,

group (44)

Gen 33:8 send this whole **g** ⌊of people
50:9 It was a very large **g**.
Num 2:9 will be the first **g** to move out.
2:16 be the second **g** to move out.
2:24 will be the third **g** to move out.
2:31 They will be the last **g** to move
16:19 LORD appeared to the whole **g**.
22:15 Balak sent a larger **g** of more
1Sm 10:5 you will meet a **g** of prophets
10:10 When Saul came to the hill, a **g**
19:20 But when they saw a **g** of
19:21 sent a third **g** of messengers,
2Sm 2:13 They sat down there, one **g** on
2:13 side of the pool and the other **g**
1Ki 10:2 with a large **g** of servants,
2Ki 1:13 The officer of the third **g** went
17:29 But each **g** ⌊that settled in
17:29 Each **g** did this in the cities
1Ch 11:42 his own **g** of thirty soldiers),
16:19 a small **g** of foreigners living in
2Ch 9:1 with a large **g** of servants,
Ezr 4:7 and the rest of their **g** wrote to
4:9 were with the others of their **g**
4:17 and the rest of their **g** living in
4:23 and their **g** hurried to Jerusalem
5:3 and their **g** went to the Jews

Ezr 5:6 Shethar Bozenai and his **g** (the
6:6 and those of your **g** (the
6:13 and their **g** did exactly what
8:15 I had this **g** gather by the river
Psa 105:12 a small **g** of foreigners living in
Jer 41:8 However, ten men from the **g**
Dan 6:6 satraps went to the king as a **g**.
6:11 times the men came in as a **g**
Luk 24:22 women from our **g** startled us.
Act 2:41 people were added ⌊to the **g**⌋.
2:47 and they were added to the **g**.
4:32 The whole **g** of believers lived
6:5 pleased the whole **g**.
11:26 and taught a large **g** of people.
17:4 especially a large **g** of Greeks
19:7 twelve men were in the **g**.
Gal 1:1 apostle ⌊chosen⌋ not by any **g**
1:14 of other Jews in my age **g**

grouped (5)

Num 24:2 saw Israel's camp **g** by tribes.
1Ch 6:19 They are **g** by families:
7:2 They were soldiers **g**
7:4 So in addition to these men **g**
23:24 who were **g** according to their

groups (29)

Exo 6:26 of Egypt in organized family **g**."
7:4 of Egypt in organized family **g**.
12:17 of Egypt in organized family **g**.
12:41 left Egypt in organized family **g**.
12:51 of Egypt in organized family **g**.
18:21 them in charge of **g** of 1,000,
18:25 them in charge of **g** of 1,000,
Num 2:17 will stay in the middle of the **g**.
33:1 left Egypt in organized **g** under
Dtr 1:15 them in charge of **g** of 1,000,
1Sm 10:19 by your tribes and family **g**."
2Sm 2:13 Both **g** met at the pool of
2Ki 11:7 Then your two **g** who
1Ch 24:3 descendants into **g** for service.
24:5 Both **g** were divided impartially
24:19 These were their priestly **g**
2Ch 35:4 ready with the family **g**
Ezr 6:18 the Levites to their **g** ⌊to lead⌋
9:1 separate from the neighboring **g**
9:2 the neighboring **g** of people.
Neh 12:24 stood in **g** across from one
12:28 So the **g** of singers came
Psa 44:2 shattered many **g** of people,
Mar 6:39 all of them to sit down in **g**
6:40 They sat down in **g** of
Luk 9:14 them sit in **g** of about fifty."
Act 26:20 Both **g** were expected to
1Co 1:10 and not to split into opposing **g**.
11:18 you split up into opposing **g**.

grove (1)

Sos 6:11 I went to the walnut **g** to look at

groves (2)

Exo 23:11 your vineyards and olive **g**.
Jos 24:13 vineyards and olive **g** that you

grow (112)

Gen 2:9 God made all the trees **g** out
3:18 The ground will **g** thorns and
Num 6:5 They must let their hair **g** long.
17:5 man I choose will begin to **g**.
17:8 of Levi had not only begun to **g**,
20:5 and pomegranates won't **g** here.
Dtr 11:17 the ground won't **g** any crops,
Jdg 16:22 But his hair started to **g** back
1Sm 2:26 The boy Samuel continued to **g**
2:31 house so that no one will **g** old
2Sm 5:10 David continued to **g** more
23:4 the grass **g** from the earth.'
2Ki 2:19 and the land cannot **g** crops."
1Ch 11:9 David continued to **g** more
Job 8:11 "Can papyrus **g** up where there
8:11 rushes **g** tall without water?
14:8 If its roots **g** old in the ground
14:9 it sprout and **g** branches like
21:7 the wicked go on living, **g** old,
29:19 My roots will **g** toward the
31:40 ⌊then⌋ let it **g** thistles instead
Job 39:4 Their young are healthy and **g**
Psa 73:12 They **g** more and more wealthy.
78:6 They will **g** up and tell their
84:6 a valley where balsam trees **g**,
88:9 My eyes **g** weak because of
90:12 so that we may **g** in wisdom.
92:12 like palm trees and **g** tall like
104:14 You make grass **g** for cattle
105:24 The LORD made his people **g**
112:2 His descendants will **g** strong
147:8 grass **g** on the mountains.
Isa 1:2 children and helped them **g**,
5:6 Thorns and weeds will **g** in it,
5:27 None of them **g** tired or stumble
17:11 you will make it **g**.
32:13 where thorns and briars will **g**.
40:28 doesn't **g** tired or become
40:29 strength to those who **g** tired
40:30 Even young people **g** tired and
40:31 They will walk and won't **g**
44:14 They let them **g** strong among
44:14 and the rain makes them **g**.
55:10 They make it sprout and **g** so
55:13 Cypress trees will **g** where
55:13 Myrtle trees will **g** where briars
57:16 would **g** faint in my presence.
61:11 that makes the seed in it **g**,
Jer 4:28 and the sky will **g** black.
5:28 They **g** big and fat.
12:2 They **g**, and they produce fruit.
15:9 birth to seven sons will **g** faint
23:5 "when I will **g** a righteous
29:6 **G** in number there;
Eze 16:7 I made you **g** like a plant in the
17:8 so that it could **g** branches,
17:9 Will this vine live and **g**?
17:10 but will it live and **g**?
17:23 It will **g** branches and produce
17:24 and I make small trees **g** tall.
17:24 and I make dry trees **g**.
31:4 Water made the tree **g**,
36:8 will **g** branches and bear fruit
36:11 They will **g** and become many.
36:29 I will make the grain **g** so that
36:30 I will make fruit **g** on the trees
36:30 grow on the trees and crops **g**
44:20 heads or let their hair **g** long.
47:12 All kinds of fruit trees will **g** on
Dan 4:20 You saw an oak tree **g** and
8:4 it pleased and continued to **g**.
11:7 "At that time a shoot will **g** from
12:4 and knowledge will **g**."
Hos 1:11 and they will **g** in the land.
9:6 Weeds will **g** over their silver
9:6 Thorns will **g** over their tents.
9:12 children away before they **g** up.
10:8 Thorns and weeds will **g** over
14:7 They will **g** like grain.
Jnh 4:6 The LORD God made a plant **g**
4:10 You didn't plant it or make it **g**.
Hab 2:13 Armies that people **g** tired only
Mat 6:28 Notice how the flowers **g** in the
13:30 Let both **g** together until the
21:19 "May fruit never **g** on you
24:12 most people's love will **g** cold.
Mar 4:27 The seeds sprout and **g**,
Luk 12:27 Consider how the flowers **g**.
21:30 As soon as leaves **g** on them,
Jon 11:15 there so that you can **g** in faith.
Act 20:32 That message can help you **g**
1Co 3:6 but God made it **g**.
3:7 ⌊only⌋ God makes it **g**.
14:3 to people to help them **g**,
14:4 he helps himself **g**.
14:4 he helps the church **g**.
14:5 he says to help the church **g**.
14:12 so that you help the church **g**.
14:17 it doesn't help other people **g**.
14:26 be done to help each other **g**.
Eph 2:21 building fit together and **g** into
4:15 we will **g** up completely in our
4:16 he makes the body **g** so that it
Php 1:25 This will help you to **g** and be
Col 1:10 him in every way as you **g**
2:19 Christ makes the whole body **g**
Heb 12:15 doesn't take root and **g** up
Jas 5:7 for their precious crops to **g**.
1Pe 2:2 you will **g** in your salvation.
2Pe 3:18 But **g** in the good will and
1Jn 3:14 The person who doesn't **g** in
Jud 1:20 use your most holy faith to **g**.

grower (1)

Amo 7:14 I am a rancher and a **g** of figs.

growers (1)

Joe 1:11 Cry loudly, you grape **g**!

growing (17)

Gen 41:5 healthy heads of grain were **g**
41:22 full heads of grain **g** on a single
Lev 13:52 because the mildew is **g**.
Dtr 29:23 Nothing will be **g**. There will be
1Ki 4:33 in Lebanon to the hyssop **g** out
Psa 38:19 mortal enemies are **g** stronger.
77:2 hands in prayer without **g** tired.
Ecc 2:6 to water the forest of **g** trees.
Sos 2:1 a lily ⌊**g**⌋ in the valleys.
Jer 6:4 of evening are **g** longer.
Eze 17:6 producing branches and **g**
17:10 in the garden where it is **g**."'
31:14 Then all the other trees **g** by
Hos 14:6 They will be like **g** branches.
14:8 I am like a **g** pine tree.
Luk 13:6 "A man had a fig tree **g** in his
Php 1:9 that your love will keep on **g**

growl (5)

Job 4:10 the roar of the lion and the **g**
Isa 5:29 They **g** like a young lion.
5:29 They **g** as they snatch their
59:11 We all **g** like bears.
Amo 3:4 Does a young lion **g** in its den

growling (1)

Jer 51:38 roaring lions and **g** lion cubs.

growls (1)

Isa 31:4 **g** over its prey when a crowd of

grown (23)

Gen 30:30 you had before I came has **g**
38:14 that Shelah was **g** up now,
41:48 Joseph collected all the food **g**
Dtr 4:25 grandchildren and have **g** old
1Sm 16:22 because I have **g** fond of him."
2Sm 10:5 until your beards have **g** back,
1Ki 1:1 King David had **g** old,
12:8 the young men who had **g** up
12:10 The young men who had **g** up
1Ch 19:5 until your beards have **g** back,
23:1 When David had **g** old and had
2Ch 10:8 the young men who had **g** up
10:10 The young men who had **g** up
Psa 144:12 sons be like full-**g**, young plants.
Ecc 1:16 I thought to myself, "I have **g**
Isa 10:27 away because you have **g** fat.
43:22 Israel, you have **g** tired of me.
Eze 7:11 Violence has **g** into a weapon
Dan 8:3 the longer one had **g** up later.
Joe 1:6 They have fangs like **g** lions.
Mat 13:32 However, when it has **g**,
Act 7:17 in Egypt had **g** very large.
Rev 2:3 and have not **g** weary.

grows (18)

Gen 38:11 until my son Shelah **g** up."
Lev 13:37 spread and black hair **g** on it,
25:5 Don't harvest what **g** by itself or
25:11 Don't plant or harvest what **g**
Dtr 22:9 to give everything that **g** there
2Ki 19:29 You will eat what **g** by itself
Job 17:9 and the one with clean hands **g**
28:5 "Above the ground food **g**,
Psa 65:10 and bless what **g** in them.
84:7 Their strength **g** as they go
Pro 11:24 spends freely and yet **g** richer,
11:24 what he owes and yet **g** poorer.
Isa 24:16 treachery **g** worse and worse."
37:30 You will eat what **g** by itself
Mar 4:32 It **g** such large branches that
1Co 15:38 Each kind of seed **g** into its

2Co 10:15 confidence that as your faith **g**.
Jas 1:15 When sin **g** up, it gives birth to

growth (5)

Lev 22:23 or one that is stunted in **g** as
Pro 27:25 the tender **g** appears,
Isa 9:7 peace will have unlimited **g**.
1Co 10:23 not everything encourages **g**.
2Th 1:3 faith is showing remarkable **g**

grudge (6)

Gen 50:15 if Joseph holds a **g** against us?
Lev 19:18 Never hold a **g** against any of
Jer 3:5 He won't hold a **g** forever.
Nah 1:2 and holds a **g** against his foes.
Mar 6:19 So Herodias held a **g** against
Luk 11:53 held a terrible **g** against him.

guarantee (143)

Gen 43:9 I **g** that he will come back.
Dtr 24:6 handmill — be taken to **g** a loan.
24:17 widows' clothes to **g** a loan.
Job 17:3 Please **g** my bail yourself.
17:3 Who else will **g** it with a
Psa 33:17 Horses are not a **g** for victory.
119:122 **G** my well-being. Do not let
Pro 6:1 My son, if you **g** a loan for your
22:26 who **g** other people's loans.
Mat 3:9 I can **g** that God can raise up
5:18 I can **g** this truth: Until the earth
5:20 I can **g** that unless you live a
5:22 But I can **g** that whoever is
5:26 I can **g** this truth: You will
5:28 But I can **g** that whoever looks
5:32 But I can **g** that any man who
6:2 I can **g** this truth: That will be
6:5 I can **g** this truth: That will be
6:16 I can **g** this truth: That will be
8:10 him, "I can **g** this truth:
8:11 I can **g** that many will come
10:15 I can **g** this truth: Judgment day
10:23 I can **g** this truth: Before you
10:42 I can **g** this truth:
11:11 "I can **g** this truth: Of all the
11:22 I can **g** that judgment day will
11:24 I can **g** that judgment day will
12:6 I can **g** that something greater
12:31 So I can **g** that people will be
12:36 "I can **g** that on judgment day
13:17 I can **g** this truth: to hear what
16:18 You are Peter, and I can **g** that
16:28 I can **g** this truth: Some people
17:12 Actually, I can **g** that Elijah
17:20 I can **g** this truth: If your faith is
18:3 said to them, "I can **g** this truth:
18:10 I can **g** that their angels in
18:13 I can **g** this truth: If he finds it,
18:18 I can **g** this truth: Whatever you
18:19 "I can **g** again that if two of you
19:9 I can **g** that whoever divorces
19:23 disciples, "I can **g** this truth:
19:24 I can **g** again that it is easier
19:28 said to them, "I can **g** this truth:
21:21 them, "I can **g** this truth:
21:31 said to them, "I can **g** this truth:
21:43 That is why I can **g** that the
23:36 I can **g** this truth: The people
23:39 I can **g** that you will not see me
24:2 I can **g** this truth: Not one of
24:34 "I can **g** this truth:
24:47 I can **g** this truth: He will put
25:40 answer them, 'I can **g** this truth:
25:45 answer them, 'I can **g** this truth:
26:13 I can **g** this truth: Wherever this
26:21 he said, "I can **g** this truth:
26:29 "I can **g** that I won't drink this
26:34 to Peter, "I can **g** this truth:
26:64 But I can **g** that from now on
Mar 3:28 "I can **g** this truth: People will
8:12 I can **g** this truth: If these
9:1 said to them, "I can **g** this truth:
9:13 I can **g** that Elijah has come.
9:41 I can **g** this truth:
10:15 I can **g** this truth:
10:29 Jesus said, "I can **g** this truth:
11:23 I can **g** this truth: This is what
Mar 12:43 said to them, "I can **g** this truth:
13:30 "I can **g** this truth:
14:9 I can **g** this truth: Wherever the
14:18 Jesus said, "I can **g** this truth:
14:25 "I can **g** this truth: I won't drink
14:30 "I can **g** this truth: Tonight,
Luk 3:8 I **g** that God can raise up
4:24 added, "I can **g** this truth:
4:25 "I can **g** this truth: There were
7:9 "I can **g** that I haven't found
7:28 I can **g** that of all the people
9:27 "I can **g** this truth:
10:12 I can **g** that judgment day will
10:24 I can **g** that many prophets and
11:8 I can **g** that although he doesn't
11:51 Yes, I can **g** this truth:
12:4 "My friends, I can **g** that you
12:8 I can **g** that the Son of Man will
12:37 I can **g** this truth: He will
12:44 I can **g** this truth: He will put
12:51 I can **g** that I came to bring
12:59 I can **g** that you won't get out
13:3 I can **g** that they weren't.
13:5 I can **g** that they weren't.
13:24 I can **g** that many will try to
13:35 I can **g** that you will not see me
14:24 I can **g** that none of those
15:7 I can **g** that there will be more
15:10 So I can **g** that God's angels
17:34 "I can **g** that on that night if two
18:8 I can **g** that he will give them
18:14 "I can **g** that this tax collector
18:17 I can **g** this truth:
18:29 said to them, "I can **g** this truth:
19:26 "'I can **g** that everyone who
19:40 "I can **g** that if they are quiet,
21:3 He said, "I can **g** this truth:
21:32 "I can **g** this truth:
22:16 I can **g** that I won't eat it again
22:18 I can **g** that from now on I won't
22:34 Jesus replied, "Peter, I can **g**
22:37 I can **g** that the Scripture
23:43 said to him, "I can **g** this truth:
Jon 1:51 to Nathanael, "I can **g** this truth:
3:3 Nicodemus, "I can **g** this truth:
3:5 Nicodemus, "I can **g** this truth:
3:11 I can **g** this truth: We know
5:19 to the Jews, "I can **g** this truth:
5:24 I can **g** this truth: Those who
5:25 "I can **g** this truth: A time is
6:26 to them, "I can **g** this truth:
6:32 said to them, "I can **g** this truth:
6:47 I can **g** this truth:
6:53 told them, "I can **g** this truth:
8:34 them, "I can **g** this truth:
8:51 I can **g** this truth:
8:58 told them, "I can **g** this truth:
10:1 "I can **g** this truth: The person
10:7 emphasized, "I can **g** this truth:
12:24 I can **g** this truth: A single grain
13:16 I can **g** this truth: Slaves are
13:20 "I can **g** this truth:
13:21 He declared, "I can **g** this truth:
13:38 I can **g** this truth: No rooster
14:12 "I can **g** this truth: Those who
16:20 I can **g** this truth: You will cry
16:23 I can **g** this truth: If you ask the
21:18 I can **g** this truth: When you
Act 5:38 I can **g** that if the plan they put
2Co 1:22 has given us the Spirit as his **g**.
5:5 has given us his Spirit to **g** it.
Gal 5:2 I, Paul, can **g** that if you allow
Eph 1:14 This Holy Spirit is the **g** that
1:14 We have this **g** until we are set
Heb 6:16 Their oaths **g** what they say
7:22 way Jesus has become the **g**

guaranteed (3)

Gen 44:32 "I **g** my father that the boy
Rom 4:16 Consequently, the promise is **g**
Heb 9:15 those who are called can be **g**

guarantees (5)

Pro 11:15 Whoever **g** a stranger's loan
17:18 He **g** a loan in the presence of
20:16 on to the garment of one who **g**
Pro 27:13 on to the garment of one who **g**
Heb 8:6 God that is based on better **g**.

guard (94)

Gen 3:24 He placed them there to **g** the
37:36 officials and captain of the **g**.
39:1 officials and captain of the **g**,
40:3 prison of the captain of the **g**,
40:4 The captain of the **g** assigned
41:12 a slave of the captain of the **g**,
Num 10:25 As a rear **g** for the whole camp,
Dtr 24:8 **G** against outbreaks of serious
Jos 6:9 The rear **g** followed the ark
6:13 and the rear **g** followed the
10:18 and post a **g** there.
10:19 Cut off their rear **g**.
1Sm 26:15 why didn't you **g** your master,
26:16 You didn't **g** your master,
2Sm 20:3 put them in a house under **g**.
20:10 Amasa wasn't on his **g** against
1Ki 20:39 He said, '**G** this prisoner.
2Ki 6:10 that they would be on their **g**.
11:5 must **g** the royal palace.
11:6 You will **g** the king's residence.
11:7 on the day of worship must **g**
25:8 who was the captain of the **g**
25:10 the captain of the **g** tore down
25:11 the captain of the **g**,
25:12 The captain of the **g** left some
25:15 The captain of the **g** took all of
25:18 The captain of the **g** took the
25:20 the captain of the **g**,
1Ch 9:27 temple because they had to **g**
2Ch 23:4 of worship, must **g** the gates.
Ezr 8:26 contributions for them to **g**:
8:29 **G** them carefully. In Jerusalem,
Neh 3:29 the **g** at East Gate,
4:22 so that we can set a **g** at night
7:3 men in Jerusalem to stand **g**,
12:25 were gatekeepers standing **g** at
13:22 to cleanse themselves and **g**
Job 7:12 that you have set a **g** over me?
Psa 17:8 **G** me as if I were the pupil in
119:34 I will **g** them with all my heart.
127:1 useless for the **g** to stay alert.
138:7 you **g** my life against the anger
141:3 O LORD, set a **g** at my mouth.
Pro 2:8 in order to **g** those on paths of
2:11 Understanding will **g** you.
4:23 **G** your heart more than
7:5 in order to **g** yourself from an
Ecc 12:3 your Creator when those who **g**
Isa 21:8 I stand **g** at my post.
52:12 of Israel will **g** you from behind.
58:8 LORD will **g** you from behind.
Jer 37:13 the captain of the **g** there,
39:9 Babylon's captain of the **g**,
39:10 the captain of the **g**,
39:13 (the captain of the **g**),
40:1 the captain of the **g**,
40:2 The captain of the **g** took
40:5 The captain of the **g** gave
41:10 the captain of the **g**,
43:6 the captain of the **g**,
52:12 who was the captain of the **g**
52:14 the captain of the **g** tore down
52:15 the captain of the **g**,
52:16 the captain of the **g**,
52:19 The captain of the **g** also took
52:19 The captain of the **g** took all of
52:24 The captain of the **g** took the
52:26 the captain of the **g**,
52:30 the captain of the **g**,
Eze 28:14 I appointed an angel to **g** you.
Dan 2:14 the captain of the royal **g**,
Nah 2:1 **G** your fortress! Keep a lookout
Hab 2:1 I will stand at my **g** post.
Zec 9:8 as a **g** against those who
Mat 27:65 soldiers you want for **g** duty.
27:66 posted the soldiers on **g** duty.
Mar 6:27 Immediately, the king sent a **g**
6:27 The **g** cut off John's head in
13:9 "Be on your **g**! People will hand
13:23 Be on your **g**! I have told you
13:34 and ordered the **g** to be alert.
14:44 Arrest him, and **g** him closely

Luk 8:29 People had kept him under g.
12:15 "Be careful to g yourselves
Jon 12:25 lives in this world will g them
Act 12:4 in squads of four to g him.
23:35 Paul under g in Herod's palace.
24:23 Felix ordered the sergeant to g
Php 1:13 clear to all the soldiers who g
4:7 will g your thoughts and
1Ti 6:20 Timothy, g the Good News
2Pe 3:17 So be on your g not to be
1Jn 5:21 g yourselves from false gods.
Jud 1:24 God can g you so that you

guarded (14)

Dtr 32:10 He g them, took care of them,
Jos 24:17 He g us wherever we went,
1Sm 25:21 David had thought, "I g this
2Ki 12:9 The priests who g the entrance
Neh 11:19 and their relatives who g the
Est 2:21 eunuchs who g the entrance,
6:2 eunuchs who g the entrance,
Job 21:32 and his grave is g.
Psa 137:3 Those who g us wanted us to
Eze 27:11 from Gammad g your towers.
44:11 They could have g the gates of
Act 22:20 I approved of his death and g
28:16 but he had a soldier who g him.
1Pe 1:5 since you are g by God's

guardian (13)

Rut 4:16 and became his g.
Est 2:3 the g of the women,
2:8 the g of the women.
2:14 the g of the concubines.
2:15 the g of the women,
Psa 121:3 Your g will not fall asleep.
121:4 Indeed, the G of Israel never
121:5 The LORD is your g.
Eze 28:16 The g angel forced you out
Dan 4:13 I saw a g, a holy being,
4:23 You saw a g, a holy being,
Gal 3:24 Moses' laws served as our g.
3:25 longer under the control of a g.

guardians (5)

2Ki 10:1 and the g of Ahab's
10:5 and the g sent this message to
Dan 4:17 The g have announced this
1Co 4:15 have countless Christian g,
Gal 4:2 is placed under the control of g

guarding (6)

1Sm 7:1 occupation of g the LORD's ark.
2Sm 12:27 the fortress g its water supply.
2Ki 9:14 (Joram and all Israel were g
1Ch 9:19 had been in charge of g
Jer 4:17 them like men g a field,
Luk 22:63 The men who were g Jesus

guardposts (1)

Act 12:10 passed the first and second g

guardroom (6)

1Ki 14:28 and then returned them to the g
2Ch 12:11 and then returned them to the g
Eze 40:7 Each g was 10 ½ feet long
40:12 21 inches in front of each g.
40:13 gateway from the top of one g
40:13 to the top of the opposite g.

guardrooms (11)

Eze 40:7 There were also g.
40:7 The space between the g was
40:10 Now, there were three g on
40:12 The g were 10 ½ feet square.
40:16 The g and recessed walls
40:21 Its three g, its recessed walls,
40:29 Its g, recessed walls,
40:29 The g and the entrance hall
40:33 Its g, recessed walls,
40:33 Its g and entrance hall had
40:36 Its g, recessed walls,

guard's (2)

Gen 41:10 to the captain of the g prison
Neh 12:39 The choir stopped at G Gate

guards (61)

Jdg 7:19 just at the change of the g.
1Sm 17:6 his legs he had bronze shin g
1Ki 14:27 of the g were stationed.
14:28 g carried the shields and then
2Ki 10:25 said to the g and attendants,
10:25 threw out the bodies until the g
11:4 of the Carites and the g
11:6 be at the gate behind the g.
11:11 The g stood with their
11:12 As the g clapped their hands,
11:13 heard the noise made by the g
11:19 of the Carites and the g
1Ch 26:16 One squad of g served its
2Ch 12:10 of the g were stationed.
12:11 g carried the shields and then
Neh 4:9 we prayed to our God and set g
4:23 and the g assigned to me never
Psa 34:20 The LORD g all of his bones.
97:10 The one who g the lives of his
121:7 The LORD g you from every
121:7 from every evil. He g your life.
121:8 The LORD g you as you come
Pro 19:8 One who g understanding finds
21:23 Whoever g his mouth and his
22:5 Whoever g himself will stay far
24:12 Won't the one who g your soul
Sos 3:8 sword at his side and g against
Jer 51:12 Strengthen the g. Station
Eze 27:11 Helech were g all around your
Mat 26:58 went inside and sat with the g
28:4 The g were so deathly afraid of
28:11 some of the g went into the
Mar 14:54 He sat with the g and warmed
14:65 Even the g took him and
Luk 11:21 g his own mansion,
22:4 chief priests and the temple g
22:52 to the chief priests, temple g,
Jon 7:32 sent temple g to arrest Jesus.
7:45 When the temple g returned,
7:46 The temple g answered,
7:47 Pharisees asked the temple g,
18:3 troop of soldiers and the g from
18:12 the Jewish g arrested Jesus.
18:18 The servants and the g were
18:22 one of the g standing near
19:6 priests and the g saw Jesus,
Act 4:1 in charge of the temple g,
4:3 So the temple g arrested them.
5:22 When the temple g arrived at
5:22 The g came back and reported,
5:23 locked and the g standing at
5:24 When the officer of the temple g
5:26 Then the officer of the temple g
5:26 After all, the officer and his g
12:6 and g were in front of the door.
12:19 So he questioned the g and
16:22 and Silas and ordered ⌊the g⌋
16:35 Roman officials sent g who told
16:37 But Paul told the g,
16:38 The g reported to the officials
2Co 11:32 under King Aretas put g around

guards' (2)

2Ki 11:19 street that goes through G Gate
Neh 3:25 king's palace to the g courtyard.

Gudgodah (2)

Dtr 10:7 They moved from there to G,
10:7 and from G to Jotbathah,

guest (8)

Jdg 19:23 This man is a g in my home.
Est 5:12 I am her invited g together
Psa 5:4 Evil will never be your g.
61:4 I would like to be a g in your
Luk 19:7 They said, "He went to be the g
Act 10:6 He is a g of Simon,
10:32 He's a g in the home of Simon,
Phm 1:22 One more thing — have a g

guests (25)

1Sm 9:22 at the head of the g — about 30
1Ki 1:41 Adonijah and all his g heard
1:49 Adonijah's g were frightened,
Job 19:14 My house g have forgotten me.
Pro 9:18 that her g are in the depths of
Zep 1:7 He has invited his special g.
Mat 9:15 Jesus replied, "Can wedding g
14:6 daughter danced for his g.
14:9 because of his oath and his g,
22:10 wedding hall was filled with g.
22:11 the king came to see the g,
22:11 clothes ⌊provided for the g⌋.
Mar 2:19 Jesus replied, "Can wedding g
6:22 Herod and his g were delighted
6:26 because of his oath and his g,
Luk 5:34 "Can you force wedding g to
7:49 The other g thought,
14:1 The g were watching Jesus
14:7 Then Jesus noticed how the g
14:10 Then all the other g will see
Act 17:7 has welcomed them as his g.
28:7 for three days we were his g.
1Pe 4:9 other as g without complaining.
3Jn 1:5 especially when they're your g.
1:10 the believers ⌊we send⌋ as g.

guidance (3)

1Sm 24:20 and under your g the kingdom
2Ch 24:13 under the foremen's g.
Pro 20:18 and with g one wages war.

guide (22)

Gen 33:14 I will slowly and gently g the
Exo 15:13 Powerfully, you will g them to
Num 10:31 and you could be our g.
Job 38:32 at the right time or g Ursa Major
39:10 Can you g a wild ox in a
Psa 31:3 lead me and g me.
43:3 Let them g me. Let them bring
67:4 everyone with justice and g
73:24 With your advice you g me,
139:10 even there your hand would g
Isa 9:16 Those who g these people
28:26 God will g him in judgment,
49:10 them and g them to springs.
51:18 there was no one to g her.
57:18 I'll g them and give them rest.
58:11 The LORD will continually g
Luk 1:79 He will g us into the way of
Jon 16:13 he will g you into the full truth.
Rom 2:19 are confident that you are a g
Gal 5:18 If your spiritual nature is your g,
1Th 3:11 the Lord Jesus will g us to you.
1Ti 1:19 let their faith g their conscience

guided (20)

1Ch 13:7 Uzzah and Ahio g the cart.
2Ch 30:12 Also, God g the people of
Psa 78:14 He g them by a cloud during
78:26 blow in the heavens and g
78:52 out like sheep and g them like
78:72 With skill he g them.
107:30 He g them to the harbor they
119:149 new life g by your regulations.
119:156 new life g by your regulations.
Pro 4:11 I have g you along decent
Isa 9:16 Those who are g by them will
63:14 In this way you g your people
Mat 22:43 g by the Spirit, call him Lord?
Mar 12:36 David, g by the Holy Spirit,
Rom 8:14 Certainly, all who are g by
2Co 5:7 Indeed, our lives are g by faith,
10:2 are only g by human motives.
Php 3:16 However, we should be g by
1Pe 4:2 That way you won't be g by
4:2 Instead, you will be g by what

guideline (1)

1Co 7:17 This is the g I use in every

guides (9)

Job 37:12 He g the clouds as they churn
Psa 23:3 He g me along the paths of
Pro 11:3 Integrity g decent people,
14:8 of a sensible person g his way
Isa 3:12 My people, your g mislead you,
Mat 23:16 it will be for you, you blind g!
23:24 You blind g! You strain gnats
Act 8:31 unless someone g me?"

2Co 5:14 Clearly, Christ's love **g** us.

guiding (33)

2Sm 6:3 were **g** the new cart.
Ezr 7:6 the LORD his God was **g** him.
7:28 the LORD my God was **g** me.
8:18 God was **g** us, so Iddo and his
8:31 God was **g** us, and he rescued
Neh 2:8 because God was **g** me.)
2:18 that my God had been **g** me
Psa 103:18 to follow his **g** principles.
111:7 his **g** principles are trustworthy.
111:10 follows ⌊God's **g** principles⌋.
119:4 that your **g** principles
119:15 I want to reflect on your **g**
119:27 Help me understand your **g**
119:40 I long for your **g** principles.
119:45 I sought out your **g** principles.
119:56 have obeyed your **g** principles.
119:63 who follows your **g** principles.
119:69 ⌊yet⌋ I obey your **g** principles
119:78 ⌊yet⌋ I reflect on your **g**
119:87 But I did not abandon your **g**
119:93 never forget your **g** principles,
119:94 searched for your **g** principles.
119:100 because I have obeyed your **g**
119:104 From your **g** principles I gain
119:110 away from your **g** principles.
119:128 paths of your **g** principles.
119:134 I may obey your **g** principles.
119:141 ⌊yet⌋ I never forget your **g**
119:159 I have loved your **g** principles!
119:168 I have followed your **g**
119:173 ⌊to follow⌋ your **g** principles.
Isa 26:8 the path of your **g** principles.
26:9 When your **g** principles are on

guild (1)

1Ch 4:21 families of the **g** of linen

guilt (76)

Gen 44:16 God has uncovered our **g**.
Lev 4:3 something wrong and brings **g**
5:6 Bring your **g** offering to the
5:7 or two pigeons as a **g** offering
5:15 bring a **g** offering to the LORD.
5:16 ram sacrificed for the **g** offering
5:17 it — when you realize your **g**,
5:18 value in money for a **g** offering.
5:19 It is a **g** offering because you
6:5 day you bring your **g** offering.
6:6 bring the LORD your **g** offering,
6:17 for sin and the **g** offering.
7:1 instructions for the **g** offering.
7:5 It is a **g** offering by fire to the
7:7 for sin and the **g** offering.
7:37 offering for sin, the **g** offering,
14:12 to the LORD as a **g** offering.
14:13 do this because the **g** offering,
14:14 of the blood from the **g** offering
14:17 put the blood of the **g** offering.
14:21 and use it for his **g** offering.
14:24 take the lamb for the **g** offering
14:25 the lamb as a **g** offering.
14:25 of the blood of the **g** offering
14:28 put the blood of the **g** offering.
19:21 He must bring a ram for his **g**
22:16 pay the penalty for their **g**
26:41 hearts and accept their **g**,
26:43 They must accept their **g**
Num 5:6 When you realize your **g**,
6:12 male lamb as an offering for **g**.
18:9 offering for sin, or a **g** offering.
Dtr 19:13 The **g** of murdering an innocent
21:8 Don't let the **g** of this unsolved
21:9 is how you will get rid of the **g**
1Sm 6:3 place with a **g** offering.
6:4 "What kind of **g** offering should
6:8 you're giving him as a **g** offering
6:17 Philistines sent as a **g** offering
14:41 the people were freed ⌊from **g**⌋.
26:9 king and remained free of **g**.
2Sm 22:24 I have kept myself from **g**.
2Ki 12:16 The money from the **g** offerings
Ezr 9:6 and our **g** is so overwhelming
9:7 we have been deep in **g**.
Ezr 9:13 of our overwhelming **g**,
10:10 you have added to Israel's **g**.
10:19 their flock as an offering for **g**
Neh 4:5 Don't ignore their **g**.
Job 10:6 Is that why you look for **g** in me
10:14 and will not free me from my **g**.
Psa 18:23 I have kept myself from **g**.
25:11 name, O LORD, remove my **g**,
31:10 under ⌊the weight of⌋ my **g**,
32:5 and I did not cover up my **g**.
36:2 hate or ⌊even⌋ recognize his **g**.
38:4 My **g** has overwhelmed me.
38:18 I confess my **g**. My sin troubles
51:2 Wash me thoroughly from my **g**,
51:14 me from the **g** of murder,
59:4 or any sin, or any **g** on my part.
85:2 You removed your people's **g**.
109:14 Let the LORD remember the **g**
109:15 Let their **g** and sin always
Pro 14:9 Stubborn fools make fun of **g**,
28:17 A person burdened with the **g**
Isa 1:4 people are loaded down with **g**.
6:7 Your **g** has been taken away,
14:21 because of their ancestors' **g**.
24:6 people are punished for their **g**.
Lam 2:14 They didn't expose your **g** in
Eze 24:23 waste away because of your **g**
40:39 for sin, and **g** offerings.
42:13 and the **g** offerings.
44:29 for sin, and **g** offerings.
46:20 boil the meat for the **g** offering

guilty (97)

Gen 18:23 away the innocent with the **g**?
18:25 to treat the innocent and the **g**
18:25 to kill the innocent with the **g**.
26:10 would have made us **g** of sin."
38:26 them and said, "She's not **g**.
Exo 22:2 he is not **g** of murder.
22:3 after sunrise, he is **g** of murder.
22:9 The one whom God declares **g**
23:7 declare **g** people innocent.
34:7 never lets the **g** go unpunished,
Lev 4:13 commands, they will be **g**.
4:22 LORD his God — he will be **g**.
4:27 commands — he will be **g**.
5:2 you are unclean and will be **g**.
5:3 what you did), you will be **g**.
5:4 what you said), you will be **g**.
5:5 "So if you are **g** of any of these
5:19 you are certainly **g** as far as
6:2 you are sinning and will be **g**.
6:4 you are sinning and will be **g**.
6:7 you did that made you **g**."
17:4 is **g** of bloodshed. He has shed
17:16 they will be **g** of sin."
19:17 so that you will not be **g**
20:20 man and woman are **g** of sin.
Num 5:19 to your husband, you're not **g**.
5:28 she is not **g** and will be able to
5:31 The husband isn't **g** of doing
14:18 never lets the **g** go unpunished,
15:31 completely. He remains **g**."
35:27 the relative is not **g** of murder.
Dtr 19:10 and you won't be **g** of murder.
23:21 You would be **g** of a sin if you
23:22 you would not be **g**.
Jdg 15:3 "This time I won't be **g** when I
21:22 You won't be **g** because you
1Sm 20:1 What crime am I **g** of?
2Sm 14:32 If I'm **g** of a sin, he should kill
21:1 They are **g** of murder because
1Ki 8:32 Condemn the **g** person with the
1Ch 21:3 to make Israel **g** of ⌊this⌋ sin?"
2Ch 6:23 Repay the **g** person with the
19:10 relatives will not become **g**
19:10 you won't be **g** ⌊of anything⌋.
28:10 But aren't you also **g** of sinning
Ezr 4:19 Its inhabitants are **g** of treason
9:15 All of us are **g**. None of us can
10:19 for guilt because they were **g**.
Job 9:29 I've already been found **g**.
10:7 You know I'm not **g**,
10:15 terrible it will be for me if I'm **g**!
34:31 a person says to God, 'I am **g**,
Psa 51:5 Indeed, I was born **g**.
Psa 68:21 of those who continue to be **g**.
69:5 and the things of which I am **g**
106:6 have done wrong. We are **g**.
109:7 let him be found **g**.
Pro 21:8 The way of a **g** person is
24:24 Whoever says to a **g** person,
24:25 those who convict a **g** person,
25:22 make him feel **g** and ashamed,
30:10 and you will be found **g**."
Isa 5:23 who declare the **g** innocent for
50:9 Who will find me **g**?
Jer 2:3 All who devoured it became **g**,
3:11 less **g** than treacherous Judah.
26:15 the people living in it will be **g**
50:7 enemies say, 'We're not **g**.
51:5 although their land is **g** of
Eze 14:10 The prophet will be as **g** as
16:38 same way that those who are **g**
22:4 You are **g** because of the
25:12 and became **g** because of it.
Hos 4:15 Don't let Judah become **g** too.
5:15 until they admit that they are **g**.
12:8 no one will find us **g** of any sin.'
12:14 He will hold them **g** of murder.
13:1 Then they became **g** of
13:16 The people of Samaria are **g**
Nah 1:3 never let the **g** go unpunished.
Hab 1:11 the wind. So they will be **g**,
Mat 12:37 words you will be declared **g**."
27:24 "I won't be **g** of killing this man.
Mar 3:29 He is **g** of an everlasting sin."
Luk 23:4 find this man **g** of any crime."
23:14 and haven't found this man **g**
Jon 18:38 find this man **g** of anything.
19:4 find this man **g** of anything."
19:6 find this man **g** of anything."
19:11 handed me over to you is **g**
Act 25:11 If I am **g** and have done
Rom 12:20 make him feel **g** and ashamed."
14:22 knows is right shouldn't feel **g**.
1Co 8:7 So they feel **g** because their
Heb 10:22 to free us from a **g** conscience,
Jas 2:10 that person is **g** of breaking all
1Pe 3:18 but he suffered for **g** people so

gulf (1)

Isa 11:15 The LORD will dry up the **g** of

gullible (19)

Job 5:2 and jealousy murders a **g**
Psa 19:7 It makes **g** people wise.
119:130 it helps **g** people understand.
Pro 1:4 to give insight to **g** people,
1:22 "How long will you **g** people
1:22 people love being so **g**?
1:32 "**G** people kill themselves
7:7 I was looking at **g** people when
8:5 You **g** people, learn how to be
9:4 "Whoever is **g** turn in here!"
9:6 Stop being **g** and live.
9:13 woman Stupidity is loud, **g**,
9:16 "Whoever is **g** turn in here!"
14:15 A **g** person believes anything,
14:18 **G** people are gifted with
19:25 Strike a mocker, and a **g**
21:11 a **g** person becomes wise,
22:3 but **g** people go ahead and
27:12 **G** people go ahead ⌊and⌋

gum (2)

Gen 43:11 honey, **g**, myrrh, pistachio nuts,
Exo 30:34 spices (two kinds of **g** resin

Guni (4)

Gen 46:24 **G**, Jezer, and Shillem.
Num 26:48 of Jahzeel, the family of **G**,
1Ch 5:15 of Abdiel and grandson of **G**,
7:13 Jahziel, **G**, Jezer, and Shallum.

Gur (1)

2Ki 9:27 They shot him at **G** Pass,

Gur Baal (1)

2Ch 26:7 the Arabs who lived in **G**,

gush (4)
Psa 78:20 and water did **g** out,
104:10 You make water **g** from springs
Isa 35:6 Water will **g** out into the desert,
35:6 and streams will **g** out into the

gushed (3)
Jdg 15:19 place at Lehi, and water **g** out.
Psa 105:41 He opened a rock, and water **g**
Isa 48:21 He split a rock, and water **g** out.

gushes (1)
Jon 4:14 in them a spring that **g** up

guzzle (1)
Oba 1:16 They will drink and **g** down

H

Haahashtari (1)
1Ch 4:6 Hepher, Temeni, and **H**.

Habakkuk (2)
Hab 1:1 that the prophet **H** saw.
3:1 A prayer of the prophet **H**;

Habazziniah (1)
Jer 35:3 and the grandson of **H**,

habit (3)
Exo 21:29 the bull has had the **h** of goring,
21:36 that the bull had the **h** of goring,
Zec 8:21 "Let's make a **h** of going to ask

Habor (3)
2Ki 17:6 along the **H** River in Gozan,
18:11 along the **H** River in Gozan,
1Ch 5:26 He brought them to Halah, **H**,

Hacaliah (2)
Neh 1:1 words of Nehemiah, son of **H**:
10:1 Governor Nehemiah (son of **H**),

Hachilah (3)
1Sm 23:19 at Horesh on the hills of **H**,
26:1 at the hill of **H** near Jeshimon,"
26:3 at the hill of **H** near Jeshimon,

Hachmon (1)
1Ch 11:11 was Jashobeam, son of **H**,

Hachmoni (1)
1Ch 27:32 Jonathan and Jehiel, son of **H**,

hacked (1)
Psa 74:5 its entrance, they **h** away like

Hadad (17)
Gen 25:15 **H**, Tema, Jetur, Naphish,
36:35 After Husham died, **H**,
36:35 **H** defeated the Midianites in
36:36 After **H** died, Samlah from
1Ki 11:14 The LORD raised up **H** the
11:14 **H** was from the Edomite royal
11:17 **H** was a young boy at the time.
11:18 Pharaoh gave **H** a home,
11:19 Pharaoh approved of **H**.
11:19 So he gave **H** his sister-in-law,
11:21 When **H** heard in Egypt that
11:25 to the trouble that **H** caused,
1Ch 1:30 Mishma, Dumah, Massa, **H**,
1:46 After Husham died, **H**,
1:47 After **H** died, Samlah from
1:50 **H** succeeded him as king,
1:51 Then **H** died. The tribal leaders

Hadadezer (14)
2Sm 8:3 he defeated Zobah's King **H**,
8:5 came to help King **H** of Zobah,
8:10 him for fighting and defeating **H**
8:10 been war between **H** and Toi.)
8:12 taken from Zobah's King **H**,
10:16 **H** sent ⌞messengers⌟ to get
10:19 subject to **H** saw that Israel
1Ki 11:23 his master, King **H** of Zobah,
1Ch 18:3 he defeated King **H** at Hamath.
18:5 came to help King **H** of Zobah,
18:9 whole army of Zobah's King **H**,
18:10 him for fighting and defeating **H**
18:10 been war between **H** and Tou.)
19:19 subject to **H** saw that Israel

Hadadezer's (7)
2Sm 8:7 that belonged to **H** servants,
8:8 Betah and Berothai, **H** cities
8:9 had defeated **H** whole army,
10:16 of **H** army, leading them.
1Ch 18:7 shields that **H** servants carried,
18:8 from Tibhath and Cun, **H** cities.
19:16 of **H** army, led them.

Hadad Rimmon (1)
Zec 12:11 as intense as the mourning at **H**

Hadad's (1)
1Ki 11:19 Queen Tahpenes, to be **H** wife

Hadar (1)
Gen 36:39 **H** succeeded him as king,

Hadashah (1)
Jos 15:37 villages: Zenan, **H**, Migdalgad,

Hadassah (1)
Est 2:7 Mordecai had raised **H**,

Hadid (3)
Ezr 2:33 of Lod, **H**, and Ono: 725
Neh 7:37 of Lod, **H**, and Ono: 721
11:34 **H**, Zeboim, Neballat,

Hadlai (1)
2Ch 28:12 son of **H** (some leaders of

Hadoram (4)
Gen 10:27 **H**, Uzal, Diklah,
1Ch 1:21 **H**, Uzal, Diklah,
18:10 he sent his son **H** to greet King
2Ch 10:18 Then King Rehoboam sent **H** to

Hadrach (1)
Zec 9:1 LORD is against the land of **H**

Hagab (1)
Ezr 2:46 **H**, Shalmai, Hanan,

Hagabah (2)
Ezr 2:45 Lebanah, **H**, Akkub,
Neh 7:48 Lebanah, **H**, Shalmai,

Hagar (18)
Gen 16:1 an Egyptian slave named **H**.
16:3 Sarai took her Egyptian slave **H**
16:4 He slept with **H**, and she
16:4 When **H** realized that she was
16:6 Then Sarai mistreated **H** so
16:8 He said, "**H**, Sarai's slave,
16:13 **H** named the LORD,
16:15 **H** gave birth to Abram's son.
16:16 86 years old when **H** gave birth
21:9 saw that Abraham's son by **H**
21:14 of water and gave them to **H**,
21:17 of God called to **H** from heaven.
21:17 "What's the matter, **H**?"
25:12 Egyptian slave **H** and Abraham.
1Ch 27:31 for the flocks: Jaziz from **H**
Psa 83:6 and Ishmael, Moab and **H**,
Gal 4:24 The one woman, **H**,
4:25 **H** is Mount Sinai in Arabia.

Hagar's (2)
1Ch 5:19 **H** descendants (including Jetur,
5:20 **H** descendants and the nations

Haggai (11)
Ezr 5:1 The prophet **H** and Zechariah,
6:14 the prophet **H** and Zechariah,
Hag 1:1 his word through the prophet **H**
1:3 his word through the prophet **H**
1:12 the words of the prophet **H**
1:13 Then **H**, the messenger of the
2:1 his word through the prophet **H**
2:10 his word to the prophet **H**.
2:13 **H** asked, "Suppose a person
2:14 Then **H** answered,
2:20 The LORD spoke his word to **H**

Haggedolim (1)
Neh 11:14 of them was Zabdiel, son of **H**.

Haggi (2)
Gen 46:16 **H**, Shuni, Ezbon, Eri, Arodi,
Num 26:15 of Zephon, the family of **H**,

Haggiah (1)
1Ch 6:30 Shimea's son was **H**.

Haggiah's (1)
1Ch 6:30 **H** son was Asaiah.

Haggith (4)
2Sm 3:4 whose mother was **H**.
1Ki 1:5 Adonijah, son of **H**,
2:13 Then Adonijah, son of **H**,
1Ch 3:2 whose mother was **H**.

Haggith's (1)
1Ki 1:11 **H** son, has become king,

Hagri (1)
1Ch 11:38 of Nathan), Mibhar (son of **H**),

Hagrites (1)
1Ch 5:10 they fought a war against the **H**,

Hagrites' (2)
1Ch 5:21 the **H** livestock: 50,000
5:22 lived in the **H** land until

hail (24)
Exo 9:19 die when the **h** falls on them.'"
9:22 and **h** will fall on people,
9:23 the LORD sent thunder and **h**,
9:23 the LORD made it **h** on Egypt.
9:25 All over Egypt the **h** knocked
9:26 The only place it didn't **h** was
9:28 enough of God's thunder and **h**.
9:29 and there will be no more **h**.
9:33 The thunder and the **h** stopped,
9:34 saw that the rain, the **h**,
10:5 will eat everything left by the **h**,
10:12 land — everything left by the **h**
10:15 on the trees that the **h** had left.
Job 38:22 or seen the warehouses for **h**
Psa 78:47 He killed their vines with **h** and
78:48 He let the **h** strike their cattle
105:32 He gave them **h** and lightning
148:8 lightning and **h**, snow and fog,
Isa 28:17 **H** will sweep away your refuge
32:19 will be flattened because of **h**,
Hag 2:17 mildew and struck it with **h**.
Rev 8:7 **h** and fire were mixed with
11:19 an earthquake, and heavy **h**.
16:21 the plague of **h** was such

hailed (2)
Exo 9:24 It **h**, and lightning flashed while
9:24 and lightning flashed while it **h**.

hailstones (11)
Jos 10:11 LORD threw huge **h** on them.
10:11 More died from the **h** than from
Psa 18:12 passed by with **h** and lightning.
18:13 heard with **h** and lightning.
147:17 throws his **h** like breadcrumbs.
147:18 out his word and melts his **h**.
Isa 30:30 windstorms, rainstorms, and **h**.
Eze 13:11 will pour down, **h** will fall on it,
13:13 and **h** will destroy the wall.
38:22 I will send rainstorms, large **h**,
Rev 16:21 Large, heavy **h** fell from the sky

hailstorm (2)
Exo 9:18 send the worst **h** that has ever

Isa 28:2 He is like a **h**, a destructive

hair (102)

Gen 25:25 body was covered with **h**,
Exo 25:4 red yarn, fine linen, goats' **h**,
26:7 "Make 11 sheets of goats' **h** to
35:6 red yarn, fine linen, goats' **h**,
35:23 goats' **h**, rams' skins dyed red,
35:26 had the skill spun the goats' **h**.
36:14 made 11 sheets of goats' **h**
Lev 10:6 by leaving your **h** uncombed
13:3 If the **h** in the diseased area
13:4 and the **h** has not turned white,
13:10 that has turned the **h** white,
13:20 skin and its **h** has turned white,
13:21 the affected area and the **h**
13:25 If the **h** on the affected area has
13:26 the priest examines it and the **h**
13:30 and there is thin yellow **h** on it,
13:31 and there is no black **h** in it,
13:32 there is no yellow **h** on it,
13:36 not have to look for yellow **h**.
13:37 spread and black **h** grows
13:40 "If a man loses his **h**,
13:41 If he loses the **h** on the front of
13:45 and leave their **h** uncombed.
14:8 shave off all his **h**,
14:9 day he must shave off all the **h**
19:27 "Never shave the **h** on your
21:10 by leaving his **h** uncombed
Num 5:18 presence and loosen her **h**.
6:5 They must let their **h** grow long.
6:7 vow to God with their long **h**.
6:9 make the Nazirite's **h** unclean.
6:18 take the **h** as proof that they
6:19 they have shaved off their **h**.
31:20 of leather, goats' **h**, or wood."
Jdg 13:5 You must never cut his **h**
16:13 the seven braids of my **h**
16:17 no one has ever cut the **h** on
16:17 If my **h** is ever shaved off,
16:22 But his **h** started to grow back
20:16 a stone at a **h** and not miss.
1Sm 14:45 not a single **h** of his head will
19:13 put a goat-**h** blanket at its head
19:16 idols with the goat-**h** blanket at
2Sm 14:11 "not a **h** on your son's head will
14:26 he used to cut his **h** because it
14:26 When he cut the **h** on his head
1Ki 1:52 not one **h** on his head will fall
2Ki 9:30 on eye shadow, fixed her **h**,
Ezr 9:3 pulled **h** from my scalp and my
Neh 13:25 and pulled out their **h**.
Job 4:15 It made my **h** stand on end.
41:32 sea appears to have silvery **h**.
Psa 68:21 ⌊and destroy even⌋ the **h**
Pro 16:31 Silver **h** is a beautiful crown
20:29 of older people is their silver **h**.
Sos 4:1 Your **h** is like a flock of goats
5:2 My head is wet with dew, my **h**
5:11 His **h** is wavy, black as a
6:5 Your **h** is like a flock of goats
Isa 3:24 heads instead of beautiful **h**.
7:20 to be a razor to shave the **h**
7:20 the **h** on your legs,
46:4 Even when your **h** turns gray,
Jer 7:29 "Cut off your **h** and throw it
9:26 will punish all who shave the **h**
25:23 shave the **h** on their foreheads;
49:32 winds those who shave the **h**
Lam 4:7 Their **h** was like sapphires.
Eze 5:1 Take scales to weigh your **h**
5:2 burn one-third of your **h** in a fire
5:3 Take a few strands of **h**,
8:3 hand and grabbed me by the **h**
16:7 developed, and your **h** grew.
44:20 heads or let their **h** grow long.
44:20 They must keep the **h** on their
Dan 3:27 The **h** on their heads wasn't
4:33 wet until his **h** grew as long
7:9 as white as snow and the **h**
Zec 13:4 a prophet⌋ in a coat made of **h**.
Mat 3:4 clothes made from camel's **h**
5:36 make one **h** black or white.
6:17 your face and comb your **h**.
10:30 Every **h** on your head has been
Mar 1:6 in clothes made from camel's **h**.
Luk 7:38 she dried his feet with her **h**,
7:44 tears and dried them with her **h**.
12:7 Even every **h** on your head has
21:18 But not a **h** on your head will
Jon 11:2 and wiped his feet with her **h**.
12:3 she dried his feet with her **h**.
Act 18:18 Aquila had his **h** cut,
27:34 since not a **h** from anyone's
1Co 11:6 she should cut off her **h**.
11:6 for a woman to cut off her **h**
11:14 for a man to have long **h**?
11:15 pride to wear her **h** long?
11:15 Her **h** is given to her in place of
1Ti 2:9 not by their **h** styles or the gold
Rev 1:14 His head and his **h** were white
6:12 black as sackcloth made of **h**.
9:8 They had **h** like women's hair
9:8 They had hair like women's **h**

hairs (3)

Psa 40:12 They outnumber the **h** on my
69:4 for no reason outnumber the **h**
Isa 50:6 to those who pluck **h** out

hairstyles (1)

1Pe 3:3 Beauty doesn't come from **h**,

hairy (5)

Gen 25:25 so they named him Esau [**H**].
27:11 "My brother Esau is a **h** man,
27:23 because his hands were **h** like
2Ki 1:8 They replied, "He was **h** and
Dan 8:21 The **h** male goat is the

Hakkatan (1)

Ezr 8:12 son of **H**, with 110 males

Hakkephirim (1)

Neh 6:2 "Let's meet in **H** on the plain of

Hakkoz (5)

1Ch 24:10 the seventh for **H**, the eighth for
Ezr 2:61 the descendants of Hobaiah, **H**,
Neh 3:4 son of Uriah and grandson of **H**,
3:21 son of Uriah and grandson of **H**,
7:63 the descendants of Hobaiah, **H**,

Hakupha (2)

Ezr 2:51 Bakbuk, **H**, Harhur,
Neh 7:53 Bakbuk, **H**, Harhur,

Halah (3)

2Ki 17:6 He settled them in **H**,
18:11 He put them in **H**, along the
1Ch 5:26 He brought them to **H**,

Halak (2)

Jos 11:17 from Mount **H** which ascends
12:7 to Mount **H** which rises toward

half (124)

Gen 15:10 He cut each of them in **h** and
15:10 in half and laid each **h** opposite
15:10 he did not cut the birds in **h**.
Exo 24:6 Moses took **h** of the blood and
24:6 the other **h** against the altar.
26:9 Fold the sixth sheet in **h** ⌊to
28:16 Fold it in **h** so that it's 9 inches
30:23 myrrh; **h** as much, that is,
39:9 It was folded in **h** and was 9
Lev 6:20 He must offer **h** of it in the
6:20 morning and **h** in the evening.
Num 31:29 these things from the soldiers' **h**
31:30 From the Israelites' **h** of the
31:36 **H** of it went to the soldiers who
31:42 Moses took the Israelites' **h** of
31:47 From the Israelites' **h** Moses
32:33 and **h** of the tribe of Manasseh,
34:14 and **h** of the tribe of Manasseh
Dtr 3:12 near the Arnon Valley and **h**
3:13 all of Bashan ruled by Og to **h**
3:18 tribes of Reuben and Gad and **h**
29:8 and **h** of the tribe of Manasseh
Jos 1:12 tribes of Reuben and Gad and **h**
3:4 However, stay about **h** a mile
Jos 4:12 men of Reuben, Gad, and **h**
8:33 **H** of the people were in front of
8:33 Mount Gerizim and the other **h**
12:2 of the valley and **h** of Gilead.
12:5 and **h** of Gilead to the border of
12:6 tribes of Reuben and Gad and **h**
13:7 for the nine tribes and **h**
13:8 of Reuben and Gad with **h**
13:25 and **h** of Ammon as far as
13:29 land as an inheritance to **h**
13:29 families of that **h** of the tribe.
13:31 It also included **h** of Gilead
13:31 They were given to **h** the
18:7 tribes of Gad and Reuben and **h**
21:5 of Ephraim and Dan and **h**
21:6 and **h** of the tribe of Manasseh
21:25 **H** of the tribe of Manasseh
21:27 cities with pasturelands from **h**
22:1 tribes of Reuben and Gad and **h**
22:7 inheritance to **h** of Manasseh,
22:7 Joshua had given the other **h**
22:9 tribes of Reuben and Gad and **h**
22:10 Reuben, Gad, and **h** of the tribe
22:11 Reuben, Gad, and **h** of the tribe
22:13 tribes of Reuben and Gad and **h**
22:21 tribes of Reuben and Gad and **h**
Rut 2:17 She had about **h** a bushel of
1Sm 1:24 **h** a bushel of flour,
2Sm 10:4 shaved off **h** of each man's
13:2 with his **h** sister Tamar that
13:32 the day his **h** brother raped his
18:3 about us, and if **h** of us die,
19:40 All the troops from Judah and **h**
1Ki 3:25 Give **h** to the one and half to
3:25 to the one and **h** to the other."
10:7 I wasn't even told **h** of it.
13:8 "Even if you gave me **h** of your
16:9 the general who commanded **h**
16:21 **H** of the army followed Tibni,
16:21 The ⌊other⌋ **h** followed Omri.
16:22 But the **h** which followed Omri
16:22 the **h** which followed Tibni,
2Ki 7:1 of the best flour will sell for **h**
7:1 48 cups of barley will sell for **h**
7:16 cups of the best flour sold for **h**
7:16 and 48 cups of barley sold for **h**
7:18 cups of barley will sell for **h**
7:18 of the best flour will sell for **h**
1Ch 2:52 **h** of the Manahathites,
2:54 **h** of the Manahathites,
5:18 and **h** of the tribe of Manasseh
5:22 Reuben, Gad, and **h** of the tribe
5:23 **H** of the tribe of Manasseh
5:25 But Gad, Reuben, and **h** of the
5:26 and **h** of the tribe of Manasseh
6:61 by lot from the families of **h**
6:70 From **h** of the tribe of
6:71 from the families of **h**
12:31 From **h** of the tribe of
12:37 and **h** the tribe of Manasseh,
26:32 and **h** of the tribe of Manasseh.
27:20 son of Azaziah for **h** of the tribe
27:21 for the **h** of Manasseh in
2Ch 9:6 I wasn't even told about **h** of
Neh 3:9 an official in charge of **h** a
3:12 an official in charge of **h** a
3:16 the official in charge of **h** the
3:17 the official in charge of **h** the
3:18 the official in charge of **h** the
4:6 which was rebuilt to about **h**
4:16 From that day on, **h** of my men
4:16 and the other **h** were wearing
4:21 **H** of us held spears from early
12:32 Hoshaiah and **h** of the leaders
12:38 I followed them with the other **h**
12:40 as did I and the **h** of the leaders
13:24 **H** their children spoke the
Est 5:3 Even if it is up to **h** of the
5:6 Even if it is up to **h** of the
7:2 Even if it is up to **h** of the
Psa 55:23 will not live out **h** their days.
Isa 44:16 **H** of the wood they burn in the
44:16 Over this **h** they roast meat that
44:19 "I burned **h** of the wood in the
Eze 16:51 "'Samaria didn't commit **h** the
Dan 7:25 a time, times, and **h** of a time.

Dan 12:7 a time, times, and **h** of a time.
Zec 14:2 **H** of the people in the city will
14:4 **H** of the mountain will move
14:4 and the other **h** will move
14:8 **h** of it to the Dead Sea and the
14:8 to the Dead Sea and the other **h**
Mar 6:23 up to **h** of my kingdom."
Luk 19:8 I'll give **h** of my property to the
Jon 7:14 When the festival was **h** over,
Act 1:12 about **h** a mile away.
18:11 in Corinth for a year and a **h**
Heb 11:37 stoned to death, sawed in **h**,
Rev 8:1 in heaven for about **h** an hour.
12:14 for a time, times, and **h** a time.

halfway (4)

Exo 26:28 to the other, **h** up the frames.
27:5 so that it comes **h** up the altar.
36:33 to the other, **h** up the frames.
38:4 under the ledge, **h** up the altar.

Halhul (1)

Jos 15:58 **H**, Bethzur, Gedor,

Hali (1)

Jos 19:25 Helkath, **H**, Beten, Achshaph,

hall (57)

1Sm 9:22 his servant to the banquet **h**
1Ki 6:3 The entrance **h** in front of the
6:17 temple served as the main **h**.
7:2 He built a **h** ⌊named⌋ the
7:3 The **h** was covered with cedar
7:6 Solomon made the **H** of Pillars
7:6 In front of the **h** was an
7:6 was an entrance **h** with pillars.
7:7 He made the **H** of Justice,
7:7 The **h** was covered with cedar
7:8 location than the **H** of Justice,
7:12 temple and the entrance **h**.
7:19 entrance **h** were lily-shaped.
7:21 in the temple's entrance **h**.
10:17 The king put them in the **h**
10:21 and all the utensils for the **h**
1Ch 28:11 the plans for the entrance **h**
2Ch 3:4 The entrance **h** in front of ⌊the
3:13 their feet and faced the main **h**.
8:12 built in front of the entrance **h**.
9:16 The king put them in the **h**
9:20 and all the utensils for the **h**
15:8 front of the LORD's entrance **h**.
29:7 of the ⌊temple's⌋ entrance **h**,
29:17 into the LORD's entrance **h**,
Eze 40:7 the gateway by the entrance **h**
40:8 the entrance **h** of the gateway.
40:9 entrance **h** faced the temple.
40:14 also measured the entrance **h**.
40:14 In front of the entrance **h** to the
40:15 of the entrance **h** was 87 ½
40:16 The entrance **h** also had
40:21 and its entrance **h** were the
40:22 to it and led to its entrance **h**.
40:24 walls and its entrance **h**.
40:25 The gateway and its entrance **h**
40:26 to it and led to its entrance **h**.
40:29 and entrance **h** were the same
40:29 the entrance **h** had windows all
40:33 Its guardrooms and entrance **h**
40:34 Its entrance **h** faced the outer
40:36 and entrance **h** had windows
40:38 opened toward the entrance **h**
40:39 In the entrance **h** of the
40:40 the other side of the entrance **h**
40:48 brought me to the entrance **h**
40:49 The entrance **h** was 35 feet
40:49 on each side of the entrance **h**.
41:25 over the outer entrance **h**.
41:26 on both sides of the entrance **h**,
44:3 enter through the entrance **h**
46:2 outside through the entrance **h**
46:8 enter through the entrance **h**
Dan 5:10 herself into the banquet **h**.
Mat 22:10 And the wedding **h** was filled
25:10 with him into the wedding **h**,
Act 19:9 in the lecture **h** of Tyrannus.

hallelujah (27)

Psa 104:35 my soul! **H**!
105:45 and follow his teachings. **H**!
106:1 **H**! Give thanks to the LORD
106:48 all the people say amen. **H**!
111:1 **H**! I will give thanks to the
112:1 **H**! Blessed is the person who
113:1 **H**! You servants of the LORD,
113:9 home a joyful mother. **H**!
115:18 the LORD now and forever. **H**!
116:19 in the middle of Jerusalem. **H**!
117:2 faithfulness endures forever. **H**!
135:1 **H**! Praise the name of the
135:21 one who lives in Jerusalem. **H**!
146:1 **H**! Praise the LORD, my soul!
146:10 throughout every generation. **H**
147:1 **H**! It is good to sing psalms to
147:20 he has handed down. **H**!
148:1 **H**! Praise the LORD from the
148:14 who are close to him. **H**!
149:1 **H**! Sing a new song to the
149:9 to all his godly ones. **H**!
150:1 **H**! Praise God in his holy place.
150:6 breathes praise the LORD! **H**!
Rev 19:1 crowd in heaven, saying, "**H**!
19:3 A second time they said, "**H**!
19:4 "Amen! **H**!"
19:6 of loud thunder, saying, "**H**!

Hallohesh (1)

Neh 10:24 **H**, Pilha, Shobek,

Hallohesh's (1)

Neh 3:12 Next to them Shallum, **H** son,

halls (3)

Eze 40:30 There were entrance **h** all
40:31 The entrance **h** faced the outer
40:33 and entrance **h** were the same

Ham (14)

Gen 5:32 father of Shem, **H**, and Japheth.
6:10 He had three sons: Shem, **H**,
7:13 sons Shem, **H**, and Japheth,
9:18 were Shem, **H**, and Japheth.
9:19 **H** was the father of Canaan.
9:22 **H**, father of Canaan, saw his
10:1 sons Shem, **H**, and Japheth,
10:1 Shem, **H** and Japheth had
14:5 Karnaim, the Zuzim at **H**,
1Ch 1:4 Noah: Shem, **H**, and Japheth.
Psa 78:51 the ones born in the tents of **H**
105:23 as a foreigner in the land of **H**.
105:27 amazing things in the land of **H**.
106:22 miracles in the land of **H**,

Haman (52)

Est 3:1 Later, King Xerxes promoted **H**.
3:1 (**H** was the son of Hammedatha
3:1 He gave **H** a position higher in
3:2 kneeling and bowing to **H** with
3:4 So they informed **H** to see if
3:5 When **H** saw that Mordecai did
3:5 bow to him, **H** was infuriated.
3:6 So **H** planned to wipe out
3:7 the lot) was thrown in front of **H**
3:8 Now, **H** told King Xerxes,
3:10 his signet ring and gave it to **H**,
3:10 (**H** was the son of Hammedatha
3:11 The king told **H**, "You can keep
3:15 So the king and **H** sat down to
4:7 of silver that **H** had promised
5:4 come today with **H** to a dinner I
5:5 "Bring **H** right away,
5:5 So the king and **H** came to the
5:8 Your Majesty, come with **H** to
5:9 When **H** left that day,
5:9 But when **H** saw Mordecai at
5:9 **H** was furious with Mordecai.
5:10 However, **H** controlled himself.
5:11 Then **H** began to relate in detail
5:12 **H** went on to say, Queen Esther
5:14 **H** liked the idea, so he had the
6:4 At that moment, **H** came
6:5 "**H** happens to be standing in
Est 6:6 So **H** came in. The king then
6:6 **H** thought to himself,
6:7 So **H** told the king,
6:10 The king told **H**, "Hurry,
6:11 So **H** took the robe and the
6:12 but **H** hurried home.
6:13 There, **H** began to relate in
6:14 arrived and quickly took **H**
7:1 So the king and **H** came to
7:6 enemy is this wicked man **H**!"
7:6 Then **H** became panic-stricken
7:7 But **H** stayed to beg Queen
7:8 **H** was falling on the couch
7:9 The 75-foot pole **H** made for
8:1 Xerxes gave the property of **H**,
8:2 which he had taken from **H**,
8:3 and to undo the evil plot of **H**,
8:5 the plot of **H** (who was
9:10 These were the ten sons of **H**,
9:24 It was because **H**,
9:24 (**H** was the son of Hammedatha
9:24 **H** had the Pur (which means
9:25 that the evil plan **H** had plotted
9:25 As a result, they hung **H** and

Haman's (10)

Est 3:12 All **H** orders were written to the
7:8 and servants covered **H** face
7:9 is still standing at **H** house."
7:10 So servants hung **H** ⌊dead
8:2 in charge of **H** property
8:7 "I have given **H** property to
8:7 and **H** ⌊dead body⌋ was hung
9:12 out 500 men and **H** 10 sons.
9:13 Let them hang **H** ten sons on
9:14 And so they hung **H** ten sons

Hamath (36)

Num 13:21 Desert of Zin to the border of **H**.
34:8 Hor to the border of **H** so that
Jos 13:5 Hermon to the border of **H**.
Jdg 3:3 Baal Hermon to the border of **H**
2Sm 8:9 When King Toi of **H** heard that
1Ki 8:65 between⌋ the border of **H**
2Ki 14:25 boundaries from the border of **H**
14:28 he recovered Damascus and **H**
17:24 from Babylon, Cuthah, Avva, **H**,
17:30 people from **H** made Ashima.
18:34 are the gods of **H** and Arpad?
19:13 Where is the king of **H**,
23:33 the territory of **H** during his
25:21 at Riblah in the territory of **H**.
1Ch 13:5 near Egypt to the border of **H**
18:3 defeated King Hadadezer at **H**.
18:9 When King Tou of **H** heard that
2Ch 7:8 between⌋ the border of **H**
8:4 built all the storage cities in **H**.
Isa 10:9 Isn't **H** like Arpad?
11:11 **H**, and the islands of the sea.
36:19 are the gods of **H** and Arpad?
37:13 Where is the king of **H**,
Jer 39:5 at Riblah in the territory of **H**.
49:23 "**H** and Arpad are worried
52:9 king of Babylon at Riblah in **H**,
52:27 at Riblah in the territory of **H**.
Eze 47:15 the way to Hethlon and **H** Pass.
47:16 borders of Damascus and **H**.
47:17 The border of **H** will lie to the
47:20 up to a point opposite **H** Pass.
48:1 the road to Hethlon to **H** Pass
48:1 border of Damascus near **H**,
Amo 6:2 from there to the great city of **H**.
6:14 you from the border of **H**
Zec 9:2 and also **H**, which borders on it,

Hamathites (2)

Gen 10:18 the Zemarites, and the **H**.
1Ch 1:16 the Zemarites, and the **H**.

Hamath Zobah (1)

2Ch 8:3 went to **H** and conquered it.

Hamites (1)

1Ch 4:40 and quiet because the **H** used

Hammath (2)

Jos 19:35 Zer, **H**, Rakkath, Chinnereth,
1Ch 2:55 the Kenites who came from **H**.

Hammedatha (5)

Est 3:1 (Haman was the son of **H** and
3:10 (Haman was the son of **H** and
8:5 Haman (who was the son of **H**
9:10 who was the son of **H** and the
9:24 (Haman was the son of **H** and

hammer (9)

Num 16:38 **H** them into thin metal sheets
Jdg 4:21 quietly toward him with a **h**
5:26 for a workman's **h** with the
1Ki 6:7 No **h**, chisel, or any other iron
Isa 2:4 They will **h** their swords into
Jer 23:29 like fire or like a **h** that shatters
50:23 The **h** of the whole earth is
Joe 3:10 **H** your plowblades into swords
Mic 4:3 They will **h** their swords into

hammered (17)

Exo 25:18 Make two angels out of **h** gold
25:31 and petals must be **h** out of one
25:36 branches should also be **h** out
37:7 made two angels out of **h** gold
37:17 and petals were **h** out of one
37:22 The buds and branches were **h**
39:3 They **h** the gold into thin
Num 8:4 to bottom, was **h** out of gold.
10:2 two trumpets out of **h** silver.
16:39 were then **h** into thin metal
Jdg 4:21 She **h** the tent peg through his
1Ki 6:32 The gold was **h** onto the
10:16 200 large shields of **h** gold,
10:17 300 small shields of **h** gold,
2Ch 9:15 200 large shields of **h** gold,
9:16 300 small shields of **h** gold,
Jer 10:9 **H** silver is brought from

hammers (2)

Isa 44:12 coals and shape them with **h**,
Jer 10:4 fasten them ⌊together⌋ with **h**

Hammolecheth (1)

1Ch 7:18 Bedan's sister **H** gave birth to

Hammon (2)

Jos 19:28 Abdon, Rehob, **H**, Kanah,
1Ch 6:76 **H** with its pastureland,

Hammoth Dor (1)

Jos 21:32 for murderers), **H**, and Kartan.

Hammuel (1)

1Ch 4:26 Mishma's son was **H**.

Hammuel's (1)

1Ch 4:26 **H** son was Zaccur.

Hamonah (1)

Eze 39:16 (A city named **H** will also be

Hamor (12)

Gen 33:19 He bought it from the sons of **H**,
34:2 of the local ruler **H** the Hivite,
34:4 Shechem said to his father **H**,
34:6 So Shechem's father **H** came to
34:8 **H** told them. "My son Shechem
34:13 gave Shechem and his father **H**
34:18 proposal seemed good to **H**
34:20 So **H** and his son Shechem
34:24 to the city gate agreed with **H**
34:26 including **H** and his son
Jos 24:32 had bought from the sons of **H**,
Jdg 9:28 Serve the descendants of **H**,

Hamor's (1)

Act 7:16 in Shechem from **H** sons

hampered (1)

Pro 4:12 your stride will not be **h**.

Hamran (1)

1Ch 1:41 Dishon's sons were **H**,

Ham's (3)

Gen 10:6 **H** descendants were Cush,
10:20 These were **H** descendants by
1Ch 1:8 **H** descendants were Cush,

Hamul (3)

Gen 46:12 of Perez were Hezron and **H**.
Num 26:21 of Hezron and the family of **H**.
1Ch 2:5 sons were Hezron and **H**.

Hamutal (3)

2Ki 23:31 His mother was **H**,
24:18 His mother was **H**,
Jer 52:1 His mother's name was **H**,

Hanamel (4)

Jer 32:7 'Jeremiah, your cousin **H**,
32:8 my cousin **H** came to me in the
32:9 in Anathoth from my cousin **H**
32:12 in the presence of my cousin **H**

Hanan (12)

1Ch 8:23 Abdon, Zichri, **H**,
8:38 Sheariah, Obadiah, and **H**.
9:44 Sheariah, Obadiah, and **H**.
11:43 **H** (son of Maacah),
Ezr 2:46 Hagab, Shalmai, **H**,
Neh 7:49 **H**, Giddel, Gahar,
8:7 Kelita, Azariah, Jozabad, **H**,
10:10 Hodiah, Kelita, Pelaiah, **H**,
10:22 Pelatiah, **H**, Anaiah,
10:26 Ahiah, **H**, Anan,
13:13 and I appointed **H**,
Jer 35:4 the side room of the sons of **H**.

Hananel (4)

Neh 3:1 then as far as the Tower of **H**.
12:39 and by the Tower of **H** and the
Jer 31:38 the Tower of **H** to Corner Gate.
Zec 14:10 and from the Tower of **H** to the

Hanani (11)

1Ch 25:4 **H**, Eliathah, Giddalti,
25:25 The eighteenth chose **H**,
2Ch 16:7 At that time the seer **H** came to
16:10 He was so angry with **H** that he
16:10 Hanani that he put **H** in prison.
19:2 Jehu, son of the seer **H**,
20:34 the records of Jehu, son of **H**,
Ezr 10:20 of Immer: **H** and Zebadiah
Neh 1:2 one of my brothers, **H**,
7:2 put my brother **H** and Hananiah
12:36 and **H** with the musical

Hananiah (29)

1Ch 3:19 sons were Meshullam and **H**,
8:24 **H**, Elam, Anthothijah,
25:4 **H**, Hanani, Eliathah, Giddalti,
25:23 The sixteenth chose **H**,
2Ch 26:11 They were commanded by **H**,
Ezr 10:28 **H**, Zabbai, and Athlai
Neh 3:8 Next to him **H**, a perfume
3:30 After him **H**, Shelemiah's son,
7:2 I put my brother Hanani and **H**,
7:2 **H** was a trustworthy man,
10:23 Hoshea, **H**, Hasshub,
12:12 Meraiah; from Jeremiah, **H**;
12:41 and **H** with trumpets,
Jer 28:1 the prophet **H**, son of Azzur,
28:5 replied to the prophet **H**
28:10 Then the prophet **H** took the
28:11 **H** said in front of all the people,
28:12 After the prophet **H** broke the
28:13 "Tell **H**, 'This is what the
28:15 Jeremiah told the prophet **H**,
28:15 **H**, the LORD hasn't sent you.
28:17 So the prophet **H** died in the
36:12 Zedekiah (son of **H**),
37:13 Shelemiah and grandson of **H**,
Dan 1:6 **H**, Mishael, and Azariah.
1:7 To **H** he gave the name
1:11 **H**, Mishael, and Azariah.
1:19 no one like Daniel, **H**, Mishael,
2:17 home and told his friends **H**,

Hananiah's (1)

1Ch 3:21 **H** sons were Pelatiah and

Hanani's (2)

1Ki 16:1 **H** son, against Baasha.
16:7 **H** son, against Baasha and his

hand (521)

Gen 14:22 "I now raise my **h** and
21:18 Take him by the **h**,
22:10 up the knife and took it in his **h**
22:12 "Do not lay a **h** on the boy,"
24:18 quickly lowered her jar to her **h**
25:26 his brother was born with his **h**
35:18 Benjamin [Son of My Right **H**].
38:18 that's in your **h**," she answered.
38:28 one of them put out his **h**.
38:29 As he pulled back his **h**,
38:30 born with the red yarn on his **h**.
39:12 and left his clothes in her **h**.
40:11 Pharaoh's cup was in my **h**,
40:11 I put the cup in Pharaoh's **h**."
40:13 cup in his **h** as you used
40:21 put the cup in Pharaoh's **h**.
48:14 He put his right **h** on Ephraim's
48:14 He put his left **h** on Manasseh's
48:17 his father had put his right **h**
48:17 So he took his father's **h** in
48:18 Put your right **h** on his head."
49:8 Your **h** will be on the neck of
49:16 "Dan will **h** down decisions for
Exo 4:2 "What's that in your **h**?"
4:6 "Put your **h** inside your shirt."
4:6 and when he took his **h** out,
4:7 "Now put your **h** back inside
7:17 With this staff in my **h**,
7:19 staff and stretch out your **h** over
8:17 Aaron held out the staff in his **h**
8:19 "This is the **h** of God!"
9:22 "Lift your **h** toward the sky,
10:12 "Stretch out your **h** over Egypt
10:21 "Lift your **h** toward the sky,
10:22 Moses lifted his **h** toward the
12:11 your shepherd's staff in your **h**.
13:3 The LORD used his mighty **h**
13:9 will be ⌊like⌋ a mark on your **h**
13:9 the LORD used his mighty **h**
13:14 'The LORD used his mighty **h**
13:16 will be ⌊like⌋ a mark on your **h**
13:16 the LORD used his mighty **h**
14:16 stretch out your **h** over the sea,
14:21 Then Moses stretched out his **h**
14:26 "Stretch out your **h** over the sea
14:27 Moses stretched his **h** over the
15:6 Your right **h**, O LORD,
15:6 Your right **h**, O LORD,
15:12 You stretched out your right **h**.
15:20 took a tambourine in her **h**.
17:9 I will hold in my **h** the staff God
17:12 Aaron held up one **h**,
17:16 He said, "Because a **h** was
21:24 a **h** for a hand, a foot for a foot,
21:24 a hand for a **h**, a foot for a foot,
32:11 your great power and mighty **h**?
33:22 and cover you with my **h** until
33:23 Then I will take my **h** away,
35:25 which they had made by **h**.
Lev 1:4 Place your **h** on the animal's
3:2 Place your **h** on the animal's
3:8 Place your **h** on the animal's
3:13 Place your **h** on its head.
4:4 He will place his **h** on the
4:24 He will place his **h** on the
4:29 He will place his **h** on the
4:33 He will place his **h** on the
14:15 and pour it into his own left **h**.
14:16 finger in the oil in his left **h**,
14:17 of the oil that is still in his **h**
14:18 put the rest of the oil in his **h**
14:26 the olive oil into his own left **h**.
14:28 some of the oil that is in his **h**
14:29 pour the rest of the oil in his **h**

Lev 21:19 or a crippled **h** or foot,
Num 6:19 unleavened bread and **h** them
14:30 I raised my **h** and swore an
20:11 Moses raised his **h** and hit the
21:2 "If you will **h** these people over
21:34 I'll **h** him, all his troops, and his
22:29 If I had a sword in my **h**,
25:7 took a spear in his **h**,
27:18 and place your **h** on him.
Dtr 1:27 He wanted to **h** us over to the
2:24 I'm going to **h** King Sihon of
2:30 in order to **h** him over
3:2 I'll **h** him, all his troops, and his
4:34 your God used his mighty **h**
5:15 your God used his mighty **h**
6:21 the LORD used his mighty **h**
7:8 So he used his mighty **h** to
7:19 He used his mighty **h** and
7:23 The LORD your God will **h**
7:24 He will **h** their kings over to
9:26 power and used your mighty **h**
11:2 his mighty **h** and powerful arm.
19:12 from that city and **h** him over
19:21 tooth for a tooth, a **h** for a hand,
19:21 tooth for a tooth, a hand for a **h**,
23:14 you and **h** your enemies over
23:25 you may pick grain by **h**.
25:12 cut off her **h**. Have no pity on her
26:8 the LORD used his mighty **h**
31:5 The LORD will **h** them over to
32:40 I raise my **h** toward heaven and
34:12 Moses used his mighty **h** to do
Jos 5:13 of him with a sword in his **h**.
6:2 "I am about to **h** Jericho,
7:7 Was it to **h** us over to the
8:1 I am about to **h** the king of Ai,
8:7 The LORD your God will **h** it
8:18 "Hold out the spear in your **h**
8:19 soon as he stretched out his **h**.
8:26 Joshua did not lower his **h**
20:5 the leaders must not **h** him over
Jdg 1:2 I am about to **h** the Canaanites
3:21 Ehud reached with his left **h**,
3:28 The LORD will **h** your enemy
4:7 I will **h** him over to you.'"
4:14 This is the day the LORD will **h**
4:21 him with a hammer in her **h**.
5:26 for a tent peg with one **h**,
6:21 tip of the staff that was in his **h**.
7:2 you for me to **h** Midian over
7:7 save you and **h** Midian over
7:9 I will **h** it over to you.
7:14 God is going to **h** Midian and
7:15 The LORD will **h** Midian's
11:30 He said, "If you will really **h**
15:12 to tie you up and **h** you over
15:13 only tie you up and **h** you over
16:24 of so many, into our very **h**!"
16:26 who was leading him by the **h**,
16:29 With his right **h** on one column
18:10 God will **h** it over to you.
20:13 Now **h** over those worthless
20:28 Tomorrow I will **h** them over to
1Sm 2:13 a three-pronged fork in his **h**.
3:13 I told him that I would **h** down a
6:9 we'll know it wasn't his **h** that
14:19 your **h** ⌊from the ephod⌋."
14:26 But no one put his **h** to his
14:27 tip of the staff he had in his **h**
14:37 Will you **h** them over to Israel?"
14:43 the tip of the staff I had in my **h**.
17:40 With a sling in his **h**,
17:46 Today the LORD will **h** you
17:47 He will **h** all of you over to us."
17:50 didn't have a sword in his **h**.
17:57 the Philistine's head in his **h**.
18:10 Now, Saul had a spear in his **h**.
18:17 "I must not lay a **h** on him.
19:9 house with his spear in his **h**.
22:6 site with his spear in his **h**
23:11 Will the citizens of Keilah **h** me
23:12 "Will the citizens of Keilah **h**
23:12 "They will **h** you over,"
23:20 We will **h** him over to you."
24:4 'I'm going to **h** your enemy over
24:6 raise my **h** against His Majesty,
1Sm 24:10 'I will not raise my **h** against
24:11 border of your robe is in my **h**!
24:12 I will not lay a **h** on you.
24:13 But I will not lay a **h** on you.
28:19 reasons the LORD will **h** you
28:19 And then the LORD will **h**
30:15 you won't kill me or **h** me over
2Sm 5:19 Will you **h** them over to me?"
5:19 I will certainly **h** the Philistines
18:12 of 25 pounds of silver in my **h**,
18:12 I wouldn't raise my **h** against
20:8 the sword dropped ⌊into his **h**⌋.
20:9 with his right **h** to kiss him.
20:10 the sword in Joab's ⌊left⌋ **h**.
21:20 six fingers on each **h** and six
23:6 they cannot be picked by **h**.
23:10 Philistines until his **h** got tired
23:21 Egyptian had a spear in his **h**.
1Ki 8:15 with his **h** he carried it out.
8:24 With your **h** you carried it out
8:41 mighty **h**, and powerful arm.
8:46 with them and **h** them over
18:9 wrong to make you **h** me over
18:44 "A little cloud like a man's **h** is
20:13 I will **h** it over to you today.
20:28 I will **h** over their entire army to
22:6 "The Lord will **h** over Ramoth
22:12 The LORD will **h** it over to
22:15 The LORD will **h** it over to
2Ki 4:29 my shepherd's staff in your **h**,
5:11 wave his **h** over the ⌊infected⌋
10:15 "If you are, give me your **h**."
10:15 When he gave Jehu his **h**,
11:8 have his weapons in his **h**.
13:16 "Take the bow in your **h**."
18:21 If you lean on it, it stabs your **h**
1Ch 11:23 like a weaver's beam in his **h**.
14:10 Will you **h** them over to me?"
14:10 I will **h** them over to you."
20:6 six fingers on each **h** and six
21:16 had a sword in his **h**
28:19 written for me by the LORD's **h**.
2Ch 6:4 with his **h** he carried it out.
6:15 With your **h** you carried it out
6:32 mighty **h**, and powerful arm.
6:36 with them and **h** them over
12:5 I will **h** you over to Shishak."
18:5 "God will **h** over Ramoth to
18:11 The LORD will **h** it over to
23:7 have his weapon in his **h**.
25:20 because he wanted to **h** over
26:19 held an incense burner in his **h**,
Neh 1:10 great power and your strong **h**.
4:17 loads did the work with one **h**
4:23 each kept our weapons at **h**.
6:5 held in his **h** an unsealed letter.
Est 5:2 that was in his **h** to Esther.
Job 1:11 But now stretch out your **h**,
1:12 you must not lay a **h** on him!"
2:5 But stretch out your **h**,
7:2 Like a hired **h**, he eagerly looks
8:20 a helping **h** to wicked people.
9:33 between us to put his **h**
15:23 that his ruin is close at **h**.
15:25 He stretches out his **h** against
19:21 because God's **h** has struck me
21:5 ⌊your⌋ **h** over ⌊your⌋ mouth.
26:13 With his **h** he stabbed the
29:20 bow in my **h** will remain new.'
30:21 your mighty **h** you assault me.
30:24 out his **h** against one who
31:25 because my **h** had found great
31:27 I threw them a kiss with my **h**,
40:4 I will put my **h** over my mouth.
40:14 your right **h** can save you.
41:8 Lay your **h** on it. Think of the
Psa 10:12 Lift your **h**, O God. Do not
18:35 Your right **h** supports me.
20:6 mighty deeds of his powerful **h**.
21:8 Your **h** will discover all your
21:8 Your powerful **h** will find all
32:4 Day and night your **h** laid
37:24 the LORD holds on to his **h**.
38:2 Your **h** has struck me hard.
39:10 you struck me with your **h**.
44:3 It was your right **h**,
Psa 44:11 You **h** us over to be butchered
45:4 Let your right **h** teach you
45:9 takes her place at your right **h**
48:10 Your right **h** is filled with
51:4 So you **h** down justice when
60:5 ⌊us⌋ with your powerful **h**,
63:8 Your right **h** supports me.
73:23 You hold on to my right **h**.
74:11 Why do you hold back your **h**,
74:11 especially your right **h**?
74:19 Do not **h** over the soul of your
75:8 A cup is in the LORD's **h**.
76:5 warriors were able to lift a **h**.
77:20 and Aaron take them by the **h**.
80:15 of what your right **h** planted,
89:13 Your **h** is strong. Your right hand
89:13 Your right **h** is lifted high.
89:21 My **h** is ready to help him.
89:25 I will put his ⌊left⌋ **h** on the
89:25 and his right **h** on the rivers.
89:42 You held the right **h** of his
89:43 took his sword out of his **h**
95:4 In his **h** are the deep places of
98:1 His right **h** and his holy arm
104:28 You open your **h**, and they are
106:26 Raising his **h**, he swore that he
108:6 ⌊us⌋ with your powerful **h**,
118:15 The right **h** of the LORD
118:16 The right **h** of the LORD is held
118:16 The right **h** of the LORD
119:173 Let your **h** help me because I
121:5 is the shade over your right **h**.
127:4 like arrows in the **h** of a warrior.
136:12 with a mighty **h** and a powerful
137:5 let my right **h** forget ⌊how to
138:7 You stretch out your **h**,
138:7 and your right **h** saves me.
139:5 You lay your **h** on me.
139:10 even there your **h** would guide
139:10 me and your right **h** would hold
145:16 You open your **h**, and you
Pro 3:16 life is in ⌊wisdom's⌋ right **h**.
3:16 In ⌊wisdom's⌋ left **h** are riches
4:9 It will **h** you a beautiful crown."
6:5 like a gazelle from the **h**
6:5 a bird from the **h** of a hunter.
17:16 a fool have money in his **h**
26:9 a thorn stuck in a drunk's **h**,
27:16 up olive oil with his right **h**.
30:4 the wind in the palm of his **h**?
30:32 put your **h** over your mouth.
Ecc 2:24 this comes from the **h** of God.
Sos 2:6 His left **h** is under my head.
2:6 His right **h** caresses me.
5:4 My beloved put his **h** through
8:3 His left **h** is under my head.
8:3 His right **h** caresses me.
8:6 as a ring on your **h**.
Isa 6:6 In his **h** was a burning coal that
8:11 said with his powerful **h** on me.
11:15 He will wave his **h** over the
13:2 Signal them with your **h** to
13:7 That is why every **h** will hang
19:4 I will **h** over the Egyptians to a
23:11 The LORD has stretched his **h**
31:3 the LORD uses his powerful **h**,
34:17 and his **h** divides up ⌊the land⌋
36:6 If you lean on it, it stabs your **h**
40:12 the sea with the palm of his **h**
40:12 sky with the length of his **h**?
41:10 you with my victorious right **h**.
41:13 hold your right **h** and say to
42:6 I will take hold of your **h**.
44:5 Another will write on his **h**,
44:20 "Isn't what I hold in my right **h**
45:1 I have held him by his right **h**
48:13 My **h** laid the foundation of the
48:13 My right **h** stretched out the
49:2 and hid me in the palm of his **h**.
49:22 I will lift my **h** ⌊to signal⌋ the
51:16 you in the palm of my **h**.
51:17 from the cup in the LORD's **h**.
51:18 no one to take her by the **h**.
51:22 I'm taking from your **h** the cup
62:3 be a beautiful crown in the **h**
62:3 crown in the **h** of your God.

Isa 62:8 has sworn with his right **h**
63:12 to support the right **h** of Moses?
Jer 1:9 the LORD stretched out his **h**
6:9 pass your **h** over its branches
15:17 I sat alone because your **h** was
18:21 **h** their children over to famine.
20:4 I will **h** all of Judah over to the
20:5 I will **h** all the riches of this city
21:5 and rage with my powerful **h**
21:7 I will **h** over Judah's King
22:24 the signet ring on my right **h**,
22:24 I will pull you off my **h**.
22:25 I will **h** you over to those who
25:15 Take from my **h** this cup filled
25:17 took the cup from the LORD's **h**.
25:28 to take the cup from your **h**
29:21 I'm going to **h** them over to King
31:32 when I took them by the **h**
32:3 I'm going to **h** this city over to
32:21 with a mighty **h** and a powerful
32:28 I'm going to **h** this city over to
34:2 I'm going to **h** this city over to
34:18 I will **h** over the people who
34:19 I will **h** over the officials of
34:20 I will **h** them over to their
34:21 I will **h** King Zedekiah of Judah
38:16 I will not kill you or **h** you over
38:19 The Babylonians may **h** me
43:3 you against us in order to **h**
44:30 I'm going to **h** Pharaoh Hophra,
46:26 I'll **h** them over to those who
48:37 There are gashes on every **h**
51:7 a golden cup in the LORD's **h**.
Lam 2:3 He withdrew his right **h** when
2:4 Like an opponent his right **h**
2:8 He didn't take his **h** away until
3:57 Be close at **h** when I call to
4:6 one human **h** touching it.
Eze 2:9 As I looked, I saw a **h**
7:17 Every **h** will hang limp,
7:21 I will **h** their jewels over to
8:3 out what looked like a **h**
8:11 an incense burner in his **h**,
11:9 I will **h** you over to foreigners,
16:39 I will **h** you over to your lovers.
20:5 I raised my **h** and swore an
20:23 I raised my **h** and swore an
20:33 I will rule you with a mighty **h**
20:34 scattered you with my mighty **h**
21:11 to be placed in the **h**.
21:31 I will **h** you over to cruel
23:28 I'm going to **h** you over to those
23:31 why I will put her cup in your **h**.
23:46 **H** them over to terror and
25:4 That is why I'm going to **h** you
25:7 against you and **h** you over
25:10 I will **h** the Moabites and the
30:22 make the sword fall from his **h**.
30:24 I will put my sword in his **h**,
30:25 I will put my sword in the **h**
34:10 I will demand that they **h** over
36:7 I raise my **h** and swear that the
37:17 that they will be one in your **h**.
37:19 which is in Ephraim's **h**,
37:19 They will be one in my **h**.'
37:20 you hold the sticks in your **h**,
39:3 knock the bow out of your left **h**
39:3 drop the arrows in your right **h**.
44:12 So I raised my **h** and swore
47:3 With a measuring line in his **h**,
47:14 I raised my **h** and swore that I
Dan 5:5 the fingers of a person's **h**
5:5 The king watched as the **h**
5:24 So he sent the **h** to write this
9:15 out of Egypt with your strong **h**
10:10 Then a **h** touched me and
12:7 He raised his right **h** and left
12:7 raised his right hand and left **h**
Hos 11:3 I took them by the **h**.
11:8 How can I **h** you over,
Amo 1:6 captive in order to **h** them over
5:19 who goes home and puts his **h**
6:8 So I will **h** over the city and
7:7 he had a plumb line in his **h**.
9:2 my **h** will take them from there.
Oba 1:14 Don't **h** over their survivors
Jnh 4:11 tell their right **h** from their left."
Hab 2:16 The cup in the LORD's right **h**
3:4 of light ⌊stream⌋ from his **h**.
Zec 2:1 with a measuring line in his **h**.
4:10 plumb line in Zerubbabel's **h**.
8:4 Each will have a cane in **h**
11:6 I am going to **h** the people over
13:7 Then I will turn my **h** against
14:13 will grab the **h** of another,
Mat 3:12 winnowing shovel is in his **h**,
5:25 he will **h** you over to the judge.
5:25 Then the judge will **h** you over
5:30 And if your right **h** leads you to
6:3 don't let your left **h** know what
6:3 what your right **h** is doing.
8:15 Jesus touched her **h**,
9:18 Come, lay your **h** on her,
9:25 Jesus went in, took her **h**,
10:17 Watch out for people who will **h**
10:19 When they **h** you over ⌊to the
10:21 "Brother will **h** over brother to
10:21 a father will **h** over his child.
12:10 with a paralyzed **h** was there.
12:13 to the man, "Hold out your **h**."
12:49 Pointing with his **h** at his
18:8 "If your **h** or your foot causes
20:19 and **h** him over to foreigners.
24:9 "Then they will **h** you over to
24:48 On the other **h**, that servant,
26:15 "What will you pay me if I **h**
26:23 who has dipped his **h** into
27:29 and put a stick in his right **h**.
Mar 1:31 Jesus went to her, took her **h**,
3:1 had a paralyzed **h** was there.
3:3 the man with the paralyzed **h**,
3:5 told the man, "Hold out your **h**."
3:5 it out, and his **h** became normal
5:4 often been chained **h** and foot.
5:41 Jesus took the child's **h** and
7:32 They begged Jesus to lay his **h**
8:23 Jesus took the blind man's **h**
9:27 Jesus took his **h** and helped
9:43 "So if your **h** causes you to
10:33 him to death and **h** him over
13:9 People will **h** you over to the
13:11 When they take you away to **h**
13:12 "Brother will **h** over brother to
13:12 a father will **h** over his child.
14:20 someone dipping his **h** into the
15:1 and **h** him over to Pilate.
Luk 3:17 winnowing shovel is in his **h**
6:6 A man whose right **h** was
6:8 the man with the paralyzed **h**,
6:10 to the man, "Hold out your **h**."
6:10 so, and his **h** became normal
8:29 He was chained **h** and foot.
8:54 But Jesus took her **h** and
12:45 On the other **h**, that servant
12:58 The judge will **h** you over to an
20:20 so that they could **h** him over
21:12 They will **h** you over to their
22:21 "The **h** of the one who will
Jon 10:12 A hired **h** isn't a shepherd and
10:13 The hired **h** is concerned about
20:25 and put my **h** into his side."
20:27 Take your **h**, and put it into my
Act 3:7 took hold of the man's right **h**
9:41 Peter took her **h** and helped her
12:17 Peter motioned with his **h** to
13:16 motioned with his **h**,
19:33 Alexander motioned with his **h**
21:11 Then they will **h** him over to
21:40 and motioned with his **h**
25:11 no one can **h** me over to them
28:3 The snake bit Paul's **h** and
28:4 the snake hanging from his **h**,
Rom 3:4 "So you **h** down justice when
1Co 5:5 **h** such a person over to Satan
12:15 a foot says, "I'm not a **h**,
12:21 An eye can't say to a **h**,
15:24 Christ will **h** over the kingdom
16:21 this greeting with my own **h**.
Col 4:18 this greeting with my own **h**.
2Th 3:17 this greeting with my own **h**.
Phm 1:19 I'm writing this with my own **h**.
Heb 8:9 when I took them by the **h**
1Jn 2:8 On the other **h**, I'm writing to
Jud 1:9 But Michael didn't dare to **h**
Rev 1:16 In his right **h** he held seven
1:17 Then he laid his right **h** on me
1:20 stars that you saw in my right **h**
2:1 the seven stars in his right **h**,
5:1 I saw a scroll in the right **h** of
5:7 took the scroll from the right **h**
8:4 went up from the angel's **h**
10:2 opened scroll in his **h**.
10:5 raised his right **h** to heaven.
10:8 the opened scroll from the **h**
10:10 small scroll from the angel's **h**
14:9 on his forehead or his **h**,
14:14 and a sharp sickle in his **h**.
17:4 In her **h** she was holding a gold
20:1 pit and a large chain in his **h**.

hand-crafted (1)

Num 31:51 took all the **h** gold articles from

hand-cut (2)

Isa 9:10 we will rebuild with **h** stones.
Amo 5:11 build houses from **h** stones,

handed (125)

Gen 14:20 who has **h** your enemies over
Exo 32:3 earrings and **h** them to Aaron.
Num 21:3 listened to the Israelites and **h**
Dtr 3:3 So the LORD our God also **h**
Jos 10:8 I have **h** them over to you.
10:12 The day the LORD **h** the
10:19 your God has **h** them over
10:30 The LORD also **h** Libnah and
10:32 The LORD **h** Lachish over to
11:8 The LORD **h** them over to
20:9 Then he will not be **h** over to
21:44 The LORD **h** all their enemies
24:8 However, I **h** them over to you.
24:11 But I **h** them over to you.
Jdg 1:4 and the LORD **h** the
2:14 He **h** them over to people who
2:23 He had not **h** them over to
3:10 The LORD **h** King Cushan
6:1 So the LORD **h** them over to
6:13 has abandoned us and has **h**
8:3 God **h** Oreb and Zeeb,
11:21 But the LORD God of Israel **h**
11:32 The LORD **h** the people of
12:3 The LORD **h** them over to me.
13:1 So the LORD **h** them over to
16:23 They said, "Our god **h** Samson,
Rut 2:14 and he **h** her some roasted
1Sm 12:9 So he **h** them over to Sisera,
14:10 that the LORD has **h** them over
14:12 post⌋ because the LORD has **h**
24:10 saw how the LORD **h** you over
24:18 When the LORD **h** me over to
26:23 The LORD **h** you over to me
30:23 He has protected us and **h** the
2Sm 3:8 and I haven't **h** you over to
13:11 When she **h** it to him to eat,
18:28 He has **h** over the men who
21:9 The king **h** them over to the
2Ki 17:20 **h** them over to those who
1Ch 5:20 nations with them were **h** over
2Ch 13:16 and God **h** them over to Judah.
16:8 he **h** them over to you.
18:14 They will be **h** over to you."
24:24 but the LORD **h** Joash's large
28:5 So the LORD his God **h** him
28:5 He also **h** him over to the king
28:9 of your ancestors **h** Judah over
36:17 God **h** all of them over to him.
Ezr 5:12 he **h** them over to King
9:7 our priests have been **h** over
Neh 9:24 You **h** the Canaanite kings and
9:27 You **h** them over to their
9:30 So you **h** them over to the
Est 2:18 and he **h** out gifts from his royal
Job 9:24 The earth is **h** over to the
16:11 God **h** me over to unjust people
Psa 31:8 You have not **h** me over to the
78:61 captive and **h** his glory over
106:41 He **h** them over to other nations
147:20 the decisions he has **h** down.

Isa 34:2 He has **h** them over to be
41:2 Nations are **h** over to him.
42:24 away as loot and **h** Israel over
Jer 12:7 I have **h** the people I love over
21:7 They will be **h** over to King
21:10 It will be **h** over to the king of
26:24 So Jeremiah was not **h** over to
27:6 Now I have **h** all these
32:4 He will certainly be **h** over to
32:24 the city will be **h** over to the
32:25 although the city was **h** over to
32:36 and plagues it will be **h** over to
32:43 said that it has been **h** over
34:3 be captured and **h** over
37:17 You will be **h** over to the king
38:3 This city will certainly be **h**
38:18 this city will be **h** over to the
38:20 "You will not be **h** over to them.
39:14 of the prison and **h** him over
39:17 You will not be **h** over to those
44:30 just as I **h** over King Zedekiah
46:24 They will be **h** over to the
Lam 1:14 The Lord has **h** me over to
2:7 He **h** the walls of Zion's
Eze 16:27 and I **h** you over to your greedy
21:11 The sword has been **h** over to
23:9 "That is why I **h** her over to her
23:24 I have **h** you over to them for
31:11 So I **h** it over to a mighty ruler
35:12 have been deserted and **h** over
39:23 face from them and **h** them over
Dan 1:2 The Lord **h** King Jehoiakim of
7:25 The holy people will be **h** over
7:26 But judgment will be **h** down,
Amo 1:9 The Tyrians have **h** all the
Mat 17:22 betrayed and **h** over to people.
18:34 so angry that he **h** him over
26:2 the Son of Man will be **h** over
26:45 of Man to be **h** over to sinners.
27:2 and **h** him over to Pilate,
27:18 Pilate knew that they had **h**
27:26 had Jesus whipped and **h** over
Mar 9:31 will be betrayed and **h** over
14:41 of Man to be **h** over to sinners.
15:10 chief priests had **h** Jesus over
15:15 had Jesus whipped and **h** over
Luk 9:44 betrayed and **h** over to people."
18:32 He will be **h** over to foreigners.
24:7 'The Son of Man must be **h**
Jon 18:30 we wouldn't have **h** him over to
18:35 and the chief priests **h** you over
18:36 to keep me from being **h** over
19:11 That's why the man who **h** me
19:16 Then Pilate **h** Jesus over to
Act 3:13 You **h** Jesus over to Pilate.
22:3 in the strict rules **h** down by our
23:33 to the governor and **h** Paul over
28:17 the customs **h** down by our
28:17 and I've been **h** over to the
Rom 4:25 Jesus, our Lord, was **h** over to
8:32 his own Son but **h** him over ⌊to
1Co 11:2 traditions that I **h** down to you.
2Co 4:11 we are constantly **h** over to
1Ti 1:20 whom I have **h** over to Satan in
1Pe 1:18 from the worthless life **h** down

handful (11)

Exo 9:8 "Take a **h** of ashes from a kiln,
Lev 2:2 Take from this a **h** of flour with
5:12 The priest will take a **h** of it.
6:15 One of them will remove a **h** of
9:17 He took a **h** of grain and burned
Num 5:26 The priest will take a **h** of the
1Ki 17:12 I have one **h** of flour in a jar and
20:10 left from Samaria to give a **h**
Ecc 4:6 One **h** of peace and quiet is
5:15 won't even be able to take a **h**
Rom 11:16 If the first **h** of dough is holy,

handfuls (3)

Lev 16:12 and two **h** of finely ground,
Ecc 4:6 and quiet is better than two **h**
Eze 13:19 in front of my people for a few **h**

handicapped (2)

Luk 14:13 the **h**, the lame, and the blind.
Luk 14:21 Bring back the poor, the **h**,

handing (1)

Jos 8:18 because I am **h** Ai over to you."

handiwork (1)

Isa 45:11 me orders concerning my **h**?

handkerchief (1)

Jon 11:44 his face was wrapped with a **h**.

handkerchiefs (1)

Act 19:12 People would take **h** and

handle (8)

Num 8:26 you will **h** the Levites' duties."
Dtr 1:18 you how to **h** these situations.
19:5 the head flies off the **h**,
Jdg 3:22 Even the **h** went in after the
2Ch 25:5 those who could **h** a spear and
Zep 1:11 and all who **h** money will
Col 2:21 will tell you, "Don't **h** this!
1Ti 5:17 leaders who **h** their duties well.

handles (2)

Sos 5:5 on the **h** of the lock.
Isa 45:9 say to you, "There are no **h**"?

handmill (3)

Num 11:8 then grind it in a **h** or crush it in
Dtr 24:6 Never let a family's **h** for
24:6 flour — or even part of a **h** —

handmills (1)

Exo 11:5 female slaves who use their **h**,

handout (1)

Act 3:3 he asked them for a **h**.

handouts (1)

Act 3:2 There he would beg for **h** from

hand's (1)

Job 7:1 like a hired **h** daily ⌊work⌋?

hands (338)

Gen 5:29 and painful labor of our **h** since
19:16 his two daughters by their **h**,
27:16 from the young goats on his **h**
27:22 "but the **h** are Esau's."
27:23 because his **h** were hairy like
27:23 hairy like his brother Esau's **h**.
48:14 But Israel crossed his **h** and
Exo 9:29 I'll spread out my **h** to the
9:33 Moses spread out his **h** to the
15:17 that you built with your own **h**,
17:11 long as Moses held up his **h**,
17:11 as soon as he put his **h** down,
17:12 Moses' **h** felt heavy.
17:12 His **h** remained steady until
29:10 will place their **h** on its head.
29:15 will place their **h** on its head.
29:19 will place their **h** on its head.
29:24 Put all of these in the **h** of
29:25 Then take them from their **h**,
30:19 it for washing their **h** and feet.
30:21 they will wash their **h** and feet
40:31 water to wash their **h** and feet.
Lev 4:15 congregation will place their **h**
8:14 sons placed their **h** on its head.
8:18 and his sons placed their **h**
8:22 and his sons placed their **h**
8:27 placed all these things in the **h**
8:28 Then he took them from their **h**
9:22 Then Aaron raised his **h**
15:11 without first rinsing his **h**,
16:21 Aaron will place both **h** on its
24:14 ⌊my name⌋ must lay their **h**
25:28 what he sold stays in the **h** of
Num 5:18 In her **h** he will put the offering
5:18 The priest will hold in his **h** the
8:10 will place their **h** on them.
8:12 "The Levites will place their **h**
24:10 He clapped his **h** and said,
27:23 Moses placed his **h** on Joshua
35:21 to death with your bare **h**,
Dtr 4:28 stone gods made by human **h**.
7:16 the LORD your God **h** over
20:13 When the LORD your God **h**
21:6 victim must wash their **h** over
21:10 LORD your God **h** them over
32:41 and take justice into my own **h**.
33:3 All your holy ones are in your **h**.
34:9 Moses had laid his **h** on him.
Jdg 7:6 men lapped water with their **h**
7:19 they were holding in their **h**.
7:20 held the torches in their left **h**
7:20 in their right **h** so that they
8:7 When the LORD **h** Zebah and
11:34 with tambourines in her **h**.
14:6 With his bare **h**, he tore the lion
14:9 scraped ⌊the honey⌋ into his **h**
15:14 and those on his **h** snapped.
16:18 with the money in their **h**.
19:27 with her **h** on the doorstep.
1Sm 5:4 Dagon's head and his two **h**
12:5 you've found nothing in my **h**."
17:22 left the supplies behind in the **h**
18:25 fall into the **h** of the Philistines.
23:7 has delivered him into my **h**.
28:17 torn the kingship out of your **h**
28:21 "and I took my life in my **h**
2Sm 3:34 Your **h** were not tied.
4:12 cut off their **h** and feet,
13:19 put her **h** on her head,
22:21 because my **h** are clean.
22:35 He trains my **h** for battle so that
24:14 let us fall into the LORD's **h**
24:14 don't let me fall into human **h**."
1Ki 8:22 out his **h** toward heaven
8:38 out their **h** toward this temple.
8:54 with his **h** stretched out toward
11:12 it away from the **h** of your son.
11:31 the kingdom out of Solomon's **h**
2Ki 4:34 his **h** on the boy's hands.
4:34 his hands on the boy's **h**.
9:35 except her skull, feet, and **h**.
10:24 I'm putting in your **h** escape,
11:11 with their weapons in their **h**.
11:12 As the guards clapped their **h**,
13:16 Elisha laid his **h** on the king's
13:16 laid his hands on the king's **h**.
19:18 statues made by human **h**.
1Ch 12:2 either their right or their left **h**.
21:13 let me fall into the LORD's **h**
21:13 don't let me fall into human **h**."
29:12 power and strength in your **h**,
29:14 what has come from your **h**.
2Ch 6:12 stretched out his **h** ⌊to pray⌋.
6:13 out his **h** toward heaven.)
6:29 out their **h** toward this temple.
13:8 which has been placed in the **h**
29:23 who laid their **h** on them.
32:19 of the gods made by human **h**
35:11 the blood with their **h** while
Ezr 7:14 which you hold in your **h**.
7:25 hold in your **h** — will appoint
9:5 stretched out my **h** to the LORD
10:19 They shook **h** as a pledge that
Neh 8:6 as they raised their **h** and then
Job 4:3 When **h** were weak,
5:18 but his **h** make you well.
9:30 and cleanse my **h** with bleach,
10:3 by rejecting the work of your **h**
10:7 one to rescue me from your **h**.
10:8 "Your **h** formed me and made
12:9 that the LORD's **h** made it?
12:10 every human body are in his **h**.
13:14 and taking my life in my own **h**.
14:15 the person your **h** have made.
16:11 me into the **h** of wicked people.
16:17 although my **h** have done
17:9 with clean **h** grows stronger.
20:10 His own **h** will have to give
27:23 It claps its **h** over him.
29:9 put their **h** over their mouths.
30:2 me was the strength of their **h**?
31:7 or my **h** are stained ⌊with sin⌋,
34:19 because his **h** made them all.
34:20 away but not by human **h**.
34:37 He claps his **h** to insult us.
36:32 He fills his **h** with lightning and

Psa 7:3 if I have done this — if my **h** are
8:6 him rule what your **h** created.
9:16 by the work of his own **h**.
18:20 because my **h** are clean.
18:24 he can see that my **h** are clean.
18:34 He trains my **h** for battle so that
19:1 what his **h** have made.
22:8 "Put yourself in the LORD's **h**.
22:16 have pierced my **h** and feet.
24:4 ⌊The one who⌋ has clean **h**
26:6 I will wash my **h** in innocence.
26:10 Evil schemes are in their **h**.
26:10 Their right **h** are full of bribes.
28:2 when I lift my **h** toward your
28:4 for what their **h** have done,
28:5 done or what his **h** have made.
31:5 Into your **h** I entrust my spirit.
31:15 My future is in your **h**.
36:11 people step on me or the **h**
44:20 our God or stretched out our **h**
47:1 Clap your **h**, all you people.
58:2 and your **h** spread violence.
63:4 I will lift up my **h** ⌊to pray⌋ in
68:31 Sudan will stretch out its **h** to
71:4 My God, free me from the **h** of
73:13 washing my **h** of any blame.
74:11 Take your **h** out of your
77:2 At night I stretched out my **h** in
81:6 His **h** were freed from the
88:9 I stretch out my **h** to you ⌊in
91:12 They will carry you in their **h**
92:4 about the works of your **h**.
95:5 and his **h** formed the dry land.
98:8 Let the rivers clap their **h** and
102:25 are the works of your **h**.
115:4 They were made by human **h**.
115:7 They have **h**, but they cannot
119:48 I lift my **h** ⌊in prayer⌋ because
119:73 Your **h** created me and made
119:109 take my life into my own **h**,
128:2 your own **h** have provided.
134:2 Lift your **h** toward the holy
135:15 They were made by human **h**.
138:8 go of what your **h** have made.
140:4 Protect me from the **h** of
141:2 Let the lifting up of my **h** in
143:5 what your **h** have made.
143:6 I stretch out my **h** to you in
144:1 who trained my **h** to fight and
144:7 Stretch out your **h** from above.
144:7 waters and from foreigners' **h**.
144:8 Their right **h** take false pledges.
144:11 rescue me from foreigners' **h**.
144:11 Their right **h** take false pledges.
149:6 two-edged swords in their **h**
Pro 1:24 I stretched out my **h** to you,
6:3 fallen into your neighbor's **h**:
6:17 **h** that kill innocent people,
10:4 Lazy **h** bring poverty,
10:4 but hard-working **h** bring riches
12:14 what his **h** have accomplished.
12:24 Hard-working **h** gain control,
12:24 but lazy **h** do slave labor.
14:1 tears it down with her own **h**.
21:25 because his **h** refuse to work.
30:28 A lizard you can hold in your **h**,
31:13 care⌋ and works with willing **h**.
31:19 "She puts her **h** on the distaff,
31:20 She opens her **h** to oppressed
Ecc 4:5 folds his **h** and wastes away.
7:26 Even her **h** are ⌊like⌋ chains.
9:1 are in God's **h**. No one knows
10:18 house leaks because of idle **h**.
11:6 and don't let your **h** rest until
Sos 5:5 My **h** dripped with myrrh,
5:14 His **h** are disks of gold set with
7:1 like the work of an artist's **h**.
Isa 1:15 stretch out your **h** ⌊in prayer⌋,
1:15 I will not listen because your **h**
2:8 and they worship what their **h**
5:12 or see what his **h** have done.
10:5 is the staff in the Assyrians' **h**.
10:13 with my own two powerful **h**.
11:8 put their **h** into vipers' nests.
17:8 to the altars made by their **h**
19:25 the work of my **h** Assyria,
Isa 25:11 Moabites will stretch out their **h**
25:11 who stretch out their **h** to swim.
25:11 the movements of their **h**.
29:23 the children I made with my **h**,
31:7 that your sinful **h** have made.
31:8 swords not made by human **h**.
31:8 Swords not made by human **h**
35:3 Strengthen limp **h**.
37:19 statues made by human **h**.
45:12 the heavens with my own **h**.
49:4 my case is in the LORD's **h**,
49:16 you on the palms of my **h**.
51:23 I will put it in the **h** of those
55:12 all the trees will clap their **h**.
56:2 and his **h** from doing anything
59:3 Your **h** are stained with blood,
59:6 Their **h** have committed acts of
60:21 the honored work of my **h**.
64:8 We are the work of your **h**.
65:2 I stretched out my **h** all day
Jer 1:16 what their **h** have made.
2:37 with your **h** over your head,
4:31 They are stretching out their **h**,
6:24 Our **h** hang limp. We are gripped
10:3 The **h** of craftsmen prepare
18:6 like the clay in the potter's **h**.
19:7 of their enemies and with the **h**
25:6 the idols your **h** have shaped.
25:7 the idols your **h** have shaped
26:14 "My life is in your **h**.
38:5 answered, "He's in your **h**.
40:4 the chains from your **h**.
Lam 1:10 The enemies laid their **h** on all
1:14 tied together by God's own **h**.
1:17 Zion holds out its **h**.
2:19 Lift up your **h** to him ⌊in prayer⌋
3:41 Let us raise our hearts and **h** to
3:64 for what their own **h** have done.
4:2 like those made by a potter's **h**.
4:10 The **h** of loving mothers
5:12 leaders are hung by their **h**.
Eze 1:8 They had human **h** under their
6:11 Clap your **h**, stomp your feet,
10:2 and fill your **h** with burning
10:7 This angel put them in the **h** of
10:8 like human **h** under their wings.
10:12 bodies, their backs, **h**, wings,
10:21 what looked like human **h**.
21:7 People's **h** will hang limp,
21:11 to be placed in the **h** of killers.
21:14 Clap your **h**! Let the sword strike
21:17 I will also clap my **h** and rest
23:37 Their **h** are covered with blood.
23:45 adultery and their **h** are covered
25:6 You clapped your **h** and
28:9 in the **h** of those who kill you.
28:10 You will die at the **h** of
Dan 10:10 made my **h** and knees shake.
11:11 fall into the southern king's **h**.
Hos 14:3 the things our **h** have made are
Mic 5:13 what your **h** have made.
7:3 Their **h** are skilled in doing evil.
7:16 They will put their **h** over their
Nah 3:19 about you will clap their **h**.
Zec 4:9 "Zerubbabel's **h** have laid the
4:9 and his **h** will finish it.
8:13 Let your **h** work hard.
Mat 4:6 They will carry you in their **h**
15:2 wash their **h** before they eat."
15:20 washing one's **h** doesn't make
18:8 or injured than to have two **h**
22:13 'Tie his **h** and feet,
27:24 some water and washed his **h**
Mar 5:4 he snapped the chains off his **h**
5:23 Come, lay your **h** on her so that
6:5 there except to lay his **h**
7:2 ate without washing their **h**.
7:3 have properly washed their **h**.
7:5 wash their **h** before they eat!"
8:23 eyes and placed his **h** on him.
8:25 Then Jesus placed his **h** on
9:43 life disabled than to have two **h**
10:16 them by placing his **h** on them.
14:58 one not made by human **h**.'"
16:18 They will place their **h** on the
Luk 4:11 They will carry you in their **h**
Luk 4:40 He placed his **h** on each of
13:13 He placed his **h** on her,
23:46 into your **h** I entrust my spirit."
24:39 Look at my **h** and feet,
24:40 he showed them his **h** and feet.
24:50 raised his **h** and blessed them.
Jon 11:44 wound around his feet and **h**,
13:9 Wash my **h** and my head too!"
20:20 he showed them his **h** and his
20:25 I see the nail marks in his **h**,
20:27 finger here, and look at my **h**.
21:18 you will stretch out your **h**,
Act 6:6 who prayed and placed their **h**
8:17 John placed their **h** on them,
8:18 placed their **h** on them.
8:19 so that anyone I place my **h**
9:12 named Ananias place his **h**
9:17 After he placed his **h** on Saul,
12:6 His **h** were bound with two
12:7 the chains fell from Peter's **h**.
13:3 and Manaen placed their **h** on
19:6 Paul placed his **h** on them,
21:11 tied his own feet and **h** with it.
28:8 placed his **h** on him,
Rom 10:21 long I have stretched out my **h**
2Co 5:1 that isn't made by human **h**.
Gal 2:9 So they shook **h** with Barnabas
Eph 4:28 good with their **h** so that they'll
Col 2:11 performed by human **h**.
1Ti 2:8 They should raise their **h** in
4:14 spiritual leaders placed their **h**
5:22 be in a hurry to place your **h**
2Ti 1:6 from God when I placed my **h**
Heb 1:10 With your own **h** you made the
9:11 that was not made by human **h**
9:24 a holy place made by human **h**.
10:31 Falling into the **h** of the living
Rev 7:9 palm branches in their **h**,
13:16 to be branded on their right **h**
20:4 branded on their foreheads or **h**

handshake (4)

Job 17:3 else will guarantee it with a **h**?
Pro 6:1 yourself for a stranger with a **h**,
17:18 sense closes a deal with a **h**.
22:26 who make deals with a **h**,

handsome (11)

Gen 39:6 Joseph was well-built and **h**.
1Sm 9:2 He had a son named Saul, a **h**,
9:2 in Israel was more **h** than Saul.
16:12 and a **h** appearance.
16:18 has a way with words, he is **h**,
2Sm 23:21 And he killed a **h** Egyptian.
1Ki 1:5 son of Haggith, was very **h**.
Psa 45:2 You are the most **h** of Adam's
Sos 1:16 You are **h**, my beloved,
Isa 33:17 Your eyes will see how **h** the
Eze 23:6 They were all **h** young men

Hanes (1)

Isa 30:4 messengers have reached **H**,

hang (18)

Gen 40:19 head and **h** your dead body
Exo 26:9 the sixth sheet in half ⌊to **h**⌋
26:12 half-sheet should **h** over
26:13 That part should **h** over each
26:32 Use gold hooks to **h** it on four
26:33 **H** the canopy from the
40:3 and **h** the canopy over the ark.
Est 7:9 king responded, "**H** him on it!"
9:13 Let them **h** Haman's ten sons
Job 3:5 Let a dark cloud **h** over it.
Pro 6:21 **H** them around your neck.
Isa 13:7 is why every hand will **h** limp,
22:24 They will **h** on him the whole
33:23 Your ropes **h** loose,
Jer 6:24 Our hands **h** limp. We are
Eze 7:17 Every hand will **h** limp,
15:3 a peg from it to **h** things on?
21:7 People's hands will **h** limp,

hanged (2)

2Sm 17:23 Then he **h** himself,
Mat 27:5 went away, and **h** himself.

hanging (10)

Exo 36:38 five posts with hooks for ⌊**h**⌋
Dtr 28:66 Your life will always be **h** by a
2Sm 18:9 So he was left **h** in midair
18:10 "I saw Absalom **h** in a tree."
Est 6:4 ask the king about **h** Mordecai
Isa 22:25 and everything **h** on it will be
Eze 41:25 There was a wooden roof **h**
Luk 23:39 One of the criminals **h** there
Act 5:30 You murdered Jesus by **h** him
28:4 saw the snake **h** from his hand,

hangs (5)

Exo 28:25 ⌊so that the breastplate **h**⌋
30:6 of the canopy which ⌊**h**⌋ over
Num 4:5 down the canopy that **h** over
Job 26:7 He **h** the earth on nothing
Ecc 8:6 human tragedy **h** over people.

Hannah (15)

1Sm 1:2 had two wives, one named **H**,
1:2 had children, but **H** had none.
1:5 also give one portion to **H**
1:7 Whenever **H** went to the
1:7 and **H** would cry and not eat.
1:8 her, "**H**, why are you crying?
1:9 One day, after **H** had
1:12 While **H** was praying a long
1:15 "No, sir," **H** responded,
1:19 made love to his wife **H**,
1:20 **H** became pregnant and gave
1:22 But **H** didn't go. She told her
1:26 "Sir," **H** said, "as sure as you
2:1 **H** prayed out loud,
2:21 The LORD came to **H**.

Hannathon (1)

Jos 19:14 the border turns north to **H**

Hanniel (2)

Num 34:23 **H**, son of Ephod, the leader of
1Ch 7:39 Ulla's sons were Arah, **H**,

Hanoch (6)

Gen 25:4 Epher, **H**, Abida, and Eldaah.
46:9 The sons of Reuben were **H**,
Exo 6:14 were **H**, Pallu, Hezron,
Num 26:5 of Reuben were the family of **H**,
1Ch 1:33 Epher, **H**, Abida, and Eldaah.
5:3 were **H**, Pallu, Hezron,

Hanun (12)

2Sm 10:1 and his son **H** became king in
10:2 "I will show kindness to **H** as
10:2 to comfort **H** after his father's
10:3 princes asked their master **H**,
10:4 So **H** took David's men,
1Ch 19:2 "I will show kindness to **H**
19:2 to comfort **H** after his father's
19:3 the Ammonite princes asked **H**,
19:4 So **H** took David's men,
19:6 So **H** and the Ammonites sent
Neh 3:13 **H** and the people of Zanoah
3:30 son, and **H**, Zalaph's sixth son,

Hapharaim (1)

Jos 19:19 **H**, Shion, Anaharath,

happen (161)

Gen 41:36 of famine that will **h** in Egypt.
42:4 that something would **h** to him.
49:1 and let me tell you what will **h**
Exo 2:4 to see what would **h** to him.
8:23 This miraculous sign will **h**
21:13 intentionally, but God let it **h**,
30:12 Then no plague will **h** to them
Dtr 4:30 and all these things **h** to you,
7:13 This will all **h** in the land the
18:22 and what he says doesn't **h**
29:20 in this book will **h** to him.
30:1 spoken about will **h** to you.
31:17 terrible disasters will **h** to them.
31:21 terrible disasters **h** to them,
31:29 days to come disasters will **h**
32:20 find out what will **h** to them.
Dtr 32:29 and realize what will **h** to them!
Jos 24:12 These things didn't **h** because
Jdg 9:24 Jerubbaal's 70 sons would **h**
20:3 such an evil thing could **h**."
20:12 an evil thing **h** among you?
1Sm 2:34 What is going to **h** to your two
9:6 Everything he says is sure to **h**.
10:7 When these signs **h** to you,
2Sm 12:12 but I will make this **h** in broad
18:22 Joab again, "Whatever may **h**,
23:5 Truly, he makes these things **h**.
1Ki 1:27 Did you allow this to **h** without
13:32 in the cities of Samaria will **h**."
14:3 tell you what will **h** to the boy."
14:14 This will **h** today. It will happen
14:14 today. It will **h** right now.
18:12 This is what will **h**:
21:29 I will not let any evil **h** to his
2Ki 7:2 "Could this **h** even if the LORD
7:18 This will **h** about this time
7:19 "Could this **h** even if the LORD
19:25 Now I make it **h** so that you
24:3 LORD had commanded it to **h**.
2Ch 25:20 (God made this **h** because he
Ezr 4:14 something **h** that will dishonor
Job 13:13 may **h** to me ⌊happen⌋!
13:13 may happen to me ⌊**h**⌋!
15:32 It will **h** before his time has
21:17 often does disaster **h** to them?
Psa 73:17 what would **h** to them.
Ecc 1:9 before will **h** ⌊again⌋.
3:15 Whatever is going to **h** ⌊in the
3:22 to see what will **h** after them?
10:14 or what will **h** after ⌊death⌋.
11:2 what disaster may **h** on earth.
Isa 5:19 One of Israel **h** quickly so that
7:7 It won't take place; it won't **h**.
14:24 "It will **h** exactly as I've
24:2 The same will **h** to people and
29:5 All of this will **h** suddenly,
29:8 This is what will **h** to the
37:26 Now I make it **h** so that you
41:22 can tell us what's going to **h**.
41:23 Tell us what's going to **h** so
42:9 new things before they **h**.
44:7 Then let him predict what will **h**
45:11 me about what is going to **h**
47:9 In one day both of these will **h**
47:9 All this will **h** to you in spite of
47:11 But evil will **h** to you.
48:3 I revealed to you what would **h**.
48:5 to you what would **h** long ago.
48:5 have commanded them to **h**."
60:22 will make it **h** quickly."
Jer 5:12 Nothing bad will **h** to us.
5:13 so let what they say **h** to them."
6:18 what will **h** to them.
13:22 "Why do these things **h** to me?"
15:4 This will **h** because of what
16:9 This will **h** in your lifetime,
19:8 at all the disasters that **h** to it.
23:17 "Nothing bad will **h** to you."
32:44 This will **h** in the territory of
39:16 things will **h** as you watch.
44:29 threats of disaster will **h** to you.
51:60 that would **h** to Babylon.
Eze 7:26 disaster will **h** after another.
12:11 What I have done will **h** to you.
12:25 Everything that I say will **h**
12:25 and it will **h** during your
12:27 that Ezekiel sees won't **h**
12:27 What he prophecies will **h** in
12:28 Whatever I say will **h**,
16:16 Such things shouldn't **h**.
20:32 you have in mind will never **h**.
24:14 It will **h**, and I will do it. I will
39:8 It will **h**! declares the Almighty
Dan 2:28 what is going to **h**
2:29 thoughts about what would **h** in
2:29 told you what is going to **h**.
2:45 God has told you what will **h**
8:19 "I will tell you what will **h** in
8:26 it is about things that will **h**
9:27 This will **h** along with
9:27 been determined that this will **h**
10:14 to explain to you what will **h**
Hos 10:15 This is what will **h** to you,
Joe 2:2 Nothing like this will ever **h**
Amo 7:3 "This won't **h**," the LORD said.
7:6 "This won't **h** either,"
Jnh 4:2 isn't this what I said would **h**
4:5 to see what would **h** to the city.
Mic 3:11 Nothing bad will **h** to us."
Nah 1:9 This trouble will never **h** again.
Hab 2:3 The vision will still **h** at the
2:3 It will certainly **h**. It won't be late
Zec 4:10 when little things began to **h**?
6:15 This will **h** if you obey the
Mat 12:45 That is what will **h** to the evil
13:49 The same thing will **h** at the
16:22 This must never **h** to you!"
21:21 into the sea,' and it will **h**.
24:3 "Tell us, when will this **h**?
24:6 These things must **h**,
24:21 will certainly never **h** again.
26:54 fulfilled that say this must **h**?"
Mar 10:32 what was going to **h** to him.
11:23 believes what he says will **h**:
11:32 ⌊then what will **h**⌋?"
13:4 "Tell us, when will this **h**?
13:7 These things must **h**,
13:19 and will certainly never **h**
13:29 when you see these things **h**,
Luk 1:38 you've said **h** to me."
21:7 "Teacher, when will this **h**?
21:9 These things must **h** first,
21:12 "Before all these things **h**,
21:26 fearfully wait for what will **h**
21:28 "When these things begin to **h**,
21:31 when you see these things **h**,
21:36 everything that is about to **h**
22:49 saw what was going to **h**.
23:31 what will **h** to a dry one?"
Jon 5:14 worse doesn't **h** to you."
14:29 When it does **h**, you will
18:4 that was going to **h** to him.
Act 8:24 things you said will **h** to me."
12:11 are expecting to **h** to me."
13:40 the prophets said may **h** to you.
20:22 know what will **h** to me there.
26:22 and Moses said would **h**.
28:6 saw nothing unusual **h** to him,
1Co 15:23 This will **h** to each person in
15:52 It will **h** in an instant,
2Th 1:10 ⌊This will **h**⌋ on that day when
Jas 1:11 The same thing will **h** to rich
3:10 and sisters, this should not **h**!
4:14 know what will **h** tomorrow.
1Pe 1:7 This will **h** when Jesus Christ
4:18 what will **h** to the godless
2Pe 2:6 of what is going to **h** to them.
Rev 1:1 the things that must **h** soon.
1:19 is going to **h** after these things.
4:1 you what must **h** after this."
22:6 the things that must **h** soon.

happened (182)

Gen 14:13 Abram the Hebrew what had **h**.
18:10 Sarah **h** to be listening at the
29:13 Jacob told Laban all that had **h**.
30:29 done for you and what has **h**
34:7 This shouldn't have **h**.
41:13 What he told us **h**:
42:29 told him all that had **h** to them.
Exo 9:18 worst hailstorm that has ever **h**
32:1 "We don't know what has **h** to
32:23 'We don't know what's **h** to this
Lev 10:16 tried to find out what had **h**
10:19 and look what **h** to me.
16:16 These sins **h** because the
Num 9:20 The same thing **h** when the
Dtr 2:23 The same thing **h** to the
4:32 as great as this ever **h** before,
29:22 see the plagues that have **h**
31:17 'Haven't these disasters **h** to us
Jos 2:23 everything that had **h** to them.
11:1 of Hazor heard ⌊what had **h**⌋.
Jdg 6:13 why has all this **h** to us?
6:38 And that is what **h**.
19:30 "Never has such a thing **h** or
21:3 why has this **h** among us?
Rut 1:22 They **h** to enter Bethlehem just

Rut 2:3 Now it **h** that she ended up in
1Sm 1:7 This **h** year after year.
4:7 Nothing like this has ever **h**
4:16 "What **h**, son?" Eli asked.
6:9 but what **h** to us was an
10:9 That day all these signs **h**.
10:11 "What has **h** to the son of Kish?
20:26 "Something has **h** to him so
25:37 his wife told him what had **h**.
2Sm 1:4 "What **h**?" David asked him.
1:6 "I **h** to be on Mount Gilboa.
10:5 David was told ⌊what had **h**⌋,
18:9 Absalom **h** to come
20:1 from the tribe of Benjamin **h** to
1Ki 10:25 This **h** year after year.
12:24 What has **h** is my doing."
15:28 The assassination **h** in Asa's
21:1 This is what **h** next.
2Ki 3:20 That is what **h** in the morning.
7:14 told them to find out what **h**.
7:18 (It **h** exactly as the man of God
7:20 So this is what **h** to the king's
15:12 It **h** exactly as the LORD had
18:12 This **h** because they refused to
19:35 It **h** that night. The LORD's
24:3 Without a doubt, this **h** to
1Ch 16:40 This **h** on the altar of burnt
19:5 people told David ⌊what had **h**⌋
29:8 Whoever **h** to have precious
29:30 and the things that **h** to him,
2Ch 9:24 This **h** year after year.
11:4 What has **h** is my doing."
12:2 This **h** because all Israel was
20:27 ⌊what had **h** to⌋ their enemies.
26:19 This **h** in front of the priests in
29:36 Everything had **h** so quickly.
30:26 Nothing like this had **h** in
32:31 the miraculous sign that had **h**
36:21 This **h** so that the LORD's
Ezr 3:8 This **h** in the second month of
9:13 "After all that has **h** to us
Neh 9:33 everything that has **h** to us.
Est 4:7 everything that had **h** to him.
6:13 everything that had **h** to him.
9:1 the exact opposite **h**:
9:26 seen and what had **h** to them —
Job 2:11 terrible things that had **h** to him
Psa 44:17 Although all of this **h** to us,
119:56 This has **h** to me because I
Ecc 1:9 Whatever has **h** before will
3:15 Whatever has **h** ⌊in the past⌋
3:15 the future⌋ has already **h** ⌊in
6:10 Whatever has **h** ⌊in the past⌋
Isa 20:6 'Look at what has **h** to our
43:18 Forget what **h** in the past,
43:26 Remind me ⌊of what **h**⌋.
44:7 Let him tell me what **h** when I
46:10 you things that had not yet **h**,
48:3 Suddenly, I acted, and they **h**.
48:5 you about them before they **h**.
51:19 many disasters have **h** to you.
51:19 and war have **h** to you.
Jer 8:15 but nothing good has **h**.
32:24 have threatened to do has **h**,
38:7 The king **h** to be sitting at
40:3 That is why this has **h** to you.
Lam 5:1 O LORD, what has **h** to us.
Eze 16:19 This is what **h**, declares the
Dan 3:8 After that **h**, some astrologers
4:28 this **h** to King Nebuchadnezzar.
5:21 This **h** until he realized that the
9:12 anything ever **h** like what has
9:12 like what has **h** to Jerusalem.
9:13 This entire disaster **h** to us,
Joe 1:2 Nothing like this has ever **h** in
2:2 Nothing like this has ever **h**.
Amo 1:1 This **h** two years before the
Jnh 1:8 why has this disaster **h** to us?
Mat 1:22 All this **h** so that what the Lord
18:31 with him saw what had **h**
21:4 This **h** so that what the prophet
24:21 a kind of misery that has not **h**
26:56 All of this has **h** so that what
27:3 regretted what had **h** when he
28:11 priests everything that had **h**.
Mar 5:14 reported everything that had **h**.
Mar 5:14 came to see what had **h**.
5:16 who saw this told what had **h**
5:33 She knew what had **h** to her.
6:52 didn't understand what had **h**
7:26 The woman **h** to be Greek,
13:19 of misery that has not **h** from
Luk 1:65 about everything that had **h**.
2:20 Everything **h** the way the angel
8:34 of the pigs saw what had **h**,
8:35 people went to see what had **h**.
8:56 not to tell anyone what had **h**.
13:2 "Do you think that this **h** to
23:47 army officer saw what had **h**,
23:48 all of them saw what had **h**,
24:12 wondering what had **h**.
24:14 about everything that had **h**.
24:18 know what has **h** recently?"
24:19 "What **h**?" he asked. They said
24:19 "We were discussing what **h** to
24:21 third day since everything **h**.
24:35 two disciples told what had **h**
24:36 were talking about what had **h**,
Jon 1:28 This **h** in Bethany on the east
5:9 That **h** on a day of worship.
14:22 what has **h** that you are going
19:36 This **h** so that the Scripture
21:1 the disciples. This is what **h**.
Act 2:31 about that before it ever **h**.
2:43 signs **h** through the apostles.
3:10 to see what had **h** to him.
4:21 praising God for what had **h**,
5:7 She didn't know what had **h**.
5:11 about what had **h** were terrified.
5:24 about what could have **h**.
7:2 This **h** before Abraham lived in
7:40 'We don't know what has **h** to
9:35 of Sharon saw what had **h**
10:16 This **h** three times.
10:37 know what **h** throughout Judea.
11:4 them point by point what had **h**.
11:10 This **h** three times.
11:15 This was the same thing that **h**
11:28 This **h** while Claudius was
12:3 This **h** during the days of
12:12 Peter realized what had **h**,
12:18 uproar over what had **h** to Peter.
13:12 the governor saw what had **h**,
13:32 promised our ancestors has **h**.
14:1 The same thing **h** in the city of
15:7 you know what **h** some time
17:17 with anyone who **h** to be there.
19:21 After all these things had **h**,
28:8 His father **h** to be sick in bed.
28:9 After that had **h**, other sick
Rom 9:10 The same thing **h** to Rebekah.
1Co 10:11 These things **h** to make them
2Co 12:2 I don't know whether this **h** to
12:4 I don't know whether this **h** to
Gal 1:16 When this **h**, I didn't talk it over
1:24 God for what had **h** to me.
4:15 What **h** to your positive
Php 1:12 that what **h** to me has helped to
Col 2:12 This **h** when you were placed
1Th 3:4 as you know, that's what **h**.
2Ti 3:11 and sufferings which **h**
Heb 7:20 None of this **h** without an oath.
12:17 anything to change what had **h**.
2Pe 3:4 by saying, "What's **h** to his
Jud 1:7 What **h** to Sodom and
Rev 16:17 the temple, and said, "It has **h**!"
21:6 He said to me, "It has **h**!

happening (19)

1Sm 5:7 of Ashdod realized what was **h**,
Neh 4:11 "Before they know what is **h** or
Est 2:11 was and what was **h** to her.
Isa 43:19 It is already **h**. Don't you
Jer 5:30 and disgusting is **h** in the land:
48:19 who are escaping what is **h**.
Mat 24:39 not aware of what was **h** until
27:54 and the other things **h**.
Luk 9:7 about everything that was **h**.
15:26 and asked what was **h**.
18:36 he tried to find out what was **h**.
Act 8:13 impressive things that were **h**.
12:9 was doing was actually **h**.
Act 14:14 and Paul heard what was **h**,
Gal 4:29 That's exactly what's **h** now.
Eph 6:21 will tell you everything that is **h**
Col 4:7 you everything that is **h** to me.
4:9 about everything that's **h** here.
1Pe 4:12 something strange is **h** to you,

happens (35)

Gen 37:20 see what **h** to his dreams."
44:29 me too and anything **h** to him,
Exo 22:3 But if it **h** after sunrise,
Num 5:21 people to see what **h** when
Dtr 8:14 When this **h**, be careful that
19:9 If this **h**, you may add three
21:14 But if it **h** that you are no longer
22:23 another man. If this **h** in a city,
25:9 "This is what **h** to a man who
2Sm 15:15 "No matter what **h**,
18:23 "Whatever **h**, I'd like to run,"
Est 6:5 "Haman **h** to be standing in the
Job 3:25 What I dread **h** to me.
8:13 The same thing **h** to all who
18:20 are shocked by what **h** to him.
18:21 This is what **h** to the homes of
Pro 1:19 This is what **h** to everyone
10:24 wicked people dread **h** to them,
Ecc 9:3 of everything that **h** under
9:6 anything that **h** under the sun.
Hos 9:7 ⌊When this **h**,⌋ Israel will
Mat 24:25 I've told you this before it **h**.
Mar 13:23 told you everything before it **h**.
Luk 1:20 to talk until the day this **h**.
12:54 to be a rainstorm,' and it **h**.
12:55 to be hot,' and that's what **h**.
Jon 13:19 I'm telling you now before it **h**.
13:19 Then, when it **h**, you will
14:29 telling you this now before it **h**.
16:4 when it **h** you'll remember what
Rom 2:16 This **h** as they face the day
2:29 is something that **h**
1Co 6:6 and this **h** in front of
Col 3:11 Where this **h**, there is no Greek
1Th 5:18 Whatever **h**, give thanks,

happier (3)

Mat 18:13 he is **h** about it than about the
2Co 7:7 This made me even **h**.
3Jn 1:4 Nothing makes me **h** than to

happily (10)

1Ki 4:20 They ate and drank and lived **h**.
Psa 66:1 Shout **h** to God, all the earth!
81:1 Shout **h** to the God of Jacob.
95:1 Let's shout **h** to the rock of our
95:2 Let's shout **h** to him with
98:4 Shout **h** to the LORD,
98:6 Shout **h** in the presence of the
100:1 Shout **h** to the LORD,
Zep 3:14 Sing **h**, people of Zion!
3:17 He **h** rejoices over you,

happiness (24)

Job 21:13 They spend their days in **h**,
21:16 isn't their **h** in their own power?
21:25 never having tasted **h**,
Psa 106:5 find joy in our people's **h**,
Pro 17:20 A twisted mind never finds **h**,
23:26 your eyes find **h** in my ways.
Isa 9:3 the nation and increase its **h**.
24:11 and the earth's **h** is banished.
35:10 Everlasting **h** will be on their
51:11 Everlasting **h** will be on their
Jer 7:34 banish the sounds of joy and **h**
16:9 stop to the sounds of joy and **h**
25:10 them the sounds of joy and **h**,
33:11 the sounds of joy and **h** and the
Lam 3:17 I have forgotten what **h** is.
Joe 1:16 **H** and rejoicing disappear from
Mat 25:21 and share your master's **h**.'
25:23 and share your master's **h**.'
Luk 15:7 that there will be more **h**
Jon 16:20 but your pain will turn to **h**.
16:22 will take that **h** away from you.
Act 14:17 food and your lives with **h**."
1Co 12:26 all the others share in its **h**.
2Ti 1:4 so that I can be filled with **h**.

Happizzez (1)

1Ch 24:15 the eighteenth for **H**,

happy (117)

Dtr 15:16 your family and is **h** with you.
24:5 and make his new wife **h**.
28:47 a joyful and **h** heart when you
Jdg 9:13 makes gods and humans **h**,
9:16 made Abimelech king, ⌊be **h**.⌋
9:16 him as he deserved, be **h**.
9:19 then be **h** with Abimelech and
9:19 let Abimelech be **h** with you.
2Ki 20:13 Hezekiah was so **h** with them
Est 5:9 he was **h** and feeling good.
8:16 So the Jews were cheerful, **h**,
8:17 the Jews were **h** and joyful,
Job 6:10 I would be **h** despite my
8:21 and your lips with **h** shouting.
21:12 and they are **h** with the music
21:23 altogether **h** and contented.
22:26 Then you will be **h** with the
27:10 Can he be **h** with the Almighty?
33:32 Speak, because I'd be **h** if you
Psa 35:27 Let those who are **h** when I am
35:27 He is **h** when his servant has
37:4 Be **h** with the LORD,
40:8 I am **h** to do your will,
51:16 You are not **h** with any
62:4 They are **h** to lie. They bless
112:1 who fears the LORD and is **h**
119:16 Your laws make me **h**.
119:24 written instructions make me **h**.
119:35 because I am **h** with them.
119:47 which I love, make me **h**.
119:70 I am **h** with your teachings.
119:77 your teachings make me **h**.
119:92 teachings had not made me **h**,
119:143 ⌊still⌋ make me **h**.
119:174 and your teachings make me **h**.
Pro 8:30 I made him **h** day after day,
10:1 A wise son makes his father **h**,
15:20 A wise son makes his father **h**,
16:13 Kings are **h** with honest words,
17:5 Whoever is **h** ⌊to see
24:17 Do not be **h** when your enemy
29:3 wisdom makes his father **h**,
Ecc 4:16 will come later will not be **h**
7:14 When times are good, be **h**.
11:9 make you **h** when you're young.
Isa 9:3 It will be **h** in your presence
9:17 That is why the Lord isn't **h**
13:17 for silver and aren't **h** with gold.
24:7 All **h** people groan.
30:29 Your hearts will be **h** like
32:13 Mourn for all the **h** homes in a
39:2 Hezekiah was so **h** with them
56:7 mountain and make them **h**
66:10 be **h** and rejoice with her.
Jer 14:10 So the LORD isn't **h** with them.
20:15 who made my father very **h**
31:4 and you will go dancing with **h**
31:7 Sing a **h** song about Jacob.
49:25 **h** city abandoned?
50:11 "You are **h** and excited.
Lam 1:21 They are **h** that you did it.
3:36 The Lord isn't **h** to see ⌊these
Eze 24:25 It makes them **h** and proud.
35:15 You were **h** when the land of
Hos 7:3 "They make kings **h** with the
7:3 They make officials **h** with the
Oba 1:12 misfortune or be **h** when
Jnh 4:6 was very **h** with the plant.
Hab 1:15 So they rejoice and are **h**.
3:18 I will be **h** with the LORD.
Zec 8:19 as well as **h** festivals
Luk 6:23 Rejoice then, and be very **h**!
10:17 70 disciples came back very **h**.
10:20 However, don't be **h** that evil
10:20 Be **h** that your names are
13:17 But the entire crowd was **h**
15:5 When he finds it, he's **h**.
15:10 angels are **h** about one person
15:32 something to be **h** about.
Jon 4:36 who harvests it are **h** together.
8:56 He saw it and was **h**."
Jon 16:20 but the world will be **h**.
16:21 anymore because she's **h** that
16:22 Then you will be **h**,
16:24 that you can be completely **h**.
Act 5:41 They were **h** to have been
8:8 that city was extremely **h**.
12:14 she was so **h** that instead of
Rom 12:12 Be **h** in your confidence,
12:15 Be **h** with those who are happy.
12:15 Be happy with those who are **h**.
15:10 be **h** together with his people!"
16:19 and this makes me **h** for you.
1Co 7:30 Those who are **h** should live
7:30 was nothing to be **h** about.
13:6 It isn't **h** when injustice is done,
13:6 but it is **h** with the truth.
2Co 1:24 with you so that you will be **h**.
2:3 those who should make me **h**.
2:3 makes me **h** also makes you
2:3 me happy also makes you **h**.
7:4 I'm encouraged and feel very **h**.
7:9 But I'm **h** now, not because I
7:13 to see how **h** Titus was.
Php 1:18 and I'm **h** about that.
1:18 Yes, I will continue to be **h**
Col 1:24 I am **h** to suffer for you now.
2:5 I'm **h** to see how orderly you
Heb 13:5 Be **h** with what you have
Jas 1:2 be very **h** when you are tested
5:13 If you are **h**, sing psalms.
1Pe 1:6 You are extremely **h** about
1:8 You are extremely **h** with joy
4:13 but be **h** as you share Christ's
2Jn 1:4 I was very **h** to find some of
3Jn 1:3 I was very **h** when some
Rev 19:7 Let us rejoice, be **h**,

Hara (1)

1Ch 5:26 Habor, **H**, and the Gozan River.

Haradah (2)

Num 33:24 Shepher and set up camp at **H**.
33:25 They moved from **H** and set up

Haran (22)

Gen 11:26 father of Abram, Nahor, and **H**.
11:27 father of Abram, Nahor, and **H**.
11:27 **H** was the father of Lot.
11:28 **H** died in Ur of the Chaldeans,
11:29 was Milcah, daughter of **H**.
11:29 (**H** was the father of Milcah and
11:31 his grandson Lot (son of **H**),
11:31 When they came as far as **H**,
11:32 lived 205 years and died in **H**.
12:4 75 years old when he left **H**.
12:5 they had acquired in **H**.
27:43 away to my brother Laban in **H**.
28:10 and traveled toward **H**.
29:4 "We're from **H**," they replied.
2Ki 19:12 rescue Gozan, **H**, Rezeph,
1Ch 2:46 was the mother of **H**,
2:46 **H** was the father of Gazez.
23:9 Shelomith, Haziel, and **H**.
Isa 37:12 rescue Gozan, **H**, Rezeph,
Eze 27:23 **H**, Canneh, Eden, Assyria, and
Act 7:2 before Abraham lived in **H**.
7:4 and lived in the city of **H**.

Haraphah (7)

2Sm 21:16 descendant of **H** named Benob,
21:18 another descendant of **H**.
21:20 also was a descendant of **H**.
21:22 descendants of **H** from Gath,
1Ch 20:4 a descendant of **H**,
20:6 also was a descendant of **H**.
20:8 descendants of **H** from Gath,

Harar (1)

2Sm 23:11 the son of Agee from **H**.

Hararite (4)

2Sm 23:33 (⌊son of⌋ Shammah the **H**),
23:33 Ahiam (son of Sharar the **H**),
1Ch 11:34 Jonathan (son of Shage the **H**),
11:35 Ahiam (son of Sachar the **H**),

harass (1)

Psa 56:2 They **h** me. There are so many

harassing (2)

Psa 56:1 because people are **h** me.
57:3 disgraces the one who is **h** me.

Harbona (2)

Est 1:10 **H**, Bigtha, Abagtha, Zethar,
7:9 **H**, one of the eunuchs present

harbor (4)

Psa 107:30 He guided them to the **h** they
Isa 23:10 You no longer have a **h**.
Act 27:12 Since the **h** was not a good
27:12 (Phoenix is a **h** that faces the

harbors (1)

Act 27:8 came to a port called Fair **H**.

hard (124)

Gen 3:17 Through **h** work you will eat
18:14 Is anything too **h** for the LORD?
19:9 They pushed **h** against Lot and
31:6 that I have worked as **h** as
31:42 seen my misery and **h** work,
33:13 If they're driven too **h** for even
Exo 1:13 Israelites to work **h** as slaves.
1:14 gave them were brutally **h**.
Lev 26:19 land will be as **h** as cement.
26:20 You will work **h** for nothing
Dtr 1:17 any case that's too **h** for you,
17:8 may be a case that is too **h**
28:23 below will be as **h** as iron.
28:33 your **h** work have produced.
28:48 put a heavy burden of **h** work
30:11 I'm giving you today isn't too **h**
Jdg 7:13 of bread hit that tent so **h** that
16:29 he pushed **h** against them.
Rut 2:16 Don't give her a **h** time about it."
1Sm 6:5 will no longer be so **h** on you,
14:24 soldiers were driven **h** that day.
1Ki 12:4 Reduce the **h** work and lighten
20:37 him **h** and wounded him.
2Ch 10:4 Reduce the **h** work and lighten
32:5 Hezekiah worked **h**.
Job 9:29 should I work so **h** for nothing?
14:14 long as my **h** labor continues.
23:2 I try **h** to control my sighing.
Psa 38:2 Your hand has struck me **h**.
107:12 he humbled them with **h** work.
118:13 They pushed **h** to make me fall,
127:2 It is useless to work **h** for the
Pro 5:10 and you will have to work **h**
10:22 and **h** work adds nothing to it.
14:23 In **h** work there is always
Ecc 1:3 gain from all their **h** work under
2:10 my reward for all my **h** work.
2:11 and all the **h** work
2:18 which I had worked so **h** under
2:19 the sun for which I worked so **h**
2:20 had worked so **h** under the sun.
2:21 had worked **h** with wisdom,
2:22 get from all of their **h** work
3:9 people gain from their **h** labor?
3:13 from every kind of **h** work.
4:4 Then I saw that all **h** work and
4:6 than two handfuls of **h** work
4:8 So there is no end to all the **h**
4:8 why they are working so **h**
4:9 a good reward for their **h** work.
5:15 with them from all their **h** work.
5:16 from working so **h** for the wind?
5:18 the good in all our **h** work under
5:19 to rejoice in their own **h** work.
6:7 that people work so **h**
8:15 they work **h** during their brief
8:17 However **h** a person may
9:9 you get for the **h** work that you
10:15 themselves out with **h** work,
Isa 5:28 horses' hoofs are as **h** as flint.
14:3 from the **h** slavery you were
40:2 it that its time of **h** labor is over
49:4 "I have worked **h** for nothing.
Jer 14:19 Why have you struck us so **h**

Jer 32:17 Nothing is too **h** for you.
32:27 Nothing is too **h** for me.
Eze 3:5 to people whose language is **h**
3:6 language is **h** to understand,
3:9 I will make you as **h** as a
29:18 his army fight **h** against Tyre.
Dan 4:9 No secret is too **h** for you ⌊to
Mic 4:13 I will make your horns as **h** as
4:13 and your hoofs as **h** as bronze.
Hag 1:11 and on all your **h** work."
Zec 7:12 They made their hearts as **h** as
8:13 Let your hands work **h**.
Mat 13:15 close-minded and **h** of hearing.
19:23 It will be **h** for a rich person to
20:12 even though we worked **h** all
23:4 They make loads that are **h** to
25:24 I knew that you are a **h** person
Mar 10:23 "How **h** it will be for rich people
10:24 how **h** it is to enter the kingdom
14:72 Then Peter began to cry very **h**.
Luk 5:5 we worked **h** all night and
11:46 with loads that are **h** to carry.
12:47 to do it will receive a **h** beating.
13:24 "Try **h** to enter through the
18:24 "How **h** it is for rich people to
21:23 land will suffer very **h** times,
22:44 So he prayed very **h** in anguish.
Jon 4:38 people have done the **h** work,
6:60 "What he says is **h** to accept.
Act 12:5 the church was praying very **h**
20:35 that by working **h** like this we
26:14 It's **h** for ⌊a mortal like⌋ you to
28:27 close-minded and **h** of hearing.
Rom 16:6 who has worked very **h** for you.
16:12 who have worked **h** for the
16:12 has worked very **h** for the Lord.
1Co 15:58 You know that the **h** work you
16:12 I tried **h** to get him to visit you
16:16 shares their labor and **h** work.
2Co 6:5 riots, **h** work, sleepless nights,
11:27 Because I've had to work so **h**,
Gal 4:11 Maybe the **h** work I spent on
Eph 4:28 and, instead, they must work **h**.
Php 1:23 I find it **h** to choose between
2:22 and son we worked **h** together
Col 1:29 I work **h** and struggle to do this
2:1 I want you to know how **h** I
4:13 I assure you that he works **h**
1Th 1:3 your love is working **h**,
3:10 We pray very **h** night and day
2Th 3:8 Instead, we worked **h** and
1Ti 4:10 Certainly, we work **h** and
5:17 true if they work **h** at teaching
2Ti 1:17 he searched **h** for me and found
Heb 5:11 explaining it to you is **h**.
6:11 you're working **h** so that you
1Pe 4:18 If it's **h** for the person who has
2Pe 3:16 his letters are **h** to understand.
Rev 2:2 done — how **h** you have worked
14:13 "Let them rest from their **h** work

hardened (2)
Psa 26:9 my soul along with **h** sinners
Zep 1:12 satisfied with their **h** lifestyle,

hardens (2)
Job 38:30 The water **h** like a stone,
38:38 when the dirt **h** into clumps and

harder (6)
Exo 5:9 Make the work **h** for these
Job 37:6 and to the pouring rain, 'Rain **h**!'
Isa 13:12 I will make people **h** to find
Eze 3:9 as a diamond, **h** than stone.
Jnh 1:13 Instead, the men tried to row **h**
1Co 15:10 I worked **h** than all the others.

hard-fought (1)
Eze 29:18 for their **h** battle against Tyre.

hardheaded (3)
Isa 48:4 Like iron, you are **h**.
Eze 3:7 Israel are very stubborn and **h**.
3:8 stubborn and as **h** as they are.

hard-hearted (2)
Dtr 15:8 Never be **h** and tight-fisted with
Pro 28:14 whoever is **h** falls into disaster.

hard-pressed (2)
1Sm 13:6 because the army was **h**,
Isa 8:21 when they are **h** and hungry.

hardship (7)
Dtr 15:18 it won't be a **h** for you.
Psa 119:143 Trouble and **h** have found me,
Isa 30:6 they experience distress and **h**.
Lam 3:5 me with bitterness and **h**.
2Co 8:13 have relief while you have **h**.
12:10 mistreatment, **h**, persecution,
Heb 10:32 You endured a lot of **h** and pain.

hardships (11)
Exo 18:8 all the **h** they had had on the
Num 20:14 You know all the **h** we've had.
Dtr 28:53 Because of the **h** your enemies
28:55 because of the **h** your enemies
28:57 because of the **h** your enemies
Neh 9:32 Do not consider all the **h** that
9:32 The **h** have come to our kings,
Psa 60:3 your people experience **h**.
132:1 David and all the **h** he endured.
Isa 30:20 may give you troubles and **h**.
Jer 19:9 and **h** that their enemies

hard-working (7)
1Ki 11:28 was a very able and **h** man.
Pro 10:4 but **h** hands bring riches.
12:24 **H** hands gain control,
12:27 a **h** person becomes wealthy.
13:4 of **h** people is satisfied.
21:5 The plans of a **h** person lead to
2Ti 2:6 A **h** farmer should have the first

Hareph (1)
1Ch 2:51 first settled Bethlehem, and **H**,

Harhaiah's (1)
Neh 3:8 **H** son, a goldsmith,

Harhas (1)
2Ki 22:14 of Tikvah and grandson of **H**.

Har Heres (1)
Jdg 1:35 were determined to live at **H**,

Harhur (2)
Ezr 2:51 Bakbuk, Hakupha, **H**,
Neh 7:53 Bakbuk, Hakupha, **H**,

Harim (10)
1Ch 24:8 the third for **H**, the fourth for
Ezr 2:32 of **H**: 320
2:39 of **H**: 1,017
10:21 From the descendants of **H**:
10:31 From the descendants of **H**:
Neh 7:35 of **H**: 320
7:42 of **H**: 1,017
10:5 **H**, Meremoth, Obadiah,
10:27 Malluch, **H**, and Baanah.
12:15 from **H**, Adna; from Meraioth,

Harim's (1)
Neh 3:11 Malchiah, **H** son, and Hasshub,

Hariph (2)
Neh 7:24 of **H**: 112
10:19 **H**, Anathoth, Nebai,

harm (60)
Gen 26:29 that you will not **h** us,
31:7 But God hasn't let him **h** me.
31:29 I have the power to **h** you.
31:52 past the pile of stones to **h** you,
31:52 of stones or marker to **h** me.
42:38 If any **h** comes to him on the
Exo 24:11 God didn't **h** these leaders of
Num 5:19 bring a curse will not **h** you.
23:23 No magic can **h** the people of
35:23 and you weren't trying to **h** him.
Dtr 20:19 Don't **h** any of its fruit trees with
Jdg 15:12 you won't **h** me yourselves."
1Sm 20:7 that he has decided to **h** me.
20:9 my father had decided to **h** you,
20:13 If my father plans to **h** you and I
20:13 may the LORD **h** me even
23:9 Saul was planning to **h** him,
24:9 that I am trying to **h** you?
24:11 to see I mean no **h** or rebellion.
25:26 who are trying to **h** you end up
26:21 I will not **h** you again,
2Sm 12:18 He may **h** ⌊himself⌋."
14:10 He'll never **h** you again."
14:11 doing more **h** by destroying my
20:6 do us more **h** than Absalom.
1Ch 16:22 ones or **h** my prophets.'
Ezr 4:22 suffer any more **h**?
Neh 6:2 They were planning to **h** me.
Est 9:2 who were planning to **h** them.
Job 5:19 no **h** will touch you:
31:29 celebrated when **h** came to him
Psa 7:14 is pregnant with **h**,
23:4 you are with me, I fear no **h**.
38:12 Those who are out to **h** me talk
91:10 No **h** will come to you.
105:15 ones or **h** my prophets."
Pro 12:21 No ⌊lasting⌋ **h** comes to a
19:23 rest easy without suffering **h**.
Isa 27:3 night so that no one will **h** it.
43:2 and the flames will not **h** you.
Jer 10:5 They can't **h** you. They can't do
21:10 I've decided to **h** this city,
25:6 Then I won't **h** you.
25:7 brought⌋ **h** upon yourselves.'
39:12 Don't **h** him in any way,
Dan 1:8 mind not to **h** himself by eating
1:8 for permission not to **h** himself
Act 18:10 No one will attack you or **h** you.
1Co 8:12 and **h** their weak consciences,
11:17 it results in more **h** than good.
2Co 7:9 so we haven't done you any **h**.
2Ti 4:14 did me a great deal of **h**.
4:18 Lord will rescue me from all **h**
1Pe 3:13 Who will **h** you if you are
3:14 of those who want to **h** you.
1Jn 5:18 and the evil one can't **h** them.
Rev 7:2 who had been allowed to **h**
7:3 "Don't **h** the land, the sea,
9:4 were told not to **h** any grass,
9:4 They could **h** only the people

harmed (6)
Jos 2:19 anyone inside your house is **h**.
1Sm 28:10 you will not be **h** if you do this."
Pro 3:30 no reason if he has not **h** you.
Dan 3:27 They saw that the fire had not **h**
Act 28:5 snake into the fire and wasn't **h**.
2Co 11:29 is caught in a trap, I'm also **h**.

harmful (3)
2Ki 4:41 there was nothing **h** in the pot.
Rom 13:10 never does anything that is **h**
1Ti 6:9 and **h** desires which drown

harming (2)
1Sm 25:34 who has kept me from **h** you,
Jer 7:19 "But they are ⌊**h**⌋ themselves

harmony (7)
Job 22:21 "Be in **h** and at peace with
Psa 133:1 and sisters live together in **h**!
Act 4:32 group of believers lived in **h**.
Rom 12:16 Live in **h** with each other.
15:5 allow you to live in **h** with each
Php 2:2 and the same love, living in **h**,
1Pe 3:8 everyone must live in **h**,

harms (2)
Pro 8:36 sins against me **h** himself.
31:12 She helps him and never **h** him

Harnepher (1)
1Ch 7:36 Zophah's sons were Suah, **H**,

harness (4)
Job 41:13 Who can approach it with a **h**?

Jas 5:4 people who **h** your fields shout

harvesting (9)

Gen 8:22 planting and **h**, cold and heat,
45:6 years without plowing or **h**.
Exo 34:21 of plowing or **h** you must not
Dtr 16:9 from the time you start **h** grain.
24:19 must do when you're **h** wheat
1Sm 6:13 of Beth Shemesh were **h** wheat
2Sm 21:9 when people started **h** barley.
Isa 17:5 That time will be like **h**
Rev 14:16 and the **h** of the earth was

harvests (8)

Gen 41:47 the land produced large **h**.
2Ch 32:28 sheds to store his **h** of grain,
Pro 14:4 of an ox produces plentiful **h**.
Jer 12:13 were disappointed by their **h**
Amo 9:13 will catch up to the one who **h**,
Jon 4:36 The person who **h** the crop is
4:36 the grain and the person who **h**
4:37 and another person **h**.'

Hasadiah (1)

1Ch 3:20 **H**, and Jushab Hesed.

Hashabiah (15)

1Ch 6:45 who was the son of **H**,
9:14 and great-grandson of **H**),
25:3 Shimei, **H**, Mattithiah.
25:19 The twelfth chose **H**,
26:30 From Hebron's descendants **H**
27:17 for the tribe of Levi: **H**,
2Ch 35:9 and **H**, Jeiel, and Jozabad,
Ezr 8:19 They also brought **H**,
8:24 **H**, and 10 of their relatives.
Neh 3:17 Next to him **H**, the official in
10:11 Mica, Rehob, **H**,
11:15 who was the son of **H**,
11:22 who was the son of **H**,
12:21 from Hilkiah, **H**; from Jedaiah,
12:24 heads of the Levites were **H**,

Hashabnah (1)

Neh 10:25 Rehum, **H**, Maaseiah,

Hashabneiah (1)

Neh 9:5 Bani, **H**, Sherebiah, Hodiah,

Hashabneiah's (1)

Neh 3:10 **H** son, made repairs.

Hashbaddanah (1)

Neh 8:4 Hashum, **H**, Zechariah,

Hashmonah (2)

Num 33:29 Mithcah and set up camp at **H**.
33:30 They moved from **H** and set up

Hashubah (1)

1Ch 3:20 **H**, Ohel, Berechiah, Hasadiah,

Hashum (5)

Ezr 2:19 of **H**: 223
10:33 From the descendants of **H**:
Neh 7:22 of **H**: 328
8:4 Pedaiah, Mishael, Malchiah, **H**,
10:18 Hodiah, **H**, Bezai,

Hasrah (1)

2Ch 34:22 of Tokhath and grandson of **H**.

Hassenaah (1)

Neh 3:3 The sons of **H** rebuilt Fish

Hassenuah (1)

1Ch 9:7 and great-grandson of **H**),

Hasshub (5)

1Ch 9:14 were Shemaiah (son of **H**,
Neh 3:11 Malchiah, Harim's son, and **H**,
3:23 After them Benjamin and **H**
10:23 Hoshea, Hananiah, **H**,
11:15 who was the son of **H**,

Hassophereth (1)

Ezr 2:55 of Sotai, **H**, Peruda,

hastily (2)

Lev 5:4 "If you **h** take a vow about
Pro 26:2 so a **h** spoken curse does not

hasty (1)

Job 5:13 of schemers prove to be **h**.

Hasupha (2)

Ezr 2:43 of Ziha, **H**, Tabbaoth,
Neh 7:46 of Ziha, **H**, Tabbaoth,

hatch (3)

Psa 84:3 There they **h** their young near
Isa 34:15 there, lay eggs, and **h** them.
59:5 They **h** viper eggs and weave

hatched (1)

Isa 59:5 a poisonous snake is **h**.

hatches (1)

Jer 17:11 is like a partridge that **h** eggs

hatchets (1)

Psa 74:6 paneling with axes and **h**.

hate (118)

Gen 26:27 since you **h** me and sent me
34:30 and the Perizzites, **h** me.
Exo 5:21 Pharaoh and his officials **h** us.
18:21 men who **h** corruption.
20:5 generation of those who **h** me.
Lev 19:17 "Never **h** another Israelite.
26:17 Those who **h** you will be your
Num 10:35 Make those who **h** you run
35:20 someone you **h** by shoving him
Dtr 5:9 generation of those who **h** me.
7:15 he will strike all those who **h**
30:7 those who **h** you and persecute
32:41 and pay back those who **h** me.
33:11 attack them and **h** them so that
Jos 20:5 He didn't even **h** the person he
Jdg 11:7 leaders, "Don't you **h** me?
14:16 She said, "You **h** me!
2Sm 5:8 the blind who **h** me by using
19:6 You love those who **h** you and
19:6 hate you and **h** those who love
1Ki 22:8 son of Imlah, but I **h** him.
2Ch 1:11 the death of those who **h** you.
18:7 son of Imla, but I **h** him.
19:2 love those who **h** the LORD?
Job 7:16 I **h** my life; I do not want to live
8:22 Those who **h** you will be
9:21 way of knowing it. I **h** my life!
10:1 "I **h** my life. I will freely express
Psa 5:5 You **h** all troublemakers.
9:13 because of those who **h** me.
21:8 hand will find all who **h** you.
31:6 I **h** those who cling to false
34:21 and those who **h** righteous
35:19 Do not let those who **h** me for
36:2 flatters himself and does not **h**
38:19 Many **h** me for no reason.
44:7 You put to shame those who **h**
44:10 Those who **h** us rob us at will.
50:17 You **h** discipline. You toss my
68:1 Those who **h** him will flee from
69:4 Those who **h** me for no reason
69:14 rescued from those who **h** me
81:15 Those who **h** the LORD would
83:2 Those who **h** you hold their
86:17 that those who **h** me may see
89:23 and defeat those who **h** him.
97:10 who love the LORD **h** evil.
101:3 I **h** what unfaithful people do.
118:7 defeat of those who **h** me.
119:104 That is why I **h** every path that
119:113 I **h** two-faced people,
119:128 I **h** every pathway that leads to
119:163 I **h** lying; I am disgusted with it.
120:6 long with those who **h** peace.
129:5 to shame all those who **h** Zion.
139:21 Shouldn't I **h** those who hate
Psa 139:21 I hate those who **h** you,
139:22 I **h** them with all my heart.
Pro 1:22 How long will you fools **h**
8:13 To fear the LORD is to **h** evil.
8:13 I **h** pride, arrogance,
8:36 those who **h** me love death."
9:8 a mocker, or he will **h** you.
10:12 **H** starts quarrels, but love
15:17 juicy steaks where there is **h**.
25:17 see too much of you and **h** you.
26:24 Whoever is filled with **h**
28:16 but those who **h** unjust gain
29:10 Bloodthirsty people **h** an
Ecc 2:17 So I came to **h** life because
2:18 I came to **h** everything for
3:8 a time to love and a time to **h**,
9:6 Their love, their **h**,
Isa 1:14 I **h** your New Moon Festivals
61:8 I **h** robbery and wrongdoing.
66:5 Your relatives, who **h** you and
Jer 12:8 They roar at me, so I **h** them.
44:4 these detestable things that I **h**.
Eze 6:9 They will **h** themselves for the
16:37 you and **h** you gather around.
16:57 Those around you **h** you.
22:7 People in you **h** their fathers
23:28 to hand you over to those you **h**
35:6 you don't **h** murdering people,
36:31 and you will **h** yourselves for
Dan 4:19 were about those who **h** you
Amo 5:10 Israel, you **h** anyone who
5:15 **H** evil and love good.
5:21 I **h** your festivals; I despise
6:8 and I **h** his palaces.
Mic 3:2 You **h** good and love evil.
Zec 8:17 I **h** all these things,
Mal 2:16 "I **h** divorce," says the LORD
2:16 "I **h** the person who covers
Mat 5:43 and **h** your enemy.'
6:24 He will **h** the first master and
10:22 Everyone will **h** you because
24:9 All nations will **h** you because
24:10 will betray and **h** each other.
Mar 13:13 Everyone will **h** you because
Luk 1:71 from the power of all who **h** us.
6:22 Blessed are you when people **h**
6:27 Be kind to those who **h** you.
16:13 He will **h** the first master and
21:17 Everyone will **h** you because
Jon 3:20 People who do what is wrong **h**
7:7 The world cannot **h** you,
12:25 and those who **h** their lives in
15:25 'They **h** me for no reason.'
Act 13:10 You **h** everything that has
Rom 7:15 Instead, I do what I **h**.
7:17 one who is doing the things I **h**,
12:9 **H** evil. Hold on to what is good.
1Jn 2:9 light but **h** other believers are
2:11 Those who **h** other believers
Rev 2:6 this in your favor — you **h** what
2:6 I also **h** what they're doing.
17:16 you saw will **h** the prostitute.

hated (42)

Gen 27:41 So Esau **h** Jacob because of
37:4 They **h** Joseph and couldn't
37:5 they **h** him even more.
37:8 They **h** him even more for his
Dtr 4:42 they had never **h** could flee
9:28 He **h** them. That's why he
19:4 kills someone he never **h**
19:6 because in the past he never **h**
Jdg 15:2 "I thought you **h** her.
2Sm 13:22 He **h** Amnon for raping his
22:18 and from those who **h** me,
22:41 and I destroyed those who **h**
Est 9:1 those who **h** them.
9:5 pleased to those who **h** them.
9:16 75,000 of those who **h** them,
Psa 18:17 and from those who **h** me,
18:40 and I destroyed those who **h**
25:19 how they have **h** me with
26:5 I have **h** the mob of evildoers
45:7 is right and **h** what is wrong.
55:12 If someone who **h** me had
105:25 so that they **h** his people,

Psa 106:10 power of the one who **h** them.
106:41 those who **h** them ruled them.
Pro 1:29 because they **h** knowledge and
5:12 "Oh, how I **h** discipline!
14:17 a person who plots evil is **h**.
14:20 A poor person is **h** even by his
Isa 60:15 have been abandoned and **h**;
Hos 9:15 I **h** the people there.
Mal 1:3 but Esau I **h**. I turned his
Luk 19:14 of his own country **h** him.
Jon 15:18 realize that it **h** me before it
15:18 that it hated me before it **h** you.
15:24 But now they have seen and **h**
17:14 But the world has **h** them
Rom 9:13 "I loved Jacob, but I **h** Esau."
Eph 5:29 No one ever **h** his own body.
Tit 3:3 We were **h**, and we hated each
3:3 and we **h** each other.
Heb 1:9 is right and **h** what is wrong.
Rev 18:2 and every unclean and **h** beast.

hateful (1)

Psa 109:3 surround me with **h** words.

hatefully (2)

Eze 23:29 They will treat you **h** and take
35:11 you acted **h** toward them.

haters (1)

Rom 1:30 slanderers, **h** of God,

hates (30)

Exo 23:5 who **h** you has collapsed
Dtr 1:27 and said, "The LORD **h** us!
7:10 pay back everyone who **h** him.
7:10 to pay back anyone who **h** him.
12:31 He **h** it! They even burn their
16:22 things the LORD your God **h**.
19:11 someone **h** another person,
Job 33:20 so that their whole being **h** food
34:17 Should anyone who **h** justice
Psa 11:5 but he **h** wicked people and the
41:7 Everyone who **h** me whispers
Pro 6:16 are six things that the LORD **h**,
11:15 but whoever **h** the closing of a
12:1 but whoever **h** correction is a
13:5 A righteous person **h** lying,
13:24 refuses to spank his son **h** him,
15:10 Anyone who **h** a warning will
15:27 but whoever **h** bribes will live.
19:7 family of a poor person **h** him.
26:28 A lying tongue **h** its victims,
29:24 Whoever is a thief's partner **h**
30:17 that makes fun of a father and **h**
Jon 7:7 but it **h** me because I say that
15:18 "If the world **h** you,
15:19 and that's why the world **h** you.
15:23 The person who **h** me also
15:23 hates me also **h** my Father.
1Jn 3:13 don't be surprised if the world **h**
3:15 Everyone who **h** another
4:20 but **h** another believer is a liar.

Hathach (5)

Est 4:5 Then Esther called for **H**,
4:6 So **H** went out to Mordecai in
4:8 **H** was supposed to show it to
4:9 So **H** returned and told Esther
4:10 Esther spoke to **H** and

Hathath (1)

1Ch 4:13 Othniel were **H** and Meonothai.

hating (1)

Eze 17:19 my promise and **h** my treaty.

Hatipha (2)

Ezr 2:54 Neziah, and **H**.
Neh 7:56 Neziah, and **H**.

Hatita (2)

Ezr 2:42 Akkub, **H**, and Shobai: 139
Neh 7:45 Akkub, **H**, and Shobai: 138

hatred (11)

2Sm 13:15 developed an intense **h** for her.
2Sm 13:15 His **h** for her was greater than
Psa 25:19 have hated me with vicious **h**!
109:5 and with **h** instead of love.
Pro 10:18 Whoever conceals **h** has lying
26:26 His **h** is deceitfully hidden,
Ecc 9:1 whether there will be love or **h**.
Gal 5:20 idolatry, drug use, **h**,
Eph 4:31 loud quarreling, cursing, and **h**.
Col 3:8 **h**, cursing, obscene language,
Jas 4:4 ⌊evil⌋ world is **h** toward God?

hats (2)

Isa 3:20 **h**, ankle bracelets, blouses,
Dan 3:21 clothes, **h**, and other clothing.

Hattil (2)

Ezr 2:57 Shephatiah, **H**, and Ami.
Neh 7:59 Shephatiah, **H**, and Amon.

Hattush (5)

1Ch 3:22 Shemaiah's six sons were **H**,
Ezr 8:3 from the family of David: **H**,
Neh 3:10 Next to them **H**, made repairs.
10:4 **H**, Shebaniah, Malluch,
12:2 Amariah, Malluch, **H**,

haughty (1)

Rom 1:30 slanderers, haters of God, **h**,

haul (1)

Eze 32:3 and they will **h** you up in a net.

Hauran (2)

Eze 47:16 which is on the border of **H**.
47:18 run between **H** and Damascus.

Havilah (7)

Gen 2:11 one that winds throughout **H**,
10:7 Seba, **H**, Sabtah, Raamah,
10:29 Ophir, **H**, and Jobab.
25:18 from the region of **H** to Shur,
1Sm 15:7 the Amalekites from **H** to Shur,
1Ch 1:9 **H**, Sabta, Raama, and Sabteca.
1:23 Ophir, **H**, and Jobab. All these

Havvoth Jair (4)

Num 32:41 called them **H** [Settlements of
Dtr 3:14 in Bashan he named **H**
Jdg 10:4 still called **H** to this day
1Ch 2:23 Aram captured **H** with Kenath

hawk's (1)

Job 28:7 No **h** eye has ever seen it.

hay (4)

Job 5:26 a ripe old age like a stack of **h**
6:5 an ox make a sound over its **h**?
Isa 33:11 You will be pregnant with **h**.
1Co 3:12 stones, wood, **h**, or straw.

Hazael (22)

1Ki 19:15 anoint **H** as king of Aram.
2Ki 8:8 The king told **H**, "Take a
8:9 **H** went to meet Elisha.
8:12 **H** asked. Elisha answered, "I
8:13 But **H** asked, "How can a dog
8:14 **H** left Elisha and went to his
8:14 **H** answered, "He told me that
8:15 But the next day **H** took a
8:15 **H** ruled as king in his place.
8:28 Joram to fight against King **H**
8:29 fought against King **H** of Aram.)
9:14 Gilead against King **H** of Aram.
9:15 while fighting King **H** of Aram.)
10:32 **H** defeated Jehu's army
12:17 At this time King **H** of Aram
12:18 these things to King **H** of Aram,
13:3 put it at the mercy of King **H**
13:22 King **H** of Aram oppressed
13:24 King **H** of Aram died,
2Ch 22:5 of Israel to fight against King **H**
22:6 fought against King **H** of Aram.)
Amo 1:4 send a fire on the house of **H**

Hazael's (2)

1Ki 19:17 from **H** sword, Jehu will kill
2Ki 13:3 and **H** son Benhadad as long

Hazaiah (1)

Neh 11:5 who was the son of **H**,

Hazar Addar (1)

Num 34:4 goes to **H** and on to Azmon

Hazar Enan (2)

Num 34:9 goes to Ziphron and ends at **H**
34:10 extends from **H** to Shepham

Hazar Enon (2)

Eze 47:17 Mediterranean Sea to **H** on the
48:1 Hethlon to Hamath Pass and **H**

Hazar Gaddah (1)

Jos 15:27 **H**, Heshmon, Beth Pelet

Hazarmaveth (2)

Gen 10:26 of Almodad, Sheleph, **H**, Jerah,
1Ch 1:20 of Almodad, Sheleph, **H**, Jerah,

Hazar Shual (4)

Jos 15:28 **H**, Beersheba, Biziothiah
19:3 **H**, Balah, Ezem
1Ch 4:28 lived in Beersheba, Moladah, **H**
Neh 11:27 in **H**, in Beersheba and its

Hazar Susah (1)

Jos 19:5 Ziklag, Beth Marcaboth, **H**

Hazar Susim (1)

1Ch 4:31 Beth Marcaboth, **H**, Beth Biri,

Hazazon Tamar (2)

Gen 14:7 Amorites who were living at **H**
2Ch 20:2 crowd is already in **H**

Hazelelponi (1)

1Ch 4:3 Their sister's name was **H**.

Hazer Hatticon (1)

Eze 47:16 will run to **H**, which is on the

Hazeroth (5)

Num 11:35 the people moved to **H**,
12:16 the people moved from **H** and
33:17 and set up camp at **H**.
33:18 They moved from **H** and set up
Dtr 1:1 near Laban, **H**, and Di Zahab.

Haziel (1)

1Ch 23:9 sons: Shelomith, **H**, and Haran.

Hazo (1)

Gen 22:22 Kesed, **H**, Pildash, Jidlaph,

Hazor (18)

Jos 11:1 King Jabin of **H** heard ⌊what
11:10 turned back and captured **H**.
11:10 (**H** was formerly the head of all
11:11 Joshua also burned **H**.
11:13 an exception and burned **H**.
12:19 king of Madon, the king of **H**,
15:23 Kedesh, **H**, Ithnan,
15:25 Kerioth Hezron (now called **H**),
19:36 Adamah, Ramah, **H**,
Jdg 4:2 who ruled at **H**, to defeat them.
4:17 this because King Jabin of **H**
1Sm 12:9 commander of the army of **H**,
1Ki 9:15 and ⌊the cities of⌋ **H**,
2Ki 15:29 Kedesh, **H**, Gilead, Galilee,
Neh 11:33 **H**, Ramah, Gittaim,
Jer 49:28 of **H** that King Nebuchadnezzar
49:30 place to hide, inhabitants of **H**,
49:33 **H** will be a place where only

Hazor Hadattah (1)

Jos 15:25 **H**, Kerioth Hezron (now called

head (283)

Gen 3:15 He will crush your **h**,
28:11 that place, put it under his **h**,
28:18 stone he had put under his **h**.
40:16 baked goods were on my **h**.

Gen 40:17 out of the basket on my **h**."
40:19 days Pharaoh will cut off your **h**
47:31 his face at the **h** of his bed.
48:14 his right hand on Ephraim's **h**,
48:14 his left hand on Manasseh's **h**,
48:17 his right hand on Ephraim's **h**,
48:17 Ephraim's **h** to Manasseh's.
48:18 Put your right hand on his **h**."
49:26 rest on the **h** of Joseph,
Exo 22:1 make up for the loss with five **h**
28:32 Make an opening for the **h** in
29:7 pour it on his **h**, and anoint him.
29:10 will place their hands on its **h**.
29:15 will place their hands on its **h**.
29:17 with the other pieces and the **h**.
29:19 will place their hands on its **h**.
Lev 1:4 your hand on the animal's **h**.
1:8 will also lay the pieces, the **h**,
1:12 The priest will lay the **h** and
3:2 your hand on the animal's **h**.
3:8 your hand on the animal's **h**.
3:13 Place your hand on its **h**.
4:4 place his hand on the bull's **h**.
4:11 meat, **h**, legs, internal organs,
4:15 place their hands on the bull's **h**
4:24 place his hand on the goat's **h**
4:29 his hand on the animal's **h**
4:33 his hand on the animal's **h**
5:8 neck without pulling its **h** off.
8:12 of the anointing oil on Aaron's **h**
8:14 placed their hands on its **h**.
8:18 their hands on the ram's **h**.
8:20 Moses burned the **h** with the
8:22 their hands on the ram's **h**.
9:13 in pieces and included the **h**.
13:12 covers the whole person from **h**
13:29 some disease on the **h** or chin,
13:30 a disease on the **h** or the chin.
13:41 the hair on the front of his **h**,
13:44 of the skin disease on his **h**.
14:9 shave off all the hair on his **h**,
14:18 of the oil in his hand on the **h**
14:29 of the oil in his hand on the **h**
16:21 will place both hands on its **h**.
16:21 transfer them to the goat's **h**.
21:4 As the **h** of your people,
24:14 must lay their hands on his **h**.
27:32 Every tenth **h** of cattle or sheep
Num 1:4 must be the **h** of a household.
6:9 days later he must shave his **h**
6:11 must dedicate his **h** again.
17:3 one staff for the **h** of each tribe.
25:15 (Zur was the **h** of a family from
Dtr 14:1 shaving bald spots on your **h**.
19:5 the **h** flies off the handle,
21:12 She must shave her **h**,
28:13 The LORD will make you the **h**,
28:35 of your feet to the top of your **h**.
28:44 They will be the **h**,
33:20 They can tear off an arm or a **h**.
Jos 11:10 (Hazor was formerly the **h** of all
22:14 a leader of a household and **h**
Jdg 5:26 She crushed his **h**.
9:53 that hit Abimelech on the **h**
16:17 has ever cut the hair on my **h**.
1Sm 1:11 will never be used on his **h**."
2:1 My **h** is lifted to the LORD.
2:10 and lifts the **h** of his Messiah."
4:12 clothes torn and dirt on his **h**.
5:4 Dagon's **h** and his two hands
9:2 He stood a **h** taller than
9:22 hall and had them sit at the **h**
10:1 poured it on Saul's **h**,
10:23 he was a **h** taller than everyone
14:45 not a single hair of his **h** will
15:17 you were the **h** of Israel's tribes.
17:5 had a bronze helmet on his **h**,
17:7 The **h** of his spear was made
17:38 a bronze helmet on David's **h**
17:46 you down and cut off your **h**.
17:51 was dead by cutting off his **h**.
17:54 David took the Philistine's **h**
17:57 the Philistine's **h** in his hand.
19:13 put a goat-hair blanket at its **h**,
19:16 the goat-hair blanket at its **h**.
26:7 stuck in the ground near his **h**.
1Sm 26:11 take that spear near his **h**
26:12 the jar of water near Saul's **h**,
26:16 of water that were near his **h**."
31:9 They cut off his **h** and stripped
2Sm 1:2 and he had dirt on his **h**.
1:10 the crown that was on his **h**
2:16 grabbed his opponent by the **h**,
3:29 May the blame fall on the **h** of
4:7 killed him, and cut off his **h**.)
4:7 They took his **h** and traveled
4:8 They brought Ishbosheth's **h** to
4:8 "Here is the **h** of Ishbosheth,
4:12 Then they took Ishbosheth's **h**
12:30 took the gold crown from the **h**
12:30 king and put it on his own **h**.
13:19 Tamar put ashes on her **h**,
13:19 put her hands on her **h**,
14:11 "not a hair on your son's **h** will
14:25 had no blemish from **h** to toe.
14:26 When he cut the hair on his **h**
15:30 He covered his **h** and walked
15:32 and he had dirt on his **h**.
16:9 go over there and tear off his **h**."
18:9 Absalom's **h** became caught in
20:21 "His **h** will be thrown to you
20:22 They cut off Sheba's **h** and
1Ki 1:52 not one hair on his **h** will fall to
10:19 of the throne was a calf's **h**.
16:18 the palace over his own **h**.
19:6 he saw near his **h** some bread
2Ki 4:19 he said to his father, "My **h**!
4:19 My **h**!" The father told his
6:5 the ax **h** fell into the water.
6:6 place and made the ax **h** float.
6:25 severe that a donkey's **h** sold
6:31 me dead if the **h** of Elisha,
6:32 sent someone to tear off my **h**?
9:3 of oil, pour it on his **h**, and say,
9:6 poured olive oil on his **h**
1Ch 5:15 was the **h** of their families.
9:34 These **h** Levites lived in
10:9 stripped him and took his **h**
10:10 of their gods and fastened his **h**
16:5 Asaph was the **h**; then Jeiel,
20:2 took the gold crown from the **h**
20:2 king and put it on David's **h**.
26:10 Shimri was the **h**, although he
26:10 His father appointed him **h**.
26:12 their **h** men were assigned
26:31 Jeriah was the **h** of Hebron's
27:3 and he was **h** of all of the
27:5 He was the **h**, and in his unit
29:11 are honored as **h** of all things.
2Ch 11:22 as family **h** and prince among
Neh 7:5 God put the idea into my **h** that
Est 2:17 he put the royal crown on her **h**
6:8 that has a royal crest on its **h**.
6:12 in despair and covered his **h**.
9:25 should turn back on his own **h**.
Job 1:20 ⌊in grief⌋, and shaved his **h**.
2:7 of his feet to the top of his **h**.
10:15 I dare not lift up my **h**.
16:4 you and shake my **h** at you.
19:9 has taken the crown off my **h**.
20:6 and his **h** touches the clouds,
29:3 made his lamp shine on my **h**,
31:36 place it on my **h** like a crown.
41:7 or its **h** with fishing spears?
Psa 3:3 You hold my **h** high.
7:16 lands back on his own **h**.
21:3 a crown of fine gold on his **h**.
23:5 You anoint my **h** with oil.
27:6 Now my **h** will be raised above
40:12 outnumber the hairs on my **h**.
60:7 Ephraim is the helmet on my **h**.
64:8 sees them will shake his **h**.
69:4 outnumber the hairs on my **h**.
108:8 Ephraim is the helmet on my **h**.
110:7 He will hold his **h** high.
112:9 His **h** is raised in honor.
133:2 scented oil on the **h**,
140:7 you have covered my **h** in the
141:5 It is like lotion for my **h**.
141:5 My **h** will not refuse it,
Pro 1:9 are a graceful garland on your **h**
4:9 a graceful garland for your **h**.
Pro 10:6 Blessings cover the **h** of a
11:26 a blessing will be upon the **h**
30:31 a king at the **h** of his army.
Ecc 2:14 person uses the eyes in his **h**,
9:8 go without lotion on your **h**.
Sos 2:6 His left hand is under my **h**.
5:2 My **h** is wet with dew,
5:11 His **h** is the finest gold.
7:5 You hold your **h** as high as
8:3 His left hand is under my **h**.
Isa 1:5 Your whole **h** is infected.
1:6 to the top of your **h** there is no
7:20 to shave the hair on your **h**,
9:14 off from Israel both **h** and tail,
9:15 and honored leaders are the **h**.
15:2 Every **h** is shaved bald,
58:5 Is fasting just bowing your **h**
59:17 a helmet of salvation on his **h**.
Jer 2:37 with your hands over your **h**,
9:1 "I wish that my **h** were ⌊filled
16:6 or shave his own **h** for them.
18:16 be stunned and shake his **h**.
31:19 I hung my **h** in shame.
47:5 will shave its **h** in mourning.
48:37 "Every **h** is shaved,
Lam 3:54 Water flowed over my **h**.
5:16 crown has fallen from our **h**.
Eze 5:1 to shave your **h** and beard.
7:18 and every **h** will be shaved.
8:3 me by the hair on my **h**.
16:12 a beautiful crown on your **h**.
16:25 also built worship sites at the **h**
16:31 build your platforms at the **h**
29:18 Every soldier's **h** was worn
38:10 time ideas will enter your **h**,
Dan 1:10 he would have my **h** cut off."
2:32 The **h** of this statue was made
2:38 You are the **h** of gold.
2:48 province of Babylon and **h**
4:9 **h** of the magicians,
5:11 made him **h** of the magicians,
7:9 the hair on his **h** was like pure
7:20 about the ten horns on its **h**
Amo 8:10 waist and shave everyone's **h**.
9:1 Cut off everyone's **h**.
Jnh 2:5 was wrapped around my **h**.
4:8 beat down on Jonah's **h** so that
Mic 1:16 Shave your **h** in mourning for
Hab 3:13 stripping him bare from **h** to toe
Zec 1:21 that no one could lift up his **h**.
3:5 "Put a clean turban on his **h**."
3:5 put a clean turban on his **h**
6:11 and put it on the **h** of Chief
Mat 5:36 don't swear an oath by your **h**.
10:30 on your **h** has been counted.
14:8 "Give me the **h** of John the
14:10 He had John's **h** cut off in
14:11 So the **h** was brought on a
26:7 perfume and poured it on his **h**.
27:29 into a crown, placed it on his **h**,
27:30 kept hitting him on the **h** with it.
27:37 written accusation above his **h**.
Mar 4:28 blade appears, then the **h**,
4:28 then the **h** full of grain.
6:16 "I had John's **h** cut off,
6:24 Her mother said, "Ask for the **h**
6:25 "I want you to give me the **h** of
6:27 ordered him to bring John's **h**.
6:27 guard cut off John's **h** in prison.
6:28 Then he brought the **h** on a
12:4 They hit the servant on the **h**
14:3 poured the perfume on his **h**.
15:17 and placed it on his **h**.
15:19 They kept hitting him on the **h**
Luk 7:46 didn't put any olive oil on my **h**.
9:9 "I had John's **h** cut off.
12:7 Even every hair on your **h** has
21:18 not a hair on your **h** will be lost.
Jon 13:9 Wash my hands and my **h** too!"
19:2 into a crown, placed it on his **h**,
19:30 Then he bowed his **h** and died.
20:7 cloth that had been on Jesus' **h**.
20:12 was where Jesus' **h** had been,
Act 27:34 since not a hair from anyone's **h**
1Co 11:4 Every man who covers his **h**
11:5 has her **h** uncovered while she

1Co 11:5 woman who has her **h** shaved.
11:6 if a woman doesn't cover her **h**,
11:6 cut off her hair or shave her **h**,
11:6 she should cover her **h**.
11:7 A man should not cover his **h**.
11:10 wear something on her **h**
11:13 to God with her **h** uncovered?
12:21 the **h** can't say to the feet,
Eph 1:10 Then Christ would be the **h** of
1:22 He has made Christ the **h** of
4:15 to Christ, who is the **h**.
5:23 The husband is the **h** of his
5:23 of his wife as Christ is the **h**
Col 1:18 He is also the **h** of the church,
2:19 hold on to ⌊Christ,⌋ the **h**.
2Ti 4:5 keep a clear **h** in everything.
Rev 1:14 His **h** and his hair were white
10:1 there was a rainbow over his **h**.
12:1 a crown of 12 stars on her **h**.
14:14 He had a gold crown on his **h**
19:12 On his **h** are many crowns.

headbands (4)

Dtr 6:8 wear them as **h** as a reminder.
11:18 wear them as **h** as a reminder.
Isa 3:18 **h**, crescent-shaped necklaces,
Mat 23:5 They make their **h** large and

headdresses (1)

Isa 3:23 mirrors, underwear, **h**,

headed (9)

Num 14:40 Early the next morning they **h**
14:44 But they **h** into the mountain
Jdg 8:4 Gideon and his 300 men **h**
1Ki 10:22 The king had a fleet **h** for
1Ch 7:11 They **h** families that produced
Jon 20:3 other disciple **h** for the tomb.
Act 14:26 they took a boat and **h** home
18:18 they took a boat **h** for Syria
Rom 9:22 they are **h** for destruction?

headfirst (4)

Psa 37:24 he will not be thrown down **h**
Pro 10:8 will be thrown down **h**.
10:10 will be thrown down **h**.
Act 1:18 a piece of land where he fell **h**

heads (156)

Gen 41:5 Seven good, healthy **h** of grain
41:6 Seven other **h** of grain,
41:7 The thin **h** of grain swallowed
41:7 the seven full, healthy **h**.
41:22 full **h** of grain growing on a
41:23 Seven other **h** of grain,
41:24 The thin **h** of grain swallowed
41:24 swallowed the seven good **h**.
41:26 and the seven good **h** of grain
41:27 The seven empty **h** of grain
Exo 6:14 These were the **h** of the
6:25 These were the **h** of Levite
9:31 the barley had formed **h**
Lev 21:5 shaving bald spots on your **h**,
Num 1:16 and **h** of the divisions of Israel.
6:5 no razor may touch their **h**.
6:18 Nazirites will shave their **h** at
7:2 Then the leaders of Israel, the **h**
8:12 will place their hands on the **h**
10:4 the **h** of the divisions of Israel,
24:17 He will crush the **h** of the
30:1 Moses said to the **h** of the
31:26 and the **h** of the families of the
32:28 and the family **h** of the tribes of
36:1 The **h** of the households
Dtr 1:15 So I took the **h** of your tribes
5:23 all the leaders and **h** of your
29:10 The **h** of your tribes,
32:42 My sword will cut off the **h** of
Jos 7:6 They put dust on their **h** and
14:1 and the **h** of Israel's tribes
22:21 of Manasseh answered the **h**
22:30 and the **h** of the divisions of
Jdg 7:25 they brought the severed **h**
2Sm 15:30 troops with him covered their **h**
1Ki 8:1 all the **h** of the tribes,
2Ki 10:6 bring the **h** of your master's
2Ki 10:7 They put the **h** in baskets and
10:8 "They've brought the **h** of the
19:21 shake their **h** behind your back.
1Ch 5:24 These were the **h** of
5:24 were famous **h** of their families.
7:2 These men were **h** of the
7:3 of them were **h** ⌊of families⌋.
7:7 They were **h** of families and
7:9 to their ancestry (the **h**
7:40 were Asher's descendants — **h**
8:6 who were **h** of the families
8:10 sons became **h** of families.
8:13 Beriah and Shema were the **h**
8:28 These were the **h** of families
8:28 They were the **h** of families.
9:9 All of these men were **h** of their
9:13 Their relatives who were **h** of
9:33 the musicians who were the **h**
9:34 They were the **h** of the Levite
12:19 They said, "It will cost us our **h**
15:12 He said to them, "You are the **h**
23:9 were the **h** of Ladan's families.
23:24 The **h** of their families were
24:4 **h** than Ithamar's descendants,
26:21 were the **h** of Ladan's families:
26:26 King David, the **h** of families,
26:32 who were **h** of families.
27:1 is a list of Israelite family **h**,
2Ch 1:2 and the **h** of Israel's families.
5:2 all the **h** of the tribes,
19:8 and family **h** from Israel to
26:12 The total number of family **h**
Ezr 1:5 Then the **h** of the families of
2:68 When some of the **h** of the
3:12 and the **h** of the families who
4:2 Zerubbabel and the **h**
4:3 and the rest of the **h** of Israel's
9:6 sins have piled up over our **h**,
10:16 men who were **h** of families.
Neh 7:70 Some of the **h** of the families
7:71 Some of the **h** of the families
9:1 and threw dirt on their **h**.
10:34 decide the order in which the **h**
11:13 the **h** of the families,
12:22 ⌊The names of⌋ the family **h** of
12:23 ⌊The names of⌋ the family **h**
12:24 The **h** of the Levites were
Job 2:12 They threw dust on their **h**.
24:24 They wither like **h** of grain.
Psa 22:7 They shake their **h** and say,
24:7 Lift your **h**, you gates. Be lifted,
24:9 Lift your **h**, you gates. Be lifted,
44:14 that people shake their **h** at us.
66:12 You let people ride over our **h**.
68:21 Certainly, God will crush the **h**
68:21 destroy even⌋ the hair on the **h**
74:13 You smashed the **h** of sea
74:14 You crushed the **h** of Leviathan
83:2 who hate you hold their **h** high.
109:25 look at me and shake their **h**.
110:6 earth he will crush ⌊their⌋ **h**.
140:9 Let the **h** of those who surround
Isa 3:17 sores ⌊to appear⌋ on the **h**
3:24 They will have bald **h** instead
22:12 for shaving your **h** and for
29:10 He will cover your **h**.
29:10 (Your **h** are the seers.)
35:10 will be on their **h** ⌊as
37:22 shake their **h** behind your back.
51:11 will be on their **h** ⌊as
Jer 13:18 crowns have fallen off your **h**."
14:3 They cover their **h**,
14:4 They cover their **h**.
22:10 Don't shake your **h** at them.
23:19 down on the **h** of the wicked.
30:23 down on the **h** of the wicked.
48:27 you shake your **h** in contempt.
Lam 2:10 They throw dirt on their **h** and
2:10 bow their **h** to the ground.
2:15 They hiss and shake their **h** at
Eze 1:22 a dome was spread over the **h**
1:25 dome over their **h** as they stood
1:26 Above the dome over their **h**
10:1 I looked at the dome over the **h**
13:18 of every size for people's **h**.
23:15 and flowing turbans on their **h**.
Eze 23:42 and beautiful crowns on their **h**.
24:23 Leave your turbans on your **h**
27:30 They put dust on their **h** and
27:31 They shaved their **h** because
32:27 were placed under their **h**.
44:18 wear linen turbans on their **h**
44:20 "They must not shave their **h**
44:20 the hair on their **h** trimmed.
Dan 3:27 hair on their **h** wasn't singed,
7:6 The animal also had four **h**.
Amo 2:7 They stomp the **h** of the poor
6:1 and for the **h** of the leading
Mat 12:1 hungry and began to pick the **h**
17:8 As they raised their **h**,
27:39 They shook their **h**
Mar 2:23 began to pick the **h** of grain.
15:29 They shook their **h** and said,
Luk 6:1 were picking the **h** of grain,
Act 21:24 the expenses to shave their **h**.
Rev 4:4 had gold crowns on their **h**.
9:7 that looked like gold on their **h**.
9:17 The horses had **h** like lions.
9:19 (Their tails have **h** like snakes
12:3 fiery red serpent with seven **h**,
12:3 and seven crowns on its **h**.
13:1 It had ten horns, seven **h**,
13:1 were insulting names on its **h**.
13:3 One of the beast's **h** looked
17:3 It had seven **h** and ten horns.
17:7 and the beast with the seven **h**
17:9 The seven **h** are seven
18:19 Then they threw dust on their **h**
20:4 of those whose **h** had been cut

headstrong (1)

1Sm 17:28 overconfident and **h** you are.

heal (47)

Num 12:13 LORD, "Please, God, **h** her!"
Dtr 32:39 I wound, and I **h**, and no one
2Ki 5:11 and **h** the skin disease.
8:29 to Jezreel to let his wounds **h**.
20:5 Now I'm going to **h** you.
20:8 sign that the LORD will **h** me
2Ch 7:14 and **h** their country.
22:6 to Jezreel to let his wounds **h**.
36:16 He could no longer **h** them.
Psa 6:2 **H** me, O LORD, because my
41:4 **H** my soul because I have
60:2 **H** the cracks in it because it is
Pro 4:22 and they **h** the whole body.
Ecc 3:3 a time to kill and a time to **h**,
Isa 19:22 he will also **h** them.
19:22 to their prayers and **h** them.
30:26 his people's injuries and **h**
57:18 ⌊sinful⌋ ways, but I'll **h** them.
57:19 "I'll **h** them," says the LORD.
58:8 and you will **h** quickly.
61:1 He has sent me to **h** those who
Jer 14:19 us so hard that we cannot **h**?
15:18 wound incurable, refusing to **h**?
17:14 **H** me, O LORD, and I will be
30:13 No medicine will **h** you.
30:17 health and **h** your wounds,"
33:6 "But I will **h** this city and
33:6 I will **h** its people, and I will
51:9 We wanted to **h** Babylon,
Lam 2:13 as the sea. Who can **h** you?
Eze 30:21 so it can't **h** and be strong
Hos 5:13 cure them or **h** their wounds.
6:1 torn us to pieces, he will **h** us.
7:1 "Whenever I want to **h** Israel,
Zec 11:16 He will not **h** those that have
Mat 8:7 "I'll come to **h** him."
12:10 Jesus whether it was right to **h**
Mar 3:2 to see whether he would **h**
Luk 5:17 had the power of the Lord to **h**.
6:7 to see whether he would **h**
10:9 **H** the sick that are there,
13:32 of people and **h** people today
14:3 "Is it right to **h** on the day of
Jon 4:47 with him to **h** his son who
1Co 12:9 Spirit gives the ability to **h**.
Heb 12:13 get worse. Instead, let it **h**.
Rev 22:2 of the tree will **h** the nations.

healed (33)

Gen 20:17 and God **h** Abimelech,
Lev 13:18 "If a boil on the skin has **h**
13:37 hair grows on it, the scab is **h**.
14:3 him. If the person is **h**,
1Sm 6:3 Then you will be **h**,
2Ch 30:20 to Hezekiah and **h** the people.
Psa 30:2 to you for help, and you **h** me.
107:20 sent his message and **h** them.
Pro 3:8 ⌊Then⌋ your body will be **h**,
Isa 6:10 and return and be **h**."
Jer 17:14 me, O LORD, and I will be **h**.
30:13 argues that you should be **h**.
51:8 Maybe it can be **h**.
51:9 but it couldn't be **h**.
Eze 34:4 **h** those that were sick,
Hos 11:3 didn't realize that I had **h** them.
Mat 8:8 and my servant will be **h**.
8:13 that moment the servant was **h**.
19:2 and he **h** them there.
21:14 courtyard, and he **h** them.
Luk 13:14 on one of those days to be **h**.
14:4 **h** him, and sent him away.
17:15 one of them saw that he was **h**,
22:51 the servant's ear and **h** him.
Jon 5:10 told the man who had been **h**,
5:13 But the man who had been **h**
Act 3:16 was **h**, as all of you saw.
4:14 the man who was **h** standing
4:22 (The man who was **h** by this
Jas 5:16 other so that you will be **h**.
1Pe 2:24 His wounds have **h** you.
Rev 13:3 but its fatal wound was **h**.
13:12 whose fatal wound was **h**.

healer (1)

Psa 147:3 He is the **h** of the

healing (17)

Pro 12:18 words of wise people bring **h**.
13:17 a dependable envoy brings **h**.
Isa 53:5 received **h** from his wounds.
Jer 8:15 We hoped for a time of **h**,
14:19 We hope for a time of **h**,
30:12 Your injury is beyond **h**.
Eze 47:12 the leaves will be used for **h**."
Mal 4:2 Righteousness will rise with **h**
Mat 13:15 they never return to me for **h**!'
Luk 13:14 was irritated with Jesus for **h**
Jon 5:16 because he kept **h** people
12:40 they never turn to me for **h**!"
Act 4:30 Show your power by **h**,
10:38 such as **h** everyone who was
28:27 they never turn to me for **h**."'
1Co 12:28 those who have the gift of **h**,
12:30 or have gifts of **h**? Can all of

heals (2)

Exo 15:26 I am the LORD, who **h** you."
Psa 103:3 one who **h** all your diseases,

health (10)

Psa 41:3 You will restore this person to **h**
90:10 or even 80 if we are in good **h**.
Pro 1:12 like those in good **h** who go
Isa 38:16 You give me **h** and keep me
Jer 8:22 Then why hasn't the **h** of my
30:17 I'll restore your **h** and heal your
33:6 heal this city and restore it to **h**.
Mar 3:4 to give a person back his **h** or
Luk 6:9 to give a person his **h** or to
8:36 demon-possessed man to **h**.

healthier (1)

Dan 1:15 After ten days they looked **h**

healthy (28)

Gen 41:5 Seven good, **h** heads of grain
41:7 the seven full, **h** heads.
Exo 1:19 They are so **h** that they have
4:7 it was **h** again like the rest of
1Sm 16:12 He had a **h** complexion,
17:42 man with a **h** complexion
2Ki 5:10 your skin will be **h** and clean."
5:14 His skin became **h** again like a
Job 18:7 "His **h** stride is shortened,
21:24 and his bones are strong and **h**.
39:4 Their young are **h** and grow up
Psa 38:3 No **h** spot is left on my body
38:7 and no **h** spot is left on my
73:4 Their bodies are **h**.
92:14 They are always **h** and fresh.
Pro 14:30 heart makes for a **h** body,
16:24 to the spirit and **h** for the body.
Isa 1:6 your head there is no **h** spot left
59:10 dead people among **h** people.
Eze 30:22 the **h** one and the broken one.
Dan 1:4 to be young men who were **h**,
Mat 9:12 "**H** people don't need a doctor;
12:13 normal again, as **h** as the other.
Mar 2:17 "**H** people don't need a doctor;
Luk 5:31 "**H** people don't need a doctor;
7:10 they found the servant **h** again.
Act 4:10 in your presence with a **h** body
3Jn 1:2 other way and that you're **h**.

heap (3)

1Sm 2:8 lifts the needy from the trash **h**
2Sm 18:17 and piled a large **h** of stones
Psa 113:7 the needy from a garbage **h**.

heaps (5)

Exo 8:14 were piled into countless **h**,
2Ch 31:6 piled these holy things in **h**.
31:8 and the leaders saw the **h**,
31:9 and the Levites about the **h**.
Neh 4:2 the stones out of the rubbish **h**,

hear (284)

Gen 4:23 Wives of Lamech, **h** what I say!
21:26 You didn't tell me, and I didn't **h**
23:10 the city gate could **h** him.
23:13 of that region could **h** him.
Exo 4:11 humans unable to talk or **h**?
15:14 People will **h** of it and tremble.
18:9 Jethro was delighted ⌊to **h**⌋
19:9 the people will **h** me speaking
22:23 be sure that I will **h** their cry.
32:18 of a wild celebration that I **h**."
Num 10:5 When they **h** the trumpet
14:13 if the Egyptians **h** about it?
23:18 **H** me, son of Zippor!
30:7 her husband may **h** about it but
30:11 Her husband may **h** about it but
Dtr 1:16 "**H** the cases that your people
1:17 too hard for you, and I will **h** it."
1:45 didn't listen to you or **h** you.
2:25 When they **h** about you,
4:6 When they **h** about all these
4:10 and I will let them **h** my words.
4:28 These gods can't see, **h**,
4:36 He let you **h** his voice from
5:25 If we continue to **h** the voice of
13:11 All Israel will **h** about it and be
13:12 You may **h** that the residents in
13:13 You may **h** that these people
17:13 When all the people **h** about it,
18:16 You said, "We never want to **h**
19:20 rest of the people **h** about this,
25:1 The judges will **h** the case and
29:4 eyes that see, or ears that **h**.
29:19 Someone may **h** the conditions
30:12 for us so that we can **h**
30:13 to get it for us so that we can **h**
31:11 so that they can **h** them.
31:13 must **h** them and learn to fear
32:1 **h** the words from my mouth.
33:7 "**H** the cry of Judah,
Jos 6:5 When you **h** a long blast on the
Jdg 5:28 Why don't I **h** the clatter of his
13:23 let us see or **h** all these things
14:13 "Tell us your riddle! Let's **h** it!"
1Sm 2:23 I **h** about your wicked ways
2:24 Sons, the report that I **h** the
15:14 this sound of cows that I **h**?"
25:7 I **h** that your sheepshearers are
2Sm 5:24 When you **h** the sound of
15:3 appointed anyone to **h** it."
15:10 "When you **h** the sound of the
15:35 When you **h** anything from the
15:36 to report to me anything you **h**."
2Sm 16:21 Then all Israel will **h** about
17:5 and let us **h** what he,
17:9 others will definitely **h** about it
19:35 Can I still **h** the singing of men
22:45 As soon as they **h** of me,
1Ki 4:34 every nation to **h** his wisdom;
5:7 Hiram was very glad to **h** what
8:30 **H** the plea for mercy that your
8:30 **H** us ⌊when we pray⌋ to
8:30 where you live. **H** and forgive.
8:32 then **h** ⌊that person⌋ in heaven,
8:34 then **h** ⌊them⌋ in heaven,
8:36 then **h** ⌊them⌋ in heaven.
8:38 ⌊**h**⌋ every prayer for mercy,
8:39 **H** ⌊them⌋ in heaven,
8:41 "People will **h** about your great
8:43 **h** ⌊them⌋ in heaven,
8:45 then **h** their prayer for mercy in
8:49 **h** their prayer for mercy.
22:19 "Then **h** the word of the LORD.
2Ki 7:6 army **h** what sounded like
7:10 and we didn't see or **h** anyone.
19:7 a spirit in him so that he will **h**
20:16 "**H** the word of the LORD!
23:2 temple so that they could **h** it.
1Ch 14:15 As you **h** the sound of
2Ch 6:21 **H** the plea for mercy that your
6:21 **H** us in heaven, the place
6:21 where you live. **H** and forgive.
6:23 then **h** ⌊that person⌋ in heaven,
6:25 then **h** ⌊them⌋ in heaven,
6:27 then **h** ⌊them⌋ in heaven.
6:29 ⌊**h**⌋ every prayer for mercy
6:30 **H** ⌊them⌋ in heaven,
6:33 then **h** ⌊them⌋ in heaven,
6:35 then **h** their prayer for mercy in
6:39 **h** their prayer for mercy.
7:14 then I will **h** ⌊their prayer⌋ from
18:18 "Then **h** the word of the LORD.
19:6 He will be with you when you **h**
20:9 and you will **h** us and save us.'
34:30 temple so that they could **h** it.
Neh 4:4 prayed,⌋ "Our God, **h** us.
4:20 When you **h** the trumpet,
Est 1:20 kingdom, great as it is, will **h** it.
Job 3:18 There they do not **h** the
13:17 my words. **H** my declaration.
26:14 We ⌊only⌋ **h** a whisper of him!
27:9 Will God **h** his cry when
29:23 They were as eager to **h** me as
Psa 4:1 pity on me, and **h** my prayer!
5:3 morning, O LORD, **h** my voice.
17:1 **H** my plea for justice,
17:6 **H** what I have to say.
18:44 As soon as they **h** of me,
27:7 **H**, O LORD, when I cry aloud.
28:2 **H** my prayer for mercy when I
30:10 **H**, O LORD, and have pity on
34:2 oppressed will **h** it and rejoice.
34:15 His ears **h** their cry for help.
38:13 am like a person who cannot **h**
38:14 I am like one who cannot **h**
51:8 Let me **h** ⌊sounds of⌋ joy and
54:2 O God, **h** my prayer,
58:5 so that it cannot **h** the voice of
59:7 ⌊They think,⌋ "Who will **h** us?"
64:1 **H** my voice, O God, when I
77:1 would open his ears to ⌊**h**⌋ me.
84:8 of armies, **h** my prayer.
85:8 I want to **h** what God the LORD
88:2 Turn your ear to **h** my cries.
92:11 My ears **h** ⌊the cries⌋ of
94:9 Do you think he can't **h**?
102:1 O LORD, **h** my prayer,
115:6 have ears, but they cannot **h**.
119:149 with your mercy, **h** my voice.
130:2 O Lord, **h** my voice.
135:17 have ears, but they cannot **h**.
140:6 O LORD, open your ears to **h**
143:1 Open your ears to **h** my urgent
143:8 Let me **h** about your mercy in
Pro 15:23 A person is delighted to **h** an
22:17 Open your ears, and **h** the
Ecc 7:21 or you may **h** your own servant
Sos 2:8 I **h** my beloved's voice.
2:14 your figure and **h** your voice.

Sos 8:13 to your voice, let me **h** ....
Isa 6:10 their eyes, **h** with their ears,
11:3 or decide by what his ears **h**.
21:3 I'm disturbed by what I **h**.
24:16 From the ends of the earth we **h**
28:14 So **h** the word of the LORD,
28:23 Pay attention, and **h** me!
29:18 the deaf will **h** the words
30:10 Tell us what we want to **h**.
30:21 You will **h** a voice behind you
32:3 who can **h** will pay attention.
32:9 women. **H** what I say,
33:13 **H** what I have done,
37:7 a spirit in him so that he will **h**
39:5 Isaiah said to Hezekiah, "**H** the
42:20 are open, but you **h** nothing.
43:9 Let the people **h** them.
48:8 been open to **h** them before.
51:4 Open your ears to **h** me,
59:1 to save or his ear too deaf to **h**.
59:2 face so that he doesn't **h** you.
60:18 No longer will you **h** about
65:24 they're still speaking, I will **h**.
Jer 4:19 I can't keep quiet because I **h** a
4:21 must I see the battle flag and **h**
4:31 I **h** a woman in labor.
4:31 I **h** the woman cry with anguish
5:21 **H** this, you stupid and
5:21 have ears, but you cannot **h**.
9:10 No one can **h** the sound of
9:20 open your ears to **h** his words.
20:16 May he **h** a cry of alarm in the
29:12 pray to me, and I will **h** you.
30:5 "We **h** cries of fear,
33:9 All the nations on earth will **h**
33:10 But once again you will **h**
33:11 You will **h** those who bring
36:3 nation of Judah will **h** about all
42:14 **h** the sound of a ram's horn,
47:3 They will **h** the sound of
Eze 12:2 have ears, but they can't **h**
26:15 when they **h** about your defeat.
33:4 If the people **h** the horn and
33:30 'Let's go and **h** the word that
36:15 I will no longer let you **h** the
Dan 3:5 When you **h** the sound of rams'
3:15 When you **h** the sound of the
5:23 These gods can't see, **h**,
Hos 10:14 So your army will **h** the noise
Nah 2:13 and no one will ever **h** the
3:19 All who **h** the news about you
Zec 7:11 ears so that they couldn't **h**.
7:12 as flint so that they couldn't **h**
Mat 10:27 what you **h** whispered.
11:4 tell John what you **h** and see:
11:5 deaf people **h** again,
11:5 poor people **h** the Good News.
12:19 and no one will **h** his voice in
12:42 earth to **h** Solomon's wisdom.
13:13 They **h**, but they don't listen.
13:14 'You will **h** clearly but never
13:15 Their ears never **h**.
13:16 and your ears because they **h**.
13:17 to **h** what you hear but didn't
13:17 to hear what you **h** but didn't
13:17 what you hear but didn't **h** it.
21:16 They said to him, "Do you **h**
22:22 They were surprised to **h** this.
24:6 "You will **h** of wars and rumors
27:13 "Don't you **h** how many
Mar 4:12 They **h** clearly but don't
4:15 Whenever they **h** the word,
4:16 Whenever they **h** the word,
4:18 thornbushes. They **h** the word,
4:20 They **h** the word, accept it,
7:35 man could **h** and talk normally.
7:37 He makes the deaf **h** and the
13:7 "When you **h** of wars and
14:11 They were pleased to **h** what
Luk 4:22 They were amazed to **h** the
5:15 Large crowds gathered to **h**
6:18 They wanted to **h** him and be
7:22 deaf people **h** again,
7:22 poor people **h** the Good News.
8:10 don't see, and when they **h**,
8:12 They **h** the word, but then the
Luk 8:13 with joy whenever they **h** it,
8:14 are people who **h** the word,
8:15 people who also **h** the word.
8:21 my brothers are those who **h**
10:24 to see and **h** what you've seen
11:28 how blessed are those who **h**
11:31 earth to **h** Solomon's wisdom.
16:2 'What's this I **h** about you?
19:48 the people were eager to **h** him.
21:9 "When you **h** of wars and
21:38 get up early to **h** him speak
Jon 3:8 You **h** its sound, but you don't
5:25 now here) when the dead will **h**
5:28 all the dead will **h** his voice,
9:27 Why do you want to **h** the story
11:42 known that you always **h** me.
14:24 make up what you **h** me say.
18:20 publicly for everyone to **h**.
Act 2:8 Why do we **h** them speaking in
2:11 We **h** these men in our own
8:30 ran to the carriage and could **h**
10:22 to his home to **h** what you have
13:7 Saul because he wanted to **h**
13:44 gathered to **h** the Lord's word.
15:7 who aren't Jewish could **h**
17:21 to tell or **h** something new
17:32 "We'll **h** you talk about this
19:26 and you see and **h** what this
21:22 They will certainly **h** that you're
22:14 and to **h** him speak to you.
23:35 he said, "I'll **h** your case when
25:22 "I would like to **h** the man."
25:22 "You'll **h** him tomorrow."
28:22 However, we would like to **h**
28:26 "You will **h** clearly but never
28:27 Their ears never **h**.
Rom 10:14 How can they **h** if no one tells
10:18 "Didn't they **h** that message?"
11:8 and their ears don't **h**!"
1Co 11:18 In the first place, I **h** that when
11:18 I believe some of what I **h**.
12:17 were an eye, how could it **h**?
Eph 4:29 say will help those who **h** you.
Php 1:27 I'll **h** all about you.
1:27 I'll **h** that you are firmly united
1:30 Now you **h** that I'm still
2Th 3:11 We **h** that some of you are not
1Ti 4:16 yourself and those who **h** you.
2Ti 4:3 tell them what they want to **h**.
4:17 News for all the nations to **h**.
Phm 1:5 I **h** about your faithfulness to
Heb 3:7 "If you **h** God speak today,
3:15 "If you **h** God speak today,
4:7 "If you **h** God speak today,
12:19 they begged not to **h** it say
1Pe 3:12 His ears **h** their prayer.
3Jn 1:4 than to **h** that my children
Rev 1:3 as well as those who **h** the
9:20 which cannot see, **h**, or walk.
22:17 Let those who **h** this say,

heard (645)

Gen 3:8 the man and his wife **h** the
3:10 "I **h** you in the garden.
14:14 When Abram **h** that his
16:11 because the LORD has **h** your
17:20 I have **h** your request about
21:17 God **h** the boy crying,
21:17 God has **h** the boy crying from
24:30 wrists and **h** her tell what
24:52 servant **h** their answer,
27:6 "I've just **h** your father speaking
27:34 When Esau **h** these words from
29:13 As soon as Laban **h** the news
29:33 the LORD has **h** that I'm
30:6 He has **h** my prayer and has
31:1 Jacob **h** that Laban's sons
34:5 Jacob **h** that Shechem had
34:7 as soon as they **h** the news.
35:22 and Israel **h** about it.
37:17 I **h** them say, 'Let's go to
37:21 When Reuben **h** this,
39:15 As soon as he **h** me scream,
39:19 When Potiphar **h** his wife's
41:15 I **h** that when you are told a
42:2 I've **h** there's grain for sale in
Gen 43:25 because they had **h** they were
45:2 loudly that the Egyptians **h** him,
45:2 Pharaoh's household **h** about it.
45:16 When Pharaoh's household **h**
Exo 2:15 When Pharaoh **h** what Moses
2:24 God **h** their groaning,
3:7 and I have **h** them crying out
3:9 I have **h** the cry of the people of
4:31 When they **h** that the LORD
6:5 Now I have **h** the groaning of
16:7 because he has **h** you
16:8 The LORD has **h** you
16:9 He has **h** you complaining.'"
16:12 "I've **h** the Israelites
18:1 **h** about everything God had
19:16 from a ram's horn ⌊was **h**⌋.
20:18 All the people **h** the thunder
20:18 They **h** the blast of the ram's
23:13 or let them be **h** on your lips.
24:8 on everything you have just **h**."
28:35 of the bells must be **h** when
32:17 Then Joshua **h** the noise of the
33:4 When the people **h** this bad
Lev 10:20 When Moses **h** this,
24:14 All who **h** him curse ⌊my
Num 7:89 he **h** the voice speaking to him
11:1 When the LORD **h** them,
11:10 Moses **h** people from every
11:18 **h** them crying and saying,
12:2 The LORD **h** their complaint.
14:14 LORD, they have already **h**
14:15 then the nations who have **h**
14:27 I've **h** the complaints the
16:4 As soon as Moses **h** this,
16:34 when they **h** their screams.
20:16 he **h** us, sent a messenger,
21:1 **h** that the Israelites were
22:36 When Balak **h** that Balaam had
30:14 to her when he **h** about it.
33:40 **h** that the Israelites were
Dtr 1:34 When the LORD **h** what you
4:12 You **h** a voice speaking but
4:32 anything like it ever been **h** of?
4:33 Have any ⌊other⌋ people ever **h**
4:36 and you **h** him speak from the
5:23 But when you **h** the voice
5:24 We've **h** his voice come from
5:26 Who has ever **h** the voice of
5:28 When the LORD **h** the words
5:28 "I have **h** what these people
9:2 You've also **h** it said,
13:2 may be gods you've never **h** of.)
13:13 may be gods you've never **h** of.)
26:7 of our ancestors, and he **h** us.
29:26 were gods they never **h** of,
32:17 to gods they never **h** of.
Jos 2:10 We've **h** how the LORD dried
2:10 We've also **h** what you did to
2:10 We've **h** how you destroyed
2:11 When we **h** about it,
5:1 the Mediterranean Sea **h** that
6:20 very loudly when they **h**
9:1 River **h** about these events,
9:3 in Gibeon **h** what Joshua had
9:9 We **h** stories about him and
9:10 We also **h** everything he did to
9:16 the Israelites **h** that these
10:1 of Jerusalem **h** that Joshua had
10:1 He also **h** that the people of
11:1 King Jabin of Hazor **h** ⌊what
14:12 You **h** that the people of Anak
22:11 The rest of the Israelites **h**
22:12 the people of Israel **h** about it,
22:30 of the divisions of Israel **h** what
24:27 It has **h** all the words which the
Jdg 7:13 When Gideon got there, he **h** a
7:15 When Gideon **h** the dream and
8:3 When they **h** what Gideon said,
9:30 Zebul, Shechem's ruler, **h** what
9:46 of Shechem's Tower **h** about
17:2 I even **h** you put a curse on
20:3 The people of Benjamin **h** that
Rut 1:6 were still in Moab she **h** that
1Sm 1:13 Her voice couldn't be **h**;
2:22 and he had **h** everything that
4:6 As the Philistines **h** the noise,

1Sm 4:19 When she **h** the news that the
7:7 When the Philistines **h** that the
7:7 The Israelites **h** ⌊about the
8:21 When Samuel **h** everything the
11:6 When he **h** this news,
13:3 and the Philistines **h** about it.
14:22 the mountains of Ephraim **h** that
14:27 Jonathan hadn't **h** that his
17:11 Israelites **h** what this Philistine
17:23 and David **h** them.
17:28 **h** David talking to the men.
22:1 rest⌋ of his family **h** about it,
22:6 Saul **h** that David and his men
23:10 I have actually **h** that Saul is
23:11 Saul come here as I have **h**?
23:25 Saul **h** about it and pursued
25:4 he **h** that Nabal was shearing
25:39 When David **h** Nabal was dead,
31:11 living in Jabesh Gilead **h** what
2Sm 3:28 Later when David **h** about it,
4:1 When Saul's son Ishbosheth **h**
5:17 When the Philistines **h** that
5:17 But David **h** about it and went
7:22 as we have **h** with our own
8:9 When King Toi of Hamath **h**
10:7 After David **h** about this,
11:26 When Uriah's wife **h** that her
13:21 When King David **h** about this,
13:30 David **h** this rumor:
18:5 All the troops **h** him give all the
18:12 We **h** the order the king gave
19:2 because all the troops **h** that
22:7 He **h** my voice from his temple,
22:14 Most High made his voice **h**.
24:25 So the LORD **h** the prayers for
1Ki 1:11 "Haven't you **h** that Adonijah,
1:41 Adonijah and all his guests **h**
1:41 When Joab **h** the sound of the
1:45 That is the sound you **h**.
2:29 After King Solomon **h** that Joab
2:41 After Solomon **h** that Shimei
3:28 All Israel **h** about the decision
4:34 who had **h** about his wisdom.
5:1 when he **h** that Solomon had
9:3 "I have **h** your prayer for mercy
10:1 The queen of Sheba **h** about
10:6 She told the king, "What I **h** in
10:7 surpass the stories I've **h**.
11:21 When Hadad **h** in Egypt that
12:2 When he **h** ⌊about Rehoboam⌋,
12:20 When all Israel **h** that
13:4 When King Jeroboam **h** the
13:26 back from the road **h** about it,
14:6 Ahijah **h** her footsteps when
15:21 When Baasha **h** the news,
16:16 When the army **h** that Zimri had
17:22 The LORD **h** Elijah's request,
18:13 Haven't you **h** what I did when
18:13 Haven't you **h** how I hid 100 of
19:13 When Elijah **h** it, he wrapped
20:12 Benhadad **h** this as he and his
20:31 "We have **h** that the kings of
21:16 When he **h** about Naboth's
21:27 When Ahab **h** these things,
2Ki 3:21 All the people of Moab **h** that
5:8 **h** that the king of Israel had torn
6:30 When the king **h** the woman
9:30 Jezebel **h** about it.
11:13 When Athaliah **h** the noise
13:4 and the LORD **h** him because
19:1 King Hezekiah **h** the message,
19:4 LORD your God may have **h** all
19:4 that the LORD your God **h**.
19:6 the message that you **h** when
19:8 He had **h** that the king left
19:9 Now, Sennacherib **h** that King
19:11 You **h** what the kings of
19:20 of Assyria. I have **h** you.
19:25 "'Haven't you **h**? I did this long
20:5 David says: I've **h** your prayer.
20:12 he **h** that Hezekiah had
22:11 When the king **h** what the book
22:18 says about the words you **h**:
22:19 when you **h** my words against
25:23 and their men **h** that
1Ch 10:11 Gilead **h** about everything
1Ch 14:8 When the Philistines **h** that
14:8 But David **h** about it and went
17:20 as we have **h** with our own
18:9 When King Tou of Hamath **h**
19:8 After David **h** about this,
2Ch 7:12 He said to Solomon, "I have **h**
9:1 The queen of Sheba **h** about
9:5 She told the king, "What I **h** in
9:6 surpassed the stories I've **h**.
10:2 When he **h** ⌊about Rehoboam⌋,
15:8 When Asa **h** the prophet
16:5 When Baasha **h** the news,
20:29 in that area when they **h** how
23:12 When Athaliah **h** the people
30:27 Their voices were **h**,
34:19 When the king **h** what the
34:26 says about the words you **h**:
34:27 when you **h** my words against
Ezr 3:13 The noise was **h** from far away.
4:1 of Judah and Benjamin **h** that
9:3 When I **h** this, I tore my clothes
Neh 1:4 to the king when I **h** this.
2:10 the Ammonite servant **h** this,
2:19 Geshem the Arab **h** about this,
4:1 When Sanballat **h** we were
4:7 and the people from Ashdod **h**
4:15 When our enemies **h** that we
5:6 I became furious when I **h** their
6:1 and the rest of our enemies **h**
6:16 all our enemies **h** about this,
8:2 could understand what they **h**.
9:9 and you **h** them crying at the
9:27 You **h** them from heaven.
9:28 and you **h** them from heaven.
12:43 could be **h** from far away.
13:1 They **h** the passage that no
13:3 the people **h** this Teaching,
Est 1:18 and Media who have **h** what
2:8 and decree were **h**,
Job 2:11 When Job's three friends **h**
3:7 Let no joyful singing be **h** in it.
4:12 and **h** something whispered
4:16 of my eyes. I **h** a soft voice:
13:1 My ear has **h** and understood it.
16:2 "I have **h** many things like this
20:3 I have **h** criticism that makes
28:22 'We've **h** a rumor about it.'
29:11 "⌊Any⌋ ears that **h** me blessed
37:4 back when his thunder is **h**.
42:5 I had **h** about you with my own
Psa 6:8 because the LORD has **h** the
6:9 The LORD has **h** my plea for
10:17 You have **h** the desire of
18:6 He **h** my voice from his temple,
18:13 Most High made his voice **h**
19:3 without their voices being **h**.
22:24 The LORD **h** when that
28:6 He has **h** my prayer for mercy!
31:13 I have **h** the whispering of
31:22 But you **h** my pleas for mercy
34:6 The LORD **h** him and saved
40:1 He turned to me and **h** my cry
44:1 we have **h** it with our own ears.
48:8 things we had only **h** about,
61:5 O God, you have **h** my vows.
62:11 I have **h** it ⌊said⌋ twice:
66:8 Make the sound of his praise **h**.
66:19 But God has **h** me.
68:33 He makes his voice **h**,
78:3 things that we have **h** and
78:21 When the LORD **h** this,
78:59 When God **h**, he became
78:63 virgins **h** no wedding songs.
81:5 I **h** a message I did not
102:20 He **h** the groans of the
106:44 suffering when he **h** their cry
118:15 joyful singing and victory is **h**
132:6 Now, we have **h** about the ark
138:4 because they have **h** the
Ecc 12:13 After having **h** it all,
Sos 2:12 mourning dove is **h** in our land.
Isa 5:7 for righteousness but **h** only
5:9 With my own ears I **h** the
6:8 Then I **h** the voice of the Lord,
15:4 Their voices are **h** as far away
16:6 We've **h** of the arrogance of
Isa 16:6 We've **h** of their boasting,
21:10 I make known to you what I **h**
28:22 because I have **h** that the
30:30 will make his majestic voice **h**.
37:1 King Hezekiah **h** the message,
37:4 LORD your God may have **h**
37:4 that the LORD your God **h**.
37:6 the message that you **h** when
37:8 He had **h** that the king left
37:9 Now, Sennacherib **h** that King
37:9 When he **h** this, he again sent
37:11 You **h** what the kings of
37:26 "'Haven't you **h**? I did this long
38:5 David says: I've **h** your prayer.
39:1 He had **h** that Hezekiah had
40:21 Haven't you **h**? Haven't you
40:28 Haven't you **h**? The eternal God,
41:26 No one **h** your words.
42:2 make his voice **h** in the streets.
48:6 You've **h** these words.
48:7 You haven't **h** about them
48:8 You have never **h** about them.
52:15 things that they had never **h**.
58:4 you from being **h** in heaven.
64:4 No one has ever **h**,
65:19 will no longer be **h** in the city.
66:8 Who has **h** of such a thing?
66:19 coastlands who have not **h**
Jer 3:21 The sound of crying is **h** on the
4:5 Make it **h** in Jerusalem.
4:15 A message is **h** from Dan,
5:20 and make this **h** in Judah:
6:7 and destruction can be **h** in it.
6:24 We have **h** the news about
8:16 The snorting of horses can be **h**
9:16 and their ancestors haven't **h** of.
9:19 sound of crying is **h** from Zion.
14:18 through a land they haven't **h** of.
15:14 in a land that you haven't **h** of,
16:13 and your ancestors haven't **h** of.
17:4 in a land that you haven't **h** of.
18:13 has ever **h** anything like this.
19:4 other gods that they hadn't **h** of.
20:1 **h** Jeremiah prophesying these
20:10 I have **h** many ⌊people⌋
22:28 another land they've never **h** of?
23:25 "I've **h** the prophets who speak
26:7 and all the people **h** Jeremiah
26:10 When the officials of Judah **h**
26:11 city as you yourselves have **h**."
26:12 that you have **h** me say against
26:21 and officials **h** what Uriah said,
26:21 But Uriah **h** about it and fled in
30:19 of laughter will be **h** from there.
31:15 A sound is **h** in Ramah,
31:18 "I have certainly **h** Ephraim
36:11 **h** Baruch read from the scroll
36:13 he **h** Baruch read from
36:16 When they **h** everything,
36:24 they **h** everything being read.
37:5 Jerusalem **h** this news,
38:1 Malchiah) **h** that Jeremiah was
38:2 They **h** Jeremiah say,
38:7 **h** that they had put Jeremiah in
38:27 because they hadn't **h** his
40:7 who were in the field **h** that
40:11 and in all the other countries **h**
41:11 who were with him **h** about all
44:3 you nor your ancestors **h** of.
46:12 The nations have **h** of your
48:5 down to Horonaim they have **h**
48:29 "We have **h** about the
48:34 "The cry will be **h** from
48:34 It will be **h** from Zoar to
49:14 I **h** a message from the LORD.
49:21 of their crying will be **h** at
49:23 are worried because they **h**
50:43 The king of Babylon has **h**
50:46 will be **h** among the nations."
51:46 or be afraid when rumors are **h**
51:54 of agony are **h** from Babylon.
51:54 terrible destruction are **h** from
51:55 The noise will be **h**
Lam 1:21 "All my enemies have **h** that I
1:21 All my enemies have **h** about
Eze 1:24 I **h** the sound of their wings.

Eze 1:28 and I **h** someone speaking.
2:2 and I **h** him speaking to me.
3:12 and behind me I **h** a loud
3:13 I also **h** the noise of the wings
9:1 Then I **h** the LORD call out
10:5 angels' wings was **h** as far as
10:13 I **h** that the wheels were called
19:4 The nations **h** about him,
19:9 his roar wouldn't be **h** anymore
23:42 "I **h** the noise from a carefree
26:13 your harps will no longer be **h**.
32:9 countries that you haven't **h** of.
33:5 They **h** the sound of the horn
35:12 **h** all the insults that you spoke
35:13 talked against me. I **h** you.
43:6 I **h** someone speaking to me
Dan 3:7 As soon as they **h** the sound of
5:14 I've **h** that you have the spirit of
5:16 I have **h** that you can interpret
6:14 displeased when he **h** this.
8:13 Then I **h** a holy one speaking.
8:16 I **h** a man in Ulai [Gate] call
10:9 I **h** the man speak,
10:12 God has **h** everything that you
11:38 a god his ancestors never **h** of.
12:7 I **h** the man dressed in linen
12:8 I **h** him, but I did not
Oba 1:1 We have **h** a message from the
Jnh 2:2 for help, and you **h** my cry.
Hab 3:2 I have **h** the report about you.
3:16 I have **h**, so there's trembling
Zep 2:8 "I have **h** the insults from Moab
Zec 1:4 who **h** the earlier prophets
7:14 nations they hadn't even **h** of.
8:23 because we have **h** that God is
Mat 2:3 and all Jerusalem **h** about this,
2:9 After they had **h** the king,
2:18 "A sound was **h** in Ramah,
2:22 But when he **h** that Archelaus
4:12 When Jesus **h** that John had
5:21 "You have **h** that it was said to
5:27 "You have **h** that it was said,
5:33 "You have **h** that it was said to
5:38 "You have **h** that it was said,
5:43 "You have **h** that it was said,
6:7 think they'll be **h** if they talk
8:10 was amazed when he **h** this.
9:12 When Jesus **h** that,
11:2 When John was in prison, he **h**
12:24 When the Pharisees **h** this,
14:1 **h** the news about Jesus.
14:13 When Jesus **h** about John,
14:13 The crowds **h** about this and
15:12 **h** your statement they
17:6 were terrified when they **h** this
19:22 When the young man **h** this,
19:25 than ever when they **h** this.
20:24 other ten apostles **h** about this,
20:30 When they **h** that Jesus was
21:45 Pharisees **h** his illustrations,
22:33 the crowds who **h** his teaching.
22:34 When the Pharisees **h** that
26:65 just **h** him dishonor God!
27:47 standing there **h** him say that,
Mar 2:17 When Jesus **h** that,
3:8 they had **h** about everything
3:21 When his family **h** about it,
5:27 Since she had **h** about Jesus,
6:2 He amazed many who **h** him.
6:14 King Herod **h** about Jesus,
6:16 But when Herod **h** about it,
6:29 John's disciples **h** about this,
6:55 place where they **h** he was.
7:25 an evil spirit **h** about Jesus.
10:22 When the man **h** that,
10:41 other ten apostles **h** about it,
10:47 When he **h** that Jesus from
11:14 His disciples **h** this.
11:18 chief priests and scribes **h** him,
12:34 When Jesus **h** how wisely the
14:58 "We **h** him say, 'I'll tear down
14:64 You've **h** him dishonor God!
15:35 standing there **h** him say that,
16:11 believe her when they **h** that
Luk 1:13 God has **h** your prayer.
1:41 When Elizabeth **h** the greeting,
Luk 1:44 As soon as I **h** your greeting,
1:58 Her neighbors and relatives **h**
1:66 Everyone who **h** about it
2:18 Everyone who **h** the
2:20 they had seen and **h**.
2:47 stunned everyone who **h** him.
4:21 today when you **h** me read it."
4:23 that we've **h** you've done
4:28 furious when they **h** this.
7:3 The officer had **h** about Jesus
7:9 officer when he **h** these words.
7:22 what you have seen and **h**:
7:29 tax collectors, **h** John.
8:50 When Jesus **h** this,
9:7 Herod the ruler **h** about
10:24 hear what you've seen and **h**,
12:3 have said in the dark will be **h**
14:15 of those eating with him **h** this.
15:25 he **h** music and dancing.
16:14 **h** all this and were making
18:22 When Jesus **h** this,
18:23 When the official **h** this,
18:26 Those who **h** him asked,
18:36 When he **h** the crowd going by,
20:16 Those who **h** him said,
22:71 We've **h** him say it ourselves."
23:6 When Pilate **h** that,
23:8 He had **h** about Jesus and
Jon 1:37 When the two disciples **h** John
1:40 the two disciples who **h** John
3:32 tells what he has seen and **h**.
4:1 that the Pharisees had **h** that
4:42 We have **h** him ourselves,
4:47 The official **h** that Jesus had
5:37 You have never **h** his voice,
6:60 many of Jesus' disciples **h** him,
7:32 The Pharisees **h** the crowd
7:40 After some of the crowd **h**
8:38 what you've **h** from your father."
8:40 you the truth that I **h** from God.
9:32 no one has ever **h** of anyone
9:35 Jesus **h** that the Jews had
9:40 who were with Jesus **h** this.
11:4 When Jesus **h** the message,
11:6 Yet, when Jesus **h** that
11:20 When Martha **h** that Jesus was
11:29 When Mary **h** this,
12:12 festival **h** that Jesus was
12:18 Because the crowd **h** that
12:29 The crowd standing there **h** the
12:34 "We have **h** from the Scriptures
14:28 You **h** me tell you,
15:15 that I've **h** from my Father.
18:21 Question those who **h** what I
19:8 When Pilate **h** them say that,
19:12 When Pilate **h** what Jesus
19:13 When Pilate **h** what they said,
21:7 When Simon Peter **h** that it
Act 2:6 gathered when they **h** the wind.
2:37 When the people **h** this,
4:4 But many of those who had **h**
4:20 about what we've seen and **h**."
4:24 When the apostles **h** this,
5:5 When Ananias **h** Peter say this,
5:5 Everyone who **h** about his
5:11 else who **h** about what had
5:24 and the chief priests **h** this,
5:33 the men on the council **h** this,
6:11 These men said, "We **h** him
6:14 We **h** him say that Jesus from
7:12 When Jacob **h** that Egypt had
7:34 I've **h** their groaning and have
8:14 apostles in Jerusalem **h** that
9:4 He fell to the ground and **h** a
9:7 They **h** the voice but didn't see
9:13 Ananias replied, "Lord, I've **h** a
9:21 Everyone who **h** him was
9:38 When the disciples **h** that Peter
10:31 God has **h** your prayer and has
10:44 everyone who **h** his message.
10:46 They **h** these non-Jewish
11:1 Judea **h** that people who
11:7 I also **h** a voice telling me,
11:18 When the others **h** this,
13:48 were pleased with what they **h**
14:14 Paul **h** what was happening,
Act 15:24 We have **h** that some
16:38 When the Roman officials **h**
17:8 were upset when they **h** this.
17:32 When the people of the court **h**
18:8 Many Corinthians who **h** Paul
18:26 Priscilla and Aquila **h** him,
19:2 we've never even **h** of the Holy
19:5 After they **h** this, they were
19:10 lived in the province of Asia **h**
19:17 city of Ephesus **h** about this.
19:28 workers and the others **h** this,
21:12 When we **h** this, we and the
21:20 leaders **h** about everything,
22:2 When the mob **h** him speak to
22:7 I fell to the ground and **h** a
22:15 what you have seen and **h**.
22:26 When the sergeant **h** this,
23:16 But Paul's nephew **h** about the
25:20 to have his case **h** there.
26:14 and I **h** a voice asking me in
28:15 Believers in Rome **h** that we
Rom 10:14 they have not **h** his message?
10:17 and the message that is **h** is
15:21 who never **h** will understand."
16:19 Everyone has **h** about your
1Co 2:9 eye has seen, no ear has **h**,
5:1 This kind of sin is not even **h**
2Co 6:2 "At the right time I **h** you.
12:4 where he **h** things that can't
Gal 1:13 You **h** about the way I once
1:13 You **h** how I violently
1:14 You also **h** how I was far
1:23 only thing they had **h** was this:
3:2 or by believing what you **h**?
3:5 through believing what you **h**?
Eph 1:13 You **h** and believed the
1:15 I, too, have **h** about your faith in
3:2 Certainly, you have **h** how God
3:3 You have **h** that he let me
4:21 You have certainly **h** his
Php 2:26 is troubled because you **h** that
4:9 what you **h** and saw me do.
Col 1:4 we have **h** about your faith
1:5 Some time ago you **h** about
1:6 you from the first day you **h** it.
1:9 since the day we **h** about you.
1:23 You've **h** this Good News of
1Th 1:8 who have **h** about your faith
2Ti 1:13 consider what you **h** me say to
2:2 You've **h** my message,
Heb 2:1 attention to what we have **h**.
2:3 Then those who **h** him
3:16 Who **h** God and rebelled?
4:2 We have **h** the same Good
4:2 News that your ancestors **h**.
4:2 didn't help those who **h**
4:6 Those who **h** the Good News
5:7 and he was **h** because of his
12:19 your ancestors **h** that voice,
Jas 5:4 The Lord of Armies has **h** the
5:11 You have **h** about Job's
2Pe 1:18 We **h** that voice speak to him
2:8 torture to him as he saw and **h**
1Jn 1:1 We have **h** it. We have seen it.
1:3 is the life we have seen and **h**.
1:5 This is the message we **h** from
2:7 you've already **h**.
2:18 You've **h** that an antichrist is
2:24 that the message you **h** from
3:11 The message that you have **h**
4:3 that you have **h** is coming.
2Jn 1:6 and you have **h** this from the
Rev 1:10 I **h** a loud voice behind me like
3:3 what you received and **h**.
4:1 I **h** the first voice like a trumpet
5:11 Then I **h** the voices of many
5:13 I **h** every creature in heaven,
6:1 I **h** one of the four living
6:3 I **h** the second living creature
6:5 I **h** the third living creature say,
6:6 I **h** what sounded like a voice
6:7 I **h** the voice of the fourth living
7:4 I **h** how many were sealed:
8:13 and I **h** it say in a loud voice,
9:13 I **h** a voice from the four horns
9:16 I **h** how many there were.

Rev 10:4 I **h** a voice from heaven say,
10:8 The voice which I had **h** from
11:12 The witnesses **h** a loud voice
12:10 Then I **h** a loud voice in
14:2 Then I **h** a sound from heaven
14:2 The sound I **h** was like the
14:13 I **h** a voice from heaven saying,
16:1 I **h** a loud voice from the
16:5 Then I **h** the angel of the water
16:7 Then I **h** the altar answer,
18:4 I **h** another voice from heaven
18:22 and trumpeters will never be **h**
18:22 will never be **h** in it again.
18:23 and grooms will never be **h**
19:1 After these things I **h** what
19:6 I **h** what sounded like the noise
21:3 I **h** a loud voice from the throne
22:8 John, **h** and saw these things.
22:8 When I had **h** and seen them,

hearing (12)

Gen 29:33 So she named him Simeon [**H**].
1Sm 4:14 **H** the cry, Eli asked, "What is
Ezr 4:23 hurried to Jerusalem after **h**
Amo 8:11 there will be a famine of **h** the
Mat 13:15 close-minded and hard of **h**.
Luk 9:9 Who is this person I'm **h** so
Jon 7:51 without first **h** that person's side
11:41 I thank you for **h** me.
Act 2:33 is what you're seeing and **h**.
28:27 close-minded and hard of **h**.
Rom 10:17 comes from **h** the message,
2Ti 4:16 At my first **h** no one stood up in

hears (44)

Gen 16:11 will name him Ishmael [God **H**],
21:6 and everyone who **h** about this
Exo 17:14 and make sure that Joshua **h** it,
Num 24:4 the message of the one who **h**
24:16 the message of the one who **h**
30:4 to her when he **h** about it,
30:5 objects when he **h** about it,
30:8 objects when he **h** about it,
30:12 cancels it when he **h** about it,
Dtr 21:21 When all Israel **h** about it,
Jos 7:9 who lives in the land **h** about it,
1Sm 1:20 named him Samuel [God **H**],
3:11 ears of everyone who **h** it ring.
16:2 "When Saul **h** about it,
2Ki 21:12 ears of everyone who **h** about
Job 34:28 and he **h** the cry of those who
Psa 4:3 The LORD **h** me when I call to
34:17 The LORD **h** and rescues them
65:2 You are the one who **h** prayers.
97:8 Zion **h** about this and rejoices.
116:1 LORD because he **h** my voice,
145:19 He **h** their cries for help and
Pro 15:29 but he **h** the prayers of
20:12 The ear that **h**, the eye that
25:10 Otherwise, when he **h** about it,
Isa 30:19 As soon as he **h** you,
Jer 19:3 ears of everyone who **h** about
23:18 and sees and **h** his word?
Dan 3:10 an order that everyone who **h**
Mat 7:24 "Therefore, everyone who **h**
7:26 "Everyone who **h** what I say
13:19 Someone **h** the word about the
13:20 ground ⌊is the person who⌋ **h**
13:22 person who⌋ **h** the word.
13:23 ground ⌊is the person who⌋ **h**
28:14 "If the governor **h** about it,
Luk 6:47 comes to me, **h** what I say,
6:49 The person who **h** ⌊what I
10:16 "The person who **h** you hears
10:16 person who hears you **h** me,
Jon 12:47 If anyone **h** my words and
16:13 He will speak what he **h** and
2Co 12:6 what he sees or **h** about me,
Rev 22:18 I warn everyone who **h** the

heart (255)

Gen 34:8 "My son Shechem has his **h**
Exo 28:29 the sons of Israel over his **h** as
28:30 will be over Aaron's **h** when
28:30 always be carrying over his **h**
Dtr 4:29 search for him with all your **h**
6:5 LORD your God with all your **h**,
6:6 Take to **h** these words that I
7:7 The LORD set his **h** on you
8:5 Learn this lesson by **h**:
10:12 and worship him with all your **h**
10:15 The LORD set his **h** on your
11:13 and serve him with all your **h**
11:18 Take these words of mine to **h**
13:3 really love him with all your **h**
21:11 captives and have your **h** set
26:16 obey them with all your **h**
28:47 and happy **h** when you had
30:1 Take them to **h** when you are
30:2 and obey him with all your **h**
30:6 LORD your God with all your **h**
30:10 LORD your God with all your **h**
30:14 mouth and in your **h** so that you
Jos 2:11 we heard about it, we lost **h**.
5:1 So they lost **h** and had no
7:5 Israel's troops lost **h** and were
22:5 him with all your **h** and soul."
23:14 You know with all your **h** and
Jdg 5:9 My **h** goes out to Israel's
16:15 me when your **h** isn't mine?
1Sm 1:15 pouring out my **h** to the LORD.
2:1 "My **h** finds joy in the LORD.
13:14 for a man after his own **h**.
16:7 but the LORD looks into the **h**."
25:37 Nabal's **h** failed, and he could
2Sm 3:21 rule everything your **h** desires."
13:33 You shouldn't burden your **h**
17:10 Even the bravest man with a **h**
18:14 them into Absalom's **h** while
22:46 Foreigners will lose **h**,
1Ki 2:44 Shimei, you know in your **h** all
3:9 Give me a **h** that listens so that
3:12 understanding **h** so that there
8:17 "My father David had his **h** set
8:18 'Since you had your **h** set on
9:3 My eyes and my **h** will always
9:4 (with a sincere and upright **h**),
11:9 because his **h** had turned from
2Ki 22:19 You had a change of **h** and
23:3 laws with all his **h** and soul.
23:25 to the LORD with all his **h**,
1Ch 22:7 "I had my **h** set on building a
28:2 I had my **h** set on building the
28:9 because he searches every **h**
29:17 With an honest **h** I have
2Ch 1:11 this request is from your **h**.
6:7 "My father David had his **h** set
6:8 'Since you had your **h** set on
7:16 My eyes and my **h** will always
15:12 with all their **h** and soul.
22:9 the LORD with all his **h**.
32:31 that was in Hezekiah's **h**.
34:27 You had a change of **h** and
34:31 laws with all his **h** and soul.
Neh 9:8 You found that his **h** was
Job 9:4 "God is wise in **h** and mighty
10:13 But in your **h** you hid these
11:13 "If you want to set your **h** right,
19:27 My **h** fails inside me!
20:20 will never know peace in his **h**.
22:22 and keep his words in your **h**.
23:12 treasured his words in my **h**.
29:13 the widow's **h** sing for joy.
31:7 or my **h** has followed ⌊the
31:27 so that my **h** was secretly
33:3 words are straight from the **h**,
37:1 "My **h** pounds because of this
38:36 Who put wisdom in the **h** or
Psa 4:7 You put more joy in my **h** than
9:1 thanks, O LORD, with all my **h**.
13:2 sorrow in my **h** day after day?
13:5 My **h** finds joy in your
15:2 speaks the truth within his **h**.
16:9 That is why my **h** is glad and
17:3 You have probed my **h**.
18:45 Foreigners will lose **h**,
19:8 They make the **h** rejoice.
19:14 and the thoughts from my **h**
22:14 My **h** is like wax. It has melted
24:4 has clean hands and a pure **h**
25:17 Relieve my troubled **h**,
26:2 closely into my **h** and mind.
Psa 27:3 my **h** will not be afraid.
27:8 my **h** said to you, "O LORD,
27:14 and let your **h** be courageous.
28:7 My **h** trusted him, so I received
28:7 My **h** is triumphant;
31:24 and let your **h** be courageous.
36:1 rebellion in the depths of his **h**:
37:4 give you the desires of your **h**.
37:31 of his God are in his **h**.
38:10 My **h** is pounding. I have lost my
39:3 My **h** burned like a fire flaring
40:10 righteousness deep in my **h**.
40:12 on my head. I have lost **h**.
41:6 His **h** collects gossip.
45:1 My **h** is overflowing with good
45:5 Your arrows are sharp in the **h**
51:10 Create a clean **h** in me,
51:17 a broken and sorrowful **h**.
55:4 My **h** is in turmoil. The terrors
55:21 but there is war in his **h**.
57:7 My **h** is confident, O God.
57:7 My **h** is confident. I want to sing
61:2 to you when I begin to lose **h**.
64:6 and the human **h** are a mystery!
69:20 Insults have broken my **h**,
73:21 When my **h** was filled with
86:11 Focus my **h** on fearing you.
86:12 thanks to you with all my **h**,
89:50 in my **h** ⌊the insults⌋ from
101:5 a conceited look or arrogant **h**.
102:4 My **h** is beaten down and
108:1 My **h** is confident, O God.
109:22 I can feel the pain in my **h**.
111:1 to the LORD with all my **h**
112:7 His **h** remains secure,
112:8 His **h** is steady, and he is not
119:11 your promise in my **h** so that
119:34 I will guard them with all my **h**.
119:36 Direct my **h** toward your written
119:58 With all my **h** I want to win
119:69 principles with all my **h**.
119:80 Let my **h** be filled with integrity
119:111 They are the joy of my **h**.
119:145 I have called out with all my **h**.
119:161 words that fill my **h** with terror.
131:1 LORD, my **h** is not conceited.
135:9 and amazing things into the **h**
138:1 thanks to you with all my **h**.
139:22 I hate them with all my **h**.
143:4 begin to lose hope and my **h** is
Pro 2:1 if you take my words ⌊to **h**⌋
2:10 Wisdom will come into your **h**.
3:3 them on the tablet of your **h**.
3:5 Trust the LORD with all your **h**,
4:21 Keep them deep within your **h**
4:23 Guard your **h** more than
5:12 How my **h** despised correction!
6:21 Fasten them on your **h** forever.
6:25 not desire her beauty in your **h**.
7:3 them on the tablet of your **h**.
7:23 until an arrow pierces his **h**,
7:25 Do not let your **h** be turned to
8:5 get a **h** that has understanding.
11:29 a slave to the wise in **h**.
12:20 Deceit is in the **h** of those who
13:12 hope makes one sick at **h**,
14:10 The **h** knows its own
14:13 while laughing a **h** can ache,
14:14 A **h** that turns ⌊from God⌋
14:30 A tranquil **h** makes for a
14:33 Wisdom finds rest in the **h** of
15:11 how much more the human **h**!
15:13 A joyful **h** makes a cheerful
15:15 but a cheerful **h** has a continual
15:28 The **h** of a righteous person
15:30 in the eye delights the **h**.
16:1 The plans of the **h** belong to
16:5 Everyone with a conceited **h** is
16:23 A wise person's **h** controls his
17:22 A joyful **h** is good medicine,
18:12 a person's **h** is arrogant,
19:3 and his **h** rages against the
19:21 Many plans are in the human **h**,
20:5 A motive in the human **h** is like
20:9 "I've made my **h** pure.
21:1 The king's **h** is like streams of

Pro 22:11 Whoever loves a pure **h** and
22:15 is firmly attached to a child's **h**.
23:15 My son, if you have a wise **h**,
23:15 my **h** will rejoice as well.
23:16 My **h** rejoices when you speak
23:17 Do not envy sinners in your **h**.
23:26 My son, give me your **h**.
24:32 I observed ⌊this⌋, I took it to **h**.
25:20 to one who has an evil **h**.
26:23 talk that covers up an evil **h**.
26:25 disgusting things in his **h**.
27:9 and incense make the **h** glad,
27:11 and make my **h** glad so that I
27:19 a person is reflected by his **h**.
28:26 Whoever trusts his own **h** is a
31:11 trusts her with ⌊all⌋ his **h**,
Ecc 1:13 With all my **h** I used wisdom to
7:2 is alive should take this to **h**!
7:3 the **h** can be joyful.
7:21 everything that people say to **h**,
10:2 A wise person's **h** leads the
10:2 The **h** of a fool leads the wrong
11:9 Follow wherever your **h** leads
Sos 5:4 My **h** throbbed for him.
8:6 me as a signet ring on your **h**,
Isa 1:5 Your whole **h** is failing.
7:4 Don't lose **h** because of the
15:5 My **h** cries out for Moab.
16:11 That is why my **h** mourns for
42:25 but they did not take it to **h**.
60:5 and your **h** will be thrilled with
63:15 Where is the longing of your **h**
66:14 When you see it, your **h** will
Jer 3:15 you shepherds after my own **h**.
4:14 wash the evil from your **h** so
4:18 It is bitter. It breaks your **h**."
4:19 My **h** is beating wildly!
4:19 My **h** is pounding! I can't keep
8:18 me. I am sick at **h**!
12:11 but no one takes this to **h**.
17:5 and whose **h** turns away from
31:20 That is why my **h** longs for him,
32:41 With all my **h** and soul I will
Lam 1:20 My **h** is pounding because I've
1:22 so much and feel so sick at **h**."
2:11 My **h** is poured out on the
2:19 Pour your **h** out like water in
3:13 from his quiver into my **h**.
Eze 3:10 take to **h** everything I have
21:6 groan with a breaking **h** and
36:26 I will give you a new **h** and put
Joe 2:12 "return to me with all your **h**—
Zep 3:14 and rejoice with all your **h**,
Zec 9:9 Rejoice with all your **h**,
Mat 5:28 committed adultery in his **h**.
6:21 Your **h** will be where your
12:40 the Son of Man will be in the **h**
22:37 Lord your God with all your **h**,
Mar 12:30 Lord your God with all your **h**,
12:33 To love him with all your **h**,
Luk 2:19 all these things in her **h**
2:35 a sword will pierce your **h**."
2:51 all these things in her **h**.
10:27 Lord your God with all your **h**,
12:34 Your **h** will be where your
Jon 1:18 is closest to the Father's **h**,
Act 2:26 That is why my **h** is glad and
13:22 is a man after my own **h**.
21:13 like this and breaking my **h**?
Rom 2:29 that happens in a person's **h**.
10:8 in your mouth and in your **h**."
Php 1:7 have a special place in my **h**.
1Ti 1:5 is for love to flow from a pure **h**,
3:1 If anyone sets his **h** on being a
2Ti 2:22 worship the Lord with a pure **h**.
Heb 3:12 unbelieving **h** that turns away
10:22 a sincere **h** and strong faith.
1Pe 1:22 love that comes from the **h**.

heartache (5)

Pro 10:10 winks with his eye causes **h**.
15:13 but with a **h** comes depression.
17:25 A foolish son is a **h** to his
Ecc 1:18 of wisdom ⌊comes⌋ a lot of **h**.
Rom 9:2 deep sorrow and endless **h**.

heartaches (1)

Psa 32:10 Many **h** await wicked people,

heartbroken (3)

Gen 6:6 on the earth, and he was **h**.
1Sm 2:33 his eyes fail, and he will be **h**.
2Sm 1:26 I am **h** over you, my brother

heartless (3)

Mat 19:8 your wives because you're **h**.
Mar 10:5 for you because you're **h**.
Act 7:51 you be so **h** and disobedient?

heart's (7)

Rut 3:7 and drunk to his **h** content, so
Psa 20:4 He will give you your **h** desire
21:2 You gave him his **h** desire.
38:8 I roar because my **h** in turmoil.
Isa 66:11 You will nurse to your **h** delight
Jer 15:16 are my joy and my **h** delight,
Rom 10:1 my **h** desire and prayer to God

hearts (118)

Gen 8:21 even though from birth their **h**
Exo 35:21 whose **h** moved them came
Lev 26:41 humble their uncircumcised **h**
Dtr 10:16 your uncircumcised **h**,
30:6 God will circumcise your **h**
30:6 your hearts and the **h**
30:17 But your **h** might turn away,
31:21 I know what their **h** are set on
1Sm 10:26 whose **h** God had touched.
2Sm 15:6 So Absalom stole the **h** of the
15:13 "The **h** of the people of Israel
1Ki 2:4 to me with all their **h** and lives,
8:39 (You know what is in their **h**,
8:39 what is in the **h** of all people.)
8:58 May he bend our **h** toward him.
8:61 May your **h** be committed to the
8:66 They rejoiced with cheerful **h**
18:37 you are winning back their **h**."
1Ch 16:10 Let the **h** of those who seek the
22:19 So dedicate your **h** and lives to
29:17 that you examine **h** and delight
29:18 their **h** directed toward you.
2Ch 6:30 (You know what is in their **h**,
6:30 know what is in people's **h**).
7:10 They rejoiced with cheerful **h**
16:9 those whose **h** are committed
20:33 still didn't have their **h** set
30:19 those who have their **h** set on
Job 1:5 and cursed God in their **h**."
36:13 have godless **h** remain angry.
Psa 5:9 Destruction comes from their **h**
14:1 Godless fools say in their **h**,
28:3 but have evil in their **h**.
33:15 The one who formed their **h**
33:21 In him our **h** find joy.
34:18 to those whose **h** are humble.
37:15 own swords will pierce their **h**,
44:18 Our **h** never turned away.
44:21 he knows the secrets in our **h**?
53:1 Godless fools say in their **h**,
55:15 homes as well as in their **h**.
62:4 but in their **h** they curse.
62:8 Pour out your **h** in his presence.
69:32 May the **h** of those who look to
78:8 Their **h** were not loyal.
78:37 Their **h** were not loyal to him.
84:5 Their **h** are on the road ⌊that
95:10 'They are a people whose **h**
104:15 make wine to cheer human **h**,
104:15 bread to strengthen human **h**.
105:3 Let the **h** of those who seek the
119:70 Their **h** are cold and
140:2 They plan evil things in their **h**.
Pro 10:20 The **h** of wicked people are
17:3 but the one who purifies **h** ⌊by
21:2 but the LORD weighs **h**.
24:12 won't the one who weighs **h**
Ecc 5:20 occupied with the joy in their **h**.
9:3 the **h** of mortals are full of evil.
9:3 Madness is in their **h** while
11:9 You should let your **h** make
Isa 7:2 the **h** of the king and his people
9:9 and conceited **h** they will say,
29:13 But their **h** are far from me,
30:29 Your **h** will be happy like
51:7 have my teachings in your **h**.
59:13 and uttered lies in our **h**.
65:14 of the gladness in their **h**.
Jer 4:4 rid of the foreskins of your **h**,
9:26 all Israel has uncircumcised **h**."
12:2 but their **h** are far from you.
17:1 point on the tablet of their **h**
17:10 search minds and test **h**.
31:33 those teachings on their **h**.
Lam 2:18 The **h** of Jerusalem's people
3:41 Let us raise our **h** and hands to
5:15 There is no joy left in our **h**.
Eze 6:9 I was hurt by their adulterous **h**,
11:19 I will remove their stubborn **h**
11:19 and give them obedient **h**.
14:5 I will do this to recapture the **h**
18:31 Get yourselves new **h** and new
20:16 their **h** chased disgusting idols.
21:7 their **h** will lose courage,
21:15 gates so that their **h** will sink
25:15 taken revenge with spiteful **h**.
33:31 but in their **h** they chase
36:26 I will remove your stubborn **h**
36:26 hearts and give you obedient **h**.
Joe 2:13 Tear your **h**, not your clothes.
Nah 2:10 **H** are melting. Knees are
Zec 7:12 They made their **h** as hard as
10:7 Their **h** will be glad as if they
10:7 Their **h** will find joy in the
Mat 7:15 but in their **h** they are vicious
15:8 but their **h** are far from me.
Mar 7:6 but their **h** are far from me.
Luk 8:15 it in their good and honest **h**
16:15 God knows what's in your **h**.
Act 7:39 and in their **h** they turned back
Rom 2:15 Teachings are written in their **h**.
5:5 has been poured into our **h** by
8:27 The one who searches our **h**
1Co 14:25 The secrets in their **h** will
2Co 3:2 in our **h** that everyone knows
3:3 but on tablets of human **h**.
6:11 have a place for you in our **h**.
6:13 Make a place for us in your **h**
7:2 Open your **h** to us.
7:3 that you are in our **h** so that we
Eph 5:19 music to the Lord with your **h**.
Col 3:16 Sing to God in your **h**.
1Ti 6:10 people who have set their **h**
Heb 3:10 'Their **h** continue to stray,
8:10 those teachings on their **h**.
10:16 will put my teachings in their **h**
2Pe 1:19 morning star to rise in your **h**.
Rev 2:23 who searches **h** and minds.

hearts' (2)

Eze 24:21 It's your **h** desire. So the sons
24:25 It is their **h** desire and the thing

heat (28)

Gen 8:22 cold and **h**, summer and winter,
30:38 When they were in **h** and came
30:41 stronger of the flocks were in **h**,
30:42 the flocks in **h** were weak,
31:40 The scorching **h** during the day
Dtr 28:22 **h** waves, drought, and ruined
1Ki 8:37 Plant diseases, **h** waves,
2Ch 6:28 Plant diseases, **h** waves,
Job 6:17 In the **h** their riverbeds dry up.
24:19 ⌊Just as⌋ drought and **h** steal
Psa 19:6 Nothing is hidden from its **h**.
32:4 shriveled in the summer **h**.
Isa 4:6 It will be a shelter from the **h**
18:4 will be like scorching **h**
18:4 dew in the **h** of the harvest.
25:4 and shade from the **h**.
25:5 like **h** in a dry land.)
25:5 like **h** that is ⌊reduced⌋
Jer 2:24 sniffing the wind while in **h**.
17:8 be afraid in the **h** of summer.
25:38 been ruined because of the **h**
36:30 out and exposed to the **h**
Lam 5:9 our lives in the **h** of the desert.
5:10 from the burning **h** of starvation

Zec 14:6 be neither **h** nor freezing cold.
Act 28:3 The **h** forced a poisonous
Jas 1:11 sun rises with its scorching **h**
Rev 7:16 burning **h** will ever overcome

heated (4)

Job 41:20 a boiling pot **h** over brushwood.
Psa 58:9 pot is **h** by burning twigs.
Dan 3:19 should be **h** seven times hotter
Hos 7:4 They are like a **h** oven,

heathen (1)

Mat 18:17 deal with him as you would a **h**

heathens (1)

Mat 6:7 don't ramble like **h** who think

heaven (478)

Gen 1:1 God created heaven **a** earth.
2:1 **H** and earth and everything in
2:4 This is the account of **h** and
2:4 LORD God made earth and **h**.
14:19 Maker of **h** and earth.
14:22 Maker of **h** and earth,
19:24 sulfur and fire rain out of **h**
21:17 of God called to Hagar from **h**.
22:11 called to him from **h** and said,
22:15 Abraham from **h** a second time
24:3 to swear by the LORD God of **h**
24:7 "The LORD God of **h** took me
28:12 with its top reaching up to **h**.
28:17 of God and the gateway to **h**!"
Exo 16:4 send you food from **h** like rain.
20:11 In six days the LORD made **h**,
20:22 I have spoken to you from **h**.
31:17 because the LORD made **h**
Dtr 2:25 all the people under **h** terrified
3:24 What kind of god is there in **h**
4:25 I call **h** and earth as witnesses
4:32 Search from one end of **h** to the
4:36 He let you hear his voice from **h**
4:39 the LORD is God in **h** above
10:14 that the sky, the highest **h**,
17:3 or the whole army of **h**.
26:15 down from your holy place in **h**.
30:12 It's not in **h**. You don't have to
30:12 "Who will go to **h** to get this
30:19 I call on **h** and earth as
31:28 these words and call on **h**
32:1 Listen, **h**, and I will speak.
32:40 I raise my hand toward **h** and
33:13 the best gift **h** can send,
Jos 2:11 God is the God of **h** and earth.
Jdg 5:20 The stars fought from **h**.
13:20 As the flame went up toward **h**
1Sm 5:12 the cry of the city went up to **h**.
2Sm 22:14 The LORD thundered from **h**.
1Ki 8:22 out his hands toward **h**
8:23 there is no god like you in **h**
8:27 If **h** itself, the highest heaven,
8:27 If heaven itself, the highest **h**,
8:30 Hear us ⌊when we pray⌋ to **h**,
8:32 then hear ⌊that person⌋ in **h**,
8:34 then hear ⌊them⌋ in **h**,
8:36 then hear ⌊them⌋ in **h**.
8:39 Hear ⌊them⌋ in **h**, where you
8:43 hear ⌊them⌋ in **h**, the place
8:45 hear their prayer for mercy in **h**,
8:49 then in **h**, the place where you
8:54 hands stretched out toward **h**.
22:19 and the entire army of **h** was
2Ki 1:10 fire will come from **h** and burn
1:10 Then fire came from **h** and
1:12 fire will come from **h** and burn
1:12 Then God's fire came from **h**
1:14 Fire has come from **h** and
2:1 was going to take Elijah to **h**
2:11 Elijah went to **h** in a windstorm.
17:16 prayed to the entire army of **h**.
19:15 You made **h** and earth.
21:3 and served the entire army of **h**.
21:5 altars for the entire army of **h**.
23:4 and the entire army of **h**.
23:5 and the entire army of **h**.
1Ch 21:16 standing between **h** and earth.
21:26 him by ⌊sending⌋ fire from **h**
1Ch 29:11 because everything in **h** and on
2Ch 2:6 him a temple when **h** itself,
2:6 the highest **h**, cannot hold him?
6:13 out his hands toward **h**.)
6:14 there is no god like you in **h** or
6:18 If **h** itself, the highest heaven,
6:18 If heaven itself, the highest **h**,
6:21 Hear us in **h**, the place where
6:23 then hear ⌊that person⌋ in **h**,
6:25 then hear ⌊them⌋ in **h**,
6:27 then hear ⌊them⌋ in **h**.
6:30 Hear ⌊them⌋ in **h**, where you
6:33 then hear ⌊them⌋ in **h**,
6:35 hear their prayer for mercy in **h**,
6:39 then in **h**, the place where you
7:1 fire came down from **h** and
7:14 I will hear ⌊their prayer⌋ from **h**,
18:18 and the entire army of **h** was
20:6 aren't you the God in **h**?
28:9 in a rage that reaches up to **h**.
30:27 went to God's holy place in **h**.
32:20 about this and called to **h**.
33:3 and served the entire army of **h**.
33:5 altars for the entire army of **h**.
36:23 The LORD God of **h** has given
Ezr 1:2 The LORD God of **h** has given
5:11 of the God of **h** and earth.
5:12 made the God of **h** angry,
6:9 to the God of **h** — young bulls,
6:10 that please the God of **h**
7:12 the Teachings of the God of **H**:
7:21 the Teachings of the God of **H**,
7:23 Whatever the God of **h** has
7:23 for the temple of the God of **h**.
9:6 overwhelming that it reaches **h**.
Neh 1:4 to fast and pray to the God of **h**.
1:5 I said, "LORD God of **h**,
2:4 So I prayed to the God of **h**,
2:20 "The God of **h** will give us
9:6 You made **h**, the highest
9:6 made heaven, the highest **h**,
9:6 the armies of **h** worship you.
9:13 You came from **h** to Mount
9:13 and spoke with them from **h**.
9:15 You gave them bread from **h** to
9:27 You heard them from **h**.
9:28 and you heard them from **h**.
Job 1:16 "A fire from God fell from **h** and
11:8 wisdom is⌋ higher than **h**.
16:19 My witness is in **h**,
20:27 **H** exposes his sin.
26:11 The pillars of **h** tremble and are
28:24 observe everything under **h**.
37:3 lightning everywhere under **h**.
38:37 or pour out the water jars of **h**
41:11 under **h** belongs to me!
Psa 2:4 The one enthroned in **h** laughs.
11:4 The LORD's throne is in **h**.
14:2 The LORD looks down from **h**
20:6 will answer him from his holy **h**
33:13 The LORD looks down from **h**.
50:4 He summons **h** and earth to
53:2 God looks down from **h** on
57:3 He sends his help from **h** and
68:33 rides through the ancient **h**,
68:33 ancient heaven, the highest **h**.
69:34 Let **h** and earth, the seas,
73:9 They verbally attack **h**,
73:25 anyone else in **h** or on earth.
76:8 From **h** you announced a
78:23 and opened the doors of **h**.
78:24 eat and gave them grain from **h**.
80:14 Look from **h** and see!
85:11 looks down from **h**.
89:29 his throne like the days of **h**.
89:37 be like a faithful witness in **h**."
102:19 From **h** he looked at the earth.
103:19 LORD has set his throne in **h**.
105:40 filled them with bread from **h**.
110:1 "Sit in the highest position in **h**
113:6 down to look at **h** and earth.
115:3 Our God is in **h**. He does
115:15 the maker of **h** and earth.
115:16 The highest **h** belongs to the
119:89 your word is established in **h**
121:2 the maker of **h** and earth.
Psa 123:1 one who sits enthroned in **h**.
124:8 the maker of **h** and earth.
134:3 the maker of **h** and earth,
135:6 does whatever he wants in **h**
136:26 Give thanks to the God of **h**
139:8 If I go up to **h**, you are there. If I
144:5 O LORD, bend your **h** low,
146:6 who made **h**, earth, the sea,
148:4 Praise him, you highest **h** and
148:13 His glory is above **h** and earth.
Pro 30:4 "Who has gone up to **h** and
Ecc 1:13 everything done under **h**.
2:3 during their brief lives under **h**.
3:1 time for every activity under **h**:
5:2 Since God is in **h** and you are
Isa 1:2 Listen, **h**, and pay attention,
13:5 from the ends of **h**.
13:13 I will make **h** tremble,
14:12 How you have fallen from **h**,
14:13 You thought, "I'll go up to **h** and
24:21 punish heaven's armies in **h**
37:16 You made **h** and earth.
38:14 were tired from looking up to **h**.
58:4 you from being heard in **h**.
63:15 Look down and see from **h**,
65:17 I will create a new **h** and a new
66:1 LORD says: **H** is my throne.
66:22 "The new **h** and earth that I am
Jer 2:12 Be horrified over this, **h**.
7:18 make cakes for the queen of **h**.
10:11 from the earth and from under **h**
10:11 they didn't make **h** and earth.
19:13 incense to the entire army of **h**
23:24 "I fill **h** and earth!" declares the
32:17 'Almighty LORD, you made **h**
33:22 like the stars of **h** that cannot
33:25 or made laws for **h** and earth.
44:17 burn incense to the queen of **h**
44:18 incense to the queen of **h**
44:19 incense to the queen of **h**,
44:25 burn incense to the queen of **h**
49:36 four corners of **h** against Elam
51:15 out **h** by his understanding.
51:48 Then **h** and earth and
51:53 of Babylon might go up to **h**.
Lam 2:1 Israel's beauty from **h** to earth.
3:41 hearts and hands to God in **h**.
3:50 looks down from **h** and sees.
3:66 out from under the LORD's **h**."
Eze 8:3 me between **h** and earth.
Dan 2:18 told them to ask the God of **h**
2:19 So Daniel praised the God of **h**.
2:28 But there is a God in **h** who
2:37 The God of **h** has given you a
2:44 the God of **h** will establish a
4:13 come down from **h**.
4:23 come down from **h**.
4:26 as you realize that **h** rules.
4:31 a voice said from **h**,
4:34 looked up to **h**, I thanked the
4:35 he wishes with the army of **h**
4:37 and give glory to the King of **H**.
5:23 greater than the Lord of **H**.
6:27 signs and amazing things in **h**
7:2 saw the four winds of **h** stirring
7:13 I saw among the clouds in **h**
7:27 of all the kingdoms under **h**,
8:8 to the four winds of **h**.
8:10 until it reached the army of **h**.
8:10 It threw some of the army of **h**,
11:4 of the four winds of **h**.
12:7 his right hand and left hand to **h**
Amo 9:2 Even if they go up to **h**,
9:6 one who builds stairs up to **h**
Jnh 1:9 the LORD, the God of **h**.
Mic 6:6 I bow in front of the God of **h**?
Zec 2:6 you to the four winds of **h**.
6:5 "They are the four spirits of **h**.
Mal 3:10 if I won't open the windows of **h**
Mat 3:2 the kingdom of **h** is near."
3:17 Then a voice from **h** said,
4:17 the kingdom of **h** is near!"
5:3 kingdom of **h** belongs to them.
5:10 kingdom of **h** belongs to them.
5:12 you have a great reward in **h**!
5:16 do and praise your Father in **h**.

Mat 5:19 in the kingdom of **h**.
5:19 great in the kingdom of **h**.
5:20 never enter the kingdom of **h**.
5:34 Don't swear an oath by **h**,
5:45 are children of your Father in **h**.
5:48 as your Father in **h** is perfect.
6:1 If you do, your Father in **h** will
6:9 should pray: Our Father in **h**,
6:10 done on earth as it is done in **h**.
6:20 treasures for yourselves in **h**,
7:11 Father in **h** give good things
7:21 will enter the kingdom of **h**,
7:21 what my Father in **h** wants.
8:11 and Jacob in the kingdom of **h**.
10:7 'The kingdom of **h** is near.'
10:32 my Father in **h** that person who
10:33 But I will tell my Father in **h**
11:11 the kingdom of **h** is greater than
11:12 the kingdom of **h** has been
11:23 will you be lifted to **h**?
11:25 Lord of **h** and earth,
12:50 my Father in **h** wants is my
13:11 kingdom of **h** has been given
13:24 He said, "The kingdom of **h** is
13:31 He said, "The kingdom of **h** is
13:33 "The kingdom of **h** is like yeast
13:44 "The kingdom of **h** is like a
13:45 "Also, the kingdom of **h** is like
13:47 "Also, the kingdom of **h** is like
13:52 of the kingdom of **h** is like
14:19 he looked up to **h** and blessed
16:1 them a miraculous sign from **h**.
16:17 but my Father in **h** revealed it
16:19 the keys of the kingdom of **h**.
16:22 He said, "**H** forbid,
18:1 greatest in the kingdom of **h**?"
18:3 never enter the kingdom of **h**.
18:4 greatest in the kingdom of **h**.
18:10 their angels in **h** always see
18:10 face of my Father, who is in **h**.
18:14 your Father in **h** does not want
18:19 my Father in **h** will accept it.
18:23 "That is why the kingdom of **h**
18:35 That is what my Father in **h**
19:12 because of the kingdom of **h**.
19:21 and you will have treasure in **h**.
19:23 to enter the kingdom of **h**.
20:1 "The kingdom of **h** is like a
21:9 Hosanna in the highest **h**!"
21:25 right to baptize come from **h**
21:25 'from **h**,' he will ask us,
22:2 "The kingdom of **h** is like a
22:30 they are like the angels in **h**.
22:44 "Take the highest position in **h**
23:9 only one Father, and he is in **h**.
23:13 people out of the kingdom of **h**.
23:22 And to swear an oath by **h** is to
24:36 Even the angels in **h** and the
25:1 the kingdom of **h** will be like
25:14 "The kingdom of **h** is like a
26:64 in the highest position in **h**.
26:64 be coming on the clouds of **h**."
28:2 Lord had come down from **h**,
28:18 He said, "All authority in **h** and
Mar 1:10 he saw **h** split open and the
1:11 A voice from **h** said,
6:41 he looked up to **h** and blessed
7:34 Then he looked up to **h**,
8:11 a miraculous sign from **h**.
10:21 and you will have treasure in **h**.
11:10 Hosanna in the highest **h**!"
11:25 Then your Father in **h** will
11:30 right to baptize come from **h**
11:31 'from **h**,' he will ask,
12:25 they are like the angels in **h**.
12:36 "Take the highest position in **h**
13:32 Even the angels in **h** and the
14:62 in the highest position in **h**.
14:62 coming with the clouds of **h**."
16:19 the Lord was taken to **h**,
Luk 2:14 "Glory to God in the highest **h**,
2:15 left them and went back to **h**.
3:21 he was praying, **h** opened,
3:22 A voice from **h** said,
6:23 You have a great reward in **h**.
9:16 the two fish, looked up to **h**,
Luk 9:51 for Jesus to be taken to **h**.
9:54 want us to call down fire from **h**
10:15 will you be lifted to **h**?
10:18 Satan fall from **h** like lightning.
10:20 your names are written in **h**."
10:21 Lord of **h** and earth,
11:13 more will your Father in **h** give
11:16 some miraculous sign from **h**.
12:33 in **h** that never loses
12:33 In **h** thieves and moths can't
15:7 happiness in **h** over one person
15:18 I've sinned against **h** and you.
15:21 I've sinned against **h** and you.
18:13 He wouldn't even look up to **h**.
18:22 and you will have treasure in **h**.
19:38 Peace in **h**, and glory in the
19:38 and glory in the highest **h**."
20:4 come from **h** or from humans?"
20:5 'from **h**,' he will ask,
20:42 "Take the highest position in **h**
22:43 Then an angel from **h** appeared
22:69 be in the highest position in **h**."
24:49 until you receive power from **h**."
24:51 left them and was taken to **h**.
Jon 1:32 come down as a dove from **h**
3:12 I tell you about things in **h**?
3:13 No one has gone to **h** except
3:13 Son of Man, who came from **h**.
3:27 has been given to them from **h**.
3:31 The person who comes from **h**
6:31 gave them bread from **h** to eat.'"
6:32 didn't give you bread from **h**,
6:32 gives you the true bread from **h**.
6:33 is the man who comes from **h**
6:38 I haven't come from **h** to do
6:41 am the bread that came from **h**."
6:42 he say now, 'I came from **h**'?"
6:50 comes from **h** so that whoever
6:51 living bread that came from **h**.
6:58 is the bread that came from **h**.
12:28 A voice from **h** said,
17:1 Jesus looked up to **h** and said,
Act 1:2 until the day he was taken to **h**.
1:2 Before he was taken to **h**,
1:9 he was taken to **h**.
1:11 who was taken from you to **h**,
1:11 way that you saw him go to **h**."
2:34 David didn't go up to **h**,
3:21 **H** must receive Jesus until the
7:49 Lord says, "**H** is my throne.
7:55 He looked into **h**, saw God's
7:56 So Stephen said, "Look, I see **h**
9:3 a light from **h** suddenly flashed
11:9 "A voice spoke from **h** a
14:17 He gives you rain from **h** and
17:24 in it is the Lord of **h** and earth.
22:6 a bright light from **h** suddenly
26:19 the vision I saw from **h**,
Rom 1:18 God's anger is revealed from **h**
8:34 has the highest position in **h**.
10:6 who will go up to **h**," (that is,
1Co 8:5 say that there are gods in **h**
15:47 The second man came from **h**.
15:48 The people in **h** are like the
15:48 like the man who came from **h**.
15:49 of the man who came from **h**.
2Co 5:1 It is an eternal house in **h** that
5:2 on the house we will have in **h**.
12:2 the third **h** fourteen years ago.
Gal 1:8 is one of us or an angel from **h**.
Eph 1:3 blessing that **h** has to offer.
1:10 of everything in **h** and on earth.
1:20 him the highest position in **h**.
2:6 us a position in **h** with him.
3:10 in **h** know his infinite
3:15 from whom all the family in **h**
6:9 master in **h** who has authority
Php 2:10 name of Jesus everyone in **h**,
3:20 We, however, are citizens of **h**.
3:20 coming from **h** as our Savior.
Col 1:5 which is kept safe for you in **h**.
1:16 He created all things in **h** and
1:20 on earth and in **h** back
1:23 throughout all creation under **h**.
4:1 you also have a master in **h**.
1Th 1:10 wait for his Son to come from **h**.
1Th 4:16 The Lord will come from **h** with
2Th 1:7 ⌞coming⌟ from **h** with his
1Ti 3:16 and was taken to **h** in glory.
Heb 1:3 the one next to the Father in **h**.
1:13 "Sit in the highest position in **h**
7:26 has the highest position in **h**.
8:1 the throne of majesty in **h**.
8:5 a shadow, of what is in **h**.
9:23 The copies of the things in **h**
9:24 Instead, he went into **h** to
9:25 However, Christ didn't go into **h**
10:12 the highest position in **h**.
12:2 the highest position in **h**,
12:23 (whose names are written in **h**).
12:25 who warns us from **h**.
Jas 5:12 take an oath on anything in **h**
1Pe 1:4 inheritance is kept in **h** for you,
1:12 who was sent from **h**,
3:22 Christ has gone to **h** where he
2Pe 1:18 to him from **h** when we were
3:5 **h** and earth existed a long time
3:7 By God's word, the present **h**
3:10 On that day **h** will pass away
3:12 When that day comes, **h** will
3:13 God has promised — a new **h**
Rev 3:12 down out of **h** from my God),
4:1 saw a door standing open in **h**.
4:2 I saw a throne in **h**,
5:3 No one in **h**, on earth, or under
5:13 I heard every creature in **h**,
8:1 there was silence in **h** for about
10:1 angel come down from **h**.
10:4 I heard a voice from **h** say,
10:5 land raised his right hand to **h**.
10:6 who created **h** and everything
10:8 which I had heard from **h** spoke
11:12 a loud voice from **h** calling
11:12 They went up to **h** in a cloud,
11:13 gave glory to the God of **h**.
11:15 there were loud voices in **h**,
11:19 God's temple in **h** was opened,
12:7 Then a war broke out in **h**.
12:8 longer any place for them in **h**.
12:10 Then I heard a loud voice in **h**,
13:6 tent — those who are living in **h**.
13:13 makes fire come down from **h**
14:2 Then I heard a sound from **h**
14:7 the one who made **h** and earth,
14:13 I heard a voice from **h** saying,
14:17 came out of the temple in **h**.
15:1 I saw another sign in **h**.
15:5 God's promise was open in **h**.
16:11 and cursed the God of **h** for
18:1 another angel come from **h**.
18:4 another voice from **h** saying,
18:5 Her sins are piled as high as **h**,
18:20 "Gloat over it, **h**, God's people,
19:1 noise from a large crowd in **h**,
19:11 I saw **h** standing open.
19:14 The armies of **h**, wearing pure,
20:1 an angel coming down from **h**,
20:9 Fire came from **h** and burned
21:1 I saw a new **h** and a new earth,
21:1 because the first **h** and earth
21:2 down from God out of **h**,
21:10 down from God out of **h**.

heavenly (22)

Jdg 5:20 Sisera from their **h** paths.
Psa 29:1 to the LORD, you **h** beings.
89:6 Who among the **h** beings is
148:2 Praise him, his entire **h** army.
Sos 6:10 awe-inspiring like those **h**
Mat 6:14 your **h** Father will also forgive
6:26 Yet, your **h** Father feeds them.
6:32 and your **h** Father certainly
15:13 "Any plant that my **h** Father did
Luk 9:31 They appeared in **h** glory and
1Co 15:40 There are **h** bodies and earthly
15:40 **H** bodies don't all have the
Eph 6:7 you were serving your **h** master
6:8 You know that your **h** master
6:12 that control evil in the **h** world.
Php 3:14 the prize that God's **h** call offers
2Ti 4:18 me safely to his **h** kingdom.
Heb 3:1 are holy partners in a **h** calling.

Heb 6:4 They experienced the **h** gift
9:23 But the **h** things themselves
11:16 a better country — a **h** country.
12:22 to the **h** Jerusalem.

heaven's (1)

Isa 24:21 the LORD will punish **h** armies

heavens (78)

Gen 49:25 blessings from the **h** above,
Dtr 28:12 The LORD will open the **h**,
33:26 He rides through the **h** to help
1Sm 2:10 He thunders at them from the **h**.
2Sm 22:8 foundations of the **h** trembled.
22:10 He spread apart the **h** and
1Ch 16:26 The LORD made the **h**.
16:31 Let the **h** rejoice and the earth
2Ch 2:12 He made the **h** and the earth
Job 9:8 He stretches out the **h** by
14:12 does not rise until the **h** cease
15:15 and the **h** are not pure in his
22:12 "Isn't God high above in the **h**?
26:7 "He stretches out his **h** over
35:5 "Look at the **h** and see.
Psa 8:1 Your glory is sung above the **h**.
8:3 When I look at your **h**,
18:9 He spread apart the **h** and
18:13 The LORD thundered in the **h**.
19:1 The **h** declare the glory of God,
19:4 up a tent in the **h** for the sun,
19:6 It rises from one end of the **h**.
33:6 The **h** were made by the word
36:5 your mercy reaches to the **h**,
50:6 The **h** announce his
57:5 you be honored above the **h**,
57:10 your mercy is as high as the **h**.
57:11 you be honored above the **h**,
71:19 righteousness reaches to the **h**,
78:26 the east wind blow in the **h**
78:69 holy place to be like the high **h**,
89:2 stands firm in the **h**."
89:5 O LORD, the **h** praise your
89:11 The **h** are yours. The earth is
96:5 The LORD made the **h**.
96:11 Let the **h** rejoice and the earth
97:6 The **h** tell about his
102:25 Even the **h** are the works of
103:11 As high as the **h** are above the
104:2 You stretch out the **h** as though
108:4 your mercy is higher than the **h**.
108:5 you be honored above the **h**,
113:4 His glory is above the **h**.
136:5 to the one who made the **h** by
148:1 Praise the LORD from the **h**.
150:1 Praise him in his mighty **h**.
Pro 3:19 he established the **h**.
8:27 "When he set up the **h**,
25:3 ⌊Like⌋ the high **h** and the deep
Isa 34:4 The **h** will be rolled up like a
34:5 covered ⌊with blood⌋ in the **h**,
42:5 The LORD God created the **h**
44:23 Sing with joy, you **h**,
44:24 I stretched out the **h** by myself.
45:8 Rain down from above, you **h**,
45:12 I stretched out the **h** with my
45:18 The LORD created the **h**.
48:13 right hand stretched out the **h**.
49:13 Sing with joy, you **h**!
50:3 I clothe the **h** in darkness and
51:13 He stretched out the **h** and laid
51:16 I stretched out the **h**,
55:9 "Just as the **h** are higher than
64:1 only you would split open the **h**
Jer 31:37 Only if the **h** could be
Hab 3:3 His splendor covers the **h**.
Hag 2:21 to shake the **h** and the earth.
Zec 12:1 LORD — who spread out the **h**,
Mat 3:16 Suddenly, the **h** were opened,
5:18 the earth and the **h** disappear,
24:35 earth and the **h** will disappear,
Mar 13:31 earth and the **h** will disappear,
Luk 16:17 is easier for the earth and the **h**
21:33 earth and the **h** will disappear,
Eph 4:10 went up above all the **h** so that
Heb 1:10 own hands you made the **h**.
4:14 who has gone through the **h**.

Rev 12:12 **h** and those who live in them.

heavier (5)

Dtr 25:13 a **h** one and a lighter one.
1Ki 12:10 'My little finger is **h** than my
2Ch 10:10 'My little finger is **h** than my
Job 6:3 then they would be **h** than the
Pro 27:3 a stubborn fool is **h** than both.

heaviest (3)

1Sm 31:3 The **h** fighting was against
2Sm 11:15 line where the fighting is **h**.
1Ch 10:3 The **h** fighting was against

heavily (3)

Psa 32:4 night your hand laid **h** on me.
88:7 Your rage lies **h** on me.
Pro 28:16 taxes ⌊his people⌋ **h**,

heavy (37)

Exo 17:12 Moses' hands felt **h**.
19:16 lightning with a **h** cloud over
Dtr 28:48 The LORD will put a **h** burden
1Sm 4:17 troops suffered **h** casualties.
4:18 (The man was old and **h**.)
2Sm 14:26 because it became **h** for him.
1Ki 5:15 men who carried **h** loads,
12:4 made us carry a **h** burden.
12:4 work and lighten the **h** burden
12:11 If my father put a **h** burden on
12:14 my father made your burden **h**,
18:41 like a **h** rain ⌊is coming⌋."
18:45 and there was a **h** rain.
2Ch 2:2 70,000 men to carry **h** loads,
2:18 He made 70,000 of them carry **h**
10:4 made us carry a **h** burden.
10:4 work and lighten the **h** burden
10:11 If my father put a **h** burden on
10:14 my father made your burden **h**,
Ezr 10:9 shivering because of the **h** rain.
Neh 5:18 were already carrying a **h** load.
Psa 38:4 Like a **h** load, it is more than I
Pro 27:3 A stone is **h**, and sand weighs
Isa 18:4 like **h** dew in the heat of the
24:20 disobedience weighs **h** on it.
30:27 His burden is **h**. His lips are
46:2 able to escape with **h** loads.
47:6 You placed a **h** burden on old
Lam 1:14 My rebellious acts are a **h**
3:7 He has put **h** chains on me.
Eze 27:25 like a ship filled with **h** cargo
Mic 6:13 to strike you with **h** blows
Zec 12:3 make Jerusalem a stone too **h**
Mat 11:28 are tired from carrying **h** loads,
Act 27:10 to face a disaster and **h** losses
Rev 11:19 an earthquake, and **h** hail.
16:21 Large, **h** hailstones fell from the

Heber (10)

Gen 46:17 of Beriah were **H** and Malchiel.
Num 26:45 Beriah were the family of **H**
Jdg 4:11 **H** the Kenite had separated
4:11 **H** went as far away as the oak
4:17 the wife of **H** the Kenite.
5:24 Jael, wife of **H** the Kenite,
1Ch 4:18 **H**, who first settled Soco,
7:31 sons were **H** and Malchiel,
7:32 **H** was the father of Japhlet,
8:17 Meshullam, Hizki, **H**,

Heber's (2)

Jdg 4:17 of Hazor and **H** family were
4:21 **H** wife, took a tent peg and

Hebrew (30)

Gen 14:13 the **H** what had happened.
39:14 My husband brought this **H**
39:17 "The **H** slave you brought here
41:12 A young **H**, a slave of the
Exo 1:15 of Egypt told the **H** midwives,
1:16 "When you help the **H** women
1:19 "**H** women are not like
1:22 Nile every ⌊**H**⌋ boy that was
2:6 "This is one of the **H** children."
2:7 go and get one of the **H** women
2:11 He saw a **H**, one of his own

Exo 2:13 he saw two **H** men fighting.
2:13 are you beating another **H**?"
3:22 "Every **H** woman should ask
21:2 "Whenever you buy a **H** slave,
Dtr 15:12 Whenever **H** men or women are
1Sm 4:6 this shouting in the **H** camp?"
Jer 34:9 supposed to free his **H** slaves,
Jnh 1:9 Jonah answered them, "I'm a **H**.
Jon 5:2 a pool called Bethesda in **H**.
19:13 (In **H** it is called Gabbatha.)
19:17 (In **H** this place is called
19:20 The notice was written in **H**,
20:16 around and said to him in **H**,
Act 21:40 Paul spoke to them in the **H**
22:2 heard him speak to them in **H**,
26:14 I heard a voice asking me in **H**,
Php 3:5 I'm a pure-blooded **H**.
Rev 9:11 In **H** he is called Abaddon,
16:16 is called Armageddon in **H**.

Hebrews (17)

Gen 40:15 from the land of the **H**,
43:32 found it offensive to eat with **H**.
Exo 3:18 'The LORD God of the **H** has
5:3 "The God of the **H** has met
7:16 'The LORD God of the **H** sent
9:1 the LORD God of the **H** says:
9:13 the LORD God of the **H** says:
10:3 the LORD God of the **H** says:
1Sm 4:9 or else you will serve the **H** as
13:3 Saul announced, "Listen, **H**!"
13:7 Some **H** crossed the Jordan
13:19 kept the **H** from making swords
14:11 some **H** are coming out of the
14:21 The **H** who had been with the
29:3 "What are these **H** doing here?"
Jer 34:14 any **H** who sold themselves
2Co 11:22 Are they **H**? So am I. Are they

Hebrew-speaking (1)

Act 6:1 complained about the **H** Jews.

Hebron (73)

Gen 13:18 trees belonging to Mamre at **H**.
23:2 Arba (that is, **H**) in Canaan.
23:19 east of Mamre (that is, **H**).
35:27 city, Kiriath Arba (that is, **H**).
37:14 away from the **H** Valley.
Exo 6:18 Amram, Izhar, **H**, and Uzziel.
Num 3:19 Amram, Izhar, **H**, and Uzziel
3:27 Amram, Izhar, **H**, and Uzziel.
13:22 the Negev and came to **H**,
13:22 (**H** was built seven years
Jos 10:3 message⌋ to King Hoham of **H**,
10:5 **H**, Jarmuth, Lachish,
10:23 **H**, Jarmuth, Lachish,
10:36 from Eglon to **H** and attacked it.
10:39 its king that he had done to **H**
11:21 in **H**, Debir, and Anab,
12:10 of Jerusalem, the king of **H**,
14:13 gave him **H** as his inheritance.
14:14 **H** is still the inheritance of
14:15 In the past **H** was called Kiriath
15:13 the city of Arba (now called **H**).
15:14 descendants of Anak from **H**.
15:54 Kiriath Arba (now called **H**),
20:7 and Kiriath Arba (now called **H**)
21:11 This is the city of **H** located in
21:13 those two tribes were **H** (a city
Jdg 1:10 the Canaanites who lived at **H**.
1:10 (In the past **H** was called
1:20 **H** was given to Caleb,
16:3 to the top of the hill facing **H**.
1Sm 30:31 **H**, and to all the places David
2Sm 2:1 "To **H**," the LORD replied.
2:3 settled in the towns around **H**.
2:4 the people of Judah came to **H**
2:11 In **H** David was king over the
2:13 David's officers also left ⌊**H**⌋.
2:32 and arrived at **H** by daybreak.
3:2 to David while he was in **H**.
3:5 to David while he was in **H**.
3:19 went directly to David in **H**
3:20 with 20 men to David in **H**,
3:22 was no longer with David in **H**.
3:27 When Abner returned to **H**,

2Sm 3:32 They buried Abner in **H**.
4:1 heard that Abner had died in **H**,
4:8 head to David at **H**.
4:12 dead bodies by the pond in **H**.
4:12 buried it in Abner's tomb in **H**.
5:1 of Israel came to David at **H**.
5:3 leaders of Israel had come to **H**.
5:3 an agreement with them at **H**
5:5 In **H** he ruled Judah for seven
5:13 after he had come there from **H**,
15:7 "Let me go to **H** and keep the
15:9 king told him. So he went to **H**.
15:10 has become king in **H**.'"
1Ki 2:11 He ruled for 7 years in **H** and for
1Ch 2:42 who first settled **H**.
3:1 born to him while he was in **H**:
3:4 Six sons were born to him in **H**,
6:2 Amram, Izhar, **H**, and Uzziel.
6:18 Amram, Izhar, **H**, and Uzziel.
6:55 They were given **H** in the
6:57 descendants were given **H** as
11:1 gathered around David at **H**.
11:3 leaders of Israel had come to **H**.
11:3 an agreement with them at **H**
12:23 The men joined David at **H** to
12:38 with a single purpose to **H**—
23:12 Amram, Izhar, **H**, and Uzziel.
26:23 of Amram, Izhar, **H**, and Uzziel,
29:27 He ruled for 7 years in **H** and for
2Ch 11:10 Zorah, Aijalon, and **H**.

Hebronite (1)

Num 26:58 the **H** family, the Mahlite family,

Hebron's (10)

1Ch 2:43 **H** sons were Korah,
15:9 Leading **H** descendants was
23:19 **H** first son was Jeriah;
24:23 Jeriah (for **H** descendants),
24:23 **H** descendants⌟), Jahaziel (the
24:23 **H** descendants⌟), Jekameam
24:23 (the fourth ⌞of **H** descendants⌟),
26:30 From **H** descendants
26:31 the head of **H** descendants.
26:31 the ancestry of **H** descendants

hedge (2)

Pro 15:19 lazy people is like a thorny **h**,
Isa 5:5 I will tear away its **h** so that it

heel (6)

Gen 3:15 and you will bruise his **h**."
25:26 hand holding on to Esau's **h**,
25:26 so he was named Jacob [**H**].
Job 18:9 A trap catches his **h**.
Psa 41:9 has lifted his **h** against me.
Hos 12:3 held on to his brother's **h** while

heels (3)

Gen 49:17 that bites a horse's **h** so that its
49:19 he will strike back at their **h**.
Pro 22:4 On the **h** of humility (the fear of

Hegai (4)

Est 2:3 the care of the king's eunuch **H**,
2:8 were placed in the care of **H**.
2:8 and placed in the care of **H**,
2:15 for what the king's eunuch **H**,

heifer (5)

Gen 15:9 "Bring me a three-year-old **h**,
Dtr 21:3 must choose a **h** that has never
21:4 that city will bring the **h** down
21:6 their hands over the dead **h**.
1Sm 16:2 "Take a **h** with you and say,

heifer's (1)

Dtr 21:4 they must break the **h** neck

height (6)

Neh 4:6 to about half its ⌞original⌟ **h**.
Job 20:6 If his **h** reaches to the sky and
Pro 14:29 temper is the **h** of stupidity.
Eze 31:14 arrogant because of their **h**,
43:13 This was the **h** of the altar:
Rev 21:16 and **h** were the same.

heights (7)

Dtr 32:13 He made them ride on the **h** of
Job 39:27 and makes its nest on the **h**?
Psa 148:1 Praise him in the **h** above.
Ecc 12:5 when someone is afraid of **h**
Isa 37:24 I'll come to its most distant **h**
58:14 I will make you ride on the **h** of
Jer 4:11 "A hot wind from the **h** will

heir (16)

Gen 15:3 of my household will be my **h**."
15:4 "This man will not be your **h**.
15:4 Your own son will be your **h**."
17:18 "Why not let Ishmael be my **h**?"
Num 5:8 But there may be no **h** to whom
2Sm 14:7 who ⌞now⌟ would be the **h**.' In
1Ki 1:48 let me see the **h** to my throne."'
2:4 you will never fail to have an **h**
8:25 'You will never fail to have an **h**
9:5 'You will never fail to have an **h**
2Ch 6:16 'You will never fail to have an **h**
7:18 'You will never fail to have an **h**
Mat 21:38 to one another, 'This is the **h**.
Mar 12:7 to one another, 'This is the **h**.
Luk 20:14 They said, 'This is the **h**.
Gal 4:1 As long as an **h** is a child,

heirs (17)

1Ki 14:8 kingdom away from David's **h**
2Ki 10:1 had 70 male **h** in Samaria.
10:2 "Your master's **h** are with you,
10:3 most honest of your master's **h**,
10:6 the heads of your master's **h**
10:6 The 70 male **h** were staying
10:7 they slaughtered all 70 **h**.
10:8 the heads of the king's **h**."
Jer 49:1 Doesn't it have any **h**?
Amo 7:9 Jeroboam's **h** with my sword."
Act 3:25 of the prophets and the **h**
Rom 4:14 Moses' Teachings are the **h**,
8:17 we are also God's **h**.
8:17 we are **h** together with him.
Gal 3:29 Abraham's descendants and **h**,
4:7 God has also made you **h**.
Tit 3:7 we have become **h** who have

Helah (1)

1Ch 4:5 had two wives, **H** and Naarah.

Helah's (1)

1Ch 4:7 **H** sons were Zereth,

Helam (2)

2Sm 10:16 came to **H** with Shobach,
10:17 Jordan River, and came to **H**.

Helbah (1)

Jdg 1:31 Achzib, **H**, Aphek, or Rehob.

Helbon (1)

Eze 27:18 They exchanged wine from **H**

held (94)

Gen 21:8 Abraham **h** a big feast.
Exo 4:4 back into a staff as he **h** it.
8:6 So Aaron **h** his staff over the
8:17 When Moses told him, Aaron **h**
10:13 Moses **h** his staff over the land
16:36 at that time **h** 20 quarts.)
17:11 As long as Moses **h** up his
17:12 Aaron **h** up one hand,
17:12 and Hur **h** up the other.
26:24 These will be **h** together at the
26:24 at the bottom and **h** tightly at
36:29 They were **h** together at the
36:29 at the bottom and **h** tightly at
39:21 the ephod and was **h** in place.
Jos 8:18 So Joshua **h** out his spear.
20:4 to the city, where court is **h**,
Jdg 7:20 They **h** the torches in their left
21:19 LORD's festival is **h** at Shiloh.
Rut 1:14 but Ruth **h** on to her tightly.
3:15 So she **h** it tight while he
4:16 took the child, **h** him on her lap,
1Sm 23:7 a double door ⌞**h** shut by⌟
1Sm 25:24 let me be **h** responsible for this
2Sm 14:9 "Let me be **h** responsible for
14:9 father's family be **h** responsible.
1Ki 3:15 and fellowship offerings and **h**
3:20 She **h** him in her arms.
7:26 It **h** 12,000 gallons.
7:38 Each basin **h** 240 gallons.
1Ch 28:1 David **h** a meeting in
2Ch 4:5 It **h** 18,000 gallons.
11:12 So Rehoboam **h** on to Judah
26:19 Uzziah, who **h** an incense
Neh 4:17 one hand and **h** their weapons
4:21 Half of us **h** spears from early
6:5 his servant **h** in his hand an
13:14 for the worship that is **h** there."
Est 1:3 he **h** a banquet in the third year
1:5 the king **h** a banquet lasting
1:5 This banquet was **h** in the
1:9 Queen Vashti also **h** a banquet
1:14 had access to the king and **h**
2:18 Then the king **h** a great
5:2 So the king **h** out the golden
8:4 The king **h** out his golden
Job 29:9 Princes **h** back ⌞their⌟ words
Psa 89:42 You **h** the right hand of his
106:46 all those who **h** them captive.
107:10 They were **h** in iron chains
118:16 The right hand of the LORD is **h**
Pro 9:12 alone will be **h** responsible.
Sos 3:4 I **h** on to him and would not let
Isa 3:9 faces will be **h** against them.
40:12 Who has **h** the dust of the earth
42:14 I kept quiet and **h** myself back.
45:1 I have **h** him by his right hand
63:9 He always **h** them and carried
Jer 4:10 a sword is **h** at their throats."
29:14 where you are being **h** captive.
33:1 Jeremiah was still being **h**
48:39 ridiculed and something **h**
51:35 of Babylon be **h** responsible
Lam 2:4 an opponent his right hand **h**
Eze 31:15 springs and **h** back
Hos 12:3 Their ancestor Jacob **h** on to
Jnh 2:6 where bars **h** me forever.
Mat 12:13 The man **h** it out, and it
23:35 As a result, you will be **h**
23:36 The people living now will be **h**
Mar 3:5 The man **h** it out, and his hand
6:19 So Herodias **h** a grudge against
Luk 5:29 Levi **h** a large reception at his
11:51 will be **h** responsible for this.
11:53 the scribes and the Pharisees **h**
Jon 2:6 Each jar **h** 18 to 27 gallons.
19:29 on a hyssop stick and **h**
Act 5:3 You've **h** back some of the
17:17 He **h** discussions in the
17:17 He also **h** discussions every
19:9 He took his disciples and **h**
25:21 He asked to be **h** in prison and
25:21 So I ordered him to be **h** in
27:32 the soldiers cut the ropes that **h**
27:40 they untied the ropes that **h**
1Co 11:27 way will be **h** responsible
2Ti 4:16 that it won't be **h** against them.
Jud 1:6 He **h** angels for judgment on
1:6 They were **h** in darkness,
Rev 1:16 his right hand he **h** seven stars,
5:8 Each **h** a harp and a gold bowl
6:5 and its rider **h** a scale.
9:14 the four angels who are **h** at
10:2 He **h** a small, opened scroll in
17:1 One of the seven angels who **h**

Heldai (2)

1Ch 27:15 by **H** from Netophah.
Zec 6:10 an offering from the exiles **H**,

Heleb (1)

2Sm 23:29 **H** (son of Baanah) from

Helech (1)

Eze 27:11 "'People from Arvad and **H**

Heled (1)

1Ch 11:30 Maharai from Netophah, **H** (son

Helek (2)

Num 26:30 family of Iezer, the family of **H**,
Jos 17:2 **H**, Asriel, Shechem, Hepher,

Helem (1)

Zec 6:14 crown will be a reminder to **H**,

Helem's (1)

1Ch 7:35 His brother **H** sons were

Heleph (1)

Jos 19:33 Their border starts from **H** at

Helez (5)

2Sm 23:26 **H** the Paltite, Ira (son of Ikkesh)
1Ch 2:39 Azariah was the father of **H**.
2:39 **H** was the father of Eleasah.
11:27 from Harod, **H** the Pelonite,
27:10 **H**, a Pelonite from the

Heliopolis (2)

Isa 19:18 of the cities will be called **H**.
Eze 30:17 The young men from **H** and

Helkai (1)

Neh 12:15 Harim, Adna; from Meraioth, **H**;

Helkath (2)

Jos 19:25 Their territory included **H**,
21:31 **H**, and Rehob.

hell (35)

Dtr 32:22 that will burn to the depths of **h**.
Job 11:8 deeper than ⌊the depths⌋ of **h**.
Psa 49:14 Like sheep, they are driven to **h**
49:15 me back from the power of **h**
86:13 me from the depths of **h**.
139:8 If I make my bed in **h**,
Pro 5:5 Her steps lead straight to **h**.
7:27 Her home is the way to **h** and
9:18 guests are in the depths of **h**.
15:24 to turn him away from **h** below.
23:14 you will save his soul from **h**.
27:20 **H** and decay are never
Mat 5:29 to have all of it thrown into **h**.
5:30 than to have all of it go into **h**.
10:28 both body and soul in **h**.
11:23 No, you will go down to **h**!
16:18 And the gates of **h** will not
23:15 twice as fit for **h** as you are.
23:33 escape being condemned to **h**?
Mar 9:43 to have two hands and go to **h**,
9:45 two feet and be thrown into **h**.
9:47 two eyes and be thrown into **h**.
9:48 In **h** worms that eat the body
Luk 10:15 No, you will go to **h**!
12:5 you into **h** after killing you.
16:23 He went to **h**, where he was
Gal 1:8 you should be condemned to **h**,
1:9 should be condemned to **h**.
Jas 3:6 and is itself set on fire from **h**.
2Pe 2:4 He threw them into **h**,
Jud 1:23 them from the fire ⌊of **h**⌋.
Rev 1:18 I have the keys of death and **h**.
6:8 **H** followed him. They were
20:13 Death and **h** gave up their dead.
20:14 Death and **h** were thrown into

hellfire (2)

Mat 5:22 a fool will answer for it in **h**.
18:9 two eyes and be thrown into **h**.

hello (1)

Mat 26:49 "**H**, Rabbi!" and kissed him.

helmet (7)

1Sm 17:5 He had a bronze **h** on his head,
17:38 he put a bronze **h** on David's
Psa 60:7 Ephraim is the **h** on my head.
108:8 Ephraim is the **h** on my head.
Isa 59:17 like a coat of armor and a **h**
Eph 6:17 Also take salvation as your **h**
1Th 5:8 the hope of salvation as a **h**.

helmets (5)

2Ch 26:14 spears, **h**, armor, bows,
Jer 46:4 positions, and put on your **h**.
Eze 23:24 and large shields and with **h**.
27:10 their shields and **h** inside you.
38:5 will have shields and **h**.

Helon (5)

Num 1:9 Eliab, son of **H**, from the tribe of
2:7 of Zebulun is Eliab, son of **H**.
7:24 of Zebulun, Eliab, son of **H**,
7:29 the gifts from Eliab, son of **H**.
10:16 Eliab, son of **H**,

help (405)

Gen 21:1 The LORD came to **h** Sarah
21:18 Come on, **h** the boy up!
49:24 limber because of the **h**
Exo 1:16 "When you **h** the Hebrew
2:23 and their cries for **h** went up to
4:12 Now go, and I will **h** you speak
4:15 I will **h** both of you speak,
13:19 will definitely come to **h** you.
18:22 yourself by letting them **h** you.
23:5 Be sure to **h** him with his
31:6 from the tribe of Dan, to **h** him.
36:1 They will do this with the **h** of
Lev 11:47 These instructions **h** you
14:57 **h** you distinguish between
19:31 psychics or mediums to get **h**.
25:35 cannot support himself, **h** him.
26:23 "If this discipline does not **h**
Num 1:4 man from each tribe will **h** you.
1:5 of the men who will **h** you:
11:17 They will **h** you take care of
18:2 tribe to join you and **h** you
18:6 among the Israelites to **h** you.
Dtr 1:38 because he will **h** Israel take
3:28 and he will **h** them take
18:11 ask ghosts or spirits for **h**,
22:4 Make sure you **h** him get it
22:24 in a city and didn't scream for **h**.
22:27 She may have screamed for **h**,
31:7 You will **h** them take
32:30 and the LORD gave them no **h**.
32:38 Let them come to **h** you!
33:7 **H** them against their enemies."
33:26 through the heavens to **h** you.
Jos 1:6 because you will **h** these
1:14 You must **h** your relatives
10:4 "Come, **h** me destroy Gibeon
10:6 **H** us because all the Amorite
10:33 Gezer had come to **h** Lachish.
Jdg 3:9 cried out to the LORD for **h**.
3:13 and the Amalekites to **h** him,
3:15 cried out to the LORD for **h**.
4:3 cried out to the LORD for **h**.
5:23 did not come to **h** the LORD,
5:23 to **h** the LORD and his heroes."
6:6 and cried out to the LORD for **h**.
6:7 cried out to the LORD for **h**
7:23 and all Manasseh to **h** pursue
7:24 were also summoned to **h**.
8:8 the people there for the same **h**.
10:10 cried out to the LORD for **h**.
10:12 you cried out to me for **h**.
10:14 Cry out for **h** to the gods you
12:2 I asked you for **h**, but you didn't
18:22 together to **h** him catch up
Rut 1:6 had come to **h** his people
1Sm 7:12 Ebenezer [Rock of H] and said,
12:21 They can't **h** or rescue you,
14:45 done this with God's **h** today."
2Sm 8:5 came to **h** King Hadadezer
10:11 my ⌊troops⌋, be ready to **h** me.
10:11 ⌊troops⌋, I'll come to **h** you.
10:19 to **h** the Ammonites anymore.
14:4 "**H** ⌊me⌋, Your Majesty,"
15:34 then you'll ⌊**h** me by⌋ undoing
18:3 to send us **h** from the city."
21:17 of Zeruiah, came to **h** David.
22:7 I called to my God for **h**.
22:7 my cry for **h** reached his ears.
22:36 Your **h** makes me great.
1Ki 8:28 Listen to my cry for **h** as I pray
2Ki 6:26 to him, "**H** me, Your Majesty!"
6:27 "If the LORD doesn't **h** you,
6:27 help you, how can I **h** you?
6:33 longer for the LORD ⌊to **h** us⌋?"
14:26 No slave or free person could **h**
15:19 and **h** strengthen his hold
23:29 (the king of Egypt) came to **h**
1Ch 5:20 and received **h** while fighting
12:17 "If you've come to **h** me as
12:18 Success to those who **h** you,
12:19 (However, David didn't **h** the
12:22 day, men came to **h** David until
18:5 came to **h** King Hadadezer
19:12 my ⌊troops⌋, be ready to **h** me.
19:12 for your ⌊troops⌋, I'll **h** you.
19:19 willing to **h** the Ammonites.
22:17 of Israel to **h** his son Solomon.
23:32 place and to **h** their relatives,
2Ch 6:19 Listen to my cry for **h** as I pray
14:11 you who can **h** those who are
14:11 **H** us, LORD our God,
16:12 of asking the LORD for **h**,
19:2 "Why do you **h** wicked people
20:3 to ask for the LORD's **h**.
20:4 gathered to seek the LORD's **h**.
25:8 God has the power to **h** you
25:20 sought **h** from Edom's gods.)
28:16 time King Ahaz sent for **h** from
28:21 But that didn't **h** him.
28:23 to them so that they will **h** me."
29:34 But the priests needed more **h**
32:8 our God is on our side to **h**
Ezr 2:68 to **h** rebuild God's temple
4:2 They told them, "We want to **h**
6:8 decree about how you must **h**
8:22 armed escort with cavalry to **h**
Neh 3:12 with the **h** of his daughters.
6:16 this work with the **h** of our God.
13:13 of Mattaniah to **h** them.
Est 4:14 someone else will **h** and
Job 5:4 His children are far from **h**.
5:8 "But I would seek God's **h** and
7:13 My bed may **h** me bear my
15:3 argue with words that don't **h**,
15:3 with speeches that don't **h**
19:7 Indeed, I cry, '**H**! I'm being
19:7 I call for **h**, but there is no
20:10 will have to ask the poor for **h**.
24:12 Wounded people cry for **h**,
29:12 the poor who called ⌊for **h**⌋
29:12 who had no one to **h** them.
30:13 is there to **h** me against them.
30:20 "I call to you for **h**,
30:24 calls for **h** in his disaster.
30:28 up in public and call for **h**.
31:16 eyes stop ⌊looking for **h**⌋,
35:9 people makes them call for **h**.
36:13 They don't even call for **h** when
36:19 Will all your mighty strength **h**
Psa 5:2 Pay attention to my cry for **h**,
9:10 those who seek your **h**.
12:1 **H**, O LORD. No godly person is
14:2 anyone who seeks **h** from God.
18:6 I cried to my God for **h**.
18:6 my cry for **h** reached his ears.
18:41 They cried out for **h**,
20:2 He will send you **h** from his
22:11 and there is no one to **h**.
22:19 Come quickly to **h** me,
22:24 person cried out to him for **h**.
27:9 You have been my **h**.
28:2 mercy when I call to you for **h**,
28:7 trusted him, so I received **h**.
30:2 I cried out to you for **h**,
31:22 when I cried out to you for **h**.
33:17 cannot **h** someone escape.
33:20 He is our **h** and our shield.
34:4 I went to the LORD for **h**.
34:10 seek the LORD's **h** have all
34:15 His ears hear their cry for **h**.
35:2 small and large. Arise to **h** me.
38:22 Come quickly to **h** me,
39:12 Open your ear to my cry for **h**.
40:1 to me and heard my cry for **h**.
40:13 Come quickly to **h** me,
40:17 You are my **h** and my savior.

Psa 44:26 **H** us! Rescue us because of
46:1 an ever-present **h** in times of
46:5 God will **h** it at the break of
53:2 anyone who seeks **h** from God.
57:3 He sends his **h** from heaven
59:4 Wake up, and **h** me;
60:11 Give us **h** against the enemy
61:1 Listen to my cry for **h**,
63:7 You have been my **h**.
69:3 am exhausted from crying for **h**
69:6 let those who come to you for **h**
69:32 look to God for **h** be refreshed.
70:1 Come quickly to **h** me,
70:5 You are my **h** and my savior.
71:12 come quickly to **h** me.
72:12 needy person who cries for **h**
72:12 person who has no one's **h**.
77:2 I went to the Lord for **h**.
79:9 **H** us, O God, our savior, for the
80:14 Come to **h** this vine.
82:4 **H** them escape the power of
83:16 that they must look to you for **h**.
88:13 I cry out to you for **h**,
89:21 My hand is ready to **h** him.
94:17 LORD had not come to **h** me,
102:1 let my cry for **h** come to you.
106:4 Come to **h** me with your
106:44 when he heard their cry for **h**.
107:12 but no one was there to **h** them.
108:12 Give us **h** against the enemy
109:10 Let them seek **h** far from their
109:26 **H** me, O LORD my God.
119:27 **H** me understand your guiding
119:34 **H** me understand so that I can
119:73 **H** me understand so that I may
119:86 persecute me with lies. **H** me!
119:116 **H** me God, as you promised,
119:125 **H** me understand so that I may
119:144 **H** me understand ⌊them⌋ so
119:147 and I cried out for **h**.
119:169 Let my cry for **h** come into your
119:169 **H** me understand as you
119:173 Let your hand **h** me because I
119:175 Let your regulations **h** me.
121:1 Where can I find **h**?
121:2 My **h** comes from the LORD,
124:8 Our **h** is in the name of the
142:6 Pay attention to my cry for **h**
145:19 cries for **h** and saves them.
146:3 mortals who cannot **h** you.
146:5 are those who receive **h** from
Pro 9:12 your wisdom will **h** you.
11:4 Riches are of no **h** on the day
27:6 by a friend are intended to **h**,
28:17 No one will **h** him.
Ecc 4:10 If one falls, the other can **h** his
4:10 There is no one to **h** him get up.
7:19 Wisdom will **h** a wise person
7:19 than ten rulers can **h** a city.
Isa 8:19 "Ask for **h** from the mediums
8:19 ask their God for **h** instead?
8:19 ask the dead to **h** the living?
10:3 Where will you run for **h**?
15:8 Cries for **h** echo throughout the
20:6 We ran ⌊to Egypt⌋ for **h** to be
22:5 crying for **h** in the mountains.
23:17 the LORD will come to **h** Tyre.
30:5 that nation can't **h** them.
30:5 can't give aid or **h** to them.
30:6 to a nation that can't **h** them.
30:7 Egypt's **h** is completely
30:19 pity on you when you cry for **h**.
31:1 for those who go to Egypt for **h**,
31:2 those who **h** troublemakers.
31:3 one who gives **h** will stumble,
31:3 one who receives **h** will fall.
38:14 O Lord! Please **h** me!
41:6 People **h** their neighbors and
41:10 I will **h** you. I will support you
41:13 'Don't be afraid; I will **h** you.'
41:14 people of Israel, I will **h** you,"
44:2 in the womb, and will **h** you.
46:7 If they cry to it for **h**,
49:8 day of salvation I will **h** you.
57:12 but they won't **h** you.
57:13 When you cry for **h**,

Isa 58:7 Don't refuse to **h** your relatives.
58:9 You will cry for **h**, and he will
59:16 sees that there's no one to **h**.
63:5 I looked, but there was no **h**.
64:4 You **h** those who wait for you.
Jer 2:8 statues that couldn't **h** them.
2:11 something that doesn't **h** them.
7:8 It's a lie that cannot **h** you.
10:21 don't look to the LORD for **h**.
11:14 when they call to me for **h**
14:9 a strong man who cannot **h**?
14:12 I won't listen to their cries for **h**.
23:32 They don't **h** these people at
37:7 army has come out to **h** you.
38:4 is not trying to **h** these people;
47:4 might have escaped to get **h**.
50:32 and there will be no one to **h**
Lam 1:7 enemies with no one to **h** them.
3:8 Even when I cry and call for **h**,
3:25 anyone who seeks **h** from him.
3:56 Listen to my cry ⌊for **h**⌋.
4:17 trying in vain to find **h**.
Eze 13:9 They will not **h** my people
14:3 be allowed to ask me for **h**?
14:4 to a prophet ⌊to ask for my **h**⌋.
14:7 to a prophet to ask for my **h**,
14:10 you are when you ask for his **h**.
16:49 They didn't **h** the poor and the
17:17 Pharaoh will not be able to **h**
18:6 worship sites or look for **h** from
18:12 He looks to idols for **h**.
18:15 worship sites or look for **h** from
20:1 came to ask for the LORD's **h**.
20:3 you coming to ask me for **h**?
20:3 not be allowed to ask me for **h**.'
20:7 idols that you look to for **h**.
20:8 idols that they looked to for **h**.
20:24 disgusting idols for **h**.
20:31 you be allowed to ask me for **h**,
20:31 be allowed to ask me for **h**.
21:21 ask his household gods for **h**,
29:16 they turned to Egypt ⌊for **h**⌋.
33:25 You look to your idols for **h**.
39:14 With the **h** of others they will
Dan 9:3 God and looked to him for **h**.
10:13 came to **h** me because I was
11:17 But this will not succeed or **h**
11:33 "People who are wise will **h**
11:34 they will get a little **h**,
11:39 With the **h** of a foreign god,
11:45 there will be no one to **h** him."
Hos 4:12 ask their wooden idols for **h**.
5:13 to ask the great king for **h**.
7:10 your God or look to him for **h**.
7:11 Egypt and run to Assyria for **h**.
Joe 1:14 and cry to the LORD for **h**.
1:19 O LORD, I cry to you for **h**!
Amo 5:2 There is no one to **h** them.
9:4 on them and not **h** them.
Jnh 1:5 they cried to their gods for **h**.
1:14 So they cried to the LORD for **h**:
2:2 my ⌊watery⌋ grave I cried for **h**,
3:8 Cry loudly to God for **h**.
Nah 3:9 Put and the Lybians were her **h**.
Hab 1:2 long, O LORD, am I to cry for **h**,
Zep 1:6 the LORD or ask him for **h**."
Mat 8:5 officer came to beg him for **h**.
9:34 out of people with the **h**
12:24 only with the **h** of Beelzebul,
12:27 people with the **h** of Beelzebul,
12:28 if I force demons out with the **h**
15:25 down, and said, "Lord, **h** me!"
25:44 or in prison and didn't **h** you?'
26:53 legions of angels to **h** me now?
Mar 3:22 out of people with the **h**
7:11 have used to **h** them is corban
9:22 yourself in our place, and **h** us!"
9:24 **H** my lack of faith."
14:7 and can **h** them whenever you
Luk 1:54 "He remembered to **h** his
4:38 They asked Jesus to **h** her.
5:7 other boat to come and **h** them.
6:33 If you **h** those who help you,
6:33 If you help those who **h** you,
6:35 love your enemies, **h** them,
7:4 "He deserves your **h**.

Luk 10:37 was kind enough to **h** him."
10:40 by myself? Tell her to **h** me."
11:15 only with the **h** of Beelzebul,
11:19 out with the **h** of Beelzebul,
11:20 if I force out demons with the **h**
18:7 they cry out to him for **h** day
18:7 Is he slow to **h** them?
19:44 time when God came to **h** you."
Jon 6:21 So they were willing to **h**
Act 3:7 hand and began to **h** him up.
7:35 and to rule them with the **h**
7:45 They did this with Joshua's **h**
9:38 to Joppa! We need your **h**!"
11:29 whatever they could afford to **h**
12:20 They enlisted the **h** of Blastus
13:5 John Mark had gone along to **h**
16:9 "Come to Macedonia to **h** us."
18:27 kindness enabled him to **h**
20:20 you anything that would **h** you,
20:32 That message can **h** you grow
20:35 like this we should **h** the weak.
21:28 shouting, "Men of Israel, **h**!
27:34 Eating will **h** you survive,
Rom 12:8 in need, **h** them cheerfully.
15:25 going to Jerusalem to bring **h**
15:27 their earthly wealth to **h** them.
15:31 will accept the **h** I bring.
16:2 because she has provided **h** to
1Co 4:17 to you to **h** you remember my
9:13 Don't those who **h** at the altar
12:28 then those who **h** others,
13:3 none of these things will **h** me.
14:3 to people to **h** them grow,
14:5 he says to **h** the church grow.
14:12 so that you **h** the church grow.
14:17 it doesn't **h** other people grow.
14:26 be done to **h** each other grow.
2Co 1:11 since you are also joining to **h**
8:23 partner and coworker to **h** you.
9:2 know how willing you are to **h**,
10:8 gave us this authority to **h** you,
10:15 of us to give us the **h** we need
11:9 I didn't bother any of you for **h**.
12:13 that I didn't bother you for **h**?
12:14 and I won't bother you for **h**.
13:4 we will live for you with his **h**.
13:8 the truth but only to **h** the truth.
13:10 gave us this authority to **h** you,
Gal 6:1 should **h** that person turn
6:2 **H** carry each other's burdens.
Eph 4:29 that you can give **h** wherever
4:29 That way, what you say will **h**
Php 1:19 through the **h** that comes from
1:25 This will **h** you to grow and be
2:25 personal representative to **h** me
2:30 up for the **h** you couldn't give
4:3 to **h** these women.
1Th 5:14 are discouraged, **h** the weak,
2Th 1:11 he will **h** you accomplish every
1:11 desire and **h** you do everything
1Ti 5:5 asking for his **h** night and day.
5:16 she should **h** them.
5:16 and can **h** widows who have
2Ti 1:14 With the **h** of the Holy Spirit
1:18 possible to **h** me in Ephesus.
2:7 The Lord will **h** you understand
Tit 3:1 them and be ready to **h** them
Heb 2:18 he is able to **h** others when
4:2 But the message didn't **h** those
4:16 which will **h** us at the right
6:10 and you continue to **h** them.
13:9 rules that don't **h** those who
1Pe 1:2 with the Spirit's **h** so that you
2:12 on the day he comes to **h** you.
1Jn 3:17 bother to **h** the other believer?
3Jn 1:7 and they didn't accept any **h**
Jud 1:20 Pray with the Holy Spirit's **h**.

helped (34)

Gen 41:51 because God **h** him forget all
Num 7:2 those tribal leaders who **h**
Jdg 9:24 Citizens of Shechem had **h**
1Sm 7:12 "Until now the LORD has **h** us."
1Ki 2:7 They **h** me when I was fleeing
2Ki 10:15 Jehu **h** him up into the chariot.
1Ch 12:21 They **h** David fight raiding

1Ch 15:26 Because God **h** the Levites
2Ch 18:31 cried out, the LORD **h** him.
20:23 they **h** destroy one another.
26:7 God **h** him when he attacked
29:34 So their relatives, the Levites, **h**
32:3 the city. They **h** him do it.
Job 26:2 "You have **h** the person who
Psa 83:8 They **h** the descendants of Lot.
86:17 have **h** me and comforted me.
118:13 but the LORD **h** me.
Isa 1:2 children and **h** them grow,
Jer 2:37 You will not be **h** by them."
Mat 23:30 we would not have **h** to murder
Mar 1:31 took her hand, and **h** her get up.
5:26 she had not been **h** at all.
9:27 Jesus took his hand and **h** him
Luk 19:35 and **h** Jesus onto it.
Act 9:8 Saul was **h** up from the ground.
9:36 She always **h** people and gave
9:41 Peter took her hand and **h** her
18:28 In public Apollos **h** them by
21:8 seven men who **h** the apostles.
1Co 3:5 They are servants who **h** you
2Co 6:2 the day of salvation I **h** you."
Php 1:12 what happened to me has **h**
Heb 6:10 You **h** his holy people,
Rev 12:16 The earth **h** the woman by

helper (19)

Gen 2:18 I will make a **h** who is right for
2:20 But the man found no **h** who
Exo 18:4 was Eliezer [My God Is a **H**],
18:4 "My father's God was my **h**.
Psa 10:14 have been the **h** of orphans.
30:10 O LORD, be my **h**!
54:4 God is my **h**! The Lord is the
115:9 He is your **h** and your shield.
115:10 He is your **h** and your shield.
115:11 He is your **h** and your shield.
118:7 LORD is on my side as my **h**.
Hos 13:9 You are against me, your **h**.
Jon 14:16 and he will give you another **h**
14:17 That **h** is the Spirit of Truth.
14:26 However, the **h**, the Holy Spirit,
15:26 "The **h** whom I will send to you
15:26 This **h**, the Spirit of Truth who
16:7 the **h** won't come to you.
Heb 13:6 "The Lord is my **h**.

helpers (2)

Job 9:13 Even Rahab's **h** bow humbly in
Act 19:22 So he sent two of his **h**,

helpful (4)

Rut 2:10 "Why are you so **h**?
1Co 6:12 but not everything is **h**.
10:23 but not everything is **h**.
2Co 8:10 because it will be **h** to you.

helping (10)

1Sm 4:20 the women **h** her said,
1Ch 12:18 because your God is **h** you."
2Ch 28:23 of the kings of Aram are **h** them.
Job 8:20 of integrity or give a **h** hand
Psa 22:1 Why are you so far away from **h**
Act 26:22 "God has been **h** me to this
Rom 12:8 If it is **h** people in need,
2Co 9:1 anything further to you about **h**
1Ti 5:10 needs, **h** the suffering,
Heb 2:16 rather than **h** angels.

helpless (9)

Dtr 32:10 them because they were **h**.
Job 6:13 Am I not completely **h**?
Psa 41:1 who has concern for **h** people.
79:8 because we are **h**.
Dan 10:8 deathly pale, and I was **h**.
10:16 overwhelmed me, and I'm **h**.
Mat 5:3 recognize they are spiritually **h**.
9:36 They were troubled and **h** like
Rom 5:6 while we were still **h**,

helps (23)

Gen 41:51 Manasseh [He **H** Me Forget],
49:25 God of your father who **h** you,
Dtr 33:29 He is a shield that **h** you and a
2Sm 23:5 everything that **h** me,
Psa 37:40 The LORD **h** them and rescues
119:130 it **h** gullible people understand.
Pro 11:17 A merciful person **h** himself,
16:21 sweetly **h** others learn.
16:23 what he says **h** others learn.
31:12 She **h** him and never harms
Isa 40:11 He gently **h** the sheep and their
50:7 The Almighty LORD **h** me.
50:9 The Almighty LORD **h** me.
Mat 12:27 who **h** your followers force
Luk 11:18 Beelzebul **h** me force demons
11:19 who **h** your followers force
Rom 8:26 the same time the Spirit also **h**
1Co 14:4 he **h** himself grow.
14:4 he **h** the church grow.
1Ti 4:8 Training the body **h** a little,
4:8 but godly living **h** in every way.
Tit 3:8 is good and **h** other people.
Heb 2:16 So Jesus **h** Abraham's

hem (7)

Exo 28:33 All around the **h** of the robe
28:34 all around the **h** of the robe.
39:24 On the **h** of the robe they made
39:25 all around the **h** of the robe.
39:26 a pomegranate all around the **h**
1Sm 15:27 Saul grabbed the **h** of his robe,
Eze 5:3 them in the **h** of your clothes.

Hemam (1)

Gen 36:22 sons of Lotan were Hori and **H**.

Heman (15)

1Ki 4:31 Ezrahite, or **H**, Calcol, or Darda,
1Ch 2:6 **H**, Calcol, and Dara — five in all.
6:33 The musician **H** was from
6:33 **H** was the son of Joel,
15:17 So the Levites appointed **H**,
15:19 The musicians **H**, Asaph,
16:41 and his relatives were **H**,
16:42 Also, **H** and Jeduthun played
25:1 the sons of Asaph, **H**,
25:4 the sons of **H** were Bukkiah,
25:5 the sons of the king's seer **H**.
25:5 So God gave **H** 14 sons and 3
25:6 Asaph, Jeduthun, and **H**.
2Ch 5:12 Asaph, **H**, Jeduthun, their sons,
35:15 places as David, Asaph, **H**,

Heman's (3)

1Ch 6:39 **H** relative Asaph stood on his
6:44 one of **H** relatives descended
2Ch 29:14 From **H** descendants were

Hemdan (1)

Gen 36:26 **H**, Eshban, Ithran, and Cheran.

hemorrhoids (3)

Dtr 28:27 He will strike you with **h**,
1Sm 6:11 models of their **h** on the cart.
6:17 The gold **h** which the

hen (3)

Zec 6:14 and **H** (son of Zephaniah) in the
Mat 23:37 the way a **h** gathers her chicks
Luk 13:34 the way a **h** gathers her chicks

Hena (3)

2Ki 18:34 of Sepharvaim, **H**, and Ivvah?
19:13 of Sepharvaim, **H**, and Ivvah?'"
Isa 37:13 of Sepharvaim, **H**, and Ivvah?'"

Henadad (1)

Neh 10:9 Binnui (of the sons of **H**),

Henadad's (3)

Ezr 3:9 descendants joined **H** family
Neh 3:18 This included Binnui, **H** son,
3:24 After him Binnui, **H** son, made

henna (3)

Sos 1:14 My beloved is a bouquet of **h**
4:13 **h** flowers and nard,
7:11 the night among the **h** flowers.

Hepher (9)

Num 26:32 and the family of **H**.
26:33 (Zelophehad, son of **H**,
27:1 son of **H**, grandson of Gilead,
Jos 12:17 king of Tappuah, the king of **H**,
17:2 Shechem, **H**, and Shemida.
17:3 Zelophehad, son of **H**,
1Ki 4:10 and the entire region of **H**.
1Ch 4:6 **H**, Temeni, and Haahashtari.
11:36 **H** the Mecherathite,

Hephzibah (1)

2Ki 21:1 His mother's name was **H**.

herald (1)

Dan 3:4 The **h** called out loudly,

herb (1)

Luk 11:42 and every garden **h**.

herbs (3)

Exo 12:8 bitter **h** and unleavened bread.
Num 9:11 unleavened bread and bitter **h**.
Sos 5:13 that produces scented **h**.

herd (12)

Gen 18:7 Then Abraham ran to the **h** and
32:16 servants in charge of each **h**.
Dtr 16:2 animal from your flock or **h** as
Jdg 6:25 a bull from your father's **h**,
Psa 68:30 the **h** of bulls with the calves of
Mat 8:30 A large **h** of pigs was feeding
8:31 send us into that **h** of pigs."
8:32 Suddenly, the whole **h** rushed
Mar 5:11 A large **h** of pigs was feeding
5:13 The **h** of about two thousand
Luk 8:32 A large **h** of pigs was feeding
8:33 Then the **h** rushed down the

herders (5)

Gen 13:7 broke out between Abram's **h**
13:7 Abram's herders and Lot's **h**.
13:8 between us or between our **h**.
26:20 The **h** from Gerar quarreled
26:20 Gerar quarreled with Isaac's **h**,

herding (2)

Jdg 3:31 a sharp stick used for **h** oxen.
Amo 7:15 the LORD took me away from **h**

herds (28)

Gen 26:14 many flocks, **h**, and servants,
30:40 So he made separate **h** for
32:16 a distance between the **h**."
32:19 the others who followed the **h**.
33:14 and gently guide the **h** that are
45:10 as well as your flocks, your **h**,
46:32 brought their flocks and **h**
46:34 'We have taken care of **h** all
47:1 **h**, and everything they have.
Exo 10:9 our flocks and **h** with us.
10:24 flocks and **h** must stay behind."
12:32 Take your flocks and **h**,
34:3 Even the flocks and **h** may not
Num 11:22 flocks and **h** were butchered
Dtr 7:13 will bless your **h** with calves,
8:13 Your **h** and flocks,
12:21 slaughter an animal from the **h**
15:19 firstborn male from your **h**
28:51 no calves from your **h**,
Jos 22:8 large **h** of livestock,
1Ch 27:29 for the **h** grazing in Sharon:
27:29 Shitrai from Sharon for the **h** in
2Ch 26:10 because he had a lot of **h**
Pro 27:23 pay close attention to your **h**.
Ecc 2:7 I owned more **h** and flocks than
Jer 3:24 worked for, their flocks and **h**,
49:32 Their large **h** will be taken as
Joe 1:18 **H** of cattle wander around

here I am (18)

Gen 22:1 "Yes, **h**!" he answered.
24:13 **H** standing by the spring,
27:1 Esau answered, "**H**.
31:11 And I answered, 'Yes, **h**.'

Gen 46:2 "**H**," he answered.
Exo 3:4 Moses answered, "**H**!"
Num 11:21 Moses said, "**H** with 600,000
1Sm 3:4 called Samuel. "**H**," Samuel
3:5 Eli and said, "**H**. You called me
3:6 Eli, and said, "**H**. You called me
3:8 Eli, and said, "**H**. You called me
3:16 my son!" he said. "**H**," he
12:3 **H**. Testify against me in front of
Isa 6:8 I said, "**H**. Send me!"
52:6 I am the one who says, "**H**!"
58:9 and he will say, "**H**!"
65:1 I said, "**H**! Here I am!" to a nation
65:1 I said, "Here I am! **H**!" to a nation

Heres (1)

Jdg 8:13 the battle through the **H** Pass

Heresh (1)

1Ch 9:15 Bakbakkar, **H**, Galal,

Hereth (1)

1Sm 22:5 David went to the forest of **H**.

Hermas (1)

Rom 16:14 Phlegon, Hermes, Patrobas, **H**,

Hermes (2)

Act 14:12 as Zeus and Paul as **H**
Rom 16:14 Greet Asyncritus, Phlegon, **H**,

Hermogenes (1)

2Ti 1:15 including Phygelus and **H**.

Hermon (15)

Dtr 3:8 the Arnon Valley to Mount **H**.
3:9 (The Sidonians call Mount **H**
4:48 Mount Siyon (that is, Mount **H**).
Jos 11:3 the foot of Mount **H** in Mizpah.
11:17 Valley at the foot of Mount **H**.
12:1 the Arnon Valley to Mount **H**,
12:5 He ruled Mount **H**, Salecah,
13:5 Baal Gad at the foot of Mount **H**
13:11 and Maacath, all of Mount **H**,
1Ch 5:23 Hermon, Senir, and Mount **H**.
Psa 42:6 on the peaks of **H**,
89:12 Mount Tabor and Mount **H** sing
133:3 It is like dew on ⌊Mount⌋ **H**,
Sos 4:8 mountain peaks in Senir and **H**,
Eze 27:5 from pine trees on Mount **H**.

hero (4)

1Sm 17:51 saw their **h** had been killed,
Psa 52:1 the evil you've done, you **h**?
Pro 16:32 get angry slowly than to be a **h**.
Zep 3:17 He is a **h** who saves you.

Herod (59)

Mat 2:1 in Judea when **H** was king.
2:3 When King **H** and all
2:7 Then **H** secretly called the
2:12 in a dream not to go back to **H**.
2:13 because **H** intends to search
2:15 He stayed there until **H** died.
2:16 When **H** saw that the wise men
2:19 After **H** was dead, an angel of
2:22 succeeded his father **H** as king
14:1 At that time **H**, ruler of Galilee,
14:3 **H** had arrested John,
14:3 **H** did this for Herodias,
14:4 John had been telling **H**,
14:5 So **H** wanted to kill John.
14:6 When **H** celebrated his
14:6 **H** was so delighted with her
Mar 6:14 King **H** heard about Jesus,
6:16 But when **H** heard about it,
6:17 **H** had sent men who had
6:17 **H** did that for Herodias,
6:18 John had been telling **H**,
6:20 because **H** was afraid of John.
6:20 **H** knew that John was a fair
6:21 **H** gave a dinner for his top
6:22 **H** and his guests were
8:15 Pharisees and the yeast of **H**!"
Luk 1:5 When **H** was king of Judea,
3:1 **H** ruled Galilee, and his brother
Luk 3:19 spoke out against the ruler **H**
3:19 because **H** had married his
3:19 He also spoke out against **H**
3:20 So **H** added one more evil to all
9:7 **H** the ruler heard about
9:9 **H** said, "I had John's head cut
9:9 So **H** wanted to see Jesus.
13:31 **H** wants to kill you."
23:7 he sent Jesus to **H**.
23:7 **H** ruled Galilee and was in
23:8 **H** was very pleased to see
23:9 **H** asked Jesus many
23:11 **H** and his soldiers treated
23:12 So **H** and Pilate became
23:15 Neither could **H**. So he sent this
Act 4:27 "In this city **H** and Pontius
12:1 About that time King **H** devoted
12:4 After capturing Peter, **H** had
12:4 **H** wanted to bring Peter to trial
12:6 The night before **H** was going
12:11 his angel to rescue me from **H**
12:19 **H** searched for Peter but
12:19 Then **H** left Judea and went to
12:20 **H** was very angry with the
12:20 were going to meet with **H**.
12:20 the help of Blastus to ask **H**
12:20 their cities depended on **H**
12:21 **H**, wearing his royal clothes,
12:23 an angel from the Lord killed **H**
12:23 **H** was eaten by maggots,
13:1 friend of **H** since childhood),

Herodias (4)

Mat 14:3 Herod did this for **H**,
Mar 6:17 Herod did that for **H**,
6:19 So **H** held a grudge against
Luk 3:19 his own sister-in-law, **H**.

Herodias' (2)

Mat 14:6 **H** daughter danced for his
Mar 6:22 **H** daughter, came in and

Herodion (1)

Rom 16:11 Greet **H**, who is Jewish by

Herod's (6)

Mat 22:16 to him along with **H** followers.
Mar 3:6 and with **H** followers they
6:21 finally came on **H** birthday.
12:13 and some of **H** followers
Luk 8:3 was **H** administrator; Susanna;
Act 23:35 Paul under guard in **H** palace

heroes (5)

Jdg 5:23 to help the LORD and his **h**."
Ecc 9:11 fast runners, or the battle by **h**.
Isa 3:2 will take their⌋ **h** and soldiers,
5:22 who are **h** at drinking wine,
33:7 **H** cry in the streets.

heroic (11)

1Ki 15:23 else about Asa — all his **h** acts,
16:5 he did and his **h** acts — written
16:27 he did and his **h** acts — written
22:45 about Jehoshaphat — the **h** acts
2Ki 10:34 all his **h** acts — written in the
13:8 his **h** acts — written in the
13:12 his **h** acts when he fought
14:15 his **h** acts when he fought
14:28 his **h** acts when he fought,
20:20 all his **h** acts and how he made
Psa 24:8 The LORD, **h** in battle!

herons (5)

Lev 11:19 storks, all types of **h**,
Dtr 14:18 storks, all types of **h**,
Isa 14:23 become the possession of **h**.
34:11 Pelicans and **h** will take
Zep 2:14 Even pelicans and **h** will nest

Heshbon (38)

Num 21:25 including **H** and all its villages,
21:26 **H** was the city of King Sihon of
21:27 the poets say: "Come to **H**!
21:28 Fire came out of **H**,
21:30 From **H** to Dibon they all died.
Num 21:34 the Amorites, who ruled in **H**."
32:3 **H**, Elealeh, Sebam, Nebo,
32:37 Reuben rebuilt the cities of **H**,
Dtr 1:4 of the Amorites, who ruled in **H**,
2:24 going to hand King Sihon of **H**,
2:26 messengers to King Sihon of **H**
2:30 But King Sihon of **H** wouldn't
3:2 the Amorites, who ruled in **H**."
3:6 as we did to King Sihon of **H**.
4:46 of the Amorites, who ruled in **H**.
29:7 King Sihon of **H** and King Og of
Jos 9:10 King Sihon of **H** and King Og of
12:2 Amorite king who lived in **H**.
12:5 to the border of King Sihon of **H**.
13:10 Sihon's capital was **H**.
13:17 It included **H** and all its cities
13:21 of the Amorites, who ruled in **H**.
13:26 It extended from **H** to Ramath
13:27 the kingdom of King Sihon of **H**.
21:39 **H**, and Jazer.
Jdg 11:19 Sihon ruled from **H**.
11:26 Israel has now lived in **H**,
1Ch 6:81 **H** with its pastureland,
Neh 9:22 the land of the king of **H**,
Sos 7:4 Your eyes are like pools in **H**,
Isa 15:4 **H** and Elealeh also cry out.
16:8 The fields of **H** and the
16:9 with my tears, **H** and Elealeh.
Jer 48:2 The people in **H** will plan
48:34 "The cry will be heard from **H**
48:45 exhausted in the shadow of **H**.
48:45 A fire will come out of **H** and a
49:3 Cry loudly, **H**, because Ai is

Heshmon (1)

Jos 15:27 Hazar Gaddah, **H**, Beth Pelet,

hesitate (3)

Job 30:10 distance from me and don't **h**
Pro 23:13 Do not **h** to discipline a child.
Act 10:20 Don't **h** to go with these men.

hesitated (1)

Gen 19:16 When he **h**, the men grabbed

hesitation (3)

Dtr 15:10 to give to them without any **h**.
Psa 119:60 Without any **h** I hurry to obey
Act 11:12 to go with them without any **h**.

Heth (2)

Gen 10:15 of Sidon his firstborn, then **H**,
1Ch 1:13 of Sidon his firstborn, then **H**,

Hethlon (2)

Eze 47:15 Sea all the way to **H**
48:1 It will extend from the road to **H**

Hezekiah (132)

2Ki 16:20 His son **H** succeeded him as
18:1 for three years when King **H**,
18:2 **H** was 25 years old when he
18:5 **H** trusted the LORD God of
18:5 the kings of Judah was like **H**.
18:14 Then King **H** of Judah sent this
18:14 Assyria demanded that King **H**
18:15 **H** gave him all the silver that
18:16 At that time **H** stripped ⌊the
18:16 ⌊Earlier⌋ **H** had them covered
18:17 to King **H** at Jerusalem.
18:18 When they called for King **H**,
18:19 He said to them, "Tell **H**,
18:22 worship and altars **H** got rid of.
18:29 Don't let **H** deceive you.
18:30 Don't let **H** get you to trust the
18:31 Don't listen to **H**, because this
18:32 Don't listen to **H** when he tries
18:37 went to **H** with their clothes
19:1 When King **H** heard the
19:3 "This is what **H** says:
19:9 sent messengers to **H**,
19:10 "Tell King **H** of Judah,
19:14 **H** took the letters from the
19:20 sent a message to **H**,
19:29 this will be a sign for you, **H**:
20:1 In those days **H** became sick

2Ki 20:2 **H** turned to the wall and prayed
20:5 "Go back and say to **H**,
20:8 **H** asked Isaiah, "What is the
20:10 **H** replied, "It's easy for the
20:12 sent letters and a present to **H**
20:12 he heard that **H** had been sick.
20:13 **H** was so happy with them that
20:13 **H** showed them everything in
20:14 came to King **H** and asked,
20:14 **H** answered, "They came to
20:15 **H** answered, "They saw
20:16 Isaiah said to **H**, "Hear the
20:19 **H** said to Isaiah, "The LORD's
20:20 Isn't everything else about **H**,
20:21 **H** lay down in death with his
21:3 that his father **H** had destroyed.
1Ch 3:13 Ahaz's son was **H**.
4:41 In the days of King **H** of Judah,
2Ch 28:27 His son **H** succeeded him as
29:1 **H** began to rule as king when
29:18 Then they went to King **H**.
29:20 in the morning **H** gathered
29:21 **H** told the priests, to sacrifice
29:27 Then **H** ordered the sacrificing
29:30 Then King **H** and the leaders
29:31 **H** said, "You have dedicated
29:36 **H** and all the people were
30:1 **H** sent a message to all Israel
30:18 **H** prayed for them:
30:20 The LORD listened to **H** and
30:22 **H** spoke encouraging words to
30:24 King **H** of Judah provided 1,000
31:2 **H** assigned the priests and the
31:8 When **H** and the leaders saw
31:9 **H** asked the priests and the
31:11 Then **H** told them to prepare
31:13 King **H** and Azariah,
31:20 This is what **H** did throughout
31:21 **H** incorporated Moses'
32:1 After everything **H** had done so
32:2 When **H** saw that Sennacherib
32:5 **H** worked hard. He rebuilt all
32:8 by what King **H** of Judah said.
32:9 he sent his officers to King **H** of
32:11 Isn't **H** misleading you and
32:12 Isn't this the same **H** who got
32:15 Don't let **H** deceive you or
32:16 LORD God and his servant **H**.
32:20 Then King **H** and the prophet
32:22 So the LORD saved **H** and the
32:23 presents to King **H** of Judah.
32:24 In those days **H** became sick
32:25 But **H** was conceited,
32:26 **H** and the people living in
32:27 **H** became richer and was
32:30 **H** was the one who stopped
32:30 **H** succeeded in everything he
32:32 Everything else about **H**,
32:33 **H** lay down in death with his
32:33 When **H** died, all of Judah and
33:3 that his father **H** had torn down.
Ezr 2:16 of Ater, that is, **H**: 98
Neh 7:21 of Ater, that is, **H**: 98
10:17 Ater, **H**, Azzur,
Pro 25:1 by the men of King **H** of Judah.
Isa 1:1 Uzziah, Jotham, Ahaz, and **H**.
36:2 to King **H** at Jerusalem.
36:4 He said to them, "Tell **H**,
36:7 worship and altars **H** got rid of.
36:7 **H** told Judah and Jerusalem,
36:14 Don't let **H** deceive you.
36:15 Don't let **H** get you to trust the
36:16 Don't listen to **H**, because this
36:18 Don't let **H** mislead you by
36:22 went to **H** with their clothes
37:1 When King **H** heard the
37:3 "This is what **H** says:
37:9 he again sent messengers to **H**,
37:10 "Tell King **H** of Judah,
37:14 **H** took the letter from the
37:21 sent a message to **H**,
37:30 this will be a sign for you, **H**:
38:1 In those days **H** became sick
38:2 **H** turned to the wall and prayed
38:5 "Go and say to **H**, 'This is
38:22 **H** asked, "What is the sign that
Isa 38:9 King **H** of Judah wrote this after
39:1 sent letters and a present to **H**.
39:1 He had heard that **H** had been
39:2 **H** was so happy with them that
39:2 **H** showed them everything in
39:3 came to King **H** and asked,
39:3 **H** answered, "They came to
39:4 **H** answered, "They saw
39:5 Isaiah said to **H**, "Hear the
39:8 **H** said to Isaiah, "The LORD's
Jer 15:4 son of **H**, did in Jerusalem.
26:18 at the time of Judah's King **H**
26:19 Did Judah's King **H** and all the
26:19 **H** feared the LORD and sought
Hos 1:1 and **H** were kings of Judah and
Mic 1:1 and **H** were kings of Judah.
Zep 1:1 of Amariah, son of **H**.
Mat 1:9 Ahaz the father of **H**,
1:10 **H** the father of Manasseh,

Hezekiah's (10)

2Ki 18:9 In **H** fourth year as king (which
18:10 Samaria was taken in **H** sixth
18:13 In **H** fourteenth year as king,
19:5 So King **H** men went to Isaiah.
1Ch 3:13 **H** son was Manasseh.
2Ch 32:17 **H** God cannot rescue his
32:26 anger on them during **H** time
32:31 everything that was in **H** heart
Isa 36:1 In **H** fourteenth year as king,
37:5 So King **H** men went to Isaiah.

Hezion (1)

1Ki 15:18 Tabrimmon and grandson of **H**.

Hezir (2)

1Ch 24:15 the seventeenth for **H**,
Neh 10:20 Magpiash, Meshullam, **H**,

Hezrai (1)

2Sm 23:35 **H** from Carmel, Paarai from

Hezro (1)

1Ch 11:37 **H** from Carmel, Naari (son of

Hezron (19)

Gen 46:9 Hanoch, Pallu, **H**, and Carmi.
46:12 of Perez were **H** and Hamul.
Exo 6:14 Hanoch, Pallu, **H**, and Carmi.
Num 26:6 the family of **H**, and the family
26:21 of Perez were the family of **H**
Jos 15:3 From there it goes to **H**,
Rut 4:18 Perez was the father of **H**.
4:19 **H** was the father of Ram.
1Ch 2:5 sons were **H** and Hamul.
2:9 sons born to **H** were Jerahmeel,
2:21 Afterwards, **H** slept with the
2:21 **H** had married her when he
2:24 After **H** died in Caleb
2:25 son of **H**) fathered Ram (his
4:1 **H**, Carmi, Hur, and Shobal.
5:3 Hanoch, Pallu, **H**, and Carmi.
Mat 1:3 Perez was the father of **H**,
1:3 **H** the father of Ram,
Luk 3:33 of Arni, son of **H**, son of Perez,

Hezron's (2)

1Ch 2:18 **H** son was Caleb. Caleb and his
2:24 **H** wife Abijah gave birth to

hid (40)

Gen 3:8 So they **h** from the LORD God
3:10 because I was naked, so I **h**."
Exo 2:2 beautiful he was and **h** him
2:12 the Egyptian to death and **h**
3:6 Moses **h** his face because he
Jos 6:17 her will live because she **h**
6:25 in Israel today because she **h**
8:9 sent them out, and they **h**.
10:16 The five kings ran away and **h**
Jdg 4:18 and she **h** him under a tent
9:5 survived because he **h**.
1Sm 13:6 hard-pressed, they **h** in caves,
20:19 So go to the place where you **h**
20:24 So David **h** in the countryside.
1Ki 18:13 Haven't you heard how I **h** 100
1Ki 18:13 I **h** 50 prophets in each cave
20:30 He came to the city and **h** in an
2Ki 6:29 but she **h** her son."
7:8 They went away and **h** them.
7:8 went away, and **h** them.
11:2 and in a bedroom she **h** him
1Ch 21:20 four sons who were with him **h**,
2Ch 22:11 she **h** Joash from Athaliah.
Job 10:13 your heart you **h** these things.
Psa 30:7 When you **h** your face,
35:7 For no reason they **h** their net
35:8 the net that they **h** catch them.
Isa 49:2 like a sharp sword and **h** me
49:2 a sharpened arrow and **h** me
54:8 I **h** my face from you for a
57:17 punished them, **h** ⌊from them⌋,
Jer 18:22 a pit to catch me and **h** snares
Eze 39:23 So I **h** my face from them and
39:24 and I **h** my face from them.
Dan 10:7 and they quickly **h** themselves.
Mat 25:18 and **h** his master's money.
25:25 So I **h** your two thousand
Act 1:9 A cloud **h** him so that they
Col 1:26 In the past God **h** this mystery,
Rev 6:15 and free people **h** themselves

Hiddai (1)

2Sm 23:30 **H** from the Gaash ravines,

hidden (66)

Dtr 29:29 Some things are **h**.
33:19 the treasures **h** in the sand."
Jos 2:4 the two men inside and **h** them.
1Sm 25:20 down a **h** mountain path when
2Sm 17:9 He has already **h** in one of the
18:13 wouldn't stay **h** from the king."
1Ki 18:4 Obadiah had **h** 100 prophets in
2Ki 4:27 The LORD has **h** the reason
11:3 but was **h** with her in the
2Ch 22:12 He was **h** in God's temple for
Job 3:23 whose paths have been **h**,
6:16 They are **h** by snow.
11:7 you discover God's **h** secrets,
12:22 He uncovers mysteries ⌊**h**⌋ in
14:13 and keep me **h** there until your
18:10 A rope is **h** on the ground for
28:11 they bring **h** treasures to light.
28:21 It is **h** from the eyes of every
28:21 **h** even from the birds in the air.
40:13 and cover their faces in the **h**
Psa 9:15 they have **h** ⌊to trap others⌋.
10:11 He has **h** his face.
19:6 Nothing is **h** from its heat.
19:12 Forgive my **h** faults.
22:24 He has not **h** his face from that
27:5 He keeps me **h** in his tent.
38:9 has not been **h** from you.
40:10 I have not **h** your mercy and
69:5 I am guilty are not **h** from you.
78:2 what has been **h** long ago,
81:7 I was **h** in thunder,
139:15 My bones were not **h** from you
142:3 ⌊My enemies⌋ have **h** a trap for
Pro 2:4 for it as if it were **h** treasure,
26:26 His hatred is deceitfully **h**,
Isa 29:14 intelligent people will be **h**."
30:20 will no longer be **h** from you.
40:27 "My way is **h** from the LORD,
42:22 trapped in pits and **h** in prisons.
45:3 dark places and **h** stockpiles.
45:15 are a God who has **h** himself.
48:6 **h** things that you do not know.
64:7 You have **h** your face from us.
65:16 They are **h** from my eyes.
Jer 16:17 Their wickedness can't be **h**;
36:26 had **h** Baruch and Jeremiah.
41:8 and honey **h** in the country."
Eze 28:3 no secret can be **h** from you.
Dan 2:22 He reveals deeply **h** things.
Oba 1:6 Even your **h** treasures will be
Hab 3:4 That is where his power is **h**.
Mat 5:14 A city cannot be **h** when it is
13:35 I will tell what has been **h**
Mar 4:22 There is nothing **h** that will not
Luk 8:17 There is nothing **h** that will not
9:45 The meaning was **h** from them

Luk 19:42 But now it is **h**, so you cannot
1Co 2:7 It is a wisdom that has been **h**,
4:5 will also bring to light what is **h**
2Co 4:3 it is **h** from those who are
Eph 3:9 kept it **h** in the past.
Col 2:3 God has **h** all the treasures of
3:3 have died, and your life is **h**
1Ti 5:25 aren't obvious can't remain **h**.
Rev 1:20 The **h** meaning of the seven
2:17 I will give some of the **h**

hide (80)

Gen 4:14 I have to **h** from you and
18:17 The LORD said, "I shouldn't **h**
Exo 2:3 When she couldn't **h** him any
Jos 2:16 **H** there for three days until they
7:19 Don't **h** anything from me."
8:12 and had them **h** between Bethel
Jdg 6:11 out wheat in a winepress to **h**
21:20 "**H** in the vineyards and
1Sm 3:17 "Please don't **h** anything from
3:17 you dead if you **h** anything
20:2 Why should my father **h** this
20:5 But let me go and **h** in the
1Ki 17:3 and **h** beside the Cherith River,
22:25 you go into an inner room to **h**."
2Ki 7:12 so they've left the camp to **h** in
2Ch 18:24 you go into an inner room to **h**."
Job 3:10 I came⌋ or **h** my eyes from
13:20 that I won't have to **h** from you:
13:24 Why do you **h** your face ⌊from
14:13 I wish you would **h** me in
23:6 Would he sue me and **h** behind
27:11 I will not **h** what the Almighty
34:22 where troublemakers can **h**.
40:13 **H** them completely in the dust,
41:7 Can you fill its **h** with harpoons
41:13 Who can skin its **h**?
Psa 10:1 Why do you **h** yourself in times
13:1 How long will you **h** your face
17:8 **H** me in the shadow of your
17:9 **H** me from wicked people who
27:9 Do not **h** your face from me.
31:20 You **h** them in the secret place
44:24 Why do you **h** your face?
51:9 **H** your face from my sins,
55:1 Do not **h** from my plea for
55:12 then I could **h** from him.
56:6 They attack, and then they **h**.
64:2 **H** me from the secret plots of
69:17 so do not **h** your face from me.
78:4 We will not **h** them from our
88:14 Why do you **h** your face from
89:46 Will you **h** yourself forever?
102:2 Do not **h** your face from me
104:29 You **h** your face, and they are
119:19 Do not **h** your commandments
139:11 If I say, "Let the darkness **h** me
140:3 Their lips **h** the venom of
143:7 Do not **h** your face from me,
Pro 1:11 Let's **h** to ambush innocent
22:3 foresee trouble and **h** ⌊from it⌋.
25:2 It is the glory of God to **h** things
27:12 people foresee trouble and **h**.
28:12 people **h** themselves.
28:28 wicked people rise, people **h**.
Isa 2:10 Go in among the rocks and **h**
3:9 don't even bother to **h** them.
16:3 **H** the fugitives. Don't betray the
26:20 **H** for a little while until his fury
29:15 who try to **h** their plans from
59:2 and your sins have made him **h**
Jer 16:17 They can't **h** anything from me.
23:24 "No one can **h** so that I can't
33:5 I will **h** my face from this city
36:19 "You and Jeremiah must **h**.
38:14 "Don't **h** anything from me."
38:25 Don't **h** anything from us,
49:8 **H** in deep caves, inhabitants of
49:10 They won't be able to **h**.
49:30 Find a place to **h**, declares the
50:2 Don't **h** anything. Say, 'Babylon
Eze 39:29 I will no longer **h** my face from
Amo 9:3 Even if they **h** on top of Mount
9:3 Even if they **h** from me at the
Mic 3:4 He will **h** his face from you at
Luk 8:47 woman saw that she couldn't **h**.
Rom 3:13 Their lips **h** the venom of
Heb 4:13 No creature can **h** from God.
11:23 Faith led Moses' parents to **h**
1Pe 2:16 Live as free people, but don't **h**
Rev 6:16 and **h** us from the face of the

hides (10)

Job 20:12 is sweet in his mouth and he **h**
34:29 If he **h** his face, who can see
Psa 10:9 He **h** there to catch oppressed
27:5 He **h** me in his shelter when
Pro 12:16 a sensible person **h** the insult.
12:23 ⌊discreetly⌋ **h** knowledge,
Ecc 6:4 The darkness then **h** its name.
Isa 8:17 I will wait for the LORD, who **h**
Luk 8:16 "No one lights a lamp and **h** it
11:33 "No one lights a lamp and **h** it

hiding (40)

Dtr 7:20 those who were **h** from you.
Jos 8:7 you come out of **h** and capture
8:13 and the other troops were **h**
8:19 The men who were **h** got up as
8:21 who had been **h** had captured
10:17 They are **h** in the cave at
10:27 cave where they had been **h**
Jdg 6:2 The Israelites made **h** places
16:9 Some men were **h** in the
1Sm 10:22 "He's **h** among the baggage."
14:11 out of the holes they were **h** in."
14:22 men of Israel who had been **h**
19:2 Go into **h**, and stay out of sight.
23:19 They said, "David is **h** with us
23:23 Watch and learn about all the **h**
23:23 places where he may be **h**,
26:1 "David is **h** at the hill of
2Ki 6:9 The Arameans are **h** there."
2Ch 22:9 him while he was **h** in Samaria.
Job 20:26 Total darkness waits in **h** for
24:4 people of the country go into **h**.
40:21 in a **h** place among reeds
Psa 10:8 From his **h** places he kills
10:9 He lies in his **h** place like a
17:12 lion crouching in **h** places.
18:11 made the darkness his **h** place,
32:7 You are my **h** place.
64:4 people from their **h** places.
119:114 You are my **h** place and my
Pro 1:18 They go into **h** only to lose
Sos 2:14 My dove, in the **h** places of the
Isa 4:6 refuge and **h** place from storms
28:15 and falsehood is our **h** place."
28:17 will wash away your **h** place.
32:2 the wind and a **h** place from
Jer 49:10 I will find their **h** places.
Lam 3:10 to ambush me, like a lion in **h**.
Mic 7:17 out of their **h** places trembling.
Mat 11:25 for **h** these things from wise
Luk 10:21 for **h** these things from wise

Hiel (1)

1Ki 16:34 In Ahab's time **H** from Bethel

Hierapolis (1)

Col 4:13 the people in Laodicea and **H**.

Higgaion (1)

Psa 9:16 of his own hands. **H** Selah

high (229)

Gen 6:15 75 feet wide, and 45 feet **h**.
7:17 that it rose **h** above the ground.
7:19 The water rose very **h** above
7:19 It covered all the **h** mountains
14:18 He was a priest of God Most **H**.
14:19 is Abram by God Most **H**,
14:20 Blessed is God Most **H**,
14:22 to the LORD God Most **H**,
34:12 give her as **h** as you want.
Exo 25:10 inches wide, and 27 inches **h**.
25:23 inches wide, and 27 inches **h**.
27:1 feet square, and 4 ½ feet **h**.
27:18 75 feet wide, and 7 ½ feet **h**,
30:2 inches square and 36 inches **h**.
37:1 inches wide, and 27 inches **h**.
37:10 inches wide, and 27 inches **h**.
37:25 inches square and 36 inches **h**.
38:1 ½ feet square and 4 ½ feet **h**.
38:18 30 feet long and 7 ½ feet **h**,
Num 24:16 knowledge from the Most **H**,
35:25 death of the **h** priest who was
35:28 until the death of the **h** priest.
35:32 before the death of the **h** priest.
Dtr 3:5 were fortified with **h** walls
12:2 sites on the **h** mountains,
26:19 Then he will place you **h**
28:1 God will place you **h** above all
28:52 all your cities until the **h**,
32:8 When the Most **H** gave nations
Jdg 9:7 he went to a **h** spot on Mount
2Sm 22:14 The Most **H** made his voice
22:17 He reached down from **h** above
22:34 me sure footing on **h** places.
1Ki 6:2 30 feet wide, and 45 feet **h**.
6:10 annex 7 ½ feet **h** alongside
6:20 30 feet wide, and 30 feet **h**.
6:26 Each was 15 feet **h**.
7:2 75 feet wide, and 45 feet **h**.
7:15 Each was 27 feet **h** and 18 feet
7:16 Each capital was 7 ½ feet **h**.
7:19 ⌊Each⌋ was six feet **h**.
7:23 It was round, 7 ½ feet **h**,
7:27 6 feet square and 4 ½ feet **h**.
7:32 Each wheel was two feet **h**.
8:13 have built you a **h** temple,
14:23 poles to worship on every **h** hill
2Ki 17:10 Asherah on every **h** hill
19:23 I'll ride up the **h** mountains,
25:17 One pillar was 27 feet **h** and
25:17 on it that was 4 ½ feet **h**.
2Ch 3:4 of the temple) and 30 feet **h**.
3:15 each pillar was 7 ½ feet ⌊**h**⌋.
4:1 30 feet wide, and 15 feet **h**.
4:2 It was round, 7 ½ feet **h**,
6:2 But I have built you a **h** temple,
6:13 ½ feet wide, and 4 ½ feet **h**.
33:14 and he built it very **h**.
Ezr 6:3 It should be 90 feet **h** and 90
Neh 9:5 and lifted **h** above all blessing
Est 5:14 "Have a pole set up, 75 feet **h**,
Job 5:11 He places lowly people up **h**.
21:22 Can anyone judge the Most **H**?
22:12 "Isn't God **h** above in the
22:12 Look how **h** the highest stars
25:2 He establishes peace in his **h**
31:2 from the Almighty on **h**?
35:5 the clouds **h** above you.
39:27 your order that the eagle flies **h**
41:34 It looks down on all **h** things.
Psa 3:3 You hold my head **h**.
7:7 Take your seat **h** above them.
7:17 the name of the LORD Most **H**.
9:2 to praise your name, O Most **H**.
18:13 The Most **H** made his voice
18:16 He reached down from **h** above
18:33 me sure footing on **h** places.
21:7 the mercy of the Most **H**,
27:5 He sets me **h** on a rock.
46:4 place where the Most **H** lives.
47:2 fear the LORD, the Most **H**.
50:14 keep your vows to the Most **H**.
57:2 I call to God Most **H**,
57:10 because your mercy is as **h** as
61:2 to the rock that is **h** above me.
62:4 force him out of his **h** position.
66:17 **H** praise was on my tongue.
68:29 temple **h** above Jerusalem.
73:11 the Most **H** know anything?"
77:10 of the Most **H** is no longer
78:17 the desert against the Most **H**.
78:35 the Most **H** was their defender.
78:56 They tested God Most **H** and
78:69 place to be like the **h** heavens,
82:6 You are all sons of the Most **H**.
83:2 hate you hold their heads **h**.
83:18 You alone are the Most **H** God
87:5 The Most **H** will make it
89:13 Your right hand is lifted **h**.
89:27 He will be the Most **H** to the
89:42 the right hand of his enemies **h**
91:1 of the Most **H** will remain

Psa 91:9 made the Most **H** your home.
92:1 to praise your name, O Most **H**.
97:9 You, O LORD, the Most **H**,
99:2 He is **h** above all people.
102:19 from his holy place **h** above.
103:11 As **h** as the heavens are above
104:18 The **h** mountains are for wild
107:11 the advice given by the Most **H**.
107:23 who do business on the **h**
107:25 and it made the waves rise **h**.
107:41 But now he lifts needy people **h**
110:7 He will hold his head **h**.
113:4 The LORD is **h** above all the
113:5 He is seated on his **h** throne.
118:16 hand of the LORD is held **h**.
138:6 though the LORD is **h** above,
139:6 It is so **h** I cannot reach it.
148:13 his name is **h** above all others.
149:6 Let the **h** praises of God be in
Pro 8:2 takes its stand on **h** ground,
9:14 She is enthroned on the **h**
17:19 city gate **h** invites destruction.
18:11 strong city and is like a **h** wall
25:3 ⸤Like⸥ the **h** heavens and the
30:19 making its way through **h** seas,
Ecc 10:6 are often given **h** positions,
10:16 the **h** officials throw parties
10:17 and when the **h** officials eat at
Sos 7:5 You hold your head as **h** as
Isa 2:11 **H** and mighty people will be
2:14 against all the **h** mountains and
2:15 against every **h** tower and
2:17 and **h** and mighty people will
6:1 I saw the Lord sitting on a **h**
14:14 I'll be like the Most **H**."
16:3 At **h** noon make your shadow
25:12 down Moab's **h** fortified walls,
26:5 brought down those who live **h**
30:13 your sin will be like a **h** wall
30:25 lofty mountain and every **h** hill.
30:28 It rises neck **h**, sifting the
30:33 deep and wide and piled **h**
32:15 Spirit is poured on us from on **h**.
33:5 honored because he lives on **h**.
33:16 This person will live on **h**.
37:24 I'll ride up the **h** mountains,
40:9 Go up a **h** mountain,
57:7 You've made your bed on a **h**
57:15 The **H** and Lofty One lives
57:15 I live in a **h** and holy place.
Jer 2:20 like a prostitute on every **h** hill
3:6 She went up every **h** mountain
17:2 beside large trees on **h** hills
49:16 you build your nest as **h** as
51:58 and its **h** gates will be set on
52:21 One pillar was 27 feet **h** and 18
52:22 that was on it was 7 ½ feet **h**
Lam 3:35 presence of the Most **H** God,
3:38 the mouth of the Most **H** God.
Eze 6:13 They will lie on every **h** hill,
17:22 it on a **h** and lofty mountain.
17:23 I will plant it on a **h** mountain in
20:28 When they saw any **h** hill or
20:40 the **h** mountain of Israel,
24:9 I, too, will pile the wood **h**.
24:10 Pile it **h**, and light the fire.
27:26 took you out to the **h** seas,
34:6 mountains and on every **h** hill.
40:2 me down on a very **h** mountain.
40:5 ½ feet thick and 10 ½ feet **h**.
40:42 3 feet wide, and 21 inches **h**.
41:3 The entrance was 10 ½ feet **h**
41:22 5 feet **h** and 3 ½ feet wide.
43:13 of the altar was 21 inches **h**
43:14 lower ledge it was 3 ½ feet **h**,
43:14 the upper ledge it was 7 feet **h**
43:15 were burned was 7 feet **h**.
Dan 2:6 gifts, awards, and **h** honors.
3:1 made a gold statue 90 feet **h**
3:26 of the Most **H** God — come
4:2 things the Most **H** God did
4:17 that the Most **H** has power over
4:24 The Most **H** has decided to
4:25 that the Most **H** has power over
4:32 that the Most **H** has power over
4:34 I thanked the Most **H**,

Dan 5:18 "Your Majesty, the Most **H** God
5:21 that the Most **H** God has power
7:18 Most **H** will take possession
7:22 the holy people of the Most **H**.
7:25 speak against the Most **H** God,
7:25 the holy people of the Most **H**,
7:27 the holy people of the Most **H**.
11:39 He will give **h** honors to those
Hos 7:16 They don't return to the Most **H**
11:7 Even if they call to the Most **H**,
Amo 4:13 He walks on the **h** places of
Oba 1:3 You make your home up **h**.
1:4 Even though you fly **h** like an
Hab 2:9 in order to set his nest up **h**
3:10 Its waves rise up **h**.
Zep 1:16 against the **h** corner towers.
Zec 4:7 What a **h** mountain you are!
Mat 4:8 took him to a very **h** mountain
17:1 up a **h** mountain where they
26:9 have been sold for a **h** price,
Mar 5:7 Son of the Most **H** God?
9:2 and John and led them up a **h**
14:5 have been sold for a **h** price,
Luk 1:32 called the Son of the Most **H**.
1:35 and the power of the Most **H**
1:76 called a prophet of the Most **H**.
4:5 The devil took him to a **h** place
4:38 was sick with a **h** fever.
6:35 the children of the Most **H** God.
8:28 Son of the Most **H** God?
Jon 12:5 this perfume sold for a **h** price
Act 7:48 "However, the Most **H** doesn't
13:50 women of **h** social standing
16:17 are servants of the Most **H** God.
Eph 3:18 long, **h**, and deep his love is.
Heb 7:1 and priest of the Most **H** God.
Jas 4:10 Then he will give you a **h**
Rev 14:20 out of the winepress as **h** as
18:5 sins are piled as **h** as heaven,
18:19 because of that city's **h** prices.
21:10 away to a large, **h** mountain.
21:12 **h** wall with 12 gates.

higher (14)

Num 23:3 Then Balaam went off to a **h**
Dtr 28:43 you will rise **h** and higher,
28:43 you will rise higher and **h**,
2Ki 25:28 him a special position **h** than
Neh 8:5 Ezra, standing **h** than all the
Est 3:1 He gave Haman a position **h** in
Job 11:8 wisdom is⸥ **h** than heaven.
Psa 108:4 because your mercy is **h** than
Isa 55:9 "Just as the heavens are **h**
55:9 so my ways are **h** than your
55:9 are **h** than your thoughts."
Jer 52:32 him a special position **h** than
Eze 41:7 grew wider as it went **h**.
Dan 3:30 and Abednego to **h** positions in

highest (56)

Dtr 10:14 that the sky, the **h** heaven,
1Ki 8:27 If heaven itself, the **h** heaven,
2Ch 2:6 the **h** heaven, cannot hold him?
6:18 If heaven itself, the **h** heaven,
Neh 9:6 made heaven, the **h** heaven,
Est 1:14 to the king and held the **h** rank
Job 22:12 Look how high the **h** stars are!
Psa 43:4 to God my ⸤**h**⸥ joy,
68:18 You went to the **h** place.
68:33 ancient heaven, the **h** heaven.
73:28 united with God is my **h** good.
97:9 You are **h**. You are above all the
110:1 "Sit in the **h** position in heaven
115:16 The **h** heaven belongs to the
137:6 consider Jerusalem my **h** joy.
148:4 Praise him, you **h** heaven and
Pro 9:3 She calls from the **h** places in
Isa 2:2 will be established as the **h**
10:33 The **h** trees will be cut down.
17:6 left at the top of the **h** branch,
Jer 49:16 cliffs and occupy the **h** places
Eze 17:4 It broke off the **h** twig and
17:22 I will break off the **h** twig and
Mic 4:1 will be established as the **h**
Mat 4:5 and had him stand on the **h** part
5:22 will answer for it in the **h** court.

Mat 21:9 Hosanna in the **h** heaven!"
22:44 "Take the **h** position in heaven
26:64 the Son of Man in the **h** position
Mar 11:10 Hosanna in the **h** heaven!"
12:36 "Take the **h** position in heaven
14:62 the Son of Man in the **h** position
16:19 where God gave him the **h**
Luk 2:14 "Glory to God in the **h** heaven,
4:9 and had him stand on the **h** part
19:38 and glory in the **h** heaven."
20:42 "Take the **h** position in heaven
22:66 Jesus in front of their **h** court
22:69 be in the **h** position in heaven."
Act 2:33 to give Jesus the **h** position.
2:34 "Take my **h** position of power
5:31 Jesus the **h** position as leader
Rom 8:34 Christ has the **h** position in
Eph 1:20 him the **h** position in heaven.
4:8 "When he went to the **h** place,
Col 3:1 Christ holds the **h** position.
Heb 1:3 he received the **h** position,
1:13 "Sit in the **h** position in heaven
7:26 has the **h** position in heaven.
8:1 has received the **h** position,
10:12 the **h** position in heaven.
12:2 Then he received the **h**
Jas 2:8 this law from the **h** authority:
1Pe 2:13 the **h** position of authority.
3:22 he has the **h** position that God
2Pe 1:4 that are of the **h** value.

highest-ranking (1)

1Ch 26:24 He was the **h** official in charge

high-grade (3)

1Ki 7:9 were built with **h** stone blocks.
7:10 **h** stones (some 12 feet long,
7:11 beams and **h** stone blocks,

high-ranking (1)

Act 8:27 The man was a eunuch, a **h**

highway (12)

Num 20:17 We'll stay on the king's **h** and
21:22 We'll stay on the king's **h** until
Jdg 21:19 east of the **h** going from Bethel
Psa 68:4 Make a **h** for him to ride through
Pro 15:19 decent people is an ⸤open⸥ **h**.
16:17 The **h** of decent people turns
Isa 11:16 There will be a **h** for the
19:23 When that day comes, a **h** will
35:8 A **h** will be there, a roadway.
40:3 Make a straight **h** in the
62:10 Build up the **h**! Clear away the
Jer 31:21 Remember the **h**, the road on

highways (5)

Isa 33:8 **H** are deserted. Travelers stop
49:11 and my **h** will be restored.
59:7 and destruction are on their **h**.
59:8 There's no justice on their **h**.
Jer 18:15 side roads and not on major **h**.

hiked (1)

1Ki 18:46 He **h** up his robe and ran ahead

Hilen (1)

1Ch 6:58 **H** with its pastureland,

Hilkiah (34)

2Ki 18:18 palace and was the son of **H**,
18:26 Then Eliakim (son of **H**),
18:37 palace and was the son of **H**,
22:4 "Go to the chief priest **H**.
22:8 The chief priest **H** told the
22:8 **H** gave the book to Shaphan,
22:10 "The priest **H** has given me a
22:12 gave an order to the priest **H**,
22:14 So the priest **H**, Ahikam,
23:4 king ordered the chief priest **H**,
23:4 the priests who served under **H**,
23:24 the book that the priest **H** found
1Ch 6:13 Shallum was the father of **H**.
6:13 **H** was the father of Azariah.
6:45 who was the son of **H**,
9:11 Azariah was the son of **H**,

1Ch 26:11 other sons were **H** (the second
2Ch 34:9 They came to the chief priest **H**
34:14 the priest **H** found the book of
34:15 **H** told the scribe Shaphan,
34:15 **H** gave the book to Shaphan.
34:18 "The priest **H** has given me a
34:20 the king gave an order to **H**,
34:22 So **H** and the king's officials
35:8 **H**, Zechariah, and Jehiel,
Ezr 7:1 who was the son of **H**,
Neh 8:4 Shema, Anaiah, Uriah, **H**,
11:11 Seraiah, who was the son of **H**,
12:7 Sallu, Amok, **H**, and Jedaiah.
12:21 from **H**, Hashabiah;
Isa 22:20 my servant Eliakim, son of **H**.
36:3 palace and was the son of **H**,
36:22 of the palace and was son of **H**,
Jer 1:1 words of Jeremiah, son of **H**.

Hilkiah's (1)

Jer 29:3 Elasah and **H** son Gemariah,

hill (48)

Gen 14:6 and the Horites in the **h** country
Exo 17:9 I will stand on top of the **h**.
17:10 and Hur went to the top of the **h**.
Jos 5:3 Israel at the **H** of Circumcision.
24:33 He was buried on the **h** that
Jdg 7:1 camp was north of him at the **h**
15:17 Ramath Lehi [Jawbone **H**].
16:3 the top of the **h** facing Hebron.
1Sm 7:1 into Abinadab's house on the **h**.
9:11 As they were going up the **h** to
10:5 you will come to the **h** of God,
10:10 When Saul came to the **h**,
17:3 were stationed on a **h**
17:3 Israelites were stationed on a **h**
26:1 "David is hiding at the **h** of
26:3 camped by the road at the **h**
26:13 of the **h** some distance away.
2Sm 2:24 they came to the **h** of Ammah,
2:25 their position on top of a **h**.
6:3 from Abinadab's home on the **h**.
1Ki 11:7 worship site on the **h** east
14:23 to worship on every high **h**
16:24 Omri bought a **h** from Shemer
16:24 He fortified the **h** and built the
2Ki 1:9 Elijah sitting on top of a **h**,
1:13 of the third group went up the **h**
17:10 Asherah on every high **h**
23:13 part of the **H** of Destruction.
23:16 saw the tombs on the **h** there,
Sos 4:6 of myrrh and the **h** of incense.
Isa 5:1 had a vineyard on a fertile **h**.
30:17 like a signpost on a **h**.
30:25 mountain and every high **h**.
31:4 to fight for Mount Zion and its **h**.
40:4 Every mountain and **h** will be
49:9 find pastures on every bare **h**.
Jer 2:20 like a prostitute on every high **h**
16:16 them on every mountain and **h**
31:39 there straight to the **H** of Gareb,
32:44 the mountains, in the **h** country,
Eze 6:13 They will lie on every high **h**,
20:28 When they saw any high **h** or
34:6 mountains and on every high **h**.
34:26 and the places around my **h**.
Mic 1:4 water pouring down a steep **h**.
Mat 5:14 when it is located on a **h**.
Luk 3:5 Every mountain and **h** will be
4:29 Their city was built on a **h** with

Hillel (1)

Jdg 12:13 After Elon, Abdon, son of **H**,

hills (81)

Gen 12:8 He moved on to the **h** east of
14:10 but the other kings fled to the **h**.
19:17 Run for the **h**, or you'll be swept
19:19 I can't run as far as the **h**.
49:26 and the riches of the ancient **h**.
Num 23:9 I look at them from the **h**.
Dtr 8:7 through the valleys and **h**.
8:9 to mine copper ore in the **h**.
11:11 is a land with **h** and valleys,
12:2 the high mountains, on the **h**,
Dtr 33:15 the best from the ancient **h**,
Jos 11:21 and in all the **h** of Judah and
1Sm 23:19 at Horesh on the **h** of Hachilah,
26:20 hunting a partridge in the **h**."
2Sm 1:19 lies dead on your **h**.
1:25 On your **h** Jonathan was killed!
1Ki 4:8 in charge of the **h** of Ephraim,
12:25 rebuilt Shechem in the **h**
20:23 "Their god is a god of the **h**.
20:28 that the LORD is a god of the **h**
22:17 in the **h** like sheep without
2Ki 2:16 dropped him on one of the **h**
5:22 of the prophets in the **h**
16:4 which were on **h** and under
1Ch 6:67 pastureland in the **h** of Ephraim,
12:8 as fast as gazelles on the **h**.
2Ch 18:16 in the **h** like sheep without
20:33 sites on the **h** were not torn
21:11 of worship in the **h** of Judah.
27:4 He built cities in the **h** of Judah,
28:4 which were on **h** and under
Job 15:7 Were you delivered before the **h**
40:20 The **h** bring it food,
Psa 50:10 the cattle on a thousand **h**,
65:12 The **h** are surrounded with joy.
72:3 and the **h** bring righteousness.
114:4 The **h** jumped like lambs.
114:6 **H**, what made you jump like
148:9 mountains and all **h**,
Pro 8:25 in their places and before the **h**,
27:25 are gathered on the **h**.
Sos 2:8 mountains, racing over the **h**.
Isa 2:2 and raised above the **h**.
2:14 mountains and all the lofty **h**,
5:25 The **h** tremble, and dead
7:25 to go to all the **h** which used
40:12 scale and the **h** on a balance?
41:15 You will turn the **h** into straw.
42:15 lay waste to mountains and **h**.
54:10 and the **h** may shake,
55:12 The mountains and the **h** will
65:7 and slandered me on the **h**.
Jer 3:2 "Look at the bare **h**,
3:21 of crying is heard on the **h**.
3:23 Truly, the noise from the **h**,
4:24 and the **h** are swaying.
7:29 song of mourning on the bare **h**,
12:12 swarm all over the bare **h**
13:27 a shameless prostitute on the **h**
14:6 donkeys stand on the bare **h**.
17:2 beside large trees on high **h**
49:16 the highest places in the **h**.
50:6 They go from mountains to **h**.
Eze 6:3 says to the mountains and **h**
22:9 at the worship sites on the **h**,
32:5 I will scatter your flesh on the **h**
35:8 in battle will fall on your **h**
36:4 says to the mountains and **h**,
36:6 Tell the mountains and **h** and
Hos 4:13 incense on the **h** under oaks,
10:8 and to the **h**, "Fall on us!"
Joe 3:18 Milk will flow on the **h**.
Amo 9:13 and flow from all the **h**.
Mic 4:1 and raised above the **h**.
6:1 and let the **h** listen to your
Nah 1:5 The **h** melt. The earth draws
Hab 3:6 The ancient **h** sink.
Zep 1:10 from the **h**," declares the LORD.
Hag 1:11 land, the **h**, and on the grain,
Mat 18:12 he leave the 99 sheep in the **h**
Luk 23:30 and to the **h**, 'Cover us!'

hillside (1)

2Sm 16:13 walking along the **h** parallel

hilltops (2)

1Ki 12:31 built worship sites on **h**.
Isa 41:18 will make rivers flow on bare **h**.

hinder (1)

1Co 9:12 with anything in order not to **h**

hindquarters (2)

1Ki 7:25 and their **h** were toward the
2Ch 4:4 and their **h** were toward the

hinges (1)

Pro 26:14 ⌊As⌋ a door turns on its **h**,

Hinnom (3)

Jos 15:8 that overlooks the valley of **H**
18:16 It descends to the valley of **H**,
Neh 11:30 Beersheba to the Valley of **H**.

hip (6)

Gen 32:25 the socket of Jacob's **h** so that
32:31 was limping because of his **h**.
32:32 thigh attached to the **h** socket
32:32 the socket of Jacob's **h** at
2Sm 20:8 and strapped over it at his **h**
Dan 5:6 His **h** joints became loose,

hips (2)

Isa 11:5 will be the belt around his **h**.
Dan 2:32 Its stomach and **h** were made

Hirah (3)

Gen 38:1 Adullam whose name was **H**.
38:12 he and his friend **H** from
38:20 Judah sent his friend **H** to

Hiram (27)

2Sm 5:11 Then King **H** of Tyre sent
1Ki 5:1 King **H** of Tyre sent his
5:1 **H** had always been David's
5:2 Solomon sent word to **H**,
5:7 **H** was very glad to hear what
5:7 **H** responded, "May the LORD
5:8 **H** sent men to Solomon to say,
5:10 So **H** gave Solomon all the
5:11 Solomon gave **H** 120,000
5:11 Solomon paid **H** this much
5:12 between **H** and Solomon,
7:13 had **H** brought from Tyre.
7:14 **H** was the son of a widow from
7:14 **H** was highly skilled,
7:21 **H** set up the pillars in the
7:23 **H** made a pool from cast metal.
7:36 **H** engraved angels,
7:38 **H** also made ten bronze basins.
7:40 **H** also made pots,
7:40 So **H** finished all the work for
7:45 **H** made all these utensils out
9:11 he gave King **H** of Tyre 20
9:11 (**H** had supplied Solomon with
9:12 **H** left Tyre to see the cities
9:14 **H** had sent the king 9,000
9:27 **H** sent his own servants ⌊who
1Ch 14:1 King **H** of Tyre sent

Hiram's (3)

1Ki 5:18 **H** workmen, and men from
10:11 **H** fleet that brought gold from
10:22 for Tarshish with **H** fleet.

hire (7)

Dtr 15:18 twice as much to **h** someone
1Sm 2:5 Those who were well-fed **h**
1Ch 19:6 pounds of silver to **h** chariots
Isa 7:20 "On that day the Lord will **h** the
46:6 They **h** a goldsmith.
Zec 8:10 was no money to **h** any person
Mat 20:1 out at daybreak to **h** workers

hired (29)

Exo 12:45 "No **h** worker may eat it.
Lev 19:13 you owe a **h** worker overnight.
25:6 female slaves, your **h** workers,
25:40 He will be like a **h** worker or a
25:50 like the wages of a **h** worker.
25:53 serve his buyer as a **h** worker.
Dtr 23:4 They even **h** Balaam,
24:14 Don't withhold pay from **h**
Jdg 9:4 With the silver, Abimelech **h**
18:4 him and added, "Micah **h** me,
2Sm 10:6 So they **h** the Arameans from
2Ki 7:6 "The king of Israel has **h** the
1Ch 19:7 They **h** 32,000 chariots and the
2Ch 24:12 and they **h** masons and
24:12 They also **h** men who worked
25:6 He also **h** 100,000 soldiers

Neh 6:12 Tobiah and Sanballat had **h**
6:13 He was **h** to intimidate me into
13:2 Instead, they **h** Balaam to
Job 7:1 like a **h** hand's daily ⌊work⌋?
7:2 Like a **h** hand, he eagerly looks
Jer 46:21 Egypt's **h** soldiers are like
Mat 20:7 "'No one has **h** us,'
20:10 who had been **h** first came,
Mar 1:20 father Zebedee and the **h** men
Luk 15:17 'How many of my father's **h**
15:19 Make me one of your **h** men."'
Jon 10:12 A **h** hand isn't a shepherd and
10:13 The **h** hand is concerned about

hires (1)
Pro 26:10 is one who **h** fools or drifters.

hiss (8)
Jer 19:8 will become something to **h** at.
19:8 by it will be stunned and **h**
46:22 Egypt will **h** like a snake as it
49:17 will be horrified and **h** at all its
50:13 will be horrified and **h** at all its
Lam 2:15 They **h** and shake their heads
2:16 They **h** and grit their teeth.
Zep 2:15 All who pass by it will **h** and

hissed (2)
Jer 18:16 something to be **h** at forever.
29:18 cursed, ridiculed, and **h** at,

historian (9)
2Sm 8:16 Jehoshaphat was the royal **h**.
20:24 son of Ahilud, was the royal **h**.
1Ki 4:3 son of Ahilud, was the royal **h**.
2Ki 18:18 who was the royal **h** and the
18:37 who was the royal **h** and the
1Ch 18:15 Jehoshaphat was the royal **h**.
2Ch 34:8 the royal **h** and son of Joahaz,
Isa 36:3 who was the royal **h** and the
36:22 who was the royal **h** and the

historic (1)
Neh 2:20 claim or **h** right in Jerusalem."

historical (1)
Gal 4:24 I'm going to use these **h** events

history (10)
Exo 9:18 since the beginning of its **h**.
2Ch 13:22 he said — is written in the **h** by
Ezr 4:15 city has a **h** of rebelliousness.
4:19 that this city has a long **h**
Est 10:2 are recorded in the **h** of the
Isa 41:4 determined the course of **h** from
Dan 2:21 times and periods of **h**.
1Co 10:11 living in the closing days of **h**.
Eph 1:10 He planned to bring all of **h** to
3:11 This was God's plan for all of **h**

hit (24)
Exo 21:19 the one who **h** him must not be
Num 20:11 Moses raised his hand and **h**
22:23 Balaam **h** the donkey to get it
22:25 So Balaam **h** the donkey again.
22:27 Balaam became so angry he **h**
22:28 to make you **h** me three times?"
22:32 "Why have you **h** your donkey
Jdg 7:13 the loaf of bread **h** that tent so
9:53 millstone that **h** Abimelech
1Ki 22:34 aimed his bow at random and **h**
2Ch 18:33 aimed his bow at random and **h**
Job 36:32 and orders it to **h** the target.
Psa 91:12 you never **h** your foot against
Mat 4:6 you never **h** your foot against
26:67 **h** him with their fists,
26:68 tell us who **h** you."
Mar 12:4 They **h** the servant on the head
14:65 They covered his face and **h**
Luk 4:11 you never **h** your foot against
22:64 "Tell us who **h** you."
Jon 18:23 why do you **h** me?"
Act 16:23 After they had **h** Paul and Silas
27:17 Fearing that they would **h** the
27:29 Fearing we might **h** rocks,

hitch (2)
1Sm 6:7 **H** the cows to the cart.
2Ki 9:21 "**H** the horses to the chariot,"

hitched (1)
1Sm 6:10 dairy cows, **h** them to a cart,

hits (6)
Exo 21:15 Whoever **h** his father or mother
21:18 men quarrel and one **h**
21:20 "Whenever an owner **h** his
21:26 "Whenever an owner **h** his
22:2 breaking in and **h** him so that
Dtr 19:5 **h**, and kills the other person.

hitting (2)
Mat 27:30 they took the stick and kept **h**
Mar 15:19 They kept **h** him on the head

Hittite (26)
Gen 25:9 son of Zohar the **H**.
26:34 daughter of Beeri the **H**.
26:34 daughter of Elon the **H**.
27:46 "I can't stand **H** women!
27:46 If Jacob marries a **H** woman
36:2 daughter of Elon the **H**;
49:29 in the field of Ephron the **H**.
49:30 from Ephron the **H** to use as a
50:13 this tomb from Ephron the **H**.
1Sm 26:6 Ahimelech the **H** and Abishai,
2Sm 11:3 Eliam and wife of Uriah the **H**."
11:6 "Send me Uriah the **H**."
11:17 died — including Uriah the **H**.
11:21 man Uriah the **H** is also dead."'
11:24 man Uriah the **H** also is dead."
12:9 You had Uriah the **H** killed in
12:10 and took the wife of Uriah the **H**
23:39 Uriah the **H** — 37 in all.
1Ki 10:29 to all the **H** and Aramean kings.
11:1 He loved **H** women and women
15:5 matter concerning Uriah the **H**
2Ki 7:6 king of Israel has hired the **H**
1Ch 11:41 Uriah the **H**, Zabad (son of
2Ch 1:17 to all the **H** and Aramean kings.
Eze 16:3 and your mother was a **H**.
16:45 Your mother was a **H**,

Hittites (32)
Gen 15:20 the **H**, the Perizzites,
23:3 dead wife and spoke to the **H**,
23:5 The **H** answered Abraham,
23:7 got up in front of the **H**,
23:10 was sitting among the **H**.
23:16 amount stated in front of the **H**:
23:18 The **H** together with all who
23:20 and its cave were sold by the **H**
25:10 had bought from the **H**.
49:32 in it were bought from the **H**."
Exo 3:8 **H**, Amorites, Perizzites,
3:17 **H**, Amorites, Perizzites,
13:5 **H**, Amorites, Hivites,
23:23 **H**, Perizzites, Canaanites,
23:28 and **H** out of your way.
33:2 **H**, Perizzites, Hivites,
34:11 **H**, Perizzites, Hivites,
Num 13:29 The **H**, Jebusites, And the
Dtr 7:1 the **H**, Girgashites, Amorites,
20:17 You must claim the **H**,
Jos 1:4 River (the country of the **H**) ⌊on
3:10 **H**, Hivites, Perizzites,
9:2 the kings of the **H**,
11:3 the Amorites, **H**, Perizzites,
12:8 and the Negev ⌊that the⌋ **H**,
24:11 **H**, Girgashites, Hivites,
Jdg 1:26 man went to the land of the **H**.
3:5 **H**, Amorites, Perizzites,
1Ki 9:20 The Amorites, **H**, Perizzites,
2Ch 8:7 The **H**, Perizzites, Hivites,
Ezr 9:1 **H**, Perizzites, Jebusites,
Neh 9:8 **H**, Amorites, Perizzites,

Hivite (2)
Gen 34:2 of the local ruler Hamor the **H**,
36:2 granddaughter of Zibeon the **H**;

Hivites (23)
Gen 10:17 the **H**, the Arkites, the Sinites,
Exo 3:8 **H**, and Jebusites live.
3:17 Perizzites, **H**, and Jebusites,
13:5 Amorites, **H**, and Jebusites.
23:23 Canaanites, **H**, and Jebusites.
23:28 ahead of you to force the **H**,
33:2 Perizzites, **H**, and Jebusites.
34:11 Hittites, Perizzites, **H**,
Dtr 7:1 Canaanites, Perizzites, **H**,
20:17 Canaanites, Perizzites, **H**,
Jos 3:10 **H**, Perizzites, Girgashites,
9:2 Perizzites, **H**, and Jebusites.)
9:7 The men of Israel said to the **H**,
11:3 and the **H** at the foot of Mount
11:19 where the **H** lived.
12:8 Canaanites, Perizzites, **H**,
24:11 **H**, and Jebusites fought you.
Jdg 3:3 and the **H** who lived on Mount
3:5 Perizzites, **H**, and Jebusites.
2Sm 24:7 Tyre and all the cities of the **H**
1Ki 9:20 Hittites, Perizzites, **H**,
1Ch 1:15 the **H**, the Arkites, the Sinites,
2Ch 8:7 The Hittites, Perizzites, **H**,

Hizki (1)
1Ch 8:17 Meshullam, **H**, Heber,

Hizkiah (1)
1Ch 3:23 were Elioenai, **H**, and Azrikam.

hoard (1)
Ecc 5:13 downfall of those who **h** them.

hoarded (2)
Ecc 5:14 These **h** riches were then lost
Isa 23:18 It won't be stored or **h**.

hoards (1)
Pro 11:26 will curse the one who **h** grain,

hoarse (1)
Psa 69:3 My throat is **h**. My eyes are

Hobab (3)
Num 10:29 said to his brother-in-law **H**,
10:30 **H** answered, "No, I won't go.
Jdg 4:11 Kenites (the descendants of **H**,

Hobah (1)
Gen 14:15 pursuing them all the way to **H**,

Hobaiah (2)
Ezr 2:61 the descendants of **H**,
Neh 7:63 the descendants of **H**,

hobbling (1)
Pro 7:22 like a ram **h** into captivity

Hod (1)
1Ch 7:37 Bezer, **H**, Shamma, Shilsha,

Hodaviah (4)
1Ch 3:24 Elioenai's seven sons were **H**,
5:24 Jeremiah, **H**, and Jahdiel.
9:7 of Meshullam, grandson of **H**,
Ezr 2:40 and Kadmiel, that is, of **H**: 74

Hodeiah (1)
Neh 7:43 of Kadmiel ⌊and⌋ of **H**:

Hodesh (1)
1Ch 8:9 he and his wife **H** had the

Hodiah (5)
Neh 8:7 **H**, Maaseiah, Kelita, Azariah,
9:5 Sherebiah, **H**, Shebaniah,
10:10 **H**, Kelita, Pelaiah, Hanan,
10:13 **H**, Bani, and Beninu.
10:18 **H**, Hashum, Bezai,

Hodiah's (1)
1Ch 4:19 The sons of **H** wife, the sister

hoed (1)

Isa 5:6 It will never be pruned or **h**.

hoes (2)

2Sm 12:31 work with saws, **h**, and axes.
1Ch 20:3 work with saws, **h**, and axes.

Hoglah (4)

Num 26:33 Noah, **H**, Milcah, and Tirzah.)
27:1 Noah, **H**, Milcah, and Tirzah.
36:11 Mahlah, Tirzah, **H**,
Jos 17:3 Noah, **H**, Milcah, and Tirzah.

Hoham (1)

Jos 10:3 message⌋ to King **H** of Hebron,

hold (151)

Gen 43:9 You can **h** me responsible for
Exo 6:5 the Egyptians **h** in slavery,
8:5 '**H** your staff over the rivers,
8:16 '**H** out your staff and strike the
9:2 to **h** them ⌊in slavery⌋,
10:7 "How long will this man **h** us in
17:9 I will **h** in my hand the staff
25:27 They are to **h** the poles for
26:29 gold rings to **h** the crossbars,
28:28 the belt of the ephod and will **h**
30:4 molding on opposite sides to **h**
36:34 gold rings to **h** the crossbars.
37:14 were put close to the rim to **h**
37:27 molding on opposite sides to **h**
38:5 He cast four rings to **h** the
Lev 19:18 Never **h** a grudge against any
23:24 first day of the seventh month **h**
Num 5:18 The priest will **h** in his hands
29:35 "On the eighth day you must **h**
Dtr 16:8 and on the seventh day **h** a
Jos 8:18 "**H** out the spear in your hand
Jdg 16:3 took **h** of the doors,
Rut 3:15 you're wearing and **h** it tight."
1Sm 17:35 I took **h** of its mane,
2Sm 2:14 the young men **h** a contest."
15:5 take **h** of him, and kiss him.
19:19 Don't **h** it against me or even
20:9 He took **h** of Amasa's beard
22:17 high above and took **h** of me.
1Ki 1:50 and took **h** of the horns of the
8:27 highest heaven, cannot **h** you,
8:64 was too small to **h** all of them.
18:32 a trench that could **h** 12 quarts
2Ki 4:16 you will **h** a baby boy in your
4:27 she took **h** of his feet.
6:32 **H** it shut because the king will
15:19 his **h** on the kingdom.
19:32 **h** a shield in front of it,
1Ch 29:12 You **h** power and strength in
2Ch 2:6 highest heaven, cannot **h** him?
6:18 highest heaven, cannot **h** you,
7:7 was not able to **h** all of them.
32:27 for himself to **h** silver,
Ezr 7:14 which you **h** in your hands.
7:25 wisdom — the Teachings you **h**
9:8 and to give us a secure **h**
Job 9:13 God does not **h** back his anger.
37:4 He doesn't **h** the lightning back
Psa 3:3 You **h** my head high.
18:16 high above and took **h** of me.
35:3 **H** your spear to block the way
73:23 You **h** on to my right hand.
74:11 Why do you **h** back your hand,
79:8 Do not **h** the crimes of our
83:2 hate you **h** their heads high.
84:11 He does not **h** back any
94:18 continued to **h** me up.
110:7 He will **h** his head high.
116:3 of the grave took **h** of me.
119:17 to me so that I may live and **h**
119:57 I promised to **h** on to your
119:67 but now I **h** on to your word.
119:117 **H** me, and I will be safe, and I
139:10 right hand would **h** on to me.
Pro 3:18 for those who take firm **h** of it.
3:27 Do not **h** back anything good
20:16 **H** on to the garment of one who
20:16 and **h** responsible the person
Pro 21:26 gives and does not **h** back.
27:13 **H** on to the garment of one who
27:13 and **h** responsible the person
30:28 A lizard you can **h** in your
31:19 and her fingers **h** a spindle.
Ecc 7:18 It's good to **h** on to the one and
Sos 7:5 You **h** your head as high as
7:5 locks could **h** a king captive.
7:8 climb the palm tree and take **h**
Isa 22:11 between the two walls to **h**
37:33 **h** a shield in front of it,
41:13 I, the LORD your God, **h** your
42:6 I will take **h** of your hand.
44:20 "Isn't what I **h** in my right hand
48:9 For my glory's sake I'll **h** my
54:2 of your tent, and don't **h** back.
58:1 Don't **h** back! Raise your voice
63:15 compassion? Don't **h** back.
64:7 calls on your name or tries to **h**
64:12 things, LORD, will you **h** back?
Jer 2:13 broken cisterns that can't **h**
3:5 He won't **h** a grudge forever.
6:23 Its people take **h** of bows and
31:34 no longer **h** their sins against
50:42 They will take **h** of bows and
Eze 3:18 but I will **h** you responsible for
3:20 I will **h** you responsible for their
17:3 It took **h** of the top of a cedar
17:22 will take **h** of the top of a cedar
30:21 be strong enough to **h** a sword.
33:6 I will **h** him responsible for their
33:8 and I will **h** you responsible for
37:20 When you **h** the sticks in your
45:11 ephah and the bath should **h**
Dan 2:43 but they will not **h** together any
11:6 She won't **h** on to her power,
Hos 12:14 He will **h** them guilty of murder.
Amo 7:8 "I'm going to **h** a plumb line in
Jnh 1:14 Don't **h** us responsible for the
2:8 Those who **h** on to worthless
Zec 8:23 among the nations will take **h**
Mat 12:11 wouldn't you take **h** of it and lift
12:13 "**H** out your hand."
14:31 out, caught **h** of him, and said,
26:50 came forward, took **h** of Jesus,
28:9 and took **h** of his feet.
Mar 3:5 "**H** out your hand."
10:13 to Jesus to have him **h** them.
14:46 Some men took **h** of Jesus and
Luk 1:66 "What does the future **h** for this
6:10 "**H** out your hand."
7:14 to the open coffin, took **h** of it,
14:4 So Jesus took **h** of the man,
18:15 to Jesus to have him **h** them.
Jon 20:17 told her, "Don't **h** on to me.
Act 2:24 death had no power to **h** him.
3:7 Peter took **h** of the man's right
5:2 They agreed to **h** back some of
7:60 don't **h** this sin against them."
19:38 days and officials to **h** court.
Rom 11:22 kind to you if you continue to **h**
12:9 **H** on to what is good.
1Co 15:2 by this Good News if you **h**
2Co 5:19 He didn't **h** people's faults
Php 2:16 as you **h** firmly to the word of
Col 2:19 He doesn't **h** on to ⌊Christ,⌋
1Th 5:21 **H** on to what is good.
2Th 2:15 firmly **h** on to the traditions we
1Ti 6:12 Take **h** of everlasting life to
6:19 In this way they take **h** of what
Heb 3:14 only if we continue to **h**
4:14 We need to **h** on to our
6:18 who have taken refuge in him **h**
8:12 no longer **h** their sins against
10:17 "I will no longer **h** their sins
10:23 We must continue to **h** firmly to
2Pe 2:9 He also knows how to **h**
Rev 2:13 You **h** on to my name and have
2:24 in Thyatira — all who don't **h**
2:25 Just **h** on to what you have
3:11 **H** on to what you have so that
12:17 keep God's commands and **h**
19:10 of the Christians who **h**

holding (25)

Gen 25:26 was born with his hand **h**
Lev 11:36 However, a spring or a cistern **h**
Num 5:25 the grain offering she was **h**,
Jos 8:26 did not lower his hand **h**
Jdg 7:19 jars they were **h** in their hands.
1Sm 25:36 he was **h** a banquet in his
1Ki 1:51 He is **h** on to the horns of the
Neh 4:16 body armor and **h** spears,
Job 2:9 "Are you still **h** on to your
11:14 If you're **h** on to sin,
Psa 119:9 ⌊He can do it⌋ by **h** on to your
Jer 6:11 I am tired of **h** it in.
20:9 I wear myself out **h** it in,
30:6 do I see every strong man **h** his
Eze 8:11 Each of them was **h** an
40:3 The man was **h** a linen tape
Col 2:23 But they have no value for **h**
2Th 2:7 until the person now **h**
2Pe 2:4 and is **h** them for judgment.
2:13 They take pleasure in **h** wild
Rev 7:1 They were **h** back the four
7:9 **h** palm branches in their hands,
15:2 They were **h** God's harps
17:4 In her hand she was **h** a gold
20:1 **h** the key to the bottomless pit

holds (26)

Gen 50:15 "What if Joseph **h** a grudge
Num 15:23 you through Moses **h** as true
Est 4:11 Only if the king **h** out the
Job 2:3 And he still **h** on to his
8:15 If one **h** on to it, it will not
12:15 When he **h** back the waters,
18:9 his heel. A snare **h** him.
20:13 it and won't let go of it and he **h**
26:8 He **h** the water in his thick
Psa 37:24 headfirst because the LORD **h**
Pro 11:24 while another **h** back what he
15:18 but one who **h** his temper
26:24 but inside he **h** on to deceit.
Isa 56:2 things and the person who **h**
Lam 1:17 Zion **h** out its hands.
Eze 23:32 because this cup **h** so much.
Amo 1:5 Aven Valley and the one who **h**
1:8 in Ashdod and the one who **h**
Nah 1:2 against his enemies and **h**
Col 1:17 and **h** everything together.
3:1 Christ **h** the highest position.
2Th 2:6 what it is that now **h** him back,
Heb 1:3 He **h** everything together
1Pe 2:13 He **h** the highest position of
Rev 2:1 The one who **h** the seven stars
2:12 The one who **h** the sharp

hole (8)

Dtr 23:13 outside to squat, dig a **h** with it.
2Ki 12:9 drilled a **h** in its lid,
Job 30:14 They come through a wide **h**
Psa 7:15 Then he falls into the **h** that he
Eze 8:7 I saw a **h** in the wall.
12:5 Dig a **h** through the wall of your
12:7 In the evening I dug a **h** through
Mat 25:18 dug a **h** in the ground,

holes (12)

Jdg 7:24 Capture the watering **h** as far
7:24 They captured the watering **h**
1Sm 14:11 out of the **h** they were hiding
Job 30:6 riverbeds, in **h** in the ground,
Isa 2:19 caves in the rocks and into **h**
7:19 and at all the water **h**.
11:8 Infants will play near cobras' **h**.
Eze 12:12 People will dig **h** in the wall to
Amo 9:11 I will repair the **h** in it.
Mat 8:20 Jesus told him, "Foxes have **h**,
Luk 9:58 Jesus told him, "Foxes have **h**,
Heb 11:38 in caves and **h** in the ground.

holiday (4)

Est 2:18 He also declared that day a **h**
8:17 feasting and enjoying a **h**.
9:19 day of the month of Adar a **h**
9:22 joy and their mourning into a **h**.

holier (2)

Isa 65:5 I'm **h** than you are."
Rom 14:5 that one day is **h** than another.

holiest (4)

Num 18:29 contribute the best and **h** parts
Eze 42:13 the LORD eat the **h** offerings.
42:13 keep the **h** offerings there:
48:12 It will be the **h** part of land,

holiness (18)

Exo 15:11 are glorious because of your **h**
Lev 10:3 'I will show my **h** among those
22:32 I will show my **h** among the
2Ch 20:21 him for the beauty of his **h**.
Psa 30:4 his **h** by giving thanks.
60:6 the following through his **h**:
89:35 On my **h** I have taken an oath
93:5 O LORD, **h** is what makes your
108:7 the following through his **h**:
Eze 36:23 I will reveal the **h** of my great
36:23 because I will reveal my **h**
38:23 show my greatness and my **h**.
44:19 transfer the **h** from their clothes
46:20 won't transfer **h** to the people.
Amo 4:2 has taken an oath on his **h**:
1Co 1:30 our **h**, and our ransom from sin.
2Co 1:12 a God-given **h** and sincerity,
1Ti 2:15 lives in faith, love, and **h**.

hollow (4)

Exo 27:8 of boards so that it's **h** inside.
38:7 boards so that it was **h** inside.
Jdg 15:19 So God split open the **h** place
Jer 52:21 It was three inches thick and **h**.

Holon (3)

Jos 15:51 Goshen, **H**, and Giloh.
21:15 **H**, Debir,
Jer 48:21 plain: to **H**, Jahzah, Mephaath,

holy (964)

Gen 2:3 day and set it apart as **h**,
31:13 a stone marker for a **h** purpose
Exo 3:5 you are standing is **h** ground.
12:16 You must have a **h** assembly
15:13 you will guide them to your **h**
15:17 the **h** place that you built with
16:23 a **h** day of worship dedicated to
19:6 of priests and my **h** nation.'
19:10 set themselves apart as **h**.
19:22 set themselves apart as **h**,
19:23 the mountain and consider it **h**."
20:8 by observing it as a **h** day.
20:11 and set this day apart as **h**.
22:31 "You must be my **h** people.
25:8 "Then have them make a **h**
26:33 mark off the most **h** place from
26:33 holy place from the **h** place.
26:34 on the ark in the most **h** place.
28:2 Make **h** clothes for your brother
28:3 will set him apart as **h** when
28:4 They will make these **h**
28:29 Aaron goes into the **h** place,
28:35 presence in the **h** place so that
28:36 a signet ring): **H** to the LORD.
28:38 their **h** offerings — whatever
28:43 serve as priests in the **h** place.
29:6 and fasten the **h** crown to it.
29:21 and their clothes will be **h**.
29:27 Set apart as **h** the breast that is
29:29 "Aaron's **h** clothes will belong
29:30 to serve in the **h** place — will
29:31 and boil its meat in a **h** place.
29:33 because the offerings are **h**.
29:34 not be eaten because it is **h**.
29:37 the altar apart for its **h** purpose.
29:37 Then the altar will be most **h**.
29:37 the altar will become **h**.
29:43 glory will make this place **h**.
29:44 the altar for their **h** purposes.
29:44 his sons apart for their **h** duties
30:10 It is most **h** to the LORD."
30:13 standard weight of the **h** place.
30:24 weight of the **h** place —
30:25 make these into a **h** oil,
30:25 This will be the **h** oil used for
30:29 them for their **h** purpose.
30:29 Then they will be most **h**,
Exo 30:29 touches them will become **h**.
30:30 set them apart for their **h** duties
30:31 this will be my **h** oil used only
30:32 It is **h**, and you must treat it as
30:32 and you must treat it as **h**.
30:35 seasoned with salt, pure and **h**.
30:36 You must treat it as most **h**.
30:37 Treat it as **h** to the LORD.
31:10 the special clothes — the **h**
31:11 incense for the **h** place.
31:13 the LORD who makes you **h**.
31:14 worship because it is **h** to you.
31:15 It is **h** to the LORD.
35:2 but the seventh day is a **h** day
35:19 duties in the **h** place — both
35:19 holy place — both the **h** clothes
35:21 and to make the **h** clothes.
36:1 for constructing the **h** place."
36:3 of constructing the **h** place.
36:4 on the **h** place stopped what
36:6 contribution to the **h** place."
37:29 had a perfumer make the **h** oil
38:24 the **h** place weighed over
38:24 standard weight of the **h** place.
38:25 standard weight of the **h** place.
38:27 the 100 bases for the **h** place
39:1 for official duties in the **h** place.
39:1 They also made the **h** clothes
39:30 medallion (the **h** crown) out
39:30 a signet ring): **H** to the LORD.
39:41 as priests in the **h** place — both
39:41 holy place — both the **h** clothes
40:9 furnishings. Then it will be **h**.
40:10 and it will be most **h**.
40:13 dress Aaron in the **h** clothes,
Lev 2:3 It is very **h**, set apart from the
2:10 It is very **h**, set apart from the
4:6 the canopy in the **h** place.
5:15 any of the LORD's **h** things,
5:15 standards of the **h** place.
5:16 Pay for whatever **h** things you
6:16 unleavened bread in a **h** place,
6:17 It is very **h** like the offering for
6:18 who touches it will become **h**."
6:25 is slaughtered. It is very **h**.
6:26 for sin will eat it in a **h** place,
6:27 that touches its meat will be **h**.
6:27 he must wash them in a **h**
6:29 the offering for sin. It is very **h**.
6:30 was brought into the **h** place
7:1 the guilt offering. It is very **h**.
7:6 It will be eaten in a **h** place.
7:6 in a holy place. It is very **h**.
8:9 gold medallion (the **h** crown)
8:12 to set him apart for his **h** duties.
8:15 and declared it **h** so that priests
10:4 from in front of the **h** place.
10:10 difference between what is **h**
10:12 to the altar because it is very **h**.
10:13 Eat it in a **h** place because it is
10:17 offering for sin in the **h** place?
10:17 It is very **h** and was given to
10:18 not brought inside the **h** place,
11:44 You must live **h** lives.
11:44 Be **h** because I am holy.
11:44 Be holy because I am **h**.
11:45 Be **h** because I am holy.
11:45 Be holy because I am **h**.
12:4 She must not touch anything **h**
12:4 holy or go into the **h** place until
14:13 the lamb in the **h** place where
14:13 to the priest. It is very **h**.
16:2 go into the **h** place whenever
16:3 order to come into the **h** place:
16:4 He must put on a **h** linen robe
16:4 These are **h** clothes.
16:16 committed against the **h** place.
16:17 time Aaron enters the **h** place
16:19 will cleanse it and declare it **h**.
16:20 with the LORD at the **h** place,
16:23 put on to go into the **h** place,
16:24 He will wash his body in the **h**
16:27 was brought into the **h** place
16:32 will put on the **h** linen clothes
16:33 with the LORD at the **h** place,
19:2 of Israel: Be **h** because I,
Lev 19:2 I, the LORD your God, am **h**.
19:8 they have dishonored what is **h**
19:24 all the fruit will be a **h** offering
19:30 worship and respect my **h** tent.
20:3 made my **h** tent unclean,
20:3 and dishonored my **h** name.
20:7 "Live **h** lives. Be holy because I
20:7 Be **h** because I am the LORD
20:8 LORD who sets you apart as **h**.
20:26 Be my **h** people because I,
20:26 because I, the LORD, am **h**.
21:6 "Be God's **h** men, and don't
21:6 Be **h** because you bring
21:7 a priest is God's **h** man.
21:8 Be **h** because you offer the
21:8 Be **h** because I, the LORD,
21:8 because I, the LORD, am **h**.
21:8 I set you apart as **h**.
21:12 He must not leave the **h** tent of
21:15 set him apart as **h**."
21:22 the food of his God — what is **h**
21:22 is holy and what is very **h**.
21:23 He must never dishonor the **h**
21:23 set them apart as **h**."
22:2 respect the **h** offerings which
22:2 will not dishonor my **h** name.
22:3 comes near the **h** offerings the
22:4 eat any of the **h** offerings until
22:6 He must not eat any of the **h**
22:7 Then he may eat the **h**
22:9 they dishonored a **h** offering.
22:9 who sets them apart as **h**.
22:10 must never eat any **h** offering,
22:12 taken from the **h** contributions.
22:14 "Those who eat a **h** offering by
22:14 must give another **h** offering
22:15 Priests must not dishonor the **h**
22:16 eaten the priests' **h** offerings.
22:16 who sets them apart as **h**."
22:32 Never dishonor my **h** name.
22:32 who sets you apart as **h**.
23:2 which you must announce as **h**
23:3 you don't work, a **h** assembly.
23:4 festivals with **h** assemblies,
23:7 day there will be a **h** assembly.
23:8 day there will be a **h** assembly.
23:20 will be **h** and will belong to the
23:21 that there will be a **h** assembly
23:24 It will be a memorial day, a **h**
23:27 There will be a **h** assembly.
23:35 day there will be a **h** assembly.
23:36 day there will be a **h** assembly.
23:37 Announce them as **h**
24:9 They will eat it in a **h** place.
24:9 It is very **h**, set apart from the
25:10 Set apart the fiftieth year as **h**,
25:12 jubilee (year) will be **h** to you.
26:2 worship and respect my **h** tent.
27:3 standard weight of the **h** place.
27:9 it will be considered **h**.
27:10 then both animals will be **h**.
27:14 to the LORD as something **h**,
27:16 to the LORD as something **h**,
27:21 it will be **h** like a field claimed
27:22 to the LORD as something **h**.
27:23 on that day as something **h**,
27:25 standard weight of the **h** place.
27:26 it cannot be set apart as **h**.
27:28 dedicated in that way is very **h**.
27:30 is **h** and belongs to the LORD.
27:32 or sheep that you counted is **h**
27:33 and its substitute will be **h**.
Num 3:13 I set apart as **h** every firstborn
3:28 They were in charge of the **h**
3:31 utensils used in the **h** place,
3:32 were in charge of the **h** place.
3:38 They were in charge of the **h**
3:47 standard weight of the **h** place)
3:50 standard weight of the **h** place.
4:4 take care of the most **h** things.
4:12 that are used in the **h** place,
4:15 finished covering the **h** things
4:15 come to carry all the **h** articles.
4:15 must never touch the **h** things,
4:16 the **h** place and its contents."
4:19 come near the most **h** things:

Num 4:19 sons will go into the **h** place
4:20 not go in to look at the **h** things,
5:9 and above the **h** offerings that
5:10 Each person's **h** offerings will
5:17 Then the priest will take **h**
6:5 as Nazirites, they will be **h**.
6:8 they will be **h** to the LORD.
6:20 They are **h** and belong to the
7:9 they took care of the **h** things.
7:9 They had to carry the **h** things
7:13 standard weight of the **h** place.
7:19 standard weight of the **h** place.
7:25 standard weight of the **h** place.
7:31 standard weight of the **h** place.
7:37 standard weight of the **h** place.
7:43 standard weight of the **h** place.
7:49 standard weight of the **h** place.
7:55 standard weight of the **h** place.
7:61 standard weight of the **h** place.
7:67 standard weight of the **h** place.
7:73 standard weight of the **h** place.
7:79 standard weight of the **h** place.
7:85 standard weight of the **h** place.
7:86 standard weight of the **h** place.
8:17 I set them apart as **h** to me.
8:19 they come near the **h** place."
10:21 who carried the **h** things,
11:18 They must be set apart as **h**.
15:40 and you will be **h** to your God.
16:3 in the whole community is **h**,
16:5 who belongs to him, who is **h**,
16:7 will choose the man who is **h**.
16:37 burners have become **h**.
16:38 and lost their lives are **h**,
18:1 any sins against the **h** place.
18:3 the furnishings in the **h** place,
18:5 of the work done at the **h** place
18:7 who comes near ⌊the **h** place
18:8 descendants all the **h** gifts from
18:9 That part of the most **h**
18:9 as a most **h** offering will belong
18:10 Eat it in a most **h** place.
18:10 You must consider it **h**.
18:16 standard weight of the **h** place.
18:17 They are **h**. Throw the blood
18:19 and your daughters all the **h**
18:32 You won't be dishonoring the **h**
19:20 He has made the **h** place of the
20:12 show the Israelites how **h** I am!
20:13 he showed them he was **h**.
27:14 didn't show the people how **h**
28:7 Pour it out to the LORD in a **h**
28:18 day there will be a **h** assembly.
28:25 you must have a **h** assembly.
28:26 you must have a **h** assembly.
29:1 you must have a **h** assembly.
29:7 you must have a **h** assembly.
29:12 you must have a **h** assembly.
31:6 Phinehas took with him the **h**
35:25 was anointed with the **h** oil.
Dtr 5:12 the day of worship as a **h** day.
7:6 You are a **h** people,
12:26 Take the **h** things and the
14:2 You are people who are **h** to
14:21 But you are people who are **h**
22:9 that grows there to the **h** place.
23:14 your camp must always be **h**.
26:13 "Nothing is left of the **h** offering
26:14 I didn't eat any of this **h** offering
26:15 Look down from your **h** place in
26:19 and you will be a people **h** to
28:9 will be the LORD's **h** people,
32:51 show the Israelites how **h** I am.
33:2 tens of thousands of **h** ones.
33:3 All your **h** ones are in your
Jos 3:5 to make yourselves **h**
5:15 where you are standing is **h**."
6:19 made of bronze and iron are **h**
7:13 to make yourselves **h**.
24:19 "Since the LORD is a **h** God,
24:26 oak tree at the LORD's **h** place.
1Sm 2:2 There is no one **h** like the
6:20 before the LORD, this **h** God?
7:1 son Eleazar the **h** occupation
16:5 to make yourselves **h**,
21:4 "But there is **h** bread for the

1Sm 21:5 men's bodies are kept **h** even
21:5 will their bodies be **h** today?"
21:6 So the priest gave him **h**
1Ki 6:16 inner room, the most **h** place.
7:50 ⌊room⌋ (the most **h** place),
7:51 He brought the **h** things that
8:4 and all the **h** utensils in it ⌊to
8:6 temple (the most **h** place) under
8:8 seen in the **h** place by anyone
8:10 the priests left the **h** place,
8:64 LORD's temple as a **h** place.
9:3 you have built is **h** so that my
9:7 this temple that I declared **h**
15:15 his father had set apart as **h**.
2Ki 4:9 "I know he's a **h** man of God.
10:20 Jehu said, "Call a **h** assembly
12:4 "⌊Collect⌋ all the **h**
19:22 It is the **H** One of Israel!
1Ch 6:49 all the work in the most **h** place
9:29 the **h** utensils, the flour, wine,
15:12 to make yourselves **h**.
15:14 the Levites made themselves **h**
16:10 Brag about his **h** name.
16:29 Worship the LORD in ⌊his⌋ **h**
16:35 give thanks to your **h** name
22:19 Start building the **h** place of the
22:19 and God's **h** utensils into
23:13 the most **h** things ⌊to God⌋,
23:28 to ensure that all the **h** things
23:32 tent of meeting and the **h** place
24:5 were officers for the **h** place
28:10 build the temple as his **h** place.
29:3 else I gathered for the **h** temple.
29:16 temple for your **h** name is from
2Ch 3:8 He made the most **h** place.
3:10 In the most **h** place he made
4:22 ⌊room⌋ (the most **h** place),
5:1 He brought the **h** things that
5:5 and all the **h** utensils in it ⌊to
5:7 temple (the most **h** place) under
5:9 seen in the **h** place by anyone
5:11 to make themselves **h**
5:12 When the priests left the **h**
7:7 LORD's temple as a **h** place.
7:16 this temple **h** so that my
7:20 this temple that I declared **h**
8:11 LORD's ark has come are **h**."
15:18 his father had set apart as **h**.
20:8 lived in it and built a **h** temple
23:6 may enter because they are **h**,
24:7 and used all the **h** things
26:18 who have been given the **h**
26:18 Get out of the **h** place because
29:5 LORD God of your ancestors **h**.
29:5 corrupted from the **h** place.
29:7 burnt offerings in the **h** place
29:15 to make themselves **h**.
29:17 to make the LORD's temple **h**.
29:19 them and made them **h**.
29:21 the **h** place, and Judah.
29:33 The animals dedicated as **h**
29:34 could make themselves **h**.
29:34 in making themselves **h** than
30:3 to make themselves **h**
30:8 Come to his **h** place that he
30:8 place that he made **h** forever.
30:15 to make themselves **h**.
30:17 had not made themselves **h**.
30:17 their lambs **h** for the LORD.
30:19 as required for the **h** place."
30:24 to make themselves **h**.
30:27 to God's **h** place in heaven.
31:6 a tenth of the **h** things they had
31:6 piled these **h** things in heaps.
31:14 LORD and the **h** gifts dedicated
31:18 in keeping themselves **h**
31:18 themselves holy for the **h** work.
35:3 to make themselves **h**
35:3 "Put the **h** ark in the temple that
35:5 Stand in the **h** place
35:6 to make yourselves **h**,
35:13 They boiled the **h** offerings in
36:14 the temple in Jerusalem **h**,
36:17 young men in their **h** temple.
Ezr 2:63 eat any of the most **h** food until
3:5 and all the other **h** festivals

Ezr 8:28 "You and the utensils are **h** to
9:2 They have mixed our **h** race
9:8 a secure hold on his **h** place.
Neh 7:65 eat any of the most **h** food until
8:9 "This is a **h** day for the LORD
8:10 Today is a **h** day for the Lord.
8:11 Today is a **h** day. Don't be sad."
9:14 You taught them about your **h**
10:31 of worship or any other **h** day.
10:33 for the **h** gifts and offerings for
10:39 the utensils of the **h** place are
11:1 to live in Jerusalem, the **h** city.
11:18 in the **h** city totaled 284.
12:47 They set aside **h** gifts for ⌊the
12:47 and the Levites set aside **h**
13:22 to keep the day of worship **h**.
Job 5:1 To which of the **h** ones will
6:10 the words of the **H** One.
15:15 If God doesn't trust his **h** ones,
Psa 2:6 king on Zion, my **h** mountain."
3:4 me from his **h** mountain.
5:7 I will bow toward your **h**
11:4 The LORD is in his **h** temple.
15:1 Who may live on your **h**
16:3 Those who lead **h** lives on
16:10 or allow your **h** one to decay.
20:2 send you help from his **h** place
20:6 He will answer him from his **h**
22:3 Yet, you are **h**, enthroned on
24:3 Who may stand in his **h** place?
28:2 toward your most **h** place.
29:2 Worship the LORD in ⌊his⌋ **h**
33:21 In his **h** name we trust.
34:9 Fear the LORD, you **h** people
43:3 Let them bring me to your **h**
46:4 the **h** place where the Most
47:8 He sits upon his **h** throne.
48:1 His **h** mountain is in the city of
51:11 not take your **H** Spirit from me.
63:2 So I look for you in the **h** place
65:4 from your **h** temple.
68:5 The God who is in his **h**
68:17 ⌊The God of⌋ Sinai is in his **h**
68:24 God, my king, into the **h** place.
68:35 is awe-inspiring in his **h** place.
71:22 O **H** One of Israel.
73:17 Only when I came into God's **h**
74:3 everything in the **h** temple.
74:7 They burned your **h** place to
77:13 O God, your ways are **h**!
78:41 and they pushed the **H** One of
78:54 He brought them into his **h** land
78:69 He built his **h** place to be like
79:1 have dishonored your **h** temple.
87:1 ⌊stands⌋ on **h** mountains.
89:5 in the assembly of the **h** ones.
89:7 in the council of the **h** ones.
89:18 belongs to the **H** One of Israel.
89:20 I anointed him with my **h** oil.
96:6 Strength and beauty are in his **h**
96:9 the LORD in ⌊his⌋ **h** splendor.
97:12 as you remember how **h** he is.
98:1 His right hand and his **h** arm
99:3 great and fearful name. He is **h**!
99:5 down at his footstool. He is **h**!
99:9 Bow at his **h** mountain.
99:9 The LORD our God is **h**!
102:19 from his **h** place high above.
103:1 Praise his **h** name,
105:3 Brag about his **h** name.
105:42 He remembered his **h** promise
106:16 the LORD's **h** one.
106:47 give thanks to your **h** name
110:3 to you in **h** splendor like dew
111:9 His name is **h** and terrifying.
114:2 Judah became his **h** place and
134:2 your hands toward the **h** place,
138:2 will bow toward your **h** temple.
145:21 will praise his **h** name forever
150:1 Praise God in his **h** place.
Pro 9:10 of the **H** One is understanding.
20:25 "This is a **h** offering!"
30:3 I don't have knowledge of the **H**
Ecc 8:10 to go in and out of the **h** place.
Isa 1:4 They have despised the **H** One
4:3 in Jerusalem will be called **h**,

Isa 5:16 The **h** God will show himself
5:16 will show himself to be **h** when
5:19 Let the plan of the **H** One of
5:24 the word of the **H** One of Israel.
6:3 each other and said, "**H**, holy,
6:3 **h**, holy is the LORD of Armies!
6:3 **h** is the LORD of Armies!
6:13 The **h** seed will be the land's
8:13 that the LORD of Armies is **h**.
10:17 Its **H** One will become a fire.
10:20 the **H** One of Israel.
11:9 anywhere on my **h** mountain.
12:6 The **H** One of Israel is great.
13:3 I've commanded my **h** ones.
16:12 They will come into the **h**
17:7 and their eyes will look to the **H**
23:18 to the LORD for his **h** purpose.
27:13 the **h** mountain in Jerusalem.
29:19 find joy in the **H** One of Israel.
29:23 acknowledge my name as **h**.
29:23 They will treat the **H** One of
29:23 the Holy One of Jacob as **h**.
30:11 Get the **H** One of Israel out of
30:12 This is what the **H** One of
30:15 the **H** One of Israel,
31:1 They don't look to the **H** One of
35:8 It will be called the **H** Road.
37:23 It is the **H** One of Israel!
40:25 is my equal?" asks the **H** One.
41:14 the **H** One of Israel.
41:16 and praise the **H** One of Israel.
41:20 that the **H** One of Israel has
43:3 the **H** One of Israel,
43:14 the **H** One of Israel,
43:15 I am the LORD, your **H** One,
43:28 the leaders of the **h** place.
45:11 The LORD is the **H** One and
47:4 Our defender is the **H** One of
48:2 ⌊citizens⌋ of the **h** city.
48:17 the **H** One of Israel,
49:7 defender of Israel, its **H** One.
49:7 The **H** One of Israel has
52:1 **h** city of Jerusalem.
52:10 The LORD will show his **h**
54:5 Your defender is the **H** One of
55:5 because of the **H** One of Israel.
56:7 Then I will bring them to my **h**
57:13 land and inherit my **h** mountain.
57:15 and his name is **h**.
57:15 I live in a high and **h** place.
58:13 as you please on my **h** day,
58:13 the LORD's **h** day honorable,
60:9 the **H** One of Israel,
60:13 come to beautify my **h** place,
60:14 the city of the **H** One of Israel.
62:9 drink wine in my **h** courtyards.
62:12 They will be called **H** People,
63:10 and offended his **H** Spirit.
63:11 who put his **H** Spirit in them?
63:15 from your **h** and beautiful
63:18 Your **h** people possessed the
63:18 have trampled on your **h** place.
64:10 Your **h** cities have become a
64:11 Our **h** and beautiful temple,
65:11 and forgotten my **h** mountain.
65:25 anywhere on my **h** mountain,"
66:17 People make themselves **h**
66:20 and camels to my **h** mountain,
Jer 1:5 set you apart for my **h** purpose.
17:12 Our **h** place is a glorious
17:22 the day of worship as a **h** day,
17:24 of worship as a **h** day by not
17:27 of worship as a **h** day by not
23:9 because of the LORD and his **h**
25:30 from his **h** dwelling place.
31:23 of righteousness, **h** mountain."
31:40 will be **h** to the LORD.
50:29 the **H** One of Israel.
51:5 abandoning the **H** One of Israel.
51:51 have gone into the **h** places
Lam 1:10 the nations enter the **h** place.
2:7 altar and disowned his **h** place.
2:20 be killed in the Lord's **h** place?
Eze 5:11 dishonored my **h** worship place
7:24 and their **h** places will be
8:6 to go far away from my **h** place.

Eze 9:6 Start with my **h** place."
20:12 that I, the LORD, made them **h**.
20:20 Set apart certain **h** days to
20:39 no longer dishonor my **h** name
20:40 worship me on my **h** mountain,
20:40 and all your **h** gifts.
20:41 you I will reveal myself as **h**
21:2 preach against the **h** places.
22:8 You have despised my **h**
22:26 and dishonor my **h** things.
22:26 distinguish between what is **h**
23:38 They have polluted my **h**
23:39 they came into my **h** place and
24:21 going to dishonor my **h** place.
24:21 You brag that my **h** place gives
25:3 You were glad when my **h**
28:14 You were on God's **h** mountain.
28:18 You dishonored your own **h**
28:22 you and show you how **h** I am.
28:25 I will show that I am **h** as the
36:20 they dishonored my **h** name.
36:21 concerned about my **h** name
36:22 but for the sake of my **h** name,
37:26 and put my **h** place among
37:28 have set Israel apart as **h**,
37:28 because my **h** place will be
38:16 I will use you for my **h** purpose
39:7 I will make my **h** name known
39:7 dishonor my **h** name again.
39:7 the **H** One in Israel.
39:25 I will stand up for my **h** name.
39:27 nations will see that I am **h**.
41:1 brought me into the **h** place
41:2 the length of the **h** place.
41:4 room at the end of the **h** place.
41:4 "This is the most **h** place."
41:15 The **h** place and the most holy
41:15 the most **h** place were paneled.
41:17 the door to the most **h** place
41:21 The doorframes in the **h** place
41:21 In front of the most **h** place was
41:23 The **h** place and the most holy
41:23 The holy place and the most **h**
41:25 on the doors of the **h** place as
42:13 face the open area are **h** rooms.
42:13 Because these rooms are **h**,
42:14 the priests enter the **h** place,
42:14 they must not go out of the **h**
42:14 These clothes are **h**.
42:20 It separated what was **h** from
43:7 dishonor my **h** name by acting
43:8 They dishonored my **h** name
43:12 top of the mountain is most **h**.
43:21 outside the **h** place.
44:1 outer east gate of the **h** place,
44:5 and leaves from the **h** place.
44:7 foreigners into my **h** place.
44:8 didn't take care of my **h** things.
44:9 may not enter my **h** place.
44:11 have served in my **h** place.
44:13 come near any of my **h** things
44:13 things or my most **h** things.
44:15 took care of my **h** place when
44:16 They may enter my **h** place,
44:19 in the side rooms of the **h** place
44:23 difference between what is **h**
44:24 They must observe **h** days to
44:27 inner courtyard of the **h** place
44:27 place to serve in the **h** place,
45:1 The entire area will be **h**.
45:2 square will be for the **h** place
45:3 The **h** place, that is, the most
45:3 place, that is, the most **h** place,
45:4 This **h** part of the land will
45:4 who serve in the **h** place,
45:4 be the location for the **h** place.
45:6 located alongside the **h** area.
45:7 land on both sides of the **h** area
45:7 western boundary of the **h** area,
45:7 eastern boundary of the **h** area,
45:18 remove sin from the **h** place.
47:12 water flows from the **h** place.
48:8 and the **h** place will be in the
48:10 This **h** area will belong to the
48:10 The LORD's **h** place will be in
48:11 They took care of my **h** place.

Eze 48:14 land is the LORD's and it is **h**.
48:18 of the land borders the **h** area
48:21 and west side of the **h** area
48:21 eastward from the **h** area
48:21 and the **h** area with the holy
48:21 and the holy area with the **h**
Dan 4:8 The spirit of the **h** gods is in
4:9 I know the spirit of the **h** gods
4:13 I saw a guardian, a **h** being,
4:17 The **h** ones have announced
4:18 because the spirit of the **h** gods
4:23 You saw a guardian, a **h** being,
5:11 has the spirit of the **h** gods.
7:18 But the **h** people of the Most
7:21 war against the **h** people
7:22 judged in favor of the **h** people
7:22 The time came when the **h**
7:25 oppress the **h** people of the
7:25 The **h** people will be handed
7:27 will be given to the **h** people of
8:11 him and wrecked his **h** place.
8:13 Then I heard a **h** one speaking.
8:13 Another **h** one said to the one
8:13 the surrender of the **h** place,
8:14 Then the **h** place will be made
8:24 along with some **h** people.
9:16 Jerusalem, your **h** mountain.
9:17 look favorably on your **h** place,
9:20 about my God's **h** mountain
9:24 for your people and your **h** city.
9:24 and to anoint the Most **H** One.
9:26 The city and the **h** place will
11:28 to fight against the **h** promise.
11:30 Angry at the **h** promise,
11:30 who abandon the **h** promise.
11:31 His forces will dishonor the **h**
11:45 seas at a beautiful **h** mountain.
12:7 When the power of the **h**
Hos 11:9 I am the **H** One among you,
11:12 against the **H** One who is
Joe 2:1 the alarm on my **h** mountain.
2:16 Prepare them for a **h** meeting.
3:17 I live on my **h** mountain,
3:17 Jerusalem will be **h**.
Amo 2:7 They dishonor my **h** name.
7:9 and the **h** places of Israel will
7:13 because this is the king's **h**
Oba 1:16 drank on my **h** mountain,
1:17 It will be **h**. The descendants of
Jnh 2:4 I ever see your **h** temple again?'
2:7 came to you in your **h** temple.
Mic 1:2 be a witness from his **h** temple.
3:5 But they declare a **h** war
Hab 1:12 O LORD, my God, my **H** One?
2:20 The LORD is in his **h** temple.
3:3 The **H** One comes from Mount
Zep 3:4 priests contaminate what is **h**.
3:11 act proud on my **h** mountain.
Hag 2:12 meat set aside for a **h** purpose
2:12 does that make the food **h**?"
Zec 2:12 Judah as his own in the **h** land
2:13 out from his **h** dwelling place."
8:3 will be called the **h** mountain.
14:5 and all the **h** ones will be with
14:20 On that day "**H** to the LORD"
14:21 and in Judah will be **h**
Mal 2:11 Judah has dishonored the **h**
Mat 1:18 was pregnant by the **H** Spirit.
1:20 She is pregnant by the **H** Spirit.
3:11 you with the **H** Spirit and fire.
4:5 devil took him into the **h** city
6:9 let your name be kept **h**.
7:6 "Don't give what is **h** to dogs or
12:32 against the **H** Spirit will not
23:17 temple that made the gold **h**?
23:19 the altar that makes the gift **h**?
24:15 will stand in the **h** place.
27:52 and the bodies of many **h**
27:53 and they went into the **h** city
28:19 and of the **H** Spirit.
Mar 1:8 baptize you with the **H** Spirit."
1:24 you are — the **H** One of God!"
3:29 But whoever curses the **H**
6:20 that John was a fair and **h** man,
8:38 he comes with the **h** angels
12:36 David, guided by the **H** Spirit,

Mar 13:11 but the **H** Spirit will.
Luk 1:15 He will be filled with the **H**
1:35 "The **H** Spirit will come to you,
1:35 Therefore, the **h** child
1:41 Elizabeth was filled with the **H**
1:49 things to me. His name is **h**.
1:67 the **H** Spirit and prophesied,
1:70 his **h** prophets long ago.
1:72 and remembered his **h** promise,
1:75 by being **h** and honorable as
2:23 to be set apart as **h** to the Lord."
2:25 The **H** Spirit was with Simeon
3:16 you with the **H** Spirit and fire.
3:22 and the **H** Spirit came down to
4:1 Jesus was filled with the **H**
4:34 you are — the **H** One of God!"
9:26 the Father and the **h** angels.
10:21 In that hour the **H** Spirit filled
11:2 let your name be kept **h**.
11:13 in heaven give the **H** Spirit
12:10 dishonors the **H** Spirit will not
12:12 At that time the **H** Spirit will
Jon 1:33 who baptizes with the **H** Spirit.'
6:69 that you are the **H** One of God."
10:36 God set me apart for this **h**
14:26 the helper, the **H** Spirit,
17:11 **H** Father, keep them safe by
17:17 "Use the truth to make them **h**.
17:19 I'm dedicating myself to this **h**
17:19 will use the truth to be **h**.
20:22 "Receive the **H** Spirit.
Act 1:2 through the **H** Spirit
1:5 be baptized by the **H** Spirit."
1:8 power when the **H** Spirit comes
1:16 "Brothers, what the **H** Spirit
2:4 were filled with the **H** Spirit
2:27 or allow your **h** one to decay.
2:33 has poured out the **H** Spirit as
2:38 Then you will receive the **H**
3:14 man who was **h** and innocent.
3:21 his **h** prophets long ago.
4:8 he was filled with the **H** Spirit,
4:25 You said through the **H** Spirit,
4:27 against your **h** servant Jesus,
4:30 name of your **h** servant Jesus."
4:31 were filled with the **H** Spirit
5:3 you could deceive the **H** Spirit?
5:32 and so is the **H** Spirit,
6:5 full of faith and the **H** Spirit,
6:13 bad things about the **h** place
7:33 you're standing is **h** ground.
7:51 always opposed the **H** Spirit,
7:55 Stephen was full of the **H** Spirit.
8:15 would receive the **H** Spirit.
8:16 (Before this the **H** Spirit had not
8:17 received the **H** Spirit.
8:19 on will receive the **H** Spirit."
9:17 to be filled with the **H** Spirit."
9:31 and the comfort of the **H** Spirit.
10:22 A **h** angel told him to summon
10:38 from Nazareth with the **H** Spirit
10:44 the **H** Spirit came to everyone
10:45 the gift of the **H** Spirit had been
10:47 They have received the **H**
11:15 "When I began to speak, the **H**
11:16 will be baptized by the **H** Spirit.'
11:24 and he was full of the **H** Spirit
13:2 and fasting, the **H** Spirit said,
13:4 Saul were sent by the **H** Spirit,
13:9 was filled with the **H** Spirit.
13:35 not allow your **h** one to decay.'
13:52 to be full of joy and the **H** Spirit.
15:8 by giving them the **H** Spirit as
15:8 as he gave the **H** Spirit to us.
15:28 The **H** Spirit and we have
16:6 because the **H** Spirit kept them
19:2 "Did you receive the **H** Spirit
19:2 even heard of the **H** Spirit."
19:6 the **H** Spirit came to them,
20:23 However, the **H** Spirit warns
20:28 which the **H** Spirit has placed
20:32 shared by all of God's **h** people.
21:11 "The **H** Spirit says,
21:28 made this **h** place unclean."
26:18 who are made **h** by believing
28:25 "How well the **H** Spirit spoke to

Rom 1:2 prophets in the **H** Scriptures.
1:4 In his spiritual, **h** nature he was
1:7 has called to be his **h** people.
5:5 into our hearts by the **H** Spirit,
6:19 This leads you to live **h** lives.
6:22 This results in a **h** life and,
7:12 So Moses' Teachings are **h**,
7:12 and the commandment is **h**,
9:1 The **H** Spirit, along with my
11:16 If the first handful of dough is **h**,
11:16 the whole batch of dough is **h**.
11:16 If the root is **h**, the branches are
11:16 the branches are **h**.
14:17 the joy that the **H** Spirit gives.
15:13 by the power of the **H** Spirit.
15:16 made **h** by the Holy Spirit.
15:16 made holy by the **H** Spirit.
16:2 shows you are God's **h** people.
16:16 Greet each other with a **h** kiss.
1Co 1:2 was made **h** by Christ Jesus
1:2 and called to be God's **h** people
3:17 him because God's temple is **h**.
3:17 You are that **h** temple!
6:1 it in front of God's **h** people?
6:11 been washed and made **h**,
6:19 that belongs to the **H** Spirit?
6:19 The **H** Spirit, whom you
7:14 unbelieving husband is made **h**
7:14 an unbelieving wife is made **h**
7:34 things so that she may be **h**
12:3 except by the **H** Spirit.
14:33 the churches of God's **h** people,
16:20 Greet each other with a **h** kiss.
2Co 1:1 all God's **h** people everywhere
6:6 the **H** Spirit's presence ⌊in our
7:1 body and spirit and live a **h** life
8:4 to his **h** people ⌊in Jerusalem⌋.
13:12 one another with a **h** kiss.
13:12 All of God's **h** people greet you.
13:13 and the **H** Spirit's presence be
Eph 1:1 To God's **h** and faithful people
1:4 chose us through Christ to be **h**
1:13 sealed with the **H** Spirit whom
1:14 This **H** Spirit is the guarantee
2:21 and grow into a **h** temple
3:5 to his **h** apostles and prophets.
4:24 truly righteous and **h**.
4:30 Don't give God's **H** Spirit any
5:3 behavior for God's **h** people.
5:26 the church **h** by cleansing it,
5:27 wrinkle — **h** and without faults.
Col 1:2 To God's **h** and faithful people,
2:16 observance of annual **h** days,
3:12 As **h** people whom God has
1Th 1:5 with power, with the **H** Spirit,
1:6 of joy that the **H** Spirit gives.
3:13 he will strengthen you to be **h**.
3:13 comes with all God's **h** people.
4:4 done in a **h** and honorable way,
4:7 sexually immoral but to be **h**.
4:8 who gives you his **H** Spirit.
5:23 who gives peace make you **h**
5:26 and sisters with a **h** kiss.
2Th 1:10 honored among all his **h** people
1Ti 1:9 think nothing is **h** or sacred,
4:5 and prayer set it apart as **h**.
2Ti 1:9 saved us and called us to be **h**,
1:14 With the help of the **H** Spirit
3:2 have no respect for what is **h**,
3:15 have known the **H** Scriptures.
Tit 3:5 in which the **H** Spirit gives
Heb 2:4 and with other gifts from the **H**
2:11 Jesus, who makes people **h**,
2:11 and all those who are made **h**
3:1 Brothers and sisters, you are **h**
3:7 As the **H** Spirit says,
6:2 setting people apart for **h** tasks,
6:4 gift and shared in the **H** Spirit.
6:10 You helped his **h** people,
6:19 goes into the ⌊**h**⌋ place behind
7:26 need a chief priest who is **h**,
8:2 He serves as priest of the **h**
9:1 It also had a **h** place on earth.
9:2 tent was called the **h** place.
9:3 tent called the most **h** place.
9:8 The **H** Spirit used this to show

Heb 9:8 into the most **h** place was not
9:12 He went into the most **h** place
9:13 made their bodies **h** and clean.
9:24 Christ didn't go into a **h** place
9:25 priest went into the **h** place
10:10 We have been set apart as **h**
10:15 The **H** Spirit tells us the same
10:19 confidently go into the **h** place.
10:29 that made him **h**) as no different
12:10 that we can become **h** like him.
12:14 and try to live **h** lives,
13:11 of animals into the **h** place as
13:12 suffered to make the people **h**
13:24 leaders and all God's **h** people.
1Pe 1:2 and chose you to live **h** lives
1:12 had spoken, the **H** Spirit,
1:15 who called you is **h** you must
1:15 you is holy you must be **h**
1:16 Scripture says, "Be **h**,
1:16 "Be holy, because I am **h**."
2:5 being built into a **h** priesthood.
2:9 a royal priesthood, a **h** nation,
3:5 After all, this is how **h** women
2Pe 1:18 with him on the **h** mountain.
1:21 Instead, it was given by the **H**
2:21 backs on the **h** life God told
3:2 in the past by the **h** prophets
3:11 So think of the kind of **h** and
1Jn 2:20 The **H** One has anointed you,
Jud 1:3 to God's **h** people once
1:14 thousands of his **h** angels.
1:20 use your most **h** faith to grow.
1:20 Pray with the **H** Spirit's help.
Rev 3:7 The one who is **h**,
4:8 they were singing, "**H**, holy,
4:8 they were singing, "Holy, **h**,
4:8 **h** is the Lord God Almighty,
5:8 the prayers of the God's **h**
6:10 "**H** and true Master,
11:2 and they will trample the **h** city
11:18 the prophets, your **h** people,
13:7 war against God's **h** people
13:10 In this situation God's **h** people
14:10 in the presence of the **h** angels
14:12 In this situation God's **h** people,
15:4 You are the only **h** one,
16:5 the one who was, the **h** one,
17:6 the blood of God's **h** people
19:8 that God's **h** people do that
20:6 Blessed and **h** are those who
20:9 the camp of God's **h** people
21:2 Then I saw the **h** city,
21:10 He showed me the **h** city,
21:26 of the nations into the **h** city.
22:11 and let **h** people continue to be
22:11 holy people continue to be **h**."
22:19 of life and the **h** city that are

Homam (1)

1Ch 1:39 Lotan's sons were Hori and **H**.

home (346)

Gen 12:1 and your father's **h**.
18:33 Abraham returned **h**.
19:2 why don't you come to my **h**
19:3 with him and went into his **h**.
20:13 God had me leave my father's **h**
23:4 a stranger with no permanent **h**.
24:7 took me from my father's **h**
24:27 has led me on this trip to the **h**
24:38 Instead, go to my father's **h** and
28:2 Go to the **h** of Bethuel,
28:21 if I return safely to my father's **h**
29:13 him and brought him into his **h**.
30:25 "Let me go **h** to my own
31:30 you have left for your father's **h**
31:55 Laban left and went back **h**.
34:5 kept quiet until they came **h**.
34:26 from Shechem's **h** and left.
35:27 Jacob came **h** to his father
38:11 "Return to your father's **h**.
38:11 went to live in her father's **h**.
39:16 her until his master came **h**.
43:14 and Benjamin ⌊**h**⌋ with you.
43:26 When Joseph came **h**,
44:30 If I come ⌊**h**⌋ without the boy

Exo 2:18 you come **h** so early today?"
3:22 and any woman living in her **h**
12:23 come into your **h** to kill you.
16:5 they prepare what they bring **h**,
18:23 settled so that they can go **h**."
Lev 12:4 Then she must stay at **h** for 33
12:5 Then she must stay at **h** for 66
22:13 back to live in her father's **h**,
25:29 "If anyone sells a **h** in a walled
25:35 stranger without a permanent **h**
25:47 a permanent **h** among you may
Num 24:11 Go **h**! I said I'd reward you
24:25 got up and went back **h**,
30:16 daughters still living at **h**.
Dtr 6:7 them when you're at **h** or away,
11:19 them when you're at **h** or away,
20:5 not dedicated it, you may go **h**.
20:6 the grapes, you may go **h**.
20:7 not married her, you may go **h**.
20:8 your courage, you may go **h**.
21:12 Bring her into your **h**.
22:2 take the animal **h** with you.
22:8 death at your **h** if someone falls
24:5 one year he is free to stay at **h**
32:25 and even at **h** there will be
33:18 yourselves when you stay at **h**.
Jos 9:12 was warm when we left **h**
20:6 Then he may go back to his **h**
22:4 So return **h**, to the land that is
22:7 When Joshua sent them **h**,
Jdg 2:6 sent the people of Israel **h**.
7:3 back **h**.'" So 22,000 men went
7:3 So 22,000 men went back **h**,
7:7 All the other men should go **h**."
7:8 sent the other men of Israel **h**,
8:29 son of Joash, went **h** to live.
9:5 went to his father's **h** in Ophrah.
9:55 was dead, they all went **h**.
11:34 went to his **h** in Mizpah,
14:2 He went **h** and told his father
17:4 Both were placed in Micah's **h**.
18:26 he turned around and went **h**.
19:2 him and went to her father's **h**,
19:3 persuade her to come back **h**.
19:9 you can start out early to go **h**."
19:15 to take them **h** for the night.
19:18 offered to take me into his **h**.
19:23 This man is a guest in my **h**.
19:28 her on the donkey and left for **h**.
19:29 When he arrived **h**,
21:23 who were dancing and went **h**.
21:24 and family. They all went **h**.
Rut 1:8 go back to your mother's **h**.
1:9 you may find security in a **h**
3:1 shouldn't I try to look for a **h**
4:11 who is coming into your **h**,
4:13 Then Boaz took Ruth **h**,
1Sm 1:19 Then they returned **h** to Ramah.
2:11 Elkanah went **h** to Ramah.
2:20 Then they would go **h**.
7:17 he would return **h** to Ramah.
10:26 Saul also went **h** to Gibeah.
13:2 the rest of the people he sent **h**.
15:34 Saul went to his **h** at Gibeah.
23:18 and Jonathan went **h**.
24:22 Then Saul went **h**,
25:1 buried him at his **h** in Ramah.
25:6 May you, your **h**, and all you
25:35 and told her, "Go **h** in peace.
25:36 was holding a banquet in his **h**.
26:25 while Saul returned **h**.
2Sm 3:16 "Go **h**," Abner told him.
3:16 Abner told him. So he went **h**.
3:22 and Joab were coming **h** from
4:5 came to Ishbosheth's **h** at the
4:11 man on his own bed in his **h**?
6:3 brought it from Abinadab's **h**
6:4 brought it from Abinadab's **h**,
6:10 Instead, he rerouted it to the **h**
6:11 ark of the LORD stayed at the **h**
6:12 has blessed Obed Edom's **h**
6:19 Then all the people went **h**.
9:4 "He is at the **h** of Machir,
9:5 sent men to get him from the **h**
9:12 **h** became Mephibosheth's
11:4 period.) Then she went **h**.
2Sm 11:8 "Go **h**," David said to Uriah,
11:9 mercenaries. He didn't go **h**.
11:10 "Uriah didn't go **h**," David
11:10 Why didn't you go **h**?"
11:13 mercenaries. He didn't go **h**.
11:27 for her and brought her to his **h**,
12:3 and she grew up in his **h** with
12:15 Then Nathan went **h**.
12:20 Then he went **h** and asked for
13:7 brother Amnon's **h**," he said,
13:8 went to her brother Amnon's **h**.
13:20 So Tamar stayed there at the **h**
14:8 "Go **h**," the king told the
14:31 went to Absalom at his **h**.
15:12 to come from his **h** in Giloh.
17:18 left quickly and came to the **h**
17:20 came to the woman at her **h**.
17:23 and went **h** to his own city.
19:24 king left until he came **h** safely.
19:30 me that you've come **h** safely."
19:39 Then Barzillai went back **h**.
20:22 from the city and went **h**.
1Ki 1:53 "Go **h**," Solomon told him.
2:34 him at his **h** in the desert.
5:14 Lebanon and two months at **h**.
8:13 a **h** for you to live in
11:18 Pharaoh gave Hadad a **h**,
11:22 that makes you eager to go **h**?"
12:16 So Israel went **h** to their own
12:24 Everyone, go **h**. What has
12:24 They returned **h**,
13:7 man of God, "Come **h** with me;
13:15 "Come **h** with me, and eat a
13:18 He said, 'Bring him **h** with you
13:19 him and ate and drank in his **h**.
14:4 and came to the **h** of Ahijah.
14:12 "Get up, and go **h**.
14:17 across the threshold of her **h**,
17:13 Go **h**, and do as you've said.
20:43 of Israel went **h** to Samaria.
21:4 Ahab went **h** because of what
22:17 Let each one go **h** in peace."
22:27 water until I come **h** safely.'"
2Ki 3:27 So they went **h** to their own
5:9 at the entrance to Elisha's **h**.
6:32 Elisha was sitting in his **h** with
8:3 the woman came **h** from
8:21 and his troops fled **h**.
14:10 Enjoy your fame, but stay **h**.
16:11 returned **h** from Damascus.
19:36 He went **h** to Nineveh and
1Ch 7:23 tragedy had come to his **h**.
13:7 a new cart from Abinadab's **h**.
13:13 bring God's ark to his **h**,
13:13 Instead, he rerouted it to the **h**
13:14 God's ark stayed at the **h** of
16:43 Then all the people went **h**.
2Ch 6:2 a **h** for you to live in
10:16 So all Israel went **h** to their
11:4 Everyone, go **h**. What has
18:16 Let each one go **h** in peace.'"
18:26 water until I return **h** safely.'"
19:1 safely to his **h** in Jerusalem.
25:10 with Judah and returned **h**.
25:19 Stay **h**! Why must you invite
28:9 the army coming **h** to Samaria.
28:12 those coming **h** from the army.
Neh 3:10 repairs across from his own **h**.
3:23 made repairs next to his **h**.
3:24 on a section from Azariah's **h**
3:28 repairs across from his own **h**.
3:29 repairs across from his own **h**.
5:13 may God brush off from **h** and
6:10 I went to the **h** of Shemaiah,
Est 5:10 He went **h** and sent for his
6:12 but Haman hurried **h**.
Job 1:10 his **h**, and everything he has?
1:13 wine in their oldest brother's **h**,
1:18 wine at their oldest brother's **h**
2:11 each of them came from his **h**
7:10 He doesn't come back **h** again,
8:6 by rebuilding your **h**.
17:13 If I look for the grave as my **h**
18:15 Sulfur is scattered over his **h**.
20:9 His **h** will not look at him again.
38:19 Where is the **h** of darkness
Job 38:20 may know the path to its **h**?
Psa 68:12 The women who remained at **h**
74:2 where you have made your **h**.
76:2 is in Salem. His **h** is in Zion.
79:7 They have destroyed his **h**.
84:3 Even sparrows find a **h**,
91:9 made the Most High your **h**.
101:2 live in my own **h** with integrity.
101:7 things will not stay in my **h**.
104:3 You lay the beams of your **h** in
104:13 mountains from your **h** above.
112:3 and riches will be in his **h**.
113:9 woman who is in a childless **h**
126:6 will come **h** singing,
128:3 like a fruitful vine inside your **h**.
132:13 He wants it for his **h**.
Pro 3:33 the **h** of righteous people.
7:11 Her feet will not stay at **h**.
7:19 because my husband's not **h**.
7:20 He won't be **h** for a couple of
7:27 Her **h** is the way to hell and
14:1 of women builds up her **h**,
15:31 be at **h** among wise people.
17:13 evil will never leave his **h**.
19:14 **H** and wealth are inherited from
21:9 of a roof than to share a **h**
21:20 treasure and wealth are in the **h**
24:15 do not lie in ambush at the **h** of
25:24 of a roof than to share a **h**
27:8 husband wandering from his **h**.
27:10 Do not go to a relative's **h** when
30:26 they make their **h** in the rocks.
Isa 3:7 any food or a coat in my **h**.
14:17 didn't let his prisoners go **h**?"
32:16 and righteousness will be at **h**
34:13 It will become a **h** for jackals
35:7 and rushes in the **h** of jackals.
37:37 He went **h** to Nineveh and
Jer 2:34 them for breaking in to your **h**.
9:11 a pile of rubble, a **h** for jackals.
16:8 "Don't even go into a **h** where
22:27 won't be allowed to come **h**."
31:23 **h** of righteousness,
39:14 of Shaphan, to take him **h**.
Eze 3:24 He said, "Go into your **h**,
8:1 I was sitting in my **h**.
17:12 He brought them **h** with him to
17:23 bird will nest in it and find a **h**
27:4 Your **h** is the sea. "'Your
36:8 My people will come **h** soon.
44:30 a blessing to rest on your **h**.
Dan 2:17 Then Daniel went **h** and told
4:4 was living comfortably at **h**.
Amo 5:19 It is like a person who goes **h**
Oba 1:3 You make your **h** up high.
Zep 3:20 At that time I will bring you **h**.
Hag 1:9 When you bring something **h**,
Mat 2:23 and made his **h** in a city called
4:13 left Nazareth and made his **h**
8:6 my servant is lying at **h**
9:6 up your stretcher, and go **h**."
9:7 So the man got up and went **h**.
12:44 'I'll go back to the **h** I left.'
13:52 of heaven is like a **h** owner.
15:32 exhausted on their way **h**."
25:35 and you took me into your **h**.
26:6 in Bethany in the **h** of Simon,
Mar 2:1 report went out that he was **h**.
2:11 up, pick up your cot, and go **h**!"
3:20 Then Jesus went **h**.
5:19 "Go **h** to your family,
5:35 from the synagogue leader's **h**.
5:38 When they came to the **h** of the
6:10 "Whenever you go into a **h**,
7:17 had left the people and gone **h**,
7:30 The woman went **h** and found
8:3 If I send them **h** before they've
8:26 told him when he sent him **h**,
9:33 While Jesus was at **h**,
10:29 Anyone who gave up his **h**,
13:34 As he left **h**, he put his
14:3 in Bethany at the **h** of Simon,
15:21 into Jerusalem from his **h**
16:12 as they were walking to their **h**
Luk 1:23 service were over, he went **h**.
1:28 When the angel entered her **h**,

Luk 1:40 **h** and greeted Elizabeth.
1:56 months and then went back **h**.
2:43 was over, they left for **h**.
5:24 up your stretcher, and go **h**."
5:25 Praising God, he went **h**.
5:29 reception at his **h** for Jesus.
6:48 to lay the foundation of his **h**.
8:39 "Go **h** to your family,
8:41 begged Jesus to come to his **h**.
8:49 from the synagogue leader's **h**.
9:4 When you go into a **h**,
10:38 welcomed him into her **h**.
11:24 'I'll go back to the **h** I left.'
12:45 is taking a long time to come **h**.
14:1 Jesus went to eat at the **h**
15:6 goes **h**. Then he calls his
15:13 for a country far away from **h**.
15:27 'Your brother has come **h**.
15:30 and when he came **h**,
16:9 be welcomed into an eternal **h**.
16:27 Lazarus back to my father's **h**.
17:19 told the man, "Get up, and go **h**!
18:14 that this tax collector went **h**
18:29 Anyone who gave up his **h**,
19:6 to welcome Jesus into his **h**.
Jon 4:50 Jesus told him, "Go **h**.
7:53 Then each of them went **h**.
8:35 doesn't live in the **h** forever,
11:20 to meet him. Mary stayed at **h**.
11:28 she went back **h** and
14:23 and make our **h** with them.
19:27 lived with that disciple in his **h**.
20:10 So the disciples went back **h**.
Act 1:20 'Let his **h** be deserted,
8:3 out of one **h** after another
8:27 to worship was on his way **h**.
10:2 He and everyone in his **h** were
10:22 him to summon you to his **h**
10:30 days ago I was praying at **h**.
10:32 He's a guest in the **h** of Simon,
11:12 and we visited Cornelius' **h**.
11:13 an angel standing in his **h**.
11:14 you and everyone in your **h**.'
12:12 he went to the **h** of Mary,
12:12 at her **h** and were praying.
14:26 they took a boat and headed **h**
16:15 she invited us to stay at her **h**.
16:15 then stay at my **h**."
16:32 the jailer and everyone in his **h**.
16:34 and Silas upstairs into his **h**
17:5 They attacked Jason's **h** and
18:7 synagogue and went to the **h**
18:26 they took him ⌊**h**⌋ with them
20:12 The people took the boy **h**.
21:6 and the disciples went back **h**.
21:8 next day we went to Philip's **h**
21:16 They took us to Mnason's **h**,
1Co 7:37 decision is to keep her ⌊at **h**⌋
11:34 should eat at **h** so that you
14:35 should ask their husbands at **h**.
Heb 11:13 with no permanent **h** on earth.
2Jn 1:10 don't take him into your **h** or
Rev 18:2 has become a **h** for demons.
21:3 God will make his **h** with them,

homeland (4)

2Sm 15:19 an exile from your **h**.
Jer 22:10 won't come back to see their **h**.
50:16 people and flee to his own **h**
Zep 3:7 Then their **h** would not be

homeless (2)

Isa 58:7 take the poor and **h** into your
1Co 4:11 dressed, roughly treated, and **h**.

homemakers (1)

Tit 2:5 to teach young women to be **h**,

homeowner (3)

Mat 24:43 You realize that if a **h** had
Luk 12:39 you realize that if the **h** had
13:25 After the **h** gets up and closes

homer (2)

Eze 45:11 the same as one-tenth of a **h**.
45:11 The **h** must be the standard

homes (68)

Exo 8:9 frogs will leave you and your **h**.
8:11 frogs will leave you, your **h**,
8:21 The **h** of the Egyptians will be
12:27 in Egypt and spared our **h** when
35:3 light a fire in any of your **h**
Lev 23:17 two loaves of bread from your **h**
25:23 strangers without permanent **h**.
Num 32:18 We will not return to our **h** until
Jos 22:6 and they went to their **h**.
22:8 "Return to your **h** with your vast
1Sm 10:25 sent the people back to their **h**.
2Sm 18:17 fled and went back to their **h**.
19:8 and went back to their own **h**.
2Ki 13:5 They were able to live in their **h**
14:12 and the Judeans fled to their **h**.
1Ch 7:28 The land and **h** of Ephraim's
29:15 foreigners without permanent **h**
2Ch 25:22 and the Judeans fled to their **h**.
Neh 3:23 repairs across from their own **h**.
4:14 your wives, and your **h**."
5:3 and our **h** in order to get some
5:11 orchards, and their **h** today.
7:3 and others in front of their **h**."
Job 1:4 used to go to each other's **h**,
3:15 who filled their **h** with silver.
18:21 This is what happens to the **h**
21:9 Their **h** are free from fear,
22:18 Yet, he filled their **h** with good
Psa 49:11 graves have become their **h**
49:14 away from their comfortable **h**.
55:15 because evil lives in their **h** as
84:10 live inside wicked people's **h**.
104:17 Storks makes their **h** in fir trees.
109:10 help far from their ruined **h**.
Pro 1:13 fill our **h** with stolen goods.
Isa 13:21 Their **h** will be full of owls.
32:13 Mourn for all the happy **h** in a
32:18 in safe **h** and quiet places of
65:22 They will not build **h** and have
Jer 9:19 because our **h** have been torn
10:22 and make them **h** for jackals.
10:25 They have destroyed their **h**.
12:16 will build **h** among my people.
17:22 not bring anything out of your **h**
18:22 Make them cry out from their **h**
30:18 show compassion on their **h**.
39:8 royal palace and the people's **h**,
Lam 5:2 Our **h** have been turned over to
Eze 11:3 'It's almost time to rebuild **h**.
23:47 and daughters and burn their **h**.
26:12 and tear down your delightful **h**.
28:26 They will build **h** and plant
33:30 and in the doorways of their **h**.
45:4 will use this place for their **h**,
48:15 left for cities, **h**, and pastures.
Dan 4:21 made their **h** in its branches.
Hos 11:11 own **h**," declares the LORD.
Mic 2:9 people out of their pleasant **h**
Zep 1:13 Their **h** will be demolished.
Mat 19:29 And everyone who gave up **h**,
25:38 stranger and take you into our **h**
25:43 you didn't take me into your **h**.
Mar 10:30 They will certainly receive **h**,
Luk 16:4 me into their **h** when I've lost
Act 2:46 as they ate at each other's **h**
1Co 11:22 Don't you have **h** in which to
1Ti 5:14 have children, manage their **h**,
2Ti 3:6 Some of these men go into **h**

homesick (1)

Gen 31:30 home because you were so **h**.

homestead (1)

Isa 27:10 The **h** is left deserted,

hometown (11)

Jdg 8:27 an idol and placed it in his **h**,
1Sm 20:6 let him run to Bethlehem, his **h**,
28:3 and buried him in his **h** Ramah.
Mat 13:54 Jesus went to his **h** and taught
13:57 prophet isn't honored is in his **h**
Mar 6:1 that place and went to his **h**.
6:4 prophet isn't honored is in his **h**,
Luk 2:39 and Mary returned to their **h**
4:23 'Do all the things in your **h** that
4:24 prophet isn't accepted in his **h**.
Jon 1:44 the **h** of Andrew and Peter.)

homosexual (1)

Jud 1:7 and engaged in **h** activities.

homosexuals (2)

1Co 6:9 those who commit adultery, **h**,
1Ti 1:10 for **h**, for kidnappers, for liars,

honest (35)

Gen 42:11 We're **h** men, not spies."
42:19 If you are **h** men, you will let
42:31 to him, 'We're **h** men, not spies.
42:33 how I'll know that you're **h** men:
42:34 that you're not spies but **h** men.
Exo 23:7 Don't kill innocent or **h** people,
Lev 19:36 Use **h** scales, honest weights,
19:36 Use honest scales, **h** weights,
19:36 weights, and **h** measures.
Dtr 9:5 you're so **h** that you're entering
25:15 Use accurate and **h** weights
2Ki 10:3 choose the best and most **h** of
12:15 because they were **h** people.
22:7 Since the workmen are **h**,
1Ch 29:17 With an **h** heart I have willingly
Job 6:25 How painful an **h** discussion
31:6 let God weigh me on **h** scales,
Psa 112:5 He earns an **h** living.
Pro 11:18 righteousness earns **h** pay.
12:22 but **h** people are his delight.
13:6 Righteousness protects the **h**
14:25 An **h** witness saves lives,
16:11 **H** balances and scales belong
16:13 Kings are happy with **h** words,
Isa 48:1 but you are not **h** or sincere.
Jer 4:2 in an **h**, fair, and right way,
8:6 but they weren't **h**.
Eze 45:10 You must have **h** scales and
45:10 have honest scales and **h** dry
Hos 2:19 I will be **h** and faithful to you.
Luk 8:15 it in their good and **h** hearts
Rom 3:4 God is **h**, and everyone else is
2Co 6:8 dishonest although we are **h**,
Php 1:18 whether with **h** or dishonest
1Th 2:10 are witnesses of how pure, **h**,

honestly (8)

Jos 2:14 we'll treat you kindly and **h**
Pro 10:9 Whoever lives **h** will live
12:17 A truthful witness speaks **h**,
16:8 gained **h** than many gained
28:18 Whoever lives **h** will be safe.
Isa 57:2 everyone who has lived **h** will
Jer 23:28 word should **h** speak my word.
Mic 2:7 good for those who live **h**?

honesty (6)

Gen 30:33 My **h** will speak for itself
1Ch 29:17 hearts and delight in **h**.
Psa 25:21 Integrity and **h** will protect me
Pro 29:14 a king judges the poor with **h**,
Isa 59:14 and **h** can't come in.
Mal 2:6 lived with me in peace and **h**

honey (62)

Gen 43:11 Take a little balm, a little **h**,
Exo 3:8 flowing with milk and **h** where
3:17 land flowing with milk and **h**.'"
13:5 land flowing with milk and **h**,
16:31 tasted like wafers made with **h**.
33:3 land flowing with milk and **h**.
Lev 2:11 Never burn yeast or **h** as an
20:24 a land flowing with milk and **h**.
Num 13:27 a land flowing with milk and **h**.
14:8 a land flowing with milk and **h**!
16:13 flowing with milk and **h** only
16:14 a land flowing with milk and **h**
Dtr 6:3 a land flowing with milk and **h**,
8:8 The land has **h** and olive trees
11:9 a land flowing with milk and **h**.
26:9 land flowing with milk and **h**.
26:15 with milk and **h** that you have
27:3 a land flowing with milk and **h**,
31:20 a land flowing with milk and **h**.

Dtr 32:13 He gave them **h** from rocks and
Jos 5:6 flowing with milk and **h** which
Jdg 14:8 a swarm of bees and some **h**
14:9 He scraped ⌊the **h**⌋ into his
14:9 gave them some of the **h** to eat.
14:18 "What is sweeter than **h**?
1Sm 14:25 and there was **h** on the ground.
14:26 the **h** was flowing.
14:29 when I tasted a little of this **h**?
14:43 "I tasted a little **h** on the tip of
2Sm 17:29 **h**, buttermilk, sheep,
1Ki 14:3 and a jar of **h** with you,
2Ki 18:32 olive trees, olive oil, and **h**.
2Ch 31:5 new wine, fresh olive oil, **h**,
Job 20:17 the rivers of **h** and buttermilk.
Psa 19:10 They are sweeter than **h**,
81:16 them with **h** from a rock."
119:103 It tastes sweeter than **h**.
Pro 5:3 adulterous woman drip with **h**.
16:24 Pleasant words are ⌊like⌋ **h**
24:13 Eat **h**, my son, because it is
24:13 **H** that flows from the
25:16 When you find **h**, eat only as
25:27 Eating too much **h** is not good,
27:7 One who is full despises **h**,
Sos 4:11 Your lips drip **h**, my bride.
4:11 **H** and milk are under your
5:1 eat my honeycomb with my **h**.
Isa 7:15 He will eat cheese and **h** until
7:22 the land will eat cheese and **h**.
Jer 11:5 a land flowing with milk and **h**,
32:22 land flowing with milk and **h**.
41:8 and **h** hidden in the country."
Eze 3:3 as sweet as **h** in my mouth.
16:13 Your food was flour, **h**,
16:19 You gave flour, olive oil, and **h**
20:6 a land flowing with milk and **h**.
20:15 a land flowing with milk and **h**.
27:17 baked goods, **h**, olive oil,
Mat 3:4 of locusts and wild **h**.
Mar 1:6 and ate locusts and wild **h**.
Rev 10:9 as sweet as **h** in your mouth."
10:10 It was as sweet as **h** in my

honeycomb (5)

1Sm 14:27 his hand and dipped it in the **h**.
Psa 19:10 even the drippings from a **h**.
Pro 16:24 ⌊like⌋ honey from a **h** — sweet
24:13 flows from the **h** tastes sweet.
Sos 5:1 I will eat my **h** with my honey.

honeycombs (1)

1Sm 14:25 The entire land had **h**,

honor (208)

Gen 30:20 This time my husband will **h**
30:20 So she named him Zebulun [**H**].
Exo 5:1 to celebrate a festival in my **h**."
8:9 "You may have the **h** of
10:9 festival in the LORD's **h**."
12:14 festival in the LORD's **h**.
12:27 sacrifice in the LORD's **h**.
13:6 festival in the LORD's **h**.
14:4 his entire army, I will receive **h**,
14:17 I will receive **h** because of
15:2 father's God, and I will **h** him.
20:12 "**H** your father and your mother,
23:14 a pilgrimage festival in my **h**.
28:2 Aaron to give him dignity and **h**.
28:40 will give them dignity and **h**.
32:5 be a festival in the LORD's **h**."
Lev 19:32 and **h** older people.
25:2 celebrate a year to **h** the LORD.
25:4 It will be a year to **h** the LORD.
26:34 land will enjoy its time ⌊to **h**
26:34 its time ⌊to **h** the LORD⌋.
26:35 it will celebrate the time ⌊to **h**
26:43 will enjoy its time to **h** the
Dtr 5:16 "**H** your father and your mother
15:2 proclaimed in the LORD's **h**.
16:1 **H** the LORD your God by
26:19 give you praise, fame, and **h**,
Jos 3:7 "Today I will begin to **h** you in
7:19 give **h** and praise to the LORD
Jdg 9:9 which people use to **h** gods
13:17 come true, we will **h** you."
Jdg 18:29 They named the city Dan in **h**
1Sm 2:29 Why do you **h** your sons more
2:30 I promise that I will **h** those
2:30 I will honor those who **h** me,
15:12 to set up a monument in his **h**.
15:30 Now please **h** me in front of the
1Ki 3:13 for — riches and **h** — so that
2Ki 10:20 a holy assembly to **h** Baal."
1Ch 17:18 light of the **h** ⌊you have given⌋
29:12 Riches and **h** are in front of you.
29:25 gave him royal **h** like no king
29:28 life was full of wealth and **h**.
2Ch 1:11 didn't ask for riches, fortunes, **h**
1:12 and **h** like no other king before
16:14 they burned a bonfire in his **h**.
17:5 he had a lot of riches and **h**.
18:2 and cattle for a banquet in **h**
21:19 a bonfire in his **h** as they had
26:18 God will not **h** you for this."
Est 1:20 wives will **h** their husbands,
Job 17:4 That is why you will not **h**
19:9 He has stripped me of my **h**.
36:7 with kings to **h** them forever.
Psa 4:2 are you going to insult my **h**?
7:5 Let him lay my **h** in the dust.
8:5 crowned him with glory and **h**.
30:1 I will **h** you highly,
34:3 us highly **h** his name together.
37:34 and he will **h** you by giving you
50:15 and you will **h** me."
79:9 our sins for the **h** of your name.
84:11 The LORD grants favor and **h**.
86:9 O Lord. They will **h** you.
86:12 I will **h** you forever
91:15 I will save you and **h** you.
99:5 Highly **h** the LORD our God.
99:9 Highly **h** the LORD our God.
112:9 His head is raised in **h**.
118:28 My God, I **h** you highly.
138:5 "The LORD's **h** is great!"
145:5 I will think about the glorious **h**
145:12 the glorious **h** of your kingdom.
149:9 This is an **h** that belongs to all
Pro 3:9 **H** the LORD with your wealth
3:16 left hand are riches and **h**.
3:35 Wise people will inherit **h**,
4:8 It will bring you **h** when you
8:18 I have riches and **h**,
14:28 A large population is an **h** for a
15:33 and humility comes before **h**.
18:12 but humility comes before **h**.
21:21 find life, righteousness, and **h**.
22:4 are riches and **h** and life.
25:27 for **h** is not honorable.
26:1 so **h** is not right for a fool.
26:8 so is giving **h** to a fool.
29:23 but a humble spirit gains **h**.
30:32 a godless fool as to **h** yourself,
Ecc 6:2 and **h** so that he doesn't lack
10:1 outweighs wisdom ⌊and⌋ **h**.
Isa 2:10 and the **h** of his majesty.
2:19 terrifying presence and the **h**
2:21 terrifying presence and the **h**
14:18 have been buried with **h**,
16:14 "Moab's **h** will be despised
17:3 will share Israel's **h**," declares
17:4 "When that day comes, the **h** of
21:16 All of Kedar's **h** will be gone in
22:23 and he will be a source of **h** for
24:15 **H** the LORD in the east.
24:15 **H** the name of the LORD God
24:16 we hear songs of praise that **h**
25:1 I will highly **h** you;
25:3 why strong people will **h** you,
29:13 me with their mouths and **h** me
43:20 and ostriches will **h** me.
43:23 for your burnt offerings or **h** me
45:4 I have given you a title of **h**,
58:13 if you **h** it by not going your
60:7 So I will **h** my beautiful temple.
60:9 their gold comes with them to **h**
60:13 and I will **h** the place where my
Jer 13:11 bring fame, praise, and **h** to me.
13:16 **H** the LORD your God before it
30:19 I'll bring them **h**, and they won't
33:9 my source of joy, praise, and **h**.
Jer 48:18 down from your place of **h**
Lam 1:8 Everyone who used to **h** it now
4:16 did they **h** their older leaders."
Dan 2:37 you power, strength, and **h**.
3:12 They don't **h** your gods or
3:14 is it true that you don't **h** my
3:17 If our God, whom we **h**,
3:18 we'll never **h** your gods or
3:28 that they would not have to **h**
4:30 power and for my glorious **h**."
4:36 My royal **h** and glory were also
4:37 will praise, **h**, Everything he
5:18 a kingdom, might, **h**, and glory.
5:20 His **h** was taken away from
5:23 You didn't **h** God, who has
7:14 He was given power, **h**,
11:36 He will highly **h** himself above
11:38 he will **h** the god of fortresses.
11:38 expensive things he will **h**
Hos 10:1 they set up ⌊to **h** other gods⌋.
Hab 1:7 their own kind of justice and **h**.
Zec 6:13 temple and receive royal **h**.
12:7 Judah's tents first so that the **h**
12:7 of David's family and the **h**
12:7 be greater than the **h** of Judah.
Mal 1:6 if I am a father, where is my **h**?
2:2 if you won't consider giving **h**
Mat 15:4 For example, God said, '**H**
15:6 does not have to **h** his father.
15:8 'These people **h** me with their
19:19 **H** your father and mother.
22:8 invited don't deserve the **h**.
23:6 They love the place of **h** at
Mar 7:6 'These people **h** me with their
7:10 For example, Moses said, '**H**
10:19 **H** your father and mother."
12:39 and the places of **h** at dinners.
Luk 14:7 always chose the places of **h**.
14:8 don't take the place of **h**.
14:9 to take the place of least **h**.
14:10 take the place of least **h**.
14:11 Those who **h** themselves will
18:20 **H** your father and your mother."
20:46 and the places of **h** at dinners.
Jon 5:23 so that everyone will **h** the Son
5:23 the Son as they **h** the Father.
5:23 Whoever doesn't **h** the Son
5:23 doesn't honor the Son doesn't **h**
8:49 I **h** my Father, but you dishonor
12:26 the Father will **h** them.
Act 15:14 those who would **h** his name.
Rom 1:5 This is for the **h** of his name.
2:7 those who search for glory, **h**,
2:10 But there will be glory, **h**,
4:20 Instead, giving **h** to God ⌊for
11:13 I bring **h** to my ministry.
13:7 If you owe someone **h**,
13:7 someone honor, **h** that person.
14:6 they observe it to **h** the Lord.
14:6 they **h** the Lord as they eat,
14:6 Vegetarians also **h** the Lord
14:7 we don't live to **h** ourselves,
14:7 and we don't die to **h** ourselves.
14:8 If we live, we **h** the Lord,
14:8 and if we die, we **h** the Lord.
1Co 12:23 are the ones we give special **h**.
12:24 together and given special **h**
2Co 1:20 people also **h** God by saying,
9:13 You will **h** God through this
Eph 6:2 "**H** your father and mother
Php 1:20 I will speak very boldly and **h**
2:9 given him an exceptional **h** —
2:29 Make sure you **h** people like
1Ti 5:3 **H** widows who have no
5:17 Give double **h** to spiritual
6:16 **H** and power belong to him
Heb 2:7 crowned him with glory and **h**.
2:9 him crowned with glory and **h**
5:4 No one takes this **h** for himself.
1Pe 1:7 praise, glory, and **h** to God.
2:7 This **h** belongs to those who
2:17 **H** everyone. Love your brothers
2:17 Fear God. **H** the emperor.
3:7 **H** your wives as those who
5:6 right time comes he will **h** you.
2Pe 1:17 when he received **h**

Rev 4:9 living creatures give glory, **h**,
4:11 you deserve to receive glory, **h**,
5:12 strength, **h**, glory, and praise."
5:13 to the lamb be praise, **h**, glory,
7:12 wisdom, thanks, **h**, power,

honorable (23)

Dtr 32:4 He is **h** and reliable.
33:21 the LORD considers fair and **h**."
1Ki 1:42 "You're an **h** man, so you must
1:52 he will behave like an **h** man,
2:32 Joab killed two **h** men who
1Ch 4:9 Jabez was more **h** than his
2Ch 18:1 was wealthy and **h**
Pro 20:3 Avoiding a quarrel is **h**.
25:27 searching for honor is not **h**.
Ecc 6:3 didn't even get an **h** burial ⌊after
8:10 people given an ⌊**h**⌋ burial.
Isa 32:8 But **h** people act honorably and
32:8 and stand firm for what is **h**.
58:13 and the LORD's holy day **h**,
Eze 31:18 tree in Eden has ever been as **h**
Mat 1:19 Her husband Joseph was an **h**
Luk 1:75 by being holy and **h** as long as
2:25 He lived an **h** and devout life.
14:10 move to a more **h** place.'
1Co 12:23 that we think are less **h** are
Php 4:8 true, **h**, fair, pure, acceptable,
1Th 4:4 to be done in a holy and **h** way,
Heb 13:4 Marriage is **h** in every way,

honorably (2)

Isa 32:8 But honorable people act **h** and
Heb 13:18 we want to live **h** in every way.

honored (63)

Gen 34:19 He was the most **h** person in
45:13 Tell my father how greatly **h** I
Exo 14:18 I am the LORD when I am **h**
Jos 4:14 On that day the LORD **h**
1Sm 22:14 He's **h** in your own household.
2Sm 6:22 I will be **h** by these slave girls
23:19 and was **h** more than they
23:23 He was **h** more than the thirty,
2Ki 5:1 was respected and highly **h** by
1Ch 11:21 although he was **h** more than
11:25 He was **h** more than the thirty,
22:5 and **h** in all other countries.
29:11 and you are **h** as head of all
2Ch 32:27 richer and was highly **h**.
32:33 the people in Jerusalem **h** him.
Job 14:21 His sons are **h**, and he doesn't
Psa 18:46 May God my Savior be **h**.
57:5 May you be **h** above the
57:11 May you be **h** above the
92:8 are highly **h** forever.
108:5 May you be **h** above the
Pro 13:18 constructive criticism will be **h**.
27:18 protects his master is **h**.
Isa 2:11 day the LORD alone will be **h**.
2:17 day the LORD alone will be **h**.
3:8 They are defiant in his **h**
5:13 **H** men will starve,
5:14 very wide so that **h** people
5:16 The LORD of Armies will be **h**
9:15 Respected and **h** leaders are
12:4 that his name is highly **h**.
23:8 Its traders are among the **h**
23:9 to humiliate all the **h** people
26:15 You are **h**. You have extended
33:5 The LORD is **h** because he
43:4 you are **h** and I love you.
52:13 praised, and highly **h**.
55:5 One of Israel. He has **h** you."
60:9 because he has **h** you.
60:21 the **h** work of my hands.
63:14 to make an **h** name for yourself.
Jer 4:2 and they will be **h** by me."
17:12 highly **h** from the beginning.
Eze 39:13 The people of Israel will be **h**
Dan 4:34 and I praised and **h** the one
Hag 1:8 I will be **h**," declares the LORD.
Mat 13:57 only place a prophet isn't **h** is
23:12 humbles himself will be **h**.
Mar 6:4 only place a prophet isn't **h** is
Luk 1:52 He **h** humble people.
14:10 guests will see how you are **h**.
14:11 humble themselves will be **h**."
18:14 humbles himself will be **h**."
Jon 4:44 had said that a prophet is not **h**
1Co 4:10 You are **h**, but we are
2Co 6:8 as we are slandered and **h**,
Php 2:9 the name **h** above all other
2Th 1:10 he comes to be **h** among all his
1:12 Jesus will be **h** among you.
1:12 you will be **h** by him.
3:1 rapidly and that it will be **h**
2Ti 2:20 Some objects are **h** when they
2:21 dishonorable people will be **h**.

honoring (2)

2Sm 10:3 "Do you think David is **h** your
1Ch 19:3 "Do you think David is **h** your

honors (11)

Jdg 4:9 But you won't win any **h** for the
Psa 15:4 by God but **h** those who fear
50:23 thanks as a sacrifice **h** me.
Pro 14:31 is kind to the needy **h** him.
Isa 49:5 (The LORD **h** me, and my God
Dan 2:6 you gifts, awards, and high **h**.
11:39 He will give high **h** to those
Mal 1:6 A son **h** his father,
1:6 and a servant **h** his master.
Mat 23:12 Whoever **h** himself will be
Luk 18:14 Everyone who **h** himself will

hoofs (18)

Lev 11:3 that have completely divided **h**
11:4 their cud or have divided **h**,
11:4 cud but do not have divided **h**.)
11:5 cud but do not have divided **h**.)
11:6 cud but do not have divided **h**.)
11:7 pigs have completely divided **h**
11:26 All animals whose **h** are not
Dtr 14:6 that have completely divided **h**
14:7 have completely divided **h**.
14:7 they don't have divided **h**.
14:8 (Although their **h** are divided,
Jdg 5:22 Then the horses' **h** pounded.
Psa 69:31 ox or a bull with horns and **h**.
Isa 5:28 Their horses' **h** are as hard as
Eze 26:11 With his horses' **h** he will
32:13 The feet of humans and the **h**
Mic 4:13 as iron and your **h** as hard as
Zec 11:16 fat animals and tear off their **h**.

hook (5)

2Ki 19:28 I will put my **h** in your nose and
2Ch 33:11 put a **h** in his nose,
Job 41:2 nose or pierce its jaw with a **h**?
Isa 37:29 I will put my **h** in your nose and
Mat 17:27 go to the sea and throw in a **h**.

hooks (19)

Exo 26:32 Use gold **h** to hang it on four
26:37 Make gold **h** for this screen.
27:10 The **h** and bands on the posts
27:11 The **h** and bands on the posts
27:17 silver **h**, and bronze bases.
36:36 They made gold **h** for the posts,
36:38 also made five posts with **h**
38:10 The **h** and bands on the posts
38:11 The **h** and bands on the posts
38:12 The **h** and bands on the posts
38:17 The **h** and bands on the posts
38:19 The **h** and bands on the posts
38:28 pounds of silver to make the **h**
Eze 19:4 brought him with **h** to Egypt.
19:9 With **h** they put him in a cage
29:4 "'I will put **h** in your jaws and
38:4 I will turn you around and put **h**
40:43 Double-pronged **h**,
Amo 4:2 you will be taken away on **h**,

hoopoes (2)

Lev 11:19 storks, all types of herons, **h**,
Dtr 14:18 storks, all types of herons, **h**,

hop (1)

Lev 11:21 their legs to **h** on the ground.

hope (150)

Gen 49:18 "I wait with **h** for you to rescue
Rut 1:12 If I said that I still have **h** ....
3:14 "I **h** that no one will ever know
2Sm 16:4 "I **h** to remain in your good
1Ch 29:15 There's no **h** ⌊for them⌋.
Ezr 10:2 there is still **h** for Israel.
Job 3:9 Let it **h** for light and receive
4:6 lifetime of integrity give you **h**?
5:16 Then the poor have **h** while
7:6 They are spent without **h**.
8:13 The **h** of the godless dies.
11:18 confident because there's **h**,
11:20 Their only **h** is to take their last
13:15 I would have no **h** ⌊left⌋.
14:7 There is **h** for a tree when it is
14:19 and you destroy a mortal's **h**.
17:15 then where is my **h**?
17:15 Can you see any **h** left in me?
17:16 Will **h** go down with me to the
17:16 Will my **h** rest with me in the
19:10 He uproots my **h** like a tree.
27:8 After all, what **h** does the
41:9 Certainly, any **h** ⌊of defeating
41:9 ⌊of defeating it⌋ is a false **h**.
Psa 9:18 Nor will the **h** of oppressed
27:14 Wait with **h** for the LORD.
27:14 Yes, wait with **h** for the LORD.
31:24 Be strong, all who wait with **h**
33:18 who wait with **h** for his mercy
33:22 since we wait with **h** for you.
37:9 but those who wait with **h** for
37:34 Wait with **h** for the LORD,
38:15 But I wait with **h** for you,
39:7 I waiting for? My **h** is in you!
42:5 Put your **h** in God,
42:11 Put your **h** in God,
43:5 Put your **h** in God,
52:9 I will wait with **h** in your good
62:5 because my **h** comes from him.
62:10 Do not **h** to gain anything
65:5 the **h** of all the ends of the earth
69:6 not let those who wait with **h**
71:5 You are my **h**, O Almighty
71:14 But I will always have **h**.
77:3 I begin to lose **h** as I think
107:5 They began to lose **h**.
112:10 The **h** that wicked people have
119:43 My **h** is based on your
119:49 Through it you gave me **h**.
119:74 because my **h** is based on your
119:81 My **h** is based on your word.
119:114 My **h** is based on your word.
119:116 turn my **h** into disappointment.
119:147 My **h** is based on your word.
119:166 I have waited with **h** for you to
130:5 and with **h** I wait for his word.
130:7 put your **h** in the LORD,
131:3 Israel, put your **h** in the LORD
142:3 When I begin to lose **h**,
143:4 That is why I begin to lose **h**
146:5 Their **h** rests on the LORD their
147:11 who wait with **h** for his mercy.
Pro 10:28 The **h** of righteous people
11:7 a wicked person, **h** vanishes.
11:23 but the **h** of wicked people
13:12 Delayed **h** makes one sick at
19:18 your son while there is still **h**.
23:18 and your **h** will never be cut off.
24:14 and your **h** will never be cut off.
26:12 There is more **h** for a fool than
29:20 There is more **h** for a fool than
Ecc 9:4 are among the living have **h**,
Isa 8:17 of Jacob. I will **h** in him.
20:5 because Sudan was their **h**
20:6 at what has happened to our **h**.
26:8 we wait with **h** for you,
33:2 We wait with **h** for you.
40:31 of those who wait with **h**
49:23 Those who wait with **h** for me
51:5 coastlands put their **h** in me,
59:9 We **h** for light, but we walk in
59:9 We **h** for brightness,
59:11 We **h** for justice, but there is
59:11 We **h** for salvation,

Isa 60:9 coastlands wait with **h** for me.
Jer 14:8 You are Israel's **h**, the one who
14:19 We **h** for peace, but no good
14:19 We **h** for a time of healing,
14:22 We have **h** in you because you
17:13 O LORD, the **H** of Israel,
23:16 They fill you with false **h**.
29:11 give you a future filled with **h**.
31:17 Your future is filled with **h**,
50:7 the **h** of their ancestors.'
Lam 3:18 live⌋ and my **h** in the LORD.'
3:21 "The reason I can ⌊still⌋ find **h**
3:24 That is why I find **h** in him.'
3:26 "It is good to continue to **h** and
3:29 Maybe a reason to **h** exists.
Eze 7:27 and princes will give up **h**.
13:6 Then they **h** that their message
19:5 saw that there was no more **h**.
37:11 and our **h** has vanished.
Hos 2:15 of Achor [Disaster] a door of **h**.
12:6 wait with **h** for your God.
Mic 5:7 They do not put their **h** in
Zec 9:5 because its **h** will fade.
9:12 you captives who have **h**.
Mat 12:21 will have **h** because of him."
Act 16:19 her owners realized that their **h**
24:15 I **h** for the same thing my
27:20 we finally began to lose any **h**
27:31 you have no **h** of staying alive."
Rom 4:18 there was nothing left to **h** for,
8:20 it to frustration did so in the **h**
8:24 were saved with this **h** in mind.
8:24 If we **h** for something we
8:24 already see, it's not really **h**.
8:25 But if we **h** for what we don't
15:12 and he will give the nations **h**."
15:13 May God, the source of **h**,
15:13 Then you will overflow with **h**
15:24 so I **h** to see you when I come
15:24 I **h** that you will support my trip
1Co 13:13 remain: faith, **h**, and love.
15:19 If Christ is our **h** in this life only,
16:7 I **h** to spend some time with
2Co 1:13 I **h** you will understand this as
5:11 and I **h** that you also know
13:6 I **h** that you will realize that we
Eph 1:12 who had already focused our **h**
2:12 You had no **h** and were in the
4:4 you were called to share one **h**.
Php 1:20 I eagerly expect and **h** that I
2:19 I **h** that the Lord Jesus will
2:23 I **h** to send him as soon as I
Col 1:5 because of the **h** which is kept
1:5 time ago you heard about this **h**
1:23 solid foundation of the **h** that
1:27 giving you the **h** of glory.
1Th 2:19 Who is our **h**, joy, or prize that
4:13 other people who have no **h**.
5:8 love as a breastplate and the **h**
2Th 2:16 encouragement and good **h**.
1Ti 3:14 I **h** to visit you soon.
Tit 2:13 time we can expect what we **h**
Phm 1:22 I **h** that, because of your
Jas 5:8 Don't give up **h**. The Lord will
2Jn 1:12 Instead, I **h** to visit and talk
3Jn 1:14 I **h** to visit you very soon.

hoped (7)

Isa 5:7 He **h** for justice but saw only
Jer 8:15 We **h** for peace, but nothing
8:15 We **h** for a time of healing,
Luk 23:8 had heard about Jesus and **h**
Act 27:12 They **h** to reach the city of
Rom 4:18 Abraham still **h** and believed.
Gal 2:4 They **h** to find a way to control

hopeless (1)

Isa 57:10 You didn't think that it was **h**.

hopelessly (1)

Sos 5:8 will tell him I am **h** lovesick.

hopes (4)

2Ki 4:28 I said, 'Don't raise my **h**.'"
Luk 3:15 People's **h** were rising as they
Act 28:20 because of what Israel **h** for."
Rom 8:24 Who **h** for what can be seen?

Hophni (6)

1Sm 1:3 two sons, **H** and Phinehas,
2:12 Eli's sons, **H** and Phinehas,⌋
2:34 two sons, **H** and Phinehas,
4:4 two sons, **H** and Phinehas,
4:11 sons, **H** and Phinehas, died.
4:17 two sons, **H** and Phinehas,

Hophra (1)

Jer 44:30 I'm going to hand Pharaoh **H**,

hoping (6)

Job 6:8 would give me what I'm **h** for,
6:11 I have ⌊left⌋ that I can go on **h**?
Dan 2:9 **h** that things will change.
Luk 24:21 We were **h** that he was the one
Act 24:26 At the same time, Felix was **h**
1Co 13:7 never stops **h**, never gives up.

Hor (12)

Num 20:22 Kadesh and came to Mount **H**.
20:23 At Mount **H**, near the border of
20:25 his son Eleazar up on Mount **H**.
20:27 saw them go up on Mount **H**.
21:4 they moved from Mount **H**,
33:37 and set up camp at Mount **H**
33:38 Aaron went up on Mount **H**.
33:39 old when he died on Mount **H**.
33:41 They moved from Mount **H** and
34:7 Mediterranean Sea to Mount **H**,
34:8 and from Mount **H** to the border
Dtr 32:50 brother Aaron died on Mount **H**

Horam (1)

Jos 10:33 At that time King **H** of Gezer

Horeb (17)

Exo 3:1 of the desert, he came to **H**,
17:6 you there by a rock at Mount **H**.
33:6 After they left Mount **H**,
Dtr 1:2 11 days to go from Mount **H**
1:6 At Mount **H** the LORD our God
1:19 So we left Mount **H**,
4:10 the LORD your God at Mount **H**.
4:15 to you from the fire at Mount **H**.
5:2 a promise to us at Mount **H**.
9:8 Even at Mount **H** you made the
18:16 of the assembly at Mount **H**.
29:1 LORD gave them at Mount **H**.
1Ki 8:9 tablets Moses put there at **H**,
19:8 and nights until he came to **H**,
2Ch 5:10 Moses placed there at **H**,
Psa 106:19 At Mount **H** they made ⌊a
Mal 4:4 I gave to him at **H** for all Israel.

Horem (1)

Jos 19:38 Yiron, Migdal El, **H**,

Horesh (4)

1Sm 23:15 Saul had come to kill him at **H**
23:16 Jonathan came to David at **H**.
23:18 David stayed in **H**,
23:19 with us in fortified camps at **H**

Hor Haggidgad (2)

Num 33:32 and set up camp at **H**
33:33 They moved from **H** and set up

Hori (3)

Gen 36:22 of Lotan were **H** and Hemam.
Num 13:5 Shaphat, son of **H**,
1Ch 1:39 sons were **H** and Homam.

Horite (4)

Gen 36:20 were the sons of Seir the **H**,
36:21 These **H** tribal leaders were the
36:29 were the **H** tribal leaders:
36:30 These were the **H** tribal leaders

Horites (3)

Gen 14:6 and the **H** in the hill country of
Dtr 2:12 The **H** used to live in Seir,
2:22 he wiped out the **H** so that

horizon (8)

Gen 1:6 "Let there be a **h** in the middle
1:7 So God made the **h** and
1:7 water above and below the **h**.
1:8 ⌊what was above⌋ the **h** sky.
Neh 1:9 the most distant point on the **h**,
Job 26:10 He marks the **h** on the surface
Pro 8:27 When he traced the **h** on the
Dan 12:3 like the brightness on the **h**.

Hormah (9)

Num 14:45 and defeated them at **H**.
21:3 **H** [Claimed for Destruction].
Dtr 1:44 you from Seir all the way to **H**.
Jos 12:14 the king of **H**, the king of Arad,
15:30 Eltolad, Chesil, **H**,
19:4 Elto Lad, Bethul, **H**,
Jdg 1:17 **H** [Claimed for Destruction].
1Sm 30:30 **H**, Borashan, Athach,
1Ch 4:30 Bethuel, **H**, Ziklag,

horn (59)

Exo 19:13 when the ram's **h** sounds
19:16 from a ram's **h** ⌊was heard⌋.
19:19 As the sound of the **h** grew
20:18 heard the blast of the ram's **h**
27:2 Make a **h** at each of its four
38:2 He made a **h** at each of its four
Jos 6:5 you hear a long blast on the **h**,
Jdg 3:27 he blew a ram's **h** in the
6:34 So Gideon blew the ram's **h** to
1Sm 13:3 of the ram's **h** throughout
2Sm 2:28 So Joab blew a ram's **h**,
15:10 hear the sound of the ram's **h**,
18:16 Joab blew the ram's **h** to stop
20:1 blew a ram's **h** ⌊to announce⌋,
20:22 He blew the ram's **h**,
1Ki 1:34 Then blow the ram's **h** and say,
1:39 They blew the ram's **h**,
1:41 Joab heard the sound of the **h**,
2Ki 9:13 They blew a ram's **h** and said,
Job 39:24 trust the sound of the ram's **h**.
39:25 As often as the **h** sounds,
Psa 47:5 up with the sound of a ram's **h**.
81:3 Blow the ram's **h** on the day of
98:6 and the playing of a ram's **h**.
132:17 There I will make a **h** sprout up
Isa 18:3 someone blows a ram's **h**,
27:13 On that day a ram's **h** will be
58:1 Raise your voice like a ram's **h**.
Jer 4:5 Say, "Blow the ram's **h**
4:19 I hear a ram's **h** sounding
6:1 Blow the ram's **h** in Tekoa.
6:17 to the sound of the ram's **h**.
42:14 hear the sound of a ram's **h**,
48:25 "Moab's **h** is cut off,
51:27 Blow the ram's **h** among the
Eze 7:14 They have blown a ram's **h**,
33:3 he will blow his **h** to warn the
33:4 If the people hear the **h** and
33:5 They heard the sound of the **h**
33:6 coming and doesn't blow his **h**
Dan 7:8 horns, another **h**, a little horn,
7:8 a little **h**, came up among them.
7:8 This **h** had eyes like human
7:11 words that the **h** was speaking.
7:20 about the other **h** that had come
7:20 That **h** had eyes and a mouth
7:21 I saw that **h** making war
8:5 prominent **h** between its eyes.
8:8 his large **h** broke off.
8:9 of the horns came a small **h**.
8:12 The **h** was successful in
8:21 and the large **h** between its
8:22 The **h** broke off, and four horns
Hos 5:8 "Blow the ram's **h** in Gibeah.
8:1 the alarm on the ram's **h**.
Joe 2:1 Blow the ram's **h** in Zion.
2:15 Blow the ram's **h** in Zion.
Amo 3:6 If a ram's **h** sounds an alarm in
Zec 9:14 LORD will blow the ram's **h**

hornets (1)

Jos 24:12 I sent **h** ahead of you to force

horns (94)

Gen 22:13 ram behind him caught by its **h**
Exo 27:2 The four **h** and the altar must
29:12 and put it on the **h** of the altar
30:2 The **h** and altar must be made
30:3 the top, the sides, and the **h**.
30:10 LORD by putting blood on its **h**.
37:25 The **h** and altar were made out
37:26 and the **h** — and he put a gold
38:2 He made the four **h** and the
Lev 4:7 put some of the blood on the **h**
4:18 also put some blood on the **h**
4:25 his finger and put it on the **h**
4:30 his finger and put it on the **h**
4:34 his finger and put it on the **h**
8:15 the blood and put it on the **h**
9:9 in the blood and put it on the **h**
16:18 it all around the **h** of the altar.
23:24 by the blowing of rams' **h**.
25:9 rams' **h** throughout the country
Dtr 33:17 Their **h** will be like the horns of
33:17 Their horns will be like the **h** of
Jos 6:4 Seven priests will carry rams' **h**
6:4 while the priests blow their **h**.
6:6 carry seven rams' **h** ahead
6:8 the seven rams' **h** ahead
6:8 off as they blew their **h**.
6:9 of the priests, who blew their **h**.
6:9 continued to blow their **h**.
6:13 the seven rams' **h** were ahead
6:13 The priests blew their **h** as
6:13 while the **h** blew continually.
6:16 the priests blew their rams' **h**.
6:20 heard the blast of the rams' **h**,
Jdg 7:8 all the supplies and rams' **h**.
7:16 He gave them each rams' **h**
7:18 those with me blow our rams' **h**,
7:19 They blew their rams' **h** and
7:20 also blew their rams' **h**
7:20 their left hands and the rams' **h**
7:22 kept on blowing their rams' **h**,
2Sm 6:15 joy and the sounding of rams' **h**.
1Ki 1:50 took hold of the **h** of the altar.
1:51 He is holding on to the **h** of the
2:28 and clung to the **h** of the altar.
22:11 made iron **h** and said,
22:11 With these **h** you will push the
1Ch 15:28 joy and the sounding of rams' **h**,
2Ch 15:14 of trumpets and rams' **h**.
18:10 made iron **h** and said,
18:10 With these **h** you will push the
Psa 22:21 mouth of the lion and from the **h**
69:31 ox or a bull with **h** and hoofs.
118:27 branches to the **h** of the altar.
150:3 Praise him with sounds from **h**.
Jer 4:21 and hear the sound of rams' **h**?
17:1 and on the **h** of their altars.
Eze 34:21 all the sick sheep with your **h**.
43:15 There were four **h** above it.
43:20 and put it on the altar's four **h**,
Dan 3:5 you hear the sound of rams' **h**,
3:7 they heard the sound of rams' **h**,
3:10 who hears the sound of rams' **h**,
3:15 hear the sound of the rams' **h**,
7:7 I had seen before. It had ten **h**.
7:8 I was thinking about the **h**,
7:8 It uprooted three of the other **h**.
7:20 wanted to know about the ten **h**
7:20 and made three of the **h** fall out.
7:24 The ten **h** are ten kings that
8:3 The ram had two long **h**,
8:7 It broke both of the ram's **h**.
8:8 In its place grew four **h**.
8:9 Out of one of the **h** came a
8:22 and four **h** replaced it.
Amo 2:2 and rams' **h** are blowing.
3:14 The **h** of the altar will be cut off
Mic 4:13 I will make your **h** as hard as
Zep 1:16 a day of rams' **h** and battle
Zec 1:18 up and saw four animal **h**.
1:19 "What do these **h** mean?"
1:19 He said to me, "These are the **h**
1:21 He answered, "Those **h**
1:21 to throw down the **h** of the
1:21 The nations raised their **h** to
Rev 5:6 He had seven **h** and seven
9:13 I heard a voice from the four **h**
12:3 with seven heads, ten **h**,
13:1 It had ten **h**, seven heads,
13:1 and ten crowns on its **h**.
13:11 and it had two **h** like a lamb.
17:3 It had seven heads and ten **h**.
17:7 and the ten **h** that carries her.
17:12 "The ten **h** that you saw are ten
17:16 The ten **h** and the beast you

Horonaim (4)

Isa 15:5 the destruction on the way to **H**.
Jer 48:3 People will cry out from **H**,
48:5 On the road down to **H** they
48:34 It will be heard from Zoar to **H**

Horonite (2)

Neh 2:10 But when Sanballat the **H** and
2:19 When Sanballat the **H**,

horrible (115)

Num 21:29 How **h** it is for you,
Psa 40:2 He pulled me out of a **h** pit,
120:5 How **h** it is to live as a
Ecc 10:16 How **h** it will be for any country
Isa 1:4 "How **h** it will be for a nation
1:24 "How **h** it will be when I take
3:9 How **h** it will be for these
3:11 How **h** it will be for the wicked!
5:8 How **h** it will be for you who
5:11 How **h** it will be for those who
5:18 How **h** it will be for those who
5:20 How **h** it will be for those who
5:21 How **h** it will be for those who
5:22 How **h** it will be for those who
10:1 How **h** it will be for those who
10:5 "How **h** it will be for Assyria!
17:12 How **h** it will be for many
18:1 How **h** it will be for the land of
24:16 How **h** it is for me!
28:1 How **h** it will be for the arrogant
29:1 How **h** it will be for you Ariel,
29:15 How **h** it will be for those who
30:1 The LORD declares, "How **h** it
31:1 How **h** it will be for those who
33:1 How **h** it will be for you,
33:1 How **h** it will be for you,
45:9 How **h** it will be for the one
45:10 How **h** it will be for the one
Jer 4:13 How **h** it will be for us!
4:31 "How **h** it is for us!
5:30 "Something **h** and disgusting is
6:4 How **h** it will be for us.
13:27 How **h** it will be for you,
16:4 They will die **h** deaths.
18:13 Israel have done a very **h** thing.
22:13 "How **h** it will be for the person
22:18 "How **h** it is for my brother and
22:18 "How **h** it is for my master and
23:1 "How **h** it will be for the
23:14 I see something **h**.
48:1 How **h** it will be for Nebo;
48:46 How **h** it will be for you,
49:17 will become something **h**.
50:27 How **h** it will be for them when
51:37 place for jackals, something **h**,
Eze 2:10 and **h** things written on it.
5:15 ridiculed and something **h**.
13:3 How **h** it will be for the foolish
13:18 How **h** it will be for women
16:23 "'How **h**! How horrible it will be
16:23 How **h** it will be for you!
24:6 How **h** it will be for that city of
24:9 How **h** it will be for that city of
34:2 How **h** it will be for the
Hos 6:10 "I have seen **h** things in the
7:13 "How **h** it will be for these
9:12 Yes, how **h** it will be for them
Amo 5:18 How **h** it will be for those who
6:1 How **h** it will be for those who
6:3 How **h** it will be for those who
6:4 How **h** it will be for those who
6:5 How **h** it will be for those who
6:6 How **h** it will be for those who
6:13 How **h** it will be for those who
Amo 8:14 ⌊How **h** it will be for⌋ those
Mic 2:1 How **h** it will be for those who
Nah 3:1 How **h** it will be for that city of
Hab 2:6 "'How **h** it will be for the one
2:9 "'How **h** it will be for the one
2:12 "'How **h** it will be for the one
2:15 "'How **h** it will be for the one
2:19 'How **h** it will be for the one
Zep 2:5 How **h** it will be for those who
3:1 How **h** it will be for that
Zec 11:17 "How **h** it will be for the foolish
Mat 11:21 "How **h** it will be for you,
11:21 How **h** it will be for you,
18:7 How **h** it will be for the world
18:7 How **h** it will be for the person
23:13 "How **h** it will be for you,
23:15 "How **h** it will be for you,
23:16 "How **h** it will be for you,
23:23 "How **h** it will be for you,
23:25 "How **h** it will be for you,
23:27 "How **h** it will be for you,
23:29 "How **h** it will be for you,
24:19 "How **h** it will be for the women
26:24 But how **h** it will be for that
Mar 13:17 "How **h** it will be for the women
14:21 But how **h** it will be for that
Luk 6:24 "But how **h** it will be for those
6:25 How **h** it will be for those who
6:25 How **h** it will be for those who
6:26 How **h** it will be for you when
10:13 "How **h** it will be for you,
10:13 How **h** it will be for you,
11:42 "How **h** it will be for you
11:43 "How **h** it will be for you
11:44 How **h** it will be for you!
11:46 Jesus said, "How **h** it will be
11:47 "How **h** it will be for you!
11:52 "How **h** it will be for you
17:1 But how **h** it will be for the
21:23 "How **h** it will be for women
22:22 But how **h** it will be for that
1Co 9:16 How **h** it will be for me if I don't
Jud 1:11 How **h** it will be for them!
Rev 12:12 How **h** it is for the earth and the
16:2 **H**, painful sores appeared on
18:10 far away and say, 'How **h**,
18:10 how **h** it is for that important
18:16 saying, 'How **h**, how horrible
18:16 saying, 'How horrible, how **h**
18:19 crying and mourning, 'How **h**,
18:19 how **h** for that important city.

horrified (7)

Jer 2:12 Be **h** over this, heaven.
34:17 the kingdoms of the world **h** at
49:17 who passes by it will be **h**
50:13 passes by Babylon will be **h**
Eze 27:35 who live on the coasts are **h**
28:19 nations who knew you are **h**
Dan 8:27 The vision **h** me because I

horrifying (5)

Jer 15:4 I will make these people a **h**
24:9 I will make them a **h** sight to
29:18 I will make them a **h** sight to
49:13 It will become something **h**,
51:42 What a **h** sight Babylon will be

horror (7)

Dtr 28:25 You will become a thing of **h** to
28:37 You will become a thing of **h**.
Job 18:20 in the east are seized with **h**.
Psa 55:5 **H** has overwhelmed me.
Eze 7:18 and **h** will cover them.
Mat 26:65 tore his robes ⌊in **h**⌋ and said,
Mar 14:63 his clothes ⌊in **h**⌋ and said,

horrors (3)

Dtr 32:25 even at home there will be **h**.
Psa 116:3 The **h** of the grave took hold of
Isa 42:25 out his burning anger and the **h**

horse (30)

1Ki 10:29 15 pounds of silver and each **h**
20:20 on a **h** with the cavalry.
2Ki 14:20 They brought him back by **h**,

2Ch 1:17 15 pounds of silver and each **h**
23:15 her as she entered **H** Gate
25:28 They brought him back by **h**
Neh 3:28 Above **H** Gate the priests made
Est 6:8 the king has worn and a **h** that
6:9 Give the robe and the **h** to one
6:9 and have him ride on the **h**
6:10 take the robe and the **h** as you
6:11 Haman took the robe and the **h**.
Job 39:18 It laughs at the **h** and its rider
39:19 "Can you give strength to a **h** or
39:24 Anxious and excited, the **h**
39:25 horn sounds, the **h** says, 'Aha!'
Psa 32:9 be stubborn like a **h** or mule.
Pro 21:31 The **h** is made ready for the
26:3 A whip is for the **h**,
Jer 31:40 as far as the corner of **H** Gate
Zec 1:8 I saw a man riding on a red **h**.
10:3 them like his splendid war **h**."
12:4 that day I will strike every **h**
Rev 6:2 and there was a white **h**,
6:4 A second **h** went out.
6:5 and there was a black **h**,
6:8 and there was a pale **h**,
19:11 There was a white **h**,
19:19 the rider on the **h** and his army.
19:21 The rider on the **h** killed the

horseback (2)

Act 23:23 infantrymen, 70 soldiers on **h**,
23:32 soldiers on **h** travel with Paul.

horse-drawn (1)

Exo 14:9 including all his **h** chariots and

horsefly (1)

Jer 46:20 but a **h** from the north will

horsemen (16)

Gen 50:9 Chariots and **h** went with him.
Jos 24:6 and **h** chased your ancestors
1Sm 13:5 had 30,000 chariots, 6,000 **h**,
2Sm 1:6 and the chariots and **h** were
8:4 David took 1,700 **h** and 20,000
10:18 chariot drivers and 40,000 **h**.
1Ch 18:4 took 1,000 chariots, 7,000 **h**,
Isa 21:7 He will see chariots, pairs of **h**,
21:9 come chariots and **h** in pairs."
22:6 manned chariots, and **h**.
22:7 and **h** will stand ready in front
Jer 46:4 Mount up, you **h**. Take your
46:9 Go into battle, you **h**.
Eze 23:12 They were mounted **h**,
Hos 1:7 or **h** to rescue them."
Amo 2:15 **H** will not be able to save

horse's (2)

Gen 49:17 that bites a **h** heels so that its
Rev 14:20 winepress as high as a **h** bridle

horses (155)

Gen 47:17 food in exchange for their **h**,
Exo 9:3 including your **h**, donkeys,
14:23 and all Pharaoh's **h**,
15:1 He has thrown **h** and their
15:19 When Pharaoh's **h**,
15:21 He has thrown **h** and their
Dtr 11:4 army, its **h** and chariots.
17:16 never own a large number of **h**
17:16 return to Egypt to get more **h**.
20:1 you may see **h**, chariots,
Jos 11:4 They also had **h** and chariots.
11:6 You must disable their **h** so
11:9 Joshua disabled their **h** and
Jdg 5:22 The mighty war **h** galloped on
1Sm 8:11 serve on his chariots and **h**,
2Sm 8:4 but 100 of their **h** so that they
15:1 Absalom acquired a chariot, **h**,
1Ki 1:5 So he got a chariot and **h** and
4:26 had stalls for 40,000 chariot **h**.
4:28 and straw for the chariot **h**
9:19 cities for his war **h**,
10:25 spices, **h**, and mules.
10:26 army⌋ with chariots and war **h**.
10:26 chariots and 12,000 war **h**.
10:28 Solomon's **h** were imported
1Ki 10:29 the same price they obtained **h**
18:5 then we can keep the **h** and
20:1 along with their **h** and chariots.
20:21 went out and destroyed the **h**
20:25 Recruit an army with as many **h**
22:4 My **h** will do what your horses
22:4 My horses will do what your **h**
2Ki 2:11 a fiery chariot with fiery **h**
2:12 Israel's chariot and **h**!"
3:7 My **h** will do what your horses
3:7 My horses will do what your **h**
5:9 Naaman came with his **h** and
6:14 So the king sent **h** and chariots
6:15 went outside, he saw troops, **h**,
6:17 was full of fiery **h** and chariots.
7:6 chariots, **h**, and a large army.
7:7 as it was with its tents, **h**,
7:10 The **h** and donkeys were still
7:13 take five of the **h** that are left
7:14 they took two chariots with **h**,
9:21 "Hitch the **h** to the chariot,"
9:33 on the wall and the **h**.
9:33 The **h** trampled her.
10:2 **h**, fortified cities, and weapons.
11:16 to the street where the **h** enter
13:7 no army left except for 50 **h**,
13:14 Israel's chariot and **h**!"
18:23 I'll give you 2,000 **h** if you can
18:24 trust Egypt for chariots and **h**?
23:11 He removed the **h** that Judah's
1Ch 18:4 but 100 of their **h** so that they
19:6 to hire chariots and **h** from
2Ch 1:14 army⌋ with chariots and war **h**.
1:14 chariots and 12,000 war **h**.
1:16 Solomon's **h** were imported
1:17 the same price they obtained **h**
8:6 all the cities for his war **h**,
9:24 spices, **h**, and mules.
9:25 4,000 stalls for **h** and chariots,
9:25 and chariots, and 12,000 war **h**.
9:28 **H** were imported for Solomon
12:3 had 1,200 chariots, 60,000 **h**,
Ezr 2:66 They had 736 **h**, 245 mules,
Neh 7:68 They had 736 **h**, 245 mules,
Est 8:10 who rode special **h** bred
8:14 rode the king's fastest **h**.
Psa 20:7 on chariots and others on **h**,
33:17 **H** are not a guarantee for
76:6 chariot riders and **h** were put to
147:10 He finds no joy in strong **h**,
Ecc 10:7 I have seen slaves sitting on **h**
Isa 2:7 Their land is filled with **h**,
28:28 but his **h** won't crush it.
30:16 said, "No, we'll flee on **h**."
30:16 "We'll ride on fast **h**."
31:1 Egypt for help, who rely on **h**,
31:1 depend on very strong war **h**.
31:3 Their **h** are flesh and blood,
36:8 I'll give you 2,000 **h** if you can
36:9 trust Egypt for chariots and **h**?
43:17 He leads chariots and **h**,
63:13 Like **h** in the wilderness,
66:20 "They will come on **h**,
Jer 4:13 His **h** are faster than eagles.
6:23 They ride on **h**. They march like
8:6 like **h** charging into battle.
8:16 The snorting of **h** can be heard
12:5 how can you compete with **h**?
17:25 ride in chariots and on **h** along
22:4 in chariots and on **h** along
46:4 Harness your **h**. Mount up, you
47:3 the sound of galloping war **h**,
50:37 A sword will kill their **h**,
50:42 They will ride **h**. They are ready
51:21 I will use you to crush **h** and
51:27 Bring up **h** like a swarm of
Eze 17:15 messengers to Egypt to get **h**
23:6 young men who rode on **h**.
23:20 semen was like that of **h**.
23:23 All of them ride on **h**.
26:7 He will bring **h**, chariots,
26:7 chariots, war **h**, many people,
26:10 He will have so many **h** that
26:10 The noise from the war **h**,
27:14 Beth Togarmah exchanged **h**,
27:14 exchanged horses, war **h**,
Eze 38:4 forces, with **h** and riders.
38:15 All of you will ride on **h**.
39:20 will be filled with **h** and riders,
Dan 11:40 chariots, **h**, and many ships.
Hos 1:7 **h**, or horsemen to rescue them
14:3 We won't ride on **h** anymore.
Joe 2:4 The soldiers look like **h**.
2:4 They run like war **h**.
Amo 4:10 along with your captured **h**.
6:12 Do **h** run on rocks?
Mic 1:13 Harness the **h** to the chariots,
5:10 "I will destroy your **h** and
Nah 3:2 **H** gallop! Chariots bounce along
3:3 **H** charge! Swords flash! Spears
Hab 1:8 Their **h** will be faster than
3:8 ⌊why⌋ do you ride your **h**,
3:15 You march with your **h** into the
Hag 2:22 and the **h** will fall along with
Zec 1:8 red, chestnut, and white **h**.
1:9 "What do these **h** mean,
1:10 "They're the **h** the LORD has
6:2 The first chariot had red **h**.
6:2 The second had black **h**.
6:3 The third had white **h**.
6:3 the fourth had strong, spotted **h**
6:4 "What do these **h** mean,
6:6 The chariot with the black **h** is
6:6 and the white **h** are following
6:7 When these strong **h** went out,
9:10 Ephraim or war **h** in Jerusalem.
10:5 to shame those who ride on **h**.
12:4 but I will strike all the **h** of the
14:15 plague will also affect **h**,
14:20 be written on the bells of the **h**.
Jas 3:3 We put bits in the mouths of **h**
Rev 9:7 The locusts looked like **h**
9:9 with many **h** rushing into battle.
9:16 The soldiers on **h** numbered
9:17 In the vision that I had, the **h**
9:17 The **h** had heads like lions.
9:19 The power of these **h** is in their
18:13 **h**, wagons, slaves (that is,
19:14 follow him on white **h**.
19:18 warriors, **h** and their riders,

horses' (3)

Jdg 5:22 Then the **h** hoofs pounded.
Isa 5:28 Their **h** hoofs are as hard as
Eze 26:11 With his **h** hoofs he will

Hosah (4)

Jos 19:29 The border then turns to **H** and
1Ch 16:38 (Jeduthun's son) and **H** were
26:11 13 sons and relatives of **H**.
26:16 Shuppim and **H** were chosen

Hosah's (2)

1Ch 26:10 of Merari there were **H** sons.
26:11 **H** other sons were Hilkiah (the

Hosanna (6)

Mat 21:9 "**H** to the Son of David!
21:9 **H** in the highest heaven!"
21:15 "**H** to the Son of David!"
Mar 11:9 him were shouting, "**H**!
11:10 **H** in the highest heaven!"
Jon 12:13 They were shouting, "**H**!

Hosea (6)

Hos 1:1 LORD spoke his word to **H**,
1:2 the LORD first spoke to **H**,
1:3 So **H** married Gomer,
1:4 The LORD told **H**, "Name him
1:6 The LORD told **H**, "Name her
Rom 9:25 As God says in **H**:

Hoshaiah (2)

Neh 12:32 **H** and half of the leaders of
Jer 43:2 Azariah (son of **H**),

Hoshaiah's (1)

Jer 42:1 Johanan and **H** son Jezaniah

Hoshama (1)

1Ch 3:18 Jekamiah, **H**, and Nedabiah.

Hoshea (14)

Num 13:8 **H**, son of Nun, from the tribe of
13:16 But Moses gave **H**,
Dtr 32:44 Moses came with **H**,
2Ki 15:30 **H**, son of Elah, plotted against
15:30 **H** attacked him and killed him.
15:30 **H** began to rule as king in his
17:1 king of Judah, **H**, son of Elah,
17:3 of Assyria defeated **H**,
17:4 The king of Assyria found **H** to
17:4 (**H** had sent messengers to
18:1 King **H**, son of Elah, had been
18:9 year in the reign of King **H**,
1Ch 27:20 for the tribe of Ephraim: **H**,
Neh 10:23 **H**, Hananiah, Hasshub,

Hoshea's (2)

2Ki 17:6 In **H** ninth year as king of Israel,
18:10 was **H** ninth year as king

hospitable (4)

Rom 12:13 people who are in need. Be **h**.
1Ti 3:2 be **h**, and be able to teach.
5:10 done: raising children, being **h**,
Tit 1:8 Instead, he must be **h**,

hospitality (2)

Heb 13:2 Don't forget to show **h** to
13:2 some believers have shown **h**

host (4)

Luk 14:9 Then your **h** would say to you,
14:10 Then, when your **h** comes,
Jon 2:10 the **h** serves cheap wine.
Rom 16:23 He is **h** to me and the whole

hostages (2)

2Ki 14:14 He also took **h**. Then he
2Ch 25:24 He also took **h**. Then he

hostile (8)

Gen 3:15 woman **h** toward each other.
3:15 **h** toward each other.
Est 8:11 and province that is **h** to them,
Jer 4:16 "**H** troops are coming from a
Hos 9:7 and they are very **h**.
9:8 and people are **h** in the temple
Rom 8:7 has a **h** attitude toward God.
Col 1:21 you did showed your **h** attitude.

hostility (4)

Psa 78:49 and **h** against them.
102:10 because of your **h** and anger,
Eph 2:14 the wall of **h** that kept them
2:16 on which he killed the **h**.

hot (30)

Gen 36:24 (Anah found the **h** springs in
Exo 16:21 When the sun was **h**,
1Sm 11:9 by the time the sun gets **h**,
11:11 until it got **h** that day.
1Ki 19:6 some bread baked on **h** stones
2Ki 23:26 the LORD still didn't turn his **h**,
Job 37:17 clothes are **h** and sweaty,
Psa 102:3 My bones burn like **h** coals.
120:4 sharpened arrows and red-**h**
Pro 6:28 Can anyone walk on red-**h** coals
19:19 A person who has a **h** temper
Isa 5:25 burns **h** against his people,
35:7 Then the **h** sand will become a
49:10 **h** wind strike them.
Jer 4:11 "A **h** wind from the heights will
Lam 5:10 Our skin is as **h** as an oven
Eze 24:11 on the coals so that it gets **h**
Dan 3:22 was so extremely **h** that
Hos 7:4 an oven so **h** that a baker
7:6 They become **h** like an oven
7:7 They are all as **h** as an oven.
Jnh 4:8 God made a **h** east wind blow.
Luk 12:55 'It's going to be **h**,' and that's
2Co 12:20 **h** tempers, selfish ambition,
Eph 4:31 bitterness, **h** tempers, anger,
Col 3:8 **h** tempers, hatred, cursing,
1Ti 4:2 scarred as if branded by a red-**h**
Rev 3:15 that you are neither cold nor **h**.
3:15 I wish you were cold or **h**.
3:16 are lukewarm and not **h** or cold,

Hotham (2)

1Ch 7:32 **H**, and their sister Shua.
11:44 Jeiel (sons of **H** from Aroer),

hothead (3)

Pro 15:18 A **h** stirs up a fight,
22:24 never keep company with a **h**,
29:22 and a **h** does much wrong.

Hothir (2)

1Ch 25:4 Mallothi, **H**, and Mahazioth.
25:28 The twenty-first chose **H**,

hotter (1)

Dan 3:19 seven times **h** than normal.

hottest (3)

Gen 18:1 of his tent during the **h** part
2Sm 4:5 Ishbosheth's home at the **h** time
Neh 7:3 not be opened at the **h** time

hour (19)

Psa 90:4 past — like an **h** in the night.
Lam 2:19 every **h** on the hour.
2:19 every hour on the **h**.
Mat 6:27 "Can any of you add a single **h**
20:12 have worked only one **h**.
24:36 when that day or **h** will come.
25:13 you don't know the day or the **h**.
26:40 stay awake with me for one **h**?
Mar 13:32 when that day or **h** will come.
14:37 you stay awake for one **h**?
Luk 10:21 In that **h** the Holy Spirit filled
12:25 "Can any of you add an **h** to
12:39 had known at what **h**
22:59 About an **h** later another person
24:33 That same **h** they went back to
Act 16:33 At that **h** of the night,
Rev 8:1 in heaven for about half an **h**.
9:15 who were ready for that **h**,
17:12 kings with the beast for one **h**.

hours (8)

1Sm 11:11 camp during the morning **h**
Psa 63:6 Through the long **h** of the night,
119:148 throughout the nighttime **h**
Pro 7:9 in the dark **h** of the night.
Isa 21:4 The twilight **h** I longed for
Jon 11:9 there twelve **h** of daylight?
Act 5:7 About three **h** later Ananias'
19:34 kept doing this for about two **h**.

house (476)

Gen 19:4 of Sodom surrounded the **h**.
19:10 pulled Lot into the **h** with them,
19:11 were in the doorway of the **h**,
24:23 there is room in your father's **h**
24:31 I have straightened up the **h**
24:32 So the man went into the **h**.
27:15 which she had in the **h**,
28:17 Certainly, this is the **h** of God
28:19 that place Bethel [**H** of God].
28:22 a marker will be the **h** of God,
31:37 you find anything from your **h**?
33:17 where he built a **h** for himself
35:7 El Bethel [God of the **H** of God].
35:15 with him Bethel [**H** of God].
39:2 He worked in the **h** of his
39:5 Potiphar owned in his **h**
39:8 himself with anything in the **h**.
39:9 No one in this **h** is greater than
39:11 One day he went into the **h** to
43:16 to the man in charge of his **h**,
43:16 "Take these men to my **h**.
43:17 and took them to Joseph's **h**.
43:18 had been brought to Joseph's **h**.
43:19 the man in charge of Joseph's **h**
43:24 the brothers into Joseph's **h**.
43:26 gifts they had brought to the **h**.
44:1 the man in charge of his **h**,
44:4 to the man in charge of his **h**,
44:8 or gold from your master's **h**?
44:14 Joseph's **h** while Joseph was
Exo 12:22 may leave the **h** until morning.
12:30 in every **h** someone had died.
12:46 must be eaten inside one **h**.
12:46 any of the meat outside the **h**.
22:7 are stolen from that person's **h**:
22:8 the owner of the **h** must be
23:19 from your soil to the **h**
34:26 from your soil to the **h**
Lev 14:34 mildew may appear in a **h**.
14:35 The owner of that **h** must come
14:35 that looks like mildew in his **h**.
14:36 the priest examines the **h**,
14:36 in the **h** will become unclean.
14:36 will go inside to examine the **h**.
14:38 will go out to the door of the **h**
14:38 close up the **h** for seven days.
14:39 the walls of the **h** has spread,
14:41 entire inside of the **h** scraped.
14:42 and the **h** must be plastered
14:43 again in the **h** after all this,
14:44 of mildew, the **h** is unclean.
14:45 The **h** — stones, wood, and all
14:46 Whoever goes into the **h** any
14:47 Whoever sleeps or eats in the **h**
14:48 has not spread in the **h** after
14:48 priest must declare the **h** clean.
14:49 use them to make the **h** clean.
14:51 sprinkle the **h** seven times.
14:52 and the red yarn to make the **h**
14:53 peace with the LORD for the **h**,
18:9 or not she was born in your **h**.
25:30 the **h** in the city belongs to the
25:33 If any Levite buys back a **h**,
25:33 in the jubilee the purchased **h**
27:14 "If you give your **h** to the LORD
Num 30:3 who still lives in her father's **h**,
Dtr 7:26 a disgusting idol into your **h**.
20:5 "If you have built a new **h** but
21:13 Then she may live in your **h**
22:8 Whenever you build a new **h**,
22:21 to the entrance of her father's **h**.
22:21 was still living in her father's **h**.
23:18 earned by prostitution into the **h**
24:1 and makes her leave his **h**.
24:2 man after she leaves his **h**.
24:10 don't go into his **h** to take a
25:14 kinds of measures in your **h**,
26:13 the holy offering stored in my **h**.
28:30 You will build a **h**,
Jos 2:1 to Jericho and entered the **h**
2:3 the men who came to your **h**.
2:15 since her **h** was built into
2:18 your father's family into your **h**.
2:19 Whoever leaves your **h** will be
2:19 inside your **h** is harmed.
6:17 Rahab and all who are in the **h**
6:22 "Go to the prostitute's **h**.
9:23 carriers for the **h** of my God."
Jdg 6:19 Then Gideon went into his **h**
11:7 throw me out of my father's **h**?
11:31 comes out of the doors of my **h**
12:1 Now we're going to burn your **h**
14:19 and he went to his father's **h**.
17:8 He came to Micah's **h** in the
18:2 They came to Micah's **h** in the
18:3 While they were at Micah's **h**,
18:13 of Ephraim as far as Micah's **h**.
18:15 stopped and entered Micah's **h**
18:18 these men entered Micah's **h**
18:19 to be a priest for one man's **h**
18:22 some distance from Micah's **h**,
18:31 there the whole time the **h**
19:3 her husband into her father's **h**.
19:18 Now I'm going to the LORD's **h**,
19:21 So he took the Levite to his **h**
19:22 from the city surrounded the **h**
19:22 the owner of the **h**,
19:22 who came to your **h** so that we
19:26 of the **h** where her husband
19:27 opened the doors of the **h**,
19:27 was lying at the door of the **h**
20:5 They surrounded the **h** where
20:8 go to his tent or return to his **h**.
1Sm 1:7 Hannah went to the LORD's **h**,
1:24 to the LORD's **h** at Shiloh while
2:31 of your father's **h** so that no

1Sm	3:15	the doors of the LORD's **h**.
	7:1	and brought it into Abinadab's **h**
	9:18	tell me where the seer's **h** is."
	18:10	He began to prophesy in his **h**
	19:9	while he was sitting in his **h**
	19:11	messengers to watch David's **h**
	20:16	the LORD punish David's **h**."
	21:15	man have to come into my **h**?"
2Sm	4:6	when they came into the **h** as
	4:7	(They had come into the **h**
	6:12	ark of God from Obed Edom's **h**
	6:21	or anyone in your father's **h**,
	7:1	King David was living in his **h**,
	7:2	I'm living in a **h** made of cedar,
	7:5	will build me a **h** to live in?
	7:6	I haven't lived in a **h** from the
	7:7	didn't build me a **h** of cedar?'
	7:11	you that I will make a **h** for you.
	7:13	He will build a **h** for my name,
	7:16	Your royal **h** will remain in my
	7:18	"and why is my **h** so important
	7:19	about the distant future of my **h**.
	7:25	made to me and my **h** forever.
	7:26	And the **h** of your servant David
	7:27	'I will build a **h** for you.'
	7:29	Now, please bless my **h** so
	7:29	With your blessing my **h** will
	11:11	Should I then go to my **h** to eat
	12:8	I gave you your master Saul's **h**
	12:8	I gave you the **h** of Israel and
	12:10	warfare will never leave your **h**
	12:20	the LORD's **h** and worshiped.
	14:24	should return to his own **h**.
	14:24	So Absalom returned to his **h**
	15:17	they stopped at the last **h**.
	16:3	"He said, 'Today the **h** of Israel
	19:5	Then Joab came into the **h**.
	19:11	reached the king at his **h**.
	19:20	I've come as the first of all the **h**
	20:3	put them in a **h** under guard.
	23:5	"Truly, God considers my **h** to
1Ki	2:36	"Build a **h** for yourself in
	3:1	he finished building his own **h**,
	3:1	his own house, the LORD's **h**,
	3:17	and I live in the same **h**.
	3:17	she was with me in the **h**.
	3:18	the two of us were in the **h**.
	9:10	the two houses (the LORD's **h**
	9:15	drafted to build the LORD's **h**,
	9:15	house, his own **h**, the Millo,
	12:16	Now look after your own **h**,
	14:10	bring disaster on Jeroboam's **h**.
	14:10	destroy every male in his **h**,
	14:10	I will burn down Jeroboam's **h**.
	14:11	If anyone from Jeroboam's **h**
	14:13	the only one in Jeroboam's **h**
	14:14	king will destroy Jeroboam's **h**.
	16:9	drunk in Tirzah at Arza's **h**.
	16:10	Zimri entered Arza's **h**,
	17:17	who owned the **h** got sick.
	17:23	from the upstairs room of the **h**,
	21:2	garden because it is near my **h**.
	21:21	every male in Ahab's ⌊**h**⌋,
	21:22	son) and like the **h** of Baasha,
	21:24	If anyone from Ahab's ⌊**h**⌋ dies
2Ki	4:2	what do you have in your **h**?"
	4:2	"I have nothing in the **h** except
	4:9	he regularly travels past our **h**.
	4:11	One day he came ⌊to their **h**⌋,
	4:32	When Elisha came to the **h**,
	5:11	at least come out ⌊of his **h**⌋,
	5:24	and put them away in the **h**.
	6:32	ahead of him ⌊to Elisha's **h**⌋.
	8:3	the king about her **h** and land.
	8:5	the king about her **h** and land.
	9:6	got up and went into the **h**.
	15:5	the king lived in a separate **h**.
1Ch	6:48	duties in the tent, the **h** of God.
	9:23	gatekeepers for the LORD's **h**,
	15:25	promise from Obed Edom's **h**.
	17:1	David was living in his **h**,
	17:1	"I'm living in a **h** made of cedar,
	17:4	You must not build this **h** for
	17:5	I haven't lived in a **h** from the
	17:6	didn't build me a **h** of cedar?'
	17:10	will build a **h** for you.
1Ch	17:12	He will build a **h** for me,
	17:14	place him in my royal **h** forever,
	17:16	"and why is my **h** so important
	17:17	about the distant future of my **h**.
	17:23	made to me and my **h** forever.
	17:24	And the **h** of David,
	17:25	me that you will build me a **h**.
	17:27	pleased to bless my **h** so that
2Ch	8:1	20 years to build the LORD's **h**
	8:1	LORD's house and his own **h**.
	10:16	Now look after your own **h**.
	22:10	royal family of the **h** of Judah.
	26:21	he lived in a separate **h** and
Ezr	3:8	site⌋ of God's **h** in Jerusalem.
	3:8	the work on the LORD's **h**.
	3:9	those working on God's **h**.
	3:11	the foundation for the **h**
	6:11	on a beam torn from his own **h**
	6:11	own house and his **h** should
Neh	2:8	and for the **h** I'll move into."
	3:20	the Angle to the door of the **h**
	3:21	from the door of Eliashib's **h**
	3:21	to the end of Eliashib's **h**.
	6:10	who was confined to his **h**,
	6:10	"Let's meet in the **h** of God,
Est	1:22	be the ruler in his own **h**
	7:9	is still standing at Haman's **h**."
Job	1:19	struck the four corners of the **h**.
	5:3	but I quickly cursed his **h**.
	5:24	You will inspect your **h** and
	8:15	If one leans on his **h**,
	8:17	They cling to a stone **h**.
	19:14	My **h** guests have forgotten me.
	20:19	He has taken by force a **h** that
	20:28	A flood will sweep away his **h**,
	21:28	'Where is the **h** of the
	27:18	He builds his **h** like a moth,
	29:18	'I may die in my own **h**,
	42:11	They ate with him at his **h**,
Psa	5:7	But I will enter your **h** because
	23:6	I will remain in the LORD's **h**
	26:8	I love the **h** where you live,
	27:4	to remain in the LORD's **h** all
	36:8	with the rich foods in your **h**,
	42:4	it in a procession to God's **h**.
	45:10	and forget your father's **h**.
	49:16	when the greatness of his **h**
	52:8	a large olive tree in God's **h**.
	55:14	and walk into God's **h**
	65:4	with good food from your **h**,
	69:9	Indeed, devotion for your **h** has
	84:4	are those who live in your **h**.
	84:10	to my God's **h** than live inside
	91:10	will come near your **h**.
	92:13	are planted in the LORD's **h**.
	93:5	holiness is what makes your **h**
	116:19	the courtyards of the LORD's **h**,
	118:26	bless you from the LORD's **h**.
	122:1	"Let's go to the **h** of the LORD."
	122:9	For the sake of the **h** of the
	127:1	the LORD does not build the **h**,
	132:3	"I will not step inside my **h**,
	134:1	all who stand in the **h** of the
	135:2	who are standing in the **h** of the
	135:2	courtyards of the **h** of our God.
Pro	2:18	Her **h** sinks down to death.
	3:33	The LORD curses the **h** of
	5:10	to work hard in a pagan's **h**.
	6:31	up all the possessions in his **h**.
	7:6	From a window in my **h** I
	7:8	and walking toward her **h**
	9:1	Wisdom has built her **h**.
	9:14	sits at the doorway of her **h**.
	15:6	Great treasure is in the **h** of a
	15:25	The LORD tears down the **h** of
	21:12	person wisely considers the **h**
	24:3	With wisdom a **h** is built.
	24:15	person. Do not rob his **h**.
	24:27	Afterwards, build your **h**.
	25:17	in your neighbor's **h** too often.
Ecc	5:1	when you go to the **h** of God.
	10:18	A **h** leaks because of idle
	12:3	those who guard the **h** tremble,
Sos	1:17	will be the walls of our **h**.
	3:4	brought him into my mother's **h**
	8:2	bring you into my mother's **h**.
Isa	2:2	mountain of the LORD's **h** will
	2:3	to the **h** of the God of Jacob.
	5:8	you who acquire **h** after house
	5:8	you who acquire house after **h**
	22:8	weapons in the **H** of the Forest.
	22:22	I will place the key of the **h** of
	24:10	to every **h** is barred shut.
	56:5	Inside my **h** and within my
	56:7	them happy in my **h** of prayer.
	56:7	because my **h** will be called a
	56:7	my house will be called a **h**
	58:7	poor and homeless into your **h**,
	66:1	Where can you build a **h** or
Jer	7:2	at the gate of the LORD's **h**,
	7:10	presence in the **h** that is called
	7:11	The **h** that is called by my
	7:14	now do to the **h** that is called
	7:30	idols in the **h** that is called
	11:15	to be in my **h** when they do
	16:5	Don't go into a **h** where people
	18:2	"Go to the potter's **h**.
	18:3	I went to the potter's **h**,
	20:6	and all those who live in your **h**
	22:13	who builds his **h** dishonestly
	22:14	He says, 'I will build a large **h**
	36:22	king was in his winter **h** sitting
	37:15	in the scribe Jonathan's **h**,
	37:20	me to the scribe Jonathan's **h**,
	38:26	to Jonathan's **h** to die there.'"
Eze	12:5	hole through the wall of your **h**,
Dan	6:10	been signed, he went to his **h**.
	6:10	An upper room in his **h** had
Amo	1:4	I will send a fire on the **h** of
	5:6	spread like a fire through the **h**
	6:9	If ten people are left in one **h**,
	6:10	the dead bodies out of the **h**
	6:10	someone who is inside the **h**,
Mic	4:1	mountain of the LORD's **h** will
	4:2	to the **h** of the God of Jacob.
Zep	1:9	and all who fill their master's **h**
Hag	1:2	to rebuild the **h** of the LORD."
	1:4	while this **h** lies in ruins?
	1:8	get lumber, and build the **h**.
	1:9	"It's because my **h** lies in ruins
	1:9	is busy working on your own **h**.
	1:14	them ⌊to rebuild his **h**⌋.
	1:14	began working on the **h**
	2:3	the faithful few who saw this **h**
	2:7	Then I will fill this **h** with glory,
	2:9	This new **h** will be more
	2:18	when the foundation of the **h**
Zec	1:16	My **h** will be rebuilt in it,
	4:9	laid the foundation of this **h**,
	5:11	"They are going to build a **h** for
	5:11	When the **h** is ready,
	6:10	same day go to the **h** of Josiah,
	7:3	asked the priests from the **h**
	8:9	when the foundation for the **h**
	9:8	I will camp in front of my **h** as a
	11:13	the potter at the **h** of the LORD.
	13:6	'I was hurt at my friend's **h**.'
	14:20	And the cooking pots in the **h**
	14:21	be any Canaanite in the **h**
Mal	1:10	the doors ⌊to my **h**⌋ so that you
	3:10	that there may be food in my **h**.
Mat	2:11	When they entered the **h**,
	5:15	shines on everyone in the **h**.
	7:24	person who built a **h** on rock.
	7:25	blew and beat against that **h**.
	7:26	person who built a **h** on sand.
	7:27	Winds blew and struck that **h**.
	8:8	to have you come into my **h**.
	8:14	When Jesus went to Peter's **h**,
	9:10	having dinner at Matthew's **h**.
	9:23	to the ⌊synagogue⌋ leader's **h**.
	9:28	Jesus went into a **h**,
	10:12	When you go into a **h**,
	10:14	leave that **h** or city,
	10:25	the owner of the **h** Beelzebul,
	12:4	read how he went into the **h**
	12:29	anyone go into a strong man's **h**
	12:29	Then he can go through his **h**
	12:44	it finds the **h** unoccupied,
	13:1	That same day Jesus left the **h**
	13:36	he went into the **h**.
	13:57	hometown and in his own **h**."

Mat 17:25 Peter went into the **h**.
21:13 'My **h** will be called a house of
21:13 will be called a **h** of prayer,'
23:38 Your **h** will be abandoned,
24:43 let the thief break into his **h**.
26:18 with my disciples at your **h**.'"
Mar 1:29 they went directly to the **h** of
2:15 was having dinner at Levi's **h**.
2:26 read how he went into the **h**
3:27 can go into a strong man's **h**
3:27 go through the strong man's **h**
5:39 When he came into the **h**,
6:4 and in his own **h**."
7:24 he was staying in a **h** there.
9:28 When Jesus went into a **h**,
10:10 When they were in a **h**,
11:4 It was tied to the door of a **h**.
11:17 'My **h** will be called a house of
11:17 'My house will be called a **h** of
13:35 the owner of the **h** will return.
14:14 When he goes into a **h**,
Luk 2:49 I had to be in my Father's **h**?"
4:38 and went to Simon's **h**.
5:18 They tried to take him into the **h**
5:19 find a way to get him into the **h**
6:4 how he went into the **h** of God,
6:48 pushed against that **h**.
6:48 But the **h** couldn't be washed
6:49 it is like someone who built a **h**
6:49 and that **h** quickly collapsed
7:6 He was not far from the **h** when
7:6 to have you come into my **h**.
7:10 had been sent returned to the **h**,
7:36 Jesus went to the Pharisee's **h**
7:37 was eating at the Pharisee's **h**.
7:44 I came into your **h**.
8:27 He would not stay in a **h** but
8:51 Jesus went into the **h**.
10:5 Whenever you go into a **h**,
10:5 'May there be peace in this **h**.'
10:7 around from one **h** to another.
11:7 answer you from inside his **h**,
11:17 A **h** divided against itself falls.
11:25 When it comes, it finds the **h**
11:37 him to have lunch at his **h**.
12:39 have let him break into his **h**.
13:35 Your **h** will be abandoned.
14:21 master of the **h** became angry.
14:23 the people to come to my **h**.
15:8 she light a lamp, sweep the **h**,
15:25 he was coming back to the **h**,
15:28 and wouldn't go into the **h**.
16:20 to the gate of the rich man's **h**.
19:5 I must stay at your **h** today."
19:46 'My **h** will be a house of prayer,'
19:46 'My house will be a **h** of prayer,'
22:10 Follow him into the **h** he enters.
22:11 Tell the owner of the **h** that the
22:54 him away to the chief priest's **h**.
Jon 2:16 my Father's **h** a marketplace!"
2:17 for your **h** will consume me."
11:31 Mary in the **h** saw her get
12:3 of the perfume filled the **h**.
14:2 My Father's **h** has many rooms.
18:28 was taken from Caiaphas' **h**
20:26 disciples were again in the **h**,
Act 2:2 the whole **h** where they were
5:42 courtyard and from **h** to house,
5:42 courtyard and from house to **h**,
7:47 the one who built a **h** for God.
7:48 live in a **h** built by humans,
7:49 What kind of **h** are you going to
9:11 Go to Judas' **h** on Straight
9:17 left and entered Judas' **h**.
10:6 whose **h** is by the sea."
10:17 by Cornelius found Simon's **h**
10:23 the men to come into the **h**
10:25 was about to enter Cornelius' **h**,
10:27 he entered Cornelius' **h** and
11:11 arrived at the **h** where we were
16:40 they went to Lydia's **h**.
18:7 His **h** was next door to the
19:16 of that **h** naked and wounded.
20:20 publicly and from **h** to house.
20:20 publicly and from house to **h**.
Rom 16:5 the church that meets in their **h**.
1Co 10:27 you ⌊to his **h** for dinner⌋,
16:19 in their **h** send their warmest
2Co 5:1 It is an eternal **h** in heaven that
5:2 since we long to put on the **h**
5:4 do want to put on the eternal **h**.
Col 4:15 the church that meets in her **h**.
1Ti 5:13 they learn to go around from **h**
5:13 house to **h** since they have
2Ti 2:20 In a large **h** there are not only
Phm 1:2 the church that meets in your **h**.
Heb 3:2 when he served in God's **h**.
3:3 builder of a **h** is praised more
3:3 is praised more than the **h**.
3:4 After all, every **h** has a builder,
10:21 priest in charge of God's **h**.
1Pe 2:5 a spiritual **h** that is being built

housed (1)

Neh 3:31 as far as the building that **h**

household (79)

Gen 12:17 LORD struck Pharaoh and his **h**
14:14 trained men, born in his own **h**,
15:2 of Damascus will inherit my **h**.
15:3 so this member of my **h** will be
17:12 whether he is born in your **h** or
17:13 Every male born in your **h** or
17:23 everyone born in his **h**,
17:23 money — every male in his **h** —
17:27 All the men of his **h**,
17:27 whether born in the **h** or bought
20:18 any woman in Abimelech's **h**
24:2 servant of his **h** who was
24:28 mother's **h** about these things.
31:14 anything left in our father's **h**
31:41 I've been with your **h** 20 years
36:6 all the members of his **h**,
39:4 He put him in charge of his **h**
39:5 LORD blessed the Egyptian's **h**
39:11 of the **h** servants were there.
39:14 she called her **h** servants and
45:2 and Pharaoh's **h** heard about it.
45:8 lord over his entire **h**,
45:16 When Pharaoh's **h** heard the
46:27 people in Jacob's **h** who went
50:8 Joseph's **h**, his brothers,
50:8 and his father's **h** also went
Exo 12:3 his family — one animal per **h**.
12:4 A **h** may be too small to eat a
12:4 That **h** and the one next door
12:48 First, every male in the **h** must
20:17 neighbor's **h** away from him.
23:12 The slaves born in your **h** and
Lev 22:11 anyone born in his **h** may eat
Num 1:4 men must be the head of a **h**.
1:18 his genealogy by family and **h**.
2:2 the flag that symbolizes its **h**.
2:34 with his own family and **h**.
12:7 most faithful person in my **h**.
18:11 Anyone in your **h** who is clean
18:13 Anyone in your **h** who is clean
Dtr 5:21 long for your neighbor's **h**,
Jos 7:14 and the **h** the LORD selects
7:18 Then he had Zabdi's **h** come
22:14 Each man was a leader of a **h**
Jdg 17:5 made an ephod and **h** idols.
18:14 and **h** idols in these houses?
18:17 the **h** idols, and the metal idol.
18:18 the **h** idols, and the metal idol,
18:20 He took the ephod, the **h** idols,
1Sm 1:21 and his entire **h** again went
2:36 left from your **h** will bow down
3:13 judgment against his **h**
22:14 He's honored in your own **h**.
25:17 and his whole **h** are doomed.
2Sm 12:11 against you within your own **h**,
15:16 and his whole **h** followed him
2Ki 10:11 of Ahab's **h** who was left
20:1 final instructions to your **h**,
Neh 13:8 So I threw all of Tobiah's **h**
Job 7:10 and his **h** doesn't recognize
Psa 50:9 young bull from your **h**
Ecc 2:7 slaves were born in my **h**.
Isa 22:18 a disgrace to your master's **h**.
22:23 of honor for his father's **h**.
22:24 whole weight of his father's **h**,
Isa 38:1 final instructions to your **h**,
Jer 12:6 of your father's **h** betray you.
38:17 You and your **h** will live.
Eze 21:21 ask his **h** gods for help,
Hab 2:9 to get things for his own **h**
2:10 for your **h** by cutting off
3:13 the leader of the wicked **h**,
Mat 12:25 And every city or **h** divided
Mar 3:25 And if a **h** is divided against
3:25 that **h** will not last.
Act 10:7 Cornelius called two of his **h**
Heb 3:5 a faithful servant in God's **h**.
3:6 son in charge of God's **h**.
3:6 We are his **h** if we continue to

households (41)

Gen 47:24 fields and as food for your **h**."
Exo 6:25 heads of Levite **h** listed by their
Num 1:2 of Israel by families and **h**.
1:20 The roster of families and **h** for
1:22 The roster of families and **h** for
1:24 The roster of families and **h** for
1:26 The roster of families and **h** for
1:28 The roster of families and **h** for
1:30 The roster of families and **h** for
1:32 The roster of families and **h** for
1:34 The roster of families and **h** for
1:36 The roster of families and **h** for
1:38 The roster of families and **h** for
1:40 The roster of families and **h** for
1:42 The roster of families and **h** for
1:45 Israelites were registered by **h**.
1:47 But the **h** from the tribe of Levi
2:32 of Israelites, counted by **h**.
3:15 the Levites by **h** and families.
3:20 were the **h** of Levite families.
3:24 the Gershonite **h** was Eliasaph,
3:30 families and **h** was Elizaphan,
3:35 families and **h** was Zuriel,
4:2 List them by families and **h**.
4:22 List them by **h** and families.
4:29 the Merarites by families and **h**.
4:34 by their families and **h**.
4:38 registered by families and **h**.
4:40 were listed by families and **h**.
4:42 registered by families and **h**.
4:46 were listed by families and **h**.
7:2 the heads of the **h** — those tribal
18:31 So you and your **h** may eat it
26:2 community of Israel by **h**.
34:14 The **h** from the tribes of
36:1 The heads of the **h** whose
36:1 leaders of the other Israelite **h**.
Jos 2:13 brothers, sisters, and their **h**,
7:14 selects will come forward by **h**,
1Ch 4:38 of people in their **h** increased.
Jer 6:12 Their **h**, their fields, and their

houses (84)

Gen 34:29 and looted everything in the **h**.
Exo 8:3 into the **h** of your officials,
8:13 The frogs died in the **h**,
8:21 your people, and your **h**.
8:24 Pharaoh's palace and into the **h**
10:6 They will fill your **h** and the
10:6 will fill your houses and the **h**
12:7 of the **h** where they will
12:13 But the blood on your **h** will be
12:15 yeast that you have in your **h**.
12:19 should be no yeast in your **h**
12:22 of the doorframes ⌊of your **h**⌋.
12:27 The LORD passed over the **h**
Lev 14:55 that infects clothing or **h**
25:31 However, **h** in villages without
25:33 because the **h** in the Levite
Dtr 6:9 on the doorframes of your **h**
6:11 Your **h** will be filled with all
8:12 You will build nice **h** and live
11:20 on the doorframes of your **h**
19:1 and live in their cities and **h**.
26:12 of that year's crops ⌊in your **h**⌋.
Jdg 18:14 household idols in these **h**?
1Ki 9:10 the two **h** (the LORD's house
20:6 palace and your servants' **h**.
2Ki 23:7 He tore down the **h** of the male
25:9 and all the **h** in Jerusalem.

Neh 7:4 and no **h** were being built.
9:25 They took possession of **h**
Job 4:19 live in clay **h** that have their
4:19 Those **h** can be crushed
15:28 in **h** that are doomed to be piles
24:16 In the dark, they break into **h**,
Pro 14:11 The **h** of wicked people will be
Ecc 2:4 I built **h** for myself.
Isa 3:14 Your **h** are filled with goods
5:9 "Many **h** will become empty.
5:9 Large, beautiful **h** will be
6:11 the **h** have no people,
13:16 Their **h** will be looted and their
22:10 will count the **h** in Jerusalem.
22:10 You will tear down those **h** in
65:21 They will build **h** and live there.
Jer 5:7 crowds to the **h** of prostitutes.
5:27 their **h** are filled with deceit.
19:13 The **h** in Jerusalem,
19:13 the **h** of the kings of Judah,
19:13 and all the rooftops of the **h**
29:5 Build **h**, and live in them.
29:28 Build **h**, and live in them.
32:15 My people will again buy **h**,
32:29 They will burn down the **h** of
33:4 The **h** in this city and the
33:5 Now their **h** are filled with the
35:7 Never build any **h** or plant any
35:9 built **h** to live in, or owned
52:13 and all the **h** in Jerusalem.
Lam 1:20 Inside the **h** it's like death.
Eze 7:24 take possession of people's **h**.
16:41 They will burn your **h** and
Dan 2:5 and your **h** will be turned into
3:29 Their **h** will be turned into piles
Hos 7:1 They break into **h** and steal.
Joe 2:9 They climb into **h**.
Amo 3:15 I will tear down winter **h** as
3:15 houses as well as summer **h**.
3:15 **H** ⌊decorated⌋ with ivory will
5:11 That is why you build **h** from
6:11 the command to level big **h**
6:11 big houses and flatten little **h**.
Mic 2:2 They desire ⌊people's⌋ **h**,
Zep 1:13 They will build **h**, but they
2:7 lie down in the **h** of Ashkelon.
Hag 1:4 paneled **h** while this house
Zec 5:4 and it will enter the **h** of thieves
5:4 the houses of thieves and the **h**
5:4 It will stay in their **h** and
14:2 will be captured, the **h** looted,
Mat 24:17 to get anything out of their **h**.
Mar 12:40 rob widows by taking their **h**
13:15 to get anything out of their **h**.
Luk 17:31 their belongings out of their **h**.
20:47 rob widows by taking their **h**
Act 4:34 people sold land or **h** and

housetops (2)

Mat 10:27 Shout from the **h** what you hear
Luk 12:3 will be shouted from the **h**.

hovering (2)

Gen 1:2 of God was **h** over the water.
Isa 31:5 defend Jerusalem like a **h** bird.

hovers (1)

Dtr 32:11 up its nest, **h** over its young,

howl (7)

Dtr 32:10 barren place where animals **h**.
Job 30:7 They **h** in bushes and huddle
Psa 59:6 They **h** like dogs. They prowl
59:14 They **h** like dogs. They prowl
Isa 13:22 Hyenas will **h** in Babylon's
13:22 and jackals will **h** in its
Zep 1:11 "**H**, inhabitants of the Mortar,

howling (2)

Amo 1:14 day of battle and winds are **h**
Zep 1:10 a **h** from the Second Part of the

Hozai (1)

2Ch 33:19 it are written in the records of **H**

hubs (1)

1Ki 7:33 and **h** were all cast metal.

huddle (1)

Job 30:7 **h** together under thornbushes.

hug (2)

Job 24:8 They **h** the rocks because they
Ecc 3:5 a time to **h** and a time to stop

huge (16)

Gen 41:49 Joseph stored up grain in **h**
Jos 10:11 the LORD threw **h** hailstones
2Sm 18:17 threw him into a **h** pit in the
Isa 34:6 a **h** slaughter in the land of
56:11 These dogs have **h** appetites.
Eze 39:17 It will be a **h** feast on the
Mat 12:40 was in the belly of a **h** fish
Mar 5:24 A **h** crowd followed Jesus and
13:1 look at these **h** stones and
Luk 5:29 A **h** crowd of tax collectors and
Act 19:24 His business brought a **h** profit
1Ti 6:6 A godly life brings **h** profits to
Rev 8:8 something like a **h** mountain
8:10 a **h** star flaming like a torch fell
12:3 a **h** fiery red serpent with seven
12:9 The **h** serpent was thrown

hugged (3)

Gen 29:13 He **h** and kissed him and
33:4 Esau **h** him, threw his arms
48:10 and Israel **h** them and kissed

hugging (1)

Ecc 3:5 to hug and a time to stop **h**,

Hukok (2)

Jos 19:34 and from there to **H**.
1Ch 6:75 **H** with its pastureland,

Hul (2)

Gen 10:23 were Uz, **H**, Gether, and Mash.
1Ch 1:17 Uz, **H**, Gether, and Meshech.

Huldah (6)

2Ki 22:14 went to talk to the prophet **H**.
22:14 **H** was living in the Second
22:18 ⌊**H** added,⌋ "But tell Judah's
2Ch 34:22 the prophet **H** about this matter.
34:22 **H** was living in the Second
34:26 ⌊**H** added,⌋ "Tell Judah's king

human (153)

Gen 6:17 sky — every living, breathing **h**.
7:21 along with every **h**.
9:6 Whoever sheds **h** blood,
Exo 12:12 both **h** and animal.
13:2 whether **h** or animal."
13:15 male in Egypt — **h** and animal.
Lev 5:3 by touching **h** uncleanness
7:21 anything unclean, **h** or animal,
Num 3:13 whether **h** or animal.
8:17 whether **h** or animal,
18:15 firstborn male, **h** or animal,
19:11 dead body of any **h** being will
19:13 the dead body of a **h** being
19:16 anyone who touches a **h** bone
19:18 who has touched a **h** bone
Dtr 4:28 stone gods made by **h** hands.
2Sm 24:14 But don't let me fall into **h**
1Ki 13:2 **H** bones will be burned on
2Ki 19:18 statues made by **h** hands.
23:14 and filled their places with **h**
23:20 altars and then burned **h** bones
1Ch 21:13 But don't let me fall into **h**
2Ch 19:6 you aren't doing it for a **h** but for
32:8 The king of Assyria has **h**
32:19 of the gods made by **h** hands
Job 4:17 Can ⌊any⌋ **h** being be pure to
9:32 A **h** like me cannot answer
10:4 Do you actually have **h** eyes?
12:10 the spirit in every **h** body are
14:10 But a **h** dies and is powerless.
15:7 "Were you the first **h** to be
16:21 my witness will plead for a **h**
Job 22:2 "Can a **h** be of any use to God
34:20 taken away but not by **h** hands.
Psa 60:11 **h** assistance is worthless.
64:6 **H** nature and the human heart
64:6 Human nature and the **h** heart
103:15 **H** life is as short-lived as grass.
104:15 make wine to cheer **h** hearts,
104:15 and bread to strengthen **h**
108:12 **h** assistance is worthless.
115:4 They were made by **h** hands.
119:134 Save me from **h** oppression so
135:15 They were made by **h** hands.
Pro 8:31 and delighted in the **h** race.
15:11 how much more the **h** heart!
19:21 Many plans are in the **h** heart,
20:5 A motive in the **h** heart is like
30:2 a dumb animal than a **h** being.
30:2 I don't ⌊even⌋ have **h**
Ecc 3:21 Who knows whether a **h** spirit
8:6 Yet, a terrible **h** tragedy hangs
Isa 13:12 gold and **h** beings more rare
31:8 swords not made by **h** hands.
31:8 Swords not made by **h** hands
37:19 statues made by **h** hands.
44:11 themselves are only **h**.
52:14 that he will hardly look like a **h**.
Jer 17:9 "The **h** mind is the most
49:18 No **h** will stay there,"
49:33 No **h** will stay there.
50:40 No **h** will stay there,"
51:43 lives and where no **h** travels.
Lam 4:6 without one **h** hand touching it.
Eze 1:8 They had **h** hands under their
1:10 creature had the face of a **h**.
1:26 a figure that looked like a **h**.
4:12 using **h** excrement for fuel."
4:15 in place of **h** excrement.
8:2 something that looked like a **h**.
10:8 looked like **h** hands under their
10:14 the second was the face of a **h**,
10:21 were what looked like **h** hands.
28:2 But you're only **h** and not a god,
28:9 You will be a **h**, not a god,
29:11 No **h** or animal will walk
39:15 the land and see a **h** bone,
Dan 4:16 Let its **h** mind be changed,
4:17 has power over **h** kingdoms.
4:25 has power over **h** kingdoms
4:32 has power over **h** kingdoms
5:21 has power over **h** kingdoms.
7:4 to stand on two feet like a **h**
7:4 and was given a **h** mind.
7:8 This horn had eyes like **h** eyes
8:25 though not by any **h** power.
10:16 like a **h** touched my lips.
10:18 looked like a **h** touched me,
11:2 looked like a **h** continued,⌋
12:1 looked like a **h** continued,⌋
Hos 11:4 them with cords of **h** kindness,
11:9 I am God, not a **h**. I am the Holy
13:2 "They offer **h** sacrifices and
Mat 12:12 Certainly, a **h** is more valuable
16:17 No **h** revealed this to you,
Mar 7:8 of God to follow **h** traditions."
14:58 one not made by **h** hands."'
Jon 1:13 way — from a **h** impulse
1:14 The Word became **h** and lived
2:25 to tell him about **h** nature.
5:34 I don't depend on **h** testimony.
7:46 "No **h** has ever spoken like this
Act 5:38 put into action is of **h** origin,
14:11 come to us, and they look **h**."
14:15 We're **h** beings like you.
17:29 of **h** imagination and skill.
Rom 1:3 In his **h** nature he was a
6:19 I'm speaking in a **h** way
8:3 the weakness our **h** nature has.
8:3 to have a **h** nature as sinners
9:5 according to his **h** nature.
1Co 1:25 God's nonsense is wiser than **h**
1:25 is stronger than **h** strength.
1:26 of you were wise from a **h** point
2:5 not be based on **h** wisdom
3:3 and living by **h** standards?
4:3 **h** court should cross-examine
9:8 I merely stating some **h** rule?

1Co 10:18 people of Israel from a **h** point
12:14 As you know, the **h** body is not
2Co 1:12 It was not by **h** wisdom that we
3:3 stone but on tablets of **h** hearts.
5:1 that isn't made by **h** hands.
5:16 think of anyone from a **h** point
5:16 If we did think of Christ from a **h**
10:2 are only guided by **h** motives.
10:3 Of course we are **h**,
Gal 1:11 spread is not a **h** message.
3:3 up doing things in a **h** way?
Eph 6:7 not merely serving **h** masters.
6:12 match against a **h** opponent.
Php 2:7 by having a **h** appearance.
Col 2:8 Such a person follows **h**
2:11 performed by **h** hands.
1Th 2:15 enemies of the whole **h** race
4:8 is not rejecting **h** authority
1Ti 2:5 God and humans — a **h**,
3:16 He appeared in his **h** nature,
Heb 7:16 he met **h** requirements,
8:2 by the Lord and not by any **h**.
9:11 that was not made by **h** hands
9:24 a holy place made by **h** hands.
Jas 5:17 Elijah was **h** like us.
1Pe 2:13 the authority of **h** governments
4:2 by sinful **h** desires as you
2Pe 2:16 spoke with a **h** voice and
1Jn 4:2 Christ has come as a **h** has
4:3 Christ has come as a **h** has
5:9 We accept **h** testimony.
Rev 4:7 the third had a face like a **h**,
9:7 Their faces were like **h** faces.
13:18 because it is a **h** number.
21:17 According to **h** measurement,

humanity (25)

Job 34:11 God will repay **h** for what it has
34:15 and **h** would return to dust.
Psa 22:6 I am scorned by **h** and
Pro 3:4 in the sight of God and **h**.
29:26 but justice for **h** comes from the
30:14 earth and people from among **h**.
Isa 49:26 Then all **h** will know that I am
66:24 All **h** will be disgusted by them.
Jer 32:27 "I am the LORD God of all **h**.
49:15 nations and despised among **h**.
Zec 9:2 (The eyes of **h** and of all the
Jon 1:4 and that life was the light for **h**.
17:2 him authority over all **h** so that
Act 17:26 he has made every nation of **h**
Rom 5:15 If **h** died as the result of one
5:15 have been showered on **h**.
5:19 disobedience **h** became sinful,
5:19 obedience **h** will receive God's
2Co 5:19 restore his relationship with **h**.
Eph 2:15 create one new **h** in himself.
Tit 3:4 kindness and love for **h** appear,
Heb 9:28 to take away the sins of **h**,
Rev 9:15 released to kill one-third of **h**.
9:18 mouths — killed one-third of **h**.
14:4 were bought from among **h** as

human's (1)

Job 10:5 Are your years like a **h** years

humans (102)

Gen 1:26 "Let us make **h** in our image,
1:27 So God created **h** in his image.
5:1 When God created **h**,
5:2 them and called them **h** when
6:2 of other **h** were beautiful.
6:3 will not struggle with **h** forever,
6:4 with the daughters of other **h**
6:5 The LORD saw how evil **h** had
6:6 was sorry that he had made **h**
6:7 face of the earth these **h** that
6:7 I will wipe out not only **h**,
7:23 **H**, domestic animals,
8:21 curse the ground because of **h**,
9:6 by **h** his blood will be shed,
9:6 the image of God, God made **h**.
Exo 4:11 "Who gave **h** their mouths?
4:11 Who makes **h** unable to talk or
Num 23:19 He is not like **h**. He doesn't
Jdg 9:9 use to honor gods and **h**,
Jdg 9:13 makes gods and **h** happy,
1Sm 2:9 because **h** cannot succeed by
16:7 God does not see as **h** see.
16:7 **H** look at outward appearances,
2Sm 23:3 'The one who rules **h** with
Job 20:4 from the time **h** were placed on
28:3 ⌊H⌋ bring an end to darkness
28:9 "**H** exert their power on the
28:28 So he told **h**, 'The fear of the
32:8 However, there is in **h** a Spirit,
32:13 Let God, not **h**, defeat him.'
38:26 a desert where there are no **h**,
Psa 78:25 **H** ate the bread of the mighty
78:60 where he had lived among **h**.
82:7 You will certainly die like **h**
104:14 and make vegetables for **h**
135:8 He killed **h** and animals alike.
144:3 O LORD, what are **h** that you
144:4 **H** are like a breath of air.
Pro 16:1 plans of the heart belong to **h**,
Ecc 3:18 "God is going to test **h** in order
3:19 **H** and animals have the same
3:19 **H** have no advantage over
9:12 **h** are trapped by a disaster
Isa 29:13 is ⌊based on⌋ rules made by **h**.
31:3 The Egyptians are **h**,
45:12 the earth and created **h** on it.
51:12 die, of **h**, who are like grass?
Jer 7:20 this place, on **h** and animals,
10:23 O LORD, I know that the way **h**
10:23 **H** do not direct their steps as
17:5 is the person who trusts **h**,
25:31 He will judge all **h**.
Eze 1:5 They were shaped like **h**,
32:13 The feet of **h** and the hoofs of
Dan 2:11 and they don't live with **h**."
2:34 stone was cut out, but not by **h**.
2:45 from a mountain, but not by **h**.
Amo 4:13 He reveals his thoughts to **h**.
Mic 5:7 They do not put their hope in **h**
Zep 1:3 put an end to **h** and animals.
1:17 "I will bring such distress on **h**
Hag 1:11 produces, on **h** and animals,
Mat 9:8 for giving such authority to **h**.
15:9 are rules made by **h**.'"
16:23 thinks but the way **h** think."
21:25 come from heaven or from **h**?"
21:26 But if we say, 'from **h**,' we're
Mar 7:7 teachings are rules made by **h**.'
8:33 thinks but the way **h** think."
11:30 come from heaven or from **h**?
11:32 But if we say, 'from **h**,' ⌊then
14:58 down this temple made by **h**,
Luk 16:15 What is important to **h** is
20:4 come from heaven or from **h**?"
20:6 we say, 'from **h**,' everyone will
Jon 5:41 "I don't accept praise from **h**.
8:15 You judge the way **h** do.
Act 7:48 live in a house built by **h**,
17:24 live in shrines made by **h**,
17:25 and he isn't served by **h** as if
19:26 gods made by **h** are not gods.
Rom 1:23 that looked like mortal **h**,
3:5 (I'm arguing the way **h** would.)
1Co 3:4 you acting like ⌊sinful⌋ **h**?
10:13 which is unusual for **h**.
13:1 speak in the languages of **h**
15:39 **H** have one kind of flesh,
2Co 10:3 but we don't fight like **h**.
10:4 in our fight are not made by **h**.
12:4 things that **h** cannot put into
Php 2:7 by becoming like other **h**,
Col 3:23 master and not merely for **h**.
1Th 2:13 realized it wasn't the word of **h**.
1Ti 2:5 mediator between God and **h** —
Heb 5:1 chief priest is chosen from **h**
1Pe 2:4 stone who was rejected by **h**
4:6 that they could be judged like **h**
2Pe 1:21 ever originated from **h**.
1:21 Spirit as **h** spoke under God's
Rev 16:18 earthquake since **h** have been
18:13 wagons, slaves (that is, **h**).
21:3 "God lives with **h**!

humble (72)

Exo 10:3 How long will you refuse to **h**
Lev 16:29 foreigners must **h** themselves.
16:31 You will **h** yourselves.
23:27 **H** yourselves, and bring the
23:29 Those who do not **h**
23:32 **H** yourselves starting on the
26:41 Then, if they **h** their
Num 12:3 (Moses was a very **h** man,
12:3 more **h** than anyone else on
29:7 You must **h** yourselves.
Dtr 8:2 He did this in order to **h** you
8:16 He did this in order to **h** you
2Sm 22:28 You save **h** people,
1Ki 12:7 **h** yourself, and speak gently,
2Ki 8:9 "Your **h** servant King Benhadad
2Ch 7:14 will **h** themselves,
33:23 He didn't **h** himself in front of
36:12 evil and didn't **h** himself
Ezr 8:21 so that we might **h** ourselves
Job 22:29 Then he will save the **h** person.
40:12 who are arrogant, and **h** them.
Psa 18:27 You save **h** people,
25:9 He leads **h** people to do what
34:18 to those whose hearts are **h**.
138:6 he sees **h** people ⌊close up⌋,
Pro 3:34 he is gracious to **h** people.
6:3 neighbor's hands: **H** yourself,
11:2 but wisdom remains with **h**
14:21 one who is kind to **h** people.
16:19 Better to be **h** with lowly
29:23 but a **h** spirit gains honor.
Isa 11:4 fair decisions for the **h** people
13:11 an end to arrogant people and **h**
14:32 and his **h** people will find
25:11 ⌊The LORD⌋ will **h** those
29:19 **H** people again will find joy in
49:13 compassion on his **h** people.
51:21 Listen to this, you **h** people
57:15 those who are crushed and **h**.
57:15 the spirit of those who are **h**
58:5 Should people **h** themselves
58:10 needs of⌋ those who are **h**,
61:1 deliver good news to **h** people.
66:2 attention to those who are **h**
Eze 22:29 They do wrong to **h** people and
Dan 5:22 You didn't remain **h**,
7:24 and he will **h** three kings.
10:12 day you decided to **h** yourself
Amo 2:7 They push the **h** out of the way.
Nah 1:12 I will not **h** you again.
Zep 2:3 Search for the LORD, all you **h**
3:12 a **h** and poor people.
Zec 9:9 He is **h** and rides on a donkey,
Mat 10:42 Whoever gives any of my **h**
11:29 because I am gentle and **h**.
Luk 1:48 favorably on me, his **h** servant.
1:52 He honored **h** people.
14:11 but people who **h** themselves
Act 2:46 They were joyful and **h** as they
Rom 12:16 but be friendly to **h** people.
2Co 10:1 I'm the one who is **h** when I'm
12:21 my God may **h** me.
Eph 4:2 Be **h** and gentle in every way.
Php 3:21 he will change our **h** bodies
Col 3:12 kind, **h**, gentle, and patient.
Jas 1:9 **H** believers should be proud
1:9 being **h** makes them important.
1:10 being rich should make them **h**.
4:6 but he is kind to **h** people."
4:10 **H** yourselves in the Lord's
1Pe 3:8 have compassion, and be **h**.
5:5 the arrogant but favors the **h**.

humbled (33)

2Ki 22:19 change of heart and **h** yourself
2Ch 12:6 and the king **h** themselves.
12:7 that they had **h** themselves,
12:7 "They have **h** themselves.
12:12 After Rehoboam **h** himself,
13:18 So the Israelites were **h** at that
28:19 The LORD **h** Judah because of
30:11 and Zebulun **h** themselves and
32:26 **h** themselves when they
33:12 God to be kind and **h** himself
33:19 The things he did before he **h**
33:23 father Manasseh had **h** himself.
34:27 change of heart and **h** yourself

2Ch 34:27 You **h** yourself, tore your
Psa 35:13 I **h** myself with fasting.
107:12 So he **h** them with hard work.
Isa 2:9 Everyone will be **h**.
2:11 of arrogant people will be **h**.
2:12 of themselves (they will be **h**),
2:17 and mighty people will be **h**.
5:15 Everyone will be **h**.
5:15 of arrogant people will be **h**.
9:1 God **h** the lands of Zebulun
26:16 They were **h** by oppression,
Jer 44:10 You have not **h** yourselves
Nah 1:12 Though I have **h** you,
Mat 23:12 honors himself will be **h**,
Luk 14:11 honor themselves will be **h**,
18:14 who honors himself will be **h**,
Act 8:33 When he **h** himself,
2Co 11:7 Did I commit a sin when I **h**
Php 2:8 He **h** himself by becoming
1Pe 5:6 Be **h** by God's power so that

humbles (4)

1Sm 2:7 He **h** ⌊people⌋; he also
Psa 68:30 until it **h** itself with pieces of
Mat 23:12 and whoever **h** himself will be
Luk 18:14 but the person who **h** himself

humbling (2)

1Ki 21:29 "Do you see how Ahab is **h**
21:29 Because he's **h** himself in my

humbly (7)

Job 9:13 Even Rahab's helpers bow **h** in
Jer 42:9 "You sent me to **h** plead your
Dan 9:20 I **h** placed my request about my
Mic 6:8 and to live **h** with your God.
Act 20:19 I **h** served the Lord,
Php 2:3 Instead, **h** think of others as
Jas 1:21 **H** accept the word that God

humiliate (5)

Pro 25:10 he hears about it, he will **h** you,
29:23 A person's pride will **h** him,
Isa 23:9 all arrogant people and to **h** all
50:6 away from those who **h** me
Dan 4:37 and he can **h** those who act

humiliated (16)

Dtr 25:3 he would be publicly **h**.
1Sm 20:34 had been **h** by his own
2Sm 6:22 Even if I am **h** in your eyes,
10:5 because they were deeply **h**.
1Ch 19:5 because they were deeply **h**.
2Ch 32:21 **H**, Sennacherib returned to his
Ezr 9:7 taken captive, robbed, and **h**,
Psa 69:6 who come to you for help be **h**
69:19 insulted, put to shame, and **h**.
107:39 few in number and were **h**
136:23 us when we were **h** —
Jer 15:9 She will die, ashamed and **h**,
31:19 I was so ashamed and **h**,
Eze 17:14 so that it would remain a **h**
Zec 10:11 The pride of Assyria will be **h**,
Mal 2:9 and I have **h** you in front of all

humiliation (2)

Psa 69:7 **H** has covered my face.
71:13 covered with disgrace and **h**.

humility (10)

Psa 45:4 of truth, **h**, and righteousness.
Pro 15:33 and **h** comes before honor.
18:12 but **h** comes before honor.
22:4 On the heels of **h** (the fear of
Zep 2:3 Search for **h**. Maybe you will
Mar 15:19 in front of him with false **h**.
Col 2:18 one who delights in ⌊false⌋ **h**
2:23 worship, ⌊false⌋ **h**,
Jas 3:13 way with the **h** that comes from
1Pe 5:5 must serve each other with **h**,

humps (1)

Isa 30:6 and their treasures on the **h**

Humtah (1)

Jos 15:54 **H**, Kiriath Arba (now called

hunchback (1)

Lev 21:20 who is a **h** or dwarf,

hunched (1)

Luk 13:11 She was **h** over and couldn't

hundred (38)

Gen 8:13 the first month of Noah's six **h**
26:12 harvested a **h** times as much
45:22 but he gave Benjamin three **h**
Exo 12:37 There were about six **h**
Lev 26:8 of you will chase a **h** of them,
26:8 and a **h** of you will chase ten
Jdg 7:6 Three **h** men lapped water with
1Sm 14:14 men within about a **h** yards.
22:2 about four **h** men with him.
23:13 about six **h** in all, left Keilah.
25:13 About four **h** men went with
25:13 while two **h** men stayed with
2Sm 15:11 Two **h** men invited from
24:3 the people a **h** times over,
1Ki 7:20 Two **h** pomegranates in rows
2Ki 4:43 I set this in front of a **h** people?"
1Ch 21:3 his people a **h** times over.
Neh 3:1 as far as the Tower of the **H**,
12:39 and the Tower of the **H**,
Pro 17:10 more than a **h** lashes impress
Ecc 6:3 Suppose he had a **h** children
8:12 A sinner may commit a **h**
Isa 65:20 Whoever lives to be a **h** years
65:20 Whoever dies before he is a **h**
Mat 13:8 They produced one **h**,
13:23 They produce one **h**,
19:29 will receive a **h** times more
Mar 4:8 or one **h** times as much as was
4:20 or one **h** times as much as was
10:30 will certainly receive a **h** times
Luk 7:41 owed him five **h** silver coins,
8:8 they produced a **h** times as
16:6 'Eight **h** gallons of olive oil.'
16:6 Sit down, and write "four **h**!"'
16:7 and write "eight **h**!"'
Act 5:36 and about four **h** men joined
13:20 He did all this in about four **h**
Rom 4:19 he was about a **h** years old,

hundreds (3)

Mat 14:24 now **h** of yards from shore,
18:28 who owed him **h** of dollars.
Mar 6:40 down in groups of **h** and fifties.

hundredth (1)

Gen 7:11 second month of the six **h** year

hung (39)

Gen 40:22 But he **h** the chief baker just as
41:13 but he **h** the baker on a pole."
Exo 27:10 ⌊**h**⌋ on 20 posts ⌊set in⌋ 20
27:12 wide and have curtains ⌊**h**⌋
27:14 curtains ⌊**h** on⌋ three posts
27:16 ⌊**h**⌋ on four posts ⌊set in⌋ four
38:10 ⌊**h**⌋ on 20 posts ⌊set in⌋ 20
38:12 feet long and had curtains ⌊**h**⌋
38:14 ½ feet wide with curtains ⌊**h**⌋
38:19 It was **h** on four posts ⌊set in⌋
39:18 ⌊so that the breastplate **h**⌋
40:21 the ark into the tent and **h**
Dtr 21:23 never leave his dead body **h**
21:23 anyone whose body is **h**
Jos 8:29 Joshua **h** the king of Ai's ⌊dead
10:26 Joshua put them to death and **h**
2Sm 4:12 and **h** their dead bodies by the
21:12 where the Philistines had **h**
Neh 6:1 at that time I had not yet **h**
7:1 rebuilt and I had **h** the doors.
Est 2:23 of Bigthan and Teresh were **h**
5:14 Mordecai's ⌊dead body⌋ **h** on it.
7:10 So servants **h** Haman's ⌊dead
8:7 Haman's ⌊dead body⌋ was **h**
9:14 And so they **h** Haman's ten
9:25 As a result, they **h** Haman and
Psa 137:2 We **h** our lyres on willow trees.
Sos 4:4 to soldiers are **h** on it.
Jer 31:19 I **h** my head in shame.
Lam 5:12 ⌊Our⌋ leaders are **h** by their
Eze 27:10 They **h** their shields and
27:11 They **h** their shields all around
Mat 18:6 large stone **h** around his neck.
Mar 9:42 large stone **h** around his neck.
Luk 17:2 a large stone **h** around his neck
21:34 **h** over, and worried about life.
Act 10:39 People **h** him on a cross and
17:5 characters who **h** around
Gal 3:13 "Everyone who is **h** on a tree is

hunger (15)

Dtr 8:3 So he made you suffer from **h**
1Sm 2:5 who were hungry **h** no more.
2Ch 32:11 abandoning you to die from **h**
Neh 9:15 from heaven to satisfy their **h**
Job 18:12 **H** undermines his strength.
30:3 Shriveled up from need and **h**,
38:39 and satisfy the **h** of her cubs
Psa 147:14 borders and satisfies your ⌊**h**⌋
Pro 16:26 because his **h** drives him on.
Lam 2:19 who faint from **h** at every street
Eze 7:19 It will no longer satisfy their **h**
34:29 will no longer experience **h**
Hos 9:4 food will only satisfy their **h**.
Mat 5:6 Blessed are those who **h** and
Rom 8:35 **h**, nakedness, danger,

hungry (60)

Lev 26:26 You will eat and go away **h**.
Dtr 12:20 You will say, "I'm **h** for meat."
28:48 even though you are already **h**,
1Sm 2:5 but those who were **h** hunger
2Sm 17:29 "The troops in the desert are **h**,
Job 5:5 fool gathers, **h** people eat.
22:7 and you take food away from **h**
24:10 They are **h**, yet they carry
Psa 34:10 Young lions go **h** and may
50:12 If I were **h**, I would not tell you,
107:5 They were **h** and thirsty.
107:9 who were **h** with good food.
107:36 he settles those who are **h**,
146:7 gives food to those who are **h**.
Pro 6:30 despise a thief who is **h** when
19:15 and an idle person will go **h**.
25:21 If your enemy is **h**,
27:7 but to one who is **h**,
Isa 8:21 they are hard-pressed and **h**.
8:21 When they are **h**, they will be
9:20 gobbles up food and is still **h**.
29:8 They will be like **h** people who
29:8 and wake up to find they're **h**.
32:6 They let people go **h** and
44:12 They get **h**, and their strength
49:10 They will never be **h** or thirsty,
58:7 Share your food with the **h**,
58:10 food to ⌊feed⌋ those who are **h**
65:13 will eat, but you will be **h**.
Jer 42:14 sound of a ram's horn, or be **h**.
Eze 18:7 gives food to people who are **h**,
18:16 gives food to people who are **h**,
Mic 6:14 So you will always be **h**.
Nah 3:15 Multiply like **h** locusts!
Mat 4:2 the end of that time, he was **h**.
12:1 His disciples were **h** and
12:3 when he and his men were **h**?
15:32 want to send them away **h**,
21:18 to the city, he became **h**.
25:35 I was **h**, and you gave me
25:37 when did we see you **h** and
25:42 I was **h**, and you gave me
25:44 when did we see you **h** or
Mar 2:25 men were in need and were **h**?
11:12 left Bethany, Jesus became **h**.
Luk 1:53 He fed **h** people with good food.
4:2 they were over, he was **h**.
6:3 when he and his men were **h**?
6:21 Blessed are those who are **h**.
6:25 They will be **h**. How horrible it
15:16 and he was so **h** that he would
Jon 6:35 to me will never become **h**,
Act 10:10 He became **h** and wanted to
Rom 12:20 But, "If your enemy is **h**,
1Co 4:11 To this moment, we are **h**,
11:21 So one person goes **h** and
11:34 Whoever is **h** should eat at
2Co 11:27 been **h** and thirsty,

Php 4:12 live when I'm full or when I'm **h**,
Rev 7:16 They will never be **h** or thirsty

hunt (9)
Gen 27:3 country and **h** some wild game
27:5 went into the open country to **h**
Lev 17:13 "If Israelites or foreigners **h** any
Job 10:16 ferocious lion you **h** me down.
38:39 "Can you **h** prey for the lioness
Psa 140:11 Let evil **h** down violent people
Pro 2:4 as if it were money and **h**
Isa 7:24 with bows and arrows ⌊to **h**⌋
Jer 16:16 and they will **h** for them on

hunted (8)
Gen 27:19 Sit up and eat this meat I've **h**
27:31 eat some of the meat I've **h** for
27:33 "Who **h** game and brought it to
Isa 13:14 They'll be like **h** gazelle and
Lam 3:52 for no reason **h** me like
Eze 19:3 to tear apart the animals he **h**.
19:6 to tear apart the animals he **h**.
Act 26:11 I **h** them down in cities outside

hunter (6)
Gen 10:9 He was a mighty **h** whom the
10:9 a mighty **h** whom the LORD
25:27 Esau became an expert **h**,
Pro 6:5 a gazelle from the hand of a **h**
6:5 like a bird from the hand of a **h**.
12:27 A lazy **h** does not catch his

hunter's (1)
Psa 124:7 like a bird caught in a **h** trap.

hunters (2)
Jer 16:16 that, I will send for many **h**,
Lam 1:6 any strength ahead of the **h**.

hunters' (1)
Psa 91:3 will rescue you from **h** traps

hunting (4)
Gen 27:3 Now take your **h** equipment,
27:30 brother Esau came in from **h**.
1Sm 26:20 for one flea like someone **h**
Lam 4:19 Those who were **h** us were

hunts (3)
Pro 6:26 but a married woman **h** for
13:21 Disaster **h** down sinners,
Mic 5:8 When a lion **h**, it tramples ⌊its

Hupham (1)
Num 26:39 and the family of **H**.

Huppah (1)
1Ch 24:13 the thirteenth for **H**,

Huppim (1)
Gen 46:21 Ehi, Rosh, Muppim, **H**, and Ard.

Huppites (2)
1Ch 7:12 The Shuppites and **H** were Ir's
7:15 wife from the **H** and Shuppites.

Hur (15)
Exo 17:10 and **H** went to the top of the hill.
17:12 So Aaron and **H** took a rock,
17:12 and **H** held up the other.
24:14 Aaron and **H** are here with you.
31:2 son of Uri and grandson of **H**,
35:30 son of Uri and grandson of **H**,
38:22 son of Uri and grandson of **H**,
Num 31:8 Evi, Rekem, Zur, **H**, and Reba.
Jos 13:21 Evi, Rekem, Zur, **H**, and Reba.
1Ch 2:19 She gave birth to **H**.
2:20 **H** was the father of Uri,
2:50 The sons of **H**, the firstborn son
4:1 Hezron, Carmi, **H**, and Shobal.
4:4 These were the sons of **H**,
2Ch 1:5 son of Uri and grandson of **H**,

Hurai (1)
1Ch 11:32 **H** from the Gaash ravines,

Huram (13)
1Ch 8:5 Gera, Shephuphan, and **H**.
2Ch 2:3 Solomon sent word to King **H**
2:11 Then King **H** of Tyre responded
2:12 **H** added, "May the LORD God
2:14 **H** knows how to work with
4:2 **H** made a pool from cast metal.
4:6 **H** also made ten basins for
4:7 **H** made ten gold lamp stands
4:11 **H** also made the pots,
4:11 So **H** finished the work for King
4:16 **H** made all of them out of
8:2 rebuilt the cities **H** gave him,
8:18 **H** sent his own servants and

Huram Abi (1)
2Ch 2:13 skill and intelligence — **H** Abi

Huram's (2)
2Ch 9:10 **H** servants and Solomon's
9:21 to Tarshish with **H** sailors.

Huri (1)
1Ch 5:14 who was the son of **H**,

hurl (2)
2Ch 26:15 arrows and **h** large stones.
Psa 144:6 **H** bolts of lightning,

hurled (3)
1Sm 17:49 out a stone, **h** it from his sling,
2Sm 16:13 Shimei cursed, **h** stones,
Psa 89:44 to his splendor and **h** his throne

hurls (1)
Job 27:22 It **h** itself at him without mercy.

hurried (10)
Gen 18:6 So Abraham **h** into the tent to
43:30 sight of his brother, he **h** away,
Jos 4:10 The people **h** to the other side.
2Sm 19:16 **h** down with the people of
Ezr 4:23 and their group **h** to Jerusalem
Est 3:15 The messengers **h** out as the
6:12 but Haman **h** home.
Mat 28:8 They **h** away from the tomb
Mar 6:25 So the girl **h** back to the king
Luk 1:39 Soon afterward, Mary **h** to a

hurries (1)
Hab 2:3 It **h** toward its goal.

hurry (47)
Gen 19:14 He said, "**H**! Get out of this
31:21 So he left in a **h** with all that
31:22 told that Jacob had left in a **h**.
45:9 "**H** back to my father,
45:13 **H** and bring my father here!"
Exo 12:11 You must eat it in a **h**.
Dtr 16:3 because you left Egypt in a **h**.)
Jos 2:5 If you **h**, you'll catch up with
10:13 day the sun was in no **h** to set.
Jdg 9:48 He told his men, "**H** and do
1Sm 9:12 **H**! He ⌊just⌋ went into the city
20:38 **H** up! Don't stand there!"
2Sm 4:4 She was in a **h** when she left,
2Ki 7:15 had thrown away in their **h**.
2Ch 26:20 Uzziah was in a **h** to get out
35:21 God told me to **h**. God is with
Est 6:10 The king told Haman, "**H**,
Psa 55:8 I would **h** to find shelter from
59:4 They **h** to take positions
119:60 Without any hesitation I **h** to
Pro 1:16 to do evil and **h** to shed blood.
19:2 person in a **h** makes mistakes.
21:5 is ⌊always⌋ in a **h** ends up
25:8 Do not be in a **h** to go to court.
28:20 but anyone in a **h** to get rich
28:22 A stingy person is in a **h** to get
Ecc 5:2 Don't be in a **h** to talk.
8:3 Don't be in a **h** to leave the
Isa 5:19 They say, "Let God **h** and
49:17 Your children will **h** back.
52:12 You will not go away in a **h**,
59:7 They **h** to shed innocent blood.
Joe 3:11 **H** from every direction,
Nah 2:5 They **h** to Nineveh's wall.
Zec 2:6 "**H**, hurry! Flee from the land of
2:6 "Hurry, **h**! Flee from the land of
2:7 **H**, Zion! Escape,
Luk 15:22 father said to his servants, '**H**!
Jon 13:27 So Jesus told him, "**H**!
Act 9:38 begged Peter, "**H** to Joppa!
12:7 woke him up, and said, "**H**!
20:16 He was in a **h** to get to
22:18 He told me, '**H**! Get out of
1Ti 5:22 Don't be in a **h** to place your
2Ti 4:9 **H** to visit me soon.
4:21 **H** to visit me before winter
Tit 3:12 **h** to visit me in the city of

hurrying (2)
Exo 5:13 The slave drivers kept **h** them.
1Sm 23:26 David was **h** to get away from

Hur's (1)
Neh 3:9 Next to them Rephaiah, **H** son,

hurt (38)
Gen 37:22 in the desert, but don't **h** him."
37:27 Let's not **h** him, because he is
Ezr 4:13 this will **h** the king's income.
Psa 15:4 even though he is **h** by it.
105:18 They **h** his feet with shackles,
Pro 3:23 and you will not **h** your foot.
9:7 warns a wicked person gets **h**.
Ecc 8:9 has authority to **h** others.
10:9 in a stone quarry may get **h**.
Isa 11:9 They will not **h** or destroy
27:7 Will the LORD **h** Israel as he
27:7 Israel as he **h** others who hurt
27:7 as he hurt others who **h** them?
28:13 That is why they will be **h**,
65:25 "They will not **h** or destroy
Jer 31:28 and to wreck, ruin, and **h** them.
38:4 he's trying to **h** them."
Eze 6:9 I was **h** by their adulterous
18:17 He refuses to **h** the poor.
28:24 no longer be **h** by prickly thorns
Dan 6:22 so that they couldn't **h** me.
Zec 13:6 'I was **h** at my friend's house.'
Mat 26:22 Feeling deeply **h**, they asked
Mar 3:5 He was deeply **h** because their
14:19 Feeling **h**, they asked him one
16:18 poison, it will not **h** them.
Luk 10:19 Nothing will **h** you.
Act 16:28 as he could, "Don't **h** yourself!
20:38 seeing Paul again **h** them most
2Co 7:12 or the man who was **h** by it.
10:8 to help you, not to **h** you.
13:10 to help you, not to **h** you.
Eph 4:29 that would **h** ⌊another person⌋.
Rev 2:11 the victory will never be **h** by
9:10 They had the power to **h**
9:19 which they use to **h** people.)
11:5 If anyone wants to **h** them,
11:5 If anyone wants to **h** them,

hurting (1)
Luk 4:35 and came out without **h** him.

hurts (2)
Pro 11:17 but a cruel person **h** himself.
Rom 14:15 you eat **h** another Christian,

husband (120)
Gen 3:6 She also gave some to her **h**,
3:16 Yet, you will long for your **h**,
16:3 and gave her to her **h** Abram
18:12 What's more, my **h** is old!"
29:32 now my **h** will love me!"
29:34 She said, "Now at last my **h**
30:15 it enough that you took my **h**?
30:18 I gave my slave to my **h**."
30:20 This time my **h** will honor me
39:14 My **h** brought this Hebrew here
Exo 21:22 the woman's **h** to demand.
Num 5:14 "A **h** may have a fit of jealousy
5:19 been unfaithful to your **h**,
5:27 by being unfaithful to her **h**,
5:29 to her **h** and becomes unclean.

Num 5:30 you what to do when a **h** has
5:31 The **h** isn't guilty of doing
30:7 her **h** may hear about it but say
30:8 But if her **h** objects when he
30:11 Her **h** may hear about it but
30:12 But if her **h** cancels it when he
30:12 Her **h** has canceled it,
30:13 "A **h** decides whether or not his
Dtr 21:13 you will become **h** and wife.
22:19 The **h** ruined the reputation of
24:1 This is what you must do if a **h**
24:3 If her second **h** doesn't love her
24:4 her first **h** is not allowed to
25:11 comes to rescue her **h** from
28:56 stingy toward the **h** she loves
Jdg 11:39 and she never had a **h**.
13:6 The woman went to tell her **h**.
13:9 But her **h** Manoah was not with
13:10 woman ran quickly to tell her **h**.
14:15 "Trick your **h** into solving the
19:3 her **h** went to persuade her to
19:3 She took her **h** into her father's
19:26 of the house where her **h** was
19:27 Her **h** got up in the morning,
20:4 the **h** of the murdered woman,
Rut 1:3 Naomi's **h** Elimelech died,
1:5 without her two sons or her **h**.
1:9 security in a home with a **h**."
1:12 And if I had a **h** tonight ....
2:11 mother-in-law after your **h** died.
1Sm 1:8 Her **h** Elkanah would ask her,
1:22 She told her **h**, "I'll wait until
1:23 her **h** Elkanah told her.
2:19 year when she went with her **h**
4:19 and her **h** were dead,
4:21 father-in-law and her **h** ⌊died⌋.
25:19 didn't tell her **h** Nabal about it.
2Sm 3:15 to take her from her **h** Paltiel,
3:16 Her **h** went with her and cried
11:26 that her **h** Uriah was dead,
14:5 "I'm a widow; my **h** is dead.
17:3 as a bride is returned to her **h**.
2Ki 4:1 to Elisha, "Sir, my **h** is dead!
4:9 She told her **h**, "I know he's a
4:14 has no son, and her **h** is old."
4:22 She called her **h** and said,
4:23 Her **h** asked, "Why are you
4:26 her **h**, and the boy are doing."
Est 1:22 "Let every **h** be the ruler in his
Pro 2:17 who leaves ⌊her **h**,⌋ the
6:34 The **h** will show no mercy
12:4 character is the crown of her **h**,
27:8 so is a **h** wandering from his
31:11 Her **h** trusts her with ⌊all⌋ his
31:23 "Her **h** is known at the city
31:28 Her children and her **h** stand up
Isa 47:9 of your children and your **h**.
54:5 Your **h** is your Maker.
Jer 3:1 her first **h** shouldn't go back to
3:14 "I'm your **h**. I will take you, one
3:20 like a wife who betrays her **h**,
31:32 although I was a **h** to them,"
Eze 16:32 who prefers strangers to her **h**.
16:45 She rejected her **h** and her
Hos 2:2 no longer treats me like her **h**.
2:7 'I'll go back to my first **h**.
2:16 will call me her **h**," declares
Mat 1:16 who was the **h** of Mary.
1:19 Her **h** Joseph was an
Mar 10:2 "Can a **h** divorce his wife?"
10:12 If a wife divorces her **h** and
Luk 2:36 Her **h** had died seven years
8:3 Joanna, whose **h** Chusa was
Jon 4:16 Jesus told her, "Go to your **h**,
4:17 replied, "I don't have a **h**."
4:17 you say that you don't have a **h**.
4:18 man you have now isn't your **h**.
Act 5:9 "How could you and your **h**
5:9 Those who buried your **h** are
5:10 and buried her next to her **h**.
Rom 7:2 by law to her **h** as long as
7:2 But if her **h** dies, that marriage
7:3 man while her **h** is still alive,
7:3 But if her **h** dies, she is free
1Co 7:2 woman should have her own **h**.
7:4 her own body, but her **h** does.
1Co 7:4 In the same way, a **h** doesn't
7:10 A wife shouldn't leave her **h**.
7:11 single or make up with her **h**.
7:11 a **h** should not divorce his wife.
7:13 she should not divorce her **h**.
7:14 Actually, the unbelieving **h** is
7:14 is made holy because of her **h**.
7:16 whether you will save your **h**?
7:16 How do you as a **h** know
7:34 how she can please her **h**.
7:39 remain with her **h** as long as
7:39 If her **h** dies, she is free to
11:3 a **h** has authority over his wife,
Gal 4:27 than the woman who has a **h**."
Eph 5:23 The **h** is the head of his wife
5:33 But every **h** must love his wife
1Th 4:4 should know that finding a **h**
1Ti 5:9 Any widow who had only one **h**
Rev 21:2 like a bride ready for her **h**.

husband's (9)

Num 5:13 man without her **h** knowledge.
5:15 because of the **h** jealousy,
5:18 because of the **h** jealousy).
Dtr 25:5 Her **h** brother must marry her
2Sm 14:7 They will not let my **h** name or
Pro 6:34 jealousy arouses a **h** fury.
7:19 because my **h** not home.
Isa 54:4 of your **h** death anymore.
Jon 1:13 or from a **h** desire ⌊to have

husbands (20)

Num 30:16 gave Moses for **h** and wives,
Rut 1:11 womb who could be your **h**?
Est 1:17 and they will despise their **h**.
1:20 all the wives will honor their **h**,
Jer 18:21 Their **h** will be put to death.
44:19 you think our **h** didn't approve?"
Eze 16:45 They rejected their **h** and their
Amo 4:1 You say to your **h**,
Jon 4:18 You've had five **h**, and the man
1Co 7:3 **H** and wives should satisfy
14:35 should ask their **h** at home.
Eph 5:25 **H**, love your wives as Christ
5:28 So **h** must love their wives as
5:33 wives should respect their **h**.
Col 3:19 **H**, love your wives, and don't
Tit 2:4 love to their **h** and children,
Heb 13:4 so **h** and wives should be
1Pe 3:1 Some **h** may not obey God's
3:2 Their **h** would see how pure
3:7 **H**, in a similar way, live with

husbands' (6)

Eph 5:22 your **h** authority as you have
5:24 their **h** authority in everything.
Col 3:18 under your **h** authority.
Tit 2:5 under their **h** authority.
1Pe 3:1 under your **h** authority.
3:5 under their **h** authority

Hush (2)

Amo 6:10 "**H**," he will add. "We shouldn't
8:3 scattered everywhere. **H**!"

Hushah (4)

2Sm 21:18 Sibbecai from **H** killed Saph,
1Ch 4:4 and Ezer was the father of **H**.
20:4 Sibbecai from **H** killed Sippai,
27:11 a descendant of Zerah from **H**,

Hushai (14)

2Sm 15:32 **H** from Archi's family was there
15:37 So **H**, David's friend, went to
16:16 When David's friend **H** from
16:17 Absalom asked **H**.
16:18 **H** answered Absalom,
17:5 Absalom said, "Please call **H**,
17:6 When **H** arrived, Absalom said
17:7 **H** said to Absalom.
17:14 "The advice of **H** from Archi's
17:15 Then **H** told the priests Zadok
23:27 Mebunnai (son of **H**),
1Ki 4:16 Baana, son of **H**, was in charge
1Ch 11:29 Sibbecai (son of **H**),
27:33 **H**, a descendant of Archi,

Husham (4)

Gen 36:34 After Jobab died, **H** from the
36:35 After **H** died, Hadad, son of
1Ch 1:45 After Jobab died, **H** from the
1:46 After **H** died, Hadad, son of

hushed (1)

Job 29:10 The voices of nobles were **h**,

Hushim (3)

Gen 46:23 The son of Dan was **H**.
1Ch 8:8 his wives **H** and Baara.
8:11 He and **H** were the parents of

Hushites (1)

1Ch 7:12 The **H** were descendants of

husks (16)

Rut 2:17 separated the grain from its **h**.
3:2 separating the barley from its **h**
Job 13:25 or trying to chase dry **h**?
21:18 straw in the wind or like **h** that
Psa 1:4 Instead, they are like **h** that the
35:5 Let them be like **h** blown by the
83:13 like **h** in the wind.
Isa 17:13 will be chased away like **h**
29:5 Your many foes will be like **h**
Dan 2:35 They became like **h** on a
Amo 8:6 We can sell the **h** mixed in
Zep 2:2 day passes like windblown **h**,
Mat 3:12 but he will burn the **h** in a fire
Luk 3:17 but he will burn the **h** in a fire
6:1 heads of grain, removing the **h**,
22:31 farmer separates wheat from **h**.

hut (1)

Isa 1:8 My people Zion are left like a **h**

hyenas (3)

Isa 13:22 **H** will howl in Babylon's
34:14 **H** will meet with jackals.
Jer 50:39 desert animals will live with **h**.

Hymenaeus (2)

1Ti 1:20 people are **H** and Alexander,
2Ti 2:17 **H** and Philetus are like that.

hymn (3)

Psa 26:7 so that I may loudly sing a **h** of
Mat 26:30 After they sang a **h**,
Mar 14:26 After they sang a **h**,

hymns (7)

Neh 12:8 in charge of the thanksgiving **h**.
12:24 from one another to sing **h**
12:27 joyfully with **h** of thanksgiving,
12:46 the songs of praise and **h**
Act 16:25 were praying and singing **h**
Eph 5:19 by reciting psalms, **h**,
Col 3:16 Use psalms, **h**, and spiritual

hypocrisy (6)

Pro 11:3 but **h** leads treacherous people
Mat 23:28 are full of **h** and lawlessness.
Mar 12:15 Jesus recognized their **h**,
Luk 12:1 I'm talking about their **h**.
Gal 2:13 also joined him in this **h**.
1Pe 2:1 kind of deception, **h**, jealousy,

hypocrite (3)

Mat 7:5 You **h**! First remove the beam
Luk 6:42 You **h**! First remove the beam
Act 23:3 "God will strike you, you **h**!

hypocrites (17)

Psa 26:4 I will not be found among **h**.
Hos 10:2 They are **h**. Now they must take
Mat 6:2 This is what **h** do in the
6:5 "When you pray, don't be like **h**.
6:16 stop looking sad like **h**.
15:7 You **h**! Isaiah was right when he
22:18 "Why do you test me, you **h**?
23:13 You **h**! You lock people out of
23:15 You **h**! You cross land and sea
23:23 You **h**! You give ⌊God⌋

Mat 23:25 You **h**! You clean the outside of
23:27 You **h**! You are like
23:29 You **h**! You build tombs for the
24:51 assign him a place with the **h**.
Mar 7:6 about you **h** in Scripture:
Luk 12:56 You **h**! You can forecast the
13:15 The Lord said, "You **h**!

hyssop (12)

Exo 12:22 Take the branch of a **h** plant,
Lev 14:4 and a **h** sprig to use for the
14:6 and the **h** sprig and dip them
14:49 and a **h** sprig and use them to
14:51 wood, the **h** sprig, the red yarn,
14:52 bird, the cedar wood, the **h**,
Num 19:6 some cedar wood, a **h** sprig,
19:18 is clean will take a sprig of **h**,
1Ki 4:33 in Lebanon to the **h** growing out
Psa 51:7 Purify me from sin with **h**,
Jon 19:29 in the vinegar on a **h** stick
Heb 9:19 and **h** and sprinkled the scroll

I

I am (442)

Gen 9:9 "**I** going to make my promise
9:11 **I** making my promise to you.
9:12 the sign of the promise **I** giving
9:17 sign of the promise **I** making
15:1 **I** your shield. Your reward will
15:7 said to him, "**I** the LORD,
17:1 "**I** God Almighty.
17:8 **I** also giving this land where
18:17 "I shouldn't hide what **I** going to
22:16 and said, "**I** taking an oath on
26:24 "**I** the God of your father
26:24 because **I** with you.
28:13 it, saying, "**I** the LORD,
28:15 Remember, **I** with you and will
31:13 **I** the God who appeared to you
35:1 **I** the God who appeared to you
35:11 "**I** God Almighty.
46:3 "**I** God, the God of your
Exo 3:6 **I** the God of your ancestors,
3:10 **I** sending you to Pharaoh so
3:14 Moses, "**I** Who I Am.
3:14 answered Moses, "I Am Who **I**.
3:14 '**I** has sent me to you.'"
6:2 to Moses, "**I** the LORD.
6:6 the Israelites, '**I** the LORD.
6:7 You will know that **I** the LORD
6:8 own possession. **I** the LORD.'"
6:29 said to Moses, "**I** the LORD.
7:5 The Egyptians will know that **I**
7:17 will recognize that **I** the LORD:
10:2 will all know that **I** the LORD."
12:12 ⌊because⌋ **I** the LORD.
14:4 will know that **I** the LORD."
14:17 **I** making the Egyptians so
14:18 The Egyptians will know that **I**
14:18 I am the LORD when **I** honored
15:26 because **I** the LORD,
16:12 Then you will know that **I** the
19:9 The LORD said to Moses, "**I**
20:2 "**I** the LORD your God,
22:27 I will listen because **I**
25:9 like the plans **I** showing you.
29:46 They will know that **I** the
29:46 **I** the LORD their God."
31:13 so that you will know that **I**
32:10 I'm so angry with them **I** going
33:17 because **I** pleased with you,
Lev 11:44 **I** the LORD your God.
11:44 Be holy because **I** holy.
11:45 reason ⌊again⌋: **I** the LORD.
11:45 Be holy because **I** holy.
14:34 come to Canaan that **I** going
18:2 **I** the LORD your God.
18:3 **I** bringing you to Canaan.
18:4 **I** the LORD your God.
18:5 life through them. **I** the LORD.
18:6 to you by blood. **I** the LORD.
18:21 name of your God. **I** the LORD.

Lev 18:24 the nations which **I** forcing out
18:30 **I** the LORD your God."
19:3 **I** the LORD your God.
19:4 **I** the LORD your God.
19:10 **I** the LORD your God.
19:12 name of your God. **I** the LORD.
19:14 fear your God. **I** the LORD.
19:16 neighbor's life. **I** the LORD.
19:18 you love yourself. **I** the LORD.
19:25 **I** the LORD your God.
19:28 never get a tattoo. **I** the LORD.
19:30 my holy tent. **I** the LORD.
19:31 **I** the LORD your God.
19:32 for your God. **I** the LORD.
19:34 **I** the LORD your God.
19:36 **I** the LORD your God who
19:37 and live by them. **I** the LORD."
20:7 Be holy because **I** the LORD
20:8 **I** the LORD who sets you apart
20:22 the land **I** bringing you to live in
20:23 of the people **I** forcing out
20:24 **I** the LORD your God who
21:12 oil of his God. **I** the LORD.
22:2 my holy name. **I** the LORD.
22:3 from my presence. **I** the LORD.
22:8 him unclean. **I** the LORD.
22:9 The priests must do what Ider,
22:9 **I** the LORD, who sets them
22:16 **I** the LORD, who sets them
22:30 of it until morning. **I** the LORD.
22:31 my commands. **I** the LORD.
22:32 **I** the LORD, who sets you apart
22:33 Iought you out of Egypt to be
22:33 to be your God. **I** the LORD."
23:10 When you come to the land **I**
23:22 **I** the LORD your God."
23:43 **I** the LORD your God."
24:22 because **I** the LORD your God."
25:17 because **I** the LORD your God.
25:38 **I** the LORD your God,
25:55 **I** the LORD your God."
26:1 because **I** the LORD your God.
26:2 my holy tent. **I** the LORD.
26:13 **I** the LORD your God.
26:44 because **I** the LORD their God.
26:45 looked on. **I** the LORD."
Num 3:13 will be mine. **I** the LORD."
3:41 **I** the LORD. Take the Levites for
3:45 will be mine. **I** the LORD.
10:10 **I** the LORD your God."
15:41 **I** the LORD your God,
15:41 **I** the LORD your God."
18:8 The LORD said to Aaron, "**I**
18:8 **I** giving you and your
18:11 **I** giving these to you,
18:12 "**I** also giving you the first of
18:19 **I** giving you, your sons,
18:20 **I** your possession and your
18:21 "**I** giving the Levites
20:12 show the Israelites how holy **I**!
27:14 how holy **I** when they were
Dtr 4:1 listen to the laws and rules **I**
4:8 teachings **I** giving you today?
5:6 "**I** the LORD your God,
29:6 so that you would know that **I**
32:39 See, **I** the only God.
32:51 show the Israelites how holy **I**.
Jos 1:2 River into the land that **I** going
3:7 do this to let them know that **I**
5:14 **I** here as the commander of the
6:2 "**I** about to hand Jericho,
8:1 **I** about to hand the king of Ai,
8:18 because **I** handing Ai over to
11:6 afraid of them because **I** going
Jdg 1:2 **I** about to hand the Canaanites
6:10 '**I** the LORD your God.
6:14 you have. **I** sending you."
1Sm 3:11 "**I** going to do something in
3:12 On that day **I** going to do to Eli
1Ki 11:31 **I** going to tear the kingdom out
20:13 you will know that **I** the LORD."
20:28 you will know that **I** the LORD."
21:21 So **I** going to bring evil on you.
Psa 35:3 to my soul, "**I** your savior."
40:8 **I** happy to do your will,
46:10 Then you will know that **I** God.

Psa 50:7 against you: **I** God, your God!
50:8 **I** not criticizing you for your
81:10 **I** the LORD your God,
Isa 27:4 **I** no longer angry. If only thorns
28:16 **I** going to lay a rock in Zion,
29:14 That is why **I** going to do
41:4 be there to the end. **I** the one!"
41:10 because **I** with you.
41:10 be intimidated; **I** your God.
41:15 "**I** going to make you into a
42:1 with whom **I** pleased.
42:8 **I** the LORD; that is my name.
43:2 go through the sea, **I** with you.
43:3 **I** the LORD your God,
43:5 because **I** with you.
43:10 in me and understand that **I**
43:12 are my witnesses that **I** God,"
43:15 **I** the LORD, your Holy One,
43:19 **I** going to do something new.
44:6 **I** the first and the last,
45:5 **I** the LORD, and there is no
45:6 **I** the LORD, and there is no
45:18 the LORD says: **I** the LORD,
45:22 of the earth, because **I** God,
46:9 the first events, because **I** God,
46:9 **I** God, and there's no one like
48:11 **I** doing this for myself,
48:12 **I** the one. I am the first and the
48:12 **I** the first and the last.
48:17 **I** the LORD your God.
49:23 you will know that **I** the LORD.
49:26 will know that **I** the LORD,
51:15 **I** the LORD your God who stirs
52:6 ⌊they will know⌋ that **I** the one
57:6 Do you think **I** pleased with all
57:15 But **I** with those who are
58:9 "Here **I**!" Get rid of that yoke.
60:16 you will know that **I** the LORD,
63:1 **I** coming to announce my
63:1 **I** powerful enough to save
65:1 I said, "Here **I**! Here I am!" to a
65:1 Here **I**!" to a nation that didn't
66:18 **I** coming to gather the nations
66:22 heaven and earth that **I** about
Jer 1:8 **I** with you, and I will rescue
1:12 **I** watching to make sure that
1:15 **I** going to call every family and
1:19 **I** with you, and I will rescue
2:9 "That is why **I** bringing charges
2:9 "and **I** bringing charges against
8:17 "**I** going to send snakes
9:15 **I** going to feed these people
10:18 This is what the LORD says: **I**
12:14 **I** going to uproot those
15:20 **I** with you, and I will save you
21:8 **I** going to give you the choice
23:23 "**I** a God who is near.
23:23 **I** also a God who is far away,"
24:7 desire to know that **I** the LORD.
25:29 **I** going to bring disaster on the
30:11 **I** with you, and I will rescue
32:27 "**I** the LORD God of all
32:37 **I** going to gather the people
34:17 Now **I** going to free you,"
34:22 **I** going to give a command,"
35:17 **I** going to bring on Judah and
42:19 know that **I** warning you today.
44:27 **I** going to watch over them.
44:27 **I** going to watch over them to
46:28 "**I** with you. I will completely
49:5 **I** going to bring terror on you
50:9 **I** going to stir up an alliance of
50:18 **I** going to punish the king of
51:25 "**I** against you, Babylon,
51:36 This is what the LORD says: **I**
Eze 2:3 He said to me, "Son of man, **I**
2:4 **I** sending you to these defiant
2:8 and eat what **I** giving to you."
3:5 **I** not sending you to people
3:5 **I** sending you to Israel.
3:6 **I** not sending you to nations
4:16 **I** going to cut off the bread
6:3 **I** going to attack you with a
6:7 you will know that **I** the LORD.
6:10 Then you will know that **I** the
6:13 you will know that **I** the LORD.

Eze 6:14 will know that I the LORD.'"
7:4 you will know that I the LORD.
7:9 Then you will know that I the
7:9 that I am the LORD and that I
7:27 will know that I the LORD."
11:10 you will know that I the LORD.
11:12 you will know that I the LORD.
12:11 'I your warning sign.
12:15 they will know that I the LORD,
12:16 will know that I the LORD.'"
12:20 will know that I the LORD.'"
13:9 you will know that I the LORD.
13:14 you will know that I the LORD.
13:21 you will know that I the LORD.
13:23 will know that I the LORD.'"
14:8 you will know that I the LORD.
15:7 they will know that I the LORD,
16:62 you will know that I the LORD.
17:24 field will know that I the LORD.
20:5 "I the LORD your God."
20:7 I the LORD your God."
20:19 I the LORD your God.
20:20 you so that you will know that I
20:26 would know that I the LORD.'
20:38 you will know that I the LORD.
20:42 you will know that I the LORD,
20:44 you will know that I the LORD,
20:47 I about to set fire to you to
21:3 the LORD says: I against you.
22:16 you will know that I the LORD."
22:26 So I dishonored among the
23:49 that I the Almighty LORD."
24:24 that I the Almighty LORD.'"
24:27 will know that I the LORD."
25:5 you will know that I the LORD.
25:7 you will know that I the LORD.
25:11 they will know that I the LORD.
25:17 will know that I the LORD.'"
26:3 says: I against you, Tyre.
26:6 they will know that I the LORD.
28:7 That is why I going to bring
28:22 will know that I the LORD,
28:22 you and show you how holy I.
28:23 they will know that I the LORD.
28:24 know that I the Almighty LORD.
28:25 I will show that I holy as the
28:26 Then they will know that I the
29:6 will know that I the LORD.
29:8 I going to attack you with a
29:9 you will know that I the LORD.
29:21 will know that I the LORD."
30:8 they will know that I the LORD,
30:19 they will know that I the LORD,
30:25 they will know that I the LORD,
30:26 will know that I the LORD."
32:15 they will know that I the LORD.'
33:29 will know that I the LORD,
34:10 I against the shepherds.
34:27 they will know that I the LORD,
34:31 You are mortal, and I your God,
35:4 you will know that I the LORD.
35:9 you will know that I the LORD.
35:15 will know that I the LORD.'"
36:6 I speaking in my anger and fury
36:9 I for you. I will turn to you, and
36:11 you will know that I the LORD.
36:22 I about to do something,
36:23 will know that I the LORD,
36:38 will know that I the LORD."
37:6 will know that I the LORD.'"
37:13 you will know that I the LORD,
38:3 says: I against you, Gog,
38:23 will know that I the LORD.'"
39:1 says: I against you, Gog,
39:6 they will know that I the LORD.
39:7 will know that I the LORD,
39:19 that I preparing for you.
39:22 people of Israel will know that I
39:27 Many nations will see that I
39:28 my people will know that I
39:28 and Iought them back again to
44:28 I their inheritance. Don't give
Dan 11:2 "What I about to tell you is the
Hos 1:7 I will rescue them because I
1:9 and I no longer your God.
11:8 my mind. I deeply moved.
Hos 11:9 I God, not a human. I am the
11:9 I the Holy One among you,
12:9 I the LORD your God.
13:4 "I the LORD your God.
14:8 I like a growing pine tree.
Joe 2:19 "I going to send grain,
2:27 You will know that I in Israel.
2:27 I the LORD your God,
3:7 I going to make them leave the
3:17 "You will know that I the LORD
Amo 2:13 I going to crush you as an
3:2 That is why I going to punish
6:8 I disgusted with Jacob's pride,
6:14 I going to lead a nation to
7:14 I a rancher and a grower of figs.
Mic 3:8 But I filled with the power of
Nah 2:13 "I against you, Nineveh,"
Hab 1:5 I going to do something in your
1:6 I going to send the
Hag 1:13 to the people, "I with you,
2:4 "Work, because I with you,"
2:6 I going to shake the sky and
2:21 'I going to shake the heavens
Zec 3:9 I engraving an inscription on it,"
8:2 I very jealous about Zion.
8:2 I fiercely possessive of it.
8:7 I going to save my people from
10:6 because I the LORD their God,
11:6 I going to hand the people over
Mal 1:6 So if I a father, where is my
1:6 If I a master, where is my
1:14 I a great king," says the LORD
Mat 3:17 my Son with whom I pleased."
11:29 because I gentle and humble.
16:15 "But who do you say I?"
17:5 love and with whom I pleased.
18:20 I there among them."
22:32 'I the God of Abraham,
26:32 "But after I brought back to life,
26:64 Jesus answered him, "Yes, I.
27:11 "Yes, I," Jesus answered.
27:43 'I the Son of God.'"
28:20 "And remember that I always
Mar 1:2 The prophet Isaiah wrote, "I
1:11 I pleased with you."
8:27 "Who do people say I?"
8:29 "But who do you say I?" Peter
12:26 'I the God of Abraham,
14:28 "But after I brought back to life,
14:62 Jesus answered, "Yes, I,
15:2 "Yes, I," Jesus answered him.
Luk 3:22 I pleased with you."
7:27 'I sending my messenger
9:18 "Who do people say I?"
9:20 do you say I?" Peter answered,
22:70 "You're right to say that I."
23:3 "Yes, I," Jesus answered.
Jon 4:26 Jesus told her, "I he,
4:26 and I speaking to you now."
6:35 "I the bread of life.
6:41 "I the bread that came from
6:48 "I the bread of life.
6:51 I the living bread that came
7:29 I know him because I from him
8:12 "I the light of the world.
8:24 you don't believe that I the one,
8:25 Jesus told them, "I whom I
8:28 then you'll know that I the one
8:40 I a man who has told you the
8:58 Abraham was ever born, I."
10:7 I the gate for the sheep.
10:9 I the gate. Those who enter the
10:11 "I the good shepherd.
10:14 "I the good shepherd.
10:38 in me and that I in the Father."
11:25 Jesus said to her, "I the one
11:25 back to life, and I life itself.
12:27 "I too deeply troubled now to
12:46 I the light that has come into
13:13 right because that's what I.
13:19 you will believe that I the one.
14:3 If I to prepare a place for you,
14:3 so that you will be where I.
14:4 to the place where I going."
14:6 him, "I the way, the truth,
14:10 Don't you believe that I in the
Jon 14:11 Believe me when I say that I in
14:11 me because of the things I.
14:12 will do the things that I doing.
14:12 greater things because I going
14:20 that day you will know that I
14:20 you are in me and that I in you.
14:28 the Father is greater than I.
14:31 and that I doing exactly what
15:1 Jesus said,, "I the true vine,
15:5 "I the vine. You are the
15:5 Those who live in me while Ive
15:11 that you will be as joyful as I,
16:7 However, I telling you the truth:
16:7 But if I, I will send him to you.
17:21 are in me and I in you.
17:23 I in them, and you are in me.
17:24 to be with me, to be where I.
18:5 Jesus told them, "I he."
18:6 When Jesus told them, "I he,"
18:8 "I told you that I he.
20:17 'I going to my Father and
20:21 so I sending you."
Act 7:32 'I the God of your ancestors
13:41 I going to do something in your
26:15 Lord answered, 'I Jesus,
26:17 people to whom I sending you.
Rom 9:33 As Scripture says, "I placing
1Pe 1:16 "Be holy, because I holy."
2:6 That is why Scripture says, "I
Rev 1:8 "I the A and the Z,"
1:17 I the first and the last,
1:18 but now I alive forever.
2:23 the churches will know that I
3:11 I coming soon! Hold on to what
16:15 "See, I coming like a thief.
21:5 "I making everything new."
21:6 I the A and the Z, the beginning
22:13 I the A and the Z, the first and
22:16 I the root and descendant of
22:16 I the bright morning star."

Ibhar (3)

2Sm 5:15 I, Elishua, Nepheg, Japhia,
1Ch 3:6 I, Elishama, Eliphelet,
14:5 I, Elishua, Elpelet,

Ibleam (3)

Jos 17:11 possessed Beth Shean and I
Jdg 1:27 I, and Megiddo or their villages.
2Ki 9:27 at Gur Pass, which is near I.

Ibneiah (1)

1Ch 9:8 I (son of Jeroham),

Ibniah (1)

1Ch 9:8 and great-grandson of I),

Ibri (1)

1Ch 24:27 Shoham, Zaccur, and I (for

Ibsam (1)

1Ch 7:2 Jeriel, Jahmai, I, and Shemuel.

Ibzan (3)

Jdg 12:8 I from Bethlehem judged Israel.
12:10 When I died, he was buried in
12:11 After I, Elon from the tribe of

ice (3)

Job 6:16 They are dark with i.
37:10 God's breath produces i,
38:29 From whose womb came the i,

Ichabod (1)

1Sm 4:21 She called the boy I [No Glory],

Ichabod's (1)

1Sm 14:3 the son of I brother Ahitub,

Iconium (8)

Act 13:51 feet and went to the city of I.
14:1 thing happened in the city of I.
14:3 Barnabas stayed in the city of I
14:4 the people of I were divided.
14:19 cities of Antioch and I arrived
14:21 back to the cities of Lystra, I,

Act 16:2 The believers in Lystra and I
2Ti 3:11 cities of Antioch, I, and Lystra.

Idalah (1)

Jos 19:15 Shimron, I, and Bethlehem.

Idbash (1)

1Ch 4:3 in Etam: Jezreel, Ishma, and I.

Iddo (15)

1Ki 4:14 Ahinadab, son of I,
1Ch 6:21 Joah's son was I. Iddo's son
27:21 half of Manasseh in Gilead: I,
2Ch 9:29 and in I the seer's visions
12:15 and the records of the seer I
13:22 in the history by the prophet I.
Ezr 5:1 and Zechariah, grandson of I,
6:14 Zechariah, the grandson of I.
8:17 I sent them to I, the leader in
8:17 I told them to tell I and his
8:18 God was guiding us, so I and
Neh 12:4 I, Ginnethoi, Abijah,
12:16 from I, Zechariah; Meshullam;
Zec 1:1 and the grandson of I.
1:7 and the grandson of I.

Iddo's (1)

1Ch 6:21 I son was Zerah. Zerah's son

idea (15)

Gen 41:37 and all his servants liked the i.
43:22 We have no i who put our
Num 16:28 things and that it wasn't my i:
Dtr 1:14 agreed that this was a good i.
1:23 It seemed like a good i to me.
Rut 2:22 "It's a good i, my daughter,
1Sm 9:10 his servant, "That's a good i!
20:39 The boy had no i what was
2Sm 13:33 your heart with the i that all
Neh 7:5 Then my God put the i into my
Est 5:14 Haman liked the i,
Luk 1:3 I thought it would be a good i
Jon 13:2 the devil had already put the i
Act 5:3 fill you with the i that you could
25:11 I don't reject the i of dying.

ideas (4)

Eze 13:3 They follow their own i,
38:10 At that time i will enter your
Mar 6:2 did this man get these i?
Act 17:19 new i that you're teaching?

identical (4)

Exo 26:17 with two i pegs. Make all the
36:22 with two i pegs. They made all
1Ki 7:18 the capitals i to each other.
7:37 i in size and shape.

identify (1)

Gal 3:19 They were added to i what

idiots (1)

Jer 10:8 They are complete i.

idle (5)

Dtr 32:47 think these words are i talk.
Job 35:13 doesn't listen to i complaints.
Pro 14:23 but i talk leads only to poverty.
19:15 and an i person will go hungry.
Ecc 10:18 A house leaks because of i

idleness (1)

Pro 31:27 she does not eat the bread of i.

idly (1)

Isa 58:13 and by not talking i,

idol (35)

Exo 34:17 "Never make an i.
Dtr 7:26 Never bring a disgusting i into
7:26 you and the i will be destroyed.
9:12 made an i for themselves."
Jdg 8:27 used the gold to make an i
17:3 I want to make a carved i and a
17:3 a carved idol and a metal i.
17:4 He made a carved i and a
Jdg 17:4 a carved idol and a metal i.
18:14 ephod, a carved i, a metal idol,
18:14 ephod, a carved idol, a metal i,
18:17 They took the carved i,
18:17 idols, and the metal i.
18:18 house and took the carved i,
18:18 idols, and the metal i,
18:20 and the carved i and went with
18:30 up the carved i for themselves.
18:31 the carved i Micah had made.
1Ki 11:5 disgusting i of the Ammonites).
11:7 for Chemosh (the disgusting i
11:7 disgusting i of the Ammonites).
2Ki 21:7 Manasseh had an i of Asherah
2Ch 33:7 had a carved i made.
33:15 rid of the foreign gods and the i
Psa 106:19 worshiped an i made of metal.
Isa 46:7 They set the i in its place,
48:14 What i has revealed such
66:3 someone who worships an i.
Eze 8:3 That was where an i that stirs
8:5 I saw the i that stirs up
Hos 8:5 Get rid of your calf-shaped i,
8:6 Samaria's calf-shaped i was
10:5 the calf-shaped i at Beth Aven.
Amo 8:14 the i of Samaria, and say,
Hab 2:18 in a carved i when its maker

idolaters (2)

Rev 21:8 sexual sinners, sorcerers, i,
22:15 sexual sinners, murderers, i,

idolatry (4)

1Sm 15:23 and i are arrogance.
2Ki 9:22 continues her i and witchcraft?"
Eze 23:49 they will pay for their sin of i.
Gal 5:20 i, drug use, hatred, rivalry,

idols (187)

Gen 31:19 Rachel stole her father's i.
31:34 Rachel had taken the i and had
31:35 he didn't find the i.
Exo 20:4 Never make your own carved i
Lev 17:7 must stop sacrificing to goat i
19:4 worthless gods or cast metal i.
26:1 "Never make worthless i or set
26:30 bodies on top of your dead i.
Num 33:52 rid of all their stone and metal i,
Dtr 4:16 and make your own carved i.
4:23 Don't make your own carved i
4:25 corrupt and make carved i
5:8 Never make your own carved i
7:5 Asherah, and burn their i.
7:25 Burn their i. Don't ever long for
7:25 the silver and gold on these i
7:25 Besides, these i are disgusting
12:3 Asherah, cut down their i,
29:17 disgusting gods and i made
32:16 they worshiped worthless i.
32:21 they worshiped worthless i.
Jdg 3:19 at the stone i near Gilgal ⌊and
3:26 He went past the stone i and
17:5 an ephod and household i.
18:14 and household i in these
18:17 the ephod, the household i,
18:18 the ephod, the household i,
18:20 the ephod, the household i,
1Sm 19:13 Then Michal took some i,
19:13 covered the i with a garment.
19:16 and there in the bed were the i
2Sm 5:21 The Philistines left their i there,
5:21 and his men carried the i away.
1Ki 14:9 You made other gods, metal i,
14:24 in the temples of i throughout
15:12 got rid of the i his father had
16:13 because of their worthless i.
16:26 Israel to sin with worthless i,
21:26 as a result of worshiping i as
2Ki 17:12 They served i, although the
17:15 They went after worthless i
17:15 became as worthless as the i.
17:41 but also served their own i.
21:11 sin by ⌊worshiping⌋ his i.
21:21 prayed to the i his father had
23:24 psychics, family i, other idols,
23:24 psychics, family idols, other i,
1Ch 10:9 Philistine territory to tell their i
16:26 all the gods of the nations are i.
2Ch 11:15 calf statues he had made as i.
15:8 away the detestable i from all
24:18 their ancestors and worshiped i
28:2 of Israel and even made metal i
33:19 worship sites and set up i
33:22 Amon sacrificed to all the i his
34:3 carved i, and metal idols.
34:3 carved idols, and metal i.
34:4 carved i, and metal idols.
34:4 carved idols, and metal i.
34:7 poles and i into powder,
34:33 i throughout Israelite territory.
Job 36:14 prostitutes in the temples of i.
Psa 78:58 because they worshiped i.
96:5 all the gods of the nations are i.
97:7 Everyone who worships i and
106:36 and they worshiped their i,
106:38 sacrificed to the i of Canaan.
115:4 Their i are made of silver and
115:8 Those who make i end up like
135:15 The i of the nations are made
135:18 Those who make i end up like
Isa 2:8 Their land is filled with i,
2:18 i will disappear completely.
2:20 silver and gold i that they made
10:10 kingdoms which have i.
10:11 I will do to Jerusalem and its i
10:11 I've done to Samaria and its i."
19:1 Egypt's i will tremble in his
19:3 They will turn to i,
21:9 All the i they worship lie
30:22 dishonor your silver-plated i
31:7 silver and gold i that your sinful
40:19 Craftsmen make i.
40:20 to set up i that will not
41:22 "Bring ⌊your i⌋ so they can tell
41:22 Explain past events that your i
42:8 else or the praise I deserve to i.
42:17 Then those who trust i and
44:9 All who make i are nothing.
44:10 making gods or casting metal i.
44:13 so the i can live in shrines.
45:16 Those who make i will be
45:20 Ignorant people carry wooden i
48:5 My carved i and my metal idols
48:5 My carved idols and my metal i
57:6 Your i are among the smooth
57:8 You've set up your i beside
57:8 uncovered yourself to the i.
57:13 your collection of i save you.
Jer 2:5 They followed worthless i and
4:1 if you take your disgusting i out
7:30 "They set up their detestable i
8:19 make me furious with their i,
10:8 learn nonsense from wooden i.
10:9 The clothing for the i is blue
10:14 are put to shame by their i.
16:18 detestable and disgusting i."
18:15 as an offering to worthless i,
25:6 about the i your hands have
25:7 about the i your hands have
32:34 They set up their detestable i
50:2 Its i will be filled with terror.'
50:38 Babylon is a land of i,
51:17 are put to shame by their i.
51:47 when I will punish Babylon's i.
51:52 "when I will punish their i,
Eze 6:4 will kill people in front of your i.
6:5 of Israel in front of your i,
6:6 Your i will be smashed and
6:9 which lusted after i.
6:13 beside the i around their altars.
6:13 offerings to their disgusting i.
8:10 and all the i in the nation of
11:21 detestable and disgusting i,
14:3 people are devoted to their i,
14:4 an Israelite is devoted to i
14:4 the answer that his many i
14:5 because of their disgusting i.'
14:6 Turn away from your i,
14:7 me by devoting himself to i
16:17 and made male i for yourself.
16:18 and covered the i with them.
16:20 sacrificed them as food to i.

Eze 16:21 them as burnt offerings to i.
16:36 and to all your disgusting i.
16:36 sacrificed their blood to these i.
18:6 sites or look for help from the i
18:12 He looks to i for help.
18:15 sites or look for help from the i
20:7 "Get rid of the detestable i that
20:7 with the disgusting i of Egypt.
20:8 detestable i that they looked
20:8 the disgusting i of Egypt.
20:16 hearts chased disgusting i.
20:18 with their disgusting i.
20:24 ancestors' disgusting i for help.
20:30 detestable i like a prostitute?
20:31 with all your disgusting i
20:39 Serve your disgusting i.
20:39 your gifts and your disgusting i.
22:3 yourself with disgusting i.
22:4 disgusting i you have made.
22:9 in you eat food sacrificed to i at
23:7 dishonored herself with the i
23:30 dishonored yourself with their i.
23:37 commit adultery with their i.
23:37 to for me as burnt offerings to i.
23:39 their children to their i,
30:13 put an end to the i in Memphis.
33:25 You look to your i for help.
36:18 dishonored the land with their i.
36:25 will cleanse you from all your i.
37:23 themselves with their i,
44:10 wandered off to follow their i.
44:12 by standing in front of their i
Hos 3:4 and without ephods or family i.
4:12 ask their wooden i for help.
4:17 have chosen to worship i.
5:11 are determined to chase i.
8:4 They chose to make i with
9:10 Peor and worshiped shameful i.
11:2 and they burned incense to i.
13:2 They make i from silver for
13:2 These i are skillfully made.
13:2 and kiss calf-shaped i."
14:8 have nothing more to do with i.
Jnh 2:8 i abandon their loyalty
Mic 1:7 All its i will be smashed to
5:13 I will destroy your i and your
Nah 1:14 the wooden and metal i from
Hab 2:18 worthless i that cannot speak.
Zec 10:2 The i speak lies. The
13:2 away the names of the i from
Rom 2:22 As you treat i with disgust,
Rev 2:14 them to eat food sacrificed to i
2:20 and to eat food sacrificed to i.
9:20 worshiping demons and i made

idols' (2)
1Sm 31:9 good news in their i temples
2Ch 30:14 people got rid of the i altars

Idumea (1)
Mar 3:8 Jerusalem, I, and from across

Iezer (1)
Num 26:30 of Gilead were the family of I,

Igal (3)
Num 13:7 I, son of Joseph, from the tribe
2Sm 23:36 I (son of Nathan) from Zobah,
1Ch 3:22 I, Bariah, Neariah, and Shaphat.

Igdaliah's (1)
Jer 35:4 (He was I son, the man of God.)

ignorance (2)
Eph 4:18 of their i and stubbornness.
1Pe 2:15 God wants you to silence the i

ignorant (13)
Psa 14:4 so i that they do not call on the
53:4 so i that they do not call on
Pro 9:13 Stupidity is loud, gullible, and i.
Isa 45:20 I people carry wooden idols
Jer 10:14 Everyone is stupid and i.
51:17 Everyone is stupid and i.
Hos 4:6 my people because they are i.
Rom 2:20 an instructor of i people,
2Co 1:8 we don't want you to be i about
2:11 not i about Satan's scheming.
1Th 4:13 we don't want you to be i about
Heb 5:2 be gentle with people who are i
2Pe 3:16 I people and people who aren't

ignorantly (1)
1Ti 1:13 I acted i in my unbelief.

ignore (12)
Lev 5:2 swarming creature — and then i
5:3 of any kind and then i
5:4 (as some people do) and then i
20:4 If the common people i those
Jos 23:16 When you i the conditions
Neh 4:5 Don't i their guilt, and don't let
Est 3:3 do you i the king's command?"
Eze 22:26 They i the days to worship me.
24:14 I will not i you, pity you,
33:4 If the people hear the horn and i
Tit 2:15 Don't let anyone i you.
2Pe 3:8 Dear friends, don't i this fact:

ignored (18)
Dtr 32:18 (You i the rock who fathered
Jos 7:11 They have i the requirements
7:15 He has i the LORD's
1Ki 12:8 But he i the advice the older
12:13 He i the advice the older
1Ch 13:3 which we i while Saul was
2Ch 10:8 But he i the advice the older
10:13 He i the older leaders' advice.
Est 9:28 of Purim must not be i among
Psa 44:17 We never i your promise.
Pro 1:25 You i all my advice.
Isa 40:27 my rights are i by my God"?
Eze 33:5 of the horn but i its warning.
Dan 9:11 All Israel has i your teachings
Luk 11:42 But you have i justice and the
1Co 14:38 what I write should be i.
Heb 8:9 so I i them, says the Lord.
12:2 death on the cross and i

ignores (8)
Pro 10:3 but he intentionally i the
10:17 but whoever i a warning strays.
13:18 to a person who i discipline,
15:32 Whoever i discipline despises
28:27 Whoever i the poor receives
Mat 18:17 If he i these witnesses,
18:17 If he also i the community,
1Co 14:38 But whoever i what I write

ignoring (3)
Luk 11:42 things without i the others.
Rom 2:23 God by i Moses' Teachings?
2Pe 3:5 They are deliberately i one fact:

Iim (1)
Jos 15:29 Baalah, I, Ezem,

Ijon (3)
1Ki 15:20 He conquered I, Dan, Abel Beth
2Ki 15:29 Pileser of Assyria took I,
2Ch 16:4 He conquered I, Dan,

Ikkesh (3)
2Sm 23:26 Ira (son of I) from Tekoa,
1Ch 11:28 Ira (son of I) from Tekoa,
27:9 Ira, the son of I from Tekoa,

Ilai (1)
1Ch 11:29 I (descendant of Ahohi),

ill (4)
Gen 48:1 was told, "Your father is i."
2Ki 13:14 Elisha became fatally i.
Psa 41:3 person to health when he is i.
Gal 4:13 you the Good News I was i.

illegal (44)
1Ki 11:7 Then Solomon built an i
12:32 He appointed priests from the i
13:2 from the i worship sites who
13:32 and all the i worship sites
13:33 priests for the i worship sites.
13:34 Appointing i priests became
15:14 Although the i worship sites
22:44 But the i worship sites were
2Ki 12:3 But the i places of worship
14:4 But the i places of worship
15:4 But the i places of worship
15:35 But the i places of worship
16:4 offering at the i worship sites,
17:9 They built for themselves i
17:11 At all the i places of worship,
17:29 They put them at the i places
17:32 at their i places of worship.
18:4 He got rid of the i places of
21:3 He rebuilt the i places of
23:5 to sacrifice at the i places
23:9 The priests of the i worship
23:13 The king made the i places of
23:19 all the temples at the i places
23:20 priests of the i worship sites
2Ch 11:15 priests for the i worship sites
14:5 He got rid of the i places of
15:17 Although the i worship sites in
17:6 He also got rid of the i places
20:33 But the i worship sites on the
21:11 Jehoram made i places of
28:4 offering at the i worship sites,
31:1 and tore down the i places of
33:3 He rebuilt the i places of
33:17 to sacrifice at the i places
33:19 where he built i worship sites
34:3 by destroying the i places
Psa 78:58 of their i worship sites.
Eze 16:24 platforms and i worship sites
16:31 and place your i worship sites
16:39 tear down your i worship sites.
18:6 He doesn't eat at the i
18:11 He eats at the i mountain
18:15 He doesn't eat at the i
Hos 10:8 The i worship sites of Aven

illegally (1)
2Ch 27:2 he didn't i enter the LORD's

illegitimate (1)
Jon 8:41 "We're not i children.

illicit (2)
Dtr 23:2 A man born from an i union
Gal 5:19 i sex, perversion, promiscuity,

illness (6)
Dtr 7:15 you from having any kind of i.
2Ki 8:8 'Will I recover from this i?'"
8:9 he will recover from this i."
Mar 5:29 She felt cured from her i.
5:34 Be cured from your i."
Gal 4:14 Even though my i was difficult

illnesses (1)
Luk 8:2 from evil spirits and various i.

illusions (1)
Isa 30:10 what we want to hear. See i.

illustrate (4)
Psa 78:2 will open my mouth to i points.
Mat 13:35 will open my mouth to i points.
Jon 16:25 examples to i these things.
Gal 4:24 women i two arrangements.

illustrates (2)
Mat 13:19 seed planted along the road i.
Luk 8:11 "This is what the story i:

illustrating (1)
Mat 13:34 not tell them anything without i

illustration (28)
Eze 17:2 Give this i to the nation of
Mat 13:24 Jesus used another i.
13:31 Jesus used another i.
13:33 He used another i.
13:36 "Explain what the i of the
15:15 "Explain this i to us."
21:33 "Listen to another i.
Mar 3:23 them together and used this i:

Mar 4:34 to them without using an **i**.
7:17 asked him about this **i**.
12:1 Then, using this **i**,
12:12 he had directed this **i** at them.
Luk 6:39 Jesus also gave them this **i**:
8:4 he used this story as an **i**:
12:16 Then he used this **i**.
12:41 did you use this **i** just for us or
13:6 Then Jesus used this **i**:
14:7 So he used this **i** when he
15:3 spoke to them using this **i**:
18:1 Jesus used this **i** with his
18:9 Jesus also used this **i** with
19:11 attention, he used this **i**.
19:28 After Jesus had given this **i**,
20:9 Then, using this **i**,
20:19 he had directed this **i** at them.
21:29 Jesus used this story as an **i**.
Jon 10:6 Jesus used this **i** as he talked
Gal 4:24 these historical events as an **i**.

illustrations (10)

Mat 13:3 Then he used stories as **i** to
13:10 "Why do you use stories as **i**
13:34 Jesus used **i** to tell the crowds
13:53 Jesus had finished these **i**,
21:45 and the Pharisees heard his **i**,
22:1 Again Jesus used stories as **i**
Mar 4:2 He used stories as **i** to teach
4:13 any of the stories I use as **i**?
4:33 them using many **i** like these.
Luk 5:36 He also used these **i**:

Illyricum (1)

Rom 15:19 Christ from Jerusalem to **I**.

I'm (254)

Gen 6:7 I sorry that I made them."
6:13 Now I going to destroy them
6:17 I about to send a flood on the
12:7 "I going to give this land to
21:18 because I going to make him
Exo 4:23 So now I going to kill your
7:17 I going to strike the Nile,
16:4 "I going to send you food from
23:20 "I going to send a Messenger
32:10 I so angry with them I am going
33:12 and I pleased with you.'
34:10 "I making my promise again.
34:27 basis of these words I making
Lev 25:2 come into the land I giving you,
Num 13:2 which I giving to the Israelites.
15:2 settled in the land I giving you,
15:18 the land where I taking you
18:26 which I giving you as your
20:12 into the land I giving them."
20:24 cannot enter the land I giving
25:12 So tell Phinehas that I making
Dtr 2:5 because I not giving you any of
2:9 I not giving you any of Ar as
2:19 I not giving you any of the land
2:24 I going to hand King Sihon of
5:31 in the land which I giving them
9:23 of the land I giving you."
32:49 the land of Canaan that I giving
32:52 the land I giving the Israelites."
1Sm 16:1 I sending you to Jesse in
23:4 I giving you the power to defeat
24:4 'I going to hand your enemy
2Sm 15:26 'I not pleased with you,'
24:12 I offering you three choices.
1Ki 3:12 So I going to do what you've
3:12 I giving you a wise and
3:13 I also giving you what you
2Ki 19:7 I going to put a spirit in him so
20:5 Now I going to heal you.
21:12 I going to bring such a disaster
22:16 I going to bring disaster on this
22:20 That is why I going to bring
22:20 I going to bring you to your
22:20 see any of the disaster I going
1Ch 21:10 I offering you three choices.
2Ch 34:24 I going to bring disaster on this
34:28 That is why I going to bring
34:28 I going to bring you to your
34:28 see any of the disaster I going
Job 42:7 "I very angry with you and your
Isa 1:11 I not pleased with the blood of
1:14 and I tired of putting up with
5:13 don't understand what I doing.
13:17 I going to stir up the Medes
37:7 I going to put a spirit in him so
38:5 I going to give you more
51:22 I taking from your hand the cup
65:18 rejoice forever in what I going
65:18 because I going to create
Jer 3:12 because I merciful,' declares
3:14 "I your husband. I will take you,
4:6 I bringing disaster and
5:14 I going to put my words in your
5:15 Nation of Israel, I going to bring
6:19 I going to bring disaster on
6:20 I not pleased with your
6:21 I going to lay stumbling blocks
11:11 I going to bring a disaster on
11:22 I going to punish them.
13:13 I going to make everyone who
15:6 I tired of showing compassion
16:5 I taking my peace,
16:9 I going to put a stop to the
16:16 "I going to send for many
18:11 I going to prepare a disaster
19:3 I going to bring such a disaster
19:15 I going to bring on this city and
20:4 I going to make you terrify
21:4 I going to take your weapons
21:13 "'I against you, Jerusalem.
23:30 "I against the prophets who
23:31 "I against the prophets who
23:32 I against those who prophesy
25:9 so I going to send for all the
25:9 I going to destroy them and turn
25:15 whom I sending you drink from
25:16 of the wars that I going
25:27 of the wars that I going
25:29 I declaring war on all those
28:16 I going to remove you from the
29:17 I going to send them wars,
29:21 I going to hand them over to
29:23 I a witness, declares the
29:32 see the blessings that I going
30:10 I going to rescue you from a
30:10 I going to rescue your
30:18 I going to bring the captives
32:3 I going to hand this city over to
32:28 I going to hand this city over to
34:2 I going to hand this city over to
36:5 Jeremiah told Baruch, "I no
39:16 I going to carry out my threat
42:11 I with you. I will save you and
43:10 I going to send for my servant
44:11 I going to bring disaster on you
44:30 I going to hand Pharaoh
45:5 because I going to bring
46:25 "I going to punish Amon,
46:27 I going to rescue you and your
49:35 I going to break the bows of
50:31 "I against you, you arrogant
Eze 3:3 eat this scroll I giving you,
8:18 take action because I angry,
13:8 That is why I against you,
13:20 I against the magic charms that
20:49 say that I only telling stories."
21:4 I going to kill the righteous
22:19 That is why I going to gather
23:22 I going to stir up your lovers
23:28 I going to hand you over to
24:16 with one blow I going to take
24:21 I going to dishonor my holy
25:4 That is why I going to hand
25:9 That is why I going to open up
25:16 I going to use my power
26:7 From the north I going to bring
28:22 says: I against you, Sidon.
29:3 says: I against you, Pharaoh,
29:10 That is why I against you and
29:19 I going to give Egypt to King
30:22 I against Pharaoh,
35:3 I against you, Mount Seir.
36:32 I want you to know that I not
39:17 for the sacrifice that I preparing
40:4 attention to everything I going
Eze 44:5 and listen to everything I going
Hos 2:14 "That is why I going to win her
10:10 will punish them when I ready.
Amo 5:21 I not pleased with your
7:8 Then the Lord said, "I going to
9:9 I going to give the order.
Mic 2:3 I planning a disaster to punish
Zec 1:14 I very jealous about Jerusalem
1:15 and I very angry with the
2:9 I going to shake my fist at the
2:10 I going to come and live
3:8 I going to bring my servant,
11:16 I about to place a shepherd in
12:2 "I going to make Jerusalem
Mal 1:10 I not pleased with you,"
2:3 "I going to punish your
2:3 I going to spread excrement on
3:1 "I going to send my messenger,
4:5 "I going to send you the
Mat 8:3 him, and said, "I willing.
10:16 "I sending you out like sheep
11:10 'I sending my messenger
20:22 you drink the cup that I going
23:34 I sending you prophets,
26:38 so great that I feel as if I dying.
Mar 1:41 him, and said, "I willing.
2:11 "I telling you to get up,
5:41 I telling you to get up!"
10:38 you drink the cup that I going
10:38 that I going to receive?"
10:39 will drink the cup that I going
10:39 baptism that I going to receive.
13:37 I telling everyone what I'm
13:37 everyone what I telling you:
14:34 so great that I feel as if I dying.
Luk 7:14 He said, "Young man, I telling
7:47 That's why I telling you that her
10:3 I sending you out like lambs
12:1 I talking about their hypocrisy.
12:5 I warning you to be afraid of
16:9 ⌊Jesus continued,⌋ "I telling
22:27 But I among you as a servant.
22:29 a kingdom, I giving it to you.
24:49 "I sending you what my Father
Jon 4:35 I telling you to look and see
5:34 I telling you this to save you.
6:46 I saying that no one has seen
7:8 I not going to this festival right
7:34 You can't go where I going.
7:36 'You can't go where I going'?
8:14 I came from and where I going.
8:14 I came from or where I going
8:21 He said, "I going away,
8:21 You can't go where I going.
8:22 'You can't go where I going'?
8:23 I from above. You're from this
8:23 I not from this world.
8:37 you don't like what I saying
8:38 What I saying is what I have
8:42 I here, and I came from God.
8:46 If I telling the truth,
8:49 answered, "I not possessed.
9:5 As long as I in the world,
9:5 I light for the world."
10:36 you say that I dishonoring God
10:36 'I the Son of God'?
10:37 If I not doing the things my
10:38 But if I doing those things and
10:38 believe the things that I doing.
11:11 and I going to Bethany to wake
11:15 but I glad that I wasn't there so
13:7 don't know now what I doing.
13:18 "I not talking about all of you.
13:19 I telling you now before it
13:33 I telling you what I told the
13:33 but you can't go where I going
13:34 "I giving you a new
13:36 now to the place where I going.
14:2 I have told you that I going
14:10 What I telling you doesn't come
14:25 "I have told you this while I still
14:27 "I leaving you peace.
14:27 I giving you my peace.
14:28 me tell you, 'I going away,
14:28 but I coming back to you.'
14:28 you would be glad that I going

Mat 20:27 Whoever wants to be most i
22:38 This is the greatest and most i
23:17 What is more i, the gold or the
23:19 What is more i, the gift or the
23:23 These are the most i things in
Mar 6:21 the most i people of Galilee.
9:35 be the most i person must take
10:44 Whoever wants to be most i
12:28 is the most i of them all?"
12:29 "The most i is, 'Listen, Israel,
12:31 The second most i
12:33 love yourself is more i than all
15:43 and was an i member
Luk 7:28 Yet, the least i person in the
14:8 Maybe someone more i than
16:15 What is i to humans is
Jon 4:12 You're not more i than our
7:37 On the last and most i day of
19:31 day was an especially i day
Act 5:36 He claimed that he was i,
25:2 The chief priests and the other i
25:23 officers and the most i men
26:22 that I can stand and testify to i
1Co 3:7 nor the one who waters is i
14:5 has revealed is more i than
15:3 I passed on to you the most i
2Co 11:7 so that you could become i?
Gal 2:2 those recognized as i people
2:6 as i people didn't add
2:9 i people) acknowledged that
6:3 you're i when you're really
Eph 6:3 This is an i commandment
Heb 2:3 if we reject the i message,
7:4 see how i Melchizedek was.
7:7 No one can deny that the more i
7:7 blesses the less i person.
8:11 All of them from the least i to
8:11 to the most i will all know
Jas 1:9 being humble makes them i.
1:18 make us his most i creatures.
3:5 it can brag about doing i things.
Rev 6:15 the i people, the generals,
11:8 street of the i city where their
11:18 if they are i or unimportant,
13:16 beast forces all people — i
16:19 The i city split into three parts,
17:18 The woman you saw is the i
18:10 how horrible it is for that i city,
18:16 how horrible for that i city
18:18 there ever a city as i as this?'
18:19 how horrible for that i city.
18:21 "The i city Babylon will be
18:23 Its merchants were the i
19:18 both i or insignificant people."
20:12 both i and unimportant people,

imported (7)

1Ki 10:12 like this i ⌊into Israel⌋,
10:28 Solomon's horses were i from
10:29 Each chariot was i from Egypt
2Ch 1:16 Solomon's horses were i from
1:17 They i each chariot from Egypt
9:28 Horses were i for Solomon from
Isa 17:10 have set out the i grapevines.

impose (1)

Jer 19:9 hardships that their enemies i

imposed (1)

2Co 2:6 The majority of you have i a

impossible (31)

Gen 20:18 (The LORD had made it i for
Exo 32:9 and they are i to deal with.
33:3 because you are i to deal with,
33:5 'You are i to deal with.
34:9 Even though we are i to deal
Dtr 9:6 You are i to deal with!
9:13 and they are i to deal with.
10:16 and don't be i to deal with any
31:27 You are i to deal with.
2Sm 13:2 It seemed i for him to be alone
2Ki 17:14 They became as i to deal with
2Ch 30:8 Don't be i to deal with like your
36:13 became so stubborn and so i
Neh 9:29 became i to deal with,
Job 37:7 He makes it i to do anything so
Psa 142:4 Escape is i for me.
Jer 7:26 You became i to deal with,
17:23 They were i to deal with and
19:15 They've become i to deal with,
Zec 8:6 It may seem i to the few
8:6 but will it seem i to me?
Mat 17:20 Nothing will be i for you."
19:26 "It is i for people ⌊to save
Mar 10:27 "It's i for people ⌊to save
10:27 but it's not i for God to save
Luk 1:37 But nothing is i for God."
18:27 "The things that are i for people
Rom 8:3 It is i to do what God's
11:33 are so deep that it is i
1Co 15:12 back from the dead is i?
1Th 2:18 but Satan made that i.

impress (1)

Pro 17:10 than a hundred lashes i a fool.

impresses (1)

Pro 17:10 A reprimand i a person who

impression (1)

Ecc 9:13 and it made a deep i on me.

impressive (11)

2Sm 23:10 So the LORD won an i victory
23:12 So the LORD won an i victory.
1Ki 9:8 as i as it is, will be appalled.
1Ch 11:14 saved ⌊them⌋ with an i victory.
2Ch 7:21 Everyone passing by this i
Dan 4:3 His miraculous signs are i.
4:30 palace by my own i power
7:8 a mouth that spoke i things.
7:11 because of the i words that
7:20 a mouth that spoke i things.
Act 8:13 miracles and i things that were

imprison (6)

Mat 16:19 Whatever you i, God will
16:19 you imprison, God will i.
18:18 this truth: Whatever you i,
18:18 you imprison, God will i.
Act 9:2 and i them in Jerusalem.
22:19 synagogue to synagogue to i

imprisoned (2)

Ezr 7:26 be i or be sentenced to die.
2Ti 2:9 However, God's word is not i.

imprisonment (3)

2Ki 25:27 the thirty-seventh year of the i
Jer 52:31 the thirty-seventh year of the i
Act 20:23 warns me in every city that i

imprisonments (1)

2Co 6:5 beatings, i, riots, hard work,

imprisons (1)

Job 11:10 If God comes along and i

improper (1)

1Co 11:27 the Lord's cup in an i way will

improve (1)

2Co 13:11 Make sure that you i.

improvement (1)

2Co 13:9 We are also praying for your i.

impulse (1)

Jon 1:13 physical way — from a human i

impure (7)

Act 10:14 anything that is i or unclean."
10:15 God has made clean are i."
10:28 longer call anyone i or unclean.
11:8 I've never put anything i or
11:9 God has made clean are i.'
2Co 2:17 go around selling an i word
2Pe 2:10 along the path of i desires

impurities (6)

Pro 25:4 Take the i out of silver,
Isa 1:25 will remove your i with bleach.
1:25 I will get rid of all your i.
Jer 6:29 because the i can't be removed.
Eze 22:18 are like the i left from silver.
24:11 Its i will melt away,

impurity (2)

Lev 14:19 is being cleansed from his i.
Mat 23:27 bones and every kind of i.

Imrah (1)

1Ch 7:36 Suah, Harnepher, Shual, Beri, I,

Imri (2)

1Ch 9:4 and great-grandson of I.
Neh 3:2 Zaccur, son of I, was next to

Imri's (1)

1Ch 9:4 (I father was Bani.)

inaccurate (2)

Mic 6:10 use i weights and measures.
6:11 and bags filled with i weights.

inappropriate (1)

2Co 6:14 Stop forming i relationships

incense (163)

Exo 25:6 oil and for the sweet-smelling i,
25:38 The tongs and i burners must
27:3 bowls, forks, and i burners.
30:1 of acacia wood for burning i.
30:7 must burn sweet-smelling i
30:8 lamps at dusk, he must burn i.
30:8 For generations to come an i
30:9 "Never burn any unauthorized i
30:27 all the utensils, the altar for i,
30:35 perfumer make it into fragrant i,
30:37 Never make any i for
31:8 all its utensils, the altar for i,
31:11 and the sweet-smelling i for the
35:8 oil and for the sweet-smelling i,
35:15 the altar for i with its poles,
35:15 the sweet-smelling i,
35:28 and the sweet-smelling i.
37:23 and the i burners out of pure
37:25 of acacia wood for burning i.
37:29 for the pure, sweet-smelling i.
38:3 bowls, forks, and i burners.
39:38 the sweet-smelling i,
40:5 Put the gold altar for i in front of
40:27 burned sweet-smelling i on it,
Lev 2:1 olive oil on it, and put i on it.
2:2 flour with olive oil, and all the i.
2:15 olive oil on it, and place i on it.
2:16 and all the i as a reminder.
4:7 of the altar for sweet-smelling i
5:11 put olive oil on it or add i to it,
6:15 with the olive oil and all the i.
10:1 and Abihu each took an i burner
10:1 put burning coals and i in it.
16:12 He will take an i burner full of
16:12 finely ground, sweet-smelling i.
16:13 Then he will put the i on the
16:13 The cloud of i will cover the
24:7 Lay pure i on top of each stack.
24:7 The i on the bread will be a
26:30 cut down your i altars,
Num 4:16 the sweet-smelling i,
7:14 weighed 4 ounces, filled with i;
7:20 weighed 4 ounces, filled with i;
7:26 weighed 4 ounces, filled with i;
7:32 weighed 4 ounces, filled with i;
7:38 weighed 4 ounces, filled with i;
7:44 weighed 4 ounces, filled with i;
7:50 weighed 4 ounces, filled with i;
7:56 weighed 4 ounces, filled with i;
7:62 weighed 4 ounces, filled with i;
7:68 weighed 4 ounces, filled with i;
7:74 weighed 4 ounces, filled with i;
7:80 weighed 4 ounces, filled with i;
7:86 The 12 gold dishes filled with i
16:6 this tomorrow: Take i burners,
16:7 and put burning coals and i in
16:17 Each man will take his i burner
16:17 incense burner and put i in it.

Num 16:17 They will offer all 250 **i** burners
16:17 Then you and Aaron offer your **i**
16:18 So each man took his **i** burner,
16:18 put burning coals and **i** in it,
16:35 250 men who were offering **i**.
16:37 to take the **i** burners out of the
16:37 coals and **i** somewhere else,
16:37 because the **i** burners have
16:38 The **i** burners of these men
16:39 the bronze **i** burners which had
16:39 The **i** burners were then
16:40 Aaron can come near to burn **i**
16:46 "Take your **i** burner,
16:46 coals from the altar and **i** in it,
16:47 Aaron took his **i** burner,
16:47 He put **i** on the incense burner
16:47 He put incense on the **i** burner
Dtr 33:10 They burn **i** for you to smell
1Sm 2:28 offerings on my altar, to burn **i**,
1Ki 3:3 he still sacrificed and burned **i**
7:50 **i** burners of pure gold,
11:8 his foreign wives who burned **i**
22:44 and burn **i** at these worship
2Ki 12:3 and burn **i** at these worship
14:4 and burn **i** at these worship
15:4 and burn **i** at these worship
15:35 and burn **i** at these worship
16:4 sacrifices and burned **i** as
18:4 had been burning **i** to it.
25:15 guard took all of the **i** burners
1Ch 6:49 offerings and on the altar for **i**.
9:29 wine, olive oil, **i**, and spices.
28:18 the refined gold for the altar of **i**.
2Ch 2:4 burn sweet-smelling **i** in his
4:22 **i** burners of pure gold,
13:11 They offer sweet-smelling **i**
14:5 of worship and the altars for **i**
26:16 into the LORD's temple to burn **i**
26:16 to burn incense on the **i** altar.
26:18 you have no right to burn **i** as
26:18 given the holy task of burning **i**.
26:19 Uzziah, who held an **i** burner in
26:19 as Uzziah was at the **i** altar.
28:4 sacrifices and burned **i** as
29:7 and didn't burn **i** or sacrifice
30:14 They got rid of all the altars for **i**
34:4 He cut down the **i** altars that
34:7 and cut down all the **i** altars
Neh 13:5 store grain offerings, **i**, utensils,
13:9 temple, the offerings, and the **i**.
Psa 141:2 accepted as sweet-smelling **i**
Pro 27:9 Perfume and **i** make the heart
Sos 3:6 with myrrh and **i** made from
4:6 of myrrh and the hill of **i**.
4:14 and all kinds of **i**, myrrh, aloes,
Isa 1:13 Your **i** is disgusting to me,
17:8 poles or **i** altars which their
27:9 Asherah or **i** altars are left
43:23 you by requiring **i** offerings.
60:6 They will bring gold and **i**.
65:3 and burnt **i** on brick altars.
65:7 They burnt **i** on the mountains
66:3 Whoever burns **i** is like
Jer 1:16 burned **i** to other gods,
6:20 **I** that comes from Sheba is no
7:9 burn **i** as an offering to Baal,
11:17 him furious by burning **i** as
17:26 grain offerings, and **i**.
18:15 They burn **i** as an offering to
19:4 unrecognizable by burning **i** as
19:13 is because people burned **i**
32:29 going up to the roofs to burn **i**
41:5 brought grain offerings and **i**
44:3 They went to burn **i** and serve
44:5 and wouldn't stop burning **i** as
44:8 make me angry by burning **i**
44:15 that their wives were burning **i**
44:17 We will burn **i** to the queen of
44:18 But since we stopped burning **i**
44:19 "When we burned **i** to the
44:21 remember that you burned **i**
44:23 You burned **i** as offerings to
44:25 We will burn **i** to the queen of
52:19 pans, **i** burners, bowls, pots,
Eze 6:4 and your **i** burners will be
6:6 Your **i** burners will be cut down,
Eze 8:11 Each of them was holding an **i**
8:11 and a cloud of **i** went up.
16:18 olive oil and **i** in their presence.
23:41 They put my **i** and my olive oil
Hos 2:13 for all the times she burned **i** as
4:13 and they burn **i** on the hills
11:2 and they burned **i** to idols.
Hab 1:16 sacrifice to their nets and burn **i**
Mal 1:11 **I** and pure offerings will be
Luk 1:9 into the Lord's temple to burn **i**.
1:10 outside while he was burning **i**.
1:11 Then, to the right of the **i** altar,
Heb 9:4 It contained the gold **i** burner
Rev 5:8 a harp and a gold bowl full of **i**,
8:3 angel came with a gold **i** burner
8:3 He was given a lot of **i** to offer
8:4 The smoke from the **i** went up
8:5 The angel took the **i** burner,
18:13 cinnamon, spices, **i**,

inches (41)

Exo 25:10 ark of acacia wood 45 **i** long,
25:10 27 **i** wide, and 27 inches high.
25:10 27 inches wide, and 27 **i** high.
25:17 ark out of pure gold 45 **i** long
25:17 45 inches long and 27 **i** wide.
25:23 table of acacia wood 36 **i** long,
25:23 18 **i** wide, and 27 inches high.
25:23 18 inches wide, and 27 **i** high.
25:25 Make a rim three **i** wide around
26:13 There will be 18 **i** left over on
26:16 be 15 feet long and 27 **i** wide,
28:16 Fold it in half so that it's 9 **i**
30:2 Make it 18 **i** square and 36
30:2 18 inches square and 36 **i** high.
36:21 was 15 feet long and 27 **i** wide,
37:1 out of acacia wood 45 **i** long,
37:1 27 **i** wide, and 27 inches high.
37:1 27 inches wide, and 27 **i** high.
37:6 mercy out of pure gold 45 **i** long
37:6 45 inches long and 27 **i** wide.
37:10 out of acacia wood 36 **i** long,
37:10 18 **i** wide, and 27 inches high.
37:10 18 inches wide, and 27 **i** high.
37:12 He made a rim 3 **i** wide around
37:25 It was 18 **i** square and 36
37:25 18 inches square and 36 **i** high.
39:9 in half and was 9 **i** square.
1Ki 7:26 The pool was three **i** thick.
2Ch 4:5 The pool was three **i** thick.
Psa 39:5 of my days ⌊only⌋ a few **i**.
Jer 52:21 It was three **i** thick and hollow.
Eze 40:12 There was a barrier about 21 **i**
40:42 long, 3 feet wide, and 21 **i** high.
40:43 hooks, three **i** long,
43:13 measuring stick was 21 **i** long.)
43:13 The base of the altar was 21 **i**
43:13 21 inches high and 21 **i** wide.
43:13 was a rim measuring 9 **i** wide.
43:14 was 7 feet high and 21 **i** wide.
43:17 around that was 10 ½ **i** wide.
43:17 Its base was 21 **i**. The steps to

incident (4)

Num 25:18 They plotted to trick you in the **i**
25:18 caused by the **i** at Peor."
31:16 LORD in the **i** that took place
Hos 10:9 ever since the **i** at Gibeah.

incinerator (2)

Mat 6:30 tomorrow it's thrown into an **i**.
Luk 12:28 tomorrow it's thrown into an **i**.

include (13)

Gen 46:26 This didn't **i** the wives of
Lev 21:2 These relatives **i** your mother,
Num 1:49 the tribe of Levi or **i** them
Dtr 14:7 They **i** camels, rabbits,
Jdg 8:26 This did not **i** the half-moon
2Ki 22:6 workers **i** the carpenters,
1Ch 21:6 Joab didn't **i** Levi and Benjamin
Jer 20:5 This will **i** all its produce,
Eze 16:29 your acts of prostitution to **i**
46:7 each ram the offering must **i**
Mat 14:21 (This number does not **i** the
15:38 (This number does not **i** the
1Ti 5:11 Don't **i** younger widows ⌊on

included (37)

Gen 23:18 His property **i** the field with the
Lev 9:13 cut in pieces and **i** the head.
Dtr 3:17 Their land **i** the plains around
4:49 It **i** all the plains on the east
Jos 12:2 This **i** the middle of the valley
12:3 It **i** the eastern plains from the
12:8 It **i** the mountains, foothills,
13:10 It **i** all the cities of King Sihon
13:11 It also **i** Gilead, the territory of
13:17 It **i** Heshbon and all its cities
13:21 It also **i** all the cities of the
13:23 It **i** cities with their villages.
13:25 Their territory **i** Jazer,
13:27 Jordan Valley it **i** Beth Haram,
13:28 It **i** cities with their villages.
13:30 from Mahanaim and **i** all
13:31 It also **i** half of Gilead with
15:46 This **i** all the cities with their
19:8 and Ramath Negev were also **i**.
19:18 Their territory **i** Jezreel,
19:25 Their territory **i** Helkath,
19:41 of their inheritance **i** Zorah,
Jdg 20:17 not **i**) totaled 400,000 soldiers
1Ch 26:8 Obed Edom's family **i** 62 men.
27:24 the report from it was never **i**
2Ch 20:34 which is **i** in the Book of the
34:11 (These workers **i** carpenters
Neh 3:11 made repairs on a section that **i**
3:18 This **i** Binnui, Henadad's son,
8:2 This **i** men, women, and any
10:28 These people **i** the priests,
Job 3:6 Let it not be **i** in the days of the
Eze 41:13 This **i** the open area with the
Mic 5:2 are too small to be **i** among
Act 1:1 This **i** everything from the
Rom 11:25 God's non-Jewish people are **i**.
Rev 20:6 and holy are those who are **i**

includes (18)

Num 31:28 This **i** people, cattle, donkeys,
31:30 This **i** people, cattle, donkeys,
34:3 "The southern side **i** part of the
Dtr 22:9 This **i** the crop you planted and
Jos 13:2 The land that is left **i** all the
13:4 This territory **i** all the land of
13:5 It also **i** the land of the people
19:15 This also **i** Kattath,
19:29 The territory **i** Meheleb,
23:4 This **i** the territory of all the
1Ch 29:30 It **i** everything about his reign,
2Ch 29:18 This **i** the altar for burnt
33:19 This **i** all his sins and
Ezr 7:13 This also **i** the priests and
Ecc 12:14 This **i** every secret thing,
Jnh 3:7 This **i** all people, animals,
Luk 11:51 This **i** the murders from Abel to
2Th 1:10 This **i** you because you

including (61)

Gen 7:21 on the earth died, **i** birds,
14:16 **i** women and soldiers.
34:26 **i** Hamor and his son Shechem.
44:16 **i** the one who had the cup."
Exo 9:3 **i** your horses, donkeys,
10:5 **i** every tree still standing in the
11:5 **i** every firstborn domestic
14:9 Pharaoh's army, **i** all his
27:19 **i** all the pegs for the tent and
Lev 6:10 **i** his linen undergarments.
Num 1:50 **i** the equipment for the tent and
15:26 **i** foreigners who are living
18:4 **i** all the maintenance work for
21:25 **i** Heshbon and all its villages,
31:11 **i** all the people and animals,
31:26 **i** the people and animals you
31:47 **i** people and animals,
Dtr 3:6 every city, **i** men, women,
13:15 everyone in it, **i** the animals,
20:14 **i** all its goods, as your loot.
33:17 to push away nations **i** those at
Jos 8:35 of Israel, **i** women, children,
13:9 **i** the city in the middle of the
13:16 **i** the city in the middle of the

Jos 20:9 i the foreigners living among
24:18 i the Amorites who lived in this
Jdg 21:10 i the women and children.
Rut 4:11 at the gate, i the leaders, said,
1Sm 6:18 i walled cities and farm
7:3 i the statues of the goddess
18:5 all the people, i Saul's officials.
25:13 And everyone, i David,
30:1 had raided the Negev, i Ziklag.
30:18 had taken, i his two wives.
2Sm 11:17 and died — i Uriah the Hittite.
1Ki 7:9 i the large courtyard,
19:1 i how he had executed all the
2Ki 8:6 i whatever her property
24:4 i the innocent blood he had
1Ch 5:19 Hagar's descendants (i Jetur,
2Ch 8:15 i the ⌊temple's⌋ finances.
32:32 i his devotion to God,
33:18 about Manasseh — i his prayer
35:26 about Josiah — i his devotion
Ezr 7:7 Some Israelites (i priests,
9:1 i the priests and Levites,
Neh 3:17 i Rehum (Bani's son),
8:13 i the priests and the Levites,
Jer 43:6 i the prophet Jeremiah and
44:24 to all the people, i the women,
Eze 16:54 have done, i comforting them.
41:14 of the temple, i the open area,
Dan 11:22 i the prince of the promise.
Luk 7:29 "All the people, i tax collectors,
23:49 All his friends, i the women
Act 1:14 i Mary (the mother of Jesus),
Rom 16:2 help to many people, i me.
2Th 2:9 i miraculous and wonderful
2Ti 1:15 i Phygelus and Hermogenes.
3Jn 1:12 Everyone, i the truth itself,
Rev 20:12 were opened, i the Book of Life.

inclusion (1)

Rom 11:12 So the i of Jewish people will

income (21)

Gen 47:22 received an i from Pharaoh,
47:22 and they lived on that i.
Num 18:21 one-tenth of every Israelite's i.
18:24 one-tenth of the Israelites' i.
18:26 the Israelites' i which I'm giving
18:26 of that i as your contribution
18:28 contribute one-tenth of your i
18:28 receive from the Israelites' i.
Dtr 12:6 one-tenth of your i,
12:11 one-tenth of your i,
14:24 carry a tenth of your i that far.
14:25 the tenth part of your i for silver.
Ezr 4:13 this will hurt the king's i.
Pro 3:9 first and best part of all your i.
15:6 trouble comes along with the i
Ecc 5:10 never be satisfied with more i.
Amo 4:4 tenth of your i every three days.
Mal 3:8 your i and other contributions.
3:10 "Bring one-tenth of your i into
Luk 18:12 I give you a tenth of my entire i.'
Act 19:25 a good i from this business,

incomplete (4)

1Co 13:9 Our knowledge is i and our
13:9 what God has revealed is i.
13:10 then what is i will no longer be
13:12 Now my knowledge is i.

incorporated (1)

2Ch 31:21 Hezekiah i Moses' Teachings

increase (42)

Gen 1:22 fertile, i in number, fill the sea,
1:28 fertile, i in number, fill the earth
3:16 He said to the woman, "I will i
8:17 Be fertile, i in number,
9:1 i in number, and fill the earth.
9:7 Be fertile, and i in number.
9:7 Spread over the earth, and i."
17:20 and i the number of his
26:24 I will bless you and i the
28:3 and i the number of your
35:11 Be fertile, and i in number.
48:4 'I will make you fertile and i the
Exo 1:10 or they'll i in number.
Lev 26:21 I will i the punishment for your
Dtr 1:10 your population i so that you
6:3 you and your population will i
7:13 and i the number of your
8:1 and your population will i.
8:13 everything else you have will i.
13:17 he will make your population i,
30:16 your population will i,
Psa 4:7 their grain and new wine i.
62:10 When riches i, do not depend
119:32 continue to i my understanding.
Pro 28:28 righteous people i.
29:2 When righteous people i,
29:16 When wicked people i,
Ecc 5:11 As the number of goods i,
Isa 9:3 the nation and i its happiness.
Jer 3:16 and your population will i in the
23:3 will be fertile and i in number.
Eze 36:10 I will i the number of people
36:11 I will i the number of people
37:26 make them i in number,
Amo 8:5 the bushel baskets, i the cost,
Jon 3:30 He must i in importance,
Rom 5:20 were added to i the failure.
6:1 so that God's kindness will i?
2Co 8:7 and your love for us i,
9:10 In your lives he will i the things
Php 4:17 looking for your resources to i.
1Th 3:12 the Lord will greatly i your love

increased (13)

Gen 6:1 The number of people i all over
7:17 The water i and lifted the ship
Exo 1:12 the more they i in number and
1:20 So the people i in number and
23:30 way until you have i enough
1Ch 4:38 of people in their households i.
Psa 3:1 look how my enemies have i!
25:19 my enemies have i in number,
Eze 16:25 You i your acts of prostitution.
16:29 So you i your acts of
Act 9:31 The number of people i as
Rom 5:20 the failure. But where sin i,
5:20 God's kindness i even more.

increases (8)

Psa 12:8 i among Adam's descendants.
49:16 the greatness of his house i.
Pro 10:31 of a righteous person i wisdom,
29:16 people increase, crime i,
Isa 5:14 is why the grave's appetite i.
40:29 to those who grow tired and i
Mar 4:24 This is the way knowledge i.
Rom 3:7 If my lie i the glory that God

increasing (4)

Job 10:17 You keep i your anger toward
2Co 3:18 into his image with ever-i glory
2Th 1:3 your love for each other is i.
2Pe 1:8 these qualities and they are i,

incurable (6)

2Ch 21:18 with an i intestinal disease.
Isa 17:11 pile on a day of grief and i pain.
Jer 15:18 pain unending and my wound i,
17:9 It is i. No one can understand
30:12 LORD says: Your wound is i.
Mic 1:9 Samaria's wounds are i.

indecent (3)

Dtr 24:1 found out something i about her
Rom 1:27 Men commit i acts with men,
1:28 So they do these i things.

indefinite (1)

Gen 13:15 for an i period of time.

independent (4)

Jdg 18:7 people of Sidon and totally i.
18:28 was far from Sidon and totally i.
2Ki 8:22 Judah's rule and is still i today.
2Ch 21:10 Judah's rule and is still i today.

India (2)

Est 1:1 127 provinces from I to Sudan.
Est 8:9 127 provinces from I to Sudan.

indicate (1)

Eze 21:22 The omens will i that he

indicated (2)

Jnh 1:7 and the dice i that Jonah was
Jon 12:33 he i how he was going to die.

indifference (1)

Pro 1:32 themselves because of their i.

indirect (1)

2Ki 3:9 and the king of Edom took an i

individual (2)

1Co 12:27 each of you is an i part of it.
Gal 1:1 ⌊chosen⌋ not by any group or i

individuals (8)

Mat 22:16 You don't favor i because of
Mar 12:14 You don't favor i because of
Act 15:24 We have heard that some i
Rom 12:5 even though we are many i,
12:5 Christ makes us one body and i
1Co 10:17 although we are many i.
11:28 With this in mind, i must
2Ti 2:2 message to faithful i who will

indoors (2)

Exo 9:19 and everything else you have i.
9:20 servants and cattle i quickly.

inexperienced (4)

1Ki 3:7 although I'm young and i,
1Ch 22:5 son Solomon is young and i,
29:1 has chosen, is young and i.
2Ch 13:7 young and i to challenge them.

infancy (1)

2Ti 3:15 From i you have known the

infant (2)

Isa 65:20 There will no longer be an i
Luk 2:12 You will find an i wrapped in

infantry (1)

Jer 46:6 "The i can't flee. The warriors

infantrymen (2)

Act 23:23 and told them, "I want 200 i,
23:31 So the i did as they had been

infants (13)

1Sm 15:3 and women, i and children,
22:19 children and i, cows, donkeys,
2Ch 20:13 from Judah, their i, wives,
Job 3:16 I would be like i who never
Psa 8:2 mouths of little children and i,
Isa 11:8 I will play near cobras' holes.
Lam 2:11 Little children and i faint in the
4:4 The tongues of nursing i stick
Joe 2:16 even the nursing i.
Mat 21:16 mouths of little children and i,
Luk 18:15 Some people brought i to
18:16 But Jesus called the i to him
1Co 3:1 You were i in your faith in

infected (2)

2Ki 5:11 his hand over the ⌊i⌋ place,
Isa 1:5 Your whole head is i.

infectious (12)

Lev 13:2 turns into an i skin disease,
13:3 it is an i skin disease.
13:8 It is an i skin disease.
13:9 anyone has an i skin disease,
13:15 It is an i skin disease.
13:20 An i skin disease has
13:25 an i skin disease has
13:25 It is an i skin disease.
13:27 It is an i skin disease.
13:44 down with an i skin disease.
14:32 one who has an i skin disease
Num 12:10 covered with an i skin disease.

infects (1)
Lev 14:55 that **i** clothing or houses

inferior (5)
Job 12:3 I am not **i** to you. But who
13:2 as you do. I am not **i** to you.
Dan 2:39 Another kingdom, **i** to yours,
2Co 11:5 I don't think I'm **i** in any way to
12:11 Even if I'm nothing, I wasn't **i** in

infested (2)
Psa 105:31 and gnats **i** their whole territory
Hag 2:17 I **i** all your work with blight and

inflammation (1)
Dtr 28:22 and **i**; heat waves, drought,

inflict (1)
Jdg 20:31 They started to **i** casualties as

inflicted (5)
2Sm 7:14 rod and with blows **i** by people.
2Ki 15:5 The LORD **i** the king with a
2Ch 26:20 the LORD had **i** him ⌊with
Isa 30:26 and heal the wounds he **i**.
58:3 Why have we **i** pain on

inflicts (1)
Job 16:14 He **i** wound after wound on me.

influence (5)
Pro 20:1 under their **i** is unwise.
Rom 3:19 to everyone under their **i**,
6:2 can we still live under sin's **i**?
7:5 we were living under the **i**
Col 2:20 were still under the world's **i**.

influenced (6)
Dtr 13:8 Don't be **i** by any of these
1Co 3:1 as people still **i** by your corrupt
3:3 because you're still **i** by your
3:3 aren't you **i** by your corrupt
Gal 5:7 you from being **i** by the truth?
Eph 4:14 We will no longer be **i** by

influences (1)
Isa 2:6 they are filled with Eastern **i**.

influencing (1)
Gal 5:8 the person who is **i** you do not

influential (18)
Job 1:3 He was the most **i** person in
12:21 He pours contempt on **i** people
21:28 is the house of the **i** person?
Psa 47:9 The **i** people from the nations
76:12 cuts short the lives of **i** people.
83:11 Treat their **i** people as you
107:40 He poured contempt on their **i**
113:8 He seats them with **i** people,
113:8 with the **i** leaders of his people.
118:9 the LORD than to trust **i** people.
119:23 Even though **i** people plot
119:161 **I** people have persecuted me
146:3 Do not trust **i** people,
Ecc 10:7 on horses and **i** people going
Lam 1:6 Its **i** people were like deer that
2:9 Its king and **i** people are
Act 28:17 Paul invited the most **i** Jews
28:23 of **i** Jews ⌊than expected⌋

inform (6)
Rut 4:4 So I said that I would **i** you.
1Sm 22:17 was fleeing, they didn't **i** me.
Ezr 4:14 are sending this letter to **i** you
Est 4:8 to show it to Esther to **i**
Jer 51:31 They **i** the king of Babylon that
Mat 16:21 began to **i** his disciples that

information (12)
Dtr 1:22 ahead of us to gather **i** about
Jos 2:2 to gather **i** about our land."
2:3 They came here to gather **i**
1Ch 10:13 He asked a medium to request **i**
10:14 He didn't request **i** from the
Ezr 5:10 For your **i**, we also asked them
Luk 1:2 They received their **i** from
Act 23:15 that you need more **i** from Paul.
23:15 get more accurate **i** about him.
23:20 more accurate **i** about him.
23:22 not to tell this **i** to anyone else.
25:15 brought me some **i** about him

informed (14)
1Sm 22:8 and no one **i** me when my son
22:8 No one felt sorry for me and **i**
1Ki 20:17 They **i** him that some men had
Est 2:22 out about it and **i** Queen Esther.
3:4 So they **i** Haman to see if
3:6 had **i** him about Mordecai's
4:4 and **i** her ⌊about Mordecai⌋.
4:7 Mordecai **i** him about
6:2 Mordecai had **i** him that Bigthan
Isa 40:14 Who **i** him about the way to
Dan 9:22 He **i** me, "Daniel, this time I
Act 23:30 Since I was **i** that there was a
25:2 leaders **i** Festus about their
1Co 10:28 it because of the one who **i** you

infrequent (1)
1Sm 3:1 LORD was rare; visions were **i**.

infuriated (2)
Est 3:5 and bow to him, Haman was **i**.
Psa 106:29 They **i** God by what they did,

ingredients (1)
1Ch 23:29 responsible for mixing the **i**

inhabitants (34)
Jos 8:24 had finished killing all the **i**
8:26 destroyed all the **i** of Ai.
2Ch 21:11 This caused the **i** of Jerusalem
21:13 have caused Judah and the **i** of
33:9 misled Judah and the **i**
34:9 and from the **i** of Jerusalem.
35:18 and the **i** of Jerusalem.
Ezr 4:6 an accusation against the **i**
4:19 Its **i** are guilty of treason and
Neh 10:28 themselves from the **i**
10:30 our daughters to marry the **i**
10:31 If the **i** of the land bring
Isa 5:3 you **i** of Jerusalem and Judah,
18:3 all you **i** of the world who live
21:14 you **i** of the land of Tema.
23:2 silent, you **i** of the coastland,
23:6 you **i** of the seacoast!
33:24 sins of its **i** will be forgiven.
Jer 4:4 of Judah and **i** of Jerusalem.
46:19 Pack your bags, **i** of Egypt,
49:8 Hide in deep caves, **i** of Dedan.
49:30 Find a place to hide, **i** of Hazor,
Lam 4:21 **i** of the country of Uz.
Eze 7:7 is coming to you, **i** of the land.
Joe 1:2 your ears, all **i** of this land!
Mic 1:11 and ashamed, **i** of Shaphir.
1:11 Don't come out, **i** of Zaanan.
1:12 anxiously for good, **i** of Maroth.
1:13 to the chariots, **i** of Lachish.
1:15 against the **i** of Mareshah.
Hab 2:8 to lands, cities, and all their **i**.
2:17 to lands, cities, and all their **i**.
Zep 1:11 "Howl, **i** of the Mortar,
Zec 2:7 Escape, you **i** of Babylon!

inhabited (13)
Job 37:12 over the face of the **i** earth
Psa 107:4 road without finding an **i** city.
107:7 that went straight to an **i** city.
Pro 8:31 found joy in his **i** world,
Isa 13:20 It will never be **i** again,
44:26 about Jerusalem, "It will be **i**."
45:18 be empty but formed it to be **i**.
Jer 50:39 It will no longer be **i** or lived in
Eze 34:13 and in all the **i** places of the
36:10 The cities will be **i**,
Zec 2:4 'Jerusalem will be **i** like an
7:7 its surrounding cities were **i**
7:7 and the foothills were still **i**?'"

inherit (36)
Gen 15:2 Damascus will **i** my household.
31:14 father's household for us to **i**?
48:6 They will **i** the land listed
Jos 19:49 the land they were to **i**,
1Sm 2:8 and even to make them **i**
2Ki 2:9 Elisha answered, "Let me **i** a
Psa 25:13 his descendants will **i** the land.
37:9 for the LORD will **i** the land.
37:11 Oppressed people will **i** the
37:22 blessed by him will **i** the land.
37:29 Righteous people will **i** the
69:36 of his servants will **i** it.
Pro 3:35 Wise people will **i** honor,
28:10 people will **i** good things.
Isa 49:8 them **i** the desolate inheritance.
57:13 land and **i** my holy mountain.
65:9 one who will **i** my mountains
65:9 My chosen ones will **i** them.
Eze 45:1 lots for the property you will **i**.
46:17 his sons can **i** his property.
Mat 5:5 They will **i** the earth.
19:29 more and will **i** eternal life.
25:34 **I** the kingdom prepared for you
Mar 10:17 should I do to **i** eternal life?"
Luk 10:25 what must I do to **i** eternal life?"
18:18 what must I do to **i** eternal life?"
Rom 4:13 that he would **i** the world.
1Co 6:9 that wicked people won't **i**
6:10 or who rob people will not **i** the
15:50 Flesh and blood cannot **i** the
15:50 cannot **i** what doesn't decay.
Gal 5:21 do things like that will not **i**
Eph 1:18 wealth that God's people will **i**.
Col 1:12 which is what God's people **i**.
1Pe 3:9 you were called to **i** a blessing.
Rev 21:7 the victory will **i** these things.

inheritance (131)
Gen 21:10 son must never share the **i**
25:32 "What good is my **i** to me?"
Num 34:2 as your **i** has these borders:
Dtr 18:2 The LORD will be their **i**,
21:16 father to give his sons their **i**,
Jos 13:6 must distribute the land as an **i**
13:7 It will be an **i** for the nine tribes
13:8 had received their **i** east
13:14 did not give any land as an **i**
13:15 Moses gave some land as an **i**
13:23 This was Reuben's **i** for its
13:24 Moses gave some land as an **i**
13:28 This was Gad's **i** for its
13:29 Moses gave some land as an **i**
13:31 son of Manasseh, ⌊for their **i**⌋.
13:33 did not give any land as an **i**
14:3 two-and-a-half tribes their **i** east
14:3 He did not give any land as an **i**
14:9 on will be a permanent **i**
14:13 and gave him Hebron as his **i**.
14:14 Hebron is still the **i** of Caleb,
16:4 received this land as their **i**.
16:8 This is the land given as an **i**
17:4 land as an **i** among our male
17:4 So they gave them an **i** among
17:6 were given an **i** along
17:14 us only one region for an **i**?
18:2 yet received any land as their **i**.
18:4 shows ⌊the borders of⌋ their **i**.
18:7 because their **i** is to serve the
18:7 have received the **i** that
18:20 borders surrounding the **i** given
18:28 is Benjamin's **i** for its families.
19:1 Their **i** was within Judah.
19:2 In their **i** they received 13 cities
19:8 This is the **i** of the tribe of
19:9 Simeon's **i** was a part of
19:9 its **i** inside Judah's borders.
19:10 The border of their **i** goes as far
19:16 their villages are the **i** given
19:23 with their villages are the **i**
19:31 with their villages are the **i**
19:39 with their villages are the **i**
19:41 of their **i** included Zorah,
19:48 with their villages are the **i**
19:49 their territory as an **i** to Joshua,

Jos 21:3 from the Israelites' **i**.
22:7 given land in Bashan as an **i**
23:4 nations that still remain as an **i**
Jdg 11:2 "You'll get no **i** from our father.
18:1 received land as an **i** among
Rut 4:5 This keeps the **i** in the dead
4:6 If I did, I would ruin my **i**.
4:10 to keep the **i** in the dead man's
1Sm 26:19 having a share of the LORD's **i**.
2Sm 14:16 my son from ⌞our⌟ God-given **i**.'
20:1 We won't receive an **i** from
1Ki 8:36 gave to your people as an **i**.
12:16 We won't receive an **i** from
1Ch 16:18 It is your share of the **i**.'
28:8 it as an **i** to your descendants.
2Ch 6:27 gave to your people as an **i**.
10:16 We won't receive an **i** from
Ezr 9:12 a long-lasting **i** to your children.'
Job 20:29 the **i** God has appointed for
27:13 the **i** that tyrants receive from
31:2 What would be my **i** from the
42:15 them and their brothers an **i**.
Psa 2:8 give you the nations as your **i**
16:5 The LORD is my **i** and my cup.
16:6 my **i** is something beautiful.
17:14 from mortals who enjoy their **i**
37:9 will be cut off ⌞from their **i**⌟.
37:18 Their **i** will last forever.
47:4 He chooses our **i** for us,
61:5 You have given me the **i** that
73:26 of my life and my **i** forever.
78:55 land of the nations as their **i**.
105:11 It is your share of the **i**."
111:6 lands of other nations as an **i**.
119:57 You are my **i**, O LORD.
127:3 Children are an **i** from the
135:12 He gave their land as an **i**,
135:12 an **i** to his people Israel.
136:21 He gave their land as an **i** —
136:22 as an **i** for his servant Israel —
142:5 my own **i** in this world of the
Pro 8:21 to give an **i** to those who love
13:22 Good people leave an **i** to their
17:2 share the **i** with the brothers.
20:21 An **i** quickly obtained in the
Ecc 7:11 Wisdom is as good as an **i**.
Isa 49:8 them inherit the desolate **i**.
54:17 This is the **i** of the LORD's
58:14 I will feed you with the **i** of your
Jer 12:14 neighbors who take the **i** that
12:15 I will return them to their **i** and
17:4 You will lose the **i** that I gave
49:1 the god Milcom taken over the **i**
49:2 will take possession of its **i**,
Eze 36:12 and you will be their **i**.
44:28 "The priests will have no **i**.
44:28 I am their **i**. Don't give them any
46:16 because it is their **i**.
46:18 give his own property as an **i**
47:14 So this land will be your **i**.
47:22 lots with you for their **i** among
47:23 will receive their share of the **i**
48:29 you will divide as your **i** among
Dan 12:13 and you will rise for your **i** at
Mic 2:2 and his family, a man and his **i**.
Zec 8:12 people all these things as an **i**.
Mal 1:3 into a wasteland and left his **i**
Mat 21:38 Let's kill him and get his **i**.'
Mar 12:7 and the **i** will be ours.'
Luk 12:13 my share of the **i** that our father
12:14 judge or to divide ⌞your **i**⌟?"
20:14 him so that the **i** will be ours.'
Act 13:19 their land to his people as an **i**.
20:32 give you the **i** that is shared
Gal 3:18 If we have to gain the **i** by
3:18 However, God freely gave the **i**
4:30 woman must never share the **i**
Eph 1:14 that we will receive our **i**.
3:6 the same **i** as Jewish people
5:5 wealth) can have any **i**
Col 3:24 give you an **i** as your reward.
Heb 9:15 be guaranteed an **i** that will last
11:8 that he would receive as an **i**.
1Pe 1:4 life which has an **i** that can't
1:4 That **i** is kept in heaven for you,

inherited (19)

Num 36:7 tribal land **i** from his ancestors.
36:8 the land **i** from his ancestors.
Jos 13:14 of Israel are what the Levites **i**,
13:33 God of Israel is what they **i**,
14:1 the people of Israel **i** in Canaan.
14:2 The land **i** by the
15:20 This is the land **i** by the
16:5 of the land they **i** is from Ataroth
24:32 **i** by Joseph's descendants.
Jdg 2:6 of the territory they had **i**.
2:9 within the territory he had **i**.
1Ki 21:3 what I **i** from my ancestors."
21:4 "I will not give you what I **i**
Neh 11:20 Everyone lived on his own **i**
Job 7:3 and I have **i** nights filled with
Psa 105:44 and they **i** what others had
Pro 19:14 and wealth are **i** from fathers,
Jer 16:19 "Our ancestors have **i** lies,
Lam 5:2 "The land we **i** has been turned

inherits (3)

Num 36:8 A woman who **i** land in any of
36:9 tribe must keep the land it **i**."
Pro 11:29 upon his family **i** ⌞only⌟ wind,

initial (1)

2Sm 17:9 are killed in the **i** attack,

injure (1)

Exo 21:22 do whenever men fight and **i**

injured (14)

Exo 21:19 If the **i** man can get up again
21:19 He must pay the **i** man for the
21:23 If anyone is **i**, the offender must
22:10 dies, is **i**, or is captured in war,
22:14 and it is **i** or dies while the
2Ki 1:2 room in Samaria and **i** himself.
Ecc 10:9 Whoever splits wood may be **i**.
Eze 34:4 or bandaged those that were **i**.
34:16 bandage those that are **i**,
Mic 4:6 and those whom I have **i**.
Zec 12:3 try to lift it will be severely **i**.
Mat 18:8 to enter life disabled or **i** than
Luk 20:12 But they **i** this one and threw
Heb 12:13 so that your **i** leg won't get

injures (4)

Exo 21:18 or with his fist and **i** him so that
Lev 24:19 Whoever **i** a neighbor must
24:20 Whoever **i** another person must
Job 5:18 God **i**, but he bandages.

injuries (2)

Exo 21:22 If there are no other **i**,
Isa 30:26 will bandage his people's **i**

injury (5)

Lev 24:19 receive the same **i** in return —
24:20 receive the same **i** in return.
2Ki 1:2 if I will recover from this **i**."
Jer 30:12 Your **i** is beyond healing.
30:15 your **i** that can't be cured?

injustice (11)

Job 6:29 Don't permit any **i**. Change your
6:30 Is there **i** on my tongue,
11:14 and don't let **i** live in your tent.
Psa 7:3 if my hands are stained with **i**,
7:11 who is angered by **i** every day.
Pro 13:11 through **i** dwindles away,
16:8 than many gained through **i**.
22:8 Whoever plants **i** will harvest
Jer 22:13 and his upper rooms through **i**.
Amo 5:10 who speaks out against **i**.
1Co 13:6 It isn't happy when **i** is done,

ink (2)

Jer 36:18 and I wrote it on the scroll in **i**."
2Co 3:3 are a letter written not with **i**

inlaid (1)

Sos 3:10 Its inside — with **i** scenes of

in-law (1)

2Ch 18:1 and became Ahab's **i**.

in-laws (1)

Gen 19:12 have anyone else here — any **i**,

inlets (1)

Jdg 5:17 and remained along the **i**.

inn (2)

Luk 2:7 any room for them in the **i**.
10:34 brought him to an **i**,

inner (95)

Exo 26:1 "Make the **i** tent with ten
26:7 an outer tent over the **i** tent.
26:11 to link the **i** tent together as
26:12 hang over the back of the **i** tent.
26:13 side in order to cover the **i** tent.
26:15 of acacia wood for the **i** tent.
26:17 Make all the frames for the **i**
26:18 for the south side of the **i** tent.
26:20 For the north side of the **i** tent
26:23 at the far end of the **i** tent.
26:26 frames on one side of the **i** tent,
26:27 on the far end of the **i** tent,
26:30 "Set up the **i** tent according to
26:35 on the north side of the **i** tent,
28:39 "Make the specially woven **i**
35:11 the **i** tent, the outer tent,
36:8 the workers made the **i** tent
36:13 together so that the **i** tent was
36:14 an outer tent over the **i** tent.
36:18 to link the **i** tent together as
36:20 of acacia wood for the **i** tent.
36:22 frames for the **i** tent this same
36:23 for the south side of the **i** tent.
36:25 For the north side of the **i** tent
36:28 at the far end of the **i** tent.
36:31 frames on one side of the **i** tent,
36:32 on the far side of the **i** tent,
39:27 They wove **i** robes out of fine
39:32 So all the work on the **i** tent
39:33 to Moses — the **i** tent,
39:40 the service of the **i** tent (the tent
40:19 the outer tent over the **i** tent
Num 3:7 needs to be done for the **i** tent.
3:8 needs to be done for the **i** tent.
3:25 were in charge of the **i** tent,
3:26 that surrounds the **i** tent
3:36 of the framework of the **i** tent,
4:25 sheets that are part of the **i** tent
4:25 They will also carry the **i** cover
4:31 the framework for the **i** tent,
1Ki 6:5 building and the **i** sanctuary.
6:16 He built it to serve as an **i** room,
6:19 He prepared the **i** room of the
6:20 The **i** room was 30 feet long,
6:21 front of the **i** room which was
6:22 altar in the **i** room with gold.
6:23 In the **i** room he made two
6:27 Solomon put the angels in the **i**
6:29 into the walls all around the **i**
6:30 He covered the floor of the **i**
6:31 the entrance to the **i** room out
6:36 He built the **i** courtyard with
7:9 saws on their **i** and outer faces.
7:12 like the **i** courtyard of the
7:49 the north in front of the **i** room),
7:50 doors of the **i** ⌞room⌟ (the most
8:6 to its place in the **i** room
8:8 standing in front of the **i** room,
20:30 to the city and hid in an **i** room.
22:25 you go into an **i** room to hide."
2Ki 9:2 Take him into an **i** room.
1Ch 28:11 upper rooms, **i** rooms,
2Ch 3:16 He made chains for the **i** room
4:20 directed in front of the **i** room),
4:22 the gold doors of the **i** ⌞room⌟
5:7 to its place in the **i** room
5:9 standing in front of the **i** room,
18:24 you go into an **i** room to hide."
Psa 139:13 You alone created my **i** being.
Jer 23:18 Who is in the LORD's **i** circle
23:22 If they had been in my **i** circle,

Eze 8:3 the north gate of the **i** courtyard
8:16 Then he brought me into the **i**
10:3 A cloud filled the **i** courtyard.
40:15 part to the front of the **i** part
40:19 to the outside of the **i** courtyard.
40:23 The **i** courtyard had a gateway
40:27 The **i** courtyard had a gateway
40:28 me to the **i** courtyard through
40:30 halls all around the **i** courtyard.
40:32 the east side of the **i** courtyard.
40:44 Outside the gateways to the **i**
40:44 the singers in the **i** courtyards.
42:3 Opposite the **i** courtyard was
42:15 finished measuring the **i** part
43:5 brought me into the **i** courtyard.
44:17 the gateways to the **i** courtyard,
44:17 the gateways to the **i** courtyard
44:21 when they enter the **i** courtyard.
44:27 When he enters the **i** courtyard
45:19 the gateways of the **i** courtyard.
46:1 The east gate of the **i** courtyard
Rom 7:22 God's standards in my **i** being.
Eph 3:16 I pray that he would give you **i**
Heb 13:9 Gaining **i** strength from God's

innermost (6)

Psa 5:1 Consider my **i** thoughts.
Pro 18:8 go down into a person's **i** being.
20:27 It searches his entire **i** being.
20:30 Such beatings cleanse the **i**
26:22 go down into a person's **i** being.
Dan 2:30 would know your **i** thoughts.

innkeeper (2)

Luk 10:35 coins and gave them to the **i**.
10:35 He told the **i**, 'Take care of him.

innocence (3)

Gen 20:5 I did this in all **i** and with a
Psa 17:2 Let the verdict of my **i** come
26:6 I will wash my hands in **i**.

innocent (94)

Gen 18:23 away the **i** with the guilty?
18:24 What if there are 50 **i** people in
18:24 sake of the 50 **i** people who are
18:25 to treat the **i** and the guilty alike
18:25 the guilty alike and to kill the **i**
18:26 The LORD said, "If I find 50 **i**
18:28 what if there are 45 **i** people?
20:4 destroy a nation even if it's **i**?
44:16 How can we prove we're **i**?
Exo 23:7 Don't kill **i** or honest people,
23:7 never declare guilty people **i**.
Num 23:10 me die the death of **i** people.
35:24 in order to decide if you ⌊are **i**⌋
35:25 ⌊If you are **i**,⌋ the community
Dtr 19:10 That way, **i** people won't be
19:13 The guilt of murdering an **i**
27:25 money to kill an **i** person will
1Sm 19:5 sin by shedding David's **i** blood
25:26 kept you from spilling **i** blood
2Sm 3:28 my kingdom and I are forever **i**
4:11 wicked men who kill an **i** man
14:9 Majesty and your throne are **i**."
22:24 I was **i** as far as he was
22:26 with **i** warriors you are
22:26 innocent warriors you are **i**,
1Ki 2:31 You can remove the **i** blood —
8:32 declare the **i** person innocent.
8:32 declare the innocent person **i**.
2Ki 10:9 He told the people, "You are **i**.
21:16 Manasseh also killed a lot of **i**
24:4 including the **i** blood he had
24:4 He had a lot of **i** people in
2Ch 6:23 declare the **i** person innocent.
6:23 declare the innocent person **i**.
Job 4:7 "Now think about this: Which **i**
9:23 he makes fun of the despair of **i**
9:28 that you won't declare me **i**.
11:4 and, 'As you can see, I'm **i**.'
17:8 the **i** against godless people.
22:19 and the **i** made fun of them by
22:30 He will rescue one who is not **i**.
27:17 and the **i** will divide the silver
Psa 10:8 hiding places he kills **i** people.
Psa 15:5 a bribe against an **i** person.
17:15 your face when I am declared **i**.
18:23 I was **i** as far as he was
18:25 with **i** people you are innocent,
18:25 with innocent people you are **i**,
35:27 I am declared **i** joyfully sing
37:18 daily ⌊struggles⌋ of **i** people.
37:37 Notice the **i** person,
64:4 to shoot at **i** people from their
69:27 Do not let them be found **i**.
94:21 condemn **i** people to death.
106:38 They shed **i** blood,
Pro 1:11 hide to ambush **i** people for fun.
6:17 hands that kill **i** people,
10:29 is a fortress for an **i** person
11:5 The righteousness of **i** people
11:20 with those whose ways are **i**.
17:26 To punish an **i** person is not
18:5 depriving an **i** person of justice.
24:24 "You are **i**," will be cursed by
28:10 but **i** people will inherit good
29:10 people hate an **i** person,
Isa 5:23 who declare the guilty **i** for a
50:8 who pronounces me **i** is near.
59:7 They hurry to shed **i** blood.
Jer 2:34 blood from poor and **i** people
2:35 spite of all this you say, 'I'm **i**.
19:4 with the blood of **i** people.
22:3 Don't kill **i** people in this place.
22:17 You kill **i** people and violently
26:15 be guilty of killing an **i** person.
Eze 16:51 you make your sisters look **i**.
16:52 They look like they are **i**
16:52 your sisters look like they are **i**.
Dan 6:22 because he considered me **i**.
Joe 3:19 They murdered **i** people in their
Jnh 1:14 for the death of an **i** man,
Mat 10:16 as snakes but as **i** as doves.
12:5 day of worship yet remain **i**?
12:7 not have condemned **i** people.
12:37 words you will be declared **i**,
23:35 accountable for all the **i** blood
27:4 sinned by betraying an **i** man."
27:19 It said, "Leave that **i** man alone.
Luk 23:47 "Certainly, this man was **i**!"
Act 3:14 the man who was holy and **i**.
18:6 I'm **i**. From now on I'm going to
2Co 7:11 people who are **i** in this matter.
Php 2:15 you will be blameless and **i**.
Heb 7:26 **i**, pure, set apart from sinners,
1Pe 3:18 He was an **i** person,

innocently (3)

2Sm 15:11 They went **i**, knowing nothing
Psa 84:11 blessing from those who live **i**.
Pro 19:1 a poor person who lives **i** than

insane (6)

1Sm 21:13 and acted **i** ⌊as long as
21:14 Don't you see ⌊that he's⌋ **i**?
21:15 that he can show me he is **i**?
Jer 25:16 they will stagger and go **i**
51:7 is why the nations have gone **i**.
2Co 11:23 It's **i** to say it, but I'm a far better

insanity (1)

2Pe 2:16 the prophet to continue his **i**.

inscribe (1)

Isa 30:8 and **i** it in a book so that it will

inscribed (6)

Exo 31:18 stone tablets **i** by God himself.
32:16 God's writing **i** on the tablets.
Dtr 9:10 stone tablets **i** by God himself.
Job 19:23 I wish they were **i** on a scroll.
Dan 10:21 I will tell you what is **i**
2Co 3:7 brought death was **i** on stone.

inscription (2)

Dan 5:24 he sent the hand to write this **i**.
Zec 3:9 I am engraving an **i** on it,"

insect (3)

Lev 11:20 "Every swarming, winged **i**
11:23 Every kind of winged **i** that
Dtr 14:19 Every swarming, winged **i** is

insects (2)

Lev 11:21 However, you may eat winged **i**
Mal 3:11 Then, for your sake, I will stop **i**

insensitive (1)

Psa 119:70 Their hearts are cold and **i**,

inseparable (1)

Job 41:17 They are locked together and **i**.

inserted (1)

Exo 40:18 up the frames, **i** the crossbars,

insides (2)

Job 30:27 My **i** are churning and won't
Psa 38:7 My **i** are filled with burning

insight (32)

Dtr 4:6 of the world your wisdom and **i**.
1Ki 4:29 gave Solomon wisdom — keen **i**
1Ch 22:12 The LORD will give you **i** and
26:14 a counselor who displayed **i**,
27:32 man who possessed **i**,
2Ch 2:12 David a wise son who has **i**
Job 12:12 who has had many days has **i**.
12:13 Advice and **i** are his.
26:12 With his **i** he killed Rahab ⌊the
34:35 His words show no **i**.'
38:4 Tell me if you have ⌊such⌋ **i**.
Psa 119:99 I have more **i** than all my
Pro 1:4 to give **i** to gullible people,
2:3 if indeed you call out for **i**,
5:2 with foresight and speak with **i**.
8:12 "I, Wisdom, live with **i**,
12:8 will be praised based on his **i**,
Jer 3:15 feed you with knowledge and **i**.
Dan 1:20 that required wisdom and **i**,
2:21 to those who have **i**.
5:11 he was found to have **i**,
5:14 of the gods and that you have **i**,
9:22 time I have come to give you **i**.
10:1 was given **i** during the vision.
Hos 14:9 A person with **i** will recognize
1Co 4:10 but you have **i** because of
Eph 1:8 us every kind of wisdom and **i**
1:18 Then you will have deeper **i**.
Php 1:9 of your knowledge and **i**.
Col 1:9 kind of spiritual wisdom and **i**.
Jas 3:13 any of you have wisdom and **i**?
Rev 13:18 Let the person who has **i** figure

insightful (1)

Dtr 4:6 "What wise and **i** people there

insights (1)

Psa 49:3 the **i** I have carefully

insignificant (6)

1Sm 2:30 me will be considered **i**.
9:21 My family is the most **i** of all
Job 40:4 "I'm so **i**. How can I answer
Rom 8:18 present sufferings **i** compared
1Co 6:2 aren't you capable of judging **i**
Rev 19:18 both important or **i** people."

insincere (1)

Php 1:17 But the others are **i**.

insist (12)

Exo 5:8 but **i** that they make the same
1Ch 21:24 King David told Ornan, "I **i**
Job 7:20 do to you since you **i**
Pro 24:21 who always **i** upon change,
Luk 6:30 don't **i** on getting it back.
Gal 2:14 So how can you **i** that people
5:3 Again, I **i** that everyone who
Php 3:2 of those who **i** on circumcision.
1Ti 4:11 **I** on these things and teach
5:7 **I** on these things so that
6:14 I **i** that, until our Lord Jesus
Tit 3:8 I want you to **i** on these things

insisted (9)

Gen 19:3 But he **i** so strongly that they

Gen 33:11 Esau took it because Jacob **i**.
1Ch 15:2 Then David **i** that only the
Luk 22:59 an hour later another person **i**,
Act 11:2 the believers who **i** on
12:15 But she **i** that Peter was at the
16:15 my home." She **i**. So we did.
Gal 2:12 He was afraid of those who **i**
1Th 2:11 encouraged you. Yet, we **i** that

inspect (2)

Job 5:24 You will **i** your house and find
7:18 ⌊What is he⌋ that you should **i**

inspected (1)

Exo 39:43 Moses **i** all the work and saw

inspection (1)

Neh 3:31 merchants across from **i** Gate

inspired (7)

2Ch 36:22 The LORD **i** the king to make
Ezr 1:1 The LORD **i** the king to make
1:5 God had **i** — came forward
Neh 2:12 anyone what my God had **i** me
Psa 36:1 There is an **i** truth about the
Hag 1:14 The LORD **i** them ⌊to rebuild
2Ti 3:16 Scripture passage is **i** by God.

inspires (1)

Job 35:10 who **i** songs in the night,

installation (1)

Exo 29:33 LORD at their ordination and **i**.

installed (1)

Psa 2:6 "I have **i** my own king on Zion,

instance (2)

Ecc 2:12 For **i**, what can the man who
Luk 12:58 For **i**, when an opponent brings

instant (5)

Num 16:21 and I'll destroy them in an **i**."
16:45 let me destroy them in an **i**!"
Jer 4:20 Their curtains are torn in an **i**.
Luk 4:5 kingdoms of the world in an **i**.
1Co 15:52 It will happen in an **i**,

instinct (3)

Pro 30:27 them divide into swarms by **i**.
2Pe 2:12 which are creatures of **i** that are
Jud 1:10 which are creatures of **i**,

instruct (13)

Exo 18:20 You must **i** them in the laws
Dtr 4:36 heaven so that he could **i** you.
24:8 as the Levitical priests **i** you.
Psa 32:8 LORD says,⌋ "I will **i** you.
94:12 and **i** from your teachings.
Rom 15:14 you are able to **i** each other.
1Co 4:14 ashamed but to **i** you as my
11:17 I have no praise for you as I **i**
Col 1:28 message about Christ as we **i**
3:16 and **i** yourselves about ⌊God's⌋
1Th 5:12 work among you and **i** you.
5:14 to **i** those who are not living
2Th 3:15 but **i** them like brothers and

instructed (19)

Exo 16:28 commanded and **i** you to do?
Jos 19:50 as the LORD had **i** them to do.
21:3 So, as the LORD had **i**,
22:9 had **i** them through Moses.
1Ki 2:1 he **i** his son Solomon,
12:12 as the king had **i** them.
2Ki 5:14 as the man of God had **i** him.
12:2 as long as the priest Jehoiada **i**
1Ch 15:22 Chenaniah, a Levite leader, **i**
2Ch 10:12 as the king had **i** them.
30:16 as **i** by Moses' Teachings.
35:3 He told the Levites, who **i** all
35:6 as the LORD **i** ⌊us⌋ through
Job 4:3 you have **i** many people:
Pro 21:11 and when a wise person is **i**,
Isa 40:13 of the LORD or **i** him as his
Mar 6:8 He **i** them to take nothing along

Act 18:25 He had been **i** in the Lord's way
20:31 Remember that I **i** each of you

instruction (8)

Exo 24:12 have written for the people's **i**."
Job 22:22 Accept **i** from his mouth,
Pro 19:27 If you stop listening to **i**,
31:26 on her tongue there is tender **i**.
Isa 29:24 who complain will accept **i**.
Lam 2:9 There is no longer any **i** ⌊from
Mal 2:7 will seek **i** from his mouth.
Eph 6:4 up in Christian discipline and **i**.

instructions (125)

Gen 26:5 laws, and **i** I gave him."
49:29 Then he gave them these **i**,
49:33 Jacob finished giving these **i**
Exo 12:24 "You must follow these **i**.
12:49 The same **i** apply to
16:4 or not they will follow my **i**.
18:16 I tell them God's laws and **i**."
36:6 So Moses gave **i** to have the
39:1 the LORD's **i** to Moses.
39:5 the LORD's **i** to Moses.
39:7 the LORD's **i** to Moses.
39:21 the LORD's **i** to Moses.
39:26 the LORD's **i** to Moses.
39:29 the LORD's **i** to Moses.
39:31 the LORD's **i** to Moses.
39:32 all the LORD's **i** to Moses.
39:42 the LORD's **i** to Moses.
39:43 they had followed the LORD's **i**.
40:19 Moses followed the LORD's **i**.
40:21 Moses followed the LORD's **i**.
40:23 following the LORD's **i**.
40:25 following the LORD's **i**.
40:27 following the LORD's **i**.
40:29 Moses followed the LORD's **i**.
40:32 Moses followed the LORD's **i**.
Lev 6:9 These are the **i** for the burnt
6:14 "These are the **i** for the grain
6:25 These are the **i** for the offering
7:1 "These are the **i** for the guilt
7:7 "The same **i** apply to the
7:11 "These are the **i** for the
7:37 These are the **i** for the burnt
11:46 "These are the **i** about animals,
11:47 These **i** help you distinguish
12:7 "These are the **i** for the woman
13:59 "These are the **i** for deciding
14:2 "These are the **i** for making a
14:32 These are the **i** for one who
14:54 "These are the **i** for any kind of
14:57 These **i** for skin diseases and
15:32 "These are the **i** for any man
18:30 So you must follow my **i**.
26:46 These are the laws, rules, and **i**
Num 5:29 "These are the **i** for how to deal
5:30 do everything these **i** tell him
6:13 "These are the **i** for Nazirites
6:21 "These are the **i** for those who
6:21 the requirements of these **i**
8:24 "These are the **i** for the Levites:
15:16 The **i** and rules are the same
15:29 You must give the same **i** to
19:14 "These are your **i** for when a
27:19 give him his **i** in their presence.
27:23 Joshua and gave him his **i** as
34:2 "Give the Israelites these **i**.
Dtr 1:16 Also at that time I gave these **i**
2:4 Give the people these **i**:
3:28 Give **i** to Joshua. Encourage
12:28 Be sure you obey all these **i** I'm
17:10 Follow all their **i** carefully.
31:14 and I will give him his **i**."
33:3 at your feet to receive your **i**.
1Sm 15:11 me and did not carry out my **i**."
15:13 I carried out the LORD's **i**."
15:22 To follow **i** is better than to
15:24 the LORD's command or your **i**.
2Sm 17:23 He gave **i** to his family.
1Ki 2:3 and written **i** as they are
18:36 done all these things by your **i**.
2Ki 11:12 the crown and the religious **i**,
20:1 Give final **i** to your household,
22:3 the LORD's temple with these **i**:

2Ki 23:3 and obey his commands, **i**,
1Ch 15:15 according to the LORD's **i**.
23:27 David's last **i** were to count the
2Ch 13:11 We're following the **i** the LORD
23:11 the crown and the religious **i**,
30:5 the written **i** said they should.
30:18 but not in the way the written **i**
34:31 and obey his commands, **i**,
Ezr 3:10 the LORD according to the **i**
Psa 19:8 The **i** of the LORD are correct.
25:10 to his promise and written **i**.
68:11 The Lord gives **i**. The women
78:5 He established written **i** for
78:56 They did not obey his written **i**.
81:5 These are the **i** God set in
99:7 They obeyed his written **i** and
119:2 those who obey his written **i**.
119:14 by⌋ your written **i** more than
119:22 I have obeyed your written **i**.
119:24 your written **i** make me happy.
119:31 clung tightly to your written **i**.
119:36 written **i** rather than getting
119:46 I will speak about your written **i**
119:59 my feet back to your written **i**.
119:79 come to know your written **i**.
119:88 so that I may obey the written **i**,
119:95 to understand your written **i**.
119:99 because your written **i** are in
119:111 Your written **i** are mine forever.
119:119 is why I love your written **i**.
119:125 come to know your written **i**.
119:129 Your written **i** are miraculous.
119:138 You have issued your written **i**.
119:144 Your written **i** are always right.
119:146 that I can obey your written **i**.
119:152 your written **i** that you made
119:157 turned away from your written **i**
119:167 I have obeyed your written **i**.
119:168 principles and your written **i**,
132:12 promise and my written **i** that
Isa 8:16 Tie up the written **i**.
8:20 teachings and to the written **i**.
38:1 Give final **i** to your household,
Jer 35:18 Jonadab, followed all his **i**,
44:23 teachings, decrees, or written **i**.
Mat 10:5 twelve out with the following **i**:
11:1 his twelve disciples these **i**,
Act 1:2 he gave **i** through the Holy
17:15 they took **i** back to Silas and
Col 4:10 have received **i** about Mark.
Heb 7:11 based on **i** they received.
8:4 the **i** that Moses gave.
11:22 give them **i** about burying his

instructor (1)

Rom 2:20 an **i** of ignorant people,

instructors (1)

Pro 5:13 did I keep my ear open to my **i**.

instrument (2)

Psa 92:3 on a ten-stringed **i** and a harp
Eze 33:32 or a musician who plays an **i**.

instruments (20)

2Sm 6:5 kinds of **i** made from cypress
1Ch 16:42 and the ⌊other⌋ musical **i** that
23:5 with the **i** David had made
2Ch 5:13 and other musical **i**,
7:6 musical **i** which King David
23:13 accompanied by musical **i**.
29:26 Levites stood with David's **i**,
29:27 by trumpets and the **i**
30:21 They played the LORD's **i**
Neh 12:36 with the musical **i** of David,
Psa 33:3 and joyfully on stringed **i**.
45:8 of stringed **i** delights you.
150:4 him with stringed **i** and flutes.
Isa 38:20 so let us play stringed **i**.
Dan 3:5 time with all other kinds of **i**,
3:7 harps with all other kinds of **i**,
3:10 kinds of **i** should bow down
3:15 time with all other kinds of **i**,
Hab 3:19 the choir director; on stringed **i**.
1Co 14:7 Musical **i** like the flute or harp

insult (26)

Job 34:37 He claps his hands to **i** us.
Psa 4:2 are you going to **i** my honor?
44:16 of the words of those who **i**
69:9 and the insults of those who **i**
74:10 will the enemy **i** us?
74:22 Remember how godless fools **i**
79:12 of insults they used to **i** you,
102:8 All day long my enemies **i** me.
Pro 12:16 a sensible person hides the **i**.
18:3 and **i** comes along with
Eze 8:17 Look how they **i** me in the
Dan 11:18 king makes and even **i** him.
Mat 5:11 are you when people **i** you,
Luk 6:22 hate you, avoid you, **i** you,
6:28 Pray for those who **i** you.
11:45 you talk this way, you **i** us too."
18:32 fun of him, **i** him, spit on him,
Act 19:37 rob temples or **i** our goddess.
Rom 15:3 "The insults of those who **i**
1Pe 4:4 Unbelievers **i** you now
2Pe 2:10 afraid to **i** the ⌊Lord's⌋ glory.
2:12 These false teachers **i** what
Jud 1:8 Lord's authority, and **i** his glory.
1:10 people don't understand, they **i**.
Rev 13:6 It opened its mouth to **i** God,
13:6 to **i** his name and his tent —

insulted (29)

Jdg 8:15 You **i** me when you said,
1Sm 17:45 of Israel, whom you have **i**.
Neh 1:3 serious troubles and being **i**.
2:17 and we will no longer be **i**."
4:5 They have **i** you in front of
Job 19:3 You have **i** me ten times now.
Psa 55:12 If an enemy had **i** me,
69:10 and fasted, but I was **i** for it.
69:19 You know that I have been **i**,
74:18 how the enemy **i** you,
89:50 how your servant has been **i**.
89:51 Your enemies **i** ⌊me⌋.
89:51 They **i** your Messiah every
Isa 51:7 be afraid of being **i** by people.
Jer 15:15 that I've been **i** because of you.
Eze 20:27 Your ancestors **i** me again
36:6 you have been **i** by the nations.
36:7 which surround you will be **i**.
Dan 9:16 are **i** by everyone around
Zep 2:8 They **i** my people and bragged
2:10 because they **i** the people who
Mat 27:39 Those who passed by **i** him.
Mar 15:29 Those who passed by **i** him.
Luk 22:65 They also **i** him in many other
23:39 there **i** Jesus by saying,
Act 18:6 they opposed him and **i** him.
Heb 10:33 were publicly **i** and mistreated.
11:26 He thought that being **i** for
1Pe 4:14 If you are **i** because of the

insulting (11)

1Sm 18:8 considered this saying to be **i**.
Mat 5:22 believer an **i** name will answer
27:44 crucified with him were **i** him
Mar 15:32 crucified with him were **i** him.
Act 13:45 They used **i** language to
23:4 "You're **i** God's chief priest!"
1Th 2:2 we suffered rough and **i**
2Pe 2:11 don't bring an **i** judgment
Rev 13:1 There were **i** names on its
13:5 to speak arrogant and **i** things.
17:3 beast covered with **i** names.

insults (29)

Num 15:30 does something wrong **i**
1Sm 25:39 who defended me against the **i**
Neh 4:4 Turn their **i** back on them,
Psa 22:7 **I** pour from their mouths.
69:7 for your sake I have endured **i**.
69:9 and the **i** of those who insult
69:20 **I** have broken my heart,
79:12 times the number of **i** they used
89:50 my heart ⌊the **i**⌋ from so many
109:25 the victim of my enemies' **i**.
119:22 Remove the **i** and contempt
119:39 Take away **i**, which I dread,
Psa 119:42 for the one who **i** me since
Pro 14:31 oppresses the poor **i** his maker,
17:5 of a poor person **i** his maker.
Jer 20:8 has made me the object of **i**
Lam 3:30 them and take their fill of **i**.
3:61 Listen to their **i**, all their plots
Eze 21:28 the Ammonites and their **i**:
34:29 suffer the **i** of other nations.
35:12 heard all the **i** that you spoke
36:15 no longer let you hear the **i** from
Dan 11:18 will silence the **i** that
Hos 12:14 will pay them back for their **i**.
Zep 2:8 "I have heard the **i** from Moab
Rom 15:3 "The **i** of those who insult you
1Ti 3:7 the victim of disgraceful **i** that
Heb 10:29 and he **i** the Spirit that God
13:13 and endure the **i** he endured.

intact (1)

1Sm 5:4 The rest of Dagon's body was **i**.

integrity (39)

Gen 6:9 and was a man of **i** among
17:1 Live in my presence with **i**.
Dtr 18:13 You must have **i** ⌊in dealing⌋
Jos 24:14 him with **i** and faithfulness.
Jdg 9:16 sincerity and **i** when you made
9:19 and **i** toward Jerubbaal
Job 1:1 He was a man of **i**:
1:8 He is a man of **i**: He is decent,
2:3 He is a man of **i**: He is decent,
4:6 lifetime of **i** give you hope?
8:20 does not reject a person of **i**
9:20 corrupt even if I am a man of **i**.
9:21 If I am a man of **i**, I have no
9:22 the man of **i** and the wicked.'
12:4 A man of **i**, a man who is
22:3 when you follow the path of **i**?
27:5 never give up my claim of **i**.
31:6 and he will know I have **i**.
Psa 7:8 of the world. according to my **i**.
15:2 The one who walks with **i**,
25:21 **I** and honesty will protect me
26:1 because I have walked with **i**
26:11 But I walk with **i**. Rescue me,
41:12 You defend my **i**, and you set
101:2 to understand the path to **i**.
101:2 live in my own home with **i**.
101:6 who lives with **i** will serve me.
119:1 are those whose lives have **i**,
119:80 Let my heart be filled with **i** in
Pro 2:7 shield for those who walk in **i**
2:21 People of **i** will remain in it.
11:3 **I** guides decent people,
20:7 lives on the basis of his **i**.
28:6 a poor person who has **i** than
2Pe 1:3 us by his own glory and **i**.
1:4 Through his glory and **i** he has
1:5 make every effort to add **i** to
1:5 and to **i** add knowledge;
Rev 19:11 With **i** he judges and wages

intellectual (4)

1Co 1:17 I didn't use **i** arguments.
2:4 with persuasive **i** arguments.
2:13 on **i** arguments like people
2Co 10:5 and all their **i** arrogance that

intelligence (4)

2Ch 2:12 wise son who has insight and **i**
2:13 with skill and **i** — Huram Abi.
Isa 29:14 The **i** of their intelligent people
1Co 1:19 the **i** of intelligent people."

intelligent (13)

Gen 41:33 look for a wise and **i** man
41:39 is no one as wise and **i** as you.
Dtr 1:13 are wise, **i**, and experienced,
Job 34:2 your ears to me, you **i** men.
Pro 17:28 He is considered **i** if he keeps
Ecc 9:11 **I** people don't necessarily have
Isa 29:14 The intelligence of their **i**
Dan 1:4 in all subjects, well-informed, **i**,
Mat 11:25 things from wise and **i** people
Luk 10:21 things from wise and **i** people
Act 13:7 was associated with an **i** man,
1Co 1:19 I will reject the intelligence of **i**
10:15 I'm talking to **i** people.

intend (12)

Jos 20:5 the relative because he didn't **i**
2Ch 13:8 Do you now **i** to challenge the
28:10 Now you **i** to enslave the men
28:13 Do you **i** to add to all our sins?
29:10 Now I **i** to make a pledge to the
Isa 10:7 But that's not what they **i** to do.
Jer 26:3 my plan about the disaster I **i**
Hos 10:4 promises they don't **i** to keep.
Luk 22:48 do you **i** to betray the Son of
Jon 7:35 "Where does this man **i** to go
2Co 8:21 We **i** to do what is right,
Gal 5:17 always do what you **i** to do.

intended (20)

Jos 22:12 They **i** to wage war against
Jdg 20:5 They **i** to kill me, but instead,
2Sm 21:16 captured David and **i** to kill him.
2Ch 32:1 He **i** to conquer them himself.
Pro 27:6 made by a friend are **i** to help,
Isa 14:24 "It will happen exactly as I've **i**.
46:10 and I'll do everything I **i** to do."
Jer 26:19 his plan about the disaster he **i**
Luk 4:29 They **i** to throw him off of it.
10:1 city and place that he **i** to go.
Jon 6:15 Jesus realized that the people **i**
Act 20:7 Since he **i** to leave the next
Rom 7:10 the commandment which was **i**
2Co 9:5 be the blessing it was **i** to be,
1Ti 1:8 used as they were **i** to be used.
1:9 must realize that laws are not **i**
1:9 Laws are **i** for lawbreakers and
1:10 Laws are **i** for people involved
1:11 Moses' Teachings were **i** to be
Jud 1:3 Dear friends, I had **i** to write to

intends (8)

Jer 23:20 has done everything he **i** to do.
26:13 plan about the disaster that he **i**
30:24 has done everything he **i** to do.
49:20 Edom and the things he **i**
49:30 against you and **i** to attack you.
50:45 Babylon and the things he **i**
Mat 2:13 because Herod **i** to search for
Eph 1:11 everything work the way he **i**.

intense (4)

1Sm 14:52 There was **i** warfare with the
2Sm 13:15 Now, Amnon developed an **i**
Zec 12:11 in Jerusalem will be as **i** as
Act 26:7 worship with **i** devotion day

intent (3)

Psa 25:14 to them the **i** of his promise.
Pro 21:27 if they bring it with evil **i**.
Jon 5:18 His reply made the Jews more **i**

intention (2)

Jos 22:23 If we built an altar with the **i** of
1Th 5:9 It was not God's **i** that we

intentionally (2)

Exo 21:13 If it wasn't done **i**, but God let it
Pro 10:3 but he **i** ignores the desires of a

intentions (3)

1Ki 8:18 for my name, your **i** were good.
2Ch 6:8 for my name, your **i** were good.
Heb 4:12 a person's thoughts and **i**.

intercede (1)

Isa 59:16 that there's no one to **i**.

intercedes (5)

Isa 53:12 He **i** for those who are
Rom 8:26 But the Spirit **i** along with our
8:27 The Spirit **i** for God's people
8:34 Christ also **i** for us.
Heb 7:25 he always lives and **i** for them.

intercessions (1)

1Ti 2:1 to make petitions, prayers, **i**,

intercourse (52)

Gen 24:16 had ever had sexual **i** with her.
Exo 19:15 by having sexual **i**."
22:16 and has sexual **i** with her,
22:19 "Whoever has sexual **i** with an
Lev 15:18 "When a man has sexual **i**
15:24 If a man has sexual **i** with her
15:33 for any man who has sexual **i**
18:6 "Never have sexual **i** with
18:7 "Never have sexual **i** with your
18:7 Never have sexual **i** with her.
18:8 Never have sexual **i** with your
18:9 Never have sexual **i** with your
18:10 Never have sexual **i** with your
18:11 Never have sexual **i** with a
18:12 Never have sexual **i** with your
18:13 Never have sexual **i** with your
18:14 Never have sexual **i** with the
18:15 Never have sexual **i** with your
18:15 Never have sexual **i** with her.
18:16 Never have sexual **i** with your
18:17 Never have sexual **i** with a
18:18 and have sexual **i** with her.
18:19 "Never have sexual **i** with a
18:20 Never have sexual **i** with your
18:22 Never have sexual **i** with a
18:23 Never have sexual **i** with any
18:23 to an animal for sexual **i**.
19:20 "If a man has sexual **i** with a
20:11 Whoever has sexual **i** with his
20:12 If a man has sexual **i** with his
20:13 When a man has sexual **i** with
20:15 A man who has sexual **i** with
20:17 and has sexual **i** does a
20:17 He has had sexual **i** with his
20:18 If a man has sexual **i** with a
20:18 have had sexual **i** in blood.
20:19 Never have sexual **i** with your
20:19 Whoever has sexual **i** with a
20:20 Whoever has sexual **i** with his
Num 5:13 and may have had sexual **i**
5:19 no other man has had sexual **i**
5:20 had sexual **i** with another man,
Dtr 22:22 man is caught having sexual **i**
22:23 do when a man has sexual **i**
22:29 the man who had sexual **i** with
27:20 "Whoever has sexual **i** with
27:21 "Whoever has sexual **i** with
27:22 "Whoever has sexual **i** with
27:23 "Whoever has sexual **i** with
1Sm 21:4 haven't had sexual **i** today."
Eze 18:6 wife or have sexual **i**
Luk 1:34 I've never had sexual **i**."

interest (23)

Exo 22:25 a moneylender. Charge no **i**.
Lev 25:36 Don't collect **i** or make any
25:37 Never collect any kind of **i** on
Dtr 23:19 Israelite any **i** on money,
23:20 You may charge a foreigner **i**,
2Sm 19:43 "We have ten times your **i** in
Neh 5:7 I told them, "You are charging **i**
5:10 we must stop charging them **i**.
5:11 Also, you must return the **i** on
Est 3:8 So it is not in your **i** to tolerate
Psa 15:5 The one who does not collect **i**
Pro 28:8 loans and **i** collects them
Eze 18:8 He doesn't lend money for **i** or
18:13 He lends money for **i** and
18:17 He doesn't charge **i** or make
22:12 You collect **i** and make
Dan 11:37 He will have no **i** in the gods of
11:37 He will have no **i** in any god,
Mat 25:27 my money back with **i**.
Luk 19:23 I could have collected it with **i**.'
Act 9:27 Then Barnabas took an **i** in
Php 2:20 a genuine **i** in your welfare.
4:10 you again showed **i** in me.

interested (2)

Job 21:21 How can he be **i** in his family
Php 4:10 You were **i** but did not have an

interests (3)

Php 2:4 only about your own **i**,
2:4 concerned about the **i** of others.
2:21 else looks after his own **i**,

interfere (3)

Ezr 6:7 Don't **i** with the work on God's
Act 11:17 So who was I to **i** with God?
1Pe 3:7 nothing will **i** with your prayers.

interfering (1)

2Th 3:11 so you go around **i** in other

interior (2)

1Ki 6:6 The **i** of the lowest story of
Act 19:1 Paul traveled through the **i**

intermarried (1)

Psa 106:35 they **i** with other nations.

intermarry (4)

Gen 34:9 **I** with us; give your daughters
Jos 23:12 if you **i** with them or associate
1Ki 11:2 "Never **i** with them.
Ezr 9:14 commandments again and **i**

intermarrying (1)

Dan 2:43 of the kingdom will mix by **i**,

internal (17)

Exo 29:13 the fat that covers the **i** organs,
29:17 wash the **i** organs and legs,
29:22 the fat that covers the **i** organs,
Lev 1:9 Wash the **i** organs and legs.
1:13 Wash the **i** organs and legs.
3:3 the fat that covers the **i** organs
3:9 the fat that covers the **i** organs.
3:14 the fat that covers the **i** organs
4:8 the fat that covers the **i** organs,
4:11 legs, **i** organs, and excrement)
7:3 the fat covering the **i** organs,
8:16 the fat that was on the **i** organs,
8:21 He washed the **i** organs and
8:25 all the fat on the **i** organs,
9:14 He washed the **i** organs and
Act 1:18 and all his **i** organs came out.
1Pe 3:4 Rather, beauty is something **i**

interpret (8)

Dan 2:4 and we'll **i** it for you."
5:12 He has the ability to **i** dreams,
5:16 I have heard that you can **i**
Mat 16:3 but you cannot **i** the signs of
1Co 12:10 Another can **i** languages.
12:30 languages or **i** languages?
14:5 This is true unless he can **i**
14:27 and someone must **i** what each

interpretation (5)

Gen 40:22 as Joseph had said in his **i**.
Jdg 7:15 heard the dream and its **i**,
1Co 14:13 language should pray for an **i**
14:26 another language, or an **i**.
2Pe 1:20 is a matter of one's own **i**.

interpreter (2)

Gen 42:23 he was speaking through an **i**.
1Co 14:28 But if an **i** isn't present,

interpreters (1)

Jer 27:9 **i** of dreams, fortunetellers,

interrupted (3)

Ezr 6:8 men so that the work is not **i**.
10:2 **i** by saying to Ezra,
Est 7:5 Then King Xerxes **i** Queen

intertwined (1)

Job 40:17 ligaments of its thighs are **i**.

intestinal (2)

2Ch 21:15 You will suffer from a chronic **i**
21:18 with an incurable **i** disease.

intestines (4)

2Sm 20:10 and his **i** poured out on the
2Ch 21:15 disease until your **i** come out."
21:19 his **i** fell out because of his
Zep 1:17 dust and their **i** like manure.

intimate (1)

Pro 3:32 The LORD's **i** advice is with

intimidate (6)

Neh 6:9 They were all trying to **i** us.
6:13 He was hired to **i** me into doing
6:14 who have been trying to **i** me."
6:19 Tobiah kept sending letters to **i**
Isa 41:23 to **i** us and make us afraid.
Php 1:28 So don't let your opponents **i**

intimidated (1)

Isa 41:10 Don't be **i**; I am your God. I will

intoxicated (3)

Pro 5:19 Always be **i** with her love.
5:20 Why should you, my son, be **i**
Sos 5:1 Drink and become **i** with

introducing (1)

Rom 16:1 With this letter I'm **i** Phoebe to

introduction (1)

1Co 16:3 I will give letters of **i** to the

invade (19)

Exo 10:12 They will **i** Egypt and eat up
Dtr 1:41 easily **i** the mountain region.
Jos 2:18 When we **i** your land,
Jdg 11:12 "Why did you **i** my land and
2Ki 13:20 raiding parties used to **i**
2Ch 20:10 However, you didn't let Israel **i**
32:1 of Assyria came to **i** Judah.
33:11 of the king of Assyria **i** Judah.
Dan 11:9 He will **i** the southern kingdom
11:13 After a few years he will **i** with
11:17 northern king will decide to **i**
11:17 decent men will **i** with him.
11:21 He will **i** when people are
11:24 he will **i** the richest parts of the
11:29 time he will again **i** the south,
11:40 He will **i** countries,
11:41 He will **i** the beautiful land,
Joe 3:17 Foreigners will never **i** it again.
Mic 5:5 When the Assyrians **i** our land

invaded (7)

Exo 10:14 They **i** all of Egypt and landed
Dtr 1:43 and **i** the mountain region.
1Ki 15:17 King Baasha of Israel **i** Judah
2Ch 16:1 King Baasha of Israel **i** Judah
28:17 The Edomites had again **i** and
Psa 79:1 O God, the nations have **i** the
Jer 35:11 of Babylon **i** this land,

invader (2)

Isa 21:1 an **i** will come from the desert,
Dan 11:16 The **i** will do as he pleases,

invaders (1)

Lam 4:12 enemies or **i** would ever get

invent (3)

Psa 58:2 No, you **i** new crimes on earth,
Dan 11:24 He will **i** new ways of
Mic 2:1 it will be for those who **i** trouble

invented (1)

1Ki 12:33 he had **i** for the Israelites.

inventive (1)

2Ch 26:15 designed by **i** people.

inventory (2)

Exo 38:21 An **i** was ordered by Moses
Ezr 1:9 This is the **i**: gold dishes:

invents (1)

Psa 36:4 He **i** trouble while lying on his

invest (1)

Luk 19:13 '**i** this money until I come back.'

invested (2)

Mat 25:16 received ten thousand dollars **i**
25:27 then you should have **i** my

investigate (3)

Dtr 17:4 are told about it, **i** it thoroughly.
Ezr 10:16 the tenth month to **i** the matter.
Pro 25:2 but the glory of kings to **i** them.

investigated (3)

Est 2:23 When the report was **i** and
Job 29:16 I carefully **i** cases brought by
1Pe 1:10 researched and **i** this salvation.

investigating (1)

Jdg 6:29 While they were **i** the matter,

investigation (2)

Dtr 13:14 Then make a thorough **i**.
19:18 judges must make a thorough **i**.

investing (1)

Luk 19:15 much each one has made by **i**.'

invisible (5)

Rom 1:20 of the world, God's **i** qualities,
Col 1:15 He is the image of the **i** God,
1:16 and on earth, visible and **i**.
1Ti 1:17 **i**, and only God. Amen.
Heb 11:27 could actually see the **i** God.

invitation (2)

1Ch 13:2 we will send ⌊an **i**⌋ to the rest
Luk 11:37 So Jesus accepted the **i**.

invite (19)

Exo 2:20 Go, **i** him to supper."
34:15 they may **i** you to eat the meat
Dtr 33:19 They will **i** nations to their
Jdg 8:1 You didn't **i** us to go fight
14:15 Did the two of you **i** us ⌊just to
1Sm 16:3 **I** Jesse to the sacrifice.
1Ki 1:10 But he didn't **i** the prophet
1:26 But he didn't **i** me or the priest
12:20 they sent men to **i** him to the
2Ki 14:10 Why must you **i** disaster and
2Ch 25:19 Why must you **i** disaster and
Job 1:4 They would send someone to **i**
Psa 65:4 is the person you choose and **i**
Eze 23:40 even sent messengers to **i** men
Zec 3:10 "each of you will **i** your
Mat 22:9 **I** everyone you find to the
Luk 14:12 "When you **i** people for lunch or
14:12 don't **i** only your friends,
14:13 **i** the poor, the handicapped,

invited (41)

Gen 29:22 So Laban **i** all the people of
31:54 He **i** his relatives to eat the
Num 25:2 who **i** the people to the
1Sm 9:13 Then those who are **i** may eat.
9:24 When I **i** people to the feast,
16:5 Jesse and his sons and **i** them
2Sm 13:23 He **i** all the king's sons.
13:24 your officials are **i** ⌊to feast⌋
15:11 Two hundred men **i** from
1Ki 1:9 He had **i** all his brothers,
1:19 He has **i** all the king's sons,
1:19 hasn't **i** your servant Solomon.
1:25 He **i** all the king's sons,
12:3 for Jeroboam and **i** him back.
2Ki 4:8 She had **i** him to eat ⌊with her⌋.
2Ch 10:3 for Jeroboam and **i** him back.
30:1 He **i** them to come to the
Est 2:18 He **i** all his officials and his
5:12 And again tomorrow I am her **i**
Lam 2:22 You have **i** those who terrorize
2:22 as though they were **i** to a
Zep 1:7 He has **i** his special guests.
Mat 22:3 to those who had been **i**
22:4 tell the people who had been **i**,
22:8 but those who were **i** don't
22:14 "Therefore, many are **i**,
Luk 7:36 One of the Pharisees **i** Jesus
7:39 The Pharisee who had **i** Jesus
Luk 11:37 After Jesus spoke, a Pharisee **i**
14:8 more important than you was **i**.
14:10 So when you're **i**, take the
14:12 Then he told the man who had **i**
14:16 banquet and **i** many people.
14:17 to tell those who were **i**,
14:24 none of those **i** earlier will taste
Jon 2:2 his disciples had been **i** too.
Act 8:31 So he **i** Philip to sit with him in
13:42 the people **i** them to speak on
16:15 she **i** us to stay at her home.
28:17 After three days Paul **i** the most
Rev 19:9 'Blessed are those who are **i** to

invites (5)

Pro 10:14 mouth of a stubborn fool **i** ruin.
17:19 his city gate high **i** destruction.
18:6 and his mouth **i** a beating.
Luk 14:8 "When someone **i** you to a
1Co 10:27 If an unbeliever **i** you ⌊to his

inviting (1)

Jdg 12:1 fight against Ammon without **i**

involve (1)

Dtr 17:8 It may **i** murder, assault, or a

involved (19)

Num 15:26 since all the people were **i** in
Dtr 19:17 The two people **i** must stand in
Jdg 12:2 "My people and I were **i** in a
Ezr 10:13 are so many of us who are **i**
Psa 131:1 I am not **i** in things too big or
141:4 to become **i** with wickedness,
Pro 26:17 ⌊so⌋ is a bystander who gets **i**
Hos 5:2 You are deeply **i** in sin.
Act 18:14 kind of misdemeanor or crime **i**,
18:15 who gets **i** in those things."
19:19 Many of those who were **i** in
2Co 12:21 in which they have been **i**.
Gal 3:20 there is only one person **i**,
Eph 5:5 well that no person who is **i**
Php 1:30 You are **i** in the same struggle
1:30 you hear that I'm still **i** in it.
1Ti 1:10 Laws are intended for people **i**
5:13 but they also gossip and get **i**
2Pe 2:20 But if they get **i** in this filth

involvement (2)

Luk 23:19 been thrown into prison for his **i**
Act 19:18 openly admitted their **i**

involves (2)

2Ch 19:10 even if the case **i** bloodshed or
1Jn 4:18 because fear **i** punishment.

involving (4)

Dtr 21:5 decision is final in all cases **i**
1Ch 26:32 overseers in every matter **i** God
2Ch 19:11 you in every matter **i** the LORD.
19:11 of every matter **i** the king.

inwardly (5)

Mar 2:8 At once, Jesus knew **i** what
Rom 2:29 Rather, a person is a Jew **i**,
8:23 first of God's gifts, also groan **i**.
2Co 4:16 **i** we are renewed day by day.
7:5 and **i** we have fears.

Iob (1)

Gen 46:13 Tola, Puvah, **I**, and Shimron.

Iphdeiah (1)

1Ch 8:25 **I**, and Penuel.

Iphtah (1)

Jos 15:43 **I**, Ashnah, Nezib,

Iphtah El (2)

Jos 19:14 and ends at the valley of **I**.
19:27 and the valley of **I** in the north

Ira (6)

2Sm 20:26 And **I**, a descendant of Jair,
23:26 **I** (son of Ikkesh) from Tekoa,
23:38 **I** (descendant of Ithra),
1Ch 11:28 **I** (son of Ikkesh) from Tekoa,
11:40 **I** (descendant of Ithra),
27:9 **I**, the son of Ikkesh from

Irad (2)

Gen 4:18 To Enoch was born **I**.
4:18 **I** was the father of Mehujael.

Iram (2)

Gen 36:43 Magdiel, and **I**. These were the
1Ch 1:54 Magdiel, and **I**. These were the

Ir Hamelah (1)

Jos 15: 62Nibshan, **I**, and En Gedi

Iri (1)

1Ch 7:7 Uzzi, Uzziel, Jerimoth, and **I**.

Irijah (3)

Jer 37:13 whose name was **I**,
37:14 But **I** wouldn't listen to him.
37:14 **I** arrested Jeremiah and took

Ir Moab (1)

Num 22: 36went out to meet him at **I**,

iron (90)

Gen 4:22 who made bronze and **i** tools.
Num 31:22 Any gold, silver, bronze, **i**,
35:16 "But if any of you uses an **i**
Dtr 3:11 His bed was made of **i** and
4:20 out of Egypt, the **i** smelter,
8:9 The land has rocks with **i** ore,
27:5 Don't use an **i** chisel on the
28:23 below will be as hard as **i**.
33:25 gates be made of **i** and copper.
Jos 6:19 made of bronze and **i** are holy
6:24 made of bronze and **i** into
8:31 on which no **i** chisels had been
17:16 have chariots made of **i**."
17:18 and have chariots made of **i**."
22:8 bronze, **i**, and loads of clothing.
Jdg 1:19 who had chariots made of **i**.
4:3 had 900 chariots made of **i**
4:13 (900 chariots made of **i**)
1Sm 17:7 was made of 15 pounds of **i**.
2Sm 23:7 touches them uses **i** ⌊tools⌋
1Ki 6:7 or any other **i** tool made a
8:51 from the middle of an **i** smelter.
22:11 made **i** horns and said,
1Ch 22:3 prepared a large quantity of **i**
22:14 and so much bronze and **i** that
22:16 The gold, silver, bronze, and **i**
29:2 objects, **i** for iron objects,
29:2 objects, iron for **i** objects,
29:7 and 7,500,000 pounds of **i** for
2Ch 2:7 and **i** as well as purple,
2:14 **i**, stone, wood, purple, violet,
18:10 made **i** horns and said,
24:12 hired men who worked with **i**
Job 19:24 rock with an **i** stylus and lead.
20:24 person flees from an **i** weapon,
28:2 **I** is taken from the ground,
40:18 They are like **i** bars.
41:27 It considers **i** to be like straw
Psa 2:9 break them with an **i** scepter.
105:18 and cut into his neck with an **i**
107:10 They were held in **i** chains
107:16 gates and cut **i** bars in two.
149:8 and their leaders in **i** shackles,
Pro 27:17 ⌊As⌋ **i** sharpens iron,
27:17 ⌊As⌋ iron sharpens **i**,
Isa 44:12 Blacksmiths shape **i** into tools.
45:2 and cut through the **i** bars.
48:4 Like **i**, you are hardheaded.
60:17 I will bring silver instead of **i**,
60:17 and **i** instead of stone.
Jer 1:18 an **i** pillar, and a bronze wall.
6:28 They are all like bronze and **i**.
11:4 which was an **i** smelter.
15:12 (No one can break **i**,
15:12 iron, **i** from the north,
17:1 sin is written with an **i** pen.
28:13 but I will replace it with an **i**
28:14 I will put an **i** yoke on the
Eze 4:3 Then take an **i** pan,

Eze 22:18 of them are like copper, tin, **i**,
22:20 People gather silver, copper, **i**,
27:12 They exchanged silver, **i**,
27:19 They exchanged wrought **i**,
Dan 2:33 Its legs were made of **i**.
2:33 Its feet were made partly of **i**
2:35 Then all at once, the **i**,
2:40 It will be as strong as **i**.
2:40 (**I** smashes and shatters
2:40 As **i** crushes things,
2:41 partly potters' clay and partly **i**.
2:41 has some of the firmness of **i**.
2:41 **i** was mixed with clay.
2:42 The toes were partly **i** and
2:43 **i** was mixed with clay.
2:43 any more than **i** can mix
2:45 It smashed the **i**, bronze, clay,
4:15 Secure it with an **i** and bronze
4:23 Secure it with an **i** and bronze
5:4 bronze, **i**, wood, or stone.
5:23 gold, bronze, **i**, wood, or stone.
7:7 and had large **i** teeth.
7:19 It was very terrifying and had **i**
Mic 4:13 make your horns as hard as **i**
Act 12:10 and came to the **i** gate that led
1Ti 4:2 as if branded by a red-hot **i**.
Rev 2:27 rule the nations with **i** scepters
9:9 They had breastplates like **i**.
12:5 the nations with an **i** scepter.
18:12 costly wood, bronze, **i**, marble,
19:15 He will rule them with an **i**

irons (1)
Act 16:24 with their feet in leg **i**.

iron-spiked (1)
Amo 1:3 with **i** threshing sledges.

Ir Peel (1)
Jos 18:27 Rekem, **I**, Taralah,

irritable (2)
1Co 13:5 It isn't **i**. It doesn't keep track of
Tit 1:7 not be a stubborn or **i** person.

irritated (15)
Lev 13:2 or an **i** area on his skin that
13:4 But if the **i** area is white and
13:23 But if the **i** area has not spread,
13:28 If the **i** area does not spread but
13:38 has white **i** areas of skin,
13:39 If the **i** areas on the skin are
14:56 is a sore, a rash, or an **i** area.
Pro 12:16 When a stubborn fool is **i**,
Mat 20:24 they were **i** with the two
21:15 the Son of David!" they were **i**.
26:8 The disciples were **i** when
Mar 10:14 Jesus saw this, he became **i**.
10:41 they were **i** with James and
14:4 Some who were there were **i**
Luk 13:14 The synagogue leader was **i**

Ir Shemesh (1)
Jos 19:41 Zorah, Eshtaol, **I**,

Iru (1)
1Ch 4:15 were **I**, Elah, and Naam.

Isaac (141)
Gen 17:19 will name him **I** [He Laughs].
17:21 But I will make my promise to **I**.
21:3 named his newborn son **I**.
21:4 When **I** was eight days old,
21:5 old when his son **I** was born.
21:8 On the day **I** was weaned,
21:9 the Egyptian was laughing at **I**.
21:10 the inheritance with my son **I**."
21:12 through **I** your descendants will
22:2 your son, your only son **I**,
22:3 of his servants and his son **I**.
22:6 offering and gave it to his son **I**.
22:7 **I** spoke up and said,
22:7 **I** asked, "We have the burning
22:9 Then he tied up his son **I** and
24:4 and get a wife for my son **I**."
24:14 have chosen for your servant **I**.
Gen 24:62 **I** had just come back from Beer
24:63 Toward evening **I** went out into
24:64 When Rebekah saw **I**,
24:66 The servant reported to **I**
24:67 **I** took her into his mother
24:67 So **I** was comforted after his
25:5 left everything he had to **I**.
25:6 sent them away from his son **I**
25:9 His sons **I** and Ishmael buried
25:11 God blessed his son **I**,
25:19 the account of Abraham's son **I**
25:19 Abraham was the father of **I**.
25:20 **I** was 40 years old when he
25:21 **I** prayed to the LORD for his
25:26 **I** was 60 years old when they
25:28 Because **I** liked to eat the meat
26:1 So **I** went to King Abimelech of
26:2 LORD appeared to **I** and said,
26:6 So **I** lived in Gerar.
26:7 **I** answered, "She's my sister."
26:8 and saw **I** caressing his wife
26:9 Abimelech called for **I** and said,
26:9 **I** answered him, "I thought I
26:12 **I** planted ⌊crops⌋ in that land.
26:16 Finally, Abimelech said to **I**,
26:17 So **I** moved away.
26:20 So **I** named the well Esek
26:21 So **I** named it Sitnah
26:24 night the LORD appeared to **I**,
26:25 So **I** built an altar there and
26:26 came from Gerar to see **I**.
26:27 **I** asked them, "Why have you
26:30 **I** prepared a special dinner for
26:31 Then **I** sent them on their way,
26:35 These women brought **I** and
27:1 When **I** was old and going
27:2 **I** said, "I'm old. I don't know
27:5 Rebekah was listening while **I**
27:20 **I** asked his son, "How did you
27:21 Then **I** said to Jacob,
27:22 **I** felt ⌊his skin⌋. "The voice is
27:25 **I** said, "Bring me some of the
27:25 Jacob brought it to **I**,
27:26 Then his father **I** said to him,
27:27 When **I** smelled his clothes,
27:30 **I** finished blessing Jacob.
27:32 his father **I** asked him.
27:33 violently all over, **I** asked,
27:35 **I** said, "Your brother came and
27:37 **I** answered Esau, "I have made
27:39 His father **I** answered him,
27:46 Rebekah said to **I**,
28:1 **I** called for Jacob and blessed
28:5 **I** sent Jacob to Paddan Aram.
28:6 Esau learned that **I** had
28:6 He learned that **I** had blessed
28:8 Esau realized that his father **I**
28:13 Abraham and the God of **I**.
31:18 back to his father **I** in Canaan.
31:42 of Abraham and the Fear of **I**,
31:53 oath by the Fear of his father **I**
32:9 and God of my father **I**!
35:12 that I gave to Abraham and **I**.
35:27 came home to his father **I**
35:27 Abraham and **I** had lived there
35:28 **I** was 180 years old
46:1 to the God of his father **I**.
48:15 and my father **I** walked,
48:16 Abraham and my father **I**.
49:31 **I** and his wife Rebekah are
50:24 give to Abraham, **I**, and Jacob."
Exo 2:24 to Abraham, **I**, and Jacob.
3:6 God of Abraham, **I**, and Jacob."
3:15 God of Abraham, **I**, and Jacob,
3:16 **I**, and Jacob, appeared to me.
4:5 **I**, and Jacob, appeared to you."
6:3 I appeared to Abraham, **I**,
6:8 give to Abraham, **I**, and Jacob.
32:13 **I**, and Israel. You took an oath,
33:1 **I**, and Jacob with an oath,
Lev 26:42 to Jacob, **I**, and Abraham.
Num 32:11 **I**, and Jacob with an oath.
Dtr 1:8 **I**, and Jacob, and to you,
6:10 Abraham, **I**, and Jacob.
9:5 Abraham, **I**, and Jacob.
9:27 Abraham, **I**, and Jacob.
Dtr 29:13 **I**, and Jacob with an oath.
30:20 Abraham, **I**, and Jacob.
34:4 oath to Abraham, **I**, and Jacob.
Jos 24:3 I also gave him **I**.
24:4 To **I** I gave Jacob and Esau.
1Ki 18:36 God of Abraham, **I**, and Israel,
2Ki 13:23 to Abraham, **I**, and Jacob.
1Ch 1:28 sons were **I** and Ishmael.
1:34 Abraham was the father of **I**.
16:16 and his sworn promise to **I**.
29:18 Abraham, **I**, and Israel,
2Ch 30:6 God of Abraham, **I**, and Israel.
Psa 105:9 and his sworn oath to **I**.
Jer 33:26 **I**, and Jacob. However,
Amo 7:9 The worship sites of **I** will be
7:16 against the descendants of **I**.'
Mat 1:2 Abraham was the father of **I**,
1:2 **I** the father of Jacob,
8:11 They will eat with Abraham, **I**,
22:32 'I am the God of Abraham, **I**,
Mar 12:26 God of Abraham, **I**, and Jacob.'
Luk 3:34 son of Jacob, son of **I**,
13:28 **I**, Jacob, and all the prophets.
20:37 God of Abraham, **I**, and Jacob.
Act 3:13 of our ancestors Abraham, **I**,
7:8 Abraham's son **I** was born,
7:8 **I** did the same to his son
7:32 God of Abraham, **I**, and Jacob.'
Rom 9:7 "Through **I** your descendants
9:10 pregnant by our ancestor **I**.
Gal 4:28 children of the promise like **I**.
Heb 11:9 as did **I** and Jacob,
11:17 faith led him to offer his son **I**.
11:18 Through **I** your descendants
11:19 God could bring **I** back from
11:19 Abraham did receive **I** back
11:20 Faith led **I** to bless Jacob and
Jas 2:21 when he offered his son **I** as

Isaac's (4)
Gen 26:19 **I** servants dug in the valley and
26:20 with **I** herders, claiming,
26:32 That same day **I** servants
1Ch 1:34 **I** sons were Esau and Israel.

Isaiah (59)
2Ki 19:2 to the prophet **I**, son of Amoz.
19:5 King Hezekiah's men went to **I**.
19:6 **I** answered them, "Say this to
19:20 Then **I**, son of Amoz, sent a
20:1 The prophet **I**, son of Amoz,
20:4 **I** hadn't gone as far as the
20:7 Then **I** said, "Get a fig cake,
20:8 Hezekiah asked **I**,
20:9 **I** said, "This is your sign from
20:11 Then the prophet **I** called on
20:14 Then the prophet **I** came to
20:15 **I** asked, "What did they see in
20:16 **I** said to Hezekiah,
20:19 Hezekiah said to **I**,
2Ch 26:22 is recorded by the prophet **I**,
32:20 Hezekiah and the prophet **I**,
32:32 in the vision of the prophet **I**,
Isa 1:1 This is the vision which **I**,
2:1 This is the message which **I**,
7:3 Then the LORD said to **I**,
7:13 descendants of David," **I** said.
13:1 is the divine revelation which **I**,
20:2 At that time the LORD told **I**,
20:2 **I** did this and walked around
20:3 "My servant **I** has gone
37:2 to the prophet **I**, son of Amoz.
37:5 King Hezekiah's men went to **I**.
37:6 **I** answered them, "Say this to
37:21 Then **I**, son of Amoz, sent a
38:1 The prophet **I**, son of Amoz,
38:4 the LORD spoke his word to **I**,
38:21 Then **I** said, "Take a fig cake,
38:7 ⌊**I** said,⌋ "This is your sign
39:3 Then the prophet **I** came to
39:4 **I** asked, "What did they see in
39:5 **I** said to Hezekiah,
39:8 Hezekiah said to **I**,
Mat 3:3 **I** the prophet spoke about this
4:14 So what the prophet **I** had said
8:17 So what the prophet **I** had said

Mat 12:17 So what the prophet I had said
15:7 I was right when he prophesied
Mar 1:2 The prophet I wrote,
7:6 Jesus told them, "I was right
Luk 3:4 As the prophet I wrote in his
4:17 him the book of the prophet I.
Jon 1:23 as the prophet I said."
12:38 of the prophet I came true:
12:39 because, as I also said,
12:41 I said this because he had
Act 8:28 reading the prophet I out loud.
8:30 reading the prophet I out loud.
28:25 ancestors through the prophet I
Rom 9:27 I also says about Israel:
9:29 This is what I predicted:
10:16 I asks, "Lord, who has
10:20 I said very boldly, "I was found
10:21 Then I said about Israel,
15:12 Again, I says, "There will be a

Isaiah's (1)

Mat 13:14 So they make I prophecy come

Iscah (1)

Gen 11:29 was the father of Milcah and I.)

Iscariot (11)

Mat 10:4 Simon the Zealot and Judas I,
26:14 the one named Judas I,
Mar 3:19 and Judas I (who later betrayed
14:10 Judas I, one of the twelve
Luk 6:16 and Judas I (who became a
22:3 Then Satan entered Judas I,
Jon 6:71 meant Judas, son of Simon I.
12:4 One of his disciples, Judas I,
13:2 mind of Judas, son of Simon I.
13:26 it to Judas, son of Simon I.
14:22 Judas (not I) asked Jesus,

Ishbah (1)

1Ch 4:17 to Miriam, Shammai, and I,

Ishbak (2)

Gen 25:2 Medan, Midian, I, and Shuah.
1Ch 1:32 Medan, Midian, I, and Shuah.

Ishbosheth (12)

2Sm 2:8 took Saul's son I and brought
2:10 Saul's son I was 40 years old
2:12 son I went from Mahanaim
2:15 (representing Saul's son I),
3:7 I asked Abner, "Why did you
3:11 I couldn't respond to a single
3:14 to Saul's son I to say,
3:15 So I sent men to take her from
4:1 When Saul's son I heard that
4:5 I was taking his midday nap
4:7 the house while I was sleeping
4:8 "Here is the head of I,

Ishbosheth's (4)

2Sm 3:8 I question made Abner very
4:5 came to I home at the hottest
4:8 They brought I head to David at
4:12 Then they took I head and

Ishhod (1)

1Ch 7:18 Hammolecheth gave birth to I,

Ishi (2)

1Ch 2:31 Appaim's son was I,
5:24 Epher, I, Eliel, Azriel, Jeremiah,

Ishi's (3)

1Ch 2:31 and I son was Sheshan,
4:20 I sons were Zoheth and Ben
4:42 I sons Pelatiah, Neariah,

Ishma (1)

1Ch 4:3 in Etam: Jezreel, I, and Idbash.

Ishmael (52)

Gen 16:11 will name him I [God Hears],
16:15 Abram named him I.
16:16 old when Hagar gave birth to I.
17:18 "Why not let I be my heir?"
17:20 heard your request about I.
17:23 So Abraham took his son I,
17:25 His son I was 13 years old
17:26 his son I were circumcised.
21:11 by this because of his son I.
25:9 His sons Isaac and I buried
25:12 of Abraham's son I.
25:13 names of the sons of I listed
25:16 These are the sons of I and
25:17 I lived 137 years. Then he took
28:9 So he went to I and married
28:9 daughter of Abraham's son I
36:3 also Basemath, daughter of I
2Sm 17:25 named Ithra, a descendant of I.
2Ki 25:23 They were I (son of Nethaniah),
25:25 In the seventh month I (son of
1Ch 1:28 sons were Isaac and I.
1:31 These were the sons of I.
2:17 was Jether, a descendant of I.
8:38 Bocheru, I, Sheariah, Obadiah,
9:44 Bocheru, I, Sheariah, Obadiah,
27:30 a descendant of I for the
2Ch 19:11 Zebadiah, who is the son of I
23:1 I, son of Jehohanan, Azariah,
Ezr 10:22 I, Nethanel, Jozabad,
Psa 83:6 the tents from Edom and I,
Jer 40:8 I (son of Nethaniah),
40:14 of the Ammonites has sent I,
40:15 "Let me kill I, Nethaniah's son.
40:16 you are saying about I is a lie."
41:1 In the seventh month I (son of
41:2 I, son of Nethaniah, and the ten
41:3 I also killed all the Jews who
41:6 I, son of Nethaniah, left Mizpah
41:7 When they came into the city, I,
41:8 from the group had said to I,
41:9 Now, the cistern where I threw
41:9 I, son of Nethaniah, filled it
41:10 Then I took captive the rest of
41:10 I, son of Nethaniah, took them
41:11 heard about all the crimes I,
41:12 all their men and went to fight I.
41:13 were with I saw Kareah's son
41:14 Then all the people I had taken
41:15 I and eight of his men escaped
41:16 whom he had rescued from I,
41:16 after I had killed Gedaliah,
41:18 because I had killed Gedaliah

Ishmaelites (6)

Gen 37:25 they saw a caravan of I coming
37:27 Let's sell him to the I.
37:28 They sold him to the I for eight
37:28 The I took him to Egypt.
39:1 bought him from the I who had
Jdg 8:24 (Their enemies, the I,

Ishmael's (2)

Gen 25:13 Nebaioth (I firstborn), Kedar,
1Ch 1:29 I firstborn was Nebaioth,

Ishmaiah (2)

1Ch 12:4 I from Gibeon (one of the thirty
27:19 for the tribe of Zebulun: I,

Ishmerai (1)

1Ch 8:18 I, Izliah, and Jobab.

Ishpah (1)

1Ch 8:16 Michael, I, and Joha.

Ishpan (1)

1Ch 8:22 Shashak's sons were I,

Ishvah (2)

Gen 46:17 Imnah, I, Ishvi, and Beriah.
1Ch 7:30 Asher's sons were Imnah, I,

Ishvi (4)

Gen 46:17 Imnah, Ishvah, I, and Beriah.
Num 26:44 family of Imnah, the family of I,
1Sm 14:49 Saul's sons were Jonathan, I,
1Ch 7:30 Imnah, Ishvah, I, and Beriah.

island (28)

Jer 47:4 who is left from the i of Crete.
Act 4:36 been born on the i of Cyprus.
13:4 there sailed to the i of Cyprus.
13:6 They went through the whole i
13:7 who was the governor of the i.
15:39 and sailed to the i of Cyprus.
16:11 straight to the i of Samothrace.
20:15 we approached the i of Chios.
20:15 day we went by the i of Samos,
21:1 sailed straight to the i of Cos.
21:1 The next day we sailed to the i
21:3 We could see the i of Cyprus
21:16 Mnason was from the i of
27:4 on the northern side of the i
27:7 the south side of the i of Crete.
27:12 and is located on the i of Crete.)
27:14 a northeaster) blew from the i.
27:16 side of a small i called Cauda,
27:26 we will run aground on some i."
28:1 out that the i was called Malta.
28:2 The people who lived on the i
28:4 people who lived on the i saw
28:7 who was the governor of the i,
28:9 other sick people on the i went
28:11 had spent the winter at the i.
Rev 1:9 I was ⌊exiled⌋ on the i of
6:14 Every mountain and i was
16:20 Every i vanished, and the

islands (9)

Est 10:1 the country and the i of the sea.
Psa 72:10 and the i bring presents.
97:1 Let all the i be joyful.
Isa 11:11 and the i of the sea.
40:15 The weight of the i is like fine
42:15 I will turn rivers into i.
49:1 Listen to me, you i.
Jer 31:10 Tell it to the distant i.
Eze 26:18 end will terrify the i in the sea.

Ismachiah (1)

2Ch 31:13 Jozabad, Eliel, I, Mahath,

isolated (1)

Isa 27:10 The fortified city is i.

isolation (9)

Lev 13:4 put him in i for seven days.
13:5 the priest must put him in i for
13:11 Without putting him in i,
13:21 put him in i for seven days.
13:26 put him in i for seven days.
13:31 disease in i for seven days.
13:33 the person with the scab in i
Num 12:14 She must be put in i outside
12:15 So Miriam was put in i outside

Israel (2018)

Gen 32:28 be Jacob but I [He Struggles
32:32 even today the people of I do
33:20 named it God Is the God of I.
35:10 but your name will be I."
35:10 So he named him I.
35:21 I moved on again and put up
35:22 While I was living in that
35:22 and I heard about it.
36:31 any king ruled the people of I:
37:3 I loved Joseph more than all
37:13 I then said to Joseph,
37:14 So I said, "See how your
43:2 from Egypt, I said to his sons,
43:6 I asked, "Why have you made
43:8 Then Judah said to his father I,
43:11 Then their father I said to them,
45:28 I said. "My son Joseph is still
46:1 I moved with all he had.
46:2 God spoke to I in a vision that
46:28 I sent Judah ahead of him to
46:29 and went to meet his father I.
46:30 I said to Joseph, "Now that I've
47:29 I was about to die.
47:31 Then I bowed down in prayer
48:2 I gathered his strength and sat
48:8 When I saw Joseph's sons,
48:9 Then I said, "Please bring
48:10 and I hugged them and kissed
48:11 I said to Joseph, "I never

Gen 48:14 But I crossed his hands and
48:20 I will speak this blessing,
48:20 In this way I put Ephraim ahead
48:21 Then I said to Joseph,
49:2 Listen to your father I.
49:7 them among ⌊the tribes of⌋ I.
49:16 people as one of the tribes of I.
49:24 of the Shepherd, the Rock of I,
49:28 These are the 12 tribes of I and
50:2 So the doctors embalmed I.
Exo 1:1 names of the sons of I (that is,
1:7 But the descendants of I had
3:9 heard the cry of the people of I.
3:10 bring my people I out of Egypt."
3:11 the people of I out of Egypt?"
3:13 "Suppose I go to the people of I
3:14 you must say to the people of I:
3:15 you must say to the people of I:
3:16 "Go, assemble the leaders of I.
3:18 "The leaders of I will listen to
3:21 kind to the people of I so that,
4:22 I is my firstborn son.
4:29 the leaders of the people of I.
4:31 concerned about the people of I
5:1 what the LORD God of I says:
5:2 Why should I obey him and let I
5:2 and I won't let I go."
11:2 the people ⌊of I⌋ that each man
11:7 between Egypt and I.
12:3 Tell the whole community of I:
12:6 of I must slaughter their
12:15 day must be excluded from I.
12:19 from the community of I,
12:21 called for all the leaders of I.
12:47 "The whole community of I
14:5 slaves because we've let I go."
14:25 The LORD is fighting for I!
14:28 cavalry that had followed I into
14:30 That day the LORD saved I
14:30 and I saw the Egyptians lying
15:22 Moses led I away from the Red
17:5 of the leaders of I with you,
17:6 the leaders of I watched him.
17:8 fought I at Rephidim.
17:11 held up his hands, I would win,
18:1 for Moses and his people I
18:1 had brought I out of Egypt.
18:8 and the Egyptians for I,
18:9 things the LORD had done for I
18:11 who treated I with contempt.
18:12 Aaron and all the leaders of I
19:2 I had moved from Rephidim
24:4 stones for the 12 tribes of I.
24:10 They saw the God of I.
28:9 the names of the sons of I
28:11 the names of the sons of I
28:21 correspond to the 12 sons of I,
28:29 of the sons of I over his heart
32:4 Then they said, "I,
32:8 They've said, 'I, here are your
32:13 Abraham, Isaac, and I.
32:27 what the LORD God of I says:
34:23 the LORD God of I.
34:27 a promise to I and to you."
39:6 the names of the sons of I.
39:14 to the 12 sons of I,
Lev 4:13 "If the whole congregation of I
9:1 his sons and the leaders of I.
16:5 from the congregation of I as
16:17 sins of the entire assembly of I.
17:5 that the people of I must take
17:12 I have said to the people of I:
17:14 I have said to the people of I:
19:2 the whole congregation of I:
23:42 Everyone born in I must live in
23:43 how I made the people of I live
24:10 from the tribe of Dan in I) and
24:23 Moses spoke to the people of I.
Num 1:2 community of I by families
1:3 everyone in I who is eligible
1:16 and heads of the divisions of I.
1:19 Moses registered the men of I
1:44 and the 12 leaders of I,
1:53 angry with the community of I.
3:13 as holy every firstborn in I,
4:46 and the leaders of I registered
Num 7:2 Then the leaders of I,
7:84 the gifts from the leaders of I
8:9 the whole community of I.
8:17 Every firstborn in I,
8:20 and the whole community of I
10:4 the heads of the divisions of I,
10:29 has promised good things to I."
10:36 the countless thousands of I!"
13:26 and the whole community of I
14:5 of I assembled there.
14:7 to the whole community of I,
14:10 of I talked about stoning
15:25 for the whole community of I.
15:26 So the whole community of I
16:9 the God of I has separated you
16:9 the rest of the community of I?
16:25 the leaders of I followed him.
16:40 altar will remind I that no one
16:41 community of I complained
18:14 "Anything in I that is claimed
19:9 be kept by the community of I
19:13 must be excluded from I,
20:1 community of I came into
20:14 is what your brother I says:
20:21 refused to let I go through their
20:22 The whole community of I left
21:17 Then I sang this song about
21:21 Then I sent messengers to say
21:23 Sihon wouldn't let I pass
21:23 out into the desert to attack I.
21:23 they fought against I.
21:24 But I defeated them in battle
21:25 I took all those Amorite cities,
21:31 So I settled in the land of the
22:2 saw all that I had done to the
23:7 'Come, condemn I.'
23:10 one-fourth of the people of I?
23:21 misfortune for the people of I.
23:23 magic can harm the people of I.
23:23 it will be said of Jacob and I:
24:1 the LORD wanted to bless I,
24:5 the places where you live, I.
24:17 A scepter will rise from I.
24:18 So I will become wealthy.
25:1 While I was staying at Shittim,
25:3 the LORD became angry with I.
25:4 the LORD's anger away from I."
25:5 Moses said to the judges of I,
25:6 community of I while they were
26:2 community of I by households.
27:20 community of I will obey him.
27:21 community of I will go into
30:1 to the heads of the tribes of I,
31:4 from each of the tribes of I."
31:5 the divisions of I — 12,000 men
31:12 and the community of I at the
32:4 won for the community of I,
32:14 the LORD angry with I again.
32:22 military duty to the LORD and I.
32:28 family heads of the tribes of I.
36:3 men from the other tribes of I.
36:8 any of the tribes of I may marry
Dtr 1:38 because he will help I take
2:12 as I did in the land that the
4:1 I, listen to the laws and rules I
4:44 Moses taught the people of I.
4:46 Moses and I defeated him after
5:1 Moses summoned all I and
5:1 all Israel and said to them: I,
6:3 Listen, I, and be careful to obey
6:4 Listen, I: The LORD is our God.
9:1 Listen, I, you're about to cross
10:12 I, what does the LORD your
13:11 All I will hear about it and be
17:4 thing has been done in I,
17:12 You must get rid of this evil in I.
17:20 will rule for a long time in I.
18:6 your cities in I may come from
19:13 person must be removed from I.
19:13 Then things will go well for I.
20:3 He should tell them, "Listen, I,
21:8 make peace with your people I,
21:8 remain among your people I."
21:21 When all I hears about it,
22:21 such a godless act in I:
22:22 You must get rid of this evil in I.
Dtr 25:6 that his name won't die out in I.
25:7 his brother's name continue in I
25:10 Then in I his family will be
26:15 Bless your people I and the
27:1 Moses and the leaders of I told
27:9 Levitical priests said to all I,
27:9 Israel, "Be quiet and listen, I.
27:14 declare to all the people of I
29:2 summoned all the people of I
29:10 and all the men of I are here.
29:21 him out from all the tribes of I
31:7 to him in the presence of all I,
31:9 and to all the leaders of I.
31:30 congregation of I listened,
32:8 to the number of the sons of I.
32:45 reciting all these words to I,
33:5 together with all the tribes of I.
33:10 rules and give I your teachings.
33:16 who are like princes in I.
33:21 of the people and did for I what
33:24 most blessed of the sons of I.
33:28 So I will live securely.
33:29 You are blessed, I!
34:10 another prophet in I like Moses,
Jos 1:2 going to give the people of I.
3:7 in front of all the people of I.
3:9 Joshua said to the people of I,
3:12 from each of the 12 tribes of I.
3:17 whole nation of I had crossed
4:5 one for each tribe of I.
4:7 reminder for the people of I."
4:8 The people of I did as Joshua
4:8 one for each of the tribes of I.
4:12 ahead of the people of I.
4:21 He said to the people of I,
4:22 should be told that I crossed
5:1 left to face the people of I.
5:2 and circumcise the men of I."
5:3 and circumcised the men of I at
5:10 The people of I camped at
5:12 The people of I never had
6:18 and disaster on the camp of I.
6:23 a place outside the camp of I.
6:24 Then I burned the city and
6:25 She still lives in I today
7:1 The people of I proved to be
7:1 angry with the people of I.
7:6 Joshua and the leaders of I
7:8 Lord, what else can I say after I
7:11 I has sinned. They have ignored
7:12 "The people of I will not be
7:12 the people of I are now claimed
7:13 This is what the LORD God of I
7:13 what I claimed for myself, I.
7:15 and done a godless thing in I.'"
7:16 He had I come forward by
7:19 praise to the LORD God of I!
7:20 against the LORD God of I.
7:23 Joshua and all the people of I.
7:24 Joshua and all I took Achan
7:25 And all I stoned Achan and his
8:10 Then he and the leaders of I
8:14 the plains to meet I for battle,
8:15 Joshua and all I pretended to
8:17 they all went after I.
8:17 unprotected as they chased I.
8:21 When Joshua and all I saw
8:22 between the battle lines of I.
8:22 So I attacked them on both
8:24 I had finished killing all the
8:27 I took the loot and the livestock
8:30 Ebal to the LORD God of I.
8:31 had commanded the people of I
8:32 There in front of the people of I
8:33 All the people of I,
8:33 bless the people of I this way.
8:35 of the whole assembly of I,
9:2 together to fight Joshua and I.
9:6 told Joshua and the men of I,
9:7 The men of I said to the
9:18 them to the LORD God of I.
9:19 them to the LORD God of I,
9:26 not let the people of I kill them.
10:1 peace with the people of I
10:4 Joshua and the people of I."
10:10 enemy into disorder in front of I

Jos	10:12	Amorites over to the people of **I**,
	10:12	LORD while **I** was watching,
	10:14	because the LORD fought for **I**.
	10:15	Then Joshua and all **I** returned
	10:24	he called for all the men of **I**.
	10:29	Joshua and all **I** marched from
	10:30	Libnah and its king over to **I**.
	10:31	Joshua and all **I** marched from
	10:32	handed Lachish over to **I**.
	10:34	Joshua and all **I** marched from
	10:36	Then Joshua and all **I** marched
	10:38	Then Joshua and all **I** went
	10:40	God of **I** had commanded.
	10:42	LORD God of **I** fought for Israel.
	10:42	LORD God of Israel fought for **I**.
	10:43	Then Joshua and all **I** returned
	11:5	of Merom in order to fight **I**.
	11:6	I am going to give them to **I**.
	11:8	LORD handed them over to **I**,
	11:13	**I** did not burn cities built on
	11:14	The people of **I** took all the loot
	11:16	the mountains and foothills of **I**.
	11:19	the people of **I** except Gibeon,
	11:19	**I** captured everything in battle.
	11:20	fighting against **I** so that
	11:21	in all the hills of Judah and **I**.
	11:22	people of Anak remained in **I**.
	11:23	He gave it to **I** as a possession,
	12:1	that the people of **I** defeated.
	12:1	**I** also took possession of their
	12:6	the people of **I** defeated them.
	12:7	and the people of **I** defeated.
	12:7	gave it as a possession to **I**,
	13:6	people of **I** everyone who lives
	13:6	inheritance to **I** by drawing lots,
	13:13	So they still live in **I** today.
	13:14	to the LORD God of **I** are what
	13:22	the people of **I** also killed
	13:33	The LORD God of **I** is what
	14:1	that the people of **I** inherited
	14:5	So the people of **I** divided the
	14:10	It's been 45 years since **I**
	14:14	loyal to the LORD God of **I**.
	18:1	The whole congregation of **I**
	18:2	seven tribes in **I** who had not
	18:10	the land among the tribes of **I**.
	19:49	the people of **I** also gave land
	19:51	that the tribes of **I** drew by lot.
	20:2	"Tell the people of **I**,
	21:43	So the LORD gave **I** the whole
	21:45	given the nation of **I** came true.
	22:12	When the people of **I** heard
	22:12	the whole congregation of **I**
	22:14	one from each tribe in **I**,
	22:14	head of a family division in **I**.
	22:16	against the God of **I**?' Today
	22:18	the whole congregation of **I**.
	22:20	the whole congregation of **I**?
	22:21	the heads of the divisions of **I**.
	22:22	He knows, so let **I** know!
	22:24	have with the LORD God of **I**?
	22:30	of the divisions of **I** heard what
	22:31	rescued the people of **I** from
	22:32	Reuben and Gad in Gilead to **I**
	22:33	The people of **I** were satisfied
	23:2	and officers of **I** together.
	24:1	tribes of **I** together at Shechem.
	24:2	what the LORD God of **I** says:
	24:9	King Zippor of Moab, fought **I**.
	24:23	over to the LORD God of **I**."
	24:31	**I** served the LORD as long as
	24:31	the LORD had done for **I**,
	24:32	which the people of **I** had
Jdg	2:4	this to all the people of **I**,
	2:6	sent the people of **I** home.
	2:7	works the LORD had done for **I**.
	2:10	or with what he had done for **I**.
	2:11	The people of **I** did what the
	2:14	angry with the people of **I**.
	2:20	LORD became angry with **I**.
	2:22	I will test the people of **I** with
	3:5	So the people of **I** lived among
	3:6	**I** also served their gods.
	3:7	The people of **I** did what the
	3:8	angry with the people of **I**.
	3:8	So **I** served Cushan
Jdg	3:9	Then the people of **I** cried out
	3:10	he became the judge of **I**.
	3:12	Once again, the people of **I** did
	3:12	Eglon of Moab stronger than **I**,
	3:12	because **I** did what the LORD
	3:15	Then the people of **I** cried out
	3:27	So the troops of **I** came down
	3:30	was crushed by **I** that day.
	3:31	So he, too, rescued **I**.
	4:1	After Ehud died, the people of **I**
	4:3	The people of **I** cried out to the
	4:3	oppressed **I** for 20 years.
	4:4	was the judge in **I** at that time.
	4:5	The people of **I** would come to
	4:6	"The LORD God of **I** has given
	4:23	God used the people of **I** to
	5:2	Men in **I** vowed to fight,
	5:3	music to the LORD God of **I**.
	5:5	presence of the LORD God of **I**.
	5:7	Villages in **I** were deserted —
	5:7	took a stand as a mother of **I**.
	5:8	was seen among 40,000 in **I**.
	5:11	victories for his villages in **I**.
	6:1	The people of **I** did what the
	6:2	power was too strong for **I**.
	6:3	Whenever **I** planted crops,
	6:4	They left nothing for **I** to live on
	6:7	When the people of **I** cried out
	6:8	what the LORD God of **I** says:
	6:14	"You will rescue **I** from Midian
	6:15	How can I rescue **I**?
	6:36	you would rescue **I** through me.
	6:37	you will rescue **I** through me,
	7:2	**I** might brag and say,
	7:8	sent the other men of **I** home,
	7:14	of Gideon, son of Joash, from **I**.
	7:15	back to the camp of **I** and said,
	7:23	The men of **I** were summoned
	8:22	The men of **I** said to Gideon,
	8:25	The men of **I** answered,
	8:27	All **I** chased after it there as
	8:28	was crushed by the people of **I**,
	8:33	the people of **I** chased after
	8:35	all the good he had done for **I**.
	9:22	ruled **I** for three years.
	9:55	When the people of **I** saw that
	10:1	of Dodo, came to rescue **I**.
	10:2	He judged **I** for 23 years.
	10:3	He judged **I** for 22 years.
	10:6	The people of **I** again did what
	10:7	angry with the people of **I**.
	10:8	the people of **I** that year.
	10:9	So **I** suffered a great deal.
	10:10	Then the people of **I** cried out
	10:11	LORD said to the people of **I**,
	10:15	The people of **I** said to the
	10:16	bear to have **I** suffer any longer.
	10:17	The people of **I** also gathered
	11:4	Ammon waged war with **I**.
	11:5	the Ammonites attacked **I**,
	11:13	the people of **I** left Egypt,
	11:15	The people of **I** didn't take
	11:16	When the people of **I** left Egypt,
	11:17	The people of **I** sent
	11:17	people of **I** remained at Kadesh.
	11:19	"Then the people of **I** sent
	11:19	The people of **I** said to him,
	11:20	at Jahaz and attacked **I**.
	11:21	But the LORD God of **I** handed
	11:21	and all his people over to **I**.
	11:21	**I** defeated them and took
	11:22	**I** took all the Amorite territory
	11:23	"The LORD God of **I** forced the
	11:23	out of the way of his people **I**.
	11:25	he ever have a case against **I**?
	11:25	Or did he ever fight against **I**?
	11:26	**I** has now lived in Heshbon,
	11:27	will decide today whether **I**
	11:33	crushed by the people of **I**.
	11:39	So the custom began in **I**
	11:40	year the girls in **I** would go out
	12:7	Jephthah judged **I** for six years.
	12:8	Ibzan from Bethlehem judged **I**.
	12:9	He judged **I** for seven years.
	12:11	the tribe of Zebulun judged **I**.
	12:11	He judged **I** for ten years.
Jdg	12:13	from Pirathon judged **I**.
	12:14	He judged **I** for eight years.
	13:1	The people of **I** again did what
	13:5	He will begin to rescue **I** from
	14:4	the Philistines were ruling **I**.)
	15:20	Samson judged **I** for 20 years
	16:31	had judged **I** for 20 years.
	17:6	In those days **I** didn't have a
	18:1	In those days **I** didn't have a
	18:1	the tribes of **I** as they should
	18:19	for a tribe in **I** and its families?"
	19:1	In those days when **I** didn't
	19:29	throughout the territories of **I**.
	19:30	time the people of **I** came out
	20:1	All the people of **I** from Dan to
	20:3	Benjamin heard that **I** had come
	20:3	The people of **I** said,
	20:6	throughout the territory of **I**.
	20:6	and godless thing in **I**.
	20:7	All you people of **I**,
	20:10	all the men from the tribes of **I**
	20:10	the godless thing they did in **I**."
	20:11	So all the men of **I** assembled.
	20:12	The tribes of **I** sent men
	20:13	of this kind of evil in **I**."
	20:13	refused to listen to the men of **I**.
	20:14	to go to war with the men of **I**.
	20:17	The men of **I** (Benjamin not
	20:18	The men of **I** went to Bethel.
	20:20	So the men of **I** went to war
	20:25	men from **I** who were armed
	20:26	Then all the men of **I** and all
	20:28	So the people of **I** asked the
	20:29	Then **I** placed troops in
	20:30	On the third day the men of **I**
	20:31	They killed about 30 men from **I**
	20:32	But the men of **I** had said,
	20:33	So the men of **I** left their
	20:35	defeated them in front of **I**.
	20:38	The men of **I** had arranged with
	20:39	Then the men of **I** would turn
	20:39	killed about 30 men of **I**.
	20:39	"**I** is completely defeated,
	20:41	the men of **I** turned around,
	20:42	They turned in front of **I** toward
	20:42	**I** slaughtered whoever came
	20:45	But the men of **I** killed 5,000
	20:48	Then the men of **I** went back to
	21:1	The men of **I** had taken this
	21:3	"LORD God of **I**, why has this
	21:3	tribe be missing today in **I**?"
	21:5	"Is there any family from **I** that
	21:6	The people of **I** felt sorry for
	21:6	tribe has been excluded from **I**.
	21:8	"Is there any family from **I** that
	21:15	the unity of the tribes of **I**.
	21:17	No tribe of **I** should be wiped
	21:18	The people of **I** have taken an
	21:24	At that time the people of **I** left.
	21:25	In those days **I** didn't have a
Rut	2:12	reward from the LORD God of **I**,
	4:7	be in **I** concerning buying back
	4:7	was publicly approved in **I**.)
	4:11	of whom built our family of **I**.
	4:14	name will be famous in **I**.
1Sm	1:17	the God of **I** grant your request.
	2:14	the people of **I** who came there
	2:22	that his sons were doing to all **I**
	2:28	out of all the tribes of **I**
	2:28	that the people of **I** burned
	2:29	offered by my people **I**?
	2:30	the LORD God of **I** declares:
	2:32	spite of the good that I do for **I**,
	3:11	"I am going to do something in **I**
	3:20	All **I** from Dan to Beersheba
	3:21	And Samuel spoke to all **I**.
	4:1	**I** went to fight against the
	4:2	their troops to meet **I** in battle.
	4:2	the Philistines defeated **I** and
	4:3	the leaders of **I** asked,
	4:5	all **I** shouted so loudly that the
	4:10	fought and defeated **I**.
	4:17	"**I** fled from the Philistines,"
	4:18	He had judged **I** for 40 years.
	5:7	"The ark of the God of **I** must
	5:8	do with the ark of the God of **I**?"

1Sm 5:8 "The ark of the God of I must
5:8 the ark of the God of I there.
5:10 the ark of the God of I here
5:11 the ark of the God of I away,"
6:3 returning the ark of the God of I
6:5 and give glory to the God of I.
7:2 nation of I mournfully sought
7:3 told the entire nation of I,
7:6 So Samuel judged I in Mizpah.
7:7 rulers came to attack I.
7:9 to the LORD on behalf of I,
7:10 came to fight against I.
7:10 that they were defeated by I.
7:14 took from I were returned
7:14 from Israel were returned to I.
7:14 And I recovered the territory
7:14 between I and the Amorites.
7:15 Samuel judged I as long as he
7:16 and Mizpah in order to judge I
7:17 There, too, he judged I.
8:1 made his sons judges over I.
8:4 Then all the leaders of I
8:22 Samuel told the people of I,
9:2 No man in I was more
9:9 (Formerly in I, when a person
9:16 him to be ruler of my people I.
9:20 have all that is desirable in I?
9:21 the smallest tribe of I.
10:1 you to be ruler of his people I.
10:18 what the LORD God of I says:
10:18 I brought I out of Egypt and
10:20 all the tribes of I come forward,
11:1 and allow no one to rescue I.
11:2 eye and bring disgrace on all I."
11:3 throughout the territory of I.
11:7 throughout the territory of I
11:8 were 300,000 troops from I
11:13 today the LORD saved I."
12:1 Then Samuel said to all I,
13:1 was king of I ⌊forty-two⌋ years.
13:2 Saul chose 3,000 men from I;
13:4 (So all I listened.) "I, Saul, have
13:4 and now I has become
13:5 assembled to fight against I.
13:13 kingdom over I permanently.
13:19 be found in the entire land of I.
13:20 Everyone in I had to go to the
14:12 handed the troops over to I."
14:18 the ephod in front of I that day.
14:22 When all the men of I who had
14:23 So the LORD saved I that day.
14:37 Will you hand them over to I?"
14:39 the LORD and Savior of I lives,
14:40 Saul told all I, "You stand on
14:41 said to the LORD, "O God of I,
14:41 son Jonathan's, LORD God of I,
14:41 But if it is in your people I,
14:45 has won this great victory in I?
14:47 taken over the kingdom of I,
14:48 He rescued I from the enemies
15:1 anoint you king of his people I.
15:2 Amalek for what they did to I.
15:17 LORD anointed you king of I.
15:26 LORD rejects you as king of I."
15:28 kingdom of I from you today.
15:29 In addition, the Glory of I does
15:30 of my people and in front of I.
15:35 that he had made Saul king of I.
16:1 have rejected him as king of I?
17:2 So Saul and the army of I
17:19 Saul and all the soldiers of I,
17:21 I and the Philistines formed
17:24 all the men of I saw Goliath,
17:25 The men of I said,
17:25 keeps coming to challenge I.
17:45 the God of the army of I,
17:46 will know that I has a God.
17:52 Then the soldiers of I and
18:16 Everyone in I and Judah loved
18:18 or my father's family in I that
18:30 still went out ⌊to fight I⌋.
19:5 and the LORD gave all I a great
20:12 "As the LORD God of I ⌊is my
23:10 David said, "LORD God of I,
23:11 LORD God of I, please tell me."
23:17 You will rule I, and I will be

1Sm 24:2 the best-trained men from all I
24:14 has the king of I come out?
24:20 the kingdom of I will prosper.
25:1 Samuel died, and all I gathered
25:30 and makes you ruler of I,
25:32 be the LORD God of I,
25:34 swear — as the LORD God of I,
26:15 Is there anyone like you in I?
26:20 The king of I has come to
27:1 up looking all over I for me,
27:12 own people in I despise him.
28:1 their army to fight against I.
28:3 and all I had mourned for him
28:19 LORD will hand you and I over
29:1 and I camped at the spring in
29:3 the servant of King Saul of I,
30:25 this a rule and a custom in I as
31:1 were fighting against I,
31:1 the men of I fled from the
31:7 When the people of I on the
31:7 saw that the men of I had fled
2Sm 1:3 the camp of I," he answered.
1:12 and the nation of I had been
1:19 "Your glory, I, lies dead on your
1:24 Daughters of I, cry over Saul,
2:9 and Benjamin, that is, all I.
2:10 old when he became king of I.
2:17 Abner and the men of I.
2:28 They didn't chase or fight I
3:10 establish David's throne over I
3:12 you and bring all I to you."
3:17 message to the leaders of I:
3:18 'I will save my people I from
3:19 Hebron to tell him everything I
3:21 so that I can gather all I for you,
3:37 That day all the people of I
3:38 a great man, has fallen in I?
4:1 and all I was alarmed.
5:1 All the tribes of I came to David
5:2 the one who led I in battle.
5:2 be shepherd of my people I,
5:2 people Israel, the leader of I.'"
5:3 All the leaders of I had come to
5:3 they anointed David king of I.
5:5 33 years over all I and Judah.
5:12 established him as king of I
5:12 famous for the sake of I,
5:17 had been anointed king of I,
6:1 all the best soldiers in I,
6:5 David and the entire nation of I
6:15 He and the entire nation of I
6:21 he appointed me leader of I,
7:6 house from the day I took I out
7:7 any of the judges of I whom
7:7 of my people I why they didn't
7:8 be the leader of my people I.
7:10 make a place for my people I
7:11 judges to rule my people I.
7:23 Who is like your people I?
7:24 You created the people of I to
7:26 of Armies is God over I.' And
7:27 You, LORD of Armies, God of I,
8:15 So David ruled all I.
10:9 he took the select troops of I
10:15 Realizing that I had defeated
10:18 The Arameans fled from I,
10:19 saw that I had defeated them,
10:19 they made peace with I and
11:11 "The ark and ⌊the army of⌋ I
12:7 what the LORD God of I says:
12:7 I anointed you king over I and
12:8 you the house of I and Judah.
12:12 broad daylight in front of all I."
13:12 That shouldn't be done in I.
13:13 one of the godless fools in I!
14:25 Now, no one in all I was
15:2 which tribe in I he was from,
15:6 the hearts of the people of I.
15:10 to all the tribes of I and said,
15:13 people of I are with Absalom."
16:3 "He said, 'Today the house of I
16:18 and all I have chosen.
16:21 Then all I will hear about how
16:22 concubines in plain sight of I.
17:4 Absalom and all the leaders of I
17:10 because all I knows that your

2Sm 17:13 If he retreats into a city, all I
17:14 and all the people of I said,
17:15 Absalom and the leaders of I
17:24 Absalom and all the men of I
18:6 went out to the country to fight I
18:16 troops returned from pursuing I
18:17 Meanwhile, all I fled and went
19:8 Meanwhile, I had fled and went
19:9 all the tribes of I were arguing
19:11 What all I was saying reached
19:22 Should anyone in I be killed
19:22 I know that I'm king of I again?
19:40 half of the troops from I brought
19:41 Then all the people of I kept
19:42 answered the people of I,
19:43 The people of I answered the
19:43 harshly than the people of I.
20:1 Everyone to his own tent, I!"
20:2 So all the people of I left David
20:14 through all the tribes of I
20:19 to destroy a mother city in I?
21:2 Gibeonites were not a part of I
21:2 destroy them for I and Judah.)
21:4 us wants to kill ⌊anyone⌋ in I."
21:15 between the Philistines and I.
21:17 The lamp of I must never be
21:21 When he challenged I,
23:3 The God of I spoke to them.
23:3 The rock of I told me,
23:9 When the soldiers from I
24:1 The LORD became angry with I
24:1 David to turn against I.
24:1 count I and Judah."
24:2 "Go throughout the tribes of I
24:4 order⌋ to count the people of I.
24:9 In I there were 800,000
24:25 and the plague on I stopped.
1Ki 1:3 So they searched throughout I
1:20 All I is looking to you,
1:30 to you by the LORD God of I.
1:34 anoint him king of I there.
1:35 to be the leader of I and Judah."
1:48 'Praise the LORD God of I who
2:4 have an heir on the throne of I.'
2:11 He ruled as king of I for 40
2:15 All I expected me to be their
3:28 All I heard about the decision
4:1 Solomon was the king of all I,
4:7 12 district governors in I.
4:20 The people of Judah and I
4:25 Judah and I (from Dan to
5:13 30,000 men from all over I
6:1 480 years after I left Egypt.
6:1 fourth year of his reign over I.
8:1 the respected leaders of I,
8:2 All the people of I gathered
8:3 all the leaders of I had arrived,
8:5 from I were offering countless
8:14 assembly of I while they were
8:15 be to the LORD God of I.
8:16 since I brought my people I out
8:16 city in any of the tribes of I as
8:16 David to rule my people I.'
8:17 the name of the LORD God of I.
8:20 and I sit on the throne of I as
8:20 the name of the LORD God of I.
8:22 of the entire assembly of I,
8:23 and said, "LORD God of I,
8:25 "Now, LORD God of I,
8:25 throne of I if your descendants
8:26 "So now, God of I,
8:30 for mercy that your people I
8:33 may defeat your people I
8:34 the sins of your people I,
8:36 of your servants, your people I.
8:38 person or by all the people in I,
8:43 and fear you like your people I
8:55 the entire assembly of I,
8:56 He has given his people I rest,
8:59 his people I justice every day
8:62 Then the king and all I offered
8:63 all the people of I dedicated
8:65 At that time Solomon and all I
8:66 servant David and his people I.
9:5 royal dynasty over I forever as
9:5 have an heir on the throne of I.'

1Ki 9:7 then I will cut I out of the land I
9:7 I will be an example and an
10:9 has put you on the throne of I.
10:9 eternal love for the people of I,
10:10 brought ⌊into I⌋ as those that
10:12 like this imported ⌊into I⌋,
11:2 had said to the people of I,
11:9 turned from the LORD God of I,
11:16 (Joab and all I stayed there six
11:25 He ruled Aram and despised I.
11:31 what the LORD God of I says:
11:32 chosen from all the tribes of I.
11:37 You will be king of I.
11:38 And I will give you I.
11:42 over all I was 40 years.
12:1 because all I had gone
12:3 ⌊I⌋ sent for Jeroboam and
12:3 the entire assembly of I went
12:16 When all I saw that the king
12:16 To your own tents, I!
12:16 So I went home to their own
12:18 Rehoboam sent Adoram to I.
12:19 I has rebelled against David's
12:20 When all I heard that Jeroboam
12:20 They made him king of all I.
12:21 to fight against the people of I
12:24 against your relatives from I.
12:28 I, here are your gods who
14:7 what the LORD God of I says:
14:7 you a leader over my people I.
14:10 whether slave or freeman in I.
14:13 All I will mourn for him and
14:13 God of I found anything good.
14:14 will appoint a king over I.
14:15 "The LORD will strike I like
14:15 He will uproot I from this good
14:16 So the LORD will desert I
14:16 sins which he led I to commit."
14:18 All I buried him and mourned
14:19 official records of the kings of I.
14:21 chose from all the tribes of I,
15:9 twentieth year as king of I,
15:16 King Baasha of I as long as
15:17 King Baasha of I invaded
15:19 with King Baasha of I so that
15:20 armies to attack the cities of I.
15:25 began to rule I in Asa's second
15:26 leading I into the same sins.
15:28 succeeded Nadab as king of I.
15:30 sins which he led I to commit.
15:30 the LORD God of I furious.
15:31 records of the kings of I?
15:33 began to rule I in Tirzah.
15:34 and led I into committing
16:2 you leader of my people I.
16:5 records of the kings of I?
16:8 began to rule I in Asa's
16:10 succeeded Elah as king ⌊of I⌋.
16:13 They sinned, led I to sin,
16:13 and made the LORD God of I
16:14 records of the kings of I?
16:16 of the army, king of I.
16:19 like Jeroboam and led I to sin.
16:20 records of the kings of I?
16:21 Then the army of I was divided
16:23 Omri began to rule I in Asa's
16:26 He sinned and led I to sin with
16:26 the LORD God of I furious.
16:27 records of the kings of I?
16:29 began to rule I in Asa's
16:33 LORD God of I furious than all
16:33 the kings of I who came before
17:1 as the LORD God of I whom I
17:14 This is what the LORD God of I
18:17 you troublemaker of I?"
18:18 "I haven't troubled I.
18:19 Order all I to gather around me
18:31 "Your name will be I.")
18:36 God of Abraham, Isaac, and I,
18:36 today that you are God in I
19:16 son of Nimshi, as king of I.
19:18 But I still have 7,000 people in I
20:2 into the city to King Ahab of I.
20:4 The king of I answered,
20:7 Then the king of I called for all
20:11 The king of I answered,

1Ki 20:13 to King Ahab of I and said,
20:20 and I pursued them.
20:21 The king of I went out and
20:22 came to the king of I and said,
20:26 and went to Aphek to fight I.
20:28 He said to the king of I,
20:31 that the kings of I are merciful.
20:31 and go to the king of I.
20:32 went to the king of I and said,
20:40 The king of I told him,
20:41 The king of I recognized him
20:43 the king of I went home to
21:7 "Aren't you king of I?
21:18 "Go, meet King Ahab of I,
21:21 whether slave or freeman in I.
21:22 me furious. You led I to sin."
21:26 confiscated their land for I.)
22:1 no war between Aram and I.
22:2 went to visit the king of I.
22:3 The king of I asked his staff,
22:4 Jehoshaphat told the king of I,
22:5 said to the king of I,
22:6 So the king of I called 400
22:8 The king of I told Jehoshaphat,
22:9 The king of I called for an
22:10 The king of I and King
22:18 The king of I said to
22:26 The king of I then said,
22:29 So the king of I and King
22:30 The king of I told Jehoshaphat,
22:30 So the king of I disguised
22:31 anyone except the king of I."
22:32 "He must be the king of I."
22:33 that he wasn't the king of I.
22:34 the king of I between his scale
22:39 records of the kings of I?
22:41 Ahab's fourth year as king of I.
22:44 made peace with the king of I.
22:51 became king of I in Samaria
22:51 Ahaziah ruled I for two years.
22:52 (Nebat's son) who led I to sin.
22:53 the LORD God of I furious,
2Ki 1:1 Moab rebelled against I.
1:3 think⌋ there is no God in I?
1:6 think⌋ there is no God in I?
1:16 is no God in I whose word you
1:18 records of the kings of I?
3:1 became king of I in Samaria
3:3 (Nebat's son) led I to commit.
3:4 king of I 100,000 male lambs
3:5 against the ⌊new⌋ king of I.
3:9 So the king of I, the king of
3:10 The king of I said,
3:11 of the king of I answered,
3:12 of Judah, the king of I,
3:13 Elisha asked the king of I,
3:13 The king of I answered him,
3:24 I went after the Moabites and
3:25 Then I tore down the cities,
5:2 brought back a little girl from I.
5:4 what the girl from I had said.
5:5 send a letter to the king of I."
5:6 the letter to the king of I.
5:7 When the king of I read the
5:8 heard that the king of I had torn
5:8 out that there is a prophet in I."
5:12 water than any of the rivers in I.
5:15 except the God of I.
6:8 of Aram was fighting against I,
6:9 a message to the king of I,
6:10 Then the king of I would send
6:11 us is ⌊a spy⌋ for the king of I?"
6:12 Elisha, the prophet in I,
6:12 tells the king of I everything
6:21 When the king of I saw them,
6:26 As the king of I was walking
7:6 "The king of I has hired the
8:16 as king of I when Jehoram,
8:18 the ways of the kings of I,
8:25 king of I when Jehoram's son
8:26 granddaughter of King Omri of I
9:3 anointed you king of I.' Then
9:6 what the LORD God of I says:
9:6 LORD's people, ⌊king⌋ of I.
9:8 whether slave or freeman in I.
9:12 I have anointed you king of I.'"

2Ki 9:14 (Joram and all I were guarding
9:21 King Joram of I and King
9:29 Ahab's son, was king of I.)
10:28 rid of Baal worship throughout I
10:29 Jeroboam (Nebat's son) led I
10:30 will sit on the throne of I."
10:31 of the LORD God of I.
10:31 that Jeroboam led I to commit.
10:34 records of the kings of I?
10:36 Jehu ruled as king of I in
12:1 seventh year as king of I,
13:1 to rule in Samaria as king of I.
13:2 (Nebat's son) led I to commit.
13:3 the LORD became angry with I
13:4 king was oppressing I.
13:6 his dynasty led I to commit.
13:8 records of the kings of I?
13:10 began to rule I in Samaria.
13:11 that Jeroboam led I to commit.
13:12 records of the kings of I?
13:13 with the kings of I in Samaria.
13:14 King Jehoash of I visited him,
13:16 Then Elisha told the king of I,
13:18 he told the king of I.
13:22 of Aram oppressed I as long as
13:25 and recovered those cities of I.
14:1 king of I when King Amaziah,
14:8 and grandson of Jehu of I,
14:8 to declare war on I.
14:9 King Jehoash of I sent this
14:11 So King Jehoash of I attacked,
14:12 I defeated the army of Judah,
14:13 King Jehoash of I captured
14:15 records of the kings of I?
14:16 with the kings of I in Samaria.
14:17 son King Jehoash of I.
14:23 son King Jeroboam of I began
14:24 (Nebat's son) led I to commit.
14:25 God of I predicted through his
14:26 everyone in I was suffering.
14:26 or free person could help I.
14:28 and Hamath for I — written
14:28 records of the kings of I?
14:29 his ancestors, the kings of I.
15:1 year as king of I,
15:8 son Zechariah was king of I
15:9 (Nebat's son) led I to commit.
15:11 official records of the kings of I.
15:12 will sit on the throne of I."
15:15 official records of the kings of I.
15:17 began to rule as king of I.
15:18 (Nebat's son) led I to commit.
15:20 from all the wealthy men in I.
15:21 records of the kings of I?
15:23 Pekahiah was king of I in
15:24 (Nebat's son) led I to commit.
15:26 official records of the kings of I.
15:27 began to rule I in Samaria.
15:28 (Nebat's son) led I to commit.
15:29 In the days of King Pekah of I,
15:31 official records of the kings of I.
15:32 ruled I, Jotham, son of Azariah,
16:1 as king of I when King Ahaz,
16:3 the example of the kings of I
16:5 son of Remaliah of I,
16:7 of Aram and I who are attacking
17:1 to rule as king of I in Samaria.
17:2 the kings of I before him had
17:6 ninth year as king of I,
17:13 The LORD had warned I and
17:18 became so angry with I that
17:20 and finally turned away from I.
17:21 When he tore I away from the
17:21 the people of I made Jeroboam
17:21 Jeroboam forced I away from
17:23 the LORD turned away from I
17:23 So the people of I were taken
17:34 of Jacob (whom he named I).
17:35 the LORD made a promise to I,
17:40 The people of I had refused to
18:1 had been king in I for three
18:5 trusted the LORD God of I.
18:9 son of Elah of I) King
18:10 ninth year as king of I).
19:15 "LORD of Armies, God of I,
19:20 what the LORD God of I says:

2Ki 19:22 It is the Holy One of I!
21:3 as King Ahab of I had done.
21:7 from all the tribes of I.
21:9 Manasseh misled I so that they
21:12 the LORD God of I,
22:15 what the LORD God of I says:
22:18 the LORD God of I says about
23:13 King Solomon of I had built
23:15 who had made I sin.
23:19 The kings of I had built these
23:22 of the judges who governed I
23:22 of the kings of I and Judah.
23:27 out of my sight as I put I out
24:13 King Solomon of I had made
1Ch 1:34 Isaac's sons were Esau and I.
1:43 any king ruled the people of I:
2:7 who caused trouble for I by
4:10 Jabez prayed to the God of I,
5:17 Judah and King Jeroboam of I.
5:26 Then the God of I led King Pul
6:38 who was the son of I.
6:49 sins to make I acceptable
7:29 son of I, live in these cities.
9:1 All I was recorded in the
9:1 of the Kings of I and Judah.
10:1 the Philistines fought against I,
10:1 the men of I fled from the
10:7 When all the people of I in the
11:1 All I gathered around David at
11:2 you were the one who led I on
11:2 be shepherd of my people I,
11:2 the leader of my people I.'"
11:3 All the leaders of I had come to
11:3 they anointed David king of I,
11:4 David and all I went to
11:10 and with all I they made him
11:10 to the LORD's word to I.
12:32 and knew what I should do.
12:38 to make David king of all I.
12:38 The rest of I also had agreed to
12:40 because I was celebrating.
13:2 told the whole assembly of I,
13:2 our relatives in every region of I
13:5 So David gathered all I from the
13:6 David and all I went to Baalah
13:8 David and all I were
14:2 established him as king of I
14:2 made famous for the sake of I,
14:8 had been anointed king of I,
15:3 David called together all I at
15:12 the ark of the LORD God of I
15:14 the ark of the LORD God of I.
15:25 So David, the leaders of I,
15:28 All I brought the ark of the
16:3 to every person in I — both men
16:4 praise to the LORD God of I.
16:13 you descendants of I,
16:17 as an everlasting promise to I,
16:36 LORD God of I from everlasting
16:40 Teachings that he gave I.
17:5 day I brought I out ⌊of Egypt⌋
17:6 the places I've moved with all I,
17:6 any of the judges of I whom
17:7 be the leader of my people I.
17:9 make a place for my people I
17:10 judges to rule my people I.
17:21 Who is like your people I?
17:22 You made the people of I to be
17:24 the God of I, is Israel's God.'
18:14 So David ruled all I.
19:10 he took the select troops of I
19:16 Realizing that I had defeated
19:18 The Arameans fled from I,
19:19 saw that I had defeated them,
20:7 When he challenged I,
21:1 Satan attempted to attack I by
21:2 count I from Beersheba to Dan.
21:3 Why do you wish to make I
21:4 So Joab left, went throughout I,
21:5 In I there were 1,100,000 men
21:7 so he struck I ⌊with a plague⌋.
21:12 the whole country of I.' Decide
21:14 the LORD sent a plague on I,
22:2 foreigners living in I to gather.
22:6 a temple for the LORD God of I.
22:9 I will give I peace and quiet.
1Ch 22:10 kingdom permanently over I.'"
22:12 you to take charge of I
22:13 commanded Moses to give to I.
22:17 ordered all the leaders of I
23:1 his son Solomon king of I.
23:2 He gathered all the officials of I
23:25 "The LORD God of I has given
24:19 God of I had commanded him.
26:29 outside ⌊the temple⌋ in I.
26:30 were appointed to serve I west
27:16 were in charge of the tribes of I:
27:23 that the people of I would
27:24 God was angry with I because
28:1 for all the leaders of I —
28:4 the LORD God of I chose me
28:4 me to be king of I permanently.
28:4 the tribe of Judah to lead ⌊I⌋.
28:4 to make me king of all I.
28:5 of the LORD's kingdom to rule I.
28:8 I order you⌋ in the sight of I
29:6 the leaders of the tribes of I,
29:10 you be praised, LORD God of I,
29:18 Abraham, Isaac, and I,
29:21 and many sacrifices for all I.
29:23 and all I obeyed him.
29:25 powerful, as all I could see.
29:25 The people of I gave him royal
29:25 like no king of I before him ever
29:26 son of Jesse, had ruled all I.
29:27 He ruled as king of I for 40
29:30 I, and all the other kingdoms.
2Ch 1:2 Solomon spoke to all I — to the
1:13 to Jerusalem. And he ruled I.
2:4 always to be celebrated by I.)
2:12 the LORD God of I be praised.
2:17 were foreigners in the land of I,
5:2 the respected leaders of I,
5:3 All the men of I gathered
5:4 all the leaders of I had arrived,
5:6 from I were offering countless
6:3 from I while they were
6:4 be to the LORD God of I.
6:5 since I brought my people I out
6:5 any city from the tribes of I as
6:5 to be prince over my people I.
6:6 David to rule my people I.'
6:7 the name of the LORD God of I.
6:10 and I sit on the throne of I as
6:10 the name of the LORD God of I.
6:11 the LORD's promise to I there."
6:12 of the entire assembly of I,
6:14 He said, "LORD God of I,
6:16 "Now, LORD God of I,
6:16 throne of I if your descendants
6:17 "So now, LORD God of I,
6:21 for mercy that your people I
6:24 may defeat your people I
6:25 the sins of your people I,
6:27 of your servants, your people I.
6:29 person or by all the people in I,
6:33 and fear you like your people I
7:6 all I was standing ⌊there⌋.
7:8 At that time Solomon and all I
7:10 Solomon, and his people I.
7:18 fail to have an heir ruling I.'
7:20 then I will uproot I from the land
8:11 in the palace of King David of I
9:8 God's love for the people of I,
9:9 of spices ⌊in I⌋ as those that
9:30 over all I for 40 years.
10:1 because all I had gone
10:3 ⌊I⌋ sent for Jeroboam and
10:3 Jeroboam and all I went to
10:16 When all I saw that the king
10:16 Everyone to his own tent, I!
10:16 So all I went home to their own
10:19 I has rebelled against David's
11:1 to fight against I and return the
11:3 and all I in Judah and
11:13 of I sided with Rehoboam.
11:16 People from every tribe of I
11:16 the LORD God of I followed
12:1 he and all I abandoned the
12:2 This happened because all I
12:6 Then the commanders of I and
12:13 chose from all the tribes of I,
2Ch 13:4 "Jeroboam and all I,
13:5 that the LORD God of I gave
13:5 of Israel gave the kingdom of I
13:12 Men of I, don't wage war
13:15 attacked Jeroboam and all I
13:17 of the best men of I were killed.
15:3 For a long time I was without
15:4 turned to the LORD God of I.
15:9 to him from I when they saw
15:13 to the LORD God of I were
15:17 sites in I were not taken
16:1 King Baasha of I invaded
16:3 with King Baasha of I so that
16:4 armies to attack the cities of I.
16:11 of the Kings of Judah and I.
17:1 ⌊to wage war⌋ against I.
17:4 did not do what I was doing.
18:3 King Ahab of I asked King
18:3 Jehoshaphat told the king of I,
18:4 said to the king of I,
18:5 So the king of I called 400
18:7 The king of I told Jehoshaphat,
18:8 The king of I called for an
18:9 The king of I and King
18:17 The king of I said to
18:19 deceive King Ahab of I so that
18:25 The king of I then said,
18:28 So the king of I and King
18:29 The king of I told Jehoshaphat,
18:29 So the king of I disguised
18:30 anyone except the king of I."
18:31 "He must be the king of I."
18:32 wasn't the king of I.
18:33 the king of I between his scale
19:8 and family heads from I to
20:10 However, you didn't let I
20:19 up to praise the LORD God of I
20:34 in the Book of the Kings of I.
20:35 himself with King Ahaziah of I,
21:2 sons of King Jehoshaphat of I.
21:4 and some of the officials of I.
21:6 the ways of the kings of I,
21:13 the ways of the kings of I.
22:5 with Ahab's son King Joram of I
23:2 the leaders of the families of I,
24:5 and collect money throughout I
24:6 the assembly had required I
24:9 I to make contributions.)
24:16 of the good he had done in I
25:6 hired 100,000 soldiers from I
25:7 because the LORD isn't with I.
25:9 silver I gave the troops from I?"
25:17 and grandson of Jehu of I,
25:17 to declare war on I.
25:18 King Jehoash of I sent this
25:21 So King Jehoash of I attacked,
25:22 I defeated the army of Judah,
25:23 King Jehoash of I captured
25:25 son King Jehoash of I.
25:26 of the Kings of Judah and I?
27:7 of the Kings of I and Judah.
28:2 the example of the kings of I
28:5 him over to the king of I,
28:13 The LORD is very angry with I
28:19 because of King Ahaz of I.
28:23 But they ruined him and all I.
28:26 of the Kings of Judah and I.
28:27 into the tombs of the kings of I.
29:7 the holy place to the God of I.
29:10 to the LORD God of I so that
29:24 peace with the LORD for I.
29:24 for sin should be for all I.
29:27 instruments of King David of I.
30:1 sent a message to all I
30:1 Passover of the LORD God of I.
30:5 throughout I from Beersheba
30:5 Passover of the LORD God of I.
30:6 throughout I and Judah.
30:6 God of Abraham, Isaac, and I.
30:25 the whole assembly from I,
30:25 the foreigners who came from I,
30:26 the days of King Solomon of I.
31:6 The people of I and Judah who
31:8 the LORD and his people I.
32:17 cursing the LORD God of I.
32:32 of the kings of Judah and I.

2Ch 33:3 as King Ahab of I had done.
33:7 from all the tribes of I.
33:8 I will never again remove I from
33:16 to serve the LORD God of I.
33:18 of the LORD God of I — are
33:18 in the records of the kings of I.
34:7 incense altars everywhere in I.
34:9 from all who were left in I,
34:21 behalf of those who are left in I
34:23 what the LORD God of I says:
34:26 the LORD God of I says about
34:33 He made all people found in I
35:3 who instructed all I and
35:3 son of David and king of I,
35:3 your God and his people I.
35:4 in the records of King David of I
35:5 relatives, the people ⌊of I⌋.
35:18 this been celebrated in I during
35:18 Samuel or the kings of I,
35:18 the people of I who could be
35:25 This became a tradition in I.
35:27 of the kings of I and Judah.
36:8 of the Kings of I and Judah.
36:13 turn back to the LORD God of I.
Ezr 1:3 a temple for the LORD God of I.
3:2 built an altar for the God of I.
3:10 instructions of King David of I.
3:11 toward I endures forever."
4:1 a temple for the LORD God of I,
4:3 it alone for the LORD God of I,
5:11 years ago by a great king of I.
6:14 as the God of I had ordered
6:16 Then the people of I,
6:17 goat for each of the tribes of I.
6:21 to worship the LORD God of I.
6:22 the temple of God, the God of I.
7:6 the LORD God of I had given.
7:10 their rules and regulations in I.
7:11 commands and laws for I:
7:15 contributed to the God of I,
7:28 So I gathered leaders in I to go
8:18 of Mahli, Levi, and I.
8:35 burnt offerings to the God of I:
8:35 12 bulls for all I, 96 rams,
9:1 me and said, "The people of I,
9:4 at the words of the God of I.
9:15 LORD God of I, because you
10:2 there is still hope for I.
10:5 and all the rest of I swear to do
Neh 2:10 of I so much assistance.
7:73 and the rest of I settled in their
7:73 the people of I were in their
8:1 had commanded I ⌊to follow⌋.
8:14 that the people of I should live
8:17 the people of I had not done
9:2 of I separated themselves from
10:33 that make peace with God for I,
13:18 more angry with I by treating
13:26 that King Solomon of I sinned?
13:26 and God made him king of all I.
Psa 14:7 If only salvation for I would
14:7 will rejoice. I will be glad.
22:3 enthroned on the praises of I.
22:23 all you descendants of I.
25:22 Rescue I, O God, from all its
41:13 Thank the LORD God of I
50:7 Listen, I, and I will testify
53:6 If only salvation for I would
53:6 will rejoice. I will be glad.
59:5 LORD God of Armies, God of I,
68:8 in the presence of the God of I.
68:26 the source of I, with the choirs.
68:34 His majesty is over I,
68:35 God, the God of I, He gives
69:6 because of me, O God of I.
71:22 to praise you, O Holy One of I.
72:18 the LORD God, the God of I,
73:1 God is truly good to I,
76:1 His name is great in I.
78:5 He gave his teachings to I.
78:21 and his anger flared up at I
78:31 the best young men in I.
78:41 the Holy One of I to the limit.
78:55 He settled the tribes of I in their
78:59 He completely rejected I.
78:71 of the people of Jacob, of I,
Psa 80:1 your ears, O Shepherd of I,
81:4 This is a law for I,
81:8 I, if you would only listen to
81:11 I wanted nothing to do with me.
81:13 If only I would follow me!
81:16 But I would feed I with the
83:4 that the name of I will no longer
89:18 belongs to the Holy One of I.
105:10 as an everlasting promise to I,
105:12 While the people of I were few
105:23 Then I came to Egypt.
105:37 He brought I out with silver and
105:38 Egyptians were terrified of I,
105:38 so they were glad when I left.
106:48 LORD God of I from everlasting
114:1 When I left Egypt,
114:2 and I became his kingdom.
115:9 I, trust the LORD. He is your
115:12 will bless the descendants of I.
118:2 I should say, "His mercy
121:4 Indeed, the Guardian of I never
122:4 that city because it is a law in I
124:1 (I should repeat this.)
125:5 Let there be peace in I!
128:6 Let there be peace in I!
129:1 (I should repeat this.)
130:7 O I, put your hope in the LORD,
130:8 He will rescue I from all its
131:3 I, put your hope in the LORD
135:4 to be his own and chose I
135:12 an inheritance to his people I.
135:19 Descendants of I, praise the
136:11 He brought I out from among
136:14 He led I through the middle of it
136:22 inheritance for his servant I —
147:2 the outcasts of I together.
147:19 and judicial decisions to I.
148:14 faithful ones, for the people of I,
149:2 Let I find joy in their creator.
Pro 1:1 David's son who was king of I,
Ecc 1:12 been king of I in Jerusalem.
Sos 3:7 from the army of I surround it.
Isa 1:3 But I doesn't know ⌊its owner⌋.
1:4 despised the Holy One of I.
1:24 the Mighty One of I,
5:7 of Armies is the nation of I,
5:19 Let the plan of the Holy One of I
5:24 the word of the Holy One of I.
8:14 block for both kingdoms of I.
8:18 We are signs and symbols in I
9:8 The message is against I.
9:11 Rezin's oppressors against I
9:12 They will devour I with open
9:14 will cut off from I both head
10:20 on the LORD, the Holy One of I.
10:22 Although your people I may be
11:12 He will gather the outcasts of I
11:16 like there was for I when
12:6 The Holy One of I is great.
14:1 for Jacob and again choose I.
14:2 The nation of I will possess
17:6 declares the LORD God of I.
17:7 will look to the Holy One of I.
19:24 When that day comes, I will be
19:25 my possession I are blessed."
21:10 LORD of Armies, the God of I.
21:17 LORD God of I has spoken.
24:15 God of I along the coastlands.
27:6 I will blossom, bud, and fill the
27:7 Will the LORD hurt I as he hurt
27:8 He punished I by sending it
27:12 People of I, you will be
29:19 find joy in the Holy One of I.
29:23 stand in terror of the God of I.
30:11 Get the Holy One of I out of our
30:12 is what the Holy One of I says:
30:15 LORD, the Holy One of I, says:
30:29 mountain, to the rock of I.
31:1 don't look to the Holy One of I.
31:6 You people of I, return to the
37:16 "LORD of Armies, God of I,
37:21 what the LORD God of I says:
37:23 It is the Holy One of I!
40:27 I, why do you say, "My way is
41:8 "But you are my servant I,
41:14 You people of I, I will help
Isa 41:14 Defender, the Holy One of I.
41:16 and praise the Holy One of I.
41:17 I, the God of I, will not abandon
41:20 the Holy One of I has created it.
42:24 away as loot and handed I over
43:1 created Jacob and formed I.
43:3 the Holy One of I, your Savior.
43:14 the Holy One of I, says:
43:15 One, the Creator of I, your King
43:22 I, you have grown tired of me.
43:28 I will set up I for ridicule.
44:1 Jacob, I, whom I have chosen.
44:5 and he will adopt the name of I.
44:21 Jacob: You are my servant, I.
44:21 I, I will not forget you.
44:23 He will display his glory in I.
45:3 the LORD God of I,
45:4 Jacob, I, my chosen one,
45:11 Holy One and the Maker of I.
45:15 You are the God of I,
45:17 I has been saved by the LORD
45:25 All the descendants of I will be
46:3 people left of the nation of I.
46:13 for Zion and bring my glory to I.
47:4 defender is the Holy One of I.
48:1 You are given the name of I.
48:1 You acknowledge the God of I,
48:2 You depend on the God of I.
48:12 Listen to me, Jacob, I,
48:17 the Holy One of I, says:
49:3 "You are my servant I.
49:5 back to him and gather I to him.
49:6 brings back those in I whom
49:7 The LORD is the defender of I,
49:7 Holy One of I has chosen you.
52:12 The God of I will guard you
54:5 defender is the Holy One of I.
55:5 because of the Holy One of I.
56:8 the scattered people of I,
60:9 your God, the Holy One of I,
60:14 the city of the Holy One of I.
63:7 good things for the nation of I
63:16 us and I doesn't pay attention
66:20 the people of I who bring their
Jer 2:3 I was set apart for the LORD.
2:4 the families in the nation of I.
2:14 "Are the people of I slaves?
2:16 have cracked your skulls, I.
2:26 so the nation of I will feel
2:31 a land of thick darkness, for I?
3:6 you see what unfaithful I did?
3:8 that I sent unfaithful I away
3:8 that I gave I her divorce papers.
3:11 "Unfaithful I was less guilty
3:12 north: "'Come back, unfaithful I
3:18 will live with the nation of I.
3:20 you, nation of I, betrayed me,"
3:21 the pleading of the people of I.
4:1 I, if you come back to me,
5:11 The nations of I and Judah are
5:15 Nation of I, I'm going to bring a
6:9 few of I like someone picks
7:3 of Armies, the God of I, says:
7:12 of the evil done by my people I.
7:21 of Armies, the God of I, says:
9:15 of Armies, the God of I, says:
9:26 all I has uncircumcised hearts."
10:1 has spoken to you, nation of I.
10:16 He made everything, and I is
11:3 the LORD, the God of I, says:
11:10 The nations of I and Judah
11:17 because of the evil things that I
12:14 that I gave my people I:
13:11 have made the entire nation of I
13:12 what the LORD God of I says:
16:9 of Armies, the God of I, says:
16:14 brought the people of I out
16:15 brought the people of I out
16:16 they will catch the people of I.
17:13 O LORD, the Hope of I,
18:6 "Nation of I, can't I do with you
18:6 Nation of I, you are like the
18:13 The people of I have done a
19:3 of Armies, the God of I, says:
19:15 of Armies, the God of I, says:
21:4 what the LORD God of I says:

Jer	23:2	the LORD God of I,
	23:6	and I will live in safety.
	23:7	brought the people of I out
	23:8	of the nation of I out
	23:13	and led my people I astray.
	24:5	what the LORD God of I says:
	25:15	This is what the LORD God of I
	25:27	the God of I, says: Drink,
	27:4	of Armies, the God of I, says:
	27:21	LORD of Armies, the God of I,
	28:2	of Armies, the God of I, says:
	28:14	of Armies, the God of I, says:
	29:4	LORD of Armies, the God of I,
	29:8	of Armies, the God of I, says:
	29:21	LORD of Armies, the God of I,
	29:23	have done shameful things in I.
	29:25	of Armies, the God of I, says:
	30:2	what the LORD God of I says:
	30:3	"when I will bring my people I
	30:4	spoke about I and Judah:
	30:10	Don't be terrified, I.
	31:1	the God of all the families of I,
	31:2	I went to find its rest.
	31:4	be rebuilt, my dear people I.
	31:7	the remaining few from I."
	31:9	I will be a Father to I,
	31:10	the people of I will gather them
	31:21	Come back, my dear people I,
	31:23	of Armies, the God of I, says:
	31:27	I will plant the nations of I
	31:31	a new promise to I and Judah.
	31:33	will make to I after those days,"
	32:14	of Armies, the God of I, says:
	32:15	of Armies, the God of I, says:
	32:20	you are still doing them in I.
	32:30	the people of I and Judah have
	32:30	The people of I have made me
	32:32	"The people of I and Judah
	32:36	what the LORD God of I says:
	33:4	This is what the LORD God of I
	33:5	The people of I fought the
	33:7	I will restore Judah and I and
	33:14	that I made to I and Judah.
	33:17	sitting on the throne of I.
	34:2	what the LORD God of I says:
	34:13	what the LORD God of I says:
	35:13	of Armies, the God of I, says:
	35:17	of Armies, the God of I, says:
	35:18	of Armies, the God of I, says:
	35:19	of Armies, the God of I, says:
	36:2	I have dictated to you about I,
	37:7	what the LORD God of I says:
	38:17	of Armies, the God of I, says:
	39:16	of Armies, the God of I, says:
	41:9	against King Baasha of I.
	42:9	This is what the LORD God of I
	42:15	of Armies, the God of I, says:
	42:18	of Armies, the God of I, says:
	43:10	of Armies, the God of I, says:
	44:2	of Armies, the God of I, says:
	44:7	of Armies, the God of I, says:
	44:11	of Armies, the God of I, says:
	44:25	of Armies, the God of I, says:
	45:2	what the LORD God of I says
	46:25	of Armies, the God of I, says,
	46:27	Don't be terrified, I.
	48:1	the God of I, says about Moab:
	48:13	nation of I was ashamed when
	48:27	you laugh at the people of I?
	49:1	Doesn't I have any children?
	49:2	Then I will take possession of
	50:4	"the people of I and Judah will
	50:17	"The people of I are like
	50:18	of Armies, the God of I, says:
	50:19	I will bring the people of I back
	50:29	the LORD, the Holy One of I.
	50:33	All the people of I and Judah
	50:34	to bring rest to the land of I
	51:5	I and Judah haven't been
	51:5	abandoning the Holy One of I.
	51:19	He made everything, and I is
	51:33	of Armies, the God of I, says:
Lam	2:5	He swallowed up I.
Eze	2:3	sending you to the people of I.
	3:1	Then speak to the people of I."
	3:4	go to the people of I,
Eze	3:5	I am sending you to I.
	3:7	But the people of I will refuse
	3:7	All the people of I are very
	3:17	watchman over the people of I.
	4:3	is a sign for the people of I.
	4:4	of the nation of I yourself.
	4:5	for the sins of the nation of I.
	4:13	the people of I will eat unclean
	5:4	the whole nation of I.
	6:2	look toward the mountains of I,
	6:3	Say this, 'You mountains of I,
	6:5	dead bodies of the people of I
	6:11	because the people of I have
	7:2	to the people in the land of I:
	7:21	will dishonor the people of I.
	7:22	face away from the people of I,
	8:6	what the people of I are doing?
	8:6	The people of I are doing very
	8:9	the people of I are doing here."
	8:10	all the idols in the nation of I.
	8:12	of the nation of I are doing
	9:3	Then the glory of the God of I
	9:8	who is left in I while you pour
	9:9	wickedness of the nations of I
	10:19	the God of I was above them.
	10:20	that I saw under the God of I at
	11:5	saying these things, nation of I.
	11:13	all the remaining people in I?"
	11:15	and about the entire nation of I.
	11:17	I will give them the land of I.
	11:22	the God of I was above them.
	12:6	a sign to warn the nation of I."
	12:9	didn't the rebellious nation of I
	12:10	the people of I who live there.'
	12:19	Jerusalem and in the land of I:
	12:22	is this proverb you have in I:
	12:23	quote it in I.' Instead, tell them,
	12:27	the people of I are saying,
	13:2	against the prophets of I.
	13:4	I, your prophets are like foxes
	13:5	the wall for the nation of I.
	13:5	So I will not be protected in
	13:7	Prophets of I, haven't you seen
	13:9	in the records of the nation of I.
	13:9	They won't even enter I.
	13:16	The prophets of I who
	14:5	the hearts of the nation of I.
	14:6	"So tell the nation of I,
	14:7	who lives in I deserts me by
	14:9	you from among my people I.
	14:11	Then the people of I will no
	17:2	illustration to the nation of I.
	17:9	"Tell the nation of I,
	17:23	plant it on a high mountain in I.
	18:2	this proverb about the land of I:
	18:3	no longer use this proverb in I.
	18:6	from the idols of the nation of I.
	18:15	from the idols of the nation of I.
	18:25	Listen, nation of I, isn't my way
	18:29	"But the nation of I says,
	18:29	Isn't my way fair, nation of I?
	18:30	people of I," declares the
	18:31	do you want to die, nation of I?
	19:1	funeral song for the princes of I.
	19:9	anymore on the mountains of I.
	20:1	some of the leaders of I came
	20:3	speak to the leaders of I.
	20:5	LORD says: When I chose I,
	20:13	"'But the people of I rebelled
	20:27	"Speak to the nation of I,
	20:30	"Tell the nation of I,
	20:31	to ask me for help, nation of I?
	20:38	You will never enter I.
	20:39	"'Nation of I, this is what the
	20:40	"'The entire nation of I,
	20:40	the high mountain of I,
	20:42	I will bring you to the land of I,
	20:44	that you have done, nation of I,
	21:2	Prophesy against the land of I.
	21:3	Tell the land of I, 'This is what
	21:12	and against all the princes of I.
	21:25	and wicked prince of I,
	22:6	"'See how all the princes of I
	22:18	"Son of man, the people of I
	24:21	'Tell the nation of I,
	25:3	when the land of I was ruined,
Eze	25:6	felt contempt for the land of I.
	25:14	I will use my people I to take
	27:17	Judah and I traded with you.
	28:24	The nation of I will no longer
	28:25	When I gather the people of I
	28:25	The people of I will live in their
	29:6	walking stick to the nation of I.
	29:7	When I grabbed you,
	29:16	The nation of I will never trust
	29:16	The people of I will remember
	29:21	the people of I strong again,
	33:7	a watchman for the people of I.
	33:10	say to the people of I,
	33:11	you want to die, people of I?'
	33:20	Yet, the people of I say,
	33:20	by your own ways, people of I."
	33:24	the ruined cities in I are saying,
	33:28	The mountains of I will
	34:2	against the shepherds of I.
	34:2	shepherds of I who have been
	34:13	of them on the mountains of I,
	34:14	graze on the mountains of I.
	34:14	pastures in the mountains of I.
	34:30	the people of I, are my people,
	35:5	always been an enemy of I.
	35:5	You deserted the people of I in
	35:10	two nations, I and Judah,
	35:12	spoke about the mountains of I.
	35:15	when the land of I became
	36:1	prophesy to the mountains of I.
	36:1	Tell them, 'Mountains of I,
	36:4	"'Mountains of I, listen to the
	36:6	"So prophesy about I.
	36:8	"'But you, mountains of I,
	36:8	and bear fruit for my people I.
	36:10	All the people of I,
	36:12	I will bring people, my people I,
	36:17	when the people of I lived in
	36:22	"So tell the people of I,
	36:22	to do something, people of I.
	36:32	of your ways, people of I.
	36:37	I will also let the people of I
	37:11	all the people of I are like these
	37:12	I will bring you to I.
	37:16	people of I associated with it.'
	37:19	and the tribes of I associated
	37:22	the land on the mountains of I.
	37:28	have set I apart as holy,
	38:8	brought to the mountains of I,
	38:14	At that time my people I will
	38:16	You will attack my people I
	38:17	my servants the prophets of I.
	38:18	that Gog attacks the land of I,
	38:19	earthquake in the land of I.
	39:2	you attack the mountains of I.
	39:4	will die on the mountains of I
	39:7	known among my people I,
	39:7	the LORD, the Holy One in I.
	39:9	Those living in the cities of I
	39:11	give Gog a burial place in I.
	39:12	The people of I will be burying
	39:13	The people of I will be honored
	39:17	feast on the mountains of I.
	39:22	the people of I will know that
	39:23	people of I went into captivity
	39:25	for the whole nation of I.
	39:29	out my Spirit on the nation of I,
	40:2	In visions, God brought me to I
	40:4	Tell the nation of I everything
	43:2	I saw the glory of the God of I
	43:7	Then the people of I and their
	43:10	this temple to the people of I.
	44:2	God of I entered through it.
	44:6	Tell the rebellious people of I,
	44:6	that you have done, people of I.
	44:10	from me when I wandered off
	44:12	and by making I fall into sin.
	44:22	only virgins from the nation of I
	44:28	them any possessions in I.
	44:29	Everything in I that is devoted
	45:6	belong to all the people of I.
	45:8	will belong to the prince in I.
	45:8	to each tribe of the nation of I.
	45:9	enough of you, you princes of I.
	45:15	the well-watered pastures of I.
	45:16	contribution to the prince in I.

Eze 45:17 festivals of the nation of I.
45:17 the LORD for the nation of I.
47:13 among the 12 tribes of I.
47:18 Gilead and the land of I.
47:21 for each of the tribes of I.
47:22 among the tribes of I.
48:19 all the tribes in I will farm it.
48:29 among the tribes of I,
48:31 be named after the tribes of I.
Dan 9:11 All I has ignored your
9:20 and the sins of my people I.
Hos 1:1 son of Joash, was king of I.
1:4 put an end to the kingdom of I.
1:6 no longer love the nation of I.
1:11 The people of Judah and I will
2:19 "I, I will make you my wife
4:5 your mother, ⌊the nation of I⌋.
4:15 "I, you act like a prostitute.
4:16 "The people of I are as
5:1 Pay attention, nation of I!
5:3 and I isn't a stranger to me.
5:3 a prostitute, and I is unclean.
5:5 I and Ephraim stumble
5:9 known among the tribes of I.
6:10 horrible things in the nation of I
6:10 a prostitute, and I is unclean.
7:1 "Whenever I want to heal I,
7:10 I, your arrogance testifies
8:1 The people of I have rejected
8:6 calf-shaped idol was made in I.
8:7 "The people of I plant the wind,
8:8 I will be swallowed up.
8:9 "The people of I went to
8:14 The people of I have built
9:1 I, don't rejoice. Don't celebrate
9:7 this happens,⌋ I will know it.
9:10 LORD said,⌋ "When I found I,
10:1 The people of I are like vines
10:6 I will be ashamed because of
10:8 I sins there. Thorns and weeds
10:9 I, you have sinned ever since
10:15 At daybreak, the king of I will
11:1 "When I was a child,
11:8 How can I hand you over, I?
11:12 The nation of I surrounds me
12:12 I worked to get a wife;
12:13 to bring the people of I out
13:1 of Ephraim were important in I.
13:9 You are destroying yourself, I.
14:1 I, return to the LORD your God.
14:5 be like dew to the people of I.
Joe 2:27 You will know that I am in I.
3:16 a stronghold for the people of I.
Amo 1:1 He saw ⌊a vision⌋ about I
2:6 Because I has committed three
2:6 The people of I sell the
2:11 Isn't that so, people of I?
3:14 On the day I punish I for its
4:5 This is what you people of I
4:12 This is what I will do to you, I.
4:12 This is what I will do to you, I!
5:1 I sing about you, nation of I:
5:2 The people of I have fallen,
5:3 ⌊only⌋ 10 left for the nation of I.
5:4 LORD says to the nation of I:
5:7 You, I, turn justice into poison
5:10 I, you hate anyone who speaks
5:25 desert for 40 years, nation of I?
6:1 to whom the nation of I comes.
6:14 nation to attack you, nation of I,
7:8 in the middle of my people I.
7:9 and the holy places of I will be
7:10 message to King Jeroboam of I.
7:10 you among the people of I.
7:11 and that I cannot avoid being
7:15 'Prophesy to my people I.'
7:16 'Stop prophesying against I,
7:17 I cannot avoid being taken from
8:2 "My people I are now ripe.
9:7 You people of I are like the
9:7 Didn't I bring I from Egypt?
9:9 I will sift the nation of I out of
9:14 I will restore my people I.
9:15 I will plant the people of I in
Oba 1:16 As you, I, drank on my holy
1:20 Exiles from I will take
Mic 1:13 The rebellious acts of I are
1:14 will betray the kings of I.
1:15 The glory of I will come to
2:12 together the few people left in I.
3:1 you rulers of the nation of I.
3:8 ⌊the nation of⌋ I about its sins.
3:9 you rulers of the nation of I.
5:1 will strike the judge of I
5:3 the LORD will abandon I until
5:3 will return to the people of I.
6:2 is arguing his case against I.
Zep 2:9 LORD of Armies, the God of I,
3:13 The faithful few in I will not do
3:14 Shout loudly, I! Celebrate and
3:15 The king of I, the LORD,
Zec 1:19 Judah, I, and Jerusalem."
8:13 of Judah and people of I,
9:2 and of all the tribes of I are
11:14 between Judah and I.
12:1 the word of the LORD about I.
Mal 1:1 his word to I through Malachi.
1:5 'Even outside the borders of I
2:11 been done in I and Jerusalem.
2:16 says the LORD God of I.
4:4 I gave to him at Horeb for all I.
Mat 2:6 He will shepherd my people I."
2:20 and his mother, and go to I.
2:21 and his mother, and went to I.
8:10 as great as this in anyone in I.
9:33 seen anything like this in I!"
10:6 the lost sheep of the nation of I.
10:23 gone through every city in I,
15:24 lost sheep of the nation of I."
15:31 So they praised the God of I.
19:28 judging the twelve tribes of I.
27:9 the price the people of I had
Mar 12:29 most important is, 'Listen, I,
15:32 Let the Messiah, the king of I,
Luk 1:16 He will bring many people in I
1:54 to help his servant I forever.
1:68 "Praise the Lord God of I!
1:80 he appeared to the people of I.
2:25 the one who would comfort I.
2:32 bring glory to your people I."
2:34 that many people in I will
4:25 There were many widows in I
4:27 people with skin diseases in I
7:9 found faith as great as this in I."
22:30 judge the twelve tribes of I."
24:21 was the one who would free I.
Jon 1:31 to show him to the people of I."
1:49 You are the king of I!"
3:10 a well-known teacher of I.
12:13 name of the Lord, the king of I!"
Act 1:6 to restore the kingdom to I?"
2:22 "Men of I, listen to what I say:
2:36 "All the people of I should
3:12 he said to the people, "Men of I,
4:10 You and all the people of I
4:27 people and the people of I.
5:21 all the leaders of I.
5:31 to lead the people of I to him,
5:35 said to the council, "Men of I,
7:42 desert for 40 years, nation of I?
9:15 and to the people of I.
10:36 sent his word to the people of I
13:16 "Men of I and converts to
13:17 The God of the people of I
13:23 come to I from David's
13:24 told everyone in I about
21:28 shouting, "Men of I, help!
28:20 because of what I hopes for."
Rom 9:6 not everyone descended from I
9:6 from Israel is part of I
9:27 Isaiah also says about I:
9:27 "Although the descendants of I
9:31 The people of I tried to gain
10:19 Again I ask, "Didn't I
10:21 Then Isaiah said about I,
11:1 God rejected his people I?"
11:2 he complains to God about I?
11:7 It means that I has never
11:7 of the rest of I were closed,
11:11 So I ask, "Has I stumbled so
11:15 It means that I has come back
11:26 In this way I as a whole will be
1Co 10:18 Look at the people of I from a
2Co 3:7 the people of I couldn't look at
3:13 He didn't want the people of I to
Gal 6:16 They are the I of God.
Eph 2:12 excluded from citizenship in I,
Php 3:5 I'm a descendant of I.
Heb 8:8 a new promise to I and Judah.
8:10 will make to I after those days,
Rev 2:14 Balak trapped the people of I
7:4 every tribe of the people of I:
21:12 The names of the 12 tribes of I

Israelite (75)

Exo 5:14 drivers had placed I foremen
5:15 Then the I foremen complained
5:19 The I foremen realized they
10:7 Let the I men go to worship the
12:19 whether he is an I or not.
14:20 Egyptian camp and the I camp.
24:5 Then he sent young I men,
35:1 Moses assembled the whole I
35:4 Then Moses said to the whole I
35:20 whole I community left Moses.
35:29 Every I man and woman who
Lev 17:3 Any I who slaughters a bull,
19:17 "Never hate another I.
24:10 a quarrel with an I in the camp.
24:11 The I woman's son began
24:22 you are a foreigner or an I,
25:35 "If an I becomes poor and
25:39 "If an I becomes poor and sells
25:47 The poor I may sell himself to
Num 10:28 which the I armies broke camp
11:16 "Bring me 70 I men who you
14:1 Then all the people in the I
15:30 "But any native-born I or
16:2 men were joined by 250 I men,
25:6 One of the I men brought a
25:8 into the tent after the I man.
25:14 The name of the I man who
26:51 number of I men was 601,730.
32:18 until every I has received his
36:1 of the other I households.
36:7 Every I must keep the tribal
36:8 In this way every I keeps the
36:9 Each I tribe must keep the land
Dtr 1:16 an I and a non-Israelite.
15:3 debt another I still owes you.
18:15 you a prophet, an I like me.
18:18 them a prophet, an I like you.
19:18 he testified against the other I,
22:3 or anything else that another I
22:19 the reputation of an I virgin.
23:17 No I man or woman should
23:19 Never charge another I any
23:20 a foreigner interest, but not an I.
24:7 kidnaps another I must die.
25:3 If an I were given more than
Jos 10:11 hailstones than from I swords.
21:1 the families of the other I tribes
Jdg 20:24 On the second day the I troops
1Sm 4:10 Every ⌊I⌋ soldier fled to his
4:10 30,000 I foot soldiers died.
17:10 "I challenge the I battle line
28:4 assembled the whole I army,
28:17 given it to your fellow I David.
1Ki 8:1 the leaders of the I families.
15:27 and the I forces were attacking
16:16 the I troops in the camp made
16:17 Omri and the I troops with him
20:15 he counted all the I soldiers.
20:27 When the I ⌊troops⌋ had been
1Ch 27:1 This is a list of I family heads,
2Ch 5:2 the leaders of the I families.
34:33 idols throughout I territory.
Ezr 2:2 This is the number of I men
10:1 a large crowd of I men,
Neh 7:7 This is the number of I men
Eze 14:4 Suppose an I is devoted to
14:4 will give that I an answer,
14:7 Suppose an I or a foreigner
Jon 1:47 is a true I who is sincere."
Act 3:22 you a prophet, an I like me.
7:24 When he saw an I man being
7:24 an Egyptian, he defended the I.
7:37 you a prophet, an I like me.'

Rom 11:1 I'm an **I** myself, a descendant
Heb 13:11 burned outside the **I** camp.

Israelite's (3)

Num 18:21 one-tenth of every **I** income.
Dtr 22:1 If you see another **I** ox or
22:4 If you see another **I** donkey or

Israelites (536)

Gen 47:27 So the **I** settled in Egypt in the
Exo 1:9 "There are too many **I**,
1:12 the more the **I** were oppressed,
1:13 So they forced the **I** to work
2:23 The **I** still groaned because
2:25 God saw the **I** ⌊being
6:5 heard the groaning of the **I**,
6:6 "Tell the **I**, 'I am the LORD.
6:9 Moses reported this to the **I**.
6:11 to let the **I** leave his country."
6:12 "The **I** wouldn't listen to me.
6:13 to Moses and Aaron about the **I**
6:13 them to bring the **I** out of Egypt.
6:26 "Bring the **I** out of Egypt in
6:27 Egypt) to let the **I** leave Egypt.
7:2 to let the **I** leave the country.
7:4 I will bring my people, the **I**,
7:5 and bring the **I** out of there."
9:4 belonging to the **I** will die.'"
9:26 of Goshen, where the **I** lived.
9:35 and would not let the **I** go,
10:20 so he did not let the **I** go.
10:23 But all the **I** had light where
11:7 But where the **I** are,
11:10 let the **I** leave his country.
12:27 passed over the houses of the **I**
12:28 The **I** did as the LORD had
12:31 He said, "You and the **I** must
12:35 The **I** did what Moses had told
12:36 So the **I** stripped Egypt of its
12:37 The **I** left Rameses to go to
12:40 The **I** had been living in Egypt
12:42 (All **I** in future generations must
12:48 the Passover like native-born **I**.
12:49 to native-born **I** as well as
12:50 All the **I** did as the LORD had
12:51 the LORD brought all the **I** out
13:2 offspring among the **I** is mine,
13:18 The **I** were ready for battle
13:19 had made the **I** solemnly swear
14:2 "Tell the **I** to go back and set
14:3 Pharaoh will think, 'The **I** are
14:4 So that is what the **I** did.
14:8 stubborn that he pursued the **I**,
14:9 The Egyptians pursued the **I**.
14:10 As Pharaoh approached, the **I**
14:10 the **I** cried out to the LORD.
14:15 Tell the **I** to start moving.
14:16 Then the **I** will go through the
14:17 that they will follow the **I**.
14:19 who had been in front of the **I**,
14:19 moved from in front of the **I**
14:22 and the **I** went through the
14:29 Meanwhile, the **I** had gone
14:31 When the **I** saw the great
15:1 Then Moses and the **I** sang
15:19 However, the **I** had gone
16:1 The whole community of **I**
16:3 The **I** said to them,
16:6 and Aaron said to all the **I**,
16:9 "Tell the whole community of **I**,
16:10 to the whole community of **I**,
16:12 "I've heard the **I** complaining.
16:15 When the **I** saw it,
16:17 So that is what the **I** did.
16:31 The **I** called the food manna.
16:35 The **I** ate manna for 40 years
17:1 The whole community of **I** left
17:7 because the **I** complained
18:25 capable men from all the **I**
19:1 months after the **I** left Egypt,
19:3 of Jacob. Tell the **I**,
19:6 words you must speak to the **I**."
20:22 is what you must say to the **I**:
21:1 decisions to be used by the **I**:
24:11 harm these leaders of the **I**.
24:17 To the **I**, the glory of the LORD
Exo 25:2 "Tell the **I** to choose something
25:22 you all my commands for the **I**.
27:20 you must command the **I** to
27:21 is a permanent law among the **I**
28:1 continued,⌋ "Out of all the **I**,
28:12 as reminders of who the **I** are.
28:30 the LORD's⌋ decisions for the **I**.
28:38 when the **I** bring their holy
29:28 It is a permanent law that the **I**
29:43 I will also meet with the **I** there,
29:45 "Then I will live among the **I**
30:12 you take a census of the **I**,
30:16 Take the money the **I** give to
30:16 It will be a reminder for the **I** in
30:31 "Say to the **I**, 'For generations
31:13 "Say to the **I**, 'Be sure to
31:16 The **I** must observe this day of
31:17 sign between me and the **I**,
32:20 and made the **I** drink it.
33:5 had said to Moses, "Tell the **I**,
33:6 left Mount Horeb, the **I** no
34:30 When Aaron and all the **I**
34:32 all the other **I** came near him,
34:34 he came out and told the **I** what
35:30 Then Moses said to the **I**,
36:3 contributions the **I** had brought
39:7 as a reminder of who the **I** are.
39:32 The **I** followed all the LORD's
39:42 The **I** had done all the work
40:17 year ⌊after the **I** had left Egypt⌋.
40:36 the **I** would break camp.
40:38 In this way all the **I** could see
Lev 1:2 "Tell the **I**: If any of you bring a
4:2 "Tell the **I**: If a person
7:23 "Tell the **I**: Never eat any fat
7:29 "Tell the **I**: Anyone who offers
7:34 the fellowship offerings of the **I**,
7:36 The LORD commanded the **I** to
7:38 time that he commanded the **I**
9:3 Also tell the **I**: 'Take a male
10:6 All the other **I** may cry over the
10:11 Also teach the **I** all the laws
10:14 fellowship offerings from the **I**.
11:2 "Tell the **I**: Here are the kinds
12:2 "Tell the **I**: When a woman
15:2 "Tell the **I**: If a man has a
15:31 "You must separate the **I** from
16:16 sins the **I** committed against
16:16 because the **I** were unclean
16:19 Because the **I** made it unclean,
16:21 all the things the **I** did wrong.
16:29 the seventh month both native **I**
16:34 for all the sins the **I** committed."
17:2 and all the **I** that this is what
17:8 "Tell them: If **I** or foreigners
17:10 "If **I** or foreigners eat any blood,
17:13 "If **I** or foreigners hunt any
17:15 "Native **I** or foreigners who eat
18:2 "Tell the **I**: I am the LORD your
20:2 "Tell the **I**: If Israelites or
20:2 "Tell the Israelites: If **I** or
21:24 and his sons and to all the **I**.
22:2 offerings which the **I** set apart
22:3 the holy offerings the **I** set apart
22:15 offerings that the **I** contribute
22:18 Aaron, his sons, and all the **I**:
22:18 **I** or foreigners may bring burnt
22:32 show my holiness among the **I**.
23:2 "Tell the **I**: These are the
23:10 "Tell the **I**: When you come to
23:24 "Tell the **I**: On the first day of
23:34 "Tell the **I**: The fifteenth day of
23:44 So Moses told the **I** about the
24:2 "Command the **I** to bring you
24:8 reminder of my promise to the **I**
24:15 "Also tell the **I**: Those who
24:16 whether they are **I** or foreigners
24:23 The **I** did as the LORD
25:2 "Tell the **I**: When you come
25:33 are their property among the **I**.
25:46 do not treat the **I** harshly.
25:55 "The **I** belong to me as
26:46 gave to the **I** through Moses
27:2 "Tell the **I**: If any of you makes
27:34 Moses on Mount Sinai for the **I**.
Num 1:45 So the **I** were registered by
Lev 1:47 along with the other **I**.
1:49 in the census with the other **I**.
1:52 "The other **I** will camp with
1:54 The **I** did everything as the
2:2 "The **I** will put up their tents
2:32 This is the total number of **I**,
2:33 along with the other **I**.
2:34 So the **I** did everything as the
3:8 of meeting and work for the **I**,
3:9 will be the only **I** given to them.
3:12 "Out of all the **I**, I have taken
3:38 holy place on behalf of the **I**.
3:40 firstborn male of the **I** who is at
3:41 be substitutes for all firstborn **I**.
3:41 for all firstborn animals of the **I**
3:42 registered all the firstborn **I** as
3:45 substitutes for all the firstborn **I**
3:46 firstborn male **I** than there are
3:48 It will buy back those **I** who
3:49 from the **I** who outnumbered
3:50 firstborn **I** weighed 34 pounds,
5:2 "Command the **I** to send
5:4 So the **I** did as the LORD had
5:6 "Tell the **I**: If you do something
5:9 holy offerings that the **I** bring
5:12 "Speak to the **I** and tell them:
6:2 "Speak to the **I** and tell them:
6:23 is how you will bless the **I**.
6:27 use my name to bless the **I**,
8:6 Levites from the rest of the **I**,
8:10 and the **I** will place their hands
8:11 LORD as an offering from the **I**.
8:14 the Levites from the other **I**,
8:16 They will be the only **I** given to
8:16 firstborn male offspring of the **I**.
8:18 for all the firstborn sons of the **I**.
8:19 The Levites will be the only **I** I
8:19 They will work for the **I** at the
8:19 peace with the LORD for the **I**.
8:19 Then no plague will strike the **I**
9:1 year after the **I** left Egypt,
9:2 "The **I** must celebrate the
9:4 So Moses told the **I** to
9:5 The **I** did everything as the
9:7 of the **I** bring their offerings?"
9:9 said to Moses, "Tell the **I**:
9:14 to foreigners and native-born **I**."
9:17 the **I** would break camp,
9:17 the **I** would set up camp.
9:18 At the LORD's command the **I**
9:19 the **I** obeyed the LORD's
9:22 the **I** would stay in the same
10:12 So the **I** moved from the Desert
11:4 Some foreigners among the **I**
11:4 Even the **I** started crying again
13:2 which I'm giving to the **I**.
13:3 of them were leaders of the **I**.
13:24 of grapes the **I** cut off there.
13:32 spread lies among the **I** about
14:27 I've heard the complaints the **I**
14:39 told these things to all the **I**,
14:45 mountains, attacked the **I**,
15:2 "Speak to the **I** and tell them:
15:13 All native-born **I** must do it this
15:18 "Speak to the **I** and tell them:
15:29 they are native-born **I** or not.
15:32 While the **I** were in the desert,
15:38 "Speak to the **I** and tell them:
16:34 All the **I** around them ran away
16:38 This will be a sign to the **I**."
17:2 "Speak to the **I**, and get 12
17:5 the **I** make against you
17:6 So Moses spoke to the **I**.
17:9 and showed them to all the **I**.
17:12 The **I** said to Moses,
18:5 my anger against the **I** again.
18:6 other Levites from among the **I**
18:8 gifts from the **I** as your share.
18:11 by the **I** are also yours.
18:19 holy contributions the **I** bring
18:20 own as the other **I** will have.
18:20 and your property among the **I**.
18:22 The other **I** must never again
18:23 no property as the other **I** will.
18:24 Levites what the **I** contribute
18:24 no property as the other **I** do."

Lev 18:32 holy offerings given by the **I**,
19:2 Tell the **I** to bring you a red
19:10 be a permanent law for the **I**
20:3 had died when the other **I** died
20:12 You didn't show the **I** how holy
20:13 where the **I** complained about
20:19 The **I** replied, "We'll stay on the
20:21 the **I** turned around and went a
20:24 enter the land I'm giving the **I**.
20:29 and all the **I** mourned for Aaron
21:1 heard that the **I** were coming on
21:2 Then the **I** made this vow to
21:3 The LORD listened to the **I** and
21:6 and many of the **I** died.
21:10 The **I** moved and set up camp
21:32 the **I** captured its cities and
21:33 came out to fight the **I** at Edrei.
21:35 The **I** defeated him,
22:1 Then the **I** moved and set up
22:3 because there were so many **I**.
23:13 where you can see the **I**.
25:3 Since the **I** joined in
25:8 **I** were experiencing stopped.
25:11 turned my fury away from the **I**.
25:13 peace with the LORD for the **I**."
26:3 the priest Eleazar spoke to the **I**
26:4 These are the **I** who came from
26:62 counted along with the other **I**,
26:63 added up the total number of **I**
26:64 a single one of the **I** Moses
27:8 "Tell the **I**: If a man dies and
27:11 This will be a rule for the **I**,
27:12 look at the land I will give the **I**.
28:2 "Give this command to the **I**:
29:40 Moses told the **I** everything the
31:2 for what they did to the **I**.
31:9 The **I** took the Midianite
31:16 advice and caused the **I**
31:54 meeting as a reminder to the **I**.
32:6 the rest of the **I** go to war?
32:9 the rest of the **I** from entering
32:13 the LORD was angry with the **I**,
32:17 of the other **I** until we have
33:1 places where the **I** set up camp
33:3 The **I** boldly left in full view of
33:5 The **I** moved from Rameses
33:38 year after the **I** had left Egypt.
33:40 heard that the **I** were coming.)
33:51 "Tell the **I**, 'You will be
34:2 "Give the **I** these instructions.
34:13 Moses commanded the **I**,
34:29 to divide Canaan for the **I**.
35:2 "Tell the **I** to give the Levites
35:8 the property of the other **I** must
35:10 "Tell the **I**: When you cross the
35:15 will be places of refuge for **I**,
35:34 I, the LORD, live among the **I**."
36:2 you to give the **I** their land by
36:5 So Moses gave the **I** a
36:7 In this way no land of the **I** will
36:13 gave the **I** through Moses
Dtr 1:1 He spoke to all the **I**.
1:3 Moses told the **I** everything the
1:5 The **I** were east of the Jordan
1:16 it is ⌊a dispute⌋ between two **I**
3:18 River⌋ ahead of the other **I**.
3:20 with the other **I** until they take
4:45 and rules Moses gave the **I**
10:6 The **I** moved from the wells of
11:6 In the middle of all the **I** the
15:7 do whenever there are poor **I**
15:9 might be stingy toward poor **I**
15:11 to other **I** who are poor
18:1 their own like the rest of the **I**.
18:2 of their own like the other **I**.
20:8 ruin the morale of the other **I**."
24:14 whether they are **I** or foreigners
29:1 Moses to give to the **I** in Moab.
31:1 continued to speak to all the **I**:
31:11 all the **I** will come into the
31:19 this song, teach it to the **I**,
31:19 a witness for me against the **I**.
31:22 this song and taught it to the **I**.
31:23 because you will bring the **I**
32:49 that I'm giving the **I** as their own
32:51 You didn't show the **I** how holy
Dtr 32:52 enter the land I'm giving the **I**."
33:1 blessed the **I** with this blessing
34:8 The **I** mourned for Moses in the
34:9 The **I** obeyed him and did what
34:12 that were seen by all the **I**.
Jos 2:2 "Some **I** have entered the city
3:1 He and all the **I** left Shittim.
4:14 in the presence of all the **I**.
4:14 As long as Joshua lived, the **I**
5:1 River so that the **I** could cross.
5:6 For 40 years the **I** wandered
6:1 the people were afraid of the **I**.
8:20 had no place to go, since the **I**,
8:24 Then the **I** went back to Ai and
8:33 whether foreigners or native **I**,
9:16 the **I** heard that these people
9:17 The **I** broke camp.
9:18 The **I** didn't destroy these other
10:11 As they fled from the **I** down
10:20 Joshua and the **I** defeated them
10:21 to speak against any of the **I**.
10:28 and the **I** killed its people and
11:8 and the **I** defeated them.
11:8 The **I** chased them as far as
13:13 But the **I** did not force out the
17:13 When the **I** became strong
18:3 So Joshua asked the **I**,
20:9 as cities of refuge for all **I**,
21:8 The **I** gave these cities with
21:41 owned by the **I** there were 48
22:9 left the rest of the **I** at Shiloh
22:11 The rest of the **I** heard about it
22:13 The **I** sent Phinehas,
23:1 the LORD gave the **I** peace
Jdg 1:1 After Joshua's death the **I**
1:28 When the **I** were strong enough
2:12 The **I** abandoned the LORD
2:15 Whenever the **I** went to war,
2:17 The **I** chased after other gods
2:18 appointed judges for the **I**,
3:1 to test all the **I** who had not
3:4 nations were left to test the **I**,
3:6 The **I** allowed their sons and
3:13 and they defeated the **I** and
3:14 The **I** served King Eglon of
4:24 The **I** became stronger and
6:2 The **I** made hiding places in
6:6 So the **I** became very poor
8:34 The **I** did not remember the
11:20 But Sihon did not trust the **I**
19:12 They're not **I**. We'll go on to
20:19 The **I** got up early in the
20:20 The **I** formed their battle line
20:23 The **I** went and cried in the
20:35 On that day the **I** slaughtered
20:36 The **I** had allowed the men of
20:36 The **I** relied on those waiting in
1Sm 6:6 they send the **I** on their way?
7:4 So the **I** got rid of the statues of
7:5 "Gather all the **I** together at
7:6 So the **I** gathered together at
7:7 heard that the **I** had gathered at
7:7 The **I** heard ⌊about the
7:8 The **I** said to Samuel,
10:18 He said to the **I**, "This is what
11:1 There was no one among the **I**
13:6 When the **I** saw they were in
14:21 now joined the **I** who were
15:2 after the **I** came from Egypt.
15:6 You were kind to all the **I** when
17:3 and the **I** were stationed on a
17:8 stood and called to the **I**,
17:11 When Saul and all the **I** heard
17:53 When the **I** came back from
2Sm 6:19 to the whole crowd of **I**,
7:7 places I've moved with all the **I**,
15:6 This is what he did for all **I**
17:26 The **I** and Absalom camped in
20:19 We are peaceful and faithful **I**.
21:2 Although the **I** had sworn ⌊to
24:15 among the **I** from that morning
1Ki 6:13 I will live among the **I** and
8:9 a promise to the **I** after they left
8:41 So when people who are not **I**
9:20 because the **I** had not been
9:20 them. They were not **I**,
1Ki 9:22 didn't make any of the **I** slaves.
12:17 But Rehoboam ruled the **I** who
12:33 he had invented for the **I**.
16:26 and the **I** made the LORD God
18:20 Ahab sent word to all the **I** and
19:10 The **I** have abandoned your
19:14 The **I** have abandoned your
20:27 The **I**, while camped opposite
20:29 The **I** killed 100,000 Aramean
2Ki 3:24 the **I** attacked them,
3:24 and they fled from the **I**.
3:27 was bitter anger against the **I**.
7:13 the rest of the **I** who are dying.
8:12 the evil you will do to the **I**:
10:21 sent messengers to all the **I**.
13:5 So the LORD gave the **I**
13:23 was kind and merciful to the **I**
13:23 He didn't want to destroy the **I**,
17:6 captured Samaria and took the **I**
17:7 The **I** sinned against the LORD
17:9 The **I** secretly did things
17:22 The **I** followed all the sins
17:24 of Samaria in place of the **I**.
18:4 that time the **I** had been burning
18:11 The king of Assyria took the **I**
21:9 destroyed when the **I** arrived
1Ch 5:25 these people as the **I** arrived.
6:64 So the **I** gave the Levites the
9:1 The **I** were taken away to
9:2 their own cities were ⌊some⌋ **I**,
21:1 provoking David to count the **I**.
21:14 on Israel, and 70,000 **I** died.
2Ch 5:10 a promise to the **I** after they left
6:32 "People who are not **I** will
7:3 When all the **I** saw the fire
8:2 and he had **I** live in them.
8:7 because the **I** had not been
8:7 destroy them. They were not **I**,
8:9 didn't make any of the **I** slaves
10:17 But Rehoboam ruled the **I** who
10:18 sent Hadoram to the **I**.
13:16 The **I** fled from Judah's ⌊army⌋,
13:18 So the **I** were humbled at that
20:10 The **I** turned away from them
28:8 The **I** captured 200,000 women,
30:6 The king's order said, "**I**,
30:21 So the **I** in Jerusalem
31:1 When this was over, all the **I**
31:1 The **I** destroyed all of these
31:1 Then all the **I** returned to their
31:5 the **I** brought plenty of offerings
33:9 destroyed when the **I** arrived
35:6 ⌊the lambs⌋ for the other **I** as
35:17 The **I** who were present
Ezr 2:59 they couldn't prove they were **I**
2:61 prove their families were **I**⌊:
2:70 All the other **I** settled in their
3:1 (The **I** had already settled in
6:21 The lambs were eaten by the **I**
7:7 Some **I** (including priests,
7:13 a decree that any **I** who are
8:25 and all the **I** had contributed for
9:2 The **I** and their sons have
10:25 From the other **I**: From the
Neh 1:6 night about your servants the **I**.
1:6 I confess the sins that we **I**
7:61 they couldn't prove they were **I**
7:63 ⌊couldn't prove they were **I**⌊:
9:1 When the **I** assembled on the
9:22 kingdoms and nations to the **I**
9:25 The **I** captured fortified cities
10:39 The **I** and the Levites should
11:3 Some **I**, priests, Levites,
11:20 The rest of the **I**, priests,
12:47 all the **I** were giving gifts for the
13:2 they didn't welcome the **I** with
13:2 hired Balaam to curse the **I**.
13:3 the non-Israelites from the **I**.
Psa 103:7 He let the **I** know the things he
105:40 The **I** asked, and he brought
Isa 10:20 At that time the remaining few **I**,
17:9 because of the **I** will
Jer 40:3 you **I** have sinned against
51:49 of Babylon have killed many **I**
Eze 20:9 by bringing the **I** out of Egypt.
20:10 "So I brought the **I** out of Egypt

Eze 20:14 me bring the I out ⌊of Egypt⌋.
20:22 me bring the I out ⌊of Egypt⌋.
37:16 'For Judah and for the I who
37:21 I will take the I out of the
43:7 I will live among the I forever.
44:9 lives among the I may not enter
44:15 the I wandered away from
47:22 Think of them as I.
48:11 wander away with the I as
Dan 1:3 to bring some of the I,
9:7 and all the I whom you
Hos 1:10 "Yet, the I will become as
3:1 her as I, the LORD, love the I,
3:4 In the same way, the I will wait
3:5 After that, the I will turn and
4:1 to the word of the LORD, you I.
13:2 People say this about the I:
Joe 3:2 They scattered the I,
Amo 3:1 have spoken against you I,
3:12 so the I living in Samaria will
Act 7:23 to visit his own people, the I.
7:26 day Moses saw two I fighting,
7:35 "This is the Moses whom the I
7:37 the same Moses who told the I,
Rom 9:4 They are I, God's adopted
11:25 The minds of some I have
2Co 11:22 Are they I? So am I. Are they
Heb 11:22 speak about the I leaving Egypt
11:30 after the I marched around them

Israelites' (19)

Exo 9:6 but none of the I animals died.
9:7 one of the I animals had died.
Lev 25:36 God by respecting other I lives
Num 18:24 one-tenth of the I income.
18:26 of the I income which I'm giving
18:28 you receive from the I income.
22:41 see the outskirts of the I camp
31:30 From the I half of the loot,
31:42 Moses took the I half of the loot
31:47 From the I half Moses
36:4 When the I jubilee year comes,
Dtr 33:24 May they be the I favorite tribe
Jos 21:3 from the I inheritance
1Ki 14:24 had forced out of the I way
2Ki 16:3 had forced out of the I way
17:8 had forced out of the I way.
21:2 had forced out of the I way
2Ch 28:3 had forced out of the I way
33:2 had forced out of the I way

Israel's (119)

Gen 34:7 I family by raping Jacob's
37:3 had been born in I old age.
42:5 I sons left with the others who
45:21 I sons did as they were told.
46:5 I sons put their father Jacob,
46:8 names of I descendants (Jacob
46:28 When I family arrived in the
48:10 I eyesight was failing because
48:13 facing I left, and Manasseh on
48:13 facing I right, and brought them
50:25 Joseph made I sons swear an
Exo 6:14 I firstborn, were Hanoch,
9:4 distinguish between I livestock
24:1 and 70 of I leaders come up the
24:9 and 70 of I leaders
Num 1:20 of Reuben, I firstborn son,
24:2 looked up, and saw I camp
26:5 Reuben was I firstborn.
Dtr 33:28 Dew will drip from I skies
Jos 7:5 I troops lost heart and were
14:1 and the heads of I tribes
22:11 near the Jordan River on I side.
24:1 together I leaders, chiefs,
Jdg 3:2 teach I descendants about war,
5:9 goes out to I commanders,
18:29 of their ancestor Dan, I son.
20:2 The leaders of all I tribes took
20:21 slaughtered 22,000 of I men
20:22 But I troops got reinforcements
20:31 went out to attack I troops
20:34 Then 10,000 of I best men
1Sm 4:21 saying, "I glory is gone,"
4:22 "I glory is gone because the
1Sm 7:11 I soldiers left Mizpah,
7:13 didn't come into I territory
11:15 Saul and all of I soldiers
14:24 I soldiers were driven hard that
15:2 They blocked I way after the
15:17 you were the head of I tribes.
17:26 and gets rid of I disgrace?
18:6 Women from all of I cities
26:2 him 3,000 of I best-trained men
28:19 the LORD will hand I army over
2Sm 6:20 "How dignified I king was
10:17 he assembled I army, crossed
11:1 and I army ⌊to war⌋.
16:15 Absalom and all I troops came
17:11 is to gather all I troops from Dan
18:7 David's men defeated I army,
20:23 put in charge of I whole army.
21:5 staying anywhere in I territory
23:1 the singer of I psalms:
1Ki 2:5 commanders of I army—Abner
2:32 and the commander of I army)
8:37 may blockade I city gates.
8:52 your people I plea so that you
11:25 Rezon was I rival as long as
12:30 them became ⌊I⌋ sin.
22:17 said, "I saw I troops scattered
2Ki 2:12 I chariot and horses!"
3:6 to prepare I army for war.
3:24 the Moabites came to I camp,
6:23 didn't raid I territory anymore.
10:32 to take away some of I territory.
10:32 army throughout I territory
13:14 I chariot and horses!"
14:25 He restored I boundaries from
14:27 to wipe out I name completely,
17:19 lived according to I customs
17:20 I descendants, made them suffer
21:8 I will never again make I feet
1Ch 2:1 These were I sons: Reuben,
5:1 the sons of Reuben, I firstborn.
5:3 I firstborn, were Hanoch,
6:49 holy place and removed I sins
17:24 is I God.' And the house of
19:17 he assembled I army, crossed
22:1 I altar for burnt offerings will
27:22 the commanders of I tribes
2Ch 1:2 and the heads of I families
6:28 may blockade I city gates.
18:16 said, "I saw I troops scattered
20:7 in this country out of I way?
20:29 waged war against I enemies
25:7 I army must not go with you,
Ezr 4:3 heads of I families told them,
5:1 name of I God, who was over
8:29 and the leaders of I families.
10:10 now you have added to I guilt
Psa 98:3 and faithful to I descendants.
Isa 4:2 the pride and joy of I survivors
7:1 King Rezin and I King Pekah,
10:17 I light will become a flame.
17:3 will share I honor," declares
44:6 The LORD is I king and
56:10 ⌊I⌋ watchmen are blind.
Jer 3:10 Even after all this, I treacherous
14:8 You are I hope, the one who
31:36 will I descendants stop being a
31:37 ever reject all of I descendants
50:20 "people will look for I crimes,
Lam 2:1 He has thrown down I beauty
2:3 anger he cut off all of I strength.
Eze 8:4 There I saw the glory of I God
8:11 drawings stood 70 of I leaders.
11:10 I will judge you at I borders.
11:11 I will judge you at I borders
14:1 Some of I leaders came to me
Hos 1:5 On that day I will break I bows
5:5 The people of I arrogance
Joe 1:10 I fields are ruined, and the
Amo 1:1 Uzziah and I King Jeroboam,
Mic 1:5 of Jacob's crime and I sin.
5:2 Yet, from you I future ruler will
Nah 2:2 I glory, although enemies have
Mat 27:42 So he's I king! Let him come
Rom 11:11 By I failure, salvation has
11:15 If I rejection means that the
11:15 what does I acceptance mean?

Issachar (38)

Gen 30:18 So she named him I [Reward].
35:23 Levi, Judah, I, and Zebulun.
46:13 The sons of I were Tola,
49:14 "I is a strong donkey,
Exo 1:3 I, Zebulun, and Benjamin;
Num 1:8 son of Zuar, from the tribe of I;
1:28 for the descendants of I listed
1:29 for the tribe of I was 54,400.
2:5 to them will be the tribe of I.
2:5 for the people of I is Nethanel,
7:18 the leader from the tribe of I,
10:15 commanded the army of I.
13:7 of Joseph, from the tribe of I;
26:23 The families descended from I
26:25 These were the families of I.
34:26 the leader of the tribe of I;
Dtr 27:12 I, Joseph, and Benjamin.
33:18 and you people of I,
Jos 17:10 and I its eastern border.
17:11 In I and Asher, En Dor,
19:17 the families descended from I.
19:23 for the families of the tribe of I.
21:6 the families of the tribes of I,
21:28 given to them from the tribe of I
Jdg 10:1 Tola was from I and lived in
1Ki 4:17 was in charge of I.
15:27 son of Ahijah from the tribe of I,
1Ch 2:1 Levi, Judah, I, Zebulun,
6:62 by lot from the tribes of I,
6:72 From the tribe of I,
12:40 as far as the territories of I,
26:5 (the sixth), I (the seventh),
27:18 brothers for the tribe of I:
2Ch 30:18 from Ephraim, Manasseh, I,
Eze 48:25 I will have one part of the land
48:26 one part of the land and border I
48:33 I Gate, and Zebulun Gate.
Rev 7:7 12,000 from the tribe of I,

Issachar's (4)

Jdg 5:15 I commanders were with
1Ch 7:1 I four sons were Tola,
7:5 all of I families) were fighting
12:32 From I descendants there were

Isshiah (6)

1Ch 7:3 Michael, Obadiah, Joel, and I.
12:6 Elkanah, I, Azarel, Joezer,
23:20 was Micah; his second was I.
24:21 I (⌊for Amram's descendants⌋
24:25 through Micah's brother I).
Ezr 10:31 Eliezer, I, Malchiah, Shemaiah,

issue (5)

Est 1:19 Your Majesty, i a royal decree.
1:20 When you i your decree,
Pro 17:9 bringing up the i separates
Dan 6:8 Your Majesty, i this decree,
Act 21:14 we dropped the i and said,

issued (9)

2Ch 24:8 The king i an order,
24:9 Then they i a proclamation in
Ezr 6:12 I, Darius, have i a decree.
7:13 I have i a decree that any
Est 3:15 The decree was also i at the
4:8 the decree that was i in Susa.
8:14 The decree was i also in the
Psa 119:138 You have i your written
Dan 2:13 So a decree was i that the

issues (1)

Pro 18:18 ⌊i⌋ between powerful people.

issuing (3)

Ezr 6:8 I am i this decree about how
6:11 I am also i a decree that if
Est 9:14 i a decree in Susa.

Italian (1)

Act 10:1 army officer in the I Regiment.

Italy (4)

Act 18:2 they had recently come from I

Act 27:1 that we should sail to **I**,
27:6 that was on its way to **I**
Heb 13:24 are with us from **I** greet you.

itching (1)
Dtr 28:27 and **i** that won't go away.

item (1)
Lev 6:4 the lost **i** you found,

items (7)
Exo 35:29 was willing brought all these **i**
35:29 They brought these **i** to be
2Ch 29:16 took the unclean **i** outside
Ezr 8:29 LORD's temple, weigh these **i**.
8:30 responsible for bringing these **i**
Eze 27:13 and bronze **i** for your goods.
Heb 9:10 and **i** used in various

Ithai (1)
1Ch 11:31 **I** (son of Ribai) from Gibeah in

Ithamar (17)
Exo 6:23 Nadab, Abihu, Eleazar, and **I**.
28:1 Abihu, Eleazar, and **I** to you.
38:21 Levites under the direction of **I**,
Lev 10:6 and his sons Eleazar and **I**:
10:12 surviving sons Eleazar and **I**,
10:16 angry with Eleazar and **I**,
Num 3:2 firstborn), Abihu, Eleazar, and **I**
3:4 So only Eleazar and **I** served
4:28 **I**, son of the priest Aaron,
4:33 **I**, son of the priest Aaron,
7:8 to do under the direction of **I**,
26:60 Nadab, Abihu, Eleazar, and **I**.
1Ch 6:3 Nadab, Abihu, Eleazar, and **I**.
24:1 and Abihu, Eleazar and **I**.
24:2 Eleazar and **I** served as priests.
24:6 for Eleazar, another for **I**.
Ezr 8:2 Gershom from the family of **I**:

Ithamar's (4)
1Ch 24:3 and **I** descendant Ahimelech
24:4 **I** descendants, they were divided
24:4 and **I** descendants had 8 family
24:5 Eleazar's and **I** descendants

Ithiel (1)
Neh 11:7 who was the son of **I**,

Ithlah (1)
Jos 19:42 Shaalabbin, Aijalon, **I**,

Ithmah (1)
1Ch 11:46 (sons of Elnaam), **I** from Moab,

Ithnan (1)
Jos 15:23 Kedesh, Hazor, **I**,

Ithra (5)
2Sm 17:25 was the son of a man named **I**,
23:38 Ira (descendant of **I**),
23:38 Gareb (descendant of **I**),
1Ch 11:40 Ira (descendant of **I**),
11:40 Gareb (descendant of **I**),

Ithran (3)
Gen 36:26 Eshban, **I**, and Cheran.
1Ch 1:41 Eshban, **I**, and Cheran.
7:37 Shilsha, **I**, and Beera.

Ithream (2)
2Sm 3:5 The sixth was **I**, ⌊born⌋ to
1Ch 3:3 The sixth was **I**, ⌊born⌋ to

Ithrites (1)
1Ch 2:53 Jearim, the **I**, the Puthites,

Ittai (9)
2Sm 15:18 all the Pelethites, **I**,
15:19 The king asked **I** from Gath,
15:21 But **I** answered the king,
15:22 So David told **I**, "Go ahead and
15:22 So **I** from Gath marched on
18:2 the last third under **I** from Gath.
18:5 ordered Joab, Abishai, and **I**,
18:12 king gave you, Abishai, and **I**:
23:29 **I** (son of Ribai) from Gibeah in

Iturea (1)
Luk 3:1 Philip ruled **I** and Trachonitis.

ivory (13)
1Ki 10:18 The king also made a large **i**
10:22 silver, **i**, apes, and monkeys.
22:39 the **i** palace he built,
2Ch 9:17 The king also made a large **i**
9:21 silver, **i**, apes, and monkeys.
Psa 45:8 From **i** palaces the music of
Sos 5:14 of **i** covered with sapphires.
7:4 Your neck is like an **i** tower.
Eze 27:6 of Cyprus. It had **i** set in it.
27:15 and they brought you **i** and
Amo 3:15 Houses ⌊decorated⌋ with **i** will
6:4 for those who sleep on **i** beds.
Rev 18:12 articles made of **i** and very

Ivvah (3)
2Ki 18:34 of Sepharvaim, Hena, and **I**?
19:13 of Sepharvaim, Hena, and **I**?'"
Isa 37:13 of Sepharvaim, Hena, and **I**?'"

Iye Abarim (2)
Num 22:11 and set up camp at **I** in the
33:44 and set up camp at **I** on the

Iyim (1)
Num 33:45 They moved from **I** and set up

Izhar (10)
Exo 6:18 Amram, **I**, Hebron, and Uzziel.
6:21 The sons of **I** were Korah,
Num 3:19 Amram, **I**, Hebron, and Uzziel
3:27 Amram, **I**, Hebron, and Uzziel.
16:1 Korah (son of **I**), Dathan and
1Ch 6:2 Kohath's sons were Amram, **I**,
6:18 Kohath's sons were Amram, **I**,
6:38 who was the son of **I**,
23:12 had four sons: Amram, **I**,
26:23 Amram, **I**, Hebron, and Uzziel,

Izhar's (3)
1Ch 23:18 **I** only son was Shelomith.
24:22 **I** descendants through
26:29 From **I** descendants

Izliah (1)
1Ch 8:18 Ishmerai, **I**, and Jobab.

Izohar (1)
1Ch 4:7 Helah's sons were Zereth, **I**,

Izrahiah (1)
1Ch 7:3 five descendants of Uzzi were **I**

Izrahiah's (1)
1Ch 7:3 Izrahiah and **I** sons Michael,

Izrah's (1)
1Ch 27:8 Shamhuth, **I** descendant, was

Izri (1)
1Ch 25:11 The fourth chose **I**,

Izziah (1)
Ezr 10:25 **I**, Malchiah, Mijamin, Eleazar,

J

Jaakan(3)
Num 33:31 and set up camp at Bene **J**.
33:32 They moved from Bene **J** and
1Ch 1:42 sons were Bilhan, Zaavan, **J**.

Jaakanites (1)
Dtr 10:6 the wells of the **J** to Moserah.

Jaakobah (1)
1Ch 4:36 Elioenai, **J**, Jeshohaiah,

Jaala (1)
Neh 7:58 **J**, Darkon, Giddel,

Jaalah (1)
Ezr 2:56 **J**, Darkon, Giddel,

Jaar (1)
Psa 132:6 We have found it in **J**.

Jaare Oregim (1)
2Sm 21:19 son of **J** from Bethlehem,

Jaareshiah (1)
1Ch 8:27 **J**, Elijah, and Zichri.

Jaasau (1)
Ezr 10:37 Mattaniah, Mattenai, **J**

Jaasiel (2)
1Ch 11:47 and **J** the Mezobaite.
27:21 of Benjamin: **J**, son of Abner

Jaazaniah (4)
2Ki 25:23 and **J** from Beth Maacah and
Jer 35:3 I took **J**, who was the son of
Eze 8:11 **J**, son of Shaphan,
11:1 saw among them Azzur's son **J**

Jaazaniah's (1)
Jer 35:3 and I took **J** brothers and all his

Jaaziah (2)
1Ch 24:26 and Merari's son **J**,
24:27 through his son **J**),

Jaaziel (1)
1Ch 15:18 **J**, Shemiramoth, Jehiel, Unni,

Jabal (1)
Gen 4:20 Adah gave birth to **J**.

Jabbok (7)
Gen 32:22 the shallow part of the **J** River.
Num 21:24 the Arnon Valley to the **J** River.
Dtr 2:37 along the bank of the **J** River
3:16 is the border) to the **J** River,
Jos 12:2 the Arnon Valley to the **J** River,
Jdg 11:13 the Arnon River to the **J** River
11:22 the Arnon River to the **J** River

Jabesh (11)
1Sm 11:1 All the men of **J** said to
11:3 The leaders of **J** told him,
11:5 the news about the men of **J**.
11:9 When the men of **J** received
31:12 They came back to **J** and
31:13 under the tamarisk tree in **J**.
2Ki 15:10 Shallum, son of **J**,
15:13 Shallum, son of **J**,
15:14 attacked Shallum (son of **J**),
1Ch 10:12 his sons and brought them to **J**.
10:12 bones under the oak tree in **J**.

Jabesh Gilead (13)
Jdg 21:8 No one from **J** had
21:9 no one there from **J**.
21:10 and kill the people of **J**,
21:12 Among the people of **J**
21:14 women from **J** who had
1Sm 11:1 and gone to **J**.
11:1 Ammonite blockaded **J**.
11:9 to say to the men of **J**:
31:11 When the people living in **J**
2Sm 2:4 "The people of **J** were
2:5 to the people of **J**.
21:12 from the citizens of **J**.
1Ch 10:11 When all the people of **J**

Jabez (4)
1Ch 2:55 of scribes who lived at **J**.
4:9 **J** was more honorable than his
4:9 had named him **J** [Painful],
4:10 **J** prayed to the God of Israel,

Jabin (6)

Jos 11:1 King J of Hazor heard what
Jdg 4:2 LORD used King J of Canaan,
4:3 King J had 900 chariots made
4:17 Sisera did this because King J
4:23 the power of King J of Canaan.
Psa 83:9 to Sisera and J at the Kishon

Jabin's (2)

Jdg 4:2 The commander of King J army
4:7 of J army), his chariots,

Jabneel (2)

Jos 15:11 and comes out at J.
19:33 It continues to Adami Nekeb, J,

Jabneh (1)

2Ch 26:6 walls of Gath, J, and Ashdod.

Jacan (1)

1Ch 5:13 Sheba, Jorai, J, Zia, and Eber.

Jachin (6)

Exo 6:15 Ohad, J, Zohar, and Shaul,
1Ki 7:21 named it J [He Establishes].
1Ch 9:10 were Jedaiah, Jehoiarib, J,
24:17 the twenty-first for J,
2Ch 3:17 He named the one on the right J
Neh 11:10 Jedaiah (son of Joiarib), J,

jacinth (3)

Exo 28:19 In the third row put j,
39:12 In the third row they put j,
Rev 21:20 green quartz, the eleventh j,

jackal (1)

Mic 1:8 I will cry like a j and mourn like

jackals (15)

Job 30:29 I'm a brother to j and a
Psa 44:19 you crushed us in a place for j
63:10 bodies will be left as food for j.
Isa 13:22 and j will howl in its luxurious
34:13 It will become a home for j and
34:14 Hyenas will meet with j.
35:7 and rushes in the home of j.
43:20 Wild animals, j, and ostriches
Jer 9:11 a pile of rubble, a home for j.
10:22 and make them homes for j.
14:6 They sniff the air like j.
49:33 be a place where only j live.
51:37 become a dwelling place for j,
Lam 4:3 Even j offer their breasts to
Mal 1:3 to the j in the desert.

Jacob (362)

Gen 25:26 and so he was named J [Heel].
25:27 J remained a quiet man,
25:28 However, Rebekah loved J.
25:29 Once, J was preparing a meal
25:30 So Esau said to J,
25:31 J responded, "First, sell me
25:33 "First, swear an oath," J said.
25:34 Then J gave Esau a meal of
27:6 Rebekah said to her son J,
27:11 J said to his mother Rebekah,
27:15 put them on her younger son J.
27:17 Then she gave her son J the
27:19 J answered his father,
27:21 Then Isaac said to J,
27:22 So J went over to his father.
27:23 He didn't recognize J,
27:24 "I am," J answered.
27:25 J brought it to Isaac,
27:25 J also brought him wine,
27:30 Isaac finished blessing J.
27:30 J had barely left when his
27:36 "Isn't that why he's named J?
27:41 So Esau hated J because of
27:41 Then I'll kill my brother J."
27:42 she sent for her younger son J
27:46 If J marries a Hittite woman
28:1 Isaac called for J and blessed
28:5 Isaac sent J to Paddan Aram.
28:5 J went to live with Laban,
Gen 28:5 was the mother of J and Esau.
28:6 that Isaac had blessed J
28:6 that Isaac had blessed J
28:7 He also learned that J had
28:10 J left Beersheba and traveled
28:16 Then J woke up from his sleep
28:18 Early the next morning J took
28:20 Then J made a vow:
29:1 J continued on his trip and
29:4 J asked some people,
29:6 J asked them. "He's fine," they
29:10 J saw Rachel, daughter of his
29:11 Then J kissed Rachel and
29:12 When J told Rachel that he
29:13 news about his sister's son J,
29:13 Then J told Laban all that had
29:14 J stayed with him for a whole
29:18 J loved Rachel. So he offered,
29:20 J worked seven years in return
29:21 end of the seven years J said
29:23 Leah and brought her to J.
29:23 J slept with her. When morning
29:25 J asked Laban. "Didn't I work for
29:28 That's what J did. He finished
29:30 J slept with Rachel too.
30:1 could not have children for J,
30:1 She said to J, "Give me
30:2 J became angry with Rachel
30:4 and J slept with her.
30:5 she gave birth to a son for J.
30:7 birth to a second son for J.
30:9 and gave her to J as his wife.
30:10 Zilpah gave birth to a son for J.
30:12 birth to her second son for J.
30:15 Rachel said, "Very well, J can
30:16 As J was coming in from the
30:17 gave birth to her fifth son for J.
30:19 gave birth to her sixth son for J.
30:25 to Joseph, J said to Laban,
30:29 J responded, "You know how
30:31 me anything," J answered.
30:36 three days away from J.
30:36 J continued to take care of the
30:37 Then J took fresh-cut branches
30:40 J separated the rams from the
30:41 J would lay the branches in the
30:42 and the stronger ones to J.
30:43 J became very wealthy.
31:1 J heard that Laban's sons were
31:1 "J has taken everything that
31:3 Then the LORD said to J,
31:4 So J sent a message to Rachel
31:11 of God called to me, 'J!' And
31:17 Then J put his children and his
31:20 J also tricked Laban the
31:22 Laban was told that J had left
31:23 He and his relatives pursued J
31:24 not to say anything at all to J."
31:25 Laban finally caught up with J,
31:25 J had put up his tents in the
31:26 Then Laban asked J,
31:29 not to say anything at all to J.'
31:31 J answered Laban,
31:32 (J didn't know that Rachel had
31:36 Then J became angry and
31:36 J demanded of Laban.
31:43 Then Laban answered J,
31:45 J took a stone and set it up as
31:46 Then J said to his relatives,
31:47 but J called it Galeed.
31:51 Laban said to J, "Here is the
31:53 So J swore this oath by the
32:1 As J went on his way,
32:2 When he saw them, J said,
32:3 J sent messengers ahead of
32:4 this is what J has to say,
32:6 messengers came back to J,
32:7 J was terrified and distressed.
32:9 Then J prayed, "God of my
32:18 they belong to your servant J.
32:18 J is right behind us."'
32:20 'J is right behind us.
32:21 So J sent the gift ahead of him
32:24 So J was left alone.
32:25 that he could not win against J,
32:26 But J answered, "I won't let
Gen 32:27 name?" "J," he answered.
32:28 "Your name will no longer be J
32:29 J said, "Please tell me your
32:29 Then he blessed J there.
32:30 So J named that place Peniel
33:1 J saw Esau coming with 400
33:4 Then Esau ran to meet J.
33:5 given me, sir," J answered.
33:10 J said, "No, please take the gift
33:11 So Esau took it because J
33:13 J said to him, "Sir, you know
33:15 J asked. "I only want to win
33:17 But J moved on to Succoth
33:18 J came safely to the city of
34:1 Dinah, daughter of Leah and J,
34:5 J heard that Shechem had
34:5 so J kept quiet until they came
34:6 father Hamor came to J
34:30 Then J said to Simeon and
35:1 Then God said to J,
35:2 So J said to his family and
35:4 So they gave J all the foreign
35:4 J buried these things under the
35:6 J and all the people who were
35:7 had revealed himself to J when
35:8 So J called it the Tree of
35:9 appeared once more to J after
35:10 said to him, "Your name is J.
35:10 You will no longer be called J,
35:14 So J set up a memorial,
35:15 J named the place where God
35:20 Then J set up a stone as a
35:22 heard about it. J had 12 sons.
35:27 J came home to his father
35:29 sons Esau and J buried him.
36:6 land away from his brother J.
37:1 J continued to live in the land
37:2 This is the account of J and
37:34 his grief, J tore his clothes,
42:1 When J found out that grain
42:4 J wouldn't send Joseph's
42:29 to their father J in Canaan,
42:36 Their father J said to them,
42:38 J replied, "My son will not go
45:25 to their father J in Canaan.
45:26 J was stunned and didn't
46:2 said, "J, Jacob!" "Here I am,"
46:2 that night and said, "Jacob, J!"
46:5 So J left Beersheba.
46:5 Israel's sons put their father J,
46:6 J and all his family arrived in
46:8 of Israel's descendants (J
46:15 of the sons Leah gave to J
46:18 birth to these children for J.
46:22 of Rachel who were born to J.
46:25 gave birth to these sons for J.
47:7 Joseph brought his father J
47:7 J blessed Pharaoh.
47:9 J answered Pharaoh,
47:10 Then J blessed Pharaoh and
47:28 J lived in Egypt 17 years,
48:1 and Ephraim to see J.
48:2 When J was told, "Your son
48:3 J said to Joseph,
48:15 Then J blessed Joseph,
49:1 J called for his sons and said,
49:2 around and listen, sons of J.
49:7 them among the sons of J
49:24 the help of the Mighty One of J,
49:33 When J finished giving these
50:4 When the time of mourning for J
50:24 give to Abraham, Isaac, and J."
Exo 1:1 J) who came with him to Egypt
2:24 to Abraham, Isaac, and J.
3:6 God of Abraham, Isaac, and J."
3:15 and J, has sent me to you.
3:16 Isaac, and J, appeared to me.
4:5 Isaac, and J, appeared to you."
6:3 and J as God Almighty,
6:8 give to Abraham, Isaac, and J.
19:3 say to the descendants of J.
33:1 and J with an oath,
Lev 26:42 will remember my promise to J,
Num 23:7 'Come, curse J for me,'
23:10 The descendants of J are like
23:21 for the descendants of J.

Num 23:23 curse the descendants of **J**.
23:23 it will be said of **J** and Israel:
24:5 How beautiful are your tents, **J**,
24:17 A star will come from **J**.
24:19 He will rule from **J** and destroy
32:11 and **J** with an oath.
Dtr 1:8 Isaac, and **J**, and to you,
6:10 Abraham, Isaac, and **J**.
9:5 Abraham, Isaac, and **J**.
9:27 Abraham, Isaac, and **J**.
29:13 and **J** with an oath.
30:20 Abraham, Isaac, and **J**.
32:9 **J** was his own possession.
33:4 belong to the assembly of **J**.
33:10 They teach **J** your rules and
34:4 oath to Abraham, Isaac, and **J**.
Jos 24:4 To Isaac I gave **J** and Esau.
24:4 **J** and his sons went to Egypt.
24:32 of ground **J** had bought from
1Sm 12:8 your ancestors went with **J**
2Sm 23:1 whom the God of **J** anointed,
1Ki 18:31 had spoken his word to **J**:
2Ki 13:23 to Abraham, Isaac, and **J**.
17:34 to the descendants of **J** (whom
1Ch 16:13 you descendants of **J**,
16:17 He confirmed it as a law for **J**,
Psa 14:7 of his people, **J** will rejoice.
20:1 of the God of **J** will protect you.
22:23 All you descendants of **J**,
24:6 for the face of the God of **J**.
44:4 You won those victories for **J**.
46:7 The God of **J** is our stronghold.
46:11 The God of **J** is our stronghold.
47:4 the pride of **J**, whom he loved.
53:6 of his people, **J** will rejoice.
59:13 they will know that God rules **J**
75:9 music to praise the God of **J**.
76:6 your stern warning, O God of **J**,
77:15 descendants of **J** and Joseph.
78:21 His fire burned against **J** and
78:71 the shepherd of the people of **J**,
79:7 They have devoured **J**.
81:1 Shout happily to the God of **J**.
81:4 decision from the God of **J**.
84:8 Open your ears, O God of **J**.
85:1 You restored the fortunes of **J**.
87:2 more than any other place in **J**.
94:7 The God of **J** doesn't even pay
99:4 done what is fair and right for **J**.
105:6 you descendants of **J**,
105:10 He confirmed it as a law for **J**,
105:23 **J** lived as a foreigner in the
114:7 in the presence of the God of **J**.
132:2 vow to the Mighty One of **J**:
132:5 place for the Mighty One of **J**."
135:4 The LORD chose **J** to be his
146:5 receive help from the God of **J**.
147:19 He speaks his word to **J**,
Isa 2:3 to the house of the God of **J**.
2:5 Come, descendants of **J**,
2:6 the descendants of **J**,
8:17 face from the descendants of **J**.
9:8 sent a message against **J**.
10:21 A few, the remaining few of **J**,
14:1 will have compassion for **J**
14:1 with the descendants of **J**.
27:6 In times to come **J** will take
27:9 of **J** are covered up.
29:22 about the descendants of **J**:
29:22 **J** will no longer be ashamed.
29:23 treat the Holy One of **J** as holy.
40:27 **J**, why do you complain?
41:8 Israel, **J**, whom I have chosen,
41:14 Don't be afraid, **J**, you worm.
42:24 Who gave **J** away as loot and
43:1 The LORD created **J** and
43:22 **J**, you have not prayed to me.
43:28 I will claim **J** for destruction.
44:1 But now listen, my servant **J**,
44:2 afraid, my servant **J**, Jeshurun,
44:5 will call on the name of **J**.
44:21 Remember these things, **J**:
44:23 The LORD has reclaimed **J**.
45:4 For the sake of my servant **J**,
46:3 Listen to me, descendants of **J**,
48:1 to this, descendants of **J**!
Isa 48:12 Listen to me, **J**, Israel, whom I
48:20 has reclaimed his servant **J**.
49:5 servant in order to bring **J** back
49:6 who restores the tribes of **J**
49:26 the Mighty One of **J**,
58:1 of **J** about their sins.
58:14 inheritance of your ancestor **J**.
59:20 to those in **J** who turn from
60:16 the Mighty One of **J**,
Jer 2:4 of the LORD, descendants of **J**,
5:20 this to the descendants of **J**,
10:25 devoured the descendants of **J**.
30:7 for the descendants of **J**,
30:10 "Don't be afraid, my servant **J**,"
30:10 The descendants of **J** will
31:7 Sing a happy song about **J**.
31:11 will free the descendants of **J**
33:26 reject the descendants of **J**
33:26 of Abraham, Isaac, and **J**.
46:27 "Don't be afraid, my servant **J**.
46:28 Don't be afraid, my servant **J**,"
Lam 1:17 has given this order about **J**:
2:3 a raging fire in ⌊the land of⌋ **J**,
Eze 28:25 the land I gave to my servant **J**.
37:25 land that I gave my servant **J**,
Hos 10:11 **J** must break up the ground.
12:2 against Judah and punishes **J**
12:3 Their ancestor **J** held on to his
12:3 When **J** became a man,
12:4 **J** cried and pleaded with him.
12:4 **J** found him at Bethel,
12:12 **J** fled to the country of Syria.
Amo 3:13 against the descendants of **J**,
7:2 descendants of⌊ **J** survive?
7:5 descendants of⌊ **J** survive?
9:8 destroy the descendants of **J**,
Oba 1:10 of the violence you did to **J**,
1:17 The descendants of **J** will get
1:18 The descendants of **J** will be
Mic 2:7 the descendants of **J** be asked:
2:12 I will surely gather all of you, **J**.
3:1 I said: Listen, you leaders of **J**,
3:8 of⌊ **J** about their crimes
3:9 of the descendants of **J**,
4:2 to the house of the God of **J**.
5:7 Then the few people left from **J**
5:8 The few people left from **J** will
7:20 You will be faithful to **J**.
Mal 1:2 declares the LORD. "I loved **J**,
3:6 of **J** haven't been destroyed
Mat 1:2 Isaac the father of **J**,
1:2 **J** the father of Judah and his
1:15 Matthan the father of **J**.
1:16 **J** was the father of Joseph,
8:11 and **J** in the kingdom of
22:32 of Abraham, Isaac, and **J**.' He's
Mar 12:26 God of Abraham, Isaac, and **J**.'
Luk 3:34 son of **J**, son of Isaac, son of
13:28 Isaac, **J**, and all the prophets.
20:37 God of Abraham, Isaac, and **J**.
Jon 4:5 piece of land that **J** had given
4:12 important than our ancestor **J**,
Act 3:13 and **J** has glorified his servant
7:8 did the same to his son **J**,
7:8 and **J** did the same to his
7:12 When **J** heard that Egypt had
7:14 Joseph sent for his father **J**
7:15 So **J** went to Egypt,
7:32 Abraham, Isaac, and **J**.' Moses
7:46 place for the family of **J**.
Rom 9:13 The Scriptures say, "I loved **J**,
11:26 remove godlessness from **J**.
Heb 11:9 as did Isaac and **J**,
11:20 led Isaac to bless **J** and Esau.
11:21 While **J** was dying,

Jacob's (49)

Gen 27:22 "The voice is **J**," he said,
31:33 So Laban went into **J** tent, into
32:25 he touched the socket of **J** hip
32:32 touched the socket of **J** hip at
34:3 very fond of **J** daughter Dinah.
34:7 **J** sons came in from the open
34:7 family by raping **J** daughter.
34:13 Then **J** sons gave Shechem
34:19 such pleasure in **J** daughter.
Gen 34:25 two of **J** sons, Simeon and
34:27 Then **J** sons stripped the
35:23 Leah were **J** firstborn Reuben,
35:26 These were **J** sons, who were
46:8 Reuben was **J** firstborn
46:19 The sons of **J** wife Rachel
46:26 The total number of **J** direct
46:26 include the wives of **J** sons
46:27 in **J** household who went
50:10 ceremony to mourn **J** death.
50:12 **J** sons did for him what he had
Exo 1:5 of **J** descendants was 70.
Dtr 33:28 **J** spring will be ⌊left⌋ alone in
1Ki 18:31 the tribes named after **J** sons.
Psa 78:5 instructions for **J** people.
114:1 when **J** family left people who
Isa 10:20 the survivors of **J** descendants
17:4 the honor of **J** people will fade
29:22 **J** face will no longer turn pale.
41:21 best arguments," says **J** king
45:19 I didn't say to **J** descendants,
65:9 **J** descendant, one who will
Jer 10:16 **J** God isn't like them.
30:18 the captives back to **J** tents
46:27 Then **J** descendants will again
51:19 **J** God isn't like them.
Lam 2:2 of **J** pastures without any pity.
Eze 20:5 to the descendants of **J** family.
39:25 I will bring back **J** captives
Amo 6:8 I am disgusted with **J** pride,
8:7 an oath by **J** pride: "I will never
Oba 1:11 strangers carried off **J** wealth.
Mic 1:5 All this is because of **J** crime
1:5 What is **J** crime? Isn't it
Nah 2:2 The LORD will restore **J** glory
Mal 1:2 "Wasn't Esau **J** brother?"
2:12 he exclude them from **J** tents
Luk 1:33 will be king of **J** people forever,
Jon 4:6 **J** Well was there. Jesus sat
Act 7:9 "**J** sons were jealous of their

Jada (2)

1Ch 2:28 sons were Shammai and **J**.
2:32 The sons of **J** (Shammai's

Jaddai (1)

Ezr 10:43 Zebina, **J**, Joel, and Benaiah

Jaddua (3)

Neh 10:21 Meshezabel, Zadok, **J**,
12:11 Jonathan was the father of **J**.
12:22 and **J** were recorded until the

Jadon (1)

Neh 3:7 Gibeon and **J** from Meronoth,

Jael (6)

Jdg 4:17 fled on foot toward the tent of **J**,
4:18 When **J** came out ⌊of her tent⌋,
4:21 exhaustion, **J**, Heber's wife,
4:22 When **J** came out ⌊of her tent⌋,
5:6 son of Anath, in the days of **J**,
5:24 **J**, wife of Heber the Kenite,

jagged (1)

Job 39:28 Its fortress is on a **j** peak.

Jagur (1)

Jos 15:21 their villages: Kabzeel, Eder, **J**,

Jahath (8)

1Ch 4:2 was the father of **J**.
4:2 **J** was the father of Ahumai and
6:20 Libni's son was **J**.
6:43 who was the son of **J**,
23:10 Shimei's sons were **J**,
23:11 **J** was the first, and Ziza was
24:22 **J** (for Izhar's descendants
2Ch 34:12 under the supervision of **J**

Jahath's (1)

1Ch 6:20 **J** son was Zimmah.

Jahaz (7)

Num 21:23 When Sihon's troops came to **J**,
Dtr 2:32 out to meet us in battle at **J**.

Jos 13:18 J, Kedemoth, Mephaath,
21:36 with pasturelands: Bezer, J,
Jdg 11:20 at J and attacked Israel.
Isa 15:4 are heard as far away as J.
Jer 48:34 from Heshbon to Elealeh and J.

Jahaziel (7)

1Ch 12:4 leaders), Jeremiah, J, Johanan,
16:6 The priests Benaiah and J
23:19 was Amariah; his third was J;
24:23 J (the third of Hebron's
2Ch 20:14 the LORD's Spirit came to J.
20:15 J said, "Pay attention to me,
Ezr 8:5 son of J, with 300 males

Jahdai's (1)

1Ch 2:47 J sons were Regem,

Jahdiel (1)

1Ch 5:24 Jeremiah, Hodaviah, and J.

Jahdo (1)

1Ch 5:14 great-grandson of J,

Jahleel (2)

Gen 46:14 were Sered, Elon, and J.
Num 26:26 and the family of J.

Jahmai (1)

1Ch 7:2 Jeriel, J, Ibsam, and Shemuel.

Jahzah (2)

1Ch 6:78 J with its pastureland,
Jer 48:21 plain: to Holon, J, Mephaath,

Jahzeel (2)

Gen 46:24 The sons of Naphtali were J,
Num 26:48 Naphtali were the family of J,

Jahzeiah (2)

Ezr 10:15 son, and J, Tikvah's son,
10:15 supported Jonathan and J.)

Jahzerah (1)

1Ch 9:12 (son of Adiel, grandson of J,

Jahziel (1)

1Ch 7:13 Naphtali's sons were J,

jail (12)

Gen 42:17 he put them in j for three days.
Exo 12:29 firstborn son of the prisoner in j,
Isa 24:22 be gathered like prisoners in a j
Act 4:3 they put Peter and John in j
5:18 and putting them in the city j.
16:23 they threw them in j and
16:26 shook the foundations of the j.
16:29 torches and rushed into the j.
16:37 a trial and have thrown us in j,
16:39 So the officials went to the j
16:39 Paul and Silas out of the j,
16:40 After Paul and Silas left the j,

jailer (9)

Act 16:23 them in jail and ordered the j
16:24 So the j followed these orders
16:27 The j woke up and saw the
16:29 The j asked for torches and
16:32 spoke the Lord's word to the j
16:33 At that hour of the night, the j
16:33 The j and his entire family
16:35 sent guards who told the j,
16:36 The j reported this order to Paul

Jair (11)

Num 32:41 Havvoth Jair [Settlements of J].
Dtr 3:14 J, a descendant of Manasseh,
Jos 13:30 60 settlements of J that were
Jdg 10:3 J from Gilead became a judge.
10:4 J had 30 sons who rode on 30
10:5 J died and was buried in
2Sm 20:26 And Ira, a descendant of J,
1Ki 4:13 he had the settlements of J,
1Ch 2:22 Segub was the father of J,
20:5 Elhanan, son of J, killed Lahmi,
Est 2:5 He was the son of J,

Jairus (2)

Mar 5:22 leader named J also arrived.
Luk 8:41 A man named J, a synagogue

Jakeh (1)

Pro 30:1 The words of Agur, son of J.

Jakim (2)

1Ch 8:19 Shimei's sons were J,
24:12 for Eliashib, the twelfth for J,

Jakin (2)

Gen 46:10 Ohad, J, Zohar, and Shaul,
Num 26:12 family of Jamin, the family of J,

Jalam (4)

Gen 36:5 birth to Jeush, J, and Korah.
36:14 She gave birth to Jeush, J,
36:18 Jeush, J, and Korah.
1Ch 1:35 Reuel, Jeush, J, and Korah.

Jalon (1)

1Ch 4:17 Jether, Mered, Epher, and J.

Jambres (2)

2Ti 3:8 Jannes and J opposed Moses,
3:9 the stupidity of Jannes and J,

James (41)

Mat 4:21 two other brothers, J and John,
10:2 J and his brother John,
10:3 J (son of Alphaeus),
13:55 Aren't his brothers' names J,
17:1 six days Jesus took Peter, J,
17:1 and John (the brother of J) and
27:56 (the mother of J and Joseph),
Mar 1:19 he saw J and John,
1:29 J and John went with them.
3:17 J and his brother John
3:18 J (son of Alphaeus),
5:37 the two brothers J and John.
6:3 and the brother of J,
9:2 days Jesus took only Peter, J,
10:35 J and John, sons of Zebedee,
10:41 were irritated with J and John.
13:3 buildings, Peter, J, John,
14:33 He took Peter, J, and John with
15:40 mother of young J and Joseph),
16:1 Mary (the mother of J),
Luk 5:10 J and John, who were
6:14 J, John, Philip, Bartholomew,
6:15 J (son of Alphaeus),
6:16 Judas (son of J), and Judas
8:51 J, and the child's parents.
9:28 and J with him and went up a
9:54 J and John, his disciples,
24:10 and Mary (the mother of J).
Act 1:13 J, Andrew, Philip, Thomas,
1:13 J (son of Alphaeus),
1:13 and Judas (son of J) went to
12:2 He had J, the brother of John,
12:17 He added, "Tell J and the other
15:13 J responded, "Brothers,
21:18 Paul went with us to visit J.
1Co 15:7 Next he appeared to J.
Gal 1:19 I only saw J, the Lord's brother.
2:9 J, Cephas, and John (who
2:12 some men J had sent from
Jas 1:1 From J, a servant of God and
Jud 1:1 of Jesus Christ and brother of J.

Jamin (6)

Gen 46:10 Jemuel, J, Ohad, Jakin, Zohar,
Exo 6:15 J, Ohad, Jachin, Zohar,
Num 26:12 of Nemuel, the family of J,
1Ch 2:27 were Maaz, J, and Eker.
4:24 Simeon's sons were Nemuel, J,
Neh 8:7 J, Akkub, Shabbethai, Hodiah,

Jamlech (1)

1Ch 4:34 Meshobab, J, Joshah (son of

Janai (1)

1Ch 5:12 descended from Gad's sons J

Janim (1)

Jos 15:53 J, Beth Tappuah, Aphekah,

Jannai (1)

Luk 3:24 son of J, son of Joseph,

Jannes (2)

2Ti 3:8 As J and Jambres opposed
3:9 the stupidity of J and Jambres,

Janoah (3)

Jos 16:6 Shiloh and passes east to J.
16:7 From J it descends to Ataroth
2Ki 15:29 J, Kedesh, Hazor, Gilead,

Japheth (9)

Gen 5:32 the father of Shem, Ham, and J.
6:10 three sons: Shem, Ham, and J.
7:13 his sons Shem, Ham, and J,
9:18 ship, were Shem, Ham, and J.
9:23 Shem and J took a blanket and
9:27 God expand the territory of J.
10:1 and J, and their descendants.
10:1 Shem, Ham and J had children
1Ch 1:4 Noah: Shem, Ham, and J.

Japheth's (3)

Gen 10:2 J descendants were Gomer,
10:21 Shem, J older brother,
1Ch 1:5 J descendants were Gomer,

Japhia (5)

Jos 10:3 King J of Lachish,
19:12 and then ascends toward J.
2Sm 5:15 Ibhar, Elishua, Nepheg, J,
1Ch 3:7 Nogah, Nepheg, J,
14:6 Nogah, Nepheg, J,

Japhlet (2)

Jos 16:3 west to the border of J
1Ch 7:32 Heber was the father of J,

Japhlet's (2)

1Ch 7:33 J sons were Pasach,
7:33 These were J sons

jar (30)

Gen 24:14 have a drink from your j?' If
24:15 Rebekah came with her j on
24:16 filled her j, and came back.
24:18 She quickly lowered her j to
24:20 So she quickly emptied her j
24:45 Rebekah came with her j on
24:46 quickly lowered her j and said,
Exo 16:33 Moses said to Aaron, "Take a j,
16:34 Aaron put the j of manna in
1Sm 26:11 his head and that j of water,
26:12 David took the spear and the j
26:16 at the king's spear and the j
1Ki 14:3 and a j of honey with you,
17:12 I have one handful of flour in a j
17:14 the j of flour will never be
17:16 The j of flour never became
19:6 on hot stones and a j of water.
2Ki 2:20 Elisha said, "Bring me a new j,
4:2 house except a j of olive oil."
Jer 19:1 Go and buy a clay j from a
19:10 "Then smash the j in front of
19:11 potter's j was smashed beyond
32:14 Put them in a clay j so that
48:11 are like wine left to settle in a j.
48:11 poured from one j to another.
48:38 break Moab like a j that no one
Jon 2:6 Each j held 18 to 27 gallons.
4:28 Then the woman left her water j
19:29 A j filled with vinegar was
Heb 9:4 In the ark were the gold j filled

Jarah (2)

1Ch 9:42 Ahaz was the father of J.
9:42 J was the father of Alemeth,

Jared (7)

Gen 5:15 he became the father of J.
5:16 After he became the father of J,

Gen 5:18 When **J** was 162 years old,
5:19 **J** lived 800 years and had other
5:20 **J** lived a total of 962 years;
1Ch 1:2 Kenan, Mahalalel, **J**,
Luk 3:37 son of **J**, son of Mahalaleel,

Jarha (2)

1Ch 2:34 an Egyptian slave named **J**.
2:35 Sheshan let **J** marry one of his

Jarib (3)

1Ch 4:24 Jamin, **J**, Zerah, and Shaul.
Ezr 8:16 Elnathan, **J**, Elnathan, Nathan,
10:18 Eliezer, **J**, and Gedaliah,

Jarmuth (7)

Jos 10:3 of Hebron, King Piram of **J**,
10:5 Jerusalem, Hebron, **J**, Lachish,
10:23 Hebron, **J**, Lachish, and Eglon.
12:11 the king of **J**, the king of
15:35 **J**, Adullam, Socoh, Azekah,
21:29 **J**, and En Gannim.
Neh 11:29 in En Rimmon, Zorah, **J**,

Jaroah (1)

1Ch 5:14 the son of Huri, grandson of **J**,

jars (14)

Jdg 7:16 horns and **j** with torches inside.
7:19 the **j** they were holding
7:20 rams' horns and broke their **j**.
Rut 2:9 When you're thirsty, go to the **j**
1Ki 18:34 He said, "Fill four **j** with water.
Job 38:37 pour out the water **j** of heaven
Isa 22:24 from bowls to **j** of every kind."
Jer 40:10 and put them in storage **j**.
48:12 people to pour Moab out of its **j**
51:34 He has turned us into empty **j**.
Mar 7:4 wash their cups, **j**, brass pots,
Jon 2:6 Six stone water **j** were there.
2:7 "Fill the **j** with water."
2:7 servers filled the **j** to the brim.

Jashar (2)

Jos 10:13 this recorded in the Book of **J**?
2Sm 1:18 (It is recorded in the Book of **J**.)

Jashobeam (3)

1Ch 11:11 of David's fighting men was **J**,
12:6 and **J** (Korah's descendants),
27:2 **J**, son of Zabdiel, was in

Jashub (3)

Num 26:24 the family of **J**, and the family
1Ch 7:1 Tola, Puah, **J**, and Shimron.
Ezr 10:29 Adaiah, **J**, Sheal, and Jeremoth

Jashubi Lehem (1)

1Ch 4:22 Saraph ruled Moab and **J**

Jason (4)

Act 17:6 they dragged **J** and some other
17:7 and **J** has welcomed them as
17:9 But after they had made **J** and
Rom 16:21 so do Lucius, **J**, and Sosipater,

Jason's (1)

Act 17:5 They attacked **J** home and

Jathniel (1)

1Ch 26:2 (the third), **J** (the fourth),

Jattir (4)

Jos 15:48 villages: Shamir, **J**, Socoh,
21:14 **J**, Eshtemoa,
1Sm 30:27 Ramoth in the Negev, **J**,
1Ch 6:57 Libnah with its pastureland, **J**,

Javan (3)

Gen 10:2 **J**, Tubal, Meshech, and Tiras.
1Ch 1:5 **J**, Tubal, Meshech, and Tiras.
Isa 66:19 Lud, Meshech, Rosh, Tubal, **J**,

Javan's (2)

Gen 10:4 **J** descendants were the
1Ch 1:7 **J** descendants were the

javelin (4)

1Sm 17:6 and on his back a bronze **j**.
17:45 me with sword and spear and **j**,
Job 39:23 with the flashing spear and **j**.
41:29 and it laughs at a rattling **j**.

jaw (1)

Job 41:2 or pierce its **j** with a hook?

jawbone (5)

Jdg 15:15 Samson found the **j** from a
15:16 "With a **j** from a donkey,
15:16 With a **j** from a donkey,
15:17 he threw the **j** away.
15:17 that place Ramath Lehi [**J** Hill].

jaws (5)

Dtr 18:3 the shoulder, **j**, and stomach.
Job 36:16 he lured you away from the **j** of
Pro 30:14 and whose **j** are ⌊like⌋ knives,
Eze 29:4 "'I will put hooks in your **j** and
38:4 around and put hooks in your **j**.

Jazer (13)

Num 21:32 After Moses sent spies to **J**,
32:1 They saw that the regions of **J**
32:3 "Ataroth, Dibon, **J**,
32:35 Atroth Shophan, **J**,
Jos 13:25 Their territory included **J**,
21:39 Heshbon, and **J**.
2Sm 24:5 they went to Gad and to **J**.
1Ch 6:81 and **J** with its pastureland.
26:31 were found at **J** in Gilead.
Isa 16:8 ⌊once⌋ reached as far as **J**
16:9 of Sibmah as **J** cries
Jer 48:32 I will cry for you as **J** cries.
48:32 reached as far as the sea of **J**.

Jaziel (1)

1Ch 15:20 Zechariah, **J**, Shemiramoth,

Jaziz (1)

1Ch 27:31 for the flocks: **J** from Hagar

jealous (23)

Gen 26:14 the Philistines became **j** of him.
30:1 and she became **j** of her sister.
37:11 So his brothers were **j** of him,
Dtr 32:21 not my people to make them **j**
Isa 11:13 Ephraim won't be **j** of Judah,
Eze 35:11 When you were angry and **j**,
Nah 1:2 God is **j**. The LORD takes
Zec 1:14 I'm very **j** about Jerusalem and
8:2 I am very **j** about Zion.
Mat 27:18 to him because they were **j**.
Mar 15:10 to him because they were **j**.
Act 5:17 with him were extremely **j**.
7:9 "Jacob's sons were **j** of their
13:45 they became very **j**.
17:5 Then the Jews became **j**.
Rom 10:19 "I will make you **j** of people
11:11 to make the Jewish people **j**.
11:14 I can make my people **j**
1Co 3:3 When you are **j** and quarrel
10:22 we trying to make the Lord **j**?
13:4 Love isn't **j**. It doesn't sing its
Tit 3:3 We were mean and **j**.
Jas 3:14 But if you are bitterly **j** and

jealousy (18)

Num 5:14 "A husband may have a fit of **j**
5:15 because of the husband's **j**,
5:18 because of the husband's **j**).
5:29 for how to deal with **j**.
5:30 when a husband has a fit of **j**
Job 5:2 and **j** murders a gullible person.
Pro 6:34 because **j** arouses a husband's
14:30 but **j** is ⌊like⌋ bone cancer.
27:4 but who can survive **j**?
Isa 11:13 Ephraim's **j** will vanish,
Act 8:23 see that you are bitter with **j**
Rom 13:13 and **j** cannot be part of our
2Co 12:20 **j**, hot tempers, selfish ambition,
Gal 5:20 rivalry, **j**, angry outbursts,
Php 1:15 because of their **j** and envy.

1Ti 6:4 This produces **j**, rivalry,
Jas 3:16 Wherever there is **j** and rivalry,
1Pe 2:1 **j**, and every kind of slander.

Jearim (1)

Jos 15:10 Mount **J** (now called Chesalon).

Jeatherai (1)

1Ch 6:21 Zerah's son was **J**.

Jeberechiah (1)

Isa 8:2 Uriah and Zechariah (son of **J**)."

Jebus (7)

Jos 15:63 out the people of **J** who lived
18:16 the south slope of the city of **J**,
18:28 **J** (now called Jerusalem),
Jdg 19:10 He left and traveled as far as **J**
19:11 By the time they were near **J**,
19:11 "Let's go spend the night in **J**."
1Ch 11:4 went to Jerusalem (that is, **J**).

Jebusite (7)

Jos 15:8 slope of the **J** city Jerusalem.
2Sm 24:16 threshing floor of Araunah the **J**
1Ch 11:6 "Whoever is the first to kill a **J**
21:15 threshing floor of Ornan the **J**.
21:28 threshing floor of Ornan the **J**,
2Ch 3:1 threshing floor of Ornan the **J**.
Zec 9:7 and Ekron will be like a **J**.

Jebusite's (2)

2Sm 24:18 Araunah the **J** threshing floor."
1Ch 21:18 at Ornan the **J** threshing floor.

Jebusites (28)

Gen 10:16 also the **J**, the Amorites,
15:21 the Girgashites, and the **J**."
Exo 3:8 Perizzites, Hivites, and **J** live.
3:17 Perizzites, Hivites, and **J**,
13:5 Amorites, Hivites, and **J**.
23:23 Canaanites, Hivites, and **J**.
33:2 Perizzites, Hivites, and **J**.
34:11 and **J** out of your way.
Num 13:29 The Hittites, **J**, and Amorites
Dtr 7:1 and **J** — seven nations larger
20:17 and **J** for the LORD and
Jos 3:10 and **J** out of your way.
9:2 Perizzites, Hivites, and **J**.)
11:3 the **J** in the mountains,
12:8 and **J** ⌊had possessed⌋.
24:11 Hivites, and **J** fought you.
Jdg 1:21 not force out the **J** who lived
1:21 The **J** still live with the tribe of
3:5 Perizzites, Hivites, and **J**.
2Sm 5:6 to Jerusalem to attack the **J**,
5:6 The **J** told David, "You will
5:8 "Whoever wants to defeat the **J**
1Ki 9:20 and **J** had been left ⌊in the
1Ch 1:14 also the **J**, the Amorites,
11:4 The **J** were living in that region.
2Ch 8:7 and **J** had been left ⌊in the
Ezr 9:1 **J**, Ammonites, Moabites,
Neh 9:8 Hittites, Amorites, Perizzites, **J**,

Jechoniah (2)

Mat 1:11 Josiah was the father of **J** and
1:12 After the exile to Babylon, **J**

Jecoliah (2)

2Ki 15:2 mother was **J** from Jerusalem.
2Ch 26:3 mother was **J** from Jerusalem.

Jeconiah (2)

1Ch 3:16 Jehoiakim's son was **J**,
3:17 of the prisoner **J** were his son

Jedaiah (13)

1Ch 4:37 great-grandson of **J**,
9:10 From the priests were **J**,
24:7 for Jehoiarib, the second for **J**,
Ezr 2:36 the descendants of **J** (through
Neh 3:10 Next to them **J**, made repairs
7:39 the descendants of **J** (through
11:10 **J** (son of Joiarib), Jachin,
12:6 Shemaiah, Joiarib, **J**,

Neh 12:7 Sallu, Amok, Hilkiah, and J.
12:19 from Joiarib, Mattenai; from J,
12:21 Hilkiah, Hashabiah; from J,
Zec 6:10 exiles Heldai, Tobijah, and J,
6:14 reminder to Helem, Tobijah, J,

Jediael (4)

1Ch 7:6 sons: Bela, Becher, and J.
11:45 J (son of Shimri) and his
12:20 J, Michael, Jozabad, Elihu,
26:2 (the firstborn), J (the second),

Jediael's (2)

1Ch 7:10 J son was Bilhan.
7:11 men were J descendants.

Jedidah (1)

2Ki 22:1 His mother was J,

Jedidiah (1)

2Sm 12:25 baby J [The LORD's Beloved].

Jeduthum (1)

Neh 11:17 who was the son of J.

Jeduthun (9)

1Ch 9:16 and great-grandson of J),
16:41 his relatives were Heman, J,
16:42 Heman and J played trumpets,
25:1 and J to serve as prophets with
25:3 the sons of J were Gedaliah,
25:3 by their father, the prophet J.
25:6 fathers Asaph, J, and Heman.
2Ch 5:12 Asaph, Heman, J, their sons,
35:15 king's seer J had commanded.

Jeduthun's (3)

1Ch 16:38 Obed Edom (J son) and Hosah
16:42 J sons were stationed at the
2Ch 29:14 From J descendants were

Jegar Sahadutha (1)

Gen 31:47 Laban called it J [Witness Pile],

Jehallelel (1)

2Ch 29:12 of Abdi, and Azariah, son of J.

Jehallelel's (1)

1Ch 4:16 J sons were Ziph,

Jehdeiah (2)

1Ch 24:20 J (for Amram's descendants
27:30 the donkeys: J from Meronoth

Jehezkel (1)

1Ch 24:16 the twentieth for J,

Jehiah (1)

1Ch 15:24 Obed Edom and J were

Jehiel (15)

1Ch 15:18 J, Unni, Eliab, Benaiah,
15:20 J, Unni, Eliab, Maaseiah,
16:5 J, Mattithiah, Eliab, Benaiah,
23:8 J was the first, then Zetham,
26:21 heads of Ladan's families: J
27:32 Jonathan and J, son of
29:8 stones gave them to J,
2Ch 21:2 J, Zechariah, Azariahu,
29:14 were J and Shimei.
31:13 appointed J, Azaziah, Nahath,
35:8 Hilkiah, Zechariah, and J,
Ezr 8:9 son of J, with 210 males
10:2 Then Shecaniah, son of J,
10:21 Shemaiah, J, and Uzziah
10:26 J, Abdi, Jeremoth, and Elijah

Jehiel's (1)

1Ch 26:22 ⌊and⌋ J sons Zetham and Joel.

Jehizkiah (1)

2Ch 28:12 J, son of Shallum, and Amasa,

Jehoaddah (2)

1Ch 8:36 Ahaz was the father of J.
8:36 J was the father of Alemeth,

Jehoaddan (1)

2Ch 25:1 mother was J from Jerusalem.

Jehoaddin (1)

2Ki 14:2 mother was J from Jerusalem.

Jehoahaz (17)

2Ki 10:35 His son J succeeded him as
13:1 year as king of Judah when J,
13:4 Then J pleaded with the LORD,
13:7 J had no army left except for
13:8 Isn't everything else about J —
13:9 J lay down in death with his
13:22 Israel as long as J ruled.
13:25 Then Jehoash, son of J,
13:25 had taken from his father J.
14:8 son of J and grandson of Jehu
23:30 of the land took Josiah's son J,
23:31 J was 23 years old when he
23:34 He took J away to Egypt,
2Ch 25:17 son of J and grandson of Jehu
36:1 of the land took Josiah's son J
36:2 J was 23 years old when he
36:4 Neco took J away to Egypt.

Jehoahaz's (5)

2Ki 13:10 J son Jehoash began to rule
14:1 J son King Jehoash was in his
14:17 death of J son King Jehoash
2Ch 25:25 death of J son King Jehoash
36:4 made J brother Eliakim king

Jehoash (22)

2Ki 13:9 His son J ruled as king in his
13:10 Jehoahaz's son J began to rule
13:12 Isn't everything else about J —
13:13 J lay down in death with his
13:14 King J of Israel visited him,
13:25 Then J, son of Jehoahaz,
13:25 J defeated Benhadad three
14:1 Jehoahaz's son King J was in
14:8 sent messengers to King J,
14:9 King J of Israel sent this
14:11 So King J of Israel attacked,
14:13 King J of Israel captured King
14:15 Isn't everything else about J —
14:16 J lay down in death with his
14:17 son King J of Israel.
14:27 through Jeroboam, son of J.
2Ch 25:17 sent messengers to King J,
25:18 King J of Israel sent this
25:20 to hand over the Judeans to J
25:21 So King J of Israel attacked,
25:23 King J of Israel captured King
25:25 son King J of Israel.

Jehoash's (1)

2Ki 14:23 when J son King Jeroboam

Jehohan (1)

2Ch 28:12 Then Azariah, son of J,

Jehohanan (8)

1Ch 26:3 Elam (the fifth), J (the sixth),
2Ch 17:15 Commander J (with 280,000),
23:1 son of J, Azariah, son of Obed,
Ezr 10:6 and went to the room of J,
10:28 of Bebai: J, Hananiah, Zabbai,
Neh 6:18 In addition, Tobiah's son J had
12:13 Meshullam; from Amariah, J;
12:42 J, Malchiah, Elam, and Ezer.

Jehoiada (50)

2Sm 20:23 Benaiah, son of J,
23:20 Benaiah, son of J,
23:22 that Benaiah, son of J, did.
1Ki 1:8 Benaiah (son of J),
1:32 Nathan, and Benaiah, son of J."
1:36 Benaiah, son of J,
1:38 Benaiah (son of J),
1:44 Benaiah (son of J),
2:25 this task to Benaiah, son of J.
2:29 Benaiah, son of J, to kill Joab.
2:34 Then Benaiah, son of J,
2:35 appointed Benaiah, son of J,
1Ki 2:46 orders to Benaiah, son of J.
4:4 Benaiah, son of J,
2Ki 11:4 J sent for the company
11:9 the priest J had ordered them.
11:9 duty and came to the priest J.
11:12 Then J brought out the king's
11:15 Then the priest J ordered the
11:17 J made a promise to the LORD
12:2 as the priest J instructed him.
12:7 So King Joash called for J and
12:9 Then the priest J took a box,
1Ch 11:22 Benaiah, son of J,
11:24 that Benaiah, son of J, did.
12:27 as well as J (leader of Aaron's
27:5 son of the priest J.
27:34 J (son of Benaiah) and Abiathar
2Ch 22:11 and wife of J the priest.
23:1 J strengthened his position by
23:3 Then J said to them,
23:8 the priest J had ordered them.
23:8 J had not dismissed the
23:9 J gave the commanders the
23:11 and J and his sons made him
23:14 Then the priest J brought the
23:16 J made a promise to the LORD
23:18 Next, J appointed officials to
23:19 J appointed gatekeepers for the
24:2 as long as the priest J lived.
24:3 J got Joash two wives,
24:6 king called for the chief priest J
24:12 The king and J would give the
24:14 of the money to the king and J,
24:14 As long as J lived,
24:15 When J was old and had lived
24:20 son of the priest J,
24:22 J, had been to him. Instead,
24:25 the son of the priest J.
Jer 29:26 priest instead of J so that there

Jehoiada's (4)

2Sm 8:18 J son Benaiah was
1Ki 1:26 who is J son, or your servant
1Ch 18:17 J son Benaiah was
2Ch 24:22 Instead, he killed J son.

Jehoiakim (39)

2Ki 23:34 changed Eliakim's name to J.
23:35 J gave Pharaoh the silver and
23:36 J was 25 years old when he
23:37 J did what the LORD
24:1 and J became subject to him
24:1 Then J turned against him and
24:2 and Ammonites against J to
24:5 Isn't everything else about J —
24:6 J lay down in death with his
24:19 considered evil, as J had done.
1Ch 3:15 the second was J,
2Ch 36:4 changed Eliakim's name to J.
36:5 J was 25 years old when he
36:6 of Babylon attacked J
36:8 Everything else about J — the
Jer 1:3 The LORD also spoke when J,
22:18 what the LORD says about J,
22:24 son of Judah's King J,
24:1 (son of King J of Judah),
25:1 all the people of Judah when J,
26:1 his word when Judah's King J,
26:21 When King J and all his
26:22 King J sent soldiers to Egypt:
26:23 Egypt and took him to King J.
27:19 son of King J of Judah,
28:4 son of King J of Judah,
35:1 Jeremiah during the reign of J,
36:1 the fourth year of the reign of J,
36:9 of the fifth year of the reign of J,
36:28 that King J of Judah burned.
36:29 Say about King J of Judah,
36:30 says about King J of Judah:
36:32 was on the scroll that King J
37:1 succeeded Jehoiakin, son of J.
45:1 during the fourth year that J,
46:2 during the fourth year that J,
52:2 considered evil, as J had done.
Dan 1:1 of the reign of King J of Judah,
1:2 The Lord handed King J of

Jehoiakim's (2)

2Ki 24:1 During **J** reign King
1Ch 3:16 **J** son was Jeconiah,

Jehoiakin (25)

2Ki 24:6 and his son **J** succeeded him
24:8 **J** was 18 years old when he
24:9 **J** did what the LORD
24:12 King **J** of Judah, his mother,
24:12 the king of Babylon captured **J**.
24:15 He took **J** to Babylon as a
25:27 of King **J** of Judah,
25:27 freed King **J** of Judah from
25:29 **J** no longer wore prison
2Ch 36:8 His son **J** succeeded him as
36:9 **J** was eight years old when he
36:10 Nebuchadnezzar sent for **J**
Est 2:6 along with Judah's King **J**,
Jer 22:24 LORD, "even though you, **J**,
22:28 This **J** is like a rejected and
22:30 Write this about **J**:
24:1 of Babylon took **J** (son
27:19 King Nebuchadnezzar took **J**,
28:4 also bring back to this place **J**,
29:2 (This was after King **J** and his
37:1 Zedekiah succeeded **J**,
52:31 of King **J** of Judah,
52:31 freed King **J** of Judah and
52:33 **J** no longer wore prison
Eze 1:2 fifth year of the exile of King **J**,

Jehoiakin's (2)

2Ki 24:17 King **J** Uncle Mattaniah king
2Ch 36:10 Nebuchadnezzar made **J** uncle

Jehoiarib (2)

1Ch 9:10 were Jedaiah, **J**, Jachin,
24:7 The first lot drawn was for **J**,

Jehonadab (4)

2Ki 10:15 he met **J**, son of Rechab,
10:15 "I am," **J** answered.
10:16 So he had **J** ride on his chariot.
10:23 Jehu and **J**, son of Rechab,

Jehonathan (2)

2Ch 17:8 **J**, Adonijah, Tobijah,
Neh 12:18 Shammua; from Shemaiah, **J**;

Jehoram (19)

1Ki 22:50 His son **J** succeeded him as
2Ki 8:16 year as king of Israel when **J**,
8:16 **J** ruled while Jehoshaphat was
8:21 **J** took all his chariots to attack
8:23 Isn't everything else about **J** —
8:24 **J** lay down in death with his
11:2 daughter of King **J** and sister of
12:18 **J**, and Ahaziah of Judah,
2Ch 17:8 and the priests Elishama and **J**.
21:1 His son **J** succeeded him as
21:3 gave the kingdom to **J**,
21:4 After **J** had taken over his
21:5 **J** was 32 years old when he
21:9 **J** took all his chariot
21:10 Libnah rebelled because **J** had
21:11 **J** made illegal places of
21:16 the people of Sudan to attack **J**.
21:18 After this, the LORD struck **J**
22:11 was the daughter of King **J**

Jehoram's (9)

2Ki 8:20 During **J** time Edom rebelled
8:25 **J** son Ahaziah became king
8:29 Then **J** son Ahaziah went to
2Ch 21:8 During **J** time Edom rebelled
21:17 They even took **J** sons and
21:17 was Ahaziah, **J** youngest son.
22:1 **J** youngest son Ahaziah king
22:1 So **J** son Ahaziah became king
22:6 Then **J** son Ahaziah went to

Jehoshaphat (94)

2Sm 8:16 Ahilud's son **J** was the royal
20:24 **J**, son of Ahilud, was the royal
1Ki 4:3 **J**, son of Ahilud, was the royal
1Ki 4:17 **J**, son of Paruah, was in
15:24 His son **J** succeeded him as
22:2 In the third year King **J** of
22:4 Then he asked **J**, "Will you go
22:4 **J** told the king of Israel,
22:5 Then **J** said to the king of
22:7 But **J** asked, "Isn't there a
22:8 The king of Israel told **J**,
22:8 **J** answered, "The king must
22:10 The king of Israel and King **J** of
22:18 The king of Israel said to **J**,
22:29 So the king of Israel and King **J**
22:30 The king of Israel told **J**,
22:32 the chariot commanders saw **J**,
22:32 But when **J** cried out,
22:41 **J**, son of Asa, became king of
22:42 **J** was 35 years old when he
22:43 **J** carefully followed the
22:44 **J** made peace with the king of
22:45 Isn't everything else about **J** —
22:48 **J** made Tarshish-style ships to
22:49 son of Ahab, said to **J**,
22:49 in the ships." But **J** refused.
22:50 **J** lay down in death with his
2Ki 3:7 message to King **J** of Judah:
3:7 **J** answered, "I'll go. I will do
3:8 **J** answered, "The road through
3:11 But **J** asked, "Isn't there a
3:12 **J** said, "The LORD's word is
3:12 So King **J** of Judah,
3:14 my respect for King **J** of Judah.
8:16 son of King **J** of Judah,
8:16 Jehoram ruled while **J** was still
9:2 son of **J** and grandson of
9:14 So Jehu, son of **J** and
12:18 the gifts his ancestors Kings **J**,
1Ch 3:10 was Asa. Asa's son was **J**.
18:15 Ahilud's son **J** was the royal
2Ch 17:1 Asa's son **J** succeeded him as
17:1 **J** strengthened himself to
17:3 The LORD was with **J**,
17:3 **J** didn't dedicate his life to
17:4 **J** did not do what Israel was
17:5 people of Judah gave gifts to **J**,
17:10 they didn't wage war against **J**.
17:12 So **J** became more and more
18:1 **J** was wealthy and honorable
18:2 for a banquet in honor of **J**
18:2 And Ahab persuaded **J** to
18:3 of Israel asked King **J** of Judah,
18:3 **J** told the king of Israel,
18:4 Then **J** said to the king of
18:6 But **J** asked, "Isn't there a
18:7 The king of Israel told **J**,
18:7 **J** answered, "The king must
18:9 The king of Israel and King **J** of
18:17 The king of Israel said to **J**,
18:28 So the king of Israel and King **J**
18:29 The king of Israel told **J**,
18:31 the chariot commanders saw **J**,
18:31 But when **J** cried out,
18:32 realized that **J** wasn't
19:1 King **J** of Judah returned safely
19:2 the seer Hanani, asked King **J**,
19:4 While **J** was living in
19:8 In Jerusalem **J** also appointed
20:1 came to wage war against **J**.
20:2 Some men reported to **J**,
20:3 Frightened, **J** decided to ask
20:5 **J** stood in front of the people.
20:15 in Jerusalem, and King **J**.
20:18 **J** bowed down with his face
20:20 **J** stopped and said,
20:25 When **J** and his troops came to
20:27 They rejoiced while **J** led them.
20:31 **J** ruled as king of Judah.
20:32 **J** carefully followed the
20:34 Everything else about **J** from
20:35 After this, King **J** of Judah
20:36 **J** joined him in making ships to
20:37 prophesied against **J**.
21:1 **J** lay down in death with his
21:2 sons of **J**: Azariah, Jehiel,
21:2 the sons of King **J** of Israel.
21:3 But **J** gave the kingdom to
21:12 the ways of your father **J**
2Ch 22:9 **J** dedicated his life to serving
Joe 3:2 them down to the valley of **J**.
3:12 Come to the valley of **J**.
Mat 1:8 Asa the father of **J**,
1:8 **J** the father of Joram,

Jehoshaphat's (6)

1Ki 22:51 **J** seventeenth year as king
2Ki 3:1 **J** eighteenth year as king
1Ch 3:11 **J** son was Joram. Joram's son
2Ch 17:5 established **J** power over
20:30 **J** kingdom was peaceful,
22:9 "Ahaziah is **J** grandson.

Jehosheba (1)

2Ki 11:2 But **J**, daughter of King

Jehoshebath (2)

2Ch 22:11 But **J**, daughter of the king and
22:11 **J** was the daughter of King

Jehozabad (4)

2Ki 12:21 and **J**, son of Shomer,
1Ch 26:4 **J** (the second), Joah (the third),
2Ch 17:18 and next to him was **J** (with
24:26 named Shimeath, and **J**,

Jehozadak (8)

1Ch 6:14 Seraiah was the father of **J**.
6:15 **J** was taken captive when the
Hag 1:1 Joshua (who was the son of **J**).
1:12 Joshua (who was the son of **J**),
1:14 Joshua (who was the son of **J**),
2:2 Joshua (who is the son of **J**),
2:4 "Chief Priest Joshua (son of **J**),
Zec 6:11 Chief Priest Joshua, son of **J**.

Jehu (71)

1Ki 16:1 The LORD spoke his word to **J**,
16:7 his word to the prophet **J**,
16:12 spoken through the prophet **J**.
19:16 Anoint **J**, son of Nimshi,
19:17 Hazael's sword, **J** will kill him.
2Ki 9:2 you arrive there, look for **J**,
9:5 **J** asked, "Which one of us?"
9:6 **J** got up and went into the
9:11 **J** came out to his master's
9:12 **J** replied, "We talked for a
9:13 ram's horn and said, "**J** is king!"
9:14 So **J**, son of Jehoshaphat and
9:15 Then **J** said, "If you want me to
9:16 So **J** got on his chariot and
9:18 driver rode off, met **J**, and said,
9:18 everything alright?'" **J** replied,
9:19 everything alright?'" **J** replied,
9:20 like **J**, grandson of Nimshi."
9:21 of Judah went to meet **J**,
9:22 When Joram saw **J**,
9:22 "Is everything alright, **J**?"
9:22 **J** answered, "How can
9:24 But **J** took his bow and shot
9:25 Then **J** said to his attendant
9:27 **J** pursued him and ordered,
9:30 When **J** arrived in Jezreel,
9:31 When **J** entered the gateway,
9:36 **J** said, "The LORD spoke
10:1 So **J** wrote letters to the
10:5 sent this message to **J**:
10:7 and sent them to **J** in Jezreel.
10:8 **J** said, "Put them in two piles
10:11 **J** also killed every member of
10:12 Then **J** left for Samaria.
10:14 **J** ordered, "Capture them!"
10:15 **J** greeted him and asked,
10:15 So **J** said, "If you are,
10:15 When he gave **J** his hand,
10:15 When he gave Jehu his hand, **J**
10:16 **J** said, "Come with me.
10:17 they arrived in Samaria, **J** killed
10:18 Then **J** brought all the people
10:18 but **J** will serve him a lot.
10:19 (**J** was deceiving them).
10:20 **J** said, "Call a holy assembly
10:21 **J** sent messengers to all the
10:22 Then **J** told the man in charge
10:23 **J** and Jehonadab, son of

2Ki 10:24 But J had stationed 80 of his
10:25 J said to the guards and
10:28 So J got rid of Baal worship
10:29 But J did not turn away from
10:30 The LORD said to J,
10:31 But J didn't wholeheartedly
10:34 Isn't everything else about J—
10:35 J lay down in death with his
10:36 J ruled as king of Israel in
13:1 when Jehoahaz, son of J,
14:8 and grandson of J of Israel,
15:12 as the LORD had told J:
1Ch 2:38 Obed was the father of J.
2:38 J was the father of Azariah.
4:35 Joel, J (son of Joshibiah,
12:3 Beracah and J from Anathoth,
2Ch 19:2 J, son of the seer Hanani,
20:34 is written in the records of J,
22:7 He went with Joram to meet J,
22:7 (The LORD had anointed J to
22:8 When J was executing
22:9 They brought him to J and
25:17 and grandson of J of Israel,

Jehubbah (1)
1Ch 7:34 were Rohgah, J, and Aram.

Jehucal (1)
Jer 37:3 King Zedekiah sent J (son of

Jehud (1)
Jos 19:45 J, Bene Berak, Gath Rimmon,

Jehudi (5)
Jer 36:14 Then all the officials sent J,
36:14 J said to Baruch, "Bring the
36:21 Then the king sent J to get the
36:21 J read it to the king and all the
36:23 As J read three or four columns,

Jehu's (7)
1Ki 19:17 from J sword, Elisha will kill
2Ki 9:17 Jezreel saw J troops coming.
10:14 ⌊J men⌋ captured and
10:32 Hazael defeated J army
12:1 rule in J seventh year as king
2Ch 22:9 and J men captured him while
Hos 1:4 while I will punish J family

Jeiel (13)
1Ch 5:7 The first was J, then Zechariah
8:29 J, who first settled Gibeon,
9:35 J, who first settled Gibeon,
11:44 Shama and J (sons of Hotham
15:18 J were appointed gatekeepers.
15:21 Mikneiah, Obed Edom, J,
16:5 then J, Shemiramoth, Jehiel,
16:5 and J with harps and lyres.
2Ch 20:14 great-grandson of J,
26:11 organized by the scribe J
29:13 were Shimri and J.
35:9 Hashabiah, J, and Jozabad,
Ezr 10:43 J, Mattithiah, Zabad, Zebina,

Jekabzeel (1)
Neh 11:25 in J and its villages,

Jekameam (2)
1Ch 23:19 was Jahaziel; his fourth was J.
24:23 J (the fourth ⌊of Hebron's

Jekamiah (3)
1Ch 2:41 Shallum was the father of J.
2:41 J was the father of Elishama.
3:18 J, Hoshama, and Nedabiah.

Jekuthiel (1)
1Ch 4:18 who first settled Soco, and J,

Jemimah (1)
Job 42:14 named the first ⌊daughter⌋ J,

Jemuel (2)
Gen 46:10 The sons of Simeon were J,
Exo 6:15 The sons of Simeon were J,

Jephthah (31)
Jdg 11:1 J was a soldier from the region
11:2 sons grew up, they threw J out.
11:3 J fled from his brothers.
11:3 men gathered around J
11:5 Gilead's leaders went to get J
11:6 They said to J, "Come and be
11:7 But J replied to Gilead's
11:8 Gilead's leaders answered J,
11:9 J told them, "If you take me
11:10 Gilead's leaders said to J,
11:11 J went with them, and the
11:11 So J went to Mizpah and
11:12 J sent messengers to the king
11:14 J again sent messengers to the
11:15 "This is what J says:
11:28 to the message J sent him.
11:29 the LORD's Spirit came over J.
11:29 J went through Gilead,
11:30 J made a vow to the LORD.
11:32 So J went to fight against
11:34 When J went to his home in
11:34 J had no other sons or
11:40 the praises of the daughter of J,
12:1 They said to J, "Why did you
12:2 J answered, "My people and I
12:4 Then J gathered all the men of
12:7 J judged Israel for six years.
12:7 Then J of Gilead died and was
12:8 After J, Ibzan from Bethlehem
1Sm 12:11 sent Jerubbaal, Bedan, J,
Heb 11:32 Samson, J, David, Samuel,

Jephthah's (2)
Jdg 11:1 J father was named Gilead.
11:13 J messengers, "When

Jephunneh (16)
Num 13:6 Caleb, son of J, from the tribe
14:6 of Nun) and Caleb (son of J),
14:30 enter it except Caleb (son of J)
14:38 and Caleb (son of J) survived.
26:65 ones left were Caleb (son of J)
32:12 Only Caleb (son of J the
34:19 their names: Caleb, son of J,
Dtr 1:36 except Caleb, son of J.
Jos 14:6 Caleb, son of J and grandson
14:13 blessed Caleb, son of J,
14:14 son of J and grandson of
15:13 Joshua gave Caleb, son of J,
21:12 son of J, as his possession.
1Ch 4:15 The sons of Caleb, son of J,
6:56 were given to Caleb, son of J.
7:38 Jether's sons were J,

Jerah (2)
Gen 10:26 Sheleph, Hazarmaveth, J,
1Ch 1:20 Sheleph, Hazarmaveth, J,

Jerahmeel (8)
1Sm 27:10 the descendants of J live,"
1Ch 2:9 sons born to Hezron were J,
2:25 J (the firstborn son of Hezron)
2:26 J had another wife.
2:27 firstborn son of J) were Maaz,
2:33 were the descendants of J.
24:29 J (for ⌊Mahli's⌋ descendants
Jer 36:26 The king commanded J (the

Jerahmeelites (1)
1Sm 30:29 the cities belonging to the J,

Jerahmeel's (1)
1Ch 2:42 (J brother) were his firstborn

Jered (1)
1Ch 4:18 wife was the mother of J,

Jeremai (1)
Ezr 10:33 J, Manasseh, and Shimei

Jeremiah (174)
2Ki 23:31 daughter of J from Libnah.
24:18 daughter of J from Libnah.
1Ch 5:24 J, Hodaviah, and Jahdiel.
12:4 leaders), J, Jahaziel, Johanan,
12:10 Mishmannah. The fifth was J.
12:13 The tenth was J. The eleventh
2Ch 35:25 J sang a funeral song about
36:12 himself in front of the prophet J,
36:21 words spoken through J would
36:22 spoken through J was about
Ezr 1:1 spoken through J was about
Neh 10:2 Seraiah, Azariah, J,
12:1 and Jeshua: Seraiah, J, Ezra,
12:12 Meraiah; from J, Hananiah;
12:34 and J also followed.
Jer 1:1 ⌊These are⌋ the words of J,
1:2 The LORD spoke his word to J
1:3 continued to speak to J until
1:6 I, J, said, "Almighty LORD,
1:11 asked, "J, what do you see?"
1:17 Brace yourself, J! Stand up, and
6:27 "J, I have put you in charge of
7:1 The LORD spoke his word to J.
7:16 "J, don't pray for these people.
7:27 "J, you will say all these
11:1 that the LORD spoke to J.
11:14 J, don't pray for these people.
11:19 Let's cut J off from this world of
14:1 his word to J about the drought.
18:1 The LORD spoke his word to J.
18:18 "Let's plot against J,
19:14 Then J left Topheth,
20:1 J prophesying these things.
20:2 Pashhur struck the prophet J
20:3 day when Pashhur took J out
20:3 out of prison, J said to him,
21:1 The LORD spoke his word to J
21:1 son of Maaseiah, to J.
21:3 J responded to them,
23:37 "J, say this to the prophets,
24:3 me, "What do you see, J?"
25:1 The LORD spoke his word to J
25:2 The prophet J spoke to all the
25:13 everything that J prophesied
26:7 and all the people heard J
26:8 But as soon as J finished
26:9 the people crowded around J
26:12 Then J said to all the officials
26:20 this city and this land as J did.
26:24 son of Shaphan, supported J.
26:24 So J was not handed over to
27:1 the LORD spoke his word to J.
28:5 The prophet J replied to the
28:10 of the prophet J and broke it.
28:11 Then the prophet J went on his
28:12 off the neck of the prophet J,
28:12 the LORD spoke his word to J.
28:15 Then J told the prophet
29:1 The prophet J sent a letter from
29:27 you arrested J from Anathoth?
29:28 That's why J sent this
29:29 read this letter to the prophet J.
29:30 the LORD spoke his word to J.
30:1 The LORD spoke his word to J.
32:1 The LORD spoke his word to J
32:2 The prophet J was locked up
32:3 Zedekiah of Judah locked up J,
32:6 J said, "The LORD spoke his
32:7 'J, your cousin Hanamel,
32:26 The LORD spoke his word to J.
33:1 While J was still being held in
33:19 The LORD spoke his word to J.
33:23 the LORD spoke his word to J.
34:1 The LORD spoke his word to J
34:6 The prophet J told all these
34:8 The LORD spoke his word to J
34:12 The LORD spoke his word to J.
35:1 The LORD spoke his word to J
35:3 who was the son of J and the
35:12 the LORD spoke his word to J.
35:18 Then J said to the family of
36:1 the LORD spoke his word to J.
36:4 Then J called Baruch,
36:4 J dictated everything that the
36:5 J told Baruch, "I'm no longer
36:8 the prophet J commanded him.
36:10 containing the words of J.
36:17 Did J dictate it to you?"
36:19 "You and J must hide.

Jer 36:26 Baruch and the prophet **J**.
36:26 had hidden Baruch and **J**.
36:27 written and that **J** had dictated,
36:27 the LORD spoke his word to **J**.
36:29 this scroll, and you asked **J**,
36:32 Then **J** took another scroll and
36:32 As **J** dictated, Baruch wrote on
37:2 spoken through the prophet **J**.
37:3 of Maaseiah) to the prophet **J**.
37:4 **J** was still free to come and go
37:6 his word to the prophet **J**.
37:12 So **J** wanted to leave
37:13 arrested the prophet **J**.
37:14 **J** answered, "That's a lie!
37:14 Irijah arrested **J** and took him to
37:15 so angry with **J** that they beat
37:16 **J** went into a prison cell,
37:17 Then King Zedekiah sent for **J**,
37:17 **J** answered, "Yes! There is a
37:18 Then **J** asked King Zedekiah,
37:21 the command to have **J** put
37:21 So **J** stayed in the courtyard of
38:1 heard that **J** was speaking
38:2 They heard **J** say,
38:6 So they took **J** and threw him
38:6 They used ropes to lower **J**
38:6 and **J** sank in the mud.
38:7 heard that they had put **J** in the
38:9 done to the prophet **J** is wrong.
38:10 and lift the prophet **J** out of the
38:11 with ropes to **J** in the cistern.
38:12 Melech from Sudan said to **J**,
38:12 you from the ropes." **J** did.
38:13 They used the ropes to pull **J**
38:13 Then **J** stayed in the courtyard
38:14 Zedekiah sent for the prophet **J**
38:14 a question," the king said to **J**.
38:15 **J** answered Zedekiah,
38:16 secretly swore an oath to **J**,
38:17 **J** said to Zedekiah,
38:19 King Zedekiah answered **J**,
38:20 **J** said, "You will not be handed
38:24 Zedekiah said to **J**,
38:27 All the officials came to **J** and
38:28 **J** stayed in the courtyard of the
39:11 an order concerning **J**.
39:13 the king of Babylon sent for **J**.
39:14 They took **J** out of the
39:15 While **J** was still confined in
40:1 word to **J** after Nebuzaradan,
40:1 Nebuzaradan found **J** in chains
40:2 The captain of the guard took **J**
40:5 The captain of the guard gave **J**
40:6 **J** went to Gedaliah,
42:1 came to the prophet **J**.
42:4 The prophet **J** answered them,
42:5 They said to **J**, "May the LORD
42:7 the LORD spoke his word to **J**.
42:8 So **J** called Kareah's son
42:9 **J** said to them, "You sent me to
43:1 So **J** finished telling all the
43:2 the arrogant people said to **J**,
43:6 the prophet **J** and Baruch,
43:8 his word to **J** in Tahpanhes.
44:1 The LORD spoke his word to **J**
44:15 Pathros in Egypt answered **J**.
44:20 Then **J** said to all the people,
44:24 Then **J** said to all the people,
45:1 that the prophet **J** spoke
45:1 scroll as **J** dictated them during
45:1 was king of Judah. **J** said,
46:1 the prophet **J** about the nations.
46:13 message to the prophet **J** about
47:1 message to the prophet **J** about
49:34 to the prophet **J** about Elam.
50:1 through the prophet **J**.
51:59 that the prophet **J** gave
51:60 **J** wrote on a scroll all the
51:61 **J** said to Seraiah, "When you
51:64 on it.'" The words of **J** end here.
52:1 daughter of **J** from Libnah.
Dan 9:2 prophet **J** that Jerusalem would
Mat 2:17 the prophet **J** came true:
16:14 still others **J** or one of the
27:9 Then what the prophet **J** had

Jeremoth (7)

1Ch 7:8 Omri, **J**, Abijah, Anathoth,
8:14 brothers were Shashak and **J**.
23:23 three sons: Mahli, Eder, and **J**.
25:22 The fifteenth chose **J**,
Ezr 10:26 Jehiel, Abdi, **J**, and Elijah
10:27 Mattaniah, **J**, Zabad, and Aziza
10:29 Adaiah, Jashub, Sheal, and **J**

Jeriah (3)

1Ch 23:19 Hebron's first son was **J**;
24:23 **J** (for Hebron's descendants),
26:31 **J** was the head of Hebron's

Jeriah's (1)

1Ch 26:32 **J** relatives were 2,700 skilled

Jeribai (1)

1Ch 11:46 Eliel the Mahavite, **J** and

Jericho (71)

Num 22:1 and set up camp across from **J**,
26:3 the Jordan River across from **J**.
26:63 the Jordan River across from **J**.
31:12 the Jordan River across from **J**.
33:48 the Jordan River across from **J**.
33:50 the Jordan River across from **J**,
34:15 Jordan River across from **J**."
35:1 the Jordan River across from **J**.
36:13 the Jordan River across from **J**.
Dtr 32:49 Nebo in Moab, across from **J**.
34:1 top of Pisgah, across from **J**.
34:3 Plain — the valley of **J** (the City
Jos 2:1 especially the city of **J**."
2:1 So they went to **J** and entered
2:2 The king of **J** was told,
2:3 So the king of **J** sent
2:16 three days until they return to **J**.
2:22 the king's men returned to **J**.
3:16 River⌋ directly opposite **J**.
4:13 to the plains of **J** for battle.
4:19 camp at Gilgal, just east of **J**.
5:10 camped at Gilgal in the **J** plain.
5:13 When Joshua was near **J**,
6:1 **J** was bolted and barred shut
6:2 "I am about to hand **J**,
6:25 Joshua had sent to look at **J**.
6:26 comes to rebuild the city of **J**.
7:2 Joshua sent men from **J** to Ai.
8:2 Ai and its king that you did to **J**
9:3 Joshua had done to **J** and Ai,
10:1 same way he had destroyed **J**
10:28 he had done to the king of **J**.
10:30 he had done to the king of **J**.
12:9 the king of **J**, the king of Ai
13:32 east of the Jordan River near **J**.
16:1 goes from the Jordan River at **J**
16:1 at Jericho to the springs of **J**
16:1 the desert that goes up from **J**,
16:7 Ataroth and Naarah, touches **J**,
18:12 goes up the slope north of **J**,
18:21 **J**, Beth Hoglah, Emek Keziz,
20:8 of the Jordan River, east of **J**.
24:11 the Jordan River and came to **J**.
24:11 The citizens of **J**, the Amorites,
2Sm 10:5 "Stay in **J** until your beards
1Ki 16:34 time Hiel from Bethel rebuilt **J**.
2Ki 2:4 the LORD is sending me to **J**."
2:4 So they went to **J**.
2:5 were in **J** approached Elisha.
2:15 who were at **J** saw him from
2:18 They returned to Elisha in **J**,
2:19 of the city ⌊of **J**⌋ told Elisha,
25:4 the road to the plain ⌊of **J**⌋.
25:5 up with him in the plain of **J**.
1Ch 6:78 Jordan River and across from **J**:
19:5 "Stay in **J** until your beards
2Ch 28:15 and brought them to **J** (the City
Ezr 2:34 of **J**: 345
Neh 3:2 The men from **J** were
7:36 of **J**: 345
Jer 39:4 the road to the plain ⌊of **J**⌋.
39:5 with Zedekiah in the plain of **J**.
52:7 the road to the plain ⌊of **J**⌋.
52:8 up with him in the plain of **J**.
Mat 20:29 As they were leaving **J**,
Mar 10:46 Then they came to **J**.
10:46 many people were leaving **J**,
Luk 10:30 man went from Jerusalem to **J**.
18:35 As Jesus came near **J**,
19:1 Jesus was passing through **J**.
Heb 11:30 Faith caused the walls of **J** to

Jeriel (1)

1Ch 7:2 Rephaiah, **J**, Jahmai, Ibsam,

Jerimoth (8)

1Ch 7:7 Ezbon, Uzzi, Uzziel, **J**, and Iri.
12:5 Eluzai, **J**, Bealiah, Shemariah,
24:30 Mahli, Eder, and **J** (for Mushi's
25:4 **J**, Hananiah, Hanani, Eliathah,
27:19 of Naphtali: **J**, son of Azriel
2Ch 11:18 Mahalath, daughter of **J**.
11:18 (**J** was the son of David and
31:13 **J**, Jozabad, Eliel, Ismachiah,

Jerioth (1)

1Ch 2:18 Azubah had a son named **J**.

Jeroboam (86)

1Ki 11:26 There was also **J**,
11:28 Solomon saw that **J** was a
11:28 So he put **J** in charge of all
11:29 At that time **J** left Jerusalem.
11:31 He told **J**, "Take 10 pieces
11:40 Then Solomon tried to kill **J**,
11:40 but **J** fled to King Shishak of
12:2 **J** (Nebat's son) was still in
12:3 ⌊Israel⌋ sent for **J** and invited
12:3 **J** and the entire assembly of
12:12 So **J** and all the people came
12:15 made to **J** (Nebat's son) through
12:20 Israel heard that **J** had returned
12:25 **J** rebuilt Shechem in the hills
12:31 **J** built worship sites on
12:32 **J** appointed a festival on the
13:1 When he arrived, **J** was
13:4 When King **J** heard the man of
13:33 **J** didn't change his evil ways,
14:1 At that time Abijah, son of **J**,
14:2 **J** told his wife, "Go to Shiloh,
14:7 Tell **J**, 'This is what the LORD
14:19 Everything else concerning **J**,
14:20 **J** ruled for 22 years.
14:30 Rehoboam and **J** as long as
15:1 of the reign of **J** (Nebat's son),
15:7 war between Abijam and **J**.
15:25 Nadab, son of **J**, began to rule
15:34 He lived like **J** and led Israel
16:2 But you have lived like **J**.
16:3 the family of **J** (Nebat's son).
16:19 Zimri lived like **J** and led Israel
16:26 exactly like **J** (Nebat's son).
16:31 same sins as **J** (Nebat's son).
21:22 the family of **J** (Nebat's son)
22:52 and of **J** (Nebat's son) who
2Ki 3:3 the sins that **J** (Nebat's son) led
9:9 the family of **J** (Nebat's son)
10:29 the sins that **J** (Nebat's son) led
10:31 from the sins that **J** led Israel
13:2 the sins that **J** (Nebat's son) led
13:6 turn away from the sins that **J**
13:11 the sins that **J** led Israel
13:13 Then **J** claimed the throne.
14:16 His son **J** succeeded him as
14:23 when Jehoash's son King **J**
14:23 **J** ruled for 41 years.
14:24 the sins that **J** (Nebat's son) led
14:27 he saved them through **J**,
14:28 Isn't everything else about **J** —
14:29 **J** lay down in death with his
15:9 the sins that **J** (Nebat's son) led
15:18 the sins that **J** (Nebat's son) led
15:24 the sins that **J** (Nebat's son) led
15:28 the sins that **J** (Nebat's son) led
17:21 the people of Israel made **J**
17:21 **J** forced Israel away from the
17:22 all the sins **J** committed
23:15 made by **J** (Nebat's son),
1Ch 5:17 of Judah and King **J** of Israel.
2Ch 9:29 visions about **J** (son of Nebat)?

2Ch 10:2 **J** (Nebat's son) was still in
10:3 ⌊Israel⌋ sent for **J** and invited
10:3 **J** and all Israel went to speak
10:12 So **J** and all the people came
10:15 made to **J** (Nebat's son) through
11:4 back from their attack on **J**.
11:14 and Jerusalem because **J**
11:15 Instead, **J** appointed ⌊his own⌋
12:15 Rehoboam and **J** as long as
13:1 year of the reign of **J**,
13:2 was war between Abijah and **J**.
13:3 while **J** arranged to oppose him
13:4 He called out, "**J** and all Israel,
13:6 But **J** (Nebat's son) rebelled
13:8 the gold calves that **J** made
13:13 But **J** had set an ambush to
13:15 God attacked **J** and all Israel in
13:19 Abijah pursued **J** and captured
13:20 **J** never regained power during
13:20 The LORD caused **J** to
13:20 to become sick, and **J** died.
Hos 1:1 kings of Judah and when **J**,
Amo 1:1 Uzziah and Israel's King **J**,
7:10 a message to King **J** of Israel.
7:11 Amos says that **J** will be killed

Jeroboam's (21)

1Ki 13:34 the sin of **J** family so that
14:4 **J** wife did this. She left, went to
14:5 "**J** wife is coming to ask you
14:6 You're **J** wife. Why are you
14:10 I will bring disaster on **J** house.
14:10 I will burn down **J** house.
14:11 If anyone from **J** house dies in
14:13 He is the only one of **J** family
14:13 He was the only one in **J** house
14:14 That king will destroy **J** house.
14:16 desert Israel because of **J** sins,
14:17 **J** wife got up, left, and went to
15:9 In **J** twentieth year as king of
15:29 everyone else in **J** family.
15:30 This was because of **J** sins
16:7 were like ⌊the sin of⌋ **J** family.
16:7 Baasha destroyed **J** family
2Ki 15:1 In **J** twenty-seventh year as
15:8 **J** son Zechariah was king of
2Ch 13:13 So **J** army was in front of
Amo 7:9 I will attack **J** heirs with my

Jeroham (8)

1Sm 1:1 He was the son of **J**,
1Ch 6:27 Eliab's son was **J**.
6:34 who was the son of **J**,
9:8 Ibneiah (son of **J**), Elah (son of
9:12 priests were Adaiah (son of **J**,
27:22 son of **J** These were the
2Ch 23:1 Azariah, son of **J**, Ishmael,
Neh 11:12 He was the son of **J**,

Jeroham's (3)

1Ch 6:27 **J** son was Elkanah.
8:26 **J** sons were Shamsherai,
12:7 **J** sons from Gedor.

Jerubbaal (9)

Jdg 6:32 Gideon "**J**" [Let Baal Defend
7:1 **J** (that is, Gideon) and all the
8:29 **J**, son of Joash, went home to
8:35 kind to the family of **J** (that is,
9:1 Abimelech, son of **J** [Gideon],
9:16 If you treated **J** and his family
9:19 sincerity and integrity toward **J**
9:57 of Jotham, son of **J**, came true.
1Sm 12:11 "Then the LORD sent **J**,

Jerubbaal's (5)

Jdg 9:2 Do you really want all of **J** 70
9:5 his 70 brothers, **J** sons.
9:5 But Jotham, **J** youngest son,
9:24 **J** 70 sons would happen
9:28 Isn't he **J** son, and isn't Zebul

Jerubbesheth's (1)

2Sm 11:21 Who killed **J** son Abimelech?

Jeruel (1)

2Ch 20:16 valley in front of the **J** Desert.

Jerusalem (867)

Jos 10:1 King Adoni Zedek of **J** heard
10:3 So King Adoni Zedek of **J** sent
10:5 So the five Amorite kings of **J**,
10:23 they brought him the kings of **J**,
12:10 the king of **J**, the king of
15:8 slope of the Jebusite city **J**.
15:63 people of Jebus who lived in **J**.
15:63 still live with Judah in **J** today.
18:28 Jebus (now called **J**),
Jdg 1:7 brought Adoni Bezek to **J**,
1:8 The men of Judah attacked **J**
1:21 the Jebusites who lived in **J**.
1:21 the tribe of Benjamin in **J** today.
19:10 as far as Jebus (now called **J**).
1Sm 17:54 head and brought it to **J**,
2Sm 5:5 In **J** he ruled for 33 years over
5:6 The king and his men went to **J**
5:9 He built the city ⌊of **J**⌋ around
5:13 and wives from **J** after
5:14 of the children born to him in **J**:
6:2 Judah to bring God's ark ⌊to **J**⌋.
8:7 and he brought them to **J**.
8:13 region as he returned ⌊to **J**⌋.
9:13 who was disabled, lived in **J**.
10:5 and then return ⌊to **J**⌋."
10:14 Ammonites and returned to **J**.
11:1 while David stayed in **J**.
11:12 So Uriah stayed in **J** that day
12:31 and all the troops returned to **J**.
14:23 and brought Absalom back to **J**.
14:28 Absalom stayed in **J** two full
15:8 LORD will bring me back to **J**,
15:11 men invited from **J** went
15:14 men who were with him in **J**,
15:29 back to **J** and stayed there.
15:37 as Absalom was entering **J**.
16:3 "He's staying in **J**," Ziba
16:15 all Israel's troops came to **J**,
17:20 servants returned to **J**.
19:19 I committed the day you left **J**.
19:25 When he came from **J** to meet
19:33 I'll provide for you in **J**."
19:34 go with Your Majesty to **J**.
20:2 from the Jordan River to **J**.
20:3 David came to his palace in **J**,
20:7 They left **J** to pursue Sheba,
20:22 went back to the king in **J**.
24:8 they came to **J** after 9 months
24:16 out his arm to destroy **J**,
1Ki 2:11 in Hebron and for 33 years in **J**.
2:36 "Build a house for yourself in **J**,
2:38 So Shimei stayed in **J** for a
2:41 that Shimei had gone from **J**
3:1 and the wall around **J**.
3:15 He went to **J** and stood in front
8:1 came to King Solomon in **J**
9:15 house, the Millo, the walls of **J**,
9:19 ⌊else⌋ he wanted to build in **J**,
10:2 She arrived in **J** with a large
10:26 and ⌊others⌋ with himself in **J**.
10:27 as common in **J** as stones,
11:7 site on the hill east of **J**
11:13 sake and for the sake of **J**,
11:29 At that time Jeroboam left **J**.
11:32 of my servant David and **J**,
11:36 a lamp in my presence in **J**,
11:42 reign in **J** over all Israel
12:18 fast as he could and fled to **J**.
12:21 When Rehoboam came to **J**,
12:27 in the LORD's temple in **J**.
12:28 worshiping in **J** long enough.
14:21 He ruled for 17 years in **J**,
14:25 Shishak of Egypt attacked **J**.
15:2 He ruled for three years in **J**.
15:4 God made Abijam a lamp in **J**.
15:4 rule after him and protected **J**.
15:10 He ruled 41 years in **J**.
22:42 and he ruled for 25 years in **J**.
2Ki 8:17 and he ruled for 8 years in **J**.
8:26 and he ruled for one year in **J**.
9:28 brought him in a chariot to **J**.
2Ki 12:1 and he ruled for 40 years in **J**.
12:17 also determined to attack **J**.
12:18 who called off the attack on **J**.
14:2 and he ruled for 29 years in **J**.
14:2 mother was Jehoaddin from **J**.
14:13 Beth Shemesh and went to **J**.
14:13 around **J** from Ephraim Gate
14:19 Conspirators in **J** plotted
14:20 and he was buried in **J**,
15:2 and he ruled for 52 years in **J**.
15:2 mother was Jecoliah from **J**.
15:33 He ruled for 16 years in **J**.
16:2 He ruled for 26 years in **J**.
16:5 came to wage war against **J**.
18:2 and he ruled for 29 years in **J**.
18:17 Lachish to King Hezekiah at **J**.
18:22 He told Judah and **J**,
18:22 "Worship at this altar in **J**."'
18:35 then rescue **J** from my control?"
19:10 you by saying that **J** will not
19:21 My people in **J** shake their
19:31 few people will go out from **J**,
21:1 and he ruled for 55 years in **J**.
21:4 "I will put my name in **J**."
21:7 this temple and **J** from all
21:12 to bring such a disaster on **J**
21:13 I will measure **J** with the
21:13 I will wipe out **J** in the same
21:16 from one end of **J** to the other.
21:19 and he ruled for 2 years in **J**.
22:1 he was king for 31 years in **J**.
22:14 living in the Second Part of **J**.
23:1 of Judah and **J** to join him.
23:2 everyone living in **J**,
23:4 burned the utensils outside **J**
23:5 of Judah and all around **J**.
23:6 to the Kidron Valley outside **J**.
23:9 gone to the LORD's altar in **J**.
23:13 of worship east of **J** unclean.
23:20 He went back to **J**.
23:23 celebrated in **J** for the LORD.
23:24 in the land of Judah and in **J**.
23:27 I will reject **J**, the city that I
23:30 brought it from Megiddo to **J**.
23:31 he was king for 3 months in **J**.
23:33 of Hamath during his reign in **J**
23:36 he was king for 11 years in **J**.
24:4 of innocent people in **J** killed,
24:8 was king for three months in **J**.
24:8 daughter of Elnathan from **J**.
24:10 of Babylon attacked **J**.
24:14 He captured all **J**, all the
24:15 of the land from **J** as captives
24:18 and he ruled for 11 years in **J**.
24:20 LORD became angry with **J**
25:1 of Babylon attacked **J**
25:8 the king of Babylon, came to **J**.
25:9 and all the houses in **J**.
25:10 tore down the walls around **J**.
1Ch 3:4 He ruled for 33 years in **J**.
3:5 were born to David in **J**:
6:10 the temple Solomon built in **J**.)
6:15 and **J** away into captivity.
6:32 built the LORD's temple in **J**.
8:28 of families. They lived in **J**.
8:32 lived next to their relatives in **J**.
9:3 **J** was settled by descendants
9:9 A total of 956 of them lived in **J**.
9:13 God's temple and settled in **J**.
9:34 These head Levites lived in **J**.
9:38 lived next to their relatives in **J**.
11:4 and all Israel went to **J** (that is,
11:6 was the first to go ⌊into **J**⌋,
11:8 built the city ⌊of **J**⌋ around it,
13:6 to bring God's ark ⌊to **J**⌋.
14:3 David married more wives in **J**
14:4 who were born to him in **J**:
15:3 called together all Israel at **J**
18:7 and he brought them to **J**.
19:5 and then return ⌊to **J**⌋."
19:15 So Joab returned to **J**.
20:1 while David stayed in **J**.
20:3 and all the troops returned to **J**.
21:4 Israel, and returned to **J**.
21:15 also sent a Messenger to **J**
21:16 hand and stretched it over **J**.

1Ch 23:25 He will now live in **J** forever.
28:1 David held a meeting in **J** for
29:27 years in Hebron and for 33 in **J**.
2Ch 1:4 He had put up a tent for it in **J**.)
1:13 of worship in Gibeon to **J**.
1:14 and ⌊others⌋ with himself in **J**.
1:15 as common in **J** as stones,
2:7 provided for me in Judah and **J**.
2:16 can take it ⌊from there⌋ to **J**."
3:1 to build the LORD's temple in **J**
5:2 They came to **J** to take the ark
6:6 But now I've chosen **J** to be a
8:6 ⌊else⌋ he wanted to build in **J**,
9:1 So she came to **J** to test him
9:25 and ⌊others⌋ with himself in **J**.
9:27 as common in **J** as stones,
9:30 Solomon ruled in **J** over all
10:18 fast as he could and fled to **J**.
11:1 When Rehoboam came to **J**,
11:5 Rehoboam lived in **J** and built
11:14 and went to Judah and **J**
11:16 the Levitical priests to **J**
12:2 Shishak of Egypt attacked **J**.
12:4 in Judah and then came to **J**.
12:5 of Judah who had gathered in **J**
12:7 Shishak to pour my anger on **J**.
12:9 Shishak of Egypt attacked **J**
12:13 his position in **J** and ruled.
12:13 He ruled for 17 years in **J**,
13:2 He ruled for three years in **J**.
14:15 Then it returned to **J**.
15:10 they gathered in **J**.
17:13 soldiers with him in **J**.
19:1 safely to his home in **J**.
19:4 Jehoshaphat was living in **J**,
19:8 In **J** Jehoshaphat also
19:8 decide cases. They lived in **J**.
20:15 everyone living in **J**,
20:17 the LORD for you, Judah and **J**.
20:18 in **J** immediately bowed down
20:20 of Judah and those living in **J**.
20:27 All the men of Judah and **J**
20:27 and Jerusalem returned to **J**.
20:28 to the LORD's temple in **J**.
20:31 and he ruled for 25 years in **J**.
21:5 and he ruled for 8 years in **J**.
21:11 caused the inhabitants of **J**
21:13 Judah and the inhabitants of **J**
21:20 and he ruled for 8 years in **J**.
22:1 The people of **J** made
22:2 and he ruled for one year in **J**.
23:2 of Israel, and came to **J**.
24:1 and he ruled for 40 years in **J**.
24:6 from Judah and **J**?
24:9 in Judah and **J** that
24:18 God's anger upon Judah and **J**.
24:23 They came to Judah and **J** and
24:23 loot they took from Judah and **J**
25:1 and he ruled for 29 years in **J**.
25:1 mother was Jehoaddan from **J**.
25:23 Shemesh and brought him to **J**.
25:23 around **J** from Ephraim Gate
25:27 conspirators in **J** plotted
26:3 and he ruled for 52 years in **J**.
26:3 mother was Jecoliah from **J**.
26:9 Uzziah built towers in **J** at
26:15 In **J** he made machines
27:1 He ruled for 16 years in **J**.
27:8 He ruled for 16 years in **J**.
28:1 He ruled for 26 years in **J**.
28:10 and women of Judah and **J**.
28:24 for himself on every corner in **J**.
28:27 and was buried in the city of **J**
29:1 He ruled for 29 years in **J**.
29:8 was angry with Judah and **J**.
30:1 come to the LORD's temple in **J**
30:2 and the whole assembly in **J**
30:3 the people hadn't gathered in **J**.
30:5 everyone to come to **J**
30:11 themselves and came to **J**.
30:13 Many people gathered in **J** to
30:14 rid of the ⌊idols'⌋ altars in **J**.
30:21 So the Israelites in **J**
30:26 The city of **J** was filled with
30:26 this had happened in **J** since
31:4 He told the people living in **J** to
2Ch 32:2 come to wage war against **J**,
32:9 in Judah who were in **J** to say:
32:10 confident as you live in **J** while
32:12 altars and told Judah and **J**,
32:18 who were on the wall of **J**.
32:19 They spoke about the God of **J**
32:22 in **J** from King Sennacherib
32:23 Many people still went to **J** to
32:25 him, with Judah, and with **J**.
32:26 in **J** humbled themselves when
32:33 the people in **J** honored him.
33:1 and he ruled for 55 years in **J**.
33:4 "My name will be in **J** forever."
33:7 this temple and **J** from all
33:9 the inhabitants of **J** so that they
33:13 him back to his kingdom in **J**.
33:15 the LORD's mountain and in **J**.
33:21 and he ruled for 2 years in **J**.
34:1 he was king for 31 years in **J**.
34:3 he began to make Judah and **J**
34:5 So he made Judah and **J** clean.
34:7 Then he went back to **J**.
34:9 and from the inhabitants of **J**.
34:22 living in the Second Part of **J**.
34:29 of Judah and **J** to join him.
34:30 everyone living in **J**,
34:32 also made all those found in **J**
34:32 Then the people of **J** lived
35:1 the Passover for the LORD in **J**.
35:18 and the inhabitants of **J**.
35:24 the chariot and brought him to **J**
35:24 and **J** mourned for Josiah.
36:1 and made him king in **J**
36:2 he was king in **J** for 3 months.
36:3 removed him from office in **J**
36:4 Eliakim king of Judah and **J**
36:5 and he ruled for 11 years in **J**.
36:9 three months and ten days in **J**.
36:10 Zedekiah king of Judah and **J**.
36:11 and he ruled for 11 years in **J**.
36:14 had made the temple in **J** holy,
36:23 a temple for him in **J** (which is
Ezr 1:2 a temple for him in **J** (which is
1:3 You may go to **J** (which is in
1:3 He is the God who is in **J**.
1:4 to be used in God's temple in **J**.
1:5 rebuild the LORD's temple in **J**.
1:7 had taken these utensils from **J**
1:11 exiles left Babylon to go to **J**.
2:1 exiles returned to **J** and Judah.
2:68 to the LORD's temple in **J**,
3:1 people gathered together in **J**.
3:8 back from exile to **J**) began
3:8 ⌊the site⌋ of God's house in **J**.
4:6 the enemies of Judah and **J**
4:6 the inhabitants of Judah and **J**.
4:8 of⌋ **J** to King Artaxerxes.
4:12 to us from you are now in **J**.
4:20 **J** has had powerful kings who
4:23 their group hurried to **J** after
4:24 God's temple in **J** was stopped.
5:1 to the Jews in Judah and **J**
5:2 to rebuild God's temple in **J**.
5:14 them out of God's temple in **J**
5:15 Place them in the temple in **J**.
5:16 foundation of God's temple in **J**.
5:17 temple of God to be rebuilt in **J**.
6:3 God's temple in **J**.
6:5 them out of God's temple in **J**
6:5 proper place in the temple in **J**.
6:9 Also, whatever the priests in **J**
6:12 the temple of the God in **J**.
6:18 of God in **J** by following
7:7 and temple servants) went to **J**
7:8 fifth month, Ezra arrived in **J**.
7:9 the fifth month, he arrived in **J**,
7:13 to go with you to **J** may go.
7:14 the situation in Judah and **J**
7:15 the God whose temple is in **J**.
7:16 for the temple of their God in **J**.
7:17 of the temple of your God in **J**.
7:19 be presented to the God of **J**.
7:27 LORD's temple in **J** beautiful.
8:29 In **J**, inside the storerooms of
8:30 to the temple of our God in **J**.
8:31 day of the first month to go to **J**.
Ezr 8:32 When we reached **J**,
9:9 protective wall in Judah and **J**.
10:7 throughout Judah and **J** that all
10:7 former exiles must gather in **J**.
10:9 gathered within three days in **J**.
Neh 1:2 survived captivity and about **J**.
1:3 The wall of **J** has been broken
2:11 I went to **J** and was there for
2:12 had inspired me to do for **J**.
2:13 walls of **J** were broken down
2:17 **J** is in ruins, and its gates are
2:17 Let's rebuild the wall of **J**,
2:20 or claim or historic right in **J**."
3:8 They left out part of **J** as far as
3:9 in charge of half a district of **J**,
3:12 in charge of half a district of **J**,
4:7 of **J** was making progress
4:8 to attack **J** to create confusion.
4:22 stay overnight in **J** so that we
6:7 to announce about you in **J**,
7:2 of the fortress, in charge of **J**.
7:3 I told them, "The gates of **J**
7:3 Order some of the men in **J** to
7:6 They returned to **J** and Judah.
8:15 throughout all their cities and **J**:
11:1 of the people settled in **J**.
11:1 one out of every ten to live in **J**,
11:2 willingly offered to live in **J**.
11:3 the province who settled in **J**.
11:4 and of Benjamin settled in **J**.
11:6 in **J** were 468 outstanding
11:22 of the Levites in **J** was Uzzi,
12:27 When the wall of **J** was going
12:27 lived and had them come to **J**
12:28 from the countryside around **J**,
12:29 for themselves around **J**.
12:43 The sound of rejoicing in **J**
13:6 was taking place, I wasn't in **J**.
13:7 I went to **J** and discovered the
13:15 and brought them into **J**
13:16 who lived in **J** were bringing
13:16 the people of Judah, even in **J**.
13:19 when the gates of **J** were
13:20 spent the night outside **J**.
Est 2:6 taken captive from **J** together
Psa 51:18 Rebuild the walls of **J**.
68:29 of your temple high above **J**.
79:1 They have left **J** in ruins.
79:3 your people around **J** as though
102:21 in Zion and his praise in **J**
116:19 house, in the middle of **J**.
122:2 standing inside your gates, **J**.
122:3 **J** is built to be a city where the
122:6 Pray for the peace of **J**:
125:2 ⌊As⌋ the mountains surround **J**,
128:5 you may see **J** prospering all
135:21 Thank the one who lives in **J**.
137:5 If I forget you, **J**, let my right
137:6 don't consider **J** my highest joy.
137:7 did the day **J** ⌊was captured⌋.
147:2 The LORD is the builder of **J**.
147:12 Praise the LORD, **J**!
Ecc 1:1 son of David and the king in **J**.
1:12 have been king of Israel in **J**.
1:16 who ⌊has ruled⌋ **J** before me.
2:7 than anyone in **J** before me.
2:9 than anyone in **J** before me.
Sos 1:5 Young women of **J**,
2:7 Young women of **J**,
3:5 Young women of **J**,
3:10 by the young women of **J**.
5:8 Young women of **J**,
5:16 young women of **J**.
6:4 love, like Tirzah, lovely like **J**,
8:4 Young women of **J**,
Isa 1:1 saw about Judah and **J** at the
2:1 saw about Judah and **J**.
2:3 of the LORD will go out from **J**.
3:1 is going to take from **J** and
3:8 **J** has stumbled, and Judah has
4:3 and whoever remains in **J** will
4:3 recorded among the living in **J**.
4:4 will clean bloodstains from **J**
5:3 you inhabitants of **J** and Judah,
7:1 went to **J** to attack it,
8:14 a snare for those who live in **J**.

Isa 10:10 statues than **J** or Samaria.
10:11 I will do to **J** and its idols what
10:12 work on Mount Zion and in **J**,
10:32 at the mountain of **J**.
22:10 You will count the houses in **J**.
22:21 a father to those who live in **J**
24:23 rule on Mount Zion and in **J**.
27:13 on the holy mountain in **J**.
28:14 who rule the people in **J**.
30:19 You will live in Zion, in **J**.
31:5 of Armies will defend **J** like
31:9 in Zion and his furnace is in **J**.
33:20 Your eyes will see **J** as a
36:2 Lachish to King Hezekiah at **J**.
36:7 Hezekiah told Judah and **J**,
36:20 then rescue **J** from my control?"
37:10 you by saying that **J** will not
37:22 My people in **J** shake their
37:32 few people will go out from **J**,
40:2 "Speak tenderly to **J** and
40:9 Call out with a loud voice, **J**.
41:27 I gave **J** a messenger with the
44:26 He says about **J**, "It will be
44:28 He says about **J**, "It will be
51:17 Stand up, **J**! You drank from the
52:1 beautiful clothes, holy city of **J**.
52:2 Get up, captive **J**. Free yourself
52:9 into shouts of joy, ruins of **J**.
52:9 his people. He will reclaim **J**.
62:6 watchmen on your walls, **J**.
62:7 any rest until he establishes **J**
64:10 a desert. **J** is a wasteland.
65:18 because I'm going to create **J**
65:19 I will rejoice about **J** and be
66:10 All who love **J**, be happy and
66:13 You will be comforted in **J**.
66:20 **J**," declares the LORD.
Jer 1:3 people of **J** were taken away
2:2 "Go and announce to **J**,
3:17 At that time they will call **J** the
3:17 All nations will gather in **J**
4:3 to the people of Judah and to **J**:
4:4 of Judah and inhabitants of **J**.
4:5 Make it heard in **J**.
4:10 deceived these people and **J**.
4:11 said to these people and to **J**:
4:14 **J**, wash the evil from your heart
4:16 Bring them to the attention of **J**.
5:1 Walk around the streets of **J**.
5:1 Then I will forgive **J**.
6:1 Run away from **J**! Blow the
6:6 up dirt mounds to attack **J**.
6:7 so **J** keeps its evil fresh.
6:8 Pay attention to my warning, **J**,
7:17 Judah and in the streets of **J**?
7:34 of Judah and in the streets of **J**,
8:1 of the others who lived in **J** will
8:5 The people of **J** turned away
9:11 I will turn **J** into a pile of rubble,
11:2 and to those who live in **J**.
11:6 of Judah and in the streets of **J**:
11:9 and among those who live in **J**.
11:12 and those who live in **J** will cry
11:13 have set up many altars ⌊in **J**⌋
11:13 altars as there are streets in **J**.
13:13 live in **J** will become drunk.
13:27 horrible it will be for you, **J**!
14:2 Their cry goes up from **J**.
14:16 thrown out into the streets of **J**.
15:4 son of Hezekiah, did in **J**.
15:5 No one will take pity on you, **J**.
17:19 Then stand at every gate in **J**.
17:20 and all those who live in **J**,
17:21 bring it through the gates of **J**.
17:25 Judah and those who live in **J**.
17:26 of Judah, from all around **J**,
17:27 anything through the gates of **J**
17:27 burn down the palaces in **J**,
18:11 and to those who live in **J**,
19:3 Judah and those who live in **J**.
19:7 the plans of Judah and **J**
19:13 The houses in **J**, the houses of
21:13 "'I'm against you, **J**.
22:19 thrown outside the gates of **J**.
23:14 this⌋ about the prophets of **J**:
23:14 The prophets of **J** commit

Jer 23:14 live in **J** are like Gomorrah."
23:15 The prophets of **J** have spread
24:1 and the builders from **J** into
24:8 the remaining few in **J** who
25:2 and to everyone who lived in **J**.
25:18 **J** and the cities of Judah as
26:18 **J** will become a pile of rubble,
27:3 to King Zedekiah of Judah in **J**.
27:18 and in **J** to be taken away to
27:19 into captivity from **J** to Babylon
27:19 all the nobles of Judah and **J**.
27:21 royal palace of Judah, and in **J**:
29:1 Jeremiah sent a letter from **J**
29:1 as captives from **J** to Babylon.
29:2 the leaders of Judah and **J**,
29:2 and metal workers left **J**.)
29:4 captive from **J** to Babylon:
29:20 sent away from **J** to Babylon.
29:25 to all the people who are in **J**,
32:2 of Babylon was blockading **J**.
32:32 and those who live in **J**
32:44 of Benjamin, in the region of **J**,
33:9 Then **J** will be my source of
33:9 blessings that I will give to **J**.
33:10 the streets of **J** are deserted.
33:13 in the area around **J**,
33:16 saved and **J** will live securely.
33:16 **J** will be called The LORD Our
34:1 that he ruled were attacking **J**
34:6 to King Zedekiah of Judah in **J**.
34:7 of Babylon was attacking **J**
34:8 all the people in **J** promised
34:19 the officials of Judah and **J**,
35:11 'Let's go to **J** ⌊to escape⌋ the
35:11 That's why we are living in **J**."
35:13 Judah and those who live in **J**,
35:17 on all those who live in **J** all
36:9 a time for all the people in **J**
36:9 from any city in Judah to **J**
36:31 on those who live in **J**,
37:4 The people of **J** hadn't put him
37:5 blockading **J** heard this news,
37:5 they retreated from **J**.
37:11 army had retreated from **J**
37:12 So Jeremiah wanted to leave **J**
38:28 until the day **J** was captured.
39:1 of Babylon attacked **J**
39:8 they tore down the walls of **J**.
40:1 along with the captives of **J**
42:18 out on those who live in **J**,
44:2 all the disasters I brought on **J**
44:6 Judah and on the streets of **J**.
44:9 Judah and on the streets of **J**?
44:13 as I punished **J** with wars,
44:17 Judah and on the streets of **J**.
44:21 and on the streets of **J** along
51:35 **J** says, "May the people of
51:50 distant land, and think about **J**.
52:1 and he ruled for 11 years in **J**.
52:3 LORD became angry with **J**
52:4 of Babylon attacked **J**
52:12 the king of Babylon, came to **J**.
52:13 and all the houses in **J**.
52:14 tore down the walls around **J**.
52:29 took 832 people from **J**.
Lam 1:1 "Look how deserted **J** is!
1:2 **J** cries bitterly at night with
1:7 **J** remembers all the treasures
1:8 **J** has sinned so much that it
1:8 **J** groans and turns away.
1:10 **J** has seen the nations enter
1:17 **J** has become a filthy thing
2:10 The young women of **J** bow
2:13 can I show you, people of **J**?
2:17 down without any pity, ⌊**J**⌋.
4:12 ever get through the gates of **J**.
Eze 4:1 and draw a map of **J** on it.
4:7 face toward the blockaded **J**.
4:8 have finished attacking ⌊**J**⌋.
4:16 to cut off the bread supply in **J**.
5:5 LORD says: This is **J**!
5:6 The people of **J** have rebelled
5:7 ⌊People of **J**,⌋ you have
8:3 He took me to **J**, to the
9:4 "Go throughout the city of **J**,
9:8 you pour out your anger on **J**?"

Eze 11:15 the people who live in **J** are
11:15 The people who live in **J** say,
12:10 about the prince from **J**
12:19 about the people who live in **J**
13:16 who prophesied to **J** are gone.
14:21 terrible punishments against **J**.
14:22 disasters that I will bring on **J**,
15:6 who live in **J** to punish them.
15:7 turn against the people of **J**.
16:2 make known to the people of **J**
16:3 LORD says to the people of **J**:
17:12 'The king of Babylon came to **J**
21:2 "Son of man, turn to **J**,
21:20 Judah and the fortified city of **J**.
21:22 he should go to the right, to **J**.
22:3 ⌊**J**,⌋ you are the city that
22:19 I'm going to gather you in **J**.
23:4 and Oholibah represents **J**.
23:46 the people of Samaria and **J**⌋.
24:2 has surrounded **J** this very day.
26:2 Tyre said this about **J**:
33:21 a refugee from **J** came to me.
36:38 like the sheep in **J** during the
40:1 years after **J** was captured.
40:1 and he brought me to **J**.
43:3 when he came to destroy **J**
Dan 1:1 came to **J** and attacked it.
5:2 had taken from the temple in **J**
5:3 taken from God's temple in **J**.
6:10 opened in the direction of **J**.
9:2 of years that **J** would remain
9:2 Jeremiah that **J** would remain
9:7 men of Judah, the citizens of **J**,
9:12 like what has happened to **J**.
9:16 city, **J**, your holy mountain.
9:16 **J** and your people are insulted
9:25 to restore and rebuild **J** until
9:25 **J** will be restored and rebuilt
Joe 2:32 will be on Mount Zion and in **J**.
3:1 the captives of Judah and **J**.
3:6 sold the people of Judah and **J**
3:16 his voice will thunder from **J**.
3:17 **J** will be holy. Foreigners will
3:20 will live in **J** from now on.
Amo 1:2 and his voice thunders from **J**.
2:5 burn down the palaces of **J**.
Oba 1:11 his gates and threw dice for **J**.
1:20 Exiles from **J** who are in
Mic 1:1 saw about Samaria and **J**.
1:5 worship place? Isn't it **J**?
1:9 the gates of my people in **J**.
1:12 will come on the gates of **J**.
3:10 and **J** on wickedness.
3:12 **J** will become a pile of rubble,
4:2 of the LORD will go out from **J**.
4:8 You, **J**, watchtower of the flock,
4:8 will return to the people of **J**.
Zep 1:4 against those who live in **J**.
1:12 "At that time I will search **J**
3:14 with all your heart, people of **J**.
3:16 On that day **J** will be told,
Zec 1:12 you show compassion to **J**
1:14 very jealous about **J** and Zion,
1:16 returned to **J** with compassion.
1:16 line will be used to rebuild **J**.
1:17 Zion and will again choose **J**."
1:19 scattered Judah, Israel, and **J**."
2:2 "I am going to measure **J** to
2:4 '**J** will be inhabited like an
2:12 land and will again choose **J**.
3:2 the LORD, who has chosen **J**,
7:7 when **J** and its surrounding
8:3 will return to Zion and live in **J**.
8:3 **J** will be called the City of
8:4 will again sit in the streets of **J**.
8:8 and they will live in **J**.
8:15 but this time to do good to **J**
8:22 seek the LORD of Armies in **J**
9:9 Shout in triumph, people of **J**!
9:10 in Ephraim or war horses in **J**.
12:2 "I'm going to make **J** like a cup
12:2 will attack Judah along with **J**.
12:3 On that day I will make **J** a
12:3 will gather ⌊to fight⌋ against **J**."
12:5 'The people who live in **J** are
12:6 But the people of **J** will remain

Zec 12:6 will remain safe in **J**.
12:7 of those who live in **J** will not
12:8 who live in **J** so that even
12:9 all the nations who attack **J**.
12:10 and on those who live in **J**.
12:11 On that day the mourning in **J**
13:1 and for those who live in **J**
14:2 all the nations to **J** for battle.
14:4 Mount of Olives, just east of **J**.
14:8 water will flow out from **J**,
14:10 Geba to Rimmon, south of **J**.
14:10 **J** will rise and remain on its
14:11 **J** will live securely.
14:12 have gone to war against **J**.
14:14 Judah will also fight in **J**.
14:16 that attacked **J** will come every
14:17 on the earth won't go to **J**
14:18 of Egypt won't go or enter **J**,
14:21 Yes, every pot in **J** and in
Mal 2:11 has been done in Israel and **J**.
3:4 The offerings from Judah and **J**
Mat 2:1 men from the east arrived in **J**.
2:3 When King Herod and all **J**
3:5 **J**, all Judea, and the whole
4:25 the Ten Cities, **J**, Judea,
5:35 which is his footstool, or by **J**,
15:1 scribes came from **J** to Jesus.
16:21 disciples that he had to go to **J**.
20:17 Jesus was on his way to **J**,
20:18 "We're going to **J**. There the Son
21:1 When they came near **J** and
21:10 When Jesus came into **J**,
23:37 "**J**, Jerusalem, you kill the
23:37 "Jerusalem, **J**, you kill the
Mar 1:5 and all the people of **J** went
3:8 **J**, Idumea, and from across the
3:22 who had come from **J** said,
7:1 from **J** gathered around Jesus.
10:32 were on their way to **J**.
10:32 ⌊that he was going to **J**⌋.
10:33 "We're going to **J**. There the Son
11:1 When they came near **J**,
11:11 Jesus came into **J** and went
11:15 When they came to **J**,
11:27 and his disciples returned to **J**.
15:21 coming ⌊into **J**⌋ from his home
15:41 women who had come to **J**
Luk 2:22 Joseph and Mary went to **J**.
2:25 man named Simeon was in **J**.
2:38 to all who were waiting for **J**
2:41 Jesus' parents would go to **J**
2:43 boy Jesus stayed behind in **J**,
2:45 they went back to **J** to look for
4:9 Then the devil took him into **J**
5:17 Galilee and Judea and from **J**.
6:17 come from all over Judea, **J**,
9:31 he was about to fulfill in **J**.
9:51 he was determined to go to **J**.
9:53 he was on his way to **J**.
10:30 "A man went from **J** to Jericho.
13:4 than other people living in **J**?
13:22 after another on his way to **J**.
13:33 for a prophet to die outside **J**.
13:34 "**J**, Jerusalem, you kill the
13:34 "Jerusalem, **J**, you kill the
17:11 and Galilee on his way to **J**.
18:31 said to them, "We're going to **J**.
19:11 Jesus was getting closer to **J**,
19:28 he continued on his way to **J**.
21:20 see armies camped around **J**,
21:21 Those of you in **J** should leave
21:24 Nations will trample **J** until the
23:7 and was in **J** at that time.
23:26 Simon was coming into **J**.
23:28 and said, "You women of **J**,
24:13 was about seven miles from **J**.
24:18 "Are you the only one in **J** who
24:33 same hour they went back to **J**.
24:47 beginning in the city of **J**.
24:52 as they went back to **J**.
Jon 1:19 sent priests and Levites from **J**
2:13 so Jesus went to **J**.
2:23 While Jesus was in **J** at the
4:20 that people must worship in **J**."
4:21 Father on this mountain or in **J**.
4:45 he had done at the festival in **J**,
Jon 5:1 Later, Jesus went to **J** for a
5:2 Near Sheep Gate in **J** was a
7:25 the people who lived in **J** said,
10:22 place in **J** during the winter.
11:18 (Bethany was near **J**,
11:55 came from the countryside to **J**
12:12 that Jesus was coming to **J**.
Act 1:4 he ordered them not to leave **J**
1:8 to testify about me in **J**,
1:12 Then they returned to **J** from
1:12 It is near **J**, about half a mile
1:19 Everyone living in **J** knows
2:5 every nation were living in **J**.
2:14 Judea and everyone living in **J**!
4:5 and scribes met in **J**.
4:16 everyone in **J** knows about.
5:16 Crowds from the cities around **J**
5:28 Yet, you've filled **J** with your
6:7 disciples in **J** grew very large.
8:1 out against the church in **J**.
8:14 When the apostles in **J** heard
8:25 villages on their way back to **J**.
8:26 goes south from **J** to Gaza."
8:27 man who had come to **J**
9:2 Christ⌋ and imprison them in **J**.
9:13 has done to your people in **J**.
9:21 the one named Jesus in **J**?
9:21 to the chief priests ⌊in **J**⌋?"
9:26 After Saul arrived in **J**,
9:28 Then Saul went throughout **J**
10:39 the land of the Jews and in **J**.
11:2 when Peter went to **J**,
11:22 reached the church in **J**,
11:27 some prophets came from **J**
11:30 and Saul to the leaders ⌊in **J**⌋.
12:25 ⌊to the leaders in **J**⌋,
12:25 returned ⌊to Antioch⌋ from **J**.
13:13 them there and went back to **J**.
13:27 The people who live in **J** and
13:31 with him to **J** from Galilee.
15:2 of the others were sent to **J**
15:3 sent Paul and Barnabas ⌊to **J**⌋.
15:4 The church in **J**, the apostles,
15:33 sent them back to **J**
16:4 spiritual leaders in **J** had made
18:22 He went ⌊to **J**⌋, greeted the
19:21 Paul decided to go to **J** by
20:16 He was in a hurry to get to **J** for
20:22 am determined to go to **J** now.
21:4 tell Paul not to go to **J**.
21:11 'This is how the Jews in **J** will
21:12 begged Paul not to go to **J**.
21:13 ready not only to be tied up in **J**
21:15 we got ready to go to **J**.
21:17 When we arrived in **J**,
21:31 a report that all **J** was rioting.
22:3 from Gamaliel here in **J**.
22:5 them back to **J** to punish them.
22:17 "After that, I returned to **J**.
22:18 Get out of **J** immediately.
23:11 told the truth about me in **J**.
24:11 for yourself that I went to **J**
25:1 from the city of Caesarea to **J**.
25:3 of having Paul brought to **J**.
25:3 kill Paul as he traveled to **J**.
25:6 Festus stayed in **J** for eight or
25:7 come from **J** surrounded him.
25:9 "Are you willing to go to **J** to be
25:15 When I went to **J**, the chief
25:20 Paul if he would like to go to **J**
25:24 All the Jews in **J** and Caesarea
26:4 with my own people and in **J**.
26:10 That is what I did in **J**.
26:11 down in cities outside ⌊**J**⌋.
26:20 people in Damascus and **J**
28:17 Yet, I'm a prisoner from **J**,
Rom 15:19 about Christ from **J** to Illyricum.
15:25 Right now I'm going to **J** to
15:26 a debt to the Christians in **J**,
15:26 poor among the Christians in **J**.
15:27 wealth of the Christians in **J**.
15:28 over to the Christians in **J**,
15:31 Pray that God's people in **J**
1Co 16:1 for God's people ⌊in **J**⌋:
16:3 send your gift to **J** with them.
2Co 8:4 to his holy people ⌊in **J**⌋.
2Co 9:1 helping the Christians ⌊in **J**⌋.
Gal 1:17 I didn't even go to **J** to see
1:18 three years later I went to **J** to
2:1 Then 14 years later I went to **J**
2:12 had sent ⌊from **J**⌋ arrived.
4:25 She is like **J** today because
4:26 But the **J** that is above is free,
Heb 12:22 living God, to the heavenly **J**.
13:12 suffered outside the gates of **J**.
Rev 3:12 (the New **J** coming down out
21:2 I saw the holy city, New **J**,
21:10 He showed me the holy city, **J**,

Jerusalem's (13)

2Ch 36:19 tore down **J** walls, burned
Isa 22:11 You didn't look to **J** Maker.
62:1 For **J** sake I will not rest,
66:12 nurse and be carried in **J** arms
Jer 1:15 at the entrance of **J** gates.
5:10 "Go among **J** rows of
13:9 and **J** extreme arrogance.
Lam 1:2 All of **J** friends have betrayed it
1:7 and they laughed at **J** downfall
1:9 **J** own filth ⌊covers⌋ its
2:15 their heads at **J** people: 'Is this
2:18 The hearts of **J** people cried
4:13 of the sins of **J** prophets

Jerusha (1)

2Ki 15:33 His mother was **J**,

Jerushah (1)

2Ch 27:1 His mother was **J**,

Jesarelah (1)

1Ch 25:14 The seventh chose **J**,

Jeshaiah (7)

1Ch 3:21 sons were Pelatiah and **J**.
25:3 Zeri, **J**, Shimei, Hashabiah,
25:15 The eighth chose **J**,
26:25 his grandson was **J**;
Ezr 8:7 from the family of Elam: **J**,
8:19 also brought Hashabiah, **J** (who
Neh 11:7 who was the son of **J**,

Jeshaiah's (2)

1Ch 3:21 **J** son was Rephaiah.
Ezr 8:19 20 of **J** relatives and their sons,

Jeshanah (1)

2Ch 13:19 its villages, **J** and its villages,

Jeshebeab (1)

1Ch 24:13 the fourteenth for **J**,

Jesher (1)

1Ch 2:18 Her other sons were **J**,

Jeshimon (6)

Num 21:20 Mount Pisgah overlooks **J**.
23:28 which overlooks **J**.
1Sm 23:19 hills of Hachilah, south of **J**.
23:24 in the plains south of **J**.
26:1 of Hachilah near **J**," they said.
26:3 at the hill of Hachilah near **J**,

Jeshishai (1)

1Ch 5:14 son of Michael, grandson of **J**,

Jeshohaiah (1)

1Ch 4:36 Elioenai, Jaakobah, **J**,

Jeshua (28)

1Ch 24:11 the ninth for **J**, the tenth for
2Ch 31:15 Eden, Miniamin, **J**,
Ezr 2:2 They went with Zerubbabel, **J**,
2:6 that is, of **J** and Joab: 2,812
2:36 (through the family of **J**) 973
2:40 descendants of **J** and Kadmiel,
3:2 Then Jozadak's son **J** and his
3:8 **J** (who was Jozadak's son),
3:9 Then **J** with his sons and
4:3 But Zerubbabel, **J**,
5:2 was Shealtiel's son, and **J**,
10:18 a descendant of **J** (who was

Neh 7:7 They went with Zerubbabel, **J**,
7:11 that is, of **J** and Joab: 2,818
7:39 (through the family of **J**):
7:43 the descendants of **J**,
8:7 The Levites — **J**, Bani,
8:17 From the time of **J** (son of Nun)
9:4 Then **J**, Bani, Kadmiel,
9:5 Then the Levites — **J**,
10:9 **J** (son of Azaniah),
11:26 in **J**, Moladah, and Beth Pelet,
12:1 (Shealtiel's son) and **J**:
12:7 their relatives at the time of **J**.
12:8 The Levites were **J**,
12:10 **J** was the father of Joiakim.
12:24 and **J** (son of Kadmiel).
12:26 son of **J**, grandson of Jozadak,

Jeshua's (2)

Ezr 8:33 The Levites, **J** son Jozabad,
Neh 3:19 Next to him Ezer, **J** son, the

Jeshurun (4)

Dtr 32:15 **J** got fat and disrespectful.
33:5 The LORD was king of **J** when
33:26 no one like your God, **J**!
Isa 44:2 Jacob, **J**, whom I have chosen.

Jesimiel (1)

1Ch 4:36 Asaiah, Adiel, **J**, Benaiah, and

Jesse (35)

Rut 4:17 He became the father of **J**,
4:22 Obed was the father of **J**.
4:22 **J** was the father of David.
1Sm 16:1 I'm sending you to **J** in
16:3 Invite **J** to the sacrifice.
16:5 performed the ceremonies for **J**
16:8 Then **J** called Abinadab and
16:9 Then **J** had Shammah come to
16:10 So **J** brought seven ⌊more⌋ of
16:10 but Samuel told **J**,
16:11 youngest one," **J** answered.
16:11 Samuel told **J**, "Send someone
16:12 So **J** sent for him. He had a
16:19 sent messengers to **J** to say,
16:20 **J** took six bushels of bread,
16:22 Saul sent ⌊this message⌋ to **J**,
17:12 a son of a man named **J** from
17:12 **J** had eight sons, and in Saul's
17:17 **J** told his son David,
17:20 and went, as **J** ordered him.
17:58 your servant **J** of Bethlehem,"
2Sm 23:1 son of **J** — the declaration by
1Ch 2:12 and Obed was the father of **J**.
2:13 **J** was the father of Eliab (his
12:18 We are with you, son of **J**.
29:26 David, son of **J**, had ruled all
2Ch 11:18 the daughter of Eliab, son of **J**.)
Psa 72:20 The prayers by David, son of **J**,
Isa 11:1 come out from the stump of **J**,
11:10 At that time the root of **J** will
Mat 1:5 Obed was the father of **J**,
1:6 **J** the father of King David.
Luk 3:32 son of **J**, son of Obed, son of
Act 13:22 have found that David, son of **J**,
Rom 15:12 "There will be a root from **J**.

Jesse's (14)

1Sm 16:18 "I know one of **J** sons from
17:13 **J** three oldest sons joined
20:27 "Why hasn't **J** son come to the
20:30 know you've sided with **J** son.
20:31 As long as **J** son lives on earth,
22:7 Will **J** son give every one of
22:8 a loyalty pledge with **J** son.
22:9 "I saw **J** son when he came to
22:13 "Why did you and **J** son plot
25:10 "Who is **J** son? So many
2Sm 20:1 an inheritance from **J** son.
1Ki 12:16 an inheritance from **J** son.
1Ch 10:14 kingship over to David, **J** son
2Ch 10:16 an inheritance from **J** son.

Jesus (1607)

Mat 1:1 This is the list of ancestors of **J**
1:16 Mary was the mother of **J**,
1:18 The birth of **J** Christ took place
1:21 will name him **J** [He Saves],
1:25 Joseph named the child **J**.
2:1 **J** was born in Bethlehem in
3:13 Then **J** appeared. He came from
3:15 **J** answered him, "This is the
3:16 After **J** was baptized,
4:1 Then the Spirit led **J** into the
4:2 **J** did not eat anything for 40
4:4 **J** answered, "Scripture says,
4:6 He said to **J**, "If you are the
4:7 **J** said to him, "Again,
4:10 **J** said to him, "Go away,
4:12 When **J** heard that John had
4:17 **J** began to tell people,
4:19 **J** said to them, "Come,
4:21 As **J** went on, he saw two
4:22 and their father and followed **J**.
4:23 **J** went all over Galilee.
4:24 The news about **J** spread
5:1 When **J** saw the crowds,
7:28 When **J** finished this speech,
8:1 When **J** came down from the
8:2 The man said to **J**,
8:3 **J** reached out, touched him,
8:4 **J** said to him, "Don't tell
8:5 When **J** went to Capernaum,
8:7 **J** said to him, "I'll come to heal
8:10 **J** was amazed when he heard
8:13 **J** told the officer, "Go!
8:14 When **J** went to Peter's house,
8:15 **J** touched her hand,
8:18 Now, when **J** saw a crowd
8:20 **J** told him, "Foxes have holes,
8:22 But **J** told him, "Follow me,
8:24 Yet, **J** was sleeping.
8:26 **J** said to them, "Why do you
8:31 The demons begged **J**,
8:32 **J** said to them, "Go!"
8:34 from the city went to meet **J**.
9:1 **J** got into a boat, crossed the
9:2 When **J** saw their faith,
9:4 **J** knew what they were
9:9 When **J** was leaving that place,
9:9 **J** said to him, "Follow me!"
9:10 Later **J** was having dinner at
9:10 to eat with **J** and his disciples.
9:12 When **J** heard that,
9:14 John's disciples came to **J**.
9:15 **J** replied, "Can wedding
9:18 leader came to **J** while
9:18 down in front of **J** and said,
9:19 **J** and his disciples got up and
9:20 a woman came up behind **J**
9:22 When **J** turned and saw her he
9:23 **J** came to the ⌊synagogue⌋
9:25 **J** went in, took her hand,
9:27 When **J** left that place,
9:28 **J** went into a house,
9:32 people brought a man to **J**.
9:35 **J** went to all the towns and
10:1 **J** called his twelve disciples
10:4 who later betrayed **J**.
10:5 **J** sent these twelve out with
11:1 After **J** finished giving his
11:3 to ask **J**, "Are you the one who
11:4 **J** answered John's disciples,
11:7 As they were leaving, **J** spoke
11:20 Then **J** denounced the cities
11:25 At that time **J** said,
12:1 Then on a day of worship **J**
12:3 **J** asked them, "Haven't you
12:9 **J** moved on from there and
12:10 The people asked **J** whether it
12:11 **J** said to them, "Suppose one
12:14 left and plotted to kill **J**.
12:22 Then some people brought **J** a
12:22 **J** cured him so that he could
12:25 Since **J** knew what they were
12:46 While **J** was still talking to the
13:1 That same day **J** left the house
13:11 **J** answered, "Knowledge about
13:24 **J** used another illustration.
13:31 **J** used another illustration.
13:34 **J** used illustrations to tell the
13:36 When **J** had sent the people
Mat 13:52 So **J** said to them,
13:53 When **J** had finished these
13:54 **J** went to his hometown and
13:57 But **J** said to them,
14:1 heard the news about **J**.
14:12 Then they went to tell **J**.
14:13 When **J** heard about John,
14:14 When **J** got out of the boat,
14:16 **J** said to them, "They don't
14:18 **J** said, "Bring them to me."
14:22 **J** quickly made his disciples
14:27 Immediately, **J** said,
14:29 **J** said, "Come!" So Peter got
14:29 walked on the water toward **J**.
14:31 Immediately, **J** reached out,
14:33 down in front of **J** and said,
14:35 The men there recognized **J**
15:1 came from Jerusalem to **J**.
15:16 **J** said, "Don't you understand
15:21 **J** left that place and went to the
15:24 **J** responded, "I was sent only
15:26 **J** replied, "It's not right to take
15:28 Then **J** answered her,
15:29 **J** moved on from there and
15:32 **J** called his disciples and said,
15:34 **J** asked them, "How many
15:39 **J** stepped into the boat and
16:1 and Sadducees came to test **J**.
16:6 **J** said to them, "Be careful!
16:8 **J** knew about their
16:13 When **J** came to the region of
16:17 **J** replied, "Simon, son of
16:21 From that time on **J** began to
16:23 But **J** turned and said to Peter,
16:24 Then **J** said to his disciples,
17:1 After six days **J** took Peter,
17:3 them and were talking with **J**.
17:4 Peter said to **J**, "Lord, it's good
17:7 But **J** touched them and said,
17:8 they saw no one but **J**.
17:9 the mountain, **J** ordered them,
17:11 **J** answered, "Elijah is coming
17:14 a man came up to **J**,
17:17 **J** replied, "You unbelieving and
17:18 **J** ordered the demon to come
17:19 Then the disciples came to **J**
17:22 together in Galilee, **J** told them,
17:25 he could speak, **J** asked him,
17:26 **J** said to him, "Then the family
18:1 disciples came to **J** and asked,
18:21 Then Peter came to **J** and
18:22 **J** answered him, "I tell you,
19:1 When **J** finished speaking,
19:4 **J** answered, "Haven't you read
19:8 **J** answered them, It was never
19:13 brought little children to **J**
19:14 **J** said, "Don't stop children
19:15 After **J** blessed them,
19:16 a man came to **J** and said,
19:17 **J** said to him, "Why do you ask
19:18 **J** said, "Never murder.
19:21 **J** said to him, "If you want to
19:23 **J** said to his disciples,
19:26 **J** looked at them and said,
19:28 **J** said to them, "I can
20:17 When **J** was on his way to
20:20 of Zebedee's sons came to **J**
20:22 **J** replied, "You don't realize
20:23 **J** said to them, "You will drink
20:25 **J** called the apostles and said,
20:29 a large crowd followed **J**.
20:30 When they heard that **J** was
20:32 **J** stopped and called them.
20:34 **J** felt sorry for them,
21:1 **J** sent two disciples ahead of
21:6 did as **J** had directed them.
21:7 coats on them for **J** to sit on.
21:10 When **J** came into Jerusalem,
21:11 "This is the prophet **J** from
21:12 **J** went into the temple
21:16 **J** replied, "Yes, I do. Have you
21:18 as **J** returned to the city,
21:21 **J** answered them, "I can
21:23 Then **J** went into the temple
21:24 **J** answered them, "I, too,
21:27 So they answered **J**,

Mat 21:27 **J** told them, "Then I won't tell
21:31 **J** said to them, "I can
21:42 **J** asked them, "Have you never
22:1 Again **J** used stories as
22:15 planned to trap **J** into saying
22:18 **J** recognized their evil plan,
22:23 come back to life, came to **J**.
22:29 **J** answered, "You're mistaken
22:34 heard that **J** had silenced
22:35 tested **J** by asking,
22:37 **J** answered him, "'Love the
22:41 still gathered, **J** asked them,
23:1 Then **J** said to the crowds and
24:1 As **J** left the temple courtyard
24:2 **J** said to them, "You see all
24:3 As **J** was sitting on the Mount
24:4 **J** answered them, "Be careful
26:1 When **J** finished saying all
26:4 They made plans to arrest **J** in
26:6 **J** was in Bethany in the home
26:7 While **J** was sitting there,
26:10 Since **J** knew what was going
26:16 looked for a chance to betray **J**.
26:17 the disciples went to **J**.
26:19 The disciples did as **J** had
26:20 When evening came, **J** was at
26:23 **J** answered, "Someone who
26:25 "Yes, I do," **J** replied.
26:26 **J** took bread and blessed it.
26:31 Then **J** said to them,
26:34 **J** replied to Peter, "I can
26:36 Then **J** went with the disciples
26:47 while **J** was still speaking,
26:49 stepped up to **J** and said,
26:50 **J** said to him, "Friend, why are
26:50 came forward, took hold of **J**,
26:51 of the men with **J** pulled out his
26:52 Then **J** said to him,
26:55 At that time **J** said to the crowd,
26:57 Those who had arrested **J** took
26:59 testimony to use against **J**
26:62 priest stood up and said to **J**,
26:63 But **J** was silent. Then the chief
26:64 **J** answered him, "Yes, I am.
26:69 were with **J** the Galilean."
26:71 was with **J** from Nazareth."
26:75 remembered what **J** had said:
27:1 people decided to execute **J**.
27:3 who had betrayed **J**,
27:3 he saw that **J** was condemned.
27:11 **J** stood in front of the governor,
27:11 "Yes, I am," **J** answered.
27:14 But **J** said absolutely nothing
27:17 want me to free Barabbas or **J**,
27:18 that they had handed **J** over
27:20 and the execution of **J**.
27:22 "Then what should I do with **J**,
27:26 But he had **J** whipped and
27:27 governor's soldiers took **J** into
27:31 finished making fun of **J**,
27:37 It read, "This is **J**, the king of
27:46 About three o'clock **J** cried out
27:48 on a stick and offered **J** a drink.
27:50 Then **J** loudly cried out once
27:54 officer and those watching **J**
27:55 They had followed **J** from
27:57 had become a disciple of **J**.
27:58 and asked for the body of **J**.
28:5 I know you're looking for **J**,
28:9 **J** met them and greeted them.
28:10 Then **J** said to them,
28:16 Galilee where **J** had told them
28:18 When **J** came near,
Mar 1:1 the Good News about **J** Christ,
1:9 At that time **J** came from
1:10 As **J** came out of the water,
1:14 **J** went to Galilee and told
1:17 **J** said to them, "Come,
1:19 As **J** went on a little farther,
1:20 men in the boat and followed **J**.
1:21 On the next day of worship, **J**
1:24 want with us, **J** from Nazareth?
1:25 **J** ordered the spirit,
1:30 they did was to tell **J** about her.
1:31 **J** went to her, took her hand,
1:35 **J** went to a place where he

Mar 1:38 **J** said to them, "Let's go
1:40 fell to his knees and begged **J**,
1:41 **J** felt sorry for him,
1:43 **J** sent him away at once and
1:45 widely that **J** could no longer
2:1 Several days later **J** came
2:2 **J** was speaking ⌊God's⌋ word
2:4 they could not bring him to **J**
2:4 over the place where **J** was.
2:5 When **J** saw their faith,
2:8 At once, **J** knew inwardly what
2:13 **J** went to the seashore again.
2:14 When **J** was leaving,
2:14 **J** said to him, "Follow me!"
2:15 Later **J** was having dinner at
2:15 were followers of **J** were eating
2:17 When **J** heard that,
2:18 Some people came to **J** and
2:19 **J** replied, "Can wedding
2:23 Once on a day of worship **J**
2:25 **J** asked them, "Haven't you
3:1 **J** went into a synagogue again.
3:2 were watching **J** closely.
3:5 **J** was angry as he looked
3:6 immediately plotted to kill **J**.
3:7 **J** left with his disciples for the
3:9 **J** told his disciples to have a
3:13 **J** went up a mountain,
3:16 Simon (whom **J** named Peter),
3:17 whom **J** named Boanerges,
3:19 Iscariot (who later betrayed **J**).
3:20 Then **J** went home.
3:20 crowd gathered so that **J**
3:23 **J** called them together and
3:30 **J** said this because the scribes
3:32 crowd sitting around **J** told him,
4:1 **J** began to teach again by the
4:11 **J** replied to them, "The mystery
4:13 **J** asked them, "Don't you
4:21 **J** said to them, "Does anyone
4:26 **J** said, "The kingdom of God is
4:30 **J** asked, "How can we show
4:33 **J** spoke ⌊God's⌋ word to them
4:35 **J** said to his disciples,
4:36 Leaving the crowd, they took **J**
5:2 As **J** stepped out of the boat,
5:6 The man saw **J** at a distance.
5:6 So he ran ⌊to **J**⌋, bowed down
5:7 **J**, Son of the Most High God?
5:8 shouted this because **J** said,
5:9 **J** asked him, "What is your
5:9 He told **J**, "My name is Legion
5:10 He begged **J** not to send them
5:13 **J** let them do this. The evil
5:15 They came to **J** and saw the
5:17 Then the people began to beg **J**
5:18 As **J** stepped into the boat,
5:19 But **J** would not allow it.
5:20 He began to tell how much **J**
5:21 **J** again crossed to the other
5:22 When he saw **J**, he quickly
5:23 He begged **J**, "My little
5:24 **J** went with the man.
5:24 A huge crowd followed **J** and
5:27 Since she had heard about **J**,
5:30 At that moment **J** felt power
5:34 **J** told her, "Daughter, your faith
5:35 While **J** was still speaking to
5:36 When **J** overheard what they
5:37 **J** allowed no one to go with
5:38 **J** saw a noisy crowd there.
5:41 **J** took the child's hand and
5:43 **J** ordered them not to let
6:1 **J** left that place and went to his
6:4 But **J** told them, "The only
6:6 Then **J** went around to the
6:14 King Herod heard about **J**,
6:30 apostles gathered around **J**.
6:31 and **J** and the apostles didn't
6:34 When **J** got out of the boat,
6:37 **J** replied, "You give them
6:45 **J** quickly made his disciples
6:48 **J** saw that they were in a lot of
6:54 the people recognized **J**.
7:1 Jerusalem gathered around **J**.
7:5 and the scribes asked **J**,

Mar 7:6 **J** told them, "Isaiah was right
7:18 **J** said to them, "Don't you
7:19 (By saying this, **J** declared all
7:24 **J** left that place and went to the
7:25 had an evil spirit heard about **J**.
7:27 **J** said to her, "First, let the
7:29 **J** said to her, "Because you
7:31 **J** then left the neighborhood of
7:32 They begged **J** to lay his hand
7:33 **J** took him away from the
7:36 **J** ordered the people not to tell
7:37 **J** completely amazed the
8:1 **J** called his disciples and said
8:5 **J** asked them, "How many
8:10 After that, **J** and his disciples
8:11 The Pharisees went to **J** and
8:15 **J** warned them, "Be careful!
8:17 **J** knew what they were saying
8:22 brought a blind man to **J**.
8:22 They begged **J** to touch him.
8:23 **J** took the blind man's hand
8:23 **J** asked him, "Can you see
8:25 Then **J** placed his hands on
8:26 **J** told him when he sent him
8:27 Then **J** and his disciples went
8:33 **J** turned, looked at his
8:33 **J** said, "Get out of my way,
8:34 Then **J** called the crowd to
9:2 After six days **J** took only
9:4 them and were talking with **J**.
9:5 Peter said to **J**, "Rabbi,
9:8 saw no one with them but **J**.
9:9 **J** ordered them not to tell
9:12 **J** said to them, "Elijah is
9:15 were very surprised to see **J**
9:16 **J** asked the scribes,
9:19 **J** said to them, How long must I
9:20 As soon as the spirit saw **J**,
9:21 **J** asked his father,
9:23 **J** said to him, "As far as
9:25 When **J** saw that a crowd was
9:27 **J** took his hand and helped him
9:28 When **J** went into a house,
9:30 **J** did not want anyone to know
9:33 While **J** was at home,
9:38 John said to **J**, "Teacher,
9:39 **J** said, "Don't stop him! No one
10:1 **J** left there and went into the
10:3 **J** answered them,
10:5 **J** said to them, "He wrote this
10:13 brought little children to **J**
10:14 When **J** saw this, he became
10:16 **J** put his arms around the
10:17 As **J** was coming out to the
10:17 He asked **J**, "Good Teacher,
10:18 **J** said to him, "Why do you call
10:21 **J** looked at him and loved him.
10:23 **J** looked around and said to his
10:24 But **J** said to them again,
10:27 **J** looked at them and said,
10:29 **J** said, "I can guarantee this
10:32 **J** and his disciples were on
10:32 **J** was walking ahead of them.
10:35 sons of Zebedee, went to **J**.
10:38 **J** said, "You don't realize what
10:39 **J** told them, "You will drink the
10:42 **J** called the apostles and said,
10:46 As **J**, his disciples, and many
10:47 When he heard that **J** from
10:47 to shout, "**J**, Son of David,
10:49 **J** stopped and said,
10:50 coat, jumped up, and went to **J**.
10:51 **J** asked him, "What do you
10:52 **J** told him, "Go, your faith has
10:52 and he followed **J** on the road.
11:1 **J** sent two of his disciples
11:6 them as **J** had told them.
11:7 They brought the donkey to **J**,
11:11 **J** came into Jerusalem and
11:12 left Bethany, **J** became hungry.
11:15 **J** went into the temple
11:19 (Every evening **J** and his
11:20 While **J** and his disciples were
11:21 ⌊what **J** had said⌋,
11:21 so he said to **J**, "Rabbi, look!
11:22 **J** said to them, "Have faith in

Mar 11:27 **J** and his disciples returned to
11:29 **J** said to them, "I'll ask you a
11:33 So they answered **J**,
11:33 **J** told them, "Then I won't tell
12:1 illustration, **J** spoke to them.
12:13 some of Herod's followers to **J**.
12:15 **J** recognized their hypocrisy,
12:17 **J** said to them, "Give the
12:18 come back to life, came to **J**.
12:24 **J** said to them, "Aren't you
12:28 One of the scribes went to **J**
12:28 how well **J** answered them,
12:29 **J** answered, "The most
12:32 The scribe said to **J**,
12:34 When **J** heard how wisely the
12:35 While **J** was teaching in the
12:41 As **J** sat facing the temple
13:1 As **J** was going out of the
13:2 **J** said to him, "Do you see
13:3 As **J** was sitting on the Mount
13:5 **J** answered them, "Be careful
14:1 underhanded way to arrest **J**
14:3 **J** was in Bethany at the home
14:3 While **J** was sitting there,
14:6 **J** said, "Leave her alone!
14:10 to the chief priests to betray **J**.
14:11 for a chance to betray **J**.
14:12 The disciples asked **J**,
14:16 everything as **J** had told them.
14:17 When evening came, **J** arrived
14:18 were at the table eating, **J** said,
14:22 **J** took bread and blessed it.
14:27 Then **J** said to them,
14:30 **J** said to Peter, "I can
14:43 while **J** was still speaking,
14:45 stepped up to **J** and said,
14:46 took hold of **J** and arrested him.
14:48 **J** asked them, "Have you come
14:51 young man was following **J**.
14:53 The men took **J** to the chief
14:55 for some testimony against **J**
14:60 up in the center and asked **J**,
14:62 **J** answered, "Yes, I am,
14:67 were with **J** from Nazareth!"
14:72 Peter remembered that **J** said
15:1 council decided to tie **J** up,
15:2 "Yes, I am," **J** answered him.
15:5 But **J** no longer answered
15:10 chief priests had handed **J** over
15:15 But he had **J** whipped and
15:16 The soldiers led **J** into the
15:20 finished making fun of **J**,
15:22 They took **J** to Golgotha
15:34 At three o'clock **J** cried out in a
15:36 on a stick and offered **J** a drink.
15:37 Then **J** cried out in a loud
15:39 who stood facing **J** saw how
15:43 to ask for the body of **J**.
15:44 Pilate wondered if **J** had
15:44 the officer to ask him if **J** was,
15:45 assured him that **J** was dead,
15:47 watched where **J** was laid.
16:1 spices to go and anoint **J**.
16:6 looking for **J** from Nazareth,
16:9 After **J** came back to life early
16:12 Later **J** appeared to two
16:14 Still later **J** appeared to the
16:15 Then **J** said to them,
Luk 1:31 birth to a son, and name him **J**.
2:21 was circumcised and named **J**.
2:22 They took **J** to present him to
2:27 were bringing the child **J** into
2:38 She spoke about **J** to all who
2:43 The boy **J** stayed behind in
2:49 **J** said to them, "Why were you
2:52 **J** grew in wisdom and maturity.
3:21 baptized, **J**, too, was baptized.
3:23 **J** was about 30 years old when
3:23 **J**, so people thought, was the
4:1 **J** was filled with the Holy
4:2 those days **J** ate nothing,
4:4 **J** answered him, 'A person
4:8 **J** answered him, 'Worship the
4:9 He said to **J**, "If you are the
4:12 **J** answered him, "It has been
4:13 devil had finished tempting **J**

Luk 4:14 **J** returned to Galilee.
4:16 Then **J** came to Nazareth,
4:20 **J** closed the book,
4:24 Then **J** added, "I can guarantee
4:29 forced **J** out of the city,
4:30 But **J** walked right by them and
4:31 **J** went to Capernaum,
4:34 want with us, **J** from Nazareth?
4:35 **J** ordered the spirit,
4:38 **J** left the synagogue and went
4:38 They asked **J** to help her.
4:41 But **J** ordered them not to
5:1 One day **J** was standing by the
5:2 **J** saw two boats on the shore.
5:3 So **J** got into the boat that
5:3 Then **J** sat down and taught
5:8 he knelt in front of **J** and said,
5:10 **J** told Simon, "Don't be afraid.
5:11 left everything, and followed **J**.
5:12 One day **J** was in a city where
5:12 When the man saw **J**,
5:12 He begged **J**, "Sir, if you want
5:13 **J** reached out, touched him,
5:14 **J** ordered him, "Don't tell
5:15 The news about **J** spread even
5:17 One day when **J** was teaching,
5:17 **J** had the power of the Lord to
5:18 house and put him in front of **J**.
5:19 (They lowered him in front of **J**.
5:20 When **J** saw their faith,
5:22 **J** knew what they were
5:27 After that, **J** left. He saw a tax
5:27 **J** said to him, "Follow me!"
5:29 reception at his home for **J**.
5:31 **J** answered them, those who are
5:34 **J** asked them, "Can you force
6:1 Once, on a day of worship, **J**
6:3 **J** answered them, "Haven't you
6:6 On another day of worship, **J**
6:7 were watching **J** closely.
6:8 But **J** knew what they were
6:9 Then **J** said to them,
6:11 other what they could do to **J**.
6:12 At that time **J** went to a
6:14 They were Simon (whom **J**
6:17 **J** came down from the
6:20 **J** looked at his disciples and
6:39 **J** also gave them this
7:1 When **J** had finished
7:3 The officer had heard about **J**
7:3 They were to ask **J** to come
7:4 They came to **J** and begged,
7:6 **J** went with them. He was not
7:6 the officer sent friends to tell **J**,
7:9 **J** was amazed at the officer
7:11 **J** went to a city called Nain.
7:15 and **J** gave him back to his
7:17 This news about **J** spread
7:20 The men came to **J** and said,
7:21 At that time **J** was curing many
7:22 **J** answered John's disciples,
7:24 **J** spoke to the crowds about
7:36 One of the Pharisees invited **J**
7:36 **J** went to the Pharisee's house
7:37 found out that **J** was eating at
7:39 who had invited **J** saw this
7:40 **J** spoke up, "Simon, I have
7:41 So **J** said, "Two men owed
7:43 **J** said to him, "You're right!"
7:48 Then **J** said to her,
7:50 **J** said to the woman,
8:1 After this, **J** traveled from one
8:3 support for **J** and his disciples.
8:4 had come to **J** from every city,
8:10 **J** answered, "Knowledge about
8:20 Someone told **J**, "Your mother
8:22 One day **J** and his disciples
8:23 sailing along, **J** fell asleep.
8:27 When **J** stepped out on the
8:28 When he saw **J**, he shouted,
8:28 **J**, Son of the Most High God?
8:29 **J** ordered the evil spirit to come
8:30 **J** asked him, "What is your
8:31 The demons begged **J** not to
8:32 The demons begged **J** to let
8:35 They came to **J** and found the

Luk 8:36 the people how **J** had restored
8:37 of the Gerasenes asked **J**
8:37 **J** got into a boat and started
8:38 But **J** sent the man away and
8:39 people how much **J** had done
8:40 When **J** came back,
8:41 bowed down in front of **J**.
8:41 He begged **J** to come to his
8:42 As **J** went, the people were
8:44 She came up behind **J**,
8:45 **J** asked, "Who touched me?"
8:46 **J** said, "Someone touched me.
8:48 **J** told her, "Daughter, your faith
8:49 While **J** was still speaking to
8:50 When **J** heard this,
8:51 **J** went into the house.
8:52 **J** said, "Don't cry! She's not
8:54 But **J** took her hand and called
8:56 **J** ordered them not to tell
9:1 **J** called the twelve apostles
9:9 So Herod wanted to see **J**.
9:10 and told **J** everything they had
9:13 **J** replied, "You give them
9:18 Once when **J** was praying
9:22 **J** said that the Son of Man
9:28 said this, **J** took Peter, John,
9:29 While **J** was praying,
9:33 him, Peter said to **J**, "Teacher,
9:36 they saw that **J** was alone.
9:37 a large crowd met **J**.
9:41 **J** answered, "You unbelieving
9:42 While he was coming to **J**,
9:42 **J** ordered the evil spirit to
9:43 all the things that **J** was doing.
9:47 **J** knew what they were
9:50 **J** said to him, "Don't stop him!
9:51 time was coming closer for **J**
9:57 along the road, a man said to **J**,
9:58 **J** told him, "Foxes have holes,
9:60 But **J** told him, "Let the dead
9:62 **J** said to him, "Whoever starts
10:18 **J** said to them, "I watched
10:21 the Holy Spirit filled **J** with joy.
10:21 **J** said, "I praise you, Father,
10:25 Teachings stood up to test **J**.
10:26 **J** answered him, "What is
10:28 **J** told him, "You're right!
10:29 So he asked **J**, "Who is my
10:30 **J** replied, "A man went from
10:37 **J** told him, "Go and imitate his
10:38 **J** went into a village.
11:1 Once **J** was praying in a
11:2 **J** told them, "When you pray,
11:5 **J** said to his disciples,
11:14 **J** was forcing a demon out of a
11:16 Others wanted to test **J** and
11:17 Since **J** knew what they were
11:27 While **J** was speaking,
11:28 **J** replied, "Rather, how blessed
11:29 gathering around him, **J** said,
11:37 After **J** spoke, a Pharisee
11:37 So **J** accepted the invitation.
11:38 to see that **J** didn't wash before
11:46 **J** said, "How horrible it will be
11:53 When **J** left, the scribes and
12:1 **J** spoke to his disciples and
12:14 **J** said to him, "Who appointed
12:22 Then **J** said to his disciples,
12:54 **J** said to the crowds,
13:1 to **J** about some Galileans
13:2 **J** replied to them, "Do you think
13:6 Then **J** used this illustration:
13:10 **J** was teaching in a synagogue
13:12 When **J** saw her, he called her
13:14 leader was irritated with **J**
13:18 **J** asked, "What is the kingdom
13:22 Then **J** traveled and taught in
13:31 time some Pharisees told **J**,
13:32 **J** said to them, "Tell that fox
14:1 On a day of worship **J** went to
14:1 were watching **J** very closely.
14:3 **J** reacted by asking the
14:4 So **J** took hold of the man,
14:5 **J** asked them, "If your son or
14:7 Then **J** noticed how the guests
14:15 So he said to **J**, "The person

Luk	14:16	**J** said to him, "A man gave a
	14:25	crowds were traveling with **J**.
	15:1	and sinners came to listen to **J**.
	15:3	**J** spoke to them using this
	15:11	Then **J** said, "A man had two
	16:1	Then **J** said to his disciples,
	16:9	**J** continued, "I'm telling you
	16:15	So **J** said to them,
	17:1	**J** told his disciples,
	17:11	**J** traveled along the border
	17:13	and shouted, "**J**, Teacher,
	17:17	**J** asked, "Weren't ten men
	17:19	**J** told the man, "Get up, and go
	17:20	The Pharisees asked **J** when
	17:22	**J** said to his disciples,
	17:37	**J** told them, "Vultures will
	18:1	**J** used this illustration with his
	18:9	**J** also used this illustration
	18:15	people brought infants to **J**
	18:16	But **J** called the infants to him
	18:18	An official asked **J**,
	18:19	**J** said to him, "Why do you call
	18:22	When **J** heard this,
	18:24	**J** watched him and said,
	18:27	**J** said, "The things that are
	18:29	**J** said to them, "I can
	18:31	**J** took the twelve apostles
	18:35	As **J** came near Jericho,
	18:37	The people told him that **J** from
	18:38	the blind man shouted, "**J**,
	18:40	**J** stopped and ordered them to
	18:40	man came near, **J** asked him,
	18:42	**J** told him, "Receive your sight!
	18:43	He followed **J** and praised God.
	19:1	**J** was passing through Jericho.
	19:3	He tried to see who **J** was.
	19:3	and he couldn't see **J** because
	19:4	and climbed a fig tree to see **J**,
	19:5	When **J** came to the tree,
	19:6	to welcome **J** into his home.
	19:9	Then **J** said to Zacchaeus,
	19:11	**J** was getting closer to
	19:11	While **J** had the people's
	19:28	After **J** had given this
	19:29	**J** sent two of his disciples
	19:32	The men **J** sent found it as he
	19:35	They brought the donkey to **J**,
	19:35	and helped **J** onto it.
	19:39	in the crowd said to **J**,
	19:40	**J** replied, "I can guarantee that
	19:45	**J** went into the temple
	19:47	**J** taught in the temple courtyard
	20:1	One day **J** was teaching the
	20:3	**J** answered them, "I, too,
	20:8	**J** told them, "Then I won't tell
	20:9	**J** spoke to the people:
	20:17	Then **J** looked straight at them
	20:27	come back to life, came to **J**.
	20:34	**J** said to them, "In this world
	20:41	**J** said to them, "How can
	20:45	**J** said to the disciples,
	21:1	Looking up, **J** saw people,
	21:5	with beautiful gifts. So **J** said,
	21:8	**J** said, "Be careful that you are
	21:10	Then **J** continued,
	21:29	Then **J** used this story as an
	21:37	During the day **J** would teach
	22:2	looking for some way to kill **J**.
	22:4	them how he could betray **J**.
	22:6	for an opportunity to betray **J**
	22:8	**J** sent Peter and John and told
	22:13	They found everything as **J**
	22:14	**J** and the apostles were at the
	22:15	**J** said to them, "I've had a deep
	22:19	Then **J** took bread and spoke a
	22:25	**J** said to them, "The kings of
	22:34	**J** replied, "Peter, I can
	22:35	Then **J** said to them,
	22:38	Then **J** said to them,
	22:39	**J** went out of the city to the
	22:45	When **J** ended his prayer,
	22:47	He came close to **J** to kiss him.
	22:48	**J** said to him, "Judas, do you
	22:49	The men who were with **J** saw
	22:51	But **J** said, "Stop! Then he
	22:52	Then **J** said to the chief priests,
Luk	22:54	So they arrested **J** and led him
	22:56	"This man was with **J**."
	22:63	The men who were guarding **J**
	22:66	They brought **J** in front of their
	22:67	**J** said to them, "If I tell you,
	22:70	**J** answered them, "You're right
	23:2	began to accuse **J** by saying,
	23:3	"Yes, I am," **J** answered.
	23:7	he sent **J** to Herod.
	23:8	was very pleased to see **J**.
	23:8	He had heard about **J** and
	23:9	Herod asked **J** many questions,
	23:9	but **J** wouldn't answer him.
	23:10	their accusations against **J**.
	23:11	Herod and his soldiers treated **J**
	23:20	Pilate wanted to free **J**,
	23:23	They shouted that **J** had to be
	23:25	them do what they wanted to **J**.
	23:26	As the soldiers led **J** away,
	23:26	and made him carry it behind **J**.
	23:27	A large crowd followed **J**.
	23:28	**J** turned to them and said,
	23:34	Then **J** said, "Father,
	23:39	there insulted **J** by saying,
	23:42	Then he said, "**J**, remember me
	23:43	**J** said to him, "I can guarantee
	23:46	**J** cried out in a loud voice,
	23:52	and asked for the body of **J**.
	23:55	with **J** from Galilee followed
	24:3	not find the body of the Lord **J**.
	24:8	what **J** had told them.
	24:15	While they were talking, **J**
	24:19	happened to **J** from Nazareth.
	24:25	Then **J** said to them,
	24:28	**J** acted as if he were going
	24:35	they had recognized **J** when
	24:36	**J** stood among them.
	24:41	Then **J** asked them,
	24:47	the authority of **J** people must
	24:50	Then **J** took them to a place
Jon	1:17	into existence through **J** Christ.
	1:29	John saw **J** coming toward him
	1:36	John saw **J** walk by.
	1:37	John say this, they followed **J**.
	1:38	**J** turned around and saw them
	1:39	**J** told them, "Come, and you
	1:40	heard John and followed **J**.
	1:42	Andrew brought Simon to **J**.
	1:42	**J** looked at Simon and said,
	1:43	The next day **J** wanted to go to
	1:45	He is **J**, son of Joseph,
	1:47	**J** saw Nathanael coming
	1:48	Nathanael asked **J**,
	1:48	**J** answered him, "I saw you
	1:49	Nathanael said to **J**,
	1:50	**J** replied, "You believe
	1:51	**J** said to Nathanael,
	2:2	**J** and his disciples had been
	2:4	**J** said to her, "Why did you
	2:7	**J** told the servers, "Fill the jars
	2:8	**J** said to them, "Pour some,
	2:11	was the place where **J** began
	2:12	After this, **J**, his mother,
	2:13	so **J** went to Jerusalem.
	2:18	The Jews reacted by asking **J**,
	2:19	**J** replied, "Tear down this
	2:21	But the temple **J** spoke about
	2:22	this statement that **J** had made.
	2:23	While **J** was in Jerusalem at
	2:24	**J**, however, was wary of these
	3:2	He came to **J** one night and
	3:3	**J** replied to Nicodemus,
	3:5	**J** answered Nicodemus,
	3:10	**J** told Nicodemus,
	3:22	Later, **J** and his disciples went
	4:1	**J** knew that the Pharisees had
	4:2	**J** was not baptizing people.
	4:4	**J** had to go through Samaria.
	4:6	**J** sat down by the well
	4:7	**J** said to her, "Give me a drink
	4:10	**J** replied to her, "If you only
	4:13	**J** answered her,
	4:15	The woman told **J**,
	4:16	**J** told her, "Go to your husband,
	4:17	**J** told her, "You're right when
	4:19	The woman said to **J**,
Jon	4:21	**J** told her, "Believe me. A time
	4:26	**J** told her, "I am he, and I am
	4:30	left the city and went to meet **J**.
	4:32	**J** told them, "I have food to eat
	4:34	**J** told them, "My food is to do
	4:39	in that city believed in **J**
	4:40	when the Samaritans went to **J**,
	4:41	because of what **J** said.
	4:43	in Samaria, **J** left for Galilee.
	4:44	**J** had said that a prophet is not
	4:45	But when **J** arrived in Galilee,
	4:46	**J** returned to the city of Cana in
	4:47	The official heard that **J** had
	4:47	So he went to **J** and asked him
	4:48	**J** told the official, "If people
	4:50	**J** told him, "Go home. Your son
	4:50	The man believed what **J** told
	4:53	same time that **J** had told him,
	4:54	miracle that **J** performed after
	5:1	Later, **J** went to Jerusalem for a
	5:6	**J** saw the man lying there and
	5:6	So **J** asked the man,
	5:7	The sick man answered **J**,
	5:8	**J** told the man, "Get up,
	5:13	healed didn't know who **J** was.
	5:13	(**J** had withdrawn from the
	5:14	Later, **J** met the man in the
	5:15	Jews and told them that **J** was
	5:16	The Jews began to persecute **J**
	5:17	**J** replied to them, "My Father is
	5:19	**J** said to the Jews,
	6:1	**J** later crossed to the other side
	6:3	**J** went up a mountain and sat
	6:5	As **J** saw a large crowd
	6:6	**J** asked this question to test
	6:10	**J** said, "Have the people sit
	6:11	**J** took the loaves, gave thanks,
	6:12	**J** told his disciples,
	6:14	saw the miracle **J** performed,
	6:15	**J** realized that the people
	6:17	By this time it was dark, and **J**
	6:19	they saw **J** walking on the sea.
	6:20	**J** told them, "It's me. Don't be
	6:21	So they were willing to help **J**
	6:22	and that **J** had not stepped
	6:24	that neither **J** nor his disciples
	6:24	city of Capernaum to look for **J**.
	6:26	**J** replied to them, "I can
	6:28	The people asked **J**,
	6:29	**J** replied to them, "God wants
	6:32	**J** said to them, "I can
	6:35	**J** told them, "I am the bread of
	6:41	began to criticize **J** for saying,
	6:42	They asked, "Isn't this man **J**,
	6:43	**J** responded, "Stop criticizing
	6:53	**J** told them, "I can guarantee
	6:59	**J** said this while he was
	6:61	**J** was aware that his disciples
	6:61	So **J** asked them, "Did what I
	6:64	"**J** knew from the beginning
	6:66	had led before they followed **J**.
	6:67	So **J** asked the twelve
	6:68	Simon Peter answered **J**,
	6:70	**J** replied, "I chose all twelve of
	6:71	**J** meant Judas, son of Simon
	6:71	would later betray **J**.
	7:1	**J** later traveled throughout
	7:6	**J** told them, "Now is not the
	7:9	**J** stayed in Galilee.
	7:10	gone to the festival, **J** went.
	7:11	The Jews were looking for **J** in
	7:12	The crowds argued about **J**.
	7:14	**J** went to the temple courtyard
	7:16	**J** responded to them,
	7:21	**J** answered them, "I performed
	7:28	Then, while **J** was teaching in
	7:32	sent temple guards to arrest **J**.
	7:33	**J** said, "I will still be with you
	7:37	**J** was standing in the temple
	7:39	**J** said this about the Spirit,
	7:39	be after **J** had been glorified.
	7:40	After some of the crowd heard **J**
	7:43	were divided because of **J**.
	7:45	"Why didn't you bring **J**?"
	7:50	who had previously visited **J**.
	8:1	**J** went to the Mount of Olives.

Jon	8:4	and asked **J**, "Teacher,
	8:6	**J** bent down and used his
	8:9	**J** was left alone with the
	8:10	Then **J** straightened up and
	8:11	**J** said, "I don't condemn you
	8:12	**J** spoke to the Pharisees again.
	8:14	**J** replied to them, "Even if I
	8:19	**J** replied, "You don't know me
	8:20	**J** spoke these words while he
	8:21	**J** spoke to the Pharisees again.
	8:23	**J** said to them, "You're from
	8:25	you say you are?" **J** told them,
	8:28	So **J** told them, "When you
	8:30	As **J** was saying this,
	8:31	So **J** said to those Jews who
	8:33	They replied to **J**, "We are
	8:34	**J** answered them, "I can
	8:39	The Jews replied to **J**,
	8:39	**J** told them, "If you were
	8:41	The Jews said to **J**,
	8:42	**J** told them, "If God were your
	8:48	The Jews replied to **J**,
	8:49	**J** answered, "I'm not
	8:52	The Jews told **J**, "Now we
	8:54	**J** said, "If I bring glory to
	8:57	The Jews said to **J**,
	8:58	**J** told them, "I can guarantee
	8:59	picked up stones to throw at **J**.
	8:59	However, **J** was concealed,
	9:1	As **J** walked along,
	9:3	**J** answered, "Neither this man
	9:6	After **J** said this, he spit on the
	9:11	"The man people call **J** mixed
	9:14	The day when **J** mixed the
	9:22	who acknowledged that **J** was
	9:35	**J** heard that the Jews had
	9:35	So when **J** found the man,
	9:37	**J** told him, "You've seen him.
	9:38	bowed in front of **J** and said,
	9:39	Then **J** said, "I have come into
	9:40	who were with **J** heard this.
	9:41	**J** told them, "If you were blind,
	10:6	**J** used this illustration as he
	10:7	**J** emphasized, "I can
	10:19	because of what **J** said.
	10:23	**J** was walking on Solomon's
	10:25	**J** answered them, "I've told
	10:31	some rocks to stone **J** to death.
	10:32	**J** replied to them, "I've shown
	10:33	The Jews answered **J**,
	10:34	**J** said to them, "Don't your
	10:39	Jews tried to arrest **J** again,
	10:41	Many people went to **J**.
	10:42	people there believed in **J**.
	11:3	sent a messenger to tell **J**,
	11:4	When **J** heard the message,
	11:5	**J** loved Martha, her sister,
	11:6	Yet, when **J** heard that Lazarus
	11:7	**J** said to his disciples,
	11:9	**J** answered, "Aren't there
	11:11	After **J** said this, he told his
	11:13	**J** meant that Lazarus was
	11:13	but the disciples thought **J**
	11:14	Then **J** told them plainly,
	11:16	so that we, too, can die with **J**."
	11:17	When **J** arrived, he found that
	11:20	heard that **J** was coming,
	11:21	Martha told **J**, "Lord, if you had
	11:23	**J** told Martha, "Your brother will
	11:24	Martha answered **J**,
	11:25	**J** said to her, "I am the one
	11:29	got up quickly and went to **J**.
	11:30	(**J** had not yet come into the
	11:32	When Mary arrived where **J**
	11:33	When **J** saw her crying,
	11:34	So **J** asked, "Where did you
	11:35	**J** cried.
	11:36	"See how much **J** loved him."
	11:38	**J** went to the tomb.
	11:39	**J** said, "Take the stone away."
	11:39	dead man's sister, told **J**, "Lord,
	11:40	**J** said to her, "Didn't I tell you
	11:41	**J** looked up and said,
	11:43	After **J** had said this,
	11:44	**J** told them, "Free Lazarus,
	11:45	seen what **J** had done believed
Jon	11:46	and told them what **J** had done.
	11:51	he prophesied that **J** would die
	11:52	He prophesied that **J** wouldn't
	11:52	but that **J** would die to bring
	11:53	council planned to kill **J**.
	11:54	So **J** no longer walked openly
	11:56	they looked for **J** and asked
	11:57	knew where **J** was should tell
	12:1	**J** arrived in Bethany.
	12:1	Lazarus, whom **J** had brought
	12:2	was prepared for **J** in Bethany.
	12:2	one of the people eating with **J**.
	12:7	**J** said to Judas, "Leave her
	12:9	of Jews found out that **J** was
	12:9	went there not only to see **J**
	12:9	whom **J** had brought back to
	12:11	the Jews and believing in **J**.
	12:12	heard that **J** was coming
	12:14	**J** obtained a donkey and sat on
	12:16	However, when **J** was glorified,
	12:17	who had been with **J** when
	12:18	Because the crowd heard that **J**
	12:21	we would like to meet **J**."
	12:22	told Andrew, and they told **J**.
	12:23	**J** replied to them, "The time
	12:30	**J** replied, "That voice wasn't
	12:35	**J** answered the crowd,
	12:36	After **J** had said this,
	12:37	Although they had seen **J**
	12:42	Many rulers believed in **J**.
	12:44	Then **J** said loudly,
	13:1	Before the Passover festival, **J**
	13:1	**J** loved his own who were in
	13:2	put the idea of betraying **J** into
	13:3	**J** knew that. He also knew that
	13:6	When **J** came to Simon Peter,
	13:7	**J** answered Peter,
	13:8	Peter told **J**, "You will never
	13:8	**J** replied to Peter, "If I don't
	13:9	Simon Peter said to **J**,
	13:10	**J** told Peter, "People who have
	13:11	(**J** knew who was going to
	13:12	After **J** had washed their feet
	13:21	**J** was deeply troubled.
	13:22	which one of them **J** meant.
	13:23	the one whom **J** loved,
	13:24	"Ask **J** whom he's talking
	13:25	Leaning close to **J**,
	13:26	**J** answered, "He's the one to
	13:26	So **J** dipped the bread and
	13:27	So **J** told him, "Hurry! Do what
	13:28	No one at the table knew why **J**
	13:29	So some thought that **J** was
	13:31	When Judas was gone, **J** said,
	13:33	**J** said, "Dear children, I will
	13:36	**J** answered him, "You can't
	13:37	Peter said to **J**, "Lord,
	13:38	**J** replied, "Will you give your
	14:6	**J** answered him, "I am the way,
	14:8	Philip said to **J**, "Lord, show us
	14:9	**J** replied, "I have been with all
	14:22	Judas (not Iscariot) asked **J**,
	14:23	**J** answered him, "Those who
	15:1	⌊Then **J** said,⌋ "I am the true
	16:1	⌊**J** continued,⌋ "I have said
	16:19	**J** knew they wanted to ask him
	16:31	**J** replied to them, "Now you
	17:1	After saying this, **J** looked up
	17:3	and **J** Christ, whom you sent.
	18:1	After **J** finished his prayer,
	18:2	knew the place because **J** and
	18:4	**J** knew everything that was
	18:5	"**J** from Nazareth."
	18:5	**J** told them, "I am he." Judas,
	18:6	When **J** told them,
	18:7	**J** asked them again,
	18:7	They said, "**J** from Nazareth."
	18:8	**J** replied, "I told you that I am
	18:9	In this way what **J** had said
	18:11	**J** told Peter, "Put your sword
	18:12	the Jewish guards arrested **J**.
	18:12	arrested Jesus. They tied **J** up
	18:15	another disciple followed **J**.
	18:15	So that disciple went with **J**
	18:19	The chief priest questioned **J**
	18:20	**J** answered him, "I have
Jon	18:22	When **J** said this, one of the
	18:22	near **J** slapped his face
	18:23	**J** replied to him, "If I've said
	18:24	Annas sent **J** to Caiaphas,
	18:24	**J** was still tied up.
	18:26	I see you with **J** in the garden?"
	18:28	Early in the morning, **J** was
	18:32	In this way what **J** had
	18:33	called for **J**, and asked him,
	18:34	**J** replied, "Did you think of that
	18:36	**J** answered, "My kingdom
	18:37	**J** replied, "You're correct in
	19:1	Then Pilate had **J** taken away
	19:5	**J** went outside. He was wearing
	19:6	priests and the guards saw **J**,
	19:9	the palace again and asked **J**,
	19:9	But **J** didn't answer him.
	19:10	So Pilate said to **J**,
	19:11	**J** answered Pilate,
	19:12	When Pilate heard what **J** said,
	19:13	he took **J** outside and sat on
	19:16	Then Pilate handed **J** over to
	19:16	So the soldiers took **J**.
	19:18	The soldiers crucified **J** and
	19:18	**J** was in the middle.
	19:19	notice read, "**J** from Nazareth,
	19:20	because the place where **J**
	19:23	the soldiers had crucified **J**,
	19:26	**J** saw his mother and the
	19:28	After this, when **J** knew that
	19:30	After **J** had taken the vinegar,
	19:32	who had been crucified with **J**.
	19:33	When the soldiers came to **J**
	19:38	(Joseph was a disciple of **J** but
	19:39	had first come to **J** at night,
	19:40	two men took the body of **J**
	19:41	place where **J** was crucified.
	19:42	Joseph and Nicodemus put **J**
	20:2	other disciple, whom **J** loved.
	20:9	meant when it said that **J** had
	20:12	the body of **J** had been lying.
	20:14	and saw **J** standing there.
	20:14	she didn't know that it was **J**.
	20:15	**J** asked her, "Why are you
	20:16	**J** said to her, "Mary!"
	20:17	**J** told her, "Don't hold on to me.
	20:19	**J** stood among them and said
	20:21	**J** said to them again,
	20:24	wasn't with them when **J** came.
	20:26	**J** stood among them and said,
	20:27	Then **J** said to Thomas,
	20:28	Thomas responded to **J**,
	20:29	**J** said to Thomas,
	20:30	**J** performed many other
	20:31	that you will believe that **J** is
	21:1	Later, by the Sea of Tiberias, **J**
	21:2	disciples of **J** were together.
	21:4	**J** stood on the shore.
	21:4	didn't realize that it was **J**.
	21:5	**J** asked them, "Friends,
	21:7	The disciple whom **J** loved
	21:10	**J** told them, "Bring some of the
	21:12	**J** told them, "Come,
	21:13	**J** took the bread, gave it to
	21:14	This was the third time that **J**
	21:15	**J** asked Simon Peter,
	21:15	**J** told him, "Feed my lambs."
	21:16	**J** asked him again,
	21:16	**J** told him, "Take care of my
	21:17	**J** asked him a third time,
	21:17	Peter felt sad because **J** had
	21:17	**J** told him, "Feed my sheep.
	21:19	**J** said this to show by what
	21:19	After saying this, **J** told Peter,
	21:20	the disciple whom **J** loved.
	21:21	saw him, he asked **J**, "Lord,
	21:22	**J** said to Peter, "If I want him to
	21:23	But **J** didn't say that he
	21:23	What **J** said was, "If I want him
	21:25	**J** also did many other things.
Act	1:1	I wrote about what **J** began to
	1:3	After his death **J** showed the
	1:4	**J** said to them, "I've told you
	1:7	**J** told them, "You don't need to
	1:11	**J**, who was taken from you to
	1:14	Mary (the mother of **J**),

Act 1:16 Judas led the men to arrest **J**.
1:20 as a witness that **J** came back
1:21 of the men who accompanied **J**
1:21 that the Lord **J** was among us.
1:22 the day that **J** was taken from
2:22 **J** from Nazareth was a man
2:23 Teachings, you crucified **J**,
2:25 meant when he said about **J**:
2:32 "God brought this man **J** back
2:33 God used his power to give **J**
2:33 **J** has also received and has
2:36 a doubt that God made **J**,
2:38 in the name of **J** Christ so that
3:6 Through the power of **J** Christ
3:13 has glorified his servant **J**.
3:13 You handed **J** over to Pilate.
3:16 We believe in the one named **J**.
3:20 He will send you **J**,
3:21 Heaven must receive **J** until
4:2 come back to life through **J**.
4:10 of **J** Christ from Nazareth.
4:10 You crucified **J** Christ,
4:12 the power of the one named **J**
4:13 these men had been with **J**.
4:17 anyone about the one named **J**.
4:18 them never to teach about **J**
4:27 against your holy servant **J**,
4:30 name of your holy servant **J**."
4:33 that the Lord **J** had come back
5:12 common faith in **J** as they met
5:30 You murdered **J** by hanging
5:31 God used his power to give **J**
5:40 speak about the one named **J**,
5:41 dishonor for speaking about **J**.
5:42 News that **J** is the Messiah.
6:14 We heard him say that **J** from
7:55 and **J** in the position of
7:59 "Lord **J**, welcome my spirit."
8:12 and the one named **J** Christ,
8:16 in the name of the Lord **J**.)
8:35 official the Good News about **J**.
9:5 The person replied, "I'm **J**,
9:17 said, "Brother Saul, the Lord **J**,
9:20 in their synagogues that **J** was
9:21 the one named **J** in Jerusalem?
9:22 that **J** was the Messiah.
9:27 spoken about the one named **J**
9:34 **J** Christ makes you well.
10:36 of peace through **J** Christ.
10:36 This **J** Christ is everyone's
10:38 You know that God anointed **J**
10:38 **J** went everywhere and did
10:38 **J** did these things because
10:39 We can testify to everything **J**
10:41 He showed **J** to witnesses,
10:41 who ate and drank with **J** after
10:42 'God has appointed **J** to judge
10:43 named **J** receive forgiveness
10:48 in the name of **J** Christ.
11:17 believed in the Lord **J** Christ.
11:20 about the Lord **J** to Greeks.
13:23 "God had the Savior, **J**,
13:24 Before **J** began his ministry,
13:27 rulers didn't know who **J** was.
13:27 So they condemned **J** and
13:33 by bringing **J** back to life.
13:34 "God stated that he brought **J**
13:38 I'm telling you that through **J**
13:39 in **J** receives God's approval.
15:11 believe that the Lord **J** saves
15:26 the one named **J** Christ.
16:7 Spirit of **J** wouldn't allow this.
16:18 you in the name of **J** Christ
16:31 "Believe in the Lord **J**,
17:3 come back to life, and that **J**,
17:7 whose name is **J**."
17:18 telling the Good News about **J**
18:5 the Jews that **J** is the Messiah.
18:25 He accurately taught about **J**
18:28 from the Scriptures that **J** is
19:4 told people to believe in **J**,
19:5 in the name of the Lord **J**.
19:13 to use the name of the Lord **J**
19:13 ⌊to come out⌋ in the name of **J**,
19:15 answered them, "I know **J**,
19:17 awe for the name of the Lord **J**

Act 20:21 act and to believe in our Lord **J**.
20:24 I received from the Lord **J** —
20:35 the words that the Lord **J** said,
21:13 the one named **J**."
22:8 'I'm **J** from Nazareth,
24:24 him talk about faith in Christ **J**.
25:19 man named **J** who had died.
25:19 Paul claimed that **J** is alive.
26:9 the one named **J** of Nazareth.
26:11 them to curse ⌊the name of **J**⌋.
26:15 "The Lord answered, 'I am **J**,
28:23 about **J** from Moses' Teachings
28:31 boldly about the Lord **J** Christ.
Rom 1:1 Paul, a servant of **J** Christ,
1:3 his Son, our Lord **J** Christ.
1:6 called to belong to **J** Christ.)
1:7 and the Lord **J** Christ are yours.
1:8 First, I thank my God through **J**
2:16 when God, through Christ **J**,
3:22 through faith in **J** Christ.
3:24 through the price Christ **J** paid
3:26 of people who believe in **J**.
4:24 in the one who brought **J**,
4:25 **J**, our Lord, was handed over to
5:1 our Lord **J** Christ has done.
5:11 In addition, our Lord **J** Christ
5:15 of one person, **J** Christ,
5:17 of one person, **J** Christ.
5:21 because of **J** Christ our Lord.
6:3 into Christ **J** were baptized into
6:11 in the power Christ **J** gives you.
6:23 life found in Christ **J** our Lord.
7:25 I thank God that our Lord **J**
8:1 in Christ **J** can no longer
8:2 who gives life through Christ **J**,
8:11 of the one who brought **J** back
8:38 which Christ **J** our Lord shows
10:9 If you declare that **J** is Lord,
13:14 live like the Lord **J** Christ did,
14:14 The Lord **J** has given me the
15:5 the example of Christ **J**.
15:6 and Father of our Lord **J** Christ.
15:16 to be a servant of Christ **J** to
15:17 So Christ **J** gives me the right
15:30 you through our Lord **J** Christ
16:3 in the service of Christ **J**.
16:20 will of our Lord **J** be with you!
16:25 message I tell about **J** Christ.
16:27 to him through **J** Christ forever!
1Co 1:1 to be an apostle of Christ **J** by
1:2 that was made holy by Christ **J**
1:2 the name of our Lord **J** Christ.
1:3 and the Lord **J** Christ are yours!
1:4 Christ **J** has shown you
1:5 Through Christ **J** you have
1:7 eagerly for our Lord **J** Christ
1:8 on the day of our Lord **J** Christ.
1:9 with his Son **J** Christ our Lord.
1:10 in the name of our Lord **J** Christ
1:30 You are partners with Christ **J**
1:30 **J** has become our wisdom sent
2:2 only one subject — **J** Christ,
3:11 and that foundation is **J** Christ.
4:15 the Good News about Christ **J**.
5:4 Then, in the name of our Lord **J**,
6:11 in the name of the Lord **J** Christ
8:6 is only one Lord, **J** Christ.
9:1 Haven't I seen **J** our Lord?
11:23 the Lord **J** took bread
12:3 Spirit says, "**J** is cursed."
12:3 No one can say, "**J** is Lord,"
15:31 you which Christ **J** our Lord has
15:57 through our Lord **J** Christ.
16:23 will of the Lord **J** be with you.
16:24 Through Christ **J** my love is
2Co 1:1 an apostle of Christ **J** by the
1:2 and the Lord **J** Christ are yours!
1:3 and Father of our Lord **J** Christ!
1:14 proud on the day of our Lord **J**.
1:19 God's Son, **J** Christ,
4:5 It is about **J** Christ as the Lord.
4:10 carry around the death of **J**
4:10 that the life of **J** is also shown
4:11 that the life of **J** is also shown
4:14 who brought the Lord **J** back
4:14 bring us back to life through **J**.

2Co 8:9 kindness of our Lord **J** Christ.
11:4 about another **J** whom we didn't
11:31 God and Father of the Lord **J**,
13:5 people in whom **J** Christ lives?
13:13 May the Lord **J** Christ's good
Gal 1:1 or individual but by **J** Christ
1:3 Father and our Lord **J** Christ!
1:12 but **J** Christ revealed it to me.
2:4 the freedom Christ **J** gives us.
2:16 only by believing in **J** Christ.
2:16 So we also believed in **J** Christ
3:14 of the world through **J** Christ
3:22 a promise based on faith in **J**
3:26 by believing in Christ **J**.
3:28 are all the same in Christ **J**.
4:14 messenger or Christ **J** himself.
5:6 to Christ **J** is concerned,
5:24 Those who belong to Christ **J**
6:14 the cross of our Lord **J** Christ.
6:17 the scars of **J** on my body.
6:18 May the good will of our Lord **J**
Eph 1:1 an apostle of Christ **J** by God's
1:2 and the Lord **J** Christ are yours!
1:3 and Father of our Lord **J** Christ!
1:5 to adopt us through **J** Christ.
1:15 about your faith in the Lord **J**
1:17 the God of our Lord **J** Christ,
2:6 to life together with Christ **J**
2:7 He did this through Christ **J** out
2:10 He has created us in Christ **J** to
2:13 But now through Christ **J** you,
2:20 Christ **J** himself is the
3:1 am the prisoner of Christ **J** for
3:6 that God made in Christ **J**.
3:11 out through Christ **J** our Lord.
3:21 in the church and in Christ **J**
4:21 his ways. The truth is in **J**.
5:20 in the name of our Lord **J** Christ
6:23 and the Lord **J** Christ give our
6:24 love for our Lord **J** Christ.
Php 1:1 servants of Christ **J**.
1:1 who is united with Christ **J**.
1:2 and the Lord **J** Christ are yours!
1:6 on the day of Christ **J**.
1:8 all the compassion of Christ **J**,
1:11 **J** Christ will fill your lives with
1:19 from the Spirit of **J** Christ.
1:26 have pride in Christ **J** with me.
2:5 same attitude that Christ **J** had.
2:10 so that at the name of **J**
2:11 and confess that **J** Christ is
2:19 I hope that the Lord **J** will allow
2:21 not after those of **J** Christ.
3:3 Spirit and take pride in Christ **J**.
3:8 off knowing Christ **J** my Lord.
3:12 But I run to win that which **J**
3:14 heavenly call offers in Christ **J**.
3:20 We look forward to the Lord **J**
4:7 and emotions through Christ **J**.
4:19 a glorious way through Christ **J**.
4:21 who believes in Christ **J**.
4:23 May the good will of our Lord **J**
Col 1:1 an apostle of Christ **J** by God's
1:3 the Father of our Lord **J** Christ,
1:4 about your faith in Christ **J**
2:6 You received Christ **J** the Lord,
3:17 done in the name of the Lord **J**,
4:11 **J**, called Justus, also greets
4:12 Epaphras, a servant of Christ **J**
1Th 1:1 Father and the Lord **J** Christ.
1:3 in our Lord **J** Christ is enduring.
1:10 His Son is **J**, whom he brought
1:10 **J** is the one who rescues us
2:14 that are united with Christ **J**.
2:15 who killed the Lord **J** and the
2:19 presence of our Lord **J** when
3:11 Father and the Lord **J** will guide
3:13 Father when our Lord **J** comes
4:1 because of the Lord **J** we ask
4:2 gave you through the Lord **J**.
4:14 We believe that **J** died and
4:14 We also believe that, through **J**,
4:14 They will come back with **J**.
5:9 through our Lord **J** Christ.
5:18 will in Christ **J** that you do
5:23 when our Lord **J** Christ comes.

1Th 5:28 The good will of our Lord **J**
2Th 1:1 Father and the Lord **J** Christ.
1:2 and the Lord **J** Christ are yours!
1:7 when the Lord **J** is revealed,
1:8 Good News about our Lord **J**.
1:12 way the name of our Lord **J** will
1:12 of the good will of **J** Christ,
2:1 our Lord **J** Christ's coming
2:8 and the Lord **J** will destroy him
2:8 When the Lord **J** comes,
2:14 the glory of our Lord **J** Christ.
2:16 Together with our Lord **J** Christ
3:6 in the name of our Lord **J** Christ
3:12 people by the Lord **J** Christ
3:18 The good will of our Lord **J**
1Ti 1:1 an apostle of Christ **J** by the
1:1 and Christ **J** our confidence.
1:2 Father and Christ **J** our Lord are
1:12 I thank Christ **J** our Lord that he
1:14 that Christ **J** shows people.
1:15 Christ **J** came into the world to
1:16 mercy so that Christ **J** could
2:5 humans — a human, Christ **J**.
3:13 a result of their faith in Christ **J**.
4:6 of Christ **J** when you point
5:21 in the sight of God, Christ **J**,
6:3 words of our Lord **J** Christ
6:13 and in the sight of Christ **J**,
6:14 until our Lord **J** Christ appears,
2Ti 1:1 an apostle of Christ **J** by God's
1:2 Father and Christ **J** our Lord.
1:9 God planned that Christ **J**
1:10 coming of our Savior Christ **J**,
1:13 With faith and love for Christ **J**,
2:1 in the kindness of Christ **J**.
2:3 like a good soldier of Christ **J**.
2:8 Always think about **J** Christ.
2:10 receive salvation from Christ **J**
3:12 in Christ **J** will be persecuted.
3:15 saved through faith in Christ **J**.
4:1 presence of God and Christ **J**,
4:1 I do this because Christ **J** will
Tit 1:1 God and an apostle of **J** Christ.
1:4 and from Christ **J** our Savior are
2:13 great God and Savior, **J** Christ.
3:6 us through **J** Christ our Savior.
Phm 1:1 who is a prisoner for Christ **J**,
1:3 and the Lord **J** Christ are yours!
1:5 your faithfulness to the Lord **J**
1:9 and now a prisoner for Christ **J**,
1:23 because of Christ **J** like I am,
1:25 of our Lord **J** Christ be yours.
Heb 2:9 **J** was made a little lower than
2:10 it was the right time to bring **J**,
2:11 **J**, who makes people holy,
2:11 That is why **J** isn't ashamed to
2:13 In addition, **J** says,
2:13 And **J** says, "I am here with the
2:14 **J** took on flesh and blood to be
2:16 So **J** helps Abraham's
2:18 Because **J** experienced
3:1 So look carefully at **J**,
3:2 **J** is faithful to God,
3:3 **J** deserves more praise than
4:14 That person is **J**, the Son of
5:7 life on earth, **J** prayed to God,
5:8 Although **J** was the Son ⌊of
6:20 where **J** went before us on our
7:21 but **J** became a priest when
7:22 In this way **J** has become the
7:24 But **J** lives forever,
7:27 **J** brought the sacrifice for the
8:6 **J** has been given a priestly
10:10 holy because **J** Christ did what
10:19 because of the blood of **J** we
10:20 **J** has opened a new and living
12:2 We must focus on **J**,
12:3 Think about **J**, who endured
12:24 You have come to **J**,
13:8 **J** Christ is the same yesterday,
13:12 That is why **J** suffered outside
13:15 Through **J** we should always
13:20 of the sheep, our Lord **J**,
13:21 May he work in us through **J**
13:21 belongs to **J** Christ forever.
Jas 1:1 of God and of the Lord **J** Christ.
Jas 2:1 our glorious Lord **J** Christ by not
2:7 curse the good name ⌊of **J**⌋,
1Pe 1:1 an apostle of **J** Christ.
1:2 that you are obedient to **J** Christ
1:3 and Father of our Lord **J** Christ!
1:3 because **J** Christ has come
1:7 when **J** Christ appears again.
1:13 when **J** Christ appears again.
2:5 God accepts through **J** Christ.
3:21 It saves you through **J** Christ,
4:11 receives glory through **J** Christ.
4:11 Glory and power belong to **J**
5:10 has called you through Christ **J**
2Pe 1:1 servant and apostle of **J** Christ.
1:1 our God and Savior, **J** Christ.
1:2 your knowledge about **J**,
1:8 about our Lord **J** Christ is living
1:11 of our Lord and Savior **J** Christ.
1:14 Our Lord **J** Christ has made
1:16 coming of our Lord **J** Christ,
2:20 our Lord and Savior **J** Christ
3:18 of our Lord and Savior **J** Christ.
1Jn 1:3 and with his Son **J** Christ.
1:7 And the blood of his Son **J**
2:1 does sin, we have **J** Christ,
2:22 but the person who rejects **J** as
3:23 the one named **J** Christ,
4:2 declares that **J** Christ has come
4:3 declare that **J** Christ has come
4:15 in those who declare that **J** is
5:1 Everyone who believes that **J**
5:5 person who believes that **J** is
5:6 This Son of God is **J** Christ,
5:20 who is real, his Son **J** Christ.
5:20 This **J** Christ is the real God
2Jn 1:3 the Father and from **J** Christ,
1:7 They refuse to declare that **J**
Jud 1:1 From Jude, a servant of **J**
1:1 and who are kept safe for **J**
1:4 only Master and Lord, **J** Christ.
1:17 of our Lord **J** Christ told you
1:21 the mercy of our Lord **J** Christ
1:25 through **J** Christ our Lord.
Rev 1:1 is the revelation of **J** Christ.
1:2 the testimony about **J** Christ.
1:5 and from **J** Christ, the witness,
1:9 and endurance because of **J**.
1:9 and the testimony about **J**.
12:17 hold on to the testimony of **J**.
14:12 and keep their faith in **J**,
17:6 of those who testify about **J**.
19:10 hold on to the testimony of **J**.
19:10 because the testimony of **J** is
20:4 of their testimony about **J**
22:16 "I, **J**, have sent my angel to
22:20 Amen! Come, Lord **J**!
22:21 The good will of the Lord **J** be

Jesus' (41)

Mat 2:1 After **J** birth wise men from the
8:23 **J** disciples went with him as
17:2 **J** appearance changed in front
27:32 forced him to carry **J** cross
28:13 that **J** disciples had come at
Mar 6:14 because **J** name had become
9:2 **J** appearance changed in front
15:21 forced him to carry **J** cross
Luk 2:33 **J** father and mother were
2:41 Every year **J** parents would go
5:30 complained to **J** disciples.
8:35 he was sitting at **J** feet.
9:31 **J** approaching death
9:32 they saw **J** glory and the two
17:16 He quickly bowed at **J** feet and
24:13 two of **J** disciples were going
Jon 2:1 **J** mother was there.
2:3 **J** mother said to him,
6:8 One of **J** disciples, Andrew,
6:60 When many of **J** disciples
6:66 **J** speech made many of his
7:3 So **J** brothers told him,
12:3 nard and poured it on **J** feet.
12:16 At first **J** disciples didn't know
12:41 because he had seen **J** glory
13:3 had put everything in **J** control.
19:25 **J** mother, her sister,
Jon 19:25 were standing beside **J** cross
19:34 of the soldiers stabbed **J** side
19:38 Pilate to let him remove **J** body.
19:38 permission to remove **J** body.
20:7 cloth that had been on **J** head.
20:12 One angel was where **J** head
20:26 A week later **J** disciples were
21:20 who leaned against **J** chest at
21:23 die spread among **J** followers.
Act 5:28 **J** name when you teach.
13:34 and that **J** body never decayed.
2Co 4:11 over to death for **J** sake so that
Gal 3:1 Wasn't Christ **J** crucifixion
2Ti 1:1 Christ **J** promise of life.

Jether (8)

Jdg 8:20 Then he told **J**, his firstborn
8:20 But **J** didn't draw his sword.
1Ki 2:5 of Ner, and Amasa, son of **J**.
2:32 Amasa (who was the son of **J**
1Ch 2:17 whose father was **J**,
2:32 brother) were **J** and Jonathan.
2:32 **J** died without children.
4:17 Ezrah's sons were **J**,

Jether's (1)

1Ch 7:38 **J** sons were Jephunneh,

Jetheth (2)

Gen 36:40 and name: Timna, Alvah, **J**,
1Ch 1:51 of Edom were Timna, Aliah, **J**,

Jethro (11)

Exo 3:1 the sheep of his father-in-law **J**,
4:18 back to his father-in-law **J**.
4:18 **J** said to Moses, "You may go."
18:1 Moses' father-in-law **J**,
18:2 his father-in-law **J** had taken
18:5 Moses' father-in-law **J** brought
18:6 **J** had sent word to Moses,
18:7 the ground and kissed **J**.
18:9 **J** was delighted ⌊to hear⌋
18:12 Then **J**, Moses' father-in-law,
18:27 So **J** went back to his own

Jetur (3)

Gen 25:15 Hadad, Tema, **J**, Naphish,
1Ch 1:31 **J**, Naphish, and Kedemah.
5:19 descendants (including **J**,

Jeuel (2)

1Ch 9:6 descendants of Zerah were **J**
Ezr 8:13 Eliphelet, **J**, and Shemaiah,

Jeush (9)

Gen 36:5 Oholibamah gave birth to **J**,
36:14 She gave birth to **J**,
36:18 **J**, Jalam, and Korah.
1Ch 1:35 Reuel, **J**, Jalam, and Korah.
7:10 Bilhan's sons were **J**,
8:39 **J** (the second son),
23:10 Jahath, Zina, **J**, and Beriah.
23:11 **J** and Beriah didn't have many
2Ch 11:19 **J**, Shemariah, and Zaham.

Jeuz (1)

1Ch 8:10 **J**, Sachia, and Mirmah. All of

Jew (21)

Est 2:5 of Susa there was a **J** from
3:4 had told them that he was a **J**.
5:13 I see Mordecai the **J** sitting at
6:10 Do this for Mordecai the **J** who
8:7 Esther and Mordecai the **J**,
9:29 and Mordecai the **J** wrote
9:31 Mordecai the **J** and Queen
10:3 Mordecai the **J** was ranked
Jer 34:9 to keep another **J** as a slave.
Zec 8:23 take hold of the clothes of a **J**.
Jon 3:25 **J** about purification ceremonies.
18:35 Pilate answered, "Am I a **J**?
Act 18:24 A **J** named Apollos,
19:34 that Alexander was a **J**,
21:39 Paul answered, "I'm a **J**,
22:3 "I'm a **J**. I was born and raised
Rom 2:17 You call yourself a **J**,

Rom 2:28 A person is not a **J** because of
2:29 a person is a **J** inwardly,
3:1 advantage, then, in being a **J**?
Col 3:11 there is no Greek or **J**,

jewel (2)

Pro 17:8 A bribe seems like a **j** to the
Isa 13:19 Babylon, the **j** of the kingdoms,

jeweler (2)

Exo 28:11 the same way a **j** engraves
38:23 He was a **j**, carpenter, designer,

jewelers (1)

Exo 35:35 They can do the work of **j**,

jewelry (21)

Gen 24:53 took out gold and silver **j**
Exo 3:22 in her home for silver and gold **j**
11:2 Egyptians for silver and gold **j**."
12:35 and silver **j** and for clothes.
33:4 No one wore any **j**.
33:5 Now take off your **j**,
33:6 Israelites no longer wore their **j**.
35:22 and brought all kinds of gold **j**:
Num 31:50 the LORD the gold **j** that each
2Sm 1:24 who put gold **j** on your clothes.
Jer 2:32 young woman can't forget her **j**
4:30 dress in red and put on gold **j**?
Eze 16:11 I gave you **j**. I put bracelets on
16:13 So you wore gold and silver **j**.
16:17 beautiful gold and silver **j** that
16:39 take away your beautiful **j**,
Hos 2:13 She put on her rings and **j**,
1Ti 2:9 by their hair styles or the gold **j**,
1Pe 3:3 hairstyles, gold **j**, or clothes.
Rev 17:4 gold **j**, gems, and pearls.
18:16 gold **j**, gems, and pearls.

jewels (13)

Job 28:17 Nor can gold ornaments, **j**,
Pro 3:15 is more precious than **j**.
8:11 wisdom is better than **j**.
20:15 There are gold and plenty of **j**,
31:10 She is worth far more than **j**.
Isa 49:18 "you will wear all of them like **j**
61:10 like a bride with her **j**.
Eze 7:20 were proud of their beautiful **j**
7:20 That is why I will make their **j**
7:21 I will hand their **j** over to
23:26 and take away your beautiful **j**.
23:40 their eyes, and put on their **j**.
Zec 9:16 in his land like **j** in a crown.

Jewish (140)

Ezr 6:8 help the **J** leaders rebuild God's
6:14 So the **J** leaders continued to
Neh 5:1 publicly about their **J** relatives.
5:8 back our **J** relatives who had
5:8 Now you are selling your **J**
5:17 I fed 1 50 **J** leaders and their
Est 6:13 If Mordecai is of **J** descent,
Mat 10:5 go among people who are not **J**
10:17 hand you over to the **J** courts
28:15 spread among the **J** people
Mar 7:3 like all other **J** people,
13:9 hand you over to the **J** courts
14:55 **J** council were searching
15:1 The whole **J** council decided
15:43 member of the **J** council.
Luk 7:3 Jesus and sent some **J** leaders
23:50 He was a member of the **J**
23:51 He was from the **J** city of
Jon 2:6 used for **J** purification rituals.
2:13 The **J** Passover was near,
3:1 and a member of the **J** council.
4:9 "How can a **J** man like you ask
5:1 to Jerusalem for a **J** festival.
6:4 The time for the **J** Passover
7:2 The time for the **J** Festival of
11:51 would die for the **J** nation.
11:53 From that day on, the **J** council
11:55 The **J** Passover was near.
18:12 Then the army officer and the **J**
19:21 The chief priests of the **J**
19:40 was the **J** custom for burial.
Jon 19:42 since that day was the **J** day of
Act 2:5 Devout **J** men from every
2:10 We're **J** people, converts to
4:5 The next day the **J** rulers,
5:21 called together the **J** council,
6:12 and brought him in front of the **J**
10:2 many gifts to poor **J** people
10:22 Also, the **J** people respect him.
10:28 how wrong it is for a **J** man
10:45 on people who were not **J**.
11:1 were not **J** had accepted God's
11:18 also led people who are not **J**
11:19 God's word only to **J** people.
12:11 the **J** people are expecting
13:6 In Paphos they met a **J** man
13:31 to the **J** people about him.
14:2 some people who were not **J**
14:5 people and the **J** people
14:27 given people who were not **J**
15:5 "People who are not **J** must be
15:7 people who aren't **J** could hear
15:8 who aren't **J** by giving them
15:9 doesn't discriminate between **J**
15:17 who aren't **J** over whom my
16:1 mother was a **J** believer,
16:13 we thought **J** people gathered
18:2 In Corinth he met a **J** man
18:6 going to people who are not **J**."
19:14 sons of Sceva, a **J** chief priest,
21:11 over to people who are not **J**."
21:21 children or follow **J** customs.
21:28 to turn against the **J** people,
22:5 to take to the **J** community
22:21 away to people who aren't **J**.'"
22:30 priests and the entire **J** council
23:1 Paul stared at the **J** council
23:20 Paul to the **J** council tomorrow.
23:28 So I took him to their **J** council
23:29 disputes about **J** teachings.
24:24 his wife Drusilla, who was **J**.
25:2 **J** leaders informed Festus
25:8 "I haven't broken any **J** law or
25:15 the chief priests and the **J**
25:17 "So the **J** leaders came to
26:17 I will rescue you from the **J**
26:20 that I first told to the **J** people
26:23 to **J** and non-Jewish people."
28:17 anything against the **J** people
28:21 The **J** leaders told Paul,
28:21 and no **J** person who has come
Rom 3:29 God of people who are not **J**?
9:3 who, like me, are **J** by birth.
10:1 on behalf of the **J** people is that
11:11 come to people who are not **J**
11:11 to make the **J** people jealous.
11:12 The fall of the **J** people made
11:12 who are not **J** spiritually rich.
11:12 So the inclusion of **J** people
11:13 I speak to you who are not **J**.
11:13 sent to people who are not **J**,
11:23 If **J** people do not continue in
11:28 The Good News made the **J**
11:30 disobedience of the **J** people.
11:31 In the same way, the **J** people
15:8 a servant for the **J** people
15:8 the ancestors of the **J** people.
15:9 People who are not **J** praise
15:16 Jesus to people who are not **J**.
15:18 who are not **J** to obedience.
16:7 who are **J** by birth like me.
16:11 who is **J** by birth like me.
16:21 who are **J** by birth like me.
1Co 1:23 This offends **J** people and
1:23 sense to people who are not **J**.
9:20 I became **J** for Jewish people.
9:20 I became Jewish for **J** people.
10:32 whether they are **J**,
12:13 Whether we are **J** or Greek,
2Co 11:24 Five times the **J** leaders had
Gal 1:13 when I followed the **J** religion.
1:14 in following the **J** religion.
1:16 who are not **J** that his Son
2:2 among people who are not **J**.
2:8 apostle to **J** people also made
2:8 to people who are not **J**.
2:9 the people who are not **J**
Gal 2:9 would work among **J** people.
2:12 who were not **J** until some men
2:12 with people who were not **J**.
2:13 The other **J** Christians also
2:14 in front of everyone, "You're **J**,
2:14 live like a person who is not **J**.
2:14 who are not **J** must live like
2:15 We are **J** by birth, not sinners
6:13 did this to follow **J** laws.
Eph 2:11 you were not **J** physically.
2:14 In his body he has made **J** and
2:15 so that he could take **J**
2:18 So **J** and non-Jewish people
3:1 for those of you who are not **J**.
3:6 that people who are not **J** have
3:6 inheritance as **J** people do.
3:8 Christ to people who are not **J**.
Php 3:6 approval by keeping **J** laws,
Col 4:11 from the **J** religion who are
1Th 2:16 who are not **J** how they can
1Ti 2:7 who are not **J** about faith
Tit 1:14 pay attention to **J** myths
Rev 3:9 They claim that they are **J**,

Jews (251)

Ezr 3:8 and the rest of the **J**,
4:12 you should know that the **J**
4:13 the **J** will no longer pay taxes,
4:23 forced the **J** to stop rebuilding.
5:1 prophesied to the **J** in Judah
5:3 and their group went to the **J**
5:4 They also asked the **J** for the
5:5 But the leaders of the **J** were
6:7 Let the governor of the **J** and
Neh 1:2 I asked them about the **J** who
2:16 I hadn't yet told the **J**,
4:1 enraged and made fun of the **J**.
4:2 "What do these miserable **J**
4:12 **J** who were living near our
6:6 that you and the **J** are planning
13:23 In those days I saw some **J**
13:25 So I reprimanded those **J**,
Est 3:6 Mordecai's people — all the **J**
3:10 the enemy of the **J**.
3:13 and destroy all the **J** — young
4:3 the **J** went into mourning,
4:7 king's treasury to destroy the **J**.
4:8 to exterminate the **J**.
4:13 safer than all the rest of the **J**.
4:14 else will help and rescue the **J**,
4:16 "Assemble all the **J** in Susa.
8:1 the enemy of the **J**,
8:3 his conspiracy against the **J**.
8:5 the order to destroy the **J**
8:7 because he tried to kill the **J**.
8:8 what you think is best for the **J**
8:9 ordered was written to the **J**
8:9 and to the **J** in their own script
8:11 had given permission for the **J**
8:13 On that day the **J** were to be
8:16 So the **J** were cheerful,
8:17 the **J** were happy and joyful,
8:17 people pretended to be **J**
8:17 they were terrified of the **J**.
9:1 when the enemies of the **J**
9:1 The **J** overpowered those who
9:2 The **J** assembled in their cities
9:3 king's treasurers assisted the **J**
9:5 Then with their swords, the **J**
9:6 In the fortress of Susa the **J**
9:10 and the enemy of the **J**.
9:10 But the **J** did not seize any of
9:12 "In the fortress of Susa the **J**
9:13 allow the **J** in Susa to do
9:15 The **J** in Susa also assembled
9:16 The other **J** who were in the
9:18 But the **J** in Susa had
9:19 That is why the **J** who live in
9:20 sent official letters to all the **J**
9:22 the **J** freed themselves from
9:23 So the **J** accepted as tradition
9:24 the enemy of all the **J**,
9:24 had plotted against the **J** to
9:25 against the **J** should turn back
9:26 So the **J** called these days
9:27 the **J** established a tradition for

Est 9:28 not be ignored among the J,
9:30 peace and security to all the J
10:3 popular with, all of the other J,
10:3 for the welfare of his fellow J.
Jer 32:12 of all the J who were sitting
38:19 "I'm afraid of the J who have
40:11 all the J who were in Moab,
40:12 So all the J returned from all
40:15 All the J who have gathered
41:3 Ishmael also killed all the J
44:1 Jeremiah about all the J living
52:28 year as king, he took 3,023 J.
52:30 of the guard, took away 745 J.
Dan 3:8 brought charges against the J.
3:12 There are certain J whom you
Mat 2:2 born to be the king of the J?
27:11 "Are you the king of the J?"
27:29 "Long live the king of the J!"
27:37 is Jesus, the king of the J."
Mar 15:2 "Are you the king of the J?"
15:9 free the king of the J for you?"
15:12 I do with the king of the J?"
15:18 "Long live the king of the J!"
15:26 It read, "The king of the J."
Luk 23:3 "Are you the king of the J?"
23:37 "If you're the king of the J,
23:38 "This is the king of the J."
Jon 1:19 answer when the J sent priests
2:18 The J reacted by asking Jesus,
2:20 The J said, "It took forty-six
4:9 (J, of course, don't associate
4:20 But you J say that people must
4:22 We ⌊J⌋ know what we're
4:22 salvation comes from the J.
5:10 So the J told the man who had
5:12 The J asked him, "Who is the
5:15 The man went back to the J
5:16 The J began to persecute
5:18 His reply made the J more
5:19 Jesus said to the J,
6:41 The J began to criticize Jesus
6:52 The J began to quarrel with
7:1 Judea because J there wanted
7:11 The J were looking for Jesus
7:13 they were afraid of the J.
7:15 The J were surprised and
7:30 The J tried to arrest him but
7:35 The J said among themselves,
7:35 with the J who are scattered
8:22 Then the J asked,
8:25 The J asked him, "Who did
8:27 (The J didn't know that he was
8:31 So Jesus said to those J who
8:39 The J replied to Jesus,
8:41 The J said to Jesus,
8:48 The J replied to Jesus,
8:52 The J told Jesus, "Now we
8:57 The J said to Jesus,
8:59 Then some of the J picked up
9:18 the J didn't believe that the
9:22 they were afraid of the J.
9:22 The J had already agreed to
9:24 So once again the J called the
9:26 The J asked him, "What did he
9:28 The J yelled at him,
9:34 The J answered him,
9:35 Jesus heard that the J had
10:19 The J were divided because of
10:24 The J surrounded him.
10:31 The J had again brought some
10:33 The J answered Jesus,
10:39 The J tried to arrest Jesus
11:8 not long ago the J wanted to
11:19 Many J had come to Martha
11:31 The J who were comforting
11:33 and the J who were crying with
11:36 The J said, "See how much
11:37 But some of the J asked,
11:45 Many J who had visited Mary
11:54 walked openly among the J.
12:9 A large crowd of J found out
12:11 people were leaving the J
13:33 I'm telling you what I told the J.
18:14 who had advised the J that
18:20 where all the J gather.
18:28 The J wouldn't go into the
Jon 18:30 The J answered Pilate,
18:31 Pilate told the J, "Take him,
18:31 The J answered him,
18:33 "Are you the king of the J?"
18:36 being handed over to the J.
18:38 he went out to the J again and
18:39 free the king of the J for you?"
18:40 The J shouted again,
19:3 "Long live the king of the J!"
19:4 outside again and told the J,
19:5 Pilate said to the J,
19:7 The J answered Pilate,
19:12 But the J shouted,
19:14 Pilate said to the J,
19:15 Then the J shouted,
19:19 Nazareth, the king of the J."
19:20 Many J read this notice,
19:21 king of the J!' Instead, write,
19:21 that he is the king of the J.'"
19:31 the J didn't want the bodies to
19:38 he was afraid of the J).
20:19 they were afraid of the J.
Act 6:1 Greek-speaking J complained
6:1 about the Hebrew-speaking J.
6:1 The Greek-speaking J claimed
9:22 and he confused the J living in
9:23 Later the J planned to murder
9:29 argued with Greek-speaking J,
10:39 Jesus did in the land of the J
12:3 he saw how this pleased the J,
13:43 many J and converts to
13:45 When the J saw the crowds,
13:48 The people who were not J
13:50 But J stirred up devout women
14:1 of J and Greeks believed.
14:2 But the J who refused to
14:4 Some were for the J,
14:19 However, J from the cities of
15:9 faith as he has cleansed us J.
16:3 him because of the J who lived
16:20 of trouble in our city. They're J,
17:4 Some of the J were persuaded
17:5 Then the J became jealous.
17:13 But when the J in
17:17 in the synagogue with J
18:2 Claudius had ordered all J
18:4 He tried to win over J and
18:5 He assured the J that Jesus is
18:12 the J had one thought in mind.
18:14 when Gallio said to the J,
18:14 that I put up with you J.
18:19 had a discussion with the J.
18:20 The J asked him to stay longer,
18:28 and that the J were wrong.
19:10 for two years so that all the J
19:13 Some J used to travel from
19:13 These J would say,
19:17 All the J and Greeks living in
19:33 so the J pushed him to the
20:3 he found out that the J were
20:19 when the J plotted against me.
20:21 I warned J and Greeks to
21:11 'This is how the J in
21:20 how many thousands of J are
21:21 the J living among non-Jewish
21:27 the J from the province of Asia
22:12 All the J living in Damascus
22:30 the J had against Paul.
23:12 In the morning the J formed a
23:20 "The J have planned to ask
23:27 The J had seized this man and
24:5 He starts quarrels among all J
24:9 The J supported Tertullus'
24:19 But some J from the province
24:27 (Since Felix wanted to do the J
25:3 The J had a plan to ambush
25:7 the J who had come from
25:9 wanted to do the J a favor.
25:10 done anything wrong to the J,
25:24 All the J in Jerusalem and
26:2 that the J brought against me.
26:4 "All the J know how I lived the
26:7 Your Majesty, the J are making
26:21 For this reason the J took me
28:17 invited the most influential J
28:19 But when the J objected,
Act 28:23 J ⌊than expected⌋ went
28:25 The J, unable to agree among
28:28 to people who are not J.
Rom 1:16 J first and Greeks as well.
2:9 for J first and Greeks as well.
2:10 for J first and Greeks as well.
3:9 accused everyone (both J
3:29 Is God only the God of the J?
9:24 whether we are J or not.
10:12 between J and Greeks.
1Co 1:22 J ask for miraculous signs,
1:24 But to those J and Greeks who
Gal 1:14 how I was far ahead of other J
2:14 not Jewish must live like J?"
3:28 There are neither J nor Greeks,
1Th 2:14 those churches did from the J
2:16 The result is that those J
Rev 2:9 who claim to be J slander you.

Jezaniah (2)

Jer 40:8 of Ephai from Netophah, and J,
42:1 Johanan and Hoshaiah's son J

Jezebel (18)

1Ki 16:31 He also married J,
18:4 (When J was killing the
18:13 heard what I did when J killed
19:1 Ahab told J everything Elijah
19:2 Then J sent a messenger to
21:5 His wife J came to him and
21:7 His wife J said to him,
21:8 So J wrote letters,
21:11 there — did what J asked them
21:14 sent ⌊this message⌋ to J:
21:15 J received the message and
21:23 spoke ⌊through Elijah⌋ about J:
21:23 "The dogs will eat J inside the
2Ki 9:7 I will get revenge on J for
9:10 Dogs will eat J inside the
9:30 in Jezreel, J heard about it.
9:37 be able to say that this is J.'"
Rev 2:20 You tolerate that woman J,

Jezebel's (4)

1Ki 18:19 of Asherah who eat at J table.
2Ki 9:36 He said, 'Dogs will eat J body
9:37 J corpse will be like manure on
Rev 2:24 J teaching, who haven't learned

Jezer (3)

Gen 46:24 Jahzeel, Guni, J, and Shillem.
Num 26:49 the family of J, and the family
1Ch 7:13 Jahziel, Guni, J, and Shallum.

Jeziel (1)

1Ch 12:3 Azmaveth's sons J and Pelet,

Jezrahiah (1)

Neh 12:42 sang under the direction of J.

Jezreel (48)

Jos 15:56 J, Jokdeam, Zanoah,
17:16 and in the valley of J have
19:18 Their territory included J,
Jdg 6:33 and camped in the valley of J.
1Sm 25:43 also married Ahinoam of J.
27:3 Ahinoam from J and Abigail
29:1 camped at the spring in J.
29:11 while the Philistines went to J.
30:5 Ahinoam from J and Abigail
2Sm 2:2 Ahinoam from J and Abigail
2:9 J, Ephraim, and Benjamin,
3:2 ⌊born⌋ to Ahinoam from J.
4:4 and Jonathan came from J.
1Ki 4:12 was near Zarethan, below J,
18:45 into his chariot to go back to J.
18:46 of Ahab until they came to J.
21:1 Naboth from J had a vineyard
21:1 had a vineyard in J next
21:4 Naboth from J had told him.
21:6 "I talked to Naboth from J.
21:7 belonging to Naboth from J."
21:15 which Naboth from J refused
21:23 Jezebel inside the walls of J.
2Ki 8:29 King Joram returned to J to let
8:29 son Ahaziah went to J

2Ki 9:10 Jezebel inside the walls of **J**.
9:15 King Joram had returned to **J**
9:15 the city to take the news to **J**."
9:16 on his chariot and drove to **J**
9:17 tower in **J** saw Jehu's troops
9:21 that belonged to Naboth from **J**.
9:25 that belonged to Naboth from **J**.
9:30 When Jehu arrived in **J**,
9:36 body inside the walls of **J**.
9:37 fields surrounding **J** so that no
10:1 letters to the officials of **J**,
10:6 heirs to me in **J** about this time
10:7 and sent them to Jehu in **J**.
10:11 household who was left in **J**:
1Ch 3:1 ⌊born⌋ to Ahinoam from **J**.
4:3 in Etam: **J**, Ishma, and Idbash.
2Ch 22:6 Joram returned to **J** to let his
22:6 son Ahaziah went to **J**
Hos 1:4 told Hosea, "Name him **J**.
1:4 people they slaughtered at **J**.
1:5 and arrows in the valley of **J**."
1:11 The day of **J** will be a great
2:22 will produce many crops, **J**.

Jidlaph (1)

Gen 22:22 Kesed, Hazo, Pildash, **J**,

jingling (2)

Isa 3:16 **j** the ankle bracelets on their
3:18 things: **j** anklets, headbands,

Joab (133)

2Sm 2:13 Zeruiah's son **J** and David's
2:14 Abner said to **J**, "Let's have the
2:14 men hold a contest." **J** agreed.
2:18 there: **J**, Abishai, and Asahel.
2:22 How could I look your brother **J**
2:24 But **J** and Abishai chased
2:26 Then Abner called to **J**,
2:27 **J** answered, "I solemnly swear,
2:28 So **J** blew a ram's horn,
2:30 **J** returned from chasing Abner.
2:32 Then **J** and his men marched
3:22 Just then David's men and **J**
3:23 When **J** came back with the
3:24 Then **J** went to the king and
3:26 **J** sent messengers after Abner.
3:27 **J** took him aside in the
3:29 the blame fall on the head of **J**
3:30 (**J** and his brother Abishai
3:31 David told **J** and all the people
8:16 Zeruiah's son **J** was in charge
10:7 he sent **J** and all the elite
10:9 When **J** saw he was under
10:11 **J** said, "If the Arameans are too
10:13 Then **J** and his troops
10:14 So **J** stopped his campaign
11:1 David sent **J**, his mercenaries,
11:6 David sent a messenger to **J**,
11:6 So **J** sent Uriah to David.
11:7 David asked him how **J** and
11:11 and my commander **J** and Your
11:14 David wrote a letter to **J**
11:16 Since **J** had kept the city under
11:17 the city came out and fought **J**.
11:18 Then **J** sent ⌊a messenger⌋ to
11:22 to David everything **J** told him
11:25 is what you are to say to **J**,
12:26 Meanwhile, **J** fought against
14:1 **J**, Zeruiah's son, knew the king
14:2 So **J** sent ⌊someone⌋ to Tekoa
14:3 Then **J** told her exactly what to
14:19 "Did **J** put you up to this?"
14:19 Yes, your servant **J** ordered me
14:20 Your servant **J** has done this to
14:21 Then the king told **J**,
14:22 **J** quickly bowed down with his
14:23 So **J** went to Geshur and
14:29 So Absalom sent for **J** in order
14:29 but **J** refused to come.
14:31 Then **J** immediately went to
14:32 Absalom answered **J**,
14:33 **J** went to the king and told him
18:5 The king ordered **J**,
18:10 A man who saw this told **J**,
18:11 **J** said to the man who told him.
2Sm 18:12 But the man told **J**,
18:14 Then **J** said, "I shouldn't waste
18:16 **J** blew the ram's horn to stop
18:20 But **J** told him, "You won't be
18:21 Then **J** said to a man from
18:21 touching the ground in front of **J**
18:22 Zadok's son, spoke to **J** again,
18:22 **J** asked. "You won't be
18:23 "Run," **J** told him. So Ahimaaz
18:29 when **J** sent me away,
19:1 **J** was told, "The king is crying
19:5 Then **J** came into the house.
20:8 **J** wore a military uniform,
20:9 **J** asked Amasa. He took hold of
20:10 **J** stabbed him in the stomach,
20:10 Then **J** and his brother Abishai
20:11 "Anyone who favors **J** and is
20:11 David's side should follow **J**."
20:13 everyone followed **J** and
20:15 All the troops with **J** were
20:16 Tell **J** to come here so that I
20:17 and she asked, "Are you **J**?"
20:20 **J** answered, I don't wish to
20:21 "That's fine," the woman told **J**.
20:22 Sheba's head and threw it to **J**.
20:22 **J** went back to the king in
20:23 Now, **J** was put in charge of
23:37 armorbearer for Zeruiah's son **J**
24:2 King David said to **J**,
24:3 **J** responded to the king,
24:4 However, the king overruled **J**
24:9 **J** reported the census figures to
1Ki 1:7 his actions with **J** (son
1:19 and **J** the commander of the
1:41 When **J** heard the sound of the
2:5 "You know what **J** (Zeruiah's
2:5 **J** killed them. When there was
2:22 The priest Abiathar and **J**
2:28 The news reached **J**.
2:28 So **J** fled to the LORD's tent
2:29 After King Solomon heard that **J**
2:29 son of Jehoiada, to kill **J**.
2:30 he told **J**, "The king says,
2:30 **J** answered, "I'll die here."
2:30 to the king what **J** had said
2:31 the blood which **J** shed — from
2:32 **J** killed two honorable men
2:32 **J** did this without my father's
2:33 for their blood will fall on **J**
2:34 went and attacked **J**,
2:35 to replace **J** as commander of
11:15 **J**, the commander of the army,
11:16 (**J** and all Israel stayed there
11:21 with his ancestors and that **J**,
1Ch 2:16 were Abishai, **J**, and Asahel.
4:14 Seraiah was the father of **J**,
11:6 Zeruiah's son **J** was the first to
11:8 **J** rebuilt the rest of the city.
11:39 armorbearer for Zeruiah's son **J**
18:15 Zeruiah's son **J** was in charge
19:8 he sent **J** and all the elite
19:10 When **J** saw he was under
19:12 **J** said, "If the Arameans are too
19:14 Then **J** and his troops
19:15 So **J** returned to Jerusalem.
20:1 **J** led the army ⌊to war⌋.
20:1 **J** defeated Rabbah and tore it
21:2 David said to **J** and the leaders
21:3 **J** responded, "May the LORD
21:4 However, the king overruled **J**.
21:4 So **J** left, went throughout
21:5 **J** reported the census figures to
21:6 **J** didn't include Levi and
26:28 and **J** (son of Zeruiah) had
27:24 **J**, son of Zeruiah, started to
27:34 **J** was the commander of the
Ezr 2:6 that is, of Jeshua and **J**: 2,812
8:9 from the family of **J**:
Neh 7:11 that is, of Jeshua and **J**: 2,818

Joab's (21)

1Sm 26:6 son and **J** brother, "Who will go
2Sm 3:27 the blood of **J** brother Asahel.
3:29 of **J** family who have oozing
14:30 **J** field is next to mine.
14:30 **J** servants came to him ⌊in
2Sm 17:25 to take **J** place as commander
17:25 and sister of **J** mother Zeruiah.)
18:2 **J** command, another third under
18:2 another third under **J** brother
18:15 Then ten of **J** armorbearers
19:13 unless you are given **J** place
20:7 So **J** men, the Cherethites,
20:10 the sword in **J** ⌊left⌋ hand.
20:11 One of **J** young men stood
20:15 **J** army came and attacked him
23:18 **J** brother Abishai, was the
23:24 the thirty was **J** brother Asahel.
1Ch 11:20 **J** brother Abishai was the
11:26 men were **J** brother Asahel,
19:15 fled from **J** brother Abishai and
27:7 Asahel, **J** brother, was in

Joah (11)

2Ki 18:18 Shebnah the scribe, and **J**,
18:26 and **J** said to the field
18:37 Shebna the scribe, and **J**,
1Ch 6:21 Zimmah's son was **J**.
26:4 **J** (the third), Sachar (the fourth
2Ch 29:12 Gershon's descendants were **J**,
29:12 of Zimmah, and Eden, son of **J**.
34:8 the mayor of the city, and **J**,
Isa 36:3 Shebna the scribe, and **J**,
36:11 Then Eliakim, Shebna, and **J**
36:22 Shebna the scribe, and **J**,

Joahaz (1)

2Ch 34:8 the royal historian and son of **J**,

Joah's (1)

1Ch 6:21 **J** son was Iddo. Iddo's son was

Joanan (1)

Luk 3:27 son of **J**, son of Rhesa, son of

Joanna (2)

Luk 8:3 **J**, whose husband Chusa was
24:10 were Mary from Magdala, **J**,

Joash (45)

Jdg 6:11 to **J** from Abiezer's family.
6:29 "Gideon, son of **J**, did this."
6:30 Then the men of the city told **J**,
6:31 But **J** said to everyone
7:14 of Gideon, son of **J**, from Israel.
8:13 Gideon, son of **J**, returned from
8:29 Jerubbaal, son of **J**,
8:32 Gideon, son of **J**, died at a very
8:32 tomb of his father **J** at Ophrah,
1Ki 22:26 of the city, and to **J**, the prince.
2Ki 11:2 took Ahaziah's son **J**.
11:2 Athaliah. So **J** wasn't killed
11:19 Then **J** sat on the royal throne.
11:21 **J** was seven years old when
12:1 **J** began to rule in Jehu's
12:2 **J** did what the LORD
12:4 **J** told the priests, "⌊Collect⌋ all
12:7 So King **J** called for Jehoiada
12:18 So King **J** of Judah took all the
12:19 Isn't everything else about **J** —
13:1 Ahaziah's son King **J** of Judah
14:1 Amaziah, son of **J** of Judah,
14:3 his father **J** had done.
14:13 son of **J** and grandson of
1Ch 3:11 Ahaziah's son was **J**.
4:22 Jokim, **J**, Saraph, and the men
7:8 Becher's sons were Zemirah, **J**,
12:3 Ahiezer was the leader, then **J**
27:28 Gedor for storing olive oil: **J**
2Ch 18:25 of the city, and to **J**, the prince.
22:11 took Ahaziah's son **J**.
22:11 she hid **J** from Athaliah.
22:12 **J** was with the priests.
24:1 **J** was 7 years old when he
24:2 **J** did what the LORD
24:3 Jehoiada got **J** two wives,
24:3 and **J** had sons and daughters.
24:4 After this, **J** wanted to renovate
24:22 King **J** did not remember how
24:23 the Aramean army attacked **J**.
24:24 ⌊the LORD's⌋ judgment on **J**.
24:25 They killed **J** in his bed.

2Ch 25:23 son of **J** and grandson of
Hos 1:1 son of **J**, was king of Israel.
Amo 1:1 King Jeroboam, son of **J**.

Joash's (10)

Jdg 6:11 **J** son Gideon was beating out
2Ki 12:6 But by **J** twenty-third year as
12:21 **J** officials Jozacar,
13:10 In **J** thirty-seventh year as king
14:17 **J** son King Amaziah of Judah
14:23 **J** son Amaziah was in his
1Ch 3:12 **J** son was Amaziah.
2Ch 24:24 but the LORD handed **J** large
24:24 **J** soldiers had abandoned
25:25 **J** son King Amaziah of Judah

Job; job (86)

Exo 36:7 more than enough to do the **j**.
Jdg 8:21 It's a man's **j**!" So Gideon got up
2Ch 19:11 Be strong, and do your **j**.
Ezr 5:8 are doing an excellent **j**
Neh 4:15 person performed his own **j**.
Job 1:1 A man named **J** lived in Uz.
1:5 **J** would send for them in order
1:5 **J** thought, "My children may
1:5 **J** offered sacrifices for them all
1:8 thought about my servant **J**?
1:9 "Haven't you given **J** a reason
1:14 a messenger came to **J**.
1:20 **J** stood up, tore his robe ⌊in
1:22 Through all this **J** did not sin or
2:3 thought about my servant **J**?
2:7 LORD's presence and struck **J**
2:8 **J** took a piece of broken
2:11 with **J** and comfort him.
3:1 After all this, **J** ⌊finally⌋
3:2 **J** said,
4:1 from Teman replied ⌊to **J**⌋,
6:1 Then **J** replied ⌊to his friends⌋,
8:1 from Shuah replied ⌊to **J**⌋,
9:1 Then **J** replied ⌊to his friends⌋,
11:1 from Naama replied ⌊to **J**⌋,
12:1 Then **J** replied ⌊to his friends⌋,
15:1 from Teman replied ⌊to **J**⌋,
16:1 Then **J** replied ⌊to his friends⌋,
18:1 from Shuah replied ⌊to **J**⌋,
19:1 Then **J** replied ⌊to his friends⌋,
20:1 from Naama replied ⌊to **J**⌋,
21:1 Then **J** replied ⌊to his friends⌋,
22:1 from Teman replied ⌊to **J**⌋,
23:1 Then **J** replied ⌊to his friends⌋,
25:1 from Shuah replied ⌊to **J**⌋,
26:1 Then **J** replied ⌊to his friends⌋,
27:1 **J** continued his poems and
29:1 **J** continued his poems and
32:1 three men stopped answering **J**
32:1 Job because **J** thought
32:2 became very angry with **J**
32:2 with Job because **J** thought
32:4 Elihu waited as they spoke to **J**
32:6 replied ⌊to **J**⌋, "I am young,
32:12 but none of you refuted **J**.
32:14 **J** did not choose his words to
33:1 "Please, **J**, listen to my words
33:31 "Pay attention, **J**! Listen to me!
34:1 to speak ⌊to **J** and his friends⌋,
34:5 because **J** has said,
34:7 What person is like **J**,
34:35 '**J** speaks without knowledge.
34:36 "My Father, let **J** be thoroughly
35:1 to speak ⌊to **J** and his friends⌋,
35:16 **J** opens his mouth for no good
36:1 continued to speak ⌊to **J**⌋,
37:14 "Open your ears to this, **J**.
38:1 Then the LORD answered **J**
40:1 The LORD responded to **J**,
40:3 **J** answered the LORD,
40:6 Then the LORD responded to **J**
42:1 Then **J** answered the LORD,
42:7 had said those things to **J**,
42:7 me as my servant **J** has done.
42:8 Go to my servant **J**,
42:8 My servant **J** will pray for you.
42:8 me as my servant **J** has done."
42:10 After **J** prayed for his friends,
42:16 **J** lived 140 years after this.
Job 42:17 Then at a very old age, **J** died.
Ecc 2:26 he gives the **j** of gathering and
Jer 50:25 LORD of Armies has a **j**
Eze 14:14 and **J** — were in that country,
14:16 and **J** could rescue their own
14:18 and **J** could rescue their sons
14:20 Noah, Daniel, and **J** could,
Mat 24:46 doing this **j** when he comes.
25:21 "His master replied, 'Good **j**!
25:23 "His master replied, 'Good **j**!
Luk 12:43 doing this **j** when he comes.
14:30 to build but couldn't finish the **j**.'
15:15 So he got a **j** from someone in
16:3 My master is taking my **j** away
16:4 homes when I've lost my **j**.'
19:17 "The king said to him, 'Good **j**!
Eph 4:16 each and every part does its **j**,

Jobab (9)

Gen 10:29 Ophir, Havilah, and **J**.
36:33 After Bela died, **J**, son of Zerah
36:34 After **J** died, Husham from the
Jos 11:1 he sent messengers to King **J**
1Ch 1:23 Ophir, Havilah, and **J**.
1:44 After Bela died, **J**, son of Zerah
1:45 After **J** died, Husham from the
8:9 **J**, Zibia, Mesha, Malcam,
8:18 Ishmerai, Izliah, and **J**.

Job's (12)

Job 1:13 One day when **J** sons and
2:10 Through all this **J** lips did not
2:11 When **J** three friends heard
31:40 This is the end of **J** words
32:3 very angry with **J** three friends
32:15 "**J** friends have been
42:9 the LORD accepted **J** prayer
42:10 the LORD restored **J** prosperity
42:12 latter years of **J** life more than
42:15 as beautiful as **J** daughters.
Jas 5:11 have heard about **J** endurance.
5:11 that the Lord ended **J** suffering

jobs (2)

Exo 1:14 All the **j** the Egyptians gave
2Ch 34:13 the workmen on the various **j**.

Jochebed (2)

Exo 6:20 married his father's sister **J**.
Num 26:59 name of Amram's wife was **J**,

Joda (1)

Luk 3:26 son of Josech, son of **J**,

Joed (1)

Neh 11:7 who was the son of **J**,

Joel (20)

1Sm 8:2 of his firstborn son was **J**;
1Ch 4:35 **J**, Jehu (son of Joshibiah,
5:8 and great-grandson of **J**).
5:12 from Gad's first son **J**.
6:28 Samuel's sons were **J**,
6:33 Heman was the son of **J**,
6:36 who was the son of **J**,
7:3 Obadiah, **J**, and Isshiah.
11:38 **J** (son of Nathan), Mibhar (son
15:7 Gershom's descendants was **J**,
15:11 Asaiah, **J**, Shemaiah, Eliel,
15:17 appointed Heman, son of **J**,
23:8 the first, then Zetham, and **J**.
26:22 Jehiel's sons Zetham and **J**.
27:20 Manasseh: **J**, son of Pedaiah
2Ch 29:12 Amasai, and **J**, son of Azariah.
Ezr 10:43 Zebina, Jaddai, **J**, and Benaiah
Neh 11:9 **J**, son of Zichri, was in charge,
Joe 1:1 is what the LORD said to **J**,
Act 2:16 the prophet **J** spoke about:

Joelah (1)

1Ch 12:7 and **J** and Zebadiah,

Joel's (1)

1Ch 5:4 **J** son was Shemaiah.

Joezer (1)

1Ch 12:6 Elkanah, Isshiah, Azarel, **J**,

Jogbehah (2)

Num 32:35 Atroth Shophan, Jazer, **J**,
Jdg 8:11 east of Nobah and **J**,

Jogli (1)

Num 34:22 Bukki, son of **J**, the leader of

Joha (2)

1Ch 8:16 Michael, Ishpah, and **J**.
11:45 and his brother **J** the Tizite,

Johanan (25)

2Ki 25:23 Nethaniah), **J** (son of Kareah),
1Ch 3:15 Josiah's firstborn son was **J**,
3:24 Akkub, **J**, Delaiah, and Anani.
6:9 Azariah was the father of **J**.
6:10 **J** was the father of Azariah.
12:4 **J**, and Jozabad from Gederah,
12:12 The eighth was **J**.
Ezr 8:12 from the family of Azgad: **J**,
Neh 12:22 the time of Eliashib, Joiada, **J**,
12:23 of Chronicles until the time of **J**,
Jer 40:8 **J** and Jonathan (sons of
40:13 Kareah's son **J** and all the army
40:15 Then **J**, Kareah's son,
40:16 son of Ahikam, told **J**,
41:11 When Kareah's son **J** and all
41:13 Ishmael saw Kareah's son **J**
41:14 and ran to Kareah's son **J**.
41:15 of his men escaped from **J**
41:16 Then Kareah's son **J** and all
41:16 **J** brought back men,
42:1 along with Kareah's son **J**
42:8 called Kareah's son **J**,
43:2 of Hoshaiah), **J** (son of Kareah),
43:4 So **J** (son of Kareah),
43:5 **J** (son of Kareah) and all the

John (159)

Mat 3:1 Later, **J** the Baptizer appeared
3:4 **J** wore clothes made from
3:13 River to be baptized by **J**.
3:14 But **J** tried to stop him and said,
3:15 Then **J** gave in to him.
4:12 When Jesus heard that **J** had
4:21 other brothers, James and **J**,
10:2 James and his brother **J**,
11:2 When **J** was in prison,
11:4 and tell **J** what you hear and
11:7 spoke to the crowds about **J**.
11:10 **J** is the one about whom
11:11 is greater than **J** the Baptizer.
11:11 of heaven is greater than **J**.
11:12 From the time of **J** the Baptizer
11:13 prophesied up to the time of **J**.
11:14 **J** is the Elijah who was to
11:18 "**J** came neither eating nor
14:2 "This is **J** the Baptizer!
14:3 Herod had arrested **J**,
14:4 **J** had been telling Herod,
14:5 So Herod wanted to kill **J**.
14:5 they thought **J** was a prophet.
14:8 "Give me the head of **J** the
14:13 When Jesus heard about **J**,
16:14 say you are **J** the Baptizer,
17:1 and **J** (the brother of James)
17:13 talking about **J** the Baptizer.
21:26 people think of **J** as a prophet."
21:32 **J** came to you and showed you
Mar 1:4 **J** the Baptizer was in the
1:6 **J** was dressed in clothes made
1:9 Galilee and was baptized by **J**
1:14 After **J** had been put in prison,
1:19 he saw James and **J**,
1:29 James and **J** went with them.
3:17 James and his brother **J**
5:37 the two brothers James and **J**.
6:14 Some people were saying, "**J**
6:17 sent men who had arrested **J**,
6:18 **J** had been telling Herod,
6:19 held a grudge against **J**
6:20 because Herod was afraid of **J**.

Mar 6:20 Herod knew that **J** was a fair
6:20 When he listened to **J**,
6:24 for the head of **J** the Baptizer."
6:25 you to give me the head of **J**
8:28 say you are **J** the Baptizer,
9:2 and **J** and led them up a high
9:38 **J** said to Jesus, "Teacher,
10:35 James and **J**, sons of
10:41 irritated with James and **J**.
11:32 All the people thought of **J** as a
13:3 buildings, Peter, James, **J**,
14:33 He took Peter, James, and **J**
Luk 1:13 and you will name him **J**.
1:60 His name will be **J**."
1:63 and wrote, "His name is **J**."
1:80 The child **J** grew and became
3:2 priests that God spoke to **J**,
3:3 **J** traveled throughout the region
3:7 coming to be baptized by **J**.
3:15 whether **J** was the Messiah.
3:16 **J** replied to all of them,
3:19 **J** spoke out against the ruler
3:20 he locked **J** in prison.
5:10 James and **J**, who were
6:14 James, **J**, Philip, Bartholomew,
7:18 Then **J** called two of his
7:20 "**J** the Baptizer sent us to ask
7:22 and tell **J** what you have seen
7:24 spoke to the crowds about **J**.
7:27 **J** is the one about whom
7:28 no one is greater than **J**.
7:28 of God is greater than **J**.
7:29 tax collectors, heard **J**.
7:29 right by letting **J** baptize them.
7:33 **J** the Baptizer has come
8:51 him except Peter, **J**, James,
9:7 saying that **J** had come back
9:19 say you are **J** the Baptizer,
9:28 said this, Jesus took Peter, **J**,
9:49 **J** replied, "Master, we saw
9:54 James and **J**, his disciples,
11:1 pray as **J** taught his disciples."
16:16 ⌊in force⌋ until the time of **J**.
20:6 that **J** was a prophet."
20:7 they didn't know who gave **J**
22:8 Jesus sent Peter and **J** and
Jon 1:6 God sent a man named **J** to be
1:7 **J** came to declare the truth
1:8 **J** was not the light,
1:15 (**J** declared the truth about him
1:20 **J** didn't refuse to answer.
1:21 **J** answered, "No, I'm not."
1:21 the prophet?" **J** replied, "No."
1:23 **J** said, "I'm a voice crying out
1:25 They asked **J**, "Why do you
1:26 **J** answered them, "I baptize
1:28 where **J** was baptizing.
1:29 **J** saw Jesus coming toward
1:32 **J** said, "I saw the Spirit come
1:35 The next day **J** was standing
1:36 **J** saw Jesus walk by.
1:36 **J** said, "Look! This is the Lamb
1:37 When the two disciples heard **J**
1:40 heard **J** and followed Jesus.
1:42 said, "You are Simon, son of **J**.
3:23 **J** was baptizing in Aenon,
3:23 came to **J** to be baptized,
3:24 since **J** had not yet been put in
3:26 So they went to **J** and asked
3:27 **J** answered, "People can't
4:1 more disciples than **J**.
5:33 sent people to **J** ⌊the Baptizer⌋,
5:35 **J** was a lamp that gave off
10:40 where **J** first baptized people.
10:41 "**J** didn't perform any miracles,
10:41 but everything **J** said about this
21:15 Simon Peter, "Simon, son of **J**,
21:16 son of **J**, do you love me?"
21:17 son of **J**, do you love me?"
Act 1:5 **J** baptized with water,
1:13 **J**, James, Andrew, Philip,
1:22 that **J** was baptizing people
3:1 Peter and **J** were going to the
3:3 that Peter and **J** were about
3:4 Peter and **J** stared at him.
3:8 He went with Peter and **J** into
Act 3:11 wouldn't let go of Peter and **J**.
4:1 Peter and **J** while they were
4:2 Peter and **J** were teaching the
4:3 they put Peter and **J** in jail until
4:6 Caiaphas, **J**, Alexander,
4:7 They made Peter and **J** stand
4:13 Peter and **J** had no education
4:14 standing with Peter and **J**,
4:15 So they ordered Peter and **J** to
4:18 They called Peter and **J** and
4:19 Peter and **J** answered them,
4:21 any way to punish Peter and **J**.
4:23 Peter and **J** were released,
8:14 they sent Peter and **J** to them.
8:15 Peter and **J** went to Samaria
8:17 Then Peter and **J** placed their
8:18 So he offered Peter and **J**
10:37 began in Galilee after **J** spread
11:16 '**J** baptized with water,
12:2 He had James, the brother of **J**,
13:24 **J** ⌊the Baptizer⌋ told everyone
13:25 When **J** was finishing his work,
18:25 about the baptism **J** performed.
19:4 **J** told people to believe in
Gal 2:9 James, Cephas, and **J** (who
Rev 1:1 his angel to his servant **J**.
1:2 **J** testified about what he saw:
1:4 From **J** to the seven churches
1:9 I am **J**, your brother. I share
22:8 I, **J**, heard and saw these

John Mark (6)

Act 12:12 the mother of **J**.
12:25 They brought **J** with them.
13:5 **J** had gone along to help
13:13 **J** deserted them there and
15:37 wanted to take **J** along.
15:38 **J** had deserted them in

John's (24)

Mat 9:14 Then **J** disciples came to
9:18 he was talking to **J** disciples.
11:4 Jesus answered **J** disciples,
14:10 He had **J** head cut off in prison.
14:12 **J** disciples came for the body
21:25 Did **J** right to baptize come
Mar 2:18 **J** disciples and the Pharisees
2:18 "Why do **J** disciples and the
6:16 "I had **J** head cut off,
6:27 ordered him to bring **J** head.
6:27 guard cut off **J** head in prison.
6:29 When **J** disciples heard about
11:30 Did **J** right to baptize come
Luk 5:33 They said to him, "**J** disciples
7:18 **J** disciples told him about all
7:22 Jesus answered **J** disciples,
7:24 When **J** messengers had left,
9:9 "I had **J** head cut off.
20:4 did **J** right to baptize come from
Jon 1:19 This was **J** answer when the
3:25 Some of **J** disciples had an
5:36 on my behalf than **J** testimony.
Act 19:3 They answered, "**J** baptism.
19:4 Paul said, "**J** baptism was a

Joiada (5)

Neh 3:6 **J**, Paseah's son, Besodeiah's
12:10 Eliashib was the father of **J**.
12:11 **J** was the father of Jonathan.
12:22 time of Eliashib, **J**, Johanan,
13:28 (**J** was the son of the chief

Joiada's (2)

Neh 13:28 Even one of **J** sons was a
13:28 I chased **J** son away from me.

Joiakim (4)

Neh 12:10 Jeshua was the father of **J**.
12:10 **J** was the father of Eliashib.
12:12 At the time of **J**, these were the
12:26 They lived in the days of **J**,

Joiarib (5)

Ezr 8:16 were leading men) and for **J**
Neh 11:5 who was the son of **J**,
11:10 Jedaiah (son of **J**),
Neh 12:6 Shemaiah, **J**, Jedaiah,
12:19 from **J**, Mattenai; from Jedaiah,

join (54)

Gen 34:30 If they **j** forces against me and
49:6 Do not let me **j** their assembly.
49:29 "I am about to **j** my ancestors
Exo 1:10 they will **j** our enemies,
23:1 Don't **j** forces with wicked
Num 18:2 your ancestor's tribe to **j** you
18:4 They will **j** you and do
20:24 "Aaron must now **j** his
20:26 there and **j** ⌊his ancestors⌋."
27:13 After you see it, you, too, will **j**
31:2 After that you will **j** your
Dtr 13:9 Then all the other people will **j**
17:7 then all the other people will **j**
23:1 penis is cut off may never **j**
23:2 from an illicit union may not **j**
23:2 No descendant of his may **j** the
23:3 or Moabites may not **j**
23:3 one descendant of theirs may **j**
23:4 They cannot **j** because they
23:8 Their grandchildren may **j** the
32:50 you will die and **j** your
1Ki 1:8 fighting men did not **j** Adonijah.
2Ki 23:1 Judah and Jerusalem to **j** him.
1Ch 12:8 Some men left Gad to **j** David
12:17 then you may **j** me.
12:19 ⌊Saul's army⌋ to **j** David when
12:20 Manasseh deserted to **j** him:
13:2 so that they may **j** us.
2Ch 18:3 ⌊We will **j**⌋ your troops in
34:29 Judah and Jerusalem to **j** him.
34:32 in Jerusalem and Benjamin **j**
Est 9:27 for anyone who would **j** them.
Psa 1:1 or **j** the company of mockers.
49:19 he must **j** the generation of his
94:21 They **j** forces to take the lives
Pro 1:14 **J** us. We'll split the loot equally."
Ecc 9:3 After that, they **j** the dead.
Isa 14:1 Foreigners will **j** them and
Eze 26:20 who descend to the grave to **j**
31:14 the earth to **j** those who have
31:16 to the grave to **j** those who had
31:17 in the grave to **j** others killed
32:19 down and **j** the godless people.'
37:17 Then **j** both sticks together so
Dan 11:34 who are not sincere will **j** them.
Zec 2:11 On that day many nations will **j**
Act 5:13 other people dared to **j** them,
9:26 he tried to **j** the disciples.
17:4 Jews were persuaded to **j** Paul
17:15 and Timothy to **j** Paul as soon
Rom 15:30 to **j** me in my struggle.
2Ti 1:8 Instead, by God's power, **j** me
2:3 **J** me in suffering like a good
1Pe 4:4 that you no longer **j** them

joined (39)

Gen 14:3 The five kings **j** forces and met
25:8 he **j** his ancestors in death.
25:17 He **j** his ancestors in death.
35:29 He **j** his ancestors in death at a
49:33 He took his last breath and **j**
Num 14:35 who have **j** forces against me.
16:2 These four men were **j** by 250
16:11 followers have **j** forces against
25:3 Since the Israelites **j** in
25:5 must kill the men who have **j**
26:9 They **j** Korah's followers when
27:3 followers who **j** forces against
Jos 9:2 they **j** together to fight Joshua
Jdg 2:10 That whole generation had **j**
1Sm 14:21 stationed in the camp now **j**
17:13 Jesse's three oldest sons **j**
17:14 The three oldest **j** Saul's army.
22:2 or bitter about life **j** him,
2Ki 23:3 all the people **j** in the promise.
1Ch 12:23 The men **j** David at Hebron to
2Ch 20:36 Jehoshaphat **j** him in making
Ezr 3:9 **j** Henadad's family
Neh 10:29 They **j** their relatives,
Job 41:17 Each is **j** to the other.
Psa 83:8 Even Assyria has **j** them.
106:28 They **j** in worshiping the god

Isa 14:20 You won't be **j** by the kings in
56:3 Foreigners who have **j** the
56:6 ⌊the foreigners who have **j**
Mat 19:6 what God has **j** together."
Mar 10:9 what God has **j** together."
Act 1:14 They were **j** by some women,
1:14 and they were **j** by his brothers.
1:26 and **j** the eleven apostles.
5:36 about four hundred men **j** him.
16:22 The crowd **j** in the attack
17:34 Some men **j** him and became
20:6 Five days later we **j** them in
Gal 2:13 Jewish Christians also **j** him

joining (1)

2Co 1:11 since you are also **j** to help us

joins (2)

1Ch 12:19 deserts and **j** his master Saul.")
Hos 7:5 and the king **j** mockers.

joint (2)

Psa 22:14 and all my bones are out of **j**.
Eph 4:16 it through the support of every **j**

joints (3)

Dan 5:6 His hip **j** became loose,
Col 2:19 given by the **j** and ligaments.
Heb 4:12 the place where **j** and marrow

Jokdeam (1)

Jos 15:56 Jezreel, **J**, Zanoah,

joke (4)

Job 30:9 I have become a **j** to them.
Eze 22:4 nations and a **j** in every land.
Hab 1:10 of kings and treat rulers as a **j**.
Mar 15:29 their heads and said, "What a **j**!

jokes (3)

Jer 10:15 They are worthless **j**.
51:18 They are worthless **j**.
Eph 5:4 or obscene **j** should be

Jokim (1)

1Ch 4:22 **J**, Joash, Saraph, and the men

joking (3)

Gen 19:14 But they thought he was **j**.
Pro 26:19 and says, "I was only **j**!"
Act 17:32 some began **j** about it,

jokingly (1)

Act 2:13 Others said **j**, "They're drunk

Jokmeam (2)

1Ki 4:12 to Abel Meholah and over to **J**.)
1Ch 6:68 **J** with its pastureland,

Jokneam (3)

Jos 12:22 the king of **J** in Carmel,
19:11 and the river near **J**.
21:34 with pasturelands: **J**, Kartah,

Jokshan (3)

Gen 25:2 **J**, Medan, Midian, Ishbak,
25:3 **J** was the father of Sheba and
1Ch 1:32 **J**, Medan, Midian, Ishbak,

Jokshan's (1)

1Ch 1:32 **J** sons were Sheba and Dedan.

Joktan (5)

Gen 10:25 His brother's name was **J**.
10:26 **J** was the father of Almodad,
1Ch 1:19 His brother's name was **J**.
1:20 **J** was the father of Almodad,
1:23 All these were sons of **J**.

Joktan's (1)

Gen 10:29 These were **J** sons

Joktheel (2)

Jos 15:38 Dilean, Mizpah, **J**,
2Ki 14:7 He gave it the name **J**,

Jonadab (12)

2Sm 13:3 had a friend by the name of **J**,
13:3 **J** was a very clever man.
13:5 Then **J** told him, "Lie down on
13:32 Then **J**, the son of David's
13:35 Then **J** told the king,
Jer 35:6 because our ancestor **J**,
35:8 have obeyed our ancestor **J**,
35:10 our ancestor **J** ordered
35:14 **J**, Rechab's son, ordered his
35:16 The descendants of **J**,
35:18 the order of your ancestor **J**,
35:19 A descendant of **J**,

Jonah (33)

2Ki 14:25 predicted through his servant **J**,
Jnh 1:1 The LORD spoke his word to **J**,
1:3 **J** immediately tried to run away
1:5 Now, **J** had gone below deck
1:7 that **J** was responsible.
1:9 **J** answered them, "I'm a
1:10 They asked **J**, "Why have you
1:11 So they asked **J**, "What should
1:15 Then they took **J** and threw
1:17 sent a big fish to swallow **J**.
1:17 **J** was inside the fish for three
2:1 From inside the fish **J** prayed
2:2 **J** prayed: "I called to the LORD
2:10 and it spit **J** out onto the shore.
3:1 the LORD spoke his word to **J**
3:3 **J** immediately went to Nineveh
3:4 **J** entered the city and walked
4:1 **J** was very upset about this,
4:5 **J** left the city and sat down
4:6 made a plant grow up beside **J**
4:6 **J** was very happy with the
4:9 Then God asked **J**,
4:9 **J** answered, "I have every right
Mat 12:39 get is the sign of the prophet **J**.
12:40 Just as **J** was in the belly of a
12:41 when **J** spoke his message.
12:41 someone greater than **J** is here!
16:4 they will be given is that of **J**."
16:17 replied, "Simon, son of **J**,
Luk 11:29 they will get is the sign of **J**.
11:30 Just as **J** became a miraculous
11:32 when **J** spoke his message,
11:32 someone greater than **J** is here!

Jonah's (1)

Jnh 4:8 The sun beat down on **J** head

Jonam (1)

Luk 3:30 son of **J**, son of Eliakim,

Jonathan (112)

Jdg 18:30 **J** (son of Gershom and
1Sm 13:2 stationed with **J** at Gibeah
13:3 **J** defeated the Philistine troops
13:16 Saul, his son **J**, and the troops
13:22 who were with Saul and **J**.
13:22 Saul and his son **J** had them.
14:1 One day Saul's son **J** said to
14:1 But **J** didn't tell his father ⌊he
14:3 troops didn't know **J** had left.
14:4 pass where **J** searched
14:6 **J** said to his armorbearer,
14:8 **J** continued, "Listen,
14:12 of the military post said to **J**
14:12 **J** told his armorbearer,
14:13 **J** climbed up ⌊the cliff⌋,
14:13 **J** struck down the Philistines.
14:14 In their first slaughter **J** and his
14:17 They looked and found that **J**
14:21 who were with Saul and **J**.
14:27 **J** hadn't heard that his father
14:29 **J** answered, "My father has
14:39 even if it is my son **J** ⌊who did
14:40 and my son **J** and I will stand
14:41 **J** and Saul were chosen,
14:42 me and my son **J**," Saul said.
14:42 Then **J** was chosen.
14:43 "Tell me," Saul asked **J**.
14:43 So **J** told him, "I tasted a little
14:44 this curse if you do not die, **J**!"
1Sm 14:45 "Should **J** die after he has won
14:45 troops rescued **J** from death.
14:49 Saul's sons were **J**,
18:1 After that, **J** became David's
18:3 So **J** made a pledge of mutual
18:4 **J** took off the coat he had on
19:1 Saul told his son **J** and all his
19:1 But Saul's son **J** was very fond
19:4 So **J** spoke well of David to his
19:6 Saul listened to **J**,
19:7 **J** told David all of this.
19:7 Then **J** took David to Saul.
20:1 Ramah, came to **J**, and asked,
20:2 **J** answered, You're not going to
20:3 '**J** must not know about this.
20:4 **J** said to David, "I'll do
20:9 **J** answered, If I knew for sure
20:11 **J** said, "Let's go out into the
20:12 ⌊is my witness⌋," **J** continued,
20:17 Once again **J** swore an oath to
20:18 Moon Festival," **J** told him,
20:25 seat by the wall, while **J** stood.
20:27 Saul asked his son **J**,
20:28 **J** answered Saul,
20:30 Then Saul got angry with **J**.
20:30 he called **J**. "I know you've
20:32 **J** asked his father,
20:33 Then **J** knew his father was
20:34 **J** got up from the table very
20:34 because **J** had been humiliated
20:35 In the morning **J** went out to the
20:35 **J** had a young boy with him.
20:36 and **J** shot the arrow over him.
20:37 landed⌋, **J** called after him,
20:38 **J** added, "Quick! Hurry up!
20:39 but **J** and David understood.
20:40 Then **J** gave his weapons to
20:42 **J** told David. "We have both
20:42 and **J** went into the city.
23:16 Saul's son **J** came to David at
23:18 in Horesh, and **J** went home.
31:2 They killed **J**, Abinadab,
2Sm 1:4 and his son **J** are dead too."
1:5 Saul and his son **J** are dead?"
1:12 his son **J**, the LORD's army,
1:17 for Saul and his son **J**.
1:23 Saul and **J** were loved and
1:25 On your hills **J** was killed!
1:26 over you, my brother **J**.
4:4 In addition, Saul's son **J** had a
4:4 Saul and **J** came from Jezreel.
9:3 "**J** has a son who is disabled,"
9:6 When Mephibosheth (son of **J**
15:27 and Abiathar's son **J** with you.
15:36 and Abiathar has **J**.
17:17 **J** and Ahimaaz were waiting at
17:18 But a young man saw **J** and
17:20 "Where are Ahimaaz and **J**?"
21:7 name between David and **J**,
21:12 of Saul and of his son **J** from
21:13 up the bones of Saul and **J**,
21:14 the bones of Saul and his son **J**
21:21 When he challenged Israel, **J**,
23:33 **J** ⌊son of⌋ Shammah the
1Ki 1:42 He was still speaking when **J**,
1:43 **J** answered Adonijah.
1Ch 2:32 brother) were Jether and **J**.
8:33 Saul was the father of **J**,
9:39 Saul was the father of **J**,
10:2 They killed **J**, Abinadab,
11:34 **J** (son of Shage the Hararite),
20:7 When he challenged Israel, **J**,
27:25 watchtowers: **J**, son of Uzziah
27:32 David's uncle **J**, an educated
27:32 **J** and Jehiel, son of Hachmoni,
Ezr 8:6 Ebed, son of **J**, with 50 males
10:15 (Only **J**, Asahel's son,
10:15 supported **J** and Jahzeiah.)
Neh 12:11 Joiada was the father of **J**.
12:11 **J** was the father of Jaddua.
12:14 from Malluchi, **J**; Joseph;
12:35 who was the son of **J**,
Jer 40:8 Johanan and **J** (sons of

Jonathan's (14)

1Sm 14:41 If this sin is mine or my son **J**,

1Sm 20:16 At that time, if J name is cut off
20:37 where J arrow ⌊had landed⌋,
20:38 J young servant gathered the
2Sm 1:22 J bow did not turn away,
9:1 can show kindness for J sake?
9:7 kindness for your father J sake.
21:7 J son and Saul's grandson,
1Ch 2:33 J sons were Peleth and Zaza.
8:34 J son was Meribbaal,
9:40 J son was Meribbaal,
Jer 37:15 J house, which had been
37:20 return me to the scribe J house,
38:26 not to send me back to J house

Joppa (17)

Jos 19:46 the border passing in front of J.
2Ch 2:16 send them to you in J by sea.
Ezr 3:7 Lebanon to J as King Cyrus
Jnh 1:3 He went to J and found a ship
Act 9:36 Tabitha lived in the city of J.
9:38 Lydda is near the city of J.
9:38 They begged Peter, "Hurry to J!
9:42 spread throughout the city of J,
9:43 Peter stayed in J for a number
10:5 now to the city of J,
10:8 to them and sent them to J.
10:9 way and coming close to J,
10:23 disciples from J went along.
10:32 So send messengers to J,
11:5 "I was praying in the city of J
11:12 Six believers ⌊from J⌋ went
11:13 'Send messengers to J,

Jorah (1)

Ezr 2:18 of J: 112

Jorai (1)

1Ch 5:13 J, Jacan, Zia, and Eber.

Joram (36)

2Sm 8:10 he sent his son J to greet King
8:10 J brought articles of gold,
2Ki 1:17 J succeeded him as king
3:1 J, son of Ahab, became king of
3:3 J would not turn away from
3:6 King J immediately left
3:8 J asked, "Which road should
8:16 J (Ahab's son) was in his fifth
8:25 J (Ahab's son) was in his
8:28 went with Ahab's son J
8:28 the Arameans wounded J.
8:29 King J returned to Jezreel to let
8:29 to Jezreel to see Ahab's son J,
9:14 of Nimshi, plotted against J.
9:14 (J and all Israel were guarding
9:15 But King J had returned to
9:16 to Jezreel because J was lying
9:16 of Judah had come to see J.)
9:17 So J said, "Take a chariot
9:19 Then J sent out a second
9:21 to the chariot," J ordered.
9:21 When that was done, King J of
9:22 When J saw Jehu,
9:23 As J turned his chariot around
9:24 his bow and shot J between
9:29 in the eleventh year that J,
1Ch 3:11 Jehoshaphat's son was J.
26:25 his great-grandson was J.
2Ch 22:5 went with Ahab's son King J
22:5 the Arameans wounded J.
22:6 J returned to Jezreel to let his
22:6 to Jezreel to see Ahab's son J,
22:7 downfall when he went to J.
22:7 He went with J to meet Jehu,
Mat 1:8 Jehoshaphat the father of J,
1:8 J the father of Uzziah,

Joram's (2)

1Ch 3:11 J son was Ahaziah.
26:25 J son was Zichri; his grandson

Jordan (204)

Gen 13:10 He saw that the whole J Plain
13:11 Lot chose the whole J Plain for
32:10 when I crossed the J River,
50:10 on the east side of the J River,
50:11 side of the J was named Abel
Num 13:29 Sea and all along the J River."
22:1 of Moab east of the J River.
26:3 near the J River across from
26:63 near the J River across from
31:12 near the J River across from
32:5 Don't make us cross the J
32:19 on the other side of the J River,
32:19 our land here, east of the J."
32:21 Have them cross the J,
32:29 presence and cross the J River
32:32 of is here, east of the J."
33:48 near the J River across from
33:49 the plains of Moab along the J.
33:50 near the J River across from
33:51 'You will be crossing the J
34:12 goes along the J River so that
34:15 east of the J River across from
35:1 near the J River across from
35:10 When you cross the J River
35:14 three on the east side of the J
36:13 near the J River across from
Dtr 1:1 in the desert east of the J River,
1:5 were east of the J River
2:29 until we cross the J River into
3:8 kings east of the J River,
3:17 the plains around the J River.
3:18 they cross ⌊the J River⌋ ahead
3:20 on the other side of the J River.
3:21 ⌊of the J River⌋ where you're
3:25 other side of the J River — those
3:27 but you will never cross the J
3:28 people across ⌊the J River⌋,
4:14 after you cross ⌊the J River⌋
4:21 that I wouldn't cross the J River
4:22 land and not cross the J River,
4:26 on the other side of the J River.
4:41 on the east side of the J River.
4:46 they were east of the J River
4:47 who were east of the J River.
4:49 east side of the J River as far
9:1 about to cross the J River.
11:8 you've crossed ⌊the J River⌋.
11:30 are on the west side of the J,
11:31 You're about to cross the J
12:10 But you will cross the J River
27:2 "The day you cross the J River
27:4 After you cross the J River,
27:12 After you cross the J River,
30:18 of when you cross the J River.
31:2 that I cannot cross the J River.
31:13 of when you cross the J River."
32:47 of when you cross the J River."
34:3 the Negev, and the J Plain —
Jos 1:2 must cross the J River into
1:11 days you will cross the J River
1:14 gave you east of the J River.
1:15 land east of the J River which
2:7 place to cross the J River.
2:10 who ruled east of the J River.
2:23 crossed the J River,
3:1 They came to the J River,
3:8 into the water of the J River,
3:11 ahead of you into the J River.
3:13 will stand in the water of the J.
3:14 camp to cross the J River.
3:15 (The J overflows all its banks
3:15 came to the edge of the J River
3:16 the J River⌋ directly opposite
3:17 in the middle of the J until
3:17 Israel had crossed the J River
4:1 finished crossing the J River.
4:3 stones from the middle of the J,
4:5 "Go to the middle of the J
4:7 'The water of the J River was
4:7 When the ark crossed the J,
4:8 from the middle of the J as
4:9 in the middle of the J River,
4:10 standing in the middle of the J.
4:16 to come out of the J River."
4:17 "Come out of the J."
4:18 came out of the middle of the J.
4:18 the water of the J returned to its
4:19 people came out of the J River.
4:20 they had taken from the J.
4:22 that Israel crossed the J River
Jos 4:23 your God dried up the J ahead
5:1 kings west of the J River
5:1 had dried up the J River so that
7:7 people across the J River?
7:7 live on the other side of the J!
9:1 west of the J River heard about
9:10 of the Amorites east of the J,
12:1 the land east of the J River that
12:7 west of the J River that Joshua
13:8 inheritance east of the J River,
13:23 territory was the J River.
13:27 In the J Valley it included Beth
13:27 The J River served as its
13:32 east of the J River near Jericho.
14:3 inheritance east of the J River.
15:5 as the mouth of the J River.
15:5 Dead Sea at the mouth of the J
16:1 goes from the J River at Jericho
16:7 and ends at the J River.
17:5 and Bashan east of the J River.
18:7 on the east side of the J River."
18:12 northern border starts at the J,
18:19 at the south end of the J River.
18:20 The J River is its eastern
19:22 and ends at the J River.
19:33 and ends at the J River.
19:34 and Judah in the east at the J.
20:8 on the east side of the J River,
22:4 gave you east of the J River.
22:7 their relatives west of the J.
22:10 the region of the J that was still
22:10 built an altar by the J River.
22:11 It's in the region near the J
22:25 The LORD has made the J
23:4 from the J River westward
24:8 on the east side of the J River.
24:11 "Then you crossed the J River
Jdg 3:28 crossings of the J River that led
5:17 remained east of the J River.
6:33 crossed ⌊the J River⌋,
7:24 as Beth Barah and the J River."
7:24 as Beth Barah and the J River.
7:25 on the other side of the J River.
8:4 men headed toward the J River.
10:8 all who lived east of the J River
10:9 Ammon also crossed the J
11:13 Jabbok River and the J River.
11:22 from the desert to the J River.
12:1 They crossed ⌊the J River⌋ to
12:5 of the J River leading back
12:6 crossings of the J River.
1Sm 11:1 east of the J River whose right
13:7 Some Hebrews crossed the J
31:7 and across the J River saw that
2Sm 2:29 They crossed the J River and
10:17 crossed the J River,
17:22 him left to cross the J River.
17:22 everyone had crossed the J
17:24 with him crossed the J River.
19:15 king came back to the J River,
19:15 bring him across the J River.
19:17 rushed to the J River across
19:18 was going to cross the J River.
19:31 with the king to the J River
19:36 I'll just cross the J River with
19:39 the troops crossed the J River,
19:41 and men across the J River?"
20:2 from the J River to Jerusalem.
24:5 They crossed the J River and
1Ki 2:8 came to meet me at the J River,
7:46 the J Valley between Succoth
17:3 which is east of the J River.
17:5 which is east of the J River.
2Ki 2:6 is sending me to the J River."
2:7 Elisha stood by the J River.
2:13 and stood on the bank of the J
5:10 seven times in the J River,
5:14 in the J River seven times,
6:2 Let's go to the J River.
6:4 They came to the J River and
7:15 them as far as the J River
10:33 east of the J River:
1Ch 6:78 land east of the J River
12:15 these men crossed the J River
12:37 the east side of the J River,
19:17 Israel's army, crossed the J,

1Ch 26:30 serve Israel west of the **J** River.
2Ch 4:17 the **J** Valley between Succoth
Job 40:23 when the **J** rushes against its
Psa 42:6 remember you in the land of **J**,
114:3 The **J** River turned back.
114:5 **J** River, what made you turn
Isa 9:1 to the land across the **J** River,
Jer 12:5 in the jungle along the **J** River?
49:19 the **J** River into pastureland.
50:44 the **J** River into pastureland.
Eze 47:8 down into the **J** Valley,
47:18 The **J** River will serve as the
Zec 11:3 banks of the **J** are destroyed.
Mat 3:5 and the whole **J** Valley went to
3:6 he baptized them in the **J** River.
3:13 He came from Galilee to the **J**
4:15 across the **J** River,
4:25 and from across the **J** River.
19:1 the other side of the **J** River
Mar 1:5 he baptized them in the **J** River.
1:9 baptized by John in the **J** River.
3:8 and from across the **J** River,
10:1 the other side of the **J** River.
Luk 3:3 the region around the **J** River.
4:1 Spirit as he left the **J** River.
Jon 1:28 on the east side of the **J** River,
3:26 on the other side of the **J** River?
10:40 He went back across the **J**

Jorim (1)

Luk 3:29 son of **J**, son of Matthat,

Jorkeam (1)

1Ch 2:44 who first settled **J**.

Josech (1)

Luk 3:26 Semein, son of **J**, son of Joda,

Joseph (260)

Gen 30:24 She named him **J** [May He
30:25 After Rachel gave birth to **J**,
33:2 and Rachel and **J** last.
33:7 Finally, **J** and Rachel came
35:24 Rachel were **J** and Benjamin.
37:2 **J** was a seventeen-year-old
37:2 **J** told his father about the bad
37:3 Israel loved **J** more than all his
37:3 sons because **J** had been born
37:3 So he made **J** a special robe
37:4 They hated **J** and couldn't
37:5 **J** had a dream and when he
37:13 Israel then said to **J**,
37:13 **J** responded, "I'll go."
37:14 Then he sent **J** away from the
37:14 When **J** came to Shechem,
37:16 **J** replied, "I'm looking for my
37:17 'Let's go to Dothan.'" So **J** went
37:21 he tried to save **J** from their
37:22 Reuben wanted to rescue **J**
37:23 So when **J** reached his
37:28 the brothers pulled **J** out of the
37:29 and saw that **J** was no longer
37:33 **J** must have been torn to
37:36 Midianites sold **J** to Potiphar,
39:1 **J** had been taken to Egypt.
39:2 The LORD was with **J**,
39:4 Potiphar liked **J** so much that
39:5 household because of **J**.
39:6 **J** was well-built and
39:7 master's wife began to desire **J**,
39:8 But **J** refused and said to her,
39:10 Although she kept asking **J**
39:20 While **J** was in prison,
39:21 The LORD also put **J** on good
39:22 So the warden placed **J** in
39:22 **J** became responsible for
39:23 because the LORD was with **J**
40:3 place where **J** was a prisoner.
40:4 the guard assigned them to **J**,
40:6 When **J** came to them in the
40:8 **J** asked them. "Why don't you
40:9 cupbearer told **J** his dream.
40:12 what it means," **J** said to him.
40:16 that the meaning **J** had given
40:16 So he said to **J**, "I had a dream
40:18 is what it means," **J** replied.
Gen 40:22 chief baker just as **J** had said
40:23 cupbearer didn't remember **J**.
41:14 Then Pharaoh sent for **J**,
41:15 Pharaoh said to **J**,
41:16 **J** answered Pharaoh,
41:17 Then Pharaoh said to **J**,
41:25 Then **J** said to Pharaoh,
41:39 Then Pharaoh said to **J**,
41:41 Then Pharaoh said to **J**,
41:42 He had **J** dressed in robes of
41:43 Pharaoh put **J** in charge of
41:44 He also said to **J**, no one
41:45 Pharaoh named **J**
41:45 **J** traveled around Egypt.
41:46 **J** was 30 years old when he
41:48 **J** collected all the food grown
41:49 **J** stored up grain in huge
41:50 **J** had two sons by Asenath,
41:51 **J** named his firstborn son
41:54 began as **J** had said they
41:55 to all the Egyptians, "Go to **J**!
41:56 **J** opened all the storehouses
41:57 The whole world came to **J** in
42:6 As governor of the country, **J**
42:7 As soon as **J** saw his brothers,
42:8 Even though **J** recognized his
42:14 as I told you," **J** said to them.
42:18 On the third day **J** said to them,
42:23 They didn't know that **J** could
42:25 **J** gave orders to fill their bags
42:36 **J** is no longer with us,
43:15 presented themselves to **J**.
43:16 When **J** saw Benjamin with
43:17 So the man did as **J** said and
43:26 When **J** came home,
43:29 As **J** looked around,
43:34 **J** had portions of food brought
43:34 So they ate and drank with **J**
44:1 **J** commanded the man in
44:2 He did what **J** told him.
44:4 far from the city when **J** said
44:14 house while **J** was still there.
44:15 **J** asked them, "What have you
44:17 But **J** said, "I would never think
44:18 Judah went up to **J** and said,
45:1 **J** could no longer control his
45:1 No one else was there when **J**
45:3 **J** said to his brothers,
45:3 said to his brothers, "I am **J**!
45:4 **J** said to his brothers.
45:4 they did so, he said, "I am **J**,
45:9 'This is what your son **J** says,
45:17 So Pharaoh said to **J**,
45:21 **J** gave them wagons and
45:24 So **J** sent his brothers on their
45:26 They told him, "**J** is still alive!
45:27 father everything **J** had said
45:27 he saw the wagons **J** had sent
45:28 "My son **J** is still alive.
46:4 **J** will close your eyes when
46:19 Rachel were **J** and Benjamin.
46:20 were born to **J** by Asenath,
46:27 **J** had two sons who were born
46:28 sent Judah ahead of him to **J**
46:29 **J** prepared his chariot and went
46:30 Israel said to **J**, "Now that I've
46:31 Then **J** said to his brothers and
47:1 **J** went and told Pharaoh,
47:5 Then Pharaoh said to **J**,
47:7 Then **J** brought his father
47:11 As Pharaoh had ordered, **J** had
47:12 **J** also provided his father,
47:14 **J** collected all the money that
47:15 all the Egyptians came to **J**.
47:16 **J** replied, "If you don't have any
47:17 brought their livestock to **J**,
47:20 **J** bought all the land in Egypt
47:21 All over Egypt **J** moved the
47:23 **J** said to the people,
47:26 **J** made a law concerning the
47:29 He called for his son **J** and
47:30 do as you say," **J** answered.
47:31 So **J** swore to him.
48:1 Later **J** was told, "Your father is
48:2 "Your son **J** is here to see you,"
48:3 Jacob said to **J**, "God Almighty
Gen 48:9 **J** answered his father.
48:10 So **J** brought his sons close to
48:11 Israel said to **J**, "I never
48:12 **J** took them off his father's lap
48:13 Then **J** took both of them,
48:15 Then Jacob blessed **J**,
48:17 When **J** saw that his father had
48:21 Then Israel said to **J**,
49:22 "**J** is a fruitful tree,
49:26 blessings rest on the head of **J**,
50:1 **J** threw himself on his father,
50:2 Then **J** ordered the doctors in
50:4 **J** spoke to the Pharaoh's
50:7 So **J** left to bury his father.
50:10 **J** took seven days to mourn his
50:14 After **J** had buried his father,
50:15 So they thought, "What if **J**
50:16 sent a messenger to **J** to say,
50:17 is what you should say to **J**,
50:17 **J** cried when he got their
50:19 **J** said to them, "Don't be afraid!
50:22 **J** and his father's family stayed
50:22 **J** lived to be 110 years old.
50:23 were adopted by **J** at birth.
50:24 At last **J** said to his brothers,
50:25 **J** made Israel's sons swear an
50:26 **J** died when he was 110 years
Exo 1:5 **J** was already in Egypt.
1:6 Eventually, **J**, all his brothers,
1:8 who knew nothing about **J**,
13:19 took the bones of **J** with him,
13:19 because **J** had made the
13:19 **J** had said, "God will definitely
Num 1:32 descendants of **J** — those from
13:7 Igal, son of **J**, from the tribe of
13:11 from the tribe of **J** (that is,
26:28 The families descended from **J**
26:37 the families descended from **J**.
27:1 families of Manasseh, son of **J**.
32:33 the tribe of Manasseh, son of **J**,
36:12 of Manasseh, son of **J**.
Dtr 27:12 Issachar, **J**, and Benjamin.
33:13 About the tribes of **J** he said,
33:16 come to the tribes of **J**.
Jos 16:1 The lot was drawn for **J**.
17:17 said to the descendants of **J**,
Jdg 1:22 The descendants of **J** also
1:35 the tribes of **J** became stronger,
2Sm 19:20 all the house of **J** to meet you."
1Ki 11:28 forced labor from the tribes of **J**.
1Ch 2:2 Dan, **J**, Benjamin, Naphtali,
5:1 However, **J** couldn't be listed in
5:2 **J** received the rights as
7:29 The descendants of **J**,
25:2 **J**, Nethaniah, and Asharelah.
25:9 The first lot drawn chose **J**,
Ezr 10:42 Shallum, Amariah, and **J**
Neh 12:14 Jonathan; from Shebaniah, **J**;
Psa 77:15 descendants of Jacob and **J**.
78:67 He rejected the tent of **J**.
80:1 descendants of **J** like sheep,
81:5 place for **J** when Joseph rose
81:5 place for Joseph when **J** rose
105:17 He sent **J**, who was sold as a
105:21 He made **J** the master of his
105:22 **J** trained the king's officers the
Eze 37:16 for **J** and for all the people of
47:13 of Israel. **J** gets two parts.
48:32 on the east side will be **J** Gate,
Amo 5:6 a fire through the house of **J**
5:15 pity on the faithful few of **J**.
6:6 ruin of the descendants of **J**.
Oba 1:18 The descendants of **J** will be
Mat 1:16 Jacob was the father of **J**,
1:18 been promised to **J** in marriage.
1:19 Her husband **J** was an
1:20 **J** had this in mind when an
1:20 The angel said to him, "**J**,
1:24 When **J** woke up, he did what
1:25 **J** named the child Jesus.
2:13 angel of the Lord appeared to **J**
2:14 **J** got up, took the child and his
2:19 in a dream to **J** in Egypt.
2:21 **J** got up, took the child and his
2:22 **J** was afraid to go there.
13:55 James, **J**, Simon, and Judas?

Mat 27:56 (the mother of James and J),
27:57 a rich man named J arrived.
27:59 J took the body and wrapped it
Mar 6:3 James, J, Judas, and Simon?
15:40 mother of young James and J),
15:43 when J arrived. He was from the
15:43 J boldly went to Pilate's
15:45 Pilate let J have the corpse.
15:46 J had purchased some linen
Luk 1:27 descendant of David named J.
2:4 So J went from Nazareth,
2:4 J, a descendant of King David,
2:5 J went there to register with
2:16 quickly and found Mary and J
2:22 J and Mary went to Jerusalem.
2:27 Mary and J were bringing the
2:38 she came up to Mary and J
2:39 J and Mary returned to their
3:23 was the son of J, son of Eli,
3:24 Melchi, son of Jannai, son of J,
3:30 Judah, son of J, son of Jonam,
23:50 His name was J. He was a
23:55 followed closely behind J.
Jon 1:45 He is Jesus, son of J,
4:5 Jacob had given to his son J.
19:38 Later J from the city of
19:38 (J was a disciple of Jesus but
19:38 Jesus' body. So J removed it.
19:39 went with J and brought 75
19:42 J and Nicodemus put Jesus in
Act 1:23 These men were J (who was
4:36 J, a descendant of Levi,
7:9 were jealous of their brother J.
7:9 But God was with J
7:10 When J stood in the presence
7:10 God gave J divine favor and
7:13 J told his brothers who he was,
7:14 J sent for his father Jacob and
7:18 who knew nothing about J,
Heb 11:22 While J was dying,
Rev 7:8 12,000 from the tribe of J,

Joseph's (45)

Gen 37:4 J brothers saw that their father
37:31 So they took J robe, killed a
37:35 This is how J father cried over
39:3 J master saw that the LORD
39:6 left all that he owned in J care.
39:16 She kept J clothes with her
39:20 So J master arrested him and
39:23 to anything under J care
41:42 ring and put it on J finger.
42:3 Ten of J brothers went to buy
42:4 Jacob wouldn't send J brother
42:6 So when J brothers arrived,
43:17 said and took them to J house
43:18 had been brought to J house.
43:19 to the man in charge of J house
43:24 took the brothers into J house.
43:25 gifts ready for J return at noon,
44:14 at J house while Joseph was
45:16 news that J brothers had come,
48:8 When Israel saw J sons, he
50:8 J household, his brothers,
50:15 J brothers realized what their
Num 1:10 Manasseh are J descendants.
34:24 Ephraim are J descendants.
36:1 (families of J descendants)
36:5 tribe of J descendants is right.
Jos 14:4 because J descendants,
14:4 J descendants gave the
16:1 The border of J territory goes
16:4 So J sons, Manasseh and
17:1 Manasseh was J firstborn.
17:2 of J son Manasseh listed by
17:14 J descendants asked Joshua,
17:16 J descendants responded,
18:5 and J descendants will stay
18:11 lies between Judah's and J.
24:32 J bones, which the people of
24:32 inherited by J descendants
1Ch 5:1 J sons, because he dishonored
Eze 37:19 I will take J stick, which is in
Zec 10:6 I will rescue J people.
Luk 4:22 They said, "Isn't this J son?
Jon 6:42 "Isn't this man Jesus, J son?

Act 7:13 Pharaoh learned about J family
Heb 11:21 him to bless each of J sons.

Joses (1)

Mar 15:47 of J) watched where Jesus

Joshah (1)

1Ch 4:34 J (son of Amaziah),

Joshaphat (2)

1Ch 11:43 and J the Mithnite,
15:24 The priests Shebaniah, J,

Joshaviah (1)

1Ch 11:46 Jeribai and J (sons of Elnaam),

Joshbekashah (2)

1Ch 25:4 Ezer, J, Mallothi, Hothir,
25:24 The seventeenth chose J,

Josheb Basshebeth (1)

2Sm 23:8 J from Tahkemon's family was

Joshibiah (1)

1Ch 4:35 Joel, Jehu (son of J,

Joshua (223)

Exo 17:9 Moses said to J, Then fight the
17:10 J did as Moses told him and
17:13 So J defeated the Amalekite
17:14 and make sure that J hears it,
24:13 set out with his assistant J,
32:17 Then J heard the noise of the
33:11 his assistant, J, son of Nun,
Num 11:28 So J, son of Nun, who had
13:16 son of Nun, the name J.
14:6 J (son of Nun) and Caleb (son
14:30 Jephunneh) and J (son of Nun).
14:38 only J (son of Nun) and Caleb
26:65 Jephunneh) and J (son of Nun).
27:18 to Moses, "Take J, son of Nun,
27:21 At his command J and the
27:22 He took J and made him stand
27:23 Moses placed his hands on J
32:12 the Kenizzite) and J (son
32:28 priest Eleazar, J (son of Nun),
34:17 the priest Eleazar and J,
Dtr 1:38 But your assistant J,
3:21 I also gave J this command:
3:28 Give instructions to J.
31:3 J will also cross the river
31:7 Then Moses called for J and
31:14 Call for J. Both of you come to
31:14 Moses and J came to the tent
31:23 LORD gave this command to J,
34:9 J, son of Nun, was filled with
Jos 1:1 said to Moses' assistant J,
1:10 Then J ordered the officers of
1:12 Next, J said to the tribes of
1:16 The people responded to J,
2:1 From Shittim J, son of Nun,
2:23 and returned to J, son of Nun.
2:24 They told J, "The LORD has
3:1 J got up early the next morning.
3:5 J told the people, "Perform the
3:6 J also told the priests,
3:7 Then the LORD said to J,
3:9 So J said to the people of
3:10 J continued, "This is how you
4:1 The LORD had told J,
4:4 J called the 12 men whom he
4:8 of Israel did as J had ordered.
4:8 Jordan as the LORD had told J.
4:9 J also set 12 stones in the
4:10 the LORD had ordered J
4:10 This was as Moses had told J.
4:14 that day the LORD honored J
4:14 As long as J lived,
4:15 The LORD said to J,
4:17 So J ordered the priests,
4:20 At Gilgal J set up the 12
5:2 that time the LORD spoke to J,
5:3 So J made flint knives and
5:4 the reason J circumcised them:
5:7 So J circumcised them.
5:9 The LORD said to J,

Jos 5:9 So J named the place Gilgal,
5:13 When J was near Jericho,
5:13 J went up to him and asked,
5:14 Immediately, J bowed with his
5:15 of the LORD's army said to J,
5:15 So J did as he was told.
6:2 The LORD said to J,
6:6 J, son of Nun, summoned the
6:8 After J had given orders to the
6:10 J ordered the troops,
6:12 J got up early in the morning.
6:16 J said to the troops,
6:22 But J said to the two spies,
6:25 J spared the prostitute Rahab,
6:25 hid the messengers J had sent
6:26 At that time J pronounced this
6:27 So the LORD was with J,
7:2 J sent men from Jericho to Ai.
7:3 They came back to J and told
7:6 J and the leaders of Israel tore
7:7 J said, "Almighty LORD,
7:10 The LORD said to J,
7:16 J got up early in the morning.
7:19 J said to Achan, "Son,
7:20 Then Achan answered J,
7:22 J sent messengers,
7:23 from the tent and brought it to J
7:24 J and all Israel took Achan
7:25 Then J said, "Why did you
8:1 The LORD said to J,
8:3 So J and all the soldiers
8:3 J picked 30,000 of his best
8:9 So J sent them out,
8:9 J spent the night with the
8:10 J got up early in the morning
8:12 J had taken about five
8:13 That night J went down into
8:14 just where ⌊J⌋ expected.
8:15 J and all Israel pretended to be
8:16 As they chased J,
8:18 Then the LORD said to J,
8:18 So J held out his spear.
8:21 When J and all Israel saw that
8:23 of Ai alive and brought him to J.
8:26 J did not lower his hand
8:27 the LORD had commanded J.
8:28 So J burned Ai and made it a
8:29 J hung the king of Ai's ⌊dead
8:29 When the sun went down, J
8:30 At that time J built an altar on
8:34 Afterwards, J read all the
8:35 J read ⌊Moses' Teachings⌋ in
9:2 together to fight J and Israel.
9:3 Gibeon heard what J had done
9:6 They came to J in the camp at
9:6 They told J and the men of
9:8 They responded to J,
9:8 J asked them, "Who are you,
9:15 So J made peace with them by
9:22 J sent for the people of Gibeon
9:24 They answered J,
9:26 So J rescued them and did not
9:27 But that day J made them
10:1 heard that J had captured Ai
10:4 it has made peace with J
10:6 sent this message to J at
10:7 So J, with all his soldiers and
10:8 The LORD told J, "Don't be
10:9 So J marched all night from
10:12 J spoke to the LORD while
10:15 Then J and all Israel returned
10:17 Someone told J, "The five
10:18 J replied, "Roll large stones
10:20 J and the Israelites defeated
10:21 whole army returned safely to J
10:22 J said, "Open the cave,
10:24 When they brought them to J,
10:25 J told them, "Don't be afraid or
10:26 After this, J put them to death
10:27 When the sun went down, J
10:28 day J captured Makkedah,
10:29 J and all Israel marched from
10:31 J and all Israel marched from
10:33 But J killed him and his troops.
10:34 J and all Israel marched from
10:36 Then J and all Israel marched

Jos 10:38 Then **J** and all Israel went
10:40 So **J** captured the whole land —
10:41 So **J** defeated the people from
10:42 **J** captured all these kings and
10:43 Then **J** and all Israel returned
11:6 The LORD told **J**, "Don't be
11:7 **J** and all his troops arrived
11:9 **J** disabled their horses and
11:10 Then **J** turned back and
11:11 **J** also burned Hazor.
11:12 So **J** captured all these cities
11:13 However, **J** made an exception
11:15 So **J** carried out what the
11:16 **J** took all this land,
11:18 **J** waged war with all these
11:21 At that time **J** also wiped out
11:21 **J** claimed them for the LORD
11:23 **J** captured the whole land as
12:7 west of the Jordan River that **J**
12:7 **J** gave it as a possession to
13:1 **J** was old, near the end of his
14:1 priest Eleazar, **J** (son of Nun),
14:6 of Judah came to **J** at Gilgal.
14:13 So **J** blessed Caleb,
15:13 **J** gave Caleb, son of
17:4 **J** (son of Nun), and the leaders.
17:14 Joseph's descendants asked **J**,
17:15 **J** replied, "If there are so many
17:17 Then **J** said to the
18:3 So **J** asked the Israelites,
18:8 As the men got ready to go, **J**
18:9 Then they returned to **J** at the
18:10 So **J** drew lots for them in the
18:10 There **J** divided the land
19:49 territory as an inheritance to **J**,
19:51 priest Eleazar, **J** son of Nun,
20:1 The LORD said to **J**,
21:1 Eleazar, to **J** (son of Nun),
22:1 **J** summoned the tribes of
22:6 Then **J** blessed them.
22:7 and **J** had given the other half
22:7 When **J** sent them home,
23:1 **J** was old, near the end of his
24:1 **J** gathered all the tribes of
24:2 **J** said to all the people,
24:19 But **J** answered the people,
24:21 The people answered **J**,
24:22 **J** said to the people,
24:24 The people replied to **J**,
24:25 That day **J** made an agreement
24:26 **J** wrote these things in the
24:27 **J** told all the people,
24:28 Then **J** sent the people away,
24:29 the LORD's servant **J**,
24:31 served the LORD as long as **J**
Jdg 2:6 Now, **J** sent the people of
2:8 The LORD's servant **J**,
2:21 the nations **J** left behind when
2:23 had not handed them over to **J**
1Sm 6:14 The cart came into the field of **J**
6:18 the field of **J** of Beth Shemesh.
1Ki 16:34 had spoken this through **J**,
2Ki 23:8 at the entrance of the Gate of **J**,
1Ch 7:27 was Nun. Nun's son was **J**.
Hag 1:1 to the chief priest **J** (who was
1:12 the chief priest **J** (who was the
1:14 the chief priest **J** (who was the
2:2 the chief priest **J** (who is the
2:4 "Chief Priest **J** (son of
Zec 3:1 Then he showed me **J**,
3:3 **J** was wearing filthy clothes
3:4 "Then he said to **J**,
3:6 of the LORD advised **J**,
3:8 "Listen, Chief Priest **J** and your
3:9 stone I have set in front of **J**.
6:11 it on the head of Chief Priest **J**,
Luk 3:29 son of **J**, son of Eliezer, son of
Heb 4:8 If **J** had given the people rest,

Joshua's (5)

Jdg 1:1 After **J** death the Israelites
2:7 the LORD throughout **J** lifetime
Zec 3:1 was standing at **J** right side
3:4 "Remove **J** filthy clothes.
Act 7:45 They did this with **J** help when

Josiah (59)

1Ki 13:2 His name will be **J**.
13:2 Here on you **J** will sacrifice the
2Ki 21:24 They made his son **J** king in
21:26 His son **J** succeeded him as
22:1 **J** was 8 years old when he
22:2 **J** did what the LORD
23:2 **J** read everything written in the
23:4 **J** burned the utensils outside
23:10 **J** also made Topheth in the
23:14 **J** crushed the sacred stones,
23:16 When **J** turned and saw the
23:18 So **J** said, "Let him rest.
23:19 **J** also got rid of all the temples
23:24 **J** also got rid of the mediums,
23:25 No king before **J** had turned to
23:25 No other ⌊king⌋ was like **J**.
23:28 Isn't everything else about **J** —
23:29 King **J** went to attack Necoh.
23:30 They buried **J** in his tomb.
23:34 king in place of his father **J**
1Ch 3:14 Amon's son was **J**.
2Ch 33:25 They made his son **J** king in
34:1 **J** was 8 years old when he
34:8 temple clean, **J** sent Shaphan,
34:33 **J** got rid of all the disgusting
35:1 **J** celebrated the Passover for
35:2 **J** appointed the priests to their
35:7 **J** provided the people with
35:16 as King **J** had commanded.
35:18 the Passover as **J** celebrated
35:20 After all this, when **J** had
35:20 **J** went to attack him.
35:21 sent messengers to **J** to say,
35:22 But **J** would not stop his attack.
35:23 Some archers shot King **J**.
35:24 and Jerusalem mourned for **J**.
35:25 sang a funeral song about **J**.
35:25 funeral songs about **J** today.
35:26 Everything else about **J** —
Jer 1:2 word to Jeremiah when King **J**,
1:3 when Jehoiakim, son of **J**,
1:3 ⌊another⌋ son of **J**,
3:6 When **J** was king,
22:18 son of Judah's King **J**:
25:1 when Jehoiakim, son of **J**,
25:3 from the time that **J**,
26:1 son of **J**, began to rule.
27:1 son of King **J** of Judah,
35:1 son of King **J** of Judah.
36:1 son of King **J** of Judah,
36:2 during the reign of **J** until today.
36:9 son of King **J** of Judah,
37:1 son of **J**, to be king of Judah.
45:1 son of **J**, was king of Judah.
46:2 son of **J**, was king of Judah.
Zep 1:1 in the days of Judah's King **J**,
Zec 6:10 same day go to the house of **J**,
Mat 1:10 Amon the father of **J**.
1:11 **J** was the father of Jechoniah

Josiah's (9)

2Ki 22:3 In **J** eighteenth year as king of
23:23 **J** reign, this Passover was
23:29 In **J** days Pharaoh Necoh (the
23:30 the land took **J** son Jehoahaz,
23:34 made **J** son Eliakim king
1Ch 3:15 **J** firstborn son was Johanan,
2Ch 35:19 of **J** reign, this Passover was
36:1 the land took **J** son Jehoahaz
Jer 22:11 about King **J** son Shallum,

Josiphiah (1)

Ezr 8:10 son of **J**, with 160 males

Jotbah (1)

2Ki 21:19 daughter of Haruz from **J**.

Jotbathah (3)

Num 33:33 and set up camp at **J**.
33:34 They moved from **J** and set up
Dtr 10:7 and from Gudgodah to **J**,

Jotham (28)

Jdg 9:5 But **J**, Jerubbaal's youngest
9:7 When **J** was told about this,
9:21 Then **J** ran away quickly.
9:57 So the curse of **J**, son of
2Ki 15:5 The king's son **J** was in charge
15:7 His son **J** succeeded him as
15:30 son of **J**, was king of Judah.
15:32 ruled Israel, **J**, son of Azariah,
15:35 **J** built the Upper Gate of the
15:36 Isn't everything else about **J** —
15:38 **J** lay down in death with his
16:1 when King Ahaz, son of **J**,
1Ch 2:47 Jahdai's sons were Regem, **J**,
3:12 Azariah's son was **J**.
5:17 records in the days of King **J**
2Ch 26:21 His son **J** was in charge of the
26:23 His son **J** succeeded him as
27:1 **J** was 25 years old when he
27:3 **J** built the Upper Gate of the
27:6 **J** grew powerful because he
27:7 Everything else about **J** — all
27:9 **J** lay down in death with his
Isa 1:1 Uzziah, **J**, Ahaz, and Hezekiah.
7:1 When Ahaz, son of **J** and
Hos 1:1 Beeri, when Uzziah, **J**, Ahaz,
Mic 1:1 from Moresheth, when **J**, Ahaz,
Mat 1:9 Uzziah the father of **J**,
1:9 **J** the father of Ahaz,

Jotham's (1)

1Ch 3:13 **J** son was Ahaz. Ahaz's son

journey (14)

Gen 19:2 you can continue your **j**."
Num 10:33 them a distance of three days' **j**
Dtr 8:2 your God led you on your **j**
10:11 "Lead the people on their **j**.
28:68 to Egypt in ships on a **j** that
Jdg 18:5 God if our **j** will be successful."
18:6 The LORD approves of your **j**."
1Sm 19:23 He continued his **j**,
2Sm 11:10 "Didn't you just come from a **j**?
1Ki 19:7 or your **j** will be too much for
Ezr 8:21 him for a safe **j** for ourselves,
8:23 and asked our God for a safe **j**,
Pro 16:9 A person may plan his own **j**,
Mic 6:5 Remember ⌊your **j**⌋ from

journeyed (1)

Isa 57:9 You've **j** to the king with

journeys (1)

Isa 57:10 tired yourself out with many **j**.

joy (192)

1Sm 2:1 "My heart finds **j** in the LORD.
2Sm 6:15 of the LORD with shouts of **j**
1Ch 15:28 promise with shouts of **j**
16:27 Strength and **j** are where he is.
16:33 in the forest will sing with **j**
2Ch 23:18 made these offerings with **j**
30:21 for seven days with great **j**.
30:26 of Jerusalem was filled with **j**.
Ezr 3:12 Many others shouted for **j**.
Neh 8:10 Don't be sad because the **j** you
Est 9:22 that month their grief turned to **j**
Job 8:19 That is its **j** in this life,
20:5 and the **j** of the godless person
20:18 He will get no **j** from the profits
29:13 the widow's heart sing for **j**.
33:26 God's face and shout for **j** as
38:7 the sons of God shouted for **j**?
39:13 the ostrich flap its wings in **j**,
39:21 It paws in strength and finds **j**
Psa 4:7 You put more **j** in my heart than
5:11 Let them sing with **j** forever.
9:2 I will find **j** and be glad about
9:14 and find **j** in your salvation.
13:5 heart finds **j** in your salvation.
16:3 noble ones who fill me with **j**.
16:11 Complete **j** is in your presence.
21:1 The king finds **j** in your
21:1 What great **j** he has in your
21:6 with the **j** of your presence.
27:6 offer sacrifices with shouts of **j**
30:5 is a song of **j** in the morning.
30:11 and clothed me with **j**

Psa 32:11 Be glad and find **j** in the LORD,
32:11 Sing with **j**, all whose motives
33:21 In him our hearts find **j**.
35:9 My soul will find **j** in the LORD
42:4 ⌊I sang⌋ songs of **j** and
43:4 to God my ⌊highest⌋ **j**,
45:7 companions, with the oil of **j**.
45:15 With **j** and delight they are
46:4 is a river whose streams bring **j**
48:2 Its beautiful peak is the **j** of the
51:8 ⌊sounds of⌋ **j** and gladness.
51:12 Restore the **j** of your salvation
63:11 But the king will find **j** in God.
64:10 Righteous people will find **j** in
65:12 The hills are surrounded with **j**.
68:3 Let them overflow with **j**.
68:30 the people who find **j** in war.
71:23 My lips will sing with **j** when I
84:2 My whole body shouts for **j** to
85:6 your people may find **j** in you?
86:4 Give me **j**, O Lord, because I
89:16 They find **j** in your name all
92:4 You made me find **j** in what
97:11 for righteous people and **j**
97:12 Find **j** in the LORD,
104:31 May the LORD find **j** in what
104:34 I will find **j** in the LORD.
105:43 brought his people out with **j**,
105:43 chosen ones with a song of **j**.
106:5 find **j** in our people's happiness,
119:14 I find **j** in the way ⌊shown by⌋
119:14 instructions more than I find **j**
119:111 They are the **j** of my heart.
119:162 I find **j** in your promise like
132:9 Let your godly ones sing with **j**.
137:6 Jerusalem my highest **j**.
147:10 He finds no **j** in strong horses,
149:2 Let Israel find **j** in their creator.
149:5 them sing for **j** on their beds.
Pro 1:22 long will you mockers find **j**
2:14 from those who find **j** in the
8:31 found **j** in his inhabited world,
10:28 righteous people ⌊leads to⌋ **j**,
11:10 there are songs of **j**.
12:20 but **j** belongs to those who
14:10 and no stranger can share its **j**.
14:13 and **j** can end in grief.
17:21 of a godless fool has no **j**.
18:2 A fool does not find **j** in
Ecc 2:26 and **j** to anyone who pleases
5:20 with the **j** in their hearts.
8:15 This **j** will stay with them
Isa 4:2 pride and **j** of Israel's survivors.
8:6 water of Shiloah and find **j**
12:3 With **j** you will draw water from
12:6 Shout loudly, and sing with **j**,
13:3 They find **j** in my triumphs.
14:7 It breaks out into shouts of **j**.
16:9 The shouts of **j** for your ripened
16:10 **J** and delight have vanished
16:10 put an end to the shouts of **j**.
24:11 All **j** passes away,
24:14 They shout for **j**. From the sea
26:19 will wake up and shout for **j**,
29:19 Humble people again will find **j**
29:19 The poorest of people will find **j**
35:2 It will rejoice and sing with **j**.
35:6 cannot speak will shout for **j**.
35:10 come to Zion singing with **j**.
41:16 But you will find **j** in the LORD
42:11 who live in Sela sing for **j**.
44:23 Sing with **j**, you heavens,
44:23 Break into shouts of **j**,
48:20 Shout for **j** as you tell it and
49:13 Sing with **j**, you heavens!
49:13 Break into shouts of **j**,
51:3 **J** and gladness will be found in
51:11 come to Zion singing with **j**.
52:9 Break out into shouts of **j**,
54:1 Sing with **j**, you childless
54:1 Break into shouts of **j**,
55:12 You will go out with **j** and be
55:12 hills will break into songs of **j**
58:14 then you will find **j** in the
60:5 your heart will be thrilled with **j**,
60:15 a **j** for all generations.
Isa 61:3 the oil of **j** instead of ⌊tears of⌋
61:7 You will have everlasting **j**.
61:10 I will find **j** in the LORD.
65:18 delight and its people to be a **j**.
66:5 then we will see your **j**."
Jer 7:34 I will banish the sounds of **j**
15:16 Your words are my **j** and my
16:9 to put a stop to the sounds of **j**
25:10 the sounds of **j** and happiness,
31:12 They will come and shout for **j**
31:13 I will turn their mourning into **j**.
31:13 I will give them **j** in place of
33:9 will be my source of **j**,
33:11 the sounds of **j** and happiness
48:33 **J** and gladness have
48:33 on grapes with shouts of **j**.
48:33 but not shouts of **j**.
Lam 2:15 the **j** of the whole world?'
5:15 There is no **j** left in our hearts.
Eze 7:7 will be no **j** in the mountains.
36:5 of my land with wholehearted **j**
Joe 1:12 Yes, the **j** of these people has
2:23 be glad and find **j** in the LORD
Hab 3:18 I will truly find **j** in God,
Zep 3:17 over you with shouts of **j**.
Zec 2:10 Sing for **j** and rejoice,
10:7 hearts will find **j** in the LORD.
Mat 2:10 They were overwhelmed with **j**
13:20 and accepts it at once with **j**.
28:8 the tomb with fear and great **j**
Mar 4:16 they accept it at once with **j**.
Luk 1:14 He will be your pride and **j**,
1:44 I felt the baby jump for **j**.
1:47 My spirit finds its **j** in God,
1:58 and they shared her **j**.
2:10 that will fill everyone with **j**.
8:13 They welcome the word with **j**
10:21 Holy Spirit filled Jesus with **j**.
24:41 disciples were overcome with **j**
Jon 3:29 This is the **j** that I feel.
15:11 and your **j** will be complete.
17:13 have the same **j** that I have.
Act 2:28 presence there is complete **j**.'
13:52 continued to be full of **j**
15:3 This story brought great **j** to all
Rom 14:17 as well as the **j** that the Holy
15:13 fill you with **j** and peace
15:32 God I may come to you with **j**
2Co 8:2 their overflowing **j**,
Gal 5:22 **j**, peace, patience, kindness,
Php 1:4 pray for all of you, I do it with **j**.
2:2 Then fill me with **j** by having
2:17 Yet, I am filled with **j**,
2:17 and I share that **j** with all of
2:18 you also should be filled with **j**
2:18 joy and share that **j** with me.
2:28 In this way you will have the **j**
4:1 You are my **j** and my crown.
4:10 The Lord has filled me with **j**
Col 1:11 endure everything with **j**.
1Th 1:6 word with the kind of **j** that
2:19 Who is our hope, **j**,
2:20 You are our glory and **j**!
3:9 enough for all the **j** you give
Phm 1:7 a lot of **j** and encouragement.
Heb 1:9 companions, with the oil of **j**."
12:2 He saw the **j** ahead of him,
12:11 to cause more pain than **j**.
Jas 4:9 mourning and your **j** into gloom
1Pe 1:8 You are extremely happy with **j**
4:13 Then you will also be full of **j**
1Jn 1:4 can be completely filled with **j**.
2Jn 1:12 will be completely filled with **j**.
Jud 1:24 can be full of **j** as you stand

joyful (42)

Dtr 28:47 the LORD your God with a **j**
1Sm 18:6 **j** music, and triangles.
1Ch 15:16 to produce **j** music for singing.
Ezr 3:13 between the **j** shouts
6:22 the LORD had made them **j**.
Neh 8:12 They had a big, **j** celebration
8:17 There was a big, **j** celebration.
Est 8:16 happy, **j**, and successful.
8:17 the Jews were happy and **j**,
Job 3:7 Let no **j** singing be heard in it.
Psa 35:9 and be **j** about his salvation.
47:1 to God with a loud, **j** song.
47:5 has gone up with a **j** shout.
63:5 sing ⌊your⌋ praise with **j** lips.
89:16 are **j** in your righteousness
97:1 Let all the islands be **j**.
98:4 Break out into **j** singing,
100:2 Come into his presence with a **j**
107:22 Let them tell in **j** songs what he
113:9 in a childless home a **j** mother.
118:15 The sound of **j** singing and
126:2 and our tongues with **j** songs.
Pro 12:25 encouraging word makes him **j**.
15:13 A **j** heart makes a cheerful face,
17:22 A **j** heart is good medicine,
Ecc 7:3 a sad face, the heart can be **j**.
Sos 3:11 his day of **j** delight.
Isa 23:12 "You will no longer be **j**,
24:8 **J** tambourine music stops.
24:8 **J** harp music stops.
32:13 all the happy homes in a **j** city.
35:10 They will be glad and **j**.
51:11 They will be glad and **j**.
Zec 8:19 the tenth month will become **j**
Jon 15:11 this so that you will be as **j** as
Act 2:46 They were **j** and humble as
Php 1:25 to grow and be **j** in your faith.
2:29 him a **j** Christian welcome.
3:1 and sisters, be **j** in the Lord.
4:4 Always be **j** in the Lord!
4:4 I'll say it again: Be **j**!
1Th 5:16 Always be **j**.

joyfully (35)

Lev 26:34 Then the land will **j** celebrate
Dtr 32:43 **J** sing with the LORD's people,
2Sm 6:12 Then David **j** went to get the
1Ch 15:25 and the army's commanders **j**
29:22 and drank as they **j** celebrated
2Ch 29:30 They **j** sang praises,
30:23 So they **j** celebrated for seven
Neh 12:27 to celebrate the dedication **j**
Psa 20:5 We will **j** sing about your
33:1 **J** sing to the LORD,
33:3 and **j** on stringed instruments.
35:27 I am declared innocent **j** sing
51:14 **j** about your righteousness!
59:16 In the morning I will **j** sing
63:7 shadow of your wings, I sing **j**.
65:8 and evening sunset sing **j**.
67:4 the nations be glad and sing **j**
71:23 have rescued, also will sing **j**.
81:1 Sing **j** to God, our strength.
89:12 Hermon sing your name **j**.
90:14 mercy so that we may sing **j**
92:4 I will sing **j** about the works of
95:1 Come, let's sing **j** to the LORD.
96:12 trees in the forest will sing **j**
98:8 and the mountains sing **j**
126:5 they plant will **j** sing while they
132:16 Then its godly ones will sing **j**.
145:7 and they will **j** sing about your
Isa 24:14 From the sea they sing **j** about
52:8 voices and shout together **j**.
Jer 31:7 Sing **j** for the leader of the
Luk 19:38 They shouted **j**, "Blessed is
Act 8:39 The official **j** continued on his
Heb 12:22 of angels **j** gathered together
13:17 so that they may do this work **j**

joyous (2)

Psa 32:7 You surround me with **j** songs
Isa 5:14 Those who are noisy and **j** will

Jozabad (10)

1Ch 12:4 and **J** from Gederah,
12:20 **J**, Jediael, Michael, Jozabad,
12:20 Michael, **J**, Elihu, and Zillethai.
2Ch 31:13 **J**, Eliel, Ismachiah, Mahath,
35:9 and Hashabiah, Jeiel, and **J**,
Ezr 8:33 The Levites, Jeshua's son **J**,
10:22 Nethanel, **J**, and Elasah
10:23 From the Levites: **J**,
Neh 8:7 Kelita, Azariah, **J**, Hanan,
11:16 Shabbethai and **J**,

Jozacar (1)

2Ki 12:21 Joash's officials J,

Jozadak (1)

Neh 12:26 son of Jeshua, grandson of J,

Jozadak's (4)

Ezr 3:2 Then J son Jeshua and his
3:8 Jeshua (who was J son), and
5:2 who was J son, began to
10:18 of Jeshua (who was J son)

Jubal (1)

Gen 4:21 His brother's name was J.

jubilee (24)

Lev 25:10 This is your j year.
25:11 fiftieth year will be your j year.
25:12 The j ⌊year⌋ will be holy to
25:13 "In this j year every slave will
25:15 the number of years since the j.
25:15 of crops ⌊until the next j⌋.
25:16 still many years ⌊until the j⌋,
25:16 only a few years ⌊until the j⌋,
25:28 of the buyer until the year of j.
25:28 In the j it will be released,
25:30 It will not be released in the j.
25:31 They will be released in the j.
25:33 in the j the purchased house in
25:40 with you until the year of j.
25:50 was bought until the year of j.
25:52 few years left until the year of j,
25:54 will be released in the year of j.
27:17 you give your field in the j year,
27:18 give the field after the j year,
27:18 years left until the next j year.
27:21 field is released in the j year,
27:23 the field's value until the j year.
27:24 In the j year the field will go
Num 36:4 the Israelites' j year comes,

Jucal (1)

Jer 38:1 J (son of Shelemiah),

Judah (809)

Gen 29:35 So she named him J [Praise].
35:23 Levi, J, Issachar, and Zebulun.
37:26 J asked his brothers,
38:1 About that time J left his
38:2 There J met the daughter of a
38:6 J chose a wife for his firstborn
38:8 Then J said to Onan,
38:11 Then J said to his
38:12 When J had finished mourning,
38:15 When J saw her, he thought
38:20 J sent his friend Hirah to
38:22 So he went back to J and said,
38:23 Then J said, "Let her keep
38:24 three months later J was told,
38:24 J ordered, "Bring her out to be
38:26 J recognized them and said,
38:26 J never made love to her again.
43:3 J said to him, "The man gave
43:8 Then J said to his father Israel,
44:14 J and his brothers arrived at
44:16 J asked. "How else can we
44:18 Then J went up to Joseph and
46:12 The sons of J were Er,
46:28 Israel sent J ahead of him to
49:8 "J, your brothers will praise
49:9 J, you are a lion cub. You have
49:10 will never depart from J nor
Exo 1:2 Reuben, Simeon, Levi, and J;
31:2 of Hur, from the tribe of J.
35:30 of Hur, from the tribe of J.
38:22 of Hur, from the tribe of J,
Num 1:7 Amminadab, from the tribe of J;
1:26 for the descendants of J listed
1:27 for the tribe of J was 74,600.
2:3 the armies led by J will camp
2:3 for the people of J is Nahshon,
7:12 Amminadab, from the tribe of J.
13:6 Jephunneh, from the tribe of J;
26:19 Er and Onan were sons of J,
26:20 The families descended from J
Num 26:22 These were the families of J.
34:19 Jephunneh, from the tribe of J;
Dtr 27:12 Levi, J, Issachar, Joseph,
33:7 he said about the tribe of J:
33:7 "Hear the cry of J, O LORD,
34:2 all the territory of J as far as the
Jos 7:1 and a member of the tribe of J,
7:16 The tribe of J was selected.
7:17 the families of J come forward,
7:18 Achan from the tribe of J was
11:21 in all the hills of J and Israel.
14:6 Then the people of J came to
15:1 for the families of the tribe of J.
15:12 These are the borders around J
15:13 land among the people of J as
15:20 by the families of the tribe of J.
15:21 they gave the tribe of J 29
15:33 In the foothills they gave J 14
15:37 They also gave J 16 other
15:42 their villages were given to J:
15:45 J also received Ekron with its
15:48 In the mountains they gave J
15:52 They also gave J nine other
15:59 villages that were given to J.
15:60 villages ⌊were given to J⌋.
15:61 In the desert J was given six
15:63 However, J was not able to
15:63 live with J in Jerusalem today.
18:5 J will stay within its territory in
18:14 Kiriath Jearim), a city of J.
19:1 Their inheritance was within J.
19:9 because J had more land
19:34 and J in the east at the Jordan.
20:7 mountains of J were chosen as
21:4 13 cities from the tribes of J,
21:9 from the tribes of J and Simeon
21:11 located in the mountains of J.
Jdg 1:3 The tribe of J said to the tribe
1:3 of Simeon went along with J.
1:8 The men of J attacked
1:9 After that, the men of J went to
1:16 went with the people of J from
1:16 of Palms into the desert of J.
1:16 they lived with the people of J
1:17 The tribe of J went to fight
1:18 J also captured Gaza,
1:19 with the men of J so that they
10:9 River to fight the tribes of J,
15:9 camped in J, and overran Lehi.
15:10 The men of J asked,
15:11 So 3,000 men from J went to
15:12 So the men from J told him,
17:7 man from Bethlehem in J.
17:7 belongs to the family of J.)
17:8 This man left Bethlehem in J to
17:9 a Levite from Bethlehem in J.
18:12 camped at Kiriath Jearim in J.
19:1 a woman from Bethlehem in J
19:2 to Bethlehem in J.
19:18 on our way from Bethlehem in J
19:18 I had gone to Bethlehem in J.
20:18 answered, "J will go first."
Rut 1:1 A man from Bethlehem in J
1:2 Bethlehem in the territory of J.
1:7 the road to the territory of J.
4:12 Tamar gave birth to for J."
1Sm 11:8 Israel and 30,000 troops from J.
15:4 and 10,000 men from J.
17:1 at Socoh, which is in J,
17:12 and the city of Bethlehem in J.
17:52 soldiers of Israel and J rose up,
18:16 in Israel and J loved David,
22:5 "Go to the land of J."
23:3 afraid of staying here in J.
23:23 among all the families of J."
27:6 to the kings of J today.)
27:10 "the Negev in J," or "the portion
30:14 live, the territory of J,
30:16 territory and from the land of J.
30:26 to his friends, the leaders of J.
2Sm 1:18 this kesheth to the people of J."
2:1 I go to one of the cities of J?"
2:4 Then the people of J came to
2:4 to be king over the tribe of J.
2:7 the tribe of J has anointed me
2:10 the tribe of J followed David.
2Sm 2:11 was king over the tribe of J
3:10 over Israel and J from Dan
5:5 In Hebron he ruled J for seven
5:5 33 years over all Israel and J.
6:2 people with him left Baalah in J
11:11 ⌊the army of⌋ Israel and J are
12:8 you the house of Israel and J.
19:11 "Ask the leaders of J,
19:14 All the people of J were in total
19:15 and the people of J came to
19:16 down with the people of J
19:40 All the troops from J and half of
19:41 our cousins, the people of J,
19:42 All the people of J answered
19:43 answered the people of J,
19:43 But the people of J spoke
20:2 But the people of J remained
20:4 "Call the people of J together
20:5 Amasa went to call J together,
21:2 destroy them for Israel and J.)
24:1 count Israel and J."
24:7 to Beersheba in the Negev of J.
24:9 and in J there were 500,000.
1Ki 1:9 ⌊other⌋ sons, all the men of J,
1:35 to be the leader of Israel and J."
4:20 The people of J and Israel
4:25 As long as Solomon lived, J
12:17 who lived in the cities of J.
12:20 Only the tribe of J remained
12:21 he gathered all the people of J
12:23 the people of J and Benjamin,
12:27 King Rehoboam of J,
12:27 return to King Rehoboam of J."
12:32 just like the festival in J.
13:1 A man of God from J had come
13:12 man of God from J had taken.)
13:14 man of God who came from J?"
14:21 son of Solomon, ruled J.
14:22 The people of J did what the
14:24 The people of J did all the
14:29 records of the kings of J?
15:1 Abijam began to rule J.
15:7 records of the kings of J?
15:9 Asa began to rule as king of J.
15:17 Baasha of Israel invaded J
15:17 or coming from King Asa of J.
15:22 King Asa drafted everyone in J
15:23 records of the kings of J?
15:25 Asa's second year as king of J.
15:28 in Asa's third year as king of J.
15:33 In Asa's third year as king of J,
16:10 year as king of J.
16:23 thirty-first year as king of J.
16:29 thirty-eighth year as king of J.
19:3 He came to Beersheba in J
22:2 King Jehoshaphat of J went
22:10 Jehoshaphat of J were dressed
22:29 King Jehoshaphat of J went
22:41 became king of J in Ahab's
22:45 records of the kings of J?
22:51 seventeenth year as king of J.
2Ki 3:1 eighteenth year as king of J.
3:7 to King Jehoshaphat of J:
3:9 the king of Israel, the king of J,
3:12 So King Jehoshaphat of J,
3:14 for King Jehoshaphat of J.
8:16 son of King Jehoshaphat of J,
8:16 was still king of J.
8:19 LORD didn't want to destroy J.
8:20 time Edom rebelled against J
8:23 records of the kings of J?
8:25 son Ahaziah became king of J.
9:16 (King Ahaziah of J had come to
9:21 and King Ahaziah of J went
9:27 King Ahaziah of J saw this,
9:29 (Ahaziah had become king of J
10:13 relatives of King Ahaziah of J.
12:18 So King Joash of J took all the
12:18 Jehoram, and Ahaziah of J,
12:19 records of the kings of J?
13:1 Ahaziah's son King Joash of J
13:1 as king of J when Jehoahaz,
13:10 thirty-seventh year as king of J,
13:12 King Amaziah of J — written
14:1 Amaziah, son of Joash of J,
14:9 message to King Amaziah of J:

2Ki 14:10 defeat and take J with you?"
14:11 and King Amaziah of J met him
14:11 in battle at Beth Shemesh in J.
14:12 Israel defeated the army of J,
14:13 and grandson of Ahaziah of J,
14:15 King Amaziah of J — written
14:17 Joash's son King Amaziah of J
14:18 records of the kings of J?
14:21 the people of J took Azariah,
14:22 it to J after King Amaziah
14:23 king of J when Jehoash's son
15:1 began to rule as king of J.
15:6 records of the kings of J?
15:8 thirty-eighth year as king of J,
15:13 thirty-ninth year as king of J.
15:17 thirty-ninth year as king of J,
15:23 fiftieth year as king of J,
15:27 fifty-second year as king of J,
15:30 son of Jotham, was king of J.
15:32 began to rule as king of J.
15:36 records of the kings of J?
15:37 son of Remaliah, to attack J.
16:1 began to rule as king of J.
16:19 records of the kings of J?
17:1 twelfth year as king of J,
17:13 Israel and J through every kind
17:18 Only the tribe of J was left.
17:19 Even J didn't obey the
18:1 Hezekiah, son of Ahaz of J,
18:5 kings of J was like Hezekiah.
18:13 cities of J and captured them.
18:14 Then King Hezekiah of J sent
18:14 of J pay 22,500 pounds
18:22 He told J and Jerusalem,
19:10 "Tell King Hezekiah of J,
19:30 the nation of J who escape will
20:20 records of the kings of J?
21:11 "King Manasseh of J has done
21:11 Manasseh has also made J sin
21:12 on Jerusalem and J that
21:16 addition to his sin that he led J
21:17 records of the kings of J?
21:25 official record of the kings of J?
22:3 eighteenth year as king of J,
22:13 of the people, all of J, and me,
22:16 that the king of J has read.
23:1 all the respected leaders of J
23:2 The king, everyone in J,
23:5 the kings of J had appointed
23:5 of worship in the cities of J
23:8 out of the cities of J from Geba
23:17 man of God who came from J
23:22 of the kings of Israel and J.
23:24 could be seen in the land of J
23:26 burning anger from J.
23:27 "I will put J out of my sight as I
23:28 records of the kings of J?
24:1 of Babylon attacked J,
24:2 Jehoiakim to destroy J as
24:3 this happened to J because the
24:3 the people of J from his sight
24:5 records of the kings of J?
24:12 King Jehoiakin of J,
24:20 angry with Jerusalem and J
25:21 So the people of J were
25:22 people in the land of J.
25:27 of King Jehoiakin of J,
25:27 King Jehoiakin of J from prison.
1Ch 2:1 Levi, J, Issachar, Zebulun,
2:4 J had five sons in all.
4:21 of Shelah, son of J, were Er,
4:27 as large as the people of J.
4:41 the days of King Hezekiah of J,
5:2 Even though J was more
5:17 in the days of King Jotham of J
6:15 used Nebuchadnezzar to take J
6:55 in the territory of J as well as
6:65 by name from the tribes of J,
9:1 of the Kings of Israel and J.
9:3 settled by descendants of J,
9:4 of Perez, son of J, was Uthai,
12:16 men of Benjamin and J came
12:39 in J had provided enough
13:6 in Kiriath Jearim, which is in J,
21:5 and in J there were 470,000
27:18 for the tribe of J: Elihu, one of
1Ch 28:4 He had chosen the tribe of J to
28:4 From the families of J he
2Ch 2:7 for me in J and Jerusalem.
9:11 seen anything like them in J.
10:17 who lived in the cities of J.
11:1 the people of J and Benjamin,
11:3 all Israel in J and Benjamin.
11:5 and built fortified cities in J.
11:10 cities in J and Benjamin.
11:12 held on to J and Benjamin.
11:14 land and property and went to J
11:17 of J by supporting Rehoboam,
11:23 every region of J and Benjamin,
12:4 captured the fortified cities in J
12:5 leaders of J who had gathered
12:12 So things went well in J.
13:1 Abijah began to rule J.
13:13 army was in front of J,
13:15 and the men of J shouted.
13:15 Israel in front of Abijah and J.
13:16 God handed them over to J.
13:18 and the men of J won because
14:4 He told the people of J to
14:5 for incense in all the cities of J.
14:6 He built fortified cities in J
14:7 So Asa told J, "Let's build
14:12 army in front of Asa and J.
15:2 you men from J and Benjamin.
15:8 detestable idols from all of J,
15:9 gathered all the people from J
15:15 All the people of J were
16:1 Baasha of Israel invaded J
16:1 or coming from King Asa of J.
16:6 took everyone in J to Ramah.
16:7 Hanani came to King Asa of J
16:11 of the Kings of J and Israel.
17:2 in all the fortified cities of J
17:2 and placed military posts in J
17:5 All the people of J gave gifts to
17:6 to the goddess Asherah in J.
17:7 to teach in the cities of J.
17:9 They taught in J. They had the
17:9 the people in all the cities of J.
17:10 to all the kingdoms around J.
17:12 supplies were stored in J.
17:13 of food in the cities of J
17:19 the fortified cities throughout J.
18:3 asked King Jehoshaphat of J,
18:9 Jehoshaphat of J were dressed
18:28 King Jehoshaphat of J went
19:1 King Jehoshaphat of J returned
19:5 in each fortified city of J.
19:11 and the leader of the tribe of J,
20:3 announced a fast throughout J.
20:4 The people of J gathered to
20:4 They came from every city in J.
20:13 All the people from J,
20:15 to me, everyone from J,
20:17 for you, J and Jerusalem.
20:18 Everyone from J and the
20:20 people of J and those living in
20:22 Seir who had come into J.
20:24 The people of J went to the
20:27 All the men of J and Jerusalem
20:31 Jehoshaphat ruled as king of J.
20:35 King Jehoshaphat of J allied
21:3 along with fortified cities in J.
21:8 time Edom rebelled against J
21:11 of worship in the hills of J.
21:11 So he led J astray.
21:12 or the ways of King Asa of J.
21:13 have caused J and the
21:17 They fought against J,
22:1 son Ahaziah became king of J.
22:10 royal family of the house of J.
23:2 They went around J,
23:2 Levites from all the cities of J
24:5 "Go to the cities of J,
24:6 from J and Jerusalem?
24:9 they issued a proclamation in J
24:17 After he died, the officials of J
24:18 anger upon J and Jerusalem.
24:23 They came to J and Jerusalem
24:23 all the loot they took from J
25:5 Amaziah called the people of J
25:5 for all of J and Benjamin.
2Ch 25:10 with J and returned home.
25:13 the towns in J from Samaria
25:17 King Amaziah of J sent
25:18 message to King Amaziah of J:
25:19 defeat and take J with you?"
25:21 and King Amaziah of J met him
25:21 in battle at Beth Shemesh in J.
25:22 Israel defeated the army of J,
25:23 and grandson of Ahaziah of J,
25:25 Joash's son King Amaziah of J
25:26 of the Kings of J and Israel?
25:28 the city of J with his ancestors.
26:1 All the people of J took Uzziah,
26:2 it to J after King Amaziah
27:4 He built cities in the hills of J,
27:7 of the Kings of Israel and J.
28:6 killed 120,000 soldiers in J
28:8 also took a lot of goods from J
28:9 your ancestors handed J over
28:10 women of J and Jerusalem.
28:17 J and captured prisoners.
28:18 the foothills and the Negev in J.
28:19 The LORD humbled J because
28:19 had spread sin throughout J
28:25 And in each city of J,
28:26 of the Kings of J and Israel.
29:8 angry with J and Jerusalem.
29:21 kingdom, the holy place, and J.
30:1 a message to all Israel and J
30:6 throughout Israel and J.
30:12 God guided the people of J so
30:24 King Hezekiah of J provided
30:25 The whole assembly from J,
30:25 and those who lived in J
31:1 there went to the cities in J.
31:1 and the altars throughout J,
31:6 The people of Israel and J who
31:6 living in the cities of J brought
31:20 Hezekiah did throughout J.
32:1 of Assyria came to invade J.
32:8 what King Hezekiah of J said.
32:9 officers to King Hezekiah of J
32:9 all of the people in J who were
32:12 and told J and Jerusalem,
32:23 presents to King Hezekiah of J.
32:25 with J, and with Jerusalem.
32:32 of the kings of J and Israel.
32:33 When Hezekiah died, all of J
33:9 Manasseh misled J and the
33:11 of the king of Assyria invade J.
33:14 in every fortified city in J.
33:16 And he told J to serve the
34:3 he began to make J and
34:5 made J and Jerusalem clean.
34:9 in the tribes of J and Benjamin,
34:11 that the kings of J had allowed
34:21 are left in Israel and J and me,
34:24 that was read to the king of J.
34:29 all the respected leaders of J
34:30 The king, everyone in J,
35:18 it with priests, Levites, all of J,
35:21 your quarrel with me, king of J?
35:24 All J and Jerusalem mourned
35:27 of the kings of Israel and J.
36:4 brother Eliakim king of J
36:8 of the Kings of Israel and J.
36:10 king of J and Jerusalem.
36:23 in Jerusalem (which is in J).
Ezr 1:2 in Jerusalem (which is in J).
1:3 go to Jerusalem (which is in J)
1:5 the families of J and Benjamin,
1:8 for Prince Sheshbazzar of J.
2:1 returned to Jerusalem and J.
4:1 When the enemies of J and
4:4 discouraged the people of J
4:5 people of J from carrying out
4:6 the enemies of J and
4:6 inhabitants of J and Jerusalem.
5:1 prophesied to the Jews in J
5:8 we went to the province of J,
6:7 of J rebuild God's temple
7:14 to evaluate the situation in J
9:9 wall in J and Jerusalem.
10:7 a proclamation throughout J
10:9 Then all the men of J and
10:23 Pethahiah, J, and Eliezer

Neh	1:2	arrived with some men from **J**.
	2:5	my request, let me go to **J**,
	2:7	safe conduct until I arrive in **J**.
	4:10	Then the people of **J** said,
	5:14	years that I was governor of **J**,
	6:7	'There's a king in **J**!' This
	6:17	In those days the nobles of **J**
	6:18	Many in **J** had promised to
	7:6	returned to Jerusalem and **J**.
	11:3	settled in the cities of **J**.
	11:4	Some of the descendants of **J**
	11:4	descendants of **J** were Athaiah,
	11:9	charge, and **J**, son of Senuah,
	11:20	lived in all the cities of **J**.
	11:25	Some people of **J** lived in
	11:36	Some divisions of Levites in **J**
	12:8	Sherebiah, **J**, and Mattaniah,
	12:31	Then I had the leaders of **J**
	12:32	the leaders of **J** followed them.
	12:34	**J**, Benjamin, Shemaiah,
	12:36	Gilalai, Maai, Nethanel, **J**,
	12:44	The people of **J** were pleased
	13:12	Then all **J** brought a tenth of all
	13:15	In those days I saw people in **J**
	13:16	of worship to the people of **J**,
	13:17	I reprimanded the nobles of **J**
	13:24	the language of **J** well enough
Psa	48:11	glad and the cities of **J** rejoice
	60:7	on my head. **J** is my scepter.
	68:27	⌊next⌋ the leaders of **J** with
	69:35	he will rebuild the cities of **J**.
	76:1	God is known in **J**.
	78:68	but he chose the tribe of **J**,
	97:8	The people of **J** are delighted
	108:8	on my head. **J** is my scepter.
	114:2	**J** became his holy place and
Pro	25:1	the men of King Hezekiah of **J**.
Isa	1:1	saw about **J** and Jerusalem at
	2:1	saw about **J** and Jerusalem.
	3:1	Jerusalem and **J** every kind
	3:8	has stumbled, and **J** has fallen,
	5:3	inhabitants of Jerusalem and **J**,
	5:7	and the people of **J** are the
	7:1	of Uzziah, was king of **J**,
	7:6	'Let's march against **J**,
	7:17	Ephraim broke away from **J**.
	8:8	It will sweep through **J**.
	9:21	Together they attack **J**.
	11:12	the scattered people of **J** from
	11:13	Ephraim won't be jealous of **J**,
	11:13	and **J** won't oppose Ephraim.
	19:17	The land of **J** will terrify the
	19:17	they are reminded of **J**,
	22:8	will remove the defenses of **J**.
	22:21	and to the nation of **J**.
	26:1	will be sung in the land of **J**:
	30:5	the people of **J** will be put to
	36:1	cities of **J** and captured them.
	36:7	Hezekiah told **J** and Jerusalem,
	37:10	"Tell King Hezekiah of **J**,
	37:31	the nation of **J** who escape will
	38:9	King Hezekiah of **J** wrote this
	40:9	Tell the cities of **J**:
	44:26	He says about the cities of **J**,
	48:1	You are descended from **J**.
	65:9	inherit my mountains from **J**.
Jer	1:2	his thirteenth year as king of **J**.
	1:3	was king of **J** and during the
	1:3	son of Josiah, was king of **J**.
	1:15	the city and all the cities of **J**.
	2:28	gods as you have cities, **J**!
	3:7	treacherous sister **J** saw her.
	3:8	**J** saw that I sent unfaithful
	3:8	But treacherous **J**,
	3:10	Israel's treacherous sister **J**
	3:11	less guilty than treacherous **J**.
	3:18	In those days the nation of **J**
	4:3	LORD says to the people of **J**
	4:4	people of **J** and inhabitants of
	4:5	Report this message in **J**.
	4:16	cries against the cities of **J**.
	4:17	because **J** has rebelled against
	5:11	The nations of Israel and **J** are
	5:20	and make this heard in **J**:
	7:2	all you people of **J** who go
	7:17	they are doing in the cities of **J**
Jer	7:30	The people of **J** have done
	7:34	In the cities of **J** and in the
	8:1	the kings and the leaders of **J**,
	9:11	I will destroy the cities of **J** so
	9:26	I will punish Egypt, **J**,
	11:2	and tell them to the people of **J**
	11:6	these things in the cities of **J**
	11:9	exists among the people of **J**
	11:10	The nations of Israel and **J**
	11:12	Then the cities of **J** and those
	11:13	**J**, you have as many gods as
	11:17	that Israel and **J** have done.
	12:14	people of **J** from among them.
	13:11	and the entire nation of **J** cling
	13:19	All the people of **J** will be
	14:2	**J** mourns; its gates fall apart.
	14:2	The people of **J** sit in mourning
	14:19	you completely rejected **J**?
	17:19	where the kings of **J** go in and
	17:20	of the LORD, you kings of **J**,
	17:20	all the people of **J**,
	17:25	along with the people of **J**
	17:26	will come from the cities of **J**,
	18:11	"Now say to the people of **J**
	19:3	you kings of **J** and those who
	19:4	and the kings of **J** have
	19:7	I will smash the plans of **J** and
	19:13	the houses of the kings of **J**,
	20:4	I will hand all of **J** over to the
	20:5	the treasures of the kings of **J**.
	21:11	to the nation of the king of **J**,
	22:1	to the palace of the king of **J**,
	22:2	these gates, and you, king of **J**,
	22:6	the palace of the king of **J**:
	22:11	his father as king of **J**
	22:30	David's throne and rule **J** again.
	23:6	In his lifetime, **J** will be saved,
	24:1	(son of King Jehoiakim of **J**),
	24:1	of Judah), the princes of **J**,
	24:5	The captives of **J**,
	24:8	abandon King Zedekiah of **J**,
	25:1	people of **J** when Jehoiakim,
	25:2	spoke to all the people of **J**
	25:3	year as king of **J** until today,
	25:18	Jerusalem and the cities of **J**
	26:2	who come from the cities of **J**
	26:10	When the officials of **J** heard
	26:18	and said to all the people of **J**,
	26:19	all the people of **J** put Micah
	27:1	son of King Josiah of **J**,
	27:3	Zedekiah of **J** in Jerusalem.
	27:12	to King Zedekiah of **J**,
	27:18	in the royal palace of **J**,
	27:19	son of King Jehoiakim of **J**,
	27:19	the nobles of **J** and Jerusalem.
	27:21	in the royal palace of **J**,
	28:1	the rule of King Zedekiah of **J**,
	28:4	son of King Jehoiakim of **J**,
	28:4	and all the captives of **J** who
	29:2	the leaders of **J** and Jerusalem,
	29:3	whom King Zedekiah of **J** had
	29:22	all the captives from **J** who are
	30:3	and **J** back from captivity.
	30:4	spoke about Israel and **J**:
	31:23	once again use this saying in **J**
	31:24	**J** and all its cities will live
	31:27	plant the nations of Israel and **J**
	31:31	a new promise to Israel and **J**.
	32:1	tenth year as king of **J**.
	32:2	in the palace of the king of **J**.
	32:3	When King Zedekiah of **J**
	32:4	King Zedekiah of **J** will not
	32:30	the people of Israel and **J** have
	32:32	"The people of Israel and **J**
	32:35	I didn't make **J** sin.
	32:44	of Jerusalem, in the cities of **J**,
	33:4	of the kings of **J** have been torn
	33:7	I will restore **J** and Israel and
	33:10	The cities of **J** and the streets
	33:13	and in the cities of **J**,
	33:14	that I made to Israel and **J**.
	33:16	In those days **J** will be saved
	34:2	Go to King Zedekiah of **J**,
	34:4	King Zedekiah of **J**.
	34:6	Zedekiah of **J** in Jerusalem.
	34:7	cities of **J** that were left.
Jer	34:19	officials of **J** and Jerusalem,
	34:21	I will hand King Zedekiah of **J**
	34:22	I will destroy the cities of **J** so
	35:1	son of King Josiah of **J**.
	35:13	Tell the people of **J** and those
	35:17	I am going to bring on **J** and on
	36:1	son of King Josiah of **J**,
	36:2	dictated to you about Israel, **J**,
	36:3	Maybe the nation of **J** will hear
	36:6	people of **J** when they come
	36:9	son of King Josiah of **J**,
	36:9	was coming from any city in **J**
	36:28	King Jehoiakim of **J** burned.
	36:29	Say about King Jehoiakim of **J**,
	36:30	about King Jehoiakim of **J**:
	36:31	and on the people of **J** all the
	36:32	Jehoiakim of **J** had burned.
	37:1	son of Josiah, to be king of **J**.
	37:7	Say this to the king of **J**,
	39:1	ninth year as king of **J**,
	39:4	When King Zedekiah of **J** and
	39:6	slaughtered all the leaders of **J**.
	39:10	had nothing in the land of **J**.
	40:1	and **J** who were being
	40:5	to govern the cities of **J**.
	40:11	had left a few survivors in **J**
	40:12	They came to **J** and to
	40:15	is left of **J** would disappear."
	42:15	you people who are left in **J**.
	42:19	you people who are left in **J** not
	43:4	They didn't stay in **J**.
	43:5	who were left in **J** to Egypt.
	43:5	who had come back to **J** from
	43:9	the people of **J** watch you.
	44:2	and on all the cities of **J**.
	44:6	to burn in the cities of **J**
	44:7	and babies from **J** until none
	44:9	by the kings of **J** and their
	44:9	and by you and your wives in **J**
	44:11	on you and destroy all of **J**.
	44:12	I will take away from **J** those
	44:14	None of the people of **J** who
	44:14	Egypt will survive or return to **J**,
	44:17	officials did in the cities of **J**
	44:21	incense in the cities of **J**
	44:24	all you people of **J** who are in
	44:26	all you people of **J** who live in
	44:26	'that no one from **J** who lives
	44:27	In Egypt the people from **J** will
	44:28	wars will return to **J** from Egypt.
	44:28	Then all the people of **J** who
	44:30	over King Zedekiah of **J**
	45:1	son of Josiah, was king of **J**.
	46:2	son of Josiah, was king of **J**.
	49:34	the rule of King Zedekiah of **J**,
	50:4	"the people of Israel and **J** will
	50:33	of Israel and **J** are oppressed.
	51:5	Israel and **J** haven't been
	51:59	with King Zedekiah of **J**
	52:3	angry with Jerusalem and **J**
	52:10	all the officials of **J** at Riblah.
	52:27	So the people of **J** were
	52:31	of King Jehoiakin of **J**,
	52:31	freed King Jehoiakin of **J** and
Lam	1:3	"**J** has been exiled after
	1:15	the people of **J** in a winepress.
	2:2	down the fortified cities of **J**
	2:2	He brought the kingdom ⌊of **J**⌋
	2:5	people of **J** mourn and moan.
	5:11	are the girls in the cities of **J**.
Eze	4:6	for the sins of the nation of **J**
	8:17	people of **J** have done these
	9:9	of Israel and **J** is terrible.
	17:13	the leading citizens from **J**
	17:15	But the king of **J** rebelled
	17:15	Will the king of **J** succeed?
	17:16	the king of **J** will die in
	17:16	who appointed him king of **J**.
	17:16	The king of **J** broke his
	17:18	The king of **J** broke the
	21:20	mark the road that leads to **J**
	25:3	the nation of **J** went into exile.
	25:8	"The nation of **J** is like all the
	25:12	took revenge on the nation of **J**
	27:17	**J** and Israel traded with you.
	35:10	two nations, Israel and **J**,

Eze 37:16 'For J and for the Israelites
48:7 J will have one part of the land
48:8 gift for the LORD will border J
48:31 Gate, J Gate, and Levi Gate.
Dan 1:1 reign of King Jehoiakim of J,
1:2 handed King Jehoiakim of J
2:25 from J who can explain
5:13 my grandfather brought from J?
6:13 one of the captives from J,
9:7 But we — the men of J,
Hos 1:1 and Hezekiah were kings of J
1:7 will love the descendants of J.
1:11 The people of J and Israel will
4:15 Don't let J become guilty too.
5:5 and J stumbles with them.
5:10 The leaders of J are like those
5:12 I will destroy the nation of J as
5:13 sick and when J saw his own
5:14 a young lion to the nation of J.
6:4 What should I do with you, J?
6:11 "Yet, J, I have set a harvest
8:14 The people of J have built
10:11 J must plow. Jacob must break
11:12 J rebels against God,
12:2 LORD brings charges against J
Joe 3:1 captives of J and Jerusalem.
3:6 You sold the people of J and
3:8 daughters to the people of J.
3:18 will flow in all the brooks of J.
3:19 the nations were cruel to J.
3:20 People will always live in J.
Amo 2:4 Because J has committed
2:4 The people of J have rejected
2:5 I will send a fire on J and burn
7:12 "You seer, run away to J!
Oba 1:12 the people of J are destroyed.
Mic 1:1 and Hezekiah were kings of J.
1:9 about Samaria⌋ will come to J.
Nah 1:12 Though I have humbled you, J,
1:15 Celebrate your festivals, J!
Zep 1:4 "I will use my power against J
2:7 faithful few from the nation of J.
Hag 1:1 and was governor of J)
1:14 and was governor of J),
2:2 Shealtiel and is governor of J),
2:21 to Zerubbabel (governor of J),
Zec 1:12 Jerusalem and the cities of J?
1:19 the nations⌋ that scattered J,
1:21 "Those horns scattered J so
1:21 horns to scatter the land of J."
2:12 The LORD will claim J as his
8:13 Just as you, people of J and
8:15 Jerusalem and the people of J.
8:19 festivals for the nation of J.
9:7 left for our God like a tribe in J,
9:13 I will bend J as my bow and
10:3 of his flock, the people of J.
10:6 will strengthen the people of J.
11:14 between J and Israel.
12:2 attack J along with Jerusalem.
12:4 will watch over the people of J,
12:5 Then the leaders of J will think
12:6 I will make the leaders of J like
12:7 be greater than the honor of J.
14:5 at the time of King Uzziah of J.
14:14 J will also fight in Jerusalem.
14:21 every pot in Jerusalem and in J
Mal 2:11 J has been unfaithful!
2:11 J has dishonored the holy
3:4 The offerings from J and
Mat 1:2 the father of J and his brothers.
1:3 J and Tamar were the father
2:6 Bethlehem in the land of J,
2:6 least among the leaders of J.
Luk 1:39 city in the mountain region of J.
3:30 son of Simeon, son of J,
3:33 Hezron, son of Perez, son of J,
Heb 7:14 Lord came from the tribe of J.
8:8 a new promise to Israel and J.
Rev 5:5 The Lion from the tribe of J,
7:5 from the tribe of J were sealed,

Judah's (61)

Gen 38:12 After a long time J wife, the
38:12 the men were shearing J sheep
Num 2:9 troops in J camp is 186,400.
Num 10:14 J descendants broke camp first.
Jos 18:11 lies between J and Joseph's.
19:9 of J because Judah had more
19:9 its inheritance inside J borders
Jdg 1:2 "J troops will go first.
1:4 J troops went into battle,
1:6 J troops chased him,
1:7 J troops brought Adoni Bezek
1:11 From there J troops went to
1Ki 2:32 and the commander of J army).
12:23 "Speak to J King Rehoboam,
16:8 twenty-sixth year as J king.
16:15 year as J king, Zimri ruled
2Ki 8:22 Edom rebelled against J rule
22:18 "But tell J king who sent you
23:11 that J kings had dedicated
23:12 the altars that J kings had
25:4 All J soldiers left on the road of
1Ch 2:3 J sons were Er, Onan,
2:3 considered Er, J firstborn, evil,
2:4 Tamar, J daughter-in-law, gave
2:4 gave birth to J sons Perez and
2:10 of Nahshon, leader of J people
4:1 J descendants were Perez,
12:24 From J descendants there
2Ch 11:3 "Speak to J King Rehoboam,
13:14 When J soldiers looked around,
13:16 Israelites fled from J ⌊army⌋,
17:14 J regimental commanders were
21:10 Edom rebelled against J rule
22:8 he found J leaders (Ahaziah's
34:26 ⌊Huldah added,⌋ "Tell J king
Ezr 3:9 J descendants joined Henadad's
Neh 11:24 J son, was the king's adviser
Est 2:6 along with J King Jehoiakin,
Isa 11:13 and J opponents will come to
Jer 1:18 up to J kings, its officials,
10:22 Its army will destroy J cities
13:9 how I will destroy J arrogance
15:4 of what J King Manasseh,
17:1 ⌊The LORD says,⌋ "J sin is
21:7 hand over J King Zedekiah,
22:18 son of J King Josiah:
22:24 son of J King Jehoiakim,
26:1 word when J King Jehoiakim,
26:18 at the time of J King Hezekiah
26:19 Did J King Hezekiah and all
38:22 left in the palace of J king will
50:20 They will look for J sins, but
52:7 and all J soldiers fled.
Eze 8:1 J leaders were sitting in front of
37:19 and I will put them with J stick.
48:22 What is between J and
Amo 1:1 the reigns of J King Uzziah
Mic 1:5 What is J worship place?
5:2 to be included among J cities.
Zep 1:1 in the days of J King Josiah,
Zec 12:7 "The LORD will save J tents

Judaism (12)

Act 2:10 Jewish people, converts to J,
6:5 who had converted to J in the
13:16 of Israel and converts to J,
13:26 of Abraham and converts to J —
13:43 many Jews and converts to J
16:14 She was a convert to J from
17:4 Greeks who had converted to J
17:17 with Jews and converts to J.
18:4 who had converted to J.
18:7 who was a convert to J.
26:3 custom and controversy in J.
Tit 1:10 especially converts from J,

Judas (45)

Mat 10:4 the Zealot and J Iscariot,
13:55 James, Joseph, Simon, and J?
26:14 the one named J Iscariot,
26:25 Then J, who betrayed him,
26:47 J, one of the twelve apostles,
26:49 Then J quickly stepped up to
27:3 Then J, who had betrayed
Mar 3:19 and J Iscariot (who later
6:3 James, Joseph, J, and Simon?
14:10 J Iscariot, one of the twelve
14:11 pleased to hear what J had
14:43 J, one of the twelve apostles,
Mar 14:45 Then J quickly stepped up to
Luk 6:16 J (son of James), and Judas
6:16 Judas (son of James), and J
22:3 Then Satan entered J Iscariot,
22:4 J went to the chief priests and
22:6 So J promised to do it.
22:47 The man called J,
22:48 Jesus said to him, "J,
Jon 6:71 Jesus meant J, son of Simon
6:71 J, who was one of the twelve
12:4 One of his disciples, J Iscariot,
12:6 (J didn't say this because he
12:7 Jesus said to J, "Leave her
13:2 Jesus into the mind of J,
13:26 the bread and gave it to J,
13:27 after J took the piece of bread,
13:29 J had the moneybag.
13:30 J took the piece of bread and
13:31 When J was gone,
14:22 J (not Iscariot) asked Jesus,
18:2 J, who betrayed him, knew the
18:3 So J took a troop of soldiers
18:5 J, who betrayed him,
Act 1:13 and J (son of James) went to
1:16 David in Scripture about J had
1:16 J led the men to arrest Jesus.
1:25 who is to take the place of J as
1:25 since J abandoned his position
5:37 J from Galilee appeared and
15:22 They chose J (called
15:27 We have sent J and Silas to
15:32 J and Silas, who were also
15:33 After J and Silas had stayed in

Judas' (2)

Act 9:11 Go to J house on Straight
9:17 left and entered J house.

Jude (1)

Jud 1:1 From J, a servant of Jesus

Judea (44)

Mat 2:1 in J when Herod was
2:5 "In Bethlehem in J.
2:22 his father Herod as king of J,
3:1 appeared in the desert of J.
3:5 Jerusalem, all J, and the whole
4:25 the Ten Cities, Jerusalem, J,
19:1 Jordan River to the territory of J
24:16 those of you in J should flee to
Mar 1:5 All J and all the people of
3:7 A large crowd from Galilee, J,
10:1 went into the territory of J along
13:14 those of you in J should flee to
Luk 1:5 When Herod was king of J,
1:65 the mountain region of J,
3:1 Pilate was governor of J.
4:44 in the synagogues of J.
5:17 every village in Galilee and J
6:17 They had come from all over J,
7:17 Jesus spread throughout J
21:21 Then those of you in J should
23:5 stirs up the people throughout J
Jon 4:47 had returned from J to Galilee.
4:54 come back from J to Galilee.
7:1 He didn't want to travel in J
7:3 and go to J so that your
11:7 "Let's go back to J."
Act 1:8 throughout J and Samaria,
2:9 J, Cappadocia, Pontus,
2:14 "Men of J and everyone living
8:1 throughout J and Samaria.
9:31 Then the church throughout J,
10:37 what happened throughout J.
11:1 throughout J heard that people
11:29 to help the believers living in J.
12:19 Then Herod left J and went to
15:1 Some men came from J and
21:10 named Agabus arrived from J.
25:1 his duties in the province of J,
26:20 the whole country of J.
28:21 any letters from J about you,
Rom 15:31 those people in J who refuse
2Co 1:16 have you support my trip to J.
Gal 1:22 The churches of Christ in J
1Th 2:14 of God in J that are united

Judean (10)

2Sm 3:8 behaving like some **J** dog?"
2Ki 18:26 Don't speak to us in the **J**
18:28 loudly in the **J** language,
1Ch 4:18 His **J** wife was the mother of
2Ch 32:18 loudly in the **J** language
Isa 36:11 Don't speak to us in the **J**
36:13 loudly in the **J** language,
Luk 2:4 to a **J** city called Bethlehem.
Jon 3:22 went to the **J** countryside,
4:3 So he left the **J** countryside

Judeans (14)

2Ki 14:12 and the **J** fled to their homes.
16:6 Rezin of Aram drove the **J** out
19:35 When the **J** got up early in the
25:25 men to kill Gedaliah and the **J**
2Ch 14:8 Asa had an army of 300,000 **J**
23:8 So the Levites and all the **J** did
25:12 The **J** captured another 10,000
25:20 he wanted to hand over the **J**
25:22 and the **J** fled to their homes.
28:8 from their relatives ⌊the **J**⌋.
Neh 4:16 leaders stood behind all the **J**
Isa 37:36 When the **J** got up early in the
Jer 32:32 and the **J** and those who live in
Dan 1:6 these young men were some **J**:

judge (166)

Gen 18:25 Won't the **j** of the whole earth
19:9 Now he wants to be our **j**!
31:53 of their father — **j** between us."
Exo 2:14 "Who made you our ruler and **j**?
5:21 what you have done and **j** you!
Lev 19:15 **J** your neighbor fairly.
Dtr 1:16 **J** each case fairly,
16:18 They are to **j** the people fairly.
17:9 priests and the **j** who is serving
17:12 the LORD your God) or the **j**,
25:2 the **j** will order him to lie down.
25:2 Then the **j** will have him
32:36 The LORD will **j** his people
Jdg 2:18 he was with each **j**.
2:18 as long as that **j** was alive.
2:19 But after each **j** died,
3:10 he became the **j** of Israel.
4:4 She was the **j** in Israel at that
10:3 Jair from Gilead became a **j**.
11:27 The LORD is the **j** who will
1Sm 7:16 and Mizpah in order to **j** Israel
8:5 Now appoint a king to **j** us so
8:6 to request a king to **j** them.
8:20 Our king will **j** us, lead us out
24:15 So the LORD must be the **j**.
2Sm 15:4 someone would make me **j**
1Ki 3:9 so that I can **j** your people
3:9 After all, who can **j** this great
7:7 on his throne and served as **j**.
1Ch 12:17 ancestors see this and **j** you."
16:33 when he comes to **j** the earth.
2Ch 1:10 After all, who can **j** this great
1:11 and knowledge to **j** my people,
19:6 When you **j**, you aren't doing it
20:12 Won't you **j** them? We don't
Job 9:15 to plead for mercy from my **j**.
19:29 you will know there is a **j**."
21:22 Can anyone **j** the Most High?
22:13 Can he **j** ⌊anything⌋ from
Psa 7:8 **J** me, O LORD, according to
7:11 God is a fair **j**, a God who is
9:4 down on your throne as a fair **j**.
26:1 **J** me favorably, O LORD,
35:24 **J** me by your righteousness,
43:1 **J** me, O God, and plead my
50:4 and earth to **j** his people:
50:6 because God is the **j**.
51:4 you are blameless when you **j**.
58:1 **j** Adam's descendants fairly?
67:4 because you **j** everyone
72:2 so that he may **j** your people
75:2 the right time, I will **j** fairly.
75:7 God alone is the **j**.
76:9 when you rose to **j**,
82:2 long are you going to **j** unfairly?
82:8 **J** the earth, because all the
Psa 94:2 Arise, O **J** of the earth.
96:10 He will **j** people fairly.
96:13 He is coming to **j** the earth.
96:13 He will **j** the world with
98:9 he is coming to **j** the earth.
98:9 He will **j** the world with justice
Pro 20:8 on his throne to **j** sifts out every
24:23 partiality as a **j** is not good.
31:9 Speak out, **j** fairly,
Ecc 3:17 I thought to myself, "God will **j**
12:14 God will certainly **j** everything
Isa 2:4 Then he will **j** disputes
3:13 He stands to **j** his people.
5:3 **j** between me and my vineyard!
11:3 He will not **j** by what his eyes
11:4 He will **j** the poor justly.
28:6 spirit of justice to those who **j**.
28:7 They swerve as they **j**.
33:22 The LORD is our **j**.
66:16 The LORD will **j** with fire,
66:16 and he will **j** all people with his
Jer 11:20 O LORD of Armies, you **j** fairly
21:12 **J** fairly every morning.
22:3 **J** fairly, and do what is right.
25:31 He will **j** all humans.
Eze 7:3 I will **j** you for the way you
7:8 I will **j** you for the way you
7:27 deserve and **j** them as they
11:10 I will **j** you at Israel's borders.
11:11 I will **j** you at Israel's borders.
17:20 I will take you to Babylon and **j**
18:30 "That is why I will **j** each of
20:4 "Will you **j** them? Will you judge
20:4 Will you **j** them, son of man?
21:30 were born, there I will **j** you.
22:2 "Will you **j**, son of man?
22:2 Will you **j** the city of murderers?
23:36 will you **j** Oholah and Oholibah
33:20 I will **j** each of you by your own
34:17 I will **j** disputes between one
34:20 I will **j** disputes between the fat
34:22 I will **j** between one sheep and
Joe 3:2 I will **j** them there. They
3:12 There I will sit to **j** all the
Mic 4:3 Then he will **j** disputes
5:1 Enemies will strike the **j** of
Mal 3:5 "I will come to **j** you.
Mat 5:25 he will hand you over to the **j**.
5:25 Then the **j** will hand you over
7:2 standard you use to **j** others.
Luk 12:14 "Who appointed me to be your **j**
12:56 reason you don't know how to **j**
12:57 So why don't you **j** for
12:58 he will drag you in front of a **j**.
12:58 The **j** will hand you over to an
18:2 He said, "In a city there was a **j**
18:4 "For a while the **j** refused to do
18:6 to what the dishonest **j** thought.
19:22 'I'll **j** you by what you've said,
22:30 will also sit on thrones and **j**
Jon 5:22 "The Father doesn't **j** anyone.
7:24 Instead, **j** correctly."
7:51 Teachings enable us to **j**
7:51 We can't **j** a person without
8:15 You **j** the way humans do.
8:15 humans do. I don't **j** anyone.
8:16 Even if I do **j**, my judgment is
8:50 who wants it, and he is the **j**.
9:39 have come into this world to **j**:
12:48 what I say have a **j** appointed
12:48 that I have spoken will **j** them
Act 7:27 'Who made you our ruler and **j**?
7:35 made you our ruler and **j**?' This
10:42 'God has appointed Jesus to **j**
17:31 set a day when he is going to **j**
18:15 I don't want to be a **j** who gets
23:3 You sit there and **j** me by
24:10 "I know that you have been a **j**
25:9 charges with me as your **j**?"
Rom 2:1 who you are, if you **j** anyone,
2:1 When you **j** another person,
2:1 you, the **j**, do the same things.
2:3 When you **j** people for doing
2:16 will **j** people's secret thoughts.
3:6 God be able to **j** the world?
1Co 4:5 Therefore, don't **j** anything
1Co 5:12 Isn't it your business to **j** those
5:13 God will **j** those who are
6:2 God's people will **j** the world?
6:2 So if you're going to **j** the world,
6:3 you know that we will **j** angels,
10:15 **J** for yourselves what I'm
11:13 **J** your own situation.
Col 2:16 Therefore, let no one **j** you
2Ti 4:1 who is going to **j** those who are
4:8 The Lord, who is a fair **j**,
Heb 10:30 "The Lord will **j** his people."
12:23 You have come to a **j** (the God
13:4 God will **j** those who commit
Jas 4:11 Those who slander and **j** other
4:11 slander and **j** God's teachings.
4:11 If you **j** God's teachings,
4:12 There is only one teacher and **j**.
4:12 who are you to **j** your neighbor?
5:9 Realize that the **j** is standing at
1Pe 4:5 to the one who is ready to **j**
Jud 1:15 He has come to **j** all these
Rev 6:10 how long before you **j** and take
14:7 the time has come for him to **j**.
20:4 sat on them were allowed to **j**.

judged (45)

Gen 30:6 "Now God has **j** in my favor.
Jdg 10:2 He **j** Israel for 23 years.
10:3 He **j** Israel for 22 years.
12:7 Jephthah **j** Israel for six years.
12:8 Ibzan from Bethlehem **j** Israel.
12:9 He **j** Israel for seven years.
12:11 the tribe of Zebulun **j** Israel.
12:11 He **j** Israel for ten years.
12:13 from Pirathon **j** Israel.
12:14 He **j** Israel for eight years.
15:20 Samson **j** Israel for 20 years
16:31 Samson had **j** Israel for 20
1Sm 4:18 He had **j** Israel for 40 years.
7:6 So Samuel **j** Israel in Mizpah.
7:15 Samuel **j** Israel as long as he
7:17 There, too, he **j** Israel.
Psa 9:19 nations be **j** in your presence.
Isa 53:8 arrested, taken away, and **j**.
Jer 51:9 God has **j** Babylon.
Eze 7:27 them as they have **j** others.
36:19 I **j** them based on the way that
Dan 7:22 came and **j** in favor of the holy
Mat 7:1 so that you will not be **j**.
7:2 Otherwise, you will be **j** by the
Luk 6:37 and you will never be **j**.
Jon 5:24 They won't be **j** because they
5:29 come back to life and will be **j**.
12:31 "This world is being **j** now.
16:11 ruler of this world has been **j**.
Act 8:33 he was not **j** fairly.
Rom 2:12 and still sins will be **j** by them.
3:7 why am I still **j** as a sinner?
14:10 stand in front of God to be **j**.
1Co 5:3 I have already **j** the man who
10:29 Why should my freedom be **j**
11:31 we would not be **j**.
Heb 9:27 and after that they are **j**.
Jas 2:12 are going to be **j** by laws that
3:1 teach will be **j** more severely.
1Pe 4:6 they could be **j** like humans
2Pe 3:7 people will be **j** and destroyed.
Rev 11:18 has come for the dead to be **j**:
16:5 you have **j** these things.
20:12 The dead were **j** on the basis
20:13 People were **j** based on what

judge's (1)

Jon 19:13 outside and sat on the **j** seat

judges (70)

Gen 30:6 So she named him Dan [He **J**].
Num 25:5 So Moses said to the **j** of Israel,
Dtr 1:16 these instructions to your **j**:
16:18 Appoint **j** and officers for your
19:17 in front of the priests and **j** who
19:18 The **j** must make a thorough
21:2 your leaders and **j** must go and
25:1 The **j** will hear the case and
33:22 the tribe of Dan [He **J**] he said,
Jos 8:33 and **j** were standing on

Jos 23:2 j, and officers of Israel together.
24:1 leaders, chiefs, j, and officers,
Jdg 2:16 Then the LORD would send j
2:17 people wouldn't listen to the j.
2:18 But when the LORD appointed j
Rut 1:1 days when the j were ruling,
1Sm 2:10 The LORD j the ends of the
8:1 he made his sons j over Israel.
8:2 They were j in Beersheba.
2Sm 7:7 did I ever ask any of the j of
7:11 ever since I appointed j to rule
2Ki 23:22 of the j who governed Israel
1Ch 17:6 did I ever ask any of the j of
17:10 ever since I appointed j to rule
23:4 appointed to be officers and j,
26:29 They served as officials and j
2Ch 1:2 and battalions, j, every prince,
19:5 He appointed j in the country,
19:6 He told the j, "Pay attention to
Ezr 7:25 in your hands — will appoint j
10:14 meet with the leaders and j
Job 9:24 He covers the faces of its j.
12:17 and makes fools out of j.
Psa 7:8 The LORD j the people of the
9:8 He alone j the world with
9:8 He j ⌊its⌋ people fairly.
58:11 There is a God who j on earth."
94:15 The decisions of j will again
141:6 When their j are thrown off a
148:11 officials and all j on the earth,
Pro 8:16 so do nobles and all fair j.
29:14 When a king j the poor with
Ecc 11:9 things when he j everyone.
Isa 1:26 I will give you j like you had
3:2 and soldiers, j and prophets,
5:16 will be honored when he j.
16:5 He j and searches for justice.
29:21 those who lay traps for j,
40:23 makes earthly j worth nothing.
Eze 18:8 and he j everyone fairly.
44:24 the priests must act as j
Dan 3:2 advisers, treasurers, j, officers,
3:3 advisers, treasurers, j, officers,
Hos 7:7 They consume their j ⌊like⌋ a
13:10 in all your cities are your j?
Amo 2:3 I will take their j away from
Mic 7:3 J accept bribes. Powerful
Zep 3:3 Its j are ⌊like⌋ wolves in the
Mat 12:27 That's why they will be your j.
Luk 11:19 That's why they will be your j.
Jon 16:8 the world that God j it.
16:11 the world that God j it,
Act 13:20 "After that he gave his people j
1Co 6:4 a low opinion of to be your j?
11:32 But when the Lord j us,
Heb 4:12 God's word j a person's
1Pe 1:17 He is the God who j all people
2:23 to the one who j fairly.
Rev 18:8 God, who j her, is powerful.
19:11 integrity he j and wages war.

judging (11)

Mat 7:1 "Stop j so that you will not be
16:3 can forecast the weather by j
19:28 j the twelve tribes of Israel.
27:19 While Pilate was j the case,
Luk 6:37 "Stop j, and you will never be
12:56 can forecast the weather by j
Jon 7:24 Stop j by outward appearance!
1Co 5:12 do I have any business j those
6:2 of j insignificant cases?
11:31 we were j ourselves correctly,
Jas 4:11 Instead, you are j them.

judgment (84)

Exo 6:6 arm and with mighty acts of j.
Num 33:4 a mighty act of j on their gods.
1Sm 3:13 j against his household
25:33 May your good j be blessed.
29:9 "I admit that in my j you're as
2Ch 22:8 When Jehu was executing j
24:24 out ⌊the LORD's⌋ j on Joash.
Job 12:20 the good j of respected leaders.
23:7 and I would escape my j
24:1 to him see his days ⌊of j⌋?
34:23 in order to bring him to divine j.
36:17 But you are given the j evil
36:17 A fair j will be upheld.
37:23 is great in power and j,
Psa 1:5 will not be able to stand in the j
7:6 You have already pronounced j.
9:7 He has set up his throne for j.
9:16 The LORD is known by the j
82:1 pronounces j among the gods:
110:6 He will pass j on the nations
119:66 use⌋ good j and knowledge,
143:2 Do not take me to court for j,
149:9 to carry out the j that is written
Pro 16:10 he cannot voice a wrong j.
Isa 4:4 from Jerusalem with a spirit of j
28:26 God will guide him in j,
41:1 Let us come together for j.
58:2 disregarded God's j ⌊on them⌋.
Jer 48:21 "J has come to all the cities on
48:47 The j against Moab ends here.
51:9 Babylon. Its j is complete.
Dan 2:14 spoke to him using shrewd j.
5:11 found to have insight, good j,
5:12 j, and an extraordinary spirit.
5:14 that you have insight, good j,
7:26 But j will be handed down,
Amo 7:4 LORD was calling for j by fire.
Hab 1:12 the Babylonians to bring j.
Zep 3:5 He brings his j to light every
Mat 10:15 I can guarantee this truth: J
11:22 I can guarantee that j day will
11:24 I can guarantee that j day will
12:36 "I can guarantee that on j day
12:41 up with you at the time of j
12:42 up at the time of j with you.
Luk 10:12 I can guarantee that j day will
10:14 J day will be better for Tyre
11:31 will stand up at the time of j
11:32 will stand up at the time of j
Jon 5:22 He has entrusted j entirely to
5:27 the Son authority to pass j
8:16 Even if I do judge, my j is valid
8:16 I make my j with the Father
Act 24:25 self-control, and the coming j,
Rom 1:32 Although they know God's j
2:2 We know that God's j is right
2:3 think you will escape God's j?
2:16 I am spreading to make that j.
3:19 is brought under the j of God.
12:3 lead you to use good j based
1Co 11:29 a j against himself when
11:34 a gathering that brings j on you.
2Co 5:10 appear in front of Christ's j seat.
Gal 5:10 will suffer God's j regardless
2Th 1:5 proves that God's j is right
1Ti 3:2 use good j, be respectable,
5:24 going ahead of them to j.
2Ti 1:7 of power, love, and good j.
Tit 1:8 use good j, be fair and moral,
2:2 good character, to use good j,
2:5 to use good j, and to be morally
2:6 young men to use good j.
Heb 6:2 back to life, and eternal j.
10:27 is left is a terrifying wait for j
Jas 2:13 Mercy triumphs over j.
1Pe 4:17 has come for the j to begin,
2Pe 2:4 and is holding them for j.
2:9 for punishment on the day of j.
2:11 don't bring an insulting j
1Jn 4:17 with confidence to the day of j.
Jud 1:6 He held angels for j on the
1:9 dare to hand down a j against
Rev 17:1 I will show you the j of that
18:10 In one moment j has come to it!'

judgments (18)

2Sm 22:23 because all his j are in front of
1Ch 16:12 he did and the j he pronounced,
16:14 His j are pronounced
Psa 10:5 Your j are beyond his
18:22 because all his j are in front of
36:6 your j like the deep ocean.
48:11 rejoice because of your j.
97:8 Judah are delighted with your j,
105:5 and the j he pronounced,
105:7 His j are pronounced
Hos 6:5 My j shined on you like light.
Zep 3:15 has reversed the j against you.
Jon 5:30 ⌊to the Father⌋, I make my j.
5:30 My j are right because I don't
Jas 2:4 a corrupt standard to make j?
Rev 15:4 they know about your fair j."
16:7 your j are true and fair."
19:2 His j are true and fair.

judicial (1)

Psa 147:19 laws and j decisions to Israel.

Judith (1)

Gen 26:34 was 40 years old, he married J,

jug (5)

1Ki 17:12 in a jar and a little oil in a j.
17:14 and the j will always contain
17:16 and the j always contained
Mar 14:13 a man carrying a j of water.
Luk 22:10 a man carrying a j of water.

jugful (1)

Amo 6:6 those who drink wine by the j.

juice (4)

Num 6:3 or any kind of grape j,
18:27 floor or j from the winepress.
Sos 8:2 some j squeezed from my
Isa 65:8 When someone finds j for new

juicy (1)

Pro 15:17 love than j steaks where there

Julia (1)

Rom 16:15 Greet Philologus and J,

Julius (2)

Act 27:1 His name was J, and he
27:3 J treated Paul kindly and

jump (8)

Exo 8:4 The frogs will j on you,
Psa 114:6 what made you j like rams?
114:6 what made you j like lambs?
Zep 1:9 day I will punish all who j over
Mat 4:6 "If you are the Son of God, j!
Luk 1:44 I felt the baby j for joy.
4:9 are the Son of God, j from here!
Act 27:43 could swim to j overboard first

jumped (5)

Psa 114:4 The mountains j like rams.
114:4 The hills j like lambs.
Mar 10:50 coat, j up, and went to Jesus.
Jon 21:7 had taken off and j into the sea.
Act 14:10 The man j up and began to

jumping (1)

Act 3:8 The man was walking, j,

jumps (1)

Job 37:1 because of this and j out

jungle (3)

Jer 12:5 how can you live in the j along
49:19 a lion coming out of the j along
50:44 a lion coming out of the j along

Junias (1)

Rom 16:7 Greet Andronicus and J,

Jushab Hesed (1)

1Ch 3:20 Berechiah, Hasadiah, and J.

just (178)

Gen 8:21 living creature as I have j done.
15:12 As the sun was j about to set,
18:19 by doing what is right and j.
19:23 The sun had j risen over the
24:62 Isaac had j come back from
27:4 meal for me, j the way I like it.
27:6 "I've j heard your father
27:9 j the way he likes it.
27:13 J obey me and go!
27:14 j the way his father liked it.
29:15 Then Laban said to him, "J

Gen 40:22 But he hung the chief baker **j**
41:21 They looked **j** as sick as
41:28 "It's **j** as I said to Pharaoh.
42:14 "It's **j** as I told you,"
48:5 will be mine **j** as Reuben
Exo 5:13 **j** as when you had straw."
5:17 ⌊**J** plain⌋ lazy!" Pharaoh
12:32 **J** go! And bless me, too!"
14:3 are ⌊**j**⌋ wandering around.
14:24 **J** before dawn, the LORD
24:8 everything you have **j** heard."
27:8 It must be made **j** as you were
28:27 This will be close to the seam **j**
28:28 This will attach it **j** above the
38:18 **j** like the curtains of the
39:20 This was close to the seam **j**
39:21 was attached **j** above
Num 11:15 why don't you **j** kill me?
11:19 They won't eat it **j** for one or
14:3 bringing us to this land — **j**
20:4 assembly into this desert **j**
21:5 you make us leave Egypt — **j**
22:5 "A nation has **j** come here from
22:11 'Some people have **j** come
32:14 "You're **j** like your parents!
Jos 1:18 **J** be strong and courageous!"
2:5 dark and the gate was **j** about
3:7 know that I am with you **j** as
4:19 at Gilgal, **j** east of Jericho.
8:6 'They're running away from us **j**
8:14 **j** where ⌊Joshua⌋ expected.
18:15 The southern border begins **j**
Jdg 7:19 of the midnight watch **j** at
9:2 sons to rule you or **j** one man?
9:18 over the citizens of Shechem **j**
13:10 the other day has **j** appeared
13:23 or hear all these things **j** now."
14:15 Did the two of you invite us ⌊**j**⌋
15:15 from a donkey that had **j** died.
16:13 Samson replied, "**J** weave the
16:28 God, give me strength **j** one
18:9 "Don't **j** sit there! Go at once and
18:12 This is why the place **j** west of
19:20 **J** don't spend the night in the
19:24 **J** don't do such a godless thing
20:39 **j** like in the first battle."
21:23 The men of Benjamin did **j** that.
Rut 1:13 up and stay single **j** for them?
1:22 to enter Bethlehem **j** when
2:4 **J** then, Boaz was coming from
2:7 She **j** sat down this minute in
2:19 **J** where did you work?
4:1 **J** then, the relative about whom
1Sm 8:8 They're doing **j** what they've
9:12 He ⌊**j**⌋ went into the city today
11:5 **J** then Saul was coming from
17:28 You came here **j** to see the
17:33 You're **j** a boy, but he's been a
20:2 It's **j** not that way."
2Sm 3:22 **J** then David's men and Joab
11:4 (She had **j** cleansed herself
11:10 "Didn't you **j** come from a
13:35 have come. It's **j** as I said."
15:20 You came to us **j** yesterday.
19:36 I'll **j** cross the Jordan River with
1Ki 2:38 "I'll do **j** what Your Majesty
2:42 I'll do **j** what you said'?
3:18 **J** the two of us were in the
12:32 **j** like the festival in Judah.
21:11 They did **j** as she had written
21:19 Have you murdered someone **j**
2Ki 5:22 He says, '**J** now two young
9:26 '**J** as I saw the blood of Naboth
Neh 5:5 Our children are **j** like theirs.
Est 2:4 and so he did **j** that.
4:13 "Do not imagine that **j** because
4:17 Mordecai did **j** as Esther had
9:22 They were to observe them **j**
Job 24:19 ⌊**J** as⌋ drought and heat steal
30:20 I stand up, but you **j** look at me.
35:2 'My case is more **j** than God's,'
39:11 Can you trust it **j** because it's
Psa 9:4 You have defended my **j** cause:
35:25 **j** what we wanted!"
37:6 your **j** cause like the noonday
Pro 2:9 understand what is right and **j**
Pro 6:10 "**J** a little sleep, just a little
6:10 a little sleep, **j** a little slumber,
6:10 a little slumber, **j** a little nap."
7:2 Follow my teachings **j** as you
14:24 of fools is **j** that — stupidity!
21:7 they refuse to do what is **j**.
24:33 "**J** a little sleep, just a little
24:33 a little sleep, **j** a little slumber,
24:33 a little slumber, **j** a little nap."
29:7 A righteous person knows the **j**
Ecc 3:19 One dies **j** like the other.
7:12 Wisdom protects us **j** as
11:5 **J** as you don't know how the
12:10 The spokesman tried to find **j**
Sos 3:4 I had **j** left them when I found
Isa 4:1 **J** let us marry you for your
28:9 To children **j** weaned from
28:9 To those **j** taken from their
39:8 He added, "**J** let there be peace
49:6 "You are not **j** my servant who
55:9 "**J** as the heavens are higher
58:2 They ask me for **j** decrees.
58:5 Is fasting **j** bowing your head
Jer 4:6 Don't **j** stand there!
8:14 Why are we **j** sitting here?
20:15 the news that he had **j** become
44:30 **j** as I handed over King
51:50 Don't **j** stand there.
Eze 23:44 Oholah and Oholibah **j** as they
40:23 opposite the north gate **j** like
Dan 4:33 **J** then the prediction about
4:36 **J** then my mind came back to
Mic 2:11 They would be **j** the type of
Hab 2:19 **J** look at it! It's covered with
Zep 3:8 The LORD declares, "**J** wait!
Zec 8:8 who is faithful and **j**.
8:13 **J** as you, people of Judah and
14:4 **j** east of Jerusalem.
Mat 5:45 whether they are **j** or unjust.
8:8 But **j** give a command,
9:18 "My daughter **j** died.
12:40 **J** as Jonah was in the belly of
13:40 **J** as weeds are gathered and
14:36 begged him to let them touch **j**
18:22 "I tell you, not **j** seven times,
24:27 again **j** as lightning flashes
26:47 **J** then, while Jesus was still
26:65 You've **j** heard him dishonor
26:74 **J** then a rooster crowed.
Mar 4:36 took Jesus along in a boat **j** as
5:28 "If I can **j** touch his clothes,
5:36 "Don't be afraid! **J** believe."
5:39 isn't dead. She's **j** sleeping."
14:43 **J** then, while Jesus was still
14:72 **J** then a rooster crowed a
16:2 when the sun had **j** come up.
16:7 **j** as he told them."
Luk 7:7 But **j** give a command,
8:50 **J** believe, and she will get
8:52 not dead. She's **j** sleeping."
11:30 **J** as Jonah became a
12:41 did you use this illustration **j**
22:60 **J** then, while he was still
23:54 and the day of worship was **j**
Jon 5:28 be surprised at what I've **j** said.
18:27 and **j** then a rooster crowed.
21:10 "Bring some of the fish you've **j**
Act 7:51 You're **j** like your ancestors.
27:33 **J** before daybreak Paul was
Rom 2:29 not **j** a written rule.
1Co 4:20 God's kingdom is not **j** talk,
7:6 What I have **j** said is not meant
9:26 as if I were **j** shadow boxing.
10:24 and not **j** about themselves.
Eph 2:3 anger **j** like everyone else.
Col 4:1 Masters, be **j** and fair to your
1Th 3:6 But Timothy has **j** now come
3:12 else, **j** as we love you.
2Pe 2:18 who have **j** escaped from those
Rev 2:25 **J** hold on to what you have
18:7 Now give her **j** as much torture

justice (130)

Exo 23:2 with the majority to pervert **j**.
23:6 "Never deny **j** to poor people in
23:8 those who can see and deny **j**
Lev 19:15 corrupt when administering **j**.
19:35 **j** concerning length,
Dtr 10:18 orphans and widows receive **j**.
16:19 Never pervert **j**. Instead, be
16:19 blind wise people and deny **j**
16:20 Strive for nothing but **j** so that
24:17 foreigners and orphans of **j**.
27:19 or widows of **j** will be cursed."
32:41 sword and take **j** into my own
1Sm 8:3 bribes and denied people **j**.
2Sm 15:4 would make sure that he got **j**."
23:3 who rules humans with **j** rules
1Ki 7:7 He made the Hall of **J**,
7:8 location than the Hall of **J**,
8:59 his people Israel **j** every day as
10:9 maintain **j** and righteousness."
2Ch 9:8 maintain **j** and righteousness."
Job 8:3 Does God distort **j**,
9:19 If it is about **j**, who will charge
16:18 let my cry ⌊for **j**⌋ be stopped.
19:7 I call for help, but there is no **j**.
29:14 I practiced **j**, and it was my
32:9 They don't understand what **j** is
34:12 Almighty will never pervert **j**.
34:17 Should anyone who hates **j** be
36:6 He grants **j** to those who are
40:8 "Would you undo my **j**?
Psa 10:18 in order to provide **j** for orphans
17:1 Hear my plea for **j**,
33:5 loves righteousness and **j**.
37:28 The LORD loves **j**,
45:6 your kingdom is a scepter for **j**.
51:4 So you hand down **j** when you
67:4 you judge everyone with **j**
72:1 O God, give the king your **j**
72:2 oppressed ⌊people⌋ with **j**.
72:4 May he grant **j** to the people
89:14 Righteousness and **j** are the
94:15 are decent will pursue **j**.
97:2 Righteousness and **j** are the
98:9 He will judge the world with **j**
99:4 strength is that he loves **j**.
101:1 I will sing about mercy and **j**.
106:3 Blessed are those who defend **j**
111:7 works are done with truth and **j**.
119:84 those who persecute me to **j**?
122:5 The court of **j** sits there.
135:14 The LORD will provide **j** for his
146:7 He brings about **j** for those who
Pro 1:3 and **j** and fairness —
2:8 to guard those on paths of **j**
8:20 on the paths of **j**,
13:23 away where there is no **j**.
17:23 a bribe to corrupt the ways of **j**.
18:5 an innocent person of **j**.
19:28 A worthless witness mocks **j**,
21:15 When **j** is done, a righteous
25:5 and **j** will make his throne
28:5 Evil people do not understand **j**,
29:4 By means of **j**, a king builds up
29:26 but **j** for humanity comes from
31:5 and change the standard of **j**
Ecc 3:16 There is wickedness where **j**
5:8 being oppressed, denied **j**,
Isa 1:17 Seek **j**. Arrest oppressors.
1:21 She was full of **j**, But now
1:27 be pardoned by ⌊the LORD's⌋ **j**,
5:7 He hoped for **j** but saw only
9:7 He will uphold it with **j** and
10:2 They deprive the poor of **j**.
11:5 **J** will be the belt around his
16:5 He judges and searches for **j**.
28:6 He will give a spirit of **j** to
28:17 I will make **j** a measuring line
29:21 deny **j** to people who are in the
30:18 The LORD is a God of **j**.
32:1 and officials will rule with **j**.
32:7 when needy people plead for **j**.
32:16 Then **j** will live in the
33:5 Zion with **j** and righteousness.
42:1 He will bring **j** to the nations.
42:3 He will faithfully bring about **j**.
42:4 or crushed until he has set up **j**
51:4 My **j** will become a light for the
51:5 I will bring **j** to people.
56:1 the LORD says: Preserve **j**,

Isa 59:4 No one calls for **j**, and no one
59:8 There's no **j** on their highways.
59:9 That is why **j** is far from us,
59:11 We hope for **j**, but there is none.
59:14 **J** is turned back, Truth has
59:15 he's angry because there's no **j**.
61:8 I, the LORD, love **j**.
Jer 5:4 and the **j** that God demands.
5:5 and the **j** that God demands."
9:24 and **j** on the earth. This kind of
12:1 want to talk to you about your **j**.
30:11 I will correct you with **j**.
46:28 I will correct you with **j**.
Lam 3:36 or deprive people of **j** in court.
Amo 5:7 You, Israel, turn **j** into poison
5:15 Then you will be able to have **j**
5:24 But let **j** flow like a river and
6:12 Yet, you have turned **j** into
Mic 3:1 You should know **j**.
3:8 Spirit, with **j**, and with strength.
3:9 You despise **j** and pervert
3:11 leaders exchange **j** for bribes.
Hab 1:4 and **j** is never carried out.
1:4 so that when **j** is carried out,
1:7 their own kind of **j** and honor.
Zep 2:3 in the land who carry out his **j**.
Zec 7:9 Armies says: Administer real **j**,
Mal 2:17 or "Where is the God of **j**?"
Mat 12:18 will announce **j** to the nations.
12:20 until he has made **j** victorious.
23:23 But you have neglected **j**,
Luk 11:42 But you have ignored **j** and the
18:3 to him and saying, 'Give me **j**.'
18:5 I'll have to give her **j**.
18:7 chosen people **j** when they cry
18:8 that he will give them **j** quickly.
Act 17:31 going to judge the world with **j**,
28:4 but **j** won't let him live."
Rom 3:4 "So you hand down **j** when you
3:26 shows that he is a God of **j**,
Heb 1:8 your kingdom is a scepter for **j**.

justify (3)

Luk 10:29 man wanted to **j** his question.
16:15 "You try to **j** your actions in
Jon 2:18 us to **j** what you're doing?"

justly (1)

Isa 11:4 He will judge the poor **j**.

Justus (2)

Act 1:23 also known as **J**) and Matthias.
Col 4:11 Jesus, called **J**, also greets

Juttah (2)

Jos 15:55 Maon, Carmel, Ziph, **J**,
21:16 Ain, **J**, and Beth Shemesh.

K

Kabal Am (1)

2Ki 15:10 attacked him at **K**,

Kabzeel (3)

Jos 15:21 their villages: **K**, Eder, Jagur,
2Sm 23:20 was from **K** and was a brave
1Ch 11:22 was from **K** and was a brave

Kadesh (18)

Gen 14:7 came to En Mishpat (that is, **K**),
16:14 there between **K** and Bered.
20:1 settled between **K** and Shur.
Num 13:26 whole community of Israel at **K**
20:1 and they stayed at **K**.
20:14 Moses sent messengers from **K**
20:16 "Now we're here in **K**,
20:22 community of Israel left **K**
27:14 was the oasis of Meribah at **K**
33:36 Geber and set up camp at **K**
33:37 They moved from **K** and set up
Dtr 1:46 That's why you stayed in **K** as
32:51 me at the oasis of Meribah at **K**
Jdg 11:16 to the Red Sea and came to **K**.
Jdg 11:17 people of Israel remained at **K**.
Psa 29:8 the wilderness of **K** tremble.
Eze 47:19 the oasis at Meribah in **K** along
48:28 to the oasis at Meribah in **K**,

Kadesh Barnea (10)

Num 32:8 did when I sent them from **K**
34:4 then goes past Zin and ends at **K**
Dtr 1:2 from Mount Horeb to **K** by way
1:19 At last we came to **K**.
2:14 from the time we left **K** until we
9:23 when the LORD sent you from **K**,
Jos 10:41 defeated the people from **K**
14:6 man of God, at **K** about you and
14:7 servant Moses sent me from **K**
15:3 Zin and goes up south of **K**.

Kadmiel (8)

Ezr 2:40 descendants of Jeshua and **K**,
3:9 his sons and relatives and **K**
Neh 7:43 of **K** and of Hodeiah:
9:4 Then Jeshua, Bani, **K**,
9:5 Then the Levites — Jeshua, **K**,
10:9 (of the sons of Henadad), **K**,
12:8 Binnui, **K**, Sherebiah, Judah,
12:24 and Jeshua (son of **K**).

Kadmonites (1)

Gen 15:19 Kenites, the Kenizzites, the **K**,

Kain (1)

Jos 15:57 **K**, Gibeah, and Timnah.

Kallai (1)

Neh 12:20 from Sallai, **K**; from Amok,

Kamon (1)

Jdg 10:5 Jair died and was buried in **K**.

Kanah (3)

Jos 16:8 goes west along the **K** River
17:9 southward to the **K** River.
19:28 Abdon, Rehob, Hammon, **K**,

Kareah (5)

2Ki 25:23 Johanan (son of **K**),
Jer 40:8 and Jonathan (sons of **K**),
43:2 Johanan (son of **K**),
43:4 So Johanan (son of **K**),
43:5 Johanan (son of **K**) and all the

Kareah's (9)

Jer 40:13 **K** son Johanan and all the
40:15 Then Johanan, **K** son, secretly
40:16 **K** son, "Don't do that!
41:11 When **K** son Johanan and all
41:13 Ishmael saw **K** son Johanan
41:14 and ran to **K** son Johanan.
41:16 Then **K** son Johanan and all
42:1 along with **K** son Johanan
42:8 called **K** son Johanan,

Karka (1)

Jos 15:3 up to Addar, around to **K**,

Karkor (1)

Jdg 8:10 Zebah and Zalmunna were in **K**

Karnaim (1)

Amo 6:13 to capture **K** by ourselves."

Kartah (1)

Jos 21:34 pasturelands: Jokneam, **K**,

Kartan (1)

Jos 21:32 Hammoth Dor, and **K**.

Kattath (1)

Jos 19:15 This also includes **K**,

katydid (1)

Lev 11:22 cricket, **k**, or grasshopper.

Kedar (9)

Gen 25:13 firstborn), **K**, Adbeel, Mibsam,
1Ch 1:29 then **K**, Adbeel, Mibsam,
Psa 120:5 or to stay in the tents of **K**.
Isa 42:11 the settlements of **K** praise him.
60:7 All of the flocks from **K** will
Jer 2:10 Send ⌞someone⌟ to **K**,
49:28 This is about the tribe of **K** and
49:28 says: Get ready, attack **K**,
Eze 27:21 Arabia and all the officials of **K**

Kedar's (3)

Sos 1:5 **K** tents, like Solomon's curtains.
Isa 21:16 All of **K** honor will be gone in
21:17 **K** mighty archers, will be few.

Kedem (3)

Jdg 6:3 and **K** came and damaged the
6:33 and **K** combined their armies,
7:12 Midian, Amalek, and all of **K**

Kedemah (2)

Gen 25:15 Tema, Jetur, Naphish, and **K**.
1Ch 1:31 Jetur, Naphish, and **K**.

Kedemoth (4)

Dtr 2:26 From the desert of **K**,
Jos 13:18 Jahaz, **K**, Mephaath,
21:37 **K**, and Mephaath.
1Ch 6:79 **K** with its pastureland and

Kedem's (1)

Jdg 8:10 that was left of **K** entire army.

Kedesh (12)

Jos 12:22 the king of **K**, the king of
15:23 **K**, Hazor, Ithnan,
19:37 **K**, Edrei, En Hazor,
20:7 **K** in Galilee in the mountains
21:32 **K** in Galilee (a city of refuge for
Jdg 4:6 from **K** in Naphtali.
4:9 started out for **K** with Barak.
4:10 and Naphtali together at **K**.
4:11 oak tree at Zaanannim near **K**
2Ki 15:29 **K**, Hazor, Gilead, Galilee,
1Ch 6:72 they received **K** with its
6:76 they received **K** in Galilee with

keen (1)

1Ki 4:29 God gave Solomon wisdom — **k**

keep (291)

Gen 6:19 the ship in order to **k** them alive
14:21 and **k** everything else for
18:19 and his family after him to **k**
24:19 "I'll also **k** drawing water for
26:3 I will **k** the oath that I swore to
32:16 and **k** a distance between the
33:9 **K** what you have, Brother."
38:23 "Let her **k** what I gave her,
41:9 a promise I failed to **k**.
42:1 "Why do you **k** looking at each
50:20 This was to **k** many people
Exo 5:17 "That's why you **k** saying,
12:42 generations must **k** watch
16:19 "No one may **k** any of it until
16:23 Save all that's left over, and **k**
21:36 its owner didn't **k** it confined,
22:7 ⌞other⌟ valuables to **k** for him,
22:10 kind of animal to **k** for him,
27:21 and his descendants must **k**
28:32 all around it to **k** it from tearing.
39:23 all around it to **k** it from tearing.
Lev 19:13 Never **k** the pay you owe a
24:3 Aaron must **k** the lamps lit in
24:4 Aaron must **k** the lamps on the
26:9 and I will **k** my promise to you.
Num 11:13 They **k** crying for me to give
15:8 other kind of sacrifice — to **k**
17:10 and **k** it there as a sign to warn
22:16 Don't let anything **k** you from
30:9 woman must **k** her vow
30:13 not his wife has to **k** any vow
30:14 that she must **k** her vow
30:14 She must **k** it because he said
36:7 Every Israelite must **k** the tribal
36:9 Each Israelite tribe must **k** the
Dtr 2:29 We'll **k** going until we cross the
2:36 had walls that could **k** us out.

Dtr 4:31 that he swore he would **k**.
7:9 **K** in mind that the LORD your
7:12 the LORD your God will **k** his
7:15 The LORD will **k** you from
11:18 of mine to heart and **k** them
17:19 He must **k** it with him and read
22:2 **K** it until the owner comes
23:21 your God expects you to **k** it.
24:12 If the person is poor, don't **k** the
28:41 but you won't be able to **k** them
Jos 22:5 and **k** his commands.
23:6 you must be very strong to **k**
Jdg 3:19 The king replied, "**K** quiet!"
18:19 They told him, "**K** quiet!
19:5 "Eat something to **k** up your
19:8 "Eat something to **k** up your
Rut 4:10 to **k** the inheritance in the dead
1Sm 1:21 To **k** his vow, the man Elkanah
1:23 May the LORD **k** his word."
2:28 ancestors the right to **k** portions
10:3 **K** going until you come to the
2Sm 7:25 "Now, LORD God, **k** the
14:11 LORD your God in order to **k**
14:14 He never plans to **k** a banished
15:7 "Let me go to Hebron and **k** the
15:22 "Go ahead and **k** marching."
18:18 He said, "I have no son to **k** the
19:29 "Why do you **k** talking about it?
21:5 He planned to wipe us out to **k**
1Ki 1:2 in your arms and **k** you warm."
2:4 because the LORD will **k**
2:43 Why didn't you **k** your oath to
6:12 and **k** my commands,
8:23 You **k** your promise of mercy to
8:25 "Now, LORD God of Israel, **k**
8:58 him and **k** his commands,
8:58 our ancestors ⌞to **k**⌟.
8:61 laws and **k** his commands as
9:4 and **k** my laws and rules,
9:6 me and do not **k** my commands
11:11 that I commanded you to **k**,
11:33 I consider right or **k** my laws
15:17 Ramah to **k** anyone from going
18:5 then we can **k** the horses and
2Ki 7:4 us something to **k** us alive,
1Ch 17:23 "Now, LORD, faithfully **k** the
29:18 **K** their hearts directed toward
2Ch 6:14 You **k** your promise of mercy to
6:16 "Now, LORD God of Israel, **k**
16:1 Ramah to **k** anyone from going
Ezr 4:5 They bribed officials to **k** the
4:21 **K** this city from being rebuilt
9:1 have failed to **k** themselves
Neh 1:5 you faithfully **k** your promise
5:9 our God to **k** our enemies from
5:13 who refuses to **k** this promise.
9:20 You didn't **k** your manna to
9:32 You faithfully **k** your promises.
13:22 and guard the gates to **k**
Est 3:11 "You can **k** your silver and do
Job 4:2 But who can **k** from talking?
5:19 He will **k** you safe from six
7:11 So I won't **k** my mouth shut,
10:16 You **k** working your miracles
10:17 You **k** finding new witnesses
10:17 You **k** increasing your anger
10:17 You **k** bringing new armies
13:5 I wish you would **k** silent.
14:13 in Sheol and **k** me hidden there
14:16 you will not **k** ⌞a record of⌟ my
16:3 that you **k** on answering ⌞me⌟?
22:22 and **k** his words in your heart.
22:27 and you will **k** your vow to him.
30:10 they **k** their distance from me
31:20 my sheep didn't **k** him warm ....)
33:31 **K** quiet, and let me speak.
33:33 **K** quiet, and I'll teach you
41:5 you play with it like a bird or **k**
Psa 12:7 You will **k** each one safe from
16:8 I always **k** the LORD in front of
19:13 **K** me from sinning.
31:20 You **k** them in a shelter,
33:19 death and **k** them alive during
34:13 **K** your tongue from saying evil
38:11 and my friends **k** their distance
41:2 protect him and **k** him alive.
Psa 50:14 and **k** your vows to the Most
50:18 You **k** company with people
56:12 I will **k** my vows by offering
61:8 as I **k** my vows day after day.
66:13 I will **k** my vows to you,
76:11 LORD your God, and **k** them.
77:4 (You **k** my eyelids open.)
81:9 Never **k** any strange god
83:1 Do not **k** quiet, O God.
101:4 I will **k** far away from devious
116:14 I will **k** my vows to the LORD
116:18 I will **k** my vows to the LORD
119:9 How can a young person **k** his
119:38 **K** your promise to me so that I
119:106 I took an oath, and I will **k** it.
140:1 **K** me safe from violent people.
140:4 **K** me safe from violent people.
141:3 **K** watch over the door of my
141:9 **K** me away from the trap they
143:11 O LORD, **k** me alive for the
Pro 3:1 and **k** my commands in mind,
3:26 He will **k** your foot from getting
4:13 **K** it because it is your life.
4:15 away from it, and **k** on walking.
4:21 **K** them deep within your heart
5:13 nor did I **k** my ear open to my
6:24 to **k** you from an evil woman
11:13 in spirit can **k** a secret.
19:7 his friends **k** their distance from
20:13 **K** your eyes open,
22:18 It is pleasant if you **k** them in
22:24 and never **k** company with a
23:19 My son, listen, be wise, and **k**
27:27 and to **k** your servant girls
30:7 Don't **k** them from me before I
30:8 **K** vanity and lies far away from
Ecc 3:6 a time to **k** and a time to throw
3:7 a time to **k** quiet and a time to
4:11 together, they can **k** warm,
4:11 but how can one person **k**
5:4 don't be slow to **k** it because
5:4 like fools. **K** your promise.
5:5 than to make one and not **k** it.
12:13 and **k** his commands,
Isa 7:21 On that day a person will **k**
18:4 I will **k** quiet and watch from
38:16 give me health and **k** me alive.
43:6 to the south, "Do not **k** them."
47:7 consider these things or **k**
47:11 won't know how to **k** it away.
47:12 **K** practicing your spells and
47:14 There are no glowing coals to **k**
56:4 castrated men who **k** my days
56:6 All of them will **k** the day of
Jer 4:19 I can't **k** quiet because I hear a
11:5 I will **k** the oath I made to your
11:6 of this promise, and **k** them.
11:8 because they did not **k** all the
11:8 that I commanded them to **k**."
14:10 They don't **k** their feet where
15:17 I didn't **k** company with those
16:12 evil ways that **k** you from
17:15 People **k** asking me,
23:17 They **k** saying to those who
29:10 I will **k** my promise to you and
33:14 "when I will **k** the promise that
34:9 No one was supposed to **k**
34:10 and not to **k** them as slaves
42:4 I won't **k** anything from you."
44:7 Why do you **k** destroying men,
44:25 **K** your vows, and do what you
47:6 long will you **k** on fighting?
48:10 Cursed are those who **k** their
49:11 and I will **k** them alive.
Lam 1:11 for food to **k** themselves alive.
1:16 comfort I need to **k** me alive.
1:19 for food to **k** themselves alive.
3:21 hope is that I **k** this one thing
3:49 My eyes will **k** flowing without
Eze 17:18 the treaty that he pledged to **k**.
18:16 He doesn't **k** the security for a
20:37 punishment and make you **k**
22:30 walls to defend the land and **k**
42:13 the priests **k** the holiest
44:20 They must **k** the hair on their
Dan 5:17 told the king, "**K** your gifts.
Dan 5:19 he wanted to **k** alive.
7:18 of the kingdom and **k**
9:4 You **k** your promise and show
12:4 **k** these words secret,
Hos 5:4 done **k** them from returning
10:4 promises they don't intend to **k**.
13:2 They **k** on sinning more and
Joe 2:8 They **k** in their own lines.
2:20 "I will **k** the northern ⌞army⌟ far
Amo 3:8 Who can **k** from prophesying?
9:4 I will **k** my eyes on them so
Jnh 2:9 I will **k** my vow. Victory belongs
Mic 7:5 **K** your mouth shut even when
Nah 1:15 **K** your vows! This wickedness
2:1 **K** a lookout on the road!
Hab 1:13 Why do you **k** watching
1:17 Will they **k** on emptying their
Hag 1:6 have enough to **k** you warm.
Mat 23:16 a person must **k** his oath.'
23:18 a person must **k** his oath.'
26:43 they couldn't **k** their eyes open.
Mar 1:25 "**K** quiet, and come out of him!"
7:9 order to **k** your own traditions!
14:40 they couldn't **k** their eyes open.
Luk 1:45 the Lord would **k** his promise
4:35 "**K** quiet, and come out of him!"
4:42 they tried to **k** him from leaving.
8:15 But they **k** it in their good and
18:5 Otherwise, she'll **k** coming to
Jon 10:24 "How long will you **k** us in
11:37 sight **k** Lazarus from dying?"
17:11 Holy Father, **k** them safe by the
18:36 my followers would fight to **k**
Act 5:38 "We should **k** away from these
8:36 What can **k** me from being
15:20 them to **k** away from things
16:23 the jailer to **k** them under tight
23:35 orders to **k** Paul under guard
24:4 I don't want to **k** you too long.
25:4 soon and would **k** Paul there.
26:6 now because I expect God to **k**
26:7 I expect God to **k** his promise.
27:42 to **k** them from swimming
Rom 1:31 any sense, don't **k** promises,
14:22 **k** it between yourself and God.
1Co 7:37 If his decision is to **k** her ⌞at
13:5 It doesn't **k** track of wrongs.
14:34 the women must **k** silent.
14:39 and don't **k** anyone from
2Co 12:7 Therefore, to **k** me from
12:7 torments me to **k** me from being
Php 1:9 I pray that your love will **k** on
4:1 Therefore, dear friends, **k** your
4:8 Finally, brothers and sisters, **k**
Col 3:2 **K** your mind on things above,
4:2 **K** praying. Pay attention when
1Th 2:16 because they try to **k** us from
3:8 long as you **k** your relationship
4:3 It is God's will that you **k** away
5:22 **K** away from every kind of evil.
5:23 May he **k** your whole being —
1Ti 5:22 **K** yourself morally pure.
6:9 rich **k** falling into temptation.
2Ti 4:5 But you must **k** a clear head in
Phm 1:13 I wanted to **k** him here with me.
Heb 11:11 that God would **k** his promise.
12:13 **K** walking along straight paths
1Pe 2:11 I'm encouraging you to **k** away
3:10 days must **k** their tongues from
3:16 **K** your conscience clear.
4:7 and **k** your minds clear so that
5:8 **K** your mind clear,
2Pe 1:10 If you **k** doing this,
1Jn 3:3 in Christ **k** themselves pure,
Jud 1:6 who didn't **k** their position
Rev 3:10 I will **k** you safe during the time
3:18 that you may **k** your shameful,
7:1 earth to **k** them from blowing
11:6 in order to **k** rain from falling
12:17 the ones who **k** God's
14:12 who obey his commands and **k**
20:3 the pit over the serpent to **k**

keeper (3)

1Ch 9:21 was the **k** at the entrance to the
Act 19:35 city of the Ephesians is the **k**

Act 19:35 knows that Ephesus is the **k**

keeping (23)

Gen 41:49 finally gave up **k** any records
Dtr 23:21 your God, don't avoid **k** it.
1Sm 25:33 Also, may you be blessed for **k**
1Ch 23:29 the ingredients and **k** track
2Ch 31:18 be faithful in **k** themselves holy
Est 8:14 in **k** with the king's command.
Psa 25:7 Remember me, O LORD, in **k**
51:1 in **k** with your mercy.
51:1 In **k** with your unlimited
73:13 I've received no reward for **k**
106:45 In **k** with his rich mercy,
119:149 In **k** with your mercy,
119:159 O LORD, in **k** with your mercy,
143:12 In **k** with your mercy,
Lam 3:32 he will have compassion in **k**
Eze 17:14 only survive by **k** the treaty.
Dan 11:14 your own people will rebel in **k**
Act 15:29 by **k** away from food sacrificed
1Co 7:19 But **k** what God commands is
Php 2:2 and **k** one purpose in mind.
3:6 approval by **k** Jewish laws,
1Ti 2:11 in **k** with her position.
5:2 while **k** yourself morally pure.

keeps (31)

Lev 15:31 anything that **k** them from being
Num 14:27 that **k** complaining about me?
23:19 he makes a promise, he **k** it.
36:8 In this way every Israelite **k** the
Dtr 7:9 He is a faithful God, who **k** his
Rut 4:5 This **k** the inheritance in the
1Sm 10:2 He **k** asking, "What can I do
17:25 He **k** coming to challenge
1Ki 3:23 "This one **k** saying,
3:23 and that one **k** saying,
Job 3:26 And trouble **k** coming!"
5:12 He **k** shrewd people from
33:18 He **k** their souls from the pit
34:29 If he **k** quiet, who can condemn
Psa 27:5 He **k** me hidden in his tent.
146:9 But he **k** wicked people from
Pro 11:12 who has understanding **k** quiet.
17:9 but whoever **k** bringing up the
17:28 to be wise if he **k** silent.
17:28 if he **k** his lips sealed.
21:23 and his tongue **k** himself out
31:27 She **k** a close eye on the
Ecc 5:20 because God **k** them occupied
Isa 56:2 Blessed is the one who **k** the
58:4 The way you fast today **k** you
Jer 6:7 As a well **k** its water fresh,
6:7 so Jerusalem **k** its evil fresh.
Mat 15:23 She **k** shouting behind us."
Luk 23:2 He **k** them from paying taxes to
1Co 1:9 God faithfully **k** his promises.
10:13 who faithfully **k** his promises,

Kehelathah (2)

Num 33:22 Rissah and set up camp at **K**.
33:23 They moved from **K** and set up

Keilah (18)

Jos 15:44 **K**, Achzib, and Mareshah.
1Sm 23:1 are fighting against **K**?
23:2 the Philistines, and save **K**."
23:3 we'll be⌋ if we go to **K** against
23:4 He said, "Go to **K**.
23:5 David and his men went to **K**,
23:5 the people who lived in **K**.
23:6 son Abiathar fled to David at **K**,
23:7 was told that David went to **K**,
23:8 to go to war and blockade **K**,
23:10 that Saul is going to come to **K**
23:11 Will the citizens of **K** hand me
23:12 "Will the citizens of **K** hand me
23:13 about six hundred in all, left **K**.
23:13 "David has escaped from **K**!"
1Ch 4:19 first settled **K** of the Garmites
Neh 3:17 charge of half the district of **K**,
3:18 charge of half the district of **K**.

Kelaiah (1)

Ezr 10:23 **K** (that is, Kelita), Pethahiah,

Kelita (3)

Ezr 10:23 (that is, **K**), Pethahiah, Judah,
Neh 8:7 **K**, Azariah, Jozabad, Hanan,
10:10 Hodiah, **K**, Pelaiah, Hanan,

Kemuel (3)

Gen 22:21 (his brother), **K** (father of Aram
Num 34:24 **K**, son of Shiphtan, the leader
1Ch 27:17 son of **K** for the family of Aaron:

Kenan (6)

Gen 5:9 he became the father of **K**.
5:10 After he became the father of **K**,
5:12 When **K** was 70 years old,
5:13 **K** lived 840 years and had
5:14 **K** lived a total of 910 years;
1Ch 1:2 **K**, Mahalalel, Jared,

Kenath (2)

Num 32:42 Nobah captured **K** and its
1Ch 2:23 captured Havvoth Jair with **K**

Kenaz (12)

Gen 36:11 Omar, Zepho, Gatam, and **K**.
36:15 were Teman, Omar, Zepho, **K**,
36:42 **K**, Teman, Mibzar,
Jos 14:6 Jephunneh and grandson of **K**,
14:14 Jephunneh and grandson of **K**,
15:17 son of Caleb's brother **K**,
Jdg 1:13 of Caleb's younger brother **K**,
3:9 of Caleb's younger brother **K**.
3:11 Then Othniel, son of **K**,
1Ch 1:36 **K** and Amalek, son of Timna.
1:53 **K**, Teman, Mibzar,
4:15 Elah's son was **K**.

Kenaz's (1)

1Ch 4:13 **K** sons were Othniel and

Kenite (4)

Jdg 1:16 of Moses' father-in-law, the **K**,
4:11 Heber the **K** had separated from
4:17 the wife of Heber the **K**.
5:24 Jael, wife of Heber the **K**,

Kenites (8)

Gen 15:19 It is the land of the **K**,
Num 24:21 Then he saw the **K** and
Jdg 4:11 the other **K** (the descendants
1Sm 15:6 Then Saul said to the **K**,
15:6 So the **K** left the Amalekites.
27:10 of the Negev where the **K** live."
30:29 the cities belonging to the **K**,
1Ch 2:55 These people are the **K** who

Kenizzite (1)

Num 32:12 Caleb (son of Jephunneh the **K**)

Kenizzites (1)

Gen 15:19 the **K**, the Kadmonites,

kept (172)

Gen 6:20 will come to you to be **k** alive.
8:5 The water **k** decreasing until
8:7 It **k** flying back and forth until
12:9 Abram **k** moving toward the
16:2 "The LORD has **k** me from
20:6 "In fact, I **k** you from sinning
30:2 who has **k** you from having
34:5 so Jacob **k** quiet until they
37:11 but his father **k** thinking about
39:9 He's **k** nothing back from me
39:10 Although she **k** asking Joseph
39:16 She **k** Joseph's clothes with
39:20 the king's prisoners were **k**.
41:35 to be **k** for food in the cities.
43:7 They answered, "The man **k**
Exo 5:13 slave drivers **k** hurrying them.
12:42 That night the LORD **k** watch
16:20 They **k** part of it until morning,
16:32 two quarts of manna to be **k**
16:33 to be **k** for your descendants."
16:34 of God's promise to be **k** there,
20:21 The people **k** their distance
21:29 but has not **k** it confined,
Exo 36:3 But the people still **k** bringing
Lev 6:9 while the altar fire is **k** burning.
24:12 They **k** him in custody until the
Num 5:13 She may have **k** it secret if
15:34 They **k** him in custody until
19:9 They will be **k** by the
30:4 her vow or oath must be **k**.
30:5 or oath doesn't have to be **k**.
30:7 her vow or oath must be **k**.
30:11 her vow or oath must be **k**.
30:12 in her vow or oath has to be **k**.
31:53 Each soldier **k** his own loot.
Dtr 7:8 the LORD loved you and **k**
Jos 14:10 The LORD has **k** me alive as
22:3 You have carefully **k** the
Jdg 5:29 But she **k** repeating to herself,
7:8 but the 300 men who stayed **k**
7:21 While each man **k** his position
7:22 The 300 men **k** on blowing
7:25 at the Winepress of Zeeb and **k**
8:4 but they **k** pursuing the enemy.
21:14 Gilead who had been **k** alive.
1Sm 1:5 even though the LORD had **k**
3:3 where the ark of God was **k**.
9:24 Samuel said, "This was **k** in
13:19 In this way the Philistines **k**
17:54 but he **k** Goliath's armor in his
18:2 (From that day on Saul **k** David
18:9 From that day on Saul **k** an eye
18:13 So he **k** David away.
21:5 "Of course women have been **k**
21:5 The young men's bodies are **k**
25:26 "The LORD has **k** you from
25:34 who has **k** me from harming
25:39 of Nabal and **k** me from doing
28:23 his officers and the woman **k**
2Sm 11:16 Since Joab had **k** the city
13:34 When the servant who **k** watch
15:12 with Absalom **k** getting larger.
19:41 Then all the people of Israel **k**
22:22 because I have **k** the ways of
22:24 I have **k** myself from guilt.
22:44 You **k** me as the leader of
1Ki 3:22 The first woman **k** on saying,
8:20 The LORD has **k** the promise
8:24 You have **k** your promise to my
18:4 each cave and **k** them alive by
22:35 and the king was **k** propped up
2Ki 2:17 But the disciples **k** urging him
4:5 The children **k** bringing
4:5 and she **k** pouring.
1Ch 21:20 but Ornan **k** on threshing the
2Ch 1:9 Now, LORD God, you've **k** the
6:10 The LORD has **k** the promise
6:15 You have **k** your promise to my
Neh 4:23 We each **k** our weapons at
6:19 Tobiah **k** sending letters to
9:8 You **k** your promise because
Est 7:4 I would have **k** silent because
Job 15:18 was not **k** secret from their
29:8 young men saw me and **k** out
31:33 like Adam and **k** my sin
31:34 terrified me so that I **k** quiet
Psa 18:21 because I have **k** the ways of
18:23 I have **k** myself from guilt.
32:3 When I **k** silent ⌊about my
37:28 They will be **k** safe forever,
39:2 I **k** silent, although it did me no
56:8 (You have **k** a record of my
56:13 You have **k** my feet from
65:1 ⌊made⌋ to you must be **k**.
66:9 He has **k** us alive and has not
116:4 But I **k** calling on the name of
116:10 I **k** my faith even when I said,
119:101 I have **k** my feet ⌊from
130:3 would be able to stand if you **k**
131:2 Instead, I have **k** my soul calm
Pro 7:14 Today I **k** my vows.
Isa 24:16 But I **k** saying, "I'm wasting
38:17 You have saved me and **k** me
42:14 I **k** quiet and held myself back.
Jer 5:25 Your sins have **k** good things
34:18 They have not **k** the terms of
44:25 and you have **k** them.
Lam 3:17 "My soul has been **k** from
4:18 ⌊The enemy⌋ **k** tracking us

Eze 31:14 were **k** from becoming arrogant
44:2 through it. It must be **k** shut.
Dan 5:19 and he **k** alive whomever he
7:28 I turned pale. I **k** this to myself.
12:9 These words are to be **k** secret
Amo 2:4 and haven't **k** his laws.
Mic 6:16 You have **k** Omri's laws and all
Mat 6:9 let your name be **k** holy.
27:30 they took the stick and **k** hitting
27:36 sat there and **k** watch over him.
Mar 1:45 But people still **k** coming to
4:22 There is nothing **k** secret that
5:32 But he **k** looking around to see
6:41 He broke the loaves apart and **k**
7:24 it couldn't be **k** a secret.
9:10 They **k** in mind what he said
14:11 So he **k** looking for a chance to
15:19 They **k** hitting him on the head
Luk 8:17 There is nothing **k** secret that
8:29 People had **k** him under guard.
9:16 He broke the loaves apart and **k**
11:2 let your name be **k** holy.
11:52 and you've **k** out those who
13:16 Satan has **k** her in this
18:3 also a widow who **k** coming
19:20 I've **k** it in a cloth for
22:6 He **k** looking for an opportunity
Jon 5:16 because he **k** healing people
7:11 They **k** asking, "Where is that
17:12 While I was with them, I **k**
Act 2:44 believers **k** meeting together,
9:1 Saul **k** threatening to murder
12:5 So Peter was **k** in prison,
12:16 But Peter **k** knocking.
13:38 Sins **k** you from receiving
14:18 they hardly **k** the crowd from
16:6 Spirit **k** them from speaking
16:18 She **k** doing this for many days.
19:34 They **k** doing this for about two
20:7 he **k** talking until midnight.
26:7 to be **k** as they worship
Rom 1:13 until now I have been **k** from
5:13 But no record of sin can be **k**
11:4 God said, "I've **k** 7,000 people
15:22 This is what has so often **k** me
16:25 the mystery that was **k**
2Co 3:13 He **k** covering his face with a
11:9 I **k** myself from being a
Gal 3:23 We were **k** under control by
Eph 2:14 of hostility that **k** them apart.
3:9 **k** it hidden in the past.
Php 2:27 on me and **k** me from having
Col 1:5 of the hope which is **k** safe
2Ti 4:7 the race. I have **k** the faith.
1Pe 1:4 That inheritance is **k** in heaven
1:11 the Spirit of Christ **k** referring
3:19 victory to the spirits **k** in prison.
2Pe 2:17 darkness has been **k** for them.
3:5 and was **k** alive by water.
3:7 They are being **k** until the day
Jud 1:1 and who are **k** safe for Jesus
1:13 gloomy darkness is **k** forever.
Rev 3:4 who have **k** their clothes clean.

Keren Happuch (1)

Job 42:14 second Cassia, and the third **K**.

Kerioth (2)

Jer 48:24 **K**, Bozrah, and on all the cities
Amo 2:2 burn down the palaces of **K**.

Kerioth Hezron (1)

Jos 15:25 Hazor Hadattah, **K** (now called

kernels (1)

Mat 13:26 wheat came up and formed **k**,

Keros (2)

Ezr 2:44 **K**, Siaha, Padon,
Neh 7:47 **K**, Sia, Padon,

Kesed (1)

Gen 22:22 **K**, Hazo, Pildash, Jidlaph,

kesheth (1)

2Sm 1:18 He said, "Teach this **k** to the

kettle (4)

Lev 6:28 Any copper **k** in which the
1Sm 2:14 into the pot, **k**, cauldron, or pan.
Job 41:31 up the ocean like a boiling **k**.
Mic 3:3 like stew meat for a **k**.

kettles (1)

2Ch 35:13 the holy offerings in pots, **k**,

Keturah (5)

Gen 25:1 and his wife's name was **K**.
25:2 **K** gave birth to these sons of
25:4 were the descendants of **K**.
1Ch 1:32 **K**, Abraham's concubine,
1:33 these were descendants of **K**.

key (7)

Dtr 32:34 lock and **k** in my storehouses?
Jdg 3:25 So they took the **k** and opened
Isa 22:22 I will place the **k** of the house
Luk 11:52 You have taken away the **k**
Rev 3:7 who has the **k** of David,
9:1 The star was given the **k** to the
20:1 holding the **k** to the bottomless

keyhole (1)

Sos 5:4 put his hand through the **k**.

keys (2)

Mat 16:19 I will give you the **k** of the
Rev 1:18 I have the **k** of death and hell.

Kezib (1)

Gen 38:5 Shelah. He was born at **K**.

Kibroth Hattaavah (5)

Num 31:34 place was called **K** [Graves of
11:35 From **K** the people moved to
33:16 of Sinai and set up camp at **K**.
33:17 moved from **K** and set up camp
Dtr 9:22 at Taberah, Massah, and **K**.

Kibzaim (1)

Jos 21:22 **K**, and Beth Horon.

kick (1)

Luk 1:41 she felt the baby **k**.

kicking (2)

Eze 16:6 by you and saw you **k** around
16:22 **k** around in your own blood.

kidnap (1)

2Sm 19:41 **k** you and bring Your Majesty

kidnapped (2)

Gen 40:15 I was **k** from the land of the
Exo 21:16 whether he has sold the **k**

kidnapper (1)

Dtr 24:7 The **k** must die, whether he

kidnappers (1)

1Ti 1:10 for homosexuals, for **k**, for liars,

kidnaps (2)

Exo 21:16 "Whoever **k** another person
Dtr 24:7 Whoever **k** another Israelite

kidneys (17)

Exo 29:13 and the two **k** with the fat on
29:22 the two **k** with the fat on them,
Lev 3:4 and the two **k** with the fat on
3:4 of the liver along with the **k**.
3:10 Also remove the two **k** with the
3:15 and the two **k** with the fat on
3:15 of the liver along with the **k**.
4:9 and the two **k** with the fat on
4:9 the lobe of the liver and the **k**
7:4 and the two **k** with the fat on
7:4 of the liver along with the **k**.
8:16 and the two **k** with their fat,
8:25 the two **k** with their fat,
9:10 the altar he burned the fat, **k**,
9:19 the **k**, and the lobe of the liver)

Job 16:13 He slashes open my **k** without
Isa 34:6 with the fat of rams' **k**.

Kidron (12)

2Sm 15:23 was crossing the **K** Valley,
1Ki 2:37 cross the brook in the **K** Valley,
15:13 and burned it in the **K** Valley.
2Ki 23:4 an open field near the **K** Brook.
23:6 **K** Valley outside Jerusalem.
23:6 He burned it in the **K** Valley,
23:12 their rubble in the **K** Valley.
2Ch 15:16 and burned it in the **K** Valley.
29:16 outside the city to the **K** Brook.
30:14 dumping them in the **K** Valley.
Jer 31:40 the whole area to the **K** Valley,
Jon 18:1 the other side of the **K** Valley.

kids (4)

Dtr 7:13 your flocks with lambs and **k**.
28:4 flocks will have lambs and **k**.
28:18 will have few lambs and **k**.
28:51 and no lambs or **k** from your

kill (315)

Gen 4:14 who finds me will **k** me!"
4:15 meeting him would not **k** him.
8:21 I will never again **k** every living
12:12 Then they'll **k** me but let you
18:25 and the guilty alike and to **k**
26:7 men of that place would **k** him
27:41 Then I'll **k** my brother Jacob."
27:42 himself by planning to **k** you.
37:18 they plotted to **k** him.
37:20 Let's **k** him, throw him into one
37:21 "Let's not **k** him," he said.
49:9 have come back from the **k**,
Exo 1:16 If it's a boy, **k** it, but if it's a girl,
2:14 Are you going to **k** me as you
4:19 who wanted to **k** you are dead."
4:23 going to **k** your firstborn son.'"
4:24 met Moses and tried to **k** him.
5:3 If we don't go, he may **k** us
5:21 given them an excuse to **k** us."
9:15 have used my power to **k** you
12:12 and **k** every firstborn male,
12:21 and **k** the Passover animal.
12:23 Egypt to **k** the Egyptians.
12:23 come into your home to **k** you.
19:22 or the LORD will violently **k**
19:24 or he will violently **k** them."
21:14 that he plans to **k** his neighbor,
23:7 Don't **k** innocent or honest
32:12 'He was planning all along to **k**
32:27 and **k** your relatives,
Lev 14:5 someone to **k** one bird over
14:50 He must **k** the one bird over a
20:15 You must **k** the animal,
20:16 you must **k** both the woman
23:30 I will **k** those who do any work
Num 11:15 why don't you just **k** me?
14:15 But if you **k** all these people at
16:13 with milk and honey only to **k**
22:29 I'd **k** you right now."
25:5 "Each of you must **k** the men
25:17 as your enemies, and **k** them
31:17 So **k** all the Midianite boys and
35:16 weapon to **k** another person,
35:17 and uses it to **k** another person,
35:18 and uses it to **k** another person,
35:19 the murderer, he must **k** him.
35:21 the death must **k** you when
35:22 **k** someone who wasn't
35:22 at him but didn't mean to **k** him.
Dtr 13:15 you must **k** the residents of that
20:13 **k** every man in that city with
27:25 "Whoever accepts money to **k**
32:25 Foreign wars will **k** off their
32:39 I **k**, and I make alive. I wound,
Jos 9:26 let the people of Israel **k** them.
20:5 because he didn't intend to **k**
Jdg 8:18 of men did you **k** at Tabor?"
8:19 I would not have to **k** you now."
8:20 "Get up and **k** them!"
9:54 "Take your sword and **k** me!
12:6 they would grab him and **k** him
13:23 "If the LORD wanted to **k** us,

Jdg 15:13 We certainly won't **k** you."
16:2 "We'll **k** him at dawn."
20:5 They intended to **k** me,
21:10 They ordered them, "Go and **k**
1Sm 2:25 the LORD wanted to **k** them.
5:10 the God of Israel here to **k** us."
5:11 its own place so that it won't **k**
11:12 have them, and we'll **k** them."
15:3 but **k** men and women,
16:2 Saul hears about it, he'll **k** me."
17:9 If he can fight me and **k** me,
17:9 if I overpower him and **k** him,
19:1 and all his officers to **k** David.
19:2 father Saul is trying to **k** you.
19:11 watch David's house and **k** him
19:15 in his bed so that I can **k** him."
19:17 Why should I **k** you?'"
20:1 father that he's trying to **k** me?
20:8 any crime, **k** me yourself.
20:33 was determined to **k** David.
22:17 "Turn and **k** the LORD's priests
23:15 had come to **k** him at Horesh
24:10 Although I was told to **k** you,
24:11 of your robe and didn't **k** you,
24:18 over to you, you didn't **k** me.
26:9 "Don't **k** him!" David told
26:15 came to **k** His Royal Majesty.
30:15 front of God that you won't **k** me
2Sm 1:9 stand over me and **k** me.
2:22 "Why should I **k** you?
4:8 Saul who tried to **k** you,"
4:11 I reward wicked men who **k**
11:21 millstone at him and **k** him?
11:25 because a sword can **k** one
12:9 You used the Ammonites to **k**
13:28 Then **k** him. Don't be afraid. I've
14:7 brother so that we can **k** him
14:32 of a sin, he should **k** me."
16:11 and blood, is trying to **k** me.
17:2 him will flee, but I'll **k** only him.
21:4 "And none of us wants to **k**
21:16 David and intended to **k** him.
23:8 He used a spear to **k** 800 men
23:18 used his spear to **k** 300 men.
1Ki 2:26 to die, but I won't **k** you at this
2:29 son of Jehoiada, to **k** Joab.
2:31 **K** him, and bury him. You can
2:32 He used his sword to **k** Abner
2:46 went to attack and **k** Shimei.
3:26 Please don't **k** him!"
3:27 Don't **k** him. She is his mother."
11:40 Solomon tried to **k** Jeroboam,
12:27 Then they will **k** me and return
17:18 me of my sin and **k** my son?
18:12 Then he will **k** me.
18:14 Elijah is here. He will **k** me."
19:17 sword, Jehu will **k** him.
19:17 sword, Elisha will **k** him.
20:36 a lion will **k** you when you
2Ki 5:7 Can I **k** someone and then
6:21 "Master, should I **k** them?
6:21 I kill them? Should I **k** them?"
6:22 answered, "Don't **k** them.
6:22 Do you **k** everyone you take
7:4 But if they **k** us, we'll die
8:12 **k** their best young men,
10:25 and attendants, "**K** them.
10:25 So they used swords to **k** the
11:8 **K** anyone who tries to break
11:15 Use your sword to **k** anyone
17:25 sent lions to **k** some of them.
25:25 with ten men to **k** Gedaliah
1Ch 11:6 "Whoever is the first to **k** a
11:11 He used his spear to **k** 300
11:20 used his spear to **k** 300 men,
2Ch 23:7 **K** anyone who tries to come
23:14 Use your sword to **k** anyone
23:14 (The priest had said, "Don't **k**
30:17 So the Levites had to **k** the
Neh 4:11 We'll **k** them and bring the work
6:10 are coming at night to **k** you."
Est 2:21 and planned to **k** King Xerxes.
3:6 himself to **k** only Mordecai.
3:13 were ordered to wipe out, **k**,
8:7 because he tried to **k** the Jews.
8:11 themselves, to wipe out, to **k**,
Est 9:2 Xerxes to **k** those who were
Job 13:15 If God would **k** me,
24:14 they **k** the poor and needy.
27:14 swords will **k** them,
Psa 34:21 Evil will **k** wicked people,
37:14 bend their bows to **k** oppressed
37:32 person and seeks to **k** him.
59:11 Do not **k** them. Otherwise, my
78:62 He let swords **k** his people.
94:6 They **k** widows and foreigners,
106:26 he swore that he would **k** them
106:27 **k** their descendants among the
139:19 you would **k** wicked people,
Pro 1:11 set an ambush to **k** someone.
1:32 "Gullible people **k** themselves
6:17 hands that **k** innocent people,
21:25 of a lazy person will **k** him
Ecc 3:3 a time to **k** and a time to heal,
Isa 11:4 He will **k** the wicked with the
14:30 famine and **k** off your survivors.
21:15 from swords ready to **k**,
27:1 He will **k** that monster which
27:7 Will he **k** them as he killed
65:15 The Almighty LORD will **k** you
Jer 2:34 You didn't **k** them for breaking
4:30 they want to **k** you.
7:6 or **k** anyone in this place.
11:21 of Anathoth want to **k** you.
11:21 of the LORD, or we'll **k** you."
15:3 "I will send swords to **k**,
18:23 know that they plan to **k** me.
19:7 of those who want to **k** them.
19:9 when they want to **k** them."
20:4 enemies' swords will **k** them,
20:4 Babylon or **k** them with swords.
21:7 enemies who want to **k** them.
21:7 Nebuchadnezzar will **k** them
22:3 Don't **k** innocent people in this
22:17 You **k** innocent people and
22:25 to those who want to **k** you,
25:31 He will **k** the wicked,
29:21 I will **k** them as you watch.
34:20 enemies who want to **k** them,
34:21 enemies who want to **k** them
38:15 "If I answer you, you'll **k** me.
38:16 As the LORD lives, I will not **k**
38:16 these men who want to **k** you."
38:25 from us, or we'll **k** you.'
40:14 Nethaniah's son, to **k** you?"
40:15 "Let me **k** Ishmael,
40:15 Why should he **k** you?
41:8 said to Ishmael, "Don't **k** us!
41:8 alone and didn't **k** them along
43:3 Then they will **k** us or take us
43:11 He will **k** in battle those who
44:30 to those who want to **k** him,
44:30 to those who wanted to **k** him.'"
46:14 will **k** those around you.'
46:26 to those who want to **k** them,
49:37 of those who want to **k** them.
50:27 **K** all their young bulls.
50:35 "A sword will **k** the
50:35 "A sword will **k** their officials
50:36 A sword will **k** the false
50:36 A sword will **k** their soldiers
50:37 A sword will **k** their horses,
Lam 1:20 streets swords **K** my children.
Eze 5:16 I will shoot to **k** you.
5:17 and wars to **k** you.
6:4 I will **k** people in front of your
6:12 Plagues will **k** those who are
9:5 him throughout the city and **k**.
9:6 **K** old men, young men,
13:19 You **k** people who shouldn't
17:17 blockades to **k** many people.
21:3 sword out of its scabbard and **k**
21:4 I'm going to **k** the righteous
21:10 It's sharpened to **k** and
21:15 like lightning. It's polished to **k**.
21:22 give the order to **k**,
21:28 a sword is drawn ready to **k**.
22:9 They want to **k** people.
23:25 and **k** everyone who remains.
23:47 will stone them and **k** them
23:47 The mob will **k** their sons and
26:11 He will **k** your people in battle,
Eze 28:9 you face those who **k** you.
28:9 in the hands of those who **k**
29:8 I will **k** people and animals.
30:15 and I will **k** many people in
32:15 and I will **k** all the people who
Dan 2:13 and his friends and **k** them.
2:14 was leaving to **k** the wise
5:19 whomever he wanted to **k**,
Hos 9:16 I would **k** their dear children."
Amo 2:3 I will **k** all their officials at the
9:1 I will **k** with a sword all who
9:4 command a sword to **k** them.
Oba 1:14 crossroads to **k** their refugees.
Nah 2:13 and a sword will **k** your young
Hab 1:17 **k** nations without mercy?
Hag 2:22 They will **k** one another with
Zec 11:5 Those who buy them will **k**
Mat 2:13 search for the child and **k** him."
2:16 He sent soldiers to **k** all the
2:20 Those who tried to **k** the child
10:21 their parents and **k** them.
10:28 Don't be afraid of those who **k**
10:28 the body but cannot **k** the soul.
12:14 left and plotted to **k** Jesus.
14:5 So Herod wanted to **k** John.
17:23 They will **k** him, but on the
21:38 Let's **k** him and get his
23:34 You will **k** and crucify some of
23:37 "Jerusalem, Jerusalem, you **k**
24:9 who will torture and **k** you.
26:4 underhanded way and to **k** him.
Mar 3:6 immediately plotted to **k** Jesus.
6:19 John and wanted to **k** him.
9:31 They will **k** him, but on the
10:34 on him, whip him, and **k** him.
11:18 they looked for a way to **k** him.
12:7 Let's **k** him, and the inheritance
13:12 their parents and **k** them.
14:1 to arrest Jesus and to **k** him.
Luk 12:4 afraid of those who **k** the body.
13:31 Herod wants to **k** you."
13:34 "Jerusalem, Jerusalem, you **k**
15:23 Bring the fattened calf, **k** it,
18:33 whip him, and **k** him.
19:27 **K** them in front of me.'"
19:44 the ground and **k** your people.
19:47 looked for a way to **k** him.
20:14 Let's **k** him so that the
21:16 betray you and **k** some of you.
22:2 for some way to **k** Jesus.
Jon 7:1 Jews there wanted to **k** him.
7:19 So why do you want to **k** me?"
7:20 Who wants to **k** you?"
7:25 this the man they want to **k**?
8:22 "Is he going to **k** himself?
8:37 However, you want to **k** me
8:40 But now you want to **k** me.
10:10 A thief comes to steal, **k**,
11:53 council planned to **k** Jesus.
12:10 planned to **k** Lazarus too.
19:15 the Jews shouted, "**K** him!
19:15 **K** him! Crucify him!" Pilate
Act 7:28 Do you want to **k** me as you
10:13 **K** these animals, and eat
11:7 **K** these animals, and eat them.'
13:28 find any good reason to **k** him,
16:27 and was about to **k** himself.
20:3 Jews were plotting to **k** him.
21:31 people were trying to **k** Paul,
21:36 behind them shouting, "**K** him!"
22:22 they began to shout, "**K** him!
23:15 We'll be ready to **k** him before
25:3 a plan to ambush and **k** Paul as
27:42 The soldiers had a plan to **k**
1Ti 1:9 for those who **k** their fathers,
Heb 11:28 would not **k** the firstborn sons.
Rev 2:23 I will **k** her children.
6:8 earth to **k** people using wars,
9:5 were not allowed to **k** them.
9:15 to **k** one-third of humanity.
11:7 conquer them, and **k** them.

killed (387)

Gen 4:8 his brother Abel and **k** him.
4:11 of your brother whom you **k**.
4:23 I **k** a man for bruising me,

Gen 4:25 since Cain **k** him."
9:11 will all life be **k** by floodwaters.
20:11 I'd be **k** because of my wife.
26:9 I would be **k** because of her."
31:39 that was **k** by wild animals.
34:25 They **k** every man
37:31 took Joseph's robe, **k** a goat,
Exo 2:14 kill me as you **k** the Egyptian?"
2:15 he tried to have him **k**.
12:27 spared our homes when he **k**
12:29 At midnight the LORD **k** every
13:15 the LORD **k** every firstborn
22:13 If it was **k** by a wild animal,
22:13 for an animal that has been **k**.
22:24 and have you **k** in combat.
22:31 has been **k** by wild animals
32:35 So the LORD **k** people
Lev 7:24 or is **k** by wild animals
14:6 of the bird that was **k** over
14:51 the blood of the bird that was **k**.
17:15 or is **k** by another animal
22:8 or is **k** by wild animals.
Num 3:13 The day I **k** every firstborn
8:17 The day I **k** every firstborn
16:41 have **k** the LORD's people."
19:16 touches someone who was **k**
19:18 someone who has been **k**
22:33 I would certainly have **k** you by
25:14 of the Israelite man who was **k**
25:15 woman who was **k** was Cozbi,
25:18 who was **k** on the day of the
31:7 Moses, and **k** every man.
31:8 Among those **k** were the five
31:8 They also **k** Balaam,
31:19 "Everyone who **k** a person or
33:4 whom the LORD had **k** in a
35:23 and someone is **k**.
Dtr 4:42 Those who unintentionally **k**
19:5 The one who accidentally **k**
19:6 he never hated the person he **k**.
19:10 innocent people won't be **k** in
25:18 exhausted and **k** all those who
32:42 blood from those who were **k**
Jos 6:21 With their swords they **k** men
7:5 The men of Ai **k** about
8:24 to Ai and **k** everyone left there.
10:28 and the Israelites **k** its people
10:30 He **k** all the people.
10:32 it on the next day and **k** all
10:33 But Joshua **k** him and his
10:35 They captured it that day and **k**
10:37 villages and **k** its king
10:39 villages and **k** everyone.
11:10 He **k** its king with a sword.
11:17 all their kings and **k** them.
13:22 people of Israel also **k** Balaam,
19:47 and **k** everyone there.
20:5 even hate the person he **k**.
Jdg 1:8 They **k** everyone there and set
1:10 There they **k** Sheshai,
1:25 the city and **k** everyone there.
3:29 At that time they **k** about ten
3:31 He **k** 600 Philistines with a
4:16 whole army was **k** in combat.
7:25 They **k** Oreb at the Rock of
8:17 down the tower of Penuel and **k**
8:21 So Gideon got up and **k** them.
9:40 Many were **k** at the entrance of
9:45 He captured the city and **k** the
9:54 'A woman **k** Abimelech.'" His
9:56 when he **k** his 70 brothers.
14:8 to look at the lion he had **k**.
14:19 he went to Ashkelon and **k** 30
15:15 He picked it up and **k** 1,000
15:16 I've **k** a thousand men."
16:30 So he **k** more Philistines when
18:27 **k** them all with swords,
20:31 They **k** about 30 men from
20:37 out in the city and **k** everyone.
20:39 had already **k** about 30 men
20:45 But the men of Israel **k** 5,000
20:45 2,000 and **k** them near Gidom.
20:46 with swords were **k** that day.
20:48 They **k** all the people and
21:16 in Benjamin have been **k**?"
1Sm 4:2 and **k** about 4,000 soldiers

1Sm 7:11 and **k** them as far as Beth Car.
11:13 "No one will be **k** today,
14:14 **k** about twenty men
14:30 have **k** more Philistines."
17:35 of its mane, struck it, and **k** it.
17:36 I have **k** lions and bears,
17:50 down and **k** the Philistine,
17:51 saw their hero had been **k**,
19:5 He risked his life and **k** the
19:6 LORD lives, he will not be **k**."
20:32 "Why should he be **k**?
21:9 whom you **k** in the Elah Valley,
22:18 and that day he **k** 85 men
22:19 He also **k** the people of Nob,
22:19 he **k** men and women,
22:21 Saul had **k** the LORD's priests.
28:9 to trap me and have me **k**?"
30:2 who were there, they **k** no one.
31:1 from the Philistines and were **k**
31:2 They **k** Jonathan, Abinadab,
2Sm 1:10 "So I stood over him and **k** him,
1:16 'I **k** the LORD's anointed king.'"
1:22 From the blood of those **k** and
1:25 On your hills Jonathan was **k**!
2:31 However, David's officers had **k**
3:30 (Joab and his brother Abishai **k**
3:30 he had **k** their brother Asahel
4:7 They stabbed him, **k** him,
4:10 I **k** him in Ziklag to reward him
6:7 so God **k** him there for his lack
8:2 lengths which were to be **k**,
8:5 David **k** 22,000 of them.
10:18 and David **k** 700 chariot drivers
11:21 Who **k** Jerubbesheth's son
12:9 had Uriah the Hittite **k** in battle.
13:30 "Absalom has **k** all the king's
13:32 the king's sons, have been **k**.
14:6 them. One **k** the other.
14:7 'Give us the man who **k** his
17:9 If some of our soldiers are **k** in
18:15 attacked him, and **k** him.
19:22 anyone in Israel be **k** today?
19:28 You could have **k** anyone in
21:1 guilty of murder because they **k**
21:9 They were **k** at the beginning
21:12 the day they **k** Saul at Gilboa.
21:17 the Philistine and **k** him.
21:18 Sibbecai from Hushah **k** Saph,
21:19 Bethlehem, **k** Goliath of Gath.
21:21 David's brother Shimei, **k** him.
21:22 and David and his men **k** them.
23:10 he attacked and **k** Philistines
23:20 He **k** two distinguished
23:20 He also went into a pit and **k** a
23:21 And he **k** a handsome
23:21 from him, and **k** him with it.
1Ki 1:51 that he will not have me **k**.'"
2:5 Joab **k** them. When there was
2:8 I won't have you **k**.'
2:25 Benaiah attacked and **k**
2:32 Joab **k** two honorable men who
2:34 went and attacked Joab, **k** him,
9:16 and **k** the Canaanites living
11:15 went to bury those **k** in battle
11:15 in battle and **k** every male
11:24 after David **k** the men of Zobah.
13:24 on the road and **k** him.
13:26 It tore him to pieces and **k** him
15:29 As soon as he was king, he **k**
16:10 and **k** him in Asa's
16:11 he **k** Baasha's entire family.
16:16 ⌊against the king⌋ and **k** him,
18:9 hand me over to Ahab to be **k**?
18:13 what I did when Jezebel **k**
20:20 Each officer **k** his opponent.
20:29 The Israelites **k** 100,000
20:36 a lion found him and **k** him.
20:42 God and should have been **k**.
22:20 will attack and be **k** at Ramoth
2Ki 3:23 another and have **k** each other.
10:9 against my master and **k** him.
10:9 But who **k** all these men?
10:11 Jehu also **k** every member of
10:17 Jehu **k** the rest of Ahab's
11:2 She saved him from being **k**
11:2 So Joash wasn't **k**

2Ki 11:15 "She must not be **k** in the
11:16 and there she was **k**.
11:18 and his statues and **k** Mattan,
11:20 because they had **k** Athaliah
12:20 against him and **k** him at Beth
14:5 officials who had **k** his father,
14:7 Amaziah **k** 10,000 Edomites in
14:19 after him and **k** him there.
15:10 him at Kabal Am, **k** him,
15:14 (son of Jabesh), **k** him,
15:25 Pekah **k** him and succeeded
15:30 attacked him and **k** him.
16:9 to Kir as captives, and **k** Rezin.
19:35 out and **k** 185,000 ⌊soldiers⌋
21:16 Manasseh also **k** a lot of
21:23 plotted against him and **k** him
21:24 Then the people of the land **k**
23:29 him at Megiddo, Pharaoh **k** him
24:4 people in Jerusalem **k**,
1Ch 2:3 so the LORD **k** Er.
4:41 down tents and **k** the Meunites.
4:43 They **k** the Amalekites who
5:22 Many were **k** in battle because
7:21 sons Ezer and Elead were **k** by
10:1 from the Philistines and were **k**
10:2 They **k** Jonathan, Abinadab,
10:14 So the LORD **k** him and turned
11:22 He **k** two distinguished
11:22 also went into a cistern and **k**
11:23 He **k** an eight-foot-tall Egyptian.
11:23 from him, and **k** him with it.
13:10 angry with Uzzah and **k** him
18:5 David **k** 22,000 of them.
18:12 Zeruiah's son Abishai **k** 18,000
19:18 and David **k** 7,000 chariot
19:18 David also **k** Shophach.
20:4 Sibbecai from Hushah **k** Sippai,
20:5 Elhanan, son of Jair, **k** Lahmi,
20:7 David's brother Shimea, **k** him.
20:8 and David and his men **k** them.
2Ch 13:17 the best men of Israel were **k**.
15:13 God of Israel were to be **k**.
18:19 will attack and be **k** at Ramoth
21:13 You have **k** your brothers,
22:1 camp with the Arabs had **k** all
22:8 Ahaziah, and he **k** them.
22:9 They brought him to Jehu and **k**
22:11 She saved him from being **k**
22:11 from Athaliah. So he wasn't **k**.
23:15 and they **k** her there.
23:17 and his statues and **k** Mattan,
23:21 because they had **k** Athaliah
24:22 Instead, he **k** Jehoiada's son.
24:25 They **k** Joash in his bed.
25:3 he executed the officials who **k**
25:11 he **k** 10,000 men from Seir.
25:13 They **k** 3,000 people and took
25:16 you want me to have you **k**?"
25:27 after him and **k** him there.
28:6 **k** 120,000 soldiers in Judah
28:7 from Ephraim, **k** Maaseiah,
28:9 You **k** them in a rage that
29:9 Our fathers were **k** in battle,
32:21 some of his own sons **k** him
33:24 plotted against him and **k** him
33:25 Then the people of the land **k**
Ezr 6:20 They **k** the Passover lambs for
Neh 9:26 and **k** your prophets who
Est 7:4 be wiped out, **k**, and destroyed.
9:6 the fortress of Susa the Jews **k**
9:7 They also **k** Parshandatha,
9:11 that day the number of those **k**
9:12 of Susa the Jews have **k**
9:15 month of Adar and **k** 300 men
9:16 They **k** 75,000 of those who
Job 15:22 ⌊to be **k**⌋ with a sword.
26:12 With his insight he **k** Rahab
Psa 44:22 Indeed, we are being **k** all day
78:31 He **k** their strongest men and
78:34 When he **k** ⌊some of⌋ them,
78:47 He **k** their vines with hail and
88:5 like those who have been **k**
105:36 He **k** all the firstborn sons,
118:18 but he did not allow me to be **k**.
135:8 He is the one who **k** every
135:8 He **k** humans and animals

Psa 135:10 nations and **k** mighty kings:
136:10 Give thanks to the one who **k**
136:18 He **k** mighty kings — because
Pro 7:26 and she has **k** all too many.
Isa 10:4 to fall with those who are **k**.
14:19 those who were **k** in battle.
14:20 your land and **k** your people.
22:2 people weren't **k** with swords.
27:7 Will he kill them as he **k**
31:8 Then Assyrians will be **k** with
34:7 Wild oxen will be **k** with them,
37:36 out and **k** 185,000 ⌊soldiers⌋
53:8 He was **k** because of my
Jer 2:30 You **k** my prophets like a
9:1 dear people who have been **k**.
14:18 I see those **k** because of war.
20:17 If only he had **k** me while I was
25:33 On that day those **k** by the
33:5 bodies of their own people I **k**
41:2 their swords, and **k** Gedaliah,
41:3 Ishmael also **k** all the Jews
41:9 of the men he had **k** was
41:16 after Ishmael had **k** Gedaliah,
41:18 Ishmael had **k** Gedaliah whom
43:11 are supposed to be **k** in battle.
51:49 Babylon have **k** many Israelites
51:49 have **k** many people throughout
Lam 2:4 He **k** all the beautiful people.
2:20 priests and prophets be **k**
2:21 You **k** them on the day of your
3:43 You **k** without pity.
4:9 Those who were **k** with
Eze 4:14 by itself or was **k** by other wild
5:11 things, I will have you **k**.
6:7 People will be **k**, and they will
6:13 "Those who are **k** will lie
9:7 So they went out and **k** the
11:6 You have **k** many people in
16:36 You also **k** your children and
22:4 of the people you have **k**.
23:10 and **k** her with a sword.
30:8 and all her defenders will be **k**.
31:17 grave to join others **k** in battle.
31:18 people who were **k** in battle,
32:20 those who were **k** in battle.
32:21 people who were **k** in battle.'
32:22 They have been **k** in battle.
32:23 They have been **k** in battle.
32:24 They have been **k** in battle.
32:25 They were **k** in battle because
32:26 They were **k** in battle because
32:28 those who were **k** in battle.
32:29 those who were **k** in battle.
32:30 those who were **k** in battle.
32:31 who have been **k** in battle,
32:32 people who were **k** in battle,"
33:27 ruined cities will be **k** in battle.
35:8 with those who have been **k**.
35:8 Those **k** in battle will fall on
37:9 people who were **k** so that they
39:18 All of them will be **k** like rams,
39:23 They were **k** in battle.
44:31 naturally or was **k** by other wild
Dan 2:13 the wise advisers were to be **k**,
3:22 and Abednego were **k** by the
5:19 Nebuchadnezzar **k** whomever
5:30 Belshazzar of Babylon was **k**.
7:11 until the animal was **k**.
Hos 6:5 I **k** you with the words from my
9:13 bring out their children to be **k**."
13:16 They will be **k** in war,
Amo 4:10 With swords I **k** your best
7:11 says that Jeroboam will be **k**
7:17 will be **k** with swords.
9:10 they will be **k** with swords.
Nah 3:3 Many are **k**! Dead bodies pile
Zep 1:11 who handle money will be **k**.
Mat 16:21 He would be **k**, but on the third
21:35 and beat one, **k** another,
21:39 out of the vineyard, and **k** him.
22:6 them, and then **k** them.
22:7 **k** those murderers,
26:52 a sword will be **k** by a sword.
Mar 8:31 He would be **k**, but after three
12:5 and they **k** that servant.
12:5 they beat, and others they **k**.
Mar 12:8 So they took him, **k** him,
Luk 9:22 He would be **k**, but on the third
11:51 who was **k** between the altar
15:27 So your father has **k** the
15:30 you **k** the fattened calf for him.'
20:15 out of the vineyard and **k** him.
22:7 the Passover lamb had to be **k**.
Act 3:15 and you **k** the source of life.
5:36 He was **k**, and all his followers
7:28 Do you want to kill me as you **k**
7:52 They **k** those who predicted
10:39 hung him on a cross and **k** him,
12:23 an angel from the Lord **k** Herod
22:20 about you, was being **k**,
23:12 before they had **k** Paul.
23:14 any food before we've **k** Paul.
26:10 I voted to have them **k** every
Rom 7:11 deceived me and then **k** me.
8:36 "We are being **k** all day long
11:3 "Lord, they've **k** your prophets
1Co 10:9 They were **k** by snakes.
2Co 4:9 We're captured, but we're not **k**.
6:9 are punished, but we are not **k**.
Gal 2:19 standards, those laws **k** me.
Eph 2:16 on which he **k** the hostility.
1Th 2:15 who **k** the Lord Jesus and the
Heb 11:31 She was not **k** with those who
11:37 and **k** with swords.
12:4 but your struggles haven't **k**
2Pe 2:12 are born to be caught and **k**.
Rev 2:13 my faithful witness who was **k**
6:11 would be **k** as they had been
6:11 be killed as they had been **k**.
9:18 **k** one-third of humanity.
11:5 he must be **k** the same way.
11:13 7,000 people were **k** by the
13:10 If anyone is **k** with a sword,
13:10 with a sword he must be **k**.
19:21 The rider on the horse **k** the
19:21 flesh of those who had been **k**.

killer (2)

Exo 21:13 the **k** should flee to a place I
Jdg 16:24 destroyer of our land and **k** of

killers (1)

Eze 21:11 to be placed in the hands of **k**.

killing (27)

Gen 37:26 "What will we gain by **k** our
Jos 8:24 Israel had finished **k** all the
1Sm 14:13 behind him, finished **k** them.
14:20 soldiers **k** their fellow soldiers
17:57 returned from **k** the Philistine,
2Sm 3:37 for **k** Ner's son Abner.
8:13 himself by **k** 18,000 Edomites
23:12 defended it by **k** Philistines.
24:17 who had been **k** the people,
1Ki 17:20 I'm staying with by **k** her son?"
18:4 (When Jezebel was **k** the
2Ki 17:26 Now the lions are **k** them
1Ch 11:14 defended it by **k** Philistines.
Est 9:5 **k** them, destroying them,
Jer 26:15 living in it will be guilty of **k**
48:10 who keep their swords from **k**.
50:21 Claim them for me by **k** them
Eze 9:8 As they were **k** people,
14:19 out my fury on it by **k** people
21:14 It's the sword for **k**.
21:14 the sword for **k** many people.
Mat 27:24 "I won't be guilty of **k** this man.
27:25 "The responsibility for **k** him
Mar 14:12 **K** the Passover lamb was
Luk 12:5 throw you into hell after **k** you.
Jon 5:18 the Jews more intent on **k** him.
Act 7:24 took revenge by **k** the Egyptian.

kills (32)

Gen 4:15 Anyone who **k** Cain will suffer
9:5 ⌊who **k**⌋ another person.
Exo 21:12 someone and **k** him must
21:29 and it **k** a man or a woman,
21:35 "Whenever one person's bull **k**
Lev 24:17 "Whoever **k** another person
24:18 Whoever **k** an animal must
24:21 Whoever **k** an animal must
Lev 24:21 Whoever **k** a person must be
Num 35:11 Anyone who unintentionally **k**
35:15 Anyone who unintentionally **k**
35:20 If any of you **k** someone you
35:27 the city of refuge and **k** you,
35:30 "Whoever **k** another person will
Dtr 19:3 Whoever **k** someone may run
19:4 A person who unintentionally **k**
19:5 and **k** the other person.
27:24 "Whoever **k** another person
Jos 20:3 **k** someone may run
20:4 "'A person who **k** someone
20:9 Anyone who accidentally **k**
1Sm 2:6 "The LORD **k**, and he gives
17:25 man who **k** this Philistine very
17:26 the man who **k** this Philistine
17:27 the man who **k** Goliath would
Job 4:9 with his breath and **k** them
5:2 anger **k** a stubborn fool,
20:16 A viper's fang **k** him.
Psa 10:8 places he **k** innocent people.
Isa 66:3 Whoever **k** a bull is like
66:3 like someone who **k** a person.
Eze 33:6 enemy comes and **k** someone,

Kilmad (1)

Eze 27:23 and **K** traded with you.

kiln (3)

Exo 9:8 a handful of ashes from a **k**,
9:10 They took ashes from a **k** and
19:18 like the smoke from a **k**,

Kinah (1)

Jos 15:22 **K**, Dimonah, Adadah,

kind (186)

Gen 6:21 Take every **k** of food that can
7:2 with you seven pairs of every **k**
7:2 of each) and one pair of every **k**
7:3 take seven pairs of every **k** of
8:19 one **k** after another.
19:19 and though you've been very **k**
24:27 The LORD hasn't failed to be **k**
46:33 'What **k** of work do you do?'
47:3 "What **k** of work do you do?"
Exo 1:14 mortar and bricks and every **k**
3:21 I will make the Egyptians **k** to
11:3 LORD made the Egyptians **k**
22:10 or any other **k** of animal to keep
25:3 This is the **k** of contribution
33:19 I will be **k** to anyone I want to.
35:5 who is willing bring this **k**
Lev 5:3 human uncleanness of any **k**
11:22 You may eat any **k** of locust,
11:23 Every **k** of winged insect that
14:54 are the instructions for any **k**
22:25 Never bring any **k** of castrated
25:37 Never collect any **k** of interest
27:9 "If ⌊the vow⌋ is to give the **k** of
Num 6:3 or any **k** of grape juice,
6:25 smile on you and be **k** to you.
15:3 or any other **k** of sacrifice.
15:8 the LORD or make any other **k**
31:30 and every other **k** of animal.
Dtr 3:24 What **k** of god is there in
7:15 from having any **k** of illness.
14:20 you may eat any ⌊other **k** of⌋
28:61 will also bring you every **k**
29:18 source of this **k** of bitter poison.
Jos 2:12 by the LORD that you'll be as **k**
Jdg 8:18 "What **k** of men did you kill at
8:35 And they were not **k** to the
20:13 death to rid ourselves of this **k**
Rut 1:8 May the LORD be as **k** to you
2:2 of anyone who will be **k** to me.
2:20 LORD hasn't stopped being **k**
1Sm 1:18 you continue to be **k** to me,"
4:8 the Egyptians with every **k**
6:4 The Philistines asked, "What **k**
15:6 You were **k** to all the Israelites
20:8 Now, be **k** to me. After all, you
20:15 never stop being **k** to my
25:8 Be **k** to my young men,
2Sm 13:18 daughters wore this **k** of robe.)
14:22 I know that you have been **k**

1Ki 2:7 "Be **k** to the sons of Barzillai
9:13 "What **k** of cities have you
2Ki 9:11 "You know the man and the **k**
13:23 But the LORD was **k** and
17:13 and Judah through every **k**
1Ch 12:33 battle with every **k** of weapon.
22:15 men skilled in every **k** of work.
2Ch 15:6 them with every **k** of trouble.
24:22 how **k** Zechariah's father,
33:12 the LORD his God to be **k**
Ezr 9:8 the LORD our God has been **k**
Neh 13:15 and every other **k** of load.
13:22 since you are very **k**."
Job 23:13 "But God is one of a **k**.
Psa 109:12 Let no one be **k** to him
109:16 he did not remember to be **k**.
119:17 Be **k** to me so that I may live
119:58 Be **k** to me as you promised.
Pro 14:21 one who is **k** to humble people.
14:31 but whoever is **k** to the needy
24:4 are filled with every **k** of riches,
28:8 for the one who is **k** to the poor.
30:11 A certain **k** of person curses
30:12 A certain **k** of person thinks he
30:13 A certain **k** of person looks
30:14 A certain **k** of person,
Ecc 2:5 I planted every **k** of fruit tree in
3:13 from every **k** of hard work.
Isa 3:1 Jerusalem and Judah every **k**
22:24 from bowls to jars of every **k**."
30:18 LORD is waiting to be **k** to you.
58:5 Is this the **k** of fasting I have
58:6 This is the **k** of fasting I have
Jer 9:24 This **k** of bragging pleases me,
Eze 8:10 with drawings of every **k**
8:10 every **k** of disgusting animal,
16:34 are a different **k** of prostitute.
17:23 Every **k** of bird will nest in it
23:24 with their own **k** of punishment.
28:13 You were covered with every **k**
39:17 Tell every **k** of bird and every
39:20 and soldiers of every **k**,
Dan 1:9 God made the chief-of-staff **k**
Hab 1:7 They will carry out their own **k**
Zep 2:14 along with animals of every **k**.
Hag 2:12 food, wine, oil, or any **k** of food,
Zec 1:13 using **k** and comforting words.
7:9 and **k** to each other.
Mal 1:9 try asking God to be **k** to you.
Mat 4:24 those who suffered from any **k**
8:27 "What **k** of man is this?
23:27 bones and every **k** of impurity.
24:21 a **k** of misery that has not
Mar 6:2 Who gave him this **k** of
9:29 He told them, "This **k** of spirit
Luk 1:58 the Lord had been very **k** to her,
4:36 "What **k** of command is this?
6:27 Be **k** to those who hate you.
6:35 After all, he is **k** to unthankful
7:42 he was **k** enough to cancel
10:37 "The one who was **k** enough to
12:15 from every **k** of greed.
23:8 him perform some **k** of miracle.
Jon 5:42 But I know what **k** of people
14:27 I don't give you the **k** of peace
21:19 said this to show by what **k**
Act 7:49 What **k** of house are you going
18:14 "If there were some **k** of
19:3 Paul asked them, "What **k** of
20:32 message that tells how **k** he is.
28:2 island were unusually **k** to us.
Rom 2:4 who is very **k** to you,
6:4 should live a new **k** of life.
9:15 "I will be **k** to anyone I want to.
9:18 if God wants to be **k** to anyone,
11:22 Look at how **k** and how severe
11:22 but **k** to you if you continue to
12:1 This **k** of worship is
1Co 1:5 and knowledge of every **k**.
2:1 mystery as if it were some **k**
3:13 That fire will determine what **k**
5:1 This **k** of sin is not even heard
8:13 I will never eat that **k** of food so
12:24 don't need this **k** of treatment.
13:4 Love is **k**. Love isn't jealous. It
15:35 With what **k** of body will they
1Co 15:38 Each **k** of seed grows into its
15:39 Humans have one **k** of flesh,
15:41 The sun has one **k** of splendor,
15:41 has another **k** of splendor,
15:41 have still another **k** of splendor.
Gal 1:6 a different **k** of good news.
Eph 1:8 kindness by giving us every **k**
4:1 encourage you to live the **k** of
4:19 They practice every **k** of
4:32 Be **k** to each other,
5:3 perversion of any **k**,
5:27 without any **k** of stain or
6:18 Use every **k** of prayer and
6:18 Use every **k** of effort and make
6:18 kind of effort and make every **k**
Php 2:22 But you know what **k** of person
4:14 Nevertheless, it was **k** of you
Col 1:9 of his will through every **k**
1:10 this so that you will live the **k**
1:10 you grow in producing every **k**
3:7 used to live that **k** of sinful life.
3:12 **k**, humble, gentle, and patient.
4:6 Everything you say should be **k**
1Th 1:5 same way you know what **k**
1:6 God's word with the **k**
5:22 Keep away from every **k** of evil.
2Th 2:9 He will use every **k** of power,
1Ti 1:14 Our Lord was very **k** to me.
2Ti 2:24 he must be **k** to everyone.
3:11 You also know about the **k** of
Tit 2:1 Tell believers to live the **k** of
2:5 to be homemakers, to be **k**,
Heb 7:11 speak about another **k** of priest.
7:11 speak about another **k** of priest,
7:12 When a different **k** of
8:1 We do have this **k** of chief
Jas 2:14 Can this **k** of faith save him?
3:6 The tongue is that **k** of flame.
3:15 That **k** of wisdom doesn't come
3:16 is disorder and every **k** of evil.
4:6 but he is **k** to humble people."
1Pe 1:14 don't live the **k** of lives you
2:1 So get rid of every **k** of evil,
2:1 every **k** of deception,
2:1 and every **k** of slander.
2:18 owners who are good and **k**,
5:9 through the same **k** of suffering
2Pe 2:5 who told people about the **k**
3:11 So think of the **k** of holy and
1Jn 2:5 obeys what Christ says is the **k**
5:17 Every **k** of wrongdoing is sin,

kindles (1)

Isa 64:2 Be like the fire that **k**

kindly (11)

Jos 2:14 we'll treat you **k** and honestly
Jdg 1:24 and we'll treat you **k**."
1Sm 20:12 If he does feel **k** toward you,
Ezr 7:28 powerful officials treat me **k**.
9:9 the kings of Persia treat us **k**.
Job 6:14 treat a troubled person **k**,
31:18 my birth I treated the widow **k**.)
Jer 24:5 I will look **k** on them.
Hos 14:2 all our sins, and **k** receive us.
Act 27:3 Julius treated Paul **k** and
28:7 welcomed us and treated us **k**,

kindness (102)

Gen 21:23 been living the same **k** that
24:12 Show your **k** to Abraham.
24:14 shown your **k** to my master."
24:49 show my master true **k** so that
Rut 2:13 may your **k** to me continue.
3:10 This last **k** — that you didn't go
1Sm 20:14 me that you will ⌋ show me **k**
2Sm 2:5 you because you showed **k**
2:6 the LORD always show you **k**.
9:1 show **k** for Jonathan's sake?"
9:3 to whom I can show God's **k**?"
9:7 "I will certainly show you **k** for
10:2 David thought, "I will show **k** to
10:2 father Nahash showed me **k**.
15:20 LORD⌋ always show you **k**."
1Ch 19:2 David thought, "I will show **k** to
19:2 father Nahash showed me **k**.
2Ch 32:25 didn't repay the LORD for his **k**.
Job 24:21 men show no **k** to widows.
Psa 31:19 Your **k** is so great!
90:17 Let the **k** of the Lord our God be
119:124 Treat me with **k**, and teach me
141:5 strike me or correct me out of **k**.
Pro 19:6 Many try to win the **k** of a
Isa 54:8 you with everlasting **k**," says
54:10 but my **k** will never depart from
Jer 31:3 continue to show you my **k**.
Hos 11:4 them with cords of human **k**,
Jon 1:14 a glory full of **k** and truth.
1:17 but **k** and truth came into
Act 11:23 God had done for them out of **k**.
15:11 he saves them — through his **k**
18:27 God's **k** enabled him to help
20:24 to the Good News of God's **k**.
Rom 1:5 him we have received God's **k**
2:4 that it is God's **k** that is trying
3:24 freely by an act of his **k** through
5:15 it is certainly true that God's **k**
5:15 and the gift given through the **k**
5:17 receive God's overflowing **k**
5:20 God's **k** increased even more.
5:21 God's **k** would rule by bringing
6:1 so that God's **k** will increase?
11:5 that God has chosen by his **k**.
11:6 If they were chosen by God's **k**,
11:6 God's **k** wouldn't be kindness.
11:6 God's kindness wouldn't be **k**.
11:22 continue to hold on to his **k**.
12:3 Because of the **k** that God has
12:6 God in his **k** gave each of us
1Co 15:10 But God's **k** made me what I
15:10 and that **k** was not wasted on
15:10 but God's **k** was with me.
2Co 1:12 we have lived but by God's **k**.
4:15 as God's **k** overflows in the
6:1 we urge you not to let God's **k**
6:6 purity, knowledge, patience, **k**,
8:1 know how God showed his **k**
8:4 in the ministry of God's **k**
8:6 his work of God's **k** among you
8:7 in this work of God's **k**.
8:9 You know about the **k** of our
8:19 us and bring this gift of God's **k**.
9:8 his constantly overflowing **k**.
9:14 of the extreme **k** that God has
10:1 the gentleness and **k** of Christ.
12:9 "My **k** is all you need.
Gal 1:6 who called you in his **k**,
1:15 and who called me by his **k**,
2:21 I don't reject God's **k**.
5:22 **k**, goodness, faithfulness,
Eph 1:6 so that the **k** he had given us in
1:7 because of his overflowing **k**.
1:8 He poured out his **k** by giving
2:5 (It is God's **k** that saved you.)
2:7 to show his extremely rich **k**
2:8 you through faith as an act of **k**.
3:2 of bringing his **k** to you.
3:7 through God's **k** freely given
3:8 Yet, God showed me his **k** by
Col 1:6 what God's **k** truly means.
3:16 yourselves about ⌊God's⌋ **k**.
2Th 2:16 loved us and by his **k** gave
1Ti 1:14 Through his **k** he brought me to
2Ti 1:9 because of his own plan and **k**.
1:9 Jesus would show us God's **k**.
2:1 in the **k** of Christ Jesus.
Tit 2:11 After all, God's saving **k** has
3:4 God our Savior made his **k**
3:7 As a result, God in his **k** has
Heb 2:9 Through God's **k** he died on
4:16 to the throne of God's **k**
4:16 to receive mercy and find **k**,
10:29 that God gave us out of his **k**.
12:15 Make sure that everyone has **k**
13:9 strength from God's **k** is good
Jas 4:6 God shows us even more **k**.
1Pe 1:10 about God's **k** that would come
1:13 in what God's **k** will bring you
3:7 life-giving **k** so that nothing
5:10 God, who shows you his **k**
Jud 1:4 They use God's **k** as an

kinds (61)

Gen 40:17 The top basket contained all **k**
Exo 30:34 one part fragrant spices (two **k**
35:22 alike — came and brought all **k**
35:35 They can do all **k** of trades.
Lev 11:2 Here are the **k** of land animals
11:4 these are the **k** you must never
11:9 "Here are the **k** of creatures that
11:13 "Here are the **k** of birds you
19:19 different **k** of animals.
19:19 Never plant two **k** of crops in
19:19 made from two **k** of material.
19:23 into the land and plant all **k**
Num 11:4 craving for ⌊other **k** of⌋ food.
Dtr 6:11 houses will be filled with all **k**
14:4 Here are the ⌊**k** of⌋ animals
14:7 not eat these ⌊**k** of⌋ animals.
25:14 Never have two **k** of measures
2Sm 6:5 the LORD's presence with all **k**
1Ki 7:14 and knowledgeable about all **k**
2Ki 8:9 with him a present and all **k**
17:32 they also appointed all **k** of
1Ch 12:37 to fight with all **k** of weapons.
22:15 You have many **k** of workers:
2Ch 2:14 also knows how to make all **k**
32:27 and all **k** of valuables.
Neh 13:16 in fish and all **k** of goods.
13:20 and those who sell all **k**
Psa 119:14 than I find joy in all **k** of riches.
144:13 be filled with all **k** of crops.
Pro 1:13 We'll find all **k** of valuable
Sos 4:14 and all **k** of incense,
7:13 and at our door are all **k** of
Eze 47:10 As many **k** of fish will be there
47:12 All **k** of fruit trees will grow on
Dan 1:17 to understand all **k** of literature.
1:17 could also understand all **k**
3:5 with all other **k** of instruments,
3:7 with all other **k** of instruments,
3:10 the same time with all other **k**
3:15 with all other **k** of instruments,
Amo 6:5 Like David, they write all **k** of
Mat 5:11 and say all **k** of evil things
13:47 It gathered all **k** of fish.
Act 10:12 In the sheet were all **k** of
Rom 1:29 lives are filled with of all **k**
3:2 There are all **k** of advantages.
7:8 and made me have all **k**
14:2 that they can eat all **k** of food.
14:6 When people eat all **k** of foods,
1Co 12:10 Another can speak in different **k**
Eph 4:14 and carried about by all **k**
1Ti 6:10 is the root of all **k** of evil.
2Ti 3:6 sins and led by all **k** of desires.
Tit 3:3 We were slaves to many **k** of
Heb 13:9 Don't get carried away by all **k**
13:16 These are the **k** of sacrifices
Jas 3:7 have tamed all **k** of animals,
1Pe 1:6 you have to suffer different **k**
Rev 18:12 all **k** of citron wood,
21:19 decorated with all **k** of gems:
22:2 It produced 12 **k** of fruit.

king (2269)

Gen 14:1 At that time ⌊four kings⌋ — **K**
14:1 **K** Arioch of Ellasar,
14:1 **K** Chedorlaomer of Elam,
14:1 and **K** Tidal of Goiim —
14:2 against ⌊five kings⌋ — **K** Bera
14:2 **K** Birsha of Gomorrah,
14:2 **K** Shinab of Admah,
14:2 **K** Shemeber of Zeboiim,
14:2 and the **k** of Bela (that is,
14:9 They fought against **K**
14:9 of Elam, **K** Tidal of Goiim,
14:9 **K** Amraphel of Shinar,
14:9 and **K** Arioch of Ellasar — four
14:17 the **k** of Sodom came out to
14:18 Then **K** Melchizedek of Salem
14:21 The **k** of Sodom said to Abram,
14:22 Abram said to the **k** of Sodom,
20:2 So **K** Abimelech of Gerar sent
26:1 So Isaac went to **K** Abimelech
26:8 **K** Abimelech of the Philistines
36:31 ruled Edom before any **k** ruled
Gen 36:33 succeeded him as **k**.
36:34 succeeded him as **k**.
36:35 of Bedad succeeded him as **k**.
36:36 Masrekah succeeded him as **k**.
36:37 the river succeeded him as **k**.
36:38 succeeded him as **k**.
36:39 Hadar succeeded him as **k**,
37:8 "Are you going to be our **k** or
40:1 their master, the **k** of Egypt.
40:5 and the baker for the **k**
41:46 of Pharaoh (the **k** of Egypt).
49:20 provide delicacies fit for a **k**.
Exo 1:8 Then a new **k**, who knew
1:15 Then the **k** of Egypt told the
1:17 God and didn't obey the **k**
1:18 So the **k** of Egypt called for the
2:23 the **k** of Egypt died.
3:18 the leaders must go to the **k**
3:19 I know that the **k** of Egypt will
5:4 The **k** of Egypt said to them,
6:11 "Go tell Pharaoh (the **k** of
6:13 and Pharaoh (the **k** of Egypt).
6:27 Aaron — told Pharaoh (the **k**
6:29 Tell Pharaoh (the **k** of Egypt)
14:5 When Pharaoh (the **k** of Egypt)
14:8 LORD made Pharaoh (the **k**
15:18 will rule as **k** forever and ever."
Num 20:14 from Kadesh to the **k** of Edom.
21:1 When the Canaanite **k** of Arad,
21:21 messengers to say to **K** Sihon
21:26 Heshbon was the city of **K**
21:26 He had fought the former **k** of
21:29 become prisoners of **K** Sihon
21:33 **K** Og of Bashan and all his
21:34 Do to him what you did to **K**
22:4 son of Zippor, was **k** of Moab.
22:10 son of **K** Zippor of Moab,
23:7 The **k** of Moab summoned me
23:21 is with them, praised as their **k**.
24:7 Their **k** will be greater than
32:33 the kingdoms of **K** Sihon of the
32:33 Sihon of the Amorites and **K** Og
33:40 (The Canaanite **k** of Arad,
Dtr 1:4 after he had defeated **K** Sihon
1:4 and **K** Og of Bashan,
2:24 I'm going to hand **K** Sihon of
2:26 I sent messengers to **K** Sihon
2:30 But **K** Sihon of Heshbon
3:1 **K** Og of Bashan and all his
3:2 Do to him what you did to **K**
3:3 our God also handed **K** Og
3:6 we did to **K** Sihon of Heshbon.
3:11 (Of the Rephaim only **K** Og of
4:46 in the land of **K** Sihon of the
4:47 of his land and the land of **K** Og
7:8 under Pharaoh (the **k** of Egypt).
11:3 did in Egypt to Pharaoh (the **k**
17:14 "Let's have our own **k** like all
17:15 Be sure to appoint the **k** the
17:15 Never let a foreigner be **k**,
17:16 The **k** must never own a large
17:17 The **k** must never have a large
17:18 When he becomes **k**,
28:36 lead you and the **k** you choose
29:7 you came to this place, **K** Sihon
29:7 King Sihon of Heshbon and **K**
31:4 nations what he did to **K** Sihon
31:4 he did to King Sihon and **K** Og
33:5 The LORD was **k** of Jeshurun
Jos 2:2 The **k** of Jericho was told,
2:3 So the **k** of Jericho sent
6:2 am about to hand Jericho, its **k**,
8:1 I am about to hand the **k** of Ai,
8:2 thing to Ai and its **k** that you did
8:2 you did to Jericho and its **k**.
8:14 When the **k** of Ai saw the main
8:14 However, the **k** didn't know
8:23 But they captured the **k** of Ai
8:29 Joshua hung the **k** of Ai's
9:10 **K** Sihon of Heshbon and King
9:10 King Sihon of Heshbon and **K**
10:1 **K** Adoni Zedek of Jerusalem
10:1 destroyed Jericho and its **k**.
10:3 So **K** Adoni Zedek of
10:3 ⌊this message⌋ to **K** Hoham
10:3 **K** Piram of Jarmuth,
Jos 10:3 **K** Japhia of Lachish,
10:3 and **K** Debir of Eglon:
10:28 its people and **k** with swords.
10:28 He did the same thing to the **k**
10:28 he had done to the **k** of Jericho.
10:30 handed Libnah and its **k** over
10:30 He did the same thing to the **k**
10:30 he had done to the **k** of Jericho.
10:33 At that time **K** Horam of Gezer
10:37 villages and killed its **k**
10:39 He captured it and its **k** and all
10:39 thing to Debir and its **k** that
11:1 **K** Jabin of Hazor heard ⌊what
11:1 So he sent messengers to **K**
11:10 He killed its **k** with a sword.
12:2 Sihon was the Amorite **k** who
12:4 The territory of **K** Og of Bashan
12:5 border of **K** Sihon of Heshbon.
12:9 the **k** of Jericho, the king of Ai
12:9 the **k** of Ai (near Bethel),
12:10 the **k** of Jerusalem,
12:10 of Jerusalem, the **k** of Hebron,
12:11 the **k** of Jarmuth, the king of
12:11 of Jarmuth, the **k** of Lachish,
12:12 the **k** of Eglon, the king of
12:12 king of Eglon, the **k** of Gezer,
12:13 the **k** of Debir, the king of
12:13 king of Debir, the **k** of Geder,
12:14 the **k** of Hormah, the king of
12:14 king of Hormah, the **k** of Arad,
12:15 the **k** of Libnah, the king of
12:15 of Libnah, the **k** of Adullam,
12:16 the **k** of Makkedah,
12:16 of Makkedah, the **k** of Bethel,
12:17 the **k** of Tappuah, the king of
12:17 of Tappuah, the **k** of Hepher,
12:18 the **k** of Aphek, the king of
12:18 king of Aphek, the **k** of Sharon,
12:19 the **k** of Madon, the king of
12:19 king of Madon, the **k** of Hazor,
12:20 the **k** of Shimron Meron,
12:20 the **k** of Achshaph,
12:21 the **k** of Taanach, the king of
12:21 of Taanach, the **k** of Megiddo,
12:22 the **k** of Kedesh, the king of
12:22 the **k** of Jokneam in Carmel,
12:23 the **k** of Dor in Naphoth Dor,
12:23 the **k** of Goiim in Gilgal,
12:24 the **k** of Tirzah. The total was
13:10 It included all the cities of **K**
13:21 the whole kingdom of **K** Sihon
13:27 the rest of the kingdom of **K**
13:30 (the whole kingdom of **K** Og
24:9 son of **K** Zippor of Moab,
Jdg 3:8 He used **K** Cushan Rishathaim
3:10 The LORD handed **K** Cushan
3:12 So the LORD made **K** Eglon of
3:14 The Israelites served **K** Eglon
3:15 payment to **K** Eglon of Moab.
3:17 the tax payment to **K** Eglon.
3:19 The **k** replied, "Keep quiet!"
3:20 He said to the **k**, "I have a
3:20 As the **k** rose from his throne,
4:2 So the LORD used **K** Jabin of
4:2 The commander of **K** Jabin's
4:3 **K** Jabin had 900 chariots made
4:17 Sisera did this because **K**
4:23 power of **K** Jabin of Canaan.
8:5 and I'm pursuing **K** Zebah and
8:5 and **K** Zalmunna of Midian."
8:12 He captured **K** Zebah and King
8:12 He captured King Zebah and **K**
9:6 and proclaimed Abimelech **k**.
9:8 someone to be **k** over them.
9:8 said to the olive tree, 'Be our **k**!'
9:10 'You come and be our **k**!'
9:12 'You come and be our **k**!'
9:14 'You come and be our **k**!'
9:15 want to anoint me to be your **k**,
9:16 when you made Abimelech **k**,
9:18 **k** over the citizens of Shechem
11:12 messengers to the **k** of Ammon.
11:12 They asked the **k**,
11:13 The **k** of Ammon answered
11:14 messengers to the **k** of Ammon.
11:17 messengers to the **k** of Edom.

Jdg 11:17 But the **k** of Edom wouldn't
11:17 messengers to the **k** of Moab.
11:19 sent messengers to **K** Sihon
11:25 son of **K** Zippor of Moab,
11:28 But the **k** of Ammon didn't
17:6 days Israel didn't have a **k**.
18:1 days Israel didn't have a **k**.
19:1 when Israel didn't have a **k**,
21:25 days Israel didn't have a **k**.
1Sm 2:10 He gives strength to his **K** and
8:5 Now appoint a **k** to judge us so
8:6 it wrong for them to request a **k**
8:9 them about the rights of a **k**."
8:10 asked him for a **k** everything
8:11 "These are the rights of a **k**:
8:18 of the **k** whom you have
8:19 They said, "No, we want a **k**!
8:20 Our **k** will judge us,
8:22 and give them a **k**."
10:16 said ⌊about his becoming **k**⌋.
10:19 Place a **k** over us.'
10:24 shouted, "Long live the **k**!"
11:1 **K** Nahash of Ammon was
11:1 whose right eye **K** Nahash
11:15 they confirmed Saul as their **k**.
12:1 me and appointed a **k** over you.
12:2 here is the **k** who will lead you.
12:3 and in front of his anointed **k**.
12:5 and his anointed **k** is a witness
12:9 and to the **k** of Moab.
12:12 But when you saw **K** Nahash
12:12 a **k** should rule over us,'
12:12 LORD your God was your **k**.
12:13 here is the **k** you have chosen,
12:13 the LORD has put a **k** over you.
12:14 then you and your **k** will follow
12:17 when you asked for a **k**."
12:19 other sins by asking for a **k**."
12:25 you and your **k** will be wiped
13:1 years old when he became **k**,
13:1 and he was **k** of Israel
15:1 LORD sent me to anoint you **k**
15:8 He captured **K** Agag of Amalek
15:11 "I regret that I made Saul **k**.
15:17 LORD anointed you **k** of Israel.
15:20 brought ⌊back⌋ **K** Agag of
15:23 he rejects you as **k**."
15:26 rejects you as **k** of Israel."
15:32 "Bring me **K** Agag of Amalek,"
15:35 he had made Saul **k** of Israel.
16:1 rejected him as **k** of Israel?
16:1 one of his sons to be **k**."
16:6 presence is his anointed **k**."
17:25 The **k** will make the man who
17:56 The **k** said, "Find out whose
18:6 cities came to meet **K** Saul.
18:22 Tell him, 'The **k** likes you,
18:25 "Tell David, 'The **k** doesn't want
18:27 them out for the **k** so that David
20:24 **K** Saul sat down to eat the
20:31 nor your right to be **k** is secure.
21:2 "The **k** ordered me to do
21:10 he came to **K** Achish of Gath.
21:11 the **k** of ⌊his⌋ country?
21:12 terrified of **K** Achish of Gath.
22:3 He asked the **k** of Moab,
22:4 brought them to the **k** of Moab,
22:11 Then the **k** sent for the priest
22:11 All of them came to the **k**.
22:14 Ahimelech asked the **k**,
22:17 the **k** said to the runners
22:18 So the **k** said to Doeg,
24:6 the LORD's anointed **k**,
24:14 Against whom has the **k** of
24:20 that you certainly will rule as **k**,
26:9 attacked the LORD's anointed **k**
26:11 attack the LORD's anointed **k**.
26:14 "Who is calling the **k**?"
26:15 you guard your master, the **k**?
26:16 the LORD's anointed **k**.
26:20 The **k** of Israel has come to
26:23 attack the LORD's anointed **k**.
27:2 with his 600 men to **K** Achish
28:13 be afraid," the **k** said to her.
29:3 the servant of **K** Saul of Israel,
2Sm 1:14 the LORD's anointed **k**?"

2Sm 1:16 killed the LORD's anointed **k**.'"
2:4 and anointed David to be **k** over
2:7 has anointed me to be their **k**."
2:9 Abner made him **k** of Gilead,
2:10 when he became **k** of Israel.
2:11 In Hebron David was **k** over the
3:3 of **K** Talmai) from Geshur.
3:17 wanted to make David your **k**.
3:23 "Ner's son Abner came to the **k**,
3:24 Joab went to the **k** and asked,
3:31 **K** David followed the open
3:32 The **k** cried loudly at Abner's
3:33 The **k** sang a funeral song for
3:36 of everything the **k** did.
3:37 knew the **k** wasn't responsible
3:38 The **k** said to his officers,
3:39 though I'm the anointed **k**.
4:8 to kill you," they told the **k**.
5:3 **K** David made an agreement
5:3 they anointed David **k** of Israel.
5:4 years old when he became **k**,
5:6 The **k** and his men went to
5:11 Then **K** Hiram of Tyre sent
5:12 had established him as **k**
5:17 had been anointed **k** of Israel,
6:12 **K** David was told, "The LORD
6:16 and saw **K** David leaping
6:20 dignified Israel's **k** was today!
7:1 While **K** David was living in
7:2 So the **k** said to the prophet
7:3 Nathan told the **k**, because the
7:18 **K** David went into the tent and
8:3 defeated Zobah's **K** Hadadezer,
8:5 came to help **K** Hadadezer
8:8 **K** David also took a large
8:9 When **K** Toi of Hamath heard
8:10 his son Joram to greet **K** David
8:11 **K** David dedicated these
8:12 from Zobah's **K** Hadadezer,
9:2 the **k** asked him. "⌊Yes,⌋ I am,"
9:4 the **k** asked. Ziba replied, "He is
9:5 So **K** David sent men to get
9:9 Then the **k** called for Ziba,
10:1 Later the **k** of Ammon died,
10:1 Hanun became **k** in his place.
10:5 The **k** said to them,
10:6 ⌊the army of⌋ the **k** of Maacah
11:8 and the **k** sent a present to him.
11:19 telling the **k** about the battle,
11:20 the **k** may become angry.
11:21 If the **k** asks this, then say,
12:7 I anointed you **k** over Israel and
12:30 from the head of Rabbah's **k**
13:6 and the **k** came to see him.
13:6 Amnon asked the **k**,
13:13 Speak to the **k**. He won't refuse
13:21 When **K** David heard about this,
13:24 went to the **k** and said,
13:25 the **k** answered Absalom.
13:26 go with you?" the **k** asked him.
13:31 The **k** stood up, tore his
13:35 Then Jonadab told the **k**,
13:36 The **k** and all his men also
13:37 fled to Geshur's **K** Talmai,
13:37 But the **k** mourned for his son
13:39 **K** David began to long for
14:1 knew the **k** was still thinking
14:3 Go to the **k**, and tell him this
14:4 from Tekoa came to the **k**
14:5 The **k** asked her, "What can I
14:8 the **k** told the woman.
14:9 from Tekoa said to the **k**,
14:10 The **k** said, "If anyone says
14:15 'I will speak to the **k** about this.
14:15 Maybe the **k** will do something
14:16 Maybe the **k** will listen and
14:18 The **k** said to the woman,
14:19 the **k** asked. The woman
14:21 Then the **k** told Joab,
14:22 and he blessed the **k**.
14:24 But the **k** said, He will not see
14:24 his house and didn't see the **k**.
14:28 full years without seeing the **k**.
14:29 in order to send him to the **k**,
14:32 I wanted to send you to the **k**
14:32 Let me see the **k** now!

2Sm 14:33 Joab went to the **k** and told him
14:33 The **k** then called for Absalom,
14:33 who came to the **k** and bowed
14:33 And the **k** kissed Absalom.
15:2 a case to be tried by **K** David,
15:3 but the **k** hasn't appointed
15:6 all Israelites who came to the **k**
15:7 later Absalom said to the **k**,
15:9 "Go in peace," the **k** told him.
15:10 has become **k** in Hebron.'"
15:16 The **k** left on foot, and his
15:16 whom the **k** left behind
15:17 As the **k** and his troops were
15:18 Gath were marching past the **k**.
15:19 The **k** asked Ittai from Gath,
15:19 and stay with **K** Absalom.
15:21 But Ittai answered the **k**,
15:21 as the LORD and the **k** live:
15:23 The **k** was crossing the Kidron
15:25 The **k** told Zadok, "Take God's
15:27 the **k** asked Zadok the priest.
16:3 the **k** asked. "He's staying in
16:3 Ziba answered the **k**.
16:4 The **k** told Ziba, "In that case
16:5 When **K** David came to
16:8 whom you succeeded as **k**.
16:9 Zeruiah's son, asked the **k**,
16:10 But the **k** said, "You don't think
16:14 The **k** and all the people with
16:16 he said, "Long live the **k**!
16:16 live the king! Long live the **k**!"
17:17 and they were to go and tell **K**
17:21 and went and told **K** David.
18:2 the **k** said to the troops.
18:4 think best," the **k** responded.
18:4 So the **k** stood by the gate
18:5 The **k** ordered Joab,
18:12 heard the order the **k** gave you,
18:13 stay hidden from the **k**."
18:19 "Let me run and bring the **k** the
18:21 tell the **k** what you saw."
18:25 called and alerted the **k**.
18:25 "If he's alone," the **k** said,
18:26 The **k** said, "This one is also
18:27 "He's a good man," the **k** said.
18:28 Ahimaaz came up to the **k**,
18:29 the **k** asked. Ahimaaz
18:30 and stand here," the **k** said.
18:32 the **k** asked. The Sudanese
18:33 The **k** was shaken ⌊by the
19:1 Joab was told, "The **k** is crying
19:2 heard that the **k** was grieving
19:4 The **k** covered his face and
19:8 The **k** sat in the gateway.
19:8 "The **k** is sitting in the
19:8 they came to the **k**.
19:9 "The **k** rescued us from our
19:10 about bringing back the **k**?"
19:11 reached the **k** at his house.
19:11 So **K** David sent ⌊this
19:11 last ⌊tribe⌋ to bring the **k** back
19:12 be the last to bring back the **k**?'
19:14 they sent the **k** this message:
19:15 The **k** came back to the Jordan
19:15 came to Gilgal to meet the **k**
19:16 of Judah to meet **K** David.
19:17 Jordan River across from the **k**.
19:18 do anything else the **k** wanted.
19:18 bowed down in front of the **k**
19:19 He pleaded with the **k**,
19:21 the LORD's anointed **k**?"
19:22 Don't I know that I'm **k** of Israel
19:23 The **k** promised Shimei,
19:23 and the **k** swore to it.
19:24 went to meet the **k**.
19:24 from the day the **k** left until
19:25 from Jerusalem to meet the **k**,
19:25 meet the king, the **k** asked him,
19:26 I'll ride on it and go with the **k**.'
19:28 the right to complain to the **k**."
19:29 The **k** asked him, "Why do you
19:30 Mephibosheth told the **k**.
19:31 came from Rogelim with the **k**
19:32 he had provided the **k** with food
19:33 The **k** told Barzillai,
19:38 go across with me," the **k** said.

2Sm 19:39 and then the **k** crossed.
19:39 The **k** kissed Barzillai and
19:40 The **k** crossed the river to
19:40 Israel brought the **k** across.
19:41 of Israel kept coming to the **k**.
19:42 "Because the **k** is our relative.
19:43 ten times your interest in the **k**
19:43 suggest bringing back our **k**?"
20:2 loyal to their **k** ⌊on his way⌋
20:4 The **k** told Amasa,
20:21 has rebelled against **K** David.
20:22 back to the **k** in Jerusalem.
21:2 The **k** called the Gibeonites
21:4 The **k** asked, "What are you
21:5 They answered the **k**,
21:6 them ⌊to you⌋," the **k** said.
21:7 But the **k** spared Mephibosheth
21:8 The **k** took Armoni and
21:9 The **k** handed them over to the
21:14 did everything the **k** ordered.
22:51 gives great victories to his **k**.
24:2 **K** David said to Joab,
24:3 Joab responded to the **k**,
24:4 However, the **k** overruled Joab
24:4 So they left the **k** ⌊in order⌋ to
24:9 the census figures to the **k**:
24:20 looked down and saw the **k**
24:20 the ground in front of the **k**.
24:23 Araunah gave to the **k** and said,
24:24 the **k** said to Araunah.
1Ki 1:1 **K** David had grown old,
1:3 and brought her to the **k**.
1:4 but the **k** did not make love to
1:5 was boasting that he was **k**.
1:11 Haggith's son, has become **k**,
1:13 Go to **K** David and ask him,
1:13 Solomon will be **k** after you,
1:13 Why is Adonijah acting as **k**?'
1:14 you're still there talking to the **k**
1:15 Bathsheba went to the **k** in his
1:15 The **k** was very old,
1:16 bowed down in front of the **k**.
1:16 do you want?" the **k** asked.
1:17 Solomon will be **k** after you,
1:18 Adonijah has become **k**,
1:22 she was still talking to the **k**,
1:23 The servants told the **k**,
1:23 When he came to the **k**,
1:24 that Adonijah will be **k** after you
1:25 'Long live **K** Adonijah!'
1:28 Then **K** David answered,
1:30 son Solomon will be **k** after me.
1:31 the ground in front of the **k**.
1:31 "May Your Majesty, **K** David,
1:32 **K** David said, "Summon the
1:32 So they came to the **k**,
1:34 prophet Nathan anoint him **k**
1:34 'Long live **K** Solomon!'
1:35 He will be **k** in place of me.
1:36 of Jehoiada, answered the **k**.
1:37 be an even greater **k** than you,
1:37 king than you, **K** David."
1:38 put Solomon on **K** David's mule
1:39 "Long live **K** Solomon!"
1:43 "His Majesty **K** David has
1:43 David has made Solomon **k**.
1:44 The **k** has sent the priest
1:45 have anointed him **k** at Gihon.
1:47 His Majesty **K** David,
1:47 The **k** himself bowed down on
1:51 is afraid of you, **K** Solomon.
1:51 'Make **K** Solomon swear to me
1:53 **K** Solomon sent men to take
1:53 down in front of **K** Solomon.
2:8 and said, 'As long as I'm **k**,
2:11 He ruled as **k** of Israel for 40
2:15 expected me to be their **k**.
2:17 He said, "Please ask **K**
2:18 "I will talk to the **k** for you."
2:19 Bathsheba went to **K** Solomon
2:19 The **k** got up to meet her and
2:20 "Ask, Mother," the **k** told her.
2:22 **K** Solomon then said,
2:23 **K** Solomon took an oath by the
2:25 **K** Solomon gave this task to
2:26 The **k** told the priest Abiathar,

1Ki 2:29 After **K** Solomon heard that
2:30 "The **k** says, 'Come out.'" "No,"
2:30 So Benaiah reported to the **k**
2:31 The **k** answered, "Do as he
2:35 The **k** then appointed Benaiah,
2:35 **K** Solomon also replaced
2:36 The **k** summoned Shimei and
2:39 slaves fled to Gath's **K** Achish,
2:45 But **K** Solomon is blessed,
2:46 Then the **k** gave orders to
2:46 Solomon's power as **k** was
3:1 of Pharaoh (the **k** of Egypt).
3:4 **K** Solomon went to Gibeon to
3:7 you've made me **k** in place of
3:13 honor — so that no other **k** will
3:16 two prostitutes came to the **k**
3:22 So they argued in front of the **k**.
3:23 The **k** said, "This one keeps
3:24 So the **k** told his servants to
3:26 She said to the **k**, "Please, sir,
3:27 The **k** replied, "Give the living
3:28 about the decision the **k** made.
3:28 respected the **k** very highly,
4:1 When **K** Solomon was the king
4:1 Solomon was the **k** of all Israel,
4:7 were to provide food for the **k**
4:19 the territory of **K** Sihon the
4:19 Sihon the Amorite and **K** Og
4:27 every year for **K** Solomon
5:1 **K** Hiram of Tyre sent his
5:1 Solomon had been anointed **k**
5:13 **K** Solomon forced 30,000 men
5:17 The **k** commanded them to
6:2 The temple that **K** Solomon
7:13 **K** Solomon had Hiram brought
7:14 He came to **K** Solomon and did
7:40 all the work for **K** Solomon
7:45 temple at **K** Solomon's request.
7:46 The **k** cast them in foundries in
7:51 All the work **K** Solomon did on
8:1 They came to **K** Solomon in
8:2 gathered around **K** Solomon at
8:5 while **K** Solomon with the
8:14 Then the **k** turned around and
8:62 Then the **k** and all Israel
8:63 So the **k** and all the people of
8:64 On that day the **k** designated
8:66 They blessed the **k** and went
9:11 ⌊When **K** Solomon had
9:11 he gave **K** Hiram of Tyre 20
9:14 Hiram had sent the **k** 9,000
9:15 whom **K** Solomon drafted
9:16 (The **k** of Egypt captured
9:26 **K** Solomon also built a fleet
9:28 and brought it to **K** Solomon.
10:3 too difficult for the **k** to answer.
10:6 She told the **k**, "What I heard in
10:9 he has made you **k** so that you
10:10 She gave the **k** 9,000 pounds
10:10 of Sheba gave **K** Solomon.
10:12 With the sandalwood the **k**
10:13 **K** Solomon gave the queen of
10:16 **K** Solomon made 200 large
10:17 The **k** put them in the hall
10:18 The **k** also made a large ivory
10:21 All **K** Solomon's cups were
10:22 The **k** had a fleet headed for
10:23 In wealth and wisdom **K**
10:27 The **k** made silver as common
11:1 **K** Solomon loved many foreign
11:18 to Pharaoh (the **k** of Egypt).
11:23 **K** Hadadezer of Zobah,
11:26 but he rebelled against the **k**.
11:27 when he rebelled against the **k**:
11:37 You will be **k** of Israel.
11:40 but Jeroboam fled to **K** Shishak
11:43 succeeded him as **k**.
12:1 to Shechem to make him **k**.
12:2 he had fled from **K** Solomon.
12:6 **K** Rehoboam sought advice
12:12 as the **k** had instructed them.
12:13 The **k** answered the people
12:15 The **k** refused to listen to the
12:16 When all Israel saw that the **k**
12:16 the people answered the **k**,
12:18 Then **K** Rehoboam sent

1Ki 12:18 So **K** Rehoboam got on his
12:20 They made him **k** of all Israel.
12:23 to Judah's **K** Rehoboam,
12:27 **K** Rehoboam of Judah,
12:27 to **K** Rehoboam of Judah."
12:28 the **k** made two golden calves.
13:4 When **K** Jeroboam heard the
13:6 Then the **k** asked the man of
13:6 and the **k** was able to use his
13:7 The **k** told the man of God,
13:8 The man of God told the **k**,
13:11 words he had spoken to the **k**.
14:2 who told me I would be **k** of
14:14 will appoint a **k** over Israel.
14:14 That **k** will destroy Jeroboam's
14:20 Nadab succeeded him as **k**.
14:25 **K** Shishak of Egypt attacked
14:27 So **K** Rehoboam made bronze
14:28 Whenever the **k** went into the
14:31 Abijam succeeded him as **k**.
15:8 son Asa succeeded him as **k**.
15:9 twentieth year as **k** of Israel,
15:9 began to rule as **k** of Judah.
15:16 between Asa and **K** Baasha
15:17 **K** Baasha of Israel invaded
15:17 or coming from **K** Asa of Judah.
15:18 **K** Asa sent them to Damascus
15:18 to Aram's **K** Benhadad,
15:19 Now break your treaty with **K**
15:20 did what **K** Asa requested.
15:22 Then **K** Asa drafted everyone
15:22 **K** Asa used the materials to
15:24 succeeded him as **k**.
15:25 second year as **k** of Judah.
15:28 Asa's third year as **k** of Judah.
15:28 Nadab as **k** of Israel.
15:29 As soon as he was **k**,
15:33 Asa's third year as **k** of Judah,
16:6 son Elah succeeded him as **k**.
16:8 twenty-sixth year as Judah's **k**.
16:10 year as **k** of Judah.
16:10 Elah as **k** ⌊of Israel⌋.
16:15 year as Judah's **k**,
16:16 had plotted ⌊against the **k**⌋
16:16 of the army, **k** of Israel.
16:21 and wanted to make him **k**.
16:22 Tibni died, and Omri became **k**.
16:23 thirty-first year as **k** of Judah.
16:28 son Ahab succeeded him as **k**.
16:29 thirty-eighth year as **k** of Judah.
16:31 daughter of **K** Ethbaal of Sidon.
19:15 anoint Hazael as **k** of Aram.
19:16 son of Nimshi, as **k** of Israel.
20:1 **K** Benhadad of Aram gathered
20:2 into the city to **K** Ahab
20:4 The **k** of Israel answered,
20:7 Then the **k** of Israel called for
20:11 The **k** of Israel answered,
20:13 Then a prophet came to **K**
20:20 **K** Benhadad of Aram escaped
20:21 The **k** of Israel went out and
20:22 Then the prophet came to the **k**
20:22 When spring comes, the **k** of
20:23 Meanwhile, the officers of **K**
20:28 He said to the **k** of Israel,
20:31 and go to the **k** of Israel.
20:32 They went to the **k** of Israel
20:38 waited for the **k** by the road.
20:39 When the **k** passed by,
20:40 The **k** of Israel told him,
20:41 The **k** of Israel recognized him
20:43 Resentful and upset, the **k** of
21:1 palace of **K** Ahab of Samaria.
21:7 "Aren't you **k** of Israel?
21:10 him of cursing God and the **k**.
21:13 of cursing God and the **k**.
21:18 "Go, meet **K** Ahab of Israel,
22:2 In the third year **K** Jehoshaphat
22:2 went to visit the **k** of Israel.
22:3 The **k** of Israel asked his staff,
22:3 it back from the **k** of Aram?"
22:4 told the **k** of Israel,
22:5 Then Jehoshaphat said to the **k**
22:6 So the **k** of Israel called 400
22:8 The **k** of Israel told
22:8 "The **k** must not say that."

1Ki 22:9 The **k** of Israel called for an
22:10 The **k** of Israel and King
22:10 The king of Israel and **K**
22:13 prophets have all told the **k**
22:15 When he came to the **k**,
22:15 the **k** asked him, "Micaiah,
22:16 The **k** asked him, "How many
22:18 The **k** of Israel said to
22:26 The **k** of Israel then said,
22:27 Say, 'This is what the **k** says:
22:29 So the **k** of Israel and King
22:29 So the king of Israel and **K**
22:30 The **k** of Israel told
22:30 So the **k** of Israel disguised
22:31 The **k** of Aram had given orders
22:31 anyone except the **k** of Israel."
22:32 "He must be the **k** of Israel."
22:33 that he wasn't the **k** of Israel.
22:34 his bow at random and hit the **k**
22:35 and the **k** was kept propped up
22:37 When the **k** was dead,
22:40 Ahaziah succeeded him as **k**.
22:41 became **k** of Judah in Ahab's
22:41 fourth year as **k** of Israel.
22:44 peace with the **k** of Israel.
22:47 There was no **k** in Edom;
22:50 Jehoram succeeded him as **k**.
22:51 became **k** of Israel in Samaria
22:51 year as **k** of Judah.
2Ki 1:2 During the rebellion **K** Ahaziah
1:3 of the **k** of Samaria,
1:5 returned, the **k** asked them,
1:6 "Go back to the **k** who sent
1:7 The **k** asked them,
1:8 from Tishbe," the **k** answered.
1:9 The **k** sent an army officer with
1:9 God, the **k** says, 'Come down."
1:11 The **k** sent another officer with
1:11 this is what the **k** says:
1:13 The **k** sent a third officer with
1:15 up and went with him to the **k**.
1:16 Elijah told the **k**, "This is what
1:17 Joram succeeded him as **k**
3:1 Joram, son of Ahab, became **k**
3:1 eighteenth year as **k** of Judah.
3:4 **K** Mesha of Moab raised sheep.
3:4 year⌋ he had to pay the **k**
3:5 But when Ahab died, the **k** of
3:5 against the ⌊new⌋ **k** of Israel.
3:6 **K** Joram immediately left
3:7 He sent this message to **K**
3:7 "The **k** of Moab has rebelled
3:9 So the **k** of Israel, the king of
3:9 king of Israel, the **k** of Judah,
3:9 and the **k** of Edom took an
3:10 The **k** of Israel said,
3:11 One of the officials of the **k** of
3:12 So **K** Jehoshaphat of Judah,
3:12 of Judah, the **k** of Israel,
3:12 and the **k** of Edom went to
3:13 Elisha asked the **k** of Israel,
3:13 The **k** of Israel answered him,
3:14 for **K** Jehoshaphat of Judah.
3:26 When the **k** of Moab saw he
3:26 break through to the **k** of Edom.
3:27 have succeeded him as **k**,
4:13 would like us to speak to the **k**
5:5 The **k** of Aram said,
5:5 send a letter to the **k** of Israel."
5:6 the letter to the **k** of Israel.
5:7 When the **k** of Israel read the
5:8 heard that the **k** of Israel had
5:8 he sent a messenger to the **k**.
6:8 Whenever the **k** of Aram was
6:9 a message to the **k** of Israel,
6:10 Then the **k** of Israel would
6:11 The **k** of Aram was very angry
6:11 is ⌊a spy⌋ for the **k** of Israel?"
6:12 tells the **k** of Israel everything
6:13 The **k** said, "Find out where he
6:13 The **k** was told, "He is in
6:14 So the **k** sent horses and
6:21 When the **k** of Israel saw them,
6:23 So the **k** prepared a great feast
6:24 Later **K** Benhadad of Aram
6:26 As the **k** of Israel was walking
2Ki 6:28 Then the **k** asked her,
6:30 When the **k** heard the woman
6:32 The **k** had sent one of his men
6:32 Hold it shut because the **k** will
7:2 the **k** was leaning answered
7:6 "The **k** of Israel has hired the
7:12 So the **k** got up at night and
7:14 and the **k** sent them to follow
7:15 returned and told the **k** about it.
7:17 The **k** appointed the servant on
7:17 when the **k** came to him.
7:18 as the man of God told the **k**,
8:3 appeal to the **k** about her house
8:4 The **k** was talking to Gehazi,
8:5 While Gehazi was telling the **k**
8:5 appeal to the **k** about her house
8:6 When the **k** asked the woman
8:6 So the **k** assigned to her an
8:7 **K** Benhadad of Aram,
8:8 The **k** told Hazael,
8:9 "Your humble servant **K**
8:13 you will become **k** of Aram."
8:15 and smothered the **k** with it.
8:15 Hazael ruled as **k** in his place.
8:16 son) was in his fifth year as **k**
8:16 son of **K** Jehoshaphat of Judah,
8:16 was still **k** of Judah.
8:20 Judah and chose its own **k**.
8:24 Ahaziah succeeded him as **k**.
8:25 was in his twelfth year as **k**
8:25 Ahaziah became **k** of Judah.
8:26 of **K** Omri of Israel.
8:28 Joram to fight against **K** Hazael
8:29 **K** Joram returned to Jezreel to
8:29 he fought against **K** Hazael
9:3 I have anointed you **k** of Israel.'
9:6 I have anointed you **k** of the
9:6 LORD's people, ⌊**k**⌋ of Israel.
9:12 have anointed you **k** of Israel.'"
9:13 horn and said, "Jehu is **k**!"
9:14 against **K** Hazael of Aram.
9:15 But **K** Joram had returned to
9:15 while fighting **K** Hazael
9:15 "If you want me to be **k**,
9:16 (**K** Ahaziah of Judah had come
9:18 Jehu, and said, "The **k** asks,
9:19 to them, he said, "The **k** asks,
9:21 When that was done, **K** Joram
9:21 King Joram of Israel and **K**
9:27 When **K** Ahaziah of Judah saw
9:29 (Ahaziah had become **k** of
9:29 Ahab's son, was **k** of Israel.)
10:5 We won't make anyone **k**.
10:13 he found some relatives of **K**
10:13 to greet the families of the **k**
10:35 Jehoahaz succeeded him as **k**.
10:36 Jehu ruled as **k** of Israel in
11:2 But Jehosheba, daughter of **K**
11:7 of worship must guard the **k** at
11:8 Surround the **k**. Each man
11:8 with the **k** wherever he goes."
11:10 that had belonged to **K** David
11:11 were stationed around the **k**
11:12 and made him **k** by anointing
11:12 they said, "Long live the **k**!"
11:14 She looked, and the **k** was
11:17 to the LORD on behalf of the **k**
11:17 between the **k** and the people.
11:19 and they brought the **k** from the
12:1 seventh year as **k** of Israel,
12:6 Joash's twenty-third year as **k**,
12:7 So **K** Joash called for Jehoiada
12:17 At this time **K** Hazael of Aram
12:18 So **K** Joash of Judah took all
12:18 He sent these things to **K**
12:21 Amaziah succeeded him as **k**.
13:1 Ahaziah's son **K** Joash of
13:1 in his twenty-third year as **k**
13:1 to rule in Samaria as **k** of Israel.
13:3 put it at the mercy of **K** Hazael
13:4 **k** was oppressing Israel.
13:7 foot soldiers because the **k**
13:9 ruled as **k** in his place.
13:10 year as **k** of Judah,
13:12 he fought against **K** Amaziah
13:14 **K** Jehoash of Israel visited him,
2Ki 13:16 Then Elisha told the **k** of Israel,
13:16 So the **k** picked up the bow.
13:17 So the **k** opened it.
13:17 Elisha said, and the **k** shot.
13:18 So the **k** took them.
13:18 he told the **k** of Israel.
13:18 The **k** stomped three times and
13:22 **K** Hazael of Aram oppressed
13:24 **K** Hazael of Aram died,
13:24 Benhadad succeeded him as **k**.
14:1 Jehoahaz's son **K** Jehoash
14:1 was in his second year as **k**
14:1 king of Israel when **K** Amaziah,
14:5 killed his father, the former **k**.
14:8 sent messengers to **K** Jehoash,
14:9 **K** Jehoash of Israel sent this
14:9 this message to **K** Amaziah
14:11 So **K** Jehoash of Israel
14:11 and **K** Amaziah of Judah met
14:13 **K** Jehoash of Israel captured
14:13 of Israel captured **K** Amaziah,
14:15 he fought against **K** Amaziah
14:16 Jeroboam succeeded him as **k**.
14:17 Joash's son **K** Amaziah of
14:17 son **K** Jehoash of Israel.
14:21 and made him **k** in place of his
14:22 after **K** Amaziah lay down
14:23 was in his fifteenth year as **k**
14:23 Jehoash's son **K** Jeroboam
14:29 Zechariah succeeded him as **k**.
15:1 year as **k** of Israel,
15:1 began to rule as **k** of Judah.
15:5 The LORD inflicted the **k** with
15:5 lasted until the day the **k** died.
15:5 So the **k** lived in a separate
15:7 Jotham succeeded him as **k**.
15:8 thirty-eighth year as **k** of Judah,
15:8 son Zechariah was **k**
15:10 and succeeded him as **k**.
15:13 became **k** in Azariah's
15:13 thirty-ninth year as **k** of Judah.
15:14 and succeeded him as **k**.
15:17 thirty-ninth year as **k** of Judah,
15:17 began to rule as **k** of Israel.
15:19 **K** Pul of Assyria came to
15:20 of silver for the **k** of Assyria.
15:20 Then the **k** of Assyria left the
15:22 Pekahiah succeeded him as **k**.
15:23 fiftieth year as **k** of Judah,
15:23 Pekahiah was **k** of Israel in
15:25 him and succeeded him as **k**.
15:27 fifty-second year as **k** of Judah,
15:29 In the days of **K** Pekah of
15:29 **K** Tiglath Pileser of Assyria
15:30 Hoshea began to rule as **k** in
15:30 son of Jotham, was **k** of Judah.
15:32 the second year that **K** Pekah,
15:32 began to rule as **k** of Judah.
15:37 LORD began to use **K** Rezin
15:38 son Ahaz succeeded him as **k**.
16:1 in his seventeenth year as **k**
16:1 as king of Israel when **K** Ahaz,
16:1 began to rule as **k** of Judah.
16:5 Then **K** Rezin of Aram and
16:5 Then King Rezin of Aram and **K**
16:6 At that time **K** Rezin of Aram
16:7 Ahaz sent messengers to **K**
16:8 palace and sent them to the **k**
16:9 The **k** of Assyria listened to
16:10 Then **K** Ahaz went to
16:10 to meet **K** Tiglath Pileser
16:10 So **K** Ahaz sent the priest
16:11 the model **K** Ahaz sent from
16:12 When the **k** came from
16:12 The **k** approached the altar and
16:15 **K** Ahaz gave this command to
16:16 what **K** Ahaz had commanded.
16:17 **K** Ahaz cut off the side panels
16:18 outer entrance for the **k** from
16:18 this to please the **k** of Assyria.
16:20 Hezekiah succeeded him as **k**.
17:1 twelfth year as **k** of Judah,
17:1 began to rule as **k** of Israel in
17:3 **K** Shalmaneser of Assyria
17:4 The **k** of Assyria found Hoshea
17:4 had sent messengers to **K** Dais

2Ki 17:4 payments to the **k** of Assyria.)
17:4 So the **k** of Assyria arrested
17:5 Then the **k** of Assyria attacked
17:6 ninth year as **k** of Israel,
17:6 the **k** of Assyria captured
17:7 of Pharaoh (the **k** of Egypt).
17:21 Jeroboam (Nebat's son) **k**.
17:24 The **k** of Assyria brought
17:26 said to the **k** of Assyria,
17:27 The **k** of Assyria gave this
18:1 **K** Hoshea, son of Elah,
18:1 had been **k** in Israel for three
18:1 three years when **K** Hezekiah,
18:1 began to rule as **k**.
18:5 No **k** among all the kings of
18:7 He rebelled against the **k** of
18:9 In Hezekiah's fourth year as **k**
18:9 year in the reign of **K** Hoshea,
18:9 son of Elah of Israel) **K**
18:10 year as **k** (which was Hoshea's
18:10 ninth year as **k** of Israel).
18:11 The **k** of Assyria took the
18:13 fourteenth year as **k**,
18:13 **K** Sennacherib of Assyria
18:14 Then **K** Hezekiah of Judah
18:14 sent this message to the **k**
18:14 So the **k** of Assyria demanded
18:14 demanded that **K** Hezekiah
18:16 the gold to the **k** of Assyria.
18:17 Then the **k** of Assyria sent his
18:17 to **K** Hezekiah at Jerusalem.
18:18 they called for **K** Hezekiah,
18:19 'This is what the great **k**,
18:19 king, the **k** of Assyria, says:
18:21 This is what Pharaoh (the **k** of
18:23 my master, the **k** of Assyria.
18:28 "Listen to the great **k**,
18:28 the great king, the **k** of Assyria.
18:29 This is what the **k** says:
18:30 the control of the **k** of Assyria.'
18:31 because this is what the **k** of
18:33 countries from the **k** of Assyria?
18:36 the **k** commanded them not
19:1 When **K** Hezekiah heard the
19:4 His master, the **k** of Assyria,
19:5 So **K** Hezekiah's men went to
19:8 returned and found the **k**
19:8 heard that the **k** left Lachish.
19:9 Now, Sennacherib heard that **K**
19:10 "Tell **K** Hezekiah of Judah,
19:10 the control of the **k** of Assyria.
19:13 Where is the **k** of Hamath,
19:13 king of Hamath, the **k** of Arpad,
19:13 and the **k** of the cities of
19:20 You prayed to me about **K**
19:32 says about the **k** of Assyria:
19:36 Then **K** Sennacherib of Assyria
19:37 succeeded him as **k**.
20:6 city from the control of the **k**
20:7 boil so that the **k** will get well."
20:12 At that time Baladan's son, **K**
20:14 Isaiah came to **K** Hezekiah
20:18 the palace of the **k** of Babylon.'"
20:21 succeeded him as **k**.
21:3 goddess Asherah as **K** Ahab
21:11 "**K** Manasseh of Judah has
21:18 son Amon succeeded him as **k**.
21:24 had plotted against **K** Amon.
21:24 his son Josiah **k** in his place.
21:26 Josiah succeeded him as **k**.
22:1 and he was **k** for 31 years in
22:3 In Josiah's eighteenth year as **k**
22:9 went to the **k** and reported,
22:10 the scribe Shaphan told the **k**,
22:10 And Shaphan read it to the **k**.
22:11 When the **k** heard what the
22:12 Then the **k** gave an order to the
22:16 written in the book that the **k**
22:18 "But tell Judah's **k** who sent
22:20 So they reported this to the **k**.
23:1 Then the **k** sent for all the
23:2 The **k**, everyone in Judah,
23:3 The **k** stood beside the pillar
23:4 Then the **k** ordered the chief
23:12 The **k** tore them down from
23:13 The **k** made the illegal places

2Ki 23:13 **K** Solomon of Israel had built
23:21 The **k** ordered all the people to
23:23 year of **K** Josiah's reign,
23:25 No **k** before Josiah had turned
23:25 No other **k** was like Josiah.
23:29 days Pharaoh Necoh (the **k**
23:29 of Egypt) came to help the **k**
23:29 **K** Josiah went to attack Necoh.
23:30 and made him **k** in place of his
23:31 years old when he became **k**,
23:31 and he was **k** for 3 months in
23:34 made Josiah's son Eliakim **k**
23:36 and he was **k** for 11 years in
24:1 During Jehoiakim's reign **K**
24:6 Jehoiakin succeeded him as **k**.
24:7 The **k** of Egypt didn't leave his
24:7 country again because the **k**
24:7 had belonged to the **k** of Egypt.
24:8 old when he began to rule as **k**.
24:8 He was **k** for three months in
24:10 At that time the officers of **K**
24:11 **K** Nebuchadnezzar of Babylon
24:12 **K** Jehoiakin of Judah,
24:12 surrendered to the **k** of Babylon
24:12 the **k** of Babylon captured
24:13 the furnishings that **K** Solomon
24:16 The **k** of Babylon brought all
24:17 The **k** of Babylon made King
24:17 The king of Babylon made **K**
24:17 Jehoiakin's Uncle Mattaniah **k**
24:20 Zedekiah rebelled against the **k**
25:1 **K** Nebuchadnezzar of Babylon
25:2 Zedekiah's eleventh year as **k**.
25:4 the **k** took the road to the plain
25:5 army pursued **K** Zedekiah
25:6 Babylonians captured the **k**,
25:6 brought him to the **k** of Babylon
25:8 year as **k** of Babylon,
25:8 an officer of the **k** of Babylon,
25:11 surrendered to the **k** of Babylon
25:19 5 men who had access to the **k**
25:20 them and brought them to the **k**
25:21 The **k** of Babylon executed
25:22 **K** Nebuchadnezzar of Babylon
25:23 and their men heard that the **k**
25:24 serve the **k** of Babylon,
25:27 imprisonment of **K** Jehoiakin
25:27 **K** Evil Merodach of Babylon,
25:27 freed **K** Jehoiakin of Judah
25:30 The **k** of Babylon gave him a
1Ch 1:43 ruled Edom before any **k** ruled
1:44 succeeded him as **k**.
1:45 succeeded him as **k**.
1:46 succeeded him as **k**,
1:47 Masrekah succeeded him as **k**.
1:48 the river succeeded him as **k**.
1:49 succeeded him as **k**.
1:50 Hadad succeeded him as **k**,
3:2 of **K** Talmai) from Geshur.
4:23 They lived there with the **k** and
4:31 cities until David became **k**.
4:41 In the days of **K** Hezekiah of
5:6 **K** Tiglath Pilneser of Assyria
5:17 records in the days of **K** Jotham
5:17 and **K** Jeroboam of Israel.
5:26 Then the God of Israel led **K**
5:26 of Assyria (**K** Tiglath Pilneser
11:3 they anointed David **k** of Israel,
11:10 they made him **k** according
12:31 by name to make David **k**.
12:38 to Hebron — to make David **k**
12:38 had agreed to make David **k**.
13:3 we ignored while Saul was **k**."
14:1 **K** Hiram of Tyre sent
14:2 had established him as **k**
14:8 had been anointed **k** of Israel,
15:29 and saw **K** David dancing
16:31 'The LORD rules as **k**!'
17:16 Then **K** David went into the
18:3 **K** Hadadezer at Hamath.
18:5 came to help **K** Hadadezer
18:9 When **K** Tou of Hamath heard
18:9 army of Zobah's **K** Hadadezer,
18:10 son Hadoram to greet **K** David
18:11 **K** David dedicated all the
19:1 Later **K** Nahash of Ammon died,

1Ch 19:1 his son became **k** in his place.
19:5 The **k** said to them,
19:7 hired 32,000 chariots and the **k**
20:2 from the head of Rabbah's **k**
21:4 However, the **k** overruled Joab.
21:24 "No," **K** David told Ornan,
23:1 his son Solomon **k** of Israel.
24:6 names in the presence of the **k**,
24:31 drew them in front of **K** David,
25:6 under the direction of the **k**.
26:26 dedicated to God that **K** David,
26:30 and they served the **k**.
26:32 **K** David appointed them to be
26:32 matter involving God or the **k**
27:1 officers who were serving the **k**
27:24 the official records of **K** David.
27:25 in charge of **K** David's property:
28:1 army units that served the **k**,
28:1 livestock belonging to the **k**
28:4 God of Israel chose me to be **k**
28:4 to make me **k** of all Israel.
29:1 Then **K** David said to the
29:9 **K** David was also overjoyed,
29:20 in front of the LORD and the **k**.
29:22 made David's son Solomon **k**.
29:23 sat on the LORD's throne as **k**
29:24 all of **K** David's sons pledged
29:24 their loyalty to **K** Solomon.
29:25 gave him royal honor like no **k**
29:27 He ruled as **k** of Israel for 40
29:28 Solomon succeeded him as **k**.
29:29 Everything about **K** David from
2Ch 1:8 you've made me **k** in his place.
1:9 You've made me **k** of people
1:11 over whom I made you **k**.
1:12 and honor like no other **k** before
1:15 The **k** made silver and gold as
2:3 Solomon sent word to **K** Huram
2:11 Then **K** Huram of Tyre
2:11 he made you their **k**."
2:12 earth and has given **K** David
4:11 the work for **K** Solomon
4:16 temple at **K** Solomon's request.
4:17 The **k** cast them in foundries in
5:3 Israel gathered around the **k** at
5:6 while **K** Solomon and the
6:3 Then the **k** turned around and
7:4 Then the **k** and all the people
7:5 **K** Solomon offered 22,000
7:5 So the **k** and all the people
7:6 which **K** David made
8:10 charge of **K** Solomon's projects:
8:11 live in the palace of **K** David
8:18 and brought it to **K** Solomon.
9:5 She told the **k**, "What I heard in
9:8 put you on his throne to be **k**
9:8 and made you **k** over them so
9:9 She gave the **k** 9,000 pounds
9:9 of Sheba gave **K** Solomon.
9:11 With the sandalwood the **k**
9:12 **K** Solomon gave the queen of
9:15 **K** Solomon made 200 large
9:16 The **k** put them in the hall
9:17 The **k** also made a large ivory
9:20 All **K** Solomon's cups were
9:21 The **k** had ships going to
9:22 In wealth and wisdom **K**
9:27 The **k** made silver as common
9:31 succeeded him as **k**.
10:1 to Shechem to make him **k**.
10:2 he had fled from **K** Solomon.
10:6 **K** Rehoboam sought advice
10:12 as the **k** had instructed them.
10:13 The **k** answered them harshly.
10:15 The **k** refused to listen to the
10:16 When all Israel saw that the **k**
10:16 the people answered the **k**,
10:18 Then **K** Rehoboam sent
10:18 So **K** Rehoboam got on his
11:3 to Judah's **K** Rehoboam,
11:22 Rehoboam could make him **k**.
12:2 **K** Shishak of Egypt attacked
12:6 and the **k** humbled themselves.
12:9 **K** Shishak of Egypt attacked
12:10 So **K** Rehoboam made bronze
12:11 Whenever the **k** went into the

2Ch 12:13 **K** Rehoboam strengthened his
12:16 Abijah succeeded him as **k**.
14:1 son Asa succeeded him as **k**.
15:16 **K** Asa also removed his
16:1 **K** Baasha of Israel invaded
16:1 or coming from **K** Asa of Judah.
16:2 to Aram's **K** Benhadad.
16:3 Now break your treaty with **K**
16:4 did what **K** Asa requested.
16:6 Then **K** Asa took everyone in
16:7 the seer Hanani came to **K** Asa
16:7 you depended on the **k**
16:7 the army of the **k** of Aram has
17:1 succeeded him as **k**.
17:19 were the men who served the **k**
17:19 to those whom the **k** put
18:3 **K** Ahab of Israel asked King
18:3 King Ahab of Israel asked **K**
18:3 told the **k** of Israel,
18:4 Then Jehoshaphat said to the **k**
18:5 So the **k** of Israel called 400
18:7 The **k** of Israel told
18:7 "The **k** must not say that."
18:8 The **k** of Israel called for an
18:9 The **k** of Israel and King
18:9 The king of Israel and **K**
18:12 prophets have all told the **k**
18:14 When he came to the **k**,
18:14 the **k** asked him, "Micaiah,
18:15 The **k** asked him, "How many
18:17 The **k** of Israel said to
18:19 'Who will deceive **K** Ahab of
18:25 The **k** of Israel then said,
18:26 Say, 'This is what the **k** says:
18:28 So the **k** of Israel and King
18:28 So the king of Israel and **K**
18:29 The **k** of Israel told
18:29 So the **k** of Israel disguised
18:30 The **k** of Aram had given orders
18:30 anyone except the **k** of Israel."
18:31 "He must be the **k** of Israel."
18:32 wasn't the **k** of Israel.
18:33 his bow at random and hit the **k**
18:34 and the **k** propped himself up in
19:1 **K** Jehoshaphat of Judah
19:2 asked **K** Jehoshaphat,
19:11 of every matter involving the **k**.
20:15 and **K** Jehoshaphat.
20:31 ruled as **k** of Judah.
20:35 After this, **K** Jehoshaphat of
20:35 allied himself with **K** Ahaziah
21:1 Jehoram succeeded him as **k**.
21:2 of **K** Jehoshaphat of Israel.
21:5 years old when he became **k**,
21:8 Judah and chose its own **k**.
21:12 or the ways of **K** Asa of Judah.
21:20 years old when he became **k**,
22:1 youngest son Ahaziah **k**
22:1 Ahaziah became **k** of Judah.
22:5 went with Ahab's son **K** Joram
22:5 Israel to fight against **K** Hazael
22:6 he fought against **K** Hazael
22:9 family was able to rule as **k**.
22:11 daughter of the **k** and sister of
22:11 was the daughter of **K** Jehoram
23:3 made an agreement with the **k**
23:3 He should be **k**, as the LORD
23:7 Levites should surround the **k**.
23:7 with the **k** wherever he goes."
23:9 that had belonged to **K** David
23:10 were stationed around the **k**
23:11 made him **k** by anointing him.
23:11 They said, "Long live the **k**!"
23:12 running and praising the **k**,
23:13 She looked, and the **k** was
23:16 to the LORD on behalf of the **k**
23:20 and they brought the **k** from the
23:20 royal palace and seated the **k**
24:6 So the **k** called for the chief
24:8 The **k** issued an order,
24:12 The **k** and Jehoiada would
24:14 money to the **k** and Jehoiada,
24:17 of Judah bowed in front of the **k**
24:17 Then the **k** listened to their
24:22 **K** Joash did not remember how
24:23 to the **k** of Damascus.

2Ch 24:27 Amaziah succeeded him as **k**.
25:3 killed his father, the former **k**.
25:16 was talking, the **k** asked him,
25:16 make you an adviser to the **k**?
25:17 **K** Amaziah of Judah sent
25:17 sent messengers to **K** Jehoash,
25:18 **K** Jehoash of Israel sent this
25:18 this message to **K** Amaziah
25:21 So **K** Jehoash of Israel
25:21 and **K** Amaziah of Judah met
25:23 **K** Jehoash of Israel captured
25:23 of Israel captured **K** Amaziah,
25:25 Joash's son **K** Amaziah of
25:25 son **K** Jehoash of Israel.
26:1 and made him **k** in place of his
26:2 after **K** Amaziah lay down
26:13 the **k** against the enemy.
26:18 They opposed **K** Uzziah.
26:21 **K** Uzziah had a skin disease
26:23 Jotham succeeded him as **k**.
27:5 He fought with the **k** of the
27:8 old when he began to rule as **k**.
27:9 son Ahaz succeeded him as **k**.
28:5 him over to the **k** of Aram,
28:5 him over to the **k** of Israel,
28:16 At that time **K** Ahaz sent for
28:19 Judah because of **K** Ahaz
28:20 **K** Tillegath Pilneser of Assyria
28:21 gave them to the **k** of Assyria.
28:22 When he had this trouble, **K**
28:27 Hezekiah succeeded him as **k**.
29:1 Hezekiah began to rule as **k**
29:3 first month of his first year as **k**,
29:18 Then they went to **K** Hezekiah.
29:19 and all the utensils **K** Ahaz
29:23 offering for sin in front of the **k**
29:24 The **k** had said that the burnt
29:27 of **K** David of Israel.
29:29 the **k** and everyone who was
29:30 Then **K** Hezekiah and the
30:2 The **k**, his officials, and the
30:4 The **k** and the whole assembly
30:6 took letters from the **k**
30:12 out the command which the **k**
30:24 **K** Hezekiah of Judah provided
30:26 days of **K** Solomon of Israel.
31:13 **K** Hezekiah and Azariah,
32:1 **K** Sennacherib of Assyria
32:7 frightened or terrified by the **k**
32:8 The **k** of Assyria has human
32:8 by what **K** Hezekiah
32:9 After this, while **K** Sennacherib
32:9 he sent his officers to **K**
32:10 "This is what **K** Sennacherib of
32:11 us from the **k** of Assyria?'
32:20 Then **K** Hezekiah and the
32:22 Jerusalem from **K** Sennacherib
32:23 presents to **K** Hezekiah
32:33 succeeded him as **k**.
33:3 goddess Asherah as **K** Ahab
33:11 the army commanders of the **k**
33:20 son Amon succeeded him as **k**.
33:25 had plotted against **K** Amon.
33:25 his son Josiah **k** in his place.
34:1 and he was **k** for 31 years in
34:3 In his twelfth year as **k**,
34:16 the book to the **k** and reported,
34:18 the scribe Shaphan told the **k**,
34:18 And Shaphan read it to the **k**.
34:19 When the **k** heard what the
34:20 Then the **k** gave an order to
34:24 that was read to the **k** of Judah.
34:26 "Tell Judah's **k** who sent you
34:28 So they reported this to the **k**.
34:29 Then the **k** sent for all the
34:30 The **k**, everyone in Judah,
34:31 The **k** stood in his place and
35:3 son of David and **k** of Israel,
35:4 listed in the records of **K** David
35:10 as the **k** had ordered.
35:16 as **K** Josiah had commanded.
35:20 **K** Neco of Egypt came to fight
35:21 quarrel with me, **k** of Judah?
35:23 Some archers shot **K** Josiah.
35:23 The **k** told his officers,
36:1 son Jehoahaz and made him **k**

2Ch 36:2 years old when he became **k**,
36:2 and he was **k** in Jerusalem for
36:3 The **k** of Egypt removed him
36:4 The **k** of Egypt made
36:4 Jehoahaz's brother Eliakim **k**
36:6 **K** Nebuchadnezzar of Babylon
36:8 Jehoiakin succeeded him as **k**.
36:9 old when he began to rule as **k**.
36:9 He was **k** for three months and
36:10 In the spring **K**
36:10 Jehoiakin's uncle Zedekiah **k**
36:13 against **K** Nebuchadnezzar.
36:17 So he had the Babylonian **k**
36:18 and the treasures of the **k** and
36:20 The **k** of Babylon took those
36:22 Cyrus' first year as **k** of Persia.
36:22 The LORD inspired the **k** to
36:23 This is what **K** Cyrus of Persia
Ezr 1:1 Cyrus' first year as **k** of Persia.
1:1 The LORD inspired the **k** to
1:2 This is what **K** Cyrus of Persia
1:7 **K** Cyrus brought out the
1:8 **K** Cyrus of Persia put the
2:1 (**K** Nebuchadnezzar of Babylon
3:7 Lebanon to Joppa as **K** Cyrus
3:10 of **K** David of Israel.
4:2 since the time of **K** Esarhaddon
4:3 as **K** Cyrus of Persia ordered
4:5 throughout the reign of **K** Cyrus
4:5 the reign of **K** Darius of Persia.
4:7 Artaxerxes was **k** of Persia.
4:8 of Jerusalem to **K** Artaxerxes.
4:11 sent to him: To **K** Artaxerxes,
4:14 happen that will dishonor the **k**.
4:16 We want the **k** to know that if
4:17 Then the **k** sent this reply:
4:22 Why should I, the **k**,
4:23 a copy of **K** Artaxerxes' letter.
4:24 second year as **k** of Persia.
5:6 of that river) sent to **K** Darius.
5:7 following report: To **K** Darius,
5:11 years ago by a great **k** of Israel.
5:12 he handed them over to **K**
5:13 in the first year of the reign of **K**
5:17 **K** Cyrus gave permission
6:1 Then **K** Darius gave the order
6:3 Cyrus' first year as **k** From:
6:3 as king From: **K** Cyrus Subject:
6:10 the life of the **k** and his sons.
6:12 cause the downfall of each **k**
6:13 what **K** Darius had ordered.
6:15 sixth year of **K** Darius' reign.
6:22 The LORD had made the **k** of
7:1 during the reign of **K**
7:6 The **k** gave Ezra everything he
7:7 Artaxerxes' seventh year as **k**.
7:11 that **K** Artaxerxes gave Ezra
7:12 **k** of kings To: Ezra the priest,
7:14 I, the **k**, and my seven advisers
7:15 the silver and gold that the **k**
7:21 I, **K** Artaxerxes, order all the
7:28 He made the **k**, his advisers,
8:1 the reign of **K** Artaxerxes:
8:22 I was ashamed to ask the **k** for
8:22 We had already told the **k**,
8:25 the contributions that the **k**,
Neh 1:1 twentieth year as **k**,
1:4 I was cupbearer to the **k** when I
1:11 make this man, **K** Artaxerxes,
2:1 twentieth year as **k**,
2:1 wine was brought for the **k**,
2:1 of wine and gave it to the **k**.
2:2 The **k** asked me, "Why do you
2:3 "May the **k** live forever!"
2:3 I said to the **k**. "Why shouldn't I
2:4 the **k** asked me. So I prayed to
2:5 and I asked the **k**, "If it pleases
2:6 beside him, the **k** asked me,
2:7 I also asked the **k**,
2:8 (The **k** let me have the letters,
2:9 (The **k** had sent army officers
2:18 me and what the **k** had told me.
2:19 going to rebel against the **k**?"
5:14 from the twentieth year of **K**
6:6 you want to become their **k**.
6:7 'There's a **k** in Judah!'

Neh	6:7	report will get back to the **k**.
	7:6	**K** Nebuchadnezzar of Babylon
	9:22	the land of the **k** of Heshbon,
	9:22	the land of **K** Og of Bashan.
	11:23	were under orders from the **k**,
	13:6	In the thirty-second year of **K**
	13:6	in Babylon, I returned to the **k**.
	13:6	Later, I asked the **k** for
	13:26	like these that **K** Solomon
	13:26	There wasn't a **k** like him
	13:26	and God made him **k** of all
Est	1:2	At the time when **K** Xerxes sat
	1:5	the **k** held a banquet lasting
	1:7	The **k** also provided plenty of
	1:8	(The **k** had ordered all the
	1:9	at the royal palace of **K** Xerxes.
	1:10	On the seventh day when the **k**
	1:10	who served under **K** Xerxes,
	1:11	Queen Vashti in front of the **k**,
	1:12	the **k** became very angry,
	1:13	Now, the **k** usually asked for
	1:14	and Medes had access to the **k**
	1:14	The **k** asked these wise men
	1:15	not obey **K** Xerxes' command,
	1:16	up in the presence of the **k**
	1:16	not only against the **k** but also
	1:16	in every province of **K** Xerxes.
	1:17	They will say, '**K** Xerxes
	1:19	appear in front of **K** Xerxes.
	1:21	The **k** and his officials
	1:21	and so the **k** did as Memucan
	2:1	Later, when **K** Xerxes got over
	2:2	young virgins for the **k**.
	2:4	The **k** liked the suggestion,
	2:6	with Judah's **K** Jehoiakin,
	2:6	whom **K** Nebuchadnezzar of
	2:12	turn to go to **K** Xerxes after she
	2:13	woman would go to the **k**.
	2:14	She never went to the **k** again
	2:14	again unless the **k** desired her
	2:15	turn came to go to the **k**,
	2:16	So Esther was taken to **K**
	2:17	Now, the **k** loved Esther more
	2:18	Then the **k** held a great
	2:21	and planned to kill **K** Xerxes.
	2:22	Then Esther told the **k**,
	3:1	**K** Xerxes promoted Haman.
	3:2	because the **k** had commanded
	3:7	In Xerxes' twelfth year as **k**,
	3:8	Now, Haman told **K** Xerxes,
	3:10	At that, the **k** removed his
	3:11	The **k** told Haman,
	3:12	signed in the name of **K** Xerxes
	3:15	hurried out as the **k** told them.
	3:15	So the **k** and Haman sat down
	4:8	command her to go to the **k**,
	4:11	that no one approaches the **k**
	4:11	Only if the **k** holds out the
	4:16	After that, I will go to the **k**,
	5:1	The **k** was sitting on the royal
	5:2	When the **k** saw Queen Esther
	5:2	So the **k** held out the golden
	5:3	Then the **k** asked her,
	5:5	The **k** replied, "Bring Haman
	5:5	So the **k** and Haman came to
	5:6	the **k** asked Esther,
	5:11	and all about how the **k**
	5:12	except me to come with the **k**
	5:12	guest together with the **k**.
	5:14	and in the morning ask the **k** to
	5:14	Then go with the **k** to the
	6:1	That night the **k** could not
	6:1	and they were read to the **k**.
	6:2	a rebellion against **K** Xerxes.
	6:3	The **k** asked, "How did I
	6:4	The **k** asked, "Who is in the
	6:4	the **k** about hanging Mordecai
	6:5	"Let him come in," the **k** said.
	6:6	The **k** then asked him,
	6:6	for the man whom the **k** wishes
	6:6	"Whom would the **k** wish to
	6:7	So Haman told the **k**,
	6:8	a royal robe that the **k** has worn
	6:8	a horse that the **k** has ridden,
	6:9	on the man whom the **k** wishes
	6:9	whom the **k** wishes to reward.'"
Est	6:10	The **k** told Haman,
	6:11	whom the **k** wishes to reward."
	7:1	So the **k** and Haman came to
	7:2	the **k** asked Esther,
	7:5	Then **K** Xerxes interrupted
	7:6	presence of the **k** and queen.
	7:7	The **k** was furious as he got up
	7:7	because he saw that the **k** had
	7:8	When the **k** returned from the
	7:8	The **k** thought, "Is he even
	7:8	Then the **k** passed sentence
	7:9	the eunuchs present with the **k**,
	7:9	up for the well-being of the **k**,
	7:9	The **k** responded, "Hang him
	7:10	Then the **k** got over his raging
	8:1	On that same day **K** Xerxes
	8:1	Also, Mordecai came to the **k**
	8:2	Then the **k** took off his signet
	8:3	Esther spoke again to the **k**.
	8:4	The **k** held out his golden
	8:4	up and stood in front of the **k**.
	8:7	**K** Xerxes said to Queen Esther
	8:10	Mordecai wrote in **K** Xerxes'
	8:11	that the **k** had given permission
	8:12	all the provinces of **K** Xerxes,
	8:15	the presence of the **k** wearing
	9:2	all the provinces of **K** Xerxes
	9:11	of Susa was reported to the **k**.
	9:12	So the **k** said to Queen Esther,
	9:14	The **k** commanded this,
	9:20	all the provinces of **K** Xerxes,
	10:1	**K** Xerxes levied a tax on the
	10:2	whom the **k** had promoted,
	10:3	second only to **K** Xerxes.
Job	15:24	him like a **k** ready for battle.
	18:14	marched off to the **k** of terrors.
	29:25	I lived like a **k** among his
	34:18	anyone ⌊even⌋ say to a **k**,
	41:34	It is **k** of everyone who is
Psa	2:6	installed my own **k** on Zion,
	5:2	my **k** and my God,
	10:16	The LORD is **k** forever and
	18:50	gives great victories to his **k**.
	20:6	give victory to his anointed **k**.
	20:9	Give victory to the **k**,
	21:1	The **k** finds joy in your strength,
	21:7	Indeed, the **k** trusts the LORD,
	24:7	so that the **k** of glory may come
	24:8	Who is this **k** of glory?
	24:9	so that the **k** of glory may come
	24:10	Who, then, is this **k** of glory?
	24:10	of Armies is the **k** of glory!
	29:10	The LORD sits enthroned as **k**
	33:16	No **k** achieves a victory with a
	44:4	You alone are my **k**,
	45:1	I will direct my song to the **k**.
	45:11	The **k** longs for your beauty.
	45:13	The daughter of the **k** is
	45:14	she is brought to the **k**.
	45:15	They enter the palace of the **k**.
	47:2	He is the great **k** of the whole
	47:6	Make music to praise our **k**.
	47:7	God is the **k** of the whole earth.
	48:2	It is the city of the great **k**.
	61:6	upon days to the life of the **k**.
	63:11	But the **k** will find joy in God.
	68:24	God, my **k**, into the holy place.
	72:1	O God, give the **k** your justice
	74:12	long ago God has been my **k**,
	84:3	my **k** and my God.
	89:18	Our **k** belongs to the Holy One
	93:1	The LORD rules as **k**!
	95:3	and a great **k** above all gods.
	96:10	"The LORD rules as **k**!"
	97:1	The LORD rules as **k**.
	98:6	in the presence of the **k**,
	99:1	The LORD rules as **k**.
	105:20	The **k** sent someone to release
	135:11	**K** Sihon of the Amorites,
	135:11	the Amorites, **K** Og of Bashan,
	136:19	**K** Sihon of the Amorites —
	136:20	and **K** Og of Bashan — because
	145:1	praise you, my God, the **k**.
	146:10	The LORD rules as **k** forever.
	149:2	of Zion rejoice over their **k**.
Pro	1:1	son who was **k** of Israel,
Pro	14:28	population is an honor for a **k**,
	14:35	A **k** is delighted with a servant
	16:15	When the **k** is cheerful,
	19:12	The rage of a **k** is like the roar
	20:2	The rage of a **k** is like the roar
	20:8	A **k** who sits on his throne to
	20:26	A wise **k** scatters the wicked
	20:28	Mercy and truth protect a **k**,
	22:11	has a **k** as his friend.
	24:21	Fear the **k** as well.
	25:1	men of **K** Hezekiah of Judah.
	25:5	away from the presence of a **k**,
	25:6	about yourself in front of a **k**
	29:4	a **k** builds up a country,
	29:14	When a **k** judges the poor with
	30:22	a slave when he becomes **k**,
	30:27	Locusts have no **k**,
	30:31	a **k** at the head of his army.
	31:1	The sayings of **K** Lemuel,
Ecc	1:1	David and the **k** in Jerusalem.
	1:12	I, the spokesman, have been **k**
	2:12	man who replaces the **k** do?
	4:13	foolish **k** who won't take
	4:14	came out of prison to rule as **k**,
	5:9	Yet, a **k** is an advantage for a
	9:14	and a powerful **k** came to
	10:16	any country where the **k** used
	10:17	is blessed when the **k** is from
	10:20	Don't curse the **k** even in your
Sos	1:4	The **k** has brought me into his
	1:12	While the **k** is at his table,
	3:9	**K** Solomon had a carriage
	3:11	out and look at **K** Solomon!
	7:5	locks could hold a **k** captive.
Isa	6:1	In the year **K** Uzziah died,
	6:5	I have seen the **k**, the LORD of
	7:1	of Uzziah, was **k** of Judah,
	7:1	Aram's **K** Rezin and Israel's
	7:1	Rezin and Israel's **K** Pekah,
	7:2	the hearts of the **k** and his
	7:6	set up Tabeel's son as its **k**.'
	7:17	will bring⌋ the **k** of Assyria.
	7:20	that day the Lord will hire the **k**
	8:4	away to the **k** of Assyria."
	8:7	of the Euphrates River — the **k**
	8:21	cursing their **k** and God.
	10:12	he will punish the **k** of Assyria
	10:13	The **k** will say, "I did this with
	14:4	Then you will mock the **k** of
	14:28	in the year **K** Ahaz died.
	16:5	LORD will set up a trusted **k**.
	19:4	A strong **k** will rule them,"
	20:1	In the year when **K** Sargon of
	20:4	The **k** of Assyria will lead
	20:6	rescued from the **k** of Assyria.
	23:15	the lifetime of one **k**.
	30:33	It was made ready for the **k**.
	32:1	A **k** will rule with fairness,
	33:17	see how handsome the **k** is.
	33:22	The LORD is our **k**.
	36:1	fourteenth year as **k**,
	36:1	**K** Sennacherib of Assyria
	36:2	Then the **k** of Assyria sent his
	36:2	to **K** Hezekiah at Jerusalem.
	36:4	'This is what the great **k**,
	36:4	king, the **k** of Assyria, says:
	36:6	This is what Pharaoh (the **k** of
	36:8	my master, the **k** of Assyria.
	36:13	"Listen to the great **k**,
	36:13	the great king, the **k** of Assyria.
	36:14	This is what the **k** says:
	36:15	the control of the **k** of Assyria.'
	36:16	because this is what the **k** of
	36:18	countries from the **k** of Assyria?
	36:21	the **k** commanded them not
	37:1	When **K** Hezekiah heard the
	37:4	His master, the **k** of Assyria,
	37:5	So **K** Hezekiah's men went to
	37:8	returned and found the **k**
	37:8	heard that the **k** left Lachish.
	37:9	Now, Sennacherib heard that **K**
	37:10	"Tell **K** Hezekiah of Judah,
	37:10	the control of the **k** of Assyria.
	37:13	Where is the **k** of Hamath,
	37:13	king of Hamath, the **k** of Arpad,
	37:13	and the **k** of the cities of

Isa 37:21 **K** Sennacherib of Assyria.
37:33 says about the **k** of Assyria:
37:37 Then **K** Sennacherib of Assyria
37:38 succeeded him as **k**.
38:6 the control of the **k** of Assyria."'
38:21 boil so that the **k** will get well."
38:9 **K** Hezekiah of Judah wrote this
39:1 At that time Baladan's son, **K**
39:3 Isaiah came to **K** Hezekiah
39:7 the palace of the **k** of Babylon."'
41:21 arguments," says Jacob's **k**.
43:15 the Creator of Israel, your **K**.
44:6 is Israel's **k** and defender.
52:7 Zion that its God rules as **k**.
57:9 You've journeyed to the **k** with
Jer 1:2 to Jeremiah when **K** Josiah,
1:2 thirteenth year as **k** of Judah.
1:3 was **k** of Judah and during the
1:3 son of Josiah, was **k** of Judah.
3:6 When Josiah was **k**,
4:9 "the **k** and the leaders will lose
8:19 Isn't Zion's **k** still there?"
10:7 O **K** of the Nations.
10:10 is the living God and eternal **k**.
13:18 Say to the **k** and his mother,
15:4 of what Judah's **K** Manasseh,
20:4 Judah over to the **k** of Babylon.
21:1 **K** Zedekiah sent Pashhur,
21:2 because **K** Nebuchadnezzar of
21:4 these weapons to fight the **k**
21:7 hand over Judah's **K** Zedekiah,
21:7 They will be handed over to **K**
21:10 over to the **k** of Babylon,
21:11 to the nation of the **k** of Judah,
22:1 to the palace of the **k** of Judah,
22:2 gates, and you, **k** of Judah,
22:6 the palace of the **k** of Judah:
22:11 about **K** Josiah's son Shallum,
22:11 who succeeded his father as **k**
22:15 Do you think you're a better **k**
22:18 son of Judah's **K** Josiah:
22:24 son of Judah's **K** Jehoiakim,
22:25 those you fear — **K**
22:30 will succeed him as **k**.
23:5 He will be a **k** who will rule
24:1 **K** Nebuchadnezzar of Babylon
24:1 Jehoiakin (son of **K** Jehoiakim
24:8 I will abandon **K** Zedekiah of
25:1 was in his fourth year as **k**.
25:1 was **k** of Babylon.)
25:3 was in his thirteenth year as **k**
25:9 my servant **K** Nebuchadnezzar
25:11 These nations will serve the **k**
25:12 I will punish the **k** of Babylon
25:19 Pharaoh **k** of Egypt,
25:26 Last of all, the **k** of Sheshach
26:1 when Judah's **K** Jehoiakim,
26:18 the time of Judah's **K** Hezekiah
26:19 Did Judah's **K** Hezekiah and all
26:21 When **K** Jehoiakim and all his
26:21 the **k** wanted to put him to
26:22 **K** Jehoiakim sent soldiers to
26:23 and took him to **K** Jehoiakim.
26:23 The **k** executed Uriah and
27:1 son of **K** Josiah of Judah,
27:3 who have come to **K** Zedekiah
27:6 my servant **K** Nebuchadnezzar
27:8 surrender to **K** Nebuchadnezzar
27:9 never serve the **k** of Babylon.
27:11 a nation surrenders to the **k**
27:12 I spoke the same message to **K**
27:12 "Surrender to the **k** of Babylon,
27:13 don't serve the **k** of Babylon.
27:14 never serve the **k** of Babylon.
27:17 Instead, serve the **k** of Babylon,
27:19 "Babylon's **K** Nebuchadnezzar
27:19 son of **K** Jehoiakim of Judah,
28:1 early in the rule of **K** Zedekiah
28:1 month of his fourth year as **k**,
28:2 the yoke of the **k** of Babylon.
28:3 temple that **K** Nebuchadnezzar
28:4 son of **K** Jehoiakim of Judah,
28:4 So I will break the yoke of the **k**
28:11 I will break the yoke of **K**
28:14 will serve **K** Nebuchadnezzar
29:2 (This was after **K** Jehoiakin

Jer 29:3 whom **K** Zedekiah of Judah
29:3 had sent to **K** Nebuchadnezzar
29:16 says about the **k** who sits
29:21 over to **K** Nebuchadnezzar
29:22 whom the **k** of Babylon burned
30:9 your God and David your **k**.
32:1 tenth year as **k** of Judah.
32:1 eighteenth year as **k**.)
32:2 At that time the army of the **k** of
32:2 in the palace of the **k** of Judah.
32:3 When **K** Zedekiah of Judah
32:3 city over to the **k** of Babylon,
32:4 **K** Zedekiah of Judah will not
32:4 over to the **k** of Babylon.
32:28 and **K** Nebuchadnezzar
32:36 over to the **k** of Babylon.'
34:1 when **K** Nebuchadnezzar
34:2 Go to **K** Zedekiah of Judah,
34:2 city over to the **k** of Babylon,
34:3 You will see the **k** of Babylon
34:4 **K** Zedekiah of Judah.
34:6 all these things to **K** Zedekiah
34:7 did this when the army of the **k**
34:8 to Jeremiah after **K** Zedekiah
34:21 I will hand **K** Zedekiah of
34:21 to the army of the **k** of Babylon,
35:1 son of **K** Josiah of Judah.
35:11 But when **K** Nebuchadnezzar
36:1 son of **K** Josiah of Judah,
36:9 son of **K** Josiah of Judah,
36:16 "We must tell the **k** everything."
36:20 they went to the **k** in the
36:21 Then the **k** sent Jehudi to get
36:21 Jehudi read it to the **k** and all
36:21 the officials standing by the **k**.
36:22 and the **k** was in his winter
36:23 the **k** would cut them off with a
36:24 The **k** and all his attendants
36:25 and Gemariah urged the **k** not
36:26 The **k** commanded Jerahmeel
36:27 After the **k** burned up the scroll
36:28 on the scroll that **K** Jehoiakim
36:29 Say about **K** Jehoiakim of
36:29 "Why did you write that the **k** of
36:30 LORD says about **K** Jehoiakim
36:32 on the scroll that **K** Jehoiakim
37:1 **K** Nebuchadnezzar of Babylon
37:1 son of Josiah, to be **k** of Judah.
37:3 **K** Zedekiah sent Jehucal (son
37:7 Say this to the **k** of Judah,
37:17 Then **K** Zedekiah sent for
37:17 and the **k** asked him privately
37:17 over to the **k** of Babylon."
37:18 Jeremiah asked **K** Zedekiah,
37:19 who told you that the **k**
37:21 **K** Zedekiah gave the command
38:3 to the army of the **k** of Babylon,
38:4 Then the officials said to the **k**,
38:5 **K** Zedekiah answered,
38:7 The **k** happened to be sitting at
38:8 to the **k** at Benjamin Gate.
38:10 Then the **k** gave Ebed Melech
38:14 **K** Zedekiah sent for the prophet
38:14 the **k** said to Jeremiah.
38:16 So **K** Zedekiah secretly swore
38:17 the officers of the **k** of Babylon,
38:18 the officers of the **k** of Babylon,
38:19 **K** Zedekiah answered
38:22 in the palace of Judah's **k** will
38:22 the officers of the **k** of Babylon.
38:23 captured by the **k** of Babylon,
38:25 'Tell us what you said to the **k**
38:25 to the king and what the **k** said
38:26 'I asked the **k** not to send me
38:27 exactly what the **k** had told him
38:27 his conversation with the **k**.
39:1 ninth year as **k** of Judah,
39:1 **K** Nebuchadnezzar of Babylon
39:2 Zedekiah's eleventh year as **k**,
39:3 Then all the officers of the **k** of
39:3 the officers of the **k** of Babylon.
39:4 When **K** Zedekiah of Judah
39:5 **K** Nebuchadnezzar at Riblah
39:5 The **k** of Babylon passed
39:6 The **k** of Babylon slaughtered
39:11 **K** Nebuchadnezzar of Babylon

Jer 39:13 all the other leaders of the **k**
40:5 whom the **k** of Babylon
40:7 in the field heard that the **k**
40:9 serve the **k** of Babylon,
40:11 other countries heard that the **k**
40:14 "Do you know that **K** Baalis of
41:2 the man whom the **k**
41:9 same one that **K** Asa made as
41:9 his defense against **K** Baasha
41:18 killed Gedaliah whom the **k**
42:11 be afraid of the **k** of Babylon,
43:10 my servant **K** Nebuchadnezzar
44:30 Pharaoh Hophra, **k** of Egypt,
44:30 just as I handed over **K**
44:30 of Judah to **K** Nebuchadnezzar
45:1 son of Josiah, was **k** of Judah.
46:2 of Pharaoh Neco, **k** of Egypt.
46:2 **K** Nebuchadnezzar of Babylon
46:2 son of Josiah, was **k** of Judah.
46:13 coming of **K** Nebuchadnezzar
46:17 **k** of Egypt, is a big windbag.
46:18 "As I live," declares the **k**,
46:26 to **K** Nebuchadnezzar of
48:15 be slaughtered," declares the **k**,
49:28 Hazor that **K** Nebuchadnezzar
49:30 **K** Nebuchadnezzar of Babylon
49:34 Early in the rule of **K** Zedekiah
49:38 and destroy its **k** and officials,
50:17 them was the **k** of Assyria.
50:17 **K** Nebuchadnezzar of Babylon.
50:18 I am going to punish the **k** of
50:18 as I punished the **k** of Assyria.
50:43 The **k** of Babylon has heard
51:28 Prepare the **k** of the Medes,
51:31 They inform the **k** of Babylon
51:34 **K** Nebuchadnezzar of Babylon
51:57 wake up," declares the **k**,
51:59 to Babylon with **K** Zedekiah
52:3 Zedekiah rebelled against the **k**
52:4 **K** Nebuchadnezzar of Babylon
52:5 Zedekiah's eleventh year as **k**.
52:8 army pursued **K** Zedekiah
52:9 Babylonians captured the **k**
52:9 king and brought him to the **k**
52:9 where the **k** of Babylon passed
52:10 The **k** of Babylon slaughtered
52:11 The **k** of Babylon took him to
52:12 year as **k** of Babylon,
52:12 an officer of the **k** of Babylon,
52:15 surrendered to the **k** of Babylon
52:20 that **K** Solomon had made
52:25 7 men who had access to the **k**
52:26 them and brought them to the **k**
52:27 The **k** of Babylon executed
52:28 In his seventh year as **k**,
52:30 twenty-third year as **k**,
52:31 imprisonment of **K** Jehoiakin
52:31 **K** Evil Merodach of Babylon,
52:31 freed **K** Jehoiakin of Judah and
52:34 The **k** of Babylon gave him a
Lam 2:9 Its **k** and influential people are
4:20 the LORD anointed ⌊as **k**⌋,
Eze 1:2 of the exile of **K** Jehoiakin,
17:12 Tell them, 'The **k** of Babylon
17:12 to Jerusalem and captured its **k**
17:15 But the **k** of Judah rebelled
17:15 of Judah rebelled against the **k**
17:15 Will the **k** of Judah succeed?
17:16 the **k** of Judah will die in
17:16 of the **k** who appointed him
17:16 who appointed him **k** of Judah.
17:16 The **k** of Judah broke his
17:16 his treaty with the **k** of Babylon.
17:18 The **k** of Judah broke the
19:9 brought him to the **k** of Babylon
21:19 mark two roads that the **k** of
21:20 Mark the road that the **k** and his
21:21 The **k** of Babylon will stop
21:23 But the **k** of Babylon will
24:2 The **k** of Babylon has
26:7 to bring **K** Nebuchadnezzar
26:7 He is the greatest **k**.
29:2 turn to Pharaoh, **k** of Egypt,
29:3 you, Pharaoh, **k** of Egypt.
29:18 "Son of man, **K**
29:19 I'm going to give Egypt to **K**

Eze 30:10 I will use **K** Nebuchadnezzar of
30:21 the arm of Pharaoh, **k** of Egypt.
30:22 against Pharaoh, **k** of Egypt.
30:24 I will make the arms of the **k** of
30:25 the arms of the **k** of Babylon,
30:25 in the hand of the **k** of Babylon.
31:2 say to Pharaoh, **k** of Egypt,
32:2 song for Pharaoh, **k** of Egypt.
32:11 The sword of the **k** of Babylon
37:22 One **k** will rule all of them.
37:24 servant David will be their **k**,
Dan 1:1 In the third year of the reign of **K**
1:1 **K** Nebuchadnezzar of Babylon
1:2 The Lord handed **K** Jehoiakim
1:3 The **k** told Ashpenaz,
1:5 The **k** arranged for them to get
1:5 they were to serve the **k**.
1:10 "I'm afraid of my master, the **k**.
1:10 The **k** determined what you
1:19 The **k** talked to them and found
1:19 So these four men served the **k**.
1:20 Whenever the **k** asked them
1:21 year of **K** Cyrus ⌊of Persia⌋.
2:2 The **k** sent for the magicians,
2:2 So they came to the **k**.
2:3 The **k** said to them,
2:4 spoke to the **k** in Aramaic,
2:5 The **k** answered the
2:8 The **k** replied, "I'm sure you're
2:10 astrologers answered the **k**,
2:10 "No one on earth can tell the **k**
2:10 No other **k**, no matter how great
2:12 This made the **k** so angry and
2:16 Daniel went and asked the **k** to
2:23 us what the **k** wants to know."
2:24 whom the **k** had appointed to
2:24 Take me to the **k**, and I'll
2:25 took Daniel to the **k**.
2:25 He told the **k**, "I've found one of
2:26 The **k** asked Daniel (who had
2:27 Daniel answered the **k**,
2:27 can tell the **k** this secret.
2:28 He will tell **K** Nebuchadnezzar
2:37 you are the greatest **k**.
2:46 **K** Nebuchadnezzar
2:47 The **k** said to Daniel,
2:48 Then the **k** promoted Daniel
3:1 **K** Nebuchadnezzar made a
3:2 **K** Nebuchadnezzar sent
3:3 **K** Nebuchadnezzar had set
3:5 that **K** Nebuchadnezzar has set
3:7 **K** Nebuchadnezzar had set
3:9 addressed **K** Nebuchadnezzar,
3:13 they were brought to the **k**.
3:16 answered **K** Nebuchadnezzar,
3:25 The **k** replied, "But look, I see
3:28 They disobeyed the **k** and
3:30 Then the **k** promoted Shadrach,
4:1 From **K** Nebuchadnezzar.
4:18 **K** Nebuchadnezzar,
4:28 All this happened to **K**
4:30 The **k** thought, "Look how great
4:31 "**K** Nebuchadnezzar,
4:37 give glory to the **K** of Heaven.
5:1 **K** Belshazzar threw a large
5:3 The **k**, his nobles, wives,
5:5 The **k** watched as the hand
5:6 Then the **k** turned pale,
5:7 The **k** screamed for the
5:8 writing or tell the **k** its meaning.
5:9 **K** Belshazzar was terrified,
5:10 The discussion between the **k**
5:11 **K** Nebuchadnezzar,
5:13 So Daniel was taken to the **k**.
5:13 The **k** asked him, "Are you
5:17 Daniel told the **k**, "Keep your
5:30 That night **K** Belshazzar of
6:2 that the **k** wouldn't be cheated.
6:3 The **k** thought about putting
6:6 and satraps went to the **k** as
6:6 "May **K** Darius live forever!
6:7 and mayors agree that the **k**
6:12 to the **k** about his decree.
6:12 The **k** answered, "That's true.
6:14 The **k** was very displeased
6:15 gathered in front of the **k**.

Dan 6:15 or statute the **k** makes can
6:16 So the **k** gave the order,
6:16 The **k** told Daniel, "May your
6:17 The **k** put his seal on the stone,
6:18 Then the **k** went to his palace
6:19 the **k** got up and quickly went
6:20 the **k** called to Daniel with
6:21 Daniel said to the **k**,
6:23 The **k** was overjoyed and had
6:24 The **k** ordered those men who
6:25 Then **K** Darius wrote to the
7:1 first year as **k** of Babylon,
7:24 Another **k** will rise to power
8:1 In Belshazzar's third year as **k**,
8:21 between its eyes is its first **k**.
8:22 be as strong as the first **k** was.
8:23 a stern-looking **k** who
8:27 I got up and worked for the **k**.
10:1 Cyrus' third year as **k** of Persia,
11:1 the Mede's first year as **k**,
11:3 Then a warrior-**k** will come.
11:5 "The southern **k** will be strong,
11:6 will go to the northern **k**
11:7 the stronghold of the northern **k**
11:8 more years than the northern **k**.
11:11 The southern **k** will be
11:11 will go to fight the northern **k**,
11:12 the southern **k** will become
11:13 "The northern **k** will return and
11:14 rebel against the southern **k**,
11:15 Then the northern **k** will come,
11:17 "Then the northern **k** will
11:17 He will give the southern **k** his
11:18 that the northern **k** makes
11:20 "Another **k** will take his place.
11:20 But in a few days the **k** will be
11:25 courage against the southern **k**,
11:25 But the southern **k** won't be
11:28 The northern **k** will return to his
11:36 "The **k** will do as he pleases.
11:40 In the end times the southern **k**
11:40 The northern **k** will rush at him
Hos 1:1 son of Joash, was **k** of Israel.
3:5 their God and David their **k**.
5:13 to ask the great **k** for help.
5:13 But the **k** couldn't cure them or
7:5 and the **k** joins mockers.
10:3 So they'll say, "We have no **k**
10:3 Even if we had a **k**,
10:6 as a present to the great **k**.
10:7 The **k** of Samaria will be
10:15 At daybreak, the **k** of Israel will
13:10 "Where, now, is your **k**,
13:11 I gave you a **k** when I was
Amo 1:1 the reigns of Judah's **K** Uzziah
1:1 and Israel's **K** Jeroboam,
1:15 Their **k** will go into captivity
2:1 have cremated Edom's **k**.
5:26 of ⌊the god⌋ Sikkuth as your **k**
7:1 followed the harvest for the **k**.
7:10 sent a message to **K** Jeroboam
Jnh 3:6 news reached the **k** of Nineveh,
3:7 "This is an order from the **k**
Mic 2:13 Their **k** will travel in front of
4:9 Don't you have a **k**?
6:5 My people, remember what **K**
Nah 3:18 Your shepherds, **k** of Assyria,
Zep 1:1 the days of Judah's **K** Josiah,
3:15 The **k** of Israel, the LORD,
Hag 1:1 in Darius' second year as **k**,
1:15 in Darius' second year as **k**.
2:10 in Darius' second year as **k**,
Zec 1:1 of Darius' second year as **k**,
1:7 in Darius' second year as **k**,
7:1 in Darius' fourth year as **k**,
9:5 Gaza will lose its **k**.
9:9 Your **K** is coming to you:
11:6 to their neighbors and their **k**,
14:5 at the time of **K** Uzziah
14:9 The LORD will be **k** over all
14:16 every year to worship the **k**,
14:17 to Jerusalem to worship the **k**,
Mal 1:14 I am a great **k**," says the LORD
Mat 1:6 Jesse the father of **K** David.
2:1 in Judea when Herod was **k**.
2:2 one who was born to be the **k**

Mat 2:3 When **K** Herod and all
2:9 After they had heard the **k**,
2:22 his father Herod as **k** of Judea,
5:35 which is the city of the great **K**.
14:9 The **k** regretted his promise.
18:23 heaven is like a **k** who wanted
21:5 'Your **k** is coming to you.
22:2 heaven is like a **k** who planned
22:7 "The **k** became angry.
22:8 "Then the **k** said to his
22:11 "When the **k** came to see the
22:13 Then the **k** told his servants,
25:34 "Then the **k** will say to those
25:40 "The **k** will answer them,
25:41 "Then the **k** will say to those
27:11 "Are you the **k** of the Jews?"
27:29 "Long live the **k** of the Jews!"
27:37 the **k** of the Jews."
27:42 So he's Israel's **k**! Let him come
Mar 6:14 **K** Herod heard about Jesus,
6:22 The **k** told the girl,
6:25 So the girl hurried back to the **k**
6:26 The **k** deeply regretted his
6:27 Immediately, the **k** sent a guard
15:2 "Are you the **k** of the Jews?"
15:9 "Do you want me to free the **k**
15:12 I do with the **k** of the Jews?"
15:18 "Long live the **k** of the Jews!"
15:26 It read, "The **k** of the Jews."
15:32 Let the Messiah, the **k** of Israel,
Luk 1:5 When Herod was **k** of Judea,
1:33 Your son will be **k** of Jacob's
2:4 a descendant of **K** David,
14:31 "Or suppose a **k** is going to
14:31 going to war against another **k**.
14:31 a **k** with 20,000 soldiers?
14:32 while the other **k** is still far
19:12 country to be appointed **k**,
19:14 don't want this man to be our **k**.'
19:15 "After he was appointed **k**,
19:17 "The **k** said to him,
19:19 "The **k** said to this servant,
19:22 "The **k** said to him,
19:24 The **k** told his men,
19:27 didn't want me to be their **k**.
19:38 "Blessed is the **k** who comes
23:2 he says that he is Christ, a **k**."
23:3 "Are you the **k** of the Jews?"
23:37 "If you're the **k** of the Jews,
23:38 "This is the **k** of the Jews."
Jon 1:49 You are the **k** of Israel!"
6:15 him by force and make him **k**.
12:13 of the Lord, the **k** of Israel!"
12:15 Your **k** is coming. He is riding
18:33 "Are you the **k** of the Jews?"
18:37 asked him, "So you are a **k**?"
18:37 correct in saying that I'm a **k**.
18:39 Would you like me to free the **k**
19:3 "Long live the **k** of the Jews!"
19:12 Anyone who claims to be a **k**
19:14 Jews, "Look, here's your **k**!"
19:15 "Should I crucify your **k**?"
19:15 emperor is the only **k** we have!"
19:19 the **k** of the Jews."
19:21 'The **k** of the Jews!'
19:21 that he is the **k** of the Jews.'"
Act 7:10 of Pharaoh (the **k** of Egypt),
7:18 Then a different **k**,
7:19 This **k** was shrewd in the way
12:1 About that time **K** Herod
13:21 the people demanded a **k**,
13:22 Saul and made David their **k**.
17:7 saying that there is another **k**,
25:13 Later **K** Agrippa and Bernice
25:14 Festus told the **k** about Paul's
25:24 Then Festus said, "**K** Agrippa
25:26 especially to you, **K** Agrippa.
26:1 Paul acknowledged **K** Agrippa
26:2 **K** Agrippa, I think I'm fortunate
26:19 I saw from heaven, **K** Agrippa.
26:26 I can easily speak to a **k** who
26:27 **K** Agrippa, do you believe the
26:30 The **k**, the governor, Bernice,
2Co 11:32 The governor under **K** Aretas
1Ti 1:17 belong forever to the eternal **k**,
6:15 He is the **K** of kings and Lord of

Heb 7:1 Melchizedek was **k** of Salem
7:2 means **k** of righteousness.
7:2 He is also called **k** of Salem
7:2 (which means **k** of peace).
Rev 9:11 The **k** who ruled them was the
11:15 will rule as **k** forever and ever."
11:17 and have begun ruling as **k**.
15:3 fair and true, **K** of the Nations.
17:11 and is no longer is the eighth **k**.
17:14 is Lord of lords and **K** of kings.
19:6 the Almighty, has become **k**.
19:16 **K** of Kings and Lord of Lords.

kingdom (309)

Gen 10:10 ⌊cities⌋ in his **k** were Babylon,
20:9 a serious sin on me and my **k**?
Exo 19:6 You will be my **k** of priests and
Num 24:7 and their **k** will be considered
Dtr 3:4 the **k** of Og in Bashan.
3:10 cities of Og's **k** in Bashan.
Jos 13:12 (the whole **k** of Og in Bashan).
13:21 the whole **k** of King Sihon of
13:27 the rest of the **k** of King Sihon
13:30 all of Bashan (the whole **k**
1Sm 13:13 your **k** over Israel permanently.
13:14 But now your **k** will not last.
14:47 had taken over the **k** of Israel,
15:28 "The LORD has torn the **k** of
18:8 thing left for David is my **k**."
24:20 and under your guidance the **k**
2Sm 3:28 my **k** and I are forever innocent
7:12 I will establish his **k**.
7:13 the throne of his **k** forever.
8:6 in the Aramean **k** of Damascus,
16:3 me back my grandfather's **k**.'"
20:1 have no share in David's **k**.
1Ki 10:20 had been made for any other **k**.
11:11 I will certainly tear the **k** away
11:13 I will not tear the whole **k** away
11:24 and ruled a **k** in Damascus.
11:31 I am going to tear the **k** out of
11:34 not take the whole **k** from him.
11:35 But I will take the **k** away from
12:16 share do we have in David's **k**?
12:21 and return the **k** to Rehoboam,
12:26 He said to himself, "The **k** will
14:8 I tore the **k** away from David's
18:10 for you in every region and **k**.
18:10 my master made that **k** or
2Ki 14:5 he had a firm control over the **k**,
15:19 strengthen his hold on the **k**.
20:13 and every corner of his **k**.
1Ch 11:10 power with him in his **k**,
14:2 that his **k** was made famous
16:20 and from one **k** to another.
17:11 I will establish his **k**.
18:6 in the Aramean **k** of Damascus,
22:10 his **k** permanently over Israel.'"
28:5 of the LORD's **k** to rule Israel.
28:7 I will establish his **k** forever if
29:11 The **k** is yours, LORD, and you
2Ch 1:1 his position over the **k**.
9:19 had been made for any other **k**.
10:16 share do we have in David's **k**?
11:1 and return the **k** to Rehoboam.
11:17 So they strengthened the **k** of
12:1 had established his **k**
13:5 LORD God of Israel gave the **k**
13:8 to challenge the LORD's **k**,
14:5 The **k** was at peace during his
17:5 power over the **k**.
20:30 Jehoshaphat's **k** was peaceful,
21:3 gave the **k** to Jehoram,
21:4 had taken over his father's **k**,
25:3 he had firm control over the **k**,
29:21 as an offering for sin for the **k**,
32:15 No god of any nation or **k** could
33:13 him back to his **k** in Jerusalem.
36:22 throughout his whole **k**
Ezr 1:1 throughout his whole **k**
7:13 any Israelites who are in my **k**
Neh 9:35 When they lived in their own **k**
Est 1:4 the enormous wealth of his **k**
1:14 held the highest rank in the **k**.
1:20 your whole **k**, great as it is,
2:3 in all the provinces of your **k**
Est 3:6 Jews in the entire **k** of Xerxes.
3:8 in all the provinces of your **k**.
5:3 Even if it is up to half of the **k**,
5:6 Even if it is up to half of the **k**,
7:2 Even if it is up to half of the **k**,
9:30 provinces of the **k** of Xerxes.
Psa 22:28 because the **k** belongs to the
45:6 The scepter in your **k** is a
103:19 His **k** rules everything.
105:13 from one **k** to another.
114:2 place and Israel became his **k**.
145:11 talk about the glory of your **k**.
145:12 the glorious honor of your **k**.
145:13 Your **k** is an everlasting
145:13 kingdom is an everlasting **k**.
Ecc 4:14 born in poverty in that same **k**.
Isa 9:7 establish David's throne and **k**.
17:3 and the **k** will disappear from
19:2 **k** against kingdom.
19:2 kingdom against **k**.
34:12 There are no nobles to rule a **k**.
39:2 and every corner of his **k**.
Jer 1:15 to call every family and **k** from
18:7 and destroy a nation or a **k**.
18:9 build and plant a nation or a **k**.
Lam 2:2 He brought the **k** ⌊of Judah⌋
Eze 29:14 There they will be a weak **k**.
29:15 They will be the weakest **k**,
Dan 1:20 and psychics in his whole **k**.
2:37 of heaven has given you a **k**.
2:39 Another **k**, inferior to yours,
2:39 Then there will be a third **k**,
2:39 a third kingdom, a **k** of bronze,
2:40 There will also be a fourth **k**.
2:40 this fourth **k** will smash and
2:41 be a divided **k** which has some
2:42 Part of the **k** will be strong,
2:43 So the two parts of the **k** will
2:44 establish a **k** that will never
4:3 His **k** is an eternal kingdom.
4:3 His kingdom is an eternal **k**.
4:18 wise advisers in my **k** can't tell
4:26 your **k** will be restored to you
4:31 The **k** has been taken from you.
4:34 forever and his **k** lasts from one
4:36 I was given back my **k** and
5:7 the third-highest ruler in the **k**."
5:11 There's a man in your **k** who
5:16 the third-highest ruler in the **k**."
5:18 Nebuchadnezzar a **k**,
5:26 numbered the days of your **k**
5:28 Divided — your **k** will be
5:29 the third-highest ruler in the **k**.
5:31 the Mede took over the **k**.
6:1 satraps to rule throughout the **k**
6:3 him in charge of the whole **k**.
6:4 Daniel of in his duties for the **k**.
6:26 of my **k** people should tremble
6:26 His **k** will never be destroyed.
7:14 given power, honor, and a **k**.
7:14 His **k** will never be destroyed.
7:18 will take possession of the **k**
7:22 took possession of the **k**.
7:24 will rise to power from that **k**.
7:27 The **k**, along with the power
7:27 Their **k** is eternal. All other
8:21 male goat is the **k** of Greece,
9:1 made ruler of the **k** of Babylon.
10:13 of the Persian **k** opposed me
11:2 against the **k** of Greece.
11:4 his **k** will be broken into pieces
11:9 He will invade the southern **k**
11:17 with the power of his entire **k**,
11:17 order to destroy the southern **k**.
11:21 the **k** using false promises.
Hos 1:4 put an end to the **k** of Israel.
Amo 9:8 have my eyes on this sinful **k**.
Oba 1:21 The **k** will belong to the
Mic 4:8 The **k** will return to the people
Mat 3:2 because the **k** of heaven is
4:17 because the **k** of heaven is
4:23 spread the Good News of the **k**.
5:3 The **k** of heaven belongs to
5:10 The **k** of heaven belongs to
5:19 unimportant in the **k** of heaven.
5:19 called great in the **k** of heaven.
Mat 5:20 never enter the **k** of heaven.
6:10 Let your **k** come. Let your will
6:33 be concerned about his **k** and
7:21 will enter the **k** of heaven,
8:11 and Jacob in the **k** of heaven.
8:12 The citizens of that **k** will be
9:35 spread the Good News of the **k**.
10:7 'The **k** of heaven is near.'
11:11 least important person in the **k**
11:12 the **k** of heaven has been
12:25 "Every **k** divided against itself
12:26 How, then, can his **k** last?
12:28 then the **k** of God has come to
13:11 about the mysteries of the **k**
13:19 hears the word about the **k**
13:24 He said, "The **k** of heaven is
13:31 He said, "The **k** of heaven is
13:33 "The **k** of heaven is like yeast
13:38 are those who belong to the **k**.
13:41 in his **k** that causes people
13:43 like the sun in their Father's **k**.
13:44 "The **k** of heaven is like a
13:45 "Also, the **k** of heaven is like a
13:47 "Also, the **k** of heaven is like a
13:52 has become a disciple of the **k**
16:19 the keys of the **k** of heaven.
16:28 Son of Man coming in his **k**."
18:1 is greatest in the **k** of heaven?"
18:3 never enter the **k** of heaven.
18:4 the greatest in the **k** of heaven.
18:23 "That is why the **k** of heaven is
19:12 because of the **k** of heaven.
19:14 these are part of the **k** of God."
19:23 person to enter the **k** of heaven.
19:24 person to enter the **k** of God."
20:1 "The **k** of heaven is like a
20:21 the other at your left in your **k**."
21:31 prostitutes are going into the **k**
21:43 why I can guarantee that the **k**
22:2 "The **k** of heaven is like a king
23:13 people out of the **k** of heaven.
24:7 nation and **k** against kingdom.
24:7 nation and kingdom against **k**.
24:14 "This Good News about the **k**
25:1 "When the end comes, the **k** of
25:14 "The **k** of heaven is like a man
25:34 Inherit the **k** prepared for you
26:29 with you in my Father's **k**."
Mar 1:15 and the **k** of God is near.
3:24 If a **k** is divided against itself,
3:24 itself, that **k** cannot last.
4:11 "The mystery about the **k** of
4:26 Jesus said, "The **k** of God is
4:30 "How can we show what the **k**
6:23 up to half of my **k**."
9:1 will not die until they see the **k**
9:47 It is better for you to enter the **k**
10:14 these are part of the **k** of God.
10:15 Whoever doesn't receive the **k**
10:23 people to enter the **k** of God!"
10:24 hard it is to enter the **k** of God!
10:25 person to enter the **k** of God."
11:10 David's **k** that is coming!
12:34 not too far from the **k** of God."
13:8 nation and **k** against kingdom.
13:8 nation and kingdom against **k**.
14:25 new wine in the **k** of God."
15:43 was waiting for the **k** of God.
Luk 1:33 and his **k** will never end."
4:43 tell the Good News about the **k**
6:20 The **k** of God is theirs.
7:28 least important person in the **k**
8:1 the Good News about God's **k**.
8:10 about the mysteries of the **k**
9:2 the message about the **k**
9:11 to them about the **k** of God,
9:27 die until they see the **k** of God."
9:60 and tell about the **k** of God."
9:62 back is not fit for the **k** of God."
10:9 'The **k** of God is near you!'
10:11 But realize that the **k** of God is
11:2 be kept holy. Let your **k** come.
11:17 "Every **k** divided against itself
11:18 how can his **k** last?
11:20 then the **k** of God has come to
12:31 be concerned about his **k**.

Luk 12:32 is pleased to give you the **k**.
13:18 "What is the **k** of God like?
13:20 can I compare the **k** of God to?
13:28 They'll be in the **k** of God,
13:29 and will eat in the **k** of God.
14:15 will be at the banquet in the **k**
16:16 Good News about the **k** of God,
17:20 asked Jesus when the **k**
17:20 the coming of the **k** of God.
17:21 the **k** of God is within you."
18:16 these are part of the **k** of God.
18:17 Whoever doesn't receive the **k**
18:24 people to enter the **k** of God!
18:25 person to enter the **k** of God."
18:29 because of the **k** of God
19:11 the people thought that the **k**
21:10 nation and **k** against kingdom.
21:10 nation and kingdom against **k**.
21:31 you know that the **k** of God is
22:16 its fulfillment in the **k** of God."
22:18 wine until the **k** of God comes."
22:29 as my Father has given me a **k**,
22:30 and drink at my table in my **k**.
23:42 me when you enter your **k**."
23:51 was waiting for the **k** of God.
Jon 3:3 No one can see the **k** of God
3:5 No one can enter the **k** of God
18:36 Jesus answered, "My **k** doesn't
18:36 If my **k** belonged to this world,
18:36 My **k** doesn't have its origin on
Act 1:3 with them about the **k** of God.
1:6 going to restore the **k** to Israel?"
8:12 the Good News about the **k**
14:22 a lot to enter the **k** of God."
19:8 them about the **k** of God.
20:25 I told about the **k** ⌊of God⌋ will
28:23 Paul was explaining the **k** of
28:31 the message about God's **k**
Rom 14:17 God's **k** does not consist of
14:17 Rather, God's **k** consists of
1Co 4:20 God's **k** is not just talk,
6:9 won't inherit the **k** of God?
6:10 will not inherit the **k** of God.
15:24 Christ will hand over the **k** to
15:50 cannot inherit the **k** of God.
Gal 5:21 will not inherit the **k** of God.
Eph 5:5 have any inheritance in the **k**
Col 1:13 and has brought us into the **k**
4:11 working with me for God's **k**.
1Th 2:12 calls you into his **k** and glory.
4:15 will not go ⌊into his **k**⌋ ahead
2Th 1:5 are considered worthy of his **k**.
2Ti 4:18 me safely to his heavenly **k**.
Heb 1:8 The scepter in your **k** is a
12:28 that we have a **k** that cannot
Jas 2:5 in faith and to receive the **k** that
2Pe 1:11 of entering into the eternal **k**
Rev 1:6 and has made us a **k**,
5:10 You made them a **k** and priests
11:15 "The **k** of the world has
11:15 of the world has become the **k**
12:10 salvation, power, **k** of our God,
13:2 The serpent gave its power, **k**,
16:10 Its **k** turned dark. People
17:17 So they will give their **k** to the

kingdoms (66)

Num 32:33 the **k** of King Sihon of the
Dtr 3:21 will do the same to all of the **k**
28:25 horror to all the **k** in the world.
Jos 11:10 the head of all these **k**.)
1Ki 4:21 Solomon ruled all the **k** from
4:21 These **k** paid taxes and were
2Ki 19:15 You alone are God of all the **k**
19:19 control so that all the **k**
1Ch 29:30 and all the other **k**.
2Ch 17:10 came to all the **k** around Judah.
20:6 You rule all the **k** of the nations.
20:29 of the LORD came over the **k**
36:23 heaven has given me all the **k**
Ezr 1:2 heaven has given me all the **k**
Neh 9:22 You gave **k** and nations to the
Psa 46:6 are in turmoil, and **k** topple.
68:32 You **k** of the world,
79:6 on the **k** that have not called
102:22 when nations and **k** gather to
Psa 135:11 and all the **k** in Canaan.
Isa 8:14 block for both **k** of Israel.
10:10 My power has reached **k** which
13:4 It is the sound of **k** and nations
13:19 Babylon, the jewel of the **k**,
14:16 earth tremble, who shook the **k**,
23:11 hand over the sea to shake **k**.
23:17 a prostitute for all the world's **k**.
37:16 You alone are God of the **k** of
37:20 control so that all the **k**
47:5 longer be called the queen of **k**.
60:12 Nations and **k** that do not serve
Jer 1:10 you in charge of nations and **k**.
10:7 in the nations or in all their **k**.
15:4 a horrifying sight to all the **k**
24:9 a horrifying sight to all the **k**
25:26 one after another — all the **k** of
27:8 "'Suppose nations or **k** won't
28:8 many countries and great **k**.
29:18 a horrifying sight to all the **k**
34:1 and all the **k** and people that he
34:17 I will make all the **k** of the
49:28 the tribe of Kedar and the **k**
51:20 I will use you to destroy **k**.
51:27 Tell the **k** of Ararat,
Eze 37:22 or be divided into two **k**.
Dan 2:40 and crush all the other **k**.
2:44 It will smash all the other **k**
4:17 High has power over human **k**.
4:25 High has power over human **k**
4:32 High has power over human **k**
5:21 God has power over human **k**.
7:17 animals are four **k** that will rise
7:23 the fourth of these **k** on earth.
7:23 will be different from all other **k**.
7:27 of all the **k** under heaven,
8:20 that you saw represents the **k**
8:22 Four **k** will come out of that
8:23 "In the last days of those **k**,
Amo 6:2 Are you better than these **k**?
Nah 3:5 body and **k** your disgrace.
Zep 3:8 to bring **k** together,
Hag 2:22 I will overthrow the thrones of **k**
Mat 4:8 and showed him all the **k**
Luk 4:5 place and showed him all the **k**
4:6 the power and glory of these **k**.
Heb 11:33 Through faith they conquered **k**

king's (221)

Gen 14:17 Valley (that is, the **K** Valley)
39:20 the **k** prisoners were kept.
40:1 Later the **k** cupbearer and his
Num 20:17 We'll stay on the **k** highway
21:22 We'll stay on the **k** highway
Jos 2:7 The **k** men pursued them on
2:7 As soon as the **k** men had left,
2:22 days until the **k** men returned
2:22 The **k** men had searched for
Jdg 8:18 Each one looked like a **k** son.
1Sm 18:18 I should be the **k** son-in-law?
18:22 Become the **k** son-in-law.'"
18:23 to become the **k** son-in-law?
18:26 to become the **k** son-in-law.
18:27 could become the **k** son-in-law.
20:5 sit and eat at the **k** ⌊table⌋.
21:8 the **k** business was urgent."
22:17 "But the **k** men refused to
25:36 It was like a **k** banquet.
26:16 Look at the **k** spear and the jar
26:22 "Here's the **k** spear.
2Sm 9:11 table as one of the **k** sons
9:13 He always ate at the **k** table
13:4 the **k** son, so worn out morning
13:18 The **k** virgin daughters wore
13:23 He invited all the **k** sons
13:27 all ⌊the rest of⌋ the **k** sons go
13:29 Then all the **k** sons got up,
13:30 has killed all the **k** sons,
13:32 all the **k** sons, have been
13:33 that all the **k** sons are dead,
13:35 "The **k** sons have come.
13:36 the **k** sons arrived and cried
15:15 The **k** servants told him,
16:2 donkeys are for the **k** family
18:12 my hand against the **k** son.
18:18 it up for himself in the **k** valley.
2Sm 18:20 because the **k** son is dead."
19:18 river to bring over the **k** family
19:42 Did we eat the **k** food, or did he
1Ki 1:4 She became the **k** servant and
1:9 the **k** ⌊other⌋ sons,
1:9 of Judah, and the **k** officials
1:19 He has invited all the **k** sons,
1:25 He invited all the **k** sons, the
1:44 have put him on the **k** mule
4:5 of Nathan, was the **k** adviser
10:28 The **k** traders bought them
2Ki 5:1 **k** army, was respected
7:20 happened to the **k** servant:
9:34 After all, she was a **k** daughter.
10:8 of the **k** heirs." Jehu said,
11:2 killed with the **k** other sons,
11:4 and showed them the **k** son
11:6 You will guard the **k** residence
11:12 brought out the **k** son, gave him
12:10 the **k** scribe and the chief priest
13:16 laid his hands on the **k** hands
15:5 The **k** son Jotham was in
16:15 the **k** burnt offerings and grain
19:6 **k** assistants slandered me.
24:15 also took the **k** mother, wives,
25:4 two walls beside the **k** garden.
25:29 in the **k** presence as long as
1Ch 9:18 were stationed at the **k** gate
21:6 was disgusted with the **k** order
25:2 a prophet under the **k** direction.
25:5 the sons of the **k** seer Heman.
27:32 were in charge of the **k** sons
27:33 Ahithophel was the **k** adviser.
27:33 of Archi, was the **k** friend
29:6 of the **k** work gave generously.
2Ch 1:16 The **k** traders bought them
8:15 No one neglected the **k** orders
22:11 killed with the **k** other sons,
23:3 "Here is the **k** son.
23:11 brought out the **k** son, gave him
24:11 brought the box to the **k** officers
24:11 the **k** scribe and the chief
24:21 and by the **k** order they stoned
26:11 one of the **k** officials
28:7 who was the **k** son, Azrikam,
28:7 was the **k** second-in-command
29:15 Then they obeyed the **k** order
29:25 lyres as David, the **k** seer Gad,
30:6 The **k** order said, "Israelites,
31:3 set aside part of the **k** property
32:21 in the Assyrian **k** camp.
34:22 So Hilkiah and the **k** officials
35:7 animals were the **k** property.
35:15 and the **k** seer Jeduthun had
Ezr 4:13 this will hurt the **k** income
5:17 to search the **k** archives
6:4 The **k** palace will pay for it.
6:8 out of the **k** own money from
7:20 You may use the **k** treasury to
7:23 angry with the **k** empire
7:26 and the **k** orders should
7:27 He put this into the **k** mind to
7:28 and all the **k** powerful officials
8:36 exiles delivered the **k** orders
8:36 king's orders to the **k** satraps
Neh 2:9 and gave them the **k** letters.
2:14 I arrived at **K** Pool, but the
3:15 by the **K** Garden as far as
3:25 that projects from the **k** palace
5:4 money to pay the **k** taxes
11:24 was the **k** adviser on all
Est 1:5 garden of the **k** palace
1:12 refused the **k** command that
1:18 talk back to all the **k** officials.
1:22 to all the **k** provinces,
2:2 So the **k** personal staff said to
2:3 the care of the **k** eunuch Hegai,
2:8 When the **k** announcement and
2:8 also was taken to the **k** palace
2:9 servants from the **k** palace.
2:13 to the **k** palace was given
2:14 of the **k** eunuch Shaashgaz,
2:15 for what the **k** eunuch Hegai,
2:19 was sitting at the **k** gate
2:21 sitting at the **k** gate, Bigthan
2:21 two of the **k** eunuchs who

Est 2:23 written up in the **k** presence
3:2 All the **k** advisers were at the
3:2 were at the **k** gate, kneeling
3:3 Then the **k** advisers at the
3:3 at the **k** gate asked Mordecai,
3:3 do you ignore the **k** command?
3:6 Because the **k** advisers had
3:12 the **k** scribes were summoned.
3:12 were written to the **k** satraps,
3:12 and sealed with the **k** ring
3:13 to all the **k** provinces.
4:2 went right up to the **k** gate.
4:3 touched by the **k** command
4:5 one of the **k** eunuchs appointed
4:6 city square in front of the **k** gate
4:7 to pay into the **k** treasury
4:11 "All the **k** advisers and the
4:11 in the **k** provinces know that no
4:11 to enter the **k** presence
4:13 you are in the **k** palace you will
5:1 of the **k** palace, facing
5:1 facing the **k** throne room.
5:9 at the **k** gate, neither getting up
5:11 the officials and the **k** advisers
5:13 the Jew sitting at the **k** gate.
6:2 two of the **k** eunuchs who
6:3 The **k** personal staff replied,
6:4 the courtyard to the **k** palace
6:5 The **k** staff answered him,
6:9 to one of the **k** officials, who is
6:9 The **k** servants are also to
6:10 the Jew who sits at the **k** gate.
6:12 Mordecai returned to the **k** gate
6:14 the **k** eunuchs arrived and
8:8 for the Jews in the **k** name.
8:8 it also with the **k** signet ring,
8:8 is written in the **k** name
8:8 with the **k** signet ring cannot
8:9 the **k** scribes were summoned.
8:10 with the **k** signet ring.
8:14 rode the **k** fastest horses.
8:14 keeping with the **k** command.
8:17 city where the **k** message
9:1 the **k** command and decree
9:3 and the **k** treasurers assisted
9:4 important man in the **k** palace.
9:12 in the rest of the **k** provinces!
9:16 **k** provinces had also assembled
9:25 this came to the **k** attention,
Psa 45:5 in the heart of the **k** enemies.
72:1 the **k** son your righteousness
99:4 The **k** strength is that he loves
105:22 Joseph trained the **k** officers
Pro 16:10 divine revelation is on a **k** lips,
16:14 A **k** anger announces death,
21:1 The **k** heart is like streams of
Ecc 4:15 young man, the **k** successor
8:2 you to obey the **k** commands
8:3 a hurry to leave the **k** service.
8:4 Since a **k** word has such
Isa 37:6 **k** assistants slandered me.
Jer 26:10 they went from the **k** palace to
36:12 room in the **k** palace where all
36:26 (the **k** son), Seraiah (son
38:6 cistern of Malchiah, the **k** son.
39:4 by way of the **k** garden through
41:1 and of the **k** officers) went
41:10 He captured the **k** daughters
43:6 and the **k** daughters.
52:7 two walls beside the **k** garden.
52:33 in the **k** presence as long as
Lam 4:20 live in our **k** shadow among
Eze 19:14 could be used as a **k** scepter.
Dan 1:4 able to serve in the **k** palace.
1:5 allowance of the **k** rich food
1:8 by eating the **k** rich food
1:8 food and drinking the **k** wine.
1:13 who are eating the **k** rich food.
1:15 had been eating the **k** rich food.
1:16 took away the **k** rich food
2:15 "Why is the **k** decree so
2:49 With the **k** permission, Daniel
2:49 But Daniel stayed at the **k** court
3:22 The **k** order was so urgent and
3:27 The **k** satraps, governors,
5:8 All the **k** wise advisers came,
Dan 11:6 The southern **k** daughter will
11:11 fall into the southern **k** hands
11:26 People who eat the **k** rich food
Hos 7:5 On the day of the **k** celebration,
Amo 7:13 because this is the **k** holy
7:13 holy place and the **k** palace.
Zep 1:8 the **k** sons, and all who dress
Zec 14:10 Hananel to the **k** winepresses
Mat 22:6 **k** servants, mistreated them,
Act 12:20 charge of the **k** living quarters.)
Heb 11:23 not afraid to disobey the **k** order
11:27 being afraid of the **k** anger.

kings (336)

Gen 14:1 At that time ⌊four **k**⌋ — King
14:2 went to war against ⌊five **k**⌋ —
14:3 The five **k** joined forces and
14:8 Then the **k** of Sodom,
14:9 of Ellasar — four **k** against five.
14:10 As the **k** of Sodom and
14:10 but the other **k** fled to the hills.
14:11 So the four **k** took all the
14:14 and pursued the four **k** all the
17:6 Many nations and **k** will come
17:16 and **k** will come from her."
35:11 and **k** will come from you.
36:31 These were the **k** who ruled
Num 31:8 those killed were the five **k**
Dtr 3:8 land of the two Amorite **k** east
3:21 God has done to these two **k**.
4:47 the two **k** of the Amorites who
7:24 He will hand their **k** over to you,
Jos 2:10 the two **k** of the Amorites,
5:1 All the Amorite **k** west of the
5:1 and all the Canaanite **k** along
9:1 When all the **k** west of the
9:2 (They were the **k** in the
9:2 the **k** of the Hittites,
9:10 everything he did to the two **k**
10:5 the five Amorite **k** of Jerusalem,
10:6 all the Amorite **k** who live
10:16 The five **k** ran away and hid in
10:17 "The five **k** have been found.
10:22 and bring me the five **k**!"
10:23 brought him the **k** of Jerusalem,
10:24 feet on the necks of these **k**."
10:39 Hebron and Libnah and their **k**.
10:42 Joshua captured all these **k**
11:1 Jobab of Madon and to the **k**
11:2 messengers to the northern **k**
11:5 All these **k** camped together by
11:12 all these cities and their **k**.
11:17 all their **k** and killed them.
11:18 waged war with all these **k**
12:1 These are the **k** of the land
12:7 These are the **k** of the land
12:8 ⌊had possessed⌋. The **k** were
12:24 The total was 31 **k**.
24:12 of you to force out the two **k**
Jdg 1:7 Adoni Bezek said, "Seventy **k**
5:3 Listen, you **k**! Open your ears,
5:19 **K** came and fought.
5:19 Then the **k** of Canaan fought.
8:26 worn by the **k** of Midian,
1Sm 10:18 all the **k** who were oppressing
14:47 Edom, the **k** of Zobah,
27:6 to the **k** of Judah today.)
2Sm 10:19 When all the **k** who were
11:1 In the spring, the time when **k**
1Ki 4:24 to Gaza and all of its **k**.
4:34 they came from all the **k** of the
10:15 traders' profits, all the Arab **k**,
10:23 all the ⌊other⌋ **k** of the world.
10:29 to all the Hittite and Aramean **k**.
14:19 records of the **k** of Israel.
14:29 records of the **k** of Judah?
15:7 records of the **k** of Judah?
15:23 records of the **k** of Judah?
15:31 records of the **k** of Israel?
16:5 records of the **k** of Israel?
16:14 records of the **k** of Israel?
16:20 records of the **k** of Israel?
16:25 than all ⌊the **k**⌋ before him.
16:27 records of the **k** of Israel?
16:30 He was worse than all ⌊the **k**⌋
16:33 of Israel furious than all the **k**
1Ki 20:1 With him were 32 **k** along with
20:16 with the 32 **k** who were his
20:24 Remove all of the **k** from their
20:31 "We have heard that the **k** of
22:39 records of the **k** of Israel?
22:45 records of the **k** of Judah?
2Ki 1:18 records of the **k** of Israel?
3:21 heard that the **k** had come
3:23 The **k** have been fighting one
7:6 hired the Hittite and Egyptian **k**
8:18 the ways of the **k** of Israel,
8:23 records of the **k** of Judah?
10:4 They said, "If two **k** couldn't
10:34 records of the **k** of Israel?
12:18 his ancestors **K** Jehoshaphat,
12:19 records of the **k** of Judah?
13:8 records of the **k** of Israel?
13:12 records of the **k** of Israel?
13:13 and was buried with the **k**
14:15 records of the **k** of Israel?
14:16 and was buried with the **k**
14:18 records of the **k** of Judah?
14:28 records of the **k** of Israel?
14:29 his ancestors, the **k** of Israel.
15:6 records of the **k** of Judah?
15:11 records of the **k** of Israel.
15:15 records of the **k** of Israel.
15:21 records of the **k** of Israel?
15:26 records of the **k** of Israel.
15:31 records of the **k** of Israel.
15:36 records of the **k** of Judah?
16:3 followed the example of the **k**
16:7 Come and save me from the **k**
16:19 records of the **k** of Judah?
17:2 but he didn't do what the **k** of
17:8 They also did what their **k**
18:5 No king among all the **k** of
19:11 You heard what the **k** of
19:17 It is true, LORD, that the **k** of
20:20 records of the **k** of Judah?
21:17 records of the **k** of Judah?
21:25 record of the **k** of Judah?
23:5 the pagan priests whom the **k**
23:11 that Judah's **k** had dedicated
23:12 the altars that Judah's **k** had
23:19 The **k** of Israel had built these
23:22 during the entire time of the **k**
23:28 records of the **k** of Judah?
24:5 records of the **k** of Judah?
25:25 a descendant of the **k**) went
25:28 than the other **k** who were
1Ch 1:43 These were the **k** who ruled
9:1 in the Book of the **K**
16:21 He warned **k** about them:
19:9 Rehob and the **k** who had come
19:16 the **k** sent ⌊messengers⌋ to get
19:19 When all the **k** who were
20:1 In the spring, the time when **k**
2Ch 1:17 to all the Hittite and Aramean **k**.
9:14 All the Arab **k** and governors of
9:22 all the ⌊other⌋ **k** of the world.
9:23 All the **k** of the world wanted to
9:26 He ruled all the **k** from the
12:8 me and serving foreign **k**."
16:11 is written in the Book of the **K**
20:34 in the Book of the **K** of Israel.
21:6 the ways of the **k** of Israel,
21:13 the ways of the **k** of Israel.
21:20 but not in the tombs of the **k**.
24:16 in the City of David with the **k**
24:25 bury him in the tombs of the **k**.
24:27 made in the Book of the **K**.
25:26 written in the Book of the **K** of
26:23 tombs that belonged to the **k**.
27:7 is written in the Book of the **K**
28:2 followed the example of the **k**
28:16 for help from the **k** of Assyria.
28:23 He thought, "The gods of the **k**
28:26 is written in the Book of the **K**
28:27 into the tombs of the **k** of Israel.
30:6 the power of the **k** of Assyria.
32:4 They said, "Why should the **k**
32:32 and in the records of the **k** of
33:18 in the records of the **k** of Israel.
34:11 of the buildings that the **k**
35:18 Samuel or the **k** of Israel.

2Ch 35:27 written in the records of the **k**
36:8 is written in the Book of the **K**
Ezr 4:15 a threat to **k** and provinces.
4:19 history of uprisings against **k**.
4:20 Jerusalem has had powerful **k**
6:14 and Artaxerxes (the **k** of
7:12 From: Artaxerxes, king of **k** To:
9:7 Our **k** and our priests have
9:7 been handed over to foreign **k**
9:9 Instead, he has made the **k** of
Neh 9:24 You handed the Canaanite **k**
9:32 hardships have come to our **k**,
9:32 people from the time of the **k**
9:34 Our **k**, leaders, priests,
9:37 land⌋ go to the **k** you put over
9:37 These **k** have control over our
Est 10:2 recorded in the history of the **k**
Job 3:14 I would be with the **k** and the
36:7 seats them on thrones with **k**
Psa 2:2 **K** take their stands.
2:10 Now, you **k**, act wisely.
45:9 The daughters of **k** are among
48:4 The **k** have gathered.
68:12 "The **k** of the armies flee;
68:14 scattering **k** there like snow
68:29 **K** will bring you gifts because
72:10 May the **k** from Tarshish and
72:10 May the **k** from Sheba and
72:11 May all **k** worship him.
76:12 He terrifies the **k** of the earth.
89:27 Most High to the **k** of the earth.
102:15 All the **k** of the earth will fear
105:14 He warned **k** about them:
110:5 He will crush **k** on the day of
119:46 in the presence of **k**
135:10 nations and killed mighty **k**:
136:17 one who defeated powerful **k** —
136:18 He killed mighty **k** — because
138:4 All the **k** of the earth will give
144:10 the one who gives victory to **k**.
148:11 **k** of the earth and all its people,
149:8 to put their **k** in chains and their
Pro 8:15 Through me **k** reign,
16:12 Wrongdoing is disgusting to **k**
16:13 **K** are happy with honest words,
22:29 He will serve **k**. He will not
25:2 glory of **k** to investigate them.
25:3 the mind of **k** is unsearchable.
31:3 your power to those who ruin **k**.
31:4 "It is not for **k**, Lemuel. It is not
31:4 It is not for **k** to drink wine or for
Ecc 2:8 treasures of **k** and provinces.
Isa 1:1 at the time of **K** Uzziah,
7:16 the land of the two **k** who terrify
10:8 'Aren't all our commanders **k**?
14:9 It raises all who were **k** of the
14:18 All the **k** of the nations,
14:20 You won't be joined by the **k** in
19:11 a descendant of ancient **k**"?
23:8 the city that produced **k**?
24:21 heaven and earth's **k** on earth.
37:11 You heard what the **k** of
37:18 It is true, LORD, that the **k** of
41:2 He defeats **k**. With his sword he
45:1 strip **k** of their power,
49:7 **K** will see ⌊you⌋ and stand.
49:23 Then **k** will be your foster
52:15 **K** will shut their mouths
60:3 and **k** will come to the
60:10 and their **k** will serve you.
60:11 with their **k** led as prisoners.
62:2 All **k** will see your glory.
Jer 1:18 able to stand up to Judah's **k**,
2:26 Their **k**, princes, priests,
8:1 "At that time the bones of the **k**
13:13 The **k** who sit on David's
17:19 where the **k** of Judah go in and
17:20 of the LORD, you **k** of Judah,
17:25 If you do this, then the **k** and
19:3 you **k** of Judah and those who
19:4 and the **k** of Judah have
19:13 the houses of the **k** of Judah,
20:5 the treasures of the **k** of Judah.
22:4 If you do what I say, then the **k**
25:14 Many nations and great **k** will
25:18 as well as its **k** and officials.
Jer 25:20 all the **k** of the land of Uz;
25:20 all the **k** of Philistia,
25:22 all the **k** of Tyre and Sidon,
25:22 and the **k** on the seacoast;
25:24 all the **k** of Arabia,
25:24 and all the **k** of the foreign
25:25 all the **k** of Zimri, all the kings
25:25 of Zimri, all the **k** of Elam,
25:25 and all the **k** of Media;
25:26 all the **k** of the north,
27:3 messages to the **k** of Edom,
27:7 Then many nations and great **k**
32:32 people, their **k** and officials,
33:4 city and the palaces of the **k**
34:5 the **k** who lived before you.
44:9 by the **k** of Judah and their
44:17 to her as our ancestors, our **k**,
44:21 your **k** and your officials,
46:25 Pharaoh, Egypt, its gods, its **k**,
50:41 A great nation and many **k** will
51:11 will stir up the spirit of the **k**
52:32 than the other **k** who were
Lam 2:6 He expelled **k** and priests
4:12 Neither the **k** of the earth nor
Eze 7:27 **K** will mourn, and princes will
19:11 used to make scepters for **k**.
27:33 You made the **k** of the earth
27:35 Their **k** are terribly afraid.
28:17 you in front of the **k** so that they
32:10 Their **k** will shudder when I
32:29 "Edom is there with its **k** and
43:7 Israel and their **k** will no longer
43:7 with the dead bodies of their **k**.
43:9 bodies of their **k** far away from
Dan 2:21 He removes **k** and establishes
2:44 "At the time of those **k**,
2:47 of gods, the Lord over **k**.
7:24 The ten horns are ten **k** that
7:24 He will be different from the **k**
7:24 and he will humble three **k**.
9:6 spoke in your name to our **k**,
9:8 We, our **k**, leaders,
10:13 left alone with the **k** of Persia.
11:2 Three more **k** will rule Persia.
11:6 and northern **k** will make
11:27 The two **k** will both plan to do
Hos 1:1 and Hezekiah were **k** of Judah
3:4 long time without **k** or officials,
7:3 "They make **k** happy with the
7:7 All their **k** die in battle,
8:4 "They chose their own **k**,
8:4 own kings, **k** I didn't approve.
8:10 the burdens of **k** and princes.
13:10 'Give us **k** and officials!'
Mic 1:1 and Hezekiah were **k** of Judah.
1:14 will betray the **k** of Israel.
Hab 1:10 They will make fun of **k** and
Mat 10:18 in front of governors and **k**
17:25 From whom do the **k** of the
Mar 13:9 in front of governors and **k**
Luk 10:24 many prophets and **k** wanted
21:12 They will drag you in front of **k**
22:25 Jesus said to them, "The **k** of
Act 4:26 **K** take their stand.
9:15 to **k**, and to the people of Israel.
1Co 4:8 You've become **k** without us!
4:8 I wish you really were **k** so that
4:8 so that we could be **k** with you.
Col 1:16 Whether they are **k** or lords,
1Ti 6:15 He is the King of **k** and Lord of
Heb 7:1 returning from defeating the **k**.
Rev 1:5 and the ruler over the **k** of the
5:10 will rule as **k** on the earth."
6:15 Then the **k** of the earth,
10:11 nations, languages, and **k**."
16:12 a road for the **k** from the east.
16:14 These spirits go to the **k** of the
16:16 The spirits gathered the **k** at
17:2 The **k** of the earth had sex with
17:10 They are also seven **k**.
17:11 It belongs with the seven **k**
17:12 saw are ten **k** who have not
17:12 receive authority to rule as **k**
17:14 is Lord of lords and King of **k**.
17:18 dominates the **k** of the earth."
18:3 The **k** of the earth had sex with
Rev 18:9 "The **k** of the earth who had
19:16 King of **K** and Lord of Lords.
19:18 Eat the flesh of **k**, generals,
19:19 the beast, the **k** of the earth,
21:24 and the **k** of the earth will bring
22:5 will rule as **k** forever and ever.

kings' (2)

Job 12:18 He loosens **k** belts and strips
Psa 105:30 even in the **k** bedrooms

kingship (11)

1Sm 10:25 the laws concerning **k**
11:14 there acknowledge ⌊Saul's⌋ **k**."
28:17 The LORD has torn the **k** out of
2Sm 3:10 'I, the LORD, will transfer the **k**
5:12 Israel and made his **k** famous
16:8 The LORD is giving the **k** to
1Ki 2:15 "You know the **k** was mine.
2:15 But the **k** has been turned over
2:22 the same as giving him the **k**.
1Ch 10:14 killed him and turned the **k** over
12:23 at Hebron to turn Saul's **k** over

Kir (6)

2Ki 3:25 Soldiers surrounded **K**
16:9 the people to **K** as captives,
Isa 15:1 In a single night **K** in Moab is
22:6 **K** uncovers its shields.
Amo 1:5 Aram will go into captivity at **K**.
9:7 and the Arameans from **K**?

Kir Hareseth (5)

2Ki 3:25 ⌊in the walls⌋ of **K** were left.
Isa 16:7 grieve over the raisin cakes of **K**
16:11 My soul mourns for **K**.
Jer 48:31 I will moan for the people of **K**
48:36 like a flute for the people of **K**.

Kiriath (1)

Jos 18:28 Jerusalem), Gibeath, and **K**.

Kiriathaim (6)

Num 32:37 cities of Heshbon, Elealeh, **K**,
Jos 13:19 **K**, Sibmah, Zereth Shahar on
1Ch 6:76 and **K** with its pastureland.
Jer 48:1 **K** will be put to shame;
48:23 **K**, Beth Gamul, Beth Meon,
Eze 25:9 Jeshimoth, Baal Meon, and **K**.

Kiriath Arba (8)

Gen 23:2 She died in **K** (that is, Hebron)
35:27 city, **K** (that is, Hebron).
Jos 14:15 In the past Hebron was called **K**.
15:54 Humtah, **K** (now called Hebron
20:7 and **K** (now called Hebron)
21:11 They gave them **K** (Arba was
Jdg 1:10 Hebron was called **K**)
Neh 11:25 people of Judah lived in **K**

Kiriath Baal (2)

Jos 15:60 The two cities of **K** (now
Jos 18:14 and ends at **K** (now called

Kiriath Huzoth (1)

Num 22:39 Balaam went with Balak to **K**

Kiriath Jearim (19)

Jos 9:17 and **K** two days later.
15:9 Baalah (now called **K**).
15:60 Baal (now called **K**)
18:14 Baal (now called **K**),
18:15 begins just outside **K**
Jos 18:12 They camped at **K** in
18:12 just west of **K** is still
1Sm 6:21 to the people living at **K**
7:1 The men of **K** came to
7:2 ark came to stay at **K**.
1Ch 2:50 who first settled **K**,
2:52 who first settled **K**,
2:53 the families of **K**,
13:5 bring God's ark from **K**.
13:6 went to Baalah in **K**,
2Ch 1:4 God's ark from **K**
Ezr 2:25 of **K**, Chephirah,
Neh 7:29 of **K**, Chephirah,

Jer 26:20 of Shemaiah, from **K**.

Kiriath Sannah (1)

Jos 15:49 **K** (now called Debir),

Kiriath Sepher (4)

Jos 15:15 (In the past Debir was called **K**
15:16 anyone who attacks **K**
Jdg 1:11 (In the past Debir was called **K**
1:12 to whoever defeats **K**

Kish (23)

1Sm 9:1 Benjamin whose name was **K**.
9:1 **K** was a powerful man.
9:3 to Saul's father **K** were lost,
9:3 Kish were lost, **K** told Saul,
10:11 has happened to the son of **K**?
10:21 Then Saul, the son of **K**,
14:51 **K** (Saul's father) and Ner
2Sm 21:14 in the tomb of Saul's father **K**.
1Ch 8:30 then Zur, **K**, Baal, Nadab,
8:33 Ner was the father of **K**.
8:33 **K** was the father of Saul.
9:36 then Zur, **K**, Baal, Nadab,
9:39 Ner was the father of **K**.
9:39 **K** was the father of Saul.
12:1 banished by Saul, son of **K**.
23:21 sons were Eleazar and **K**.
23:22 Their cousins, the sons of **K**,
24:29 descendants through **K**),
26:28 the seer, Saul (son of **K**),
2Ch 29:12 Merari's descendants were **K**,
Est 2:5 and the great-grandson of **K**.
2:6 (**K** had been taken captive from
Act 13:21 God gave them Saul, son of **K**,

Kishi (1)

1Ch 6:44 Ethan was the son of **K**,

Kishion (2)

Jos 19:20 Rabbith, **K**, Ebez,
21:28 tribe of Issachar: **K**, Daberath,

Kishon (6)

Jdg 4:7 troops to you at the **K** River.
4:13 to come to the **K** River.
5:21 The **K** River swept them away
5:21 away — that old river, the **K**.
1Ki 18:40 and Elijah took them to the **K**
Psa 83:9 to Sisera and Jabin at the **K**

Kislon (1)

Num 34:21 Elidad, son of **K**, from the tribe

kiss (23)

Gen 27:26 "Come here and give me a **k**,
27:27 He went over and gave him a **k**.
31:28 You didn't even let me **k** my
2Sm 15:5 take hold of him, and **k** him.
20:9 with his right hand to **k** him.
1Ki 19:20 "Please let me **k** my father and
Job 31:27 I threw them a **k** with my hand,
Psa 2:12 **K** the Son, or he will become
Pro 5:3 Her **k** is smoother than oil,
24:26 is ⌊like⌋ a **k** on the lips.
Sos 1:2 Let him **k** me with the kisses of
8:1 on the street, I would **k** you,
Hos 13:2 and **k** calf-shaped idols."
Mat 26:48 He said, "The one I **k** is the
Mar 14:44 He said, "The one I **k** is the
Luk 7:45 You didn't give me a **k**.
22:47 He came close to Jesus to **k**
22:48 the Son of Man with a **k**?"
Rom 16:16 Greet each other with a holy **k**.
1Co 16:20 Greet each other with a holy **k**.
2Co 13:12 one another with a holy **k**.
1Th 5:26 and sisters with a holy **k**.
1Pe 5:14 each other with a **k** of love.

kissed (22)

Gen 29:11 Then Jacob **k** Rachel and
29:13 He hugged and **k** him and
31:55 Early the next morning Laban **k**
33:4 arms around him, and **k** him.
45:15 He **k** all his brothers and cried
48:10 and Israel hugged them and **k**
Gen 50:1 cried over him, and **k** him.
Exo 4:27 the mountain of God, he **k** him.
18:7 the ground and **k** Jethro.
Rut 1:9 When she **k** them goodbye,
1:14 Then Orpah **k** her
1Sm 10:1 Saul's head, **k** him, and said,
20:41 Then they **k** each other and
2Sm 14:33 And the king **k** Absalom.
19:39 The king **k** Barzillai and
1Ki 19:18 whose mouths have not **k** him."
Psa 85:10 and peace have **k**.
Mat 26:49 Rabbi!" and **k** him.
Mar 14:45 "Rabbi!" and **k** him.
Luk 7:38 **k** them over and over again,
15:20 arms around him, and **k** him.
Act 20:37 arms around Paul and **k** him.

kisses (3)

Pro 7:13 She grabs him and **k** him and
27:6 but an enemy's **k** are too much
Sos 1:2 Let him kiss me with the **k** of

kissing (1)

Luk 7:45 she has not stopped **k** my feet.

kitchens (1)

Eze 46:24 "These are the **k** where the

kites (2)

Lev 11:14 **k**, all types of buzzards,
Dtr 14:13 buzzards, all types of **k**,

Kitron (1)

Jdg 1:30 who lived at **K** or Nahalol.

Kiyyun (1)

Amo 5:26 as your king and the star **K**,

knead (2)

Gen 18:6 of flour, **k** it, and make bread."
Jer 7:18 and women **k** dough to make

kneaded (2)

1Sm 28:24 She took flour, **k** it,
2Sm 13:8 She took dough, **k** it,

knee (2)

Isa 45:23 "Every **k** will bow to me and
Eze 7:17 and every **k** will be as weak as

kneel (11)

Gen 24:11 The servant had the camels **k**
Jdg 7:5 those who **k** down to drink."
Est 3:2 But Mordecai would not **k** and
3:5 saw that Mordecai did not **k**
Job 31:10 and let other ⌊men⌋ **k** over her.
39:3 They **k** down to give birth and
Psa 22:29 who go down to the dust will **k**
72:9 May the people of the desert **k**
95:6 Let's **k** in front of the LORD,
Eph 3:14 This is the reason I **k** in the
Php 2:10 and in the world below will **k**

kneeled (1)

2Ch 29:29 with him **k** and bowed down.

kneeling (3)

1Ki 8:54 where he had been **k** with his
Est 3:2 **k** and bowing to Haman with
Mar 15:19 and **k** in front of him with false

knees (18)

Dtr 28:35 The LORD will afflict your **k**
Jdg 11:35 You've brought me to my **k**!
1Ki 19:18 Israel whose **k** have not knelt
Job 3:12 Why did **k** welcome me?
4:4 When **k** were weak,
Psa 17:13 Bring them to their **k**!
20:8 will sink to their **k** and fall,
109:24 My **k** give way because I have
Isa 35:3 limp hands. Steady weak **k**.
66:12 arms and cuddled on her **k**.
Eze 21:7 and their **k** will become as
47:4 The water came up to my **k**.
Dan 5:6 and his **k** knocked against
6:10 each day he got down on his **k**
Dan 10:10 made my hands and **k** shake.
Nah 2:10 **K** are knocking. Every stomach
Mar 1:40 The man fell to his **k** and
Heb 12:12 your tired arms and weak **k**.

knelt (31)

Gen 24:26 The man **k**, bowing to the
24:48 I **k**, bowing down to the LORD.
43:28 Then they **k**, bowing down.
Exo 4:31 had seen their misery, they **k**,
12:27 Egyptians.'" Then the people **k**,
34:8 Immediately, Moses **k**,
Num 22:31 So Balaam **k**, bowing with his
Jdg 7:6 All the rest of the men **k** down
1Sm 24:8 David **k** down with his face
28:14 Saul **k** down with his face
1Ki 1:16 Bathsheba **k** and bowed down
19:18 Israel whose knees have not **k**
2Ki 1:13 group went up the hill and **k**
1Ch 29:20 God of their ancestors and **k**
2Ch 6:13 He stood on the platform, **k** in
7:3 they **k** down with their faces on
Ezr 9:5 with my clothes torn, I **k** down,
Dan 8:17 and immediately **k** down.
Mat 17:14 up to Jesus, **k** in front of him,
27:29 They **k** in front of him and
Mar 10:17 man came running to him and **k**
Luk 5:8 he **k** in front of Jesus and said,
7:38 and **k** at his feet. She was
22:41 throw, **k** down, and prayed,
Jon 11:32 she **k** at his feet and said,
Act 7:60 Then he **k** down and shouted,
9:40 He **k** and prayed. Then he
16:29 He was trembling as he **k** in
20:36 he **k** down and prayed with all
21:5 We **k** on the beach,
Rom 11:4 have not **k** to worship Baal."

knew (104)

Gen 8:11 Then Noah **k** that the water
38:9 But Onan **k** that the
Exo 1:8 who **k** nothing about Joseph,
2:14 thought that everyone **k** what
38:23 and he **k** how to embroider
Num 22:37 You **k** I'd be able to reward
Dtr 11:28 other gods you never **k**.
13:6 and your ancestors never **k**.
28:33 People you never **k** will eat
28:36 and your ancestors never **k**.
28:64 you nor your ancestors ever **k**.
Jos 24:31 who outlived him and who **k**
Jdg 13:21 Then Manoah **k** that this had
1Sm 3:13 because he **k** about his sons'
3:20 to Beersheba **k** Samuel was
20:9 If I **k** for sure that my father had
20:33 Then Jonathan **k** his father
22:15 I **k** nothing at all about this."
22:17 "When they **k** David was
22:22 David told Abiathar, "I **k** that
26:12 No one saw them, **k** about it,
28:14 Then Saul **k** it was Samuel.
2Sm 1:10 since I **k** he couldn't survive
3:37 day all the people of Israel **k**
11:16 Uriah at the place where he **k**
14:1 Joab, Zeruiah's son, **k** the king
1Ch 12:32 times and **k** what Israel should
2Ch 33:13 Then Manasseh **k** that the
Neh 4:15 that we **k** about their plots
9:10 you **k** how arrogantly they
Est 1:14 wise men who **k** the times,
Job 23:3 "If only I **k** where I could find
31:21 because I **k** that others would
Psa 55:13 my best friend, one I **k** so well!
Ecc 12:9 taught the people what he **k**.
Isa 48:7 that you already **k** about them.
Jer 1:5 you in the womb, I **k** you.
32:8 Then I **k** that the LORD had
41:4 before anyone **k** about it,
44:15 Then all the men who **k** that
Eze 28:19 All the nations who **k** you are
Dan 1:20 he found that they **k** ten times
5:22 even though you **k** all this.
Jnh 1:10 They **k** that he was running
4:2 I **k** that you are a merciful and
Mat 9:4 Jesus **k** what they were
12:15 He **k** about this, so he left that

Mat 12:25 Since Jesus **k** what they were
16:8 Jesus **k** about their
21:45 they **k** that he was talking
25:24 I **k** that you are a hard person to
25:26 If you **k** that I harvest where I
26:10 Since Jesus **k** what was going
27:18 Pilate **k** that they had handed
Mar 1:34 After all, they **k** who he was.
2:8 At once, Jesus **k** inwardly
5:33 She **k** what had happened to
6:20 Herod **k** that John was a fair
8:17 Jesus **k** what they were
12:12 They **k** that he had directed
15:10 Pilate **k** that the chief priests
Luk 4:41 they **k** he was the Messiah.
5:22 Jesus **k** what they were
6:8 But Jesus **k** what they were
8:53 because they **k** she was dead.
9:47 Jesus **k** what they were
11:17 Since Jesus **k** what they were
12:47 "The servant who **k** what his
19:22 You **k** that I was a tough
19:22 You **k** that I take what isn't
20:19 They **k** that he had directed
Jon 2:9 who had poured the water **k**.
2:25 He **k** what people were really
4:1 Jesus **k** that the Pharisees had
4:10 "If you only **k** what God's gift is
5:6 the man lying there and **k** that
6:6 him but already **k** what to do.
6:64 "Jesus **k** from the beginning
8:19 If you **k** me, you would also
11:57 whoever **k** where Jesus was
13:1 Jesus **k** that the time had come
13:3 Jesus **k** that. He also knew that
13:3 He also **k** that he had come
13:11 (Jesus **k** who was going to
13:28 No one at the table **k** why
16:19 Jesus **k** they wanted to ask
17:25 Yet, I **k** you, and these
18:2 Judas, who betrayed him, **k** the
18:4 Jesus **k** everything that was
19:28 After this, when Jesus **k** that
21:12 They **k** he was the Lord.
Act 2:30 David was a prophet and **k** that
2:31 David **k** that the Messiah
3:10 They **k** that he was the man
7:18 who **k** nothing about Joseph,
16:3 he **k** that Timothy's father
18:24 an eloquent speaker and **k** how
18:25 about Jesus but **k** only about
24:22 Felix **k** the way ⌊of Christ⌋
Rom 1:21 They **k** God but did not praise
8:29 he already **k** his people
11:2 people whom he **k** long ago.
2Co 1:13 you already **k** before you read
1Pe 1:2 God the Father **k** you long ago

knife (6)

Gen 22:6 the burning coals and the **k**.
22:10 Next, Abraham picked up the **k**
Exo 4:25 Then Zipporah took a flint **k**,
Jdg 19:29 he arrived home, he got a **k**.
Pro 23:2 and put a **k** to your throat if you
Jer 36:23 cut them off with a scribe's **k**

knitted (4)

Lev 13:48 that is woven or **k** from linen or
13:58 from the woven or **k** clothing
13:59 that is woven or **k** from linen
Psa 139:13 You **k** me together inside my

knives (4)

Jos 5:2 spoke to Joshua, "Make flint **k**,
5:3 So Joshua made flint **k** and
Ezr 1:9 30 silver dishes: 1,000 **k**: 29
Pro 30:14 and whose jaws are ⌊like⌋ **k**,

knock (9)

Dtr 24:20 never **k** down all of them.
Job 9:17 He would **k** me down with a
Psa 58:6 **k** the teeth out of their mouths.
Eze 34:21 and you **k** down all the sick
39:3 Then I will **k** the bow out of
Mat 7:7 **K**, and the door will be opened
Luk 11:9 **K**, and the door will be opened
Luk 12:36 door at their master's **k** when
13:25 **k** at the door, and say, 'Sir,

knocked (8)

Exo 9:25 All over Egypt the hail **k** down
1Ch 4:41 the men listed here **k** down
Job 4:10 lions have had their teeth **k** out.
Dan 5:6 his knees **k** against each other.
10:17 the wind has been **k** out of me."
Luk 9:42 the demon **k** the boy to the
Jon 2:15 coins and **k** over their tables.
Act 12:13 Peter **k** on the door of the

knocking (4)

Sos 5:2 My beloved is **k**. Open to me,
Nah 2:10 Knees are **k**. Every stomach
Act 12:16 But Peter kept **k**. When they
Rev 3:20 I'm standing at the door and **k**.

knocks (3)

Exo 21:27 If the owner **k** out the tooth of
Mat 7:8 and for the one who **k**,
Luk 11:10 and for the person who **k**,

know (939)

Gen 4:9 "I don't **k**," he answered.
12:11 "I **k** that you're a beautiful
15:13 God said to Abram, "You can **k**
16:5 I **k** that I gave my slave to you,
18:21 are true. If not, I will **k** it."
19:33 He didn't **k** when she came to
19:35 He didn't **k** when she came to
20:6 "Yes, I **k** that you did this with
21:26 "I don't **k** who did this.
22:12 Now I **k** that you fear God,
24:14 This way I'll **k** that you've
24:49 so that I will **k** what to do."
27:2 I don't **k** when I'm going to die.
28:16 in this place, and I didn't **k** it!"
29:5 asked them, "Do you **k** Laban,
30:26 You **k** how much work I've
30:29 Jacob responded, "You **k** how
31:6 You **k** that I have worked as
31:32 (Jacob didn't **k** that Rachel had
33:13 Jacob said to him, "Sir, you **k**
38:16 Since he didn't **k** she was his
41:39 God has let you **k** all this,
42:7 But he acted as if he didn't **k**
42:23 They didn't **k** that Joseph could
42:33 'This is how I'll **k** that you're
42:34 Then I'll **k** that you're not spies
43:7 How could we possibly **k** he
44:15 Don't you **k** that a man like me
44:27 'You **k** that my wife ⌊Rachel⌋
47:18 "you **k** that our money is gone,
48:19 father refused and said, "I **k**,
48:19 and said, "I know, Son, I **k**!
Exo 3:7 I **k** how much they're suffering.
3:19 I **k** that the king of Egypt will
4:14 I **k** he can speak well.
5:2 I don't **k** the LORD,
6:7 You will **k** that I am the LORD
7:5 The Egyptians will **k** that I am
8:10 so that you will **k** that there is
8:22 This way you will **k** that I,
9:14 This is how you will **k** that
9:29 This is how you will **k** that the
9:30 But I **k** that you and your
10:2 This is how you will all **k** that I
10:10 I **k** you're up to no good!
10:26 and we won't **k** what we'll need
14:4 and the Egyptians will **k** that I
14:18 The Egyptians will **k** that I am
16:6 "In the evening you will **k** that
16:12 Then you will **k** that I am the
16:15 because they didn't **k** what it
18:11 Now I **k** that the LORD is
23:9 You **k** what it's like to be
29:46 They will **k** that I am the LORD
31:13 to come so that you will **k** that
32:1 They said to him, "We don't **k**
32:22 "You **k** that these people are
32:23 They said to me, 'We don't **k**
33:12 but you haven't let me **k** whom
33:12 also said, 'I **k** you by name,
33:13 your ways so that I can **k** you
Exo 33:16 How will anyone ever **k** you're
33:17 and I **k** you by name."
34:29 the LORD, but he didn't **k** it.
35:35 They **k** how to embroider violet,
35:35 They **k** how to weave yarn on
36:1 They will **k** how to do all the
Lev 5:1 what you saw or what you **k**,
5:3 (although you **k** what you did),
5:4 (although you **k** what you said),
5:17 but you didn't **k** it — when you
5:18 you didn't **k** what you did),
Num 10:31 You **k** where we can set up
11:16 men who you **k** are leaders
14:34 suffer for your sins and **k** what
16:28 "This is how you will **k** that the
16:30 then you'll **k** that these men
20:14 You **k** all the hardships we've
22:6 I **k** that whomever you bless is
22:34 I didn't **k** you were standing
35:23 However, you didn't **k** the
Dtr 1:39 who are still too young to **k** the
3:19 I **k** you have a lot of livestock.
4:35 things so that you would **k** that
8:2 He wanted to **k** whether or not
9:2 You **k** all about them.
20:20 trees that you **k** are not fruit
22:2 you or you don't **k** who owns it,
22:3 that you don't **k** what to do.
28:33 As long as you live, you will **k**
29:6 I did this so that you would **k**
29:16 You **k** how we lived in Egypt
31:13 who don't **k** these teachings,
31:21 I **k** what their hearts are set on
31:27 I **k** how rebellious you are.
31:29 I **k** that after I die you will
33:9 They said that they didn't **k**
Jos 2:4 But I didn't **k** where they had
2:5 I don't **k** where they went.
2:9 She said to them, "I **k** the
3:4 so that you will **k** which way
3:7 I will do this to let them **k** that I
3:10 "This is how you will **k** that the
4:24 would **k** his mighty power
8:14 However, the king didn't **k** there
14:6 "You **k** what the LORD said to
22:22 He knows, so let Israel **k**!
22:31 "Today we **k** the LORD is
23:13 then you should **k** that the
23:14 You **k** with all your heart and
Jdg 6:37 then I'll **k** that you will rescue
14:4 His father and mother didn't **k**
14:18 you wouldn't **k** my riddle now."
15:11 "Don't you **k** that the
17:13 Then Micah said, "Now I **k** that
18:14 "Do you **k** that there's an ephod,
Rut 2:11 people that you didn't **k** before.
3:3 Don't let him **k** that you're there
3:14 "I hope that no one will ever **k**
3:18 until you **k** how it turns out.
4:4 Then I will **k** that I am next in
1Sm 6:3 and you will **k** why he would
6:9 But if not, we'll **k** it wasn't his
14:3 didn't **k** Jonathan had left.
16:18 One of the officials said, "I **k**
17:28 I **k** how overconfident and
17:46 The whole world will **k** that
17:47 gathered here will **k** that
17:55 live, Your Majesty, I don't **k**."
20:3 must not **k** about this.
20:7 then you'll **k** for sure that he
20:30 "I **k** you've sided with Jesse's
21:2 'No one must **k** anything about
22:3 with you until I **k** what God is
23:1 David was asked, "Did you **k**
24:11 you should **k** and be able to
24:20 Now I **k** that you certainly will
28:1 "You need to **k** that you and
28:2 "you will then **k** what I can do."
28:9 The woman told him, "You **k**
2Sm 1:5 "How do you **k** Saul and his
2:26 Don't you **k** this will end in
3:25 Certainly you must **k** that Ner's
3:38 "Don't you **k** that today a leader,
7:20 since you **k** me so well!
11:20 Didn't you **k** they would shoot
14:22 He said, "Today I **k** that you

2Sm	15:20	I don't even **k** where I'm going?
	17:8	"You **k** your father and his men.
	18:29	but I didn't **k** what it meant."
	19:20	I **k** I've sinned. Today I've come
	19:22	Don't I **k** that I'm king of Israel
	22:44	I did not **k** will serve me.
	24:2	That way I will **k** how many
1Ki	1:11	doesn't ⌊even⌋ **k** about it?
	1:18	and you don't ⌊even⌋ **k**
	2:5	"You **k** what Joab (Zeruiah's
	2:9	You are wise and **k** what to do
	2:15	"You **k** the kingship was mine.
	2:44	Shimei, you **k** in your heart all
	5:3	"You **k** that my father David
	5:6	You **k** we don't have any
	8:39	(You **k** what is in their hearts,
	8:39	because you alone **k** what is in
	8:43	of the world may **k** your name
	8:60	people of the world will **k** that
	18:37	these people will **k** that you,
	20:13	Then you will **k** that I am the
	20:28	Then you will **k** that I am the
	22:3	"Do you **k** that Ramoth in
2Ki	2:3	They asked him, "Do you **k**
	2:3	He answered, "Yes, I **k**.
	2:5	They asked, "Do you **k** that the
	2:5	He answered, "Yes, I **k**.
	4:1	You **k** how he feared the LORD.
	4:9	"I **k** he's a holy man of God.
	5:15	"Now I **k** that there's no god in
	7:12	said, "They **k** we're starving,
	8:12	Elisha answered, "I **k** the evil
	9:11	He answered, "You **k** the man
	17:26	in the cities of Samaria don't **k**
	17:26	them because they don't **k**
	19:19	on earth will **k** that you alone
	19:27	I **k** when you ⌊get up⌋ and sit
1Ch	17:18	and since you **k** me so well!
	21:2	I may **k** how many ⌊people⌋
	28:9	learn to **k** your father's God.
	29:17	I **k**, my God, that you examine
2Ch	1:11	God replied to Solomon, "I **k**
	2:7	He should **k** how to make
	2:8	I **k** that your servants are
	6:29	all who **k** suffering or pain,
	6:30	(You **k** what is in their hearts,
	6:30	because you alone **k** what is in
	6:33	of the world may **k** your name
	13:5	Don't you **k** that the LORD God
	20:12	We don't **k** what to do,
	25:16	He said, "I **k** that God has
	32:13	Don't you **k** what I and my
Ezr	4:12	Your Majesty, you should **k**
	4:13	You should also **k** that if this
	4:16	We want the king to **k** that if
	5:8	Your Majesty should **k** that we
	7:25	who **k** your God's Teachings
	7:25	who doesn't **k** the Teachings.
Neh	2:16	The officials didn't **k** where I
	4:11	"Before they **k** what is
Est	4:11	king's provinces **k** that no one
Job	3:8	the day (those who **k** how
	5:24	"You will **k** peace in your tent.
	8:9	yesterday, and we **k** nothing.
	9:2	"Yes, I **k** that this is true.
	9:28	I **k** that you won't declare me
	9:35	But I **k** that I am not like that."
	10:2	Let me **k** why you are
	10:7	You **k** I'm not guilty,
	10:13	I **k** this is what you did.
	11:6	and you would **k** that God
	11:8	of hell. What can you **k**?
	12:3	who doesn't **k** these things?
	12:9	What creature doesn't **k** that the
	13:2	all, I **k** it as well as you do.
	13:18	I **k** that I will be declared
	14:21	and he doesn't **k** it.
	15:9	What do you **k** that we don't
	15:9	do you know that we don't **k**?
	18:21	to those who do not **k** God."
	19:6	then I want you to **k** that God
	19:25	But I **k** that my defender lives,
	19:29	Then you will **k** there is a
	20:4	"Don't you **k** that from ancient
	20:20	He will never **k** peace in his
	21:14	We don't want to **k** your ways.
Job	21:19	person so that he would **k** that
	21:27	"You see, I **k** your thoughts and
	22:13	You ask, 'What does God **k**?
	23:5	I want to **k** the words he would
	24:16	They do not ⌊even⌋ **k** the light,
	30:23	I **k** you will lead me to death,
	31:6	and he will **k** I have integrity.
	32:6	was afraid to tell you what I **k**.
	32:10	Let me tell you what I **k**.'
	32:17	I'll tell you what I **k**.
	32:22	I don't **k** how to flatter.
	34:33	Tell me what you **k**.
	37:15	Do you **k** how God controls
	37:16	Do you **k** how the clouds drift
	38:5	Certainly, you **k**! Who stretched
	38:18	Tell me, if you **k** all of this!
	38:20	so that you may **k** the path to
	38:21	You must **k** because you were
	38:33	Do you **k** the laws of the sky or
	39:1	"Do you **k** the time when the
	39:2	months they are pregnant or **k**
	42:2	"I **k** that you can do everything
	42:3	too mysterious for me to **k**.
Psa	4:3	**K** that the LORD singles out
	9:10	Those who **k** your name trust
	9:20	Let the nations **k** that they are
	18:43	I did not **k** will serve me:
	20:6	Now I **k** that the LORD will
	35:11	me things I **k** nothing about.
	36:10	your mercy to those who **k** you
	38:9	You **k** all my desires,
	39:4	that I may **k** how temporary my
	40:9	You **k** that, O LORD.
	41:11	When you do this, I **k** that you
	46:10	Then you will **k** that I am God.
	50:11	I **k** every bird in the mountains.
	56:9	This I **k**: God is on my side.
	59:13	Then they will **k** that God rules
	69:5	O God, you **k** my stupidity,
	69:19	You **k** that I have been insulted,
	73:11	"What does God **k**?"
	73:11	"Does the Most High **k**
	78:6	next generation would **k** them.
	79:6	the nations that do not **k** you,
	82:5	Wicked people do not **k** or
	88:12	Will anyone **k** about your
	89:15	Blessed are the people who **k**
	91:14	you because you **k** my name.
	92:6	A stupid person cannot **k** and a
	94:10	Do you think he doesn't **k**
	103:7	He let Moses **k** his ways.
	103:7	He let the Israelites **k** the
	109:27	Then they will **k** that this is
	119:75	I **k** that your regulations are fair,
	119:79	to **k** your written instructions.
	119:125	to **k** your written instructions.
	135:5	I **k** that the LORD is great,
	139:1	examined me, and you **k** me.
	139:2	You alone **k** when I sit down
	139:4	you **k** all about it, LORD.
	139:23	me, O God, and **k** my mind.
	139:23	Test me, and **k** my thoughts.
	140:12	I **k** that the LORD will defend
	142:3	you ⌊already⌋ **k** what I am
	143:8	Let me **k** the way that I should
	147:20	The other nations do not **k** the
Pro	4:19	They do not **k** what makes
	9:18	But he does not **k** that the
	24:12	you say, "We didn't **k** this,"
	24:12	one who guards your soul **k** it?
	27:1	because you do not **k** what
	30:4	Certainly, you must **k**!
Ecc	1:17	⌊Now⌋ I **k** that this is ⌊like⌋
	8:5	mind of a wise person will **k**
	8:7	They don't **k** what the future
	8:12	Still, I **k** with certainty that it
	8:17	a wise person claims to **k**,
	9:5	The living **k** that they will die,
	9:5	but the dead don't **k** anything.
	10:15	because they don't even **k** the
	11:2	because you don't **k** what
	11:5	Just as you don't **k** how the
	11:6	You don't **k** whether this field or
Sos	1:8	If you do not **k**, most beautiful
	6:12	I did not **k** that I had become
Isa	1:3	Oxen **k** their owners,
Isa	1:3	and donkeys **k** where their
	1:3	Israel doesn't **k** ⌊its owner⌋.
	3:12	and you don't **k** which way to
	9:9	who live in Samaria will **k** it.
	19:21	The Egyptians will **k** the LORD
	37:20	on earth will **k** that you alone
	37:28	I **k** when you ⌊get up⌋ and sit
	40:21	Don't you **k**? Haven't you heard?
	40:28	Don't you **k**? Haven't you heard?
	41:20	People will see and **k**.
	41:22	them and **k** what their outcome
	41:23	so that we may **k** that you are
	41:26	so that we could **k** it?
	43:10	my servant so that you can **k**
	44:8	is no ⌊other⌋ rock; I **k** of none.
	44:9	do not see or **k** anything,
	44:18	They don't **k** or understand
	45:3	Then you will **k** that I,
	45:4	although you don't **k** me.
	45:5	although you don't **k** me,
	45:6	west people will **k** that there is
	47:11	You won't **k** how to keep it
	48:4	I **k** that you are stubborn.
	48:6	hidden things that you do not **k**.
	48:8	I **k** that you've acted very
	49:23	Then you will **k** that I am the
	49:26	Then all humanity will **k** that I
	50:4	so I will **k** how to encourage
	50:7	I **k** that I will not be put to
	51:7	people who **k** righteousness,
	52:6	my people will **k** my name.
	52:6	⌊they will **k**⌋ that I am the one
	55:5	a nation that you don't **k**,
	55:5	and a nation that doesn't **k** you
	56:10	None of them **k** anything.
	58:2	day and want to **k** my ways.
	59:8	They don't **k** the way of peace.
	59:8	on them will never **k** peace.
	59:12	We **k** our wrongdoings.
	60:16	Then you will **k** that I am the
	63:16	Even though Abraham doesn't **k**
Jer	1:6	I do not **k** how to speak.
	2:8	with my teachings didn't **k** me.
	2:19	You should **k** and see how evil
	4:22	They don't **k** me. They are
	4:22	and they don't **k** how to do
	5:4	They don't **k** the way of the
	5:5	They **k** the way of the LORD
	5:15	You don't **k** the language of this
	6:15	They don't even **k** how to
	6:27	You will **k** how to test their
	7:9	other gods that you do not **k**.
	8:7	Even storks **k** when it's time to
	8:7	and cranes **k** when it's time to
	8:7	But my people don't **k** that I,
	8:12	They don't even **k** how to
	9:3	and they don't **k** me,"
	9:24	that they understand and **k** me.
	10:23	O LORD, I **k** that the way
	10:25	on the nations who don't **k** you
	11:19	I didn't **k** that they were plotting
	12:3	You **k** me, O LORD. You see
	12:4	They think that God doesn't **k**
	13:12	'We **k** that every bottle will be
	15:15	You should **k** that I've been
	16:21	Then they will **k** that my name
	17:16	You **k** what came out of my
	18:23	**k** that they plan to kill me.
	22:16	this what it means to **k** me?"
	24:7	I will give them the desire to **k**
	26:15	But **k** for certain that if you put
	29:11	I **k** the plans that I have for you,
	29:23	I **k** what they have done.
	31:34	by saying, '**K** the LORD.'
	31:34	will **k** me," declares the LORD,
	33:3	things that you do not **k**.
	36:19	let anyone **k** where you are."
	38:24	"Don't let anyone **k** about this
	40:14	They asked him, "Do you **k**
	40:15	No one will **k** about it.
	42:19	You need to **k** that I am
	42:22	But now, you need to **k** that
	44:28	Egypt will **k** whose words have
	44:29	that you will **k** that my threats
	48:30	I **k** how arrogant they are,"
	50:24	be caught, but you won't **k** it.

Eze 5:13 you will **k** that I, the LORD,
6:7 Then you will **k** that I am the
6:10 Then you will **k** that I am the
6:13 Then you will **k** that I am the
6:14 Then they will **k** that I am the
7:4 Then you will **k** that I am the
7:9 Then you will **k** that I am the
7:27 Then they will **k** that I am the
11:5 But I **k** what's going through
11:10 Then you will **k** that I am the
11:12 Then you will **k** that I am the
12:15 Then they will **k** that I am the
12:16 Then they will **k** that I am the
12:20 Then they will **k** that I am the
13:9 Then you will **k** that I am the
13:14 Then you will **k** that I am the
13:21 Then you will **k** that I am the
13:23 Then you will **k** that I am the
14:8 Then you will **k** that I am the
14:23 Then you will **k** that everything
15:7 Then they will **k** that I am the
16:62 and you will **k** that I am the
17:12 'Don't you **k** what this means?'
17:21 Then you will **k** that I,
17:24 the trees in the field will **k** that
20:12 us so that they would **k** that I,
20:20 and you so that you will **k** that
20:26 them so that they would **k** that
20:38 Then you will **k** that I am the
20:42 Then you will **k** that I am the
20:44 Then you will **k** that I am the
20:48 Then everyone will **k** that I,
21:5 Then everyone will **k** that I,
22:16 Then you will **k** that I am the
22:22 Then you will **k** that I,
23:49 Then they will **k** that I am the
24:24 Then you will **k** that I am the
24:27 Then they will **k** that I am the
25:5 Then you will **k** that I am the
25:7 Then you will **k** that I am the
25:11 Then they will **k** that I am the
25:14 Edomites will **k** my revenge,
25:17 Then they will **k** that I am the
26:6 Then they will **k** that I am the
28:22 Then people will **k** that I am
28:23 Then they will **k** that I am the
28:24 Then they will **k** that I am the
28:26 Then they will **k** that I am the
29:6 those living in Egypt will **k** that
29:9 Then you will **k** that I am the
29:16 Then they will **k** that I am the
29:21 Then they will **k** that I am the
30:8 Then they will **k** that I am the
30:19 Then they will **k** that I am the
30:25 Then they will **k** that I am the
30:26 Then they will **k** that I am the
32:15 Then they will **k** that I am the
33:29 Then people will **k** that I am
33:33 true — these people will **k** that
34:27 Then they will **k** that I am the
34:30 Then they will **k** that I,
35:4 Then you will **k** that I am the
35:9 Then you will **k** that I am the
35:12 Then you will **k** that I,
35:15 Then you will **k** that I am the
36:11 Then you will **k** that I am the
36:23 Then the nations will **k** that I
36:32 I want you to **k** that I'm not
36:36 nations that are left will **k** that I,
36:38 Then they will **k** that I am the
37:3 I answered, "Only you **k**,
37:6 Then you will **k** that I am the
37:13 you will **k** that I am the LORD,
37:14 Then you will **k** that I,
37:28 Then the nations will **k** that I,
38:14 live safely, and you will **k** it.
38:16 land so that nations will **k** me.
38:23 Then they will **k** that I am the
39:6 Then they will **k** that I am the
39:7 Then the nations will **k** that I
39:22 the people of Israel will **k** that I
39:23 Then the nations will **k** that the
39:28 Then my people will **k** that I
Dan 2:3 I want to **k** what the dream
2:8 some time because you **k** that
2:9 Then I'll **k** that you can explain
Dan 2:23 us what the king wants to **k**."
2:30 **k** your innermost thoughts.
3:18 But if he doesn't, you should **k**,
4:9 I **k** the spirit of the holy gods is
4:17 every living creature will **k** that
5:9 His nobles didn't **k** what to do.
5:23 can't see, hear, or **k** anything.
7:19 Then I wanted to **k** the truth
7:20 I also wanted to **k** about the ten
10:20 He asked, "Do you **k** why I
11:32 But the people who **k** their God
Hos 2:20 Then you will **k** the LORD.
5:3 I **k** Ephraim, and Israel isn't a
5:4 and they don't **k** the LORD.
6:3 Let's get to **k** the LORD.
6:6 I want you to **k** me,
8:4 own princes, princes I didn't **k**.
9:7 this happens,⌋ Israel will **k** it.
Joe 2:27 You will **k** that I am in Israel.
3:17 "You will **k** that I am the LORD
Amo 3:10 destructive acts don't **k** how
5:12 I **k** that your crimes are
Oba 1:7 and you won't even **k** about it.
Jnh 1:12 I **k** that I'm responsible for this
Mic 3:1 You should **k** justice.
4:12 They don't **k** the thoughts of the
6:5 to Gilgal so that you may **k**
Zec 2:9 Then you will **k** that the LORD
2:11 Then you will **k** that the LORD
4:5 "Don't you **k** what they mean?"
4:9 Then you will **k** that the LORD
4:13 He asked me, "Don't you **k**
6:15 Then you will **k** the LORD of
Mal 2:4 Then you will **k** that I sent you
Mat 6:3 don't let your left hand **k** what
7:11 Even though you're evil, you **k**
7:16 You will **k** them by what they
7:20 So you will **k** them by what
8:9 As you **k**, I'm in a chain of
9:6 I want you to **k** that the Son of
9:30 "Don't let anyone **k** about this!"
10:33 Father in heaven that I don't **k**
10:33 others that he doesn't **k** me.
15:17 Don't you **k** that whatever goes
20:25 "You **k** that the rulers of nations
21:27 answered Jesus, "We don't **k**."
22:16 we **k** that you tell the truth and
22:29 mistaken because you don't **k**
24:32 you **k** that summer is near.
24:33 you **k** that he is near,
24:36 in heaven and the Son don't **k**.
24:42 because you don't **k** on what
25:12 'I don't even **k** who you are!'
25:13 because you don't **k** the day or
26:2 "You **k** that the Passover will
26:34 times that you don't **k** me."
26:35 I'll never say that I don't **k** you!"
26:70 "I don't **k** what you're talking
26:72 "I don't **k** the man!"
26:74 "I don't **k** the man!"
26:75 times that you don't **k** me."
27:65 tomb as secure as you **k** how."
28:5 I **k** you're looking for Jesus,
Mar 1:24 I **k** who you are — the Holy One
2:10 I want you to **k** that the Son of
4:27 although the man doesn't **k**
5:43 not to let anyone **k** about this.
7:18 Don't you **k** that whatever goes
7:24 He didn't want anyone to **k** that
9:6 (Peter didn't **k** how to respond.
9:30 anyone to **k** where he was
10:19 You **k** the commandments:
10:42 "You **k** that the acknowledged
11:33 answered Jesus, "We don't **k**."
12:14 we **k** that you tell the truth.
12:24 mistaken because you don't **k**
13:28 you **k** summer is near.
13:29 you **k** that he is near,
13:32 in heaven and the Son don't **k**.
13:33 You don't **k** the exact time.
13:35 because you don't **k** when the
14:30 times that you don't **k** me."
14:31 never say that I don't **k** you."
14:40 They didn't even **k** what they
14:68 it by saying, "I don't **k** him,
14:71 "I don't **k** this man you're
Mar 14:72 times that you don't **k** me."
Luk 1:4 In this way you will **k** that what
1:77 You will make his people **k**
2:43 but his parents didn't **k** it.
4:34 I **k** who you are — the Holy One
5:24 I want you to **k** that the Son of
7:8 As you **k**, I'm in a chain of
7:39 he would **k** what sort of woman
8:46 I **k** power has gone out of me."
9:7 He didn't **k** what to make of it.
9:33 Peter didn't **k** what he was
9:45 They didn't **k** what he meant.
11:13 Even though you're evil, you **k**
12:9 that I don't **k** those people who
12:9 tell others that they don't **k** me.
12:18 He said, 'I **k** what I'll do.
12:48 But the servant who didn't **k**
12:56 But for some reason you don't **k**
13:25 'I don't **k** who you are.'
13:27 'I don't **k** who you are.
16:4 I **k** what I'll do so that people
18:20 You **k** the commandments:
18:34 they didn't **k** what he meant.
19:15 I want to **k** how much each one
20:7 they didn't **k** who gave John
20:21 we **k** that you're right in what
21:30 you **k** without being told that
21:31 you **k** that the kingdom of God
22:34 times that you don't **k** me."
22:57 saying, "I don't **k** him, woman."
22:60 But Peter said, "I don't **k** what
22:61 times that you don't **k** me."
23:34 They don't **k** what they're
24:18 doesn't **k** what has happened
Jon 1:26 Someone you don't **k** is
1:31 I didn't **k** who he was.
1:33 I didn't **k** who he was.
1:33 you'll **k** that person is the one
1:48 "How do you **k** anything about
2:9 He didn't **k** where it had come
3:2 we **k** that God has sent you as
3:8 but you don't **k** where the wind
3:11 We **k** what we're talking about,
3:31 **k** nothing but what is on earth,
4:22 You don't **k** what you're
4:22 We ⌊Jews⌋ **k** what we're
4:25 "I **k** that the Messiah is coming.
4:32 to eat that you don't **k** about."
4:42 and we **k** that he really is the
5:13 healed didn't **k** who Jesus was.
5:32 and I **k** that what he says about
5:42 But I **k** what kind of people you
6:42 Don't we **k** his father and
6:69 Besides, we believe and **k** that
7:17 the will of God will **k** if what
7:26 Can it be that the rulers really **k**
7:27 However, we **k** where this man
7:27 no one will **k** where he is from."
7:28 he said loudly, "You **k** me,
7:28 and you **k** where I come from.
7:28 He's the one you don't **k**.
7:29 I **k** him because I am from him
7:49 it doesn't **k** Moses' Teachings."
8:14 is true because I **k** where
8:14 However, you don't **k** where I
8:19 "You don't **k** me or my Father.
8:19 you would also **k** my Father."
8:27 (The Jews didn't **k** that he was
8:28 then you'll **k** that I am the one
8:32 You will **k** the truth,
8:37 I **k** that you're Abraham's
8:44 He doesn't **k** what the truth is.
8:52 "Now we **k** that you're
8:55 However, I **k** him. If I would say
8:55 If I would say that I didn't **k** him,
8:55 But I do **k** him, and I do what
9:12 The man answered, "I don't **k**."
9:20 His parents replied, "We **k** that
9:21 But we don't **k** how he got his
9:24 We **k** that this man who gave
9:25 "I don't **k** if he's a sinner or not.
9:25 But I do **k** one thing.
9:29 We **k** that God spoke to Moses,
9:29 but we don't **k** where this man
9:30 You don't **k** where he's from.
9:31 We **k** that God doesn't listen to

Jon 10:14 I **k** my sheep as the Father
10:14 My sheep **k** me as I know the
10:14 know me as I **k** the Father.
10:27 and I **k** who they are.
10:38 Then you will **k** and recognize
11:22 But even now I **k** that God will
11:24 Martha answered Jesus, "I **k**
11:49 "You people don't **k** anything.
12:16 At first Jesus' disciples didn't **k**
12:27 deeply troubled now to **k** how
12:35 don't **k** where they're going.
12:50 I **k** that what he commands is
13:7 "You don't **k** now what I'm
13:18 I **k** the people I've chosen to
13:35 Everyone will **k** that you are
13:38 three times that you don't **k** me.
14:4 You **k** the way to the place
14:5 we don't **k** where you're going.
14:5 So how can we **k** the way?"
14:7 you will also **k** my Father.
14:7 From now on you **k** him
14:9 Don't you **k** me yet,
14:17 because it doesn't see or **k** him.
14:17 You **k** him, because he lives
14:20 On that day you will **k** that I am
14:31 However, I want the world to **k**
15:15 because a servant doesn't **k**
15:21 since they don't **k** the one who
16:30 Now we **k** that you know
16:30 we know that you **k** everything.
17:3 This is eternal life: to **k** you,
17:7 Now they **k** that everything you
17:8 and they **k** for sure that I came
17:25 the world didn't **k** you.
18:21 They **k** what I've said."
19:4 him out to you to let you **k** that
19:10 Don't you **k** that I have the
20:2 and we don't **k** where they've
20:9 They didn't **k** yet what
20:13 and I don't **k** where they've put
20:14 she didn't **k** that it was Jesus.
21:15 you **k** that I love you."
21:16 you **k** that I love you."
21:17 to him, "Lord, you **k** everything.
21:17 You **k** that I love you."
21:24 We **k** that what he says is true.
Act 1:7 "You don't need to **k** about
1:24 you **k** everyone's thoughts.
2:22 You **k** that through this man
2:36 of Israel should **k** beyond
3:16 man, whom you **k**, was healed,
3:17 "And now, brothers, I **k** that like
3:17 you didn't **k** what you were
4:9 You want to **k** how he was
5:7 didn't **k** what had happened.
6:3 people **k** are spiritually wise.
7:40 They told Aaron, 'We don't **k**
8:34 "I would like to **k** who the
10:29 I want to **k** why you sent for
10:37 You **k** what happened
10:38 You **k** that God anointed Jesus
13:27 rulers didn't **k** who Jesus was.
15:7 you **k** what happened some
17:20 like to **k** what they mean."
17:30 when people didn't **k** any better.
19:15 answered them, "I **k** Jesus,
19:25 Demetrius said, "Men, you **k**
19:32 Most of the people didn't even **k**
20:18 "You **k** how I spent all my time
20:22 I don't **k** what will happen to
20:25 "Now I **k** that none of you
20:29 I **k** that fierce wolves will come
20:34 You **k** that I worked to support
21:24 Then everyone will **k** that what
22:14 has chosen you to **k** his will,
22:19 "I said, 'Lord, people here **k**
23:5 I didn't **k** that he is the chief
23:28 I wanted to **k** what they had
24:10 Paul responded, "I **k** that you
25:10 as you **k** very well.
26:4 "All the Jews **k** how I lived the
26:5 They **k** that I lived my life as a
26:27 I **k** you believe them!"
27:23 I **k** this because an angel from
28:22 We **k** that everywhere people
28:28 "You need to **k** that God has

Rom 1:13 I want you to **k**, brothers and
1:32 Although they **k** God's
2:2 We **k** that God's judgment is
2:18 **k** what he wants,
3:19 We **k** that whatever is in
5:3 We **k** that suffering creates
6:3 Don't you **k** that all of us who
6:6 We **k** that the person we used
6:9 We **k** that Christ, who was
6:16 Don't you **k** that if you offer to
7:14 I **k** that God's standards are
7:18 I **k** that nothing good lives in
8:22 We **k** that all creation has been
8:26 because we don't **k** how to
8:28 We **k** that all things work
11:2 Don't you **k** what Elijah says in
13:11 You **k** the times in which we
15:29 I **k** that when I come to you I
1Co 2:12 from God so that we could **k**
3:16 Don't you **k** that you are God's
4:19 Then I'll **k** what these arrogant
5:6 Don't you **k** that a little yeast
6:2 Don't you **k** that God's people
6:3 Don't you **k** that we will judge
6:9 Don't you **k** that wicked people
6:19 Don't you **k** that your body is a
7:16 How do you as a wife **k**
7:16 How do you as a husband **k**
8:1 We **k** that we all have
8:2 Those who think they **k**
8:4 We **k** that the false gods in this
10:1 I want you to **k**, brothers and
12:2 You **k** that when you were
12:3 So I want you to **k** that no one
12:14 As you **k**, the human body is
14:9 how will anyone **k** what you're
14:11 If I don't **k** what a language
14:16 don't **k** what you're saying.
14:35 If they want to **k** anything they
15:34 Some people don't **k** anything
15:58 You **k** that the hard work you
16:15 You **k** that the family of
2Co 1:7 We **k** that as you share our
2:4 but to let you **k** how much
2:14 clear what it means to **k** Christ.
4:14 We **k** that the one who brought
5:1 We **k** that if the life we live
5:6 We **k** that as long as we are
5:11 As people who **k** what it
5:11 that you also **k** what we are.
8:1 we want you to **k** how God
8:9 You **k** about the kindness of
9:2 I **k** how willing you are to help,
10:10 I **k** that someone is saying that
11:6 I **k** what I'm talking about.
12:2 I **k** a follower of Christ who
12:2 I don't **k** whether this happened
12:3 I **k** that this person
12:4 I don't **k** whether this happened
Gal 1:11 I want you to **k**, brothers and
1:22 in Judea didn't **k** me personally.
2:16 Yet, we **k** that people don't
4:8 When you didn't **k** God,
4:9 But now you **k** God,
4:13 You **k** that the first time I
Eph 1:17 as you come to **k** Christ better.
1:18 You will **k** the confidence that
1:19 You will also **k** the unlimited
3:3 You have heard that he let me **k**
3:10 heaven **k** his infinite wisdom.
3:19 You will **k** Christ's love,
5:5 You **k** very well that no person
6:8 You **k** that your heavenly
6:9 You **k** that there is one master
6:21 that you will **k** how I'm getting
6:22 that you may **k** how we're doing
Php 1:12 I want you to **k**, brothers and
1:16 out of love **k** that God has
1:19 I **k** that I will be set free through
1:22 I don't **k** which I would prefer.
1:25 Since I'm convinced of this, I **k**
2:22 But you **k** what kind of person
4:5 Let everyone **k** how
4:6 But in every situation let God **k**
4:12 I **k** how to live in poverty or
4:15 You Philippians also **k** that in

Col 1:6 At that time you came to **k**
1:27 throughout the world to **k**
2:1 I want you to **k** how hard I work
3:24 You **k** that your real master will
4:1 because you **k** that you also
4:6 thought out so that you **k** how
4:8 so that you may **k** how we are
1Th 1:4 because we **k** that God loves
1:5 We **k** this because the Good
1:5 In the same way you **k** what
2:1 You **k**, brothers and sisters,
2:2 As you **k**, we suffered rough
2:5 As you **k**, we never used
2:11 You **k** very well that we treated
3:3 You **k** that we're destined to
3:4 And as you **k**, that's what
4:2 You **k** what orders we gave
4:4 Each of you should **k** that
4:5 way of people who don't **k** God.
5:2 You **k** very well that the day of
2Th 2:6 You **k** what it is that now holds
3:7 You **k** what you must do to
1Ti 1:8 We **k** that Moses' Teachings
3:5 (If a man doesn't **k** how to
3:15 I want you to **k** how people
4:3 who believe and **k** the truth.
2Ti 1:12 I **k** whom I trust. I'm convinced
1:15 You **k** that everyone in the
1:18 You **k** very well that he did
2:23 You **k** they cause quarrels.
2:25 act and lead them to **k** the truth.
3:10 But you **k** all about my
3:11 You also **k** about the kind of
3:14 You **k** who your teachers were.
Tit 1:16 They claim to **k** God,
3:11 You **k** that people like this are
Phm 1:21 And I **k** that you will do even
Heb 5:14 are trained by practice to **k**
8:11 by saying, '**K** the Lord.'
8:11 the most important will all **k** me
10:30 We **k** the God who said,
10:34 since you **k** that you have a
12:17 You **k** that afterwards,
13:2 to believers you don't **k**.
13:23 You **k** that Timothy,
Jas 1:3 You **k** that such testing of your
1:5 wisdom to **k** what you should
3:1 You **k** that we who teach will
4:4 Don't you **k** that love for this
4:14 You don't **k** what will happen
1Pe 1:14 because you didn't **k** any better.
2Pe 1:12 although you already **k** about
1:14 I **k** that I will die soon.
2:20 People can **k** our Lord and
2:21 that God approves of than to **k**
3:17 you already **k** these things.
1Jn 2:3 We are sure that we **k** Christ if
2:4 person who says, "I **k** him,"
2:5 That's how we **k** we are in
2:11 They don't **k** where they're
2:13 because you **k** Christ who has
2:14 because you **k** the Father.
2:14 because you **k** Christ,
2:18 That's how we **k** it's the end of
2:21 to you because you **k** the truth,
2:21 because you don't **k** the truth.
2:21 You **k** that no lie ever comes
2:29 If you **k** that Christ has God's
2:29 you also **k** that everyone who
3:2 We do **k** that when Christ
3:5 You **k** that Christ appeared in
3:14 We **k** that we have passed
3:15 and you **k** that a murderer
3:19 This is how we will **k** that we
3:24 We **k** that he lives in us
4:8 doesn't love doesn't **k** God,
4:13 We **k** that we live in him and
5:2 We **k** that we love God's
5:13 that they will **k** that they have
5:15 We **k** that he listens to our
5:15 So we **k** that we already have
5:18 We **k** that those who have
5:19 We **k** that we are from God,
5:20 We **k** that the Son of God has
5:20 us understanding so that we **k**
3Jn 1:2 I **k** that you are spiritually well.

3Jn 1:12 and you **k** that what we say is
Jud 1:5 you about what you already **k**:
1:10 they **k** to destroy themselves.
Rev 2:2 I **k** what you have done — how
2:2 I also **k** that you cannot tolerate
2:9 I **k** how you are suffering,
2:9 I also **k** that those who claim to
2:13 I **k** where you live.
2:19 I **k** what you do. I know your
2:19 I **k** your love, faith, service,
2:19 I also **k** that what you are doing
2:23 Then all the churches will **k**
3:1 I **k** what you have done.
3:3 You don't **k** when I will come.
3:8 I **k** what you have done.
3:15 I **k** what you have done,
7:14 I answered him, "Sir, you **k**."
15:4 because they **k** about your fair

knowing (13)

Gen 3:5 be like God, **k** good and evil."
2Sm 3:26 Sirah without David **k** about it.
15:11 They went innocently, **k**
2Ki 4:39 stew without **k** what they were.
Job 9:5 mountains without their **k** it,
9:21 I have no way of **k** it.
Psa 39:6 riches without **k** who will get
Ecc 6:8 a poor person have in **k** how
Luk 11:44 them without **k** what they are."
Php 3:8 better off **k** Christ Jesus my
Heb 11:8 own country without **k** where
1Pe 5:9 **k** that other believers
Rev 12:12 **k** that he has little time left."

knowledge (129)

Gen 2:9 tree of life and the tree of the **k**
2:17 never eat from the tree of the **k**
Num 5:13 man without her husband's **k**.
24:16 receives **k** from the Most High,
1Sm 2:3 the LORD is a God of **k**,
1Ki 2:32 did this without my father's **k**.
2Ch 1:10 Give me wisdom and **k** so that
1:11 you've asked for wisdom and **k**
1:12 So wisdom and **k** will be given
Ezr 7:11 a man with a thorough **k** of the
Job 21:22 "Can anyone teach God **k**?
33:3 and I sincerely speak the **k**
34:35 'Job speaks without **k**.
35:16 a lot without having any **k**."
36:3 I will get my **k** from far away
36:12 die like those who have no **k**.
38:2 do not show any **k** ⌊about it⌋?
42:3 having any **k** ⌊about it⌋?'
Psa 19:2 night shares **k** with the next
119:66 ⌊to use⌋ good judgment and **k**,
139:6 Such **k** is beyond my grasp.
Pro 1:4 to give **k** and foresight to the
1:7 the LORD is the beginning of **k**.
1:22 How long will you fools hate **k**?
1:29 because they hated **k** and did
2:5 and you will find the **k** of God.
2:6 come **k** and understanding.
2:10 **K** will be pleasant to your soul.
3:20 By his **k** the deep waters were
8:9 to those who have acquired **k**.
8:10 and my **k** rather than fine gold,
8:12 and I acquire **k** and foresight.
9:10 The **k** of the Holy One is
10:14 Those who are wise store up **k**,
11:9 people are rescued by **k**.
12:23 person ⌊discreetly⌋ hides **k**,
13:16 sensible person acts with **k**,
14:6 but **k** comes easily to a person
14:7 will not receive **k** from his lips.
14:18 people are crowned with **k**.
15:2 give good expression to **k**,
15:7 lips of wise people spread **k**,
15:14 understanding searches for **k**,
17:27 Whoever has **k** controls his
18:15 has understanding acquires **k**.
18:15 ears of wise people seek **k**.
19:2 A person without **k** is no good.
19:25 and he will gain more **k**.
19:27 will stray from the words of **k**.
20:15 the lips of **k** are precious gems.
21:11 is instructed, he gains **k**.
Pro 22:12 LORD's eyes watch over **k**,
22:17 your mind on the **k** I give you.
22:20 previously with advice and **k**
23:12 listen carefully to words of **k**.
24:4 With **k** its rooms are filled with
24:5 but a person with **k** is even
24:14 The **k** of wisdom is like that for
28:2 has understanding and **k** will
30:3 I don't have **k** of the Holy One.
Ecc 1:16 with wisdom and **k**."
1:17 wisdom and **k** as well as
1:18 The greater ⌊your⌋ **k**,
2:21 with wisdom, **k**, and skill. Yet,
2:26 God gives wisdom, **k**,
9:10 there is no work, planning, **k**,
Isa 11:2 the Spirit of **k** and fear of the
11:9 world will be filled with the **k**
33:6 of salvation are wisdom and **k**.
40:14 Who taught him **k**?
44:19 No one has enough **k** or
44:25 turn their **k** into foolishness.
47:10 Your wisdom and **k** have led
Jer 3:15 feed you with **k** and insight.
Dan 1:17 God gave these four men **k**,
2:21 to those who are wise and **k**
5:12 was found to have **k**,
12:4 everywhere, and **k** will grow."
Hos 4:1 and no **k** of God in the land.
Hab 2:14 earth will be filled with the **k**
Mal 2:7 priest's lips should preserve **k**.
Mat 13:11 Jesus answered, "**K** about the
13:12 will be given ⌊more **k**⌋,
Mar 4:24 ⌊**K**⌋ will be measured out to
4:24 This is the way **k** increases.
4:25 will be given ⌊more **k**⌋.
Luk 8:10 Jesus answered, "**K** about the
8:18 will be given ⌊more **k**⌋.
11:52 away the key that unlocks **k**.
11:52 entrance into ⌊**k**⌋ yourselves,
Rom 2:20 you have the full content of **k**
11:33 God's riches, wisdom, and **k**
14:14 Lord Jesus has given me the **k**
15:14 you have all the **k** you need
1Co 1:5 in speech and **k** of every kind.
8:1 We know that we all have **k**.
8:1 **K** makes people arrogant,
8:10 sees you, who have this **k**,
8:11 In that case, your **k** is ruining a
12:8 the ability to speak with **k**.
13:2 all mysteries and have all **k**.
13:8 There is the gift of **k**,
13:9 Our **k** is incomplete and our
13:12 Now my **k** is incomplete.
13:12 Then I will have complete **k** as
13:12 as God has complete **k** of me.
14:6 **k**, prophecy, or doctrine to you.
2Co 4:6 to light the **k** about God's glory
6:6 ⌊People can see⌋ our purity, **k**,
8:7 speak, your **k**, your dedication,
10:5 that oppose the **k** of God.
Eph 3:19 which goes far beyond any **k**.
4:13 and in our **k** about God's Son,
Php 1:9 because of your **k** and insight.
Col 1:9 ask ⌊God⌋ to fill you with the **k**
1:10 good work by this **k** about God.
2:3 of wisdom and **k** in Christ.
3:10 is continually renewed in **k**
1Ti 6:20 claims of false **k** that people
6:21 Although some claim to have **k**,
Tit 1:1 people to faith and to the **k**
Phm 1:6 come to have a complete **k**
2Pe 1:2 through your **k** about Jesus,
1:3 was given to us through **k**
1:5 and to integrity add **k**;
1:6 to **k** add self-control;
1:8 it demonstrates that your **k**
3:18 But grow in the good will and **k**
1Jn 2:20 so all of you have **k**.

knowledgeable (4)

Exo 31:3 and **k** in all trades.
35:31 and **k** in all trades.
1Ki 7:14 and **k** about all kinds of bronze
Dan 1:4 **k** in all subjects, well-informed,

known (115)

Gen 36:8 who was also **k** as Edom,
Exo 6:3 but I didn't make myself **k** to
21:36 However, if it was **k** that the
34:14 he is **k** for not tolerating rivals.)
Lev 4:14 they have done becomes **k**,
Num 12:6 I make myself **k** to them in
Dtr 9:24 the LORD as long as I've **k** you.
Jdg 3:2 at least those who had **k**
1Sm 10:11 When all who had **k** him before
2Sm 7:21 You made it **k** to me.
7:23 to make his name **k**,
1Ki 18:36 make **k** today that you are God
1Ch 16:8 Make **k** among the nations
17:19 made this great thing **k** to me.
17:21 to make your name **k**,
Ezr 8:3 whose genealogies were **k**
Est 2:7 Hadassah, also **k** as Esther,
Job 18:17 and his reputation will not be **k**
42:11 had previously **k** him came
Psa 9:16 The LORD is **k** by the
16:11 make the path of life **k** to me.
25:4 Make your ways **k** to me,
31:7 You have **k** the troubles in my
32:5 I made my sins **k** to you,
67:2 your ways will be **k** on earth,
76:1 God is **k** in Judah.
77:14 strength **k** among the nations.
78:3 we have heard and **k** about,
78:5 to make them **k** to their children
92:15 They make it **k** that the LORD
98:2 has made his salvation **k**.
105:1 Make **k** among the nations
106:8 make his mighty power **k**.
145:12 in order to make **k** your mighty
Pro 1:23 I will make my words **k** to you.
20:11 Even a child makes himself **k**
22:19 I have made them **k** to you,
24:8 do evil will be **k** as a schemer.
31:23 "Her husband is **k** at the city
Ecc 6:5 seen the sun or **k** anything,
6:10 Mortals are already **k** for what
Isa 12:4 Make his deeds **k** among the
12:5 this be **k** throughout the earth.
19:21 the LORD will make himself **k**
21:10 I make **k** to you what I heard
38:19 faithfulness **k** to their children.
44:8 Didn't I make this **k** to you long
48:3 and I made them **k**.
48:8 You have never **k** about them.
61:9 Then their offspring will be **k**
64:2 down to make your name **k**
66:14 of the LORD will be made **k**
Jer 7:32 will no longer be **k** as Topheth
7:32 it will be **k** as Slaughter Valley.
16:21 and my strength **k** to them.
46:14 Make it **k** in Memphis and in
Eze 16:2 "Son of man, make **k** to the
20:5 I made myself **k** to them in
20:9 I made myself **k** to them by
20:11 and made my rules **k** to them.
34:29 will give them a place that is **k**
39:7 I will make my holy name **k**
Hos 5:9 I will make the truth **k** among
13:4 You have **k** no god besides me.
Amo 3:2 I have **k** no one else but you.
Zec 14:7 There will be one day — a day **k**
Mat 7:23 them publicly, 'I've never **k** you.
10:26 is secret will be made **k**.
12:7 If you had **k** what 'I want
24:43 homeowner had **k** at what time
Luk 6:44 Each tree is **k** by its fruit.
12:2 is secret will be made **k**.
12:39 homeowner had **k** at what hour
19:42 He said, "If you had only **k**
Jon 1:18 Father's heart, has made him **k**.
7:4 he wants to be **k** publicly.
8:55 Yet, you haven't **k** him.
11:42 I've **k** that you always hear me.
14:7 If you have **k** me, you will also
15:15 friends because I've made **k**
16:3 to you because they haven't **k**
17:6 "I made your name **k** to the
17:25 and these ⌊disciples⌋ have **k**
17:26 made your name **k** to them,

Jon 17:26 and I will make it **k** so that the
Act 1:23 and was also **k** as Justus)
2:28 make the path of life **k** to me.
13:9 But Saul, also **k** as Paul,
15:18 that have always been **k**!'
26:5 They've **k** me for a long time
Rom 1:19 What can be **k** about God is
7:7 For example, I wouldn't have **k**
15:20 the name of Christ was not **k**.
16:26 but now is publicly **k**.
1Co 2:8 the rulers of this world has **k** it.
2:11 In the same way, no one has **k**
2:16 "Who has **k** the mind of the
8:3 they are **k** by God.
14:25 in their hearts will become **k**,
15:1 I'm making **k** to you the Good
Eph 3:5 this mystery was not **k** by
1Ti 6:15 right time God will make this **k**.
2Ti 3:15 From infancy you have **k** the
Tit 1:6 His children shouldn't be **k** for
Heb 11:24 faith led him to refuse to be **k**
11:39 All these people were **k** for
1Pe 1:12 has now made **k** to you by
1:20 He is the lamb who was **k** long
1:20 good he became publicly **k**
2Pe 2:21 better for them never to have **k**
1Jn 3:6 haven't seen or **k** Christ.
4:16 We have **k** and believed that
Rev 2:17 a name that is **k** only to the
3:1 You are **k** for being alive,
10:7 he had made this Good News **k**

knows (106)

Gen 3:5 "God **k** that when you eat it
3:22 since he **k** good and evil.
44:15 out because he **k** the future?"
Exo 31:5 He **k** how to cut and set stones
35:33 He **k** how to cut and set stones
Num 15:24 and no one else **k** about it,
Dtr 21:1 If no one **k** who committed the
34:6 Even today no one **k** where his
Jos 22:22 He **k**, so let Israel know! If our
Rut 3:11 The whole town **k** that you are
1Sm 20:3 "Your father certainly **k** that you
23:17 Even my father Saul **k** this."
25:11 coming from who **k** where?"
2Sm 12:22 I thought, 'Who **k**?
14:20 who **k** everything on earth."
17:10 because all Israel **k** that your
2Ch 2:14 Huram **k** how to work with gold,
2:14 He also **k** how to make all
Est 4:14 And who **k**, you may have
Job 11:11 He **k** who the scoundrels are.
15:23 He **k** that his ruin is close at
23:10 ⌞I can't find him⌟ because he **k**
28:7 No bird of prey **k** the way to it.
28:13 No mortal **k** where it is.
28:23 He **k** where it lives
34:25 He **k** what they do,
36:4 The one who **k** everything is
37:16 of the one who **k** everything),
Psa 1:6 The LORD **k** the way of
37:18 The LORD **k** the daily
44:21 since he **k** the secrets in our
74:9 No one **k** how long this will
94:11 The LORD **k** that people's
103:14 He certainly **k** what we are
104:19 which **k** when to set.
Pro 14:10 The heart **k** its own bitterness,
21:24 His arrogance **k** no limits.
24:5 A strong man **k** how to use his
24:22 Who **k** what misery both may
29:7 A righteous person **k** the just
Ecc 2:19 Who **k** whether that person will
3:21 Who **k** whether a human spirit
6:12 Who **k** what may be good for
7:22 Your conscience **k** that you
8:1 Who **k** how to explain things?
9:1 No one **k** whether there will be
9:12 No one **k** when his time will
10:14 No one **k** what the future will
Isa 7:15 and honey until he **k** how
7:16 Indeed, before the boy **k** how to
8:4 Before the boy **k** how to say
Jer 48:17 and everyone who **k** its fame.
Dan 2:22 He **k** what is in the dark,
Joe 2:14 Who **k**? He may reconsider and
Jnh 3:9 Who **k**? God may reconsider his
Nah 1:7 He **k** those who seek shelter in
3:17 No one **k** where they've gone.
Mat 6:8 Your Father **k** what you need
6:32 Father certainly **k** you need all
11:27 Only the Father **k** the Son.
11:27 And no one **k** the Father
24:36 "No one **k** when that day or
24:36 Only the Father **k**.
Mar 13:32 "No one **k** when that day or
13:32 Only the Father **k**.
Luk 10:22 Only the Father **k** who the Son
10:22 And no one **k** who the Father is
12:30 your Father **k** you need them.
16:15 But God **k** what's in your
Jon 10:14 my sheep as the Father **k** me.
14:21 Whoever **k** and obeys my
17:23 In this way the world **k** that you
19:35 What he says is true, and he **k**
Act 1:19 in Jerusalem **k** about this.
4:16 everyone in Jerusalem **k** about.
15:8 who **k** everyone's thoughts,
19:35 everyone **k** that this city of the
19:35 Everyone **k** that Ephesus is the
26:26 king who **k** about these things.
Rom 8:27 searches our hearts **k** what
11:34 "Who **k** how the Lord thinks?
14:22 what he **k** is right shouldn't
1Co 2:11 After all, who **k** everything
3:20 "The Lord **k** that the thoughts of
8:7 But not everyone **k** this.
2Co 3:2 that everyone **k** and reads.
5:11 God already **k** what we are,
11:11 God **k** that I do love you.
11:31 **k** that I'm not lying.
12:2 or spiritually. Only God **k**.
12:4 or spiritually. Only God **k**.
Gal 4:9 God, or rather, God **k** you.
Php 3:10 that **k** Christ. Faith knows the
3:10 Faith **k** the power that his
2Ti 2:19 "The Lord **k** those who belong
Heb 7:3 No one **k** anything about
7:3 No one **k** when he was born or
7:14 Everyone **k** that our Lord came
Jas 4:17 Whoever **k** what is right but
2Pe 2:9 Since the Lord did all this, he **k**
2:9 He also **k** how to hold immoral
1Jn 3:20 conscience and **k** everything.
4:6 The person who **k** God listens
4:7 been born from God and **k** God.
2Jn 1:1 Everyone who **k** the truth also
Rev 19:12 but only he **k** what it is.

Koa (1)

Eze 23:23 men from Pekod, Shoa, and **K**,

Kohath (26)

Gen 46:11 were Gershon, **K**, and Merari.
Exo 6:16 order: Gershon, **K**, and Merari.
6:18 The sons of **K** were Amram,
6:18 **K** lived 133 years.
Num 3:17 Gershon, **K**, and Merari were
3:19 and Uzziel were the sons of **K**.
3:27 To **K** belonged the families
3:27 the families descended from **K**.
3:29 The families descended from **K**
4:2 who are descended from **K**.
16:1 a descendant of **K** and Levi.
26:57 of Gershon, the family of **K**,
26:58 **K** was the ancestor of Amram.
Jos 21:4 families of **K** that were chosen
21:10 who were from the families of **K**
21:20 were from the families of **K**.
21:26 to the rest of the families of **K**.
1Ch 6:1 Levi's sons were Gershon, **K**,
6:16 Levi's sons were Gershom, **K**,
6:38 who was the son of **K**,
6:54 the family descended from **K**.
23:6 of Levi's sons (Gershon, **K**,
23:12 **K** had four sons: Amram, Izhar,
24:20 Levi's descendants ⌞from **K**⌟:
2Ch 20:19 descendants of **K** and Korah,
34:12 Meshullam (descendants of **K**).

Kohathite (4)

Num 3:30 The leader of the **K** families
4:18 "Don't let the **K** families from
4:37 in the **K** families who served
1Ch 9:32 Some of their **K** relatives were

Kohathites (8)

Num 4:4 "This is the work the **K** will do
4:15 the **K** will come to carry all the
4:15 The **K** will carry all the things
4:20 But the **K** must not go in to look
4:34 the **K** by their families
4:37 Moses and registered the **K**.
7:9 none of these gifts to the **K**,
10:21 Then the **K**, who carried the

Kohath's (11)

Jos 21:5 The rest of **K** descendants
1Ch 6:2 **K** sons were Amram,
6:18 **K** sons were Amram,
6:22 These were **K** descendants:
6:22 **K** son was Amminadab.
6:33 Heman was from **K** family line.
6:61 The rest of **K** descendants
6:66 **K** descendants had cities chosen
6:70 of the rest of **K** descendants
15:5 Leading **K** descendants was
2Ch 29:12 From **K** descendants were

Kolaiah (1)

Neh 11:7 who was the son of **K**,

Kolaiah's (1)

Jer 29:21 says about **K** son Ahab and

Korah (29)

Gen 36:5 birth to Jeush, Jalam, and **K**.
36:14 Jeush, Jalam, and **K** for Esau.
36:16 **K**, Gatam, and Amalek.
36:18 Jeush, Jalam, and **K**.
Exo 6:21 The sons of Izhar were **K**,
6:24 The sons of **K** were Assir,
6:24 the families descended from **K**.
Num 16:1 **K** (son of Izhar), Dathan and
16:1 (**K** was a descendant of Kohath
16:5 Then he said to **K** and all his
16:6 **K**, you and all your followers
16:8 Moses also said to **K**,
16:16 Moses said to **K**, Aaron will
16:19 When **K** had gathered all his
16:24 Move away from the tents of **K**,
16:27 away from the tents of **K**,
16:32 the followers of **K**,
16:40 die like **K** and his followers.
16:49 who had died because of **K**.
26:10 swallowed them along with **K**.
26:11 descendants of **K** didn't die.)
1Ch 1:35 Reuel, Jeush, Jalam, and **K**.
2:43 Hebron's sons were **K**,
6:22 Amminadab's son was **K**.
6:37 who was the son of **K**,
9:19 great-grandson of **K**) and the
9:29 Other descendants of **K** were
2Ch 20:19 descendants of Kohath and **K**,
Jud 1:11 **K** and destroyed themselves.

Korahite (1)

Num 26:58 family, and the **K** family.

Korah's (9)

Num 26:9 They joined **K** followers when
27:3 **K** followers who joined forces
1Ch 6:22 was Korah. **K** son was Assir.
9:19 **K** descendants) were responsible
9:31 **K** descendant, was entrusted
12:6 Jashobeam (**K** descendants),
26:1 For **K** descendants there was
26:4 ⌞Also for **K** descendants⌟ there
26:19 **K** and Merari's descendants.

Kore (4)

1Ch 9:19 Shallum (son of **K**,
26:1 Meshelemiah, the son of **K**,
2Ch 31:14 **K**, son of Imnah the Levite,
31:16 men who served under **K** were

koum (1)

Mar 5:41 and said to her, "Talitha, **k**!"

Koz (1)

1Ch 4:8 **K** was the father of Anub and

Kue (4)

1Ki 10:28 imported from Egypt and **K**.
10:28 traders bought them from **K**
2Ch 1:16 imported from Egypt and **K**.
1:16 traders bought them from **K**

Kushaiah (1)

1Ch 15:17 they appointed Ethan, son of **K**.

L

Laadah (1)

1Ch 4:21 **L**, who first settled Mareshah,

Laban (56)

Gen 24:29 a brother whose name was **L**.
24:30 Immediately, **L** ran out to the
24:33 "Speak up," **L** said.
24:50 **L** and Bethuel answered,
25:20 and sister of **L** the Aramean.
27:43 away to my brother **L** in Haran.
28:2 the daughters of your uncle **L**.
28:5 Jacob went to live with **L**,
29:5 asked them, "Do you know **L**,
29:10 daughter of his uncle **L**,
29:13 As soon as **L** heard the news
29:13 Then Jacob told **L** all that had
29:14 **L** said to him, "You are my own
29:15 Then **L** said to him,
29:16 **L** had two daughters.
29:19 **L** responded, "It's better that I
29:21 seven years⌋ Jacob said to **L**,
29:22 So **L** invited all the people of
29:24 (**L** had given his slave Zilpah
29:25 Jacob asked **L**. "Didn't I work for
29:26 **L** answered, "It's not our
29:28 Then **L** gave his daughter
29:29 (**L** had given his slave Bilhah
29:30 for **L** another seven years.
30:25 to Joseph, Jacob said to **L**,
30:27 **L** replied, "Listen to me.
30:31 **L** asked, "What should I give
30:34 **L** answered, "Agreed. We'll do
30:35 However, that same day **L** took
30:42 the weaker ones belonged to **L**
31:2 He also noticed that **L** did not
31:12 seen everything that **L** is doing
31:19 When **L** went to shear his
31:20 Jacob also tricked **L** the
31:22 Two days later **L** was told that
31:23 **L** caught up with him in the
31:24 God came to **L** the Aramean in
31:25 When **L** finally caught up with
31:25 So **L** and his relatives put up
31:26 Then **L** asked Jacob,
31:31 Jacob answered **L**,
31:33 So **L** went into Jacob's tent,
31:34 **L** rummaged through the whole
31:35 So even though **L** had made a
31:36 angry and confronted **L**.
31:36 Jacob demanded of **L**.
31:43 Then **L** answered Jacob,
31:47 ⌊In his language⌋ **L** called it
31:48 **L** said, "This pile of stones
31:51 **L** said to Jacob, "Here is the
31:55 Early the next morning **L**
31:55 Then **L** left and went back
32:4 'I've been living with **L** and
46:18 whom **L** gave to his daughter
46:25 whom **L** gave to his daughter
Dtr 1:1 Tophel, and near **L**, Hazeroth,

Laban's (6)

Gen 29:10 with his uncle **L** sheep.
29:10 and watered his uncle **L** sheep
30:36 take care of the rest of **L** flocks
30:40 striped or black in **L** flocks.
30:40 did not add them to **L** flocks
31:1 Jacob heard that **L** sons were

labor (53)

Gen 3:16 pain and your **l** when you give
5:29 from the work and painful **l**
35:16 Rachel went into **l** and was
35:16 and was having severe **l** pains.
Exo 1:11 oppress them through forced **l**.
2:11 them suffering under forced **l**.
6:7 the forced **l** of the Egyptians.
Dtr 20:11 to do forced **l** and serve you.
Jos 16:10 they are required to do forced **l**.
17:13 the Canaanites do forced **l**,
Jdg 1:28 the Canaanites do forced **l**.
1:30 and were made to do forced **l**.
1:33 Anath were made to do forced **l**.
1:35 made the Amorites do forced **l**.
1Sm 4:19 she went into **l** prematurely and
2Sm 20:24 was in charge of forced **l**.
1Ki 4:6 was in charge of forced **l**.
5:14 was in charge of forced **l**.
9:21 drafted them for slave **l**.
11:28 in charge of all forced **l** from
12:18 He was in charge of forced **l**,
2Ch 8:8 drafted them for slave **l**.
10:18 He was in charge of forced **l**,
Job 14:14 as long as my hard **l** continues.
39:1 the does when they are in **l**?
39:11 so strong or leave your **l** to it?
Psa 48:6 a woman experiences during **l**.
Pro 12:24 but lazy hands do slave **l**.
Ecc 3:9 people gain from their hard **l**?
Sos 8:5 mother went into **l** with you.
8:5 There she went into **l** and gave
Isa 3:10 will taste the fruit of their **l**.
23:4 "I've never been in **l** or given
26:17 and cry out in their **l** pains.
26:18 we writhed with **l** pains only to
31:8 will be made to do forced **l**.
40:2 it that its time of hard **l** is over
45:10 you go through **l** pains for me?"
66:7 Before a woman goes into **l**,
66:7 Before she has **l** pains,
66:8 When Zion went into **l**,
Jer 4:31 I hear a woman in **l**.
13:21 grip you like a woman in **l**?
31:8 pregnant women and those in **l**.
49:24 grip them like a woman in **l**.
50:43 him as pain grips a woman in **l**.
Lam 1:1 Now it does forced **l**.
Mic 4:9 grips you like a woman in **l**.
4:10 and groan like a woman in **l**.
1Co 4:12 ourselves out doing physical **l**.
16:16 shares their **l** and hard work.
1Th 5:3 It will be as sudden as **l** pains
Rev 12:2 She cried out from **l** pains and

laborer (2)

Gen 49:15 and will become a slave **l**.
Job 14:6 he loves life as a **l** loves work.

laborer's (1)

Pro 16:26 A **l** appetite works to his

laborers (1)

1Ki 9:15 This is the record of the forced **l**

labors (1)

Psa 104:13 earth with the fruits of your **l**.

laced (1)

Jon 19:40 They **l** the strips with spices.

Lachish (24)

Jos 10:3 of Jarmuth, King Japhia of **L**,
10:5 Jerusalem, Hebron, Jarmuth, **L**,
10:23 Hebron, Jarmuth, **L**, and Eglon.
10:31 marched from Libnah to **L**,
10:32 The LORD handed **L** over to
10:33 of Gezer had come to help **L**.
10:34 Israel marched from **L** to Eglon,
10:35 same way he had destroyed **L**.
12:11 king of Jarmuth, the king of **L**,
15:39 **L**, Bozkath, Eglon,
2Ki 14:19 against him, so he fled to **L**.
14:19 But they sent men to **L** after
18:14 to the king of Assyria at **L**:
18:17 with a large army from **L**
19:8 had heard that the king left **L**.
2Ch 11:9 Adoraim, **L**, Azekah,
25:27 Amaziah fled to **L**,
25:27 but they sent men to **L** after him
32:9 royal forces were attacking **L**,
Neh 11:30 villages, in **L** and its fields,
Isa 36:2 with a large army from **L**
37:8 had heard that the king left **L**.
Jer 34:7 and the cities of **L** and Azekah.
Mic 1:13 to the chariots, inhabitants of **L**.

lack (20)

Gen 27:39 place where you live will **l**
2Sm 6:7 him there for his **l** of respect.
Job 39:13 or do its wings **l** feathers?
Pro 5:23 He will die for his **l** of
31:11 he does not **l** anything good.
Ecc 6:2 and honor so that he doesn't **l**
Isa 34:16 Not one will **l** a mate,
Jer 47:3 Fathers who **l** courage
Eze 4:17 of each other because of the **l**
Mat 13:58 there because of their **l** of faith.
Mar 9:24 Help my **l** of faith."
Luk 22:35 you didn't **l** anything,
Rom 4:20 God's promise out of a **l** of faith.
1Co 1:7 Therefore, you don't **l** any gift
7:5 so that Satan doesn't use your **l**
7:19 and the **l** of it is nothing.
2Co 6:5 sleepless nights, and **l** of food.
2Ti 3:3 and **l** normal affection for their
3:3 **l** self-control, be brutal,
Heb 5:13 All those who live on milk **l** the

lacks (3)

Pro 11:22 woman who **l** good taste.
25:28 ⌊so⌋ is a person who **l**
28:27 gives to the poor **l** nothing.

Ladan (5)

1Ch 7:26 Tahan's son was **L**.
23:7 **L** and Shimei were Gershon's
23:8 **L** had three sons: Jehiel was
26:21 also⌋ the descendants of **L**,
26:21 ⌊Those who served⌋ for **L**,

Ladan's (3)

1Ch 7:26 **L** son was Ammihud.
23:9 were the heads of **L** families
26:21 were the heads of **L** families:

ladies (1)

Psa 45:9 kings are among your noble **l**.

lady (2)

2Jn 1:1 To the chosen **l** and her
1:5 Dear **l**, I'm now requesting that

Lael (1)

Num 3:24 was Eliasaph, son of **L**.

lagging (1)

Dtr 25:18 all those who were **l** behind.

Lahad (1)

1Ch 4:2 was the father of Ahumai and **L**.

Lahmas (1)

Jos 15:40 Cabbon, **L**, Chitlish,

Lahmi (1)

1Ch 20:5 Elhanan, son of Jair, killed **L**,

Lahmi's (1)

1Ch 20:5 (The shaft of **L** spear was like

laid (83)

Gen 9:23 Japheth took a blanket and **l**
15:10 in half and **l** each half opposite
22:9 tied up his son Isaac and **l** him
Lev 9:14 organs and the legs and **l** them
Dtr 34:9 because Moses had **l** his
Jos 2:6 flax which she had **l** up there.)

Jos 7:23 Then they l it out in the
23:13 a whip l to your sides,
1Sm 9:24 up the leg and thigh and l
9:24 "This was kept in order to be l
19:13 some idols, l them in the bed,
2Sm 22:16 of the earth were l bare at
1Ki 3:20 Then she l her dead son in my
6:37 of the LORD's temple was l.
13:29 man of God, l it on the donkey,
13:30 He l the body of the man of
17:19 and l him on his own bed.
2Ki 4:21 She took him upstairs and l
9:13 took off his coat and l
13:16 Elisha l his hands on the king's
2Ch 3:3 This is how Solomon l the
8:16 the LORD's temple was l until
16:14 They l him on a bed full of
29:23 who l their hands on them.
Ezr 3:6 temple had not yet been l.
3:10 The builders l the foundation of
3:11 house of the LORD had been l.
5:8 and with wooden beams l
5:16 Then Sheshbazzar l the
6:3 Its foundation should be l.
Neh 3:3 They l its beams and set its
3:6 They l its beams and set its
Job 6:2 if only my misery could be l on
10:18 anyone had l eyes on me.
38:4 "Where were you when I l the
38:6 Who l its cornerstone
Psa 18:15 of the earth were l bare at your
24:2 He l its foundation on the seas
31:4 that they have secretly l for me.
32:4 Day and night your hand l
39:10 the sickness you l upon me.
66:11 You have l burdens on our
85:3 You l aside all your fury.
89:40 and have l his fortified cities
102:25 Long ago you l the foundation
140:5 Arrogant people have l a trap
Pro 3:19 By Wisdom the LORD l the
Isa 14:32 LORD has l Zion's foundation,
15:1 In a single night Ar in Moab is l
15:1 In a single night Kir in Moab is l
24:3 The earth will be completely l
44:28 "Your foundation will be l."
48:13 My hand l the foundation of the
49:17 Those who destroyed you and l
51:13 stretched out the heavens and l
51:16 l the foundations of the earth,
53:6 and the LORD has l all our sins
Jer 48:8 and the plain will be l waste
Lam 1:10 The enemies l their hands on
3:28 the LORD has l these burdens
Eze 32:32 all his soldiers will be l among
40:42 On these tables the priests l
Hag 2:15 were before one stone was l
2:18 the house of the LORD was l.
Zec 4:9 "Zerubbabel's hands have l the
8:9 of the LORD of Armies was l.
12:1 l the foundation of the earth,
Mat 15:30 They l them at his feet,
27:60 Then he l it in his own new
Mar 6:29 they came for his body and l it
15:46 Then he l the body in a tomb,
15:47 watched where Jesus was l.
16:6 Look at the place where they l
Luk 2:7 him in strips of cloth and l him
23:26 They l the cross on him and
23:53 Then he l the body in a tomb
23:55 and how his body was l in it.
Act 9:37 prepared for burial and was l
13:36 He was l to rest with his
Rom 15:20 foundation which others had l.
1Co 3:11 than the one that is already l,
Heb 1:10 in the beginning you l the
Rev 1:17 Then he l his right hand on me

lain (1)

1Ki 11:21 in Egypt that David had l down

lair (2)

Jer 4:7 A lion has come out of its l.
25:38 He has left his l like a lion.

lairs (3)

Job 37:8 their dens and stay in their l.
38:40 ready to ambush from their l?
Sos 4:8 and Hermon, from the l of lions,

Laish (6)

Jdg 18:7 there and came to the city of L.
18:9 replied, "Get up, let's attack L.
18:14 the land around L spoke up.
18:27 priest and went to the city of L.
18:29 the city was called L.
2Sm 3:15 her husband Paltiel, son of L.

Laishah (1)

Isa 10:30 in L and miserable Anathoth!

Laish's (1)

1Sm 25:44 L son, who was from Gallim.

lake (11)

Dtr 33:23 will take possession of the l
Job 14:11 As water drains out of a l,
Luk 8:22 cross to the other side of the l."
8:23 storm came across the l.
8:33 the cliff into the l and drowned.
Rev 19:20 into the fiery l of burning sulfur.
20:10 thrown into the fiery l of sulfur,
20:14 hell were thrown into the fiery l.
20:14 (The fiery l is the second
20:15 Life were thrown into the fiery l.
21:8 find themselves in the fiery l

lakes (2)

Psa 107:35 He changes deserts into l and
Isa 41:18 I will turn deserts into l.

Lakkum (1)

Jos 19:33 to Adami Nekeb, Jabneel, to L,

lamb (98)

Gen 22:7 but where is the l for the burnt
22:8 "God will provide a l for the
30:32 or spotted sheep, every black l,
30:33 spotted or any l that isn't black
30:35 white on it), and every black l.
Exo 12:3 month each man must take a l
12:5 You may choose a l or a young
12:21 He said to them, "Pick out a l
29:40 With the first l make an offering
29:41 Offer the other l at dusk,
Lev 3:7 If your offering is a l,
4:32 "If someone brings a l as his
4:35 the fat of the l is removed from
9:3 a calf and a l (each
12:6 she must bring a one-year-old l
12:8 If she cannot afford a l,
14:10 female l that has no
14:13 He will slaughter the l in the
14:21 he must take one male l,
14:24 The priest will take the l for the
14:25 He will slaughter the l as a
22:27 "When a calf, a l, or a goat is
23:12 one-year-old male l that has no
Num 6:12 bring a one-year-old male l as
6:14 a one-year-old male l as a burnt
6:14 a one-year-old female l as an
7:15 and a one-year-old male l as a
7:21 and a one-year-old male l as a
7:27 and a one-year-old male l as a
7:33 and a one-year-old male l as a
7:39 and a one-year-old male l as a
7:45 and a one-year-old male l as a
7:51 and a one-year-old male l as a
7:57 and a one-year-old male l as a
7:63 and a one-year-old male l as a
7:69 and a one-year-old male l as a
7:75 and a one-year-old male l as a
7:81 and a one-year-old male l as a
28:7 of one quart of wine for each l.
28:8 Offer the other l at dusk along
28:13 and with each one-year-old l a
28:14 and with each l 1 quart of wine.
1Sm 7:9 Then Samuel took a l,
2Sm 12:3 had only one little female l that
12:4 So he took the poor man's l
2Sm 12:6 four times the price of the l
2Ch 30:15 slaughtered the Passover l
35:1 The Passover l was
35:6 Slaughter the Passover l,
Psa 119:176 wandered away like a lost l.
Isa 53:7 He was led like a l to the
66:3 Whoever sacrifices a l is like
Jer 11:19 I was like a trusting l brought to
Eze 46:7 and with each l the offering
46:13 "'Prepare a year-old l that has
46:15 Prepare the l, the grain offering,
Mar 14:12 Killing the Passover l was
Luk 22:7 Bread when the Passover l had
22:8 prepare the Passover l for us to
Jon 1:29 This is the L of God who takes
1:36 This is the L of God."
Act 8:32 "He was led like a l to the
1Co 5:7 Christ, our Passover l,
1Pe 1:19 the l with no defects or
1:20 He is the l who was known
Rev 5:6 I saw a l standing in the center
5:6 The l looked like he had been
5:8 When the l had taken the scroll,
5:12 "The l who was slain deserves
5:13 throne and to the l be praise,
6:1 I watched as the l opened the
6:3 When the l opened the second
6:5 When the l opened the third
6:7 When the l opened the fourth
6:9 When the l opened the fifth
6:12 I watched as the l opened the
6:16 and from the anger of the l,
7:9 in front of the throne and the l.
7:10 sits on the throne, and to the l!"
7:14 them white in the blood of the l.
7:17 The l in the center near the
12:11 because of the blood of the l
13:8 That book belongs to the l who
13:11 and it had two horns like a l.
14:1 I looked, and the l was
14:4 They follow the l wherever he
14:4 offered to God and to the l.
14:10 of the holy angels and the l.
15:3 Moses and the song of the l.
17:14 will go to war against the l.
17:14 The l will conquer them
19:7 it's time for the marriage of the l
21:9 you the bride, the wife of the l."
21:14 apostles of the l were written
21:22 and the l are its temple.
21:23 The l was its lamp.
22:1 the throne of God and the l.
22:3 The throne of God and the l

lamb's (2)

Rev 19:9 to the l wedding banquet."'
21:27 names are written in the l Book

lambs (101)

Gen 21:28 seven female l from the flock.
21:29 seven female l you have set
21:30 "Accept these l from me so that
Exo 29:38 two one-year-old l.
Lev 14:10 take two male l that have no
14:12 will take one of the male l
23:18 one-year-old l that have no
23:19 sin and two one-year-old l as
23:20 All this, along with the two l,
Num 7:17 and five one-year-old male l as
7:23 and five one-year-old male l as
7:29 and five one-year-old male l as
7:35 and five one-year-old male l as
7:41 and five one-year-old male l as
7:47 and five one-year-old male l as
7:53 and five one-year-old male l as
7:59 and five one-year-old male l as
7:65 and five one-year-old male l as
7:71 and five one-year-old male l as
7:77 and five one-year-old male l as
7:83 and five one-year-old male l as
7:87 12 one-year-old male l,
7:88 and 60 one-year-old male l.
28:3 two one-year-old l that have no
28:9 two one-year-old l that have no
28:11 and seven one-year-old l that
28:19 and seven one-year-old l,

Num 28:21 8 cups for each of the seven **l**.
28:27 and seven one-year-old **l**.
28:29 8 cups for each of the seven **l**.
29:2 and seven one-year-old **l** that
29:4 8 cups for each of the seven **l**.
29:8 and seven one-year-old **l**,
29:10 8 cups for each of the seven **l**.
29:13 and 14 one-year-old **l**,
29:15 each of the 14 one-year-old **l**.
29:17 and 14 one-year-old **l** that have
29:18 each of the bulls, rams, and **l**.
29:20 and 14 one-year-old **l** that have
29:21 each of the bulls, rams, and **l**.
29:23 and 14 one-year-old **l** that have
29:24 each of the bulls, rams, and **l**.
29:26 and 14 one-year-old **l** that have
29:27 each of the bulls, rams, and **l**.
29:29 and 14 one-year-old **l** that have
29:30 each of the bulls, rams, and **l**.
29:32 and 14 one-year-old **l** that have
29:33 each of the bulls, rams, and **l**.
29:36 and seven one-year-old **l** that
29:37 for the bull, the ram, and the **l**.
Dtr 7:13 and your flocks with **l** and kids.
28:4 flocks will have **l** and kids.
28:18 flocks will have few **l** and kids.
28:51 and no **l** or kids from your
32:14 He gave them fat from **l**,
1Sm 15:9 the fattened animals, the **l**,
2Ki 3:4 king of Israel 100,000 male **l**
1Ch 29:21 rams, 1,000 **l**, wine offerings,
2Ch 29:21 bulls, seven rams, seven **l**,
29:22 After that, they slaughtered the **l**
29:32 70 bulls, 100 rams, and 200 **l**.
30:17 had to kill the Passover **l**
30:17 and couldn't make their **l** holy
35:6 and prepare ⌊the **l**⌋ for the other
35:11 slaughtered the Passover **l**.
35:11 while the Levites skinned the **l**.
35:13 They roasted the Passover **l**
Ezr 6:9 rams, **l**, wheat, salt, wine,
6:17 100 bulls, 200 rams, and 400 **l**.
6:20 They killed the Passover **l** for
6:21 The **l** were eaten by the
7:17 to buy bulls, rams, **l**, grain,
8:35 for all Israel, 96 rams, 77 **l**,
Job 21:11 out ⌊to play⌋ like a flock of **l**,
Psa 78:71 ewes that had **l** so that David
114:4 The hills jumped like **l**.
114:6 what made you jump like **l**?
144:13 give birth to thousands of **l**,
Pro 27:26 **L** ⌊will provide⌋ you with
Isa 1:11 blood of bulls, **l**, or male goats.
5:17 Then **l** will graze as if they
11:6 Wolves will live with **l**.
11:6 and year-old **l** will be together,
16:1 Send **l** to the ruler of the land.
16:1 Send **l** from Sela through the
34:6 with the blood of **l** and goats,
40:11 He gathers the **l** in his arms.
40:11 helps the sheep and their **l**.
65:25 Wolves and **l** will feed together,
Jer 31:12 and olive oil, **l** and calves.
51:40 them to be slaughtered like **l**,
Eze 27:21 They traded **l**, rams, and male
39:18 be killed like rams, **l**, goats,
46:4 to the LORD six **l** that have no
46:5 is to be brought with the **l** must
46:6 must be one young bull, six **l**,
46:11 But with the **l**, the prince may
Hos 4:16 can the LORD feed them like **l**
Amo 6:4 and eat **l** from their flocks
Luk 10:3 you out like **l** among wolves.
Jon 21:15 Jesus told him, "Feed my **l**."

lame (29)

Lev 21:18 anyone who is blind or **l**,
Dtr 15:21 But if an animal is **l** or blind or
2Sm 5:6 Even the blind and the **l** could
5:8 the Jebusites must reach the **l**
5:8 "The blind and the **l** will not get
Job 29:15 I was feet for the **l** person.
Pro 25:19 a broken tooth and a **l** foot,
26:7 ⌊Like⌋ a **l** person's limp legs,
Isa 33:23 **L** people will carry off your loot.
35:6 Then those who are **l** will leap
Jer 31:8 Blind people and **l** people will
Mic 4:6 "I will gather those who are **l**.
4:7 I will change those who are **l**
Zep 3:19 I will rescue those who are **l**.
Mal 1:8 When you bring a **l** or a sick
1:13 "You bring stolen, **l**,
Mat 11:5 **l** people are walking,
15:30 bringing with them the **l**,
15:31 disabled cured, the **l** walking,
21:14 Blind and **l** people came to him
Mar 9:45 It is better for you to enter life **l**
Luk 7:22 **l** people are walking,
14:13 the **l**, and the blind.
14:21 the blind, and the **l**.'
Jon 5:3 **l**, or paralyzed — used to lie.
Act 3:2 a man who had been **l** from
3:2 men would put the **l** man at
8:7 and **l** people were cured.
14:8 A man who was born **l** was in

Lamech (12)

Gen 4:18 Methushael was the father of **L**.
4:19 **L** married two women,
4:23 **L** said to his wives,
4:23 Wives of **L**, hear what I say!
4:24 7 times, then **L**, 77 times."
5:25 he became the father of **L**.
5:26 After he became the father of **L**,
5:28 When **L** was 182 years old,
5:30 After **L** became the father of
5:31 **L** lived a total of 777 years;
1Ch 1:3 Enoch, Methuselah, **L**,
Luk 3:36 of Shem, son of Noah, son of **L**,

lamp (88)

Exo 25:31 "Make a **l** stand out of pure
25:31 The **l** stand, its base, and its
25:33 coming out of the **l** stand is
25:34 The **l** stand itself is to have
25:35 coming out of the **l** stand.
25:36 of pure gold as the **l** stand.
25:37 and set them on the **l** stand so
25:39 of pure gold to make the **l** stand
26:35 and put the **l** stand opposite the
30:27 the **l** stand and all the utensils,
31:8 the pure ⌊gold⌋ **l** stand and all
35:14 the **l** stand used for the light
37:17 He made the **l** stand out of pure
37:17 The **l** stand, its base, and its
37:19 out of the **l** stand had three
37:20 The **l** stand itself had four
37:21 coming out of the **l** stand.
37:22 of pure gold as the **l** stand.
37:24 The **l** stand and all the utensils
39:37 the pure ⌊gold⌋ **l** stand with its
40:4 Bring in the **l** stand,
40:24 He placed the **l** stand in the
Lev 24:2 virgin olive oil for the **l** stand so
24:4 on the pure gold **l** stand lit
Num 3:31 the table, the **l** stand, the altars,
4:9 cloth and cover the **l** stand,
4:10 Then they will put the **l** stand
8:2 the seven lamps on the **l** stand,
8:3 set up the lamps on the **l** stand
8:4 This is how the **l** stand was
8:4 The whole **l** stand,
1Sm 3:3 The **l** in God's temple hadn't
2Sm 21:17 The **l** of Israel must never be
22:29 O LORD, you are my **l**.
1Ki 7:49 **l** stands of pure gold (five on
11:36 David will always have a **l**
15:4 made Abijam a **l** in Jerusalem.
2Ki 4:10 and **l** stand there for him.
8:19 his descendants a ⌊shining⌋ **l**.
1Ch 28:15 the weight of the gold **l** stands
28:15 the weight of gold for each **l**
28:15 of silver for each silver **l** stand
28:15 of each **l** stand for worship),
2Ch 4:7 Huram made ten gold **l** stands
4:20 **l** stands and lamps of pure gold
13:11 The lamps on the gold **l** stand
21:7 his descendants a ⌊shining⌋ **l**.
Job 18:6 and the **l** above him is snuffed
21:17 "How often is the **l** of the
29:3 when he made his **l** shine on
Psa 18:28 O LORD, you light my **l**.
119:105 Your word is a **l** for my feet and
132:17 I will prepare a **l** for my
Pro 6:23 because the command is a **l**,
13:9 but the **l** of wicked people will
20:20 The **l** of the person who curses
20:27 A person's soul is the LORD's **l**.
31:18 Her **l** burns late at night.
Jer 52:19 bowls, pots, **l** stands, dishes,
Dan 5:5 wall opposite the **l** stand
Zec 4:2 I answered, "I see a solid gold **l**
4:2 seven spouts for each **l** that is
4:11 the left of the **l** stand mean?"
Mat 5:15 No one lights a **l** and puts it
5:15 everyone who lights a **l** puts
5:15 a lamp puts it on a **l** stand.
6:22 "The eye is the **l** of the body.
Mar 4:21 "Does anyone bring a **l** into a
4:21 Isn't it put on a **l** stand?
Luk 8:16 "No one lights a **l** and hides it
8:16 everyone who lights a **l** puts
8:16 lamp puts it on a **l** stand so that
11:33 "No one lights a **l** and hides it
11:33 everyone who lights a **l** puts
11:33 lamp puts it on a **l** stand so that
11:34 "Your eye is the **l** of your body.
11:36 as bright as a **l** shining on you."
15:8 Doesn't she light a **l**,
Jon 5:35 John was a **l** that gave off
Heb 9:2 The **l** stand, the table, and the
Rev 1:12 I saw seven gold **l** stands.
1:13 Son of Man among the **l** stands.
1:20 the seven gold **l** stands is this:
1:20 and the seven **l** stands are the
2:1 among the seven gold **l** stands,
2:5 and take your **l** stand from its
11:4 and the two **l** stands standing
21:23 The lamb was its **l**.

lamps (45)

Exo 25:6 olive oil for the **l**, spices for the
25:37 "Make seven **l**, and set them
27:20 oil so that the **l** won't go out.
27:21 descendants must keep the **l** lit
30:7 when he takes care of the **l**.
30:8 when Aaron lights the **l** at dusk,
35:8 olive oil for the **l**, spices for the
35:14 its **l** and the olive oil for the
35:14 lamps and the olive oil for the **l**,
35:28 and the olive oil for the **l**,
37:23 He made the seven **l**,
39:37 ⌊gold⌋ lamp stand with its **l**
39:37 the olive oil for the **l**,
40:4 lamp stand, and set up the **l**.
40:25 He set up the **l** in the LORD's
Lev 24:2 stand so that the **l** won't go out.
24:3 Aaron must keep the **l** lit in the
24:4 Aaron must keep the **l** on the
Num 4:9 as well as the **l**, tongs, trays,
4:9 for the olive oil used in the **l**.
4:16 be in charge of the oil for the **l**,
8:2 When you set up the seven **l**
8:3 So Aaron set up the **l** on the
1Ki 7:49 room), flowers, **l**, gold tongs,
1Ch 28:15 and their gold **l** (⌊that is,⌋
28:15 for each lamp stand and its **l**),
28:15 lamp stand and its **l** (according
2Ch 4:20 lamp stands and **l** of pure gold
4:21 flowers, **l**, pure gold tongs,
13:11 The **l** on the gold lamp stand
29:7 extinguished the **l**,
Pro 21:4 which are the **l** of wicked
24:20 and the **l** of wicked people will
Jer 25:10 of mills, and the light of **l**.
Zep 1:12 I will search Jerusalem with **l**
Zec 4:2 a bowl on top and seven **l** on it.
Mat 25:1 They took their oil **l** and went
25:3 foolish bridesmaids took their **l**,
25:4 took along extra oil for their **l**.
25:7 woke up and got their **l** ready.
25:8 Our **l** are going out.'
Luk 12:35 and have your **l** burning.
Act 20:8 (Many **l** were lit in the upstairs
Rev 18:23 Light from **l** will never shine in
22:5 will not need any light from **l**

lance (1)

Job 41:26 Neither will a spear, l,

land (1306)

Gen 1:9 and let the dry l appear."
1:10 God named the dry l earth.
1:30 as food to every l animal,
2:5 there was no one to farm the l.
2:12 (The gold of that l is pure.
2:15 the Garden of Eden to farm the l
4:3 some crops from the l as
4:14 have forced me off this l today.
4:16 in Nod [The L of Wandering],
7:22 on dry l (every living,
8:3 began to recede from the l.
8:7 the water on the l had dried up.
8:9 dove couldn't find a place to l
8:13 the water on the l had dried up.
8:14 second month the l was dry.
10:11 He went from that l to Assyria
11:28 of the Chaldeans, his native l.
12:1 "Leave your l, your relatives,
12:1 Go to the l that I will show you.
12:6 Abram traveled through the l
12:6 the Canaanites were in the l.
12:7 "I'm going to give this l to your
12:10 There was a famine in the l.
13:9 Isn't all this l yours also?
13:15 I will give all the l you see to
13:17 and forth across the entire l
15:7 to give you this l so that you
15:13 will live in a l that is not
15:18 He said, "I will give this l to
15:18 This is the l from the river of
15:19 It is the l of the Kenites,
17:8 I am also giving this l where
19:23 risen over the l as Lot came
19:28 and Gomorrah and all the l
19:28 he saw smoke rising from the l
20:15 said, "Look, here's my l.
21:23 Show me and the l where
21:32 back to the l of the Philistines.
21:34 time in the l of the Philistines.
23:15 The l is worth ten pounds of
24:4 Instead, you will go to the l of
24:5 to come back to this l with me?
24:5 back to the l you came from?"
24:7 from my father's home and the l
24:7 'I will give this l to your
24:37 in whose l I'm living.
25:6 his son Isaac to a l in the east.
26:1 There was a famine in the l in
26:3 Live here in this l for a while,
26:12 Isaac planted ⌊crops⌋ in that l.
26:22 and we will prosper in this l."
28:4 of the l where you are
28:4 the l that God gave to
28:13 I will give the l on which you
28:15 also bring you back to this l
29:1 and came to the l in the east.
31:3 "Go back to the l of your
31:13 Now leave this l, and go back
31:13 back to the l of your relatives.'"
32:9 'Go back to your l and to your
33:19 Then he bought the piece of l
34:10 and the l will be yours.
34:21 so let them live in our l and
34:21 plenty of room in this l for them.
35:6 Bethel) in the l of Canaan.
35:12 I will give you the l that I gave
35:12 this l to your descendants."
36:6 went to another l away from his
36:20 the people living in that l:
36:30 tribal leaders in the l of Seir.
36:34 Husham from the l of the
37:1 to live in the l of Canaan,
40:15 I was kidnapped from the l of
41:30 and the famine will ruin the l.
41:31 was plenty of food in the l,
41:34 appoint supervisors over the l
41:36 Then the l will not be ruined by
41:47 the l produced large harvests.
41:52 him children in the l where
42:30 "The governor of that l spoke
42:33 "Then the governor of that l
Gen 43:1 The famine was severe in the l.
43:11 of the best products of the l
45:6 The famine has been in the l
45:10 Live in the l of Goshen,
45:18 give you the best l in Egypt.
45:18 can enjoy the best food in the l.'
47:4 We have come to live in this l
47:6 live in the best part of the l.
47:18 except our bodies and our l.
47:19 Do you want the l to be ruined?
47:19 Take us and our l in exchange
47:19 Pharaoh's slaves and our l will
47:20 Joseph bought all the l in
47:20 The l became Pharaoh's.
47:22 But he didn't buy the priests' l
47:22 why they didn't sell their l.
47:23 you and your l for Pharaoh,
47:23 Plant crops in the l.
47:26 made a law concerning the l
47:26 Only the l of the priests didn't
48:4 I will give this l to your
48:6 They will inherit the l listed
48:21 back to the l of your fathers.
49:15 good and that the l is pleasant,
50:24 of you and take you out of this l
50:24 take you out of this land to the l
Exo 1:7 and strong that the l was filled
2:15 and settled in the l of Midian.
3:8 and to bring them from that l
3:8 them from that land to a good l
3:8 It is a l flowing with milk and
3:17 your misery in Egypt to the l
3:17 a l flowing with milk and
5:5 many people there are in the l!
6:4 the l where they lived as
6:8 I will bring you to the l I
8:5 This will bring frogs onto the l.'"
8:6 up and covered the l of Egypt.
8:7 and brought frogs onto the l.
8:14 and the l began to stink
8:22 I, the LORD, am here in this l.
9:24 was the worst storm in all the l
10:5 They will cover the l so that
10:12 plant in the l — everything left
10:13 his staff over the l of Egypt,
10:13 east blow over the l all that day
11:5 of Pharaoh who rules the l,
12:25 When you enter the l that the
12:29 son of Pharaoh who ruled the l
13:3 you left Egypt, the l of slavery.
13:5 that he would give you the l
13:5 When he brings you into that l
13:11 the LORD brings you to the l
20:12 may live for a long time in the l
23:11 you must leave the l unplowed
23:23 and will bring you to ⌊the l of⌋
23:26 No woman in your l will
23:29 the l would be deserted,
23:30 to take possession of the l.
23:31 in the l under your control,
23:33 Never let them live in your l,
32:12 them out ⌊of our l⌋.' Don't
32:13 to your descendants all the l
33:1 Go to the l I promised to
33:3 Go to that l flowing with milk
34:12 live in the l where you're going.
34:15 with those who live in that l.
34:24 away your l while you're gone
Lev 11:2 Here are the kinds of l animals
18:25 The l has become unclean.
18:25 The l will vomit out those who
18:27 The people of the l who were
18:27 the l has become unclean.
18:28 If you make the l unclean,
19:9 you harvest the grain in your l,
19:23 "When you come into the l and
19:33 a foreigner living in your l.
20:22 the l I am bringing you to live in
20:24 you that you will take their l.
20:24 It is a l flowing with milk and
22:24 things to an animal in your l.
23:10 When you come to the l I am
23:22 you harvest the grain in your l,
23:39 gathered what the l produces,
25:2 When you come into the l I'm
25:2 the l will celebrate a year to
Lev 25:4 will be a festival year for the l.
25:5 year will be a festival for the l.
25:6 Whatever the l produces during
25:7 and the wild animals in your l.
25:7 Everything the l produces will
25:10 to everyone living in the l.
25:11 grapes from the vines in the l.
25:18 you will live securely in the l.
25:19 The l will give you its products,
25:21 that the l will produce enough
25:22 on what the l already produced.
25:22 until the l produces more.
25:23 "L must never be sold
25:23 because the l is mine.
25:31 belonging to the fields of the l.
26:4 The l will produce its crops,
26:5 and live securely in your l.
26:6 "I will bring peace to your l.
26:6 there will be no war in your l.
26:19 have no rain, and your l will
26:20 because your l will produce no
26:32 I will make your l so deserted
26:34 "Then the l will enjoy its time
26:34 and you are in your enemies' l.
26:34 Then the l will joyfully
26:36 those who are left in the l
26:38 The l of their enemies will
26:42 I will also remember the l.
26:43 The l, abandoned by them,
26:44 Even when they are in the l of
27:30 of what comes from the l,
Num 11:12 way to the l you promised their
13:16 Moses sent to explore the l.
13:18 See what the l is like and
13:19 Is the l they live in good or
13:20 Does the l have trees or not?
13:20 back some fruit from the l."
13:21 So the men explored the l from
13:25 came back from exploring the l.
13:26 them the fruit from the l.
13:27 "We went to the l where you
13:27 It really is a l flowing with milk
13:30 and take possession of the l.
13:32 about the l they had explored.
13:32 They said, "The l we explored
14:3 bringing us to this l — just
14:6 those who had explored the l,
14:7 "The l we explored is very
14:8 he will bring us into this l and
14:8 This is a l flowing with milk
14:9 be afraid of the people of the l.
14:14 the people who live in this l?
14:16 to bring these people into the l
14:22 the desert will see the l which
14:24 I'll bring him to the l he already
14:30 swore an oath to give you this l
14:31 them into the l you rejected,
14:34 For 40 days you explored the l.
14:36 sent to explore the l died
14:37 by spreading lies about the l.
14:38 men who went to explore the l,
15:2 settled in the l I'm giving you,
15:18 When you enter the l where I'm
15:19 eat any of the food from the l,
16:13 brought us out of a l flowing
16:14 brought us into a l flowing
18:13 in their l that they bring
18:20 "You will have no l or property
20:12 into the l I'm giving them."
20:24 since he cannot enter the l I'm
21:24 took possession of their l from
21:26 Moab and had taken all his l up
21:31 settled in the l of the Amorites.
21:34 and his l over to you.
21:35 they took possession of his l.
22:5 in the l where his people lived.
26:53 "The l these people will
26:54 Give more l to larger tribes and
26:54 land to larger tribes and less l
26:54 in giving l to each tribe.
26:55 But the l must be divided by
26:55 The tribes will receive their l
26:56 the l must be divided by
26:62 were given no l of their own.
27:12 and take a look at the l I will
32:4 the l that the LORD won for the

Num	32:5	Please give us this **l** as our
	32:7	them from entering the **l**
	32:8	Barnea to take a look at the **l**.
	32:9	Eshcol Valley and saw the **l**.
	32:9	from entering the **l** that
	32:11	will see the **l** I promised
	32:12	of Nun) will get to see the **l**.
	32:17	we have brought them to their **l**.
	32:18	has received his own **l**.
	32:19	won't take possession of any **l**
	32:19	We already have our **l** here,
	32:22	and the **l** is conquered.
	32:22	This **l** will be your own
	32:29	with you and you conquer the **l**,
	32:30	the **l** they will take possession
	32:32	but the **l** we will take
	32:33	Og of Bashan — the whole **l**
	33:53	Take possession of the **l** and
	33:54	Divide the **l** among your
	33:54	Give more **l** to larger families
	33:54	to larger families and less **l**
	33:54	The **l** must be given to each
	33:55	out those who live in the **l**,
	33:55	with you over the **l** you live in.
	34:2	When you enter Canaan, the **l**
	34:12	"This will be your **l** and the
	34:13	"This is the **l** you will divide by
	34:13	has commanded that this **l** will
	34:14	have already received their **l**.
	34:15	tribes received **l** east
	34:17	who will divide the **l** for you:
	34:18	from each tribe to divide the **l**.
	35:4	"The **l** around the cities that
	35:8	amount of **l** each tribe owns.
	35:32	and live on his own **l** before
	35:33	"You must not pollute the **l**
	35:33	Murder is what pollutes the **l**.
	35:33	The **l** where a murder was
	35:34	Never make the **l** where you
	36:2	their **l** by drawing lots.
	36:2	commanded you to give the **l**
	36:3	Their **l** will be taken away from
	36:3	ancestors and added to the **l**
	36:3	we will have lost part of our **l**.
	36:4	their **l** will be added to that of
	36:4	Then part of the **l** of our
	36:7	In this way no **l** of the Israelites
	36:7	the tribal **l** inherited from his
	36:8	A woman who inherits **l** in any
	36:8	keeps the **l** inherited from his
	36:9	No **l** may pass from one tribe to
	36:9	tribe must keep the **l** it inherits."
	36:12	So their **l** stayed in the tribe of
Dtr	1:7	Mediterranean coast (the **l**
	1:8	I'm giving you this **l**.
	1:8	and take possession of the **l**
	1:21	your God is giving you this **l**.
	1:22	information about the **l** for us.
	1:25	They reported, "The **l** that the
	1:35	will ever see the good **l** that
	1:36	and I will give the **l** that he set
	1:38	Israel take possession of the **l**.
	1:39	good and evil, will enter that **l**.
	2:5	you any of their **l** — not even
	2:12	of Esau claimed their **l**,
	2:12	as Israel did in the **l** that the
	2:19	I'm not giving you any of the **l**
	2:20	This **l** was thought of as the
	2:20	land was thought of as the **l**
	2:21	the Ammonites claimed their **l**
	2:22	descendants claimed their **l**
	2:29	cross the Jordan River into the **l**
	2:31	Take possession of his **l**."
	2:37	you to go anywhere near the **l**
	2:37	So you didn't enter the **l** along
	3:2	and his **l** over to you.
	3:8	We took the **l** of the two
	3:12	we took possession of this **l**.
	3:12	of Reuben and Gad the **l** north
	3:13	be called the **l** of the Rephaim.
	3:17	Their **l** included the plains
	3:18	has given you this **l** so that you
	3:20	they take possession of the **l**
	3:20	go back to the **l** I gave you."
	3:25	go over and see the beautiful **l**
	3:27	You may look at the **l**,
Dtr	3:28	possession of the **l** you see."
	4:1	take possession of the **l** that
	4:5	them when you've entered the **l**
	4:14	and take possession of the **l**.
	4:21	River and enter the good **l**
	4:22	I'm going to die in this **l** and not
	4:22	take possession of that good **l**.
	4:25	and have grown old in that **l**,
	4:26	from the **l** you're going
	4:38	way to bring you into their **l**
	4:38	This **l** is your own possession
	4:40	will live for a long time in the **l**.
	4:40	your God is giving you the **l**
	4:46	in the **l** of King Sihon of the
	4:47	They took possession of his **l**
	4:47	of his land and the **l**
	4:48	This **l** went from Aroer on the
	5:16	will go well for you in the **l**
	5:31	to obey in the **l** which I'm giving
	5:33	a long time in the **l** that you are
	6:1	Obey them after you enter the **l**
	6:3	will increase in a **l** flowing
	6:10	God will bring you into the **l**
	6:10	This **l** will have large,
	6:18	of that good **l** which
	6:23	bring us here and give us this **l**
	7:1	bring you to the **l** you're about
	7:13	will bless your **l** with produce:
	7:13	This will all happen in the **l** the
	8:1	take possession of the **l** that
	8:7	is bringing you into a good **l**.
	8:7	It is a **l** with rivers that don't dry
	8:8	The **l** has wheat and barley,
	8:8	The **l** has honey and olive
	8:9	The **l** will have enough food for
	8:9	The **l** has rocks with iron ore,
	8:10	LORD your God for the good **l**
	8:15	desert — a thirsty and arid **l**,
	8:20	other nations as you enter the **l**.
	9:3	will take possession of their **l**
	9:4	to take possession of this **l**."
	9:5	to take possession of their **l**.
	9:6	you this good **l** to possess.
	9:23	of the **l** I'm giving you."
	9:28	able to bring them to the **l**
	10:7	a **l** with rivers that don't dry up.
	10:9	is why the tribe of Levi has no **l**
	10:11	and take possession of the **l**
	11:8	of the **l** once you've crossed
	11:9	also live for a long time in the **l**
	11:9	their descendants — a **l** flowing
	11:10	The **l** you're about to enter and
	11:10	of isn't like the **l** you left
	11:11	The **l** you're about to enter is a
	11:11	land you're about to enter is a **l**
	11:12	It is a **l** the LORD your God
	11:14	I will send rain on your **l** at the
	11:17	disappear from this good **l**
	11:21	live for a long time in this **l** that
	11:23	of ⌐the **l** belonging to¬ people
	11:25	you wherever you go in this **l**.
	11:29	you into the **l** you're about
	11:31	and take possession of the **l**
	12:1	must faithfully obey in the **l** that
	12:1	as long as you live in the **l**.
	12:10	Jordan River and settle in the **l**
	12:12	cities because they have no **l**
	12:19	as long as you live in your **l**.
	12:29	of their **l** and live there.
	13:7	one end of the **l** to the other.)
	14:27	They have no **l** of their own as
	14:29	come because they have no **l**
	15:4	will certainly bless you in the **l**
	15:7	in one of your cities in the **l** that
	15:11	always be poor people in the **l**.
	16:4	be no yeast anywhere in your **l**
	16:20	take possession of the **l** that
	17:14	You will enter the **l** that the
	18:1	tribe of Levi — will receive no **l**
	18:2	So the Levites will have no **l** of
	18:9	When you come to the **l** that
	19:1	living in the **l** that he's giving
	19:2	set aside three cities in the **l**
	19:3	cities and divide the **l** that
	19:8	He may give you the whole **l**
	19:10	won't be killed in the **l** that
Dtr	19:14	on any property in the **l** that
	21:1	lying in a field in the **l** that
	21:4	to a location where the **l** hasn't
	21:23	The **l** that the LORD your God
	23:20	do once you've entered the **l**
	24:4	Don't pollute with sin the **l** that
	25:15	live for a long time in the **l** that
	25:19	around you in the **l** that
	26:1	take possession of the **l** that
	26:2	from the fields in the **l** that
	26:3	that I have come to the **l** that
	26:9	and gave us this **l** flowing
	26:15	people Israel and the **l** flowing
	27:2	Jordan River and enter the **l** that
	27:3	is giving you a **l** flowing
	27:3	After you're in that **l**,
	28:4	Your **l** will have crops.
	28:8	God will bless you in the **l** that
	28:11	produce many crops in the **l**
	28:12	He will send rain on your **l** at
	28:18	Your **l** will have few crops.
	28:21	you out of the **l** you're about
	28:33	never knew will eat what your **l**
	28:52	down everywhere in your **l**.
	28:52	cities everywhere in the **l** that
	28:63	You will be torn out of the **l**
	29:8	We took their **l** and gave it to
	29:22	that have happened in this **l**
	29:24	the LORD done this to their **l**?
	29:27	LORD became angry with this **l**
	29:28	these people from their **l**
	30:5	to the **l** your ancestors owned.
	30:16	you in the **l** that you're about
	30:18	time in the **l** that you're going
	30:20	a long life for you in the **l** that
	31:3	will take possession of their **l**.
	31:7	with these people into the **l** that
	31:7	them take possession of the **l**.
	31:13	as you live in the **l** that you are
	31:16	When these people enter the **l**
	31:20	I will bring them into the **l** that I
	31:20	a **l** flowing with milk and
	31:21	I bring them into the **l** that
	31:23	the Israelites into the **l** that
	32:8	Most High gave nations their **l**,
	32:10	found his people in a desert **l**,
	32:43	make peace for his people's **l**.
	32:47	a long time in the **l** that you are
	32:49	Take a look at the **l** of Canaan
	32:52	You may see the **l** from a
	32:52	but you may not enter the **l** I'm
	33:13	bless their **l** with ⌐water,¬
	33:14	LORD bless their **l** with crops,
	33:16	May the LORD bless their **l**
	33:20	gives the people of Gad more **l**.
	33:21	the best **l** for themselves.
	33:21	a commander's piece of **l** was
	33:23	of the lake and the **l** south of it."
	33:28	spring will be ⌐left¬ alone in a **l**
	34:1	LORD showed him the whole **l**.
	34:4	"This is the **l** I promised with
Jos	1:2	the Jordan River into the **l** that
	1:6	people take possession of the **l**
	1:11	to take possession of the **l**
	1:13	your God will give you this **l** —
	1:14	and livestock may stay in the **l**
	1:15	take possession of the **l** the
	1:15	take possession of the **l** east
	2:2	gather information about our **l**."
	2:3	information about the entire **l**."
	2:9	the LORD will give you this **l**.
	2:14	the LORD gives us this **l**."
	2:18	When we invade your **l**,
	4:18	their feet stepped onto dry **l**,
	5:6	not let them see this **l** flowing
	5:11	some of the produce of the **l**,
	6:27	fame spread throughout the **l**.
	7:9	lives in the **l** hears about it,
	8:1	people, city, and **l** over to you.
	9:24	Moses to give you the whole **l**
	10:40	So Joshua captured the whole **l**
	11:16	Joshua took all this **l**,
	11:16	all the **l** of Goshen,
	11:17	The **l** extended from Mount
	11:23	Joshua captured the whole **l**
	11:23	So the **l** had peace.

Jos 12:1 These are the kings of the l
12:6 Then he gave their l as a
12:7 These are the kings of the l
13:1 and there is a lot of l left to be
13:2 The l that is left includes all
13:4 This territory includes all the l
13:5 It also includes the l of the
13:6 you must distribute the l as an
13:7 So divide this l. It will be an
13:14 Moses did not give any l as an
13:15 Moses gave some l as an
13:24 Moses gave some l as an
13:29 Moses gave some l as an
13:32 This is the l that Moses
13:33 Moses did not give any l as an
14:1 This is the l that the people of
14:2 The l inherited by the
14:3 He did not give any l as an
14:4 were not given a share of the l.
14:5 people of Israel divided the l as
14:7 Kadesh Barnea to explore the l.
14:9 'The l your feet walked on will
14:15 So the l had peace.
15:13 a share of l among the people
15:19 you've given me some dry l,
15:20 This is the l inherited by the
16:4 this l as their inheritance.
16:5 The eastern border of the l they
16:8 This is the l given as an
17:2 The l was given to the rest of
17:4 Moses to give us some l as
17:5 Ten portions of l went to
17:5 besides the l of Gilead and
17:8 (The l of Tappuah belongs to
17:12 determined to stay in this l.
17:15 for yourselves there in the l
18:1 The l was under their control.
18:2 any l as their inheritance.
18:3 time conquering the l which
18:4 They will survey the l and
18:5 They will divide the l into
18:6 the seven parts of the l
18:8 to write a description of the l.
18:8 He said, "Go survey the l.
18:9 The men surveyed the l.
18:9 The l was divided into seven
18:10 There Joshua divided the l
19:9 because Judah had more l than
19:49 finally received the l they were
19:49 the people of Israel also gave l
19:51 This is the l that the tribes of
19:51 divided the l by drawing lots.
19:51 So they finished dividing the l.
21:43 LORD gave Israel the whole l
22:4 So return home, to the l that is
22:4 It is the l that the LORD's
22:7 Moses had given l in Bashan
22:7 the other half of the tribe their l
22:19 If your l is unclean,
22:19 come over here to the LORD's l.
22:33 the l where they were
23:5 You will take their l as the
23:13 of you are left in this good l that
23:15 you from this good l that
23:16 disappear from the good l
24:8 "After that I brought you to the l
24:8 So you took their l,
24:13 So I gave you a l that you
24:15 Amorites in whose l you live,
24:18 the Amorites who lived in this l.
24:30 He was buried on his own l at
Jdg 1:15 you've given me some dry l,
1:26 The man went to the l of the
1:27 determined to live in this l.
2:1 you out of Egypt into the l that
2:2 the people who live in this l.
3:11 there was finally peace in the l
3:30 peace in the l for 80 years.
5:31 So the l had peace for 40 years.
6:4 enemy used to camp on the l
6:5 They came into the l only to
6:9 of your way. I gave you their l.
6:10 in whose l you will live.'
8:28 So the l had peace for 40 years
9:45 and scattered salt all over the l.
10:8 east of the Jordan River in the l

Jdg 11:3 He went to live in the l of Tob.
11:5 get Jephthah from the l of Tob.
11:12 "Why did you invade my l and
11:13 left Egypt, they took my l.
11:15 didn't take away the l belonging
11:19 us go through your l to our own.
11:21 and took possession of all the l
16:24 destroyer of our l and killer of
18:1 time they had not received l as
18:2 sent to spy throughout the l
18:2 "Go and explore the l!"
18:9 We saw the l. It's very good!
18:9 Go at once and take the l.
18:10 The l is wide open to you.
18:14 the l around Laish spoke
18:17 throughout the l went inside.
18:30 in that l were taken captive.
Rut 1:1 there was a famine in the l.
1Sm 13:3 the ram's horn throughout the l,
13:19 be found in the entire l of Israel.
14:25 The entire l had honeycombs,
14:46 returned to their own l.
22:5 "Go to the l of Judah."
28:3 (Saul had rid the l of mediums
28:9 "You know that Saul rid the l of
30:16 were spread out all over the l,
30:16 territory and from the l of Judah
2Sm 4:11 his murder and rid the l of you."
9:7 I will give back to you all the l
9:10 your servants should farm the l
15:4 would make me judge in the l.
19:29 and Ziba should divide the l."
21:10 She wouldn't let any birds l on
21:14 Jonathan in the l of Benjamin,
21:14 answered the prayers for the l.
24:13 famine come to you and your l,
24:13 be a three-day plague in your l?
1Ki 2:26 "Go to your l in Anathoth.
8:34 and bring them back to the l
8:36 Then send rain on the l,
8:37 "There may be famine in the l.
8:40 as long as they live in the l
8:47 and plead with you in the l
8:48 their attitude toward you in the l
8:48 if they pray to you toward the l
9:7 then I will cut Israel out of the l
9:8 things to this l and this temple?'
9:20 had been left ⌊in the l⌋
9:21 who were still in the l.
11:18 home, a food allowance, and l.
14:15 Israel from this good l which
14:24 of idols throughout the l.
15:12 temple prostitutes out of the l
17:7 no rain had fallen in the l.
17:14 the LORD sends rain on the l,
21:26 confiscated their l for Israel.)
22:46 He rid the l of the male temple
2Ki 2:19 and the l cannot grow crops."
3:19 to ruin every good piece of l."
8:3 the king about her house and l.
8:5 the king about her house and l.
11:14 All the people of the l were
11:18 Then all the people of the l
11:19 and all the people of the l,
11:20 of the l were celebrating.
16:15 of all the people of the l.
17:11 had removed from the l ahead
17:23 of Israel were taken from their l
19:37 and escaped to the l of Ararat.
21:8 feet wander from the l that
21:9 the Israelites arrived in the l.
21:24 Then the people of the l killed
23:24 gods that could be seen in the l
23:30 Then the people of the l took
23:35 gold from the people of the l
24:14 people of the l were left.
24:15 and the leading citizens of the l
25:12 of the poorest people in the l
25:21 captives when they left their l.
25:22 people in the l of Judah.
1Ch 1:45 Husham from the l of the
4:40 The l was vast, peaceful,
4:41 They lived in that l in place of
5:22 lived in the Hagrites' l until
5:23 lived in the l from Bashan
5:25 of the people of the l as if they

1Ch 6:78 Merari's descendants received l
7:28 The l and homes of Ephraim's
16:19 of foreigners living in that l,
21:12 sword — a plague in the l
21:22 "Let me have the l this
28:8 be able to possess this good l
2Ch 2:17 foreigners in the l of Israel,
6:25 and bring them back to the l
6:27 Then send rain on the l,
6:28 "There may be famine in the l.
6:31 as long as they live in the l
6:37 and plead with you in the l
6:38 you in the l where they are
6:38 if they pray to you toward the l
7:20 I will uproot Israel from the l
7:21 things to this l and this temple?'
8:7 had been left ⌊in the l⌋
8:8 who were still in the l.
9:14 of the l also brought gold
11:14 The priests abandoned their l
14:1 In Asa's time the l had peace
14:6 because the l had peace.
15:5 everyone living in the l had
20:11 us out of your l that you gave
23:13 All the people of the l were
23:20 and all the people of the l,
23:21 of the l were celebrating.
30:9 They will return to this l.
32:4 brook that flowed through the l.
32:31 sign that had happened in the l,
33:8 remove Israel from the l that
33:9 the Israelites arrived in the l.
33:25 Then the people of the l killed
34:8 reign as he was making the l
36:1 Then people of the l took
36:21 The l had its years of rest and
36:21 ⌊the l had its⌋ 70 years of rest.
Ezr 6:21 of the non-Jews in the l
9:11 'The l you are going to take
9:12 the good things the l produces,
9:12 and be able to give this l as a
10:11 from the people of this l
Neh 4:4 and let them be robbed in the l
5:16 and we bought no l.
9:8 a promise to him to give the l
9:10 and all the people in his l
9:15 of the l that you swore
9:22 possession of the l of Sihon,
9:22 the l of the king of Heshbon,
9:22 and the l of King Og of Bashan.
9:23 You brought them into the l you
9:24 took possession of the l.
9:24 Canaanites, who lived in the l.
9:25 fortified cities and a rich l.
9:35 fertile l which was set in front
9:36 In the l you gave our ancestors,
9:37 The many products ⌊from our l⌋
10:28 from the inhabitants of the l
10:30 to marry the inhabitants of the l
10:31 If the inhabitants of the l bring
11:30 So they settled in the l from
Job 1:10 have spread out over the l.
10:21 before I go away to a l of
10:22 to a dismal l of long shadows
14:19 wash away soil from the l,
15:19 (The l was given to them alone,
15:19 stranger passed through their l.
15:29 won't spread out over the l.
22:8 A strong person owns the l.
24:18 Their property is cursed in the l
30:8 forced out of the l with whips.
31:38 "If my l has cried out against
38:26 to bring rain on a l where no
41:33 Nothing on l can compare to it.
Psa 10:16 have vanished from his l.
25:13 descendants will inherit the l.
35:20 the peaceful people in the l.
37:3 Live in the l, and practice being
37:9 for the LORD will inherit the l.
37:11 people will inherit the l
37:22 by him will inherit the l.
37:29 people will inherit the l
37:34 honor you by giving you the l.
41:2 He will be blessed in the l.
42:6 you in the l of Jordan,
44:2 forced nations ⌊out of the l⌋,

Psa 44:3 they took possession of the l.
60:2 You made the l quake.
63:1 parched l where there is no
66:6 He turned the sea into dry l.
68:6 must live in an unproductive l.
68:9 You watered the l with plenty
68:9 it when your l was exhausted.
72:6 like showers that water the l.
72:16 there be plenty of grain in the l.
74:8 meeting place of God in the l.
74:20 dark corner of the l is filled
78:12 miracles in the l of Egypt,
78:54 He brought them into his holy l,
78:55 their way and gave them the l
79:1 the nations have invaded the l
80:9 that it took root and filled the l.
85:1 You favored your l,
85:9 ⌊this⌋ glory will remain in our l.
85:12 and our l will produce crops.
95:5 and his hands formed the dry l.
101:6 people in the l so that they
101:8 all the wicked people in the l
105:11 "I will give you the l of Canaan.
105:12 of foreigners living in that l,
105:16 He brought famine to the l.
105:23 as a foreigner in the l of Ham.
105:27 amazing things in the l of Ham.
105:28 and made ⌊their l⌋ dark.
105:30 He made their l swarm with
105:32 of rain throughout their l.
105:35 devoured all the plants in the l.
105:36 the first ones born in the l when
106:22 miracles in the l of Ham,
106:24 ⌊to enter⌋ the pleasant l.
106:38 The l became polluted with
125:3 to govern the l set aside
135:12 He gave their l as an
136:21 He gave their l as an
137:4 the LORD's song in a foreign l?
139:9 rays of the morning sun ⌊or⌋ l
143:6 Like parched l, my soul thirsts
Pro 2:21 Decent people will live in the l.
2:22 people will be cut off from the l
8:26 when he had not yet made l or
10:30 will not continue to live in the l.
12:11 Whoever works his l will have
28:19 Whoever works his l will have
30:16 the grave, a barren womb, a l
31:23 he sits with the leaders of the l.
Sos 2:12 Blossoms appear in the l.
2:12 mourning dove is heard in our l.
Isa 1:19 you will eat the best from the l.
2:7 Their l is filled with silver and
2:7 Their l is filled with horses,
2:8 Their l is filled with idols,
4:2 The fruit of the l will be the
5:8 have to live by yourself in the l.
5:30 If they look at the l,
6:11 the l is completely desolate.
6:12 of the l will be abandoned.
6:13 the l will be burned again.
7:16 the l of the two kings who
7:22 Everyone who is left in the l
7:24 hunt⌋ because the whole l will
8:21 They will pass through the l
9:1 no more gloom for the l that is
9:1 to the l across the Jordan River,
9:2 live in the l of death's shadow.
9:19 The l is scorched by the fury of
13:5 army is coming from a distant l,
13:14 people and flee to his own l.
14:2 female slaves in the LORD's l.
14:20 you have destroyed your l
14:25 I'll crush Assyria on my l.
15:8 echo throughout the l of Moab.
16:1 Send lambs to the ruler of the l.
18:1 How horrible it will be for the l
18:2 whose l is divided by rivers.
18:7 whose l is divided by rivers.
19:17 The l of Judah will terrify the
21:1 the desert, from a terrifying l.
21:14 inhabitants of the l of Tema.
22:18 you far away into another l.
23:13 Look at the l of the
23:13 Assyria gave this l to the
25:5 like heat in a dry l.)
Isa 26:1 will be sung in the l of Judah:
26:10 what is wrong in the upright l
26:18 able to bring salvation to the l,
28:22 to destroy the whole l.
32:2 of a large rock in a weary l.
32:13 Mourn for my people's l where
33:17 You will see a l that stretches
34:6 huge slaughter in the l of Edom.
34:7 Their l will be drenched with
34:9 Its l will become blazing tar.
34:11 will take possession of the l.
34:17 and his hand divides up ⌊the l⌋
35:1 The desert and the dry l will be
35:2 Like a lily the l will blossom.
37:38 and escaped to the l of Ararat.
41:18 I will turn dry l into springs.
43:19 I will make rivers on dry l.
43:20 I will make rivers on the dry l
44:3 thirsty ground and rain on dry l.
46:11 for my plan from a faraway l.
49:8 You will restore the l.
49:12 will come from the l of Sinim.
49:19 and demolished and your l is
57:13 trusts me will possess the l
60:6 camels will cover your ⌊l⌋,
60:18 hear about violence in your l
60:21 will possess the l permanently.
61:7 measure of wealth in your l.
62:4 and your l will no longer be
62:4 and your l will be named
62:4 and your l will be married.
63:18 holy people possessed the l
65:16 asks for a blessing in the l will
65:16 an oath in the l will swear by
Jer 1:14 on all those who live in the l.
1:18 able to stand up to the whole l.
2:2 into a l that couldn't be farmed.
2:6 a l of drought and the shadow
2:7 I brought them into a fertile l to
2:7 came and made my l unclean.
2:15 Young lions have turned the l
2:31 a l of thick darkness,
3:1 The l would become
3:2 You have polluted the l with
3:9 she polluted the l and
3:16 will increase in the l," declares
3:18 will come together from the l
3:18 the land of the north to the l that
3:19 and give you a pleasant l,
4:5 the ram's horn throughout the l.
4:7 left his place to destroy your l.
4:20 The whole l is ruined.
4:26 I see that the fertile l has
5:19 served foreign gods in your l.
5:19 in a l that isn't yours."
5:30 is happening in the l:
6:8 I will make your l desolate,
6:8 a l where no one will live.
6:12 in the l," declares the LORD.
6:20 from a distant l is no good
7:7 in the l that I gave permanently
7:34 because the l will be a
8:16 makes the whole l tremble.
8:16 They are coming to devour the l
8:19 people comes from a distant l:
9:3 Lies and dishonesty rule the l.
9:12 The l dies; it has been ruined
9:19 We must leave our l because
10:18 who live in the l at this time
10:22 uproar is coming from the l
11:5 and give them a l flowing
11:5 the l you still have today."'" I
12:4 How long will the l mourn?
12:11 The whole l is destroyed,
12:12 them from one end of the l
13:13 who lives in this l drunk.
14:4 there has been no rain in the l.
14:8 you be like a stranger in the l,
14:15 be no wars or famines in this l.
14:18 through a l they haven't heard
15:14 enemies in a l that you haven't
16:3 who have children in this l:
16:6 young alike will die in this l.
16:13 So I will throw you out of this l
16:13 out of this land into a l that you
16:15 the people of Israel out of the l
Jer 16:15 bring them back to the l that
16:18 they have polluted my l.
17:4 enemies in a l that you haven't
17:6 in a salty l where no one can
18:16 Their l will become desolate
22:12 and he will never see this l
22:26 and your mother into another l.
22:27 You will want to return to this l,
22:28 another l they've never heard
22:29 O l, land, land! Listen to the
22:29 O land, l, land! Listen to the
22:29 O land, land, l! Listen to the
23:5 do what is fair and right in the l.
23:8 the nation of Israel out of the l
23:8 they will live in their own l.
23:10 The l is filled with adulterers.
23:10 The l mourns because of the
23:15 godlessness throughout the l.
24:6 I will bring them back to this l.
24:8 who stayed behind in this l,
24:10 they disappear from the l that
25:5 and live in the l that the LORD
25:9 from the north to attack this l,
25:11 This whole l will be ruined and
25:13 I will bring on that l all the
25:20 all the kings of the l of Uz;
25:30 He roars against his l.
25:38 Their l has been ruined
26:17 of the leaders in the l got up
26:20 city and this l as Jeremiah did.
27:11 I will let it stay in its own l.
27:11 People will farm the l and live
30:3 I will bring them back to the l
31:8 "I will bring them from the l of
31:16 return from the l of the enemy.
32:15 and vineyards in this l.'
32:22 You gave them the l that you
32:22 the l flowing with milk and
32:41 faithfully plant them in this l.
32:43 You have said that this l is a
32:43 once again buy fields in this l.
33:11 will restore the fortunes of the l
33:15 do what is fair and right in the l.
35:7 long time in the l where you are
35:11 of Babylon invaded this l,
35:15 Then you will live in the l that I
36:29 certainly come to destroy this l
37:7 will go back to Egypt, its own l.
37:19 wouldn't attack you and this l?
39:10 had nothing in the l of Judah.
40:4 The whole l is yours.
40:6 people who were left in the l.
41:2 had appointed to govern the l.
41:18 had appointed to govern the l.
42:10 Suppose you stay in this l.
42:12 on you and return you to your l.
42:13 'We won't stay in this l,' and
44:21 and the people in the l?
44:22 That is why your l has become
44:22 No one lives in that l today.
46:16 to the l where we were born,
46:27 descendants from a faraway l,
46:27 from the l where you are
47:2 It will overflow the l and
47:2 lives in the l will cry loudly.
50:1 spoke about Babylon and the l
50:3 and destroy its l so that no
50:8 Leave the l of the Babylonians.
50:18 the king of Babylon and his l as
50:21 "Attack the l of Merathaim and
50:22 and great destruction fills the l.
50:25 do in the l of the Babylonians.
50:34 in order to bring rest to the l
50:38 Babylon is a l of idols,
50:45 things he intends to do to the l
51:2 to winnow it and strip its l bare.
51:4 will lie dead in their own l.
51:5 although their l is guilty of
51:9 abandon it and go to our own l.
51:43 It will become a desert, a l
51:46 when rumors are heard in the l.
51:46 Rumors of violence are in the l.
51:46 against another are in the l.
51:50 the LORD in a distant l,
51:52 will moan everywhere in the l.
51:54 from the l of the Babylonians.

Jer 52:16 of the poorest people in the l
52:27 captives as they left their l.
Lam 2:3 a raging fire in ⌊the l of⌋ Jacob,
5:2 "The l we inherited has been
Eze 5:16 and more famines into your l,
6:14 against them and destroy the l,
7:2 ⌊the people in⌋ the l of Israel:
7:7 inhabitants of the l.
7:23 The l is filled with murder,
8:12 LORD has abandoned this l.'"
8:17 Yet, they also fill the l with
9:9 The l is filled with murder,
9:9 the LORD has abandoned the l
11:15 This l has been given to us as
11:17 I will give them the l of Israel.
12:6 face so that you won't see the l.
12:12 so that he cannot see the l.
12:13 the l of the Babylonians,
12:19 "Tell the people of this l,
12:19 Jerusalem and in the l of Israel:
16:3 your ancestors were in the l
16:27 I took away some of your l,
16:29 of prostitution to include the l
18:2 proverb about the l of Israel:
19:7 The l and everyone living in it
19:13 in a dry and waterless l.
20:6 them out of Egypt to a l that
20:6 This l is the most beautiful
20:6 land is the most beautiful l,
20:6 a l flowing with milk and
20:15 not bring them into the l that
20:15 This l is the most beautiful
20:15 land is the most beautiful l,
20:15 a l flowing with milk and
20:28 I brought them to the l that I
20:38 I will bring you out of the l
20:40 of Israel, everyone in the l,
20:42 I will bring you to the l of Israel,
20:42 the l that I promised to give
20:47 It will burn the whole l from the
21:2 Prophesy against the l of Israel.
21:3 Tell the l of Israel,
21:30 in the l where you were born,
21:32 You will die in the l.
22:4 nations and a joke in every l.
22:24 'You are an unclean l that has
22:30 in the walls to defend the l
23:48 a stop to the sinning in the l,
25:3 when the l of Israel was ruined,
25:4 They will possess your l.
25:6 felt contempt for the l of Israel.
25:13 I will turn the l into ruins from
26:20 your place in the l of the living.
28:25 of Israel will live in their own l,
28:25 the l I gave to my servant
29:14 the l they came from.
30:5 and people from the promised l
30:11 will be brought to destroy the l.
30:11 and fill the l with dead bodies.
30:12 up the Nile River and sell the l
30:12 have foreigners destroy the l
31:12 fell in every ravine in the l.
32:8 will bring darkness over your l,
32:15 I will take everything in the l,
32:23 people in the l of the living.
32:24 once terrified people in the l
32:25 they terrified others in the l
32:26 others in the l of the living.
32:27 others in the l of the living.
32:32 I terrified people in the l of the
33:24 and he was given the l.
33:24 Certainly the l has been given
33:25 Should the l be given to you?
33:26 Should the l be given to you?'
33:28 I will turn the l into a barren
33:29 when I make the l a barren
34:13 and bring them to their own l.
34:13 all the inhabited places of the l.
34:14 They will rest on the good l
34:25 animals from the l so that my
34:27 the l will yield crops,
34:27 sheep will live safely in their l.
34:29 experience hunger in the l,
35:10 along with their l, belong to us.
35:15 You were happy when the l of
36:5 have taken possession of my l
Exe 36:5 out the people and took their l.'
36:17 people of Israel lived in their l,
36:18 they poured out blood on the l
36:18 the l with their idols.
36:20 yet they had to leave his l.'
36:24 bring you back to your own l.
36:28 Then you will live in the l that I
36:36 crops in the l that was empty.
37:14 I will place you in your own l.
37:21 and bring them to their own l.
37:22 them into one nation in the l
37:25 They will live in the l that I
37:25 the l where their ancestors
38:2 turn to Gog from the l of Magog
38:8 you will attack a l that has
38:9 like a storm and cover the l like
38:11 You will say, "I'll attack a l
38:16 like a cloud that covers the l.
38:16 I will let you attack my l so that
38:18 that Gog attacks the l of Israel,
38:19 earthquake in the l of Israel.
39:12 months to make the l clean.
39:14 be chosen to go through the l
39:15 Whenever they go through the l
39:16 way they will cleanse the l.'
39:26 When they live safely in a l
39:28 them back again to their l.
45:1 "'Divide the l by drawing lots
45:4 This holy part of the l will
45:7 "The prince will have all the l
45:7 his l will extend to the
45:7 his l will extend to the eastern
45:8 This l will belong to the prince
45:8 They will give l to each tribe of
47:8 "This water flows through the l
47:13 These are the borders of the l
47:14 Divide the l equally.
47:14 swore that I would give the l
47:14 So this l will be your
47:15 is the northern border for the l:
47:18 Gilead and the l of Israel.
47:21 Divide this l among yourselves
47:22 This l will be for you.
48:1 Dan will have one part of the l.
48:2 Asher will have one part of the l
48:3 will have one part of the l
48:4 will have one part of the l
48:5 will have one part of the l
48:6 will have one part of the l
48:7 will have one part of the l
48:8 The l that you set aside as a
48:9 This special l that you set
48:11 This l that has been set apart
48:12 a special portion from the l.
48:12 It will be the holiest part of l,
48:12 next to the l belonging to the
48:13 Alongside the l belonging to
48:13 priests will be the l belonging
48:14 have the best part of the l,
48:14 because the l is the LORD's
48:15 A strip of l, 8,750 feet wide by
48:18 The rest of the l borders the
48:18 This l will be 17,500 feet on its
48:20 You must give this l as a
48:21 This l will extend eastward
48:22 the prince's part of the l.
48:23 will have one part of the l.
48:24 will have one part of the l
48:25 will have one part of the l
48:26 will have one part of the l
48:27 Gad will have one part of the l
48:29 This is the l you will divide as
Dan 8:9 and the beautiful l.
11:10 ⌊enemy⌋ and pass through its l.
11:16 rise to power in the beautiful l
11:39 and distribute l for a price.
11:40 and pass through their l.
11:41 He will invade the beautiful l,
Hos 1:2 The people in this l have acted
1:11 and they will grow in the l.
2:3 turn her into a dry and barren l,
2:23 I will plant my people in the l.
4:1 against those who live in the l:
4:1 no knowledge of God in the l.
4:3 That is why the l is drying up,
9:3 won't stay in the LORD's l.
Hos 10:1 The more their l produced,
13:5 of you in the desert, in a dry l.
Joe 1:2 all inhabitants of this l!
1:6 A strong nation attacked my l.
1:14 everyone who lives in the l.
2:1 lives in the l should tremble,
2:3 In front of it the l is like the
2:3 Behind it the l is like a barren
2:18 became concerned about his l,
2:20 force it into a dry and barren l.
2:21 L, do not be afraid. Be glad and
3:2 They divided my l.
3:6 send them far away from their l.
3:19 innocent people in their l.
Amo 2:10 of the l of the Amorites.
3:5 Does a bird l in a trap on the
3:11 An enemy will surround your l,
4:6 with no food in your entire l.
5:2 lie abandoned in their own l.
5:17 through your l ⌊with death⌋.
7:2 eating every plant in the l,
7:4 the ocean and burned up the l.
7:11 taken from its l into exile."
7:17 Your l will be surveyed and
7:17 you will die in an unclean l.
7:17 taken from its l into exile."
8:8 The l will tremble because of
8:8 The entire l will rise like the
8:11 send a famine throughout the l.
9:15 the people of Israel in their l,
9:15 uprooted again from the l that
Oba 1:7 will force you to leave your l.
1:20 They will possess l as far as
Jnh 1:9 who made the sea and the l."
Mic 5:5 the Assyrians invade our l
5:6 when they come into our l
5:11 I will destroy the cities in your l
Hab 3:9 You split the l with rivers.
Zep 2:3 all you humble people in the l
2:5 the l of the Philistines:
3:8 The whole l will be consumed
Hag 1:11 I called for a drought on the l,
2:4 Everyone in the l, be strong,"
2:6 the sea and the dry l.
Zec 1:21 horns to scatter the l of Judah."
2:6 Flee from the l of the north,
2:12 Judah as his own in the holy l
7:5 "Tell all the people of the l and
7:14 They left behind a l so ruined
7:14 a pleasant l into a wasteland."
8:7 my people from the l where
8:7 sun rises and from the l where
8:12 The l will yield its crops.
9:1 of the LORD is against the l
9:16 sparkle in his l like jewels
11:6 pity on those who live in the l.
11:6 who will crush the l.
11:16 to place a shepherd in the l.
12:12 The l will mourn, each family
13:2 names of the idols from the l.
13:2 the unclean spirit from the l.
13:5 I've owned this l since I was a
13:8 "Throughout the l two-thirds
Mal 1:4 'the Wicked L' and 'the people
3:11 destroy the produce of your l.
3:12 you will be a delightful l," says
4:6 my l by destroying you."
Mat 2:6 Bethlehem in the l of Judah,
4:15 "L of Zebulun and land of
4:15 of Zebulun and l of Naphtali,
4:16 in a l overshadowed by death."
23:15 You cross l and sea to recruit a
27:45 over the whole l until three
Mar 6:47 and he was alone on the l.
15:33 over the whole l until three
Luk 12:16 He said, "A rich man had l that
21:23 the l will suffer very hard times,
23:44 darkness came over the entire l
Jon 4:5 Sychar was near the piece of l
Act 1:18 he bought a piece of l where
1:19 call that piece of l Akeldama,
4:24 made the sky, the l, the sea,
4:34 From time to time, people sold l
4:37 He had some l. He sold it and
5:3 money you received for the l.
5:4 While you had the l,

Act 5:8 did you sell the l for that price?"
7:3 God told him, 'Leave your l
7:3 Go to the l that I will show you.'
7:4 there to this l where we now
7:5 give Abraham anything in this l
7:5 But God promised to give this l
7:45 they brought it into this l.
7:45 took possession of the l from
10:39 to everything Jesus did in the l
13:19 in Canaan and gave their l
14:15 made the sky, the l, the sea,
27:27 that we were approaching l.
27:39 they couldn't recognize the l,
Rom 9:28 carry out his sentence on the l,
Heb 11:29 the Red Sea as if it were dry l.
Rev 7:1 them from blowing on the l,
7:2 allowed to harm the l and sea,
7:3 "Don't harm the l, the sea,
10:2 on the sea and his left on the l.
10:5 sea and on the l raised his right
10:8 on the sea and on the l."

landed (5)

Exo 10:14 They invaded all of Egypt and l
1Sm 20:37 Jonathan's arrow ⌊had⌋ l,
Mat 14:34 the sea and l at Gennesaret.
Luk 8:26 They l in the region of the
Act 21:3 We l at the city of Tyre,

landmarks (1)

Jer 31:21 Set up l! Put up road signs!

landowner (3)

Mat 20:1 heaven is like a l who went out
21:33 A l planted a vineyard.
21:36 So the l sent more servants.

landowners (1)

2Ki 24:16 all 7,000 of the prominent l,

land's (3)

Isa 6:13 holy seed will be the l stump.
26:15 extended all the l boundaries
Zec 3:9 "I will remove this l sin in a

lands (28)

Gen 26:3 I will give all these l to you
26:4 in the sky and give all these l
Lev 26:39 are left will waste away in the l
26:41 them and bring them into the l
Dtr 31:4 the Amorites and to their l when
Jos 12:1 took possession of their l from
12:7 ⌊Their l extended⌋ from Baal
1Ch 14:17 fame spread through all l,
Ezr 4:10 and the rest of the l west
Psa 7:16 His mischief l back on his own
49:11 named their l after themselves,
65:8 The l of the morning sunrise
105:44 He gave them the l of ⌊other⌋
106:27 them throughout various l.
111:6 his people by giving them the l
Isa 9:1 God humbled the l of Zebulun
23:7 its people to settle in distant l?
30:6 "My people travel through l
Jer 12:14 those neighbors from their l.
12:15 their inheritance and to their l.
16:15 of the north and all the l where
23:8 of the north and all the l where
27:10 you to be taken far from your l.
32:37 the people from all the l where
Oba 1:19 will take possession of the l
Hab 1:6 of l that don't belong
2:8 and violence done to l,
2:17 and violence done to l,

language (57)

Gen 10:5 had its own l and families.
11:1 The whole world had one l
11:6 are one people with one l.
11:7 and mix up their l so that they
11:9 there the LORD turned the l
31:47 ⌊In his l⌋ Laban called it Jegar
Dtr 28:49 whose l you won't understand.
2Ki 18:26 to us in the Judean l as long as
18:28 shouted loudly in the Judean l,
2Ch 32:18 shouted loudly in the Judean l
Ezr 4:7 translated into the Aramaic l.
Neh 13:24 Half their children spoke the l
13:24 they couldn't understand the l
Est 1:22 in each province in their own l:
3:12 in each province in their own l.
8:9 to each people in their own l,
8:9 their own script and their own l.
Psa 55:9 Completely confuse their l,
114:1 people who spoke a foreign l,
Isa 19:18 have people that speak the l
28:11 them by speaking in a foreign l.
33:19 with an unrecognizable l,
33:19 with a foreign l that you can't
36:11 to us in the Judean l as long as
36:13 shouted loudly in the Judean l,
66:18 to gather the nations of every l.
Jer 5:15 You don't know the l of this
Eze 3:5 you to people whose l is hard
3:6 you to nations whose l is hard
Dan 1:4 They were to be taught the l
3:4 of every province, nation, and l!
3:7 and l bowed down and
3:29 or l who say anything
4:1 nation, and l in the world.
5:19 and l trembled and were
6:25 and l all over the world:
7:14 and l were to serve him.
Zec 8:23 from every l found among
Jon 8:43 you understand the l I use?
Act 13:45 They used insulting l to
14:11 shouted in the Lycaonian l,
21:40 spoke to them in the Hebrew l.
1Co 5:11 gods, use abusive l, get drunk,
6:10 who use abusive l,
14:2 a person speaks in another l,
14:4 a person speaks in another l,
14:11 If I don't know what a l means,
14:13 speaks in another l should pray
14:14 If I pray in another l,
14:19 thousand words in another l.
14:26 another l, or an interpretation.
Col 3:8 obscene l, and all similar sins.
2Ti 3:2 and use abusive l.
Rev 5:9 They are from every tribe, l,
7:9 nation, tribe, people, and l.
13:7 tribe, people, l, and nation.
14:6 nation, tribe, l, and people.

languages (28)

Gen 10:20 and l within their countries
10:31 and l within their countries
Neh 13:24 of Ashdod or one of the other l,
Mar 16:17 They will speak new l.
Act 2:4 began to speak in other l as
2:11 We hear these men in our own l
10:46 people speaking in other l
19:6 and they began to talk in other l
1Co 12:10 speak in different kinds of l.
12:10 Another can interpret l.
12:28 can speak in a number of l.
12:30 other l or interpret languages?
12:30 other languages or interpret l?
13:1 I may speak in the l of humans
13:8 is the gift of speaking in other l,
14:5 of you could speak in other l,
14:5 person who speaks in other l.
14:6 to you speaking in other l,
14:10 No matter how many different l
14:18 I speak in other l more than any
14:21 people who speak foreign l
14:22 So the gift of speaking in other l
14:23 place and you speak in other l.
14:27 If people speak in other l,
14:39 from speaking in other l.
Rev 10:11 people, nations, l, and kings."
11:9 of the people, tribes, l,
17:15 people, crowds, nations, and l.

lanterns (1)

Jon 18:3 They were carrying l,

Laodicea (7)

Col 2:1 for the people of L,
4:13 the people in L and Hierapolis.
4:15 our brothers and sisters in L,
4:16 read it in the church at L.
4:16 you also read the letter from L.
Rev 1:11 Sardis, Philadelphia, and L."
3:14 messenger of the church in L,

lap (6)

Gen 48:12 took them off his father's l
Jdg 7:5 "Separate those who l water
16:19 put Samson to sleep on her l.
Rut 4:16 the child, held him on her l,
2Ki 4:20 The boy sat on her l until noon,
Pro 6:27 Can a man carry fire in his l

lapped (2)

Jdg 7:6 Three hundred men l water
7:7 "With the 300 men who l water

Lappidoth (1)

Jdg 4:4 Deborah, wife of L,

large (276)

Gen 1:21 created the l sea creatures,
29:2 saw a well with a l stone over
30:30 came has grown to a l amount.
30:43 He had l flocks, male and
41:47 the land produced l harvests.
50:9 It was a very l group.
Exo 7:9 and it will become a l snake."
7:10 and it became a l snake.
7:12 and they all became l snakes.
12:38 along with l numbers of sheep,
Lev 26:9 Your families will be l,
Num 13:28 have walls and are very l.
26:56 the tribes are l or small,
32:1 and Gad had a l number
Dtr 3:5 We also captured a l number of
6:10 This land will have l,
12:2 and under every l tree.
17:16 The king must never own a l
17:17 The king must never have a l
26:5 a great, powerful, and l nation.
27:2 set up some l stones and cover
Jos 7:26 They made such a l pile of
8:29 of the city and made a l pile
10:2 because Gibeon was a l city.
10:18 Joshua replied, "Roll l stones
10:27 hiding and put l stones over
14:12 still there and that they have l,
22:8 l herds of livestock,
22:10 was very l and highly visible.
24:26 Then he took a l stone and set
1Sm 6:14 and stopped there by a l rock.
6:15 and put them on the l rock.)
6:18 The l rock on which they put
14:33 Roll a l rock over to me now."
2Sm 8:8 King David also took a l
12:2 The rich man had a very l
18:9 the tangled branches of a l tree.
18:17 and piled a l heap of stones
20:8 When they were at the l rock in
1Ki 4:13 60 l cities with walls and
5:17 commanded them to quarry l,
7:9 including the l courtyard,
7:10 foundation was made with l,
7:12 The l courtyard had three
8:65 A l crowd had come from ⌊the
10:2 in Jerusalem with a l group
10:2 a very l quantity of gold,
10:10 a very l quantity of spices,
10:10 Never again was such a l
10:11 Ophir also brought a l quantity
10:16 King Solomon made 200 l
10:18 The king also made a l ivory
14:23 and ⌊put up⌋ l stones
14:23 high hill and under every l tree.
20:13 Have you seen this l army?
2Ki 4:38 "Put a l pot on the fire,
6:14 and a l fighting unit there.
7:6 chariots, horses, and a l army.
10:26 Then they brought out the l
16:4 on hills and under every l tree.
17:10 high hill and under every l tree.
18:17 with a l army from Lachish
1Ch 4:27 family didn't become as l as
12:22 an army as l as God's army.
18:8 David also took a l quantity of
22:3 David prepared a l quantity of

1Ch 22:5 magnificent, l, famous, praised,
2Ch 2:9 build will be l and astonishing.
4:9 courtyard and the l courtyard
7:8 A very l crowd had come from
9:1 She arrived with a l group of
9:1 a l quantity of gold,
9:9 a very l quantity of spices,
9:9 Never was there such a l
9:15 King Solomon made 200 l
9:17 The king also made a l ivory
13:8 You are a l crowd,
14:8 who were armed with l shields
14:11 can fight against a l ⌊army⌋.
14:11 we go against this l crowd.
16:8 Sudanese and Libyans a l army
17:13 He had l supplies of food in the
20:2 "A l crowd is coming against
20:12 to face this l crowd that is
20:15 or terrified by this l crowd.
23:9 the small and l shields that had
24:24 but the LORD handed Joash's l
26:15 shoot arrows and hurl l stones.
28:4 on hills and under every l tree.
30:5 celebrated it in l numbers as
30:13 They formed a l assembly.
30:24 So a l number of priests were
31:5 They brought l quantities,
32:4 A l crowd gathered as they
Ezr 5:8 The temple is being built with l
6:4 with three rows of l stones and
10:1 a l crowd of Israelite men,
10:13 But the crowd is too l,
Neh 3:27 from the l projecting tower as
5:2 "We have l families!
5:7 I arranged for a l meeting to
7:4 The city was l and wide-open.
12:31 and I arranged two l choirs to
13:5 had provided a l room for
Est 8:15 and white robe, a l gold crown,
Job 1:3 and a l number of servants.
12:23 He makes nations l and leads
22:25 gold and your l supply of silver.
31:34 because I dreaded the l,
36:18 Don't let a l bribe turn you ⌊to
Psa 5:12 Like a l shield, you surround
33:16 a victory with a l army.
35:2 ⌊both⌋ small and l.
35:18 you thanks in a l gathering.
37:35 himself out like a l cedar tree.
52:8 But I am like a l olive tree in
68:11 the good news are a l army.
104:24 What a l number of things you
104:25 living things both l and small.
148:7 Praise him, l sea creatures and
Pro 14:28 A l population is an honor for a
Isa 2:16 against all the l ships of
5:9 L, beautiful houses will be
6:12 and a l area in the middle of the
8:1 "Take a l writing tablet,
13:4 It is like the sound of a l army.
30:23 your cattle will graze in l
32:2 and the shade of a l rock
33:23 A l amount of loot will be
36:2 with a l army from Lachish
57:5 trees and under every l tree.
Jer 2:20 high hill and under every l tree.
3:6 and under every l tree,
3:13 to strangers under every l tree.
11:16 The LORD called you a l olive
17:2 goddess Asherah beside l trees
22:14 He says, 'I will build a l house
31:8 A l crowd will return here.
40:12 They gathered a l harvest of
41:12 him at the l pool in Gibeon.
43:9 "Take some l stones,
46:3 "Get your l and small shields
49:32 Their l herds will be taken as
Eze 1:18 wheels were l and frightening.
6:13 and under every l tree and
17:3 A l eagle came to Lebanon.
17:3 It had l wings with long,
17:7 "There was another l eagle
17:7 large eagle with l wings
17:17 Even with a l army and many
23:24 wagons and with a l number
23:24 around with small and l shields

Eze 23:42 A l number of people came
31:5 Its branches became l and long
37:10 of them to form a very l army.
38:4 They will carry l and small
38:13 to carry away l amounts
38:15 You will be a l crowd and a
38:19 On that day there will be a l
38:22 rainstorms, l hailstones, fire,
39:9 will burn small and l shields,
45:7 His territory will be as l as the
Dan 2:31 You saw a l statue.
2:35 a l mountain which filled
5:1 King Belshazzar threw a l
7:3 Four l animals, each one
7:7 and had l iron teeth.
7:17 He said, "These four l animals
8:8 his l horn broke off.
8:21 and the l horn between its eyes
11:10 They will assemble a l number
11:11 who will raise a l army that will
11:13 he will invade with a l army
11:22 He will overwhelm l forces and
11:25 "With a l army he will summon
11:25 will prepare for war with a l,
Joe 2:2 A l and mighty army will
2:11 His forces are very l.
2:25 (They are the l army that I sent
Jnh 3:3 Nineveh was a very l city.
Hab 2:5 He has a l appetite like the
Zec 14:4 forming a very l valley from
14:14 a very l amount of gold,
Mat 4:25 L crowds followed him.
8:1 l crowds followed him.
8:30 A l herd of pigs was feeding in
9:37 his disciples, "The harvest is l,
13:2 around him was so l that
13:32 It becomes a tree that is l
13:33 a woman mixed into a l amount
14:14 of the boat, he saw a l crowd.
15:30 A l crowd came to him,
15:37 and filled seven l baskets.
16:10 how many l baskets you filled?
18:6 sea with a l stone hung around
19:2 L crowds followed him,
20:29 a l crowd followed Jesus.
23:5 They make their headbands l
25:21 put you in charge of a l amount.
25:23 put you in charge of a l amount.
26:47 A l crowd carrying swords and
27:60 After rolling a l stone against
28:12 soldiers a l amount of money
Mar 2:13 L crowds came to him,
3:7 A l crowd from Galilee,
4:1 A very l crowd gathered around
4:32 It grows such l branches that
5:11 A l herd of pigs was feeding on
5:21 A l crowd gathered around him
6:34 he saw a l crowd and felt sorry
8:1 there was once again a l crowd
8:8 and filled seven l baskets.
8:20 how many l baskets did you fill
9:14 they saw a l crowd around
9:42 sea with a l stone hung around
12:37 The l crowd enjoyed listening
12:41 Many rich people put in l
13:2 "Do you see these l buildings?
14:15 and show you a l room.
16:4 It was a very l stone.
Luk 2:13 Suddenly, a l army of angels
5:6 they caught such a l number of
5:9 amazed to see the l number
5:15 L crowds gathered to hear him
5:29 Levi held a l reception at his
6:17 A l crowd of his disciples and
6:38 A l quantity, pressed together,
7:11 His disciples and a l crowd
7:12 A l crowd from the city was
8:4 When a l crowd had gathered
8:32 A l herd of pigs was feeding on
9:37 a l crowd met Jesus.
10:2 He told them, "The harvest is l,
13:21 a woman mixed into a l amount
14:16 "A man gave a l banquet and
14:25 L crowds were traveling with
17:2 sea with a l stone hung around
22:12 show you a l furnished room.

Luk 23:27 A l crowd followed Jesus.
Jon 5:3 Under these porches a l
6:2 A l crowd followed him
6:5 As Jesus saw a l crowd
12:9 A l crowd of Jews found out
12:12 On the next day the l crowd
21:11 net was filled with 153 l fish,
Act 6:7 in Jerusalem grew very l.
6:7 A l number of priests accepted
7:17 in Egypt had grown very l.
9:25 him in a l basket through
10:11 like a l linen sheet being
11:5 I saw something like a l linen
11:21 and a l number of people
11:24 A l crowd believed in the Lord.
11:26 whole year and taught a l group
14:1 in such a way that a l crowd
17:4 especially a l group of Greeks
19:26 He has won over a l crowd that
27:17 Fearing that they would hit the l
Rom 9:33 a l rock that people find
Gal 6:11 Look at how l the letters ⌊in
2Ti 2:20 In a l house there are not only
Jas 3:5 A l forest can be set on fire by
1Pe 2:8 a stone that people trip over, a l
Rev 6:4 So he was given a l sword.
7:9 After these things I saw a l
9:2 like the smoke from a l furnace.
12:14 the two wings of the l eagle
16:21 L, heavy hailstones fell from
18:6 in her own cup twice as l as
18:21 that was like a l millstone.
19:1 the loud noise from a l crowd
19:6 like the noise from a l crowd,
20:1 the bottomless pit and a l chain
20:11 I saw a l, white throne and the
21:10 me by his power away to a l,
21:12 It had a l, high wall with 12

larger (17)

Gen 1:16 the l light to rule the day and
Num 14:12 and I'll make you into a nation l
22:15 Balak sent a l group of more
26:54 Give more land to l tribes and
33:54 Give more land to l families
35:8 Take more cities from l tribes
Dtr 7:1 Jebusites — seven nations l
9:1 be forcing out nations that are l
9:14 I'll make you into a nation l
20:1 and armies l than yours.
25:14 a l one and a smaller one.
Jos 10:2 one of the royal cities, l than Ai.
2Sm 15:12 with Absalom kept getting l.
2Ch 3:5 He paneled the l building with
Dan 11:13 return and raise an army l than
Amo 6:2 Is their territory l than yours?
Act 28:23 On a designated day a l

large-scale (1)

Zec 14:13 On that day a l panic from the

largest (4)

2Ki 17:9 to the ⌊l⌋ fortified city.
18:8 to the ⌊l⌋ fortified city all
Pro 6:35 The l bribe will not satisfy him.
Luk 7:43 who had the l debt canceled."

Lasea (1)

Act 27:8 The port was near the city of L.

Lasha (1)

Gen 10:19 and Zeboiim as far as L.

lashes (5)

Dtr 25:2 him beaten with as many l as
25:3 Forty l may be given,
Job 5:21 "When the tongue l out,
Pro 17:10 than a hundred l impress a fool.
2Co 11:24 had me beaten with 39 l;

last (151)

Gen 19:34 L night I went to bed with my
25:8 Then he took his l breath,
25:17 Then he took his l breath and
29:34 She said, "Now at l my
31:29 L night the God of your father

Gen 31:42 and l night he made it right."
33:2 and Rachel and Joseph l.
35:18 As she took her l breath,
35:29 when he took his l breath and
49:33 He took his l breath and joined
50:24 At l Joseph said to his brothers,
Lev 8:33 not until the l day of your
23:34 It will l seven days.
23:36 This is the l festival of the year.
26:5 Threshing time will l until
26:5 gathering will l until planting.
Num 2:31 They will be the l group to
10:25 descendants broke camp l
14:33 your unfaithfulness until the l
Dtr 1:19 At l we came to Kadesh
2:16 When the l of these soldiers
33:25 May your strength l as long as
Jos 12:4 He was the l of the Rephaim.
13:12 He was the l of the Rephaim.
17:11 The l three are on mountain
21:40 They were the l of the families
Rut 3:10 This l kindness — that you
1Sm 13:14 now your kingdom will not l.
15:16 what the LORD told me l night."
2Sm 15:17 they stopped at the l house.
18:2 and the l third under Ittai from
19:11 'Why should you be the l
19:12 Why should you be the l to
23:1 These are the l words of David:
2Ki 8:1 and it will l seven years."
1Ch 23:27 David's l instructions were to
29:29 David from first to l is written
2Ch 9:29 acts from first to l is written
12:15 Rehoboam from first to l written
16:11 Asa from first to l is written
20:34 from first to l is written
35:27 and his acts from first to l — are
Neh 8:18 day of the festival to the l day,
Job 3:11 and breathe my l breath when
10:18 I wish I had breathed my l
11:20 Their only hope is to take their l
14:10 A person breathes his l breath,
15:29 and his wealth won't l.
20:21 His prosperity won't l.
27:5 Until I breathe my l breath,
31:39 made its owners breathe their l,
Psa 30:5 Weeping may l for the night,
37:18 Their inheritance will l forever.
74:9 one knows how long this will l.
75:8 will have to drink every l drop.
78:69 the earth which he made to l
81:15 punishment would l forever.
89:2 "Your mercy will l forever.
89:4 I built your throne to l
89:36 His dynasty will l forever.
111:8 They l forever and ever.
119:152 that you made them to l forever.
146:4 they breathe their l breath,
Pro 12:19 but lies l only a moment.
27:24 Nor does a crown l from one
28:2 knowledge will it l a long time.
Ecc 3:14 God does will l forever.
5:18 At l I have seen what is good
Isa 2:2 In the l days the mountain of
40:8 but the word of our God will l
44:6 I am the first and the l,
48:12 I am the first and the l.
51:6 But my salvation will l forever,
51:8 my righteousness will l forever,
51:8 l throughout every generation.
Jer 15:9 grow faint and breathe her l.
23:20 In the l days you will
25:26 L of all, the king of Sheshach
30:24 In the l days you will
32:14 so that they will l a long time.
48:47 will restore Moab in the l days,"
50:17 The l to gnaw at their bones
Lam 1:19 leaders breathed their l breath
2:16 At l we have seen it!'
Eze 4:5 each year its punishment will l.
16:60 it a promise that will l forever.
37:26 This promise will l forever.
Dan 3:16 "We don't need to answer your l
8:19 what will happen in the l days,
8:23 "In the l days of those
10:14 to your people in the l days,
Dan 11:6 and the alliance won't l.
11:24 But this will l only for a little
Hos 3:5 for his blessings in the l days.
Mic 4:1 In the l days the mountain of
Mat 12:25 divided against itself will not l.
12:26 How, then, can his kingdom l?
19:30 many who are first will be l,
19:30 many who are l will be first.
20:8 Start with the l, and end with
20:12 They said, 'These l workers
20:14 I want to give this l worker as
20:16 "In this way the l will be first,
20:16 and the first will be l."
22:27 At l the woman died.
26:60 At l two men came forward.
27:64 Then the l deception will be
Mar 3:24 that kingdom cannot l.
3:25 that household will not l.
3:26 and is divided, he cannot l.
4:17 They l for a short time.
9:35 person must take the l place
10:31 But many who are first will be l,
10:31 and the l will be first."
12:22 L of all, the woman died.
Luk 11:18 how can his kingdom l?
13:7 'For the l three years I've come
13:30 Some who are l will be first,
13:30 some who are first will be l."
Jon 6:39 them back to life on the l day.
6:40 them back to life on the l day."
6:44 people back to life on the l day.
6:54 them back to life on the l day.
7:37 On the l and most important
11:24 come back to life on the l day,
12:48 will judge them on the l day.
15:16 to produce fruit that will l,
Act 2:17 'In the l days, God says, I will
27:23 I serve stood by me l night.
Rom 1:10 God will now at l make
1Co 4:9 placed us apostles l in line,
15:8 L of all, he also appeared to
15:26 The l enemy he will destroy is
15:45 The l Adam became a
15:52 at the sound of the l trumpet.
2Co 4:18 But things that can't be seen l
8:10 L year you were not only
9:2 their collection since l year,"
1Th 2:16 So at l they are receiving
2Ti 3:1 In the l days there will be
Heb 1:2 In these l days he has spoken
9:15 inheritance that will l forever.
Jas 5:3 up riches in these l days.
1Pe 1:20 known in the l period of time.
2Pe 3:3 In the l days people who follow
Jud 1:18 "In the l times people who
Rev 1:17 I am the first and the l,
2:8 The first and the l,
15:1 with the l seven plagues which
21:9 of the l seven plagues came
22:13 A and the Z, the first and the l,

lasted (5)

2Ki 15:5 with a skin disease that l until
25:2 The blockade of the city l until
Jer 5:15 It is a nation that has l a long
52:5 The blockade of the city l until
Luk 23:44 the entire land and l until three

lasting (9)

1Sm 25:28 give you, sir, a l dynasty,
2Sm 23:5 because he has made a l
Est 1:5 held a banquet l seven days.
Psa 119:165 There is l peace for those who
Pro 8:18 l wealth and righteousness.
12:21 No l harm comes to a
Jer 14:13 will give you l peace in this
Eze 45:21 a festival l seven days when
Act 24:2 leadership we have l peace

lasts (18)

Lev 15:25 If her period l longer than usual,
Job 20:5 person l only a moment?
Psa 30:5 His anger l only a moment.
30:5 His favor l a lifetime.
52:1 mercy of God l all day long!
Pro 12:19 The word of truth l forever,
Ecc 1:4 but the earth l forever.
Dan 4:3 His power l from one
4:34 because his power l forever
4:34 kingdom l from one generation
6:26 His power l to the end of
Mat 13:21 he l only a little while.
Luk 1:50 l throughout every generation.
Jon 6:27 Instead, work for the food that l
1Co 7:29 While it l, those who are
2Ti 2:10 Jesus with glory that l forever.
Heb 10:12 and this sacrifice l forever.
1Pe 1:25 the word of the Lord l forever."

Latin (1)

Jon 19:20 in Hebrew, L, and Greek.

latrine (2)

2Ki 10:27 of Baal and made it into a l.
10:27 a latrine. It is still a l today.

lattice (3)

Jdg 5:28 as she peered through the l.
2Ki 1:2 Ahaziah fell through a window l
Sos 2:9 looking through the l.

latticed (1)

1Ki 6:4 He also made l windows for

laugh (21)

Gen 18:13 "Why did Sarah l and say,
18:15 LORD said, "Yes, you did l."
21:6 hears about this will l with me.
Jdg 16:25 and he made them l.
2Ki 19:21 Zion despise you and l at you.
Job 5:22 "You will be able to l at
30:1 are younger than I am l at me.
Psa 52:6 They will l at you and say,
59:8 O LORD, you l at them.
Pro 1:26 I will l at your calamity.
Ecc 3:4 a time to cry and a time to l,
Isa 37:22 Zion despise you and l at you.
Jer 15:17 company with those who l
48:26 and people will l at them.
48:27 People of Moab, didn't you l at
51:39 so that they will shout and l.
Eze 5:15 will ridicule you and l at you.
27:36 among the nations l at you.
Mic 7:8 Don't l at me, my enemies.
Hab 1:10 They will l at every fortified
Luk 6:21 who are crying. They will l.

laughed (7)

Gen 17:17 He l as he thought to himself,
18:12 And so Sarah l to herself,
18:15 Sarah denied that she had l.
Lam 1:7 they l at Jerusalem's downfall.
Mat 9:24 sleeping." But they l at him.
Mar 5:40 They l at him. So he made all of
Luk 8:53 They l at him because they

laughing (4)

Gen 21:9 the Egyptian was l at Isaac.
Pro 14:13 Even while l a heart can ache,
Isa 28:22 Now stop l, or your chains will
Luk 6:25 it will be for those who are l.

laughingstock (5)

Gen 38:23 or we'll become a l.
Job 12:4 I am a l to my neighbors.
12:4 is righteous, has become a l.
17:6 "Now he has made me a l for
Lam 3:14 I have become a l to all my

laughs (7)

Gen 17:19 you will name him Isaac [He L].
Job 39:7 It l at the noise of the city and
39:18 It l at the horse and its rider
39:22 It l at fear, is afraid of nothing,
41:29 and it l at a rattling javelin.
Psa 2:4 The one enthroned in heaven l.
37:13 The Lord l at him because he

laughter (10)

Gen 21:6 "God has brought me l,
Job 8:21 He will fill your mouth with l
Psa 126:2 our mouths were filled with l

Pro 10:23 Like the l of a fool when he
Ecc 2:2 "L doesn't make any sense.
7:3 Sorrow is better than l because,
7:6 The l of a fool is like the
10:19 A meal is made for l,
Jer 30:19 and the sound of l will be heard
Jas 4:9 Turn your l into mourning and

laundryman's (3)

2Ki 18:17 Pool on the road to the L Field
Isa 7:3 Pool on the road to the L Field
36:2 Pool on the road to L Field

law (56)

Gen 47:26 Joseph made a l concerning
Exo 12:14 This is a permanent l for
12:17 This is a permanent l for future
12:24 They are a permanent l for you
27:21 This is a permanent l among
28:43 "This is a permanent l for him
29:9 this is a permanent l.
29:28 It is a permanent l that the
30:21 This will be a permanent l for
Lev 3:17 This is a permanent l for
6:18 It is a permanent l for
6:22 This is a permanent l of the
7:34 This is a permanent l for
7:36 This is a permanent l for
10:9 This is a permanent l for
10:15 This will be a permanent l,
16:29 will be a permanent l for you:
16:31 It is a permanent l.
16:34 "This permanent l tells you
17:7 This is a permanent l for the
23:14 It is a permanent l for
23:21 It is a permanent l for
23:31 It is a permanent l for
23:41 This is a permanent l for
24:3 It is a permanent l for
24:9 This is a permanent l."
Num 10:8 This will be a permanent l for
15:15 There is one l for the whole
15:15 It is a permanent l for future
18:23 This is a permanent l for future
19:10 This will be a permanent l for
19:21 will be a permanent l for them.
Dtr 17:13 will never defy ⌊God's l⌋ again.
1Ch 16:17 He confirmed it as a l for Jacob,
Neh 13:5 These things belonged by l to
Est 4:11 By l that person must be put to
Job 22:4 and bring you into a court of l
Psa 81:4 This is a l for Israel,
94:20 Are wicked rulers who use the l
105:10 He confirmed it as a l for Jacob,
122:4 go to that city because it is a l
148:6 He made it a l that no one can
Pro 19:16 Whoever obeys the l preserves
Dan 6:8 According to the l of the Medes
6:12 According to the l of the Medes
6:15 have a l that no decree
Jon 18:31 and try him by your l."
19:7 answered Pilate, "We have a l,
19:7 and by that l he must die
Act 25:8 "I haven't broken any Jewish l
Rom 2:14 they are a l to themselves even
7:2 a married woman is bound by l
7:2 that marriage l is no longer in
7:3 she is free from this l,
Jas 2:8 right if you obey this l from
2:9 and this l convicts you of being

lawbreakers (1)

1Ti 1:9 are intended for l and rebels,

lawgiver (1)

Isa 33:22 The LORD is our l.

lawlessness (2)

Mat 23:28 you are full of hypocrisy and l.
24:12 there will be more and more l,

law's (2)

Gal 2:19 l standards, those laws killed
3:11 obeying the l standards since,

laws (196)

Gen 26:5 l, and instructions I gave him."
Exo 15:25 There the LORD set down l
15:26 commands and obey all his l,
18:16 them God's l and instructions."
18:20 You must instruct them in the l
Lev 10:11 teach the Israelites all the l that
19:19 "Obey my l. Never crossbreed
19:37 "Obey all my l and all my rules,
20:8 Obey my l, and live by them.
20:22 "If you carefully obey all my l
25:18 "Obey my l, and carefully
26:3 I will do if you will live by my l
26:15 if you reject my l and look at
26:43 looked at my l with disgust.
26:46 These are the l, rules,
Num 30:16 These are the l the LORD gave
Dtr 4:1 Israel, listen to the l and rules I
4:5 I have taught you l and rules as
4:6 Faithfully obey these l.
4:6 they hear about all these l,
4:8 great nation has such fair l
4:14 me to teach you the l
4:40 Obey his l and commands
4:45 are the commandments, l,
5:1 listen to the l and rules I'm
5:31 give you all the commands, l,
6:1 These are the commands, l,
6:2 All of you must obey all his l
6:3 and be careful to obey these l.
6:17 God and the regulations and l
6:20 "What do these regulations, l,
6:24 us to obey all these l
6:24 These l are for our own good
6:25 If we faithfully obey all these l
7:11 So obey the commands, l,
8:11 and l that I'm giving you today.
10:13 commands and l that I'm giving
11:1 Always obey his l,
11:32 be careful to obey all the l and
12:1 Here are the l and rules you
16:12 and obey these l carefully.
17:19 found in these teachings and l.
26:16 you to obey these l and rules.
26:17 obey his l, commands,
27:10 and l which I'm giving
28:15 all his commands and l that
28:45 or follow his commands and l,
30:10 and l that are written
30:16 l, and rules. Then you will live,
Jos 24:25 for the people and set up l
1Sm 10:25 Samuel explained the l
10:25 He wrote the l on a scroll,
2Sm 22:23 not turned away from his l.
1Ki 2:3 Obey his directions, l,
3:14 if you follow me and obey my l
6:12 If you live by my l,
8:58 his commands, l, and rules,
8:61 Then you will live by his l and
9:4 and keep my l and rules,
9:6 keep my commands and l that
11:11 for my promises or my l that
11:33 I consider right or keep my l
11:34 obeyed my commands and l.
11:38 I consider right by obeying my l
2Ki 17:37 Faithfully obey the l,
23:3 and l with all his heart and
1Ch 22:13 if you will carefully obey the l
28:7 to obey my commands and l,
29:19 and l and do everything to build
2Ch 7:17 and obey my l and rules,
7:19 my commands and l that
19:8 to administer the LORD's l
34:31 and l with all his heart and
Ezr 7:11 commands and l for Israel:
Neh 1:7 obeyed the commandments, l,
9:13 good l and commandments.
9:14 gave them commandments, l,
Est 3:8 Their l differ from those of all
Job 38:33 Do you know the l of the sky or
Psa 18:22 not turned away from his l.
89:31 if they violate my l and do not
99:7 instructions and the l that
105:45 so that they would obey his l
119:5 so that I can obey your l.
Psa 119:8 I will obey your l. Never
119:12 O LORD. Teach me your l.
119:16 Your l make me happy.
119:23 against me, I reflect on your l.
119:26 me. Teach me your l.
119:33 how to live by your l,
119:48 I will reflect on your l.
119:54 Your l have become like
119:64 fills the earth. Teach me your l.
119:68 good things. Teach me your l.
119:71 to suffer in order to learn your l.
119:80 in regard to your l so that
119:83 I have not forgotten your l.
119:112 I have decided to obey your l.
119:117 I will always respect your l.
119:118 who wander away from your l,
119:124 and teach me your l.
119:135 and teach me your l.
119:145 I want to obey your l.
119:155 have not searched for your l.
119:171 because you teach me your l.
147:19 his l and judicial decisions to
Pro 8:15 and rulers decree fair l.
Isa 10:1 be for those who make unjust l
24:5 teachings, violated his l,
Jer 31:36 Only if these l stop working,
33:25 with day and night or made l
Eze 5:6 my rules and my l more than
5:6 and they don't live by my l.
5:7 You haven't lived by my l or
11:12 You haven't lived by my l,
11:20 Then they will live by my l and
18:9 rules and obeys my l faithfully.
18:17 my rules and lives by my l.
18:21 He obeys all my l and does
20:11 I gave them my l and made my
20:13 They didn't live by my l,
20:16 and they didn't live by my l.
20:18 "Don't live by the l of your
20:19 Live by my l. Obey my rules
20:21 They didn't live by my l,
20:24 and they rejected my l.
20:25 I also allowed them to follow l
36:27 will enable you to live by my l,
37:24 and they will obey my l.
44:24 make decisions based on my l.
Dan 7:25 the appointed times and l.
9:5 your commandments and l.
Hos 4:2 People break ⌊my l⌋,
Amo 2:4 and haven't kept his l.
Mic 6:16 You have kept Omri's l and all
Zec 1:6 Didn't my warnings and my l,
Mal 3:7 have turned away from my l
Jon 5:18 Not only did he break the l
Rom 2:12 Whoever sins without having l
2:12 And whoever has l from God
2:13 People who merely listen to l
2:13 people who do what those l
2:14 who don't have l from God do
2:14 they don't have any l from God.
2:17 rely on the l in Moses'
2:23 As you brag about the l in
2:25 valuable if you follow Moses' l.
2:25 If you don't follow those l,
4:15 The l in Moses' Teachings
4:15 But where l don't exist,
5:13 world before there were any l.
5:13 be kept when there are no l.
6:14 you're not controlled by l,
6:15 we are not controlled by l
7:1 that l have power over people
7:4 you have died to the l in
7:5 Stirred up by Moses' l,
7:6 died to those l that bound us.
7:7 Are Moses' l sinful?
7:7 sin if those l hadn't shown
7:8 Clearly, without l sin is dead.
7:9 time I was alive without any l.
10:5 approval by following his l.
10:5 "The person who obeys l will
10:5 live because of the l he obeys."
1Co 9:20 who are subject to those l.
Gal 2:19 standards, those l killed me.
2:21 God's approval by obeying l,
3:12 L have nothing to do with faith,
3:12 "Whoever obeys l will live

Gal 3:12 live because of the l he obeys."
3:13 that God's l bring by becoming
3:17 This is what I mean: The l
3:18 by following those l,
3:19 is the purpose of the l given to
3:19 Moses' l did this until the
3:21 Does this mean, then, that the l
3:21 If those l could give us life,
3:23 by Moses' l until this faith
3:24 Before Christ came, Moses' l
4:4 under the control of God's l.
4:5 controlled by these l so that we
4:21 by Moses' l should tell me
5:4 by obeying his l have been cut
5:18 you are not subject to Moses' l.
5:23 There are no l against things
6:13 did this to follow Jewish l.
Php 3:6 approval by keeping Jewish l,
3:9 approval by obeying his l.
Col 2:14 written l God had established.
1Ti 1:9 a person must realize that l are
1:9 L are intended for lawbreakers
1:10 L are intended for people
Jas 2:10 all of God's l except one,
2:11 a person who disobeys God's l.
2:12 judged by l that bring freedom.

lawsuit (2)

Mic 6:2 Listen to the LORD's l,
6:2 The LORD has filed a l against

lawsuits (2)

Hos 10:4 That's why l spring up like
1Co 6:7 you have l against each other.

lawyer (1)

Tit 3:13 Give Zenas the l and Apollos

lay (103)

Gen 9:21 and l naked inside his tent.
22:12 "Do not l a hand on the boy,"
28:11 his head, and l down there.
30:41 Jacob would l the branches in
30:42 he didn't l down the branches.
Lev 1:7 will start a fire on the altar and l
1:8 will also l the pieces,
1:12 The priest will l the head and
1:17 Then the priest will l the bird
3:5 Then Aaron's sons will l them
4:10 The priest will l them on the
6:12 He will l the burnt offering on
24:7 L pure incense on top of each
24:14 ⌊my name⌋ must l their hands
Num 22:27 it l down under Balaam.
Jos 6:26 firstborn son to l the foundation.
Jdg 5:27 He l between her feet!
Rut 3:7 so he went and l at the edge of
3:7 uncovered his feet, and l down.
3:14 So Ruth l at his feet until
1Sm 3:5 So Samuel went back and l
3:9 "So Samuel went and l down
17:52 Wounded Philistines l on the
18:17 "I must not l a hand on him.
19:24 of Samuel and l there naked all
24:12 I will not l a hand on you.
24:13 But I will not l a hand on you.
2Sm 12:16 he fasted and l on the ground
13:6 So Amnon l down and acted
13:31 and l down on the ground.
1Ki 2:10 David l down in death with his
11:43 Solomon l down in death with
13:31 L my bones beside his bones.
14:20 Then he l down in death with
14:31 Rehoboam l down in death
15:8 Abijam l down in death with
15:24 Asa l down in death with his
16:6 Baasha l down in death with
16:28 Omri l down in death with his
18:23 it into pieces, l it on the wood,
19:5 Then he l down and slept
21:4 from my ancestors.") So Ahab l
21:27 He fasted, l in sackcloth,
22:40 Ahab l down in death with his
22:50 Jehoshaphat l down in death
2Ki 4:29 L my staff on the boy's face."
4:34 Then he l on the boy,
2Ki 8:24 Jehoram l down in death with
10:35 Jehu l down in death with his
13:9 Jehoahaz l down in death with
13:13 Jehoash l down in death with
14:16 Jehoash l down in death with
14:22 after King Amaziah l down
14:29 Jeroboam l down in death with
15:7 Azariah l down in death with
15:22 Menahem l down in death with
15:38 Jotham l down in death with
16:20 Ahaz l down in death with his
20:21 Hezekiah l down in death with
21:18 Manasseh l down in death with
24:6 Jehoiakim l down in death with
2Ch 9:31 Solomon l down in death with
12:16 Rehoboam l down in death
14:1 Abijah l down in death with his
16:13 Asa l down in death with his
21:1 Jehoshaphat l down in death
26:2 after King Amaziah l down
26:23 Uzziah l down in death with
27:9 Jotham l down in death with
28:27 Ahaz l down in death with his
32:33 Hezekiah l down in death with
33:20 Manasseh l down in death with
36:21 While it l in ruins, ⌊the land
Job 1:12 but you must not l a hand on
22:24 and l your gold down in the
41:8 L your hand on it. Think of the
Psa 5:3 In the morning I l my needs in
7:5 Let him l my honor in the dust.
22:15 You l me down in the dust of
38:12 Those who seek my life l traps
50:21 argue my point with you and l
104:3 You l the beams of your home
139:5 You l your hand on me.
Isa 28:16 I am going to l a rock in Zion,
29:21 those who l traps for judges,
34:15 there, l eggs, and hatch them.
42:15 I will l waste to mountains and
Jer 2:20 You l down and acted like a
6:21 I'm going to l stumbling blocks
17:11 that hatches eggs it did not l.
Eze 6:5 I will l the dead bodies of the
19:2 She l down among the lions.
23:18 and she l around naked.
Mat 9:18 Come, l your hand on her,
23:4 that are hard to carry and l them
Mar 5:23 Come, l your hands on her so
6:5 there except to l his hands
7:32 They begged Jesus to l his
Luk 6:48 who dug down to bedrock to l
14:29 Otherwise, if you l a foundation
Act 27:30 they were going to l out
1Co 3:10 the gift that God gave me to l
3:11 After all, no one can l any other

layer (6)

Exo 16:13 in the morning there was a l
16:14 was covered with a thin l
Lev 9:19 the tail, the l of fat, the kidneys,
1Ki 7:12 of cut stone blocks and a l
Psa 107:34 and fertile ground into a l of salt
Pro 31:21 has a double l of clothing.

layers (1)

1Ki 7:12 The large courtyard had three l

laying (2)

1Ki 16:34 L the foundation cost him his
1Pe 2:6 "I am l a chosen and precious

layman (1)

Lev 22:12 if a priest's daughter marries a l,

laypeople (5)

Lev 22:10 "L must never eat any holy
2Ch 35:12 to give them to the l according
35:12 The l could then present them
Ezr 8:15 I noticed l and priests there,
Neh 10:34 We priests, Levites, and l have

layperson (1)

Lev 22:13 But a l must never eat it.

lays (1)

Job 39:14 It l its eggs on the ground and

Lazarus (26)

Luk 16:20 named L who was regularly
16:21 L would have eaten any
16:21 L was covered with sores,
16:23 he saw Abraham and L.
16:24 Send L to dip the tip of his
16:27 to send L back to my father's
Jon 11:1 L, who lived in Bethany,
11:2 Her brother L was the one who
11:5 loved Martha, her sister, and L.
11:6 Jesus heard that L was sick,
11:11 "Our friend L is sleeping,
11:13 Jesus meant that L was dead,
11:13 that L was only sleeping.
11:14 told them plainly, "L has died,
11:15 grow in faith. Let's go to L."
11:17 he found that L had been in the
11:34 "Where did you put L?"
11:37 man sight keep L from dying?"
11:43 as he could, "L, come out!"
11:44 Jesus told them, "Free L,
12:1 L, whom Jesus had brought
12:2 Martha served the dinner, and
12:9 to see Jesus but also to see L,
12:10 priests planned to kill L too.
12:11 L was the reason why many
12:17 Jesus when he called L from

Lazarus' (1)

Luk 16:25 while L life was filled with

laziness (2)

Pro 19:15 L throws one into a deep sleep,
Ecc 10:18 A roof sags because of l.

lazy (26)

Exo 5:8 They're l! That's why they're
5:17 "You're l! ⌊Just plain⌋ lazy!"
5:17 Just plain⌋ l!" Pharaoh
Pro 6:6 Consider the ant, you l bum.
6:9 will you lie there, you l bum?
10:4 L hands bring poverty,
10:26 so is the l person to those who
12:24 but l hands do slave labor.
12:27 A l hunter does not catch his
13:4 A l person craves food and
15:19 The path of l people is like a
18:9 Whoever is l in his work is
19:24 A l person puts his fork in his
20:4 A l person does not plow in the
21:25 The desire of a l person will
22:13 A l person says, "There's a
24:30 I passed by a l person's field,
26:13 A l person says, "There's a
26:14 so the l person turns on his
26:15 A l person puts his fork in his
26:16 A l person thinks he is wiser
Mat 25:26 'You evil and l servant!
Rom 12:11 Don't be l in showing your
Tit 1:12 animals, and l gluttons."
Heb 5:11 since you have become too l
6:12 Then, instead of being l,

lead (109)

Exo 13:17 God didn't l them on the road
13:21 in a column of smoke to l them
15:10 They sank like l in the raging
15:13 "Lovingly, you will l the people
32:1 Make gods who will l us."
32:23 gods for us. They will l us.'
32:34 L the people to the place I told
33:12 telling me to l these people,
34:16 they'll l your sons to do the
Num 27:17 who will l them in and out ⌊of
31:22 silver, bronze, iron, tin, or l—
Dtr 3:28 because he will l these people
10:11 "L the people on their journey.
13:5 He was trying to l you away
13:10 were trying to l you away from
20:9 appoint commanders to l them.
28:36 The LORD will l you and the
31:2 I'm not able to l you anymore.

Jdg 4:7 I will l Sisera (the commander
20:32 "Let's flee in order to l them
1Sm 8:20 will judge us, l us out ⌊to war⌋,
12:2 here is the king who will l you.
30:15 "Will you l me to these troops?"
30:15 and I'll l you to these troops."
2Sm 17:11 L them into battle yourself.
2Ki 4:24 she told her servant, "L on.
6:19 Follow me, and I will l you to
1Ch 28:4 the tribe of Judah to l ⌊Israel⌋.
2Ch 1:10 so that I may l these people.
8:14 ⌊The Levites⌋ were to l in
Ezr 6:18 Levites to their groups ⌊to l⌋
Neh 12:46 for the singers to l ⌊in singing⌋
Est 6:13 certainly l to your downfall."
Job 19:24 a rock with an iron stylus and l.
30:23 I know you will l me to death,
38:20 so that you may l it to its
Psa 5:8 O LORD, l me in your
16:3 Those who l holy lives on
25:5 L me in your truth and teach me
27:11 L me on a level path because I
31:3 l me and guide me.
42:4 to walk with the crowd and l
48:14 He will l us beyond death."
60:9 Who will l me to Edom?
61:2 L me to the rock that is high
108:10 Who will l me to Edom?
119:35 L me on the path of your
125:5 the LORD will l them away
139:24 Then l me on the everlasting
143:10 May your good Spirit l me on
143:11 l me out of trouble.
Pro 2:18 Her ways l to the souls of the
3:17 and all its paths l to peace.
5:5 Her steps l straight to hell.
6:22 walk around, they will l you.
21:5 person l to prosperity,
Ecc 5:13 Riches l to the downfall of
Sos 8:2 I would l you. I would bring you
Isa 9:16 these people l them astray.
11:6 and little children will l them.
19:14 So they l the Egyptians astray
20:4 The king of Assyria will l away
30:28 of the people to l them astray.
42:16 I will l the blind on unfamiliar
42:16 I will l them on unfamiliar
44:20 misguided minds l them astray.
48:17 I l you where you should go.
49:10 on them will l them
Jer 6:29 make the fire melt away the l.
7:6 not follow other gods that l you
23:32 up and l my people astray
31:9 I will l them beside streams on
50:8 the male goats that l the flock.
51:27 a commander to l the attack.
Eze 22:18 and l in a smelting furnace.
22:20 gather silver, copper, iron, l,
27:12 and l for your merchandise.
34:15 care of my sheep and l them
38:4 I will l you out with all your
39:2 I will turn you around and l you.
Dan 12:3 Those who l many people to
Hos 2:14 I will l her into the desert.
Amo 6:14 I am going to l a nation to
Mic 1:13 You were the first to l the
2:13 will open the way and l them.
2:13 The LORD will l the people.
5:4 ⌊He will l them⌋ with the
6:4 and Miriam to l you.
Zec 5:7 A l cover ⌊on the basket⌋ was
5:8 and forced the l cover down
Mat 7:13 the gate and road that l
7:14 narrow gate and the road that l
Mar 15:1 to tie Jesus up, l him away,
Luk 6:39 one blind person l another?
Jon 10:16 I must l them. They, too, will
Act 5:31 He did this to l the people of
7:40 So make gods who will l us.'
13:11 He tried to find people to l him.
Rom 2:4 kindness that is trying to l you
12:3 Instead, your thoughts should l
12:8 leadership, l enthusiastically.
Eph 4:14 clever strategies to l us astray.
1Ti 2:15 if they l respectable lives in
2Ti 2:25 they think and act and l them
Tit 1:1 I was sent to l God's chosen
1Jn 5:16 a sin that doesn't l to death,
5:16 sins that don't l to death.
5:17 are sins that don't l to death.
Rev 7:17 He will l them to springs filled

leader (125)

Gen 23:6 You are a mighty l among us.
Exo 22:28 God or curse a l of your people.
Lev 4:22 "When a l unintentionally does
4:26 LORD for what the l did wrong,
4:26 and the l will be forgiven.
Num 2:3 The l for the people of Judah is
2:5 The l for the people of Issachar
2:7 The l for the people of Zebulun
2:10 The l for the people of Reuben
2:12 The l for the people of Simeon
2:14 The l for the people of Gad is
2:18 The l for the people of Ephraim
2:20 The l for the people of
2:22 The l for the people of
2:25 The l for the people of Dan is
2:27 The l for the people of Asher is
2:29 The l for the people of Naphtali
3:24 The l of the Gershonite
3:30 The l of the Kohathite families
3:32 The chief l of the Levites was
3:35 The l of the Merarite families
7:3 leaders and one ox from each l.
7:11 "Each day a different l will
7:18 the l from the tribe of Issachar,
7:24 On the third day the l of the
7:30 On the fourth day the l of the
7:36 On the fifth day the l of the
7:42 On the sixth day the l of the
7:48 On the seventh day the l of the
7:54 On the eighth day the l of the
7:60 On the ninth day the l of the
7:66 On the tenth day the l of the
7:72 On the eleventh day the l of the
7:78 On the twelfth day the l of the
13:2 Send one l from each of their
14:4 "Let's choose a l and go back
17:2 one from the l of each of their
17:6 one from the l of each of their
25:14 (Salu was the l of a family from
25:18 daughter of a Midianite l,
34:18 You must also take one l from
34:22 the l of the tribe of Dan;
34:23 the l of the tribe of Manasseh;
34:24 the l of the tribe of Ephraim;
34:25 the l of the tribe of Zebulun;
34:26 the l of the tribe of Issachar;
34:27 the l of the tribe of Asher;
34:28 the l of the tribe of Naphtali."
Jos 22:14 Each man was a l of a
Jdg 11:9 them to me, I will be your l."
11:11 him their l and commander.
1Sm 19:20 with Samuel serving as their l,
2Sm 3:38 "Don't you know that today a l,
5:2 people Israel, the l of Israel.'"
6:21 and he appointed me l of Israel,
7:8 so that you could be the l
22:44 You kept me as the l of nations.
23:8 from Tahkemon's family was l
23:18 was the l of the thirty.
1Ki 1:35 I have appointed him to be the l
11:24 gathered men and became the l
14:7 made you a l over my people
16:2 from the dust and made you l
21:9 Seat Naboth as l of the people.
21:12 seated as the l of the people.
2Ki 9:20 The troop's l is driving like a
20:5 to Hezekiah, l of my people,
1Ch 2:10 l of Judah's people.
5:6 He was l of the tribe of Reuben.
11:2 the l of my people Israel.'"
11:11 of Hachmon, the l of the three.
11:20 brother Abishai was the l
11:42 the tribe of Reuben (who was l
12:3 Ahiezer was the l,
12:18 gave Amasai, the l of the thirty,
12:27 as well as Jehoiada (l of
15:22 Chenaniah, a Levite l,
15:27 the l of the musicians'
17:7 so that you could be the l
1Ch 29:22 they anointed Solomon to be l
2Ch 13:12 God is with us as our l.
19:11 is the son of Ishmael and the l
Ezr 8:17 them to Iddo, the l in Casiphia.
Neh 9:17 stubborn and appointed a l
11:17 the l who led the prayer of
11:17 The Levite l Bakbukiah was
Job 29:25 I sat as their l. I lived like a king
Psa 18:43 You made me the l of nations.
148:14 has given his people a strong l,
Pro 28:16 A l without understanding
Isa 3:6 You'll be our l. This pile of ruins
3:7 make me a l of our family."
7:8 and the l of Damascus is
7:9 and the l of Samaria is
55:4 a l and a commander for
Jer 30:21 Their l will be someone from
31:7 Sing joyfully for the l of the
49:19 Is there any l who can stand up
50:44 Is there any l who can stand up
Eze 38:7 You will be their l.
Hos 1:11 appoint one l for themselves,
Hab 3:13 You crush the l of the wicked
3:14 You pierce the l of his gang
Zec 10:4 a battle bow, from them every l.
Mat 2:6 A l will come from you.
9:18 A ⌊synagogue⌋ l came to
23:10 Don't make others call you a l,
23:10 because you have only one l,
Mar 5:22 A synagogue l named Jairus
5:35 They told the synagogue l,
5:36 he told the synagogue l,
5:38 to the home of the synagogue l,
Luk 8:41 named Jairus, a synagogue l,
8:50 he told the synagogue l,
13:14 The synagogue l was irritated
13:14 The l told the crowd,
22:26 and your l must be like a
Act 5:31 position as l and savior.
18:8 The synagogue l Crispus and
18:17 Sosthenes, the synagogue l,
1Ti 5:19 against a spiritual l unless
Tit 1:6 A spiritual l must have a good
1Pe 5:1 spiritual l who also witnessed
2Jn 1:1 From the church l.
3Jn 1:1 From the church l.

leader's (3)

Mat 9:23 to the ⌊synagogue⌋ l house.
Mar 5:35 from the synagogue l home.
Luk 8:49 from the synagogue l home.

leaders (386)

Gen 25:16 and camps — 12 l of their tribes.
36:15 These were the tribal l among
36:16 These were the tribal l
36:17 These were the tribal l among
36:17 These were the tribal l
36:18 These were the tribal l among
36:18 These were the tribal l
36:19 is, Edom), who were tribal l.
36:21 These Horite tribal l were the
36:29 These were the Horite tribal l:
36:30 These were the Horite tribal l in
36:40 tribal l descended from Esau,
36:43 These were the tribal l of Edom
50:7 the l in his palace staff,
50:7 and all the l of Egypt went with
Exo 3:16 "Go, assemble the l of Israel.
3:18 "The l of Israel will listen to
3:18 Then you and the l must go to
4:29 Egypt⌋ and assembled all the l
12:21 called for all the l of Israel.
15:15 The tribal l of Edom will be
16:22 All the l of the community
17:5 "Bring some of the l of Israel
17:6 Moses did this while the l of
18:12 Aaron and all the l of Israel
19:7 went down and called for the l
24:1 and 70 of Israel's l come up the
24:9 and 70 of Israel's l.
24:11 God didn't harm these l of the
24:14 He said to the l, "Wait here for
34:31 so Aaron and all the l of the
35:27 The l brought onyx stones and
Lev 4:15 The l of the congregation will

Lev 9:1 and his sons and the **l** of Israel.
Num 1:16 the **l** of their ancestors' tribes,
1:44 and the 12 **l** of Israel,
4:34 Moses, Aaron, and the **l** of the
4:46 and the **l** of Israel registered
7:2 Then the **l** of Israel,
7:2 those tribal **l** who helped
7:3 one wagon from every two **l**
7:10 The **l** also brought offerings for
7:84 These were the gifts from the **l**
10:4 If only one trumpet blows, the **l**,
11:16 men who you know are **l**
11:24 He gathered 70 of the **l** of the
11:25 on Moses and put it on the 70 **l**.
11:26 were on the list with the other **l**
11:30 Then Moses and the **l** went
13:3 of them were **l** of the Israelites.
16:2 well-known **l** of the community,
16:25 and the **l** of Israel followed him.
17:6 Their **l** gave him 12 staffs,
22:4 said to the **l** of Midian,
22:7 The **l** of Moab and Midian left,
25:4 "Take all the **l** of the people,
27:2 of him, the priest Eleazar, the **l**,
31:13 and all the **l** of the community
32:2 and the **l** of the community,
36:1 and spoke to Moses and the **l**
Dtr 1:13 I'll appoint them to be your **l**."
5:23 all the **l** and heads of your
19:12 If someone does this, the **l** of
21:2 your **l** and judges must go and
21:3 the **l** from that city must choose
21:4 The **l** of that city will bring the
21:6 All the **l** from the city which
21:19 mother must take him to the **l**
21:20 They will say to the **l** of the
22:15 go to the city gate where the **l**
22:16 The girl's father will tell the **l**,
22:17 cloth in front of the **l** of the city.
22:18 The **l** of that city must take the
25:7 she must go to the **l** of the city
25:8 Then the **l** of the city must
25:9 to him in the presence of the **l**.
27:1 Moses and the **l** of Israel told
29:10 The heads of your tribes, your **l**,
31:9 and to all the **l** of Israel.
31:28 Assemble all the **l** of your
32:7 and your **l** to tell you.
33:5 king of Jeshurun when the **l**
33:21 They were **l** of the people and
Jos 7:6 Joshua and the **l** of Israel tore
8:10 Then he and the **l** of Israel led
8:33 native Israelites, the **l**, officers,
9:11 Our **l** and everyone who lives
9:15 The **l** of the congregation
9:18 because the **l** of the
9:18 complained about the **l**.
9:19 But all the **l** said to them,
9:21 The **l** said that they should be
9:21 congregation, as the **l** had said.
13:21 him and Midian's **l** — Evi,
13:22 Along with these **l**,
17:4 Joshua (son of Nun), and the **l**.
19:51 and the **l** of the families divided
20:4 and present his case to the **l** of
20:5 the **l** must not hand him over to
21:1 Then the **l** of the families of
21:1 and to the **l** of the families of
22:14 Ten **l**, one from each tribe in
22:15 When they arrived these **l** said
22:30 the **l** of the congregation,
22:32 and the **l** returned from Reuben
23:2 So he called all the **l**,
24:1 He called together Israel's **l**,
24:31 long as Joshua and the older **l**,
Jdg 2:7 of the **l** who had outlived
8:14 77 officials and **l** of Succoth.
8:16 So Gideon took the **l** of the city
9:51 and **l** of the town fled to it.
10:18 The **l** of the people of Gilead
11:5 Gilead's **l** went to get Jephthah
11:7 Jephthah replied to Gilead's **l**,
11:8 Gilead's **l** answered Jephthah,
11:10 Gilead's **l** said to Jephthah,
20:2 The **l** of all Israel's tribes took
21:16 The **l** of the congregation

Rut 4:2 chose ten men who were **l**
4:4 and in the presence of the **l**
4:9 Then Boaz said to the **l** and to
4:11 the gate, including the **l**, said,
1Sm 4:3 the **l** of Israel asked,
8:4 Then all the **l** of Israel gathered
11:3 The **l** of Jabesh told him,
14:38 So Saul ordered all the **l** of the
15:30 please honor me in front of the **l**
16:4 to Bethlehem, the **l** of the city,
29:2 The Philistine **l** were marching
30:26 to his friends, the **l** of Judah.
2Sm 3:17 message to the **l** of Israel:
5:3 All the **l** of Israel had come to
12:17 The older **l** in his palace stood
17:4 Absalom and all the **l** of Israel
17:15 advised Absalom and the **l**
19:11 "Ask the **l** of Judah,
1Ki 8:1 the respected **l** of Israel,
8:1 and the **l** of the Israelite
8:3 When all the **l** of Israel had
12:6 from the older **l** who had served
12:8 the advice the older **l** gave him.
12:13 the advice the older **l** gave him.
20:7 king of Israel called for all the **l**
20:8 All the **l** and all the people told
21:8 sent them to the respected **l**
21:11 Naboth's city — the respected **l**
21:14 Then the **l** sent ⌊this
2Ki 6:32 in his home with the ⌊city's⌋ **l**.
6:32 Elisha asked the **l**,
10:1 of Jezreel, the respected **l**,
10:5 of the city, the respected **l**,
19:2 and the **l** of the priests,
23:1 king sent for all the respected **l**
1Ch 1:51 The tribal **l** of Edom were
1:54 were the tribal **l** of Edom.
4:38 are mentioned by name were **l**
7:40 and distinguished **l**.
11:3 All the **l** of Israel had come to
12:4 fighting men and one of their **l**),
12:32 were 200 **l** who understood
15:16 David told the Levite **l** to
15:25 So David, the **l** of Israel,
21:2 David said to Joab and the **l** of
21:16 David and the **l** were dressed
22:17 David ordered all the **l** of Israel
24:4 descendants had 16 family **l**
24:4 descendants had 8 family **l**.
24:6 and the family **l** of the priests
24:20 ⌊The following men were **l**⌋ for
24:26 The following men were **l** from
24:31 and the **l** of the families of the
27:4 (Mikloth was one of its **l**.)
28:1 in Jerusalem for all the **l**
28:1 all the leaders of Israel — the **l**
28:1 the **l** of the army units that
28:8 Now, ⌊**l**, I order you⌋ in the
28:21 In addition, all the **l** and people
29:6 Then the **l** of the families,
29:6 the **l** of the tribes of Israel,
29:9 that the **l** gave so generously
29:24 All the **l** and soldiers and all of
2Ch 5:2 the respected **l** of Israel,
5:2 and the **l** of the Israelite
5:4 When all the **l** of Israel had
10:6 from the older **l** who had served
10:8 the advice the older **l** gave him.
12:5 came to Rehoboam and the **l**
22:8 he found Judah's **l** (Ahaziah's
23:2 all the cities of Judah and the **l**
24:23 and destroyed all the people's **l**.
28:12 son of Hadlai (some **l** of
28:14 and the loot in front of the **l**
29:20 Hezekiah gathered the **l**
29:30 Then King Hezekiah and the **l**
30:12 the king and the **l** gave from
30:24 The **l** provided 1,000 bulls and
31:8 When Hezekiah and the **l** saw
32:31 When the **l** of Babylon sent
34:29 king sent for all the respected **l**
35:9 the **l** of the Levites,
Ezr 5:5 But the **l** of the Jews were
5:9 We asked their **l** the following
5:10 of the men who were their **l**.
6:7 governor of the Jews and the **l**

Ezr 6:8 Jewish **l** rebuild God's temple:
6:14 So the Jewish **l** continued to
7:28 So I gathered **l** in Israel to go
8:1 These are the **l** of the families
8:24 Then I selected 12 **l** from the
8:29 and the **l** of Israel's families."
9:1 the **l** came to me and said,
9:2 Furthermore, the **l** and officials
10:5 Ezra got up and made the **l**,
10:8 come within three days as the **l**
10:14 Let our **l** represent the whole
10:14 woman must meet with the **l**
Neh 2:16 priests, the **l**, the other officials,
4:14 the **l**, and the rest of the people,
4:16 The **l** stood behind all the
4:19 I told the nobles, the **l**,
5:7 confronted the nobles and the **l**.
5:17 I fed 1 50 Jewish **l** and their
7:5 I should gather the nobles, **l**,
8:13 On the second day the **l** of the
9:32 **l**, priests, prophets, ancestors,
9:34 Our kings, **l**, priests,
9:38 Our **l**, Levites, and priests are
10:14 These were the **l** of the people:
11:1 The **l** of the people settled in
11:16 and Jozabad, Levite **l**,
12:7 These were the **l** of the priests
12:12 were the priests who were the **l**
12:31 Then I had the **l** of Judah come
12:32 Hoshaiah and half of the **l** of
12:40 as did I and the half of the **l**
13:11 I reprimanded the **l**.
Job 12:20 good judgment of respected **l**.
12:24 common sense of a country's **l**
Psa 68:27 ⌊next⌋ the **l** of Judah with their
68:27 ⌊then⌋ the **l** of Zebulun,
68:27 ⌊then⌋ the **l** of Naphtali.
83:11 Treat all their **l** like Zebah and
105:22 taught his respected **l** wisdom.
107:32 in the company of respected **l**.
113:8 the influential **l** of his people.
149:8 and their **l** in iron shackles,
Pro 31:23 he sits with the **l** of the land.
Isa 3:3 military **l** and civilian leaders,
3:3 military leaders and civilian **l**,
3:4 "I will make boys their **l**.
3:14 his case to the respected **l**
9:15 Respected and honored **l** are
14:9 all who were **l** on earth.
19:11 The **l** of Zoan are nothing but
19:13 The **l** of Zoan are acting
19:13 The **l** of Memphis are led
19:13 The **l** who are the cornerstones
19:15 No one — **l** or followers,
21:5 Get up, you **l**! Prepare your
22:3 All your **l** fled together and
24:4 The great **l** of the earth waste
24:23 the presence of his respected **l**.
37:2 and the **l** of the priests,
43:28 That is why I will corrupt the **l**
Jer 4:9 "the king and the **l** will lose
8:1 of the kings and the **l** of Judah,
19:1 Take along some of the **l** of the
19:1 and some of the **l** of the priests.
25:34 in the dust, you **l** of the flock.
25:35 no escape for the **l** of the flock.
25:36 shepherds are crying and the **l**
26:17 Then some of the **l** in the land
29:1 to the rest of the **l** among
29:2 the **l** of Judah and Jerusalem,
39:6 slaughtered all the **l** of Judah.
39:13 and all the other **l** of the king of
Lam 1:19 My priests and **l** breathed their
2:2 ⌊of Judah⌋ and its **l** down
2:10 The respected **l** of Zion's
4:16 nor did they honor their older **l**.
5:12 ⌊Our⌋ **l** are hung by their
5:12 ⌊Our⌋ older **l** are shown no
5:14 ⌊Our⌋ older **l** have stopped
Eze 7:26 the advice of **l** will disappear.
8:1 Judah's **l** were sitting in front of
8:11 drawings stood 70 of Israel's **l**.
8:11 was standing with the **l**.
8:12 do you see what the **l** of the
11:1 They were **l** of the people.
14:1 Some of Israel's **l** came to me

Eze 17:12 and captured its king and its l.
20:1 some of the l of Israel came to
20:3 speak to the l of Israel.
22:27 Your l are like wolves that tear
Dan 9:6 name to our kings, l, ancestors,
9:8 We, our kings, l, and ancestors
11:41 But Edom, Moab, and the l of
Hos 5:10 The l of Judah are like those
Joe 1:2 Listen to this, you l!
1:14 Gather the l and everyone who
2:16 Assemble the l. Gather the
Mic 3:1 I said: Listen, you l of Jacob,
3:9 Listen to this, you l of the
3:11 Your l exchange justice for
5:5 seven shepherds and eight l.
Zec 12:5 Then the l of Judah will think
12:6 "On that day I will make the l
Mat 2:6 least among the l of Judah.
15:14 They are blind l. When one
16:21 to suffer a lot because of the l,
21:23 The chief priests and the l of
26:3 Then the chief priests and the l
26:47 priests and l of the people.
26:57 and the l had gathered together.
27:1 all the chief priests and the l
27:3 back to the chief priests and l.
27:12 While the chief priests and l
27:20 But the chief priests and l
27:41 the scribes and the l made fun
28:12 gathered together with the l
Mar 8:31 he would be rejected by the l,
11:27 and the l came to him.
12:13 The l sent some of the
14:43 and l of the people.
14:53 All the chief priests, l,
15:1 came to a decision with the l
Luk 7:3 and sent some Jewish l to him.
9:22 He would be rejected by the l,
19:47 and the l of the people looked
20:1 and l came up to him.
22:52 and l who had come for him,
22:66 the council of the people's l,
Act 4:5 next day the Jewish rulers, l,
4:8 "Rulers and l of the people,
4:23 the chief priests and l had said.
5:21 that is, all the l of Israel.
6:12 people, the l, and the scribes.
9:2 to the synagogue l
11:30 Saul to the l ⌊in Jerusalem⌋.
12:25 ⌊to the l in Jerusalem⌋,
13:15 the synagogue l sent ⌊a
14:23 each church choose spiritual l,
14:23 and fasting they entrusted the l
15:2 and spiritual l about this claim.
15:4 and the spiritual l welcomed
15:6 The apostles and spiritual l
15:22 the apostles, the spiritual l,
15:22 were l among the believers.
15:23 the apostles and the spiritual l,
16:4 that the apostles and spiritual l
20:17 and called the spiritual l
21:18 All the spiritual l were present.
21:20 When the spiritual l heard
22:5 council of our l can prove that
23:14 to the chief priests and l ⌊of
24:1 city of Caesarea with some l
25:2 Jewish l informed Festus about
25:15 the Jewish l brought me some
25:17 "So the Jewish l came to
28:21 The Jewish l told Paul,
2Co 11:24 Five times the Jewish l had
1Th 5:12 for those l who work among
1Ti 4:14 spiritual l placed their hands
5:17 Give double honor to spiritual l
5:20 Reprimand those l who sin.
5:20 so that the other l will also
Tit 1:5 be done — appointing spiritual l
Heb 13:7 Remember your l who have
13:17 Obey your l, and accept their
13:24 Greet all your l and all God's
Jas 5:14 call for the church l.
1Pe 5:1 I appeal to your spiritual l.
5:5 under the authority of spiritual l.
Rev 4:4 and on these thrones sat 24 l
4:10 the 24 l bow in front of the one
5:5 Then one of the l said to me,
Rev 5:6 four living creatures and the l.
5:8 creatures and the 24 l bowed
5:11 and the l surrounding the
5:14 the l bowed and worshiped.
7:11 around the throne with the l
7:13 One of the l asked me,
11:16 Then the 24 l, who were sitting
14:3 four living creatures, and the l.
19:4 The 24 l and the 4 living

leaders' (1)

2Ch 10:13 He ignored the older l advice

leadership (3)

Num 33:1 in organized groups under the l
Act 24:2 through your wise l we have
Rom 12:8 If it is l, lead enthusiastically.

leading (26)

Jos 2:7 men pursued them on the road l
Jdg 12:5 of the Jordan River l back
16:26 young man who was l him by
2Sm 10:16 of Hadadezer's army, l them.
15:2 up early and stand by the road l
23:13 three of the thirty l men came
23:24 ⌊The thirty l men were⌋
1Ki 15:26 l Israel into the same sins.
2Ki 9:27 he fled on the road l to Beth
24:15 and the l citizens of the land
1Ch 11:15 Once three of the thirty l men
15:5 L Kohath's descendants was
15:6 L Merari's descendants was
15:7 L Gershom's descendants was
15:8 L Elizaphan's descendants
15:9 L Hebron's descendants was
15:10 L Uzziel's descendants was
2Ch 23:13 The singers were l the
Ezr 8:16 and Meshullam (who were l
Psa 68:27 the youngest, is l them,
Pro 15:33 is discipline ⌊l to⌋ wisdom,
Eze 17:13 away the l citizens from Judah
40:20 l to the outer courtyard.
Amo 6:1 for the heads of the l nations,
Luk 22:47 twelve apostles, was l them.
Act 16:12 Philippi is a l city in that part of

leads (47)

Dtr 27:18 "Whoever l blind people in the
Job 12:17 He l counselors away barefoot
12:19 He l priests away barefoot and
12:23 nations large and l them away.
Psa 23:2 He l me beside peaceful
25:9 He l humble people to do what
37:8 preoccupied. It only l to evil.
68:6 He l prisoners out of prison into
80:1 the one who l ⌊the
84:5 are on the road ⌊that l to you⌋.
95:7 in his care, the flock that he l.
119:104 I hate every path that l to lying.
119:128 every pathway that l to lying.
Pro 7:27 home is the way to hell and l
10:28 The hope of righteous people ⌊l
11:3 but hypocrisy l treacherous
11:19 As righteousness l to life,
12:26 wicked people l others astray.
14:23 but idle talk l only to poverty.
15:24 life for a wise person l upward
16:29 his neighbor and l him
19:23 The fear of the LORD l to life,
22:16 to the rich certainly l to poverty.
28:10 Whoever l decent people into
Ecc 7:10 It isn't wisdom that l you to ask
10:2 A wise person's heart l the right
10:2 heart of a fool l the wrong way.
11:9 Follow wherever your heart l
Sos 2:4 He l me into a banquet room
Isa 43:17 He l chariots and horses,
Jer 6:16 Ask which way l to blessings.
Eze 21:20 and mark the road that l to
Hos 4:12 of prostitution l them astray.
Mat 5:30 And if your right hand l you to
15:14 one blind person l another,
Jon 10:3 sheep by name and l them out
Rom 6:16 sin be your master l to death.
6:16 your master l to God's approval.
6:19 This l you to live holy lives.
Rom 8:6 nature's attitude l to death.
8:6 the spiritual nature's attitude l
8:15 of slaves that l you into fear
2Co 2:14 But I thank God, who always l
7:10 they think and act and l them
Eph 5:18 which l to wild living.
Tit 1:1 the knowledge of the truth that l
1Jn 5:16 There is a sin that l to death.

leaf (4)

Gen 8:11 was a freshly plucked olive l.
Lev 26:36 The sound of a wind-blown l
Job 13:25 to make a fluttering l tremble
Pro 11:28 will flourish like a green l.

leaf-scattered (1)

Sos 1:16 The l ground will be our couch.

leafy (4)

Lev 23:40 the branches of l trees and
Eze 6:13 large tree and every l oak.
20:28 saw any high hill or any l tree,
Mar 11:8 Others cut l branches in the

Leah (29)

Gen 29:16 name of the older one was L,
29:17 L had attractive eyes,
29:23 evening he took his daughter L
29:23 he realized it was L.
29:24 to his daughter L as her slave.)
29:28 He finished the week with L.
29:30 He loved Rachel more than L.
29:31 the LORD saw L was unloved,
29:32 L became pregnant and gave
30:9 When L saw that she had
30:11 L said, "I've been lucky!"
30:13 L said, "I've been blessed!
30:14 brought them to his mother L.
30:14 Rachel said to L, "Please give
30:15 L replied, "Isn't it enough that
30:16 L went out to meet him.
30:18 L said, "God has given me my
30:20 L said, "God has presented me
31:4 a message to Rachel and L
31:14 Rachel and L answered him,
33:1 divided the children among L,
33:2 L and her children after them,
33:7 Likewise, L and her children
34:1 Dinah, daughter of L and Jacob,
35:23 The sons of L were Jacob's
46:15 of the sons L gave
46:18 Laban gave to his daughter L.
49:31 I also buried L there.
Rut 4:11 like Rachel and L,

Leah's (6)

Gen 30:10 L slave Zilpah gave birth to a
30:12 L slave Zilpah gave birth to her
30:17 God answered L prayer.
31:33 into L tent, and into the tent of
31:33 He came out of L tent and went
35:26 The sons of L slave Zilpah

leaks (1)

Ecc 10:18 A house l because of idle

lean (6)

Jdg 16:26 so that I can l against them."
2Ki 7:17 on whose arm he used to l
18:21 If you l on it, it stabs your hand
Psa 109:24 My body has become l,
Pro 4:27 Do not l to the right or to the left.
Isa 36:6 If you l on it, it stabs your hand

leaned (4)

Isa 30:12 and deceit, and l on them.
Eze 29:7 When they l on you,
Jon 21:20 He was the one who l against
Heb 11:21 He l on the top of his staff and

leaning (4)

2Sm 1:6 Saul was there l on his spear,
2Ki 7:2 arm the king was l answered
Psa 62:3 as though he were a l wall or a
Jon 13:25 L close to Jesus, that disciple

leans (2)
2Ki 5:18 to worship, l on my arm,
Job 8:15 If one l on his house,

leap (4)
Job 39:20 Can you make it l like a locust,
Isa 35:6 who are lame will l like deer,
Joe 2:5 As they l on mountaintops,
Mal 4:2 You will go out and l like

leaping (1)
2Sm 6:16 window and saw King David l

learn (60)
Lev 23:43 generations to come may l how
Dtr 4:10 Then they will l to fear me as
5:1 L them and faithfully obey
8:5 L this lesson by heart:
14:23 Then you will l to fear the
17:19 He will l to fear the LORD his
18:9 never l the disgusting
31:12 Have them listen and l to fear
31:13 must hear them and l to fear the
1Sm 23:23 Watch and l about all the
2Sm 3:25 and l everything you're doing!"
1Ki 8:43 Israel and l also that this
1Ch 28:9 l to know your father's God.
2Ch 6:33 Israel and l that this temple
12:8 his servants so that they can l
Job 5:27 Listen to it, and l it for yourself."
Psa 64:9 They will l from what he has
78:6 Children yet to be born would l
79:10 Let us watch as the nations l
119:7 to you as I l your regulations,
119:71 to suffer in order to l your laws.
119:73 I may l your commandments.
Pro 1:5 will listen and continue to l,
8:5 l how to be sensible.
9:9 and he will l more.
12:1 loves discipline loves to l,
16:21 sweetly helps others l.
16:23 what he says helps others l.
19:25 gullible person may l a lesson.
22:25 or you will l his ways and set a
Isa 1:17 L to do good. Seek justice.
26:9 those who live in the world l to
26:10 they do not l to do what is right.
Jer 6:18 Listen, you nations, and l,
10:2 Don't l the practices of the
10:8 They l nonsense from wooden
12:16 Suppose they l carefully the
32:33 but they refused to listen and l.
35:13 'Won't you ever l your lesson
Dan 9:25 L, then, and understand that
10:12 of your God so that you could l
Hos 4:6 You have refused to l,
6:3 Let's l about the LORD.
Mat 9:13 L what this means:
11:29 your shoulders, and l from me,
24:32 "L from the story of the fig tree.
Mar 13:28 "L from the story of the fig tree.
1Co 4:6 You should l from us not to go
8:2 something still have a lot to l.
14:31 everyone will l and be
2Co 1:9 stop trusting ourselves and l
Gal 2:4 They slipped in as spies to l
3:2 I want to l only one thing from
1Ti 2:4 to be saved and to l the truth.
2:11 A woman must l in silence,
5:4 of a widow must first l
5:13 At the same time, they l to go
Tit 3:14 Our people should also l how
Heb 12:11 But later on, those who l from
Rev 14:3 on earth could l the song.

learned (38)
Gen 28:6 Esau l that Isaac had blessed
28:6 He l that Isaac had blessed
28:7 He also l that Jacob had
30:27 I've l from the signs I've seen
Dtr 11:2 today the discipline you l from
1Sm 23:9 When David l that Saul was
29:8 "What have you l about me
Neh 13:10 I l that the Levites had not been
Job 8:8 out what their ancestors had l.
Psa 95:10 They have not l my ways.'
106:35 They l to do what other nations
119:152 Long ago I l from your written
Pro 24:32 I saw it and l my lesson.
30:3 I haven't l wisdom.
Ecc 7:25 I l that wickedness is stupid
Isa 53:11 he has l through suffering.
Eze 19:3 He l to tear apart the animals
19:6 He l to tear apart the animals
28:16 You l to be violent,
Dan 6:10 When Daniel l that the
9:2 l from the Scriptures the
Mat 2:16 the exact time he had l from
Jon 6:45 Those who do what they have l
Act 7:13 l about Joseph's family.
Rom 3:17 They have not l to live in
16:17 is not the same as you have l.
Eph 4:20 you l from Christ's teachings.
Php 3:16 by what we have l so far.
4:9 Practice what you've l and
4:11 I've l to be content in whatever
4:12 I've l the secret of how to live
Col 1:7 You l about this Good News
2Ti 3:14 continue in what you have l
Heb 3:10 and they have not l my ways.'
5:8 he l to be obedient through his
10:26 after we have l the truth,
10:32 when you first l the truth.
Rev 2:24 who haven't l what are called

learning (2)
Pro 4:3 When I was a boy l from my
2Co 7:7 his arrival but also by l about

lease (1)
Mat 21:41 Then he will l the vineyard to

leased (3)
Mat 21:33 Then he l it to vineyard
Mar 12:1 Then he l it to vineyard
Luk 20:9 l it to vineyard workers,

leash (1)
Job 41:5 or keep it on a l for your girls?

least (69)
Exo 30:14 Everyone counted who is at l
38:26 who was at l 20 years old:
Num 1:3 who is at l 20 years old.
1:18 Each man at l 20 years old
1:20 who was at l 20 years old
1:22 who was at l 20 years old
1:24 who were at l 20 years old
1:26 who were at l 20 years old
1:28 who were at l 20 years old
1:30 who were at l 20 years old
1:32 who were at l 20 years old
1:34 who were at l 20 years old
1:36 who were at l 20 years old
1:38 who were at l 20 years old
1:40 who were at l 20 years old
1:42 who were at l 20 years old
1:45 men who were at l 20 years old
3:15 who is at l one month old."
3:22 all the males at l one month old
3:28 The number of all the males at l
3:34 all the males at l one month old
3:39 every male who was at l one
3:40 who is at l one month old,
3:43 males at l one month old
14:29 All of you who are at l 20 years
23:25 then at l don't bless them!"
26:2 List those who are at l 20 years
26:4 "Take a census of those at l
26:62 males at l one month old
Dtr 1:17 Listen to the l important people
Jdg 3:2 at l those who had known
6:15 I'm the l important member of
16:28 with the Philistines for at l one
2Ki 5:11 he would at l come out of
1Ch 12:14 The l able one was in
23:3 Every male Levite who was at l
23:24 temple was at l 20 years old.
23:27 who were at l 20 years old.
2Ch 25:5 who were at l 20 years old
31:16 who were at l three years old.
31:17 who were at l 20 years old.
Ezr 3:8 who were at l 20 years old
Psa 115:13 from the l important to the most
Jer 6:13 "All of them, from the l
8:10 All of them, from the l important
31:34 All of them, from the l important
42:1 from the l important to the most
42:8 and all the people from the l
44:12 All of them, from the l important
50:12 will be the l important nation.
Jnh 3:5 important to the l important,
Mat 2:6 you are by no means l among
11:11 Yet, the l important person in
24:44 return when you l expect him.
Luk 7:28 Yet, the l important person in
9:48 The one who is l among all of
12:40 return when you l expect him."
14:9 to take the place of l honor.
14:10 take the place of l honor.
Jon 10:38 then at l believe the things that
Act 5:15 that at l Peter's shadow might
1Co 6:5 Don't you have at l one wise
9:2 at l I'm an apostle to you.
9:22 order to save at l some of them.
15:9 I'm the l of the apostles.
2Co 2:17 At l we don't go around selling
Eph 3:8 I am the l of all God's people.
1Ti 5:9 and is at l 60 years old
Heb 8:11 All of them from the l important

leather (29)
Exo 25:5 rams' skins dyed red, fine l,
26:14 that put a cover made of fine l.
28:32 edge (like a l collar) all around
35:7 rams' skins dyed red, fine l,
35:23 or fine l brought them.
36:19 they put a cover made of fine l.
39:23 edge (like a l collar) all around
39:34 the cover made of fine l,
Lev 11:32 article, clothing, l, a sack,
13:48 linen or wool or on any l article,
13:52 piece of clothing or the l article
13:56 it out of the clothing or the l.
13:57 burn the clothing or the l article
13:58 clothing or any l article when
13:59 wool or in any l article is clean
15:17 Any clothes or any l with
Num 4:6 will put a covering of fine l.
4:8 will cover all this with fine l.
4:10 under a covering of fine l
4:11 and cover the cloth with fine l.
4:12 cover that with fine l,
4:14 a covering of fine l over all this.
4:25 the outer cover of fine l that
31:20 and everything made of l,
2Ki 1:8 "He was hairy and had a l belt
Jer 27:2 Make l straps and a wooden
Eze 16:10 dress on you and fine l sandals
Mat 3:4 hair and had a l belt around his
Mar 1:6 He wore a l belt around his

leatherworker (3)
Act 9:43 of days with Simon, a l.
10:6 He is a guest of Simon, a l,
10:32 a l who lives by the sea.'

leave (280)
Gen 2:24 That is why a man will l his
6:16 Make a roof for the ship, and l
12:1 "L your land, your relatives,
18:5 After that you can l,
18:16 Then the men got up to l.
20:13 When God had me l my father's
28:15 because I will not l you until
31:13 Now l this land, and go back to
31:27 Why did you l secretly and
33:15 Esau said, "Then let me l
42:15 that you won't l this place
42:33 L one of your brothers with me.
44:22 'The boy can't l his father.
45:1 "Have everyone l me!"
Exo 1:10 and l the country."
2:20 Why did you l the man there?
3:21 of Israel so that, when you l,
3:21 you will not l empty-handed.
6:11 let the Israelites l his country."

Exo 6:27 to let the Israelites **l** Egypt.
7:2 let the Israelites **l** the country.
8:9 Then the frogs will **l** you and
8:11 The frogs will **l** you,
8:29 "As soon as I **l** you,
11:8 After that I will **l**." Burning with
11:10 let the Israelites **l** his country.
12:10 Don't **l** any of it until morning.
12:22 No one may **l** the house until
12:31 "You and the Israelites must **l**
12:33 begged the people to **l**
14:12 tell you in Egypt, '**L** us alone!
16:29 the seventh day you may not **l**.
21:2 In the seventh year he may **l**
21:3 he must **l** by himself.
21:3 his wife may **l** with him.
21:4 the slave must **l** by himself.
21:5 I don't want to **l** as a free man,'
23:5 under its load, don't **l** it there.
23:11 in the seventh year you must **l**
23:11 may eat what the poor people **l**.
32:10 Now **l** me alone. I'm so angry
33:1 out of Egypt must **l** this place.
33:15 don't make us **l** this place.
Lev 7:15 Never **l** any of it until morning.
8:33 You will not **l** the entrance to
10:7 You must not **l** the entrance to
13:45 and **l** their hair uncombed.
16:23 holy place, and **l** them there.
19:10 **L** them for poor people and
21:12 He must not **l** the holy tent of
22:30 Never **l** any of it until morning.
23:22 **L** it for poor people and
Num 9:12 You must never **l** any of the
10:31 "Please don't **l** us.
11:20 'Why did we ever **l** Egypt?'"
20:5 Why did you make us **l** Egypt
20:17 the king's highway and never **l**
21:5 "Why did you make us **l** Egypt
Dtr 2:27 and won't ever **l** the road.
9:12 He told me, "**L** right away.
9:14 **L** me alone! I'll destroy them
15:16 "I don't want to **l** you,"
15:17 slave ⌊if she doesn't want to **l**⌋.
16:4 Never **l** until morning any of the
21:23 never **l** his dead body hung on
24:1 and makes her **l** his house.
24:19 **L** it there for foreigners,
24:20 **L** some for foreigners,
24:21 **L** some for foreigners,
28:51 They'll **l** you no grain,
31:6 He won't abandon you or **l** you."
31:8 He won't abandon you or **l** you.
Jos 6:1 No one could enter or **l**.
8:35 He did not **l** out one word from
11:15 He did not **l** out anything the
Jdg 6:18 Don't **l** until I come back.
7:3 should **l** Mount Gilead
16:17 my strength will **l** me.
19:5 got up early in the morning to **l**,
19:7 When the Levite started to **l**,
19:8 the Levite got up early to **l**.
19:9 The Levite started to **l** with his
19:9 It's too late ⌊to **l**⌋ now.
19:27 and was about to **l**.
Rut 1:16 "Don't force me to **l** you.
2:8 and don't even **l** this one.
2:16 grain out of the bundles and **l**
1Sm 6:7 and **l** them in their stall.
10:2 When you **l** me today,
10:9 Saul turned around to **l** Samuel,
14:36 And let's not **l** any of them
15:27 When Samuel turned to **l**,
17:28 "and with whom did you **l**
25:22 May God punish me if I **l** even
28:22 will have strength when you **l**."
29:7 So **l** peacefully without doing
29:10 and **l** when it's light."
30:22 his wife and children and **l**."
2Sm 2:19 and refused to **l** him alone.
2:21 Abner told him, "**L** me alone!
12:10 So warfare will never **l** your
13:9 "Have everyone **l** me,"
15:14 Let's **l** right away, or he'll catch
16:11 **L** him alone. Let him curse,
17:1 12,000 men and **l** tonight

2Sm 17:21 "**L** right away," they told David.
1Ki 2:2 "I'm about to **l** this world.
2:36 Don't **l** ⌊the city⌋ to go
2:37 But the day you **l** and cross the
8:57 May he never **l** us or abandon
11:22 "But let me **l** anyway."
12:5 He said to them, "**L** and come
15:19 so that he will **l** me alone."
17:3 "**L** here, turn east, and hide
18:12 what will happen: When I **l** you,
18:44 and **l** before the rain delays
20:36 will kill you when you **l** me."
22:24 "How did the LORD's Spirit **l**
2Ki 4:27 man of God said, "**L** her alone.
4:30 I will not **l** without you."
9:2 get up and **l** his companions.
9:3 Then open the door and **l**
10:14 They didn't **l** any survivors.
18:14 Go away, and **l** me alone.
24:7 The king of Egypt didn't **l** his
1Ch 28:8 to possess this good land and **l**
2Ch 16:3 so that he will **l** me alone."
35:15 They didn't need to **l** their work,
Ezr 9:8 God has been kind enough to **l**
Neh 6:3 should the work stop while I **l**
9:19 The column of smoke didn't **l**
9:19 The column of fire didn't **l** them
Job 7:16 **L** me alone because my days
10:20 So stop ⌊this⌋, and **l** me alone.
21:14 they say to God, '**L** us alone.
22:17 They told God, '**L** us alone!
39:4 They **l** and don't come back.
39:11 it's so strong or **l** your labor
Psa 17:14 and they **l** what remains to their
27:9 Do not **l** me! Do not abandon
37:8 go of anger, and **l** rage behind.
41:8 He will never **l** his sickbed."
49:10 They **l** their riches to others.
55:11 and fraud never **l** the streets.
119:121 Do not **l** me at the mercy of
139:19 people would **l** me alone.
141:8 Do not **l** me defenseless.
Pro 3:3 Do not let mercy and truth **l** you
8:33 Do not **l** my ways.
13:22 Good people **l** an inheritance to
17:13 evil will never **l** his home.
22:10 a mocker, and conflict will **l**.
27:22 his stupidity will not **l** him.
Ecc 2:18 because I will have to **l** it to the
5:15 They will **l** as naked as they
5:16 They **l** exactly as they came.
8:3 Don't be in a hurry to **l** the
Isa 10:3 Where will you **l** your wealth?
48:20 **L** Babylon; flee from the
49:17 laid waste to you will **l** you.
59:21 put in your mouth will not **l** you.
Jer 2:37 You will also **l** this place with
5:6 All who **l** the cities will be torn
9:19 We must **l** our land because
14:9 by your name. Don't **l** us!
26:2 Don't **l** out a single word.
37:9 that the Babylonians will **l** you.
37:9 They will not **l** you.
37:12 So Jeremiah wanted to **l**
43:12 He will **l** Egypt peacefully.
49:9 won't they **l** a few grapes
50:8 **L** the land of the Babylonians.
50:26 and don't **l** anyone behind.
51:45 "**L** it, my people! Run for your
51:50 who escaped from the sword, **l**!
Eze 9:7 with dead people, and then **l**."
10:16 the wheels didn't **l** their side.
12:3 Let the people see you **l** in the
12:4 evening let them see you **l** like
12:5 of your house, and **l** through it.
12:12 his shoulders in the dark and **l**.
16:39 and **l** you naked and bare.
23:29 They will **l** you naked and bare.
24:23 **L** your turbans on your heads
29:5 I will **l** you in the desert,
36:20 yet they had to **l** his land.'
42:14 courtyard until they **l** behind
44:3 gateway and **l** the same way."
44:19 They must **l** their clothes in the
46:2 of the gateway and then **l**.
46:8 must enter and **l** the same way.

Eze 46:9 gate to worship must **l** through
46:9 the south gate must **l** through
46:9 They must not **l** through the
46:9 They must **l** through the
46:10 When they **l**, he must leave.
46:10 When they leave, he must **l**.
Dan 4:15 But **l** the stump and its roots in
4:23 But **l** the stump and its roots in
11:44 He will **l** very angry to destroy
Hos 2:3 I will **l** her as naked as the day
4:17 to worship idols. **L** them alone!
9:12 will be for them when I **l** them.
Joe 1:4 What young locusts **l**,
1:4 What mature locusts **l**,
1:4 What adult locusts **l**,
2:7 They do not **l** their places.
2:14 and change his plan and **l**
2:16 Grooms **l** their rooms.
2:16 Brides **l** their chambers.
3:7 I am going to make them **l** the
Amo 4:3 Each of you will **l** ⌊the city⌋
Oba 1:5 won't they **l** a few grapes
1:7 All your allies will force you to **l**
Jnh 1:2 "**L** at once for the important city,
3:2 "**L** at once for the important city,
Mic 2:13 out, go through the gate, and **l**.
4:10 Now you will **l** the city,
Zep 3:3 They **l** nothing to gnaw on for
3:12 So with you I will **l** a faithful
Mal 4:1 "It won't **l** a single root or
Mat 5:24 **l** your gift at the altar.
8:34 begged him to **l** their territory.
9:24 He said to them, "**L**!
10:11 them until you **l** ⌊that place⌋.
10:14 **l** that house or city,
15:14 **L** them alone! They are blind
18:12 Won't he **l** the 99 sheep in the
19:5 'That's why a man will **l** his
22:9 Go where the roads **l** the city.
27:19 "**L** that innocent man alone.
27:49 The others said, "**L** him alone!
Mar 5:17 to beg Jesus to **l** their territory.
6:10 until you're ready to **l** that place.
6:11 **l** and shake the dust from your
6:33 But many people saw them **l**
10:7 That's why a man will **l** his
11:19 his disciples would **l** the city.)
14:6 Jesus said, "**L** her alone!
Luk 2:29 are allowing your servant to **l**
4:39 ordered the fever to **l**,
5:8 of Jesus and said, "**L** me, Lord!
8:37 Gerasenes asked Jesus to **l**
9:4 stay there until you're ready to **l**.
9:5 don't welcome you, **l** that city,
9:42 ordered the evil spirit to **l**.
10:10 people don't welcome you, **l**.
15:4 Doesn't he **l** the 99 sheep
21:21 of you in Jerusalem should **l** it.
Jon 6:67 "Do you want to **l** me too?
7:3 brothers told him, "**L** this place,
11:31 saw her get up quickly and **l**.
12:7 said to Judas, "**L** her alone!
13:1 had come for him to **l** this world
14:18 "I will not **l** you all alone.
14:31 Get up! We have to **l**."
16:28 I'm going to **l** the world and go
16:32 own way and **l** me all alone.
Act 1:4 he ordered them not to **l**
4:15 they ordered Peter and John to **l**
5:38 We should **l** them alone.
7:3 '**L** your land and your relatives.
7:7 After that, they will **l** that
9:40 made everyone **l** the room.
16:36 So you can **l** peacefully now."
16:39 they asked them to **l** the city.
18:2 had ordered all Jews to **l** Rome.
19:12 and evil spirits would **l** them.
20:7 Since he intended to **l** the next
20:29 will come to you after I **l**,
1Co 5:10 you would have to **l** this world.
7:10 A wife shouldn't **l** her husband.
7:15 But if the unbelieving partners **l**
Eph 5:31 That's why a man will **l** his
Php 1:23 I would like to **l** this life and be
Heb 11:27 Faith led Moses to **l** Egypt
13:5 "I will never abandon you or **l**

Rev 3:12 They will never **l** it again.
11:2 **L** that out, because it is given
17:16 They will **l** her abandoned and

leavened (1)

Dtr 16:3 Never eat **l** bread with the meat

leaves (35)

Gen 3:7 They sewed fig **l** together and
44:22 If the boy **l** him, his father will
Num 27:8 If a man dies and **l** no sons,
Dtr 24:2 man after she **l** his house.
Jos 2:19 Whoever **l** your house will be
1Sm 6:20 will he go when he **l** us?"
Job 41:32 It **l** a shining path behind it so
Psa 1:3 and whose **l** do not wither.
41:6 ⌊Then⌋ he **l** to tell others.
58:8 like a snail that **l** behind
Pro 2:17 who **l** ⌊her husband,⌋
15:10 ⌊burden⌋ to anyone who **l**
28:3 like a driving rain that **l** no food.
Isa 1:30 You will be like an oak whose **l**
34:4 The stars will fall like **l** from a
64:6 All of us shrivel like **l**,
Jer 3:1 divorces his wife and she **l** him
8:13 and the **l** have dried up.
17:8 Its **l** will turn green.
Eze 17:9 All the **l** on its branches will
44:5 enters the temple and **l** from
46:12 When he **l**, the gate must be
47:12 Their **l** won't wither,
47:12 and the **l** will be used for
Dan 4:12 It had beautiful **l** and plenty of
4:14 Strip off its **l**! Scatter its fruit!
4:21 It had beautiful **l** and plenty of
Mat 21:19 and found nothing on it but **l**.
24:32 tender and it sprouts **l**,
Mar 11:13 he saw a fig tree with **l**.
11:13 he found nothing but **l** because
12:19 'If a man dies and **l** a wife but
13:28 tender and it sprouts **l**,
Luk 21:30 As soon as **l** grow on them,
Rev 22:2 The **l** of the tree will heal the

leaving (38)

Gen 31:20 by not telling him he was **l**.
31:27 didn't even tell me you were **l**.
45:24 As they were **l**, he said to them,
Exo 9:17 still blocking my people from **l**.
13:4 month of Abib, you are **l** Egypt.
14:8 who were boldly **l** Egypt.
Lev 10:6 "Do not mourn by **l** your hair
21:10 He must never mourn by **l** his
Num 1:1 in the second year after **l** Egypt.
21:35 all his troops, **l** no survivors.
Dtr 3:3 defeated him, **l** no survivors.
Jdg 16:4 After ⌊**l** Gaza⌋, he fell in love
1Sm 8:8 I took them out of Egypt — **l** me
25:10 nowadays are **l** their masters.
2Sm 3:26 After **l** David, Joab sent
15:17 the king and his troops were **l**
2Ch 20:20 As they were **l**, "Listen to me,
Ezr 1:4 people who are **l** with silver,
Ecc 8:8 prevent the spirit of life from **l**.
Dan 2:14 was **l** to kill the wise advisers
Mat 9:9 When Jesus was **l** that place,
9:32 As they were **l**, some people
11:7 As they were **l**, Jesus spoke to
20:29 As they were **l** Jericho,
26:44 After **l** them again,
Mar 2:14 When Jesus was **l**,
4:36 **L** the crowd, they took Jesus
10:46 many people were **l** Jericho,
Luk 4:42 they tried to keep him from **l**.
9:33 Moses and Elijah were **l** him,
9:39 **l** the child worn out.
Jon 12:11 why many people were **l**
14:27 "I'm **l** you peace. I'm giving you
Act 13:42 were **l** the synagogue,
26:31 As they were **l**, they said to
27:4 **L** Sidon, we sailed on the
Heb 11:22 about the Israelites **l** Egypt
1Jn 2:19 But by **l** they made it clear that

Lebanah (2)

Ezr 2:45 **L**, Hagabah, Akkub,
Neh 7:48 **L**, Hagabah, Shalmai,

Lebanese (2)

2Ch 2:8 are skilled **L** lumberjacks.
Sos 7:4 a **L** tower facing Damascus.

Lebanon (68)

Dtr 1:7 and into **L** as far as the
3:25 those beautiful mountains in **L**."
11:24 will be from the desert to **L**,
Jos 1:4 nearby **L** to the Euphrates River
9:2 coast as far as **L**,
11:17 as Baal Gad in the **L** Valley at
12:7 from Baal Gad in the valley of **L**
13:5 all **L** eastward from Baal Gad
13:6 lives in the mountains from **L**
Jdg 3:3 on Mount **L** from Mount Baal
9:15 and burn up the cedars of **L**.'
1Ki 4:33 trees — from the cedar in **L**
5:6 cut down cedars from **L** for me.
5:9 workers will bring logs from **L**
5:14 sent a shift of 10,000 men to **L**
5:14 would spend one month in **L**
7:2 a hall ⌊named⌋ the Forest of **L**.
9:19 to build in Jerusalem, **L**,
10:17 he called the Forest of **L**.
10:21 the Forest of **L** were fine gold.
2Ki 14:9 "A thistle in **L** sent a message
14:9 sent a message to a cedar in **L**.
14:9 but a wild animal from **L** came
19:23 up the slopes of **L**.
2Ch 2:8 and sandalwood from **L**.
2:16 all the lumber you need in **L**.
8:6 to build in Jerusalem, **L**,
9:16 hall ⌊named⌋ the Forest of **L**.
9:20 the Forest of **L** were fine gold.
25:18 "A thistle in **L** sent a message
25:18 sent a message to a cedar in **L**.
25:18 but a wild animal from **L** came
Ezr 3:7 men would bring by sea from **L**
Psa 29:5 LORD splinters the cedars of **L**.
29:6 He makes **L** skip along like a
72:16 its fruit like ⌊the treetops of⌋ **L**.
92:12 grow tall like the cedars in **L**.
104:16 the cedars in **L** which he
Sos 3:9 for himself from the wood of **L**.
4:8 You will come with me from **L**,
4:8 from **L** as my bride.
4:11 is like the fragrance of **L**.
4:15 of living water flowing from **L**.
5:15 His form is like **L**, choice as
Isa 2:13 and mighty cedars of **L**
10:34 **L** will fall in front of the Mighty
14:8 The cedars of **L** say,
29:17 In a very short time **L** will be
33:9 **L** is ashamed and is decaying.
35:2 It will have the glory of **L**,
37:24 up the slopes of **L**.
40:16 All the trees in **L** are not
Jer 18:14 The rocky slopes of **L** are
22:6 Gilead to me, like the top of **L**.
22:20 "Go to **L** and cry! Raise your
22:23 You live in **L** and have your
Eze 17:3 A large eagle came to **L**.
27:5 They took cedar trees from **L** to
31:3 It was a cedar in **L** with fine
31:15 I made **L** mourn for the tree,
31:16 choicest and best trees of **L**,
Hos 14:5 firmly rooted like cedars from **L**
14:6 be fragrant like cedars from **L**.
14:7 as famous as the wines from **L**.
Nah 1:4 The flowers of **L** wither.
Hab 2:17 The violence done to **L** will
Zec 10:10 bring them to Gilead and to **L**,
11:1 Open your doors, **L**,

Lebanon's (1)

Isa 60:13 "**L** glory will come to you:

Lebaoth (1)

Jos 15:32 **L**, Shilhim, Ain, and Rimmon.

Leb Kamai (1)

Jer 51:1 against the people who live in **L**.

Lebonah (1)

Jdg 21:19 to Shechem, and south of **L**."

Lecah (1)

1Ch 4:21 who first settled **L**,

lecture (1)

Act 19:9 in the **l** hall of Tyrannus.

led (168)

Gen 24:27 The LORD has **l** me on this trip
24:48 The LORD **l** me in the right
Exo 3:1 As he **l** the sheep to the far
13:18 So God **l** the people around the
15:22 Moses **l** Israel away from the
19:17 Then Moses **l** the people out of
32:1 who **l** us out of Egypt.
Num 2:3 the armies **l** by Judah will
2:10 "On the south side the armies **l**
2:18 "On the west side the armies **l**
2:25 "On the north side the armies **l**
10:14 the armies **l** by Judah's
10:18 the armies **l** by Reuben's
10:22 the armies **l** by Ephraim's
10:25 the armies **l** by Dan's
Dtr 6:23 The LORD **l** us out of there to
8:2 years the LORD your God **l** you
8:15 He was the one who **l** you
13:13 have been **l** away from the
29:5 For 40 years I **l** you through the
32:12 the LORD alone **l** his people.
Jos 8:10 he and the leaders of Israel **l**
24:3 I **l** him through all of Canaan
24:5 with plagues. Later I **l** you out.
24:6 When I **l** your ancestors out of
Jdg 3:27 with him, and he **l** them.
3:28 of the Jordan River that **l**
9:39 Then Gaal **l** citizens of
20:31 troops and were **l** away from
1Sm 10:5 They will be **l** by men playing
12:2 I have **l** you from my youth until
18:13 David **l** the troops out ⌊to
18:16 because he **l** them in and out
30:16 The Egyptian **l** him ⌊to them⌋.
2Sm 5:2 you were the one who **l** Israel
1Ki 10:19 Six steps **l** to the throne.
14:16 which he **l** Israel to commit."
15:30 and the sins which he **l** Israel
15:34 He lived like Jeroboam and **l**
16:2 You have **l** my people to sin,
16:13 They sinned, **l** Israel to sin,
16:19 Jeroboam and **l** Israel to sin.
16:26 He sinned and **l** Israel to sin
20:19 district governors **l** an attack,
21:22 You **l** Israel to sin."
22:52 son) who **l** Israel to sin.
2Ki 3:3 Jeroboam (Nebat's son) **l** Israel
6:19 So he **l** them into Samaria.
10:29 Jeroboam (Nebat's son) **l** Israel
10:31 Jeroboam **l** Israel to commit.
13:2 Jeroboam (Nebat's son) **l** Israel
13:6 and his dynasty **l** Israel
13:11 the sins that Jeroboam **l** Israel
14:24 (Nebat's son) **l** Israel to commit.
15:9 (Nebat's son) **l** Israel to commit.
15:18 (Nebat's son) **l** Israel to commit.
15:24 (Nebat's son) **l** Israel to commit.
15:28 (Nebat's son) **l** Israel to commit.
17:21 from the LORD and **l** them
21:16 In addition to his sin that he **l**
1Ch 4:42 and Uzziel **l** 500 of Simeon's
5:26 Then the God of Israel **l** King
8:7 Gera **l** the rest of them away as
11:2 you were the one who **l** Israel
19:16 of Hadadezer's army, **l** them.
20:1 Joab **l** the army ⌊to war⌋.
2Ch 9:18 Six steps **l** to the throne,
20:27 while Jehoshaphat **l** them.
20:35 who **l** him to do evil.
21:11 So he **l** Judah astray.
22:3 him advice that **l** him to sin.
25:11 courageously **l** his troops.
Ezr 9:2 the leaders and officials have **l**
Neh 9:12 You **l** them during the day by a
9:19 but it **l** them on their way.

Neh 11:17 the leader who l the prayer of
12:36 Ezra the scribe l them.
13:26 non-Israelite wives l him to sin.
Job 36:18 Be careful that you are not l
Psa 77:20 a shepherd, you l your people.
78:13 He divided the sea and l them
78:52 But he l his own people out
78:53 He l them safely. They had no
106:9 He l them through deep water
107:7 He l them on a road that went
107:28 He l them from their troubles.
136:14 He l Israel through the middle
136:16 Give thanks to the one who l
Ecc 4:16 everyone whom he l.
Isa 19:13 of Memphis are l astray.
47:10 knowledge have l you astray,
48:21 They weren't thirsty when he l
53:7 He was l like a lamb to the
55:12 will go out with joy and be l out
60:11 with their kings l as prisoners.
63:13 Where is the one who l them
Jer 2:6 He l us through the desert,
2:17 LORD your God when he l you
23:13 by Baal and l my people Israel
50:6 shepherds have l them astray.
Eze 20:10 out of Egypt and l them into
37:2 He l me all around them.
40:22 Seven steps went up to it and l
40:24 Then the man l me to the south
40:26 Seven steps went up to it and l
40:31 and eight steps l up to each
40:34 and eight steps l up to the
40:37 and eight steps l up to the
40:49 Steps l up to it. Pillars stood by
42:1 Then the man l me out toward
42:15 he l me out through the east
46:21 Then the man l me to the outer
47:2 Then he l me through the north
47:3 third of a mile and l me through
47:4 third of a mile and l me through
47:4 third of a mile and l me through
47:7 Then the man l me back along
Hos 11:4 I l them with cords of human
Amo 2:4 They have been l astray by
2:10 I l you through the desert for 40
Mat 2:9 The star they had seen rising l
4:1 Then the Spirit l Jesus into the
17:1 brother of James) and l them up
27:2 They tied him up, l him away,
27:31 Then they l him away to
Mar 8:23 blind man's hand and l him out
9:2 and John and l them up a high
15:16 The soldiers l Jesus into the
15:20 Then they l him out to crucify
Luk 4:1 The Spirit l him while he was
4:29 and l him to the cliff.
22:54 So they arrested Jesus and l
23:26 As the soldiers l Jesus away,
23:32 were l away to be executed
Jon 6:66 they had l before they followed
Act 1:16 Judas l the men to arrest
5:19 to their cell and l them out
5:37 Galilee appeared and l people
7:36 This is the man who l our
7:40 who l us out of Egypt.
8:32 "He was l like a lamb to the
9:8 l him into Damascus.
11:18 "Then God has also l people
12:10 came to the iron gate that l into
21:38 and l four thousand terrorists
22:11 So the men who were with me l
Rom 6:19 This l you to live disobedient
1Co 12:2 every time you were l to
2Co 7:9 distress I caused you has l you
8:6 This l us to urge Titus to finish
12:21 who formerly l sinful lives
13:2 who formerly l sinful lives as
2Ti 3:6 with sins and l by all kinds
Heb 3:16 All those whom Moses l out of
6:6 Therefore, they cannot be l a
11:4 Faith l Abel to offer God a
11:7 Faith l Noah to listen when
11:8 Faith l Abraham to obey when
11:9 Faith l Abraham to live as a
11:17 faith l him to offer his son
11:20 Faith l Isaac to bless Jacob
Heb 11:21 While Jacob was dying, faith l
11:22 While Joseph was dying, faith l
11:23 Faith l Moses' parents to hide
11:24 When Moses grew up, faith l
11:27 Faith l Moses to leave Egypt
11:28 Faith l Moses to establish the
11:31 Faith l the prostitute Rahab to

ledge (8)

Exo 27:5 Put the grate under the l of the
38:4 ⌊and put it⌋ under the l,
Eze 43:14 on the ground to the lower l
43:14 and from the lower l to the
43:14 the lower ledge to the upper l
43:17 The upper l was also square.
43:20 on the four corners of the l,
45:19 on the four corners of the l of

ledger (2)

Luk 16:6 'Take my master's l.
16:7 manager told him, 'Take the l,

ledges (1)

1Ki 6:6 Solomon made l all around the

leech (1)

Pro 30:15 The bloodsucking l has two

leeks (1)

Num 11:5 l, onions, and garlic we had?

left (738)

Gen 4:16 Then Cain l the LORD's
7:23 with him in the ship were l.
12:4 So Abram l, as the LORD had
12:4 75 years old when he l Haran.
13:1 Abram l Egypt with his wife
13:9 If you go to the l, I'll go to the
13:9 go to the right, I'll go to the l."
13:14 After Lot l, the LORD said to
14:11 as well as all their food, and l.
17:22 with Abraham, he l him.
18:33 speaking to Abraham, he l.
19:30 Lot l Zoar because he was
21:14 So she l and wandered around
21:32 l and went back to the land of
22:19 together they l for Beersheba.
23:3 Then Abraham l the side of his
24:10 of his master's camels and l,
24:61 Then Rebekah and her maids l.
24:61 servant took Rebekah and l.
25:5 Abraham l everything he had to
25:34 and then he got up and l.
26:31 and they l peacefully.
27:30 Jacob had barely l when his
27:37 What is l for me to do for you,
28:7 and had l for Paddan Aram.
28:10 Jacob l Beersheba and
31:14 "Is there anything l in our
31:21 So he l in a hurry with all that
31:22 told that Jacob had l in a hurry.
31:30 Now you have l for your father's
31:31 "I l because I was afraid.
31:55 Then Laban l and went back
32:24 So Jacob was l alone.
34:26 from Shechem's home and l.
38:1 About that time Judah l his
38:19 After she got up and l,
39:6 So he l all that he owned in
39:12 "But he ran outside and l his
39:13 but had l his clothes behind,
39:15 he ran outside and l his clothes
39:18 he ran outside and l his clothes
41:46 He l Pharaoh and traveled all
42:5 Israel's sons l with the others
42:26 grain on their donkeys and l.
42:38 and he's the only one l.
44:20 only one of his mother's sons l,
45:25 So they l Egypt and came to
46:5 So Jacob l Beersheba.
47:10 Jacob blessed Pharaoh and l.
47:18 There's nothing l to bring you
48:13 on his right, facing Israel's l,
48:13 and Manasseh on his l,
48:14 He put his l hand on
50:7 So Joseph l to bury his father.
Gen 50:8 their cattle were l in Goshen.)
Exo 5:20 As they l Pharaoh,
8:9 The only ones l will be those
8:11 The only frogs l will be those
8:12 Moses and Aaron l Pharaoh,
8:30 Moses l Pharaoh and prayed to
8:31 The swarms of flies l Pharaoh,
8:31 his people. Not one fly was l.
9:21 seriously l their servants
9:33 As soon as he l Pharaoh and
10:5 They will eat everything l by
10:6 Moses turned and l Pharaoh.
10:12 land — everything l by the hail.
10:15 on the trees that the hail had l.
10:15 Nothing green was l on any
10:18 Moses l Pharaoh and prayed to
10:19 was l anywhere in Egypt.
10:26 one animal must be l behind.
11:8 with anger, Moses l Pharaoh.
12:10 Anything l over in the morning
12:37 The Israelites l Rameses to go
12:41 all the LORD's people l Egypt
13:3 the day when you l Egypt,
13:8 did for us when we l Egypt.'
13:18 for battle when they l Egypt.
14:22 wall on their right and on their l.
14:29 wall on their right and on their l.
16:1 month after they had l Egypt.
16:23 Save all that's l over,
17:1 whole community of Israelites l
19:1 after the Israelites l Egypt,
23:15 that was when you l Egypt.
23:18 festivals should never be l over
26:13 There will be 18 inches l over
29:32 and the bread ⌊l⌋ in the basket.
29:34 is l over until morning,
33:6 After they l Mount Horeb,
34:25 Festival should be l over
35:20 Israelite community l Moses.
40:17 the Israelites had l Egypt⌋.
Lev 2:13 promise must never be l out
6:10 he will remove the ashes l
7:17 on the third day any meat l over
8:32 any meat or bread that is l over.
10:12 "Take the grain offering l over
14:15 and pour it into his own l hand.
14:16 finger in the oil in his l hand,
14:26 olive oil into his own l hand.
19:6 day burn whatever is l over.
19:9 what is l after you're finished.
23:22 what is l after you're finished.
25:27 Then he will pay what is l to
25:51 If there are many years l,
25:52 If there are only a few years l
26:36 fill with despair those who are l
26:39 Those who are l will waste
27:18 on the number of years l until
Num 9:1 year after the Israelites l Egypt,
10:11 the ⌊column of⌋ smoke l the
10:33 So they l the mountain of the
12:9 was angry with them, so he l.
12:10 When the smoke l the tent,
14:19 time they l Egypt until now."
20:22 community of Israel l Kadesh
22:7 leaders of Moab and Midian l,
22:21 he saddled his donkey and l
22:26 room to turn to the right or the l
24:19 whoever is l in their cities."
25:7 So he l the assembly,
26:65 The only ones l were Caleb
27:3 for his own sin and l no sons.
31:32 This is the loot that was l from
33:1 set up camp after they l Egypt
33:3 The Israelites boldly l in full
33:38 after the Israelites had l Egypt.
Dtr 1:3 year ⌊after they had l Egypt⌋,
1:19 So we l Mount Horeb,
1:24 They l and went into the
2:14 time we l Kadesh Barnea until
2:15 until none were l in the camp.
3:11 only King Og of Bashan was l.
4:27 and only a few of you will be l
4:45 Israelites after they had l Egypt.
4:46 defeated him after they l Egypt.
7:20 There will be no one l — not
9:7 the day you l Egypt until you

Dtr 9:28 the country we **l** will say,
11:10 like the land you **l** in Egypt.
16:3 of misery because you **l** Egypt
16:3 remember the day you **l** Egypt.
16:6 you did it when you **l** Egypt.
26:13 "Nothing is **l** of the holy offering
28:54 and the children he still has **l**.
28:55 It will be all that he has **l**,
28:62 But only a few of you will be **l**,
32:36 is gone and that no one is **l**,
33:28 Jacob's spring will be ⌊**l**⌋
Jos 2:5 was just about to close, they **l**.
2:7 soon as the king's men had **l**,
2:10 front of you when you **l** Egypt.
2:11 There was no courage **l** in any
3:1 and all the Israelites **l** Shittim.
5:1 lost heart and had no courage **l**
5:4 the desert after they **l** Egypt.
5:5 The men who **l** Egypt had been
5:6 their soldiers who **l** Egypt died.
8:17 Not one man was **l** in Ai or
8:17 So the city was **l** unprotected
8:24 Ai and killed everyone **l** there.
8:29 on a pole and **l** him there until
9:12 was warm when we **l** home
11:22 Some of them were **l** in Gaza,
13:1 a lot of land **l** to be conquered.
13:2 The land that is **l** includes all
22:9 half of the tribe of Manasseh **l**
23:7 get mixed up with the nations **l**
23:13 eyes until none of you are **l**
Jdg 2:21 nations Joshua **l** behind when
3:1 the nations the LORD **l** behind
3:2 The LORD **l** them to teach
3:3 He **l** the five rulers of the
3:4 These nations were **l** to test
3:19 all his advisers **l** the room.
3:21 Ehud reached with his **l** hand,
3:23 Ehud **l** the room. (He had closed
3:23 doors of the room before he **l**.)
5:13 men who were **l** came down.
6:4 They **l** nothing for Israel to live
7:3 and 10,000 were **l**.
7:20 They held the torches in their **l**
8:10 This was all that was **l** of
11:13 the people of Israel **l** Egypt,
11:16 the people of Israel **l** Egypt,
14:8 ⌊On his way⌋ he **l** the road to
16:19 because his strength had **l** him.
16:20 that the LORD had **l** him.)
16:29 hand on one column and his **l**
17:8 This man **l** Bethlehem in Judah
18:7 The five men **l** there and came
18:11 from the tribe of Dan **l** Zorah
18:21 When they **l**, they put their
18:24 What do I have **l**? How can you
19:2 She **l** him and went to her
19:10 He **l** and traveled as far as
19:28 on the donkey and **l** for home.
20:33 men of Israel **l** their positions.
21:7 wives for the men who are **l**?
21:16 wives for the men who are **l**,
21:24 that time the people of Israel **l**.
Rut 1:3 and she was **l** alone with her
1:5 So Naomi was **l** alone,
1:7 So she **l** the place where she
2:2 There I will gather the grain **l**
2:3 gathered the grain **l** behind by
2:11 They told me how you **l** your
2:14 wanted and had some **l** over.
2:18 what she had **l** over from lunch
1Sm 2:36 Then anyone who is **l** from
6:12 the road and didn't turn right or **l**
7:11 Israel's soldiers **l** Mizpah,
9:25 Then they **l** the worship site for
11:11 no two of them were **l** together.
13:15 Samuel **l** Gilgal. The rest of the
13:17 Raiding parties **l** the Philistine
14:3 didn't know Jonathan had **l**.
14:17 see who has **l** ⌊our camp⌋."
15:6 the Kenites **l** the Amalekites.
15:12 Then he **l** there and went to
16:13 Then Samuel **l** for Ramah.
16:14 the LORD's Spirit had **l** Saul,
16:23 and the evil spirit **l** him.
17:22 David **l** the supplies behind in
1Sm 18:8 The only thing **l** for David is my
18:12 was with David but had **l** Saul.
20:41 When the boy had **l**,
20:42 forever."' So David **l**,
21:10 That day David **l**. He was ⌊still⌋
23:13 six hundred in all, **l** Keilah.
23:24 They **l** for Ziph ahead of Saul.
24:7 Saul **l** the cave and went out
24:8 Later, David got up, **l** the cave,
25:34 had one of his men **l** at dawn."
26:12 near Saul's head, and they **l**.
27:9 he **l** no man or woman alive.
28:8 Saul **l** with two men and came
28:20 He also had no strength **l**,
28:25 ate and **l** that ⌊same⌋ night.
30:9 where some were **l** behind.
30:13 "My master **l** me behind
2Sm 2:13 officers also **l** ⌊Hebron⌋.
3:21 Abner, who **l** peacefully.
3:23 and Abner **l** peacefully."
4:4 She was in a hurry when she **l**,
5:21 The Philistines **l** their idols
6:2 He and all the people with him **l**
9:1 David asked, "Is there anyone **l**
9:3 "Is there someone **l** in Saul's
11:8 Uriah **l** the royal palace,
11:22 The messenger **l**, and when he
13:9 So everyone **l** him.
13:30 and not a single one is **l**."
14:7 burning coal that is **l** for me.
15:16 The king **l** on foot,
15:16 whom the king **l** behind
16:21 father's concubines whom he **l**
17:12 of his men will be **l** ⌊alive⌋.
17:18 So both of them **l** quickly and
17:21 After Absalom's servants **l**,
17:22 and all the troops with him **l**
17:23 he saddled his donkey, **l**,
18:9 So he was **l** hanging in midair
19:9 from Absalom and **l** the country
19:19 the day you **l** Jerusalem.
19:24 from the day the king **l** until
20:2 So all the people of Israel **l**
20:3 the ten concubines he had **l**
20:7 They **l** Jerusalem to pursue
20:10 the sword in Joab's ⌊**l**⌋ hand.
21:2 of Israel but were **l** over from
24:4 So they **l** the king ⌊in order⌋ to
1Ki 2:42 Didn't I warn you that if you **l**
6:1 480 years after Israel **l** Egypt.
7:21 he set up the pillar on the **l**
7:47 Solomon **l** all the products
8:9 the Israelites after they **l** Egypt.
8:10 When the priests **l** the holy
9:12 Hiram **l** Tyre to see the cities
9:20 and Jebusites had been **l** ⌊in
11:18 They **l** Midian and went to
11:29 time Jeroboam **l** Jerusalem.
11:32 He will have one tribe ⌊**l**⌋
12:5 tomorrow." So the people **l**.
12:25 Then he **l** that place and built
13:10 So the man of God **l** on another
13:24 The man of God **l**.
14:4 She **l**, went to Shiloh,
14:17 Jeroboam's wife got up, **l**,
15:18 the silver and gold that was **l**
16:17 troops with him **l** Gibbethon
17:5 Elijah **l** and did what the word
17:17 that finally no life was **l** in him.
19:3 Judah and **l** his servant there.
19:10 I'm the only one **l**, and they're
19:14 I'm the only one **l**, and they're
19:20 So Elisha **l** the oxen,
19:21 Elisha **l** him, took two oxen,
19:21 Then he **l** to follow and assist
20:9 do this."' The messengers **l**
20:10 be enough dust **l** from Samaria
20:36 When the friend **l**, a lion found
22:19 near him on his right and his **l**.
22:46 who were **l** there from
2Ki 1:4 will die there."' Then Elijah **l**.
2:1 Elijah and Elisha **l** Gilgal.
2:8 The water divided to their **l** and
2:14 it divided to his **l** and his right,
2:25 He **l** that place, went to Mount
3:6 King Joram immediately **l**
2Ki 3:25 walls⌋ of Kir Hareseth were **l**.
4:5 So she **l** him and closed the
4:21 the man of God, **l** ⌊the room⌋,
4:37 She took her son and **l**.
4:43 and even have some **l** over."
4:44 They ate and had some **l** over,
5:5 When Naaman **l**, he took 750
5:11 Naaman became angry and **l**.
5:12 he turned around and **l** in anger.
5:19 After Elisha had **l** him and gone
5:24 dismissed the men, and they **l**.
5:27 When he **l** Elisha, Gehazi had
7:10 Even the tents were **l** exactly
7:12 so they've **l** the camp to hide in
7:12 'When they've **l** the city,
7:13 of the horses that are **l** here.
8:3 Philistine territory but **l** again
8:6 produced from the day she **l**
8:14 Hazael **l** Elisha and went to his
9:10 Then he opened the door and **l**.
10:11 who was **l** in Jezreel:
10:11 Not one of them was **l**.
10:12 Then Jehu **l** for Samaria.
10:15 When he **l** that place,
10:17 member who was **l** in Samaria.
13:7 Jehoahaz had no army **l**
15:20 king of Assyria **l** the country.
17:18 Only the tribe of Judah was **l**.
19:4 for the few people who are **l**."
19:8 He had heard that the king **l**
19:36 King Sennacherib of Assyria **l**.
20:17 to Babylon. Nothing will be **l**.
21:15 their ancestors **l** Egypt until this
23:8 (The worship site was to the **l**
23:18 So they **l** his bones with the
24:14 people of the land were **l**.
25:4 All Judah's soldiers **l** on the
25:11 captured the few people **l** in the
25:12 The captain of the guard **l**
25:21 captives when they **l** their land.
25:26 and the army commanders **l**
1Ch 4:43 the Amalekites who were **l**.
6:44 On the **l** was Ethan,
12:2 either their right or their **l** hands
12:8 Some men **l** Gad to join David
14:12 The Philistines **l** their gods
16:37 David **l** Asaph and his relatives
16:38 David also **l** Obed Edom and
16:39 David **l** Zadok and his priestly
21:4 So Joab **l**, went throughout
21:21 So he **l** the threshing floor and
27:1 for a month at a time and then **l**.
2Ch 3:17 the right and the other on the **l**.
3:17 the one on the **l** Boaz [In Him
5:10 the Israelites after they **l** Egypt.
5:12 the priests **l** the holy place,
8:7 and Jebusites had been **l** ⌊in
10:5 tomorrow." So the people **l**.
16:2 the silver and gold that was **l**
18:18 standing on his right and his **l**.
18:23 did the Spirit go when he **l** me
21:17 The only son **l** was Ahaziah,
24:25 they **l** him suffering from many
28:14 So the army **l** the prisoners and
31:10 and there's a lot **l** over."
32:31 in the land, God **l** him.
34:9 from all who were **l** in Israel,
34:21 "On behalf of those who are **l**
Ezr 1:11 him when the exiles **l** Babylon
2:1 They were the ones who **l** the
4:16 you will have nothing **l** ⌊of your
7:1 of Persia, Ezra **l** Babylon.
7:9 He had **l** Babylon on the first
8:1 of those who **l** Babylon
8:31 Then we **l** the Ahava River on
9:14 us and no survivors are **l**.
10:6 Then Ezra **l** the front of God's
Neh 3:8 They **l** out part of Jerusalem as
5:13 brushed off and **l** with nothing."
6:1 and that no gaps had been **l**
7:6 They were the ones who **l** the
8:4 stood beside him on his **l**.
12:38 The other choir went to the **l**.
13:10 had **l** for their own fields.
Est 5:9 When Haman **l** that day,
8:14 They **l** quickly, in keeping with

Job 1:12 Satan **l** the LORD's presence.
2:7 Satan **l** the LORD's presence
6:11 What strength do I have ⌊**l**⌋
13:15 I would have no hope ⌊**l**⌋.
17:15 Can you see any hope **l** in me?
20:21 "Nothing is **l** for him to eat.
20:26 Whatever is **l** in his tent will be
22:20 up what ⌊little⌋ they had **l**.'
23:12 I have not **l** his commands
27:3 long as there is one breath ⌊**l**⌋
27:19 his eyes, nothing will be **l**.
31:7 "If my steps have **l** the
Psa 12:1 No godly person is **l**.
38:3 No healthy spot is **l** on my
38:7 healthy spot is **l** on my body.
38:10 Even the light of my eyes has **l**
39:4 number of days I have **l** so that
44:18 Our feet never **l** your path.
50:22 will be no one **l** to rescue you.
59:13 them until not one of them is **l**.
63:10 Their dead bodies will be **l** as
79:1 They have **l** Jerusalem in ruins.
89:25 I will put his ⌊**l**⌋ hand on the
105:38 they were glad when Israel **l**.
114:1 When Israel **l** Egypt,
114:1 when Jacob's family **l** people
119:84 What is **l** of my life?
Pro 3:16 In ⌊wisdom's⌋ **l** hand are
4:27 not lean to the right or to the **l**.
25:28 city broken into ⌊and⌋ **l** without
Ecc 10:6 and rich people are **l** to fill
Sos 2:6 His **l** hand is under my head.
3:4 I had just **l** them when I found
5:6 I almost died when he **l**.
8:3 His **l** hand is under my head.
Isa 1:6 head there is no healthy spot **l**
1:8 My people Zion are **l** like a hut
1:9 If the LORD of Armies hadn't **l**
4:3 Then whoever is **l** in Zion and
5:8 after field until there's nothing **l**
6:13 if one out of ten people is **l** in it,
6:13 oak is cut down, a stump is **l**.
7:22 Everyone who is **l** in the land
9:20 On the **l**, another eats and is
10:4 Nothing's **l** but to crouch among
11:16 remaining few of his people **l**
15:6 and nothing green is **l**.
16:14 like workers count the years **l**
17:6 Only two or three olives are **l** at
18:6 They will be **l** for the birds of
21:11 how much of the night is **l**?
21:11 how much of the night is **l**?"
21:16 the years **l** on their contracts.
24:6 and only a few people are **l**.
24:12 The city is **l** in ruins.
24:13 shaken or like what's **l** after
27:9 or incense altars are **l** standing.
27:10 The homestead is **l** deserted,
28:8 There isn't a clean place **l**.
30:14 and nothing will be **l** of it.
30:17 Then you will be **l** alone like a
30:21 it turns to the right or to the **l**."
37:4 for the few people who are **l**."
37:8 He had heard that the king **l**
37:37 King Sennacherib of Assyria **l**.
39:6 to Babylon. Nothing will be **l**.
46:3 the few people **l** of the nation of
49:21 I was **l** alone. Where have they
54:3 spread out to the right and **l**.
Jer 2:15 and everyone has **l**.
4:7 He has **l** his place to destroy
7:25 ancestors **l** Egypt until now,
7:32 no other place will be **l**.
10:20 My children have **l** me and
12:7 I have **l** my own people.
12:11 They've **l** it a wasteland.
15:6 You have **l** me," declares the
19:14 Then Jeremiah **l** Topheth,
22:11 king of Judah and **l** this place:
25:20 and the people **l** in Ashdod;
25:38 He has **l** his lair like a lion.
27:18 to allow the utensils that are **l**
27:19 utensils that are **l** in this city.
27:21 about the utensils that are **l**
29:2 and metal workers **l**
29:32 from his family will be **l** alive.
Jer 34:7 cities of Judah that were **l**.
37:10 a few badly wounded men **l**
38:4 the soldiers who are **l**
38:8 Ebed Melech **l** the royal palace
38:22 All the women who are **l** in the
39:4 They **l** the city at night by way
39:9 captured the few people **l** in the
39:10 **l** some poor people who had
40:6 people who were **l** in the land.
40:11 that the king of Babylon had **l**
40:15 What is **l** of Judah would
41:6 **l** Mizpah to meet them,
41:8 So he **l** them alone and didn't
41:10 who had been **l** at Mizpah.
41:10 them captive and **l** for Ammon.
41:17 When they **l** Gibeon,
42:2 God for all of us who are **l** here.
42:2 there are only a few of us **l**.
42:15 you people who are **l** in Judah.
42:19 has told you people who are **l**
43:5 took all the people who were **l**
43:6 had **l** with Gedaliah,
44:7 from Judah until none are **l**?
44:12 from Judah those who are **l**,
47:4 and anyone who is **l** from
47:5 you people **l** on the plains?
48:11 Its people are like wine **l** to
52:7 They **l** the city at night through
52:15 captured the few people **l** in the
52:16 **l** some of the poorest people in
52:27 captives as they **l** their land.
Lam 1:13 He has **l** me devastated.
3:11 and **l** me with nothing.
5:15 There is no joy **l** in our hearts.
Eze 1:10 From the **l**, each one had the
3:12 which **l** this place."
4:4 "Then lie on your **l** side and
5:10 whoever is **l** to the wind.
6:12 and anyone who is **l** and has
7:11 None of the people will be **l**.
7:11 and nothing of value will be **l**.
9:8 killing people, I was **l** alone.
9:8 you destroy everyone who is **l**
10:7 The person took them and **l**.
10:18 Then the glory of the LORD **l**
10:19 I was watching them as they **l**
11:23 The LORD's glory **l** the middle
11:24 Then the vision I saw **l** me.
21:16 Cut to the **l** or wherever your
22:18 like the impurities **l** from silver.
23:25 and burn down whatever is **l**.
24:21 that you **l** behind will die
25:16 people that are **l** on the coast.
28:17 you to the ground and **l** you
31:12 out from under its shade and **l**.
36:36 nations that are **l** will know that
39:3 the bow out of your **l** hand
39:28 I **l** none of them behind.
48:15 long, will be **l** for cities, homes,
48:21 Whatever is **l** on the east side
Dan 4:26 and the tree's roots were to be **l**,
7:7 and trampled whatever was **l**.
7:19 and trampled whatever was **l**.
10:8 So I was **l** alone to see this
10:8 I had no strength **l** in me.
10:13 help me because I was **l** alone
10:17 I have no strength **l**,
12:7 He raised his right hand and **l**
Hos 5:6 can't find him. He has **l** them.
Joe 1:7 and **l** the branches bare.
Amo 4:6 I **l** you with nothing to eat in
4:6 I **l** you with no food in your
5:3 to war will have ⌊only⌋ 100 **l**.
5:3 off to war will have ⌊only⌋ 10 **l**
6:9 If ten people are **l** in one house,
9:1 kill with a sword all who are **l**.
Oba 1:18 There will be no one **l** among
Jnh 4:5 Jonah **l** the city and sat down
4:11 tell their right hand from their **l**.
Mic 2:12 the few people **l** in Israel.
5:7 Then the few people **l** from
5:8 The few people **l** from Jacob
Zep 2:9 and those who are **l** in my
3:6 Not a single person will be **l**.
Hag 2:19 Is there any seed **l** in the barn?
Zec 2:3 who was speaking with me **l**.
Zec 4:3 the bowl and the other on its **l**."
4:11 olive trees at the right and the **l**
7:14 They **l** behind a land so ruined
9:7 only a few of them will be **l**
11:9 that are **l** devour each other."
12:6 nations to the right and to the **l**.
12:14 families that are **l** ⌊will mourn⌋,
13:8 Yet, one-third will be **l** in it.
14:16 Everyone who is **l** from all the
Mal 1:3 wasteland and **l** his inheritance
Mat 2:12 So they **l** for their country by
2:13 After they had **l**, an angel of the
2:14 and **l** for Egypt that night.
2:22 in a dream, he **l** for Galilee
4:11 Then the devil **l** him,
4:13 He **l** Nazareth and made his
4:20 They immediately **l** their nets
4:22 and they immediately **l** the boat
6:3 don't let your **l** hand know what
8:23 went with him as he **l** in a boat.
9:27 When Jesus **l** that place,
12:14 The Pharisees **l** and plotted to
12:15 about this, so he **l** that place.
12:44 go back to the home I **l**.' When
13:1 That same day Jesus **l** the
13:53 illustrations, he **l** that place.
14:13 he **l** in a boat and went to a
15:21 Jesus **l** that place and went to
16:4 Then he **l** them standing there
19:1 he **l** Galilee and traveled along
20:21 other at your **l** in your kingdom.
20:23 grant you a seat at my right or **l**.
21:17 He **l** them and went out of the
22:22 Then they **l** him alone and
22:25 he **l** his widow to his brother.
24:1 As Jesus **l** the temple
24:2 one of these stones will be **l**
24:40 and the other one will be **l**.
24:41 and the other one will be **l**.
25:33 his right but the goats on his **l**.
25:41 king will say to those on his **l**,
27:38 his right and the other on his **l**.
Mar 1:18 They immediately **l** their nets
1:20 and they **l** their father Zebedee
1:29 After they **l** the synagogue,
1:45 When the man **l**, he began to
2:2 There was no room **l**,
3:6 The Pharisees **l**, and with
3:7 Jesus **l** with his disciples for
5:20 So the man **l**. He began to tell
6:1 Jesus **l** that place and went to
7:17 When he had **l** the people and
7:24 Jesus **l** that place and went to
7:29 demon has **l** your daughter."
7:31 Jesus then **l** the neighborhood
8:13 Then he **l** them there.
9:30 They **l** that place and were
10:1 Jesus **l** there and went into the
10:37 the other at your **l** in your glory.
10:40 grant you a seat at my right or **l**.
11:12 when they **l** Bethany,
12:12 So they **l** him alone and went
13:2 one of these stones will be **l**
13:34 As he **l** home, he put his
14:16 The disciples **l**. They went into
14:52 but he **l** the linen sheet behind
15:27 his right and the other on his **l**.
Luk 1:38 Then the angel **l** her.
2:15 The angels **l** them and went
2:37 Anna never **l** the temple
2:43 was over, they **l** for home.
4:1 with the Holy Spirit as he **l**
4:13 the devil **l** him until another
4:38 Jesus **l** the synagogue and
5:11 the boats to shore, **l** everything,
5:27 After that, Jesus **l**.
5:28 So Levi got up, **l** everything,
7:24 John's messengers had **l**,
8:39 So the man **l**. He went through
10:30 and **l** him for dead.
10:40 care that my sister has **l** me
11:24 'I'll go back to the home I **l**.'
11:53 When Jesus **l**, the scribes and
12:13 inheritance that our father **l** us."
15:13 gathered his possessions and **l**
15:14 He had nothing **l** when a

Luk 17:29 on the day that Lot l Sodom,
17:34 and the other one will be l.
17:35 and the other one will be l."
18:28 Then Peter said, "We've l
19:13 ⌊Before he l,⌋ he called ten of
19:44 One stone will not be l on top
20:31 widow, died, and l no children.
21:6 one of these stones will be l
22:13 The disciples l. They found
23:33 his right and the other on his l.
24:9 The women l the tomb and
24:51 he l them and was taken to
Jon 4:3 So he l the Judean countryside
4:28 Then the woman l her water jar
4:30 The people l the city and went
4:43 Jesus l for Galilee.
4:50 what Jesus told him and l.
4:52 "The fever l him yesterday
8:9 the scribes and Pharisees l.
8:9 Jesus was l alone with the
8:29 He hasn't l me by myself.
8:59 and he l the temple courtyard.
11:54 Instead, he l Bethany and went
12:36 he was concealed as he l.
16:28 I l the Father and came into the
19:23 His robe was l over.
Act 2:31 that the Messiah wouldn't be l
5:41 The apostles l the council
7:4 "Then Abraham l the country of
7:29 Moses quickly l Egypt and
7:58 The witnesses l their coats
9:17 Ananias l and entered Judas'
10:7 After saying this, the angel l.
10:23 The next day Peter l with them.
11:25 Then Barnabas l Antioch to go
12:10 The angel suddenly l Peter.
12:17 Then he l and went
12:19 Then Herod l Judea and went
13:14 Paul and Barnabas l Perga and
14:20 next day Paul and Barnabas l
15:40 Paul chose Silas and l after the
16:18 the evil spirit l her.
16:40 After Paul and Silas l the jail,
16:40 encouraged them, and then l.
17:15 When the men l Athens,
17:33 this response, Paul l the court.
18:1 After this, Paul l Athens and
18:7 Then he l the synagogue and
18:18 Paul l ⌊for Ephesus⌋.
18:19 where Paul l Priscilla and
18:21 As he l, he told them, "I'll come
19:9 the way ⌊of Christ⌋, he l them.
20:1 and l for Macedonia.
20:11 time, until sunrise, and then l.
21:1 When we finally l them,
21:3 Cyprus as we passed it on our l
24:27 he l Paul in prison.)
25:14 "Felix l a man here in prison.
25:20 these things l me puzzled.
27:40 They cut the anchors free and l
28:25 l after Paul had quoted this
Rom 4:18 When there was nothing l to
9:29 "If the Lord of Armies hadn't l
11:3 I'm the only one l, and they're
11:5 there are now a few l that God
1Co 10:1 that all our ancestors ⌊who l
Php 4:15 when I l the province of
1Ti 1:6 Some people have l these
2Ti 4:13 bring the warm coat I l with
4:20 of Corinth and I l Trophimus
Tit 1:5 I l you in Crete to do what still
Heb 2:8 control, nothing was l out.
10:27 All that is l is a terrifying wait
11:8 Abraham l his own country
11:15 the country that they had l,
1Pe 2:21 He l you an example so that
2:23 he didn't make any threats but l
2Pe 2:15 These false teachers have l
1Jn 2:19 They l us. However, they were
Rev 3:2 that are l which are about
10:2 the sea and his l on the land.
12:12 that he has little time l."

left-handed (2)
Jdg 3:15 It was Ehud, a l man from the
20:16 the best 700 were l.

leftover (10)
Job 24:6 They pick the l grapes in the
Mat 14:20 they picked up the l pieces,
15:37 The disciples picked up the l
Mar 6:43 they picked up the l pieces,
8:8 The disciples picked up the l
8:19 did you fill with l pieces?"
8:20 did you fill with l pieces?"
Luk 9:17 they picked up the l pieces,
Jon 6:12 "Gather the l pieces so that
6:13 The disciples gathered the l

leg (3)
1Sm 9:24 So the cook picked up the l
Act 16:24 with their feet in l irons.
Heb 12:13 your injured l won't get worse.

legal (10)
Exo 21:1 "Here are the l decisions to be
24:3 LORD's words and l decisions.
Jdg 4:5 come to her for l decisions.
12:2 I were involved in a l dispute
Rut 4:7 In order to make every matter l,
Job 23:6 hide behind great l maneuvers?
Psa 81:4 This is a law for Israel, a l
Act 19:38 a l complaint against anyone,
19:39 you must settle the matter in a l
22:25 "Is it l for you to whip a Roman

legion (3)
Mar 5:9 "My name is L [Six Thousand],
5:15 possessed by the l of demons.
Luk 8:30 "L [Six Thousand]."

legions (1)
Mat 26:53 to send more than twelve l

legs (24)
Exo 25:26 where the four l are.
29:17 wash the internal organs and l,
37:13 where the four l were.
Lev 1:9 Wash the internal organs and l.
1:13 Wash the internal organs and l.
4:11 meat, head, l, internal organs,
8:21 the internal organs and the l.
9:14 the internal organs and the l
11:21 that swarm if they use their l
11:42 creature with many l that goes
Dtr 28:35 will afflict your knees and l
1Sm 17:6 On his l he had bronze shin
Pro 26:7 ⌊Like⌋ a lame person's limp l,
Sos 5:15 His l are columns of marble set
Isa 7:20 on your head, the hair on your l,
47:2 Uncover your l, and cross the
Eze 1:7 Their l were straight,
Dan 2:33 Its l were made of iron.
10:6 His arms and l looked like
Amo 3:12 As a shepherd rescues two l or
Zec 11:16 those that have broken their l
Jon 19:31 to have the men's l broken
19:32 The soldiers broke the l of the
19:33 they didn't break his l.

Lehabites (2)
Gen 10:13 Anamites, L, Naphtuhites,
1Ch 1:11 Anamites, L, Naphtuhites,

Lehi (5)
Jdg 15:9 in Judah, and overran L.
15:14 When he came to L,
15:19 open the hollow place at L,
15:19 It is still there at L today.
2Sm 23:11 Philistines had gathered at L,

lema (2)
Mat 27:46 voice, "Eli, Eli, l sabachthani?"
Mar 15:34 "Eloi, Eloi, l sabachthani?"

Lemuel (2)
Pro 31:1 The sayings of King L,
31:4 "It is not for kings, L.

lend (7)
Exo 22:25 "If you l money to my people —
Dtr 15:8 and freely l them as much as
Eze 18:8 He doesn't l money for interest
Luk 6:34 If you l anything to those from
6:34 Sinners also l to sinners to get
6:34 sinners to get back what they l.
6:35 and l to them without

lender (1)
Pro 22:7 and a borrower is a slave to a l.

lenders (1)
Isa 24:2 and sellers, l and borrowers,

lending (1)
Neh 5:10 and I are l money and grain to

lends (4)
Psa 37:26 always generous and l freely.
112:5 is generous and l willingly.
Pro 19:17 Whoever has pity on the poor l
Eze 18:13 He l money for interest and

length (17)
Gen 23:1 This was the l of her life.
47:9 "The l of my stay on earth has
Exo 26:13 on each side because of the l
Lev 19:35 justice concerning l,
Num 6:12 as a Nazirite for the same l
2Sm 8:2 and one l which was to be
1Ki 6:3 the temple was the same l as
11:42 The l of Solomon's reign in
2Ch 3:11 The combined l of the angels'
Psa 39:5 Indeed, you have made the l of
Isa 40:12 or measured the sky with the l
Eze 40:15 The total l of the gateway from
40:20 Then the man measured the l
41:2 Then he measured the l of the
41:8 It measured the full l of the
41:15 He also measured the l of the
Rev 21:16 Its l, width, and height were the

lengthen (2)
Isa 54:2 L your tent ropes, and drive in
Php 3:13 look back, I l my stride, and

lengthening (1)
Psa 109:23 I fade away like a l shadow.

lengthens (1)
Pro 10:27 The fear of the LORD l ⌊the

lengths (1)
2Sm 8:2 He measured two l which were

lent (1)
Jer 15:10 I have never l or borrowed

lentils (4)
Gen 25:34 Esau a meal of bread and l.
2Sm 17:28 flour, roasted grain, beans, l,
23:11 there was a field of ripe l.
Eze 4:9 l, millet, and winter wheat.

leopard (4)
Jer 5:6 A l will lie in ambush outside
Dan 7:6 It looked like a l. On its back it
Hos 13:7 Like a l I will wait by the road
Rev 13:2 beast that I saw was like a l.

leopards (4)
Sos 4:8 from the mountains of l.
Isa 11:6 L will lie down with goats.
Jer 13:23 skin or l change their spots?
Hab 1:8 horses will be faster than l

Leshem (1)
Jos 19:47 went up and attacked L,

lesson (7)
Dtr 8:5 Learn this l by heart:
Jdg 8:16 taught them a l using thorns
Pro 19:25 a gullible person may learn a l.
24:32 I saw it and learned my l.
Jer 31:19 After I was taught a l,
35:13 'Won't you ever learn your l
Luk 4:16 He stood up to read the l.

lessons (1)

Hos 12:10 I taught **l** through the prophets.

letter (63)

2Sm 11:14 In the morning David wrote a **l**
11:15 In the **l** he wrote, "Put Uriah on
2Ki 5:5 I will also send a **l** to the king
5:6 He brought the **l** to the king of
5:6 my officer Naaman with this **l**.
5:7 the king of Israel read the **l**,
10:2 As soon as this **l** reaches you,
10:6 So he wrote them a second **l**.
10:7 When the **l** came to the men,
2Ch 2:11 by sending a **l** that said,
21:12 Then a **l** came to him from the
Ezr 4:6 Judah and Jerusalem wrote a **l**
4:7 The **l** was written with the
4:8 another **l** against ⌊the people
4:11 This is the copy of the **l** they
4:14 are sending this **l** to inform you
4:18 The **l** you sent me has been
4:23 a copy of King Artaxerxes' **l**.
5:6 Here is a copy of the **l**
7:11 This is a copy of the **l** that King
Neh 2:8 Also, let me have a **l**
2:8 In the **l** order him to give me
6:5 held in his hand an unsealed **l**.
Est 9:25 in the well-known **l**,
9:26 was said in this **l** — both what
9:29 to establish with this second **l**
Isa 37:14 Hezekiah took the **l** from the
Jer 29:1 The prophet Jeremiah sent a **l**
29:3 He sent the **l** with Shaphan's
29:3 in Babylon. The **l** said:
29:29 priest Zephaniah read this **l**
Act 15:20 Instead, we should write a **l**
15:23 They wrote this **l** for them to
15:30 together and delivered the **l**.
15:31 When the people read the **l**,
21:25 non-Jewish believers a **l**
23:25 The officer wrote a **l** to the
23:33 they delivered the **l** to the
23:34 the governor had read the **l**,
Rom 15:15 However, I've written you a **l**,
16:1 With this **l** I'm introducing
16:22 I, Tertius, who wrote this **l**,
1Co 5:9 In my **l** to you I told you not to
2Co 3:2 You're our **l** of recommendation
3:3 It's clear that you are Christ's **l**,
3:3 You are a **l** written not with ink
3:3 a **l** written not on tablets of
4:2 is our ⌊**l** of⌋ recommendation.
7:8 If my **l** made you
7:8 But since my **l** did make you
13:10 That's why I'm writing this **l**
Col 4:16 After you have read this **l**,
4:16 also read the **l** from Laodicea.
1Th 5:27 I order you to read this **l** to all
2Th 2:2 or **l** that the day of the Lord has
2:15 we spoke to you or in our **l**.
3:14 listen to what we say in this **l**.
3:17 In every **l** that I send,
Heb 13:22 I have written you a short **l**.
1Pe 5:12 I've written this short **l** to you
2Pe 3:1 this is the second **l** I'm writing
2Jn 1:12 I would prefer not to write a **l**.
3Jn 1:9 I wrote a **l** to the congregation.

letters (36)

1Ki 21:8 So Jezebel wrote **l**,
21:9 In these **l** she wrote:
21:11 had written in the **l** she sent.
2Ki 10:1 So Jehu wrote **l** to the officials
10:1 in Samaria. The **l** read,
19:14 Hezekiah took the **l** from the
20:12 sent **l** and a present to
2Ch 30:1 all Israel and Judah and wrote **l**
30:6 Messengers took **l** from the
32:17 Sennacherib wrote **l** cursing
32:17 These **l** said, "As the gods of
Neh 2:7 let me have **l** addressed to the
2:7 In the **l** tell them to grant me
2:8 (The king let me have the **l**,
2:9 and gave them the king's **l**.
6:17 of Judah sent many **l** to Tobiah,
Neh 6:17 sent many **l** back to them.
6:19 kept sending **l** to intimidate me.
Est 9:20 things down and sent official **l**
Isa 39:1 sent **l** and a present to
Jer 29:25 You sent **l** in your own name to
29:25 to all the priests. These **l** said:
Act 9:2 and asked him to write **l** of
22:5 In fact, they even gave me **l** to
28:21 "We haven't received any **l**
1Co 16:3 When I come, I will give **l** of
2Co 3:1 people, need **l** that recommend
3:1 us to you or **l** from you that
10:9 trying to frighten you with my **l**.
10:10 is saying that my **l** are powerful
10:11 about in our **l** when we weren't
Gal 6:11 Look at how large the **l** ⌊in
2Pe 3:1 In both **l** I'm trying to refresh
3:16 about this subject in all his **l**.
3:16 Some things in his **l** are hard to
3:16 distort what Paul says in his **l**

Letushites (1)

Gen 25:3 the **L**, and the Leummites.

Leummites (1)

Gen 25:3 the Letushites, and the **L**.

level (14)

Jos 4:18 returned to its seasonal flood **l**.
2Sm 20:15 and it stood **l** with the outer
Psa 26:12 My feet stand on **l** ground.
27:11 Lead me on a **l** path because I
65:10 ⌊with rain⌋ and **l** their clumps
143:10 good Spirit lead me on **l** ground.
Isa 25:12 high fortified walls, **l** them,
26:7 The path of the righteous is **l**.
40:4 Steep places will be made **l**.
Jer 31:9 streams on a **l** path where they
Eze 13:14 I will **l** it and expose its
Amo 6:11 the command to **l** big houses
Luk 6:17 them and stood on a **l** place.
19:44 They will **l** you to the ground

leveled (5)

2Ki 19:17 that the kings of Assyria have **l**
Isa 32:19 the city will be completely **l**.
37:18 of Assyria have **l** every country.
Jer 51:58 thick walls of Babylon will be **l**,
Luk 3:5 mountain and hill will be **l**.

levels (2)

Isa 26:5 He **l** it. He levels it to the ground
26:5 He **l** it to the ground and throws

Levi (66)

Gen 29:34 So she named him **L**
34:25 of Jacob's sons, Simeon and **L**,
34:30 Jacob said to Simeon and **L**,
34:31 Simeon and **L** asked,
35:23 Simeon, **L**, Judah, Issachar,
46:11 The sons of **L** were Gershon,
49:5 "Simeon and **L** are brothers.
Exo 1:2 Reuben, Simeon, **L**,
6:16 names of the sons of **L** listed
6:16 and Merari. **L** lived 137 years.
6:19 descended from **L** listed
Num 1:47 tribe of **L** were not registered
1:49 "Don't register the tribe of **L** or
3:6 "Bring the tribe of **L**,
3:17 and Merari were the sons of **L**.
16:1 a descendant of Kohath and **L**.
17:3 Aaron's name on the staff for **L**
17:8 for the tribe of **L** had not only
26:57 The families descended from **L**
26:58 These were the families of **L**:
26:59 a descendant of **L**,
Dtr 10:8 LORD set apart the tribe of **L**
10:9 This is why the tribe of **L** has
18:1 the whole tribe of **L** — will
21:5 the descendants of **L**,
27:12 **L**, Judah, Issachar, Joseph,
33:8 About the tribe of **L** he said,
Jos 13:14 an inheritance to the tribe of **L**.
13:33 an inheritance to the tribe of **L**.
21:1 of the families of **L** came
21:10 of Kohath in the tribe of **L**.
Jos 21:27 who were in the tribe of **L**,
21:34 who were from the tribe of **L**,
21:40 the last of the families of **L**.
1Ki 12:31 descended from **L** to be priests.
1Ch 2:1 **L**, Judah, Issachar, Zebulun,
6:38 who was the son of **L**,
6:43 who was the son of **L**.
6:47 who was the son of **L**.
21:6 Joab didn't include **L** and
23:14 counted with the tribe of **L**.
24:6 and a descendant of **L**.
27:17 for the tribe of **L**: Hashabiah,
Ezr 8:18 of Mahli, **L**, and Israel.
Psa 135:20 Descendants of **L**,
Eze 43:19 men from the tribe of **L**,
48:31 Gate, Judah Gate, and **L** Gate.
Zec 12:13 the family of **L** by itself,
Mal 2:4 my promise to **L** will continue,"
2:5 "I promised **L** life and peace.
2:8 the promise made to **L**," says
Mar 2:14 he saw **L**, son of Alphaeus,
2:14 So **L** got up and followed him.
Luk 3:24 son of Matthat, son of **L**,
3:29 Jorim, son of Matthat, son of **L**,
5:27 a tax collector named **L** sitting
5:28 So **L** got up, left everything,
5:29 **L** held a large reception at his
Act 4:36 Joseph, a descendant of **L**,
Heb 7:5 tribe of **L** who become priests
7:6 was not from the tribe of **L**,
7:9 **L** was giving a tenth of
7:9 **L** gave, although later his
7:10 Even though **L** had not yet
7:20 The men from the tribe of **L**
Rev 7:7 12,000 from the tribe of **L**,

Leviathan (9)

Job 3:8 to wake up **L**) curse that night.
41:1 "Can you pull **L** out ⌊of the
41:10 is brave enough to provoke **L**.
41:18 When **L** sneezes, it gives out a
41:25 mighty are afraid when **L** rises.
Psa 74:14 You crushed the heads of **L**
104:26 Ships sail on it, and **L**,
Isa 27:1 powerful sword to punish **L**,
27:1 snake, **L**, that twisting snake.

Leviathan's (1)

Job 41:12 about **L** limbs, its strength,

levied (1)

Est 10:1 King Xerxes **l** a tax on the

Levi's (20)

Exo 2:1 A man from **L** family married a
Num 4:18 from **L** tribe be destroyed.
Jos 14:3 as an inheritance to **L** tribe,
18:7 **L** tribe has no separate region
21:3 **L** descendants were given the
21:8 **L** descendants by drawing lots,
21:20 **L** descendants who were from
21:41 cities in all for **L** descendants
1Ch 6:1 **L** sons were Gershon,
6:16 **L** sons were Gershom,
6:19 are the descendants of **L** sons.
6:54 where **L** descendants lived,
12:26 From **L** descendants there
23:6 on which of **L** sons (Gershon,
23:24 These were **L** descendants,
24:20 **L** descendants ⌊from Kohath⌋:
24:26 **L** descendants from Merari:
24:30 These were **L** descendants
Mal 3:3 He will purify **L** sons and refine
Mar 2:15 was having dinner at **L** house.

Levite (51)

Exo 2:1 family married a **L** woman.
4:14 about your brother Aaron the **L**?
6:25 These were the heads of **L**
Lev 25:33 If any **L** buys back ⌊a house⌋,
25:33 because the houses in the **L**
Num 3:20 the households of **L** families.
26:62 The total number of all the ⌊**L**⌋
Dtr 18:6 A **L** from any of your cities in
Jos 21:4 Aaron the **L** received 13 cities
Jdg 17:7 He was a **L** but was living in

Jdg 17:9 The man told him, "I'm a **L** from
17:10 The **L** accepted the offer
17:12 Micah ordained the **L**.
17:13 I have a **L** for my priest."
18:4 The **L** told them what Micah
18:15 house and greeted the young **L**.
19:1 there was a **L** who lived in a
19:4 He made the **L** stay there with
19:7 When the **L** started to leave,
19:8 the **L** got up early to leave.
19:9 The **L** started to leave with his
19:10 But the **L** refused to spend
19:12 The **L** told him, "We'll never go
19:15 The **L** entered Gibeah and sat
19:18 The **L** replied, "We're on our
19:21 So he took the **L** to his house
19:25 So the **L** grabbed his
19:28 The **L** said to her, "Get up!
20:4 The **L**, the husband of the
1Ch 9:18 gatekeepers for the **L** quarters.
9:26 The four chief **L** gatekeepers
9:31 Mattithiah, a **L**, the firstborn son
9:33 the heads of the **L** families.
9:34 They were the heads of the **L**
15:12 are the heads of the **L** families.
15:16 David told the **L** leaders to
15:22 Chenaniah, a **L** leader,
23:3 Every male **L** who was at least
26:20 Ahijah, a **L**, was in charge of
2Ch 20:14 a **L** descended from Asaph.)
31:2 Each priest or **L** was put in a
31:12 The **L** Conaniah was in charge
31:14 Kore, son of Imnah the **L**,
31:19 pasturelands of every **L** city.
34:9 the money that the **L**
Ezr 7:24 **L**, singer, gatekeeper, servant,
10:15 and Shabbethai, the **L**,
Neh 11:16 and Jozabad, **L** leaders,
11:17 The **L** leader Bakbukiah was
13:13 and Pedaiah the **L**,
Luk 10:32 Then a **L** came to that place.

Levite's (2)

Jdg 18:3 recognized the young **L** voice.
19:11 The **L** servant said to him,

Levites (252)

Exo 32:26 all the **L** gathered around him.
32:28 The **L** did what Moses told
38:21 and carried out by the **L** under
Lev 25:32 "The **L** always have the right to
Num 1:50 Put the **L** in charge of the tent
1:50 The **L** will carry the tent and all
1:51 the **L** will take it down.
1:53 The **L** will camp all around the
1:53 So the **L** will be in charge of
2:17 the **L** will stay in the middle of
2:33 the **L** were not registered along
3:9 Give the **L** to Aaron and his
3:9 The **L** will be the only
3:12 I have taken the **L** to be
3:12 among them. The **L** are mine,
3:15 "Count the **L** by households
3:32 leader of the **L** was Eleazar,
3:39 The grand total of **L** that Moses
3:41 Take the **L** for me to be
3:41 Also take the animals of the **L**
3:45 "Take the **L** to be substitutes
3:45 and the animals of the **L**
3:45 The **L** will be mine.
3:46 male Israelites than there are **L**.
3:48 who outnumber the **L**."
3:49 who outnumbered the **L**.
4:2 "Take a census of the **L** who
4:46 total of all the **L** whom Moses,
7:5 Give them to the **L** to use
7:6 oxen and gave them to the **L**.
8:6 "Separate the **L** from the rest of
8:9 Bring the **L** to the front of the
8:10 Then bring the **L** into the
8:11 Aaron will present the **L** to the
8:12 "The **L** will place their hands
8:12 peace with the LORD for the **L**.
8:13 Make the **L** stand in front of
8:14 you will separate the **L** from
8:14 and the **L** will be mine.
Num 8:15 the **L** may come and do their
8:18 So I have taken the **L** as
8:19 The **L** will be the only
8:20 Moses to do to the **L**.
8:21 The **L** performed the
8:22 After that, the **L** came and did
8:24 are the instructions for the **L**:
8:26 They may assist the other **L** in
16:8 said to Korah, "Listen, you **L**!
16:10 and all the other **L** near himself,
18:2 Bring the other **L** from your
18:6 I have chosen the other **L** from
18:21 "I am giving the **L** one-tenth of
18:23 Only the **L** will do the work at
18:24 Instead, I will give the **L** what
18:26 "Speak to the **L** and say to
31:30 Give them to the **L** who are in
31:47 Then he gave all this to the **L**
35:2 "Tell the Israelites to give the **L**
35:2 They must also give the **L** the
35:3 Then the **L** will have cities to
35:4 give the **L** will extend 1,500
35:6 "Six of the cities you give the **L**
35:6 also give the **L** 42 other cities.
35:7 cities with pastureland to the **L**.
35:8 The cities you give the **L** from
Dtr 12:12 and female slaves, and the **L**.
12:12 (The **L** live in your cities
12:18 and the **L** who live in your
12:19 Don't forget to take care of the **L**
14:27 to take care of the **L** who live
14:29 The **L** may also come because
16:11 the **L** who live in your cities,
16:14 the **L**, foreigners, orphans,
18:2 So the **L** will have no land of
18:5 your God has chosen the **L**
18:7 like all the other **L** who do their
26:11 Then you, the **L**, and the
26:12 what you have stored to the **L**,
26:13 I distributed it to the **L**,
27:14 The **L** will declare to all the
31:25 He gave this command to the **L**
Jos 13:14 Israel are what the **L** inherited,
14:4 The **L** were not given a share
14:4 descendants gave the **L** cities
1Sm 6:15 (The **L** had already taken down
2Sm 15:24 Zadok and all the **L** with him
1Ki 8:4 priests and the **L** carried them
1Ch 6:48 Their relatives, the **L**,
6:64 So the Israelites gave the **L** the
9:2 the **L**, and the temple servants.
9:14 From the **L** descended from
9:34 head **L** lived in Jerusalem.
13:2 Israel and to the priests and **L**
15:2 that only the **L** carry God's ark
15:4 Aaron's descendants and the **L**.
15:11 and Abiathar and for the **L** Uriel,
15:14 So the priests and the **L** made
15:15 The **L** carried God's ark on their
15:17 So the **L** appointed Heman,
15:26 Because God helped the **L**
15:27 as were all the **L** who carried
15:27 the ⌊**L** who were⌋ singers,
16:4 David appointed some **L** to
16:41 and the rest of the **L** who had
23:2 of Israel and the priests and **L**.
23:6 David organized the **L** into
23:26 The **L** will no longer have to
23:27 to count the **L** who were at
24:6 leaders of the priests and **L**.
24:31 families of the priests and **L**.
25:6 All these ⌊**L**⌋ sang at the
26:17 the east side there were six **L**.
26:18 on the west there were four **L** at
28:13 the divisions of priests and **L**.
28:21 divisions of the priests and **L**
2Ch 5:4 the **L** picked up the ark.
5:5 priests and the **L** carried them
5:12 All the **L** who were musicians
7:6 So were the **L** who had the
7:6 The priests were opposite the **L**
8:14 and the ⌊divisions of⌋ **L**
8:14 ⌊The **L**⌋ were to lead in
8:15 orders to the priests or the **L**
11:13 The priests and **L** in every
13:9 and you forced out the **L** so that
2Ch 13:10 and the **L** assist them.
17:8 them were the **L** Shemaiah,
19:8 also appointed some **L**,
19:11 The **L** will serve as officers of
20:19 The **L**, descendants of Kohath
23:2 gathered the **L** from all the
23:4 the priests and **L** who are on
23:6 the priests and the **L** who are
23:7 The **L** should surround the king
23:8 So the **L** and all the Judeans
23:18 direction of the priests and **L**.
24:5 gathered the priests and the **L**
24:5 But the **L** didn't do it
24:6 "Why didn't you require the **L** to
24:11 Whenever the **L** brought the
29:4 He brought the priests and **L**
29:5 said to them, "Listen to me, **L**.
29:12 So the **L** started to work.
29:16 Then the **L** took the unclean
29:25 He had the **L** stand in the
29:26 The **L** stood with David's
29:30 and the leaders told the **L**
29:34 So their relatives, the **L**,
29:34 The **L** were more diligent in
30:15 priests and **L** were ashamed,
30:16 blood they received from the **L**.
30:17 So the **L** had to kill the
30:21 Each day the **L** and priests
30:22 words to all the **L** who had
30:25 from Judah, the priests, the **L**,
31:2 priests and the **L** to divisions.
31:4 to give the priests and **L**
31:9 and the **L** about the heaps.
31:17 and to the **L** who were at
31:18 The priests and **L** were
31:18 The priests and **L** had to be
31:19 in the genealogies of the **L**.
34:12 (**L** descended from Merari),
34:12 The **L**, who were skilled
34:13 Some of the **L** served as
34:30 in Jerusalem, the priests, the **L**,
35:3 He told the **L**, who instructed
35:5 Let the **L** be considered a part
35:8 to the people, priests, and **L**.
35:9 the leaders of the **L**,
35:9 gave the **L** 5,000 sheep and
35:10 positions with the **L** according
35:11 while the **L** skinned the lambs.
35:12 The **L** did the same with the
35:14 So the **L** prepared ⌊the
35:15 because their relatives, the **L**,
35:18 it with priests, **L**, all of Judah,
Ezr 1:5 and the **L** — everyone God had
2:40 These **L** returned from exile:
2:70 The priests, the **L**,
3:8 rest of the Jews, (the priests, **L**,
3:8 They began by appointing the **L**
3:9 their sons and relatives, the **L**,
3:10 and the **L** who were Asaph's
3:12 But many of the priests, **L**,
6:16 of Israel, the priests, the **L**,
6:18 to their divisions and the **L**
6:20 Since the priests and **L** had
7:7 **L**, singers, gatekeepers,
7:13 also includes the priests and **L**.
8:15 but I didn't find any **L**.
8:20 had appointed to work for the **L**.
8:29 in front of the chief priests, **L**,
8:30 So the priests and the **L** took
8:33 The **L**, Jeshua's son Jozabad,
9:1 including the priests and **L**,
10:5 made the leaders, priests, **L**,
10:23 From the **L**: Jozabad, Shimei,
Neh 3:17 After him the **L**, made repairs.
7:1 and the **L** were assigned their
7:43 These **L** returned from exile:
7:73 The priests, **L**, the singers,
8:7 The **L** — Jeshua, Bani,
8:9 and the **L** who taught the
8:11 So the **L** calmed all the people
8:13 including the priests and the **L**,
9:4 on the stairs built for the **L**
9:5 Then the **L** — Jeshua,
9:38 Our leaders, **L**, and priests are
10:9 These were the **L**:
10:28 **L**, gatekeepers, singers,

Neh 10:34 We priests, **L**, and laypeople
10:37 We will bring for the **L**
10:37 because the **L** are the ones
10:38 be with the **L** when they collect
10:38 Then the **L** should bring
10:39 The Israelites and the **L** should
11:3 Some Israelites, priests, **L**,
11:15 These were the **L**:
11:18 All the **L** in the holy city totaled
11:20 and **L** lived in all the cities of
11:22 The man in charge of the **L** in
11:36 Some divisions of **L** in Judah
12:1 These are the priests and **L**
12:8 The **L** were Jeshua,
12:22 of the family heads of the **L**
12:23 heads of the **L** were recorded
12:24 heads of the **L** were Hashabiah,
12:27 they went to wherever the **L**
12:30 the **L** cleansed themselves.
12:44 for the priests and **L** from
12:44 ministry of the priests and **L**.
12:47 for the daily support of the **L**,
12:47 and the **L** set aside holy gifts
13:5 belonged by law to the **L**,
13:10 I learned that the **L** had not
13:10 So each of the **L** and singers,
13:11 So I brought the **L** back
13:22 Then I told the **L** to cleanse
13:29 you made to the priests and **L**."
13:30 duties to the priests and **L**.
Isa 52:11 Make yourselves pure, you **L**
66:21 and **L**," declares the LORD.
Jer 33:22 David and the **L** who serve me
Eze 40:46 They are the only **L** who are
44:10 "'Some **L** went far away from
44:15 "'But the priests who are **L** and
45:5 will belong to the **L** who serve
48:11 with the Israelites as the **L** did.
48:12 to the land belonging to the **L**.
48:13 be the land belonging to the **L**.
Jon 1:19 priests and **L** from Jerusalem

Levites' (3)

Num 3:38 who tried to do the **L** duties had
8:26 you will handle the **L** duties.
Eze 48:22 So the **L** property and the city's

Levitical (16)

Dtr 17:9 Go to the **L** priests and the
17:18 he should have the **L** priests
18:1 The **L** priests — in fact,
24:8 as the **L** priests instruct you.
27:9 Then Moses and the **L** priests
31:9 to the **L** priests who carried
Jos 3:3 and the **L** priests who carry
8:33 They faced the **L** priests who
2Ch 11:16 of Israel followed the **L** priests
30:27 Then the **L** priests blessed the
Jer 33:18 The **L** priests will never fail to
33:21 the **L** priests could also
Heb 7:11 The people established the **L**
7:11 If the work of the **L** priests had
7:11 not a **L** priest like Aaron.
8:6 superior to the **L** priests' work.

liability (1)

Exo 21:28 bull's owner is free from any **l**.

liar (13)

Job 24:25 who can prove I'm a **l** and
34:6 I'm considered a **l** in spite of
Pro 17:4 A **l** opens his ears to a
19:22 it is better to be poor than a **l**.
30:6 and you will be found to be a **l**.
Jon 8:44 He's a **l** and the father of lies.
8:55 I would be a **l** like all of you.
Rom 3:4 and everyone else is a **l**,
1Jn 1:10 we turn God into a **l** and his
2:4 obey his commandments is a **l**.
2:22 Who is a **l**? Who else but the
4:20 hates another believer is a **l**.
5:10 God have made God a **l**.

liars (11)

Psa 26:4 I did not sit with **l**, and I will not
58:3 From their birth **l** go astray.
63:11 but the mouths of **l** will be shut.
Isa 57:4 children, descendants of **l**?
Mic 2:11 **L** and frauds may go around
Act 6:12 The **l** stirred up trouble among
1Ti 1:10 for kidnappers, for **l**,
Tit 1:12 "Cretans are always **l**,
Rev 2:2 have discovered that they are **l**.
21:8 and all **l** will find themselves in
21:27 and no **l** will ever enter it.

liberty (1)

Lev 25:10 and proclaim **l** to everyone

Libnah (19)

Num 33:20 Perez and set up camp at **L**.
33:21 They moved from **L** and set up
Jos 10:29 Makkedah to **L** and attacked it.
10:30 The LORD also handed **L** and
10:30 same thing to the king of **L** that
10:31 marched from **L** to Lachish,
10:32 same way he had captured **L**.
10:39 to Hebron and **L** and their kings
12:15 the king of **L**, the king of
15:42 to Judah: **L**, Ether, Ashan,
21:13 city of refuge for murderers), **L**,
2Ki 8:22 At that time **L** also rebelled.
19:8 of Assyria fighting against **L**.
23:31 daughter of Jeremiah from **L**.
24:18 daughter of Jeremiah from **L**.
1Ch 6:57 **L** with its pastureland,
2Ch 21:10 **L** rebelled because Jehoram
Isa 37:8 of Assyria fighting against **L**.
Jer 52:1 daughter of Jeremiah from **L**.

Libni (6)

Exo 6:17 families were **L** and Shimei.
Num 3:18 **L** and Shimei were the sons of
3:21 descended from **L** and Shimei.
1Ch 6:17 Gershom's sons: **L** and Shimei.
6:20 Gershom's son was **L**.
6:29 Mahli's son was **L**.

Libni's (2)

1Ch 6:20 **L** son was Jahath.
6:29 **L** son was Shimei.

Libnite (1)

Num 26:58 families of Levi: the **L** family,

library (1)

Ezr 6:1 the order to search the **l** where

Libya (3)

Dan 11:43 **L** and Sudan will surrender to
Act 2:10 the country near Cyrene in **L**.
27:17 sandbank off the shores of **L**,

Libyans (3)

2Ch 12:3 and an army of countless **L**,
16:8 Weren't the Sudanese and **L** a
Eze 30:5 Put, Lud, all the Arabs, the **L**,

lick (6)

1Ki 21:19 the dogs will **l** up your blood."'
Psa 68:23 the tongues of your dogs may **l**
72:9 May his enemies **l** the dust.
Isa 49:23 They will **l** the dust at your feet.
Mic 7:17 They will **l** dust like snakes,
Luk 16:21 and dogs would **l** them.

licked (2)

1Ki 21:19 At the place where the dogs **l**
22:38 The dogs **l** up his blood,

lid (2)

Num 19:15 Every container without a **l**
2Ki 12:9 drilled a hole in its **l**,

Lidbir (1)

Jos 13:26 as far as the border of **L**.

lie (138)

Exo 20:16 "Never **l** when you testify about
Lev 6:2 if you **l** to your neighbor about
6:2 if you **l** about something stolen
6:3 that someone lost and **l** about
19:11 "Never steal, **l**, or deceive your
26:6 You will **l** down with no one to
Num 21:15 to the site of Ar and **l** along
23:24 It doesn't **l** down until it eats its
24:9 His people **l** down and rest
Dtr 6:7 when you **l** down or get up.
11:19 when you **l** down or get up.
25:2 judge will order him to **l** down.
31:16 "Soon you are going to **l** down
Rut 3:4 his feet, and **l** down there.
3:13 **L** down until morning."
1Sm 3:9 "Go, **l** down," Eli told Samuel.
15:29 the Glory of Israel does not **l** or
2Sm 7:12 time comes for you to **l** down
8:2 made the Moabites **l** down on
11:13 But that evening Uriah went to **l**
13:5 "**L** down on your bed.
1Ki 1:2 She can **l** in your arms and
1:21 like criminals when you **l** down
2Ki 4:16 Don't **l** to me. You're a man of
Job 6:28 I won't **l** to your face.
7:4 When I **l** down, I ask,
7:21 Soon I'll **l** down in the dust.
11:19 You will **l** down with no one to
20:11 will **l** down with him in the
21:26 Together they **l** down in the
24:7 All night they **l** naked without a
29:19 and dew will **l** on my branches
38:40 crouch in their dens and **l** ready
Psa 3:5 I **l** down and sleep.
4:2 is empty and seek what is a **l**?
4:8 in peace the moment I **l** down
23:2 He makes me **l** down in green
24:4 long for what is false or **l** when
57:4 I must **l** down with man-eating
59:3 They **l** in ambush for me right
62:4 They are happy to **l**.
63:6 As I **l** on my bed, I remember
88:5 been killed and **l** in graves,
89:33 or allow my truth to become a **l**.
89:35 I will not **l** to David.
102:7 I **l** awake. I am like a lonely bird
104:22 they gather and **l** down in their
Pro 3:24 When you **l** down,
3:24 As you **l** there, your sleep will
6:9 How long will you **l** there,
6:22 When you **l** down,
12:22 Lips that **l** are disgusting to the
14:5 trustworthy witness does not **l**,
15:11 If Sheol and Abaddon **l** open in
24:15 You wicked one, do not **l** in
Ecc 4:11 if two people **l** down together,
Sos 1:7 Where does your flock **l** down
Isa 5:25 and dead bodies **l** like garbage
6:11 he replied, "Until the cities **l**
11:6 Leopards will **l** down with
11:7 young will **l** down together.
13:21 animals will **l** down there.
14:30 and the needy will **l** down in
17:2 which will **l** down in them.
21:9 All the idols they worship **l**
26:19 Those who **l** dead in the dust
27:10 They will **l** down. They will
28:1 where they **l** drunk from wine.
29:4 you will speak as you **l** on the
34:10 Edom will **l** in ruins for
43:17 (They **l** down together and do
51:20 They **l** sleeping at every street
51:23 They said to you, "**L** down so
53:9 and had never spoken a **l**.
56:10 They **l** around dreaming;
63:8 children who will not **l** to me."
Jer 3:25 We must **l** down in our shame
5:2 they **l** when they take this oath.
5:6 A leopard will **l** in ambush
5:12 They **l** about the LORD and
5:26 They **l** in ambush like bird
7:4 the LORD's temple!" It's a **l**.
7:8 It's a **l** that cannot help you.
7:9 **l** when you take oaths,
23:14 commit adultery and live a **l**.
23:26 continue to **l** and deceive?
28:15 made these people believe a **l**.
29:31 He has made you believe a **l**.
37:14 Jeremiah answered, "That's a **l**!
40:16 saying about Ishmael is a **l**."

Jer 49:13 will l in ruins permanently.
51:4 They will l dead in their own
51:47 and all its soldiers will l dead.
Lam 2:21 Young and old l on the ground
Eze 4:4 "Then l on your left side and
4:4 days as you l on that side.
4:6 you will l down again,
6:13 "Those who are killed will l
6:13 They will l on every high hill,
13:19 You l to my people who are
29:12 Egypt's cities will l in ruins.
30:7 Egypt's cities will l in ruins.
31:18 You will l among the godless
32:20 "The Egyptians will l among
32:21 and you now l with the godless
32:25 They l among the dead.
32:27 They don't l with the godless
32:28 and you will l with those who
32:29 but now they l with those who
32:29 They l there with the godless
32:30 Now they l with those who
47:17 The border of Hamath will l to
Hos 6:9 are like gangs of robbers who l
7:6 oven while they l in ambush.
10:4 They l when they take oaths,
Amo 5:2 They l abandoned in their own
Mic 7:2 All people l in ambush to
Hab 2:3 It won't be a l. If it's delayed,
Zep 2:7 In the evening they will l down
2:14 Flocks will l down in it along
3:13 graze their sheep and l down,
Mat 5:11 insult you, persecute you, l,
Jon 5:3 or paralyzed — used to l.
8:44 Whenever he tells a l,
Act 5:4 You didn't l to people but to
6:11 they bribed some men to l.
Rom 1:25 exchanged God's truth for a l.
3:7 If my l increases the glory that
Gal 1:20 that what I'm writing is not a l.)
Col 3:9 Don't l to each other.
2Th 2:11 so that they will believe a l.
1Ti 1:10 for those who l when they take
Heb 6:18 God cannot l when he takes an
1Jn 2:21 You know that no l ever comes
2:27 is true and contains no l.
Rev 11:8 Their dead bodies will l on the
14:5 They've never told a l.
22:15 and all who l in what they say

lied (7)

Dtr 19:18 If it is found that the witness l
Jos 7:11 but they have also l.
Psa 78:36 him with their mouths and l
119:78 because they l about me,
Isa 57:11 fear so much that you l to me?
Act 6:13 Some witnesses stood up and l
1Co 15:15 witnesses who l about God

lies (103)

Gen 49:9 He l down and rests like a lion.
Exo 5:9 will be too busy to listen to l."
23:7 Avoid telling l. Don't kill
Lev 15:4 makes everything he l
15:20 Everything she l on or sits on
15:24 Any bed he l on will become
15:26 any bed she l on or anything
26:34 the LORD⌋ while it l deserted
26:35 All the days it l deserted,
26:43 it l deserted without them.
Num 13:32 So they began to spread l
14:33 the last of your bodies l dead
14:37 by spreading l about the land.
23:19 He tells no l. He is not like
Jos 18:11 Their territory l between
Jdg 16:10 fun of me by telling me l.
16:13 fun of me by telling me l.
Rut 3:4 When he l down, notice the
2Sm 1:19 l dead on your hills.
19:27 He told you l about me,
1Ki 22:22 be a spirit that tells l through
22:23 a spirit that makes them tell l.
2Ch 18:21 be a spirit that tells l through
18:22 a spirit that makes them tell l.
Job 13:4 But you are smearing me with l.
14:12 so each person l down and
31:5 "If I have walked with l or my
36:4 Certainly, my words are not l.
40:21 It l down under the lotus plants
Psa 5:6 You destroy those who tell l.
7:14 and gives birth to l.
10:9 He l in his hiding place like a
40:4 people or those who follow l.
59:12 they speak curses and l.
88:7 Your rage l heavily on me.
101:7 The one who tells l will not
119:29 Turn me away from a life of l.
119:69 have smeared me with l,
119:86 people persecute me with l.
119:118 because their l mislead them.
144:8 Their mouths speak l.
144:11 Their mouths speak l.
Pro 6:19 witness spitting out l,
12:19 but l last only a moment.
14:5 a dishonest witness breathes l.
14:25 one who tells l is dangerous.
19:5 who tells l will not escape.
19:9 One who tells l will die.
29:12 If a ruler pays attention to l,
30:8 Keep vanity and l far away
Sos 1:13 of myrrh that l at night between
Isa 5:18 who string people along with l
9:15 who teach l are the tail.
18:1 whirring wings which l beyond
24:10 The ruined city l desolate.
28:15 we have taken refuge in our l,
28:17 sweep away your refuge of l,
32:7 order to ruin poor people with l,
59:3 You speak l, and you mutter
59:4 arguments and speak l.
59:13 and uttered l in our hearts.
Jer 5:31 Prophets prophesy l.
8:8 to turn these teachings into l.
9:3 L and dishonesty rule the land.
9:5 train their tongues to speak l.
14:14 "These are the l that the
16:19 "Our ancestors have inherited l,
20:6 whom you prophesied these l."
23:25 heard the prophets who speak l
23:32 my people astray with their l
27:10 They are prophesying l to you.
27:14 They are prophesying l to you.
27:15 They prophesy l in my name.
27:16 They are prophesying l to you.
29:9 These people are prophesying l
29:21 who prophesy l to you in my
29:23 neighbors' wives and spoke l
Lam 5:18 on Mount Zion, which l in ruins.
Eze 13:8 and your visions are l.
13:22 righteous people with your l,
21:29 you and prophesy l about you.
22:28 visions and by prophesying l.
32:23 Assyria's army l around its
Dan 11:27 sit at the same table and tell l.
Hos 7:3 happy with the l they tell.
7:13 but they tell l about me.
10:13 the fruit that your l produced.
11:12 "Ephraim surrounds me with l.
Mic 6:12 who live in the city speak l,
Nah 3:1 It is completely full of l and
Hab 2:18 a molded statue, a teacher of l,
Zep 3:13 Israel will not do wrong, tell l,
Hag 1:4 while this house l in ruins?
1:9 "It's because my house l in
Zec 10:2 The idols speak l.
13:3 to live because you speak l
Jon 8:44 He's a liar and the father of l.
Eph 4:25 So then, get rid of l.
2Th 2:9 signs. But they will be l.
1Ti 4:2 These people will speak l
Tit 1:2 eternal life. God, who never l,
Heb 12:1 We must run the race that l
1Jn 4:6 Spirit of truth from the spirit of l.

life (783)

Gen 2:7 the breath of l into his nostrils.
2:9 The tree of l and the tree of the
3:17 from it every day of your l.
3:20 Adam named his wife Eve [L]
3:22 fruit from the tree of l and eat.
3:24 to guard the way to the tree of l.
7:3 to preserve animal l all over
7:11 six hundredth year of Noah's l,
9:4 with blood in it. (Blood is l.)
9:5 demand your blood for your l.
9:5 I will demand the l of any
9:11 Never again will all l be killed
9:15 become a flood to destroy all l.
9:17 I am making to all l on earth."
19:19 very kind to me by saving my l,
19:20 Then my l will be saved."
23:1 This was the length of her l.
25:8 After a long and full l,
32:30 but my l was saved."
38:7 So the LORD took away his l.
38:10 LORD took away Onan's l too.
43:9 can blame me the rest of my l.
44:30 "Our father's l is wrapped up
44:30 is wrapped up with the boy's l.
44:32 can blame me the rest of my l,
47:9 The years of my l have been
48:15 has been my shepherd all my l
Exo 21:6 Then he will be his slave for l.
21:23 offender must pay a l for a life,
21:23 offender must pay a life for a l,
21:30 the bull's owner may save his l
23:26 I will let you live a normal l
30:12 LORD a ransom for his l when
Lev 17:11 because blood contains l.
17:14 This is because the l of any
17:14 because the l of any creature is
18:5 You will have l through them.
19:16 endanger your neighbor's l.
24:18 animal must replace it, l for life.
24:18 animal must replace it, life for l.
Num 16:22 the breath of l to everyone!
27:16 the breath of l to everyone.
35:31 payment in exchange for the l
Dtr 5:33 l will go well for you,
12:23 because blood contains l.
12:23 Never eat the l with the meat.
15:17 and he will be your slave for l.
17:19 with him and read it his entire l.
19:4 of these cities to save his l.
19:5 of these cities and save his l.
19:6 him and take his l even though
19:11 him, attacks him, takes his l,
19:21 ⌊Take⌋ a l for a life,
19:21 ⌊Take⌋ a life for a l,
20:16 you must not spare anyone's l
28:66 Your l will always be hanging
28:66 will never feel sure of your l.
30:15 Today I offer you l and
30:19 I have offered you l or death,
30:19 Choose l so that you and your
30:20 This will be your way of l,
30:20 and it will mean a long l for you
32:18 forgot the God who gave you l.)
32:47 They are your l! By these words
Jos 2:19 be responsible for his own l.
4:24 your God every day of your l."
13:1 near the end of his l.
13:1 near the end of your l,
23:1 near the end of his l.
23:2 near the end of my l.
Jdg 5:18 risked his l on the battlefield.
8:28 for 40 years during Gideon's l.
9:17 He risked his l and rescued
12:3 I risked my l and went to fight
14:17 she made his l miserable.
16:16 Every day she made his l
Rut 1:20 has made my l very bitter.
4:15 He will bring you a new l and
1Sm 1:28 to the LORD for his whole l."
2:6 LORD kills, and he gives l.
2:33 will die in the prime of l.
19:5 He risked his l and killed the
22:2 or bitter about l joined him,
22:23 The one who is seeking my l
22:23 life is ⌊also⌋ seeking your l.
24:11 me in order to take my l.
25:29 pursued you and sought your l,
25:29 your l is wrapped in the bundle
25:29 bundle of l which comes from
26:21 you valued my l today.
26:24 great value on your l today,
26:24 place great value on my l
28:2 make you my bodyguard for l."
28:21 "and I took my l in my hands

2Sm	6:23	was childless her entire **l**.
	14:7	because he took his brother's **l**.
	14:19	"I solemnly swear on your **l**,
	17:3	Since you will be seeking the **l**
	19:5	"They saved your **l** and the
	19:7	you've had in your entire **l**."
1Ki	1:12	about how to save your **l**
	1:12	save your life and your son's **l**.
	1:29	has saved my **l** from all trouble
	2:23	pay with his **l** for this request!
	3:11	for this and not for a long **l**,
	3:14	I will also give you a long **l**."
	15:5	him to do his entire **l** (except
	15:14	to the LORD his entire **l**.
	17:17	He got so sick that finally no **l**
	17:21	this child's **l** return to him."
	17:22	and the child's **l** returned to him
	19:2	tomorrow I don't take your **l**
	19:3	Elijah fled to save his **l**.
	19:4	"Take my **l**! I'm no better than
	19:10	and they're trying to take my **l**."
	19:14	and they're trying to take my **l**."
	20:39	you will pay for his **l** with your
	20:39	pay for his life with your own **l**
	20:42	For that reason your **l** will be
	20:42	will be taken in place of his **l**
2Ki	1:13	please treat my **l** and the lives
	1:14	my **l** as something precious."
	4:31	there was no sound or sign of **l**.
	5:7	and then bring him back to **l**?
	8:1	son he had brought back to **l**,
	8:5	brought a dead child back to **l**,
	8:5	Elisha brought back to **l**."
	13:21	came back to **l** and stood up.
	15:18	During his entire **l** he never
1Ch	28:9	If you dedicate your **l** to serving
	29:28	His long **l** was full of wealth
2Ch	1:11	You didn't even ask for a long **l**.
	15:17	⌊to the LORD⌋ his entire **l**.
	17:3	didn't dedicate his **l**
	17:4	Instead, he dedicated his **l** to
	19:3	your **l** to serving God."
	21:19	as his **l** was coming to an end,
	22:9	Jehoshaphat dedicated his **l** to
	25:15	"Why do you dedicate your **l** to
	26:5	He dedicated his **l** to serving
	26:5	As long as he dedicated his **l**
	27:7	his wars and his **l** — is written
	31:21	worship and dedicated his **l**
	34:3	he began to dedicate his **l** to
Ezr	6:10	of heaven and pray for the **l**
	8:22	everyone who dedicates his **l**
Neh	5:15	before me had made **l** difficult
	6:11	into the temple to save his **l**?
	9:6	You give **l** to them all,
	9:29	he will find **l** in them.
Est	7:3	you, Your Majesty, spare my **l**.
	7:3	And spare the **l** of my people.
	7:7	to beg Queen Esther for his **l**,
Job	2:4	give everything he has for his **l**.
	2:6	but you must spare his **l**!"
	3:20	give light to one in misery and **l**
	6:11	I would want to prolong my **l**?
	7:7	my **l** is only a breath,
	7:16	I hate my **l**; I do not want to live
	8:19	That is its joy in this **l**,
	9:21	way of knowing it. I hate my **l**!
	10:1	"I hate my **l**. I will freely
	10:12	You gave me **l** and mercy.
	10:20	"Isn't my **l** short enough?
	11:17	Then your **l** will be brighter
	11:17	The darkness in your **l** will
	12:5	"A person who has an easy **l**
	12:10	The **l** of every living creature
	13:14	I can chew and taking my **l**
	14:6	Meanwhile, he loves **l** as a
	24:22	will never feel secure about **l**.
	27:2	who has made my **l** bitter:
	27:8	when God takes away his **l**?
	29:2	"If only my **l** could be like it
	29:4	in the prime of my **l** ⌊again⌋,
	30:16	"Now my **l** is pouring out of me.
	31:30	down a curse on his **l**) ....
	33:4	of the Almighty gives me **l**.
	33:28	and my **l** will see the light.'
	33:30	them with the light of **l**.
Job	42:12	latter years of Job's **l** more than
Psa	7:5	Let him trample my **l** into the
	11:3	⌊of **l**⌋ are undermined,
	11:7	He loves a righteous way of **l**.
	16:11	You make the path of **l** known
	17:13	my **l** from wicked people.
	17:14	their inheritance only in this **l**.
	21:4	He asked you for **l**.
	21:4	You gave him a long **l**,
	22:20	my **l** from vicious dogs.
	23:6	to me all the days of my **l**,
	25:13	He will enjoy good things in **l**,
	25:20	Protect my **l**, and rescue me!
	26:9	hardened sinners or my **l** along
	27:4	house all the days of my **l**
	30:3	You called me back to **l** from
	31:10	My **l** is exhausted from sorrow,
	31:13	They were plotting to take my **l**.
	34:12	Which of you wants a full **l**?
	35:4	Let those who seek my **l** be put
	35:17	my precious **l** from the lions.
	36:9	the fountain of **l** is with you.
	38:12	Those who seek my **l** lay traps
	39:4	about the end of my **l**.
	39:4	know how temporary my **l** is.
	39:5	My **l** span is nothing compared
	39:10	My **l** is over because you
	40:14	all those who seek to end my **l**
	42:8	a prayer to the God of my **l**.
	49:7	or pay God a ransom for his **l**.
	54:3	Ruthless people seek my **l**.
	54:4	Lord is the provider for my **l**.
	56:6	step as they wait to take my **l**.
	56:13	your presence, in the light of **l**.
	61:6	Add days upon days to the **l** of
	63:3	mercy is better than **l** ⌊itself⌋.
	63:9	try to destroy my **l** will go into
	64:1	Protect my **l** from a terrifying
	69:28	be erased from the Book of **L**.
	70:2	Let those who seek my **l** be
	71:10	me as they plot to take my **l**.
	71:20	You restore me to **l** again.
	73:13	no reward for keeping my **l** pure
	73:26	remains the foundation of my **l**
	74:19	Do not forget the **l** of your
	80:18	Give us **l** again, and we will
	86:14	of ruthless people seeks my **l**.
	88:3	and my **l** comes closer to the
	89:47	Remember how short my **l** is!
	91:16	I will satisfy you with a long **l**.
	102:24	me now in the middle of my **l**.
	102:27	and your **l** will never end.
	103:4	the one who rescues your **l**
	103:5	the one who fills your **l** with
	103:15	Human **l** is as short-lived as
	104:33	to the LORD throughout my **l**.
	119:9	young person keep his **l** pure?
	119:25	me a new **l** as you promised.
	119:29	Turn me away from a **l** of lies.
	119:30	have chosen a **l** of faithfulness.
	119:37	Give me a new **l** in your ways.
	119:40	a new **l** in your righteousness.
	119:50	Your promise gave me a new **l**.
	119:59	I have thought about my **l**,
	119:84	What is left of my **l**?
	119:88	Give me a new **l** through your
	119:93	gave me a new **l** through them.
	119:107	Give me a new **l**, O LORD,
	119:109	I always take my **l** into my own
	119:149	O LORD, give me a new **l**
	119:154	me a new **l** as you promised.
	119:156	Give me a new **l** guided by
	119:159	your mercy, give me a new **l**.
	119:168	because my whole **l** is in front
	119:175	Let my soul have new **l** so that
	121:7	every evil. He guards your **l**.
	128:5	all the days of your **l**.
	133:3	the blessing of eternal **l**.
	138:7	you guard my **l** against the
	139:16	Every day ⌊of my **l**⌋ was
	143:3	He has ground my **l** into the dirt
	144:4	Their **l** span is like a fleeting
	146:2	the LORD throughout my **l**.
Pro	1:19	Greed takes away his **l**.
	2:9	fair — every good course ⌊in **l**⌋.
	2:19	they ever reach the paths of **l**.
Pro	3:2	they will bring you long **l**,
	3:16	Long **l** is in ⌊wisdom's⌋ right
	3:18	⌊Wisdom⌋ is a tree of **l** for
	3:22	Then they will mean **l** for you,
	4:10	will multiply the years of your **l**.
	4:13	Keep it because it is your **l**.
	4:22	because they are **l** to those
	4:23	source of your **l** flows from it.
	5:6	even think about the path of **l**.
	6:23	from discipline are the path of **l**
	6:26	woman hunts for ⌊your⌋ **l** itself.
	7:23	that it will cost him his **l**.
	8:35	Whoever finds me finds **l** and
	9:11	years will be added to your **l**.
	10:11	person is a fountain of **l**,
	10:16	righteous person's reward is **l**.
	10:17	discipline is on the way to **l**,
	11:19	As righteousness leads to **l**,
	11:30	a righteous person is a tree of **l**,
	12:10	cares ⌊even⌋ about the **l**
	12:28	Everlasting **l** is on the way of
	13:3	his mouth protects his own **l**.
	13:6	protects the honest way of **l**,
	13:8	riches are the ransom for his **l**,
	13:12	a fulfilled longing is a tree of **l**.
	13:14	wise person are a fountain of **l**
	14:8	person guides his way of **l**,
	14:27	of the LORD is a fountain of **l**
	15:4	A soothing tongue is a tree of **l**,
	15:24	The path of **l** for a wise person
	16:15	the king is cheerful, there is **l**,
	16:17	his way preserves his own **l**.
	16:22	Understanding is a fountain of **l**
	16:31	crown found in a righteous **l**.
	18:21	has the power of **l** and death,
	19:3	person turns his **l** upside down,
	19:16	obeys the law preserves his **l**,
	19:20	may be wise the rest of your **l**.
	19:23	The fear of the LORD leads to **l**,
	20:2	makes him angry forfeits his **l**.
	21:21	and mercy will find **l**,
	21:29	but a decent person's way of **l**
	22:4	are riches and honor and **l**.
	23:12	Live a more disciplined **l**,
	29:10	people seek ⌊to protect⌋ his **l**.
	29:24	a thief's partner hates his own **l**.
	31:12	harms him all the days of her **l**.
Ecc	2:17	So I came to hate **l** because
	2:23	Their entire **l** is filled with pain,
	3:19	have the same breath ⌊of **l**⌋.
	3:19	All ⌊of **l**⌋ is pointless.
	3:20	All ⌊**l**⌋ goes to the same place.
	3:20	All ⌊**l**⌋ comes from the ground,
	3:22	because that is their lot ⌊in **l**⌋.
	5:18	That is our lot ⌊in **l**⌋.
	5:19	ability⌋ to accept their lot in **l**,
	6:8	have in knowing how to face **l**?
	7:12	of wisdom is that it gives **l**
	7:15	seen it all in my pointless **l**:
	8:8	the spirit of **l** from leaving.
	8:12	crimes and yet live a long **l**.
	8:15	the enjoyment ⌊of **l**⌋.
	9:9	Enjoy **l** with your wife,
	9:9	during all your brief, pointless **l**.
	9:9	you your pointless **l** under
	9:9	This is your lot ⌊in **l**⌋ and what
	10:19	and wine makes **l** pleasant,
	11:5	know how the breath of **l** enters
	12:7	and the breath of **l** goes back to
Isa	2:22	Their **l** is in their nostrils.
	38:10	thought that in the prime of my **l**
	38:10	be robbed of the rest of my **l**.
	38:12	My **l** was over. You rolled it up
	38:12	You rolled up my **l** like a
	38:12	You ended my **l** in one day.
	38:13	You ended my **l** in one day.
	38:15	I will be careful the rest of my **l**
	42:5	He gave **l** to the people who
	43:4	will be the price I pay for your **l**.
	53:10	When the LORD has made his **l**
	53:12	because he poured out his **l** in
	65:20	man who doesn't live a long **l**.
Jer	18:20	They dig a pit to take my **l**.
	21:8	you the choice of **l** or death.
	26:14	"My **l** is in your hands.
	38:16	"The LORD gave us **l**.

Jer	39:18	You will escape with your l
	45:5	let you escape with your l.'"
	51:13	The thread of your l has been
Lam	2:19	to him ⌊in prayer⌋ for the l
	3:24	'The LORD is my lot ⌊in l⌋.
	3:58	O LORD. Reclaim my l.
	4:20	who is the breath of our l,
	5:21	Give us back the l we had long
Eze	18:4	The l of every person belongs
	33:15	lives by the rules of l,
	37:10	Then they came to l and stood
	47:9	the river flows, it will bring l.
Dan	5:23	who has power over your l and
Jnh	1:14	let us die for taking this man's l.
	2:5	me, threatening my l.
	2:7	"As my l was slipping away,
	4:3	So now, LORD, take my l.
Hab	1:14	like schools of sea l that have
	2:10	and forfeiting your own l.
	2:19	but there's absolutely no l in it."
Mal	2:5	"I promised Levi l and peace.
Mat	5:20	you live a l that has God's
	6:25	Isn't l more than food and the
	6:27	hour to your l by worrying?
	7:14	the road that lead to l are full
	9:25	and the girl came back to l.
	10:8	bring the dead back to l,
	10:39	to preserve his l will lose it,
	10:39	but the person who loses his l
	11:5	people are brought back to l,
	13:22	But the worries of l and the
	14:2	He has come back to l.
	16:21	he would be brought back to l.
	16:26	person give in exchange for l?
	17:9	has been brought back to l."
	17:23	he will be brought back to l."
	18:8	It is better for you to enter l
	18:9	It is better for you to enter l with
	19:16	should I do to gain eternal l?"
	19:17	If you want to enter into l,
	19:29	more and will inherit eternal l.
	20:19	he will be brought back to l."
	20:28	to serve and to give his l as
	22:23	will never come back to l,
	22:28	when the dead come back to l,
	22:30	When people come back to l,
	22:31	the dead coming back to l?
	25:46	approval will go into eternal l."
	26:32	after I am brought back to l,
	27:50	once again and gave up his l.
	27:52	who had died came back to l.
	27:53	after he had come back to l,
	27:63	days I will be brought back to l.'
	27:64	been brought back to l.' Then
	28:6	He has been brought back to l
	28:7	he has been brought back to l.
Mar	4:19	but the worries of l,
	6:14	Baptizer has come back to l.
	6:16	and he has come back to l!"
	8:31	days he would come back to l.
	8:37	person give in exchange for l?
	9:9	Son of Man had come back to l.
	9:10	he meant by "come back to l."
	9:31	day he will come back to l."
	9:43	It is better for you to enter l
	9:45	It is better for you to enter l
	10:17	should I do to inherit eternal l?"
	10:30	times as much here in this l.
	10:30	they will receive eternal l.
	10:34	days he will come back to l."
	10:45	to serve and to give his l as
	12:18	will never come back to l,
	12:23	When the dead come back to l,
	12:25	When the dead come back to l,
	12:26	that the dead come back to l?
	14:28	after I am brought back to l,
	16:6	He has been brought back to l.
	16:9	After Jesus came back to l
Luk	2:25	an honorable and devout l.
	7:3	come and save the servant's l.
	7:14	telling you to come back to l!"
	7:22	people are brought back to l,
	7:37	A woman who lived a sinful l
	8:14	but as l goes on the worries,
	8:14	and pleasures of l choke them.
	8:15	good despite what l may bring.
Luk	8:55	She came back to l and got up
	9:7	that John had come back to l.
	9:8	long ago had come back to l.
	9:19	long ago has come back to l."
	9:22	day he would come back to l.
	10:25	must I do to inherit eternal l?"
	10:28	Do this, and l will be yours."
	12:15	L is not about having a lot of
	12:19	Take l easy, eat, drink,
	12:20	I will demand your l from you
	12:23	L is more than food,
	12:25	an hour to your l by worrying?
	14:14	approval come back to l."
	15:24	dead and has come back to l.
	15:32	dead but has come back to l.
	16:9	When l is over, you will be
	16:25	that you had a l filled with good
	16:25	while Lazarus' l was filled with
	16:31	if someone comes back to l.'"
	18:18	must I do to inherit eternal l?"
	18:30	many times as much in this l
	18:30	life and will receive eternal l
	18:33	day he will come back to l."
	20:27	will never come back to l,
	20:33	when the dead come back to l,
	20:35	worthy to come back to l
	20:36	who have come back to l.
	20:37	that the dead come back to l.
	21:19	endurance you will save your l.
	21:34	and worried about l.
	24:6	He has been brought back to l!
	24:7	and come back to l on the third
	24:34	Lord has really come back to l
	24:46	that he would come back to l
Jon	1:4	He was the source of l,
	1:4	and that l was the light for
	2:22	After he came back to l,
	3:15	in him will have eternal l."
	3:16	not die but will have eternal l.
	3:36	in the Son has eternal l,
	3:36	rejects the Son will not see l.
	4:14	that gushes up to eternal l."
	4:36	is gathering grain for eternal l.
	5:21	the dead and gives them l,
	5:21	the Son gives l to anyone he
	5:24	sent me will have eternal l.
	5:24	already passed from death to l.
	5:26	The Father is the source of l,
	5:26	Son to be the source of l too.
	5:29	will come back to l and live.
	5:29	done evil will come back to l
	5:39	the source of eternal l in them.
	5:40	come to me to get ⌊eternal⌋ l.
	6:27	the food that lasts into eternal l.
	6:33	and gives l to the world."
	6:35	"I am the bread of l.
	6:39	me to bring them back to l
	6:40	believe in him to have eternal l.
	6:40	me to bring them back to l
	6:44	bring these people back to l
	6:47	Every believer has eternal l.
	6:48	"I am the bread of l.
	6:51	The bread I will give to bring l
	6:53	have the source of l in you.
	6:54	drink my blood have eternal l,
	6:54	and I will bring them back to l
	6:57	The Father who has l sent me,
	6:63	L is spiritual. Your physical
	6:63	doesn't contribute to that l.
	6:63	to you are spiritual. They are l.
	6:68	Your words give eternal l.
	8:12	follows me will have a l filled
	8:34	Whoever lives a sinful l is a
	10:10	so that my sheep will have l
	10:11	gives his l for the sheep.
	10:15	So I give my l for my sheep.
	10:17	loves me because I give my l
	10:18	No one takes my l from me.
	10:18	I give my l of my own free will.
	10:18	have the authority to give my l,
	10:18	to take my l back again.
	10:28	and I give them eternal l.
	11:23	brother will come back to l."
	11:24	know that he'll come back to l
	11:24	everyone will come back to l."
	11:25	who brings people back to l,
Jon	11:25	back to life, and I am l itself.
	12:1	Jesus had brought back to l,
	12:9	Jesus had brought back to l.
	12:17	back to l reported what they
	12:25	guard them for everlasting l.
	12:50	what he commands is eternal l.
	13:37	I'll give my l for you."
	13:38	"Will you give your l for me?
	14:6	am the way, the truth, and the l.
	15:13	is to give your l for your friends.
	17:2	so that he can give eternal l
	17:3	This is eternal l: to know you,
	20:9	Jesus had to come back to l.
	20:31	and so that you will have l by
	21:14	after he had come back to l.
Act	1:1	from the beginning ⌊of his l⌋
	1:20	that Jesus came back to l.
	2:24	God raised him from death to l
	2:28	You make the path of l known
	2:31	Messiah would come back to l,
	2:32	this man Jesus back to l.
	3:12	by our own power or godly l?
	3:15	and you killed the source of l.
	3:15	But God brought him back to l,
	3:26	brought his servant back to l
	4:2	come back to l through Jesus.
	4:10	God has brought him back to l.
	4:33	Lord Jesus had come back to l.
	5:20	everything about l ⌊in Christ⌋."
	5:30	brought him back to l.
	8:33	generation will talk about his l
	10:40	but God brought him back to l
	10:41	Jesus after he came back to l.
	11:18	and act and have eternal l."
	13:30	But God brought him back to l,
	13:33	by bringing Jesus back to l.
	13:34	that he brought Jesus back to l
	13:37	the man God brought back to l
	13:46	unworthy of everlasting l,
	13:48	for everlasting l believed.
	17:3	and come back to l,
	17:18	people would come back to l.
	17:25	He gives everyone l,
	17:31	by bringing that man back to l."
	17:32	a person had come back to l,
	20:24	place any value on my own l.
	23:6	the dead will come back to l."
	23:8	the dead won't come back to l
	24:15	without it will come back to l.
	24:21	the dead will come back to l.'"
	26:5	that I lived my l as a Pharisee.
	26:8	bring dead people back to l?
	26:23	be the first to come back to l
	27:22	No one will lose his l.
Rom	1:4	way when he came back to l.
	2:7	He will give everlasting l to
	4:17	of the God who gives l
	4:24	Jesus, our Lord, back to l.
	4:25	brought back to l so that we
	5:10	the l his Son lived will save us.
	5:17	gift of his approval will rule in l
	6:4	brought back from death to l by
	6:4	should live a new kind of l.
	6:5	we come back to l as he did.
	6:9	who was brought back to l,
	6:22	This results in a holy l and,
	6:22	life and, finally, in everlasting l.
	6:23	gives is everlasting l found
	7:4	one who was brought back to l.
	7:10	bring me l actually brought me
	8:2	who gives l through Christ
	8:6	attitude leads to l and peace.
	8:11	brought Jesus back to l live
	8:11	Christ back to l will also make
	8:34	he was brought back to l.
	8:38	can't be separated by death or l,
	10:9	that God brought him back to l,
	11:3	and they're trying to take my l."
	11:15	that Israel has come back to l.
	14:9	died and came back to l so that
1Co	3:22	Cephas, the world, l or death,
	4:15	in the Christian l by telling you
	4:17	my Christian way of l as
	6:3	not to mention things in this l?
	6:4	have cases dealing with this l,
	6:12	to gain control over my l.

1Co 7:17 Everyone should live the l that
7:35 you how to live a noble l
15:4 He was brought back to l on
15:8 fetus ⌊who was given⌋ l.
15:12 has been brought back to l,
15:13 dead can't be brought back to l,
15:13 Christ hasn't come back to l.
15:14 If Christ hasn't come back to l,
15:15 that he brought Christ back to l.
15:15 the dead don't come back to l,
15:15 didn't bring Christ back to l.
15:16 if the dead don't come back to l,
15:16 hasn't come back to l either.
15:17 If Christ hasn't come back to l,
15:19 Christ is our hope in this l only,
15:20 have died to come back to l.
15:21 also brought l back from death.
15:29 the dead ⌊will come back to l⌋.
15:29 If the dead can't come back to l,
15:29 if they can ⌊come back to l⌋?
15:35 do the dead come back to l?
15:36 plant doesn't come to l unless
15:42 when the dead come back to l.
15:42 When it comes back to l,
15:43 When it comes back to l,
15:44 It comes back to l as a spiritual
15:52 the dead will come back to l.
2Co 1:9 who brings the dead back to l.
3:6 but the Spirit brings l.
4:10 in our bodies so that the l
4:11 for Jesus' sake so that the l
4:12 but l is at work in you.
4:14 Jesus back to l will also bring
4:14 us back to l through Jesus.
5:1 We know that if the l we live
5:4 Then ⌊eternal⌋ l will put an
5:15 was brought back to l for them.
6:15 share l with an unbeliever?
7:1 body and spirit and live a holy l
Gal 1:1 who brought him back to l —
2:20 The l I now live I live by
3:15 an example from everyday l.
3:21 If those laws could give us l,
5:16 Live your l as your spiritual
6:8 you will harvest everlasting l.
6:9 will receive ⌊everlasting l⌋ at
Eph 1:20 when he brought him back to l
2:6 God has brought us back to l
4:1 the kind of l which proves that
4:18 They are excluded from the l
5:2 He gave his l for us as an
5:25 the church and gave his l for it.
6:3 may have a long l on earth."
6:4 your children bitter about l.
Php 1:21 everything to me in this l,
1:22 If I continue to live in this l,
1:23 I would like to leave this l and
1:24 it's better that I remain in this l.
2:16 you hold firmly to the word of l.
2:17 My l is being poured out as a
2:30 He risked his l and almost died
3:10 that his coming back to l gives
3:11 come back to l from the dead.
4:3 names are in the Book of L.
Col 1:18 the first to come back to l so
2:12 you were also brought back to l
2:12 who brought him back to l.
3:1 brought back to l with Christ,
3:3 You have died, and your l is
3:4 When Christ your l appears,
3:7 used to live that kind of sinful l.
3:9 used to be and the l you used
1Th 1:10 whom he brought back to l.
4:1 God-pleasing l even more than
4:12 Then your way of l will win
4:14 Jesus died and came back to l.
4:16 in Christ will come back to l.
5:10 whether we are awake in this l
2Th 2:13 you to be saved through a l
3:6 who doesn't live a disciplined l
3:7 a disciplined l among you.
1Ti 2:2 and peaceful l always lived
4:7 train yourself to live a godly l.
4:8 living has the promise of l now
4:10 and struggle to live a godly l,
4:15 Devote your l to them so that
1Ti 4:16 Focus on your l and your
6:5 They think that a godly l is a
6:6 A godly l brings huge profits to
6:11 of: a godly l, faith, love,
6:12 Take hold of everlasting l to
6:13 who gives l to everything,
6:19 take hold of what l really is.
2Ti 1:1 Christ Jesus' promise of l.
1:10 brought eternal l into full view.
2:8 He was brought back to l and
2:18 have already come back to l.
3:5 will appear to have a godly l,
3:10 my way of l, my purpose,
3:12 Those who try to live a godly l
3:16 and training them for a l that
4:6 My l is coming to an end,
Tit 1:1 the truth that leads to a godly l.
1:2 on the confidence of eternal l.
1:2 promised this eternal l before
2:1 the kind of l that goes along
3:7 that we have everlasting l.
Phm 1:19 that you owe me your l.
Heb 1:12 and your l will never end.
5:7 During his l on earth,
6:2 dead people coming back to l,
7:16 that comes from a l that cannot
11:35 that they might gain eternal l.
11:40 would gain eternal l with them.
12:23 and have gained eternal l.
13:20 back to l through the blood of
Jas 1:12 they will receive the crown of l
1:18 God decided to give us l
4:14 What is l? You are a mist that is
1Pe 1:3 We have been born into a new l
1:3 Christ has come back to l.
1:4 We have been born into a new l
1:15 holy in every aspect of your l.
1:18 the worthless l handed down
1:21 who brought Christ back to l
2:24 we could live a l that has
3:10 who want to live a full l
3:16 the good Christian l you live
3:18 brought to l through his spirit.
3:21 who came back from death to l.
2Pe 1:3 us everything we need for l
1:9 qualities aren't present in your l,
2:5 the kind of l that has God's
2:21 the way of l that God approves
2:21 on the holy l God told them
1Jn 1:1 The Word of l existed from the
1:2 This l was revealed to us.
1:2 about this eternal l that was
1:3 This is the l we have seen and
2:25 us the promise of eternal l.
3:8 The person who lives a sinful l
3:14 have passed from death to l,
3:15 murderer doesn't have eternal l.
3:16 that Christ gave his l for us.
4:9 we could have l through him.
5:11 God has given us eternal l,
5:11 and this l is found in his Son.
5:12 who has the Son has this l.
5:12 Son of God doesn't have this l.
5:13 know that they have eternal l.
5:16 God would give that person l.
5:20 is the real God and eternal l.
Jud 1:21 Christ to give you eternal l.
Rev 1:5 the first to come back to l,
2:7 of eating from the tree of l,
2:10 I will give you the crown of l.
3:5 their names from the Book of L.
7:17 filled with the water of l,
11:11 After 3 ½ days the breath of l
12:11 They didn't love their l so much
13:8 is not written in the Book of L.
17:8 written in the Book of L when
20:5 that people come back to l.
20:6 that people come back to l.
20:12 including the Book of L.
20:15 the Book of L were thrown into
21:6 filled with the water of l
21:27 lamb's Book of L will enter it.
22:1 a river filled with the water of l,
22:2 was a tree of l visible from both
22:14 have the right to the tree of l
22:17 who want the water of l take
Rev 22:19 away his portion of the tree of l

lifeboat (3)

Act 27:16 barely got control of the ship's l.
27:30 They let the l down into the
27:32 cut the ropes that held the l

life-giving (8)

Pro 15:31 The ear that listens to a l
Jer 2:13 the fountain of l water.
17:13 the fountain of l water.
Act 7:38 Moses received l messages to
Rom 5:18 and everyone received God's l
1Co 15:45 The last Adam became a l
2Co 2:16 to others we are a l fragrance.
1Pe 3:7 share God's l kindness so that

lifeless (1)

Jer 16:18 my property with the l statues

life's (1)

Psa 27:1 The LORD is my l fortress.

lifestyle (4)

Pro 1:31 They will eat the fruit of their l.
Zep 1:12 satisfied with their hardened l,
Luk 15:13 everything he had on a wild l.
2Pe 2:7 Lot was distressed by the l of

lifestyles (2)

Tit 1:6 wild l or being rebellious.
1Jn 2:16 and extravagant l — comes

lifetime (16)

Gen 26:15 during his father Abraham's l.
26:18 during his father Abraham's l.
Num 3:4 served as priests during the l
Jdg 2:7 the LORD throughout Joshua's l
1Ki 11:12 But I will not do it in your l
21:29 evil on it during his son's l."
Job 4:6 give you confidence and your l
Psa 30:5 His favor lasts a l.
Isa 23:15 for 70 years, the l of one king.
Jer 16:9 This will happen in your l,
17:11 During his l, he will lose his
22:30 He won't prosper in his l.
23:6 In his l, Judah will be saved,
Eze 12:25 and it will happen during your l,
Joe 1:2 has ever happened in your l
1:2 lifetime or in your ancestors' l.

lifetimes (1)

Jdg 2:7 lifetime and throughout the l

lift (28)

Exo 9:22 "L your hand toward the sky,
10:21 "L your hand toward the sky,
2Sm 22:49 You l me up above my
Job 10:15 I dare not l up my head.
Psa 10:12 L your hand, O God. Do not
18:48 You l me up above my
24:7 L your heads, you gates.
24:9 L your heads, you gates.
25:1 To you, O LORD, I l my soul.
28:2 when I l my hands toward your
63:4 I will l up my hands ⌊to pray⌋
76:5 warriors were able to l a hand.
86:4 because I l my soul to you.
119:48 I l my hands ⌊in prayer⌋
134:2 L your hands toward the holy
Isa 10:26 so he will l it as he did in
46:7 They l it on their shoulders and
49:22 I will l my hand ⌊to signal⌋ the
Jer 38:10 and l the prophet Jeremiah out
38:13 pull Jeremiah up and l him out
Lam 2:19 L up your hands to him ⌊in
Nah 3:5 "I will l up your dress over your
Zec 1:21 that no one could l up his head.
12:3 heavy for all the nations to l.
12:3 All who try to l it will be
Mat 12:11 you take hold of it and l it out?
23:4 they are not willing to l a finger
Luk 11:46 But you won't l a finger to carry

lifted (30)

Gen 7:17 The water increased and l the

Gen 45:27 him back, his spirits were l.
Exo 9:23 When Moses l his staff toward
10:22 Moses l his hand toward the
17:16 "Because a hand was l against
1Sm 2:1 My head is l to the LORD.
2Ki 2:16 Maybe the LORD's Spirit l him
Neh 9:5 is praised and l high above all
Job 4:4 you l him up with your words.
Psa 24:7 Be l, you ancient doors, so that
24:9 Be l, you ancient doors, so that
41:9 has l his heel against me.
89:13 Your right hand is l high.
Pro 14:3 words a whip is l against him,
Isa 33:10 Now I will be l up."
Eze 3:12 Then the Spirit l me,
3:14 Then the Spirit l me and took
10:16 When the angels l their wings
10:19 The angels l their wings and
11:1 Then the Spirit l me and took
11:24 the Spirit l me and brought me
43:5 The Spirit l me and brought me
Dan 7:4 plucked off and it was l off
Mat 11:23 will you be l to heaven?
Luk 10:15 will you be l to heaven?
Jon 3:14 "As Moses l up the snake ⌊on
3:14 so the Son of Man must be l up.
8:28 "When you have l up the Son
12:32 When I have been l up from the
12:34 'The Son of Man must be l up

lifting (1)

Psa 141:2 Let the l up of my hands in

lifts (8)

1Sm 2:8 He l the needy from the trash
2:10 gives strength to his King and l
Job 5:11 He l those who mourn to safety.
Psa 107:41 But now he l needy people
113:7 He l the poor from the dust.
113:7 He l the needy from a garbage
Pro 14:34 Righteousness l up a nation,
Isa 10:15 move the person who l it.

ligaments (4)

Job 40:17 The l of its thighs are
Eze 37:6 I will put l on you, and cover
37:8 I saw that l were on them,
Col 2:19 unity given by the joints and l.

light (238)

Gen 1:3 Then God said, "Let there be l!"
1:3 there be light!" So there was l.
1:4 God saw the l was good.
1:4 the l from the darkness.
1:5 God named the l day,
1:16 the larger l to rule the day and
1:16 to rule the day and the smaller l
1:17 in the sky to give l to the earth,
1:18 and to separate the l from the
Exo 10:23 But all the Israelites had l
13:21 fire to give them l so that they
25:37 so that they l up ⌊the area⌋
35:3 Never l a fire in any of your
35:14 the lamp stand used for the l
Num 8:2 they should l up the area in
8:3 lamps on the lamp stand to l up
Jdg 19:26 still there when it became l.
1Sm 14:36 until the l of dawn.
29:10 and leave when it's l."
2Sm 14:20 the matter in a different l.
22:29 LORD turns my darkness into l.
23:4 He is like the morning l as the
2Ki 7:9 until morning when it's l out,
1Ch 17:18 "What more can I do for you in l
Ezr 9:8 Our God has made our eyes l
Neh 9:12 a column of fire to give them l
9:19 but it gave them l to see the
Job 3:4 Let no l shine on it.
3:9 Let it hope for l and receive
3:9 Let it not see the first l of dawn
3:16 infants who never saw the l.
3:20 "Why give l to one in misery
3:23 Why give l to those whose
10:22 confusion where l is as bright
12:22 and brings gloom into the l.
12:25 grope in the dark with no l,
Job 17:12 L has nearly become darkness.
18:5 "Indeed, the l of the wicked is
18:6 The l in his tent becomes dark,
18:18 He will be driven from the l into
22:28 and l will shine on your path.
24:13 those who rebel against the l.
24:16 They do not ⌊even⌋ know the l,
25:3 on whom his l does not rise?
26:10 boundary where l meets dark.
28:11 they bring hidden treasures to l.
29:3 through the dark in his l.
30:26 When I looked for l,
31:26 If I saw the l shine or the moon
33:28 and my life will see the l.'
33:30 enlighten them with the l of life.
37:3 His l flashes to the ends of the
37:22 A golden l comes from the
38:15 people are deprived of their l,
38:19 way to the place where l lives?
38:24 the place where l is scattered
41:18 it gives out a flash of l.
Psa 4:6 Let the l of your presence shine
13:3 L up my eyes, or else I will die
18:28 O LORD, you l my lamp.
18:28 God turns my darkness into l.
26:3 I walk in the l of your truth.
27:1 The LORD is my l and my
36:9 In your l we see light.
36:9 In your light we see l.
37:6 righteousness shine like a l,
38:10 Even the l of my eyes has left
43:3 Send your l and your truth.
44:3 and the l of your presence ⌊that
49:19 who will never see l ⌊again⌋.
56:13 in your presence, in the l of life.
78:14 by a fiery l throughout the night
89:15 They walk in the l of your
90:8 sins in the l of your presence.
97:4 His flashes of lightning l up the
97:11 L dawns for righteous people
104:2 You cover yourself with l as
105:39 and a fire to l up the night.
112:4 L will shine in the dark for a
118:27 and he has given us l.
119:105 for my feet and a l for my path.
119:130 word is a doorway that lets in l,
139:11 me and let the l around me turn
139:12 Darkness and l are the same
Pro 4:18 of righteous people is like the l
6:23 the teachings are a l,
13:9 The l of righteous people
Ecc 2:13 over foolishness as l has
11:7 L is sweet, and it is good for
12:2 before the sun, the l, the moon,
12:3 out of the windows see a dim l.
Isa 2:5 let's live in the l of the LORD.
5:20 who turn darkness into l and
5:20 into light and l into darkness,
5:30 Even the l will be darkened by
9:2 in darkness will see a bright l.
9:2 The l will shine on those who
10:17 Israel's l will become a flame.
13:10 won't show their l anymore.
30:26 Then the l of the moon will be
30:26 of the moon will be like the l
30:26 The l of the sun will be seven
30:26 like the l of seven days.
42:6 as my l to the nations.
42:16 I will turn darkness into l in
45:7 I make l and create darkness.
49:6 I have also made you a l for the
50:10 in darkness and have no l trust
50:11 But all of you l fires and arm
50:11 So walk in your own l and
51:4 will become a l for the people.
58:8 Then your l will break through
58:10 then your l will rise in the dark,
59:9 We hope for l, but we walk in
60:1 Your l has come, and the glory
60:3 Nations will come to your l,
60:19 The sun will no longer be your l
60:19 of the moon give you l,
60:19 will be your everlasting l.
60:20 will be your everlasting l,
Jer 7:18 gather wood, fathers l fires,
13:16 You will look for l,
Jer 25:10 and the l of lamps.
31:35 the sun to be a l during
50:32 I will l a fire in their cities that
Lam 3:2 walk in darkness instead of l.
Eze 1:4 surrounded by a bright l.
1:27 A bright l surrounded him.
24:10 Pile it high, and l the fire.
32:7 "'When I put out your l,
Dan 2:22 and l lives with him.
5:27 a scale and found to be too l.
6:19 At dawn, as soon as it was l,
Hos 6:5 judgments shined on you like l.
Amo 5:18 is one of darkness and not l.
5:20 brings darkness and not l.
5:20 It is pitch black, with no l.
Mic 7:8 in the dark, the LORD is my l.
7:9 He will bring me into the l,
Hab 3:4 Rays of l ⌊stream⌋ from his
3:11 They scatter at the l of your
Zep 3:5 judgment to l every morning.
Zec 14:7 It will be l even in the evening.
Mal 1:10 so that you could not l fires
Mat 4:16 darkness have seen a bright l.
4:16 A l has risen for those who live
5:14 "You are l for the world.
5:15 Then its l shines on everyone
5:16 In the same way let your l
6:22 whole body will be full of l.
6:23 If the l in you is darkness,
11:30 is easy and my burden is l."
17:2 and his clothes as white as l.
24:29 the moon will not give l,
Mar 4:22 secret that will not come to l.
13:24 the moon will not give l,
Luk 1:79 He will give l to those who live
2:9 of the Lord filled the area with l,
2:32 He is a l that will reveal
8:16 who come in will see the l.
8:17 secret that will not come to l.
11:33 who come in will see its l.
11:34 your whole body is full of l.
11:35 So be careful that the l in you
11:36 If your whole body is full of l
12:48 will receive a l beating.
15:8 Doesn't she l a lamp,
Jon 1:4 that life was the l for humanity.
1:5 The l shines in the dark,
1:7 about the l so that everyone
1:8 John was not the l,
1:8 to declare the truth about the l.
1:9 The real l, which shines on
3:19 The l came into the world.
3:19 loved the dark rather than the l
3:20 do what is wrong hate the l
3:20 the light and don't come to the l.
3:21 is true come to the l so that
5:35 a lamp that gave off brilliant l.
5:35 enjoyed the pleasure of his l.
8:12 said, "I am the l of the world.
8:12 me will have a life filled with l
9:5 I'm l for the world."
11:9 they see the l of this world.
11:10 they have no l in themselves."
12:35 "The l will still be with you for
12:35 Walk while you have l so that
12:36 While you have the l,
12:36 believe in the l so that you will
12:36 whose lives show the l."
12:46 I am the l that has come into
Act 9:3 a l from heaven suddenly
12:7 and his cell was filled with l.
13:11 unable to see the l of day."
13:47 'I have made you a l for the
22:6 a bright l from heaven suddenly
22:9 who were with me saw the l
22:11 "I was blind because the l had
26:13 I saw a l that was brighter than
26:13 The l came from the sky and
26:18 turn them from darkness to l
26:23 back to life and would spread l
Rom 2:19 a l to those in the dark,
13:12 weapons that belong to the l.
13:13 people who live in the l of day.
1Co 4:5 He will also bring to l what is
2Co 4:4 As a result, they don't see the l
4:6 said that l should shine out

2Co 4:6 out of darkness has given us l.
4:6 For that reason we bring to l
4:17 Our suffering is l and temporary
6:14 Can l have anything in
11:14 himself as an angel of l.
Eph 5:8 the Lord has filled you with l.
5:8 Live as children who have l.
5:9 L produces everything that is
5:13 L exposes the true character of
5:14 because l makes everything
Col 1:12 made you able to share the l,
1Th 5:5 You belong to the day and the l
1Ti 6:16 He lives in l that no one can
Heb 6:4 Some people once had God's l.
1Pe 2:9 darkness into his marvelous l.
2Pe 1:19 as you would to a l that shines
1Jn 1:5 are reporting to you: God is l,
1:7 But if we live in the l in the
1:7 same way that God is in the l,
2:8 the true l is already shining.
2:9 who say that they are in the l
2:10 other believers live in the l.
2:10 faith of those who live in the l.
Rev 8:12 There was no l for one-third of
18:23 L from lamps will never shine
21:11 Its l was like a valuable gem,
21:23 any sun or moon to give it l
21:23 the glory of God gave it l.
21:24 The nations will walk in its l,
22:5 and they will not need any l

lighten (5)

1Ki 12:4 Reduce the hard work and l the
12:9 people who are asking me to l
2Ch 10:4 Reduce the hard work and l the
10:9 people who are asking me to l
Jnh 1:5 throw the cargo overboard to l

lightened (1)

Act 27:38 they l the ship by dumping the

lighter (1)

Dtr 25:13 a heavier one and a l one.

lightheaded (1)

Isa 29:8 and wake up to find they're l

lighting (1)

Exo 27:20 "For the l, you must command

lightly (1)

2Co 1:17 think that I made these plans l,

lightning (46)

Exo 9:23 and l struck the earth.
9:24 and l flashed while it hailed.
19:16 there was thunder and l with a
20:18 the thunder and saw the l.
2Sm 22:13 in front of him, he made l.
22:15 He flashed streaks of l and
Job 36:30 he scatters his flashes of l
36:32 He fills his hands with l and
37:3 He flashes his l everywhere
37:4 He doesn't hold the l back
37:11 scatters his l from the clouds.
37:15 and makes the l flash from his
38:35 Can you send l flashes so that
Psa 18:12 by with hailstones and l.
18:13 heard with hailstones and l.
18:14 He flashed streaks of l and
29:7 LORD strikes with flashes of l.
77:18 Streaks of l lit up the world.
78:48 bolts of l strike their livestock.
97:4 His flashes of l light up the
105:32 He gave them hail and l
135:7 who makes l for the
144:6 Hurl bolts of l, and scatter them.
148:8 l and hail, snow and fog,
Jer 10:13 He makes l flash with the rain.
51:16 He sends l with the rain.
Eze 1:4 with flashing l surrounded by
1:4 The middle of the l looked like
1:13 and l came out of the fire.
1:14 ran back and forth like l.
21:10 kill and polished to flash like l.
21:15 It's ready to flash like l.
21:28 to destroy and flash like l.
Dan 10:6 His face looked like l.
Nah 2:4 They look like torches, like l,
Hab 3:11 at the bright l of your spear.
Zec 9:14 and his arrow will go out like l.
Mat 24:27 just as l flashes from east
28:3 He was as bright as l,
Luk 10:18 Satan fall from heaven like l.
17:24 will be like l that flashes from
24:4 as l suddenly stood beside
Rev 4:5 L, noise, and thunder came
8:5 noise, l, and an earthquake.
11:19 There was l, noise, thunder,
16:18 There was l, noise, thunder,

lights (14)

Gen 1:14 Then God said, "Let there be l
1:15 They will be l in the sky to
1:16 God made the two bright l:
Exo 30:8 Also, when Aaron l the lamps
Psa 136:7 to the one who made the great l
Jer 4:23 I see the sky. Its l are gone.
31:35 moon and stars to be l during
Eze 32:8 I will darken all the l shining in
Mat 5:15 No one l a lamp and puts it
5:15 Instead, everyone who l a lamp
Luk 8:16 "No one l a lamp and hides it
8:16 Instead, everyone who l a lamp
11:33 "No one l a lamp and hides it or
11:33 Instead, everyone who l a lamp

liked (8)

Gen 25:28 Because Isaac l to eat the
27:14 just the way his father l it.
39:4 Potiphar l Joseph so much that
41:37 and all his servants l the idea.
Est 2:4 The king l the suggestion,
2:15 Everyone who saw Esther l
5:14 Haman l the idea, so he had
Mar 6:20 and yet he l to listen to him.

likeness (8)

Gen 1:26 humans in our image, in our l.
5:1 he made them in the l of God.
5:3 father ⌊of a son⌋ in his own l,
1Co 15:49 As we have worn the l of the
15:49 we will also wear the l of the
Heb 1:3 of God's glory and the exact l
10:1 They aren't an exact l of those
Jas 3:9 who were created in God's l.

likes (2)

Gen 27:9 just the way he l it.
1Sm 18:22 Tell him, 'The king l you,

Likhi (1)

1Ch 7:19 Ahian, Shechem, L, and Aniam.

lilies (6)

Sos 2:16 grazes his flock among the l.
4:5 gazelles grazing among the l.
5:13 His lips are l that drip with
6:2 in the gardens and gather l.
6:3 grazes his flock among the l.
7:2 bundle of wheat enclosed in l.

lily (3)

Sos 2:1 a l ⌊growing⌋ in the valleys.
2:2 Like a l among thorns,
Isa 35:2 Like a l the land will blossom.

lily's (2)

1Ki 7:26 shaped like a l bud.
2Ch 4:5 shaped like a l bud.

lily-shaped (2)

1Ki 7:19 in the entrance hall were l.
7:22 There were l capitals at the top

limb (6)

Jdg 19:29 and cut her l from limb into
19:29 her limb from l into 12 pieces.
Dan 2:5 you will be torn l from limb,
2:5 you will be torn limb from l,
3:29 will be torn l from limb.
3:29 will be torn limb from l.

limber (1)

Gen 49:24 and his arms remained l

limbs (5)

Job 17:7 Now all my l are like a shadow.
18:13 eats away at the l of his body.
41:12 be silent about Leviathan's l,
Ecc 11:5 the breath of life enters the l
Jer 13:22 torn off and your l are bare.

limit (12)

Num 11:23 "Is there a l to the LORD's
Job 14:5 by you, and you set his l,
25:3 Is there any ⌊l to the⌋ number
28:3 ⌊there⌋ and search to the l
38:10 when I set a l for it and put up
Psa 78:41 the Holy One of Israel to the l.
119:96 I have seen a l to everything
119:96 your commandments have no l.
147:5 is no l to his understanding.
Pro 8:29 when he set a l for the sea so
Ecc 5:2 l the number of your words.
Jon 3:34 gives him the Spirit without l.

limited (1)

Lam 3:22 His compassion is never l.

limitless (1)

1Ki 4:29 keen insight and a mind as l as

limits (4)

1Sm 9:27 were going toward the city l,
Job 11:7 able to find the Almighty's l?
Pro 21:24 His arrogance knows no l.
Jer 5:28 Their evil deeds have no l.

limp (6)

Pro 26:7 ⌊Like⌋ a lame person's l legs,
Isa 13:7 is why every hand will hang l,
35:3 Strengthen l hands.
Jer 6:24 Our hands hang l. We are
Eze 7:17 Every hand will hang l,
21:7 People's hands will hang l,

limping (1)

Gen 32:31 He was l because of his hip.

line (51)

Gen 19:32 our family l through our father."
19:34 our family l through our father."
Dtr 25:9 continue his brother's family l."
Jos 22:25 River a dividing l between
Jdg 20:20 their battle l facing Gibeah.
20:22 They formed their battle l
20:30 They formed their battle l
20:33 They formed their battle l at
Rut 4:4 I will know that I am next in l
1Sm 3:14 oath concerning Eli's family l:
4:12 of Benjamin ran from the front l
4:16 I fled from the front l today."
17:2 They formed a battle l to fight
17:8 "Why do you form a battle l?
17:10 "I challenge the Israelite battle l
17:20 to the battle l shouting their war
17:22 ran to the battle l,
17:48 ran toward the opposing battle l
2Sm 10:8 Ammonites formed a battle l at
10:17 The Arameans formed a battle l
11:15 "Put Uriah on the front l where
22:30 you I can attack a l of soldiers.
1Ki 6:15 he began to l the inside walls
13:2 a son born in David's family l.
2Ki 21:13 with the measuring l used
21:13 Samaria and the plumb l used
1Ch 6:33 was from Kohath's family l.
19:9 Ammonites formed a battle l at
19:17 David formed a battle l against
Job 6:4 God's terrors l up in battle
38:5 stretched a measuring l over it?
Psa 18:29 you I can attack a l of soldiers.
Isa 28:17 will make justice a measuring l
28:17 and righteousness a plumb l.
34:11 He will stretch the measuring l
34:11 line of chaos and the plumb l
34:17 for them with a measuring l.

Jer 31:39 A measuring **l** will stretch from
Lam 2:8 He marked it off with a **l**.
Eze 47:3 With a measuring **l** in his hand,
Amo 7:7 built with the use of a plumb **l**,
7:7 he had a plumb **l** in his hand.
7:8 I answered, "A plumb **l**."
7:8 "I'm going to hold a plumb **l** in
Zec 1:16 A measuring **l** will be used to
2:1 with a measuring **l** in his hand.
4:10 when they see the plumb **l**
Act 19:27 will discredit our **l** of work,
27:28 So they threw a **l** with a weight
27:28 This time the **l** sank 90 feet.
1Co 4:9 placed us apostles last in **l**,

lined (1)

Mar 4:1 the entire crowd **l** the shore.

linen (105)

Gen 41:42 dressed in robes of fine **l**
Exo 25:4 red yarn, fine **l**, goats' hair,
26:1 sheets made from fine **l** yarn.
26:31 an angel design into fine **l** yarn.
26:36 a screen out of fine **l** yarn,
27:9 curtains made out of fine **l** yarn,
27:16 screen made from fine **l** yarn,
27:18 with ⌊curtains⌋ made of fine **l**
28:4 another specially woven **l** robe,
28:5 and bright red yarn, and fine **l**.
28:6 the ephod out of fine **l** yarn.
28:15 red yarn and out of fine **l** yarn.
28:39 woven inner robe of fine **l**.
28:39 Make the turban of fine **l**,
28:40 "Also make **l** robes,
28:42 "Make **l** undergarments to
29:5 put them on Aaron — the **l** robe,
29:8 Dress them in their **l** robes,
35:6 red yarn, fine **l**, goats' hair,
35:23 red yarn, fine **l**, goats' hair,
35:25 and bright red yarn, and fine **l**,
35:35 and bright red yarn on fine **l**.
36:8 sheets made from fine **l** yarn
36:35 bright red yarn and fine **l** yarn.
36:37 made a screen out of fine **l** yarn
38:9 curtains made out of fine **l** yarn,
38:16 were made out of fine **l** yarn.
38:18 ⌊fabric made from⌋ fine **l** yarn.
38:23 and bright red yarn on fine **l**.
39:2 the ephod out of fine **l** yarn
39:3 and throughout the fine **l**.
39:8 red yarn, and of fine **l** yarn.
39:27 wove inner robes out of fine **l**
39:28 beautiful turbans out of fine **l**.
39:28 and belt out of fine **l** yarn.
40:14 and dress them in their **l** robes.
Lev 6:10 priest must put on his **l** clothes,
6:10 including his **l** undergarments.
8:7 He put the **l** robe on Aaron and
8:13 He put **l** robes on them,
10:5 men were still in their **l** robes.
13:48 that is woven or knitted from **l**
13:59 that is woven or knitted from **l**
16:4 He must put on a holy **l** robe
16:4 robe and wear **l** undergarments.
16:4 He must wear a **l** belt and
16:23 take off the **l** clothes he had put
16:32 He will put on the holy **l** clothes
Dtr 22:11 of wool and **l** woven together.
Jdg 14:12 I'll give you 30 **l** shirts and 30
1Sm 2:18 ⌊already⌋ wearing a **l** ephod.
22:18 wearing the **l** priestly ephod.
2Sm 6:14 Wearing a **l** ephod,
1Ch 4:21 families of the guild of **l**
15:27 was dressed in a fine **l** robe,
15:27 David also wore a **l** ephod.
2Ch 2:14 violet, and dark red cloth, and **l**.
3:14 and dark red cloth and of **l** and
5:12 were dressed in fine **l**
Est 1:6 had white and violet **l** curtains.
1:6 made of white and purple fine **l**.
8:15 and a purple outer robe of fine **l**.
Pro 7:16 colored sheets of Egyptian **l**.
31:13 "She seeks out wool and **l**
31:22 ⌊made of⌋ **l** and purple cloth.
31:24 "She makes **l** garments and
Isa 22:21 I will dress him in your **l** robe
Jer 13:1 LORD said to me: "Buy a **l** belt.
Eze 9:2 dressed in **l** who was carrying
9:3 dressed in **l** who was carrying
9:11 Then the person dressed in **l**
10:2 said to the person dressed in **l**,
10:6 the person dressed in **l**
10:7 of the person dressed in **l**.
16:10 I dressed you in fine **l** and
16:13 You were dressed in fine **l**,
27:7 fine embroidered **l** from Egypt.
27:16 richly woven cloth, **l**, coral,
40:3 The man was holding a **l** tape
44:17 they must wear **l** clothes.
44:18 They must wear **l** turbans on
44:18 heads and **l** undergarments.
Dan 10:5 I saw a man dressed in **l**,
12:6 dressed in **l** clothes who was
12:7 I heard the man dressed in **l**
Hos 2:5 wool and **l**, olive oil and wine.'
2:9 away the wool and the **l** that
Mat 27:59 wrapped it in a clean **l** cloth.
Mar 14:51 He had nothing on but a **l** sheet.
14:52 but he left the **l** sheet behind
15:46 had purchased some **l** cloth.
Luk 23:53 the cross, he wrapped it in **l**.
24:12 and saw only the strips of **l**.
Jon 19:40 and bound it with strips of **l**.
20:5 He saw the strips of **l** lying
20:6 saw the strips of **l** lying there.
20:7 wasn't lying with the strips of **l**
Act 10:11 a large **l** sheet being lowered
11:5 I saw something like a large **l**
Rev 15:6 shining **l** with gold belts around
18:12 pearls, fine **l**, purple cloth, silk,
18:16 city which was wearing fine **l**,
19:8 of wearing dazzling, pure **l**."
19:8 This fine **l** represents the
19:14 heaven, wearing pure, white **l**,

linenworkers (1)

Isa 19:9 **L** and weavers will be

lines (11)

Jos 8:22 between the battle **l** of Israel.
1Sm 17:21 their battle **l** facing each other.
17:23 came from the battle **l** of the
17:25 coming ⌊from the Philistine **l**⌋?
2Ki 8:21 broke through their **l**,
2Ch 14:10 two armies set up their battle **l**
21:9 night and broke through their **l**.
Psa 16:6 Your boundary **l** mark out
Isa 19:8 All who cast their **l** into the
44:13 blocks of wood with ⌊chalk⌋ **l**.
Joe 2:8 They keep in their own **l**.

lingering (1)

Dtr 28:59 and severe and **l** diseases.

link (4)

Exo 26:6 Use them to **l** the ⌊two sets of⌋
26:11 put them through the loops to **l**
36:13 They used them to **l** the ⌊two
36:18 made 50 bronze fasteners to **l**

Linus (1)

2Ti 4:21 Eubulus, Pudens, **L**,

lion (81)

Gen 49:9 Judah, you are a **l** cub.
49:9 He lies down and rests like a **l**.
Num 23:24 and is as ferocious as a **l**.
24:9 lie down ⌊and⌋ rest like a **l**.
Dtr 33:20 They wait there like a **l**.
33:22 "The people of Dan are a **l** cub.
Jdg 14:5 a young roaring **l** met Samson.
14:6 he tore the **l** apart as if it were a
14:8 he left the road to look at the **l**
14:18 What is stronger than a **l**?"
1Sm 17:34 Whenever a **l** or a bear came
17:37 who saved me from the **l** and
2Sm 17:10 a heart like a **l** would lose his
23:20 went into a pit and killed a **l**
1Ki 13:24 A **l** found him ⌊as he traveled⌋
13:24 The donkey and the **l** were
13:25 the road and the **l** standing by
13:26 The LORD gave him to the **l**.
1Ki 13:28 and the **l** standing beside it.
13:28 The **l** had not eaten the body,
20:36 a **l** will kill you when you leave
20:36 a **l** found him and killed him.
1Ch 11:22 into a cistern and killed a **l**
Job 4:10 Though the roar of the **l** and the
4:10 of the ferocious **l** ⌊is loud⌋,
10:16 ferocious **l** you hunt me down.
28:8 No ferocious **l** has ever passed
Psa 7:2 Like a **l** they will tear me to
10:9 lies in his hiding place like a **l**
17:12 Each one of them is like a **l**
17:12 and like a young **l** crouching
22:21 Save me from the mouth of the **l**
Pro 19:12 of a king is like the roar of a **l**,
20:2 of a king is like the roar of a **l**.
22:13 "There's a **l** outside!
26:13 "There's a ferocious **l** out on
26:13 There's a **l** loose in the streets!"
28:15 ⌊Like⌋ a roaring **l** and a
30:30 a **l**, mightiest among animals,
Ecc 9:4 dog is better than a dead **l**.
Isa 5:29 They growl like a young **l**.
15:9 A **l** will attack the fugitives
31:4 to me: A **l**, even a young lion,
31:4 to me: A lion, even a young **l**,
38:13 I cried out until morning as if a **l**
Jer 2:30 my prophets like a raging **l**.
4:7 A **l** has come out of its lair.
5:6 That is why a **l** from the forest
12:8 have turned on me like a **l**
25:38 He has left his lair like a **l**.
49:19 their places like a **l** coming out
50:44 their places like a **l** coming out
51:38 lions and growling **l** cubs.
Lam 3:10 ambush me, like a **l** in hiding.
Eze 1:10 each one had the face of a **l**.
10:14 the third was the face of a **l**,
19:3 she raised became a young **l**.
19:5 and raised him into a young **l**.
19:6 He became a young **l**,
32:2 'You think you are like a **l**
41:19 and the face of a **l**,
Dan 7:4 The first animal was like a **l**,
Hos 5:14 I will be like a **l** to Ephraim and
5:14 to Ephraim and like a young **l**
11:10 follow me when I roar like a **l**.
13:7 So I will be like a **l**.
13:8 Like a **l** I will devour you.
Amo 3:4 Does a **l** roar in the forest if it
3:4 Does a young **l** growl in its den
3:8 The **l** has roared. Who isn't
5:19 person who flees from a **l** only
Mic 5:8 They will be like a **l** among
5:8 like a young **l** among flocks of
5:8 When a **l** hunts, it tramples ⌊its
Nah 2:11 Where are the **l**, the lioness,
2:11 and the **l** cub who moved about
2:12 The **l** tore its prey to pieces to
1Pe 5:8 around like a roaring **l** as
Rev 4:7 first living creature was like a **l**,
5:5 The **L** from the tribe of Judah,
10:3 in a loud voice as a **l** roars.

lioness (9)

Gen 49:9 He is like a **l**. Who dares to
Num 23:24 is a nation that attacks like a **l**
24:9 They are like a **l**. Who dares to
Job 4:11 the cubs of the **l** are scattered.
38:39 "Can you hunt prey for the **l**
Isa 5:29 They roar like a **l**. They growl
Eze 19:2 Say: Your mother was like a **l**.
19:5 The **l** waited until she saw that
Nah 2:11 Where are the lion, the **l**,

lionesses (1)

Isa 30:6 Lions and **l** live there.

lion's (5)

Jdg 14:8 some honey in the **l** dead body.
14:9 it out of the **l** dead body.
Amo 3:12 of an ear out of a **l** mouth, so
2Ti 4:17 I was snatched out of a **l** mouth
Rev 13:2 Its mouth was like a **l** mouth.

lions (48)

1Sm 17:36 I have killed **l** and bears,
2Sm 1:23 than eagles and stronger than **l**.
1Ki 7:29 the panels set in frames were **l**,
7:29 Above and below the **l** and the
7:36 Hiram engraved angels, **l**,
10:19 Two **l** stood beside the
10:20 Twelve **l** stood on six steps,
2Ki 17:25 So the LORD sent **l** to kill
17:26 of that country, so he sent **l**.
17:26 Now the **l** are killing them
1Ch 12:8 They looked like **l** and were as
2Ch 9:18 Two **l** stood beside the
9:19 Twelve **l** stood on six steps,
Job 4:10 the young **l** have had their teeth
4:11 The old **l** die without any prey
Psa 22:13 me like ferocious, roaring **l**.
34:10 Young **l** go hungry and may
35:17 my precious life from the **l**.
57:4 My soul is surrounded by **l**.
57:4 lie down with man-eating **l**.
91:13 You will step on **l** and cobras.
91:13 trample young **l** and snakes.
104:21 The young **l** roar for their prey
Pro 28:1 people are as bold as **l**.
Sos 4:8 and Hermon, from the lairs of **l**,
Isa 11:6 Calves, young **l**, and year-old
11:7 **L** will eat straw like oxen.
30:6 **L** and lionesses live there.
35:9 **L** won't be there. Wild animals
65:25 **l** will eat straw like oxen,
Jer 2:15 Young **l** have roared very
2:15 Young **l** have turned the land
50:17 sheep that **l** have chased.
51:38 Its people are like roaring **l** and
Eze 19:2 She lay down among the **l**.
19:6 and he prowled among the **l**.
22:25 Your princes are like roaring **l**
Dan 6:20 able to save you from the **l**?
6:24 the **l** attacked them and
6:27 He saved Daniel from the **l**.
Joe 1:6 They have teeth like **l**.
1:6 They have fangs like grown **l**.
Nah 2:11 that feeding place for young **l**?
2:13 a sword will kill your young **l**.
Zep 3:3 Its officials are ⌊like⌋ roaring **l**.
Zec 11:3 The young **l** are roaring,
Heb 11:33 They shut the mouths of **l**,
Rev 9:17 The horses had heads like **l**.

lions' (9)

Psa 58:6 the young **l** teeth, O LORD.
Dan 6:7 will be thrown into a **l** den
6:12 will be thrown into a **l** den?"
6:16 him and thrown into the **l** den.
6:19 and quickly went to the **l** den
6:22 shut the **l** mouths so that they
6:24 were thrown into the **l** den.
Nah 2:11 Where is the **l** den, that feeding
Rev 9:8 hair and teeth like **l** teeth

lip (1)

Psa 12:3 LORD cut off every flattering **l**

lips (78)

Exo 23:13 or let them be heard on your **l**.
Lev 13:45 They must cover their upper **l**
1Sm 1:13 only her **l** were moving.
Job 2:10 Through all this Job's **l** did not
8:21 and your **l** with happy shouting.
15:6 Your **l** testify against you.
16:5 and my quivering **l** could ease
27:4 my **l** will not say anything
33:3 the knowledge that is on my **l**.
Psa 12:2 They speak with flattering **l**.
12:4 With **l** such as ours,
16:4 offerings of blood or use my **l**
17:1 comes⌋ from **l** free from deceit.
21:2 not refuse the prayer from his **l**.
31:18 ⌊their⌋ lying **l** be speechless,
34:13 your **l** from speaking deceitful
40:9 I will not close my **l**.
45:2 Grace is poured on your **l**.
51:15 O Lord, open my **l**,
59:7 mouths — swords from their **l**!
Psa 59:12 and the words on their **l**.
63:3 My **l** will praise you because
63:5 sing ⌊your⌋ praise with joyful **l**.
66:14 the vows made by my **l** and
71:23 My **l** will sing with joy when I
119:13 With my **l** I have repeated
119:171 Let my **l** pour out praise
120:2 LORD, rescue me from lying **l**
140:3 Their **l** hide the venom of
141:3 watch over the door of my **l**.
Pro 4:24 speech far away from your **l**.
5:3 The **l** of an adulterous woman
7:21 With her smooth **l**,
8:6 and my **l** will say what is right.
8:7 is disgusting to my **l**.
10:13 Wisdom is found on the **l** of a
10:18 conceals hatred has lying **l**.
10:19 whoever seals his **l** is wise.
10:21 The **l** of a righteous person
10:32 The **l** of a righteous person
12:22 **L** that lie are disgusting to the
14:7 receive knowledge from his **l**.
15:7 The **l** of wise people spread
16:10 revelation is on a king's **l**,
16:30 Whoever bites his **l** has
17:4 pays attention to wicked **l**.
17:28 if he keeps his **l** sealed.
18:7 His **l** are a trap to his soul.
20:15 but the **l** of knowledge are
24:2 and their **l** talk trouble.
24:26 is ⌊like⌋ a kiss on the **l**.
24:28 and do not deceive with your **l**.
27:2 and not from your own **l**.
Ecc 10:12 a fool's **l** are self-destructive.
Sos 4:3 Your **l** are like scarlet thread.
4:11 Your **l** drip honey, my bride.
5:13 His **l** are lilies that drip with
7:9 beloved and glides over the **l**
Isa 6:5 passes through my **l** is sinful.
6:5 live among people with sinful **l**.
6:7 "This has touched your **l**.
11:4 with the breath from his **l**.
29:13 and honor me with their **l**.
30:27 His **l** are filled with fury.
57:19 I'll create praise on their **l**:
Jer 7:28 and vanished from their **l**.'
12:2 speak well of you with their **l**,
Dan 10:16 like a human touched my **l**.
Hos 14:2 we'll praise you with our **l**.
Hab 3:16 At the report my **l** quivered.
Zep 3:9 I will give all people pure **l**
Mal 2:6 unjust was found on his **l**.
2:7 "A priest's **l** should preserve
Mat 15:8 people honor me with their **l**,
Mar 7:6 people honor me with their **l**,
Luk 4:22 words flowing from his **l**.
Rom 3:13 Their **l** hide the venom of
1Pe 3:10 and their **l** from speaking

liquid (5)

Lev 11:34 Any **l** that you drink from that
19:35 length, weight, or measuring **l**.
Sos 5:5 were drenched with **l** myrrh,
Eze 45:10 and honest dry and **l** measures.
45:11 The dry and **l** measures must

liquor (19)

Lev 10:9 any wine or **l** when you go
Num 6:3 must never drink wine, **l**,
6:3 vinegar made from wine or **l**,
Dtr 14:26 **l** — whatever you choose.
29:6 bread and drank no wine or **l**.
Jdg 13:4 Don't drink any wine or **l** or eat
13:7 So don't drink any wine or **l** or
13:14 drink any wine or **l**,
Pro 20:1 **l** ⌊makes them⌋ noisy,
31:4 wine or for rulers to crave **l**.
31:6 Give **l** to a person who is dying
Isa 24:9 **L** tastes bad to its drinkers.
28:7 and wobble from too much **l**.
28:7 They stagger from too much **l**
28:7 They wobble because of their **l**.
29:9 You stagger, but not from **l**.
56:12 and we'll fill ourselves with **l**.
Mic 2:11 to you about wine and **l**."
Luk 1:15 never drink wine or any other **l**.

list (19)

Num 1:2 **L** every man by name
1:3 **L** them by divisions.
3:1 This is the **l** of Aaron and
3:40 and make a **l** of their names.
4:2 **L** them by families and
4:22 **L** them by households and
11:26 They were on the **l** with the
26:2 **L** those who are at least 20
26:53 must be divided using the **l**
33:1 This is a **l** of all the places
33:2 as they traveled. This is the **l**:
1Ch 1:29 This is their **l** of descendants:
25:1 This is the **l** of the men who
27:1 This is a **l** of Israelite family
Ezr 1:8 So Mithredath made a **l** of them
Psa 87:4 and Sudan to the **l** of those
Mat 1:1 This is the **l** of ancestors of
1Ti 5:9 be put on your **l** ⌊of widows⌋.
5:11 younger widows ⌊on your **l**⌋.

listed (39)

Gen 10:32 sons **l** by their genealogies,
25:13 names of the sons of Ishmael **l**
25:16 names **l** by their settlements
36:43 the tribal leaders of Edom **l** by
48:6 They will inherit the land **l**
Exo 6:16 the names of the sons of Levi **l**
6:17 The sons of Gershon **l** by their
6:19 from Levi **l** in birth order.
6:25 households **l** by their families.
Num 1:18 Then his name was **l**.
1:20 **l** every man by name who was
1:22 registered and **l** every man by
1:24 for the descendants of Gad **l**
1:26 for the descendants of Judah **l**
1:28 the descendants of Issachar **l**
1:30 the descendants of Zebulun **l**
1:32 those from Ephraim — **l**
1:34 the descendants of Manasseh **l**
1:36 the descendants of Benjamin **l**
1:38 for the descendants of Dan **l**
1:40 for the descendants of Asher **l**
1:42 the descendants of Naphtali **l**
3:43 They were **l** by name.
4:36 They were **l** by families.
4:40 They were **l** by families and
4:44 They were **l** by families.
4:46 They were **l** by families and
14:29 who were registered and **l**,
26:57 descended from Levi were **l** as
Jos 17:2 Manasseh **l** by their families.
1Ch 4:41 the men **l** here knocked down
5:1 However, Joseph couldn't be **l**
8:28 of families **l** by their ancestry.
2Ch 17:14 They are **l** by families.
31:19 families and to everyone **l**
35:4 which are **l** in the records of
Ezr 8:20 These were all **l** by name.
10:16 (They were all ⌊**l**⌋ by name.)
Psa 69:28 be **l** with righteous people.

listen (474)

Gen 4:23 "Adah and Zillah, **l** to me!
21:12 **L** to what Sarah says because
23:6 "**L** to us, sir. You are a mighty
23:8 to let me bury my wife, **l** to me.
23:11 "No, sir, **l** to me. I'm giving you
23:13 "If you would only **l** to me.
23:15 "Sir, **l** to me. The land is worth
27:8 Now **l** to me, Son,
30:27 Laban replied, "**L** to me.
37:6 "Please **l** to the dream I had.
37:9 "**L**," he said, "I had another
42:21 us for mercy, but we wouldn't **l**.
42:22 But you wouldn't **l**.
49:2 "Gather around and **l**,
49:2 **L** to your father Israel.
Exo 3:18 leaders of Israel will **l** to you.
4:1 never believe me or **l** to me!"
4:9 miraculous signs or **l** to you,
5:9 will be too busy to **l** to lies."
6:9 But they would not **l** to him
6:12 "The Israelites wouldn't **l** to me.
6:12 Why would Pharaoh **l** to me?

Exo	6:30	"Why would Pharaoh l to me?"
	7:4	Pharaoh will not l to you.
	7:13	and would not l to them,
	7:22	to be stubborn and would not l
	8:15	stubborn and would not l
	8:19	to be stubborn and would not l
	9:12	so he wouldn't l to Moses and
	11:9	"Pharaoh will not l to you.
	15:26	He said, "If you will l carefully
	16:20	some of them didn't l to Moses.
	18:19	Now l to me, and I'll give you
	20:19	"You speak to us, and we'll l.
	22:27	When he cries out to me, I will l
	23:21	attention to him, and l to him.
	23:22	But if you will l to him and do
Lev	26:14	"If you will not l to me and
	26:18	"If you still will not l to me,
	26:21	"If you resist and don't l to me,
	26:27	"If in spite of this you do not l
Num	12:6	He said, "L to my words:
	13:30	to be quiet and l to Moses.
	16:8	Moses also said to Korah, "L,
	20:10	said to them, "L, you rebels,
	23:18	"Stand up, Balak, and l!
Dtr	1:17	L to the least important people
	1:17	people the same way you l
	1:43	I told you, but you wouldn't l.
	1:45	but the LORD didn't l to you or
	3:26	so he wouldn't l to me.
	4:1	Israel, l to the laws and rules I
	5:1	l to the laws and rules I'm
	5:27	⌊Moses,⌋ go and l to
	5:27	tells you. We'll l and obey."
	6:3	L, Israel, and be careful to obey
	6:4	L, Israel: The LORD is our God.
	7:12	If you l to these rules and
	9:1	L, Israel, you're about to cross
	13:2	But don't l to that prophet or
	13:4	l to what he says, serve him,
	13:8	of these people or l to them.
	13:18	God will do this if you l to him,
	15:5	He will bless you only if you l
	18:14	nations you are forcing out l
	18:15	You must l to him.
	18:19	Whoever refuses to l to the
	20:3	He should tell them, "L,
	21:18	he still won't l to them.
	23:5	God refused to l to Balaam.
	26:17	and rules, and l to him.
	27:9	Israel, "Be quiet and l, Israel.
	30:17	and you might not l.
	31:12	Have them l and learn to fear
	31:28	As they l, I will speak these
	32:1	L, heaven, and I will speak.
Jos	3:9	and l to the words of the LORD
	24:10	But I refused to l to Balaam.
Jdg	2:17	But the people wouldn't l to the
	5:3	L, you kings! Open your ears,
	5:11	L to the voices of those singing
	5:16	Was it to l to the shepherds
	7:11	L to what people are saying.
	9:7	He shouted to them, "L to me,
	9:7	so that God might l to you.
	11:17	of Edom wouldn't l to them.
	11:28	But the king of Ammon didn't l
	19:25	But the men refused to l to him.
	20:13	men of Benjamin refused to l
Rut	2:8	Boaz said to Ruth, "L,
1Sm	2:25	But they wouldn't l to their
	8:7	The LORD told Samuel, "L to
	8:9	L to them now, but be sure to
	8:19	people refused to l to Samuel.
	8:22	The LORD told him, "L to them,
	13:3	Saul announced, "L, Hebrews!"
	14:8	Jonathan continued, "L,
	15:1	Now l to the LORD's words.
	22:7	He said to his officials, "L here,
	22:12	Saul said, "L here,
	24:9	"Why do you l to rumors that I
	25:24	Please l to my words.
	26:19	please l to my words.
	28:18	you today because you didn't l
	28:22	Now please l to me.
2Sm	12:18	and he wouldn't l to us.
	13:14	But Amnon wouldn't l to her.
	13:16	But he wouldn't l to her.
2Sm	14:16	Maybe the king will l and
	20:16	called from the city, "L, listen!
	20:16	called from the city, "Listen, l!
	20:17	"L to what I have to say,"
1Ki	8:28	L to my cry for help as I pray to
	8:29	L to me as I pray toward this
	8:52	Israel's plea so that you will l
	10:24	The whole world wanted to l to
	12:15	The king refused to l to the
	12:16	the king refused to l to them,
	20:8	people told him, "Don't l to him.
2Ki	7:1	"L to the word of the LORD!
	10:6	my side and ready to l to me,
	14:11	But Amaziah wouldn't l.
	17:14	But they refused to l.
	17:40	people of Israel had refused to l
	18:28	"L to the great king,
	18:31	Don't l to Hezekiah,
	18:32	Don't l to Hezekiah when he
	19:16	ear toward me, LORD, and l.
	19:16	L to the message that
	22:19	So I will l ⌊to you⌋,
1Ch	28:2	of them and said, "L to me,
2Ch	6:19	L to my cry for help as I pray to
	6:20	L to me as I pray toward this
	9:7	of you and l to your wisdom!
	9:23	kings of the world wanted to l
	10:15	The king refused to l to the
	10:16	the king refused to l to them,
	13:4	and all Israel, l to me!
	15:2	Asa and said to him, "L to me,
	20:20	stopped and said, "L to me,
	24:19	but they wouldn't l.
	25:16	you refuse to l to my advice."
	25:20	But Amaziah wouldn't l.
	28:11	L to me. Return these prisoners
	29:5	He said to them, "L to me,
	34:27	So I will l ⌊to you⌋,
	35:22	He refused to l to Neco's words,
Neh	8:11	all the people by saying, "L.
	9:17	They refused to l. They forgot
	9:29	to deal with, and wouldn't l.
	9:30	However, they wouldn't l.
Job	5:27	L to it, and learn it for yourself."
	9:16	believe that he would l to me.
	13:6	Please l to my argument,
	13:17	"L carefully to my words.
	15:8	Did you l in on God's council
	15:17	"I'll tell you; l to me!
	21:2	"L carefully to my words,
	22:27	and he will l to you,
	31:35	someone who would l to me!
	32:10	"That is why I say, 'L to me!
	33:1	"Please, Job, l to my words
	33:31	L to me! Keep quiet, and let me
	33:33	If not, you l to me. Keep quiet,
	34:2	"L to my words, you wise men.
	34:10	have understanding, l to me.
	34:16	"If you understand, l to this.
	34:34	the wise people who l to me,
	35:13	"Surely, God doesn't l to idle
	36:10	He makes them l to his
	36:11	"If righteous people l and serve
	36:12	But if they don't l, they will
	37:2	L! Listen to the roar of God's
	37:2	L to the roar of God's voice,
	39:7	of the city and doesn't ⌊even⌋ l
	42:4	"⌊You said,⌋ 'L now,
Psa	34:11	Come, children, l to me.
	39:12	L to my prayer, O LORD.
	45:10	L, daughter! Look closely!
	49:1	L to this, all you people.
	50:7	"L, my people, and I will
	50:7	L, Israel, and I will testify
	55:19	God will l. The one who has sat
	61:1	L to my cry for help,
	66:16	Come and l, all who fear God,
	68:33	L! He makes his voice heard,
	81:8	L, my people, and I will warn
	81:8	if you would only l to me!
	81:11	"But my people did not l to me.
	81:13	only my people would l to me!
	95:7	only you would l to him today!
	141:6	they will l to what I have to
	143:1	O LORD, l to my prayer.
Pro	1:5	a wise person will l and
Pro	1:8	l to your father's discipline,
	1:24	"I called, and you refused to l.
	4:1	l to ⌊your⌋ father's discipline,
	4:10	son, l and accept my words,
	5:7	But now, sons, l to me,
	5:13	I didn't l to what my teachers
	7:24	Now, sons, l to me.
	8:6	L! I am speaking about noble
	8:32	"Now, sons, l to me.
	8:33	L to discipline, and become
	13:1	does not l to reprimands.
	19:20	L to advice and accept
	23:12	and l carefully to words of
	23:19	My son, l, be wise, and keep
	23:22	L to your father since you are
	28:9	of someone who refuses to l
Ecc	5:1	It is better to go there and l than
	7:5	It is better to l to wise people
Sos	5:2	L! My beloved is knocking.
Isa	1:2	L, heaven, and pay attention,
	1:10	L to the word of the LORD,
	1:15	I will not l because your hands
	6:9	'No matter how closely you l,
	7:13	"L now, descendants of
	8:9	L, all you distant parts of the
	13:4	L to the noise on the
	18:3	L when someone blows a
	28:12	But they weren't willing to l.
	28:23	Open your ears, and l to me!
	30:9	children who refuse to l to the
	32:9	Get up, and l to me,
	33:15	He refuses to l to those who
	34:1	Come close, you nations, and l.
	34:1	and everything on it will l.
	36:13	"L to the great king,
	36:16	Don't l to Hezekiah,
	37:17	ear toward me, LORD, and l.
	37:17	L to the entire message that
	41:1	"Be silent and l to me,
	42:18	L, you deaf people. Look,
	42:23	Who among you will l to this?
	42:23	attention and l in the future?
	44:1	But now l, my servant Jacob,
	46:3	L to me, descendants of Jacob,
	46:12	L to me, you stubborn people
	47:8	Now then, l to this,
	48:1	L to this, descendants of
	48:12	L to me, Jacob, Israel, whom I
	48:14	together, all of you, and l.
	48:16	L to this: From the beginning I
	49:1	L to me, you islands.
	50:4	wake me to l like a student.
	51:1	L to me, you people who
	51:7	L to me, you people who know
	51:21	L to this, you humble people
	52:8	L! Your watchmen raise their
	55:1	"L! Whoever is thirsty, come to
	55:2	L carefully to me: Eat what is
	55:3	L so that you may live!
	65:12	I spoke, but you didn't l.
	66:4	I spoke, but they didn't l.
	66:5	L to the word of the LORD,
	66:6	L to the uproar from the city.
	66:6	L to the sound from the temple.
Jer	2:4	L to the word of the LORD,
	6:10	Who will l? Their ears are
	6:18	L, you nations, and learn,
	6:19	L, earth! I'm going to bring
	7:2	'L to the word of the LORD,
	7:13	again and again, you did not l.
	7:16	because I will not l to you.
	9:20	L to the word of the LORD,
	10:1	L to the message that the
	11:2	"L to the terms of this promise,
	11:3	Cursed is anyone who doesn't l
	11:6	L to the terms of this promise,
	11:11	cry out to me, I won't l to them.
	11:14	I won't l when they call to me
	12:17	But suppose they don't l.
	13:10	people refuse to l to me.
	13:11	However, they wouldn't l.
	13:15	L, and pay attention! Don't be
	13:17	If you won't l, I will cry secretly
	14:12	I won't l to their cries for help.
	17:20	"L to the word of the LORD,
	17:23	not l or accept discipline.

Jer 17:24 "you must **l** to me and not bring
17:27 But you must **l** to me and
18:19 and **l** to what my accusers say.
19:3 "**L** to the word of the LORD,
21:11 '**L** to the word of the LORD,
22:2 "**L** to the word of the LORD,
22:21 but you said that you wouldn't **l**.
22:21 were young. You don't **l** to me.
22:29 **L** to the word of the LORD.
23:16 Don't **l** to what the prophets are
25:8 You did not **l** to my words,
26:3 Maybe they'll **l**, and they'll turn
26:4 Suppose you don't **l** to me and
26:5 Suppose you don't **l** to the
26:5 even though you didn't **l**.
26:13 and **l** to the LORD your God.
27:9 Don't **l** to prophets,
27:14 Don't **l** to the prophets who tell
27:16 Don't **l** to the prophets who tell
27:17 Don't **l** to them. Instead, serve
28:7 But now **l** to this message that
28:15 Hananiah, "Now **l**, Hananiah,
29:8 Don't even **l** to your own
29:19 They didn't **l** to me,
29:19 but they refused to **l**,
29:20 So **l** to the word of the LORD,
31:10 **l** to the word of the LORD.
32:33 but they refused to **l** and learn.
34:4 "**L** to the word of the LORD,
34:14 refused to obey me or **l** to me.
35:14 but you have refused to **l** to me.
35:15 However, you refused to **l** to
35:16 but you refuse to **l** to me.
35:17 to them, but they didn't **l**.
36:25 he refused to **l** to them.
36:31 They refused to **l**. So I will bring
37:2 and the common people didn't **l**
37:14 But Irijah wouldn't **l** to him.
37:20 now, Your Majesty, please **l**,
38:15 you won't **l** to me."
42:2 "Please **l** to our request,
42:15 **l** to the word of the LORD,
43:7 They didn't **l** to the LORD,
44:5 But you wouldn't **l** or pay
44:16 "We won't **l** to the message
44:24 "**L** to the word of the LORD,
44:26 But **l** to the word of the LORD,
49:20 **L** to the plans that the LORD is
50:28 **L**! Fugitives and refugees from
50:45 **L** to the plans that the LORD is
Lam 1:18 Please **l**, all you people,
3:56 **L** to my cry ⌊for help⌋.
3:61 **L** to their insults, all their plots
Eze 2:5 these rebellious people **l** or not,
2:7 to them whether they **l** or not,
2:8 son of man, **l** to what I say.
3:6 they will certainly **l** to you.
3:7 people of Israel will refuse to **l**
3:7 because they refuse to **l** to me.
3:10 spoken to you, and **l** closely.
3:11 Whether they **l** or not,
3:17 **L** to what I say, and warn them
3:27 Some will **l**, and some will
3:27 and some will refuse to **l**.
6:3 **l** to the word of the Almighty
8:18 in my ears, I won't **l** to them."
13:2 '**L** to the word of the LORD.
13:19 my people who are willing to **l**.
16:35 "'**L** to the word of the LORD,
18:25 **L**, nation of Israel, isn't my way
20:8 me and refused to **l** to me.
20:39 you will not **l** to me.
20:47 '**L** to the word of the LORD.
25:3 Tell the Ammonites, '**L** to the
33:7 **L** to what I say, and warn them
33:31 They **l** to what you say,
33:32 They **l** to your words,
34:7 **l** to the word of the LORD.
34:9 **l** to the word of the LORD.
36:1 **l** to the word of the LORD.
36:4 "'Mountains of Israel, **l** to the
37:4 **l** to the word of the LORD.
40:4 and **l** with your ears.
44:5 Look, and **l** to everything I'm
44:5 **L** to all the rules and
Dan 4:31 Nebuchadnezzar, **l** to this:
Dan 9:11 and refused to **l** to you.
9:17 **l** to my prayer and request.
9:18 Open your ears and **l**,
9:19 **L** to us, Lord. Forgive us, Lord.
Hos 4:1 **L** to the word of the LORD,
5:1 "**L** to this, you priests!
9:17 they refused to **l** to him.
Joe 1:2 **L** to this, you leaders!
Amo 3:1 **L** to this message which I,
3:13 **L**, and testify against the
4:1 **L** to this message,
5:1 **L** to this message,
5:23 I won't **l** to the music of your
7:16 "Now **l** to the word of the
8:4 **L** to this, those who trample on
Mic 1:2 **L**, all you people! earth and all
3:1 Then I said: **L**, you leaders of
3:9 **L** to this, you leaders of the
6:1 Now **l** to what the LORD is
6:1 let the hills **l** to your request.
6:2 **L** to the LORD's lawsuit,
6:2 **L**, you strong foundations of the
6:9 "**L**, you tribe assembled in the
7:7 will wait for my God to **l** to me.
Hab 1:2 cry for help, but you will not **l**?
Zep 1:14 **L**! Warriors will cry out bitterly
2:14 **L**! A bird will sing in a window.
Zec 1:4 But they didn't **l** or pay attention
3:8 "**L**, Chief Priest Joshua and
7:13 "When I called, they wouldn't **l**.
7:13 now when they call, I won't **l**,
11:3 **L**! The shepherds are crying,
11:3 **L**! The young lions are roaring,
Mal 2:2 If you won't **l** and if you won't
Mat 10:11 look for people who will **l** to
10:14 doesn't welcome you or **l**
11:15 Let the person who has ears **l**!
13:3 He said, "**L**! A farmer went to
13:9 Let the person who has ears **l**!"
13:13 They hear, but they don't **l**.
13:18 "**L** to what the story about the
13:43 Let the person who has ears **l**!
15:10 "**L** and try to understand!
17:5 whom I am pleased. **L** to him!"
18:16 But if he does not **l**,
21:33 "**L** to another illustration.
24:25 **L**! I've told you this before it
Mar 4:3 "**L**! A farmer went to plant seed.
4:9 the person who has ears **l**!"
4:23 Let the person who has ears **l**!"
6:11 don't welcome you or **l** to you,
6:20 and yet he liked to **l** to him.
7:14 to them, "**L** to me, all of you,
7:16 Let the person who has ears **l**!"
9:7 whom I love. **L** to him!"
12:29 most important is, '**L**, Israel,
15:35 him say that, they said, "**L**!
Luk 8:8 the person who has ears **l**!"
8:18 "So pay attention to how you **l**!
9:35 I have chosen. **L** to him!"
9:44 "**L** carefully to what I say.
14:35 the person who has ears **l**!"
15:1 and sinners came to **l** to Jesus.
16:29 Your brothers should **l** to them!'
16:31 'If they won't **l** to Moses'
22:31 Lord said,⌋ "Simon, Simon, **l**!
Jon 5:24 Those who **l** to what I say and
5:30 As I **l** ⌊to the Father⌋,
6:60 wants to **l** to him anymore?"
9:27 told you, but you didn't **l**.
9:31 that God doesn't **l** to sinners.
10:20 Why do you **l** to him?"
Act 2:22 "Men of Israel, **l** to what I say:
3:22 **L** to everything he tells you.
3:23 Those who won't **l** to that
4:19 whether God wants people to **l**
7:2 "Brothers and fathers, **l** to me.
7:57 shouted and refused to **l**.
10:33 now in the presence of God to **l**
13:16 converts to Judaism, **l** to me.
15:13 responded, "Brothers, **l** to me.
22:1 "Brothers and fathers, **l** as I
24:4 Please **l** to us. We will be brief.
26:3 I ask you to **l** patiently to me.
28:28 are not Jews. They will **l**."
Rom 2:13 People who merely **l** to laws
1Co 14:21 even then they will not **l** to me,
2Co 6:2 **L**, now is God's acceptable
2Th 3:14 be that some people will not **l**
2Ti 4:3 come when people will not **l**
4:4 People will refuse to **l** to the
Heb 11:7 Faith led Noah to **l** when God
12:25 refuse to **l** when God speaks.
12:25 when they refused to **l** to God,
13:22 to **l** patiently to my encouraging
Jas 1:19 Everyone should be quick to **l**,
1:22 Don't merely **l** to it,
1:25 that don't merely **l** and forget;
2:5 **L**, my dear brothers and sisters!
1Jn 4:6 belong to God doesn't **l** to us.
Rev 2:7 "Let the person who has ears **l**
2:11 Let the person who has ears **l**
2:17 Let the person who has ears **l**
2:29 Let the person who has ears **l**
3:6 Let the person who has ears **l**
3:13 Let the person who has ears **l**
3:22 Let the person who has ears **l**
13:9 If anyone has ears, let him **l**:

listened (52)

Gen 3:17 Then he said to the man, "You **l**
Exo 7:16 So far you have not **l**.
9:20 of Pharaoh's court who **l**
18:24 Moses **l** to his father-in-law and
24:7 and read it while the people **l**.
Num 21:3 The LORD **l** to the Israelites
Dtr 9:19 once more the LORD **l** to me.
10:10 Once again the LORD **l** to me
31:30 whole congregation of Israel **l**,
32:44 of this song as the people **l**.
1Sm 12:1 "I have **l** to everything you
13:4 (So all Israel **l**.) "I, Saul, have
15:24 of the people and **l** to them.
19:6 Saul **l** to Jonathan,
25:35 I've **l** to what you've said and
28:21 "I **l** to you," she told him, "and I
28:23 urging him until he **l** to them.
2Ki 16:9 The king of Assyria **l** to him
2Ch 24:17 Then the king **l** to their advice.
30:20 The LORD **l** to Hezekiah and
33:13 accepted his prayer and **l**
Neh 8:3 All the people **l** to the Book of
8:9 people were crying as they **l**
9:3 ⌊they **l** as⌋ the Book of the
Job 29:21 "People **l** to me eagerly,
32:11 I **l** for you to share your
33:8 and I **l** to your words.
Psa 66:18 Lord would not have **l** ⌊to me⌋.
Ecc 9:16 and no one **l** to what he said.
Isa 48:18 If only you had **l** to my
Jer 8:6 I have paid attention and **l**,
25:3 but you have not **l**.
25:4 you haven't **l** or paid attention
25:7 But you haven't **l** to me,
42:4 "I have **l** to your request.
Eze 3:21 certainly live because they **l**
Dan 1:14 The supervisor **l** to them about
9:6 We haven't **l** to your servants
9:10 We never **l** to you or lived by
9:14 But we never **l** to you.
10:9 and as I **l** to his words,
Mal 3:16 the LORD paid attention and **l**.
Mar 6:20 When he **l** to John,
Luk 5:1 him as they **l** to God's word.
10:39 the Lord's feet and **l** to him talk.
Act 5:21 after they had **l** to the angel,
7:54 council members **l** to Stephen,
8:6 They **l** to him and saw the
14:9 He **l** to what Paul was saying.
15:12 They **l** to Barnabas and Paul
22:22 Up to that point the mob **l**.
24:24 He sent for Paul and **l** to him

listening (23)

Gen 18:10 Sarah happened to be **l** at the
27:5 Rebekah was **l** while Isaac
1Sm 3:9 I'm **l**. "So Samuel went and lay
3:10 "Speak. I'm **l**."
2Sm 20:17 "I'm **l**," he answered.
1Ki 10:8 front of you, **l** to your wisdom!
2Ki 18:26 there are people on the wall **l**."
Neh 13:1 read while the people were **l**.

Pro 19:27 If you stop l to instruction,
Sos 8:13 while your friends are l to your
Isa 36:11 there are people on the wall l."
Eze 9:5 he said to the others as I was l,
Zec 8:9 you people who are presently l
Mar 4:24 attention to what you're l to!
12:37 large crowd enjoyed l to him.
Luk 2:46 among the teachers, l to them,
6:27 "But I tell everyone who is l:
20:45 While all the people were l,
Act 16:14 She was l because the Lord
16:25 other prisoners were l to them.
26:29 to God that you and everyone l
Gal 4:21 Are you really l to what Moses'
2Ti 2:14 only destroys those who are l.

listens (25)

1Ki 3:9 Give me a heart that l so that I
1Ch 28:8 congregation) and as our God l
Psa 55:17 and he l to my voice.
69:33 The LORD l to needy people.
Pro 1:33 But whoever l to me will live
8:34 is the person who l to me,
12:15 but a person who l to advice is
13:1 A wise son l to his father's
15:31 The ear that l to a life-giving
15:32 but the person who l to
18:13 an answer before he l is stupid
21:28 but a person who l to advice
25:12 to the ear of one who l.
Jer 23:18 attention and l to his word?
Mat 10:13 If it is a family that l to you,
18:15 If he l to you, you have won
Jon 3:29 who stands and l to him,
9:31 Instead, he l to people who are
18:37 belongs to the truth l to me."
Jas 1:23 If someone l to God's word but
1Jn 4:5 and the world l to them.
4:6 person who knows God l to us.
5:14 We are confident that God l to
5:15 We know that he l to our
Rev 3:20 If anyone l to my voice and

lit (11)

Exo 14:20 and it l up the night.
27:21 must keep the lamps l
Lev 24:3 Aaron must keep the lamps l in
24:4 on the pure gold lamp stand l
1Sm 14:27 it to his mouth, his eyes l up.
14:29 See how my eyes l up when I
Psa 77:18 Streaks of lightning l up the
Isa 50:11 among the torches you have l.
Luk 22:55 Some men had l a fire in the
Act 20:8 (Many lamps were l in the
Rev 18:1 and his glory l up the earth.

literature (2)

Dan 1:4 and l of the Babylonians.
1:17 to understand all kinds of l.

littered (1)

2Ki 7:15 saw how the whole road was l

little (164)

Gen 18:4 let someone bring a l water?
30:30 The l that you had before I
43:2 back and buy us a l more food."
43:11 Take a l balm, a little honey,
43:11 Take a little balm, a l honey,
44:25 back and buy us a l more food.'
Exo 16:18 gathered less didn't have too l.
23:30 L by little I will force them out
23:30 Little by l I will force them out
Lev 11:17 l owls, cormorants, great owls,
Dtr 1:39 Although you thought the l
7:22 L by little he will force these
7:22 Little by l he will force these
14:16 l owls, great owls, barn owls,
28:38 but harvest l because locusts
Jdg 4:19 "Please give me a l water to
1Sm 14:29 when I tasted a l of this honey?
14:43 "I tasted a l honey on the tip of
2Sm 12:3 but the poor man had only one l
1Ki 2:20 "I'm asking you for one l thing,"
12:10 'My l finger is heavier than my
17:12 of flour in a jar and a l oil
1Ki 18:44 "A l cloud like a man's hand is
2Ki 5:2 they had brought back a l girl
5:14 again like a l child's skin.
8:12 smash their l children,
10:18 He said, "Ahab served Baal a l,
2Ch 10:10 'My l finger is heavier than my
12:7 In a l while I will give them an
Ezr 8:21 for ourselves, for our l ones,
Job 10:20 me alone. Let me smile a l
21:11 They send their l children out
22:20 up what l they had left.'
24:24 be prosperous for a l while,
36:2 "Be patient with me a l longer,
Psa 8:2 From the mouths of l children
8:5 You have made him a l lower
37:10 In a l while a wicked person
37:16 The l that the righteous person
137:9 one who grabs your l children
Pro 6:10 "Just a l sleep, just a little
6:10 a little sleep, just a l slumber,
6:10 a little slumber, just a l nap."
13:11 but whoever gathers l by little
13:11 gathers little by l has plenty.
15:16 Better to have a l with the fear
23:8 You will vomit the l bit you
24:33 "Just a l sleep, just a little
24:33 a little sleep, just a l slumber,
24:33 a little slumber, just a l nap."
Ecc 5:12 whether they eat a l or a lot.
10:1 A l foolishness outweighs
Sos 2:15 the l foxes that ruin vineyards.
8:8 We have a l sister,
Isa 3:16 taking short l steps,
11:6 and l children will lead them.
13:16 Their l children will be
22:24 offspring and all the l utensils,
26:20 Hide for a l while until his fury
32:10 In a l less than a year you
63:18 the land for a l while.
Jer 48:4 Its l ones will cry out.
49:20 He will surely drag away the l
50:45 He will surely drag away the l
Lam 2:11 L children and infants faint in
2:19 life of your l children who faint
4:4 L children beg for bread,
Eze 11:16 sanctuary for a l while among
16:47 It only took you a l time to be
Dan 7:8 a l horn, came up among them.
11:24 But this will last only for a l
11:34 they will get a l help,
Hos 1:4 In a l while I will punish Jehu's
Amo 6:11 houses and flatten l houses.
Nah 3:10 Even her l children were
Hag 1:6 but you harvested l.
1:9 but you received a l.
2:6 says: Once again, in a l while,
Zec 1:15 I was only a l angry,
4:10 Who despised the day when l
13:7 my hand against the l ones."
Mat 6:30 people who have so l faith?
8:26 you cowards have so l faith?"
11:25 revealing them to l children.
13:5 where there was l soil.
13:21 he lasts only a l while.
14:31 "You have so l faith!
16:8 You have so l faith!
17:20 "Because you have so l faith.
18:2 He called a l child and had him
18:3 and become like l children,
18:4 Whoever becomes like this l
18:6 "These l ones believe in me.
18:10 not to despise these l ones.
18:14 not want one of these l ones
19:13 Then some people brought l
21:16 'From the mouths of l children
26:39 After walking a l farther,
26:73 After a l while the men
Mar 1:19 As Jesus went on a l farther,
5:23 "My l daughter is dying.
5:41 which means, "L girl,
5:43 He also told them to give the l
7:25 A woman whose l daughter
7:30 and found the l child lying
9:36 Then he took a l child and had
9:42 "These l ones believe in me.
10:13 Some people brought l children
Mar 10:15 of God as a l child receives
14:35 After walking a l farther,
14:70 After a l while the men
Luk 5:3 asked him to push off a l from
7:47 But whoever receives l
7:47 little forgiveness loves very l."
9:47 So he took a l child and had
9:48 "Whoever welcomes this l
10:21 revealing them to l children.
12:28 people who have so l faith?
12:32 Don't be afraid, l flock.
15:29 given me so much as a l goat
16:10 be trusted with very l can also
16:10 with very l is dishonest
17:2 to cause one of these l ones
18:17 of God as a l child receives
19:17 be trusted with a l money.
22:58 A l later someone else saw
Jon 4:49 with me before my l boy dies."
7:33 still be with you for a l while.
12:35 still be with you for a l while.
13:33 still be with you for a l while.
14:19 In a l while the world will no
16:16 "In a l while you won't see me
16:16 Then in a l while you will see
16:17 He tells us that in a l while we
16:17 Then he tells us that in a l
16:18 when he says, 'In a l while'?
16:19 'In a l while you won't see me,
16:19 and in a l while you will see
Act 5:34 be taken outside for a l while.
27:28 They waited a l while and did
1Co 4:3 It means very l to me that you
5:6 Don't you know that a l yeast
2Co 8:15 and those who gathered a l
8:15 a little didn't have too l."
10:8 So, if I brag a l too much about
11:1 I want you to put up with a l
11:16 fool so that I can also brag a l.
Gal 5:9 A l yeast spreads through the
Eph 4:14 we will no longer be l children,
Php 4:12 too much or when I have too l.
1Th 2:17 from you for a l while.
1Ti 4:8 Training the body helps a l,
5:23 Instead, drink a l wine for your
Heb 2:7 You made him a l lower than
2:9 Jesus was made a l lower than
11:25 pleasures of sin for a l while.
Jas 3:5 can be set on fire by a l flame.
1Pe 1:6 of trouble for a l while now.
5:10 you as you suffer for a l while.
Rev 3:8 You only have a l strength,
6:11 They were told to rest a l
12:12 knowing that he has l time left."
17:10 he must remain for a l while.
20:3 it must be set free for a l while.

live (1054)

Gen 3:14 of animals as long as you l.
3:22 Then he would l forever."
4:20 He was the first person to l in
6:3 They will l 120 years."
9:27 May he l in the tents of Shem.
12:12 they'll kill me but let you l.
12:13 and because of you I will l."
13:18 his tents and went to l by
15:13 that your descendants will l
17:1 L in my presence with integrity.
20:7 will pray for you, and you will l.
20:15 L anywhere you like."
26:3 L here in this land for a while,
27:39 "The place where you l will
27:40 You will use your sword to l,
28:5 Jacob went to l with Laban,
31:32 them will not be allowed to l.
34:10 You can l with us,
34:10 L here, move about freely in
34:16 and we'll l with you and
34:21 so let them l in our land and
34:22 These people will consent to l
34:23 Then they'll l with us."
35:1 "Go to Bethel and l there.
36:7 possessions to l together.
37:1 Jacob continued to l in the land
38:11 L as a widow until my son
38:11 So Tamar went to l in her

Gen	42:18	them, "Do this, and you will **l**.
	45:10	**L** in the land of Goshen,
	45:10	**L** there with your children and
	46:34	say this⌋ so that you may **l**
	47:4	We have come to **l** in this land
	47:4	So please let us **l** in Goshen."
	47:6	your father and your brothers **l**
	47:6	Let them **l** in Goshen.
	47:11	had his father and his brothers **l**
	49:13	"Zebulun will **l** by the coast.
Exo	1:16	kill it, but if it's a girl, let it **l**."
	1:17	They let the boys **l**.
	1:18	Why have you let the boys **l**?"
	1:22	but to let every girl **l**.
	3:8	Hivites, and Jebusites **l**.
	8:22	That is where my people **l**.
	12:20	Wherever you **l**, you must eat
	15:17	the place where you **l**,
	15:25	laws and rules for them to **l** by,
	18:20	show them how to **l**,
	19:13	or a person, it must not **l**.
	20:12	so that you may **l** for a long
	21:35	they must sell the **l** bull and
	22:18	"Never let a witch **l**.
	23:26	I will let you **l** a normal life
	23:33	Never let them **l** in your land,
	25:8	and I will **l** among them.
	29:45	"Then I will **l** among the
	29:46	so that I might **l** among them.
	32:8	way I commanded them to **l**.
	33:20	no one may see me and **l**."
	34:12	make a treaty with those who **l**
	34:15	make a treaty with those who **l**
Lev	3:17	to come wherever you **l**:
	7:26	animal no matter where you **l**.
	11:9	are the kinds of creatures that **l**
	11:44	You must **l** holy lives.
	13:46	They must **l** outside the camp.
	14:8	days he will **l** outside his tent.
	18:3	You used to **l** in Egypt.
	18:3	Don't **l** the way the Egyptians
	18:3	Don't **l** the way the Canaanites
	18:3	Never **l** by their standards.
	18:4	and **l** by my standards.
	18:5	**L** by my standards,
	18:25	will vomit out those who **l** in it.
	18:26	**L** by my standards,
	18:30	Don't **l** by the standards of the
	19:37	and all my rules, and **l** by them.
	20:7	"**L** holy lives. Be holy because I
	20:8	Obey my laws, and **l** by them.
	20:22	the land I am bringing you to **l**
	22:13	and comes back to **l** in her
	23:3	day of worship wherever you **l**.
	23:14	to come wherever you **l**.
	23:21	to come wherever you **l**.
	23:31	to come wherever you **l**.
	23:42	**L** in booths for seven days.
	23:42	born in Israel must **l** in booths
	23:43	I made the people of Israel **l**
	25:18	Then you will **l** securely in the
	25:19	you want and **l** there securely.
	25:22	⌊again⌋ in the eighth year but **l**
	25:35	He must **l** with you as a
	26:3	will do if you will **l** by my laws
	26:5	You will eat all you want and **l**
	26:12	So I will **l** among you and be
	26:13	over you and made you **l** as
Num	5:3	where I **l** among you unclean."
	6:2	make a special vow to **l** as
	13:19	Is the land they **l** in good or
	13:28	But the people who **l** there are
	13:29	The Amalekites **l** in the Negev.
	13:29	and Amorites **l** in the mountain
	13:29	And the Canaanites **l** along the
	13:32	that devours those who **l** there.
	14:14	Egyptians tell the people who **l**
	14:21	But as I **l** and as the glory of
	14:28	So tell them, 'As I **l**,
	14:30	to give you this land to **l** in.
	19:10	the foreigners who **l** with them.
	21:8	is bitten can look at it and **l**."
	24:5	and the places where you **l**,
	24:21	have a permanent place to **l**.
	24:23	Who will **l** when God decides
	31:15	did you let all the women **l**?"
Num	32:17	Meanwhile our families will **l** in
	32:17	the other people who **l** here.
	33:52	out all the people who **l** there.
	33:53	of the land and **l** there,
	33:55	do not force out those who **l**
	33:55	with you over the land you **l** in.
	35:3	the Levites will have cities to **l**
	35:25	You must **l** there until the death
	35:29	generations wherever you **l**.
	35:32	must never go back and **l**
	35:33	pollute the land where you **l**.
	35:34	land where you and I **l** unclean.
	35:34	**l** among the Israelites."
Dtr	2:4	of Esau, who **l** in Seir.
	2:10	The Emites used to **l** there.
	2:12	The Horites used to **l** in Seir,
	2:20	Rephaim who used to **l** there,
	2:29	of Esau, who **l** in Seir,
	2:29	who **l** in Ar, did for us.
	4:1	Obey them so that you will **l**
	4:9	your memory as long as you **l**.
	4:10	me as long as they **l** on earth,
	4:26	You won't **l** very long there.
	4:27	the LORD will force you to **l**.
	4:40	You will **l** for a long time in the
	4:40	the land for as long as you **l**.
	5:16	Then you will **l** for a long time,
	5:24	that people can **l** even if God
	5:29	as long as they **l**!
	5:33	Then you will continue to **l**,
	5:33	and you will **l** for a long time in
	6:2	As long as you **l**, you,
	6:2	and you will **l** a long time.
	6:24	good as long as we **l** so that
	8:1	Then you will **l**, and your
	8:3	you that a person cannot **l**
	8:12	nice houses and **l** in them.
	9:12	way I commanded them to **l**.
	9:16	the LORD commanded you to **l**.
	11:9	Then you will also **l** for a long
	11:21	you and your children will **l**
	11:28	I'm commanding you to **l** today,
	11:30	region of the Canaanites who **l**
	11:31	possession of it and **l** there,
	12:1	as long as you **l** in the land.
	12:5	a place out of all your tribes to **l**
	12:10	you so that you will **l** securely.
	12:11	a place where his name will **l**.
	12:12	(The Levites **l** in your cities
	12:15	In whatever city you **l**,
	12:18	and the Levites who **l** in your
	12:19	as long as you **l** in your land.
	12:29	of their land and **l** there.
	13:7	around you, who **l** near or far,
	13:12	your God is giving you to **l**
	14:2	of all the people who **l** on earth,
	14:21	give it to the foreigners who **l**
	14:23	your God as long as you **l**.
	14:27	take care of the Levites who **l**
	14:29	and widows who **l** in your
	16:2	will choose for his name to **l**.
	16:3	bread so that, as long as you **l**,
	16:6	will choose for his name to **l**.
	16:11	the Levites who **l** in your cities,
	16:11	and widows who **l** among you.
	16:11	will choose for his name to **l**.
	16:14	widows who **l** in your cities.
	16:20	but justice so that you will **l**
	17:14	possession of it and **l** there.
	19:1	You will force them out and **l** in
	19:9	his directions as long as you **l**.
	21:13	Then she may **l** in your house
	22:2	If the owner doesn't **l** near you
	22:7	and you will **l** for a long time.
	23:6	or friendship as long as you **l**.
	23:16	Let him stay with you ⌊and **l**⌋
	25:5	When brothers **l** together and
	25:15	Then you will **l** for a long time
	26:2	will choose for his name to **l**.
	26:11	and the foreigners who **l**
	28:29	As long as you **l**, you will be
	28:30	but you won't **l** in it.
	28:33	As long as you **l**, you will
	28:43	who **l** among you will
	28:66	You will **l** in terror day and
	30:6	all your soul, and you will **l**.
Dtr	30:16	Then you will **l**, and the LORD
	30:18	You will not **l** for a long time in
	30:19	and your descendants will **l**.
	31:12	as well as the foreigners who **l**
	31:13	your God as long as you **l**
	31:29	I have commanded you to **l**.
	32:40	As surely as I **l** forever,
	32:47	words you will be able to **l**
	33:6	"May the tribe of Reuben **l** and
	33:12	beloved people will **l** securely
	33:25	strength last as long as you **l**.
	33:28	So Israel will **l** securely.
Jos	1:5	successfully as long as you **l**.
	2:24	The people who **l** there are
	6:17	are in the house with her will **l**
	7:7	I wish we had been content to **l**
	9:15	treaty which allowed them to **l**.
	9:20	We must let them **l** to avoid
	9:21	they should be allowed to **l**.
	9:22	'We **l** very far away from you,'
	9:22	when you **l** here with us?
	9:24	and destroy all who **l** there.
	10:6	all the Amorite kings who **l**
	13:13	So they still **l** in Israel today.
	14:4	gave the Levites cities to **l**
	15:63	So they still **l** with Judah in
	16:10	So the Canaanites still **l** in
	17:7	people who **l** in En Tappuah.
	20:4	give him a place to **l** with them.
	21:2	we should receive cities to **l**
	24:13	cities to **l** in that you hadn't
	24:15	Amorites in whose land you **l**,
Jdg	1:21	The Jebusites still **l** with the
	1:27	determined to **l** in this land.
	1:29	the Canaanites continued to **l**
	1:30	the Canaanites continued to **l**
	1:32	the tribe of Asher continued to **l**
	1:33	So they continued to **l** with the
	1:35	determined to **l** at Har Heres,
	2:2	a treaty with the people who **l**
	5:23	curse those who **l** there!
	6:4	They left nothing for Israel to **l**
	6:10	in whose land you will **l**.' But
	8:19	if you had let them **l**,
	8:29	son of Joash, went home to **l**.
	9:41	continued to **l** at Arumah.
	9:41	not let them **l** in Shechem.
	11:3	He went to **l** in the land of Tob.
	13:12	how should the boy **l** and what
	15:8	Then he went to **l** in a cave in
	17:8	in Judah to **l** wherever
	17:9	I'm going to **l** wherever I can
	17:11	and agreed to **l** with Micah.
	18:1	was looking for a place to **l**.
Rut	1:1	with his wife and two sons to **l**
	2:23	to **l** with her mother-in-law.
1Sm	1:26	Hannah said, "as sure as you **l**,
	2:30	father's family would always **l**
	2:32	no one in your family will **l** to
	2:35	and he will always **l** as my
	10:24	shouted, "Long **l** the king!"
	12:11	so that you could **l** securely.
	17:55	swear, as you **l**, Your Majesty,
	20:3	as the LORD and you **l**,
	20:14	But as long as I **l**, ⌊promise me
	22:5	"Don't **l** in your fortified camp,"
	25:6	Say to him, 'May you **l** ⌊long⌋!
	25:26	as the LORD and you **l**,
	25:28	found in you as long as you **l**.
	27:5	towns so that I can **l** there.
	27:5	Why should I **l** in the royal city
	27:10	descendants of Jerahmeel **l**,"
	27:10	the Negev where the Kenites **l**."
	30:14	Negev where the Cherethites **l**,
	31:7	came to **l** in these cities.
2Sm	4:3	They still **l** there today.
	7:5	will build me a house to **l** in?
	7:10	They will **l** in their own place
	12:22	to me and let the child **l**.'
	15:21	as the LORD and the king **l**:
	16:16	he said, "Long **l** the king!
	16:16	live the king! Long **l** the king!"
	19:34	"I don't have much longer to **l**.
	24:3	and may Your Majesty ⌊**l**⌋ to
1Ki	1:25	'Long **l** King Adonijah!'
	1:31	Majesty, King David, **l** forever!"

1Ki 1:34 'Long l King Solomon!'
1:39 "Long l King Solomon!"
3:13 be like you as long as you l.
3:17 this woman and I l in the same
6:12 If you l by my laws,
6:13 I will l among the Israelites and
8:12 "The LORD said he would l in
8:13 for you to l in permanently."
8:27 "Does God really l on earth?
8:30 the place where you l.
8:36 Teach them the proper way to l.
8:39 ⌊them⌋ in heaven, where you l.
8:40 Then, as long as they l in the
8:43 the place where you l.
8:49 the place where you l,
8:61 Then you will l by his laws
17:5 He went to l by the Cherith
20:31 Maybe he'll let you l."
20:32 'Please let me l.'" Ahab asked,
2Ki 2:2 the LORD lives and as you l,
2:4 the LORD lives and as you l,
2:6 the LORD lives and as you l,
4:30 as the LORD and you l,
6:2 make a place for us to l there."
7:4 to keep us alive, we'll l.
8:2 She and her family went to l in
10:19 Whoever is missing will not l."
11:12 they said, "Long l the king!"
13:5 They were able to l in their
16:6 to Elath and still l there today.
17:25 When they first came to l there,
17:28 Samaria went to l in Bethel.
17:34 They don't fear the LORD or l
18:32 L! Don't die! Don't listen to
19:26 Those who l in these cities are
20:6 I'll give you 15 more years to l.
20:19 and security as long as I l?"
21:22 and didn't l the LORD's way.
22:19 place and those who l here.
22:19 I had said that those who l here
25:24 L in this country, serve the king
1Ch 4:40 the Hamites used to l there.
4:41 today no Meunites l there.)
4:43 descendants still l there today.
7:29 son of Israel, l in these cities.
10:7 came to l in these cities.
17:4 build this house for me to l in.
17:9 They will l in their own place
22:18 He put the people who l in this
23:25 will now l in Jerusalem forever.
2Ch 2:3 he could build a palace to l in.
6:1 "The LORD said he would l in
6:2 for you to l in permanently."
6:18 "Does God really l on earth
6:21 the place where you l.
6:27 Teach them the proper way to l.
6:30 ⌊them⌋ in heaven, where you l.
6:31 Then, as long as they l in the
6:33 the place where you l.
6:39 the place where you l,
8:2 and he had Israelites l in them.
8:11 He said, "My wife will not l in
17:6 He had the confidence to l the
17:6 way the LORD wanted him to l.
23:11 They said, "Long l the king!"
27:6 he was determined to l as
32:10 are you so confident as you l
34:27 place and those who l here.
34:28 and those who l here.'" So they
34:31 He said he would l by the
Ezr 7:10 LORD's Teachings, l by them,
7:25 your God's Teachings and l ⌊in
Neh 2:3 "May the king l forever!"
5:9 Shouldn't you l in the fear of our
8:14 the people of Israel should l
11:1 of every ten to l in Jerusalem,
11:1 nine-tenths were supposed to l
11:2 offered to l in Jerusalem.
11:31 Benjamin's descendants l in
Est 4:11 golden scepter to him will he l.
9:19 That is why the Jews who l in
Job 4:19 will he accuse those who l
7:16 I do not want to l forever.
11:14 don't let injustice l in your tent.
18:19 survivor where he used to l.
21:28 tent where wicked people l?'
Job 27:6 won't accuse me as long as I l.
28:12 Where does understanding l?
28:20 Where does understanding l?
29:25 I decided how they should l.
30:6 They have to l in dry riverbeds,
32:9 merely because they l long.
36:6 allow the wicked person to l.
36:11 they will l out their days in
36:14 or they l on as male prostitutes
39:6 I gave it the desert to l in and
Psa 4:8 enable me to l securely.
15:1 Who may l on your holy
22:26 praise him. May you l forever.
24:1 The world and all who l in it
25:8 sinners the way they should l.
26:8 I love the house where you l,
33:8 Let all who l in the world stand
33:14 down upon all who l on earth.
34:12 Who would like to l long
37:3 L in the land, and practice
37:27 evil, do good, and l forever.
37:29 land and l there permanently.
49:1 all who l in the world —
49:9 in order to l forever and never
55:23 people will not l out half their
63:4 I will thank you as long as I l.
65:4 you choose and invite to l
65:8 Those who l at the ends of the
68:6 but rebellious people must l in
68:16 where God has chosen to l?
68:16 the LORD will l there forever.
68:18 so that the LORD God may l
69:35 His servants will l there and
69:36 Those who love him will l
71:3 Be a rock on which I may l,
71:18 Let me l to tell the people of
72:15 May he l long. May the gold
74:7 place where you l among us.
83:7 along with those who l in Tyre.
84:4 Blessed are those who l in
84:10 than l inside wicked people's
84:11 from those who l innocently.
86:11 so that I may l in your truth.
88:12 place where forgotten people l?
89:30 and do not l by my rules,
90:9 We l out our years like one
98:7 and those who l in it roar like
101:2 I will l in my own home with
101:6 so that they may l with me.
104:12 The birds l by the streams.
104:33 to praise my God as long as I l.
107:36 and they build cities to l in.
116:2 I will call on him as long as I l
118:17 I will not die, but I will l and tell
119:17 Be kind to me so that I may l
119:33 how to l by your laws,
119:77 reach me so that I may l,
119:116 you promised, so that I may l.
119:144 ⌊them⌋ so that I will l.
120:5 How horrible it is to l as a
128:1 fear the LORD and l his way.
128:6 May you l to see your
133:1 sisters l together in harmony!
140:13 people will l in your presence.
143:3 He has made me l in dark
146:2 to praise my God as long as I l.
Pro 1:33 But whoever listens to me will l
2:21 Decent people will l in the land.
4:4 commands so that you may l.
7:2 commands so that you may l.
8:12 "I, Wisdom, l with insight,
9:6 Stop being gullible and l.
9:11 You will l longer because of
10:9 lives honestly will l securely,
10:30 not continue to l in the land.
15:27 but whoever hates bribes will l.
21:9 Better to l on a corner of a roof
21:19 Better to l in a desert than with
23:12 L a more disciplined life,
25:24 Better to l on a corner of a roof
28:16 hate unjust gain will l longer.
Ecc 6:12 pointless days they l?
8:12 a hundred crimes and yet l
8:13 They will not l any longer.
11:8 Even though people may l for
Isa 1:21 But now murderers l there!
Isa 2:3 so that we may l by them."
2:5 let's l in the light of the LORD.
5:8 and you have to l by yourself
5:9 be without people to l in them.
6:5 I l among people with sinful
8:14 for those who l in Jerusalem.
9:1 where foreigners l.
9:2 light will shine on those who l
9:9 Ephraim and the people who l
10:24 My people who l in Zion,
10:31 those who l in Gebim take
11:6 Wolves will l with lambs.
13:20 and no one will l in it for
13:21 Ostriches will l there,
18:3 of the world who l on the earth.
20:6 those who l on this coastland
22:21 be like a father to those who l
23:18 will belong to those who l
24:5 earth is polluted by those who l
24:6 That is why those who l on the
24:17 store for those who l on earth.
26:5 brought down those who l high
26:9 those who l in the world learn
26:19 Your dead will l. Their corpses
26:21 place to punish those who l
30:6 Lions and lionesses l there.
30:6 and poisonous snakes l there.
30:14 big enough to carry l coals from
30:19 You will l in Zion, You won't cry
32:16 Then justice will l in the
32:18 My people will l in a peaceful
33:14 Can any of us l through a fire
33:14 Can any of us l through a fire
33:15 right and speaks the truth will l.
33:16 This person will l on high.
34:11 Owls and crows will l there.
34:17 and l there for generations.
37:27 Those who l in these cities are
38:5 to give you 15 more years to l.
38:16 people l in spite of such things,
38:16 and I have the will to l in spite
38:20 We l our lives in the LORD's
39:8 and security as long as I l."
40:22 and those who l on it are like
40:22 spreads it out like a tent to l in.
42:7 and bring those who l in
42:10 all the creatures that l in them,
42:10 and all who l on them.
42:11 Let those who l in the desert
42:11 Let those who l in the
42:11 Let those who l in Sela sing for
42:24 They didn't want to l his way.
44:13 so the idols can l in shrines.
45:22 all who l at the ends of the
47:8 You l securely and say to
47:8 I won't l as a widow.
49:18 "I solemnly swear as I l,"
49:20 Make room for me to l here."
51:3 He will comfort all those who l
51:6 and those who l there will die
51:13 Why should you l in constant
52:4 to Egypt to l there as foreigners.
55:3 Listen so that you may l!
57:15 I l in a high and holy place.
58:12 of Streets Where People L.
59:18 who l on the coastlands.
65:9 My servants will l there.
65:20 or an old man who doesn't l
65:21 will build houses and l there.
65:22 homes and have others l there.
65:22 My people will l as long as
Jer 1:14 on all those who l in the land.
3:18 days the nation of Judah will l
4:7 and no one will l in them.
4:29 and no one will l in it.
6:8 a land where no one will l.
6:12 my power against those who l
6:16 L that way, and find a resting
6:16 that you wouldn't l that way.
7:3 Change the way you l and act,
7:3 and I will let you l in this place.
7:5 really change the way you l
7:7 Then I will let you l in this
7:23 L the way I told you to live so
7:23 Live the way I told you to l so
8:3 want to die rather than l where

Jer 9:11 so that no one can l there.
9:26 the hair on their foreheads or l
10:18 going to throw out those who l
11:2 to those who l in Jerusalem.
11:9 those who l in Jerusalem.
11:12 cities of Judah and those who l
12:5 how can you l in the jungle
13:13 and all those who l in
17:6 He will l in the dry places in
17:6 salty land where no one can l.
17:20 all those who l in Jerusalem,
17:25 and those who l in Jerusalem.
18:11 to those who l in Jerusalem,
18:12 We'll l the way we want to.
19:3 and those who l in Jerusalem.
19:12 place and to those who l in it,
20:6 and all those who l in your
21:6 I will defeat those who l in this
21:9 Those who l in this city will
21:9 to the Babylonians will l.
22:23 You l in Lebanon and have
22:24 "As I l," declares the LORD,
23:6 and Israel will l in safety.
23:8 At that time they will l in their
23:14 commit adultery and l a lie.
23:14 and those who l in Jerusalem
23:17 They tell all who l by their own
25:5 and l in the land that the LORD
25:29 war on all those who l on earth,
25:30 all those who l on earth.
27:11 People will farm the land and l
27:17 the king of Babylon, and l.
29:5 Build houses, and l in them.
29:16 and about all the people who l
29:28 Build houses, and l in them.
30:19 The people who l there will
31:24 its cities will l there together.
31:24 and shepherds will also l there.
32:19 reward them for the way they l
32:32 and those who l in Jerusalem
32:37 and make them l here securely.
32:39 will fear me as long as they l.
33:10 that no people or animals l in it.
33:10 No people or animals l there.
33:12 where no people or animals l,
33:16 and Jerusalem will l securely.
34:16 had set free to l their own lives.
34:22 so that no one will l there."
35:7 You must always l in tents so
35:7 live in tents so that you may l
35:9 built houses to l in,
35:10 We l in tents, and we have
35:13 and those who l in Jerusalem,
35:15 Then you will l in the land that
35:17 Judah and on all those who l
36:31 on those who l in Jerusalem,
38:2 to the Babylonians will l.
38:17 the king of Babylon, you will l,
38:17 You and your household will l.
38:20 go well for you, and you will l.
40:5 L among the people with him,
40:9 L in this country, serve the king
40:10 I'm going to l in Mizpah and
40:10 L in the cities you have taken
42:15 and you go and l there.
42:17 people who decide to go and l
42:18 on those who l in Jerusalem,
42:22 where you want to go and l."
43:2 we must not go to l in Egypt.
44:8 where you have come to l.
44:12 determined to go to l in Egypt.
44:14 people of Judah who went to l
44:14 where they long to return and l.
44:23 You didn't l by his teachings,
44:26 people of Judah who l in Egypt.
44:28 people of Judah who went to l
46:18 "As I l," declares the king,
46:26 Afterward, they will l in peace
47:2 cities and those who l in them.
48:28 L among the cliffs.
48:43 store for those who l in Moab,"
49:1 people l in Gad's cities?
49:2 where the people of Ammon l.
49:16 You l on rocky cliffs and
49:18 No one will l there.
49:20 to do to those who l in Teman.

Jer 49:20 of the people who l in Teman.
49:31 or bars. Its people l alone.
49:33 a place where only jackals l.
49:33 No one will l there.
50:3 land so that no one will l in it.
50:13 No one will l in Babylon
50:21 and the people who l in Pekod.
50:34 to the people who l in Babylon.
50:39 animals will l with hyenas.
50:39 Desert owls will also l there.
50:40 No one will l there.
51:1 the people who l in Leb Kamai.
51:12 the people who l in Babylon.
51:13 Babylon, you l beside many
51:24 and all the people who l
51:29 so that no one will l there.
51:35 The people who l in Zion say,
51:62 no person or animal will l here,
Lam 1:3 Its people l among the
3:6 He has made me l in darkness,
3:18 'I've lost my strength to l, and
4:20 We had thought that we would l
Eze 2:6 and you l among scorpions.
3:21 they will certainly l because
5:6 and they don't l by my laws.
5:11 "As I l, declares the Almighty
6:6 Wherever people l,
6:8 "But I will let some people l.
7:13 Sellers will not l long enough
7:13 none of the people will l.
11:15 "Son of man, the people who l
11:15 The people who l in Jerusalem
11:20 Then they will l by my laws
12:10 the people of Israel who l there.'
12:19 says about the people who l
12:20 The cities where people l will
13:19 lives of people who shouldn't l.
14:16 As I l, declares the Almighty
14:18 As I l, declares the Almighty
14:20 As I l, declares the Almighty
14:22 you will see how they l.
14:23 when you see how they l.
15:6 so I will take the people who l
16:6 own blood. I said to you, "L."
16:48 As I l, declares the Almighty
17:9 Will this vine l and grow?
17:10 but will it l and grow?
17:16 "'As I l, declares the Almighty
17:19 Almighty LORD says: As I l,
18:3 As I l, declares the Almighty
18:9 He will certainly l," declares
18:13 Will this person l?
18:13 He will not l. He has done all
18:17 He will certainly l.
18:19 He will certainly l.
18:21 He will certainly l.
18:22 He will l because of the right
18:23 turn from their evil ways and l.
18:24 Will he l? All the right things
18:27 what is fair and right, he will l.
18:28 He will certainly l.
20:3 As I l, declares the Almighty
20:11 If people obey them they will l.
20:13 They didn't l by my laws,
20:13 If people obey them, they will l.
20:16 and they didn't l by my laws.
20:18 "Don't l by the laws of your
20:19 L by my laws. Obey my rules
20:21 They didn't l by my laws,
20:21 If people obey them, they will l.
20:25 rules by which they could not l.
20:31 "'As I l, declares the Almighty
20:33 "'As I l, declares the Almighty
22:3 murders people who l in you.
22:6 all the princes of Israel who l
22:9 People who l in you eat food
22:11 Other men who l in you have
26:15 The people who l on the coast
26:18 will make the people who l by
26:20 I will make you l below the
27:35 All those who l on the coasts
28:25 The people of Israel will l in
28:26 They will l there in safety.
28:26 They will l in safety when I
29:11 and no one will l there for 40
30:9 in ships to terrify those who l

Eze 32:15 kill all the people who l there.
33:10 of them. How can we l?'"
33:11 "Tell them, 'As I l,
33:11 to turn from their ways and l.
33:12 person will not l when he sins.'
33:13 person that he will certainly l.
33:15 Then he will certainly l.
33:16 He will certainly l.
33:19 he will l because of it.
33:24 "Son of man, those who l in the
33:27 Almighty LORD says: As I l,
34:8 As I l, declares the Almighty
34:25 so that my sheep can l safely
34:27 and my sheep will l safely in
34:28 They will l safely.
35:6 That is why, as I l,
35:11 That is why, as I l,
36:10 number of people who l on you.
36:10 Israel, all of them, will l on you.
36:11 and animals that l on you.
36:11 I will let people l on you as in
36:27 I will enable you to l by my
36:28 Then you will l in the land that
37:3 can these bones l?"
37:5 to enter you, and you will l.
37:6 breath in you, and you will l.
37:9 were killed so that they will l.'"
37:14 my Spirit in you, and you will l.
37:24 They will l by my rules,
37:25 They will l in the land that I
37:25 and their grandchildren will l in
38:8 and all of them l there safely.
38:11 peaceful people who l safely.
38:11 All of them l without walls,
38:12 and they l in the world."
38:14 my people Israel will l safely,
39:6 and on those who l safely
39:26 When they l safely in a land
43:7 This is where I will l among
43:9 I will l among them forever.
45:5 so that they have cities to l in.
47:22 residents who l among you
Dan 2:4 Majesty, may you l forever!
2:11 and they don't l with humans."
2:38 and birds, wherever they l.
3:9 Majesty, may you l forever!
4:12 Birds came to l in its branches.
4:25 forced away from people and l
4:32 forced away from people and l
4:35 and with those who l on earth.
5:10 Majesty, may you l forever!
6:6 "May King Darius l forever!
6:21 Majesty, may you l forever!
7:12 but they were allowed to l for a
12:2 Some will wake up to l forever,
Hos 2:18 so people can l safely.
4:1 charges against those who l
6:2 that we may l in his presence.
10:5 Those who l in Samaria fear
12:9 I will make you l in tents again
13:13 have the opportunity to l again,
14:7 They will l again in God's
14:9 Righteous people l by them.
Joe 3:17 I l on my holy mountain,
3:20 People will always l in Judah.
3:20 People will l in Jerusalem from
Amo 4:1 you cows of Bashan who l on
5:4 Search for me and l!
5:6 Search for the LORD and l!
5:11 but you will not l in them.
5:14 of evil so that you may l.
9:5 and all who l on it mourn.
9:14 the ruined cities and l in them.
Oba 1:3 You l on rocky cliffs.
1:17 "But refugees will l on Mount
Mic 2:7 good for those who l honestly?
4:2 so that we may l by them."
4:5 All the nations l by the names
4:5 but we will l by the name of the
4:10 l in the open fields,
5:4 They will l in safety because
6:8 and to l humbly with your God.
6:12 Those who l in the city speak
7:13 a wasteland for those who l
7:14 They l alone in the woods,
Nah 1:5 The world and all who l in it

Hab 2:4 But the righteous person will l
Zep 1:4 those who l in Jerusalem.
1:13 but they won't l in them.
1:18 to those who l on earth.
2:5 it will be for those who l
2:9 as I l," declares the LORD of
2:15 the city that used to l securely,
Hag 1:4 "Is it time for you to l in your
Zec 2:10 to come and l among you,
2:11 I will l among you.
3:7 If you l according to my ways
8:3 to Zion and l in Jerusalem.
8:8 and they will l in Jerusalem.
9:6 A mixed race will l in Ashdod,
10:9 They will l with their children
10:12 They will l in his name,"
11:6 longer have pity on those who l
12:5 'The people who l in
12:7 and the honor of those who l
12:8 LORD will defend those who l
12:10 on those who l in Jerusalem.
13:1 family and for those who l
13:3 'You don't deserve to l because
14:11 People will l there,
14:11 Jerusalem will l securely.
Mat 4:4 'A person cannot l on bread
4:15 where foreigners l!
4:16 A light has risen for those who l
5:20 can guarantee that unless you l
9:18 hand on her, and she will l."
21:32 way that God wants you to l,
27:29 "Long l the king of the Jews!"
Mar 5:23 so that she may get well and l."
9:50 Have salt within you, and l in
12:44 everything she had to l on."
15:18 "Long l the king of the Jews!"
Luk 1:75 and honorable as long as we l.
1:79 He will give light to those who l
4:4 cannot l on bread alone.'"
7:25 wear splendid clothes and l
11:31 with the men who l today.
15:14 He had nothing to l on.
20:35 to come back to life and l
21:4 everything she had to l on."
21:35 all people who l on the earth.
Jon 4:50 Your son will l." The man
4:53 had told him, "Your son will l."
5:25 those who respond to it will l.
5:29 will come back to life and l.
6:51 eats this bread will l forever.
6:56 and drink my blood l in me,
6:56 live in me, and I l in them.
6:57 and I l because of the Father.
6:57 on me will l because of me.
6:58 Those who eat this bread will l
7:35 Does he mean that he'll l with
8:12 and will never l in the dark."
8:31 "If you l by what I say,
8:35 A slave doesn't l in the home
11:25 Those who believe in me will l
12:46 in me will not l in the dark.
14:19 You will l because I live.
14:19 You will live because I l.
15:4 L in me, and I will live in you.
15:4 Live in me, and I will l in you.
15:4 fruit unless you l in me.
15:5 Those who l in me while I live
15:5 Those who live in me while I l
15:6 Whoever doesn't l in me is
15:7 If you l in me and what I say
15:9 has loved me. So l in my love.
15:10 you will l in my love.
15:10 and in that way I l in his love.
19:3 "Long l the king of the Jews!"
21:22 "If I want him to l until I come
21:23 "If I want him to l until I come
Act 1:20 and let no one l there,'
7:4 to this land where we now l.
7:48 the Most High doesn't l in a
13:10 way the Lord wants people to l.
13:27 The people who l in Jerusalem
14:16 all people to l as they pleased.
17:24 He doesn't l in shrines made by
17:26 nation of humanity to l all over
17:26 boundaries within which to l.
17:28 Certainly, we l, move,

Act 22:22 been allowed to l this long!"
25:24 not be allowed to l any longer.
28:4 but justice won't let him l."
28:16 was allowed to l by himself,
28:30 Paul rented a place to l for two
Rom 1:15 why I'm eager to tell you who l
1:17 will l because of faith."
3:17 have not learned to l in peace.
6:2 we still l under sin's influence?
6:4 should l a new kind of life.
6:8 that we will also l with him.
6:19 led you to l disobedient lives.
6:19 This leads you to l holy lives.
8:4 Therefore, we, who do not l by
8:5 Those who l by the corrupt
8:5 But those who l by the spiritual
8:11 Jesus back to life l in you?
8:12 we have no obligation to l the
8:12 our corrupt nature wants us to l.
8:13 If you l by your corrupt nature,
8:13 of the body, you will l.
10:5 person who obeys laws will l
12:16 L in harmony with each other.
12:18 l in peace with everyone.
13:3 Would you like to l without
13:13 We should l decently,
13:13 as people who l in the light of
13:14 l like the Lord Jesus Christ did,
14:7 It's clear that we don't l to honor
14:8 If we l, we honor the Lord,
14:8 So whether we l or die,
14:11 "As certainly as I l,
15:5 allow you to l in harmony with
1Co 5:11 in the Christian faith but l
7:12 and she is willing to l with him,
7:13 and he is willing to l with her,
7:15 has called you to l in peace.
7:17 Everyone should l the life that
7:29 those who are married should l
7:30 tears should l as though they
7:30 Those who are happy should l
7:30 should l as though they
7:35 I'm showing you how to l a
8:6 from him, and we l for him.
8:6 and we l because of him."
15:52 so that they can l forever.
15:53 into a body that will l forever.
15:54 into a body that will l forever,
2Co 1:13 this as long as you l,
5:1 We know that if the life we l
5:8 We are confident and prefer to l
5:8 this body and to l with the Lord.
5:9 Whether we l in the body or
5:15 those who l should no longer
5:15 who live should no longer l
6:16 "I will l and walk among them.
7:1 body and spirit and l
7:3 that we will l and die together.
10:13 city of Corinth, where you l.
12:9 that Christ's power will l in me.
13:4 but by God's power we will l
13:11 same attitude and l in peace.
Gal 2:14 but you l like a person who is
2:14 not Jewish must l like Jews?"
2:16 their own efforts to l according
2:16 their own efforts to l according
2:19 I l in a relationship with God.
2:20 I no longer l, but Christ lives in
2:20 The life I now l I live by
2:20 The life I now live I l by
3:2 your own efforts to l according
3:10 their own efforts to l according
3:11 will l because of faith."
3:12 "Whoever obeys laws will l
5:16 L your life as your spiritual
5:25 If we l by our spiritual nature,
Eph 2:10 in Christ Jesus to l lives filled
3:17 Then Christ will l in you
4:1 encourage you to l the kind of
4:17 name not to l any longer like
5:2 L in love as Christ also loved
5:8 L as children who have light.
5:15 be very careful how you l.
5:15 Don't l like foolish people but
Php 1:20 as always, whether I l or die.
1:22 If I continue to l in this life,

Php 1:25 I know that I will continue to l
1:27 L as citizens who reflect the
3:17 pay attention to those who l by
3:18 that many l as the enemies of
4:12 I know how to l in poverty or
4:12 secret of how to l when I'm full
Col 1:10 We ask this so that you will l
1:19 to have all of himself l in Christ.
2:6 continue to l as Christ's people.
2:20 you let others tell you how to l?
3:7 You used to l that kind of sinful
3:9 to be and the life you used to l,
3:16 wisdom and richness l in you.
1Th 2:12 you should l in a way that
4:11 make it your goal to l quietly,
5:4 you don't l in the dark.
5:10 we will l together with him.
5:13 L in peace with each other.
2Th 3:6 with any believer who doesn't l
1Ti 1:16 believe in him and l forever.
3:15 of God's family must l.
4:7 train yourself to l a godly life.
4:10 we work hard and struggle to l
2Ti 2:11 we will l with him.
3:12 Those who try to l a godly life
Tit 2:1 Tell believers to l the kind of
2:3 Tell older women to l their
2:12 so that we can l self-controlled,
3:14 that they can l productive lives.
Heb 1:11 but you will l forever.
5:13 All those who l on milk lack
10:38 who has God's approval will l
11:9 Faith led Abraham to l as a
12:9 of spirits, so that we will l?
12:14 Try to l peacefully with
12:14 and try to l holy lives,
13:18 we want to l honorably
Jas 4:15 we will l and carry out our
1Pe 1:2 and chose you to l holy lives
1:14 don't l the kind of lives you
1:17 if you call God your Father, l
your time as
2:12 L decent lives among
2:16 L as free people, but don't hide
2:24 we could l a life that has God's
3:1 they l without saying anything.
3:7 Husbands, in a similar way, l
3:8 everyone must l in harmony,
3:10 "People who want to l a full life
3:16 the good Christian life you l
4:2 sinful human desires as you l
4:6 earthly lives and l like God
2Pe 2:18 from those who l in error.
2:21 the holy life God told them to l.
3:11 and godly lives you must l
1Jn 1:6 relationship with God" and yet l
1:7 But if we l in the light in the
2:6 Those who say that they l in
2:6 say that they live in him must l
2:10 who love other believers l
2:10 faith of those who l in the light.
2:11 believers are in the dark and l
2:24 you will also l in the Son and
2:27 So l in Christ as he taught you
2:28 Now, dear children, l in Christ.
3:4 Those who l sinful lives are
3:6 Those who l in Christ don't go
3:9 from God don't l sinful lives.
3:9 and they can't l sinful lives.
3:17 a person has enough to l
3:24 commandments l in God,
4:13 We know that we l in him and
4:15 Son of God, and they l in God.
4:16 Those who l in God's love live
4:16 who live in God's love l in God,
2Jn 1:6 Love means that we l by doing
1:6 were commanded to l in love,
Rev 2:13 I know where you l.
12:12 and those who l in them.
14:6 News to spread to those who l
20:5 The rest of the dead did not l

lived (348)

Gen 4:16 left the LORD's presence and l
5:4 he l 800 years and had other
5:5 Adam l a total of 930 years;

Gen 5:7 Seth l 807 years and had other
5:8 Seth l a total of 912 years;
5:10 Enosh l 815 years and had
5:11 Enosh l a total of 905 years;
5:13 Kenan l 840 years and had
5:14 Kenan l a total of 910 years;
5:16 Mahalalel l 830 years and had
5:17 Mahalalel l a total of 895 years;
5:19 Jared l 800 years and had other
5:20 Jared l a total of 962 years;
5:23 Enoch l a total of 365 years.
5:26 Methuselah l 782 years and
5:27 Methuselah l a total of 969
5:30 he l 595 years and had other
5:31 Lamech l a total of 777 years;
6:12 all people on earth l evil lives.
9:28 Noah l 350 years after the flood.
9:29 Noah l a total of 950 years;
10:30 The region where they l
11:11 Shem l 500 years and had
11:13 Arpachshad l 403 years and
11:15 Shelah l 403 years and had
11:17 Eber l 430 years and had other
11:19 Peleg l 209 years and had
11:21 Reu l 207 years and had other
11:23 Serug l 200 years and had
11:25 Nahor l 119 years and had
11:32 Terah l 205 years and died in
13:12 Abram l in Canaan,
13:12 while Lot l among the cities of
13:13 (The people who l in Sodom
16:3 After Abram had l in Canaan for
19:25 all who l in the cities,
19:30 where they l in a cave.
21:20 He l in the desert and became
21:21 He l in the desert of Paran,
21:34 Abraham l a long time in the
23:1 Sarah l to be 127 years old.
25:7 Abraham l 175 years.
25:17 Ishmael l 137 years.
25:18 His descendants l as nomads
26:6 So Isaac l in Gerar.
26:17 in the Gerar Valley and l there.
35:27 Abraham and Isaac had l there
36:8 l in the mountains of Seir.
36:43 by the places where they l
37:1 where his father had l.
47:22 and they l on that income.
47:28 Jacob l in Egypt 17 years,
47:28 so he l a total of 147 years.
50:22 Joseph l to be 110 years old.
Exo 6:4 land where they l as foreigners.
6:16 and Merari. Levi l 137 years.
6:18 Kohath l 133 years.
6:20 Amram l 137 years.
9:26 where the Israelites l.
Lev 18:30 people who l there before you.
26:35 celebrated while you l there.
Num 13:22 Sheshai, and Talmai l.
14:45 who l there came down
20:15 and we l there for many years.
21:1 who l in the Negev,
21:9 they were bitten, and they l.
21:25 all its villages, and l in them.
22:5 in the land where his people l.
31:10 cities where the Midianites l
32:40 of Manasseh), and they l there.
33:40 who l in the Negev,
Dtr 1:44 The Amorites who l there came
2:8 of Esau, who l in Seir.
2:22 of Esau, who l in Seir.
2:23 happened to the Avvites who l
4:33 God speak from a fire and l?
5:26 from a fire, as we did, and l?
26:5 to Egypt and l as foreigners.
29:16 You know how we l in Egypt
Jos 2:15 (She l in the city wall.)
4:14 As long as Joshua l,
9:16 their neighbors and l with them.
11:19 where the Hivites l.
12:2 Amorite king who l in Heshbon.
12:4 of King Og of Bashan who l
13:21 who l in that country.
15:63 of Jebus who l in Jerusalem.
16:10 the Canaanites who l in Gezer.
19:50 He rebuilt the city and l there.

Jos 24:2 l on the other side of the
24:7 Then you l in the desert for a
24:8 the land of the Amorites who l
24:18 including the Amorites who l in
Jdg 1:9 to fight the Canaanites who l
1:10 Canaanites who l at Hebron.
1:16 There they l with the people of
1:17 defeated the Canaanites who l
1:21 Jebusites who l in Jerusalem.
1:29 the Canaanites who l in Gezer.
1:30 force out those who l at Kitron
1:31 force out those who l at Acco
1:33 those who l at Beth Shemesh
3:3 and the Hivites who l on Mount
3:5 So the people of Israel l among
4:2 who l at Harosheth Haggoyim.
9:21 He went to Beerah and l there
10:1 Tola was from Issachar and l
10:8 they oppressed all who l east
11:21 of the Amorites who l there.
11:26 Israel has now l in Heshbon,
18:7 that the people there l without
18:28 of Dan rebuilt the city and l in it.
19:1 there was a Levite who l in a
19:16 of Ephraim but l in Gibeah.
19:16 The other people who l there
21:23 rebuilt their cities and l in them.
Rut 1:2 the country of Moab and l there
1:4 They l there for about ten years.
1Sm 7:13 as long as Samuel l.
7:15 judged Israel as long as he l.
14:52 Philistines as long as Saul l.
19:18 to the pastures and l there.
23:5 the people who l in Keilah.
23:14 David l in fortified camps in the
23:14 and he l in fortified camps in
27:8 (They l in the territory which
27:11 as he l in Philistine territory.
2Sm 5:6 who l in that region.
5:9 David l in the fortress and
7:6 I haven't l in a house from the
9:12 Everyone who l at Ziba's home
9:13 was disabled, l in Jerusalem.
20:3 So they l like widows in
1Ki 3:3 Solomon loved the LORD and l
3:6 He l in your presence with truth
4:20 They ate and drank and l
4:21 to Solomon as long as he l.
4:24 So he l in peace with all the
4:25 As long as Solomon l,
4:25 Dan to Beersheba) l securely,
11:20 and Genubath l in the palace
11:25 rival as long as Solomon l.
12:17 ruled the Israelites who l
12:25 the hills of Ephraim and l there.
14:30 Jeroboam as long as they l.
15:16 of Israel as long as they l.
15:21 Ramah and l in Tirzah.
15:32 and Baasha as long as they l.
15:34 He l like Jeroboam and led
16:2 But you have l like Jeroboam.
16:19 Zimri l like Jeroboam and led
16:26 He l exactly like Jeroboam
21:11 and nobles who l there — did
2Ki 4:8 where a rich woman l.
13:3 Benhadad as long as they l.
14:17 of Judah l 15 years after
15:5 So the king l in a separate
17:8 and l by the customs of the
17:19 LORD their God but l according
17:24 over Samaria and l in its cities.
17:29 this in the cities where they l:
20:3 remember how I've l faithfully
21:21 He l like his father in every
22:2 He l in the ways of his
25:29 king's presence as long as he l.
25:30 food allowance as long as he l.
1Ch 2:55 of scribes who l at Jabez.
4:23 They were the potters who l at
4:23 They l there with the king and
4:28 descendants l in Beersheba,
4:33 places were where they l,
4:41 They l in that land in place of
5:8 Reuben's descendants l in
5:9 Some of them l eastward as far
5:10 and l in their tents throughout

1Ch 5:11 Gad's descendants l next to
5:16 They l in Gilead, in Bashan
5:22 half of the tribe of Manasseh l
5:23 Half of the tribe of Manasseh l
6:54 where Levi's descendants l,
6:62 of Manasseh that l in Bashan.
8:13 of the families who l in Aijalon.
8:28 They l in Jerusalem.
8:29 settled Gibeon, l in Gibeon,
8:32 They l next to their relatives in
9:9 of 956 of them l in Jerusalem.
9:16 who l in the villages belonging
9:33 They l in rooms in the temple
9:34 head Levites l in Jerusalem.
9:35 settled Gibeon, l in Gibeon,
9:38 They l next to their relatives in
11:7 David l in the fortress,
17:5 I haven't l in a house from the
23:1 old and had l out his years,
2Ch 10:17 ruled the Israelites who l
11:5 Rehoboam l in Jerusalem and
11:17 ⌞those⌟ three years they l
11:17 way David and Solomon had l.
12:15 Jeroboam as long as they l.
13:22 else about Abijah — how he l
17:3 who l in the old way like his
17:4 God and l by God's commands.
19:8 They l in Jerusalem.
20:8 His descendants have l in it
20:18 Judah and the people who l
21:16 and the Arabs who l near
24:2 long as the priest Jehoiada l.
24:14 As long as Jehoiada l,
24:15 old and had l out his years,
25:25 of Judah l 15 years after
26:7 the Arabs who l in Gur Baal,
26:21 he l in a separate house and
30:25 those who l in Judah rejoiced.
31:19 priests who l in the
34:2 He l in the ways of his
34:32 Then the people of Jerusalem l
34:33 As long as he l, they didn't stop
Neh 3:22 After him the priests who l in
8:17 made booths and l in them.
9:24 Canaanites, who l in the land.
9:35 When they l in their own
11:3 They l on their own property in
11:20 and Levites l in all the cities of
11:20 Everyone l on his own
11:21 But the temple servants l on
11:25 Many people l in villages that
11:25 Some people of Judah l in
12:26 They l in the days of Joiakim,
12:27 went to wherever the Levites l
13:16 People from Tyre who l in
Job 1:1 A man named Job l in Uz.
21:31 tell him to his face how he l?
29:25 I l like a king among his troops,
38:21 were born then and have l such
42:16 Job l 140 years after this.
Psa 78:60 where he had l among humans.
105:23 Jacob l as a foreigner in the
107:10 Those who l in the dark,
120:6 I have l too long with those
Ecc 6:3 he had a hundred children and l
6:3 how long he would have l,
Isa 1:21 and righteousness l in her.
38:3 remember how I've l faithfully
57:2 everyone who has l honestly
Jer 8:1 the bones of the others who l
25:2 everyone who l in Jerusalem.
34:5 the kings who l before you.
39:14 So he l among the people.
40:6 at Mizpah and l with him
44:10 You haven't feared me or l your
44:15 and all the people who l at
44:17 and we l comfortably and saw
48:11 "Moab has l securely ever
50:39 inhabited or l in for generations.
52:33 king's presence as long as he l.
52:34 food allowance as long as he l.
Eze 3:15 to the exiles who l by the
5:7 You haven't l by my laws or
5:7 You haven't even l up to the
7:3 you for the way you have l,
7:4 back for the way you have l

Eze 7:8 you for the way you have l,
7:9 back for the way you have l
11:12 You haven't l by my laws,
16:46 She and her daughters l north
20:43 will remember the way you l
23:5 Assyrian lovers who l nearby.
24:14 you because of the way you l
26:17 those who l by the coast.
31:6 powerful nations l in its shade.
31:13 wild animals l in its branches.
31:17 All who l in its shadow were
35:9 Your cities will not be l in.
36:17 when the people of Israel l in
36:17 dishonored it by the way they l
36:19 based on the way that they l
36:33 your cities to be l in again,
37:25 land where their ancestors l.
47:22 children while they l with you.
Dan 4:21 Wild animals l under it,
5:21 He l with wild donkeys,
7:9 who has l for endless years,
7:13 who has l for endless years,
7:22 who has l for endless years,
9:10 We never listened to you or l
Zec 9:5 Ashkelon will no longer be l in.
Mal 2:6 He l with me in peace and
Mat 1:11 They l at the time when the
4:16 The people who l in darkness
5:12 The prophets who l before you
23:30 Then you say, 'If we had l at
Mar 5:3 and l among the tombs.
Luk 1:80 He l in the desert until the day
2:3 where their ancestors had l.
2:25 He l an honorable and devout
7:37 A woman who l a sinful life in
8:27 in a house but l in the tombs.
Jon 1:14 human and l among us.
7:25 Some of the people who l in
7:42 of Bethlehem, where David l?
11:1 Lazarus, who l in Bethany,
11:1 Mary and her sister Martha l,
12:1 had brought back to life, l there.
19:27 From that time on she l with
Act 4:32 group of believers l in harmony.
7:2 before Abraham l in Haran.
7:4 left the country of Chaldea and l
7:29 Moses quickly left Egypt and l
8:9 A man named Simon l in that
9:10 A disciple named Ananias l in
9:31 of people increased as people l
9:32 he came to those who l in the
9:35 Everyone who l in the city of
9:36 A disciple named Tabitha l in
10:1 A man named Cornelius l in the
13:17 while they l as foreigners
16:1 a disciple named Timothy l.
16:3 him because of the Jews who l
17:21 Everyone who l in Athens
18:11 Paul l in Corinth for a year and
19:10 all the Jews and Greeks who l
21:12 we and the believers who l
22:12 named Ananias l in Damascus.
26:4 "All the Jews know how I l the
26:5 They know that I l my life as a
28:2 The people who l on the island
28:4 When the people who l on the
Rom 5:10 the life his Son l will save us.
2Co 1:12 proud of the way that we have l
1:12 We have l with a God-given
1:12 human wisdom that we have l
Gal 1:13 about the way I once l when
Eph 2:3 All of us once l among these
5:8 Once you l in the dark,
2Th 3:7 We l a disciplined life among
1Ti 2:2 quiet and peaceful life always l
2Ti 1:5 That faith first l in your
Heb 11:9 He l in tents, as did Isaac and
11:38 in deserts and mountains and l
Jas 5:5 You have l in luxury and
1Pe 1:14 the kind of lives you once l.
1:14 Once you l to satisfy your
2Pe 2:7 and l in sexual freedom.
2:8 he l among the people of
1Jn 2:6 must live the same way he l.
Rev 13:14 wounded by a sword and yet l.
18:9 who had sex with her and l
Rev 20:4 They l and ruled with Christ for

liver (11)

Exo 29:13 organs, the lobe of the l,
29:22 organs, the lobe of the l,
Lev 3:4 Also cut off the lobe of the l
3:10 along with the lobe of the l.
3:15 Also remove the lobe of the l
4:9 lobe of the l and the kidneys
7:4 remove the lobe of the l along
8:16 organs, the lobe of the l,
8:25 organs, the lobe of the l,
9:10 and lobe of the l from the
9:19 and the lobe of the l)

livers (1)

Eze 21:21 and examine animal l.

lives (339)

Gen 6:12 all people on earth lived evil l.
9:3 Everything that l and moves
19:17 angels⌋ said, "Run for your l!
42:15 as surely as Pharaoh l,
42:16 as surely as Pharaoh l,
45:5 sent me ahead of you to save l.
45:7 on the earth and to save your l
46:34 taken care of herds all our l,
47:25 have saved our l," they said.
Exo 1:14 They made their l bitter with
30:15 and make your l acceptable
30:16 the sins in their l are removed."
Lev 11:44 You must live holy l.
20:7 "Live holy l. Be holy because I
25:36 by respecting other Israelites' l.
Num 16:38 sinned and lost their l are holy,
23:9 I see a nation that l by itself,
30:3 who still l in her father's house,
Dtr 4:42 of these cities and save their l.
6:24 so that he will preserve our l.
14:9 may eat of every creature that l
22:19 divorce her as long as he l.
22:29 divorce her as long as he l.
33:12 l on the mountain slopes."
Jos 2:14 "We pledge our l for your lives.
2:14 "We pledge our lives for your l.
6:25 She still l in Israel today
7:9 Canaanites and everyone who l
9:11 leaders and everyone who l
9:24 because we feared for our l.
13:6 people of Israel everyone who l
Jdg 8:19 swear, as the LORD l,
10:18 rule everyone who l in Gilead."
11:8 of everyone who l in Gilead."
18:25 your family will lose your l."
Rut 3:13 swear, as the LORD l,
1Sm 1:11 him to you for as long as he l.
14:39 the LORD and Savior of Israel l,
14:45 swear, as the LORD l,
19:6 swear, as the LORD l,
20:21 I swear it, as the LORD l.
20:31 long as Jesse's son l on earth,
22:22 for all the l of your family.
25:29 But he will dispose of the l of
25:34 l — if you hadn't come to meet
26:10 as the LORD l," David added,
26:16 swear, as the LORD l,
28:10 swear, as the LORD l,
29:4 He'll do it with the l of our men!
29:6 swear, as the LORD l,
2Sm 2:27 "I solemnly swear, as God l,
4:11 swear, as the LORD l,
12:5 as the LORD l," he said to
14:11 as the LORD l," he said,
19:5 "They saved your life and the l
22:38 return until I had ended their l.
22:39 I ended their l by shattering
22:47 The LORD l! Thanks be to my
23:17 of men who risked their l!"
1Ki 1:29 saved my life from all trouble l,
2:4 to me with all their hearts and l,
2:24 who has established me l,
11:34 him to be ruler as long as he l
15:6 Rehoboam throughout their l.
17:1 God of Israel whom I serve l,
17:12 as the LORD your God l,
18:10 as the LORD your God l,
1Ki 18:15 of Armies whom I serve l,
19:2 took the l of Baal's prophets."
21:18 of Israel, who l in Samaria.
22:14 swear, as the LORD l,
2Ki 1:13 please treat my life and the l of
2:2 as the LORD l and as you live,
2:4 as the LORD l and as you live,
2:6 as the LORD l and as you live,
3:14 of Armies whom I serve l,
5:16 as the LORD whom I serve l,
5:20 As sure as the LORD l,
7:7 and donkeys and ran for their l.)
10:24 will pay for their l with yours."
1Ch 11:19 these men who risked their l?
11:19 They had to risk their l to get
15:13 We hadn't dedicated our l to
22:19 So dedicate your hearts and l
28:8 God listens to dedicate your l
2Ch 14:4 of Judah to dedicate their l
14:7 we have dedicated our l
14:7 We have dedicated our l to him,
15:2 If you will dedicate your l to
15:12 one another to dedicate their l
15:13 who refused to dedicate their l
18:13 swear, as the LORD l,
29:31 "You have dedicated your l to
30:19 hearts set on dedicating their l
Neh 9:35 turn away from their wicked l.
Job 15:28 He l in ruined cities where no
18:15 Fire l in his tent. Sulfur is
19:25 But I know that my defender l,
22:8 A privileged person l in it.
23:3 I would go where he l.
28:23 He knows where it l
33:18 the pit and their l from crossing
33:22 Their l come close to those
38:19 way to the place where light l?
38:26 rain on a land where no one l,
Psa 16:3 Those who lead holy l on earth
18:37 return until I had ended their l.
18:46 The LORD l! Thanks be to my
46:4 place where the Most High l.
55:15 because evil l in their homes
68:6 out of prison into productive l,
72:13 will save the l of the needy.
73:1 to those whose l are pure.
73:5 They have no drudgery in their l
75:3 the earth and everyone who l
76:12 He cuts short the l of influential
78:50 He let the plague take their l.
85:6 Won't you restore our l again so
90:10 Each of us l for 70 years — or
91:1 Whoever l under the shelter of
94:21 They join forces to take the l of
97:10 The one who guards the l of
101:6 The person who l with integrity
119:1 those whose l have integrity,
135:21 the one who l in Jerusalem.
Pro 1:18 into hiding only to lose their l.
10:9 Whoever l honestly will live
10:9 but whoever l dishonestly will
14:2 Whoever l right fears the LORD,
14:25 An honest witness saves l,
19:1 Better to be a poor person who l
20:7 A righteous person l on the
22:23 their case and will take the l
28:18 Whoever l honestly will be
28:18 Whoever l dishonestly will fall
Ecc 2:3 their brief l under heaven.
3:12 enjoy what is good in their l.
5:17 spend their entire l in darkness,
5:18 during the brief l God gives us.
5:20 much thought to their brief l
6:6 Even if the rich person l two
8:13 Their l are like shadows,
8:15 their brief l which God has
Isa 5:18 whose l are sinful.
8:18 who l on Mount Zion.
27:1 He will kill that monster which l
33:5 honored because he l on high.
33:24 No one who l ⌊in Zion⌋ will
38:20 We live our l in the LORD's
57:15 High and Lofty One l forever,
57:16 the l of those I've made,
65:20 no longer be an infant who l
65:20 Whoever l to be a hundred

Jer 2:6 No one l there or travels there."
4:2 "As the LORD l ..."
5:2 People say, "As the LORD l ..."
12:16 in my name, 'As the LORD l ...'
13:13 going to make everyone who l
16:14 of Egypt. As the LORD l ....'
16:15 As the LORD l ....' They will say
17:21 If you value your l,
18:11 change your l, and do good.'
20:13 He has rescued the l of needy
21:9 You will escape with your l.
22:6 into cities that no one l in.
23:7 out of Egypt. As the LORD l ...'
23:8 As the LORD l ...' At that time
31:12 Their l will be like
34:16 had set free to live their own l.
38:2 They will escape with their l.
38:16 As the LORD l, I will not kill
44:10 or lived your l by my teachings
44:22 No one l in that land today.
44:26 'that no one from Judah who l
44:26 "As the Almighty LORD l ..."
46:19 a pile of rubble where no one l.
47:2 will cry out and everyone who l
48:6 Run for your l! Run like a wild
50:35 everyone who l in Babylon,"
51:6 Run for your l! You shouldn't die
51:37 of contempt, where no one l.
51:43 a land where no one l and
51:45 Run for your l! Run from the
Lam 2:12 Their l dwindle away in their
5:9 we have to risk our l in the heat
Eze 3:18 ways in order to save their l.
12:19 everyone who l there is violent.
13:18 You want to control the l of my
13:19 and you spare the l of people
13:22 wicked ways to save their l.
14:7 an Israelite or a foreigner who l
16:46 She l south of you with her
18:9 He l by my rules and obeys my
18:17 He obeys my rules and l by my
32:10 tremble in fear for their own l.
33:15 l by the rules of life,
44:9 Any godless foreigner who l
Dan 2:22 and light l with him.
3:28 and risked their l so that they
4:34 honored the one who l forever,
4:35 Everyone who l on earth is
12:7 oath by the one who l forever.
Hos 4:3 and everyone who l in it is
4:15 the oath, 'As the LORD l ...'
Joe 1:14 the leaders and everyone who l
2:1 Everyone who l in the land
3:21 The LORD l in Zion!
Amo 8:8 Everyone who l in it will mourn.
8:14 swear, Dan, as your god l ...."
Mat 14:15 "No one l around here,
15:33 in this place where no one l?"
16:25 Those who want to save their l
16:25 But those who lose their l for
16:26 whole world and lose their l?
23:21 it and by the one who l there.
Mar 6:35 "No one l around here,
8:4 in this place where no one l?"
8:35 Those who want to save their l
8:35 But those who lose their l for
8:36 whole world yet lose their l?
Luk 9:12 No one l around here."
9:24 Those who want to save their l
9:24 But those who lose their l for
9:25 lose their l by destroying them?
10:6 If a peaceful person l there,
14:26 as well as their own l,
17:33 Those who try to save their l
17:33 who lose their l will save them.
Jon 6:66 go back to the l they had led
8:34 Whoever l a sinful life is a
11:26 Everyone who l and believes
12:25 Those who love their l will
12:25 and those who hate their l in
12:36 become people whose l show
14:10 The Father, who l in me,
14:17 You know him, because he l
15:7 in me and what I say l in you,
Act 10:32 leatherworker who l by the sea.'
14:17 He fills you with food and your l
Act 15:26 and Paul have dedicated their l
26:20 prove they had changed their l.
27:10 and it will affect our l."
Rom 1:29 Their l are filled with of all
6:10 But now he l, and he lives for
6:10 now he lives, and he l for God.
6:19 led you to live disobedient l.
6:19 This leads you to live holy l.
7:17 but sin that l in me is doing
7:18 know that nothing good l in me;
7:18 nothing good l in my corrupt
7:20 Sin that l in me is doing it.
8:9 But if God's Spirit l in you,
8:10 However, if Christ l in you,
8:11 alive by his Spirit who l in you.
13:13 jealousy cannot be part of our l.
16:4 They risked their l to save me.
1Co 3:16 and that God's Spirit l in you?
6:19 received from God, l in you.
7:39 her husband as long as he l.
2Co 4:15 kindness overflows in the l
5:7 our l are guided by faith,
6:4 Instead, our l demonstrate that
6:6 Spirit's presence in our l,
9:10 In your l he will increase the
12:21 many who formerly led sinful l
13:2 formerly led sinful l as well as
13:4 but by God's power he l.
13:5 people in whom Jesus Christ l?
Gal 2:20 longer live, but Christ l in me.
5:25 then our l need to conform to
Eph 2:10 us in Christ Jesus to live l filled
2:22 into a place where God l.
Php 1:11 Jesus Christ will fill your l with
1:11 Your l will then bring glory and
Col 1:10 live the kind of l that prove you
2:9 All of God l in Christ's body,
1Th 2:8 News of God but also our l.
2Th 3:5 May the Lord direct your l as
3:11 you are not living disciplined l.
3:11 interfering in other people's l.
1Ti 2:15 they lead respectable l in faith,
5:6 But the widow who l for
6:16 He l in light that no one can
2Ti 1:5 convinced that it also l in you.
1:14 of the Holy Spirit who l in us,
Tit 2:3 Tell older women to live their l
2:12 It trains us to avoid ungodly l
2:12 and godly l in this present
3:14 that they can live productive l.
Heb 2:15 who were slaves all their l
6:19 sure and strong anchor for our l.
7:8 but we are told that he l.
7:24 But Jesus l forever,
7:25 do this because he always l
12:14 and try to live holy l,
13:7 about how their l turned out,
Jas 3:6 The tongue sets our l on fire,
4:5 It says, "The Spirit that l in us
4:8 Clean up your l, you sinners,
1Pe 1:2 and chose you to live holy l
1:2 good will and peace fill your l!
1:14 don't live the kind of l you once
2:12 decent l among unbelievers.
2:25 shepherd and bishop of your l.
3:2 pure and reverent their l are.
3:15 But dedicate your l to Christ as
4:2 live the rest of your l on earth.
4:6 like humans in their earthly l
4:6 live like God in their spiritual l.
2Pe 1:2 your l through your knowledge
3:11 holy and godly l you must live
3:13 that has God's approval l.
1Jn 2:14 strong and God's word l in you.
2:17 does what God wants l forever.
2:24 from the beginning l in you.
2:24 If that message l in you,
2:27 received from Christ l in you.
3:4 Those who live sinful l are
3:8 The person who l a sinful life
3:9 born from God don't live sinful l
3:9 What God has said l in them,
3:9 and they can't live sinful l.
3:16 give our l for other believers.
3:24 and God l in them.
3:24 We know that he l in us
1Jn 4:12 love each other, God l in us,
4:13 that we live in him and he l
4:15 God l in those who declare that
4:16 and God l in them.
4:18 The person who l in fear
2Jn 1:2 because of the truth which l
Jud 1:2 and love fill your l!
1:23 be stained by their sinful l.
Rev 2:13 your presence, where Satan l.
4:9 the one who l forever and ever,
4:10 worship the one who l forever
10:6 oath by the one who l forever
15:7 who l forever and ever,
21:3 "God l with humans!

livestock (56)

Gen 4:20 to live in tents and have l.
13:2 very rich because he had l,
29:7 "It isn't time yet to gather the l.
30:29 to your l under my care.
31:9 has taken away your father's l
31:18 He drove all his l ahead of him
31:18 He took his own l that he had
33:17 and made shelters for his l.
34:5 His sons were with his l out in
34:23 Won't their l, their personal
36:7 pastureland for all of their l.
46:6 They also took their l and the
46:32 They take care of l.
47:6 put them in charge of my l."
47:16 more money, give me your l,
47:17 they brought their l to Joseph,
47:17 food in exchange for all their l.
47:18 and you have all our l.
Exo 9:3 bring a terrible plague on your l,
9:4 distinguish between Israel's l
9:4 Israel's livestock and the l
9:6 All the l of the Egyptians died,
9:19 send servants to bring your l
10:26 All our l must go with us.
17:3 and our l die of thirst?"
22:5 "Whenever someone lets his l
34:19 the firstborn males of all your l,
Num 20:19 and if we or our l drink any of
31:9 took all their animals, their l,
32:1 Gad had a large number of l.
32:1 Gilead were a good place for l.
32:4 is a good place for l.
32:4 Gentlemen, we have l.
32:16 to build stone fences for our l
32:26 Our children, our wives, our l,
Dtr 3:19 I know you have a lot of l.
3:19 Your wives, children, and l
Jos 1:14 Your wives, children, and l
8:2 its loot and l for yourselves.
8:27 Israel took the loot and the l of
11:14 the loot and l from these cities.
21:2 in and pasturelands for our l."
22:8 large herds of l, silver, gold,
Jdg 6:5 they came with their l and their
18:21 l, and property in front of them.
1Sm 23:5 the Philistines, drove off their l,
1Ch 5:9 they had so much l in Gilead.
5:21 confiscated the Hagrites' l:
7:21 when they came to take their l.
28:1 all the property and l belonging
Ezr 1:4 with silver, gold, supplies, l,
1:6 silver and gold, supplies, l,
Neh 9:37 do as they please with our l.
Job 1:15 They took the l and massacred
Psa 66:15 you a sacrifice of fattened l
78:48 bolts of lightning strike their l.

living (393)

Gen 1:24 every type of l creature:
1:30 crawls on the earth — every l,
2:7 The man became a l being.
3:20 the mother of every l person.
6:17 people under the sky — every l,
6:19 Bring two of every l creature
7:4 of the earth every l creature that
7:15 A pair of every l,
7:22 Everything on dry land (every l
7:23 Every l creature on the face of
8:21 I will never again kill every l
9:10 and every l being that is with

Gen 9:10 ship — every l thing on earth.
9:12 to you and every l being that is
9:15 to you and every l animal.
9:16 to every l animal on earth."
13:7 were also l in that area.)
14:7 who were l at Hazazon Tamar.
14:12 since he was l in Sodom.
14:13 He was l next to the oak trees
16:14 of the L One Who Watches
17:8 this land where you are l — all
19:29 to the cities where he was l.
20:1 While he was l in Gerar,
21:23 the land where you've been l
24:3 Canaanites among whom I'm l.
24:37 in whose land I'm l.
24:40 'I have been l the way the
24:62 since he was l in the Negev.
25:6 But while he was still l,
28:4 the land where you are now l,
32:4 'I've been l with Laban and
34:30 You've made the people l in the
35:22 While Israel was l in that
36:20 the people l in that land:
50:11 When the Canaanites l there
Exo 2:22 a foreigner l in another country.
3:22 neighbor and any woman l
10:23 had light where they were l.
12:40 The Israelites had been l in
18:3 a foreigner l in another country.
20:10 and the foreigners l in your city
22:21 you were foreigners l in Egypt.
23:9 you were foreigners l in Egypt.
23:31 I will put the people l in the
Lev 11:10 all swarming creatures l
11:46 and every l creature that swims
14:4 will order someone to get two l,
14:6 The priest will take the l bird,
14:6 and dip them and the l bird
14:7 Then he will let the l bird fly
14:51 and the l bird and dip them in
14:52 the l bird, the cedar wood,
14:53 Then he will let the l bird fly
16:20 he will bring the l goat forward.
18:18 While your wife is l,
19:33 a foreigner l in your land.
19:34 Foreigners l among you will be
19:34 you were foreigners l in Egypt.
20:2 If Israelites or foreigners l
25:10 proclaim liberty to everyone l
25:45 from the foreigners l among you
25:47 and your relative l with him
Num 9:14 "Foreigners l with you may
13:18 the people l there are strong
14:25 and Canaanites are l
15:14 are visiting you or l among you
15:15 foreigners who are l with you.
15:16 foreigners who are l with you."
15:26 who are l among them,
30:16 young daughters still l at home.
Dtr 1:7 and go to everyone l on the
5:14 animals — even the foreigners l
5:26 voice of the l God speak from
5:32 Never stop l this way.
9:4 "Because we've been l right,
9:5 It's not because you've been l
9:6 It's not because you've been l
10:19 you were foreigners l in Egypt.
11:6 and every l creature with them.
18:6 come from where he has been l
19:1 destroy all the nations that are l
22:21 while she was still l in her
23:7 foreigners l in their country.
24:14 are Israelites or foreigners l
28:43 The ⌊standard of l for the⌋
28:43 while your ⌊standard of l⌋ will
31:16 enter the land and are l among
Jos 3:10 know that the l God is among
8:35 and foreigners l among them.
9:3 When the people l in Gibeon
9:7 "What if you're l in this area?
10:1 of Israel and were l with them.
10:40 He claimed every l creature for
15:15 against the people l in Debir.
17:1 of the people l in Gilead,
17:11 villages and the people l in Dor,
17:16 Besides, all the Canaanites l in

Jos 20:9 the foreigners l among them.
22:33 the land where they were l.
Jdg 1:11 to fight the people l at Debir.
1:19 could not force out the people l
5:24 blessed woman l in a tent.
17:7 Levite but was l in Bethlehem.
18:30 for Dan's tribe until the people l
Rut 1:7 place where she had been l,
2:20 kind to people — l or dead."
1Sm 6:21 to the people l at Kiriath Jearim
17:26 the army of the l God?"
17:36 the army of the l God."
22:4 him as long as David was l
31:11 When the people l in Jabesh
2Sm 1:23 well-liked while they were l.
7:1 While King David was l in his
7:2 I'm l in a house made of cedar,
11:11 Majesty's mercenaries are l
11:11 as sure as you're l,
15:8 I made a vow while I was l at
18:18 ⌊While he was still l,⌋
1Ki 3:25 he said, "Cut the l child in two.
3:26 give her the l child.
3:27 The king replied, "Give the l
9:16 killed the Canaanites l there.
13:11 An old prophet was l in Bethel.
13:25 where the old prophet was l.
15:26 evil, l as his father did,
21:8 and nobles l in Naboth's city.
2Ki 4:13 She answered, "I'm already l
19:4 sent him to defy the l God.
19:16 sent to defy the l God.
22:14 Huldah was l in the Second
22:16 on the people l here according
23:2 everyone l in Jerusalem,
1Ch 8:6 were heads of the families l
8:13 forced out the people l in Gath.
11:4 Jebusites were l in that region.
16:19 of foreigners l in that land,
17:1 When David was l in his
17:1 "I'm l in a house made of cedar,
22:2 David ordered the foreigners l
2Ch 15:5 because everyone l in the land
19:4 was l in Jerusalem,
19:10 Warn your relatives l in other
20:7 force those who were l in this
20:15 everyone l in Jerusalem,
20:20 and those l in Jerusalem.
28:18 They captured and began l in
31:4 He told the people l in
31:6 of Israel and Judah who were l
32:22 Hezekiah and the people l
32:26 Hezekiah and the people l in
34:2 and never stopped l this way.
34:22 Huldah was l in the Second
34:24 on the people l here according
34:30 everyone l in Jerusalem,
Ezr 1:4 wherever they may be l,
4:17 rest of their group l in Samaria,
Neh 3:26 the temple servants who were l
3:30 made repairs across from his l
4:12 Jews who were l near our
Job 12:10 The life of every l creature and
14:14 a person dies, will he go on l?
21:7 "Why do the wicked go on l,
26:5 and so do the creatures l there.
28:13 be found in this world of the l.
28:21 from the eyes of every l being,
30:23 appointed for all l beings."
34:15 all l beings would die together,
Psa 27:13 the LORD in this world of the l.
42:2 thirsts for God, for the l God.
52:5 roots out of this world of the l.
84:2 shouts for joy to the l God.
89:48 Can a mortal go on l and never
102:6 like an owl l in the ruins.
102:28 servants will go on l ⌊here⌋.
104:25 l things both large and small.
105:12 of foreigners l in that land,
107:34 of the people l there.
112:5 He earns an honest l.
116:9 presence in this world of the l.
136:25 He gives food to every l
142:5 in this world of the l."
145:16 the desire of every l thing.
145:21 and all l creatures will praise

Pro 18:20 His talking provides him a l.
27:10 A neighbor l nearby is better
Ecc 4:2 already died, rather than the l,
4:15 I saw all l people moving about
7:15 Wicked people go on l in spite
9:4 are among the l have hope,
9:4 because a l dog is better than a
9:5 The l know that they will die,
Sos 4:15 a well of l water flowing from
8:13 Young woman l in the gardens,
Isa 4:3 among the l in Jerusalem.
6:11 in ruins with no one l in them,
8:19 they ask the dead to help the l?
24:1 and scatter the people l on it.
37:4 sent him to defy the l God.
37:17 sent to defy the l God.
38:19 Those who are l praise you as
Jer 10:10 He is the l God and eternal
11:19 this world of the l so that we
17:25 will always have people l in it.
23:36 twist the words of the l God,
24:8 and those who are l in Egypt.
25:20 foreign people l among them;
25:24 foreign people l in the desert;
26:9 of rubble with no one l here?"
26:15 and the people l in it will be
32:43 people or animals l in it.
35:11 why we are l in Jerusalem."
44:1 Jeremiah about all the Jews l
44:13 I will punish those l in Egypt
49:31 Attack the nation l peacefully
Lam 3:39 "Why should any l mortal (any
4:12 kings of the earth nor anyone l
Eze 1:1 while I was l among the exiles
1:5 looked like four l creatures.
1:13 The l creatures looked like
1:13 forth between the l creatures.
1:14 The l creatures ran back and
1:15 As I looked at the l creatures,
1:19 When the l creatures moved,
1:19 When the l creatures rose from
1:20 because the spirit of the l
1:21 because the spirit of the l
1:22 the heads of the l creatures.
3:13 of the l creatures touching one
3:20 If righteous people turn from l
10:15 These were the l creatures that
10:17 The spirit of the l creatures
10:20 These are the l creatures that I
12:2 "Son of man, you are l among
19:7 The land and everyone l in it
20:9 the nations where they were l.
20:38 out of the land where you are l.
26:19 that have no one l in them.
26:20 your place in the land of the l.
29:6 Then all those l in Egypt will
32:23 people in the land of the l.
32:24 people in the land of the l.
32:25 others in the land of the l.
32:26 others in the land of the l.
32:27 others in the land of the l.
32:32 people in the land of the l.
36:35 and have people l in them."
38:12 ruins that people are l in again.
39:9 Those l in the cities of Israel
47:23 tribe among whom they are l,
Dan 4:4 was l comfortably at home.
4:4 while l in my palace.
4:12 It fed every l creature.
4:17 that every l creature will know
6:20 servant of the l God!
6:26 the l God who continues
Hos 1:10 'You are the children of the l
Amo 1:5 I will cut off those l in Aven
1:8 I will cut off those l in Ashdod
3:12 so the Israelites l in Samaria
Jnh 1:8 What do you do for a l?
Mic 7:13 the people l there have done.
Zep 2:5 so that no one will be l there."
3:6 No one will be l there.
Zec 14:8 On that day l water will flow
Mat 11:16 the people who are l now?
16:16 the Son of the l God!"
22:32 God of the dead but of the l."
23:36 The people l now will be held
26:63 "Swear an oath in front of the l

Mar 12:27 the God of the dead but of the l.
Luk 7:31 the people who are l now?
11:29 "The people l today are evil.
11:30 sign to the people l today.
11:32 with the people l today.
11:32 condemn the people l today.
11:50 So the people l now will be
11:51 The people l today will be held
12:56 judge the time in which you're l.
13:4 other people l in Jerusalem?
20:38 the God of the dead but of the l.
20:38 In God's sight all people are l."
24:5 among the dead for the l one?
Jon 4:10 He would have given you l
4:11 you going to get this l water?
6:51 I am the l bread that came from
7:38 As Scripture says, 'Streams of l
Act 1:19 Everyone l in Jerusalem
2:5 nation were l in Jerusalem.
2:14 and everyone l in Jerusalem!
7:6 would be foreigners l
9:22 and he confused the Jews l in
10:42 to judge the l and the dead.'
11:29 to help the believers l in Judea.
12:20 charge of the king's l quarters.)
14:15 worthless gods to the l God.
14:15 The l God made the sky,
16:14 and sold purple dye for a l.
18:3 they made tents for a l as
19:17 All the Jews and Greeks l in
21:21 l among non-Jewish people
22:12 All the Jews l in Damascus
Rom 1:18 the truth by their immoral l.
5:21 This results in our l forever
6:11 dead to sin's power but l
7:5 While we were l under the
9:26 be called children of the l God."
12:1 your bodies as l sacrifices,
13:11 the times ⌊in which we are l⌋.
14:9 Lord of both the l and the dead.
14:15 you are no longer l by love.
1Co 3:3 and l by human standards?
9:14 News should earn their l from
10:11 as a warning for us who are l
15:6 (Most of these people are still l,
15:45 became a l being."
2Co 1:8 wondered if we could go on l.
3:3 but with the Spirit of the l God,
5:6 know that as long as we are l
5:6 we are l away from the Lord.
5:10 done while l in their bodies.
5:17 old way of l has disappeared.
5:17 A new way of l has come into
6:9 as you see, we go on l.
6:16 we are the temple of the l God.
Gal 6:9 allow ourselves to get tired of l
Eph 4:22 to change the way you were l.
5:18 which leads to wild l.
Php 2:2 the same love, l in harmony,
3:5 When it comes to l up to
Col 1:27 which is Christ l in you,
1Th 1:9 gods to serve the real, l God
2:9 and what we did to earn a l.
3:8 Now we can go on l as long as
4:1 and encourage you to excel in l
4:11 and earn your own l,
5:14 those who are not l right,
2Th 3:11 you are not l disciplined lives.
1Ti 3:15 is the church of the l God,
4:8 but godly l helps in every way.
4:8 Godly l has the promise of life
4:10 our confidence in the l God.
2Ti 4:1 going to judge those who are l
Heb 3:12 that turns away from the l God.
4:12 God's word is l and active.
9:14 Now we can serve the l God.
10:20 Jesus has opened a new and l
10:31 Falling into the hands of the l
11:13 that they were l as strangers
12:22 to the city of the l God,
Jas 3:13 Show this by l the right way
1Pe 2:4 You are coming to Christ, the l
2:5 You come to him as l stones,
4:4 in the same excesses of wild l.
4:5 to judge the l and the dead.
2Pe 1:8 Christ is l and productive.
2Jn 1:4 to find some of your children l
3Jn 1:3 told us that you are l according
1:4 that my children are l according
Rev 1:18 the l one. I was dead, but now I
3:10 world to test those l on earth.
4:6 were four l creatures covered
4:7 The first l creature was like a
4:8 Each of the four l creatures had
4:9 Whenever the l creatures give
5:6 throne with the four l creatures
5:8 the four l creatures and the 24
5:11 the four l creatures,
5:14 The four l creatures said,
6:1 I heard one of the four l
6:3 the second l creature say,
6:5 I heard the third l creature say,
6:6 from among the four l creatures
6:7 of the fourth l creature say,
6:10 and take revenge on those l
7:2 east with the seal of the l God.
7:11 leaders and the four l creatures.
8:9 of the creatures that were l
8:13 catastrophe for those l on earth,
11:10 Those l on earth will gloat over
11:10 had tormented those l on earth.
13:6 those who are l in heaven.
13:8 Everyone l on earth will
13:12 makes the earth and those l
13:14 It deceives those l on earth
13:14 It tells those l on earth to make
14:3 the four l creatures,
15:7 One of the four l creatures gave
16:3 and every l thing in the sea
17:2 and those l on earth became
17:8 Those l on earth, will be
18:17 and everyone who made their l
19:4 The 24 leaders and the 4 l

lizard (1)

Pro 30:28 A l you can hold in your hands,

lizards (2)

Lev 11:29 moles, mice, and all types of l:
11:30 geckos, monitors, l,

load (8)

Gen 45:17 'L up your animals,
Exo 5:11 but your work l will not be
23:5 you has collapsed under its l,
Neh 5:18 already carrying a heavy l.
13:15 and every other kind of l.
Psa 38:4 Like a heavy l, it is more than I
Isa 46:1 a l for weary people.
Jnh 1:5 overboard to lighten the ship's l.

loaded (6)

Gen 42:26 they l their grain on their
44:13 Then each one l his donkey
1Sm 25:18 cakes and l them on donkeys.
2Sm 16:1 They were l with 200 loaves of
2Ki 8:9 He had l the goods on 40
Isa 1:4 ⌊Its⌋ people are l down with

loads (15)

Jos 22:8 bronze, iron, and l of clothing.
1Ki 5:15 men who carried heavy l,
2Ch 2:2 70,000 men to carry heavy l,
2:18 70,000 of them carry heavy l,
Neh 4:17 who were carrying l did
13:15 saw them bringing in l of wine,
13:15 They piled the l on donkeys
13:19 to make sure that no l could
Job 37:11 Yes, he l the thick clouds with
Isa 46:2 able to escape with heavy l.
Lam 5:13 boys stagger under l of wood.
Mat 11:28 are tired from carrying heavy l,
23:4 They make l that are hard to
Luk 11:46 You burden people with l that
11:46 a finger to carry any of these l.

loaf (17)

Exo 29:23 take a round l of bread,
Lev 7:14 offering you must bring one l
8:26 He took a l of unleavened
Jdg 7:13 There was a l of barley bread
7:13 the l of bread hit that tent so
1Sm 2:36 front of him to get a coin or a l
2Sm 6:19 and women — one l of bread,
1Ki 17:13 But first make a small l and
1Ch 16:3 men and women — a l of bread,
Pro 6:26 price is ⌊only⌋ a l of bread,
Jer 37:21 He gave him a l of bread every
Hos 7:8 are like a half-baked l of bread.
Mar 8:14 bread along and had only one l
Luk 4:3 stone to become a l of bread."
Jon 21:9 and they saw a l of bread.
1Co 10:17 Because there is one l,
10:17 All of us share one l.

Lo Ammi (1)

Hos 1:9 Name him L [Not My People].

loan (21)

Dtr 15:2 If you've made a l,
24:6 be taken to guarantee a l.
24:10 When you make a l to your
24:11 you're making the l will bring
24:17 clothes to guarantee a l.
Job 22:6 goods as security for a l
24:3 widow's ox as security for a l.
24:9 baby as security for a l.
Psa 15:5 does not collect interest on a l
Pro 6:1 My son, if you guarantee a l for
11:15 a stranger's l will get into
17:18 He guarantees a l in the
20:16 who guarantees a stranger's l,
20:16 the person who makes a l
22:27 have no money to pay back a l,
27:13 who guarantees a stranger's l,
27:13 the person who makes a l
Eze 18:7 gives him as security for a l.
18:12 return the security for a l.
18:16 doesn't keep the security for a l.
33:15 He returns the security for a l,

loans (8)

Dtr 15:6 You will make l to many
28:12 You will be able to make l to
28:44 will be able to make l to you,
28:44 won't be able to make l to them.
Neh 5:7 "You are charging interest on l
Pro 22:26 who guarantee other people's l.
28:8 wealthy through ⌊unfair⌋ l
Hab 2:6 makes himself wealthy on l.

loaves (40)

Exo 29:2 and bake some l of bread,
Lev 7:12 and l made from flour mixed
23:17 Bring two l of bread from your
Num 11:8 cook it in a pot or make round l
1Sm 10:3 will be carrying three l of bread,
10:4 and give you two l of bread,
17:17 of roasted grain and these ten l
21:3 Give me five l of bread or
25:18 quickly took 200 l of bread,
2Sm 16:1 loaded with 200 l of bread,
1Ki 14:3 Take ten l of bread,
2Ki 4:42 harvested grain, 20 barley l,
Eze 4:12 as you would eat barley l.
Mat 4:3 stones to become l of bread."
12:4 men had no right to eat those l.
14:17 "All we have here are five l of
14:19 After he took the five l and the
14:19 He broke the l apart,
15:34 "How many l of bread do you
15:36 He took the seven l and the
16:9 Don't you remember the five l
16:10 Don't you remember the seven l
Mar 2:26 He had no right to eat those l.
6:38 "How many l do you have?
6:38 "Five l of bread and two fish."
6:41 After he took the five l and the
6:41 He broke the l apart and kept
6:52 happened with the l of bread.
8:5 "How many l of bread do you
8:6 He took the seven l and gave
8:19 When I broke the five l for the
8:20 "When I broke the seven l for
Luk 6:4 He had no right to eat those l.
9:13 "We have five l of bread and
9:16 Then he took the five l and the
9:16 He broke the l apart and kept

Luk 11:5 let me borrow three l of bread.
Jon 6:9 "A boy who has five l of barley
6:11 Jesus took the l, gave thanks,
6:26 much of those l as you wanted.

lobe (17)

Exo 29:13 organs, the l of the liver,
29:22 organs, the l of the liver,
Lev 3:4 Also cut off the l of the liver
3:10 along with the l of the liver.
3:15 Also remove the l of the liver
4:9 He will also remove the l of the
7:4 He will also remove the l of the
8:16 organs, the l of the liver,
8:23 and put it on Aaron's right ear l,
8:25 organs, the l of the liver,
9:10 and l of the liver from the
9:19 and the l of the liver)
14:14 and put it on the right ear l,
14:17 in his hand on the right ear l,
14:25 and put it on the right ear l,
14:28 is in his hand on the right ear l,
Dtr 15:17 pierce it through his ear l into

lobes (2)

Exo 29:20 and put it on the right ear l of
Lev 8:24 of the blood on their right ear l,

local (2)

Gen 34:2 When Shechem, son of the l
Job 31:34 of the ⌊l⌋ mobs terrified me

located (6)

Jos 21:11 This is the city of Hebron l in
Eze 8:3 stirs up ⌊God's⌋ anger was l.
45:6 It will be l alongside the holy
Mat 5:14 be hidden when it is l on a hill.
Jon 19:41 A garden was l in the place
Act 27:12 and northwest winds and is l

location (6)

Dtr 21:4 to a l where the land hasn't
1Ki 7:8 were in a different l than
2Ki 2:19 "This city's l is as good as you
1Ch 17:5 from one l ⌊to another⌋.
Eze 45:4 and it will be the l for the holy
Jon 19:17 out ⌊of the city⌋ to a l called

lock (4)

Dtr 32:34 this what I've stored under l
Job 24:16 by day they l themselves in.
Sos 5:5 on the handles of the l.
Mat 23:13 You l people out of the

locked (18)

Jdg 3:23 (He had closed and l the doors
3:24 surprised that the doors were l.
9:51 They l the door behind them
Job 41:17 are l together and inseparable.
Psa 77:9 Has he l up his compassion
Pro 18:19 and disputes are like the l gate
Sos 4:12 my sister is a garden that is l,
4:12 is locked, a garden that is l,
Isa 24:22 in a jail and l in prison.
Jer 13:19 cities in the Negev will be l up,
32:2 The prophet Jeremiah was l up
32:3 When King Zedekiah of Judah l
Luk 3:20 he l John in prison.
11:7 The door is already l,
Jon 20:19 were together behind l doors
20:26 Even though the doors were l,
Act 5:23 "We found the prison securely l
26:10 I l many Christians in prison.

locks (8)

Dtr 33:25 May the l and bolts of your
Neh 3:3 its doors, l, and bars in place.
3:6 its doors, l, and bars in place.
3:13 its doors, l, and bars in place,
3:14 He rebuilt it and set its doors, l,
3:15 its doors, l, and bars in place.
Sos 7:5 Your flowing l could hold a
Eze 38:11 All of them live without walls, l,

locust (3)

Exo 10:19 Not one l was left anywhere in
Lev 11:22 You may eat any kind of l,
Job 39:20 Can you make it leap like a l,

locusts (38)

Exo 10:4 I will bring l into your country.
10:12 your hand over Egypt to bring l.
10:13 the east wind had brought the l.
10:14 there been so many l like this,
10:19 It picked up the l and blew
Dtr 28:38 but harvest little because l will
Jdg 6:5 Like swarms of l, they came
7:12 in the valley like a swarm of l.
1Ki 8:37 heat waves, funguses, l,
2Ch 6:28 heat waves, funguses, l,
Psa 78:46 and their produce to l.
105:34 countless l and grasshoppers came.
Pro 30:27 L have no king, yet all of them
Isa 33:4 Like swarming l, people rush
Jer 46:23 They are more numerous than l
51:14 They will swarm like l.
51:27 up horses like a swarm of l.
Joe 1:4 What young l leave,
1:4 locusts leave, mature l will eat.
1:4 What mature l leave,
1:4 locusts leave, adult l will eat.
1:4 What adult l leave,
2:25 for the years that the mature l,
2:25 the adult l, the grasshoppers,
2:25 and the young l ate your crops.
Amo 4:9 L repeatedly devoured your
7:1 He was preparing swarms of l
7:2 When the l had finished eating
Nah 3:15 It will consume you like l.
3:15 Multiply like l! Multiply like
3:15 Multiply like hungry l!
3:16 ⌊They are⌋ like l that attack
3:17 Your officers are like l,
3:17 are like swarms of l that settle
Mat 3:4 consisted of l and wild honey.
Mar 1:6 waist and ate l and wild honey.
Rev 9:3 L came out of the smoke onto
9:7 The l looked like horses

Lod (4)

1Ch 8:12 Ono, L, and Lod's villages).
Ezr 2:33 of L, Hadid, and Ono: 725
Neh 7:37 of L, Hadid, and Ono: 721
11:35 L, Ono, and in the valley of the

Lo Debar (4)

2Sa 9:4 Machir, Ammiel's son, in L."
9:5 of Ammiel's son Machir in L
17:27 Machir, son of Ammiel from L,
Amo 6:13 for those who rejoice over L

Lod's (1)

1Ch 8:12 built Ono, Lod, and L villages)

lodge (1)

Isa 10:29 mountain pass and l at Geba

lofty (6)

Isa 2:14 mountains and all the l hills,
6:1 sitting on a high and l throne.
30:25 streams on every l mountain
57:7 bed on a high and l mountain.
57:15 The High and L One lives
Eze 17:22 it on a high and l mountain.

log (2)

Amo 4:11 You were like a burning l
Zec 3:2 Isn't this man like a burning l

logs (8)

1Ki 5:8 to the cedar and cypress l.
5:9 My workers will bring l from
5:18 the stone and prepared the l
2Ki 6:2 Each of us can get some l and
1Ch 22:4 David so many cedar l that
22:4 that the l couldn't be counted.
Isa 7:4 These two are smoldering l.'
30:33 high with plenty of burning l.

Lois (1)

2Ti 1:5 first lived in your grandmother L

lonely (3)

Psa 25:16 I am l and oppressed.
68:6 God places l people in
102:7 I am like a l bird on a rooftop.

loner (1)

Pro 18:1 A l is out to get what he wants

long (538)

Gen 3:14 of animals as l as you live.
3:16 Yet, you will l for your husband,
6:4 These children were famous l
6:5 All day l their deepest thoughts
6:15 the ship is to be 450 feet l,
8:22 As l as the earth exists,
21:34 Abraham lived a l time in the
25:8 After a l and full life,
26:8 he had been there a l time,
37:3 a special robe with l sleeves.
37:23 his special robe with l sleeves.
37:32 the special robe with l sleeves
37:34 and mourned for his son a l
38:12 After a l time Judah's wife,
43:10 If we hadn't waited so l,
46:29 cried on his shoulder a l time.
Exo 2:23 After a l time passed,
10:3 How l will you refuse to
10:7 "How l will this man hold us in
14:20 came near the other all night l.
16:28 "How l will you refuse to do
17:11 As l as Moses held up his
19:13 ram's horn sounds a l blast."
20:12 so that you may live for a l time
25:10 ark of acacia wood 45 inches l,
25:17 ark out of pure gold 45 inches l
25:23 of acacia wood 36 inches l,
26:2 Each sheet will be 42 feet l
26:8 the 11 sheets will be 45 feet l
26:16 Each frame is to be 15 feet l
27:9 courtyard should be 150 feet l
27:11 should be the same: 150 feet l,
27:18 courtyard should be 150 feet l,
36:9 Each sheet was 42 feet l and 6
36:15 of the 11 sheets was 45 feet l
36:21 Each frame was 15 feet l and
37:1 out of acacia wood 45 inches l,
37:6 out of pure gold 45 inches l
37:10 out of acacia wood 36 inches l,
38:9 of the courtyard was 150 feet l
38:11 north side was also 150 feet l
38:12 The west side was 75 feet l
38:18 It was 30 feet l and 7 ½ feet
Lev 13:46 As l as they have the skin
15:25 she will be unclean as l as she
15:26 As l as she has a discharge,
Num 6:4 As l as they are Nazirites,
6:5 "As l as they are under the
6:5 They must let their hair grow l.
6:7 vow to God with their l hair.
6:8 As l as they are Nazirites,
9:10 body or is away on a l trip.
9:18 As l as the ⌊column of⌋ smoke
9:19 stayed over the tent for a l time,
9:22 as l as the ⌊column of⌋ smoke
14:11 "How l will these people treat
14:11 How l will they refuse to trust
14:27 "How l must I put up with this
Dtr 1:6 at this mountain l enough.
1:46 in Kadesh as l as you did.
2:1 For a l time we traveled around
2:3 around this region l enough.
3:11 and was more than 13 feet l
4:9 your memory as l as you live.
4:10 to fear me as l as they live
4:26 You won't live very l there.
4:32 distant past, l before your time.
4:40 You will live for a l time in the
4:40 the land for as l as you live.
5:16 Then you will live for a l time,
5:21 "Never l for your neighbor's
5:29 as l as they live!
5:33 and you will live for a l time in
6:2 As l as you live, you,
6:2 and you will live a l time.
6:24 our own good as l as we live

Dtr 7:10 He never takes l to pay back
7:25 Don't ever l for the silver and
9:24 the LORD as l as I've known
11:9 Then you will also live for a l
11:12 He watches over it all year l.
11:21 children will live for a l time
11:21 your ancestors — as l as there's
12:1 You must obey them as l as
12:19 of the Levites as l as you live
14:23 your God as l as you live.
16:3 bread so that, as l as you live,
17:20 will rule for a l time in Israel.
19:9 his directions as l as you live.
20:19 you blockade a city for a l time
22:7 and you will live for a l time.
22:19 divorce her as l as he lives.
22:29 divorce her as l as he lives.
23:6 or friendship as l as you live.
25:15 Then you will live for a l time
28:29 As l as you live, you will be
28:32 eyes looking for them all day l,
28:33 As l as you live, you will know
30:18 You will not live for a l time in
30:20 and it will mean a l life for you
31:13 your God as l as you live
32:7 Remember a time l ago.
32:47 will be able to live for a l time
33:12 will shelter them all day l,
33:25 strength last as l as you live.
Jos 1:5 successfully as l as you live.
4:14 As l as Joshua lived,
6:5 When you hear a l blast on the
9:13 we have come such a l way."
11:18 with all these kings for a l time.
18:3 "How l are you going to waste
23:1 A l time afterward,
24:2 L ago your ancestors,
24:7 lived in the desert for a l time.
24:31 Israel served the LORD as l as
Jdg 2:18 their enemies as l as that judge
5:28 "Why is his chariot taking so l?
9:45 attacked the city all day l.
1Sm 1:11 I will give him to you for as l as
1:12 While Hannah was praying a l
1:14 "How l are you going to stay
7:2 A l time passed after the ark
7:13 as l as Samuel lived.
7:15 judged Israel as l as he lived.
10:24 shouted, "L live the king!"
14:52 Philistines as l as Saul lived.
16:1 "How l are you going to mourn
20:14 But as l as I live, ⌊promise me
20:31 As l as Jesse's son lives on
21:13 and acted insane ⌊as l as
22:4 and they stayed with him as l
24:13 like people used to say l ago,
25:6 Say to him, 'May you live ⌊l!
25:7 missing as l as they've been
25:16 day and night as l as we were
25:28 found in you as l as you live.
27:11 This was his practice as l as
2Sm 2:26 How l will it be before you will
12:22 "As l as the child was alive,
13:39 King David began to l for
14:2 for the dead for a l time.
16:16 he said, "L live the king!
16:16 live the king! L live the king!"
1Ki 1:25 'L live King Adonijah!'
1:34 'L live King Solomon!'
1:39 "L live King Solomon!"
2:8 and said, 'As l as I'm king,
2:38 in Jerusalem for a l time.
3:11 for this and not for a l life,
3:13 be like you as l as you live.
3:14 then I will also give you a l
4:21 to Solomon as l as he lived.
4:25 As l as Solomon lived,
6:2 for the LORD was 90 feet l,
6:20 The inner room was 30 feet l,
6:24 of the angels was 7 ½ feet l.
7:2 It was 150 feet l, 75 feet wide,
7:6 the Hall of Pillars 75 feet l
7:10 stones (some 12 feet l,
7:10 12 feet long, others 15 feet l).
8:8 The poles were so l that their
8:40 Then, as l as they live in the

1Ki 11:25 Rezon was Israel's rival as l
11:34 I will allow him to be ruler as l
12:28 in Jerusalem l enough.
14:30 Jeroboam as l as they lived.
15:16 of Israel as l as they lived.
15:32 and Baasha as l as they lived.
17:15 and her family had food for a l
18:21 "How l will you try to have it
2Ki 9:22 be alright as l as your mother
11:12 they said, "L live the king!"
12:2 as l as the priest Jehoiada
13:3 Benhadad as l as they lived.
13:22 Israel as l as Jehoahaz ruled.
18:26 language as l as there are
19:25 I did this l ago. I planned it in
20:19 and security as l as I live?"
25:29 presence as l as he lived.
25:30 allowance as l as he lived.
1Ch 7:22 Ephraim mourned a l time,
29:28 His l life was full of wealth and
2Ch 1:11 You didn't even ask for a l life.
3:3 It was 90 feet l and 35 feet
3:8 It was as l as the temple was
3:8 the temple was wide, 30 feet l.
3:11 of the angels was 7 ½ feet l
3:11 Its other wing was 7 ½ feet l
3:12 of the angels was 7 ½ feet l
3:12 Its other wing was 7 ½ feet l
3:15 They were 53 feet l,
4:1 made a bronze altar 30 feet l,
5:9 The poles were so l that their
6:13 a bronze platform 7 ½ feet l,
6:31 Then, as l as they live in the
12:15 Jeroboam as l as they lived.
15:3 For a l time Israel was without
23:11 They said, "L live the king!"
24:2 as l as the priest Jehoiada
24:14 As l as Jehoiada lived,
26:5 As l as he dedicated his life to
34:33 As l as he lived, they didn't
Ezr 4:19 that this city has a l history
Neh 2:6 "How l will you be gone,
12:46 L ago in the time of David and
Job 3:5 Let the darkness and l
3:21 to those who l for death but it
7:4 But the evening is l,
7:19 stop looking at me l enough
8:2 "How l will you say these
8:2 How l will your words be so
10:22 to a dismal land of l shadows
14:2 shadow; he doesn't stay l.
14:14 relief to come as l as my hard
14:15 You will l for the person your
18:2 "How l before your words will
19:2 "How l will you torment me and
27:3 'As l as there is one breath
27:6 won't accuse me as l as I live.
32:9 merely because they live l.
38:21 and have lived such a l time!
Psa 4:2 You important people, how l
4:2 How l are you going to love
6:3 But you, O LORD, how l ...?
12:5 safety for those who l for it."
13:1 How l, O LORD? Will you
13:1 How l will you hide your face
13:2 How l must I make decisions
13:2 How l will my enemy triumph
21:4 You gave him a l life,
24:4 and a pure heart and does not l
25:5 I wait all day l for you.
32:3 of my groaning all day l.
34:12 Who would like to live l
35:17 O Lord, how l will you look on?
35:28 about your praise all day l.
38:12 All day l they think of ways to
42:3 People ask me all day l,
42:10 They ask me all day l,
44:1 in their day, in days l ago.
44:8 All day l we praise our God.
44:15 All day l my disgrace is in front
44:22 we are being killed all day l
52:1 mercy of God lasts all day l!
56:1 All day l warriors oppress me.
56:2 All day l my enemies spy on
56:5 All day l my enemies twist my
62:3 How l will all of you attack a

Psa 62:3 How l will you try to murder
63:4 So I will thank you as l as I
63:6 Through the l hours of the night
71:8 with your glory all day l.
71:15 about your salvation all day l.
71:24 your righteousness all day l,
72:5 May they fear you as l as the
72:15 May he live l. May the gold from
72:15 ⌊they⌋ praise him all day l.
72:17 May his name continue as l as
73:14 ⌊with problems⌋ all day l,
73:25 As l as I have you,
74:2 L ago you made it your own.
74:9 one knows how l this will last.
74:10 How l, O God, will the enemy
74:12 And yet, from l ago God has
74:22 fools insult you all day l.
77:5 the days of old, the years l ago.
78:2 what has been hidden l ago,
78:69 he made to last for a l time.
79:5 How l, O LORD? Will you
80:4 how l will you smolder in anger
82:2 "How l are you going to judge
82:2 How l are you going to side
86:3 I call out to you all day l.
88:9 All day l I call out to you,
88:17 around me all day l like water.
89:16 find joy in your name all day l.
89:46 How l, O LORD? Will you hide
89:46 How l will your anger continue
90:9 out our years like one ⌊l⌋ sigh.
90:13 How l ...? Change your plans
91:16 I will satisfy you with a l life.
93:2 Your throne was set in place a l
94:3 How l, O LORD, will wicked
94:3 people triumph? How l?
102:8 All day l my enemies insult me.
102:25 L ago you laid the foundation of
104:33 to praise my God as l as I live.
116:2 I will call on him as l as I live
119:40 I l for your guiding principles.
119:52 your regulations from l ago,
119:97 are in my thoughts all day l.
119:131 I l for your commandments.
119:152 L ago I learned from your
120:6 I have lived too l with those
129:3 made l slashes ⌊like furrows⌋."
143:3 like those who have died l ago.
143:5 I remember the days l ago.
143:8 because I l for you.
146:2 to praise my God as l as I live.
Pro 1:22 "How l will you gullible people
1:22 How l will you mockers find
1:22 How l will you fools hate
3:2 they will bring you l life,
3:16 L life is in ⌊wisdom's⌋ right
6:9 How l will you lie there,
7:19 He has gone on a l trip.
8:22 already possessed me l ago,
21:26 All day l he feels greedy,
28:2 knowledge will it last a l time.
Ecc 1:10 already been here l before us.
2:16 fool will be remembered for l,
6:3 No matter how l he would have
8:12 crimes and yet live a l life.
Isa 1:26 you judges like you had l ago,
6:11 I asked, "How l, O Lord?"
22:11 the one who formed it l ago.
24:22 After a l time they'll be
25:1 out your plans from l ago.
26:9 With my soul I l for you at night.
30:33 Topheth was prepared l ago.
36:11 language as l as there are
37:26 I did this l ago. I planned it in
39:8 and security as l as I live."
42:14 I have been silent for a l time.
43:18 not dwell on events from l ago.
44:7 I established my people l ago.
44:8 make this known to you l ago?
45:21 past and predicted it l ago?
46:10 From l ago I told you things
48:5 you what would happen l ago.
49:19 devoured you will be l gone.
51:9 up as you did in days l past,
51:9 as in generations l ago.
52:5 my name is cursed all day l.

Isa 57:11 I've been silent for a l time.
61:4 the places destroyed l ago.
64:5 continued to sin for a l time.
65:2 out my hands all day l
65:5 like a smoldering fire all day l.
65:20 man who doesn't live a l life.
65:22 people will live as l as trees,
Jer 2:20 "L ago you broke off your yoke,
4:21 How l must I see the battle flag
5:15 nation that has lasted a l time.
7:7 to your ancestors l ago.
12:4 How l will the land mourn?
12:4 How l will the plants in every
20:7 I've been made fun of all day l.
20:8 insults and contempt all day l.
23:26 How l will these prophets
28:8 L ago, the prophets who
29:28 You will be captives a l time.
30:20 will be like they were l ago.
31:22 How l will you wander around,
32:14 so that they will last a l time.
32:39 will fear me as l as they live.
35:7 so that you may live for a l time
37:16 and he stayed there a l time.
44:14 where they l to return and live.
46:26 live in peace as they did l ago,"
47:5 How l will you cut yourselves,
47:6 how l will you keep on
52:33 presence as l as he lived.
52:34 allowance as l as he lived.
Lam 1:13 He has made me sick all day l.
2:17 the threat he announced l ago.
3:3 me again and again all day l.
3:6 those who died a l time ago.
3:14 All day l they make fun of
3:62 directed against me all day l.
5:20 us for such a l time?
5:21 Give us back the life we had l
Eze 7:13 Sellers will not live l enough to
12:27 sees won't happen for a l time.
17:3 It had large wings with l,
26:20 to join the people of l ago.
31:5 branches became large and l
31:7 beautiful with its l branches.
38:8 After a l time you will be called
38:8 have been ruined for a l time.
38:17 You are the one I spoke about l
40:5 stick that was 10 ½ feet l.
40:7 guardroom was 10 ½ feet l
40:11 and the gateway was 23 feet l.
40:18 It was as wide as it was l.
40:21 The gateway was 87 ½ feet l
40:25 It was 87 ½ feet l and 44 feet
40:29 The gateway was 87 ½ feet l
40:30 They were all 44 feet l and 9
40:33 The gateway was 87 ½ feet l
40:36 The gateway was 87 ½ feet l
40:42 They were 3 feet l,
40:43 hooks, three inches l,
40:47 a perfect square — 175 feet l
40:49 The entrance hall was 35 feet l
41:2 It was 70 feet l and 35 feet
41:4 It was 35 feet l and 35 feet
41:12 and it was 157 ½ feet l.
41:13 It was 175 feet l. This included
41:13 All together it was 175 feet l.
41:15 It was 175 feet l. The holy place
42:2 that faced north was 175 feet l
42:4 17 ½ feet wide and 175 feet l.
42:8 courtyard was 87 ½ feet l.
42:8 the temple were 175 feet l.
42:11 These side rooms were as l
42:16 It was 875 feet l according to
42:17 It was 875 feet l according to
42:18 It was 875 feet l according to
42:19 It was 875 feet l according to
42:20 The wall was 875 feet l and
43:13 stick was 21 inches l.)
43:16 21 feet wide and 21 feet l.
43:17 It was 24 ½ feet l and 24 ½
44:20 heads or let their hair grow l.
45:1 Set aside an area 43,750 feet l
45:3 off an area 43,750 feet l
45:5 An area 43,750 feet l and
45:6 feet wide and 43,750 feet l as
46:22 of the courtyard were 60 feet l
Eze 48:8 and it will be as l as one of the
48:9 the LORD will be 43,750 feet l
48:10 side it will be 43,750 feet l.
48:10 side it will be 43,750 feet l.
48:13 It will be 43,750 feet l and
48:15 feet wide by 43,750 feet l,
48:16 north side it will be 7,875 feet l.
48:16 side it will be 7,875 feet l.
48:21 Both of these areas are as l as
48:30 north side will be 7,875 feet l.
48:32 east side will be 7,875 feet l.
48:33 south side will be 7,875 feet l.
48:34 west side will be 7,875 feet l.
Dan 4:33 grew as l as eagles' feathers
4:33 nails grew as l as birds' claws.
8:3 The ram had two l horns,
8:13 "How l will the things in this
12:6 "How l will it be until these
Hos 3:3 "You must wait for me a l time.
3:4 the Israelites will wait a l time
7:6 All night l their anger smolders,
8:5 How l will they remain
Joe 1:20 Even wild animals l for you.
Amo 5:18 it will be for those who l
5:18 Why do you l for that day?
8:14 "I solemnly swear as l as there
9:11 them as they were a l time ago.
Mic 5:2 the distant past, to days l ago.
7:20 an oath to our ancestors l ago.
Hab 1:2 How l, O LORD, am I to cry for
2:6 How l will this go on?'
Zec 2:2 see how wide and how l it is."
5:2 "It's 30 feet l and 15 feet wide."
Mal 3:4 in the past, as in years l ago.
Mat 11:21 they thought and acted l ago
17:17 How l must I be with you?
17:17 How l must I put up with you?
20:6 here all day l without work?'
23:5 the tassels on their shawls l.
24:48 may think that it will be a l time
25:19 "After a l time the master of
27:29 "L live the king of the Jews!"
Mar 1:35 In the morning, l before sunrise
2:19 As l as they have the groom
8:3 Some of them have come a l
9:19 How l must I be with you?
9:19 How l must I put up with you?
9:21 "How l has he been like this?"
12:38 like to walk around in l robes,
12:40 houses and then say l prayers
15:18 "L live the king of the Jews!"
Luk 1:21 was staying in the temple so l.
1:70 through his holy prophets l ago.
1:75 and honorable as l as we live.
8:27 not worn clothes for a l time.
8:29 controlled the man for a l time.
9:8 prophets from l ago had come
9:19 prophets from l ago has come
9:41 How l must I be with you and
10:13 L ago they would have worn
12:45 his master is taking a l time
17:22 time will come when you will l
20:9 and went on a l trip.
20:46 They like to walk around in l
20:47 houses and then say l prayers
23:8 For a l time he had wanted to
Jon 5:6 he had been sick for a l time.
9:5 As l as I'm in the world,
10:24 They asked him, "How l will
11:8 not l ago the Jews wanted to
14:9 been with all of you for a l time.
19:3 "L live the king of the Jews!"
Act 3:21 through his holy prophets l ago.
8:11 had amazed them for a l time
14:3 the city of Iconium for a l time.
14:28 They stayed for a l time with
15:32 spoke a l time to encourage
20:11 with the people for a l time,
21:38 started a revolution not l ago
22:22 been allowed to live this l!"
24:4 I don't want to keep you too l.
26:5 They've known me for a l time
28:6 But after they had waited a l
Rom 1:11 I l to see you to share a
7:1 people only as l as they are
7:2 by law to her husband as l as
Rom 8:36 "We are being killed all day l
10:21 "All day l I have stretched out
11:2 people whom he knew l ago.
11:13 As l as I am an apostle sent to
15:4 Everything written l ago was
16:25 kept in silence for a very l time
1Co 7:39 with her husband as l as
11:14 for a man to have l hair?
11:15 pride to wear her hair l?
2Co 1:13 this as l as you live,
5:2 since we l to put on the house
5:6 We know that as l as we are
Gal 4:1 As l as an heir is a child,
Eph 3:18 l, high, and deep his love is.
6:3 and you may have a l life on
Php 1:8 I l to see every one of you.
1Th 3:8 Now we can go on living as l
1Ti 6:8 As l as we have food and
Heb 7:23 There was a l succession of
10:2 would have stopped l ago.
1Pe 1:2 God the Father knew you l ago
1:10 L ago they spoke about God's
1:20 who was known l ago before
3:20 like those who disobeyed l ago
2Pe 1:13 As l as I'm still alive,
2:3 The verdict against them from l
3:5 and earth existed a l time ago.
Jud 1:4 Not l ago they were
Rev 6:10 how l before you judge and
9:6 They will l to die, but death
21:16 It was as wide as it was l.
21:16 It was 12,000 stadia l.

longed (6)

Psa 107:30 to the harbor they had l for.
119:174 I have l for you to save me,
Isa 21:4 The twilight hours I l for make
Jer 17:16 and I have not l for the day of
Eze 23:21 So she l to do the sinful things
Mat 13:17 and many of God's people l

longer (256)

Gen 4:12 it will no l yield its best for you.
17:5 So your name will no l be
32:28 "Your name will no l be Jacob
35:10 You will no l be called Jacob,
37:29 that Joseph was no l there,
42:13 the other one is no l with us."
42:32 One is no l with us.
42:36 Joseph is no l with us,
42:36 Simeon is no l with us,
45:1 Joseph could no l control his
49:4 You will no l be first because
Exo 1:12 couldn't stand them any l.
2:3 she couldn't hide him any l,
5:10 I'm no l giving you straw.
9:28 don't have to stay here any l."
33:6 no l wore their jewelry.
Lev 15:25 If her period lasts l than usual,
26:13 so that you are no l slaves
26:31 I will no l accept the soothing
Dtr 10:16 impossible to deal with any l.
21:13 and no l wear the clothes she
21:14 that you are no l pleased
24:1 her and she no l pleased him.)
32:5 they are no l his children.
Jos 22:23 intention of no l following him,
Jdg 2:14 They could no l stand up
2:21 I will no l force out the nations
10:16 bear to have Israel suffer any l.
1Sm 1:18 She was no l sad.
6:5 Maybe he will no l be so hard
10:2 Your father no l cares about
2Sm 3:22 so he was no l with David in
7:10 The wicked will no l oppress
19:28 So I no l have the right to
19:34 "I don't have much l to live.
20:3 He provided for them but no l
20:5 but he took l to do it than David
1Ki 11:4 He was no l committed to the
2Ki 6:33 Why should I wait any l for the
25:29 Jehoiakin no l wore prison
1Ch 17:9 The wicked will no l frighten
19:19 And the Arameans were no l
23:26 The Levites will no l have to
2Ch 12:12 the LORD was no l angry with

2Ch 35:3 carried on your shoulders any l.
36:16 He could no l heal them.
Ezr 4:13 the Jews will no l pay taxes,
Neh 2:17 and we will no l be insulted."
13:21 After that, they no l came on
Job 7:8 over me will no l see me.
11:9 It is l than the earth and wider
30:11 they are no l restrained in my
36:2 "Be patient with me a little l,
Psa 40:12 with me so that I can no l see.
72:7 until the moon no l ⌊shines⌋.
74:9 We no l see miraculous signs.
77:10 Most High is no l the same."
78:32 and they no l believed in his
83:4 Israel will no l be remembered."
88:5 whom you no l remember,
102:11 like a shadow that is getting l,
103:16 and there is no l any sign of it.
104:35 May there no l be any wicked
Pro 9:11 You will live l because of me,
28:16 who hate unjust gain will live l.
Ecc 4:13 who won't take advice any l.
8:13 They will not live any l.
Isa 7:8 so that it will no l be a nation.
7:25 And you will no l be able to go
10:20 descendants will no l depend
17:1 "Damascus will no l be a city.
23:10 You no l have a harbor.
23:12 "You will no l be joyful,
24:9 People no l drink wine when
26:14 They are no l alive.
26:21 on it and will no l cover up its
27:4 I am no l angry. If only thorns
29:22 Jacob will no l be ashamed.
29:22 Jacob's face will no l turn pale.
30:20 But your teacher will no l be
32:5 Godless fools will no l be
33:8 People are no l respected.
33:19 You will no l see those savage
41:12 to nothing and no l exist.
47:1 You will no l be called soft and
47:5 You will no l be called the
52:1 people will no l come to you.
60:18 No l will you hear about
60:19 The sun will no l be your light
60:20 Your sun will no l go down,
62:4 You will no l be called
62:4 and your land will no l be
65:19 Screaming and crying will no l
65:20 There will no l be an infant
Jer 2:31 around and no l come to me?
3:12 I will no l frown on you
3:12 'I will no l be angry with you.
3:16 "People will no l talk about the
3:16 It will no l come to mind.
3:17 They will no l follow their own
6:4 of evening are growing l.
7:32 "when that place will no l be
16:13 because I will no l have pity
16:14 "when people will no l begin
19:6 when this place will no l be
20:9 "I can forget the LORD and no l
20:9 but I can't do it any l.
23:4 My sheep will no l be afraid or
23:7 people's oaths will no l be,
30:8 Foreigners will no l make you
31:29 people will no l say,
31:34 No l will each person teach his
31:34 and I will no l hold their sins
33:24 and they no l consider them a
36:5 Jeremiah told Baruch, "I'm no l
44:22 The LORD could no l bear the
48:2 People will no l praise Moab.
49:7 Is there no l any wisdom in
50:39 It will no l be inhabited or lived
51:44 Nations will no l stream to
52:33 Jehoiakin no l wore prison
Lam 2:9 There is no l any instruction
4:15 'They can't stay here any l.'
4:16 He will no l look favorably on
4:16 They no l respected the priests,
5:14 men no l play their music.
Eze 7:19 It will no l satisfy their hunger
12:23 You will no l quote it in Israel.'
12:24 There will no l be any false
12:28 that I say will no l be delayed.
Eze 13:21 power so that they will no l
13:23 That is why you will no l see
14:11 will no l wander away from
14:11 They will no l dishonor me
16:41 and you will no l pay others.
16:42 I will no l be angry.
18:3 you will no l use this proverb in
19:14 It no l has any strong branches
20:39 You will no l dishonor my holy
21:32 You will no l be remembered.
25:10 So the Ammonites will no l be
26:13 your harps will no l be heard.
26:21 and you will no l exist.
28:9 You will no l say that you are a
28:24 The nation of Israel will no l be
31:14 and their tops were no l
33:22 I spoke, and I was no l quiet.
33:28 People will no l brag about its
34:10 and they will no l take care of
34:10 sheep will no l be their food.
34:22 and they will no l be prey.
34:28 They will no l be prey to the
34:28 wild animals will no l eat them.
34:29 They will no l experience
34:29 and they will no l suffer the
36:12 You will no l take their children
36:14 So you will no l devour your
36:15 I will no l let you hear the
36:15 You will no l suffer the
36:30 will no l suffer disgrace among
36:34 It will no l remain empty for
37:22 They will no l be two nations
37:23 They will no l dishonor
39:29 I will no l hide my face from
43:7 will no l dishonor my holy
45:8 Then my princes will no l
Dan 8:3 one l than the other,
8:3 though the l one had grown up
11:4 It will no l be like his empire,
Hos 1:6 I will no l love the nation of
1:6 I will no l forgive them.
1:9 You are no l my people,
1:9 and I am no l your God.
2:2 She no l acts like my wife.
2:2 She no l treats me like her
2:16 "She will no l call me her
14:4 I will no l be angry with them.
Joe 1:9 wine offerings are no l brought
2:10 and the stars no l shine.
2:19 I will no l make you a disgrace
3:15 The stars will no l shine.
Amo 7:8 I will no l overlook what they
8:2 I will no l overlook what they
Jnh 1:2 people that I can no l overlook
Mic 2:3 You will no l be able to walk
5:13 You will no l worship what
Nah 1:14 You will no l have
Zep 1:6 LORD and those who no l seek
3:11 On that day you will no l be
Zec 1:12 how much l until you show
9:5 Ashkelon will no l be lived in.
11:6 The LORD declares, "I will no l
13:2 They will no l be remembered.
14:21 On that day there will no l be
Mal 2:13 because he no l pays attention
Mat 5:13 It is no l good for anything
19:6 So they are no l two but one.
Mar 1:45 Jesus could no l enter any city
5:3 No one could restrain him any l,
7:12 he no l has to do anything for
10:8 So they are no l two but one.
15:5 Jesus no l answered anything,
Luk 16:2 manage my property any l.'
Jon 4:42 "Our faith is no l based on
11:54 So Jesus no l walked openly
14:19 the world will no l see me,
14:30 so I won't talk with you much l.
17:11 I won't be in the world much l,
Act 1:9 so that they could no l see him.
10:28 should no l call anyone impure
18:18 in Corinth quite a while l,
18:20 The Jews asked him to stay l,
19:22 while he stayed l in the
25:24 not be allowed to live any l.
Rom 6:6 this we are no l slaves to sin.
6:9 Death no l has any power over
Rom 7:2 that marriage law is no l in
7:17 So I am no l the one who is
7:20 I am no l the one who is doing
8:1 Jesus can no l be condemned.
14:15 you are no l living by love.
1Co 12:15 Would that mean it's no l part of
12:16 Would that mean it's no l part of
13:8 but it will no l be used.
13:8 but it will no l be used.
13:10 is incomplete will no l be used.
13:11 I no l used childish ways.
15:18 believers in Christ no l exist.
2Co 5:15 those who live should no l live
Gal 2:20 I no l live, but Christ lives in
3:18 then it no l comes to us
3:25 we are no l under the control of
4:7 So you are no l slaves but
Eph 2:19 That is why you are no l
4:14 Then we will no l be little
4:14 We will no l be influenced by
4:17 to live any l like other people
4:19 Since they no l have any
1Th 3:1 because we couldn't wait any l
3:5 But when I couldn't wait any l,
Phm 1:16 no l as a slave but better than a
Heb 7:23 priest died he could no l serve.
8:11 No l will each person teach his
8:12 and I will no l hold their sins
10:17 Then he adds, "I will no l hold
10:18 there is no l any need to
Jas 4:11 you are no l following them.
1Pe 4:1 suffered physically no l sins.)
4:4 that you no l join them
Rev 6:11 They were told to rest a little l
12:8 and there was no l any place
16:20 mountains could no l be seen.
17:8 beast which once was, is no l,
17:8 is no l, and will come again.
17:11 The beast that was and is no l
22:3 There will no l be any curse.

longing (5)

Psa 119:20 endless l for your regulations.
Pro 13:12 but a fulfilled l is a tree of life.
Isa 63:15 Where is the l of your heart and
Php 2:26 He has been l to see all of you
Heb 11:16 Instead, these men were l for a

long-lasting (1)

Ezr 9:12 give this land as a l inheritance

longs (8)

Job 7:2 Like a slave, he l for shade.
Psa 42:1 As a deer l for flowing streams,
42:1 so my soul l for you,
45:11 The king l for your beauty.
63:1 My body l for you in a dry,
84:2 My soul l and yearns for the
Sos 7:10 my beloved's, and he l for me.
Jer 31:20 That is why my heart l for him,

long-sleeved (2)

2Sm 13:18 (She was wearing a l gown.
13:19 tore the l gown she had on,

long-time (1)

Eze 25:15 tried to destroy their l enemies.

long-winded (1)

Job 16:3 Will ⌊your⌋ l speeches never

look (448)

Gen 2:9 These trees were nice to l at,
3:6 was good to eat, nice to l at,
4:6 and why do you l
13:14 to Abram, "L north, south, east,
15:5 "Now l up at the sky and count
18:31 "L now, if I may be so bold as
19:8 "L, I have two daughters who
19:17 Don't l behind you,
19:20 L, there's a city near enough to
20:15 Abimelech said, "L,
31:12 He said, 'L up and see that all
34:21 L, there's plenty of room in this
37:19 They said to each other, "L,
39:14 servants and said to them, "L!

Gen 40:7 do you l so unhappy today?"
41:33 "Pharaoh should l for a wise
Exo 1:16 l at the child when you deliver
3:6 he was afraid to l at God.
5:5 Then Pharaoh added, "L how
14:11 L what you've done by bringing
33:21 Then the LORD said, "L,
Lev 10:19 and l what happened to me.
13:4 and does not l deeper than
13:31 and it does not l deeper than
13:32 and the scab does not l deeper
13:34 skin and does not l deeper than
13:36 the priest does not have to l for
13:55 If it doesn't l any different and
26:11 and I will never l at you with
26:15 if you reject my laws and l at
26:30 I will l at you with disgust.
26:44 I will not reject them or l at
27:33 You must not l to see if it is
Num 4:20 Kohathites must not go in to l at
6:26 The LORD will l on you with
11:6 Everywhere we l there's
15:39 Whenever you l at the threads
21:8 Anyone who is bitten can l at it
23:9 I l at them from the hills.
24:1 he didn't l for omens as he had
24:17 I l at someone who is not
27:12 and take a l at the land I will
32:8 Barnea to take a l at the land.
Dtr 3:27 and l west, north, south,
3:27 You may l at the land,
4:29 But if you l for the LORD your
26:15 L down from your holy place in
28:23 sky above will l like bronze,
32:49 Take a l at the land of Canaan
Jos 2:1 told them, "Go, l at that country,
6:25 Joshua had sent to l at Jericho.
7:2 to them, "Go, l at that country."
9:12 L at it now! It's dry and
9:13 L at them now! See how they
14:10 "So l at me. The LORD has kept
14:10 So now l at me today.
22:28 'L at the model of the LORD's
Jdg 6:15 L at my whole family.
9:36 the troops, he said to Zebul, "L,
9:36 of the mountains l like men
14:8 his way⌋ he left the road to l at
16:10 Delilah told Samson, "L,
Rut 1:15 Naomi said, "L, Go back with
3:1 shouldn't I try to l for a home
1Sm 1:11 if you will l at my misery,
9:3 and go l for the donkeys."
9:8 again answered Saul, "L, here!
10:14 "To l for the donkeys,
12:3 I take a bribe from anyone to l
14:11 The Philistines said, "L,
14:17 "L around," Saul told the troops
16:7 "Don't l at his appearance or
16:7 Humans l at outward
16:16 why don't you command us to l
17:42 Philistine got a good l at David,
20:21 Now, if I tell the boy, 'L,
21:14 said to his officers, "L at him!
23:25 and his men came to l for him,
24:11 My master, l at this!
26:16 L at the king's spear and the jar
2Sm 2:22 How could I l your brother Joab
7:2 said to the prophet Nathan, "L,
9:8 "Who am I that you would l at
14:30 "L, Joab's field is next to mine.
20:3 concubines he had left to l after
1Ki 3:21 I took a good l at him and
12:16 Now l after your own house,
17:23 He said, "L! Your son is alive."
18:43 and l toward the sea."
2Ki 2:16 "Don't send them ⌊to l.⌋"
3:14 I wouldn't even bother to l at
7:13 Let's send them to take a l."
9:2 you arrive there, l for Jehu,
18:21 Now, l! When you trust Egypt,
2Ch 10:16 Now l after your own house,
25:19 become arrogant enough to l
Ezr 9:6 I am embarrassed to l at you.
9:15 L at us. All of us are guilty.
Neh 2:2 "Why do you l so sad?
2:3 "Why shouldn't I l sad when
Neh 9:36 L ⌊at us⌋ now. We're slaves! In
Job 6:19 Caravans from Tema l for them.
6:28 now, if you're willing, l at me.
7:8 Your eye will l for me,
10:6 Is that why you l for guilt in me
10:15 while I l on my misery.
11:18 and you will l around and rest
14:6 L away from him, and he will
16:19 Even now, l! My witness is in
17:13 If I l for the grave as my home
19:5 yourselves l better than me
20:9 home will not l at him again.
21:5 L at me, and be shocked,
22:12 L how high the highest stars
22:26 Almighty and l up toward God.
30:20 I stand up, but you just l at me.
31:1 Then how can I l with lust at a
31:35 L, here is my signature! Let the
32:3 They made it l as if God were
35:5 "L at the heavens and see.
36:20 Don't l forward to the night,
36:30 L, he scatters his flashes of
37:21 People can't l at the sun when
40:11 L at all who are arrogant,
40:12 L at all who are arrogant,
40:15 "L at Behemoth, which I made
40:16 L at the strength in its back
Psa 3:1 O LORD, l how my enemies
8:3 When I l at your heavens,
9:13 L at what I suffer because of
13:3 L at me! Answer me, O LORD
18:27 you bring down a conceited l.
20:3 all your grain offerings and l
22:26 Those who l to the LORD will
25:18 L at my misery and suffering,
26:2 L closely into my heart and
34:5 All who l to him will be radiant.
35:17 O Lord, how long will you l on?
36:12 L at the troublemakers who
37:37 and l at the decent person,
39:13 L away from me so that I may
45:10 L closely! Turn your ear ⌊toward
52:7 "L at this person who refused
63:2 So I l for you in the holy place
68:16 Why do you l with envy,
69:32 May the hearts of those who l
73:12 L how wicked they are!
80:14 L from heaven and see!
80:16 the threatening l on your face.
83:2 L, your enemies are in an
83:16 so that they must l to you for
84:9 L at our shield, O God.
84:9 L with favor on the face of your
91:8 You only have to l with your
92:9 Now l at your enemies,
92:9 Now l at your enemies.
101:5 a conceited l or arrogant heart.
104:27 All of them l to you to give
109:25 They l at me and shake their
112:8 In the end he will l triumphantly
113:6 He bends down to l at heaven
119:153 L at my misery, and rescue me,
121:1 I l up toward the mountains.
123:1 I l up to you, to the one who
131:1 My eyes do not l down on
141:8 My eyes l to you, I have taken
142:4 L to my right and see that no
145:15 eyes of all creatures l to you,
Pro 1:28 They will l for me,
4:25 Let your eyes l straight ahead
21:4 A conceited l and an arrogant
23:31 Do not l at wine because it is
23:35 I'm going to l for another drink."
Ecc 1:14 L at it! It's all pointless. ⌊It's
2:11 But when I turned to l at all that
4:1 Next, I turned to l at all the acts
4:1 L at the tears of those who
4:7 Next, I turned to l at something
5:11 ⌊the opportunity⌋ to l at them?
6:9 It is better to l at what is in front
8:1 and it changes one's grim l.
8:16 study wisdom and how to l at
12:3 ⌊and⌋ those who l out of the
Sos 1:15 L at you! You are beautiful, my
1:15 L at you! You are so beautiful!
1:16 L at you! You are handsome, my
Sos 2:8 L! Here he comes, sprinting
2:9 L! There he stands behind our
2:11 L! The winter is past. The rain
3:2 I will l for the one I love.
3:7 L! Solomon's sedan chair! Sixty
3:11 come out and l at King
3:11 L at his crown, the crown his
4:1 L at you! You are beautiful, my
4:1 L at you! You are so beautiful.
6:1 We will l for him with you.
6:11 I went to the walnut grove to l
6:13 back so that we may l at you!
6:13 Why do you l at me,
6:13 as you l at the dance of
8:1 no one would l down on me.
Isa 3:9 The l on their faces will be
5:11 for those who get up early to l
5:26 L, they are coming very
5:30 If they l at the land,
6:9 No matter how closely you l,
8:21 Then they will l up,
8:22 They will l at the earth and see
10:33 Now l! The Almighty LORD of
12:2 L! God is my Savior. I am
13:8 They'll l at one another in
13:18 nor will they l with pity on
14:16 they l at you closely and say,
17:7 they will l to their Maker,
17:7 and their eyes will l to the Holy
17:8 They won't l to the altars made
18:3 L when someone raises a flag
20:6 'L at what has happened to our
21:9 L! Here come chariots and
22:8 You will l for weapons in the
22:11 You didn't l to Jerusalem's
22:17 L, mighty man! The LORD will
23:13 L at the land of the
26:9 my spirit I eagerly l for you.
29:20 All who l for ways to do wrong
30:2 They l for shelter under
30:2 Pharaoh's protection and l
31:1 They don't l to the Holy One of
33:15 He doesn't l for evil things to
33:20 L at Zion, the city of our
36:6 L! When you trust Egypt, you're
40:26 L at the sky and see.
41:27 I was the first to tell Zion, 'L,
41:28 When I l, there is no one.
42:18 L, you blind people, so that you
48:6 Now l at all this. Won't you
49:18 L up, look around, and watch!
49:18 Look up, l around, and watch!
51:1 L to the rock from which you
51:2 L to Abraham, your ancestor,
51:6 L at the sky. Look at the earth
51:6 L at the earth below.
52:14 that he won't l like any other
52:14 he will hardly l like a human.
53:2 that would make us l at him.
58:2 They l for me every day and
60:4 "L up, look around, and watch.
60:4 "Look up, l around,
63:15 L down and see from heaven,
64:9 Now l, we are all your people.
65:6 "L! It is written in front of me. I
66:24 Then they will go out and l at
Jer 2:23 L how you've behaved in the
2:24 All who l for you won't get tired.
2:33 You carefully planned ways to l
3:2 "L at the bare hills,
3:3 Yet, you have the shameless l
5:1 L around, and think about these
5:3 LORD, your eyes l for the truth.
6:16 Stand at the crossroads and l.
10:21 They don't l to the LORD for
11:16 that has beautiful fruit to l at.
13:16 You will l for light,
13:20 L up, and see those who are
24:5 I will l kindly on them.
29:13 When you l for me,
32:4 in person and l him
39:12 "Take him, and l after him.
40:4 come, and I'll l after you.
45:5 Don't l for them, because I'm
48:17 Say, 'L at the strong staff,
48:39 'L how Moab is defeated!

Jer 50:20 "people will l for Israel's
50:20 They will l for Judah's sins,
Lam 1:1 "L how deserted Jerusalem is!
1:9 'O LORD, l at my suffering,
1:11 l and see how despised I am!'"
1:12 L and see if there's any pain
1:18 you people, and l at my pain.
2:1 "L how the Lord has covered
2:20 "O LORD, l and consider:
3:40 Let us l closely at our ways
3:59 L at the wrong that has been
3:60 L at all their malice,
3:63 L at them! Whether they are
4:1 "L how the gold has become
4:16 He will no longer l favorably on
5:1 Take a l at our disgrace!
Eze 6:2 "Son of man, l toward the
7:25 People will l for peace,
8:5 l toward the north."
8:17 L how they insult me in the
13:17 "Son of man, l at the women
16:51 you make your sisters l
16:52 They l like they are innocent
16:52 your sisters l like they are
18:6 mountain worship sites or l
18:15 mountain worship sites or l
20:7 the detestable idols that you l
20:40 There I will l for your offerings,
21:21 Then he will l for omens.
26:21 People will l for you,
27:10 Their victories made you l
33:25 You l to your idols for help.
34:11 and I will l after them.
34:12 so I will l after my sheep.
34:16 I will l for those that are lost,
40:4 "Son of man, l with your eyes,
44:5 L, and listen to everything I'm
Dan 1:10 If he sees that you l worse than
1:13 us on the basis of how we l."
3:25 The king replied, "But l,
4:30 "L how great Babylon is!
9:17 l favorably on your holy place,
9:18 Open your eyes and l at our
Hos 3:5 the Israelites will turn and l to
5:15 they will eagerly l for me."
7:10 turn to the LORD your God or l
Joe 2:4 The soldiers l like horses.
Amo 5:22 I won't even l at the fellowship
6:2 Go to Calneh and l.
9:3 I will l for them and take them
Mic 7:7 I will l to the LORD.
7:10 Now I l at them. They are
Nah 2:4 They l like torches,
3:6 I will make you l like a fool.
3:11 Even you will l for a fortress
3:13 L at your soldiers; The gates of
Hab 1:5 L among the nations and
1:13 eyes are too pure to l at evil.
2:4 "L at the proud person.
2:19 Just l at it! It's covered with gold
3:10 The mountains l at you.
Hag 2:3 How does it l to you now?
Zec 3:9 "L at the stone I have set in
5:5 He said, "L up, and see what's
5:6 the people's sins l like all over
6:8 Then he called out to me, "L!
9:9 L! Your King is coming to you:
12:10 They will l at me, whom they
Mal 2:15 what does the same ⌊God⌋ l
Mat 5:32 makes her l as though she
5:32 way makes himself l as though
6:26 "L at the birds. They don't plant,
10:11 l for people who will listen to
11:3 should we l for someone else?"
11:19 and people say, 'L at him!
12:2 saw this, they said to him, "L!
12:39 of an evil and unfaithful era l
12:41 But l, someone greater than
12:42 But l, someone greater than
12:49 at his disciples, he said, "L,
16:4 "Evil and unfaithful people l for
18:12 the 99 sheep in the hills to l
19:27 Then Peter replied to him, "L,
23:27 graves that l beautiful
23:28 So on the outside you l as
28:1 Mary went to l at the tomb.
Mar 2:24 The Pharisees asked him, "L!
3:34 a circle around him, he said, "L,
8:24 They l like trees walking
11:21 so he said to Jesus, "Rabbi, l!
12:15 me a coin so that I can l at it."
12:40 to make themselves l good.
13:1 l at these huge stones and
15:4 L how many accusations
16:6 L at the place where they laid
16:12 He did not l as he usually did.
Luk 2:44 they started to l for him among
2:45 back to Jerusalem to l for him.
7:19 should we l for someone else?"
7:20 we l for someone else?'"
7:34 and you say, 'L at him!
8:10 When they l, they don't see,
9:38 I beg you to l at my son.
11:29 They l for a miraculous sign.
11:31 But l, someone greater than
11:32 But l, someone greater than
13:6 He went to l for fruit on the tree
13:7 last three years I've come to l
15:4 grazing in the pasture and l
15:8 and l for the coin carefully until
18:13 He wouldn't even l up to
19:20 the other servant said, 'Sir, l!
20:47 to make themselves l good.
21:29 "L at the fig tree or any other
22:38 The disciples said, "Lord, l!
24:12 He bent down to l inside and
24:39 L at my hands and feet,
Jon 1:29 him the next day and said, "L!
1:36 John said, "L! This is the Lamb
4:35 I'm telling you to l and see that
5:44 each other's praise and don't l
6:24 of Capernaum to l for Jesus.
7:26 But l at this! He's speaking in
7:34 You will l for me, but you won't
7:36 he says, 'You will l for me,
8:21 and you'll l for me.
12:19 L! The whole world is following
13:33 You will l for me, but you can't
19:5 Pilate said to the Jews, "L,
19:14 Pilate said to the Jews, "L,
19:26 He said to his mother, "L,
19:27 he said to the disciple, "L,
19:37 "They will l at the person
20:27 and l at my hands.
Act 3:4 "L at us!" Peter said.
7:31 As he went closer to l at the
7:32 and didn't dare to l at the bush.
7:56 So Stephen said, "L,
8:36 The official said to Philip, "L,
11:25 the city of Tarsus to l for Saul.
13:41 'L, you mockers! Be amazed
14:11 and they l human."
17:27 so that they would l for God,
23:15 You have to make it l as
23:20 They're going to make it l as
Rom 5:6 L at it this way: At the right
11:22 L at how kind and how severe
1Co 1:22 and Greeks l for wisdom,
4:9 for people and angels to l at.
7:27 Don't l for another one.
10:18 L at the people of Israel from a
15:32 to the way people l at things?
2Co 3:7 Israel couldn't l at Moses' face.
4:18 We don't l for things that can be
7:11 l at how much devotion it
10:7 L at the plain facts!
Gal 6:11 L at how large the letters ⌊in
Php 3:13 This is what I do: I don't l back,
3:20 We l forward to the Lord Jesus
Col 2:23 These things l like wisdom
1Ti 4:12 Don't let anyone l down on you
Heb 3:1 So l carefully at Jesus,
8:7 no one would l for another one.
1Pe 1:12 even the angels want to l into.
2Pe 3:12 as you l forward to the day of
3:13 But we l forward to what God
3:14 with this to l forward to,
1Jn 3:21 we can boldly l to God
4:17 So we l ahead with confidence
Jud 1:21 Remain in God's love as you l
Rev 1:7 L! He is coming in the clouds.
3:20 L, I'm standing at the door and
Rev 5:3 open the scroll or l inside it.
5:4 to open the scroll or l inside it.
9:6 At that time people will l for
11:9 and nations will l at the

looked (206)

Gen 8:13 the top of the ship, l out,
13:10 Then Lot l in the direction of
18:2 Abraham l up, and suddenly he
18:16 they l toward Sodom.
19:26 Lot's wife l back and turned
19:28 When he l toward Sodom and
22:13 When Abraham l around,
24:63 When he l up, he saw camels
26:8 of the Philistines l out
29:2 He l around, and out in a field
31:10 I l up and saw that the male
41:21 They l just as sick as before.
43:29 As Joseph l around,
43:33 They l at each other in
Exo 2:6 the basket, l at the baby,
2:12 He l all around, and when he
3:2 Moses l, and although the bush
4:6 It l as ⌊flaky as⌋ snow.
14:10 the Israelites l up and saw that
14:24 Just before dawn, the LORD l
16:10 they l toward the desert.
24:17 the glory of the LORD l like a
34:30 and all the Israelites l at Moses
Lev 26:43 my rules and l at my laws
26:45 be their God while nations l on.
Num 11:7 seeds and l like resin.
13:33 how we must have l to them."
17:9 They l at them, and each man
21:9 People l at the bronze snake
24:2 l up, and saw Israel's camp
Jos 5:13 he l up and saw a man
7:2 So the men went and l at Ai.
8:20 When the men of Ai l back,
Jdg 5:28 Sisera's mother l through her
8:18 Each one l like a king's son."
1Sm 6:13 When they l up and saw the
6:19 Shemesh because they l inside
10:21 They l for him but couldn't find
14:17 They l and found that Jonathan
24:8 When Saul l back,
28:5 When Saul l at the Philistine
2Sm 1:7 When he l back and saw me,
2:20 When Abner l back,
6:16 Saul's daughter Michal l out of
13:34 servant who kept watch l up,
17:20 The servants l for them but did
18:24 As he l, he saw a man running
22:42 They l, but there was no one to
22:42 They l to the LORD,
24:20 When Araunah l down and saw
1Ki 18:43 He went up, l, ⌊came back,⌋
19:6 When he l, he saw near his
2Ki 9:30 and l out of a second-story
9:32 or three eunuchs l out at him.
11:14 She l, and the king was
1Ch 12:8 They l like lions and were as
15:29 Saul's daughter Michal l out of
21:16 When David l up, he saw the
21:21 Ornan l up and saw him.
2Ch 13:14 Judah's soldiers l around,
20:24 watchtower in the desert and l
23:13 She l, and the king was
Neh 4:14 I l them over and proceeded to
Job 16:9 My opponent l sharply at me.
30:26 evil came. When I l for light,
36:25 Mortals have l at it from a
Psa 69:20 I l for sympathy, but there was
69:20 I l for people to comfort me,
78:34 their sins and eagerly l for God.
102:19 "The LORD l down from his
102:19 From heaven he l at the earth.
114:3 The Red Sea l at this and ran
Pro 7:6 house I l through my screen.
7:15 Eagerly, I l for you,
Ecc 7:29 but they l for many ways ⌊to
Sos 3:1 Night after night on my bed I l
3:1 I l for him but did not find him.
3:2 I l for him but did not find him.
5:6 I l for him, but I did not find him.
Isa 63:5 I l, but there was no help. I was

Jer 31:26 At this, I woke up and l around.
Lam 1:7 Their opponents l on,
Eze 1:4 As I l, I saw a storm coming
1:4 lightning l like glowing metal.
1:5 I saw what l like four living
1:10 Their faces l like this:
1:11 That is what their faces l like.
1:13 The living creatures l like
1:15 As I l at the living creatures,
1:16 This is how the wheels l and
1:16 were made: They l like beryl.
1:16 All four wheels l the same.
1:16 They l like a wheel within a
1:22 It l like dazzling crystal.
1:26 was something that l like
1:26 a figure that l like a human.
1:27 Then I saw what he l like from
1:27 He l like glowing bronze with
1:27 the waist down, he l like fire.
1:28 The brightness all around him l
2:9 As I l, I saw a hand stretched
8:2 As I l, I saw something that
8:2 I saw something that l like a
8:2 waist down its body l like fire,
8:2 its body l like glowing metal.
8:3 It stretched out what l like a
8:5 So I l toward the north,
8:7 As I l, I saw a hole in the wall.
8:10 So I went in and l.
10:1 As I l at the dome over the
10:1 I saw something that l like a
10:8 have what l like human hands
10:9 As I l, I saw four wheels
10:9 The wheels l like beryl.
10:10 All four wheels l the same.
10:21 were what l like human hands.
10:22 Their faces l exactly like the
16:8 went by you again and l at you.
20:8 the detestable idols that they l
20:24 and they l to their ancestors'
22:30 "I l for someone among you
23:15 All of them l like Babylonian
34:4 those that strayed away or l
34:6 No one searched or l for them.
37:8 As I l, I saw that ligaments
40:2 some buildings that l like those
40:3 I saw a man who l like he was
44:4 When I l, I saw the LORD's
Dan 1:15 After ten days they l healthier
2:31 in front of you, and it l terrifying.
4:34 l up to heaven, I thanked the
7:5 It l like a bear. It was raised on
7:6 It l like a leopard. On its back it
8:3 I l up and saw a single ram
8:15 I saw someone who l like a
9:3 I turned to the Lord God and l
10:5 When I l up, I saw a man
10:6 His face l like lightning.
10:6 His arms and legs l like
10:16 Then someone who l like a
10:18 Again, the person who l like a
11:2 ⌊The person who l like a
12:1 ⌊The person who l like a
12:5 When I, Daniel, l up,
Zec 1:18 I l up and saw four animal
2:1 I l up and saw a man with a
5:1 I l up again and saw a flying
5:9 I l up and saw two women
6:1 I l up again and saw four
Mat 14:19 he l up to heaven and blessed
19:26 Jesus l at them and said,
26:16 From then on, he l for a chance
Mar 3:5 Jesus was angry as he l
6:41 he l up to heaven and blessed
7:34 Then he l up to heaven,
8:24 The man l up and said,
8:33 Jesus turned, l at his disciples,
9:8 Suddenly, as they l around,
9:26 The boy l as if he were dead,
10:21 Jesus l at him and loved him.
10:22 When the man heard that, he l
10:23 Jesus l around and said to his
10:27 Jesus l at them and said,
11:11 where he l around at
11:18 they l for a way to kill him.
14:67 She l at him and said,
Mar 16:4 When they l up, they saw that
Luk 1:48 because he has l favorably on
6:10 He l around at all of them and
6:20 Jesus l at his disciples and
9:16 the two fish, l up to heaven,
16:23 As he l up, in the distance he
18:9 of them while they l down
19:5 he l up and said, "Zacchaeus,
19:47 and the leaders of the people l
20:17 Then Jesus l straight at them
22:61 Then the Lord turned and l
24:17 They stopped and l very sad.
Jon 1:42 Jesus l at Simon and said,
11:41 Jesus l up and said,
11:56 they l for Jesus and asked
17:1 Jesus l up to heaven and said,
20:5 He bent over and l inside the
20:11 stood there and cried as she l
20:11 she bent over and l inside.
Act 2:3 Tongues that l like fire
6:15 him and saw that his face l like
7:55 He l into heaven, saw God's
11:6 I l into the sheet very closely
16:10 we immediately l for a way to
17:21 Everyone who lived in Athens l
Rom 1:23 that l like mortal humans,
Rev 4:3 The one sitting there l like gray
4:3 throne which l like an emerald.
5:6 The lamb l like he had been
6:2 Then I l, and there was a white
6:5 I l, and there was a black
6:8 I l, and there was a pale horse,
9:7 The locusts l like horses
9:7 to have crowns that l like gold
9:17 and their riders l like this:
13:3 One of the beast's heads l like
14:1 I l, and the lamb was standing
14:14 Then I l, and there was a white
15:2 Then I saw what l like a sea of
15:5 After these things I l,

looking (89)

Gen 37:15 "What are you l for?"
37:16 "I'm l for my brothers.
42:1 do you keep l at each other?
43:30 l for a place to cry.
Exo 25:20 l at the throne of mercy.
37:9 l at the throne of mercy.
Dtr 22:2 it until the owner comes l for it.
28:32 You will strain your eyes l for
Jdg 4:22 the man you've been l for."
14:4 The LORD was l for an
15:2 Isn't her younger sister better l?
18:1 days the tribe of Dan was l
1Sm 10:2 the donkeys you went l for.
27:1 Then Saul will give up l all
1Ki 1:20 All Israel is l to you,
20:7 how this man is l for trouble.
2Ki 2:24 L back, he saw them and
6:19 you to the man you're l for."
9:32 L up at the window,
19:22 Who are you l at so arrogantly?
2Ch 15:15 They took great pleasure in l
20:12 what to do, so we're l to you."
Job 7:19 Why don't you stop l at me long
24:5 out to do their work, l for food.
31:16 widow's eyes stop ⌊l for help⌋,
33:10 God is only l for an excuse to
Psa 69:3 strained ⌊from⌋ l for my God.
119:82 have become strained from l
119:123 My eyes are strained from l for
119:123 for you to save me and from l
Pro 7:7 I was l at gullible people when
8:17 Those eagerly l for me will find
17:24 but the eyes of a fool ⌊are⌋ l
21:6 They are l for death.
Ecc 3:6 a time to start l and a time to
3:6 looking and a time to stop l,
6:9 is in front of you than to go l
Sos 2:9 l through the lattice.
Isa 37:23 Who are you l at so arrogantly?
38:14 My eyes were tired from l up to
41:17 poor and needy are l for water,
65:1 by those who weren't l for me.
Jer 45:5 Are you l for great things for
46:5 They flee without l back.
Lam 1:19 l for food to keep themselves
Dan 4:10 while I was asleep: I was l,
Mal 3:1 Then the Lord you are l for will
Mat 6:16 stop l sad like hypocrites.
12:43 it goes through dry places l for
24:26 don't go out ⌊l for him⌋.
28:5 I know you're l for Jesus,
Mar 1:37 "Everyone is l for you."
3:32 brothers are outside l for you."
3:34 Then l at those who sat in a
5:32 But he kept l around to see the
14:1 priests and the scribes were l
14:11 So he kept l for a chance to
16:6 You're l for Jesus from
Luk 2:48 been worried sick l for you!"
2:49 "Why were you l for me?
11:24 it goes through dry places l for
21:1 L up, Jesus saw people,
22:2 priests and the scribes were l
22:6 He kept l for an opportunity to
24:5 "Why are you l among the dead
Jon 1:38 "What are you l for?"
4:23 The Father is l for people like
6:26 You're not l for me because you
6:26 You are l for me because you
7:11 The Jews were l for Jesus in
7:18 speak their own thoughts are l
13:22 The disciples began l at each
18:4 "Who are you l for?"
18:7 "Who are you l for?"
18:8 So if you are l for me,
20:15 Who are you l for?"
Act 1:11 from Galilee standing here l at
10:19 "Three men are l for you.
10:21 "I'm the man you're l for.
13:25 I'm not the person you're l for.
17:23 your city and l closely at
Rom 10:20 by those who weren't l for me.
Php 4:17 It's not that I'm l for a gift.
4:17 I'm l for your resources to
Heb 11:14 make it clear that they are l
11:26 He was l ahead to his reward.
13:14 but we are l for the city that we
2Pe 2:14 They're always l for an
2:14 They can't stop l for sin as they

lookout (2)

Psa 10:8 eyes are on the l for victims.
Nah 2:1 Keep a l on the road!

looks (42)

Lev 13:3 and the diseased area l deeper
13:5 If the disease l the same and
13:20 If it l deeper than the rest of the
13:25 the affected area l deeper than
13:30 If it l deeper than the rest of the
14:35 is something that l like mildew
1Sm 16:7 but the LORD l into the heart."
17:42 healthy complexion and good l.
2Sm 14:25 for his good l as much as
15:25 If the LORD l favorably on me,
Job 7:2 he eagerly l for his pay.
39:8 and l for anything green.
41:34 It l down on all high things.
Psa 14:2 The LORD l down from heaven
33:13 The LORD l down from heaven.
33:14 he l down upon all who live on
53:2 God l down from heaven on
85:11 l down from heaven.
104:32 He l at the earth, and it
Pro 11:27 but whoever l for evil finds it.
12:26 A righteous person l out for his
17:11 A rebel l for nothing but evil.
20:4 He l for something in the
25:23 tongue brings angry l.
30:13 A certain kind of person l
Ecc 11:4 Whoever l at the clouds will
Sos 2:4 into a banquet room and l at me
6:10 She l like the dawn.
Isa 52:14 His l will be so disfigured that
Lam 3:50 until the LORD l down from
Eze 18:12 He l to idols for help.
34:12 As a shepherd l after his flock
Dan 3:25 The fourth one l like a son of
Mat 5:28 can guarantee that whoever l at
Luk 9:62 "Whoever starts to plow and l

Jon 9:9 "No, he isn't, but he l like him."
Rom 2:28 a matter of how the body l.
Php 2:21 Everyone else l after his own
Heb 10:29 That person l at the blood of
Jas 1:23 he is like a person who l at his
1:24 forgets what he l like.
1Pe 5:8 like a roaring lion as he l

loom (5)

Exo 35:35 how to weave yarn on a l.
Jdg 16:13 with the other threads in the l."
16:14 tied his braids to the l shuttle.
16:14 the threads out of the l shuttle.
Isa 38:12 You cut me off from the l.

loops (7)

Exo 26:4 Make 50 violet l along the edge
26:5 the l opposite each other.
26:10 Make 50 l along the edge of the
26:11 and put them through the l to
36:11 Then they made 50 violet l
36:12 the l opposite each other.
36:17 Then they made 50 l along the

loose (13)

Exo 23:4 ox or donkey wandering l,
Psa 129:4 He has cut me l from the ropes
Pro 2:16 from a l woman with her
5:20 and fondle a l woman's breast?
6:24 the smooth talk of a l woman.
7:5 from a l woman with her
23:27 A l woman is a narrow well.
26:13 There's a lion l in the streets!"
Isa 5:27 belts on their waists aren't l
7:25 be a place for turning oxen l
33:23 Your ropes hang l,
Dan 5:6 His hip joints became l,
Act 16:26 all the prisoners' chains came l.

loosen (2)

Num 5:18 LORD's presence and l her hair.
Isa 58:6 L the chains of wickedness,

loosened (1)

Job 4:21 the ropes of their tent been l?

loosens (1)

Job 12:18 He l kings' belts and strips

loot (71)

Exo 15:9 I'll divide the l! I'll take all I
Num 31:9 and their valuables as l.
31:11 Then they took everything as l,
31:12 the l, and everything to Moses,
31:26 need to count all the l,
31:27 Divide the l between the
31:29 from the soldiers' half of the l,
31:30 From the Israelites' half of the l,
31:32 This is the l that was left from
31:42 half of the l from the soldiers.
31:53 Each soldier kept his own l.
Dtr 2:35 However, we did l the cities
3:7 However, we did l the cities,
20:14 all its goods, as your l.
Jos 7:21 about one pound among the l.
7:22 The l was buried inside with
7:23 They took the l from the tent
8:2 However, you may take its l
8:27 Israel took the l and the
11:14 people of Israel took all the l
22:8 Divide the l from your enemies
Jdg 5:19 they didn't carry off any rich l.
5:30 really finding and dividing the l:
8:24 me the earrings from your l."
8:25 man took the earrings from his l
1Sm 30:16 much l from Philistine territory
30:19 the l or anything else they had
30:20 "This is David's l."
30:22 any of the l we recovered.
30:26 he sent part of the l to his
30:26 "Here is a gift for you from the l
1Ch 26:27 donated some of the l taken
2Ch 15:11 a part of the l they had brought
20:25 his troops came to take the l,
20:25 three days collecting the l.
24:23 The Arameans sent all the l
2Ch 28:14 army left the prisoners and the l
28:15 and gave clothes from the l
Pro 1:14 We'll split the l equally."
Isa 8:4 and the l from Samaria will
9:3 or rejoice when dividing l.
10:6 to take their belongings, l them,
11:14 Together they will l the people
33:4 You nations, your l is gathered
33:4 people rush for your l.
33:23 A large amount of l will be
33:23 people will carry off your l.
42:22 They have become l with no
42:24 Who gave Jacob away as l
49:24 Can l be taken away from
49:25 L will be taken away from
Jer 15:13 wealth and treasures as l as
17:3 and all your treasures into l.
20:5 Their enemies will l them,
49:28 and l the people from the east.
49:32 large herds will be taken as l.
50:10 All who l them will get
Eze 7:21 jewels over to foreigners as l
25:7 you over to the nations as l.
26:12 His troops will l your riches
29:19 its prized possessions, and l it.
38:12 come to rob them and l them.
39:10 They will l those who looted
Dan 11:24 He will distribute l and wealth
Amo 3:11 and l your palaces.
Mic 4:13 You will claim their l for the
Hab 2:8 All the rest of the people will l
Zep 2:9 few of my people will l them,
Zec 2:9 their own slaves will l them.
14:1 when the l you have taken
Luk 11:22 trusted and will divide the l.

looted (23)

Gen 34:27 sons stripped the corpses and l
34:29 and children and l everything
1Sm 14:48 who l their possessions.
17:53 they l all the goods in the
2Ki 7:16 So the people went out and l
17:20 to those who l their property,
2Ch 14:14 The army l all the cities
Isa 10:13 I've l treasuries. I've brought
13:16 Their houses will be l and their
17:14 be the fate of those who l us,
42:22 these people are robbed and l.
Jer 30:16 Those who l you will be looted.
30:16 Those who looted you will be l.
50:11 You have l the people who
50:37 treasures, and they will be l.
Eze 39:10 will loot those who l them,
Dan 11:33 They will be captured and l.
Oba 1:6 your hidden treasures will be l.
Nah 2:2 although enemies have l it and
Hab 2:8 You have l many nations.
Zep 1:13 Their wealth will be l.
Zec 2:8 me to the nations who l you.
14:2 will be captured, the houses l,

looter (1)

Jdg 5:30 cloth for the neck of the l."

looters (2)

Jer 12:12 L swarm all over the bare hills
Oba 1:5 "If thieves or l come to you

looting (4)

Isa 8:1 'Maher Shalal Hash Baz' [The L
Jer 48:3 "L and great destruction!"
Eze 23:46 Hand them over to terror and l.
45:9 Stop your violence and l,

LORD; Lord; lord (6970)

Gen 2:4 at the time when the L God
2:5 because the L God hadn't sent
2:7 Then the L God formed the
2:8 The L God planted a garden in
2:9 The L God made all the trees
2:15 Then the L God took the man
2:16 The L God commanded the
2:18 Then the L God said,
2:19 The L God had formed all the
2:21 So the L God caused him to
2:21 the L God took out one of the
Gen 2:22 Then the L God formed a
3:1 animals the L God had made.
3:8 the L God walking around
3:8 So they hid from the L God
3:9 The L God called to the man
3:13 Then the L God asked the
3:14 So the L God said to the snake,
3:21 The L God made clothes from
3:22 Then the L God said,
3:23 So the L God sent the man out
4:1 the man that the L promised."
4:3 the land as an offering to the L.
4:4 The L approved of Abel and his
4:6 Then the L asked Cain,
4:9 The L asked Cain,
4:10 The L asked, "What have you
4:13 But Cain said to the L,
4:15 So the L said to him,
4:15 The L gave Cain a sign so that
4:26 people began to worship the L.
5:29 hands since the L has cursed
6:3 Then the L said, "My Spirit will
6:5 The L saw how evil humans
6:6 The L was sorry that he had
6:8 But the L was pleased with
7:1 The L said to Noah,
7:5 that the L commanded him.
7:16 Then the L closed the door
8:20 Noah built an altar to the L.
8:21 The L smelled the soothing
9:26 Praise the L, the God of Shem!
10:9 hunter whom the L blessed.
10:9 a mighty hunter whom the L
11:5 The L came down to see the
11:6 The L said, "They are one
11:8 So the L scattered them all
11:9 because there the L turned the
11:9 From that place the L scattered
12:1 The L said to Abram,
12:4 as the L had told him,
12:7 Then the L appeared to Abram
12:7 he built an altar there to the L,
12:8 He also built an altar to the L
12:8 there and worshiped the L.
12:17 However, the L struck Pharaoh
13:4 There Abram worshiped the L.
13:10 (This was before the L
13:13 terrible sins against the L.)
13:14 the L said to Abram,
13:18 There he built an altar for the L.
14:22 swear to the L God Most High,
15:1 Later the L spoke his word to
15:2 Abram asked, "Almighty L,
15:4 Suddenly, the L spoke his
15:6 Then Abram believed the L,
15:6 and the L regarded that faith to
15:7 Then the L said to him,
15:7 LORD said to him, "I am the L,
15:8 Abram asked, "Almighty L,
15:18 At that time the L made a
16:2 So Sarai said to Abram, "The L
16:5 May the L decide who is right
16:7 The Messenger of the L found
16:9 The Messenger of the L said to
16:10 The Messenger of the L also
16:11 Then the Messenger of the L
16:11 because the L has heard your
16:13 Hagar named the L,
17:1 the L appeared to him.
18:1 The L appeared to Abraham by
18:10 The L said, "I promise I'll come
18:13 The L asked Abraham,
18:14 Is anything too hard for the L?
18:15 But the L said, "Yes, you did
18:17 The L said, "I shouldn't hide
18:19 the way of the L by doing what
18:19 In this way I, the L,
18:20 The L also said, "Sodom and
18:22 standing in front of the L.
18:26 The L said, "If I find 50
18:28 The L answered, "I will not
18:33 When the L finished speaking
19:13 The complaints to the L
19:13 are so loud that the L has sent
19:14 because the L is going to
19:16 because the L wanted to spare

Gen 19:24 Then the L made burning sulfur
19:27 he had stood in front of the L.
20:4 near her, so he asked, "L,
20:18 (The L had made it impossible
21:1 The L came to help Sarah and
21:33 and worshiped the L,
22:11 But the Messenger of the L
22:14 that place The L Will Provide.
22:14 "On the mountain of the L it
22:15 Then the Messenger of the L
22:16 my own name, declares the L,
24:1 and the L had blessed him in
24:3 I want you to swear by the L
24:7 "The L God of heaven took me
24:12 Then he prayed, "L,
24:21 or not the L had made his
24:26 The man knelt, bowing to the L
24:27 He said, "Praise the L,
24:27 The L hasn't failed to be kind
24:27 The L has led me on this trip to
24:31 you whom the L has blessed.
24:35 "The L has blessed my master,
24:35 The L has given him sheep
24:40 the way the L wants me to.
24:40 The L will send his angel with
24:42 'L God of my master Abraham,
24:44 let her be the woman the L has
24:48 I knelt, bowing down to the L.
24:48 I praised the L, the God of my
24:48 The L led me in the right
24:50 "This is from the L.
24:51 as the L has said."
24:52 he bowed down to the L.
24:56 "Don't delay me now that the L
25:21 Isaac prayed to the L for his
25:21 The L answered his prayer,
25:22 So she went to ask the L.
25:23 The L said to her, Two nations
26:2 The L appeared to Isaac and
26:12 the L had blessed him.
26:22 "Now the L has made room for
26:24 That night the L appeared to
26:25 altar there and worshiped the L.
26:28 "We have seen that the L is
26:29 Now you are blessed by the L."
27:7 presence of the L before I die.'
27:20 "The L your God brought it to
27:27 country that the L has blessed.
28:13 The L was standing above it,
28:13 above it, saying, "I am the L,
28:16 the L is in this place,
28:21 then the L will be my God.
29:31 When the L saw Leah was
29:32 the L has seen my misery;
29:33 She said, "Certainly, the L has
29:35 "This time I will praise the L."
30:24 "May the L give me another
30:27 seen that the L has blessed me
30:30 The L has blessed you
31:3 Then the L said to Jacob,
31:49 "May the L watch between you
32:9 L, you said to me, 'Go back to
38:7 Er angered the L. So the LORD
38:7 So the L took away his life.
38:10 What Onan did angered the L
38:10 that the L took away Onan's
39:2 The L was with Joseph,
39:3 Joseph's master saw that the L
39:3 and that the L made everything
39:5 From that time on the L
39:21 the L was with him.
39:21 The L reached out to him with
39:21 The L also put Joseph on good
39:23 care because the L was
45:8 l over his entire household,
45:9 "God has made me l of Egypt.
49:18 hope for you to rescue me, O L.
Exo 3:2 The Messenger of the L
3:4 When the L saw that Moses
3:7 The L said, "I have seen the
3:15 The L God of your ancestors,
3:16 'The L God of your ancestors,
3:18 'The L God of the Hebrews has
3:18 sacrifices to the L our God.'
4:1 'The L didn't appear to you.'"
4:2 Then the L asked him,

Exo 4:3 The L said, "Throw it on the
4:4 Then the L said to Moses,
4:5 ⌊The L explained,⌋
4:5 the people that the L God
4:6 The L said to him,
4:7 inside your shirt," the L said.
4:8 ⌊Then the L said,⌋
4:10 Moses said to the L,
4:10 L, I'm not a good speaker.
4:11 The L asked him, "Who gave
4:11 them blind? It is I, the L!
4:13 But Moses said, "Please, L,
4:14 Then the L became angry with
4:19 Now, the L had said to Moses
4:21 The L said to Moses,
4:22 'This is what the L says:
4:24 The L met Moses and tried to
4:26 So the L let him alone.
4:27 Meanwhile, the L had told
4:28 everything the L had sent him
4:28 the L had commanded him
4:30 them everything the L had said
4:31 When they heard that the L
5:1 "This is what the L God of
5:2 Pharaoh asked, "Who is the L?
5:2 I don't know the L,
5:3 sacrifices to the L our God.
5:17 us go offer sacrifices to the L.'
5:21 So they said, "May the L see
5:22 went back to the L and asked,
6:1 Then the L said to Moses,
6:2 spoke to Moses, "I am the L.
6:3 to them by my name, the L.
6:6 "Tell the Israelites, 'I am the L.
6:7 know that I am the L your God,
6:8 own possession. I am the L.'"
6:10 Then the L spoke to Moses,
6:12 But Moses protested to the L,
6:13 The L spoke to Moses and
6:26 and Moses to whom the L said,
6:28 At that time the L spoke to
6:29 He said to Moses, "I am the L.
6:30 But Moses said to the L,
7:1 The L answered Moses,
7:5 will know that I am the L when
7:6 as the L had commanded them.
7:8 The L said to Moses and
7:10 did as the L had commanded.
7:13 as the L had predicted.
7:14 Then the L said to Moses,
7:16 Say to him, 'The L God of the
7:17 Here is what the L says:
7:17 will recognize that I am the L:
7:19 The L said to Moses,
7:20 did as the L had commanded.
7:22 as the L had predicted.
7:25 after the L struck the Nile.
8:1 Then the L said to Moses,
8:1 'This is what the L says:
8:5 Then the L said to Moses,
8:8 "Pray that the L will take the
8:8 go to offer sacrifices to the L."
8:10 is no one like the L our God.
8:12 Moses prayed to the L about
8:13 The L did what Moses asked.
8:15 as the L had predicted.
8:16 Then the L said to Moses,
8:19 as the L had predicted.
8:20 Then the L said to Moses,
8:20 'This is what the L says:
8:22 I, the L, am here in this land.
8:24 The L did what he said.
8:26 The sacrifices we offer to the L
8:27 sacrifices to the L our God,
8:28 sacrifices to the L your God
8:29 I will pray to the L.
8:29 go to offer sacrifices to the L."
8:30 Pharaoh and prayed to the L.
8:31 The L did what Moses asked.
9:1 Then the L said to Moses,
9:1 'This is what the L God of the
9:3 the L will bring a terrible plague
9:4 But the L will distinguish
9:5 The L set a definite time.
9:6 The next day the L did as he
9:8 Then the L said to Moses and

Exo 9:12 But the L made Pharaoh
9:12 as the L had predicted to
9:13 Then the L said to Moses,
9:13 'This is what the L God of the
9:22 Then the L said to Moses,
9:23 the L sent thunder and hail,
9:23 So the L made it hail on Egypt.
9:27 "The L is right, and my people
9:28 Pray to the L. We've had enough
9:29 I'll spread out my hands to the L
9:29 that the earth belongs to the L.
9:30 still don't fear the L God."
9:33 out his hands to the L in prayer.
9:35 as the L had predicted through
10:1 Then the L said to Moses,
10:2 will all know that I am the L."
10:3 "This is what the L God of the
10:7 go to worship the L their God.
10:8 "Go, worship the L your God,"
10:10 Pharaoh said to them, "The L
10:11 men may go to worship the L,
10:12 The L said to Moses,
10:13 and the L made a wind from the
10:16 "I have sinned against the L
10:17 Pray to the L your God to take
10:18 Pharaoh and prayed to the L.
10:19 Then the L changed the wind
10:20 But the L made Pharaoh
10:21 Then the L said to Moses,
10:24 and said, "Go, worship the L!
10:25 have to make to the L our God.
10:26 for worshiping the L our God,
10:27 But the L made Pharaoh
11:1 Then the L said to Moses,
11:3 The L made the Egyptians kind
11:4 "This is what the L says:
11:7 you will see that the L shows
11:9 The L had said to Moses,
11:10 the L made Pharaoh stubborn,
12:1 The L said to Moses and Aaron
12:12 ⌊because⌋ I am the L.
12:23 The L will go throughout Egypt
12:25 the land that the L will give you
12:27 The L passed over the houses
12:28 The Israelites did as the L had
12:29 At midnight the L killed every
12:31 worship the L as you asked.
12:36 The L made the Egyptians
12:42 That night the L kept watch to
12:42 since it is dedicated to the L.)
12:43 The L said to Moses and
12:50 All the Israelites did as the L
12:51 That very day the L brought all
13:1 The L spoke to Moses,
13:3 The L used his mighty hand to
13:5 The L swore to your ancestors
13:8 this because of what the L did
13:9 of the L are ⌊always⌋
13:9 Because the L used his mighty
13:11 "When the L brings you to the
13:12 firstborn male offspring to the L
13:12 your animals belongs to the L.
13:13 donkey back from the L.
13:13 firstborn son back from the L.
13:14 'The L used his mighty hand to
13:15 the L killed every firstborn male
13:15 every firstborn male to the L
13:15 firstborn son back from the L.'
13:16 because the L used his mighty
13:21 By day the L went ahead of
14:1 Then the L said to Moses,
14:4 will know that I am the L."
14:8 The L made Pharaoh (the king
14:10 the Israelites cried out to the L.
14:13 Stand still, and see what the L
14:14 The L is fighting for you!
14:15 Then the L said to Moses,
14:18 will know that I am the L when
14:21 All that night the L pushed
14:24 Just before dawn, the L looked
14:25 The L is fighting for Israel!
14:26 Then the L said to Moses,
14:27 but the L swept them into the
14:30 That day the L saved Israel
14:31 power the L had used against
14:31 they feared the L and believed

Exo 15:1 sang this song to the L:
15:1 "I will sing to the L.
15:2 The L is my strength and my
15:3 The L is a warrior!
15:3 The L is his name.
15:6 Your right hand, O L,
15:6 Your right hand, O L,
15:11 like you among the gods, O L?
15:16 until your people pass by, O L,
15:17 the place where you live, O L,
15:17 built with your own hands, O L.
15:18 The L will rule as king forever
15:19 the L made the water of the sea
15:21 sang to them: "Sing to the L.
15:25 Moses cried out to the L,
15:25 and the L showed him a piece
15:25 There the L set down laws and
15:26 carefully to the L your God
15:26 because I am the L,
16:3 "If only the L had let us die in
16:4 The L said to Moses,
16:6 it was the L who brought you
16:7 you will see the glory of the L,
16:8 Moses also said, "The L will
16:8 The L has heard you
16:8 about us but about the L."
16:10 they saw the glory of the L in
16:11 The L said to Moses,
16:12 that I am the L your God.'"
16:15 "It's the food the L has given
16:16 is what the L has commanded:
16:23 "This is what the L said:
16:23 of worship dedicated to the L.
16:25 of worship dedicated to the L.
16:28 The L said to Moses,
16:29 Remember: The L has given
16:32 is what the L has commanded:
16:34 as the L commanded Moses.
17:1 as the L commanded them.
17:2 Why are you testing the L?"
17:4 So Moses cried out to the L,
17:5 The L answered Moses,
17:7 and because they tested the L,
17:7 "Is the L with us or not?"
17:14 The L said to Moses,
17:15 called it The L Is My Banner.
18:1 how the L had brought Israel
18:8 everything the L had done
18:8 and how the L had saved them.
18:9 the good things the L had done
18:10 He said, "Thank the L!
18:11 Now I know that the L is
19:3 and the L called to him from the
19:7 that the L had commanded him.
19:8 do everything the L has said."
19:8 their answer back to the L.
19:9 The L said to Moses,
19:9 Moses told the L what the
19:10 So the L said to Moses,
19:11 On that day the L will come
19:18 because the L had come down
19:20 The L came down on top of
19:21 The L said to him,
19:21 ⌊the boundary⌋ to see the L,
19:22 near the L must set themselves
19:22 or the L will violently kill them."
19:23 Moses said to the L,
19:24 The L said to him,
19:24 boundary to come up to the L,
20:2 "I am the L your God,
20:5 because I, the L your God,
20:7 "Never use the name of the L
20:7 The L will make sure that
20:10 dedicated to the L your God.
20:11 In six days the L made heaven,
20:11 That's why the L blessed the
20:12 in the land the L your God is
20:22 The L said to Moses,
21:1 ⌊The L continued,⌋
22:1 ⌊The L continued,⌋
22:11 swearing an oath to the L that
22:20 to any god except the L must
23:1 ⌊The L continued,⌋
23:17 presence of the Master, the L.
23:19 to the house of the L your God.
23:25 You must serve the L your God,

Exo 24:1 The L said to Moses,
24:2 Moses may come near the L,
24:3 "We will do everything the L
24:5 fellowship offerings to the L.
24:7 do everything the L has said."
24:8 promise that the L has made
24:12 The L said to Moses,
24:16 The glory of the L settled on
24:16 and on the seventh day the L
24:17 the glory of the L looked like a
25:1 The L said to Moses,
26:1 ⌊The L continued,⌋
27:1 ⌊The L continued,⌋
28:1 ⌊The L continued,⌋
28:36 on a signet ring): Holy to the L.
28:38 so that the L will accept their
29:1 ⌊The L continued,⌋
29:18 an offering by fire to the L.
29:24 who will offer them to the L.
29:25 an offering by fire to the L.
29:26 and present it to the L.
29:27 breast that is offered to the L
29:28 their contribution to the L from
29:33 with the L at their ordination
29:36 to make peace with the L.
29:37 the altar make peace with the L
29:41 an offering by fire to the L.
29:46 know that I am the L their God.
29:46 I am the L their God."
30:1 ⌊The L continued,⌋
30:10 with the L by putting blood
30:10 altar to make peace with the L.
30:10 It is most holy to the L."
30:11 Then the L said to Moses,
30:12 each person must pay the L a
30:13 silver is a contribution to the L.
30:14 give this contribution to the L.
30:15 given to make peace with the L
30:15 your lives acceptable to the L.
30:16 give to make peace with the L,
30:17 The L said to Moses,
30:20 burn an offering by fire to the L,
30:22 The L said to Moses,
30:34 The L said to Moses,
30:37 Treat it as holy to the L.
31:1 The L said to Moses,
31:12 The L said to Moses,
31:13 that I am the L who makes you
31:15 It is holy to the L. Whoever
31:17 because the L made heaven
31:18 The L finished speaking to
32:7 The L said to Moses,
32:9 The L added, "I've seen these
32:11 pleaded with the L his God.
32:11 "L," he said, "why are you so
32:14 So the L reconsidered his
32:27 "This is what the L God of
32:30 go up the mountain to the L.
32:30 peace with the L for your sin."
32:31 went back to the L and said,
32:33 The L answered Moses,
32:35 So the L killed people because
33:1 Then the L said to Moses,
33:5 The L had said to Moses,
33:9 while the L spoke with Moses.
33:11 The L would speak to Moses
33:12 Moses said to the L,
33:14 The L answered, "My presence
33:17 The L answered Moses,
33:19 The L said, "I will let all my
33:19 I will call out my name 'the L.' I
33:21 Then the L said, "Look,
34:1 The L said to Moses,
34:4 as the L had commanded him,
34:5 The L came down in a cloud
34:5 called out his name "the L."
34:6 calling out, "The L, the LORD,
34:6 calling out, "The LORD, the L,
34:9 Then he said, "L, please go
34:10 The L said, "I'm making my
34:14 because the L is a God who
34:23 the L God of Israel.
34:26 to the house of the L your God.
34:27 Then the L said to Moses,
34:28 Moses was there with the L 40
34:29 from speaking with the L,

Exo 34:32 to do everything the L told him
34:35 in again to speak with the L.
35:1 "These are the things the L
35:2 It is dedicated to the L.
35:4 is what the L has commanded:
35:5 a special contribution to the L.
35:5 kind of contribution to the L:
35:10 the L has commanded:
35:21 their contributions to the L.
35:22 gold and offered them to the L.
35:24 it as their contribution to the L.
35:29 all these items to the L as
35:29 the L had commanded through
35:30 "The L has chosen Bezalel,
35:31 The L has filled Bezalel with
35:34 Also, the L has given Bezalel
35:35 The L has made these men
36:1 work as the L has commanded.
36:1 to whom the L has given
36:2 to whom the L had given these
36:5 the work the L commanded
38:22 the L had commanded Moses.
38:24 presented to the L used
38:29 to the L weighed 5,310 pounds.
39:30 on a signet ring): Holy to the L.
40:1 Then the L said to Moses,
40:16 as the L commanded him.
40:34 the glory of the L filled the tent.
40:35 the glory of the L filled the tent.
Lev 1:1 The L called Moses and spoke
1:2 of you bring a sacrifice to the L,
1:3 so that the L will accept you.
1:4 to make peace with the L.
1:9 a soothing aroma to the L.
1:13 a soothing aroma to the L.
1:14 "If your offering to the L is a
1:17 a soothing aroma to the L."
2:1 ⌊The L continued,⌋
2:1 bring a grain offering to the L,
2:2 a soothing aroma to the L.
2:8 "Bring the L the grain offering
2:9 a soothing aroma to the L.
2:11 that you bring to the L must
2:11 or honey as an offering to the L.
2:12 You may bring them to the L as
2:14 a grain offering to the L from
2:16 It is an offering by fire to the L."
3:1 ⌊The L continued,⌋
3:4 and offer them by fire to the L.
3:5 a soothing aroma to the L.
3:6 offering of sheep to the L,
3:7 you must bring it to the L.
3:9 and offer it by fire to the L.
3:11 an offering by fire to the L.
3:12 you must bring it to the L.
3:15 as an offering by fire to the L.
3:16 an offering by fire to the L.
3:16 All the fat belongs to the L.
4:1 The L spoke to Moses,
4:3 as an offering for sin to the L.
4:20 will make peace with the L
4:22 commands of the L his God —
4:26 will make peace with the L
4:31 for a soothing aroma to the L.
4:31 will make peace with the L
4:35 with the offering by fire to the L.
4:35 will make peace with the L
5:1 ⌊The L continued,⌋
5:6 Bring your guilt offering to the L
5:6 will make peace with the L
5:7 you must bring to the L two
5:10 will make peace with the L
5:12 of the offering by fire to the L
5:13 will make peace with the L
5:14 The L spoke to Moses,
5:15 bring a guilt offering to the L.
5:16 to make peace with the L
5:18 will make peace with the L
5:19 as far as the L is concerned."
6:1 The L spoke to Moses,
6:2 "If any of you sin against the L
6:6 Then bring the L your guilt
6:7 will make peace with the L.
6:8 The L spoke to Moses,
6:15 It is a soothing aroma to the L.
6:18 the offering by fire to the L.

Lev 6:19 The **L** spoke to Moses,
6:20 his sons must bring to the **L**
6:21 as a soothing aroma to the **L**.
6:22 is a permanent law of the **L**:
6:24 The **L** spoke to Moses,
6:30 to make peace with the **L**.
7:1 ⌊The **L** continued,⌋
7:5 a guilt offering by fire to the **L**.
7:7 to make peace with the **L**.
7:11 that you must bring to the **L**.
7:14 must bring one loaf to the **L** as
7:22 The **L** spoke to Moses,
7:25 sacrificed by fire to the **L** must
7:28 The **L** spoke to Moses,
7:29 Anyone who offers the **L** a
7:29 that sacrifice as a gift to the **L**.
7:30 by fire made to the **L** yourself.
7:30 breast and present it to the **L**.
7:35 sacrifices by fire made to the **L**.
7:35 them to serve the **L** as priests.
7:36 The **L** commanded the
7:38 On Mount Sinai the **L** gave
8:1 The **L** spoke to Moses,
8:4 did as the **L** commanded him,
8:5 "The **L** has commanded that
8:9 the **L** had commanded Moses.
8:13 the **L** had commanded Moses.
8:15 it to make peace with the **L**.
8:17 as the **L** commanded him.
8:21 altar as the **L** commanded him.
8:21 an offering by fire to the **L**.
8:27 things to the **L** as an offering.
8:28 a soothing aroma to the **L**.
8:29 and presented it to the **L**.
8:29 as the **L** had commanded.
8:34 I did today what the **L**
8:34 make peace with the **L** for you.
8:35 and serve as the **L** tells you.
8:36 **L** commanded through Moses.
9:4 The **L** will appear to you
9:6 Moses said, "The **L** has
9:7 to make peace with the **L**
9:7 to make peace with the **L** for
9:7 for them as the **L** commanded."
9:10 the **L** had commanded Moses.
9:21 to the **L** as Moses commanded.
10:2 A fire flashed from the **L** and
10:2 died in the presence of the **L**.
10:3 is exactly what the **L** said:
10:6 If you do, you will die and the **L**
10:6 may cry over the fire the **L** sent,
10:7 because the **L** has anointed
10:8 The **L** spoke to Aaron,
10:12 from the offering by fire to the **L**
10:13 by fire to the **L** that belongs
10:14 the breast presented ⌊to the **L**⌋
10:15 the breast presented ⌊to the **L**⌋,
10:15 and present them to the **L**.
10:15 as the **L** has commanded."
10:17 peace with the **L** for them.
10:19 would the **L** have approved?"
11:1 The **L** spoke to Moses and
11:44 I am the **L** your God.
11:45 the reason ⌊again⌋: I am the **L**.
12:1 The **L** spoke to Moses,
12:7 make peace with the **L** for her.
12:8 make peace with the **L** for her,
13:1 The **L** spoke to Moses and
14:1 The **L** spoke to Moses,
14:12 oil and present them to the **L** as
14:18 he will make peace with the **L**
14:19 sin to make peace with the **L**
14:20 will make peace with the **L**
14:21 peace with the **L** for himself,
14:24 oil and present them to the **L**.
14:31 will make peace with the **L**
14:33 The **L** spoke to Moses and
14:53 He will make peace with the **L**
15:1 The **L** spoke to Moses and
15:15 will make peace with the **L**
15:30 will make peace with the **L**
16:1 The **L** spoke to Moses after
16:2 The **L** said, "Tell your brother
16:6 he will make peace with the **L**
16:8 One lot will be for the **L** and the
16:9 goat chosen by lot for the **L** as

Lev 16:10 order to make peace with the **L**
16:11 he will make peace with the **L**
16:16 he will make peace with the **L**
16:17 will make peace with the **L**
16:18 make peace with the **L** there
16:20 making peace with the **L** at
16:24 to make peace with the **L**
16:27 make peace with the **L** for sins.
16:30 will make peace with the **L**
16:33 and will make peace with the **L**
16:33 He will make peace with the **L**
16:34 to make peace with the **L** once
16:34 the **L** had commanded Moses.
17:1 The **L** spoke to Moses,
17:2 is what the **L** has commanded:
17:4 Offer it to the **L** in front of the
17:5 fields and bring them to the **L**.
17:5 as fellowship offerings to the **L**.
17:6 as a soothing aroma to the **L**.
17:9 meeting to offer them to the **L**,
18:1 The **L** spoke to Moses,
18:2 I am the **L** your God.
18:4 I am the **L** your God.
18:5 life through them. I am the **L**.
18:6 to you by blood. I am the **L**.
18:21 name of your God. I am the **L**.
18:30 I am the **L** your God."
19:1 The **L** spoke to Moses,
19:2 I, the **L** your God, am holy.
19:3 I am the **L** your God.
19:4 I am the **L** your God.
19:5 a fellowship offering to the **L**,
19:8 what is holy to the **L**.
19:10 I am the **L** your God.
19:12 name of your God. I am the **L**.
19:14 fear your God. I am the **L**.
19:16 your neighbor's life. I am the **L**.
19:18 you love yourself. I am the **L**.
19:21 for his guilt offering to the **L** at
19:22 them to make peace with the **L**
19:24 holy offering of praise to the **L**.
19:25 I am the **L** your God.
19:28 never get a tattoo. I am the **L**.
19:30 my holy tent. I am the **L**.
19:31 I am the **L** your God.
19:32 for your God. I am the **L**.
19:34 I am the **L** your God.
19:36 I am the **L** your God who
19:37 and live by them. I am the **L**."
20:1 The **L** spoke to Moses,
20:7 because I am the **L** your God.
20:8 I am the **L** who sets you apart
20:24 I am the **L** your God who
20:26 because I, the **L**, am holy.
21:1 The **L** spoke to Moses,
21:6 bring sacrifices by fire to the **L**.
21:8 Be holy because I, the **L**,
21:12 oil of his God. I am the **L**.
21:15 I, the **L**, set him apart as holy."
21:16 The **L** spoke to Moses,
21:21 bring sacrifices by fire to the **L**.
21:23 I, the **L**, set them apart as holy."
22:1 The **L** spoke to Moses,
22:2 my holy name. I am the **L**.
22:3 the Israelites set apart for the **L**,
22:3 from my presence. I am the **L**.
22:8 make him unclean. I am the **L**.
22:9 I am the **L**, who sets them apart
22:15 Israelites contribute to the **L**.
22:16 I am the **L**, who sets them apart
22:17 The **L** spoke to Moses,
22:18 bring burnt offerings to the **L**
22:21 A person may bring the **L** a
22:22 Never bring the **L** an animal
22:22 Never give the **L** any of these
22:24 Never bring the **L** an animal
22:26 The **L** spoke to Moses,
22:27 as a sacrifice by fire to the **L**.
22:29 a thank offering to the **L**,
22:30 of it until morning. I am the **L**.
22:31 my commands. I am the **L**.
22:32 I am the **L**, who sets you apart
22:33 to be your God. I am the **L**."
23:1 The **L** spoke to Moses,
23:2 appointed festivals with the **L**,
23:8 Bring the **L** a sacrifice by fire

Lev 23:9 The **L** spoke to Moses,
23:11 He will present it to the **L** so
23:12 as a burnt offering to the **L**.
23:13 sacrifice by fire made to the **L**,
23:15 an offering presented to the **L**)
23:16 a new grain offering to the **L**.
23:17 your homes to present to the **L**.
23:17 first harvested grain for the **L**.
23:18 will be a burnt offering to the **L**.
23:18 a soothing aroma to the **L**.
23:20 grain as an offering to the **L**.
23:22 I am the **L** your God."
23:23 The **L** spoke to Moses,
23:25 a sacrifice by fire to the **L**."
23:26 The **L** spoke to Moses,
23:27 and bring the **L** a sacrifice by
23:28 peace with the **L** your God.
23:33 The **L** spoke to Moses,
23:34 the Festival of Booths to the **L**.
23:36 bring a sacrifice by fire to the **L**.
23:36 Bring the **L** a sacrifice by fire.
23:37 sacrifices by fire to the **L**.
23:38 your freewill offerings to the **L**.
23:40 the presence of the **L** your God
23:43 I am the **L** your God."
24:1 The **L** spoke to Moses,
24:7 an offering by fire to the **L**.
24:12 until the **L** told them what
24:13 The **L** spoke to Moses,
24:22 because I am the **L** your God."
24:23 as the **L** commanded Moses.
24:23 as the **L** commanded Moses.
25:1 The **L** spoke to Moses on
25:2 celebrate a year to honor the **L**.
25:4 It will be a year to honor the **L**.
25:17 because I am the **L** your God.
25:38 I am the **L** your God,
25:55 I am the **L** your God."
26:1 ⌊The **L** continued,⌋
26:1 because I am the **L** your God.
26:2 my holy tent. I am the **L**.
26:13 I am the **L** your God.
26:34 its time ⌊to honor the **L**⌋ while
26:34 its time ⌊to honor the **L**⌋.
26:35 the time ⌊to honor the **L**⌋
26:43 its time to honor the **L** while
26:44 because I am the **L** their God.
26:45 nations looked on. I am the **L**."
26:46 and instructions that the **L** gave
27:1 The **L** spoke to Moses,
27:2 ⌊to give a person⌋ to the **L**,
27:9 that people offer to the **L**,
27:11 cannot be brought to the **L** as
27:14 "If you give your house to the **L**
27:16 to the **L** as something holy,
27:21 like a field claimed by the **L**.
27:22 to the **L** as something holy.
27:23 belonging to the **L**.
27:26 animal already belongs to the **L**
27:26 it belongs to the **L**.
27:28 everything dedicated to the **L**
27:28 It belongs to the **L**.
27:30 is holy and belongs to the **L**.
27:32 is holy and belongs to the **L**.
27:34 These are the commands the **L**
Num 1:1 The **L** spoke to Moses in the
1:19 as the **L** had commanded him.
1:48 The **L** had said to Moses,
1:53 In this way ⌊the **L**⌋ won't be
1:54 as the **L** commanded Moses.
2:1 The **L** spoke to Moses and
2:33 As the **L** had commanded
2:34 the **L** had commanded Moses.
3:1 at the time when the **L** spoke
3:5 The **L** said to Moses,
3:11 The **L** said to Moses,
3:13 They will be mine. I am the **L**."
3:14 The **L** said to Moses in the
3:16 So Moses did what the **L** said
3:40 The **L** said to Moses,
3:41 I am the **L**. Take the Levites for
3:42 as the **L** commanded him.
3:44 The **L** said to Moses,
3:45 will be mine. I am the **L**.
3:51 Then Moses did what the **L**
4:1 The **L** said to Moses and

Num 4:17 The **L** said to Moses and
4:21 The **L** said to Moses,
4:37 Moses and Aaron did as the **L**
4:41 Moses and Aaron did as the **L**
4:45 Moses and Aaron did as the **L**
4:49 as the **L** commanded Moses.
5:1 The **L** said to Moses,
5:4 So the Israelites did as the **L**
5:5 The **L** said to Moses,
5:6 have been unfaithful to the **L**.
5:8 wrong must be given to the **L**
5:8 which makes peace with the **L**.
5:11 The **L** said to Moses:
5:21 may the **L** make you an
5:21 The **L** will make your uterus
5:25 was holding, present it to the **L**,
6:1 The **L** said to Moses,
6:2 as a Nazirite dedicated to the **L**.
6:5 dedicated to the **L** as Nazirites,
6:6 dedicated to the **L** as Nazirites,
6:8 they will be holy to the **L**.
6:11 will make peace with the **L**
6:12 dedicate himself to the **L** as
6:14 bring these offerings to the **L**:
6:16 bring these offerings to the **L**
6:17 a fellowship offering to the **L**,
6:20 them as an offering to the **L**.
6:21 to bring their offerings to the **L**
6:22 The **L** said to Moses,
6:24 The **L** will bless you and
6:25 The **L** will smile on you and be
6:26 The **L** will look on you with
7:3 brought these gifts to the **L**:
7:4 The **L** said to Moses,
7:11 The **L** said to Moses,
7:89 of meeting to speak with the **L**,
7:89 how the **L** spoke with Moses.
8:1 The **L** said to Moses,
8:3 as the **L** commanded Moses.
8:4 one the **L** had shown Moses.
8:5 The **L** said to Moses,
8:11 present the Levites to the **L** as
8:12 one as a burnt offering to the **L**.
8:12 with the **L** for the Levites.
8:13 them as an offering to the **L**.
8:19 will make peace with the **L**
8:20 what the **L** commanded Moses
8:21 them as an offering to the **L**
8:21 and made peace with the **L**
8:22 the **L** had commanded Moses.
8:23 The **L** said to Moses,
9:1 the **L** spoke to Moses in the
9:5 the **L** had commanded Moses.
9:7 us bring our offerings to the **L** at
9:8 out what the **L** commands you
9:9 Then the **L** said to Moses,
9:13 bring your offering to the **L** at
9:23 that the **L** had given through
10:1 The **L** said to Moses,
10:9 Then the **L** your God will
10:10 I am the **L** your God."
10:13 that the **L** had given through
10:29 to the place the **L** promised
10:29 because the **L** has promised
10:32 the good things the **L** gives us."
10:33 they left the mountain of the **L**
10:35 Moses would say, "Arise, O **L**!
10:36 he would say, "Return, O **L**,
11:1 to the **L** about their troubles.
11:1 When the **L** heard them,
11:1 and fire from the **L** began to
11:2 Moses prayed to the **L**,
11:3 from the **L** burned among them
11:10 The **L** became very angry,
11:11 So he asked, "**L**, why have you
11:16 The **L** answered Moses,
11:18 I, the **L**, heard them crying and
11:20 they rejected the **L** who is here
11:23 The **L** asked Moses,
11:24 told the people what the **L** said.
11:25 Then the **L** came down in the
11:29 and that the **L** would put his
11:31 The **L** sent a wind from the sea
11:33 chew it — the **L** became angry
12:2 They asked, "Did the **L** speak
12:2 The **L** heard their complaint.

Num 12:4 Suddenly, the **L** said to Moses,
12:5 Then the **L** came down in the
12:6 prophets of the **L** among you,
12:8 He even sees the form of the **L**.
12:9 The **L** was angry with them,
12:13 So Moses cried to the **L**,
12:14 The **L** replied to Moses,
13:1 The **L** said to Moses,
14:3 Why is the **L** bringing us to this
14:8 If the **L** is pleased with us,
14:9 Don't rebel against the **L**,
14:9 and the **L** is with us.
14:10 they all saw the glory of the **L**
14:11 The **L** said to Moses,
14:13 But Moses said to the **L**,
14:14 **L**, they have already heard that
14:16 'The **L** wasn't able to bring
14:17 "**L**, let your power be as great
14:18 'The **L** ... patient, forever loving
14:20 The **L** said, "I forgive them,
14:21 and as the glory of the **L** fills
14:26 Then the **L** said to Moses and
14:28 them, 'As I live, declares the **L**,
14:35 I, the **L**, have spoken. I swear I
14:36 in front of the **L** from a plague.
14:40 Now we'll go to the place the **L**
14:42 enemies because the **L** is not
14:43 have turned away from the **L**,
14:43 the **L** will not be with you."
15:1 The **L** said to Moses,
15:3 bring offerings by fire to the **L**.
15:3 are a soothing aroma to the **L**.
15:4 offering must also give the **L**
15:7 as a soothing aroma to the **L**.
15:8 bull as a burnt offering to the **L**
15:10 a soothing aroma to the **L**.
15:13 a soothing aroma to the **L**.
15:14 a soothing aroma to the **L**,
15:15 As far as the **L** is concerned,
15:17 The **L** said to Moses,
15:19 of it as a contribution to the **L**.
15:21 as a contribution to the **L**.
15:22 commands the **L** gave Moses.
15:23 (Everything the **L** commanded
15:23 day the **L** gave the commands.)
15:24 a soothing aroma to the **L**,
15:25 will make peace with the **L**
15:25 these two offerings to the **L**
15:28 to make peace with the **L**
15:30 something wrong insults the **L**
15:31 has despised the word of the **L**
15:35 Then the **L** said to Moses,
15:36 as the **L** commanded Moses.
15:37 The **L** said to Moses,
15:41 I am the **L** your God,
15:41 I am the **L** your God."
16:3 and the **L** is among them.
16:5 "In the morning the **L** will show
16:5 Only the person the **L** chooses
16:7 Then the **L** will choose the
16:9 The **L** has brought you near
16:11 joined forces against the **L**!
16:15 angry and said to the **L**,
16:17 250 incense burners to the **L**.
16:19 the glory of the **L** appeared to
16:20 The **L** said to Moses and
16:23 Then the **L** said to Moses,
16:28 will know that the **L** sent me
16:29 then the **L** hasn't sent me.
16:30 But if the **L** does something
16:30 treated the **L** with contempt."
16:35 Fire came from the **L** and
16:36 Then the **L** said to Moses,
16:38 they were offered to the **L**.
16:40 that the **L** had given through
16:40 near to burn incense to the **L**.
16:42 and the glory of the **L** appeared.
16:44 The **L** said to Moses,
16:46 to make peace with the **L**
16:46 The **L** is showing his anger;
16:47 peace with the **L** for the people.
17:1 The **L** said to Moses,
17:10 The **L** said to Moses,
17:11 Moses did exactly what the **L**
18:1 The **L** said to Aaron,
18:6 They are a gift given to the **L** to

Num 18:8 The **L** said to Aaron,
18:12 of the produce they give the **L**:
18:13 that they bring to the **L** is yours.
18:14 is claimed by the **L** is yours.
18:15 that is brought to the **L** is yours.
18:17 a soothing aroma to the **L**.
18:19 the Israelites bring to the **L**.
18:20 The **L** said to Aaron,
18:24 contribute to the **L** — one-tenth
18:25 The **L** said to Moses,
18:26 as your contribution to the **L**.
18:28 of your income to the **L** out
18:29 best and holiest parts to the **L**.
19:1 The **L** said to Moses and
19:20 the holy place of the **L** unclean.
20:6 glory of the **L** appeared to them.
20:7 The **L** said to Moses,
20:12 But the **L** said to Moses and
20:13 complained about the **L**
20:16 When we cried out to the **L**,
20:23 the **L** said to Moses and Aaron,
20:27 did as the **L** commanded.
21:2 made this vow to the **L**:
21:3 The **L** listened to the Israelites
21:6 So the **L** sent poisonous
21:7 we criticized the **L** and you.
21:7 Pray to the **L** so that he will
21:8 The **L** said to Moses,
21:14 the Book of the Wars of the **L**:
21:16 This is the well where the **L**
21:34 The **L** said to Moses,
22:8 to you what the **L** tells me."
22:13 because the **L** has refused to
22:18 command of the **L** my God no
22:19 and I'll find out what else the **L**
22:22 So the Messenger of the **L**
22:23 Messenger of the **L** standing
22:24 Messenger of the **L** stood there.
22:25 saw the Messenger of the **L**,
22:26 Then the Messenger of the **L**
22:27 saw the Messenger of the **L**,
22:28 Then the **L** made the donkey
22:31 Then the **L** let Balaam see the
22:31 of the **L** who was standing
22:32 Messenger of the **L** asked him,
22:34 said to the Messenger of the **L**,
22:35 The Messenger of the **L** said to
23:3 Maybe the **L** will come and
23:5 The **L** told Balaam,
23:8 whom the **L** hasn't condemned?
23:12 "I must say what the **L** tells me
23:16 The **L** came to Balaam and told
23:17 "What did the **L** say?"
23:21 The **L** their God is with them,
23:26 must do whatever the **L** says?"
24:1 When Balaam saw that the **L**
24:6 like aloes planted by the **L**,
24:11 but the **L** has made you lose
24:13 I must say only what the **L**
25:3 the **L** became angry with Israel.
25:4 The **L** said to Moses,
25:10 Then the **L** said to Moses,
25:13 with the **L** for the Israelites."
25:16 The **L** said to Moses,
26:1 After the plague the **L** said to
26:4 as the **L** commanded Moses."
26:52 Then the **L** said to Moses,
26:65 The **L** had said, "They must all
27:3 joined forces against the **L**.
27:5 brought their case to the **L**,
27:6 and the **L** said to him,
27:11 as the **L** commanded Moses."
27:12 The **L** said to Moses,
27:15 Moses said to the **L**,
27:16 "**L**, you are the God who gives
27:18 So the **L** said to Moses,
27:22 did as the **L** commanded him.
27:23 as the **L** had told him.
28:1 The **L** said to Moses,
28:3 fire that you must bring to the **L**.
28:6 an offering by fire to the **L**.
28:7 Pour it out to the **L** in a holy
28:8 a soothing aroma to the **L**.
28:11 first of every month bring the **L**
28:13 an offering by fire to the **L**.
28:15 goat must be offered to the **L** as

Num 28:19 bring the L an offering by fire,
28:22 sin to make peace with the L.
28:24 a soothing aroma to the L.
28:26 Bring the L your new grain
28:27 aroma to the L — two young
28:30 goat to make peace with the L.
29:1 ⌊The L continued,⌋
29:2 a soothing aroma to the L,
29:5 sin to make peace with the L.
29:6 an offering by fire to the L.
29:11 sin to make peace with the L)
29:12 festival to the L for seven days.
29:13 a soothing aroma to the L,
29:36 a soothing aroma to the L,
29:39 bring to the L at your festivals.
29:39 you vowed to give to the L,
29:40 the L had commanded him.
30:1 "This is what the L has
30:2 If a man makes a vow to the L
30:3 might make a vow to the L that
30:5 The L will free her ⌊from this
30:8 The L will free her ⌊from this
30:12 and the L will free her ⌊from
30:16 These are the laws the L gave
31:1 The L said to Moses,
31:3 The L will use them to get
31:7 as the L commanded Moses,
31:16 to be unfaithful to the L
31:25 The L said to Moses,
31:28 Collect a tax for the L.
31:29 as a contribution to the L.
31:31 as the L commanded Moses.
31:37 675 went to the L as taxes.
31:38 72 went to the L as taxes.
31:39 61 went to the L as taxes.
31:40 32 went to the L as taxes.
31:41 as the L had commanded him.
31:47 as the L commanded him.
31:50 have brought as gifts to the L
31:50 to make peace with the L."
31:52 All the gold contributed to the L
32:4 the land that the L won for the
32:7 the land the L has given them.
32:9 land that the L had given them.
32:10 That day the L became angry
32:12 wholeheartedly followed the L.
32:13 Since the L was angry with the
32:14 trying to make the L angry
32:21 and fight until the L forces out
32:22 military duty to the L and Israel.
32:23 will be sinning against the L.
32:31 we will do as the L has said.
33:4 whom the L had killed in a
33:50 The L said to Moses on the
34:1 The L said to Moses,
34:13 The L has commanded that
34:16 The L said to Moses,
34:29 These are the men the L
35:1 The L spoke to Moses on the
35:9 The L said to Moses,
35:33 with the L except through
35:34 I, the L, live among the
36:2 They said, "Sir, the L
36:2 The L also commanded you to
36:5 a command from the L.
36:6 This is what the L commands
36:10 as the L commanded Moses.
36:13 and rules the L gave
Dtr 1:3 the L had commanded him
1:6 At Mount Horeb the L our God
1:8 of the land the L swore
1:10 The L your God has made your
1:11 May the L God of your
1:19 as the L our God had
1:20 which the L our God is giving
1:21 The L your God is giving you
1:21 Take possession of it, as the L
1:25 "The land that the L our God is
1:26 the command of the L your God
1:27 and said, "The L hates us!
1:30 The L your God, who is going
1:31 There you saw how the L your
1:32 you didn't trust the L your God,
1:34 When the L heard what you
1:36 wholeheartedly followed the L."
1:37 The L became angry with me
Dtr 1:41 "We have sinned against the L.
1:41 We'll go and fight, as the L our
1:42 But the L said to me,
1:45 came back, you cried to the L,
1:45 but the L didn't listen to you or
2:1 Red Sea as the L had told me.
2:2 The L said to me,
2:7 The L your God has blessed
2:7 For 40 years now the L your
2:9 The L said to me, "Don't bother
2:12 the land that the L gave them.
2:13 Then the L said, "Now cross
2:14 as the L had sworn they would.
2:15 In fact, it was the L himself
2:17 the L said to me,
2:21 But the L wiped them out
2:22 The L did the same thing for
2:24 ⌊The L continued,⌋
2:29 into the land the L our God is
2:30 The L your God made him
2:31 The L said to me, "I have
2:33 The L our God gave Sihon to
2:36 The L our God gave us all of
2:37 But the L our God had
3:2 The L said to me, "Don't be
3:3 So the L our God also handed
3:18 "The L your God has given you
3:20 of the land the L your God is
3:21 that the L your God has
3:21 The L will do the same to all of
3:22 because the L your God
3:23 Then I pleaded with the L:
3:24 "Almighty L, you have ⌊only⌋
3:26 The L was angry with me
4:1 of the land that the L God
4:2 of the L your God that
4:3 you saw what the L did at Baal
4:3 The L your God destroyed
4:4 But you were loyal to the L
4:5 as the L my God commanded
4:7 to them as the L our God is
4:10 in front of the L your God at
4:10 The L had said to me,
4:12 The L spoke to you from the
4:13 The L told you about the terms
4:14 The L also commanded me to
4:15 You didn't see the L the day he
4:19 The L your God has given
4:20 But you are the people the L
4:21 The L was angry with me
4:21 So the L your God took an oath
4:23 that the L your God made
4:23 anything the L your God has
4:24 The L your God is a raging fire,
4:25 If you do this thing that the L
4:27 The L will scatter you among
4:27 where the L will force you
4:29 But if you look for the L your
4:30 come back to the L your God
4:31 The L your God is a merciful
4:34 The L your God used his
4:35 would know that the L is God.
4:39 and never forget that the L is
4:40 The L your God is giving you
5:2 The L our God made a promise
5:4 The L spoke to you face to
5:5 I stood between the L and you
5:5 to tell you the word of the L,
5:5 on the mountain. The L said:
5:6 "I am the L your God,
5:9 because I, the L your God,
5:11 "Never use the name of the L
5:11 The L will make sure that
5:12 This is what the L your God
5:14 dedicated to the L your God.
5:15 and that the L your God used
5:15 This is why the L your God
5:16 mother as the L your God has
5:16 in the land the L your God is
5:22 commandments the L spoke
5:24 You said, "The L our God has
5:25 hear the voice of the L our God,
5:27 that the L our God says.
5:27 Then tell us whatever the L our
5:28 When the L heard the words
5:32 So be careful to do what the L
Dtr 5:33 Follow all the directions the L
6:1 and rules the L your God
6:2 must fear the L your God.
6:3 as the L God of your ancestors
6:4 Listen, Israel: The L is our God.
6:4 The L is the only God.
6:5 Love the L your God with all
6:10 The L your God will bring you
6:12 that you don't forget the L,
6:13 You must fear the L your God,
6:15 If you do, the L your God will
6:15 because the L your God,
6:16 Never test the L your God as
6:17 commands of the L your God
6:18 Do what the L considers right
6:18 land which the L promised
6:19 You will see the L expel your
6:20 and rules which the L our God
6:21 but the L used his mighty hand
6:22 Right before our eyes the L did
6:23 The L led us out of there to
6:24 The L our God commanded us
6:25 the presence of the L our God,
7:1 The L your God will bring you
7:2 When the L your God gives
7:2 have been claimed by the L.
7:4 Then the L will get very angry
7:6 who belong to the L your God.
7:7 The L set his heart on you and
7:8 because the L loved you
7:9 Keep in mind that the L your
7:12 the L your God will keep his
7:13 in the land the L will give you,
7:15 The L will keep you from
7:16 people the L your God hands
7:18 Remember what the L your
7:19 the amazing things the L did.
7:20 The L your God will spread
7:21 because the L your God is with
7:23 The L your God will hand
7:25 disgusting to the L your God.
8:1 of the land that the L promised
8:2 for 40 years the L your God led
8:3 every word that the L speaks.
8:5 The L your God was
8:6 commands of the L your God.
8:7 The L your God is bringing you
8:10 thank the L your God for the
8:11 you don't forget the L your God.
8:14 and forget the L your God,
8:18 But remember the L your God
8:19 that if you forget the L your God
8:20 The L is going to destroy other
8:20 you don't obey the L your God.
9:3 Realize today that the L your
9:3 them as the L promised you.
9:4 When the L your God expels
9:4 the L brought us here to take
9:4 that the L is forcing them
9:5 wicked that the L your God is
9:5 It's also because the L wants
9:6 right that the L your God is
9:7 you made the L your God angry
9:7 You've rebelled against the L
9:8 you made the L so angry that
9:9 of the promise that the L made
9:10 Then the L gave me the two
9:10 all the words that the L spoke
9:11 the L gave me the two stone
9:13 The L also said to me,
9:16 sinned against the L your God.
9:16 the way the L commanded you
9:18 myself down in front of the L.
9:18 You did what the L considered
9:19 once more the L listened to me.
9:20 The L also became very angry
9:22 You also made the L angry at
9:23 When the L sent you from
9:23 the word of the L your God.
9:24 You've rebelled against the L
9:25 myself down in front of the L
9:25 40 nights because the L said
9:26 I prayed to the L and said,
9:26 LORD and said, "Almighty L,
9:28 "The L wasn't able to bring
10:1 At that time the L said to me,

Dtr 10:4 The L wrote on these tablets
10:4 Then the L gave them to me.
10:5 They are still there, where the L
10:8 At that time the L set apart the
10:9 The L your God is their only
10:10 Once again the L listened to
10:11 The L said to me, "Lead the
10:12 Israel, what does the L your
10:13 The L wants you to obey his
10:14 belong to the L your God.
10:15 The L set his heart on your
10:17 The L your God is God of gods
10:17 is God of gods and L of lords,
10:20 Fear the L your God,
10:22 Now the L your God has made
11:1 Love the L your God,
11:2 learned from the L your God.
11:4 the L destroyed them forever.
11:7 things that the L did.
11:9 time in the land the L swore
11:12 It is a land the L your God
11:13 love the L your God,
11:17 The L will become angry with
11:17 good land the L is giving you.
11:21 in this land that the L swore
11:22 Love the L your God,
11:23 Then the L will force all these
11:25 As the L your God promised,
11:27 of the L your God that
11:28 commands of the L your God,
11:29 When the L your God brings
11:31 of the land the L your God is
12:1 obey in the land that the L God
12:4 Never worship the L your God
12:5 The L your God will choose a
12:7 the presence of the L your God,
12:7 because the L your God has
12:9 the property the L your God is
12:10 in the land the L your God is
12:11 Then the L your God will
12:11 you vow to bring to the L.
12:12 of the L your God along
12:14 the place that the L will choose
12:15 from what the L your God has
12:18 presence of the L your God at
12:18 There in the presence of the L
12:20 The L your God will expand
12:21 If the place the L your God
12:21 flocks that the L has given you.
12:25 what the L considers right.
12:26 to the place the L will choose.
12:27 on the altar of the L your God.
12:27 the altar of the L your God,
12:28 what the L your God considers
12:29 The L your God will destroy
12:31 Never worship the L your God
12:31 gods is disgusting to the L.
13:3 The L your God is testing you
13:4 Worship the L your God,
13:5 against the L your God,
13:5 directions the L your God gave
13:10 you away from the L your God,
13:12 cities which the L your God is
13:13 have been led away from the L
13:16 burnt offering to the L your God
13:17 Then the L will stop being
13:18 The L your God will do this if
14:1 the children of the L your God.
14:2 who are holy to the L your God.
14:2 the L has chosen you to be his
14:3 that is disgusting to the L.
14:21 who are holy to the L your God.
14:23 the presence of the L your God
14:23 Then you will learn to fear the L
14:24 But the place the L your God
14:25 and go to the place the L your
14:26 the presence of the L your God.
14:29 Then the L your God will bless
15:4 because the L your God will
15:5 carefully to the L your God
15:6 The L your God will bless you,
15:7 the land that the L your God is
15:9 complain to the L about you,
15:10 When you do this, the L your
15:14 to them as the L your God has
15:15 Egypt and the L your God freed

Dtr 15:18 Besides, the L your God will
15:19 and flocks to the L your God.
15:20 the presence of the L your God
15:20 in the place the L will choose.
15:21 sacrifice it to the L your God.
16:1 Honor the L your God by
16:1 In the month of Abib the L your
16:2 sacrifice to the L your God.
16:2 Do this at the place where the L
16:5 of the cities the L your God is
16:6 where the L your God will
16:7 and eat it at the place the L
16:8 dedicated to the L your God.
16:10 of Weeks to the L your God.
16:10 blessings the L your God has
16:11 of the L your God along
16:11 at the place the L your God will
16:15 dedicated to the L your God
16:15 because the L your God will
16:16 presence of the L your God at
16:16 of the L without an offering.
16:17 blessings the L your God has
16:18 city that the L your God is
16:20 the land that the L your God is
16:21 the altar for the L your God,
16:22 things the L your God hates.
17:1 a sacrifice to the L your God.
17:2 In one of the cities the L your
17:2 what the L considers evil.
17:8 place that the L your God will
17:10 place that the L will choose.
17:12 (who serves the L your God)
17:14 the land that the L your God is
17:15 the king the L your God will
17:16 The L has told you,
17:19 He will learn to fear the L his
18:1 has been sacrificed to the L.
18:2 The L will be their inheritance,
18:5 Out of all your tribes, the L your
18:5 in the name of the L forever.
18:6 to the place the L will choose.
18:7 the name of the L his God like
18:9 the land that the L your God is
18:12 things is disgusting to the L.
18:12 The L your God is forcing
18:13 dealing with the L your God.
18:14 But the L your God won't let
18:15 The L your God will send you
18:16 This is what you asked the L
18:16 hear the voice of the L our God
18:17 The L told me, "What they've
18:21 that the L didn't speak this
18:22 then it didn't come from the L.
19:1 The L your God will destroy all
19:2 the land that the L your God is
19:3 the land that the L your God is
19:8 The L your God may expand
19:9 you — to love the L your God
19:10 the land that the L your God is
19:14 the land that the L your God is
20:1 because the L your God,
20:4 The L your God is going with
20:13 When the L your God hands
20:14 goods that the L your God has
20:16 nations that the L your God is
20:17 and Jebusites for the L and
20:17 as the L your God has
20:18 will sin against the L your God.
21:1 the land that the L your God is
21:5 The L your God has chosen
21:8 L, make peace with your
21:8 with the L despite the murder.
21:9 what the L considers right.
21:10 and the L your God hands
21:23 The land that the L your God is
22:5 is disgusting to the L your God.
23:1 join the assembly of the L.
23:2 not join the assembly of the L.
23:2 of the L for ten generations.
23:3 not join the assembly of the L.
23:3 of the L for ten generations.
23:5 But the L your God refused to
23:5 because the L your God loves
23:8 may join the assembly of the L.
23:14 The L your God moves around
23:14 This way, the L will never see

Dtr 23:18 the house of the L your God as
23:18 disgusting to the L your God.
23:20 Then the L your God will bless
23:21 make a vow to the L your God,
23:21 The L your God expects you to
23:23 your vow to the L your God.
24:4 the land that the L your God is
24:9 Remember what the L your
24:13 the presence of the L your God.
24:15 complain to the L about you,
24:18 Egypt and the L your God freed
24:19 Then the L your God will bless
25:15 the land that the L your God is
25:16 is disgusting to the L.
25:19 So when the L your God gives
26:1 the land that the L your God is
26:2 the land that the L your God is
26:2 where the L your God will
26:3 "I declare today to the L your
26:3 the land that the L is giving us,
26:4 of the altar of the L your God.
26:5 the presence of the L your God:
26:7 We cried out to the L God of
26:8 Then the L used his mighty
26:10 the fields you gave me, L."
26:10 the presence of the L your God
26:11 which the L your God has
26:13 say to the L your God,
26:14 I have obeyed the L my God.
26:16 Today the L your God is
26:17 declared that the L is your God
26:18 Today the L has declared that
26:19 people holy to the L your God,
27:2 the land that the L your God is
27:3 The L God of your ancestors is
27:5 dedicated to the L your God.
27:6 the altar of the L your God.
27:6 on it to the L your God.
27:7 the presence of the L your God.
27:9 the people of the L your God.
27:10 Obey the L your God and
27:15 anything disgusting to the L
28:1 Carefully obey the L your God,
28:1 If you do, the L your God will
28:2 you obey the L your God:
28:7 The L will defeat your enemies
28:8 The L will bless your barns
28:8 The L your God will bless you
28:9 commands of the L your God
28:11 The L will give you plenty of
28:11 in the land the L will give you,
28:12 The L will open the heavens,
28:13 The L will make you the head,
28:13 of the L your God that
28:15 Obey the L your God,
28:20 The L will send you curses,
28:20 will do by abandoning the L.
28:21 The L will send one plague
28:22 The L will strike you with
28:24 The L will send dust storms
28:25 The L will let your enemies
28:27 The L will strike you with the
28:28 The L will strike you with
28:35 The L will afflict your knees
28:36 The L will lead you and the
28:37 All the nations where the L will
28:45 because you didn't obey the L
28:47 You didn't serve the L your God
28:48 whom the L will send against
28:48 The L will put a heavy burden
28:49 The L will bring against you a
28:52 the land that the L your God is
28:53 whom the L your God has
28:58 name: the L your God.
28:59 If so, the L will strike you and
28:61 The L will also bring you every
28:62 you didn't obey the L your God.
28:63 At one time the L was more
28:63 Now the L will be more than
28:64 Then the L will scatter you
28:65 There the L will give you an
28:68 The L will bring you back to
29:1 that the L commanded Moses
29:1 the promise the L gave them at
29:2 eyes everything that the L did
29:4 But to this day the L hasn't

Dtr 29:6 know that I am the L your God.
29:10 the presence of the L your God.
29:12 promise that the L your God is
29:13 With this promise the L will
29:15 the presence of the L our God
29:18 who turns from the L our God
29:19 After all, ⌊the L would never⌋
29:20 The L will never be willing to
29:20 The L will erase ⌊every
29:21 And the L will single him out
29:22 the diseases the L sent here.
29:23 cities the L destroyed in fierce
29:24 "Why has the L done this to
29:25 the promise of the L God
29:26 gods the L didn't permit them to
29:27 So the L became angry with
29:28 the L uprooted these people
29:29 They belong to the L our God.
30:1 where the L your God will
30:2 return to the L your God
30:4 the L your God will gather you
30:5 The L your God will bring you
30:5 and the L will make you more
30:6 The L your God will
30:6 You will love the L your God
30:7 Then the L your God will put
30:8 You will again obey the L and
30:9 The L your God will give you
30:9 The L will again delight in
30:10 and return to the L your God
30:16 Love the L your God,
30:16 and the L your God will bless
30:20 Love the L your God,
30:20 you in the land that the L swore
31:2 Besides, the L has told me that
31:3 The L your God is the one who
31:3 ahead of you, as the L told you.
31:4 The L will do to those nations
31:5 The L will hand them over to
31:6 The L your God is the one who
31:7 land that the L will give them,
31:8 The L is the one who is going
31:11 presence of the L your God at
31:12 and learn to fear the L your God
31:13 learn to fear the L your God as
31:14 The L said to Moses,
31:15 Then the L appeared in a
31:16 The L said to Moses,
31:23 The L gave this command to
31:26 the promise of the L your God,
31:27 you are rebelling against the L.
31:29 make the L furious by doing
32:3 will proclaim the name of the L.
32:6 Is this how you repay the L,
32:12 so the L alone led his people.
32:19 The L saw this and rejected
32:27 It wasn't the L who did all this!'"
32:30 them and the L gave them no
32:36 The L will judge his people
32:48 same day the L said to Moses,
33:2 "The L came from Sinai.
33:5 The L was king of Jeshurun
33:7 "Hear the cry of Judah, O L,
33:11 L, bless them with strength and
33:12 The L will shelter them all day
33:13 "May the L bless their land
33:14 May the L bless their land with
33:16 May the L bless their land with
33:21 Israel what the L considers fair
33:29 a nation saved by the L?
34:1 The L showed him the whole
34:4 Then the L said to him,
34:5 As the L had predicted,
34:9 the L had commanded through
34:10 whom the L dealt with face to
34:11 He was the one the L sent to
Jos 1:1 the L said to Moses' assistant
1:9 because the L your God is with
1:11 of the land the L your God is
1:13 Moses said, 'The L your God
1:15 of the land the L your God is
1:17 May the L your God be with
2:9 She said to them, "I know the L
2:10 We've heard how the L dried up
2:10 you destroyed them for the L.
2:11 The L your God is the God of
Jos 2:12 Please swear by the L that
2:14 and honestly when the L gives
2:24 They told Joshua, "The L has
3:3 the promise of the L your God
3:5 tomorrow the L will do miracles
3:7 Then the L said to Joshua,
3:9 to the words of the L your God."
3:11 the ark of the promise of the L
3:13 who carry the ark of the L,
3:13 the L of the whole earth,
4:1 The L had told Joshua,
4:5 of the ark of the L your God.
4:8 as the L had told Joshua.
4:10 the L had ordered Joshua
4:13 the river in front of the L
4:14 On that day the L honored
4:15 The L said to Joshua,
4:23 The L your God dried up the
4:24 The L did this so that everyone
4:24 fear the L your God every
5:1 heard that the L had dried up
5:2 At that time the L spoke to
5:6 because they disobeyed the L.
5:6 The L swore that he would not
5:9 The L said to Joshua,
6:2 The L said to Joshua,
6:8 ahead of the L marched off as
6:16 because the L has given you
6:17 city has been claimed by the L.
6:17 in it belongs to the L.
6:18 by the L for destruction,
6:18 will be destroyed by the L.
6:18 that is claimed by the L,
6:19 are holy and belong to the L.
6:21 everything in it for the L.
6:26 "The L will curse whoever
6:27 So the L was with Joshua,
7:1 the things claimed by the L.
7:1 that had been claimed by the L.
7:1 So the L became angry with
7:7 Joshua said, "Almighty L,
7:8 L, what else can I say after
7:10 The L said to Joshua,
7:13 This is what the L God of
7:14 The tribe the L selects will
7:14 Then the family the L selects
7:14 and the household the L
7:15 what the L has claimed.
7:19 give honor and praise to the L
7:20 I have sinned against the L
7:23 it out in the presence of the L.
7:25 The L will bring disaster on
7:26 Then the L withdrew his
8:1 The L said to Joshua,
8:7 The L your God will hand it
8:8 Do what the L says.
8:18 Then the L said to Joshua,
8:27 the L had commanded Joshua.
8:30 Ebal to the L God of Israel.
8:31 made burnt offerings to the L
9:9 because the L your God has
9:14 they did not ask the L about it.
9:18 oath about them to the L God
9:19 oath about them to the L God
9:24 "We were told that the L your
10:1 Ai and claimed it for the L
10:8 The L told Joshua,
10:10 The L threw the enemy into
10:11 the L threw huge hailstones on
10:12 The day the L handed the
10:12 Joshua spoke to the L while
10:14 The L did what a man told him
10:14 because the L fought for Israel.
10:19 because the L your God has
10:25 because this is what the L will
10:28 He claimed them for the L by
10:30 The L also handed Libnah and
10:32 The L handed Lachish over to
10:35 He claimed it for the L by
10:37 for the L by destroying them.
10:39 all for the L by destroying them.
10:40 for the L by destroying it,
10:40 as the L God of Israel had
10:42 campaign because the L God
11:6 The L told Joshua,
11:8 The L handed them over to
Jos 11:9 as the L had told him.
11:11 for the L by destroying them
11:12 He claimed them for the L by
11:15 what the L had commanded his
11:15 the L had commanded Moses.
11:20 The L made their enemies
11:21 Joshua claimed them for the L
11:23 as the L had promised Moses.
13:1 So the L said to him,
13:14 The sacrifices offered to the L
13:14 as the L had promised them.
13:33 The L God of Israel is what
14:2 the L had commanded through
14:5 the L had commanded Moses.
14:6 "You know what the L said to
14:8 loyal to the L my God.
14:9 loyal to the L my God.'
14:10 The L has kept me alive as he
14:10 when the L made this promise
14:12 region which the L spoke
14:12 If the L is with me,
14:14 loyal to the L God of Israel.
15:13 Judah as the L had told them.
17:4 They said, "The L commanded
17:4 relatives as the L had required.
17:14 because the L has blessed us."
18:3 the land which the L God
18:6 the presence of the L our God.
18:7 is to serve the L as priests.
18:8 of the L here in Shiloh."
18:10 the presence of the L in Shiloh.
19:50 as the L had instructed them to
19:51 in the presence of the L at
20:1 The L said to Joshua,
21:2 They said to them, "The L
21:3 So, as the L had instructed,
21:8 as the L had commanded
21:43 So the L gave Israel the whole
21:44 The L allowed them to have
21:44 The L handed all their enemies
21:45 promise that the L had given
22:3 commands of the L your God.
22:4 "Now the L your God has given
22:5 Love the L your God,
22:9 as the L had instructed them
22:16 from following the L by building
22:16 have rebelled against the L!
22:18 away from following the L!
22:18 Today you rebel against the L,
22:19 Don't rebel against the L or
22:19 to the altar of the L our God.
22:20 the things claimed by the L?
22:20 Didn't the L become angry with
22:22 "The L is ⌊the only true⌋ God!
22:22 The L is ⌊the only true⌋ God!
22:22 rebellious or unfaithful to the L,
22:23 let the L punish us.
22:24 have with the L God of Israel?
22:25 The L has made the Jordan
22:25 no connection with the L!' So
22:25 from worshiping the L.
22:27 in the presence of the L
22:27 have no connection with the L!'
22:29 for us to rebel against the L
22:29 from following the L by building
22:29 to the altar of the L our God that
22:31 "Today we know the L is
22:31 an unfaithful act against the L.
22:34 Us That the L Is ⌊the Only
23:1 A long time afterward, the L
23:3 everything the L your God did
23:3 The L your God fought for you!
23:5 The L your God will expel
23:5 You will take their land as the L
23:8 be loyal to the L your God,
23:9 The L has forced important and
23:10 That was because the L your
23:11 careful to love the L your God.
23:13 know that the L your God will
23:13 land that the L your God has
23:14 which the L your God has
23:15 "Every good word the L your
23:15 In the same way the L will
23:16 on you by the L your God
23:16 the L will be angry with you.
24:2 "This is what the L God of

Jos	24:7	ancestors cried out to the **L**,
	24:14	"Fear the **L**, and serve him with
	24:14	and serve only the **L**.
	24:15	if you don't want to serve the **L**,
	24:15	and I will still serve the **L**."
	24:16	for us to abandon the **L**
	24:17	The **L** our God brought us and
	24:18	The **L** forced out all the people
	24:18	We, too, will serve the **L**,
	24:19	"Since the **L** is a holy God,
	24:20	If you abandon the **L** and serve
	24:21	We will ⌞only⌟ serve the **L**!"
	24:22	have chosen to serve the **L**."
	24:23	over to the **L** God of Israel."
	24:24	"We will serve the **L** our God
	24:27	the words which the **L** spoke
	24:31	Israel served the **L** as long as
	24:31	everything the **L** had done
Jdg	1:1	the Israelites asked the **L**,
	1:2	The **L** answered, I am about to
	1:4	and the **L** handed the
	1:17	it for the **L** by destroying it.
	1:19	The **L** was with the men of
	1:22	and the **L** was with them.
	2:1	The Messenger of the **L** went
	2:4	While the Messenger of the **L**
	2:5	offered sacrifices there to the **L**.
	2:7	The people served the **L**
	2:7	works the **L** had done
	2:10	personal experience with the **L**
	2:11	did what the **L** considered evil.
	2:12	The Israelites abandoned the **L**
	2:12	and that made the **L** angry.
	2:13	They abandoned the **L** to serve
	2:14	So the **L** became angry with
	2:15	the power of the **L** brought
	2:15	This was what the **L** said he
	2:16	Then the **L** would send judges
	2:18	But when the **L** appointed
	2:18	The **L** rescued them from their
	2:18	The **L** was moved by the
	2:20	The **L** became angry with
	2:23	So the **L** let these nations stay.
	3:1	These are the nations the **L** left
	3:2	The **L** left them to teach Israel's
	3:4	the **L** had given their
	3:7	did what the **L** considered evil.
	3:7	They forgot the **L** their God and
	3:8	The **L** became angry with the
	3:9	Israel cried out to the **L** for help.
	3:9	The **L** sent a savior to rescue
	3:10	The **L** handed King Cushan
	3:12	did what the **L** considered evil.
	3:12	So the **L** made King Eglon of
	3:12	did what the **L** considered evil.
	3:15	Israel cried out to the **L** for help.
	3:15	The **L** sent a savior to rescue
	3:28	The **L** will hand your enemy
	4:1	did what the **L** considered evil.
	4:2	So the **L** used King Jabin of
	4:3	Israel cried out to the **L** for help.
	4:6	She told him, "The **L** God of
	4:9	because the **L** will use a
	4:14	This is the day the **L** will hand
	4:14	The **L** will go ahead of you."
	4:15	The **L** threw Sisera,
	5:2	Praise the **L**! Men in Israel
	5:3	I will sing a song to the **L**.
	5:3	music to the **L** God of Israel.
	5:4	O **L**, when you went out from
	5:5	in the presence of the **L** God
	5:5	presence of the **L** God of Israel.
	5:9	who volunteered. Praise the **L**!
	5:11	repeat the victories of the **L**,
	5:23	said the Messenger of the **L**.
	5:23	did not come to help the **L**,
	5:23	to help the **L** and his heroes."
	5:31	your enemies die like that, O **L**.
	5:31	But may those who love the **L**
	6:1	did what the **L** considered evil.
	6:1	So the **L** handed them over to
	6:6	and cried out to the **L** for help.
	6:7	of Israel cried out to the **L**
	6:8	the **L** sent a prophet to them.
	6:8	He said, "This is what the **L**
	6:10	'I am the **L** your God.
Jdg	6:11	The Messenger of the **L** came
	6:12	The Messenger of the **L**
	6:12	"The **L** is with you,
	6:13	But if the **L** is with us,
	6:13	The **L** brought us out of Egypt
	6:13	But now the **L** has abandoned
	6:14	The **L** turned to him and said,
	6:16	The **L** replied, "I will be with
	6:19	to the Messenger of the **L** under
	6:20	Messenger of the **L** told him,
	6:21	Then the Messenger of the **L**
	6:21	Then the Messenger of the **L**
	6:22	been the Messenger of the **L**.
	6:22	So he said, "**L** God!
	6:22	of the **L** face to face."
	6:23	The **L** said to him,
	6:24	built an altar there to the **L**.
	6:24	He called it The **L** Calms.
	6:25	That same night the **L** said to
	6:26	build an altar to the **L** your God
	6:27	and did what the **L** had told him
	7:2	The **L** said to Gideon,
	7:4	The **L** said to Gideon,
	7:5	The **L** said to him,
	7:7	Then the **L** said to Gideon,
	7:9	That night the **L** said to Gideon,
	7:15	he worshiped the **L**.
	7:15	The **L** will hand Midian's camp
	7:18	'For the **L** and for Gideon!'"
	7:20	sword for the **L** and for Gideon!"
	7:22	and the **L** caused the whole
	8:7	When the **L** hands Zebah and
	8:19	solemnly swear, as the **L** lives,
	8:23	The **L** will rule you."
	8:34	not remember the **L** their God,
	10:6	did what the **L** considered evil.
	10:6	They abandoned the **L** and did
	10:7	The **L** became angry with the
	10:10	Israel cried out to the **L** for help.
	10:11	The **L** said to the people of
	10:15	people of Israel said to the **L**,
	10:16	they had and served the **L**.
	10:16	So the **L** could not bear to have
	11:9	and the **L** gives them
	11:10	"The **L** is a witness between
	11:11	things in the presence of the **L**.
	11:21	But the **L** God of Israel handed
	11:23	"The **L** God of Israel forced the
	11:24	everything the **L** our God took
	11:27	The **L** is the judge who will
	11:30	Jephthah made a vow to the **L**.
	11:31	Ammon will belong to the **L**.
	11:32	The **L** handed the people of
	11:35	a foolish promise to the **L**.
	11:36	you made a promise to the **L**.
	11:36	since the **L** has punished your
	12:3	The **L** handed them over to me.
	13:1	did what the **L** considered evil.
	13:1	So the **L** handed them over to
	13:3	The Messenger of the **L**
	13:8	Manoah pleaded with the **L**,
	13:8	with the LORD, "Please, **L**,
	13:13	of the **L** answered Manoah,
	13:15	said to the Messenger of the **L**,
	13:16	Messenger of the **L** responded,
	13:16	sacrifice it to the **L**."
	13:16	it was the Messenger of the **L**.)
	13:17	asked the Messenger of the **L**,
	13:18	Messenger of the **L** asked him,
	13:19	and sacrificed them to the **L**
	13:19	**L** did something miraculous.
	13:20	the Messenger of the **L** went up
	13:21	The Messenger of the **L** didn't
	13:21	been the Messenger of the **L**.
	13:23	"If the **L** wanted to kill us,
	13:24	and the **L** blessed him.
	14:4	that the **L** was behind this.
	14:4	The **L** was looking for an
	15:18	he called out to the **L** and said,
	16:20	realize that the **L** had left him.)
	16:28	Then Samson called to the **L**,
	16:28	to the LORD, "Almighty **L**,
	17:2	"The **L** bless you, my son!"
	17:3	"I dedicate this silver to the **L**
	17:13	"Now I know that the **L** will be
	18:6	The **L** approves of your
Jdg	20:1	united in the presence of the **L**.
	20:18	The **L** answered, "Judah will
	20:23	presence of the **L** until evening.
	20:23	They asked the **L**,
	20:23	The **L** answered, "Go fight
	20:26	cried in the presence of the **L**
	20:26	fellowship offerings to the **L**.
	20:28	people of Israel asked the **L**,
	20:28	The **L** answered, "Go!
	20:35	So the **L** defeated them in front
	21:3	"**L** God of Israel, why has this
	21:5	in the presence of the **L**?"
	21:5	of the **L** at Mizpah must
	21:7	We swore to the **L** that we
	21:8	presence of the **L** at Mizpah?"
	21:11	for the **L** by destroying them."
	21:15	because the **L** had broken
Rut	1:6	she heard that the **L** had come
	1:8	May the **L** be as kind to you as
	1:9	May the **L** repay each of you so
	1:13	because the **L** has sent me
	1:17	May the **L** strike me down if
	1:21	I went away full, but the **L** has
	1:21	when the **L** has tormented me
	2:4	"May the **L** be with all of you!"
	2:4	"May the **L** bless you!"
	2:12	May the **L** reward you for what
	2:12	a rich reward from the **L** God
	2:20	"May the **L** bless him.
	2:20	The **L** hasn't stopped being
	3:10	"May the **L** bless you,
	3:13	solemnly swear, as the **L** lives,
	4:11	May the **L** make this wife,
	4:12	whom the **L** will give you
	4:13	He slept with her, and the **L**
	4:14	said to Naomi, "Praise the **L**,
1Sm	1:3	worship and sacrifice to the **L**
	1:3	served there as priests of the **L**.
	1:5	even though the **L** had kept her
	1:6	Because the **L** had made her
	1:10	prayed to the **L** while she cried.
	1:11	made this vow, "**L** of Armies,
	1:12	a long time in front of the **L**,
	1:15	pouring out my heart to the **L**.
	1:19	and worshiped in front of the **L**.
	1:19	and the **L** remembered her.
	1:20	"I asked the **L** for him."
	1:21	the annual sacrifice to the **L**.
	1:22	him and present him to the **L**,
	1:23	May the **L** keep his word."
	1:26	next to you and prayed to the **L**.
	1:27	and the **L** granted my request.
	1:28	I am giving him to the **L**.
	1:28	He will be dedicated to the **L**
	1:28	And they worshiped the **L** there
	2:1	"My heart finds joy in the **L**.
	2:1	My head is lifted to the **L**.
	2:2	There is no one holy like the **L**.
	2:2	There is no one but you, O **L**.
	2:3	of your mouth because the **L** is
	2:6	"The **L** kills, and he gives life.
	2:7	The **L** causes poverty and
	2:10	"Those who oppose the **L** are
	2:10	The **L** judges the ends of the
	2:11	⌞Samuel⌟ served the **L** under
	2:12	they had no faith in the **L**.
	2:17	was a serious matter to the **L**,
	2:17	made to the **L** with contempt.
	2:18	to serve in front of the **L**.
	2:20	"May the **L** give you children
	2:20	which she has given to the **L**."
	2:21	The **L** came to Hannah.
	2:21	grew up in front of the **L**.
	2:24	of the **L** spreading isn't good!
	2:25	a person sins against the **L**,
	2:25	warning — the **L** wanted
	2:26	favor of the **L** and the people.
	2:27	"This is what the **L** says:
	2:30	the **L** God of Israel declares:
	2:30	"But now the **L** declares:
	3:1	was serving the **L** under Eli.
	3:1	a prophecy from the **L** was rare;
	3:3	in the temple of the **L** where
	3:4	Then the **L** called Samuel.
	3:6	The **L** called Samuel again.
	3:7	had no experience with the **L**,

1Sm 3:7 because the word of the **L** had
3:8 The **L** called Samuel a third
3:8 Then Eli realized that the **L**
3:9 he calls you, say, 'Speak, **L**.
3:10 The **L** came and stood there.
3:11 Then the **L** said to Samuel,
3:17 "What did the **L** tell you?"
3:18 Eli replied, "He is the **L**.
3:19 The **L** was with him and didn't
3:21 The **L** continued to appear in
3:21 since the **L** revealed himself to
3:21 through the word of the **L**.
4:3 "Why has the **L** used the
4:4 the ark of the promise of the **L**
5:6 The **L** dealt harshly with the
5:9 the **L** threw the city into a great
6:1 The ark of the **L** had been in
6:2 we do with the ark of the **L**?
6:8 Take the ark of the **L**,
6:11 They put the ark of the **L** and
6:14 as a burnt offering to the **L**.
6:15 ⌊from the cart⌋ the ark of the **L**
6:15 and sacrifices to the **L** that day.
6:17 as a guilt offering to the **L** were
6:18 they put the ark of the **L** is
6:19 looked inside the ark of the **L**.
6:19 because the **L** struck them
6:20 "Who can stand before the **L**,
6:21 brought back the ark of the **L**.
7:2 Israel mournfully sought the **L**.
7:3 to the **L** wholeheartedly,
7:3 Make a commitment to the **L**,
7:4 Astarte and served only the **L**.
7:5 and I will pray to the **L** for you."
7:6 poured it out in front of the **L**,
7:6 have sinned against the **L**."
7:8 Don't stop crying to the **L** our
7:9 it as a burnt offering to the **L**.
7:9 Samuel cried to the **L** on behalf
7:9 and the **L** answered him.
7:10 On that day the **L** thundered
7:12 now the **L** has helped us."
7:13 The **L** restrained the Philistines
7:17 Ramah he built an altar to the **L**.
8:6 So Samuel prayed to the **L**.
8:7 The **L** told Samuel,
8:10 king everything the **L** had said.
8:18 The **L** will not answer you
8:21 he reported it privately to the **L**.
8:22 The **L** told him, "Listen to them,
9:15 Now, the **L** had revealed the
9:17 noticed Saul, the **L** told him,
10:1 "The **L** has anointed you to be
10:1 This will be the sign that the **L**
10:17 presence of⌊ the **L** at Mizpah.
10:18 "This is what the **L** God of
10:19 Now then, stand in front of the **L**
10:22 They asked the **L** again,
10:22 The **L** answered, "He's hiding
10:24 see whom the **L** has chosen?
10:25 he placed in front of the **L**.
11:7 became terrified by the **L**,
11:13 today the **L** saved Israel."
11:15 fellowship offerings to the **L**.
12:3 against me in front of the **L**
12:5 Samuel told them, "The **L** is a
12:6 Samuel told the people, "The **L**
12:7 I put you on trial in front of the **L**
12:7 the righteous things the **L** did
12:8 they cried out to the **L**,
12:8 The **L** settled them in this
12:9 But they forgot the **L** their God.
12:10 they cried out to the **L** and said,
12:10 We have abandoned the **L** and
12:11 "Then the **L** sent Jerubbaal,
12:12 though the **L** your God was
12:13 the **L** has put a king over you.
12:14 If you fear the **L**, serve him,
12:14 king will follow the **L** your God.
12:15 But if you don't obey the **L**,
12:15 then the **L** will be against you
12:16 this great thing the **L** is going
12:17 I will call on the **L**,
12:18 Then Samuel called on the **L**.
12:18 That day the **L** sent thunder
12:18 that all the people feared the **L**

1Sm 12:19 "Pray to the **L** your God for us
12:20 But don't turn away from the **L**.
12:20 serve the **L** wholeheartedly.
12:22 the **L** will not abandon his
12:22 because the **L** wants to make
12:23 to sin against the **L** by failing
12:24 Fear the **L**, and serve him
13:13 command of the **L** your God.
13:13 ⌊If you had,⌋ the **L** would have
13:14 The **L** has searched for a man
13:14 The **L** has appointed him as
13:14 follow the command of the **L**."
14:6 Maybe the **L** will act on our
14:6 The **L** can win a victory with a
14:10 that the **L** has handed them
14:12 because the **L** has handed
14:23 So the **L** saved Israel that day.
14:33 against the **L** by eating meat
14:34 But don't sin against the **L** by
14:35 Saul built an altar to the **L**;
14:35 he had built an altar to the **L**.
14:39 I solemnly swear, as the **L** and
14:41 Then Saul said to the **L**,
14:41 son Jonathan's, **L** God of Israel,
14:45 solemnly swear, as the **L** lives,
15:1 Samuel told Saul, "The **L** sent
15:2 This is what the **L** of Armies
15:10 Then the **L** spoke to Samuel:
15:11 and he prayed to the **L** all night.
15:13 who said, "The **L** bless you.
15:15 to sacrifice to the **L** your God.
15:16 "and let me tell you what the **L**
15:17 The **L** anointed you king of
15:18 And the **L** sent you on a
15:19 Why didn't you obey the **L**?
15:19 what the **L** considers evil?"
15:20 "But I did obey the **L**," Saul told
15:20 "I went where the **L** sent me,
15:21 to sacrifice to the **L** your God
15:22 Then Samuel said, "Is the **L** as
15:23 you rejected the word of the **L**,
15:25 so that I may worship the **L**."
15:26 rejected what the **L** told you.
15:26 So the **L** rejects you as king of
15:28 Samuel told him, "The **L** has
15:30 let me worship the **L** your God."
15:31 and Saul worshiped the **L**.
15:33 the presence of the **L** at Gilgal.
15:35 And the **L** regretted that he had
16:1 The **L** asked Samuel,
16:2 The **L** said, "Take a heifer with
16:2 'I've come to sacrifice to the **L**.'
16:4 Samuel did what the **L** told him.
16:5 have come to sacrifice to the **L**.
16:7 But the **L** told Samuel,
16:7 but the **L** looks into the heart."
16:8 But Samuel said, "The **L** has
16:9 "The **L** has not chosen this one
16:10 "The **L** has not chosen ⌊any
16:12 The **L** said, "Go ahead,
16:14 spirit from the **L** tormented him
16:18 and the **L** is with him."
17:37 David added, "The **L**,
17:37 "and may the **L** be with you."
17:45 in the name of the **L** of Armies,
17:46 Today the **L** will hand you over
17:47 that the **L** can save without
17:47 because the **L** determines
18:12 because the **L** was with David
18:14 because the **L** was with him.
18:28 Saul realized that the **L** was
19:5 and the **L** gave all Israel a great
19:6 solemnly swear, as the **L** lives,
19:9 Then an evil spirit from the **L**
20:3 as the **L** and you live,
20:8 into an agreement with the **L**.
20:12 "As the **L** God of Israel ⌊is my
20:13 may the **L** harm me even more.
20:13 May the **L** be with you as he
20:14 me kindness because of the **L**.
20:15 The **L** will wipe each of
20:16 the **L** punish David's house."
20:21 I swear it, as the **L** lives.
20:22 because the **L** has sent you
20:23 and the **L** is ⌊a witness⌋
20:42 The **L** will be ⌊a witness⌋

1Sm 22:10 Ahimelech prayed to the **L** for
23:2 David asked the **L**,
23:2 "Go," the **L** told David,
23:4 David asked the **L** again,
23:4 and the **L** answered him.
23:10 David said, "**L** God of Israel,
23:11 **L** God of Israel, please tell me."
23:11 will come," the **L** answered.
23:12 you over," the **L** answered.
23:16 David's ⌊faith⌋ in the **L**.
23:21 Saul responded, "The **L** bless
24:4 "Today is the day the **L** referred
24:10 Today you saw how the **L**
24:12 May the **L** decide between you
24:12 May the **L** take revenge on you
24:15 So the **L** must be the judge.
24:18 When the **L** handed me over to
24:19 The **L** will repay you
24:21 Swear an oath to the **L** for me
25:26 "The **L** has kept you from
25:26 as the **L** and you live,
25:28 The **L** will certainly give you,
25:29 comes from the **L** your God.
25:30 When the **L** does all the good
25:31 When the **L** has given you
25:32 "Blessed be the **L** God of
25:34 But I solemnly swear — as the **L**
25:38 About ten days later the **L**
25:39 "Blessed be the **L**,
25:39 The **L** has turned Nabal's own
26:10 as the **L** lives," David added,
26:10 "the **L** will strike him.
26:12 The **L** had made them fall into
26:16 solemnly swear, as the **L** lives,
26:19 If the **L** has turned you against
26:19 let them be cursed by the **L**.
26:23 The **L** will reward any person
26:23 The **L** handed you over to me
26:24 may the **L** place great value on
28:6 He prayed to the **L**,
28:6 but the **L** didn't answer him
28:10 solemnly swear, as the **L** lives,
28:16 when the **L** has turned against
28:17 The **L** has done to you
28:17 The **L** has torn the kingship out
28:18 The **L** is doing this to you
28:19 For the same reasons the **L**
28:19 And then the **L** will hand
29:6 solemnly swear, as the **L** lives,
30:6 strength in the **L** his God.)
30:8 Then David asked the **L**,
30:8 "Pursue them," the **L** told him.
30:23 which the **L** has given us.
2Sm 2:1 After this, David asked the **L**,
2:1 "Go," the **L** answered him.
2:1 "To Hebron," the **L** replied.
2:5 He said to them, "May the **L**
2:6 May the **L** always show you
3:9 what the **L** had promised him
3:10 'I, the **L**, will transfer the
3:18 Do it now, because the **L** said
3:28 "As far as the **L** is concerned,
3:39 May the **L** repay this evildoer
4:8 "Today the **L** has given Your
4:11 The **L** has rescued me from
4:11 solemnly swear, as the **L** lives,
5:2 The **L** has said to you,
5:3 them at Hebron in front of the **L**.
5:10 powerful because the **L** God
5:12 So David realized that the **L**
5:19 David asked the **L**,
5:19 The **L** answered David,
5:20 Perazim [The **L** Overwhelms]
5:20 He said, "The **L** has
5:23 David asked the **L**,
5:24 act immediately because the **L**
5:25 David did as the **L** ordered him
6:2 by the name of the **L** of Armies,
6:7 The **L** became angry with
6:8 David was angry because the **L**
6:9 was afraid of the **L** that day.
6:9 "How can the ark of the **L** come
6:10 wouldn't bring the ark of the **L**
6:11 The ark of the **L** stayed at the
6:11 and the **L** blessed Obed Edom
6:12 King David was told, "The **L**

2Sm 6:13 the ark of the **L** had gone six
6:15 of Israel brought the ark of the **L**
6:16 When the ark of the **L** came to
6:18 in the name of the **L** of Armies.
6:21 slave girls but in front of the **L**.
7:1 the **L** gave him peace with all
7:3 because the **L** is with you."
7:4 But that same night the **L**
7:5 'This is what the **L** says:
7:8 'This is what the **L** of Armies
7:11 I, the **L**, tell you that I will make
7:18 the tent and sat in front of the **L**.
7:18 Almighty **L**," he asked,
7:19 to be a small act, Almighty **L**.
7:19 Almighty **L**, this is the teaching
7:20 David, say to you, Almighty **L**,
7:22 is why you are great, **L** God.
7:24 And you, **L**, became their God.
7:25 "Now, **L** God, keep the
7:26 'The **L** of Armies is God over
7:27 You, **L** of Armies, God of Israel,
7:28 "Almighty **L**, you are God,
7:29 Indeed, you, Almighty **L**,
8:6 the **L** gave him victories.
8:11 these articles to the **L**,
8:14 the **L** gave him victories.
10:12 and the **L** will do what he
11:27 But the **L** considered David's
12:1 So the **L** sent Nathan to David.
12:5 swear, as the **L** lives,"
12:7 "This is what the **L** God of
12:11 "This is what the **L** says:
12:13 "I have sinned against the **L**."
12:13 Nathan replied, "The **L** has
12:14 contempt for the **L** by this affair,
12:15 The **L** struck the child that
12:22 The **L** may be gracious to me
12:24 The **L** loved the child
14:11 please pray to the **L** your God
14:11 swear, as the **L** lives," he said,
14:17 May the **L** your God be with
15:7 keep the vow I made to the **L**.
15:8 I said, 'If the **L** will bring me
15:8 I will serve the **L**.'"
15:20 May the **L** always show you
15:21 as the **L** and the king live:
15:25 If the **L** looks favorably on me,
15:31 So David prayed, "**L**,
16:8 The **L** is paying you back for
16:8 The **L** is giving the kingship to
16:10 If the **L** has told him,
16:11 Let him curse, since the **L** has
16:12 Maybe the **L** will see my
16:18 to be with the one whom the **L**,
17:14 (The **L** had commanded
18:19 news that the **L** has freed him
18:28 Ahimaaz said, "May the **L** your
18:31 "Today the **L** has freed you
19:7 I swear to you by the **L** that if
20:19 up what belongs to the **L**?"
21:1 The **L** answered, "It's because
21:3 bless what belongs to the **L**?"
21:6 Saul whom the **L** had chosen.)
22:1 David sang this song to the **L**
22:1 when the **L** rescued him from
22:2 He said, The **L** is my rock and
22:4 The **L** should be praised.
22:7 I called on the **L** in my distress.
22:14 The **L** thundered from heaven.
22:19 but the **L** became my defense.
22:21 The **L** rewarded me because of
22:22 I have kept the ways of the **L**
22:25 The **L** paid me back because
22:29 O **L**, you are my lamp.
22:29 The **L** turns my darkness into
22:31 The promise of the **L** has
22:32 Who is God but the **L**?
22:42 They looked to the **L**,
22:47 The **L** lives! Thanks be to my
22:50 I will give thanks to you, O **L**,
23:2 "The Spirit of the **L** spoke
23:10 So the **L** won an impressive
23:12 So the **L** won an impressive
23:16 an offering to the **L** and said,
23:17 that I would do this, **L**.
24:1 The **L** became angry with

2Sm 24:3 "May the **L** your God multiply
24:10 David said to the **L**,
24:10 **L**, please forgive me because I
24:11 the **L** spoke his word to the
24:12 'This is what the **L** says:
24:15 So the **L** sent a plague among
24:16 the **L** changed his mind about
24:16 The Messenger of the **L** was at
24:17 he said to the **L**, "I've sinned.
24:18 set up an altar for the **L** at
24:19 as the **L** had commanded him.
24:21 and to build an altar for the **L**.
24:23 "May the **L** your God accept
24:24 I won't offer the **L** my God burnt
24:25 David built an altar for the **L**
24:25 So the **L** heard the prayers for
1Ki 1:17 took an oath to the **L** your God.
1:29 as the **L** who has saved my life
1:30 I swore to you by the **L** God
1:36 "The **L** your God says so too.
1:37 As the **L** has been with you,
1:48 and said, 'Praise the **L** God of
2:3 your duty to the **L** your God.
2:4 because the **L** will keep
2:8 took an oath by the **L** and said,
2:15 my brother because the **L** gave
2:23 took an oath by the **L** and said,
2:24 The **L** set me on my father
2:24 So I solemnly swear, as the **L**
2:26 the ark of the Almighty **L** ahead
2:29 to the altar in the tent of the **L**,
2:30 came to the tent of the **L**,
2:32 The **L** will repay him for the
2:33 receive peace from the **L**."
2:42 you take an oath by the **L**?
2:43 you keep your oath to the **L**
2:44 The **L** is going to pay you back
2:45 be firmly established by the **L**."
3:2 the name of the **L** had not yet
3:3 Solomon loved the **L** and lived
3:5 In Gibeon the **L** appeared to
3:7 "**L** my God, although I'm young
3:10 The **L** was pleased that
5:3 the name of the **L** our God until
5:3 God until the **L** let him defeat
5:4 But the **L** my God has
5:5 the name of the **L** my God as
5:5 LORD my God as the **L** spoke
5:7 "May the **L** be praised today.
5:12 The **L** gave Solomon wisdom
6:2 built for the **L** was 90 feet
6:11 The **L** spoke to Solomon,
8:9 where the **L** made a promise to
8:12 Then Solomon said, "The **L**
8:15 "Thanks be to the **L** God of
8:17 the name of the **L** God of Israel.
8:18 the **L** said to my father David,
8:20 The **L** has kept the promise he
8:20 of Israel as the **L** promised.
8:20 the name of the **L** God of Israel.
8:23 and said, "**L** God of Israel,
8:25 "Now, **L** God of Israel,
8:28 Nevertheless, my **L** God,
8:44 and they pray to you, O **L**,
8:53 After all, you, **L** God,
8:54 this prayer for mercy to the **L**,
8:56 "Thanks be to the **L**!
8:57 May the **L** our God be with us
8:59 which I have prayed to the **L**
8:59 be near the **L** our God day
8:60 will know that the **L** is God
8:61 be committed to the **L** our God.
8:62 offered sacrifices to the **L**.
8:63 as fellowship offerings to the **L**.
8:64 in front of the **L** was too small
8:65 Egypt to be near the **L** our God
8:66 blessings the **L** had given his
9:2 Then the **L** appeared to him a
9:3 The **L** said to him,
9:8 'Why did the **L** do these things
9:9 abandoned the **L** their God,
9:9 That is why the **L** brought this
9:25 on the altar he built for the **L**.
10:1 reputation to the name of the **L**.)
10:9 Thank the **L** your God,
11:2 about which the **L** had said

1Ki 11:4 committed to the **L** his God as
11:6 did what the **L** considered evil.
11:6 follow the **L** as his father
11:9 So the **L** became angry with
11:9 heart had turned from the **L**
11:11 The **L** told Solomon,
11:14 The **L** raised up Hadad the
11:31 because this is what the **L** God
12:15 the **L** was directing these
12:24 This is what the **L** says:
12:24 they obeyed the word of the **L**.
12:24 as the **L** told them.
13:2 By a command of the **L**,
13:2 This is what the **L** says:
13:3 "This is the sign that the **L** will
13:6 an appeal to the **L** your God,
13:6 God made an appeal to the **L**,
13:9 When the **L** spoke to me,
13:17 When the **L** spoke to me,
13:18 spoke the word of the **L** to me.
13:20 the **L** spoke his word to the old
13:21 The **L** also called to the man of
13:21 "This is what the **L** says:
13:21 that the **L** your God gave
13:26 The **L** gave him to the lion.
13:26 the word of the **L** had told him."
13:32 by a command of the **L** against
14:5 However, the **L** had told Ahijah,
14:7 'This is what the **L** God of
14:11 The **L** has said this!
14:13 house in whom the **L** God
14:14 The **L** will appoint a king over
14:15 "The **L** will strike Israel like
14:15 and made the **L** furious.
14:16 So the **L** will desert Israel
14:18 him as the **L** had said through
14:21 the city that the **L** chose from
14:21 the city where the **L** put his
14:22 did what the **L** considered evil.
14:24 that the **L** had forced out
15:3 committed to the **L** his God as
15:4 But for David's sake the **L** his
15:5 The **L** did this because David
15:5 did what the **L** considered right:
15:5 anything the **L** commanded him
15:11 did what the **L** considered right,
15:14 to the **L** his entire life.
15:26 did what the **L** considered evil,
15:29 spare a soul, as the **L** had spoken
15:30 Those sins made the **L** God of
15:34 did what the **L** considered evil.
16:1 The **L** spoke his word to Jehu,
16:7 In addition, the **L** spoke his
16:7 which the **L** considered evil.
16:7 which made the **L** furious,
16:7 The **L** was also furious
16:12 as the **L** had spoken through
16:13 and made the **L** God of Israel
16:19 things the **L** considered evil.
16:25 did what the **L** considered evil.
16:26 and the Israelites made the **L**
16:30 did what the **L** considered evil.
16:33 He did more to make the **L** God
16:34 The **L** had spoken this through
17:1 as the **L** God of Israel whom I
17:2 Then the **L** spoke his word to
17:5 word of the **L** had told him.
17:8 Then the **L** spoke his word to
17:12 as the **L** your God lives,
17:14 This is what the **L** God of
17:14 Until the **L** sends rain on the
17:16 as the **L** had promised through
17:20 Then he called to the **L**,
17:20 to the LORD, "**L** my God,
17:21 three times and called to the **L**,
17:21 to the LORD, "**L** my God,
17:22 The **L** heard Elijah's request,
17:24 word of the **L** from your mouth
18:1 the **L** spoke his word to Elijah:
18:3 a devout worshiper of the **L**.
18:10 as the **L** your God lives,
18:12 "I have been faithful to the **L**
18:15 as the **L** of Armies whom I
18:21 If the **L** is God, follow him;
18:22 only surviving prophet of the **L**,
18:24 I will call on the name of the **L**.

1Ki 18:31 (The L had spoken his word to
18:36 He said, "L God of Abraham,
18:37 Answer me, L! Answer me!
18:37 people will know that you, L,
18:38 So a fire from the L fell down
18:39 "The L is God!" they said. "The
18:39 they said. "The L is God!"
19:4 had enough now, L," he said.
19:7 The angel of the L came back
19:9 Then the L spoke his word to
19:10 answered, "L God of Armies,
19:11 out and stand in front of the L
19:11 As the L was passing by,
19:11 shattered rocks ahead of the L.
19:11 But the L was not in the wind.
19:11 But the L wasn't in the
19:12 But the L wasn't in the fire.
19:14 answered, "L God of Armies,
19:15 The L told him, "Go back to the
20:13 "This is what the L says:
20:13 you will know that I am the L."
20:14 "This is what the L says:
20:28 "This is what the L says:
20:28 the Arameans said that the L is
20:28 you will know that I am the L."
20:35 the word of the L had told him.
20:36 "Since you didn't obey the L,
20:42 "This is what the L says:
21:3 Naboth told Ahab, "The L has
21:17 Then the L spoke his word to
21:19 'This is what the L asks:
21:19 'This is what the L says:
21:20 to do what the L considers evil.
21:23 Then the L also spoke
21:25 do what the L considered evil.
21:26 (The L confiscated their land
21:28 Then the L spoke his word to
22:5 find out what the word of the L
22:6 "The L will hand over Ramoth
22:7 "Isn't there a prophet of the L
22:8 can ask the L through Micaiah,
22:11 "This is what the L says:
22:12 The L will hand it over to you."
22:14 solemnly swear, as the L lives,
22:14 him whatever the L tells me."
22:15 The L will hand it over to you."
22:17 The L said, 'These ⌊sheep⌋
22:19 "Then hear the word of the L.
22:19 I saw the L sitting on his
22:20 The L asked, 'Who will
22:21 stood in front of the L,
22:21 "'How?' the L asked.
22:22 "The L said, 'You will succeed
22:23 "So, the L has put into the
22:23 The L has spoken evil about
22:28 then the L wasn't speaking
22:38 as the L had predicted.
22:43 did what the L considered right.
22:52 did what the L considered evil.
22:53 and made the L God of Israel
2Ki 1:3 Then the angel of the L said to
1:4 This is what the L says:
1:6 'This is what the L says:
1:15 The angel of the L told Elijah,
1:16 "This is what the L says:
1:17 So Ahaziah died as the L had
2:1 When the L was going to take
2:2 because the L is sending me
2:2 as the L lives and as you live,
2:3 "Do you know that the L is
2:4 please stay here because the L
2:4 as the L lives and as you live,
2:5 "Do you know that the L is
2:6 because the L is sending me
2:6 as the L lives and as you live,
2:14 "Where is the L God of Elijah?"
2:21 "This is what the L says:
3:2 did what the L considered evil,
3:10 The L has put the three of us at
3:11 "Isn't there a prophet of the L
3:13 The L has called the three of
3:14 as the L of Armies whom I
3:16 "This is what the L says:
3:18 The L considers that an easy
4:1 You know how he feared the L.
4:27 The L has hidden the reason

2Ki 4:30 as the L and you live,
4:33 and prayed to the L.
4:43 "This is what the L says:
4:44 as the L had predicted.
5:1 The L had given Aram a victory
5:11 on the name of the L his God,
5:16 as the L whom I serve lives,
5:17 I will sacrifice to the L alone.
5:18 May the L forgive me when my
5:18 When I do this, may the L
5:20 As sure as the L lives,
6:17 Then Elisha prayed, "L,
6:17 The L opened the servant's
6:18 Elisha prayed to the L,
6:18 The L struck them with
6:20 into Samaria, Elisha said, "L,
6:20 The L opened their eyes and
6:27 "If the L doesn't help you,
6:33 severe famine is from the L.
6:33 longer for the L ⌊to help us⌋?"
7:1 "Listen to the word of the L!
7:1 This is what the L says:
7:2 if the L poured rain through
7:6 (The L had made the Aramean
7:16 as the L had predicted.
7:19 if the L poured rain through
8:1 The L has decided to send a
8:8 Ask the L through him,
8:10 although the L has shown me
8:13 Elisha answered, "The L has
8:18 did what the L considered evil.
8:19 But for David's sake the L
8:19 The L had told David that he
8:27 did what the L considered evil,
9:3 'This is what the L says:
9:6 "This is what the L God of
9:12 'This is what the L says:
9:25 The L revealed this prophecy
9:26 in this field,' declares the L.
9:26 the field as the L predicted."
9:36 Jehu said, "The L spoke
10:10 of the L spoken about Ahab's
10:10 The L will do what he said
10:16 how devoted I am to the L."
10:17 as the L had told Elijah.
10:23 are no worshipers of the L here
10:30 The L said to Jehu,
10:31 the teachings of the L God
10:32 So in those days the L began
11:17 made a promise to the L
12:2 did what the L considered right,
12:18 had dedicated to the L,
12:18 he had dedicated to the L,
13:2 did what the L considered evil.
13:3 So the L became angry with
13:4 Jehoahaz pleaded with the L,
13:4 and the L heard him because
13:5 So the L gave the Israelites
13:11 He did what the L considered
13:23 But the L was kind and
14:3 did what the L considered right,
14:24 did what the L considered evil.
14:25 to the Dead Sea as the L God
14:26 The L did this because he saw
14:27 Since the L had said he was
15:3 did what the L considered right,
15:5 The L inflicted the king with a
15:9 did what the L considered evil,
15:12 It happened exactly as the L
15:18 did what the L considered evil.
15:24 did what the L considered evil.
15:28 did what the L considered evil.
15:34 did what the L considered right,
15:37 In those days the L began to
16:2 He didn't do what the L his God
16:3 that the L had forced out
16:14 bronze altar dedicated to the L.
17:2 did what the L considered evil,
17:7 sinned against the L their God,
17:8 that the L had forced out
17:9 against the L their God that
17:11 that the L had removed from
17:11 things and made the L furious.
17:12 although the L had said,
17:13 The L had warned Israel and
17:14 refused to trust the L their God.

2Ki 17:15 although the L had commanded
17:16 commands of the L their God:
17:17 what the L considered evil,
17:18 The L became so angry with
17:19 commands of the L their God
17:20 So the L rejected all of Israel's
17:21 forced Israel away from the L
17:23 Finally, the L turned away from
17:25 they didn't worship the L.
17:25 So the L sent lions to kill some
17:28 them how to worship the L.
17:32 people were worshiping the L,
17:33 They worshiped the L but also
17:34 They don't fear the L or live by
17:34 or commands that the L gave to
17:35 When the L made a promise to
17:36 Instead, worship the L,
17:36 Bow down to the L,
17:39 worship the L your God,
17:41 nations worshiped the L
18:3 did what the L considered right,
18:5 Hezekiah trusted the L God of
18:6 He was loyal to the L and
18:6 that the L had given through
18:7 so the L was with him.
18:12 refused to obey the L their God
18:22 "We're trusting the L our God."
18:25 destroy this place without the L
18:25 The L said to me, 'Attack this
18:30 get you to trust the L by saying,
18:30 'The L will certainly rescue us,
18:32 'The L will rescue us.'
18:35 Could the L then rescue
19:4 The L your God may have
19:4 The L your God may punish
19:4 that the L your God heard.
19:6 'This is what the L says:
19:14 them out in front of the L
19:15 and prayed to the L,
19:15 "L of Armies, God of Israel,
19:16 Turn your ear toward me, L,
19:16 Open your eyes, L,
19:17 It is true, L, that the kings of
19:19 Now, L our God, rescue us
19:19 that you alone are the L God."
19:20 "This is what the L God of
19:21 This is the message that the L
19:23 you defy the L and say,
19:31 The L is determined to do this.'
19:32 "This is what the L says about
19:33 declares the L of Armies.
20:1 "This is what the L says:
20:2 to the wall and prayed to the L,
20:3 "Please, L, remember how I've
20:4 when the L spoke his word
20:5 'This is what the L God of your
20:8 "What is the sign that the L
20:9 "This is your sign from the L
20:11 prophet Isaiah called on the L,
20:11 and the L made the shadow
20:16 "Hear the word of the L!
20:17 The L says, 'The days are
21:2 He did what the L considered
21:2 that the L had forced out
21:4 where the L had said,
21:6 things that made the L furious.
21:7 where the L had said to David
21:9 that the L had destroyed when
21:10 Then the L spoke through his
21:12 the L God of Israel,
21:16 to commit in front of the L,
21:20 did what the L considered evil,
21:22 He abandoned the L God of his
22:2 did what the L considered right.
22:13 ask the L about the words in
22:15 "This is what the L God of
22:16 'This is what the L says:
22:18 to me to ask the L a question,
22:18 'This is what the L God of
22:19 in front of the L when you heard
22:19 listen ⌊to you⌋, declares the L.
23:3 made a promise to the L that
23:3 that he would follow the L
23:16 This fulfilled the word of the L
23:19 places to make the L furious.
23:21 Passover for the L their God as

2Ki 23:23 in Jerusalem for the **L**.
23:25 Josiah had turned to the **L**
23:26 But the **L** still didn't turn his hot
23:27 The **L** had said, "I will put
23:32 did what the **L** considered evil,
23:37 did what the **L** considered evil,
24:2 The **L** sent raiding parties of
24:2 as the **L** had predicted through
24:3 because the **L** had commanded
24:4 and the **L** refused to forgive
24:9 did what the **L** considered evil,
24:13 As the **L** had predicted,
24:19 did what the **L** considered evil,
24:20 The **L** became angry with
1Ch 2:3 The **L** considered Er,
2:3 evil, so the **L** killed Er.
6:15 the **L** used Nebuchadnezzar
9:20 and the **L** was with him.)
10:13 of his unfaithfulness to the **L**:
10:13 did not obey the word of the **L**.
10:14 request information from the **L**.
10:14 So the **L** killed him and turned
11:2 The **L** your God has said to
11:3 them at Hebron in front of the **L**.
11:3 as the **L** had spoken through
11:9 more powerful because the **L**
11:14 So the **L** saved ⌊them⌋ with an
11:18 it out ⌊as an offering⌋ to the **L**
12:23 to David, as the **L** had said.
13:2 "If you approve and if the **L** our
13:6 (The **L** is enthroned over the
13:10 The **L** became angry with
13:11 David was angry because the **L**
13:14 and the **L** blessed Obed
14:2 So David realized that the **L**
14:10 The **L** answered him,
14:11 Perazim [The **L** Overwhelms].
14:17 and the **L** made all the nations
15:2 the **L** had chosen them
15:12 Then bring the ark of the **L** God
15:13 the **L** our God struck us.
15:14 the ark of the **L** God of Israel.
16:2 the people in the name of the **L**.
16:4 praise to the **L** God of Israel.
16:7 songs of thanks to the **L**:
16:8 "Give thanks to the **L**.
16:10 those who seek the **L** rejoice.
16:11 Search for the **L** and his
16:14 "He is the **L** our God.
16:23 "Sing to the **L**, all the earth!
16:23 that the **L** saves his people.
16:25 "The **L** is great! He should be
16:26 The **L** made the heavens.
16:28 "Give to the **L**, you families of
16:28 Give to the **L** glory and power.
16:29 Give to the **L** the glory his
16:29 Worship the **L** in ⌊his⌋ holy
16:31 'The **L** rules as king!'
16:33 in the presence of the **L** when
16:34 "Give thanks to the **L** because
16:36 Thanks be to the **L** God of
16:36 said amen and praised the **L**.
16:40 burnt offerings to the **L**.
16:41 thanks to the **L** ⌊by singing,⌋
17:4 'This is what the **L** says:
17:7 'This is what the **L** of Armies
17:10 I even tell you that I, the **L**,
17:16 the tent and sat in front of the **L**.
17:16 "Who am I, **L** God,"
17:17 **L** God, you've shown me the
17:19 **L**, you've done this great thing
17:20 "**L**, there is no one like you,
17:22 And you, **L**, became their God.
17:23 "Now, **L**, faithfully keep the
17:24 say, 'The **L** of Armies,
17:26 "Almighty **L**, you are God.
17:27 Indeed, you, **L**, have blessed it.
18:6 the **L** gave him victories.
18:11 and bronze to the **L**,
18:13 the **L** gave him victories.
19:13 and the **L** will do what he
21:3 Joab responded, "May the **L**
21:9 The **L** spoke to Gad,
21:10 'This is what the **L** says:
21:11 "This is what the **L** says:
21:12 Messenger of the **L** destroying

1Ch 21:14 So the **L** sent a plague on
21:15 the **L** reconsidered and
21:15 The Messenger of the **L** was
21:16 he saw the Messenger of the **L**
21:17 **L** my God, let your punishment
21:18 up an altar for the **L** at Ornan
21:22 I'll build an altar for the **L** on it.
21:24 take what is yours for the **L**
21:26 David built an altar for the **L**
21:26 He called on the **L**,
21:26 and the **L** answered him by
21:27 So the **L** spoke to the
21:28 when David saw the **L** had
22:1 "This is where the **L** God's
22:5 that will be built for the **L** must
22:6 a temple for the **L** God of Israel.
22:7 a temple for the name of the **L**,
22:8 But the **L** spoke his word to me
22:11 the **L** will be with you.
22:11 the temple of the **L** your God as
22:12 The **L** will give you insight and
22:12 Teachings of the **L** your God.
22:13 the **L** commanded Moses
22:16 May the **L** be with you."
22:18 "Isn't the **L** your God with you?
22:18 by the **L** and his people.
22:19 lives to serving the **L** your God.
22:19 holy place of the **L** God so that
23:5 were appointed to praise the **L**
23:13 to offer sacrifices to the **L**,
23:25 David had said, "The **L** God of
23:30 praise to the **L** every morning.
23:31 to stand in front of the **L**
24:19 as the **L** God of Israel had
25:3 They thanked and praised the **L**
25:7 skilled musicians for the **L**.
26:30 They did everything the **L**
27:23 because the **L** had promised
28:4 Yet, from my entire family the **L**
28:5 And of all my sons (the **L** has
28:8 everything the **L** your God has
28:9 Serve the **L** wholeheartedly
28:10 So be careful, because the **L**
28:20 The **L** God, my God, will be
29:1 for a person but for the **L** God.
29:5 himself to the **L** today?"
29:9 and wholeheartedly to the **L**.
29:10 he praised the **L** while the
29:10 you be praised, **L** God of Israel,
29:11 glory, and majesty are yours, **L**,
29:11 The kingdom is yours, **L**,
29:16 "**L**, our God, all this wealth that
29:18 **L** God of our ancestors
29:20 "Praise the **L** your God!"
29:20 assembly praised the **L** God
29:20 in front of the **L** and the king.
29:21 day they sacrificed to the **L**.
29:21 burnt offerings to the **L**:
29:22 celebrated in front of the **L**.
29:25 The **L** made Solomon
2Ch 1:1 The **L** his God was with him
1:5 the assembly worshiped the **L**.
1:9 Now, **L** God, you've kept the
2:4 for the name of the **L** my God.
2:4 appointed by the **L** our God.
2:11 "Because the **L** loves his
2:12 Huram added, "May the **L** God
3:1 where the **L** appeared to his
5:10 where the **L** made a promise to
5:13 and thanked the **L** in unison.
5:13 they sang in praise to the **L**:
6:1 Then Solomon said, "The **L**
6:4 "Thanks be to the **L** God of
6:7 the name of the **L** God of Israel.
6:8 the **L** said to my father David,
6:10 The **L** has kept the promise he
6:10 of Israel as the **L** promised.
6:10 the name of the **L** God of Israel.
6:14 He said, "**L** God of Israel,
6:16 "Now, **L** God of Israel,
6:17 "So now, **L** God of Israel,
6:19 Nevertheless, my **L** God,
6:41 **L** God — you and the ark of
6:41 Clothe your priests, **L** God,
6:42 **L** God, do not reject your
7:3 worshiped and praised the **L**,

2Ch 7:4 offered sacrifices to the **L**.
7:5 sheep as sacrifices to the **L**.
7:6 David made for praising the **L**
7:7 in front of the **L** was not able
7:10 the **L** had given David,
7:12 Then the **L** appeared to him at
7:21 They will ask, 'Why did the **L**
7:22 'They abandoned the **L** God of
8:12 burnt offerings to the **L**
8:14 were to lead in praising ⌊the **L**⌋
9:8 Thank the **L** your God,
9:8 on behalf of the **L** your God.
10:15 the **L** was directing these
11:4 This is what the **L** says:
11:4 they obeyed the word of the **L**.
11:16 determined to seek the **L** God
11:16 to sacrifice to the **L** God
12:2 all Israel was not loyal to the **L**.
12:5 "This is what the **L** says:
12:6 "The **L** is right!" they said.
12:7 When the **L** saw that they had
12:12 the **L** was no longer angry with
12:13 the city that the **L** chose from
12:13 the city where the **L** put his
12:14 himself to serving the **L**.
13:5 Don't you know that the **L** God
13:10 "However, the **L** is our God.
13:10 The priests who serve the **L**
13:11 offerings to the **L** every
13:11 instructions the **L** our God gave
13:12 don't wage war against the **L**
13:14 They cried out to the **L**,
13:18 because they trusted the **L** God
13:20 The **L** caused Jeroboam to
14:2 Asa did what the **L** his God
14:4 their lives to serving the **L** God
14:6 years because the **L** gave him
14:7 lives to serving the **L** our God.
14:11 Asa called on the **L** his God.
14:11 He said, "**L**, there is no one
14:11 Help us, **L** our God,
14:11 You are the **L** our God.
14:12 The **L** attacked the Sudanese
14:13 It was crushed in front of the **L**
14:14 the cities were afraid of the **L**.
15:2 The **L** is with you when you
15:4 they turned to the **L** God of
15:9 God, the **L**, was with him.)
15:11 that day they sacrificed to the **L**
15:12 their lives to serving the **L** God
15:13 their lives to the **L** God
15:14 their oath to the **L** with shouts,
15:15 pleasure in looking for the **L**,
15:15 So the **L** surrounded them with
15:17 ⌊to the **L**⌋ his entire life.
16:7 not depend on the **L** your God,
16:8 when you depended on the **L**,
16:12 Instead of asking the **L** for help,
17:3 The **L** was with Jehoshaphat,
17:5 So the **L** established
17:6 live the way the **L** wanted him
17:10 Fear of the **L** came to all the
17:16 who volunteered to serve the **L**
18:4 find out what the word of the **L**
18:6 "Isn't there a prophet of the **L**
18:7 can ask the **L** through Micaiah,
18:10 "This is what the **L** says:
18:11 The **L** will hand it over to you."
18:13 solemnly swear, as the **L** lives,
18:16 The **L** said, 'These sheep have
18:18 "Then hear the word of the **L**.
18:18 I saw the **L** sitting on his
18:19 The **L** asked, 'Who will
18:20 stood in front of the **L**,
18:20 "How?' the **L** asked.
18:21 "The **L** said, 'You will succeed
18:22 "So the **L** has put into the
18:22 The **L** has spoken evil about
18:27 then the **L** wasn't speaking
18:31 cried out, the **L** helped him.
19:2 and love those who hate the **L**?
19:4 the people back to the **L** God
19:6 it for a human but for the **L**.
19:7 have the fear of the **L** in you.
19:7 The **L** our God is never unjust.
19:9 of the **L** and with faithfulness.

2Ch 19:10 become guilty in front of the L.
19:11 in every matter involving the L.
19:11 May the L be with those who
20:6 "L God of our ancestors,
20:13 were standing in front of the L.
20:15 This is what the L says to you:
20:17 see the victory of the L for you,
20:17 The L is with you."
20:18 bowed down in front of the L.
20:19 stood up to praise the L God of
20:20 Trust the L your God,
20:21 people to sing to the L
20:21 "Thank the L because his
20:22 the L set ambushes against the
20:26 they thanked the L there,
20:27 The L gave them a reason to
20:29 The fear of the L came over the
20:29 how the L waged war against
20:32 did what the L considered right.
20:37 He said, "The L will destroy
21:6 did what the L considered evil.
21:7 But the L, recalling the promise
21:7 The L had told David that he
21:10 had abandoned the L God
21:12 It read, "This is what the L God
21:14 The L will strike a great blow
21:16 The L prompted the Philistines
21:18 After this, the L struck Jehoram
22:4 did what the L considered evil,
22:7 (The L had anointed Jehu to
22:9 his life to serving the L
23:3 He should be king, as the L
23:16 made a promise to the L
23:18 burnt offerings to the L as
24:2 did what the L considered right,
24:9 should be brought to the L.
24:18 the temple of the L God
24:19 The L sent them prophets to
24:20 The L has abandoned you
24:22 "May the L see ⌊this⌋ and get
24:24 but the L handed Joash's large
24:24 had abandoned the L God
25:2 did what the L considered right,
25:7 because the L isn't with Israel.
25:9 "The L can give you much
25:15 The L became angry with
25:27 turned away from the L,
26:4 did what the L considered right,
26:5 his life to serving the L,
26:5 the L gave him success.
26:16 was unfaithful to the L his God.
26:18 incense as an offering to the L.
26:18 The L God will not honor you
26:20 because the L had inflicted him
27:2 did what the L considered right,
27:6 live as the L his God wanted.
28:1 do what the L considered right,
28:3 that the L had forced out
28:5 So the L his God handed him
28:6 they had abandoned the L God
28:9 A prophet of the L named Oded
28:9 He said to them, "The L God of
28:10 against the L your God?
28:11 because the L is very angry
28:13 for this sin against the L.
28:13 The L is very angry with Israel
28:19 The L humbled Judah because
28:19 and was unfaithful to the L.
28:22 more unfaithful to the L.
28:25 So he made the L God of his
29:2 did what the L considered right,
29:5 make the temple of the L God
29:6 what the L our God considered
29:8 So the L was angry with Judah
29:10 to make a pledge to the L God
29:11 The L has chosen you to stand
29:24 peace with the L for Israel.
29:25 This command came from the L
29:27 the songs to the L started.
29:30 told the Levites to praise the L
29:31 dedicated your lives to the L.
29:32 were burnt offerings to the L.
30:1 Passover of the L God of Israel.
30:5 the Passover of the L God
30:6 return to the L God of Abraham,
30:7 were unfaithful to the L God

2Ch 30:8 Reach out for the L.
30:8 Serve the L your God,
30:9 When you return to the L,
30:9 The L your God is merciful and
30:17 make their lambs holy for the L.
30:18 "May the good L forgive
30:19 May the L God of their
30:20 The L listened to Hezekiah and
30:21 priests praised the L in song.
30:22 had the skills to serve the L.
30:22 their sins to the L God
31:6 dedicated to the L their God.
31:8 they praised the L and his
31:10 The L has blessed his people,
31:14 the offerings made to the L
31:20 right and true to the L his God.
32:8 but the L our God is on our side
32:11 'The L our God will rescue us
32:16 said more against the L God
32:17 wrote letters cursing the L God
32:21 The L sent an angel who
32:22 So the L saved Hezekiah and
32:22 The L gave them peace with
32:23 Jerusalem to bring gifts to the L
32:24 He prayed to the L,
32:25 so he didn't repay the L for his
32:25 The L became angry with him,
32:26 So the L didn't vent his anger
33:2 He did what the L considered
33:2 that the L had forced out
33:4 where the L had said,
33:6 things that made the L furious.
33:9 that the L had destroyed when
33:10 When the L spoke to
33:11 So the L made the army
33:12 he begged the L his God to be
33:13 He prayed to the L,
33:13 and the L accepted his prayer
33:13 The L brought him back to his
33:13 knew that the L is God.
33:16 to serve the L God of Israel.
33:17 only to the L their God.
33:18 to him in the name of the L God
33:22 did what the L considered evil,
33:23 in front of the L as his father
34:2 did what the L considered right.
34:8 the temple of the L his God.
34:21 ask the L about the words in
34:21 of the L by doing everything
34:23 "This is what the L God of
34:24 'This is what the L says:
34:26 to me to ask the L a question,
34:26 'This is what the L God of
34:27 listen ⌊to you⌋, declares the L.
34:31 made a promise to the L that
34:31 that he would follow the L
34:33 in Israel serve the L their God.
34:33 they didn't stop following the L
35:1 for the L in Jerusalem.
35:3 make themselves holy to the L,
35:3 Serve the L your God and his
35:6 as the L instructed ⌊us⌋
35:12 present them to the L as written
35:16 day for the worship of the L.
36:5 He did what the L his God
36:9 did what the L considered evil.
36:12 He did what the L his God
36:12 who spoke for the L.
36:13 turn back to the L God of Israel.
36:14 Although the L had made the
36:15 The L God of their ancestors
36:16 until the L became angry
36:22 The promise the L had spoken
36:22 The L inspired the king to
36:23 The L God of heaven has
36:23 May the L God be with all of
Ezr 1:1 The promise the L had spoken
1:1 The L inspired the king to
1:2 The L God of heaven has
1:3 build a temple for the L God
3:3 on it to the L every morning
3:5 the other holy festivals of the L,
3:5 offerings brought to the L.
3:6 these burnt offerings to the L
3:10 to praise the L according
3:11 and gave thanks to the L,

Ezr 3:11 "Praise the L," because the
3:11 house of the L had been laid.
4:1 a temple for the L God of Israel,
4:3 We must build it alone for the L
6:21 to worship the L God of Israel.
6:22 because the L had made them
6:22 The L had made the king of
7:6 which the L God of Israel had
7:6 because the L his God was
7:27 Thanks be to the L God of our
7:28 because the L my God was
8:28 the utensils are holy to the L.
8:28 freewill offerings to the L God
8:35 were burnt offerings for the L.
9:5 stretched out my hands to the L
9:8 the L our God has been kind
9:15 L God of Israel, because you
10:3 as my l ⌊Ezra⌋ and the others
10:11 Confess to the L God of your
Neh 1:5 I said, "L God of heaven,
1:11 L, please pay attention to my
4:14 and awe-inspiring the L is.
5:13 said amen and praised the L.
8:1 which the L had commanded
8:6 Ezra thanked the L,
8:6 ground and worshiped the L.
8:9 a holy day for the L your God.
8:10 Today is a holy day for the L.
8:10 have in the L is your strength."
8:14 Teachings that the L had given
9:3 of the L their God was
9:3 and worshiped the L their God.
9:4 cried loudly to the L their God.
9:5 and thank the L your God:
9:6 You alone are the L.
9:7 You are the L, the God who
10:29 regulations of the L our Lord.
10:29 regulations of the LORD our L.
10:34 on the altar of the L our God at
Job 1:6 came to stand in front of the L,
1:7 The L asked Satan,
1:7 Satan answered the L,
1:8 The L asked Satan,
1:9 Satan answered the L,
1:12 The L told Satan, but you must
1:21 The L has given, and the
1:21 and the L has taken away!
1:21 the name of the L be praised."
2:1 came to stand in front of the L,
2:2 The L asked Satan,
2:2 Satan answered the L,
2:3 The L asked Satan,
2:4 Satan answered the L,
2:6 The L told Satan, "He is in your
28:28 'The fear of the L is wisdom!
38:1 Then the L answered Job out
40:1 The L responded to Job,
40:3 Job answered the L,
40:6 Then the L responded to Job
42:1 Then Job answered the L,
42:7 After the L had said those
42:7 the L said to Eliphaz from
42:9 did what the L had told them
42:9 the L accepted Job's prayer.
42:10 the L restored Job's prosperity
42:11 for all the evil the L had brought
42:12 The L blessed the latter years
Psa 1:2 in the teachings of the L
1:6 The L knows the way of
2:2 plans together against the L
2:4 The L makes fun of them.
2:11 Serve the L with fear,
3:1 O L, look how my enemies
3:3 But you, O L, are a shield that
3:4 I call aloud to the L,
3:5 I wake up again because the L
3:7 Arise, O L! Save me, O my
3:8 Victory belongs to the L!
4:3 Know that the L singles out
4:3 The L hears me when I call to
4:5 righteousness by trusting the L.
4:6 presence shine on us, O L.
4:8 down because you alone, O L,
5:1 your ears to my words, O L.
5:3 In the morning, O L,
5:6 The L is disgusted with

Psa 5:8 O L, lead me in your
5:12 bless righteous people, O L.
6:1 O L, do not punish me in your
6:2 Have pity on me, O L,
6:2 Heal me, O L, because my
6:3 But you, O L, how long ...?
6:4 Come back, O L. Rescue me.
6:8 because the L has heard the
6:9 The L has heard my plea for
6:9 The L accepts my prayer.
7:1 O L my God, I have taken
7:3 O L my God, if I have done this
7:6 Arise in anger, O L.
7:8 The L judges the people of the
7:8 Judge me, O L, according to
7:17 I will give thanks to the L for
7:17 the name of the L Most High.
8:1 O L, our Lord, how majestic is
8:1 O LORD, our L, how majestic
8:9 O L, our Lord, how majestic is
8:9 O LORD, our L, how majestic
9:1 I will give ⌊you⌋ thanks, O L,
9:7 Yet, the L is enthroned forever.
9:9 The L is a stronghold for the
9:10 know your name trust you, O L,
9:11 Make music to praise the L,
9:13 Have pity on me, O L.
9:16 The L is known by the
9:19 Arise, O L. Do not let mortals
9:20 Strike them with terror, O L.
10:1 Why are you so distant, L?
10:3 but he curses the L.
10:12 Arise, O L! Lift your hand, O
10:16 The L is king forever and ever.
10:17 of oppressed people, O L.
11:1 I have taken refuge in the L.
11:4 The L is in his holy temple.
11:5 The L tests righteous people,
11:7 The L is righteous.
12:1 Help, O L. No godly person is
12:3 May the L cut off every
12:5 I will now arise," says the L.
12:6 The promises of the L are pure,
12:7 O L, you will protect them.
13:1 How long, O L? Will you forget
13:3 Answer me, O L my God!
13:6 I will sing to the L because he
14:2 The L looks down from heaven
14:4 that they do not call on the L?
14:6 because the L is their refuge.
14:7 When the L restores the
15:1 O L, who may stay in your
15:4 honors those who fear the L.
16:2 I said to the L, "You are my
16:2 to the LORD, "You are my L.
16:5 The L is my inheritance and
16:7 I will praise the L, who advises
16:8 I always keep the L in front of
17:1 Hear my plea for justice, O L.
17:13 Arise, O L; confront them!
17:14 rescue me from mortals, O L,
18:1 I love you, O L, my strength.
18:2 The L is my rock and my
18:3 The L should be praised.
18:6 I called on the L in my distress.
18:13 The L thundered in the
18:15 bare at your stern warning, O L,
18:18 but the L came to my defense.
18:20 The L rewarded me because of
18:21 I have kept the ways of the L
18:24 The L paid me back because
18:28 O L, you light my lamp.
18:30 The promise of the L has
18:31 Who is God but the L?
18:41 They cried out to the L,
18:46 The L lives! Thanks be to my
18:49 I will give thanks to you, O L,
19:7 teachings of the L are perfect.
19:7 of the L is dependable.
19:8 instructions of the L are correct
19:8 command of the L is radiant.
19:9 The fear of the L is pure.
19:9 The decisions of the L are true.
19:14 O L, my rock and my defender.
20:1 The L will answer you in times
20:5 The L will fulfill all your

Psa 20:6 Now I know that the L will give
20:7 in the name of the L our God.
20:9 Give victory to the king, O L.
21:1 finds joy in your strength, O L.
21:7 Indeed, the king trusts the L,
21:9 The L will swallow them up in
21:13 Arise, O L, in your strength.
22:8 Let the L save him!
22:19 Do not be so far away, O L.
22:23 All who fear the L,
22:24 The L has not despised or
22:24 The L heard when that
22:25 of those who fear the L.
22:26 Those who look to the L will
22:27 remember and return to the L.
22:28 the kingdom belongs to the L
22:30 that will be told about the L.
23:1 The L is my shepherd.
24:5 receive a blessing from the L
24:8 The L, strong and mighty!
24:8 The L, heroic in battle!
24:10 The L of Armies is the king of
25:1 To you, O L, I lift my soul.
25:4 O L, and teach me your paths.
25:6 Remember, O L, They have
25:7 Remember me, O L,
25:8 The L is good and decent.
25:10 Every path of the L is ⌊one of⌋
25:11 For the sake of your name, O L,
25:12 is this person that fears the L?
25:12 He is the one whom the L will
25:14 The L advises those who fear
25:15 My eyes are always on the L.
26:1 Judge me favorably, O L,
26:2 Examine me, O L,
26:6 walk around your altar, O L,
26:8 O L, I love the house where
26:12 I will praise the L with the
27:1 The L is my light and my
27:1 The L is my life's fortress.
27:3 have confidence ⌊in the L⌋.
27:4 asked one thing from the L.
27:6 make music to praise the L.
27:7 Hear, O L, when I cry aloud.
27:8 "O L, I will seek your face."
27:10 the L will take care of me.
27:11 Teach me your way, O L.
27:13 I will see the goodness of the L
27:14 Wait with hope for the L.
27:14 Yes, wait with hope for the L.
28:1 O L, I call to you. O my rock,
28:5 The L will tear them down and
28:6 Thank the L! He has heard my
28:7 The L is my strength and my
28:8 The L is the strength of his
29:1 Give to the L, you heavenly
29:1 Give to the L glory and power.
29:2 Give to the L the glory his
29:2 Worship the L in ⌊his⌋ holy
29:3 The voice of the L rolls over
29:3 The L shouts over raging water.
29:4 The voice of the L is powerful.
29:4 The voice of the L is majestic.
29:5 The voice of the L breaks the
29:5 The L splinters the cedars of
29:7 The voice of the L strikes with
29:8 The voice of the L makes the
29:8 The L makes the wilderness of
29:9 The voice of the L splits the
29:10 The L sat enthroned over the
29:10 The L sits enthroned as king
29:11 The L will give power to his
29:11 The L will bless his people
30:1 I will honor you highly, O L,
30:2 O L my God, I cried out to you
30:3 O L, you brought me up from
30:4 Make music to praise the L,
30:7 O L, by your favor you have
30:8 I will cry out to you, O L.
30:8 I will plead to the L for mercy:
30:10 Hear, O L, and have pity on
30:10 O L, be my helper!
30:12 O L my God, I will give thanks
31:1 I have taken refuge in you, O L.
31:5 You have rescued me, O L,
31:6 to false gods, but I trust the L.

Psa 31:9 Have pity on me, O L,
31:14 I trust you, O L. I said, "You are
31:17 O L, I have called on you,
31:21 Thank the L! He has shown me
31:23 Love the L, all you godly ones!
31:23 The L protects faithful people,
31:24 who wait with hope for the L,
32:2 whom the L never accuses
32:5 to confess them to you, O L.
32:8 ⌊The L says,⌋ "I will instruct
32:10 those who trust the L.
32:11 Be glad and find joy in the L,
33:1 Joyfully sing to the L,
33:1 Praising ⌊the L⌋ is proper for
33:2 thanks with a lyre to the L.
33:4 The word of the L is correct,
33:5 The L loves righteousness and
33:6 were made by the word of the L
33:8 Let all the earth fear the L.
33:10 The L blocks the plans of the
33:12 the nation whose God is the L.
33:13 The L looks down from heaven.
33:20 We wait for the L. He is our help
33:22 Let your mercy rest on us, O L,
34:1 I will thank the L at all times.
34:2 My soul will boast about the L.
34:4 I went to the L for help.
34:6 The L heard him and saved
34:7 The Messenger of the L camps
34:8 and see that the L is good.
34:9 Fear the L, you holy people
34:11 will teach you the fear of the L.
34:16 The L confronts those who do
34:17 The L hears and rescues them
34:18 The L is near to those whose
34:19 but the L rescues him from all
34:20 The L guards all of his bones.
34:22 The L protects the souls of his
35:1 O L, attack those who attack
35:5 of the L chases them.
35:6 of the L pursues them.
35:9 My soul will find joy in the L
35:10 All my bones will say, "O L,
35:17 O L, how long will you look
35:22 You have seen it, O L.
35:22 O L, do not be so far away from
35:23 O my God and my L.
35:24 righteousness, O L my God.
35:27 say, "The L is great.
36:5 O L, your mercy reaches to the
36:6 save people and animals, O L.
37:3 Trust the L, and do good things.
37:4 Be happy with the L,
37:5 Entrust your ways to the L.
37:7 Surrender yourself to the L,
37:9 with hope for the L will inherit
37:13 The L laughs at him because
37:17 but the L continues to support
37:18 The L knows the daily
37:23 steps are directed by the L,
37:23 and the L delights in his way.
37:24 headfirst because the L holds
37:28 The L loves justice,
37:33 But the L will not abandon him
37:34 Wait with hope for the L,
37:39 people comes from the L.
37:40 The L helps them and rescues
38:1 O L, do not angrily punish me
38:9 You know all my desires, O L,
38:15 I wait with hope for you, O L.
38:15 You will answer, O L,
38:21 Do not abandon me, O L.
38:22 Come quickly to help me, O L,
39:4 "Teach me, O L, about the end
39:7 And now, L, what am I waiting
39:12 Listen to my prayer, O L.
40:1 I waited patiently for the L.
40:3 They will trust the L.
40:4 places his confidence in the L
40:5 things, O L my God.
40:9 You know that, O L.
40:11 your compassion from me, O L.
40:13 O L, please rescue me!
40:13 Come quickly to help me, O L!
40:16 say, "The L is great!"
40:17 May the L think of me.

Psa 41:1 The L will rescue him in times
41:2 The L will protect him and
41:3 The L will support him on his
41:4 I said, "O L, have pity on me!
41:10 Have pity on me, O L!
41:13 Thank the L God of Israel
42:8 The L commands his mercy
44:23 Why are you sleeping, O L?
45:11 He is your L. Worship him.
46:7 The L of Armies is with us.
46:8 Come, see the works of the L,
46:11 The L of Armies is with us.
47:2 We must fear the L,
47:5 The L has gone up with the
48:1 The L is great. He should be
48:8 in the city of the L of Armies,
50:1 The L, the only true God,
51:15 O L, open my lips, and my
54:4 The L is the provider for my life.
54:6 thanks to your good name, O L.
55:9 confuse their language, O L,
55:16 and the L saves me.
55:22 Turn your burdens over to the L
56:10 I praise the word of the L.
57:9 to you among the people, O L.
58:6 the young lions' teeth, O L.
59:3 Fierce men attack me, O L,
59:5 O L God of Armies,
59:8 O L, you laugh at them.
59:11 Bring them down, O L,
62:12 Mercy belongs to you, O L.
64:10 people will find joy in the L
66:18 the L would not have listened
68:4 The L is his name.
68:11 The L gives instructions.
68:16 the L will live there forever.
68:17 The L is among them.
68:18 so that the L God may live
68:19 Thanks be to the L,
68:20 The Almighty L is our escape
68:22 The L said, "I will bring them
68:26 Thank God, the L,
68:32 Make music to praise the L.
69:6 O Almighty L of Armies.
69:13 you at an acceptable time, O L.
69:16 Answer me, O L, because your
69:31 This will please the L more
69:33 The L listens to needy people.
70:1 Come quickly to help me, O L!
70:5 my savior. O L, do not delay!
71:1 I have taken refuge in you, O L.
71:5 are my hope, O Almighty L.
71:16 mighty deeds of the Almighty L.
72:18 Thank the L God, the God of
73:20 he wakes up, so you, O L,
73:28 I have made the Almighty L my
74:18 the enemy insulted you, O L.
76:11 Make vows to the L your God,
77:2 I went to the L for help.
77:7 Will the L reject ⌊me⌋ for all
77:11 remember the deeds of the L.
78:21 When the L heard this,
78:65 Then the L woke up like one
78:71 people who belonged to the L.
79:5 How long, O L? Will you remain
79:12 they used to insult you, O L.
80:4 O L God, commander of
80:19 O L God, commander of
81:10 I am the L your God,
81:15 Those who hate the L would
83:16 faces blush with shame, O L,
83:18 Your name is the L.
84:1 place is lovely, O L of Armies!
84:3 near your altars, O L of Armies,
84:8 O L God, commander of
84:11 The L God is a sun and shield.
84:11 The L grants favor and honor.
84:12 O L of Armies, blessed is the
85:1 You favored your land, O L.
85:7 Show us your mercy, O L,
85:8 to hear what God the L says,
85:12 The L will certainly give us
86:1 your ear ⌊toward me⌋, O L.
86:3 Have pity on me, O L,
86:4 Give me joy, O L, because I lift
86:5 You, O L, are good and

Psa 86:6 your ears to my prayer, O L.
86:8 No god is like you, O L.
86:9 will bow in your presence, O L.
86:11 Teach me your way, O L,
86:12 with all my heart, O L my God.
86:15 But you, O L, are a
86:17 You, O L, have helped me and
87:1 ⌊The city⌋ the L has founded
87:2 The L loves the city of Zion
87:4 ⌊The L says,⌋ "I will add
87:6 The L will record this in the
88:1 O L God, my savior, I cry out to
88:9 day long I call out to you, O L.
88:13 I cry out to you for help, O L,
88:14 do you reject my soul, O L?
89:1 evidence of your mercy, O L.
89:5 O L, the heavens praise your
89:6 skies can compare with the L?
89:6 heavenly beings is like the L?
89:8 O L God of Armies,
89:8 Mighty L, even your
89:15 the light of your presence, O L.
89:18 Our shield belongs to the L.
89:46 How long, O L? Will you hide
89:49 the evidence of your mercy, L?
89:50 Remember, O L, how your
89:52 Thank the L forever.
90:1 O L, you have been our refuge
90:13 Return, L! How long ...? Change
90:17 Let the kindness of the L our
91:2 I will say to the L, "⌊You are⌋
91:9 You, O L, are my refuge!
92:1 is good to give thanks to the L,
92:4 in what you have done, O L.
92:5 are your works, O L!
92:8 But you, O L, are highly
92:9 Now look at your enemies, O L.
92:15 it known that the L is decent.
93:1 The L rules as king!
93:1 The L has clothed himself;
93:3 The ocean rises, O L.
93:4 The L above is mighty —
93:5 O L, holiness is what makes
94:1 O L, God of vengeance, O God
94:3 How long, O L, will wicked
94:5 They crush your people, O L.
94:7 say, "The L doesn't see it.
94:11 The L knows that people's
94:12 O L, blessed is the person
94:14 The L will never desert his
94:17 If the L had not come to help
94:18 O L, continued to hold me up.
94:22 The L has become my
94:23 The L our God will destroy
95:1 let's sing joyfully to the L.
95:3 The L is a great God and a
95:6 Let's kneel in front of the L,
96:1 Sing to the L a new song!
96:1 Sing to the L, all the earth!
96:2 Sing to the L! Praise his name!
96:2 that the L saves his people.
96:4 The L is great! He should be
96:5 The L made the heavens.
96:7 Give to the L, you families of
96:7 Give to the L glory and power.
96:8 Give to the L the glory he
96:9 Worship the L in ⌊his⌋ holy
96:10 "The L rules as king!"
97:1 The L rules as king.
97:5 wax in the presence of the L,
97:5 in the presence of the L of the
97:8 with your judgments, O L.
97:9 You, O L, the Most High,
97:10 those who love the L hate evil.
97:12 Find joy in the L, you righteous
98:1 Sing a new song to the L
98:2 The L has made his salvation
98:4 Shout happily to the L,
98:5 Make music to the L with a
98:6 the presence of the king, the L.
99:1 The L rules as king.
99:2 The L is mighty in Zion.
99:5 Highly honor the L our God.
99:6 They called to the L,
99:8 O L, our God, you answered
99:9 Highly honor the L our God.

Psa 99:9 The L our God is holy!
100:1 Shout happily to the L,
100:2 Serve the L cheerfully.
100:3 Realize that the L alone is God.
100:5 The L is good. His mercy
101:1 O L, I will make music to
102:1 O L, hear my prayer, and let my
102:12 But you, O L, remain forever.
102:16 When the L builds Zion,
102:18 to be created may praise the L:
102:19 "The L looked down from his
102:22 gather to worship the L."
103:1 Praise the L, my soul!
103:2 Praise the L, my soul,
103:6 The L does what is right and
103:8 The L is compassionate,
103:13 so the L has compassion for
103:19 The L has set his throne in
103:20 Praise the L, all his angels,
103:21 Praise the L, all his armies,
103:22 Praise the L, all his creatures
103:22 Praise the L, my soul!
104:1 Praise the L, my soul! O LORD
104:1 O L my God, you are very
104:24 of things you have made, O L!
104:31 glory of the L endure forever.
104:31 May the L find joy in what he
104:33 I will sing to the L throughout
104:34 I will find joy in the L.
104:35 Praise the L, my soul!
105:1 Give thanks to the L.
105:3 those who seek the L rejoice.
105:4 Search for the L and his
105:7 He is the L our God.
105:24 The L made his people grow
106:1 Give thanks to the L because
106:2 mighty things the L has done?
106:4 Remember me, O L,
106:25 They did not obey the L.
106:34 people as the L had told them.
106:40 The L burned with anger
106:47 Rescue us, O L our God,
106:48 Thanks be to the L God of
107:1 Give thanks to the L because
107:2 Let the people the L defended
107:6 distress they cried out to the L.
107:8 Let them give thanks to the L
107:13 distress they cried out to the L.
107:15 Let them give thanks to the L
107:19 distress they cried out to the L.
107:21 Let them give thanks to the L
107:24 have seen what the L can do,
107:28 distress they cried out to the L.
107:31 Let them give thanks to the L
108:3 to you among the people, O L.
109:14 Let the L remember the guilt of
109:15 on record in front of the L.
109:15 Let the L remove every memory
109:20 This is how the L rewards
109:21 O L Almighty, deal with me out
109:26 Help me, O L my God.
109:27 is your doing, that you, O L,
109:30 will give many thanks to the L.
110:1 The L said to my Lord,
110:1 The LORD said to my L,
110:2 The L will extend your
110:4 The L has taken an oath and
110:5 The L is at your right side.
111:1 I will give thanks to the L with
111:4 The L is merciful and
111:10 The fear of the L is the
112:1 is the person who fears the L
112:7 full of confidence in the L.
113:1 You servants of the L,
113:1 Praise the name of the L.
113:2 name of the L now and forever.
113:3 of the L should be praised.
113:4 The L is high above all the
113:5 Who is like the L our God?
114:7 in the presence of the L,
115:1 Don't give glory to us, O L.
115:9 Israel, trust the L. He is your
115:10 of Aaron, trust the L.
115:11 If you fear the L, trust the
115:11 you fear the LORD, trust the L.
115:12 The L, who is ⌊always⌋

Psa 115:13 will bless those who fear the L,
115:14 May the L continue to bless
115:15 You will be blessed by the L,
115:16 heaven belongs to the L,
115:17 are dead do not praise the L,
115:18 But we will thank the L now
116:1 I love the L because he hears
116:4 calling on the name of the L:
116:4 LORD: "Please, L, rescue me!"
116:5 The L is merciful and righteous.
116:6 The L protects defenseless
116:7 because the L has been good
116:12 How can I repay the L for all
116:13 and call on the name of the L.
116:14 I will keep my vows to the L in
116:15 Precious in the sight of the L is
116:16 O L, I am indeed your servant.
116:17 I will call on the name of the L.
116:18 I will keep my vows to the L in
117:1 Praise the L, all you nations!
118:1 Give thanks to the L because
118:4 who fear the L should say,
118:5 of trouble I called on the L.
118:5 The L answered me ⌊and⌋ set
118:6 The L is on my side.
118:7 The L is on my side as my
118:8 It is better to depend on the L
118:9 It is better to depend on the L
118:10 armed⌋ with the name of the L,
118:11 armed⌋ with the name of the L,
118:12 armed⌋ with the name of the L,
118:13 but the L helped me.
118:14 The L is my strength and my
118:15 hand of the L displays strength.
118:16 The right hand of the L is held
118:16 hand of the L displays strength.
118:17 and tell what the L has done.
118:18 The L disciplined me severely,
118:19 ⌊and⌋ give thanks to the L.
118:20 This is the gate of the L
118:23 The L is responsible for this,
118:24 This is the day the L has made.
118:25 We beg you, O L, save us!
118:25 We beg you, O L, give us
118:26 comes in the name of the L.
118:27 The L is God, and he has
118:29 Give thanks to the L because
119:1 follow the teachings of the L.
119:12 Thanks be to you, O L.
119:31 O L, do not let me be put to
119:33 Teach me, O L, how to live by
119:41 your blessings reach me, O L.
119:52 regulations from long ago, O L,
119:55 I remember your name, O L,
119:57 You are my inheritance, O L.
119:64 Your mercy, O L, fills the earth.
119:65 You have treated me well, O L,
119:75 your regulations are fair, O L,
119:89 O L, your word is established
119:107 Give me a new life, O L,
119:108 praise I gladly give you, O L,
119:126 It is time for you to act, O L.
119:137 You are righteous, O L,
119:145 Answer me, O L. I want to obey
119:149 O L, give me a new life guided
119:151 You are near, O L,
119:156 are many in number, O L.
119:159 O L, in keeping with your
119:166 hope for you to save me, O L.
119:169 come into your presence, O L.
119:174 longed for you to save me, O L,
120:1 I cried out to the L,
120:2 O L, rescue me from lying lips
120:3 what can the L give you?
121:2 My help comes from the L,
121:5 The L is your guardian.
121:5 The L is the shade over your
121:7 The L guards you from every
121:8 The L guards you as you come
122:1 "Let's go to the house of the L."
122:4 thanks to the name of the L.
122:9 of the house of the L our God,
123:2 so we depend on the L our God
123:3 Have pity on us, O L.
124:1 "If the L had not been on our
124:2 "If the L had not been on our

Psa 124:6 Thank the L, who did not let
124:8 help is in the name of the L,
125:1 Those who trust the L are like
125:2 so the L surrounds his people
125:4 Do good, O L, to those who are
125:5 the L will lead them away with
126:1 When the L restored the
126:2 Then the nations said, "The L
126:3 The L has done spectacular
126:4 Restore our fortunes, O L,
127:1 If the L does not build the
127:1 If the L does not protect a city,
127:2 The L gives ⌊food⌋ to those he
127:3 are an inheritance from the L.
128:1 Blessed are all who fear the L
128:4 This is how the L will bless
128:5 May the L bless you from Zion
129:4 The L is righteous.
129:8 "May you be blessed by the L"
129:8 bless you in the name of the L."
130:1 O L, out of the depths I call to
130:2 O L, hear my voice. Let your
130:3 O L, who would be able to
130:5 I wait for the L, my soul waits,
130:6 My soul waits for the L more
130:7 O Israel, put your hope in the L,
130:7 because with the L there is
131:1 O L, my heart is not conceited.
131:3 hope in the L now and forever.
132:1 O L, remember David and all
132:2 how he swore an oath to the L
132:5 until I find a place for the L,
132:8 O L, arise, and come to your
132:11 The L swore an oath to David.
132:13 The L has chosen Zion.
133:3 That is where the L promised
134:1 Praise the L, all you servants
134:1 all you servants of the L,
134:1 house of the L night after night.
134:2 holy place, and praise the L.
134:3 May the L, the maker of heaven
135:1 Praise the name of the L.
135:1 you servants of the L
135:2 standing in the house of the L,
135:3 Praise the L because he is
135:4 The L chose Jacob to be his
135:5 I know that the L is great,
135:5 that our L is greater than all the
135:6 The L does whatever he wants
135:13 O L, your name endures
135:13 O L, you will be remembered
135:14 The L will provide justice for
135:19 of Israel, praise the L.
135:19 of Aaron, praise the L.
135:20 of Levi, praise the L.
135:20 You people who fear the L,
135:20 fear the LORD, praise the L.
135:21 Thank the L in Zion.
136:1 Give thanks to the L because
136:3 Give thanks to the L of lords
137:7 O L, remember the people of
138:4 will give thanks to you, O L,
138:5 this about the ways of the L:
138:6 Even though the L is high
138:8 The L will do everything for me.
138:8 O L, your mercy endures
139:1 O L, you have examined me,
139:4 you know all about it, L.
139:21 hate those who hate you, O L?
140:1 me from evil people, O L.
140:4 hands of wicked people, O L.
140:6 I said to the L, "You are my
140:6 O L, open your ears to hear my
140:7 O L Almighty, the strong one
140:8 O L, do not give wicked people
140:12 I know that the L will defend
141:1 O L, I cry out to you,
141:3 O L, set a guard at my mouth.
141:8 eyes look to you, L Almighty.
142:1 Loudly, I cry to the L.
142:1 I plead with the L for mercy.
142:5 I call out to you, O L.
143:1 O L, listen to my prayer.
143:7 Answer me quickly, O L.
143:9 me from my enemies, O L.
143:11 O L, keep me alive for the sake

Psa 144:1 Thank the L, my rock,
144:3 O L, what are humans that you
144:5 O L, bend your heaven low,
144:15 the people whose God is the L!
145:3 The L is great, and he should
145:8 The L is merciful, patient, and
145:9 The L is good to everyone and
145:10 will give thanks to you, O L,
145:14 The L supports everyone who
145:17 The L is fair in all his ways
145:18 The L is near to everyone who
145:20 The L protects everyone who
145:21 will speak the praise of the L,
146:1 Praise the L, my soul!
146:2 I want to praise the L
146:5 hope rests on the L their God,
146:6 The L remains faithful forever.
146:7 The L sets prisoners free.
146:8 The L gives sight to blind
146:8 The L straightens ⌊the backs⌋
146:8 The L loves righteous people.
146:9 The L protects foreigners.
146:9 The L gives relief to orphans
146:10 The L rules as king forever.
147:2 The L is the builder of
147:5 Our L is great, and his power is
147:6 The L gives relief to those who
147:7 Sing to the L a song of
147:11 The L is pleased with those
147:12 Praise the L, Jerusalem!
148:1 Praise the L from the heavens.
148:5 them praise the name of the L
148:7 Praise the L from the earth.
148:13 them praise the name of the L
149:1 Sing a new song to the L.
149:4 because the L takes pleasure
150:6 that breathes praise the L!

Pro 1:7 The fear of the L is the
1:29 did not choose the fear of the L.
2:5 will understand the fear of the L
2:6 The L gives wisdom.
3:5 Trust the L with all your heart,
3:7 Fear the L, and turn away from
3:9 Honor the L with your wealth
3:11 reject the discipline of the L,
3:12 because the L warns the one
3:19 By Wisdom the L laid the
3:26 The L will be your confidence.
3:32 person is disgusting to the L.
3:33 The L curses the house of
5:21 ways are clearly seen by the L,
6:16 are six things that the L hates,
8:13 To fear the L is to hate evil.
8:22 "The L already possessed me
8:35 and obtains favor from the L.
9:10 The fear of the L is the
10:3 The L will not allow a
10:24 but ⌊the L⌋ grants the desire of
10:27 The fear of the L lengthens
10:29 The way of the L is a fortress
11:1 scales are disgusting to the L,
11:20 people are disgusting to the L,
12:2 person obtains favor from the L,
12:2 but the L condemns everyone
12:22 that lie are disgusting to the L,
14:2 Whoever lives right fears the L,
14:26 In the fear of the L there is
14:27 The fear of the L is a fountain
15:3 eyes of the L are everywhere.
15:8 people is disgusting to the L,
15:9 people is disgusting to the L,
15:11 in front of the L how much more
15:16 fear of the L than great treasure
15:25 The L tears down the house of
15:26 people are disgusting to the L,
15:29 The L is far from wicked
15:33 The fear of the L is discipline
16:1 the tongue comes from the L.
16:2 but the L weighs motives.
16:3 Entrust your efforts to the L,
16:4 The L has made everything for
16:5 heart is disgusting to the L.
16:6 peace is made with the L.
16:6 By the fear of the L,
16:7 ways are pleasing to the L,
16:9 but the L directs his steps.

Pro 16:11 and scales belong to the L.
16:20 is the person who trusts the L.
16:33 L determines every outcome
17:3 hearts ⌊by fire⌋ is the L.
17:15 people is disgusting to the L.
18:10 The name of the L is a strong
18:22 has obtained favor from the L.
19:3 his heart rages against the L.
19:14 wife comes from the L.
19:17 pity on the poor lends to the L,
19:21 the advice of the L will endure.
19:23 The fear of the L leads to life,
20:10 both are disgusting to the L.
20:12 sees — the L made them both.
20:22 Wait for the L, and he will save
20:23 weights is disgusting to the L,
20:24 The L is the one who directs a
21:2 but the L weighs hearts.
21:3 to the L than offering
21:30 ⌊can stand up⌋ against the L.
21:31 but the victory belongs to the L.
22:2 the L is the maker of them all.
22:4 (the fear of the L) are riches
22:14 The one who is cursed by the L
22:19 that your trust may be in the L.
22:23 because the L will plead their
23:17 Instead, continue to fear the L.
24:18 The L will see it, he won't like
24:21 Fear the L, my son. Fear the
25:22 and the L will reward you.
28:5 the L understand everything.
28:25 but whoever trusts the L
29:13 The L gives both of them sight.
29:25 one who trusts the L is safe.
29:26 for humanity comes from the L.
30:9 you and say, 'Who is the L?' or
31:30 fear of the L should be praised.
Sos 8:6 flames that come from the L.
Isa 1:2 The L has spoken,
1:4 They have abandoned the L.
1:9 If the L of Armies hadn't left us
1:10 Listen to the word of the L,
1:11 The L asks, "What do your
1:18 says the L. "Though your sins
1:20 The L has spoken.
1:24 That's why the L, the LORD of
1:24 why the Lord, the L of Armies,
1:28 and those who abandon the L
2:3 go to the mountain of the L,
2:3 The word of the L will go out
2:5 let's live in the light of the L.
2:6 L, you have abandoned your
2:11 On that day the L alone will be
2:12 The L of Armies will have his
2:17 On that day the L alone will be
3:1 See now, the L, the LORD of
3:1 now, the Lord, the L of Armies,
3:8 what they do is against the L.
3:13 The L takes his place in the
3:14 The L presents his case to the
3:15 The Almighty L of Armies asks,
3:16 The L adds, "The women of
3:17 The L will cause sores ⌊to
3:17 and the L will make their
3:18 On that day the L will take
4:2 the branch of the L will be
4:4 The L will wash away the filth
4:5 The L will create a cloud of
5:7 The vineyard of the L of Armies
5:9 With my own ears I heard the L
5:12 attention to what the L is doing
5:16 The L of Armies will be
5:24 rejected the teachings of the L
5:25 That's why the anger of the L
5:26 The L raises up a flag for the
6:1 I saw the L sitting on a high
6:3 holy is the L of Armies!
6:5 seen the king, the L of Armies!"
6:8 Then I heard the voice of the L,
6:11 I asked, "How long, O L?"
6:12 The L will send his people far
7:3 Then the L said to Isaiah,
7:7 is what the Almighty L says:
7:10 Again the L spoke to Ahaz,
7:11 "Ask the L your God for a sign.
7:12 wouldn't think of testing the L."

Isa 7:14 So the L himself will give you
7:17 "The L will bring on you,
7:18 On that day the L will whistle
7:20 "On that day the L will hire the
8:1 The L said to me, "Take a
8:3 The L told me, "Name him
8:5 The L spoke to me again.
8:7 That is why the L is going to
8:11 This is what the L said with
8:13 Remember that the L of Armies
8:17 I will wait for the L,
8:18 that the L has given me.
8:18 in Israel from the L of Armies,
9:7 The L of Armies is determined
9:8 The L sent a message against
9:11 The L will set Rezin's
9:13 they sought the L of Armies.
9:14 So in one day the L will cut off
9:17 That is why the L isn't happy
9:19 by the fury of the L of Armies,
10:12 When the L has finished all his
10:16 That is why the Almighty L of
10:20 They will only depend on the L,
10:23 The Almighty L of Armies will
10:24 The Almighty L of Armies says:
10:26 Then the L of Armies will raise
10:33 The Almighty L of Armies will
11:2 The Spirit of the L will rest on
11:2 of knowledge and fear of the L.
11:3 gladly bear the fear of the L.
11:9 of the L like water covering
11:11 At that time the L will use his
11:15 The L will dry up the gulf of the
12:1 will say, "I will praise you, O L.
12:2 because the L is my strength
12:4 you will say, "Praise the L.
12:5 Make music to praise the L.
13:4 The L of Armies is assembling
13:5 The L is coming with the
13:6 for the day of the L is near.
13:9 The day of the L is going to
13:13 from its place when the L
14:1 The L will have compassion
14:3 When that day comes, the L
14:5 The L has broken the staff of
14:22 declares the L of Armies.
14:22 descendants," declares the L.
14:23 declares the L of Armies.
14:24 The L of Armies has taken an
14:27 The L of Armies has planned it.
14:32 ⌊Tell them that⌋ the L has laid
16:5 Then the L will set up a trusted
16:13 This is the message that the L
16:14 But now the L says,
17:3 declares the L of Armies.
17:6 declares the L God of Israel.
17:13 But the L will yell at them,
18:4 This is what the L says to me:
18:7 gifts will be brought to the L
18:7 the name of the L of Armies is.
19:1 The L is riding on a
19:4 the Almighty L of Armies.
19:12 Let them explain what the L of
19:14 The L mixes up their minds.
19:16 and be terrified because the L
19:17 of it because of what the L
19:18 allegiance to the L of Armies.
19:19 an altar for the L will be in the
19:19 and a stone marker for the L
19:20 a sign and a witness that the L
19:20 When the people cry to the L
19:21 So the L will make himself
19:21 The Egyptians will know the L
19:21 They will make vows to the L
19:22 The L will strike Egypt with a
19:22 they will come back to the L.
19:25 The L of Armies will bless
20:2 At that time the L told Isaiah,
20:3 Then the L said, "My servant
21:6 This is what the L says to me:
21:10 I heard from the L of Armies,
21:16 This is what the L says to me:
21:17 The L God of Israel has
22:5 The Almighty L of Armies has
22:8 On that day the L will remove
22:12 On that day the Almighty L of

Isa 22:14 The L of Armies revealed this
22:14 says the Almighty L of Armies.
22:15 This is what the Almighty L of
22:17 The L will throw you out.
22:25 The L of Armies declares,
22:25 The L has spoken.
23:9 The L of Armies planned this in
23:11 The L has stretched his hand
23:17 At the end of 70 years the L
23:18 will be turned over to the L
23:18 presence of the L so that they
24:1 The L is going to turn the earth
24:3 because the L has spoken.
24:15 Honor the L in the east.
24:15 Honor the name of the L God of
24:21 On that day the L will punish
24:23 because the L of Armies will
25:1 O L, you are my God. I will
25:6 On this mountain the L of
25:8 The Almighty L will wipe away
25:8 The L has spoken.
25:9 This is the L; we have waited
25:11 ⌊The L⌋ will humble those
26:4 Trust the L always,
26:4 LORD always, because the L,
26:4 the LORD, the L alone,
26:8 we wait with hope for you, O L,
26:10 do not see the majesty of the L.
26:11 O L, your power is visible,
26:12 O L, you will establish peace
26:13 O L, our God, you are not the
26:15 have expanded the nation, O L.
26:16 O L, the people have come to
26:17 O L, when we are with you,
26:21 The L is going to come out
27:1 On that day the L will use his
27:3 I, the L, watch over it. I water it
27:7 Will the L hurt Israel as he hurt
27:12 On that day the L will begin his
27:13 will come and worship the L
28:2 The L has one who is strong
28:5 When that day comes, the L of
28:11 The L will speak to these
28:13 The L speaks utter nonsense
28:14 So hear the word of the L,
28:16 is what the Almighty L says:
28:21 The L will rise as he did on
28:22 I have heard that the Almighty L
28:29 has come from the L of Armies.
29:6 The L of Armies will punish
29:10 The L has poured out on you a
29:13 The L says, "These people
29:15 to hide their plans from the L.
29:19 again will find joy in the L.
29:22 This is what the L,
30:1 The L declares, "How horrible
30:15 This is what the Almighty L,
30:18 The L is waiting to be kind to
30:18 The L is a God of justice.
30:19 The L will certainly have pity
30:20 The L may give you troubles
30:23 The L will give you rain for the
30:26 When that day comes, the L
30:27 The name of the L is going to
30:30 The L will make his majestic
30:31 At the sound of the L,
30:32 the L will pound on them.
31:1 They don't seek the L.
31:3 When the L uses his powerful
31:4 This is what the L said to me:
31:4 So the L of Armies will come to
31:5 The L of Armies will defend
31:9 The L declares this.
32:6 They speak falsely about the L.
33:2 O L, have pity on us. We wait
33:5 The L is honored because he
33:6 fear of the L is ⌊your⌋ treasure.
33:10 The L says, "Now I will arise.
33:21 The L will be our mighty
33:22 The L is our judge.
33:22 The L is our lawgiver.
33:22 The L is our king. The LORD is
33:22 The L is our savior.
34:2 The L is angry with all the
34:6 The L will receive a sacrifice
34:8 The L will have a day of

Isa 34:16 because the L has commanded
35:2 will see the glory of the L,
35:9 ⌊by the L⌋ will walk ⌊on
35:10 ransomed by the L will return.
36:7 "We're trusting the L our God."
36:10 this country without the L
36:10 The L said to me, 'Attack this
36:15 get you to trust the L by saying,
36:15 'The L will certainly rescue us,
36:18 'The L will rescue us.'
36:20 Could the L then rescue
37:4 The L your God may have
37:4 The L your God may punish
37:4 that the L your God heard.
37:6 'This is what the L says:
37:14 He spread it out in front of the L
37:15 and prayed to the L,
37:16 "L of Armies, God of Israel,
37:17 Turn your ear toward me, L,
37:17 Open your eyes, L,
37:18 It is true, L, that the kings of
37:20 Now, L our God, rescue us
37:20 know that you alone are the L."
37:21 "This is what the L God of
37:22 This is the message that the L
37:24 you defy the L and say,
37:32 The L of Armies is determined
37:33 "This is what the L says about
37:34 declares the L of Armies.
38:1 "This is what the L says:
38:2 to the wall and prayed to the L.
38:3 "Please, L, remember how I've
38:4 Then the L spoke his word to
38:5 'This is what the L God of your
38:7 "This is your sign from the L
38:11 thought that I wouldn't see the L
38:14 I've suffered miserably, O L!
38:16 L, people live in spite of such
38:20 The L is going to rescue me,
39:5 the word of the L of Armies!
39:6 The L says, 'The days are
40:2 It has received from the L
40:3 "Clear a way for the L.
40:5 The L has spoken."
40:10 The Almighty L is coming with
40:13 has directed the Spirit of the L
40:27 "My way is hidden from the L,
40:28 The eternal God, the L,
40:31 wait with hope in the L will
41:2 to whom the L gives victory
41:4 I, the L, was there first, and I
41:13 I, the L your God, hold your
41:14 declares the L, your Defender,
41:16 But you will find joy in the L
41:17 I, the L, will answer them. I,
41:21 your case," says the L.
42:5 The L God created the
42:5 This is what the L God says:
42:6 I, the L, have called you to do
42:8 I am the L; that is my name.
42:10 Sing a new song to the L.
42:12 Let them give glory to the L
42:13 The L marches out like a
42:19 blind like the servant of the L?
42:21 The L is pleased because he
42:24 Wasn't it the L, against whom
43:1 The L created Jacob and
43:1 Now, this is what the L says:
43:3 I am the L your God,
43:10 my witnesses," declares the L.
43:11 I alone am the L, and there is
43:12 that I am God," declares the L.
43:14 This is what the L,
43:15 I am the L, your Holy One,
43:16 The L makes a path through
43:17 This is what the L says:
44:2 The L made you, formed you in
44:2 This is what the L says:
44:5 "I belong to the L."
44:6 The L is Israel's king and
44:6 He is the L of Armies.
44:6 This is what the L says:
44:23 because the L has done this.
44:23 The L has reclaimed Jacob.
44:24 The L reclaimed you.
44:24 This is what the L says:

Isa 44:24 says: I, the L, made everything.
45:1 This is what the L says about
45:3 the L God of Israel,
45:5 I am the L, and there is no
45:6 I am the L, and there is no
45:7 I, the L, do all these things.
45:8 I, the L, have created them.
45:11 The L is the Holy One and the
45:11 This is what the L says:
45:13 says the L of Armies.
45:14 This is what the L says:
45:17 been saved by the L forever.
45:18 The L created the heavens.
45:18 This what the L says:
45:18 the LORD says: I am the L,
45:19 I, the L, speak what is fair and
45:21 Wasn't it I, the L? There is no
45:24 are found in the L alone."
45:25 and they will praise the L.
47:4 His name is the L of Armies.
48:1 oaths by the name of the L.
48:2 His name is the L of Armies.
48:14 The L loves Cyrus.
48:16 Now the Almighty L has sent
48:17 This is what the L,
48:17 I am the L your God.
48:20 Say that the L has reclaimed
48:22 for the wicked," says the L.
49:1 I was born, the L chose me.
49:5 The L formed me in the womb
49:5 (The L honors me,
49:6 Now, the L says, "You are not
49:7 The L is the defender of Israel,
49:7 This is what the L says to the
49:7 The L is faithful. The Holy One
49:8 This is what the L says:
49:13 The L has comforted his
49:14 "The L has abandoned me.
49:14 My L has forgotten me."
49:18 as I live," declares the L,
49:22 is what the Almighty L says:
49:23 you will know that I am the L.
49:25 This is what the L says:
49:26 will know that I am the L,
50:1 This is what the L says:
50:4 The Almighty L will teach me
50:5 The Almighty L will open my
50:7 The Almighty L helps me.
50:9 The Almighty L helps me.
50:10 Who among you fears the L
50:10 no light trust the name of the L
51:1 what is right and seek the L.
51:3 So the L will comfort Zion.
51:3 like the garden of the L.
51:9 yourself with strength, O L!
51:10 ⌊by the L⌋ might pass through
51:11 ransomed by the L will return.
51:13 Why have you forgotten the L,
51:15 I am the L your God who stirs
51:15 My name is the L of Armies.
51:20 experience the anger of the L,
51:22 The L your God defends his
52:3 This is what the L says:
52:4 is what the Almighty L says:
52:5 asks the L. My people are taken
52:5 are screaming, declares the L.
52:8 When the L brings Zion back,
52:9 The L will comfort his people.
52:10 The L will show his holy
52:12 The L will go ahead of you.
53:6 and the L has laid all our sins
53:10 When the L has made his life a
53:10 The will of the L will succeed
54:1 of married women," says the L.
54:5 His name is the L of Armies.
54:6 "The L has called you as if you
54:8 says the L your defender.
54:10 will never change," says the L,
54:13 children will be taught by the L,
54:17 from me," declares the L.
55:5 you because of the L your God,
55:6 Seek the L while he may be
55:7 Let them return to the L,
55:8 not your ways," declares the L.
56:1 This is what the L says:
56:3 joined the L should not say,

Isa 56:3 "The L will separate us from
56:4 This is what the L says:
56:6 who have joined the L
56:8 The Almighty L, who gathers
57:19 "I'll heal them," says the L.
58:5 an acceptable day to the L?
58:8 and the glory of the L will guard
58:9 and the L will answer.
58:11 The L will continually guide
58:14 then you will find joy in the L.
58:14 The L has spoken.
59:1 The L is not too weak to save
59:13 have rebelled and denied the L.
59:15 The L sees it, and he's angry
59:19 will fear the name of the L.
59:19 The wind of the L pushes him.
59:20 from rebellion," declares the L.
59:21 promise to them," says the L.
59:21 permanently," says the L.
60:1 the glory of the L has dawned.
60:2 But the L dawns, and his glory
60:6 will sing the praises of the L.
60:9 the name of the L your God,
60:14 will call you the city of the L,
60:16 you will know that I am the L,
60:19 But the L will be your
60:20 The L will be your everlasting
60:22 At the right time I, the L,
61:1 The Spirit of the Almighty L is
61:1 because the L has anointed me
61:3 the Plantings of the L,
61:6 be called the priests of the L.
61:8 I, the L, love justice. I hate
61:9 whom the L has blessed.
61:10 I will find joy in the L.
61:11 so the Almighty L will make
62:2 name that the L will announce.
62:3 crown in the hand of the L,
62:4 The L is delighted with you,
62:6 Whoever calls on the L,
62:8 The L has sworn with his right
62:9 will eat it and praise the L.
62:11 The L has announced to the
62:12 Those Reclaimed by the L,
63:1 "It is I, the L. I am coming to
63:7 and ⌊sing⌋ the praises of the L,
63:7 everything that the L has done
63:16 to us, O L, you are our Father.
63:17 O L, why do you let us wander
64:8 But now, L, you are our Father.
64:9 Don't be too angry, L.
64:12 Despite these things, L,
65:7 of your ancestors," says the L.
65:8 This is what the L says:
65:11 You have abandoned the L and
65:13 This is what the L God says:
65:15 The Almighty L will kill you
65:23 be offspring blessed by the L.
65:23 The L will bless their
65:25 my holy mountain," says the L.
66:1 This is what the L says:
66:2 into being," declares the L.
66:5 Listen to the word of the L,
66:5 "Let the L show his glory;
66:6 It is the sound of the L paying
66:9 asks the L. "Do I cause a
66:12 This is what the L says:
66:14 The power of the L will be
66:15 The L will come with fire and
66:16 The L will judge with fire,
66:16 will be struck dead by the L.
66:17 the same time," declares the L.
66:20 like a grain offering to the L.
66:20 Jerusalem," declares the L.
66:21 and Levites," declares the L.
66:22 my presence," declares the L.
66:23 to worship me," declares the L.
Jer 1:2 The L spoke his word to
1:3 The L also spoke when
1:3 The L continued to speak to
1:4 The L spoke his word to me,
1:6 I, Jeremiah, said, "Almighty L,
1:7 But the L said to me,
1:8 rescue you," declares the L.
1:9 Then the L stretched out his
1:9 The L said to me, "Now I have

Jer 1:11 Again the L spoke his word to
1:12 Then the L said to me,
1:13 Again the L spoke his word to
1:14 Then the L said to me,
1:15 from the north," declares the L.
1:19 rescue you," declares the L.
2:1 The L spoke his word to me,
2:2 'This is what the L says:
2:3 Israel was set apart for the L.
2:3 struck them,'" declares the L.
2:4 Listen to the word of the L,
2:5 This is what the L says:
2:6 didn't ask, "Where is the L,
2:8 didn't ask, "Where is the L?"
2:9 against you," declares the L,
2:12 terribly afraid," declares the L.
2:17 the L your God when
2:19 if you abandon the L your God
2:19 the Almighty L of Armies.
2:22 declares the Almighty L.
2:29 against me," declares the L.
2:31 "Consider the word of the L,
2:37 because the L has rejected
3:1 back to me!" declares the L.
3:6 was king, the L asked me,
3:10 was deceitful," declares the L.
3:11 Then the L said to me,
3:12 It is the L speaking.
3:12 I'm merciful,' declares the L.
3:13 You have rebelled against the L
3:13 not obeyed me,' declares the L.
3:14 people," declares the L.
3:16 in the land," declares the L.
3:17 Jerusalem the throne of the L.
3:17 because the name of the L will
3:20 betrayed me," declares the L.
3:21 have forgotten the L their God.
3:22 because you are the L our God.
3:23 the L our God will rescue us.
3:25 sinned against the L our God.
3:25 haven't obeyed the L our God.
4:1 The L declares, "If you come
4:2 "As the L lives ..."
4:3 This is what the L says to the
4:4 Be circumcised by the L,
4:9 day comes," declares the L,
4:10 I said, "Almighty L,
4:17 against me," declares the L.
4:26 are torn down because of the L
4:27 This is what the L says:
5:2 People say, "As the L lives ..."
5:3 L, your eyes look for the truth.
5:4 don't know the way of the L
5:5 They know the way of the L
5:9 these things," declares the L.
5:10 they don't belong to the L.
5:11 to me," declares the L.
5:12 They lie about the L and say,
5:13 The L hasn't spoken through
5:14 This is what the L God of
5:15 to attack you, declares the L.
5:18 in those days, declares the L,
5:19 They will ask, "Why has the L
5:22 asks the L. "Don't you tremble
5:24 'We should fear the L our God.
5:29 these things," declares the L.
6:6 This is what the L of Armies
6:9 This is what the L of Armies
6:10 When the L speaks his word to
6:11 filled with the anger of the L.
6:12 live in the land," declares the L.
6:15 I punish them," says the L.
6:16 This is what the L says:
6:21 This is what the L says:
6:22 This is what the L says:
6:30 the L has rejected them."
7:1 The L spoke his word to
7:2 'Listen to the word of the L,
7:2 these gates to worship the L.
7:3 This is what the L of Armies,
7:11 you are doing,'" declares the L.
7:13 did at Shiloh,'" declares the L.
7:19 provoking me," declares the L.
7:20 is what the Almighty L says:
7:21 "This is what the L of Armies,
7:28 did not obey the L their God.

Jer 7:29 because in his anger the L has
7:30 I consider evil," declares the L.
7:32 are coming," declares the L,
8:1 The L declares, "At that time
8:3 declares the L of Armies.
8:4 'This is what the L says:
8:7 the L, am urging them to return
8:9 have rejected the word of the L.
8:12 I punish them,'" says the L.
8:13 their harvest,'" declares the L,
8:14 The L our God has condemned
8:14 we have sinned against the L.
8:17 will bite you," declares the L.
8:19 "Isn't the L in Zion?
9:3 don't know me," declares the L.
9:6 me," declares the L.
9:7 This is what the L of Armies
9:9 for these things, declares the L.
9:12 To whom has the L revealed
9:13 The L answered, They didn't
9:15 This is what the L of Armies,
9:17 This is what the L of Armies
9:20 Listen to the word of the L,
9:22 This is what the L says:
9:23 This is what the L says:
9:24 They should brag that I, the L,
9:24 pleases me, declares the L.
9:25 are coming," declares the L,
10:1 message that the L has spoken
10:2 This is what the L says:
10:6 No one is like you, O L.
10:10 But the L is the only God.
10:12 The L made the earth by his
10:16 His name is the L of Armies.
10:18 This is what the L says:
10:21 don't look to the L for help.
10:23 O L, I know that the way
10:24 Correct me, O L, but please be
11:1 This is the message that the L
11:3 'This is what the L,
11:5 today."'" I answered, "Yes, L."
11:6 The L said to me, Listen to the
11:9 The L said to me,
11:11 This is what the L says:
11:16 The L called you a large olive
11:17 The L of Armies planted you.
11:18 The L revealed their plot to me
11:20 O L of Armies, you judge fairly
11:21 This is what the L says:
11:21 prophesy in the name of the L,
11:22 This is what the L of Armies
12:1 O L, even if I would argue my
12:3 You know me, O L.
12:13 of the burning anger of the L.
12:14 "This is what I, the L,
12:16 in my name, 'As the L lives ...'
12:17 and destroy it," declares the L.
13:1 This is what the L said to me:
13:2 as the L had told me,
13:3 The L spoke his word to me
13:5 as the L had told me.
13:6 After many days the L said to
13:8 Then the L spoke his word to
13:9 "This is what the L says:
13:11 cling to me," declares the L.
13:12 'This is what the L God of
13:13 'This is what the L says:
13:14 together, declares the L.
13:15 The L has spoken.
13:16 Honor the L your God before it
13:16 You will look for light, but the L
13:25 for you," declares the L.
14:1 The L spoke his word to
14:7 Do something, L, for the sake
14:9 You, O L, are among us.
14:10 This is what the L says about
14:10 So the L isn't happy with them.
14:11 The L said to me, "Don't pray
14:13 Then I said, "Almighty L,
14:13 or famines, because I, the L,
14:14 Then the L told me,
14:15 So this is what I, the L,
14:20 O L, we realize our
14:22 But you can, O L our God.
15:1 Then the L said to me,
15:2 'This is what the L says:

Jer 15:3 punish them," declares the L.
15:6 have left me," declares the L.
15:9 their enemies," declares the L.
15:11 The L said, "I will certainly
15:15 O L, you understand.
15:16 O L God of Armies.
15:19 This is what the L says:
15:20 and rescue you, declares the L.
16:1 The L spoke his word to me.
16:3 This is what the L says about
16:5 "This is what the L says:
16:5 these people," declares the L.
16:9 This is what the L of Armies,
16:10 'Why does the L threaten us
16:10 sinned against the L our God?'
16:11 abandoned me, declares the L.
16:14 are coming," declares the L,
16:14 'The L brought the people of
16:14 out of Egypt. As the L lives ....'
16:15 But they will say, 'The L
16:15 As the L lives ....' They will say
16:16 fishermen," declares the L,
16:19 The L is my strength and my
16:21 know that my name is the L."
17:1 ⌊The L says,⌋ "Judah's sin is
17:5 "This is what the L says:
17:5 heart turns away from the L.
17:7 is the person who trusts the L.
17:7 The L will be his confidence.
17:10 I, the L, search minds and test
17:13 O L, the Hope of Israel, all who
17:13 because they abandon the L,
17:14 Heal me, O L, and I will be
17:15 "Where is the word of the L?
17:19 This is what the L said to me:
17:20 "Listen to the word of the L,
17:21 This is what the L says:
17:24 "Now," declares the L,
18:1 The L spoke his word to
18:5 The L spoke his word to me.
18:5 his word to me. The L asked,
18:11 'This is what the L says:
18:13 "This is what the L says:
18:19 Pay attention to me, O L,
18:23 But you, O L, know that they
19:1 This is what the L says:
19:3 "Listen to the word of the L,
19:3 This is what the L of Armies,
19:6 are coming, declares the L,
19:10 ⌊The L says,⌋ "Then smash
19:11 to them, 'This is what the L
19:12 who live in it, declares the L.
19:14 where the L had sent him to
19:15 "This is what the L of Armies,
20:3 "The L doesn't call you
20:4 This is what the L says:
20:7 O L, you have deceived me,
20:8 The word of the L has made
20:9 "I can forget the L and no
20:11 But the L is on my side like a
20:12 But the L of Armies examines
20:13 Sing to the L! Praise the LORD!
20:13 Praise the L! He has rescued the
20:16 the L destroyed without pity.
21:1 The L spoke his word to
21:2 "Consult the L for us,
21:2 Maybe the L will perform
21:4 'This is what the L God of
21:7 Afterwards, declares the L,
21:8 'This is what the L says:
21:10 to do good to it, declares the L.
21:11 'Listen to the word of the L,
21:12 This is what the L says:
21:13 in the plain,'" declares the L.
21:14 have done,'" declares the L.
22:1 This is what the L says:
22:2 "Listen to the word of the L,
22:3 "This is what the L says:
22:5 on myself," declares the L,
22:6 "This is what the L says about
22:8 'Why has the L done this to
22:9 the promise of the L their God.
22:11 This is what the L says about
22:16 to know me?" asks the L.
22:18 This is what the L says about
22:24 "As I live," declares the L,

Jer 22:29 Listen to the word of the L.
22:30 This is what the L says:
23:1 in my care," declares the L.
23:2 the L God of Israel,
23:2 you have done," declares the L.
23:4 be missing," declares the L.
23:5 are coming," declares the L,
23:6 The L Our Righteousness.
23:7 are coming," declares the L,
23:7 'The L brought the people of
23:7 out of Egypt. As the L lives ...'
23:8 'The L brought the
23:8 As the L lives ...' At that time
23:9 because of the L and his holy
23:11 doing evil," declares the L.
23:12 be punished," declares the L.
23:15 This is what the L of Armies
23:16 This is what the L of Armies
23:16 visions are not from the L.
23:17 who despise me, "The L says,
23:19 The storm of the L will come
23:20 The anger of the L will not turn
23:23 is far away," declares the L.
23:24 I can't see him," declares the L.
23:24 and earth!" declares the L.
23:28 to do with straw?" asks the L.
23:29 shatters a rock?" asks the L.
23:30 each other," declares the L.
23:32 they made up," declares the L.
23:32 people at all," declares the L.
23:33 'What revelation has the L
23:33 abandon you, declares the L.'
23:35 and 'What did the L say?'
23:36 God, the L of Armies, our God.
23:37 and 'What did the L say?'
23:38 'This is what the L says:
24:1 After this, the L showed me
24:3 Then the L asked me,
24:4 The L spoke his word to me,
24:5 "This is what the L God of
24:7 desire to know that I am the L.
24:8 "But this is what the L says
24:8 The L says, 'Like these bad
25:1 The L spoke his word to
25:3 the L continued to speak his
25:4 "Even though the L has sent all
25:5 and live in the land that the L
25:7 listened to me, declares the L.
25:8 "This is what the L of Armies
25:9 of Babylon, declares the L.
25:12 for their crimes, declares the L.
25:15 This is what the L God of
25:17 to whom the L sent me drink
25:27 ⌊The L said,⌋ "Say to them,
25:27 'This is what the L of Armies,
25:28 'This is what the L of Armies
25:29 declares the L of Armies.'
25:30 'The L roars from above.
25:31 the L has brought charges
25:31 kill the wicked, declares the L.'
25:32 "This is what the L of Armies
25:33 killed by the L will stretch from
25:36 because the L is stripping their
26:1 The L spoke his word when
26:2 "This is what the L says:
26:4 The L added, "Also say to
26:4 'This is what the L says:
26:8 that the L had commanded him
26:12 "The L sent me to prophesy
26:13 and listen to the L your God.
26:13 Then the L will change his
26:15 The L has certainly sent me to
26:16 in the name of the L our God."
26:18 'This is what the L of Armies
26:19 Hezekiah feared the L and
26:19 So the L changed his plan
26:20 in the name of the L.
27:1 the L spoke his word to
27:2 This is what the L said to me:
27:4 "This is what the L of Armies,
27:8 power, declares the L.
27:11 and live on it,"' declares the L.
27:13 The L has threatened the
27:15 send them, declares the L.
27:16 "This is what the L said to me:
27:18 If they are prophets and the L is

Jer 27:18 they should beg the L of
27:21 This is what the L of Armies,
27:22 I come for them, declares the L.
28:2 "This is what the L of Armies,
28:4 to Babylon, declares the L.
28:6 May the L do this! May the
28:6 May the L make your prophecy
28:9 a prophet that the L sent only if
28:11 "This is what the L says:
28:12 the L spoke his word to
28:13 'This is what the L says:
28:14 This is what the L of Armies,
28:15 the L hasn't sent you.
28:16 This is what the L says:
28:16 rebellion against the L."
29:4 This is what the L of Armies,
29:7 and pray to the L for that city.
29:8 This is what the L of Armies,
29:9 send them, declares the L.
29:10 This is what the L says:
29:11 I have for you, declares the L.
29:14 let you find me, declares the L.
29:14 scattered you, declares the L.
29:15 You've said that the L has
29:16 But this is what the L says
29:17 The L of Armies says:
29:19 listen to me, declares the L.
29:19 to listen, declares the L.
29:20 So listen to the word of the L,
29:21 This is what the L of Armies,
29:22 May the L curse you as he
29:23 I'm a witness, declares the L.
29:24 ⌊The L says,⌋ "Say to
29:25 'This is what the L of Armies,
29:26 The L made you priest instead
29:30 Then the L spoke his word to
29:31 'This is what the L says about
29:32 The L says: I will punish
29:32 my people, declares the L,
29:32 rebellion against the L."'
30:1 The L spoke his word to
30:2 "This is what the L God of
30:3 are coming," declares the L,
30:4 This is the message that the L
30:5 "This is what the L says:
30:8 declares the L of Armies,
30:9 You will serve the L your God
30:10 servant Jacob," declares the L.
30:11 rescue you," declares the L.
30:12 "This is what the L says:
30:17 your wounds," declares the L.
30:18 "This is what the L says:
30:21 to come near me?" asks the L.
30:23 The storm of the L will come
31:1 "At that time," declares the L,
31:2 This is what the L says:
31:3 The L appeared to me in a
31:6 go to Zion, to the L our God."'
31:7 This is what the L says:
31:7 say, "O L, rescue your people,
31:10 listen to the word of the L.
31:11 The L will free the
31:14 my blessings," declares the L.
31:15 This is what the L says:
31:16 This is what the L says:
31:16 for your work, declares the L.
31:17 filled with hope, declares the L.
31:18 because you are the L my God.
31:20 on him," declares the L.
31:22 The L will create something
31:23 This is what the L of Armies,
31:23 in its cities: "The L bless you,
31:27 are coming," declares the L,
31:28 to plant them," declares the L.
31:31 are coming," declares the L,
31:32 to them," declares the L.
31:33 those days," declares the L:
31:34 by saying, 'Know the L.' All
31:34 will know me," declares the L,
31:35 The L provides the sun to be a
31:35 His name is the L of Armies.
31:35 This is what the L says:
31:36 stop working, declares the L,
31:37 This is what the L says:
31:37 they have done, declares the L.
31:38 are coming," declares the L,

Jer 31:40 will be holy to the L.
32:1 The L spoke his word to
32:3 'This is what the L says:
32:5 I deal with him, declares the L.
32:6 "The L spoke his word to me.
32:8 "Then, as the L had said,
32:8 Then I knew that the L had
32:14 'This is what the L of Armies,
32:15 This is what the L of Armies,
32:16 son of Neriah, I prayed to the L.
32:17 'Almighty L, you made heaven
32:18 Your name is the L of Armies.
32:25 Yet you, Almighty L,
32:26 The L spoke his word to
32:27 "I am the L God of all humanity.
32:28 This is what the L says:
32:30 they've done," declares the L.
32:36 Now this is what the L God of
32:42 "This is what the L says:
32:44 their captivity," declares the L.
33:1 the L spoke his word to him a
33:1 him a second time. The L said,
33:2 My name is the L. This is what
33:2 This is what the L says:
33:4 This is what the L God of
33:10 "This is what the L says:
33:11 'Give thanks to the L of Armies
33:11 Armies because the L is good,
33:11 they were before," says the L.
33:12 "This is what the L of Armies
33:13 count their sheep," says the L.
33:14 are coming," declares the L,
33:16 The L Our Righteousness.
33:17 "This what the L says:
33:19 The L spoke his word to
33:20 "This is what the L says:
33:23 Then the L spoke his word to
33:24 They have said that the L has
33:25 "This is what the L says:
34:1 The L spoke his word to
34:2 "This is what the L God of
34:2 and tell him, 'The L says:
34:4 "'Listen to the word of the L,
34:4 This is what the L says about
34:5 my word, declares the L."
34:8 The L spoke his word to
34:12 The L spoke his word to
34:13 "This is what the L God of
34:17 "This is what the L says:
34:17 to free you," declares the L.
34:22 a command," declares the L.
35:1 The L spoke his word to
35:12 Then the L spoke his word to
35:13 "This is what the L of Armies,
35:13 my words? declares the L.
35:17 "'This is what the L God of
35:18 "This is what the L of Armies,
35:19 So this is what the L of Armies,
36:1 the L spoke his word to
36:4 that the L had told him,
36:7 The L has threatened these
36:8 everything that the L had said.
36:11 everything the L had said.
36:26 But the L had hidden Baruch
36:27 the L spoke his word to
36:29 'This is what the L says:
36:30 This is what the L says about
37:2 what the L had spoken through
37:3 "Please pray to the L our God
37:6 The L spoke his word to the
37:7 "This is what the L God of
37:9 "'This is what the L says:
37:17 there any message from the L?"
37:17 There is a message from the L.
38:2 "This is what the L says:
38:3 "This is what the L says:
38:16 "The L gave us life.
38:16 As the L lives, I will not kill
38:17 "This is what the L God of
38:20 Obey the L by doing what I'm
38:21 is what the L has shown me.
39:15 the L spoke his word to him.
39:15 his word to him. The L said,
39:16 'This is what the L of Armies,
39:17 will rescue you, declares the L.
39:18 trusted me, declares the L."'

Jer 40:1 The **L** spoke his word to
40:2 "The **L** your God threatened to
40:3 The **L** did as he promised
42:2 and pray to the **L** your God for
42:3 Let the **L** your God tell us
42:4 I will pray to the **L** your God as
42:4 tell you everything the **L** says.
42:5 "May the **L** be a true and
42:5 what the **L** your God tells
42:6 We will obey the **L** our God to
42:6 Yes, we will obey the **L** our
42:7 After ten days the **L** spoke his
42:9 plead your case to the **L**.
42:9 This is what the **L** God of
42:11 be afraid of him, declares the **L**.
42:13 you disobey the **L** your God.
42:15 listen to the word of the **L**,
42:15 This is what the **L** of Armies,
42:18 "This is what the **L** of Armies,
42:19 "The **L** has told you people
42:20 you sent me to the **L** your God
42:20 'Pray to the **L** our God for us,
42:20 and tell us everything that the **L**
42:21 anything the **L** your God sent
43:1 message from the **L** their God.
43:1 He told them everything the **L**
43:2 The **L** our God didn't send you
43:4 all the people didn't obey the **L**.
43:7 They didn't listen to the **L**,
43:8 Then the **L** spoke his word to
43:10 'This is what the **L** of Armies,
44:1 The **L** spoke his word to
44:2 This is what the **L** of Armies,
44:7 Now, this is what the **L** God of
44:11 This is what the **L** of Armies,
44:21 "Doesn't the **L** remember that
44:22 The **L** could no longer bear the
44:23 sinned against the **L**,
44:24 "Listen to the word of the **L**,
44:25 This is what the **L** of Armies,
44:26 But listen to the word of the **L**,
44:26 by my great name,' says the **L**,
44:26 "As the Almighty **L** lives ..."
44:29 you this sign,' declares the **L**.
44:30 This is what the **L** says:
45:2 "This is what the **L** God of
45:3 The **L** has added grief to my
45:4 'This is what the **L** says:
45:5 on all people, declares the **L**.
46:1 The **L** spoke this message to
46:5 around them," declares the **L**.
46:10 to the Almighty **L** of Armies.
46:10 The Almighty **L** of Armies will
46:13 The **L** spoke this message to
46:15 They can't stand because the **L**
46:18 whose name is the **L** of Armies,
46:23 the forest," declares the **L**,
46:25 The **L** of Armies, the God of
46:26 did long ago," declares the **L**.
46:28 servant Jacob," declares the **L**.
47:1 The **L** spoke this message to
47:2 This is what the **L** says:
47:4 The **L** will destroy the
47:6 You cry out, "Sword of the **L**,
47:7 can the sword of the **L** rest?
47:7 The **L** has ordered it to attack
48:1 This is what the **L** of Armies,
48:8 waste as the **L** has threatened.
48:12 are coming," declares the **L**,
48:15 whose name is the **L** of Armies.
48:25 arm is broken," declares the **L**.
48:26 have spoken against the **L**.
48:30 declares the **L**, "but it isn't right.
48:35 to their gods," declares the **L**.
48:38 no one wants," declares the **L**.
48:40 "This is what the **L** says:
48:42 because it spoke against the **L**.
48:43 live in Moab," declares the **L**.
48:44 to Moab," declares the **L**.
48:47 the last days," declares the **L**.
49:1 This is what the **L** says about
49:2 are coming, declares the **L**,
49:2 of its inheritance, says the **L**.
49:5 the Almighty **L** of Armies.
49:6 of Ammon, declares the **L**.
49:7 This is what the **L** of Armies

Jer 49:12 This is what the **L** says:
49:13 oath on myself, declares the **L**,
49:14 I heard a message from the **L**.
49:16 from there," declares the **L**.
49:18 will stay there," says the **L**.
49:20 Listen to the plans that the **L** is
49:26 declares the **L** of Armies.
49:28 This is what the **L** says:
49:30 of Hazor, declares the **L**.
49:31 and securely, declares the **L**.
49:32 from every side, declares the **L**.
49:34 the **L** spoke his word to the
49:35 This is what the **L** of Armies
49:37 burning anger, declares the **L**.
49:38 and officials, declares the **L**.
49:39 of Elam, declares the **L**.
50:1 This is the message that the **L**
50:4 at that time," declares the **L**,
50:4 to seek the **L** their God.
50:5 agreement with the **L**.
50:7 have sinned against the **L**,
50:7 have sinned against the **L**,
50:10 they want," declares the **L**.
50:14 have sinned against the **L**.
50:18 "This is what the **L** of Armies,
50:20 at that time," declares the **L**,
50:21 with a sword," declares the **L**.
50:24 you have opposed the **L**.
50:25 The **L** will open his armory and
50:25 because the Almighty **L** of
50:28 vengeance of the **L** our God,
50:29 They have disobeyed the **L**,
50:30 that day," declares the **L**.
50:31 the Almighty **L** of Armies.
50:33 This is what the **L** of Armies
50:34 His name is the **L** of Armies.
50:35 in Babylon," declares the **L**.
50:40 will stay there," declares the **L**.
50:45 Listen to the plans that the **L** is
51:1 This is what the **L** says:
51:5 by their God, the **L** of Armies,
51:6 time for the vengeance of the **L**.
51:10 The **L** has brought about our
51:10 in Zion what the **L** our God has
51:11 The **L** will stir up the spirit of
51:11 The **L** will avenge his temple.
51:12 The **L** will carry out his plans
51:14 The **L** of Armies has taken an
51:15 The **L** made the earth by his
51:19 His name is the **L** of Armies.
51:24 did in Zion," declares the **L**.
51:25 whole earth," declares the **L**.
51:26 ruins," declares the **L**.
51:29 The **L** carries out his plans
51:33 This is what the **L** of Armies,
51:36 This is what the **L** says:
51:39 wake up again, declares the **L**.
51:45 from the burning anger of the **L**.
51:48 will attack it," declares the **L**.
51:50 Remember the **L** in a distant
51:52 are coming," declares the **L**,
51:53 against them," declares the **L**.
51:55 The **L** will destroy Babylon.
51:56 "I, the **L**, am a God who
51:57 whose name is the **L** of Armies.
51:58 This is what the **L** of Armies
51:62 Then say, '**L**, you have
52:2 did what the **L** considered evil,
52:3 The **L** became angry with
Lam 1:5 The **L** made Zion suffer for its
1:9 'O **L**, look at my suffering,
1:10 'O **L**, they are the same people
1:11 'O **L**, look and see how
1:12 pain that the **L** has caused me,
1:14 The **L** has handed me over to
1:15 The **L** has treated all the
1:15 The **L** trampled the people of
1:17 The **L** has given this order
1:18 "The **L** is right in what he did,
1:20 "O **L**, see the distress I'm in!
2:1 "Look how the **L** has covered
2:2 The **L** swallowed up all of
2:5 The **L** became an enemy.
2:6 The **L** wiped out the memory of
2:7 The **L** rejected his altar and
2:8 The **L** planned to destroy the

Lam 2:9 ⌊The **L**⌋ destroyed and
2:9 can find no visions from the **L**.
2:17 The **L** has accomplished what
2:18 people cried out to the **L**,
2:19 water in the presence of the **L**.
2:20 "O **L**, look and consider:
3:18 ⌊to live⌋ and my hope in the **L**.'
3:24 'The **L** is my lot ⌊in life⌋.
3:25 The **L** is good to those who
3:26 silently for the **L** to save us.
3:28 because the **L** has laid these
3:31 "The **L** will not reject ⌊such⌋
3:36 The **L** isn't happy to see ⌊these
3:37 It was the **L** who gave the
3:40 them and then return to the **L**.
3:50 until the **L** looks down from
3:55 name from the deepest pit, O **L**.
3:58 Plead my case for me, O **L**.
3:59 that has been done to me, O **L**.
3:64 Pay them back, O **L**,
4:16 The **L** himself has scattered
4:20 The person the **L** anointed ⌊as
4:22 The **L** will not let you remain in
5:1 "Remember, O **L**, what has
5:19 "But you, O **L**, sit enthroned
5:21 O **L**, bring us back to you,
Eze 1:3 the **L** spoke his word to the
1:3 of the **L** came over Ezekiel.
2:4 'This is what the Almighty **L**
3:1 The **L** said to me, "Son of man,
3:11 'This is what the Almighty **L**
3:14 power of the **L** came over me.
3:16 After seven days the **L** spoke
3:22 The power of the **L** came over
3:27 is what the Almighty **L** says.'
4:1 ⌊The **L** said,⌋ "Son of man,
4:13 Then the **L** said, "In the same
4:14 I answered, "Almighty **L**,
5:1 ⌊The **L** said,⌋ "Son of man,
5:5 is what the Almighty **L** says:
5:7 is what the Almighty **L** says:
5:8 is what the Almighty **L** says:
5:11 declares the Almighty **L**,
5:13 you, you will know that I, the **L**,
5:15 I, the **L**, have spoken.
5:17 I, the **L**, have spoken."
6:1 The **L** spoke his word to me.
6:3 to the word of the Almighty **L**!
6:3 This is what the Almighty **L**
6:7 you will know that I am the **L**.
6:10 you will know that I am the **L**
6:11 is what the Almighty **L** says:
6:13 you will know that I am the **L**.
6:14 will know that I am the **L**.'"
7:1 The **L** spoke his word to me.
7:2 this is what the Almighty **L**
7:4 you will know that I am the **L**.
7:5 is what the Almighty **L** says:
7:9 you will know that I am the **L**
7:27 they will know that I am the **L**."
8:1 the Almighty **L** came over me.
8:12 'The **L** doesn't see me.
8:12 The **L** has abandoned this
9:1 Then I heard the **L** call out with
9:3 The **L** called to the person
9:4 The **L** said to that person,
9:8 I cried, "Almighty **L**,
9:9 They think that the **L** has
10:2 The **L** said to the person
10:6 After the **L** had commanded the
10:18 Then the glory of the **L** left the
11:2 Then the **L** said to me,
11:5 "This is what the **L** says:
11:7 is what the Almighty **L** says:
11:8 declares the Almighty **L**.
11:10 you will know that I am the **L**.
11:12 you will know that I am the **L**.
11:13 and cried out, "Almighty **L**,
11:14 Then the **L** spoke his word to
11:15 'They are far away from the **L**.
11:16 is what the Almighty **L** says:
11:17 is what the Almighty **L** says:
11:21 declares the Almighty **L**.'"
11:25 the **L** had shown me.
12:1 The **L** spoke his word to me.
12:8 The next morning the **L** spoke

Eze 12:10 is what the Almighty **L** says:
12:15 they will know that I am the **L**,
12:16 will know that I am the **L**.'"
12:17 The **L** spoke his word to me.
12:19 'This is what the Almighty **L**
12:20 will know that I am the **L**.'"
12:21 The **L** spoke his word to me.
12:23 is what the Almighty **L** says:
12:25 I, the **L**, will speak.
12:25 declares the Almighty **L**.'"
12:26 The **L** spoke his word to me.
12:28 is what the Almighty **L** says:
12:28 declares the Almighty **L**.'"
13:1 The **L** spoke his word to me.
13:2 'Listen to the word of the **L**.
13:3 is what the Almighty **L** says:
13:5 in battle on the day of the **L**.
13:6 They say, "The **L** said this."
13:6 But the **L** hasn't sent them.
13:7 you say, "The **L** said this,"
13:8 is what the Almighty **L** says:
13:8 declares the Almighty **L**.
13:9 you will know that I am the **L**.
13:13 is what the Almighty **L** says:
13:14 you will know that I am the **L**.
13:16 declares the Almighty **L**.'"
13:18 is what the Almighty **L** says:
13:20 is what the Almighty **L** says:
13:21 you will know that I am the **L**.
13:23 you will know that I am the **L**.'"
14:2 Then the **L** spoke his word to
14:4 'This is what the **L** says:
14:4 I, the **L**, will give that Israelite
14:6 is what the Almighty **L** says:
14:7 the **L**, will give him an answer.
14:8 you will know that I am the **L**.
14:9 the **L**, who tricked the prophet.
14:11 declares the Almighty **L**.'"
14:12 The **L** spoke his word to me.
14:14 declares the Almighty **L**.
14:16 declares the Almighty **L**,
14:18 declares the Almighty **L**,
14:20 declares the Almighty **L**,
14:21 is what the Almighty **L** says:
14:23 declares the Almighty **L**.
15:1 The **L** spoke his word to me.
15:6 is what the Almighty **L** says:
15:7 they will know that I am the **L**,
15:8 declares the Almighty **L**.
16:1 The **L** spoke his word to me.
16:3 'This is what the Almighty **L**
16:8 declares the Almighty **L**.
16:14 declares the Almighty **L**.
16:19 declares the Almighty **L**.
16:23 declares the Almighty **L**.
16:30 declares the Almighty **L**.
16:35 "'Listen to the word of the **L**,
16:36 is what the Almighty **L** says:
16:43 declares the Almighty **L**.
16:48 declares the Almighty **L**,
16:58 you have done, declares the **L**.
16:59 is what the Almighty **L** says:
16:62 you will know that I am the **L**.
16:63 declares the Almighty **L**.'"
17:1 The **L** spoke his word to me.
17:3 is what the Almighty **L** says:
17:9 is what the Almighty **L** says:
17:11 The **L** spoke his word to me.
17:16 declares the Almighty **L**,
17:19 "'So this is what the Almighty **L**
17:21 you will know that I, the **L**,
17:22 is what the Almighty **L** says:
17:24 field will know that I am the **L**.
17:24 I, the **L**, have spoken, and I will
18:1 The **L** spoke his word to me.
18:3 declares the Almighty **L**,
18:9 declares the Almighty **L**.
18:23 declares the Almighty **L**.
18:30 declares the Almighty **L**.
18:32 declares the Almighty **L**.
20:2 Then the **L** spoke his word to
20:3 is what the Almighty **L** says:
20:3 declares the Almighty **L**,
20:5 is what the Almighty **L** says:
20:5 "I am the **L** your God."
20:7 I am the **L** your God."

Eze 20:12 that I, the **L**, made them holy.
20:19 I am the **L** your God.
20:20 know that I am the **L** your God."
20:26 would know that I am the **L**.'
20:27 is what the Almighty **L** says:
20:30 is what the Almighty **L** says:
20:31 declares the Almighty **L**,
20:33 declares the Almighty **L**,
20:36 declares the Almighty **L**.
20:38 you will know that I am the **L**.
20:39 is what the Almighty **L** says:
20:40 declares the Almighty **L**.
20:42 you will know that I am the **L**,
20:44 you will know that I am the **L**,
20:44 declares the Almighty **L**.'"
20:45 The **L** spoke his word to me.
20:47 'Listen to the word of the **L**.
20:47 is what the Almighty **L** says:
20:48 that I, the **L**, started the fire.
20:49 Almighty **L**, no! The people
21:1 The **L** spoke his word to me.
21:3 'This is what the **L** says:
21:5 will know that I, the **L**,
21:7 declares the Almighty **L**."
21:8 The **L** spoke his word to me.
21:9 'This is what the **L** says:
21:13 declares the Almighty **L**.
21:17 I, the **L**, have spoken."'
21:18 The **L** spoke his word to me.
21:24 is what the Almighty **L** says:
21:26 is what the Almighty **L** says:
21:28 'This is what the Almighty **L**
21:32 I, the **L**, have spoken."'
22:1 The **L** spoke his word to me.
22:3 is what the Almighty **L** says:
22:12 declares the Almighty **L**.
22:14 I, the **L**, have spoken, and I will
22:16 you will know that I am the **L**."
22:17 Then the **L** spoke his word to
22:19 is what the Almighty **L** says:
22:22 you will know that I, the **L**,
22:23 "The **L** spoke his word to me.
22:28 is what the Almighty **L** says.'
22:28 Yet, the **L** hasn't spoken.
22:31 declares the Almighty **L**.
23:1 The **L** spoke his word to me.
23:22 is what the Almighty **L** says:
23:28 is what the Almighty **L** says:
23:32 is what the Almighty **L** says:
23:34 declares the Almighty **L**.
23:35 is what the Almighty **L** says:
23:36 The **L** said to me, "Son of man,
23:46 is what the Almighty **L** says:
23:49 know that I am the Almighty **L**."
24:1 the **L** spoke his word to me.
24:3 is what the Almighty **L** says:
24:6 is what the Almighty **L** says:
24:9 is what the Almighty **L** says:
24:14 I, the **L**, have spoken. It will
24:14 done,"' declares the Almighty **L**.
24:15 Then the **L** spoke his word to
24:20 "The **L** spoke his word to me.
24:21 is what the Almighty **L** says:
24:24 that I am the Almighty **L**.'"
24:27 they will know that I am the **L**."
25:1 The **L** spoke his word to me.
25:3 to the word of the Almighty **L**.
25:3 is what the Almighty **L** says:
25:5 you will know that I am the **L**.
25:6 is what the Almighty **L** says:
25:7 you will know that I am the **L**.
25:8 is what the Almighty **L** says:
25:11 they will know that I am the **L**.
25:12 is what the Almighty **L** says:
25:13 is what the Almighty **L** says:
25:14 declares the Almighty **L**.
25:15 is what the Almighty **L** says:
25:16 is what the Almighty **L** says:
25:17 will know that I am the **L**.'"
26:1 the **L** spoke his word to me.
26:3 is what the Almighty **L** says:
26:5 declares the Almighty **L**.
26:6 they will know that I am the **L**.
26:7 is what the Almighty **L** says:
26:14 I, the **L**, have spoken,
26:14 declares the Almighty **L**.

Eze 26:15 "This is what the Almighty **L**
26:19 is what the Almighty **L** says:
26:21 declares the Almighty **L**.
27:1 The **L** spoke his word to me.
27:3 is what the Almighty **L** says:
28:1 The **L** spoke his word to me.
28:2 is what the Almighty **L** says:
28:6 is what the Almighty **L** says:
28:10 I have spoken,"' declares the **L**.
28:11 The **L** spoke his word to me.
28:12 is what the Almighty **L** says:
28:20 The **L** spoke his word to me.
28:22 is what the Almighty **L** says:
28:22 will know that I am the **L**,
28:23 they will know that I am the **L**.
28:24 know that I am the Almighty **L**.
28:25 is what the Almighty **L** says:
28:26 that I am the **L** their God."'
29:1 the **L** spoke his word to me.
29:3 is what the Almighty **L** says:
29:6 Egypt will know that I am the **L**.
29:8 is what the Almighty **L** says:
29:9 you will know that I am the **L**.
29:13 is what the Almighty **L** says:
29:16 know that I am the Almighty **L**."
29:17 the **L** spoke his word to me.
29:19 is what the Almighty **L** says:
29:20 declares the Almighty **L**.
29:21 they will know that I am the **L**."
30:1 The **L** spoke his word to me.
30:2 is what the Almighty **L** says:
30:3 The day of the **L** is near.
30:6 "'This is what the **L** says:
30:6 declares the Almighty **L**.
30:8 they will know that I am the **L**,
30:10 is what the Almighty **L** says:
30:12 I, the **L**, have spoken.
30:13 is what the Almighty **L** says:
30:19 they will know that I am the **L**,
30:20 the **L** spoke his word to me.
30:22 is what the Almighty **L** says:
30:25 they will know that I am the **L**,
30:26 they will know that I am the **L**."
31:1 the **L** spoke his word to me.
31:10 is what the Almighty **L** says:
31:15 is what the Almighty **L** says:
31:18 declares the Almighty **L**.'"
32:1 the **L** spoke his word to me.
32:3 is what the Almighty **L** says:
32:8 declares the Almighty **L**.
32:11 is what the Almighty **L** says:
32:14 declares the Almighty **L**.
32:15 they will know that I am the **L**.'
32:16 declares the Almighty **L**.
32:17 the **L** spoke his word to me.
32:31 declares the Almighty **L**.
32:32 declares the Almighty **L**.
33:1 The **L** spoke his word to me.
33:11 declares the Almighty **L**,
33:22 the power of the **L** came over
33:22 the **L** made me speak.
33:23 The **L** spoke his word to me.
33:25 is what the Almighty **L** says:
33:27 is what the Almighty **L** says:
33:29 will know that I am the **L**,
33:30 word that has come from the **L**.'
34:1 The **L** spoke his word to me.
34:2 is what the Almighty **L** says:
34:7 listen to the word of the **L**.
34:8 declares the Almighty **L**,
34:9 listen to the word of the **L**.
34:10 is what the Almighty **L** says:
34:11 is what the Almighty **L** says:
34:15 declares the Almighty **L**.
34:17 is what the Almighty **L** says:
34:20 "'So this is what the Almighty **L**
34:24 I, the **L**, will be their God,
34:24 I, the **L**, have spoken.
34:27 they will know that I am the **L**,
34:30 know that I, the **L** their God,
34:30 declares the Almighty **L**.
34:31 declares the Almighty **L**."
35:1 The **L** spoke his word to me.
35:3 is what the Almighty **L** says:
35:4 you will know that I am the **L**.
35:6 declares the Almighty **L**,

Eze 35:9 you will know that I am the **L**.
35:10 But the **L** was there.
35:11 declares the Almighty **L**,
35:12 you will know that I, the **L**,
35:14 is what the Almighty **L** says:
35:15 you will know that I am the **L**.'"
36:1 ⌊The **L** said,⌋ "Son of man,
36:1 listen to the word of the **L**.
36:2 is what the Almighty **L** says:
36:3 is what the Almighty **L** says:
36:4 to the word of the Almighty **L**.
36:4 This is what the Almighty **L**
36:6 is what the Almighty **L** says:
36:7 is what the Almighty **L** says:
36:11 you will know that I am the **L**.
36:13 is what the Almighty **L** says:
36:14 declares the Almighty **L**.
36:15 declares the Almighty **L**.'"
36:16 The **L** spoke his word to me.
36:22 is what the Almighty **L** says:
36:23 will know that I am the **L**,
36:23 declares the Almighty **L**.
36:32 declares the Almighty **L**.
36:33 is what the Almighty **L** says:
36:36 are left will know that I, the **L**,
36:36 I, the **L**, have spoken, and I will
36:37 is what the Almighty **L** says:
36:38 they will know that I am the **L**."
37:1 The power of the **L** came over
37:1 The **L** brought me out by his
37:3 "Only you know, Almighty **L**."
37:4 listen to the word of the **L**.
37:5 This is what the Almighty **L**
37:6 you will know that I am the **L**.'"
37:9 Then the **L** said to me,
37:9 is what the Almighty **L** says:
37:11 The **L** also said to me,
37:12 is what the Almighty **L** says:
37:13 you will know that I am the **L**,
37:14 you will know that I, the **L**,
37:14 I have done it, declares the **L**.'"
37:15 The **L** spoke his word to me
37:19 is what the Almighty **L** says:
37:21 is what the Almighty **L** says:
37:28 nations will know that I, the **L**,
38:1 The **L** spoke his word to me.
38:3 is what the Almighty **L** says:
38:10 is what the Almighty **L** says:
38:14 is what the Almighty **L** says:
38:17 is what the Almighty **L** says:
38:18 declares the Almighty **L**.
38:21 declares the Almighty **L**.
38:23 will know that I am the **L**.'"
39:1 ⌊The **L** said,⌋ "Son of man,
39:1 is what the Almighty **L** says:
39:5 declares the Almighty **L**.
39:6 they will know that I am the **L**.
39:7 will know that I am the **L**,
39:8 declares the Almighty **L**.
39:10 declares the Almighty **L**.
39:13 declares the Almighty **L**.
39:17 is what the Almighty **L** says:
39:20 declares the Almighty **L**.'
39:22 know that I am the **L** their God.
39:25 is what the Almighty **L** says:
39:28 know that I am the **L** their God.
39:29 declares the Almighty **L**."
40:46 near the **L** and serve him."
41:22 that is in the presence of the **L**."
42:13 who come near the **L** eat
43:18 is what the Almighty **L** says:
43:20 and make peace with the **L**.
43:24 Offer them to the **L**.
43:24 them as burnt offerings to the **L**
43:26 make peace with the **L** at
43:27 declares the Almighty **L**."
44:2 The **L** said to me, "This gate
44:2 through it because the **L** God
44:3 food in the presence of the **L**.
44:5 The **L** said to me, "Son of man,
44:6 is what the Almighty **L** says:
44:9 is what the Almighty **L** says:
44:12 for their sins, declares the **L**.
44:15 declares the Almighty **L**.
44:27 declares the Almighty **L**.
44:29 is devoted to the **L** will belong

Eze 45:1 and 35,000 feet wide for the **L**.
45:4 who come near to serve the **L**.
45:9 is what the Almighty **L** says:
45:9 declares the Almighty **L**.
45:13 you must give to the **L**:
45:15 to make peace with the **L**,
45:15 declares the Almighty **L**.
45:17 to make peace with the **L**
45:18 is what the Almighty **L** says:
45:20 peace with the **L** for the temple.
45:23 prepare burnt offerings for the **L**
46:1 is what the Almighty **L** says:
46:3 in the presence of the **L**
46:4 The prince must offer to the **L**
46:12 or a fellowship offering to the **L**,
46:13 day as a burnt offering to the **L**.
46:14 offering dedicated to the **L**.
46:16 is what the Almighty **L** says:
47:13 is what the Almighty **L** says:
47:23 declares the Almighty **L**.
48:8 gift for the **L** will border Judah
48:9 that you set aside for the **L** will
48:20 as a special gift to the **L** along
48:29 declares the Almighty **L**.
48:35 name will be: The **L** Is There.
Dan 1:2 The **L** handed King Jehoiakim
2:47 of gods, the **L** over kings.
5:23 greater than the **L** of Heaven.
9:2 The **L** had told the prophet
9:3 So I turned to the **L** God and
9:4 I prayed to the **L** my God.
9:4 I confessed and said, "**L**,
9:7 You, **L**, are righteous. But we —
9:8 we have sinned against you, **L**.
9:9 "But you, **L** our God,
9:13 **L** our God, we never tried to
9:14 **L** our God, you are righteous in
9:15 "**L** our God, you brought your
9:16 **L**, since you are very righteous,
9:17 For your own sake, **L**,
9:19 Listen to us, **L**. Forgive us, Lord.
9:19 Forgive us, **L**. Pay attention,
9:20 in front of the **L** my God.
Hos 1:1 The **L** spoke his word to
1:2 When the **L** first spoke to
1:2 spoke to Hosea, the **L** told him,
1:2 and abandoned the **L**."
1:4 The **L** told Hosea, "Name him
1:6 The **L** told Hosea, "Name her
1:7 because I am the **L** their God.
1:9 The **L** said, "Name him Lo
2:13 She forgot me," declares the **L**.
2:16 her husband," declares the **L**.
2:20 Then you will know the **L**.
2:21 ⌊prayers⌋," declares the **L**.
3:1 Then the **L** told me,
3:1 Love her as I, the **L**,
3:5 turn and look to the **L** their God
3:5 will come trembling to the **L**
4:1 Listen to the word of the **L**,
4:1 The **L** has brought these
4:10 They have abandoned the **L**.
4:15 take the oath, 'As the **L** lives ...'
4:16 How can the **L** feed them like
5:4 and they don't know the **L**.
5:6 their cattle to search for the **L**,
5:7 have been unfaithful to the **L**,
6:1 Let's return to the **L**.
6:3 Let's learn about the **L**.
6:3 Let's get to know the **L**.
7:10 you don't turn to the **L** your God
8:13 meat of sacrifices, but I, the **L**,
9:4 pour wine offerings to the **L**,
9:10 ⌊The **L** said,⌋ "When I found
9:14 **L**, give them what they
10:3 because we didn't fear the **L**.
10:12 It's time to seek the **L**!
11:11 own homes," declares the **L**.
12:2 The **L** brings charges against
12:5 The **L** is the God of Armies.
12:5 The **L** is the name by which he
12:7 ⌊The **L** says,⌋ "The merchants
12:9 I am the **L** your God.
12:13 The **L** used a prophet to bring
12:14 of Ephraim made the **L** bitter.
12:14 The **L** will pay them back for

Hos 13:4 "I am the **L** your God.
14:1 Israel, return to the **L** your God.
14:2 Return to the **L**, and say these
14:4 ⌊The **L** says,⌋ "I will cure them
Joe 1:1 This is what the **L** said to Joel,
1:14 to the temple of the **L** your God,
1:14 and cry to the **L** for help.
1:15 The day of the **L** is near,
1:19 O **L**, I cry to you for help!
2:1 the day of the **L** is coming.
2:11 The **L** shouts out orders to his
2:11 The day of the **L** is extremely
2:12 "But even now," declares the **L**,
2:13 Return to the **L** your God.
2:14 offerings to the **L** your God.
2:17 The priests who serve the **L**
2:17 say, "Spare your people, O **L**.
2:18 Then the **L** became concerned
2:19 The **L** said to his people,
2:21 The **L** has done great things!
2:23 and find joy in the **L** your God.
2:23 The **L** has given you the
2:26 the name of the **L** your God,
2:27 I am the **L** your God,
2:31 terrifying day of the **L** comes."
2:32 calls on the name of the **L** will
2:32 will be those whom the **L** calls,
2:32 as the **L** has promised.
3:8 The **L** has spoken.
3:11 O **L**, bring your soldiers.
3:14 The day of the **L** is near in the
3:16 The **L** will roar from Zion,
3:16 The **L** will be a refuge for his
3:17 know that I am the **L** your God.
3:21 The **L** lives in Zion!
Amo 1:2 He said: The **L** roars from Zion,
1:3 This is what the **L** says:
1:5 The **L** has said this.
1:6 This is what the **L** says:
1:8 The Almighty **L** has said this.
1:9 This is what the **L** says:
1:11 This is what the **L** says:
1:13 This is what the **L** says:
1:15 The **L** has said this.
2:1 This is what the **L** says:
2:3 The **L** has said this.
2:4 This is what the **L** says:
2:6 This is what the **L** says:
2:11 The **L** has declared this.
2:16 The **L** has declared this.
3:1 to this message which I, the **L**,
3:6 hasn't the **L** done it?
3:7 Certainly, the Almighty **L**
3:8 The Almighty **L** has spoken.
3:10 do what is right, declares the **L**.
3:11 is what the Almighty **L** says:
3:12 This is what the **L** says:
3:13 declares the Almighty **L**,
3:15 be demolished, declares the **L**.
4:2 The Almighty **L** has taken an
4:3 The **L** declares this.
4:5 The Almighty **L** declares this.
4:6 return to me, declares the **L**.
4:8 return to me, declares the **L**.
4:9 return to me, declares the **L**.
4:10 return to me, declares the **L**.
4:11 return to me, declares the **L**.
4:13 name is the **L** God of Armies.
5:3 is what the Almighty **L** says:
5:4 This is what the **L** says to the
5:6 Search for the **L** and live!
5:8 His name is the **L**.
5:14 Then the **L** God of Armies will
5:15 Maybe the **L** God of Armies
5:16 This is what the **L**,
5:17 The **L** has said this.
5:18 who long for the day of the **L**!
5:18 The day of the **L** is one of
5:20 The day of the **L** brings
5:27 beyond Damascus, says the **L**,
6:8 The Almighty **L** has sworn an
6:8 The **L** God of Armies declares:
6:10 mention the name of the **L**!"
6:11 The **L** is going to give the
6:14 declares the **L** God of the
7:1 the Almighty **L** showed me:

Amo 7:2 "Almighty **L**, please forgive us!
7:3 The **L** changed his plans about
7:3 won't happen," the **L** said.
7:4 the Almighty **L** showed me:
7:4 The Almighty **L** was calling for
7:5 Then I said, "Almighty **L**,
7:6 The **L** changed his plans about
7:6 the Almighty **L** said.
7:7 The **L** was standing by a wall
7:8 Then the **L** said, "I'm going to
7:15 But the **L** took me away from
7:16 listen to the word of the **L**:
7:17 this is what the **L** says:
8:1 the Almighty **L** showed me:
8:2 Then the **L** said to me,
8:3 declares the Almighty **L**.
8:7 The **L** has sworn an oath by
8:9 declares the Almighty **L**,
8:11 declares the Almighty **L**,
8:11 of hearing the words of the **L**.
8:12 searching for the word of the **L**.
9:1 I saw the **L** standing by the
9:5 The Almighty **L** of Armies
9:6 of the earth — His name is the **L**
9:7 people from Sudan, says the **L**.
9:8 I, the Almighty **L**, have my
9:8 of Jacob, declares the **L**.
9:12 my authority, declares the **L**,
9:13 going to come, declares the **L**,
9:15 says the **L** your God.
Oba 1:1 This is what the Almighty **L**
1:1 heard a message from the **L**.
1:4 from there," declares the **L**.
1:8 mountain," declares the **L**.
1:15 "The day of the **L** is near for all
1:18 The **L** has spoken.
1:21 kingdom will belong to the **L**."
Jnh 1:1 The **L** spoke his word to Jonah,
1:3 to run away from the **L** by going
1:3 to get away from the **L**.
1:4 The **L** sent a violent wind over
1:9 I worship the **L**, the God of
1:10 was running away from the **L**,
1:14 So they cried to the **L** for help:
1:14 the LORD for help: "Please, **L**,
1:14 you, **L**, do whatever you want."
1:16 The men were terrified of the **L**.
1:16 and made vows to the **L**.
1:17 The **L** sent a big fish to
2:1 Jonah prayed to the **L** his God.
2:2 I called to the **L** in my distress,
2:6 back from the pit, O **L**, my God.
2:7 I remembered the **L**.
2:9 Victory belongs to the **L**!"
2:10 Then the **L** spoke to the fish,
3:1 Then the **L** spoke his word to
3:3 to Nineveh as the **L** told him.
4:2 So he prayed to the **L**,
4:2 So he prayed to the LORD, "**L**,
4:3 So now, **L**, take my life.
4:4 The **L** asked, "What right do
4:6 The **L** God made a plant grow
4:10 The **L** replied, "This plant grew
Mic 1:1 The **L** spoke his word to Micah,
1:2 The Almighty **L** will be a
1:2 The **L** will be a witness from
1:3 The **L** is going to come from
1:12 From the **L** disaster will come
2:3 So this is what the **L** says:
2:4 The **L** gives our people's
2:7 Has the Spirit of the **L** become
2:13 (The **L**) will open the way and
2:13 The **L** will lead the people.
3:4 Then you will cry to the **L**,
3:5 This is what the **L** says about
3:11 But they rely on the **L** when
3:11 say, "After all, the **L** is with us.
4:2 go to the mountain of the **L**,
4:2 The word of the **L** will go out
4:4 The **L** of Armies has spoken.
4:5 name of the **L** our God forever.
4:6 day comes," declares the **L**,
4:7 The **L** will rule them on Mount
4:10 There the **L** will reclaim you
4:12 don't know the thoughts of the **L**
4:13 will claim their loot for the **L**,
Mic 4:13 their wealth for the **L** of the
5:3 That is why the **L** will abandon
5:4 with the strength of the **L**,
5:4 name of the **L** his God.
5:7 people like dew from the **L**,
5:10 day comes," declares the **L**,
6:1 listen to what the **L** is saying,
6:2 The **L** has filed a lawsuit
6:5 know the victories of the **L**."
6:7 Will the **L** be pleased with
6:8 You mortals, the **L** has told you
6:8 This is what the **L** requires
6:9 The voice of the **L** calls out to
7:7 I will look to the **L**.
7:8 sit in the dark, the **L** is my light.
7:9 I have sinned against the **L**.
7:10 "Where is the **L** your God?"
7:17 presence in fear, O **L** our God.
Nah 1:1 from the **L** about Nineveh.
1:2 The **L** takes revenge.
1:2 The **L** takes revenge and is full
1:2 The **L** takes revenge against
1:3 The **L** is patient and has great
1:3 The **L** will never let the guilty
1:7 The **L** is good. (He is) a
1:9 What do you think about the **L**?
1:11 evil against the **L** sets out.
1:12 This is what the **L** says:
1:14 The **L** has given this command
2:2 The **L** will restore Jacob's glory
2:7 The **L** has determined:
2:13 declares the **L** of Armies.
3:5 declares the **L** of Armies.
Hab 1:2 How long, O **L**, am I to cry for
1:12 O **L**, my God, my Holy One?
1:12 O **L**, you have appointed the
2:2 Then the **L** answered me,
2:13 Isn't it from the **L** of Armies that
2:20 The **L** is in his holy temple.
3:2 **L**, I have heard the report about
3:2 **L**, I fear your work. In the
3:8 The **L** is not angry with the
3:18 I will be happy with the **L**.
3:19 The **L** Almighty is my strength.
Zep 1:1 This is the word that the **L**
1:1 The **L** spoke his word in the
1:2 an end to it," declares the **L**.
1:3 of the earth," declares the **L**.
1:5 to the **L** while also swearing
1:6 away from following the **L**
1:6 those who no longer seek the **L**
1:7 the presence of the Almighty **L**,
1:7 the day of the **L** is near.
1:7 The **L** has prepared a sacrifice.
1:10 from the hills," declares the **L**.
1:12 who think that the **L** won't do
1:14 frightening day of the **L** is near.
1:14 out bitterly on the day of the **L**.
1:17 have sinned against the **L**."
2:3 Search for the **L**, all you
2:5 The word of the **L** is against
2:7 The **L** their God will take care
2:9 declares the **L** of Armies,
2:10 the people who belong to the **L**
2:11 The **L** will terrify them,
2:13 The **L** will use his power
2:14 because the **L** will expose the
3:2 It does not trust the **L**.
3:5 The righteous **L** is in that city.
3:8 The **L** declares, "Just wait!
3:9 pure lips to worship the **L**
3:12 refuge in the name of the **L**.
3:15 The **L** has reversed the
3:15 The king of Israel, the **L**,
3:17 The **L** your God is with you.
3:20 before your eyes," says the **L**.
Hag 1:1 the **L** spoke his word through
1:2 "This is what the **L** of Armies
1:2 to rebuild the house of the **L**."
1:3 Then the **L** spoke his word
1:5 Now, this is what the **L** of
1:7 This is what the **L** of Armies
1:8 be honored," declares the **L**.
1:9 declares the **L** of Armies.
1:12 obeyed the **L** their God.
1:12 because the **L** their God had
Hag 1:12 the people feared the **L**.
1:13 the messenger of the **L** who
1:13 "I am with you, declares the **L**."
1:14 The **L** inspired them (to rebuild
1:14 on the house of the **L** of Armies,
2:1 the **L** spoke his word through
2:4 be strong," declares the **L**.
2:4 land, be strong," declares the **L**.
2:4 declares the **L** of Armies.
2:6 "This is what the **L** of Armies
2:7 says the **L** of Armies.
2:8 declares the **L** of Armies.
2:9 declares the **L** of Armies.
2:9 declares the **L** of Armies."
2:10 the **L** spoke his word to the
2:11 "This is what the **L** of Armies
2:14 is this nation, declares the **L**.
2:15 another in the temple of the **L**.
2:17 back to me, declares the **L**.
2:18 of the house of the **L** was laid.
2:20 The **L** spoke his word to
2:23 declares the **L** of Armies,
2:23 of Shealtiel), declares the **L**.
2:23 declares the **L** of Armies.'"
Zec 1:1 the **L** spoke his word to the
1:2 "The **L** was very angry with
1:3 'This is what the **L** of Armies
1:3 declares the **L** of Armies,
1:3 says the **L** of Armies.'
1:4 'This is what the **L** of Armies
1:4 attention to me, declares the **L**.
1:6 'The **L** of Armies has done to
1:7 the **L** spoke his word to the
1:10 "They're the horses the **L** has
1:11 of the **L** standing among
1:12 the Messenger of the **L** said,
1:12 of the LORD said, "**L** of Armies,
1:13 The **L** responded to the angel
1:14 This is what the **L** of Armies
1:16 This is what the **L** of Armies
1:16 declares the **L** of Armies.
1:17 This is what the **L** of Armies
1:17 The **L** will again comfort Zion
1:20 Then the **L** showed me four
2:5 of fire around it, declares the **L**.
2:6 of the north, declares the **L**.
2:8 This is what the **L** of Armies
2:9 Then you will know that the **L**
2:10 live among you, declares the **L**.
2:11 many nations will join the **L**
2:11 Then you will know that the **L**
2:12 The **L** will claim Judah as his
2:13 silent in the presence of the **L**.
3:1 front of the Messenger of the **L**.
3:2 The **L** said to Satan,
3:2 "I, the **L**, silence you, Satan! I,
3:2 I, the **L**, who has chosen
3:5 of the **L** was standing there.
3:6 of the **L** advised Joshua,
3:7 "This is what the **L** of Armies
3:9 declares the **L** of Armies.
3:10 declares the **L** of Armies,
4:6 "This is the word the **L** spoke
4:6 says the **L** of Armies.
4:8 Then the **L** spoke his word to
4:9 Then you will know that the **L**
4:10 (These seven eyes of the **L**
4:14 who are standing beside the **L**
5:4 declares the **L** of Armies,
6:5 in the presence of the **L**
6:9 The **L** spoke his word to me.
6:12 'This is what the **L** of Armies
6:15 Then you will know the **L** of
6:15 the **L** your God completely.'"
7:1 the **L** spoke his word to
7:2 men to ask the **L** for a blessing.
7:3 priests from the house of the **L**
7:4 Then the **L** of Armies spoke his
7:7 that the **L** announced through
7:8 Then the **L** spoke his word to
7:9 "This is what the **L** of Armies
7:12 the words that the **L** of Armies
7:12 So the **L** of Armies became
7:13 says the **L** of Armies.
8:1 The **L** of Armies spoke his
8:2 This is what the **L** of Armies

Hag 8:3 This is what the L says:
8:3 The mountain of the L of
8:4 This is what the L of Armies
8:6 This is what the L of Armies
8:6 declares the L of Armies.
8:7 This is what the L of Armies
8:9 This is what the L of Armies
8:9 for the house of the L
8:11 declares the L of Armies.
8:14 This is what the L of Armies
8:14 declares the L of Armies,
8:17 all these things, declares the L.
8:18 The L of Armies spoke his
8:19 This is what the L of Armies
8:20 This is what the L of Armies
8:21 a habit of going to ask the L
8:21 and to seek the L of Armies.
8:22 nations will come to seek the L
8:22 and to ask the L for a blessing.
8:23 This is what the L of Armies
9:1 The word of the L is against
9:2 the tribes of Israel are on the L.)
9:4 The L will take away its
9:14 The L will appear over them,
9:14 The Almighty L will blow the
9:15 The L of Armies will defend
9:16 On that day the L their God will
10:1 Ask the L for rain in the
10:1 The L makes thunderstorms.
10:3 The L of Armies takes care of
10:5 They will fight because the L
10:6 because I am the L their God,
10:7 hearts will find joy in the L.
10:11 The L will pass through a sea
10:12 "I will strengthen them in the L.
10:12 in his name," declares the L.
11:4 This is what the L my God
11:5 them will say, "Praise the L!
11:6 The L declares, "I will no
11:11 that it was the word of the L.
11:13 The L told me, "Give it to the
11:13 the potter at the house of the L.
11:15 Then the L said to me,
12:1 the word of the L about Israel.
12:1 The L — who spread out the
12:4 The L declares, "On that day I
12:5 because of the L of Armies,
12:7 "The L will save Judah's tents
12:8 On that day the L will defend
12:8 of the L ahead of them.
13:1 (The L declares,)
13:2 declares the L of Armies,
13:3 lies in the name of the L.' Then
13:7 declares the L of Armies.
13:8 The L declares, Yet, one-third
13:9 'The L is our God.'"
14:1 A day is going to come for the L
14:3 Then the L will go out and fight
14:5 The L my God will come,
14:7 day — a day known to the L —
14:9 The L will be king over all the
14:9 On that day the L will be the
14:9 the LORD will be the only L
14:12 This will be the plague the L
14:13 from the L will spread among
14:16 the king, the L of Armies,
14:17 the king, the L of Armies,
14:18 The plague the L uses to strike
14:20 On that day "Holy to the L" will
14:20 pots in the house of the L will
14:21 will be holy to the L of Armies.
14:21 in the house of the L of Armies.
Mal 1:1 The L spoke his word to Israel
1:2 "I loved you," says the L.
1:2 declares the L. "I loved Jacob,
1:4 "Yet, this is what the L of
1:4 whom the L is always angry.'
1:5 borders of Israel the L is great.'
1:6 "This is what the L of Armies
1:8 asks the L of Armies.
1:9 asks the L of Armies.
1:10 says the L of Armies,
1:11 says the L of Armies.
1:13 says the L of Armies.
1:13 them from you?" asks the L.
1:14 ones to the L instead.

Mal 1:14 says the L of Armies.
2:2 says the L of Armies,
2:4 says the L of Armies.
2:7 messenger for the L of Armies,
2:8 says the L of Armies.
2:11 the holy place that the L loves
2:12 May the L exclude anyone
2:12 offerings to the L of Armies.
2:14 It is because the L is a witness
2:16 says the L God of Israel.
2:16 says the L of Armies.
2:17 have tried the patience of the L
2:17 is considered good by the L.
3:1 Then the L you are looking for
3:1 says the L of Armies.
3:3 acceptable offerings to the L.
3:4 will be pleasing to the L as
3:5 says the L of Armies.
3:6 "I, the L, never change. That is
3:7 says the L of Armies.
3:10 says the L of Armies.
3:11 says the L of Armies.
3:12 says the L of Armies.
3:13 words against me," says the L.
3:16 Then those who feared the L
3:16 and the L paid attention and
3:16 to those who feared the L
3:17 says the L of Armies.
4:1 says the L of Armies.
4:3 says the L of Armies.
4:5 terrifying day of the L comes.
Mat 1:20 an angel of the L appeared
1:22 what the L had spoken through
1:24 he did what the angel of the L
2:13 an angel of the L appeared to
2:15 What the L had spoken through
2:19 an angel of the L appeared in a
3:3 'Prepare the way for the L!
4:7 'Never tempt the L your God.'"
4:10 Scripture says, 'Worship the L
5:33 but give to the L what you
7:21 who says to me, 'L, Lord!'
7:21 who says to me, 'Lord, L!' will
7:22 say to me on that day, 'L, Lord,
7:22 say to me on that day, 'Lord, L,
8:25 they woke him up, saying, "L!
9:28 "Yes, L," they answered.
9:38 So ask the L who gives this
11:25 L of heaven and earth,
14:28 Peter answered, "L,
14:30 He shouted, "L, save me!"
15:22 mercy on me, L, Son of David!
15:25 down, and said, "L, help me!"
15:27 She said, "You're right, L.
16:22 He said, "Heaven forbid, L!
17:4 Peter said to Jesus, "L,
18:21 to Jesus and asked him, "L,
20:30 they shouted, "L, Son of David,
20:31 even louder, "L, Son of David,
20:33 They told him, "L, we want you
21:3 tell him that the L needs them.
21:9 comes in the name of the L!
21:42 The L is responsible for this,
22:37 "'Love the L your God with all
22:43 by the Spirit, call him L?
22:44 'The L said to my Lord,
22:44 'The Lord said to my L,
22:45 If David calls him L,
23:39 comes in the name of the L!'"
24:42 on what day your L will return.
25:37 approval will reply to him, 'L,
25:44 "They, too, will ask, 'L,
26:22 don't mean me, do you, L?"
27:10 as the L had directed me."
28:2 An angel of the L had come
Mar 1:3 'Prepare the way for the L!
5:19 and tell them how much the L
7:28 She answered him, "L,
11:3 say that the L needs it.
11:9 comes in the name of the L!
12:11 The L has done this,
12:29 the L our God is the only Lord.
12:29 the Lord our God is the only L.
12:30 So love the L your God with all
12:36 'The L said to my Lord:
12:36 'The Lord said to my L:

Mar 12:37 David calls him L.
13:20 If the L does not reduce that
16:19 the L was taken to heaven,
16:20 The L worked with them.
Luk 1:11 angel of the L appeared to him.
1:15 As far as the L is concerned,
1:16 Israel back to the L their God.
1:17 He will go ahead of the L with
1:17 prepare the people for their L."
1:25 "The L has done this for me
1:28 "You are favored by the L!
1:28 The L is with you."
1:32 The L God will give him the
1:43 mother of my L is visiting me.
1:45 that the L would keep his
1:58 heard that the L had been very
1:66 clear that the L was with him.
1:68 "Praise the L God of Israel!
1:76 You will go ahead of the L to
2:9 An angel from the L suddenly
2:9 The glory of the L filled the
2:11 Today your Savior, Christ the L,
2:15 and see what the L has told
2:22 Jesus to present him to the L.
2:23 to be set apart as holy to the L."
2:26 whom the L would send.
2:29 "Now, L, you are allowing your
3:4 'Prepare the way for the L!
4:8 'Worship the L your God and
4:12 'Never tempt the L your God.'"
4:18 "The Spirit of the L is with me.
5:8 Jesus and said, "Leave me, L!
5:17 had the power of the L to heal.
6:46 "Why do you call me L but
7:13 When the L saw her,
7:19 and sent them to ask the L,
9:54 They asked, "L, do you want
10:1 After this, the L appointed 70
10:2 So ask the L who gives this
10:17 They said, "L, even demons
10:21 L of heaven and earth,
10:27 He answered, "'Love the L your
10:40 So she asked, "L, don't you
10:41 The L answered her,
11:1 of his disciples said to him, "L,
11:39 The L said to him,
12:41 Peter asked, "L, did you use
12:42 The L asked, "Who, then,
13:15 The L said, "You hypocrites!
13:35 comes in the name of the L!'"
17:5 Then the apostles said to the L,
17:6 The L said, "If you have faith
17:37 They asked him, "Where, L?"
18:6 The L added, "Pay attention to
18:41 The blind man said, "L,
19:8 stood up and said to the L,
19:8 up and said to the Lord, "L,
19:31 say that the L needs it."
19:34 answered, "The L needs it."
19:38 comes in the name of the L!
20:37 He says that the L is the God
20:42 'The L said to my Lord,
20:42 'The Lord said to my L,
20:44 David calls him L.
22:31 (Then the L said,)
22:33 But Peter said to him, "L,
22:38 The disciples said, "L,
22:49 So they asked him, "L,
22:61 Then the L turned and looked
22:61 what the L had said:
24:3 find the body of the L Jesus.
24:34 They were saying, "The L has
Jon 1:23 the way for the L straight,'
6:23 bread after the L gave thanks.
6:68 Peter answered Jesus, "L,
9:38 Jesus and said, "I believe, L."
11:2 who poured perfume on the L
11:3 "L, your close friend is sick."
11:12 His disciples said to him, "L,
11:21 Martha told Jesus, "L,
11:27 Martha said to him, "Yes, L,
11:32 said, "L, if you had been here,
11:34 They answered him, "L,
11:39 man's sister, told Jesus, "L,
12:13 comes in the name of the L,
12:38 prophet Isaiah came true: "L,

Jon 13:6 Peter, Peter asked him, "L,
13:9 Simon Peter said to Jesus, "L,
13:13 You call me teacher and L,
13:14 So if I, your L and teacher,
13:25 disciple asked, "L, who is it?"
13:36 Simon Peter asked him, "L,
13:37 Peter said to Jesus, "L,
14:5 Thomas said to him, "L,
14:8 Philip said to Jesus, "L,
14:22 (not Iscariot) asked Jesus, "L,
20:2 "They have removed the L from
20:13 "They have removed my L,
20:18 "I have seen the L."
20:20 were glad to see the L.
20:25 "We've seen the L."
20:28 "My L and my God!"
21:7 loved said to Peter, "It's the L."
21:7 Peter heard that it was the L,
21:12 They knew he was the L.
21:15 Peter answered him, "Yes, L,
21:16 Peter answered him "Yes, L,
21:17 So Peter said to him, "L,
21:20 at the supper and asked, "L,
21:21 Jesus, "L, what about him?"
Act 1:6 together, they asked him, "L,
1:21 that the L Jesus was among
1:24 Then they prayed, "L,
2:20 terrifying day of the L comes.
2:21 name of the L will be saved.'
2:25 'I always see the L in front of
2:34 'The L said to my Lord,
2:34 'The Lord said to my L,
2:36 both L and Christ."
2:39 who worships the L our God."
2:47 Every day the L saved people,
3:20 when the L will refresh you.
3:22 "Moses said, 'The L your God
4:26 plans together against the L
4:29 "L, pay attention to their threats
4:33 that the L Jesus had come
5:14 ever began to believe in the L.
5:19 But at night an angel from the L
7:31 the voice of the L said to him,
7:33 The L told him, 'Take off your
7:49 'The L says, "Heaven is my
7:59 "L Jesus, welcome my spirit."
7:60 he knelt down and shouted, "L,
8:16 in the name of the L Jesus.)
8:22 and ask the L if he will forgive
8:24 Simon answered, "Pray to the L
8:25 about the message of the L,
8:26 An angel from the L said to
8:39 the Spirit of the L suddenly
9:10 The L said to him in a vision,
9:10 Ananias answered, "Yes, L."
9:11 The L told him, "Get up! Go to
9:13 Ananias replied, "L,
9:15 The L told Ananias,
9:17 "Brother Saul, the L Jesus,
9:27 how Saul had seen the L
9:27 road and that the L had spoken
9:28 power and authority of the L.
9:31 people lived in the fear of the L
9:35 and turned to the L in faith.
9:42 many people believed in the L.
10:14 answered, "I can't do that, L!
10:33 the L has ordered you
10:36 Jesus Christ is everyone's L.
11:8 I answered, 'I can't do that, L!
11:16 that the L had said,
11:17 believed in the L Jesus Christ.
11:20 about the L Jesus to Greeks.
11:21 believed and turned to the L.
11:23 solidly committed to the L.
11:24 A large crowd believed in the L.
12:7 Suddenly, an angel from the L
12:11 "Now I'm sure that the L sent
12:17 them how the L had taken him
12:23 an angel from the L killed
13:2 worshiping the L and fasting,
13:10 the way the L wants people
13:11 The L is against you now.
13:47 The L gave us the following
13:49 The word of the L spread
14:3 They spoke boldly about the L,
14:23 entrusted the leaders to the L
Act 15:11 We certainly believe that the L
15:17 may search for the L,
15:17 for the Lord, declares the L.
15:26 dedicated their lives to our L,
16:14 because the L made her willing
16:15 that I believe in the L,
16:31 "Believe in the L Jesus,
17:24 and everything in it is the L
18:8 whole family believed in the L.
18:9 One night the L said to Paul in
19:5 in the name of the L Jesus.
19:10 of Asia heard the word of the L.
19:13 to use the name of the L Jesus
19:17 for the name of the L Jesus
19:20 word of the L was spreading
20:19 I humbly served the L,
20:19 I served the L during the
20:21 and to believe in our L Jesus.
20:24 I received from the L Jesus —
20:35 words that the L Jesus said,
21:13 die there for the sake of the L,
22:10 do you want me to do, L?' "The
22:10 "The L told me, 'Get up!
22:18 and saw the L. He told me,
22:19 "I said, 'L, people here know
22:21 "But the L told me,
23:11 The L stood near Paul the next
26:15 "The L answered, 'I am Jesus,
28:31 boldly about the L Jesus Christ.
Rom 1:3 our L Jesus Christ.
1:7 and the L Jesus Christ are
4:8 the L never considers sinful."
4:24 Jesus, our L, back to life.
4:25 Jesus, our L, was handed over
5:1 of what our L Jesus Christ has
5:11 In addition, our L Jesus Christ
5:21 because of Jesus Christ our L.
6:23 life found in Christ Jesus our L.
7:25 I thank God that our L Jesus
8:38 Christ Jesus our L shows us.
9:28 The L will carry out his
9:29 "If the L of Armies hadn't left us
10:9 If you declare that Jesus is L,
10:12 They all have the same L,
10:13 name of the L will be saved."
10:16 Isaiah asks, "L, who has
11:3 "L, they've killed your prophets
11:34 "Who knows how the L thinks?
11:35 Who gave the L something
11:35 which the L must pay back?
12:11 Use your energy to serve the L.
12:19 I will pay back, says the L."
13:14 live like the L Jesus Christ did,
14:4 The L will determine whether
14:4 the L makes him successful.
14:6 they observe it to honor the L.
14:6 they honor the L as they eat,
14:6 Vegetarians also honor the L
14:8 If we live, we honor the L,
14:8 and if we die, we honor the L.
14:8 we belong to the L.
14:9 to life so that he would be the L
14:11 certainly as I live, says the L,
14:14 The L Jesus has given me the
15:6 Father of our L Jesus Christ.
15:11 And again, "Praise the L,
15:30 I encourage you through our L
16:8 friend in the service of the L.
16:12 have worked hard for the L.
16:12 has worked very hard for the L.
16:18 are not serving Christ our L.
16:20 May the good will of our L
1Co 1:2 the name of our L Jesus Christ.
1:3 and the L Jesus Christ are
1:7 eagerly for our L Jesus Christ
1:8 the day of our L Jesus Christ.
1:9 his Son Jesus Christ our L.
1:10 the name of our L Jesus Christ
1:31 about what the L has done."
2:8 have crucified the L of glory.
2:16 known the mind of the L so that
3:5 Each did what the L gave him
3:20 Again Scripture says, "The L
4:4 the L who cross-examines me.
4:5 Wait until the L comes.
5:4 in the name of our L Jesus,
1Co 5:5 be saved on the day of the L.
6:11 the name of the L Jesus Christ
6:13 not for sexual sin but for the L,
6:13 and the L is for the body.
6:14 God raised the L, and by his
6:17 with the L becomes one spirit
7:10 along (not really I, but the L):
7:12 I (not the L) say to the rest of
7:17 life that the L gave him when
7:22 If the L called you when you
7:25 have any command from the L,
7:25 I'm a person to whom the L has
7:32 about the things of the L,
7:32 about how he can please the L.
7:35 the L without being distracted
8:6 There is only one L,
9:1 Haven't I seen Jesus our L?
9:1 the result of my work for the L?
9:14 In the same way, the L has
10:9 We shouldn't put the L to the
10:21 participate at the table of the L
10:22 trying to make the L jealous?
11:11 Yet, as believers in the L,
11:23 what I had received from the L.
11:23 the L Jesus took bread
11:32 But when the L judges us,
12:3 No one can say, "Jesus is L,"
12:5 and yet the same L is served.
14:21 not listen to me, says the L."
14:37 you is what the L commands.
15:31 Jesus our L has given me:
15:57 through our L Jesus Christ.
15:58 in the work you do for the L.
15:58 do for the L is not pointless.
16:7 but if the L lets me,
16:22 If anyone doesn't love the L,
16:22 him be cursed! Our L, come!
16:23 May the good will of the L
2Co 1:2 and the L Jesus Christ are
1:3 Father of our L Jesus Christ!
1:14 on the day of our L Jesus.
2:12 the L gave me an opportunity to
3:16 a person turns to the L,
3:17 This L is the Spirit.
3:18 This comes from the L,
4:5 is about Jesus Christ as the L.
4:14 who brought the L Jesus back
5:6 we are living away from the L.
5:8 this body and to live with the L.
5:11 what it means to fear the L,
6:17 The L says, "Get away from
6:18 The L Almighty says,
8:5 they gave themselves to the L
8:9 kindness of our L Jesus Christ.
8:19 a way that brings glory to the L
8:21 not only in the sight of the L,
10:8 authority which the L gave us,
10:8 The L gave us this authority to
10:17 about what the L has done."
10:18 but the person whom the L
11:17 say if I were speaking for the L.
11:31 God and Father of the L Jesus,
12:1 and revelations from the L.
12:8 I begged the L three times to
13:10 authority that the L gave me.
13:10 The L gave us this authority to
13:13 May the L Jesus Christ's good
Gal 1:3 Father and our L Jesus Christ!
5:10 The L gives me confidence
6:14 the cross of our L Jesus Christ.
6:18 May the good will of our L
Eph 1:2 and the L Jesus Christ are
1:3 Father of our L Jesus Christ!
1:15 about your faith in the L Jesus
1:17 the God of our L Jesus Christ,
2:21 into a holy temple in the L.
3:11 out through Christ Jesus our L.
4:1 I, a prisoner in the L,
4:5 There is one L, one faith,
5:8 but now the L has filled you
5:10 which things please the L.
5:17 but understand what the L
5:19 music to the L with your hearts.
5:20 the name of our L Jesus Christ.
6:10 receive your power from the L
6:23 May God the Father and the L

Eph 6:24 love for our **L** Jesus Christ.
Php 1:2 and the **L** Jesus Christ are
1:14 the **L** has given most of our
2:11 confess that Jesus Christ is **L**
2:19 I hope that the **L** Jesus will
2:24 But the **L** gives me confidence
3:1 and sisters, be joyful in the **L**.
3:8 off knowing Christ Jesus my **L**.
3:20 We look forward to the **L** Jesus
4:1 relationship with the **L** firm!
4:2 the attitude the **L** wants them
4:4 Always be joyful in the **L**!
4:5 you are. The **L** is near.
4:10 The **L** has filled me with joy
4:23 May the good will of our **L**
Col 1:3 Father of our **L** Jesus Christ,
1:10 that prove you belong to the **L**.
2:6 received Christ Jesus the **L**,
3:13 Forgive as the **L** forgave you.
3:17 in the name of the **L** Jesus,
3:20 This is pleasing to the **L**.
1Th 1:1 Father and the **L** Jesus Christ.
1:3 and your confidence in our **L**
1:6 You imitated us and the **L**.
2:15 who killed the **L** Jesus and the
2:19 presence of our **L** Jesus when
3:8 relationship with the **L** firm.
3:11 and the **L** Jesus will guide
3:12 We also pray that the **L** will
3:13 when our **L** Jesus comes
4:1 because of the **L** Jesus we ask
4:2 gave you through the **L** Jesus.
4:6 The **L** is the one who punishes
4:15 telling you what the **L** taught.
4:15 when the **L** comes will not
4:16 The **L** will come from heaven
4:17 in the clouds to meet the **L**
4:17 we will always be with the **L**.
5:2 the day of the **L** will come like
5:9 through our **L** Jesus Christ.
5:23 our **L** Jesus Christ comes.
5:28 The good will of our **L** Jesus
2Th 1:1 Father and the **L** Jesus Christ.
1:2 and the **L** Jesus Christ are
1:7 He will do this when the **L**
1:8 Good News about our **L** Jesus.
1:12 That way the name of our **L**
1:12 of Jesus Christ, our God and **L**,
2:1 our **L** Jesus Christ's coming
2:2 day of the **L** has already come.
2:8 and the **L** Jesus will destroy
2:8 When the **L** Jesus comes,
2:13 You are loved by the **L** and we
2:14 the glory of our **L** Jesus Christ.
2:16 with our **L** Jesus Christ,
3:3 But the **L** is faithful and will
3:4 The **L** gives us confidence that
3:5 May the **L** direct your lives as
3:6 in the name of our **L** Jesus
3:12 people by the **L** Jesus Christ
3:16 May the **L** of peace give you
3:16 The **L** be with all of you.
3:18 The good will of our **L** Jesus
1Ti 1:2 Christ Jesus our **L** are yours!
1:12 I thank Christ Jesus our **L** that
1:14 Our **L** was very kind to me.
6:3 words of our **L** Jesus Christ
6:14 I insist that, until our **L** Jesus
6:15 the King of kings and **L** of lords.
2Ti 1:2 Father and Christ Jesus our **L**.
1:8 to tell others about our **L**
1:16 May the **L** be merciful to the
1:18 May the **L** grant that
2:7 The **L** will help you understand
2:19 "The **L** knows those who
2:19 and "Whoever worships the **L**
2:22 with those who worship the **L**
2:24 A servant of the **L** must not
3:11 and the **L** rescued me from all
4:8 The **L**, who is a fair judge,
4:14 The **L** will pay him back for
4:17 However, the **L** stood by me
4:18 The **L** will rescue me from all
4:22 The **L** be with you.
Phm 1:3 and the **L** Jesus Christ are
1:5 your faithfulness to the **L** Jesus

Phm 1:20 because we're brothers in the **L**,
1:25 The good will of our **L** Jesus
Heb 1:10 God also said, "**L**,
2:3 the **L** told this saving message.
7:14 Everyone knows that our **L**
7:21 God said about him, "The **L**
8:2 of the true tent set up by the **L**
8:8 days are coming, says the **L**,
8:9 so I ignored them, says the **L**.
8:10 after those days, says the **L**:
8:11 by saying, 'Know the **L**.' All
10:16 after those days, says the **L**:
10:25 see the day of the **L** coming.
10:30 "The **L** will judge his people."
12:5 when the **L** disciplines you.
12:6 The **L** disciplines everyone he
12:14 you will not see the **L**.
13:6 "The **L** is my helper.
13:20 of the sheep, our **L** Jesus,
Jas 1:1 God and of the **L** Jesus Christ.
1:7 to receive anything from the **L**.
2:1 our glorious **L** Jesus Christ by
3:9 we praise our **L** and Father.
4:15 "If the **L** wants us to,
5:4 The **L** of Armies has heard the
5:7 patient until the **L** comes again.
5:8 The **L** will soon be here.
5:10 spoke in the name of the **L**.
5:11 You saw that the **L** ended
5:11 the **L** is compassionate
5:14 olive oil in the name of the **L**.
5:15 and the **L** will cure them.)
1Pe 1:3 Father of our **L** Jesus Christ!
1:25 the word of the **L** lasts forever."
2:3 have tasted that the **L** is good!
2:13 governments to please the **L**.
3:12 The **L** confronts those who do
3:15 your lives to Christ as **L**.
2Pe 1:2 about Jesus, our God and **L**!
1:8 about our **L** Jesus Christ is
1:11 the eternal kingdom of our **L**
1:14 Our **L** Jesus Christ has made
1:16 coming of our **L** Jesus Christ,
2:1 They will deny the **L**,
2:9 Since the **L** did all this,
2:11 against them from the **L**.
2:20 People can know our **L** and
3:2 holy prophets and what the **L**
3:8 One day with the **L** is like a
3:9 The **L** isn't slow to do what he
3:10 The day of the **L** will come like
3:18 will and knowledge of our **L**
Jud 1:4 deny our only Master and **L**,
1:5 The **L** once saved his people
1:9 "May the **L** reprimand you!"
1:14 He said, "The **L** has come with
1:17 of our **L** Jesus Christ told
1:21 the mercy of our **L** Jesus Christ
1:25 through Jesus Christ our **L**.
Rev 1:8 A and the Z," says the **L** God,
4:8 holy is the **L** God Almighty,
4:11 "Our **L** and God, you deserve
11:4 presence of the **L** of the earth.
11:8 where their **L** was crucified.
11:15 become the kingdom of our **L**
11:17 thanks to you, **L** God Almighty,
14:13 believing in the **L** are blessed."
15:3 and amazing, **L** God Almighty.
15:4 **L**, who won't fear and praise
16:7 answer, "Yes, **L** God Almighty,
17:14 conquer them because he is **L**
18:8 because the **L** God,
19:6 The **L** our God, the Almighty,
19:16 King of Kings and **L** of Lords.
21:22 because the **L** God Almighty
22:5 because the **L** God will shine
22:6 The **L** God of the spirits of the
22:20 Amen! Come, **L** Jesus!
22:21 The good will of the **L** Jesus

LORD'S; Lord's (904)

Gen 4:16 Then Cain left the **L** presence
13:10 well-watered like the **L** garden
39:5 Therefore, the **L** blessing was
Exo 9:20 **L** warning brought their servants
9:21 **L** warning seriously left their

Exo 10:9 festival in the **L** honor.
12:11 It is the **L** Passover
12:14 festival in the **L** honor
12:27 sacrifice in the **L** honor.
12:41 years all the **L** people left Egypt
12:48 to celebrate the **L** Passover.
13:6 festival in the **L** honor
16:9 'Come into the **L** presence.
16:33 and put it in the **L** presence to
17:16 was lifted against the **L** throne,
24:3 told the people all the **L** words
24:4 wrote down all the **L** words.
24:7 took the Book of the **L** Promise
27:21 **L** presence from evening until
28:12 as a reminder in the **L** presence
28:29 reminder in the **L** presence.
28:30 he comes into the **L** presence.
28:30 **L** presence, Aaron will always
28:30 determining the **L** decisions
28:35 and goes out of the **L** presence
29:11 the bull in the **L** presence at
29:23 is in the **L** presence, take
29:25 aroma in the **L** presence,
29:42 ⌞made⌟ in the **L** presence at
30:8 constantly in the **L** presence
30:16 Israelites in the **L** presence that
32:5 will be a festival in the **L** honor.
32:26 "If you're on the **L** side, come
32:29 are ordained as the **L** priests.
33:7 was seeking the **L** will used
34:24 times a year to the **L** festivals
34:34 went into the **L** presence
39:1 the **L** instructions to Moses.
39:5 the **L** instructions to Moses.
39:7 the **L** instructions to Moses.
39:21 the **L** instructions to Moses.
39:26 the **L** instructions to Moses.
39:29 the **L** instructions to Moses.
39:31 the **L** instructions to Moses.
39:32 all the **L** instructions to Moses.
39:42 the **L** instructions to Moses.
39:43 had followed the **L** instructions.
40:19 followed the **L** instructions
40:21 followed the **L** instructions
40:23 in the **L** presence, following
40:23 following the **L** instructions
40:25 in the **L** presence, following
40:25 following the **L** instructions
40:27 following the **L** instructions
40:29 followed the **L** instructions
40:32 followed the **L** instructions
40:38 So the **L** column stayed over
Lev 1:5 the bull in the **L** presence.
1:11 Slaughter it in the **L** presence
2:3 apart from the **L** offering by fire
2:10 apart from the **L** offering by fire
3:1 of cattle in the **L** presence,
4:2 of the **L** commands — this is
4:4 the bull into the **L** presence at
4:4 the bull in the **L** presence
4:6 times in the **L** presence facing
4:7 incense in the **L** presence
4:13 of the **L** commands, they will
4:15 bull's head in the **L** presence.
4:15 slaughter it in the **L** presence
4:17 times in the **L** presence facing
4:18 of the altar in the **L** presence
4:24 it in the **L** presence where
4:27 forbidden by the **L** commands
5:15 with any of the **L** holy things,
5:17 by any of the **L** commands,
6:14 bring it into the **L** presence
6:25 slaughtered in the **L** presence
7:20 eat meat from the **L** fellowship
7:21 the **L** fellowship offering must
8:26 which was in the **L** presence.
9:2 them in the **L** presence
9:4 to sacrifice in the **L** presence.
9:5 and stood in the **L** presence
9:6 that you may see the **L** glory.
9:23 Then the **L** glory appeared to
9:24 came out from the **L** presence
10:1 Then in the **L** presence they
10:19 burnt offering in the **L** presence
12:7 offer them in the **L** presence
14:11 offerings into the **L** presence at

Lev 14:16 seven times in the L presence
14:18 that person in the L presence
14:23 of meeting in the L presence
14:27 seven times in the L presence
14:29 In the L presence, the priest
14:31 So in the L presence the priest
15:14 come into the L presence at
15:15 So in the L presence, the priest
15:30 So in the L presence the priest
16:1 into the L presence and died.
16:7 them into the L presence at
16:10 for Azazel into the L presence.
16:12 which is in the L presence,
16:13 on the fire in the L presence.
16:18 altar that is in the L presence
16:30 all your sins in the L presence
17:4 the LORD in front of the L tent
17:6 the blood against the L altar at
19:22 In the L presence the priest will
23:3 It is the L day of worship
23:4 are the L appointed festivals
23:5 the evening, is the L Passover
23:6 same month is the L Festival
23:20 and will belong to the L priests
23:37 are the L appointed festivals.
23:38 This is in addition to the L days
23:39 celebrate the L festival for
23:41 It is the L festival. Celebrate it
23:44 about the L appointed festivals.
24:3 L presence from evening until
24:4 lamp stand lit in the L presence
24:6 the gold table in the L presence
24:8 the bread in the L presence.
24:9 set apart from the L offering by
24:11 son began cursing the L name
24:16 who curse the L name must
24:16 curses the L name must die.
24:23 the L name was taken outside
Num 3:4 Abihu died in the L presence
3:39 at the L command, by families,
4:7 in the L presence will also
4:49 At the L command through
5:16 and stand in the L presence
5:18 the woman into the L presence
5:30 wife stand in the L presence,
8:10 the Levites into the L presence,
8:11 will be ready to do the L work
9:14 to celebrate the L Passover.
9:18 At the L command the
9:19 obeyed the L command
9:20 At the L command they would
9:23 At the L command they set up
10:33 The ark of the L promise went
10:34 The L ⌊column of⌋ smoke was
11:23 "Is there a limit to the L power?
11:29 I wish all the L people were
13:3 So at the L command, Moses
14:41 disobeying the L command?
14:44 though the ark of the L promise
15:31 and broken the L command.
15:39 remember all the L commands
16:3 above the L assembly?
16:7 in them in the L presence.
16:16 must come into the L presence.
16:41 "You have killed the L people.
17:7 put the staffs in the L presence
17:9 the staffs from the L presence
17:13 comes near the L tent will die!
18:19 of salt in the L presence
18:28 You will give the L contribution
19:2 "This is what the L teachings
19:13 sin makes the L tent unclean.
20:3 died in the L presence
20:4 Did you bring the L assembly
20:9 ⌊the tent in⌋ the L presence as
24:13 the L command no matter how
25:4 daylight in the L presence.
25:4 This will turn the L anger away
26:9 they defied the L authority
26:61 fire in the L presence
27:17 that the L community will not
27:21 decisions in the L presence.
28:16 first month is the L Passover
31:16 The L community experienced
31:21 "This is what the L teachings
31:30 of the work done at the L tent.
Num 31:41 Moses gave the L taxes to the
31:47 of the work done at the L tent
31:54 brought it into the L presence at
32:13 in the L presence was gone.
32:20 In the L presence have all your
32:22 own property in the L presence
32:27 But in the L presence we will
32:29 for battle in the L presence
32:32 armed troops in the L presence,
33:2 At the L command Moses
33:38 At the L command the priest
Dtr 1:43 You defied the L command and
6:25 the L approval: If we faithfully
9:19 I was terrified of the L anger
10:8 carry the ark of the L promise,
10:8 to stand in the L presence
12:17 may not eat ⌊the L offerings⌋
15:2 been proclaimed in the L honor
17:2 the conditions of the L promise
18:7 do their work in the L presence
18:22 a prophet speaks in the L name
19:17 must stand in the L presence,
21:5 to bless people in the L name.
24:4 disgusting in the L presence.
28:9 You will be the L holy people,
28:10 see that you are the L people,
29:20 because the L burning anger
31:9 carried the ark of the L promise
31:25 carried the ark of the L promise:
32:9 But the L people were his
32:43 Joyfully sing with the L people,
33:12 "The L beloved people will live
33:23 of Naphtali enjoy the L favor
33:23 are filled with the L blessings.
34:5 the L servant Moses died in
Jos 1:1 death of the L servant Moses,
1:13 "Remember what the L servant
1:15 the L servant Moses gave you."
3:17 of the L promise stood firmly
4:7 front of the ark of the L promise.
4:11 the priests with the L ark
4:18 ark of the L promise came out
5:14 of the L army." Immediately,
5:15 The commander of the L army
6:6 rams' horns ahead of the L ark.
6:7 men march ahead of the L ark.
6:8 of the L promise followed them.
6:11 So the L ark went around the
6:12 The priests carried the L ark
6:13 guard followed the L ark while
6:19 must go into the L treasury.
6:24 and iron into the L treasury
7:6 the ground in front of the L ark.
7:15 has ignored the L requirements
8:31 This was as the L servant
8:33 carried the ark of the L promise.
8:33 the L servant Moses had
9:20 live to avoid ⌊the L⌋ anger
9:27 They served the L altar,
11:12 as the L servant Moses had
12:6 The L servant Moses and the
13:8 since the L servant Moses had
14:7 the L servant Moses sent me
18:7 the L servant Moses gave them
22:2 L servant Moses commanded
22:4 It is the land that the L servant
22:5 the L servant Moses gave you.
22:16 "All of the L congregation is
22:17 a plague on the L congregation
22:19 come over here to the L land.
22:19 The L tent is standing here.
22:28 'Look at the model of the L altar
22:31 of Israel from the L punishment.
24:26 the oak tree at the L holy place.
24:29 the L servant Joshua,
Jdg 2:8 The L servant Joshua,
2:17 had obeyed the L commands.
2:22 the L ways as their ancestors
3:10 When the L Spirit came over
5:11 Then the L people went down
5:13 The L people went into battle
6:34 Then the L Spirit gave Gideon
11:29 Then the L Spirit came over
13:25 The L Spirit began to stir in him
14:6 The L Spirit came over him.
14:19 When the L Spirit came over
Jdg 15:14 But the L Spirit came over him.
19:18 Now I'm going to the L house,
21:19 "Every year the L festival is
1Sm 1:7 L house, Peninnah would make
1:9 by the door of the L temple.
1:24 She brought him to the L house
2:8 pillars of the earth are the L.
3:15 the doors of the L house.
3:20 was the L appointed prophet.
4:3 of the L promise from Shiloh so
4:5 When the L ark came into the
4:6 out that the L ark had come into
5:3 the ground in front of the L ark.
5:4 the ground in front of the L ark.
6:9 this disaster is the L doing.
7:1 Jearim came to take the L ark
7:1 of guarding the L ark
10:6 Then the L Spirit will come
11:15 and there in the L presence,
12:17 L presence when you asked
13:12 but I haven't sought the L favor.'
14:3 the L priest at Shiloh.
15:1 Now listen to the L words
15:13 I carried out the L instructions.
15:24 not following the L command
16:6 here in the L presence is his
16:13 The L Spirit came over David
16:14 Now, the L Spirit had left Saul,
18:17 the L battles." (Saul thought,
20:42 an oath in the L name, saying,
21:6 been taken from the L presence
21:7 in the L presence was there.
22:17 "Turn and kill the L priests
22:17 refused to attack the L priests
22:21 Saul had killed the L priests
23:18 a pledge in the L presence.
24:6 the L anointed king,
24:6 since he is the L anointed.
24:10 because you are the L anointed.
25:28 you are fighting the L battles.
26:9 attacked the L anointed king
26:11 to attack the L anointed king.
26:16 the L anointed king.
26:19 a share of the L inheritance.
26:20 away from the L presence.
26:23 to attack the L anointed king.
28:10 the L name, "I solemnly swear,
30:26 ⌊taken from⌋ the L enemies.
2Sm 1:12 the L army, and the nation of
1:14 to destroy the L anointed king?"
1:16 'I killed the L anointed king.'"
5:12 the sake of Israel, the L people
6:5 celebrating in the L presence
6:14 David danced in the L presence
6:16 L presence, so she despised
6:17 offerings in the L presence
6:21 leader of Israel, the L people.
6:21 celebrate in the L presence,
12:20 He went into the L house and
12:25 baby Jedidiah [The L Beloved]
19:21 cursing the L anointed king?"
21:1 and David asked the L advice
21:6 the L presence at Saul's town
21:7 in the L name between David
21:9 the mountain in the L presence.
22:16 laid bare at the L stern warning,
24:14 let us fall into the L hands
1Ki 2:27 Abiathar as the L priest
2:27 the L word spoken at Shiloh
2:28 So Joab fled to the L tent and
3:1 the L house, and the wall
3:15 front of the ark of the L promise.
6:1 the L temple 480 years after
6:19 the ark of the L promise there.
6:37 of the L temple was laid.
7:12 inner courtyard of the L temple
7:40 King Solomon on the L temple:
7:45 the L temple at King Solomon's
7:48 the furnishings for the L temple
7:51 on the L temple was finished.
7:51 the storerooms of the L temple
8:1 the ark of the L promise from
8:3 the priests picked up the L ark
8:6 brought the ark of the L promise
8:10 a cloud filled the L temple
8:11 The L glory filled his temple.

1Ki 8:21 contains the **L** promise that
8:22 stood in front of the **L** altar.
8:54 he stood in front of the **L** altar,
8:63 of Israel dedicated the **L** temple
8:64 in front of the **L** temple as
9:1 finished building the **L** temple,
9:10 the two houses (the **L** house
9:15 the **L** house, his own house,
9:25 that was in the **L** presence.
10:5 **L** temple, she was breathless.
10:12 made supports for the **L** temple
12:27 go to sacrifice in the **L** temple
13:5 performed at the **L** command
13:21 the words from the **L** mouth
13:26 the words from the **L** mouth!
14:26 the treasures from the **L** temple
14:28 the **L** temple, guards carried
15:15 He brought into the **L** temple
15:18 in the treasuries of the **L** temple
18:4 **L** prophets, Obadiah had hidden
18:12 the **L** Spirit will take you away
18:13 Jezebel killed the **L** prophets?
18:13 how I hid 100 of the **L** prophets
18:18 by disobeying the **L** commands
18:30 He rebuilt the **L** altar that had
18:32 built an altar in the **L** name
18:46 The **L** power was on Elijah.
22:16 you take an oath in the **L** name
22:24 "How did the **L** Spirit leave me
2Ki 2:16 Maybe the **L** Spirit lifted him up
2:24 and cursed them in the **L** name.
3:12 "The **L** word is with him."
3:15 the **L** power came over Elisha.
9:6 king of the **L** people, ⌞king⌟
9:7 and all the **L** ⌞other⌟ servants.
11:3 hidden with her in the **L** temple
11:4 come to him in the **L** temple.
11:4 under oath in the **L** temple,
11:7 guard the king at the **L** temple
11:10 but were now in the **L** temple
11:13 she went into the **L** temple,
11:15 not be killed in the **L** temple.")
11:17 they would be the **L** people.
11:18 to be in charge of the **L** temple
11:19 the king from the **L** temple.
12:4 are brought into the **L** temple—
12:4 voluntarily to the **L** temple
12:9 one comes into the **L** temple.
12:9 was brought to the **L** temple
12:10 was donated in the **L** temple
12:11 to work on the **L** temple.
12:12 to make repairs on the **L** temple
12:13 were made for the **L** temple
12:16 not brought into the **L** temple.
12:18 the storerooms of the **L** temple
13:17 is the arrow of the **L** victory,
14:6 He obeyed the **L** command
14:14 he found in the **L** temple
15:35 the Upper Gate of the **L** temple
16:8 gold he found in the **L** temple
16:14 his altar and the **L** temple.
16:18 for the king from the **L** temple.
18:12 the **L** servant, had commanded.
18:15 could be found in the **L** temple
18:16 and doorposts of the **L** temple.
19:1 and went into the **L** temple
19:14 and went to the **L** temple.
19:35 The **L** angel went out and
20:5 you will go to the **L** temple
20:8 and that I'll go to the **L** temple
20:19 "The **L** word that you have
21:4 He built altars in the **L** temple,
21:5 two courtyards of the **L** temple,
21:22 and didn't live the **L** way
22:3 to the **L** temple with these
22:4 the **L** temple, ⌞the money⌟ that
22:5 are in charge of the **L** temple.
22:5 making repairs on the **L** temple
22:8 in the **L** temple." Hilkiah gave
22:9 are in charge of the **L** temple.
22:13 The **L** fierce anger is directed
23:2 and old) went to the **L** temple.
23:2 in the **L** temple so that they
23:4 to take out of the **L** temple all
23:7 the **L** temple, where women did
23:9 had never gone to the **L** altar

2Ki 23:11 at the entrance of the **L** temple.
23:12 two courtyards of the **L** temple.
23:24 Hilkiah found in the **L** temple
24:13 all the treasures in the **L** temple
24:13 had made for the **L** temple
25:9 He burned down the **L** temple,
25:13 bronze pillars of the **L** temple,
25:13 the bronze pool in the **L** temple.
25:16 made for the **L** temple couldn't
1Ch 6:31 the music in the **L** temple after
6:32 until Solomon built the **L** temple
9:19 the entrances to the **L** camp
9:23 for the **L** house, that is,
11:10 to the **L** word to Israel.
14:2 the sake of Israel, the **L** people
15:3 at Jerusalem to bring the **L** ark
15:15 according to the **L** instructions
15:25 **L** promise from Obed Edom's
15:26 **L** promise, they sacrificed seven
15:28 brought the ark of the **L** promise
15:29 When the ark of the **L** promise
16:4 of the **L** ark by offering prayers,
16:37 of the ark of the **L** promise, as
16:39 to serve in the **L** tent at
16:40 as written in the **L** Teachings
17:1 while the ark of the **L** promise
21:12 or three days of the **L** sword
21:13 let me fall into the **L** hands
21:18 The **L** Messenger told Gad to
21:19 Gad had told him in the **L** name
21:29 The **L** tent that Moses made in
21:30 the sword of the **L** Messenger
22:14 preparations for the **L** temple.
22:19 bring the ark of the **L** promise
22:19 that will be built for the **L** name.
23:4 **L** temple, 6,000 were appointed
23:24 in the **L** temple was at least
23:28 to serve in the **L** temple.
23:32 as they served in the **L** temple
24:19 went to serve at the **L** temple.
25:6 sang at the **L** temple under
26:12 to serve in the **L** temple
26:22 of the treasuries in the **L** temple
26:27 battle to support the **L** temple.
28:2 the ark of the **L** promise could
28:5 on the throne of the **L** kingdom
28:8 of Israel (the **L** congregation)
28:12 the courtyards of the **L** temple
28:13 for worship in the **L** temple.
28:13 for worship in the **L** temple
28:18 cover the ark of the **L** promise
28:19 written for me by the **L** hand.
28:20 on the **L** temple is finished.
29:8 for the treasury of the **L** temple
29:22 On the **L** behalf they anointed
29:23 sat on the **L** throne as king
2Ch 1:3 Moses, the **L** servant, had
1:5 made was in front of the **L** tent.
1:6 In the **L** presence Solomon
2:1 the temple for the **L** name
2:12 and can build the **L** temple
3:1 began to build the **L** temple
4:16 the **L** temple at King Solomon's
5:1 on the **L** temple was finished.
5:2 the ark of the **L** promise from
5:7 brought the ark of the **L** promise
5:13 Then the **L** temple was filled
5:14 The **L** glory filled God's temple.
6:11 which contains the **L** promise
6:12 stood in front of the **L** altar.
7:1 and the **L** glory filled the
7:2 couldn't go into the **L** temple
7:2 because the **L** glory had filled
7:2 glory had filled the **L** temple
7:3 fire come down and the **L** glory
7:6 had the **L** musical instruments
7:7 in front of the **L** temple as
7:11 Solomon finished the **L** temple
7:11 he had in mind for the **L** temple
8:1 20 years to build the **L** house
8:11 where the **L** ark has come are
8:12 to the LORD on the **L** altar that
8:16 of the **L** temple was laid until
8:16 The **L** temple was ⌞now⌟
9:4 **L** temple, she was breathless.
9:11 made gateways to the **L** temple

2Ch 11:14 rejected them as the **L** priests
12:1 abandoned the **L** teachings
12:9 the treasures from the **L** temple
12:11 the **L** temple, guards carried
13:8 the **L** kingdom, which has been
13:9 You forced out the **L** priests
14:13 The **L** army captured a lot of
15:8 He also repaired the **L** altar in
15:8 in front of the **L** entrance hall.
16:2 in the treasuries of the **L** temple
16:9 The **L** eyes scan the whole
17:9 the Book of the **L** Teachings
18:15 you take an oath in the **L** name
19:2 The **L** anger is directed toward
19:8 Israel to administer the **L** laws
20:3 decided to ask for the **L** help.
20:4 gathered to seek the **L** help.
20:5 **L** temple, Jehoshaphat stood
20:14 Then the **L** Spirit came to
20:28 to the **L** temple in Jerusalem.
23:5 the courtyards of the **L** temple
23:6 come into the **L** temple except
23:6 should follow the **L** regulations
23:12 she went into the **L** temple,
23:14 "Don't kill her in the **L** temple.")
23:16 that they would be the **L** people
23:18 in charge of the **L** temple under
23:18 in divisions for the **L** temple.
23:19 gates of the **L** temple so that no
23:20 the king from the **L** temple.
24:4 to renovate the **L** temple
24:6 The **L** servant Moses and the
24:7 the **L** temple ⌞to worship⌟ other
24:8 outside the gate of the **L** temple
24:9 (In the desert the **L** servant
24:12 were working on the **L** temple,
24:12 to renovate the **L** temple.
24:12 bronze to repair the **L** temple
24:14 make utensils for the **L** temple.
24:14 burnt offerings in the **L** temple
24:20 you breaking the **L** commands?
24:21 in the courtyard of the **L** temple
24:24 out ⌞the **L**⌟ judgment on Joash.
25:4 He obeyed the **L** command
26:16 He went into the **L** temple to
26:17 80 of the **L** courageous priests.
26:19 in the **L** temple as Uzziah was
26:21 was barred from the **L** temple.
27:2 ⌞illegally⌟ enter the **L** temple.
27:3 the Upper Gate of the **L** temple
28:21 of the things from the **L** temple,
28:24 the doors to the **L** temple.
29:3 the doors of the **L** temple
29:6 turned away from the **L** tent
29:15 the king's order from the **L** word
29:16 priests entered the **L** temple
29:16 that they found in the **L** temple.
29:17 went into the **L** entrance hall,
29:17 to make the **L** temple holy.
29:18 made all of the **L** temple clean.
29:19 They are in front of the **L** altar.
29:20 city and went to the **L** temple
29:21 the animals on the **L** altar
29:25 Levites stand in the **L** temple
29:31 thank offerings to the **L** temple.
29:35 **L** temple was reestablished.
30:1 them to come to the **L** temple
30:12 leaders gave from the **L** word
30:15 burnt offerings to the **L** temple
30:21 They played the **L** instruments
31:2 within the gates of the **L** camp
31:3 it is written in the **L** Teachings
31:4 themselves to the **L** Teachings
31:10 to the **L** temple, we have had
31:11 storerooms in the **L** temple.
31:16 who went to the **L** temple
32:12 who got rid of the **L** places
33:4 He built altars in the **L** temple,
33:5 two courtyards of the **L** temple,
33:15 and the idol in the **L** temple.
33:15 in the temple on the **L** mountain
33:16 He built the **L** altar and
34:10 were in charge of the **L** temple.
34:14 been deposited in the **L** temple,
34:14 **L** Teachings written by Moses.
34:15 in the **L** temple." Hilkiah gave

2Ch 34:17 was donated in the **L** temple
34:21 The **L** fierce anger has been
34:30 old) went up to the **L** temple.
34:30 in the **L** temple so that they
35:2 them to serve in the **L** temple
35:16 on the **L** altar as King Josiah
35:26 is written in the **L** Teachings
36:7 of the utensils of the **L** temple
36:10 utensils from the **L** temple.
36:18 the treasures from the **L** temple
36:21 **L** words spoken through
Ezr 1:5 the **L** temple in Jerusalem.
1:7 belonging to the **L** temple.
2:68 families came to the **L** temple
3:6 of the **L** temple had not yet
3:8 direct the work on the **L** house
3:10 the foundation of the **L** temple.
7:10 the **L** Teachings, live by them,
7:11 knowledge of the **L** commands
7:27 mind to make the **L** temple
8:29 **L** temple, weigh these items.
Neh 10:35 tree each year to the **L** temple
Job 1:12 Then Satan left the **L** presence
2:7 Satan left the **L** presence and
12:9 know that the **L** hands made it?
Psa 2:7 I will announce the **L** decree.
11:4 The **L** throne is in heaven.
22:8 "Put yourself in the **L** hands.
23:6 and I will remain in the **L** house
24:1 everything it contains are the **L**.
24:3 may go up the **L** mountain?
27:4 to remain in the **L** house all the
27:4 in order to gaze at the **L** beauty
33:11 The **L** plan stands firm forever.
33:18 The **L** eyes are on those who
34:3 Praise the **L** greatness with me.
34:10 but those who seek the **L** help
34:15 The **L** eyes are on righteous
37:20 The **L** enemies will vanish like
75:8 A cup is in the **L** hand.
78:4 generation about the **L** power
84:2 and yearns for the **L** courtyards.
92:13 are planted in the **L** house.
96:13 in the **L** presence because he
98:9 in the **L** presence because he
101:8 in the land to rid the **L** city
102:15 nations will fear the **L** name.
102:21 The **L** name is announced in
103:17 the **L** mercy is on those who
104:16 The **L** trees, the cedars in
105:19 The **L** promise tested him
106:16 of Aaron, the **L** holy one.
107:43 understand the **L** blessings
111:2 The **L** deeds are spectacular.
116:9 I will walk in the **L** presence in
116:19 the courtyards of the **L** house,
117:2 The **L** faithfulness endures
118:26 We bless you from the **L** house
122:4 All of the **L** tribes go to that city
137:4 How could we sing the **L** song
138:5 "The **L** honor is great!"
Pro 3:32 The **L** intimate advice is with
10:22 It is the **L** blessing that makes
16:20 to the **L** word prospers,
19:16 despises the **L** ways will
20:27 A person's soul is the **L** lamp.
21:1 Both are under the **L** control.
22:12 The **L** eyes watch over
Isa 1:27 be pardoned by ⌊the **L**⌋ justice,
1:27 by ⌊the **L**⌋ righteousness
2:2 mountain of the **L** house will
2:10 of the **L** terrifying presence
2:19 of the **L** terrifying presence
2:21 of the **L** terrifying presence
14:2 female slaves in the **L** land.
24:5 **L** teachings, violated his laws,
24:14 joyfully about the **L** majesty
25:10 The **L** power will be on this
30:9 to listen to the **L** teachings
30:29 on the way to the **L** mountain,
30:33 The **L** breath will be like a
34:6 The **L** sword is covered with
34:16 Search the **L** book, and read it.
37:1 and went into the **L** temple
37:14 and went to the **L** temple.
37:36 The **L** angel went out and

Isa 38:22 sign that I'll go to the **L** temple?
38:20 live our lives in the **L** temple
39:8 "The **L** word that you have
40:5 Then the **L** glory will be
40:7 wither when the **L** breath blows
41:20 that the **L** power has done this,
44:5 "The **L**," and he will adopt the
48:14 He will carry out the **L** plan
49:4 my case is in the **L** hands,
51:17 from the cup in the **L** hand.
52:11 the utensils for the **L** temple
53:1 the **L** power been revealed?
53:10 Yet, it was the **L** will to crush
54:17 inheritance of the **L** servants.
55:13 be a reminder of the **L** name
56:6 to love the **L** name, and to be
58:13 and the **L** holy day honorable,
61:2 the year of the **L** good will
63:7 I will acknowledge the **L** acts
63:14 were given rest by the **L** Spirit.
66:20 in clean dishes to the **L** temple
Jer 3:16 about the ark of the **L** promise.
4:8 and cry because the **L** burning
7:2 at the gate of the **L** house,
7:4 "This is the **L** temple, the
7:4 the **L** temple, the LORD's
7:4 the **L** temple!" It's a lie.
8:8 that you have the **L** teachings?
12:12 The **L** sword destroys them
13:17 tears because the **L** flock will
17:26 thank offerings to the **L** temple
19:14 in the courtyard of the **L** temple
20:1 the chief officer of the **L** temple,
20:2 Gate that was in the **L** temple
23:18 Who is in the **L** inner circle and
23:34 'This is the **L** revelation!' I will
23:35 'What is the **L** answer?' and
23:36 'This is the **L** revelation,'
23:37 'What was the **L** answer to
23:38 'This is the **L** revelation!' Then
23:38 "This is the **L** revelation!" even
24:1 figs set in front of the **L** temple
25:17 I took the cup from the **L** hand.
25:37 by the **L** burning anger.
26:2 in the courtyard of the **L** temple,
26:2 to worship in the **L** temple.
26:7 these things in the **L** temple
26:9 in the **L** name that this temple
26:9 Jeremiah in the **L** temple
26:10 king's palace to the **L** temple.
26:10 of New Gate to the **L** ⌊temple⌋
26:19 LORD and sought the **L** favor.
27:16 the utensils of the **L** temple will
27:18 that are left in the **L** temple,
27:21 that are left in the **L** temple,
28:1 spoke to me in the **L** temple.
28:3 **L** temple that King
28:5 people standing in the **L** temple
28:6 the utensils of the **L** temple
29:26 be officials for the **L** temple.
30:24 The **L** burning anger will not
31:12 the **L** blessings: fresh grain,
33:11 offerings to the **L** temple say,
35:2 the side rooms in the **L** temple,
35:4 them into the **L** temple, into
36:5 allowed to go to the **L** temple
36:6 the **L** message that you wrote
36:6 it to the people in the **L** temple.
36:7 will come into the **L** presence,
36:8 In the **L** temple he read from the
36:9 to fast in the **L** presence
36:10 to all the people in the **L** temple
36:10 of New Gate of the **L** temple
38:14 third entrance in the **L** temple.
41:5 and incense to the **L** temple
44:16 spoken to us in the **L** name
48:10 who neglect doing the **L** work.
50:13 because of the **L** anger.
50:15 Since this is the **L** vengeance,
51:7 a golden cup in the **L** hand.
51:51 the holy places of the **L** temple
52:13 He burned down the **L** temple,
52:17 bronze pillars of the **L** temple,
52:17 the bronze pool in the **L** temple.
52:20 made for the **L** temple couldn't
Lam 2:7 noise in the **L** temple as though

Lam 2:20 be killed in the **L** holy place?
2:22 on the day of the **L** anger.
3:22 the **L** mercy. We were not
3:66 out from under the **L** heaven.
4:11 The **L** fury has accomplished
4:21 The cup ⌊of the **L** fury⌋ will be
Eze 1:28 It was like the **L** glory.
3:12 "Blessed is the **L** glory, which
3:23 The **L** glory was standing there
7:19 them on the day of the **L** anger.
8:14 the north gate of the **L** temple.
8:16 inner courtyard of the **L** temple.
8:16 to the **L** temple, between
8:16 backs turned to the **L** temple.
10:4 The **L** glory rose from the
10:4 brightness of the **L** glory filled
10:19 to the east gate of the **L** temple,
11:1 to the east gate of the **L** temple.
11:5 The **L** Spirit came to me and
11:23 The **L** glory left the middle of
18:25 'The **L** way is unfair.'
18:29 'The **L** way is unfair.'
20:1 came to ask for the **L** help.
33:17 'The **L** way is unfair.'
33:20 'The **L** way is unfair.'
36:20 'These are the **L** people, yet
40:1 At that time the **L** power came
43:4 The **L** glory came into the
43:5 I saw the **L** glory fill the temple.
44:4 I looked, I saw the **L** glory fill
44:4 LORD's glory fill the **L** temple.
44:5 regulations for the **L** temple.
46:9 will enter the **L** presence at
48:10 The **L** holy place will be in the
48:14 because the land is the **L** and
Hos 8:1 down on the **L** temple like
9:3 won't stay in the **L** land.
9:4 ⌊as an offering⌋ to the **L** temple
9:5 or on the **L** festival days?
13:15 However, the **L** scorching wind
14:9 The **L** ways are right.
Joe 1:9 longer brought to the **L** temple.
1:9 the **L** servants, mourn.
3:18 will flow from the **L** temple.
Amo 2:4 have rejected the **L** Teachings
Mic 2:5 the **L** assembly will draw lots
3:8 with the power of the **L** Spirit,
4:1 mountain of the **L** house will
5:3 Then the rest of the **L** people
6:2 Listen to the **L** lawsuit, you
6:6 into the **L** presence, when
Hab 2:14 knowledge of the **L** glory like
2:16 The cup in the **L** right hand will
Zep 1:8 "On the day of the **L** sacrifice I
1:18 day of the **L** overflowing fury.
2:2 before the **L** burning anger
2:2 before the day of the **L** anger
2:3 on the day of the **L** anger
Hag 1:13 received the **L** message, said
Zec 6:12 and he will rebuild the **L** temple
6:13 He will rebuild the **L** temple
6:14 of Zephaniah) in the **L** temple
6:15 come and rebuild the **L** temple.
7:12 couldn't hear the **L** teachings,
Mal 1:7 "When you say that the **L** table
1:12 you say that the **L** table may
2:13 You cover the **L** altar with tears.
Luk 1:6 followed all the **L** commands
1:9 custom to go into the **L** temple
1:38 "I am the **L** servant.
1:46 soul praises the **L** greatness
2:23 **L** Teachings: "Every firstborn
2:24 by the **L** Teachings: "a pair
2:39 the **L** Teachings required,
4:19 the year of the **L** favor.
10:39 Mary sat at the **L** feet and
Jon 12:38 the **L** power been revealed?"
Act 5:9 agree to test the **L** Spirit?
9:1 to murder the **L** disciples.
11:21 The **L** power was with his
13:12 The **L** teachings amazed him.
13:44 city gathered to hear the **L** word
13:48 heard and praised the **L** word.
15:35 taught people about the **L** word
15:36 where we spread the **L** word.
15:40 entrusted him to the **L** care

Act 16:32 They spoke the **L** word to the
18:25 been instructed in the **L** way
21:14 "May the **L** will be done."
Rom 9:4 They have the **L** glory, the
1Co 4:17 he faithfully does the **L** work
4:19 If it's the **L** will, I'll visit you
7:22 you are the **L** free person.
7:34 about the **L** things so that she
9:2 proves that I am the **L** apostle
9:5 the **L** brothers, and Cephas do?
10:21 You cannot drink the **L** cup and
10:26 "The earth is the **L** and
11:20 possibly be eating the **L** Supper
11:26 you tell about the **L** death until
11:27 bread or drinks from the **L** cup
11:27 for the **L** body and blood.
11:29 he doesn't recognize the **L** body
16:10 He's doing the **L** work as I am,
2Co 3:17 Wherever the **L** Spirit is,
3:18 As all of us reflect the **L** glory
Gal 1:19 I only saw James, the **L** brother
Eph 4:17 you in the **L** name not
5:22 under the **L** authority
6:21 a faithful deacon in the **L** work.
Col 3:18 behavior for the **L** people
4:7 and partner in the **L** work.
4:17 that he started as the **L** servant
1Th 1:8 From you the **L** word has
5:27 In the **L** name, I order you to
2Th 1:9 separated from the **L** presence
3:1 pray that we spread the **L** word
Heb 9:4 and the ark of the **L** promise.
Jas 4:10 yourselves in the **L** presence.
1Pe 3:12 The **L** eyes are on those who
2Pe 2:10 who despise the **L** authority.
2:10 afraid to insult the ⌊**L**⌋ glory
3:15 Think of our **L** patience as an
Jud 1:8 reject the **L** authority, and insult
Rev 1:10 the Spirit's power on the **L** day.

Lords; lords (8)

Dtr 10:17 is God of gods and Lord of **l**,
Psa 136:3 Give thanks to the Lord of **l**
1Co 8:5 earth — many gods and many **l**,
Eph 1:21 all rulers, authorities, powers, **l**,
Col 1:16 Whether they are kings or **l**,
1Ti 6:15 the King of kings and Lord of **l**.
Rev 17:14 them because he is Lord of **l**
19:16 King of Kings and Lord of **L**.

Lo Ruhamah (2)

Hos 1:6 Hosea, "Name her **L** [Unloved].
1:8 After Gomer had weaned **L**,

lose (82)

Gen 27:45 Why should I **l** both of you in
42:36 "You're going to make me **l** all
43:14 If I **l** my children, I lose my
43:14 my children, I **l** my children."
45:11 to you won't **l** everything.'"
Num 24:11 has made you **l** your reward."
Dtr 20:3 Don't **l** your courage!
Jdg 18:25 your family will **l** your lives."
2Sm 17:10 like a lion would **l** his courage,
22:46 Foreigners will **l** heart,
1Ki 18:5 alive and not **l** any animals."
Ezr 10:8 then they would **l** all their
Est 6:13 "You are starting to **l** power to
Job 11:20 the wicked will **l** their eyesight.
33:20 food and they **l** their appetite
Psa 18:45 Foreigners will **l** heart,
61:2 to you when I begin to **l** heart.
71:9 me when I **l** my strength.
77:3 I begin to **l** hope as I think
107:5 They began to **l** hope.
142:3 When I begin to **l** hope,
143:4 That is why I begin to **l** hope
Pro 1:18 into hiding only to **l** their lives.
3:21 do not **l** sight of these things.
4:21 Do not **l** sight of these things.
Isa 7:4 Don't **l** heart because of the
19:3 The Egyptians will **l** courage.
Jer 4:9 the leaders will **l** their courage.
17:4 You will **l** the inheritance that I
17:11 he will **l** his wealth.
51:46 Don't **l** courage or be afraid
Eze 7:27 people will **l** their courage.
21:7 their hearts will **l** courage,
Oba 1:6 you, Esau, will **l** everything.
Zep 3:16 Zion! Do not **l** courage!"
Zec 9:5 Gaza will **l** its king.
Mal 3:11 not **l** their unripened grapes,"
Mat 5:29 It is better for you to **l** a part of
5:30 It is better for you to **l** a part of
10:39 tries to preserve his life will **l** it,
10:42 certainly never **l** his reward."
11:6 Whoever doesn't **l** his faith in
16:25 to save their lives will **l** them.
16:25 But those who **l** their lives for
16:26 whole world and **l** their lives?
18:6 causes one of them to **l** faith
18:7 it causes people to **l** their faith.
18:7 cause people to **l** their faith will
18:7 causes someone to **l** his faith!
18:8 foot causes you to **l** your faith,
18:9 eye causes you to **l** your faith,
24:10 Then many will **l** faith.
Mar 8:35 to save their lives will **l** them.
8:35 But those who **l** their lives for
8:36 whole world yet **l** their lives?
9:41 will certainly not **l** his reward."
9:42 causes one of them to **l** faith
9:43 hand causes you to **l** your faith,
9:45 foot causes you to **l** your faith,
9:47 eye causes you to **l** your faith,
Luk 7:23 Whoever doesn't **l** his faith in
9:24 to save their lives will **l** them.
9:24 But those who **l** their lives for
9:25 whole world but **l** their lives by
17:1 cause people to **l** their faith are
17:1 causes someone to **l** his faith!
17:2 of these little ones to **l** his faith.
17:33 to save their lives will **l** them,
17:33 and those who **l** their lives will
Jon 6:39 me doesn't want me to **l** any
6:61 "Did what I say make you **l**
16:1 so that you won't **l** your faith.
Act 23:11 "Don't **l** your courage!
27:20 we finally began to **l** any hope
27:22 No one will **l** his life.
Rom 14:13 have doubts or **l** their faith.
1Co 1:17 cross of Christ **l** its meaning.
8:13 other believers to **l** their faith,
8:13 other believers **l** their faith.
Heb 10:35 So don't **l** your confidence.
2Pe 2:13 and **l** what their wrongdoing
Rev 16:15 alert and doesn't **l** his clothes.

losers (1)

Exo 32:18 It's not the sound of **l** crying.

loses (10)

Lev 13:40 "If a man **l** his hair,
13:41 If he **l** the hair on the front of his
Jer 50:43 about them, and he **l** courage.
Mat 5:13 But if salt **l** its taste,
10:39 but the person who **l** his life for
Mar 9:50 But if salt **l** its taste,
Luk 12:33 in heaven that never **l** its value!
14:34 But if salt **l** its taste,
15:4 a man has 100 sheep and **l** one
15:8 has ten coins and **l** one.

losing (1)

2Ki 3:26 Moab saw he was **l** the battle,

loss (22)

Gen 31:39 I paid for the **l** myself.
Exo 21:19 pay the injured man for the **l**
21:26 to make up for the **l** of the eye.
21:27 to make up for the **l** of the tooth.
21:34 cistern must make up for the **l**.
21:36 must make up for the **l** — bull
22:1 he must make up for the **l** with
22:4 he must make up for the **l** with
22:5 up from his own field for the **l**
22:6 the fire must make up for the **l**.
22:7 he must make up for the **l** with
22:9 make up for his neighbor's **l**
22:11 have to make up for the **l**.
22:12 must make up for the owner's **l**.
22:14 must make up for the **l**.
Exo 22:15 have to make up for the **l**.
22:15 the rental fee covers the **l**.
Dtr 21:13 and mourn ⌊the **l** of⌋ her father
Isa 47:8 I won't suffer the **l** of children."
47:9 the **l** of your children and your
Act 27:21 avoided this disaster and **l**.
1Co 3:15 he will suffer ⌊the **l**⌋.

losses (1)

Act 27:10 to face a disaster and heavy **l**

lost (56)

Gen 31:40 and I **l** a lot of sleep.
Exo 14:5 We've **l** our slaves because
22:9 or any ⌊other⌋ **l** property which
Lev 6:3 find something that someone **l**
6:4 the **l** item you found,
21:7 those who have **l** their virginity,
21:14 woman who has **l** her virginity,
Num 11:6 But now we've **l** our appetite!
16:38 who sinned and **l** their lives are
17:12 We're **l**! We're all lost!
17:12 We're lost! We're all **l**!
36:3 Then we will have **l** part of our
Dtr 20:8 afraid or have **l** your courage,
22:3 another Israelite may have **l**.
32:28 My people have **l** their good
34:7 never **l** his physical strength.
Jos 2:11 we heard about it, we **l** heart.
5:1 So they **l** heart and had no
7:5 Israel's troops **l** heart and were
1Sm 9:3 to Saul's father Kish were **l**,
9:20 that were **l** three days ago
2Sm 4:1 in Hebron, he **l** his courage,
Neh 6:16 and **l** their self-confidence.
Psa 9:18 oppressed people be **l** forever.
38:10 I have **l** my strength.
40:12 on my head. I have **l** heart.
119:176 wandered away like a **l** lamb.
Ecc 5:14 hoarded riches were then **l**
Sos 4:2 and not one has **l** its young.
6:6 and not one has **l** its young.
Jer 6:26 Mourn as if you have **l** your
16:7 those who have **l** their fathers
50:6 My people have been **l** sheep.
Lam 3:18 I said, 'I've **l** my strength ⌊to
Eze 34:4 or looked for those that were **l**.
34:16 I will look for those that are **l**,
Hos 13:8 Like a bear that has **l** her cubs,
Mat 10:6 Instead, go to the **l** sheep of the
15:24 "I was sent only to the **l** sheep
18:14 one of these little ones to be **l**.
Luk 15:4 and look for the **l** sheep until
15:6 I've found my **l** sheep!'
15:9 I've found the coin that I **l**.'
15:24 He was **l** but has been found.'
15:32 He was **l** but has been found.'"
16:4 their homes when I've **l** my job.'
19:10 and to save people who are **l**."
21:18 a hair on your head will be **l**.
Jon 10:28 They will never be **l**,
17:12 except one person, became **l**.
18:9 "I **l** none of those you gave
Act 27:9 We had **l** so much time that the
27:34 from anyone's head will be **l**."
2Co 3:10 brings punishment **l** its glory
Heb 4:11 Then no one will be **l** by
1Pe 2:25 You were like **l** sheep.

Lot; lot (164)

Gen 11:27 Haran was the father of **L**.
11:31 his grandson **L** (son of Haran),
12:4 and **L** went with him.
12:5 his wife Sarai, his nephew **L**,
13:1 to the Negev. **L** was with him.
13:5 **L**, who had been traveling with
13:8 Abram said to **L**, "Please,
13:10 Then **L** looked in the direction
13:11 **L** chose the whole Jordan
13:12 Abram lived in Canaan, while **L**
13:14 After **L** left, the LORD said to
14:12 also took Abram's nephew **L**
14:16 relative **L** and his possessions.
19:1 in the evening as **L** was sitting
19:1 When **L** saw them,
19:5 They called to **L**, "Where are

Gen 19:6 Then **L** went outside and shut
19:9 They pushed hard against **L**
19:10 pulled **L** into the house with
19:12 Then the men asked **L**,
19:14 So **L** went out and spoke to the
19:15 the angels urged **L** by saying,
19:16 the LORD wanted to spare **L**.
19:18 **L** answered, "Oh no!
19:23 the land as **L** came to Zoar.
19:29 **L** was allowed to escape from
19:30 **L** left Zoar because he was
26:35 Isaac and Rebekah a **l** of grief.
31:40 and I lost a **l** of sleep.
34:30 have caused me a **l** of trouble!
Lev 16:8 One **l** will be for the LORD and
16:9 sacrifice the goat chosen by **l**
16:10 must bring the goat chosen by **l**
Dtr 2:9 it to the descendants of **L**."
2:19 of **L** as their property."
3:19 know you have a **l** of livestock.
17:17 And he must never own a **l** of
Jos 13:1 and there is a **l** of land left to be
15:1 The **l** was drawn for the
16:1 The **l** was drawn for Joseph.
17:1 The **l** was drawn for the tribe of
17:14 We have a **l** of people because
18:11 The **l** was drawn for the
19:1 The second **l** was drawn for
19:10 The third **l** was drawn for the
19:17 The fourth **l** was drawn for the
19:24 The fifth **l** was drawn for the
19:32 The sixth **l** was drawn for the
19:40 The seventh **l** was drawn for
19:51 the tribes of Israel drew by **l**.
21:10 Their **l** was the first one drawn.
21:20 Cities were chosen by **l** from
21:40 12 cities were chosen by **l**.
Jdg 20:9 We'll decide by **l** who should
2Sm 3:22 from a raid with a **l** of goods.
12:30 David also took a **l** of goods
18:29 Ahimaaz answered, "I saw a **l**
2Ki 4:13 since she has gone to a **l** of
10:18 but Jehu will serve him a **l**.
12:10 Whenever they saw a **l** of
21:16 Manasseh also killed a **l** of
24:4 He had a **l** of innocent people
1Ch 6:54 The ⌊first⌋ **l** was drawn for the
6:61 10 cities chosen by **l** from
6:62 13 cities chosen by **l** from
6:63 12 cities chosen by **l** from
6:65 ⌊them⌋ the cities chosen by **l**
6:66 had cities chosen by **l** from
20:2 David also took a **l** of goods
22:8 'You have caused a **l** of
22:8 and fought in a **l** of wars.
24:7 The first **l** drawn was for
25:9 The first **l** drawn chose Joseph,
2Ch 14:13 army captured a **l** of goods.
15:5 in the land had a **l** of turmoil.
17:5 and he had a **l** of riches and
20:25 found among them a **l** of goods,
24:11 and they saw a **l** of money,
24:11 so they collected a **l** of money.
25:13 people and took a **l** of goods.
26:10 cisterns because he had a **l**
28:8 They also took a **l** of goods
31:10 and there's a **l** left over."
32:29 had given him a **l** of property.
Est 3:7 Pur (which means the **l**) was
9:24 means the **l**) thrown ⌊in order
Job 35:16 talks a **l** without having any
Psa 83:8 helped the descendants of **L**.
Pro 27:3 and sand weighs a **l**,
Ecc 1:16 I've had a **l** of experience with
1:18 With a **l** of wisdom ⌊comes⌋ a
1:18 ⌊comes⌋ a **l** of heartache.
3:22 because that is their **l** ⌊in life⌋.
5:12 whether they eat a little or a **l**.
5:18 That is our **l** ⌊in life⌋.
5:19 ability⌋ to accept their **l** in life,
9:9 This is your **l** ⌊in life⌋ and
Jer 2:22 detergent and use a **l** of soap,
Lam 3:24 'The LORD is my **l** ⌊in life⌋.
Eze 19:10 It had a **l** of fruit and many
Dan 11:13 army and a **l** of equipment.
11:28 his country with a **l** of wealth.
Hos 9:7 They have sinned a **l**,
Mic 2:12 They will make a **l** of noise
Hag 1:6 You planted a **l**, but you
1:9 "You expected a **l**,
Mat 6:7 they'll be heard if they talk a **l**.
16:21 he would have to suffer a **l**
19:22 he owned a **l** of property.
24:21 There will be a **l** of misery at
Mar 6:34 So he spent a **l** of time
6:48 Jesus saw that they were in a **l**
8:31 of Man would have to suffer a **l**.
9:12 the Son of Man must suffer a **l**
10:22 he owned a **l** of property.
Luk 9:22 of Man would have to suffer a **l**.
10:41 and fuss about a **l** of things.
12:15 a **l** of material possessions."
12:19 "You've stored up a **l** of good
12:48 A **l** will be expected from
12:48 who has been given a **l**.
12:48 has been entrusted with a **l**.
16:10 can also be trusted with a **l**.
16:10 very little is dishonest with a **l**.
17:25 But first he must suffer a **l** and
17:28 will also be like the time of **L**.
17:29 on the day that **L** left Sodom,
Jon 8:26 I have a **l** I could say about you
8:26 I could say about you and a **l**
11:47 is performing a **l** of miracles.
12:24 it will produce a **l** of grain.
15:5 in them will produce a **l** of fruit.
15:8 Father when you produce a **l**
16:12 "I have a **l** more to tell you,
Act 1:3 Jesus showed the apostles a **l**
7:11 Canaan brought a **l** of suffering.
9:13 I've heard a **l** of people tell
14:22 "We must suffer a **l** to enter the
15:7 After a **l** of debating,
16:16 She made a **l** of money for her
16:20 "These men are stirring up a **l**
20:37 Everyone cried a **l** as they put
22:28 The officer replied, "I paid a **l** of
25:7 They made a **l** of serious
25:23 auditorium with a **l** of fanfare.
26:9 used to think that I had to do a **l**
1Co 8:2 still have a **l** to learn.
2Co 7:4 and I have a **l** of reasons to be
8:15 "Those who had gathered a **l**
11:26 Because I've traveled a **l**,
1Th 1:6 In spite of a **l** of suffering,
1Ti 1:4 and genealogies raise a **l**
6:10 caused themselves a **l** of grief.
6:18 to do a **l** of good things,
Phm 1:7 ⌊for God's people⌋ gives me a **l**
Heb 5:11 We have a **l** to explain about
10:32 You endured a **l** of hardship
Jas 3:2 All of us make a **l** of mistakes.
2Pe 2:7 Yet, God rescued **L**,
2:7 **L** was distressed by the
2Jn 1:12 I have a **l** to write to you.
3Jn 1:13 I have a **l** to write to you.
Rev 2:22 with her will also suffer a **l**,
8:3 He was given a **l** of incense to

Lotan (4)

Gen 36:20 land: **L**, Shobal, Zibeon, Anah,
36:22 The sons of **L** were Hori and
36:29 **L**, Shobal, Zibeon, Anah,
1Ch 1:38 Seir's sons were **L**,

Lotan's (3)

Gen 36:22 **L** sister was Timna.
1Ch 1:39 **L** sons were Hori and Homam.
1:39 Timna was **L** sister

lotion (3)

Psa 92:10 and soothing **l** is poured on me.
141:5 It is like **l** for my head.
Ecc 9:8 go without **l** on your head.

Lot's (4)

Gen 13:7 Abram's herders and **L** herders.
19:26 **L** wife looked back and turned
19:36 So **L** two daughters became
Luk 17:32 Remember **L** wife

lots (32)

Lev 16:8 Then Aaron must throw **l** for the
Num 26:55 must be divided by drawing **l**.
26:56 must be divided by drawing **l**."
33:54 your families by drawing **l**.
33:54 to each family by drawing **l**.
34:13 you will divide by drawing **l**.
36:2 their land by drawing **l**.
Jos 13:6 to Israel by drawing **l**,
14:2 determined by drawing **l** as
18:6 I will draw **l** for you here in the
18:8 Then I will draw **l** for you in the
18:10 So Joshua drew **l** for them in
19:51 divided the land by drawing **l**.
21:4 that were chosen by drawing **l**.
21:8 descendants by drawing **l**,
Jdg 1:3 given to us when we drew **l**,
1Ch 6:54 for them when **l** were drawn:
24:5 by drawing **l** so that there
24:31 They drew **l** as their relatives,
25:8 They drew **l** for their
26:13 They drew **l** by families,
Neh 10:34 and laypeople have drawn **l** to
10:35 We have drawn **l** to decide
10:36 we have drawn **l** to decide who
10:37 Also, we have drawn **l** to
11:1 The rest of the people drew **l** to
Pro 7:20 He took **l** of money with him.
12:21 people have **l** of trouble.
Eze 45:1 "'Divide the land by drawing **l**
47:22 Divide it by drawing **l**.
47:22 They will draw **l** with you for
Mic 2:5 LORD's assembly will draw **l**

lotus (2)

Job 40:21 It lies down under the **l** plants
40:22 **L** plants provide it with cover.

loud (74)

Gen 19:13 against its people are so **l** that
27:34 he shouted out a very **l** and
39:14 but I screamed as **l** as I could.
Exo 11:6 There will be **l** crying
12:30 There was **l** crying throughout
19:16 and a very **l** blast from a ram's
Num 11:1 people began complaining out **l**
14:1 and cried out **l** all that night.
Dtr 5:22 He spoke in a **l** voice from the
27:14 the people of Israel in a **l** voice:
1Sm 2:1 Hannah prayed out **l**,
1Ki 8:55 Then he stood and in a **l** voice
2Ch 20:19 God of Israel with very **l** songs.
Ezr 3:13 joyful shouts and the **l** sobbing
Job 2:12 They cried out **l** and wept,
4:10 of the ferocious lion ⌊is⌋ **l**,
30:31 and my flute for **l** weeping.
Psa 47:1 Shout to God with a **l**,
102:5 bones because of my **l** groans.
150:5 Praise him with **l** cymbals.
Pro 7:11 She is **l** and rebellious.
9:13 The woman Stupidity is **l**,
27:14 the morning with a **l** voice — his
Isa 29:6 and **l** noises, with windstorms,
40:9 Call out with a **l** voice,
Jer 51:55 He will silence the **l** noise
Eze 3:12 and behind me I heard a **l**
3:13 them as well as a **l** rumbling.
9:1 LORD call out with a **l** voice.
27:32 song for you with **l** crying:
Amo 5:16 There will be **l** crying in every
5:17 There will be **l** crying in every
8:3 the temple will become **l** cries,"
Zep 1:10 On that day a **l** cry will come
1:10 and a **l** crashing sound from the
Mat 24:31 his angels with a **l** trumpet call,
27:46 Jesus cried out in a **l** voice,
Mar 1:26 came out of him with a **l** shriek.
15:34 Jesus cried out in a **l** voice,
15:37 cried out in a **l** voice and died.
Luk 1:42 She said in a **l** voice,
8:28 and said in a **l** voice,
17:15 and praised God in a **l** voice.
23:46 Jesus cried out in a **l** voice,
Act 2:14 In a **l** voice he said to them,
8:28 reading the prophet Isaiah out **l**.

Act 8:30 reading the prophet Isaiah out l.
14:10 So Paul said in a l voice,
23:9 The shouting became very l.
1Co 13:1 But if I don't have love, I am a l
Eph 4:31 anger, l quarreling, cursing,
Heb 5:7 He prayed and pleaded with l
Rev 1:10 I heard a l voice behind me like
5:2 angel calling out in a l voice,
5:12 In a l voice they were singing,
6:10 They cried out in a l voice,
7:2 He cried out in a l voice to the
7:10 and crying out in a l voice,
8:13 and I heard it say in a l voice,
10:3 Then he shouted in a l voice
11:12 The witnesses heard a l voice
11:15 there were l voices in heaven,
12:10 Then I heard a l voice in
14:2 and the noise of l thunder.
14:7 The angel said in a l voice,
14:9 and said in a l voice,
14:15 He cried out in a l voice to the
14:18 This angel called out in a l
16:1 I heard a l voice from the
16:17 A l voice came from the throne
19:1 sounded like the l noise from
19:6 like the noise of l thunder,
19:17 He cried out in a l voice to all
21:3 I heard a l voice from the throne

louder (8)

Exo 19:19 of the horn grew l and louder,
19:19 of the horn grew louder and l,
1Ki 18:27 "Shout l, since he is a god.
18:28 So they shouted l.
Mat 20:31 But they shouted even l,
Mar 10:48 But he shouted even l,
15:14 But they shouted even l,
Luk 18:39 But he shouted even l,

loudest (1)

1Sm 20:41 but David cried the l.

loudly (72)

Gen 21:16 So she sat down and sobbed l.
27:38 And Esau sobbed l.
29:11 kissed Rachel and sobbed l.
45:2 He cried so l that the Egyptians
Jos 6:5 all the troops must shout very l.
6:20 So the troops shouted very l
Jdg 2:4 they began to cry l.
21:2 evening. They cried very l,
Rut 1:9 they began to cry l.
1:14 They began to cry l again.
1Sm 4:5 all Israel shouted so l that the
7:10 day the LORD thundered l at
11:4 the news, the people cried l.
24:16 David?" and Saul cried l.
28:12 she cried out l and asked,
30:4 Then David and his men cried l
2Sm 3:32 The king cried l at Abner's
13:36 king's sons arrived and cried l.
15:23 The whole country was crying l
19:4 covered his face and cried l,
1Ki 1:40 and celebrated so l that their
2Ki 18:28 stood and shouted l
2Ch 30:21 the LORD's instruments l.
32:18 officers shouted l
Ezr 3:13 the people were shouting so l.
Neh 9:4 built for the Levites and cried l
Est 4:1 the city and cried l and bitterly.
Psa 26:7 so that I may l sing a hymn of
77:1 L, I cried to God. Loudly, I cried
77:1 L, I cried to God so that he
142:1 L, I cry to the LORD. Loudly,
142:1 L, I plead with the LORD for
Isa 12:6 Shout l, and sing with joy,
13:2 Call l to them. Signal them with
13:6 Cry l, for the day of the LORD
14:31 Cry l in the gate! Cry out in the
15:5 They cry l over the destruction
23:1 Cry l, you ships of Tarshish!
23:6 Cry l, you inhabitants of the
23:14 Cry l, you ships of Tarshish,
27:13 a ram's horn will be blown l.
36:13 stood and shouted l
Jer 2:15 have roared very l at them.
Jer 4:5 Shout l and say, Let's go into
47:2 who lives in the land will cry l.
48:20 Shout l, and cry. Tell the news
49:3 Cry l, Heshbon, because Ai is
Eze 27:30 They cried l and bitterly over
Dan 3:4 The herald called out l,
4:14 He shouted l, 'Cut down the
8:16 a man in Ulai Gate call l,
Hos 10:5 The priests will cry l because
Joe 1:5 Cry l, you wine drinkers!
1:8 Cry l like a young woman who
1:11 Cry l, you grape growers!
1:13 Cry l, you servants of the altar.
Amo 5:16 professional mourners to cry l.
Jnh 3:8 Cry l to God for help.
Mic 4:9 Now why are you crying so l?
Zep 3:14 Shout l, Israel! Celebrate and
Mat 27:23 But they began to shout l,
27:50 Then Jesus l cried out once
Mar 5:38 were crying and sobbing l.
Luk 4:33 He shouted very l,
Jon 1:15 truth about him when he said l,
7:28 he said l, "You know me,
7:37 He said l, "Whoever is thirsty
11:43 he shouted as l as he could,
12:44 Then Jesus said l,
Act 4:24 they were united and l prayed
8:2 as they mourned l for him.
16:28 But Paul shouted as l as he

love (457)

Gen 4:1 Adam made l to his wife Eve.
4:17 Cain made l to his wife.
4:25 Adam made l to his wife again.
22:2 whom you l, and go to Moriah.
29:32 now my husband will l me!"
32:10 I'm not worthy of all the l and
38:26 never made l to her again.
39:21 to him with his unchanging l
47:29 "I want you to swear that you l
Exo 20:6 generations of those who l me
21:5 'I hereby declare my l for my
34:7 He continues to show his l to
Lev 19:18 Instead, l your neighbor as you
19:18 your neighbor as you l yourself.
19:34 L them as you love yourself,
19:34 Love them as you l yourself,
Num 14:19 By your great l, please forgive
Dtr 5:10 generations of those who l me
6:5 L the LORD your God with all
7:9 generations of those who l him
7:13 He will l you, bless you,
10:12 follow all his directions, l him,
10:19 So you should l foreigners,
11:1 L the LORD your God,
11:13 l the LORD your God,
11:22 L the LORD your God,
13:3 to find out if you really l him
13:6 son, or daughter, the wife you l,
19:9 I am now giving you — to l
21:15 have two wives and l one
21:15 the wife that the man doesn't l.
21:16 son of the wife he doesn't l).
21:17 son of the wife he doesn't l as
24:3 If her second husband doesn't l
30:6 You will l the LORD your God
30:16 L the LORD your God,
30:20 L the LORD your God,
33:3 You certainly l your people.
Jos 22:5 L the LORD your God,
23:11 Be very careful to l the LORD
Jdg 5:31 But may those who l the LORD
14:16 You don't really l me!
16:4 leaving Gaza, he fell in l
16:15 "How can you say that you l
1Sm 1:19 Elkanah made l to his wife
18:20 Michal fell in l with David.
20:17 because of his l for David.
2Sm 1:26 Your l was more wonderful to
1:26 to me than the l of women.
7:15 stop showing him my l as
13:1 son Amnon fell in l with Tamar,
13:4 "I'm in l with Absalom's sister
19:6 You l those who hate you and
19:6 you and hate those who l you.
1Ki 1:4 the king did not make l to her.
1Ki 3:6 "You've shown great l to my
3:6 him your great l by giving him
3:26 was deeply moved by her l
10:9 Because of your God's eternal l
11:2 was obsessed with their l.
1Ch 17:13 stop showing him my l as
2Ch 1:8 "You've shown great l to my
9:8 Because of your God's l for the
19:2 people and l those who hate
Neh 1:5 show mercy to those who l you
Job 19:19 Those I l have turned against
Psa 4:2 How long are you going to l
5:11 and let those who l your name
11:5 and the ones who l violence.
18:1 I l you, O LORD, my strength.
26:8 I l the house where you live,
31:23 L the LORD, all you godly
40:16 Let those who l your salvation
52:4 You l every destructive
69:36 Those who l him will live there.
70:4 Let those who l your salvation
91:14 Because you l me,
97:10 Let those who l the LORD hate
109:4 In return for my l, they accuse
109:5 and with hatred instead of l.
116:1 I l the LORD because he hears
119:47 Your commandments, which I l,
119:48 your commandments, which I l.
119:97 Oh, how I l your teachings!
119:113 but I l your teachings.
119:119 I l your written instructions.
119:127 I l your commandments more
119:132 do for those who l your name.
119:140 thoroughly tested, and I l it.
119:163 with it. I l your teachings.
119:165 for those who l your teachings.
122:6 "May those who l you prosper.
Pro 1:22 people l being so gullible?
4:6 L wisdom, and it will protect
5:19 be intoxicated with her l.
7:18 drink our fill of l until morning.
7:18 Let's enjoy making l,
8:17 I l those who love me.
8:17 I love those who l me.
8:21 inheritance to those who l me
8:36 All those who hate me l death."
9:8 wise person, and he will l you.
10:12 but l covers every wrong.
15:17 there is l than juicy steaks
17:9 forgives an offense seeks l,
18:21 and those who l to talk will
20:13 Do not l sleep or you will end
27:5 is better than unexpressed l.
Ecc 3:8 a time to l and a time to hate,
9:1 there will be l or hatred.
9:6 Their l, their hate, and their
9:9 life with your wife, whom you l,
Sos 1:2 Your expressions of l are better
1:3 No wonder the young women l
1:4 of l more than wine.
1:4 is that the young women l you!
1:7 Please tell me, you whom I l,
1:9 My true l, I compare you to a
1:15 You are beautiful, my true l!
2:2 so is my true l among the
2:4 room and looks at me with l.
2:5 because I am weak from l.
2:7 field that you will not awaken l
2:7 or arouse l before its proper
2:10 up, my true l, my beautiful one,
2:13 Get up, my true l, my beautiful
3:1 my bed I looked for the one I l.
3:2 I will look for the one I l.
3:3 "Have you seen the one I l?"
3:4 them when I found the one I l.
3:5 that you will not awaken l or
3:5 or arouse l before its proper
3:10 inlaid scenes of l — was made
4:1 You are beautiful, my true l.
4:7 in every way, my true l.
4:10 are your expressions of l,
4:10 your expressions of l than wine
5:1 with expressions of l!
5:2 Open to me, my true l,
6:4 You are beautiful, my true l,
7:6 are, my l, with your elegance.

Sos 7:12 There I will give you my **l**.
8:4 me that you will not awaken **l**
8:4 or arouse **l** before its proper
8:6 **L** is as overpowering as death.
8:7 water cannot extinguish **l**,
8:7 all his family's wealth for **l**,
Isa 1:23 They all **l** bribes and run after
43:4 you are honored and I **l** you.
56:6 to **l** the LORD's name,
56:10 dreaming; they **l** to sleep.
61:8 I, the LORD, **l** justice.
63:9 In his **l** and compassion he
66:10 All who **l** Jerusalem,
Jer 2:2 the **l** you had for me as a bride.
2:25 You **l** foreign gods and follow
2:33 planned ways to look for **l**.
5:31 and my people **l** this.
9:24 act out of **l**, righteousness,
11:15 "What right do these people I **l**
12:7 I have handed the people I **l**
14:10 people: They **l** to wander.
16:5 I'm taking my peace, **l**,
31:3 "I **l** you with an everlasting
31:3 love you with an everlasting **l**.
33:26 I will restore their fortunes and **l**
Lam 1:2 Out of all those who **l** the city,
1:19 I called for those who **l** me,
Eze 16:8 were old enough to make **l** to.
16:8 I promised to **l** you,
16:37 I will have all those who **l** you
23:7 those with whom she fell in **l**.
23:16 She fell in **l** with them at first
24:16 you the person you **l** the most.
24:21 It's the thing you **l** the most.
24:25 and the thing they **l** the most.
33:31 They say that they **l** me,
33:32 voice who sings **l** songs
Dan 9:4 show mercy to those who **l** you
Hos 1:6 I will no longer **l** the nation of
1:7 Yet, I will **l** the descendants of
2:4 I won't **l** her children,
2:19 you my **l** and compassion.
3:1 "**L** your wife again,
3:1 **L** her as I, the LORD, love the
3:1 as I, the LORD, **l** the Israelites,
3:1 have turned to other gods and **l**
4:1 land: "There is no faith, no **l**,
4:18 dearly **l** to act shamefully.
6:4 Your **l** is like fog in the morning.
9:15 and I won't **l** them anymore.
11:4 kindness, with ropes of **l**.
12:7 They **l** to cheat people.
14:3 are our gods. You **l** orphans."
14:4 I will **l** them freely.
Amo 4:5 you people of Israel **l** to do.
5:15 Hate evil and **l** good.
Mic 1:16 mourning for the children you **l**.
3:2 You hate good and **l** evil.
6:8 to do what is right, to **l** mercy,
Zep 3:17 renews you with his **l**,
Zec 8:19 So **l** truth and peace.
Mal 1:2 'How did you **l** us?'
Mat 3:17 whom I **l** — my Son with whom
5:43 it was said, '**L** your neighbor,
5:44 I tell you this: **L** your enemies,
5:46 If you **l** those who love you,
5:46 If you love those who **l** you,
6:24 first master and **l** the second,
12:18 whom I have chosen, whom I **l**,
17:5 whom I **l** and with whom I am
19:19 **L** your neighbor as you love
19:19 Love your neighbor as you **l**
22:37 Jesus answered him, "'**L** the
22:39 The second is like it: '**L** your
22:39 'Love your neighbor as you **l**
23:6 They **l** the place of honor at
23:7 They **l** to be greeted in the
24:12 most people's **l** will grow cold.
Mar 1:11 "You are my Son, whom I **l**.
9:7 "This is my Son, whom I **l**.
12:30 So **l** the Lord your God with all
12:31 '**L** your neighbor as you love
12:31 your neighbor as you **l** yourself.'
12:33 To **l** him with all your heart,
12:33 and to **l** your neighbor as you
12:33 as you **l** yourself is more
Luk 3:22 "You are my Son, whom I **l**.
6:27 is listening: **L** your enemies.
6:32 "If you **l** those who love you,
6:32 "If you love those who **l** you,
6:32 Even sinners **l** those who love
6:32 Even sinners love those who **l**
6:35 Rather, **l** your enemies,
7:42 you think will **l** him the most?"
7:47 Her great **l** proves that.
10:27 He answered, "'**L** the Lord your
10:27 And '**L** your neighbor as you
10:27 neighbor as you **l** yourself.'"
11:42 justice and the **l** of God.
11:43 You **l** to sit in the front seats in
16:13 first master and **l** the second,
16:14 The Pharisees, who **l** money,
20:13 I'll send my son, whom I **l**.
20:46 walk around in long robes and **l**
Jon 5:42 You don't have any **l** for God.
8:42 your Father, you would **l** me.
12:25 Those who **l** their lives will
13:34 **L** each other in the same way
13:35 of your **l** for each other."
14:15 "If you **l** me, you will obey my
14:21 Those who **l** me will have my
14:21 me will have my Father's **l**,
14:21 will **l** them and show myself to
14:23 "Those who **l** me will do what I
14:23 My Father will **l** them,
14:24 A person who doesn't **l** me
14:31 I want the world to know that I **l**
15:9 has loved me. So live in my **l**.
15:10 you will live in my **l**.
15:10 and in that way I live in his **l**.
15:12 **L** each other as I have loved
15:13 The greatest **l** you can show is
15:17 **L** each other. This is what I'm
15:19 the world would **l** you as one of
17:26 it known so that the **l** you have
21:15 do you **l** me more than the other
21:15 you know that I **l** you."
21:16 son of John, do you **l** me?"
21:16 you know that I **l** you."
21:17 son of John, do you **l** me?"
21:17 him a third time, "Do you **l** me?"
21:17 You know that I **l** you."
Act 13:34 enduring **l** promised to David.'
Rom 1:31 and don't show **l** to their own
5:5 because God's **l** has been
5:8 demonstrates God's **l** for us.
8:28 of those who **l** God — those
8:35 What will separate us from the **l**
8:35 death separate us from his **l**?
8:38 God's **l** which Christ Jesus
12:9 **L** sincerely. Hate evil. Hold on
13:8 is the debt of **l** that you owe
13:9 "**L** your neighbor as you love
13:9 "Love your neighbor as you **l**
13:10 **L** never does anything that is
13:10 **l** fulfills Moses' Teachings.
14:15 you are no longer living by **l**.
15:30 Jesus Christ and by the **l** that
1Co 2:9 prepared for those who **l** him."
4:21 that I punish you or show you **l**
8:1 but **l** builds them up.
8:3 But if they **l** God, they are
13:1 But if I don't have **l**,
13:2 But if I don't have **l**,
13:3 But if I don't have **l**,
13:4 **L** is patient. Love is kind. Love
13:4 **L** is kind. Love isn't jealous. It
13:4 **L** isn't jealous. It doesn't sing its
13:7 **L** never stops being patient,
13:8 **L** never comes to an end.
13:13 remain: faith, hope, and **l**.
13:13 But the best one of these is **l**.
14:1 Pursue **l**, and desire spiritual
16:14 Do everything with **l**.
16:22 If anyone doesn't **l** the Lord,
16:24 Through Christ Jesus my **l** is
2Co 2:4 let you know how much I **l** you.
2:8 to assure him that you **l** him.
5:14 Clearly, Christ's **l** guides us.
6:6 ⌊in our lives⌋, our sincere **l**,
8:7 and your **l** for us increase,
8:8 genuine your **l** is by pointing
2Co 8:24 men a demonstration of your **l**.
11:11 Because I don't **l** you?
11:11 God knows that I do **l** you.
12:15 Do you **l** me less because I
12:15 less because I **l** you so much?
13:11 The God of **l** and peace will be
13:13 Christ's good will, God's **l**,
Gal 5:6 that expresses itself through **l**.
5:13 serve each other through **l**.
5:14 "**L** your neighbor as you love
5:14 "Love your neighbor as you **l**
5:22 the spiritual nature produces **l**,
Eph 1:5 Because of his **l** he had
1:15 in the Lord Jesus and your **l**
2:4 because of his great **l** for us.
3:17 I also pray that **l** may be the
3:18 long, high, and deep his **l** is.
3:19 You will know Christ's **l**,
4:16 so that it builds itself up in **l**.
5:2 Live in **l** as Christ also loved
5:25 Husbands, **l** your wives as
5:28 So husbands must **l** their
5:28 as they **l** their own bodies.
5:33 But every husband must **l** his
6:23 peace and **l** along with faith.
6:24 everyone who has an undying **l**
Php 1:9 I pray that your **l** will keep on
1:16 Christ out of **l** know that God
2:1 you have any comfort from **l**?
2:2 same attitude and the same **l**,
4:1 I **l** you and miss you.
Col 1:4 faith in Christ Jesus and your **l**
1:8 and has told us about the **l** that
2:2 Because they are united in **l**,
3:19 Husbands, **l** your wives,
1Th 1:3 your **l** is working hard,
3:6 news about your faith and **l**.
3:12 Lord will greatly increase your **l**
3:12 else, just as we **l** you.
4:9 Christians should **l** each other.
4:9 has taught you to **l** each other.
4:10 In fact, you are showing **l** to all
4:10 to excel in **l** even more.
5:8 We must put on faith and **l** as a
5:13 We ask you to **l** them and think
2Th 1:3 remarkable growth and your **l**
2:10 those who refused to **l** the truth
3:5 God's **l** and Christ's endurance.
1Ti 1:5 in giving you this order is for **l**
1:14 gave me the **l** that Christ Jesus
2:15 lives in faith, **l**, and holiness.
3:3 He must not be quarrelsome or **l**
4:12 your speech, behavior, **l**, faith,
6:2 are believers whom they **l**.
6:10 Certainly, the **l** of money is the
6:11 **l**, endurance, and gentleness.
2Ti 1:7 of power, **l**, and good judgment.
1:13 With faith and **l** for Christ
2:22 Pursue faith, **l**, and peace
3:2 will be selfish and **l** money.
3:3 and have no **l** for what is good.
3:4 They will **l** pleasure rather than
3:10 my **l**, and my endurance.
4:10 He fell in **l** with this present
Tit 1:8 be hospitable, **l** what is good,
2:2 in faith, **l**, and endurance.
2:4 teach young women to show **l**
3:4 and **l** for humanity appear,
Phm 1:5 to the Lord Jesus and your **l**
1:7 Your **l** ⌊for God's people⌋ gives
1:9 an appeal on the basis of **l**.
Heb 6:10 done or the **l** you've shown
10:24 encourage each other to show **l**
13:1 Continue to **l** each other.
13:5 Don't **l** money. Be happy with
Jas 1:12 promised to those who **l** him.
2:5 promised to those who **l** him?
2:8 "**L** your neighbor as you love
2:8 "Love your neighbor as you **l**
4:4 Don't you know that **l** for this
1Pe 1:8 never seen Christ, you **l** him.
1:22 **L** each other with a warm love
1:22 Love each other with a warm **l**
1:22 As a result you have a sincere **l**
2:17 **L** your brothers and sisters in
3:8 **l** each other, have compassion,

1Pe 4:8 Above all, l each other warmly,
4:8 because l covers many sins.
5:14 each other with a kiss of l.
2Pe 1:7 and to Christian affection add l.
1:17 whom I l and in whom I
1Jn 2:5 in whom God's l is perfected.
2:10 Those who l other believers
2:15 Don't l the world and what it
2:15 Those who l the world don't
2:15 have the Father's l in them.
3:1 The Father has given us his l.
3:10 is right or l other believers isn't
3:11 the beginning is to l each other.
3:14 because we l other believers.
3:14 grow in l remains in death.
3:16 We understand what l is when
3:17 How can God's l be in that
3:18 Dear children, we must show l
3:23 and to l each other as he
4:7 Dear friends, we must l each
4:7 because l comes from God.
4:8 The person who doesn't l
4:8 know God, because God is l.
4:9 God has shown us his l by
4:10 This is l: not that we have
4:11 we must also l each other.
4:12 If we l each other, God lives in
4:12 and his l is perfected in us.
4:16 God is l. Those who live in
4:16 Those who live in God's l live
4:17 God's l has reached its goal in
4:17 like him ⌊with regard to l⌋.
4:18 No fear exists where his l is.
4:18 Rather, perfect l gets rid of fear,
4:18 in fear doesn't have perfect l.
4:19 We l because God loved us
4:20 Whoever says, "I l God,"
4:20 who don't l other believers,
4:20 they have seen, can't l God,
4:21 must also l other believers.
5:2 We know that we l God's
5:2 when we l God by obeying
5:3 To l God means that we obey
2Jn 1:1 whom I l because we share the
1:2 We l you because of the truth
1:3 who in truth and l is the
1:5 we continue to l each other.
1:5 commanded to l each other.
1:6 L means that we live by doing
1:6 were commanded to live in l,
3Jn 1:1 whom I l because we share the
1:6 the congregation about your l.
Jud 1:2 and l fill your lives!
1:21 Remain in God's l as you look
Rev 2:4 The l you had at first is gone.
2:19 I know your l, faith, service,
3:19 and discipline everyone I l.
12:11 They didn't l their life so much

loved (91)

Gen 24:67 became his wife, and he l her.
25:28 of wild animals, he l Esau.
25:28 However, Rebekah l Jacob.
29:18 Jacob l Rachel. So he offered,
29:20 days to him because he l her.
29:30 He l Rachel more than Leah.
34:3 He l the girl and spoke tenderly
37:3 Israel l Joseph more than all
37:4 that their father l him more than
Dtr 4:37 Because he l your ancestors
7:8 because the LORD l you
10:15 on your ancestors and l them.
Rut 1:8 me and to our l ones who have
1Sm 1:5 to Hannah because he l her,
16:21 Saul l him very much and
18:1 He l David as much as ⌊he
18:1 as much as ⌊he l⌋ himself.
18:3 because he l him as much
18:3 him as much as ⌊he l⌋ himself.
18:16 in Israel and Judah l David,
18:28 his daughter Michal l David.
20:17 He l David as much as ⌊he
20:17 as much as ⌊he l⌋ himself.
2Sm 1:23 Saul and Jonathan were l and
12:24 The LORD l the child
1Ki 3:3 Solomon l the LORD and lived
1Ki 11:1 King Solomon l many foreign
11:1 He l Hittite women and women
2Ch 11:21 Rehoboam l Maacah,
26:10 fields because he l the soil.
Neh 13:26 God l him, and God made him
Est 2:17 Now, the king l Esther more
Psa 38:11 My l ones and my friends keep
45:7 You have l what is right and
47:4 the pride of Jacob, whom he l.
78:68 Mount Zion which he l.
88:18 You have taken my l ones and
109:17 He l to put curses ⌊on others⌋,
119:159 See how I have l your guiding
119:167 I have l them very much.
Pro 14:20 but a rich person is l by many.
16:13 speaks what is right is l.
Jer 8:2 are the things that they had l,
Hos 2:1 call your sisters Ruhamah [L].
2:23 Those who are not l I will call
2:23 not loved I will call my l ones.
3:1 even though she is l by others
11:1 Israel was a child, I l him,
Mal 1:2 "I l you," says the LORD.
1:2 declares the LORD. "I l Jacob,
Mar 10:21 Jesus looked at him and l him.
12:6 was his son, whom he l.
Jon 3:16 God l the world this way:
3:19 Yet, people l the dark rather
11:5 Jesus l Martha, her sister,
11:36 "See how much Jesus l him."
13:1 Jesus l his own who were in
13:1 and he l them to the end.
13:23 the one whom Jesus l,
13:34 the same way that I have l you.
14:28 If you l me, you would be glad
15:9 "I have l you the same way the
15:9 same way the Father has l me.
15:12 each other as I have l you.
16:27 you because you have l me
17:23 me and that you have l them
17:23 the same way you have l me.
17:24 me because you l me before
19:26 whom he l standing there.
20:2 other disciple, whom Jesus l.
21:7 The disciple whom Jesus l
21:20 the disciple whom Jesus l.
Rom 9:13 The Scriptures say, "I l Jacob,
9:25 Those who are not l I will call
9:25 not loved I will call my l ones.
11:28 But by God's choice they are l
Gal 2:20 who l me and took the
Eph 5:2 Live in love as Christ also l us.
5:25 love your wives as Christ l the
Col 3:12 whom God has chosen and l,
2Th 2:13 You are l by the Lord and we
2:16 God our Father l us and by his
Heb 1:9 You have l what is right and
11:35 Women received their l ones
2Pe 2:15 Balaam l what his wrongdoing
1Jn 4:10 not that we have l God,
4:10 but that he l us and sent his
4:11 if this is the way God l us,
4:19 We love because God l us first.
Jud 1:1 who are l by God the Father,
Rev 3:9 and realize that I have l you.

lovely (8)

Psa 84:1 Your dwelling place is l,
Sos 1:5 I am dark and l like Kedar's
1:10 cheeks are l with ornaments,
2:14 and your figure is l."
4:3 Your mouth is l. Your temples
6:4 like Tirzah, l like Jerusalem,
Jer 6:2 "My people Zion are like l
Zec 9:17 They will be beautiful and l.

lover (1)

Isa 47:8 listen to this, you l of pleasure.

lovers (21)

Jer 3:1 a prostitute who has many l.
4:30 Your l reject you; they want to
22:20 all your l are defeated."
22:22 and your l will go into captivity.
30:14 All your l have forgotten you,
Eze 16:33 But you give gifts to all your l
Eze 16:36 you gave yourself to your l
16:37 is why I will gather all your l
16:39 I will hand you over to your l.
23:5 Assyrian l who lived nearby.
23:9 why I handed her over to her l,
23:20 She lusted after her l,
23:22 to stir up your l against you.
23:22 They are the l you turned away
Hos 2:2 Tell her to remove the l from
2:5 She said, 'I'll chase after my l.
2:7 She will run after her l,
2:10 show her naked body to her l,
2:12 that they were gifts from her l.
2:13 and she chased after her l.
8:9 sold themselves to their l.

love's (1)

Sos 8:6 L flames are flames of fire,

loves (67)

Gen 44:20 and his father l him.'
Dtr 10:18 He l foreigners and gives them
15:16 because he l you and your
21:16 son of the wife he l as if that
23:5 the LORD your God l you.
28:54 his brother, the wife he l,
28:56 toward the husband she l
Rut 4:15 Your daughter-in-law who l you
2Ch 2:11 the LORD l his people,
Job 14:6 Meanwhile, he l life as a
14:6 he loves life as a laborer l
Psa 11:7 He l a righteous way of life.
33:5 The LORD l righteousness and
37:28 The LORD l justice,
87:2 The LORD l the city of Zion
99:4 strength is that he l justice.
127:2 to those he l while they sleep.
145:20 protects everyone who l him,
146:8 The LORD l righteous people.
Pro 3:12 the LORD warns the one he l,
12:1 Whoever l discipline loves to
12:1 loves discipline l to learn,
13:24 but whoever l his son
15:9 but he l those who pursue
17:17 A friend always l, and a brother
17:19 Whoever l sin loves a quarrel.
17:19 Whoever loves sin l a quarrel.
19:8 who gains sense l himself.
21:17 Whoever l pleasure will
21:17 Whoever l wine and expensive
22:11 Whoever l a pure heart and
29:3 A person who l wisdom makes
Ecc 5:10 Whoever l money will never be
5:10 Whoever l wealth will never be
Isa 48:14 The LORD l Cyrus.
Hos 10:11 is like a trained calf that l
Mal 2:11 the holy place that the LORD l
Mat 10:37 "The person who l his father or
10:37 The person who l a son or
Luk 7:5 He l our people and built our
7:47 little forgiveness l very little."
Jon 3:35 The Father l his Son and has
5:20 The Father l the Son and
10:17 The Father l me because I give
14:21 is the person who l me.
16:27 The Father l you because you
Rom 1:7 everyone in Rome whom God l
8:37 The one who l us gives us an
13:8 The one who l another person
2Co 9:7 since God l a cheerful giver.
Eph 5:1 since you are the children he l.
5:28 A man who l his wife loves
5:28 A man who loves his wife l
5:33 love his wife as he l himself,
Col 1:13 of his Son, whom he l.
1Th 1:4 we know that God l you
Heb 12:6 Lord disciplines everyone he l.
1Jn 3:1 He l us so much that we are
4:7 Everyone who l has been born
4:16 and believed that God l us.
4:21 The person who l God must
5:1 Everyone who l the Father also
5:1 the Father also l his children.
2Jn 1:1 I'm not the only one who l you.
1:1 who knows the truth also l you.
3Jn 1:9 who l to be in charge,

Rev 1:5 ever belong to the one who l

lovesick (1)

Sos 5:8 will tell him I am hopelessly l.

lovesong (1)

Isa 5:1 Let me sing a l to my beloved

loving (7)

Num 14:18 patient, forever l....
Pro 5:19 a l doe and a graceful deer.
18:24 but a l friend can stick closer
Lam 4:10 The hands of l mothers cooked
Luk 1:78 our God is l and merciful.
Rom 12:10 to each other like a l family.
Col 3:14 Above all, be l. This ties

lovingly (3)

Exo 15:13 "L, you will lead the people
Eph 4:2 Be patient with each other and l
4:15 as we l speak the truth,

low (7)

Job 24:24 They are brought down l and
Psa 38:6 over and bowed down very l.
144:5 O LORD, bend your heaven l,
Isa 46:1 the god Nebo stoops l.
46:2 These gods stoop l and bow
Eze 17:6 grew into a l vine that spread
1Co 6:4 the church has a l opinion

low-class (1)

Act 17:5 They took some l characters

lower (26)

Gen 6:16 Build the ship with l,
Dtr 28:43 of living will sink l and lower.
28:43 of living will sink lower and l.
Jos 8:26 Joshua did not l his hand
15:19 her the upper and l springs.
16:3 of Japhlet and L Beth Horon,
18:13 south of L Beth Horon.
Jdg 1:15 her the upper and l springs.
1Ki 9:17 rebuilt Gezer, L Beth Horon,
1Ch 7:24 who built Upper and L Beth
2Ch 8:5 Horon and L Beth Horon into
Neh 3:5 However, the nobles wouldn't l
Psa 8:5 him a little l than yourself.
Ecc 10:6 and rich people are left to fill l
Isa 11:11 Upper and L Egypt,
22:9 You will store water in the L
Jer 38:6 They used ropes to l Jeremiah
Eze 40:18 The pavement in the l
40:19 from the inside of the l gateway
42:9 These l side rooms had an
43:14 on the ground to the l ledge
43:14 and from the l ledge to the
Luk 5:4 and l your nets to catch some
5:5 But if you say so, I'll l the nets."
Heb 2:7 You made him a little l than the
2:9 Jesus was made a little l than

lowered (14)

Gen 24:18 She quickly l her jar to her
24:46 She quickly l her jar and said,
44:11 Each one quickly l his sack to
1Sm 19:12 So Michal l David through a
Isa 40:4 mountain and hill will be l.
Jer 38:11 clothes from there and l them
Eze 1:24 stood still, they l their wings.
1:25 stood still with their wings l.
Mar 2:4 Then they l the cot on which
Luk 5:19 (They l him in front of Jesus.)
Act 9:25 However, Saul's disciples l
10:11 linen sheet being l by its four
11:5 linen sheet being l by its four
27:17 they l the sail and were carried

lowest (6)

Gen 3:14 You will be the l of animals as
9:25 He will be the l slave to his
1Ki 6:6 The interior of the l story of
Neh 4:13 behind the wall where it was l
Dan 4:17 He can place the l of people in
Eph 4:9 had gone down to the l parts

lowest-ranking (2)

2Ki 18:24 my master's l officers when you
Isa 36:9 my master's l officers when you

lowly (2)

Job 5:11 He places l people up high.
Pro 16:19 Better to be humble with l

loyal (25)

Dtr 4:4 But you were l to the LORD
10:20 God, worship him, be l to him,
11:22 his directions, and be l to him.
13:4 serve him, and be l to him.
30:20 God, obey him, and be l to him.
Jos 14:8 However, I was completely l to
14:9 because you were completely l
14:14 Caleb was completely l
22:5 Be l to him, and serve him with
23:8 But you must be l to the LORD
2Sm 15:10 But Absalom sent his l
16:17 "Is that how l you are to your
20:2 the people of Judah remained l
1Ki 12:20 remained l to David's dynasty.
2Ki 10:15 "Are you as l to me as I am to
18:6 He was l to the LORD and
1Ch 12:29 remained l to Saul's family.
2Ch 12:2 Israel was not l to the LORD.
Psa 78:8 Their hearts were not l.
78:37 Their hearts were not l to him.
Pro 20:6 people declare themselves l,
Isa 57:1 L people are taken away,
Eze 17:13 and made him promise to be l.
Hos 12:6 Be l and fair, and always wait
Tit 2:10 and completely l they can be.

loyalty (12)

1Sm 18:3 made a pledge of mutual l
22:8 my son entered into a l pledge
1Ch 12:33 Their l was unquestioned.
29:24 their l to King Solomon.
Psa 81:7 I tested your l at the oasis of
Pro 19:22 L is desirable in a person,
Jer 2:2 I remember the unfailing l of
Hos 6:6 I want your l, not your
10:12 and harvest the fruit that your l
Jnh 2:8 idols abandon their l to you.
Zep 1:5 who worship by swearing l
1:5 LORD while also swearing l

Lucius (3)

Act 13:1 the Black), L (from Cyrene),
13:3 fasting and praying, Simeon, L,
Rom 16:21 so do L, Jason, and Sosipater,

luck (1)

Gen 30:11 So she called him Gad [L].

lucky (1)

Gen 30:11 Leah said, "I've been l!"

Lud (5)

Gen 10:22 Arpachshad, L, and Aram.
1Ch 1:17 L, Aram, Uz, Hul, Gether,
Isa 66:19 Put and L, Meshech, Rosh,
Eze 27:10 People from Persia, L,
30:5 Sudan, Put, L, all the Arabs,

Ludites (2)

Gen 10:13 was the ancestor of the L,
1Ch 1:11 was the ancestor of the L,

Luhith (2)

Isa 15:5 go up the mountain road to L.
Jer 48:5 People go up the pass of L,

Luke (3)

Col 4:14 My dear friend L, the physician,
2Ti 4:11 Only L is with me.
Phm 1:24 and L send you greetings.

lukewarm (1)

Rev 3:16 But since you are l and not hot

lumber (7)

1Ki 9:11 as much cedar and cypress l
1Ki 15:22 the stones and l from Ramah.
2Ki 22:6 the rest of the money to buy l
2Ch 2:9 prepare plenty of l for me,
2:16 We will cut all the l you need
16:6 the stones and l from Ramah.
Hag 1:8 "Go to the mountains, get l,

lumberjack (1)

Isa 14:8 no l has come to attack us."

lumberjacks (3)

1Ki 5:6 any skilled l like those from
2Ch 2:8 are skilled Lebanese l.
2:10 I will give your l 120,000

lump (1)

Rom 9:21 use from the same l of clay.

lunatic (3)

2Ki 9:11 Why did this l come to you?"
9:20 troop's leader is driving like a l,
Jer 29:26 You should put any l who acts

lunatics (1)

1Sm 21:15 Do I have such a shortage of l

lunch (3)

Rut 2:18 what she had left over from l
Luk 11:37 a Pharisee invited him to have l
14:12 you invite people for l or dinner,

lunged (1)

Gen 19:9 hard against Lot and l forward

lunges (1)

Job 16:14 He l at me like a warrior.

lure (4)

Jos 8:6 and we will l them away from
Pro 1:10 My son, if sinners l you,
Act 20:30 They will do this to l disciples
Jas 1:14 desires as they l him away

lured (3)

Jos 8:16 they were l away from the city.
Job 36:16 "Yes, he l you away from the
2Co 11:3 somehow be l away from your

lush (1)

Zec 11:3 because the l banks of the

lust (8)

2Sm 13:15 for her was greater than the l
Job 31:1 can I look with l at a virgin?
Isa 57:5 You burn with l under oak trees
Eze 23:17 and dishonored her with their l.
24:13 to clean you of your filthy l,
Mar 7:22 shameless l, envy, cursing,
Rom 1:27 with women and burn with l
Col 3:5 sin, perversion, passion, l,

lusted (7)

Eze 6:9 which l after idols.
23:5 She l after her Assyrian lovers
23:9 to the Assyrians whom she l
23:11 Oholibah l after men more than
23:12 She l after the Assyrians who
23:20 She l after her lovers,
23:30 because you l after the nations

lustful (2)

Eze 16:26 had sex with your l neighbors,
1Th 4:5 not in the passionate, l way of

lusts (3)

Rom 1:24 this reason God allowed their l
2Ti 2:22 Stay away from l which tempt
Tit 3:3 many kinds of l and pleasures.

luxuries (1)

Rev 18:14 All your l and your splendor

luxurious (2)

Isa 13:22 will howl in its l palaces.
Rev 18:3 Her l wealth has made the

luxury (5)

Pro 19:10 **L** does not fit a fool,
Luk 7:25 clothes and live in **l** are
Jas 5:5 You have lived in **l** and
Rev 18:7 She gave herself glory and **l**.
18:9 had sex with her and lived in **l**

Luz (7)

Gen 28:19 the name of the city was **L**.
35:6 with him came to **L** (that is,
48:3 Almighty appeared to me at **L**
Jos 16:2 Bethel the border goes to **L**
18:13 slope of **L** (now called Bethel).
Jdg 1:23 the past the city was called **L**.)
1:26 he built a city and called it **L**.

Lybians (1)

Nah 3:9 Put and the **L** were her help.

Lycaonia (1)

Act 14:6 to Lystra and Derbe, cities of **L**,

Lycaonian (1)

Act 14:11 shouted in the **L** language,

Lycia (1)

Act 27:5 of Myra in the province of **L**.

Lydda (5)

Act 9:32 those who lived in the city of **L**.
9:33 In **L** Peter found a man named
9:35 who lived in the city of **L**
9:38 **L** is near the city of Joppa.
9:38 heard that Peter was in **L**,

Lydia (3)

Jer 46:9 you warriors from **L** who use
Act 16:14 woman named **L** was present.
16:15 When **L** and her family were

Lydia's (1)

Act 16:40 they went to **L** house.

lye (1)

Job 9:30 If I wash myself with **l** soap

lying (81)

Gen 4:7 But if you don't do well, sin is **l**
28:13 the land on which you are **l**
29:2 Three flocks of sheep were **l**
49:14 "Issachar is a strong donkey, **l**
Exo 14:30 and Israel saw the Egyptians **l**
Dtr 21:1 do if you find a murder victim **l**
22:4 Israelite's donkey or ox **l**
Jdg 3:25 shocked to see their ruler **l**
4:22 He saw Sisera **l** there dead
19:27 his concubine) was **l** at the
Rut 3:4 notice the place where he is **l**.
3:8 to see a woman **l** at his feet.
1Sm 3:2 One night Eli was **l** down in
5:4 were cut off ⌊and were **l**⌋
26:5 commander of the army, were **l**.
26:5 Saul was **l** in the camp,
26:7 Saul was **l** asleep inside the
26:7 the soldiers were **l** around him.
31:8 three sons **l** on Mount Gilboa.
2Sm 13:8 He was **l** down. She took
1Ki 13:18 (But the old prophet was **l**.)
13:25 who passed by saw the body **l**
2Ki 1:4 up from the bed you are **l** on.
1:6 up from the bed you are **l** on.
1:16 up from the bed you are **l** on.
4:32 boy was **l** on Elisha's bed.
9:16 Jezreel because Joram was **l**
1Ch 10:8 his sons **l** on Mount Gilboa.
2Ch 20:24 Corpses were **l** on the ground.
Est 7:8 the couch where Esther was **l**.
Job 3:13 I would now be quietly **l** down.
Psa 31:18 Let ⌊their⌋ **l** lips be
36:4 He invents trouble while **l** on
52:3 You prefer **l** to speaking the
109:2 They speak against me with **l**
119:104 I hate every path that leads to **l**.
119:128 every pathway that leads to **l**.
119:163 I hate **l**; I am disgusted with it.
Psa 120:2 O LORD, rescue me from **l** lips
Pro 6:17 arrogant eyes, a **l** tongue,
10:18 conceals hatred has **l** lips.
12:17 a **l** witness speaks deceitfully.
13:5 A righteous person hates **l**,
17:7 How much less does **l** fit a
19:5 A **l** witness will not go
19:9 A **l** witness will not go
21:6 Those who gather wealth by **l**
21:28 A **l** witness will die,
23:28 is like a robber, **l** in ambush.
23:34 You will be like someone **l**
23:34 the sea or like someone **l** down
26:28 A **l** tongue hates its victims,
Jer 43:2 said to Jeremiah, "You're **l**!
Eze 4:9 that you are **l** on your side.
29:3 are like a monster crocodile **l**
Dan 2:29 while you were **l** in bed,
9:17 which is **l** in ruins.
Hos 4:2 There is cursing, **l**,
Jnh 1:5 and was **l** there sound asleep.
Mic 7:5 a woman is **l** in your arms.
Mal 3:5 adulterers, **l** witnesses,
Mat 8:6 my servant is **l** at home
15:19 sexual sins, stealing, **l**,
28:6 see the place where he was **l**.
Mar 2:4 the paralyzed man was **l**.
7:30 home and found the little child **l**
Luk 2:12 of cloth and **l** in a manger."
2:16 who was **l** in a manger.
5:25 the stretcher he had been **l** on.
Jon 5:5 sick for 38 years, was **l** there.
5:6 Jesus saw the man **l** there and
20:5 He saw the strips of linen **l**
20:6 He saw the strips of linen **l**
20:7 It wasn't **l** with the strips of
20:12 the body of Jesus had been **l**.
21:9 they saw a fire with a fish **l** on
Rom 9:1 I'm not **l**. The Holy Spirit, along
2Co 11:31 knows that I'm not **l**.
1Ti 2:7 telling you the truth. I'm not **l**.
1Jn 1:6 and yet live in the dark, we're **l**.
Rev 3:9 they are Jewish, but they are **l**.

lyre (18)

1Sm 10:5 a tambourine, a flute, and a **l**.
16:16 a man who can play the **l** well?
16:23 David took the **l** and strummed
18:10 strummed a tune on the **l** as
Job 21:12 sing with the tambourine and **l**,
30:31 So my **l** is used for mourning
Psa 33:2 Give thanks with a **l** to the
43:4 will give thanks to you on the **l**,
49:4 riddle with the ⌊music of⌋ a **l**.
57:8 Wake up, harp and **l**!
71:22 thanks to you as I play on a **l**.
92:3 harp and with a melody on a **l**.
98:5 music to the LORD with a **l**,
98:5 with a **l** and the melody of a
108:2 Wake up, harp and **l**!
137:5 hand forget ⌊how to play the **l**⌋.
147:7 music to our God with a **l**.
Isa 23:16 "Take your **l**. Go around in the

lyres (26)

Gen 31:27 by tambourines and **l**.
2Sm 6:5 from cypress wood and with **l**,
1Ki 10:12 and **l** and harps for the singers.
1Ch 13:8 with **l**, harps, tambourines,
15:16 to play music on harps, **l**,
15:21 were appointed to play **l**
15:28 cymbals, harps, and **l**.
16:5 and Jeiel with harps and **l**.
25:1 to serve as prophets with **l**,
25:3 the LORD as they played **l**.)
25:6 They played cymbals, **l**,
2Ch 5:12 with cymbals, harps, and **l**.
9:11 and **l** and harps for the singers.
20:28 So they brought harps, **l**,
29:25 cymbals, harps, and **l** as David,
Neh 12:27 and with harps and **l**.
Psa 81:2 Play **l** and harps with their
137:2 We hung our **l** on willow trees.
149:3 to him with tambourines and **l**,
150:3 Praise him with harps and **l**.
Isa 5:12 feasts there are **l** and harps,
Isa 30:32 the sound of tambourines and **l**,
Dan 3:5 of rams' horns, flutes, **l**, harps,
3:7 of rams' horns, flutes, **l**, harps,
3:10 of rams' horns, flutes, **l**, harps,
3:15 the rams' horns, flutes, **l**, harps,

Lysanias (1)

Luk 3:1 **L** was the ruler of Abilene.

Lysias (1)

Act 24:22 "When the officer **L** arrives,

Lystra (7)

Act 14:6 they escaped to **L** and Derbe,
14:8 who was born lame was in **L**.
14:19 and Iconium arrived in **L**
14:21 went back to the cities of **L**,
16:1 of Derbe and then went to **L**,
16:2 The believers in **L** and Iconium
2Ti 3:11 of Antioch, Iconium, and **L**.

M

Maacah (24)

Gen 22:24 Gaham, Tahash, and **M**."
2Sm 3:3 whose mother was **M** (the
10:6 of the king of **M** (1,000 men),
10:8 and **M** remained by themselves
23:34 and grandson of a man from **M**),
1Ki 2:39 Gath's King Achish, son of **M**.
15:2 His mother was named **M**,
15:10 His grandmother was named **M**
15:13 his grandmother **M** from
1Ch 2:48 **M**, Caleb's concubine, was the
3:2 ⌊born⌋ to **M** (the daughter of
7:15 His wife's name was **M**.
7:16 **M**, Machir's wife, had a son,
8:29 and his wife's name was **M**.
9:35 and his wife's name was **M**.
11:43 Hanan (son of **M**),
19:6 Mesopotamia, **M**, and Zobah.
19:7 chariots and the king of **M**
27:16 Simeon: Shephatiah, son of **M**
2Ch 11:20 Mahalath, he married **M**,
11:21 Rehoboam loved **M**,
11:22 appointed Abijah, son of **M**,
15:16 his grandmother **M** from
Jer 40:8 was the son of a man from **M**.

Maacath (3)

Jos 12:5 to the border of Geshur and **M**,
13:11 of the people of Geshur and **M**,
13:13 the people of Geshur and **M**.

Maacathites (2)

Dtr 3:14 of the Geshurites and the **M**.
1Ch 4:19 and Eshtemoa of the **M**.

Maadai (1)

Ezr 10:34 of Bani: **M**, Amram, Uel,

Maadiah (1)

Neh 12:5 Mijamin, **M**, Bilgah,

Maai (1)

Neh 12:36 Gilalai, **M**, Nethanel, Judah,

Maarath (1)

Jos 15:59 **M**, Bethanoth, and Eltekon

Maasai (1)

1Ch 9:12 of Malchiah) and **M** (son

Maaseiah (22)

1Ch 15:18 **M**, Mattithiah, Eliphelehu,
15:20 Jehiel, Unni, Eliab, **M**,
2Ch 23:1 son of Obed, **M**, son of Adaiah,
26:11 scribe Jeiel and the officer **M**.
28:7 man from Ephraim, killed **M**,
34:8 **M**, the mayor of the city,
Ezr 10:18 women: **M**, Eliezer, Jarib,
10:21 **M**, Elijah, Shemaiah, Jehiel,
10:22 **M**, Ishmael, Nethanel, Jozabad,

Ezr 10:30 **M**, Mattaniah, Bezalel, Binnui,
Neh 3:23 After them Azariah, son of **M**
8:4 and **M** stood beside him on his
8:7 **M**, Kelita, Azariah, Jozabad,
10:25 Rehum, Hashabnah, **M**,
11:5 **M** was the son of Baruch,
11:7 who was the son of **M**,
12:41 **M**, Miniamin, Micaiah, Elioenai,
12:42 and **M**, Shemaiah, Eleazar,
Jer 21:1 son of **M**, to Jeremiah.
29:25 son of **M**, and to all the priests.
35:4 and above the side room of **M**,
37:3 the priest Zephaniah (son of **M**)

Maaseiah's (1)
Jer 29:21 and about **M** son Zedekiah,

Maath (1)
Luk 3:26 son of **M**, son of Mattathias,

Maaz (1)
1Ch 2:27 son of Jerahmeel) were **M**,

Maaziah (2)
1Ch 24:18 the twenty-fourth for **M**.
Neh 10:8 **M**, Bilgai, and Shemaiah.

Macedonia (25)
Act 16:9 had a vision of a man from **M**.
16:9 "Come to **M** to help us."
16:10 looked for a way to go to **M**.
16:10 us to tell the people of **M** about
16:12 a leading city in that part of **M**,
18:5 and Timothy arrived from **M**,
19:21 through **M** and Greece.
19:22 Timothy and Erastus, to **M**,
20:1 said goodbye, and left for **M**.
20:3 decided to go back through **M**.
Rom 15:26 Because the believers in **M**
1Co 16:5 I go through the province of **M**,
16:5 (I will be going through **M**.)
2Co 1:16 of Corinth to the province of **M**.
1:16 Then from **M** I had planned to
2:13 and went to the province of **M**.
7:5 we arrived in the province of **M**,
8:1 churches in the province of **M**.
9:2 believers in the province of **M**.
11:9 of **M** supplied everything
Php 4:15 when I left the province of **M** to
1Th 1:7 the province of **M** and Greece.
1:8 only through the province of **M**
4:10 throughout the province of **M**.
1Ti 1:3 was going to the province of **M**,

Macedonian (1)
Act 27:2 Aristarchus, a **M** from the city

Macedonians (3)
Act 19:29 the **M** who traveled with Paul,
Rom 15:27 These **M** and Greeks have
2Co 9:4 if any **M** come with me,

Machbannai (1)
1Ch 12:13 The eleventh was **M**.

Machbenah (1)
1Ch 2:49 who first settled **M** and Gibea.

Machi (1)
Num 13:15 Geuel, son of **M**, from the tribe

machines (2)
2Ch 26:15 In Jerusalem he made **m**
26:15 The **m** were placed on the

Machir (20)
Gen 50:23 Even the children of **M**,
Num 26:29 the family of **M** (Machir was
26:29 the family of Machir (**M** was
27:1 of Gilead, descendant of **M**,
32:39 The descendants of **M**,
32:40 people of **M** (the descendants
36:1 son of **M** and grandson of
Dtr 3:15 I gave Gilead to **M**.
Jos 13:31 given to half the families of **M**,
17:1 **M**, Manasseh's firstborn,
Jos 17:3 and great-grandson of **M**,
Jdg 5:14 Commanders from **M** went into
2Sm 9:4 "He is at the home of **M**,
9:5 of Ammiel's son **M** in Lo Debar.
17:27 from Rabbah in Ammon, and **M**,
1Ch 2:21 slept with the daughter of **M**,
2:23 people were descendants of **M**,
7:14 sons were Asriel and **M**.
7:14 **M** was the first to settle Gilead.
7:17 of **M** (son of Manasseh).

Machir's (1)
1Ch 7:16 Maacah, **M** wife, had a son,

Machnadebai (1)
Ezr 10:40 **M**, Shashai, Sharai,

Machpelah (6)
Gen 23:9 to let me have the cave of **M**
23:17 So Ephron's field at **M**,
23:19 in the cave in the field of **M**,
25:9 buried him in the cave of **M**
49:30 cave that is in the field of **M**,
50:13 in the cave in the field of **M**,

mad (1)
Dtr 28:34 you see will drive you **m**.

Madai (2)
Gen 10:2 **M**, Javan, Tubal, Meshech,
1Ch 1:5 **M**, Javan, Tubal, Meshech,

made (1387)
Gen 1:7 So God **m** the horizon and
1:16 God **m** the two bright lights:
1:16 He also **m** the stars.
1:25 God **m** every type of wild
1:31 saw everything that he had **m**
2:4 God **m** earth and heaven.
2:9 The LORD God **m** all the trees
3:1 animals the LORD God had **m**.
3:7 and **m** clothes for themselves.
3:21 The LORD God **m** clothes from
4:1 Adam **m** love to his wife Eve.
4:17 Cain **m** love to his wife.
4:22 who **m** bronze and iron tools.
4:25 Adam **m** love to his wife again.
5:1 he **m** them in the likeness of
6:6 sorry that he had **m** humans
6:7 I'm sorry that I **m** them."
7:4 living creature that I have **m**."
8:1 So God **m** a wind blow over
8:6 window he had **m** in the ship
8:20 On it he **m** a burnt offering of
9:6 image of God, God **m** humans.
13:4 where he had first **m** an altar.
14:23 be able to say, 'I **m** Abram rich.'
15:18 At that time the LORD **m** a
17:5 of Many] because I have **m** you
19:24 Then the LORD **m** burning
20:18 (The LORD had **m** it
21:27 two of them **m** an agreement.
21:32 After they **m** the treaty at
24:21 had **m** his trip successful.
24:31 up the house and **m**
24:37 My master **m** me swear this
24:56 has **m** my trip successful.
26:10 and then you would have **m** us
26:22 "Now the LORD has **m** room for
27:37 "I have **m** him your master,
27:37 and I have **m** all his brothers
28:20 Then Jacob **m** a vow:
29:31 he **m** it possible for her to have
30:22 answered her prayer and **m**
30:40 the rams from the flock and **m**
30:40 So he **m** separate herds for
31:13 holy purpose and where you **m**
31:35 So even though Laban had **m** a
31:42 and last night he **m** it right."
33:17 for himself and **m** shelters
34:30 You've **m** the people living in
35:5 As they moved on, God **m** the
37:3 So he **m** Joseph a special robe
38:26 Judah never **m** love to her
39:3 that the LORD **m** everything
39:4 much that he **m** him his trusted
Gen 39:23 with Joseph and **m** whatever
43:6 Israel asked, "Why have you **m**
43:10 we could have **m** this trip twice
44:12 Then the man **m** a thorough
45:8 He has **m** me ⌊like⌋ a father to
45:9 "God has **m** me lord of Egypt.
47:26 Joseph **m** a law concerning the
50:5 'My father **m** me swear an oath.
50:25 Joseph **m** Israel's sons swear
Exo 1:14 They **m** their lives bitter with
2:3 she took a basket **m** of
2:14 The man asked, "Who **m** you
5:21 You have **m** Pharaoh and his
6:4 I even **m** a promise to give
7:1 "I have **m** you a god to
9:12 the LORD **m** Pharaoh stubborn,
9:23 So the LORD **m** it hail on
10:1 I have **m** him and his officials
10:13 and the LORD **m** a wind from
10:20 the LORD **m** Pharaoh stubborn,
10:27 the LORD **m** Pharaoh stubborn,
11:3 The LORD **m** the Egyptians
11:10 the LORD **m** Pharaoh stubborn,
12:20 Eat nothing **m** with yeast.
12:36 The LORD **m** the Egyptians
13:3 eat anything **m** with yeast.
13:19 because Joseph had **m** the
14:8 The LORD **m** Pharaoh (the king
14:25 He **m** the wheels of their
15:19 the LORD **m** the water of the
15:26 suffer any of the diseases I **m**
16:31 like wafers **m** with honey.
20:11 six days the LORD **m** heaven,
20:24 must build an altar for me **m** out
20:25 If you build an altar for me **m**
24:8 promise that the LORD has **m**
24:10 like a pavement **m** out
25:38 burners must be **m** of pure gold
26:1 ten sheets **m** from fine linen
26:14 put a cover **m** of fine leather.
26:24 frames will be **m** this way.
27:2 and the altar must be **m** out
27:8 It must be **m** just as you were
27:9 long and have curtains **m** out
27:10 the posts should be **m** of silver.
27:11 the posts should be **m** of silver.
27:16 30-foot screen **m** from fine linen
27:18 with ⌊curtains⌋ **m** of fine linen
27:19 must be **m** of bronze.
29:2 some rings of bread **m** with
29:23 a ring of bread **m** with olive oil,
29:33 through which they **m** peace
29:42 be the daily burnt offering ⌊**m**⌋
30:2 The horns and altar must be **m**
31:17 because the LORD **m** heaven
32:4 he **m** it into a statue of a calf.
32:8 They've **m** a statue of a calf for
32:20 he took the calf they had **m**,
32:20 and **m** the Israelites drink it.
32:31 They **m** gods out of gold for
35:25 which they had **m** by hand.
35:35 The LORD has **m** these men
36:8 among the workers **m**
36:8 ten sheets **m** from fine linen
36:11 Then they **m** 50 violet loops
36:13 They also **m** 50 gold fasteners.
36:14 They **m** 11 sheets of goats' hair
36:17 Then they **m** 50 loops along
36:18 They also **m** 50 bronze
36:19 They **m** a cover out of rams'
36:19 put a cover **m** of fine leather.
36:20 They **m** a framework out of
36:22 They **m** all the frames for the
36:23 They **m** 20 frames for the south
36:24 Then they **m** 40 silver sockets
36:25 inner tent ⌊they **m**⌋ 20 frames
36:27 They **m** six frames for the far
36:28 They **m** two frames for ⌊each
36:29 corner frames were **m** this way.
36:31 They also **m** crossbars out of
36:33 They **m** the middle crossbar so
36:34 with gold and **m** gold rings
36:35 They **m** the canopy out of
36:36 They **m** four posts of acacia
36:36 They **m** gold hooks for the
36:37 They **m** a screen out of fine

Exo 36:38 They also **m** five posts with
36:38 for the posts were **m** of bronze.
37:1 Bezalel **m** the ark out of acacia
37:4 Then he **m** poles out of acacia
37:6 He **m** the throne of mercy out of
37:7 Then he **m** two angels out of
37:10 He **m** the table out of acacia
37:12 He **m** a rim 3 inches wide
37:15 These poles were **m** out of
37:16 For the table he **m** plates,
37:16 All of them were **m** out of pure
37:17 He **m** the lamp stand out of
37:23 He **m** the seven lamps,
37:24 and all the utensils were **m** out
37:25 He **m** an altar out of acacia
37:25 The horns and altar were **m** out
37:27 He **m** two gold rings and put
37:28 He **m** the poles out of acacia
38:1 He **m** the altar for burnt
38:2 He **m** a horn at each of its four
38:2 He **m** the four horns and the
38:3 He **m** all the utensils out of
38:4 He **m** a grate for the altar out of
38:6 He **m** the poles out of acacia
38:7 He **m** the altar out of boards so
38:8 He **m** the basin and stand out
38:9 He also **m** the courtyard.
38:9 long and had curtains **m** out
38:10 on the posts were **m** of silver.
38:11 on the posts were **m** of silver.
38:12 on the posts were **m** of silver.
38:16 the courtyard were **m** out
38:17 The bases for the posts were **m**
38:17 on the posts were **m** of silver.
38:17 the courtyard were **m** of silver.
38:18 the courtyard was **m** of violet,
38:18 on ⌊fabric **m** from⌋ fine linen
38:19 on the posts were **m** of silver.
38:20 courtyard were **m** of bronze.
38:22 **m** everything the LORD had
38:30 With this he **m** the bases for
39:1 and bright red yarn they **m**
39:1 They also **m** the holy clothes
39:2 They **m** the ephod out of fine
39:4 They **m** two shoulder straps
39:5 They **m** the belt that is
39:8 They **m** the breastplate as
39:8 creatively as they **m** the ephod.
39:8 It was **m** out of gold,
39:15 For the breastplate they **m**
39:16 They **m** two gold settings and
39:19 They **m** two gold rings and
39:20 They **m** two ⌊more⌋ gold rings
39:22 They **m** the robe that is worn
39:24 On the hem of the robe they **m**
39:25 They **m** bells out of pure gold
39:28 They also **m** the chief priest's
39:28 They **m** the undergarments and
39:30 They **m** the flower-shaped
39:34 the cover **m** of rams' skins
39:34 the cover **m** of fine leather,
Lev 2:4 be rings of unleavened bread **m**
2:5 will be unleavened bread **m** of
2:7 it will be **m** of flour with olive
6:7 you did that **m** you guilty."
6:17 the offerings by fire **m** to me.
6:23 Every grain offering **m** by a
7:12 and loaves **m** from flour mixed
7:30 Bring the sacrifices by fire **m** to
7:35 from the sacrifices by fire **m**
8:26 a ring of bread **m** with olive oil,
12:4 in order to be **m** clean from her
12:5 in order to be **m** clean from her
16:19 the Israelites **m** it unclean,
19:19 Never wear clothes **m** from two
20:3 **m** my holy tent unclean,
23:13 will be a sacrifice by fire **m**
23:43 to come may learn how I **m**
26:13 over you and **m** you live as
Num 4:6 will spread a cloth **m** entirely
5:8 whom the payment can be **m**.
6:3 vinegar **m** from wine or liquor,
6:15 some rings of bread **m**
6:18 proof that they had **m** this vow,
8:4 is how the lamp stand was **m**:
8:4 It was **m** exactly like the one

Num 8:15 "Once you have **m** them clean
8:21 to the LORD and **m** peace
11:8 like rich pastry **m** with olive oil.
14:37 they had returned and **m**
19:20 He has **m** the holy place of the
21:2 Then the Israelites **m** this vow
21:9 So Moses **m** a bronze snake
22:28 Then the LORD **m** the donkey
22:29 "You've **m** a fool of me!
24:11 but the LORD has **m** you lose
25:13 up for his God and he **m** peace
27:22 He took Joshua and **m** him
30:8 the vow or promise she **m**.
31:20 and everything **m** of leather,
32:13 he **m** them wander in the desert
Dtr 1:10 The LORD your God has **m**
1:15 men and **m** them officers
2:30 The LORD your God **m** him
3:11 His bed was **m** of iron and was
4:23 the LORD your God **m** to you.
4:28 stone gods **m** by human hands.
5:2 The LORD our God **m** a
8:3 So he **m** you suffer from hunger
8:15 He was the one who **m** water
9:7 Never forget how you **m** the
9:8 Even at Mount Horeb you **m** the
9:9 that the LORD **m** to you,
9:12 They've **m** an idol for
9:16 You had **m** a statue of a calf for
9:18 evil and **m** him furious.
9:21 I took that sinful calf you **m**
9:22 You also **m** the LORD angry at
10:3 I **m** an ark out of acacia wood.
10:5 the tablets in the ark I had **m**.
10:22 Now the LORD your God has **m**
15:2 If you've **m** a loan,
16:13 floor and **m** your wine,
20:11 all the people there will be **m**
22:11 Never wear clothes **m** of wool
22:17 Now he has **m** up charges
26:6 and **m** us do back-breaking
26:19 all the other nations he has **m**.
27:15 to the LORD that was **m** by
28:36 There you will worship gods **m**
28:64 There you will serve gods **m** of
29:17 gods and idols **m** of wood,
29:25 He **m** this promise to them
30:9 as he **m** your ancestors.
31:16 reject the promise I **m** to them.
32:6 who **m** you and formed you?
32:13 He **m** them ride on the heights
32:15 the God who **m** them
32:16 They **m** him furious because
32:19 daughters had **m** him angry.
32:21 They **m** him furious because
33:25 and bolts of your gates be **m**
Jos 2:17 oath which you **m** us swear,
2:20 oath which you **m** us swear."
4:19 They **m** their camp at Gilgal,
5:3 So Joshua **m** flint knives and
6:19 and gold and everything **m**
6:24 and gold and everything **m**
7:26 They **m** such a large pile of
8:28 So Joshua burned Ai and **m** it a
8:29 the entrance of the city and **m**
8:31 They **m** burnt offerings to the
9:15 So Joshua **m** peace with them
9:16 days after the treaty was **m**,
9:27 But that day Joshua **m** them
10:1 people of Gibeon had **m** peace
10:4 because it has **m** peace
11:13 However, Joshua **m** an
11:19 Not one city had **m** a peace
11:20 The LORD **m** their enemies
14:10 when the LORD **m** this promise
17:13 they **m** the Canaanites do
17:16 have chariots **m** of iron."
17:18 and have chariots **m** of iron."
22:25 The LORD has **m** the Jordan
22:28 if this statement is **m** to us or to
22:28 LORD's altar our ancestors **m**.
24:7 He **m** the sea flow back and
24:25 That day Joshua **m** an
Jdg 1:19 who had chariots **m** of iron.
1:28 they **m** the Canaanites do
1:30 to live with them and were **m**

Jdg 1:33 and Beth Anath were **m**
1:35 they **m** the Amorites do forced
2:12 and that **m** the LORD angry.
2:15 So he **m** them suffer a great
3:12 So the LORD **m** King Eglon of
3:16 Ehud **m** a two-edged dagger for
4:3 King Jabin had 900 chariots **m**
4:13 all his chariots (900 chariots **m**
6:2 The Israelites **m** hiding places
6:19 goat and unleavened bread **m**
8:33 They **m** Baal Berith their god.
9:16 when you **m** Abimelech king,
9:18 You have **m** Abimelech,
9:27 Then they **m** an offering of
11:11 and the people **m** him their
11:30 Jephthah **m** a vow to the
11:35 I **m** a foolish promise to the
11:36 you **m** a promise to the LORD.
14:17 she **m** his life miserable.
15:16 I've **m** two piles of them.
16:15 You've **m** fun of me three times
16:16 Every day she **m** his life
16:21 chains and **m** him grind grain
16:25 and he **m** them laugh.
16:25 They **m** him stand between
17:4 He **m** a carved idol and a metal
17:5 He also **m** an ephod and
18:24 away the gods I **m** as well as
18:27 of Dan took what Micah had **m**
18:31 the carved idol Micah had **m**.
19:4 He **m** the Levite stay there with
Rut 1:20 the Almighty has **m** my life very
1Sm 1:6 Because the LORD had **m** her
1:11 She **m** this vow, "LORD of
1:19 Elkanah **m** love to his wife
2:17 were treating the offerings **m**
8:1 When Samuel was old, he **m**
14:24 Saul **m** the troops swear,
15:11 "I regret that I **m** Saul king.
15:33 sword **m** women childless,
15:33 so your mother will be **m**
15:35 that he had **m** Saul king
16:21 and **m** David his armorbearer.
17:7 The head of his spear was **m**
17:16 forward and **m** his challenge.
17:51 and **m** certain the Philistine
18:3 So Jonathan **m** a pledge of
18:13 He **m** David captain of a
18:23 When Saul's officers **m** it a
20:23 We have **m** a promise to each
23:18 Both of them **m** a pledge in the
25:38 the LORD **m** him even more
26:12 The LORD had **m** them fall into
26:21 a fool and **m** a terrible mistake."
27:12 "He has definitely **m** his own
30:25 From that time on he **m** this a
2Sm 2:9 Abner **m** him king of Gilead,
3:8 Ishbosheth's question **m** Abner
3:14 I **m** a payment of 100 Philistine
5:3 King David **m** an agreement
5:12 and **m** his kingship famous
6:5 **m** from cypress wood
7:2 I'm living in a house **m** of cedar,
7:21 You **m** it known to me.
7:25 keep the promise you **m** to me
8:2 He also defeated Moab, **m** the
8:13 David **m** a name for himself by
10:6 had **m** themselves offensive
10:19 they **m** peace with Israel and
13:2 Tamar that he **m** himself sick.
13:8 **m** flat bread in front of him,
15:7 keep the vow I **m** to the LORD.
15:8 I **m** a vow while I was living at
16:21 you have **m** your father despise
19:5 "Today you have **m** all your
19:6 Today, you have **m** it clear that
22:12 He **m** the dark rain clouds his
22:13 in front of him, he **m** lightning.
22:14 Most High **m** his voice heard.
22:40 You **m** my opponents bow at
22:41 You **m** my enemies turn their
23:5 because he has **m** a lasting
1Ki 1:43 David has **m** Solomon king.
2:4 keep the promise he **m** to me:
3:7 you've **m** me king in place of
3:28 about the decision the king **m**.

1Ki 5:12 and they **m** a treaty with one
6:4 He also **m** latticed windows for
6:6 Solomon **m** ledges all around
6:7 or any other iron tool **m** a sound
6:12 I will fulfill the promise I **m**
6:23 In the inner room he **m** two
6:31 He **m** doors for the entrance to
6:32 The two doors were ⌞**m** out of⌟
6:33 In the same way he **m** square
6:34 He **m** two doors from cypress.
7:6 Solomon **m** the Hall of Pillars
7:7 He **m** the Hall of Justice,
7:10 foundation was **m** with large,
7:15 He **m** two bronze pillars.
7:16 He **m** two capitals of cast
7:17 He also **m** seven rows of
7:18 After he **m** the pillars,
7:18 After he made the pillars, he **m**
7:18 He **m** the capitals identical to
7:23 Hiram **m** a pool from cast metal.
7:27 He **m** ten bronze stands.
7:28 The stands were **m** this way:
7:30 The supports were **m** of cast
7:33 The wheels were **m** like
7:37 This is the way he **m** the ten
7:38 Hiram also **m** ten bronze
7:40 Hiram also **m** pots,
7:45 Hiram **m** all these utensils out
7:48 Solomon **m** all the furnishings
8:9 where the LORD **m** a promise
8:15 With his mouth he **m** a promise
8:20 has kept the promise he **m**.
8:21 I've **m** a place there for the ark
8:21 the LORD's promise that he **m**
8:26 may the promise you **m** to my
8:35 sin because you **m** them suffer,
8:38 **m** by one person or by all the
8:56 he **m** through his servant
9:3 for mercy that you **m** to me.
10:9 he has **m** you king so that you
10:12 the king **m** supports
10:16 King Solomon **m** 200 large
10:17 He also **m** 300 small shields of
10:18 The king also **m** a large ivory
10:20 Nothing like this had been **m**
10:27 The king **m** silver as common
10:27 and he **m** cedars as plentiful as
12:4 "Your father **m** us carry a heavy
12:14 He said, "If my father **m** your
12:15 carry out the promise he had **m**
12:20 They **m** him king of all Israel.
12:28 the king **m** two golden calves.
12:32 to the calves he had **m**.
13:6 So the man of God **m** an
13:33 but he once again **m** some men
14:7 out of the people and **m** you
14:9 You **m** other gods,
14:9 You **m** me furious and turned
14:15 and **m** the LORD furious.
14:22 Their sins **m** him more angry
14:26 gold shields Solomon had **m**.
14:27 So King Rehoboam **m** bronze
15:4 the LORD his God **m** Abijam
15:12 rid of the idols his father had **m**.
15:13 queen mother because she **m**
15:22 He **m** them carry the stones
15:30 Those sins **m** the LORD God
16:2 from the dust and **m** you leader
16:7 which **m** the LORD furious,
16:13 and **m** the LORD God of Israel
16:16 troops in the camp **m** Omri,
16:26 and the Israelites **m** the LORD
16:33 Ahab **m** poles dedicated to the
18:10 my master **m** that kingdom or
18:26 around the altar they had **m**.
18:32 He also **m** a trench that could
20:34 So Ahab **m** a treaty with
21:22 because you **m** me furious.
22:11 **m** iron horns and said,
22:12 All the other prophets **m** the
22:44 Jehoshaphat **m** peace with the
22:48 Jehoshaphat **m** Tarshish-style
22:53 and **m** the LORD God of Israel
2Ki 4:42 Shalisha brought bread **m** from
5:27 Gehazi had a disease that **m**
6:6 the water at that place and **m**

2Ki 7:6 (The LORD had **m** the Aramean
10:25 the burnt offerings had been **m**,
10:27 and the temple of Baal and **m**
11:4 He **m** an agreement with them,
11:12 and **m** him king by anointing
11:13 Athaliah heard the noise **m** by
11:17 Jehoiada **m** a promise to the
11:17 He **m** other promises between
12:13 gold and silver utensils were **m**
13:7 He had **m** them like dust that
14:21 and **m** him king in place of his
17:11 things and **m** the LORD furious.
17:15 the promise he **m** to their
17:16 They **m** two calves out of cast
17:16 They **m** a pole dedicated to the
17:17 and they **m** him furious.
17:20 descendants, **m** them suffer,
17:21 the people of Israel **m**
17:29 the people of Samaria had **m**.
17:30 Babylon **m** Succoth Benoth.
17:30 The people from Cuth **m** Nergal
17:30 The people from Hamath **m**
17:31 The people from Avva **m**
17:35 When the LORD **m** a promise
17:38 forget the promise I **m** to you.
17:40 to listen and **m** up their own
18:4 snake that Moses had **m**
18:12 of the promise he **m** to them.
19:15 You **m** heaven and earth.
19:18 statues **m** by human hands.
20:11 and the LORD **m** the shadow
20:20 his heroic acts and how he **m**
21:3 altars dedicated to Baal and **m**
21:6 things that **m** the LORD furious.
21:7 had an idol of Asherah **m**.
21:11 Manasseh has also **m** Judah
21:24 They **m** his son Josiah king in
23:3 stood beside the pillar and **m**
23:4 that had been **m** for Baal,
23:8 from Geba to Beersheba and **m**
23:10 Josiah also **m** Topheth in the
23:12 altars that Judah's kings had **m**
23:12 and the altars Manasseh had **m**
23:13 The king **m** the illegal places
23:15 **m** by Jeroboam (Nebat's
23:15 who had **m** Israel sin.
23:30 and **m** him king in place of his
23:33 Pharaoh Necoh **m** him a
23:34 Then Pharaoh Necoh **m**
24:13 King Solomon of Israel had **m**
24:17 The king of Babylon **m** King
25:15 burners and bowls that were **m**
25:16 the stands that Solomon had **m**
25:17 capital were all **m** of bronze.
1Ch 11:3 David **m** an agreement with
11:6 first to kill a Jebusite will be **m**
11:10 and with all Israel they **m** him
12:18 them and **m** them officers over
14:2 his kingdom was **m** famous
14:17 and the LORD **m** all the nations
15:14 the Levites **m** themselves holy
16:16 promise that he **m** to Abraham,
16:26 The LORD **m** the heavens.
17:1 living in a house **m** of cedar,
17:19 You **m** this great thing known
17:22 You **m** the people of Israel to
17:23 keep the promise you **m**
19:6 had **m** themselves offensive
19:19 they **m** peace with David and
21:29 The LORD's tent that Moses **m**
22:14 "Despite my troubles I've **m**
23:1 he **m** his son Solomon king of
23:5 David had **m** for praising God.
23:29 and the bread **m** in frying pans.
23:31 burnt offerings were **m**—
24:19 Their ancestor Aaron **m** these
28:2 and I have **m** preparations to
28:19 He **m** all the details of the plan
29:22 For the second time they **m**
29:25 The LORD **m** Solomon
2Ch 1:1 him and **m** him very powerful.
1:3 had **m** the tent in the desert.
1:5 had **m** was in front of the
1:8 and you've **m** me king in his
1:9 you've kept the promise you **m**
1:9 You've **m** me king of people

2Ch 1:11 over whom I **m** you king.
1:15 The king **m** silver and gold as
1:15 and he **m** cedars as plentiful as
2:11 he **m** you their king."
2:12 He **m** the heavens and the
2:18 He **m** 70,000 of them carry
3:8 He **m** the most holy place.
3:10 In the most holy place he **m**
3:14 Solomon **m** the canopy of
3:15 He **m** two pillars for the front of
3:16 He **m** chains for the inner room
3:16 He **m** 100 pomegranates and
4:1 He **m** a bronze altar 30 feet
4:2 Huram **m** a pool from cast
4:6 Huram also **m** ten basins for
4:7 Huram **m** ten gold lamp stands
4:8 He **m** ten tables and put them
4:8 And he **m** 100 gold bowls.
4:9 He also **m** the priests' courtyard
4:11 Huram also **m** the pots,
4:16 Huram **m** all of them out of
4:18 Solomon **m** so many of these
4:19 Solomon **m** all the furnishings
5:10 where the LORD **m** a promise
6:4 With his mouth he **m** a promise
6:10 has kept the promise he **m**.
6:13 (Solomon had **m** a bronze
6:17 the promise you **m** to David,
6:26 sin because you **m** them suffer,
6:29 for mercy **m** by one person
7:6 which King David **m**
7:7 the bronze altar that he had **m**
9:8 and **m** you king over
9:11 the king **m** gateways
9:15 King Solomon **m** 200 large
9:16 He also **m** 300 small shields of
9:17 The king also **m** a large ivory
9:19 Nothing like this had been **m**
9:27 The king **m** silver as common
9:27 and he **m** cedars as plentiful as
10:4 "Your father **m** us carry a heavy
10:14 He said, "If my father **m** your
10:15 carry out the promise he had **m**
11:12 He **m** the cities very secure.
11:15 calf statues he had **m** as idols.
12:1 kingdom and **m** himself strong,
12:9 gold shields Solomon had **m**.
12:10 So King Rehoboam **m** bronze
13:8 gold calves that Jeroboam **m**
15:12 They **m** an agreement with one
15:16 queen mother because she **m**
16:6 He **m** them carry the stones
18:10 **m** iron horns and said,
18:11 All the other prophets **m** the
20:36 They **m** the ships in Ezion
21:7 the promise he had **m** to David,
21:11 Jehoram **m** illegal places of
22:1 The people of Jerusalem **m**
23:3 The whole assembly **m** an
23:11 and Jehoiada and his sons **m**
23:16 Jehoiada **m** a promise to the
23:18 They **m** these offerings with
24:8 and they **m** a box and placed it
24:14 They **m** dishes and gold and
24:27 God's temple is in the notes **m**
25:20 (God **m** this happen because
26:1 and **m** him king in place of his
26:15 In Jerusalem he **m** machines
28:2 Israel and even **m** metal idols
28:20 Pilneser **m** trouble for him.
28:24 He **m** altars for himself on
28:25 And in each city of Judah, he **m**
28:25 So he **m** the LORD God of his
29:8 He **m** them something that
29:18 "We have **m** all of the LORD's
29:19 restored them and **m** them holy
29:24 the goats and **m** their blood
30:7 He **m** them something that
30:8 place that he **m** holy forever.
30:17 had not **m** themselves holy.
30:18 had not **m** themselves clean.
31:14 the freewill offerings **m** to God.
31:14 to distribute the offerings **m**
32:3 and his military staff **m** plans to
32:5 **m** the towers taller,
32:5 and **m** plenty of weapons and

2Ch	32:19	of the gods **m** by human hands
	32:28	He **m** sheds to store his
	32:28	and he **m** barns for all his cattle
	32:29	He **m** cities for himself
	33:3	gods — the Baals — and **m**
	33:6	things that **m** the LORD furious.
	33:7	Manasseh had a carved idol **m**.
	33:11	So the LORD **m** the army
	33:14	He **m** the wall go around the
	33:22	his father Manasseh had **m**,
	33:25	They **m** his son Josiah king in
	34:5	So he **m** Judah and Jerusalem
	34:31	king stood in his place and **m**
	34:32	He also **m** all those found in
	34:33	He **m** all people found in Israel
	36:1	son Jehoahaz and **m** him king
	36:4	The king of Egypt **m**
	36:10	Nebuchadnezzar **m** Jehoiakin's
	36:13	Nebuchadnezzar had **m**
	36:14	Although the LORD had **m** the
	36:14	they **m** the temple unclean.
	36:16	and **m** fun of his prophets until
	36:21	was **m** acceptable ⌊again⌋.
Ezr	1:6	them with articles **m** from silver
	1:8	So Mithredath **m** a list of them
	4:4	of Judah and **m** them afraid
	4:6	wrote a letter in which they **m**
	4:19	and a search was **m**.
	5:12	But because our ancestors **m**
	5:14	whom he had **m** governor.
	6:8	Full payment should be **m** to
	6:22	the LORD had **m** them joyful.
	6:22	The LORD had **m** the king of
	7:28	He **m** the king, his advisers,
	9:8	Our God has **m** our eyes light
	9:9	Instead, he has **m** the kings of
	10:5	Ezra got up and **m** the leaders,
Neh	2:19	they **m** fun of us and ridiculed
	3:4	grandson of Hakkoz, **m** repairs.
	3:4	of Meshezabel, **m** repairs.
	3:4	son of Baana, **m** repairs.
	3:5	the men from Tekoa **m** repairs.
	3:6	**m** repairs on Old Gate.
	3:7	**m** repairs on the wall.
	3:8	son, a goldsmith, **m** repairs.
	3:8	a perfume maker, **m** repairs.
	3:9	district of Jerusalem, **m** repairs.
	3:10	**m** repairs across from his own
	3:10	Hashabneiah's son, **m** repairs.
	3:11	**m** repairs on a section that
	3:12	**m** repairs with the help of his
	3:15	He also **m** repairs on the wall
	3:16	**m** repairs all the way to a point
	3:17	Rehum (Bani's son), **m** repairs.
	3:17	**m** repairs for his district.
	3:18	him their relatives **m** repairs.
	3:20	**m** repairs on a section from the
	3:21	**m** repairs on a section from the
	3:22	lived in that area **m** repairs.
	3:23	Hasshub **m** repairs across from
	3:23	**m** repairs next to his home.
	3:24	**m** repairs on a section from
	3:25	Palal, Uzai's son, **m** repairs
	3:26	living on the Ophel **m** repairs
	3:28	Gate the priests **m** repairs.
	3:28	Each priest **m** repairs across
	3:29	**m** repairs across from his own
	3:29	guard at East Gate, **m** repairs.
	3:30	**m** repairs across from his living
	3:31	**m** repairs as far as the building
	3:32	merchants **m** repairs between
	4:1	he became enraged and **m** fun
	5:7	charging interest on loans **m**
	5:12	Then I called the priests and **m**
	5:15	before me had **m** life difficult
	6:9	But God **m** me strong.
	8:4	on a raised wooden platform **m**
	8:16	Some **m** booths on their roofs,
	8:17	come back from exile **m** booths
	9:6	You **m** heaven, the highest
	9:6	You **m** the earth and everything
	9:8	You **m** a promise to him to give
	9:10	You **m** a name for yourself,
	9:15	hunger and **m** water flow from
	9:18	even when they **m** a metal
	9:23	You **m** their children as
Neh	9:27	who **m** them suffer.
	13:13	Since they could be trusted, I **m**
	13:25	I **m** them swear by God:
	13:26	God loved him, and God **m**
	13:29	office and the promise you **m**
Est	1:6	and marble pillars by cords **m**
	2:17	head and **m** her queen instead
	3:14	A copy of the document was **m**
	7:9	pole Haman **m** for Mordecai,
	8:13	of the document was **m** public
	9:17	fourteenth they rested and **m**
	9:18	rested on the fifteenth and **m**
Job	1:17	formed three companies and **m**
	4:3	you **m** them strong.
	4:15	It **m** my hair stand on end.
	9:9	He **m** ⌊the constellations⌋ Ursa
	9:26	like boats **m** from reeds,
	10:8	"'Your hands formed me and **m**
	10:9	Please remember that you **m**
	12:9	that the LORD's hands **m** it?
	14:15	the person your hands have **m**.
	17:6	"Now he has **m** me a
	19:4	Even if it were true that I've **m**
	19:8	He has **m** my paths dark.
	22:19	and the innocent **m** fun of them
	27:2	who has **m** my life bitter:
	28:26	when he **m** rules for the rain
	29:3	when he **m** his lamp shine on
	29:13	I **m** the widow's heart sing for
	29:17	wicked person and **m** him drop
	30:11	my cord and has **m** me suffer,
	31:1	"I have **m** an agreement with
	31:15	Didn't he who **m** me in my
	31:16	the requests of the poor or **m**
	31:39	for it and **m** its owners breathe
	32:3	They **m** it look as if God were
	33:4	"God's Spirit has **m** me.
	34:19	because his hands **m** them all.
	37:18	as firm as a mirror **m** of metal?
	38:25	"Who **m** a channel for the
	40:15	which I **m** along with you.
	41:33	to it. It was **m** fearless.
Psa	7:15	the hole that he **m** ⌊for others⌋.
	8:5	You have **m** him a little lower
	8:6	You have **m** him rule what your
	9:15	sunk into the pit they have **m**.
	18:11	He **m** the darkness his hiding
	18:13	The Most High **m** his voice
	18:39	You **m** my opponents bow at
	18:40	You **m** my enemies turn their
	18:43	You **m** me the leader of nations.
	19:1	what his hands have **m**.
	21:6	you **m** him a blessing forever.
	21:6	You **m** him glad with the joy of
	22:9	the one who **m** me feel safe at
	28:5	or what his hands have **m**.
	30:7	by your favor you have **m** my
	31:13	they **m** plans together against
	32:5	I **m** my sins known to you,
	33:6	The heavens were **m** by the
	39:5	Indeed, you have **m** the length
	40:2	a rock and **m** my steps secure.
	40:5	You have **m** many wonderful
	44:13	You **m** us a disgrace to our
	44:14	You **m** our ⌊defeat⌋ a proverb
	50:5	my godly people who have **m**
	50:21	⌊That⌋ **m** you think I was like
	60:2	You **m** the land quake.
	60:3	You have **m** your people
	65:1	and vows ⌊**m**⌋ to you must be
	66:14	the vows **m** by my lips and
	71:20	You have **m** me endure many
	73:28	I have **m** the Almighty LORD
	74:2	Long ago you **m** it your own.
	74:2	where you have **m** your home.
	74:23	Do not forget the uproar **m** by
	77:14	You have **m** your strength
	78:13	He **m** the waters stand up like
	78:16	He **m** streams come out of a
	78:16	He **m** the water flow like rivers.
	78:26	He **m** the east wind blow in the
	78:28	He **m** the birds fall in the
	78:58	They **m** him angry because of
	78:58	They **m** him furious because
	78:69	like the earth which he **m** to
	80:5	You **m** them eat tears as food.
Psa	80:5	You often **m** them drink ⌊their
	80:6	You **m** us a source of conflict
	80:6	and our enemies **m** fun of us.
	86:9	All the nations that you have **m**
	88:8	You **m** me disgusting to them.
	89:3	⌊You said,⌋ "I have **m** a
	89:11	You **m** the world and
	89:42	of his enemies high and **m** all
	90:15	days as you have **m** us suffer,
	91:9	You have **m** the Most High your
	92:4	You **m** me find joy in what you
	95:5	He **m** it, and his hands formed
	96:5	The LORD **m** the heavens.
	98:2	The LORD has **m** his salvation
	100:3	He **m** us, and we are his.
	103:14	knows what we are **m** of.
	104:24	number of things you have **m**,
	104:24	You **m** them all by wisdom.
	104:26	which you **m**, plays in it.
	104:31	find joy in what he has **m**.
	105:9	promise that he **m** to Abraham,
	105:21	He **m** Joseph the master of his
	105:24	The LORD **m** his people grow
	105:28	He sent darkness and **m** ⌊their
	105:30	He **m** their land swarm with
	106:19	At Mount Horeb they **m** ⌊a
	106:19	worshiped an idol **m** of metal.
	106:32	They **m** God angry by the
	106:33	since they **m** him bitter so that
	106:42	them and **m** them subject
	107:25	and it **m** the waves rise high.
	107:29	He **m** the storm calm down,
	107:40	and **m** them stumble around
	111:4	He has **m** his miracles
	114:5	what **m** you turn back?
	114:6	what **m** you jump like rams?
	114:6	what **m** you jump like lambs?
	115:4	Their idols are **m** of silver and
	115:4	They were **m** by human hands.
	118:24	is the day the LORD has **m**.
	119:67	Before you **m** me suffer,
	119:73	Your hands created me and **m**
	119:92	teachings had not **m** me happy,
	119:152	instructions that you **m** them
	129:3	They **m** long slashes ⌊like
	132:2	to the LORD and **m** this vow
	135:15	The idols of the nations are **m**
	135:15	They were **m** by human hands.
	136:5	to the one who **m** the heavens
	136:7	to the one who **m** the great
	138:2	You have **m** your name and
	138:3	You **m** me bold by
	138:8	go of what your hands have **m**.
	139:14	amazingly and miraculously **m**.
	139:15	when I was being **m** in secret,
	143:3	He has **m** me live in dark
	143:5	what your hands have **m**.
	145:9	for everything that he has **m**.
	145:10	Everything that you have **m**
	146:6	who **m** heaven, earth, the sea,
	148:6	He **m** it a law that no one can
Pro	7:16	I've **m** my bed, with colored
	8:26	when he had not yet **m** land or
	8:30	I **m** him happy day after day,
	11:25	generous person will be **m** rich,
	16:4	The LORD has **m** everything
	16:6	peace is **m** with the LORD.
	16:11	He **m** the entire set of weights.
	20:9	"I've **m** my heart pure.
	20:12	sees — the LORD **m** them both.
	21:31	The horse is **m** ready for the
	22:19	Today I have **m** them known to
	27:6	Wounds **m** by a friend are
	31:22	Her clothes are ⌊**m** of⌋ linen
Ecc	2:5	I **m** gardens and parks for
	2:6	I **m** pools to water the forest of
	7:14	God has **m** the one time as
	7:29	God **m** people decent,
	9:13	and it **m** a deep impression on
	10:5	an error often **m** by rulers.
	10:19	A meal is **m** for laughter,
	11:5	who **m** everything,
Sos	1:6	They **m** me the caretaker of the
	3:6	with myrrh and incense **m** from
	3:9	King Solomon had a carriage **m**
	3:10	He had its posts **m** out of silver,

Sos 3:10 scenes of love — was **m** by
Isa 2:20 and gold idols that they **m**
5:2 and **m** a winepress in it.
7:2 family that the Arameans had **m**
14:16 "Is this the man who **m** the
14:17 who **m** the world like a desert
17:8 They won't look to the altars **m**
18:2 messengers by sea in boats **m**
28:15 You say, "We **m** a treaty with
29:13 on⌞ rules **m** by humans.
29:16 Can something that has been **m**
29:23 the children I **m** with my hands,
30:33 It was **m** ready for the king.
30:33 It was **m** deep and wide and
31:7 that your sinful hands have **m**.
31:8 swords not **m** by human hands.
31:8 Swords not **m** by human hands
31:8 and their young men will be **m**
33:16 will be a fortress **m** of rock.
37:16 You **m** heaven and earth.
37:19 statues **m** by human hands.
38:8 The sun **m** a shadow that went
40:4 Steep places will be **m** level.
40:4 Rough places will be **m**
43:7 whom I formed and **m**.
44:2 The LORD **m** you,
44:22 I **m** your rebellious acts
44:24 I, the LORD, **m** everything.
45:12 I **m** the earth and created
45:18 God formed the earth and **m** it.
46:4 I **m** you and will continue to
48:3 and I **m** them known.
48:21 He **m** water flow from a rock for
49:2 He **m** my tongue like a sharp
49:2 He **m** me like a sharpened
49:6 I have also **m** you a light for the
51:10 You **m** a road in the depths of
51:23 of those who **m** you suffer.
51:23 So you **m** your back like the
53:10 When the LORD has **m** his life
54:17 No weapon that has been **m** to
55:4 I **m** him a witness to people,
57:7 You've **m** your bed on a high
57:8 You've **m** your bed with them.
57:8 You've **m** a deal with those you
57:16 the lives of those I've **m**,
59:2 and your sins have **m** him hide
59:8 They've **m** their paths crooked.
62:8 the new wine which you **m**."
63:6 In my wrath I **m** them drunk
65:4 their pots **m** broth from unclean
66:2 I have **m** all these things.
66:14 of the LORD will be **m** known
Jer 1:16 what their hands have **m**.
1:18 Today I have **m** you like a
2:7 They came and **m** my land
2:7 They **m** my property disgusting
2:28 that you **m** for yourselves?
5:22 I **m** the sand a boundary for the
7:12 where I first **m** a dwelling place
7:30 They have **m** it unclean.
10:9 all **m** by skilled workers.
10:12 The LORD **m** the earth by his
10:16 He **m** everything, and Israel is
11:4 I **m** this promise to your
11:5 I will keep the oath I **m** to your
11:10 that I **m** to their ancestors.
11:17 They have **m** him furious by
13:11 so I have **m** the entire nation of
19:4 They have **m** this place
20:7 I've been **m** fun of all day long.
20:8 The word of the LORD has **m**
20:15 Cursed is the man who **m** my
23:32 prophesy dreams they **m** up,"
23:32 "They tell the dreams they **m**
25:7 You have **m** me furious about
25:17 I **m** all the nations to whom the
25:19 ⌞I also **m** these people drink
27:6 I have even **m** wild animals
28:15 You have **m** these people
29:26 The LORD **m** you priest
29:31 He has **m** you believe a lie.
31:32 not be like the promise that I **m**
32:17 'Almighty LORD, you **m**
32:20 You **m** a name for yourself that
32:29 of people who **m** me furious by
Jer 32:30 The people of Israel have **m**
32:31 "The people in this city have **m**
32:32 and Judah have **m** me furious
33:2 "I **m** ⌞the earth⌟, formed it,
33:14 I will keep the promise that I **m**
33:25 Suppose I hadn't **m** an
33:25 with day and night or **m** laws
34:11 freed and **m** them their slaves
34:13 a condition on the promise I **m**
34:15 and you **m** a promise in my
34:18 of the promise which they **m**
41:9 same one that King Asa **m** as
44:3 and they **m** me angry.
44:19 and **m** cakes for her with her
44:25 and your wives **m** promises,
49:30 has **m** plans against you
51:7 It **m** the whole world drunk.
51:15 The LORD **m** the earth by his
51:19 He **m** everything, and Israel is
52:19 trays and bowls that were **m**
52:20 that King Solomon had **m**
52:22 They were all **m** of bronze.
Lam 1:4 young women are **m** to suffer.
1:5 The LORD **m** Zion suffer for its
1:12 like the pain that he has **m** me
1:13 He **m** it go deep into my bones.
1:13 He **m** me turn back.
1:13 He has **m** me sick all day long.
2:5 He **m** the people of Judah
2:7 The enemies **m** noise in the
2:8 He **m** the towers and walls
2:17 He **m** your enemies gloat over
3:2 me away and **m** me walk
3:4 He has **m** my flesh and my
3:6 He has **m** me live in darkness,
3:9 and **m** my paths crooked.
3:12 He has drawn his bow and **m**
3:15 He has **m** me drink wormwood.
3:45 You **m** us the scum and trash
4:2 like those **m** by a potter's
Eze 1:16 looked and how they were **m**:
1:26 like a throne **m** of sapphire.
3:17 "Son of man, I have **m** you a
6:13 places where they **m** offerings
10:1 like a throne **m** of sapphire.
12:6 I've **m** you a sign to warn the
15:5 it couldn't be **m** into anything.
16:7 I **m** you grow like a plant in the
16:16 and **m** your worship sites
16:17 given you and **m** male idols
16:43 and you **m** me very angry with
16:52 because you have **m** your
16:60 remember the promise that I **m**
17:13 **m** a treaty with him,
17:13 and **m** him promise to be loyal.
20:5 I **m** myself known to them in
20:5 I **m** a promise to them and said,
20:9 I **m** myself known to them by
20:11 I gave them my laws and **m** my
20:12 that I, the LORD, **m** them holy.
20:28 they **m** sacrifices and brought
21:23 because they have **m** treaties
22:4 disgusting idols you have **m**.
22:13 excessive profits you have **m**
22:24 You have not been **m** clean.
27:4 builders **m** your beauty perfect.
27:5 Your builders **m** all your boards
27:6 They **m** your oars from oaks in
27:6 They **m** your deck from pine
27:7 Your sails were **m** out of fine
27:10 victories **m** you look good.
27:33 You **m** the kings of the earth
28:4 you've **m** yourself rich.
28:5 you've **m** yourself very wealthy.
28:13 and your sockets were **m**
29:3 is mine. I **m** it for myself."
29:9 "The Nile River is mine. I **m** it."
29:18 of Babylon **m** his army fight
31:4 Water **m** the tree grow,
31:4 underground springs **m** it tall.
31:6 All the birds **m** their nests in its
31:9 I was the one who **m** it
31:15 to the grave, I **m** people mourn.
31:15 I **m** Lebanon mourn for the tree,
31:16 I **m** the nations tremble in fear
32:25 A bed has been **m** for Elam
Eze 33:22 the LORD **m** me speak.
34:27 the people who **m** them slaves.
40:42 There were four tables **m** of cut
41:22 and its sides were **m** of wood.
44:26 After a priest is **m** clean,
Dan 1:8 Daniel **m** up his mind not to
1:9 God **m** the chief-of-staff kind
2:12 This **m** the king so angry and
2:32 The head of this statue was **m**
2:32 and arms were **m** of silver.
2:32 and hips were **m** of bronze.
2:33 Its legs were **m** of iron.
2:33 Its feet were **m** partly of iron
2:38 He has **m** you ruler of them all.
2:48 Nebuchadnezzar **m** Daniel
3:1 King Nebuchadnezzar **m** a gold
3:15 worship the gold statue I **m**?
4:21 and birds **m** their homes in its
4:33 Dew from the sky **m** his body
4:36 and **m** extraordinarily great.
5:4 praised their gods **m** of gold,
5:11 **m** him head of the magicians,
5:23 But you **m** yourself greater than
5:23 praised your gods **m** of silver,
5:29 He **m** Daniel the third-highest
7:4 It was **m** to stand on two feet
7:20 that had come up and **m** three
8:14 will be **m** acceptable to God."
8:18 me and **m** me stand up.
9:1 was **m** ruler of the kingdom of
9:15 and **m** yourself famous even
10:5 and he had a belt **m** of gold
10:10 Then a hand touched me and **m**
11:23 alliance has been **m** with him,
12:10 Many will be purified, **m** white,
Hos 7:15 them and **m** them strong.
8:6 idol was **m** in Israel.
8:6 Skilled workers **m** it.
12:8 We've **m** a fortune.
12:14 The people of Ephraim **m** the
13:2 These idols are skillfully **m**.
14:3 our hands have **m** are our gods.
Amo 2:12 You **m** the Nazirites drink wine.
4:10 I **m** the stench from your camps
5:8 God **m** the ⌞constellations⌟
5:26 the gods you **m** for yourselves.
Jnh 1:9 He is the God who **m** the sea
1:16 They offered sacrifices and **m**
3:7 Then he **m** this announcement
4:5 He **m** himself a shelter there.
4:6 The LORD God **m** a plant grow
4:8 God **m** a hot east wind blow.
Mic 5:13 what your hands have **m**.
Zep 2:10 and **m** themselves greater than
Hag 2:5 "This is the promise I **m** to you
Zec 1:15 but they **m** things worse.
6:8 the north have **m** my Spirit rest
7:12 They **m** their hearts as hard as
8:14 your ancestors **m** me angry,
8:14 I **m** plans to destroy you,
8:15 So now I have again **m** plans,
11:10 break the promise that I had **m**
13:4 a prophet⌟ in a coat **m** of hair.
Mal 2:8 the promise **m** to Levi,"
2:9 "So I have **m** you disgusting,
Mat 2:23 and **m** his home in a city called
3:4 John wore clothes **m** from
4:13 He left Nazareth and **m** his
5:13 how will it be **m** salty again?
9:22 Your faith has **m** you well."
10:26 Whatever is secret will be **m**
11:5 skin diseases are **m** clean,
12:20 he has **m** justice victorious.
12:22 The demon **m** the man blind
13:35 hidden since the world was **m**."
14:22 Jesus quickly **m** his disciples
14:36 his clothes was **m** well.
15:9 are rules **m** by humans.'"
19:4 that the Creator **m** them male
21:33 wall around it, **m** a winepress,
23:17 temple that **m** the gold holy?
26:4 They **m** plans to arrest Jesus
27:29 They knelt in front of him and **m**
27:41 scribes and the leaders **m** fun
Mar 1:6 John was dressed in clothes **m**
2:4 they **m** an opening in the roof

Mar 2:27 of worship was **m** for people,
5:34 your faith has **m** you well.
5:40 So he **m** all of them go outside.
6:45 Jesus quickly **m** his disciples
6:56 his clothes was **m** well.
7:7 are rules **m** by humans.'
10:6 But God **m** them male and
10:52 your faith has **m** you well."
12:1 **m** a vat for the winepress,
14:3 perfume **m** from pure nard.
14:58 this temple **m** by humans,
14:58 one not **m** by human hands.'"
15:31 priests and the scribes **m** fun
Luk 1:55 This is the promise he **m** to our
1:70 He **m** this promise through his
3:5 ways will be **m** straight.
3:5 The rough roads will be **m**
5:19 They **m** an opening in the tiles
7:22 skin diseases are **m** clean,
8:48 your faith has **m** you well.
10:42 Mary has **m** the right choice,
11:14 The demon had **m** the man
11:40 Didn't the one who **m** the
11:50 prophet since the world was **m**.
12:2 Whatever is secret will be **m**
17:14 they were **m** clean.
17:17 "Weren't ten men **m** clean?
17:19 Your faith has **m** you well."
18:42 Your faith has **m** you well."
19:15 each one has **m** by investing.'
19:18 has **m** five times as much.'
22:20 new promise **m** with my blood."
22:63 were guarding Jesus **m** fun
23:11 Jesus with contempt and **m** fun
23:26 cross on him and **m** him carry
23:36 The soldiers also **m** fun of him.
Jon 1:3 that exists was **m** without him.
1:18 has **m** him known.
2:11 He **m** his glory public there,
2:15 He **m** a whip from small ropes
2:22 statement that Jesus had **m**.
5:11 "The man who **m** me well told
5:15 the man who had **m** him well.
5:18 His reply **m** the Jews more
5:18 but also he **m** himself equal to
6:66 Jesus' speech **m** many of his
7:23 you angry with me because I **m**
8:3 They **m** her stand in front of
12:3 perfume **m** from pure nard
12:40 "God blinded them and **m** them
13:18 However, I've **m** my choice so
15:15 friends because I've **m** known
17:6 "I **m** your name known to the
17:24 me before the world was **m**.
17:26 I have **m** your name known to
Act 2:36 a doubt that God **m** Jesus,
3:12 though we have **m** him walk by
3:18 But in this way God **m** the
3:25 heirs of the promise that God **m**
4:7 They **m** Peter and John stand
4:9 to know how he was **m** well.
4:24 you **m** the sky, the land,
4:27 Pontius Pilate **m** plans together
4:27 They **m** their plans against
5:27 they **m** them stand in front of
7:4 After his father died, God **m**
7:19 He **m** them abandon their
7:27 He asked Moses, 'Who **m** you
7:35 'Who **m** you our ruler and
7:41 was the time they **m** a calf.
7:41 delighted in what they had **m**.
7:43 and the statues you **m** for
9:39 Dorcas had **m** while she was
9:40 Peter **m** everyone leave the
10:15 God has **m** clean are impure."
10:26 But Peter **m** him get up.
11:9 God has **m** clean are impure.'
13:17 our ancestors and **m** them
13:22 God removed Saul and **m**
13:47 'I have **m** you a light for the
14:9 believed he could be **m** well.
14:15 The living God **m** the sky,
16:4 had **m** for the people.
16:14 because the Lord **m** her willing
16:16 She **m** a lot of money for her
17:6 "Those men who have **m**
Act 17:9 But after they had **m** Jason and
17:24 The God who **m** the universe
17:24 live in shrines **m** by humans,
17:26 From one man he has **m** every
17:29 is like an image **m** from gold,
18:3 and because they **m** tents for a
19:26 He tells people that gods **m** by
20:13 He had **m** these arrangements,
21:23 We have four men who have **m**
21:28 and has **m** this holy place
25:7 They **m** a lot of serious
25:25 But since he **m** an appeal to
26:6 that he **m** to our ancestors.
26:18 who are **m** holy by believing
28:2 They **m** a fire and welcomed
28:8 hands on him, and **m** him well.
28:9 went to Paul and were **m** well.
Rom 1:19 to them because he has **m**
1:20 clearly observed in what he **m**.
3:21 approval has been **m** plain
4:17 as Scripture says: "I have **m**
6:18 Freed from sin, you were **m**
7:8 and **m** me have all
9:20 Can an object that was **m** say
11:12 The fall of the Jewish people **m**
11:12 Their failure **m** people who are
11:28 The Good News **m** the Jewish
15:16 **m** holy by the Holy Spirit.
1Co 1:2 To God's church that was **m**
1:11 from Chloe's family have **m**
1:17 That would have **m** the cross
3:6 but God **m** it grow.
6:11 have been washed and **m** holy,
7:14 the unbelieving husband is **m**
7:14 and an unbelieving wife is **m**
9:19 I have **m** myself a slave for all
10:19 Do I mean that an offering **m** to
10:20 which people make are **m**
11:8 Clearly, man wasn't **m** from
11:25 cup is the new promise **m**
12:14 the human body is not **m** up of
12:23 parts are **m** more presentable.
15:10 But God's kindness **m** me what
15:22 so also everyone will be **m**
15:23 to him ⌊will be **m** alive⌋.
15:47 The first man was **m** from the
15:48 like the man who was **m** from
15:49 of the man who was **m** from
16:17 They have **m** up for your
2Co 1:17 You don't think that I **m** these
1:20 Certainly, Christ **m** God's many
2:2 if I had **m** you uncomfortable,
4:7 Our bodies are **m** of clay,
5:1 that isn't **m** by human hands.
7:7 This **m** me even happier.
7:8 my letter **m** you uncomfortable,
7:9 I **m** you uncomfortable,
8:2 has **m** them even more
8:4 They **m** an appeal to us,
10:4 our fight are not **m** by humans.
11:6 Timothy and I have **m** this
Gal 2:8 The one who **m** Peter an
2:8 to Jewish people also **m** me
4:7 God has also **m** you heirs.
4:23 a promise ⌊**m** to Abraham⌋.
4:24 is the arrangement **m** on Mount
Eph 1:22 He has **m** Christ the head of
2:5 but he **m** us alive together with
2:10 God has **m** us what we are.
2:12 and the pledges ⌊God **m** in
2:14 In his body he has **m** Jewish
2:15 in himself. So he **m** peace.
3:6 that God **m** in Christ Jesus.
Col 1:12 who has **m** you able to share
2:10 and God has **m** you complete
2:13 But God **m** you alive with
2:15 ⌊of their power⌋ and **m**
1Th 2:17 We have **m** every possible
2:18 but Satan **m** that impossible.
1Ti 6:12 called and about which you **m**
2Ti 2:20 there are not only objects **m**
2:20 but also those **m** of wood and
Tit 3:4 when God our Savior **m** his
Heb 1:2 God **m** his Son responsible for
1:2 whom God **m** the universe.
1:10 own hands you **m** the heavens.
Heb 2:7 You **m** him a little lower than
2:9 Jesus was **m** a little lower than
2:11 and all those who are **m** holy
6:13 God **m** a promise to Abraham.
8:9 not be like the promise that I **m**
8:13 God **m** this new promise and
9:11 was not **m** by human hands
9:13 people **m** their bodies holy
9:16 that the one who **m** it has died.
9:18 first promise was **m** with blood.
9:20 the promise God has **m** to you."
9:24 holy place **m** by human hands.
10:2 these sacrifices could have **m**
10:12 However, this chief priest **m**
10:13 enemies to be **m** his footstool.
10:23 The one who **m** the promise is
10:29 (the blood that **m** him holy) as
11:3 seen was **m** by something that
11:36 Some were **m** fun of and
12:27 will change what he has **m**.
Jas 1:17 from the Father who **m** the sun,
1Pe 1:12 has now **m** known to you by
2Pe 1:14 Our Lord Jesus Christ has **m**
1:16 on clever myths that we **m** up.
2:6 He **m** those cities an example
1Jn 2:19 But by leaving they **m** it clear
5:10 don't believe God have **m** God
Rev 1:6 and has **m** us a kingdom,
5:10 You **m** them a kingdom and
6:12 black as sackcloth **m** of hair.
7:14 their robes and **m** them white
9:20 demons and idols **m** of gold,
10:7 as he had **m** this Good News
14:7 Worship the one who **m**
14:8 She has **m** all the nations drink
17:17 God has **m** them do what he
18:3 Her luxurious wealth has **m** the
18:12 articles **m** of ivory and very
18:17 and everyone who **m** their
19:7 His bride has **m** herself ready.
21:18 Its wall was **m** of gray quartz.
21:18 The city was **m** of pure gold,
21:21 Each gate was **m** of one pearl.
21:21 The street of the city was **m** of

madly (1)

Nah 2:4 Chariots are racing **m** through

madman (1)

Pro 26:18 Like a **m** who shoots flaming

Madmannah (2)

Jos 15:31 Ziklag, **M**, Sansannah,
1Ch 2:49 who first settled **M**,

Madmen (1)

Jer 48:2 You will be silenced, city of **M**.

Madmenah (1)

Isa 10:31 The people in **M** flee;

madness (6)

Dtr 28:28 LORD will strike you with **m**,
Ecc 1:17 as well as **m** and stupidity.
2:12 wisdom, **m**, and foolishness.
7:25 is stupid and foolishness is **m**.
9:3 **M** is in their hearts while they
Zec 12:4 panic and every rider with **m**.

Madon (2)

Jos 11:1 messengers to King Jobab of **M**
12:19 the king of **M**, the king of

Magadan (1)

Mat 15:39 and came to the territory of **M**.

Magbish (1)

Ezr 2:30 of **M**: 156

Magdala (11)

Mat 27:56 them were Mary from **M**
27:61 Mary from **M** and the other
28:1 Mary from **M** and the other
Mar 15:40 them were Mary from **M**
15:47 Mary from **M** and Mary (the
16:1 was over, Mary from **M**,

Mar 16:9 appeared first to Mary from **M**,
Luk 24:10 The women were Mary from **M**,
Jon 19:25 Mary from **M** were standing
20:1 Mary from **M** went to the tomb.
20:18 Mary from **M** went to the

Magdalene (1)
Luk 8:2 were Mary, also called **M**,

Magdiel (2)
Gen 36:43 **M**, and Iram. These were the
1Ch 1:54 **M**, and Iram. These were the

maggot (1)
Job 25:6 is a mortal — who is only a **m** —

maggots (3)
Job 7:5 is covered with **m** and scabs.
Isa 14:11 **M** are spread out ⌊like a bed⌋
Act 12:23 Herod was eaten by **m**,

magic (21)
Exo 7:11 thing using their **m** spells.
7:22 thing using their **m** spells.
8:7 same thing using their **m** spells
8:18 gnats using their **m** spells,
Num 23:23 No **m** can harm the people of
Dtr 18:10 them alive, practice black **m**,
18:14 to those who practice black **m**.
Jos 13:22 who used black **m**.
1Sm 15:23 The sin of black **m** is rebellion.
2Ki 17:17 They practiced black **m** and
Isa 3:3 workers, and experts in **m**.
47:9 to you in spite of your evil **m**
47:12 your spells and your evil **m**.
Eze 13:18 for women who sew **m** charms
13:18 wrists and make **m** veils
13:20 I'm against the **m** charms that
13:21 I will tear off your **m** veils and
Nah 3:4 charming mistress of evil **m**.
3:4 and people her evil **m**."
Act 8:9 Samaria with his practice of **m**.
8:11 time with his practice of **m**.

magical (1)
Act 19:18 their involvement with **m** spells

magician (2)
Dan 2:10 asked such a thing of any **m**,
2:27 "No wise adviser, psychic, **m**,

magicians (13)
Gen 41:8 upset that he sent for all the **m**
41:24 I told this to the **m**,
Exo 7:11 These Egyptian **m** did the
7:22 But the Egyptian **m** did the
8:7 But the **m** did the same thing
8:18 The **m** also tried to produce
8:19 So the **m** said to Pharaoh,
9:11 The **m** couldn't compete with
Dan 1:20 ten times more than all the **m**
2:2 The king sent for the **m**,
4:7 The **m**, psychics, astrologers,
4:9 "Belteshazzar, head of the **m**,
5:11 made him head of the **m**,

magnificent (3)
1Ch 22:5 built for the LORD must be **m**,
Eze 17:23 It will become a **m** cedar tree.
Zec 11:13 Such a **m** price was set by

Magog (5)
Gen 10:2 **M**, Madai, Javan, Tubal,
1Ch 1:5 **M**, Madai, Javan, Tubal,
Eze 38:2 turn to Gog from the land of **M**.
39:6 I will send fire on **M** and on
Rev 20:8 go out to deceive Gog and **M**,

Magpiash (1)
Neh 10:20 **M**, Meshullam, Hezir,

Mahalaleel (1)
Luk 3:37 Jared, son of **M**, son of Cainan,

Mahalalel (7)
Gen 5:12 he became the father of **M**.
5:13 After he became the father of **M**,
5:15 When **M** was 65 years old,
5:16 **M** lived 830 years and had
5:17 **M** lived a total of 895 years;
1Ch 1:2 Kenan, **M**, Jared,
Neh 11:4 who was the son of **M**,

Mahalath (4)
Gen 28:9 went to Ishmael and married **M**,
2Ch 11:18 Rehoboam married **M**,
11:19 **M** gave birth to the following
11:20 After marrying **M**, he married

Mahanaim (14)
Gen 32:2 that place **M** [Two Camps].
Jos 13:26 and from **M** as far as the border
13:30 territory extended from **M**
21:38 city of refuge for murderers), **M**
2Sm 2:8 and brought him to **M**.
2:12 went from **M** to Gibeon.
2:29 Bithron until they came to **M**.
17:24 David had ⌊already⌋ come to **M**
17:27 When David came to **M**,
19:32 while he was staying at **M**.
1Ki 2:8 repeatedly when I went to **M**.
4:14 was in charge of **M**.
1Ch 6:80 **M** with its pastureland,
Sos 6:13 as you look at the dance of **M**?

Mahaneh Dan (2)
Jdg 13:25 he was at **M**, between Zorah
18:12 Kiriath Jearim is still called **M**

Maharai (2)
2Sm 23:28 of Ahohi), **M** from Netophah,
1Ch 11:30 **M** from Netophah, Heled (son

Mahath (3)
1Ch 6:35 who was the son of **M**,
2Ch 29:12 Kohath's descendants were **M**,
31:13 Jozabad, Eliel, Ismachiah, **M**,

Mahavite (1)
1Ch 11:46 Eliel the **M**, Jeribai and

Mahazioth (2)
1Ch 25:4 Mallothi, Hothir, and **M**.
25:30 The twenty-third chose **M**,

Maher Shalal Hash Baz (2)
Isa 8:1 write on it with a pen: '**M**
8:3 LORD told me, "Name him **M**

Mahlah (5)
Num 26:33 Their names were **M**,
27:1 Their names were **M**,
36:11 **M**, Tirzah, Hoglah, Milcah,
Jos 17:3 Their names were **M**,
1Ch 7:18 birth to Ishhod, Abiezer, and **M**.

Mahli (11)
Exo 6:19 of Merari were **M** and Mushi.
Num 3:20 **M** and Mushi were the sons of
3:33 descended from **M** and Mushi.
1Ch 6:19 sons were **M** and Mushi.
6:29 Merari's son was **M**.
6:47 who was the son of **M**,
23:21 sons were **M** and Mushi.
23:23 Mushi had three sons: **M**,
24:26 from Merari: **M**, Mushi,
24:30 **M**, Eder, and Jerimoth (for
Ezr 8:18 who was a descendant of **M**,

Mahli's (4)
1Ch 6:29 **M** son was Libni. Libni's son
23:21 **M** sons were Eleazar and Kish.
24:28 for **M** descendants),
24:29 **M** descendants through Kish),

Mahlite (1)
Num 26:58 Hebronite family, the **M** family,

Mahlon (3)
Rut 1:2 two sons were **M** and Chilion.
1:5 Then both **M** and Chilion died
4:9 that belonged to Chilion and **M**.

Mahlon's (1)
Rut 4:10 **M** widow, to keep the

Mahol's (1)
1Ki 4:31 Calcol, or Darda, **M** sons.

Mahrai (1)
1Ch 27:13 **M**, a descendant of Zerah from

Mahseiah (2)
Jer 32:12 of Neriah and grandson of **M**.
51:59 of Neriah and grandson of **M**,

maid (2)
Psa 123:2 as a **m** depends on her
Pro 30:23 a **m** when she replaces her

maids (1)
Gen 24:61 Then Rebekah and her **m** left.

main (13)
Num 20:19 "We'll stay on the **m** road,
Jos 8:13 The **m** camp was north of the
8:14 the king of Ai saw the **m** camp,
2Sm 8:1 He took control of the **m**
1Ki 6:3 hall in front of the **m** room
6:5 to the walls of the **m** building
6:17 temple served as the **m** hall.
1Ch 18:17 And David's sons were his **m**
2Ch 3:4 in front of ⌊the **m** room⌋ was 30
3:13 their feet and faced the **m** hall.
Eze 19:14 from the vine's **m** branch.
Dan 7:1 He wrote down the **m** parts of
Heb 8:1 The **m** point we want to make

mainland (2)
Eze 26:6 villages and on the **m** will die
26:8 destroy the villages on your **m**.

maintain (3)
1Ki 10:9 **m** justice and righteousness."
2Ch 9:8 **m** justice and righteousness."
Eph 4:3 do your best to **m** the unity that

maintains (1)
Pro 20:28 with mercy he **m** his throne.

maintenance (1)
Num 18:4 including all the **m** work for the

majestic (11)
Dtr 33:17 They will be as **m** as a
Job 37:4 He thunders with his **m** voice.
Psa 8:1 O LORD, our Lord, how **m** is
8:9 O LORD, our Lord, how **m** is
29:4 The voice of the LORD is **m**.
76:4 You are more **m** than the
111:3 His work is glorious and **m**.
Isa 10:18 The **m** forest and the orchard
30:30 will make his **m** voice heard.
Mic 5:4 with the **m** name of the LORD
2Pe 1:17 of our **m** God spoke these

majesty (143)
Gen 49:3 first in **m** and first in power.
Exo 15:7 With your unlimited **m**,
Dtr 33:26 In **m** he rides through the
Jdg 3:19 He said, "Your **M**, I have a
1Sm 16:16 Your **M**, why don't you
17:55 you live, Your **M**, I don't know."
22:14 Your **M**, he's your son-in-law,
23:20 Come, Your **M**, whenever you
24:6 to raise my hand against His **M**,
24:8 and called to Saul, "Your **M**!"
24:10 raise my hand against Your **M**
26:15 came to kill His Royal **M**.
26:17 Your Royal **M**," David answered
26:19 Your **M**, please listen to my
29:8 I fight your enemies, Your **M**?"
2Sm 3:21 all Israel for you, Your **M**.
4:8 given Your Royal **M** revenge
9:11 you've commanded, Your **M**."
13:24 Your **M** and your officials are
13:33 king's sons are dead, Your **M**.
14:4 "Help ⌊me⌋, Your **M**," she said.

2Sm 14:9 responsible for the sin, Your **M**.
14:9 Your **M** and your throne are
14:11 She said, "Your **M**,
14:18 "Please speak, Your **M**."
14:19 swear on your life, Your **M**,
15:34 'Your **M**, I'll be your servant.
16:4 in your good graces, Your **M**."
16:9 dead dog curse you, Your **M**?
17:16 or Your **M** and all the troops
18:28 who rebelled against Your **M**."
18:31 "Good news for Your **M**!"
19:19 or even think about it, Your **M**.
19:26 servant deceived me, Your **M**.
19:27 told you lies about me, Your **M**.
19:28 in my entire family, Your **M**.
19:34 go with Your **M** to Jerusalem.
19:35 a burden to you, Your **M**?
19:41 kidnap you and bring Your **M**
24:3 and may Your **M** ⌊live⌋ to see
24:3 But why does Your **M** wish to
24:21 "Why has Your **M** come to
24:22 said to David, "Take it, Your **M**,
1Ki 1:2 His officials told him, "Your **M**,
1:13 David and ask him, 'Your **M**,
1:18 anything about it, Your **M**.
1:20 is looking to you, Your **M**,
1:24 Nathan said, "Your **M**,
1:31 "May Your **M**, King David,
1:43 "His **M** King David has made
1:47 His **M** King David,
2:38 "I'll do just what Your **M** said."
20:4 "As you say, Your **M**.
20:9 messengers, "Tell His **M**,
2Ki 6:12 answered, "No one, Your **M**.
6:26 to him, "Help me, Your **M**!"
8:5 Gehazi said, "Your **M**,
1Ch 16:27 Splendor and **m** are in his
21:3 But, Your **M**, aren't they all your
21:23 said to David, "Take it, Your **M**,
29:11 glory, and **m** are yours, LORD,
2Ch 2:14 workmen of His **M** David,
2:15 Your **M** may now send the
25:7 came to him and said, "Your **M**,
Ezr 4:12 Your **M**, you should know that
5:8 Your **M** should know that we
5:17 If it pleases Your **M**,
Neh 2:5 "If it pleases Your **M**,
2:7 "If it pleases Your **M**,
Est 1:19 If it pleases you, Your **M**,
1:19 Furthermore, Your **M**,
2:4 who pleases you, Your **M**,
3:8 told King Xerxes, "Your **M**,
3:8 to tolerate them, Your **M**.
5:4 "If it pleases you, Your **M**,
5:8 Your **M**, come with Haman to a
5:8 I will answer you, Your **M**.
5:8 Your **M**, and if it pleases you,
5:8 and if it pleases you, Your **M**,
7:3 Your **M**, and if it pleases you,
7:3 you, Your **M**, spare my life.
7:4 troubling you about, Your **M**."
8:5 She said, "Your **M**,
8:5 in all your provinces, Your **M**.
9:13 said, "If it pleases you, Your **M**,
Job 13:11 Doesn't his **m** terrify you?
31:23 In the presence of his **m** I can
37:22 A terrifying **m** is around God.
40:10 dress yourself in **m** and dignity.
Psa 21:5 place splendor and **m** on him.
45:3 side with your splendor and **m**.
45:4 Ride on victoriously in your **m**
68:34 His **m** is over Israel,
93:1 He is clothed with **m**.
96:6 Splendor and **m** are in his
104:1 clothed with splendor and **m**.
145:5 the glorious honor of your **m**
Isa 2:10 and the honor of his **m**.
2:19 and the honor of his **m** when
2:21 and the honor of his **m** when
24:14 joyfully about the LORD's **m**.
26:10 do not see the **m** of the LORD.
35:2 the **m** of Carmel and Sharon.
35:2 of the LORD, the **m** of our God.
53:2 He had no form or **m** that would
Jer 37:20 But now, Your **M**, please listen,
38:9 "Your **M**, everything that these
Dan 2:4 "Your **M**, may you live forever!
2:7 Once more they said, "Your **M**,
2:11 you ask is difficult, Your **M**.
2:25 meaning to you, Your **M**."
2:29 Your **M**, while you were lying
2:31 "Your **M**, you had a vision.
2:37 "Your **M**, you are the greatest
2:45 happen in the future, Your **M**.
3:9 "Your **M**, may you live forever!
3:10 Your **M**, you gave an order that
3:12 didn't obey your order, Your **M**.
3:17 your power, he will, Your **M**.
3:18 you should know, Your **M**,
3:24 Your **M**," they answered.
4:22 You are that tree, Your **M**.
4:24 "This is the meaning, Your **M**.
4:24 to apply it to you, Your **M**.
4:27 "That is why, Your **M**,
5:10 The queen said, "Your **M**,
5:18 "Your **M**, the Most High God
6:7 or person except you, Your **M**,
6:8 Your **M**, issue this decree,
6:12 or person except you, Your **M**,
6:13 They replied, "Your **M**,
6:15 to him, "Remember, Your **M**,
6:21 said to the king, "Your **M**,
6:22 Your **M**, I haven't committed
Mat 6:29 in all his **m** was dressed like
Luk 12:27 in all his **m** was dressed like
Act 25:21 in prison and to have His **M**
25:25 appeal to His **M** the Emperor,
26:7 Your **M**, the Jews are making
26:13 Your **M**, at noon, while I was
Heb 8:1 the throne of **m** in heaven.
2Pe 1:16 Rather, we witnessed his **m**
Jud 1:25 and for eternity glory, **m**, power,

Majesty's (5)

2Sm 11:11 Your **M** mercenaries are living
11:24 of Your **M** mercenaries died.
15:15 we are Your **M** servants.
Ezr 5:17 send us Your **M** decision
Neh 2:8 the supervisor of Your **M** forest.

major (4)

1Sm 4:10 It was a **m** defeat in which
Job 9:9 ⌊the constellations⌋ Ursa **M**,
38:32 or guide Ursa **M** with its cubs?
Jer 18:15 roads and not on **m** highways.

majority (2)

Exo 23:2 with the **m** to pervert justice.
2Co 2:6 The **m** of you have imposed a

Makaz (1)

1Ki 4:9 who was in charge of **M**,

make (1221)

Gen 1:26 Let us **m** humans in our image,
2:18 I will **m** a helper who is right for
3:15 I will **m** you and the woman
3:15 I will **m** your descendants and
6:14 **M** yourself a ship of cypress
6:14 **M** rooms in the ship and coat it
6:16 **M** a roof for the ship,
6:18 "But I will **m** my promise to
9:9 "I am going to **m** my promise to
11:3 "Let's **m** bricks and bake them
11:4 Let's **m** a name for ourselves
12:2 I will **m** you a great nation,
12:2 I will **m** your name great,
17:7 I will **m** my promise to you and
17:19 I will **m** an everlasting promise
17:20 I will bless him, **m** him fertile,
17:20 and I will **m** him a great nation.
17:21 But I will **m** my promise to
18:6 of flour, knead it, and **m** bread."
21:13 Besides, I will **m** the slave's
21:18 because I'm going to **m** him
22:17 I will certainly bless you and **m**
24:6 "**M** sure that you do not take
24:12 **m** me successful today.
24:40 you to **m** your trip successful.
24:42 please **m** my trip successful.
26:4 I will **m** your descendants as
26:28 We'd like to **m** an agreement
Gen 28:3 bless you, **m** you fertile,
31:44 Now, let's **m** an agreement and
32:9 and I will **m** you prosperous.'
32:12 But you did say, 'I will **m** sure
32:20 "He thought, "I'll **m** peace with
35:1 **M** an altar there. I am the God
35:3 I will **m** an altar there to God,
41:34 **M** arrangements to appoint
41:43 of him and shouted, "**M** way!"
42:36 "You're going to **m** me lose all
43:14 May God Almighty **m** him
43:18 and **m** us slaves."
45:7 God sent me ahead of you to **m**
46:3 because I will **m** you a great
46:4 and I will **m** sure you come
48:4 He said to me, 'I will **m** you
48:20 'May God **m** you like Ephraim
Exo 3:21 I will **m** the Egyptians kind to
4:21 But I will **m** him stubborn so
5:7 more straw to **m** bricks as you
5:8 but insist that they **m** the same
5:9 **M** the work harder for these
5:14 were ordered to **m** yesterday
5:14 Why didn't you **m** as many as
5:16 and yet we're told to **m** bricks.
5:18 but you must still **m** the same
5:19 "Don't **m** fewer bricks each day
6:3 but I didn't **m** myself known to
6:7 Then I will **m** you my people,
7:3 But I will **m** Pharaoh stubborn.
9:16 power and **m** my name famous
10:25 burnt offerings we have to **m**
14:4 I will **m** Pharaoh so stubborn
15:26 I will never **m** you suffer any of
17:3 Was it to **m** us, our children,
17:14 and **m** sure that Joshua hears
18:22 **M** it easier for yourself by
20:4 Never **m** your own carved idols
20:7 The LORD will **m** sure that
20:23 Never **m** any gods of silver or
20:25 never **m** it with cut stone
20:25 you will **m** it unacceptable to
21:26 let the slave go free to **m** up
21:27 let the slave go free to **m** up
21:34 the owner of the cistern must **m**
21:36 the owner must **m** up for the
22:1 he must **m** up for the loss with
22:3 "A thief must **m** up for what he
22:4 he must **m** up for the loss with
22:5 he must **m** up for what the
22:5 he must **m** up from his own
22:6 who started the fire must **m** up
22:7 he must **m** up for the loss with
22:9 God declares guilty must **m** up
22:11 The neighbor doesn't have to **m**
22:12 he must **m** up for the owner's
22:13 He doesn't have to **m** up for an
22:14 the borrower must **m** up for the
22:15 the borrower doesn't have to **m**
23:27 I will **m** all your enemies flee
23:32 Never **m** a treaty with them and
23:33 or they will **m** you sin against
25:8 "Then have them **m** a holy
25:9 **M** the tent and all its
25:10 "**M** an ark of acacia wood 45
25:13 **M** poles of acacia wood,
25:17 "**M** a throne of mercy to cover
25:18 **M** two angels out of hammered
25:23 "**M** a table of acacia wood 36
25:25 **M** a rim three inches wide
25:26 **M** four gold rings for it,
25:28 **M** the poles out of acacia
25:29 **M** plates and dishes for the
25:31 "**M** a lamp stand out of pure
25:37 "**M** seven lamps, and set them
25:39 75 pounds of pure gold to **m**
25:40 Be sure to **m** them according to
26:1 ⌊The LORD continued,⌋ "**M** the
26:4 **M** 50 violet loops along the
26:6 **M** 50 gold fasteners.
26:7 "**M** 11 sheets of goats' hair to
26:10 **M** 50 loops along the edge of
26:11 **M** 50 bronze fasteners,
26:14 **M** a cover of rams' skins that
26:15 "**M** a framework out of acacia
26:17 **M** all the frames for the inner

Exo 26:18 **M** 20 frames for the south side
26:19 Then **m** 40 silver sockets at
26:20 of the inner tent **m** 20 frames
26:22 **M** six frames for the far end,
26:23 **M** two frames for ⌊each of⌋ the
26:26 "**M** crossbars out of acacia
26:29 Cover the frames with gold, **m**
26:31 "**M** a canopy of violet,
26:36 **m** a screen out of fine linen
26:37 **M** five posts of acacia wood for
26:37 **M** gold hooks for this screen.
27:1 "**M** an altar out of acacia wood.
27:2 **M** a horn at each of its four
27:3 "**M** all the utensils for it out of
27:4 "**M** a grate for it out of bronze
27:4 and **m** a bronze ring for ⌊each
27:6 "**M** poles out of acacia wood
27:8 "**M** the altar out of boards so
27:9 "**M** a courtyard for the tent.
28:2 **M** holy clothes for your brother
28:3 ability — to **m** Aaron's clothes.
28:4 are the clothes they will **m**:
28:4 They will **m** these holy clothes
28:6 "**M** the ephod out of fine linen
28:8 **M** the belt that is attached to
28:13 **M** gold settings
28:15 "**M** the breastplate for
28:15 creatively as you **m** the ephod.
28:15 **M** it out of gold, violet, purple,
28:22 "For the breastplate **m** chains
28:23 **M** two gold rings for the
28:26 **M** two gold rings, and fasten
28:27 **M** two ⌊more⌋ gold rings,
28:31 "**M** the robe that is worn with
28:32 **M** an opening for the head in
28:33 of the robe **m** pomegranates
28:36 "**M** a flower-shaped medallion
28:39 "**M** the specially woven inner
28:39 **M** the turban of fine linen,
28:40 "Also **m** linen robes,
28:42 "**M** linen undergarments to
29:36 bull as an offering to **m** peace
29:37 For seven days at the altar **m**
29:40 With the first lamb **m** an
29:40 **M** a wine offering of one quart
29:41 and with it **m** the same grain
29:43 my glory will **m** this place holy.
30:2 **M** it 18 inches square and 36
30:4 **M** two gold rings, and put them
30:5 **M** the poles out of acacia
30:10 Once a year Aaron must **m**
30:10 placed on the altar to **m** peace
30:15 This contribution is given to **m**
30:15 and **m** your lives acceptable
30:16 the Israelites give to **m** peace
30:18 "**M** a bronze basin with a
30:25 Have a perfumer **m** these into a
30:32 Never **m** any perfumed oil
30:35 Have a perfumer **m** it into
30:37 Never **m** any incense for
31:6 skill necessary to **m** everything
31:11 They will **m** all these things as
32:1 **M** gods who will lead us."
32:10 Then I'll **m** you into a great
32:13 You told them, 'I will **m** your
32:23 **M** gods for us. They will lead us.
32:30 Maybe I will be able to **m** a
32:30 for your sin and **m** peace
32:35 they had Aaron **m** the calf.
33:15 don't **m** us leave this place.
34:12 Be careful not to **m** a treaty
34:15 Be careful not to **m** a treaty
34:17 "Never **m** an idol.
35:10 you come and **m** everything
35:21 and to **m** the holy clothes.
35:29 to be used to **m** everything
36:6 "No man or woman needs to **m**
37:29 He also had a perfumer **m** the
38:28 used 44 pounds of silver to **m**
Lev 1:4 will be accepted to **m** peace
2:12 the altar to **m** a soothing aroma.
4:20 So the priest will **m** peace with
4:26 So the priest will **m** peace with
4:31 So the priest will **m** peace with
4:35 So the priest will **m** peace with
5:6 Then the priest will **m** peace

Lev 5:10 So the priest will **m** peace with
5:13 So the priest will **m** peace with
5:16 for the guilt offering to **m** peace
5:18 The priest will **m** peace with
6:7 So the priest will **m** peace with
6:30 the tent of meeting to **m** peace
7:7 belong to the priest to **m** peace
8:15 priests could use it to **m** peace
8:34 commanded me to **m** peace
9:7 and a burnt offering to **m** peace
9:7 Also **m** an offering for the
9:7 to **m** peace with the LORD for
10:12 **M** unleavened bread,
10:17 congregation and to **m** peace
12:4 days needed to **m** her clean are
12:6 "When the days needed to **m**
12:7 LORD's presence to **m** peace
12:8 So the priest will **m** peace with
13:36 will **m** another examination.
13:39 priest will **m** an examination.
14:18 So he will **m** peace with the
14:19 the offering for sin to **m** peace
14:20 So the priest will **m** peace with
14:21 present it to **m** peace with the
14:29 to be cleansed in order to **m**
14:31 the priest will **m** peace
14:49 use them to **m** the house clean.
14:52 red yarn to **m** the house clean.
14:53 He will **m** peace with the
15:15 the priest will **m** peace with the
15:30 the priest will **m** peace
15:31 die because they **m** my tent,
16:6 By doing this, he will **m** peace
16:10 to Azazel in order to **m** peace
16:11 By doing this he will **m** peace
16:16 So he will **m** peace with the
16:17 Aaron will **m** peace with the
16:18 LORD's presence and **m** peace
16:24 and for the people to **m** peace
16:27 into the holy place to **m** peace
16:30 On this day Aaron will **m**
16:30 with the LORD to **m** you clean.
16:33 and will **m** peace with the
16:33 He will **m** peace with the
16:34 law tells you how to **m** peace
17:8 If Israelites or foreigners **m**
17:11 this blood to you to **m** peace
17:11 is needed to **m** peace with me.
18:28 If you **m** the land unclean,
19:4 Never **m** any gods for
19:14 people to **m** them stumble.
19:22 priest will use them to **m** peace
19:25 Do this to **m** the trees produce
19:31 That will **m** you unclean.
21:4 That would **m** you unholy.
22:8 It will **m** him unclean.
22:16 They must **m** those people pay
23:21 **M** an announcement that there
23:28 It is a time when you **m** peace
25:36 Don't collect interest or **m** any
26:1 "Never **m** worthless idols or set
26:10 out old food supplies to **m** room
26:22 and **m** you so few that your
26:31 I will **m** your cities deserted
26:32 I will **m** your land so deserted
26:36 leaf will **m** them run.
Num 3:40 and **m** a list of their names.
5:3 They must not **m** this camp
5:21 may the LORD **m** you an
5:21 The LORD will **m** your uterus
5:22 and **m** your stomach swell
5:30 He will **m** his wife stand in the
6:2 A man or a woman may **m** a
6:7 they must not **m** themselves
6:9 dead next to a Nazirite and **m**
6:11 The priest will **m** peace with
6:16 offerings to the LORD and **m**
6:17 and **m** the grain offerings and
8:6 and **m** them clean.
8:7 you must do to **m** them clean:
8:7 **M** them shave their whole
8:12 These sacrifices will **m** peace
8:13 **M** the Levites stand in front of
8:19 They will **m** peace with the
8:21 them in order to **m** them clean.
10:2 "**M** two trumpets out of

Num 10:35 **M** those who hate you run
11:8 it in a pot or **m** round loaves
12:6 I **m** myself known to them in
14:12 and I'll **m** you into a nation
15:8 the LORD or **m** any other kind
15:20 the contribution you **m** from
15:25 The priest will **m** peace with
15:28 offer the sacrifice to **m** peace
16:46 into the community to **m** peace
16:47 the incense burner to **m** peace
17:5 the Israelites **m** against you
20:5 Why did you **m** us leave Egypt
21:5 They said, "Why did you **m** us
21:8 said to Moses, "**M** a snake,
21:17 "**M** your water spring up!
22:17 I will **m** sure you are richly
22:28 "What have I done to **m** you hit
27:19 **M** him stand in front of the
27:21 who will use the Urim to **m**
28:22 an offering for sin to **m** peace
28:30 Also bring one male goat to **m**
29:5 an offering for sin to **m** peace
29:11 offering for sin to **m** peace
30:3 might **m** a vow to the LORD
30:6 "An unmarried woman might **m**
30:10 "A married woman might **m** a
31:23 fire in order to **m** it clean.
31:50 We offer them to **m** peace with
32:5 Don't **m** us cross the Jordan
32:14 a bunch of sinners trying to **m**
35:19 avenge the death must **m** sure
35:33 committed can never **m** peace
35:34 Never **m** the land where you
Dtr 1:11 God of your ancestors **m** you
2:25 Today I will start to **m** all the
4:16 corrupt and **m** your own carved
4:16 Don't **m** statues that represent
4:20 in order to **m** you his own
4:23 Don't **m** your own carved idols
4:25 don't become corrupt and **m**
5:3 He didn't **m** this promise to our
5:8 Never **m** your own carved idols
5:11 The LORD will **m** sure that
7:2 Don't **m** any treaties with them
9:14 Then I'll **m** you into a nation
10:1 Also **m** an ark out of wood.
11:25 he will **m** people terrified of you
13:14 Then **m** a thorough
13:17 In his mercy he will **m** your
15:6 You will **m** loans to many
17:16 a large number of horses or **m**
17:18 the Levitical priests **m** him
19:18 The judges must **m** a thorough
21:7 Then they must **m** this formal
21:8 LORD, **m** peace with your
22:1 **M** sure you take it back.
22:4 **M** sure you help him get it back
22:7 You may take the chicks, but **m**
22:12 **M** tassels on the four corners of
22:14 Then he might **m** up charges
23:9 that will **m** you unclean.
23:21 If you **m** a vow to the LORD
23:22 If you didn't **m** a vow,
23:23 **M** sure you do what you said
23:23 You freely chose to **m** your
24:5 at home and **m** his new wife
24:8 **M** sure you do what I
24:10 When you **m** a loan to your
24:13 **M** sure you bring it back to him
25:9 She must **m** this formal
26:5 You will **m** this formal
28:12 You will be able to **m** loans to
28:13 The LORD will **m** you the head,
28:37 the LORD will send you will **m**
28:44 They will be able to **m** loans to
28:44 but you won't be able to **m**
28:53 will **m** you suffer during
28:55 will **m** you suffer during
28:57 will **m** you suffer during
28:63 than glad to **m** you prosperous
29:18 **M** sure there is no man,
29:18 **M** sure that no one among you
30:5 and the LORD will **m** you more
31:29 to you because you will **m**
32:21 my people to **m** them jealous
32:21 godless fools to **m** them angry.

Dtr 32:27 their enemies to **m** me angry.
32:30 people **m** ten thousand flee?
32:39 I kill, and I **m** alive.
32:43 with his enemies and **m** peace
Jos 3:5 "Perform the ceremonies to **m**
5:2 to Joshua, "**M** flint knives,
6:10 "Don't shout, **m** any noise,
7:13 to **m** yourselves holy.
9:6 **M** a treaty with us right now."
9:7 We wouldn't be able to **m** a
9:11 **M** a treaty with us right now.'"
22:28 They didn't **m** it for burnt
Jdg 2:2 You must never **m** a treaty with
5:3 I will **m** music to the LORD
6:39 Let me **m** one more test with
8:27 Gideon used the gold to **m**
9:27 in the vineyards to **m** wine.
13:16 But if you **m** a burnt offering,
14:15 invite us ⌊just to⌋ **m** us poor⌊?⌋"
17:3 I want to **m** a carved idol and a
18:25 "Don't **m** another sound,
20:38 in ambush that they would **m**
Rut 1:16 Don't **m** me turn back from
3:4 He will **m** it clear what you
4:7 In order to **m** every matter legal
4:11 May the LORD **m** this wife,
4:11 character in Ephrathah and **m**
1Sm 1:6 in order to **m** her miserable.
1:7 would **m** her miserable,
2:8 heap in order to **m** them sit
2:8 and even to **m** them inherit
2:19 His mother would **m** him a robe
2:29 I have commanded people to **m**
3:11 something in Israel that will **m**
3:14 will ever ⌊be able to⌋ **m** peace
6:5 **M** models of your tumors and
7:3 **M** a commitment to the LORD,
8:11 **m** them serve on his chariots
8:11 and **m** them run ahead of his
8:12 and to **m** weapons and
8:13 and have them **m** perfumes,
10:8 and **m** fellowship offerings.
11:1 "**M** a treaty with us,
11:2 "I'll **m** a treaty with you on this
12:22 wants to **m** you his people.
16:5 to **m** yourselves holy,
17:25 The king will **m** the man who
22:7 Will he **m** you all officers over
23:22 Please **m** more plans,
27:1 for me to do is to **m** sure that
28:2 "I will **m** you my bodyguard for
31:4 stab me, and **m** fun of me."
2Sm 3:12 "**M** an agreement with me,"
3:13 "I'll **m** an agreement with you.
3:17 wanted to **m** David your king.
3:21 They will **m** a treaty with you,
7:9 I will **m** your name famous like
7:10 I will **m** a place for my people
7:11 tell you that I will **m** a house for
7:23 free in order to **m** its people his
7:23 to **m** his name known,
12:12 but I will **m** this happen in
13:6 Tamar come and **m** some bread
15:4 "I wish someone would **m** me
15:4 and I would **m** sure that he got
15:20 Should I **m** you wander around
15:31 **m** Ahithophel's advice foolish."
17:16 but **m** sure you cross ⌊the
21:3 What should I ⌊give you⌋ to **m**
22:37 You **m** a wide path for me to
22:50 among the nations and **m**
1Ki 1:4 the king did not **m** love to her.
1:47 'May your God **m** Solomon's
1:51 '**M** King Solomon swear to me
2:42 Solomon asked him, "Didn't I **m**
5:9 and I will have them **m** them
8:32 take action, and **m** a decision.
9:22 But Solomon didn't **m** any of
11:39 I will **m** David's descendants
12:1 to Shechem to **m** him king.
13:6 "Please **m** an appeal to the
16:2 and their sins **m** me furious.
16:3 I will **m** his family like the
16:21 and wanted to **m** him king.
16:33 He did more to **m** the LORD
17:13 But first **m** a small loaf and

1Ki 17:21 please **m** this child's life return
18:9 "What have I done wrong to **m**
18:27 At noon Elijah started to **m** fun
18:36 **m** known today that you are
20:18 they have come out to **m** peace
21:22 I will **m** your family like the
22:13 **M** your message agree with
22:16 "How many times must I **m**
2Ki 3:16 **M** this valley full of ditches.
4:10 Let's **m** a small room on the
6:2 of us can get some logs and **m**
8:3 territory but left again to **m**
8:5 the mother ⌊came to⌋ **m** an
9:9 I will **m** Ahab's family like the
10:5 We won't **m** anyone king.
10:19 **M** sure no one is missing
10:23 "**M** sure that there are no
12:5 donors and use it to **m** repairs
12:7 Instead, use it to **m** repairs on
12:12 and cut stones to **m** repairs
17:3 required to **m** annual payments
17:29 continued to **m** its own gods.
18:23 **m** a deal with my master,
18:31 says: **M** peace with me!
19:25 Now I **m** it happen so that you
19:28 I will **m** you go back the way
21:8 I will never again **m** Israel's
22:17 gods in order to **m** me furious.
23:16 on the altar to **m** it unclean.
23:19 had built these places to **m**
23:26 these things to **m** him furious.
1Ch 6:49 sins to **m** Israel acceptable
10:4 men will come and **m** fun
12:31 by name to **m** David king.
12:38 to Hebron — to **m** David king
12:38 had agreed to **m** David king.
15:12 to **m** yourselves holy.
16:8 **M** known among the nations
16:9 **M** music to praise him.
16:35 name and **m** your praise our
17:8 I will **m** your name like the
17:9 I will **m** a place for my people
17:21 free in order to **m** its people his
17:21 to **m** your name known,
18:8 Solomon used it to **m** the pool,
21:3 Why do you wish to **m** Israel
25:5 to him to **m** him prominent,
28:4 he was pleased to **m** me king
29:5 to **m** gold objects, and
29:5 else the craftsmen will **m**.
29:5 Who else is willing to **m** an
29:12 and you can **m** anyone great
29:19 **M** my son Solomon completely
2Ch 2:7 He should know how to **m**
2:14 He also knows how to **m** all
2:16 Then we will **m** rafts out of it
5:11 to **m** themselves holy
6:23 take action, and **m** a decision.
7:20 I will **m** it an example and an
8:9 But Solomon didn't **m** any of
10:1 to Shechem to **m** him king.
11:22 Rehoboam could **m** him king.
14:7 "Let's build these cities and **m**
18:12 **M** your message agree with
18:15 "How many times must I **m**
21:19 His people did not **m** a bonfire
24:9 Israel to **m** contributions.)
24:14 who used it to **m** utensils for
25:16 "Did we **m** you an adviser to
28:13 You'll **m** us responsible for this
29:5 Perform the ceremonies to **m**
29:10 Now I intend to **m** a pledge to
29:15 to **m** themselves holy.
29:15 the temple to **m** it clean.
29:16 LORD's temple to **m** it clean.
29:17 performed the ceremonies to **m**
29:24 for sin at the altar to **m** peace
29:34 could **m** themselves holy.
30:3 to **m** themselves holy
30:15 to **m** themselves holy.
30:17 and couldn't **m** their lambs holy
30:24 to **m** themselves holy.
34:3 he began to **m** Judah and
34:25 gods in order to **m** me furious.
35:3 to **m** themselves holy
35:6 to **m** yourselves holy,

2Ch 36:22 **M** this announcement
Ezr 1:1 **M** this announcement
6:9 **M** sure that nothing is omitted.
6:14 continued to **m** progress
7:24 are forbidden to **m** any priest,
7:27 this into the king's mind to **m**
10:3 So we must now **m** a promise
Neh 1:11 success today and **m** this man,
4:3 "Even a fox would **m** their
8:15 branches — to **m** booths as
8:16 to get branches to **m** booths
10:33 offerings for sin that **m** peace
13:19 by the gates to **m** sure that no
Est 9:19 and in the unwalled towns **m**
Job 5:18 but his hands **m** you well.
6:5 or does an ox **m** a sound over
7:17 that you should **m** so much
7:20 Why do you **m** me your target?
11:3 others so that you can **m** fun
13:19 Who can **m** a case against me?
13:23 **M** me aware of my
13:25 Are you trying to **m** a fluttering
13:26 You **m** me suffer for the sins of
14:9 merely a scent of water will **m**
17:13 as my home and **m** my bed
19:5 If you are trying to **m**
19:18 If I stand up, they **m** fun of me.
20:2 thoughts **m** me answer,
23:13 Who can **m** him change his
29:18 but I will **m** my days as
30:9 "And now they **m** fun of me
31:15 in my mother's belly **m** them?
37:18 with him and **m** them as firm
38:27 wasteland in order to **m**
38:33 laws of the sky or **m** them rule
39:20 Can you **m** it leap like a locust,
39:26 "Does your understanding **m** a
41:4 Will it **m** an agreement with
41:28 An arrow won't **m** it run away.
42:8 Go to my servant Job, and **m** a
Psa 2:2 Rulers **m** plans together
5:8 **M** your way in front of me
7:9 but **m** the righteous person
7:17 I will **m** music to praise the
9:2 I will **m** music to praise your
9:11 **M** music to praise the LORD,
13:2 How long must I **m** decisions
16:11 You **m** the path of life known to
18:36 You **m** a wide path for me to
18:49 among the nations and **m**
19:8 They **m** the heart rejoice.
21:9 When you appear, you will **m**
21:13 We will sing and **m** music to
22:7 All who see me **m** fun of me.
25:4 **M** your ways known to me,
27:6 I will sing and **m** music to
30:4 **M** music to praise the LORD,
33:2 **M** music for him on a
36:8 and you **m** them drink from the
37:6 He will **m** your righteousness
44:10 You **m** us retreat from the
45:16 You will **m** them princes over
47:6 **M** music to praise God.
47:6 **M** music to praise our king.
47:7 **M** your best music for him!
50:18 you want to **m** friends with him.
52:7 refused to **m** God his fortress!
54:6 I will **m** a sacrifice to you along
56:7 angrily **m** the nations fall.
57:7 I want to sing and **m** music.
57:9 I want to **m** music to praise you
59:8 You **m** fun of all the nations.
59:11 **M** them wander aimlessly by
59:17 I will **m** music to praise you!
61:8 Then I will **m** music to praise
62:10 on extortion ⌊to **m** you rich⌋.
65:9 You **m** it much richer than it
66:2 **M** music to praise the glory of
66:2 **M** his praise glorious.
66:4 It will **m** music to praise you.
66:4 It will **m** music to praise your
66:8 **M** the sound of his praise
68:4 **m** music to praise his name.
68:4 **M** a highway for him to ride
68:32 **M** music to praise the Lord.
69:12 and drunkards **m** up songs

Psa 71:21 You comfort me and **m** me
71:22 I will **m** music with a harp to
71:23 sing with joy when I **m** music
73:18 places and **m** them fall into
75:3 I will **m** its foundations as solid
75:9 I will **m** music to praise the
76:11 **M** vows to the LORD your God,
78:5 our ancestors to **m** them known
83:3 They **m** plans in secret against
84:6 they **m** it a place of springs.
85:13 will go ahead of him and **m**
87:5 Most High will **m** it secure."
88:7 You **m** all your waves pound
89:4 'I will **m** your dynasty continue
89:27 Yes, I will **m** him the firstborn.
89:29 I will **m** his dynasty endure
90:15 **M** us rejoice for as many days
90:17 **M** us successful in everything
90:17 Yes, **m** us successful in
92:1 to **m** music to praise your
92:10 But you **m** me as strong as a
92:15 They **m** it known that the
94:5 They **m** those who belong to
98:4 joyful singing, and **m** music.
98:5 **M** music to the LORD with a
101:1 I will **m** music to praise you.
104:4 You **m** your angels winds and
104:10 You **m** water gush from springs
104:14 You **m** grass grow for cattle
104:14 for cattle and **m** vegetables
104:15 You **m** wine to cheer human
104:15 olive oil to **m** faces shine,
104:33 I will **m** music to praise my
105:1 **M** known among the nations
105:2 **M** music to praise him.
106:8 he could **m** his mighty power
106:47 name and **m** your praise our
108:1 I want to sing and **m** music
108:3 I want to **m** music to praise you
110:1 until I **m** your enemies your
115:7 They cannot ⌊even⌋ **m** a
115:8 Those who **m** idols end up like
118:13 They pushed hard to **m** me fall,
119:16 Your laws **m** me happy.
119:24 instructions **m** me happy.
119:47 which I love, **m** me happy.
119:75 you were right to **m** me suffer.
119:77 your teachings **m** me happy.
119:98 Your commandments **m** me
119:133 **M** my steps secure through
119:143 ⌊still⌋ **m** me happy.
119:165 can **m** those people stumble.
119:174 your teachings **m** me happy.
129:6 **M** them be like grass on a roof,
132:17 There I will **m** a horn sprout up
135:3 **M** music to praise his name
135:18 Those who **m** idols end up like
138:1 I will **m** music to praise you in
139:8 If I **m** my bed in hell,
140:3 They **m** their tongues as sharp
145:12 in order to **m** known your
146:2 I want to **m** music to praise my
147:7 **M** music to our God with a lyre.
149:3 Let them **m** music to him with
Pro 1:23 I will **m** my words known to
1:26 I will **m** fun of you when panic
3:6 he will **m** your paths smooth.
4:16 they **m** someone stumble.
14:9 Stubborn fools **m** fun of guilt,
22:26 among those who **m** deals
25:5 will **m** his throne secure.
25:22 ⌊In this way⌋ you will **m** him
27:9 Perfume and incense **m** the
27:11 Be wise, my son, and **m** my
30:26 yet they **m** their home in the
Ecc 2:2 "Laughter doesn't **m** any sense.
2:3 I explored ways to **m** myself
4:1 that **m** people suffer under
5:4 When you **m** a promise to God,
5:5 It is better not to **m** a promise
5:5 make a promise than to **m** one
7:16 Why **m** yourself miserable?
10:1 Dead flies will **m** a bottle of
10:4 If you remain calm, you can **m**
11:9 You should let your hearts **m**
11:9 But realize that God will **m** you
Ecc 12:1 They will **m** you say,
Sos 1:11 We will **m** gold ornaments with
5:9 any other beloved that you **m**
Isa 2:6 they **m** deals with foreigners.
3:4 "I will **m** boys their leaders.
3:5 The young will **m** fun of the old,
3:5 and common people will **m** fun
3:7 Don't **m** me a leader of our
3:17 will **m** their foreheads bare.
5:6 I will **m** it a wasteland.
6:10 **M** these people close-minded.
8:10 **M** plans for battle, but they will
10:1 be for those who **m** unjust laws
10:1 who **m** oppressive regulations.
10:15 Can a saw **m** itself greater than
11:4 He will **m** fair decisions for the
12:4 **M** his deeds known among the
12:4 **M** them remember that his
12:5 **M** music to praise the LORD.
13:9 He will **m** the earth desolate.
13:12 I will **m** people harder to find
13:13 I will **m** heaven tremble,
16:3 **M** a decision. At high noon
16:3 At high noon **m** your shadow
17:11 you will **m** it grow.
17:11 you will **m** it sprout.
17:12 The noise that the people **m**
17:13 The people will **m** noise like
19:21 So the LORD will **m** himself
19:21 They will **m** vows to the LORD
21:4 I longed for **m** me tremble.
21:10 I **m** known to you what I heard
23:16 **M** sweet music. Sing many
26:7 O Upright One, you **m** the road
27:5 Let them **m** peace with me.
27:5 Yes, let them **m** peace with me.
28:9 To whom will they **m** the
28:17 I will **m** justice a measuring
28:24 break up the soil and **m** furrows
29:16 its maker, "He didn't **m** me"?
29:21 those who **m** people sin with
30:1 They **m** alliances against my
30:30 The LORD will **m** his majestic
31:4 disturbed by the noise they **m**.
34:15 Owls will **m** their nests there,
36:8 **m** a deal with my master,
36:16 says: **M** peace with me!
37:26 Now I **m** it happen so that you
37:29 I will **m** you go back the way
38:8 I'm going to **m** the shadow go
38:19 Fathers **m** your faithfulness
40:3 **M** a straight highway in the
40:19 Craftsmen **m** idols.
40:19 Silversmiths **m** silver chains
41:15 "I am going to **m** you into a
41:18 I will **m** rivers flow on bare
41:18 I will **m** springs flow through
41:23 intimidate us and **m** us afraid.
42:2 He will not **m** his voice heard
42:16 I will **m** rough places smooth.
43:19 I will **m** rivers on dry land.
43:20 I will **m** rivers on the dry land
44:8 Didn't I **m** this known to you
44:9 All who **m** idols are nothing.
44:15 They also **m** gods from these
44:15 They **m** them into carved
44:17 of the wood they **m** into gods,
44:25 prophets to fail and **m** fools
44:25 I **m** wise men retreat and turn
45:7 I **m** light and create darkness.
45:7 I **m** blessings and create
45:13 I will **m** all his roads straight.
45:16 Those who **m** idols will be
46:5 compare me and **m** me equal?
49:8 You will **m** them inherit the
49:20 **M** room for me to live here."
49:26 I will **m** your oppressors eat
51:3 He will **m** its desert like Eden.
51:3 He will **m** its wilderness like
52:11 **M** yourselves pure,
53:2 form or majesty that would **m**
53:2 that would **m** us desire him.
55:3 I will **m** an everlasting promise
55:10 They **m** it sprout and grow so
56:7 mountain and **m** them happy
58:14 I will **m** you ride on the heights
Isa 59:15 evil **m** themselves victims.
60:15 But now I will **m** you a source
60:22 will **m** it happen quickly."
61:8 I will **m** an everlasting promise
61:11 so the Almighty LORD will **m**
63:12 the water in front of them to **m**
63:14 you guided your people to **m**
64:2 Come down to **m** your name
64:12 Will you be silent and **m** us
66:9 deliver and then **m** her unable
66:17 People **m** themselves holy and
66:21 "I will **m** some of them priests
66:22 I am about to **m** will continue
Jer 1:12 I am watching to **m** sure that
1:17 or I will **m** you ⌊even more⌋
3:16 it, miss it, or **m** another one.
4:5 **M** it heard in Jerusalem.
5:20 and **m** this heard in Judah:
6:8 I will **m** your land desolate,
6:13 eager to **m** money dishonestly.
6:29 blast furnace blow fiercely to **m**
7:18 and women knead dough to **m**
7:18 gods in order to **m** me furious.
8:10 eager to **m** money dishonestly.
8:19 They **m** me furious with their
10:11 they didn't **m** heaven and earth.
10:22 cities and **m** them homes
13:13 I'm going to **m** everyone who
14:22 of the nations can't **m** it rain.
15:4 I will **m** these people a
15:7 I will **m** them childless.
15:11 I will certainly **m** your enemies
15:14 I will **m** you serve your
15:20 I will **m** you like a solid bronze
16:20 "People can't **m** gods for
16:21 This time I will **m** my power
17:4 I will **m** you serve your
18:4 pot the way he wanted to **m** it.
18:11 and **m** plans against you.
18:22 **M** them cry out from their
18:23 **M** them stumble in your
19:9 I will **m** the people eat the flesh
19:12 I will **m** this city like Topheth.
20:4 I'm going to **m** you terrify
23:27 because they want to **m** my
24:9 I will **m** them a horrifying sight
25:6 Don't **m** me furious about the
25:14 and great kings will **m** slaves
25:15 and **m** all the nations to whom
27:2 **M** ⌊leather⌋ straps and a
27:5 and my powerful arm to **m**
27:7 kings will **m** him their slave.
28:6 May the LORD **m** your
28:14 I will even **m** wild animals
29:18 I will **m** them a horrifying sight
30:8 no longer **m** you serve them.
30:19 I'll **m** them numerous,
31:31 "when I will **m** a new promise
31:33 this is the promise that I will **m**
32:19 You **m** wise plans and do
32:35 I didn't **m** Judah sin.
32:37 this place and **m** them live here
32:40 I will **m** an eternal promise to
32:40 I will **m** them fear me so that
34:17 I will **m** all the kingdoms of the
42:12 I will **m** him have compassion
44:8 Why do you **m** me angry by
46:14 **M** it known in Memphis and in
46:27 and no one will **m** them afraid.
48:28 Be like doves that **m** their
49:15 "Edom, I will **m** you the
50:5 They will go there to **m** a
51:25 and **m** you a scorched
51:29 against Babylon to **m** Babylon
51:36 sea and **m** its springs dry.
51:39 for them and **m** them drunk so
51:44 I will **m** Bel spit out everything
51:57 I will **m** their officials and wise
Lam 2:13 What comparison can I **m** that
2:14 order to **m** things better again.
3:14 All day long they **m** fun of
3:63 they **m** fun of me in their songs.
3:65 **M** them stubborn. Let your
Eze 3:8 Yet, I will **m** you as stubborn
3:9 I will **m** you as hard as a
3:20 I will **m** them stumble,

Eze 3:26 I will **m** your tongue stick to the
4:9 and use them to **m** bread for
7:20 and used them to **m** disgusting
7:20 I will **m** their jewels disgusting.
13:2 Tell those who **m** up their
13:9 They will not help my people **m**
13:17 people who **m** up prophecies,
13:18 wrists and **m** magic veils
13:23 false visions or **m** predictions.
14:8 I will **m** an example of him.
14:15 that country and they **m**
15:3 people use it to **m** something?
15:3 Do they **m** a peg from it to hang
15:4 Then can it be used to **m**
15:5 How can it be used to **m**
16:2 "Son of man, **m** known to the
16:4 with water to **m** you clean.
16:8 were old enough to **m** love to.
16:26 your prostitution to **m** me angry
16:43 Didn't you **m** wicked plans in
16:51 you **m** your sisters look
16:60 and I will **m** it a promise that
16:62 Then I will **m** my promise with
17:24 and I **m** small trees grow tall.
17:24 and I **m** dry trees grow.
18:8 lend money for interest or **m**
18:17 interest or **m** excessive profits.
19:11 They were used to **m** scepters
20:28 offerings there to **m** me angry.
20:37 Then I will **m** you suffer
20:37 punishment and **m** you keep
21:19 **M** a sign, and put it where the
21:24 You **m** people remember how
22:4 That is why I will **m** you a
22:12 and **m** excessive profits.
22:12 You **m** profits by mistreating
22:27 people to **m** excessive profits.
25:7 the nations, **m** you disappear,
26:18 Your defeat will **m** the people
26:20 I will **m** you live below the
27:5 cedar trees from Lebanon to **m**
28:23 against you and **m** blood flow
29:4 put hooks in your jaws and **m**
29:12 I will **m** Egypt the most
29:15 I will **m** them so weak that they
29:21 "On that day I will **m** the
30:22 I will **m** the sword fall from his
30:24 I will **m** the arms of the king of
32:2 You **m** the streams muddy.
32:4 I will **m** birds perch on you,
32:9 "'I will **m** many people troubled
32:14 Then I will **m** its water clear
32:14 clear and **m** its streams flow
33:2 and **m** him their watchman.
33:12 will not **m** him stumble when
33:29 when I **m** the land a barren
36:11 and I will **m** you better off than
36:25 you and **m** you clean instead
36:29 I will **m** the grain grow so that
36:30 I will **m** fruit grow on the trees
36:37 ask me to **m** them as numerous
37:19 I will **m** them into one stick.
37:26 **m** them increase in number,
38:10 and you will **m** wicked plans.
39:3 your left hand and **m** you drop
39:7 I will **m** my holy name known
39:10 They will **m** fires with the
39:12 months to **m** the land clean.
39:14 through the land and **m** it clean.
43:20 sin from the altar and **m** peace
43:26 the priests should **m** peace
44:24 judges and **m** decisions based
44:25 "'A priest must not **m** himself
45:15 and fellowship offerings to **m**
45:17 and fellowship offerings to **m**
45:20 So you must **m** peace with the
47:9 The river will **m** the water in
Dan 2:9 among yourselves to **m** up
4:14 **M** the animals under it run
4:14 and **m** the birds fly from its
4:25 from the sky will **m** you wet.
6:7 agree that the king should **m**
9:23 you began to **m** your request,
11:6 kings will **m** an alliance.
11:6 to the northern king to **m** peace
11:35 and **m** them white until the end
Dan 11:37 because he will **m** himself
11:39 **m** them rulers over many
Hos 2:8 used it to **m** statues of Baal.
2:15 I will **m** the valley of Achor
2:18 "On that day I will **m** an
2:19 I will **m** you my wife forever.
5:9 I will **m** the truth known among
7:3 "They **m** kings happy with the
7:3 They **m** officials happy with
7:14 cry in their beds and **m** cuts
8:4 They chose to **m** idols with
8:11 of Ephraim build to **m** offerings
9:14 **M** the women miscarry,
9:14 or else **m** them unable to nurse
10:4 and they **m** promises they don't
11:8 How can I **m** you like Admah?
12:1 They **m** treaties with Assyria
12:9 I will **m** you live in tents again
13:2 They **m** idols from silver for
Joe 2:19 I will no longer **m** you a
3:7 I am going to **m** them leave the
Amo 6:5 for those who **m** up songs as
8:9 I will **m** the sun go down at
8:10 I will **m** that day seem like a
Oba 1:2 "Edom, I will **m** you the
1:3 You **m** your home up high.
Jnh 4:6 and **m** him more comfortable.
4:10 You didn't plant it or **m** it grow.
Mic 1:16 **M** yourselves as bald as
2:4 people will **m** fun of you.
2:12 They will **m** a lot of noise
4:4 and no one will **m** them afraid.
4:13 I will **m** your horns as hard as
6:15 You will **m** new wine,
Nah 3:6 I will **m** you look like a fool.
3:6 I will **m** you a sight to be seen.
Hab 1:3 Why do you **m** me see
1:10 They will **m** fun of kings and
1:14 You **m** all people like the fish
2:2 **M** it clear on tablets so that
2:18 to **m** worthless idols that
Zep 1:3 and the sins that **m** people fall,
2:11 because he will **m** all the gods
2:15 and **m** an obscene gesture.
3:19 I will **m** them praised and
3:20 I will **m** you famous and
Hag 2:12 does that **m** the food holy?"
2:13 does that **m** them unclean?"
2:23 I will **m** you like a signet ring,
Zec 6:11 the silver and gold, **m** a crown,
8:21 "Let's **m** a habit of going to ask
9:10 He will **m** sure there are no
12:2 "I'm going to **m** Jerusalem like
12:3 On that day I will **m** Jerusalem
12:6 "On that day I will **m** the
Mal 2:15 Didn't God **m** you one?
3:17 "On that day I will **m** them my
Mat 3:3 **M** his paths straight!'"
5:9 are those who **m** peace.
5:17 aside but to **m** them come true.
5:24 First go away and **m** peace
5:25 "**M** peace quickly with your
5:36 After all, you cannot **m** one hair
6:16 They put on sad faces to **m** it
8:2 you can **m** me clean."
12:33 "**M** a tree good, and then its
12:33 Or **m** a tree rotten, and then its
13:14 So they **m** Isaiah's prophecy
15:11 mouth doesn't **m** him unclean.
15:20 These are the things that **m** a
15:20 doesn't **m** a person unclean."
17:12 same way they're going to **m**
20:19 They will **m** fun of him,
23:4 They **m** loads that are hard to
23:5 They **m** their headbands large
23:8 But don't **m** others call you
23:10 Don't **m** others call you a
23:15 you **m** that person twice as fit
27:64 Therefore, give the order to **m**
27:65 Go and **m** the tomb as secure
28:19 **m** disciples of all nations:
Mar 1:3 **M** his paths straight!'"
1:40 you can **m** me clean."
2:22 the wine will **m** the skins burst,
7:15 the outside can **m** him unclean.
7:18 outside can't **m** him unclean?
Mar 7:23 and **m** a person unclean."
10:34 They will **m** fun of him,
12:40 to **m** themselves look good.
13:36 **M** sure he doesn't come
Luk 1:77 You will **m** his people know
2:22 by Moses' Teachings to **m**
3:4 **M** his paths straight!
5:12 you can **m** me clean."
5:37 If they do, the new wine will **m**
9:7 He didn't know what to **m** of it.
11:40 the outside **m** the inside too?
12:33 **M** yourselves wallets that don't
12:33 **M** a treasure for yourselves in
12:37 **m** them sit down at the table,
14:29 who watches will **m** fun of you.
15:19 **M** me one of your hired men.'"
16:9 you should use it to **m** friends
18:32 They will **m** fun of him,
20:26 They couldn't **m** him say
20:43 until I **m** your enemies your
20:47 to **m** themselves look good.
21:14 So **m** up your minds not to
21:34 "**M** sure that you don't become
24:11 story didn't **m** any sense,
Jon 1:23 '**M** the way for the Lord straight,
5:30 I **m** my judgments.
6:15 him by force and **m** him king.
6:61 what I say **m** you lose faith?
8:16 is valid because I don't **m**
8:16 I **m** my judgment with the
11:52 together and **m** them one.
14:23 and we will go to them and **m**
14:24 I don't **m** up what you hear me
15:2 that does produce fruit to **m**
17:17 "Use the truth to **m** them holy.
17:26 and I will **m** it known so that
Act 2:28 You **m** the path of life known to
4:26 Rulers **m** plans together
7:6 there would **m** them slaves
7:26 and he tried to **m** peace
7:40 So **m** gods who will lead us.'
7:50 Didn't I **m** all these things?'"
23:15 You have to **m** it look as
23:20 They're going to **m** it look as
Rom 1:10 God will now at last **m**
2:16 spreading to **m** that judgment.
8:11 will also **m** your mortal bodies
9:18 wants to **m** someone stubborn,
9:20 "Why did you **m** me like this?"
9:21 He can **m** something for a
10:19 "I will **m** you jealous of people
10:19 I will **m** you angry about a
11:11 who are not Jewish to **m**
11:12 of Jewish people will **m**
11:14 Perhaps I can **m** my people
12:6 **m** sure what you say agrees
12:20 If you do this, you will **m** him
14:5 must **m** his own decision.
14:13 would **m** other Christians have
16:17 and who **m** others fall away
1Co 3:13 The day will **m** what each one
4:14 I'm not writing this to **m** you
6:15 Christ's body and **m** them parts
7:11 she should stay single or **m** up
8:9 freedom you don't somehow **m**
8:13 I won't **m** other believers lose
9:27 my body with punches and **m**
10:11 These things happened to **m**
10:20 which people **m** are made
10:22 Are we trying to **m** the Lord
11:19 have to exist in order to **m**
16:10 If Timothy comes, **m** sure that
2Co 1:17 you think that when I **m** plans,
1:17 I **m** them in a sinful way?
2:3 those who should **m** me happy.
2:4 I didn't write to **m** you
2:14 God uses us to **m** clear what it
6:10 we **m** many people spiritually
6:13 **M** a place for us in your hearts
7:8 But since my letter did **m** you
8:9 in order to **m** you rich through
9:5 before I do and **m** arrangements
9:11 God will **m** you rich enough so
10:1 I, Paul, **m** my appeal to you
10:12 **m** their own recommendations.
13:11 **M** sure that you improve.

Gal 6:7 **M** no mistake about this:
6:7 You can never **m** a fool out of
6:12 These people who want to **m** a
6:17 don't **m** any trouble for me!
Eph 5:16 **M** the most of your
5:19 Sing and **m** music to the Lord
5:26 He did this to **m** the church
6:4 Fathers, don't **m** your children
6:18 Use every kind of effort and **m**
Php 2:29 **M** sure you honor people like
2:30 work of Christ in order to **m** up
3:21 bodies and **m** them like his
Col 3:21 don't **m** your children resentful,
4:4 Pray that I may **m** this mystery
4:5 **M** the most of your
4:16 **M** sure that you also read the
1Th 2:5 or schemes to **m** money.
4:11 **m** it your goal to live quietly,
5:15 **M** sure that no one ever pays
5:23 who gives peace **m** you holy
2Th 1:11 that our God will **m** you worthy
2:1 we have this request to **m** of
1Ti 2:1 I encourage you to **m** petitions,
3:8 shameful ways to **m** money.
4:12 Instead, **m** your speech,
6:5 godly life is a way to **m** a profit.
6:15 time God will **m** this known.
2Ti 3:3 They will refuse to **m** peace
Tit 1:7 shameful ways to **m** money.
1:11 shameful way they **m** money.
Phm 1:9 However, I would prefer to **m**
Heb 1:13 until I **m** your enemies your
2:17 in God's presence and **m** peace
3:1 whom we **m** our declaration
4:11 So we must **m** every effort to
6:17 He wanted to **m** this perfectly
8:1 point we want to **m** is this:
8:5 Moses was about to **m** the tent,
8:5 "Be sure to **m** everything based
8:8 when I will **m** a new promise to
8:10 this is the promise that I will **m**
9:25 went into the holy place to **m**
10:1 They can never **m** those who
10:16 is the promise that I will **m**
11:14 Those who say such things **m**
12:15 **M** sure that everyone has
12:16 **M** sure that no one commits
13:12 He suffered to **m** the people
Jas 1:8 time and can't **m** up his mind
1:10 rich should **m** them humble.
1:18 through the word of truth to **m**
1:25 teachings that **m** people free
2:4 standard to **m** judgments?
2:16 and **m** sure you eat enough."
3:2 All of us **m** a lot of mistakes.
3:2 If someone doesn't **m** any
3:3 of horses to **m** them obey us,
4:13 business, and **m** money."
1Pe 2:23 When he suffered, he didn't **m**
3:6 letting anything **m** you afraid
3:15 However, **m** your defense with
5:1 I **m** this appeal as a spiritual
5:10 strengthen you, **m** you strong,
2Pe 1:5 Because of this, **m** every effort
1:10 use more effort to **m** God's
1:15 So I will **m** every effort to see
3:14 **m** every effort to have him find
1Jn 2:24 **M** sure that the message you
Jud 1:11 into Balaam's error to **m** a profit
Rev 3:9 I will **m** those who are in
3:12 I will **m** everyone who wins the
6:4 and to **m** people slaughter one
13:14 tells those living on earth to **m**
16:12 water in the river dried up to **m**
21:3 God will **m** his home with

maker (25)

Gen 14:19 **M** of heaven and earth.
14:22 **M** of heaven and earth,
Neh 3:8 a perfume **m**, made repairs.
Job 4:17 human being be pure to his **m**?'
32:22 If I did, my **m** would soon carry
40:19 Its **m** approaches it with his
Psa 95:6 in front of the LORD, our **m**,
115:15 the **m** of heaven and earth.
121:2 the **m** of heaven and earth.
124:8 the **m** of heaven and earth.
134:3 the **m** of heaven and earth,
Pro 14:31 the poor insults his **m**,
17:5 of a poor person insults his **m**.
22:2 the LORD is the **m** of them all.
Isa 17:7 they will look to their **M**,
22:11 didn't look to Jerusalem's **M**.
27:11 That is why their **M** won't have
29:16 been made say about its **m**,
45:9 one who quarrels with his **M**.
45:11 Holy One and the **M** of Israel.
54:5 Your husband is your **M**.
Hos 8:14 and they have forgotten their **M**.
Hab 2:18 idol when its **m** has carved it?
2:18 when its **m** has molded it?
Rom 9:20 that was made say to its **m**,

makes (190)

Exo 4:11 Who **m** humans unable to talk
4:11 them sight or **m** them blind?
21:5 But if he **m** this statement:
31:13 am the LORD who **m** you holy.
Lev 6:26 The priest who **m** the offering
14:48 But if the priest comes and **m**
15:3 chronic or not **m** no difference;
15:4 has a discharge **m** everything
15:32 of semen that **m** him unclean,
18:9 It **m** no difference whether or
24:16 It **m** no difference whether they
24:22 It **m** no difference whether you
27:2 If any of you **m** a special vow
Num 5:8 to the ram which **m** peace
19:13 water to take away his sin **m**
23:19 When he **m** a promise,
30:2 If a man **m** a vow to the LORD
Dtr 8:18 is the one who **m** you wealthy.
10:18 He **m** sure orphans and
24:1 and **m** her leave his house.
Jdg 9:13 which **m** gods and humans
16:5 and find out what **m** him so
16:6 "Please tell me what **m** you so
16:15 told me what **m** you so strong."
1Sm 2:6 He **m** ⌊people⌋ go down to the
25:30 he promised and **m** you ruler
2Sm 22:34 He **m** my feet like those of a
22:36 Your help **m** me great.
23:4 The rain **m** the grass grow from
23:5 he **m** these things happen.
1Ki 11:22 you have here that **m** you eager
22:23 a spirit that **m** them tell lies.
2Ki 18:19 What **m** you so confident?
2Ch 18:22 a spirit that **m** them tell lies.
Job 9:23 he **m** fun of the despair of
12:17 away barefoot and **m** fools out
12:20 He **m** trusted advisers unable
12:23 He **m** nations important and
12:23 He **m** nations large and leads
12:24 and **m** them stumble about
12:25 and he **m** them stumble like
20:3 criticism that **m** me ashamed,
20:23 person and **m** his wrath come
27:18 a shack that a watchman **m**.
35:9 The weight of oppression **m**
35:9 The power of mighty people **m**
35:11 who **m** us wiser than the birds
36:10 He **m** them listen to his
37:7 He **m** it impossible to do
37:13 he **m** the storm appear.
37:15 how God controls them and **m**
39:27 eagle flies high and **m** its nest
40:17 It **m** its tail stiff like a cedar.
41:31 It **m** the deep sea boil like a
Psa 2:4 The Lord **m** fun of them.
7:12 he **m** it ready ⌊to shoot⌋.
11:6 He **m** them drink from a cup
15:4 The one who **m** a promise and
18:32 strength and **m** my way perfect.
18:33 He **m** my feet like those of a
18:35 Your gentleness **m** me great.
19:7 It **m** gullible people wise.
19:8 It **m** the eyes shine.
23:2 He **m** me lie down in green
29:6 He **m** Lebanon skip along like
29:8 The voice of the LORD **m** the
29:8 The LORD **m** the wilderness of
48:8 God **m** Zion stand firm forever.
52:2 Your tongue **m** up threats.
60:3 us wine that **m** us stagger.
68:33 He **m** his voice heard,
77:10 Then I said, "It **m** me feel sick
93:5 O LORD, holiness is what **m**
104:17 Storks **m** their homes in fir
107:41 and **m** their families like
113:9 He **m** a woman who is in a
135:7 He is the one who **m** the
135:7 who **m** lightning for the
147:8 He **m** grass grow on the
147:13 He **m** the bars across your
147:18 He **m** wind blow ⌊and⌋ water
Pro 4:19 know what **m** them stumble.
6:13 **m** a signal with his foot,
7:21 she **m** him give in.
10:1 A wise son **m** his father happy,
10:22 It is the LORD's blessing that **m**
11:5 people **m** their road smooth,
12:25 encouraging word **m** him joyful.
13:12 Delayed hope **m** one sick at
14:30 A tranquil heart **m** for a healthy
15:13 A joyful heart **m** a cheerful face,
15:20 A wise son **m** his father happy,
16:7 he **m** even his enemies to be at
16:14 a wise man **m** peace with him.
17:5 Whoever **m** fun of a poor
19:2 A person in a hurry **m** mistakes.
20:1 Wine ⌊**m** people⌋ mock,
20:1 liquor ⌊**m** them⌋ noisy,
20:2 Whoever **m** him angry forfeits
20:11 Even a child **m** himself known
20:16 responsible the person who **m**
23:5 It **m** wings for itself like an
27:13 responsible the person who **m**
29:3 A person who loves wisdom **m**
30:17 The eye that **m** fun of a father
31:22 She **m** quilts for herself.
31:24 "She **m** linen garments and
Ecc 8:1 Wisdom **m** one's face shine,
10:19 and wine **m** life pleasant,
Sos 5:9 what **m** your beloved better
5:9 What **m** your beloved better
Isa 8:14 But he will be a rock that **m**
36:4 What **m** you so confident?
40:23 He **m** rulers unimportant and
40:23 and **m** earthly judges worth
42:21 teachings and **m** them glorious.
43:16 The LORD **m** a path through
44:14 and the rain **m** them grow.
46:6 He **m** it into a god.
51:15 the sea and **m** its waves roar.
51:17 the cup that **m** people stagger,
51:22 the cup that **m** people stagger,
61:11 crops and like a garden that **m**
62:7 establishes Jerusalem and **m**
64:2 brushwood and **m** water boil.
Jer 5:24 He **m** sure that we have
8:16 The neighing of stallions **m** the
10:13 He **m** clouds rise from the ends
10:13 He **m** lightning flash with the
13:21 What will you say when God **m**
17:5 who **m** flesh and blood his
22:13 He **m** his neighbors work for
51:16 He **m** clouds rise from the ends
Lam 3:32 Even if he **m** us suffer,
Eze 18:13 and **m** excessive profits.
24:25 It **m** them happy and proud.
44:18 anything that **m** them sweat.
Dan 6:15 the king **m** can be changed."
11:18 insults that the northern king **m**
Hos 7:4 its flames when he **m** bread.
Amo 4:13 He **m** dawn and dusk ⌊appear⌋.
Nah 1:4 He yells at the sea and **m** it dry.
Hab 2:6 for the one who **m** himself rich
2:6 his own and **m** himself wealthy
2:15 one who **m** his neighbor drink
3:19 He **m** my feet like those of a
3:19 He **m** me walk on the
Hag 2:13 "That **m** them unclean."
Zec 10:1 The LORD **m** thunderstorms.
10:3 He **m** them like his splendid
12:2 like a cup ⌊of wine⌋ that **m** all
Mat 5:32 unfaithfulness **m** her look as
5:32 in this way **m** himself look as
5:45 He **m** his sun rise on people

Mat 15:11 that **m** a person unclean."
15:18 that's what **m** a person unclean.
23:19 or the altar that **m** the gift holy?
Mar 7:15 of a person that **m** him unclean.
7:20 of a person that **m** him unclean.
7:37 He **m** the deaf hear and the
Act 9:34 Jesus Christ **m** you well.
Rom 12:5 Christ **m** us one body and
14:4 the Lord **m** him successful.
16:19 and this **m** me happy
1Co 1:23 Jewish people and **m** no sense
3:7 because ⌞only⌟ God **m** it grow.
8:1 Knowledge **m** people arrogant,
2Co 2:3 that whatever **m** me happy also
2:3 me happy also **m** you happy.
3:5 Rather, God **m** us qualified.
10:18 It isn't the person who **m** his
11:20 When someone **m** you slaves,
13:3 he **m** his power felt among you.
Gal 2:6 they were **m** no difference
Eph 1:11 which **m** everything work the
4:16 He **m** the whole body fit
4:16 he **m** the body grow so that it
5:14 because light **m** everything
Col 2:19 Christ **m** the whole body grow
Phm 1:8 Christ **m** me bold enough to
Heb 1:7 "He **m** his messengers winds.
1:7 He **m** his servants flames of
2:11 Jesus, who **m** people holy,
6:18 takes an oath or **m** a promise.
Jas 1:9 humble **m** them important.
2Pe 3:10 Everything that **m** up the
3:12 Everything that **m** up the
3Jn 1:4 Nothing **m** me happier than to
Rev 13:12 The second beast **m** the earth
13:13 It even **m** fire come down from

Makheloth (2)

Num 33:25 Haradah and set up camp at **M**.
33:26 They moved from **M** and set up

making (80)

Gen 3:6 desirable for **m** someone wise.
9:11 I am **m** my promise to you.
9:17 the sign of the promise I am **m**
Exo 5:8 of bricks they were **m** before.
5:8 **M** fewer bricks will not be
14:17 I am **m** the Egyptians so
31:3 **m** him highly skilled,
34:10 "I'm **m** my promise again.
34:27 the basis of these words I'm **m**
35:31 **m** him highly skilled,
Lev 14:2 are the instructions for **m**
16:20 "When he finishes **m** peace
17:5 sacrifices they have been **m**
19:29 your daughter by **m** her
Num 14:27 the Israelites are **m** about me.
25:12 So tell Phinehas that I'm **m** a
Dtr 4:25 considers evil, **m** him furious,
24:11 the person to whom you're **m**
30:9 delight in **m** you as prosperous
Jos 9:15 made peace with them by **m**
22:23 we built it for **m** burnt offerings,
Jdg 16:10 you're **m** fun of me by telling
16:13 "You're still **m** fun of me by
1Sm 2:29 than me by **m** yourselves fat
8:3 to dishonest ways of **m** money.
13:19 from **m** swords and spears.
2Ki 17:4 stopped **m** annual payments
21:15 have been **m** me furious from
22:5 the workmen who are **m** repairs
1Ch 11:8 starting from the Millo and **m** a
2Ch 20:36 Jehoshaphat joined him in **m**
23:1 strengthened his position by **m**
29:34 in **m** themselves holy than
34:8 year of his reign as he was **m**
Ezr 5:8 job and **m** rapid progress.
Neh 4:7 of Jerusalem was **m** progress
6:8 You are **m** them up out of your
9:38 "We are **m** a binding agreement
13:18 Now you're **m** him even more
Job 4:18 his angels of **m** mistakes.
Pro 7:18 Let's enjoy **m** love,
30:19 an eagle **m** its way through the
30:19 a snake **m** its way over a rock,
30:19 a ship **m** its way through high
Pro 30:19 a man **m** his way with a virgin.
31:18 She sees that she is **m** a good
Sos 3:3 The watchmen **m** their rounds
5:7 The watchmen **m** their rounds
Isa 3:16 **m** seductive glances,
44:10 Nothing comes from **m** gods or
44:19 Now I am **m** the rest of the
45:9 "What are you **m**?"
57:4 Whom are you **m** fun of?
57:4 Whom are you **m** a face at?
58:5 a cattail and **m** your bed from
Jer 4:14 Don't continue **m** evil plans.
4:30 You are **m** yourself beautiful for
49:20 the LORD is **m** against Edom
50:45 the LORD is **m** against Babylon
Eze 27:11 **m** your beauty perfect.
44:12 idols and by **m** Israel fall into
Dan 7:21 I saw that horn **m** war against
Hab 2:15 **m** him drunk in order to stare at
Mat 27:31 After the soldiers finished **m**
Mar 5:39 "Why are you **m** so much noise
15:20 After the soldiers finished **m**
Luk 16:14 heard all this and were **m**
23:35 were **m** sarcastic remarks.
Jon 2:16 Stop **m** my Father's house a
4:1 had heard that he was **m**
18:29 are you **m** against this man?"
Act 12:21 sat on his throne and began **m**
16:19 hope of **m** money was gone,
19:24 was in the business of **m** silver
26:7 Your Majesty, the Jews are **m**
1Co 15:1 Brothers and sisters, I'm **m**
2Co 8:16 I thank God for **m** Titus as
Col 1:20 He did this by **m** peace through
1Th 3:5 **m** our work meaningless.
Rev 21:5 "I am **m** everything new."

Makkedah (9)

Jos 10:10 all the way to Azekah and **M**.
10:16 away and hid in the cave at **M**.
10:17 are hiding in the cave at **M**."
10:21 to Joshua in the camp at **M**.
10:28 same day Joshua captured **M**,
10:28 same thing to the king of **M** that
10:29 and all Israel marched from **M**
12:16 the king of **M**, the king of
15:41 Beth Dagon, Naamah, and **M**.

Malachi (1)

Mal 1:1 his word to Israel through **M**.

Malcam (1)

1Ch 8:9 sons: Jobab, Zibia, Mesha, **M**,

Malchiah (16)

1Ch 6:40 who was the son of **M**,
9:12 and great-grandson of **M**) and
24:9 the fifth for **M**, the sixth for
Ezr 10:25 **M**, Mijamin, Eleazar, Malchiah,
10:25 Eleazar, **M**, and Benaiah
10:31 **M**, Shemaiah, Shimeon,
Neh 3:11 **M**, Harim's son, and Hasshub,
3:14 Gate itself was repaired by **M**,
3:31 After him **M**, one of the
8:4 Pedaiah, Mishael, **M**,
10:3 Pashhur, Amariah, **M**,
11:12 who was the son of **M**.
12:42 Jehohanan, **M**, Elam, and Ezer.
Jer 21:1 sent Pashhur, son of **M**,
38:1 and Pashhur (son of **M**) heard
38:6 threw him into the cistern of **M**,

Malchiel (3)

Gen 46:17 of Beriah were Heber and **M**.
Num 26:45 of Heber and the family of **M**.
1Ch 7:31 sons were Heber and **M**,

Malchiram (1)

1Ch 3:18 then **M**, Pedaiah, Shenazzar,

Malchishua (5)

1Sm 14:49 were Jonathan, Ishvi, and **M**.
31:2 Abinadab, and **M**, Saul's sons.
1Ch 8:33 **M**, Abinadab, and Eshbaal.
9:39 **M**, Abinadab, and Eshbaal.
10:2 Abinadab, and **M**, Saul's sons.

Malchus (1)

Jon 18:10 (The servant's name was **M**.)

male (221)

Gen 1:27 He created them **m** and female.
5:2 He created them **m** and female.
6:19 They must be **m** and female.
7:2 every kind of clean animal (a **m**
7:2 animal (a **m** and a female).
7:3 pairs of every kind of bird (a **m**
7:9 to go into the ship in pairs (a **m**
7:16 A **m** and a female of every
12:16 **m** and female slaves,
17:10 Every **m** among you is to be
17:12 to come every **m** child who is
17:13 Every **m** born in your
17:14 Any uncircumcised **m** must be
17:23 bought with money — every **m**
19:4 all the young and old **m**
20:14 and **m** and female slaves and
24:35 **m** and female slaves,
30:35 striped and spotted **m** goats,
30:43 **m** and female slaves,
31:10 I looked up and saw that the **m**
31:12 'Look up and see that all the **m**
32:5 and **m** and female slaves.
32:14 female goats and 20 **m** goats,
32:14 200 female sheep and 20 **m**
32:15 20 female donkeys and 10 **m**
34:15 Every **m** must be circumcised
34:22 Every **m** must be circumcised
45:23 He sent his father ten **m**
Exo 12:5 be a one-year-old **m** that has no
12:12 Egypt and kill every firstborn **m**
12:29 LORD killed every firstborn **m**
12:44 "Any **m** slave you have bought
12:48 First, every **m** in the household
13:2 apart every firstborn **m** for me.
13:2 Every firstborn **m** offspring
13:12 sacrifice every firstborn **m**
13:12 The firstborn **m** offspring of
13:15 LORD killed every firstborn **m**
13:15 we sacrifice every firstborn **m**
20:10 your **m** and female slaves,
20:17 his **m** or female slave,
21:7 go free the way **m** slaves do.
21:20 "Whenever an owner hits his **m**
21:26 "Whenever an owner hits his **m**
21:27 knocks out the tooth of his **m**
21:32 If the bull gores a **m** or female
34:19 "Every first **m** offspring is mine,
Lev 1:3 you must offer a **m** that has no
1:10 you must bring a **m** that has no
3:1 it must be a **m** or female animal
3:6 you must bring a **m** or female
4:23 he must bring a **m** goat that has
6:18 Every **m** descendant of Aaron
6:29 Any **m** among the priests may
7:6 Any **m** among the priests may
9:3 'Take a **m** goat as an offering
9:15 He took the **m** goat for the
10:16 to the **m** goat that was
14:10 take two **m** lambs that have
14:12 will take one of the **m** lambs
14:21 he must take one **m** lamb,
16:5 He will take two **m** goats from
16:7 He must take the two **m** goats
22:19 The offering must be a **m** that
23:12 a one-year-old **m** lamb that has
23:19 Also sacrifice one **m** goat as
25:6 your **m** and female slaves,
25:44 "You may have **m** and female
Num 3:12 **m** offspring among them.
3:13 every firstborn **m** in Egypt,
3:15 Count every **m** who is at least
3:39 every **m** who was at least one
3:40 "Register every firstborn **m** of
3:46 There are 273 more firstborn **m**
6:12 He must bring a one-year-old **m**
6:14 a one-year-old **m** lamb as a
7:15 and a one-year-old **m** lamb as a
7:16 a **m** goat as an offering for sin;
7:17 bulls, five rams, five **m** goats,
7:17 and five one-year-old **m** lambs
7:21 and a one-year-old **m** lamb as a

Num 7:22 a **m** goat as an offering for sin;
7:23 bulls, five rams, five **m** goats,
7:23 and five one-year-old **m** lambs
7:27 and a one-year-old **m** lamb as a
7:28 a **m** goat as an offering for sin;
7:29 bulls, five rams, five **m** goats,
7:29 and five one-year-old **m** lambs
7:33 and a one-year-old **m** lamb as a
7:34 a **m** goat as an offering for sin;
7:35 bulls, five rams, five **m** goats,
7:35 and five one-year-old **m** lambs
7:39 and a one-year-old **m** lamb as a
7:40 a **m** goat as an offering for sin;
7:41 bulls, five rams, five **m** goats,
7:41 and five one-year-old **m** lambs
7:45 and a one-year-old **m** lamb as a
7:46 a **m** goat as an offering for sin;
7:47 bulls, five rams, five **m** goats,
7:47 and five one-year-old **m** lambs
7:51 and a one-year-old **m** lamb as a
7:52 a **m** goat as an offering for sin;
7:53 bulls, five rams, five **m** goats,
7:53 and five one-year-old **m** lambs
7:57 and a one-year-old **m** lamb as a
7:58 a **m** goat as an offering for sin;
7:59 bulls, five rams, five **m** goats,
7:59 and five one-year-old **m** lambs
7:63 and a one-year-old **m** lamb as a
7:64 a **m** goat as an offering for sin;
7:65 bulls, five rams, five **m** goats,
7:65 and five one-year-old **m** lambs
7:69 and a one-year-old **m** lamb as a
7:70 a **m** goat as an offering for sin;
7:71 bulls, five rams, five **m** goats,
7:71 and five one-year-old **m** lambs
7:75 and a one-year-old **m** lamb as a
7:76 a **m** goat as an offering for sin;
7:77 bulls, five rams, five **m** goats,
7:77 and five one-year-old **m** lambs
7:81 and a one-year-old **m** lamb as a
7:82 a **m** goat as an offering for sin;
7:83 bulls, five rams, five **m** goats,
7:83 and five one-year-old **m** lambs
7:87 12 one-year-old **m** lambs,
7:87 Twelve **m** goats were used as
7:88 24 bulls, 60 rams, 60 **m** goats,
7:88 and 60 one-year-old **m** lambs.
8:16 for every firstborn **m** offspring
8:17 every firstborn **m** in Egypt,
15:24 and a **m** goat as an offering for
18:10 Any **m** may eat it. You must
18:15 Every firstborn **m**, human or
18:15 son and the firstborn **m**
28:15 one **m** goat must be offered to
28:22 Also bring one **m** goat as an
28:30 Also bring one **m** goat to make
29:5 Also bring one **m** goat as an
29:11 Also bring one **m** goat as an
29:16 Also bring one **m** goat as an
29:19 Also bring one **m** goat as an
29:22 Also bring one **m** goat as an
29:25 Also bring one **m** goat as an
29:28 Also bring one **m** goat as an
29:31 Also bring one **m** goat as an
29:34 Also bring one **m** goat as an
29:38 Also bring one **m** goat as an
Dtr 5:14 your **m** and female slaves,
5:14 In this way your **m** and female
5:21 his **m** or female slave,
12:12 **m** and female slaves,
12:18 **m** and female slaves,
15:16 But suppose a **m** slave says to
15:19 firstborn **m** from your herds
16:11 **m** and female slaves,
16:14 **m** and female slaves,
32:14 **m** goats, and the best wheat.
Jos 17:2 These were the **m**
17:4 among our **m** relatives."
Jdg 21:11 and claim every **m**.
1Sm 8:16 He will take your **m** and female
2Sm 21:5 "Give us seven of the **m**
1Ki 11:15 and killed every **m** in Edom.
11:16 destroyed every **m** in Edom.)
14:10 I will destroy every **m** in his
14:24 There were even **m** prostitutes
15:12 He forced the **m** temple
1Ki 16:11 Baasha's **m** relatives or friends.
21:21 I will destroy every **m** in
22:46 He rid the land of the **m** temple
2Ki 3:4 king of Israel 100,000 **m** lambs
9:8 I will destroy every **m** from
10:1 Ahab had 70 **m** heirs in
10:6 The 70 **m** heirs were staying
23:7 of the **m** temple prostitutes who
1Ch 4:42 of Simeon's **m** descendants
23:3 Every **m** Levite who was at
26:30 **m** relatives were appointed to
2Ch 15:13 All people (young or old, **m** or
17:11 7,700 rams and 7,700 **m** goats.
29:21 and seven **m** goats as an
29:23 Then they brought the **m** goats
35:25 All the **m** and female singers
Ezr 2:65 In addition to the **m** and female
2:65 had 200 **m** and female singers.
6:17 They sacrificed 12 **m** goats as
8:35 and 12 **m** goats for an offering
Neh 7:67 In addition to the **m** and female
7:67 had 245 **m** and female singers.
Job 31:13 of my servants, **m** or female,
36:14 or they live on as **m** prostitutes
Psa 50:9 or a single **m** goat from your
135:8 every firstborn **m** in Egypt.
Pro 27:26 and the money from the **m**
30:31 a strutting rooster, a **m** goat,
Ecc 2:7 I bought **m** and female slaves.
2:8 I provided myself with **m** and
Isa 1:11 of bulls, lambs, or **m** goats.
14:2 will possess nations as **m**
24:2 **m** slaves and masters,
34:14 **M** goats will call to their mates.
Jer 34:9 both **m** and female.
34:10 and promised to free their **m**
34:16 You brought back the **m** and
34:16 have forced them to be your **m**
50:8 Be like the **m** goats that lead
51:40 like lambs, rams, and **m** goats.
Eze 16:17 given you and made **m** idols
27:21 lambs, rams, and **m** goats.
34:17 between rams and **m** goats.
43:22 "On the second day bring a **m**
45:23 and one **m** goat as an offering
Dan 8:5 I saw a **m** goat coming from the
8:8 The **m** goat became very
8:21 The hairy **m** goat is the
Zec 10:3 I will punish the **m** goats.
Mal 1:14 They have **m** animals in their
Mat 19:4 that the Creator made them **m**
Mar 10:6 But God made them **m** and
Jon 7:22 So you circumcise a **m** on a
7:23 If you circumcise a **m** on the

males (23)

Exo 12:48 But no uncircumcised **m** may
34:19 even the firstborn **m** of all your
Num 3:22 The total number of all the **m** at
3:28 The number of all the **m** at
3:34 The total number of all the **m** at
3:43 The total of all the firstborn **m**
26:62 all the ⌊Levite⌋ **m** at least one
2Ch 31:16 them to **m** who were at
31:19 of the offerings to all the **m**
Ezr 8:3 with 150 **m** whose genealogies
8:4 son of Zerahiah, with 200 **m**
8:5 son of Jahaziel, with 300 **m**
8:6 son of Jonathan, with 50 **m**
8:7 son of Athaliah, with 70 **m**
8:8 son of Michael, with 80 **m**
8:9 son of Jehiel, with 210 **m**
8:10 son of Josiphiah, with 160 **m**
8:11 son of Bebai, with 38 **m**
8:12 son of Hakkatan, with 110 **m**
8:13 who arrived later with 60 **m**
8:14 Uthai and Zabbud, with 70 **m**.
Psa 136:10 one who killed the firstborn **m**
Gal 3:28 nor free people, **m** nor females.

malice (1)

Lam 3:60 Look at all their **m**,

malicious (2)

Psa 35:11 **M** people bring charges against
3Jn 1:10 with saying **m** things about us.

maliciously (1)

Psa 73:8 They speak **m**. They speak

Mallothi (2)

1Ch 25:4 **M**, Hothir, and Mahazioth.
25:26 The nineteenth chose **M**,

Malluch (6)

1Ch 6:44 who was the son of **M**,
Ezr 10:29 **M**, Adaiah, Jashub, Sheal,
10:32 Benjamin, **M**, and Shemariah
Neh 10:4 Hattush, Shebaniah, **M**,
10:27 **M**, Harim, and Baanah.
12:2 Amariah, **M**, Hattush,

Malluchi (1)

Neh 12:14 from **M**, Jonathan; Joseph;

Malta (1)

Act 28:1 that the island was called **M**.

Mamre (9)

Gen 13:18 trees belonging to **M** at Hebron.
14:13 belonging to **M** the Amorite,
14:24 and **M** take their share."
18:1 the oak trees belonging to **M** as
23:17 east of **M**, was sold
23:19 east of **M** (that is, Hebron).
25:9 The cave is east of **M**.
49:30 east of **M** in Canaan,
50:13 field of Machpelah, east of **M**.

Mamre's (1)

Gen 35:27 to **M** city, Kiriath Arba (that

man (1379)

Gen 2:7 LORD God formed the **m** from
2:7 The **m** became a living being.
2:8 That's where he put the **m**
2:15 Then the LORD God took the **m**
2:16 LORD God commanded the **m**.
2:18 "It is not good for the **m** to be
2:19 Then he brought them to the **m**
2:19 Whatever the **m** called each
2:20 So the **m** named all the
2:20 But the **m** found no helper who
2:21 While the **m** was sleeping,
2:22 that he had taken from the **m**.
2:22 He brought her to the **m**.
2:23 The **m** said, "This is now bone
2:23 she was taken from **m**."
2:24 That is why a **m** will leave his
2:25 The **m** and his wife were both
3:8 the cool of the evening, the **m**
3:9 The LORD God called to the **m**
3:12 The **m** answered, the one you
3:17 Then he said to the **m**,
3:21 from animal skins for the **m**
3:22 "The **m** has become like one of
3:23 So the LORD God sent the **m**
3:23 which the **m** had been formed.
3:24 After he sent the **m** out,
4:1 She said, "I have gotten the **m**
4:23 I killed a **m** for bruising me,
4:23 a young **m** for wounding me.
6:9 God's approval and was a **m**
15:4 "This **m** will not be your heir.
17:17 born to a hundred-year-old **m**?
19:9 This **m** came here to stay
24:16 No **m** had ever had sexual
24:21 The **m** was silently watching
24:22 the **m** took out a gold nose ring
24:26 The **m** knelt, bowing to the
24:30 her tell what the **m** had said
24:30 Laban ran out to the **m** by the
24:30 He came to the **m**,
24:32 So the **m** went into the house.
24:58 "Will you go with this **m**?"
24:61 they followed the **m**.
24:65 "Who is that **m** over there
25:27 Jacob remained a quiet **m**,
26:11 "Anyone who touches this **m** or
27:11 "My brother Esau is a hairy **m**,
29:19 her to you than to any other **m**.
32:24 Then a **m** wrestled with him

Gen 32:25 When the **m** saw that he could
32:26 Then the **m** said, "Let me go;
32:27 So the **m** asked him,
32:28 The **m** said, "Your name will
32:29 The **m** answered, "Why do you
34:14 We can't give our sister to a **m**
34:19 The young **m** didn't waste any
34:25 They killed every **m**
37:2 a seventeen-year-old young **m**.
37:15 a **m** found him wandering
37:15 you looking for?" the **m** asked.
37:17 The **m** said, "They moved on
38:1 with a **m** from Adullam whose
38:2 Canaanite **m** whose name was
38:25 "I'm pregnant by the **m** who
39:2 so he became a successful **m**.
40:5 Each **m** had a dream with its
41:33 for a wise and intelligent **m**
41:38 like this — a **m** who has God's
42:11 We're all sons of one **m**.
42:13 sons of one **m** in Canaan.
42:35 each **m** found his bag of money
42:38 gray-haired old **m** to his grave!"
43:3 Judah said to him, "The **m**
43:5 The **m** said to us, 'You won't
43:6 telling the **m** you had another
43:7 They answered, "The **m** kept
43:11 then take the **m** a gift.
43:13 and go back to the **m**.
43:16 he said to the **m** in charge of
43:17 So the **m** did as Joseph said
43:19 So they came to the **m** in
43:21 and each **m** found all of his
43:24 The **m** took the brothers into
44:1 Joseph commanded the **m** in
44:4 city when Joseph said to the **m**
44:10 The **m** who has the cup will be
44:12 Then the **m** made a thorough
44:15 Don't you know that a **m** like
44:17 Only the **m** who had the cup
44:26 The **m** won't see us unless our
44:29 gray-haired old **m** to his grave.'
Exo 2:1 A **m** from Levi's family married
2:14 The **m** asked, "Who made you
2:20 Why did you leave the **m** there?
2:21 decided to stay with the **m**.
10:7 "How long will this **m** hold us
11:2 people ⌊of Israel⌋ that each **m**
12:3 of this month each **m** must take
21:2 year he may leave as a free **m**,
21:3 If he comes as a married **m**,
21:5 want to leave as a free **m**,'
21:7 "Whenever a **m** sells his
21:19 If the injured **m** can get up
21:19 He must pay the injured **m** for
21:28 "Whenever a bull gores a **m** or
21:29 and it kills a **m** or a woman,
22:16 "Whenever a **m** seduces a
33:11 as a **m** speaks to his friend.
35:29 Every Israelite **m** and woman
36:6 "No **m** or woman needs to
Lev 13:29 "If a **m** or a woman has some
13:38 "If a **m** or a woman has white
13:40 "If a **m** loses his hair,
13:44 the **m** has come down with an
15:2 "Tell the Israelites: If a **m** has a
15:4 "The **m** who has a discharge
15:7 Those who touch a **m** who has
15:8 If a **m** who has a discharge
15:9 When a **m** who has a
15:11 If a **m** who has a discharge
15:12 When a **m** who has a
15:15 the LORD for the **m** who had
15:16 "If a **m** has an emission of
15:18 "When a **m** has sexual
15:24 If a **m** has sexual intercourse
15:32 instructions for any **m** who has
15:33 for any **m** or woman who has a
15:33 or for any **m** who has sexual
16:21 A **m** will be appointed to
16:22 The **m** must release the goat in
16:26 "The **m** who released the goat
18:22 sexual intercourse with a **m** as
19:20 "If a **m** has sexual intercourse
19:20 who is engaged to another **m**
19:22 The **m** will be forgiven for this

Lev 20:10 "If a **m** commits adultery with
20:12 If a **m** has sexual intercourse
20:13 When a **m** has sexual
20:13 intercourse with another **m** as
20:14 When a **m** marries a woman
20:14 The **m** and the two women
20:15 A **m** who has sexual
20:18 If a **m** has sexual intercourse
20:20 That **m** and woman are guilty
20:21 That **m** and woman will have
20:27 "Every **m** or woman who is a
21:7 a priest is God's holy **m**.
24:10 A **m**, whose mother was
24:14 "The **m** who cursed ⌊my
24:23 So the **m** who had cursed the
25:26 If a **m** doesn't have anyone to
25:27 he will pay what is left to the **m**
27:3 you must give for a **m** from 20
27:7 For a **m** 60 years or over,
Num 1:2 List every **m** by name
1:4 One **m** from each tribe will help
1:18 Each **m** at least 20 years old
1:20 listed every **m** by name who
1:22 listed every **m** by name who
4:19 place and tell each **m** what
4:32 Tell each **m** by name the
4:49 Moses each **m** was registered
5:13 **m** without her husband's
5:19 'If no other **m** has had sexual
5:20 intercourse with another **m**,
6:2 A **m** or a woman may make a
11:27 Then a young **m** ran and told
11:28 ever since he was a young **m**,
12:3 (Moses was a very humble **m**,
15:32 they found a **m** gathering wood
15:35 "This **m** must be put to death.
16:7 will choose the **m** who is holy.
16:17 Each **m** will take his incense
16:18 So each **m** took his incense
16:22 If one **m** sins, will you be angry
17:5 The staff from the **m** I choose
17:9 and each **m** took his staff.
19:9 "A **m** who is clean will collect
24:3 This is the message of the **m**
24:15 This is the message of the **m**
25:8 the tent after the Israelite **m**.
25:8 drove the spear through the **m**
25:14 The name of the Israelite **m**
27:8 If a **m** dies and leaves no sons,
27:18 a **m** who has the Spirit,
30:2 If a **m** makes a vow to the
31:7 and killed every **m**.
31:17 who has gone to bed with a **m**.
31:18 never gone to bed with a **m**.
31:35 never gone to bed with a **m**.
36:8 may marry a **m** from any family
Dtr 16:17 Each **m** must bring a gift in
17:2 there may be a **m** or woman
17:5 then bring the **m** or woman who
20:13 kill every **m** in that city with
21:15 A **m** might have two wives and
21:15 the wife that the **m** doesn't love.
22:5 and a **m** must never wear
22:13 A **m** might marry a woman,
22:16 daughter in marriage to this **m**,
22:18 take the **m** and punish him.
22:22 If a **m** is caught having sexual
22:22 both that **m** and the woman
22:23 a **m** has sexual intercourse
22:23 who is engaged to another **m**.
22:24 The **m** must die because he
22:25 But if a **m** rapes an engaged
22:25 then only the **m** must die.
22:27 The **m** found the girl out in the
22:28 you must do when a **m** rapes
22:29 the **m** who had sexual
22:30 A **m** must never marry his
23:1 A **m** whose testicles are
23:2 A **m** born from an illicit union
23:17 No Israelite **m** or woman
24:2 She might marry another **m**
24:5 A **m** who has recently been
25:7 But if the **m** doesn't want to
25:9 "This is what happens to a **m**
25:10 of the **M** Without a Sandal.
25:11 from the **m** who is beating

Dtr 28:30 but another **m** will have sex
28:54 sensitive **m** among you will
29:18 Make sure there is no **m**,
33:1 Moses, the **m** of God,
Jos 3:12 Choose one **m** from each of the
4:2 "Choose one **m** from each of
4:5 Each **m** must take a stone on
5:13 he looked up and saw a **m**
7:14 will come forward **m** by man.
7:14 will come forward man by **m**.
7:15 The **m** who is selected,
7:17 Zerah come forward **m** by man,
7:17 Zerah come forward man by **m**,
7:18 come forward **m** by man,
7:18 come forward man by **m**,
8:17 Not one **m** was left in Ai or
10:14 The LORD did what a **m** told
14:6 said to Moses, the **m** of God,
14:15 Arba was the greatest **m**
22:14 Each **m** was a leader of a
Jdg 1:24 The spies saw a **m** coming out
1:25 But they let that **m** and his
1:26 The **m** went to the land of the
3:15 It was Ehud, a left-handed **m**
3:17 (Eglon was a very fat **m**.)
4:16 Not one **m** survived.
4:20 has been a **m** around here,
4:22 the **m** you've been looking
6:12 LORD is with you, brave **m**."
6:16 as if it were ⌊only⌋ one **m**."
7:13 he heard a **m** telling his friend a
7:13 The **m** said, "I had a strange
7:21 While each **m** kept his position
8:14 a young **m** from Succoth.
8:14 and the young **m** wrote down
8:20 he was only a young **m**.
8:25 Each **m** took the earrings from
9:2 sons to rule you or just one **m**?
11:40 the **m** from Gilead.
13:2 There was a **m** from Zorah
13:6 "A **m** of God came to me.
13:8 let the **m** of God you sent come
13:10 She said, "The **m** who came to
13:11 When he came to the **m**,
13:11 "Are you the **m** who spoke to
14:20 wife was given to his best **m**.
15:2 So I gave her to your best **m**.
15:6 son-in-law of the **m** at Timnah.
15:6 Samson did it because the **m**
15:6 and gave her to his best **m**."
16:7 I will be like any other **m**."
16:11 I will be like any other **m**."
16:17 Then I'll be like any other **m**."
16:19 She called for a **m** to shave off
16:26 Samson told the young **m** who
17:1 There was a **m** named Micah
17:7 There was a young **m** from
17:8 This **m** left Bethlehem in Judah
17:9 The **m** told him, "I'm a Levite
17:11 The young **m** became like one
17:12 So the young **m** became his
18:27 and the **m** who had become
19:16 That evening an old **m** came
19:17 So the old **m** asked,
19:20 Then the old **m** said,
19:22 They told the old **m**,
19:22 "Bring out the **m** who came to
19:23 This **m** is a guest in my home.
19:24 such a godless thing to this **m**."
21:11 who has gone to bed with a **m**,
21:12 never gone to bed with a **m**.
21:22 didn't provide a wife for each **m**
21:24 Each **m** went to his tribe and
Rut 1:1 A **m** from Bethlehem in Judah
2:1 He was a **m** of outstanding
2:5 Boaz asked the young **m** in
2:6 The young **m** answered,
2:19 May the **m** who paid attention
2:19 She said, "The **m** I worked
2:20 "That **m** is a relative of ours.
3:8 midnight the **m** was shivering.
3:16 everything the **m** had done
3:18 The **m** won't rest unless he
4:1 So the **m** came over and sat
4:3 Boaz said to the **m**,
4:4 The **m** said, "I'll buy back the

Rut	4:6	The **m** replied, "In that case I
	4:7	a **m** would take off his sandal
	4:7	and give it to the other **m**.
	4:8	So when the **m** said to Boaz,
1Sm	1:1	There was a **m** named Elkanah
	1:3	Every year this **m** would go
	1:21	To keep his vow, the **m**
	2:15	to the **m** who was sacrificing,
	2:16	If the **m** said to the servant,
	2:27	Then a **m** of God came to Eli
	2:33	Any **m** in your family whom I
	4:12	A **m** from the tribe of Benjamin
	4:13	The **m** went into the city to tell
	4:14	So the **m** went quickly to tell
	4:16	The **m** told Eli, "I'm the one
	4:18	(The **m** was old and heavy.)
	9:1	There was a **m** from the tribe of
	9:1	Kish was a powerful **m**.
	9:2	Saul, a handsome, young **m**.
	9:2	No **m** in Israel was more
	9:6	"There's a **m** of God in this city,
	9:6	a highly respected **m**.
	9:7	"what could we bring the **m**
	9:7	we can bring the **m** of God.
	9:8	I'll give it to the **m** of God.
	9:10	city where the **m** of God was.
	9:16	I will send you a **m** from
	9:17	"There's the **m** I told you about.
	9:17	This **m** will govern my people."
	9:21	Saul replied, "I am a **m** from the
	10:12	But a **m** from that place asked,
	10:27	"How can this **m** save us?"
	13:14	searched for a **m** after his own
	14:52	or any skilled fighting **m** came
	16:16	us to look for a **m** who can play
	16:17	"Please find me a **m** who can
	16:18	He's a courageous **m** and a
	17:7	The **m** who carried his shield
	17:8	Choose a **m**, and let him come
	17:10	Send out a **m** so that we can
	17:12	David was a son of a **m** named
	17:12	in Saul's day he was an old **m**.
	17:25	"Did you see that **m** coming
	17:25	The king will make the **m** who
	17:25	will give his daughter to that **m**
	17:26	"What will be done for the **m**
	17:27	how the **m** who kills Goliath
	17:30	He turned to face another **m**
	17:41	preceded by the **m** carrying his
	17:42	After all, David was a young **m**
	17:55	whose son is this young **m**?"
	17:56	whose son this young **m** is."
	17:58	son are you, young **m**?"
	20:31	him to me. He's a dead **m**!"
	21:15	that you bring this **m** so that
	21:15	Does this **m** have to come into
	25:2	Now, there was a **m** in Maon
	25:2	He was a very rich **m**.
	25:17	And he's such a worthless **m**
	26:15	asked Abner, "Aren't you a **m**?
	27:9	he left no **m** or woman alive.
	27:11	He did not bring a single **m** or
	28:14	"An old **m** is coming up,
	29:4	"Send the **m** back,"
	29:4	Is this **m** going to try to regain
	29:6	you are a dependable **m**.
	30:13	the young **m** answered.
	30:22	and worthless **m** who had gone
2Sm	1:2	On the third day a **m** came from
	1:4	The **m** answered, "The army
	1:5	David asked the young **m** who
	1:6	The young **m** answered,
	1:13	David asked the young **m** who
	1:13	And the young **m** answered,
	1:15	David's young **m** executed him
	3:38	a great **m**, has fallen in Israel?
	4:10	"I once seized a **m** who told
	4:11	men who kill an innocent **m**
	7:19	is the teaching about the **m**.
	11:3	The **m** said, "She's Bathsheba,
	11:21	'Your **m** Uriah the Hittite is also
	11:24	Your **m** Uriah the Hittite also is
	12:2	The rich **m** had a very large
	12:3	but the poor **m** had only one
	12:4	a visitor came to the rich **m**.
	12:4	The rich **m** thought it would be
2Sa	12:5	with anger against the **m**.
	12:5	"the **m** who did this certainly
	12:7	"You are the **m**!" Nathan told
	13:3	Jonadab was a very clever **m**.
	14:7	They said, 'Give us the **m** who
	14:16	from the **m** who wants to cut off
	14:21	Bring back the young **m**
	16:5	a **m** who was a distant cousin
	16:7	Get out, you bloodthirsty **m**!
	16:8	you're a bloodthirsty **m**."
	17:3	seeking the life of only one **m**,
	17:10	Even the bravest **m** with a
	17:18	But a young **m** saw Jonathan
	17:18	and came to the home of a **m**
	17:25	the son of a **m** named Ithra,
	18:5	"Treat the young **m** Absalom
	18:10	A **m** who saw this told Joab,
	18:11	Joab said to the **m** who told
	18:12	But the **m** told Joab,
	18:12	'Protect the young **m** Absalom
	18:20	"You won't be the **m** carrying
	18:21	Joab said to a **m** from Sudan,
	18:24	he saw a **m** running alone.
	18:26	saw another **m** running,
	18:26	⌊another⌋ **m** running alone."
	18:27	"He's a good **m**," the king said.
	18:29	the young **m** Absalom alright?"
	18:32	the young **m** Absalom alright?"
	18:32	you be like that young **m**!"
	19:31	Barzillai, the **m** from Gilead,
	19:32	Barzillai was an elderly **m**,
	19:32	Because he was a very rich **m**,
	20:1	A good-for-nothing **m** by the
	20:12	When the **m** saw that all the
	20:21	A **m** from the mountains of
	21:5	of the **m** who wanted
	21:20	there was a tall **m** who had a
	23:1	by the **m** whom God raised
	23:20	was a brave **m** who did many
	23:34	grandson of a **m** from Maacah),
1Ki	1:42	"You're an honorable **m**,
	1:52	behave like an honorable **m**,
	2:6	Don't let that gray-haired, old **m**
	2:9	old **m** into his grave by
	11:28	a very able and hardworking **m**.
	12:22	to Shemaiah, the **m** of God.
	13:1	A **m** of God from Judah had
	13:2	this **m** condemned the altar.
	13:3	That day the **m** of God ⌊also⌋
	13:4	King Jeroboam heard the **m**
	13:4	he pointed to the **m** across the
	13:4	that he used to point to the **m**
	13:5	was the miraculous sign the **m**
	13:6	the king asked the **m** of God,
	13:6	So the **m** of God made an
	13:7	The king told the **m** of God,
	13:8	The **m** of God told the king,
	13:10	So the **m** of God left on another
	13:11	sons told him everything the **m**
	13:12	had seen which road the **m**
	13:14	He went after the **m** of God and
	13:14	"Are you the **m** of God who
	13:16	The **m** of God said,
	13:19	The **m** of God went back with
	13:20	had brought back the **m** of God.
	13:21	also called to the **m** of God.
	13:24	The **m** of God left.
	13:26	prophet who had brought the **m**
	13:26	"It's the **m** of God who rebelled
	13:28	He found the body of the **m**
	13:29	up the body of the **m** of God,
	13:30	He laid the body of the **m** of
	13:30	tomb and mourned over the **m**,
	13:31	he had buried the **m** of God,
	13:31	me in the tomb where the **m**
	17:18	I have in common, **m** of God?
	17:24	I'm convinced that you are a **m**
	20:7	"You can see how this **m** is
	20:28	The **m** of God came again.
	20:35	but the **m** refused to punch him.
	20:37	the disciple found another **m**.
	20:37	The **m** punched him hard and
	20:39	A **m** turned around and brought
	20:42	LORD says: You let the **m** go.
	22:27	Put this **m** in prison,
	22:34	One **m** aimed his bow at
1Ki	22:36	"Every **m** to his own city!
	22:36	Every **m** to his own property!"
2Ki	1:6	They told him that a **m** came to
	1:7	"What was the **m** who told you
	1:9	"**M** of God, the king says,
	1:10	the officer, "If I'm a **m** of God,
	1:11	The officer said, "**M** of God,
	1:12	the officer, "If I'm a **m** of God,
	1:13	officer begged him, "**M** of God,
	3:25	each **m** throwing rocks on
	4:7	went and told the **m** of God.
	4:9	"I know he's a holy **m** of God.
	4:16	You're a **m** of God."
	4:21	him on the bed of the **m** of God,
	4:22	I will go quickly to the **m** of
	4:25	So she came to the **m** of God
	4:27	When she came to the **m** of
	4:27	But the **m** of God said,
	4:29	The **m** of God told Gehazi,
	4:31	back to meet the **m** of God.
	4:40	death in the pot, **m** of God!"
	4:42	A **m** from Baal Shalisha
	4:42	and fresh grain to the **m** of God.
	4:42	The **m** of God said,
	4:43	the **m** of God said.
	5:1	This **m** was a good soldier,
	5:7	This **m** sends someone to me
	5:8	But when Elisha, the **m** of God,
	5:14	as the **m** of God had instructed
	5:15	men returned to the **m** of God.
	5:20	of Elisha (the **m** of God),
	5:26	spirit when the **m** turned around
	6:6	The **m** of God asked,
	6:9	So the **m** of God would send a
	6:10	to the place that the **m**
	6:15	When the servant of the **m** of
	6:19	and I will lead you to the **m**
	7:2	answered the **m** of God,
	7:17	as the **m** of God had predicted
	7:18	(It happened exactly as the **m**
	7:19	answered the **m** of God,
	8:2	The woman did what the **m** of
	8:4	the servant of the **m** of God.
	8:7	"The **m** of God has come here."
	8:8	and meet the **m** of God.
	8:11	Then the **m** of God began to
	9:4	The young **m**, the servant of
	9:11	He answered, "You know the **m**
	10:22	Then Jehu told the **m** in charge
	11:8	Each **m** should have his
	13:19	Then the **m** of God became
	13:21	who were burying a **m** saw one
	13:21	So they quickly put the **m** into
	13:21	the **m** came back to life and
	22:15	Tell the **m** who sent you to me,
	23:16	announced by the **m** of God.
	23:17	"It's the tomb of the **m** of God
1Ch	2:21	the **m** who first settled Gilead.
	2:23	the **m** who first settled Gilead.
	11:22	was a brave **m** who did many
	17:17	the generation of the great **m**.
	20:6	there was a tall **m** who had 24
	22:9	son who will be a peaceful **m**.
	23:14	sons of Moses, the **m** of God,
	27:32	an educated **m** who possessed
2Ch	2:7	"Send me a **m** who has the
	2:13	And now, I'm sending a **m** with
	6:5	And I didn't choose any **m** to be
	8:14	the **m** of God, had commanded.
	11:2	to Shemaiah, the **m** of God.
	17:17	fighting **m** Eliada (with 200,000
	18:26	Put this **m** in prison,
	18:33	One **m** aimed his bow at
	23:7	Each **m** should have his
	25:7	But a **m** of God came to him
	25:9	Amaziah asked the **m** of God,
	25:9	The **m** of God answered,
	28:7	a fighting **m** from Ephraim,
	30:16	(Moses was a **m** of God.)
	34:23	Tell the **m** who sent you to me,
Ezr	3:2	(Moses was a **m** of God).
	5:14	to a **m** named Sheshbazzar,
	7:11	a **m** with a thorough knowledge
Neh	1:11	today and make this **m**,
	4:18	The **m** who was supposed to
	4:22	"Every **m** and his servant

Neh 6:11 "Should a **m** like me run away?
6:11 Would a **m** like me go into the
7:2 Hananiah was a trustworthy **m**,
11:14 The **m** in charge of them was
11:22 The **m** in charge of the Levites
12:24 the **m** of God, had ordered.
12:36 of David, the **m** of God.
Est 6:6 "What should be done for the **m**
6:9 Put the robe on the **m** whom
6:9 'This is what is done for the **m**
6:11 "This is what is done for the **m**
7:6 is this wicked **m** Haman!"
9:4 Mordecai was an important **m**
Job 1:1 A **m** named Job lived in Uz.
1:1 He was a **m** of integrity:
1:8 He is a **m** of integrity:
2:3 He is a **m** of integrity:
2:4 Certainly, a **m** will give
9:20 even if I am a **m** of integrity.
9:21 If I am a **m** of integrity,
9:22 'He destroys ⌊both⌋ the **m** of
12:4 A **m** of integrity, a man who is
12:4 a **m** who is righteous,
16:21 The Son of **M** will plead for his
17:10 find one wise **m** among you.
31:10 my wife grind for another ⌊**m**⌋,
38:3 Brace yourself like a **m**!
40:7 "Brace yourself like a **m**!
Psa 8:4 or the Son of **M** that you take
22:6 Yet, I am a worm and not a **m**.
34:6 Here is a poor **m** who called
80:17 Let your power rest on the **m**
80:17 the son of **m** you strengthened
88:4 I am like a **m** without any
105:17 He sent a **m** ahead of them.
127:4 The children born to a **m** when
127:5 Blessed is the **m** who has
Pro 6:27 Can a **m** carry fire in his lap
6:29 So it is with a **m** who has sex
6:33 An adulterous **m** will find
7:7 a young **m** without much sense
16:14 but a wise **m** makes peace
21:22 A wise **m** attacks a city of
24:5 A strong **m** knows how to use
30:19 a **m** making his way with a
Ecc 2:12 For instance, what can the **m**
4:13 A young **m** who is poor and
4:14 A young **m** came out of prison
4:15 with the second young **m**,
7:28 I found one **m** out of a
Sos 8:7 If a **m** exchanged all his
Isa 4:1 will grab one **m** and say,
10:13 down people like a mighty **m**.
14:16 "Is this the **m** who made the
22:15 the **m** in charge of the palace,
22:17 Look, mighty **m**! The LORD will
52:14 he won't look like any other **m**.
53:3 He was a **m** of sorrows,
62:5 As a young **m** marries a
65:20 or an old **m** who doesn't live
Jer 3:1 A saying: If a **m** divorces his
3:1 him and marries another **m**,
6:11 A **m** and his wife will be taken
14:9 like a strong **m** who cannot
15:10 I am a **m** who argues and
20:15 Cursed is the **m** who made my
20:16 May that **m** be like the cities
26:11 "This **m** is condemned to die
26:16 "This **m** should not be
26:20 There was another **m**
30:6 Can a **m** give birth to a child?
30:6 do I see every strong **m** holding
31:22 A woman will protect a **m**.
35:4 Igdaliah's son, the **m** of God.)
38:4 "Have this **m** put to death.
38:4 This **m** is not trying to help
40:8 the son of a **m** from Maacah.
41:2 So they assassinated the **m**
Lam 3:1 "I am the **m** who has
Eze 2:1 He said to me, "Son of **m**,
2:3 He said to me, "Son of **m**,
2:6 Son of **m**, don't be afraid of
2:8 But you, son of **m**,
3:1 "Son of **m**, eat what you find.
3:3 He said to me, "Son of **m**,
3:4 He said to me, "Son of **m**,

Eze 3:10 He also said to me, "Son of **m**,
3:17 "Son of **m**, I have made you a
3:25 tie you up with ropes, son of **m**,
4:1 ⌊The LORD said,⌋ "Son of **m**,
4:16 He also said to me, "Son of **m**,
5:1 ⌊The LORD said,⌋ "Son of **m**,
6:2 "Son of **m**, look toward the
7:2 "Son of **m**, this is what the
8:5 God said to me, "Son of **m**,
8:6 He asked me, "Son of **m**,
8:8 He said to me, "Son of **m**,
8:12 God asked me, "Son of **m**,
8:15 He asked me, "Son of **m**,
8:17 He asked me, "Son of **m**,
11:2 LORD said to me, "Son of **m**,
11:4 Prophesy, son of **m**."
11:15 "Son of **m**, the people who live
12:2 "Son of **m**, you are living
12:3 "Son of **m**, pack your bags as if
12:9 "Son of **m**, didn't the rebellious
12:18 "Son of **m**, shake as you eat
12:22 "Son of **m**, what is this proverb
12:27 "Son of **m**, the people of Israel
13:2 "Son of **m**, prophesy against
13:17 "Son of **m**, look at the women
14:3 "Son of **m**, these people are
14:13 "Son of **m**, suppose a country
15:2 "Son of **m**, what good is the
16:2 "Son of **m**, make known to the
17:2 "Son of **m**, tell this riddle.
20:3 "Son of **m**, speak to the leaders
20:4 Will you judge them, son of **m**?
20:27 to the nation of Israel, son of **m**.
20:46 "Son of **m**, turn to the south,
21:2 "Son of **m**, turn to Jerusalem,
21:6 "So, son of **m**, groan with a
21:9 "Son of **m**, prophesy.
21:12 "'Cry and mourn, son of **m**,
21:14 So prophesy, son of **m**.
21:19 "Son of **m**, mark two roads that
21:28 "Son of **m**, prophesy.
22:2 "Will you judge, son of **m**?
22:18 "Son of **m**, the people of Israel
22:24 "Son of **m**, tell the city,
23:2 "Son of **m**, there were once two
23:36 LORD said to me, "Son of **m**,
24:2 "Son of **m**, write down today's
24:16 "Son of **m**, with one blow I'm
24:25 "Son of **m**, on that day I will
25:2 "Son of **m**, turn to the
26:2 "Son of **m**, Tyre said this about
27:2 "Son of **m**, sing a funeral song
28:2 "Son of **m**, tell the ruler of Tyre,
28:12 "Son of **m**, sing a funeral song
28:21 "Son of **m**, turn to Sidon and
29:2 "Son of **m**, turn to Pharaoh,
29:18 "Son of **m**, Every soldier's head
30:2 "Son of **m**, prophesy. Say,
30:21 "Son of **m**, I have broken the
31:2 "Son of **m**, say to Pharaoh,
32:2 "Son of **m**, sing a funeral song
32:18 "Son of **m**, cry for the many
33:2 "Son of **m**, speak to your
33:7 "Son of **m**, I have appointed
33:10 "Son of **m**, say to the people of
33:12 "Son of **m**, say to your people,
33:24 "Son of **m**, those who live in
33:30 "Son of **m**, your people are
34:2 "Son of **m**, prophesy against
35:2 "Son of **m**, turn to Mount Seir,
36:1 ⌊The LORD said,⌋ "Son of **m**,
36:17 "Son of **m**, when the people of
37:3 Then he asked me, "Son of **m**,
37:9 Prophesy, son of **m**.
37:11 also said to me, "Son of **m**,
37:16 "Son of **m**, take a stick and
38:2 "Son of **m**, turn to Gog from the
38:14 "So prophesy, son of **m**.
39:1 ⌊The LORD said,⌋ "Son of **m**,
39:17 "Son of **m**, this is what the
40:3 I saw a **m** who looked like he
40:3 The **m** was holding a linen
40:4 He said to me, "Son of **m**,
40:5 The **m** had a measuring stick
40:6 Then the **m** went to the
40:11 Then the **m** measured the

Eze 40:17 Then the **m** brought me into the
40:19 The **m** measured the distance
40:20 Then the **m** measured the
40:23 The **m** measured the distance
40:24 Then the **m** led me to the south
40:27 The **m** measured the distance
40:28 Then the **m** brought me to the
40:32 Then the **m** brought me to the
40:35 Then the **m** brought me to the
40:45 The **m** said to me,
40:47 The **m** measured the courtyard.
40:48 Then the **m** brought me to the
41:1 Then the **m** brought me into the
41:3 Then the **m** went inside and
41:4 The **m** said to me,
41:5 Next, the **m** measured the
41:13 Then the **m** measured the
41:19 the face of a **m**, which was
41:22 Then the **m** told me,
42:1 Then the **m** led me out toward
42:13 Then the **m** said to me,
42:15 When the **m** had finished
43:1 Then the **m** took me to the east
43:6 the **m** was standing beside
43:7 voice said to me, "Son of **m**,
43:10 "Son of **m**, describe this temple
43:18 Then the **m** said to me,
43:18 the man said to me, "Son of **m**,
44:1 Then the **m** took me back to
44:4 The **m** brought me through the
44:5 "Son of **m**, pay close attention.
46:19 The **m** brought me through a
46:21 Then the **m** led me to the outer
46:24 Then the **m** said to me,
47:1 Then the **m** took me back to
47:3 the **m** went eastward.
47:6 Then he asked me, "Son of **m**,
47:7 Then the **m** led me back along
47:8 Then the **m** said to me,
Dan 5:11 There's a **m** in your kingdom
6:3 This **m**, Daniel, The king
6:5 find anything to accuse this **m**,
6:28 This **m**, Daniel,
7:13 someone like the Son of **M**.
8:15 who looked like a **m** standing
8:16 I heard a **m** in Ulai ⌊Gate⌋ call
8:16 explain the vision to this **m**."
8:17 He said to me, "Son of **m**,
9:21 I was praying, the **m** Gabriel,
10:5 I saw a **m** dressed in linen,
10:9 I heard the **m** speak,
10:11 The **m** said to me,
12:5 One **m** stood on one side of the
12:6 One of them asked the **m**
12:7 I heard the **m** dressed in linen
Hos 3:3 or offer yourself to any **m**.
7:9 old **m**, but you don't realize it.
12:3 When Jacob became a **m**,
Joe 1:8 mourning for the **m** she was
Jnh 1:14 for the death of an innocent **m**,
Mic 2:2 They cheat a **m** and his family,
2:2 a **m** and his inheritance.
5:5 This **m** will be their peace.
Zec 1:8 During that night I saw a **m**
1:10 The **m** standing among the
2:1 I looked up and saw a **m** with a
2:4 and say to that young **m**,
3:2 Isn't this **m** like a burning log
6:12 Here is the **m** whose name is
13:3 "If a **m** still prophesies,
13:7 against the **m** who is my
Mal 3:17 I will spare them as a **m**
Mat 1:19 Joseph was an honorable **m**
3:3 spoke about this **m** when
5:32 But I can guarantee that any **m**
8:2 A **m** with a serious skin
8:2 The **m** said to Jesus,
8:20 but the Son of **M** has nowhere
8:27 "What kind of **m** is this?
9:2 brought him a paralyzed **m**
9:2 he said to the **m**, "Cheer up,
9:6 that the Son of **M** has authority
9:6 he said to the paralyzed **m**,
9:7 So the **m** got up and went
9:9 he saw a **m** sitting in a tax
9:19 got up and followed the **m**.

Mat 9:32 people brought a **m** to Jesus.
9:32 The **m** was unable to talk
9:33 the **m** began to speak.
10:23 the Son of **M** will come.
10:35 I came to turn a **m** against his
11:8 A **m** dressed in fine clothes?
11:19 The Son of **M** came eating and
12:8 "The Son of **M** has authority
12:10 A **m** with a paralyzed hand
12:13 Then he said to the **m**,
12:13 The **m** held it out, and it
12:22 Jesus a **m** possessed by
12:22 The demon made the **m** blind
12:23 "Can this **m** be the Son of
12:24 "This **m** can force demons out
12:29 he must tie up the strong **m**.
12:32 word against the Son of **M** will
12:40 so the Son of **M** will be in the
12:48 He replied to the **m** speaking to
13:24 is like a **m** who planted good
13:37 the good seeds is the Son of **M**.
13:41 The Son of **M** will send his
13:44 When a **m** discovered it,
13:54 "Where did this **m** get this
13:56 did this **m** get all this?"
16:13 people say the Son of **M** is?"
16:27 The Son of **M** will come with
16:28 they see the Son of **M** coming
17:9 Wait until the Son of **M** has
17:12 to make the Son of **M** suffer."
17:14 a **m** came up to Jesus,
17:22 "The Son of **M** will be betrayed
18:12 Suppose a **m** has 100 sheep
19:3 They asked, "Can a **m** divorce
19:5 'That's why a **m** will leave his
19:7 did Moses order a **m** to give his
19:10 "If that is the only reason a **m**
19:16 Then a **m** came to Jesus and
19:18 the **m** asked. Jesus said,
19:20 The young **m** replied,
19:22 When the young **m** heard this,
19:28 When the Son of **M** sits on his
20:18 There the Son of **M** will be
20:28 same way with the Son of **M**.
21:28 A **m** had two sons.
22:12 "The **m** had nothing to say.
22:24 'If a **m** dies childless,
24:27 The Son of **M** will come again
24:30 "Then the sign of the Son of **M**
24:30 they see the Son of **M** coming
24:37 the Son of **M** comes again,
24:39 the Son of **M** comes again.
24:44 the Son of **M** will return when
25:14 of heaven is like a **m** going
25:15 He gave one **m** ten thousand
25:15 Then the **m** went on his trip.
25:31 "When the Son of **M** comes in
26:2 At that time the Son of **M** will
26:6 a **m** who had suffered from a
26:18 "Go to a certain **m** in the city,
26:24 The Son of **M** is going to die
26:24 who betrays the Son of **M**.
26:45 time is near for the Son of **M**
26:48 one I kiss is the **m** you want.
26:61 They stated, "This **m** said,
26:64 on you will see the Son of **M**
26:71 "This **m** was with Jesus from
26:72 "I don't know the **m**!"
26:74 "I don't know the **m**!"
27:4 by betraying an innocent **m**."
27:17 "Which **m** do you want me to
27:19 "Leave that innocent **m** alone.
27:24 won't be guilty of killing this **m**.
27:32 they found a **m** named Simon.
27:43 After all, this **m** said,
27:57 In the evening a rich **m** named
Mar 1:23 At that time there was a **m** in
1:26 The evil spirit threw the **m** into
1:40 Then a **m** with a serious skin
1:40 The **m** fell to his knees and
1:45 When the **m** left, he began to
2:3 to him carrying a paralyzed **m**.
2:4 the paralyzed **m** was lying.
2:5 faith, he said to the **m**, "Friend,
2:9 to say to this paralyzed **m**,
2:10 that the Son of **M** has authority
Mar 2:10 he said to the paralyzed **m**,
2:12 The **m** got up, and walked away
2:28 For this reason the Son of **M**
3:1 A **m** who had a paralyzed hand
3:2 whether he would heal the **m**
3:3 So he told the **m** with the
3:5 Then he told the **m**,
3:5 The **m** held it out, and his hand
3:27 he must tie up the strong **m**.
4:26 is like a **m** who scatters seeds
4:27 the **m** doesn't know how.
4:41 each other, "Who is this **m**?
5:2 a **m** came out of the tombs and
5:2 The **m** was controlled by an
5:6 The **m** saw Jesus at a
5:8 come out of the **m**."
5:13 evil spirits came out of the **m**
5:15 and saw the **m** who had been
5:15 The **m** was sitting there
5:16 **m** and the pigs.
5:18 the **m** who had been
5:19 Instead, he told the **m**,
5:20 So the **m** left. He began to tell
5:24 Jesus went with the **m**.
6:2 They asked, "Where did this **m**
6:20 John was a fair and holy **m**,
7:32 to him a **m** who was deaf
7:34 and said to the **m**, "Ephphatha!"
7:35 At once the **m** could hear and
8:22 brought a blind **m** to Jesus.
8:24 The **m** looked up and said,
8:25 and the **m** saw clearly.
8:31 that the Son of **M** would have
8:38 the Son of **M** will be ashamed
9:9 the Son of **M** had come back
9:12 that the Son of **M** must suffer
9:17 A **m** in the crowd answered,
9:31 He taught them, "The Son of **M**
10:4 said, "Moses allowed a **m**
10:7 That's why a **m** will leave his
10:12 and marries another **m**,
10:17 a **m** came running to him and
10:20 The **m** replied, "Teacher,
10:22 When the **m** heard that,
10:33 There the Son of **M** will be
10:45 same way with the Son of **M**.
10:49 They called the blind **m** and
10:50 The blind **m** threw off his coat,
10:51 The blind **m** said, "Teacher,
12:1 "A **m** planted a vineyard.
12:4 So the **m** sent another servant
12:5 The **m** sent another,
12:19 'If a **m** dies and leaves a wife
12:34 how wisely the **m** answered,
12:34 man answered, he told the **m**,
13:26 will see the Son of **M** coming
13:34 It is like a **m** who went on a
14:3 a **m** who had suffered from a
14:13 You will meet a **m** carrying a
14:21 The Son of **M** is going to die
14:21 who betrays the Son of **M**!
14:41 time has come for the Son of **M**
14:44 one I kiss is the **m** you want.
14:51 A certain young **m** was
14:62 and you will see the Son of **M**
14:69 "This **m** is one of them!"
14:71 this **m** you're talking about!"
15:7 There was a **m** named
15:21 A **m** named Simon from the city
15:36 The **m** said, "Let's see if Elijah
15:39 this **m** was the Son of God!"
16:5 they saw a young **m**.
16:6 The young **m** said to them,
Luk 1:15 he will be a great **m**.
1:18 I'm an old **m**, and my wife is
1:32 He will be a great **m** and will
2:25 A **m** named Simeon was in
4:33 In the synagogue was a **m**
4:35 The demon threw the **m** down
5:12 where there was a **m** covered
5:12 When the **m** saw Jesus,
5:18 men brought a paralyzed **m**
5:19 in the tiles and let the **m** down
5:21 thought, "Who is this **m**?
5:24 that the Son of **M** has authority
5:24 he said to the paralyzed **m**,
Luk 5:25 The **m** immediately stood up in
6:5 Then he added, "The Son of **M**
6:6 A **m** whose right hand was
6:7 whether he would heal the **m**
6:8 So he told the **m** with the
6:8 The **m** got up and stood there.
6:10 of them and then said to the **m**,
6:10 The **m** did so, and his hand
6:22 are committed to the Son of **M**.
7:12 The dead **m** was a widow's
7:14 He said, "Young **m**,
7:15 The dead **m** sat up and began
7:25 A **m** dressed in fine clothes?
7:34 The Son of **M** has come eating
7:39 "If this **m** really were a prophet,
7:49 "Who is this **m** who even
8:25 each other, "Who is this **m**?
8:27 a certain **m** from the city met
8:27 The **m** was possessed by
8:29 evil spirit to come out of the **m**.
8:29 evil spirit had controlled the **m**
8:33 The demons came out of the **m**
8:35 and found the **m** from whom
8:36 demon-possessed **m** to health.
8:38 The **m** from whom the demons
8:38 But Jesus sent the **m** away
8:39 So the **m** left. He went through
8:41 A **m** named Jairus,
9:22 Jesus said that the Son of **M**
9:26 the Son of **M** will be ashamed
9:38 A **m** in the crowd shouted,
9:44 The Son of **M** will be betrayed
9:57 a **m** said to Jesus,
9:58 but the Son of **M** has nowhere
9:59 He told another **m**,
9:59 But the **m** said, "Sir, first let me
10:29 But the **m** wanted to justify his
10:30 Jesus replied, "A **m** went from
10:31 When he saw the **m**,
10:32 When he saw the **m**,
10:33 came across the **m**.
10:33 he felt sorry for the **m**,
10:36 to the **m** who was attacked
11:14 forcing a demon out of a **m**.
11:14 The demon had made the **m**
11:14 the **m** began to talk.
11:21 "When a strong **m**,
11:22 But a stronger **m** than he may
11:22 Then the stronger **m** will take
11:22 in which the strong **m** trusted
11:30 so the Son of **M** will be a
12:8 the Son of **M** will acknowledge
12:10 against the Son of **M** will
12:16 He said, "A rich **m** had land
12:40 the Son of **M** will return when
13:6 "A **m** had a fig tree growing in
14:2 A **m** whose body was swollen
14:4 So Jesus took hold of the **m**,
14:12 Then he told the **m** who had
14:16 Jesus said to him, "A **m** gave a
15:2 "This **m** welcomes sinners and
15:4 "Suppose a **m** has 100 sheep
15:11 "A **m** had two sons.
16:1 "A rich **m** had a business
16:2 So the rich **m** called for his
16:18 "Any **m** who divorces his wife
16:18 The **m** who marries a woman
16:19 "There was a rich **m** who wore
16:22 The rich **m** also died and was
16:27 "The rich **m** responded,
16:30 "The rich **m** replied,
17:16 (The **m** was a Samaritan.)
17:19 Jesus told the **m**, "Get up,
17:22 one of the days of the Son of **M**,
17:24 The day of the Son of **M** will be
17:26 the Son of **M** comes again,
17:30 The day when the Son of **M** is
18:8 But when the Son of **M** comes,
18:31 the Son of **M** will come true.
18:35 a blind **m** was sitting and
18:38 Then the blind **m** shouted,
18:39 of the crowd told the blind **m**
18:40 them to bring the **m** to him.
18:40 When the **m** came near,
18:41 The blind **m** said, "Lord, I want
19:2 A **m** named Zacchaeus was

Luk	19:3	But Zacchaeus was a small **m**,
	19:10	Indeed, the Son of **M** has come
	19:14	'We don't want this **m** to be our
	19:24	give it to the **m** who has ten.'
	20:9	"A **m** planted a vineyard,
	20:28	'If a married **m** dies and has no
	21:27	will see the Son of **M** coming
	21:36	stand in front of the Son of **M**."
	22:10	and you will meet a **m** carrying
	22:22	The Son of **M** is going to die
	22:47	The **m** called Judas,
	22:48	the Son of **M** with a kiss?"
	22:56	"This **m** was with Jesus."
	22:59	"It's obvious that this **m** was
	22:69	But from now on, the Son of **M**
	23:4	"I can't find this **m** guilty of any
	23:6	if the **m** was from Galilee.
	23:14	"You brought me this **m** as
	23:14	and haven't found this **m** guilty
	23:15	So he sent this **m** back to us.
	23:15	This **m** hasn't done anything to
	23:22	I haven't found this **m**
	23:26	grabbed a **m** named Simon,
	23:41	But this **m** hasn't done anything
	23:47	this **m** was innocent!"
	23:50	There was a good **m** who had
	24:7	He said, 'The Son of **M** must
Jon	1:6	God sent a **m** named John to
	1:30	'A **m** who comes after me was
	1:45	"We have found the **m** whom
	1:51	coming down to the Son of **M**."
	3:4	be born when he's an old **m**?
	3:13	to heaven except the Son of **M**,
	3:14	so the Son of **M** must be lifted
	3:26	do you remember the **m** you
	3:29	The best **m**, who stands and
	3:34	The **m** whom God has sent
	4:9	"How can a Jewish **m** like you
	4:18	and the **m** you have now isn't
	4:29	"Come with me, and meet a **m**
	4:50	The **m** believed what Jesus
	5:5	One **m**, who had been sick for
	5:6	Jesus saw the **m** lying there
	5:6	So Jesus asked the **m**,
	5:7	The sick **m** answered Jesus,
	5:8	Jesus told the **m**, "Get up,
	5:9	The **m** immediately became
	5:10	So the Jews told the **m** who
	5:11	The **m** replied, "The man who
	5:11	The man replied, "The **m** who
	5:12	"Who is the **m** who told you to
	5:13	But the **m** who had been
	5:14	Later, Jesus met the **m** in the
	5:15	The **m** went back to the Jews
	5:15	was the **m** who had made
	5:27	because he is the Son of **M**.
	6:14	"This **m** is certainly the prophet
	6:27	This is the food the Son of **M**
	6:33	God's bread is the **m** who
	6:42	asked, "Isn't this **m** Jesus,
	6:52	They said, "How can this **m**
	6:53	eat the flesh of the Son of **M**
	6:62	What if you see the Son of **M**
	7:11	"Where is that **m**?"
	7:12	"He's a good **m**," while others
	7:15	"How can this **m** be so
	7:18	But the **m** who wants to bring
	7:23	I made a **m** entirely well
	7:25	"Isn't this the **m** they want to
	7:26	that this **m** is the Messiah?
	7:27	where this **m** comes from.
	7:31	miracles than this **m** has?"
	7:35	"Where does this **m** intend to
	7:40	"This **m** is certainly the
	7:41	"This **m** is the Messiah."
	7:46	has ever spoken like this **m**."
	8:28	you have lifted up the Son of **M**,
	8:40	I am a **m** who has told you the
	9:1	he saw a **m** who had been born
	9:2	why was this **m** born blind?
	9:3	"Neither this **m** nor his parents
	9:7	"sent.") The blind **m** washed
	9:8	"Isn't this the **m** who used to sit
	9:9	But the **m** himself said,
	9:11	He replied, "The **m** people call
	9:12	"Where is that **m**?"
Jon	9:12	The **m** answered, "I don't
	9:13	Some people brought the **m**
	9:14	dirt and gave the **m** sight was
	9:15	So the Pharisees asked the **m**
	9:15	The **m** told the Pharisees,
	9:16	"The **m** who did this is not from
	9:16	"How can a **m** who is a sinner
	9:17	They asked the **m** who had
	9:17	"What do you say about the **m**
	9:17	The **m** answered, "He's a
	9:18	that the **m** had been blind
	9:24	called the **m** who had been
	9:24	We know that this **m** who gave
	9:25	The **m** responded,
	9:27	The **m** replied, "I've already
	9:29	but we don't know where this **m**
	9:30	The **m** replied to them,
	9:33	If this **m** were not from God,
	9:35	Jews had thrown the **m** out of
	9:35	So when Jesus found the **m**,
	9:35	you believe in the Son of **M**?"
	9:36	The **m** replied, "Sir, tell me
	9:38	The **m** bowed in front of Jesus
	10:33	although you're only a **m**."
	10:41	John said about this **m** is true."
	11:37	"Couldn't this **m** who gave a
	11:37	a blind **m** sight keep Lazarus
	11:44	The dead **m** came out.
	11:47	This **m** is performing a lot of
	11:50	It is better for one **m** to die for
	12:23	for the Son of **M** to be glorified.
	12:34	'The Son of **M** must be lifted up
	12:34	Who is this 'Son of **M**'?"
	13:31	"The Son of **M** is now glorified,
	13:32	because of the Son of **M**,
	13:32	God will glorify the Son of **M**
	13:32	glorify the Son of **M** at once."
	18:14	it was better to have one **m** die
	18:26	a relative of the **m** whose ear
	18:29	you making against this **m**?"
	18:38	find this **m** guilty of anything.
	18:40	again, "Don't free this **m**!
	19:4	find this **m** guilty of anything."
	19:5	the Jews, "Look, here's the **m**!"
	19:6	find this **m** guilty of anything."
	19:11	That's why the **m** who handed
	19:12	"If you free this **m**,
	19:32	broke the legs of the first **m**
	19:32	of the other **m** who had been
Act	2:22	Jesus from Nazareth was a **m**
	2:22	You know that through this **m**
	2:32	"God brought this **m** Jesus
	3:2	At the same time, a **m** who had
	3:2	men would put the lame **m** at
	3:3	When the **m** saw that Peter and
	3:5	So the **m** watched them
	3:8	The **m** was walking,
	3:10	They knew that he was the **m**
	3:11	The **m** wouldn't let go of Peter
	3:12	are you amazed about this **m**?
	3:14	You rejected the **m** who was
	3:16	his power alone this **m**,
	4:9	good we did for a crippled **m**.
	4:10	understand that this **m** stands
	4:14	When they saw the **m** who
	4:22	(The **m** who was healed by
	5:1	A **m** named Ananias and his
	5:28	us for putting that **m** to death."
	5:37	"After that **m**, at the time of the
	6:5	who was a **m** full of faith and
	6:8	Stephen was a **m** filled with
	6:13	They said, "This **m** never
	7:22	and became a great **m**
	7:24	When he saw an Israelite **m**
	7:36	This is the **m** who led our
	7:52	those who predicted that a **m**
	7:52	betrayed and murdered that **m**.
	7:56	opened and the Son of **M**
	7:58	with a young **m** named Saul.
	8:9	A **m** named Simon lived in that
	8:10	"This **m** is the power of God,
	8:27	An Ethiopian **m** who had come
	8:27	The **m** was a eunuch,
	9:2	Saul wanted to arrest any **m** or
	9:11	and ask for a **m** named Saul
	9:12	In a vision he has seen a **m**
Act	9:13	evil things this **m** has done
	9:15	I've chosen this **m** to bring my
	9:21	They asked, "Isn't this the **m**
	9:33	In Lydda Peter found a **m**
	10:1	A **m** named Cornelius lived in
	10:5	and summon a **m** whose name
	10:21	"I'm the **m** you're looking for.
	10:22	He's a **m** who has God's
	10:26	"Stand up! I'm only a **m**."
	10:28	how wrong it is for a Jewish **m**
	10:30	Suddenly, a **m** dressed in
	10:32	and summon a **m** whose name
	11:13	and summon a **m** whose name
	11:24	Barnabas was a dependable **m**,
	12:22	voice of a god and not of a **m**!
	13:6	In Paphos they met a Jewish **m**
	13:7	with an intelligent **m**,
	13:22	is a **m** after my own heart.
	13:37	However, the **m** God brought
	14:8	A **m** who was born lame was
	14:9	and saw that the **m** believed
	14:10	The **m** jumped up and began to
	16:9	vision of a **m** from Macedonia.
	16:9	The **m** urged Paul,
	17:26	From one **m** he has made
	17:31	and he will use a **m** he has
	17:31	by bringing that **m** back to life."
	18:2	In Corinth he met a Jewish **m**
	18:7	of a **m** named Titius Justus,
	18:13	They said, "This **m** is
	19:16	Then the **m** possessed by the
	19:26	what this **m** Paul has done.
	20:9	A young **m** named Eutychus
	21:11	will tie up the **m** who owns this
	21:28	This is the **m** who teaches
	22:12	"A **m** named Ananias lived in
	22:22	doesn't need a **m** like this.
	22:26	This **m** is a Roman citizen."
	23:9	anything wrong with this **m**.
	23:17	"Take this young **m** to the
	23:18	The sergeant took the young **m**
	23:18	asked me to bring this young **m**
	23:19	The officer took the young **m**
	23:20	The young **m** answered,
	23:22	officer dismissed the young **m**
	23:27	The Jews had seized this **m**
	23:30	there was a plot against this **m**,
	24:5	We have found this **m** to be a
	25:5	if the **m** has done something
	25:14	"Felix left a **m** here in prison.
	25:17	court and summoned the **m**.
	25:19	some **m** named Jesus who
	25:22	"I would like to hear the **m**."
	25:24	to me about this **m** you see
	26:31	"This **m** isn't doing anything for
	26:32	Agrippa told Festus, "This **m**
	28:4	"This **m** must be a murderer!
	28:7	A **m** named Publius,
Rom	2:26	So if a **m** does what Moses'
	2:27	The uncircumcised **m** who
	7:3	So if she marries another **m**
	7:3	if she marries another **m**.
1Co	5:1	a **m** is actually married
	5:2	If you had been upset, the **m**
	5:3	I have already judged the **m**
	5:13	that wicked **m** from among you.
	7:2	each **m** should have his own
	7:12	If any Christian **m** is married to
	7:13	is married to a **m** who is
	7:15	circumstances a Christian **m**
	7:18	Any **m** who was already
	7:18	Any **m** who was
	7:32	An unmarried **m** is concerned
	7:33	But the married **m** is concerned
	7:39	but only if the **m** is a Christian.
	9:1	you agree that I'm a free **m**?
	11:3	has authority over every **m**,
	11:4	Every **m** who covers his head
	11:7	A **m** should not cover his head.
	11:8	Clearly, **m** wasn't made from
	11:8	woman but woman from **m**.
	11:9	**M** wasn't created for woman
	11:9	for woman but woman for **m**.
	11:12	came into existence from a **m**,
	11:14	you that it is disgraceful for a **m**
	15:21	Since a **m** brought death,

1Co 15:21 Since a man brought death, a **m**
15:45 says: "The first **m**, Adam,
15:47 The first **m** was made from the
15:47 second **m** came from heaven.
15:48 are like the **m** who was made
15:48 are like the **m** who came from
15:49 of the **m** who was made
15:49 of the **m** who came from
2Co 5:14 of the fact that one **m** has died
5:15 but for the **m** who died
7:12 I didn't write because of the **m**
7:12 wrong or the **m** who was hurt
11:2 in marriage to one **m** — Christ.
Gal 1:23 "The **m** who persecuted us is
3:9 with Abraham, the **m** of faith.
Eph 5:28 A **m** who loves his wife loves
5:31 That's why a **m** will leave his
2Th 2:3 place first, and the **m** of sin,
2:3 the **m** of destruction,
2:8 Then the **m** of sin will be
2:8 will put an end to this **m**.
2:9 The **m** of sin will come with
1Ti 2:12 or to have authority over a **m**.
3:5 (If a **m** doesn't know how to
5:1 when you correct an older **m**,
6:11 But you, **m** of God,
Phm 1:9 I, Paul, as an old **m** and now a
Heb 2:6 or the Son of **M** that you take
11:12 Yet, from this **m** came
Jas 2:2 One **m** is wearing gold rings
2:2 the other **m**, who is poor,
2:3 to the **m** wearing fine clothes
2:3 But you say to the poor **m**,
2:15 whether a **m** or a woman,
2Pe 2:7 a **m** who had his approval.
2:8 Although he was a **m** who had
Rev 1:13 like the Son of **M** among
1:17 down at his feet like a dead **m**.
14:14 who was like the Son of **M**.
16:3 like the blood of a dead **m**,

Manaen (2)

Act 13:1 **M** (a close friend of Herod
13:3 and **M** placed their hands on

manage (5)

Luk 16:2 It's obvious that you can't **m** my
1Ti 3:4 He must **m** his own family well.
3:5 know how to **m** his own family,
3:12 Deacons must **m** their children
5:14 have children, **m** their homes,

manager (10)

Luk 12:42 skilled **m** that the master will
16:1 "A rich man had a business **m**.
16:1 The **m** was accused of
16:2 So the rich man called for his **m**
16:3 "The **m** thought, 'What should I
16:5 "So the **m** called for each one
16:6 "The **m** told him, 'Take my
16:7 "The **m** told him, 'Take the
16:8 master praised the dishonest **m**
1Pe 4:10 Each of you as a good **m** must

managers (3)

1Co 4:1 Christ and **m** who are entrusted
4:2 **M** are required to be
12:28 help others, those who are **m**,

Manahath (3)

Gen 36:23 **M**, Ebal, Shepho, and Onam.
1Ch 1:40 Shobal's sons were Alian, **M**,
8:6 taken away as captives to **M**:

Manahathites (2)

1Ch 2:52 Haroeh, half of the **M**,
2:54 Joab, half of the **M**, the Zorites,

Manasseh (154)

Gen 41:51 firstborn son **M** [He Helps Me
46:20 In Egypt, **M** and Ephraim were
48:1 So he took his two sons **M** and
48:5 Ephraim and **M** will be mine
48:13 Israel's left, and **M** on his left,
48:14 although **M** was older.
48:19 **M**, too, will become a nation,
Gen 48:20 and **M**!'" In this way Israel
48:20 Israel put Ephraim ahead of **M**.
50:23 children of Machir, son of **M**,
Num 1:10 from the tribe of **M**;
1:10 **M** are Joseph's descendants.)
1:34 for the descendants of **M** listed
1:35 for the tribe of **M** was 32,200.
2:20 to them will be the tribe of **M**.
2:20 for the people of **M** is Gamaliel,
7:54 leader of the descendants of **M**,
10:23 commanded the army of **M**.
13:11 Joseph (that is, the tribe of **M**);
26:28 ⌊through⌋ **M** and Ephraim were
26:29 (from **M**) the family of Machir
26:34 These were the families of **M**.
27:1 whose father was **M**,
27:1 belonged to the families of **M**,
32:33 and half of the tribe of **M**,
32:39 son of **M**, went to Gilead,
32:40 Machir (the descendants of **M**),
32:41 Then Jair, a descendant of **M**,
34:14 and half of the tribe of **M** have
34:23 the leader of the tribe of **M**;
34:24 (**M** and Ephraim are Joseph's
36:1 of Machir and grandson of **M**,
36:12 of the descendants of **M**,
Dtr 3:13 by Og to half of the tribe of **M**.
3:14 Jair, a descendant of **M**,
3:18 of the tribe of **M** this command:
4:43 in Bashan for the tribe of **M**.
29:8 the tribe of **M** as their property.
33:17 from the tribe of **M** will
34:2 the territory of Ephraim and **M**,
Jos 1:12 Gad and half of the tribe of **M**,
4:12 and half of the tribe of **M** did as
12:6 Gad and half of the tribe of **M**.
13:7 tribes and half of the tribe of **M**."
13:8 the tribe of **M** had received their
13:29 to half of the tribe of **M**.
13:31 families of Machir, son of **M**,
14:4 descendants, **M** and Ephraim,
16:4 Joseph's sons, **M** and Ephraim,
17:1 lot was drawn for the tribe of **M**,
17:1 because **M** was Joseph's
17:2 the families descended from **M**,
17:2 Joseph's son **M** listed by their
17:3 whose father was **M**,
17:5 Ten portions of land went to **M**,
17:8 land of Tappuah belongs to **M**,
17:8 on the border of **M**,
17:10 is north ⌊of it⌋ belongs to **M**.
17:11 In Issachar and Asher, **M**
17:12 But **M** was not able to take
17:17 ⌊the tribes of⌋ Ephraim and **M**,
18:7 of the tribe of **M** have received
20:8 the tribe of **M** were chosen as
21:5 Dan and half of the tribe of **M**.
21:6 half of the tribe of **M** in Bashan.
21:25 Half of the tribe of **M** gave them
21:27 from half of the tribe of **M**:
22:1 Gad and half of the tribe of **M**.
22:7 as an inheritance to half of **M**,
22:9 and half of the tribe of **M** left
22:10 and half of the tribe of **M** came
22:11 and half of the tribe of **M** have
22:13 half of the tribe of **M** in Gilead.
22:21 half of the tribe of **M** answered
22:30 of Reuben, Gad, and **M** said,
22:31 tribes of Reuben, Gad, and **M**,
Jdg 1:27 Now, the tribe of **M** did not
6:15 It's the weakest one in **M**.
6:35 sent messengers throughout **M**
7:23 and all **M** to help pursue the
11:29 went through Gilead, **M**,
12:4 fugitives from Ephraim and **M**."
1Ki 4:13 a descendant of **M**,
2Ki 10:33 and **M**) from Aroer,
20:21 His son **M** succeeded him as
21:1 **M** was 12 years old when he
21:3 **M**, like Ahab, worshiped and
21:7 **M** had an idol of Asherah made.
21:9 **M** misled Israel so that they did
21:11 "King **M** of Judah has done
21:11 **M** has also made Judah sin by
21:16 **M** also killed a lot of innocent
21:17 Isn't everything else about **M** —
2Ki 21:18 **M** lay down in death with his
21:20 as his father **M** had done.
23:12 and the altars **M** had made in
23:26 After all, **M** had done all these
1Ch 3:13 Hezekiah's son was **M**.
5:18 and half of the tribe of **M** had
5:22 and half of the tribe of **M** lived
5:23 Half of the tribe of **M** lived in
5:25 and half of the tribe of **M** were
5:26 of the tribe of **M** into captivity.
6:61 families of half of the tribe of **M**.
6:62 and ⌊the part of⌋ the tribe of **M**
6:70 From half of the tribe of **M**,
6:71 families of half of the tribe of **M**.
7:17 of Machir (son of **M**).
7:29 Next to **M** were Beth Shean
9:3 Benjamin, Ephraim, and **M**:
12:19 Some men from **M** had
12:20 these men from **M** deserted to
12:20 an officer over 1,000 men in **M**.
12:31 From half of the tribe of **M** there
12:37 and half the tribe of **M**,
26:32 and half of the tribe of **M**.
27:20 for half of the tribe of **M**:
27:21 for the half of **M** in Gilead:
2Ch 15:9 from Ephraim, **M**, and Simeon.
30:1 to the tribes of Ephraim and **M**.
30:10 the territories of Ephraim and **M**
30:11 some people from Asher, **M**,
30:18 Many people from Ephraim, **M**,
31:1 Benjamin, Ephraim, and **M**.
32:33 His son **M** succeeded him as
33:1 **M** was 12 years old when he
33:3 **M**, like Ahab, worshiped and
33:7 **M** had a carved idol made.
33:9 **M** misled Judah and the
33:10 When the LORD spoke to **M**
33:11 They took **M** captive,
33:13 Then **M** knew that the LORD is
33:14 After this, **M** rebuilt the outer
33:15 **M** got rid of the foreign gods
33:18 Everything else about **M** —
33:20 **M** lay down in death with his
33:22 as his father **M** had done.
33:22 idols his father **M** had made,
33:23 father **M** had humbled himself.
34:6 In the cities of **M**, Ephraim,
34:9 the tribes of **M** and Ephraim,
Ezr 10:30 Bezalel, Binnui, and **M**
10:33 Jeremai, **M**, and Shimei
Psa 60:7 **M** is mine. Ephraim is the
80:2 of Ephraim, Benjamin, and **M**.
108:8 **M** is mine. Ephraim is the
Isa 9:21 **M** is against Ephraim.
9:21 Ephraim is against **M**.
Jer 15:4 of what Judah's King **M**,
Eze 48:4 **M** will have one part of the land
48:5 part of the land and border **M**
Mat 1:10 Hezekiah the father of **M**,
1:10 **M** the father of Amon,
Rev 7:6 12,000 from the tribe of **M**,

Manasseh's (14)

Gen 48:14 He put his left hand on **M** head,
48:17 it from Ephraim's head to **M**.
Jos 16:9 for Ephraim in **M** territory
17:1 Machir, **M** firstborn, the
17:6 **M** daughters were given
17:6 to **M** other descendants.
17:7 **M** border extends from Asher
17:9 they are among **M** cities.
17:9 **M** ⌊southern⌋ border is the
2Ki 24:3 because of **M** sins — everything
1Ch 3:14 **M** son was Amon.
5:24 the heads of **M** families: Epher,
7:14 **M** sons were Asriel and Machir.
7:14 was **M** Aramean concubine.

mandrakes (6)

Gen 30:14 the fields and found some **m**.
30:14 give me some of your son's **m**."
30:15 going to take my son's **m**?"
30:15 in return for your son's **m**."
30:16 are my reward for my son's **m**.
Sos 7:13 The **m** give off a fragrance,

mane (2)
1Sm 17:35 I took hold of its **m**,
Job 39:19 its neck with a flowing **m**?

man-eating (1)
Psa 57:4 I must lie down with **m** lions.

maneuvers (1)
Job 23:6 and hide behind great legal **m**?

manger (3)
Luk 2:7 of cloth and laid him in a **m**
2:12 strips of cloth and lying in a **m**."
2:16 who was lying in a **m**.

manna (19)
Exo 16:31 Israelites called the food **m**.
16:32 Take two quarts of **m** to be
16:33 put two quarts of **m** in it,
16:34 Aaron put the jar of **m** in front of
16:35 The Israelites ate **m** for 40
16:35 They ate **m** until they came to
Num 11:6 we look there's nothing but **m**!"
11:7 (**M** was ⌊small⌋ like coriander
11:9 camp at night, **m** fell with it.)
Dtr 8:3 and then fed you with **m**,
8:16 fed you in the desert with **m**,
Jos 5:12 day after that, the **m** stopped.
5:12 of Israel never had **m** again.
Neh 9:20 didn't keep your **m** to yourself.
Psa 78:24 He rained **m** down on them to
Jon 6:31 Our ancestors ate the **m** in the
6:49 Your ancestors ate the **m** in the
Heb 9:4 were the gold jar filled with **m**,
Rev 2:17 will give some of the hidden **m**

manned (1)
Isa 22:6 **m** chariots, and horsemen.

Manoah (18)
Jdg 13:2 a man from Zorah named **M**.
13:2 **M** was from the family of Dan.
13:8 Then **M** pleaded with the
13:9 God did what **M** asked.
13:9 But her husband **M** was not
13:11 **M** immediately followed his
13:12 Then **M** asked, "When your
13:13 of the LORD answered **M**,
13:15 **M** said to the Messenger of the
13:16 (**M** did not realize that it was
13:17 Then **M** asked the Messenger
13:19 So **M** took a young goat and a
13:19 While **M** and his wife watched,
13:20 When **M** and his wife saw this,
13:21 LORD didn't appear again to **M**
13:21 Then **M** knew that this had
13:22 So **M** said to his wife,
16:31 in the tomb of his father **M**.

Manoah's (1)
Jdg 13:23 But **M** wife replied,

man's (45)
Gen 2:21 God took out one of the **m** ribs
20:7 Give the **m** wife back to him
42:25 He put each **m** money back
44:1 Put each **m** money in his sack.
Lev 15:13 "When a **m** discharge stops,
20:10 adultery with another **m** wife
Num 5:12 A **m** wife may have been
17:2 Write each **m** name on his staff.
Dtr 22:24 had sex with another **m** wife.
25:11 grabbing the other **m** genitals,
Jdg 8:21 It's a **m** job!" So Gideon got up
18:19 to be a priest for one **m** house
19:24 daughter and this **m** concubine.
Rut 1:2 The **m** name was Elimelech,
4:5 the dead **m** widow.
4:5 in the dead **m** name.
4:10 in the dead **m** name.
4:10 In this way the dead **m** name
1Sm 25:3 This **m** name was Nabal,
25:21 "I guarded this **m** stuff in the
2Sm 10:4 of each **m** beard, cut off their
12:4 So he took the poor **m** lamb
17:19 The **m** wife took a cover,
1Ki 18:44 "A little cloud like a **m** hand is
Pro 30:1 This **m** declaration: "I'm weary,
Jnh 1:14 let us die for taking this **m** life.
Mat 9:9 The **m** name was Matthew.
12:29 go into a strong **m** house
Mar 3:27 can go into a strong **m** house
3:27 go through the strong **m** house
7:33 put his fingers into the **m** ears,
7:33 he touched the **m** tongue
8:23 Jesus took the blind **m** hand
8:23 He spit into the **m** eyes and
8:25 his hands on the **m** eyes
Luk 16:1 of wasting the rich **m** property
16:20 to the gate of the rich **m** house
16:21 that fell from the rich **m** table.
Jon 9:6 he smeared it on the **m** eyes
9:18 they talked to the **m** parents,
11:39 the dead **m** sister, told Jesus,
18:17 one of this **m** disciples too?"
Act 3:7 Peter took hold of the **m** right
3:7 Immediately, the **m** feet and
1Co 11:7 woman, however, is **m** glory

mansion (1)
Luk 11:21 guards his own **m**,

mansions (1)
Amo 3:15 **M** will be demolished,

manure (13)
1Ki 14:10 It will burn like **m** until it is
2Ki 6:25 silver and a half-pint of dove **m**
9:37 Jezebel's corpse will be like **m**
Psa 83:10 They became **m** to fertilize the
Isa 25:10 that is trampled in a pile of **m**.
25:11 in the **m** like swimmers who
Jer 8:2 will become **m** on the ground.
9:22 Dead bodies will fall like **m** on
16:4 They will be like **m** on the
25:33 become like **m** on the ground.
Eze 4:15 "I will let you use cow **m** in
Zep 1:17 dust and their intestines like **m**.
Luk 14:35 for the ground or for the **m** pile.

Maon (6)
Jos 15:55 **M**, Carmel, Ziph, Juttah,
1Sm 23:24 men were in the desert of **M**,
23:25 stronghold in the desert of **M**.
23:25 David into the desert of **M**.
25:2 Now, there was a man in **M**
1Ch 2:45 Shammai's son was **M**,

Maonites (1)
Jdg 10:12 and the **M** oppressed you,

map (1)
Eze 4:1 and draw a **m** of Jerusalem on

mar (1)
Isa 24:1 He will **m** the face of the earth

Mara (1)
Rut 1:20 Call me **M** [Bitter] because the

Marah (4)
Exo 15:23 they came to **M** [Bitter Place],
15:23 why the place was called **M**.
Num 33:8 they set up camp at **M**.
33:9 They moved from **M** and came

Maralah (1)
Jos 19:11 west the border ascends to **M**

marble (6)
1Ch 29:2 different colors, gems, and **m**.
Est 1:6 rods and **m** pillars by cords
1:6 rock, white **m**, pearl-like stone,
1:6 pearl-like stone, and black **m**.
Sos 5:15 His legs are columns of **m** set
Rev 18:12 costly wood, bronze, iron, **m**,

march (23)
Num 32:17 Then we'll be ready ⌊to **m**⌋ in
Jos 1:14 all your best soldiers must **m** in
6:3 All the soldiers will **m** around
6:4 day you must **m** around
6:7 "**M** around the city.
6:7 Let the armed men **m** ahead of
8:1 with you, and **m** against Ai.
8:3 soldiers started to **m** against Ai.
Jdg 5:21 I must **m** on with strength!
Neh 12:31 thanks and **m** in procession.
Psa 118:27 **M** in a festival procession with
Pro 30:29 even four that **m** with dignity:
Isa 7:6 'Let's **m** against Judah,
Jer 6:23 They **m** like soldiers ready for
46:9 **M** into battle, you warriors,
Eze 12:3 **M** like a captive from your
Joe 2:7 They **m** straight ahead.
Oba 1:13 Don't **m** through the gates of
Nah 2:5 over themselves as they **m**.
Hab 1:6 They will **m** throughout the
3:12 You **m** through the earth with
3:15 You **m** with your horses into
Zec 9:14 blow the ram's horn and will **m**

marched (24)
Gen 14:8 Zoar) **m** out and prepared for
Jos 4:12 They **m** across in battle
6:8 of the LORD **m** off as they
6:15 They **m** around the city seven
6:15 That was the only day they **m**
8:11 All the troops with him **m** until
10:5 They **m** to Gibeon,
10:9 So Joshua **m** all night from
10:29 Joshua and all Israel **m** from
10:31 Joshua and all Israel **m** from
10:34 Joshua and all Israel **m** from
10:36 Then Joshua and all Israel **m**
15:15 From there he **m** against the
Jdg 5:4 when you **m** from the country
18:13 From there they **m** to the
1Sm 31:12 all the fighting men **m** all night
2Sm 2:29 Abner and his men **m** through
2:32 Then Joab and his men **m** all
15:22 So Ittai from Gath **m** on with all
18:4 the troops **m** out by battalions
Job 18:14 the safety of his tent and **m** off
Psa 48:4 gathered. They **m** together.
68:7 when you **m** through the desert
Heb 11:30 the Israelites **m** around them

marches (1)
Isa 42:13 The LORD **m** out like a warrior.

marching (8)
1Sm 29:2 The Philistine leaders were **m**
29:2 David and his men were **m** in
2Sm 5:24 When you hear the sound of **m**
15:18 Gath were **m** past the king.
15:22 "Go ahead and keep **m**."
1Ch 14:15 As you hear the sound of **m** in
Isa 9:5 Every warrior's boot **m** to the
41:3 He chases them, **m** by safely

Marduk (1)
Jer 50:2 **M** will be filled with terror.

mare (1)
Sos 1:9 a **m** among Pharaoh's stallions.

Mareshah (8)
Jos 15:44 Keilah, Achzib, and **M**.
1Ch 2:42 and the sons of **M**,
4:21 who first settled **M**,
2Ch 11:8 Gath, **M**, Ziph,
14:9 Zerah got as far as **M**.
14:10 in the Zephathah Valley at **M**.
20:37 son of Dodavahu from **M**,
Mic 1:15 against the inhabitants of **M**.

mariners (2)
Eze 27:27 your **m** and your sailors,
27:29 and all the **m** came down from

marital (1)
Mat 1:25 He did not have **m** relations

Mark; mark (26)
Gen 1:14 and will **m** religious festivals,
35:14 to **m** the place where God had

Exo 13:9 ⌊festival⌋ will be ⌊like⌋ a **m**
13:16 ⌊festival⌋ will be ⌊like⌋ a **m**
19:12 **M** off a boundary around the
19:23 you warned us yourself to **m** off
26:33 The canopy will **m** off the most
40:21 canopy over it to **m** off where
Psa 16:6 Your boundary lines **m** out
Isa 44:13 They **m** them with pens.
44:13 them with chisels and **m** them
Eze 9:4 and put a **m** on the foreheads of
9:6 anyone who has a **m** on him.
21:19 "Son of man, **m** two roads that
21:20 **M** the road that the king and his
21:20 and **m** the road that leads to
Nah 1:3 winds and storms **m** his path,
Act 15:39 Barnabas took **M** with him and
Rom 4:11 The **m** of circumcision is the
Col 4:10 So does **M**, the cousin of
4:10 received instructions about **M**.
1Th 4:3 away from sexual sin as a **m**
2Ti 4:11 Get **M** and bring him with you.
Phm 1:24 and my coworkers **M**,
1Pe 5:13 my son **M** send you greetings.
2Jn 1:7 This is the **m** of a deceiver and

marked (1)

Lam 2:8 He **m** it off with a line.

marker (16)

Gen 28:18 He set it up as a **m** and poured
28:22 that I have set up as a **m** will
31:13 poured olive oil on a stone **m**
31:45 a stone and set it up as a **m**.
31:51 and here is the **m** that I have
31:52 This pile of stones and this **m**
31:52 pile of stones or **m** to harm me.
35:14 set up a memorial, a stone **m**,
35:20 Jacob set up a stone as a **m**
35:20 The same **m** is at Rachel's
Dtr 19:14 neighbor's original boundary **m**
27:17 his neighbor's boundary **m** will
Pro 22:28 boundary **m** that your ancestors
23:10 move an ancient boundary **m**
Isa 19:19 and a stone **m** for the LORD
Eze 39:15 they will set up a **m** beside it

markers (4)

Job 24:2 "⌊People⌋ move boundary **m**.
Hos 5:10 those who move boundary **m**.
10:1 the more stone **m** they set up
10:2 and destroy their stone **m**.

market (3)

Jer 9:21 the young men in the **m** places.
Act 28:15 as far as the cities of Appius' **M**
1Co 10:25 in the **m** without letting your

marketplace (6)

Isa 23:3 became the **m** for the nations.
Eze 27:24 In your **m** they traded for
Mat 20:3 standing in the **m** without work.
Mar 7:4 When they come from the **m**,
Luk 7:32 like children who sit in the **m**
Jon 2:16 my Father's house a **m**!"

marketplaces (6)

Mat 11:16 like children who sit in the **m**
23:7 love to be greeted in the **m**
Mar 6:56 would put their sick in the **m**.
12:38 to be greeted in the **m**,
Luk 11:43 and to be greeted in the **m**.
20:46 and love to be greeted in the **m**,

marks (4)

Job 13:27 follow my trail by engraving **m**
26:10 He **m** the horizon on the
Psa 104:19 which **m** the seasons,
Jon 20:25 this unless I see the nail **m**

Maroth (1)

Mic 1:12 for good, inhabitants of **M**.

marriage (24)

Gen 29:26 younger daughter ⌊in **m**⌋ before
Lev 38:14 hadn't been given to him in **m**.)
20:11 wife has violated his father's **m**.
20:20 wife violates his uncle's **m**.
20:21 wife violates his brother's **m**
Dtr 22:16 "I gave my daughter in **m** to
22:21 She had sex before **m**,
1Sm 25:39 behalf to propose **m** to Abigail.
2Ki 8:27 related to Ahab's family by **m**.
Pro 2:17 and forgets her **m** vows to her
Eze 16:8 and I exchanged **m** vows with
16:59 You despised your **m** vows
Mal 2:14 the wife of your **m** vows.
Mat 1:18 been promised to Joseph in **m**.
1:19 So he decided to break the **m**
Luk 1:27 went to a virgin promised in **m**
2:5 to him in **m** and was pregnant.
Rom 7:2 But if her husband dies, that **m**
1Co 7:15 is not bound ⌊by a **m** vow⌋.
7:38 father to give his daughter in **m**,
7:38 daughter in **m** does even better.
2Co 11:2 a virgin whom I promised in **m**
Heb 13:4 **M** is honorable in every way,
Rev 19:7 glory because it's time for the **m**

marriages (1)

Neh 13:26 I said, "Wasn't it because of **m**

married (107)

Gen 4:19 Lamech **m** two women,
6:2 So they **m** any woman they
11:29 Both Abram and Nahor **m**.
19:31 We can't get **m** as other people
20:3 She's a **m** woman!"
24:67 He **m** Rebekah. She became his
25:1 Abraham **m** again,
25:20 years old when he **m** Rebekah,
26:34 was 40 years old, he **m** Judith,
26:34 He also **m** Basemath,
28:9 to Ishmael and **m** Mahalath,
38:2 He **m** her and slept with her.
Exo 2:1 family **m** a Levite woman.
6:20 Amram **m** his father's sister
6:23 Aaron **m** Elisheba,
6:25 Eleazar, son of Aaron, **m** one of
21:3 If he comes as a **m** man,
Num 12:1 Moses because he was **m**
30:10 "A **m** woman might make a
36:4 to that of the tribe they **m** into.
36:11 and Noah **m** their cousins on
36:12 They **m** within the families of
Dtr 20:7 to a woman but have not **m** her,
22:14 by saying, "I **m** this woman.
22:22 intercourse with a **m** woman,
24:5 who has recently been **m** will
Jdg 11:37 have an opportunity to get **m**."
11:38 never being able to get **m**.
12:9 His sons and daughters **m**
Rut 1:4 Each son **m** a woman from
1:4 One son **m** a woman named
1:4 and the other son **m** a woman
1:12 I am too old to get **m** again.
1Sm 18:19 she was **m** to Adriel from
25:43 David also **m** Ahinoam of
2Sm 5:13 David **m** more concubines and
1Ki 1:2 woman who has never been **m**.
4:15 **m** Solomon's daughter
16:31 He also **m** Jezebel,
1Ch 2:19 Azubah died, Caleb **m** Ephrath.
2:21 Hezron had **m** her when he
7:15 He **m** a wife from the Huppites
14:3 David **m** more wives in
23:22 the sons of Kish, **m** them.
2Ch 11:18 Rehoboam **m** Mahalath,
11:20 Mahalath, he **m** Maacah,
13:21 He **m** 14 wives and fathered 22
Ezr 2:61 and Barzillai (who had **m** one
9:2 and their sons have **m** some
10:14 everyone who has **m** a foreign
10:17 who had **m** foreign women.
10:18 the following were **m** to foreign
10:44 men had **m** foreign women.
Neh 6:18 Tobiah's son Jehohanan had **m**
7:63 and Barzillai (who had **m** one
Neh 13:23 had **m** women from Ashdod,
Pro 5:18 and enjoy the girl you **m** when
6:26 but a **m** woman hunts for
30:23 is unloved when she gets **m**,
Isa 54:1 there are children of **m** women,
54:6 a wife who **m** young and was
62:4 and your land will be named **M**.
62:4 and your land will be **m**.
Jer 29:6 Get **m**, and have sons and
29:6 and let your daughters get **m**
Eze 23:4 I **m** them, and they gave birth to
Hos 1:3 So Hosea **m** Gomer,
Mal 2:11 that the LORD loves and has **m**
Mat 1:18 But before they were **m**,
14:4 not right for you to be **m** to her."
19:10 it's better not to get **m**."
22:25 The first **m** and died.
22:28 brothers had been **m** to her."
24:38 and getting **m** until the day that
Mar 6:17 for Herodias, whom he had **m**.
6:18 "It's not right for you to be **m** to
12:20 The first got **m** and died
12:21 The second **m** her and died
12:23 The seven brothers had **m** her."
Luk 2:36 seven years after they were **m**,
3:19 had **m** his own sister-in-law,
14:20 another said, 'I recently got **m**,
17:27 and getting **m** until the day that
20:28 'If a **m** man dies and has no
20:29 The first got **m** and died
20:30 second brother **m** the widow,
20:31 seven brothers **m** the widow,
20:33 The seven brothers had **m** her."
20:34 "In this world people get **m**.
Rom 7:2 For example, a **m** woman is
1Co 5:1 a man is actually **m**
7:1 It's good for men not to get **m**.
7:8 I say to those who are not **m**,
7:9 your desires, you should get **m**.
7:12 If any Christian man is **m** to a
7:13 If any Christian woman is **m** to
7:28 But if you do get **m**,
7:28 If a virgin gets **m**, she has not
7:29 While it lasts, those who are **m**
7:33 But the **m** man is concerned
7:34 But the **m** woman is concerned
7:36 is old enough to get **m**.
7:36 If she wants to get **m**,
7:36 sinning by letting her get **m**.
7:37 she doesn't want to get **m**,
7:39 A **m** woman must remain with
1Ti 4:3 try to stop others from getting **m**

marries (15)

Gen 27:46 If Jacob **m** a Hittite woman like
Exo 21:10 If that son **m** another woman,
Lev 20:14 When a man **m** a woman and
20:21 Whoever **m** his brother's wife
22:12 a priest's daughter **m** a layman,
Num 30:6 do something. When she **m**,
Isa 62:5 As a young man **m** a woman,
Jer 3:1 leaves him and **m** another man,
Mat 5:32 Whoever **m** a woman divorced
19:9 if he **m** another woman."
Mar 10:11 wife and **m** another woman is
10:12 husband and **m** another man,
Luk 16:18 The man who **m** a woman
Rom 7:3 So if she **m** another man while
7:3 adultery if she **m** another man.

marrow (1)

Heb 4:12 place where joints and **m** meet.

marry (65)

Gen 28:1 "You are not to **m** any of the
28:6 commanded him not to **m** any
31:50 or **m** other women behind
34:8 Please let her **m** him.
34:21 We can **m** their daughters and
34:21 daughters and let them **m** ours.
Exo 22:16 pay the bride-price and **m** her.
Lev 18:18 never **m** her sister as a rival
21:7 You should never **m** prostitutes,

Lev 21:13 anointed priest must **m** a virgin.
21:14 He must never **m** a widow,
21:14 He may only **m** a virgin from
Num 36:3 Suppose they **m** men from the
36:3 the land of the tribe they **m** into.
36:6 They may **m** anyone they want
36:8 of the tribes of Israel may **m**
Dtr 7:3 Never **m** any of them.
7:3 Never let your daughters **m**
7:3 or your sons **m** their daughters.
20:7 and someone else will **m** her."
21:11 set on her, you may **m** her.
22:13 A man might **m** a woman,
22:30 A man must never **m** his
24:2 She might **m** another man after
24:4 is not allowed to **m** her again.
25:5 his widow must not **m** outside
25:5 Her husband's brother must **m**
25:7 want to **m** his brother's widow,
25:8 that he doesn't want to **m** her,
Jdg 3:6 daughters to **m** these people.
14:2 her for me so that I can **m** her."
14:3 Do you have to **m** a woman
14:8 Later he went back to **m** her.
15:2 looking? **M** her instead! "
21:1 **m** anyone from Benjamin."
21:7 any of our daughters **m** them."
1Sm 17:25 his daughter to that man to **m**
2Sm 13:13 refuse your request to **m** me."
2Ki 14:9 'Let your daughter **m** my son,'
1Ch 2:35 Sheshan let Jarha **m** one of his
2Ch 25:18 'Let your daughter **m** my son,'
Ezr 9:12 So never let your daughters **m**
9:12 or your sons **m** their daughters,
Neh 10:30 not allow our daughters to **m**
10:30 their daughters to **m** our sons.
13:25 our daughters to **m** their sons,
13:25 won't allow their daughters to **m**
Isa 4:1 Just let us **m** you for your
62:5 so your sons will **m** you.
Jer 16:2 "Don't **m**! Don't have any sons
Eze 44:22 They must not **m** widows or
44:22 They may **m** only virgins from
Hos 1:2 LORD told him, "**M** a prostitute,
Joe 1:8 the man she was going to **m**.
Mat 22:24 his brother should **m** his
22:30 come back to life, they don't **m**.
Mar 12:19 his brother should **m** his
12:25 come back to life, they don't **m**.
Luk 16:18 his wife to **m** another woman is
20:28 his brother should **m** his
20:35 in the next world will neither **m**
1Co 7:9 It is better for you to **m** than to
7:39 she is free to **m** anyone she
1Ti 5:11 to Christ, they'll want to **m**.
5:14 I want younger widows to **m**,

marrying (6)
Exo 34:16 will end up **m** their daughters.
1Ki 3:1 After **m** Pharaoh's daughter,
2Ch 11:20 After **m** Mahalath, he married
Ezr 10:2 God by **m** foreign women who
10:10 unfaithful by **m** foreign women,
Neh 13:27 by **m** non-Israelite women?"

Marsena (1)
Est 1:14 Meres, **M**, and Memucan.

marshes (2)
Jer 51:32 The enemy has burned its **m**,
Eze 47:11 and **m** won't become fresh.

Martha (16)
Luk 10:38 A woman named **M** welcomed
10:40 But **M** was upset about all the
10:41 The Lord answered her, "**M**,
10:41 Lord answered her, "Martha, **M**
Jon 11:1 Mary and her sister **M** lived,
11:5 Jesus loved **M**, her sister,
11:19 Many Jews had come to **M**
11:20 When **M** heard that Jesus was
11:21 **M** told Jesus, "Lord, if you had
11:23 Jesus told **M**, "Your brother will
11:24 **M** answered Jesus,
11:27 **M** said to him, "Yes, Lord,
11:28 After **M** had said this,
Jon 11:30 still where **M** had met him.)
11:39 **M**, the dead man's sister,
12:2 **M** served the dinner,

marvelous (1)
1Pe 2:9 out of darkness into his **m** light.

Mary (66)
Mat 1:16 who was the husband of **M**.
1:16 **M** was the mother of Jesus,
1:18 His mother **M** had been
1:18 before they were married, **M**
1:20 don't be afraid to take **M** as
1:24 He took **M** to be his wife.
2:11 the child with his mother **M**.
13:55 Isn't his mother's name **M**?
27:56 them were **M** from Magdala,
27:56 **M** (the mother of James and
27:61 **M** from Magdala and the other
27:61 the other **M** were sitting there,
28:1 **M** from Magdala and the other
28:1 Magdala and the other **M** went
Mar 6:3 this the carpenter, the son of **M**,
15:40 them were **M** from Magdala,
15:40 **M** (the mother of young James
15:47 **M** from Magdala and Mary (the
15:47 Mary from Magdala and **M** (the
16:1 was over, **M** from Magdala,
16:1 **M** (the mother of James),
16:9 first to **M** from Magdala,
Luk 1:27 The virgin's name was **M**.
1:30 told her, "Don't be afraid, **M**.
1:34 **M** asked the angel,
1:38 **M** answered, "I am the Lord's
1:39 Soon afterward, **M** hurried to a
1:46 **M** said, "My soul praises the
1:56 **M** stayed with Elizabeth about
2:5 went there to register with **M**.
2:6 the time came for **M** to have her
2:16 They went quickly and found **M**
2:19 **M** treasured all these things in
2:22 Joseph and **M** went to
2:27 **M** and Joseph were bringing
2:34 blessed them and said to **M**,
2:38 that moment she came up to **M**
2:39 Joseph and **M** returned to their
8:2 These women were **M**,
10:39 She had a sister named **M**.
10:39 **M** sat at the Lord's feet and
10:42 **M** has made the right choice,
24:10 women were **M** from Magdala,
24:10 and **M** (the mother of James).
Jon 11:1 the village where **M** and her
11:2 (**M** was the woman who
11:19 had come to Martha and **M**
11:20 **M** stayed at home.
11:28 and whispered to her sister **M**,
11:29 When **M** heard this,
11:31 Jews who were comforting **M**
11:32 When **M** arrived where Jesus
11:45 Many Jews who had visited **M**
12:3 **M** took a bottle of very
19:25 **M** (the wife of Clopas),
19:25 and **M** from Magdala were
20:1 **M** from Magdala went to the
20:11 **M**, however, stood there and
20:13 **M** told them, "They have
20:15 **M** thought it was the gardener
20:16 Jesus said to her, "**M**!"
20:16 **M** turned around and said to
20:18 **M** from Magdala went to the
Act 1:14 including **M** (the mother of
12:12 he went to the home of **M**,
Rom 16:6 Greet **M**, who has worked very

Mash (1)
Gen 10:23 were Uz, Hul, Gether, and **M**.

Mashal (1)
1Ch 6:74 they received **M** with its

mask (1)
Isa 25:7 and the **m** covering all nations.

masons (5)
2Ki 12:12 **m**, and stonecutters. They also
2Ki 22:6 carpenters, builders, and **m**.)
1Ch 14:1 along with cedarwood, **m**,
22:15 stonecutters, **m**, carpenters,
2Ch 24:12 and they hired **m** and

Masrekah (2)
Gen 36:36 Samlah from **M** succeeded him
1Ch 1:47 Samlah from **M** succeeded him

Massa (2)
Gen 25:14 Mishma, Dumah, **M**,
1Ch 1:30 Mishma, Dumah, **M**,

massacre (1)
2Sm 18:7 and the **m** was sizable that day

massacred (2)
Job 1:15 livestock and **m** the servants.
1:17 the camels and **m** the servants.

massacres (1)
2Sm 15:14 on us when he **m** the city."

Massah (5)
Exo 17:7 He named that place **M**
Dtr 6:16 your God as you did at **M**.
9:22 **M**, and Kibroth Hattaavah.
33:8 You tested your people at **M**.
Psa 95:8 like the time at **M** in the desert.

massive (1)
Jer 14:17 will suffer **m** destruction.

mast (3)
Pro 23:34 lying down on top of a ship's **m**,
Isa 33:23 your **m** isn't secure,
Eze 27:5 Lebanon to make a **m** for you.

master (171)
Gen 1:28 fill the earth, and be its **m**.
4:7 but you must **m** it."
24:9 So the servant did as his **m**
24:12 God of my **m** Abraham,
24:14 shown your kindness to my **m**."
24:27 the God of my **m** Abraham.
24:27 to be kind and faithful to my **m**.
24:35 "The LORD has blessed my **m**,
24:36 and my **m** has given that son
24:37 My **m** made me swear this
24:39 "I asked my **m**, 'What if the
24:42 'LORD God of my **m** Abraham,
24:48 the God of my **m** Abraham.
24:49 to show my **m** true kindness so
24:54 "Let me go back to my **m**."
24:56 Let me go back to my **m**."
24:65 "That is my **m**," the servant
27:29 Be the **m** of your brothers,
27:37 "I have made him your **m**,
37:19 here comes that **m** dreamer!
39:2 in the house of his Egyptian **m**.
39:3 Joseph's **m** saw that the LORD
39:8 "My **m** doesn't concern himself
39:16 her until his **m** came home.
39:20 So Joseph's **m** arrested him
40:1 and his baker offended their **m**,
44:5 Isn't this the cup that my **m**
Exo 21:4 If his **m** gives him a wife and
21:4 her children belong to the **m**,
21:5 declare my love for my **m**,
21:6 then his **m** must bring him to
21:6 The **m** must bring him to the
21:8 If she doesn't please the **m**
21:32 of silver to the slave's **m**,
23:17 into the presence of the **M**,
31:4 He's a **m** artist familiar with
34:23 into the presence of the **M**,
35:32 He's a **m** artist familiar with
35:35 They are **m** artists."
Dtr 23:15 If a slave escapes from his **m**
23:15 don't return him to his **m**.
1Sm 20:38 the arrows and came to his **m**.
24:11 My **m**, look at this! The border
25:14 from the desert to greet our **m**,
25:17 you should do because our **m**
26:15 why didn't you guard your **m**,
26:16 You didn't guard your **m**,

1Sm 30:13 "My **m** left me behind because
30:15 me or hand me over to my **m**,
2Sm 2:5 to your **m** Saul by burying
2:7 Because your **m** Saul is dead,
10:3 princes asked their **m** Hanun,
12:8 I gave you your **m** Saul's house
16:3 is your **m** Saul's grandson?"
1Ki 1:11 and our **m** David doesn't
11:23 Rezon fled from his **m**,
12:27 the former **m** of these people,
18:7 "Is it you, my **m** Elijah?"
18:8 "Tell your **m** that Elijah is
18:10 my **m** has searched for you in
18:10 my **m** made that kingdom or
18:11 'Tell your **m** that Elijah is here.'
18:14 I should tell my **m** that Elijah is
22:17 'These ⌊sheep⌋ have no **m**.
2Ki 2:3 to take your **m** from you today?"
2:5 to take your **m** from you today?"
2:12 saw this, he cried out, "**M**!
2:12 **M**! Israel's chariot and horses!"
2:16 them go and search for your **m**.
5:1 and highly honored by his **m**.
5:3 "If only my **m** were with the
5:4 Naaman went to his **m** and told
5:13 went to him and said, "**M**,
5:18 forgive me when my **m** goes
5:20 "My **m** let this Aramean
5:22 My **m** has sent me.
5:25 and stood in front of his **m**.
6:5 He cried out, "Oh no, **m**!
6:15 Elisha's servant asked, "**M**,
6:21 Elisha, "**M**, should I kill them?
6:22 let them go back to their **m**."
6:23 he sent them back to their **m**.
8:14 and went to his **m** Benhadad,
9:7 the family of your **m** Ahab.
9:31 murderer of your **m**?"
10:9 I plotted against my **m** and
13:14 cried over him, and said, "**M**!
13:14 **M**! Israel's chariot and horses!"
18:23 "Now, make a deal with my **m**,
18:27 "Did my **m** send me to tell
18:27 things only to you and your **m**?
19:4 His **m**, the king of Assyria,
19:6 "Say this to your **m**,
1Ch 12:19 deserts and joins his **m** Saul.")
2Ch 13:6 son) rebelled against his **m**.
18:16 'These sheep have no **m**.
Job 3:19 the slave is free from his **m**.
39:7 listen to the shouting of its **m**.
Psa 12:4 who can be our **m**?"
52:2 a sharp razor, you **m** of deceit.
105:21 He made Joseph the **m** of his
Pro 8:30 beside him as a **m** craftsman.
17:2 A wise slave will become **m**
27:18 protects his **m** is honored.
30:10 not slander a slave to his **m**.
Isa 19:4 the Egyptians to a harsh **m**.
26:13 you are not the only **m** to rule
36:8 "Now, make a deal with my **m**,
36:12 "Did my **m** send me to tell
36:12 things only to you and your **m**?
37:4 His **m**, the king of Assyria,
37:6 "Say this to your **m**,
51:22 This is what your **m** says:
Jer 22:18 it is for my **m** and his splendor!"
34:5 **m**," as they mourn for you.
Eze 27:9 **M** shipbuilders from Gebal
Dan 1:10 "I'm afraid of my **m**,
Hos 2:16 will no longer call me her **m**.
Mal 1:6 and a servant honors his **m**.
1:6 If I am a **m**, where is my
Mat 6:24 He will hate the first **m** and
18:25 the **m** ordered him,
18:27 "The **m** felt sorry for his
18:31 told their **m** the whole story.
18:32 "Then his **m** sent for him and
18:34 "His **m** was so angry that he
24:45 The **m** will put that person in
24:46 if his **m** finds him doing
24:48 long time before his **m** comes.
24:50 His **m** will return unexpectedly.
24:51 Then his **m** will severely
25:19 "After a long time the **m** of
25:21 "His **m** replied, 'Good job!
Mat 25:23 "His **m** replied, 'Good job!
25:26 "His **m** responded,
Luk 8:24 woke him up, and said, "**M**!
8:24 **M**! We're going to die!" Then he
9:49 John replied, "**M**, we saw
12:37 whom the **m** finds awake when
12:42 skilled manager that the **m** will
12:43 if his **m** finds him doing
12:45 may think that his **m** is taking
12:46 His **m** will return at an
12:46 Then his **m** will punish him
12:47 who knew what his **m** wanted
12:48 know ⌊what his **m** wanted⌋
14:21 back to report this to his **m**.
14:21 Then the **m** of the house
14:23 "Then the **m** told his servant,
16:3 My **m** is taking my job away
16:5 'How much do you owe my **m**?'
16:8 "The **m** praised the dishonest
16:13 He will hate the first **m** and
Jon 15:15 know what his **m** is doing.
15:20 isn't greater than his **m**.' If
Act 4:24 to God, "**M**, you made the sky,
Rom 6:16 you must obey that **m**?
6:16 Either your **m** is sin,
6:16 or your **m** is obedience.
6:16 Letting sin be your **m** leads to
6:16 Letting obedience be your **m**
Eph 6:7 were serving your heavenly **m**
6:8 You know that your heavenly **m**
6:9 You know that there is one **m**
Col 3:22 out of respect for your real **m**.
3:23 were working for your real **m**
3:24 You know that your real **m** will
3:24 It is Christ, your real **m**,
4:1 you also have a **m** in heaven.
Jud 1:4 and deny our only **M** and Lord,
Rev 6:10 a loud voice, "Holy and true **M**,

master's (32)

Gen 24:10 took ten of his **m** camels
24:10 him all of his **m** best things.
24:27 to the home of my **m** relatives.
24:36 My **m** wife Sarah gave him a
24:44 has chosen for my **m** son.
24:48 the daughter of my **m** relative
24:51 the wife of your **m** son, as
39:7 After a while his **m** wife began
40:7 in his **m** prison, "Why do you
44:8 or gold from your **m** house
1Sm 25:41 the feet of my **m** servants.
29:4 to try to regain his **m** favor?
2Sm 9:9 "I have given your **m** grandson
9:10 your **m** family will have food
9:10 However, your **m** grandson
2Ki 9:11 came out to his **m** officials.
10:2 "Your **m** heirs are with you,
10:3 most honest of your **m** heirs,
10:3 Fight for your **m** family.
10:6 bring the heads of your **m** heirs
18:24 **m** lowest-ranking officers when
Isa 22:18 a disgrace to your **m** household
36:9 **m** lowest-ranking officers when
Zep 1:9 and all who fill their **m** house
Mat 18:26 the servant fell at his **m** feet
25:18 and hid his **m** money
25:21 and share your **m** happiness.
25:23 and share your **m** happiness.
Luk 12:36 the door at their **m** knock when
16:5 for each one of his **m** debtors.
16:6 'Take my **m** ledger.
2Ti 2:21 apart for the **m** use, prepared

masters (22)

1Sm 25:10 nowadays are leaving their **m**.
Psa 123:2 As servants depend on their **m**,
Pro 25:13 He refreshes his **m**.
Isa 1:3 know where their **m** feed them.
24:2 male slaves and **m**,
24:2 female slaves and **m**,
Jer 13:21 were your friends your new **m**?
27:4 Give them an order for their **m**:
27:4 Say this to your **m**,
Mat 6:24 "No one can serve two **m**.
Luk 16:13 "A servant cannot serve two **m**.
Eph 6:5 Slaves, obey your earthly **m**
Eph 6:7 not merely serving human **m**.
Col 3:22 always obey your earthly **m**.
4:1 **M**, be just and fair to your
1Ti 6:1 respect to their own **m**.
6:2 Slaves whose **m** also believe
6:2 their **m** even though their
6:2 their **m** are also believers.
6:2 serve their **m** even better
Tit 2:9 Tell them to please their **m**,
2:10 tell slaves to show their **m** how

masters' (2)

Mat 15:27 that fall from their **m** tables.
Tit 2:9 under their **m** authority

match (3)

Eze 31:8 garden couldn't **m** its beauty.
Luk 5:36 from the new will not **m** the old.
Eph 6:12 This is not a wrestling **m**

matched (2)

Mat 2:16 This **m** the exact time he had
2Co 8:11 will be **m** by what you

mate (3)

Gen 30:41 they would **m** by the branches.
Isa 34:15 each one with its **m**.
34:16 Not one will lack a **m**,

mated (1)

Gen 30:39 they **m** in front of the branches.

material (8)

Exo 28:31 the ephod entirely of violet **m**.
36:7 The **m** they had was more than
38:21 This is the amount of **m** that
Lev 19:19 made from two kinds of **m**.
Num 4:6 cloth made entirely of violet **m**.
Luk 12:15 having a lot of **m** possessions."
12:21 treasures **m** possessions
12:33 "Sell your **m** possessions,

materials (6)

Gen 37:25 carrying the **m** for cosmetics,
1Ki 15:22 King Asa used the **m** to fortify
1Ch 22:5 ⌊the building **m**⌋ for him."
22:5 So David prepared many **m**
29:2 all my might I gathered ⌊the **m**⌋
2Ch 16:6 Asa used the **m** to fortify Geba

maternal (1)

Lev 18:13 She is your **m** aunt.

mates (2)

Isa 34:14 Male goats will call to their **m**.
Nah 2:12 It strangled ⌊the prey⌋ for its **m**.

mating (3)

Gen 31:10 "During the **m** season I had a
31:10 which were **m** were striped,
31:12 goats which are **m** are striped,

Matred (2)

Gen 36:39 daughter of **M** and
1Ch 1:50 daughter of **M** and

Matri (1)

1Sm 10:21 the family of **M** was chosen.

Mattan (3)

2Ki 11:18 and his statues and killed **M**,
2Ch 23:17 and his statues and killed **M**,
Jer 38:1 Shephatiah (son of **M**),

Mattanah (2)

Num 21:18 From the desert they went to **M**
21:19 and from **M** to Nahaliel,

Mattaniah (16)

2Ki 24:17 King Jehoiakin's Uncle **M** king
1Ch 9:15 Heresh, Galal, **M** (son of Mica,
25:4 **M**, Uzziel, Shebuel, Jerimoth,
25:16 The ninth chose **M**,
2Ch 20:14 whose father was **M**,
29:13 were Zechariah and **M**.
Ezr 10:26 **M**, Zechariah, Jehiel, Abdi,

Ezr 10:27 **M**, Jeremoth, Zabad, and Aziza
10:30 Maaseiah, **M**, Bezalel, Binnui,
10:37 **M**, Mattenai, Jaasau
Neh 11:17 **M** was the son of Mica,
11:22 who was the son of **M**,
12:8 Sherebiah, Judah, and **M**,
12:25 **M**, Bakbukiah, Obadiah,
12:35 who was the son of **M**,
13:13 of Zaccur and grandson of **M**

Mattaniah's (1)

2Ki 24:17 changed **M** name to Zedekiah.

Mattatha (1)

Luk 3:31 son of **M**, son of Nathan,

Mattathias (2)

Luk 3:25 son of **M**, son of Amos, son of
3:26 son of Maath, son of **M**,

Mattattah (1)

Ezr 10:33 **M**, Zabad, Eliphelet, Jeremai,

Mattenai (3)

Ezr 10:33 **M**, Mattattah, Zabad, Eliphelet,
10:37 Mattaniah, **M**, Jaasau
Neh 12:19 from Joiarib, **M**; from Jedaiah,

matter (71)

Gen 21:17 "What's the **m**, Hagar?"
41:32 the **m** has been definitely
Exo 7:23 the entire **m** from his mind.
19:13 No **m** whether it's an animal or
27:19 no **m** how they're used,
Lev 7:26 or animal no **m** where you live.
Num 22:18 LORD my God no **m** whether
24:13 command no **m** how good
Dtr 1:16 Judge each case fairly, no **m**
Jdg 6:29 they were investigating the **m**,
Rut 3:18 unless he settles this **m** today."
4:7 In order to make every **m** legal,
1Sm 2:17 of Eli's sons was a serious **m**
24:15 and take my side in ⌊this⌋ **m**
30:24 you have to say in this **m**?
2Sm 13:20 Don't dwell on this **m**."
14:8 to take care of this **m**."
14:20 has done this to portray the **m**
15:15 "No **m** what happens,
1Ki 2:14 Then he added, "I have a **m** ⌊to
15:5 in the **m** concerning Uriah
22:5 of the LORD is ⌊in this **m**⌋."
2Ki 6:28 asked her, "What's the **m**?"
9:18 "Why should that **m** to you?
9:19 "Why should that **m** to you?
1Ch 12:19 away after considering the **m**.
26:32 in every **m** involving God
2Ch 8:15 priests or the Levites in any **m**,
16:9 You acted foolishly in this **m**.
18:4 of the LORD is ⌊in this **m**⌋."
19:11 of you in every **m** involving
19:11 will be in charge of every **m**
25:8 no **m** how courageous you are,
31:16 genealogical records did not **m**.
34:22 prophet Huldah about this **m**.
Ezr 4:22 to neglect your duty in this **m**.
5:17 Majesty's decision on this **m**.
10:9 trembling because of this **m**
10:14 turned away from us in this **m**."
10:16 month to investigate the **m**.
Est 2:23 The **m** was written up in the
Job 9:19 If it is a **m** of strength,
Ecc 6:3 No **m** how long he would have
Isa 6:9 'No **m** how closely you listen,
6:9 No **m** how closely you look,
22:1 What's the **m** with you?
28:15 passes by, it won't **m** to us,
Dan 1:14 listened to them about this **m**
2:10 no **m** how great and powerful,
2:17 and Azariah about this **m**.
7:28 Here is the end of the **m**.
Mat 25:40 no **m** how unimportant ⌊they
25:45 no **m** how unimportant ⌊they
Act 4:15 the **m** among themselves.
19:39 you must settle the **m** in a legal
21:25 ⌊To clarify this **m**⌋ we have
Rom 2:1 No **m** who you are,
2:28 nor is circumcision a **m** of how
9:11 remain a **m** of his choice,
1Co 6:1 you go to court to settle the **m**
11:17 instruct you in the following **m**:
14:10 No **m** how many different
2Co 7:11 who are innocent in this **m**.
8:13 it's a **m** of striking a balance.
Gal 5:6 it doesn't **m** whether we are
6:15 Certainly, it doesn't **m** whether
Php 1:18 But what does it **m**?
4:12 No **m** what the situation,
2Pe 1:20 No prophecy in Scripture is a **m**
Rev 11:18 no **m** if they are important or
19:5 no **m** who you are."

matters (8)

2Sm 20:18 That's the way they settle **m**.'
Neh 11:24 on all **m** concerning the people.
Pro 24:7 **M** of wisdom are beyond the
1Co 11:34 the other **m** when I come.
2Co 11:28 Besides these external **m**,
Gal 5:6 But what **m** is a faith that
6:15 Rather, what **m** is being a new
Php 1:18 Nothing **m** except that,

Matthan (2)

Mat 1:15 Eleazar the father of **M**,
1:15 **M** the father of Jacob.

Matthat (2)

Luk 3:24 son of **M**, son of Levi, son of
3:29 of Jorim, son of **M**, son of Levi,

Matthew (6)

Mat 9:9 The man's name was **M**.
9:9 So **M** got up and followed him.
10:3 Thomas and **M** the tax
Mar 3:18 Bartholomew, **M**, Thomas,
Luk 6:15 **M**, Thomas, James (son of
Act 1:13 **M**, James (son of Alphaeus),

Matthew's (1)

Mat 9:10 was having dinner at **M** house.

Matthias (2)

Act 1:23 also known as Justus) and **M**.
1:26 **M** was chosen and joined the

Mattithiah (8)

1Ch 9:31 **M**, a Levite, the firstborn son of
15:18 **M**, Eliphelehu, and Mikneiah.
15:21 **M**, Eliphelehu, Mikneiah,
16:5 Jehiel, **M**, Eliab, Benaiah,
25:3 Shimei, Hashabiah, **M**.
25:21 The fourteenth chose **M**,
Ezr 10:43 **M**, Zabad, Zebina, Jaddai,
Neh 8:4 **M**, Shema, Anaiah, Uriah,

mattock (2)

1Sm 13:20 his plow, his **m**, ax, or sickle.
13:21 ounce of silver to sharpen a **m**

mattocks (1)

1Sm 13:21 a pim for plow blades and **m**,

mature (13)

1Ki 2:2 this world. Be strong and **m**.
Joe 1:4 **m** locusts will eat.
1:4 What **m** locusts leave,
2:25 for the years that the **m** locusts,
1Co 2:6 to speak to those who are **m**.
14:20 but think like **m** people.
Eph 4:13 until we become **m**,
Php 3:15 Whoever has a **m** faith should
Col 1:28 as **m** Christian people.
4:12 that you will continue to be **m**
Heb 5:14 solid food is for **m** people,
6:1 on to topics for more **m** people.
Jas 1:4 you will be **m** and complete,

matured (1)

Eze 16:7 You grew up, **m**, and became a

maturity (1)

Luk 2:52 Jesus grew in wisdom and **m**.

mayor (3)

2Ki 10:5 of the palace, the **m** of the city,
23:8 the gate named after the **m** of
2Ch 34:8 the **m** of the city, and Joah,

mayors (4)

Dan 3:2 **m**, military advisers, treasurers,
3:3 Then the satraps, governors, **m**,
3:27 king's satraps, governors, **m**,
6:7 and **m** agree that the king

meadow (1)

Psa 37:20 vanish like the best part of a **m**.

meadows (1)

Zep 2:6 become pastureland with **m**

meal (31)

Gen 25:29 was preparing a **m** when Esau,
25:34 Then Jacob gave Esau a **m** of
27:4 a good-tasting **m** for me,
27:7 and prepare a good-tasting **m**
27:9 them as a good-tasting **m**
27:14 She prepared a good-tasting **m**,
27:17 son Jacob the good-tasting **m**
27:31 prepared a good-tasting **m** and
31:54 relatives to eat the **m** with him.
43:16 an animal, and prepare a **m**,
Exo 12:43 may eat the Passover **m**.
12:46 "The **m** must be eaten inside
12:48 may ever eat the Passover **m**.
18:12 of Israel came to eat the **m**
1Sm 20:24 sat down to eat the festival **m**.
20:27 come to the **m** either yesterday
2Sm 12:4 sheep or cattle to prepare a **m**
13:5 She can prepare a **m** in front of
1Ki 13:15 and eat a **m**," the old prophet
Job 33:20 their appetite for a delicious **m**.
Ecc 10:19 A **m** is made for laughter,
Mat 8:15 So she got up and prepared a **m**
26:17 the Passover **m** for you?"
Mar 1:31 and she prepared a **m** for them.
14:12 the Passover **m** for you?"
14:14 **m** with my disciples?'
Luk 4:39 and prepared a **m** for them.
11:38 Jesus didn't wash before the **m**.
22:11 **m** with my disciples?'
22:14 time to eat the Passover **m**,
Heb 12:16 the firstborn son for a single **m**.

meals (5)

Exo 12:16 except to prepare your own **m**.
2Ki 25:29 and he ate his **m** in the king's
2Ch 30:22 They ate the festival **m** for
Jer 52:33 and he ate his **m** in the king's
Jud 1:12 at the special **m** you share

mean (65)

Gen 29:15 doesn't **m** that you should
40:8 no one to tell us what they **m**."
40:8 one who can tell what they **m**?"
50:15 their father's death could **m**.
Num 35:22 at him but didn't **m** to kill him.
Dtr 6:20 commanded you **m** to you?"
30:20 and it will **m** a long life for you
Jos 4:6 do these stones **m** to you?'
4:21 'What do these stones **m**?'
22:17 committed at Peor **m** nothing
1Sm 1:8 Don't I **m** more to you than ten
24:11 and be able to see I **m** no harm
25:3 but he was harsh and **m**.
2Sm 19:6 and servants **m** nothing
Psa 12:2 They say one thing but **m**
Pro 3:22 Then they will **m** life for you,
23:7 but he doesn't really **m** it.
Isa 1:11 animal sacrifices **m** to me?
Eze 18:2 "What do you **m** when you use
24:19 that you are doing **m** to us?"
37:18 'Tell us what you **m** by this.'
Zec 1:9 "What do these horses **m**,
1:9 "I will show you what they **m**."
1:19 "What do these horns **m**?"
4:4 "What do these things **m**,
4:5 "Don't you know what they **m**?"
4:11 the left of the lamp stand **m**?"

Zec 4:13 know what these things **m**?"
6:4 "What do these horses **m**,
Mat 23:16 by the temple doesn't **m** a thing.
23:18 by the altar doesn't **m** a thing.
24:6 but they don't **m** that the end
26:22 one, "You don't **m** me, do you,
26:25 "You don't **m** me, do you,
Mar 13:7 but they don't **m** that the end
14:19 one, "You don't **m** me, do you?"
Luk 20:17 does this Scripture verse **m**:
Jon 7:35 Does he **m** that he'll live with
7:36 What does he **m** when he says,
16:17 "What does he **m**?
16:18 "What does he **m** when he
Act 2:12 "What can this **m**?"
17:20 like to know what they **m**."
28:19 That doesn't **m** I have any
Rom 1:12 What I **m** is that we may be
1:29 They are **m**. They are filled with
11:7 So what does all this **m**?
11:15 does Israel's acceptance **m**?
1Co 1:12 This is what I **m**: Each of you
4:4 but that doesn't **m** I have God's
7:29 This is what I **m**, brothers and
10:19 Do I **m** that an offering made to
12:15 Would that **m** it's no longer part
12:16 Would that **m** it's no longer part
14:15 So what does this **m**?
14:26 So what does this **m**,
15:50 and sisters, this is what I **m**:
2Co 8:13 I don't **m** that others should
Gal 2:17 does that **m** that Christ
3:17 This is what I **m**: The laws
3:21 Does this **m**, then, that the
Eph 4:9 Now what does it **m** that he
Tit 3:3 We were **m** and jealous.
Jas 5:12 If you **m** yes, say yes. If you
5:12 If you **m** no, say no. Do this so

meaning (44)

Gen 21:29 "What is the **m** of these seven
40:5 dream with its own special **m**.
40:16 The chief baker saw that the **m**
41:11 Each dream had its own **m**.
2Sm 5:6 you away" (**m** that David could
Neh 8:8 and explained the **m** so that
Ecc 8:17 he will not find ⌊its **m**⌋.
Dan 2:5 tell me the dream and its **m**,
2:6 tell me the dream and its **m**,
2:6 tell me the dream and its **m**."
2:7 and we'll tell you its **m**."
2:9 you can explain its **m** to me."
2:16 could explain the dream's **m**.
2:24 explain the dream's **m** to him."
2:25 explain the dream's **m** to you,
2:26 me the dream I had and its **m**?"
2:30 so that you could be told the **m**
2:36 Now we'll tell you its **m**.
2:45 you can trust that this is its **m**."
4:6 to me to tell me the dream's **m**.
4:7 but they couldn't tell me its **m**.
4:9 Tell me the **m** of the visions I
4:18 tell me its **m** because the wise
4:19 dream and its **m** frighten you."
4:19 you and its **m** were about your
4:24 "This is the **m**, Your Majesty.
5:7 writing and tells me its **m** will
5:8 the writing or tell the king its **m**.
5:15 this writing and tell me its **m**.
5:15 But they couldn't tell me its **m**.
5:16 the writing and tell ⌊me⌋ its **m**,
5:17 for you and tell you its **m**.
5:26 This is its **m**: Numbered — God
Zec 4:12 "What is the **m** of the two
Mat 7:12 That is ⌊the **m** of⌋ Moses'
Luk 9:45 The **m** was hidden from them
24:32 the road and opened up the **m**
Act 10:17 Peter was puzzled by the **m**
13:8 them and tried to distort the **m**
1Co 1:17 the cross of Christ lose its **m**.
14:10 not one of them is without **m**.
15:14 our message has no **m** and
15:14 and your faith also has no **m**.
Rev 1:20 The hidden **m** of the seven

meaningless (3)

1Co 9:15 turn my bragging into **m** words.
Eph 5:6 deceive you with **m** words.
1Th 3:5 making our work **m**.

means (67)

Gen 40:12 "This is what it **m**," Joseph
40:18 is what it **m**," Joseph replied.
41:15 no one can tell me what it **m**.
41:15 you can say what it **m**."
Exo 12:26 what this ceremony **m** to you,
13:14 children ask you what this **m**,
28:30 carrying over his heart the ⌊**m**
Lev 17:5 ⌊This **m**⌋ that the people of
21:18 That **m** anyone who is blind or
Num 14:34 your sins and know what it **m**
30:14 this **m** he's decided that she
1Sm 6:3 but by all **m** return it to its
Est 3:7 Pur (which **m** the lot) was
9:24 Haman had the Pur (which **m**
Pro 29:4 By **m** of justice, a king builds
Jer 22:16 Isn't this what it **m** to know
Eze 17:12 you know what this **m**?' Tell
Dan 2:41 This **m** that there will be a
5:12 he will tell ⌊you⌋ what it **m**."
Mat 1:23 which **m** "God is with us."
2:6 you are by no **m** least among
9:13 Learn what this **m**:
12:7 'I want mercy, not sacrifices' **m**,
13:18 the story about the farmer **m**.
13:36 of the weeds in the field **m**."
23:16 by the gold in the temple **m**
23:18 oath by the gift on the altar **m**
27:33 Golgotha (which **m** "the place
27:46 which **m**, "My God, my God,
Mar 3:17 which **m** "Thunderbolts"),
5:41 which **m**, "Little girl, I'm telling
7:34 which **m**, "Be opened!"
15:22 Golgotha (which **m** "the place
15:34 which **m**, "My God, my God,
Jon 1:38 "Rabbi" (which **m** "teacher"),
1:41 Messiah" (which **m** "Christ").
1:42 be Cephas" (which **m** "Peter").
8:22 Is that what he **m** when he
9:7 (Siloam **m** "sent.") The blind
20:16 (This word **m** "teacher.")
Act 1:19 which **m** 'Field of Blood' in
4:36 which **m** "a person who
13:8 whose name **m** astrologer,
24:14 This **m** that I serve our
Rom 9:8 This **m** that children born by
11:7 It **m** that Israel has never
11:15 If Israel's rejection **m** that the
11:15 It **m** that Israel has come back
1Co 4:3 It **m** very little to me that you or
14:11 don't know what a language **m**,
14:15 It **m** that I will pray with my
2Co 2:14 us to make clear what it **m**
5:11 As people who know what it **m**
Eph 5:5 or greed (which **m** worshiping
Php 1:21 Christ **m** everything to me in
3:9 This **m** that I didn't receive
3:10 back to life gives and what it **m**
Col 1:6 what God's kindness truly **m**.
1:14 which **m** that our sins are
Heb 7:2 Melchizedek's name **m** king of
7:2 Salem (which **m** king of peace).
11:3 This **m** what can be seen was
Jas 4:5 think this passage **m** nothing?
1Jn 3:16 That **m** we must give our lives
5:3 To love God **m** that we obey
2Jn 1:6 Love **m** that we live by doing
Jud 1:4 to whom God **m** nothing.

meant (27)

Gen 41:8 one could tell him what they **m**.
41:12 he told each of us what they **m**.
41:24 no one could tell me what it **m**."
2Sm 18:29 but I didn't know what it **m**."
Dan 2:5 astrologers, "I **m** what I said!
2:8 you know that I **m** what I said.
7:16 So he told me what all this **m**.
Mar 8:32 them very clearly what he **m**.
9:10 what he **m** by "come back
9:32 didn't understand what he **m**
Luk 1:29 figure out what this greeting **m**.
2:50 didn't understand what he **m**.
8:9 asked him what this story **m**.
9:45 They didn't know what he **m**.
18:34 they didn't know what he **m**.
Jon 6:71 Jesus **m** Judas, son of Simon
10:6 didn't understand what he **m**.
11:13 Jesus **m** that Lazarus was
11:13 Jesus **m** that Lazarus was
12:16 what these prophecies **m**.
13:22 which one of them Jesus **m**.
16:19 yourselves what I **m** when
20:9 yet what Scripture **m** when
Act 2:25 This is what David **m** when he
1Co 5:11 Now, what I **m** was that you
7:6 What I have just said is not **m**
Heb 9:10 gifts and sacrifices were **m**

Mearah (1)

Jos 13:4 as well as **M** which belongs

measure (25)

Gen 41:49 because he couldn't **m** it all.
Exo 16:36 (Now, the standard dry **m** at
Num 35:5 Outside the city **m** off 3,000
Dtr 21:2 and judges must go and **m**
2Ki 21:13 I will **m** Jerusalem with the
Psa 60:6 I will **m** the valley of Succoth.
108:7 I will **m** the valley of Succoth.
Isa 44:13 Carpenters **m** blocks of wood
61:7 You will receive a double **m** of
61:7 why you will have a double **m**
Eze 4:11 **M** out two-thirds of a quart of
31:8 The plane trees couldn't **m** up
40:3 was holding a linen tape **m**
45:3 **M** off an area 43,750 feet long
45:11 homer must be the standard **m**.
45:14 olive oil using the standard **m**.
48:35 The city will **m** about 31,500
Hos 1:10 No one will be able to **m** them
Zec 2:2 He answered, "I am going to **m**
Mar 4:24 you by the **m** ⌊of attention⌋ you
2Co 10:12 Certainly, when they **m**
Eph 4:13 until we **m** up to Christ,
Rev 11:1 I was told, "Stand up and **m** the
11:2 But do not **m** the temple
21:15 measuring stick to **m** the city,

measured (47)

Exo 16:18 They **m** it into two-quart
Rut 3:15 So she held it tight while he **m**
2Sm 8:2 and **m** them with a rope.
8:2 He **m** two lengths which were
Job 28:25 gave the wind its force and **m**
Isa 40:12 Who has **m** the water of the
40:12 with the palm of his hand or **m**
Jer 31:37 Only if the heavens could be **m**
33:22 the seashore that cannot be **m**."
Eze 40:5 He **m** the wall. It was 10 ½ feet
40:6 He went up its steps and **m** the
40:8 He also **m** the entrance hall of
40:11 Then the man **m** the width of
40:13 He **m** the gateway from the top
40:14 He also **m** the entrance hall.
40:19 The man **m** the distance from
40:20 Then the man **m** the length and
40:23 The man **m** the distance from
40:24 He **m** its recessed walls and
40:27 The man **m** the distance from
40:28 He **m** the south gateway.
40:32 He **m** the gateway.
40:35 He **m** it. It was the same size as
40:47 The man **m** the courtyard.
40:48 and **m** its recessed walls.
41:1 holy place in the temple and **m**
41:2 Then he **m** the length of the
41:3 inside and **m** the passageway.
41:4 Then he **m** the room at the end
41:5 the man **m** the temple wall.
41:8 It **m** the full length of the
41:13 Then the man **m** the temple.
41:15 He also **m** the length of the
42:15 Then he **m** all the way around
42:16 He **m** the east side with a
42:17 He **m** the north side.
42:18 He **m** the south side.

Eze 42:19 to the west side and **m** it.
42:20 So he **m** all four sides.
47:3 He **m** off a third of a mile and
47:4 Then he **m** off another third of a
47:4 He **m** off another third of a mile
47:5 Then he **m** another third of a
Mar 4:24 ⌊Knowledge⌋ will be **m** out to
Eph 4:7 It was **m** out to us by Christ
Rev 21:16 He **m** the city with the stick.
21:17 He **m** its wall. According to

measurement (2)

2Ch 3:3 (They used the old standard **m**.)
Rev 21:17 According to human **m**,

measurements (4)

1Ki 6:25 Both had the same **m** and the
Eze 43:13 These are the **m** of the altar,
43:13 of the altar, using royal **m**.
48:16 These will be the **m** for the city:

measures (15)

Gen 18:6 "get three **m** of flour,
Lev 19:36 honest weights, and honest **m**.
Dtr 25:14 Never have two kinds of **m** in
25:15 and honest weights and **m**.
25:16 weights and **m** is disgusting
Rut 3:15 measured out six **m** of barley.
3:17 "He gave me these six **m** of
1Ch 23:29 track of all weights and **m**.
Ezr 7:22 of silver, 100 **m** of wheat,
Pro 20:10 of weights and **m** — both are
Eze 45:10 and honest dry and liquid **m**.
45:11 The dry and liquid **m** must
Mic 6:10 use inaccurate weights and **m**.
Hag 2:16 to a pile of grain ⌊to get⌋ 20 **m**,
2:16 to a wine vat to draw out 50 **m**,

measuring (23)

Lev 19:35 length, weight, or **m** liquid.
2Ki 21:13 Jerusalem with the **m** line used
Job 38:5 Who stretched a **m** line over it?
Isa 28:17 I will make justice a **m** line and
34:11 He will stretch the **m** line of
34:17 ⌊land⌋ for them with a **m** line.
Jer 31:39 A **m** line will stretch from there
Eze 40:3 tape measure and a **m** stick,
40:5 The man had a **m** stick that
41:8 the full length of the **m** rod,
42:15 When the man had finished **m**
42:16 the east side with a **m** stick.
42:16 long according to the **m** stick.
42:17 long according to the **m** stick.
42:18 long according to the **m** stick.
42:19 long according to the **m** stick.
43:13 (The royal **m** stick was 21
43:13 was a rim **m** 9 inches wide.
47:3 With a **m** line in his hand,
Zec 1:16 A **m** line will be used to rebuild
2:1 and saw a man with a **m** line
Rev 11:1 given a stick like a **m** stick.
21:15 to me had a gold **m** stick

meat (114)

Gen 9:4 "But you are not to eat **m** with
18:8 and milk, as well as the **m**,
25:28 Isaac liked to eat the **m**
27:19 Sit up and eat this **m** I've
27:31 eat some of the **m** I've hunted
Exo 12:8 The **m** must be eaten that
12:46 Never take any of the **m**
16:3 There we sat by our pots of **m**
16:8 "The LORD will give you **m** to
16:12 'At dusk you will eat **m**,
21:28 and its **m** may not be eaten.
22:31 Never eat the **m** of an animal
29:14 But burn the bull's **m**,
29:31 and boil its **m** in a holy place.
29:32 and his sons will eat the **m**
29:34 If any **m** or bread from the
34:15 eat the **m** from their sacrifices
Lev 4:11 **m**, head, legs, internal organs,
6:27 Anything that touches its **m**
7:15 "The **m** from your fellowship
7:17 third day any **m** left over from
Lev 7:18 not be accepted if any **m** from
7:19 "**M** that touches anything
7:20 Those who eat **m** from the
8:17 the rest of the bull, its skin, **m**,
8:31 "Cook the **m** at the entrance to
8:31 Take the **m** and the bread in
8:32 You must burn any **m** or bread
9:11 He burned the **m** and the skin
11:8 Never eat the **m** of these
11:11 Never eat their **m**. Consider
16:27 The skin, **m**, and excrement
19:26 "Never eat any **m** with blood
22:8 He must never eat the **m** of an
Num 9:12 any of the **m** until morning
11:4 "If only we had **m** to eat!
11:13 Where can I get **m** for all these
11:13 for me to give them **m** to eat.
11:18 Then they will eat **m**.
11:18 'If only we had **m** to eat!
11:18 So I will give them **m**.
11:21 you say, 'I will give them **m**
11:33 While the **m** was still in their
11:34 of Those Who Craved ⌊**M**⌋
11:34 had a strong craving ⌊for **m**⌋.
18:18 But the **m** is yours,
19:5 entire cow (the skin, **m**, blood,
22:40 and sent some of the **m** to
25:2 The people ate the **m** from the
Dtr 12:15 eat as much **m** as you want
12:20 will say, "I'm hungry for **m**."
12:20 eat as much **m** as you want.
12:23 Never eat the life with the **m**.
12:27 Sacrifice the **m** and the blood
12:27 but you may eat the **m**.
14:8 Never eat their **m** or touch their
16:3 with the **m** from this sacrifice.
16:4 any of the **m** you slaughter
16:7 Cook the **m**, and eat it at the
28:31 but you won't eat any of its **m**.
Jdg 6:19 He put the **m** in a basket and
6:20 "Take the **m** and the
6:21 of the LORD touched the **m**
6:21 from the rock and burned the **m**
1Sm 2:13 While the **m** was boiling,
2:15 "Give the **m** to the priest to
2:15 doesn't want boiled **m** from you.
9:23 portion of the sacrificial **m** that
14:32 The troops ate the **m** with
14:33 against the LORD by eating **m**
14:34 against the LORD by eating **m**
25:11 and my **m** that I butchered for
1Ki 17:6 brought him bread and **m**
19:21 He boiled the **m**, using the
19:21 He gave the **m** to the people to
2Ch 4:6 The priests rinsed the **m**
Psa 50:13 Do I eat the **m** of bulls or drink
78:20 us, his people, with **m**?"
78:27 He rained **m** down on them like
Pro 7:14 "I have some sacrificial **m**.
9:2 She has prepared her **m**.
23:20 those who eat too much **m**,
Isa 22:13 You will eat **m**, drink wine,
44:16 Over this half they roast **m** that
44:19 I roasted **m** and ate it.
Jer 7:21 your sacrifices, and eat the **m**.
11:15 Can the **m** from their sacrifices
Eze 4:14 No unclean **m** has ever entered
11:3 a cooking pot, and we're the **m**.'
11:7 the middle of the city are the **m**,
11:11 and you will not be the **m** in it.
24:4 Cut the **m** into pieces,
24:6 Empty the **m** out of it piece by
24:10 Cook the **m** thoroughly,
33:25 You eat **m** with blood in it.
39:17 You can eat **m** and drink blood
39:18 You can eat the **m** of warriors
39:19 You can eat the best **m** until
40:43 were for the **m** of the animals.
46:20 the priests must boil the **m**
Dan 7:5 eat as much **m** as you want."
10:3 No **m** or wine entered my
Hos 8:13 me and eat the **m** of sacrifices,
Mic 3:3 You chop them up like **m** for a
3:3 like stew **m** for a kettle.
Hag 2:12 Suppose a person carries **m**
Zec 11:16 But he will eat the **m** of the fat
Act 15:20 from eating the **m** of strangled
15:20 and from eating bloody **m**.
15:29 from eating bloody **m**,
15:29 from eating the **m** of strangled
21:25 to false gods, bloody **m**,
21:25 or the **m** of strangled animals.
Rom 14:21 thing to do is to avoid eating **m**,

meatiest (1)

Eze 24:4 Fill the pot with the **m** bones

Mebunnai (1)

2Sm 23:27 **M** (son of Hushai),

Mecherathite (1)

1Ch 11:36 Hepher the **M**, Ahijah the

Meconah (1)

Neh 11:28 and in **M** and its villages,

Medad (2)

Num 11:26 Two men, named Eldad and **M**,
11:27 "Eldad and **M** are prophesying

medallion (4)

Exo 28:36 "Make a flower-shaped **m** out
28:38 The **m** must always be on
39:30 **m** (the holy crown)
Lev 8:9 the gold **m** (the holy crown)

Medan (2)

Gen 25:2 **M**, Midian, Ishbak, and Shuah.
1Ch 1:32 **M**, Midian, Ishbak, and Shuah.

Mede (2)

Dan 5:31 Darius the **M** took over the
9:1 who was a **M** by birth,

Medeba (5)

Num 21:30 between Nophah and **M**."
Jos 13:9 whole plateau from **M** to Dibon.
13:16 and the whole plateau near **M**.
1Ch 19:7 They camped near **M**.
Isa 15:2 Moab wails over Nebo and **M**.

Mede's (1)

Dan 11:1 During Darius the **M** first year

Medes (14)

2Ki 17:6 and in the cities of the **M**.
18:11 and in the cities of the **M**.
Est 1:3 officers of the Persians and **M**,
1:14 the Persians and **M** had access
1:19 decrees of the Persians and **M**,
10:2 kings of the **M** and Persians.
Isa 13:17 to stir up the **M** against them.
Jer 51:11 the spirit of the kings of the **M**
51:28 Prepare the king of the **M**,
Dan 5:28 given to the **M** and Persians."
6:8 According to the law of the **M**
6:12 According to the law of the **M**
6:15 the **M** and Persians have a law
Act 2:9 We're Parthians, **M**,

Media (5)

Ezr 6:2 which is in the province of **M**.
Est 1:18 Persia and **M** who have heard
Isa 21:2 Surround them, **M**!
Jer 25:25 and all the kings of **M**;
Dan 8:20 the kingdoms of **M** and Persia.

mediator (4)

Job 9:33 There is no **m** between us to
Gal 3:19 through angels, using a **m**.
3:20 A **m** is not used when there is
1Ti 2:5 There is also one **m** between

medical (1)

Exo 21:19 and for all his **m** expenses.

medicine (6)

Gen 37:25 cosmetics, **m**, and embalming.
Pro 17:22 A joyful heart is good **m**,
Jer 8:22 Isn't there **m** in Gilead?
30:13 No **m** will heal you.
46:11 Go to Gilead, and get **m**,

Jer 51:8 Bring **m** for its pain.

medicines (1)

Jer 46:11 used many **m** without results;

meditate (3)

Gen 24:63 went out into the field to **m**.
1Ch 16:9 **M** on all the miracles he has
Psa 105:2 **M** on all the miracles he has

Mediterranean (35)

Exo 23:31 from the Red Sea to the **M** Sea
Num 13:29 along the coast of the **M** Sea
34:5 the border ends at the **M** Sea.
34:6 is the coastline of the **M** Sea.
34:7 border extends from the **M** Sea
Dtr 1:7 on the whole **M** coast (the land
11:24 Euphrates River to the **M** Sea.
34:2 of Judah as far as the **M** Sea,
Jos 1:4 and the **M** Sea on the west.
5:1 along the **M** Sea heard that
9:2 and along the whole **M** coast
15:4 the border ends at the **M** Sea.
15:11 The border ends at the **M** Sea.
15:12 is the coastline of the **M** Sea.
15:46 between Ekron and the **M** Sea
15:47 and the coast of the **M** Sea.
16:3 and ends at the **M** Sea.
16:8 River and ends at the **M** Sea.
17:9 which ends at the **M** Sea.
17:10 So the **M** Sea ⌊is its western
19:29 Hosah and ends at the **M** Sea.
23:4 River westward to the **M** Sea.
Psa 80:11 with its branches to the **M** Sea.
Isa 23:3 The grain of Shihor is on the **M**.
Eze 26:19 and the **M** Sea will cover you.
45:7 land will extend to the **M** Sea.
47:10 there as there are in the **M** Sea.
47:15 will run from the **M** Sea all
47:17 border will run from the **M** Sea
47:19 along the ravine to the **M** Sea.
47:20 On the west side the **M** Sea is
48:28 Brook of Egypt to the **M** Sea.
Dan 7:2 of heaven stirring up the **M** Sea.
Zec 14:8 and the other half to the **M** Sea.
Act 27:27 still drifting through the **M** Sea.

medium (2)

Lev 20:27 man or woman who is a **m**
1Ch 10:13 He asked a **m** to request

mediums (11)

Lev 19:31 "Don't turn to psychics or **m** to
20:6 condemn people who turn to **m**
1Sm 28:3 rid the land of **m** and psychics.)
28:9 rid the land of **m** and psychics.
2Ki 21:6 ⌊royal⌋ **m** and psychics.
23:24 Josiah also got rid of the **m**,
2Ch 33:6 ⌊royal⌋ **m** and psychics.
Isa 8:19 "Ask for help from the **m** and
19:3 ghosts, **m**, and fortunetellers.
Jer 27:9 Don't listen to prophets, **m**,
29:8 Don't let the prophets or the **m**

meet (119)

Gen 14:17 of Sodom came out to **m** him
18:2 he saw them, he ran to **m** them,
19:1 he got up to **m** them and bowed
24:17 The servant ran to **m** her and
24:65 through the field to **m** us?"
29:13 son Jacob, he ran to **m** him.
30:16 Leah went out to **m** him.
32:6 He is coming to **m** you with
33:4 Then Esau ran to **m** Jacob.
46:29 and went to **m** his father Israel.
Exo 4:14 already on his way to **m** you,
4:27 the LORD had told Aaron to **m**
7:15 In the morning **m** Pharaoh
18:7 went out to **m** his father-in-law.
19:17 out of the camp to **m** with God,
23:27 throw any nation you **m** into
25:22 the angels whenever I **m**
29:42 There I will **m** with you to
29:43 I will also **m** with the Israelites
30:6 I will **m** with you there in front
30:36 where I will **m** with you.
Num 10:3 the whole community will **m**
10:4 of Israel, will **m** with you.
14:35 They will **m** their end in this
17:4 of meeting where I **m** with you,
22:36 he went out to **m** him at Ir
23:3 will come and **m** with me.
23:15 your burnt offering while I **m**
31:13 outside the camp to **m** them.
Dtr 2:32 all his troops came out to **m**
Jos 8:14 toward the plains to **m** Israel
9:11 for the trip, and go **m** them.
9:12 we left home to **m** with you.
Jdg 6:35 and they went to **m** the enemy
11:31 of my house to **m** me when
11:34 daughter coming out to **m** him.
20:25 out from Gibeah to **m** them.
1Sm 4:2 their troops to **m** Israel
10:5 you will **m** a group of prophets
10:10 of prophets came to **m** him,
13:15 followed Saul to **m** the soldiers.
15:12 morning he got up to **m** Saul.
18:6 cities came to **m** King Saul.
21:1 as he went to **m** David.
25:32 who sent you today to **m** me.
25:34 hadn't come to **m** me quickly,
30:21 They came to **m** David and the
2Sm 6:20 Michal came out to **m** him.
10:5 he sent ⌊someone⌋ to **m** them
15:32 family was there to **m** him.
19:15 of Judah came to Gilgal to **m**
19:16 of Judah to **m** King David.
19:20 the house of Joseph to **m** you."
19:24 went to **m** the king.
19:25 from Jerusalem to **m** the king,
1Ki 2:8 But when he came to **m** me at
2:19 The king got up to **m** her and
18:16 Ahab went to **m** Elijah.
20:27 they went to **m** the enemy.
21:18 "Go, **m** King Ahab of Israel,
2Ki 1:3 "**M** the messengers of the king
1:6 him that a man came to **m** them
2:15 Then they went to **m** him and
4:26 Run to **m** her and ask her how
4:29 Whenever you **m** anyone,
4:31 So Gehazi came back to **m** the
8:8 and **m** the man of God.
8:9 Hazael went to **m** Elisha.
9:17 send him to **m** them,
9:21 of Judah went to **m** Jehu,
10:15 who was coming to **m** him.
16:10 to **m** King Tiglath Pileser
1Ch 12:17 David went to **m** them.
14:8 it and went out to **m** them.
19:5 he sent ⌊someone⌋ to **m** them
2Ch 22:7 He went with Joram to **m** Jehu,
28:9 He went to **m** the army coming
Ezr 10:14 a foreign woman must **m**
Neh 6:2 "Let's **m** in Hakkephirim on the
6:3 while I leave to **m** with you?"
6:10 "Let's **m** in the house of God,
Job 5:14 In the daytime they **m**
Psa 49:10 foolish and stupid people **m**
59:10 God will come to **m** me.
Pro 7:15 That's why I came to **m** you.
8:2 wayside where the roads **m**,
17:12 Better to **m** a bear robbed of its
Isa 7:3 son Shear Jashub to **m** Ahaz at
14:9 Sheol below wakes up to **m**
34:14 Hyenas will **m** with jackals.
Jer 41:6 left Mizpah to **m** them,
51:31 Runners run to **m** runners.
Dan 4:36 and nobles wanted to **m**
Amo 4:12 Prepare to **m** your God.
Zec 2:3 Another angel came out to **m**
Mal 3:14 What do we gain if we **m** his
Mat 8:34 from the city went to **m** Jesus.
25:1 and went to **m** the groom.
25:6 groom is here! Come to **m** him!'
Mar 14:13 You will **m** a man carrying a
Luk 8:19 But they couldn't **m** with him
22:10 and you will **m** a man carrying
Jon 4:29 "Come with me, and **m** a man
4:30 the city and went to **m** Jesus.
11:20 she went to **m** him.
12:13 branches and went to **m** him.
12:18 they came to **m** him.
Jon 12:21 we would like to **m** Jesus."
18:4 So he went to **m** them and
Act 12:20 were going to **m** with Herod.
20:17 leaders of the church to **m**
22:30 the entire Jewish council to **m**.
28:15 and Three Taverns to **m** us.
28:17 Jews in Rome to **m** with him.
Rom 8:4 are able to **m** God's standards.
1Th 4:17 will be taken in the clouds to **m**
2Th 2:1 and our gathering to **m** him.
Heb 4:12 place where soul and spirit **m**,
4:12 where joints and marrow **m**.

meeting (175)

Gen 4:15 that anyone **m** him would not
Exo 27:21 In the tent of **m** outside the
28:43 when they go into the tent of **m**
29:4 to the entrance of the tent of **m**,
29:10 bull to the front of the tent of **m**.
29:11 at the entrance to the tent of **m**.
29:30 one who goes into the tent of **m**
29:32 At the entrance to the tent of **m**,
29:42 at the entrance to the tent of **m**.
29:44 I will dedicate the tent of **m**
30:16 the expenses of the tent of **m**.
30:18 Put it between the tent of **m**
30:20 they go into the tent of **m**,
30:26 "Use it to anoint the tent of **m**,
30:36 of my promise in the tent of **m**,
31:7 the tent of **m**, the ark containing
33:7 He called it the tent of **m**.
33:7 the camp to the tent of **m**.
35:21 used to construct the tent of **m**,
38:8 at the entrance to the tent of **m**.
38:30 for the entrance to the tent of **m**,
39:32 (the tent of **m**) was now done.
39:40 of the inner tent (the tent of **m**)
40:2 "Set up the tent (the tent of **m**)
40:6 of the entrance to the tent of **m**.
40:7 the basin between the tent of **m**
40:12 to the entrance of the tent of **m**,
40:22 put the table in the tent of **m**
40:24 stand in the tent of **m** opposite
40:26 the gold altar in the tent of **m**
40:29 to the tent (the tent of **m**).
40:30 the basin between the tent of **m**
40:32 they went into the tent of **m**
40:34 smoke covered the tent of **m**,
40:35 couldn't go into the tent of **m**,
Lev 1:1 spoke to him from the tent of **m**.
1:3 entrance to the tent of **m** so that
1:5 at the entrance to the tent of **m**.
3:2 at the entrance to the tent of **m**.
3:8 it in front of the tent of **m**.
3:13 it in front of the tent of **m**.
4:4 at the entrance to the tent of **m**.
4:5 and bring it into the tent of **m**.
4:7 presence in the tent of **m**.
4:7 at the entrance to the tent of **m**.
4:14 bring it in front of the tent of **m**.
4:16 bull's blood into the tent of **m**.
4:18 presence in the tent of **m**.
4:18 at the entrance to the tent of **m**.
6:16 in the courtyard of the tent of **m**
6:26 in the courtyard of the tent of **m**
6:30 the holy place in the tent of **m**
8:3 at the entrance to the tent of **m**."
8:4 at the entrance to the tent of **m**.
8:31 at the entrance to the tent of **m**.
8:33 the entrance to the tent of **m**
8:35 entrance to the tent of **m** day
9:5 them in front of the tent of **m**.
9:23 Aaron went into the tent of **m**.
10:7 the entrance to the tent of **m**
10:9 when you go into the tent of **m**,
12:6 at the entrance to the tent of **m**.
14:11 at the entrance to the tent of **m**.
14:23 at the entrance to the tent of **m**
15:14 at the entrance to the tent of **m**.
15:29 at the entrance to the tent of **m**.
16:7 at the entrance to the tent of **m**.
16:16 the tent of **m** which is among
16:17 No one may be in the tent of **m**
16:20 the tent of **m**, and the altar,
16:23 Aaron will go to the tent of **m**,
16:33 the tent of **m**, and the altar.

Lev 17:4 to the entrance of the tent of **m**.
17:5 at the entrance to the tent of **m**.
17:6 at the entrance to the tent of **m**.
17:9 to the entrance of the tent of **m**
19:21 at the entrance to the tent of **m**.
24:3 In the tent of **m**, outside the
Num 1:1 spoke to Moses in the tent of **m**
2:2 their tents around the tent of **m**,
2:17 "When the tent of **m** is moved,
3:7 in front of the tent of **m**,
3:8 the furnishings in the tent of **m**
3:23 west side behind the tent of **m**.
3:25 At the tent of **m** the
3:25 for the entrance to the tent of **m**,
3:29 the south side of the tent of **m**.
3:35 the north side of the tent of **m**.
3:38 side in front of the tent of **m**.
4:3 to work at the tent of **m**.
4:4 will do in the tent of **m**:
4:15 all the things from the tent of **m**.
4:23 to serve at the tent of **m**.
4:25 the inner tent and the tent of **m**.
4:25 the inner cover for the tent of **m**,
4:25 for the entrance to the tent of **m**,
4:28 families in the tent of **m**.
4:30 to serve at the tent of **m**.
4:31 as they work at the tent of **m**:
4:33 as they work at the tent of **m**.
4:35 to work at the tent of **m**.
4:37 who served at the tent of **m**.
4:39 at the tent of **m** were registered.
4:41 who worked at the tent of **m**.
4:43 at the tent of **m** were registered.
4:47 and who carried the tent of **m**.
6:10 at the entrance to the tent of **m**.
6:13 to the entrance of the tent of **m**.
6:18 at the entrance to the tent of **m**,
7:5 the work done for the tent of **m**.
7:89 Moses went into the tent of **m**
8:9 to the front of the tent of **m**,
8:15 do their work at the tent of **m**.
8:19 the Israelites at the tent of **m**.
8:22 did their work at the tent of **m**
8:24 to serve at the tent of **m**.
8:26 in their duties at the tent of **m**,
10:3 at the entrance to the tent of **m**.
10:17 Then the tent ⌊of **m**⌋ was
10:21 the tent ⌊of **m**⌋ would already
11:16 Take them to the tent of **m**,
12:4 of you come to the tent of **m**."
14:10 ⌊shining⌋ at the tent of **m**.
16:18 at the entrance to the tent of **m**.
16:19 at the entrance to the tent of **m**,
16:42 turned toward the tent of **m**,
16:43 to the front of the tent of **m**.
16:50 at the entrance to the tent of **m**,
17:4 Put them in the tent of **m** where
18:4 is necessary for the tent of **m**,
18:6 is necessary at the tent of **m**.
18:21 work they do at the tent of **m**.
18:22 again come near the tent of **m**.
18:23 do the work at the tent of **m**.
18:31 for your work at the tent of **m**.
19:4 toward the front of the tent of **m**.
20:6 to the entrance of the tent of **m**.
25:6 at the entrance to the tent of **m**.
27:2 at the entrance to the tent of **m**.
31:54 presence at the tent of **m** as
Dtr 31:14 of you come to the tent of **m**,
31:14 Joshua came to the tent of **m**.
Jos 7:14 by tribes ⌊to the tent of **m**⌋.
18:1 and set up the tent of **m** there.
19:51 at the entrance of the tent of **m**.
1Sm 2:22 at the gate of the tent of **m**.
2Sm 7:6 in a tent, the tent ⌊of **m**⌋.
1Ki 1:50 went ⌊to the tent of **m**,⌋ and
8:4 brought the ark, the tent of **m**,
2Ki 4:38 the prophets were **m** with him,
1Ch 6:32 the tent of **m** until Solomon built
9:21 at the entrance to the tent of **m**.
17:5 moving the tent ⌊of **m**⌋ from
23:32 the regulations for the tent of **m**
28:1 David held a **m** in Jerusalem
2Ch 1:3 God's tent of **m** was there.
1:6 altar in front of the tent of **m**
1:13 went from the tent of **m** at
2Ch 5:5 brought the ark, the tent of **m**,
Neh 5:7 I arranged for a large **m** to deal
Job 15:8 listen in on God's council **m**
Psa 74:4 roared inside your **m** place.
74:8 They burned every **m** place of
Lam 5:14 leaders have stopped **m** at
Joe 2:16 Prepare them for a holy **m**.
Amo 3:3 walk together without **m** first?
Jon 11:47 and the Pharisees called a **m**
Act 1:4 while he was **m** with them,
2:44 the believers kept **m** together,
4:31 their **m** place shook.
13:43 When the **m** of the synagogue
19:25 He called a **m** of his workers
20:8 room where we were **m**.)
23:7 the men in the **m** were divided.
Gal 2:2 I did this in a private **m** with

meetings (1)

Gen 49:6 not let me attend their secret **m**.

meets (7)

Gen 32:17 "When my brother Esau **m** you
Job 26:10 boundary where light **m** dark.
Pro 7:10 with an ulterior motive **m** him.
Rom 16:5 Also greet the church that **m** in
1Co 16:19 Prisca and the church that **m**
Col 4:15 the church that **m** in her house.
Phm 1:2 church that **m** in your house.

Megiddo (12)

Jos 12:21 king of Taanach, the king of **M**,
17:11 and **M** and their villages.
Jdg 1:27 and **M** or their villages.
5:19 at Taanach by the waters of **M**.
1Ki 4:12 **M**, and all of Beth Shean.
9:15 cities of⌋ Hazor, **M**, and Gezer.
2Ki 9:27 to flee until he got to **M**,
23:29 When Pharaoh saw him at **M**,
23:30 brought it from **M** to Jerusalem.
1Ch 7:29 **M** and its villages,
2Ch 35:22 went to fight in the valley of **M**.
Zec 12:11 Rimmon in the plain of **M**.

Meheleb (1)

Jos 19:29 The territory includes **M**,

Mehetabel (3)

Gen 36:39 His wife's name was **M**,
1Ch 1:50 His wife's name was **M**,
Neh 6:10 of Delaiah and grandson of **M**.

Mehida (2)

Ezr 2:52 Bazluth, **M**, Harsha,
Neh 7:54 Bazlith, **M**, Harsha,

Mehir (1)

1Ch 4:11 was the father of **M**,

Meholah (2)

1Sm 18:19 was married to Adriel from **M**.
2Sm 21:8 son of Barzillai from **M**.

Mehujael (2)

Gen 4:18 Irad was the father of **M**.
4:18 **M** was the father of

Mehuman (1)

Est 1:10 he ordered **M**, Biztha, Harbona,

Me Jarkon (1)

Jos 19:46 **M**, and Rakkon, with the border

Melatiah (1)

Neh 3:7 Next to them **M** from Gibeon

Melchi (2)

Luk 3:24 Levi, son of **M**, son of Jannai,
3:28 son of **M**, son of Addi, son of

Melchizedek (17)

Gen 14:18 Then King **M** of Salem brought
Psa 110:4 in the way **M** was a priest."
Heb 5:6 in the way **M** was a priest."
5:10 in the way **M** was a priest.
6:20 in the way **M** was a priest.
Heb 7:1 **M** was king of Salem and
7:2 Abraham gave **M** a tenth of
7:3 Like the Son of God, **M**
7:4 can see how important **M** was.
7:6 Although **M** was not from the
7:6 Then **M** blessed Abraham,
7:8 **M** received a tenth of
7:9 say that when Abraham gave **M**
7:10 of Abraham when **M** met him.
7:11 kind of priest, a priest like **M**,
7:15 priest who is like **M** appeared.
7:17 in the way **M** was a priest."

Melchizedek's (2)

Heb 7:2 In the first place, **M** name
7:3 about **M** father, mother,

Melea (1)

Luk 3:31 son of **M**, son of Menna, son of

Melech (3)

2Ki 23:11 room of the eunuch Nathan **M**.
1Ch 8:35 Micah's sons were Pithon, **M**,
9:41 Micah's sons were Pithon, **M**,

melody (2)

Psa 92:3 a harp and with a **m** on a lyre.
98:5 a lyre and the **m** of a psalm,

melt (12)

Psa 68:2 Let wicked people **m** in God's
75:3 who lives on it begin to **m**,
97:5 The mountains **m** like wax in
Jer 6:29 to make the fire **m** away
49:23 They **m** in fear. They are
Eze 22:20 in a smelting furnace to **m** them
22:20 in the city. I will **m** you there.
22:21 and **m** you in the city.
24:11 Its impurities will **m** away,
Mic 1:4 Mountains will **m** under him
Nah 1:5 The hills **m**. The earth draws
2Pe 3:12 the universe will burn and **m**.

melted (6)

Exo 16:21 the sun was hot, it **m** away.
Job 28:2 rocks are **m** for ⌊their⌋ copper.
Psa 22:14 It has **m** within me.
107:26 Their courage **m** in ⌊the face
Eze 22:22 You will be **m** in the city like
22:22 in the city like silver that is **m**

melting (1)

Nah 2:10 Hearts are **m**. Knees are

melts (3)

Psa 46:6 The earth **m** at the sound of
147:18 his word and **m** his hailstones.
Nah 2:6 and the palace **m** away.

member (17)

Gen 15:3 so this **m** of my household will
Lev 25:47 foreigner or a **m** of his family.
Jos 7:1 and a **m** of the tribe of Judah,
Jdg 6:15 least important **m** of my family."
2Sm 23:19 didn't become a **m** of the three.
23:23 but he was not a **m** of the three.
2Ki 10:11 Jehu also killed every **m** of
10:17 every **m** who was left in
1Ch 11:21 didn't become a **m** of the three.
11:25 but he was not a **m** of the three.
27:12 Abiezer, a **m** of the tribe of
27:14 Benaiah, a **m** of the tribe of
Mar 15:43 and was an important **m**
Luk 23:50 He was a **m** of the Jewish
Jon 3:1 was a Pharisee and a **m**
Act 17:34 who was a **m** of the court,
Heb 7:13 we are talking about was a **m**

members (25)

Gen 36:6 all the **m** of his household,
Exo 9:20 Those **m** of Pharaoh's court
2Sm 3:29 May there always be **m** of
1Ch 5:23 The tribe **m** were numerous.
9:19 of Korah) and the **m**
Ecc 4:8 no children or other family **m**.
Jer 12:6 Even your relatives and **m** of

Mic 7:6 People's enemies are the **m** of
Mat 10:25 the family **m** the same name.
10:36 person's enemies will be the **m**
17:25 Is it from their family **m** or from
17:26 "Then the family **m** are exempt.
Act 7:54 As council **m** listened to
7:57 But the council **m** shouted and
7:59 While council **m** were
12:1 certain **m** of the church.
14:27 they called the **m** of the church
17:2 with the synagogue **m**.
1Co 5:1 Your own **m** are aware that
10:32 or **m** of God's church.
Eph 2:19 people and **m** of God's family.
4:25 because we are all **m** of the
1Ti 3:15 to know how people who are **m**
Heb 7:5 Moses' Teachings say that **m**
Rev 11:9 For 3 ½ days some **m** of the

memorandum (1)

Ezr 6:2 This was written on it: **M**

memorial (3)

Gen 35:14 So Jacob set up a **m**,
Lev 23:24 It will be a **m** day, a holy
Num 5:26 the grain offering as a **m** portion

memories (2)

Php 1:3 I thank my God for all the **m** I
1Th 3:6 that you always have fond **m**

memory (19)

Exo 17:14 I will completely erase any **m**
Dtr 4:9 Don't let them fade from your **m**
25:19 don't forget to erase every **m** of
29:20 The LORD will erase every **m**
32:26 erase everyone's **m** of them.
Jos 7:9 us and remove every **m**
2Sm 18:18 "I have no son to keep the **m** of
Job 18:17 All **m** about him will vanish
Psa 9:6 Even the **m** of them has faded.
31:12 I have faded from **m** as if I were
34:16 evil in order to wipe out all **m**
109:15 Let the LORD remove every **m**
Ecc 9:5 reward for the dead when the **m**
Isa 26:14 and wiped out all **m** of them.
Lam 2:6 The LORD wiped out the **m** of
Mat 26:13 will also be told in **m** of her."
Mar 14:9 will also be told in **m** of her."
2Pe 1:13 think it's right to refresh your **m**
3:1 I'm trying to refresh your **m**.

Memphis (6)

Isa 19:13 The leaders of **M** are led astray.
Jer 46:14 Make it known in **M** and in
46:19 **M** will become a dreary
Eze 30:13 put an end to the idols in **M**.
30:16 and **M** will be in trouble every
Hos 9:6 Egypt will capture them and **M**

Memucan (3)

Est 1:14 Meres, Marsena, and **M**.
1:16 Then **M** spoke up in the
1:21 and so the king did as **M**

men (1196)

Gen 12:20 Pharaoh gave his **m** orders
14:13 (These **m** were Abram's allies.)
14:14 he armed his 318 trained **m**,
14:15 He split up his **m** to attack
14:24 except what my **m** have eaten.
17:27 All the **m** of his household,
18:2 and suddenly he saw three **m**
18:16 Then the **m** got up to leave.
18:22 From there the **m** turned and
19:5 "Where are the **m** who came to
19:8 don't do anything to these **m**,
19:9 But the **m** yelled, "Get out of
19:9 treat you worse than those **m**."
19:10 The **m** inside reached out,
19:11 Then they struck all the **m** who
19:12 Then the **m** asked Lot,
19:14 and spoke to the **m** engaged
19:16 the **m** grabbed him,
19:31 No **m** are here. We can't get
Gen 20:2 of Gerar sent **m** to take Sarah.
24:32 was brought for him and his **m**
24:54 Then he and the **m** who were
24:59 Abraham's servant and his **m**.
26:7 When the **m** of that place
26:7 He thought that the **m** of that
32:6 to meet you with 400 **m**."
32:28 with God and with **m** —
33:1 saw Esau coming with 400 **m**.
33:15 leave some of my **m** with you."
34:7 The **m** felt outraged and very
34:20 their city gate to speak to the **m**
34:24 All the **m** who had come out to
34:25 while the **m** were still in pain,
38:12 the **m** were shearing Judah's
38:21 He asked the **m** of that area,
38:22 Even the **m** of that area said,
41:8 and wise **m** of Egypt.
41:43 **M** ran ahead of him and
42:11 We're honest **m**, not spies."
42:19 If you are honest **m**,
42:31 'We're honest **m**, not spies.
42:33 I'll know that you're honest **m**:
42:34 you're not spies but honest **m**.
43:15 The **m** took the gifts,
43:16 "Take these **m** to my house.
43:18 The **m** were frightened,
44:3 At dawn the **m** were sent on
44:4 "Go after those **m** at once,
46:32 The **m** are shepherds.
49:6 In their anger they murdered **m**
Exo 2:13 he saw two Hebrew **m** fighting.
4:19 because all the **m** who wanted
5:16 but your **m** are at fault."
7:11 for his wise **m** and sorcerers.
10:7 Let the Israelite **m** go to
10:11 Only the **m** may go to worship
12:37 hundred thousand **m** on foot,
15:15 The powerful **m** of Moab will
17:9 "Choose some of our **m**.
18:21 "But choose capable **m** from all
18:21 all the people, **m** who fear God,
18:21 who fear God, **m** you can trust,
18:21 **m** who hate corruption.
18:25 Moses chose capable **m** from
18:26 These **m** were the ones who
21:18 must do whenever **m** quarrel
21:22 you must do whenever **m** fight
23:17 that all your **m** must come into
24:5 Then he sent young Israelite **m**,
34:23 "Three times a year all your **m**
35:22 All who were willing — **m** and
35:35 The LORD has made these **m**
Lev 10:5 The dead **m** were still in their
20:13 both **m** are doing something
21:6 "Be God's holy **m**,
Num 1:4 Each of these **m** must be the
1:5 "Here are the names of the **m**
1:16 These were the **m** chosen from
1:17 Moses and Aaron took the **m**
1:19 So Moses registered the **m** of
1:24 Gad listed the **m** by name who
1:26 listed the **m** by name who
1:28 listed the **m** by name who
1:30 listed the **m** by name who
1:32 listed the **m** by name who
1:34 listed the **m** by name who
1:36 listed the **m** by name who
1:38 Dan listed the **m** by name who
1:40 listed the **m** by name who
1:42 listed the **m** by name who
1:45 The grand total of **m** who were
2:4 The total number of **m** in his
2:6 The total number of **m** in his
2:8 The total number of **m** in his
2:11 The total number of **m** in his
2:13 The total number of **m** in his
2:15 The total number of **m** in his
2:19 The total number of **m** in his
2:21 The total number of **m** in his
2:23 The total number of **m** in his
2:26 The total number of **m** in his
2:28 The total number of **m** in his
2:30 The total number of **m** in his
2:31 "The grand total of all the **m** in
4:3 Register all the **m** between the
Num 4:23 Register all the **m** between the
4:30 Register all the **m** between the
4:35 They registered all the **m**
4:39 All the **m** between the ages of
4:43 All the **m** between the ages of
4:47 These were the **m** between the
5:3 Send all of these unclean **m**
8:24 **M** 25 years old or older are
9:6 But there were some **m** who
11:16 "Bring me 70 Israelite **m** who
11:26 Two **m**, named Eldad and
13:2 "Send **m** to explore Canaan,
13:3 Moses sent these **m** from the
13:16 These are the names of the **m**
13:21 So the **m** explored the land
13:31 But the **m** who had gone with
14:36 So the **m** Moses sent to
14:38 Of all the **m** who went to
16:2 These four **m** were joined by
16:2 were joined by 250 Israelite **m**,
16:21 "Move away from these **m**,
16:26 the tents of these wicked **m**.
16:29 If these **m** die like all other
16:30 know that these **m** have treated
16:35 the 250 **m** who were offering
16:38 The incense burners of these **m**
22:9 "Who are these **m** with you?"
22:20 "If these **m** have come to
22:35 to Balaam, "Go with the **m**,
25:1 the **m** began to have sex with
25:5 "Each of you must kill the **m**
25:6 One of the Israelite **m** brought
26:7 total number of **m** was 43,730.
26:9 **m** chosen by the community,
26:10 the fire consumed the 250 **m**.
26:14 total number of **m** was 22,200.
26:18 total number of **m** was 40,500.
26:22 total number of **m** was 76,500.
26:25 total number of **m** was 64,300.
26:27 total number of **m** was 60,500.
26:34 total number of **m** was 52,700.
26:37 total number of **m** was 32,500.
26:41 total number of **m** was 45,600.
26:43 The total number of **m** in all the
26:47 total number of **m** was 53,400.
26:50 total number of **m** was 45,400.
26:51 of Israelite **m** was 601,730.
31:3 "Some of your **m** must get
31:4 Send 1,000 **m** from each of the
31:5 So 1,000 **m** from each tribe
31:5 Israel — 12,000 **m** ready for war.
31:6 1,000 **m** from each tribe along
31:48 companies and battalions of **m**,
32:20 all your armed **m** get ready
34:17 "These are the names of the **m**
34:29 These are the **m** the LORD
36:3 Suppose they marry **m** from the
Dtr 1:13 choose some **m** who are wise,
1:15 were wise and experienced **m**
1:22 "Let's send **m** ahead of us to
1:23 So I chose 12 of your **m**,
1:28 Our own **m** have discouraged
2:34 them for God by destroying **m**,
3:6 city, including **m**, women,
4:16 that represent **m** or women,
7:14 Your **m** and women will be
15:12 Whenever Hebrew **m** or women
16:16 Three times a year all your **m**
21:21 All the **m** of the city should
22:5 wear anything **m** would wear,
22:21 The **m** of her city must stone
23:10 If one of your **m** becomes
25:11 do when two **m** are fighting
29:10 and all the **m** of Israel are here.
31:12 Assemble the **m**, women,
32:25 Young **m** and young women
32:25 babies and gray-haired **m**.
Jos 2:1 sent out two **m** as spies.
2:3 "Bring out the **m** who came to
2:4 already taken the two **m** inside
2:4 the **m** did come here.
2:7 The king's **m** pursued them on
2:7 soon as the king's **m** had left,
2:14 The **m** promised her,
2:16 so that the **m** who are pursuing
2:17 The **m** told her, "We will be

Jos 2:22 The **m** went to the mountains
2:22 days until the king's **m** returned
2:22 The king's **m** had searched for
4:4 Joshua called the 12 **m** whom
4:12 The **m** of Reuben, Gad,
4:13 About 40,000 armed **m** crossed
5:2 and circumcise the **m** of Israel."
5:3 knives and circumcised the **m**
5:5 The **m** who left Egypt had been
5:5 However, the **m** born later,
5:8 When all the **m** had been
6:7 Let the armed **m** march ahead
6:9 The armed **m** went ahead of
6:13 The armed **m** were ahead of
6:21 they killed **m** and women,
7:2 Joshua sent **m** from Jericho to
7:2 So the **m** went and looked at
7:3 or three thousand **m** are needed
7:4 three thousand **m** were sent.
7:4 they fled from the **m** of Ai.
7:5 The **m** of Ai killed about
8:12 taken about five thousand **m**
8:19 The **m** who were hiding got up
8:20 When the **m** of Ai looked back,
8:21 saw that the **m** who had been
8:21 turned and attacked the **m** of Ai.
8:22 The **m** who had captured the
8:22 The **m** of Ai were caught
8:25 Twelve thousand **m** and
9:6 told Joshua and the **m** of Israel,
9:7 The **m** of Israel said to the
9:14 The **m** believed the evidence
10:2 All its **m** were warriors.
10:6 The **m** of Gibeon sent this
10:24 he called for all the **m** of Israel.
18:4 Choose three **m** from each tribe
18:8 As the **m** got ready to go,
18:9 The **m** surveyed the land.
Jdg 1:4 defeated 10,000 **m** at Bezek.
1:8 The **m** of Judah attacked
1:9 After that, the **m** of Judah went
1:19 The LORD was with the **m** of
1:21 The **m** of Benjamin did not
1:23 They sent **m** to spy on Bethel.
3:18 he sent back the **m** who had
3:29 of Moab's best fighting **m**.
4:6 Take 10,000 **m** from Naphtali
4:10 Ten thousand **m** went to fight
4:14 with 10,000 **m** behind him.
5:2 **M** in Israel vowed to fight,
5:13 Then those mighty **m** who
5:15 **m** had second thoughts.
5:16 **m** had second thoughts.
6:27 of his father's family and the **m**
6:28 When the **m** of the city got up
6:30 Then the **m** of the city told
7:2 "You have too many **m** with
7:3 So 22,000 **m** went back home,
7:4 "There are still too many **m**.
7:5 So Gideon took the **m** down to
7:6 Three hundred **m** lapped water
7:6 All the rest of the **m** knelt down
7:7 "With the 300 **m** who lapped
7:7 the other **m** should go home."
7:8 So Gideon sent the other **m** of
7:8 but the 300 **m** who stayed kept
7:16 Gideon divided the 300 **m** into
7:19 Gideon and his 100 **m** came to
7:22 The 300 **m** kept on blowing
7:23 The **m** of Israel were
7:24 All the **m** of Ephraim were also
8:1 The **m** from Ephraim strongly
8:4 Gideon and his 300 **m** headed
8:5 said to the **m** of Succoth,
8:5 for the **m** under my command.
8:8 that the **m** of Succoth gave.
8:10 an army of about 15,000 **m**.
8:15 Gideon went to the **m** of
8:15 **m** food before you've
8:17 and killed the **m** of that city.
8:18 "What kind of **m** did you kill at
8:22 The **m** of Israel said to Gideon,
8:25 The **m** of Israel answered,
9:4 and reckless **m** to follow him.
9:32 You and your **m** must start out
9:33 When Gaal and his **m** come

Jdg 9:36 mountains look like **m** to you."
9:48 he and all his **m** went to Mount
9:48 He told his **m**, "Hurry and do
9:49 There were about a thousand **m**
9:51 All the **m**, women, and leaders
9:57 God also paid back the **m** of
11:3 Worthless **m** gathered around
12:1 The **m** of Ephraim were
12:4 Jephthah gathered all the **m**
12:4 The **m** of Gilead defeated
12:5 The **m** of Gilead captured the
12:5 the **m** of Gilead would ask,
12:6 42,000 **m** from Ephraim died.
14:10 is what young **m** used to do.)
14:18 the **m** of the city said to him,
14:19 Ashkelon and killed 30 **m** there.
14:19 gave them to the **m** who solved
15:10 The **m** of Judah asked,
15:11 So 3,000 **m** from Judah went to
15:12 So the **m** from Judah told him,
15:15 it up and killed 1,000 **m** with it.
15:16 I've killed a thousand **m**."
15:18 into the power of godless **m**."
16:9 Some **m** were hiding in the
16:12 Some **m** were in her bedroom
16:27 were about three thousand **m**
18:2 out five qualified **m** from Zorah
18:7 The five **m** left there and came
18:8 The **m** went back to their
18:11 So 600 **m** from the tribe of Dan
18:14 Then the five **m** who had gone
18:14 said to the other **m** of Dan,
18:16 The 600 armed **m** from Dan
18:17 The five **m** who had gone to
18:17 the city with the 600 armed **m**.
18:18 When these **m** entered Micah's
18:25 or some violent **m** will attack
19:22 some worthless **m** from the city
19:25 But the **m** refused to listen to
20:10 We'll take one-tenth of all the **m**
20:11 So all the **m** of Israel
20:12 The tribes of Israel sent **m**
20:13 those worthless **m** in Gibeah.
20:13 But the **m** of Benjamin refused
20:13 to listen to the **m** of Israel.
20:14 So the **m** of Benjamin went
20:14 go to war with the **m** of Israel.
20:15 That day 26,000 **m** armed with
20:15 with 700 of Gibeah's best **m**.
20:17 The **m** of Israel (Benjamin not
20:18 The **m** of Israel went to Bethel.
20:20 So the **m** of Israel went to war
20:20 to war with the **m** of Benjamin.
20:21 That day the **m** of Benjamin
20:21 22,000 of Israel's **m**.
20:23 the **m** of Benjamin?"
20:25 18,000 **m** from Israel who
20:26 Then all the **m** of Israel and all
20:28 the **m** of Benjamin?
20:30 On the third day the **m** of Israel
20:30 went to fight the **m** of Benjamin.
20:31 The **m** of Benjamin went out to
20:31 They killed about 30 **m** from
20:32 The **m** of Benjamin shouted,
20:32 But the **m** of Israel had said,
20:33 So the **m** of Israel left their
20:34 best **m** attacked Gibeah.
20:34 But Benjamin's **m** didn't realize
20:35 25,100 **m** from Benjamin who
20:36 Then the **m** of Benjamin
20:36 Israelites had allowed the **m**
20:37 The **m** in ambush quickly
20:38 The **m** of Israel had arranged
20:39 Then the **m** of Israel would turn
20:39 The **m** of Benjamin had already
20:39 killed about 30 **m** of Israel.
20:40 the **m** of Benjamin turned
20:41 Then the **m** of Israel turned
20:41 and the **m** of Benjamin
20:42 up with the **m** of Benjamin.
20:43 They closed in on the **m** of
20:44 **m** from Benjamin who
20:45 But the **m** of Israel killed 5,000
20:46 In all, 25,000 **m** from Benjamin
20:46 They were all experienced **m**.
20:47 But 600 **m** turned and fled into

Jdg 20:48 Then the **m** of Israel went back
21:1 The **m** of Israel had taken this
21:6 the **m** of Benjamin.
21:7 wives for the **m** who are left?
21:13 sent messengers to the **m**
21:14 So the **m** of Benjamin came
21:14 These **m** were given the
21:16 wives for the **m** who are left,
21:17 Some said, "Benjamin's **m** who
21:18 whoever gives wives to the **m**
21:20 So they told the **m** of Benjamin,
21:23 The **m** of Benjamin did just
Rut 2:9 Watch where my **m** are reaping,
2:9 I have ordered my young **m** not
2:9 that the young **m** have drawn."
3:10 didn't go after the younger **m**,
4:2 Then Boaz chose ten **m** who
4:4 of these **m** sitting here
1Sm 2:17 because these **m** were treating
4:4 The troops sent some **m** who
4:9 Philistines, and act like **m**,
4:9 Act like **m** and fight."
7:1 The **m** of Kiriath Jearim came
9:4 The **m** went through the
10:2 two **m** will be at Rachel's grave
10:3 There you will find three **m** on
10:5 They will be led by **m** playing
11:1 However, seven thousand **m**
11:1 All the **m** of Jabesh said to
11:5 news about the **m** of Jabesh.
11:9 is what you are to say to the **m**
11:9 will be rescued."' When the **m**
13:2 Saul chose 3,000 **m** from Israel;
13:15 still with him — about 600 **m**.
14:2 He had with him about 600 **m**
14:6 victory with a few **m** as well as
14:12 "Come up here," the **m** of the
14:14 about twenty **m** within about
14:22 When all the **m** of Israel who
14:36 Saul said ⌊to his **m**⌋,
15:3 but kill **m** and women,
15:4 and 10,000 **m** from Judah.
17:24 When all the **m** of Israel saw
17:25 The **m** of Israel said,
17:26 David asked the **m** who were
17:28 heard David talking to the **m**.
18:5 him in charge of the fighting **m**.
18:27 David and his **m** went out and
20:31 Now, send some **m** to bring
21:2 I've stationed my young **m** at a
21:4 for the young **m** if they haven't
22:2 about four hundred **m** with him.
22:6 and his **m** had been found.
22:7 "Listen here, **m** of Benjamin!
22:17 "But the king's **m** refused to
22:18 and that day he killed 85 **m**
22:19 he killed **m** and women,
23:3 David's **m** told him,
23:5 David and his **m** went to
23:8 where David and his **m** were.
23:12 Keilah hand me and my **m** over
23:13 So David and his **m**,
23:19 Then the **m** of Ziph went to
23:24 David and his **m** were in the
23:25 When Saul and his **m** came to
23:26 and David and his **m** went on
23:26 and Saul and his **m** were going
23:26 toward David and his **m**,
24:2 best-trained **m** from all Israel
24:2 to search for David and his **m**
24:3 and his **m** were sitting further
24:4 David's **m** told him,
24:6 He said to his **m**, "It would be
24:7 So David stopped his **m** by
24:22 and David and his **m** went to
25:5 So David sent ten young **m**
25:8 Ask your young **m**,
25:8 Be kind to my young **m**,
25:9 When David's young **m** came
25:11 them to **m** coming from who
25:12 David's young **m** returned and
25:13 David told his **m**. And everyone,
25:13 About four hundred **m** went
25:13 while two hundred **m** stayed
25:14 of the young **m** told Abigail,
25:15 Those **m** were very good to us.

1Sm 25:19 she told her young **m**,
25:20 and his **m** coming toward her.
25:22 I leave even one of his **m** alive
25:25 see the young **m** you sent.
25:27 May it be given to the young **m**
25:34 had one of his **m** left at dawn."
25:39 Then David sent **m** ⌊on his
26:2 3,000 of Israel's best-trained **m**
26:16 LORD lives, you are dead **m**.
26:22 One of the young **m** should
27:2 So David went with his 600 **m**
27:3 David and his **m** stayed with
27:8 Then David and his **m** went to
28:1 know that you and your **m** will
28:8 Saul left with two **m** and came
29:2 David and his **m** were
29:4 do it with the lives of our **m**!
29:11 David and his **m** returned
30:1 when David and his **m** came to
30:3 By the time David and his **m**
30:4 Then David and his **m** cried
30:9 So David and his 600 **m** went
30:10 David and 400 **m** went in
30:10 while 200 **m** who were too
30:11 David's **m** found an Egyptian in
30:17 400 young **m** who rode away
30:20 His **m** drove the animals ahead
30:21 David came to the 200 **m** who
30:21 As David approached the **m**,
30:31 and his **m** visited from time
31:1 the **m** of Israel fled from the
31:4 or these godless **m** will come,
31:6 and all his **m** died together that
31:7 the Jordan River saw that the **m**
31:9 Then they sent **m** throughout
31:12 all the fighting **m** marched all
2Sm 1:11 All the **m** with him did the
1:15 called one of ⌊his⌋ young **m**
1:20 of godless **m** will celebrate.
2:3 David took his **m** and their
2:14 "Let's have the young **m** hold a
2:15 The **m** got up and were
2:17 and David's **m** defeated Abner
2:17 Abner and the **m** of Israel.
2:21 Catch one of the young **m**,
2:25 The **m** of Benjamin rallied
2:27 the **m** would not have stopped
2:29 Abner and his **m** marched
2:31 officers had killed 360 of the **m**
2:32 Then Joab and his **m** marched
3:15 So Ishbosheth sent **m** to take
3:20 So Abner came with 20 **m** to
3:20 had a feast for Abner and his **m**.
3:22 Just then David's **m** and Joab
3:34 one falls in front of wicked **m**.
3:39 These **m**, Zeruiah's sons,
4:2 Saul's son had two **m** who
4:11 I reward⌋ wicked **m** who kill
4:12 gave an order to his young **m**,
5:6 The king and his **m** went to
5:21 so David and his **m** carried the
6:1 soldiers in Israel, 30,000 **m**.
6:3 David and his **m** put God's ark
6:17 The **m** carrying the ark set it in
6:19 both **m** and women — one loaf
9:5 So King David sent **m** to get
10:3 your father because he sent **m**
10:3 Hasn't David sent his **m** to
10:4 So Hanun took David's **m**,
10:6 the king of Maacah (1,000 **m**),
10:6 and the **m** of Tob (12,000 men).
10:6 and the men of Tob (12,000 **m**).
10:8 and Rehob and the **m** from Tob
11:17 The **m** of the city came out and
11:23 The messenger said, "Their **m**
12:1 "There were two **m** in a certain
13:32 don't think that all the young **m**,
13:36 The king and all his **m** also
15:1 and 50 **m** to run ahead of him.
15:11 Two hundred **m** invited from
15:14 David told all his **m** who were
15:18 and all 600 **m** who had
15:22 Gath marched on with all his **m**
16:13 As David and his **m** went along
17:1 "Let me choose 12,000 **m** and
17:8 know your father and his **m**.
2Sm 17:10 father is a warrior and the **m**
17:12 Neither he nor any of his **m** will
17:21 both **m** came out of the cistern
17:24 the time Absalom and all the **m**
18:7 There David's **m** defeated
18:7 sizable that day — 20,000 **m**.
18:9 with some of David's **m**.
18:28 He has handed over the **m** who
19:5 made all your **m** feel ashamed,"
19:7 and encourage your **m**.
19:35 the singing of **m** and women?
19:41 and your family and **m** across
20:6 Take my **m** and go after him,
20:7 So Joab's **m**, the Cherethites,
20:11 One of Joab's young **m** stood
21:13 his **m** gathered the bones of
21:15 So David and his **m** went to
21:17 Then David's **m** swore an oath,
21:22 David and his **m** killed them.
23:8 names of David's fighting **m**:
23:8 to kill 800 **m** on one occasion.
23:9 one of the three fighting **m**.
23:13 of the thirty leading **m** came
23:16 So the three fighting **m** burst
23:17 This is the blood of **m** who
23:17 which the three fighting **m** did.
23:18 He used his spear to kill 300 **m**.
23:22 famous as the three fighting **m**.
23:24 ⌊The thirty leading **m** were⌋
24:9 able-bodied **m** who could serve
24:20 and his **m** coming toward him,
1Ki 1:5 a chariot and horses and 50 **m**
1:8 and David's ⌊thirty⌋ fighting **m**
1:9 all the **m** of Judah,
1:10 Benaiah, the fighting **m**,
1:53 King Solomon sent **m** to take
2:32 Joab killed two honorable **m**
5:6 So order **m** to cut down cedars
5:8 Hiram sent **m** to Solomon to
5:13 King Solomon forced 30,000 **m**
5:14 He sent a shift of 10,000 **m** to
5:15 Solomon had 70,000 **m** who
5:18 and **m** from Gebal quarried the
10:8 How blessed your **m** must be!
11:18 Taking some **m** from Paran
11:24 David killed the **m** of Zobah.
11:24 Rezon gathered **m** and became
12:8 the young **m** who had grown
12:10 The young **m** who had grown
12:14 them as the young **m** advised.
12:20 they sent **m** to invite him to the
12:31 He appointed **m** who were not
13:33 again made some **m** priests
20:17 Benhadad had sent **m** ⌊to
20:17 They informed him that some **m**
20:33 The **m**, watching for a good
21:10 Have two good-for-nothing **m**
21:11 The **m** in Naboth's city — the
21:13 The two good-for-nothing **m**
21:13 In front of the people, these **m**
2Ki 1:9 army officer with 50 **m** to Elijah.
1:10 burn up you and your 50 **m**."
1:10 up the officer and his 50 **m**.
1:11 officer with 50 **m** to Elijah.
1:12 burn up you and your 50 **m**."
1:12 up the officer and his 50 **m**.
1:13 sent a third officer with 50 **m**.
1:14 two officers and their 100 **m**.
2:8 and the two **m** crossed ⌊the
2:16 "There are 50 strong **m** here
2:17 him ⌊to send the **m**⌋ until
2:17 "They sent 50 **m** who searched
3:21 So all **m** old enough to bear
4:40 out the food for the **m** to eat.
5:15 Then he and all his **m** returned
5:22 'Just now two young **m** from
5:24 Then he dismissed the **m**,
6:13 Then I will send **m** to capture
6:20 open the eyes of these **m**,
6:32 The king had sent one of his **m**
7:3 Four **m** with skin diseases
7:8 When the **m** with skin
7:13 "Please let some **m** take five of
7:13 Those **m** will be no worse off
8:12 kill their best young **m**,
10:6 with the city's most powerful **m**.
2Ki 10:6 These **m** had raised them.
10:7 When the letter came to the **m**,
10:9 But who killed all these **m**?
10:11 all the most powerful **m**,
10:14 ⌊Jehu's **m**⌋ captured and
10:24 stationed 80 of his **m** outside.
11:9 Each commander took his **m**
12:11 to the **m** who had been
12:15 They didn't require the **m** who
14:19 But they sent **m** to Lachish
15:20 from all the wealthy **m** in Israel.
15:25 With 50 **m** from Gilead,
18:27 Didn't he send me to the **m**
19:5 Hezekiah's **m** went to Isaiah.
20:14 "What did these **m** say?
23:16 he sent **m** to take the bones out
24:16 and all the **m** who could fight in
25:19 5 **m** who had access to the
25:23 and their **m** heard that
25:23 from Beth Maacah and their **m**.
25:24 an oath to them and their **m**.
25:25 of the kings) went with ten **m**
1Ch 4:12 These were the **m** from Recah.
4:22 and the **m** of Cozeba.
4:41 the **m** listed here knocked
6:31 David put **m** in charge of the
6:33 These are the **m** who served
7:2 These **m** were heads of the
7:4 So in addition to these **m**
7:5 families) were fighting **m**.
7:7 of families and fighting **m**.
7:9 of their families and fighting **m**)
7:11 All of these **m** were Jediael's
7:11 17,200 fighting **m** who could go
7:21 and Elead were killed by the **m**
7:40 All of these **m** were Asher's
7:40 outstanding **m**, soldiers,
8:38 of these **m** were Azel's sons.
8:40 **m** were Benjamin's descendants.
9:9 All of these **m** were heads of
9:22 The **m** chosen to be
9:44 of these **m** were Azel's sons.
10:1 the **m** of Israel fled from the
10:4 Stab me, or these godless **m**
10:9 Then they sent **m** throughout
10:12 all the fighting **m** came and
11:10 of David's fighting **m**,
11:11 fighting **m** was Jashobeam,
11:11 to kill 300 **m** on one occasion.
11:12 one of the three fighting **m**.
11:15 the thirty leading **m** went down
11:19 of these **m** who risked their
11:19 which the three fighting **m** did.
11:20 He used his spear to kill 300 **m**,
11:24 famous as the three fighting **m**.
11:26 The distinguished fighting **m**
12:1 These are the **m** who came to
12:4 (one of the thirty fighting **m**
12:8 Some **m** left Gad to join David
12:14 one was in command of 100 **m**,
12:15 these **m** crossed the Jordan
12:16 Some of the **m** of Benjamin and
12:19 Some **m** from Manasseh had
12:20 these **m** from Manasseh
12:20 over 1,000 **m** in Manasseh.
12:22 From day to day, **m** came to
12:23 These are the numbers of the **m**
12:23 The **m** joined David at Hebron
12:24 there were 6,800 **m** equipped
12:27 With him there were 3,700 **m**,
12:29 there were 3,000 **m**,
13:7 David and his **m** put God's ark
14:11 So David ⌊and his **m**⌋ attacked
14:16 and his **m** defeated the
16:1 The **m** carrying the ark set it
16:3 every person in Israel — both **m**
19:3 your father because he sent **m**
19:4 So Hanun took David's **m**,
19:5 ⌊what had happened⌋ to the **m**,
20:8 These ⌊**m**⌋ were the
20:8 David and his **m** killed them.
21:5 1,100,000 **m** who could serve
22:4 The **m** of Sidon and Tyre
22:15 and **m** skilled in every kind of
24:4 had more **m** who were family
24:20 ⌊The following **m** were

1Ch 24:26 The following **m** were leaders
25:1 This is the list of the **m** who
25:9 and his relatives — 12 **m**.
25:10 and his relatives — 12 **m**.
25:11 and his relatives — 12 **m**.
25:12 and his relatives — 12 **m**.
25:13 and his relatives — 12 **m**.
25:14 and his relatives — 12 **m**.
25:15 and his relatives — 12 **m**.
25:16 and his relatives — 12 **m**.
25:17 and his relatives — 12 **m**.
25:18 and his relatives — 12 **m**.
25:19 and his relatives — 12 **m**.
25:20 and his relatives — 12 **m**.
25:21 and his relatives — 12 **m**.
25:22 and his relatives — 12 **m**.
25:23 and his relatives — 12 **m**.
25:24 and his relatives — 12 **m**.
25:25 and his relatives — 12 **m**.
25:26 and his relatives — 12 **m**.
25:27 and his relatives — 12 **m**.
25:28 and his relatives — 12 **m**.
25:29 and his relatives — 12 **m**.
25:30 and his relatives — 12 **m**.
25:31 and his relatives — 12 **m**.
26:8 Edom's family included 62 **m**.
26:9 relatives were 18 skilled **m**.
26:12 head **m** were assigned duties
26:32 relatives were 2,700 skilled **m**,
27:1 unit consisted of 24,000 **m**.
27:6 was one of the thirty fighting **m**
28:1 and the fighting **m**.
2Ch 2:2 Solomon drafted 70,000 **m** to
2:7 the skilled **m** whom my father
2:17 Solomon counted all the **m**
5:3 All the **m** of Israel gathered
9:7 How blessed your **m** must be!
10:8 the young **m** who had grown
10:10 The young **m** who had grown
10:14 them as the young **m** advised.
13:7 Worthless, good-for-nothing **m**
13:12 **M** of Israel, don't wage war
13:15 and the **m** of Judah shouted.
13:17 So Abijah and his **m** defeated
13:17 and 500 of the best **m** of Israel
13:18 and the **m** of Judah won
14:8 All of these **m** were good
14:8 men were good fighting **m**.
14:9 Sudan came with 1,000,000 **m**
15:2 Asa and all you **m** from Judah
17:14 (with 300,000 fighting **m**),
17:16 (with 200,000 fighting **m**).
17:17 Eliada (with 200,000 armed **m**
17:18 an army of 180,000 armed **m**).
17:19 These were the **m** who served
20:2 Some **m** reported to
20:27 All the **m** of Judah and
22:9 and Jehu's **m** captured him
23:8 Each took his **m** who were
24:12 They also hired **m** who worked
24:13 As the **m** worked, the project
24:24 with a small number of **m**,
24:26 These were the **m** who
25:5 he had 300,000 of the best **m**
25:7 not with these **m** from Ephraim.
25:11 he killed 10,000 **m** from Seir.
25:27 but they sent **m** to Lachish after
28:10 you intend to enslave the **m**
28:15 Then the **m** who were
29:15 These **m** gathered their
31:16 The six **m** who served under
31:19 **M** were appointed to give a
31:19 These **m** were Aaron's
34:12 The **m** did their work faithfully
35:8 the **m** in charge of God's
36:17 and execute their best young **m**
36:17 He didn't spare the best **m** or
Ezr 2:2 the number of Israelite **m** from
3:7 and olive oil to the **m** from
3:7 which the **m** would bring by
4:21 So order these **m** to stop
5:4 of the **m** who were working
5:10 record of the **m** who were their
6:8 be made to these **m** so that
8:16 (who were leading **m**)
8:17 that they should bring us **m**
Ezr 10:1 a large crowd of Israelite **m**,
10:8 and the older **m** had advised,
10:9 Then all the **m** of Judah and
10:16 Ezra the priest chose **m** who
10:17 with all the **m** who had married
10:44 All of these **m** had married
Neh 1:2 with some **m** from Judah.
2:12 a few **m** without telling anyone
3:2 The **m** from Jericho were
3:5 Next to them the **m** from Tekoa
3:7 with **m** from Gibeon and
3:27 After him the **m** from Tekoa
4:16 From that day on, half of my **m**
5:1 the **m** and their wives,
5:16 All my **m** gathered here for
6:10 Some **m** are coming at night to
7:3 Order some of the **m** in
7:7 the number of Israelite **m** from
8:2 This included **m**, women,
8:3 in front of Water Gate to the **m**,
11:6 were 468 outstanding **m**.
12:44 On that day **m** were put in
13:13 I appointed the following **m** to
13:19 I stationed some of my **m** by
Est 1:14 The king asked these wise **m**
7:4 If our **m** and women had only
9:6 killed and wiped out 500 **m**.
9:12 killed and wiped out 500 **m**
9:15 Adar and killed 300 **m** in Susa,
Job 1:15 **m** from Sheba attacked.
24:21 These **m** take advantage of
24:21 These **m** show no kindness to
24:22 mighty **m** by his power.
28:4 ⌊In this shaft⌋ **m** dangle and
29:8 young **m** saw me and kept out
29:8 Old **m** stood up straight out of
31:10 let other ⌊**m**⌋ kneel over her.
32:1 These three **m** stopped
32:5 that the three **m** had no further
34:2 to my words, you wise **m**.
34:2 ears to me, you intelligent **m**.
Psa 59:3 Fierce **m** attack me,
78:9 The **m** of Ephraim,
78:31 He killed their strongest **m** and
78:31 the best young **m** in Israel.
78:63 consumed his best young **m**,
106:16 In the camp certain **m** became
148:12 young **m** and women,
Pro 11:16 but ruthless **m** gain riches.
20:29 While the glory of young **m** is
25:1 that were copied by the **m**
Ecc 2:8 and the pleasures **m** have
12:3 strong **m** are stooped over,
Sos 2:3 beloved among the young **m**.
5:10 He stands out among 10,000 **m**.
Isa 3:25 Your mighty **m** will die in battle.
5:13 Honored **m** will starve,
9:17 isn't happy with their young **m**,
10:16 disease against brave **m**.
13:3 I've called my mighty **m** to
15:4 Moab's armed **m** cry out.
19:11 "I'm a descendant of wise **m**,
19:12 Where are your wise **m** now?
31:8 and their young **m** will be made
36:12 Didn't he send me to the **m**
37:5 Hezekiah's **m** went to Isaiah.
39:3 "What did these **m** say?
40:30 and young **m** will stumble and
44:25 I make wise **m** retreat and turn
49:24 be taken away from mighty **m**
49:25 will be freed from mighty **m**.
56:3 Castrated **m** should not say,
56:4 the castrated **m** who keep my
59:10 We grope like blind **m** along a
Jer 3:2 You have had sex with **m** in
4:17 They surround them like **m**
6:11 and on the gangs of young **m**.
8:10 will give their wives to other **m**
9:21 in the streets and the young **m**
11:22 The young **m** will die because
15:8 the mothers of young **m**.
18:21 Their young **m** will be struck
19:10 jar in front of the **m** who went
31:13 and dance along with young **m**
31:13 with young men and old **m**.
34:11 minds and took back the **m**
Jer 37:10 a few badly wounded **m** left
38:9 everything that these **m** have
38:10 "Take 30 **m** from here,
38:11 So Ebed Melech took the **m**
38:16 you over to these **m** who want
40:7 and their **m** who were
40:7 of the country's poorest **m**,
40:8 who went with their **m**
40:9 an oath to them and their **m**.
41:1 went with ten **m** to Gedaliah,
41:2 and the ten **m** who were with
41:5 80 **m** arrived from Shechem,
41:7 and his **m** slaughtered them
41:8 However, ten **m** from the group
41:9 threw all the bodies of the **m**
41:12 they took all their **m** and went
41:15 Ishmael and eight of his **m**
41:16 Johanan brought back **m**,
43:6 They took **m**, women, children,
44:7 Why do you keep destroying **m**,
44:15 Then all the **m** who knew that
44:20 both **m** and women,
48:15 Its finest young **m** will be
49:26 That is why its young **m** will
50:30 That is why their young **m** will
50:35 their officials and their wise **m**.
51:3 Don't spare Babylon's young **m**.
51:22 you to crush **m** and women.
51:22 to crush young **m** and women.
51:57 officials and wise **m** drunk,
52:25 7 **m** who had access to the
Lam 1:15 an army to defeat my young **m**.
1:18 My young women and young **m**
2:21 My young women and **m** are
5:13 ⌊Our⌋ young **m** work at the
5:14 and ⌊our⌋ young **m** no longer
Eze 8:16 were about 25 **m** who had their
9:2 So six **m** came from the upper
9:2 The **m** came in and stood by
9:6 Kill old **m**, young men,
9:6 Kill old men, young **m**,
9:6 So they started with the old **m**
11:1 Twenty-five **m** were at the
11:2 these are the **m** who plan evil
14:14 Even if these three **m** — Noah,
22:10 **M** have sex with their father's
22:11 **M** do disgusting things with
22:11 Some **m** sexually dishonor
22:11 Other **m** who live in you have
23:3 There **m** fondled and caressed
23:6 handsome young **m** who rode
23:7 all the important **m** in Assyria.
23:8 **m** went to bed with her,
23:11 Oholibah lusted after **m** more
23:12 all of them desirable young **m**.
23:14 She saw pictures of **m** carved
23:14 were figures of Babylonian **m**,
23:15 The **m** had belts around their
23:17 So these **m** came from
23:21 when young **m** caressed and
23:23 I will bring **m** from Babylon and
23:23 **m** from Pekod, Shoa, and Koa,
23:23 They are desirable young **m**,
23:23 officers and important **m**.
23:40 sent messengers to invite **m**
23:40 When the **m** arrived,
23:40 washed themselves for the **m**,
23:43 Yet, **m** continued to have sex
23:44 **M** slept with her. They slept
30:17 The young **m** from Heliopolis
33:2 country choose one of their **m**
43:19 **m** from the tribe of Levi,
Dan 1:4 They were to be young **m** who
1:6 Among these young **m** were
1:10 the other young **m** your age,
1:13 to the young **m** who are eating
1:15 the young **m** who had been
1:17 gave these four **m** knowledge,
1:18 young **m** to Nebuchadnezzar.
1:19 these four **m** served the king.
2:13 and some **m** were sent to find
3:12 These **m** didn't obey your order,
3:21 Then the three **m** were thrown
3:22 the **m** who carried Shadrach,
3:23 So these three **m** — Shadrach,
3:24 "Didn't we throw three **m** into

Dan 3:25 replied, "But look, I see four **m**.
3:27 gathered around the three **m**.
6:5 These **m** said, "We won't find
6:11 One of those times the **m** came
6:24 The king ordered those **m** who
9:7 But we — the **m** of Judah,
10:7 The **m** with me didn't see the
11:14 and violent **m** from your own
11:17 and some decent **m** will invade
12:5 I saw two **m** standing there.
Hos 4:14 The **m** go to prostitutes and
Joe 2:28 Your old **m** will dream dreams.
2:28 Your young **m** will see visions.
2:29 on both **m** and women.
Amo 2:14 Strong **m** will find that their
4:10 killed your best young **m** along
8:13 and strong young **m** will faint
Jnh 1:10 Then the **m** were terrified.
1:13 Instead, the **m** tried to row
1:16 The **m** were terrified of the
Nah 2:5 remembers his best fighting **m**.
3:10 tossed dice for her important **m**
3:10 and all her best **m** were bound
3:18 Your best fighting **m** are at rest.
Zec 3:8 These **m** are a sign of things to
7:2 and Regem Melech with their **m**
8:4 Old **m** and old women will
9:17 Young **m** will prosper on grain,
Mat 2:1 After Jesus' birth wise **m** from
2:7 secretly called the wise **m**
2:16 the wise **m** had tricked him,
2:16 had learned from the wise **m**.
8:27 The **m** were amazed and
8:28 of Galilee, two **m** met him.
8:28 the **m** were so dangerous.
8:33 the **m** possessed by demons.
9:27 two blind **m** followed him.
9:28 and the blind **m** followed him.
12:3 he and his **m** were hungry?
12:4 He and his **m** had no right to
12:41 The **m** of Nineveh will stand up
14:21 five thousand **m** had eaten.
14:33 The **m** in the boat bowed down
14:35 The **m** there recognized Jesus
15:38 Four thousand **m** had eaten.
19:12 For example, some **m** are
20:30 Two blind **m** were sitting by
23:19 You blind **m**! What is more
23:34 sending you prophets, wise **m**,
24:40 "At that time two **m** will be
26:50 Then some **m** came forward,
26:51 Suddenly, one of the **m** with
26:60 At last two **m** came forward.
26:62 these **m** testify against you?"
26:73 After a little while the **m**
27:48 One of the **m** ran at once,
Mar 1:20 father Zebedee and the hired **m**
2:3 Four **m** came to him carrying a
2:25 did when he and his **m** were
2:26 also gave some of it to his **m**?"
6:17 Herod had sent **m** who had
6:44 There were 5,000 **m** who had
11:5 some **m** standing there asked
11:6 So the **m** let them go.
14:46 Some **m** took hold of Jesus
14:53 The **m** took Jesus to the chief
14:57 Then some **m** stood up and
14:60 these **m** testify against you?"
14:70 After a little while the **m**
Luk 5:6 After the **m** had done this,
5:18 Some **m** brought a paralyzed
6:3 he and his **m** were hungry?
6:4 and gave some of it to the **m**
7:10 When the **m** who had been
7:14 and the **m** who were carrying it
7:20 The **m** came to Jesus and said,
7:41 ⌊So Jesus said,⌋ "Two **m**
9:14 were about five thousand **m**.)
9:32 Peter and the **m** with him were
9:32 the two **m** standing with him.
10:36 "Of these three **m**,
11:31 with the **m** who live today.
11:32 The **m** of Nineveh will stand up
11:32 Since the **m** of Nineveh turned
15:17 father's hired **m** have more food
15:19 Make me one of your hired **m**."'

Luk 17:12 As he went into a village, ten **m**
17:17 "Weren't ten **m** made clean?
18:10 He said, "Two **m** went into the
19:24 The king told his **m**,
19:32 The **m** Jesus sent found it as
22:49 The **m** who were with Jesus
22:55 Some **m** had lit a fire in the
22:63 The **m** who were guarding
24:4 two **m** in clothes that were as
24:5 The **m** asked the women,
24:24 Some of our **m** went to the
Jon 6:10 about 5,000 **m** in the crowd.)
8:9 beginning with the older **m**,
18:8 let these other **m** go."
18:25 Some **m** asked him,
19:18 Jesus and two other **m** there.
19:40 These two **m** took the body of
Act 1:10 Suddenly, two **m** in white
1:11 They asked, "Why are you **m**
1:16 led the **m** to arrest Jesus.
1:21 He must be one of the **m** who
1:23 that two **m** were qualified.
1:23 These **m** were Joseph (who
2:5 Devout Jewish **m** from every
2:7 "All of these **m** who are
2:11 We hear these **m** in our own
2:12 All of these devout **m** were
2:14 "**M** of Judea and everyone
2:15 These **m** are not drunk as you
2:17 Your young **m** will see visions.
2:17 Your old **m** will dream dreams.
2:18 on both **m** and women.
2:22 "**M** of Israel, listen to what I
2:23 By using **m** who don't
3:2 was being carried by some **m**.
3:2 Every day these **m** would put
3:12 said to the people, "**M** of Israel,
4:4 so the number of **m** who
4:13 They realized that these **m** had
4:16 should we do to these **m**?
5:6 Some young **m** got up,
5:10 When the young **m** came back,
5:14 More **m** and women than ever
5:21 They also sent **m** to the prison
5:25 "The **m** you put in prison are
5:26 went with some of his **m**
5:33 When the **m** on the council
5:35 to the council, "**M** of Israel,
5:35 what you do with these **m**.
5:36 four hundred **m** joined him.
5:38 away from these **m** for now.
6:3 choose seven **m** whom the
6:6 The disciples had these **m**
6:6 their hands on these seven **m**.
6:9 ⌊One day⌋ some **m** from the
6:11 Then they bribed some **m** to lie.
6:11 These **m** said, "We heard him
7:26 He said to them, '**M**,
7:27 "But one of the **m** pushed
8:2 Devout **m** buried Stephen as
8:3 He dragged **m** and women out
8:12 **m** and women believed him
9:7 Meanwhile, the **m** traveling
9:38 they sent two **m** to him.
10:9 while Cornelius' **m** were on
10:17 the **m** sent by Cornelius found
10:19 "Three **m** are looking for you.
10:20 hesitate to go with these **m**.
10:21 So Peter went to the **m**.
10:22 The **m** replied, "Cornelius,
10:23 Peter asked the **m** to come into
10:41 We apostles are those **m** who
11:3 They said, "You went to visit **m**
11:11 "At that moment three **m**
13:13 Paul and his **m** took a ship
13:16 "**M** of Israel and converts to
14:15 and said, "**M**, what are you
15:1 Some **m** came from Judea and
15:2 a fierce dispute with these **m**.
15:22 to choose some of their **m**
15:24 authorize these **m** ⌊to speak⌋.
15:25 that we should choose **m**
15:30 So the **m** were sent on their
16:17 "These **m** are servants of the
16:20 "These **m** are stirring up a lot of
16:35 "You can release those **m**

Act 17:4 wives of many prominent **m**.
17:6 They shouted, "Those **m** who
17:12 Greek **m** and women.
17:15 The **m** who escorted Paul took
17:15 When the **m** left Athens,
17:22 court and said, "**M** of Athens,
17:34 Some **m** joined him and
19:7 About twelve **m** were in the
19:24 profit for the **m** who worked
19:25 Demetrius said, "**M**,
19:29 and they dragged the two **m**
19:37 The **m** you brought here don't
19:38 If Demetrius and the **m** who
20:5 All these **m** went ahead and
20:30 Some of your own **m** will come
21:8 one of the seven **m** who helped
21:23 We have four **m** who have
21:24 Take these **m**, go through the
21:26 The next day, Paul took the **m**
21:28 shouting, "**M** of Israel, help!
22:4 I tied up **m** and women and put
22:9 "The **m** who were with me saw
22:11 So the **m** who were with me
23:2 the **m** standing near Paul
23:3 ordering these **m** to strike me!"
23:4 The **m** standing near Paul said
23:7 and the **m** in the meeting were
23:13 More than forty **m** took part in
24:20 Otherwise, these **m** who are
25:23 and the most important **m**
27:10 "**M**, we're going to face a
27:12 most of the **m** decided to sail
27:13 the **m** thought their plan would
27:17 The **m** pulled it up on deck.
27:18 that the next day the **m** began
27:21 among them and said, "**M**,
27:25 So have courage, **m**!
Rom 1:27 Likewise, their **m** have given
1:27 **M** commit indecent acts with
1:27 commit indecent acts with **m**,
1Co 7:1 It's good for **m** not to get
11:11 couldn't exist without **m**
11:11 and **m** couldn't exist without
11:12 so **m** come into existence by
2Co 8:23 The other **m** are
8:24 So give these **m** a
12:17 any of the **m** I sent you?
Gal 2:12 until some **m** James had sent
1Ti 2:8 I want **m** to offer prayers
5:1 Talk to younger **m** as if they
2Ti 3:6 Some of these **m** go into
3:8 so these **m** oppose the truth.
Tit 2:2 Tell older **m** to be sober.
2:2 Tell them to be **m** of good
2:6 Encourage young **m** to use
Heb 7:20 The **m** from the tribe of Levi
11:16 Instead, these **m** were longing
Jas 2:2 For example, two **m** come to
1Pe 3:1 Their wives could win these **m**

Menahem (7)

2Ki 15:14 Then **M**, son of Gadi,
15:16 Then **M** attacked Tiphsah,
15:17 king of Judah, **M**, son of Gadi,
15:19 So **M** gave Pul 75,000 pounds
15:20 **M** raised the money from all the
15:21 Isn't everything else about **M** —
15:22 **M** lay down in death with his

Menahem's (1)

2Ki 15:23 **M** son Pekahiah began to rule.

Menna (1)

Luk 3:31 son of Melea, son of **M**,

men's (3)

Gen 44:1 "Fill the **m** sacks with as much
1Sm 21:5 The young **m** bodies are kept
Jon 19:31 to have the **m** legs broken

menstrual (1)

Eze 36:17 as a woman's **m** period.

mention (12)

Gen 40:14 **M** me to Pharaoh, and get me
Exo 23:13 "Never **m** the names of other

Jos 23:7 Don't ever **m** the names of their
Eze 16:56 You didn't **m** your sister Sodom
16:57 You didn't **m** her before your
Amo 6:10 "We shouldn't **m** the name of
Act 4:18 Jesus or even **m** his name.
5:28 not to **m** Jesus' name when
Rom 1:9 witness that I always **m** you
1Co 6:3 not to **m** things in this life?
Phm 1:4 thank my God when I **m** you
1:19 I won't even **m** that you owe

mentioned (9)

Lev 11:24 the creatures **m** above,
1Sm 4:18 When the messenger **m** the ark
1Ch 4:38 These who are **m** by name
6:65 by lot and **m** here by name
2Ch 28:15 Then the men who were **m** by
Isa 14:20 wicked will never be **m** again.
Act 28:21 or **m** anything bad about
Eph 5:3 or greed even be **m** among you.
5:4 or obscene jokes should be **m**

Meonothai (2)

1Ch 4:13 of Othniel were Hathath and **M**.
4:14 **M** was the father of Ophrah.

Mephaath (4)

Jos 13:18 Jahaz, Kedemoth, **M**,
21:37 Kedemoth, and **M**.
1Ch 6:79 and **M** with its pastureland.
Jer 48:21 the plain: to Holon, Jahzah, **M**,

Mephibosheth (14)

2Sm 4:4 His name was **M**.)
9:6 When **M** (son of Jonathan and
9:6 "**M**!" David said to him. "Yes,
9:8 **M** bowed down ⌊again⌋ and
9:10 your master's grandson **M** will
9:11 From then on, **M** ate at David's
9:12 **M** had a young son whose
9:13 However, **M**, who was
16:4 belonged to **M** now belongs
19:24 **M**, Saul's grandson, went to
19:25 didn't you go with me, **M**?"
19:30 him take it all," **M** told the king.
21:7 But the king spared **M**,
21:8 The king took Armoni and **M**,

Mephibosheth's (2)

2Sm 9:12 Ziba's home became **M** servant
16:1 **M** servant, met him with a pair

Merab (4)

1Sm 14:49 were **M** (the firstborn daughter
18:17 "Here is my oldest daughter **M**.
18:19 Saul's daughter **M** to David,
2Sm 21:8 and five sons whom **M** (Saul's

Meraiah (1)

Neh 12:12 **M**; from Jeremiah, Hananiah;

Meraioth (7)

1Ch 6:6 Zerahiah was the father of **M**.
6:7 **M** was the father of Amariah.
6:52 Zerahiah's son was **M**.
9:11 Zadok's father was **M**,
Ezr 7:3 who was the son of **M**,
Neh 11:11 who was the son of **M**,
12:15 from Harim, Adna; from **M**,

Meraioth's (1)

1Ch 6:52 **M** son was Amariah.

Merari (20)

Gen 46:11 were Gershon, Kohath, and **M**.
Exo 6:16 order: Gershon, Kohath, and **M**.
6:19 The sons of **M** were Mahli and
Num 3:17 and **M** were the sons of Levi.
3:20 and Mushi were the sons of **M**.
3:33 To **M** belonged the families
3:33 the families descended from **M**.
26:57 and the family of **M**.
Jos 21:34 To the families of **M**,
21:40 belonged to the families of **M**.
1Ch 6:1 were Gershon, Kohath, and **M**.
6:16 were Gershom, Kohath, and **M**.
6:44 relatives descended from **M**.
6:47 who was the son of **M**,
9:14 from **M** were Shemaiah (son
23:6 or **M**) they were descended
24:26 Levi's descendants from **M**:
26:10 From the descendants of **M**
2Ch 34:12 (Levites descended from **M**),
Ezr 8:19 (who was a descendant of **M**),

Merari's (14)

Jos 21:7 **M** descendants received 12
1Ch 6:19 **M** sons were Mahli and Mushi.
6:29 These were **M** descendants:
6:29 **M** son was Mahli. Mahli's son
6:63 The families of **M** descendants
6:77 The rest of **M** descendants
6:78 **M** descendants received land
15:6 Leading **M** descendants was
15:17 **M** descendants, they appointed
23:21 **M** sons were Mahli and Mushi.
24:26 and **M** son Jaaziah,
24:27 and Ibri (for **M** descendants
26:19 Korah's and **M** descendants
2Ch 29:12 From **M** descendants were

Merarite (3)

Num 3:35 The leader of the **M** families
4:33 This is what the **M** families
4:45 registered in the **M** families.

Merarites (6)

Num 3:36 It was the duty of the **M** to be in
4:29 "Register the **M** by families and
4:42 The **M** were registered by
4:45 Moses and registered the **M**.
7:8 and eight oxen to the **M**
10:17 and the Gershonites and **M**,

Merathaim (1)

Jer 50:21 "Attack the land of **M** and the

mercenaries (8)

2Sm 11:1 battle, David sent Joab, his **m**,
11:9 palace among his superior's **m**.
11:11 and Your Majesty's **m** are living
11:13 his bed among his superior's **m**.
11:17 some of David's **m**,
11:24 the wall shot down at your **m**,
11:24 some of Your Majesty's **m** died.
15:18 All his **m** passed by him;

merchandise (10)

Neh 10:31 inhabitants of the land bring **m**
Isa 23:18 Her **m** will belong to those who
45:14 the **m** from Sudan,
Eze 27:12 and lead for your **m**.
27:14 and mules for your **m**.
27:16 and rubies for your **m**.
27:19 from Uzal traded for your **m**.
27:22 and gold for your **m**.
27:27 Your wealth, your **m**,
27:33 Your **m** was sent overseas.

merchant (3)

Pro 31:14 She is like **m** ships.
Eze 27:3 It is the **m** to the nations.
Mat 13:45 is like a **m** who was searching

merchants (24)

Gen 37:28 As the Midianite **m** were
1Ki 10:15 gold⌋ which came from the **m**,
2Ch 9:14 ⌊the gold⌋ which the **m**
Neh 3:31 and **m** across from Inspection
3:32 The goldsmiths and **m** made
13:20 Once or twice **m** and those
Job 41:6 it and divide it among the **m**?
Pro 31:24 and delivers belts to the **m**.
Isa 23:2 you **m** from Sidon.
23:8 Its **m** are princes. Its traders are
Eze 16:29 to include the land of the **m**,
17:4 and carried it to a country of **m**.
17:4 planted the twig in a city of **m**.
27:22 The **m** from Sheba and
27:23 the **m** from Sheba,
27:27 your caulkers and your **m**,
27:36 The **m** among the nations
38:13 the **m** from Tarshish,
Hos 12:7 "The **m** use dishonest scales.
Zep 1:11 because all the **m** will be
Rev 18:3 wealth has made the **m**
18:11 "The **m** of the earth cry and
18:15 her torture, the **m** who had
18:23 Its **m** were the important people

merchants' (2)

Gen 23:16 at the current **m** exchange rate.
Sos 3:6 from the **m** scented powders.

merciful (44)

Gen 43:14 May God Almighty make him **m**
Exo 33:19 I will be **m** to anyone I want to.
34:6 a compassionate and **m** God,
Dtr 4:31 LORD your God is a **m** God.
7:9 keeps his promise and is **m**
7:12 to you and be **m** to you,
2Sm 24:14 hands because he is very **m**.
1Ki 20:31 that the kings of Israel are **m**.
2Ki 13:23 But the LORD was kind and **m**
1Ch 21:13 because he is extremely **m**.
2Ch 30:9 God is **m** and compassionate.
Neh 9:17 is compassionate, **m**, patient,
9:31 a **m** and compassionate God.
Psa 25:6 compassionate and **m** deeds.
59:9 is my stronghold, my **m** God!
59:17 is my stronghold, my **m** God!
77:9 Has God forgotten to be **m**?
86:15 a compassionate and **m** God.
98:3 He has not forgotten to be **m**
103:8 is compassionate, **m**, patient,
111:4 is **m** and compassionate.
112:4 He is **m**, compassionate,
116:5 The LORD is **m** and righteous.
144:2 my **m** one, my fortress,
145:8 The LORD is **m**, patient, and
Pro 11:17 A **m** person helps himself,
14:22 while those who are **m** and
Jer 3:12 you because I'm **m**,' declares
Dan 2:18 ask the God of heaven to be **m**
Joe 2:13 He is **m** and compassionate,
Jnh 4:2 I knew that you are a **m** and
Hab 3:2 remember to be **m**.
Mar 5:19 has done for you and how **m**
Luk 1:78 our God is loving and **m**.
6:36 Be **m** as your Father is
6:36 merciful as your Father is **m**.
18:13 'God, be **m** to me, a sinner!'
Rom 9:15 I will be **m** to anyone I want to."
11:30 But now God has been **m** to
11:31 so that God may be **m**
11:32 he could be **m** to all people.
2Ti 1:16 May the Lord be **m** to the family
Heb 2:17 sisters so that he could be **m**.
Jas 5:11 Lord is compassionate and **m**.

mercifully (2)

Mat 5:7 They will be treated **m**.
18:33 the other servant as **m** as

mercy (270)

Gen 42:21 when he pleaded with us for **m**,
Exo 20:6 But I show **m** to thousands of
25:17 "Make a throne of **m** to cover
25:18 the two ends of the throne of **m**,
25:19 angels and the throne of **m** out
25:20 spread above the throne of **m**,
25:20 looking at the throne of **m**.
25:21 place the throne of **m** on top.
25:22 I will be above the throne of **m**
26:34 Put the throne of **m** that is on
30:6 in front of the throne of **m** that is
31:7 with the throne of **m** on it,
35:12 the throne of **m** and the canopy
37:6 He made the throne of **m** out of
37:7 the two ends of the throne of **m**,
37:8 angels and the throne of **m** out
37:9 spread above the throne of **m**,
37:9 looking at the throne of **m**.
39:35 its poles and the throne of **m**,
40:20 ark and placed the throne of **m**
Lev 16:2 in front of the throne of **m**
16:2 smoke above the throne of **m**.
16:13 will cover the throne of **m**,

Lev 16:14 the east side of the throne of **m**.
16:14 times in front of the throne of **m**.
16:15 sprinkle it on the throne of **m**
Num 7:89 him from above the throne of **m**
Dtr 5:10 But I show **m** to thousands of
7:2 with them or show them any **m**.
13:17 angry and will show you **m**.
13:17 In his **m** he will make your
30:3 He will have **m** on you and
Jos 9:8 to Joshua, "We're at your **m**."
9:11 Tell them, "We're at your **m**.
9:25 Now we're at your **m**.
11:20 all for destruction without **m**,
2Sm 22:51 He shows **m** to his anointed,
1Ki 8:23 You keep your promise of **m** to
8:28 attention to my prayer for **m**.
8:30 Hear the plea for **m** that your
8:38 ⌞hear⌟ every prayer for **m**,
8:45 their prayer for **m** in heaven,
8:49 hear their prayer for **m**.
8:50 them to have **m** on them
8:54 praying this prayer for **m**
9:3 "I have heard your prayer for **m**
2Ki 3:10 has put the three of us at the **m**
3:13 in order to put us at Moab's **m**."
3:18 he will put Moab at your **m**.
13:3 with Israel and put it at the **m**
1Ch 16:34 because his **m** endures forever.
16:41 "His **m** endures forever."
28:11 the room for the throne of **m**.
2Ch 5:13 his **m** endures forever."
6:14 You keep your promise of **m** to
6:19 attention to my prayer for **m**.
6:21 Hear the plea for **m** that your
6:29 ⌞hear⌟ every prayer for **m** made
6:35 their prayer for **m** in heaven,
6:39 hear their prayer for **m**.
6:42 Remember your **m** to your
7:3 his **m** endures forever."
7:6 with "his **m** endures forever"
20:21 his **m** endures forever!"
Ezr 3:11 his **m** toward Israel endures
Neh 1:5 keep your promise and show **m**
Est 4:8 to go to the king, beg him for **m**,
8:3 and begged him to have **m**
Job 8:5 plead for **m** from the Almighty,
9:15 to plead for **m** from my judge.
10:12 You gave me life and **m**.
16:13 open my kidneys without **m**
27:22 It hurls itself at him without **m**.
37:13 good of⌟ his earth, or out of **m**,
41:3 Will it plead with you for **m** or
Psa 5:7 house because of your great **m**.
6:4 Save me because of your **m**!
6:9 LORD has heard my plea for **m**.
13:5 But I trust your **m**. My heart
17:7 your miraculous deeds of **m**,
18:50 He shows **m** to his anointed,
21:7 and through the **m** of the Most
23:6 Certainly, goodness and **m** will
25:7 your **m** and your goodness.
25:10 path of the LORD is ⌞one of⌟ **m**
26:3 I see your **m** in front of me.
28:2 Hear my prayer for **m** when I
28:6 He has heard my prayer for **m**!
30:8 I will plead to the Lord for **m**:
31:7 and be glad because of your **m**.
31:16 Save me with your **m**.
31:21 shown me the miracle of his **m**
31:22 But you heard my pleas for **m**
32:10 but **m** surrounds those who
33:5 His **m** fills the earth.
33:18 who wait with hope for his **m**
33:22 Let your **m** rest on us,
36:5 your **m** reaches to the heavens,
36:7 Your **m** is so precious,
36:10 Continue to show your **m** to
40:10 I have not hidden your **m** and
40:11 May your **m** and your truth
41:2 him at the **m** of his enemies.
42:8 The LORD commands his **m**
44:26 Rescue us because of your **m**!
48:9 we carefully reflect on your **m**,
51:1 in keeping with your **m**.
52:1 The **m** of God lasts all day
52:8 I trust the **m** of God forever and
Psa 55:1 Do not hide from my plea for **m**.
57:3 God sends his **m** and his truth!
57:10 because your **m** is as high as
59:16 will joyfully sing about your **m**.
61:7 May **m** and truth protect him.
62:12 **M** belongs to you, O Lord.
63:3 because your **m** is better than
66:20 or taken away his **m** from me.
69:13 out of the greatness of your **m**,
69:16 because your **m** is good.
77:8 Has his **m** come to an end
85:7 Show us your **m**, O LORD,
85:10 **M** and truth have met.
86:5 full of **m** toward everyone who
86:6 attention when I plead for **m**.
86:13 because your **m** toward me is
88:11 Will anyone tell about your **m**
89:1 about the evidence of your **m**,
89:2 I said, "Your **m** will last forever.
89:14 **M** and truth stand in front of
89:24 My faithfulness and **m** will be
89:28 My **m** will stay with him
89:33 But I will not take my **m** away
89:49 is the evidence of your **m**,
90:14 morning with your **m** so that we
92:2 It is good to announce your **m**
94:18 are slipping," your **m**, O LORD,
100:5 His **m** endures forever.
101:1 I will sing about **m** and justice.
103:4 you with **m** and compassion,
103:11 how vast his **m** is toward those
103:17 the LORD's **m** is on those who
106:1 because his **m** endures forever.
106:7 your numerous acts of **m**,
106:45 In keeping with his rich **m**,
107:1 because his **m** endures forever.
107:8 to the LORD because of his **m**.
107:15 to the LORD because of his **m**.
107:21 to the LORD because of his **m**.
107:31 to the LORD because of his **m**.
108:4 because your **m** is higher than
109:21 Rescue me because of your **m**.
109:26 Save me because of your **m**.
115:1 of your **m** and faithfulness.
116:1 my voice, my pleas for **m**.
117:2 His **m** toward us is powerful.
118:1 because his **m** endures forever.
118:2 "His **m** endures forever."
118:3 "His **m** endures forever."
118:4 "His **m** endures forever."
118:29 because his **m** endures forever.
119:64 Your **m**, O LORD, fills the
119:76 Let your **m** comfort me as you
119:88 new life through your **m** so that
119:121 Do not leave me at the **m** of
119:149 In keeping with your **m**,
119:159 in keeping with your **m**,
119:170 Let my plea for **m** come into
130:2 ears be open to my pleas for **m**.
130:7 with the LORD there is **m**
136:1 because his **m** endures forever.
136:2 because his **m** endures forever.
136:3 because his **m** endures forever.
136:4 because his **m** endures forever.
136:5 because his **m** endures forever.
136:6 because his **m** endures forever.
136:7 because his **m** endures forever.
136:8 because his **m** endures forever.
136:9 because his **m** endures forever.
136:10 because his **m** endures forever.
136:11 because his **m** endures forever.
136:12 because his **m** endures forever.
136:13 because his **m** endures forever.
136:14 because his **m** endures forever.
136:15 because his **m** endures forever.
136:16 because his **m** endures forever.
136:17 because his **m** endures forever.
136:18 because his **m** endures forever.
136:19 because his **m** endures forever.
136:20 because his **m** endures forever.
136:21 because his **m** endures forever.
136:22 because his **m** endures forever.
136:23 because his **m** endures forever.
136:24 because his **m** endures forever.
136:25 because his **m** endures forever.
136:26 because his **m** endures forever.
Psa 138:2 because of your **m** and truth.
138:8 your **m** endures forever.
142:1 I plead with the LORD for **m**.
143:8 Let me hear about your **m** in the
143:12 In keeping with your **m**,
147:11 who wait with hope for his **m**.
Pro 3:3 Do not let **m** and truth leave
6:34 The husband will show no **m**
16:6 By **m** and faithfulness,
20:28 **M** and truth protect a king,
20:28 and with **m** he maintains his
21:21 and **m** will find life,
Isa 47:6 You showed them no **m**.
63:7 the LORD's acts of **m**,
63:7 and his unlimited **m**.
Jer 13:14 I will have no pity, **m**,
32:18 You show **m** to thousands of
33:11 because his **m** endures forever.'
37:20 and accept my plea for **m**.
Lam 3:22 the LORD's **m**. We were not
3:32 with the richness of his **m**.
Dan 9:4 keep your promise and show **m**
Mic 6:8 to do what is right, to love **m**,
7:18 you would rather show **m**.
7:20 You will have **m** on Abraham
Hab 1:17 always kill nations without **m**?
Zec 12:10 out the Spirit of blessing and **m**
Mat 5:7 are those who show **m**.
9:13 'I want **m**, not sacrifices.'
9:27 They shouted, "Have **m** on us,
12:7 you had known what 'I want **m**,
15:22 to shout, "Have **m** on me, Lord,
17:15 have **m** on my son.
20:30 Son of David, have **m** on us!"
20:31 Son of David, have **m** on us!"
23:23 justice, **m**, and faithfulness.
Mar 10:47 Son of David, have **m** on me!"
10:48 "Son of David, have **m** on me!"
Luk 1:50 For those who fear him, his **m**
1:72 He has shown his **m** to our
16:24 Have **m** on me! Send Lazarus to
17:13 Teacher, have **m** on us!"
18:38 Son of David, have **m** on me!"
18:39 "Son of David, have **m** on me!"
Rom 1:31 own families or **m** to others.
3:25 of **m** where God's approval
9:16 desire or effort, but on God's **m**.
9:23 who are objects of his **m**
15:9 praise God for his **m** as well.
1Co 7:25 whom the Lord has shown **m**,
2Co 4:1 us this ministry through his **m**.
Gal 6:16 Peace and **m** will come to rest
Eph 2:4 But God is rich in **m** because
Php 2:27 But God had **m** not only on him
1Ti 1:2 Good will, **m**, and peace from
1:13 However, I was treated with **m**
1:16 However, I was treated with **m**
2Ti 1:2 Good will, **m**, and peace from
1:18 finds **m** when that day
Tit 3:5 Instead, because of his **m** he
Heb 4:16 of God's kindness to receive **m**
9:5 overshadowing the throne of **m**.
10:28 that person was shown no **m**
Jas 2:13 No **m** will be shown to those
2:13 who show no **m** to others.
2:13 **M** triumphs over judgment.
3:17 filled with **m** and good deeds,
1Pe 1:3 birth because of his great **m**.
2:10 Once you were not shown **m**,
2:10 now you have been shown **m**.
2Jn 1:3 Good will, **m**, and peace will
Jud 1:2 May **m**, peace, and love fill
1:21 love as you look for the **m**
1:22 Show **m** to those who have
1:23 Show **m** to others,

Mered (1)

1Ch 4:17 Ezrah's sons were Jether, **M**,

Meremoth (6)

Ezr 8:33 under the supervision of **M**,
10:36 Vaniah, **M**, Eliashib,
Neh 3:4 Next to them **M**, son of Uriah
3:21 After him **M**, son of Uriah and
10:5 Harim, **M**, Obadiah,
12:3 Shecaniah, Rehum, **M**,

Meres (1)

Est 1:14 **M**, Marsena, and Memucan.

Meribah (11)

Exo 17:7 [Testing] and **M** [Complaining]
Num 20:13 the oasis of **M** [Complaining],
20:24 my command at the oasis of **M**.
27:14 (This was the oasis of **M** at
Dtr 32:51 me at the oasis of **M** at Kadesh
33:8 with them at the oasis of **M**.
Psa 81:7 ⌊loyalty⌋ at the oasis of **M**.
95:8 like ⌊my people were⌋ at **M**,
106:32 God angry by the water at **M**.
Eze 47:19 from Tamar to the oasis at **M**
48:28 to the oasis at **M** in Kadesh,

Meribbaal (4)

1Ch 8:34 Jonathan's son was **M**,
8:34 and **M** was the father of Micah.
9:40 Jonathan's son was **M**,
9:40 and **M** was the father of Micah.

Merodach Baladan (2)

2Ki 20:12 Baladan's son, King **M** of
Isa 39:1 Baladan's son, King **M** of

Merom (2)

Jos 11:5 together by the Springs of **M**
11:7 suddenly at the Springs of **M**

Meronoth (2)

1Ch 27:30 the donkeys: Jehdeiah from **M**
Neh 3:7 from Gibeon and Jadon from **M**,

Meroz (1)

Jdg 5:23 "Curse **M**!" said the Messenger

mesh (2)

Exo 27:4 a grate for it out of bronze **m**,
38:4 for the altar out of bronze **m**,

Mesha (4)

Gen 10:30 from **M** toward Sephar
2Ki 3:4 King **M** of Moab raised sheep.
1Ch 2:42 were his firstborn son **M**,
8:9 Jobab, Zibia, **M**, Malcam,

Meshach (15)

Dan 1:7 Mishael he gave the name **M**.
2:49 Daniel appointed Shadrach, **M**,
3:12 Shadrach, **M**, and Abednego.
3:13 **M**, and Abednego. Immediately,
3:14 "Shadrach, **M**, and Abednego,
3:16 Shadrach, **M**, and Abednego
3:19 anger toward Shadrach, **M**,
3:20 his army to tie up Shadrach, **M**,
3:22 men who carried Shadrach, **M**,
3:23 three men — Shadrach, **M**,
3:26 and said, "Shadrach, **M**,
3:26 Shadrach, **M**, and Abednego
3:28 of Shadrach, **M**, and Abednego.
3:29 about the God of Shadrach, **M**,
3:30 king promoted Shadrach, **M**,

Meshech (10)

Gen 10:2 Javan, Tubal, **M**, and Tiras.
1Ch 1:5 Javan, Tubal, **M**, and Tiras.
1:17 Aram, Uz, Hul, Gether, and **M**.
Psa 120:5 it is to live as a foreigner in **M**
Isa 66:19 Lud, **M**, Rosh, Tubal, Javan,
Eze 27:13 and **M** traded with you.
32:26 "**M** and Tubal are there with all
38:2 ⌊the nations of⌋ **M** and Tubal.
38:3 chief prince of **M** and Tubal.
39:1 the chief prince of **M** and Tubal.

Meshelemiah (2)

1Ch 9:21 Zechariah, son of **M**,
26:1 descendants there was **M**,

Meshelemiah's (2)

1Ch 26:2 **M** sons were Zechariah (the
26:9 **M** sons and relatives were 18

Meshezabel (3)

Neh 3:4 Berechiah and grandson of **M**,
10:21 **M**, Zadok, Jaddua,
11:24 Pethahiah, son of **M**,

Meshillemith (1)

1Ch 9:12 whose father was **M**,

Meshillemoth (2)

2Ch 28:12 son of **M**, Jehizkiah,
Neh 11:13 who was the son of **M**,

Meshobab (1)

1Ch 4:34 **M**, Jamlech, Joshah (son of

Meshullam (25)

2Ki 22:3 of Azaliah and grandson of **M**,
1Ch 3:19 sons were **M** and Hananiah,
5:13 **M**, Sheba, Jorai, Jacan, Zia,
8:17 Zebadiah, **M**, Hizki, Heber,
9:7 Benjamin were Sallu (son of **M**,
9:8 and **M** (son of Shephatiah,
9:11 son of Hilkiah, grandson of **M**,
9:12 and great-grandson of **M**,
2Ch 34:12 and Zechariah and **M**
Ezr 8:16 and **M** (who were leading men)
10:15 **M** and Shabbethai,
10:29 **M**, Malluch, Adaiah, Jashub,
Neh 3:4 Next to them **M**, son of
3:6 Joiada, Paseah's son, and **M**,
3:30 After him **M**, Berechiah's son,
6:18 had married the daughter of **M**,
8:4 and **M** stood beside him on his
10:7 **M**, Abijah, Mijamin,
10:20 Magpiash, **M**, Hezir,
11:7 who was the son of **M**,
11:11 who was the son of **M**,
12:13 from Ezra, **M**; from Amariah,
12:16 Zechariah; from Ginnethon, **M**;
12:25 Obadiah, **M**, Talmon,
12:33 Azariah, Ezra, **M**,

Meshullemeth (1)

2Ki 21:19 His mother was **M**,

Mesopotamia (3)

1Ch 19:6 from the Arameans in Upper **M**,
Act 2:9 We're people from **M**,
7:2 to our ancestor Abraham in **M**.

message (226)

Gen 31:4 So Jacob sent a **m** to Rachel
32:4 them to give this **m** to Esau,
38:25 she sent a **m** to her
50:17 cried when he got their **m**.
Exo 36:6 following **m** announced all over
Num 22:5 Balak's **m** was, "A nation has
22:10 sent them with this **m**:
23:5 and give him my **m**."
23:7 Then Balaam delivered this **m**:
23:16 and give him my **m**."
23:18 Then Balaam delivered this **m**:
24:3 and he delivered this **m**:
24:3 "This is the **m** of Balaam,
24:3 This is the **m** of the man
24:4 This is the **m** of the one who
24:15 Then Balaam delivered this **m**:
24:15 "This is the **m** of Balaam,
24:15 This is the **m** of the man
24:16 This is the **m** of the one who
24:20 and delivered this **m**:
24:21 Kenites and delivered this **m**:
24:23 He delivered this **m**:
Dtr 18:21 the LORD didn't speak this **m**?"
Jos 10:3 of Jerusalem sent ⌊this **m**⌋
10:6 The men of Gibeon sent this **m**
Jdg 3:19 I have a secret **m** for you."
3:20 "I have a **m** from God for you."
7:24 region of Ephraim with this **m**,
11:28 to the **m** Jephthah sent him.
16:18 she sent a **m** to the Philistine
1Sm 9:15 had revealed the following **m**
11:7 of Israel with the following **m**:
11:9 men of Jabesh received the **m**,
16:22 Saul sent ⌊this **m**⌋ to Jesse,
2Sm 3:17 Abner sent the following **m** to
12:25 and sent a **m** through the
15:28 until I receive a **m** from you."
18:22 why should you deliver the **m**?"
19:11 So King David sent ⌊this **m**⌋ to
19:14 So they sent the king this **m**:
1Ki 5:8 "I've received the **m** you sent
20:5 has sent this **m** to you:
20:10 sent Ahab the following **m**:
21:14 sent ⌊this **m**⌋ to Jezebel:
21:15 Jezebel received the **m** and
22:13 told the king the same good **m**.
22:13 Make your **m** agree with their
22:13 message agree with their **m**.
2Ki 3:7 He sent this **m** to King
6:9 man of God would send a **m**
10:5 guardians sent this **m** to Jehu:
14:9 Jehoash of Israel sent this **m**
14:9 "A thistle in Lebanon sent a **m**
18:14 Hezekiah of Judah sent this **m**
18:37 They told him the **m** from the
19:1 King Hezekiah heard the **m**,
19:4 him because of the **m** that
19:6 Don't be afraid of the **m** that you
19:16 Listen to the **m** that
19:20 sent a **m** to Hezekiah,
19:21 This is the **m** that the LORD
2Ch 18:12 told the king the same good **m**.
18:12 Make your **m** agree with their
18:12 message agree with their **m**.
25:18 Jehoash of Israel sent this **m**
25:18 "A thistle in Lebanon sent a **m**
30:1 Hezekiah sent a **m** to all Israel
Ezr 6:14 progress because of the **m** from
Neh 6:2 and Geshem sent this **m** to me:
6:4 They sent the same **m** to me
6:5 Sanballat sent me the same **m**
8:15 send this **m** throughout all their
Est 8:17 every city where the king's **m**
Psa 19:4 their **m** to the ends of the earth.
81:5 I heard a **m** I did not
107:20 He sent his **m** and healed them.
Pro 26:6 a fool to send a **m** cuts off his
Isa 2:1 This is the **m** which Isaiah,
9:8 LORD sent a **m** against Jacob.
9:8 The **m** is against Israel.
16:13 This is the **m** that the LORD
28:9 they make the **m** understood?
28:9 whom will they explain this **m**?
28:19 this **m** brings only terror.
36:22 They told him the **m** from the
37:1 King Hezekiah heard the **m**,
37:4 him because of the **m** that
37:6 Don't be afraid of the **m** that you
37:17 Listen to the entire **m** that
37:21 sent a **m** to Hezekiah,
37:22 This is the **m** that the LORD
53:1 Who has believed our **m**?
Jer 4:5 Report this **m** in Judah.
4:15 A **m** is heard from Dan,
7:2 announce from there this **m**:
10:1 Listen to the **m** that the LORD
11:1 This is the **m** that the LORD
13:12 "Give this **m** to them,
18:2 There I will give you my **m**."
22:1 and speak this **m** there:
23:21 yet they ran ⌊with their **m**⌋.
27:12 I spoke the same **m** to King
27:16 I also spoke this **m** to the
28:7 But now listen to this **m** that I
28:9 the LORD sent only if the **m**
29:28 why Jeremiah sent this **m**
29:31 "Send this **m** to all the
30:4 This is the **m** that the LORD
31:6 of Ephraim will call out this **m**:
36:6 the LORD's **m** that you wrote
37:17 "Is there any **m** from the
37:17 There is a **m** from the LORD.
43:1 telling all the people the **m** from
44:16 "We won't listen to the **m** that
45:1 This is the **m** that the prophet
46:1 The LORD spoke this **m** to the
46:2 This is the **m** about Egypt,
46:13 The LORD spoke this **m** to the
47:1 The LORD spoke this **m** to the
49:14 I heard a **m** from the LORD.

Jer 49:23 This is a **m** about Damascus.
50:1 This is the **m** that the LORD
51:59 This is the **m** that the prophet
Eze 13:6 that their **m** will come true.
Dan 9:23 respected. So study the **m**,
10:1 a **m** was revealed to Daniel
10:1 The **m** was true. It was about a
10:1 Daniel understood the **m**
Amo 3:1 Listen to this **m** which I,
4:1 Listen to this **m**, you cows of
5:1 Listen to this **m**, this funeral
7:10 sent a **m** to King Jeroboam of
Oba 1:1 We have heard a **m** from the
Jnh 3:2 Announce to the people the **m** I
Hag 1:13 had received the LORD's **m**,
Mat 3:1 desert of Judea. His **m** was,
10:7 As you go, spread this **m**:
11:1 to teach his **m** in their cities.
11:14 are willing to accept their **m**,
12:41 when Jonah spoke his **m**.
27:19 his wife sent him a **m**.
Luk 2:10 I have good news for you, a **m**
4:44 So he spread his **m** in the
9:2 He sent them to spread the **m**
11:32 when Jonah spoke his **m**,
Jon 1:7 believers through his **m**.
3:11 Yet, you don't accept our **m**.
3:34 God has sent speaks God's **m**.
5:38 have the Father's **m** within you,
6:61 were criticizing his **m**.
11:4 When Jesus heard the **m**,
12:38 who has believed our **m**?
17:8 because I gave them the **m**
17:8 They have accepted this **m**,
17:14 I have given them your **m**.
17:20 believe in me through their **m**.
Act 4:2 and spreading the **m** that
4:4 heard the **m** became believers,
8:25 had boldly spoken about the **m**
10:44 to everyone who heard his **m**.
11:14 He will give you a **m** that will
13:15 synagogue leaders sent ⌊a **m**⌋
13:15 The **m** said, "Brothers, if you
13:26 the **m** that God saves
14:3 who confirmed their **m** about
14:25 They spoke the **m** in the city of
17:11 very willing to receive God's **m**,
20:32 God and to his **m** that tells how
20:32 That **m** can help you grow and
23:25 governor with the following **m**:
26:20 Instead, I spread the **m** that I
26:20 I spread the same **m** to
28:31 He spread the **m** about God's
Rom 10:8 "This **m** is near you.
10:8 This is the **m** of faith that we
10:14 if they have not heard his **m**?
10:16 who has believed our **m**?"
10:17 faith comes from hearing the **m**,
10:17 and the **m** that is heard is what
10:18 "Didn't they hear that **m**?"
10:19 Israel understand ⌊that **m**⌋?"
16:25 by the Good News and the **m**
1Co 1:6 Our **m** about Christ has been
1:18 The **m** about the cross is
1:23 but our **m** is that Christ was
2:1 kind of brilliant **m** or wisdom.
2:4 I didn't speak my **m** with
2:4 I spoke my **m** with a show of
15:11 this is the **m** we brought you,
15:14 our **m** has no meaning and your
2Co 1:18 Our **m** to you isn't false;
1:19 of him our **m** was always true.
1:20 that reason, because of our **m**,
2:17 we speak the pure **m** that
4:5 Our **m** is not about ourselves.
5:19 and he has given us this **m** of
Gal 1:11 have spread is not a human **m**.
2:6 add a single thing to my **m**.
Eph 1:13 and believed the **m** of truth,
4:21 You have certainly heard his **m**
Php 1:15 Some people tell the **m** about
1:15 Others tell the **m** about him
1:16 Those who tell the **m** about
1:17 They tell the **m** about Christ out
1:18 are told the **m** about Christ,
Col 1:5 News which is the **m** of truth.
Col 1:25 work of telling you his entire **m**.
1:28 We spread the **m** about Christ
1Ti 2:6 This **m** is valid for every era.
2Ti 2:2 You've heard my **m**,
2:2 Entrust this **m** to faithful
Tit 1:2 My **m** is based on the
1:9 to the trustworthy **m** we teach.
2:8 Speak an accurate **m** that
Heb 2:2 After all, the **m** that the angels
2:3 if we reject the important **m**,
2:3 the **m** that God saved us?
2:3 the Lord told this saving **m**.
2:3 heard him confirmed that **m**.
4:2 But the **m** didn't help those who
12:24 speaks a better **m** than Abel's.
2Pe 1:16 we didn't base our **m** on clever
1Jn 1:5 This is the **m** we heard from
2:24 Make sure that the **m** you heard
2:24 If that **m** lives in you,
3:11 The **m** that you have heard

messages (6)

2Ch 36:15 sent **m** through his messengers
Jer 27:3 Then send **m** to the kings of
36:32 They added many similar **m**.
Act 7:38 Moses received life-giving **m** to
13:27 understand the prophets' **m**,
1Ti 4:13 giving encouraging **m**,

messenger (143)

Gen 16:7 The **M** of the LORD found her
16:9 The **M** of the LORD said to her,
16:10 The **M** of the LORD also said
16:11 Then the **M** of the LORD said
21:17 and the **M** of God called to
22:11 But the **M** of the LORD called
22:15 Then the **M** of the LORD called
31:11 In the dream the **M** of God
48:16 may the **M**, who has rescued
50:16 They sent a **m** to Joseph to
Exo 3:2 The **M** of the LORD appeared
14:19 The **M** of God, who had been
23:20 "I'm going to send a **M** in front
23:23 "My **M** will go ahead of you
32:34 My **M** will go ahead of you.
33:2 I will send a **M** ahead of you,
Num 20:16 LORD, he heard us, sent a **m**,
22:22 So the **M** of the LORD stood in
22:23 When the donkey saw the **M** of
22:24 Now the **M** of the LORD stood
22:25 When the donkey saw the **M** of
22:26 Then the **M** of the LORD
22:27 When the donkey saw the **M** of
22:31 the LORD let Balaam see the **M**
22:32 The **M** of the LORD asked him,
22:34 Balaam said to the **M** of the
22:35 The **M** of the LORD said to
Jdg 2:1 The **M** of the LORD went from
2:4 While the **M** of the LORD was
5:23 said the **M** of the LORD.
6:11 The **M** of the LORD came and
6:12 The **M** of the LORD appeared
6:19 and presented them to the **M**
6:20 The **M** of the LORD told him,
6:21 Then the **M** of the LORD
6:21 Then the **M** of the LORD
6:22 that this had been the **M**
6:22 I have seen the **M** of the LORD
13:3 The **M** of the LORD appeared
13:6 appearance like the **M** of God.
13:9 The **M** of God came back to
13:13 The **M** of the LORD answered
13:15 Manoah said to the **M** of the
13:16 But the **M** of the LORD
13:16 that it was the **M** of the LORD.)
13:17 Then Manoah asked the **M** of
13:18 The **M** of the LORD asked him,
13:20 the **M** of the LORD went up in
13:21 The **M** of the LORD didn't
13:21 had been the **M** of the LORD.
1Sm 4:17 Philistines," the **m** answered.
4:18 When the **m** mentioned the ark
23:27 Then a **m** came to Saul and
29:9 you're as good as God's **M**.
2Sm 11:6 Then David sent a **m** to Joab,
11:18 Then Joab sent ⌊a **m**⌋ to report
2Sm 11:19 And he commanded the **m**,
11:22 The **m** left, and when he
11:23 The **m** said, "Their men
11:25 David said to the **m**,
14:17 You are like God's **M**,
14:20 You are as wise as God's **M**,
18:21 The **m** bowed down with his
18:22 to run after the Sudanese **m**."
18:23 got ahead of the Sudanese **m**.
18:31 Then the Sudanese **m** came.
18:32 The Sudanese **m** answered,
19:27 However, you are like God's **M**.
24:16 But when the **M** stretched out
24:16 he said to the **M** who was
24:16 The **M** of the LORD was at the
24:17 When David saw the **M** who
1Ki 19:2 Jezebel sent a **m** to Elijah.
22:13 The **m** who went to call
2Ki 5:8 he sent a **m** to the king.
5:10 Elisha sent a **m** to him.
6:32 But before the **m** arrived,
6:32 When the **m** comes,
6:33 talking to them, the **m** arrived.
9:18 "The **m** you sent has reached
10:8 A **m** told him, "They've brought
1Ch 21:12 a plague in the land with the **M**
21:15 God also sent a **M** to
21:15 he said to the destroying **M**.
21:15 The **M** of the LORD was
21:16 he saw the **M** of the LORD
21:16 The **M** had a sword in his hand
21:18 The LORD's **M** told Gad to tell
21:20 turned around and seen the **M**.
21:27 So the LORD spoke to the **M**,
21:30 by the sword of the LORD's **M**.
2Ch 18:12 The **m** who went to call
Job 1:14 a **m** came to Job. He said,
1:16 another ⌊**m**⌋ came and said,
1:17 another ⌊**m**⌋ came and said,
1:18 another ⌊**m**⌋ came and said,
33:23 "If they have a **m** for them,
33:28 The **m** has freed my soul from
Psa 34:7 The **M** of the LORD camps
35:5 blown by the wind as the **M**
35:6 be dark and slippery as the **M**
Pro 13:17 An undependable **m** gets into
17:11 Therefore, a cruel **m** will be
25:13 ⌊so⌋ is a trustworthy **m** to
Ecc 5:6 the presence of a ⌊temple⌋ **m**,
Isa 41:27 I gave Jerusalem a **m** with the
42:19 or deaf like the **m** I send?
52:7 feet of the **m** who announces
63:9 and he was the **M** who saved
Jer 49:14 A **m** was sent among the
Hos 12:4 struggled with the **M** and won.
Oba 1:1 A **m** was sent among the
Nah 1:15 the feet of a **m** who announces
Hag 1:13 Then Haggai, the **m** of the
Zec 1:11 Then they reported to the **M** of
1:12 Then the **M** of the LORD said,
3:1 standing in front of the **M** of the
3:3 was standing in front of the **M**.
3:4 The **M** said to those who were
3:5 and dressed him while the **M**
3:6 The **M** of the LORD advised
12:8 like the **M** of the LORD ahead
Mal 2:7 Then, because he is the **m** for
3:1 "I'm going to send my **m**,
3:1 The **m** of the promise will
Mat 11:10 'I'm sending my **m** ahead of
Mar 1:2 "I am sending my **m** ahead of
Luk 7:27 'I am sending my **m** ahead of
Jon 1:6 a man named John to be his **m**.
11:3 So the sisters sent a **m** to tell
Act 7:30 "Forty years later, a **m**
7:35 the help of the **m** who appeared
7:38 Our ancestors and the **m** who
2Co 12:7 That problem, Satan's **m**,
Gal 4:14 me as if I were God's **m**
2Pe 2:5 Noah was his **m** who told
Rev 2:1 "To the **m** of the church in
2:8 "To the **m** of the church in
2:12 "To the **m** of the church in
2:18 "To the **m** of the church in
3:1 "To the **m** of the church in
3:7 "To the **m** of the church in

Rev 3:14 "To the **m** of the church in

messengers (114)

Gen 32:3 Jacob sent **m** ahead of him to
32:5 I've sent ⌊these **m**⌋ to tell you
32:6 When the **m** came back to
Num 20:14 Moses sent **m** from Kadesh to
21:21 Then Israel sent **m** to say to
22:5 He sent **m** to summon Balaam,
24:12 "I told the **m** you sent me,
Dtr 2:26 I sent **m** to King Sihon of
Jos 2:3 of Jericho sent **m** to Rahab,
6:17 she hid the **m** we sent.
6:25 she hid the **m** Joshua had sent
7:22 Joshua sent **m**, and they ran to
9:4 They posed as **m**.
11:1 So he sent **m** to King Jobab of
11:2 He also sent **m** to the northern
Jdg 6:35 He also sent **m** throughout
7:24 Gideon also sent **m** to the
9:31 secretly sent **m** to Abimelech.
11:12 Jephthah sent **m** to the king of
11:13 answered Jephthah's **m**,
11:14 Jephthah again sent **m** to the
11:17 The people of Israel sent **m** to
11:17 They also sent **m** to the king of
11:19 the people of Israel sent **m**
21:13 the whole congregation sent **m**
1Sm 6:21 They sent **m** to the people
11:3 that we can send **m** throughout
11:4 The **m** came to Saul's town,
11:7 and sent them by **m** throughout
11:9 They told the **m** who had come,
16:19 Saul sent **m** to Jesse to say,
19:11 Saul sent **m** to watch David's
19:14 When Saul sent **m** to get David,
19:15 Then Saul sent the **m** back to
19:16 The **m** came, and there in the
19:20 Saul sent **m** to get David.
19:20 over Saul's **m** so that they
19:21 ⌊about this⌋, he sent other **m**,
19:21 even sent a third group of **m**,
25:14 "David sent **m** from the desert
25:42 So she went with David's **m**
2Sm 2:5 So David sent **m** to the people
3:12 Then Abner sent **m** to David to
3:14 Then David sent **m** to Saul's
3:26 Joab sent **m** after Abner.
5:11 Hiram of Tyre sent **m** to David,
10:16 Hadadezer sent ⌊**m**⌋ to get
11:4 So David sent **m** and took her.
12:27 So he sent **m** to tell David,
17:16 Now send **m** quickly to tell
1Ki 20:2 He sent **m** into the city to King
20:5 But Benhadad sent **m** back ⌊to
20:9 Ahab told Benhadad's **m**,
20:9 I did everything your **m** told me
20:9 but I can't do this.'" The **m** left
2Ki 1:2 So he sent **m** ⌊to Ekron⌋.
1:3 "Meet the **m** of the king of
1:5 When the **m** returned,
1:6 Do you send **m** to seek advice
1:16 You sent **m** to seek advice
7:15 The **m** returned and told the
10:21 Jehu sent **m** to all the
14:8 Then Amaziah sent **m** to King
16:7 Ahaz sent **m** to King Tiglath
17:4 (Hoshea had sent **m** to King
19:9 sent **m** to Hezekiah,
19:14 took the letters from the **m**,
20:13 showed the **m** his warehouse:
1Ch 14:1 Hiram of Tyre sent **m** to David,
19:2 "So David sent **m** to comfort
19:16 the kings sent ⌊**m**⌋ to get
2Ch 25:17 King Amaziah of Judah sent **m**
30:6 **M** took letters from the king
30:10 So the **m** went from city to city
35:21 But Neco sent **m** to Josiah to
36:15 sent messages through his **m**
36:16 But they mocked God's **m**,
Neh 6:3 I sent **m** to tell them,
Est 3:13 **M** were sent with official
3:15 The **m** hurried out as the king
8:10 Then he sent them by **m** who
8:14 The **m** rode the king's fastest
Isa 14:32 How should we answer the **m**
Isa 18:2 It sends **m** by sea in boats
18:2 Go, swift **m**, to a tall and
23:2 Your **m** have crossed the sea.
30:4 and his **m** have reached Hanes,
33:7 **M** of peace cry bitterly.
37:9 he again sent **m** to Hezekiah,
37:14 took the letter from the **m**,
39:2 showed the **m** his warehouse:
44:26 and fulfills the plan of his **m**.
Jer 27:3 with **m** who have come to King
51:31 **M** follow messengers.
51:31 Messengers follow **m**.
Eze 17:15 of Babylon by sending his **m**
23:16 them at first sight and sent **m**
23:40 "They even sent **m** to invite
30:9 On that day I will send **m** in
Dan 3:2 King Nebuchadnezzar sent **m**
Nah 2:13 hear the voice of your **m** again."
Mat 14:35 Jesus and sent **m** all around
Luk 7:24 When John's **m** had left,
9:52 He sent **m** ahead of him.
Jon 13:16 and **m** are not superior to the
Act 10:5 Send **m** now to the city of
10:32 So send **m** to Joppa,
11:13 'Send **m** to Joppa,
19:31 who were Paul's friends sent **m**
20:17 From Miletus Paul sent **m** to
Rom 10:15 the feet of the **m** who announce
10:18 "The voice of the **m** has gone
Heb 1:7 "He makes his **m** winds.
Rev 1:20 The seven stars are the **m** of

Messiah (62)

1Sm 2:10 and lifts the head of his **M**."
Psa 2:2 and against his **M** by saying,
28:8 fortress for the victory of his **M**.
89:51 They insulted your **M** every
Mat 1:17 from the exile until the **M**.
2:4 where the **M** was supposed
16:16 answered, "You are the **M**,
16:20 tell anyone that he was the **M**.
22:42 do you think about the **M**?
23:10 have only one leader, the **M**.
24:5 They will say, 'I am the **M**,' and
24:23 tells you, 'Here is the **M**!' or
26:63 God and tell us, are you the **M**,
Mar 8:29 him, "You are the **M**!"
12:35 say that the **M** is David's son?
13:21 tells you, 'Here is the **M**!' or
14:61 him again, "Are you the **M**,
15:32 Let the **M**, the king of Israel,
Luk 2:26 die until he had seen the **M**,
3:15 whether John was the **M**.
4:41 they knew he was the **M**.
9:20 answered, "You are the **M**,
20:41 say that the **M** is David's son?
22:67 "Tell us, are you the **M**?"
23:35 If he's the **M** that God has
23:39 "So you're really the **M**,
24:26 Didn't the **M** have to suffer
24:46 "Scripture says that the **M**
Jon 1:20 them clearly, "I'm not the **M**."
1:25 you baptize if you're not the **M**
1:41 the **M**" (which means "Christ").
3:28 that I said, 'I'm not the **M**,
4:25 "I know that the **M** is coming.
4:25 (**M** is the one called Christ.)
4:29 Could he be the **M**?"
7:26 know that this man is the **M**?
7:31 "When the **M** comes,
7:41 "This man is the **M**."
7:41 can the **M** come from Galilee?
7:42 Doesn't Scripture say that the **M**
10:24 If you are the **M**, tell us
11:27 I believe that you are the **M**,
12:34 that the **M** will remain here
20:31 believe that Jesus is the **M**,
Act 2:31 David knew that the **M** would
2:31 He said that the **M** wouldn't be
3:18 sufferings of his **M** come true.
4:26 the Lord and against his **M**.'
5:42 News that Jesus is the **M**.
8:5 and told people about the **M**.
9:22 proving that Jesus was the **M**.
17:3 showed them that the **M** had
17:3 he talked about, was this **M**.
Act 18:5 the Jews that Jesus is the **M**.
18:28 Scriptures that Jesus is the **M**
26:23 They said that the **M** would
Rom 9:5 The **M** is descended from their
9:5 The **M** is God over everything,
1Jn 2:22 who rejects Jesus as the **M**?
5:1 Jesus is the **M** has been born
Rev 11:15 of our Lord and of his **M**,
12:10 authority of his **M** have come.

met (56)

Gen 14:3 five kings joined forces and **m**
32:1 God's angels **m** him.
33:8 ⌊of people and animals⌋ I **m**?"
38:2 There Judah **m** the daughter of
Exo 3:18 of the Hebrews has **m** with us.
4:24 The LORD **m** Moses and tried
4:27 When Aaron **m** Moses at the
5:3 of the Hebrews has **m** with us.
Jdg 4:18 out ⌊of her tent⌋, she **m** Sisera.
4:22 out ⌊of her tent⌋, she **m** him.
14:5 a young roaring lion **m** Samson.
15:14 the Philistines **m** him with
1Sm 9:11 they **m** girls coming out to get
25:20 path when she **m** David
2Sm 2:13 Both groups **m** at the pool of
16:1 **m** him with a pair of saddled
20:8 Amasa **m** them there.
1Ki 11:29 Ahijah from Shiloh **m** him
18:7 on the road when he **m** Elijah.
2Ki 9:18 rode off, **m** Jehu, and said,
10:15 that place, he **m** Jehonadab,
14:11 and King Amaziah of Judah **m**
2Ch 25:21 and King Amaziah of Judah **m**
Neh 8:13 **m** with Ezra the scribe to study
Psa 85:10 Mercy and truth have **m**.
Pro 26:12 Have you **m** a person who
29:20 Have you **m** a person who is
Jer 41:6 When he **m** them, he said to
44:23 That is why you have **m** with
Mat 8:28 of Galilee⌋, two men **m** him.
10:10 deserves to have his needs **m**.
28:9 Suddenly, Jesus **m** them and
Mar 5:2 out of the tombs and **m** him.
Luk 7:12 he **m** a funeral procession.
8:27 man from the city **m** him.
9:37 a large crowd **m** Jesus.
17:12 with a skin disease **m** him.
Jon 4:51 his servants **m** him and told
5:14 Later, Jesus **m** the man in the
11:30 still where Martha had **m** him.)
Act 4:5 and scribes **m** in Jerusalem.
5:12 as they **m** on Solomon's Porch.
10:25 Cornelius **m** him, bowed down,
11:26 Barnabas and Saul **m** with the
13:6 In Paphos they **m** a Jewish
15:6 and spiritual leaders **m**
16:16 a female servant **m** us.
16:40 They **m** with the believers,
18:2 In Corinth he **m** a Jewish man
19:1 He **m** some disciples in
20:7 On Sunday we **m** to break
20:14 When Paul **m** us in Assos,
Col 2:1 and for people I have never **m**.
Heb 7:1 He **m** Abraham and blessed
7:10 when Melchizedek **m** him.
7:16 he **m** human requirements,

metal (35)

Lev 19:4 worthless gods or cast **m** idols.
Num 16:38 Hammer them into thin **m**
16:39 hammered into thin **m** sheets
33:52 of all their stone and **m** idols,
Dtr 27:15 has a carved or **m** statue,
Jdg 17:3 a carved idol and a **m** idol.
17:4 a carved idol and a **m** idol.
18:14 ephod, a carved idol, a **m** idol,
18:17 idols, and the **m** idol.
18:18 idols, and the **m** idol,
1Sm 13:21 a mattock or set a **m** point
1Ki 7:23 Hiram made a pool from cast **m**.
7:24 They were cast in **m** when the
7:25 pool was set on 12 **m** bulls.
7:30 supports were made of cast **m**
7:33 and hubs were all cast **m**.
14:9 You made other gods, **m** idols,

2Ki 17:16 made two calves out of cast **m**.
2Ch 4:2 made a pool from cast **m**.
4:3 They were cast in **m** when the
4:4 pool was set on 12 **m** bulls.
28:2 Israel and even made **m** idols
34:3 carved idols, and **m** idols.
34:4 carved idols, and **m** idols.
Neh 9:18 even when they made a **m**
Job 37:18 as firm as a mirror made of **m**?
Psa 106:19 worshiped an idol made of **m**.
Isa 44:10 gods or casting **m** idols.
48:5 My carved idols and my **m**
Jer 29:2 and **m** workers left Jerusalem.)
Eze 1:4 looked like glowing **m**.
8:2 its body looked like glowing **m**.
Dan 11:8 He will take the **m** statues of
Nah 1:14 the wooden and **m** idols from
2:3 The **m** on his chariots flashes

metals (1)
Jer 10:9 and goldsmiths shape these **m**.

metalsmiths (3)
Isa 41:7 **M** encourage blacksmiths who
Jer 10:14 **M** are put to shame by their
51:17 **M** are put to shame by their

metalworker (1)
2Ti 4:14 Alexander the **m** did me a great

Methuselah (7)
Gen 5:21 he became the father of **M**.
5:22 After he became the father of **M**,
5:25 When **M** was 187 years old,
5:26 **M** lived 782 years and had
5:27 **M** lived a total of 969 years;
1Ch 1:3 Enoch, **M**, Lamech,
Luk 3:37 son of **M**, son of Enoch, son of

Methushael (2)
Gen 4:18 Mehujael was the father of **M**.
4:18 And **M** was the father of

Meunim (2)
Ezr 2:50 Asnah, **M**, Nephusim,
Neh 7:52 Besai, **M**, Nephusheshim,

Meunites (6)
1Ch 4:41 down tents and killed the **M**.
4:41 They claimed the **M** for God
4:41 (Even today no **M** live there.)
4:41 in that land in place of the **M**
2Ch 20:1 and some of the **M** came to
26:7 lived in Gur Baal, and the **M**.

Mezahab (2)
Gen 36:39 Matred and granddaughter of **M**
1Ch 1:50 Matred and granddaughter of **M**

Mezobaite (1)
1Ch 11:47 Eliel, Obed, and Jaasiel the **M**.

Mibhar (1)
1Ch 11:38 of Nathan), **M** (son of Hagri),

Mibsam (3)
Gen 25:13 firstborn), Kedar, Adbeel, **M**,
1Ch 1:29 then Kedar, Adbeel, **M**,
4:25 Shallum's son was **M**.

Mibsam's (1)
1Ch 4:25 **M** son was Mishma.

Mibzar (2)
Gen 36:42 Kenaz, Teman, **M**,
1Ch 1:53 Kenaz, Teman, **M**,

Mica (5)
2Sm 9:12 son whose name was **M**.
1Ch 9:15 Mattaniah (son of **M**,
Neh 10:11 **M**, Rehob, Hashabiah,
11:17 Mattaniah was the son of **M**,
11:22 who was the son of **M** from

Micah (26)
Jdg 17:1 There was a man named **M**
17:3 So **M** gave the 1,100 pieces of
17:4 When **M** returned the silver to
17:5 **M** owned a shrine.
17:9 **M** asked him, "Where do you
17:10 **M** told him, "Stay with me!
17:11 and agreed to live with **M**.
17:12 **M** ordained the Levite.
17:13 Then **M** said, "Now I know that
18:4 The Levite told them what **M**
18:4 for him and added, "**M** hired me
18:23 turned around and said to **M**,
18:24 **M** answered, "You've taken
18:26 **M** saw they were stronger than
18:27 The people of Dan took what **M**
18:31 the carved idol **M** had made.
1Ch 5:5 Shimei's son was **M**.
8:34 Meribbaal was the father of **M**.
9:40 Meribbaal was the father of **M**.
23:20 Uzziel's first son was **M**;
24:24 descendants through **M**),
2Ch 34:20 of Shaphan), Abdon (son of **M**),
Jer 26:18 "**M** from Moresheth prophesied
26:19 of Judah put **M** to death?
Mic 1:1 LORD spoke his word to **M**,
1:1 This is the vision that **M** saw

Micah's (14)
Jdg 17:4 Both were placed in **M** home
17:8 He came to **M** house in the
17:11 became like one of **M** sons
18:2 They came to **M** house in the
18:3 While they were at **M** house,
18:13 of Ephraim as far as **M** house
18:15 stopped and entered **M** house
18:18 these men entered **M** house
18:22 **M** house, Micah's neighbors
18:22 **M** neighbors were called
1Ch 5:5 **M** son was Reaiah.
8:35 **M** sons were Pithon,
9:41 **M** sons were Pithon,
24:25 through **M** brother Isshiah).

Micaiah (31)
1Ki 22:8 can ask the LORD through **M**,
22:9 'Get **M**, son of Imlah!"
22:13 who went to call **M** told him,
22:14 **M** answered, "I solemnly
22:15 king, the king asked him, "**M**,
22:15 **M** said to him, "Attack and you
22:17 So **M** said, "I saw Israel's
22:19 **M** added, "Then hear the word
22:24 went to **M** and struck him on
22:25 **M** answered, "You will find out
22:26 "Send **M** back to Amon,
22:28 **M** said, "If you really do come
2Ki 22:12 Achbor (son of **M**),
2Ch 13:2 His mother was named **M**,
17:7 and **M** to teach in the cities of
18:7 can ask the LORD through **M**,
18:8 'Get **M**, son of Imla!"
18:12 who went to call **M** told him,
18:13 **M** answered, "I solemnly
18:14 king, the king asked him, "**M**,
18:14 **M** said, "Attack and you will
18:16 So **M** said, "I saw Israel's
18:18 **M** added, "Then hear the word
18:23 went to **M** and struck him on
18:24 **M** answered, "You will find out
18:25 "Send **M** back to Amon,
18:27 **M** said, "If you really do come
Neh 12:35 who was the son of **M**,
12:41 **M**, Elioenai, Zechariah,
Jer 36:11 **M**, who was the son of
36:13 **M** told them everything he

mice (6)
Lev 11:29 **m**, and all types of lizards:
1Sm 6:4 gold tumors and five gold **m**
6:5 your **m** which are destroying
6:11 the box containing the gold **m**
6:18 And the number of gold **m** was
Isa 66:17 pork, disgusting things, and **m**.

Michael (18)
Num 13:13 Sethur, son of **M**, from the tribe
1Ch 5:13 relatives by families were **M**,
5:14 Gilead was the son of **M**,
6:40 who was the son of **M**,
7:3 Izrahiah and Izrahiah's sons **M**,
8:16 **M**, Ishpah, and Joha.
12:20 Jediael, **M**, Jozabad, Elihu,
27:18 of Issachar: Omri, son of **M**
2Ch 21:2 Azariahu, **M**, and Shephatiah.
Ezr 8:8 son of **M**, with 80 males
Dan 10:13 But then **M**, one of the chief
10:21 except your commander, **M**.
11:1 strengthened and defended **M**."
12:1 continued, "At that time **M**,
Jud 1:9 When the archangel **M** argued
1:9 But **M** didn't dare to hand down
1:9 Instead, **M** said, "May the Lord
Rev 12:7 **M** and his angels had to fight a

Michal (18)
1Sm 14:49 and **M** (the younger daughter).
18:20 However, Saul's daughter **M**
18:27 him his daughter **M** as his wife.
18:28 his daughter **M** loved David.
19:11 But **M**, David's wife,
19:12 So **M** lowered David through a
19:13 Then **M** took some idols,
19:14 get David, **M** said, "He's sick."
19:17 Saul asked **M**, "Why did you
19:17 **M** answered, "He told me,
25:44 Saul had given his daughter **M**,
2Sm 3:13 to see me unless you bring **M**,
3:14 "Give me my wife **M**.
6:16 Saul's daughter **M** looked out of
6:20 Saul's daughter **M** came out to
6:21 David answered **M**,
6:23 So Saul's daughter **M** was
1Ch 15:29 Saul's daughter **M** looked out of

Michmas (2)
Ezr 2:27 of **M**: 122
Neh 7:31 of **M**: 122

Michmash (9)
1Sm 13:2 were stationed with Saul at **M**
13:5 They camped at **M**,
13:11 were assembling at **M**.
13:16 the Philistines camped at **M**.
13:23 had gone out to the pass at **M**.
14:5 a pillar on the north facing **M**,
14:31 Philistines from **M** to Aijalon,
Neh 11:31 in the area of Geba, in **M**, Aija,
Isa 10:28 store their equipment at **M**.

Michmethath (2)
Jos 16:6 with **M** on the north.
17:7 extends from Asher to **M**,

Michri (1)
1Ch 9:8 of Uzzi and grandson of **M**),

midair (1)
2Sm 18:9 So he was left hanging in **m**

midday (2)
2Sm 4:5 Ishbosheth was taking his **m**
Pro 4:18 and brighter until it reaches **m**.

Middin (1)
Jos 15:61 Beth Arabah, **M**, Secacah,

middle (70)
Gen 1:6 "Let there be a horizon in the **m**
2:9 grew in the **m** of the garden.
3:3 except the tree in the **m** of the
6:16 Build the ship with lower, **m**,
29:7 "It's still the **m** of the day,"
Exo 14:22 Israelites went through the **m**
15:8 thickened in the **m** of the sea.
26:28 The **m** crossbar will run from
36:33 They made the **m** crossbar so
Num 2:17 the Levites will stay in the **m** of
16:47 and ran into the **m** of the
33:8 and went through the **m**
Dtr 3:16 from the Arnon Valley (the **m**
11:6 In the **m** of all the Israelites the
13:16 Gather their goods into the **m** of
Jos 3:17 firmly on dry ground in the **m**

Jos 4:3 to pick up 12 stones from the **m**
4:5 He said to them, "Go to the **m**
4:8 They took them from the **m** of
4:9 also set 12 stones in the **m**
4:10 ark remained standing in the **m**
4:18 promise came out of the **m**
8:13 down into the **m** of the valley.
10:13 The sun stopped in the **m** of
12:2 This included the **m** of the
13:9 including the city in the **m** of
13:16 including the city in the **m** of
Jdg 16:29 Samson felt the two **m**
2Sm 20:12 wallowing in his blood in the **m**
23:12 he stood in the **m** of the field
24:5 south of the city in the **m** of the
1Ki 6:8 A staircase went up to the **m**
8:51 brought out of Egypt from the **m**
2Ki 6:20 they were in the **m** of Samaria.
20:4 as far as the **m** courtyard when
1Ch 11:14 they stood in the **m** of the field
2Ch 6:13 He put it in the **m** of the
Neh 4:11 will be right in the **m** of them.
Est 4:1 He went into the **m** of the city
Job 1:3 influential person in the **M** East.
34:20 They die suddenly in the **m** of
Psa 78:28 He made the birds fall in the **m**
102:24 don't take me now in the **m** of
116:19 in the **m** of Jerusalem.
136:14 He led Israel through the **m** of it
138:7 I walk into the **m** of trouble,
Pro 23:34 someone lying down in the **m**
Isa 6:12 and a large area in the **m** of the
19:19 LORD will be in the **m** of Egypt,
Jer 39:3 came in and sat in **M** Gate:
51:63 to it and throw it into the **m**
Eze 1:4 The **m** of the lightning looked
5:2 of your hair in a fire in the **m**
11:7 corpses that you put in the **m**
11:23 The LORD's glory left the **m** of
15:4 both its ends and chars its **m**.
37:1 Spirit and put me down in the **m**
48:8 holy place will be in the **m** of it.
48:10 holy place will be in the **m** of it.
48:15 The city will be in the **m** of it.
Dan 3:25 walking in the **m** of the fire,
4:10 and I saw an oak tree in the **m**
9:27 In the **m** of the seven time
Amo 7:8 to hold a plumb line in the **m**
Mar 6:47 the boat was in the **m** of the
Luk 4:35 threw the man down in the **m**
12:38 blessed if he comes in the **m**
22:55 Some men had lit a fire in the **m**
Jon 19:18 Jesus was in the **m**.
Act 17:22 Paul stood in the **m** of the court

Midian (48)

Gen 25:2 Medan, **M**, Ishbak, and Shuah.
25:4 The sons of **M** were Ephah,
Exo 2:15 and settled in the land of **M**.
2:16 of the priest of **M** came.
3:1 Jethro, the priest of **M**.
4:19 LORD had said to Moses in **M**,
18:1 Jethro, the priest of **M**,
Num 22:4 said to the leaders of **M**,
22:7 The leaders of Moab and **M** left,
31:3 use them to get even with **M**.
31:7 They went to war against **M**,
31:8 were the five kings of **M** — Evi,
Jdg 6:1 them over to **M** for seven years.
6:2 protect themselves⌋ from **M**.
6:3 planted crops, **M**, Amalek,
6:6 very poor because of **M**
6:13 and has handed us over to **M**."
6:14 "You will rescue Israel from **M**
6:16 You will defeat **M** as if it were
6:33 All of **M**, Amalek, and Kedem
7:2 with you for me to hand **M** over
7:7 will save you and hand **M** over
7:8 The camp of **M** was below him
7:12 **M**, Amalek, and all of Kedem
7:13 rolling around in the camp of **M**.
7:14 God is going to hand **M** and the
7:22 caused the whole camp of **M**
7:23 to help pursue the troops of **M**.
7:24 "Go into battle against **M**.
7:25 Zeeb and kept on pursuing **M**.
Jdg 8:1 us to go fight **M** with you."
8:5 and King Zalmunna of **M**."
8:12 and King Zalmunna of **M**,
8:22 You rescued us from **M**."
8:26 clothes worn by the kings of **M**,
8:28 The power of **M** was crushed
8:28 and **M** never again became a
9:17 life and rescued you from **M**.
1Ki 11:18 They left **M** and went to Paran.
1Ch 1:32 Medan, **M**, Ishbak, and Shuah.
1:33 The sons of **M** were Ephah,
Psa 83:9 Do to them what you did to **M**,
Isa 9:4 did in the battle against⌋ **M**.
10:26 As he struck down **M** at the
60:6 camels from **M** and Ephah.
Hab 3:7 see trembling in the tents of **M**.
Act 7:29 left Egypt and lived in **M** as
7:29 In **M** he fathered two sons.

Midianite (14)

Gen 37:28 As the **M** merchants were
Num 10:29 son of Reuel the **M**,
25:6 men brought a **M** woman
25:14 with the **M** woman was Zimri,
25:15 The name of the **M** woman
25:15 of a family from the **M** tribes.)
25:18 daughter of a **M** leader,
31:9 The Israelites took the **M**
31:17 So kill all the **M** boys and
31:17 and every **M** woman who has
Jdg 7:21 everyone in the **M** camp began
7:25 the two **M** commanders.
8:11 the unsuspecting **M** army.
8:12 the whole **M** army panicked.

Midianites (9)

Gen 36:35 Hadad defeated the **M** in the
37:36 Meanwhile, in Egypt the **M**
Num 25:17 "Treat the **M** as your enemies,
31:2 "Get even with the **M** for what
31:3 to go to war against the **M**.
31:10 all the cities where the **M** lived
Jdg 6:7 of what the **M** had done
6:11 winepress to hide it from the **M**.
1Ch 1:46 who defeated the **M** in the

Midian's (5)

Jos 13:21 him and **M** leaders — Evi,
Jdg 6:2 **M** power was too strong for
7:1 **M** camp was north of him at the
7:15 The LORD will hand **M** camp
8:3 **M** commanders, over to you.

midnight (12)

Exo 11:4 About **m** I will go out among
12:29 At **m** the LORD killed every
Jdg 7:19 It was the beginning of the **m**
16:3 the prostitute⌋ only until **m**.
Rut 3:8 At **m** the man was shivering.
Psa 119:62 At **m** I wake up to give thanks
Mat 25:6 "At **m** someone shouted,
Mar 13:35 could be in the evening or at **m**
Luk 11:5 you go to him at **m** and say,
Act 16:25 Around **m** Paul and Silas were
20:7 he kept talking until **m**.
27:27 About **m** the sailors suspected

midwife (3)

Gen 35:17 of her pains, the **m** said to her,
38:28 The **m** took a piece of red yarn,
Exo 1:19 their babies before a **m** arrives."

midwives (6)

Exo 1:15 of Egypt told the Hebrew **m**,
1:17 However, the **m** feared God
1:18 king of Egypt called for the **m**.
1:19 The **m** answered Pharaoh,
1:20 God was good to the **m**.
1:21 Because the **m** feared God,

Migdal Eder (1)

Gen 35:21 and put up his tent beyond **M**

Migdal El (1)

Jos 19:38 Yiron, **M**, Horem, Beth Anath,

Migdalgad (1)

Jos 15:37 villages: Zenan, Hadashah, **M**,

Migdol (6)

Exo 14:2 between **M** and the sea.
Num 33:7 and set up camp near **M**.
Jer 44:1 the Jews living in Egypt at **M**,
46:14 announce this in **M**.
Eze 29:10 a wasteland, from **M** to Syene,
30:6 will die in war from **M** to Syene,

might (20)

Jdg 16:30 he pushed with all his **m**,
2Sm 6:14 presence with all his **m**.
1Ch 13:8 God's presence with all their **m**,
29:2 With all my **m** I gathered ⌊the
2Ch 20:6 You possess power and **m**,
Est 10:2 All his acts of power and **m**
Psa 54:1 and defend me with your **m**.
66:7 He rules forever with his **m**.
77:15 With your **m** you have
78:26 the south wind with his **m**.
145:11 of Adam about your **m**
Ecc 9:10 do it with ⌊all⌋ your **m**,
Isa 30:30 will come down with all his **m**,
33:13 Acknowledge my **m**,
40:26 of the greatness of his **m**
63:15 is your determination and **m**?
Dan 5:18 a kingdom, **m**, honor, and glory.
Zec 4:6 You won't ⌊succeed⌋ by **m** or
Eph 1:19 of his power as it works with **m**
Col 1:11 you by his glorious **m**

mightier (2)

Psa 93:4 The LORD above is mighty — **m**
93:4 **m** than the foaming waves of

mightiest (2)

Pro 30:30 a lion, **m** among animals,
Eze 32:21 The **m** warriors will say to

mighty (116)

Gen 10:8 the first **m** warrior on the earth.
10:9 He was a **m** hunter whom the
10:9 a **m** hunter whom the LORD
18:18 to become a great and **m** nation
23:6 You are a **m** leader among us.
49:24 of the help of the **M** One
Exo 6:6 and with **m** acts of judgment.
13:3 The LORD used his **m** hand to
13:9 Because the LORD used his **m**
13:14 'The LORD used his **m** hand to
13:16 because the LORD used his **m**
32:11 your great power and **m** hand?
Num 33:4 the LORD had killed in a **m** act
Dtr 3:24 deeds and the **m** acts you have
4:34 your God used his **m** hand
5:15 your God used his **m** hand
6:21 but the LORD used his **m** hand
7:8 So he used his **m** hand to bring
7:19 He used his **m** hand and
9:26 power and used your **m** hand
11:2 his great power — his **m** hand
26:8 Then the LORD used his **m**
34:12 Moses used his **m** hand to do
Jos 4:24 world would know his **m** power
Jdg 5:13 Then those **m** men who were
5:13 for me against the **m** soldiers.
5:22 The **m** war horses galloped on
1Sm 4:8 the power of these **m** gods?
2Sm 1:19 See how the **m** have fallen!
1:25 See how the **m** have fallen in
1:27 See how the **m** have fallen!
1Ki 8:41 **m** hand, and powerful arm.
2Ki 17:36 his great power and a **m** arm
1Ch 1:10 the first **m** warrior on the earth.
2Ch 6:32 **m** hand, and powerful arm.
Neh 9:32 **m**, and awe-inspiring God.
Job 5:15 needy from the power of the **m**.
9:4 wise in heart and **m** in power.
9:19 then he is the **m** one.
12:21 unbuckles the belt of the **m**.
24:22 away ⌊these⌋ **m** men by his
30:21 With your **m** hand you assault
34:17 one who is righteous and **m**?

Job 34:19 righteous and **m** does not grant
34:20 **M** people are taken away but
34:24 He breaks **m** people into
35:9 The power of **m** people makes
36:5 "Certainly, God is **m**.
36:5 He is **m** and brave.
36:19 all your **m** strength help you?
41:25 "The **m** are afraid when
Psa 20:6 his holy heaven with **m** deeds
24:8 The LORD, strong and **m**!
69:4 who want to destroy me are **m**.
71:16 I will come with the **m** deeds of
78:25 ate the bread of the **m** ones,
80:10 Its branches covered the **m**
89:8 **M** LORD, even your
89:13 Your arm is **m**. Your hand is
93:4 The LORD above is **m** —
99:2 The LORD is **m** in Zion.
103:20 you **m** beings who carry out his
106:2 Who can speak about all the **m**
106:8 make his **m** power known.
132:2 vow to the **M** One of Jacob:
132:5 place for the **M** One of Jacob."
135:10 nations and killed **m** kings:
136:12 with a **m** hand and a powerful
136:18 He killed **m** kings — because
145:4 will talk about your **m** acts.
145:12 in order to make known your **m**
150:1 Praise him in his **m** heavens.
150:2 Praise him for his **m** acts.
Pro 30:26 badgers are not a **m** species,
Isa 1:24 the **M** One of Israel,
2:11 High and **m** people will be
2:13 against all the towering and **m**
2:17 and high and **m** people will be
3:25 Your **m** men will die in battle.
9:6 **M** God, Everlasting Father,
10:13 down people like a **m** man.
10:21 will return to the **m** God.
10:34 will fall in front of the **M** One.
13:3 I've called my **m** men to carry
21:17 Kedar's **m** archers,
22:17 Look, **m** man! The LORD will
33:21 The LORD will be our **m**
49:24 Can loot be taken away from **m**
49:25 will be freed from **m** men.
49:26 the **M** One of Jacob,
53:12 give him a share among the **m**,
60:16 the **M** One of Jacob,
60:22 them will become a **m** nation.
62:8 right hand and with his **m** arm,
Jer 5:16 They are all **m** warriors.
11:16 set fire to you with a **m** storm,
21:5 powerful hand and my **m** arm.
32:18 You, God, are great and **m**.
32:19 You make wise plans and do **m**
32:21 with a **m** hand and a powerful
Eze 20:33 I will rule you with a **m** hand
20:34 scattered you with my **m** hand
31:11 So I handed it over to a **m** ruler
32:18 along with the other **m** nations.
38:15 be a large crowd and a **m** army.
Dan 4:22 strong and **m** until you reached
Joe 2:2 A large and **m** army will spread
2:5 and like a **m** army prepared for
2:11 carry out his commands are **m**.
Hab 3:15 into the **m** raging waters.
Zec 10:7 Ephraim will be like **m** warriors.
Luk 1:51 "He displayed his **m** power.
1:69 He has raised up a **m** Savior for
Eph 6:10 Lord and from his **m** strength.
Col 1:29 this while his **m** power works
2Th 1:7 from heaven with his **m** angels

migrate (1)

Jer 8:7 know when it's time to **m**.

Migron (2)

1Sm 14:2 under a pomegranate tree at **M**.
Isa 10:28 They pass through **M**.

Mijamin (4)

1Ch 24:9 for Malchiah, the sixth for **M**,
Ezr 10:25 **M**, Eleazar, Malchiah,
Neh 10:7 Meshullam, Abijah, **M**,
12:5 **M**, Maadiah, Bilgah,

Mikloth (4)

1Ch 8:32 and **M**, who was the father of
9:37 Gedor, Ahio, Zechariah, and **M**.
9:38 **M** was the father of Shimeam.
27:4 (**M** was one of its leaders.)

Mikneiah (2)

1Ch 15:18 Mattithiah, Eliphelehu, and **M**.
15:21 Mattithiah, Eliphelehu, **M**,

Milalai (1)

Neh 12:36 **M**, Gilalai, Maai, Nethanel,

Milcah (11)

Gen 11:29 name of Nahor's wife was **M**,
11:29 was the father of **M** and Iscah.)
22:20 Later Abraham was told, "**M**
22:23 **M** had these eight sons by
24:15 daughter of Bethuel, son of **M**,
24:24 son of **M** and Nahor.
24:47 son of Nahor and **M**.' "I
Num 26:33 Noah, Hoglah, **M**, and Tirzah.)
27:1 **M**, and Tirzah. They came
36:11 Mahlah, Tirzah, Hoglah, **M**,
Jos 17:3 Noah, Hoglah, **M**, and Tirzah.

Milcom (6)

1Ki 11:5 and **M** (the disgusting idol
11:33 and **M** (the god of Ammon).
2Ki 23:13 and **M** (the disgusting god of
Jer 49:1 Why, then, has the god **M**
49:3 **M** will be taken away into
Zep 1:5 swearing loyalty to the god **M**.

Milcom's (1)

Jer 49:1 Why do **M** people live in Gad's

mildew (18)

Lev 13:49 it is **m**. It must be shown to the
13:50 The priest will examine the **m**
13:52 because the **m** is growing.
13:55 and the **m** has not spread,
13:59 for deciding whether **m**
14:34 **m** may appear in a house.
14:35 that looks like **m** in his house.
14:37 He will examine the **m** area on
14:39 If the **m** in the walls of the
14:40 the stones that have the **m**
14:43 If the **m** develops again in the
14:44 If it is a spreading type of **m**,
14:48 and the **m** has not spread
14:48 house clean. The **m** is gone.
14:54 for any kind of **m** or fungus
14:57 and **m** help you distinguish
Amo 4:9 your ⌊crops⌋ with blight and **m**.
Hag 2:17 all your work with blight and **m**

mile (7)

Jos 3:4 about half a **m** behind them.
Eze 47:3 He measured off a third of a **m**
47:4 off another third of a **m**
47:4 off another third of a **m**
47:5 measured another third of a **m**.
Mat 5:41 forces you to go one **m**,
Act 1:12 about half a **m** away.

miles (4)

Mat 5:41 go two **m** with him.
Luk 24:13 about seven **m** from Jerusalem.
Jon 6:19 they had rowed three or four **m**,
11:18 not quite two **m** away.)

Miletus (4)

Act 20:15 day we arrived at the city of **M**.
20:17 From **M** Paul sent messengers
20:17 to meet with him ⌊in **M**⌋.
2Ti 4:20 I left Trophimus in the city of **M**

military (37)

Num 1:3 who is eligible for **m** duty.
1:20 old and eligible for **m** duty.
1:22 old and eligible for **m** duty.
1:24 old and eligible for **m** duty.
1:26 old and eligible for **m** duty.
1:28 old and eligible for **m** duty.
Num 1:30 old and eligible for **m** duty.
1:32 old and eligible for **m** duty.
1:34 old and eligible for **m** duty.
1:36 old and eligible for **m** duty.
1:38 old and eligible for **m** duty.
1:40 old and eligible for **m** duty.
1:42 old and eligible for **m** duty.
1:45 old and eligible for **m** duty
26:2 old and eligible for **m** duty."
31:48 officers from the **m** divisions,
32:22 You will have fulfilled your **m**
Dtr 24:5 married will be free from **m** duty
1Sm 10:5 the Philistines have a **m** post.
14:1 "Let's go to the Philistine **m**
14:4 to attack the Philistine **m** post.
14:6 "Let's go to the **m** post of these
14:12 the men of the **m** post said to
14:12 "Follow me up ⌊to the **m** post⌋
14:15 and all the troops in the **m** post.
2Sm 20:8 Joab wore a **m** uniform,
1Ch 7:40 Their **m** roster had 26,000
2Ch 17:2 of Judah and placed **m** posts
32:3 he, his officers, and his **m** staff
32:6 He appointed **m** commanders
Est 1:3 the **m** officers of the Persians
Isa 3:3 **m** leaders and civilian leaders,
Eze 23:23 **m** officers and important men.
38:4 you out with all your **m** forces,
Dan 3:2 **m** advisers, treasurers, judges,
3:3 **m** advisers, treasurers, judges,
2Ti 2:4 Whoever serves in the **m**

militia (2)

2Ki 25:19 who was in charge of the **m**,
Jer 52:25 who was in charge of the **m**,

milk (48)

Gen 18:8 Abraham took cheese and **m**,
49:12 His teeth are whiter than **m**.
Exo 3:8 It is a land flowing with **m** and
3:17 flowing with **m** and honey.'"
13:5 land flowing with **m** and honey,
23:19 a young goat in its mother's **m**.
33:3 land flowing with **m** and honey.
34:26 a young goat in its mother's **m**."
Lev 20:24 land flowing with **m** and honey.
Num 13:27 land flowing with **m** and honey.
14:8 land flowing with **m** and honey!
16:13 us out of a land flowing with **m**
16:14 us into a land flowing with **m**
Dtr 6:3 land flowing with **m** and honey,
11:9 land flowing with **m** and honey.
14:21 a young goat in its mother's **m**.
26:9 land flowing with **m** and honey.
26:15 and the land flowing with **m**
27:3 land flowing with **m** and honey,
31:20 land flowing with **m** and honey.
32:14 cows and drank **m** from sheep
Jos 5:6 see this land flowing with **m**
Jdg 4:19 But instead she gave him **m** to
5:25 She gave him **m**. She offered
1Sm 7:9 one still feeding on **m**,
Job 10:10 Didn't you pour me out like **m**
21:24 His stomach is full of **m**,
Pro 27:27 There will be enough goat **m** to
30:33 As churning **m** produces butter
Sos 4:11 Honey and **m** are under your
5:1 I will drink my wine with my **m**.
5:12 are set like doves bathing in **m**.
Isa 7:22 they will produce so much **m**.
28:9 children just weaned from **m**?
55:1 Come, buy wine and **m**.
60:16 You will drink **m** from other
Jer 11:5 land flowing with **m** and honey,
32:22 land flowing with **m** and honey.
Lam 4:7 purer than snow, whiter than **m**.
Eze 20:6 land flowing with **m** and honey.
20:15 land flowing with **m** and honey.
25:4 your crops and drink your **m**.
Joe 3:18 **M** will flow on the hills.
1Co 3:2 I gave you **m** to drink.
9:7 not drink **m** from the sheep?
Heb 5:12 You need **m**, not solid food.
5:13 All those who live on **m** lack
1Pe 2:2 as newborn babies desire **m**.

mill (5)

Jdg 16:21 him grind grain in the **m** there.
Ecc 12:3 the women at the **m** stop
12:4 the sound of the **m** is muffled,
Lam 5:13 young men work at the **m**,
Mat 24:41 women will be working at a **m**.

millet (1)

Eze 4:9 lentils, **m**, and winter wheat.

millions (1)

Mat 18:24 a servant who owed him **m** of

Millo (6)

2Sm 5:9 it from the **M** to the palace.
1Ki 9:15 the **M**, the walls of Jerusalem,
9:24 Then he built the **M**.
11:27 Solomon was building the **M**
1Ch 11:8 starting from the **M** and making
2Ch 32:5 strengthened the **M** in the City

mills (1)

Jer 25:10 and grooms, the sound of **m**,

millstone (5)

Jdg 9:53 Then a woman threw a small **m**
2Sm 11:21 Thebez throw a small **m** at him
Job 41:24 solid like a rock, solid like a **m**.
Rev 18:21 a stone that was like a large **m**.
18:22 The sound of a **m** will never be

millstones (1)

Isa 47:2 Take **m** and grind flour.

mina (1)

Eze 45:12 One **m** must weigh 60 shekels.

mind (115)

Exo 7:23 the entire matter from his **m**.
Num 23:19 He doesn't change his **m**.
Dtr 7:9 Keep in **m** that the LORD your
11:18 to heart and keep them in **m**.
28:65 will give you an unsettled **m**,
29:4 you a **m** that understands,
1Sm 9:19 I tell you all that's on your **m**.
14:7 "Do whatever you have in **m**.
15:29 does not lie or change his **m**,
15:29 a mortal who changes his **m**."
2Sm 7:3 "Do everything you have in **m**,
24:16 the LORD changed his **m** about
1Ki 4:29 insight and a **m** as limitless as
10:2 everything she had on her **m**.
1Ch 17:2 "Do everything you have in **m**,
21:15 and changed his **m** about
2Ch 7:11 everything he had in **m**
9:1 everything she had on her **m**.
Ezr 6:22 of Assyria change his **m** so that
7:27 He put this into the king's **m** to
Est 7:7 had a terrible end in **m** for him.
Job 6:29 Please change your **m**.
6:29 Change your **m** because I am
12:3 Like you, I have a **m**.
23:13 can make him change his **m**?
38:36 gave understanding to the **m**?
Psa 26:2 closely into my heart and **m**.
73:21 and my **m** was seized ⌊with
73:26 My body and **m** may waste
103:14 He bears in **m** that we are dust.
110:4 oath and will not change his **m**:
139:23 me, O God, and know my **m**.
Pro 2:2 your **m** reach for understanding
3:1 and keep my commands in **m**,
6:14 all the time with a twisted **m**.
6:18 a **m** devising wicked plans,
6:35 of money will change his **m**.
12:8 a twisted **m** will be despised.
15:14 The **m** of a person who has
17:16 have a **m** to grasp anything?
17:20 A twisted **m** never finds
18:15 The **m** of a person who has
21:10 The **m** of a wicked person
22:17 and set your **m** on the
22:18 keep them in **m** ⌊so that⌋ they
23:19 and keep your **m** going in the
25:3 so the **m** of kings is
29:17 he will give you peace of **m**.
Ecc 1:17 I've used my **m** to understand
2:3 continued to control my **m**.
7:7 and a bribe can corrupt the **m**.
8:5 The **m** of a wise person will
Sos 5:2 I sleep, but my **m** is awake.
Isa 5:19 we may see what he has in **m**.
33:18 Your **m** will be thinking of the
47:7 or keep in **m** how they would
65:17 They will not come to **m**.
Jer 2:36 You change your **m** so easily.
3:16 It will no longer come to **m**.
7:31 It never entered my **m**.
17:9 "The human **m** is the most
19:5 It never entered my **m**.
22:17 "But your eyes and your **m** are
32:35 It never entered my **m**.
Lam 3:21 that I keep this one thing in **m**:
Eze 11:5 what's going through your **m**.
20:32 What you have in **m** will never
Dan 1:8 Daniel made up his **m** not to
4:16 Let its human **m** be changed,
4:16 and give it the **m** of an animal.
4:34 and my **m** came back to me.
4:36 Just then my **m** came back to
5:21 and his **m** was changed into an
5:21 changed into an animal's **m**.
7:4 and was given a human **m**.
Hos 11:8 I have changed my **m**.
Mat 1:20 Joseph had this in **m** when an
21:29 he changed his **m** and went.
22:37 and with all your **m**.'
Mar 3:21 They said, "He's out of his **m**!"
5:15 dressed and in his right **m**.
9:10 They kept in **m** what he said
12:30 all your soul, with all your **m**,
Luk 8:35 Dressed and in his right **m**,
10:27 and with all your **m**.' And
Jon 13:2 Jesus into the **m** of Judas,
Act 7:57 Stephen with one purpose in **m**,
18:12 the Jews had one thought in **m**.
19:29 thought in **m** as they rushed
Rom 7:23 with the standards my **m** sets
7:25 to God's standards with my **m**,
8:24 saved with this hope in **m**.
8:27 knows what the Spirit has in **m**.
11:29 God never changes his **m**
14:18 Christ with this in **m** is pleasing
1Co 2:9 and no **m** has imagined the
2:16 "Who has known the **m** of the
2:16 we have the **m** of Christ.
11:28 With this in **m**,
14:14 but my **m** is not productive.
14:15 and I will pray with my **m**.
14:15 I will sing psalms with my **m**.
14:23 say that you're out of your **m**?
2Co 2:13 I didn't have any peace of **m**,
7:13 of you had put his **m** at ease.
Php 2:2 and keeping one purpose in **m**.
Col 2:18 Such a person, whose sinful **m**
3:2 Keep your **m** on things above,
2Th 1:11 With this in **m**, we always pray
2:14 With this in **m** he called you by
Heb 6:1 With this in **m**, we should stop
7:21 oath and will not change his **m**.
Jas 1:8 make up his **m** about anything.
1Pe 5:8 Keep your **m** clear,
Rev 17:9 situation a wise **m** is needed.

minding (1)

Pro 9:15 those **m** their own business,

mindless (1)

2Sm 6:20 like a **m** fool might expose

minds (53)

Gen 50:21 setting their **m** at ease.
Exo 13:17 they may change their **m** and
14:5 changed their **m** about them.
Job 17:4 You have closed their **m** so
Psa 101:4 keep far away from devious **m**.
105:25 He changed their **m** so that
Pro 12:23 but foolish **m** preach stupidity.
24:2 because their **m** plot violence,
Ecc 2:23 Even at night their **m** don't rest.
3:11 sense of eternity in people's **m**.
7:4 The **m** of wise people think
7:4 but the **m** of fools think about
Isa 6:10 understand with their **m**,
10:7 Their **m** don't work that way.
19:14 The LORD mixes up their **m**.
26:3 protect those whose **m** cannot
32:6 and their **m** plan evil in order to
44:18 And their **m** are closed,
44:20 Their own misguided **m** lead
Jer 17:10 search **m** and test hearts.
34:11 they changed their **m** and took
Eze 11:21 But as for those whose **m** are
Mat 13:15 Their **m** never understand.
21:32 your **m** and believe him.
Mar 3:5 because their **m** were closed.
6:52 Instead, their **m** were closed.)
8:17 Are your **m** closed?
Luk 21:14 So make up your **m** not to
24:45 Then he opened their **m** to
Jon 12:40 and their **m** don't understand.
Act 14:2 their **m** against the believers.
28:6 they changed their **m** and said
28:27 Their **m** never understand.
Rom 1:21 and their misguided **m** were
1:28 allowed their own immoral **m**
11:7 The **m** of the rest of Israel were
11:25 The **m** of some Israelites have
2Co 3:14 their **m** became closed.
3:15 a veil covers their **m**.
4:4 of this world has blinded the **m**
11:3 so your **m** may somehow be
Eph 4:17 Their **m** are set on worthless
Php 3:19 Their **m** are set on worldly
1Ti 6:5 corrupt **m** have been robbed
2Ti 3:8 Their **m** are corrupt,
Tit 1:15 Indeed, their **m** and their
Heb 5:14 whose **m** are trained by
10:16 and write them in their **m**."'
Jas 4:8 and clear your **m**, you doubters.
1Pe 1:13 Therefore, your **m** must be
4:7 and keep your **m** clear so that
2Pe 2:14 Their **m** are focused on their
Rev 2:23 who searches hearts and **m**.

mine (51)

Gen 31:43 Everything you see is **m**!
37:7 and suddenly **m** stood up.
48:5 will be **m** just as Reuben
Exo 13:2 among the Israelites is **m**,
19:5 though the whole world is **m**.
34:19 "Every first male offspring is **m**,
Lev 25:23 because the land is **m**.
Num 3:12 The Levites are **m**,
3:13 because every firstborn is **m**.
3:13 They will be **m**. I am the LORD."
3:45 The Levites will be **m**.
8:14 and the Levites will be **m**.
8:16 I have taken them to be **m** as
8:17 whether human or animal, is **m**.
Dtr 8:9 and you will be able to **m**
11:18 Take these words of **m** to heart
Jdg 16:15 me when your heart isn't **m**?
1Sm 14:41 If this sin is **m** or my son
20:30 are your mother's son but not **m**
2Sm 14:30 Joab's field is next to **m**.
1Ki 2:15 know the kingship was **m**.
3:26 "He won't be **m** or yours.
20:3 Your silver and gold are **m**.
20:3 wives and children are **m**."
20:5 and children are **m**.
Psa 50:10 cattle on a thousand hills, is **m**.
50:11 that moves in the fields is **m**.
50:12 and all that it contains are **m**.
60:7 Gilead is **m**. Manasseh is mine.
60:7 Manasseh is **m**. Ephraim is the
108:8 Gilead is **m**. Manasseh is mine.
108:8 Manasseh is **m**. Ephraim is the
119:111 instructions are **m** forever.
Pro 8:14 and priceless wisdom are **m**.
Sos 2:16 My beloved is **m**, and I am his.
6:3 and my beloved is **m**.
Isa 30:1 They carry out plans, but not **m**.
43:1 called you by name; you are **m**.
Jer 44:28 have come true, **m** or theirs.
Eze 16:8 You became **m**, declares the
29:3 You say, "The Nile River is **m**.

Eze 29:9 You said, "The Nile River is **m**.
Hag 2:8 The silver is **m**, and the gold is
2:8 is mine, and the gold is **m**,
Mal 3:17 "They will be **m**," says the
Mat 26:39 will be done rather than **m**."
Mar 14:36 will be done rather than **m**."
Luk 11:6 A friend of **m** on a trip has
19:22 knew that I take what isn't **m**
22:42 your will must be done, not **m**."
Jon 17:10 and everything you have is **m**.

mined (1)

Job 28:1 is a place where silver is **m**

mineshaft (1)

Job 28:4 They open up a **m** far from

mineshafts (1)

Job 28:10 They cut out **m** in the rocks.

Miniamin (3)

2Ch 31:15 Eden, **M**, Jeshua, Shemaiah,
Neh 12:17 from Abijah, Zichri; from **M**,
12:41 **M**, Micaiah, Elioenai,

ministers (1)

2Co 3:6 has also qualified us to be **m**

ministry (17)

Neh 12:44 Judah were pleased with the **m**
Luk 3:23 old when he began ⌊his **m**⌋.
Act 1:17 given an active role in this **m**.
13:24 Before Jesus began his **m**,
Rom 11:13 I bring honor to my **m**.
2Co 3:3 written as a result of our **m**.
3:7 The **m** that brought death was
3:8 Won't the **m** that brings the
3:9 If the **m** that brings punishment
3:9 then the **m** that brings God's
3:10 In fact, the **m** that brings
3:10 superior glory of the other **m**.
3:11 If that former **m** faded away
3:11 how much more does that **m**
4:1 us this **m** through his mercy.
5:18 **m** of restoring relationships.
8:4 to let them participate in the **m**

Minni (1)

Jer 51:27 Tell the kingdoms of Ararat, **M**,

Minnith (2)

Jdg 11:33 defeated them from Aroer to **M**
Eze 27:17 exchanged wheat from **M**,

minor (2)

Exo 18:22 settle all **m** cases themselves.
18:26 settled all **m** ones themselves.

mint (2)

Mat 23:23 ⌊God⌋ one-tenth of your **m**,
Luk 11:42 ⌊God⌋ one-tenth of your **m**,

minute (1)

Rut 2:7 sat down this **m** in the shelter."

miracle (13)

Psa 31:21 He has shown me the **m** of his
44:1 us about the **m** you performed
Mar 9:39 No one who works a **m** in my
Luk 23:8 him perform some kind of **m**.
Jon 2:18 "What **m** can you show us to
4:54 This was the second **m** that
6:14 saw the **m** Jesus performed,
6:30 What **m** are you going
7:21 "I performed one **m**,
12:18 Jesus had performed this **m**,
Act 4:16 Clearly, they've performed a **m**
4:17 Then the news about the **m**
4:22 healed by this **m** was over 40

miracles (96)

Exo 3:20 After all the **m** that I will do
15:11 your splendor. You perform **m**.
34:10 I will perform **m** that have never
34:10 how awesome these **m** are that
Jos 3:5 LORD will do **m** among you."
Jdg 6:13 Where are all the **m** our
13:18 It's a name that works **m**."
1Ch 16:9 on all the **m** he has done.
16:12 Remember the **m** he performed
16:24 Tell all the nations about his **m**.
Neh 9:17 They forgot the **m** you
Job 5:9 and **m** that ⌊we⌋ cannot
9:10 and **m** that cannot
10:16 working your **m** against me.
37:14 Stop and consider God's **m**.
37:16 the clouds drift (these are the **m**
Psa 9:1 about all the **m** you have done.
26:7 and tell about all your **m**.
40:5 I will tell others about your **m**,
71:17 about the **m** you have done.
72:18 who alone does **m**.
75:1 and your **m** confirm that.
75:9 But I will speak ⌊about your **m**⌋
77:11 I will remember your ancient **m**.
77:14 are the God who performs **m**.
78:11 what he had done — the **m** that
78:12 their ancestors he performed **m**
78:32 no longer believed in his **m**.
86:10 you are great, a worker of **m**.
88:10 Will you perform **m** for those
88:12 Will anyone know about your **m**
89:5 the heavens praise your **m** and
96:3 Tell all the nations about his **m**.
105:2 on all the **m** he has performed.
105:5 Remember the **m** he performed
106:7 they gave no thought to your **m**.
106:22 **m** in the land of Ham,
107:8 his **m** for Adam's descendants.
107:15 his **m** for Adam's descendants.
107:21 his **m** for Adam's descendants.
107:24 the **m** he performed in the
107:31 his **m** for Adam's descendants.
111:4 has made his **m** unforgettable.
119:27 so that I may reflect on your **m**.
Jer 21:2 the LORD will perform **m**
Dan 12:6 it be until these **m** are over?"
Joe 2:26 who has performed **m** for you.
2:30 I will work **m** in the sky and on
Mic 7:15 Let us see **m** like the time you
Mat 7:22 out demons and do many **m** by
11:20 he had worked most of his **m**
11:21 If the **m** worked in you had
11:23 If the **m** that had been worked
13:54 and the power to do these **m**?
13:58 He didn't work many **m** there
14:2 the power to perform these **m**."
21:15 the scribes saw the amazing **m**
Mar 6:2 the ability to do such great **m**?
6:5 He couldn't work any **m** there
6:14 the power to perform these **m**."
Luk 10:13 If the **m** worked in your cities
19:37 for all the **m** they had seen.
Jon 2:11 Jesus began to perform **m**.
2:23 saw the **m** that he performed.
3:2 No one can perform the **m** you
4:48 "If people don't see **m** and
6:2 because they saw the **m** that
6:26 for me because you saw **m**.
7:31 will he perform more **m** than
9:16 a sinner perform **m** like these?"
10:41 "John didn't perform any **m**,
11:47 man is performing a lot of **m**.
12:37 Jesus perform so many **m**,
20:30 Jesus performed many other **m**
20:30 Those **m** are not written in this
20:31 But these **m** have been written
Act 2:11 tell about the **m** that God has
2:19 I will work **m** in the sky and
2:22 this man God worked **m**,
4:30 by healing, performing **m**,
5:12 the apostles perform many **m**
6:8 things and performed **m**.
7:36 things and worked **m** in Egypt,
8:6 saw the **m** that he performed.
8:13 was amazed to see the **m**
14:3 will by having them perform **m**
15:12 and Paul tell about all the **m**
19:11 unusual **m** through Paul.
1Co 12:10 Another can work **m**.
12:28 then those who perform **m**,
12:29 Do all of them perform **m**
2Co 12:12 and **m** which prove that I'm an
Gal 3:5 work **m** among you through
Rev 16:14 are spirits of demons that do **m**.
19:20 false prophet who had done **m**
19:20 By these **m** the false prophet

miraculous (67)

Exo 4:8 pay attention to the first **m** sign,
4:9 believe these two **m** signs
4:17 and use it to do the **m** signs."
4:28 him to say and all the **m** signs
4:30 He also did the **m** signs for the
7:3 Even though I will do many **m**
8:23 This **m** sign will happen
10:1 do these **m** signs among them.
10:2 Egyptians and what **m** signs
Num 14:11 me in spite of all the **m** signs
14:22 saw my glory and the **m** signs
Dtr 4:34 **m** signs, amazing things,
6:22 our eyes the LORD did **m** signs
7:19 terrible plagues, the **m** signs,
11:3 You saw the **m** signs and
13:1 may predict a **m** sign or an
26:8 **m** signs, and amazing things.
29:3 terrible plagues, those **m** signs,
34:11 sent to do all the **m** signs
Jdg 13:19 the LORD did something **m**.
1Ki 13:3 ⌊also⌋ gave ⌊them⌋ a **m** sign,
13:5 This was the **m** sign the man
2Ch 32:24 him and gave him a **m** sign.
32:31 him about the **m** sign that had
Neh 9:10 You performed **m** signs and did
Job 37:5 voice thunders in **m** ways.
Psa 17:7 Reveal your **m** deeds of mercy,
40:5 You have done many **m** things,
65:8 are in awe of your **m** signs.
74:9 We no longer see **m** signs.
78:4 great deeds and the **m** things
78:43 when he performed his **m** signs
98:1 because he has done **m** things.
105:27 They displayed his **m** signs
119:18 so that I may see the **m** things
119:129 Your written instructions are **m**.
135:9 He sent **m** signs and amazing
136:4 only one who does **m** things —
139:14 Your works are **m**,
145:5 and the **m** things you have
Isa 25:1 You have done **m** things.
Jer 32:20 You performed **m** signs and
32:21 people from Egypt with **m** signs
Dan 4:2 write to you about the **m** signs
4:3 His **m** signs are impressive.
6:27 He saves, rescues, and does **m**
Mat 12:38 we want you to show us a **m**
12:39 unfaithful era look for a **m** sign.
16:1 them a **m** sign from heaven.
16:4 people look for a **m** sign.
24:24 They will work spectacular, **m**
Mar 8:11 perform a **m** sign from heaven.
13:22 They will work **m** signs and do
16:17 "These are the **m** signs that
16:20 He confirmed his word by the **m**
Luk 11:16 some **m** sign from heaven.
11:29 They look for a **m** sign.
11:30 Just as Jonah became a **m**
11:30 so the Son of Man will be a **m**
13:17 was happy about the **m** things
21:11 Terrifying sights and **m** signs
21:25 "**M** signs will occur in the sun,
Act 2:43 and **m** signs happened through
Rom 15:19 by the power of **m** and amazing
1Co 1:22 Jews ask for **m** signs,
2Th 2:9 including **m** and wonderful
Heb 2:4 they said through **m** signs,

miraculously (1)

Psa 139:14 so amazingly and **m** made.

Miriam (13)

Exo 15:20 Then the prophet **M**,
15:21 **M** sang to them: "Sing to the
Num 12:1 **M** and Aaron began to criticize
12:4 said to Moses, Aaron, and **M**,
12:5 He called to Aaron and **M**,
12:10 When the smoke left the tent, **M**
12:15 So **M** was put in isolation

Num 20:1 **M** died and was buried there.
26:59 Moses, and their sister **M**.
Dtr 24:9 the LORD your God did to **M**
1Ch 4:17 His wife gave birth to **M**,
6:3 were Aaron, Moses, and **M**.
Mic 6:4 and **M** to lead you.

Mirmah (1)

1Ch 8:10 Jeuz, Sachia, and **M**.

mirror (3)

Job 37:18 as firm as a **m** made of metal?
1Co 13:12 we see a blurred image in a **m**.
Jas 1:23 who looks at his face in a **m**,

mirrors (2)

Exo 38:8 out of the bronze **m** given by
Isa 3:23 **m**, underwear, headdresses,

miscarried (1)

Gen 31:38 Your sheep and goats never **m**,

miscarry (3)

Exo 23:26 No woman in your land will **m**
Job 21:10 birth to calves and never **m**.
Hos 9:14 Make the women **m**,

mischief (1)

Psa 7:16 His **m** lands back on his own

misdemeanor (1)

Act 18:14 "If there were some kind of **m**

miserable (14)

Jdg 14:17 because she made his life **m**.
16:16 Every day she made his life **m**
1Sm 1:6 in order to make her **m**.
1:7 Peninnah would make her **m**,
Neh 4:2 "What do these **m** Jews think
Pro 15:15 is a terrible day for a **m** person,
Ecc 7:16 Why make yourself **m**?
Isa 10:30 you people in Laishah and **m**
Jer 15:10 I'm so **m**! Why did my mother
45:3 You said, 'I'm so **m**!
Rom 7:24 What a **m** person I am!
Jas 4:9 Be **m**, mourn, and cry.
Rev 3:17 do not realize that you are **m**,
18:7 not a widow. I'll never be **m**.'

miserably (1)

Isa 38:14 I've suffered **m**, O Lord!

misery (46)

Gen 29:32 the LORD has seen my **m**;
31:42 God has seen my **m** and hard
44:34 bear to see my father's **m**!"
Exo 3:7 "I have seen the **m** of my
3:17 will take you away from your **m**
4:31 and that he had seen their **m**,
Dtr 16:3 (It is the bread of **m** because
26:7 He saw our **m**, suffering,
1Sm 1:11 if you will look at my **m**,
2Sm 16:12 the LORD will see my **m**
1Ki 17:20 have you brought **m** on the
2Ki 19:3 Today is a day filled with **m**,
Ezr 9:5 sacrifice I got up from my **m**,
Job 3:20 "Why give light to one in **m**
4:8 wickedness and planted **m**,
6:2 if only my **m** could be laid on
7:3 inherited nights filled with **m**.
10:15 disgrace while I look on my **m**.
11:16 ⌊Then⌋ you will forget your **m**
20:22 the full force of **m** comes down
20:23 Let that **m** fill his belly.
30:27 Days of **m** are ahead of me.
36:8 and tangled in ropes of **m**,
Psa 25:18 Look at my **m** and suffering,
31:7 You have seen my **m**.
44:24 you forget our suffering and **m**?
55:3 They bring **m** crashing down
55:10 Trouble and **m** are everywhere.
90:10 of them ⌊bring⌋ trouble and **m**.
107:10 shadow were prisoners in **m**.
119:50 This is my comfort in my **m**:
119:92 I would have died in my **m**.
119:153 Look at my **m**, and rescue me,
Pro 23:29 Who has **m**? Who has quarrels?
24:22 knows what **m** both may bring?
Isa 37:3 Today is a day filled with **m**,
Oba 1:13 their **m** when disaster strikes.
Mat 24:21 There will be a lot of **m** at that
24:21 a kind of **m** that has not
24:29 "Immediately after the **m** of
Mar 13:19 It will be a time of **m** that has
13:24 after the **m** of those days,
Luk 16:25 Lazarus' life was filled with **m**.
Jas 5:1 Cry and moan about the **m** that
Rev 18:7 her just as much torture and **m**.
18:8 reason her plagues of death, **m**,

misfortune (3)

Num 23:21 He sees no **m** for the people of
Job 12:5 life has no appreciation for **m**.
Oba 1:12 gloat over your relative's **m**

misguided (3)

Isa 44:20 Their own **m** minds lead them
Rom 1:21 and their **m** minds were
10:2 devoted to God, but they are **m**.

Mishael (8)

Exo 6:22 The sons of Uzziel were **M**,
Lev 10:4 Moses called **M** and Elzaphan,
Neh 8:4 Pedaiah, **M**, Malchiah,
Dan 1:6 Hananiah, **M**, and Azariah.
1:7 To **M** he gave the name
1:11 Hananiah, **M**, and Azariah.
1:19 one like Daniel, Hananiah, **M**,
2:17 told his friends Hananiah, **M**,

Mishal (2)

Jos 19:26 Allammelech, Amad, and **M**.
21:30 the tribe of Asher: **M**, Abdon,

Misham (1)

1Ch 8:12 Elpaal's sons were Eber, **M**,

Mishma (3)

Gen 25:14 **M**, Dumah, Massa,
1Ch 1:30 **M**, Dumah, Massa, Hadad,
4:25 Mibsam's son was **M**.

Mishmannah (1)

1Ch 12:10 The fourth was **M**.

Mishma's (1)

1Ch 4:26 **M** son was Hammuel.

Mishraites (1)

1Ch 2:53 the Shumathites, and the **M**.

mislead (9)

2Ki 18:32 he tries to **m** you by saying
Psa 119:118 because their lies **m** them.
Isa 3:12 My people, your guides **m** you,
19:13 of its tribes **m** the Egyptians.
36:18 Don't let Hezekiah **m** you by
Mic 3:5 the prophets who **m** my people:
Col 2:4 I say this so that no one will **m**
2Ti 3:6 **m** weak-minded women who
3:13 bad to worse as they **m** people

misleading (4)

Gen 34:13 his father Hamor a **m** answer
2Ch 32:11 Isn't Hezekiah **m** you and
Lam 2:14 Your prophets saw **m** visions
Col 2:8 a shallow and **m** philosophy.

misleads (4)

Job 12:19 and **m** those who serve
Pro 14:8 but the stupidity of fools **m**
16:29 A violent person **m** his
Rev 2:20 She teaches and **m** my

misled (6)

2Ki 21:9 Manasseh **m** Israel so that they
2Ch 33:9 Manasseh **m** Judah and the
Jer 38:22 'Your trusted friends have **m**
Lam 2:14 false prophecies that **m** you.
2Ti 3:13 people and are themselves **m**.
Tit 3:3 stupid, disobedient, and **m**.

Mispar (1)

Ezr 2:2 Bilshan, **M**, Bigvai, Rehum,

Mispereth (1)

Neh 7:7 Bilshan, **M**, Bigvai, Nehum,

Misrephoth Maim (2)

Jos 11:8 as far as Great Sidon, **M**,
13:6 mountains from Lebanon to **M**

miss (4)

Jdg 20:16 a stone at a hair and not **m**.
Psa 58:7 let their arrows **m** the target.
Jer 3:16 They won't remember it, **m** it,
Php 4:1 I love you and **m** you.

missed (3)

1Sm 20:18 "and you will be **m** when your
20:19 you will be **m** even more.
Jer 46:17 He has **m** his chance.'

misses (1)

1Sm 20:6 If your father really **m** me,

missing (17)

Num 31:49 and not one of them is **m**.
Jdg 21:3 one tribe be **m** today in Israel?"
1Sm 25:7 Nothing of theirs has been **m**
25:15 was **m** wherever we went
25:21 one of his possessions was **m**.
30:19 Nothing was **m** — young or old,
2Sm 2:30 officers and Asahel were **m**.
2Ki 10:19 Make sure no one is **m**
10:19 Whoever is **m** will not live."
Job 5:24 your house and find nothing **m**.
Isa 34:16 one of these animals will be **m**.
40:26 not one of them is **m**.
59:15 Truth is **m**. Those who turn
Jer 23:4 will be **m**," declares the LORD.
Zec 11:9 those that are **m** stay missing.
11:9 those that are missing stay **m**.
Mar 10:21 "You're still **m** one thing.

mission (8)

1Sm 15:18 And the LORD sent you on a **m**.
21:2 about this **m** I'm sending you
21:5 usual when we go ⌊on a **m**⌋.
Pro 10:26 those who send him ⌊on a **m**⌋.
Act 20:24 I want to carry out the **m** I
20:24 from the Lord Jesus — the **m**
22:21 I'll send you on a **m**.
1Th 3:2 His **m** was to strengthen and

missionaries (1)

Eph 4:11 gave apostles, prophets, **m**,

missionary (2)

Act 21:8 He was a **m** and one of the
2Ti 4:5 Do the work of a **m**.

mist (4)

Job 36:27 He distills rain from his **m**,
Isa 44:22 your sins like the morning **m**.
Jas 4:14 You are a **m** that is seen for a
2Pe 2:17 They are a **m** blown around by

mistake (8)

Gen 43:12 Maybe it was a **m**.
Lev 22:14 offering by **m** must give another
1Sm 26:21 a fool and made a terrible **m**."
Job 19:4 made a **m** without realizing it,
19:4 my **m** would affect only me.
Psa 19:12 Who can notice every **m**?
Ecc 5:6 "My promise was a **m**!"
Gal 6:7 Make no **m** about this:

mistaken (3)

Mat 22:29 Jesus answered, "You're **m**
Mar 12:24 "Aren't you **m** because you
12:27 of the living. You're badly **m**!"

mistakes (4)

Job 4:18 his angels of making **m**.
Pro 19:2 A person in a hurry makes **m**.
Jas 3:2 All of us make a lot of **m**.

Jas 3:2 If someone doesn't make any **m**

mistreat (10)

Gen 31:50 If you **m** my daughters or marry
Exo 22:21 "Never **m** or oppress foreigners
Lev 19:33 "Never **m** a foreigner living in
Dtr 21:14 You must never sell her or **m**
23:16 best to him. Never **m** him.
1Sm 25:15 They didn't **m** us, and we found
Psa 89:22 No wicked person will **m** him.
Isa 58:3 You **m** all your workers.
Jer 22:3 Don't **m** foreigners,
Act 7:6 make them slaves and **m** them

mistreated (11)

Gen 16:6 Then Sarai **m** Hagar so much
Num 16:15 And I haven't **m** any of them."
20:15 The Egyptians **m** us and our
1Sm 25:7 ⌊and⌋ we have not **m** them.
Mat 22:6 **m** them, and then killed them.
Act 7:19 He **m** our ancestors.
7:34 how my people are **m** in Egypt.
Heb 10:33 were publicly insulted and **m**.
11:37 were poor, abused, and **m**.
13:3 Remember those who are **m** as
13:3 as if you were being **m**.

mistreating (4)

Job 10:3 What do you gain by **m** me,
19:3 You're not even ashamed of **m**
Eze 22:12 profits by **m** your neighbors.
Act 12:1 attention to **m** certain members

mistreatment (1)

2Co 12:10 **m**, hardship, persecution,

mistress (4)

2Ki 5:3 The girl told her **m**,
Psa 123:2 as a maid depends on her **m**,
Pro 30:23 maid when she replaces her **m**.
Nah 3:4 this very charming **m** of evil

misunderstand (1)

Dtr 32:27 their opponents to **m** and say,

misunderstanding (1)

1Co 12:1 **m** concerning spiritual gifts.

misuse (1)

Psa 139:20 Your enemies **m** your name.

Mithcah (2)

Num 33:28 Terah and set up camp at **M**.
33:29 They moved from **M** and set up

Mithnite (1)

1Ch 11:43 and Joshaphat the **M**,

Mithredath (3)

Ezr 1:8 of Persia put the treasurer **M**
1:8 So **M** made a list of them for
4:7 Bishlam, **M**, Tabeel, and the

Mitylene (1)

Act 20:14 board and went to the city of **M**.

mix (5)

Gen 11:7 Let us go down there and **m** up
Exo 30:34 and **m** them with one part pure
Pro 23:30 wine and **m** it with everything.
Dan 2:43 will **m** by intermarrying,
2:43 more than iron can **m** with clay.

mixed (57)

Exo 29:40 offering of eight cups of flour **m**
Lev 2:4 bread made of flour **m**
2:5 made of flour **m** with olive oil.
7:10 whether **m** with olive oil or dry,
7:12 rings of unleavened bread **m**
7:12 and loaves made from flour **m**
9:4 and a grain offering **m** with
14:10 also take eight cups of flour **m**
14:21 take only eight cups of flour **m**
23:13 offering of four quarts of flour **m**
Num 7:13 dish was filled with flour **m**
7:19 dish was filled with flour **m**
Num 7:25 dish was filled with flour **m**
7:31 dish was filled with flour **m**
7:37 dish was filled with flour **m**
7:43 dish was filled with flour **m**
7:49 dish was filled with flour **m**
7:55 dish was filled with flour **m**
7:61 dish was filled with flour **m**
7:67 dish was filled with flour **m**
7:73 dish was filled with flour **m**
7:79 dish was filled with flour **m**
8:8 and the grain offering of flour **m**
15:4 offering of eight cups of flour **m**
15:6 offering of 16 cups of flour **m**
15:9 offering of 24 cups of flour **m**
28:5 offering of eight cups of flour **m**
28:9 offering of 16 cups of flour **m**
28:12 offering of 24 cups of flour **m**
28:12 cups of flour **m** with olive oil,
28:13 offering of 8 cups of flour **m**
28:20 bring grain offerings of flour **m**
28:28 bring grain offerings of flour **m**
29:3 bring grain offerings of flour **m**
29:9 bring grain offerings of flour **m**
29:14 bring grain offerings of flour **m**
Jos 23:7 Don't get **m** up with the nations
Ezr 9:2 They have **m** our holy race
Psa 75:8 is thoroughly **m** with spices.)
102:9 my tears are **m** with my drink
Pro 9:2 She has **m** her wine.
9:5 and drink the wine I have **m**.
Dan 2:41 iron was **m** with clay.
2:43 iron was **m** with clay.
Hos 8:8 It has already **m** in with the
Amo 8:6 We can sell the husks **m** in
Zec 9:6 A **m** race will live in Ashdod,
Mat 13:33 like yeast that a woman **m** into
27:34 gave him a drink of wine **m**
Mar 15:23 They tried to give him wine **m**
Luk 13:21 It's like yeast that a woman **m**
Jon 9:6 he spit on the ground and **m** the
9:11 "The man people call Jesus **m**
9:14 The day when Jesus **m** the
2Ti 2:4 in the military doesn't get **m** up
Rev 8:7 hail and fire were **m** with blood,
15:2 like a sea of glass **m** with fire.

mixes (2)

Isa 19:14 The LORD **m** up their minds.
Hos 7:8 "Ephraim **m** with other nations.

mixing (4)

Exo 8:3 into your ovens and into your **m**
Lev 6:21 pan with olive oil, **m** it well.
1Ch 23:29 they were responsible for **m** the
Isa 5:22 who are champions at **m**

mixture (7)

Exo 30:25 into a holy oil, a fragrant **m**,
1Ch 9:30 sons prepared the **m** of spices.
Isa 30:24 work the soil will eat a **m**
Eze 24:5 Bring the **m** in the pot to a boil.
24:10 the meat thoroughly, stir the **m**,
Jon 9:15 "He put a **m** of spit and dirt on
19:39 pounds of a myrrh and aloe **m**.

Mizar (1)

Psa 42:6 peaks of Hermon, on Mount **M**.

Mizpah (45)

Gen 31:49 and also **M** [Watchtower],
Jos 11:3 the foot of Mount Hermon in **M**.
11:8 and the valley of **M** in the east.
15:38 Dilean, **M**, Joktheel,
Jdg 10:17 together and camped at **M**.
11:11 So Jephthah went to **M** and
11:29 and **M** in Gilead ⌊to gather an
11:29 From **M** in Gilead Jephthah
11:34 went to his home in **M**,
20:1 and from Gilead came to **M**.
20:3 that Israel had come to **M**.
21:1 Israel had taken this oath in **M**:
21:5 of the LORD at **M** must
21:8 presence of the LORD at **M**?"
1Sm 7:5 all the Israelites together at **M**,
7:6 gathered together at **M**.
7:6 So Samuel judged Israel in **M**.
1Sm 7:7 Israelites had gathered at **M**,
7:11 Israel's soldiers left **M**,
7:12 set it up between **M** and Shen.
7:16 and **M** in order to judge Israel in
10:17 presence of the LORD at **M**.
22:3 there David went to **M** in Moab.
1Ki 15:22 fortify Geba in Benjamin and **M**.
2Ki 25:23 they went to Gedaliah at **M**.
25:25 who were with him at **M**.
2Ch 16:6 fortify Geba in Benjamin and **M**.
Neh 3:7 with men from Gibeon and **M**,
3:15 in charge of the district of **M**,
3:19 the official in charge of **M**,
Jer 40:6 at **M** and lived with him among
40:8 their men to Gedaliah at **M**:
40:10 I'm going to live in **M** and
40:12 to Judah and to Gedaliah at **M**.
40:13 country came to Gedaliah at **M**.
40:15 secretly asked Gedaliah at **M**,
41:1 Gedaliah, son of Ahikam, at **M**.
41:1 As they ate together at **M**,
41:3 with Gedaliah at **M** as well as
41:6 left **M** to meet them,
41:10 of the people who were at **M**.
41:10 people who had been left at **M**.
41:14 had taken captive at **M** turned
41:16 rest of the people of **M** whom
Hos 5:1 You set traps at **M** and spread

Mizpeh (1)

Jos 18:26 **M**, Chephirah, Mozah,

Mizzah (3)

Gen 36:13 Zerah, Shammah, and **M**.
36:17 Zerah, Shammah, and **M**.
1Ch 1:37 Zerah, Shammah, and **M**.

Mnason (1)

Act 21:16 **M** was from the island of

Mnason's (1)

Act 21:16 They took us to **M** home,

Moab (155)

Gen 19:37 to a son and named him **M**.
36:35 Midianites in the country of **M**.
Exo 15:15 powerful men of **M** will tremble.
Num 21:11 Abarim in the desert west of **M**.
21:13 between **M** and the Amorites.)
21:15 lie along the border of **M** ...."
21:20 in **M** where Mount Pisgah
21:26 had fought the former king of **M**
21:28 They destroyed Ar of **M**,
21:29 How horrible it is for you, **M**!
22:1 on the plains of **M** east of the
22:4 son of Zippor, was king of **M**.
22:7 The leaders of **M** and Midian
22:8 of **M** stayed with Balaam.
22:10 son of King Zippor of **M**,
22:36 right on the border of **M**.
23:6 with all the princes of **M**.
23:7 The king of **M** summoned me
23:17 offering with the princes of **M**.
26:3 on the plains of **M** near
26:63 on the plains of **M** near
31:12 camp on the plains of **M** near
33:44 Iye Abarim on the border of **M**.
33:48 camp on the plains of **M** near
33:49 camp on the plains of **M** along
33:50 Moses on the plains of **M** near
35:1 Moses on the plains of **M** near
36:13 Moses on the plains of **M** near
Dtr 1:5 River in **M** when Moses began
2:8 goes through the desert of **M**.
2:9 Don't bother the people of **M** or
2:18 to pass by the border of **M** at Ar.
29:1 to give to the Israelites in **M**.
32:49 to Mount Nebo in **M**,
34:1 Nebo from the plains of **M**.
34:5 servant Moses died in **M**.
34:6 He was buried in a valley in **M**,
34:8 for Moses in the plains of **M**
Jos 24:9 son of King Zippor of **M**,
Jdg 3:12 Eglon of **M** stronger than Israel,
3:14 King Eglon of **M** for 18 years.
3:15 payment to King Eglon of **M**.

Jdg 3:28 will hand your enemy **M** over
3:28 of the Jordan River that led to **M**
3:30 The power of **M** was crushed
10:6 of Aram, Sidon, **M**, Ammon,
11:15 land belonging to **M** or Ammon.
11:17 messengers to the king of **M**.
11:18 by-passing Edom and **M**.
11:18 They camped east of **M** — east
11:25 son of King Zippor of **M**,
Rut 1:1 for a while in the country of **M**.
1:2 country of **M** and lived there.
1:4 son married a woman from **M**.
1:6 back from the country of **M**.
1:6 (While they were still in **M** she
1:22 back from the country of **M**,
2:2 Ruth, who was from **M**,
2:6 Naomi from the country of **M**.
2:21 Ruth, who was from **M**,
4:3 back from the country of **M**,
1Sm 12:9 and to the king of **M**.
14:47 on every side — against **M**,
22:3 David went to Mizpah in **M**.
22:3 He asked the king of **M**,
22:4 brought them to the king of **M**,
2Sm 8:2 He also defeated **M**,
8:12 from Edom, **M**, Ammon,
23:20 distinguished soldiers from **M**.
1Ki 11:1 women and women from **M**,
11:7 (the disgusting idol of **M**)
11:33 Chemosh (the god of **M**),
2Ki 1:1 **M** rebelled against Israel.
3:4 King Mesha of **M** raised sheep.
3:5 the king of **M** rebelled against
3:7 "The king of **M** has rebelled
3:7 Will you fight **M** with me?"
3:9 took an indirect route ⌊to **M**⌋.
3:10 mercy of ⌊the people of⌋ **M**."
3:18 he will put **M** at your mercy.
3:21 All the people of **M** heard that
3:26 When the king of **M** saw he
23:13 (the disgusting god of **M**),
1Ch 1:46 Midianites in the country of **M**,
4:22 Saraph ruled **M** and Jashubi
8:8 and Baara. But later in **M**,
11:22 distinguished soldiers from **M**.
11:46 of Elnaam), Ithmah from **M**,
18:2 He also defeated **M**,
18:11 **M**, Ammon, the Philistines,
Neh 13:23 from Ashdod, Ammon, and **M**.
Psa 60:8 **M** is my washtub. I will throw
83:6 and Ishmael, **M** and Hagar,
108:9 **M** is my washtub. I will throw
Isa 11:14 will conquer Edom and **M**.
15:1 the divine revelation about **M**.
15:1 In a single night Ar in **M** is laid
15:1 In a single night Kir in **M** is laid
15:2 **M** wails over Nebo and
15:5 My heart cries out for **M**.
15:8 echo throughout the land of **M**.
15:9 will attack the fugitives from **M**
16:4 Let the fugitives from **M** stay
16:7 That is why **M** will wail.
16:7 Everyone will wail for **M**.
16:11 my heart mourns for **M** like
16:12 When the people of **M** appear
16:13 spoke about **M** in the past.
25:10 **M** will be trampled beneath him
Jer 9:26 Judah, Edom, Ammon, and **M**.
25:21 Edom, **M**, and the people of
27:3 **M**, Ammon, Tyre, and Sidon,
40:11 all the Jews who were in **M**,
48:1 God of Israel, says about **M**:
48:2 People will no longer praise **M**.
48:4 **M** will be broken. Its little ones
48:9 Put salt on **M**. It will be
48:11 "**M** has lived securely ever
48:12 I will send people to pour **M** out
48:13 Then **M** will be ashamed of
48:15 The enemy will attack **M** and
48:18 The destroyers of **M** will attack
48:20 '**M** is disgraced; it is defeated.
48:20 in Arnon that **M** is destroyed.'
48:24 and on all the cities of **M**,
48:26 "Get the people of **M** drunk;
48:27 People of **M**, didn't you laugh at
48:28 People of **M**, abandon your
Jer 48:31 That is why I will weep for **M**
48:31 for Moab and cry for all of **M**.
48:33 the orchards and fields of **M**.
48:35 I will stop those in **M** who
48:36 "That is why I moan for **M** like
48:38 People in **M** will mourn on
48:38 because I will break **M** like a
48:39 'Look how **M** is defeated!
48:39 **M** turns away in shame!'
48:39 **M** has become something
48:40 and spread their wings over **M**.
48:42 **M** will be destroyed as a
48:43 live in **M**," declares the LORD.
48:44 to **M**," declares the LORD.
48:45 foreheads of the people of **M**
48:46 horrible it will be for you, **M**.
48:47 But I will restore **M** in the last
48:47 judgment against **M** ends here.
Eze 25:8 LORD says: **M** and Seir said,
25:11 I will punish **M**. Then they will
Dan 11:41 But Edom, **M**, and the leaders
Amo 2:1 Because **M** has committed
2:2 I will send a fire on **M** and burn
2:2 **M** will die during the noise of
Mic 6:5 King Balak of **M** planned ⌊to do
Zep 2:8 "I have heard the insults from **M**
2:9 "**M** will become like Sodom,

Moabite (10)

Num 22:14 So the **M** princes went back to
22:21 and left with the **M** princes.
25:1 to have sex with **M** women
Rut 1:22 her **M** daughter-in-law,
2:6 "She's a young **M** woman who
4:5 responsibility for the **M** Ruth,
4:10 bought as my wife the **M** Ruth,
2Ki 13:20 **M** raiding parties used to
2Ch 24:26 of a **M** woman named Shimrith.
Neh 13:1 no Ammonite or **M** should ever

Moabites (24)

Gen 19:37 the ancestor of the **M** of today.
Num 22:3 The **M** were very afraid
22:3 Besides, the **M** couldn't stand
22:4 So the **M** said to the leaders of
24:17 will crush the heads of the **M**
Dtr 2:11 but the **M** called them Emites.
2:29 Seir, and the **M**, who live in Ar,
23:3 Ammonites or **M** may not join
2Sm 8:2 made the **M** lie down on the
8:2 So the **M** became David's
2Ki 3:22 When the **M** got up early in the
3:23 Now, **M**, let's take their goods!"
3:24 So when the **M** came to Israel's
3:24 after the **M** and defeated them.
24:2 of Babylonians, Arameans, **M**,
1Ch 18:2 and the **M** became David's
2Ch 20:1 Later the **M**, Ammonites,
20:10 "The Ammonites, **M**,
20:22 against the Ammonites, **M**,
20:23 Then the Ammonites and **M**
Ezr 9:1 **M**, Egyptians, and Amorites.
Isa 25:11 The **M** will stretch out their
Eze 25:10 I will hand the **M** and the
Amo 2:1 The **M** have cremated Edom's

Moab's (15)

Jos 13:32 distributed on **M** plains, east
Jdg 3:29 of **M** best fighting men.
11:18 River because it was **M** border
2Ki 3:13 in order to put us at **M** mercy.
Isa 15:4 **M** armed men cry out.
16:2 **M** daughters are like fluttering
16:6 of the arrogance of **M** people.
16:14 "**M** honor will be despised
25:12 He will bring down **M** high
Jer 48:2 will plan **M** destruction.
48:16 "**M** destruction is coming near;
48:25 "**M** horn is cut off, and its arm
48:29 the arrogance of **M** people.
48:41 On that day **M** soldiers will be
Eze 25:9 cities that protect **M** borders.

Moach's (1)

1Sm 27:2 to King Achish of Gath, **M** son

Moadiah (1)

Neh 12:17 from Miniamin, from **M**, Piltai;

moan (8)

Jer 48:31 I will **m** for the people of Kir
48:36 "That is why I **m** for Moab like
51:52 wounded will **m** everywhere
Lam 2:5 people of Judah mourn and **m**.
Eze 7:16 They will **m** like doves in the
7:16 They will **m** because of their
Mal 2:13 You **m** and groan because he
Jas 5:1 Cry and **m** about the misery

moat (1)

Dan 9:25 a city square and a **m** during

mob (22)

Job 15:34 because a **m** of godless people
30:12 me on my right side like a **m**.
Psa 22:16 A **m** has encircled me.
26:5 I have hated the **m** of evildoers
64:2 from the **m** of troublemakers.
86:14 and a **m** of ruthless people
Jer 9:2 all adulterers, a **m** of traitors.
12:6 They have also formed a **m** to
Eze 16:40 will also bring a **m** against you.
23:46 Bring together a **m** ⌊against the
23:47 Then the **m** will stone them
23:47 The **m** will kill their sons and
Act 17:5 the public square, formed a **m**,
19:40 be able to explain this **m**."
21:30 was in chaos, and a **m** formed.
21:30 The **m** grabbed Paul and
21:36 The **m** was behind them
21:40 When the **m** was silent,
22:2 When the **m** heard him speak
22:22 Up to that point the **m** listened.
22:23 The **m** was yelling,
24:18 crowd or noisy **m** was present.

mobs (1)

Job 31:34 of the ⌊local⌋ **m** terrified me so

mock (5)

Pro 9:12 If you **m**, you alone will be held
20:1 Wine ⌊makes people⌋ **m**,
Isa 14:4 Then you will **m** the king of
28:11 He will **m** them by speaking in
Eze 22:5 and those far away will **m** you.

mocked (6)

Jdg 5:18 But Zebulun **m** death,
2Ki 2:23 came out of the city and **m** him.
2Ch 36:16 But they **m** God's messengers,
Psa 119:51 Arrogant people have **m** me
Eze 23:32 You will be scorned and **m**,
36:4 become prey and are **m** by

mocker (10)

Pro 9:7 corrects a **m** receives abuse.
9:8 Do not warn a **m**, or he will
13:1 but a **m** does not listen to
14:6 A **m** searches for wisdom
15:12 A **m** does not appreciate a
19:25 Strike a **m**, and a gullible
21:11 When a **m** is punished,
21:24 conceited person is called a **m**.
22:10 Drive out a **m**, and conflict will
24:9 and a **m** is disgusting to

mockers (10)

Job 17:2 Certainly, **m** are around me.
Psa 1:1 or join the company of **m**.
35:16 With crude and abusive **m**,
Pro 1:22 How long will you **m** find joy in
3:34 When he mocks the **m**,
19:29 Punishments are set for **m** and
29:8 **M** create an uproar in a city,
Isa 29:20 **M** will be finished.
Hos 7:5 and the king joins **m**.
Act 13:41 'Look, you **m**! Be amazed and

mockery (1)

Zep 2:8 Moab and the **m** from Ammon.

mocking (3)

Gen 27:12 ⌊my skin⌋ and think I'm **m** him.
Job 21:3 I've spoken, you may go on **m**.
Pro 1:22 mockers find joy in your **m**?

mocks (4)

1Sm 2:1 My mouth **m** my enemies.
Pro 3:34 When he **m** the mockers,
19:28 A worthless witness **m** justice,
Jer 20:7 all day long. Everyone **m** me.

model (6)

Jos 22:28 'Look at the **m** of the LORD's
2Ki 16:10 Ahaz sent the priest Urijah a **m**
16:11 like the **m** King Ahaz sent
Act 7:44 He used the **m** he had seen.
1Th 1:7 This way, you became a **m** for
Heb 9:24 He didn't go into a **m** of the real

models (3)

1Sm 6:5 Make **m** of your tumors and
6:11 the gold mice and the **m**
Act 19:24 business of making silver **m**

modest (1)

1Ti 2:9 that are **m** and respectable.

moisten (1)

Eze 46:14 quarts of olive oil to **m** the flour.

moisture (2)

Job 37:11 loads the thick clouds with **m**
Luk 8:6 because they had no **m**.

Moladah (4)

Jos 15:26 Amam, Shema, **M**,
19:2 Beersheba (Sheba), **M**,
1Ch 4:28 in Beersheba, **M**, Hazar Shual,
Neh 11:26 in Jeshua, **M**, and Beth Pelet,

mold (3)

1Ki 7:37 them were cast in the same **m**,
Pro 25:4 ready for the silversmith to **m**.
Nah 3:14 the clay! Grab the brick **m**!

molded (4)

Isa 2:8 and what their fingers have **m**.
17:8 altars which their fingers **m**.
Hab 2:18 benefit is there in a **m** statue,
2:18 when its maker has **m** it?

molding (10)

Exo 25:11 and put a gold **m** around it.
25:24 and put a gold **m** around it.
25:25 put a gold **m** around the rim.
30:3 Put a gold **m** around it.
30:4 and put them below the **m** on
37:2 out and put a gold **m** around it.
37:11 gold and put a gold **m** around it.
37:12 put a gold **m** around the rim.
37:26 and he put a gold **m** around it.
37:27 rings and put them below the **m**

Molech (8)

Lev 18:21 to the god **M** ⌊by burning them
20:2 as a sacrifice to ⌊the god⌋ **M**,
20:3 gave one of their children to **M**,
20:4 who give their children to **M**
20:5 who chases after **M** as if
1Ki 11:7 and for **M** (the disgusting idol
2Ki 23:10 by burning them to the god **M**.
Jer 32:35 their sons and daughters to **M**.

moles (2)

Lev 11:29 ground are unclean for you — **m**
Isa 2:20 day people will throw to the **m**

molested (1)

Rut 2:22 else's field, you may be **m**."

Molid (1)

1Ch 2:29 She gave birth to Ahban and **M**.

mollusk (1)

Exo 30:34 resin and aromatic **m** shells),

Moloch (1)

Act 7:43 carried along the shrine of **M**,

moment (35)

Num 4:20 even for a **m**, or they will die."
Rut 3:14 At that **m** Boaz thought to
1Ki 14:12 The **m** you set foot in the city
Ezr 9:8 And now, for a brief **m**,
Est 6:4 At that **m**, Haman came through
Job 7:18 and examine him every **m**?
20:5 godless person lasts only a **m**?
Psa 4:8 I fall asleep in peace the **m** I
6:10 In a **m** they will retreat and be
30:5 His anger lasts only a **m**.
Pro 6:15 In a **m** he will be crushed
7:12 One **m** she is out on the street,
12:19 but lies last only a **m**.
Isa 54:7 abandoned you for one brief **m**,
54:8 I hid my face from you for a **m**
66:8 Can a nation be born in a **m**?
66:9 "Do I bring a mother to the **m** of
Lam 3:49 without stopping for a **m**
Mat 8:13 And at that **m** the servant was
9:22 At that very **m** the woman
15:28 At that **m** her daughter was
17:18 At that **m** the boy was cured.
Mar 5:30 At that **m** Jesus felt power had
Luk 2:38 At that **m** she came up to Mary
Act 11:11 "At that **m** three men arrived at
12:7 At that **m** the chains fell from
19:40 At this **m** we run the risk of
22:13 At that **m** my sight came back
1Co 4:11 To this **m**, we are hungry,
Gal 2:5 did not give in to them for a **m**,
Jas 4:14 for a **m** and then disappears.
Rev 11:13 At that **m** a powerful
18:10 In one **m** judgment has come to
18:17 In one **m** all this wealth has
18:19 In one **m** it has been destroyed!'

mommy (1)

Isa 8:4 to say 'Daddy' or '**M**,' the wealth

money (180)

Gen 17:12 or bought with **m** from
17:13 or bought with your **m** is
17:23 and everyone bought with **m** —
17:27 or bought with **m** from
31:15 but he has used up the **m** that
42:25 He put each man's **m** back into
42:27 His **m** was right inside his
42:28 "My **m** has been put back!
42:35 each man found his bag of **m** in
42:35 their father saw the bags of **m**,
43:12 twice as much **m** with you.
43:12 You must return the **m** that was
43:15 the gifts, twice as much **m**,
43:18 because of the **m** that was put
43:21 man found all of his **m** inside.
43:22 We also brought more **m** to buy
43:22 We have no idea who put our **m**
43:23 I received your **m**."
44:1 Put each man's **m** in his sack.
44:2 brother's sack along with the **m**
44:8 We brought the **m** we found in
47:14 Joseph collected all the **m** that
47:15 When the **m** in Egypt and
47:15 We don't have any more **m**!"
47:16 "If you don't have any more **m**,
47:18 "you know that our **m** is gone,
Exo 21:11 paying any **m** for her freedom.
21:34 He must pay **m** to the animal's
21:35 divide the **m** between them.
22:17 he must pay an amount of **m**
22:25 "If you lend **m** to my people —
30:16 Take the **m** the Israelites give
Lev 5:18 from the flock or its value in **m**
6:6 no defects or its value in **m**.
25:37 any kind of interest on your **m**
27:2 you may give **m** instead of the
Num 3:49 So Moses took this ransom **m**
3:51 and his sons this ransom **m** as
22:7 taking **m** with them to pay for
Dtr 23:18 Never bring gifts or **m** earned
23:19 Israelite any interest on **m**,
27:25 "Whoever accepts **m** to kill an
Jdg 16:18 with the **m** in their hands.
1Sm 8:3 dishonest ways of making **m**.
2Ki 12:4 temple — the **m** each person is
12:4 all the **m** brought voluntarily
12:7 Don't take any more **m** from the
12:8 neither to receive **m** from
12:9 put the **m** that was brought
12:10 Whenever they saw a lot of **m**
12:10 count the **m** that was donated
12:11 Then they would give the **m**
12:13 with the **m** that was brought.
12:14 Instead, the **m** was given to the
12:15 who were entrusted with the **m**
12:16 The **m** from the guilt offerings
15:20 Menahem raised the **m** from all
22:4 Have him count the **m** that has
22:4 ⌊the **m**⌋ that the doorkeepers
22:6 Also, use ⌊the rest of⌋ the **m** to
22:7 for the **m** you give them."
22:9 "We have taken the **m** donated
2Ch 24:5 and collect **m** throughout Israel
24:10 They brought the **m** and
24:11 and they saw a lot of **m**,
24:11 so they collected a lot of **m**.
24:12 and Jehoiada would give the **m**
24:14 they brought the rest of the **m** to
34:9 gave him the **m** that had been
34:9 the **m** that the Levite
34:10 They gave the **m** to the
34:14 When they brought out the **m**
34:17 We took the **m** that was
Ezr 3:7 So they gave **m** to the
6:8 out of the king's own **m** from
7:17 You must use this **m** to buy
Neh 5:4 "We've had to borrow **m** to pay
5:10 and I are lending **m** and grain to
5:11 return the interest on the **m**,
12:44 and a tenth of the people's **m**.
Job 42:11 Each one gave him some **m**
Pro 2:4 for wisdom as if it were **m**
6:35 No amount of **m** will change
7:20 He took lots of **m** with him.
17:16 Why should a fool have **m** in
22:27 If you have no **m** to pay back a
27:26 and the **m** from the male goats
Ecc 5:10 Whoever loves **m** will never be
5:10 will never be satisfied with **m**.
7:12 us just as **m** protects us,
10:19 but **m** is the answer for
Isa 19:10 work for **m** will be distressed.
23:17 will go back to earning **m** as
43:24 any sugar cane with ⌊your⌋ **m**
52:3 be bought back, but without **m**.
55:1 Whoever has no **m** can come,
55:2 Why do you spend **m** on what
Jer 6:13 eager to make **m** dishonestly.
8:10 eager to make **m** dishonestly.
32:9 Hanamel and gave him the **m**.
32:25 told me to buy a field with **m**
32:44 They will buy fields for **m**,
Eze 18:8 He doesn't lend **m** for interest or
18:13 He lends **m** for interest and
Amo 2:6 of Israel sell the righteous for **m**
8:6 We can buy the poor with **m**
Mic 1:7 That **m** will again pay for
3:11 prophets tell the future for **m**.
6:10 wicked people who use their **m**
Zep 1:11 all who handle **m** will be killed.
Hag 1:6 You spend **m** as fast as you
Zec 8:10 Before that time there was no **m**
Mat 19:21 Give the **m** to the poor,
20:14 Take your **m** and go!
20:15 what I want with my own **m**?
25:14 and entrusted some **m** to them.
25:15 Each was given **m** based on
25:16 dollars invested the **m** at once
25:16 at once and doubled his **m**.
25:17 same and also doubled his **m**.
25:18 and hid his master's **m**.
25:25 in the ground. Here's your **m**!'
25:27 should have invested my **m**
25:27 my **m** back with interest.
26:9 and the **m** could have been
27:5 So he threw the **m** into the
27:6 priests took the **m** and said,

Mat 27:6 because it's blood **m**."
28:12 soldiers a large amount of **m**
28:15 The soldiers took the **m** and
Mar 5:26 and had spent all her **m**,
6:8 or **m** in their pockets.
10:21 Give the **m** to the poor,
12:41 he watched how ⌊much⌋ **m**
14:5 and the **m** could have been
14:11 and promised to give him **m**.
Luk 3:13 "Don't collect more **m** than you
3:14 to get **m** from anyone."
7:41 owed a moneylender some **m**.
9:3 food, **m**, or a change of clothes.
12:33 and give the **m** to the poor.
14:28 you have enough **m** to finish it.
15:30 spent your **m** on prostitutes,
16:14 The Pharisees, who love **m**,
18:22 Distribute the **m** to the poor,
19:13 'Invest this **m** until I come
19:15 servants to whom I gave **m**.
19:17 could be trusted with a little **m**.
19:23 Then why didn't you put my **m**
22:5 agreed to give him some **m**.
Jon 12:5 for a high price and the **m** given
Act 1:18 With the **m** he received from
2:45 and distributed the **m**
3:6 "I don't have any **m**,
4:34 or houses and brought the **m**
4:35 Then the **m** was distributed to
4:37 He sold it and turned the **m**
5:2 of the **m** ⌊they had pledged⌋
5:3 some of the **m** you received
5:4 as you pleased with the **m**.
8:18 So he offered Peter and John **m**
8:20 Peter told Simon, "May your **m**
16:16 She made a lot of **m** for her
16:19 hope of making **m** was gone,
22:28 "I paid a lot of **m** to become a
24:26 Paul would give him some **m**.
Rom 15:28 officially turned the **m** over
1Co 16:1 Now, concerning the **m** to be
16:2 set aside some of your **m**
16:2 Then **m** won't have to be
Php 4:15 to share your **m** with me.
1Th 2:5 flattery or schemes to make **m**.
1Ti 3:3 not be quarrelsome or love **m**.
3:8 use shameful ways to make **m**.
6:10 Certainly, the love of **m** is the
2Ti 3:2 will be selfish and love **m**.
Tit 1:7 use shameful ways to make **m**.
1:11 shameful way they make **m**.
Heb 13:5 Don't love **m**. Be happy with
Jas 4:13 business, and make **m**."

moneybag (2)

Jon 12:6 He was in charge of the **m** and
13:29 Judas had the **m**. So some

moneychangers (1)

Jon 2:14 He also found **m** sitting there.

moneychangers' (3)

Mat 21:12 He overturned the **m** tables and
Mar 11:15 He overturned the **m** tables and
Jon 2:15 He dumped the **m** coins and

moneylender (2)

Exo 22:25 you — never act like a **m**.
Luk 7:41 men owed a **m** some money.

monitors (1)

Lev 11:30 geckos, **m**, lizards, skinks,

monkeys (2)

1Ki 10:22 gold, silver, ivory, apes, and **m**.
2Ch 9:21 gold, silver, ivory, apes, and **m**.

monopoly (1)

Job 15:8 and receive a **m** on wisdom?

monster (5)

Job 7:12 "Am I the sea or a sea **m** that
26:12 he killed Rahab ⌊the sea **m**⌋.
Isa 27:1 He will kill that **m** which lives
Jer 51:34 He has swallowed us like a **m**.
Eze 29:3 You are like a **m** crocodile

monsters (1)

Psa 74:13 heads of sea **m** in the water.

month (209)

Gen 7:11 day of the second **m**
8:4 day of the seventh **m**,
8:5 decreasing until the tenth **m**.
8:5 On the first day of the tenth **m**,
8:13 By the first day of the first **m** of
8:14 day of the second **m**
29:14 stayed with him for a whole **m**.
Exo 12:2 "This **m** will be the very first
12:2 month will be the very first **m**
12:3 On the tenth ⌊day⌋ of this **m**
12:6 the fourteenth ⌊day⌋ of this **m**."
12:18 day of the first **m** until
13:4 Today, in the **m** of Abib,
13:5 this ceremony in this **m**.
16:1 of the second **m** after they had
23:15 appointed time in the **m** of Abib,
34:18 appointed time in the **m** of Abib,
34:18 because in that **m** you came
40:2 day of the first **m** of the year.
40:17 up on the first day of the first **m**
Lev 16:29 **m** both native Israelites
23:5 fourteenth day of the first **m**,
23:6 fifteenth day of this same **m** is
23:24 first day of the seventh **m** hold
23:27 the tenth day of this seventh **m**
23:32 of the ninth day of the **m**.
23:34 day of this seventh **m** is
23:39 fifteenth day of the seventh **m**,
23:41 this festival in the seventh **m**.
25:9 the tenth day of the seventh **m**,
27:6 For a boy from one **m** to five
Num 1:1 the first day of the second **m**
1:18 the first day of the second **m**.
3:15 who is at least one **m** old."
3:22 at least one **m** old was 7,500.
3:28 at least one **m** old was 8,600.
3:34 at least one **m** old was 6,200.
3:39 who was at least one **m** old,
3:40 who is at least one **m** old,
3:43 at least one **m** old was 22,273.
9:1 In the first **m** of the second year
9:3 day of this **m** at dusk.
9:5 day of the first **m** at dusk while
9:11 day of the second **m** at dusk.
9:22 Whether it was two days, a **m**,
10:10 and on the first day of the **m**,
10:11 twentieth day of the second **m**
11:20 but for a whole **m**, until it
11:21 them meat to eat for a whole **m**!'
18:16 When they are one **m** old,
20:1 In the first **m** the whole
26:62 at least one **m** old was 23,000.
28:11 "On the first of every **m** bring
28:14 offering for every **m** of the year.
28:16 fourteenth day of the first **m** is
28:17 The fifteenth of this same **m** is
29:1 the seventh **m** you must have
29:7 the seventh **m** you must have
29:12 the seventh **m** you must have
33:3 the fifteenth day of the first **m**,
33:38 on the first day of the fifth **m**
Dtr 1:3 the first day of the eleventh **m**
16:1 Passover in the **m** of Abib.
16:1 In the **m** of Abib the LORD your
21:13 her father and mother for one **m**
33:14 the best produce of each **m**,
Jos 4:19 On the tenth day of the first **m**,
5:10 of the fourteenth day of the **m**.
1Sm 11:1 About a **m** later Nahash the
20:27 But on the second day of the **m**,
20:34 that second day of the **m**.
1Ki 4:7 food for one **m** every year.
4:27 food for one **m** every year
5:14 10,000 men to Lebanon for a **m**.
5:14 They would spend one **m** in
6:1 He began building in the **m** of
6:1 the month of Ziv (the second **m**)
6:37 In the **m** of Ziv of the fourth
6:38 In the **m** of Bul (the eighth
6:38 the month of Bul (the eighth **m**)
8:2 Booths⌋ in the **m** of Ethanim,
1Ki 8:2 of Ethanim, the seventh **m**.
12:32 fifteenth day of the eighth **m**,
12:33 fifteenth day of the eighth **m**,
2Ki 15:13 ruled for an entire **m** in Samaria
25:1 On the tenth day of the tenth **m**
25:3 the ninth day of the fourth **m**,
25:8 the seventh day of the fifth **m**
25:25 In the seventh **m** Ishmael (son
25:27 day of the twelfth **m**
1Ch 12:15 In the first **m** of the year,
27:1 each year they came for a **m** at
27:2 the one during the first **m**.
27:3 army's officers for the first **m**.
27:4 of the unit during the second **m**.
27:5 during the third **m** was Benaiah,
27:7 fourth unit during the fourth **m**,
27:8 the fifth unit during the fifth **m**.
27:9 sixth unit during the sixth **m**.
27:10 unit during the seventh **m**.
27:11 eighth unit during the eighth **m**.
27:12 ninth unit during the ninth **m**.
27:13 tenth unit during the tenth **m**.
27:14 unit during the eleventh **m**.
27:15 During the twelfth **m**,
2Ch 3:2 second day in the second **m**
5:3 ⌊of Booths⌋ in the seventh **m**.
7:10 day of the seventh **m**,
15:10 In the third **m** of the fifteenth
29:3 In the first **m** of his first year as
29:17 on the first day of the first **m**.
29:17 the sixteenth day of the first **m**.
30:2 the Passover in the second **m**.
30:13 Bread in the second **m**.
30:15 fourteenth day of the second **m**.
31:7 In the third **m** they started piling
31:7 in the seventh **m** they finished.
35:1 the fourteenth day of the first **m**
Ezr 3:1 When the seventh **m** came,
3:6 the first day of the seventh **m**,
3:8 This happened in the second **m**
6:15 on the third day of the **m**
6:19 the fourteenth day of the first **m**
7:8 In that same year in the fifth **m**,
7:9 on the first day of the first **m**,
7:9 on the first day of the fifth **m**,
8:31 on the twelfth day of the first **m**
10:9 twentieth day of the ninth **m**,
10:16 on the first day of the tenth **m**
10:17 By the first day of the first **m**,
Neh 1:1 During the **m** of Chislev,
2:1 In the **m** of Nisan, after some
6:15 twenty-fifth day of the **m** of Elul.
7:73 When the seventh **m** came,
8:1 ⌊When the seventh **m** came,⌋
8:2 the first day of the seventh **m**.
8:14 a festival in the seventh **m**.
9:1 the twenty-fourth day of this **m**,
Est 2:16 royal palace in the **m** of Tebeth,
2:16 month of Tebeth, the tenth **m**,
3:7 for every day of every **m**,
3:7 Nisan, the first **m**, until Adar,
3:7 until Adar, the twelfth **m**.
3:12 the thirteenth day of the first **m**
3:13 thirteenth day of the twelfth **m**,
3:13 twelfth month, the **m** of Adar.
8:9 day of Sivan, the third **m**,
8:12 day of Adar, the twelfth **m**.
9:1 day of Adar, the twelfth **m**,
9:15 on the fourteenth day of the **m**
9:17 thirteenth day of the **m** of Adar.
9:19 the fourteenth day of the **m**
9:21 and fifteenth days of the **m**
9:22 In that **m** their grief turned to joy
Isa 47:13 foretell the future **m** by month,
47:13 foretell the future month by **m**,
66:23 From one **m** to the next and
Jer 1:3 in the fifth **m** of the year.
28:1 in the fifth **m** of his fourth year
28:17 in the seventh **m** of that year.
36:9 In the ninth **m** of the fifth year of
36:22 It was the ninth **m**,
39:1 In the tenth **m** of Zedekiah's
39:2 On the ninth day of the fourth **m**
41:1 In the seventh **m** Ishmael (son
52:4 On the tenth day of the tenth **m**
52:6 the ninth day of the fourth **m**,

Jer 52:12 On the tenth day of the fifth **m**
52:31 twenty-fifth day of the twelfth **m**
Eze 1:1 On the fifth day of the fourth **m**
1:2 On the fifth day of the **m**,
8:1 On the fifth day of the sixth **m**
20:1 On the tenth day of the fifth **m**
24:1 On the tenth day of the tenth **m**
26:1 On the first day of the **m** in the
29:1 the twelfth day of the tenth **m**
29:17 On the first day of the first **m** in
30:20 the seventh day of the first **m**
31:1 On the first day of the third **m** in
32:1 On the first day of the twelfth **m**
32:17 On the fifteenth day of the **m** in
33:21 On the fifth day of the tenth **m**
40:1 It was the tenth day of the **m** in
45:18 On the first day of the first **m**,
45:20 on the seventh day of the **m**
45:21 the fourteenth day of the first **m**
45:25 fifteenth day of the seventh **m**,
46:6 On the first day of the **m**,
47:12 Each **m** they will produce fresh
Dan 10:4 twenty-fourth day of the first **m**,
Hag 1:1 On the first day of the sixth **m**
1:15 twenty-fourth day of the sixth **m**
2:1 day of the seventh **m**,
2:10 twenty-fourth day of the ninth **m**
2:18 day of the ninth **m**,
2:20 the twenty-fourth day of the **m**.
Zec 1:1 In the eighth **m** of Darius'
1:7 of the eleventh **m** (the month
1:7 of the eleventh month (the **m**
7:1 On the fourth day of the ninth **m**
7:1 day of the ninth month (the **m**
7:3 fast in the fifth **m** as we have
8:19 The fast in the fourth **m**,
8:19 the fast in the fifth **m**,
8:19 the fast in the seventh **m**,
8:19 and the fast in the tenth **m** will
11:8 rid of three shepherds in one **m**.
Rev 9:15 ready for that hour, day, **m**,
22:2 Each **m** had its own fruit.

monthly (10)

Lev 12:2 she is unclean for her **m** period.
12:5 be unclean as in her **m** period.
15:19 a woman has her **m** period,
15:25 days other than her **m** period,
18:19 is unclean during her **m** period.
20:18 while she has her **m** period,
Num 28:14 This will be the **m** burnt
29:6 Offer these in addition to the **m**
2Sm 11:4 herself after her **m** period.)
Jer 2:24 find you during your **m** period.

months (52)

Gen 38:24 About three **m** later Judah was
Exo 2:2 he was and hid him for three **m**.
19:1 Two **m** after the Israelites left
Jdg 11:37 Give me two **m** for my friends
11:38 and he sent her off for two **m**.
11:39 At the end of those two **m** she
19:2 she had been there four **m**,
20:47 at Rimmon Rock for four **m**.
1Sm 6:1 in Philistine territory seven **m**
27:7 territory for one year and four **m**
2Sm 2:11 for seven years and six **m**.
5:5 for seven years and six **m**.
6:11 Edom from Gath for three **m**,
24:8 after 9 **m** and 20 days.
24:13 or three **m** during which you
1Ki 5:14 in Lebanon and two **m** at home.
11:16 there six **m** until they had
2Ki 15:8 of Israel in Samaria for six **m**.
23:31 was king for 3 **m** in Jerusalem.
24:8 king for three **m** in Jerusalem.
1Ch 3:4 for seven years and six **m**.
13:14 with his family for three **m**,
21:12 or three **m** during which your
2Ch 36:2 was king in Jerusalem for 3 **m**.
36:9 He was king for three **m** and
Est 2:12 six **m** using oil of myrrh and
2:12 and six **m** using perfumes
Job 3:6 or be numbered among the **m**.
7:3 Likewise, I have been given **m**
14:5 of his **m** are determined by
Job 21:21 number of his **m** is cut short?
39:2 Can you count the **m** they are
Eze 39:12 burying them there for seven **m**
39:14 At the end of seven **m** they will
Dan 4:29 Twelve **m** later, he was
Amo 4:7 rain from falling three **m** before
Zec 7:5 and seventh **m** these past 70
Luk 1:24 didn't go out in public for five **m**.
1:26 Six **m** after Elizabeth had
1:36 is six **m** pregnant with a son in
1:56 with Elizabeth about three **m**
Jon 4:35 "Don't you say, 'In four more **m**
Act 7:20 took care of him for three **m**.
19:8 For three **m** Paul would go into
20:3 and stayed there for three **m**.
28:11 After three **m** we sailed on an
Gal 4:10 days, **m**, seasons, and years!
Heb 11:23 to hide him for three **m** after
Rev 9:5 to torture them for five **m**.
9:10 with their tails for five **m**.
11:2 trample the holy city for 42 **m**.
13:5 given authority to act for 42 **m**.

monument (4)

1Sm 15:12 went to Carmel to set up a **m**
2Sm 18:18 still called Absalom's **M** today.)
2Ki 23:17 "What is this **m** that I see?"
Isa 56:5 I will give them a **m** and a

monuments (5)

Jer 43:13 Shemesh he will break the **m**
Mic 5:13 your idols and your sacred **m**.
Mat 23:29 prophets and decorate the **m**
Luk 11:47 You build the **m** for the
11:48 prophets for whom you build **m**.

mood (1)

1Sm 25:36 He was in a good **m** and very

mooing (1)

1Sm 6:12 Continually **m**, they stayed on

moon (64)

Gen 37:9 dream: I saw the sun, the **m**,
Dtr 4:19 sky — the sun, the **m**, the stars,
17:3 to other gods, the sun, the **m**,
Jos 10:12 stand still over Gibeon, and **m**,
10:13 The sun stood still, and the **m**
1Sm 20:5 is the New **M** Festival,
20:18 is the New **M** Festival,"
20:24 the New **M** Festival came,
2Ki 4:23 It isn't a New **M** Festival or a
23:5 sun god, the **m** god, the zodiac,
1Ch 23:31 at New **M** Festivals,
2Ch 2:4 days, New **M** Festivals,
8:13 on the New **M** Festivals,
31:3 the New **M** Festivals,
Ezr 3:5 the offerings for the New **M**
Neh 10:33 and on the New **M** Festivals,
Job 25:5 Even the **m** isn't bright,
31:26 If I saw the light shine or the **m**
Psa 8:3 the **m** and the stars that you
72:5 and **m** ⌊shine⌋ — throughout
72:7 until the **m** no longer ⌊shines⌋.
74:16 You set the **m** and the sun in
81:3 horn on the day of the new **m**,
81:3 on the day of the full **m**,
89:37 Like the **m** his throne will stand
104:19 He created the **m**, which marks
121:6 nor will the **m** at night.
136:9 the **m** and stars to rule the night
148:3 Praise him, sun and **m**.
Ecc 12:2 the **m**, and the stars turn dark,
Sos 6:10 She is beautiful like the **m**,
Isa 1:13 so are your New **M** Festivals,
1:14 I hate your New **M** Festivals
13:10 The **m** won't shine.
24:23 The **m** will be embarrassed.
30:26 Then the light of the **m** will be
60:19 nor will the brightness of the **m**
60:20 nor will your **m** disappear.
Jer 8:2 and exposed to the sun, the **m**,
31:35 He orders the **m** and stars to be
Eze 32:7 and the **m** won't shine anymore.
45:17 the New **M** Festivals,
46:1 opened on the New **M** Festival.
Eze 46:3 and on New **M** Festivals.
Hos 2:11 her New **M** Festivals,
5:7 Now their New **M** ⌊Festivals⌋
Joe 2:10 The sun and the **m** turn dark,
2:31 and the **m** will become as red
3:15 The sun and the **m** will turn
Amo 8:5 "When will the New **M** Festival
Hab 3:11 The sun and the **m** stand still.
Mat 24:29 the **m** will not give light,
Mar 13:24 the **m** will not give light,
Luk 21:25 occur in the sun, **m**, and stars.
Act 2:20 and the **m** will become as red
7:42 worship the sun, **m**, and stars.
1Co 15:41 the **m** has another kind of
Col 2:16 holy days, New **M** Festivals,
Jas 1:17 made the sun, **m**, and stars.
1:17 produced by the sun and the **m**.
Rev 6:12 The full **m** turned as red as
8:12 of the sun, one-third of the **m**,
12:1 who had the **m** under her feet
21:23 city doesn't need any sun or **m**

moral (5)

Job 8:6 if you are **m** and ethical,
Pro 21:8 of those who are pure is **m**.
Tit 1:8 good judgment, be fair and **m**,
2:7 of **m** purity and dignity.
2:12 we can live self-controlled, **m**,

morale (1)

Dtr 20:8 Then you won't ruin the **m** of

morally (4)

Job 11:4 'My teaching is **m** correct,'
1Ti 5:2 while keeping yourself **m** pure.
5:22 Keep yourself **m** pure.
Tit 2:5 judgment, and to be **m** pure.

Mordecai (62)

Ezr 2:2 **M**, Bilshan, Mispar, Bigvai,
Neh 7:7 **M**, Bilshan, Mispereth, Bigvai,
Est 2:5 the tribe of Benjamin named **M**.
2:7 **M** had raised Hadassah,
2:7 **M** adopted her as his own
2:10 because **M** had ordered her not
2:11 Every day **M** would walk back
2:15 **M** had adopted her as his own
2:19 **M** was sitting at the king's gate.
2:20 as **M** had ordered her.
2:20 did whatever **M** told her,
2:21 In those days, while **M** was
2:22 But **M** found out about it and
2:22 told the king, on behalf of **M**.
3:2 But **M** would not kneel and
3:3 at the king's gate asked **M**,
3:4 since **M** had told them that he
3:5 When Haman saw that **M** did
3:6 beneath himself to kill only **M**.
4:1 When **M** found out about
4:4 and informed her ⌊about **M**⌋.
4:4 She sent clothing for **M** to put
4:5 She commanded him to go to **M**
4:6 So Hathach went out to **M** in
4:7 **M** informed him about
4:9 told Esther what **M** had said.
4:10 commanded him to say to **M**,
4:12 told **M** what Esther said.
4:13 **M** sent this answer back to
4:15 sent this reply back to **M**,
4:17 **M** did just as Esther had
5:9 But when Haman saw **M** at the
5:9 Haman was furious with **M**.
5:13 to me every time I see **M**
6:2 The records showed how **M**
6:3 reward and promote **M** for this?
6:4 ask the king about hanging **M**
6:10 Do this for **M** the Jew who sits
6:11 He put the robe on **M** and had
6:12 **M** returned to the king's gate,
6:13 are starting to lose power to **M**.
6:13 If **M** is of Jewish descent,
7:9 75-foot pole Haman made for **M**,
7:10 pole he had prepared for **M**.
8:1 Also, **M** came to the king
8:1 told him how **M** was related
8:2 from Haman, and gave it to **M**.

Est 8:2 And Esther put **M** in charge of
8:7 Queen Esther and **M** the Jew,
8:9 What **M** had ordered was
8:10 **M** wrote in King Xerxes' name
8:15 **M** went out from the presence
9:3 they were terrified of **M**.
9:4 **M** was an important man in the
9:4 since **M** was becoming more
9:20 Now, **M** wrote these things
9:23 as **M** had written to them.
9:29 daughter Queen Esther and **M**
9:30 **M** sent official documents
9:31 **M** the Jew and Queen Esther
10:2 account of the greatness of **M**,
10:3 **M** the Jew was ranked second

Mordecai's (5)

Est 2:15 daughter of Abihail, **M** uncle.
3:4 to see if **M** actions would
3:6 him about **M** nationality,
3:6 to wipe out **M** people — all
5:14 to have **M** ⌊dead body⌋ hung

Moreh (3)

Gen 12:6 belonging to **M** at Shechem.
Dtr 11:30 next to the oak trees of **M**.)
Jdg 7:1 at the hill of **M** in the valley.

Moresheth (2)

Jer 26:18 "Micah from **M** prophesied at
Mic 1:1 to Micah, who was from **M**,

Moresheth Gath (1)

Mic 1:14 give farewell gifts to **M** Gath.

Moriah (2)

Gen 22:2 whom you love, and go to **M**.
2Ch 3:1 in Jerusalem on Mount **M**,

morning (229)

Gen 1:5 then **m** — the first day.
1:8 then **m** — a second day.
1:13 then **m** — a third day.
1:19 then **m** — a fourth day.
1:23 then **m** — a fifth day.
1:31 then **m** — the sixth day.
19:2 Then early tomorrow **m** you
19:27 Early the next **m** Abraham
20:8 Early in the **m** Abimelech
21:14 Early the next **m** Abraham took
22:3 Early the next **m** Abraham
24:54 When they got up in the **m**,
26:31 Early the next **m** they
28:18 Early the next **m** Jacob took
29:23 When **m** came, he realized it
31:55 Early the next **m** Laban kissed
40:6 Joseph came to them in the **m**,
41:8 In the **m** he was so upset that
49:27 In the **m** he devours his prey.
Exo 7:15 In the **m** meet Pharaoh when
8:20 said to Moses, "Early in the **m**,
9:13 said to Moses, "Early in the **m**,
10:13 By **m** the east wind had
12:10 Don't leave any of it until **m**.
12:10 Anything left over in the **m**
12:22 may leave the house until **m**.
16:7 In the **m** you will see the glory
16:8 all the food you want in the **m**.
16:12 and in the **m** you will eat all the
16:13 and in the **m** there was a layer
16:19 one may keep any of it until **m**."
16:20 They kept part of it until **m**,
16:21 Each **m** they gathered as much
16:23 and keep it until tomorrow **m**."
16:24 until the next **m** as Moses had
18:13 Moses from **m** until evening.
18:14 you from **m** until evening?"
19:16 On the **m** of the second day,
23:18 never be left over in the **m**.
24:4 Early the next **m** he built an
27:21 presence from evening until **m**.
29:34 ordination is left over until **m**,
29:39 Offer one in the **m** and the other
29:41 and wine offering as in the **m**.
30:7 on this altar every **m** when
34:2 Be ready in the **m**.
Exo 34:4 Early the next **m** he went up on
34:25 should be left over in the **m**.
36:3 him freewill offerings every **m**.
Lev 6:12 will burn wood on it every **m**.
6:20 He must offer half of it in the **m**
7:15 Never leave any of it until **m**.
9:17 addition to the **m** burnt offering
22:30 Never leave any of it until **m**.
24:3 presence from evening until **m**.
Num 9:12 leave any of the meat until **m**
9:15 From evening until **m**,
9:21 only from evening until **m**.
9:21 the smoke moved in the **m**,
14:40 Early the next **m** they headed
16:5 "In the **m** the LORD will show
22:13 When Balaam got up in the **m**,
22:21 When Balaam got up in the **m**,
22:41 The next **m** Balak took Balaam
28:4 Offer one in the **m** and the other
28:8 as you brought in the **m**.
28:23 addition to the **m** burnt offering
Dtr 16:4 Never leave until **m** any of the
16:7 In the **m** you may go back to
28:67 In the **m** you'll say,
28:67 "If only it were **m**!"
Jos 3:1 Joshua got up early the next **m**.
6:12 Joshua got up early in the **m**.
7:14 In the **m** come forward by tribes
7:16 Joshua got up early in the **m**.
8:10 Joshua got up early in the **m**
8:14 his troops got up early in the **m**.
Jdg 6:28 of the city got up early in the **m**,
6:31 will be put to death in the **m**.
6:38 The next **m** Gideon got up
9:33 In the **m**, when the sun rises,
19:5 got up early in the **m** to leave,
19:8 On the **m** of the fifth day,
19:25 abused her all night until **m**.
19:27 Her husband got up in the **m**,
20:19 Israelites got up early in the **m**
Rut 3:13 In the **m** if he will agree to take
3:13 Lie down until **m**."
3:14 So Ruth lay at his feet until **m**.
1Sm 1:19 Early in the **m** Elkanah and his
3:15 remained in bed until **m**.
5:4 But the next **m** they saw that
9:19 In the **m** I'll let you go after I tell
11:11 camp during the **m** hours
15:12 Early in the **m** he got up to
17:16 Each **m** and evening for 40
17:20 David got up early in the **m** and
19:2 Please be careful tomorrow **m**.
19:11 house and kill him in the **m**.
20:35 In the **m** Jonathan went out to
25:22 one of his men alive in the **m**."
25:37 But in the **m**, when the effects
29:10 Get up early in the **m** with
29:10 Get up in the **m**, and leave
29:11 Early the next **m** David and his
2Sm 2:27 chasing their relatives until **m**."
11:14 In the **m** David wrote a letter to
13:4 so worn out **m** after morning?
13:4 so worn out morning after **m**?
23:4 He is like the **m** light as the
23:4 like a **m** without clouds,
24:11 When David got up in the **m**,
24:15 the Israelites from that **m** until
1Ki 3:21 When I got up in the **m** to nurse
17:6 him bread and meat in the **m**
18:26 name of Baal from **m** until noon.
2Ki 3:20 is what happened in the **m**.
3:22 got up early in the **m** as
6:15 the man of God got up in the **m**
7:9 If we wait until **m** when it's
10:8 to the gateway until **m**."
10:9 In the **m** he stood there.
16:15 must burn the **m** burnt offerings
19:35 Judeans got up early in the **m**,
1Ch 9:27 to guard it and open it every **m**.
16:40 continually, **m** and evening,
23:30 praise to the LORD every **m**.
2Ch 2:4 offerings every **m** and evening,
13:11 offerings to the LORD every **m**
20:20 They got up early in the **m** and
29:20 Early in the **m** Hezekiah
31:3 the **m** and evening offerings,
Ezr 3:3 LORD every **m** and evening.
Est 2:14 and come back in the **m**
5:14 and in the **m** ask the king to
Job 1:5 He would get up early in the **m**
4:20 From **m** to evening,
7:18 should inspect him every **m**
11:17 in your life will become like **m**.
24:17 because **m** and deep darkness
38:7 when the **m** stars sang together
38:12 you ever given orders to the **m**
Psa 5:3 In the **m**, O LORD, hear my
5:3 In the **m** I lay my needs in front
30:5 there is a song of joy in the **m**.
49:14 people will rule them in the **m**.)
55:17 **M**, noon, and night I complain
59:16 In the **m** I will joyfully sing
65:8 The lands of the **m** sunrise and
73:14 and every **m** my punishment
88:13 and in the **m** my prayer will
90:5 again in the **m** like cut grass.
90:6 In the **m** they blossom and
90:14 Satisfy us every **m** with your
92:2 announce your mercy in the **m**
101:8 Every **m** I will destroy all the
110:3 like dew in the early **m**.
130:6 those who watch for the **m**,
130:6 those who watch for the **m**.
139:9 the rays of the **m** sun ⌊or⌋ land
143:8 hear about your mercy in the **m**,
Pro 7:18 let's drink our fill of love until **m**.
27:14 his friend early in the **m**
Ecc 10:16 officials throw parties in the **m**.
11:6 Plant your seed in the **m**,
Isa 14:12 you **m** star, son of the dawn!
17:11 On the **m** you set out the
17:14 Before **m** they will be gone.
21:12 answers, "**M** is coming,
28:19 It will pass by **m** after morning,
28:19 It will pass by morning after **m**,
33:2 Be our strength in the **m**.
37:36 Judeans got up early in the **m**,
38:13 I cried out until **m** as if a lion
44:22 and your sins like the **m** mist.
50:4 **M** after morning he will wake
50:4 Morning after **m** he will wake
Jer 20:16 he hear a cry of alarm in the **m**
21:12 Judge fairly every **m**.
Lam 3:23 It is new every **m**. His
Eze 12:8 The next **m** the LORD spoke
24:18 I spoke to the people in the **m**,
24:18 The next **m** I did as I was
33:22 On the **m** the refugee arrived,
46:13 to the LORD. Do this every **m**.
46:14 a grain offering with it every **m**:
46:15 and the olive oil every **m** as a
Hos 6:3 to us as sure as the **m** comes.
6:4 Your love is like fog in the **m**.
6:4 as quickly as the **m** dew.
7:6 but in the **m** it burns like a
13:3 they will be like fog in the **m**
13:3 and like **m** dew that disappears
Amo 4:4 Bring your sacrifices every **m**.
Mic 2:1 When the **m** dawns,
Zep 3:3 nothing to gnaw on for the **m**.
3:5 his judgment to light every **m**.
Mat 14:25 three and six o'clock in the **m**,
16:3 And in the **m** you say that there
21:18 In the **m**, as Jesus returned to
27:1 Early in the **m** all the chief
28:1 as the sun rose Sunday **m**,
Mar 1:35 In the **m**, long before sunrise,
6:48 three and six o'clock in the **m**,
11:20 were walking early in the **m**,
13:35 midnight or at dawn or in the **m**.
15:1 Early in the **m** the chief priests
15:25 It was nine in the **m** when they
Luk 4:42 In the **m** he went to a place
12:38 middle of the night or toward **m**
22:66 In the **m** the council of the
24:1 Very early on Sunday **m** the
24:22 went to the tomb early this **m**
Jon 1:39 was about ten o'clock in the **m**.
8:2 Early the next **m** he returned to
18:28 Early in the **m**, Jesus was
19:14 was about six o'clock in the **m**
20:1 Early on Sunday **m**,

Act 2:15 It's only nine in the **m**.
5:21 Early in the **m**, after they had
12:18 In the **m** the soldiers were in an
16:35 In the **m** the Roman officials
23:12 In the **m** the Jews formed a
27:29 ship and prayed for **m** to come.
27:39 In the **m** they couldn't
28:23 From **m** until evening,
2Pe 1:19 for day to come and the **m** star
Rev 2:28 I will also give them the **m** star.
22:16 I am the bright **m** star."

mornings (2)

Dan 8:14 "For 2,300 evenings and **m**.
8:26 and **m** that was explained

mortal (25)

1Sm 15:29 because he is not a **m** who
Job 4:17 'Can ⌊any⌋ **m** be righteous to
7:17 "What is a **m** that you should
9:2 But how can a **m** be declared
10:4 Do you see as a **m** sees?
13:9 him as one **m** tricks another?
15:14 Why should a **m** be considered
25:6 How much less pure is a **m** —
28:13 No **m** knows where it is.
33:12 God is greater than any **m**.
Psa 8:4 what is a **m** that you remember
9:20 know that they are ⌊only⌋ **m**.
10:18 that no mere **m** will terrify them
38:19 My **m** enemies are growing
89:48 Can a **m** go on living and never
Lam 3:39 "Why should any living **m** (any
Eze 34:31 You are **m**, and I am your God,
Act 26:14 It's hard for ⌊a **m** like⌋ you to
Rom 1:23 that looked like **m** humans,
8:11 make your **m** bodies alive by
1Co 15:53 This **m** body must be changed
15:54 and this **m** body is changed
2Co 4:11 is also shown in our **m** nature.
5:4 put an end to our **m** existence.
Heb 2:6 "What is a **m** that you should

mortal's (3)

Job 7:1 "Isn't a **m** stay on earth difficult
10:5 Are your days like a **m** days?
14:19 and you destroy a **m** hope

mortals (35)

1Sm 26:19 But if mere **m** ⌊have turned you
Job 36:25 **M** have looked at it from a
Psa 9:19 Do not let **m** gain any power.
17:14 your power rescue me from **m**,
17:14 from **m** who enjoy their
49:12 But **m** will not continue here
49:20 **M**, with what they treasure,
56:11 What can **m** do to me?
76:10 Even angry **m** will praise you.
90:3 You turn **m** back into dust and
90:5 You sweep **m** away.
118:6 What can **m** do to me?
118:8 on the LORD than to trust **m**.
144:3 What are mere **m** that you
146:3 **m** who cannot help you.
Ecc 1:13 **M** are weighed down with a
2:3 whether this was good for **m**
3:10 I have seen **m** weighed down
3:11 Yet, **m** still can't grasp what
6:1 It is a terrible one for **m**.
6:10 **M** are already known for what
6:10 **M** cannot argue with the one
6:11 advantage do **m** gain from this?
6:12 be good for **m** while they are
6:12 **M** pass by like a shadow.
7:14 so that **m** cannot predict their
9:3 the hearts of **m** are full of evil.
12:5 **M** go to their eternal rest,
12:7 Then the dust ⌊of **m**⌋ goes
Isa 7:13 that you try the patience of **m**?
51:12 Why, then, are you afraid of **m**,
Mic 5:7 hope in humans or wait for **m**.
6:8 You **m**, the LORD has told you
Heb 7:28 designated **m** as chief priests
13:6 What can **m** do to me?"

mortar (5)

Gen 11:3 bricks as stones and tar as **m**.
Exo 1:14 with back-breaking work in **m**
Num 11:8 in a handmill or crush it in a **m**.
Pro 27:22 crush a stubborn fool in a **m**
Zep 1:11 "Howl, inhabitants of the **M**,

mortgage (1)

Neh 5:3 "We've had to **m** our fields,

mortician (1)

Amo 6:10 If a relative or a **m** comes to

mosaic (1)

Est 1:6 were on a **m** pavement

Moserah (1)

Dtr 10:6 wells of the Jaakanites to **M**.

Moseroth (2)

Num 33:30 and set up camp at **M**.
33:31 They moved from **M** and set up

Moses (847)

Exo 2:10 named him **M** [Pulled Out]
2:11 the course of time **M** grew up.
2:13 When **M** went there the next
2:14 Then **M** was afraid and thought
2:15 heard what **M** had done,
2:15 But **M** fled from Pharaoh and
2:15 while **M** was sitting by a well,
2:17 So **M** got up, came to their
2:21 **M** decided to stay with the
2:21 Zipporah to **M** as his wife.
2:22 **M** named him Gershom
3:1 **M** was taking care of the sheep
3:2 **M** looked, and although the
3:4 When the LORD saw that **M**
3:4 "**M**, Moses!" Moses answered,
3:4 him from the bush, "Moses, **M**!"
3:4 **M** answered, "Here I am!"
3:6 **M** hid his face because he was
3:11 But **M** said to God,
3:13 Then **M** replied to God,
3:14 God answered **M**, "I Am Who I
3:15 Again God said to **M**,
4:1 **M** protested. "They will say,
4:3 When **M** threw it on the ground,
4:4 Then the LORD said to **M**,
4:6 So **M** did this, and when he
4:7 **M** put it back, and when he
4:10 **M** said to the LORD,
4:13 But **M** said, "Please, Lord,
4:14 angry with **M** and asked,
4:18 Then **M** went back to his
4:18 **M** said to him, "Please let me
4:18 Jethro said to **M**, "You may go."
4:19 LORD had said to **M** in Midian,
4:20 So **M** took his wife and sons,
4:21 The LORD said to **M**,
4:24 The LORD met **M** and tried to
4:27 LORD had told Aaron to meet **M**
4:27 When Aaron met **M** at the
4:28 **M** told Aaron everything the
4:29 Then **M** and Aaron went ⌊to
4:30 the LORD had said to **M**.
5:1 Later **M** and Aaron went to
5:4 said to them, "**M** and Aaron,
5:20 they found **M** and Aaron
5:22 **M** went back to the LORD and
6:1 Then the LORD said to **M**,
6:2 God spoke to **M**, "I am the
6:9 **M** reported this to the Israelites
6:10 Then the LORD spoke to **M**,
6:12 But **M** protested to the LORD,
6:13 The LORD spoke to **M** and
6:20 She gave birth to Aaron and **M**.
6:26 was the same Aaron and **M**
6:27 They — this same **M** and Aaron
6:28 the LORD spoke to **M** in Egypt.
6:29 He said to **M**, "I am the LORD.
6:30 But **M** said to the LORD,
7:1 The LORD answered **M**,
7:6 **M** and Aaron did as the LORD
7:7 **M** was 80 years old and Aaron
Exo 7:8 LORD said to **M** and Aaron,
7:10 **M** and Aaron went to Pharaoh
7:14 Then the LORD said to **M**,
7:19 The LORD said to **M**,
7:20 **M** and Aaron did as the LORD
7:22 not listen to **M** and Aaron,
8:1 Then the LORD said to **M**,
8:5 Then the LORD said to **M**,
8:8 Pharaoh sent for **M** and Aaron
8:9 **M** answered Pharaoh,
8:10 **M** replied, "It will be as you
8:12 After **M** and Aaron left Pharaoh,
8:12 **M** prayed to the LORD about
8:13 The LORD did what **M** asked.
8:15 not listen to **M** and Aaron,
8:16 Then the LORD said to **M**,
8:17 When **M** told him, Aaron held
8:19 not listen to **M** and Aaron,
8:20 Then the LORD said to **M**,
8:25 Pharaoh called for **M** and Aaron
8:26 **M** replied, "It wouldn't be right
8:29 **M** answered, "As soon as I
8:30 **M** left Pharaoh and prayed to
8:31 The LORD did what **M** asked.
9:1 Then the LORD said to **M**,
9:8 the LORD said to **M** and Aaron,
9:8 and have **M** throw them up in
9:10 **M** threw the ashes up in the air,
9:11 couldn't compete with **M**
9:12 wouldn't listen to **M** and Aaron,
9:12 the LORD had predicted to **M**.
9:13 Then the LORD said to **M**,
9:22 Then the LORD said to **M**,
9:23 When **M** lifted his staff toward
9:27 Pharaoh sent for **M** and Aaron.
9:29 **M** replied, "As soon as I'm out
9:33 **M** spread out his hands to the
9:35 LORD had predicted through **M**.
10:1 Then the LORD said to **M**,
10:3 So **M** and Aaron went to
10:6 **M** turned and left Pharaoh.
10:8 So **M** and Aaron were brought
10:9 **M** answered, "Everyone!
10:11 Then **M** and Aaron were thrown
10:12 The LORD said to **M**,
10:13 **M** held his staff over the land of
10:16 Pharaoh quickly called for **M**
10:18 **M** left Pharaoh and prayed to
10:21 Then the LORD said to **M**,
10:22 **M** lifted his hand toward the
10:24 Pharaoh called for **M** and said,
10:25 But **M** said, "You must allow
10:28 Pharaoh said to **M**,
10:29 **M** answered. "You'll never see
11:1 Then the LORD said to **M**,
11:3 And **M** was highly respected
11:4 **M** said, "This is what the
11:8 with anger, **M** left Pharaoh.
11:9 The LORD had said to **M**,
11:10 **M** and Aaron showed Pharaoh
12:1 The LORD said to **M** and Aaron
12:21 Then **M** called for all the
12:28 had commanded **M** and Aaron.
12:31 Pharaoh called for **M** and Aaron
12:35 The Israelites did what **M** had
12:43 LORD said to **M** and Aaron,
12:50 had commanded **M** and Aaron.
13:1 The LORD spoke to **M**,
13:3 Then **M** said to the people,
13:19 **M** took the bones of Joseph
14:1 Then the LORD said to **M**,
14:11 They said to **M**, "Did you bring
14:13 **M** answered the people,
14:15 Then the LORD said to **M**,
14:21 Then **M** stretched out his hand
14:26 Then the LORD said to **M**,
14:27 **M** stretched his hand over the
14:31 in him and in his servant **M**.
15:1 Then **M** and the Israelites sang
15:22 **M** led Israel away from the Red
15:24 complained about **M** by asking,
15:25 **M** cried out to the LORD,
16:2 complained about **M** and Aaron.
16:4 The LORD said to **M**,
16:6 So **M** and Aaron said to all the
16:8 **M** also said, "The LORD will

Exo 16:9 **M** said to Aaron, "Tell the
16:11 The LORD said to **M**,
16:15 **M** said to them, "It's the food
16:19 Then **M** said to them,
16:20 some of them didn't listen to **M**.
16:20 So **M** was angry with them.
16:22 of the community came to **M**
16:24 morning as **M** had commanded,
16:25 "Eat it today," **M** said,
16:28 The LORD said to **M**,
16:32 **M** said, "This is what the
16:33 **M** said to Aaron, "Take a jar,
16:34 as the LORD commanded **M**.
17:2 complained to **M** by saying,
17:2 **M** said to them, "Why are you
17:3 complained to **M** and asked,
17:4 So **M** cried out to the LORD,
17:5 The LORD answered **M**,
17:6 **M** did this while the leaders of
17:9 **M** said to Joshua, Then fight the
17:10 Joshua did as **M** told him and
17:10 Amalekites, while **M**, Aaron,
17:11 As long as **M** held up his
17:14 The LORD said to **M**,
17:15 **M** built an altar and called it
18:1 everything God had done for **M**
18:2 When **M** had sent away his
18:3 [Foreigner], because **M** said,
18:5 Moses' sons and wife to **M**
18:6 Jethro had sent word to **M**,
18:7 So **M** went out to meet his
18:7 **M** bowed with his face
18:8 **M** told his father-in-law
18:13 The next day **M** was settling
18:13 The people stood around **M**
18:14 saw everything **M** was doing
18:15 **M** answered his father-in-law,
18:24 **M** listened to his father-in-law
18:25 **M** chose capable men from all
18:26 bring difficult cases to **M**,
18:27 **M** sent his father-in-law on his
19:3 Then **M** went up the mountain
19:7 So **M** went down and called for
19:8 So **M** brought their answer
19:9 The LORD said to **M**,
19:9 **M** told the LORD what the
19:10 So the LORD said to **M**,
19:14 After **M** went down the
19:15 Then **M** said to the people,
19:17 Then **M** led the people out of
19:19 and louder, **M** was speaking,
19:20 top of Mount Sinai and called **M**
19:20 the mountain. So **M** went up.
19:23 **M** said to the LORD,
19:25 So **M** went down to the people
20:19 Then they said to **M**,
20:20 **M** answered the people,
20:21 distance while **M** went closer
20:22 The LORD said to **M**,
24:1 The LORD said to **M**,
24:2 **M** may come near the LORD,
24:2 must not come along with **M**."
24:3 **M** went and told the people all
24:4 So **M** wrote down all the
24:6 **M** took half of the blood and put
24:8 **M** took the blood and sprinkled
24:9 **M** went up with Aaron,
24:12 The LORD said to **M**,
24:13 **M** set out with his assistant
24:13 and **M** went up on the mountain
24:15 So **M** went up on the mountain,
24:16 LORD called to **M** from inside
24:18 **M** entered the cloud as he went
25:1 The LORD said to **M**,
30:11 Then the LORD said to **M**,
30:17 The LORD said to **M**,
30:22 The LORD said to **M**,
30:34 The LORD said to **M**,
31:1 The LORD said to **M**,
31:12 The LORD said to **M**,
31:18 LORD finished speaking to **M**
32:1 When the people saw that **M**
32:1 what has happened to this **M**,
32:7 The LORD said to **M**,
32:11 But **M** pleaded with the LORD
32:15 **M** turned and went down the

Exo 32:17 He said to **M**, "It's the sound of
32:18 **M** replied, "It's not the sound of
32:19 In a burst of anger **M** threw
32:21 **M** asked Aaron, "What did
32:23 to this **M** who brought
32:25 When **M** saw this,
32:28 Levites did what **M** told them,
32:29 **M** said, "Today you are
32:30 The next day **M** said to the
32:31 So **M** went back to the LORD
32:33 The LORD answered **M**,
33:1 Then the LORD said to **M**,
33:5 The LORD had said to **M**,
33:7 Now, **M** used to take a tent and
33:8 Whenever **M** went out to the
33:8 to their tents and watch **M** until
33:9 As soon as **M** went into the
33:9 while the LORD spoke with **M**.
33:11 would speak to **M** personally,
33:11 Then **M** would come back to
33:12 **M** said to the LORD,
33:15 Then **M** said to him,
33:17 The LORD answered **M**,
33:18 Then **M** said, "Please let me
34:1 The LORD said to **M**,
34:4 So **M** cut two ⌊more⌋ stone
34:6 Then he passed in front of **M**,
34:8 Immediately, **M** knelt,
34:27 Then the LORD said to **M**,
34:28 **M** was there with the LORD 40
34:29 **M** came down from Mount
34:30 all the Israelites looked at **M**
34:31 **M** called to them, so Aaron and
34:31 Then **M** spoke to them.
34:33 When **M** finished speaking to
34:34 But whenever **M** went into the
34:35 Then **M** would put the veil
35:1 **M** assembled the whole
35:4 Then **M** said to the whole
35:20 Israelite community left **M**.
35:29 had commanded through **M**.
35:30 Then **M** said to the Israelites,
36:1 ⌊**M** continued,⌋ "So Bezalel
36:2 **M** called Bezalel and Oholiab
36:3 **M** turned over to them all the
36:4 They all came to **M**.
36:6 So **M** gave instructions to have
38:21 An inventory was ordered by **M**
38:22 the LORD had commanded **M**.
39:1 the LORD's instructions to **M**.
39:5 the LORD's instructions to **M**.
39:7 the LORD's instructions to **M**.
39:21 the LORD's instructions to **M**.
39:26 the LORD's instructions to **M**.
39:29 the LORD's instructions to **M**.
39:31 the LORD's instructions to **M**.
39:32 the LORD's instructions to **M**.
39:33 they brought everything to **M**
39:42 the LORD's instructions to **M**.
39:43 **M** inspected all the work and
39:43 So **M** blessed them.
40:1 Then the LORD said to **M**,
40:16 **M** did everything as the LORD
40:18 When **M** set up the tent,
40:19 **M** followed the LORD's
40:21 **M** followed the LORD's
40:22 **M** put the table in the tent of
40:26 **M** put the gold altar in the tent
40:29 **M** followed the LORD's
40:31 **M**, Aaron, and his sons used
40:32 **M** followed the LORD's
40:33 Finally, **M** finished the work.
40:35 **M** couldn't go into the tent of
Lev 1:1 The LORD called **M** and spoke
4:1 The LORD spoke to **M**,
5:14 The LORD spoke to **M**,
6:1 The LORD spoke to **M**,
6:8 The LORD spoke to **M**,
6:19 The LORD spoke to **M**,
6:24 The LORD spoke to **M**,
7:22 The LORD spoke to **M**,
7:28 The LORD spoke to **M**,
7:35 on the day **M** ordained them
7:38 gave **M** commands about these
8:1 The LORD spoke to **M**,
8:4 **M** did as the LORD

Lev 8:5 **M** told the congregation,
8:6 **M** had Aaron and his sons
8:9 the LORD had commanded **M**.
8:10 **M** took the anointing oil to
8:13 **M** had Aaron's sons come
8:13 the LORD had commanded **M**.
8:15 When it was slaughtered, **M**
8:16 **M** took all the fat that was on
8:19 **M** slaughtered it and threw the
8:20 **M** burned the head with the
8:21 Then **M** burned the whole ram
8:23 **M** slaughtered it, took some of
8:24 **M** also brought Aaron's sons
8:24 **M** threw the rest of the blood
8:27 **M** presented all these things to
8:29 **M** also took the breast from the
8:30 **M** took some of the anointing
8:31 **M** told Aaron and his sons:
8:36 LORD commanded through **M**.
9:1 On the eighth day **M**
9:5 So they took the things **M**
9:6 **M** said, "The LORD has
9:7 **M** told Aaron, "Come to the
9:10 the LORD had commanded **M**.
9:21 to the LORD as **M** commanded.
9:23 **M** and Aaron went into the tent
10:3 **M** said to Aaron, "This is
10:4 **M** called Mishael and
10:5 the camp, as **M** told them.
10:6 **M** told Aaron and his sons
10:7 with his oil." They obeyed **M**.
10:11 that I gave them through **M**."
10:12 **M** told Aaron and his surviving
10:16 **M** tried to find out what had
10:19 Aaron answered **M**,
10:20 When **M** heard this,
11:1 LORD spoke to **M** and Aaron,
12:1 The LORD spoke to **M**,
13:1 LORD spoke to **M** and Aaron,
14:1 The LORD spoke to **M**,
14:33 LORD spoke to **M** and Aaron,
15:1 LORD spoke to **M** and Aaron,
16:1 The LORD spoke to **M** after
16:34 the LORD had commanded **M**.
17:1 The LORD spoke to **M**,
18:1 The LORD spoke to **M**,
19:1 The LORD spoke to **M**,
20:1 The LORD spoke to **M**,
21:1 The LORD spoke to **M**,
21:16 The LORD spoke to **M**,
21:24 So **M** spoke to Aaron and his
22:1 The LORD spoke to **M**,
22:17 The LORD spoke to **M**,
22:26 The LORD spoke to **M**,
23:1 The LORD spoke to **M**,
23:9 The LORD spoke to **M**,
23:23 The LORD spoke to **M**,
23:26 The LORD spoke to **M**,
23:33 The LORD spoke to **M**,
23:44 So **M** told the Israelites about
24:1 The LORD spoke to **M**,
24:11 So they brought him to **M**.
24:13 The LORD spoke to **M**,
24:23 **M** spoke to the people of Israel.
24:23 as the LORD commanded **M**.
24:23 as the LORD commanded **M**.
25:1 spoke to **M** on Mount Sinai,
26:46 through **M** on Mount Sinai.
27:1 The LORD spoke to **M**,
27:34 commands the LORD gave **M**
Num 1:1 The LORD spoke to **M** in the
1:17 **M** and Aaron took the men who
1:19 So **M** registered the men of
1:44 **M**, Aaron, and the 12 leaders of
1:48 The LORD had said to **M**,
1:54 as the LORD commanded **M**.
2:1 LORD spoke to **M** and Aaron,
2:33 the LORD had commanded **M**,
2:34 the LORD had commanded **M**.
3:1 spoke to **M** on Mount Sinai.
3:5 The LORD said to **M**,
3:11 The LORD said to **M**,
3:14 The LORD said to **M** in the
3:16 So **M** did what the LORD said
3:38 **M**, Aaron, and his sons put up
3:39 grand total of Levites that **M**

Lev 3:40 The LORD said to **M**,
3:42 So **M** registered all the firstborn
3:44 The LORD said to **M**,
3:49 So **M** took this ransom money
3:50 The silver **M** collected for the
3:51 Then **M** did what the LORD
4:1 LORD said to **M** and Aaron,
4:17 LORD said to **M** and Aaron,
4:21 The LORD said to **M**,
4:34 **M**, Aaron, and the leaders of
4:37 **M** and Aaron did as the LORD
4:37 the LORD had commanded **M**
4:41 **M** and Aaron did as the LORD
4:41 the LORD had commanded **M**
4:45 **M** and Aaron did as the LORD
4:45 the LORD had commanded **M**
4:46 total of all the Levites whom **M**,
4:49 through **M** each man was
4:49 as the LORD commanded **M**.
5:1 The LORD said to **M**,
5:4 did as the LORD had told **M**.
5:5 The LORD said to **M**,
5:11 The LORD said to **M**:
6:1 The LORD said to **M**,
6:22 The LORD said to **M**,
7:1 When **M** finished setting up the
7:4 The LORD said to **M**,
7:6 **M** took the wagons and the
7:9 But **M** gave none of these gifts
7:11 The LORD said to **M**,
7:89 Whenever **M** went into the tent
7:89 how the LORD spoke with **M**.
8:1 The LORD said to **M**,
8:3 as the LORD commanded **M**.
8:4 one the LORD had shown **M**.
8:5 The LORD said to **M**,
8:20 **M**, Aaron, and the whole
8:20 what the LORD commanded **M**
8:22 the LORD had commanded **M**.
8:23 The LORD said to **M**,
9:1 the LORD spoke to **M** in the
9:4 So **M** told the Israelites to
9:5 the LORD had commanded **M**.
9:6 They came to **M** and Aaron
9:8 **M** answered them,
9:9 Then the LORD said to **M**,
9:23 the LORD had given through **M**.
10:1 The LORD said to **M**,
10:13 the LORD had given through **M**.
10:29 **M** said to his brother-in-law
10:31 But **M** said, "Please don't leave
10:35 **M** would say, "Arise, O LORD!
11:2 The people cried out to **M**,
11:2 **M** prayed to the LORD,
11:10 **M** heard people from every
11:10 and **M** didn't like it either.
11:16 The LORD answered **M**,
11:21 But **M** said, "Here I am with
11:23 The LORD asked **M**,
11:24 **M** went out and told the people
11:25 of the Spirit that was on **M**
11:27 a young man ran and told **M**,
11:29 But **M** asked him, "Do you
11:30 Then **M** and the leaders went
12:1 and Aaron began to criticize **M**
12:2 LORD speak only through **M**?
12:3 (**M** was a very humble man,
12:4 Suddenly, the LORD said to **M**,
12:7 the way I treat my servant **M**.
12:8 to criticize my servant **M**?"
12:11 So he said to **M**, "Please, sir,
12:13 So **M** cried to the LORD,
12:14 The LORD replied to **M**,
13:1 The LORD said to **M**,
13:3 So at the LORD's command, **M**
13:16 the names of the men **M** sent
13:16 But **M** gave Hoshea,
13:17 When **M** sent them to explore
13:26 They came back to **M**,
13:27 This is what they reported to **M**:
13:30 to be quiet and listen to **M**.
14:2 complained to **M** and Aaron,
14:5 Immediately, **M** and Aaron
14:10 of Israel talked about stoning **M**
14:11 The LORD said to **M**,
14:13 But **M** said to the LORD,

Lev 14:26 the LORD said to **M** and Aaron,
14:36 So the men **M** sent to explore
14:37 about **M** by spreading lies
14:39 When **M** told these things to all
14:41 But **M** asked, "Why are you
14:44 LORD's promise and **M** stayed
15:1 The LORD said to **M**,
15:17 The LORD said to **M**,
15:22 commands the LORD gave **M**.
15:23 you through **M** holds as true
15:33 wood brought him to **M**
15:35 Then the LORD said to **M**,
15:36 as the LORD commanded **M**.
15:37 The LORD said to **M**,
16:1 of Peleth) dared to challenge **M**.
16:3 came together to confront **M**
16:4 As soon as **M** heard this,
16:8 **M** also said to Korah,
16:12 Then **M** sent for Dathan and
16:15 **M** became angry and said to
16:16 **M** said to Korah, Aaron will also
16:18 and stood with **M** and Aaron at
16:19 those who opposed **M**
16:20 LORD said to **M** and Aaron,
16:23 Then the LORD said to **M**,
16:25 **M** got up and went to Dathan
16:28 **M** said, "This is how you will
16:36 Then the LORD said to **M**,
16:40 the LORD had given through **M**.
16:41 complained to **M** and Aaron.
16:42 to confront **M** and Aaron.
16:43 Then **M** and Aaron went to the
16:44 The LORD said to **M**,
16:46 **M** said to Aaron, "Take your
16:47 incense burner, as **M** told him,
16:50 time Aaron came back to **M** at
17:1 The LORD said to **M**,
17:6 So **M** spoke to the Israelites.
17:7 **M** put the staffs in the LORD's
17:8 The next day **M** went into the
17:9 **M** brought out the staffs from
17:10 The LORD said to **M**,
17:11 **M** did exactly what the LORD
17:12 The Israelites said to **M**,
18:25 The LORD said to **M**,
19:1 LORD said to **M** and Aaron,
20:2 to confront **M** and Aaron.
20:3 complained to **M** and said,
20:6 **M** and Aaron went from the
20:7 The LORD said to **M**,
20:9 **M** took his staff out of ⌊the tent
20:10 Then **M** and Aaron assembled
20:11 **M** raised his hand and hit the
20:12 the LORD said to **M** and Aaron,
20:14 **M** sent messengers from
20:23 the LORD said to **M** and Aaron,
20:27 **M** did as the Lord commanded.
20:28 **M** took off Aaron's priestly
20:28 Then **M** and Eleazar came
21:5 and criticized God and **M**.
21:7 people came to **M** and said,
21:7 So **M** prayed for the people.
21:8 The LORD said to **M**,
21:9 So **M** made a bronze snake
21:16 where the LORD said to **M**,
21:32 After **M** sent spies to Jazer,
21:34 The LORD said to **M**,
25:4 The LORD said to **M**,
25:5 So **M** said to the judges of
25:6 He did this right in front of **M**
25:10 Then the LORD said to **M**,
25:16 The LORD said to **M**,
26:1 LORD said to **M** and Eleazar,
26:3 So **M** and the priest Eleazar
26:4 as the LORD commanded **M**."
26:9 who defied **M** and Aaron's
26:52 Then the LORD said to **M**,
26:59 **M**, and their sister Miriam.
26:63 **M** and the priest Eleazar added
26:64 a single one of the Israelites **M**
27:2 to **M** and stood in front of him,
27:5 So **M** brought their case to the
27:11 as the LORD commanded **M**."
27:12 The LORD said to **M**,
27:15 **M** said to the LORD,
27:18 So the LORD said to **M**,

Lev 27:22 **M** did as the LORD
27:23 **M** placed his hands on Joshua
28:1 The LORD said to **M**,
29:40 **M** told the Israelites everything
30:1 **M** said to the heads of the
30:16 are the laws the LORD gave **M**
31:1 The LORD said to **M**,
31:3 **M** said to the people,
31:6 Then **M** sent them off to war,
31:7 as the LORD commanded **M**,
31:12 and everything to **M**,
31:13 **M**, the priest Eleazar, and all
31:14 **M** was angry with the officers
31:21 LORD's teachings told **M** to do:
31:25 The LORD said to **M**,
31:31 **M** and the priest Eleazar did as
31:31 as the LORD commanded **M**.
31:41 **M** gave the LORD's taxes to
31:42 **M** took the Israelites' half of the
31:47 From the Israelites' half **M**
31:48 battalions of men, came to **M**.
31:51 **M** and the priest Eleazar took
31:54 **M** and the priest Eleazar took
32:2 So they came to **M**,
32:6 **M** asked the tribes of Gad and
32:16 Reuben came up to **M** and said,
32:20 **M** answered, "Do what you
32:25 of Gad and Reuben said to **M**,
32:28 So **M** gave orders about them
32:29 **M** told them, "If the tribes of
32:33 So **M** gave the tribes of Gad,
32:40 So **M** gave Gilead to the
33:1 the leadership of **M** and Aaron.
33:2 At the LORD's command **M**
33:50 The LORD said to **M** on the
34:1 The LORD said to **M**,
34:13 **M** commanded the Israelites,
34:16 The LORD said to **M**,
35:1 The LORD spoke to **M** on the
35:9 The LORD said to **M**,
36:1 came and spoke to **M**
36:5 So **M** gave the Israelites a
36:10 as the LORD commanded **M**.
36:13 gave the Israelites through **M**

Dtr 1:1 This is the speech **M** gave in
1:3 **M** told the Israelites everything
1:5 River in Moab when **M** began
4:41 Then **M** set aside three cities
4:44 This is what **M** taught the
4:45 and rules **M** gave the Israelites
4:46 **M** and Israel defeated him after
5:1 **M** summoned all Israel and
5:27 ⌊**M**,⌋ go and listen to
27:1 **M** and the leaders of Israel told
27:9 Then **M** and the Levitical
27:11 That same day **M** gave the
29:1 that the LORD commanded **M**
29:2 **M** summoned all the people of
31:1 **M** continued to speak to all the
31:7 Then **M** called for Joshua and
31:9 **M** wrote down these teachings
31:10 Then **M** commanded them,
31:14 The LORD said to **M**,
31:14 **M** and Joshua came to the tent
31:16 The LORD said to **M**,
31:22 That day **M** wrote down this
31:24 Finally, **M** finished writing all
31:30 **M** recited all the words of this
32:44 **M** came with Hoshea,
32:45 When **M** had finished reciting
32:48 same day the LORD said to **M**,
33:1 **M**, the man of God, blessed the
33:4 **M** gave us these teachings.
34:1 Then **M** went up on Mount
34:5 servant **M** died in Moab.
34:7 **M** was 120 years old when he
34:8 The Israelites mourned for **M** in
34:9 because **M** had laid his hands
34:9 had commanded through **M**.
34:10 another prophet in Israel like **M**
34:12 **M** used his mighty hand to do

Jos 1:1 death of the LORD's servant **M**,
1:2 "My servant **M** is dead.
1:3 you set foot, as I promised **M**.
1:5 be with you as I was with **M**.
1:7 my servant **M** commanded you.

Jos 1:13 servant **M** commanded you.
1:13 **M** said, ‘The LORD your God
1:14 the land that **M** gave you east
1:15 LORD’s servant **M** gave you."
1:17 will obey you as we obeyed **M**.
1:17 be with you as he was with **M**.
3:7 with you just as I was with **M**.
4:10 This was as **M** had told
4:12 did as **M** had told them.
4:14 way they had respected **M**.
8:31 servant **M** had commanded
8:32 which **M** had written down.
8:33 the LORD’s servant **M** had
8:34 all been written down by **M**.
8:35 everything **M** had commanded.
9:24 God commanded his servant **M**
11:12 **M** had commanded him.
11:15 had commanded his servant **M**
11:15 what **M** had commanded him.
11:15 the LORD had commanded **M**.
11:20 as he had commanded **M**.
11:23 as the LORD had promised **M**.
12:6 The LORD’s servant **M** and the
13:8 since the LORD’s servant **M**
13:12 **M** had defeated them and
13:14 **M** did not give any land as an
13:15 **M** gave some land as an
13:21 **M** defeated him and Midian’s
13:24 **M** gave some land as an
13:29 **M** gave some land as an
13:32 This is the land that **M**
13:33 **M** did not give any land as an
14:2 had commanded through **M**.
14:3 **M** had given the two-and-a-half
14:5 the LORD had commanded **M**.
14:6 what the LORD said to **M**,
14:7 LORD’s servant **M** sent me from
14:9 On that day **M** swore this oath:
14:10 LORD made this promise to **M**.
14:11 as I was when **M** sent me out.
17:4 "The LORD commanded **M** to
18:7 LORD’s servant **M** gave them
20:2 I spoke to you through **M**.
21:2 through **M** that we should
21:8 had commanded through **M**.
22:2 servant **M** commanded you.
22:4 servant **M** gave you east
22:5 LORD’s servant **M** gave you.
22:7 **M** had given land in Bashan as
22:9 had instructed them through **M**
24:5 "Then I sent **M** and Aaron,
Jdg 1:20 As **M** had promised,
3:4 their ancestors through **M**.
18:30 of Gershom and grandson of **M**)
1Sm 12:6 "The LORD appointed **M** and
12:8 who sent **M** and Aaron to bring
1Ki 8:9 two stone tablets **M** put there at
8:53 servant **M** when you brought
8:56 his servant **M** has failed
2Ki 18:4 bronze snake that **M** had made
18:6 the LORD had given through **M**,
18:12 to obey everything that **M**,
21:8 that my servant **M** gave them."
1Ch 6:3 were Aaron, **M**, and Miriam.
6:49 servant **M** had commanded.
15:15 They used poles as **M** had
21:29 The LORD’s tent that **M** made
22:13 the LORD commanded **M**
23:13 sons were Aaron and **M**.
23:14 The sons of **M**, the man of God,
2Ch 1:3 **M**, the LORD’s servant,
5:10 two tablets **M** placed there at
8:13 Booths) as **M** had commanded.
24:6 The LORD’s servant **M** and the
24:9 servant **M** had required Israel
30:16 (**M** was a man of God.)
33:8 ⌊I gave⌋ through **M**."
34:14 Teachings written by **M**.
35:6 instructed ⌊us⌋ through **M**."
35:12 as written in the Book of **M**.
Ezr 3:2 (**M** was a man of God).
6:18 written in the Book of **M**.
Neh 1:7 us through your servant **M**.
1:8 told us through your servant **M**:
8:14 given an order through **M** that
9:14 through your servant **M**.
Neh 10:29 God’s teachings given by **M**,
13:1 On that day the Book of **M** was
Psa 77:20 You had **M** and Aaron take
99:6 **M** and Aaron were among his
103:7 He let **M** know his ways.
105:26 He sent his servant **M**,
106:16 men became envious of **M**.
106:23 them, but **M**, his chosen one,
106:32 Things turned out badly for **M**
Isa 63:11 Then his people remembered **M**
63:12 to support the right hand of **M**?
Jer 15:1 "Even if **M** and Samuel were
Dan 9:11 Teachings of your servant **M**.
Mic 6:4 I sent **M**, Aaron, and Miriam to
Mal 4:4 the teachings of my servant **M**,
Mat 8:4 Then offer the sacrifice **M**
17:3 Suddenly, **M** and Elijah
17:4 one for **M**, and one for Elijah."
19:7 did **M** order a man to give his
19:8 Jesus answered them, "**M**
22:24 "Teacher, **M** said, ‘If a man
Mar 1:44 which **M** commanded as proof
7:10 For example, **M** said,
9:4 Then Elijah and **M** appeared to
9:5 one for **M**, and one for Elijah."
10:3 command did **M** give you?"
10:4 They said, "**M** allowed a man
12:19 "Teacher, **M** wrote for us,
12:26 you read in the book of **M** that
Luk 5:14 Then offer the sacrifice as **M**
9:30 Suddenly, both **M** and Elijah
9:33 As **M** and Elijah were leaving
9:33 one for **M**, and one for Elijah."
20:28 "Teacher, **M** wrote for us,
20:37 "Even **M** showed in the
Jon 1:17 were given through **M**,
1:45 the man whom **M** wrote about
3:14 "As **M** lifted up the snake ⌊on a
5:45 **M**, the one you trust, is already
5:46 If you really believed **M**,
5:46 **M** wrote about me.
5:47 you don’t believe what **M** wrote,
6:32 **M** didn’t give you bread from
7:19 Didn’t **M** give you his
7:19 of you does what **M** taught you.
7:22 **M** gave you the teaching about
7:22 (although it didn’t come from **M**
8:5 In his teachings, **M** ordered us
9:29 We know that God spoke to **M**,
Act 3:22 "**M** said, ‘The Lord your God
6:11 heard him slander **M** and God."
6:14 the customs that **M** gave us."
7:20 "At that time **M** was born,
7:21 When **M** was abandoned
7:22 So **M** was educated in all the
7:25 **M** thought his own people
7:26 The next day **M** saw two
7:27 of the men pushed **M** aside.
7:27 He asked **M**, ‘Who made you
7:29 After he said that, **M** quickly
7:31 **M** was surprised when he saw
7:32 **M** began to tremble and didn’t
7:35 "This is the **M** whom the
7:37 This is the same **M** who told
7:38 This is the **M** who was in the
7:38 **M** received life-giving
7:40 what has happened to this **M**,
7:44 **M** built this tent exactly as
21:21 people to abandon **M**.
26:22 and **M** said would happen.
Rom 5:14 time of Adam to the time of **M**,
9:15 For example, God said to **M**,
10:5 **M** writes about receiving God’s
10:19 **M** was the first to say,
1Co 10:2 They were all united with **M** by
2Co 3:13 We are not like **M**.
3:15 when they read the books of **M**,
Gal 3:17 The laws ⌊given to **M**⌋ 430
3:19 of the laws given to **M**?
3:21 that the laws given to **M**
2Ti 3:8 and Jambres opposed **M**,
Heb 3:2 in the same way that **M** was
3:3 deserves more praise than **M**
3:5 **M** was a faithful servant in
3:16 All those whom **M** led out of
7:14 **M** never said anything about
Heb 8:4 the instructions that **M** gave.
8:5 When **M** was about to make
9:19 As Moses’ Teachings tell us, **M**
9:21 In the same way, **M** sprinkled
11:23 because they saw that **M** was
11:24 When **M** grew up, faith led him
11:27 Faith led **M** to leave Egypt
11:27 **M** didn’t give up but continued
11:28 Faith led **M** to establish the
12:21 so terrifying that even **M** said
Jud 1:9 arguing over the body of **M**.
Rev 15:3 the song of God’s servant **M**

Moses’ (150)

Exo 4:25 and touched **M** feet ⌊with it⌋.
17:12 Eventually, **M** hands felt heavy.
18:1 **M** father-in-law Jethro,
18:5 **M** father-in-law Jethro brought
18:5 Jethro brought **M** sons
18:12 Then Jethro, **M** father-in-law,
18:12 the meal with **M** father-in-law
18:14 When **M** father-in-law saw
18:17 **M** father-in-law replied,
34:35 they would see that **M** face
Lev 8:29 It was **M** share, as the LORD
Num 3:1 of Aaron and **M** descendants at
11:28 who had been **M** assistant ever
Jos 1:1 said to **M** assistant Joshua,
8:31 in the book of **M** Teachings.
8:35 Joshua read ⌊**M** Teachings⌋ in
23:6 in the Book of **M** Teachings.
Jdg 1:16 descendants of **M** father-in-law,
4:11 of Hobab, **M** father-in-law).
1Ki 2:3 are recorded in **M** Teachings.
2Ki 14:6 **M** Teachings: "Parents must
22:8 found the book of **M** Teachings
23:25 as directed in **M** Teachings.
1Ch 23:15 **M** sons were Gershom and
26:24 descendant of **M** son Gershom.
2Ch 15:3 and without **M** Teachings
19:10 derived from **M** Teachings.
23:18 as it is written in **M** Teachings.
25:4 **M** Teachings: "Parents must
30:16 as instructed by **M** Teachings.
31:21 incorporated **M** Teachings
Ezr 3:2 written in **M** Teachings.
7:6 expert in **M** Teachings, which
10:3 do what **M** Teachings tell us.
Neh 8:1 Book of **M** Teachings, which
8:3 to the Book of **M** Teachings
12:44 designated by **M** Teachings
Lam 2:9 ⌊from **M** Teachings⌋.
Dan 9:13 it was written in **M** Teachings.
Mat 5:17 came to set aside **M** Teachings
5:18 **M** Teachings before everything
7:12 ⌊the meaning of⌋ **M** Teachings
11:13 **M** Teachings prophesied up
12:5 you read in **M** Teachings that
22:35 an expert in **M** Teachings,
22:36 the greatest in **M** Teachings?
22:40 All of **M** Teachings and the
23:2 teach with **M** authority
23:23 things in **M** Teachings.
Luk 2:22 days required by **M** Teachings
2:27 what **M** Teachings required.
5:17 in **M** Teachings were present.
7:30 **M** Teachings rejected God’s plan
10:25 Then an expert in **M** Teachings
10:26 is written in **M** Teachings?
11:45 experts in **M** Teachings said
11:46 you experts in **M** Teachings!
11:52 you experts in **M** Teachings!
14:3 the experts in **M** Teachings, "Is
16:16 "**M** Teachings and the
16:17 a comma from **M** Teachings
16:29 ‘They have **M** ⌊Teachings⌋
16:31 won’t listen to **M** ⌊Teachings⌋
24:27 he began with **M** Teachings
24:44 about me in **M** Teachings,
Jon 7:23 **M** Teachings, why are you
7:49 it doesn’t know **M** Teachings.
7:51 "Do **M** Teachings enable us to
9:28 but we’re **M** disciples
Act 2:23 **M** Teachings, you crucified Jesus
5:34 expert in **M** Teachings.
6:13 holy place and **M** Teachings

Act 7:53 **M** Teachings, which were put
13:15 After reading from **M** Teachings
13:38 approval through **M** Teachings
15:1 as **M** Teachings require.
15:5 ordered to follow **M** Teachings.
15:21 After all, **M** words have been
18:13 that are against **M** Teachings.
21:20 committed to **M** Teachings
21:24 carefully follow **M** Teachings
21:28 **M** Teachings, and this temple.
22:12 who followed **M** Teachings.
23:3 and judge me by **M** Teachings
24:14 written in **M** Teachings
28:23 about Jesus from **M** Teachings
Rom 2:14 that **M** Teachings contain,
2:15 in **M** Teachings are written
2:17 **M** Teachings, brag about your
2:18 have been taught **M** Teachings
2:20 and truth in **M** Teachings
2:23 **M** Teachings, are you
2:23 God by ignoring **M** Teachings
2:25 valuable if you follow **M** laws.
2:26 what **M** Teachings demand,
2:27 **M** Teachings say will condemn
2:27 have **M** Teachings in writing.
3:19 is in **M** Teachings applies
3:20 by following **M** Teachings.
3:20 **M** Teachings show what sin is.
3:21 a way other than **M** Teachings.
3:21 **M** Teachings and the Prophets
3:31 **M** Teachings by this faith?
3:31 we are supporting **M** Teachings
4:13 **M** Teachings that Abraham
4:14 If those who obey **M** Teachings
4:15 The laws in **M** Teachings bring
4:16 by obeying **M** Teachings
7:1 are familiar with **M** Teachings.
7:4 **M** Teachings through Christ's
7:5 Stirred up by **M** laws, they did
7:7 Are **M** laws sinful?
7:7 if **M** Teachings hadn't said,
7:12 So **M** Teachings are holy,
9:4 **M** Teachings, the true worship,
9:31 by obeying **M** Teachings,
10:4 **M** Teachings so that everyone
13:8 has fulfilled **M** Teachings
13:10 love fulfills **M** Teachings
1Co 9:8 Don't **M** Teachings say the
9:9 **M** Teachings say,
9:20 subject to **M** Teachings
9:20 I'm not subject to **M** Teachings
9:21 does not have **M** Teachings
14:34 place as **M** Teachings say.
2Co 3:7 of Israel couldn't look at **M** face.
Gal 3:10 in **M** Teachings is cursed."
3:19 **M** laws did this until the
3:23 by **M** laws until this faith
3:24 **M** laws served as our guardian.
4:21 by **M** laws should tell me
4:21 to what **M** Teachings say?
5:3 **M** Teachings demand.
5:14 All of **M** Teachings are
5:18 you are not subject to **M** laws
Eph 2:15 found in **M** Teachings so that
1Ti 1:7 to be experts in **M** Teachings.
1:8 We know that **M** Teachings are
1:11 **M** Teachings were intended to
Tit 3:9 and fights about **M** Teachings.
Heb 7:5 **M** Teachings say that
7:19 **M** Teachings couldn't
7:28 **M** Teachings designated
7:28 which came after **M** Teachings,
9:19 As **M** Teachings tell us,
9:22 As **M** Teachings tell us,
10:1 **M** Teachings with their yearly
10:8 **M** Teachings require people
10:28 **M** Teachings, that person was
11:23 Faith led **M** parents to hide him

most (193)

Gen 14:18 He was a priest of God **M** High.
14:19 is Abram by God **M** High,
14:20 Blessed is God **M** High,
14:22 to the LORD God **M** High,
34:19 He was the **m** honored person
Exo 26:33 The canopy will mark off the **m**
Exo 26:34 on the ark in the **m** holy place.
29:37 Then the altar will be **m** holy.
30:10 It is **m** holy to the LORD."
30:29 Then they will be **m** holy,
30:36 You must treat it as **m** holy.
40:10 and it will be **m** holy.
Lev 16:31 This is the **m** important
Num 4:4 take care of the **m** holy things.
4:19 come near the **m** holy things:
12:7 He is the **m** faithful person in
18:9 That part of the **m** holy
18:9 to me as a **m** holy offering will
18:10 Eat it in a **m** holy place.
24:16 knowledge from the **M** High,
Dtr 1:17 to the **m** important people.
28:54 Even the **m** tender and
28:56 The **m** tender and sensitive
30:4 to the **m** distant country
32:8 When the **M** High gave nations
33:16 and the **m** plentiful crops of the
33:24 "The people of Asher are the **m**
Jdg 5:24 be the **m** blessed woman,
5:24 the **m** blessed woman living in
1Sm 9:21 My family is the **m** insignificant
2Sm 22:14 The **M** High made his voice
1Ki 3:4 it was the **m** important place
6:16 inner room, the **m** holy place.
7:50 ⌊room⌋ (the **m** holy place),
8:6 temple (the **m** holy place) under
2Ki 10:3 choose the best and **m** honest
10:6 with the city's **m** powerful men.
10:11 all the **m** powerful men,
19:23 I'll come to its **m** distant
19:23 borders and its **m** fertile forests.
1Ch 6:49 They did all the work in the **m**
12:29 though **m** of them remained
23:13 dedicate the **m** holy things ⌊to
2Ch 3:8 He made the **m** holy place.
3:10 In the **m** holy place he made
4:22 ⌊room⌋ (the **m** holy place),
5:7 temple (the **m** holy place) under
Ezr 2:63 eat any of the **m** holy food until
Neh 1:9 be driven to the **m** distant point
4:13 it was lowest and **m** exposed.
7:2 God more than **m** people do.
7:65 eat any of the **m** holy food until
Job 1:3 He was the **m** influential
3:25 What I fear **m** overtakes me.
21:22 Can anyone judge the **M** High?
Psa 7:17 the name of the LORD **M** High.
9:2 to praise your name, O **M** High.
18:13 The **M** High made his voice
21:7 the mercy of the **M** High,
28:2 toward your **m** holy place.
45:2 You are the **m** handsome of
46:4 place where the **M** High lives.
47:2 fear the LORD, the **M** High.
50:14 and keep your vows to the **M**
57:2 I call to God **M** High,
65:5 earth and of the **m** distant sea,
73:11 the **M** High know anything?"
77:10 the power of the **M** High is no
78:17 the desert against the **M** High.
78:35 that the **M** High was their
78:56 They tested God **M** High and
82:6 You are all sons of the **M** High.
83:18 You alone are the **M** High God
87:5 The **M** High will make it
89:27 He will be the **M** High to the
91:1 of the **M** High will remain
91:9 made the **M** High your home.
92:1 to praise your name, O **M** High.
97:9 You, O LORD, the **M** High,
107:11 the advice given by the **M** High.
115:13 important to the **m** important.
139:9 land on the **m** distant shore
Sos 1:1 The **m** beautiful song of
1:8 **m** beautiful of women,
5:9 **M** beautiful of women,
6:1 **m** beautiful of women?
Isa 14:14 I'll be like the **M** High."
37:24 I'll come to its **m** distant
37:24 heights and its **m** fertile forests.
41:9 you from its **m** distant places.
Jer 3:19 the **m** beautiful property among
6:13 important to the **m** important,
Jer 8:10 important to the **m** important,
9:17 Send for those who are the **m**
16:19 Nations come to you from the **m**
17:9 "The human mind is the **m**
31:34 important to the **m** important,
42:1 important to the **m** important,
42:8 important to the **m** important.
44:12 important to the **m** important,
49:35 the **m** important weapon of
Lam 3:35 presence of the **M** High God,
3:38 the mouth of the **M** High God.
Eze 7:21 as loot and to the **m** evil people
7:24 So I will send the **m** evil nation,
20:6 land is the **m** beautiful land,
20:15 land is the **m** beautiful land,
24:16 you the person you love the **m**.
24:21 It's the thing you love the **m**.
24:25 and the thing they love the **m**.
28:7 the **m** ruthless foreigners
29:12 I will make Egypt the **m**
30:7 "'Egypt will become the **m**
30:11 He and his troops, the **m**
31:12 Foreigners from the **m** ruthless
32:12 All of them will be the **m**
41:4 "This is the **m** holy place."
41:15 The holy place and the **m** holy
41:17 the door to the **m** holy place
41:21 In front of the **m** holy place was
41:23 The holy place and the **m** holy
43:12 top of the mountain is **m** holy.
44:13 things or my **m** holy things.
45:3 place, that is, the **m** holy place,
Dan 3:26 servants of the **M** High God —
4:2 things the **M** High God did
4:17 that the **M** High has power
4:22 Your power reaches the **m**
4:24 The **M** High has decided to
4:25 that the **M** High has power
4:32 that the **M** High has power
4:34 I thanked the **M** High,
5:18 "Your Majesty, the **M** High God
5:21 that the **M** High God has
7:18 But the holy people of the **M**
7:22 the holy people of the **M** High.
7:25 speak against the **M** High God,
7:25 the holy people of the **M** High,
7:27 the holy people of the **M** High.
9:24 and to anoint the **M** Holy One.
Hos 7:16 They don't return to the **M** High
11:7 Even if they call to the **M** High,
Jnh 3:5 from the **m** important to the
Mic 7:4 The **m** decent person is
Mat 11:20 cities where he had worked **m**
20:27 Whoever wants to be **m**
21:8 **M** of the people spread their
22:38 **m** important commandment.
23:23 These are the **m** important
24:12 **m** people's love will grow cold.
Mar 5:7 Son of the **M** High God?
6:21 and the **m** important people of
9:35 "Whoever wants to be the **m**
10:44 Whoever wants to be **m**
12:28 "Which commandment is the **m**
12:29 "The **m** important is,
12:31 The second **m** important
12:40 the **m** severe punishment."
Luk 1:32 called the Son of the **M** High.
1:35 and the power of the **M** High
1:42 "You are the **m** blessed of all
1:76 called a prophet of the **M** High.
6:35 the children of the **M** High God.
7:42 you think will love him the **m**?"
8:28 Son of the **M** High God?
20:47 the **m** severe punishment."
Jon 7:37 On the last and **m** important
Act 7:48 "However, the **M** High doesn't
8:1 **M** believers, except the
14:12 Paul did **m** of the talking.
16:17 are servants of the **M** High God.
19:32 **M** of the people didn't even
20:38 Paul again hurt them **m** of all.
25:6 for eight or ten days at the **m**
25:23 Roman army officers and the **m**
27:12 **m** of the men decided to sail
28:17 invited the **m** influential Jews
1Co 10:5 not pleased with **m** of them,

1Co	14:27	or three at the **m** should speak.
	15:3	I passed on to you the **m**
	15:6	(**M** of these people are still
2Co	9:2	your enthusiasm has moved **m**
Gal	2:9	recognized as the **m** important
Eph	5:16	Make the **m** of your
Php	1:14	the Lord has given **m** of our
Col	4:5	the **m** of your opportunities.
Heb	7:1	and priest of the **M** High God.
	8:11	to the **m** important will all
	9:3	tent called the **m** holy place.
	9:8	way into the **m** holy place was
	9:12	He went into the **m** holy place
Jas	1:18	us his **m** important creatures.
Jud	1:20	use your **m** holy faith to grow.

moth (4)

Job	4:19	be crushed quicker than a **m**!
	27:18	He builds his house like a **m**,
Psa	39:11	Like a **m** you eat away at what
Hos	5:12	as a **m** destroys clothing.

moth-eaten (1)

Job	13:28	wineskins, like **m** clothes.

mother (266)

Gen	2:24	man will leave his father and **m**
	3:20	because she became the **m**
	17:16	will become ⌊a **m** of⌋ nations,
	21:21	and his **m** got him a wife from
	24:53	presents to her brother and **m**.
	24:55	Her brother and **m** replied,
	24:60	become the **m** of many
	24:67	took her into his **m** Sarah's tent.
	27:11	Jacob said to his **m** Rebekah,
	27:13	His **m** responded, "Let any
	27:14	and brought them to his **m**.
	27:29	and may the sons of your **m**
	28:5	She was the **m** of Jacob and
	28:7	had obeyed his father and **m**
	30:14	He brought them to his **m** Leah.
	37:10	Will your **m** and I and your
Exo	2:8	the girl brought the baby's **m**.
	20:12	"Honor your father and your **m**,
	21:15	"Whoever hits his father or **m**
	21:17	curses his father or **m** must
Lev	18:7	sexual intercourse with your **m**.
	18:7	She is your own **m**.
	19:3	"Respect your **m** and father.
	20:9	curses his father or **m** must
	20:9	He has cursed his father or **m**
	20:14	marries a woman and her **m**,
	21:2	These relatives include your **m**,
	21:11	even for his father or **m**.
	22:27	it must stay with its **m** for
	24:10	A man, whose **m** was
Num	6:7	Even if their own father, **m**,
	11:12	Am I their **m**? Did I give birth to
Dtr	5:16	"Honor your father and your **m**
	21:13	⌊the loss of⌋ her father and **m**
	21:19	His father and **m** must take him
	22:6	If the **m** bird is sitting on the
	22:7	but make sure you let the **m** go.
	22:15	The girl's father and **m** must go
	27:16	his father or **m** will himself
	33:9	didn't know their father and **m**.
Jos	2:13	that you'll protect my father, **m**,
	2:18	Also, gather your father, **m**,
	6:23	Rahab, her father, **m**, brothers,
Jdg	5:7	took a stand as a **m** of Israel.
	5:28	Sisera's **m** looked through her
	11:1	His **m** was a prostitute.
	14:2	and told his father and **m**,
	14:3	His father and **m** asked him,
	14:4	His father and **m** didn't know
	14:5	his father and **m** to Timnah.
	14:9	he came to his father and **m**,
	14:16	even told my father and **m**,
	17:2	He told his **m**, "You were upset
	17:2	His **m** said, "The LORD bless
	17:3	pieces of silver back to his **m**.
	17:3	Then his **m** said, "I dedicate
	17:4	returned the silver to his **m**,
Rut	2:11	how you left your father and **m**
1Sm	2:5	but the **m** of many children
	2:19	His **m** would make him a robe
1Sm	15:33	so your **m** will be made
	22:3	"Please let my father and **m**
2Sm	3:3	whose **m** was Maacah (the
	3:4	whose **m** was Haggith.
	3:4	whose **m** was Abital.
	17:25	His **m** was Abigail,
	17:25	and sister of Joab's **m** Zeruiah.)
	19:37	the grave of my father and **m**.
	20:19	Are you trying to destroy a **m**
1Ki	1:5	His **m** gave birth to him after
	1:11	asked Solomon's **m** Bathsheba,
	2:13	to Bathsheba, Solomon's **m**.
	2:19	had a throne brought for his **m**,
	2:20	"Ask, **M**," the king told her.
	3:27	Don't kill him. She is his **m**."
	11:26	His **m** Zeruah was a widow.
	14:21	Rehoboam's **m** was an
	14:31	(His **m** was an Ammonite
	15:2	His **m** was named Maacah,
	15:13	from the position of queen **m**
	17:23	and gave him to his **m**.
	19:20	kiss my father and **m** goodbye.
	22:52	the example of his father and **m**
2Ki	3:2	what his father or **m** had done.
	4:19	"Carry him to his **m**."
	4:20	up and brought him to his **m**.
	4:30	The boy's **m** said, "I solemnly
	8:5	the **m** ⌊came to⌋ make an
	8:26	His **m** was Athaliah,
	9:22	your **m** continues her idolatry
	10:13	of the king and the queen **m**."
	11:1	When Ahaziah's **m**,
	12:1	His **m** was Zibiah from
	14:2	His **m** was Jehoaddin from
	15:2	His **m** was Jecoliah from
	15:33	His **m** was Jerusha,
	18:2	His **m** was Abi, daughter of
	21:19	His **m** was Meshullemeth,
	22:1	His **m** was Jedidah,
	23:31	His **m** was Hamutal,
	23:36	His **m** was Zebidah,
	24:8	His **m** was Nehushta,
	24:12	King Jehoiakin of Judah, his **m**,
	24:15	He also took the king's **m**,
	24:18	His **m** was Hamutal,
1Ch	2:17	Abigail was the **m** of Amasa,
	2:26	and she was the **m** of Onam.
	2:46	was the **m** of Haran,
	2:48	was the **m** of Sheber and
	2:49	she was the **m** of Shaaph,
	3:2	whose **m** was Haggith.
	3:5	and Solomon (the **m** of these
	4:9	His **m** had named him Jabez
	4:18	wife was the **m** of Jered,
	7:14	Their **m** was Manasseh's
2Ch	12:13	(Rehoboam's **m** was an
	13:2	His **m** was named Micaiah,
	15:16	from the position of queen **m**
	22:2	His **m** was Athaliah,
	22:3	because his **m** gave him
	22:10	When Ahaziah's **m**,
	24:1	His **m** was Zibiah from
	25:1	His **m** was Jehoaddan from
	26:3	His **m** was Jecoliah from
	27:1	His **m** was Jerushah,
	29:1	His **m** was Abijah,
Est	2:7	When her father and **m** died,
Job	1:21	"Naked I came from my **m**,
	17:14	'You are my **m** and sister,'
Psa	27:10	if my father and **m** abandon me,
	35:14	as if I were mourning for my **m**.
	51:5	when my **m** conceived me.
	113:9	in a childless home a joyful **m**.
	139:13	me together inside my **m**.
Pro	4:3	tender and only child of my **m**,
	6:20	the teachings of your **m**.
	10:1	son brings grief to his **m**.
	15:20	a foolish child despises its **m**.
	17:25	father and bitter grief to his **m**.
	19:26	away his **m** brings shame
	20:20	curses his father and **m** will
	23:22	and do not despise your **m**
	23:25	your father and your **m** be glad.
	28:24	his father or his **m** and says,
	29:15	child disgraces his **m**.
	30:11	and does not bless his **m**.
Pro	30:17	and hates to obey a **m** will
	31:1	by his **m** to discipline him.
Sos	3:11	the crown his **m** placed on him
	6:9	Her **m** thinks she is unique.
	8:5	There your **m** went into labor
Isa	45:10	or to his **m**, "Why did you go
	50:1	I got rid of your **m** because of
	66:9	"Do I bring a **m** to the moment
	66:9	"Do I cause a **m** to deliver and
	66:13	As a **m** comforts her child,
Jer	2:27	You call stone your **m**.
	13:18	Say to the king and his **m**,
	15:9	A **m** who gives birth to seven
	15:10	Why did my **m** give birth to me?
	20:14	the day that my **m** gave birth to
	20:17	Then my **m** would have been
	22:26	I will throw you and your **m**
	29:2	after King Jehoiakin and his **m**,
	50:12	But your **m** will be greatly
Eze	16:3	and your **m** was a Hittite.
	16:44	you: Like **m**, like daughter.
	16:45	Your **m** was a Hittite,
	19:2	Your **m** was like a lioness.
	19:10	Your **m** was like a grapevine
	23:2	daughters of the same **m**.
	44:25	**m**, son, daughter, brother,
Hos	2:2	"Plead with your **m**;
	2:5	Their **m** acted like a prostitute.
	4:5	So I will destroy your **m**.
Mic	5:3	Israel until the time a **m** has
	7:6	daughter rebels against her **m**.
Zec	13:3	his father and his **m**,
	13:3	Then his father and his **m**,
Mat	1:3	Tamar were the father and **m**
	1:5	were the father and **m** of Boaz.
	1:5	were the father and **m** of Obed.
	1:6	the father and **m** of Solomon.
	1:16	Mary was the **m** of Jesus,
	1:18	His **m** Mary had been promised
	2:11	saw the child with his **m** Mary.
	2:13	take the child and his **m**,
	2:14	took the child and his **m**,
	2:20	take the child and his **m**,
	2:21	took the child and his **m**,
	10:35	a daughter against her **m**,
	10:37	his father or **m** more than me
	12:46	his **m** and brothers were
	12:47	Someone told him, "Your **m**
	12:48	to him, "Who is my **m**,
	12:49	here are my **m** and my brothers
	12:50	is my brother and sister and **m**."
	14:8	Urged by her **m**, she said,
	14:11	who took it to her **m**.
	15:4	**m**' and 'Whoever curses father
	15:4	curses father or **m** must
	15:5	whoever tells his father or **m**,
	19:5	man will leave his father and **m**
	19:19	Honor your father and **m**.
	19:29	or sisters, father, **m**, children,
	20:20	Then the **m** of Zebedee's sons
	27:56	Mary (the **m** of James and
	27:56	and the **m** of Zebedee's sons.
Mar	3:31	Then his **m** and his brothers
	3:32	"Your **m** and your brothers are
	3:33	replied to them, "Who is my **m**,
	3:34	here are my **m** and my brothers
	3:35	is my brother and sister and **m**."
	5:40	he took the child's father, **m**,
	6:24	she went out and asked her **m**,
	6:24	Her **m** said, "Ask for the head
	6:28	and the girl gave it to her **m**.
	7:10	**m**' and 'Whoever curses father
	7:10	curses father or **m** must
	7:11	'If a person tells his father or **m**
	7:12	do anything for his father or **m**.'
	10:7	man will leave his father and **m**
	10:19	Honor your father and **m**."
	10:29	sisters, **m**, father, children,
	15:40	Mary (the **m** of young James
	15:47	from Magdala and Mary (the **m**
	16:1	Mary (the **m** of James),
Luk	1:43	I feel blessed that the **m** of my
	1:60	But his **m** spoke up,
	2:21	before his **m** became pregnant.
	2:22	to make a **m** clean had passed,
	2:33	Jesus' father and **m** were

Luk 2:34 them and said to Mary, his **m**,
2:48 His **m** asked him, "Son,
2:51 His **m** treasured all these
7:15 Jesus gave him back to his **m**.
8:19 His **m** and his brothers came to
8:20 Someone told Jesus, "Your **m**
8:21 He answered them, "My **m** and
11:27 "How blessed is the **m** who
12:53 A **m** will be against her
12:53 and a daughter against her **m**.
18:20 Honor your father and your **m**."
24:10 and Mary (the **m** of James).
Jon 2:1 Jesus' **m** was there.
2:3 Jesus' **m** said to him,
2:5 His **m** told the servers,
2:12 After this, Jesus, his **m**,
3:4 He can't go back inside his **m**
6:42 we know his father and **m**?
19:25 Jesus' **m**, her sister, Mary (the
19:26 Jesus saw his **m** and the
19:26 He said to his **m**, "Look,
19:27 disciple, "Look, here's your **m**!"
Act 1:14 Mary (the **m** of Jesus),
12:12 the **m** of John Mark.
16:1 Timothy's **m** was a Jewish
Rom 16:13 Christian, and his **m**,
16:13 who has been a **m** to me too.
Gal 4:26 above is free, and she is our **m**.
Eph 5:31 man will leave his father and **m**
6:2 "Honor your father and **m**
1Th 2:7 like a **m** taking care of her
2Ti 1:5 Lois and your **m** Eunice.
Heb 7:3 father, **m**, or ancestors.
Rev 17:5 the **M** of Prostitutes and

mother-in-law (17)

Dtr 27:23 intercourse with his **m** will
Rut 1:14 Orpah kissed her **m** goodbye,
2:11 for your **m** after your husband
2:18 and her **m** saw what she had
2:19 Her **m** asked her, "Where did
2:19 So Ruth told her **m** about the
2:23 continued to live with her **m**.
3:1 Naomi, Ruth's **m**, said to her,
3:6 as her **m** had directed her.
3:16 her **m** Naomi asked,
Mic 7:6 rebels against her **m**.
Mat 8:14 he saw Peter's **m** in bed with a
10:35 daughter-in-law against her **m**.
Mar 1:30 Simon's **m** was in bed with a
Luk 4:38 Simon's **m** was sick with a
12:53 A **m** will be against her
12:53 daughter-in-law against her **m**."

mother's (45)

Gen 20:12 father's daughter but not my **m**.
24:28 **m** household about these things.
24:67 comforted after his **m** death
28:2 your **m** father, and get yourself
43:29 brother Benjamin, his **m** son.
44:20 the only one of his **m** sons left,
Exo 23:19 cook a young goat in its **m** milk
34:26 a young goat in its **m** milk.
Lev 18:9 daughter or your **m** daughter.
18:13 intercourse with your **m** sister.
20:17 daughter or his **m** daughter,
20:19 intercourse with your **m** sister
Dtr 14:21 cook a young goat in its **m** milk
27:22 or his **m** daughter will be
Jdg 8:19 were my brothers, my **m** sons.
9:1 to see the uncles on his **m** side
9:1 them and his **m** whole family.
Rut 1:8 go back to your **m** home.
1Sm 20:30 act as if you are your **m** son
1Ki 22:42 His **m** name was Azubah,
2Ki 3:13 prophets or your **m** prophets."
21:1 His **m** name was Hephzibah.
2Ch 20:31 His **m** name was Azubah,
Job 31:15 me in my **m** belly make them?
Psa 22:9 me feel safe at my **m** breasts
22:10 From my **m** womb you have
50:20 You slander your own **m** son
69:8 a foreigner to my **m** sons
71:6 You took me from my **m** womb.
109:14 and not wipe out his **m** sin
131:2 child is content in its **m** arms
Pro 1:8 not neglect your **m** teachings,
Ecc 5:15 from their **m** womb naked.
11:5 its **m** womb, you also don't
Sos 3:4 him into my **m** house, into
8:1 who nursed at my **m** breasts.
8:2 bring you into my **m** house.
Isa 28:9 taken from their **m** breasts
49:1 While I was in my **m** womb, he
50:1 are your **m** divorce papers?
Jer 52:1 His **m** name was Hamutal,
Eze 16:45 You are your **m** daughter.
Hos 12:3 of them were in their **m** womb.
13:13 won't come out of its **m** womb
Mat 13:55 Isn't his **m** name Mary?

mothers (15)

Gen 32:11 me and the **m** and children too.
Exo 22:30 stay with their **m** seven days,
Isa 49:15 Although **m** may forget,
Jer 15:8 send a destroyer against the **m**
16:3 in this place and about the **m**
16:7 have lost their fathers or **m**.
Lam 2:12 They're asking their **m** for some
4:10 The hands of loving **m** cooked
5:3 Our **m** are like widows.
Eze 22:7 in you hate their fathers and **m**.
Hos 10:14 **M** and their children were
Mar 10:30 sisters, **m**, children and fields,
Luk 14:26 **m**, wives, children, brothers,
1Ti 1:9 fathers, their **m**, or other people
5:2 women as if they were your **m**,

mothers' (1)

Lam 2:12 dwindle away in their **m** arms

moths (6)

Isa 50:9 a garment. **M** will eat them.
51:8 **M** will eat them like clothing.
Mat 6:19 where **m** and rust destroy and
6:20 where **m** and rust don't destroy
Luk 12:33 In heaven thieves and **m** can't
Jas 5:2 clothes have been eaten by **m**.

motioned (8)

Luk 1:22 He **m** to them but remained
1:62 So they **m** to the baby's father
Jon 13:24 Simon Peter **m** to that disciple
Act 12:17 Peter **m** with his hand to quiet
13:16 up, **m** with his hand, and said,
19:33 Alexander **m** with his hand to
21:40 the stairs of the barracks and **m**
24:10 The governor **m** for Paul to

motive (2)

Pro 7:10 with an ulterior **m** meets him.
20:5 A **m** in the human heart is like

motives (18)

Psa 7:10 those whose **m** are decent.
11:2 at people whose **m** are decent.
32:11 all whose **m** are decent.
36:10 to those whose **m** are decent.
64:10 Everyone whose **m** are decent
94:15 and everyone whose **m** are
97:11 for those whose **m** are decent.
125:4 to those whose **m** are decent.
Pro 16:2 but the LORD weighs **m**.
Jer 11:20 fairly and test **m** and thoughts.
20:12 He sees their **m** and thoughts.
Jon 7:18 and doesn't have dishonest **m**.
1Co 4:5 the dark and reveal people's **m**.
2Co 10:2 are only guided by human **m**.
12:18 Didn't we have the same **m**
Php 1:18 with honest or dishonest **m**,
Col 3:22 Be sincere in your **m** out of
1Th 2:4 but God, who tests our **m**.

mound (2)

Dtr 13:16 It must remain a **m** of ruins and
Jos 8:28 made it a deserted **m** of ruins.

mounds (3)

Jos 11:13 did not burn cities built on **m**.
Isa 29:3 I will put up **m** of dirt around
Jer 6:6 Build up dirt **m** to attack

mount (179)

Exo 17:6 you there by a rock at **M** Horeb.
19:11 come down on **M** Sinai as all
19:18 All of **M** Sinai was covered
19:20 came down on top of **M** Sinai
19:23 people can't come up **M** Sinai,
24:16 of the LORD settled on **M** Sinai.
28:11 **M** them in gold settings,
28:20 **M** them in gold settings.
31:18 speaking to Moses on **M** Sinai.
33:6 After they left **M** Horeb,
34:2 Then come up on **M** Sinai,
34:4 morning he went up on **M** Sinai,
34:29 came down from **M** Sinai,
34:32 the LORD told him on **M** Sinai.
Lev 7:38 On **M** Sinai the LORD gave
25:1 spoke to Moses on **M** Sinai,
26:46 through Moses on **M** Sinai.
27:34 LORD gave Moses on **M** Sinai
Num 3:1 spoke to Moses on **M** Sinai.
20:22 left Kadesh and came to **M** Hor.
20:23 At **M** Hor, near the border of
20:25 his son Eleazar up on **M** Hor.
20:27 saw them go up on **M** Hor.
21:4 Then they moved from **M** Hor,
21:20 **M** Pisgah overlooks Jeshimon.
23:14 of Zophim on top of **M** Pisgah,
23:28 Balaam to the top of **M** Peor,
28:6 was established on **M** Sinai.
33:23 and set up camp at **M** Shepher.
33:24 They moved from **M** Shepher
33:37 and set up camp at **M** Hor
33:38 priest Aaron went up on **M** Hor.
33:39 old when he died on **M** Hor.
33:41 They moved from **M** Hor and
34:7 Mediterranean Sea to **M** Hor,
34:8 and from **M** Hor to the border of
Dtr 1:2 (It takes 11 days to go from **M**
1:2 Barnea by way of **M** Seir.)
1:6 At **M** Horeb the LORD our God
1:19 So we left **M** Horeb,
2:1 around the region of **M** Seir.
2:5 the region of **M** Seir as their
3:8 from the Arnon Valley to **M**
3:9 (The Sidonians call **M** Hermon
3:17 which is near **M** Pisgah on the
3:27 Go to the top of **M** Pisgah,
4:10 the LORD your God at **M** Horeb.
4:15 to you from the fire at **M** Horeb.
4:48 Valley to **M** Siyon (that is,
4:48 Siyon (that is, **M** Hermon).
4:49 foot of the slopes of **M** Pisgah.
5:2 a promise to us at **M** Horeb.
9:8 Even at **M** Horeb you made the
11:29 recite the blessing from **M**
11:29 and the curse from **M** Ebal.
18:16 of the assembly at **M** Horeb.
27:4 set up these stones on **M** Ebal,
27:12 that will stand on **M** Gerizim
27:13 tribes that will stand on **M** Ebal
29:1 LORD gave them at **M** Horeb.
32:49 to **M** Nebo in Moab,
32:50 your brother Aaron died on **M**
33:2 like sunshine from **M** Paran.
34:1 Then Moses went up on **M**
Jos 8:30 Joshua built an altar on **M** Ebal
8:33 were in front of **M** Gerizim
8:33 the other half in front of **M** Ebal.
11:3 the foot of **M** Hermon in Mizpah
11:17 The land extended from **M**
11:17 Valley at the foot of **M** Hermon.
12:1 the Arnon Valley to **M** Hermon,
12:5 He ruled **M** Hermon,
12:7 to **M** Halak which rises
13:5 Gad at the foot of **M** Hermon
13:11 and Maacath, all of **M** Hermon,
15:9 it goes to the cities of **M** Ephron
15:10 the border turns west to **M** Seir
15:10 slope of **M** Jearim (now called
15:11 to Shikkeron, on to **M** Baalah,
24:30 of Ephraim north of **M** Gaash.
Jdg 2:9 of Ephraim north of **M** Gaash.
3:3 and the Hivites who lived on **M**
3:3 Lebanon from **M** Baal Hermon
4:6 'Gather troops on **M** Tabor.

Jdg 4:12 had come to fight at **M** Tabor.
4:14 So Barak came down from **M**
7:3 should leave **M** Gilead
9:7 to a high spot on **M** Gerizim.
9:48 all his men went to **M** Zalmon.
1Sm 31:1 killed in battle on **M** Gilboa.
31:8 three sons lying on **M** Gilboa.
2Sm 1:6 "I happened to be on **M** Gilboa.
15:30 as he went up the **M** of Olives.
15:32 David came to the top ⌊of the **M**
16:1 the top ⌊of the **M** of Olives⌋,
1Ki 18:19 gather around me on **M** Carmel.
18:20 prophets together on **M** Carmel
18:43 go back to ⌊**M** Carmel⌋.
2Ki 2:25 went to **M** Carmel,
4:25 to the man of God at **M** Carmel.
19:31 escape will go out of **M** Zion.
1Ch 4:42 male descendants to **M** Seir.
5:23 Hermon, Senir, and **M** Hermon.
10:1 killed in battle on **M** Gilboa.
10:8 his sons lying on **M** Gilboa.
2Ch 3:1 in Jerusalem on **M** Moriah,
13:4 Then Abijah stood on **M**
20:10 and the people of **M** Seir have
20:22 and the people of **M** Seir who
20:23 attacked the people from **M** Seir
Neh 9:13 You came from heaven to **M**
11:21 servants lived on **M** Ophel
Psa 29:6 like a calf and **M** Sirion like
42:6 peaks of Hermon, on **M** Mizar.
48:2 **M** Zion is on the northern ridge.
48:5 ⌊When⌋ they saw ⌊**M** Zion⌋,
48:11 Let **M** Zion be glad and the
68:14 snow falling on **M** Zalmon."
74:2 This tribe is **M** Zion,
78:68 **M** Zion which he loved.
89:12 **M** Tabor and Mount Hermon
89:12 Mount Tabor and **M** Hermon
106:19 At **M** Horeb they made ⌊a
125:1 trust the LORD are like **M** Zion,
133:3 It is like dew on ⌊**M**⌋ Hermon,
Sos 4:1 goats moving down **M** Gilead.
4:8 me from the peak of **M** Amana,
7:5 your head as high as **M** Carmel.
Isa 4:5 over the whole area of **M** Zion
8:18 who lives on **M** Zion.
10:12 finished all his work on **M** Zion
16:1 desert to my people at **M** Zion.
18:7 They will be brought to **M** Zion,
24:23 of Armies will rule on **M** Zion
28:21 rise as he did on **M** Perazim.
29:8 that fight against **M** Zion.
31:4 will come to fight for **M** Zion
37:32 escape will go out from **M** Zion.
Jer 31:12 shout for joy on top of **M** Zion.
46:4 **M** up, you horsemen.
46:18 "someone who is like **M** Tabor
46:18 Someone who is like **M** Carmel
50:19 They will eat on **M** Carmel and
50:19 Mount Carmel and **M** Bashan.
Lam 5:18 Foxes roam around on **M** Zion,
Eze 27:5 from pine trees on **M** Hermon.
35:2 "Son of man, turn to **M** Seir,
35:3 says: I'm against you, **M** Seir.
35:7 I will turn **M** Seir into a barren
35:15 **M** Seir, and so will all of Edom.
Hos 5:1 spread out nets on **M** Tabor.
Joe 2:32 who escape will be on **M** Zion
Amo 1:2 and the top of ⌊**M**⌋ Carmel is
4:1 who live on **M** Samaria.
9:3 if they hide on top of **M** Carmel,
Oba 1:17 refugees will live on **M** Zion.
1:21 will come from **M** Zion
Mic 4:7 The LORD will rule them on **M**
Hab 3:3 Holy One comes from **M** Paran.
Zec 14:4 will stand on the **M** of Olives,
14:4 The **M** of Olives will be split in
Mat 21:1 Bethphage on the **M** of Olives,
24:3 was sitting on the **M** of Olives,
26:30 they went to the **M** of Olives.
Mar 11:1 at the **M** of Olives,
13:3 As Jesus was sitting on the **M**
14:26 they went to the **M** of Olives.
Luk 19:29 and Bethany at the **M**
19:37 went down the **M** of Olives.
21:37 at night he would go to the **M**
Luk 22:39 went out ⌊of the city⌋ to the **M**
Jon 8:1 Jesus went to the **M** of Olives.
Act 1:12 called the **M** of Olives.
7:30 bush in the desert of **M** Sinai.
7:38 to him on **M** Sinai were there
Gal 4:24 arrangement made on **M** Sinai.
4:25 Hagar is **M** Sinai in Arabia.
Heb 12:22 you have come to **M** Zion,
Rev 14:1 lamb was standing on **M** Zion.

mountain (222)

Gen 22:14 It is still said today, "On the **m**
31:54 offered a sacrifice on the **m**.
31:54 and spent the night on the **m**.
48:22 I'm giving you one more **m**
Exo 3:1 came to Horeb, the **m** of God.
3:12 will worship God on this **m**."
4:27 met Moses at the **m** of God,
15:17 and plant them on your own **m**,
18:5 camped near the **m** of God.
19:2 up camp there in front of the **m**.
19:3 Moses went up the **m** to God,
19:3 LORD called to him from the **m**,
19:4 and brought you to my **m**.
19:12 off a boundary around the **m**
19:12 and tell them not to go up the **m**
19:12 Those who touch the **m** must
19:13 The people may go up the **m**
19:14 After Moses went down the **m**
19:16 with a heavy cloud over the **m**,
19:17 they stood at the foot of the **m**.
19:18 Smoke rose from the **m** like the
19:18 the whole **m** shook violently.
19:20 Moses to the top of the **m**.
19:23 off a boundary around the **m**
20:18 horn and saw the **m** covered
24:1 Israel's leaders come up the **m**
24:4 built an altar at the foot of the **m**
24:12 "Come up to me on the **m**.
24:13 went up on the **m** of God.
24:15 So Moses went up on the **m**,
24:17 a raging fire on top of the **m**.
24:18 the cloud as he went up the **m**.
24:18 He stayed on the **m** 40 days
25:40 you were shown on the **m**."
26:30 you were shown on the **m**.
27:8 as you were shown on the **m**.
32:1 coming down from the **m**,
32:15 and went down the **m** carrying
32:19 them at the foot of the **m**.
32:30 Now I will go up the **m** to the
34:2 presence on the top of the **m**.
34:3 be seen anywhere on the **m**.
34:3 not graze in front of this **m**."
Num 10:33 So they left the **m** of the LORD
13:17 and then into the **m** region.
13:29 Amorites live in the **m** region.
14:40 they headed into the **m** region.
14:44 into the **m** region anyway,
20:28 died there on top of the **m**.
20:28 Eleazar came down from the **m**.
Dtr 1:6 stayed at this **m** long enough.
1:7 Go to the **m** region of the
1:19 saw on the way to the **m** region
1:20 "We have come to the **m** region
1:41 easily invade the **m** region.
1:43 and invaded the **m** region.
3:12 Valley and half of the **m** region
4:11 and stood at the foot of the **m**,
5:4 to face from the fire on the **m**.
5:5 fire and didn't go up on the **m**.
5:22 your whole assembly on the **m**.
5:23 and saw the **m** blazing
9:9 When I went up on the **m** to get
9:9 I stayed on the **m** 40 days and
9:10 to you from the fire on the **m**
9:15 and went down the **m** while
9:21 river that flowed down the **m**.
10:1 and come up to me on the **m**.
10:3 the two tablets up the **m**.
10:4 to you from the fire on the **m**
10:5 I came back down the **m** and
10:10 I stayed on the **m** 40 days and
14:5 wild goats, **m** goats, antelope,
14:5 goats, antelope, and **m** sheep.
32:50 On this **m** where you're going,
Dtr 33:12 lives on the **m** slopes."
33:19 will invite nations to their **m**,
Jos 13:19 Shahar on the **m** in the valley,
14:12 Now give me this **m** region
15:8 It then goes to the top of the **m**
15:9 From the top of that **m** the
17:11 The last three are on **m** ridges.
17:18 The **m** region will be yours as
18:14 south of the **m** that faces Beth
18:16 the foot of the **m** that overlooks
Jdg 6:2 and **m** strongholds ⌊to protect
7:24 to the whole **m** region
17:1 from the **m** region of Ephraim.
19:16 He was from the **m** region of
1Sm 14:4 of the **m** pass where Jonathan
23:25 So he went to his **m** stronghold
23:26 Saul went on one side of the **m**,
23:26 went on the other side of the **m**.
23:26 around ⌊the **m**⌋ toward David
25:20 a hidden **m** path when she
2Sm 13:34 road beside the **m** west of him.
21:9 who executed them on the **m**
1Ki 19:8 came to Horeb, the **m** of God.
19:11 in front of the LORD on the **m**."
2Ki 4:27 to the man of God at the **m**,
6:17 The **m** around Elisha was full
2Ch 33:15 LORD's **m** and in Jerusalem.
Job 14:18 As surely as a **m** falls and
39:1 when the **m** goats give birth?
Psa 2:6 own king on Zion, my holy **m**."
3:4 answers me from his holy **m**.
11:1 "Flee to your **m** like a bird?
15:1 Who may live on your holy **m**?
24:3 Who may go up the LORD's **m**?
30:7 have made my **m** stand firm.
43:3 them bring me to your holy **m**
48:1 His holy **m** is in the city of our
68:15 The **m** of Bashan is the
68:15 of Bashan is the **m** of God.
68:15 The **m** of Bashan is the
68:15 is the **m** with many peaks.
68:16 at the **m** where God has
72:16 ⌊in the breeze⌋ on the **m** tops,
78:54 to this **m** that his power had
95:4 and the **m** peaks are his.
99:9 Bow at his holy **m**.
Sos 4:6 I will go to the **m** of myrrh and
4:8 from the **m** peaks in Senir and
Isa 2:2 In the last days the **m** of the
2:3 "Let's go to the **m** of the LORD,
10:29 They go through the **m** pass
10:32 They shake their fist at the **m**
10:32 at the **m** of Jerusalem.
11:9 anywhere on my holy **m**.
14:13 I'll sit on the **m** far away in the
15:5 They go up the **m** road to
25:6 On this **m** the LORD of Armies
25:7 On this **m** he will remove the
25:10 power will be on this **m**.
27:13 on the holy **m** in Jerusalem.
30:17 like a flagpole on top of a **m**,
30:25 and streams on every lofty **m**
30:29 on the way to the LORD's **m**,
40:4 Every **m** and hill will be
40:9 Go up a high **m**, Zion. Tell the
56:7 I will bring them to my holy **m**
57:7 your bed on a high and lofty **m**.
57:13 the land and inherit my holy **m**.
65:11 LORD and forgotten my holy **m**.
65:25 on my holy **m**," says the LORD.
66:20 and camels to my holy **m**,
Jer 3:6 She went up every high **m** and
16:16 will hunt for them on every **m**
18:14 The cool **m** streams never dry
26:18 and the temple **m** will become
31:23 of righteousness, holy **m**."
51:25 you destructive **m**.
51:25 and make you a scorched **m**.
Eze 11:23 and stopped above the **m** east
17:22 plant it on a high and lofty **m**.
17:23 plant it on a high **m** in Israel.
18:6 He doesn't eat at the illegal **m**
18:11 at the illegal **m** worship sites.
18:15 He doesn't eat at the illegal **m**
20:40 will worship me on my holy **m**,
20:40 the high **m** of Israel,

Eze 28:14 You were on God's holy **m**.
28:16 down from God's **m** in disgrace.
40:2 set me down on a very high **m**.
40:2 On the south side of the **m**
43:12 the top of the **m** is most holy.
Dan 2:35 became a large **m** which filled
2:45 that you saw cut out from a **m**,
9:16 city, Jerusalem, your holy **m**.
9:20 request about my God's holy **m**
11:45 the seas at a beautiful holy **m**.
Joe 2:1 Sound the alarm on my holy **m**.
3:17 I live on my holy **m**,
Amo 6:1 secure on the **m** of Samaria,
Oba 1:8 Esau's **m**," declares the LORD.
1:9 Esau's **m** will be slaughtered.
1:16 drank on my holy **m**,
1:19 take possession of Esau's **m**.
1:21 Mount Zion to rule Esau's **m**.
Mic 3:12 and the temple **m** will become
4:1 In the last days the **m** of the
4:2 "Let's go to the **m** of the LORD,
7:12 and from **m** to mountain.
7:12 and from mountain to **m**.
Zep 3:11 you act proud on my holy **m**.
Zec 4:7 What a high **m** you are!
8:3 The **m** of the LORD of Armies
8:3 will be called the holy **m**.
14:4 Half of the **m** will move toward
Mat 4:8 devil took him to a very high **m**
5:1 he went up a **m** and sat down.
8:1 Jesus came down from the **m**,
14:23 he went up a **m** to pray by
15:29 he went up a **m** and sat there.
17:1 up a high **m** where they could
17:9 On their way down the **m**,
17:20 you can say to this **m**,
21:21 You could also say to this **m**,
28:16 eleven disciples went to the **m**
Mar 3:13 Jesus went up a **m**,
6:46 he went up a **m** to pray.
9:2 up a high **m** where they could
9:9 On their way down the **m**,
11:23 He can say to this **m**,
Luk 1:39 a city in the **m** region of Judah.
1:65 Throughout the **m** region of
3:5 Every **m** and hill will be
6:12 time Jesus went to a **m** to pray.
6:17 Jesus came down from the **m**
9:28 him and went up a **m** to pray.
9:37 had come down from the **m**,
Jon 4:20 ancestors worshiped on this **m**.
4:21 on this **m** or in Jerusalem.
6:3 Jesus went up a **m** and sat
6:15 he returned to the **m** by himself
Act 1:12 to Jerusalem from the **m** called
Heb 8:5 plan I showed you on the **m**."
12:20 even an animal touches the **m**,
2Pe 1:18 were with him on the holy **m**.
Rev 6:14 Every **m** and island was
8:8 something like a huge **m**
21:10 power away to a large, high **m**.

mountains (233)

Gen 7:19 It covered all the high **m**
8:4 came to rest in the **m** of Ararat.
8:5 the tops of the **m** appeared.
10:30 toward Sephar in the eastern **m**.
19:30 in the **m** where they lived
22:2 offering on one of the **m** that
31:21 went toward the **m** of Gilead.
31:23 up with him in the **m** of Gilead.
31:25 had put up his tents in the **m**.
31:25 their tents in the **m** of Gilead.
36:8 lived in the **m** of Seir.
36:9 of Edom in the **m** of Seir.
49:26 the blessings of the oldest **m**
Exo 32:12 all along to kill them in the **m**
Num 14:45 there came down from those **m**,
23:7 me from the eastern **m**.
27:12 "Go up into the Abarim **M**,
33:47 in the Abarim **M** east of Nebo.
33:48 They moved from the Abarim **M**
Dtr 1:7 plains, in the **m**, in the foothills,
1:24 They left and went into the **m**.
2:37 or capture the cities in the **m**.
3:25 those beautiful **m** in Lebanon."
Dtr 11:30 (These **m** are on the west side
12:2 worship sites on the high **m**,
32:22 the foundations of the **m** on fire.
32:49 "Go into the Abarim **M**,
33:15 finest fruits from the oldest **m**,
Jos 2:16 She told them, "Go to the **m** so
2:22 The men went to the **m** and
2:23 spies came down out of the **m**,
9:2 (They were the kings in the **m**,
10:6 in the **m** have united against
10:40 the whole land — the **m**,
11:2 to the northern kings in the **m**,
11:3 the Jebusites in the **m**,
11:16 took all this land, the **m**,
11:16 and the **m** and foothills of
11:21 out the people of Anak in the **m**,
12:8 It included the **m**, foothills,
13:6 lives in the **m** from Lebanon
15:48 In the **m** they gave Judah 11
16:1 and through the **m** to Bethel.
17:15 and Rephaim if the **m**
17:16 "The **m** are not enough for us
18:12 west through the **m**,
18:13 Ataroth Addar over the **m** south
19:50 Serah in the **m** of Ephraim.
20:7 in Galilee in the **m** of Naphtali,
20:7 Shechem in the **m** of Ephraim,
20:7 (now called Hebron) in the **m**
21:11 located in the **m** of Judah.
21:21 murderers) in the **m** of Ephraim
24:4 I gave Esau the **m** in Seir as
24:30 land at Timnath Serah in the **m**
24:33 Phinehas in the **m** of Ephraim.
Jdg 1:9 Canaanites who lived in the **m**,
1:19 to take possession of the **m**.
1:34 the tribe of Dan into the **m**
2:9 This was in the **m** of Ephraim
3:27 he blew a ram's horn in the **m**
3:27 down from the **m** with him,
4:5 and Bethel in the **m** of Ephraim.
5:5 and the **m** shook in the
6:2 made hiding places in the **m**,
9:25 for Abimelech on top of the **m**.
9:36 "The shadows of the **m** look
10:1 in Shamir in the **m** of Ephraim.
11:37 friends and me to walk in the **m**
11:38 and her friends went to the **m**,
12:15 in the **m** of Amalek.
17:8 came to Micah's house in the **m**
18:2 house in the **m** of Ephraim.
18:13 there they marched to the **m**
19:1 area in the **m** of Ephraim.
19:18 area in the **m** of Ephraim.
1Sm 1:1 Zophim in the **m** of Ephraim.
9:4 They went through the **m** of
13:2 and in the **m** of Bethel,
14:22 who had been hiding in the **m**
23:14 lived in fortified camps in the **m**
2Sm 1:21 You **m** in Gilboa, may there be
20:21 A man from the **m** of Ephraim
1Ki 5:15 who quarried stone in the **m**,
19:11 a fierce wind tore **m** and
2Ki 19:23 chariots I'll ride up the high **m**,
2Ch 2:2 to quarry stones in the **m**,
2:18 of them quarry stone in the **m**,
13:4 Zemaraim in the **m** of Ephraim.
15:8 captured in the **m** of Ephraim.
19:4 and the **m** of Ephraim.
26:10 and vineyard workers in the **m**
Neh 8:15 and Jerusalem: "Go to the **m**,
Job 9:5 He moves **m** without their
24:8 by the rainstorms in the **m**.
28:9 and overturn **m** at their base.
39:8 It explores the **m** for its pasture
Psa 18:7 foundations of the **m** trembled.
36:6 is like the **m** of God,
46:2 quakes or the **m** topple into
46:3 Water roars and foams, and **m**
50:11 I know every bird in the **m**.
65:6 the one who set the **m** in place
68:16 you **m** with many peaks,
72:3 May the **m** bring peace to the
76:4 majestic than the ancient **m**.
80:10 Its shade covered the **m**.
83:15 forest and flames set **m** on fire.
87:1 founded ⌊stands⌋ on holy **m**.
Psa 90:2 Before the **m** were born,
97:5 The **m** melt like wax in the
98:8 hands and the **m** sing joyfully
104:6 Water stood above the **m**
104:8 The **m** rose and the valleys
104:10 It flows between the **m**.
104:13 You water the **m** from your
104:18 The high **m** are for wild goats.
104:32 He touches the **m**,
114:4 The **m** jumped like rams.
114:6 **M**, what made you jump like
121:1 I look up toward the **m**.
125:2 the **m** surround Jerusalem,
133:3 comes down on Zion's **m**.
144:5 Touch the **m**, and they will
147:8 He makes grass grow on the **m**.
148:9 **m** and all hills, fruit trees and
Pro 8:25 I was born before the **m** were
Sos 2:8 sprinting over the **m**,
2:17 stag on the **m** that separate us!
4:8 from the **m** of leopards.
8:14 young stag on the **m** of spices.
Isa 2:2 as the highest of the **m**
2:14 against all the high **m** and all
13:4 Listen to the noise on the **m**.
14:25 I'll trample it underfoot on my **m**
17:13 husks on the **m** being blown by
18:3 raises a flag on the **m**.
18:6 for the birds of prey on the **m**
22:5 and crying for help in the **m**.
34:3 **M** will be red with their blood.
37:24 chariots I'll ride up the high **m**,
40:12 basket or weighed the **m**
41:15 You will thresh the **m** and
42:11 shout from the tops of the **m**.
42:15 I will lay waste to **m** and hills.
44:23 Break into shouts of joy, you **m**,
49:11 I will turn all my **m** into roads,
49:13 Break into shouts of joy, you **m**!
52:7 How beautiful on the **m** are the
54:10 The **m** may move,
55:12 The **m** and the hills will break
64:1 The **m** would quake at your
64:3 you came down and the **m**
65:7 They burnt incense on the **m**
65:9 will inherit my **m** from Judah.
Jer 3:23 noise from the hills, from the **m**,
4:15 comes from the **m** of Ephraim.
4:24 I see the **m**. They are shaking,
9:10 I will cry and weep for the **m**.
13:16 your feet stumble on the **m**
17:3 and on **m** in the open country.
17:26 from the **m**, and from the Negev
31:5 vineyards on the **m** of Samaria.
31:6 day when watchmen on the **m**
32:44 in the cities on the **m**,
33:13 In the cities on the **m**,
46:18 Tabor among the **m** will come.
50:6 They wander around on the **m**.
50:6 They go from **m** to hills.
50:19 eat until they are full on the **m**
Lam 4:19 They chased us in the **m** and
Eze 6:2 look toward the **m** of Israel,
6:3 Say this, 'You **m** of Israel,
6:3 Almighty LORD says to the **m**
7:7 There will be no joy in the **m**.
7:16 survive will escape to the **m**.
19:9 anymore on the **m** of Israel.
31:12 Its branches fell on the **m** and
32:6 blood all the way to the **m**.
33:28 The **m** of Israel will become so
34:6 sheep wandered over all the **m**
34:13 care of them on the **m** of Israel,
34:14 will graze on the **m** of Israel.
34:14 best pastures in the **m** of Israel.
35:8 I will fill your **m** with those who
35:12 spoke about the **m** of Israel.
36:1 prophesy to the **m** of Israel.
36:1 Tell them, '**M** of Israel,
36:4 "'**M** of Israel, listen to the word
36:4 LORD says to the **m** and hills,
36:6 Tell the **m** and hills and the
36:8 "'But you, **m** of Israel,
37:22 in the land on the **m** of Israel.
38:8 and brought to the **m** of Israel,
38:8 **m** that have been ruined for a

Eze 38:20 The **m** will be torn down,
38:21 war against Gog on all my **m**,
39:2 have you attack the **m** of Israel.
39:4 You will die on the **m** of Israel
39:17 a huge feast on the **m** of Israel.
Hos 10:8 People will say to the **m**,
Joe 2:2 will spread over the **m** like
3:18 day new wine will cover the **m**.
Amo 3:9 together on the **m** of Samaria.
4:13 God forms the **m** and creates
9:13 New wine will drip from the **m**
Jnh 2:6 I sank to the foot of the **m**.
Mic 1:4 **M** will melt under him like wax
4:1 as the highest of the **m**
6:1 your case in front of the **m**,
6:2 to the LORD's lawsuit, you **m**.
Nah 1:5 The **m** quake because of him.
1:15 There on the **m** are the feet of a
3:18 people are scattered on the **m**,
Hab 3:6 The oldest **m** break apart.
3:10 The **m** look at you.
3:19 He makes me walk on the **m**.
Hag 1:8 "Go to the **m**, get lumber,
Zec 6:1 out from between the two **m**.
6:1 They were **m** of bronze.
14:5 will flee to the valley of my **m**,
14:5 between the **m** will go as
Mal 1:3 I turned his **m** into a wasteland
Mat 24:16 in Judea should flee to the **m**.
Mar 13:14 in Judea should flee to the **m**.
Luk 21:21 in Judea should flee to the **m**.
23:30 Then people will say to the **m**,
1Co 13:2 have enough faith to move **m**.
Heb 11:38 around in deserts and **m**
Rev 6:15 and among the rocks in the **m**.
6:16 They said to the **m** and rocks,
16:20 and the **m** could no longer be
17:9 The seven heads are seven **m**

mountainside (2)

Mar 5:11 was feeding on a **m** nearby.
Luk 8:32 of pigs was feeding on a **m**.

mountainsides (1)

Mar 5:5 tombs and on the **m** screaming

mountaintop (1)

Isa 13:2 Raise a banner on the bare **m**.

mountaintops (5)

Gen 7:20 It rose 23 feet above the **m**.
Jdg 9:36 are coming down from the **m**!"
Eze 6:13 on every high hill, on all the **m**,
Hos 4:13 They offer sacrifices on **m**,
Joe 2:5 As they leap on **m**,

mounted (4)

Exo 39:6 They **m** the onyx stones in
39:13 stones were **m** in gold settings.
2Sm 13:29 got up, **m** their mules, and fled.
Eze 23:12 They were **m** horsemen,

mourn (73)

Gen 23:2 Abraham went to **m** for Sarah
27:41 "The time to **m** for my father is
37:35 I will **m** for my son until I die."
50:10 ceremony to **m** Jacob's death.
50:10 days to **m** his father's death.
Lev 10:6 "Do not **m** by leaving your hair
19:28 slash your body to **m** the dead,
21:5 "You should never **m** by
21:10 He must never **m** by leaving
Dtr 14:1 don't ⌊**m**⌋ by cutting
21:13 your house and **m** ⌊the loss of⌋
Jdg 11:37 in the mountains and **m** that
1Sm 16:1 "How long are you going to **m**
25:1 all Israel gathered to **m** for him.
2Sm 3:31 on sackcloth, and **m** for Abner."
1Ki 13:29 He came to his own city to **m**
14:13 All Israel will **m** for him and
Neh 8:9 Don't **m** or cry." All the people
Job 5:11 He lifts those who **m** to safety.
Ecc 3:4 a time to **m** and a time to
Isa 16:7 **M** and grieve over the raisin
19:8 their lines into the Nile will **m**.
32:12 Beat your breasts as you **m** for
Isa 32:13 **M** for my people's land where
32:13 **M** for all the happy homes in a
66:10 All who **m** for her, be glad with
Jer 4:8 So put on sackcloth, **m**,
4:28 The earth will **m**, and the sky
6:26 **M** as if you have lost your only
8:21 I **m**; terror grips me.
12:4 How long will the land **m**?
15:5 No one will **m** for you.
16:4 No one will **m** for them or bury
16:5 Don't go to **m** or to grieve for
16:6 No one will **m** for them or bury
16:7 comfort those who **m** the dead.
22:18 People won't **m** for him and
22:18 They won't **m** for him and say,
25:34 **M**, you shepherds, and cry.
31:18 heard Ephraim **m** and say,
34:5 master," as they **m** for you.
48:17 **M** over it, all of its neighbors
48:38 People in Moab will **m** on
49:3 put on your sackcloth, and **m**.
Lam 2:5 He made the people of Judah **m**
2:8 made the towers and walls **m**.
Eze 7:12 and sellers will not **m**,
7:27 Kings will **m**, and princes will
21:12 "'Cry and **m**, son of man,
24:16 But you must not **m**,
31:15 to the grave, I made people **m**.
31:15 I made Lebanon **m** for the tree,
32:16 They will sing it as they **m** for
Hos 10:5 The people will **m** over it.
Joe 1:9 the LORD's servants, **m**.
1:11 **M** for the wheat and the barley.
1:13 Put on your sackcloth and **m**,
Amo 5:16 They will call on farmers to **m**
8:8 Everyone who lives in it will **m**.
9:5 and all who live on it **m**.
Mic 1:8 I will **m** and cry because of
1:8 a jackal and **m** like an ostrich.
Zec 7:3 "Should we **m** and fast in the
12:10 Then they will **m** for him as
12:12 The land will **m**, each family
12:14 families that are left ⌊will **m**⌋,
Mat 5:4 Blessed are those who **m**.
Luk 6:25 They will **m** and cry.
Jas 4:9 Be miserable, **m**, and cry.
Rev 1:7 Every tribe on earth will **m**
18:9 will cry and **m** over her when
18:11 of the earth cry and **m** over her,
18:15 They will cry and **m**,

mourned (20)

Gen 37:34 and **m** for his son a long time.
50:3 The Egyptians **m** for him 70
Num 14:39 the people **m** bitterly,
20:29 and all the Israelites **m** for
Dtr 34:8 The Israelites **m** for Moses in
1Sm 6:19 The people **m** because the
15:35 though Samuel **m** over Saul.
28:3 and all Israel had **m** for him and
2Sm 1:12 They **m**, cried, and fasted until
11:26 Uriah was dead, she **m** for him.
13:37 But the king **m** for his son
1Ki 13:30 in his own tomb and **m** over
14:18 All Israel buried him and **m** for
1Ch 7:22 Their father Ephraim **m** a long
2Ch 35:24 and Jerusalem **m** for Josiah.
Neh 1:4 I **m** for days. I continued to fast
Jer 25:33 They will not be **m**,
Dan 10:2 **m** for three whole weeks.
Zec 7:5 'When you fasted and **m** in the
Act 8:2 as they **m** loudly for him.

mourner (1)

2Sm 14:2 "Please act like a **m**,

mourners (7)

Job 29:25 like one who comforts **m**.
Ecc 12:5 and **m** go out in the streets.
Isa 57:18 I'll comfort them and their **m**.
Eze 24:17 face or eat the food that **m** eat."
24:22 faces or eat the food that **m** eat.
Hos 9:4 will be like the food that **m** eat.
Amo 5:16 on professional **m** to cry loudly.

mournfully (1)

1Sm 7:2 of Israel **m** sought the LORD.

mourning (53)

Gen 15:9 ram, a **m** dove, and a pigeon."
38:12 When Judah had finished **m**,
50:4 When the time of **m** for Jacob
Lev 1:14 sacrifice a **m** dove or pigeon.
5:7 bring to the LORD two **m** doves
5:11 "But if you cannot afford two **m**
12:6 and a pigeon or a **m** dove as
12:8 she must use two **m** doves or
14:22 and two **m** doves or two
14:30 must take one of the **m** doves
15:14 day he must take two **m** doves
15:29 she must take two **m** doves
Num 6:10 day he must bring two **m** doves
Dtr 26:14 holy offering while I was in **m**.
34:8 Then the time of **m** for him was
2Sm 1:17 David wrote this song of **m** for
11:27 When her **m** was over,
14:2 and dress in **m** clothes.
14:2 like a woman who has been **m**
19:1 is crying and **m** for Absalom."
19:2 of that day was turned into **m**
Ezr 10:6 He was **m** because these
Est 4:3 the Jews went into **m**,
9:22 turned to joy and their **m** into
Job 30:31 So my lyre is used for **m** and
Psa 35:14 I walked around as if I were **m**
35:14 as if I were **m** for my mother.
38:6 All day I walk around in **m**.
42:9 Why must I walk around in **m**
43:2 Why must I walk around in **m**
Sos 2:12 The cooing of the **m** dove is
Isa 22:12 will call for crying and for **m**,
29:2 with people grieving and **m**.
Jer 7:29 Sing a song of **m** on the bare
8:7 **M** doves, swallows,
14:2 The people of Judah sit in **m**
25:36 the leaders of the flock are **m**
31:13 I will turn their **m** into joy.
47:5 Gaza will shave its head in **m**.
48:38 There will be **m** everywhere,
Lam 5:15 Our dancing has turned into **m**.
Eze 2:10 funeral songs, songs of **m**,
27:31 bitterness and with bitter **m**.
Joe 1:8 **m** for the man she was going to
2:12 with fasting, crying, and **m**."
Mic 1:11 Beth Ezel is in **m**. It will take its
1:16 Shave your head in **m** for the
Nah 2:7 Its young women will be **m**
Zec 12:11 On that day the **m** in Jerusalem
12:11 as the **m** at Hadad Rimmon
Luk 2:24 "a pair of **m** doves or two
Jas 4:9 Turn your laughter into **m** and
Rev 18:19 shouted while crying and **m**,

mourns (6)

Isa 16:11 That is why my heart **m** for
16:11 My soul **m** for Kir Hareseth.
Jer 12:11 it **m** in my presence.
14:2 Judah **m**; its gates fall apart.
23:10 The land **m** because of the
Zec 12:10 will mourn for him as one **m**

mouth (188)

Dtr 18:18 I will put my words in his **m**.
30:14 They're in your **m** and in your
32:1 hear the words from my **m**.
Jos 6:10 word come out of your **m** until
10:18 large stones against the **m**
10:27 and put large stones over the **m**
15:5 Dead Sea as far north as the **m**
15:5 Sea at the **m** of the Jordan
Jdg 9:38 "Where is your big **m** now?
1Sm 1:12 Eli was watching her **m**.
2:1 My **m** mocks my enemies.
2:3 arrogance come out of your **m**
14:26 no one put his hand to his **m**,
14:27 When he put it to his **m**,
17:35 rescued the sheep from its **m**.
2Sm 22:9 a raging fire came out of his **m**.
1Ki 8:15 With his **m** he made a promise
8:24 With your **m** you promised it.

1Ki 13:21 the words from the LORD's **m**
13:26 the words from the LORD's **m**!
17:24 the LORD from your **m** is true."
2Ki 4:34 putting his **m** on the boy's
4:34 his mouth on the boy's **m**,
19:28 nose and my bridle in your **m**.
2Ch 6:4 With his **m** he made a promise
6:15 With your **m** you promised it.
Job 3:1 Job ⌊finally⌋ opened his **m**
5:16 while wrongdoing shuts its **m**.
6:30 or is my **m** unable to tell the
7:11 So I won't keep my **m** shut,
8:21 He will fill your **m** with laughter
9:20 my own **m** would condemn me.
11:5 speak and open his **m** ⌊to talk⌋
15:6 Your ⌊own⌋ **m** condemns you,
15:13 spit these words out of your **m**?
16:5 encourage you with my **m**,
20:12 "Though evil is sweet in his **m**
20:13 he holds it on the roof of his **m**,
21:5 put ⌊your⌋ hand over ⌊your⌋ **m**.
22:22 Accept instruction from his **m**,
29:17 him drop the prey out of his **m**.
32:20 I must open my **m** and answer.
33:2 I've opened my **m**.
35:16 Job opens his **m** for no good
37:2 that comes from his **m**.
40:4 I will put my hand over my **m**.
40:23 Jordan rushes against its **m**.
41:14 Who can open its closed **m**?
41:19 Flames shoot from its **m**.
41:21 and a flame pours from its **m**.
Psa 10:7 His **m** is full of cursing,
17:3 that my **m** will not sin.
18:8 a raging fire came out of his **m**.
19:14 May the words from my **m** and
22:15 sticks to the roof of my **m**.
22:21 Save me from the **m** of the lion
32:9 need⌋ a bit and bridle in their **m**
33:6 the stars by the breath of his **m**.
34:1 My **m** will always praise him.
36:3 The words from his **m** are
37:30 The **m** of the righteous person
39:1 I will bridle my **m** while wicked
39:9 I did not open my **m** because
40:3 He placed a new song in my **m**,
49:3 My **m** will speak wise sayings,
50:16 decrees and **m** my promises!
50:19 You let your **m** say anything
51:15 my lips, and my **m** will tell about
54:2 ears to the words from my **m**.
63:5 My **m** will sing ⌊your⌋ praise
66:14 spoken by my ⌊own⌋ **m** when
66:17 With my **m** I cried out to him.
69:15 or the pit close its **m** over me.
71:8 My **m** is filled with your praise,
71:15 My **m** will tell about your
78:1 ears to the words from my **m**.
78:2 I will open my **m** to illustrate
81:10 Open your **m** wide,
109:30 With my **m** I will give many
119:13 that ⌊comes⌋ from your **m**.
119:43 single word of truth from my **m**.
119:72 from your **m** are worth more
119:88 ⌊which came⌋ from your **m**.
119:131 I open my **m** and pant because
137:6 stick to the roof of my **m** if
141:3 O LORD, set a guard at my **m**.
141:7 planted at the **m** of the grave.
145:21 My **m** will speak the praise of
Pro 2:6 From his **m** come knowledge
4:24 dishonesty from your **m**.
6:2 by the words of your own **m**,
6:12 person who has a dishonest **m**.
7:24 to the words from my **m**.
8:7 My **m** expresses the truth,
10:11 The **m** of a righteous person is
10:14 but the **m** of a stubborn fool
10:31 The **m** of a righteous person
13:3 Whoever controls his **m**
13:3 has a big **m** comes to ruin.
15:23 an answer from his own **m**,
18:4 The words of a person's **m** are
18:6 and his **m** invites a beating.
18:7 A fool's **m** is his ruin.
19:24 even bring it back to his **m**.
Pro 20:17 but afterwards his **m** will be
20:19 whose **m** is always open.
21:23 Whoever guards his **m** and his
22:14 The **m** of an adulterous woman
23:33 and your **m** will say
24:7 gate he does not open his **m**.
26:15 as he brings it back to his **m**.
26:28 and a flattering **m** causes ruin.
27:2 and not from your own **m**,
30:20 eats, wipes her **m**, and says,
30:32 put your hand over your **m**.
Ecc 5:6 Don't let your **m** talk you into
Sos 1:2 me with the kisses of his **m**.
4:3 Your **m** is lovely. Your temples
5:16 His **m** is sweet in every way.
7:9 May your **m** taste like the best
Isa 5:14 It opens its **m** very wide so that
6:7 He touched my **m** with it and
9:17 every **m** speaks foolishness.
10:14 opened its **m**, or peeped."
11:4 the earth with a rod from his **m**.
37:29 nose and my bridle in your **m**.
45:23 my righteous **m** that will not
48:3 words came out of my **m**,
51:16 I put my words in your **m** and
53:7 but he didn't open his **m**.
53:7 He didn't open his **m**.
55:11 which comes from my **m**,
59:21 I put in your **m** will not leave
Jer 1:9 his hand and touched my **m**.
1:9 I have put my words in your **m**.
5:14 to put my words in your **m** like
17:16 know what came out of my **m**.
Lam 3:38 good and bad come from the **m**
Eze 2:8 Open your **m**, and eat what I
3:2 So I opened my **m**,
3:3 as sweet as honey in my **m**.
3:26 to the roof of your **m** so that you
3:27 I will open your **m**.
4:14 meat has ever entered my **m**."
16:63 will never again open your **m**
24:27 On that very day your **m** will be
Dan 4:31 the words came out of his **m**,
7:5 ribs in its **m** between its teeth.
7:8 and a **m** that spoke impressive
7:20 That horn had eyes and a **m**
10:3 No meat or wine entered my **m**.
10:16 I opened my **m** and began to
Hos 6:5 you with the words from my **m**.
Amo 3:12 piece of an ear out of a lion's **m**,
Mic 7:5 Keep your **m** shut even when a
Nah 3:12 figs fall into the **m** of the eater.
Mal 2:6 that came from his **m** was true.
2:7 seek instruction from his **m**.
Mat 12:34 Your **m** says what comes from
13:35 "I will open my **m** to illustrate
15:11 What goes into a person's **m**
15:11 It's what comes out of the **m**
15:17 goes into the **m** goes into
15:18 But whatever goes out of the **m**
17:27 Open its **m**, and you will find a
Mar 9:18 Then he foams at the **m**,
9:20 and foamed at the **m**.
Luk 9:39 and foams at the **m**.
Jon 19:29 stick and held it to his **m**.
Act 8:32 He didn't open his **m**.
11:8 impure or unclean into my **m**.'
23:2 Paul to strike him on the **m**.
Rom 10:8 It's in your **m** and in your heart.
2Ti 4:17 was snatched out of a lion's **m**.
Jas 3:10 curses come from the same **m**.
Rev 1:16 and out of his **m** came a sharp,
2:16 with the sword from my **m**.
3:16 going to spit you out of my **m**.
10:9 as sweet as honey in your **m**."
10:10 as sweet as honey in my **m**,
12:15 The snake's **m** poured out a
12:16 the woman by opening its **m**
12:16 poured out of the serpent's **m**.
13:2 Its **m** was like a lion's mouth.
13:2 Its mouth was like a lion's **m**.
13:6 It opened its **m** to insult God,
19:15 sword comes out of his **m**
19:21 sword that came out of his **m**.

mouthful (1)

Job 23:4 I would have a **m** of arguments.

mouths (64)

Exo 4:11 "Who gave humans their **m**?
Num 11:33 still in their **m** — before they
Jdg 7:6 with their hands to their **m**.
1Ki 19:18 and whose **m** have not kissed
22:22 that tells lies through the **m**
22:23 the LORD has put into the **m** of
2Ch 18:21 that tells lies through the **m**
18:22 the LORD has put into the **m**
Job 16:10 gaped at me with wide-open **m**.
29:9 put their hands over their **m**.
29:10 stuck to the roofs of their **m**.
29:23 They opened their **m** wide as if
Psa 5:9 Nothing in their **m** is truthful.
8:2 From the **m** of little children
17:10 **m** have spoken arrogantly.
22:7 Insults pour from their **m**.
22:13 They have opened their **m** to
35:21 They open their big **m** and say
58:6 knock the teeth out of their **m**.
59:7 See what pours out of their **m** —
59:12 of⌋ the sins from their **m**
62:4 They bless with their **m**,
63:11 but the **m** of liars will be shut.
78:30 the food was still in their **m**,
78:36 They flattered him with their **m**
107:42 people will shut their **m**.
109:2 opened their **m** against me.
115:5 They have **m**, but they cannot
126:2 Then our **m** were filled with
135:16 They have **m**, but they cannot
144:8 Their **m** speak lies.
144:11 Their **m** speak lies.
Pro 10:6 covers the **m** of wicked people.
10:11 but the **m** of wicked people
10:32 but the **m** of wicked people are
15:2 but the **m** of fools pour out a
15:14 but the **m** of fools feed on
15:28 but the **m** of wicked people
19:28 and the **m** of wicked people
26:7 is a proverb in the **m** of fools.
26:9 is a proverb in the **m** of fools.
Ecc 6:7 so hard for goes into their **m**,
Isa 9:12 will devour Israel with open **m**.
29:13 people worship me with their **m**
30:28 placing a bit in the **m** of the
52:15 Kings will shut their **m**
Lam 3:29 They should put their **m** in the
4:4 stick to the roofs of their **m**
Eze 34:10 rescue my sheep from their **m**,
Dan 6:22 shut the lions' **m** so that they
Mic 7:16 put their hands over their **m**.
Zec 8:9 to the words from the **m**
9:7 remove the blood from their **m**
14:12 their tongues will rot in their **m**.
Mat 21:16 'From the **m** of little children
Rom 3:14 Their **m** are full of curses and
1Co 14:21 languages and through the **m**
Heb 11:33 They shut the **m** of lions,
Jas 3:3 We put bits in the **m** of horses
Rev 9:17 and sulfur came out of their **m**.
9:18 out of their **m** — killed one-third
9:19 of these horses is in their **m**
11:5 comes out of the witnesses' **m**
16:13 like frogs come out of the **m**

move (48)

Gen 34:10 **m** about freely in this area,
34:21 in our land and **m** about freely
42:34 and you'll be able to **m** about
48:17 his father's hand in order to **m**
Exo 14:25 off so that they could hardly **m**.
40:37 But if the column didn't **m**,
Lev 11:29 swarming creatures that **m**
11:31 the swarming creatures that **m**
Num 2:9 They will be the first group to **m**
2:16 be the second group to **m** out.
2:17 The tribes will **m** out in the
2:24 will be the third group to **m** out.
2:31 They will be the last group to **m**
4:5 the camp is supposed to **m**,
4:15 and the camp is ready to **m**,

Num 10:35 Whenever the ark started to **m**,
16:21 "**M** away from these men,
16:24 **M** away from the tents of Korah,
16:26 He said to the community, "**M**
Dtr 19:14 Never **m** your neighbor's
1Sm 25:37 and he could not **m**.
1Ch 15:14 themselves holy in order to **m**
Neh 2:8 and for the house I'll **m** into."
Job 24:2 **m** boundary markers.
31:26 light shine or the moon **m** along
Psa 31:8 in a place where I can **m** freely.
104:3 You **m** on the wings of the
Pro 22:28 Do not **m** an ancient boundary
23:10 Do not **m** an ancient boundary
Isa 10:15 A rod cannot **m** the person who
41:7 with nails so they won't **m**.
46:7 It doesn't **m** from its place.
54:10 The mountains may **m**,
Hos 5:10 who **m** boundary markers.
Hab 1:11 They will **m** quickly and pass
Zec 14:4 Half of the mountain will **m**
14:4 half will **m** toward the south.
Mat 17:20 '**M** from here to there,'
17:20 here to there,' and it will **m**.
23:4 willing to lift a finger to **m** them.
Luk 10:7 Do not **m** around from one
14:10 **m** to a more honorable place.'
Act 7:4 God made him **m** from there to
17:28 Certainly, we live, **m**,
1Co 13:2 enough faith to **m** mountains.
15:58 don't let anyone **m** you off the
2Co 5:9 we live in the body or **m** out
Heb 6:1 truths about Christ and **m**

moved (142)

Gen 11:2 As people **m** toward the east,
12:8 He **m** on to the hills east of
13:11 He **m** toward the east.
13:18 So Abram **m** his tents and went
20:1 Abraham **m** to the Negev and
26:17 So Isaac **m** away.
26:22 He **m** on from there and dug
33:17 But Jacob **m** on to Succoth
35:5 As they **m** on, God made the
35:16 Then they **m** on from Bethel.
35:21 Israel **m** on again and put up
37:17 "They **m** on from here.
43:30 Deeply **m** at the sight of his
46:1 Israel **m** with all he had.
47:21 All over Egypt Joseph **m** the
Exo 13:20 They **m** from Succoth and
14:19 the Israelites, **m** behind them.
14:19 So the column of smoke **m**
16:1 of Israelites **m** from Elim
19:2 Israel had **m** from Rephidim
35:21 whose hearts **m** them came
40:36 the ⌊column of⌋ smoke **m** from
Num 1:51 When the tent has to be **m**,
2:17 "When the tent of meeting is **m**,
9:17 Whenever the smoke **m** from
9:21 When the smoke **m** in the
9:21 when the smoke **m**,
9:22 But when the smoke **m**,
10:12 So the Israelites **m** from the
10:13 This was the first time they **m**,
10:34 by day when they **m** the camp.
11:35 the people **m** to Hazeroth,
12:16 After that, the people **m** from
16:27 So they **m** away from the tents
21:4 Then they **m** from Mount Hor,
21:10 The Israelites **m** and set up
21:11 Next they **m** from Oboth and
21:12 From there they **m** and set up
21:13 They **m** from there and set up
22:1 Then the Israelites **m** and set
22:25 it **m** over and pinned Balaam's
22:26 of the LORD **m** ahead
33:3 They **m** from Rameses on the
33:5 The Israelites **m** from Rameses
33:6 They **m** from Succoth and set
33:7 They **m** from Etham and turned
33:8 They **m** from Pi Hahiroth and
33:9 They **m** from Marah and came
33:10 They **m** from Elim and set up
33:11 They **m** from the Red Sea and
33:12 They **m** from the Desert of Sin
Num 33:13 They **m** from Dophkah and set
33:14 They **m** from Alush and set up
33:15 They **m** from Rephidim and set
33:16 They **m** from the Desert of
33:17 They **m** from Kibroth Hattaavah
33:18 They **m** from Hazeroth and set
33:19 They **m** from Rithmah and set
33:20 They **m** from Rimmon Perez
33:21 They **m** from Libnah and set up
33:22 They **m** from Rissah and set up
33:23 They **m** from Kehelathah and
33:24 They **m** from Mount Shepher
33:25 They **m** from Haradah and set
33:26 They **m** from Makheloth and
33:27 They **m** from Tahath and set up
33:28 They **m** from Terah and set up
33:29 They **m** from Mithcah and set
33:30 They **m** from Hashmonah and
33:31 They **m** from Moseroth and set
33:32 They **m** from Bene Jaakan and
33:33 They **m** from Hor Haggidgad
33:34 They **m** from Jotbathah and set
33:35 They **m** from Abronah and set
33:36 They **m** from Ezion Geber and
33:37 They **m** from Kadesh and set
33:41 They **m** from Mount Hor and set
33:42 They **m** from Zalmonah and set
33:43 They **m** from Punon and set up
33:44 They **m** from Oboth and set up
33:45 They **m** from Iyim and set up
33:46 They **m** from Dibon Gad and
33:47 They **m** from Almon Diblathaim
33:48 They **m** from the Abarim
Dtr 10:6 The Israelites **m** from the wells
10:7 They **m** from there to
Jdg 2:18 The LORD was **m** by the
9:26 his brothers **m** into Shechem.
1Sm 5:9 But after they had **m** it,
14:23 the battle **m** beyond Beth Aven.
17:48 When the Philistine **m** closer in
2Sm 7:6 Instead, I **m** around in a tent,
7:7 In all the places I've **m** with all
20:13 As soon as he was **m** from the
1Ki 3:26 alive was deeply **m** by her love
9:24 Pharaoh's daughter **m** from the
2Ki 16:14 But he **m** the bronze altar
1Ch 4:39 They **m** to the outskirts of
16:30 stands firm; it cannot be **m**.
17:6 In all the places I've **m** with all
Est 2:9 Then he **m** her and her
Job 41:23 are solid and cannot be **m**.
Psa 16:8 is by my side, I cannot be **m**.
21:7 Most High, he will not be **m**.
37:36 But he **m** on, and now there is
93:1 set in place; it cannot be **m**.
96:10 stands firm; it cannot be **m**.
Pro 10:30 person will never be **m**,
12:3 righteous people cannot be **m**.
Isa 33:20 It is a tent that can't be **m**.
Eze 1:9 and they did not turn as they **m**.
1:12 and they didn't turn as they **m**.
1:13 Fire **m** back and forth between
1:17 Whenever they **m**,
1:17 Whenever they moved, they **m**
1:17 without turning as they **m**.
1:19 When the living creatures **m**,
1:19 the wheels **m** with them.
1:21 So whenever the creatures **m**,
1:21 moved, the wheels **m**.
1:24 When the creatures **m**,
10:11 Whenever the angels **m**,
10:11 they **m** in any of the four
10:11 without turning as they **m**.
10:11 They always **m** in the direction
10:11 without turning as they **m**.
10:16 When the angels **m**,
10:16 the wheels **m** beside them.
Hos 11:8 my mind. I am deeply **m**.
Nah 2:11 and the lion cub who **m** about
Mat 11:1 he **m** on from there to teach his
12:9 Jesus **m** on from there and
15:29 Jesus **m** on from there and
Luk 2:27 **M** by the Spirit, Simeon went
Jon 11:33 he was deeply **m** and troubled.
11:38 Deeply **m** again, Jesus went to
11:41 So the stone was **m** away from
Act 2:25 I cannot be **m** because he is
27:41 ship stuck and couldn't be **m**,
2Co 9:2 and your enthusiasm has **m**
Col 1:23 in faith without being **m** from
Rev 6:14 island was **m** from its place.

movement (1)

Act 5:36 The whole **m** was a failure.

movements (2)

2Sm 3:25 to find out about your **m** and
Isa 25:11 despite the **m** of their hands.

moves (7)

Gen 8:19 and bird — everything that **m**
9:3 Everything that lives and **m**
Dtr 23:14 The LORD your God **m** around
27:17 "Whoever **m** his neighbor's
Job 9:5 He **m** mountains without their
Psa 50:11 Everything that **m** in the fields
69:34 and everything that **m** in them,

moving (9)

Gen 12:9 kept **m** toward the Negev.
13:12 **m** his tents as far as Sodom.
Exo 14:15 Tell the Israelites to start **m**.
1Sm 1:13 only her lips were **m**.
2Sm 15:23 and all the people were **m**
1Ch 17:5 **m** the tent ⌊of meeting⌋ from
Ecc 4:15 I saw all living people **m** about
Sos 4:1 of goats **m** down Mount Gilead.
6:5 of goats **m** down from Gilead.

Moza (5)

1Ch 2:46 of Haran, **M**, and Gazez.
8:36 Zimri was the father of **M**.
8:37 **M** was the father of Binea.
9:42 Zimri was the father of **M**.
9:43 **M** was the father of Binea.

Mozah (1)

Jos 18:26 Mizpeh, Chephirah, **M**,

mud (14)

Job 41:30 a threshing sledge on the **m**.
Psa 40:2 out of the **m** and clay.
69:2 I am sinking in deep **m**.
69:14 Rescue me from the **m**.
Isa 10:6 on them like **m** in the streets.
41:25 attack rulers as if they were **m**,
57:20 water throws up **m** and slime.
Jer 38:6 no water in the cistern, only **m**,
38:6 and Jeremiah sank in the **m**.
38:22 Your feet are stuck in the **m**,
Mic 7:10 trampled like **m** in the streets.
Zec 9:3 and gold like **m** in the streets.
10:5 trample the enemy in the **m**
2Pe 2:22 back to roll around in the **m**."

muddied (2)

Pro 25:26 ⌊Like⌋ a **m** spring and a
Eze 34:19 drink what your feet have **m**?

muddy (3)

Job 9:31 would plunge me into a **m** pit,
Eze 32:2 You make the streams **m**.
34:18 Must you **m** the rest of the

muffled (2)

Ecc 12:4 the sound of the mill is **m**,
Isa 29:4 Your words will be **m** by the

mulberry (1)

Luk 17:6 you could say to this **m** tree,

mule (7)

2Sm 18:9 He was riding on a **m**,
18:9 and the **m** went under the
18:9 when the **m** that was under
1Ki 1:33 Put my son Solomon on my **m**,
1:38 put Solomon on King David's **m**
1:44 have put him on the king's **m**.
Psa 32:9 be stubborn like a horse or **m**.

mules (11)

2Sm 13:29 up, mounted their **m**, and fled.

1Ki 10:25 spices, horses, and **m**.
18:5 keep the horses and **m** alive
2Ki 5:17 dirt as a pair of **m** can carry.
1Ch 12:40 donkeys, camels, **m**, and oxen.
2Ch 9:24 spices, horses, and **m**.
Ezr 2:66 They had 736 horses, 245 **m**,
Neh 7:68 They had 736 horses, 245 **m**,
Isa 66:20 on **m** and camels to my holy
Eze 27:14 and **m** for your merchandise.
Zec 14:15 horses, **m**, camels, donkeys,

multicolored (1)

Eze 27:24 and many **m** rugs with woven

multiplies (1)

Job 34:37 He **m** his words against God."

multiply (9)

2Sm 24:3 "May the LORD your God **m**
1Ch 21:3 "May the LORD **m** his people a
Psa 16:4 other gods **m** their sorrows.
107:38 and their numbers **m**,
Pro 4:10 and they will **m** the years of
Jer 33:22 I will **m** the descendants of my
Nah 3:15 **M** like locusts! Multiply like
3:15 **M** like hungry locusts!
2Co 9:10 also give you seed and **m** it.

mumble (1)

Job 27:4 will not **m** anything deceitful.'

Muppim (1)

Gen 46:21 Ehi, Rosh, **M**, Huppim, and Ard.

murder (68)

Exo 20:13 "Never **m**.
22:2 he is not guilty of **m**.
22:3 after sunrise, he is guilty of **m**.
Num 35:12 So anyone accused of **m** will
35:27 the relative is not guilty of **m**.
35:33 **M** is what pollutes the land.
35:33 The land where a **m** was
Dtr 5:17 "Never **m**.
17:8 It may involve **m**, assault, or a
19:10 and you won't be guilty of **m**.
21:1 do if you find a **m** victim lying
21:1 knows who committed the **m**,
21:6 the **m** victim must wash
21:7 "We didn't commit this **m**,
21:8 unsolved **m** remain among your
21:8 with the LORD despite the **m**.
21:9 an unsolved **m** by doing what
2Sm 4:11 I'll now seek revenge for his **m**
21:1 They are guilty of **m** because
Psa 9:12 The one who avenges **m** has
51:14 Rescue me from the guilt of **m**,
62:3 How long will you try to **m** him,
94:6 and they **m** orphans.
Pro 1:18 set an ambush for their own **m**.
28:17 with the guilt of **m** will
Jer 7:9 You steal, **m**, commit adultery,
41:4 day after the **m** of Gedaliah,
Eze 7:23 The land is filled with **m**,
9:9 The land is filled with **m**,
16:38 and **m** are punished.
22:6 used their power to **m** people.
22:12 people take bribes to **m** people.
22:27 They **m** and destroy people to
23:45 women for adultery and for **m**,
33:25 You **m** people. Should the land
35:6 **m** will pursue you.
Hos 4:2 there is one **m** after another.
6:9 They **m** on the road to
12:14 He will hold them guilty of **m**.
Joe 3:21 I will punish those who **m**."
Mic 7:2 lie in ambush to commit **m**.
Mat 5:21 to your ancestors, 'Never **m**.
15:19 Evil thoughts, **m**, adultery,
19:18 Jesus said, "Never **m**.
23:30 have helped to **m** the prophets.'
23:35 from the **m** of righteous Abel to
Mar 7:21 sexual sins, stealing, **m**,
10:19 the commandments: Never **m**.
15:7 had committed **m** during a riot.
Luk 11:49 They will **m** some of those
11:50 now will be charged with the **m**
18:20 Never **m**. Never steal. Never
23:19 place in the city and for **m**.)
Jon 16:2 people who **m** you will think
Act 9:1 Saul kept threatening to **m** the
9:23 Later the Jews planned to **m**
9:24 day and night in order to **m** him.
9:29 but they tried to **m** him.
23:27 man and were going to **m** him.
26:21 courtyard and tried to **m** me.
Rom 1:29 They are filled with envy, **m**,
3:15 They run quickly to **m** people.
13:9 adultery; never **m**; never steal;
Jas 2:11 one who said, "Never **m**."
2:11 not commit adultery but you **m**,
4:2 don't have, so you commit **m**.
1Jn 3:12 why did Cain **m** his brother?
Rev 9:21 turn away from committing **m**,

murdered (18)

Gen 49:6 In their anger they **m** men.
Jdg 20:4 the husband of the **m** woman,
1Ki 21:19 Have you **m** someone just to
Pro 22:13 I'll be **m** in the streets!"
Lam 2:22 My enemy has **m** the children I
Eze 35:6 I will let you be **m**.
Joe 3:19 They **m** innocent people in
Mat 23:31 of those who **m** the prophets.
23:35 blood of those **m** on earth,
23:35 whom you **m** between the
Luk 11:47 your ancestors who **m** them.
11:48 They **m** the prophets for whom
Act 5:30 You **m** Jesus by hanging him
7:52 who betrayed and **m** that man.
23:21 before they have **m** him.
Jas 5:6 You have condemned and **m**
1Jn 3:12 the evil one and **m** his brother.
Rev 18:24 and everyone who had been **m**

murderer (19)

Num 35:16 another person, you are a **m**.
35:17 another person, you are a **m**.
35:18 another person, you are a **m**.
35:19 must make sure a **m** is put
35:19 he catches up with the **m**,
35:21 You are a **m**. The relative who
35:21 because you are a **m**.
35:30 will be put to death as a **m** only
35:31 of a convicted **m** who has been
35:32 "An accused **m** who has fled to
35:33 through the death of the **m**.
2Ki 6:32 "Do you see how this **m** has
9:31 **m** of your master?"
Jon 8:44 The devil was a **m** from the
Act 3:14 to have a **m** given to you,
28:4 "This man must be a **m**!
1Pe 4:15 shouldn't suffer for being a **m**,
1Jn 3:15 hates another believer is a **m**,
3:15 and you know that a **m** doesn't

murderers (21)

Num 35:6 You must allow **m** to escape to
35:16 **M** must be put to death.
35:17 **M** must be put to death.
35:18 **M** must be put to death.
35:28 Accused **m** must stay in their
35:31 **M** must be put to death.
Jos 21:13 Hebron (a city of refuge for **m**)
21:21 Shechem (a city of refuge for **m**
21:27 of refuge for **m**) and Ashtaroth.
21:32 Galilee (a city of refuge for **m**),
21:38 Gilead (a city of refuge for **m**),
Job 24:14 At dawn **m** rise; they kill the
Isa 1:21 But now **m** live there!
Jer 4:31 in the presence of **m**!"
Eze 22:2 Will you judge the city of **m**?
24:6 it will be for that city of **m**,
24:9 it will be for that city of **m**.
35:6 **M** will pursue you.
Mat 22:7 his soldiers, killed those **m**,
Rev 21:8 **m**, sexual sinners, sorcerers,
22:15 sexual sinners, **m**, idolaters,

murdering (6)

Dtr 19:13 The guilt of **m** an innocent
2Ch 24:25 plotted against him for **m**
Eze 35:6 Since you don't hate **m** people,
Hos 4:2 There is cursing, lying, **m**,
Luk 23:25 put in prison for rioting and **m**,
Act 22:20 of those who were **m** him.'

murders (8)

Dtr 22:26 attacks and **m** another person.
Job 5:2 jealousy **m** a gullible person.
Isa 33:15 to those who are plotting **m**.
Eze 18:10 has a son who robs and **m**.
22:3 you are the city that **m** people
22:13 and the **m** you have committed.
Mat 5:21 Whoever **m** will answer for it in
Luk 11:51 This includes the **m** from Abel

muscle (2)

Gen 32:32 of Israel do not eat the **m**
32:32 hip at the **m** of the thigh.)

muscles (4)

Job 40:16 at the strength in its back **m**,
40:16 the power in its stomach **m**.
Eze 37:6 on you, place **m** on you,
37:8 were on them, **m** were on them,

Mushi (8)

Exo 6:19 of Merari were Mahli and **M**.
Num 3:20 Mahli and **M** were the sons of
3:33 descended from Mahli and **M**.
1Ch 6:19 sons were Mahli and **M**.
6:47 who was the son of **M**,
23:21 sons were Mahli and **M**.
23:23 **M** had three sons: Mahli, Eder,
24:26 **M**, and Merari's son Jaaziah,

Mushi's (1)

1Ch 24:30 Jerimoth (for **M** descendants).

Mushite (1)

Num 26:58 Mahlite family, the **M** family,

music (64)

Jdg 5:3 I will make **m** to the LORD God
1Sm 18:6 joyful **m**, and triangles.
2Sm 22:50 among the nations and make **m**
2Ki 3:15 me someone to play some **m**."
1Ch 6:31 put men in charge of the **m**
15:16 expected to play **m** on harps,
15:16 to produce joyful **m** for singing.
16:9 Make **m** to praise him.
Job 21:12 happy with the **m** of the flute.
Psa 7:17 I will make **m** to praise the
9:2 I will make **m** to praise your
9:11 Make **m** to praise the LORD,
18:49 among the nations and make **m**
21:13 We will sing and make **m** to
27:6 I will sing and make **m** to
30:4 Make **m** to praise the LORD,
30:12 my soul may praise you with **m**
33:2 Make **m** for him on a
45:8 From ivory palaces the **m** of
47:6 Make **m** to praise God.
47:6 Play **m** for him! Make music to
47:6 Make **m** to praise our king.
47:6 our king. Play **m** for him!
47:7 Make your best **m** for him!
49:4 riddle with the **m** of a lyre.
57:7 I want to sing and make **m**.
57:9 I want to make **m** to praise you
59:17 I will make **m** to praise you!
61:8 Then I will make **m** to praise
66:2 Make **m** to praise the glory of
66:4 It will make **m** to praise you.
66:4 It will make **m** to praise your
68:4 make **m** to praise his name.
68:32 Make **m** to praise the Lord.
71:22 I will make **m** with a harp to
71:23 sing with joy when I make **m**
75:9 I will make **m** to praise the God
81:2 harps with their pleasant **m**.
92:1 to make **m** to praise your name,
98:4 joyful singing, and make **m**.
98:5 Make **m** to the LORD with a
101:1 I will make **m** to praise you.
104:33 I will make **m** to praise my God
105:2 Make **m** to praise him.
108:1 I want to sing and make **m**

Psa 108:3 I want to make **m** to praise you
135:3 Make **m** to praise his name
138:1 I will make **m** to praise you in
146:2 I want to make **m** to praise my
147:7 Make **m** to our God with a lyre.
149:3 Let them make **m** to him with
Isa 12:5 Make **m** to praise the LORD.
14:11 down to Sheol along with the **m**
23:16 Make sweet **m**. Sing many
24:8 Joyful tambourine **m** stops.
24:8 Joyful harp **m** stops.
Lam 5:14 men no longer play their **m**.
Eze 26:13 and the **m** from your harps will
Amo 5:23 listen to the **m** of your harps.
Mat 11:17 'We played **m** for you,
Luk 7:32 'We played **m** for you,
15:25 he heard **m** and dancing.
Eph 5:19 Sing and make **m** to the Lord
Rev 14:2 like the **m** played by harpists.

musical (6)
1Ch 16:42 and the ⌊other⌋ **m** instruments
2Ch 5:13 and other **m** instruments,
7:6 **m** instruments which King
23:13 by **m** instruments.
Neh 12:36 and Hanani with the **m**
1Co 14:7 **M** instruments like the flute or

musician (3)
2Ki 3:15 While the **m** was playing,
1Ch 6:33 The **m** Heman was from
Eze 33:32 love songs or a **m** who plays

musicians (11)
1Ch 6:32 They served as **m** in the
9:33 These were the **m** who were
15:16 of their relatives to serve as **m**.
15:19 The **m** Heman, Asaph,
25:7 skilled **m** for the LORD.
25:8 the skilled ⌊**m**⌋ along with the
2Ch 5:12 Levites who were **m** — Asaph,
5:12 With the **m** were 120 priests
34:12 who were skilled **m**,
Psa 68:25 The **m** are behind them.
Rev 18:22 The sound of harpists, **m**,

musicians' (1)
1Ch 15:27 of the **m** prophetic songs.

mustache (1)
2Sm 19:24 to his feet, trimmed his **m**,

mustard (6)
Mat 13:31 is like a **m** seed that someone
17:20 faith is the size of a **m** seed,
Mar 4:31 It's like a **m** seed planted in the
4:31 The **m** seed is one of the
Luk 13:19 It's like a **m** seed that someone
17:6 have faith the size of a **m** seed,

mute (2)
Mat 15:31 to see **m** people talking,
Mar 7:37 the deaf hear and the **m** talk."

mutter (2)
Isa 8:19 who whisper and **m**."
59:3 and you **m** wicked things.

mutual (1)
1Sm 18:3 made a pledge of **m** loyalty

muzzle (3)
Dtr 25:4 Never **m** an ox when it's
1Co 9:9 "Never **m** an ox when it is
1Ti 5:18 "Never **m** an ox when it is

Myra (2)
Act 27:5 and arrived at the city of **M**
27:6 In **M** the officer found a ship

myrrh (16)
Gen 43:11 honey, gum, **m**, pistachio nuts,
Exo 30:23 12 ½ pounds of powdered **m**;
Est 2:12 six months using oil of **m** and
Psa 45:8 robes are ⌊fragrant⌋ with **m**,
Pro 7:17 I've sprinkled my bed with **m**,
Sos 1:13 My beloved is a pouch of **m**
3:6 She is perfumed with **m** and
4:6 I will go to the mountain of **m**
4:14 all kinds of incense, **m**, aloes,
5:1 I will gather my **m** with my
5:5 My hands dripped with **m**,
5:5 were drenched with liquid **m**,
5:13 lips are lilies that drip with **m**.
Mat 2:11 of gold, frankincense, and **m**.
Mar 15:23 mixed with a drug called **m**,
Jon 19:39 of a **m** and aloe mixture.

myrtle (6)
Neh 8:15 olive and wild olive, **m**, palm,
Isa 41:19 I will plant cedar, acacia, **m**,
55:13 **M** trees will grow where briars
Zec 1:8 He was standing among the **m**
1:10 The man standing among the **m**
1:11 standing among the **m** trees,

Mysia (2)
Act 16:7 They went to the province of **M**
16:8 So they passed by **M** and went

mysteries (12)
Job 12:22 He uncovers **m** ⌊hidden⌋ in the
Mat 13:11 "Knowledge about the **m** of the
13:12 who understand ⌊these **m**⌋ will
13:12 don't understand ⌊these **m**⌋.
Mar 4:25 who understand ⌊these **m**⌋ will
4:25 don't understand ⌊these **m**⌋.
Luk 8:10 "Knowledge about the **m** of the
8:18 who understand ⌊these **m**⌋ will
8:18 don't understand ⌊these **m**⌋.
1Co 4:1 are entrusted with God's **m**.
13:2 and I may understand all **m**
14:2 His spirit is speaking **m**.

mysterious (4)
Job 42:3 things too **m** for me to know.
Isa 28:21 his deeds, his **m** deeds.
Jer 33:3 I will tell you great and **m**
Dan 8:23 understands **m** things will rise

mystery (28)
Psa 64:6 and the human heart are a **m**!
Mar 4:11 Jesus replied to them, "The **m**
Luk 18:34 What he said was a **m** to them,
Rom 11:25 I want you to understand this **m**
16:25 revealing the **m** that was kept
1Co 2:1 I didn't speak about God's **m**
2:7 We speak about the **m** of God's
15:51 I'm telling you a **m**.
Eph 1:9 when he revealed the **m** of his
3:3 he let me know this **m** through
3:4 I understand the **m** about Christ
3:5 In the past, this **m** was not
3:6 This **m** is the Good News that
3:9 explain the way this **m** works.
5:32 This is a great **m**. (I'm talking
6:19 boldly when I reveal the **m**
Col 1:26 In the past God hid this **m**,
1:27 riches of this **m** — which is
2:2 He is the **m** of God.
4:3 we may tell the **m** about Christ.
4:3 It is because of this **m** that I am
4:4 Pray that I may make this **m** as
2Th 2:7 The **m** of this sin is already at
1Ti 3:9 about possessing the **m**
3:16 The **m** that gives us our
Rev 10:7 the **m** of God will be
17:5 The name was **M**:
17:7 I will tell you the **m** of the

myths (6)
1Ti 1:4 occupying themselves with **m**
1:4 These **m** and genealogies
4:7 with godless **m** that old women
2Ti 4:4 listen to the truth and turn to **m**.
Tit 1:14 pay attention to Jewish **m**
2Pe 1:16 on clever **m** that we made

N

Naam (1)
1Ch 4:15 were Iru, Elah, and **N**.

Naama (4)
Job 2:11 Bildad of Shuah, Zophar of **N**.
11:1 Zophar from **N** replied ⌊to Job⌋,
20:1 Zophar from **N** replied ⌊to Job⌋,
42:9 and Zophar of **N** went and did

Naamah (5)
Gen 4:22 Tubalcain's sister was **N**.
Jos 15:41 Gederoth, Beth Dagon, **N**,
1Ki 14:21 an Ammonite woman named **N**.
14:31 Ammonite woman named **N**.)
2Ch 12:13 Ammonite woman named **N**.)

Naaman (25)
Gen 46:21 **N**, Ehi, Rosh, Muppim, Huppim,
Num 26:40 (⌊through⌋ Ard and **N**) were
26:40 of Ard and the family of **N**.
2Ki 5:1 **N**, the commander of the
5:1 given Aram a victory through **N**
5:4 **N** went to his master and told
5:5 When **N** left, he took 750
5:6 read, "I'm sending my officer **N**
5:8 Please let **N** come to me and
5:9 **N** came with his horses and
5:11 But **N** became angry and left.
5:15 **N** stood in front of Elisha and
5:16 **N** urged him to take it,
5:17 So **N** said, "If you won't take it,
5:19 Elisha told **N**, "Go in peace."
5:20 "My master let this Aramean **N**
5:20 I'll run after **N** and get
5:21 So Gehazi went after **N**.
5:21 When **N** saw Gehazi running
5:23 **N** replied, "Please let me give
5:23 **N** urged him ⌊to take the
5:23 **N** tied up 150 pounds of silver
1Ch 8:4 Abishua, **N**, Ahoah,
8:7 **N**, Ahijah, and Gera. Gera led
Luk 4:27 But God cured no one except **N**

Naaman's (3)
2Ki 5:2 became the servant of **N** wife
5:13 But **N** servants went to him and
5:27 **N** skin disease will cling to

Naarah (3)
Jos 16:7 it descends to Ataroth and **N**,
1Ch 4:5 had two wives, Helah and **N**.
4:6 **N** gave birth to Ahuzzam,

Naarah's (1)
1Ch 4:6 These were **N** sons

Naaran (1)
1Ch 7:28 and its villages, **N** to the east,

Naari (1)
1Ch 11:37 from Carmel, **N** (son of Ezbai),

Nabal (14)
1Sm 25:3 This man's name was **N**,
25:4 he heard that **N** was shearing
25:5 visit **N**, and greet him for me.
25:9 David's young men came to **N**,
25:10 **N** answered David's servants.
25:19 tell her husband **N** about it.
25:25 worthless person **N** seriously.
25:25 His name is **N** [Godless Fool],
25:26 to harm you end up like **N**.
25:34 **N** certainly wouldn't have had
25:36 When Abigail came to **N**,
25:38 even more sick, and **N** died.
25:39 When David heard **N** was dead,
25:39 me against the insults of **N**

Nabal's (7)
1Sm 25:14 **N** wife, "David sent
25:37 **N** heart failed, and he could not
25:39 The LORD has turned **N** own
27:3 had been **N** wife) from Carmel.
30:5 had been **N** wife) from Carmel.
2Sm 2:2 had been **N** wife) from Carmel.

2Sm 3:3 had been **N** wife) from Carmel.

Naboth (15)

1Ki 21:1 **N** from Jezreel had a vineyard
21:2 Ahab told **N**, "Give me your
21:3 **N** told Ahab, "The LORD has
21:4 of what **N** from Jezreel had
21:4 ⌊**N** had said,⌋ "I will not give
21:6 "I talked to **N** from Jezreel.
21:7 belonging to **N** from Jezreel."
21:9 Seat **N** as leader of the people.
21:12 a fast and had **N** seated as
21:13 these men accused **N** of
21:14 "**N** has been stoned to death."
21:15 which **N** from Jezreel refused
2Ki 9:21 that belonged to **N** from Jezreel.
9:25 that belonged to **N** from Jezreel.
9:26 'Just as I saw the blood of **N**

Naboth's (5)

1Ki 21:8 and nobles living in **N** city
21:11 The men in **N** city — the
21:16 When he heard about **N** death,
21:18 went to confiscate **N** vineyard
21:19 the dogs licked up **N** blood,

Nacon's (1)

2Sm 6:6 they came to **N** threshing floor,

Nadab (21)

Exo 6:23 She gave birth to **N**,
24:1 "You and Aaron, **N**, Abihu,
24:9 Moses went up with Aaron, **N**,
28:1 brother Aaron and his sons **N**,
Lev 10:1 Aaron's sons **N** and Abihu each
Num 3:2 sons are **N** (the firstborn),
3:4 **N** and Abihu died in the
26:60 Aaron was the father of **N**,
26:61 But **N** and Abihu had died
1Ki 14:20 His son **N** succeeded him as
15:25 **N**, son of Jeroboam, began to
15:27 of Issachar, plotted against **N**.
15:27 city of Gibbethon while **N**
15:28 Baasha succeeded **N** as king
15:31 Isn't everything else about **N** —
1Ch 2:28 sons were **N** and Abishur.
6:3 Aaron's sons were **N**,
8:30 Abdon, then Zur, Kish, Baal, **N**,
9:36 Abdon, then Zur, Kish, Baal, **N**,
24:1 sons were **N** and Abihu.
24:2 **N** and Abihu died before their

Nadab's (1)

1Ch 2:30 **N** sons were Seled and

Naggai (1)

Luk 3:25 Nahum, son of Esli, son of **N**,

Nahalal (2)

Jos 19:15 This also includes Kattath, **N**,
21:35 Dimnah, and **N**.

Nahaliel (2)

Num 21:19 and from Mattanah to **N**,
21:19 and from **N** to Bamoth,

Nahalol (1)

Jdg 1:30 those who lived at Kitron or **N**.

Naham (1)

1Ch 4:19 Hodiah's wife, the sister of **N**,

Nahamani (1)

Neh 7:7 **N**, Mordecai, Bilshan,

Naharai (2)

2Sm 23:37 from Ammon, **N** from Beeroth,
1Ch 11:39 from Ammon, **N** from Beroth,

Nahash (14)

1Sm 11:1 King **N** of Ammon was
11:1 River whose right eye King **N**
11:1 About a month later **N** the
11:1 the men of Jabesh said to **N**,
11:2 **N** the Ammonite responded,
11:10 They said ⌊to **N**,⌋ and you may
1Sm 12:12 But when you saw King **N** of
2Sm 10:2 father **N** showed me kindness.
17:25 the daughter of **N** and sister of
17:27 son of **N** from Rabbah in
1Ch 4:12 who first settled the city of **N**.
19:1 Later King **N** of Ammon died,
19:2 father **N** showed me kindness.
19:2 territory to comfort **N**

Nahath (5)

Gen 36:13 These were Reuel's sons: **N**,
36:17 Reuel: **N**, Zerah, Shammah,
1Ch 1:37 Reuel's sons were **N**,
6:26 Zophai's son was **N**.
2Ch 31:13 **N**, Asahel, Jerimoth, Jozabad,

Nahath's (1)

1Ch 6:27 **N** son was Eliab. Eliab's son

Nahbi (1)

Num 13:14 **N**, son of Vophsi, from the tribe

Nahor (16)

Gen 11:22 he became the father of **N**.
11:23 After he became the father of **N**,
11:24 **N** was 29 years old when he
11:25 **N** lived 119 years and had
11:26 father of Abram, **N**, and Haran.
11:27 father of Abram, **N**, and Haran.
11:29 Both Abram and **N** married.
22:20 these children of your brother **N**
22:23 sons by Abraham's brother **N**.
24:15 the wife of Abraham's brother **N**
24:24 son of Milcah and **N**.
24:47 son of **N** and Milcah.'
31:53 May the God of Abraham and **N**
Jos 24:2 and his sons Abraham and **N**,
1Ch 1:26 Serug, **N**, Terah,
Luk 3:34 son of Terah, son of **N**,

Nahor's (4)

Gen 11:29 and the name of **N** wife was
22:24 **N** concubine, whose name
24:10 to Aram Naharaim, **N** city
29:5 **N** grandson?" They answered,

Nahshon (13)

Exo 6:23 of Amminadab and sister of **N**.
Num 1:7 **N**, son of Amminadab, from the
2:3 for the people of Judah is **N**,
7:12 his gifts on the first day was **N**,
7:17 These were the gifts from **N**,
10:14 **N**, son of Amminadab, was in
Rut 4:20 was the father of **N**.
4:20 **N** was the father of Salmon.
1Ch 2:10 was the father of **N**,
2:11 **N** was the father of Salma,
Mat 1:4 Amminadab the father of **N**,
1:4 **N** the father of Salmon.
Luk 3:32 Boaz, son of Salmon, son of **N**,

Nahum (2)

Nah 1:1 the vision of **N** from Elkosh.
Luk 3:25 of Amos, son of **N**, son of Esli,

nail (4)

1Sm 18:11 "I'll **n** David to the wall."
19:10 Saul tried to **n** David to the wall
26:8 Please let me **n** him to the
Jon 20:25 this unless I see the **n** marks

nailing (1)

Col 2:14 He took the charges away by **n**

nails (7)

Dtr 21:12 must shave her head, cut her **n**,
1Ch 22:3 a large quantity of iron for **n**
2Ch 3:9 The gold **n** weighed 20 ounces.
Ecc 12:11 are like **n** that have been
Isa 41:7 And they fasten things with **n**
Jer 10:4 hammers and **n** so that they
Dan 4:33 feathers and his **n** grew as long

Nain (1)

Luk 7:11 Jesus went to a city called **N**.

naked (52)

Gen 2:25 man and his wife were both **n**,
3:7 both realized that they were **n**.
3:10 I was afraid because I was **n**,
3:11 "Who told you that you were **n**?
9:21 and lay **n** inside his tent.
9:22 of Canaan, saw his father **n**.
9:23 covered their father's **n** body.
9:23 they didn't see their father **n**.
Dtr 28:48 **n**, and in need of everything.
1Sm 19:24 Samuel and lay there **n** all day
2Ch 28:15 to all the prisoners who were **n**.
Job 1:21 "**N** I came from my mother,
1:21 my mother, and **n** I will return.
24:7 All night they lie **n** without a
24:10 is why the poor go around **n**.
26:6 Sheol is **n** in God's presence,
31:19 or a poor person going **n** ....
Ecc 5:15 from their mother's womb **n**.
5:15 They will leave as **n** as they
Isa 20:2 walked around barefoot and **n**.
20:3 Isaiah has gone barefoot and **n**
20:4 They will be barefoot and **n**.
32:11 off your clothes, walk around **n**,
47:3 People will see you **n**.
57:8 You've seen them **n**.
58:7 when you see ⌊them⌋ **n**.
Lam 1:8 They've seen it **n**. Jerusalem
Eze 16:7 Yet, you were **n** and bare.
16:8 and covered your **n** body.
16:22 when you were **n** and bare,
16:36 your **n** body when you
16:37 and they will see you **n**.
16:39 and leave you **n** and bare.
18:7 clothes to those who are **n**.
18:16 clothes to those who are **n**.
23:10 They stripped her **n**,
23:18 and she lay around **n**.
23:29 They will leave you **n** and bare.
Hos 2:3 I will leave her as **n** as the day
2:9 I gave her to cover her **n** body.
2:10 I will show her **n** body to her
Amo 2:16 will run away **n** that day.
Mic 1:8 walk around barefoot and **n**.
1:11 Pass by, **n** and ashamed,
Nah 3:5 I will show nations your **n** body
Mar 14:52 sheet behind and ran away **n**.
Act 19:16 of that house **n** and wounded.
2Co 5:3 have put it on, we won't be **n**.
Rev 3:17 pitiful, poor, blind, and **n**.
3:18 **n** body from showing.
16:15 He will not have to go **n** and let
17:16 leave her abandoned and **n**.

nakedness (2)

Hab 2:15 drunk in order to stare at his **n**.'
Rom 8:35 persecution, hunger, **n**, danger,

name (732)

Gen 2:11 The **n** of the first river is
2:13 The **n** of the second river is
2:14 The **n** of the third river is Tigris.
2:19 each creature became its **n**.
4:21 His brother's **n** was Jubal.
10:25 The **n** of the one was Peleg
10:25 His brother's **n** was Joktan.
11:4 Let's make a **n** for ourselves so
11:29 The **n** of Abram's wife was
11:29 and the **n** of Nahor's wife was
12:2 I will make your **n** great,
16:11 You will **n** him Ishmael [God
17:5 So your **n** will no longer be
17:15 wife by the **n** Sarai anymore.
17:15 her **n** is Sarah [Princess].
17:19 and you will **n** him Isaac [He
21:12 will carry on your **n**.
22:16 taking an oath on my own **n**,
22:24 whose **n** was Reumah,
24:29 Rebekah had a brother whose **n**
25:1 and his wife's **n** was Keturah.
26:33 That is why the **n** of the city is
28:19 the **n** of the city was Luz.
29:16 The **n** of the older one was
29:16 and the **n** of the younger one
30:28 So he offered, "**N** your wages,

Gen 32:27 asked him, "What's your **n**?"
32:28 The man said, "Your **n** will no
32:29 "Please tell me your **n**."
32:29 "Why do you ask for my **n**?"
35:10 said to him, "Your **n** is Jacob.
35:10 but your **n** will be Israel."
36:32 The **n** of his ⌊capital⌋ city was
36:35 The **n** of his capital city was
36:39 and the **n** of his capital city
36:39 His wife's **n** was Mehetabel,
36:40 and **n**: Timna, Alvah, Jetheth,
38:1 Adullam whose **n** was Hirah.
38:2 man whose **n** was Shua.
38:6 son Er. Her **n** was Tamar.
48:16 May they be called by my **n**
49:24 because of the **n** of the
Exo 3:13 'What is his **n**?' What
3:15 This is my **n** forever.
6:3 myself known to them by my **n**,
9:16 make my **n** famous throughout
15:3 The LORD is his **n**.
18:4 The **n** of the other was Eliezer
20:7 "Never use the **n** of the LORD
20:7 uses his **n** will be punished.
20:24 to have my **n** remembered,
28:21 to the 12 sons of Israel, by **n**,
28:21 (like a signet ring) with the **n**
33:12 also said, 'I know you by **n**,
33:17 and I know you by **n**."
33:19 I will call out my **n** 'the LORD.'
34:5 called out his **n** "the LORD."
39:14 to the 12 sons of Israel, by **n**,
39:14 (like a signet ring) with the **n**
Lev 18:21 you are dishonoring the **n** of
19:12 "Never swear by my **n** in order
19:12 This dishonors the **n** of your
20:3 and dishonored my holy **n**.
21:6 and don't dishonor the **n** of your
22:2 will not dishonor my holy **n**.
22:32 Never dishonor my holy **n**.
24:11 began cursing the LORD's **n**
24:14 "The man who cursed ⌊my **n**⌋
24:14 curse ⌊my **n**⌋ must lay their
24:16 who curse the LORD's **n** must
24:16 curses the LORD's **n** must die.
24:23 LORD's **n** was taken outside
Num 1:2 List every man by **n**
1:18 Then his **n** was listed.
1:20 listed every man by **n** who was
1:22 every man by **n** who was at
1:24 the men by **n** who were at
1:26 the men by **n** who were at
1:28 the men by **n** who were at
1:30 the men by **n** who were at
1:32 the men by **n** who were at
1:34 the men by **n** who were at
1:36 the men by **n** who were at
1:38 the men by **n** who were at
1:40 the men by **n** who were at
1:42 the men by **n** who were at
3:43 They were listed by **n**.
4:32 Tell each man by **n** the things
6:27 "So whenever they use my **n** to
13:16 son of Nun, the **n** Joshua.
17:2 Write each man's **n** on his staff.
17:3 Write Aaron's **n** on the staff for
25:14 The **n** of the Israelite man who
25:15 The **n** of the Midianite woman
26:59 The **n** of Amram's wife was
27:4 Why should our father's **n** be
Dtr 3:9 Mount Hermon by the **n** Sirion,
3:14 This is still their **n** today.)
5:11 "Never use the **n** of the LORD
5:11 who uses his **n** carelessly will
6:13 take your oaths only in his **n**.
9:14 them and wipe their **n** off
10:8 and to praise his **n**,
10:20 and take your oaths in his **n**.
12:5 your tribes to live and put his **n**.
12:11 a place where his **n** will live.
12:21 chooses to put his **n** is too far
14:23 he will choose to put his **n**.
14:24 will choose to put his **n** may
16:2 will choose for his **n** to live.
16:6 will choose for his **n** to live.
16:11 will choose for his **n** to live.

Dtr 18:5 do the work of serving in the **n**
18:7 and may serve in the **n** of the
18:19 speaks in my **n** will answer
18:20 to say something in my **n** that
18:20 to say or who speaks in the **n**
18:22 prophet speaks in the LORD's **n**
21:5 bless people in the LORD's **n**.
25:6 the dead brother's **n** so that his
25:6 name so that his **n** won't die out
25:7 to let his brother's **n** continue
26:2 will choose for his **n** to live.
28:58 glorious and awe-inspiring **n**:
29:20 that person's **n** from the earth.
32:3 I will proclaim the **n** of the
Jos 5:9 the **n** it still has today.
7:9 great **n** ⌊will be remembered⌋?"
22:34 and Gad gave the altar a **n**:
Jdg 1:26 The city still has that **n** today.
13:6 and he didn't tell me his **n**.
13:17 of the LORD, "What is your **n**?
13:18 "Why do you ask for my **n**?
13:18 It's a **n** that works miracles."
16:4 Her **n** was Delilah.
Rut 1:2 The man's **n** was Elimelech,
1:2 his wife's **n** was Naomi,
4:5 in the dead man's **n**."
4:10 inheritance in the dead man's **n**.
4:10 In this way the dead man's **n**
4:11 in Ephrathah and make a **n**
4:14 The child's **n** will be famous in
4:17 So they gave him the **n** Obed.
1Sm 8:2 The **n** of his firstborn son was
8:2 the **n** of his second son was
9:1 Benjamin whose **n** was Kish.
12:22 For the sake of his great **n**,
14:4 The **n** of one ⌊cliff⌋ was
14:4 and the **n** of the other was
14:50 The **n** of Saul's wife was
14:50 The **n** of the commander of his
17:4 His **n** was Goliath from Gath.
17:45 but I come to you in the **n** of the
20:16 At that time, if Jonathan's **n** is
20:42 taken an oath in the LORD's **n**,
21:7 His **n** was Doeg. A foreman for
22:20 His **n** was Abiathar.
24:21 descendants or destroy my **n**
25:3 This man's **n** was Nabal,
25:3 and his wife's **n** was Abigail.
25:25 He is like his **n**. His name is
25:25 His **n** is Nabal [Godless Fool],
28:10 took an oath in the LORD's **n**,
2Sm 4:4 His **n** was Mephibosheth.)
6:2 (The ark is called by the **n** of
6:18 he blessed the people in the **n**
7:9 I will make your **n** famous like
7:13 He will build a house for my **n**,
7:23 to make his **n** known,
7:26 Your **n** will be respected
8:13 David made a **n** for himself by
9:2 a servant whose **n** was Ziba.
9:12 young son whose **n** was Mica.
12:25 through the prophet Nathan to **n**
13:3 a friend by the **n** of Jonadab,
14:7 will not let my husband's **n**
16:5 His **n** was Shimei,
18:18 the memory of my **n** alive."
18:18 He called the rock by his **n**,
20:1 A good-for-nothing man by the **n**
20:21 of Ephraim by the **n** of Sheba,
21:7 in the LORD's **n** between David
22:50 make music to praise your **n**.
1Ki 1:47 Solomon's **n** more famous than
3:2 because a temple for the **n**
5:3 couldn't build a temple for the **n**
5:5 of building a temple for the **n**
5:5 will build a temple for my **n**.'
8:16 to build a temple for my **n**.
8:17 on building a temple for the **n**
8:18 on building a temple for my **n**,
8:19 will build the temple for my **n**.'
8:20 I've built the temple for the **n** of
8:29 'My **n** will be there.'
8:33 turn to you, praise your **n**, pray,
8:35 this place, praise your **n**,
8:41 will hear about your great **n**,
8:41 countries because of your **n**

1Ki 8:43 of the world may know your **n**
8:43 which I built bears your **n**.
8:44 and the temple I built for your **n**,
8:48 temple I have built for your **n**,
9:3 built is holy so that my **n** may
9:7 that I declared holy for my **n**.
10:1 (He owed his reputation to the **n**
11:36 where I chose to place my **n**.
13:2 His **n** will be Josiah.
14:21 city where the LORD put his **n**.
18:24 "You call on the **n** of your gods,
18:24 but I will call on the **n** of the
18:25 Call on the **n** of your god,
18:26 and called on the **n** of Baal
18:31 "Your **n** will be Israel.")
18:32 built an altar in the LORD's **n**
21:8 signed them with Ahab's **n**,
22:16 take an oath in the LORD's **n**
22:42 His mother's **n** was Azubah,
2Ki 2:24 cursed them in the LORD's **n**.
5:11 call on the **n** of the LORD his
14:7 He gave it the **n** Joktheel,
14:7 which is still its **n** today.
14:27 wipe out Israel's **n** completely,
21:1 His mother's **n** was Hephzibah.
21:4 "I will put my **n** in Jerusalem."
21:7 I will put my **n** here forever.
23:27 where I said my **n** would be."
23:34 Eliakim's **n** to Jehoiakim.
24:17 Mattaniah's **n** to Zedekiah.
1Ch 1:19 The **n** of the one was Peleg
1:19 His brother's **n** was Joktan.
1:43 and the **n** of his ⌊capital⌋ city
1:46 and the **n** of his ⌊capital⌋ city
1:50 and the **n** of his ⌊capital⌋ city
1:50 His wife's **n** was Mehetabel,
2:26 Her **n** was Atarah, and she was
2:29 The **n** of Abishur's wife was
4:3 sister's **n** was Hazelelponi.
4:38 These who are mentioned by **n**
6:65 and mentioned here by **n** from
7:15 His wife's **n** was Maacah.
7:15 The **n** of his second son was
7:16 His brother's **n** was Sheresh,
8:29 and his wife's **n** was Maacah.
9:35 and his wife's **n** was Maacah.
12:31 who had been designated by **n**
13:6 the ark⌋ where his **n** is used.)
16:2 people in the **n** of the LORD.
16:8 Call on his **n**. Make known
16:10 Brag about his holy **n**.
16:29 LORD the glory his **n** deserves.
16:35 may give thanks to your holy **n**
16:41 been selected, chosen by **n**,
17:8 I will make your **n** like the
17:21 to make your **n** known,
17:24 Your **n** will endure and be
21:19 had told him in the LORD's **n**.
22:7 on building a temple for the **n**
22:8 not build a temple for my **n**
22:9 His **n** will be Solomon [Peace],
22:10 He will build a temple for my **n**.
22:19 will be built for the LORD's **n**."
23:13 give the blessing in his **n**.
23:24 registered by **n** as they were
28:3 not build the temple for my **n**.
29:13 and praise your wonderful **n**.
29:16 for your holy **n** is from you.
2Ch 2:1 the temple for the LORD's **n**
2:4 to build the temple for the **n**
6:5 to build a temple for my **n**.
6:6 to be a place for my **n**;
6:7 on building a temple for the **n**
6:8 on building a temple for my **n**,
6:9 will build the temple for my **n**.'
6:10 I've built the temple for the **n** of
6:20 which you said your **n** will
6:24 people turn, praise your **n**, pray,
6:26 this place, praise your **n**,
6:32 because of your great **n**,
6:33 of the world may know your **n**
6:33 which I built bears your **n**.
6:34 and the temple I built for your **n**,
6:38 temple I have built for your **n**,
7:14 who are called by my **n**,

2Ch 7:16 temple holy so that my **n** may
7:20 that I declared holy for my **n**.
12:13 city where the LORD put his **n**.
14:11 In your **n** we go against this
18:15 take an oath in the LORD's **n**
20:8 a holy temple for your **n** in it.
20:9 front of you because your **n** is
20:31 His mother's **n** was Azubah,
28:15 mentioned by **n** took charge
33:4 "My **n** will be in Jerusalem
33:7 I will put my **n** here forever.
33:18 the seers spoke to him in the **n**
36:4 Eliakim's **n** to Jehoiakim.
36:13 of allegiance to him in God's **n**.
Ezr 2:61 and took that ⌊family⌋ **n**).
5:1 Judah and Jerusalem in the **n**
6:12 May the God whose **n** is
8:20 These were all listed by **n**.
10:16 (They were all ⌊listed⌋ by **n**.)
Neh 1:9 where I chose to put my **n**.'
1:11 who want to worship your **n**.
7:63 and took that ⌊family⌋ **n**).
9:5 your glorious **n** is praised
9:7 and gave him the **n** Abraham.
9:10 You made a **n** for yourself,
9:10 a **n** which remains to this day.
Est 2:14 her and requested her by **n**.
3:12 The orders were signed in the **n**
8:8 for the Jews in the king's **n**.
8:8 is written in the king's **n**
8:10 wrote in King Xerxes' **n**
Job 1:21 May the **n** of the LORD be
Psa 5:11 who love your **n** triumph in you.
7:17 will make music to praise the **n**
8:1 how majestic is your **n**
8:9 is your **n** throughout the earth!
9:2 make music to praise your **n**,
9:10 who know your **n** trust you,
18:49 make music to praise your **n**.
20:1 The **n** of the God of Jacob will
20:5 We will wave our flags in the **n**
20:7 but we will boast in the **n** of the
22:22 tell my people about your **n**.
23:3 for the sake of his **n**.
25:11 For the sake of your **n**,
29:2 LORD the glory his **n** deserves.
31:3 For the sake of your **n**,
33:21 In his holy **n** we trust.
34:3 Let us highly honor his **n**
41:5 and when will his family **n**
44:5 With your **n** we can trample
44:20 If we forgot the **n** of our God or
45:17 I will cause your **n** to be
48:10 Like your **n**, O God, your praise
52:9 wait with hope in your good **n**.
54:1 O God, save me by your **n**,
54:6 will give thanks to your good **n**,
54:7 Your **n** rescues me from every
61:5 to those who fear your **n**.
61:8 music to praise your **n** forever,
63:4 my hands ⌊to pray⌋ in your **n**.
66:2 to praise the glory of his **n**.
66:4 make music to praise your **n**."
68:4 make music to praise his **n**.
68:4 The LORD is his **n**.
69:30 I want to praise the **n** of God
72:17 May his **n** endure forever.
72:17 May his **n** continue as long as
72:19 be to his glorious **n** forever.
74:18 godless fools despised your **n**.
74:21 needy people praise your **n**.
76:1 His **n** is great in Israel.
79:9 for the glory of your **n**.
79:9 our sins for the honor of your **n**.
83:4 out their nation so that the **n**
83:18 Your **n** is the LORD.
89:12 Hermon sing your **n** joyfully.
89:16 They find joy in your **n** all day
89:24 and in my **n** he will be
91:14 you because you know my **n**.
92:1 to make music to praise your **n**,
96:2 Praise his **n**! Day after day
99:3 to your great and fearful **n**.
100:4 thanks to him; praise his **n**.
102:8 me use my **n** as a curse.
102:15 nations will fear the LORD's **n**.
Psa 102:21 The LORD's **n** is announced in
103:1 Praise his holy **n**, all that is
105:3 Brag about his holy **n**.
106:47 may give thanks to your holy **n**
109:13 be cut off and their family **n**
109:21 out of the goodness of your **n**.
111:9 His **n** is holy and terrifying.
113:1 Praise the **n** of the LORD.
113:2 Thank the **n** of the LORD now
113:3 the **n** of the LORD should be
115:1 Instead, give glory to your **n**
116:4 But I kept calling on the **n** of
116:13 and call on the **n** of the LORD.
116:17 I will call on the **n** of the LORD.
118:10 ⌊but armed⌋ with the **n** of the
118:11 ⌊but armed⌋ with the **n** of the
118:12 ⌊So armed⌋ with the **n** of the
118:26 is the one who comes in the **n**
119:55 At night I remember your **n**,
119:132 to do for those who love your **n**.
122:4 thanks to the **n** of the LORD.
124:8 Our help is in the **n** of the
129:8 you in the **n** of the LORD."
135:1 Praise the **n** of the LORD.
135:3 Make music to praise his **n**
135:3 because his **n** is beautiful.
135:13 your **n** endures forever.
138:2 I will give thanks to your **n**
138:2 You have made your **n** and
139:20 Your enemies misuse your **n**.
140:13 will give thanks to your **n**.
142:7 I may give thanks to your **n**.
143:11 me alive for the sake of your **n**.
145:1 bless your **n** forever and ever.
145:2 praise your **n** forever and ever.
145:21 his holy **n** forever and ever.
147:4 He gives each one a **n**.
148:5 Let them praise the **n** of the
148:13 Let them praise the **n** of the
148:13 because his **n** is high above
149:3 them praise his **n** with dancing.
Pro 7:4 Give the **n** "my relative" to
10:7 The **n** of a righteous person
18:10 The **n** of the LORD is a strong
22:1 A good **n** is more desirable
30:4 What is his **n** or the name of
30:4 What is his name or the **n** of
30:9 poor and steal and give the **n**
Ecc 6:4 The darkness then hides its **n**.
6:10 ⌊in the past⌋ already has a **n**.
7:1 A good **n** is better than
Isa 4:1 Just let us marry you for your **n**.
7:14 and she will **n** him Immanuel
8:3 **N** him Maher Shalal Hash Baz.
12:4 Call on his **n**. Make his deeds
12:4 that his **n** is highly honored.
14:22 "I'll cut off the **n** of the survivors
18:7 the place where the **n** of the
24:15 Honor the **n** of the LORD God
25:1 I will praise your **n**.
26:8 to remember you and your **n**.
29:23 acknowledge my **n** as holy.
30:27 The **n** of the LORD is going to
40:26 He calls them all by **n**.
41:25 He will call on my **n** from the
42:8 I am the LORD; that is my **n**.
43:1 I have called you by **n**;
43:7 who is called by my **n**,
44:5 will call on the **n** of Jacob.
44:5 he will adopt the **n** of Israel.
45:3 have called you by **n**.
45:4 I have called you by **n**.
47:4 His **n** is the LORD of Armies.
48:1 You are given the **n** of Israel.
48:1 You take oaths by the **n** of the
48:2 His **n** is the LORD of Armies.
48:11 should my **n** be dishonored?
49:1 womb, he recorded my **n**.
50:10 and have no light trust the **n**
51:15 My **n** is the LORD of Armies.
52:5 And my **n** is cursed all day
52:6 my people will know my **n**.
54:5 His **n** is the LORD of Armies.
55:13 be a reminder of the LORD's **n**
56:5 give them a monument and a **n**.
56:5 I will give them a permanent **n**
Isa 56:6 to love the LORD's **n**,
57:15 lives forever, and his **n** is holy.
59:19 of the west will fear the **n**
60:9 comes with them to honor the **n**
62:2 You will be given a new **n** that
63:12 an everlasting **n** for himself?
63:14 make an honored **n** for yourself.
63:16 Your **n** is our Defender From
63:19 who are not called by your **n**.
64:2 Come down to make your **n**
64:7 No one calls on your **n** or tries
65:15 Your **n** will be used as a curse
65:15 call his servants by another **n**.
66:22 and your **n** will also continue
Jer 2:8 prophets prophesied in the **n**
3:17 in Jerusalem because the **n**
7:10 house that is called by my **n**.
7:11 is called by my **n** has become
7:12 a dwelling place for my **n**.
7:14 house that is called by my **n**.
7:30 house that is called by my **n**.
10:6 Your **n** is powerful.
10:16 His **n** is the LORD of Armies.
11:21 "Don't prophesy in the **n** of the
12:16 they take an oath in my **n**,
12:16 take an oath in ⌊the **n** of⌋ Baal.
14:7 for the sake of your **n**,
14:9 We are called by your **n**.
14:14 the prophets are telling in my **n**:
14:15 Yet, they prophesy in my **n** that
14:21 For the sake of your **n**,
15:16 because I am called by your **n**,
16:21 know that my **n** is the LORD."
20:9 and no longer speak his **n**."
23:6 This is the **n** that he will be
23:25 who speak lies in my **n**.
23:27 to make my people forget my **n**,
23:27 forgot my **n** because of Baal.
26:9 in the LORD's **n** that this temple
26:16 He has spoken to us in the **n** of
26:20 man prophesying in the **n**
26:20 His **n** was Uriah, son of
27:15 They prophesy lies in my **n**.
29:9 lies to you in my **n**.
29:21 prophesy lies to you in my **n**:
29:23 wives and spoke lies in my **n**.
29:25 You sent letters in your own **n**
31:35 His **n** is the LORD of Armies.
32:18 Your **n** is the LORD of Armies.
32:20 You made a **n** for yourself that
32:34 temple that is called by my **n**,
33:2 My **n** is the LORD.
34:15 temple that is called by my **n**.
37:13 whose **n** was Irijah,
44:16 spoken to us in the LORD's **n**.
44:26 'I swear by my great **n**,' says
44:26 will ever again call on my **n**
46:18 whose **n** is the LORD of
48:15 whose **n** is the LORD of
50:34 His **n** is the LORD of Armies.
51:19 His **n** is the LORD of Armies.
51:57 whose **n** is the LORD of
52:1 His mother's **n** was Hamutal,
Lam 3:55 "I call your **n** from the deepest
Eze 20:9 But I acted so that my **n** would
20:14 But I acted so that my **n** would
20:22 power so that my **n** would not
20:39 no longer dishonor my holy **n**
20:44 with you for the sake of my **n**.
22:5 Your **n** will be dishonored,
36:20 they dishonored my holy **n**.
36:21 concerned about my holy **n**
36:22 but for the sake of my holy **n**,
36:23 the holiness of my great **n**,
36:23 ⌊the **n**⌋ that you have
39:7 I will make my holy **n** known
39:7 them dishonor my holy **n** again.
39:25 I will stand up for my holy **n**.
43:7 my holy **n** by acting like
43:8 They dishonored my holy **n**
48:35 then on the city's **n** will be:
Dan 1:7 he gave the **n** Belteshazzar.
1:7 he gave the **n** Shadrach.
1:7 he gave the **n** Meshach.
1:7 And to Azariah he gave the **n**
2:20 He said, "Praise God's **n** from

Dan 9:6 who spoke in your **n** to our
9:18 and at the city called by your **n**.
9:19 people are called by your **n**."
Hos 1:4 told Hosea, "**N** him Jezreel.
1:6 "**N** her Lo Ruhamah [Unloved].
1:9 The LORD said, "**N** him Lo
12:5 The LORD is the **n** by which
Joe 2:26 You will praise the **n** of the
2:32 Then whoever calls on the **n** of
Amo 2:7 They dishonor my holy **n**.
4:13 His **n** is the LORD God of
5:8 His **n** is the LORD.
5:27 whose **n** is the God of Armies.
6:10 mention the **n** of the LORD!"
9:6 the earth — His **n** is the LORD.
Mic 4:5 but we will live by the **n** of the
5:4 with the majestic **n** of the
6:9 (The fear of your **n** is wisdom.)
Nah 1:14 descendants to carry on your **n**.
Zep 3:12 refuge in the **n** of the LORD.
Zec 5:4 those who take oaths in my **n**.
6:12 is the man whose **n** is Branch.
10:12 in his **n**," declares the LORD.
13:3 you speak lies in the **n**
14:9 Lord and his **n** the only name.
14:9 Lord and his name the only **n**.
Mal 1:6 You priests despise my **n**.
1:6 have we despised your **n**?'
1:11 my **n** will be great.
1:11 be offered everywhere in my **n**,
1:11 because my **n** will be great
1:14 the nations my **n** is respected.
2:2 giving honor to my **n**," says
2:5 me and stood in awe of my **n**.
3:16 the LORD and respected his **n**.
4:2 for you people who fear my **n**.
Mat 1:21 and you will **n** him Jesus [He
1:23 and they will **n** him Immanuel,"
5:22 an insulting **n** will answer
6:9 let your **n** be kept holy.
7:22 didn't we prophesy in your **n**?
7:22 power and authority of your **n**?'
9:9 The man's **n** was Matthew.
10:25 family members the same **n**.
13:55 Isn't his mother's **n** Mary?
18:5 like this in my **n** welcomes me.
18:20 have come together in my **n**,
19:29 or fields because of my **n** will
21:9 is the one who comes in the **n**
22:20 "Whose face and **n** is this?"
23:39 comes in the **n** of the Lord!'"
24:5 Many will come using my **n**.
27:16 prisoner by the **n** of Barabbas.
28:19 Baptize them in the **n** of the
Mar 5:9 asked him, "What is your **n**?"
5:9 He told Jesus, "My **n** is Legion
6:14 because Jesus' **n** had become
9:37 like this in my **n** welcomes me.
9:38 power and authority of your **n**.
9:39 miracle in my **n** can turn around
11:9 who comes in the **n** of the Lord!
12:16 "Whose face and **n** is this?"
13:6 Many will come using my **n**.
16:17 the power and authority of my **n**
Luk 1:13 and you will **n** him John.
1:27 The virgin's **n** was Mary.
1:31 birth to a son, and **n** him Jesus.
1:49 things to me. His **n** is holy.
1:59 They were going to **n** him
1:60 His **n** will be John."
1:61 have any relatives with that **n**."
1:62 what he wanted to **n** the child.
1:63 and wrote, "His **n** is John."
2:21 This was the **n** the angel had
8:30 asked him, "What is your **n**?"
9:48 child in my **n** welcomes me.
9:49 power and authority of your **n**.
10:17 power and authority of your **n**!"
11:2 let your **n** be kept holy.
13:35 comes in the **n** of the Lord!'"
19:38 is the king who comes in the **n**
20:24 Whose face and **n** is this?"
21:8 Many will come using my **n**.
21:12 governors because of my **n**.
23:50 His **n** was Joseph.
Jon 1:42 Your **n** will be Cephas" (which
Jon 10:3 He calls his sheep by **n** and
10:25 that I do in my Father's **n** testify
12:13 is the one who comes in the **n**
12:28 Father, give glory to your **n**."
14:13 ⌊the Father⌋ in my **n** so that
14:26 the Father will send in my **n**,
15:16 and to ask the Father in my **n**
16:23 the Father for anything in my **n**,
16:24 asked for anything in my **n**.
16:26 ask for what you want in my **n**.
17:6 "I made your **n** known to the
17:11 safe by the power of your **n**,
17:11 the **n** that you gave me,
17:12 safe by the power of your **n**,
17:12 the **n** that you gave me.
17:26 I have made your **n** known to
18:10 (The servant's **n** was Malchus.)
Act 2:21 Then whoever calls on the **n** of
2:38 you must be baptized in the **n**
4:7 "By what power or in whose **n**
4:18 Jesus or even mention his **n**.
4:30 through the power and the **n**
5:28 Jesus' **n** when you teach.
8:16 had only been baptized in the **n**
9:14 who calls on your **n** in prison."
9:15 man to bring my **n** to nations,
9:16 to suffer for the sake of my **n**."
9:36 Her Greek **n** was Dorcas.
10:5 a man whose **n** is Simon Peter.
10:32 and summon a man whose **n** is
10:48 should be baptized in the **n**
11:13 a man whose **n** is Simon Peter.
13:8 whose **n** means astrologer,
15:14 those who would honor his **n**.
15:17 over whom my **n** is spoken,
16:18 "I command you in the **n** of
17:7 whose **n** is Jesus."
19:5 they were baptized in the **n** of
19:13 They tried to use the **n** of the
19:13 come out⌋ in the **n** of Jesus,
19:17 were filled with awe for the **n**
22:16 away as you call on his **n**.'
26:11 them to curse ⌊the **n** of Jesus⌋.
27:1 His **n** was Julius, and he
Rom 1:5 This is for the honor of his **n**.
2:24 As Scripture says, "God's **n** is
9:7 will carry on your **n**."
9:17 my **n** throughout the earth."
10:13 "Whoever prays in the **n** of the
15:9 I will sing praises to your **n**."
15:20 the Good News where the **n**
1Co 1:2 everywhere who call on the **n**
1:10 I encourage all of you in the **n**
1:13 Were you baptized in Paul's **n**?
1:15 say you were baptized in my **n**.
5:4 in the **n** of our Lord Jesus,
6:11 God's approval in the **n**
Gal 3:27 **n** have clothed yourselves
Eph 3:15 and on earth receives its **n**.
4:17 you in the Lord's **n** not
5:20 Father for everything in the **n**
Php 2:9 honor — the **n** honored above
2:10 so that at the **n** of Jesus
Col 3:17 or do should be done in the **n**
1Th 5:27 In the Lord's **n**, I order you to
2Th 1:12 That way the **n** of our Lord
3:6 Brothers and sisters, in the **n** of
1Ti 6:1 one will speak evil of God's **n**
Heb 1:4 been given a **n** that is superior
2:12 tell my people about your **n**.
7:2 Melchizedek's **n** means king of
11:18 will carry on your **n**."
Jas 2:7 curse the good **n** ⌊of Jesus⌋,
2:7 the **n** that was used to bless
5:10 prophets who spoke in the **n**
5:14 olive oil in the **n** of the Lord.
1Pe 4:14 because of the **n** of Christ,
4:16 God for being called that **n**.
3Jn 1:15 Greet each of our friends by **n**.
Rev 2:3 trouble because of my **n**,
2:13 You hold on to my **n** and have
2:17 stone with a new **n** written
2:17 a **n** that is known only to the
3:8 and have not denied my **n**.
3:12 I will write on them the **n** of my
3:12 the **n** of the city of my God (the
Rev 3:12 from my God), and my new **n**.
6:8 and its rider's **n** was Death.
11:18 and those who fear your **n**,
13:6 to insult his **n** and his tent —
13:8 everyone whose **n** is not
13:17 which is the beast's **n** or the
13:17 name or the number of its **n**.
14:1 people with him who had his **n**
14:1 name and his Father's **n** written
14:11 for anyone branded with its **n**."
15:2 and the number of its **n** were
15:4 won't fear and praise your **n**?
16:9 They cursed the **n** of God,
17:5 A **n** was written on her
17:5 The **n** was Mystery:
19:12 He has a **n** written on him,
19:13 and his **n** is the Word of God.
19:16 his thigh he has a **n** written:
22:4 His **n** will be on their foreheads.

named (207)

Gen 1:5 God **n** the light day,
1:5 and the darkness he **n** night.
1:8 God **n** ⌊what was above⌋ the
1:10 God **n** the dry land earth.
1:10 which came together he **n** sea.
2:20 So the man **n** all the domestic
2:23 She will be **n** woman because
3:20 Adam **n** his wife Eve [Life]
4:17 and he **n** it Enoch after his son.
4:19 one **n** Adah and the other
4:25 birth to a son and **n** him Seth,
4:26 and he **n** him Enosh.
5:3 his own image. He **n** him Seth.
5:29 He **n** him Noah [Relief],
11:9 This is why it was **n** Babel,
16:1 an Egyptian slave **n** Hagar.
16:13 Hagar **n** the LORD,
16:14 This is why the well is **n** Beer
16:15 Abram **n** him Ishmael.
19:22 (The city is **n** Zoar [Small].)
19:37 birth to a son and **n** him Moab.
19:38 to a son and **n** him Ben Ammi.
21:3 Abraham **n** his newborn son
22:14 Abraham **n** that place The
25:25 so they **n** him Esau [Hairy].
25:26 and so he was **n** Jacob [Heel].
26:20 So Isaac **n** the well Esek
26:21 Isaac **n** it Sitnah [Accusation].
26:22 So he **n** it Rehoboth [Roomy]
26:33 So he **n** it Shibah [Oath].
27:36 "Isn't that why he's **n** Jacob?
28:19 He **n** that place Bethel [House
29:32 She **n** him Reuben [Here's My
29:33 So she **n** him Simeon [Hearing].
29:34 So she **n** him Levi [Attached].
29:35 So she **n** him Judah [Praise].
30:6 So she **n** him Dan [He Judges].
30:8 So she **n** him Naphtali [My
30:13 So she **n** him Asher [Blessing].
30:18 she **n** him Issachar [Reward].
30:20 So she **n** him Zebulun [Honor].
30:21 to a daughter and **n** her Dinah.
30:24 She **n** him Joseph [May He
31:48 This is why it was **n** Galeed
32:2 He **n** that place Mahanaim
32:30 So Jacob **n** that place Peniel
33:17 That is why the place is **n**
33:20 He set up an altar there and **n** it
35:10 So he **n** him Israel.
35:15 Jacob **n** the place where God
35:18 she **n** her son Benoni [Son of
35:18 but his father **n** him Benjamin
38:3 and gave birth to a son **n** Er.
38:4 whom she **n** Onan.
38:5 whom she **n** Shelah.
38:29 He was **n** Perez [Bursting Into].
38:30 He was **n** Zerah [Sunrise].
41:45 Pharaoh **n** Joseph
41:51 Joseph **n** his firstborn son
41:52 He **n** the second son Ephraim
50:11 was **n** Abel Mizraim[Egyptian
Exo 2:10 Pharaoh's daughter **n** him
2:22 Moses **n** him Gershom
17:7 He **n** that place Massah
18:3 was **n** Gershom [Foreigner],

Num 1:17 took the men who had been **n**
3:18 families were **n** after them.
3:19 families were **n** after them.
3:20 families were **n** after them.
11:26 Two men, **n** Eldad and Medad,
26:46 (Asher had a daughter **n** Serah.
32:42 He **n** it Nobah after himself.
Dtr 3:14 Bashan he **n** Havvoth Jair after
Jos 2:1 house of a prostitute **n** Rahab
5:9 So Joshua **n** the place Gilgal,
Jdg 8:31 That son was **n** Abimelech.
11:1 Jephthah's father was **n** Gilead.
13:2 a man from Zorah **n** Manoah.
13:24 had a son and **n** him Samson.
17:1 There was a man **n** Micah from
18:29 They **n** the city Dan in honor of
Rut 1:4 son married a woman **n** Orpah,
1:4 son married a woman **n** Ruth.
2:1 outstanding character **n** Boaz.
2:19 I worked with today is **n** Boaz."
1Sm 1:1 There was a man **n** Elkanah
1:2 had two wives, one **n** Hannah,
1:20 She **n** him Samuel [God Hears],
7:12 He **n** it Ebenezer [Rock of Help]
9:2 He had a son **n** Saul,
17:12 David was a son of a man **n**
2Sm 3:7 Saul had a concubine **n** Rizpah
4:2 One was **n** Baanah,
4:2 and the other was **n** Rechab.
12:24 David **n** him Solomon.
12:28 and it will be **n** after me."
17:25 (Amasa was the son of a man **n**
21:16 of Haraphah **n** Benob,
1Ki 7:2 He built a hall ⌊**n**⌋ the Forest of
7:21 up the pillar on the right and **n**
7:21 up the pillar on the left and **n**
9:13 So he **n** it the region of Cabul
11:20 sister had a son ⌊**n**⌋ Genubath.
14:21 Ammonite woman **n** Naamah.
14:31 Ammonite woman **n** Naamah.)
15:2 His mother was **n** Maacah,
15:10 grandmother was **n** Maacah,
16:24 He **n** the city after its former
18:31 one for each of the tribes **n** after
2Ki 17:34 of Jacob (whom he **n** Israel).
23:8 the gate **n** after the mayor of the
1Ch 2:18 Azubah had a son **n** Jerioth.
2:34 He had an Egyptian slave **n**
4:9 His mother had **n** him Jabez
4:14 (It was **n** this because they
7:16 and she **n** him Peresh.
7:23 and Ephraim **n** him Beriah
2Ch 3:17 He **n** the one on the right
9:16 king put them in the hall ⌊**n**⌋
9:20 all the utensils for the hall ⌊**n**⌋
12:13 Ammonite woman **n** Naamah.)
13:2 His mother was **n** Micaiah,
24:26 Ammonite woman **n** Shimeath,
24:26 son of a Moabite woman **n**
28:9 A prophet of the LORD **n** Oded
Ezr 5:14 them to a man **n** Sheshbazzar,
Est 2:5 tribe of Benjamin **n** Mordecai.
Job 1:1 A man **n** Job lived in Uz.
42:14 He **n** the first ⌊daughter⌋
Psa 49:11 Although they **n** their lands
Sos 1:3 (Cologne should be **n** after you.
Isa 9:6 He will be **n**: Mighty God,
62:4 But you will be **n** My Delight,
62:4 and your land will be **n** Married.
Jer 25:29 on the city that is **n** after me.
Eze 23:4 "The older girl was **n** Oholah,
23:4 younger girl was **n** Oholibah.
39:16 (A city **n** Hamonah will also be
48:31 The gates of the city will be **n**
Zec 11:7 staffs and **n** one Favor
Mat 1:25 Joseph **n** the child Jesus.
26:14 the one **n** Judas Iscariot,
27:32 way they found a man **n** Simon.
27:57 a rich man **n** Joseph arrived.
Mar 3:16 Simon (whom Jesus **n** Peter),
3:17 whom Jesus **n** Boanerges,
5:22 A synagogue leader **n** Jairus
10:46 a blind beggar **n** Bartimaeus,
15:7 There was a man **n** Barabbas
15:21 A man **n** Simon from the city of
Luk 1:5 there was a priest **n** Zechariah,
Luk 1:5 of priests **n** after Abijah.
1:27 descendant of David **n** Joseph.
2:21 was circumcised and **n** Jesus.
2:25 A man **n** Simeon was in
5:27 He saw a tax collector **n** Levi
6:14 Simon (whom Jesus **n** Peter)
8:41 A man **n** Jairus, a synagogue
10:38 A woman **n** Martha welcomed
10:39 She had a sister **n** Mary.
16:20 There was also a beggar **n**
19:2 A man **n** Zacchaeus was there.
23:26 they grabbed a man **n** Simon,
Jon 1:6 God sent a man **n** John to be
Act 3:16 We believe in the one **n** Jesus.
4:12 the power of the one **n** Jesus
4:17 anyone about the one **n** Jesus.
5:1 A man **n** Ananias and his wife
5:34 But a Pharisee **n** Gamaliel
5:40 speak about the one **n** Jesus,
7:58 coats with a young man **n** Saul.
8:9 A man **n** Simon lived in that
8:12 and the one **n** Jesus Christ,
9:10 A disciple **n** Ananias lived in
9:11 and ask for a man **n** Saul from
9:12 a man **n** Ananias place his
9:21 worshiped the one **n** Jesus
9:27 spoken about the one **n** Jesus
9:33 In Lydda Peter found a man **n**
9:36 A disciple **n** Tabitha lived in
10:1 A man **n** Cornelius lived in the
10:43 **n** Jesus receive forgiveness
11:28 One of them was **n** Agabus.
12:13 and a servant **n** Rhoda came to
13:6 met a Jewish man **n** Barjesus.
15:26 the one **n** Jesus Christ.
16:1 a disciple **n** Timothy lived.
16:14 A woman **n** Lydia was present.
17:34 and a woman **n** Damaris,
18:2 he met a Jewish man **n** Aquila
18:7 home of a man **n** Titius Justus,
18:24 A Jew **n** Apollos, who had
20:9 A young man **n** Eutychus was
21:10 a prophet **n** Agabus arrived
21:13 of the Lord, the one **n** Jesus."
22:12 "A man **n** Ananias lived in
24:1 and an attorney **n** Tertullus.
25:19 some man **n** Jesus who had
26:9 the one **n** Jesus of Nazareth.
28:7 A man **n** Publius, who was the
Eph 1:21 all other names that can be **n**,
1Jn 3:23 the one **n** Jesus Christ,
3Jn 1:7 trip to serve the one **n** Christ,
Rev 8:11 That star was **n** Wormwood.
12:9 **n** Devil and Satan,
19:11 and its rider is **n** Faithful and
20:2 **n** Devil and Satan.

namely (1)

2Sm 11:17 Some of the people, **n**,

name's (2)

Isa 48:9 For my **n** sake I'll be patient.
66:5 you for my **n** sake, say,

names (88)

Gen 25:13 These are the **n** of the sons of
25:16 and their **n** listed by their
26:18 He gave them the same **n** that
36:10 These were the **n** of Esau's
36:40 These were the **n** of the tribal
46:8 These are the **n** of Israel's
48:6 listed under their brothers' **n**.
48:16 by my name and by the **n**
Exo 1:1 These are the **n** of the sons of
1:15 whose **n** were Shiphrah and
6:16 These are the **n** of the sons of
23:13 "Never mention the **n** of other
28:9 and engrave on them the **n** of
28:10 in birth order — six of their **n**
28:11 Engrave the **n** of the sons of
28:12 this way Aaron will carry their **n**
28:29 he will be carrying the **n** of the
39:6 and engraved on them the **n** of
Num 1:5 "Here are the **n** of the men who
3:2 The **n** of Aaron's sons are
3:3 These are the **n** of Aaron's
Num 3:40 and make a list of their **n**.
13:4 These are their **n**: Shammua,
13:16 These are the **n** of the men
26:33 Their **n** were Mahlah,
26:53 the list of **n** ⌊from the census⌋.
26:55 on the **n** of their ancestors.
27:1 Their **n** were Mahlah,
32:38 Meon (whose **n** were changed),
32:38 These are the **n** they gave the
34:17 "These are the **n** of the men
34:19 These are their **n**: Caleb, son of
Dtr 7:24 will even remember their **n**.
12:3 and wipe out the **n** of their gods
Jos 17:3 Their **n** were Mahlah,
21:9 These are the **n** of the cities
23:7 Don't ever mention the **n** of
Jdg 8:14 man wrote down for him the **n**
Rut 1:2 and the **n** of their two sons
1Sm 14:49 The **n** of his two daughters
2Sm 5:14 These are the **n** of the children
7:9 your name famous like the **n**
23:8 These are the **n** of David's
1Ki 4:8 Their **n** were Benhur,
1Ch 6:17 These are the **n** of Gershom's
8:38 Their **n** were Azrikam,
9:44 Their **n** were Azrikam,
14:4 These are the **n** of the children
17:8 will make your name like the **n**
24:6 Shemaiah recorded their **n** in
Ezr 2:62 searched for their ⌊family⌋ **n**
2:62 but their **n** couldn't be found
5:4 also asked the Jews for the **n**
5:10 we also asked them for their **n**
Neh 7:64 searched for their ⌊family⌋ **n**
7:64 but their **n** couldn't be found
12:22 ⌊The **n** of⌋ the family heads of
12:23 ⌊The **n** of⌋ the family heads of
Psa 9:5 out their **n** forever and ever.
16:4 or use my lips to speak their **n**.
69:28 Let their ⌊**n**⌋ be erased from the
Pro 10:7 but the **n** of wicked people will
Isa 48:19 Their **n** would not be cut off or
Eze 48:1 These are the **n** of the tribes.
Dan 1:7 gave them ⌊Babylonian⌋ **n**:
Hos 2:17 I won't allow her to say the **n** of
2:17 will never again call out their **n**.
Mic 4:5 All the nations live by the **n** of
Zep 1:4 Baal from this place and the **n**
Zec 13:2 "I will wipe away the **n** of the
Mat 10:2 These are the **n** of the twelve
13:55 Aren't his brothers' **n** James,
Luk 10:20 Be happy that your **n** are
Act 1:26 They drew **n** to choose an
18:15 **n**, and your own teachings,
Eph 1:21 and all other **n** that can be
Php 2:9 honored above all other **n** —
4:3 whose **n** are in the Book of Life.
Heb 12:23 children (whose **n** are written
Rev 3:5 I will never erase their **n** from
11:8 The spiritual **n** of that city are
13:1 were insulting **n** on its heads.
17:3 beast covered with insulting **n**.
17:8 Those living on earth, whose **n**
20:15 Those whose **n** were not found
21:12 The **n** of the 12 tribes of Israel
21:14 The 12 **n** of the 12 apostles of
21:27 Only those whose **n** are

Naomi (29)

Rut 1:2 his wife's name was **N**,
1:5 So **N** was left alone,
1:6 **N** and her daughters-in-law
1:8 Then **N** said to her two
1:11 But **N** said, "Go back,
1:15 **N** said, "Look, Go back with
1:18 When **N** saw that Ruth was
1:19 "This can't be **N**, can it?"
1:20 "Don't call me **N** [Sweet].
1:21 Why do you call me **N** when
1:22 When **N** came back from the
2:1 **N** had a relative. He was from
2:2 who was from Moab, said to **N**,
2:2 **N** told her, "Go, my daughter."
2:6 who came back with **N** from
2:18 from lunch and gave it to **N**.
2:20 **N** said to her daughter-in-law,

Rut 2:20 Then **N** told her, "That man is a
2:22 **N** told her daughter-in-law Ruth,
3:1 **N**, Ruth's mother-in-law, said to
3:16 her mother-in-law **N** asked,
3:16 Ruth told **N** everything the man
3:18 **N** replied, "Stay here,
4:3 Boaz said to the man, "**N**,
4:5 "When you buy the field from **N**
4:9 bought from **N** all that belonged
4:14 The women said to **N**,
4:16 **N** took the child, held him on
4:17 said, "**N** has a son."

Naomi's (1)

Rut 1:3 **N** husband Elimelech died,

nap (3)

2Sm 4:5 was taking his midday **n**
Pro 6:10 a little slumber, just a little **n**."
24:33 a little slumber, just a little **n**."

Naphish (3)

Gen 25:15 Hadad, Tema, Jetur, **N**,
1Ch 1:31 Jetur, **N**, and Kedemah.
5:19 (including Jetur, **N**, and Nodab)

Naphoth Dor (2)

Jos 11:2 the foothills, and **N** in the west,
12:23 of Dor in **N**, the king of Goiim

Naphtali (52)

Gen 30:8 named him **N** [My Struggle].
35:25 slave Bilhah were Dan and **N**.
46:24 The sons of **N** were Jahzeel,
49:21 "**N** is a doe set free that has
Exo 1:4 Dan and **N**; Gad and Asher.
Num 1:15 from the tribe of **N**."
1:42 for the descendants of **N** listed
1:43 for the tribe of **N** was 53,400.
2:29 "Then ⌊will be⌋ the tribe of **N**.
2:29 for the people of **N** is Ahira,
7:78 leader of the descendants of **N**,
10:27 commanded the army of **N**.
13:14 from the tribe of **N**;
26:48 The families descended from **N**
26:50 These were the families of **N**.
34:28 the leader of the tribe of **N**."
Dtr 27:13 Asher, Zebulun, Dan, and **N**.
33:23 About the tribe of **N** he said,
33:23 "The people of **N** enjoy the
34:2 all of **N**, the territory of Ephraim
Jos 19:32 descended from the tribe of **N**.
19:39 for the families of the tribe of **N**.
20:7 Galilee in the mountains of **N**,
21:6 the tribes of Issachar, Asher, **N**,
21:32 to them from the tribe of **N**:
Jdg 1:33 The tribe of **N** did not force out
4:6 of Abinoam, from Kedesh in **N**.
4:6 Take 10,000 men from **N** and
4:10 and **N** together at Kedesh.
5:18 and **N** risked his life on the
6:35 and **N** were also summoned to
7:23 Israel were summoned from **N**,
1Ki 4:15 Ahimaaz was in charge of **N**.
7:14 of a widow from the tribe of **N**.
15:20 with the entire territory of **N**.
2Ki 15:29 and the entire territory of **N**.
1Ch 2:2 Dan, Joseph, Benjamin, **N**,
6:62 the tribes of Issachar, Asher, **N**,
6:76 From the tribe of **N**,
12:34 From **N** there were 1,000
12:40 and **N** brought food on donkeys
27:19 of Obadiah for the tribe of **N**:
2Ch 16:4 cities in the territory of **N**.
34:6 Simeon, and as far as **N**,
Psa 68:27 ⌊then⌋ the leaders of **N**.
Isa 9:1 the lands of Zebulun and **N**
Eze 48:3 **N** will have one part of the land
48:4 part of the land and border **N**
48:34 Gate, Asher Gate, and **N** Gate.
Mat 4:13 in the region of Zebulun and **N**.
4:15 "Land of Zebulun and land of **N**,
Rev 7:6 12,000 from the tribe of **N**,

Naphtali's (1)

1Ch 7:13 **N** sons were Jahziel,

Naphtuhites (2)

Gen 10:13 Anamites, Lehabites, **N**,
1Ch 1:11 Anamites, Lehabites, **N**,

Narcissus (1)

Rom 16:11 who belong to the family of **N**.

nard (4)

Sos 4:13 henna flowers and **n**,
4:14 **n** and saffron, calamus,
Mar 14:3 perfume made from pure **n**.
Jon 12:3 perfume made from pure **n**

narrow (7)

Num 22:24 through the vineyards, it was **n**,
Pro 23:27 A loose woman is a **n** well.
Isa 28:20 The blanket is too **n** to serve
Mat 7:13 "Enter through the **n** gate
7:14 But the **n** gate and the road that
7:14 Only a few people find the **n**
Luk 13:24 hard to enter through the **n** door

narrower (2)

Num 22:26 stood in a **n** place where there
Eze 42:5 third story were **n** than those

Nathan (43)

2Sm 5:14 Shobab, **N**, Solomon,
7:2 the king said to the prophet **N**,
7:3 **N** told the king, "Do everything
7:4 the LORD spoke his word to **N**:
7:17 **N** told David all these words
12:1 So the LORD sent **N** to David.
12:1 **N** came to him and said,
12:5 the LORD lives," he said to **N**,
12:7 **N** told David. "This is what the
12:13 Then David said to **N**,
12:13 **N** replied, "The LORD has
12:15 Then **N** went home.
12:25 message through the prophet **N**
23:36 Igal (son of **N**) from Zobah,
1Ki 1:8 the prophet **N**, Shimei, Rei,
1:10 he didn't invite the prophet **N**,
1:11 Then **N** asked Solomon's
1:22 the prophet **N** arrived.
1:23 "The prophet **N** is here."
1:24 **N** said, "Your Majesty,
1:32 the prophet **N**, and Benaiah,
1:34 the prophet **N** anoint him king
1:38 the priest Zadok, the prophet **N**,
1:44 the priest Zadok, the prophet **N**,
1:45 prophet **N** have anointed him
4:5 Azariah, son of **N**, was in
4:5 Zabud, son of **N**, was the
1Ch 2:36 Attai was the father of **N**.
2:36 **N** was the father of Zabad.
3:5 Shimea, Shobab, **N**,
11:38 Joel (son of **N**), Mibhar (son of
14:4 Shobab, **N**, Solomon,
17:1 he said to the prophet **N**,
17:2 **N** told David, "Do everything
17:3 night God spoke his word to **N**:
17:15 **N** told David all these words
29:29 the seer Samuel, the prophet **N**,
2Ch 9:29 in the records of **N** the prophet,
29:25 and the prophet **N** had ordered.
Ezr 8:16 Jarib, Elnathan, **N**, Zechariah,
10:39 Shelemiah, **N**, Adaiah,
Zec 12:12 the family of **N** by itself,
Luk 3:31 son of **N**, son of David,

Nathanael (7)

Jon 1:45 Philip found **N** and told him,
1:46 **N** said to Philip, "Can anything
1:47 Jesus saw **N** coming toward
1:48 **N** asked Jesus, "How do you
1:49 **N** said to Jesus, "Rabbi,
1:51 Jesus said to **N**, "I can
21:2 **N** from Cana in Galilee,

Nathan Melech (1)

2Ki 23:11 room of the eunuch **N**.

nation (262)

Gen 10:5 Each **n** had its own language
10:32 their genealogies, **n** by nation.
10:32 their genealogies, nation by **n**.
12:2 I will make you a great **n**,
15:14 I will punish the **n** they serve,
17:20 and I will make him a great **n**.
18:18 to become a great and mighty **n**
20:4 will you destroy a **n** even if it's
21:13 the slave's son into a **n** also,
21:18 to make him into a great **n**."
25:23 One **n** will be stronger than the
34:22 live with us and become one **n**
35:11 A **n** and a community of
46:3 I will make you a great **n** there.
48:19 will become a **n**, and he, too,
Exo 9:24 Egypt since it had become a **n**.
19:6 priests and my holy **n**.' These
23:27 and throw any **n** you meet into
32:10 I'll make you into a great **n**."
33:13 This **n** is your people."
34:10 never been done in any other **n**
Num 14:12 and I'll make you into a **n** larger
22:5 Balak's message was, "A **n**
23:9 I see a **n** that lives by itself,
23:24 Here is a **n** that attacks like a
Dtr 4:6 people there are in this great **n**!"
4:7 What great **n** ever had their
4:8 Or what other great **n** has such
4:34 take one **n** away from another
9:14 Then I'll make you into a **n**
15:6 but no **n** will ever rule you.
26:5 a great, powerful, and large **n**.
28:32 are given to another **n**.
28:36 king you choose to a **n** that you
28:49 against you a **n** from far away,
28:49 The **n** will swoop down on you
28:49 It will be a **n** whose language
32:21 to make them jealous and a **n**
33:29 a **n** saved by the LORD?
Jos 3:17 of the Jordan until the whole **n**
4:1 The whole **n** finished crossing
10:13 and the moon stopped until a **n**
21:45 that the LORD had given the **n**
Jdg 2:20 "Because the people of this **n**
1Sm 7:2 For 20 years the entire **n** of
7:3 told the entire **n** of Israel,
2Sm 1:12 and the **n** of Israel had been
6:5 David and the entire **n** of Israel
6:15 He and the entire **n** of Israel
7:23 It is the one **n** on earth that God
1Ki 4:34 People came from every **n** to
5:7 a wise son to rule this great **n**."
2Ki 19:30 Those few people from the **n** of
1Ch 16:20 they wandered from **n** to nation
16:20 they wandered from nation to **n**
17:21 It is the one **n** on earth that God
2Ch 15:6 One **n** crushed another nation;
15:6 One nation crushed another **n**;
32:15 No god of any **n** or kingdom
Ezr 6:12 of each king and **n** who tries
Job 34:29 can see him whether it is a **n**
Psa 33:12 Blessed is the **n** whose God is
43:1 my case against an ungodly **n**.
74:18 Remember how an entire **n** of
83:4 "Let's wipe out their **n** so that
87:4 Each **n** ⌊will claim that it⌋ was
105:13 they wandered from **n** to nation,
105:13 they wandered from nation to **n**,
147:20 nothing like this for any other **n**.
Pro 11:14 A **n** will fall when there is no
14:34 Righteousness lifts up a **n**,
Isa 1:4 it will be for a **n** that sins.
5:7 of Armies is the **n** of Israel,
7:8 so that it will no longer be a **n**.
9:3 You will expand the **n** and
10:6 send them against a godless **n**.
14:2 The **n** of Israel will possess
18:2 a strong and aggressive **n**,
18:7 a strong and aggressive **n**,
22:21 and to the **n** of Judah.
26:2 and let the righteous **n** come in,
26:2 the **n** that remains faithful.
26:15 You have expanded the **n**,
26:15 You have expanded the **n**.
30:5 because that **n** can't help them.
30:5 That **n** can't give aid or help to
30:6 of camels to a **n** that can't help

Isa 37:31 Those few people from the **n** of
46:3 people left of the **n** of Israel.
49:7 to the one scorned by the **n**,
51:4 your ears to hear me, my **n**.
55:5 You will summon a **n** that you
55:5 and a **n** that doesn't know you
58:2 They act as if they were a **n**
60:22 them will become a mighty **n**.
63:7 many good things for the **n**
65:1 to a **n** that didn't worship me.
66:8 Can a **n** be born in a moment?
66:20 your relatives from every **n** like
Jer 2:4 the families in the **n** of Israel.
2:11 Has any **n** ever exchanged
2:26 so the **n** of Israel will feel
3:18 In those days the **n** of Judah
3:18 will live with the **n** of Israel.
3:20 you, **n** of Israel, betrayed me,"
5:9 "I will punish this **n**.
5:15 **N** of Israel, I'm going to bring a
5:15 I'm going to bring a **n** from far
5:15 It is a **n** that has lasted a long
5:15 It is an ancient **n**. You don't
5:15 know the language of this **n**.
5:29 "I will punish this **n**.
6:22 A great **n** is preparing itself in
7:28 'This is the **n** that did not obey
9:9 I will punish this **n**.
10:1 has spoken to you, **n** of Israel.
12:7 "I have abandoned my **n**.
12:17 Then I will uproot that **n** and
13:11 so I have made the entire **n** of
13:11 nation of Israel and the entire **n**
18:6 "**N** of Israel, can't I do with you
18:6 **N** of Israel, you are like the
18:7 and destroy a **n** or a kingdom.
18:8 But suppose the **n** that I
18:9 and plant a **n** or a kingdom.
18:10 But suppose that **n** does what I
21:11 "Say to the **n** of the king of
23:8 the descendants of the **n**
25:12 the king of Babylon and that **n**
25:32 is spreading from **n** to nation.
25:32 is spreading from nation to **n**.
27:11 But suppose a **n** surrenders to
31:36 stop being a **n** in my presence.
33:24 no longer consider them a **n**.
36:3 Maybe the **n** of Judah will hear
48:2 "Let's destroy that **n**!"
48:13 ashamed of Chemosh as the **n**
48:42 Moab will be destroyed as a **n**,
49:31 Attack the **n** living peacefully
49:31 It is a **n** with no gates or bars.
49:36 There won't be a **n** where
50:3 A **n** from the north will attack
50:12 will be the least important **n**.
50:41 A great **n** and many kings will
Lam 4:17 We waited and waited for a **n**
Eze 2:3 They are people from a **n** that
4:4 take the punishment of the **n**
4:5 for the sins of the **n** of Israel.
4:6 punishment for the sins of the **n**
5:4 the whole **n** of Israel.
7:24 So I will send the most evil **n**,
8:10 all the idols in the **n** of Israel.
8:12 see what the leaders of the **n**
11:5 saying these things, **n** of Israel.
11:15 and about the entire **n** of Israel.
12:6 a sign to warn the **n** of Israel."
12:9 didn't the rebellious **n** of Israel
13:5 the wall for the **n** of Israel.
13:9 in the records of the **n** of Israel.
14:5 the hearts of the **n** of Israel.
14:6 "So tell the **n** of Israel,
16:14 You became famous in every **n**
17:2 illustration to the **n** of Israel.
17:9 "Tell the **n** of Israel,
18:6 from the idols of the **n** of Israel.
18:15 from the idols of the **n** of Israel.
18:25 Listen, **n** of Israel, isn't my way
18:29 "But the **n** of Israel says,
18:29 Isn't my way fair, **n** of Israel?
18:31 do you want to die, **n** of Israel?
20:27 "Speak to the **n** of Israel,
20:30 "Tell the **n** of Israel,
20:31 to ask me for help, **n** of Israel?
Eze 20:39 "'**N** of Israel, this is what the
20:40 "The entire **n** of Israel,
20:44 that you have done, **n** of Israel,
24:21 'Tell the **n** of Israel,
25:3 and when the **n** of Judah went
25:8 "The **n** of Judah is like all the
25:12 Edom took revenge on the **n** of
28:24 The **n** of Israel will no longer
29:6 walking stick to the **n** of Israel.
29:16 The **n** of Israel will never trust
31:12 from the most ruthless **n** cut
36:13 the children away from your **n**.
36:14 the children away from your **n**,
36:15 children away from your own **n**,
37:22 I will form them into one **n** in
38:6 all its troops and with the **n**
39:25 for the whole **n** of Israel.
39:29 out my Spirit on the **n** of Israel,
40:4 Tell the **n** of Israel everything
44:22 marry only virgins from the **n**
45:8 to each tribe of the **n** of Israel.
45:17 festivals of the **n** of Israel.
45:17 the LORD for the **n** of Israel.
Dan 3:4 province, **n**, and language!
3:7 people from every province, **n**,
3:29 people from every province, **n**,
4:1 **n**, and language in the world.
5:19 People from every province, **n**,
6:25 the people of every province, **n**,
7:14 People from every province, **n**,
8:22 will come out of that **n**,
Hos 1:6 no longer love the **n** of Israel.
4:5 your mother, ⌊the **n** of Israel⌋.
5:1 Pay attention, **n** of Israel!
5:12 I will destroy the **n** of Judah as
5:14 a young lion to the **n** of Judah.
6:10 horrible things in the **n** of Israel
11:12 The **n** of Israel surrounds me
Joe 1:6 A strong **n** attacked my land.
3:8 a **n** that is far away."
Amo 5:1 I sing about you, **n** of Israel:
5:3 ⌊only⌋ 10 left for the **n** of Israel.
5:4 LORD says to the **n** of Israel:
5:25 desert for 40 years, **n** of Israel?
6:1 to whom the **n** of Israel comes.
6:14 I am going to lead a **n** to attack
6:14 nation to attack you, **n** of Israel,
9:9 I will sift the **n** of Israel out of
Mic 3:1 you rulers of the **n** of Israel.
3:8 and ⌊the **n** of⌋ Israel about
3:9 you rulers of the **n** of Israel.
4:7 forced away into a strong **n**."
Hab 1:6 that fierce and reckless **n**.
Zep 2:1 together, you shameless **n**,
2:5 for the **n** from Crete.
2:7 faithful few from the **n** of Judah.
2:9 and those who are left in my **n**
2:11 every coast and **n** will bow
Hag 2:14 are unclean, and so is this **n**,
Zec 8:19 festivals for the **n** of Judah.
Mal 3:9 the whole **n** is cheating me!
Mat 10:6 the lost sheep of the **n** of Israel.
15:24 lost sheep of the **n** of Israel."
24:7 **N** will fight against nation and
24:7 Nation will fight against **n** and
25:32 The people of every **n** will be
Mar 13:8 **N** will fight against nation and
13:8 Nation will fight against **n** and
Luk 21:10 Then Jesus continued, "**N** will
21:10 "Nation will fight against **n** and
Jon 11:48 away our position and our **n**."
11:50 the whole **n** to be destroyed."
11:51 would die for the Jewish **n**.
11:52 wouldn't die merely for this **n**,
Act 2:5 men from every **n** were living
7:42 desert for 40 years, **n** of Israel?
10:35 is acceptable to him in any **n**.
13:17 a strong **n** while they lived
17:26 one man he has made every **n**
24:10 have been a judge over this **n**
Rom 1:5 who bring people from every **n**
10:19 of people who are not a **n**.
10:19 a **n** that doesn't understand."
16:26 shown to the people of every **n**
1Pe 2:9 a royal priesthood, a holy **n**,
Rev 5:9 tribe, language, people, and **n**.
Rev 7:9 a large crowd from every **n**,
13:7 tribe, people, language, and **n**.
14:6 who live on earth — to every **n**,

nationalities (2)

Est 3:8 but separate from — the **n**
3:8 differ from those of all other **n**.

nationality (5)

Est 2:10 Esther did not reveal her **n** or
2:20 her family background or **n**,
3:6 him about Mordecai's **n**,
3:8 there is a certain **n** scattered
Jnh 1:8 you from? What **n** are you?"

nations (574)

Gen 10:20 within their countries and **n**.
10:31 countries according to their **n**.
10:32 the **n** spread over
17:4 become the father of many **n**.
17:5 made you a father of many **n**.
17:6 Many **n** and kings will come
17:16 will become ⌊a mother of⌋ **n**,
18:18 nation and through him all the **n**
22:18 your descendant all the **n**
25:23 Two **n** will go their separate
26:4 your descendant all the **n**
27:29 May **n** serve you. May people
35:11 A nation and a community of **n**
48:19 will become many **n**."
Exo 19:5 then out of all the **n** you will be
34:24 I will force **n** out of your way
Lev 18:24 By these practices all the **n**
25:44 them from the **n** around you.
26:33 I will scatter you among the **n**.
26:38 will be destroyed among the **n**.
26:45 be their God while **n** looked on.
Num 14:15 then the **n** who have heard
23:9 themselves to be like other **n**.
24:8 He will devour **n** that are his
24:20 "Amalek was first among the **n**,
Dtr 4:27 will be left among the **n** where
4:29 when you are among those **n**,
4:38 He forced **n** greater and
7:1 He will force many **n** out of
7:1 and Jebusites — seven **n** larger
7:6 out of all the **n** on earth.
7:7 You were the smallest of all **n**.
7:17 "These **n** outnumber us.
7:22 little he will force these **n** out
8:20 to destroy other **n** as you enter
9:1 You'll be forcing out **n** that are
9:4 No, it's because these **n** are so
12:29 the **n** where you're going
15:6 You will make loans to many **n**,
15:6 You will rule many **n**,
17:14 like all the other **n** around us."
18:9 disgusting practices of those **n**.
18:12 your God is forcing these **n** out
18:14 These **n** you are forcing out
19:1 destroy all the **n** that are living
20:15 don't belong to the **n** nearby.
20:16 life in the cities of these **n** that
26:19 you high above all the other **n**
28:1 all the other **n** in the world.
28:12 able to make loans to many **n**
28:37 All the **n** where the LORD will
28:65 Among those **n** you will find no
29:18 to worship the gods of those **n**.
29:24 Then all the other **n** in the
30:1 you are among all the **n** where
30:3 and gather you from all the **n**
31:3 He will destroy those **n** as you
31:4 The LORD will do to those **n**
32:8 the Most High gave **n** their land
32:43 with the LORD's people, you **n**,
33:17 push away **n** including those at
33:19 They will invite **n** to their
Jos 23:3 your God did to all those **n**.
23:4 territory of the **n** that still
23:4 includes the territory of all the **n**
23:7 Don't get mixed up with the **n**
23:9 important and powerful **n** out
23:12 other **n** within your ⌊borders⌋,
24:17 as we passed through other **n**.
Jdg 2:21 I will no longer force out the **n**

Jdg 2:22 people of Israel with these **n**
2:23 So the LORD let these **n** stay.
3:1 These are the **n** the LORD left
3:4 These **n** were left to test the
1Sm 8:5 we will be like all the other **n**."
8:20 will be like all the other **n**.
2Sm 7:23 You forced **n** and their gods out
8:11 from all the **n** he conquered —
22:44 You kept me as the leader of **n**.
22:50 among the **n** and make music
1Ki 4:31 spread to all the **n** around him.
11:2 They came from the **n** about
14:24 practices done by the **n** that
2Ki 16:3 things done by the **n** that
17:8 by the customs of the **n** that
17:11 in the same way as the **n** that
17:15 like the **n** around them,
17:33 of the **n** from which they
17:41 These ⌞other⌟ **n** worshiped the
18:33 Did any of the gods of the **n**
19:12 Did the gods of the **n** which my
19:17 of Assyria have leveled **n**.
21:2 things done by the **n** that
21:9 more evil things than the **n** that
1Ch 5:20 Hagar's descendants and the **n**
14:17 LORD made all the **n** fear him.
16:8 Make known among the **n** what
16:24 all the **n** about his miracles.
16:26 all the gods of the **n** are idols.
16:28 you families of the **n**.
16:31 Say to the **n**, 'The LORD rules
16:35 save us from the **n** so that we
17:21 You forced the **n** and their gods
18:11 taken from other **n** — from
2Ch 20:6 rule all the kingdoms of the **n**.
28:3 things done by the **n** that
32:13 gods of these other **n** ever able
32:14 Were the gods of these **n** able
32:14 claimed and destroyed those **n**.
32:17 "As the gods of the **n** in other
32:23 important by all the **n**.
33:2 things done by the **n** that
33:9 more evil things than the **n** that
36:14 disgusting practices of the **n**.
Neh 1:8 I will scatter you among the **n**.
5:8 who had been sold to other **n**.
5:17 to us from the surrounding **n**.
6:6 been reported throughout the **n**
6:16 all the surrounding **n** were
9:22 You gave kingdoms and **n** to
9:30 the people in the surrounding **n**
13:26 a king like him among all **n**.
Job 12:23 He makes **n** important and then
12:23 He makes **n** large and leads
Psa 2:1 Why do the **n** gather together?
2:8 and I will give you the **n** as
9:5 You condemned **n**.
9:11 Announce to the **n** what he has
9:15 The **n** have sunk into the pit
9:17 all the **n** who forget God,
9:19 Let the **n** be judged in your
9:20 Let the **n** know that they are
10:16 The **n** have vanished from his
18:43 You made me the leader of **n**.
18:49 among the **n** and make music
22:27 from all the **n** will worship you
22:28 to the LORD and he rules the **n**.
33:10 blocks the plans of the **n**.
44:2 By your power you forced **n**
44:11 and scatter us among the **n**.
44:14 among the **n** so that people
45:5 **N** fall beneath you.
45:17 That is why the **n** will give
46:6 **N** are in turmoil, and kingdoms
46:10 I rule the **n**. I rule the earth.
47:3 and ⌞puts⌟ **n** under our feet.
47:8 God rules the **n**. He sits upon
47:9 from the **n** gather together as
56:7 O God, angrily make the **n** fall.
57:9 to praise you among the **n**
59:5 arise to punish all the **n**.
59:8 You make fun of all the **n**.
65:7 and the uproar of the **n**.
66:7 His eyes watch the **n**.
66:8 Thank our God, you **n**.
67:2 your salvation throughout all **n**.

Psa 67:4 Let the **n** be glad and sing
67:4 with justice and guide the **n**
68:30 bulls with the calves of the **n**,
72:11 May all **n** serve him.
72:17 May all **n** be blessed through
77:14 strength known among the **n**.
78:55 He forced **n** out of their way
78:55 of the **n** as their inheritance.
79:1 O God, the **n** have invaded the
79:6 Pour your fury on the **n** that do
79:10 Why should the **n** ⌞be allowed
79:10 Let us watch as the **n** learn that
80:8 forced out the **n** and planted it.
82:8 all the **n** belong to you.
86:9 All the **n** that you have made
87:6 record this in the Book of **N**:
94:10 He disciplines **n**. Do you think
96:3 all the **n** about his miracles.
96:5 all the gods of the **n** are idols.
96:7 you families of the **n**.
96:10 Say to the **n**, "The LORD rules
98:2 righteousness for the **n** to see.
102:15 The **n** will fear the LORD's
102:22 when **n** and kingdoms gather to
105:1 Make known among the **n** what
105:20 The ruler of **n** set him free.
105:44 them the lands of ⌞other⌟ **n**,
106:27 their descendants among the **n**,
106:35 they intermarried with other **n**.
106:35 They learned to do what other **n**
106:41 He handed them over to other **n**
106:47 and gather us from the **n** so that
108:3 to praise you among the **n**
110:6 He will pass judgment on the **n**
111:6 of other **n** as an inheritance.
113:4 LORD is high above all the **n**.
115:2 Why should other **n** say,
117:1 Praise the LORD, all you **n**!
118:10 All the **n** surrounded me,
126:2 Then the **n** said, "The LORD
135:10 the one who defeated many **n**
135:15 The idols of the **n** are made of
147:20 The other **n** do not know the
149:7 to take vengeance on the **n**,
Pro 24:24 people and condemned by **n**.
Isa 2:2 All the **n** will stream to it.
2:4 will judge disputes between **n**
2:4 **N** will never fight against each
5:26 up a flag for the **n** far away.
10:7 and put an end to many **n**.
10:13 eliminated the boundaries of **n**.
10:14 I've found the riches of **n** as
11:10 The **n** will come to him.
11:12 He will raise a banner for the **n**
12:4 his deeds known among the **n**.
13:4 and **n** gathering together.
14:2 Israel will possess **n** as male
14:6 They ruled **n** in anger,
14:9 of the **n** from their thrones.
14:12 you conqueror of **n**!
14:18 All the kings of the **n**,
14:26 use his power against all the **n**.
14:32 the messengers from the **n**?
16:8 Rulers of the **n** have cut off
23:3 the marketplace for the **n**.
24:13 it will be on earth among the **n**.
25:7 and the mask covering all **n**.
29:7 The armies from all the **n** will
29:8 from all the **n** that fight against
30:28 It rises neck high, sifting the **n**
33:3 **N** scatter when you attack.
33:4 You **n**, your loot is gathered as
34:1 Come close, you **n**,
34:2 LORD is angry with all the **n**.
36:18 Did any of the gods of the **n**
37:12 Did the gods of the **n** which my
40:15 The **n** are like a drop in a
40:17 All the **n** amount to nothing in
41:2 **N** are handed over to him.
42:1 He will bring justice to the **n**.
42:6 as my light to the **n**.
43:4 **N** will be the price I pay for
43:9 All **n** have gathered together,
45:1 he could conquer the **n** ahead
45:20 you refugees from the **n**.
49:6 you a light for the **n** so that you

Isa 49:22 lift my hand ⌞to signal⌟ the **n**.
52:10 his holy power to all the **n**.
52:15 He will cleanse many **n** ⌞with
54:3 will take over other **n**,
56:7 a house of prayer for all **n**.
60:2 thick darkness covers the **n**.
60:3 **N** will come to your light,
60:5 The wealth of the **n** will come
60:11 may bring you the wealth of **n**,
60:12 **N** and kingdoms that do not
60:12 The **n** will certainly be ruined.
60:16 You will drink milk from other **n**
61:6 consume the wealth of the **n**.
61:9 will be known among the **n**
61:11 praise spring up in front of all **n**.
62:2 The **n** will see your
64:2 The **n** will tremble in your
66:12 and the wealth of the **n** like
66:18 I am coming to gather the **n** of
66:19 some of their survivors to the **n**:
66:19 about my glory among the **n**.
Jer 1:5 you to be a prophet to the **n**."
1:10 in charge of **n** and kingdoms.
3:17 All **n** will gather in Jerusalem
3:19 beautiful property among the **n**.
4:2 then the **n** will be blessed,
4:7 A destroyer of **n** has set out.
4:16 Warn the **n** about these things.
5:11 The **n** of Israel and Judah are
6:18 Listen, you **n**, and learn,
9:16 I will scatter them among **n**
9:26 these **n** are circumcised,
10:2 learn the practices of the **n**.
10:2 because the **n** are frightened by
10:7 fears you, O King of the **N**.
10:7 all the wise people in the **n**
10:10 The **n** can't endure his fury.
10:25 Pour out your fury on the **n** who
11:10 The **n** of Israel and Judah have
14:22 The worthless gods of the **n**
16:19 **N** come to you from the most
18:13 Ask among the **n** if anyone has
22:8 "People from many **n** will pass
25:9 and all these surrounding **n**.
25:11 These **n** will serve the king of
25:13 prophesied against all the **n**,
25:14 Many **n** and great kings will
25:15 and make all the **n** to whom I'm
25:17 I made all the **n** to whom the
25:31 brought charges against the **n**.
26:6 cursed by all the **n** on earth.'"
27:7 All **n** will serve him,
27:7 Then many **n** and great kings
27:8 "'Suppose **n** or kingdoms won't
27:8 I will punish those **n** by wars,
27:13 The LORD has threatened the **n**
28:11 of all the **n** within two years."
28:14 of all these **n** so that they
29:14 I will gather you from all the **n**
29:18 disgrace among all the **n** where
30:11 destroy all the **n** where
31:7 joyfully for the leader of the **n**.
31:10 "You **n**, listen to the word of the
31:27 "when I will plant the **n** of
33:9 All the **n** on earth will hear
36:2 and all the other **n** from the time
44:8 ridiculed by all the **n** on earth.
46:1 prophet Jeremiah about the **n**.
46:12 The **n** have heard of your
46:28 destroy all the **n** where
49:14 was sent among the **n** to say,
49:15 will make you the smallest of **n**
50:2 "Announce this among the **n**,
50:9 up an alliance of strong **n** from
50:9 Those **n** will take up positions
50:23 desolate Babylon is of all the **n**!
50:46 cry will be heard among the **n**."
51:7 The **n** drank its wine.
51:7 is why the **n** have gone insane.
51:20 I will use you to crush **n**.
51:27 the ram's horn among the **n**.
51:27 Prepare **n** to attack Babylon.
51:28 Prepare **n** to attack Babylon.
51:42 sight Babylon will be to the **n**!
51:44 **N** will no longer stream to
51:58 The **n** wear themselves out

Lam 1:1 it was important among the **n**.
1:3 Its ⌊people⌋ live among the **n**;
1:10 Jerusalem has seen the **n** enter
2:9 are ⌊scattered⌋ among the **n**.
3:45 us the scum and trash of the **n**.
4:15 the people of the **n** said,
4:20 king's shadow among the **n**."
Eze 3:6 I am not sending you to **n**
3:6 If I send you to those **n**,
4:13 bread among the **n** where
5:5 placed it in the center of the **n**
5:6 more than the surrounding **n**.
5:7 trouble than the **n** around you.
5:7 standards of the **n** around you.
5:8 will punish you in front of the **n**.
5:14 among the **n** around you
5:15 The **n** that are around you will
6:8 escape the battle among the **n**
6:9 me among the **n** where they are
9:9 "The wickedness of the **n** of
11:12 set by the **n** around you."
11:16 them far away among the **n**
11:17 bring them together from the **n**
12:15 I will scatter them among the **n**
12:16 Wherever they go among the **n**,
19:4 The **n** heard about him,
19:8 The **n** from every region came
20:9 among the **n** where they were
20:9 While other **n** were watching,
20:14 among the **n** who had watched
20:22 among the **n** who had watched
20:23 to scatter them among the **n**
20:32 that you want to be like other **n**,
20:34 I will bring you out from the **n**
20:35 you into the desert of the **n**.
20:41 When I bring you out from the **n**
20:41 holy to the **n** that are watching.
21:23 made treaties with other **n**.
22:4 make you a disgrace to the **n**
22:15 I will scatter you among the **n**
22:16 dishonored in the sight of the **n**.
23:30 because you lusted after the **n**
25:7 hand you over to the **n** as loot.
25:7 wipe you out from among the **n**,
25:8 of Judah is like all the other **n**."
25:10 be remembered among the **n**.
26:2 gateway for the **n** is destroyed,
26:3 I will bring many **n** against you
26:5 It will become a prize for the **n**.
27:3 It is the merchant to the **n**.
27:36 The merchants among the **n**
28:7 foreigners among the **n**.
28:19 All the **n** who knew you are
28:25 from the **n** where they were
28:25 that I am holy as the **n** watch.
29:12 the Egyptians among the **n**
29:13 from the **n** where they have
29:15 they will never rule the **n** again.
29:15 they will never rule the **n** again.
30:3 a time of trouble for the **n**.
30:11 ruthless troops among the **n**,
30:23 the Egyptians among the **n**
30:26 the Egyptians among the **n**
31:6 All the powerful **n** lived in its
31:11 to a mighty ruler among the **n**,
31:12 All the **n** in the world came out
31:16 I made the **n** tremble in fear at
31:17 were scattered among the **n**.
32:2 you are like a lion among the **n**.
32:3 When many **n** gather together,
32:9 of your destruction among the **n**
32:12 ruthless warriors among the **n**.
32:16 The people from the **n** will sing
32:18 along with the other mighty **n**.
34:13 I will bring them out from the **n**,
34:28 will no longer be prey to the **n**,
34:29 suffer the insults of other **n**.
35:10 "'You said, "These two **n**,
36:3 possession of the rest of the **n**,
36:4 by the rest of the surrounding **n**
36:5 spoken against the rest of the **n**
36:6 have been insulted by the **n**.
36:7 that the **n** which surround you
36:15 you hear the insults from the **n**.
36:19 I forced them into other **n**,
36:19 became scattered among the **n**.
Eze 36:20 they went among the **n**,
36:21 the **n** wherever they went.
36:22 the **n** wherever you have
36:23 has been dishonored by the **n**,
36:23 Then the **n** will know that I am
36:24 "'I will take you from the **n** and
36:30 the **n** because of famines.
36:36 The surrounding **n** that are left
37:21 out of the **n** where they've gone.
37:22 They will no longer be two **n** or
37:28 Then the **n** will know that I,
38:2 He is the chief prince of ⌊the **n**
38:8 been gathered from many **n**
38:8 were brought there from the **n**,
38:12 who were gathered from the **n**.
38:16 land so that **n** will know me.
38:23 I will reveal myself to many **n**.
39:7 Then the **n** will know that I am
39:21 my greatness among the **n**.
39:21 All the **n** will see how I will
39:23 Then the **n** will know that the
39:27 them back from the other **n**
39:27 Many **n** will see that I am holy.
39:28 into captivity among the **n**,
Dan 12:1 have been **n** until that time.
Hos 7:8 "Ephraim mixes with other **n**.
8:8 mixed in with the other **n**.
8:10 sold themselves among the **n**,
9:1 Don't celebrate as other **n** do.
9:17 They will wander among the **n**.
Joe 2:17 Don't let the **n** ridicule them.
2:19 you a disgrace among the **n**.
3:2 I will gather all the **n**.
3:2 belong to me, among the **n**.
3:9 Announce this among the **n**:
3:11 and gather there, all you **n**.
3:12 Wake up, you **n**. Come to the
3:12 to judge all the surrounding **n**.
3:13 The **n** are very wicked.
3:19 This is because the **n** were
Amo 6:1 for the heads of the leading **n**,
6:14 God of the Armies of the **N**.
9:9 of Israel out of all the **n** as if
9:12 all the other **n** that were under
Oba 1:1 was sent among the **n** to say,
1:2 make you the smallest of **n**.
1:15 of the LORD is near for all **n**.
1:16 so all **n** will drink in turn.
Mic 4:2 Then many **n** will come and
4:3 arguments between many **n** far
4:3 **N** will never fight against each
4:5 All the **n** live by the names of
4:11 But now many **n** gather against
4:13 You will smash many **n** into
5:8 Jacob will be among the **n**,
5:15 great anger on the **n** that do not
7:16 **N** will see this and be
Nah 3:4 She used to sell **n** her
3:5 I will show **n** your naked body
Hab 1:5 Look among the **n** and watch.
1:17 always kill **n** without mercy?
2:5 He gathers all the **n** to himself.
2:8 You have looted many **n**.
2:13 and **n** exhaust themselves
3:6 a glance and startles the **n**.
3:12 You trample the **n** in anger.
Zep 3:6 "I will cut off the **n**.
3:8 I have decided to gather **n**,
Hag 2:7 I will shake all the **n**,
2:7 and the one whom all the **n**
2:22 and destroy the power of **n**.
Zec 1:15 and I'm very angry with the **n**
1:19 "These are the horns ⌊of the **n**⌋
1:21 throw down the horns of the **n**.
1:21 The **n** raised their horns to
2:8 the Glory sent me to the **n** who
2:9 going to shake my fist at the **n**,
2:11 On that day many **n** will join
7:14 to scatter them among all the **n**,
7:14 **n** they hadn't even heard of.
8:13 been a curse among the **n**,
8:22 Many people and powerful **n**
8:23 among the **n** will take hold
9:10 will announce peace to the **n**.
10:9 scattered them among the **n**,
11:10 that I had made to all the **n**.
Zec 12:3 too heavy for all the **n** to lift.
12:3 All the **n** in the world will
12:4 all the horses of the **n** blind.
12:6 burn up all the surrounding **n**
12:9 all the **n** who attack Jerusalem.
14:2 I will gather all the **n** to
14:3 out and fight against those **n** as
14:12 from the **n** that have gone
14:14 of all the surrounding **n** will
14:16 the **n** that attacked Jerusalem
14:18 to strike the **n** will affect those
14:19 the sin of all the **n** that won't go
Mal 1:11 "From the **n** where the sun
1:11 the sun rises to the **n** where
1:11 be great among the **n**," says
1:14 "Among the **n** my name is
3:12 "All **n** will call you blessed
Mat 12:18 will announce justice to the **n**.
12:21 The **n** will have hope because
20:25 "You know that the rulers of **n**
24:9 All **n** will hate you because
24:14 world as a testimony to all **n**.
28:19 make disciples of all **n**:
Mar 10:42 rulers of **n** have absolute power
11:17 for all **n**,' but you have turned
13:10 News must be spread to all **n**.
Luk 2:32 will reveal ⌊salvation⌋ to the **n**
21:24 off into all **n** as prisoners.
21:24 **N** will trample Jerusalem until
21:24 allowed for the **n** ⌊to do this⌋
21:25 The **n** of the earth will be
22:25 "The kings of **n** have power
24:47 be told to people from all **n**,
Act 4:25 'Why do the **n** act arrogantly?
7:45 land from the **n** that God forced
9:15 this man to bring my name to **n**,
13:19 Then he destroyed seven **n** in
13:46 to turn to people of other **n**.
13:47 you a light for the **n** so that you
Rom 1:13 among the rest of the **n**.
2:24 among the **n** because of you."
4:17 made you a father of many **n**."
4:17 into existence **n** that don't even
4:18 he became a father of many **n**,
15:9 give thanks to you among the **n**
15:10 Scripture says again, "You **n**,
15:11 "Praise the Lord, all you **n**!
15:12 He will rise to rule the **n**,
15:12 and he will give the **n** hope."
15:16 in order that I might bring the **n**
16:4 all the churches among the **n**.
Gal 2:15 not sinners from other **n**.
1Ti 3:16 announced throughout the **n**,
2Ti 4:17 Good News for all the **n** to hear.
Rev 2:26 I will give authority over the **n**
2:27 Those people will rule the **n**
10:11 **n**, languages, and kings."
11:2 because it is given to the **n**,
11:9 and **n** will look at the
11:18 "The **n** were angry,
12:5 who is to rule all the **n** with an
14:8 She has made all the **n** drink
15:3 is fair and true, King of the **N**.
15:4 and all the **n** will come to
16:19 and the cities of the **n** fell.
17:15 crowds, **n**, and languages.
18:3 All the **n** fell because of the
18:23 because all the **n** were
19:15 out of his mouth to defeat the **n**.
20:3 deceiving the **n** anymore until
20:8 the **n** in the four corners of the
21:24 The **n** will walk in its light,
21:26 glory and wealth of the **n** into
22:2 of the tree will heal the **n**.

native (7)

Gen 11:28 Ur of the Chaldeans, his **n** land.
Lev 16:29 seventh month both **n** Israelites
17:15 "'**N** Israelites or foreigners who
Jos 8:33 foreigners or **n** Israelites,
1Ki 7:14 His father, a **n** of Tyre,
2Ch 2:14 and his father is a **n** of Tyre.
Act 2:8 speaking in our **n** dialects?

native-born (6)

Exo 12:48 the Passover like **n** Israelites.

Exo 12:49 apply to **n** Israelites as well
Num 9:14 to foreigners and **n** Israelites."
15:13 All **n** Israelites must do it this
15:29 they are **n** Israelites or not.
15:30 "But any **n** Israelite or foreigner

natural (9)

Num 16:29 if they die a **n** death — then
Rom 1:26 exchanged **n** sexual relations
1:27 their men have given up **n**
9:8 by **n** descent ⌊from Abraham⌋
11:21 didn't spare the **n** branches,
11:24 be easier for these **n** branches
Gal 4:23 was conceived in a **n** way,
4:29 in a **n** way persecuted
1Ti 5:11 Whenever their **n** desires

naturally (9)

Lev 7:24 fat from an animal that dies **n**
17:15 body of an animal that dies **n**
22:8 meat of an animal that dies **n**
Num 19:16 who was killed or has died **n**
19:18 been killed or who has died **n**.
Dtr 14:21 eat any creature that dies **n**.
1Sm 26:10 will come when he'll die ⌊**n**⌋,
Eze 44:31 bird or animal that has died **n**
Jon 8:44 doing what comes **n** to him.

nature (59)

Psa 64:6 Human **n** and the human heart
Jon 2:25 to tell him about human **n**.
Rom 1:3 In his human **n** he was a
1:4 In his spiritual, holy **n** he was
1:20 his eternal power and divine **n**,
2:14 have laws from God do by **n**
6:19 the weakness of your corrupt **n**.
7:5 the influence of our corrupt **n**,
7:14 but I have a corrupt **n**,
7:18 good lives in my corrupt **n**.
7:25 standards with my corrupt **n**.
8:3 weakness our human **n** has.
8:3 a human **n** as sinners have
8:3 condemned sin in our corrupt **n**
8:4 who do not live by our corrupt **n**
8:4 nature but by our spiritual **n**,
8:5 Those who live by the corrupt **n**
8:5 who live by the spiritual **n** have
8:7 is so because the corrupt **n** has
8:8 the corrupt **n** can't please God.
8:9 the control of your spiritual **n**,
8:9 nature, not your corrupt **n**.
8:12 the way our corrupt **n** wants
8:13 If you live by your corrupt **n**,
8:13 But if you use your spiritual **n**
9:5 according to his human **n**.
13:14 the desires of your sinful **n**.
1Co 3:1 influenced by your corrupt **n**.
3:3 influenced by your corrupt **n**.
3:3 influenced by your corrupt **n**
5:5 destroy his corrupt **n** so that his
5:5 so that his spiritual **n** may
11:14 Doesn't **n** itself teach you that it
2Co 4:11 is also shown in our mortal **n**.
Gal 5:5 However, in our spiritual **n**,
5:13 an excuse for your corrupt **n**
5:16 as your spiritual **n** directs you.
5:16 on what your corrupt **n** wants.
5:17 What your corrupt **n** wants is
5:17 to what your spiritual **n** wants,
5:17 and what your spiritual **n** wants
5:17 to what your corrupt **n** wants.
5:18 If your spiritual **n** is your guide,
5:19 Now, the effects of the corrupt **n**
5:22 the spiritual **n** produces love,
5:24 crucified their corrupt **n** along
5:25 If we live by our spiritual **n**,
5:25 to conform to our spiritual **n**.
6:8 in ⌊the soil of⌋ your corrupt **n**,
6:8 in ⌊the soil of⌋ your spiritual **n**,
Eph 2:3 the desires of our corrupt **n**.
2:3 So, because of our **n**,
Col 2:11 was a removal of the corrupt **n**
2:13 your uncircumcised corrupt **n**.
2:23 desires of your corrupt **n**.
1Ti 3:16 He appeared in his human **n**,
1Pe 2:11 the desires of your corrupt **n**.
2Pe 1:4 you will share in the divine **n**
2:10 who follow their corrupt **n** along

nature's (4)

Rom 8:5 have the corrupt **n** attitude.
8:5 have the spiritual **n** attitude
8:6 The corrupt **n** attitude leads to
8:6 But the spiritual **n** attitude

navel (1)

Sos 7:2 Your **n** is a round bowl.

Nazarene (2)

Mat 2:23 "He will be called a **N**."
Act 24:5 He's a ringleader of the **N** sect.

Nazareth (29)

Mat 2:23 his home in a city called **N**.
4:13 He left **N** and made his home in
21:11 Jesus from **N** in Galilee."
26:71 man was with Jesus from **N**."
Mar 1:9 At that time Jesus came from **N**
1:24 want with us, Jesus from **N**?
10:47 from **N** ⌊was passing by⌋,
14:67 were with Jesus from **N**!"
16:6 You're looking for Jesus from **N**,
Luk 1:26 sent the angel Gabriel to **N**,
2:4 So Joseph went from **N**,
2:39 their hometown of **N** in Galilee.
2:51 he returned with them to **N**
4:16 Then Jesus came to **N**,
4:34 want with us, Jesus from **N**?
18:37 Jesus from **N** was passing by.
24:19 happened to Jesus from **N**.
Jon 1:45 from the city of **N**."
1:46 anything good come from **N**?"
18:5 answered him, "Jesus from **N**."
18:7 They said, "Jesus from **N**."
19:19 The notice read, "Jesus from **N**,
Act 2:22 Jesus from **N** was a man
3:6 power of Jesus Christ from **N**,
4:10 power of Jesus Christ from **N**.
6:14 that Jesus from **N** will destroy
10:38 that God anointed Jesus from **N**
22:8 told me, 'I'm Jesus from **N**,
26:9 the one named Jesus of **N**.

Nazarites (1)

Num 6:7 **N** show their vow to God with

Nazirite (7)

Num 6:2 vow to live as a **N** dedicated
6:5 as they are under the **N** vow,
6:9 suddenly drop dead next to a **N**
6:12 himself to the LORD as a **N**
Jdg 13:5 the boy will be a **N** dedicated
13:7 the boy will be a **N** dedicated
16:17 He told her, "Because I'm a **N**,

Nazirite's (1)

Num 6:9 and make the **N** hair unclean.

Nazirites (13)

Num 6:3 **N** must never drink wine,
6:4 As long as they are **N**,
6:5 dedicated to the LORD as **N**,
6:6 dedicated to the LORD as **N**,
6:8 As long as they are **N**,
6:13 for **N** who complete their
6:18 "Then the **N** will shave their
6:19 them to the **N** after they have
6:20 that, the **N** may drink wine.
6:21 LORD because they were **N**.
6:21 of these instructions for **N**
Amo 2:11 children and **N** from among
2:12 You made the **N** drink wine.

Neah (1)

Jos 19:13 where it turns to **N**.

Neapolis (1)

Act 16:11 day we sailed to the city of **N**,

Neariah (2)

1Ch 3:22 Igal, Bariah, **N**, and Shaphat.
4:42 Ishi's sons Pelatiah, **N**,

Neariah's (1)

1Ch 3:23 **N** three sons were Elioenai,

Nebai (1)

Neh 10:19 Hariph, Anathoth, **N**,

Nebaioth (5)

Gen 25:13 **N** (Ishmael's firstborn),
28:9 son Ishmael and sister of **N**,
36:3 of Ishmael and sister of **N**.
1Ch 1:29 Ishmael's firstborn was **N**,
Isa 60:7 The rams of **N** will serve you.

Neballat (1)

Neh 11:34 Hadid, Zeboim, **N**,

Nebat (2)

1Ki 11:26 who was the son of **N** and an
2Ch 9:29 about Jeroboam (son of **N**)?

Nebat's (22)

1Ki 12:2 Jeroboam (**N** son) was still in
12:15 (**N** son) through Ahijah from
15:1 (**N** son), Abijam began
16:3 the family of Jeroboam (**N** son)
16:26 exactly like Jeroboam (**N** son).
16:31 sins as Jeroboam (**N** son).
21:22 the family of Jeroboam (**N** son)
22:52 (**N** son) who led Israel
2Ki 3:3 that Jeroboam (**N** son) led
9:9 the family of Jeroboam (**N** son)
10:29 Jeroboam (**N** son) led Israel
13:2 Jeroboam (**N** son) led Israel
14:24 Jeroboam (**N** son) led Israel
15:9 Jeroboam (**N** son) led Israel
15:18 Jeroboam (**N** son) led Israel
15:24 Jeroboam (**N** son) led Israel
15:28 Jeroboam (**N** son) led Israel
17:21 made Jeroboam (**N** son) king.
23:15 (**N** son), who had made
2Ch 10:2 Jeroboam (**N** son) was still in
10:15 (**N** son) through Ahijah from
13:6 But Jeroboam (**N** son) rebelled

Nebo (13)

Num 32:3 Elealeh, Sebam, **N**, and Beon,
32:38 **N**, Baal Meon (whose names
33:47 Abarim Mountains east of **N**.
Dtr 32:49 to Mount **N** in Moab,
34:1 went up on Mount **N** from
1Ch 5:8 as far as **N** and Baal Meon.
Ezr 2:29 of **N**: 52
10:43 From the descendants of **N**:
Neh 7:33 of the other **N**: 52
Isa 15:2 wails over **N** and Medeba.
46:1 the god **N** stoops low.
Jer 48:1 How horrible it will be for **N**;
48:22 Dibon, **N**, Beth Diblathaim,

Nebuchadnezzar (97)

2Ki 24:1 Jehoiakim's reign King **N**
24:10 that time the officers of King **N**
24:11 King **N** of Babylon arrived
24:13 As the LORD had predicted, **N**
25:1 King **N** of Babylon attacked
25:22 King **N** of Babylon appointed
1Ch 6:15 captive when the LORD used **N**
2Ch 36:6 King **N** of Babylon attacked
36:7 **N** also brought some of the
36:10 In the spring King **N** sent for
36:10 **N** made Jehoiakin's uncle
36:13 also rebelled against King **N**.
36:13 **N** had made Zedekiah swear
Ezr 1:7 **N** had taken these utensils
2:1 (King **N** of Babylon had taken
5:12 he handed them over to King **N**
5:12 So **N** destroyed this temple and
5:14 (**N** had taken them out of God's
6:5 (**N** had taken them out of God's
Neh 7:6 King **N** of Babylon had taken
Est 2:6 whom King **N** of Babylon had
Jer 21:2 because King **N** of Babylon is
21:2 for us so that **N** will retreat."
21:7 will be handed over to King **N**
21:7 **N** will kill them with swords.

Jer 22:25 those you fear — King **N** of
24:1 King **N** of Babylon took
25:1 (This was the first year that **N**
25:9 my servant King **N** of Babylon,
27:6 my servant King **N** of Babylon.
27:8 surrender to King **N** of Babylon.
27:19 King **N** took Jehoiakin,
28:3 the LORD's temple that King **N**
28:11 I will break the yoke of King **N**
28:14 will serve King **N** of Babylon.
29:1 and all the people that **N** took
29:3 had sent to King **N** in Babylon.
29:21 them over to King **N** of Babylon.
32:4 He will talk to **N** in person and
32:5 **N** will take Zedekiah to
32:28 and King **N** of Babylon.
34:1 when King **N** of Babylon,
35:11 But when King **N** of Babylon
37:1 King **N** of Babylon appointed
39:1 King **N** of Babylon attacked
39:5 to Babylon's King **N** at Riblah
39:11 King **N** of Babylon gave
43:10 my servant King **N** of Babylon.
43:12 **N** will put on Egypt as his coat
44:30 Zedekiah of Judah to King **N**
46:2 King **N** of Babylon defeated his
46:13 coming of King **N** of Babylon,
46:26 to King **N** of Babylon and his
49:28 kingdoms of Hazor that King **N**
49:30 King **N** of Babylon has made
50:17 bones was King **N** of Babylon.
51:34 King **N** of Babylon has
52:4 King **N** of Babylon attacked
52:28 are the people **N** took captive:
52:29 In his eighteenth year, **N** took
Eze 26:7 north I'm going to bring King **N**
29:18 "Son of man, King **N** of
29:19 Egypt to King **N** of Babylon.
29:20 **N** and his army worked for me,
30:10 I will use King **N** of Babylon to
Dan 1:1 King **N** of Babylon came to
1:2 from God's temple over to **N**.
1:2 **N** took the utensils to the
1:18 brought all the young men to **N**.
2:28 He will tell King **N** what is
2:46 King **N** immediately bowed
2:48 **N** made Daniel governor of the
3:1 King **N** made a gold statue 90
3:2 King **N** sent messengers to
3:3 the statue King **N** had set up.
3:5 statue that King **N** has set up.
3:7 gold statue King **N** had set up.
3:9 They addressed King **N**,
3:13 **N** summoned Shadrach,
3:14 **N** asked them, "Shadrach,
3:16 Abednego answered King **N**,
3:19 **N** was so filled with anger
3:24 Then **N** was startled.
3:26 Then **N** went to the door of the
3:28 **N** said, "Praise the God of
4:1 From King **N**. To the people of
4:4 I, **N**, was living comfortably at
4:18 dream I, King **N**, had. Now you,
4:28 All this happened to King **N**.
4:31 heaven, "King **N**, listen to this:
4:33 Just then the prediction about **N**
4:34 I, **N**, looked up to heaven,
4:37 Now I, **N**, will praise, honor,
5:2 grandfather **N** had taken from
5:11 Your grandfather, King **N**,
5:18 your grandfather **N** a kingdom,
5:19 **N** killed whomever he wanted

Nebuchadnezzar's (7)

2Ki 25:8 of **N** nineteenth year as king
Jer 27:8 to them by **N** power, declares
32:1 (This was **N** eighteenth year as
52:12 of **N** nineteenth year as king
52:30 In **N** twenty-third year as king,
Dan 2:1 the second year of **N** reign,
5:22 you are one of **N** successors.

Nebushazban (1)

Jer 39:13 **N** (the chief official),

Nebuzaradan (16)

2Ki 25:8 year as king of Babylon, **N**,
25:11 **N**, the captain of the guard,
25:20 **N**, the captain of the guard,
Jer 39:9 **N**, Babylon's captain of the
39:10 But **N**, the captain of the guard,
39:11 of Babylon gave **N**
39:13 **N** (the captain of the guard),
40:1 his word to Jeremiah after **N**,
40:1 **N** found Jeremiah in chains
41:10 They were the people whom **N**,
43:6 took every person whom **N**,
52:12 year as king of Babylon, **N**,
52:15 **N**, the captain of the guard,
52:16 But **N**, the captain of the guard,
52:26 **N**, the captain of the guard,
52:30 **N**, the captain of the guard,

necessarily (4)

Ecc 9:11 Wise people don't **n** have food.
9:11 people don't **n** have riches,
9:11 and skilled people don't **n**
Rom 9:8 are not **n** God's children.

necessary (10)

Exo 31:6 every craftsman the skill **n**
36:1 LORD has given the **n** skills
Num 18:3 doing whatever work is **n** for
18:4 you and do whatever work is **n**
18:6 to do whatever work is **n** at
Neh 5:18 choice sheep was **n** every day.
Act 15:28 Do only what is **n**
Rom 13:5 it is **n** for you to obey,
Gal 2:12 that circumcision was **n**.
5:11 that circumcision is **n**,

necessity (1)

Dtr 28:57 secretly eat them out of dire **n**,

neck (41)

Gen 27:16 hands and on the back of his **n**.
27:40 and break his yoke off your **n**."
41:42 put a gold chain around his **n**.
49:8 Your hand will be on the **n** of
Exo 13:13 you must break the donkey's **n**.
34:20 you must break the donkey's **n**.
Lev 1:15 He will break its **n** and burn the
5:8 He will break the bird's **n**
Dtr 21:4 they must break the heifer's **n**.
Jdg 5:30 cloth for the **n** of the looter."
1Sm 4:18 He broke his **n**, and he died.
Job 16:12 me by the back of the **n**
39:19 to a horse or dress its **n**
41:22 Strength resides in its **n**,
Psa 69:1 water is already up to my **n**!
105:18 and cut into his **n** with an iron
Pro 1:9 ⌊golden⌋ chain around your **n**.
3:3 Fasten them around your **n**.
3:22 and they will grace your **n**.
6:21 Hang them around your **n**.
Sos 1:10 your **n** with strings of pearls.
4:4 Your **n** is like David's
7:4 Your **n** is like an ivory tower.
Isa 10:27 will be removed from your **n**.
22:22 house of David around his **n**.
30:28 It rises **n** high, sifting the
52:2 from the chains around your **n**,
66:3 someone who breaks a dog's **n**.
Jer 27:2 and strap the yoke on your **n**.
28:10 took the yoke off the **n**
28:11 of Babylon off the **n**
28:12 broke the yoke off the **n**
Lam 1:14 They were tied around my **n**.
Eze 16:11 and a necklace around your **n**.
Dan 5:7 wear a gold chain on his **n**,
5:16 wear a gold chain on your **n**,
5:29 and wear a gold chain on his **n**.
Hos 10:11 put a yoke on its beautiful **n**.
Mat 18:6 large stone hung around his **n**.
Mar 9:42 large stone hung around his **n**.
Luk 17:2 stone hung around his **n** than

neck-high (1)

Isa 8:8 and pass through; it will be **n**.

necklace (3)

Psa 73:6 they wear arrogance like a **n**
Sos 4:9 with a single strand of your **n**.
Eze 16:11 and a **n** around your neck.

necklaces (1)

Isa 3:18 crescent-shaped **n**,

necks (11)

Jos 10:24 and put your feet on the **n**
Jdg 8:21 that were on their camels' **n**.
8:26 the chains from their camels' **n**.
1Ki 20:31 put ropes around our **n**,
20:32 and put ropes around their **n**.
Jer 28:14 I will put an iron yoke on the **n**
30:8 will break the yokes off your **n**
Lam 5:5 are breathing down our **n**.
Eze 21:29 placed on the **n** of dishonest,
Hos 11:4 removed the yokes from their **n**.
Act 14:13 flowery wreaths around their **n**

Neco (4)

2Ch 35:20 King **N** of Egypt came to fight a
35:21 But **N** sent messengers to
36:4 **N** took Jehoahaz away to
Jer 46:2 about the army of Pharaoh **N**,

Necoh (5)

2Ki 23:29 In Josiah's days Pharaoh **N**
23:29 King Josiah went to attack **N**.
23:33 Pharaoh **N** made him a prisoner
23:34 Then Pharaoh **N** made Josiah's
23:35 land and give it to Pharaoh **N**.

Neco's (1)

2Ch 35:22 He refused to listen to **N** words,

Nedabiah (1)

1Ch 3:18 Jekamiah, Hoshama, and **N**.

need (123)

Gen 33:11 and has given me all that I **n**."
34:23 We only **n** to agree to do this
Exo 8:27 We **n** to travel three days into
10:26 know what we'll **n** until we get
16:4 out and gather only what they **n**
36:5 bringing much more than we **n**
Lev 26:26 Ten women will **n** only one
Num 7:5 use wherever they **n** these gifts
11:29 "Do you think you **n** to stand up
31:26 the families of the community **n**
Dtr 8:9 you will have everything you **n**.
15:8 lend them as much as they **n**.
24:15 they are poor and **n** their pay.
28:12 to many nations but won't **n**
28:48 and in **n** of everything.
Jos 7:3 "You don't **n** to send all the
9:11 'Take what you **n** for the trip,
Jdg 19:19 We have everything we **n**."
1Sm 28:1 "You **n** to know that you and
2Ch 2:16 We will cut all the lumber you **n**
35:15 They didn't **n** to leave their
Ezr 6:9 the priests in Jerusalem **n**
Neh 5:2 We **n** some grain ⌊if we are
Job 6:26 think my words **n** correction?
30:3 Shriveled up from **n** and hunger
33:7 You certainly don't **n** to be
38:41 wander around in **n** of food?
Psa 23:1 my shepherd. I am never in **n**.
32:9 ⌊They **n**⌋ a bit and bridle in
34:9 who fear him are never in **n**.
34:10 have all the good things they **n**.
73:25 As long as I have you, I don't **n**
91:5 You do not **n** to fear terrors of
Pro 6:11 and your **n** will come ⌊to you⌋
24:34 and your **n** will come like a
25:16 eat only as much as you **n**.
30:8 Feed me ⌊only⌋ the food I **n**,
Isa 21:12 If you **n** to ask, come back and
Jer 31:25 those who are weary all they **n**.
42:19 You **n** to know that I am
42:22 But now, you **n** to know that
Lam 1:16 one can give me the comfort I **n**
Eze 39:10 They will not **n** to get wood
Dan 3:16 "We don't **n** to answer your last

Mat 3:14 "I **n** to be baptized by you.
6:8 Your Father knows what you **n**
6:32 knows you **n** all of them.
9:12 people don't **n** a doctor;
14:16 "They don't **n** to go away.
19:20 What else do I **n** to do?"
25:38 into our homes or see you in **n**
25:44 or thirsty or as a stranger or in **n**
26:65 Why do we **n** any more
Mar 2:17 people don't **n** a doctor;
2:25 were in **n** and were hungry?
14:63 do we **n** any more witnesses?
Luk 5:31 people don't **n** a doctor;
10:42 There's only one thing you **n**.
11:8 and give you whatever you **n**
12:4 I can guarantee that you don't **n**
12:30 but your Father knows you **n**
14:18 bought a field, and I **n** to see it.
18:1 to show them that they **n**
18:22 "You still **n** one thing.
22:71 Then they said, "Why do we **n**
Jon 2:25 and didn't **n** anyone to tell him
6:7 Philip answered, "We would **n**
10:10 will have everything they **n**.
13:10 They **n** to have only their feet
16:30 You don't **n** to wait for
Act 1:7 Jesus told them, "You don't **n**
9:38 to Joppa! We **n** your help!"
22:22 The world doesn't **n** a man like
23:15 you **n** more information from
28:28 "You **n** to know that God has
Rom 8:26 how to pray for what we **n**.
12:8 If it is helping people in **n**,
12:13 with God's people who are in **n**.
15:14 have all the knowledge you **n**
16:2 her with anything she may **n**,
1Co 12:21 say to a hand, "I don't **n** you!"
12:21 say to the feet, "I don't **n** you!"
12:22 are the ones we really **n**.
12:24 our presentable parts don't **n**
2Co 3:1 Do we, like some people, **n**
7:1 we **n** to cleanse ourselves from
8:14 your surplus fills their **n** so that
8:14 their surplus may fill your **n**.
9:1 I don't **n** to write anything
9:8 always have everything you **n**,
9:10 and food to those who **n** to eat.
10:15 of us to give us the help we **n**
12:9 "My kindness is all you **n**.
Gal 5:25 then our lives **n** to conform to
Eph 4:28 to share with those in **n**.
Php 2:25 to help me in my **n**.
4:6 let God know what you **n**
4:11 this because I'm in any **n**.
4:19 God will richly fill your every **n**
Col 1:11 might with all the power you **n**
1Th 1:8 We don't **n** to say a thing about
3:10 you still **n** for your faith.
4:9 You don't **n** anyone to write to
4:12 on anyone else for what you **n**.
5:1 and sisters, you don't **n** anyone
Tit 3:13 will have everything they **n**.
Heb 4:14 We **n** to hold on to our
5:12 Instead, you still **n** someone to
5:12 You **n** milk, not solid food.
7:11 we wouldn't **n** to speak about
7:26 We **n** a chief priest who is holy,
7:27 We **n** a priest who doesn't have
10:18 there is no longer any **n** to
10:36 You **n** endurance so that after
Jas 1:4 and you won't **n** anything.
2Pe 1:3 has given us everything we **n**
1Jn 2:27 You don't **n** anyone to teach
3:17 notices another believer in **n**.
Rev 3:17 I don't **n** anything.' Yet, you do
13:10 **n** endurance and confidence.
14:12 faith in Jesus, **n** endurance.
21:23 The city doesn't **n** any sun or
22:5 and they will not **n** any light

needed (32)

Exo 39:40 and pegs — all the equipment **n**
Lev 12:4 the holy place until the days **n**
12:6 "When the days **n** to make her
14:32 what is **n** for his cleansing."
17:11 Blood is **n** to make peace with
Dtr 2:7 and you haven't **n** a thing.
Jos 7:3 or three thousand men are **n**
19:9 Judah had more land than it **n**.
Jdg 21:23 number of wives they **n** from
1Ki 8:59 justice every day as it is **n**.
2Ki 12:5 the temple where they are **n**."
12:12 to buy anything else that they **n**
2Ch 8:14 the priests by doing whatever **n**
29:34 But the priests **n** more help to
Neh 9:21 and they had everything they **n**.
12:45 what **n** to be done for
Mat 25:36 I **n** clothes, and you gave me
25:43 I **n** clothes, and you didn't give
Jon 13:29 telling him to buy what they **n**
Act 2:45 the money to anyone who **n** it.
4:34 None of them **n** anything.
4:35 distributed to anyone who **n** it.
17:25 by humans as if he **n** anything.
27:3 and receive any care he **n**.
28:10 put whatever we **n** on board.
2Co 11:9 was with you and **n** something,
11:9 supplied everything I **n**.
Eph 4:29 can give help wherever it is **n**.
Php 4:15 You gave me what I **n**,
Tit 1:5 you in Crete to do what still **n**
Rev 13:18 In this situation wisdom is **n**.
17:9 this situation a wise mind is **n**.

needle (3)

Mat 19:24 go through the eye of a **n** than
Mar 10:25 go through the eye of a **n** than
Luk 18:25 go through the eye of a **n** than

needs (28)

Gen 41:16 Pharaoh the answer that he **n**."
Exo 36:6 "No man or woman **n** to make
Num 3:7 doing what **n** to be done for the
3:8 doing what **n** to be done for the
4:26 will do everything that **n**
Jdg 19:20 Let me take care of your **n**.
Ezr 7:22 and as much salt as he **n**.
Psa 5:3 In the morning I lay my **n** in
132:15 certainly bless all that Zion **n**.
145:19 He fills the **n** of those who fear
Isa 58:10 to satisfy ⌊the **n** of⌋ those who
Jer 5:7 even though I satisfied their **n**.
Mat 10:10 deserves to have his **n** met.
21:3 tell him that the Lord **n** them.
Mar 11:3 say that the Lord **n** it.
Luk 19:31 say that the Lord **n** it."
19:34 answered, "The Lord **n** it."
Act 24:23 his friends take care of his **n**.
1Co 7:3 each other's ⌊sexual⌋ **n**.
2Co 9:12 not only provides for the **n**
Php 4:16 you provided for my **n** twice.
4:18 you have filled my **n**.
1Ti 5:10 taking care of believers' **n**,
2Ti 1:16 He often took care of my **n** and
Tit 3:14 when urgent **n** arise so that
Jas 1:5 If any of you **n** wisdom to know
2:15 or a woman, **n** clothes or food
2:16 for that person's physical **n**,

needy (45)

Dtr 15:11 Israelites who are poor and **n**.
24:14 workers who are poor and **n**,
1Sm 2:8 He lifts the **n** from the trash
Job 5:15 their slander and the **n** from
24:4 They force **n** people off the
24:14 they kill the poor and **n**.
29:16 I was father to the **n**.
Psa 9:18 **N** people will not always be
12:5 are robbed and **n** people groan,
35:10 and weak and **n** people from
37:14 to kill oppressed and **n** people,
40:17 But I am oppressed and **n**.
69:33 The LORD listens to **n** people.
70:5 But I am oppressed and **n**.
72:4 May he save the children of **n**
72:12 He will rescue the **n** person
72:13 will have pity on the poor and **n**
72:13 and will save the lives of the **n**.
74:21 Let weak and **n** people praise
82:4 Rescue weak and **n** people.
86:1 because I am oppressed and **n**.
107:41 But now he lifts **n** people high
109:16 "He drove oppressed, **n**,
109:22 I am oppressed and **n**.
109:31 because he stands beside **n**
113:7 He lifts the **n** from a garbage
132:15 satisfy its **n** people with food.
140:12 the cause of those who are **n**.
Pro 14:31 is kind to the **n** honors him.
31:9 of oppressed and **n** people."
31:20 stretches them out to **n** people.
Isa 10:2 of the **n** among my people.
14:30 and the **n** will lie down in
25:4 a refuge for the **n** in their
32:7 even when **n** people plead for
41:17 "The poor and **n** are looking for
Jer 20:13 He has rescued the lives of **n**
22:16 the cause of the poor and **n**.
Eze 16:49 didn't help the poor and the **n**.
18:12 He oppresses the poor and **n**.
Amo 2:6 righteous for money and the **n**
4:1 the poor and abuse the **n**.
5:12 You deny the **n** access to the
8:4 those who trample on the **n**
8:6 the poor with money and the **n**

Negev (39)

Gen 12:9 kept moving toward the **N**.
13:1 he had and went to the **N**.
13:3 He went from the **N** as far as
20:1 Abraham moved to the **N** and
24:62 since he was living in the **N**.
Num 13:17 "Go through the **N** and then into
13:22 They went through the **N** and
13:29 The Amalekites live in the **N**.
21:1 who lived in the **N**,
33:40 who lived in the **N**,
Dtr 1:7 in the foothills, in the **N**,
34:3 the **N**, and the Jordan Plain —
Jos 10:40 mountains, the **N**, the foothills,
11:16 land, the mountains, all the **N**,
12:8 and the **N** ⌊that the⌋ Hittites,
15:21 On the farthest edge of the **N**,
Jdg 1:9 the **N**, and the foothills.
1:16 of Judah in the **N** near Arad.
1Sm 27:10 answer, "the **N** in Judah,"
27:10 or "the portion of the **N** where
27:10 or "the portion of the **N** where
30:1 Amalekites had raided the **N**,
30:14 We raided the portion of the **N**
30:14 the portion of the **N** where
30:27 Bethel, Ramoth in the **N**, Jattir,
2Sm 24:7 to Beersheba in the **N** of Judah.
2Ch 28:18 the foothills and the **N** in Judah.
Psa 126:4 ⌊to dry riverbeds⌋ in the **N**.
Isa 21:1 storm sweeping through the **N**,
30:6 about the animals in the **N**.
Jer 13:19 The cities in the **N** will be
17:26 the mountains, and from the **N**.
32:44 and in the **N** because I will
33:13 in the foothills, in the **N**,
Eze 20:46 against the forest in the **N**.
20:47 Tell the forest in the **N**,
Oba 1:19 "People from the **N** will take
1:20 of the cities in the **N**.
Zec 7:7 and undisturbed and the **N**

neglect (6)

Jos 1:5 I will never **n** you or abandon
Ezr 4:22 Be careful not to **n** your duty in
Neh 10:39 We won't **n** our God's temple.
Pro 1:8 not **n** your mother's teachings,
Jer 48:10 Cursed are those who **n** doing
1Ti 4:14 Don't **n** the gift which you

neglected (5)

2Ch 8:15 No one **n** the king's orders to
Neh 13:11 is God's temple being **n**?"
Psa 119:102 I have not **n** your regulations,
Mat 23:23 But you have **n** justice,
Act 6:1 them were **n** every day when

neglecting (1)

Mat 23:23 things without **n** the others.

negligent (1)

2Ch 29:11 Don't be **n**, my sons.

Nehelam (3)
Jer 29:24 "Say to Shemaiah from **N**,
29:31 says about Shemaiah from **N**:
29:32 I will punish Shemaiah from **N**.

Nehemiah (14)
Ezr 2:2 Jeshua, **N**, Seraiah, Reelaiah,
Neh 1:1 These are the words of **N**,
3:16 After him **N**, Azbuk's son,
4:4 ⌊**N** prayed,⌋ "Our God, hear us.
6:14 ⌊**N** prayed,⌋ "My God,
7:7 Jeshua, **N**, Azariah, Raamiah,
8:9 Then **N** the governor,
10:1 Governor **N** (son of Hacaliah),
12:26 and in the days of **N** the
12:47 the time of Zerubbabel and **N**,
13:14 ⌊**N** prayed,⌋ "Remember me for
13:22 ⌊**N** prayed,⌋ "Remember me
13:29 ⌊**N** prayed,⌋ "Remember them,
13:31 ⌊**N** prayed,⌋ "Remember me,

Nehum (1)
Neh 7:7 Bigvai, **N**, and Baanah.

Nehushta (1)
2Ki 24:8 His mother was **N**,

Nehushtan (1)
2Ki 18:4 incense to it. They called it **N**.

Neiel (1)
Jos 19:27 and goes to Beth Emek and **N**.

neigh (2)
Jer 5:8 They **n** for their neighbors'
50:11 the grass and **n** like stallions.

neighbor (68)
Exo 3:22 should ask her Egyptian **n**
20:16 when you testify about your **n**.
21:14 angry that he plans to kill his **n**,
22:7 someone gives his **n** silver
22:10 someone gives his **n** a donkey,
22:11 LORD that the **n** did not take
22:11 The **n** doesn't have to make up
22:12 animal was stolen from the **n**,
22:14 borrows an animal from his **n**,
Lev 6:2 if you lie to your **n** about
6:2 stolen or seized from your **n**,
19:11 steal, lie, or deceive your **n**.
19:13 "Never oppress or rob your **n**.
19:15 Judge your **n** fairly.
19:17 Be sure to correct your **n** so
19:18 Instead, love your **n** as you
24:19 Whoever injures a **n** must
25:14 If you sell anything to your **n** or
25:15 you buy property from your **n**,
25:15 Your **n** must sell it to you
Dtr 5:20 when you testify about your **n**.
15:2 the debt your **n** still owes you.
15:2 Don't demand that your **n** or
24:10 you make a loan to your **n**,
1Sm 15:28 He has given it to your **n** who
Psa 15:3 or bring disgrace on his **n**.
101:5 who secretly slanders his **n**.
Pro 3:28 do not tell your **n**, "Go away!
3:29 wrong to your **n** while
6:1 you guarantee a loan for your **n**
6:3 yourself, and pester your **n**.
11:9 godless person can ruin his **n**,
11:12 A person who despises a **n**
12:26 person looks out for his **n**,
14:20 person is hated even by his **n**,
14:21 Whoever despises his **n** sins,
16:29 A violent person misleads his **n**
18:17 right ⌊until⌋ his **n** comes
21:10 has no consideration for his **n**.
24:28 Do not testify against your **n**
25:8 end if your **n** disgraces you?
25:9 your argument to your **n**,
25:18 false testimony against his **n**.
26:19 who tricks his **n** and says,
27:10 A **n** living nearby is better than
29:5 A person who flatters his **n** is
Isa 3:5 everyone will oppress his **n**.
Isa 19:2 **n** against neighbor,
19:2 neighbor against **n**,
Jer 9:4 **n** goes around slandering.
9:5 Everyone cheats his **n**.
Hab 2:15 who makes his **n** drink from
Zec 3:10 "each of you will invite your **n**
8:10 every person against his **n**.
Mat 5:43 that it was said, 'Love your **n**,
19:19 Love your **n** as you love
22:39 'Love your **n** as you love
Mar 12:31 'Love your **n** as you love
12:33 and to love your **n** as you love
Luk 10:27 And 'Love your **n** as you love
10:29 asked Jesus, "Who is my **n**?"
10:36 who do you think was a **n** to
Rom 13:9 "Love your **n** as you love
13:10 anything that is harmful to a **n**.
15:2 all be concerned about our **n**
Gal 5:14 "Love your **n** as you love
Jas 2:8 "Love your **n** as you love
4:12 who are you to judge your **n**?

neighborhood (2)
Rut 4:17 The women in the **n** said,
Mar 7:31 Jesus then left the **n** of Tyre.

neighboring (9)
Dtr 21:2 the body to each of the **n** cities.
Jos 10:37 They captured it and its **n**
10:39 its king and all its **n** villages
1Ki 4:24 peace with all the **n** countries.
Ezr 3:3 of the people in the **n** regions.
9:1 separate from the **n** groups
9:2 our holy race with the **n** groups
Jer 49:18 and their **n** cities when they
50:40 and their **n** cities when I,

neighbor's (23)
Exo 20:17 **n** household away from him.
20:17 to take your **n** wife, his male
22:8 or not he took his **n** valuables
22:9 must make up for his **n** loss
22:26 of your **n** clothes as collateral,
Lev 18:20 intercourse with your **n** wife
19:16 Never endanger your **n** life.
20:10 wife or with his **n** wife, both
Dtr 5:21 your **n** wife away from him.
5:21 for your **n** household, his field,
19:14 Never move your **n** original
23:24 If you go into your **n** vineyard,
23:25 If you go into your **n** grain field,
23:25 use a sickle to cut your **n** grain
27:17 his **n** boundary marker will
Job 31:9 secretly waited near my **n** door,
Pro 6:3 your **n** hands: Humble yourself,
6:29 who has sex with his **n** wife.
25:17 Do not set foot in your **n** house
Eze 18:6 He doesn't dishonor his **n** wife
18:11 He dishonors his **n** wife
18:15 He doesn't dishonor his **n** wife
33:26 You dishonor your **n** wife.

neighbors (43)
Exo 32:27 your relatives, friends, and **n**."
Jos 9:16 that these people were their **n**
Jdg 18:22 Micah's **n** were called together
18:23 Why did you call your **n**
2Ki 4:3 containers from all your **n**.
1Ch 12:40 Also, their **n** as far as the
22:18 you peace with all your **n**?
2Ch 32:22 them peace with all their **n**.
Ezr 1:6 All their **n** ⌊who were
Job 12:4 I am a laughingstock to my **n**.
Psa 28:3 speak of peace with their **n**
31:11 by my friends, even by my **n**.
44:13 made us a disgrace to our **n**
79:4 become a disgrace to our **n**,
79:12 Pay each one of our **n** back
80:6 us a source of conflict to our **n**,
Isa 41:6 People help their **n** and say to
Jer 6:21 **N** and their friends will die.
9:4 "Beware of your **n**.
9:8 People speak politely to their **n**,
9:20 Teach your **n** funeral songs.
12:14 say about all my evil **n** who
12:14 I am going to uproot those **n**
Jer 22:13 He makes his **n** work for
23:35 They should ask their **n** and
31:34 will each person teach his **n**
34:15 You agreed to free your **n**,
34:17 freed your relatives and **n**.
48:17 Mourn over it, all of its **n** and
49:10 None of their **n** will say,
Lam 1:17 His own **n** will become his
Eze 16:26 had sex with your lustful **n**,
16:57 Aram and their **n** despise you.
22:12 profits by mistreating your **n**.
Mic 7:5 Don't trust your **n**. Don't have
Zec 11:6 hand the people over to their **n**
Luk 1:58 Her **n** and relatives heard that
1:65 All their **n** were filled with awe.
14:12 family, other relatives, or rich **n**.
15:6 Then he calls his friends and **n**
15:9 she calls her friends and **n**
Jon 9:8 His **n** and those who had
Heb 8:11 will each person teach his **n**

neighbors' (4)
Psa 89:41 the object of his **n** scorn.
Jer 5:8 They neigh for their **n** wives
29:23 adultery with their **n** wives
Eze 22:11 things with their **n** wives.

neighing (1)
Jer 8:16 The **n** of stallions makes the

Nekoda (4)
Ezr 2:48 Rezin, **N**, Gazzam,
2:60 of Delaiah, Tobiah, and **N**.
Neh 7:50 Reaiah, Rezin, **N**,
7:62 of Delaiah, Tobiah, and **N**.

Nemuel (3)
Num 26:9 and **N**, Dathan, and Abiram
26:12 Simeon were the family of **N**,
1Ch 4:24 Simeon's sons were **N**,

Nepheg (4)
Exo 6:21 Izhar were Korah, **N**, and Zichri.
2Sm 5:15 Ibhar, Elishua, **N**, Japhia,
1Ch 3:7 Nogah, **N**, Japhia,
14:6 Nogah, **N**, Japhia,

nephew (5)
Gen 12:5 along his wife Sarai, his **n** Lot,
14:12 They also took Abram's **n** Lot
14:14 When Abram heard that his **n**
29:12 that he was her father's **n**
Act 23:16 But Paul's **n** heard about the

nephews (2)
1Ch 5:1 as firstborn were given to his **n**,
2Ch 22:8 (Ahaziah's **n**) who were serving

Nephilim (3)
Gen 6:4 The **N** were on the earth in
Num 13:33 We saw **N** there. (The
13:33 descendants of Anak are **N**.)

Nephtoah (2)
Jos 15:9 goes around to the spring of **N**.
18:15 to the springs of **N**.

Nephusheshim (1)
Neh 7:52 Besai, Meunim, **N**,

Nephusim (1)
Ezr 2:50 Asnah, Meunim, **N**,

Ner (7)
1Sm 14:50 the son of Saul's uncle **N**.
14:51 Kish (Saul's father) and **N**
1Ki 2:5 Abner, son of **N**, and Amasa,
2:32 Abner (who was the son of **N**
1Ch 8:33 **N** was the father of Kish.
9:39 **N** was the father of Kish.
26:28 (son of Kish), Abner (son of **N**),

Nereus (1)
Rom 16:15 Greet Philologus and Julia, **N**,

Nergal (4)

2Ki 17:30 The people from Cuth made **N**.
Jer 39:3 **N** (the quartermaster),
39:3 **N** (the quartermaster and the
39:13 **N** (the quartermaster and the

Neri (1)

Luk 3:27 son of Shealtiel, son of **N**,

Neriah (10)

Jer 32:12 son of **N** and grandson of
32:16 son of **N**, I prayed to the LORD.
36:4 called Baruch, son of **N**.
36:8 Baruch, son of **N**, did as the
36:14 Baruch, son of **N**, took the
36:32 to the scribe Baruch, son of **N**.
43:3 But Baruch, son of **N**,
43:6 Jeremiah and Baruch, son of **N**.
45:1 spoke to Baruch, son of **N**.
51:59 son of **N** and grandson of

Ner's (8)

1Sm 26:5 where Saul and **N** son Abner,
26:14 the troops and to **N** son Abner.
2Sm 2:8 **N** son Abner, commander of
2:12 **N** son Abner and the officers of
3:23 "**N** son Abner came to the king,
3:25 know that **N** son Abner came
3:28 the blood of **N** son Abner.
3:37 for killing **N** son Abner.

nervous (1)

1Co 2:3 I was afraid and very **n**.

nest (16)

Num 24:21 Your **n** is built in a rock.
Dtr 22:6 and find a **n** containing chicks
22:6 mother bird is sitting on the **n**,
32:11 Like an eagle that stirs up its **n**,
Job 39:27 makes its **n** on the heights?
Psa 84:3 find a **n** for themselves.
Pro 27:8 a bird wandering from its **n**,
Isa 10:14 of nations as one finds a **n**.
Jer 22:23 in Lebanon and have your **n**
49:16 Even though you build your **n**
Eze 17:23 Every kind of bird will **n** in it
Oba 1:4 eagle and build your **n** among
Hab 2:9 in order to set his **n** up high
Zep 2:14 pelicans and herons will **n**
Mat 13:32 for birds to **n** in its branches."
Mar 4:32 that birds can **n** in its shade."

nested (1)

Luk 13:19 and the birds **n** in its branches."

nestlings (1)

Isa 16:2 fluttering birds, like scattered **n**,

nests (8)

Psa 104:17 Birds build their **n** in them.
Isa 11:8 put their hands into vipers' **n**.
34:15 Owls will make their **n** there,
60:8 like doves to their **n**?
Jer 48:28 Be like doves that make their **n**
Eze 31:6 All the birds made their **n** in its
Mat 8:20 have holes, and birds have **n**,
Luk 9:58 have holes, and birds have **n**,

net (31)

Job 18:8 feet get him tangled in a **n** as
19:6 and surrounded me with his **n**.
Psa 9:15 Their feet are caught in the **n**
10:9 when he draws them into his **n**.
31:4 so pull me out of the **n** that they
35:7 For no reason they hid their **n**
35:8 Let the **n** that they hid catch
57:6 ⌊My enemies⌋ spread out a **n**
66:11 You have trapped us in a **n**.
140:5 have spread out a **n** with ropes.
Pro 1:17 It does no good to spread a **n**
29:5 his neighbor is spreading a **n**
Ecc 9:12 fish that are caught in a cruel **n**
Isa 51:20 like an antelope caught in a **n**.
Lam 1:13 He spread a **n** for my feet.
Eze 12:13 I will spread my **n** over him,
Eze 12:13 and he will be caught in my **n**.
17:20 I will spread my **n** over you to
19:8 They spread their **n** over him
32:3 I will spread my **n** over you,
32:3 they will haul you up in a **n**.
Hos 7:12 I will spread my **n** over you.
Mat 4:18 They were throwing a **n** into
13:47 is like a **n** that was thrown
Mar 1:16 They were throwing a **n** into
Jon 21:6 He told them, "Throw the **n** out
21:6 So they threw the **n** out and
21:8 the boat and dragged the **n** full
21:11 boat and pulled the **n** ashore.
21:11 Though the **n** was filled with
Rom 11:9 for them become a trap and a **n**,

Netaim (1)

1Ch 4:23 who lived at **N** and Gederah.

Nethanel (14)

Num 1:8 **N**, son of Zuar, from the tribe of
2:5 for the people of Issachar is **N**,
7:18 On the second day **N**,
7:23 These were the gifts from **N**,
10:15 **N**, son of Zuar, commanded the
1Ch 2:14 **N** (his fourth son), Raddai (his
15:24 **N**, Amasai, Zechariah,
24:6 Shemaiah was a son of **N**
26:4 Sachar (the fourth), **N** (the fifth
2Ch 17:7 Hail, Obadiah, Zechariah, **N**,
35:9 his brothers Shemaiah and **N**,
Ezr 10:22 **N**, Jozabad, and Elasah
Neh 12:21 Hashabiah; from Jedaiah, **N**.
12:36 Gilalai, Maai, **N**, Judah,

Nethaniah (15)

2Ki 25:23 They were Ishmael (son of **N**),
25:25 month Ishmael (son of **N**
1Ch 25:2 Joseph, **N**, and Asharelah.
25:12 The fifth chose **N**, his sons,
2Ch 17:8 **N**, Zebadiah, Asahel,
Jer 36:14 who was the son of **N**,
40:8 Ishmael (son of **N**),
41:1 month Ishmael (son of **N**
41:2 Ishmael, son of **N**,
41:6 Ishmael, son of **N**,
41:7 into the city, Ishmael, son of **N**,
41:9 Ishmael, son of **N**,
41:10 Ishmael, son of **N**,
41:11 Ishmael, son of **N**, had done,
41:16 rescued from Ishmael, son of **N**,

Nethaniah's (2)

Jer 40:14 **N** son, to kill you?"
40:15 "Let me kill Ishmael, **N** son.

Netophah (11)

2Sm 23:28 of Ahohi), Maharai from **N**,
23:29 Heleb (son of Baanah) from **N**,
2Ki 25:23 (son of Tanhumeth from **N**),
1Ch 11:30 Maharai from **N**, Heled (son of
11:30 Heled (son of Baanah) from **N**,
27:13 a descendant of Zerah from **N**,
27:15 commanded by Heldai from **N**.
Ezr 2:22 of **N**: 56
Neh 7:26 the people of Bethlehem and **N**:
12:28 from the villages of **N**,
Jer 40:8 the sons of Ephai from **N**,

Netophathites (2)

1Ch 2:54 Bethlehem, were the **N**, Atroth,
9:16 the villages belonging to the **N**).

nets (18)

Psa 141:10 people fall into their own **n**,
Isa 19:8 Those who spread their **n** on
Eze 26:5 people spread their fishing **n**.
26:14 a place to spread fishing **n**.
47:10 with their fishing **n** spread out.
Hos 5:1 spread out **n** on Mount Tabor.
Mic 7:2 They trap each other with **n**.
Hab 1:15 drag them away in **n**,
1:16 is why they sacrifice to their **n**
1:17 they keep on emptying their **n**
Mat 4:20 left their **n** and followed him.
4:21 father Zebedee preparing their **n**
Mar 1:18 left their **n** and followed him.
1:19 their **n** ⌊to go fishing⌋.
Luk 5:2 them and were washing their **n**.
5:4 and lower your **n** to catch some
5:5 if you say so, I'll lower the **n**."
5:6 of fish that their **n** began to tear.

nettles (1)

Isa 34:13 fortresses have **n** and thistles.

new (210)

Gen 27:28 and plenty of fresh grain and **n**
27:37 I've provided fresh grain and **n**
Exo 1:8 Then a **n** king, who knew
21:33 up a cistern or digs a **n** one
Lev 23:16 Then bring a **n** grain offering to
26:10 to make room for **n** ones.
Num 16:30 does something totally **n** — if
18:12 oil and the best of the **n** wine
28:26 the LORD your **n** grain offering,
Dtr 7:13 grain, **n** wine, and olive oil.
11:14 grain, **n** wine, and olive oil.
12:17 grain, **n** wine, and olive oil;
14:23 grain, **n** wine, and olive oil,
18:4 grain, **n** wine, olive oil,
20:5 "If you have built a **n** house but
22:8 Whenever you build a **n** house,
24:5 and make his **n** wife happy.
28:51 grain, no **n** wine, no olive oil,
32:17 These were **n** gods,
33:28 in a land of grain and **n** wine.
Jos 9:13 These were **n** wineskins when
Jdg 5:8 When the people chose **n** gods,
15:13 So they tied him up with two **n**
16:7 seven **n** bowstrings that are
16:8 seven **n** bowstrings that were
16:11 tightly with **n** ropes that have
16:12 So Delilah took some **n** ropes
Rut 4:15 He will bring you a **n** life and
1Sm 6:7 Now get a **n** cart ready for two
20:5 is the **N** Moon Festival,
20:18 is the **N** Moon Festival,"
20:24 When the **N** Moon Festival
2Sm 6:3 men put God's ark on a **n** cart
6:3 were guiding the **n** cart.
21:16 which he wore on a **n** belt,
1Ki 11:29 and Ahijah had on **n** clothes.
11:30 Ahijah took his **n** garment and
2Ki 2:20 Elisha said, "Bring me a **n** jar,
3:5 against the ⌊**n**⌋ king of Israel.
4:23 It isn't a **N** Moon Festival or a
18:32 country with grain and **n** wine,
1Ch 13:7 ark on a **n** cart from Abinadab's
23:31 at **N** Moon Festivals,
2Ch 2:4 **N** Moon Festivals,
8:13 on the **N** Moon Festivals,
20:5 In the **n** courtyard at the
31:3 the **N** Moon Festivals,
31:5 **n** wine, fresh olive oil, honey,
32:28 **n** wine, and fresh olive oil,
Ezr 3:5 the offerings for the **N** Moon
9:8 us **n** opportunities while we
Neh 4:2 and give them **n** strength?"
5:11 on the money, grain, **n** wine,
10:33 and on the **N** Moon Festivals,
10:37 fruit from every tree, **n** wine,
10:39 of grain, **n** wine, and olive oil.
13:5 **n** wine, and olive oil.
13:12 all the grain harvested, **n** wine,
Job 10:17 You keep finding **n** witnesses
10:17 bringing **n** armies against me.
29:20 bow in my hand will remain **n**.'
32:19 like **n** wineskins that are ready
Psa 4:7 their grain and **n** wine increase.
33:3 Sing a **n** song to him.
40:3 He placed a **n** song in my
58:2 you invent **n** crimes on earth,
81:3 horn on the day of the **n** moon,
96:1 Sing to the LORD a **n** song!
98:1 Sing a **n** song to the LORD
119:25 Give me a **n** life as you
119:37 Give me a **n** life in your ways.
119:40 Give me a **n** life in your
119:50 Your promise gave me a **n** life.
119:88 Give me a **n** life through your
119:93 gave me a **n** life through them.

Psa	119:107	Give me a **n** life, O LORD,
	119:149	O LORD, give me a **n** life
	119:154	Give me a **n** life as you
	119:156	Give me a **n** life guided by your
	119:159	your mercy, give me a **n** life.
	119:175	Let my soul have **n** life so that
	144:9	I will sing a **n** song to you.
	149:1	Sing a **n** song to the LORD.
Ecc	1:9	is nothing **n** under the sun.
	1:10	Can you say that anything is **n**?
Sos	7:13	I have saved **n** and old things
Isa	1:13	so are your **N** Moon Festivals,
	1:14	I hate your **N** Moon Festivals
	24:7	**N** wine dries up, All happy
	26:18	and no **n** people were born on
	36:17	country with grain and **n** wine,
	41:1	Let the people gain **n** strength.
	41:15	you into a **n** threshing sledge
	42:9	I will reveal **n** things before
	42:10	Sing a **n** song to the LORD.
	43:19	I am going to do something **n**.
	48:6	on I will reveal to you **n** things,
	49:26	blood as though it were **n** wine.
	62:2	You will be given a **n** name
	62:8	nor will foreigners drink the **n**
	65:8	When someone finds juice for **n**
	65:17	I will create a **n** heaven and a
	65:17	a new heaven and a **n** earth.
	66:14	you will flourish like **n** grass.
	66:22	"The **n** heaven and earth that I
Jer	8:10	and their fields to **n** owners.
	13:21	your friends your **n** masters?
	18:4	he would rework it into a **n** clay
	26:10	They sat at the entrance of **N**
	31:12	grain, **n** wine, and olive oil,
	31:22	create something **n** on earth:
	31:31	"when I will make a **n** promise
	36:10	at the entrance of **N** Gate
Lam	3:23	It is **n** every morning.
Eze	11:19	purpose and put a **n** spirit
	18:31	Get yourselves **n** hearts and
	18:31	new hearts and **n** spirits.
	36:26	I will give you a **n** heart and put
	36:26	a new heart and put a **n** spirit
	45:17	the **N** Moon Festivals,
	46:1	It must also be opened on the **N**
	46:3	and on **N** Moon Festivals.
Dan	11:24	He will invent **n** ways of
Hos	2:8	her grain, **n** wine, and olive oil.
	2:9	and my **n** wine when it's
	2:11	her **N** Moon Festivals,
	2:22	grain, **n** wine, and olive oil.
	4:11	Prostitutes, old wine, and **n**
	5:7	Now their **N** Moon ⌊Festivals⌋
	7:14	praying for grain and **n** wine.
	10:12	"Break **n** ground. Plant
Joe	1:5	**N** wine has been taken away
	1:10	The **n** wine has dried up.
	2:19	**n** wine, and olive oil to you.
	2:24	The vats will overflow with **n**
	3:18	On that day **n** wine will cover
Amo	8:5	"When will the **N** Moon
	9:13	**N** wine will drip from the
Mic	6:15	You will make **n** wine,
Hag	1:11	grain, the **n** wine, the olive oil,
	2:9	This **n** house will be more
Zec	9:17	women will prosper on **n** wine.
Mat	9:16	an old coat with a **n** piece
	9:17	Nor do people pour **n** wine into
	9:17	Rather, people pour **n** wine into
	13:52	He brings **n** and old things out
	26:29	that day when I drink **n** wine
	27:60	he laid it in his own **n** tomb,
Mar	1:27	This is a **n** teaching that has
	2:21	an old coat with a **n** piece
	2:21	Otherwise, the **n** patch will
	2:22	People don't pour **n** wine into
	2:22	Rather, **n** wine is to be poured
	14:25	that day when I drink **n** wine
	16:17	They will speak **n** languages.
Luk	1:78	A **n** day will dawn on us from
	5:36	a piece of cloth from a **n** coat
	5:36	the **n** cloth will tear the old.
	5:36	Besides, the patch from the **n**
	5:37	People don't pour **n** wine into
	5:37	If they do, the **n** wine will make
Luk	5:38	Rather, **n** wine is to be poured
	5:39	old wine wants **n** wine.
	22:20	for you is the **n** promise made
Jon	13:34	giving you a **n** commandment:
	19:41	In that garden was a **n** tomb in
Act	17:19	"Could you tell us these **n**
	17:21	hear something **n** and unusual.
Rom	1:30	They think up **n** ways to be
	6:4	should live a **n** kind of life.
	7:6	are serving in a **n** spiritual way,
	15:23	But now I have no **n**
1Co	5:7	so that you may be a **n** batch
	11:25	He said, "This cup is the **n**
2Co	3:6	to be ministers of a **n** promise,
	3:12	confidence ⌊in the **n** promise⌋,
	5:17	in Christ is a **n** creation.
	5:17	A **n** way of living has come
Gal	6:15	what matters is being a **n**
Eph	2:15	and create one **n** humanity
	4:23	you were taught to have a **n**
	4:24	to become a **n** person created
Col	2:16	**N** Moon Festivals,
	3:10	and you've become a **n** person.
	3:10	This **n** person is continually
1Ti	3:6	He must not be a **n** Christian,
Tit	3:5	gives us **n** birth and renewal.
Heb	8:8	when I will make a **n** promise
	8:13	God made this **n** promise and
	9:10	God would establish a **n** way
	9:15	he is able to bring a **n** promise
	10:20	Jesus has opened a **n** and
	12:24	who brings the **n** promise from
1Pe	1:3	God has given us a **n** birth
	1:3	We have been born into a **n** life
	1:4	We have been born into a **n** life
2Pe	3:13	has promised — a **n** heaven
	3:13	a new heaven and a **n** earth —
1Jn	2:7	to give you a **n** commandment.
	2:8	to give you a **n** commandment.
2Jn	1:5	to give you a **n** commandment.
Rev	2:17	stone with a **n** name written
	3:12	(the **N** Jerusalem coming down
	3:12	from my God), and my **n** name.
	5:9	Then they sang a **n** song,
	14:3	They were singing a **n** song in
	21:1	I saw a **n** heaven and a new
	21:1	a new heaven and a **n** earth,
	21:2	the holy city, **N** Jerusalem,
	21:5	"I am making everything **n**."

newborn (4)

Gen	21:3	named his **n** son Isaac.
1Ki	20:27	seemed like two **n** goats.
Act	7:19	their **n** babies outdoors,
1Pe	2:2	Desire God's pure word as **n**

news (97)

Gen	29:13	As soon as Laban heard the **n**
	32:5	to tell you ⌊this **n**⌋
	34:7	as soon as they heard the **n**.
	37:14	and bring some **n** back to me."
	45:16	the **n** that Joseph's brothers
Exo	33:4	the people heard this bad **n**,
1Sm	4:13	went into the city to tell the **n**.
	4:14	went quickly to tell Eli the **n**.
	4:19	When she heard the **n** that the
	11:4	they told the people the **n**,
	11:5	So they told him the **n** about
	11:6	When he heard this **n**,
	17:18	bring back some **n** about them.
	18:20	the **n** pleased him.
	23:25	David was told the **n**.
	31:9	to tell the people this good **n**
2Sm	1:5	who had brought him the **n**.
	1:13	who had brought him the **n**,
	1:20	Don't tell the **n** in Gath.
	4:4	the **n** about ⌊the death of⌋ Saul
	4:10	he was bringing good **n**.
	4:10	Ziklag to reward him for his **n**.
	18:19	bring the king the good **n** that
	18:20	the man carrying good **n** today.
	18:20	You can carry the **n** some other
	18:20	You must not deliver the **n**
	18:22	won't be rewarded for this **n**."
	18:25	"he has good **n** to tell."
	18:26	one is also bringing good **n**."
2Sm	18:27	must be coming with good **n**."
	18:31	"Good **n** for Your Majesty!"
	18:33	king was shaken ⌊by the **n**⌋.
1Ki	1:42	you must be bringing good **n**."
	2:28	The **n** reached Joab.
	14:6	told to give you some terrible **n**.
	15:21	When Baasha heard the **n**,
2Ki	7:9	This is a day of good **n**,
	7:9	Let's bring the **n** to the royal
	7:11	gatekeepers announced the **n**
	9:15	city to take the **n** to Jezreel."
1Ch	10:9	and the people this good **n**.
2Ch	16:5	When Baasha heard the **n**,
Est	1:17	The **n** of what the queen has
Psa	40:9	I will announce the good **n** of
	45:1	is overflowing with good **n**.
	68:11	who announce the good **n** are
	112:7	He is not afraid of bad **n**.
Pro	15:30	Good **n** refreshes the body.
	25:25	so is good **n** from far away.
Isa	23:5	When the **n** reaches Egypt,
	23:5	shudder over the **n** about Tyre.
	24:18	Whoever flees from **n** of a
	40:9	Tell the good **n**! Call out with a
	40:9	Tell the good **n**! Raise your
	41:27	a messenger with the good **n**.
	52:7	who announces the good **n**,
	52:7	He brings the good **n**,
	61:1	anointed me to deliver good **n**
Jer	6:24	have heard the **n** about them.
	20:15	very happy with the **n** that
	37:5	Jerusalem heard this **n**,
	48:20	Tell the **n** in Arnon that Moab is
	49:23	because they heard the bad **n**.
	50:2	the nations, and spread the **n**.
	50:46	The earth will quake at the **n**
Eze	21:7	'**N** has come that will
	24:26	come to you to tell you the **n**.
	32:9	troubled when I spread the **n**
Dan	11:44	But **n** from the east and the
Jnh	3:6	When the **n** reached the king of
Mic	1:9	⌊The **n** about Samaria⌋ will
Nah	1:15	who announces the good **n**:
	3:19	All who hear the **n** about you
Mat	4:24	The **n** about Jesus spread
	9:26	The **n** about this spread
	9:31	the **n** about him throughout
	14:1	heard the **n** about Jesus.
Mar	1:28	The **n** about him spread
	7:36	the more they spread the **n**.
Luk	1:19	sent me to tell you this good **n**.
	2:10	I have good **n** for you,
	4:14	and the **n** about him spread
	4:37	So **n** about him spread to every
	5:15	The **n** about Jesus spread
	7:17	This **n** about Jesus spread
Act	4:17	Then the **n** about the miracle
	9:42	The **n** about this spread
	10:37	spread the **n** about baptism.
	11:22	After the **n** about Antioch
2Co	11:4	tells you good **n** that is different
Gal	1:6	a different kind of good **n**.
	1:7	are calling good **n** is not really
	1:7	news is not really good **n** at all.
	1:8	Whoever tells you good **n** that
	1:9	If anyone tells you good **n** that
Php	2:19	some encouraging **n** about you.
1Th	3:1	any longer ⌊for **n** about you⌋,

next (197)

Gen	8:8	**N**, he sent out a dove to see if
	14:13	He was living **n** to the oak
	17:21	birth to him at this time **n** year."
	18:10	come back to you **n** year at this
	18:14	I will come back to you **n** year
	19:27	Early the **n** morning Abraham
	19:34	The **n** day the older daughter
	21:14	Early the **n** morning Abraham
	22:3	Early the **n** morning Abraham
	22:10	**N**, Abraham picked up the knife
	26:31	Early the **n** morning they
	28:18	Early the **n** morning Jacob took
	31:55	Early the **n** morning Laban
	40:13	In the **n** three days Pharaoh
	40:19	In the **n** three days Pharaoh
	47:18	they came to him the **n** year.

Exo 2:13 Moses went there the **n** day,
9:6 The **n** day the LORD did as he
12:4 That household and the one **n**
15:27 **N**, they went to Elim,
16:24 So they saved it until the **n**
17:16 from one generation to the **n**."
18:13 The **n** day Moses was settling
24:4 Early the **n** morning he built an
28:26 the inside edge **n** to the ephod.
32:6 Early the **n** day the people
32:30 The **n** day Moses said to the
34:4 Early the **n** morning he went up
39:19 the inside edge **n** to the ephod.
Lev 6:10 and will put them **n** to the altar.
7:16 the day you offer it or the **n** day.
10:12 and eat it **n** to the altar because
16:15 "**N**, Aaron will slaughter the
19:6 you bring it and on the **n** day.
23:32 From that evening to the **n**,
25:15 of crops until the **n** jubilee.
27:18 left until the **n** jubilee year.
Num 2:5 "**N** to them will be the tribe of
2:12 "**N** to them will be the tribe of
2:20 "**N** to them will be the tribe of
2:27 "**N** to them will be the tribe of
4:14 **N**, they will put all the
6:9 might suddenly drop dead **n**
8:8 **N**, they must take a young bull
10:18 descendants broke camp **n**.
10:22 descendants broke camp **n**.
11:32 day and night and all the **n** day
14:40 Early the **n** morning they
16:41 The **n** day the whole
17:8 The **n** day Moses went into the
21:11 **N** they moved from Oboth and
22:41 The **n** morning Balak took
Dtr 3:1 **N** we turned and followed the
11:30 **n** to the oak trees of Moreh.)
29:22 Then the **n** generation of your
31:26 and put it **n** to the ark of the
Jos 1:12 **N**, Joshua said to the tribes of
3:1 got up early the **n** morning.
10:32 He captured it on the **n** day and
Jdg 6:25 goddess Asherah that is **n** to it.
6:28 The Asherah pole **n** to it had
6:38 The **n** morning Gideon got up
9:42 The **n** day the people of
21:4 The **n** day the people got up
Rut 4:4 Then I will know that I am **n** in
1Sm 1:26 the woman who stood here **n**
5:3 Early the **n** day the people of
5:4 But the **n** morning they saw
11:11 The **n** day Saul arranged the
18:10 The **n** day an evil spirit from
20:12 "I'll find out in the **n** two or three
20:21 the arrows are **n** to you;
20:22 'The arrows are **n** to you,'
20:37 "The arrows are **n** to you!"
29:11 Early the **n** morning David and
30:17 dawn until evening the **n** day,
31:8 The **n** day, when the
2Sm 11:12 Jerusalem that day and the **n**.
14:30 Joab's field is **n** to mine.
23:9 **N** in rank to him was Eleazar,
23:11 **N** in rank to him was
1Ki 1:27 would sit on your throne **n**?"
6:5 This annex was **n** to the walls
17:1 during the **n** few years unless
21:1 This is what happened **n**.
21:1 had a vineyard in Jezreel **n**
2Ki 4:16 "At this time **n** spring,
4:17 had a son at that time **n** year,
6:29 The **n** day I told her,
8:15 But the **n** day Hazael took a
11:18 **N**, the priest appointed officials
19:29 by itself this year and **n** year.
1Ch 5:11 Gad's descendants lived **n** to
7:29 **N** to Manasseh were Beth
8:32 They lived **n** to their relatives
9:38 They lived **n** to their relatives
10:8 The **n** day, when the
11:12 **N** in rank to him was Eleazar,
29:21 The **n** day they sacrificed to
2Ch 17:15 **n** to him Commander
17:16 and **n** to him Amasiah,
17:18 and **n** to him was Jehozabad
2Ch 23:18 **N**, Jehoiada appointed officials
Neh 3:2 were rebuilding **n** to Eliashib.
3:2 son of Imri, was **n** to them.
3:4 **N** to them Meremoth,
3:4 **N** to them Meshullam,
3:4 **N** to them Zadok, son of
3:5 **N** to them the men from Tekoa
3:7 **N** to them Melatiah from
3:8 **N** to them Uzziel, a goldsmith,
3:8 **N** to him Hananiah,
3:9 **N** to them Rephaiah,
3:10 **N** to them Jedaiah,
3:10 **N** to them Hattush,
3:12 **N** to them Shallum,
3:17 **N** to him Hashabiah,
3:19 **N** to him Ezer, Jeshua's son,
3:23 made repairs **n** to his home.
Psa 19:2 One day tells a story to the **n**.
19:2 shares knowledge with the **n**
48:13 Then you can tell the **n**
68:2 presence like wax **n** to a fire.
68:27 **n** the leaders of Judah with
78:4 We will tell the **n** generation
78:6 so that the **n** generation would
109:13 wiped out by the **n** generation.
145:4 will praise your deeds to the **n**.
Pro 7:12 the **n** she is at the curb,
27:24 from one generation to the **n**.
Ecc 4:1 **N**, I turned to look at all the
4:7 **N**, I turned to look at something
Isa 37:30 and the **n** year you will eat
66:23 From one month to the **n** and
66:23 week to the **n** all people will
Jer 20:3 The **n** day when Pashhur took
35:4 It was **n** to the room of the
51:46 rumor comes the **n** year.
Lam 4:21 fury will be passed to you **n**.
Eze 12:8 The **n** morning the LORD
24:18 The **n** morning I did as I was
41:5 **N**, the man measured the
48:12 **n** to the land belonging to the
Dan 4:3 from one generation to the **n**.
4:34 from one generation to the **n**.
6:7 that for the **n** 30 days whoever
Jnh 4:7 At dawn the **n** day,
Zec 4:12 branches from the olive trees **n**
Mat 12:32 forgiven in this world or the **n**.
27:62 The **n** day, which was the day
Mar 1:21 On the **n** day of worship,
11:12 The **n** day, when they left
15:24 **N** they crucified him.
Luk 9:37 The **n** day, when they had
10:35 The **n** day the Samaritan took
13:9 Maybe **n** year it'll have figs.
13:33 today, tomorrow, and the **n** day.
20:35 live in the **n** world will neither
Jon 1:29 coming toward him the **n** day
1:35 The **n** day John was standing
1:43 The **n** day Jesus wanted to go
6:22 On the **n** day the people were
8:2 Early the **n** morning he
12:12 On the **n** day the large crowd
19:31 Since it was Friday and the **n**
Act 4:3 and John in jail until the **n** day.
4:5 The **n** day the Jewish rulers,
5:10 buried her **n** to her husband.
7:26 The **n** day Moses saw two
10:9 Around noon the **n** day,
10:23 The **n** day Peter left with them.
13:42 subject the **n** day of worship.
13:44 On the **n** day of worship,
14:20 The **n** day Paul and Barnabas
16:11 The **n** day we sailed to the city
18:7 His house was **n** door to the
20:7 he intended to leave the **n** day,
20:15 The **n** day we went by the
20:15 and on the **n** day we arrived at
21:1 The **n** day we sailed to the
21:8 The **n** day we went to Philip's
21:18 The **n** day Paul went with us to
21:26 The **n** day, Paul took the men
22:30 officer released Paul the **n** day
23:11 The Lord stood near Paul the **n**
23:32 to their barracks the **n** day
25:6 The **n** day Festus took his
25:17 The **n** day I immediately
Act 25:23 The **n** day Agrippa and Bernice
27:3 The **n** day we arrived at the
27:18 by the storm that the **n** day
28:13 The **n** day a south wind began
1Co 12:28 **n** prophets, third teachers,
15:5 **N** he appeared to the twelve
15:7 **N** he appeared to James.
Heb 1:3 the one **n** to the Father in
12:2 the one **n** to the throne of God.

Neziah (2)

Ezr 2:54 **N**, and Hatipha.
Neh 7:56 **N**, and Hatipha.

Nezib (1)

Jos 15:43 Iphtah, Ashnah, **N**,

Nibhaz (1)

2Ki 17:31 from Avva made **N** and Tartak.

Nibshan (1)

Jos 15:62 **N**, Ir Hamelah, and En Gedi.

Nicanor (1)

Act 6:5 **N**, Timon, Parmenas,

nice (4)

Gen 2:9 These trees were **n** to look at,
3:6 was good to eat, **n** to look at,
Dtr 8:12 You will build **n** houses and
Luk 6:26 says **n** things about you.

nice-looking (3)

Gen 41:2 Suddenly, seven **n**,
41:4 and skinny ate the seven **n**,
41:18 Suddenly, seven **n**,

nicknamed (1)

Jdg 6:32 So that day they **n** Gideon

Nicodemus (11)

Jon 3:1 **N** was a Pharisee and a
3:3 Jesus replied to **N**,
3:4 **N** asked him, "How can
3:5 Jesus answered **N**,
3:9 **N** replied, "How can that be?"
3:10 Jesus told **N**, "You're a
7:50 One of those Pharisees was **N**,
7:50 visited Jesus. **N** asked them,
7:52 They asked **N**, "Are you
19:39 **N**, the one who had first come
19:42 Joseph and **N** put Jesus in that

Nicolaitans (2)

Rev 2:6 you hate what the **N** are doing.
2:15 who follow what the **N** teach.

Nicolaus (1)

Act 6:5 Timon, Parmenas, and **N**,

Nicopolis (1)

Tit 3:12 hurry to visit me in the city of **N**.

night (297)

Gen 1:5 and the darkness he named **n**.
1:14 to separate the day from the **n**.
1:16 the smaller light to rule the **n**.
1:18 to dominate the day and the **n**,
8:22 day and **n** will never stop."
14:15 up his men to attack them at **n**.
19:2 to my home and spend the **n**?
19:2 "we'd rather spend the **n** in the
19:33 That **n** they gave their father
19:34 Last **n** I went to bed with my
19:35 That **n** they gave their father
20:3 to Abimelech in a dream one **n**
24:23 house for us to spend the **n**."
24:25 room for you to spend the **n**."
24:54 ate and drank and spent the **n**.
26:24 That **n** the LORD appeared to
28:11 he stopped for the **n** because
30:16 he went to bed with her that **n**.
31:24 the Aramean in a dream at **n**
31:29 Last **n** the God of your father
31:39 stolen during the day or at **n**.
31:40 the cold at **n** wore me down,

Gen 31:42 and last **n** he made it right."
31:54 spent the **n** on the mountain.
32:13 He stayed there that **n**.
32:21 he stayed in the camp that **n**.
32:22 During that **n** he got up and
40:5 of Egypt — had dreams one **n**.
41:11 both had dreams the same **n**.
42:27 where they stopped for the **n**,
43:21 When we stopped for the **n**,
46:2 in a vision that **n** and said,
Exo 4:24 the way they stopped for the **n**.
10:13 land all that day and all that **n**.
12:8 must be eaten that same **n**.
12:12 "On that same **n** I will go
12:30 Egyptians got up during the **n**.
12:31 Moses and Aaron during the **n**.
12:42 That **n** the LORD kept watch to
12:42 must keep watch on this **n**,
13:21 By **n** he went ahead of them in
13:21 could travel by day or by **n**.
13:22 of fire was always there at **n**.
14:20 came, and it lit up the **n**.
14:20 came near the other all **n** long.
14:21 All that **n** the LORD pushed
40:38 was fire in the smoke at **n**.
Lev 8:35 to the tent of meeting day and **n**
Num 9:16 At **n** the smoke covering the
9:21 Day or **n**, when the smoke
11:9 dew fell on the camp at **n**,
11:32 All that day and **n** and all the
14:1 and cried out loud all that **n**.
14:14 and in a column of fire by **n**.
22:8 "Spend the **n** here,"
22:20 That **n** God came to Balaam
Dtr 1:33 in a column of fire at **n**
16:1 brought you out of Egypt at **n**.
24:13 wears his coat to bed ⌊that **n**⌋,
28:66 You will live in terror day and **n**.
Jos 1:8 You must think about them **n**
2:1 Rahab to spend the **n** there.
6:11 and stayed there for the **n**.
8:3 soldiers and sent them out at **n**
8:9 spent the **n** with the troops.
8:13 That **n** Joshua went down into
10:9 So Joshua marched all **n** from
Jdg 6:25 That same **n** the LORD said to
6:27 of the city, so he did it at **n**.
6:40 During the **n**, God did what
7:9 That **n** the LORD said to
9:34 all his troops started out at **n**.
16:2 the place and waited all **n** at
16:2 They were quiet all **n**.
18:2 They spent the **n** there.
19:6 the **n** and enjoy yourself?"
19:7 urged him to stay another **n**,
19:9 Please stay another **n**.
19:10 refused to spend another **n**.
19:11 "Let's go spend the **n** in Jebus."
19:13 We'll spend the **n** either at
19:15 They went to spend the **n** there.
19:15 to take them home for the **n**.
19:20 Just don't spend the **n** in the
19:25 abused her all **n** until morning.
20:4 in Benjamin to spend the **n**.
20:5 ⌊where I was staying⌋ that **n**.
1Sm 3:2 One **n** Eli was lying down in
14:34 brought his ox with him that **n**
15:11 he prayed to the LORD all **n**.
15:16 what the LORD told me last **n**."
19:10 escaping ⌊from Saul⌋ that **n**.
19:24 there naked all day and all **n**.
25:16 us day and **n** as long as
26:7 among ⌊Saul's⌋ troops that **n**.
28:8 and came to the woman that **n**.
28:20 eaten anything all day or all **n**.
28:25 ate and left that ⌊same⌋ **n**.
31:12 the fighting men marched all **n**
2Sm 2:29 through the plains all that **n**.
2:32 and his men marched all **n**
4:7 head and traveled all **n** along
7:4 But that same **n** the LORD
12:16 and lay on the ground all **n**.
21:10 come near them during the **n**.
1Ki 3:5 to Solomon in a dream at **n**.
3:19 That **n** this woman's son died
3:20 So she got up during the **n** and
1Ki 8:29 **N** and day may your eyes be
8:59 the LORD our God day and **n**.
19:9 into a cave and spent the **n**.
2Ki 6:14 They came at **n** and
7:12 So the king got up at **n** and told
8:21 him, but he got up at **n**,
19:35 It happened that **n**.
25:4 through the city walls that **n**.
1Ch 9:27 They would spend the **n**
9:33 they were on duty day and **n**.
17:3 But that same **n** God spoke his
2Ch 1:7 That **n** God appeared to
6:20 Day and **n** may your eyes be
7:12 the LORD appeared to him at **n**.
21:9 but he got up at **n** and broke
Neh 1:6 I am praying to you day and **n**
2:12 During the **n** I went out with a
2:13 that **n** toward Snake Fountain
2:15 I went through the valley that **n**
4:9 guards to protect us day and **n**.
4:22 so that we can set a guard at **n**
6:10 are coming at **n** to kill you."
9:12 of smoke and during the **n** by
9:19 didn't leave them during the **n**,
13:20 spent the **n** outside Jerusalem.
13:21 "Why are you spending the **n** in
Est 6:1 That **n** the king could not sleep.
Job 3:3 I was born and the **n** that said,
3:6 "That **n** — let the blackness
3:7 Let that **n** be empty.
3:8 up Leviathan) curse that **n**.
4:13 thoughts from visions in the **n**,
5:14 in the sunlight as if it were **n**.
17:12 You say that **n** is day.
20:8 away like a vision in the **n**.
24:7 All **n** they lie naked without a
24:14 At **n** they become thieves.
27:20 snatches him away at **n**.
29:19 will lie on my branches all **n**.
30:3 and barren ground during the **n**
30:17 At **n** God pierces my bones.
31:32 never spent the **n** outside,
33:15 a prophetic vision at **n**,
34:20 suddenly in the middle of the **n**.
34:25 so he overthrows them at **n**,
35:10 who inspires songs in the **n**,
36:20 Don't look forward to the **n**,
39:9 or will it stay at **n** beside your
39:28 It perches for the **n** on a cliff.
Psa 1:2 on his teachings day and **n**.
6:6 My eyes flood my bed every **n**.
16:7 My conscience warns me at **n**.
17:3 You have confronted me at **n**.
19:2 One **n** shares knowledge with
22:2 you do not answer — also at **n**,
30:5 Weeping may last for the **n**,
32:4 Day and **n** your hand laid
42:3 tears are my food day and **n**.
42:8 and at **n** his song is with me —
55:10 Day and **n** they go around on
55:17 and **n** I complain and groan,
59:15 they will stay all **n**.
63:6 Through the long hours of the **n**
74:16 The day and the **n** are yours.
77:2 At **n** I stretched out my hands
77:6 I remember my song in the **n**
78:14 by a fiery light throughout the **n**
88:1 to you during the day and at **n**.
90:4 past — like an hour in the **n**.
91:5 not need to fear terrors of the **n**,
105:39 and a fire to light up the **n**.
119:55 At **n** I remember your name,
121:6 nor will the moon at **n**.
134:1 of the LORD **n** after night.
134:1 of the LORD night after **n**.
136:9 the moon and stars to rule the **n**
139:11 the light around me turn into **n**,
139:12 **N** is as bright as day.
Pro 7:9 in the dark hours of the **n**.
31:18 Her lamp burns late at **n**.
Ecc 2:23 Even at **n** their minds don't rest.
8:16 going without sleep day and **n**),
Sos 1:13 lies at **n** between my breasts.
3:1 **N** after night on my bed I
3:1 Night after **n** on my bed I
3:8 against the terrors of the **n**.
Sos 5:2 my hair with the dewdrops of **n**.
7:11 Let's spend the **n** among the
Isa 4:5 flame of fire during the **n** over
10:29 and lodge at Geba for the **n**.
15:1 In a single **n** Ar in Moab is laid
15:1 In a single **n** Kir in Moab is laid
16:3 your shadow as dark as **n**.
21:8 Every **n**, I stand guard at my
21:11 how much of the **n** is left?
21:11 how much of the **n** is left?"
21:12 and **n** will come again.
21:13 of Dedan will spend the **n**
26:9 With my soul I long for you at **n**.
27:3 I watch over it day and **n** so
28:19 during the day and during the **n**.
29:7 like a vision in the **n**.
30:29 song you sing on a festival **n**.
34:10 not be extinguished day or **n**,
60:11 closed day or **n** so that people
62:6 will never be silent day or **n**.
Jer 6:5 Let's attack at **n** and destroy its
9:1 so that I could cry day and **n**
14:8 traveler who stays only one **n**?
14:17 day and **n** without stopping
16:13 will serve other gods day and **n**
31:35 stars to be lights during the **n**.
33:20 with day and **n** so that they
33:25 an arrangement with day and **n**
36:30 heat of day and the cold of **n**.
39:4 They left the city at **n** by way
49:9 If thieves come during the **n**,
52:7 They left the city at **n** through
Lam 1:2 Jerusalem cries bitterly at **n**
2:18 run down like a river day and **n**.
2:19 Cry out at **n**, every hour on the
Dan 2:19 Daniel in a vision during the **n**.
5:30 That **n** King Belshazzar of
6:18 and spent the **n** without food
7:2 In my visions at **n** I,
7:7 in my vision during the **n**.
7:13 In my visions during the **n**,
Hos 4:5 and during the **n** the prophets
7:6 All **n** long their anger smolders,
Joe 1:13 Spend the **n** in sackcloth,
Amo 5:8 He turns day into **n**.
Oba 1:5 come to you during the **n**,
Zec 1:8 During that **n** I saw a man
14:7 difference between day and **n**.
Mat 2:14 and left for Egypt that **n**.
21:17 Bethany and spent the **n** there.
24:43 known at what time of the **n**
28:13 Jesus' disciples had come at **n**
Mar 4:27 He sleeps at **n** and is awake
5:5 **N** and day he was among the
Luk 2:8 their flock during the **n**.
2:37 worshiped day and **n** by fasting
5:5 we worked hard all **n** and
6:12 He spent the whole **n** in prayer
12:38 he comes in the middle of the **n**
17:34 "I can guarantee that on that **n**
18:7 out to him for help day and **n**?
21:37 But at **n** he would go to the
21:37 called) and spend the **n** there.
Jon 3:2 He came to Jesus one **n** and
9:4 The **n** when no one can do
11:10 However, those who walk at **n**
13:30 went outside. It was **n**.
19:39 had first come to Jesus at **n**,
21:3 but didn't catch a thing that **n**.
Act 5:19 But at **n** an angel from the Lord
9:24 the city gates day and **n**
9:25 an opening in the wall one **n**.
12:6 The **n** before Herod was going
16:9 During the **n** Paul had a vision
16:33 At that hour of the **n**,
17:10 Immediately when **n** came,
18:9 One **n** the Lord said to Paul in
20:31 you for three years, day and **n**,
23:11 Lord stood near Paul the next **n**
23:31 city of Antipatris during the **n**.
26:7 intense devotion day and **n**.
27:23 I serve stood by me last **n**.
27:27 On the fourteenth **n** we were
Rom 13:12 The **n** is almost over,
1Co 11:23 On the **n** he was betrayed,
2Co 11:25 on the sea for a **n** and a day.

1Th 2:9 We worked **n** and day so that
3:10 We pray very hard **n** and day
5:2 will come like a thief in the **n**.
5:5 light not to the **n** and the dark.
5:7 People who sleep, sleep at **n**;
5:7 who get drunk, get drunk at **n**.
2Th 3:8 worked hard and struggled **n**
1Ti 5:5 asking for his help **n** and day.
2Ti 1:3 remember you in my prayers **n**
Rev 4:8 Without stopping day or **n** they
7:15 They serve him day and **n** in
8:12 the day and one-third of the **n**.
12:10 one accusing them day and **n**
14:11 There will be no rest day or **n**
20:10 day and **n** forever and ever.
21:25 there won't be any **n** there.
22:5 There will be no more **n**,

nighthawks (2)

Lev 11:16 ostriches, **n**, seagulls, all types
Dtr 14:15 ostriches, **n**, seagulls, all types

nights (20)

Gen 7:4 the earth for 40 days and 40 **n**.
7:12 the earth for 40 days and 40 **n**.
Exo 24:18 the mountain 40 days and 40 **n**.
34:28 40 days and 40 **n** without food
Dtr 9:9 40 days and 40 **n** without food
9:11 end of the 40 days and 40 **n**,
9:18 and water for 40 days and 40 **n**
9:25 the LORD for 40 days and 40 **n**
10:10 mountain 40 days and 40 **n** as
1Sm 20:5 the countryside for two more **n**.
1Ki 19:8 he traveled for 40 days and **n**
Job 2:13 for seven days and seven **n**.
7:3 inherited **n** filled with misery.
Isa 65:4 and spent their **n** in caves.
Jnh 1:17 fish for three days and three **n**.
Mic 3:6 will have **n** without visions.
Mat 4:2 anything for 40 days and 40 **n**.
12:40 fish for three days and three **n**,
12:40 earth for three days and three **n**
2Co 6:5 sleepless **n**, and lack of food.

nighttime (2)

Psa 104:20 He brings darkness, and it is **n**,
119:148 throughout the **n** hours

Nile (43)

Gen 41:1 was standing by the **N** River.
41:17 standing on the bank of the **N**.
Exo 1:22 into the **N** every ⌊Hebrew⌋ boy
2:3 near the bank of the **N** River.
2:5 daughter came to the **N**
4:9 take some water from the **N**
4:9 The water you take from the **N**
7:15 when he's on his way to the **N**.
7:17 I'm going to strike the **N**,
7:18 The fish in the **N** will die,
7:18 to drink any water from the **N**.'"
7:20 his staff and struck the **N**.
7:21 The fish in the **N** died,
7:24 the Egyptians dug along the **N**
7:25 after the LORD struck the **N**.
8:3 The **N** River will swarm with
8:9 left will be those in the **N**."
8:11 left will be those in the **N**."
8:20 way when he's going to the **N**.
17:5 you used to strike the **N** River.
Isa 7:18 distant branches of the **N** River
19:5 The water in the **N** River will
19:7 The rushes by the **N**,
19:7 by the edge of the **N**,
19:7 beside the **N** will dry up,
19:8 their lines into the **N** will mourn
23:3 The harvest of the **N** River is
23:10 through your country like the **N**
Jer 2:18 to drink water from the **N** River.
46:7 rising like the **N** River,
46:8 Egypt is like the rising **N** River,
Eze 29:3 crocodile lying in the **N** River.
29:3 You say, "The **N** River is mine.
29:4 the fish in the **N** River stick
29:4 all the fish in the **N** sticking
29:5 you and all the fish from the **N**.
29:9 You said, "The **N** River is mine.
Eze 29:10 I'm against you and the **N** River.
30:12 I will dry up the **N** River and
Amo 8:8 entire land will rise like the **N**,
9:5 All of it rises like the **N** and
Nah 3:8 sits by the streams of the **N**
Zec 10:11 the deep places of the **N** River.

Nimrah (1)

Num 32:3 "Ataroth, Dibon, Jazer, **N**,

Nimrim (2)

Isa 15:6 The **N** Brook has run dry!
Jer 48:34 the streams of **N** will dry up.

Nimrod (4)

Gen 10:8 Cush was the father of **N**,
10:9 used to say, "⌊He's⌋ like **N**,
1Ch 1:10 Cush was the father of **N**,
Mic 5:6 swords and the country of **N**

Nimshi (5)

1Ki 19:16 Anoint Jehu, son of **N**,
2Ki 9:2 and grandson of **N**.
9:14 and grandson of **N**,
9:20 like Jehu, grandson of **N**."
2Ch 22:7 to meet Jehu, grandson of **N**.

Nineveh (30)

Gen 10:11 that land to Assyria and built **N**,
10:12 city between **N** and Calah.
2Ki 19:36 home to **N** and stayed there.
Isa 37:37 home to **N** and stayed there.
Jnh 1:2 once for the important city, **N**.
3:2 once for the important city, **N**.
3:3 Jonah immediately went to **N**
3:3 **N** was a very large city.
3:4 forty days **N** will be destroyed."
3:5 The people of **N** believed God.
3:6 the news reached the king of **N**,
4:11 sorry for this important city, **N**?
Nah 1:1 from the LORD about **N**.
1:8 He will put an end to **N** with a
1:9 He is the one who will bring **N**
1:10 ⌊The people of **N** will be⌋ like
1:11 From you, **N**, a person who
1:12 Though the people of **N** are
1:14 this command about you, **N**:
2:8 **N** was like a pool of water from
2:10 **N** is destroyed, deserted,
2:13 "I am against you, **N**," declares
3:5 "I am against you, **N**," declares
3:7 '**N** has been violently
3:11 Even you, **N**, will stagger like a
Zep 2:13 He will turn **N** into a deserted
Mat 12:41 The men of **N** will stand up
Luk 11:30 sign to the people of **N**,
11:32 The men of **N** will stand up at
11:32 Since the men of **N** turned to

Nineveh's (3)

Nah 1:13 But now I will break **N** yoke off
2:5 They hurry to **N** wall.
3:4 of **N** constant prostitution,

ninth (24)

Lev 23:32 on the evening of the **n** day
25:22 even in the **n** year,
Num 7:60 On the **n** day the leader of the
2Ki 17:6 In Hoshea's **n** year as king of
18:10 was Hoshea's **n** year as king
25:1 of the tenth month of the **n** year
25:3 On the **n** day of the fourth
1Ch 12:12 The **n** was Elzabad.
24:11 the **n** for Jeshua, the tenth for
25:16 The **n** chose Mattaniah,
27:12 was in charge of the **n** unit
27:12 ninth unit during the **n** month.
Ezr 10:9 twentieth day of the **n** month,
Jer 36:9 In the **n** month of the fifth year
36:22 It was the **n** month,
39:1 of Zedekiah's **n** year as king
39:2 On the **n** day of the fourth
52:4 of the tenth month of the **n** year
52:6 On the **n** day of the fourth
Eze 24:1 of the tenth month in the **n** year,
Hag 2:10 day of the **n** month
Hag 2:18 day of the **n** month,
Zec 7:1 On the fourth day of the **n**
Rev 21:20 the eighth beryl, the **n** topaz,

Nisan (2)

Neh 2:1 In the month of **N**, after some
Est 3:7 month, from **N**, the first month,

Nisroch (2)

2Ki 19:37 in the temple of his god **N**,
Isa 37:38 in the temple of his god **N**,

Noadiah (2)

Ezr 8:33 and Binnui's son **N**,
Neh 6:14 remember the female prophet **N**

Noah (53)

Gen 5:29 He named him **N** [Relief],
5:30 Lamech became the father of **N**,
5:32 When **N** was 500 years old,
6:8 the LORD was pleased with **N**.
6:9 This is the account of **N** and
6:9 **N** had God's approval and was
6:13 God said to **N**, "I have decided
6:22 **N** did this. He did everything
7:1 The LORD said to **N**,
7:5 So **N** did everything that the
7:6 **N** was 600 years old when the
7:7 **N**, his sons, his wife, and his
7:9 came to **N** to go into the ship in
7:9 as God had commanded **N**.
7:13 On that same day **N** and his
7:15 breathing animal came to **N** to
7:16 in as God had commanded **N**.
7:23 Only **N** and those with him in
8:1 God remembered **N** and all the
8:6 After 40 more days **N** opened
8:9 So it came back to **N** in the
8:11 Then **N** knew that the water
8:13 **N** opened the top of the ship,
8:15 Then God spoke to **N**,
8:18 So **N** came out with his sons,
8:20 **N** built an altar to the LORD.
9:1 God blessed **N** and his sons
9:8 also said to **N** and his sons,
9:17 So God said to **N**, "This is the
9:20 **N**, a farmer, was the first
9:24 When **N** sobered up,
9:28 **N** lived 350 years after the
9:29 **N** lived a total of 950 years;
Num 26:33 Their names were Mahlah, **N**,
27:1 Their names were Mahlah, **N**,
36:11 and **N** married their cousins on
Jos 17:3 Their names were Mahlah, **N**,
1Ch 1:4 **N**: Shem, Ham, and Japheth.
Eze 14:14 Even if these three men — **N**,
14:16 LORD, not even **N**, Daniel,
14:18 LORD, not even **N**, Daniel,
14:20 LORD, not even **N**, Daniel,
Mat 24:37 be exactly like the days of **N**.
24:38 until the day that **N** went into
Luk 3:36 son of **N**, son of Lamech,
17:26 will be like the time of **N**.
17:27 until the day that **N** went into
Heb 11:7 Faith led **N** to listen when God
11:7 Through faith **N** condemned
1Pe 3:20 the days of **N** when God waited
3:20 waited patiently while **N** built
2Pe 2:5 but he protected **N** and seven
2:5 **N** was his messenger who told

Noah's (9)

Gen 7:11 six hundredth year of **N** life, all
7:13 as well as **N** wife and his three
8:13 the first month of **N** six hundred
9:18 **N** sons, who came out of the
9:19 These were **N** three sons.
10:1 is the account of **N** sons Shem,
10:32 of **N** sons listed by their
Isa 54:9 this is like **N** floodwaters, when
54:9 **N** floodwaters would never cover

No-amon (1)

Nah 3:8 Are you better than **N**,

Nob (6)

1Sm 21:1 to the priest Ahimelech at **N**.
22:9 Ahimelech, Ahitub's son, in **N**.
22:11 who were the priests in **N**.
22:19 He also killed the people of **N**,
Neh 11:32 in Anathoth, **N**, Ananiah,
Isa 10:32 This day they stopped at **N**.

Nobah (3)

Num 32:42 **N** captured Kenath and its
32:42 He named it **N** after himself.
Jdg 8:11 east of **N** and Jogbehah,

nobility (2)

Pro 31:25 dresses with strength and **n**,
Dan 1:3 the royal family, and the **n**.

noble (14)

Ezr 4:10 and **n** Assurbanipal deported.
Est 6:9 the king's officials, who is a **n**.
Psa 16:3 on earth are the **n** ones who fill
45:9 kings are among your **n** ladies.
Pro 8:6 I am speaking about **n** things,
17:7 less does lying fit a **n** person!
17:26 To strike down **n** people is not
31:29 women have done **n** work,
Ecc 10:17 the king is from a **n** family
Sos 6:12 the chariots of my **n** people.
7:1 in their sandals, **n** daughter!
Rom 12:17 things that are considered **n**.
1Co 7:35 I'm showing you how to live a **n**
1Ti 1:18 conscience to fight this **n** war.

nobles (31)

Num 21:18 dug out by the **n** of the people
1Sm 2:8 in order to make them sit with **n**
1Ki 21:8 respected leaders and **n** living
21:11 leaders and **n** who lived there
2Ch 23:20 the **n**, the people's governors,
23:20 The **n**, the governors of the
Neh 3:5 However, the **n** wouldn't lower
4:14 and proceeded to tell the **n**,
4:19 I told the **n**, the leaders, and the
5:7 I confronted the **n** and the
6:17 In those days the **n** of Judah
6:19 The **n** were singing Tobiah's
7:5 head that I should gather the **n**,
10:29 joined their relatives, the **n**,
13:17 I reprimanded the **n** of Judah
Est 1:3 the **n** and officials of the
Job 29:10 The voices of **n** were hushed,
34:18 or to **n**, 'You wicked people!'
Pro 8:16 so do **n** and all fair judges.
Isa 32:5 fools will no longer be called **n**,
34:12 There are no **n** to rule a
Jer 27:19 to Babylon along with all the **n**
Dan 4:36 My advisers and **n** wanted to
5:1 a large banquet for 1,000 **n**
5:2 to drink from them with his **n**,
5:3 The king, his **n**, wives,
5:9 His **n** didn't know what to do.
5:10 the king and his **n** brought
5:23 You, your **n**, wives,
6:17 his ring and the rings of his **n**,
Jnh 3:7 order from the king and his **n**:

Nobles' (1)

Isa 13:2 with your hand to enter **N** Gates

nocturnal (1)

Dtr 23:10 unclean from a **n** emission,

Nod (1)

Gen 4:16 and lived in **N** [The Land

Nodab (1)

1Ch 5:19 Jetur, Naphish, and **N**)

Nogah (2)

1Ch 3:7 **N**, Nepheg, Japhia,
14:6 **N**, Nepheg, Japhia,

Nohah (1)

1Ch 8:2 **N** (his fourth son), and Rapha

noise (42)

Exo 32:17 Then Joshua heard the **n** of the
Jos 6:10 "Don't shout, make any **n**,
1Sm 4:6 As the Philistines heard the **n**,
1Ki 1:41 the reason for the **n** in the city?"
2Ki 11:13 When Athaliah heard the **n**
Ezr 3:13 The **n** was heard from far away.
Job 39:7 It laughs at the **n** of the city and
Isa 13:4 Listen to the **n** on the
17:12 The **n** that the people make
17:12 like the **n** from rushing water.
17:13 The people will make **n** like
22:2 filled with **n** and excitement.
31:4 disturbed by the **n** they make.
33:3 People flee from the **n** of
Jer 3:23 Truly, the **n** from the hills,
3:23 is the **n** of false worship.
50:22 The **n** of battle and great
51:55 He will silence the loud **n**
51:55 The **n** will be heard
Lam 2:7 The enemies made **n** in the
Eze 1:24 The sound was like the **n** of
3:13 I also heard the **n** of the wings
3:13 touching one another and the **n**
23:42 "I heard the **n** from a carefree
26:10 The **n** from the war horses,
37:7 suddenly there was a rattling **n**,
Hos 10:14 army will hear the **n** of battle.
Amo 2:2 Moab will die during the **n** of
Mic 2:12 They will make a lot of **n**
Mar 5:39 making so much **n** and crying?
Act 21:34 of the **n** and confusion,
Rev 4:5 Lightning, **n**, and thunder came
8:5 Then there was thunder, **n**,
9:9 The **n** from their wings was
11:19 There was lightning, **n**,
14:2 a sound from heaven like the **n**
14:2 noise of raging water and the **n**
16:18 There was lightning, **n**,
19:1 sounded like the loud **n** from
19:6 I heard what sounded like the **n**
19:6 like the **n** of raging waters,
19:6 like the **n** of loud thunder,

noises (1)

Isa 29:6 and loud **n**, with windstorms,

noisy (12)

Job 31:34 because I dreaded the large, **n**
Psa 68:27 of Judah with their **n** crowds,
Pro 1:21 At the corners of **n** streets she
20:1 liquor makes them **n**,
Isa 5:14 Those who are **n** and joyous
24:8 **N** celebrations cease.
32:14 **N** cities will be abandoned.
Jer 48:45 the skulls of those **n** people.
Eze 26:13 will put a stop to your **n** songs,
Mat 9:23 He saw flute players and a **n**
Mar 5:38 Jesus saw a **n** crowd there.
Act 24:18 crowd or **n** mob was present.

nomad (1)

Jer 3:2 waiting for them like a **n**

nomads (1)

Gen 25:18 His descendants lived as **n**

nonexistent (1)

2Ch 13:9 ordained as a priest of **n** gods.

non-Israelite (3)

Dtr 1:16 between an Israelite and a **n**.
Neh 13:26 But his **n** wives led him to sin.
13:27 to him by marrying **n** women?"

non-Israelites (1)

Neh 13:3 the **n** from the Israelites.

non-Jewish (22)

Act 4:27 plans together with **n** people
10:46 They heard these **n** people
14:5 found out that the **n** people
15:3 of how **n** people were turning
15:9 between Jewish and **n** people.
15:9 He has cleansed **n** people
15:12 through them among **n** people.
15:14 taking from **n** people those who
15:19 trouble **n** people who are
15:23 To their **n** brothers and sisters
21:19 through his work with **n** people.
21:21 Jews living among **n** people
21:25 we have written **n** believers
26:17 people and from the **n** people
26:20 the same message to **n** people.
26:23 light to Jewish and **n** people."
Rom 9:30 We can say that **n** people who
11:25 of God's **n** people are included.
Gal 3:8 approval to **n** people who have
Eph 2:14 Jewish and **n** people one by
2:15 take Jewish and **n** people
2:18 So Jewish and **n** people can

non-Jews (2)

Ezr 6:21 the unclean practices of the **n**
Rom 2:14 For example, whenever **n** who

non-military (1)

2Ti 2:4 get mixed up in **n** activities.

nonsense (17)

Job 21:34 with this **n** when your answers
27:12 you chatter on about such **n**?
Isa 28:10 They speak utter **n**.
28:13 LORD speaks utter **n** to them.
Jer 10:8 learn **n** from wooden idols.
Rom 1:21 their thoughts were total **n**,
1Co 1:18 message about the cross is **n**
1:20 the wisdom of the world into **n**?
1:21 So God decided to use the **n** of
1:25 God's **n** is wiser than human
1:27 what the world considers **n**
2:14 He thinks they're **n**.
3:19 The wisdom of this world is **n**
15:17 your faith is **n** and sin still has
Tit 1:10 speak **n** and deceive people.
3:9 This is useless **n**.
2Pe 2:18 They arrogantly use **n** to

noon (23)

Gen 43:16 are going to eat with me at **n**."
43:25 ready for Joseph's return at **n**,
1Ki 18:26 of Baal from morning until **n**.
18:27 At **n** Elijah started to make fun
20:16 They attacked at **n**,
2Ki 4:20 The boy sat on her lap until **n**,
Neh 8:3 From daybreak until **n**,
Psa 55:17 Morning, **n**, and night I
91:6 epidemics that strike at **n**.
Sos 1:7 does your flock lie down at **n**?
Isa 16:3 At high **n** make your shadow
59:10 We stumble at **n** as if it were
Jer 6:4 Let's attack at **n**! How horrible it
20:16 morning and a battle cry at **n**.
Amo 8:9 will make the sun go down at **n**
Zep 2:4 Ashdod will be driven out at **n**,
Mat 20:5 "He went out again about **n**
27:45 At **n** darkness came over the
Mar 15:33 At **n** darkness came over the
Luk 23:44 Around **n** darkness came over
Act 10:9 Around **n** the next day,
22:6 the city of Damascus about **n**,
26:13 Your Majesty, at **n**,

noonday (3)

Job 11:17 will be brighter than the **n** sun.
Psa 37:6 your just cause like the **n** sun.
Isa 58:10 become as bright as the **n** sun.

noontime (1)

Jer 15:8 At **n** I will send a destroyer

Noph (2)

Jer 2:16 People from **N** and Tahpanhes
44:1 Tahpanhes, **N**, and Pathros.

Nophah (1)

Num 21:30 between **N** and Medeba."

normal (7)

Exo 23:26 I will let you live a **n** life span.
Dan 3:19 seven times hotter than **n**.

Mat 12:13 and it became **n** again,
Mar 3:5 and his hand became **n** again.
8:25 His sight was **n** again.
Luk 6:10 and his hand became **n** again.
2Ti 3:3 and lack **n** affection for their

normally (3)

2Ki 11:7 Then your two groups who ⌊**n**⌋
Mar 7:35 the man could hear and talk **n**.
2Pe 2:16 A donkey, which **n** can't talk,

north (149)

Gen 13:14 to Abram, "Look **n**, south, east,
14:15 which is **n** of Damascus.
28:14 to the **n** and to the south.
Exo 14:2 Set up your camp facing **n** — by
14:9 the sea at Pi Hahiroth facing **n**.
26:20 For the **n** side of the inner tent
26:35 the canopy on the **n** side
27:11 The **n** side should be the same:
36:25 For the **n** side of the inner tent
38:11 The **n** side was also 150 feet
40:22 tent of meeting on the **n** side
Lev 1:11 LORD's presence on the **n** side
Num 2:25 "On the **n** side the armies led
3:35 They put up their tents on the **n**
35:5 and 3,000 feet on the **n** side,
Dtr 2:3 region long enough. Now go **n**.
3:12 of Reuben and Gad the land **n**
3:27 look west, **n**, south, and east.
Jos 1:4 of the Hittites) ⌊on the **n**⌋,
8:11 They camped **n** of Ai with the
8:13 The main camp was **n** of the
15:5 is the Dead Sea as far **n** as
15:5 border starts from the **n** end
15:6 It then passes **n** to Beth Arabah
15:7 goes up to Debir and turns **n**
15:8 Hinnom to the west at the **n** end
15:10 Seir and over to the **n** slope
15:11 the border goes on the **n** side
16:6 with Michmethath on the **n**.
17:10 and what is **n** ⌊of it⌋ belongs to
18:5 within their territory in the **n**.
18:12 goes up the slope **n** of Jericho,
18:16 in the **n** end of the valley of
18:17 Then it turns **n** and goes to En
18:18 Then it continues on to the **n**
18:19 The border continues to the **n**
19:14 There the border turns **n** to
19:27 the valley of Iphtah El in the **n**
24:30 of Ephraim **n** of Mount Gaash.
Jdg 2:9 of Ephraim **n** of Mount Gaash.
7:1 Midian's camp was **n** of him at
21:19 Shiloh is **n** of Bethel,
1Sm 14:5 on the **n** facing Michmash,
1Ki 7:25 Three bulls faced **n**,
7:39 temple and five on the **n** side
7:49 the south side and five on the **n**
2Ki 11:11 the south side to the **n** side
16:14 Ahaz put it on the **n** side of his
1Ch 9:24 (east, west, **n**, and south).
26:14 was chosen for the **n** side.
26:17 On the **n** there were four every
2Ch 4:4 Three bulls faced **n**,
4:6 side and five on the **n** side.
4:7 side and five on the **n** side.
4:8 side and five on the **n** side.
23:10 the south side to the **n** side
Job 37:22 golden light comes from the **n**.
Psa 89:12 You created **n** and south.
107:3 from the **n** and from the south.
Pro 25:23 ⌊As⌋ the **n** wind brings rain,
Ecc 1:6 south and shifts toward the **n**.
11:3 If a tree falls **n** or south,
Sos 4:16 Awake, **n** wind! Come, south
Isa 14:13 far away in the **n** where
14:31 Smoke comes from the **n**,
41:25 raised up someone from the **n**,
43:6 I will say to the **n**, "Give them
49:12 They will come from the **n** and
Jer 1:13 top is tilted away from the **n**."
1:14 will be poured out from the **n**
1:15 kingdom from the **n**," declares
3:12 proclaim these things to the **n**:
3:18 together from the land of the **n**
4:6 destruction from the **n**.
Jer 6:1 are coming from the **n**.
6:22 is going to come from the **n**.
10:22 coming from the land of the **n**.
13:20 who are coming from the **n**.
15:12 iron, iron from the **n**, or bronze.
16:15 of Israel out of the land of the **n**
23:8 of Israel out of the land of the **n**
25:9 for all the families from the **n**.
25:9 bring the families from the **n**
25:26 all the kings of the **n**,
31:8 them from the land of the **n**.
46:6 They stumble and fall in the **n**
46:10 them as sacrifices in the **n** by
46:20 from the **n** will attack it.
46:24 over to the people from the **n**."
47:2 Water is rising in the **n**.
50:3 A nation from the **n** will attack
50:9 of strong nations from the **n**
50:9 will be captured from the **n**.
50:41 are going to come from the **n**.
51:48 because destroyers from the **n**
Eze 1:4 saw a storm coming from the **n**.
8:3 to the entrance to the **n** gate of
8:5 look toward the **n**."
8:5 So I looked toward the **n**,
8:5 entrance to the **n** gate beside
8:14 me to the entrance of the **n** gate
9:2 came from the upper **n** gate.
16:46 her daughters lived **n** of you.
20:47 land from the south to the **n**.
21:4 from the south to the **n**.
23:24 They will attack you from the **n**,
26:7 From the **n** I'm going to bring
32:30 "All the rulers from the **n** and all
38:6 of Togarmah from the far **n**.
38:15 from your place in the far **n**
39:2 I will bring you from the far **n**
40:19 It was 175 feet from east to **n**.
40:20 was the gateway that faced **n**.
40:23 opposite the **n** gate just like
40:35 brought me to the **n** gateway.
40:40 to the **n** gateway there were
40:44 at the side of the **n** gateway.
40:44 the south gateway. It faced **n**.
40:46 The room that faces **n** is for the
41:11 There was one door to the **n**
42:1 man led me out toward the **n**
42:2 The building that faced **n** was
42:4 of these side rooms faced **n**.
42:11 of the side rooms on the **n** side.
42:12 as the doors to the **n** rooms.
42:17 He measured the **n** side.
44:4 brought me through the **n** gate
46:9 Those entering through the **n**
46:9 must leave through the **n** gate.
46:19 to the side rooms that faced **n**.
47:2 Then he led me through the **n**
47:15 On the **n** side the border will
47:17 of Hamath will lie to the **n**.
47:17 This is the **n** side.
48:10 On the **n** side it will be 43,750
48:16 On the **n** side it will be 7,875
48:17 will be 4,375 feet on the **n**,
48:30 The **n** side will be 7,875 feet
48:31 The three gates on the **n** side
Dan 8:4 I saw the ram charging west, **n**,
11:44 east and the **n** will frighten him.
Amo 8:12 sea to sea and roam from the **n**
Zep 2:13 use his power against the **n**
Zec 2:6 Flee from the land of the **n**,
6:6 horses is going toward the **n**,
6:8 Those who went to the **n** have
6:8 made my Spirit rest in the **n**."
14:4 will move toward the **n**,
Rev 21:13 three gates on the **n**,

northeaster (1)

Act 27:14 wind (called a **n**) blew from

northern (27)

Num 34:7 "The **n** border extends from the
Jos 11:2 sent messengers to the **n** kings
15:5 The **n** border starts from the
17:10 Asher its **n** border,
18:12 Their **n** border starts at the
18:19 Hoglah and ends at the **n** bay
Psa 48:2 Mount Zion is on the **n** ridge.
Eze 42:1 open area and the **n** building.
42:11 and as wide as the **n** rooms.
42:13 "The **n** and southern side
47:15 This is the **n** border for the land:
48:1 Beginning at the **n** border,
48:1 on the **n** border of Damascus
Dan 11:6 southern and **n** kings will make
11:6 daughter will go to the **n** king
11:7 He will attack the **n** army,
11:7 the stronghold of the **n** king,
11:8 for more years than the **n** king.
11:11 He will go to fight the **n** king,
11:13 "The **n** king will return and
11:15 Then the **n** king will come,
11:17 "Then the **n** king will decide to
11:18 insults that the **n** king makes
11:28 The **n** king will return to his
11:40 The **n** king will rush at him like
Joe 2:20 "I will keep the **n** ⌊army⌋ far
Act 27:4 we sailed on the **n** side of the

northward (4)

Jos 13:3 **n** as far as the border of Ekron.
19:27 From there it goes **n** to Cabul,
Jdg 1:36 Akrabbim Pass — from Selah **n**.
Job 23:9 If I go **n**, where he is at work,

northwest (1)

Act 27:12 the southwest and **n** winds

nose (15)

Gen 24:22 the man took out a gold **n** ring
24:30 He saw the **n** ring and the
24:47 "I put the ring in her **n** and the
2Ki 19:28 I will put my hook in your **n**
2Ch 33:11 put a hook in his **n**,
Job 40:24 or pierce its **n** with snares?
41:2 Can you put a ring through its **n**
Psa 10:4 He turns up his **n** ⌊and says⌋,
Pro 30:33 punching a **n** produces blood,
Sos 7:4 Your **n** is like a Lebanese
Isa 3:21 signet rings, **n** rings,
37:29 I will put my hook in your **n**
65:5 become like smoke in my **n**,
Eze 16:12 I put a ring in your **n**,
23:25 They will cut off your **n** and

noses (3)

Psa 115:6 They have **n**, but they cannot
Isa 3:16 They walk with their **n** in the
Amo 4:10 from your camps fill your **n**.

nostrils (9)

Gen 2:7 the breath of life into his **n**.
Exo 15:8 With a blast from your **n**,
2Sm 22:9 Smoke went up from his **n**,
22:16 blast of the breath from his **n**.
Job 27:3 me and God's breath fills my **n**,
41:20 Smoke comes from its **n** like a
Psa 18:8 Smoke went up from his **n**,
18:15 blast of the breath from your **n**.
Isa 2:22 Their life is in their **n**.

notable (1)

Pro 25:6 spot that belongs to **n** people,

note (8)

Psa 10:14 you have taken **n** of trouble and
Pro 24:12 who weighs hearts take **n** of it?
Mat 24:15 see this (let the reader take **n**),
28:7 Take **n** that I have told you."
Mar 13:14 not (let the reader take **n**),
2Co 10:7 he should take **n** that we also
10:11 those things should take **n**
2Th 3:14 Take **n** of them and don't

noted (1)

Luk 21:5 They **n** that it was built with

notes (2)

2Ch 24:27 God's temple is in the **n** made
1Co 14:7 If there is no difference in the **n**,

notice (19)

Rut 3:4 **n** the place where he is lying.

2Ki 3:14 bother to look at you or **n** you if
Job 9:11 and I don't even **n** him.
Psa 19:12 Who can **n** every mistake?
37:37 **N** the innocent person,
Isa 1:23 They don't **n** the widows' pleas.
Jnh 1:6 Maybe he will **n** us,
Mat 5:31 wife must give her a written **n**.'
6:28 **N** how the flowers grow in the
7:3 another believer's eye and not **n**
19:7 wife a written **n** to divorce her?"
Mar 10:4 wife a written **n** to divorce her."
15:26 There was a written **n** of the
Luk 6:41 another believer's eye and not **n**
23:38 A written **n** was placed above
Jon 19:19 Pilate wrote a **n** and put it on
19:19 The **n** read, "Jesus from
19:20 Many Jews read this **n**,
19:20 The **n** was written in Hebrew,

noticed (10)

Gen 31:2 He also **n** that Laban did not
1Sm 9:17 When Samuel **n** Saul,
18:15 Saul **n** how very successful he
Ezr 8:15 I **n** laypeople and priests there,
Jer 33:24 "Haven't you **n** what these
Mat 14:30 But when he **n** how strong the
Luk 14:7 Then Jesus **n** how the guests
21:2 He **n** a poor widow drop in two
Jon 6:22 They **n** that only one boat was
Act 17:23 I **n** an altar with this written on

notices (2)

Psa 142:4 right and see that no one **n** me.
1Jn 3:17 live on and **n** another believer

noticing (1)

Job 33:14 two ways without people **n** it:

notifying (1)

Ezr 7:24 Furthermore, we are **n** you that

notorious (2)

Rev 17:1 of that **n** prostitute who sits
19:2 He has condemned the **n**

nourish (1)

Isa 55:2 money on what cannot **n** you

nourished (2)

Dtr 33:19 They will be **n** by the
1Ti 4:6 Then you will be **n** by the

nourishing (1)

Isa 30:23 provides will be rich and **n**.

nourishment (2)

Pro 3:8 and your bones will have **n**.
Rom 11:17 You get your **n** from the roots of

nudged (1)

Act 12:7 The angel **n** Peter's side,

nuisance (1)

Mal 1:13 "You say, 'Oh what a **n** it is,'

numb (1)

Psa 38:8 I am **n** and completely

numbed (1)

Hab 1:4 That is why your teaching is **n**,

number (157)

Gen 1:22 increase in **n**, fill the sea,
1:28 increase in **n**, fill the earth,
6:1 The **n** of people increased all
8:17 Be fertile, increase in **n**,
9:1 increase in **n**, and fill the earth.
9:7 Be fertile, and increase in **n**.
17:20 and increase the **n** of his
26:24 bless you and increase the **n**
28:3 and increase the **n** of your
35:11 Be fertile, and increase in **n**.
46:15 The total **n** of these sons and
46:26 The total **n** of Jacob's direct
47:12 family with food based on the **n**
48:4 you fertile and increase the **n**
Exo 1:5 The total **n** of Jacob's
1:10 or they'll increase in **n**.
1:12 the more they increased in **n**
1:20 So the people increased in **n**
5:8 that they make the same **n**
5:18 make the same **n** of bricks."
12:4 your animal based on the **n**
23:30 have increased enough in **n**
Lev 12:2 This is the same **n** of days she
25:15 take into account the **n** of years
25:15 to you taking into account the **n**
25:16 selling you only the **n** of crops.
25:50 must take into account the **n**
25:50 will be adjusted based on the **n**
27:18 its value based on the **n**
Num 2:4 The total **n** of men in his army
2:6 The total **n** of men in his army
2:8 The total **n** of men in his army
2:11 The total **n** of men in his army
2:13 The total **n** of men in his army
2:15 The total **n** of men in his army
2:19 The total **n** of men in his army
2:21 The total **n** of men in his army
2:23 The total **n** of men in his army
2:26 The total **n** of men in his army
2:28 The total **n** of men in his army
2:30 The total **n** of men in his army
2:32 This is the total **n** of Israelites,
3:22 The total **n** of all the males at
3:28 The **n** of all the males at least
3:34 The total **n** of all the males at
7:87 The total **n** of animals for the
7:88 The total **n** of animals for
23:10 Who can count them or **n** even
26:7 The total **n** of men was 43,730.
26:14 The total **n** of men was 22,200.
26:18 The total **n** of men was 40,500.
26:22 The total **n** of men was 76,500.
26:25 The total **n** of men was 64,300.
26:27 The total **n** of men was 60,500.
26:34 The total **n** of men was 52,700.
26:37 The total **n** of men was 32,500.
26:41 The total **n** of men was 45,600.
26:43 The total **n** of men in all the
26:47 The total **n** of men was 53,400.
26:50 The total **n** of men was 45,400.
26:51 The total **n** of Israelite men
26:62 The total **n** of all the ⌊Levite⌋
26:63 Eleazar added up the total **n**
32:1 Gad had a large **n** of livestock.
Dtr 3:5 a large **n** of unwalled villages.
7:13 and increase the **n** of your
17:16 king must never own a large **n**
17:17 never have a large **n** of wives,
32:8 tribes corresponding to the **n**
33:6 their people are few in **n**."
Jdg 21:23 They captured the **n** of wives
1Sm 6:18 And the **n** of gold mice was the
6:18 mice was the same as the **n**
2Sm 12:2 The rich man had a very large **n**
15:12 and the **n** of people siding with
1Ch 4:38 and the **n** of people in their
16:19 "While they were few in **n**,
21:6 Levi and Benjamin in the **n**
2Ch 24:24 come with a small **n** of men,
26:11 based on the **n** organized by
26:12 The total **n** of family heads
30:24 So a large **n** of priests were
Ezr 2:2 This is the **n** of Israelite men
3:4 the required **n** of burnt offerings
Neh 7:7 This is the **n** of Israelite men
11:8 (The **n** of Benjamin's
Est 9:11 On that day the **n** of those
Job 1:3 and a large **n** of servants.
14:5 If the **n** of his days and the
14:5 number of his days and the **n**
21:21 when the **n** of his months is cut
25:3 Is there any ⌊limit to the⌋ **n** of
31:37 I would tell him the **n** of my
36:26 The **n** of his years cannot be
Psa 25:19 enemies have increased in **n**,
39:4 Teach me about the **n** of days I
68:17 God are twenty thousand in **n**,
79:12 back with seven times the **n**
90:12 Teach us to **n** each of our days
102:23 reduced ⌊the **n** of⌋ my days.
Psa 104:24 What a large **n** of things you
105:12 people of Israel were few in **n**,
105:24 his people grow rapidly in **n**
107:39 They became few in **n** and
109:8 Let his days be few ⌊in **n**⌋.
119:156 of compassion are many in **n**,
139:17 How vast in **n** they are!
147:4 He determines the **n** of stars.
Pro 10:27 lengthens ⌊the **n** of⌋ days,
Ecc 5:2 limit the **n** of your words.
5:11 As the **n** of goods increase,
5:11 so do the **n** of people who
Isa 16:14 In spite of their great **n**,
21:17 The remaining **n** of archers,
Jer 23:3 will be fertile and increase in **n**.
29:6 daughters. Grow in **n** there;
30:19 and their **n** won't decrease.
52:23 The total **n** of pomegranates on
Eze 23:24 and with a large **n** of troops.
23:42 A large **n** of people came from
36:10 I will increase the **n** of people
36:11 I will increase the **n** of people
37:26 make them increase in **n**,
Dan 9:2 from the Scriptures the **n**
11:10 They will assemble a large **n**
Nah 1:12 physically fit and many in **n**,
Mat 14:21 (This **n** does not include the
15:38 (This **n** does not include the
24:22 If God does not reduce the **n** of
Luk 5:6 they caught such a large **n** of
5:9 was amazed to see the large **n**
Jon 5:3 Under these porches a large **n**
Act 1:20 must be added to our **n**
4:4 so the **n** of men who believed
6:1 as the **n** of disciples grew,
6:7 and the **n** of disciples in
6:7 A large **n** of priests accepted
7:17 the **n** of our people in Egypt
9:31 The **n** of people increased as
9:43 Peter stayed in Joppa for a **n** of
11:21 and a large **n** of people
16:12 were in this city for a **n** of days.
17:12 and quite a **n** of them were
21:10 had been there for a **n** of days,
25:14 staying there for a **n** of days,
27:7 sailing slowly for a **n** of days.
27:20 For a **n** of days we couldn't see
28:23 On a designated day a larger **n**
1Co 11:30 and quite a **n** ⌊of you⌋ have
12:28 can speak in a **n** of languages.
2Co 7:5 we suffer in a **n** of ways.
12:7 because of the excessive **n**
Rev 13:17 name or the **n** of its name.
13:18 who has insight figure out the **n**
13:18 because it is a human **n**.
13:18 The beast's **n** is 666.
15:2 and the **n** of its name were

numbered (11)

Ezr 2:65 female servants who **n** 7,337,
Neh 7:67 female servants who **n** 7,337,
Job 3:6 year or be **n** among the months.
9:10 and miracles that cannot be **n**.
Psa 88:4 I am **n** with those who go into
Dan 5:25 **N**, Numbered, Weighed,
5:25 **N**, Weighed, and Divided.
5:26 This is its meaning: **N** — God
5:26 Numbered — God has **n** the
Rev 5:11 They **n** ten thousand times ten
9:16 The soldiers on horses **n**

numbers (6)

Exo 12:38 along with large **n** of sheep,
1Ch 12:23 These are the **n** of the men
23:31 **n** whenever burnt offerings
2Ch 30:5 not celebrated it in large **n** as
Psa 107:38 and their **n** multiply,
Act 16:5 faith and grew in **n** every day.

numerous (34)

Gen 22:17 your descendants as **n** as
26:4 your descendants as **n** as
Exo 1:7 They became so **n** and strong
32:13 your descendants as **n** as
Dtr 1:10 so that you are now as **n** as
1:11 you a thousand times more **n**,

Dtr 2:10 people were as strong, as **n**,
2:21 people were as strong, as **n**,
10:22 God has made you as **n** as
28:62 At one time you were as **n** as
28:63 to make you prosperous and **n**.
30:5 and **n** than your ancestors
Jos 11:4 Their troops were as **n** as the
Jdg 7:12 They were as **n** as the grains
2Sm 17:11 since they are as **n** as the sand
1Ki 3:8 They are too **n** to count or
4:20 Judah and Israel were as **n** as
1Ch 5:23 The tribe members were **n**.
27:23 of Israel would be as **n** as
2Ch 1:9 people who are as **n** as specks
Neh 9:23 You made their children as **n**
Job 29:18 my days as **n** as the sand.
Psa 106:7 They did not remember your **n**
Isa 10:22 people Israel may be as ⌊**n** as⌋
Jer 15:8 Their widows will be more **n**
30:19 I'll make them **n**, and their
46:23 They are more **n** than locusts;
Eze 36:37 to make them as **n** as sheep.
Hos 1:10 the Israelites will become as **n**
Amo 5:12 I know that your crimes are **n**
Zec 10:8 They will be as **n** as they have
Rom 9:27 of Israel are as **n** as
Heb 11:12 came descendants as **n** as
Rev 20:8 They will be as **n** as the grains

Nun (30)

Exo 33:11 assistant, Joshua, son of **N**,
Num 11:28 So Joshua, son of **N**,
13:8 Hoshea, son of **N**, from the tribe
13:16 son of **N**, the name Joshua.
14:6 Joshua (son of **N**) and Caleb
14:30 and Joshua (son of **N**).
14:38 only Joshua (son of **N**) and
26:65 and Joshua (son of **N**).
27:18 "Take Joshua, son of **N**,
32:12 and Joshua (son of **N**) will get
32:28 Joshua (son of **N**),
34:17 Eleazar and Joshua, son of **N**.
Dtr 1:38 Joshua, son of **N**, will go there.
31:23 command to Joshua, son of **N**:
32:44 came with Hoshea, son of **N**,
34:9 Joshua, son of **N**, was filled
Jos 1:1 assistant Joshua, son of **N**,
2:1 From Shittim Joshua, son of **N**,
2:23 returned to Joshua, son of **N**.
6:6 Joshua, son of **N**, He said to
14:1 Joshua (son of **N**),
17:4 Joshua (son of **N**),
19:49 to Joshua, son of **N**.
19:51 Eleazar, Joshua son of **N**,
21:1 to Joshua (son of **N**),
24:29 servant Joshua, son of **N**, died.
Jdg 2:8 servant Joshua, son of **N**,
1Ki 16:34 this through Joshua, son of **N**.
1Ch 7:27 Elishama's son was **N**.
Neh 8:17 the time of Jeshua (son of **N**)

Nun's (1)

1Ch 7:27 **N** son was Joshua.

nurse (19)

Gen 21:7 that Sarah would **n** children?
24:59 sister Rebekah and her **n** go
35:8 Rebekah's **n** Deborah died and
Exo 2:7 one of the Hebrew women to **n**
2:9 "Take this child, **n** him for me,
Num 11:12 in my arms — as a **n** carries
2Sm 4:4 His **n** picked him up and fled
1Ki 3:21 up in the morning to **n** my son,
2Ki 11:2 hid him and his **n** from Athaliah.
2Ch 22:11 and she put him and his **n** in a
Job 3:12 Why did breasts let me **n**?
Isa 49:23 and their queens will **n** you.
60:16 nations and **n** at royal breasts.
66:11 You will **n** and be satisfied
66:11 You will **n** to your heart's
66:12 You will **n** and be carried in
Lam 4:3 their breasts to **n** their young,
Hos 9:14 them unable to **n** their babies.
Luk 23:29 and who couldn't **n** a child.'

nursed (6)

Exo 2:9 She took the child and **n** him.
1Sm 1:23 The woman stayed and **n** her
Sos 8:1 one who **n** at my mother's
Lam 2:20 the children they have **n**?
2:22 the children I **n** and raised."
Luk 11:27 you and the breasts that **n** you."

nursing (9)

Gen 33:13 cattle that are **n** their young.
Dtr 32:25 will die as well as **n** babies
Job 24:9 "⌊People⌋ snatch the ⌊**n**⌋
Isa 49:15 a woman forget her **n** child?
Lam 4:4 The tongues of **n** infants stick
Joe 2:16 even the **n** infants.
Mat 24:19 pregnant or who are **n** babies
Mar 13:17 pregnant or who are **n** babies
Luk 21:23 pregnant or who are **n** babies

nuts (1)

Gen 43:11 pistachio **n**, and almonds.

Nympha (1)

Col 4:15 especially **N** and the church

O

oak (26)

Gen 12:6 the land to the **o** tree belonging
13:18 to live by the **o** trees belonging
14:13 He was living next to the **o**
18:1 by the **o** trees belonging
35:4 under the **o** tree near Shechem.
35:8 under the **o** tree outside Bethel.
Dtr 11:30 next to the **o** trees of Moreh.)
Jos 19:33 at the **o** tree at Zaanannim.
24:26 and set it up under the **o** tree at
Jdg 4:11 as the **o** tree at Zaanannim
6:11 came and sat under the **o** tree
6:19 of the LORD under the **o** tree.
9:6 They went to the **o** tree that
1Sm 10:3 you come to the **o** tree at Tabor.
1Ki 13:14 him sitting under an **o** tree.
1Ch 10:12 the bones under the **o** tree
Isa 1:30 You will be like an **o** whose
6:13 When a sacred **o** or an oak is
6:13 When a sacred oak or an **o** is
57:5 You burn with lust under **o**
Eze 6:13 large tree and every leafy **o**.
Dan 4:10 and I saw an **o** tree in the
4:14 'Cut down the **o** tree!
4:20 You saw an **o** tree grow and
4:23 He said, 'Cut down the **o** tree!
Zec 11:2 Cry, **o** trees of Bashan,

oaks (8)

Psa 29:9 voice of the LORD splits the **o**
Isa 1:29 You will be ashamed of the **o**
2:13 and all the **o** of Bashan,
44:14 Then they choose fir trees or **o**.
61:3 be called **O** of Righteousness,
Eze 27:6 your oars from **o** in Bashan.
Hos 4:13 incense on the hills under **o**,
Amo 2:9 as cedars and as strong as **o**.

oars (3)

Isa 33:21 Ships with **o** won't travel on
Eze 27:6 They made your **o** from oaks in
Act 27:40 ropes that held the steering **o**.

oasis (9)

Num 20:13 This was the **o** of Meribah
20:24 command at the **o** of Meribah.
27:14 were complaining at the **o**."
27:14 (This was the **o** of Meribah at
Dtr 32:51 were unfaithful to me at the **o**
33:8 with them at the **o** of Meribah.
Psa 81:7 ⌊loyalty⌋ at the **o** of Meribah.
Eze 47:19 from Tamar to the **o** at Meribah
48:28 from Tamar to the **o** at Meribah

oath (183)

Gen 21:23 Now, swear an **o** to me here in
21:31 both of them swore an **o** there.
22:16 and said, "I am taking an **o** on
24:2 "Take a solemn **o**.
24:7 spoke to me and swore this **o**:
24:8 then you'll be free from this **o**
24:9 commanded and swore the **o**
24:37 master made me swear this **o**:
24:41 will be free from your **o** to me.
24:41 You will also be free of your **o**
25:33 "First, swear an **o**," Jacob said.
25:33 So Esau swore an **o** to him
26:3 I will keep the **o** that I swore to
26:33 So he named it Shibah [**O**].
31:53 So Jacob swore this **o** by the
50:5 father made me swear an **o**.
50:24 to the land he swore with an **o**
50:25 made Israel's sons swear an **o**.
Exo 22:11 be settled by swearing an **o**
22:11 The owner must accept the **o**.
32:13 You took an **o**, swearing on
33:1 and Jacob with an **o**,
Lev 5:1 if you are a witness under **o**
6:3 lost and lie about it under **o**,
Num 5:21 the curse of this **o** comes true:
5:21 the priest will administer the **o**
11:12 their ancestors with an **o**?
14:30 raised my hand and swore an **o**
30:2 something or swears an **o** that
30:3 or swear an **o** that she won't
30:4 her vow or **o** must be kept.
30:5 her vow or **o** doesn't have to be
30:5 free her ⌊from this vow or **o**⌋
30:7 her vow or **o** must be kept.
30:10 or swear an **o** that she won't
30:11 her vow or **o** must be kept.
30:12 she said in her vow or **o** has
30:12 free her ⌊from this vow or **o**⌋.
30:13 vow to do something or any **o**
30:14 she must keep her vow or **o**.
32:10 angry and swore this **o**,
32:11 and Jacob with an **o**.
Dtr 1:34 he was angry and took this **o**:
4:21 LORD your God took an **o** that
6:18 to your ancestors with an **o**.
6:23 to our ancestors with an **o**.
7:8 LORD loved you and kept the **o**
8:1 to your ancestors with an **o**.
19:8 your ancestors with an **o**.
26:15 with an **o** to our ancestors."
28:9 as he promised you with an **o**.
29:13 and Jacob with an **o**.
34:4 promised with an **o** to Abraham,
Jos 2:17 "We will be free from the **o**
2:20 we will be free from the **o**
9:15 swore to it with an **o**.
9:18 had sworn an **o** about them
9:19 "We have sworn an **o** about
9:20 because of the **o** we swore."
14:9 that day Moses swore this **o**:
21:44 as he had sworn with an **o** to
23:7 gods or swear an **o** to them.
Jdg 2:15 said he would do in an **o**.
21:1 had taken this **o** in Mizpah:
21:5 They had taken a solemn **o**
21:18 taken an **o** that whoever gives
1Sm 3:14 That is why I have taken an **o**
14:26 were afraid of violating their **o**.
14:27 forced the troops to take an **o**.
14:28 the troops to take a solemn **o**:
20:3 But David took an **o**,
20:17 again Jonathan swore an **o**
20:42 "We have both taken an **o** in
24:21 Swear an **o** to the LORD for me
28:10 But Saul took an **o** in the
30:15 He answered, "Take an **o** in
2Sm 3:9 had promised him with an **o**:
3:35 But David had taken an **o**:
21:7 because of the **o** in the LORD's
21:17 Then David's men swore an **o**,
1Ki 1:17 "You took an **o** to the LORD
1:29 and he swore an **o**.
2:8 I took an **o** by the LORD and
2:23 King Solomon took an **o** by the

1Ki 2:42 "Didn't I make you take an **o** by
2:43 Why didn't you keep your **o** to
8:31 and is required to take an **o**
8:31 oath and comes to take the **o**
18:10 region take an **o** that they hadn't
22:16 must I make you take an **o**
2Ki 11:4 put them under **o** in the LORD's
25:24 Gedaliah swore an **o** to them
2Ch 6:22 and is required to take an **o**
6:22 oath and comes to take the **o**
15:14 and the people swore their **o**
15:15 overjoyed because of the **o**,
15:15 they took the **o** wholeheartedly.
18:15 must I make you take an **o**
36:13 had made Zedekiah swear an **o**
Ezr 10:5 So they took an **o**.
Neh 10:28 rest of the people took an **o**.
10:28 understanding also took an **o**.
10:29 with a curse and an **o**
Job 27:2 "I swear an **o** by God,
Psa 24:4 false or lie when he is under **o**.
63:11 Everyone who takes an **o** by
89:3 I swore this **o** to my servant
89:35 I have taken an **o** once
89:49 You swore an **o** to David on
95:11 I angrily took this solemn **o**:
105:9 and his sworn **o** to Isaac.
110:4 The LORD has taken an **o** and
119:106 I took an **o**, and I will keep it.
119:106 I took an **o** to follow your
132:2 Remember how he swore an **o**
132:11 LORD swore an **o** to David.
Pro 29:24 He will not testify under **o**.
Ecc 8:2 because of the **o** you took
Isa 14:24 of Armies has taken an **o**:
45:23 I have bound myself with an **o**.
54:9 when I swore an **o** that Noah's
54:9 So now I swear an **o** not to be
65:16 Whoever swears an **o** in the
Jer 4:2 if you take the **o**, "As the LORD
5:2 they lie when they take this **o**.
11:5 I will keep the **o** I made to your
12:16 Suppose they take an **o** in my
12:16 taught my people to take an **o**
16:14 will no longer begin an **o** with,
22:5 I will take an **o** on myself,"
32:22 land that you swore with an **o**
38:16 swore an **o** to Jeremiah,
40:9 swore an **o** to them and their
44:26 on my name and take the **o**,
49:13 I take an **o** on myself,
51:14 has taken an **o** on himself:
Eze 20:5 raised my hand and swore an **o**
20:15 I also swore an **o** to them in the
20:23 raised my hand and swore an **o**
Dan 9:11 the curses you swore in an **o**,
12:7 to heaven and swore an **o** by
Hos 4:15 Don't take the **o**, 'As the LORD
Amo 4:2 Almighty LORD has taken an **o**
6:8 has sworn an **o** on himself.
8:7 The LORD has sworn an **o** by
Mic 7:20 Abraham as you swore by an **o**
Zec 5:3 everyone who takes an **o** will
Mat 5:33 'Never break your **o**,
5:33 you swore in an **o** to give him.'
5:34 I tell you don't swear an **o** at all.
5:34 Don't swear an **o** by heaven,
5:36 And don't swear an **o** by your
14:9 But because of his **o** and his
23:16 You say, 'To swear an **o** by the
23:16 But to swear an **o** by the gold
23:16 a person must keep his **o**.'
23:18 Again you say, 'To swear an **o**
23:18 But to swear an **o** by the gift on
23:18 a person must keep his **o**.'
23:20 To swear an **o** by the altar is to
23:21 To swear an **o** by the temple is
23:22 And to swear an **o** by heaven
26:63 "Swear an **o** in front of the
26:72 denied it and swore with an **o**,
26:74 to curse and swear with an **o**,
Mar 6:23 He swore an **o** to her:
6:26 But because of his **o** and his
14:71 to curse and swear with an **o**,
Luk 1:73 the **o** that he swore to our
Act 2:30 had promised with an **o** that
1Ti 1:10 who lie when they take an **o**,
Heb 3:11 So I angrily took a solemn **o**
4:3 "So I angrily took a solemn **o**
6:13 greater on whom to base his **o**,
6:17 his promise, so he took an **o**.
6:18 cannot lie when he takes an **o**
7:20 of this happened without an **o**.
7:20 become priests without an **o**,
7:21 a priest when God took an **o**.
7:21 "The Lord has taken an **o** and
Jas 5:12 do not take an **o** on anything in
5:12 Do not take any **o**.
Rev 10:6 He swore an **o** by the one who

oaths (15)

Gen 26:31 morning they exchanged **o**.
Dtr 6:13 and take your **o** only in his
10:20 and take your **o** in his name.
Ecc 9:2 People who take **o** are treated
9:2 those who are afraid to take **o**.
Isa 48:1 You take **o** by the name of the
Jer 5:7 They took godless **o**.
7:9 lie when you take **o**,
23:7 "when people's **o** will no longer
23:8 Instead, their **o** will be,
Hos 10:4 They lie when they take **o**,
Zec 5:4 the houses of those who take **o**
Heb 6:16 When people take **o**,
6:16 they base their **o** on someone
6:16 Their **o** guarantee what they

Obadiah (22)

1Ki 18:3 Ahab sent for **O**, who was in
18:3 **O** was a devout worshiper of
18:4 **O** had hidden 100 prophets in
18:5 Ahab told **O**, "Let's go
18:6 and **O** went the other way by
18:7 **O** was on the road when he
18:7 **O** recognized him and
18:9 **O** asked, "What have I done
18:16 So **O** went to tell Ahab.
1Ch 3:21 Arnan's son was **O**.
7:3 Michael, **O**, Joel, and Isshiah.
8:38 Sheariah, **O**, and Hanan.
9:16 **O** (son of Shemaiah,
9:44 Sheariah, **O**, and Hanan.
12:9 The second was **O**.
27:19 son of **O** for the tribe of
2Ch 17:7 Hail, **O**, Zechariah, Nethanel,
34:12 and **O** (Levites descended from
Ezr 8:9 from the family of Joab: **O**,
Neh 10:5 Harim, Meremoth, **O**,
12:25 Mattaniah, Bakbukiah, **O**,
Oba 1:1 This is the vision of **O**.

Obadiah's (1)

1Ch 3:21 **O** son was Shecaniah.

Obal (1)

Gen 10:28 **O**, Abimael, Sheba,

Obed (13)

Rut 4:17 So they gave him the name **O**.
4:21 Boaz was the father of **O**.
4:22 **O** was the father of Jesse.
1Ch 2:12 Boaz was the father of **O**,
2:12 and **O** was the father of Jesse.
2:37 Ephlal was the father of **O**.
2:38 **O** was the father of Jehu.
11:47 Eliel, **O**, and Jaasiel the
26:7 brothers Rephael, **O**, Elzabad,
2Ch 23:1 Azariah, son of **O**, Maaseiah,
Mat 1:5 the father and mother of **O**.
1:5 **O** was the father of Jesse,
Luk 3:32 son of Jesse, son of **O**,

Obed Edom (14)

2Sm 6:10 it to the home of **O**,
6:11 the home of **O** from Gath
6:11 and the LORD blessed **O**
1Ch 13:13 it to the home of **O**,
13:14 stayed at the home of **O**
15:18 **O** and Jeiel were
15:21 Mikneiah, **O**, Jeiel,
15:24 **O** and Jehiah were
16:5 Eliab, Benaiah, **O**,
1Ch 16:38 David also left **O** and 68
16:38 **O** (Jeduthun's son) and
26:5 God had blessed **O**.
26:15 **O** was chosen for the
2Ch 25:24 in God's temple with **O**

Obed Edom's (7)

2Sa 6:12 "The LORD has blessed **O**
6:12 of God from **O** house
1Ch 13:14 and the LORD blessed **O**
15:25 promise from **O** house.
26:4 were **O** sons Shemaiah
26:8 were **O** descendants.
26:8 **O** family included 62

obedience (10)

1Sm 15:22 as he would be with your **o**?
Psa 51:12 me with a spirit of willing **o**.
Rom 1:5 to the **o** that is associated
5:19 and through one person's **o**
6:16 or your master is **o**.
6:16 Letting **o** be your master leads
15:18 who are not Jewish to **o**.
16:19 has heard about your **o**
16:26 them to the **o** that is associated
Heb 10:9 establish the **o** that God wants.

obedient (15)

Isa 1:19 If you are willing and **o**,
Eze 11:19 hearts and give them **o** hearts.
36:26 hearts and give you **o** hearts.
Luk 2:51 to Nazareth and was **o** to them.
Rom 6:17 have become wholeheartedly **o**
7:25 So I am **o** to God's standards
7:25 but I am **o** to sin's standards
2Co 2:9 if you would be **o** in every way.
7:15 as he remembers how **o** all
10:5 captive so that it is **o** to Christ.
10:6 have become completely **o**.
Php 2:8 himself by becoming **o**
Heb 5:8 to be **o** through his sufferings.
Jas 3:17 Then it is peaceful, gentle, **o**,
1Pe 1:2 Spirit's help so that you are **o**

obey (272)

Gen 27:13 Just **o** me and go! Get me the
27:43 So now, Son, **o** me.
49:10 comes and the people **o** him.
Exo 1:17 feared God and didn't **o**
5:2 Why should I **o** him and let
15:26 commands and **o** all his laws,
19:5 If you carefully **o** me and are
20:6 me and **o** my commandments.
24:7 They said, "We will **o** and do
Lev 18:5 my standards, and **o** my rules.
18:26 my standards, and **o** my rules.
19:19 "**O** my laws. Never crossbreed
19:37 "**O** all my laws and all my
20:8 **O** my laws, and live by them.
20:22 "If you carefully **o** all my laws
22:31 "Carefully **o** my commands.
25:18 "**O** my laws, and carefully
26:3 and carefully **o** my commands:
26:14 me and **o** all these commands,
Num 14:22 ten times and refused to **o** me.
15:39 LORD's commands and **o** them.
15:40 You will remember to **o** all my
27:20 community of Israel will **o** him.
Dtr 4:1 **O** them so that you will live
4:2 Then you will be able to **o** the
4:5 You must **o** them when you've
4:6 Faithfully **o** these laws.
4:14 you must **o** after you cross
4:30 the LORD your God and **o** him.
4:40 **O** his laws and commands
5:1 Learn them and faithfully **o**
5:10 me and **o** my commandments.
5:27 We'll listen and **o**."
5:29 and **o** all my commandments
5:31 that you must teach them to **o**
6:1 **O** them after you enter the land
6:2 All of you must **o** all his laws
6:3 and be careful to **o** these laws.
6:17 Be sure to **o** the commands of
6:24 us to **o** all these laws
6:25 If we faithfully **o** all these laws

Dtr 7:9 love him and **o** his commands.
7:11 So **o** the commands,
7:12 rules and faithfully **o** them,
8:1 Be careful to **o** every command
8:2 **o** his commands.
8:6 **O** the commands of the LORD
8:11 Don't fail to **o** his commands,
8:20 like them if you don't **o**
9:23 You didn't believe him or **o** him.
10:13 The LORD wants you to **o** his
11:1 Always **o** his laws,
11:8 **O** all the commands I'm giving
11:13 If you faithfully **o** the
11:22 Faithfully **o** all these
11:27 You'll be blessed if you **o** the
11:32 be careful to **o** all the laws and
12:1 and rules you must faithfully **o**
12:1 You must **o** them as long as
12:28 Be sure you **o** all these
13:4 fear him, **o** his commands,
13:18 **o** all the commands that I'm
15:5 faithfully **o** all these commands
16:12 and **o** these laws carefully.
17:19 faithfully **o** everything found
19:9 faithfully **o** all these commands
21:18 son who doesn't **o** them.
21:20 He won't **o** us. He eats too much
26:16 you to **o** these laws
26:16 You must faithfully **o** them with
26:17 **o** his laws, commands,
26:18 be sure to **o** his commands.
27:1 "**O** every command I'm giving
27:10 **O** the LORD your God and
27:26 "Whoever doesn't **o** every word
28:1 Carefully **o** the LORD your God,
28:2 close to you because you **o**
28:9 He will do this if you **o** the
28:13 if you faithfully **o** the
28:15 **O** the LORD your God,
28:45 because you didn't **o** the LORD
28:58 You might not faithfully **o** every
28:62 because you didn't **o** the LORD
29:9 Faithfully **o** the terms of this
29:29 We must **o** every word of these
30:2 the LORD your God and **o** him
30:8 You will again **o** the LORD and
30:10 He will do this if you **o** him and
30:12 so that we can hear it and **o** it?"
30:13 so that we can hear it and **o** it?"
30:14 heart so that you will **o** them.
30:16 and **o** his commands,
30:20 **o** him, and be loyal to him.
31:12 God and faithfully **o** every word
32:46 to faithfully **o** every word
Jos 1:17 We will **o** you as we obeyed
1:18 or does not **o** your orders will
24:24 the LORD our God and **o** him."
Jdg 2:2 But you didn't **o** me.
3:4 to find out if they would **o** the
1Sm 12:14 the LORD, serve him, **o** him,
12:15 But if you don't **o** the LORD,
15:19 Why didn't you **o** the LORD?
15:20 "But I did **o** the LORD,"
15:22 To **o** is better than sacrificing
2Sm 22:45 they hear of me, they will **o** me.
1Ki 2:3 **O** his directions, laws,
2:43 your oath to the LORD and **o**
3:14 And if you follow me and **o** my
8:23 who **o** you wholeheartedly.
11:10 did not **o** God's command.
13:21 the LORD's mouth and didn't **o**
20:36 "Since you didn't **o** the LORD,
2Ki 10:31 Jehu didn't wholeheartedly **o**
17:13 and **o** my commands and
17:19 Even Judah didn't **o** the
17:37 Faithfully **o** the laws,
18:12 because they refused to **o**
18:12 They refused to **o** everything
21:8 their ancestors if they will **o** all
21:9 (But they wouldn't **o**.)
22:13 our ancestors did not **o**
23:3 LORD and **o** his commands,
1Ch 10:13 He did not **o** the word of the
22:13 succeed if you will carefully **o**
28:7 determined to **o** my commands
29:19 that he will **o** your commands,

2Ch 6:14 who **o** you wholeheartedly.
7:17 and **o** my laws and rules,
33:8 their ancestors if they will **o** all
34:21 our ancestors did not **o**
34:31 LORD and **o** his commands,
Neh 1:5 and **o** your commandments.
1:9 to **o** my commandments,
9:16 and wouldn't **o** your commands.
9:29 not **o** your commandments.
9:34 didn't **o** your teachings.
Est 1:15 not **o** King Xerxes' command,
3:8 They do not **o** your decrees.
Psa 18:44 they hear of me, they will **o** me.
78:7 and to **o** his commands.
78:56 not **o** his written instructions.
89:31 do not **o** my commandments,
103:20 ready to **o** his spoken orders.
105:45 so that they would **o** his laws
106:25 They did not **o** the LORD.
112:1 is happy to **o** his commands.
119:2 Blessed are those who **o** his
119:5 so that I can **o** your laws.
119:8 I will **o** your laws. Never
119:33 and I will **o** them to the end.
119:60 hurry to **o** your commandments
119:69 ⌊yet⌋ I **o** your guiding
119:88 your mercy so that I may **o**
119:101 path in order to **o** your word.
119:112 I have decided to **o** your laws.
119:115 so that I can **o** the
119:129 That is why I **o** them.
119:134 I may **o** your guiding principles.
119:145 I want to **o** your laws.
119:146 can **o** your written instructions.
148:8 winds that **o** his commands,
Pro 4:4 **O** my commands so that you
6:20 **O** the command of your father,
7:2 **O** my commands so that you
30:17 fun of a father and hates to **o**
Ecc 8:2 I ⌊advise⌋ you to **o** the king's
Isa 42:24 They didn't **o** his teachings.
Jer 7:23 But I did tell them this, '**O** me,
7:24 But they didn't **o** me or pay
7:26 But you didn't **o** me or pay
7:27 but they will not **o** you.
7:28 'This is the nation that did not **o**
9:13 They didn't **o** me, and they
11:4 I said, "**O** me, and do
11:7 I solemnly warned them to **o**
11:8 But they didn't **o** me or pay
11:10 and refused to **o** my words.
16:11 They didn't **o** my teachings.
17:23 Your ancestors did not **o** me or
18:10 consider evil and doesn't **o** me.
19:15 and they refuse to **o** me."
32:23 However, they refused to **o** you
34:14 But your ancestors refused to **o**
34:17 LORD says: You didn't **o** me.
35:13 your lesson and **o** my words?
35:15 you refused to listen to me or **o**
38:20 **O** the LORD by doing what I'm
40:3 him and refused to **o** him.
42:6 We will **o** the LORD our God to
42:6 Yes, we will **o** the LORD our
42:21 but you won't **o** anything the
43:4 the people didn't **o** the LORD.
44:23 and wouldn't **o** him.
Eze 11:20 by my laws and **o** my rules.
20:11 If people **o** them they will live.
20:13 If people **o** them, they will live.
20:18 Don't **o** their rules or dishonor
20:19 **O** my rules and follow them.
20:21 and they didn't **o** my rules and
20:21 If people **o** them, they will live.
36:27 and you will **o** my rules.
37:24 and they will **o** my laws.
44:24 They must **o** my rules and my
Dan 3:12 These men didn't **o** your order,
6:13 refuses to **o** your order or the
7:27 powers will serve and **o** them."
9:4 and **o** your commandments.
Mic 5:15 the nations that do not **o** me."
Zec 6:15 This will happen if you **o** the
Mat 7:26 hears what I say but doesn't **o**
8:27 Even the wind and the sea **o**
19:17 **o** the commandments."

Mar 1:27 to evil spirits, and they **o** him."
4:41 Even the wind and the sea **o**
Luk 6:49 ⌊what I say⌋ but doesn't **o**
8:25 and the water, and they **o** him!"
10:17 even demons **o** us when we
10:20 don't be happy that evil spirits **o**
11:28 who hear and **o** God's word."
17:6 and it would **o** you.
Jon 14:15 you will **o** my commandments.
15:10 If you **o** my commandments,
15:14 if you **o** my commandments.
Act 5:29 "We must **o** God rather than
5:32 has given to those who **o** him."
7:39 were not willing to **o** him.
Rom 1:30 They don't **o** their parents,
4:14 If those who **o** Moses'
6:12 body so that you **o** its desires.
6:16 you must **o** that master?
13:1 Every person should **o** the
13:5 it is necessary for you to **o**,
Gal 2:19 When I tried to **o** the law's
3:10 "Whoever doesn't **o** everything
Eph 2:2 in people who refuse to **o** God.
5:6 to those who refuse to **o** him.
6:1 Children, **o** your parents
6:5 Slaves, **o** your earthly masters
6:5 as you are when you **o** Christ.
6:6 Don't **o** them only while you're
6:6 But **o** like slaves who belong
Col 3:6 on those who refuse to **o** him.
3:20 always **o** your parents.
3:22 always **o** your earthly masters.
3:22 Don't **o** them only while you're
1Ti 3:4 should respectfully **o** him.
6:14 you **o** this command
Tit 3:1 Believers should **o** them and
Heb 3:18 about those who didn't **o** him.
4:6 because they did not **o** God.
4:11 of those who refused to **o**.
11:8 Faith led Abraham to **o** when
11:31 those who refused to **o** God.
12:20 They couldn't **o** the command
13:17 **O** your leaders, and accept
13:17 **O** them so that they may do
Jas 2:8 You are doing right if you **o** this
3:3 of horses to make them **o** us,
1Pe 1:14 you are children who **o** God,
2:13 **O** the emperor. He holds the
2:14 Also **o** governors. They are
2:18 **O** not only those owners who
3:1 may not **o** God's word.
4:17 end for those who refuse to **o**
1Jn 2:3 if we **o** his commandments.
2:4 but doesn't **o** his
3:22 We receive it because we **o**
3:24 Those who **o** Christ's
5:3 that we **o** his commandments.
Rev 3:3 **O**, and change the way you
14:12 who **o** his commands and keep

obeyed (50)

Gen 22:18 because you have **o** me."
26:5 you because Abraham **o** me
28:7 that Jacob had **o** his father
Lev 10:7 with his oil." They **o** Moses.
Num 9:19 the Israelites **o** the LORD's
9:23 They **o** the command that the
Dtr 26:14 I have **o** the LORD my God.
33:9 But they **o** your word and were
34:9 The Israelites **o** him and did
Jos 1:17 will obey you as we **o** Moses.
22:2 You have also **o** me in
Jdg 2:17 of their ancestors who had **o**
2:20 ancestors and have not **o** me,
6:10 But you have not **o** me."
1Ki 11:34 who **o** my commands and
12:24 So they **o** the word of the
14:8 He **o** my commands and
2Ki 14:6 He **o** the LORD's command
18:6 He **o** the commands that the
1Ch 29:23 successful and all Israel **o** him.
2Ch 11:4 So they **o** the word of the
25:4 He **o** the LORD's command
29:15 Then they **o** the king's order
Neh 1:7 haven't **o** the commandments,

Psa 99:7 They o his written instructions
119:22 o your written instructions.
119:56 have o your guiding principles.
119:100 have o your guiding principles.
119:167 I have o your written
Jer 3:13 You have not o me,'
3:25 We haven't o the LORD our
35:8 have o our ancestor Jonadab,
35:10 We live in tents, and we have o
35:14 because they have o their
35:18 You o the order of your
Eze 5:7 lived by my laws or o my rules.
11:12 and you haven't o my rules.
18:19 He o my rules and followed
Hag 1:12 who returned from Babylon o
1:12 They also o the words of the
Mat 19:20 "I have o all these
Mar 10:20 I've o all these commandments
Luk 18:21 The official replied, "I've o all
Jon 15:10 I have o my Father's
Act 7:53 you haven't o those teachings."
Gal 3:21 approval because we o them.
Php 2:12 you have always o,
Heb 11:7 He o God and built a ship to
1Pe 3:6 Sarah o Abraham and spoke to
Rev 3:10 Because you have o my

obeying (13)

Num 15:22 by not o all these commands
1Ki 11:38 I consider right by o my laws
Jer 16:12 evil ways that keep you from o
Rom 4:13 So it was not by o Moses'
4:16 by o Moses' Teachings
9:31 by o Moses' Teachings,
Gal 2:21 God's approval by o laws,
3:11 receives God's approval by o
5:4 approval by o his laws have
Php 3:9 God's approval by o his laws.
1Pe 1:22 yourselves by o the truth.
1Jn 5:2 God by o his commandments.
5:3 O his commandments isn't

obeys (18)

Pro 19:16 Whoever o the law preserves
Ecc 8:5 Whoever o his commands will
Isa 50:10 the LORD and o his servant?
Eze 18:9 He lives by my rules and o my
18:17 He o my rules and lives by my
18:21 He o all my laws and does
Zep 3:2 It o no one. It does not accept
Mat 7:24 who hears what I say and o
Luk 6:47 what I say, and o it is like.
Jon 8:51 Whoever o what I say will
14:21 Whoever knows and o my
Rom 10:5 He says, "The person who o
10:5 live because of the laws he o."
Gal 3:12 "Whoever o laws will live
3:12 live because of the laws he o."
Heb 5:9 for everyone who o him.
Jas 2:10 If someone o all of God's laws
1Jn 2:5 But whoever o what Christ

Obil (1)

1Ch 27:30 for the camels: O, Jehdeiah

object (15)

Exo 32:25 and they became an o of
Num 30:11 but may say nothing and not o.
1Ki 9:7 will be an example and an o
2Ch 7:20 make it an example and an o
Psa 44:13 to our neighbors and an o
69:11 but I became the o of ridicule.
79:4 an o of ridicule and contempt to
89:41 He has become the o of his
Isa 62:7 Jerusalem and makes it an o
Jer 6:10 show contempt for it and o to it.
20:8 the LORD has made me the o
51:37 and an o of contempt,
Eze 5:14 you into a wasteland and an o
Act 10:29 That is why I didn't o to coming
Rom 9:20 Can an o that was made say to

objected (5)

Num 30:5 or oath because her father o.
Mat 16:22 took him aside and o to this.
Mar 8:32 took him aside and o to this.
Mar 8:33 and o to what Peter said.
Act 28:19 But when the Jews o,

objections (1)

Act 11:18 they had no further o.

objects (18)

Num 30:5 But if her father o when he
30:8 But if her husband o when he
1Sm 6:8 Put the gold o which you're
6:15 box which contained the gold o
1Ch 29:2 of my God: gold for gold o,
29:2 gold objects, silver for silver o,
29:2 bronze for bronze o,
29:2 bronze objects, iron for iron o,
29:2 wood for wooden o,
29:5 to make gold o, silver objects,
29:5 to make gold objects, silver o,
Isa 19:20 These o will be a sign and a
Act 17:23 closely at the o you worship,
Rom 9:22 patient with people who are o
9:23 of his glory to people who are o
Col 2:22 All of these things deal with o
2Ti 2:20 there are not only o made
2:20 Some o are honored when they

obligated (3)

1Sm 21:7 of Saul's servants who was o
2Sm 18:11 Then I would have felt o to
Rom 15:27 So they are o to use their

obligates (1)

Gal 5:3 must realize that he o himself

obligation (4)

Neh 10:32 we take upon ourselves the o
Rom 1:14 I have an o to those who are
8:12 we have no o to live the way
1Co 9:16 brag about because I have an o

Oboth (4)

Num 21:10 moved and set up camp at O.
21:11 Next they moved from O and
33:43 Punon and set up camp at O.
33:44 They moved from O and set up

obscene (3)

Zep 2:15 hiss and make an o gesture.
Eph 5:4 or o jokes should be mentioned
Col 3:8 hatred, cursing, o language,

observance (1)

Col 2:16 you eat or drink or about the o

observation (1)

2Sm 11:16 Joab had kept the city under o,

observe (31)

Exo 12:25 he promised, o this ceremony.
13:5 you must o this ceremony in
31:13 'Be sure to o my days of
31:14 "'O the day of worship
31:16 The Israelites must o this day
Lev 19:3 O my days of worship.
19:30 "O my days of worship and
23:32 o the day of worship."
26:2 O my days of worship and
Dtr 5:12 "O the day of worship as a
5:15 God has commanded you to o
Est 9:21 days they must o every year.
9:22 They were to o them just like
9:27 never fail to o these two days
Job 14:3 You o this and call me to
23:9 he is at work, I can't o him.
28:24 and o everything under heaven.
35:5 O the clouds high above you.
Psa 17:2 Let your eyes o what is fair.
Isa 42:20 but you do not o anything.
56:4 and faithfully o the conditions
56:6 unholy and will faithfully o
Jer 2:10 to Kedar, and o closely.
17:22 Do not do any work, but o the
17:24 You must o the day of worship
17:27 But you must listen to me and o
Eze 44:24 They must o holy days to
Luk 17:20 "People can't o the coming of
Rom 14:6 When people o a special day,
14:6 they o it to honor the Lord.
Gal 4:10 You religiously o days,

observed (7)

2Ch 7:9 They had o the dedication of
Est 9:28 must be remembered and o
Pro 24:32 When I o this, I took it to
Luk 23:55 They o the tomb and how his
Act 14:9 Paul o him closely and saw
Rom 1:20 have been clearly o in what he
1Jn 1:1 We o and touched it.

observing (1)

Exo 20:8 the day of worship by o

obsessed (2)

2Sm 13:2 Amnon was so o with his half
1Ki 11:2 Solomon was o with their love.

obstacle (1)

Isa 57:14 Remove every o in the way of

obstacles (1)

Eph 6:13 Once you have overcome all o,

obtain (5)

Job 28:15 You cannot o it with solid gold
Luk 20:10 to the workers to o from them
1Th 5:9 that we o salvation through our
2Th 2:14 told you so that you would o
1Pe 1:9 as you o the salvation that is

obtained (9)

1Ki 10:29 For the same price they o
2Ch 1:17 For the same price they o
11:23 allowances and o many wives
Pro 4:17 They eat food o through
4:17 drink wine o through violence.
18:22 good and has o favor from
20:21 An inheritance quickly o in the
Jon 12:14 Jesus o a donkey and sat on it,
2Pe 1:1 To those who have o a faith

obtains (3)

Pro 3:13 the one who o understanding.
8:35 me finds life and o favor from
12:2 A good person o favor from the

obvious (11)

Mat 6:16 to make it o that they're fasting.
6:18 Then your fasting won't be o.
6:18 Instead, it will be o to your
26:73 "It's o you're also one of them.
Mar 14:70 "It's o you're one of them.
Luk 16:2 It's o that you can't manage my
22:59 "It's o that this man was with
Gal 5:19 of the corrupt nature are o:
1Ti 5:24 The sins of some people are o,
5:25 things that people do are o,
5:25 aren't o can't remain hidden.

occasion (8)

1Sm 20:19 where you hid on that other o,
25:8 we have come on a special o.
2Sm 23:8 spear to kill 800 men on one o.
1Ch 11:11 spear to kill 300 men on one o.
Neh 8:4 platform made for this o.
Rom 2:15 thoughts accuse them on one o
9:21 make something for a special o
Jud 1:5 But on another o he destroyed

occasions (1)

Zec 8:19 joyful and glad o as well as

occult (1)

Act 19:19 in the o gathered their books

occupation (1)

1Sm 7:1 son Eleazar the holy o

occupied (2)

Jdg 3:13 defeated the Israelites and o
Ecc 5:20 because God keeps them o

occupy (1)

Jer 49:16 You live on rocky cliffs and o

occupying (1)

1Ti 1:4 and o themselves with myths

occur (3)

Eze 16:16 happen. They shouldn't o.
Luk 21:7 the sign when all this will o?"
21:25 "Miraculous signs will o in the

ocean (20)

2Sm 22:16 Then the o floor could be seen.
Job 28:14 The deep o says, 'It isn't in
38:16 the valleys of the o depths?
38:30 surface of the o freezes over.
41:31 It stirs up the o like a boiling
Psa 18:15 Then the o floor could be seen.
36:6 your judgments like the deep o.
69:15 Do not let the o swallow me up,
78:15 plenty to drink, an o of water.
93:3 The o rises, O LORD.
93:3 The o rises with a roar.
93:3 The o rises with its pounding
104:6 You covered the earth with an o
148:7 creatures and all the o depths,
Pro 8:27 horizon on the surface of the o,
8:28 the currents in the o,
Isa 51:10 the water of the great o?
Eze 26:19 I will bring the deep o over you,
Amo 7:4 The fire dried up the o and
Hab 3:10 The deep o roars. Its waves rise

oceans (3)

Psa 33:7 puts the o in his storehouses.
135:6 or in all the depths of the o.
Pro 8:24 I was born before there were o

Ochran (5)

Num 1:13 Pagiel, son of O, from the tribe
2:27 of Asher is Pagiel, son of O.
7:72 of Asher, Pagiel, son of O,
7:77 the gifts from Pagiel, son of O.
10:26 Pagiel, son of O,

o'clock (11)

Mat 14:25 Between three and six o in the
27:46 About three o Jesus cried out
Mar 6:48 Between three and six o in the
15:34 At three o Jesus cried out in a
Jon 1:39 was about ten o in the morning.
4:6 was about six o in the evening.
4:52 yesterday evening at seven o."
19:14 The time was about six o in
Act 3:1 courtyard for the three o prayer
10:30 three o in the afternoon.
23:23 go to Caesarea at nine o tonight

Oded (2)

2Ch 15:1 came to Azariah, son of O.
28:9 the LORD named O was there.

Oded's (1)

2Ch 15:8 Asa heard the prophet O words

odor (1)

Joe 2:20 A foul o will rise from the dead

offended (4)

Gen 40:1 and his baker o their master,
Pro 18:19 An o brother is more
Isa 63:10 But they rebelled and o his
Mat 15:12 your statement they were o?"

offender (2)

Exo 21:22 the o must pay whatever fine
21:23 the o must pay a life for a life,

offends (3)

Job 19:17 My breath o my wife.
Mic 2:10 destroyed, because it o me.
1Co 1:23 This o Jewish people and

offense (11)

Gen 31:36 "What is my o that you have
Dtr 19:15 convict someone of a crime, o,
1Sm 25:28 Please forgive my o.
2Ch 24:18 This o of theirs brought God's
Job 31:11 and that would be a criminal o.
31:28 would be a criminal o,
Psa 19:13 I will be free from any great o.
Pro 17:9 forgives an o seeks love,
19:11 credit that he overlooks an o.
Mat 13:57 So they took o at him.
Mar 6:3 So they took o at him.

offenses (1)

Ecc 10:4 you can make up for serious o.

offensive (8)

Gen 43:32 because they found it o to eat
Dtr 23:14 see anything o among you
1Sm 13:4 and now Israel has become o
2Sm 10:6 made themselves o to David.
1Ch 19:6 made themselves o to David.
Rom 9:33 a large rock that people find o.
Gal 5:11 cross wouldn't be o anymore.
1Pe 2:8 a large rock that people find o."

offer (149)

Exo 3:18 into the desert to o sacrifices
5:3 into the desert to o sacrifices
5:8 'Let us go o sacrifices to our
5:17 'Let us go o sacrifices to the
8:8 your people go to o sacrifices
8:26 The sacrifices we o to the
8:26 If they see us o sacrifices that
8:27 into the desert to o sacrifices
8:28 You may o sacrifices to the
8:29 the people go to o sacrifices
23:18 "Never o the blood of a
23:18 o anything containing yeast.
29:24 who will o them to the LORD.
29:38 "This is what you are to o on
29:39 O one in the morning and the
29:41 O the other lamb at dusk,
34:25 "Never o the blood of a
34:25 o anything containing yeast.
Lev 1:2 you must o an animal from your
1:3 you must o a male that has no
1:3 O it at the entrance to the tent
1:5 the priests, will o the blood.
2:8 O it to the priest who will bring
3:4 fat on them and o them by fire
3:9 the fellowship offering and o
6:20 He must o half of it in the
6:21 O baked pieces of the grain
7:3 He will o all the fat,
7:12 If you o it as a thank offering,
7:16 it must be eaten the day you o
7:33 When any of Aaron's sons o
9:6 you to o these sacrifices so
12:7 The priest will o them in the
15:30 The priest will o one as an
17:4 O it to the LORD in front of the
17:9 of the tent of meeting to o them
18:23 A woman must never o herself
21:8 Be holy because you o the
21:17 never bring food to o to God.
21:21 never bring food to o to God.
27:9 the kind of animal that people o
Num 6:17 o the basket of unleavened
15:7 O them as a soothing aroma to
15:9 O with the young bull a grain
15:28 The priest will o the sacrifice
16:17 They will o all 250 incense
16:17 Aaron o your incense burners."
28:4 O one in the morning and the
28:8 O the other lamb at dusk along
28:9 "On the day of worship o two
28:23 O these in addition to the
28:31 O these animals that have no
29:6 O these in addition to the
31:50 We o them to make peace with
Dtr 2:26 with the following o of peace:
17:1 Never o an ox or a sheep that
20:10 o its people a peaceful way to
20:12 If they won't accept your o of
23:6 Never o them peace or
26:14 I didn't o any of it to the dead.
30:15 Today I o you life and
Dtr 33:19 and there they will o the proper
Jdg 16:23 rulers gathered together to o
17:10 The Levite accepted the o
1Sm 1:21 household again went to o
2:19 to o the annual sacrifice.
20:29 Our relatives will o a sacrifice
2Sm 7:27 the courage to o this prayer
24:22 and o whatever you think is
24:24 I won't o the LORD my God
1Ki 13:1 at the altar to o a sacrifice.
13:2 worship sites who o sacrifices
18:36 it was time to o the sacrifice,
2Ki 5:17 I will not o any burnt offering or
10:19 have a great sacrifice to o Baal.
10:24 So they went in to o sacrifices
12:3 The people continued to o
14:4 The people continued to o
15:4 The people continued to o
15:35 The people continued to o
1Ch 21:24 and o burnt sacrifices that
23:13 to o sacrifices to the LORD,
2Ch 7:6 and which he used to o praise.
13:11 They o sweet-smelling
Ezr 6:3 as a place to o sacrifices.
6:10 Then they can o sacrifices that
7:17 and wine to o on the altar of the
Neh 4:2 Are they going to o sacrifices?
Job 6:22 or 'O me a bribe from your
15:34 the tents of those who o bribes.
21:2 that be the comfort you o me.
Psa 4:5 O the sacrifices of
27:6 I will o sacrifices with shouts
38:14 and who can o no arguments.
51:16 I would o one ⌊to you⌋.
66:15 I will o you a sacrifice of
66:15 I will o cattle and goats.
119:112 They o a reward that never
Ecc 9:2 whether they o sacrifices or
9:2 sacrifices or don't o sacrifices.
Isa 1:15 though you o many prayers,
30:5 only o shame and disgrace."
50:6 I will o my back to those who
57:7 gone to o sacrifices there.
66:12 I will o you peace like a river
Jer 16:7 No one will o food to comfort
35:2 and o them a drink of wine."
46:10 will o them as sacrifices
Lam 4:3 Even jackals o their breasts to
Eze 20:31 You o your children as
43:23 you finish removing sin, o
43:24 O them to the LORD.
43:24 on them and o them as burnt
46:4 The prince must o to the LORD
Hos 3:3 Don't be a prostitute or o
4:13 They o sacrifices on
4:14 The men go to prostitutes and o
8:13 They o sacrifices to me and
13:2 "They o human sacrifices and
Mal 1:7 "You o contaminated food on
Mat 5:24 come back and o your gift.
8:4 Then o the sacrifice Moses
Mar 1:44 Then o the sacrifices which
Luk 5:14 Then o the sacrifice as Moses
6:29 o the other cheek as well.
10:7 and drink whatever they o you.
23:36 o him some vinegar,
Act 14:13 and the crowd wanted to o
Rom 6:13 Never o any part of your body
6:13 Instead, o yourselves to God
6:13 O all the parts of your body to
6:16 Don't you know that if you o to
6:19 Now, in the same way, o all
12:1 I encourage you to o your
Eph 1:3 blessing that heaven has to o.
Php 2:17 of the sacrifice and service ⌊I o
Col 4:2 you o prayers of thanksgiving.
1Ti 2:8 men to o prayers everywhere.
Heb 5:1 to o gifts and sacrifices for sin.
5:3 he has to o sacrifices for his
8:3 priest is appointed to o gifts
8:3 this chief priest had to o
8:4 On earth ⌊other⌋ priests o gifts
10:8 Teachings require people to o.)
11:4 Faith led Abel to o God a better
11:17 faith led him to o his son Isaac.
11:17 was willing to o his only son

1Pe	2:5	So **o** spiritual sacrifices that
Rev	8:3	was given a lot of incense to **o**

offered (80)

Gen	29:18	So he **o**, "I'll work seven years
	30:28	So he **o**, "Name your wages,
	31:54	and **o** a sacrifice on the
	46:1	he **o** sacrifices to the God of
Exo	29:27	as holy the breast that is **o**
	32:8	down to it and **o** sacrifices
	35:22	these gifts of gold and **o** them
Lev	7:15	be eaten on the day it is **o**.
	10:1	they **o** this unauthorized fire.
Num	3:4	they **o** unauthorized fire
	8:8	with olive oil that is **o** with it.
	15:3	They may be **o** to fulfill a vow,
	16:38	because they were **o** to the
	23:2	and the two of them **o** a bull
	23:4	and I **o** a bull and a ram on
	23:14	He **o** a bull and a ram on each
	23:30	and he **o** a bull and a ram on
	25:2	the people to the sacrifices **o**
	26:61	they **o** unauthorized fire
	28:15	one male goat must be **o** to the
	28:24	They will be **o** in addition to
Dtr	30:19	today that I have **o** you life
Jos	13:14	The sacrifices **o** to the LORD
Jdg	2:5	They **o** sacrifices there to the
	5:25	She **o** him buttermilk in a royal
	19:15	because no one **o** to take them
	19:18	but no one has **o** to take me
	21:13	Rock and **o** them peace.
1Sm	1:4	Elkanah **o** a sacrifice,
	2:29	the sacrifices **o** by my people
1Ki	8:62	Then the king and all Israel **o**
2Ki	16:4	He **o** sacrifices and burned
1Ch	6:49	Aaron and his descendants **o**
	21:28	he **o** sacrifices there.
	29:17	willingly **o** all these things.
2Ch	6:40	to the prayers ⌊**o**⌋ in this place.
	7:4	and all the people **o** sacrifices
	7:5	King Solomon **o** 22,000 cattle
	28:4	He **o** sacrifices and burned
Ezr	1:6	everything that was freely **o**.
Neh	11:2	everyone who willingly **o**
	12:43	That day they **o** many
Job	1:5	Job **o** sacrifices for them all the
	26:3	and **o** so much assistance.
Psa	51:19	be pleased with sacrifices **o**
	51:19	bulls will be **o** on your altar.
Isa	65:3	They **o** sacrifices in gardens
	65:11	of good fortune and **o** cups full
Eze	16:18	You **o** my olive oil and incense
	16:19	You also **o** them sweet and
	16:25	You **o** your body to everyone
	20:28	There they **o** their sacrifices
	44:7	my temple when you **o** fat
	46:7	gallon of olive oil must be **o**
Jnh	1:16	They **o** sacrifices and made
Mal	1:11	offerings will be **o** everywhere
Mat	2:11	treasure chests and **o** him gifts
	26:15	They **o** him 30 silver coins.
	27:48	on a stick and **o** Jesus a drink.
Mar	15:36	Then he put it on a stick and **o**
Luk	2:24	They also **o** a sacrifice as
Act	7:41	They **o** a sacrifice to that false
	8:18	So he **o** Peter and John money
	21:26	and the sacrifice would be **o**
Rom	6:19	Clearly, you once **o** all the
1Co	8:1	Now, concerning food **o** to
	8:4	about eating food that was **o**
	8:7	believe they are eating food **o**
	8:10	that person to eat food **o**
	8:13	Therefore, if eating food ⌊**o** to
Heb	9:7	and brought blood that he **o**
	9:12	place and **o** this sacrifice once
	9:14	Through the eternal Spirit he **o**
	9:15	Because Christ **o** himself to
	10:11	He **o** the same type of sacrifice
Jas	2:21	he did when he **o** his son Isaac
	5:15	(Prayers **o** in faith will save
	5:16	Prayers **o** by those who have
Rev	8:3	He **o** it with the prayers of all of
	14:4	humanity as the first ones **o**

offering (551)

Gen	4:3	the land as an **o** to the LORD.
	4:4	approved of Abel and his **o**,
	4:5	approve of Cain and his **o**.
	8:20	On it he made a burnt **o** of each
	22:2	Sacrifice him there as a burnt **o**
	22:3	cut the wood for the burnt **o**,
	22:6	took the wood for the burnt **o**
	22:7	is the lamb for the burnt **o**?"
	22:8	provide a lamb for the burnt **o**,
	22:13	and sacrificed it as a burnt **o**
	35:14	He poured a wine **o** and olive
Exo	18:12	brought a burnt **o** and other
	23:15	into my presence without an **o**.
	29:14	the camp. It is an **o** for sin.
	29:18	It's a burnt **o**, a soothing aroma,
	29:18	an **o** by fire to the LORD.
	29:25	the altar on top of the burnt **o**.
	29:25	an **o** by fire to the LORD.
	29:36	sacrifice a young bull as an **o**
	29:36	Sacrifice this **o** for sin on the
	29:40	With the first lamb make an **o**
	29:40	Make a wine **o** of one quart of
	29:41	with it make the same grain **o**
	29:41	grain offering and wine **o** as
	29:41	an **o** by fire to the LORD.
	29:42	be the daily burnt **o** ⌊made⌋
	30:8	incense **o** must burn constantly
	30:9	Never pour a wine **o** on it.
	30:10	come — blood from the **o** must
	30:20	as priests and burn an **o** by fire
	34:20	into my presence without an **o**.
	35:29	to the LORD as a freewill **o**.
Lev	1:3	"If you bring a burnt **o** from
	1:4	The burnt **o** will be accepted to
	1:6	Skin the burnt **o**, and cut it into
	1:9	It is a burnt **o**, an offering by
	1:9	is a burnt offering, an **o** by fire,
	1:10	"If your **o** is a sheep or goat,
	1:13	It is a burnt **o**, an offering by
	1:13	is a burnt offering, an **o** by fire,
	1:14	"If your **o** to the LORD is a bird,
	1:17	It is a burnt **o**, an offering by
	1:17	is a burnt offering, an **o** by fire,
	2:1	if any of you bring a grain **o** to
	2:1	your **o** must be flour.
	2:2	It is an **o** by fire, a soothing
	2:3	The rest of the grain **o** will
	2:3	apart from the LORD's **o** by fire.
	2:4	"If you bring a grain **o** which
	2:5	If your grain **o** is prepared in a
	2:6	olive oil over it. It is a grain **o**.
	2:7	If your grain **o** is prepared in a
	2:8	"Bring the LORD the grain **o**
	2:9	will remove part of the grain **o**
	2:9	It is an **o** by fire, a soothing
	2:10	The rest of the grain **o** belongs
	2:10	apart from the LORD's **o** by fire.
	2:11	"Every grain **o** that you bring to
	2:11	or honey as an **o** to the LORD.
	2:14	"If you bring a grain **o** to the
	2:15	incense on it. It is a grain **o**.
	2:16	It is an **o** by fire to the LORD."
	3:1	your sacrifice is a fellowship **o**
	3:3	From your **o** remove the fat that
	3:5	lay them on top of the burnt **o**
	3:5	It is an **o** by fire, a soothing
	3:6	your sacrifice is a fellowship **o**
	3:7	If your **o** is a lamb,
	3:9	the fat from the fellowship **o**
	3:11	priest will burn the fellowship **o**
	3:11	an **o** by fire to the LORD.
	3:12	"If your **o** is a goat,
	3:15	the fat on them as an **o** by fire
	3:16	an **o** by fire to the LORD.
	4:3	bull that has no defects as an **o**
	4:8	the bull that is the **o** for sin,
	4:10	bull used for the fellowship **o**.
	4:14	sacrifice a bull as an **o** for sin.
	4:20	the bull used as the **o** for sin.
	4:21	It is an **o** for sin for the
	4:23	that has no defects as his **o**.
	4:24	offerings. It is an **o** for sin.
	4:25	take some of the blood of the **o**
	4:26	of the fellowship **o** is burned.
Lev	4:28	that has no defects as his **o**
	4:31	removed from the fellowship **o**.
	4:32	brings a lamb as his **o** for sin,
	4:34	some of the blood from the **o**
	4:35	it on the altar with the **o** by fire
	5:6	Bring your guilt **o** to the LORD
	5:6	sheep or goat as an **o** for sin.
	5:7	or two pigeons as a guilt **o**
	5:7	One will be an **o** for sin,
	5:7	the other a burnt **o**.
	5:8	and he will sacrifice the **o** for
	5:9	some of the blood from the **o**
	5:9	of the altar. It is an **o** for sin.
	5:10	the second bird as a burnt **o**.
	5:11	bring eight cups of flour as an **o**
	5:11	because it is an **o** for sin.
	5:12	reminder on top of the **o** by fire
	5:12	on the altar. It is an **o** for sin.
	5:13	The **o** will belong to the priest
	5:13	to the priest like the grain **o**."
	5:15	bring a guilt **o** to the LORD.
	5:16	the ram sacrificed for the guilt **o**
	5:18	its value in money for a guilt **o**.
	5:19	It is a guilt **o** because you are
	6:5	the day you bring your guilt **o**.
	6:6	bring the LORD your guilt **o**,
	6:9	for the burnt **o** that stays
	6:10	fire that consumed the burnt **o**
	6:12	He will lay the burnt **o** on the
	6:12	burn the fat of the fellowship **o**.
	6:14	the instructions for the grain **o**.
	6:15	handful of flour from the grain **o**
	6:17	It is very holy like the **o** for sin
	6:17	offering for sin and the guilt **o**.
	6:18	to come regarding the **o** by fire
	6:20	"This is the **o** that Aaron and
	6:21	baked pieces of the grain **o** as
	6:23	Every grain **o** made by a priest
	6:25	the instructions for the **o** for sin.
	6:25	The **o** for sin must be
	6:25	the burnt **o** is slaughtered.
	6:26	The priest who makes the **o** for
	6:28	piece of pottery in which the **o**
	6:28	copper kettle in which the **o**
	6:29	priests may eat the **o** for sin.
	6:30	Any **o** for sin must not be eaten
	7:1	the instructions for the guilt **o**.
	7:2	the burnt **o** is slaughtered.
	7:5	It is a guilt **o** by fire to the
	7:7	instructions apply to the **o**
	7:7	offering for sin and the guilt **o**.
	7:8	The skin of the burnt **o** belongs
	7:9	Every grain **o**, whether baked
	7:10	Every grain **o**, whether mixed
	7:11	the fellowship **o** that you must
	7:12	If you offer it as a thank **o**,
	7:13	fellowship **o** of thanksgiving.
	7:14	From every **o** you must bring
	7:14	the blood of the fellowship **o**.
	7:15	meat from your fellowship **o**
	7:16	"If your sacrificial **o** is
	7:16	you vowed or a freewill **o**,
	7:18	from the fellowship **o** is eaten
	7:20	**o** while unclean must
	7:21	the LORD's fellowship **o** must
	7:29	a fellowship **o** must bring
	7:33	and fat of the fellowship **o**,
	7:34	thigh from the contribution **o**.
	7:37	the instructions for the burnt **o**,
	7:37	the grain **o**, the offering for sin,
	7:37	the **o** for sin, the guilt offering,
	7:37	the offering for sin, the guilt **o**,
	7:37	guilt offering, the ordination **o**,
	7:37	and the fellowship **o**.
	8:2	bull that will be the **o** for sin,
	8:14	the bull that was the **o** for sin.
	8:18	forward the ram for the burnt **o**.
	8:21	It was a burnt **o**, a soothing
	8:21	an **o** by fire to the LORD.
	8:22	second ram for the ordination **o**.
	8:27	things to the LORD as an **o**.
	8:28	them on top of the burnt **o**
	8:29	from the ram of the ordination **o**
	8:31	the basket of the ordination **o**.
	9:2	no defects for yourself as an **o**
	9:2	has no defects as a burnt **o**.

Lev 9:3 a male goat as an **o** for sin,
9:3 without defects) as a burnt **o**,
9:4 and a ram as a fellowship **o**,
9:4 and a grain **o** mixed with olive
9:7 to the altar and sacrifice an **o**
9:7 an offering for sin and a burnt **o**
9:7 Also make an **o** for the people,
9:8 the calf as his own **o** for sin.
9:10 and lobe of the liver from the **o**
9:12 the animal for the burnt **o**.
9:13 They also gave him the burnt **o**,
9:14 top of the burnt **o** on the altar.
9:15 the male goat for the people's **o**
9:16 the burnt **o** and sacrificed it.
9:17 He also brought the grain **o**.
9:17 addition to the morning burnt **o**.
9:18 for the people's fellowship **o**.
9:22 He sacrificed the **o** for sin,
9:22 the offering for sin, the burnt **o**,
9:22 and the fellowship **o**.
9:24 and consumed the burnt **o**
10:12 "Take the grain **o** left over from
10:12 left over from the **o** by fire
10:13 it is the part of the **o** by fire
10:16 supposed to be the **o** for sin.
10:17 "Why didn't you eat the **o** for
10:19 "Today they sacrificed their **o**
10:19 offering for sin and their burnt **o**
10:19 If I had eaten the **o** for sin
12:6 one-year-old lamb for a burnt **o**
12:6 mourning dove as an **o** for sin.
12:8 One will be the burnt **o** and the
12:8 and the other the **o** for sin.
14:10 with olive oil for a grain **o** along
14:12 them to the LORD as a guilt **o**.
14:13 where he slaughters the **o**
14:13 offering for sin and the burnt **o**.
14:13 will do this because the guilt **o**,
14:13 guilt offering, like the **o** for sin,
14:14 of the blood from the guilt **o**
14:17 had put the blood of the guilt **o**.
14:19 priest will also sacrifice the **o**
14:19 he will slaughter the burnt **o**.
14:20 priest will sacrifice the burnt **o**
14:20 burnt offering and the grain **o**
14:21 and use it for his guilt **o**.
14:21 with olive oil as a grain **o**,
14:22 The one will be an **o** for sin
14:22 for sin and the other a burnt **o**.
14:24 will take the lamb for the guilt **o**
14:25 slaughter the lamb as a guilt **o**.
14:25 some of the blood of the guilt **o**
14:28 had put the blood of the guilt **o**.
14:31 and sacrifice it as an **o** for sin.
14:31 sacrifice it as a burnt **o** together
14:31 together with the grain **o**.
15:15 priest will sacrifice one as an **o**
15:15 sin and the other as a burnt **o**.
15:30 The priest will offer one as an **o**
15:30 sin and the other as a burnt **o**.
16:3 He must take a bull as an **o** for
16:3 for sin and a ram as a burnt **o**.
16:5 congregation of Israel as an **o**
16:5 for sin and a ram as a burnt **o**.
16:6 the bull as his own **o** for sin.
16:9 lot for the LORD as an **o** for sin.
16:11 it as his own **o** for sin.
16:15 goat for the people's **o** for sin.
16:24 out and sacrifice the burnt **o**
16:25 He will burn the fat of the **o** for
16:27 These animals were the **o** for
19:5 "When you bring a fellowship **o**
19:21 must bring a ram for his guilt **o**
19:24 year all the fruit will be a holy **o**
22:9 they dishonored a holy **o**.
22:10 must never eat any holy **o**,
22:14 "Those who eat a holy **o** by
22:14 must give another holy **o**
22:19 The **o** must be a male that has
22:21 bring the LORD a fellowship **o**
22:21 fulfill a vow or for a freewill **o**.
22:23 in growth as a freewill **o**.
22:25 from a foreigner as a food **o**
22:29 "When you sacrifice a thank **o**
23:12 as a burnt **o** to the LORD.
23:13 Bring a grain **o** of four quarts of
Lev 23:13 quart of wine for the wine **o**.
23:14 when you bring the **o** to your
23:15 of grain as an **o** presented
23:16 a new grain **o** to the LORD.
23:18 They will be a burnt **o** to the
23:19 sacrifice one male goat as an **o**
23:19 lambs as a fellowship **o**.
23:20 the first harvested grain as an **o**
24:7 an **o** by fire to the LORD.
24:9 apart from the LORD's **o** by fire.
27:11 brought to the LORD as an **o**,
Num 4:16 incense, the daily grain **o**,
5:15 of barley flour as an **o** for her.
5:15 since it is a grain **o** brought
5:15 an **o** used for a confession — to
5:18 In her hands he will put the **o**
5:18 the grain **o** brought because of
5:25 The priest will take the grain **o**
5:26 take a handful of the grain **o** as
6:11 priest will sacrifice one as an **o**
6:11 and the other one as a burnt **o**.
6:12 male lamb as an **o** for guilt.
6:14 male lamb as a burnt **o**,
6:14 female lamb as an **o** for sin,
6:14 and a ram as a fellowship **o**.
6:16 to the LORD and make the **o**
6:16 offering for sin and the burnt **o**.
6:17 the ram as a fellowship **o**
6:18 the fire under the fellowship **o**.
6:20 priest will present them as an **o**
7:13 with olive oil as a grain **o**.
7:15 male lamb as a burnt **o**;
7:16 a male goat as an **o** for sin;
7:17 male lambs as a fellowship **o**.
7:19 with olive oil as a grain **o**.
7:21 male lamb as a burnt **o**;
7:22 a male goat as an **o** for sin;
7:23 male lambs as a fellowship **o**.
7:25 with olive oil as a grain **o**.
7:27 male lamb as a burnt **o**;
7:28 a male goat as an **o** for sin;
7:29 male lambs as a fellowship **o**.
7:31 with olive oil as a grain **o**.
7:33 male lamb as a burnt **o**;
7:34 a male goat as an **o** for sin;
7:35 male lambs as a fellowship **o**.
7:37 with olive oil as a grain **o**.
7:39 male lamb as a burnt **o**;
7:40 a male goat as an **o** for sin;
7:41 male lambs as a fellowship **o**.
7:43 with olive oil as a grain **o**.
7:45 male lamb as a burnt **o**;
7:46 a male goat as an **o** for sin;
7:47 male lambs as a fellowship **o**.
7:49 with olive oil as a grain **o**.
7:51 male lamb as a burnt **o**;
7:52 a male goat as an **o** for sin;
7:53 male lambs as a fellowship **o**.
7:55 with olive oil as a grain **o**.
7:57 male lamb as a burnt **o**;
7:58 a male goat as an **o** for sin;
7:59 male lambs as a fellowship **o**.
7:61 with olive oil as a grain **o**.
7:63 male lamb as a burnt **o**;
7:64 a male goat as an **o** for sin;
7:65 male lambs as a fellowship **o**.
7:67 with olive oil as a grain **o**.
7:69 male lamb as a burnt **o**;
7:70 a male goat as an **o** for sin;
7:71 male lambs as a fellowship **o**.
7:73 with olive oil as a grain **o**.
7:75 male lamb as a burnt **o**;
7:76 a male goat as an **o** for sin;
7:77 male lambs as a fellowship **o**.
7:79 with olive oil as a grain **o**.
7:81 male lamb as a burnt **o**;
7:82 a male goat as an **o** for sin;
7:83 male lambs as a fellowship **o**.
8:8 a young bull and the grain **o**
8:8 young bull as an **o** for sin.
8:11 to the LORD as an **o** from
8:12 Sacrifice one of them as an **o**
8:12 and the other one as a burnt **o**
8:13 them as an **o** to the LORD.
8:15 and presented them as an **o**,
8:21 Aaron presented them as an **o**
Num 9:13 You didn't bring your **o** to the
15:3 to fulfill a vow, as a freewill **o**,
15:4 Whoever brings the **o** must
15:4 also give the LORD a grain **o**
15:5 sheep or goat for the burnt **o**
15:5 also give an **o** of one quart of
15:6 "With a ram, give a grain **o** of
15:7 and an **o** of 1 ¼ quarts of
15:8 a young bull as a burnt **o**
15:8 a vow or as a fellowship **o**.
15:9 with the young bull a grain **o**
15:10 Also give an **o** of two quarts of
15:10 It is an **o** by fire, a soothing
15:13 when they bring an **o** by fire,
15:14 If they bring an **o** by fire,
15:24 a young bull as a burnt **o**,
15:24 and a male goat as an **o** for sin.
15:25 an **o** by fire and an offering for
15:25 offering by fire and an **o** for sin.
15:27 be sacrificed as an **o** for sin.
16:15 "Don't accept their **o**.
16:35 250 men who were **o** incense.
18:9 It may come from a grain **o**,
18:9 an **o** for sin, or a guilt offering.
18:9 an offering for sin, or a guilt **o**.
18:9 as a most holy **o** will belong
18:17 and burn the fat as an **o** by fire,
19:9 The cow is an **o** for sin.
19:17 cow that was burned as an **o**
23:3 "Stay here beside your burnt **o**
23:6 him standing beside his burnt **o**
23:15 "Stay here beside your burnt **o**
23:17 him standing beside his burnt **o**
28:3 burnt **o** two one-year-old lambs
28:5 of them⌋ also bring a grain **o**
28:6 This is the daily burnt **o** which
28:6 This **o** is a soothing aroma,
28:6 an **o** by fire to the LORD.
28:7 Also bring a wine **o** of one
28:8 along with the same grain **o**
28:8 and wine **o** as you brought
28:8 This is an **o** by fire,
28:9 a grain **o** of 16 cups of flour
28:9 and the wine **o** that goes with
28:10 This burnt **o** is for every day of
28:11 month bring the LORD a burnt **o**
28:12 each bull there will be a grain **o**
28:12 with each ram a grain **o** of 16
28:13 one-year-old lamb a grain **o**
28:13 This is a burnt **o**, a soothing
28:13 an **o** by fire to the LORD.
28:14 The wine **o** that goes with
28:14 This will be the monthly burnt **o**
28:15 In addition to the daily burnt **o**
28:15 burnt offering with its wine **o**,
28:15 to the LORD as an **o** for sin.
28:19 bring the LORD an **o** by fire,
28:19 a burnt **o** of two young bulls,
28:22 bring one male goat as an **o**
28:23 addition to the morning burnt **o**.
28:24 in addition to the daily burnt **o**
28:24 and the wine **o** that goes
28:26 the LORD your new grain **o**,
28:27 Bring a burnt **o** as a soothing
29:2 As a burnt **o**, a soothing aroma
29:5 bring one male goat as an **o**
29:6 addition to the monthly burnt **o**
29:6 burnt offering with its grain **o**,
29:6 an **o** by fire to the LORD.
29:8 As a burnt **o**, a soothing aroma,
29:11 bring one male goat as an **o**
29:11 sin (in addition to the ⌊other⌋ **o**
29:13 As a burnt **o**, an offering by fire,
29:13 As a burnt offering, an **o** by fire,
29:16 bring one male goat as an **o**
29:19 bring one male goat as an **o**
29:22 bring one male goat as an **o**
29:25 bring one male goat as an **o**
29:28 bring one male goat as an **o**
29:31 bring one male goat as an **o**
29:34 bring one male goat as an **o**
29:36 As a burnt **o**, an offering by fire,
29:36 As a burnt offering, an **o** by fire,
29:38 bring one male goat as an **o**
Dtr 13:16 and all their goods as a burnt **o**
16:10 Bring a freewill **o** in proportion

Dtr 16:16 of the LORD without an **o**.
23:18 your God as an **o** you vowed
26:13 "Nothing is left of the holy **o**
26:14 I didn't eat any of this holy **o**
Jdg 6:26 bull and sacrifice it as a burnt **o**
6:28 been sacrificed as a burnt **o**
9:27 Then they made an **o** of praise
11:31 I will sacrifice it as a burnt **o**."
13:16 But if you make a burnt **o**,
13:19 took a young goat and a grain **o**
13:23 not have accepted our burnt **o**
13:23 our burnt offering and grain **o**.
1Sm 2:13 people who were **o** sacrifices:
3:14 No **o** or sacrifice will ever ⌊be
6:3 proper⌋ place with a guilt **o**.
6:4 "What kind of guilt **o** should we
6:8 you're giving him as a guilt **o**
6:14 cows as a burnt **o** to the LORD.
6:17 the Philistines sent as a guilt **o**
7:9 and sacrificed it as a burnt **o** to
7:10 was sacrificing the burnt **o**,
9:12 today since the people are **o**
13:9 me the animals for the burnt **o**
13:9 So he sacrificed the burnt **o**.
13:10 finished sacrificing the burnt **o**,
13:12 into sacrificing the burnt **o**."
20:6 because his relatives are **o** the
26:19 let him be satisfied with an **o**.
2Sm 15:12 Absalom was **o** sacrifices,
23:16 He poured it out ⌊as an **o**⌋ to
24:12 I'm **o** you three choices.
24:22 There are oxen for the burnt **o**,
1Ki 8:5 Israel were **o** countless sheep
12:33 his altar in Bethel to burn an **o**
18:34 Pour the water on the **o** and on
18:38 and consumed the burnt **o**,
2Ki 3:20 At the time of the grain **o**,
3:27 him on the wall as a burnt **o**.
5:17 I will not offer any burnt **o** or
16:4 and burned incense as an **o** at
16:13 He sacrificed his burnt **o** and
16:13 his burnt offering and grain **o**,
16:13 poured out his wine **o**,
16:13 of his fellowship **o** on the altar.
16:15 and the evening grain **o**,
1Ch 11:18 it out ⌊as an **o**⌋ to the LORD
16:4 of the LORD's ark by **o** prayers,
16:29 Bring an **o**, and come to him.
21:10 I'm **o** you three choices.
21:23 give you oxen for the burnt **o**,
21:23 and wheat for the grain **o**.
29:5 else is willing to make an **o**
29:17 your people here **o** so willingly
2Ch 5:6 Israel were **o** countless sheep
26:18 no right to burn incense as an **o**
28:4 and burned incense as an **o** at
29:21 and seven male goats as an **o**
29:23 brought the male goats for the **o**
29:24 and made their blood an **o**
29:28 until the burnt **o** was finished.
Ezr 6:17 12 male goats as an **o** for sin,
8:35 12 male goats for an **o** for sin.
10:19 a ram from their flock as an **o**
Job 42:8 make a burnt **o** for yourselves.
Psa 54:6 to you along with a freewill **o**.
56:12 I will keep my vows by **o**
96:8 Bring an **o**, and come into his
Pro 20:25 "This is a holy **o**!"
21:3 to the LORD than **o** a sacrifice.
Isa 40:16 are not enough to burn an **o**.
40:16 not enough for a single burnt **o**.
66:20 from every nation like a grain **o**
Jer 7:9 burn incense as an **o** to Baal,
11:17 incense as an **o** to Baal.
18:15 They burn incense as an **o** to
19:4 by burning incense as an **o**
44:5 incense as an **o** to other gods.
Eze 43:19 to the priests as an **o** for sin.
43:21 a young bull as an **o** for sin,
43:22 has no defects as an **o** for sin.
43:25 from the flock as an **o** for sin.
44:27 he must bring his **o** for sin,
45:19 take some blood from the **o**
45:22 a young bull as an **o** for sin.
45:23 one male goat as an **o** for sin.
45:24 He must also give as a grain **o**

Eze 46:4 that has no defects as a burnt **o**
46:5 The grain **o** that is to be
46:5 and the grain **o** that is to be
46:6 the burnt **o** must be one young
46:7 each ram the **o** must include
46:7 and with each lamb the **o** must
46:11 a grain **o** of a half-bushel must
46:12 prepares a freewill burnt **o**,
46:12 either a burnt **o** or a fellowship
46:12 burnt offering or a fellowship **o**
46:13 defects every day as a burnt **o**
46:14 Also, prepare a grain **o** with it
46:14 It will be a grain **o** dedicated to
46:15 Prepare the lamb, the grain **o**,
46:15 morning as a daily burnt **o**.
46:20 boil the meat for the guilt **o**
46:20 guilt offering and the **o** for sin.
Dan 8:11 took the daily burnt **o** from him
8:12 put a stop to the daily burnt **o**.
8:13 this vision — the daily burnt **o**,
11:31 take away the daily burnt **o**,
12:11 From the time the daily burnt **o**
Hos 2:13 she burned incense as an **o**
9:4 It will not be brought ⌊as an **o**⌋
Amo 4:5 Burn bread as a thank **o**.
Zep 3:10 people, will bring my **o**.
Hag 2:14 Whatever **o** they bring is
Zec 6:10 "Take an **o** from the exiles
Mal 1:8 Try **o** it to your governor.
Mat 5:23 "So if you are **o** your gift at the
Mar 7:11 is corban (that is, an **o** to God),
12:41 sat facing the temple **o** box,
Luk 21:1 their gifts into the temple **o** box.
Rom 15:16 to God as an acceptable **o**,
1Co 10:19 Do I mean that an **o** made to a
Eph 5:2 life for us as an **o** and sacrifice,
Heb 13:11 the holy place as an **o** for sin.

offerings (443)

Exo 10:25 sacrifices and burnt **o** we have
20:24 Sacrifice your burnt **o** and your
20:24 offerings and your fellowship **o**,
24:5 they sacrificed bulls as burnt **o**
24:5 and fellowship **o** to the LORD.
25:29 to be used for pouring wine **o**.
28:38 their holy **o** — whatever their
28:38 the LORD will accept their **o**.
29:28 LORD from the fellowship **o**.
29:33 They will eat those **o** through
29:33 them because the **o** are holy.
30:9 on this altar or any burnt **o**
30:9 or any burnt offerings or grain **o**
30:28 the altar for burnt **o** and all its
31:9 the altar for burnt **o** and all its
32:6 the people sacrificed burnt **o**
32:6 and brought fellowship **o**.
35:16 the altar for burnt **o** with its
36:3 him freewill **o** every morning.
37:16 to be used for pouring wine **o**.
38:1 He made the altar for burnt **o**
38:24 of gold from the **o** presented
38:29 The bronze from the **o**
40:6 "Put the altar for burnt **o** in front
40:10 Anoint the altar for burnt **o** and
40:29 He put the altar for burnt **o** at
40:29 He sacrificed burnt **o** and grain
40:29 burnt offerings and grain **o** on it
Lev 2:12 bring them to the LORD as **o**
2:13 put salt on each of your grain **o**.
2:13 never be left out of your grain **o**.
2:13 Put salt on all your **o**.
4:7 bottom of the altar for burnt **o** at
4:10 lay them on the altar for burnt **o**.
4:18 bottom of the altar for burnt **o** at
4:24 slaughters animals for burnt **o**.
4:25 the horns of the altar for burnt **o**
4:25 bottom of the altar for burnt **o**.
4:29 for burnt **o** are slaughtered.
4:30 the horns of the altar for burnt **o**
4:33 slaughters animals for burnt **o**.
4:34 the horns of the altar for burnt **o**
4:35 removed from the fellowship **o**.
6:17 share from the **o** by fire made
7:7 Both **o** belong to the priest to
7:34 From the fellowship **o** of the
7:38 commands about these **o** at

Lev 7:38 the Israelites to bring their **o**
8:28 These were ordination **o**,
8:28 ordination offerings, **o** by fire,
9:15 He brought the people's **o**.
10:14 fellowship **o** from the Israelites.
14:11 bring the person and his **o** into
17:5 as fellowship **o** to the LORD.
17:8 make burnt **o** or sacrifices
22:2 must respect the holy **o** which
22:3 comes near the holy **o** the
22:4 may eat any of the holy **o** until
22:6 not eat any of the holy **o** unless
22:7 Then he may eat the holy **o**
22:15 not dishonor the holy **o** that
22:16 have eaten the priests' holy **o**.
22:18 or foreigners may bring burnt **o**
22:18 they vowed or as freewill **o**.
23:18 With these **o** also bring grain
23:18 also bring grain and wine **o**.
23:37 Bring burnt **o**, grain offerings,
23:37 Bring burnt offerings, grain **o**,
23:37 and wine **o** — each one on its
23:38 your freewill **o** to the LORD.
Num 4:7 and pitchers for the wine **o**.
5:9 over and above the holy **o** that
5:10 Each person's holy **o** will
6:14 They must bring these **o** to the
6:15 grain **o** and wine offerings.
6:15 grain offerings and wine **o**.
6:16 "The priest will bring these **o** to
6:17 the grain **o** and wine offerings.
6:17 the grain offerings and wine **o**.
6:21 have vowed to bring their **o**
6:21 They must bring these **o** in
7:2 census — came to give their **o**.
7:10 The leaders also brought **o** for
7:87 for the burnt **o** was 12 young
7:87 along with their grain **o**.
7:87 goats were used as **o** for sin.
7:88 for fellowship **o** was 24 bulls,
9:7 won't you let us bring our **o**
9:7 of the Israelites bring their **o**?"
10:10 when you sacrifice your burnt **o**
10:10 offerings and fellowship **o**.
15:3 you may bring **o** by fire to the
15:3 They may be burnt **o** or any
15:3 or as one of your festival **o**.
15:3 or goats — **o** that are a soothing
15:24 the proper grain and wine **o**,
15:25 and they brought these two **o**
18:9 That part of the most holy **o**
18:11 taken from the **o** presented by
18:32 dishonoring the holy **o** given by
28:2 Be sure to bring me my **o** at the
28:2 They are **o** by fire,
28:3 These are the **o** by fire that you
28:10 in addition to the daily burnt **o**
28:10 offerings and the wine **o** that go
28:20 Along with them bring grain **o**
28:24 Bring all these **o** on each of the
28:24 They are **o** by fire,
28:28 Along with them bring grain **o**
28:31 defects along with their wine **o**,
28:31 in addition to the daily burnt **o**
28:31 offerings and their grain **o**."
29:3 Along with them bring grain **o**
29:6 and the daily burnt **o** with their
29:6 with their proper grain **o**
29:6 grain offerings and wine **o**.
29:9 Along with them bring grain **o**
29:11 the LORD) and the daily burnt **o**
29:11 their grain **o** and wine offerings.
29:11 their grain offerings and wine **o**.
29:14 Along with them bring grain **o**
29:16 in addition to the daily burnt **o**
29:16 their grain **o** and wine offerings.
29:16 their grain offerings and wine **o**.
29:18 the proper amount of grain **o**
29:18 of grain offerings and wine **o**
29:19 in addition to the daily burnt **o**
29:19 their grain **o** and wine offerings.
29:19 their grain offerings and wine **o**.
29:21 the proper amount of grain **o**
29:21 of grain offerings and wine **o**
29:22 in addition to the daily burnt **o**
29:22 their grain **o** and wine offerings.

Num 29:22 their grain offerings and wine **o**.
29:24 the proper amount of grain **o**
29:24 of grain offerings and wine **o**
29:25 in addition to the daily burnt **o**
29:25 their grain **o** and wine offerings.
29:25 their grain offerings and wine **o**.
29:27 the proper amount of grain **o**
29:27 of grain offerings and wine **o**
29:28 in addition to the daily burnt **o**
29:28 their grain **o** and wine offerings.
29:28 their grain offerings and wine **o**.
29:30 the proper amount of grain **o**
29:30 of grain offerings and wine **o**
29:31 in addition to the daily burnt **o**
29:31 their grain **o** and wine offerings.
29:31 their grain offerings and wine **o**.
29:33 the proper amount of grain **o**
29:33 of grain offerings and wine **o**
29:34 in addition to the daily burnt **o**
29:34 their grain **o** and wine offerings.
29:34 their grain offerings and wine **o**.
29:37 the proper amount of grain **o**
29:37 of grain offerings and wine **o**
29:38 in addition to the daily burnt **o**
29:38 their grain **o** and wine offerings.
29:38 their grain offerings and wine **o**.
29:39 "These are the **o** you must
29:39 They are the **o** you must bring
29:39 must bring in addition to the **o**
29:39 to the LORD, your freewill **o**,
29:39 freewill offerings, your burnt **o**,
29:39 burnt offerings, your grain **o**,
29:39 grain offerings, your wine **o**,
29:39 and your fellowship **o**."
Dtr 12:6 Bring him your burnt **o**,
12:6 the **o** you vow to bring,
12:6 vow to bring, your freewill **o**,
12:11 Bring your burnt **o**,
12:11 and all the best **o** you vow to
12:13 burnt **o** wherever you want.
12:17 may not eat ⌊the LORD's **o**⌋
12:17 Those **o** are: one-tenth of your
12:17 the **o** you vow to bring;
12:17 vow to bring; your freewill **o**;
12:26 Take the holy things and the **o**
12:27 and the blood of your burnt **o**
27:6 Sacrifice burnt **o** on it to the
27:7 Sacrifice fellowship **o**,
32:38 the wine from their wine **o**?
33:10 sacrifice burnt **o** on your altar.
Jos 8:31 They made burnt **o** to the
8:31 fellowship **o** on the altar.
22:23 if we built it for making burnt **o**,
22:23 grain **o**, or fellowship offerings,
22:23 grain offerings, or fellowship **o**,
22:26 not be for burnt **o** or sacrifices,
22:27 of the LORD with our burnt **o**,
22:27 and fellowship **o**.' Then
22:28 They didn't make it for burnt **o**
22:29 by building an altar for burnt **o**,
22:29 altar for burnt offerings, grain **o**
Jdg 20:26 Then they sacrificed burnt **o**
20:26 and fellowship **o** to the LORD.
21:4 **o** and fellowship offerings.
21:4 offerings and fellowship **o**.
1Sm 2:17 men were treating the **o** made
2:28 to sacrifice burnt **o** on my altar,
2:29 my sacrifices and grain **o** that
6:15 Shemesh presented burnt **o**
10:8 I will come to sacrifice burnt **o**
10:8 and make fellowship **o**.
11:15 they sacrificed fellowship **o**
13:9 offering and the fellowship **o**."
15:22 LORD as delighted with burnt **o**
2Sm 6:17 David sacrificed burnt **o** and
6:17 burnt offerings and fellowship **o**
6:18 finished sacrificing the burnt **o**
6:18 offerings and the fellowship **o**,
24:25 there and sacrificed burnt **o**
24:25 offerings and fellowship **o**.
1Ki 3:4 1,000 burnt **o** on that altar.
3:15 He sacrificed burnt **o** and
3:15 burnt offerings and fellowship **o**
8:63 120,000 sheep as fellowship **o**
8:64 He sacrificed the burnt **o**,
8:64 the burnt offerings, grain **o**,
1Ki 8:64 the fat from the fellowship **o**
9:25 year Solomon sacrificed burnt **o**
9:25 burnt offerings and fellowship **o**
10:5 and the burnt **o** that he
2Ki 10:24 to offer sacrifices and burnt **o**.
10:25 When the burnt **o** had been
12:16 The money from the guilt **o** and
12:16 the guilt offerings and the **o**
16:15 must burn the morning burnt **o**
16:15 the king's burnt **o** and grain
16:15 burnt offerings and grain **o**,
16:15 and the burnt **o**, grain offerings,
16:15 and the burnt offerings, grain **o**,
16:15 and wine **o** of all the people of
16:15 all the blood of the burnt **o**
1Ch 6:49 on the altar for burnt **o**
16:1 They presented burnt **o** and
16:1 fellowship **o** in God's presence.
16:2 had finished sacrificing burnt **o**
16:2 offerings and fellowship **o**,
16:40 ordered to sacrifice burnt **o**
16:40 the altar of burnt **o** continually,
21:26 there and sacrificed burnt **o**
21:26 offerings and fellowship **o**.
21:26 heaven on the altar for burnt **o**.
21:29 and the altar for burnt **o** were at
22:1 Israel's altar for burnt **o** will
23:29 the flour for the grain **o**,
23:31 whenever burnt **o** were made—
29:21 They sacrificed burnt **o** to the
29:21 rams, 1,000 lambs, wine **o**,
2Ch 1:6 sacrificed 1,000 burnt **o** on it.
2:4 I want to ⌊sacrifice⌋ burnt **o**
4:6 prepared for the burnt **o** in them
7:1 and consumed the burnt **o**
7:7 He sacrificed the burnt **o**,
7:7 the burnt offerings, grain **o**,
8:12 Solomon sacrificed burnt **o**
9:4 and the burnt **o** that he
13:11 They sacrifice burnt **o** to the
23:18 appointed to sacrifice burnt **o**
23:18 They made these **o** with joy
24:14 for the service and for the **o**.
24:14 they sacrificed burnt **o** in the
29:7 incense or sacrifice burnt **o**
29:18 includes the altar for burnt **o**,
29:24 king had said that the burnt **o**
29:24 that the burnt offerings and **o**
29:27 the sacrificing of burnt **o**
29:27 When the burnt **o** started,
29:29 When the burnt **o** were finished
29:31 bring sacrifices and thank **o** to
29:31 brought sacrifices and thank **o**,
29:31 was willing brought burnt **o**.
29:32 The burnt **o** brought by the
29:32 were burnt **o** to the LORD.
29:34 help to skin all the burnt **o**.
29:35 There were many burnt **o** in
29:35 to the fat of the fellowship **o**
29:35 and wine **o** that accompanied
29:35 that accompanied the burnt **o**.
30:15 Then they brought burnt **o** to
30:22 sacrificed fellowship **o**,
31:2 sacrificing burnt **o**,
31:2 sacrificing fellowship **o**,
31:3 the king's property for burnt **o**
31:3 the morning and evening **o**,
31:3 burnt **o** on the weekly worship
31:5 brought plenty of **o** from
31:10 the people started to bring the **o**
31:12 the **o** of one-tenth of the crops,
31:14 take care of the freewill **o** made
31:14 was to distribute the **o** made
31:15 They were to distribute the **o**
31:16 Kore were to distribute the **o**
31:17 They were to distribute **o** to the
31:19 to give a portion of the **o**
33:16 and sacrificed fellowship **o**
33:16 offerings and thank **o** on it.
35:7 to be sacrificed as Passover **o**
35:12 They set aside the burnt **o** to
35:13 They boiled the holy **o** in pots,
35:14 were sacrificing the burnt **o**
35:16 and the burnt **o** were sacrificed
Ezr 1:4 and freewill **o** to be used in
2:68 they contributed freewill **o** to
Ezr 3:2 it in order to sacrifice burnt **o**.
3:3 They sacrificed burnt **o** on it to
3:4 the required number of burnt **o**.
3:5 sacrificed the daily burnt **o**,
3:5 the **o** for the New Moon
3:5 and all the freewill **o** brought to
3:6 started to bring these burnt **o**
6:9 in Jerusalem need for burnt **o**
8:28 silver and gold are freewill **o**
8:35 from captivity sacrificed burnt **o**
8:35 were burnt **o** for the LORD.
Neh 10:33 and for the daily grain **o** and
10:33 offerings and daily burnt **o**,
10:33 for the holy gifts and **o** for sin
13:5 had been used to store grain **o**,
13:9 temple, the **o**, and the incense.
Job 1:5 morning and sacrifice burnt **o**
Psa 16:4 not pour out their sacrificial **o**
20:3 will remember all your grain **o**
20:3 look with favor on your burnt **o**.
40:6 pleased with sacrifices and **o**.
40:6 You did not ask for burnt **o** or
50:8 for your sacrifices or burnt **o**,
51:16 are not pleased with burnt **o**.
51:19 in the right spirit—with burnt **o**
51:19 offerings and whole burnt **o**.
66:13 into your temple with burnt **o**.
66:15 of fattened livestock for burnt **o**
Isa 1:11 I've had enough of your burnt **o**
1:13 any more worthless grain **o**.
19:21 with sacrifices and food **o**.
43:23 bring me sheep for your burnt **o**
43:23 burden you by requiring grain **o**
43:23 you by requiring incense **o**.
56:7 Their burnt **o** and their
57:6 You have given them wine **o**
57:6 and sacrificed grain **o** to them.
60:7 sacrificed as acceptable ⌊**o**⌋
66:20 of Israel who bring their grain **o**
Jer 6:20 I won't accept your burnt **o**.
7:18 They pour out wine **o** to other
7:21 Add your burnt **o** to your
7:22 about burnt **o** and sacrifices.
14:12 Even if they sacrifice burnt **o**
14:12 burnt offerings and grain **o**,
17:26 They will bring burnt **o**,
17:26 grain **o**, and incense.
17:26 They will also bring thank **o** to
19:13 out wine **o** to other gods."
32:29 pour out wine **o** to other gods.
33:11 hear those who bring thank **o**
33:18 presence to sacrifice burnt **o**,
33:18 burnt offerings, to burn grain **o**,
41:5 They brought grain **o** and
44:17 of heaven and pour out wine **o**
44:18 and pouring out wine **o** to her,
44:19 poured out wine **o** to her,
44:23 You burned incense as **o** to
44:25 and pour out wine **o** to her.'
48:35 those who bring **o** to their
52:19 and the bowls used for wine **o**.
Eze 6:13 the places where they made **o**
16:21 them as burnt **o** to idols.
20:28 sacrifices and brought **o** there
20:28 and poured out their wine **o**.
20:40 There I will look for your **o**,
23:37 to for me as burnt **o** to idols.
40:38 the animals for the burnt **o**.
40:39 were slaughtered for burnt **o**,
40:39 **o** for sin, and guilt offerings.
40:39 offerings for sin, and guilt **o**.
40:42 made of cut stone for burnt **o**.
40:42 for burnt **o** and sacrifices.
42:13 the LORD eat the holiest **o**.
42:13 priests keep the holiest **o** there:
42:13 the grain **o**, the offerings for sin,
42:13 the grain offerings, the **o** for sin,
42:13 offerings for sin, and the guilt **o**.
43:18 the rules for sacrificing burnt **o**
43:24 them as burnt **o** to the LORD.
43:27 priests must sacrifice burnt **o**
43:27 burnt offerings and fellowship **o**
44:11 the animals for the burnt **o**
44:29 They will eat grain **o**,
44:29 **o** for sin, and guilt offerings.
44:29 offerings for sin, and guilt **o**.

Eze 45:15 sacrifice them with grain **o**,
45:15 with grain offerings, burnt **o**,
45:15 and fellowship **o** to make
45:17 responsible to provide burnt **o**,
45:17 provide burnt offerings, grain **o**,
45:17 and wine **o** at the annual
45:17 He must prepare **o** for sin,
45:17 for sin, grain **o**, burnt offerings,
45:17 for sin, grain offerings, burnt **o**,
45:17 and fellowship **o** to make
45:23 he must prepare burnt **o** for the
45:25 prepare the same **o** for sin,
45:25 for sin, burnt **o**, grain offerings,
45:25 offerings, grain **o**, and olive oil.
46:2 prepare the prince's burnt **o**
46:2 offerings and fellowship **o**.
46:12 He must sacrifice burnt **o** and
46:12 offerings and fellowship **o** as
46:20 must bake grain **o** so that they
46:20 don't have to bring the **o** into
Dan 2:46 He ordered that gifts and **o** be
9:27 stop the sacrifices and food **o**.
Hos 6:6 not to give me burnt **o**.
8:11 of Ephraim build to make **o**
9:4 They won't pour wine **o** to the
Joe 1:9 Grain **o** and wine offerings are
1:9 Grain offerings and wine **o** are
1:13 Grain **o** and wine offerings are
1:13 Grain offerings and wine **o** are
2:14 Then you could give grain **o**
2:14 give grain offerings and wine **o**
Amo 4:5 and boast about your freewill **o**.
5:22 though you bring me burnt **o**
5:22 me burnt offerings and grain **o**,
5:22 even look at the fellowship **o**
5:25 bring me sacrifices and grain **o**
Mic 6:6 him year-old calves as burnt **o**?
Mal 1:10 "and I won't accept your **o**.
1:11 Incense and pure **o** will be
1:13 When you bring such **o**,
2:12 tents and from bringing **o**
2:13 longer pays attention to your **o**
2:14 "Why ⌊aren't our **o** accepted⌋?"
3:3 acceptable **o** to the LORD.
3:4 The **o** from Judah and
Mar 12:33 all the burnt **o** and sacrifices."
Act 7:42 bring me sacrifices and grain **o**
24:17 for the poor and **o** ⌊for God⌋.
Heb 10:5 did not want sacrifices and **o**,
10:6 You did not approve of burnt **o**
10:8 sacrifices, **o**, burnt offerings,
10:8 burnt **o**, and sacrifices for sin.

offers (16)

Lev 7:9 belongs to the priest who **o** it.
7:29 Anyone who **o** the LORD a
20:16 When a woman **o** herself
Psa 50:23 Whoever **o** thanks as a
Isa 66:3 Whoever **o** a grain sacrifice is
66:3 someone who ⌊**o**⌋ pig's blood.
Lam 1:2 no one **o** it comfort.
1:9 No one **o** it comfort.
1:17 No one **o** it comfort.
1:21 No one **o** me comfort.
Eze 46:16 Suppose the prince **o** one of
46:17 But suppose the prince **o** a gift
1Co 9:23 in order to share what it **o**.
Php 3:14 heavenly call **o** in Christ Jesus.
1Jn 2:15 love the world and what it **o**.
2:16 Not everything that the world **o**

office (6)

2Ch 36:3 of Egypt removed him from **o**
Neh 13:29 contaminated the priestly **o**
Isa 22:19 "I will remove you from your **o**
Mat 9:9 he saw a man sitting in a tax **o**.
Mar 2:14 of Alphaeus, sitting in a tax **o**.
Luk 5:27 named Levi sitting in a tax **o**.

officer (81)

Exo 14:7 placing an **o** in each of them.
Jdg 9:28 and isn't Zebul his **o**?
1Ki 20:20 Each **o** killed his opponent.
22:9 Israel called for an **o** and said,
2Ki 1:9 The king sent an army **o** with
1:9 When the **o** found Elijah sitting
2Ki 1:10 Elijah answered the **o**,
1:10 heaven and burned up the **o**
1:11 The king sent another **o** with
1:11 The **o** said, "Man of God,
1:12 Elijah answered the **o**,
1:12 heaven and burned up the **o**
1:13 The king sent a third **o** with 50
1:13 The **o** of the third group went
1:13 The **o** begged him,
5:6 It read, "I'm sending my **o**
15:25 His **o** Pekah, son of Remaliah,
25:8 captain of the guard and an **o**
1Ch 12:20 Each one was an **o** over 1,000
13:1 David consulted with every **o**
2Ch 18:8 Israel called for an **o** and said,
24:11 the chief priest's **o** would empty
26:11 Jeiel and the **o** Maaseiah.
Pro 6:7 Although it has no overseer, **o**,
Jer 20:1 the chief **o** of the LORD's
39:3 Samgar Nebo (the chief **o**),
52:12 captain of the guard and an **o**
Mat 5:25 will hand you over to an **o**,
8:5 a Roman army **o** came to beg
8:6 The **o** said, "Sir, my servant is
8:8 The **o** responded, "Sir, I don't
8:13 Jesus told the **o**, "Go!
27:54 An army **o** and those watching
Mar 15:39 When the **o** who stood facing
15:44 So he summoned the **o** to ask
15:45 When the **o** had assured him
Luk 7:3 The **o** had heard about Jesus
7:6 house when the **o** sent friends
7:9 Jesus was amazed at the **o**
12:58 you over to an **o** who will throw
23:47 When an army **o** saw what had
Jon 18:12 Then the army **o** and the
Act 4:1 Some priests, the **o** in charge
5:24 When the **o** of the temple
5:26 Then the **o** of the temple
5:26 After all, the **o** and his guards
10:1 He was a Roman army **o** in the
10:22 a Roman army **o**, sent us.
21:31 the **o** in charge of the Roman
21:32 When the crowd saw the **o** and
21:33 Then the **o** went to Paul,
21:33 The **o** asked who Paul was
21:34 The **o** couldn't get any facts
21:37 the barracks, he asked the **o**,
21:37 The **o** replied to Paul,
21:40 The **o** gave Paul permission to
22:24 So the **o** ordered the soldiers to
22:24 The **o** wanted to find out why
22:26 it to his commanding **o**.
22:27 The **o** went to Paul and asked
22:28 The **o** replied, "I paid a lot of
22:29 The **o** was afraid when he
22:30 The **o** wanted to find out
22:30 So the **o** released Paul the
22:30 Then the **o** brought Paul and
23:10 and the **o** was afraid that they
23:10 So the **o** ordered his soldiers to
23:15 council must go to the Roman **o**
23:17 "Take this young man to the **o**.
23:18 young man to the **o** and said,
23:19 The **o** took the young man by
23:22 The **o** dismissed the young
23:23 Then the **o** summoned two of
23:25 The **o** wrote a letter to the
24:22 "When the **o** Lysias arrives,
27:1 were turned over to an army **o**.
27:6 In Myra the **o** found a ship from
27:11 However, the **o** was persuaded
27:31 Paul told the **o** and the soldiers,
27:43 the **o** wanted to save Paul,
2Ti 2:4 pleases his commanding **o**.

officer's (1)

Luk 7:2 **o** valuable slave was sick

officers (111)

Exo 15:4 Pharaoh's best **o** were drowned
Num 11:16 you know are leaders and **o**
31:14 Moses was angry with the **o** of
31:48 Then the **o** from the military
Dtr 1:15 men and made them **o**
16:18 Appoint judges and **o** for your
Dtr 20:5 The **o** should tell the troops,
20:8 The **o** should also tell the
20:9 When the **o** finish speaking to
29:10 tribes, your leaders, your **o**,
31:28 of your tribes and your **o**
Jos 1:10 ordered the **o** of the people,
3:2 Three days later the **o** went
8:33 native Israelites, the leaders, **o**,
10:24 He told the **o** who had gone
23:2 and **o** of Israel together.
24:1 leaders, chiefs, judges, and **o**,
Jdg 5:14 The **o** from Zebulun also went.
1Sm 8:12 He will appoint them to be his **o**
18:22 Saul ordered his **o**,
18:22 and all his **o** are fond of you.
18:23 When Saul's **o** made it a point
18:24 When the **o** told Saul what
18:26 When his **o** told David this,
18:30 than the rest of Saul's **o**.
19:1 his son Jonathan and all his **o**
21:11 Achish's **o** asked, "Isn't this
21:14 Achish said to his **o**,
22:7 Will he make you all **o** over a
28:7 Saul told his **o**, "Find me a
28:7 His **o** told him, "There is a
28:23 Nevertheless, his **o** and the
28:25 she served it to Saul and his **o**.
29:3 The Philistine **o** asked,
29:3 Achish asked the Philistine **o**,
29:4 But the Philistine **o** were angry
29:4 the Philistine **o** told him.
29:9 However, the Philistine **o** said,
2Sm 2:12 Ner's son Abner and the **o** of
2:13 David's **o** also left ⌊Hebron⌋.
2:15 twelve were from David's **o**.
2:30 ⌊only⌋ 19 of David's **o** and
2:31 However, David's **o** had killed
3:38 The king said to his **o**,
1Ki 9:22 soldiers, officials, **o**, generals,
9:23 These were the **o** in charge of
11:26 He was one of Solomon's **o**,
20:12 He told his **o** to get ready.
20:14 by using the young **o** of the
20:15 Ahab counted the young **o** of
20:17 The young **o** of the district
20:19 The young **o** of the district
20:23 Meanwhile, the **o** of King
20:31 His **o** told him, "We have heard
2Ki 1:14 and burned up the first two **o**
6:8 he asked for advice from his **o**
6:11 He called his **o** and asked
6:12 One of his **o** answered,
7:12 up at night and told his **o** what
7:13 One of his **o** replied,
18:24 **o** when you trust
23:30 His **o** put his dead body in a
24:10 At that time the **o** of King
24:11 while his **o** were blockading
25:24 be afraid of the Babylonian **o**.
1Ch 12:14 of Gad were army **o**.
12:18 made them **o** over his troops.
12:28 from whose family came 22 **o**.
23:4 appointed to be **o** and judges,
24:5 lots so that there were **o**
24:5 officers for the holy place and **o**
27:1 and **o** who were serving the
27:3 was head of all of the army's **o**
27:16 The following **o** were in charge
2Ch 8:9 were the soldiers, **o**, generals,
8:10 These were the **o** in charge of
11:11 them and put army **o**
17:7 he sent his **o** Ben Hail,
19:11 The Levites will serve as **o** of
24:11 brought the box to the king's **o**
32:3 he, his **o**, and his military staff
32:9 he sent his **o** to King Hezekiah
32:16 Sennacherib's **o** said more
32:18 Sennacherib's **o** shouted loudly
35:23 The king told his **o**,
35:24 His **o** took him out of the
Neh 2:9 (The king had sent army **o** and
Est 1:3 the military **o** of the Persians
8:9 and **o** of the 127 provinces from
Psa 105:22 Joseph trained the king's **o** the
Isa 31:9 and their **o** will be frightened at
36:9 **o** when you trust

Jer 36:14 and went with him to see the o.
38:17 If you surrender to the o of the
38:18 if you don't surrender to the o
38:22 king will be brought out to the o
39:3 Then all the o of the king of
39:3 and all the rest of the o of the
41:1 family and of the king's o) went
46:26 of Babylon and his o.
51:57 their governors, o, and soldiers.
Eze 23:15 Babylonian o who were born
23:23 military o and important men.
Dan 3:2 advisers, treasurers, judges, o,
3:3 advisers, treasurers, judges, o,
11:5 but one of his o will become
Nah 3:17 Your o are like locusts,
Mar 6:21 for his top officials, army o,
Act 18:17 governor's o, took Sosthenes,
21:32 he took some soldiers and o
25:23 Roman army o and the most

officers' (2)

1Ki 10:5 his o seating arrangement,
2Ch 9:4 his o seating arrangement,

official (86)

Gen 23:18 city gate were the o witnesses
Exo 35:19 the special clothes worn for o
39:1 clothes worn for o duties
Lev 5:15 according to the o standards
1Ki 14:19 and his reign is written in the o
14:29 did — written in the o records
15:7 did — written in the o records
15:23 written in the o records
15:31 did — written in the o records
16:5 acts — written in the o records
16:14 did — written in the o records
16:20 his plot written in the o records
16:27 acts — written in the o records
22:39 written in the o records
22:45 written in the o records
2Ki 1:18 did — written in the o records
8:23 did — written in the o records
10:5 So the o in charge of the
10:34 acts — written in the o records
12:19 did — written in the o records
13:8 acts — written in the o records
13:12 Judah — written in the o records
14:15 Judah — written in the o records
14:18 written in the o records
14:28 Israel — written in the o records
15:6 did — written in the o records
15:11 is written in the o records
15:15 is written in the o records
15:21 did — written in the o records
15:26 did — is written in the o records
15:31 did — is written in the o records
15:36 did — written in the o records
16:19 did — written in the o records
20:20 written in the o records of the
21:17 written in the o records
21:25 he did — written in the o record
22:12 and the royal o Asaiah.
23:28 did — written in the o records
24:5 did — written in the o records
1Ch 9:11 the son of Ahitub (the o in
9:20 had been the o in charge of the
26:24 He was the highest-ranking o
27:24 never included in the o records
2Ch 34:20 and the royal o Asaiah.
Ezr 4:15 that you should search the o
4:15 You will find in those o records
Neh 3:9 an o in charge of half a district
3:12 an o in charge of half a district
3:14 the o in charge of the district of
3:15 Shallun, Col Hozeh's son, the o
3:16 the o in charge of half the
3:17 Next to him Hashabiah, the o
3:18 the o in charge of half the
3:19 the o in charge of Mizpah,
Est 1:22 He sent o documents to all the
2:23 king's presence in his o record
3:13 Messengers were sent with o
6:1 to bring the o daily records,
8:5 cancel the o orders
8:10 and sealed the o documents
9:20 things down and sent o letters
Est 9:30 Mordecai sent o documents
Jer 38:7 But an o in the royal palace,
39:13 Nebushazban (the chief o),
Dan 2:15 He asked Arioch, the royal o,
11:20 He will have a cruel o go out in
Luk 18:18 An o asked Jesus,
18:21 The o replied, "I've obeyed all
18:23 When the o heard this,
Jon 4:46 A government o was in Cana.
4:47 The o heard that Jesus had
4:48 Jesus told the o, "If people
4:49 The o said to him,
4:51 While the o was on his way to
4:52 The o asked them at what time
4:53 So the o and his entire family
Act 8:27 a high-ranking o in charge of all
8:28 As the o rode along in his
8:30 and could hear the o reading
8:31 The o answered, "How can I
8:32 that the o was reading:
8:34 The o said to Philip,
8:35 Philip told the o the Good
8:36 The o said to Philip,
8:38 The o ordered the carriage to
8:39 The o joyfully continued on his

officially (1)

Rom 15:28 completed and I have o turned

officials (198)

Gen 12:15 When Pharaoh's o saw her,
20:8 called together all his o.
37:36 one of Pharaoh's o and captain
39:1 one of Pharaoh's Egyptian o
40:7 So he asked these o of
45:16 and his o were pleased.
50:7 All Pharaoh's o, the leaders in
Exo 5:21 Pharaoh and his o hate us.
7:10 in front of Pharaoh and his o,
7:20 In front of Pharaoh and his o,
8:3 into the houses of your o,
8:4 and on all your o."
8:9 you, your o, and your people.
8:11 your o, and your people.
8:21 on you, your o, your people,
8:24 and into the houses of his o.
8:29 you, your o, and your people.
8:31 Pharaoh, his o, and his people.
9:14 as well as your o and people.
9:30 But I know that you and your o
9:34 He and his o continued to be
10:1 I have made him and his o
10:6 and the houses of all your o
10:7 Then Pharaoh's o asked him,
11:3 respected by Pharaoh's o
11:8 Then all these o of yours will
12:30 Pharaoh, all his o,
14:5 he and his o changed their
Dtr 29:2 Egypt to Pharaoh, to all his o,
34:11 Egypt to Pharaoh, to all his o,
Jdg 8:14 for him the names of the 77 o
1Sm 8:14 and give them to his o.
8:15 and give it to his aids and o.
16:15 Saul's o told him, "An evil spirit
16:17 Saul told his o, "Please find
16:18 One of the o said, "I know one
18:5 including Saul's o.
22:6 all his o standing around him.
22:7 He said to his o, "Listen here,
22:9 standing with Saul's o,
22:14 "But whom among all your o
2Sm 12:18 But David's o were afraid to tell
12:19 But when David saw that his o
12:21 His o asked him, "Why are you
13:24 Your Majesty and your o are
1Ki 1:2 His o told him, "Your Majesty,
1:9 men of Judah, and the king's o.
1:33 "Take my o with you.
1:47 Furthermore, the royal o have
3:15 and held a banquet for all his o.
4:2 these were his o: Azariah,
5:1 King Hiram of Tyre sent his o
9:22 Instead, they were soldiers, o,
10:5 the organization of his o and
15:18 and turned them over to his o.
2Ki 3:11 One of the o of the king of
2Ki 9:11 came out to his master's o.
10:1 wrote letters to the o of Jezreel,
11:18 Next, the priest appointed o to
12:20 His own o plotted against him
12:21 Joash's o Jozacar,
14:5 he executed the o who had
20:18 They will become o in the
21:23 Amon's o plotted against him
24:12 Judah, his mother, o, generals,
1Ch 18:17 David's sons were his main o.
23:2 He gathered all the o of Israel
26:29 They served as o and judges
28:1 the o in charge of all the
28:1 the palace o, the soldiers,
29:6 and the o in charge of the
2Ch 9:4 the organization of his o and
21:4 and some of the o of Israel.
23:18 Next, Jehoiada appointed o to
24:10 All the o and all the people
24:17 After he died, the o of Judah
24:25 His own o plotted against him
25:3 he executed the o who killed
26:11 one of the king's o.
30:2 The king, his o, and the whole
30:6 king and his o throughout Israel
32:21 exterminated all the soldiers, o,
33:24 His o plotted against him and
34:13 as scribes, o, or gatekeepers.
34:22 So Hilkiah and the king's o
35:8 His o also voluntarily gave
36:14 All the o, the priests, and the
36:18 the king and his o to Babylon.
Ezr 4:5 They bribed o to keep the
7:28 and all the king's powerful o
8:20 David and his o had appointed
8:25 the king, his advisers, his o,
8:36 These o then gave their
9:2 Furthermore, the leaders and o
Neh 2:16 The o didn't know where I had
2:16 priests, the leaders, the other o,
11:3 These were the o of the
Est 1:3 was for all his o and advisers,
1:3 the nobles and o of the
1:11 especially the o, her beauty,
1:14 These seven o of the Persians
1:16 presence of the king and the o,
1:16 king but also against all the o
1:18 Today the wives of the o in
1:18 will talk back to all the king's o.
1:21 The king and his o approved of
2:18 He invited all his o and his
3:1 than all the other o who were
3:12 and the o of every people.
5:11 him to a position over the o
6:9 the horse to one of the king's o,
9:3 All the o of the provinces,
Psa 135:9 against Pharaoh and all his o.
148:11 o and all judges on the earth,
Ecc 10:16 where the high o throw parties
10:17 and when the high o eat at
Isa 3:14 the respected leaders and the o
30:4 Although Pharaoh's o are in
32:1 and o will rule with justice.
39:7 They will become o in the
Jer 1:18 Judah's kings, its o, its priests,
21:7 Zedekiah, his o, the people,
22:2 to the word of the LORD, you o,
22:4 with their o and their people.
25:18 as well as its kings and o.
25:19 his servants, o, all his people,
26:10 When the o of Judah heard
26:11 and the prophets said to the o
26:12 Then Jeremiah said to all the o
26:16 Then the o and all the people
26:21 troops and o heard what Uriah
29:2 and his mother, the court o,
29:26 so that there would be o
32:32 The people, their kings and o,
34:10 All the o and all the people
34:19 I will hand over the o of Judah
34:19 the palace o, the priests,
34:21 of Judah and his o over
35:4 It was next to the room of the o
36:12 and all the other o were there.
36:14 Then all the o sent Jehudi,
36:19 The o said to Baruch,

Jer 36:21 king and all the o standing by
37:14 Jeremiah and took him to the o.
37:15 The o were so angry with
38:4 Then the o said to the king,
38:25 The o may find out that I've
38:27 All the o came to Jeremiah and
44:17 and our o did in the cities of
44:21 your kings and your o,
48:7 with all its priests and o.
49:3 captivity with its priests and o.
49:38 and destroy its king and o,
50:35 "A sword will kill their o and
51:23 you to crush governors and o.
51:57 I will make their o and wise
52:10 He also slaughtered all the o of
Eze 27:21 Arabia and all the o of Kedar
Dan 3:2 and all the other provincial o to
3:3 and all the other provincial o
6:2 these satraps were three o.
6:2 Daniel was one of these o.
6:2 to report to these three o so that
6:3 himself among the other o
6:4 So the other o and satraps tried
6:6 So these o and satraps went to
6:7 All the o, governors, satraps,
Hos 3:4 a long time without kings or o,
7:3 They make o happy with the
7:5 the o become drunk from wine,
7:16 Their o will die in battle
9:15 All their o are rebellious.
13:10 said, 'Give us kings and o!'
Amo 1:15 into captivity along with his o.
2:3 I will kill all their o at the same
Mic 7:3 O ask for gifts. Judges accept
Zep 1:8 sacrifice I will punish the o,
3:3 Its o are ⌊like⌋ roaring lions.
Mat 14:2 He said to his o, "This is John
20:25 their o have absolute authority
Mar 6:21 gave a dinner for his top o,
10:42 their o have absolute authority
Act 13:50 high social standing and the o
16:20 In front of the Roman o,
16:22 Then the o tore the clothes off
16:35 In the morning the Roman o
16:36 "The o have sent word to
16:37 "Roman o have had us beaten
16:38 The guards reported to the o
16:38 When the Roman o heard that
16:39 So the o went to the jail and
16:39 As the o escorted Paul and
17:6 believers in front of the city o.
17:8 The crowd and the o were
19:31 Even some o who were from
19:38 we have special days and o to
2Co 11:25 three times Roman o had me
Tit 3:1 the authority of government o.

offspring (17)

Exo 13:2 Every firstborn male o among
13:12 sacrifice every firstborn male o
13:12 The firstborn male o of each of
34:19 "Every first male o is mine,
Num 3:12 firstborn male o among them.
8:16 male o of the Israelites.
Dtr 7:14 animals will be able to have o.
28:4 Your animals will have o.
28:11 Your animals will have many o.
28:51 They'll eat the o of your
30:9 Your animals will have many o.
Psa 21:10 and their o from among Adam's
Isa 14:22 its o and descendants,"
22:24 descendants and o and all the
44:3 I will pour my Spirit on your o
61:9 Then their o will be known
65:23 because they will be o

Og (22)

Num 21:33 King O of Bashan and all his
32:33 of the Amorites and King O
Dtr 1:4 and King O of Bashan,
3:1 King O of Bashan and all his
3:3 our God also handed King O
3:4 the kingdom of O in Bashan.
3:11 (Of the Rephaim only King O of
3:13 and all of Bashan ruled by O
4:47 the land of King O of Bashan,
Dtr 29:7 Sihon of Heshbon and King O
31:4 did to King Sihon and King O
Jos 2:10 what you did to Sihon and O,
9:10 Sihon of Heshbon and King O
12:4 The territory of King O of
13:12 kingdom of O in Bashan).
13:12 O ruled in Ashtaroth and Edrei.
13:30 (the whole kingdom of King O
13:31 the royal cities of O in Bashan.
1Ki 4:19 Amorite and King O of Bashan.
Neh 9:22 the land of King O of Bashan.
Psa 135:11 King O of Bashan,
136:20 and King O of Bashan —

Og's (1)

Dtr 3:10 cities of O kingdom in Bashan.

Ohad (2)

Gen 46:10 O, Jakin, Zohar, and Shaul,
Exo 6:15 O, Jachin, Zohar, and Shaul,

Ohel (1)

1Ch 3:20 O, Berechiah, Hasadiah,

Oholah (5)

Eze 23:4 "The older girl was named O,
23:4 O represents Samaria,
23:5 O acted like a prostitute,
23:36 will you judge O and Oholibah
23:44 O and Oholibah just as they

Oholiab (5)

Exo 31:6 Also, I have appointed O,
35:34 has given Bezalel and O,
36:1 "So Bezalel and O will do the
36:2 Moses called Bezalel and O
38:23 His assistant was O,

Oholibah (7)

Eze 23:4 the younger girl was named O.
23:4 and O represents Jerusalem.
23:11 her younger sister O saw this,
23:11 O lusted after men more than
23:22 "O, this is what the Almighty
23:36 will you judge Oholah and O
23:44 Oholah and O just as they

Oholibah's (1)

Eze 23:11 O prostitution became worse

Oholibamah (8)

Gen 36:2 daughter of Elon the Hittite; O,
36:5 O gave birth to Jeush,
36:14 the sons of Esau's wife O,
36:18 descendants of Esau's wife O:
36:18 descended from Esau's wife O,
36:25 of Anah: Dishon and O,
36:41 O, Elah, Pinon,
1Ch 1:52 O, Elah, Pinon,

oil (210)

Gen 28:18 as a marker and poured olive o
31:13 where you poured olive o on a
35:14 wine offering and olive o on it.
Exo 25:6 olive o for the lamps,
25:6 spices for the anointing o and
27:20 virgin olive o so that the lamps
29:2 of bread made with olive o,
29:2 wafers brushed with olive o.
29:7 Take the anointing o,
29:21 and some of the anointing o,
29:23 ring of bread made with olive o,
29:36 Then anoint it ⌊with olive o⌋ in
29:40 with one quart of virgin olive o.
30:24 place — and 4 quarts of olive o.
30:25 make these into a holy o,
30:25 the holy o used for anointing.
30:31 this will be my holy o used
30:32 Never make any perfumed o
31:11 the anointing o, and the
35:8 olive o for the lamps,
35:8 spices for the anointing o and
35:14 and the olive o for the lamps,
35:15 with its poles, the anointing o,
35:28 the spices and the olive o
35:28 for the lamps, the anointing o,
Exo 37:29 had a perfumer make the holy o
39:37 the olive o for the lamps,
39:38 the gold altar, the anointing o,
40:9 Take the anointing o,
Lev 2:1 Pour olive o on it, and put
2:2 a handful of flour with olive o,
2:4 of flour mixed with olive o
2:4 bread brushed with olive o.
2:5 of flour mixed with olive o.
2:6 pieces and pour olive o over it.
2:7 be made of flour with olive o.
2:15 Put olive o on it, and place
2:16 will burn the flour, olive o,
5:11 Never put olive o on it or add
6:15 together with the olive o and all
6:21 it in a frying pan with olive o,
7:10 mixed with olive o or dry,
7:12 bread mixed with olive o,
7:12 bread brushed with olive o,
7:12 flour mixed well with olive o.
8:2 clothes, the anointing o,
8:10 Moses took the anointing o to
8:11 He sprinkled some of the o on
8:12 poured some of the anointing o
8:26 ring of bread made with olive o,
8:30 took some of the anointing o
9:4 offering mixed with olive o
10:7 has anointed you with his o."
14:10 cups of flour mixed with olive o
14:10 along with a quart of olive o.
14:12 lambs and the quart of olive o
14:15 also take some of the olive o
14:16 will dip his right finger in the o
14:16 some of the o seven times
14:17 put some of the o that is still
14:18 priest will put the rest of the o
14:21 of flour mixed with olive o as
14:21 grain offering, a quart of olive o,
14:24 offering and the quart of olive o
14:26 of the olive o into his own
14:27 some of the o seven times
14:28 will put some of the o that is
14:29 priest will pour the rest of the o
21:10 priest who is anointed with o
21:12 dedicated with the anointing o
23:13 flour mixed with olive o with it.
24:2 virgin olive o for the lamp stand
Num 4:9 containers for the olive o used
4:16 will be in charge of the o for the
4:16 and the anointing o.
5:15 He must not pour olive o on the
6:15 of bread made with olive o
6:15 bread brushed with olive o,
7:13 with flour mixed with olive o as
7:19 with flour mixed with olive o as
7:25 with flour mixed with olive o as
7:31 with flour mixed with olive o as
7:37 with flour mixed with olive o as
7:43 with flour mixed with olive o as
7:49 with flour mixed with olive o as
7:55 with flour mixed with olive o as
7:61 with flour mixed with olive o as
7:67 with flour mixed with olive o as
7:73 with flour mixed with olive o as
7:79 with flour mixed with olive o as
8:8 with olive o that is offered
11:8 rich pastry made with olive o.
15:4 mixed with one quart of olive o.
15:6 mixed with 1 ¼ quarts of o
15:9 with two quarts of olive o.
18:12 the best of all the olive o and
28:5 with one quart of virgin olive o.
28:9 of flour mixed with olive o,
28:12 of flour mixed with olive o,
28:12 of flour mixed with olive o,
28:13 of flour mixed with olive o.
28:20 of flour mixed with olive o.
28:28 of flour mixed with olive o.
29:3 of flour mixed with olive o.
29:9 of flour mixed with olive o.
29:14 of flour mixed with olive o.
35:25 was anointed with the holy o.
Dtr 7:13 grain, new wine, and olive o.
8:8 and olive trees for olive o.
11:14 grain, new wine, and olive o.
12:17 grain, new wine, and olive o;

Dtr 14:23 grain, new wine, and olive **o**,
18:4 grain, new wine, olive **o**,
28:40 in your country but no olive **o**
28:51 grain, no new wine, no olive **o**,
32:13 and olive **o** from solid rock.
33:24 and wash their feet in olive **o**.
Jdg 9:9 'Should I stop producing **o**,
1Sm 10:1 Samuel took a flask of olive **o**,
16:1 Fill a flask with olive **o** and go.
16:13 Samuel took the flask of olive **o**
2Sm 1:21 was never rubbed with olive **o**.
14:2 Don't rub olive **o** on yourself,
1Ki 1:39 the container of olive **o** from
5:11 120,000 gallons of pure olive **o**.
17:12 of flour in a jar and a little **o**
17:14 the jug will always contain **o**."
17:16 jug always contained olive **o**,
2Ki 4:2 house except a jar of olive **o**."
4:4 and pour **o** into all those
4:6 So the olive **o** stopped flowing.
4:7 He said, "Sell the **o**,
9:1 Take this flask of olive **o**,
9:3 Take the flask of **o**,
9:6 The prophet poured olive **o** on
18:32 trees, olive **o**, and honey. Live!
20:13 fine olive **o**, his entire armory,
1Ch 9:29 olive **o**, incense, and spices.
12:40 olive **o**, cattle, and sheep,
27:28 from Gedor for storing olive **o**:
2Ch 2:10 and 200,000 gallons of olive **o**."
2:15 send the wheat, barley, olive **o**,
11:11 food, olive **o**, and wine in them.
31:5 new wine, fresh olive **o**, honey,
32:28 new wine, and fresh olive **o**,
Ezr 3:7 and olive **o** to the men from
6:9 and olive **o** — should be
7:22 600 gallons of olive **o**,
Neh 5:11 and olive **o** you've been
10:37 and olive **o** to the priests,
10:39 of grain, new wine, and olive **o**.
13:5 new wine, and olive **o**.
13:12 and olive **o** to the storerooms.
Est 2:12 six months using **o** of myrrh
Job 24:11 They press out olive **o**
29:6 streams of olive **o** on me.
Psa 23:5 You anoint my head with **o**.
45:7 companions, with the **o** of joy.
55:21 are more soothing than **o**,
89:20 I anointed him with my holy **o**.
104:15 olive **o** to make faces shine,
109:18 like water and his bones like **o**.
133:2 scented **o** on the head,
Pro 5:3 Her kiss is smoother than **o**,
27:16 He can even pick up olive **o**
Isa 1:6 bandaged, or soothed with **o**.
39:2 fine olive **o**, his entire armory,
61:3 the **o** of joy instead of ⌊tears
Jer 31:12 and olive **o**, lambs and calves.
40:10 summer fruit, and olive **o**,
41:8 We have wheat, barley, olive **o**,
Eze 16:9 I poured olive **o** over you.
16:13 was flour, honey, and olive **o**.
16:18 You offered my olive **o** and
16:19 You gave flour, olive **o**,
23:41 and my olive **o** on their tables.
27:17 baked goods, honey, olive **o**,
32:14 make its streams flow like **o**,
45:14 percent of your olive **o** using
45:24 also give one gallon of olive **o**
45:25 grain offerings, and olive **o**.
46:5 One gallon of olive **o** must be
46:7 One gallon of olive **o** must be
46:11 One gallon of olive **o** must be
46:14 one-and-a-third quarts of olive **o**
46:15 and the olive **o** every morning
Hos 2:5 and linen, olive **o** and wine.'
2:8 grain, new wine, and olive **o**.
2:22 grain, new wine, and olive **o**.
12:1 and take olive **o** to Egypt.
Joe 1:10 The olive **o** has run out.
2:19 and olive **o** to you.
2:24 with new wine and olive **o**.
Mic 6:7 endless streams of olive **o**?
6:15 but you won't rub the **o** on your
Hag 1:11 the new wine, the olive **o**,
2:12 wine, **o**, or any kind of food,
Mat 25:1 They took their **o** lamps and
25:3 but they didn't take any extra **o**.
25:4 along extra **o** for their lamps.
25:8 'Give us some of your **o**.
25:9 someone to sell you some **o**.'
25:10 "While they were buying **o**,
Mar 6:13 out of people and poured **o**
Luk 7:46 You didn't put any olive **o** on
16:6 gallons of olive **o**.' "The
Heb 1:9 companions, with the **o** of joy."
Jas 5:14 you and anoint you with olive **o**
Rev 6:6 the olive **o** and the wine."
18:13 olive **o**, flour, wheat, cattle,

oils (2)

Isa 57:9 to the king with perfumed **o**
Amo 6:6 They rub the finest **o** all over

ointment (1)

Rev 3:18 Buy **o** to put on your eyes so

old (315)

Gen 5:3 When Adam was 130 years **o**,
5:6 When Seth was 105 years **o**,
5:9 When Enosh was 90 years **o**,
5:12 When Kenan was 70 years **o**,
5:15 Mahalalel was 65 years **o**,
5:18 When Jared was 162 years **o**,
5:21 When Enoch was 65 years **o**,
5:25 Methuselah was 187 years **o**,
5:28 Lamech was 182 years **o**,
5:32 When Noah was 500 years **o**,
7:6 Noah was 600 years **o** when
11:10 when Shem was 100 years **o**,
11:12 Arpachshad was 35 years **o**
11:14 Shelah was 30 years **o** when
11:16 Eber was 34 years **o** when he
11:18 Peleg was 30 years **o** when he
11:20 Reu was 32 years **o** when he
11:22 Serug was 30 years **o** when he
11:24 Nahor was 29 years **o** when he
11:26 Terah was 70 years **o** when he
12:4 Abram was 75 years **o** when
15:15 and be buried at a very **o** age.
16:16 Abram was 86 years **o** when
17:1 When Abram was 99 years **o**,
17:12 child who is eight days **o** must
17:24 Abraham was 99 years **o** when
17:25 Ishmael was 13 years **o** when
18:11 Abraham and Sarah were **o**.
18:12 "Now that I've become **o**,
18:12 What's more, my husband is **o**!"
18:13 have a child now that I'm **o**?'
19:4 all the young and **o** male
19:11 young and **o** alike,
19:31 younger one, "Our father is **o**.
21:2 a son for Abraham in his **o** age.
21:4 When Isaac was eight days **o**,
21:5 Abraham was 100 years **o**
21:7 I have given him a son in his **o**
23:1 Sarah lived to be 127 years **o**.
24:1 By now Abraham was **o**,
24:36 gave him a son in her **o** age,
25:8 and died at a very **o** age.
25:20 Isaac was 40 years **o** when he
25:26 Isaac was 60 years **o** when
26:34 When Esau was 40 years **o**,
27:1 When Isaac was **o** and going
27:2 Isaac said, "I'm **o**. I don't know
35:28 Isaac was 180 years **o**
35:29 in death at a very **o** age.
37:3 had been born in Israel's **o** age.
41:46 Joseph was 30 years **o** when
42:38 drive this gray-haired **o** man
44:20 'We have a father who is **o** and
44:20 to him when he was already **o**.
44:29 you'll drive this gray-haired **o**
44:31 drive our gray-haired **o** father
47:8 asked him, "How **o** are you?"
48:10 was failing because of **o** age,
50:22 Joseph lived to be 110 years **o**.
50:26 died when he was 110 years **o**.
Exo 2:10 When the child was **o** enough,
7:7 Moses was 80 years **o** and
10:9 be taking our young and **o**,
30:14 least 20 years **o** must give this
Exo 38:26 who was at least 20 years **o**:
Lev 12:3 when he is eight days **o**.
26:10 You will clear out **o** food
27:3 20 to 60 years **o** is 20 ounces
27:5 For a boy from 5 to 20 years **o**,
27:6 from one month to five years **o**,
Num 1:3 who is at least 20 years **o**.
1:18 Each man at least 20 years **o**
1:20 who was at least 20 years **o**
1:22 who was at least 20 years **o**
1:24 who were at least 20 years **o**
1:26 who were at least 20 years **o**
1:28 who were at least 20 years **o**
1:30 who were at least 20 years **o**
1:32 who were at least 20 years **o**
1:34 who were at least 20 years **o**
1:36 who were at least 20 years **o**
1:38 who were at least 20 years **o**
1:40 who were at least 20 years **o**
1:42 who were at least 20 years **o**
1:45 who were at least 20 years **o**
3:15 who is at least one month **o**."
3:22 least one month **o** was 7,500.
3:28 least one month **o** was 8,600.
3:34 least one month **o** was 6,200.
3:39 who was at least one month **o**,
3:40 who is at least one month **o**,
3:43 least one month **o** was 22,273.
8:24 Men 25 years **o** or older are
8:25 But when they're 50 years **o**,
14:29 who are at least 20 years **o**,
18:16 When they are one month **o**,
26:2 who are at least 20 years **o**
26:4 of those at least 20 years **o**,
26:62 least one month **o** was 23,000.
32:11 the people 20 years **o** or older,
33:39 Aaron was 123 years **o** when
Dtr 4:25 and have grown **o**
28:50 will show no respect for the **o**
31:2 "I'm 120 years **o** now,
34:7 Moses was 120 years **o** when
Jos 6:21 young and **o**, as well as cattle,
9:4 Their wineskins were **o**,
13:1 Joshua was **o**, near the end of
13:1 LORD said to him, "You are **o**,
14:7 I was 40 years **o** when the
14:10 at me today. I'm 85 years **o**.
23:1 Joshua was **o**, near the end of
23:2 He said to them, "I am **o**,
24:29 He was 110 years **o**.
Jdg 2:19 the people went back to their **o**
5:21 swept them away — that **o** river,
6:25 a bull that is seven years **o**.
8:32 died at a very **o** age.
19:16 That evening an **o** man came
19:17 So the **o** man asked,
19:20 Then the **o** man said,
19:22 They told the **o** man,
Rut 1:12 Go, because I am too **o** to get
4:15 and support you in your **o** age.
1Sm 2:22 Now, Eli was very **o**,
2:31 one will grow **o** in your family.
2:32 family will live to an **o** age.
4:15 (Eli was 98 years **o**,
4:18 (The man was **o** and heavy.)
8:1 When Samuel was **o**,
8:5 They told him, "You're **o**,
12:2 I am **o** and gray, but my sons
13:1 Saul was ⌊thirty⌋ years **o**
17:12 and in Saul's day he was an **o**
28:14 "An **o** man is coming up,
30:2 young and **o** women who were
30:19 was missing — young or **o**,
2Sm 2:10 was 40 years **o** when
4:4 When the boy was five years **o**,
5:4 David was 30 years **o** when he
19:32 an elderly man, 80 years **o**.
19:35 I'm 80 years **o** now.
20:18 "There's an **o** saying:
1Ki 1:1 King David had grown **o**,
1:15 The king was very **o**,
2:6 Don't let that gray-haired, **o** man
2:9 **o** man into his grave by
11:4 In his **o** age, his wives tempted
13:11 An **o** prophet was living in
13:13 The **o** prophet told his sons,

1Ki 13:14 The **o** prophet asked him,
13:15 the **o** prophet replied.
13:18 The **o** prophet said,
13:18 (But the **o** prophet was lying.)
13:20 word to the **o** prophet who had
13:23 After the **o** prophet had
13:25 where the **o** prophet was living.
13:26 When the **o** prophet who had
13:27 Then the **o** prophet told his
13:29 The **o** prophet picked up the
14:4 had failed because he was **o**.
14:21 He was 41 years **o** when he
15:23 But when he was **o**,
22:42 Jehoshaphat was 35 years **o**
2Ki 3:21 So all men **o** enough to bear
4:14 and her husband is **o**."
8:17 He was 32 years **o** when he
8:26 Ahaziah was 22 years **o** when
11:21 Joash was seven years **o**
14:2 Amaziah was 25 years **o** when
14:21 who was 16 years **o**,
15:2 He was 16 years **o** when he
15:33 He was 25 years **o** when he
16:2 Ahaz was 20 years **o** when he
18:2 Hezekiah was 25 years **o**
21:1 Manasseh was 12 years **o**
21:19 Amon was 22 years **o** when he
22:1 Josiah was 8 years **o** when he
23:2 the people (young and **o**) went
23:31 Jehoahaz was 23 years **o**
23:36 Jehoiakim was 25 years **o**
24:8 Jehoiakin was 18 years **o**
24:18 Zedekiah was 21 years **o**
1Ch 2:21 her when he was 60 years **o**.
23:1 When David had grown **o** and
23:3 least 30 years **o** was counted.
23:24 temple was at least 20 years **o**.
23:27 who were at least 20 years **o**.
27:23 count those under 20 years **o**,
29:28 He died at a very **o** age.
2Ch 3:3 the **o** standard measurement.)
12:13 He was 41 years **o** when he
15:13 All people (young or **o**,
17:3 who lived in the **o** way like his
20:31 He was 35 years **o** when he
21:5 Jehoram was 32 years **o** when
21:20 He was 32 years **o** when he
22:2 Ahaziah was 42 years **o** when
24:1 Joash was 7 years **o** when he
24:15 When Jehoiada was **o** and had
24:15 was 130 years **o** when he died.
25:1 Amaziah was 25 years **o** when
25:5 who were at least 20 years **o**
26:1 who was 16 years **o**,
26:3 Uzziah was 16 years **o** when
27:1 Jotham was 25 years **o** when
27:8 He was 25 years **o** when he
28:1 Ahaz was 20 years **o** when he
29:1 king when he was 25 years **o**.
31:15 young and **o**, by their divisions.
31:16 were at least three years **o**.
31:17 who were at least 20 years **o**.
33:1 Manasseh was 12 years **o**
33:21 Amon was 22 years **o** when he
34:1 Josiah was 8 years **o** when he
34:30 people (young and **o**) went up
36:2 Jehoahaz was 23 years **o**
36:5 Jehoiakim was 25 years **o**
36:9 Jehoiakin was eight years **o**
36:11 Zedekiah was 21 years **o**
36:17 the **o** people or the sick people.
Ezr 3:8 who were at least 20 years **o**
3:12 families who were **o** enough
Neh 3:6 made repairs on **O** Gate.
12:39 over **O** Gate and Fish Gate,
Est 3:13 all the Jews — young and **o**,
Job 4:11 The **o** lions die without any
5:26 your grave at a ripe **o** age like
14:8 If its roots grow **o** in the ground
15:10 Both the **o** and the gray-haired
21:7 wicked go on living, grow **o**,
22:15 "Are you following the **o** path
29:8 **O** men stood up straight out of
32:6 "I am young, and you are **o**.
32:9 is merely because they're **o**.
42:17 Then at a very **o** age,
Psa 37:25 been young, and now I am **o**,
71:9 Do not reject me when I am **o**
71:18 Even when I am **o** and gray,
77:5 have considered the days of **o**,
92:14 Even when they are **o**,
148:12 **o** and young together.
Pro 22:6 and even when he is **o** he will
23:22 your mother because she is **o**.
Ecc 4:13 and wise is better than an **o**,
7:10 better in the **o** days than they
Sos 7:13 I have saved new and **o** things
Isa 3:5 young will make fun of the **o**,
20:4 and the **o** — captives from
22:11 to hold the water of the **O** Pool.
46:4 Even when you're **o**,
47:6 a heavy burden on **o** people.
65:20 days or an **o** man who doesn't
65:20 to be a hundred years **o** will
65:20 he is a hundred years **o** will
Jer 6:11 away as well as very **o** people.
6:16 Ask which paths are the **o**,
16:6 "**O** and young alike will die in
31:13 with young men and **o** men.
51:22 I will use you to crush the **o**
52:1 Zedekiah was 21 years **o**
Lam 2:21 Young and **o** lie on the ground
Eze 9:6 Kill **o** men, young men,
9:6 men, **o** women, young women,
9:6 So they started with the **o** men
16:8 You were **o** enough to make
Dan 5:31 He was 62 years **o**.
Hos 4:11 Prostitutes, **o** wine,
7:9 **o** man, but you don't realize it.
Joe 2:28 Your **o** men will dream dreams.
Zec 8:4 **O** men and old women will
8:4 Old men and **o** women will
8:4 cane in hand because of **o** age.
Mat 2:16 to kill all the boys two years **o**
9:16 "No one patches an **o** coat with
9:17 new wine into **o** wineskins.
13:52 He brings new and **o** things out
Mar 2:21 "No one patches an **o** coat with
2:21 rip away some of the **o** cloth,
2:22 new wine into **o** wineskins.
5:42 (She was twelve years **o**.)
Luk 1:7 were too **o** to have children.
1:18 I'm an **o** man, and my wife is
1:36 with a son in her **o** age.
1:59 the child was eight days **o**,
2:36 She was now very **o**.
2:42 When he was 12 years **o**,
3:23 Jesus was about 30 years **o**
5:36 a new coat to patch an **o** coat.
5:36 the new cloth will tear the **o**.
5:36 the new will not match the **o**.
5:37 new wine into **o** wineskins.
5:39 drinking **o** wine wants new
5:39 says, 'The **o** wine is better!'"
8:42 who was about twelve years **o**,
Jon 3:4 be born when he's an **o** man?
8:57 "You're not even fifty years **o**.
9:21 He's **o** enough to answer for
9:23 to ask him. He's **o** enough.")
21:18 But when you're **o**,
Act 2:17 Your **o** men will dream dreams.
4:22 miracle was over 40 years **o**.)
7:23 When he was 40 years **o**,
Rom 4:19 was about a hundred years **o**,
7:6 not in an **o** way dictated by
1Co 5:7 Remove the **o** yeast ⌊of sin⌋
5:8 with the **o** yeast ⌊of sin⌋
7:36 his virgin daughter is **o** enough
2Co 5:17 The **o** way of living has
1Ti 4:7 myths that **o** women like
5:9 is at least 60 years **o** should
Phm 1:9 I, Paul, as an **o** man and now a
Heb 11:11 even though he was **o** and
1Jn 2:7 Rather, I'm giving you an **o**
2:7 It's the **o** commandment you've

older (43)

Gen 10:21 Shem, Japheth's **o** brother,
19:31 The **o** daughter said to the
19:33 Then the **o** one went to bed
19:34 The next day the **o** daughter
19:37 The **o** one gave birth to a son
25:23 and the **o** will serve the
27:1 he called his **o** son Esau and
27:15 Then Rebekah took her **o** son
27:42 told what her **o** son Esau had
29:16 The name of the **o** one was
29:26 ⌊in marriage⌋ before the **o** one.
48:14 although Manasseh was **o**.
Lev 19:32 and honor **o** people.
Num 8:24 Men 25 years old or **o** are
32:11 of the people 20 years old or **o**,
Jos 24:31 as Joshua and the **o** leaders,
2Sm 12:17 The **o** leaders in his palace
1Ki 2:22 After all, he is my **o** brother.
12:6 from the **o** leaders who had
12:8 But he ignored the advice the **o**
12:13 advice the **o** leaders gave him.
2Ch 10:6 from the **o** leaders who had
10:8 But he ignored the advice the **o**
10:13 ignored the **o** leaders' advice.
22:1 Arabs had killed all the **o** sons.
Ezr 10:8 and the **o** men had advised,
Job 15:10 They are **o** than your father.
32:4 they were **o** than he was.
Pro 20:29 the splendor of **o** people is their
Lam 4:16 nor did they honor their **o**
5:12 ⌊Our⌋ **o** leaders are shown no
5:14 ⌊Our⌋ **o** leaders have stopped
Eze 16:46 "'Your **o** sister was Samaria.
16:61 ashamed when I return your **o**
23:4 "The **o** girl was named Oholah,
Luk 15:25 "His **o** son was in the field.
15:28 "Then the **o** son became angry
Jon 8:9 beginning with the **o** men,
Rom 9:11 Rebekah was told that the **o**
1Ti 5:1 when you correct an **o** man,
5:2 **o** women as if they were your
Tit 2:2 Tell **o** men to be sober.
2:3 Tell **o** women to live their lives

oldest (14)

Gen 43:33 to their ages — from the **o**
44:12 He began with the **o** and ended
49:26 blessings of the **o** mountains
Dtr 33:15 fruits from the **o** mountains,
1Sm 17:13 Jesse's three **o** sons joined
17:14 The three **o** joined Saul's army.
17:28 Eliab, David's **o** brother,
18:17 "Here is my **o** daughter Merab.
1Ch 24:31 The families of the **o** brother
25:8 the youngest as well as the **o**,
26:13 youngest and **o** alike,
Job 1:13 wine in their **o** brother's home,
1:18 wine at their **o** brother's home
Hab 3:6 The **o** mountains break apart.

Old Testament (1)

2Co 3:14 still there when they read the **O**.

olive (192)

Gen 8:11 was a freshly plucked **o** leaf.
28:18 up as a marker and poured **o** oil
31:13 where you poured **o** oil on a
35:14 He poured a wine offering and **o**
Exo 23:11 your vineyards and **o** groves.
25:6 **o** oil for the lamps,
27:20 virgin **o** oil so that the lamps
29:2 rings of bread made with **o** oil,
29:2 wafers brushed with **o** oil.
29:23 a ring of bread made with **o** oil,
29:36 Then anoint it ⌊with **o** oil⌋ in
29:40 with one quart of virgin **o** oil.
30:24 place — and 4 quarts of **o** oil.
35:8 **o** oil for the lamps,
35:14 its lamps and the **o** oil for the
35:28 brought the spices and the **o** oil
39:37 the **o** oil for the lamps,
Lev 2:1 Pour **o** oil on it, and put
2:2 this a handful of flour with **o** oil,
2:4 made of flour mixed with **o** oil
2:4 bread brushed with **o** oil.
2:5 made of flour mixed with **o** oil.
2:6 Break it into pieces and pour **o**
2:7 it will be made of flour with **o**
2:15 Put **o** oil on it, and place
2:16 priest will burn the flour, **o** oil,
5:11 Never put **o** oil on it or add

Lev 6:15 together with the **o** oil and all
6:21 it in a frying pan with **o** oil,
7:10 whether mixed with **o** oil or dry,
7:12 bread mixed with **o** oil,
7:12 bread brushed with **o** oil,
7:12 from flour mixed well with **o** oil.
8:26 a ring of bread made with **o** oil,
9:4 a grain offering mixed with **o** oil
14:10 cups of flour mixed with **o** oil
14:10 along with a quart of **o** oil.
14:12 lambs and the quart of **o** oil
14:15 will also take some of the **o** oil
14:21 of flour mixed with **o** oil as
14:21 a grain offering, a quart of **o** oil,
14:24 offering and the quart of **o** oil
14:26 pour some of the **o** oil into his
23:13 quarts of flour mixed with **o** oil
24:2 virgin **o** oil for the lamp stand
Num 4:9 and all the containers for the **o**
5:15 He must not pour **o** oil on the
6:15 rings of bread made with **o** oil
6:15 bread brushed with **o** oil,
7:13 with flour mixed with **o** oil as
7:19 with flour mixed with **o** oil as
7:25 with flour mixed with **o** oil as
7:31 with flour mixed with **o** oil as
7:37 with flour mixed with **o** oil as
7:43 with flour mixed with **o** oil as
7:49 with flour mixed with **o** oil as
7:55 with flour mixed with **o** oil as
7:61 with flour mixed with **o** oil as
7:67 with flour mixed with **o** oil as
7:73 with flour mixed with **o** oil as
7:79 with flour mixed with **o** oil as
8:8 of flour mixed with **o** oil that is
11:8 like rich pastry made with **o** oil.
15:4 mixed with one quart of **o** oil.
15:9 mixed with two quarts of **o** oil.
18:12 the best of all the **o** oil and the
28:5 with one quart of virgin **o** oil.
28:9 cups of flour mixed with **o** oil,
28:12 cups of flour mixed with **o** oil,
28:12 cups of flour mixed with **o** oil,
28:13 8 cups of flour mixed with **o** oil.
28:20 of flour mixed with **o** oil.
28:28 of flour mixed with **o** oil.
29:3 of flour mixed with **o** oil.
29:9 of flour mixed with **o** oil.
29:14 of flour mixed with **o** oil.
Dtr 6:11 vineyards and **o** trees that you
7:13 grain, new wine, and **o** oil.
8:8 The land has honey and **o**
8:8 honey and olive trees for **o** oil.
11:14 own grain, new wine, and **o** oil.
12:17 your grain, new wine, and **o** oil;
14:23 your grain, new wine, and **o** oil,
18:4 grain, new wine, **o** oil,
28:40 You will have **o** trees
28:40 in your country but no **o** oil
28:51 no grain, no new wine, no **o** oil,
32:13 from rocks and **o** oil from solid
33:24 and wash their feet in **o** oil.
Jos 24:13 vineyards and **o** groves that
Jdg 9:8 They said to the **o** tree,
9:9 But the **o** tree responded,
15:5 Their **o** orchards also caught
1Sm 8:14 and **o** orchards and give them
10:1 Samuel took a flask of **o** oil,
16:1 Fill a flask with **o** oil and go.
16:13 Samuel took the flask of **o** oil
2Sm 1:21 was never rubbed with **o** oil.
14:2 Don't rub **o** oil on yourself,
1Ki 1:39 took the container of **o** oil from
5:11 120,000 gallons of pure **o** oil.
6:23 angels out of **o** wood.
6:31 to the inner room out of **o** wood.
6:32 were ⌊made out of⌋ **o** wood.
6:33 square doorposts out of **o** wood
17:16 the jug always contained **o** oil,
2Ki 4:2 the house except a jar of **o** oil."
4:6 So the **o** oil stopped flowing.
5:26 **o** orchards, vineyards, sheep,
9:1 Take this flask of **o** oil,
9:6 The prophet poured **o** oil on his
18:32 a country with **o** trees,
18:32 trees, **o** oil, and honey. Live!

2Ki 20:13 fine **o** oil, his entire armory,
1Ch 9:29 **o** oil, incense, and spices.
12:40 wine, **o** oil, cattle, and sheep,
27:28 for the **o** and fig trees in the
27:28 from Gedor for storing **o** oil:
2Ch 2:10 and 200,000 gallons of **o** oil."
2:15 send the wheat, barley, **o** oil,
11:11 of food, **o** oil, and wine in them.
31:5 new wine, fresh **o** oil, honey,
32:28 new wine, and fresh **o** oil,
Ezr 3:7 and **o** oil to the men from Sidon
6:9 and **o** oil — should be provided
7:22 600 gallons of **o** oil,
Neh 5:11 vineyards, their **o** orchards,
5:11 and **o** oil you've been charging
8:15 and get branches — **o** and wild
8:15 branches — olive and wild **o**,
9:25 **o** trees, and plenty of fruit trees.
10:37 and **o** oil to the priests,
10:39 of grain, new wine, and **o** oil.
13:5 harvested, new wine, and **o** oil.
13:12 and **o** oil to the storerooms.
Job 15:33 off his blossoms like an **o** tree
24:11 They press out **o** oil between
24:11 oil between rows ⌊of **o** trees⌋.
29:6 poured streams of **o** oil on me.
Psa 52:8 But I am like a large **o** tree in
104:15 **o** oil to make faces shine,
128:3 like young **o** trees around your
Pro 27:16 He can even pick up **o** oil with
Isa 17:6 They will be like an **o** tree that
24:13 They will be like an **o** tree
39:2 fine **o** oil, his entire armory,
41:19 and wild **o** trees in the desert.
Jer 11:16 The LORD called you a large **o**
31:12 and **o** oil, lambs and calves.
40:10 grapes, summer fruit, and **o** oil,
41:8 We have wheat, barley, **o** oil,
Eze 16:9 I poured **o** oil over you.
16:13 was flour, honey, and **o** oil.
16:18 You offered my **o** oil and
16:19 You gave flour, **o** oil,
23:41 They put my incense and my **o**
27:17 baked goods, honey, **o** oil,
45:14 one percent of your **o** oil using
45:24 also give one gallon of **o** oil
45:25 grain offerings, and **o** oil.
46:5 One gallon of **o** oil must be
46:7 One gallon of **o** oil must be
46:11 One gallon of **o** oil must be
46:14 one-and-a-third quarts of **o** oil
46:15 and the **o** oil every morning as
Hos 2:5 wool and linen, **o** oil and wine.'
2:8 her grain, new wine, and **o** oil.
2:22 grain, new wine, and **o** oil.
12:1 Assyria and take **o** oil to Egypt.
14:6 will be beautiful like **o** trees.
Joe 1:10 The **o** oil has run out.
2:19 new wine, and **o** oil to you.
2:24 with new wine and **o** oil.
Amo 4:9 fig trees, and **o** trees.
Mic 6:7 with endless streams of **o** oil?
Hab 3:17 even if the **o** tree fails to
Hag 1:11 grain, the new wine, the **o** oil,
2:19 and the **o** tree still haven't
Zec 4:3 There are also two **o** trees
4:11 "What do these two **o** trees at
4:12 branches from the **o** trees next
Luk 7:46 You didn't put any **o** oil on my
16:6 'Eight hundred gallons of **o** oil.'
Rom 11:17 But some of the **o** branches
11:17 off, and you, a wild **o** branch,
11:17 from the roots of the **o** tree.
11:24 been cut from a wild **o** tree,
11:24 onto the **o** tree they belong
Jas 5:14 you and anoint you with **o** oil
Rev 6:6 But do not damage the **o** oil
11:4 These witnesses are the two **o**
18:13 wine, **o** oil, flour, wheat, cattle,

olives (23)

Dtr 24:20 When you harvest **o** from your
28:40 because the **o** will fall off the
2Sm 15:30 as he went up the Mount of **O**.
15:32 of **O**⌋ where people worshiped
16:1 the top ⌊of the Mount of **O**⌋,
Isa 17:6 Only two or three **o** are left at
17:6 four or five **o** on the rest of the
Mic 6:15 You will crush **o**, but you won't
Zec 14:4 will stand on the Mount of **O**,
14:4 The Mount of **O** will be split in
Mat 21:1 Bethphage on the Mount of **O**,
24:3 was sitting on the Mount of **O**,
26:30 they went to the Mount of **O**.
Mar 11:1 and Bethany, at the Mount of **O**,
13:3 sitting on the Mount of **O** facing
14:26 they went to the Mount of **O**.
Luk 19:29 Bethany at the Mount of **O** (as
19:37 went down the Mount of **O**.
21:37 would go to the Mount of **O** (as
22:39 the city⌋ to the Mount of **O** as
Jon 8:1 Jesus went to the Mount of **O**.
Act 1:12 called the Mount of **O**.
Jas 3:12 can a fig tree produce **o**?

Olympas (1)

Rom 16:15 Nereus, and his sister, and **O**,

Omar (3)

Gen 36:11 **O**, Zepho, Gatam, and Kenaz.
36:15 were Teman, **O**, Zepho, Kenaz,
1Ch 1:36 sons were Teman and **O**,

omen (1)

Isa 20:3 years as a sign and as an **o**

omens (4)

Num 24:1 he didn't look for **o** as he had
1Sm 6:2 people skilled in explaining **o**.
Eze 21:21 Then he will look for **o**.
21:22 The **o** will indicate that he

omit (1)

Est 6:10 Do not **o** anything you have

omitted (1)

Ezr 6:9 Make sure that nothing is **o**.

Omri (17)

1Ki 16:16 troops in the camp made **O**,
16:17 **O** and the Israelite troops with
16:21 The ⌊other⌋ half followed **O**.
16:22 But the half which followed **O**
16:22 Tibni died, and **O** became king.
16:23 **O** began to rule Israel in Asa's
16:24 **O** bought a hill from Shemer for
16:25 **O** did what the LORD
16:27 Isn't everything else about **O** —
16:28 **O** lay down in death with his
16:29 Ahab, son of **O**, began to rule
16:30 Ahab, son of **O**, did what the
2Ki 8:26 of King **O** of Israel.
1Ch 7:8 **O**, Jeremoth, Abijah, Anathoth,
9:4 of Ammihud, grandson of **O**,
27:18 of Issachar: **O**, son of Michael
2Ch 22:2 the granddaughter of **O**.

Omri's (1)

Mic 6:16 You have kept **O** laws and all

On (5)

Gen 41:45 priest from the city of **O**.
41:50 priest from the city of **O**.
46:20 priest from the city of **O**.
Num 16:1 and **O** (son of Peleth) dared to
16:1 Dathan, Abiram, and **O** were

Onam (3)

Gen 36:23 Ebal, Shepho, and **O**.
1Ch 1:40 Ebal, Shephi, and **O**.
2:26 and she was the mother of **O**.

Onam's (1)

1Ch 2:28 **O** sons were Shammai and

Onan (8)

Gen 38:4 whom she named **O**.
38:8 Then Judah said to **O**,
38:9 But **O** knew that the
38:10 What **O** did angered the LORD
46:12 The sons of Judah were Er, **O**,
46:12 (Er and **O** had died in Canaan.)

Num 26:19 Er and **O** were sons of Judah,
1Ch 2:3 Judah's sons were Er, **O**,

Onan's (1)
Gen 38:10 the LORD took away **O** life too.

Onesimus (4)
Col 4:9 I'm sending **O** with him.
4:9 **O** is from your city and is our
Phm 1:10 to you for my child **O** [Useful].
1:15 Maybe **O** was gone for a while

Onesiphorus (3)
2Ti 1:16 be merciful to the family of **O**.
1:18 May the Lord grant that **O** finds
4:19 and Aquila and the family of **O**.

onions (1)
Num 11:5 leeks, **o**, and garlic we had?

Ono (5)
1Ch 8:12 and Shemed (who built **O**,
Ezr 2:33 of Lod, Hadid, and **O**:
Neh 6:2 Hakkephirim on the plain of **O**."
7:37 of Lod, Hadid, and **O**:
11:35 Lod, **O**, and in the valley of the

onyx (12)
Gen 2:12 Bdellium and **o** are also
Exo 25:7 **o** stones, and other precious
28:9 Take two **o** stones,
28:20 In the fourth row put beryl, **o**,
35:9 **o** stones, and other precious
35:27 The leaders brought **o** stones
39:6 They mounted the **o** stones in
39:13 put beryl, **o**, and gray quartz.
1Ch 29:2 **o** stones and settings,
Job 28:16 or with precious **o** or sapphire.
Eze 28:13 beryl, **o**, gray quartz, sapphire,
Rev 21:20 the fifth **o**, the sixth red quartz,

ooze (1)
Job 7:5 over with sores; then they **o**.

oozing (1)
2Sm 3:29 Joab's family who have **o** sores

open (187)
Gen 7:11 all the deep springs burst **o**.
27:3 and go out into the **o** country
27:5 When Esau went into the **o**
27:27 like the smell of **o** country that
31:4 out to the **o** country where his
34:5 livestock out in the **o** country,
34:7 in from the **o** country as soon
37:15 around in the **o** country.
Exo 9:9 boils to break into **o** sores
9:10 boils to break into **o** sores
9:21 and animals out in the **o**.
9:25 that was out in the **o**.
Lev 1:17 bird's wings to tear the bird **o**,
14:7 bird fly away into the **o** country.
14:53 from the city into the **o** country.
17:5 been making in the **o** fields
Num 24:4 ⌊into a trance⌋ with his eyes **o**:
24:16 ⌊into a trance⌋ with his eyes **o**:
Dtr 20:11 If they accept it and **o** ⌊their
28:12 The LORD will **o** the heavens,
Jos 10:22 Joshua said, "**O** the cave,
Jdg 3:25 but Eglon didn't **o** the doors.
5:3 **O** your ears, you princes! I will
15:19 So God split **o** the hollow
18:10 The land is wide **o** to you.
20:31 men from Israel in the **o** country
1Sm 30:11 an Egyptian in the **o** country
2Sm 3:31 King David followed the **o**
10:8 by themselves in the **o** country.
1Ki 11:29 were alone in the **o** country,
2Ki 6:17 please **o** his eyes so that he
6:20 **o** the eyes of these men,
8:12 rip **o** their pregnant women."
9:3 Then **o** the door and leave
13:17 Elisha said, "**O** the window
15:16 Because the city didn't **o** its
15:16 he attacked it and ripped **o** all
19:16 **O** your eyes, LORD, and see.
2Ki 23:4 Jerusalem in an **o** field near
1Ch 9:27 guard it and **o** it every morning.
19:9 by themselves in the **o** country.
2Ch 6:40 may your eyes be **o** and your
7:15 My eyes will be **o**,
Neh 1:6 **O** your eyes, and pay close
8:16 in the **o** area by Water Gate,
8:16 or in the **o** area at Ephraim
Job 11:5 speak and **o** his mouth ⌊to
16:13 He slashes **o** my kidneys
28:4 They **o** up a mineshaft far from
32:20 I must **o** my mouth and answer.
34:2 **O** your ears to me,
34:16 **O** your ears to my words!
36:16 into an **o** area where you
37:14 "**O** your ears to this,
41:14 Who can **o** its closed mouth?
Psa 5:1 **O** your ears to my words,
5:9 Their throats are **o** graves.
17:1 **O** your ears to my prayer,
35:21 They **o** their big mouths and
39:9 I did not **o** my mouth because
39:12 **O** your ear to my cry for help.
49:1 **O** your ears, all who live in the
51:15 **O** Lord, **o** my lips, and my
54:2 O God, hear my prayer, and **o**
55:1 **O** your ears to my prayer,
60:2 You split it wide **o**.
77:1 so that he would **o** his ears
77:4 (You keep my eyelids **o**.)
78:1 **O** your ears to my teachings,
78:2 I will **o** my mouth to illustrate
80:1 **O** your ears, O Shepherd of
81:10 **O** your mouth wide,
84:8 **O** your ears, O God of Jacob.
86:6 **O** your ears to my prayer,
104:28 You **o** your hand, and they are
106:17 The ground split **o** and
118:19 **O** the gates of righteousness
119:131 I **o** my mouth and pant because
130:2 Let your ears be **o** to my pleas
140:6 O LORD, **o** your ears to hear
141:1 **O** your ears to me when I cry
143:1 **O** your ears to hear my urgent
145:16 You **o** your hand, and you
Pro 4:20 **O** your ears to what I say.
5:1 **O** your ears to my
5:13 my ear **o** to my instructors.
15:11 If Sheol and Abaddon lie **o** in
15:19 people is an ⌊**o**⌋ highway.
20:13 Keep your eyes **o**,
20:19 whose mouth is always **o**.
22:17 **O** your ears, and hear the
24:7 gate he does not **o** his mouth.
27:5 **O** criticism is better than
Sos 5:2 **O** to me, my true love,
5:5 I got up to **o** for my beloved.
Isa 9:12 devour Israel with **o** mouths.
22:22 What he shuts no one will **o**.
26:2 **O** the gates, and let the
28:23 **O** your ears, and listen to me!
37:17 **O** your eyes, LORD, and see.
42:20 Your ears are **o**, but you hear
45:1 and **o** doors ahead of him so
45:8 Let the earth **o**. Let salvation
48:8 Your ears have never been **o** to
50:5 Almighty LORD will **o** my ears.
51:4 **O** your ears to hear me,
53:7 but he didn't **o** his mouth.
53:7 He didn't **o** his mouth.
55:3 **O** your ears, and come to me!
60:11 Your gates will always be **o**.
64:1 If only you would split **o** the
Jer 5:16 arrow quivers are like **o** graves.
9:20 and **o** your ears to hear his
12:5 If you stumble in **o** country,
17:3 on mountains in the **o** country.
50:25 The LORD will **o** his armory
50:26 **o** their storehouses,
Eze 2:8 **O** your mouth, and eat what I
3:27 I will **o** your mouth.
16:5 you were thrown into an **o** field.
16:63 You will never again **o** your
25:9 That is why I'm going to **o** up
26:2 its doors are swung **o** to me.
29:5 You will fall in an **o** field.
Eze 32:4 and toss you into an **o** field.
33:27 Whoever is in the **o** field will
37:12 I will **o** your graves and take
37:13 because I will **o** your graves
39:5 You will die in the **o** field
41:9 There was an **o** area between
41:11 were entrances into the **o** area.
41:11 The base of the **o** area was 9
41:12 At the far end of the **o** area,
41:13 This included the **o** area with
41:14 including the **o** area,
41:24 double doors that swung **o**.
42:1 rooms opposite both the **o** area
42:10 They faced the **o** area and the
42:13 that face the **o** area are holy
45:2 place with an **o** area 87 ½
Dan 9:18 **O** your ears and listen,
9:18 **O** your eyes and look at our
Hos 4:16 like lambs in an **o** pasture?
5:1 **O** your ears, royal family!
13:8 I will rip you **o**. Like a lion I will
13:16 women will be ripped **o**.
Joe 1:2 **O** your ears, all inhabitants of
1:19 has burned up the **o** pastures.
1:20 Fire has burned up the **o**
Amo 1:13 by ripping **o** pregnant women
Mic 2:13 ⌊The LORD⌋ will **o** the way
4:10 live in the **o** fields,
Nah 3:13 of your country are wide **o**
Zec 11:1 **O** your doors, Lebanon, so that
Mal 3:10 "See if I won't **o** the windows
Mat 13:35 "I will **o** my mouth to illustrate
17:27 **O** its mouth, and you will find a
25:11 said, 'Sir, sir, **o** the door for us!'
26:43 they couldn't keep their eyes **o**.
27:51 and the rocks were split **o**.
Mar 1:10 he saw heaven split **o** and the
14:40 they couldn't keep their eyes **o**.
Luk 7:14 He went up to the **o** coffin,
12:36 Be like servants waiting to **o**
13:25 and say, 'Sir, **o** the door for us!'
Jon 1:51 You will see the sky **o** and
Act 1:18 His body split **o**, and all his
8:32 He didn't **o** his mouth.
10:11 He saw the sky **o** and
16:26 the doors immediately flew **o**,
16:27 up and saw the prison doors **o**.
26:18 You will **o** their eyes and turn
Rom 3:13 Their throats are **o** graves.
2Co 6:11 We have been very **o** in
7:2 **O** your hearts to us.
11:26 in the **o** country, on the sea,
Heb 9:8 holy place was not **o** while
Rev 3:7 ⌊a door⌋ that no one can **o**,
4:1 a door standing **o** in heaven.
5:2 "Who deserves to **o** the scroll
5:3 or under the earth could **o** the
5:4 was found who deserved to **o**
5:5 He can **o** the scroll and the
5:9 deserve to take the scroll and **o**
15:5 promise was **o** in heaven.
19:11 I saw heaven standing **o**.
21:25 Its gates will be **o** all day.

opened (90)
Gen 3:5 you eat it your eyes will be **o**.
3:7 Then their eyes were **o**,
7:11 springs burst open. The sky **o**,
8:6 After 40 more days Noah **o** the
8:13 Noah **o** the top of the ship,
21:19 God **o** her eyes. Then she saw
41:56 Joseph **o** all the storehouses
42:27 one of them **o** his sack to feed
43:21 for the night, we **o** our sacks,
44:11 his sack to the ground and **o** it.
Exo 2:6 daughter **o** the basket,
Num 16:32 and the earth **o** up to swallow
26:10 The ground **o** up and
Dtr 11:6 the Israelites the ground **o** up
Jdg 3:25 took the key and **o** the door.
19:27 **o** the doors of the house,
1Sm 3:15 Then he **o** the doors of the
2Ki 4:35 seven times and **o** his eyes.
6:17 The LORD **o** the servant's eyes
6:20 The LORD **o** their eyes and let
9:10 Then he **o** the door and left.

2Ki 13:17 So the king **o** it. "Shoot," Elisha
2Ch 29:3 he **o** the doors of the LORD's
Neh 7:3 of Jerusalem should not be **o** at
8:5 **o** the book in front of all the
8:5 As he **o** it, all the people stood
Job 3:1 After all this, Job ⌊finally⌋ **o**
29:23 They **o** their mouths wide as if
31:32 because I **o** my door to the
32:19 of⌊ wine that has not been **o**,
33:2 I've **o** my mouth. The words are
Psa 22:13 They have **o** their mouths to
74:15 You **o** the springs and brooks.
78:23 the clouds above and **o**
105:41 He **o** a rock, and water gushed
109:2 have **o** their mouths against
Sos 5:6 I **o** for my beloved,
7:12 if the grape blossoms have **o**,
Isa 10:14 a wing, **o** its mouth, or peeped."
24:18 floodgates in the sky will be **o**,
35:5 the eyes of the blind will be **o**,
Eze 1:1 by the Chebar River, the sky **o**,
3:2 So I **o** my mouth, and he gave
24:27 very day your mouth will be **o**,
40:38 room with a door that **o** toward
44:2 will stay shut and will not be **o**.
46:1 but it must be **o** on the weekly
46:1 It must also be **o** on the New
46:12 the east gate must be **o** for him.
Dan 6:10 his house had windows that **o**
7:10 and the books were **o**.
10:16 I **o** my mouth and began to talk.
Nah 2:6 The gates of the rivers are **o**,
Zec 13:1 that day a fountain will be **o**
Mat 2:11 Then they **o** their treasure
3:16 Suddenly, the heavens were **o**,
7:7 and the door will be **o** for you.
7:8 who knocks, the door will be **o**.
27:52 The tombs were **o**,
Mar 7:34 which means, "Be **o**!"
14:3 She **o** the bottle and poured the
Luk 3:21 he was praying, heaven **o**,
4:17 He **o** it and found the place
11:9 and the door will be **o** for you.
11:10 who knocks, the door will be **o**.
24:31 Then their eyes were **o**,
24:32 with us on the road and **o** up
24:45 Then he **o** their minds to
Act 5:19 night an angel from the Lord **o**
5:23 However, when we **o** the doors,
7:56 I see heaven **o** and the Son of
9:8 When he **o** his eyes,
9:40 Tabitha **o** her eyes,
12:10 This gate **o** by itself for them,
12:16 When they **o** the door,
Heb 10:20 Jesus has **o** a new and living
Rev 3:8 See, I have **o** a door in front of
6:1 I watched as the lamb **o** the
6:3 When the lamb **o** the second
6:5 When the lamb **o** the third seal,
6:7 When the lamb **o** the fourth
6:9 When the lamb **o** the fifth seal,
6:12 I watched as the lamb **o** the
8:1 When he **o** the seventh seal,
9:2 It **o** the shaft of the bottomless
10:2 **o** scroll in his hand.
10:8 It said, "Take the **o** scroll from
11:19 God's temple in heaven was **o**,
13:6 It **o** its mouth to insult God,
20:12 Books were **o**, including the

opening (19)

Gen 6:16 and leave an 18-inch-high **o** at
29:2 with a large stone over the **o**.
29:3 stone would be rolled off the **o**
29:3 in place over the **o** of the well.
29:8 the stone is rolled off the **o**
29:10 and rolled the stone off the **o**
Exo 28:32 Make an **o** for the head in the
39:23 The **o** in the center of the robe
1Ki 7:31 Each had a 1 1 opening in the
7:31 **T** opening was round,
7:31 Around **t** opening there were
Pro 17:14 quarrel is ⌊like⌋ **o** a floodgate,
Dan 6:17 brought and placed over the **o**
Mar 2:4 they made an **o** in the roof over
Luk 5:19 They made an **o** in the tiles

Act 9:25 in a large basket through an **o**
12:14 that instead of **o** the door,
2Co 11:33 down in a basket through an **o**
Rev 12:16 the woman by **o** its mouth

openly (9)

Gen 44:18 let me speak **o** with you.
Isa 65:3 constantly and **o** provoked me.
Eze 21:24 are because you **o** do wrong.
23:18 carried out her prostitution **o**,
Mar 1:45 no longer enter any city **o**.
Jon 7:13 Yet, no one would talk **o** about
11:54 So Jesus no longer walked **o**
Act 19:18 Many believers **o** admitted their
Gal 2:11 I had to **o** oppose him because

open-minded (1)

Act 17:11 of Berea were more **o** than

opens (14)

Exo 21:33 "Whenever someone **o** up a
Num 16:30 totally new — if the ground **o** up
Job 27:19 When he **o** his eyes,
33:16 he **o** people's ears and terrifies
35:16 Job **o** his mouth for no good
36:15 and he **o** their ears through
Pro 17:4 A liar **o** his ears to a
18:16 A gift **o** doors for the one who
31:20 She **o** her hands to oppressed
Isa 5:14 It **o** its mouth very wide so that
22:22 What he **o** no one will shut.
Jon 10:3 The gatekeeper **o** the gate for
Rev 3:7 who **o** ⌊a door⌋ that no one can
3:20 to my voice and **o** the door,

Ophel (6)

2Ki 5:24 came to the **O** in Samaria,
2Ch 27:3 building of the wall at the **O**.
33:14 made the wall go around the **O**,
Neh 3:26 living on the **O** made repairs
3:27 as far as the Wall of the **O**.
11:21 servants lived on Mount **O**

Ophir (13)

Gen 10:29 **O**, Havilah, and Jobab.
1Ki 9:28 they went to **O**, got 31,500
10:11 gold from **O** also brought
10:11 and precious stones from **O**.
22:48 ships to go to **O** for gold.
1Ch 1:23 **O**, Havilah, and Jobab.
29:4 225,000 pounds of gold from **O**
2Ch 8:18 with Solomon's servants to **O**,
9:10 **O** also brought sandalwood
Job 22:24 and put your gold from **O**
28:16 be bought with the gold from **O**
Psa 45:9 hand and wears gold from **O**.
Isa 13:12 more rare than gold from **O**.

Ophni (1)

Jos 18:24 Chephar Ammoni, **O**,

Ophrah (8)

Jos 18:23 Avvim, Parah, **O**,
Jdg 6:11 the oak tree in **O** that belonged
6:24 To this day it is still in **O**,
8:27 placed it in his hometown, **O**.
8:32 tomb of his father Joash at **O**,
9:5 went to his father's home in **O**.
1Sm 13:17 turned onto the road to **O**
1Ch 4:14 Meonothai was the father of **O**.

opinion (7)

Dtr 17:9 Ask for their **o**, and they will
Pro 18:2 only in expressing his own **o**.
Rom 14:1 argument over differences of **o**.
1Co 6:4 whom the church has a low **o**
7:25 the Lord, I'll give you my **o**.
7:40 That is my **o**, and I think that I,
2Co 8:10 I'm giving you my **o** because it

opinions (2)

Jon 9:16 were divided in their **o**.
1Co 1:10 in your understanding and **o**.

opponent (10)

Exo 23:22 and an **o** to your opponents.

2Sm 2:16 Each one grabbed his **o** by the
1Ki 20:20 Each officer killed his **o**.
Job 16:9 My **o** looked sharply at me.
Ecc 4:12 two people can resist one **o**.
Lam 2:4 Like an **o** his right hand held
Mat 5:25 with your **o** while you are
Luk 12:58 For instance, when an **o** brings
Eph 6:12 match against a human **o**.
1Pe 5:8 Your **o** the devil is prowling

opponent's (1)

2Sm 2:16 stuck his sword into his **o** side,

opponents (26)

Exo 23:22 and an opponent to your **o**.
Dtr 32:27 I didn't want their **o** to
2Sm 22:40 You made my **o** bow at my feet.
22:49 You lift me up above my **o**.
Psa 8:2 built a fortress against your **o**
10:5 He spits at all his **o**.
13:4 My **o** will rejoice because I
18:39 You made my **o** bow at my feet.
18:48 You lift me up above my **o**.
27:2 My **o** and enemies stumbled
27:12 me to the will of my **o**.
31:11 a disgrace because of all my **o**.
69:19 All my **o** are in front of you.
74:4 Your **o** have roared inside your
74:23 forget the shouting of your **o**.
119:157 I have many persecutors and **o**,
Isa 1:24 when I take revenge on my **o**!
11:13 and Judah's **o** will come to an
59:18 He will pay back his **o** with
Lam 1:5 Its **o** are now in control.
1:5 ahead of their **o** into captivity.
1:7 Their **o** looked on,
1:17 neighbors will become his **o**.
2:17 raised the weapons of your **o**.
Mic 5:9 use your power against your **o**,
Php 1:28 So don't let your **o** intimidate

opportunities (5)

Ezr 9:8 given us new **o** while we were
Act 17:21 lived in Athens looked for **o**
Rom 15:23 But now I have no new **o** for
Eph 5:16 Make the most of your **o**
Col 4:5 Make the most of your **o**.

opportunity (25)

Jdg 11:37 never have an **o** to get married."
14:4 The LORD was looking for an **o**
Ezr 9:9 He did this to give us an **o** to
Ecc 5:11 all their goods⌋ except ⌊the **o**⌋
Hos 13:13 They have the **o** to live again,
Mar 6:21 An **o** finally came on Herod's
Luk 20:20 So they watched for an **o** to
21:13 It will be your **o** to testify to
22:6 He kept looking for an **o** to
Act 14:27 not Jewish the **o** to believe.
Rom 7:8 But sin took the **o** provided by
7:11 Sin, taking the **o** provided by
1Co 16:9 I have a great **o** to do effective
16:12 visit you when he has an **o**.
2Co 2:12 the Lord gave me an **o** to
5:12 but we are giving you an **o** to
6:3 We don't give people any **o** to
11:12 This will take away the **o** of
Gal 6:10 Whenever we have the **o**,
Eph 4:27 give the devil any **o** ⌊to work⌋.
Php 4:10 did not have an **o** to show it.
Col 4:3 Pray that God will give us an **o**
Heb 3:13 day while you have the **o**.
2Pe 3:9 wants all people to have an **o**
3:15 Lord's patience as an **o** ⌊for us⌋

oppose (31)

Lev 26:40 things they did to **o** me —
26:41 I will **o** them and bring them
Dtr 9:2 "Who can **o** the descendants of
Jos 1:5 No one will be able to **o** you
1Sm 2:10 "Those who **o** the LORD are
2Ch 13:3 while Jeroboam arranged to **o**
14:11 Don't let anyone successfully **o**
20:6 and no one can **o** you.
Ezr 8:22 but his power and his anger **o**
Job 9:4 Who could **o** him and win?

Psa	66:7	will not be able to o him.
	109:6	"Appoint the evil one to o him.
Pro	28:4	teachings o wicked people.
Isa	11:13	and Judah won't o Ephraim.
	41:11	Those who o you will be
Lam	1:14	me over to people I cannot o.
Dan	4:35	There is no one who can o him
	8:25	He will o the Commander of
Nah	1:6	Who can o his burning anger?
Mat	5:39	But I tell you not to o an evil
Luk	21:15	be able to o or prove wrong.
Act	17:7	All of them o the emperor's
	26:9	I had to do a lot of things to o
1Co	16:9	are many people who o me.
2Co	10:5	intellectual arrogance that o
Gal	2:11	I had to openly o him because
1Ti	6:20	use to o ⌊the Christian faith⌋.
2Ti	2:25	in correcting those who o
	3:8	so these men o the truth.
Tit	1:9	correct those who o the word.
	2:8	Then those who o us will be

opposed (14)

Num	16:19	followers — those who o Moses
2Ch	13:7	They o Rehoboam,
	26:18	They o King Uzziah.
	28:12	Ephraim) o those coming home
Ezr	10:15	Jahzeiah, Tikvah's son, o this.
Jer	50:24	because you have o the LORD.
Dan	10:13	of the Persian kingdom o me
Luk	13:17	everyone who o him felt
Act	7:51	They always o the Holy Spirit,
	13:8	o them and tried to distort the
	18:6	But they o him and insulted
Gal	5:17	They are o to each other.
2Ti	3:8	Jannes and Jambres o Moses,
	4:15	He violently o what we said.

opposes (5)

Pro	18:1	He o all sound reasoning.
Rom	13:2	government o what God has
2Th	2:4	He o every so-called god or
Jas	4:6	"God o arrogant people,
1Pe	5:5	because God o the arrogant but

opposing (3)

1Sm	17:48	David quickly ran toward the o
1Co	1:10	and not to split into o groups.
	11:18	you split up into o groups.

opposite (33)

Gen	15:10	and laid each half o the other.
Exo	26:5	placing the loops o each other.
	26:35	and put the lamp stand o the
	30:4	below the molding on o sides
	36:12	placing the loops o each other.
	37:27	below the molding on o sides
	40:24	the tent of meeting o the table,
Jos	3:16	River⌋ directly o Jericho.
	8:33	and judges were standing on o
	18:17	and from there to the region o
2Sm	2:24	o Giah on the road from Gibeon
1Ki	7:4	each other on o sides ⌊of
	7:5	each other on o sides ⌊of
	20:27	The Israelites, while camped o
	21:10	good-for-nothing men sit o him
	21:13	men came in and sat o him.
2Ch	7:6	The priests were o the Levites
Est	9:1	the exact o happened:
Eze	16:34	You are the o. You pay them,
	40:13	to the top of the o guardroom.
	40:13	from one door to the o door.
	40:23	courtyard had a gateway o
	40:27	the south side to its o gateway.
	42:1	me to the side rooms o both
	42:3	O the inner courtyard was an
	42:3	and o the pavement of the outer
	46:9	They must leave through the o
	47:20	up to a point o Hamath Pass.
Dan	5:5	and wrote on the plaster wall o
1Co	12:22	The o is true. The parts of the
2Co	2:17	The o is true. As Christ's
Php	3:9	The o is true! I have God's
	4:17	The o is true. I'm looking for

opposition (4)

Job	17:2	My eyes are focused on their o.
1Co	4:6	one of us in o to the other.
1Th	2:2	Good News in spite of strong o.
Heb	12:3	who endured o from sinners,

oppress (39)

Exo	1:11	order to o them through forced
	22:21	"Never mistreat or o foreigners,
	23:9	"Never o foreigners.
Lev	19:13	"Never o or rob your neighbor.
1Sm	12:3	Did I cheat or o anyone?
	12:4	"You didn't cheat us, o us,
2Sm	7:10	The wicked will no longer o
1Ch	16:21	didn't permit anyone to o them.
Job	37:23	righteousness, and does not o.
Psa	56:1	All day long warriors o me.
	105:14	didn't permit anyone to o them.
	119:121	the mercy of those who o me.
	119:122	Do not let arrogant people o me.
Isa	3:5	People will o each other,
	3:5	everyone will o his neighbor.
	3:12	"Children will o my people.
	19:20	because of those who o them,
	51:13	of the fury of those who o you,
	51:13	is the fury of those who o you?
	60:14	of those who o you will bow
Jer	7:6	you do not o foreigners,
	21:12	robbed from those who o them.
	22:3	robbed from those who o them.
	22:3	or widows, and don't o them.
	22:17	and violently o your people."
Eze	18:7	He doesn't o anyone.
	18:16	He doesn't o anyone.
	22:7	They o foreigners in you.
	22:7	They o orphans and widows in
	22:29	The common people o and rob
	22:29	They o foreigners for no reason.
	45:8	will no longer o my people.
Dan	7:25	o the holy people of the Most
Amo	4:1	You women o the poor and
	5:12	You o the righteous by taking
	6:14	They will o you from the border
Zec	7:10	Don't o widows, orphans,
Mal	3:5	of their wages and o widows
Jas	2:6	Don't rich people o you and

oppressed (68)

Gen	15:13	they will be o for 400 years.
Exo	1:12	the more the Israelites were o,
	2:25	saw the Israelites ⌊being o⌋
Dtr	26:6	treated us cruelly, o us,
	28:29	you will be o and robbed with
Jdg	2:18	who were tormented and o.
	4:3	of iron and had cruelly o Israel
	6:9	the power of those who o you.
	10:8	They o and crushed the people
	10:8	For 18 years they o all who
	10:12	and the Maonites o you,
1Sm	12:8	Jacob to Egypt ⌊and were o⌋,
2Ki	13:22	King Hazael of Aram o Israel
2Ch	16:10	Asa also o some of the people
Job	36:6	justice to those who are o.
Psa	9:9	LORD is a stronghold for the o,
	9:12	has remembered o people.
	9:18	Nor will the hope of o people
	10:2	arrogantly pursues o people.
	10:9	hides there to catch o people.
	10:9	He catches o people when he
	10:12	Do not forget o people!
	10:17	heard the desire of o people,
	10:18	orphans and o people so that
	12:5	"Because o people are robbed
	14:6	They put the advice of o
	22:24	with the plight of the o one.
	22:24	The LORD heard when that o
	22:26	O people will eat until they are
	25:16	pity on me. I am lonely and o.
	34:2	Those who are o will hear it
	37:11	O people will inherit the land
	37:14	and bend their bows to kill o
	40:17	But I am o and needy.
	68:10	you provided for o people.
	69:32	O people will see ⌊this⌋ and
	70:5	But I am o and needy.
Psa	72:2	your o ⌊people⌋ with justice.
	72:4	justice to the people who are o.
	72:12	help and the o person who has
	74:19	the life of your o people forever.
	74:21	Do not let o people come back
	76:9	when you rose to save every o
	82:3	the rights of the o and the poor.
	86:1	because I am o and needy.
	103:6	right and fair for all who are o.
	106:42	Their enemies o them and
	109:16	"He drove o, needy,
	109:22	I am o and needy. I can feel the
	140:12	the rights of those who are o
	146:7	justice for those who are o.
	147:6	gives relief to those who are o.
	149:4	those who are o with victory.
Pro	22:22	on the rights of an o person at
	30:14	devours o people from the earth
	31:5	of justice for all o people.
	31:9	rights of o and needy people."
	31:20	She opens her hands to o
Ecc	5:8	if you see poor people being o,
Isa	26:6	Feet trample it, the feet of the o,
	52:4	Later the Assyrians o them for
	58:6	of the yoke, let the o go free,
Jer	50:33	of Israel and Judah are o.
Eze	18:18	But his father has o others,
Hos	5:11	Ephraim is o — crushed by
Amo	8:4	those who are o in the world.
Zec	11:7	and also of the o sheep.
	11:11	and the o among the sheep

oppresses (6)

Psa	42:9	while the enemy o me?"
	43:2	while the enemy o me?
Pro	14:31	Whoever o the poor insults his
	28:3	A poor person who o poorer
Jer	30:20	punish everyone who o them.
Eze	18:12	He o the poor and needy.

oppressing (7)

Exo	3:9	how the Egyptians are o them.
Num	10:9	an enemy who is o you,
1Sm	10:18	all the kings who were o you.
	11:1	of Ammon was severely o
2Ki	13:4	the Aramean king was o Israel.
Job	13:21	Stop o me. Don't let your terror
Pro	22:16	O the poor for profit ⌊or⌋ giving

oppression (21)

Exo	6:6	bring you out from under the o
Dtr	26:7	our misery, suffering, and o.
	28:33	know nothing but o and abuse.
Job	35:9	The weight of o makes them
Psa	10:7	of cursing, deception, and o.
	55:11	O and fraud never leave the
	72:14	them from o and violence.
	73:8	They speak arrogantly about o.
	107:39	were humiliated because of o,
	119:134	Save me from human o so that
Ecc	4:1	the acts of o that make people
	7:7	O can turn a wise person into a
Isa	26:16	They were humbled by o,
	30:12	trusted o and deceit,
	54:14	You will be far from o.
	59:13	spoken about o and revolt.
Jer	6:6	There is nothing but o in it.
	9:6	O follows oppression.
	9:6	Oppression follows o.
Lam	1:7	during its suffering and o,
Amo	3:9	confusion and o in Samaria."

oppressive (1)

Isa	10:1	and who make o regulations.

oppressor (6)

Psa	72:4	needy people and crush their o.
	78:42	day he freed them from their o,
	78:61	handed his glory over to an o.
Pro	29:13	A poor person and an o have
Isa	9:4	and the stick used by their o,
Jer	25:38	because of the heat of the o,

oppressors (6)

Ecc	4:1	Their o have ⌊all⌋ the power.
Isa	1:17	Arrest o. Defend orphans.

Isa 9:11 The LORD will set Rezin's **o**
14:2 captors captive and rule their **o**.
49:26 I will make your **o** eat their own
Zec 9:8 No **o** will pass through them,

orchard (1)

Isa 10:18 The majestic forest and the **o**

orchards (8)

Jdg 15:5 Their olive **o** also caught on
1Sm 8:14 and olive **o** and give them to
2Ki 5:26 olive **o**, vineyards, sheep,
Neh 5:11 their vineyards, their olive **o**,
Isa 16:10 have vanished from the **o**.
Jer 48:33 have disappeared from the **o**
Joe 1:12 as well as all the trees in the **o**,
1:19 burned up all the trees in the **o**.

ordain (7)

Exo 28:41 his sons, anoint them, **o** them,
29:9 In this way you will **o** Aaron
29:35 Take seven days to **o** them.
Lev 8:33 It will take seven days to **o**
1Ti 4:14 their hands on you ⌊to **o** you⌋.
5:22 hands on anyone ⌊to **o** him⌋.
2Ti 1:6 my hands on you ⌊to **o** you⌋.

ordained (8)

Exo 29:29 can be anointed and **o** in them.
32:29 Moses said, "Today you are **o**
Lev 7:35 them on the day Moses **o** them
16:32 priest who is anointed and **o**
Num 3:3 who were **o** to serve as priests.
Jdg 17:5 He **o** one of his sons to be his
17:12 Micah **o** the Levite.
2Ch 13:9 and seven rams can be **o** as

order (251)

Gen 1:6 in the middle of the water in **o**
6:19 living creature into the ship in **o**
25:13 sons of Ishmael listed in the **o**
32:5 to tell you ⌊this news⌋ in **o**
45:19 "Give them this **o**:
48:17 he took his father's hand in **o**
Exo 1:11 drivers in charge of them in **o**
6:16 sons of Levi listed in birth **o**:
6:19 from Levi listed in birth **o**.
25:14 sides of the ark in **o** to carry it.
26:13 hang over each side in **o**
28:10 in birth **o** — six of their names
29:1 this is what you must do in **o** to
29:36 offering for sin on the altar in **o**
29:36 olive oil⌋ in **o** to dedicate it.
37:5 sides of the ark in **o** to carry it.
Lev 12:4 stay at home for 33 days in **o**
12:5 stay at home for 66 days in **o**
13:54 he must **o** the area to be
14:4 the priest will **o** someone to get
14:5 Then the priest will **o** someone
14:29 of the one to be cleansed in **o**
14:36 he will **o** everything taken out
14:40 the priest must **o** the stones
16:3 is what Aaron must do in **o**
16:10 it in the desert to Azazel in **o**
19:12 "Never swear by my name in **o**
22:9 The priests must do what I **o**,
22:19 or goats in **o** to be accepted.
22:21 animal that has no defects in **o**
25:10 Every slave will be freed in **o**
25:13 every slave will be freed in **o**
Num 2:17 out in the same **o** as they are
6:9 he must shave his head in **o**
8:21 with the LORD for them in **o**
10:28 This was the **o** in which the
16:13 you also have to **o** us around?
21:4 in **o** to get around Edom.
31:19 the third and seventh days in **o**
31:23 must be put through fire in **o**
31:23 put through the ritual water in **o**
35:24 must use these rules in **o**
Dtr 2:30 stubborn and overconfident in **o**
4:20 in **o** to make you his own
8:2 He did this in **o** to humble you
8:16 He did this in **o** to humble you
20:19 a city for a long time in **o**
24:6 prepare food in **o** to stay alive.
Dtr 25:2 the judge will **o** him to lie
Jos 3:8 **O** the priests who carry the ark
4:3 **O** them to pick up 12 stones
4:16 "**O** the priests who carry the
8:29 Joshua gave the **o** to take his
10:27 Joshua gave the **o** to take them
11:5 of Merom in **o** to fight Israel.
Jdg 4:6 of Israel has given you this **o**:
9:9 in **o** to rule the trees?'
9:11 sweet fruit in **o** to rule the
9:13 in **o** to rule the trees?'
16:5 We want to tie him up in **o** to
20:32 "Let's flee in **o** to lead them
Rut 4:7 In **o** to make every matter legal,
1Sm 1:6 tormented her endlessly in **o**
2:8 needy from the trash heap in **o**
7:16 and Mizpah in **o** to judge Israel
9:24 "This was kept in **o** to be laid
15:21 were claimed for God — in **o**
17:48 moved closer in **o** to attack,
24:11 are trying to ambush me in **o**
2Sm 4:12 So David gave an **o** to his
7:23 earth that God came to free in **o**
13:28 Then Absalom gave an **o** to his
13:28 I've given you the **o**,
14:8 "I will **o** someone to take care
14:11 pray to the LORD your God in **o**
14:29 So Absalom sent for Joab in **o**
17:14 defeated in **o** to ruin Absalom.)
18:5 this **o** regarding Absalom.
18:12 We heard the **o** the king gave
24:4 So they left the king ⌊in **o**⌋ to
1Ki 5:6 So **o** men to cut down cedars
5:17 expensive blocks of stone in **o**
6:19 inner room of the temple in **o**
18:6 So they split up in **o** to cover
18:19 **O** all Israel to gather around me
2Ki 3:13 has called the three of us in **o**
22:12 Then the king gave an **o** to the
22:17 sacrificed to other gods in **o**
1Ch 4:41 in place of the Meunites in **o**
13:5 to the border of Hamath in **o**
15:14 made themselves holy in **o**
17:21 earth that God came to free in **o**
21:6 disgusted with the king's **o**.
28:8 Now, ⌊leaders, I **o** you⌋ in the
2Ch 18:31 So they surrounded him in **o** to
24:8 The king issued an **o**,
24:21 and by the king's **o** they stoned
29:15 Then they obeyed the king's **o**
30:6 The king's **o** said, "Israelites,
34:20 the king gave an **o** to Hilkiah,
34:25 sacrificed to other gods in **o**
Ezr 3:2 They built it in **o** to sacrifice
4:19 I gave the **o**, and a search was
4:21 So **o** these men to stop
4:21 being rebuilt until I give the **o**.
6:1 Then King Darius gave the **o** to
7:21 I, King Artaxerxes, **o** all the
Neh 2:8 In the letter **o** him to give me
5:3 and our homes in **o** to get some
6:13 reputation in **o** to discredit me.
7:3 **O** some of the men in
8:14 given an **o** through Moses that
9:29 You warned them in **o** to bring
10:34 have drawn lots to decide the **o**
Est 8:5 He signed ⌊the **o**⌋ to destroy
9:24 means the lot) thrown ⌊in **o**
9:29 wrote with full authority in **o**
9:31 He did this in **o** to establish
Job 1:5 Job would send for them in **o** to
30:13 all traces of my path in **o**
34:23 to set a time for a person in **o**
38:27 the desolate wasteland in **o**
39:27 Is it by your **o** that the eagle
Psa 10:18 in **o** to provide justice for
27:4 all the days of my life in **o**
33:9 He gave the **o**, and there it
34:16 those who do evil in **o**
49:9 in **o** to live forever and never
71:3 You gave the **o** to save me!
73:9 and they **o** people around on
104:14 for humans to use in **o**
119:71 good that I had to suffer in **o**
119:95 people have waited for me in **o**
119:101 walking⌋ on any evil path in **o**
Psa 145:12 in **o** to make known your
Pro 2:8 in **o** to guard those on paths of
4:1 in **o** to gain understanding.
7:5 in **o** to guard yourself from an
15:24 wise person leads upward in **o**
22:21 in **o** to teach you the words of
Ecc 1:7 where the streams began in **o**
3:18 is going to test humans in **o**
7:27 added one thing to another in **o**
10:17 eat at the right time in **o**
Isa 10:6 In my fury I **o** them against the
20:4 in **o** to disgrace Egypt.
22:10 tear down those houses in **o**
23:9 of Armies planned this in **o**
32:6 and their minds plan evil in **o** to
32:7 They devise wicked plans in **o**
49:5 the womb to be his servant in **o**
Jer 7:18 offerings to other gods in **o**
7:31 the valley of Ben Hinnom in **o**
13:10 and follow other gods in **o**
18:20 and pleaded for them in **o**
27:4 Give them an **o** for their
35:6 Rechab's son, gave us this **o**:
35:14 This **o** has been carried out.
35:14 have obeyed their ancestor's **o**.
35:15 and don't follow other gods in **o**
35:18 You obeyed the **o** of your
39:11 an **o** concerning Jeremiah.
43:3 has turned you against us in **o**
50:34 take up their cause in **o**
Lam 1:17 has given this **o** about Jacob:
2:14 didn't expose your guilt in **o**
3:37 It was the Lord who gave the **o**.
Eze 3:18 change their wicked ways in **o**
21:22 rams there, give the **o** to kill,
24:8 In **o** to stir up my fury so that I
Dan 2:12 and furious that he gave an **o**
3:10 Your Majesty, you gave an **o**
3:11 ⌊Your **o** said that⌋ whoever
3:12 These men didn't obey your **o**,
3:22 The king's **o** was so urgent and
3:29 So I **o** that people from every
6:13 refuses to obey your **o** or the
6:16 So the king gave the **o**,
11:17 king his daughter as a wife in **o**
11:35 will be defeated in **o** to refine,
Amo 1:6 all the people captive in **o**
4:8 they walked to another city in **o**
9:9 I'm going to give the **o**.
Jnh 3:7 "This is an **o** from the king and
Hab 2:9 for his own household in **o**
2:15 making him drunk in **o** to stare
Mat 5:40 someone wants to sue you in **o**
6:1 your good works in public in **o**
6:2 and on the streets in **o**
8:26 Then he got up, gave an **o** to
12:44 swept clean, and in **o**.
14:28 **o** me to come to you on the
17:11 will put everything in **o** again.
19:7 did Moses **o** a man to give his
26:59 Jesus in **o** to execute him.
27:64 Therefore, give the **o** to make
Mar 3:10 up to him in **o** to touch him.
7:9 the commandments of God in **o**
9:12 will put everything in **o** again.
9:25 he gave an **o** to the evil spirit.
14:55 testimony against Jesus in **o**
Luk 8:31 begged Jesus not to **o** them
11:25 house swept clean and in **o**.
Jon 10:17 me because I give my life in **o**
Act 6:2 word in **o** to distribute food.
9:24 and night in **o** to murder him.
13:47 Lord gave us the following **o**:
16:36 The jailer reported this **o** to
17:5 it for Paul and Silas in **o**
19:13 These Jews would say, "I **o**
25:23 Festus gave the **o**,
Rom 8:17 share in Christ's suffering in **o**
8:21 free from slavery to decay in **o**
15:16 I do this in **o** that I might bring
1Co 1:28 considers to be nothing — in **o**
3:18 give up that wisdom in **o**
7:2 But in **o** to avoid sexual sins,
9:12 put up with anything in **o** not
9:15 and I haven't written this in **o** to
9:22 everything to everyone in **o**

1Co 9:23 the sake of the Good News in **o**
11:19 Factions have to exist in **o** to
14:19 in **o** to teach others in church,
2Co 8:9 your sake he became poor in **o**
12:9 in **o** that Christ's power
Gal 1:4 In **o** to free us from this present
2:16 believed in Jesus Christ in **o**
Eph 2:7 out of his generosity to us in **o**
Php 1:17 out of selfish ambition in **o**
2:30 died for the work of Christ in **o**
3:8 it all away in **o** to gain Christ
1Th 4:8 whoever rejects this ⌊**o**⌋ is not
5:27 In the Lord's name, I **o** you to
2Th 3:6 Lord Jesus Christ we **o** you not
3:8 struggled night and day in **o** not
3:10 we gave you the **o**:
3:12 We **o** and encourage such
1Ti 1:3 That way you could **o** certain
1:5 My goal in giving you this **o** is
1:18 I'm giving you this **o** about the
1:20 have handed over to Satan in **o**
Phm 1:8 me bold enough to **o** you
Heb 9:16 In **o** for a will to take effect,
10:9 did away with sacrifices in **o**
11:23 afraid to disobey the king's **o**.
1Pe 4:12 troubles that are coming in **o**
1Jn 3:5 know that Christ appeared in **o**
Jud 1:16 and flatter people in **o** to take
Rev 11:6 authority to shut the sky in **o**
12:14 wings of the large eagle in **o**
12:15 of water behind the woman in **o**

ordered (146)

Gen 26:11 So Abimelech **o** his people,
38:24 Judah **o**, "Bring her out to be
45:21 for their trip as Pharaoh had **o**.
47:11 As Pharaoh had **o**,
50:2 Then Joseph **o** the doctors in
Exo 5:14 finish all the bricks you were **o**
38:21 An inventory was **o** by Moses
Jos 1:10 Then Joshua **o** the officers of
4:8 of Israel did as Joshua had **o**.
4:10 the LORD had **o** Joshua
4:17 So Joshua **o** the priests,
6:10 Joshua **o** the troops,
18:8 Joshua **o** them to write a
Jdg 21:10 They **o** them, "Go and kill the
Rut 2:9 I have **o** my young men not to
2:15 Boaz **o** his servants,
1Sm 14:38 So Saul **o** all the leaders of the
17:20 and went, as Jesse **o** him.
18:22 Saul **o** his officers,
20:29 and my brother **o** me to be
21:2 "The king **o** me to do
2Sm 5:25 David did as the LORD **o** him
7:7 of the judges of Israel whom I **o**
13:29 to Amnon as Absalom had **o**.
14:19 Yes, your servant Joab **o** me
18:5 The king **o** Joab, Abishai,
21:14 They did everything the king **o**.
2Ki 9:21 horses to the chariot," Joram **o**.
9:27 Jehu pursued him and **o**,
10:14 Jehu **o**, "Capture them!"
11:5 He **o** them, "This is what you
11:9 the priest Jehoiada had **o** them.
11:15 Then the priest Jehoiada **o** the
23:4 Then the king **o** the chief priest
23:21 The king **o** all the people to
1Ch 14:12 so David **o** that the gods be
14:16 David did as God **o** him,
16:40 They were **o** to sacrifice burnt
17:6 of the judges of Israel whom I **o**
21:17 "I'm the one who **o** the people
22:2 David **o** the foreigners living in
22:17 David **o** all the leaders of Israel
2Ch 19:9 He **o** them, "Do this
23:8 the priest Jehoiada had **o** them.
29:25 and the prophet Nathan had **o**.
29:27 Then Hezekiah **o** the
35:10 divisions, as the king had **o**.
36:23 Then he **o** me to build a temple
Ezr 1:2 Then he **o** me to build a temple
4:3 Cyrus of Persia **o** us to do."
6:12 to be carried out exactly as **o**.
6:13 what King Darius had **o**.
6:14 as the God of Israel had **o**
Ezr 6:14 (the kings of Persia) had **o**.
Neh 5:18 days a supply of wine was **o**.
12:24 David, the man of God, had **o**.
12:45 son Solomon had **o** them to do.
13:19 I **o** the doors to be shut and not
Est 1:8 (The king had **o** all the waiters
1:10 wine, he **o** Mehuman, Biztha,
1:17 They will say, 'King Xerxes **o**
2:10 Mordecai had **o** her not to.
2:20 as Mordecai had **o** her.
3:13 ⌊The people were **o**⌋ to wipe
8:9 What Mordecai had **o** was
9:25 he **o**, in the well-known letter,
Psa 111:9 He has **o** that his promise
Jer 35:8 in everything he **o** us to do.
35:10 ancestor Jonadab **o** us to do.
35:14 Jonadab, Rechab's son, **o** his
47:7 The LORD has **o** it to attack
Eze 12:7 I did what I was **o** to do.
24:18 next morning I did as I was **o**.
Dan 2:46 He **o** that gifts and offerings be
3:19 He **o** that the furnace should be
4:6 So I **o** all the wise advisers in
5:2 Belshazzar **o** that the gold and
5:29 Then Belshazzar **o** that Daniel
6:24 The king **o** those men who had
Mat 8:18 he **o** ⌊his disciples⌋ to cross to
12:16 He also **o** them not to tell
14:9 he **o** that her wish be granted.
14:19 Then he **o** the people to sit
15:35 He **o** the crowd to sit down on
16:20 Then he strictly **o** the disciples
17:9 the mountain, Jesus **o** them,
17:18 Jesus **o** the demon to come out
18:25 the master **o** him, his wife,
27:58 Pilate **o** that it be given to him.
Mar 1:25 Jesus **o** the spirit, "Keep quiet,
4:39 **o** the wind to stop,
5:43 Jesus **o** them not to let anyone
6:27 the king sent a guard and **o**
6:39 Then he **o** all of them to sit
7:36 Jesus **o** the people not to tell
7:36 But the more he **o** them,
8:6 He **o** the crowd to sit down on
8:30 He **o** them not to tell anyone
9:9 Jesus **o** them not to tell anyone
13:34 work to each one and **o**
Luk 2:1 time the Emperor Augustus **o**
3:13 than you are **o** to collect."
4:35 Jesus **o** the spirit, "Keep quiet,
4:39 **o** the fever to leave,
4:41 But Jesus **o** them not to speak.
5:14 Jesus **o** him, "Don't tell
8:24 Then he got up and **o** the wind
8:29 Jesus **o** the evil spirit to come
8:55 He **o** her parents to give her
8:56 Jesus **o** them not to tell anyone
9:21 He **o** them not to tell this to
9:42 Jesus **o** the evil spirit to leave.
14:22 what you've **o** has been done.
17:10 done everything you're **o** to do,
18:40 Jesus stopped and **o** them to
Jon 8:5 In his teachings, Moses **o** us to
10:18 is what my Father **o** me to do."
Act 1:4 he **o** them not to leave
4:15 So they **o** Peter and John to
4:18 and John and **o** them never
5:34 He **o** that the apostles should
5:40 **o** them not to speak about the
8:38 The official **o** the carriage to
10:33 the Lord has **o** you to say."
10:42 He **o** us to warn the people,
10:48 So Peter **o** that they should be
15:5 must be circumcised and **o**
16:22 and Silas and **o** ⌊the guards⌋
16:23 they threw them in jail and **o**
18:2 Claudius had **o** all Jews
21:33 and **o** him to be tied up with
21:34 so he **o** Paul to be taken into
22:24 So the officer **o** the soldiers to
22:30 Paul the next day and **o**
23:2 The chief priest Ananias **o** the
23:10 So the officer **o** his soldiers to
23:22 the young man and **o** him not
23:30 I have also **o** his accusers to
23:31 did as they had been **o**.
Act 24:23 Felix **o** the sergeant to guard
25:21 So I **o** him to be held in prison
27:43 He **o** those who could swim to
27:44 Then he **o** the rest to follow on
Rom 16:26 The everlasting God **o** that
1Th 4:11 your own living, as we **o** you.
2Th 3:4 to do what we **o** you to do.

ordering (1)

Act 23:3 teachings by **o** these men

orderly (3)

Luk 1:3 good idea to write an **o** account
1Co 14:40 be done in a proper and **o** way.
Col 2:5 I'm happy to see how **o** you are

orders (52)

Gen 12:20 his men **o** concerning Abram.
42:25 Joseph gave **o** to fill their bags
Exo 1:17 obey the king of Egypt's **o**.
5:6 day Pharaoh gave these **o**
Num 32:28 So Moses gave **o** about them
Jos 1:18 or does not obey your **o** will
6:8 After Joshua had given **o** to the
8:4 with these **o**: "Set an ambush
8:8 These are your **o**."
1Sm 21:2 and about the **o** I've given you.
1Ki 2:46 the king gave **o** to Benaiah,
22:31 The king of Aram had given **o**
2Ch 2:1 Solomon gave **o** to begin
8:15 No one neglected the king's **o**
18:30 The king of Aram had given **o**
Ezr 6:11 if anyone tampers with my **o**,
6:12 who tries to tamper with my **o**
7:26 and the king's **o** should
8:36 exiles delivered the king's **o**
Neh 11:23 They were under **o** from the
11:23 **o** that determined which duties
Est 3:9 If you approve, have the **o** for
3:12 All Haman's **o** were written to
3:12 The **o** were signed in the name
8:5 cancel the official **o**
Job 23:14 He will carry out ⌊his⌋ **o**
36:10 to his warning and **o** them
36:32 his hands with lightning and **o**
37:12 to do everything he **o** them.
38:12 "Have you ever given **o** to the
39:25 far away — the thundering ⌊**o**⌋
Psa 103:20 beings who carry out his **o**
103:20 are ready to obey his spoken **o**.
105:28 did not rebel against his **o**.
Isa 8:10 Give **o**, but they won't be
45:11 **o** concerning my handiwork?
Jer 31:35 He **o** the moon and stars to be
32:13 Then I gave Baruch these **o**:
35:16 have carried out the **o** of their
Joe 2:11 The LORD shouts out **o** to his
Mar 1:27 He gives **o** to evil spirits,
3:12 He gave them **o** not to tell
Luk 4:36 authority and power he gives **o**
8:25 He gives **o** to the wind and the
17:9 the servant for following **o**.
Jon 11:57 had given **o** that whoever knew
Act 5:28 He said, "We gave you strict **o**
12:19 the guards and gave **o**
16:24 So the jailer followed these **o**
23:35 Then the governor gave **o** to
2Co 11:20 your property, **o** you around,
1Th 4:2 You know what **o** we gave you

ordinances (1)

2Ch 33:8 all the teachings, the **o**,

ordinary (5)

1Sm 21:4 "I don't have any **o** bread,"
21:5 holy even on **o** campaigns.
Psa 73:5 in their lives like **o** people.
Amo 8:11 It won't be an **o** famine or
1Co 1:28 what the world considers **o**

ordination (12)

Exo 29:22 (This is the ram for the **o**.)
29:26 from the ram used for Aaron's **o**
29:27 from the ram used for the **o**.
29:31 "Take the ram used for the **o**,
29:33 at their **o** and installation.

Exo 29:34 If any meat or bread from the o
Lev 7:37 the guilt offering, the o offering,
8:22 second ram for the o offering.
8:28 These were o offerings,
8:29 from the ram of the o offering
8:31 in the basket of the o offering.
8:33 the last day of your o is over.

ore (2)
Dtr 8:9 The land has rocks with iron o,
8:9 to mine copper o in the hills.

Oreb (7)
Jdg 7:25 also captured O and Zeeb,
7:25 They killed O at the Rock of
7:25 killed Oreb at the Rock of O
7:25 brought the severed heads of O
8:3 God handed O and Zeeb,
Psa 83:11 as you treated O and Zeeb.
Isa 10:26 down Midian at the Rock of O

Oren (1)
1Ch 2:25 Bunah, O, Ozem, and Ahijah.

organization (2)
1Ki 10:5 the o of his officials and the
2Ch 9:4 the o of his officials and the

organized (18)
Exo 6:26 of Egypt in o family groups."
7:4 out of Egypt in o family groups.
12:17 out of Egypt in o family groups.
12:41 left Egypt in o family groups.
12:51 out of Egypt in o family groups.
Num 33:1 left Egypt in o groups under
Jdg 20:15 from Benjamin's cities and o
1Sm 4:2 The Philistines o their troops to
15:4 Saul o the troops, and he
2Sm 10:9 troops of Israel and o them
10:10 Abishai o them for combat
1Ki 20:26 Spring came, and Benhadad o
20:27 Israelite ⌊troops⌋ had been o
1Ch 19:10 troops of Israel and o them
19:11 They o for combat against the
23:6 David o the Levites into
2Ch 25:5 He o those who were at least
26:11 based on the number o by

organs (16)
Exo 29:13 fat that covers the internal o,
29:17 wash the internal o and legs,
29:22 fat that covers the internal o,
Lev 1:9 Wash the internal o and legs.
1:13 Wash the internal o and legs.
3:3 fat that covers the internal o
3:9 fat that covers the internal o.
3:14 fat that covers the internal o,
4:8 fat that covers the internal o,
4:11 legs, internal o, and excrement)
7:3 the fat covering the internal o,
8:16 fat that was on the internal o,
8:21 He washed the internal o and
8:25 all the fat on the internal o,
9:14 He washed the internal o and
Act 1:18 and all his internal o came out.

orgy (2)
Exo 32:6 which turned into an o.
1Co 10:7 a feast which turned into an o."

origin (2)
Jon 18:36 doesn't have its o on earth."
Act 5:38 put into action is of human o,

original (6)
Dtr 19:14 Never move your neighbor's o
Ezr 3:3 rebuilt the altar on its o site,
5:15 Rebuild God's temple on its o
6:7 temple on its ⌊o⌋ foundation.
Neh 4:6 to about half its ⌊o⌋ height.
Heb 3:14 on to our o confidence until

originally (3)
Gen 13:3 Ai where his tent had been o,
Jdg 18:29 O, the city was called Laish.
Ezr 5:11 that was o built many years

originate (1)
1Co 14:36 Did God's word o with you?

originated (1)
2Pe 1:21 prophecy ever o from humans.

origins (1)
Mic 5:2 His o go back to the distant

Orion (3)
Job 9:9 Major, O, and the Pleiades,
38:31 or untie the ropes of O?
Amo 5:8 Pleiades and O.

ornament (1)
Pro 25:12 a gold ring and a fine gold o,

ornaments (6)
Jdg 8:21 Then he took the half-moon o
8:26 did not include the half-moon o,
Job 28:17 Nor can gold o, jewels,
Sos 1:10 Your cheeks are lovely with o,
1:11 We will make gold o with
7:1 curves of your thighs are like o,

Ornan (11)
1Ch 21:15 floor of O the Jebusite.
21:18 up an altar for the LORD at O
21:20 Now, O had turned around and
21:20 but O kept on threshing the
21:21 O looked up and saw him.
21:22 David said to O, "Let me have
21:23 O said to David, "Take it,
21:24 "No," King David told O,
21:25 So David gave O 15 pounds of
21:28 floor of O the Jebusite,
2Ch 3:1 floor of O the Jebusite.

Ornan's (1)
1Ch 21:20 O four sons who were with him

Orpah (2)
Rut 1:4 married a woman named O,
1:14 Then O kissed her

orphan (7)
Exo 22:22 advantage of any widow or o.
Est 2:7 because she was an o.
Job 6:27 you also throw dice for an o?
24:9 snatch the ⌊nursing⌋ o from
31:17 without letting the o eat any
31:18 (From my youth the o grew up
31:21 If I have shaken my fist at an o

orphan's (1)
Job 24:3 They drive away the o donkey.

orphans (34)
Exo 22:24 will become widows and o.
Dtr 10:18 He makes sure o and widows
14:29 Foreigners, o, and widows
16:11 in your cities, the foreigners, o,
16:14 the Levites, foreigners, o,
24:17 foreigners and o of justice.
24:19 Leave it there for foreigners, o,
24:20 Leave some for foreigners, o,
24:21 Leave some for foreigners, o,
26:12 o, and widows in your cities,
26:13 it to the Levites, foreigners, o,
27:19 deprives foreigners, o,
Job 22:9 and the arms of o are broken.
29:12 help⌋ and the o who had no
Psa 10:14 have been the helper of o.
10:18 in order to provide justice for o
82:3 Defend weak people and o.
94:6 and they murder o.
146:9 gives relief to o and widows.
Pro 23:10 or enter fields that belong to o,
Isa 1:17 Defend o. Plead the case of
1:23 They never defend o.
9:17 for their o and widows.
10:2 prey on widows and rob o.
Jer 5:28 no respect for the rights of o.
7:6 foreigners, o, and widows,
22:3 Don't mistreat foreigners, o,
49:11 "Abandon your o, and I will
Lam 5:3 We are o without a father.
Eze 22:7 They oppress o and widows in
Hos 14:3 are our gods. You love o."
Zec 7:10 Don't oppress widows, o,
Mal 3:5 and oppress widows and o.
Jas 1:27 is to take care of o and widows

ospreys (2)
Lev 11:18 barn owls, pelicans, o,
Dtr 14:17 pelicans, o, cormorants,

ostrich (2)
Job 39:13 "Does the o flap its wings in
Mic 1:8 a jackal and mourn like an o.

ostriches (7)
Lev 11:16 o, nighthawks, seagulls,
Dtr 14:15 o, nighthawks, seagulls,
Job 30:29 jackals and a companion of o.
Isa 13:21 O will live there, and wild
34:13 for jackals and a place for o.
43:20 and o will honor me.
Lam 4:3 people are as cruel as wild o.

Othni (1)
1Ch 26:7 Shemaiah's sons were O,

Othniel (9)
Jos 15:17 Then O, son of Caleb's brother
15:18 When she came to O,
Jdg 1:13 Then O, son of Caleb's
1:14 When she came to O,
3:9 It was O, son of Caleb's
3:10 and O overpowered him.
3:11 Then O, son of Kenaz, died.
1Ch 4:13 sons were O and Seraiah.
4:13 The sons of O were Hathath

Othniel's (1)
1Ch 27:15 He was O descendant.

Othni's (1)
1Ch 26:7 and O skilled brothers Rephael,

ounce (15)
Gen 24:22 ring weighing a fifth of an o
Exo 30:13 he must give one-fifth of an o of
30:13 This one-fifth of an o of silver
30:15 than one-fifth of an o of silver,
38:26 to one-fifth of an o per person,
Lev 27:6 and for a girl give about one o.
1Sm 9:8 have one-tenth of an o of silver.
13:21 and one-tenth of an o of silver
2Ki 7:1 best flour will sell for half an o
7:1 will sell for half an o of silver."
7:16 flour sold for half an o of silver,
7:16 sold for half an o of silver,
7:18 will sell for half an o of silver.
7:18 will sell for half an o of silver.
Neh 10:32 to give an eighth of an o

ounces (35)
Gen 24:22 gold bracelets weighing four o.
37:28 Ishmaelites for eight o of silver.
Exo 21:32 its owner must pay 12 o of
Lev 27:3 to 60 years old is 20 o of silver.
27:4 If it is a woman, give 12 o.
27:5 give 8 o and for a girl give 4
27:5 8 ounces and for a girl give 4 o.
27:6 give 2 o of silver and for a girl
27:7 give 6 o and for a woman give
27:7 and for a woman give 4 o.
27:16 will be worth 20 o of silver.
Num 3:47 It will cost you two o of silver
7:14 a gold dish that weighed 4 o,
7:20 a gold dish that weighed 4 o,
7:26 a gold dish that weighed 4 o,
7:32 a gold dish that weighed 4 o,
7:38 a gold dish that weighed 4 o,
7:44 a gold dish that weighed 4 o,
7:50 a gold dish that weighed 4 o,
7:56 a gold dish that weighed 4 o,
7:62 a gold dish that weighed 4 o,
7:68 a gold dish that weighed 4 o,
7:74 a gold dish that weighed 4 o,

Num 7:80 a gold dish that weighed 4 **o**,
7:86 incense weighed 4 **o** each,
18:16 fixed price of two **o** of silver,
2Sm 18:11 felt obligated to give you four **o**
1Ki 10:29 and each horse for 6 **o** of silver.
2Ki 6:25 dove manure for two **o** of silver.
15:20 Each gave 20 **o** of silver for the
2Ch 1:17 and each horse for 6 **o** of silver.
3:9 The gold nails weighed 20 **o**.
Jer 32:9 The field cost seven **o** of silver.
Eze 4:10 Eat eight **o** of food every day at
Hos 3:2 So I bought her for 23 **o** of

outbreaks (1)
Dtr 24:8 Guard against **o** of serious skin

outbursts (2)
Job 40:11 Unleash your **o** of anger.
Gal 5:20 angry **o**, selfish ambition,

outcast (1)
Jer 30:17 "People call you an **o**:

outcasts (2)
Psa 147:2 He is the one who gathers the **o**
Isa 11:12 He will gather the **o** of Israel

outcome (4)
1Sm 17:47 determines every battle's **o**.
Psa 49:13 This is the final **o** for fools and
Pro 16:33 the LORD determines every **o**.
Isa 41:22 and know what their **o** will be.

outdated (2)
Heb 8:13 that the first promise was **o**.
8:13 What is **o** and aging will soon

outdoors (4)
Gen 25:29 exhausted, came in from **o**.
Num 19:16 "Whoever is **o** and touches
Act 7:19 their newborn babies **o**,
7:21 Moses was abandoned **o**,

outdoorsman (1)
Gen 25:27 became an expert hunter, an **o**.

outer (42)
Exo 26:7 goats' hair to form an **o** tent over
26:13 the length of the **o** tent's sheets.
26:14 been dyed red for the **o** tent.
26:36 "For the entrance of the **o** tent,
35:11 the inner tent, the **o** tent,
36:14 goats' hair to form an **o** tent over
36:19 been dyed red for the **o** tent,
36:37 for the entrance to the **o** tent.
39:33 the **o** tent and all its
40:19 He spread the **o** tent over the
Num 3:25 the **o** tent and cover,
4:25 the **o** cover of fine leather that
2Sm 20:15 it stood level with the **o** wall.
1Ki 6:29 around the inner and **o** rooms
6:30 floor of the inner and **o** rooms
7:9 on their inner and **o** faces.
2Ki 16:18 He also removed the **o**
2Ch 33:14 Manasseh rebuilt the **o** wall of
Est 8:15 and a purple **o** robe of fine
Eze 10:5 heard as far as the **o** courtyard.
40:15 from the front of the **o** part
40:17 brought me into the **o** courtyard
40:20 leading to the **o** courtyard.
40:31 halls faced the **o** courtyard.
40:34 hall faced the **o** courtyard.
40:37 walls faced the **o** courtyard.
41:9 The **o** wall of the side rooms
41:25 over the **o** entrance hall.
42:1 the north to the **o** courtyard.
42:3 the **o** courtyard were corridors
42:7 side rooms and the **o** courtyard.
42:8 The row of rooms in the **o**
42:9 the **o** courtyard through them.
42:14 into the **o** courtyard until they
42:15 all the way around the **o** area.
44:1 took me back to the **o** east gate
44:19 the people in the **o** courtyard,
46:20 offerings into the **o** courtyard.
46:21 Then the man led me to the **o**
Eze 47:2 and around to the **o** east gate.
Jon 13:4 removed his **o** clothes,
13:12 feet and put on his **o** clothes,

outlet (1)
2Ch 32:30 from the upper **o** of Gihon.

outlived (2)
Jos 24:31 who **o** him and who knew
Jdg 2:7 of the leaders who had **o** him

outlying (1)
1Sm 27:5 in one of the **o** towns so that

outnumber (5)
Num 3:48 Israelites who **o** the Levites."
Dtr 7:7 even though you didn't **o** all the
7:17 "These nations **o** us.
Psa 40:12 They **o** the hairs on my head.
69:4 who hate me for no reason **o**

outnumbered (1)
Num 3:49 Israelites who **o** the Levites.

outrage (1)
Jer 15:17 You filled me with **o**.

outraged (2)
Gen 34:7 The men felt **o** and very angry
Dan 11:11 The southern king will be **o**.

outrageous (2)
Neh 9:18 They committed **o** sins.
9:26 They committed **o** sins.

outsiders (4)
1Co 14:16 how can **o** say "Amen!"
14:23 When **o** or unbelievers come in,
14:24 When unbelievers or **o** come in
Eph 2:19 are no longer foreigners and **o**

outskirts (4)
Num 11:1 people on the **o** of the camp.
22:41 From there he could see the **o**
1Sm 14:2 Saul was staying on the **o** of
1Ch 4:39 They moved to the **o** of Gedor,

outsmart (1)
Exo 1:10 We have to **o** them,

outspoken (1)
Psa 40:10 I have been **o** about your

outspread (1)
Isa 8:8 Its **o** wings will extend over

outstanding (4)
Rut 2:1 of **o** character named Boaz.
1Ch 7:40 their families, **o** men, soldiers,
Neh 11:6 in Jerusalem were 468 **o** men.
Rom 16:13 Greet Rufus, that **o** Christian,

outstretched (2)
1Ki 8:7 When the angels' **o** wings were
2Ch 5:8 The angels' **o** wings were over

outward (2)
1Sm 16:7 Humans look at **o** appearances,
Jon 7:24 Stop judging by **o** appearance!

outwardly (2)
2Co 4:16 Though **o** we are wearing out,
7:5 **O** we have conflicts,

outweighs (1)
Ecc 10:1 **o** wisdom ⌊and⌋ honor.

outwit (1)
2Co 2:11 I don't want Satan to **o** us.

oven (10)
Gen 15:17 Suddenly a smoking **o** and a
Lev 2:4 which has been baked in an **o**,
7:9 whether baked in an **o** or
11:35 If it is an **o** or a stove,
26:26 women will need only one **o**
Lam 5:10 Our skin is as hot as an **o** from
Hos 7:4 They are like a heated **o**,
7:4 an **o** so hot that a baker doesn't
7:6 They become hot like an **o**
7:7 They are all as hot as an **o**.

ovens (3)
Exo 8:3 into your **o** and into your
Neh 3:11 included the Tower of the **O**.
12:38 past the Tower of the **O**,

overboard (6)
Jnh 1:5 began to throw the cargo **o**
1:12 He told them, "Throw me **o**.
1:15 took Jonah and threw him **o**,
Act 27:18 began to throw the cargo **o**.
27:19 threw the ship's equipment **o**.
27:43 who could swim to jump **o** first

overcast (3)
Joe 2:2 a day of clouds and **o** skies.
Zep 1:15 a day of clouds and **o** skies,
Mat 16:3 because the sky is red and **o**.

overcome (11)
Psa 12:4 "We will **o** with our tongues.
55:5 Fear and trembling have **o** me.
Mic 7:19 You will **o** our wrongdoing.
Mar 4:41 They were **o** with fear and
Luk 1:12 was troubled and **o** with fear.
22:45 asleep and **o** with sadness.
24:41 The disciples were **o** with joy
Jon 16:33 I have **o** the world."
Act 20:9 Finally, **o** by sleep,
Eph 6:13 Once you have **o** all obstacles,
Rev 7:16 burning heat will ever **o** them.

overconfident (7)
Dtr 2:30 God made him stubborn and **o**
1Sm 17:28 I know how **o** and headstrong
Pro 14:16 but a fool is careless and **o**.
Isa 32:9 what I say, you **o** daughters.
32:10 In a little less than a year you **o**
32:11 Tremble, you **o** women.
Dan 5:20 conceited that he became **o**,

overflow (12)
Psa 65:12 in the desert **o** ⌊with richness⌋.
68:3 Let them **o** with joy.
78:20 and the streams did **o**.
Pro 3:10 vats will **o** with fresh wine.
Isa 8:7 It will **o** all its channels and go
8:8 It will **o** and pass through;
Jer 47:2 It will **o** the land and everything
Joe 2:24 The vats will **o** with new wine
3:13 The vats **o**. The nations are very
Zec 1:17 My cities will **o** with prosperity
Rom 15:13 Then you will **o** with hope by
Col 2:7 and **o** with thanksgiving.

overflowing (13)
Psa 45:1 My heart is **o** with good news.
124:4 An ⌊**o**⌋ stream would have
Pro 18:4 The fountain of wisdom is an **o**
Isa 30:28 His breath is like an **o** stream.
66:12 of the nations like an **o** stream.
Jer 46:8 like a river quickly **o** its banks.
47:2 It will become an **o** river.
Zep 1:15 That day will be a day of **o** fury,
1:18 on the day of the LORD's **o** fury.
Rom 5:17 who receive God's **o** kindness
2Co 8:2 tested by suffering, their **o** joy,
9:8 you his constantly **o** kindness.
Eph 1:7 because of his **o** kindness.

overflows (4)
Jos 3:15 (The Jordan **o** all its banks
Psa 23:5 my head with oil. My cup **o**.
65:11 richness **o** wherever you are.
2Co 4:15 as God's kindness **o** in the

overgrown (1)
Pro 24:31 that it was all **o** with thistles.

overhead (3)
Rev 8:13 I saw an eagle flying **o**,

Rev 14:6 I saw another angel flying **o**
19:17 voice to all the birds flying **o**,

overheard (2)

1Sm 17:31 What David said was **o** and
Mar 5:36 When Jesus **o** what they said,

overjoyed (12)

1Sm 6:13 and saw the ark, they were **o**.
11:9 the message, they were **o**.
1Ch 29:9 The people were **o** that the
29:9 King David was also **o**,
29:17 I've been **o** to see your people
2Ch 15:15 All the people of Judah were **o**
24:10 and all the people were **o**.
29:36 and all the people were **o**
Psa 126:3 things for us. We are **o**.
Dan 6:23 The king was **o** and had Daniel
Luk 24:52 him and were **o** as they went
Jon 3:29 is **o** when the groom speaks.

overlaid (4)

2Ch 3:5 cypress, **o** it with fine gold,
3:7 He also **o** the building,
3:8 He **o** it with 45,000 pounds of
3:9 He also **o** the upper rooms with

overland (1)

Act 20:13 planned to walk **o** to Assos.

overloaded (1)

Amo 2:13 I am going to crush you as an **o**

overlook (4)

Amo 7:8 I will no longer **o** what they
8:2 I will no longer **o** what they
Jnh 1:2 people that I can no longer **o**
Mic 7:18 You forgive sin and **o** the

overlooked (1)

Act 17:30 "God **o** the times when people

overlooks (6)

Num 21:20 Mount Pisgah **o** Jeshimon.
23:28 which **o** Jeshimon.
Jos 15:8 to the top of the mountain that **o**
18:16 the foot of the mountain that **o**
1Sm 13:18 road toward the region that **o**
Pro 19:11 his credit that he **o** an offense.

overnight (8)

Lev 6:9 that stays on the altar **o** while
19:13 pay you owe a hired worker **o**.
Dtr 21:23 dead body hung on a pole **o**.
24:12 coat you took as a deposit **o**.
Neh 4:22 and his servant should stay **o**
Jnh 4:10 "This plant grew up **o** and died
4:10 grew up overnight and died **o**.
Act 10:23 the house and had them stay **o**.

overpower (7)

Gen 43:18 going to attack us, **o** us,
Jdg 16:5 Find out how we can **o** him.
1Sm 17:9 But if I **o** him and kill him,
Est 9:1 the Jews expected to **o** them,
Job 14:20 You **o** him forever,
Jer 20:10 Then we can **o** him and take
Mat 16:18 And the gates of hell will not **o**

overpowered (9)

Jdg 3:10 and Othniel **o** him.
2Sm 11:23 "Their men **o** us and came to
Est 9:1 The Jews **o** those who hated
Psa 13:4 enemy will say, "I have **o** him."
129:2 but they have never **o** me.
Ecc 4:12 person may be **o** by another,
Jer 20:7 You **o** me and won.
Zep 3:19 deal with all who have **o** you.
Rev 20:2 He **o** the serpent, that ancient

overpowering (1)

Sos 8:6 Love is as **o** as death.

overpowers (1)

Isa 42:13 and **o** his enemies.

overran (2)

Jdg 15:9 camped in Judah, and **o** Lehi.
2Sm 5:22 again attacked and **o**

overripe (1)

Rev 14:15 the harvest on the earth is **o**."

overruled (2)

2Sm 24:4 However, the king **o** Joab and
1Ch 21:4 However, the king **o** Joab.

overrun (2)

Dtr 7:22 would be **o** with wild animals.
2Sm 5:18 Philistines had come and **o**

overseas (1)

Eze 27:33 Your merchandise was sent **o**.

overseer (1)

Pro 6:7 Although it has no **o**,

overseers (1)

1Ch 26:32 David appointed them to be **o**

overshadow (1)

Luk 1:35 of the Most High will **o** you.

overshadowed (4)

Mat 4:16 who live in a land **o** by death."
17:5 when a bright cloud **o** them.
Mar 9:7 Then a cloud **o** them.
Luk 9:34 saying this, a cloud **o** them.

overshadowing (3)

Exo 25:20 above the throne of mercy, **o** it.
37:9 above the throne of mercy, **o** it.
Heb 9:5 of glory ⌊with their wings⌋ **o**

overstating (1)

2Co 10:14 We're not **o** the facts.

overstep (1)

Pro 8:29 would not **o** his command,

overtake (8)

Gen 19:19 This disaster will **o** me,
Jdg 20:34 own evil was about to **o** them.
Job 27:20 Terrors **o** him like a flood.
Pro 28:22 that poverty is about to **o** him.
Ecc 9:11 events **o** all of them.
Isa 47:11 will **o** you suddenly.
Hos 10:9 War will **o** the wicked people
Mic 2:6 Disgrace will never **o** us."

overtaken (1)

Jdg 20:41 that their evil had **o** them.

overtakes (1)

Job 3:25 What I fear most **o** me.

overthrow (4)

Pro 12:7 **O** wicked people, and they are
Jer 1:10 You will destroy and **o**.
Hag 2:22 I will **o** the thrones of kingdoms
2:22 I will **o** chariots and their riders,

overthrows (1)

Job 34:25 so he **o** them at night,

overtook (1)

Jdg 20:43 They **o** them east of Gibeah.

overturn (1)

Job 28:9 rocks and **o** mountains at their

overturned (2)

Mat 21:12 He **o** the moneychangers'
Mar 11:15 He **o** the moneychangers'

overturns (1)

Pro 22:12 but he **o** the words of a

overwhelm (7)

Job 41:9 Doesn't the sight of it **o** you?
Psa 65:3 Various sins **o** me.
Dan 11:10 so that they can **o** ⌊the enemy⌋
11:22 He will **o** large forces and
11:40 will invade countries, **o** them,
Hab 2:17 done to Lebanon will **o** you,
2Co 2:7 Such distress could **o**

overwhelmed (13)

2Sm 5:20 He said, "The LORD has **o** my
22:5 of destruction had **o** me.
1Ch 14:11 God has **o** my enemies."
Job 32:15 "Job's friends have been **o** and
Psa 18:4 of destruction had **o** me.
38:4 My guilt has **o** me.
55:5 me. Horror has **o** me.
119:20 My soul is **o** with endless
Jer 8:18 Sorrow has **o** me. I am sick at
Dan 10:16 of this vision, pain has **o** me,
11:26 His army will be **o**,
Mat 2:10 They were **o** with joy to see
Mar 16:8 and trembling had **o** them.

overwhelming (10)

2Sm 5:20 in front of me like an **o** flood."
1Ch 14:11 my power like an **o** flood,
Ezr 9:6 and our guilt is so **o** that it
9:13 and because of our **o** guilt,
Pro 27:4 Anger is cruel, and fury is **o**,
Isa 28:2 like a thunderstorm, an **o** flood.
28:15 When the **o** disaster passes by,
28:18 When the **o** disaster passes by,
Rom 8:37 loves us gives us an **o** victory
2Co 3:9 God's approval has an **o** glory.

overwhelms (2)

2Sm 5:20 to Baal Perazim [The Lord **O**]
1Ch 14:11 at Baal Perazim [The Lord **O**].

owe (14)

Lev 19:13 Never keep the pay you **o** a
Dtr 18:3 This is what the people **o** the
Mat 18:28 'Pay what you **o**!' he
Luk 16:5 much do you **o** my master?'
16:7 'How much do you **o**?' "The
19:8 pay four times as much as I **o**
Rom 13:7 everyone whatever you **o** them.
13:7 If you **o** taxes, pay them. If you
13:7 If you **o** tolls, pay them. If you
13:7 If you **o** someone respect,
13:7 If you **o** someone honor,
13:8 of love that you **o** each other.
15:26 in Macedonia and Greece **o**
Phm 1:19 mention that you **o** me your life.

owed (8)

1Ki 10:1 (He **o** his reputation to the
Mat 18:24 a servant who **o** him millions of
18:28 he found a servant who **o** him
18:30 until he would repay what he **o**.
18:34 repay everything that he **o**.
Luk 7:41 ⌊So Jesus said,⌋ "Two men **o**
7:41 One **o** him five hundred silver
7:41 and the other **o** him fifty.

owes (4)

Dtr 15:2 debt your neighbor still **o** you.
15:3 another Israelite still **o** you.
Pro 11:24 another holds back what he **o**
Phm 1:18 in any way or **o** you anything,

owl (2)

Psa 102:6 I am like a desert **o**,
102:6 like an **o** living in the ruins.

owls (11)

Lev 11:17 little **o**, cormorants, great owls,
11:17 little owls, cormorants, great **o**,
11:18 barn **o**, pelicans, ospreys,
Dtr 14:16 little **o**, great owls, barn owls,
14:16 little owls, great **o**,
14:16 little owls, great owls, barn **o**,
Isa 13:21 Their homes will be full of **o**.
34:11 **O** and crows will live there.
34:14 Screech **o** will rest there and
34:15 **O** will make their nests there,
Jer 50:39 Desert **o** will also live there.

owned (21)

Gen 16:1 She **o** an Egyptian slave
24:2 was in charge of all that he **o**,
26:14 Because he **o** so many flocks,
36:43 lived and the property they **o**.
39:4 household and everything he **o**.
39:5 was on everything Potiphar **o**
39:6 So he left all that he **o** in
Dtr 30:5 to the land your ancestors **o**.
Jos 21:41 Within the territory **o** by the
Jdg 17:5 Micah **o** a shrine. He also made
1Sm 28:24 a fattened calf that she **o**.
1Ki 9:19 all the storage cities that he **o**.
17:17 the son of the woman who **o**
1Ch 13:14 family and everything he **o**.
2Ch 8:6 all the storage cities that he **o**.
Job 1:3 He **o** 7,000 sheep and goats,
Ecc 2:7 I **o** more herds and flocks than
Jer 35:9 in, or **o** vineyards, pastures,
Zec 13:5 I've **o** this land since I was a
Mat 19:22 went away sad because he **o**
Mar 10:22 because he **o** a lot of property.

owner (47)

Gen 16:4 be disrespectful to Sarai, her **o**.
16:8 "I'm running away from my **o**
16:9 "Go back to your **o**,
Exo 21:20 "Whenever an **o** hits his male
21:20 the **o** must be punished.
21:21 the **o** must not be punished.
21:26 "Whenever an **o** hits his male
21:27 If the **o** knocks out the tooth of
21:28 The bull's **o** is free from any
21:29 and the **o** has been warned but
21:29 must be stoned and its **o** must
21:30 is demanded from the **o**,
21:30 the bull's **o** may save his life
21:32 its **o** must pay 12 ounces of
21:34 the **o** of the cistern must make
21:34 pay money to the animal's **o**,
21:36 and its **o** didn't keep it confined,
21:36 the **o** must make up for the loss
22:8 If the thief is not caught, the **o**
22:11 The **o** must accept the oath.
22:14 dies while the **o** is not present,
22:15 If the **o** is with the animal,
Lev 6:5 Give it back to its **o** on the day
14:35 The **o** of that house must come
Dtr 22:2 If the **o** doesn't live near you or
22:2 Keep it until the **o** comes
32:6 Isn't he your Father and **O**,
Jdg 19:22 the **o** of the house,
19:23 The **o** went out to them.
1Ki 16:24 the city after its former **o**,
Isa 1:3 But Israel doesn't know ⌊its **o**⌋.
Eze 21:27 until its rightful **o** comes.
Mat 10:24 Nor is a slave better than his **o**.
10:25 teacher and a slave like his **o**.
10:25 If they have called the **o** of the
13:52 of heaven is like a home **o**.
20:8 "When evening came, the **o** of
20:11 they began to protest to the **o**.
20:13 "The **o** said to one of them,
21:40 "Now, when the **o** of the
Mar 12:9 "What will the **o** of the vineyard
13:35 you don't know when the **o**
14:14 tell the **o** that the teacher asks,
Luk 20:13 "Then the **o** of the vineyard
20:15 "What will the **o** of the vineyard
22:11 Tell the **o** of the house that the
Act 27:11 by what the pilot and the **o**

owner's (2)

Exo 22:12 he must make up for the **o** loss
Mat 13:27 "The **o** workers came to him

owners (11)

Job 31:39 made its **o** breathe their last,
Ecc 5:11 What do **o** gain ⌊from all their
5:14 The **o** had children,
Isa 1:3 Oxen know their **o**,
Jer 8:10 men and their fields to new **o**.
Luk 19:33 donkey, its **o** asked them,
Jon 13:16 are not superior to their **o**,
Act 16:16 for her **o** by telling fortunes.
Act 16:19 When her **o** realized that their
1Pe 2:18 under the authority of your **o**
2:18 Obey not only those **o** who are

ownership (2)

Exo 22:9 If there is a dispute over the **o**
2Co 1:22 he has put his seal ⌊of **o**⌋ on

owns (13)

Gen 23:9 cave of Machpelah that he **o** at
38:25 by the man who **o** these things.
39:8 trusts me with everything he **o**.
Num 35:8 the amount of land each tribe **o**.
Dtr 21:17 portion of whatever he **o**.
22:2 you or you don't know who **o** it,
2Sm 3:12 "Who **o** this country?"
6:12 home and everything he **o**
Job 12:16 He **o** ⌊both⌋ the deceiver and
22:8 A strong person **o** the land.
Psa 109:11 a creditor take everything he **o**.
Act 21:11 tie up the man who **o** this belt.
Gal 4:1 even though he **o** everything.

ox (31)

Exo 20:17 slave, his **o**, his donkey,
23:4 come across your enemy's **o**
23:12 Then your **o** and donkey can
Num 7:3 and one **o** from each leader.
18:17 never buy back a firstborn **o**,
22:4 us the same way an **o** eats up
Dtr 5:21 slave, his **o**, his donkey,
15:19 Never use a firstborn **o** for work
17:1 Never offer an **o** or a sheep that
18:3 whenever they sacrifice an **o**,
22:1 If you see another Israelite's **o**
22:4 Israelite's donkey or **o** lying
22:10 Never plow with an **o** and a
25:4 Never muzzle an **o** when it's
28:31 Your **o** will be butchered as
33:17 be like the horns of a wild **o**.
1Sm 12:3 Did I take anyone's **o**?
14:34 bring me your **o** or your sheep,
14:34 of the soldiers brought his **o**
Neh 5:18 Preparing one **o** and six choice
Job 6:5 or does an **o** make a sound
24:3 They take the widow's **o** as
39:9 "Will the wild **o** agree to serve
39:10 Can you guide a wild **o** in a
Psa 29:6 and Mount Sirion like a wild **o**.
69:31 more than ⌊sacrificing⌋ an **o**
Pro 14:4 **o** produces plentiful harvests.
Luk 13:15 Don't each of you free your **o** or
14:5 "If your son or your **o** falls into
1Co 9:9 "Never muzzle an **o** when it is
1Ti 5:18 "Never muzzle an **o** when it is

oxen (36)

Num 7:3 freight wagons and twelve **o**,
7:6 took the wagons and the **o**
7:7 He gave two wagons and four **o**
7:8 gave four wagons and eight **o**
Dtr 5:14 and female slaves, your **o**,
14:4 you may eat: **o**, sheep, goats,
Jdg 3:31 sharp stick used for herding **o**.
1Sm 11:5 from the field behind some **o**.
11:7 Saul took a pair of **o**,
11:7 is what will be done to the **o**
2Sm 6:6 threshing floor, the **o** stumbled.
24:22 There are **o** for the burnt
24:22 and **o** yokes for firewood."
24:24 the threshing floor and the **o**
1Ki 7:29 were lions, **o**, and angels.
19:19 plowing behind 12 pairs of **o**.
19:20 So Elisha left the **o**,
19:21 Elisha left him, took two **o**,
1Ch 12:40 camels, mules, and **o**.
13:9 threshing floor, the **o** stumbled.
21:23 I'll give you **o** for the burnt
Job 1:3 camels, 1,000 **o**, 500 donkeys,
1:14 He said, "While the **o** were
42:12 2,000 **o**, and 1,000 donkeys.
Psa 22:21 and from the horns of wild **o**.
Isa 1:3 **O** know their owners,
7:25 It will be a place for turning **o**
11:7 Lions will eat straw like **o**.
30:24 The **o** and the donkeys which
Isa 32:20 stream and those who let **o**
34:7 Wild **o** will be killed with them,
65:25 lions will eat straw like **o**,
Jer 51:23 to crush farmers and their **o**.
Amo 6:12 a farmer plow the sea with **o**?
Luk 14:19 'I bought five pairs of **o**,
1Co 9:9 God's concern isn't for **o**.

oxen's (1)

1Ki 19:21 using the **o** yoke ⌊for

Ozem (2)

1Ch 2:15 **O** (his sixth son), and David
2:25 Bunah, Oren, **O**, and Ahijah.

Ozni (1)

Num 26:16 the family of **O**, the family of

P

Paarai (1)

2Sm 23:35 from Carmel, **P** from Arabah,

pace (2)

Gen 33:14 that are in front of me at their **p**
33:14 and at the children's **p** until

pack (4)

Jer 46:19 **P** your bags, inhabitants of
Eze 12:3 "Son of man, **p** your bags as if
Zec 9:9 on a colt, a young **p** animal.
Mat 21:5 a young **p** animal.'"

Paddan (1)

Gen 48:7 As I was coming back from **P**,

Paddan Aram (10)

Gen 25:20 the Aramean from **P**
28:2 Go to **P**. Go to the home
28:5 Isaac sent Jacob to **P**.
28:6 had sent him away to **P**
28:7 mother and had left for **P**
31:18 he had accumulated in **P**
33:18 So having come from **P**,
35:9 he came back from **P**,
35:26 who were born in **P**.
46:15 Leah gave to Jacob in **P**,

Padon (2)

Ezr 2:44 Keros, Siaha, **P**,
Neh 7:47 Keros, Sia, **P**,

pagan (2)

2Ki 23:5 He got rid of the **p** priests
Zep 1:4 names of the **p** priests along

pagan's (1)

Pro 5:10 have to work hard in a **p** house

Pagiel (5)

Num 1:13 **P**, son of Ochran, from the tribe
2:27 for the people of Asher is **P**,
7:72 of Asher, **P**, son of Ochran,
7:77 These were the gifts from **P**,
10:26 **P**, son of Ochran,

Pahath Moab (5)

Ezr 2:6 of **P**, that is, of Jeshua and Joab:
8:4 from the family of **P**: Eliehoenai,
10:30 descendants of **P**: Adna, Chelal,
Neh 7:11 of **P**, that is, of Jeshua and Joab:
10:14 leaders of the people: Parosh, **P**,

Pahath Moab's (1)

Neh 3:11 and Hasshub, **P** son, made

Pai (1)

1Ch 1:50 of his ⌊capital⌋ city was **P**.

paid (63)

Gen 31:15 up the money that was **p** for us.
31:39 I **p** for the loss myself.
39:23 The warden **p** no attention to

Gen 44:4 'Why have you **p** me back with
Exo 3:16 He said, "I have **p** close
Jdg 1:7 God has **p** me back for what I
9:56 So God **p** back Abimelech for
9:57 God also **p** back the men of
Rut 2:19 May the man who **p** attention to
1Sm 25:21 Yet, he has **p** me back with
2Sm 8:2 subjects and **p** taxes ⌊to him⌋.
8:6 subjects and **p** taxes ⌊to him⌋.
22:21 are clean. He **p** me back
22:25 The LORD **p** me back because
1Ki 4:21 These kingdoms **p** taxes and
5:11 Solomon **p** Hiram this much
1Ch 18:2 subjects and **p** taxes ⌊to him⌋.
18:6 subjects and **p** taxes ⌊to him⌋.
2Ch 26:8 The Ammonites **p** taxes to
Ezr 4:14 Now, because we are **p** by
4:20 and tolls were **p** to them.
6:8 The cost ⌊for this⌋ should be **p**
Neh 5:14 I never ate any food that was **p**
Est 3:4 he **p** no attention to them.
Job 32:12 I've **p** close attention to you,
Psa 7:4 if I have **p** back my friend with
18:20 are clean. He **p** me back
18:24 The LORD **p** me back because
49:8 The price to be **p** for his soul is
66:19 He has **p** attention to my prayer.
103:10 as we deserve for our sins or **p**
Pro 1:24 and no one **p** attention.
12:14 Another is **p** according to what
Isa 40:2 and its wrongs have been **p** for.
43:3 Seba are the price I **p** for you.
52:3 but no price was **p**.
64:4 no one has **p** attention,
Jer 8:6 I have **p** attention and listened,
18:20 Good should not be **p** back
25:4 listened or **p** attention to them.
32:10 and **p** out the silver.
Eze 16:31 because you don't want to be **p**.
16:33 All prostitutes get **p**.
39:24 I **p** them back for their
Jnh 1:3 He **p** for the trip and went on
Zec 11:12 And they **p** me my wages — 30
Mal 3:16 and the LORD **p** attention and
Mat 22:5 "But they **p** no attention and
Luk 14:14 You will be **p** back when those
Jon 4:36 the crop is already getting **p**.
10:13 about what he's going to get **p**
Act 8:6 The crowds **p** close attention
8:10 children to adults **p** attention
8:11 They **p** attention to Simon
22:28 The officer replied, "I **p** a lot of
Rom 3:24 through the price Christ Jesus **p**
Gal 3:13 Christ **p** the price to free us
3:14 ⌊Christ **p** the price⌋ so that the
Php 4:18 You have **p** me in full,
Col 1:14 His Son **p** the price to free us,
3:25 who does wrong will be **p** back
Heb 9:15 Through his death he **p** the
Rev 3:8 but you have **p** attention to my

pain (69)

Gen 3:16 "I will increase your **p** and your
34:25 while the men were still in **p**,
1Ch 4:10 evil so that I will not be in **p**."
2Ch 6:29 all who know suffering or **p**,
Job 2:13 that he was in such great **p**.
6:10 happy despite my endless **p**,
7:13 bed may help me bear my **p**,'
14:22 He feels only his body's **p**.
16:5 lips could ease ⌊your **p**⌋.
16:6 If I speak, my **p** is not eased.
21:17 an angry God give them **p**?
33:19 In **p** on their sickbeds,
39:3 Then the **p** of giving birth is
Psa 38:7 are filled with burning **p**,
38:17 I am continually aware of my **p**.
39:2 in thought, my **p** grew worse.
69:26 and they talk about the **p** of
69:29 I am suffering and in **p**.
73:4 They suffer no **p**. Their bodies
109:22 I can feel the **p** in my heart.
116:3 I experienced **p** and agony.
Pro 23:35 "They strike me, but I feel no **p**.
Ecc 1:18 the greater ⌊your⌋ **p**.
2:23 Their entire life is filled with **p**,
Isa 13:8 **P** and anguish will seize them.
14:3 relief from your **p** and suffering,
17:11 a day of grief and incurable **p**.
21:3 **P** grips me like the pain of
21:3 grips me like the **p** of childbirth.
58:3 Why have we inflicted **p** on
Jer 4:19 I writhe in **p**. My heart is beating
6:24 gripped by anguish and **p** like
13:21 Won't **p** grip you like a woman
15:18 Why is my **p** unending and my
22:23 will groan when **p** strikes you,
22:23 **p** like a woman giving birth to
30:6 holding his stomach in **p** like
45:3 LORD has added grief to my **p**.
49:24 Anguish and **p** grip them like a
50:43 Anguish will grip him as **p**
51:8 Bring medicine for its **p**.
51:29 earth trembles and writhes in **p**.
Lam 1:12 Look and see if there's any **p**
1:12 if there's any pain like the **p** that
1:12 like the **p** that he has made me
1:18 you people, and look at my **p**.
Eze 30:16 Sin will be in much **p**.
Dan 10:16 **p** has overwhelmed me,
Mic 4:9 **P** grips you like a woman in
4:10 Daughter of Zion, writhe in **p**
Hab 3:10 They writhe in **p**. Floodwaters
Zec 9:5 Gaza will also be in great **p**,
Mat 4:24 from any kind of disease or **p**.
8:6 paralyzed and in terrible **p**."
8:12 cry and be in extreme **p** there.
13:42 cry and be in extreme **p** there.
13:50 cry and be in extreme **p** there.
22:13 cry and be in extreme **p** there.'
24:51 cry and be in extreme **p** there.
25:30 cry and be in extreme **p** there.'
Luk 13:28 will cry and be in extreme **p**.
Jon 16:20 You will feel **p**, but your pain
16:20 You will feel pain, but your **p**
16:21 A woman has **p** when her time
16:21 she doesn't remember the **p**
Heb 10:32 endured a lot of hardship and **p**.
12:11 to cause more **p** than joy.
Rev 9:5 Their torture was like the **p** of a
21:4 won't be any grief, crying, or **p**,

painful (11)

Gen 5:29 relief from the work and **p** labor
1Ch 4:9 had named him Jabez [**P**],
4:9 she said that his birth was **p**.
2Ch 21:19 He died a **p** death.
Job 2:7 struck Job with **p** boils from
6:25 How **p** an honest discussion
Ecc 5:13 There is a **p** tragedy that I have
5:16 This also is a **p** tragedy:
6:2 This is pointless and is a **p**
Jon 16:22 "Now you're in a **p** situation.
Rev 16:2 Horrible, **p** sores appeared on

pains (17)

Gen 35:16 and was having severe labor **p**.
35:17 During one of her **p**,
Isa 26:17 and cry out in their labor **p**.
26:18 we writhed with labor **p** only to
45:10 you go through labor **p** for me?"
54:1 women who never had birth **p**.
66:7 Before she has labor **p**,
Mat 24:8 the beginning **p** ⌊of the end⌋.
Mar 13:8 the beginning **p** ⌊of the end⌋.
Act 2:24 and destroyed the **p** of death,
Rom 8:22 has been groaning with the **p**
Gal 4:19 I am suffering birth **p** for you
4:27 who feel no **p** of childbirth!
1Th 5:3 It will be as sudden as labor **p**
1Pe 2:19 the **p** of unjust suffering.
Rev 12:2 She cried out from labor **p** and
16:11 the God of heaven for their **p**

paint (5)

Eze 13:10 the prophets cover it up with **p**.
13:11 the wall with **p** that their wall
13:12 "Where's the **p** that you used to
13:14 the prophets covered up with **p**.
13:15 those who covered it up with **p**.

painted (5)

Lam 2:14 They **p** a good picture of you.
Eze 13:15 and so are those who **p** it.
23:14 men, **p** in bright red.
23:40 for the men, **p** their eyes,
Nah 2:3 of his warriors are **p** red.

paints (1)

Jer 22:14 with cedar, and **p** them red.

pair (9)

Gen 7:2 a female of each) and one **p**
7:15 A **p** of every living,
1Sm 11:7 Saul took a **p** of oxen,
2Sm 16:1 met him with a **p** of saddled
1Ki 19:19 He was using the twelfth **p**.
2Ki 5:17 give me as much dirt as a **p**
Amo 2:6 the needy for a **p** of sandals.
8:6 the needy for a **p** of sandals.
Luk 2:24 "a **p** of mourning doves or two

pairs (11)

Gen 7:2 Take with you seven **p** of
7:3 Also, take seven **p** of every
7:9 to go into the ship in **p** (a male
Exo 25:35 a bud under each of the three **p**
37:21 a bud under each of the three **p**
Jdg 15:4 He tied them together in **p** by
1Ki 19:19 plowing behind 12 **p** of oxen.
Isa 21:7 see chariots, **p** of horsemen,
21:9 chariots and horsemen in **p**."
Luk 10:1 They were to travel in **p**.
14:19 'I bought five **p** of oxen,

palace (177)

Gen 12:15 Sarai was taken to Pharaoh's **p**.
41:40 You will be in charge of my **p**,
47:14 Then he took it to Pharaoh's **p**.
50:4 spoke to the Pharaoh's **p** staff.
50:7 the leaders in his **p** staff,
Exo 7:23 turned and went back to his **p**.
8:3 They will come into your **p**,
8:24 of flies came into Pharaoh's **p**
10:11 were thrown out of Pharaoh's **p**.
Num 22:18 "Even if Balak gave me his **p**
24:13 would give me his **p** filled
2Sm 5:8 the lame will not get into the **p**."
5:9 around it from the Millo to the **p**
5:11 They built a **p** for David.
6:20 slave girls of his **p** staff — like
11:2 on the roof of the royal **p**.
11:8 Uriah left the royal **p**,
11:9 the royal **p** among his superior's
12:17 The older leaders in his **p**
13:7 David sent for Tamar at the **p**.
15:16 left behind to take care of the **p**.
15:35 hear anything from the royal **p**,
16:21 he left to take care of the **p**.
19:11 to bring the king back to his **p**?
20:3 came to his **p** in Jerusalem,
20:3 he had left to look after the **p**
1Ki 4:6 Ahishar was in charge of the **p**.
4:7 food for the king and his **p**.
5:9 me by providing food for my **p**."
7:1 years to finish building his **p**.
7:4 on opposite sides ⌊of the **p**⌋.
7:5 on opposite sides ⌊of the **p**⌋.
9:1 the LORD's temple, the royal **p**,
9:10 LORD's house and the royal **p**).
9:24 to the **p** that Solomon had
10:4 wisdom, the **p** he built,
10:12 LORD's temple and the royal **p**,
11:20 the boy to Pharaoh in the **p**,
11:20 **p** among Pharaoh's children.
13:8 if you gave me half of your **p**,
14:26 LORD's temple and the royal **p**.
14:27 by the entrance to the royal **p**,
15:18 LORD's temple and the royal **p**
16:9 in charge of the **p** in Tirzah.)
16:18 the stronghold in the royal **p**
16:18 down the **p** over his own
18:3 who was in charge of the **p**.
20:6 my servants to search your **p**
21:1 in Jezreel next to the **p**
22:39 the ivory **p** he built,

2Ki 7:9 bring the news to the royal **p**."
7:11 the news to the royal **p**.
10:5 the official in charge of the **p**,
11:5 must guard the royal **p**.
11:16 the horses enter the royal **p**,
11:19 Guards' Gate to the royal **p**.
11:20 with a sword at the royal **p**.
12:18 LORD's temple and the royal **p**.
14:14 and in the royal **p** treasury.
15:5 Jotham was in charge of the **p**
15:25 of the royal **p** in Samaria.
16:8 in the treasury in the royal **p**
18:15 and in the royal **p** treasury.
18:18 who was in charge of the **p**
18:37 who was in charge of the **p**
19:2 who was in charge of the **p**,
20:13 them everything in his **p**
20:15 "What did they see in your **p**?"
20:15 "They saw everything in my **p**,
20:17 when everything in your **p**,
20:18 will become officials in the **p**
21:18 in the garden of his own **p**,
21:23 him and killed him in his **p**.
24:13 LORD's temple and the royal **p**.
25:9 the LORD's temple, the royal **p**,
1Ch 14:1 to build a **p** for David.
26:16 the gateway that goes to the **p**.
26:18 Levites at the gateway to the **p**
28:1 the **p** officials, the soldiers,
29:1 important because this **p** is not
29:19 to build the **p** I have planned."
2Ch 2:1 name and a royal **p** for himself.
2:3 he could build a **p** to live in.
2:12 LORD's temple and a royal **p**.
7:11 LORD's temple and the royal **p**
7:11 LORD's temple and his own **p**.
8:11 from the City of David to a **p**
8:11 "My wife will not live in the **p**
9:3 wisdom, the **p** he built,
9:11 LORD's temple and the royal **p**,
12:9 LORD's temple and the royal **p**.
12:10 by the entrance to the royal **p**,
16:2 LORD's temple and the royal **p**.
21:17 could be found in the royal **p**.
23:5 third must be at the royal **p**.
23:15 Horse Gate of the royal **p**,
23:20 Upper Gate to the royal **p**
25:24 and in the royal **p** treasury.
26:21 was in charge of the royal **p**
28:7 who was in charge of the **p**,
28:21 the royal **p**, and the princes,
33:20 They buried him in his own **p**.
33:24 him and killed him in his **p**.
36:7 put them in his **p** in Babylon.
Ezr 4:14 because we are paid by your **p**,
6:2 was found in the **p** of Ecbatana,
6:4 The king's **p** will pay for it.
Neh 3:25 that projects from the king's **p**
12:37 the wall rises past David's **p**
Est 1:5 enclosed garden of the king's **p**
1:8 ordered all the waiters in his **p**
1:9 at the royal **p** of King Xerxes.
2:8 also was taken to the king's **p**
2:9 servants from the king's **p**.
2:13 to the king's **p** was given
2:16 to King Xerxes in his royal **p**
4:13 you are in the king's **p** you will
5:1 in the courtyard of the king's **p**,
5:1 on the royal throne inside the **p**,
6:4 the courtyard to the king's **p**
7:7 and went into the **p** garden.
7:8 king returned from the **p** garden
7:8 garden to the **p** dining room,
7:8 the queen while I'm in the **p**?"
9:4 important man in the king's **p**.
Psa 45:13 king is glorious inside the **p**.
45:15 They enter the **p** of the king.
105:21 Joseph the master of his **p**
144:12 that adorn the corners of a **p**.
Isa 22:15 the man in charge of the **p**,
36:3 who was in charge of the **p**
36:22 who was in charge of the **p**
37:2 who was in charge of the **p**,
38:8 the stairway of Ahaz's upper **p**.
39:2 them everything in his **p**
39:4 "What did they see in your **p**?"
Isa 39:4 "They saw everything in my **p**,
39:6 when everything in your **p**,
39:7 will become officials in the **p**
Jer 22:1 Go to the **p** of the king of
22:4 ride through the gates of this **p**
22:5 "that this **p** will become a pile
22:6 the LORD says about the **p**
22:6 This **p** is like Gilead to me,
26:10 they went from the king's **p** to
27:18 in the royal **p** of Judah,
27:21 in the royal **p** of Judah,
32:2 This prison was in the **p** of the
34:19 the **p** officials, the priests,
36:12 room in the king's **p** where all
37:17 asked him privately in the **p**,
38:7 But an official in the royal **p**,
38:8 Ebed Melech left the royal **p**
38:11 him and went to the royal **p**,
38:22 the women who are left in the **p**
39:8 burned down the royal **p**
43:9 the Pharaoh's **p** in Tahpanhes.
52:13 the LORD's temple, the royal **p**,
Dan 1:4 able to serve in the king's **p**.
1:21 Daniel served the royal **p** until
4:4 while living in my **p**.
4:29 around the royal **p** in Babylon.
4:30 I built the royal **p** by my own
5:5 the lamp stand of the royal **p**.
6:18 Then the king went to his **p**
Amo 7:13 holy place and the king's **p**."
Nah 2:6 and the **p** melts away.
Mat 26:3 of the people gathered in the **p**
27:27 soldiers took Jesus into the **p**
Mar 15:16 into the courtyard of the **p**
Jon 18:28 house to the governor's **p**.
18:28 Jews wouldn't go into the **p**.
18:33 Pilate went back into the **p**,
19:9 He went into the **p** again and
Act 7:10 and of Pharaoh's whole **p**.
23:35 Paul under guard in Herod's **p**.
Php 4:22 those in the emperor's **p**,

palaces (36)

2Ch 36:19 burned down all its **p**,
Psa 45:8 From ivory **p** the music of
48:3 God is in its **p**. He has proved
48:13 Walk through its **p**.
122:7 walls and prosperity in your **p**."
Pro 30:28 it can even be found in royal **p**.
Isa 13:22 will howl in its luxurious **p**.
23:13 battle towers, stripped **p** bare,
25:2 and foreigners' **p** into cities that
32:14 **P** will be deserted.
34:13 Its **p** are covered with thorns.
Jer 6:5 at night and destroy its **p**.'"
9:21 our windows and entered our **p**.
17:27 burn down the **p** in Jerusalem,
30:18 and fortified **p** will be built in
33:4 houses in this city and the **p**
49:27 and burn down Benhadad's **p**."
Lam 2:5 He swallowed up all of its **p**.
2:7 He handed the walls of Zion's **p**
Hos 8:14 people of Israel have built **p**,
8:14 cities and burn down their **p**."
Amo 1:4 burn down the **p** of Ben Hadad.
1:7 of Gaza and burn down its **p**.
1:10 of Tyre and burn down its **p**.
1:12 and burn down the **p** of Bozrah.
1:14 down its **p** while troops are
2:2 and burn down the **p** of Kerioth.
2:5 burn down the **p** of Jerusalem.
3:9 Announce in the **p** of Ashdod
3:9 Ashdod and in the **p** of Egypt,
3:10 profits in their **p** through violent
3:11 your defenses, and loot your **p**.
6:8 Jacob's pride, and I hate his **p**.
Mic 5:5 our land and trample our **p**,
Mat 11:8 wear fine clothes are in royal **p**.
Luk 7:25 and live in luxury are in royal **p**.

Palal (1)

Neh 3:25 **P**, Uzai's son, made repairs

pale (13)

Lev 13:39 areas on the skin are **p** white,
13:56 that the area is **p** after washing,
Isa 29:22 face will no longer turn **p**.
Jer 30:6 Why has every face turned **p**?
Dan 5:6 Then the king turned **p**,
5:9 and his face turned **p**.
5:10 frighten you, and don't turn **p**.
7:28 by my thoughts, and I turned **p**.
10:8 My face turned deathly **p**,
Joe 2:6 Every face turns **p**.
Nah 2:10 Every face turns **p**.
Rev 6:8 and there was a **p** horse,
9:17 fiery red, **p** blue, and yellow.

Pallu (5)

Gen 46:9 Hanoch, **P**, Hezron, and Carmi.
Exo 6:14 Hanoch, **P**, Hezron, and Carmi.
Num 26:5 of Hanoch, the family of **P**,
26:8 Eliab was the son of **P**,
1Ch 5:3 Hanoch, **P**, Hezron, and Carmi.

palm (35)

Exo 15:27 were 12 springs and 70 **p** trees.
Lev 23:40 take the best fruits, **p** branches,
Num 33:9 had 12 springs and 70 **p** trees,
Jdg 4:5 She used to sit under the **P**
1Ki 6:29 He carved angels, **p** trees,
6:32 He carved angels, **p** trees,
6:32 onto the angels and the **p** trees.
6:35 angels, **p** trees, and flowers.
7:36 engraved angels, lions, **p** trees,
2Ch 3:5 the form of **p** trees and chains.
Neh 8:15 olive and wild olive, myrtle, **p**,
Psa 92:12 Righteous people flourish like **p**
Pro 30:4 has gathered the wind in the **p**
Sos 7:7 your figure is like a **p** tree,
7:8 I thought, "I will climb the **p**
Isa 9:14 both **p** branches and cattails.
40:12 the water of the sea with the **p**
49:2 sword and hid me in the **p**
51:16 and sheltered you in the **p**
Eze 40:16 Pictures of **p** trees were carved
40:22 and **p** tree pictures were the
40:26 Pictures of **p** trees were carved
40:31 Pictures of **p** trees were carved
40:34 Pictures of **p** trees were carved
40:37 Pictures of **p** trees were carved
41:18 pictures of angels and **p** trees.
41:18 **P** trees were positioned
41:19 which was turned toward a **p**
41:19 which was turned toward a **p**
41:20 Pictures of angels and **p** trees
41:25 Pictures of angels and **p** trees
41:26 small windows and **p** trees
Joe 1:12 The pomegranate, **p**,
Jon 12:13 So they took **p** branches and
Rev 7:9 holding **p** branches in their

palms (5)

Dtr 34:3 Jericho (the City of **P**) — as far
Jdg 1:16 of Judah from the City of **P** into
3:13 and occupied the City of **P**.
2Ch 28:15 (the City of **P**) near their own
Isa 49:16 I have engraved you on the **p** of

Palti (2)

Num 13:9 **P**, son of Raphu, from the tribe
1Sm 25:44 David's wife, to **P**, Laish's son,

Paltiel (2)

Num 34:26 **P**, son of Azzan, the leader of
2Sm 3:15 to take her from her husband **P**,

Paltite (1)

2Sm 23:26 Helez the **P**, Ira (son of Ikkesh)

pamper (1)

Pro 29:21 **P** a slave from childhood,

pampered (2)

Isa 32:9 and listen to me, you **p** women.
32:11 Shudder, you **p** women.

Pamphylia (5)

Act 2:10 Phrygia, **P**, Egypt, and the
13:13 arrived in Perga, a city in **P**.
14:24 through Pisidia, they went to **P**.
15:38 Mark had deserted them in **P**

Act 27:5 the provinces of Cilicia and **P**

pan (6)
Lev 2:5 is prepared in a frying **p**,
6:21 Prepare it in a frying **p** with
7:9 in a skillet or a frying **p**,
1Sm 2:14 the pot, kettle, cauldron, or **p**.
2Sm 13:9 Then she took the **p** and
Eze 4:3 Then take an iron **p**,

paneled (6)
1Ki 6:15 He **p** the inside of the temple
2Ch 3:5 He **p** the larger building with
Eze 41:15 the most holy place were **p**.
41:16 of all three stories were **p**.
41:16 up to the windows, were **p**.
Hag 1:4 live in your **p** houses while this

paneling (2)
1Ki 6:18 carved into the cedar **p** inside
Psa 74:6 They smashed all its carved **p**

panels (9)
1Ki 6:34 of the doors had two folding **p**.
7:28 They had side **p** set in frames.
7:29 On the **p** set in frames were
7:31 But **t** panels were square,
7:32 four wheels were under the **p**,
7:35 which were part of the **p**.
7:36 space on the supports and **p**.
2Ki 16:17 King Ahaz cut off the side **p** of
Jer 22:14 **p** the rooms with cedar,

panic (22)
Exo 14:24 the Egyptian camp into a **p**.
23:27 any nation you meet into a **p**.
23:28 I will spread **p** ahead of you to
Dtr 7:20 will spread **p** among them until
7:23 a great **p** until they're destroyed
28:20 LORD will send you curses, **p**,
28:28 madness, blindness, and **p**.
Jdg 4:15 and his whole army into a **p** in
1Sm 5:9 threw the city into a great **p**:
14:15 There was **p** among the army
14:15 there was a **p** sent from God.
2Sm 17:2 and I'll cause him to **p**.
Job 4:5 It touches you, and you **p**.
Psa 53:5 ⌊but⌋ there was no reason to **p**,
Pro 1:26 fun of you when **p** strikes you,
1:27 when **p** strikes you like a
Jer 30:5 cries of **p**, not cries of peace.
49:24 turn to flee, but **p** grips them.
Lam 3:47 **P** and pitfalls have found us,
Zec 12:4 I will strike every horse with **p**
14:13 On that day a large-scale **p**
Mar 16:6 man said to them, "Don't **p**!

panicked (3)
Jdg 8:12 the whole Midianite army **p**.
20:41 and the men of Benjamin **p**.
2Ki 10:4 But they **p**. They said, "If two

panic-stricken (6)
Est 7:6 Then Haman became **p** in the
Psa 14:5 There they are — **p** because
31:22 When I was **p**, I said, "I have
53:5 There they are — **p** — ⌊but⌋
116:11 I also said when I was **p**,
Mar 16:5 on the right side. They were **p**.

pans (3)
1Ch 23:29 and the bread made in frying **p**.
2Ch 35:13 and **p** and immediately served
Jer 52:19 of the guard also took **p**,

pant (3)
Job 5:5 people **p** after his wealth.
Psa 119:131 I open my mouth and **p**
Isa 42:14 I will cry out. I will gasp and **p**.

pants (1)
Job 12:18 belts and strips them of their **p**.

paper (3)
Eze 9:2 who was carrying **p** and pen.
9:3 who was carrying **p** and pen.
9:11 in linen who was carrying **p**

papers (2)
Isa 50:1 are your mother's divorce **p**?
Jer 3:8 that I gave Israel her divorce **p**.

Paphos (3)
Act 13:6 island as far as the city of **P**.
13:6 In **P** they met a Jewish man
13:13 and his men took a ship from **P**

papyrus (4)
Exo 2:3 she took a basket made of **p**
2:3 set it among the **p** plants near
2:5 the basket among the **p** plants
Job 8:11 "Can **p** grow up where there is

parade (1)
Psa 12:8 Wicked people **p** around when

paradise (4)
Sos 4:13 You are **p** that produces
Luk 23:43 you will be with me in **p**."
2Co 12:4 was snatched away to **p** where
Rev 2:7 which stands in the **p** of God,

Parah (1)
Jos 18:23 Avvim, **P**, Ophrah,

parallel (5)
2Sm 16:13 along the hillside **p** to him.
Lam 2:13 What **p** can I show you,
Eze 42:7 There was a wall which ran **p**
42:10 There were side rooms **p** to the
42:12 end of the walkway that was **p**

paralyzed (19)
1Ki 13:4 the man of God was **p** so that
Mat 4:24 those who were **p**,
8:6 my servant is lying at home **p**
9:2 Some people brought him a **p**
9:6 Then he said to the **p** man,
12:10 A man with a **p** hand was there.
Mar 2:3 came to him carrying a **p** man.
2:4 on which the **p** man was lying.
2:9 Is it easier to say to this **p** man,
2:10 Then he said to the **p** man,
3:1 who had a **p** hand was there.
3:3 told the man with the **p** hand,
Luk 5:18 Some men brought a **p** man on
5:24 Then he said to the **p** man,
6:6 right hand was **p** was there.
6:8 told the man with the **p** hand,
Jon 5:3 blind, lame, or **p** — used to lie.
Act 8:7 Many **p** and lame people were
9:33 man named Aeneas who was **p**

Paran (11)
Gen 21:21 He lived in the desert of **P**,
Num 10:12 stopped in the Desert of **P**.
12:16 set up camp in the Desert of **P**.
13:3 these men from the Desert of **P**.
13:26 at Kadesh in the Desert of **P**.
Dtr 1:1 between **P** and Tophel,
33:2 like sunshine from Mount **P**.
1Sm 25:1 David went to the desert of **P**.
1Ki 11:18 They left Midian and went to **P**.
11:18 some men from **P** with them,
Hab 3:3 Holy One comes from Mount **P**.

parched (7)
Psa 63:1 **p** land where there is no water.
143:6 Like **p** land, my soul thirsts for
Isa 5:13 people will be **p** with thirst."
29:8 lightheaded and **p** with thirst.
32:2 They will be like streams on **p**
41:17 Their tongues are **p** with thirst.
Jer 50:12 You will become a **p** desert.

parchments (1)
2Ti 4:13 scrolls and especially the **p**.

pardon (1)
Hos 11:7 he will not **p** them.

pardoned (5)
Psa 32:1 is forgiven and whose sin is **p**.
85:2 You **p** all their sins.
Isa 1:27 Zion will be **p** by ⌊the LORD's⌋
1:27 and those who return will be **p**
Rom 4:7 forgiven and whose sins are **p**.

parent (1)
Pro 17:21 The **p** of a fool has grief,

parents (51)
Exo 10:6 Your **p** and ancestors never
Num 32:14 "You're just like your **p**!
Dtr 1:31 as **p** carry their children.
8:5 as **p** discipline their children.
21:18 **P** might have a stubborn and
22:17 Then the girl's **p** must spread
24:16 **P** must never be put to death
24:16 death for the crimes of their **p**.
Jos 4:21 when children ask their **p**,
Jdg 2:19 more corruptly than their **p**.
14:6 He didn't tell his **p** what he had
1Sm 1:25 Then the **p** butchered the bull
2Ki 14:6 "**P** must never be put to death
14:6 death for the crimes of their **p**.
1Ch 8:11 He and Hushim were the **p** of
2Ch 25:4 "**P** must never be put to death
25:4 death for the crimes of their **p**.
Neh 9:23 into the land you told their **p**
Psa 78:3 things that our **p** have told us.
Pro 17:6 and **p** are the glory of their
Jer 6:21 **P** and children will stumble
13:14 I will smash **p** and children
32:18 for the wickedness of their **p**.
Eze 5:10 That is why **p** will eat their
5:10 and children will eat their **p**.
Mal 4:6 attitudes toward their **p**.
Mat 10:21 against their **p** and kill them.
Mar 13:12 against their **p** and kill them.
Luk 2:41 Every year Jesus' **p** would go
2:43 but his **p** didn't know it.
2:48 When his **p** saw him,
8:51 John, James, and the child's **p**.
8:55 He ordered her **p** to give her
18:29 up his home, wife, brothers, **p**,
21:16 "Even **p**, brothers, relatives,
Jon 9:2 Did he or his **p** sin?"
9:3 this man nor his **p** sinned.
9:18 Until they talked to the man's **p**,
9:19 They asked his **p**,
9:20 His **p** replied, "We know that
9:22 (His **p** said this because they
9:23 That's why his **p** said,
Act 7:20 His **p** took care of him for three
Rom 1:30 They don't obey their **p**,
2Co 12:14 have to provide for their **p**,
12:14 but **p** should provide for their
Eph 6:1 Children, obey your **p** because
Col 3:20 Children, always obey your **p**.
1Ti 5:4 own family by repaying their **p**.
2Ti 3:2 They will curse their **p**,
Heb 11:23 Faith led Moses' **p** to hide him

parents' (6)
Exo 20:5 I punish children for their **p** sins
34:7 grandchildren for their **p** sins
Num 14:18 for their **p** sins to the third and
Dtr 5:9 I punish children for their **p** sins
Mal 4:6 He will change **p** attitudes
Luk 1:17 He will change **p** attitudes

parks (1)
Ecc 2:5 made gardens and **p** for myself.

Parmashta (1)
Est 9:9 **P**, Arisai, Aridai, and Vaizatha.

Parmenas (1)
Act 6:5 Timon, **P**, and Nicolaus,

Parnach (1)
Num 34:25 Elizaphan, son of **P**,

Parosh (5)
Ezr 2:3 the descendants of **P**:

Ezr 8:3 Shecaniah from the family of **P**:
10:25 From the descendants of **P**:
Neh 7:8 the descendants of **P**:
10:14 **P**, Pahath Moab, Elam, Zattu,

Parosh's (1)

Neh 3:25 After him Pedaiah, **P** son,

Parshandatha (1)

Est 9:7 They also killed **P**,

part (129)

Gen 18:1 during the hottest **p** of the day.
32:22 and crossed at the shallow **p**
47:6 your brothers live in the best **p**
47:11 live in the best **p** of Egypt,
Exo 13:9 LORD are ⌞always⌟ to be a **p**
16:20 They kept **p** of it until morning,
26:13 That **p** should hang over each
30:34 "Take one **p** fragrant spices
30:34 with one **p** pure frankincense.
34:25 No **p** of the sacrifice at the
Lev 2:9 The priest will remove **p** of the
7:29 offering must bring a **p**
10:13 a holy place because it is the **p**
10:14 place because they are your **p**
11:25 Whoever carries any **p** of their
27:16 "If a person gives **p** of a field to
27:22 bought (not one that was a **p**
27:31 If you buy back any **p** of it,
Num 4:25 will carry the sheets that are **p**
15:20 Shape one **p** of your dough into
15:21 you must give one **p** of your
18:9 That **p** of the most holy
18:30 When you contribute the best **p**,
18:32 When you contribute the best **p**,
27:3 He was not a **p** of Korah's
34:3 "The southern side includes **p**
36:3 we will have lost **p** of our land.
36:4 Then **p** of the land of our
Dtr 14:25 If so, exchange the tenth **p** of
23:13 must carry a pointed stick as **p**
24:6 for grinding flour — or even **p**
Jos 19:9 Simeon's inheritance was a **p**
Jdg 17:12 his priest and a **p** of his family.
21:5 from Israel that did not take **p**
21:21 of Shiloh come out to take **p**
Rut 2:3 that she ended up in the **p**
1Sm 30:26 he sent **p** of the loot to his
2Sm 4:2 considered a **p** of Benjamin,
21:2 (The Gibeonites were not a **p**
1Ki 7:34 each stand were **p** of the stand.
7:35 which were **p** of the panels.
2Ki 22:14 in the Second **P** of Jerusalem.
23:13 They were on the southern **p** of
1Ch 6:62 and ⌞the **p** of⌟ the tribe of
2Ch 15:11 they sacrificed to the LORD a **p**
31:3 He set aside **p** of the king's
34:22 in the Second **P** of Jerusalem.
35:5 considered a **p** of each family.
Neh 3:8 They left out **p** of Jerusalem as
Job 10:8 me and made every **p** of me,
Psa 37:20 will vanish like the best **p**
59:4 or any sin, or any guilt on my **p**.
101:3 people do. I want no **p** of it.
Pro 3:9 and with the first and best **p**
Ecc 8:3 Don't take **p** in something evil,
9:6 They will never again take **p** in
Isa 14:15 to the deepest **p** of the pit.
43:24 or satisfy me with the best **p**
Jer 2:3 It was the best **p** of the harvest.
23:3 I will gather the remaining **p**
41:9 one that King Asa made as a **p**
Eze 23:19 So she took **p** in even more
40:15 from the front of the outer **p**
40:15 part to the front of the inner **p**
42:15 finished measuring the inner **p**
45:4 This holy **p** of the land will
48:1 Dan will have one **p** of the land.
48:2 Asher will have one **p** of the
48:3 Naphtali will have one **p** of the
48:4 Manasseh will have one **p** of
48:5 Ephraim will have one **p** of the
48:6 Reuben will have one **p** of the
48:7 Judah will have one **p** of the
48:12 It will be the holiest **p** of land,
Eze 48:14 not let others have the best **p**
48:22 will be between the prince's **p**
48:23 Benjamin will have one **p** of
48:24 Simeon will have one **p** of the
48:25 Issachar will have one **p** of the
48:26 Zebulun will have one **p** of the
48:27 Gad will have one **p** of the land
Dan 2:42 **P** of the kingdom will be strong,
2:42 and **p** will be brittle.
4:22 the most distant **p** of the world.
6:26 I decree that in every **p** of my
Zep 1:10 a howling from the Second **P** of
Mat 4:5 on the highest **p** of the temple.
5:29 It is better for you to lose a **p** of
5:30 It is better for you to lose a **p** of
19:14 Children like these are **p** of the
Mar 10:14 Children like these are **p** of the
Luk 4:9 had him stand on the highest **p**
18:16 Children like these are **p** of the
Jon 12:16 that they had taken **p**
Act 5:2 had pledged⌟ and turned only **p**
8:32 This was the **p** of the
16:12 city in that **p** of Macedonia,
23:13 forty men took **p** in this plot.
Rom 6:13 Never offer any **p** of your body
6:13 No **p** of your body should ever
9:6 from Israel is **p** of Israel
13:13 cannot be **p** of our lives.
1Co 9:11 is it too much if we receive **p** of
12:14 is not made up of only one **p**,
12:15 so I'm not **p** of the body!"
12:15 it's no longer **p** of the body?
12:16 so I'm not a **p** of the body!"
12:16 it's no longer **p** of the body?
12:18 So God put each and every **p**
12:19 be a body if it only had one **p**?
12:24 honor to the **p** that doesn't have
12:26 If one **p** of the body suffers,
12:26 If one **p** is praised,
12:27 of you is an individual **p** of it.
Eph 4:16 As each and every **p** does its
Php 2:17 life is being poured out as a **p**
Phm 1:12 like sending you a **p** of myself.
Heb 9:2 The first **p** of this tent was
9:2 were in this **p** of the tent.
9:3 the second curtain was the **p**
9:6 always went into the first **p**
9:7 priest went into the second **p**
9:9 The first **p** of the tent is an
9:11 human hands and that is not **p**
12:8 you aren't **p** of the family.
Jas 3:5 way the tongue is a small **p**
1Pe 4:3 and took **p** in the forbidden
1Jn 2:19 they were never really **p** of us.
2:19 that none of them were **p** of us.

Partakka (1)

Ezr 4:9 **P**, Tarpel, Persia, Erech,

parted (1)

Act 15:39 so sharply that they **p** ways.

Parthians (1)

Act 2:9 We're **P**, Medes, and Elamites.

partial (2)

Job 32:21 I won't be **p** toward anyone or
Pro 18:5 It is not good to be **p** toward a

partiality (2)

Pro 24:23 Showing **p** as a judge is not
28:21 Showing **p** is not good,

participate (5)

1Co 10:21 You cannot **p** at the table of the
2Co 8:4 begging us to let them **p** in the
8:7 the more we want you to **p** in
1Ti 5:22 Don't **p** in the sins of others.
Rev 18:4 so that you do not **p** in her sins

particular (2)

Eze 24:6 without choosing any **p** piece.
Act 28:25 left after Paul had quoted this **p**

parties (12)

1Sm 13:17 Raiding **p** left the Philistine
2Sm 4:2 who were captains of raiding **p**.
2Ki 13:20 Moabite raiding **p** used to
13:21 saw one of these raiding **p**.
24:2 sent raiding **p** of Babylonians,
1Ch 12:21 helped David fight raiding **p**
Job 1:4 where they would have **p**.
1:5 they finished having their **p**,
Ecc 10:16 officials throw **p** in the morning
Rom 13:13 Wild **p**, drunkenness,
1Pe 4:3 got drunk, went to wild **p**,
2Pe 2:13 take pleasure in holding wild **p**

partner (5)

Pro 29:24 Whoever is a thief's **p** hates his
2Co 8:23 remember that Titus is my **p**
Php 4:3 ask you, Syzugus, my true **p**,
Col 4:7 and **p** in the Lord's work.
Phm 1:17 If you think of me as your **p**,

partners (15)

Psa 94:20 things able to be your **p**?
Luk 5:7 So they signaled to their **p** in
5:7 Their **p** came and filled both
5:10 Zebedee's sons and Simon's **p**,
5:11 Simon and his **p** brought the
1Co 1:9 He called you to be **p** with his
1:30 You are **p** with Christ Jesus
7:15 But if the unbelieving **p** leave,
10:20 want you to be **p** with demons.
2Co 6:14 Can right and wrong be **p**?
Gal 2:9 agreeing to be our **p**.
Eph 5:7 Don't be **p** with them.
Php 1:7 All of you are my **p**.
Heb 3:1 you are holy **p** in a heavenly
3:14 we will remain Christ's **p** only if

partnership (1)

Php 1:5 I can do this because of the **p**

partridge (2)

1Sm 26:20 hunting a **p** in the hills."
Jer 17:11 is like a **p** that hatches eggs

parts (45)

Gen 4:4 also brought some choice **p**
Lev 10:15 These **p** will belong to you and
Num 18:29 best and holiest **p** to the LORD.
Jos 18:5 divide the land into seven **p**.
18:6 You must describe the seven **p**
18:9 divided into seven **p** according
1Ki 7:20 the bowl-shaped **p** around
Job 38:14 and ⌞**p** of it⌟ stand out like
Ecc 11:2 what you have into seven **p**,
Isa 8:9 all you distant **p** of the earth.
Jer 6:22 in the distant **p** of the earth.
16:19 to you from the most distant **p**
31:8 gather them from the farthest **p**
Eze 5:1 divide it ⌞into three even **p**⌟.
32:23 graves are in the deepest **p**
34:3 You eat the best **p** of the sheep,
47:13 Joseph gets two **p**.
Dan 2:43 So the two **p** of the kingdom
7:1 down the main **p** of the dream.
11:24 he will invade the richest **p** of
Rom 6:13 Offer all the **p** of your body to
6:19 you once offered all the **p** of
6:19 offer all the **p** of your body as
12:4 Our bodies have many **p**,
12:4 but these **p** don't all do the
15:15 **p** of which are rather bold,
1Co 6:15 realize that your bodies are **p**
6:15 Should I take the **p** of Christ's
6:15 Christ's body and make them **p**
12:12 is one unit and yet has many **p**.
12:12 As all the **p** form one body,
12:14 of only one part, but of many **p**.
12:20 there are many **p** but one body.
12:22 The **p** of the body that we think
12:23 The **p** of the body that we think
12:23 So our unpresentable **p** are
12:24 However, our presentable **p**
12:25 that all of its **p** should feel
12:26 all the other **p** share its
Eph 2:21 In him all the **p** of the building
4:9 to the lowest **p** of the earth?
5:30 We are **p** of his body.

Heb 9:6 That is how these two **p** of the
Jas 3:6 It is a world of evil among the **p**
Rev 16:19 important city split into three **p**,

party (9)

Jdg 14:10 Samson threw a **p**.
14:12 during the seven days of the **p**,
14:17 rest of the seven days of the **p**.
1Sm 14:15 The raiding **p** also trembled ⌊in
Job 1:4 took his turn having a **p**.)
Luk 16:19 Every day was like a **p** to him.
Act 5:17 chief priest and the whole **p**
15:5 But some believers from the **p**
26:5 that I followed the strictest **p** of

partying (1)

Gal 5:21 envy, drunkenness, wild **p**,

Paruah (1)

1Ki 4:17 Jehoshaphat, son of **P**,

Parvaim (1)

2Ch 3:6 it and used gold from **P**.

Pasach (1)

1Ch 7:33 Japhlet's sons were **P**,

Pas Dammim (2)

2Sa 23:9 Eleazar was with David at **P**
1Ch 11:13 Eleazar was with David at **P**

Paseah (3)

1Ch 4:12 the father of **P** and Tehinnah,
Ezr 2:49 Uzza, **P**, Besai,
Neh 7:51 Gazzam, Uzza, **P**,

Paseah's (1)

Neh 3:6 Joiada, **P** son, and Meshullam,

Pashhur (14)

1Ch 9:12 of Jeroham, grandson of **P**,
Ezr 2:38 of **P**: 1,247
10:22 From the descendants of **P**:
Neh 7:41 of **P**: 1,247
10:3 **P**, Amariah, Malchiah,
11:12 who was the son of **P**,
Jer 20:1 Now the priest, Immer's son **P**,
20:2 **P** struck the prophet Jeremiah
20:3 The next day when **P** took
20:3 "The LORD doesn't call you **P**,
20:6 And you, **P**, and all those who
21:1 when King Zedekiah sent **P**,
38:1 Gedaliah (son of **P**),
38:1 and **P** (son of Malchiah) heard

pass (70)

Exo 12:13 see the blood, I will **p** over you.
12:23 he will **p** over that doorway,
15:16 petrified until your people **p** by,
15:16 the people you purchased **p** by.
33:19 "I will let all my goodness **p** in
Num 20:18 "You may not **p** through our
20:19 We want to **p** through on foot.
20:20 "You may not **p** through."
21:23 Sihon wouldn't let Israel **p**
34:4 turns south of the Akrabbim **P**.
36:7 Israelites will **p** from one tribe
36:9 No land may **p** from one tribe to
Dtr 2:4 'You're going to **p** through the
2:18 "Today you are going to **p** by
2:30 wouldn't allow us to **p** through.
Jos 15:3 goes south of the Akrabbim **P**.
15:7 that faces the Adummim **P**,
18:17 opposite the Adummim **P**.
Jdg 1:36 the Akrabbim **P** — from Selah
8:13 the battle through the Heres **P**
1Sm 13:23 gone out to the **p** at Michmash.
14:4 **p** where Jonathan searched
2Ki 9:27 They shot him at Gur **P**,
2Ch 20:16 will be coming up the Ziz **P**.
Job 9:26 They **p** by quickly like boats
34:20 have seizures and **p** away.
Psa 57:1 until destructive storms **p** by.
80:12 All who **p** by are picking its
84:6 As they **p** through a valley
110:6 He will **p** judgment on the
129:8 Those who **p** by will never say
Pro 9:15 and calls to those who **p** by,
Ecc 6:12 Mortals **p** by like a shadow.
Isa 8:8 It will overflow and **p** through;
8:21 They will **p** through the land
10:28 They **p** through Migron.
10:29 They go through the mountain **p**
28:19 It will **p** by morning after
31:5 He will **p** over it and protect it.
51:10 the LORD⌋ might **p** through it.
Jer 1:16 I will **p** sentence on my people
4:12 I will **p** sentence on them."
6:9 picking grapes, **p** your hand
18:16 Everyone who will **p** by it will
22:8 many nations will **p** by this city
48:5 People go up the **p** of Luhith,
Lam 1:12 this affect all of you who **p** by?
Eze 47:15 way to Hethlon and Hamath **P**.
47:20 to a point opposite Hamath **P**.
48:1 the road to Hethlon to Hamath **P**
Dan 4:25 And seven time periods will **p**
4:32 And seven time periods will **p**
9:25 of seven time periods will **p**.
11:10 enemy⌋ and **p** through its land.
11:40 and **p** through their land.
Amo 5:17 because I will **p** through your
Mic 1:11 **P** by, naked and ashamed,
2:8 from those who **p** by without
Nah 1:15 This wickedness will never **p**
Hab 1:11 They will move quickly and **p**
3:10 Floodwaters **p** by.
Zep 2:15 All who **p** by it will hiss and
Zec 9:8 oppressors will **p** through them,
10:11 The LORD will **p** through a sea
Mar 6:48 He wanted to **p** by them.
15:21 As he was about to **p** by,
Jon 5:27 the Son authority to **p** judgment
1Co 7:10 I **p** this command along (not
Jas 1:12 When they **p** the test,
2Pe 3:10 On that day heaven will **p**

passage (17)

Neh 13:1 They heard the **p** that no
Eze 46:19 brought me through a **p** beside
Mar 12:10 you never read the Scripture **p**:
12:26 It's in the **p** about the bush,
Luk 4:21 Then he said to them, "This **p**
20:37 "Even Moses showed in the **p**
22:37 that the Scripture **p** which says,
Jon 19:37 Another Scripture **p** says,
Act 8:35 Starting with that **p**,
28:25 quoted this particular **p** to them
Rom 11:2 says in the Scripture **p** when
2Ti 3:16 Every Scripture **p** is inspired by
Heb 4:5 God also said in the same **p**,
4:7 David in the **p** already quoted:
10:8 In this **p** Christ first said,
Jas 2:23 The Scripture **p** came true.
4:5 think this **p** means nothing?

passageway (1)

Eze 41:3 inside and measured the **p**.

passed (52)

Gen 15:17 and a flaming torch **p** between
32:31 The sun rose as he **p** Penuel.
Exo 2:23 After a long time **p**,
7:25 Seven days **p** after the LORD
12:27 The LORD **p** over the houses
33:22 with my hand until I have **p** by.
34:6 Then he **p** in front of Moses,
Num 20:17 we've **p** through your territory."
21:22 we've **p** through your territory."
Dtr 2:8 So we **p** by our relatives,
2:14 Thirty-eight years **p** from the
29:16 we **p** through other countries
Jos 24:17 as we **p** through other nations.
Jdg 9:25 everyone who **p** by them
1Sm 7:2 A long time **p** after the ark
2Sm 2:15 and were counted as they **p** by.
2:29 the Jordan River and **p** through
15:18 All his mercenaries **p** by him;
20:14 Sheba **p** through all the tribes
1Ki 13:25 People who **p** by saw the body
20:39 When the king **p** by,
2Ki 25:6 and **p** sentence on him.
Est 7:8 Then the king **p** sentence on
Job 4:15 A spirit **p** in front of me.
15:19 stranger **p** through their land.)
28:8 lion has ever **p** over it.
Psa 18:12 those rain clouds **p** by with
89:41 (Everyone who **p** by robbed
Pro 10:25 When the storm has **p**,
24:30 I **p** by a lazy person's field,
Isa 60:15 no one has **p** through you.
Jer 34:18 two and **p** between its pieces.
34:19 people who **p** between
39:5 of Babylon **p** sentence on him.
52:9 of Babylon **p** sentence on him.
Lam 4:21 ⌊of the LORD's fury⌋ will be **p**
Eze 16:25 body to everyone who **p** by.
Mat 27:39 Those who **p** by insulted him.
Mar 15:29 Those who **p** by insulted him.
Luk 1:2 and they **p** it on to us.
2:22 to make a mother clean had **p**,
Jon 5:24 they have already **p** from death
Act 12:10 They **p** the first and second
16:8 So they **p** by Mysia and went
21:3 the island of Cyprus as we **p**
24:27 Two years **p**. Then Porcius
27:17 Then they **p** ropes under the
1Co 11:23 After all, I **p** on to you what I
15:3 I **p** on to you the most important
2Co 13:7 to prove that we've **p** the test.
1Th 2:4 do this because we **p** his test.
1Jn 3:14 We know that we have **p** from

passes (17)

Exo 33:22 When my glory **p** by,
Jos 15:3 It then **p** Zin and goes up south
15:6 It then **p** north to Beth Arabah
15:7 Then the border **p** the Springs
16:6 Shiloh and **p** east to Janoah.
Job 9:11 He **p** alongside of me,
14:20 him forever, and he **p** away.
Isa 6:5 Every word that **p** through my
24:11 All joy **p** away, and the earth's
28:15 overwhelming disaster **p** by,
28:18 overwhelming disaster **p** by,
28:19 Each time it **p** by it will take
Jer 49:17 Everyone who **p** by it will be
50:13 Everyone who **p** by Babylon
Lam 1:4 No one **p** through any of its
Eze 5:14 of everyone who **p** by you.
Zep 2:2 day **p** like windblown husks,

passing (20)

Gen 37:28 Midianite merchants were **p** by,
Jos 19:46 with the border **p** in front of
Rut 4:1 he had spoken was **p** by.
2Sm 15:23 as all the troops were **p** by.
1Ki 9:8 Everyone **p** by this temple,
19:11 As the LORD was **p** by,
2Ch 7:21 Everyone **p** by this impressive
Neh 2:14 **P** through Fountain Gate,
Job 17:11 My days are **p** by. My plans are
Jer 6:4 The day is **p**, and the shadows
Eze 36:34 empty for everyone **p** by to see.
Hos 4:3 who lives in it is **p** away.
Mat 20:30 heard that Jesus was **p** by,
Mar 9:30 and were **p** through Galilee.
10:47 from Nazareth ⌊was **p** by⌋,
Luk 18:37 Jesus from Nazareth was **p** by.
19:1 Jesus was **p** through Jericho.
1Co 7:31 in its present form is **p** away.
1Pe 1:7 than gold, and by **p** the test,
1Jn 2:17 and its evil desires are **p** away.

passion (1)

Col 3:5 sexual sin, perversion, **p**, lust,

passionate (2)

1Th 4:5 not in the **p**, lustful way of
Rev 14:8 the wine of her **p** sexual sins."

passions (4)

Ecc 9:6 hate, and their **p** have already vanished.
Rom 1:26 God allowed their shameful **p**
7:5 sinful **p** were at work
Gal 5:24 along with its **p** and desires.

Passover (90)

Exo 12:11 It is the LORD's **P**.
12:21 and kill the **P** animal.
12:27 you must answer, 'It's the **P**
12:43 "These are the rules for the **P**:
12:43 "No foreigner may eat the **P**
12:47 of Israel must celebrate the **P**.
12:48 to celebrate the LORD's **P**.
12:48 Then they may celebrate the **P**
12:48 males may ever eat the **P** meal.
34:25 No part of the sacrifice at the **P**
Lev 23:5 the evening, is the LORD's **P**.
23:11 present it on the day after **P**.
23:15 the day after **P** (the day you
Num 9:2 must celebrate the **P** at
9:3 for the celebration of the **P**."
9:4 the Israelites to celebrate the **P**,
9:6 celebrate the **P** that day.
9:10 You may still celebrate the **P**.
9:11 You must eat the **P** animal
9:12 for the **P** when you celebrate
9:13 don't bother to celebrate the **P**,
9:14 to celebrate the LORD's **P**.
28:16 the first month is the LORD's **P**.
33:3 the day after the **P**.
Dtr 16:1 your God by celebrating **P**
16:2 flock or herd as the **P** sacrifice
16:5 to slaughter the animals for **P**
16:6 slaughter your animals for **P** in
Jos 5:10 There they celebrated the **P** on
5:11 On the day after the **P**,
2Ki 23:21 all the people to celebrate the **P**
23:22 The **P** had never been
23:23 this **P** was celebrated in
2Ch 30:1 in Jerusalem to celebrate the **P**
30:2 decided to celebrate the **P**
30:5 to Jerusalem to celebrate the **P**
30:15 They slaughtered the **P** lamb
30:17 So the Levites had to kill the **P**
30:18 So they ate the **P**, but not in the
35:1 Josiah celebrated the **P** for the
35:1 The **P** lamb was slaughtered
35:6 Slaughter the **P** lamb,
35:7 to be sacrificed as **P** offerings
35:8 and 300 bulls for **P** sacrifices.
35:9 and 500 bulls as **P** sacrifices.
35:11 They slaughtered the **P** lambs.
35:13 They roasted the **P** lambs
35:16 The **P** was celebrated,
35:17 celebrated the **P** at that time.
35:18 Never had a **P** like this been
35:18 They did not celebrate the **P**
35:19 this **P** was celebrated.
Ezr 6:19 from exile celebrated the **P**.
6:20 They killed the **P** lambs for all
Eze 45:21 you will celebrate the **P**,
Mat 26:2 "You know that the **P** will take
26:17 to prepare the **P** meal for you?"
26:18 I will celebrate the **P** with my
26:19 them and prepared the **P**.
27:15 At every **P** festival the governor
Mar 14:1 It was two days before the **P**
14:12 Killing the **P** lamb was
14:12 to prepare the **P** meal for you?"
14:14 where I can eat the **P** meal
14:16 So they prepared the **P**.
15:6 At every **P** festival,
Luk 2:41 to Jerusalem for the **P** festival.
22:1 Bread, called **P**, was near.
22:7 Bread when the **P** lamb had
22:8 prepare the **P** lamb for us to
22:11 where I can eat the **P** meal
22:13 told them and prepared the **P**.
22:14 it was time to eat the **P** meal,
22:15 had a deep desire to eat this **P**
Jon 2:13 The Jewish **P** was near,
2:23 in Jerusalem at the **P** festival,
6:4 the Jewish **P** festival was near.
11:55 The Jewish **P** was near.
11:55 purify themselves before the **P**.
12:1 Six days before **P**,
12:12 to the **P** festival heard that
12:20 to worship during the **P** festival.
13:1 Before the **P** festival,
18:28 since they wanted to eat the **P**.
Jon 18:39 free one person for you at **P**.
19:14 on the Friday of the **P** festival.
Act 2:1 the fiftieth day after **P**,
12:4 in front of the people after **P**.
1Co 5:7 Christ, our **P** lamb,
Heb 11:28 led Moses to establish the **P**

past (79)

Gen 18:11 Sarah was **p** the age of
31:52 witnesses that I will not go **p**
31:52 and that you will not go **p** the
Num 34:4 It then goes **p** Zin and ends at
Dtr 4:32 Search the distant **p**,
8:4 didn't swell these **p** 40 years.
19:4 he never hated in the **p** may run
19:6 because in the **p** he never
32:7 about all the **p** generations.
Jos 14:15 In the **p** Hebron was called
15:15 (In the **p** Debir was called
Jdg 1:10 (In the **p** Hebron was called
1:11 (In the **p** Debir was called
1:23 (In the **p** the city was called
3:2 known nothing about it in the **p**.
3:26 He went **p** the stone idols and
1Sm 15:32 of death is **p**," Agag said.
2Sm 5:2 "Even in the **p** when Saul ruled
15:18 Gath were marching **p** the king.
15:34 your father's servant in the **p**,
2Ki 4:9 regularly travels **p** our house.
19:25 I planned it in the distant **p**.
1Ch 11:2 "Even in the **p** when Saul ruled,
Neh 12:37 There the wall rises **p** David's
12:38 **p** the Tower of the Ovens,
12:39 then **p** Ephraim Gate,
Job 8:7 Then what you had in the **p**
8:8 the people of **p** generations.
9:11 He goes **p** me, and I don't even
14:5 then he cannot go **p** it.
Psa 90:4 like yesterday — already **p** —
Ecc 1:11 from the **p** is remembered.
3:15 ⌞in the **p**⌟ is present now.
3:15 already happened ⌞in the **p**⌟.
3:15 God will call the **p** to account.
6:10 ⌞in the **p**⌟ already has
Sos 2:11 The winter is **p**. The rain is over
Isa 16:13 spoke about Moab in the **p**.
23:7 city founded in the distant **p**?
33:18 of the terrors ⌞in the **p**⌟.
37:26 I planned it in the distant **p**.
41:22 Explain **p** events that your
41:26 Who revealed this from the **p**
42:9 What I said in the **p** has come
43:18 Forget what happened in the **p**,
45:21 revealed this in the distant **p**
48:7 are created now, not in the **p**.
51:9 up as you did in days long **p**,
58:12 foundations of **p** generations.
63:9 them and carried them in the **p**.
63:11 Moses and the distant **p**.
65:16 **P** troubles are forgotten.
65:17 **P** things will not be
Jer 8:20 The harvest is **p**, the summer
Eze 36:11 people live on you as in the **p**,
46:21 outer courtyard and took me **p**
Mic 5:2 origins go back to the distant **p**,
Zec 7:5 months these **p** 70 years,
Mal 3:4 to the LORD as in the **p**,
Act 14:16 In the **p** God allowed all people
20:16 Paul had decided to sail **p**
27:9 day of fasting had already **p**.
Rom 3:25 with sins committed in the **p**.
11:30 In the **p**, you disobeyed God.
Gal 1:9 what we've told you in the **p**:
5:21 I've told you in the **p** and I'm
Eph 3:5 In the **p**, this mystery was not
3:9 kept it hidden in the **p**.
Col 1:26 In the **p** God hid this mystery,
1Ti 1:13 In the **p** I cursed him,
Heb 1:1 In the **p** God spoke to our
4:2 help those who heard it in the **p**
4:6 News in the **p** did not enter
10:32 Remember the **p**, when you
1Pe 3:5 expressed their beauty in the **p**.
4:3 You spent enough time in the **p**
2Pe 1:9 cleansed from your **p** sins.
2:1 among God's people ⌞in the **p**⌟,
2Pe 3:2 the words spoken in the **p** by

pastors (1)

Eph 4:11 as well as **p** and teachers as

pastry (1)

Num 11:8 It tasted like rich **p** made with

pasture (26)

Gen 47:4 in Canaan that there's no **p**
2Sm 7:8 I took you from the **p** where
1Ki 4:23 20 cows from the **p**,
1Ch 4:39 to find **p** for their flocks.
4:40 They found **p** that was rich and
4:41 order to have **p** for their flocks.
17:7 I took you from the **p** where
Job 39:8 explores the mountains for its **p**
Psa 79:13 the flock in your **p**,
Isa 5:17 as if they were in their own **p**,
65:10 Plain will be a **p** for flocks.
Jer 23:3 I will bring them back to their **p**,
25:36 the LORD is stripping their **p**.
49:20 He will surely destroy the **p**
50:7 against the LORD, their true **p**.
50:45 He will surely destroy the **p**
Lam 1:6 deer that couldn't find any **p**.
Eze 25:5 turn Rabbah into a **p** for camels,
34:14 I will feed them in good **p**,
34:18 for you to feed on the good **p**?
34:18 you trample the rest of the **p**
34:31 are the sheep in my **p**.
Hos 4:16 them like lambs in an open **p**?
Joe 1:18 There's no **p** for them.
Mic 2:12 like a flock in its **p**.
Luk 15:4 the 99 sheep grazing in the **p**

pastureland (54)

Gen 13:6 There wasn't enough **p** for both
36:7 There wasn't enough **p** for all of
Num 35:2 the **p** around those cities.
35:3 will have cities to live in and **p**
35:5 will be their **p** around the city.
35:7 48 cities with **p** to the Levites.
Jos 21:11 father) and the **p** around it.
21:42 cities had its own **p** around it.
1Ch 5:16 and in the entire **p** of Sharon to
6:55 as well as the **p** around it,
6:57 refuge, Libnah with its **p**, Jattir,
6:57 Eshtemoa with its **p**,
6:58 Hilen with its **p**, Debir with its
6:58 its pastureland, Debir with its **p**,
6:59 Ashan with its **p**, and Beth
6:59 and Beth Shemesh with its **p**.
6:60 received Geba with its **p**,
6:60 Alemeth with its **p**,
6:60 and Anathoth with its **p**.
6:67 Shechem with its **p** in the hills
6:67 of Ephraim, Gezer with its **p**,
6:68 Jokmeam with its **p**,
6:68 Beth Horon with its **p**,
6:69 Aijalon with its **p**, and Gath
6:69 and Gath Rimmon with its **p**.
6:70 they were given Aner with its **p**
6:70 and Bileam with its **p**
6:71 Golan in Bashan with its **p**
6:71 and Ashtaroth with its **p** from
6:72 received Kedesh with its **p**,
6:72 Daberath with its **p**,
6:73 Ramoth with its **p**,
6:73 and Anem with its **p**.
6:74 received Mashal with its **p**,
6:74 pastureland, Abdon with its **p**,
6:75 Hukok with its **p**, and Rehob
6:75 and Rehob with its **p**.
6:76 Kedesh in Galilee with its **p**,
6:76 Hammon with its **p**,
6:76 and Kiriathaim with its **p**.
6:77 received Rimmono with its **p**
6:77 and Tabor with its **p** from
6:78 in the wilderness with its **p**,
6:78 pastureland, Jahzah with its **p**,
6:79 Kedemoth with its **p** and
6:79 and Mephaath with its **p**.
6:80 Ramoth in Gilead with its **p**,
6:80 Mahanaim with its **p**,
6:81 Heshbon with its **p**,

1Ch 6:81 and Jazer with its **p**.
Jer 49:19 along the Jordan River into **p**.
50:44 along the Jordan River into **p**.
Eze 48:17 The city's **p** will be 4,375 feet
Zep 2:6 The seacoast will become **p**

pasturelands (21)

Jos 14:4 Levites cities to live in with **p**
21:2 live in and **p** for our livestock."
21:3 the following cities with **p** from
21:8 gave these cities with **p**
21:13 gave the following cities with **p**
21:19 In all, 13 cities with **p** were
21:21 These four cities with **p** were
21:25 gave them two cities with **p**:
21:26 In all, ten cities with **p** were
21:27 two cities with **p** from half of
21:28 Four cities with **p** were also
21:30 Another four cities with **p** were
21:32 Also three cities with **p** were
21:33 In all, 13 cities with **p** were
21:34 Zebulun gave four cities with **p**:
21:36 gave them four cities with **p**:
21:38 gave them four cities with **p**:
1Ch 6:64 Levites the cities with their **p**.
13:2 in their cities and **p** so that they
2Ch 31:19 priests who lived in the **p** of
Psa 83:12 take God's **p** for ourselves."

pastures (29)

1Sm 19:18 went to the **p** and lived there.
19:19 David was in the **p** at Ramah,
19:22 "Over there in the **p** at Ramah."
19:23 he went toward the **p** at Ramah,
19:23 he came to the **p** at Ramah.
20:1 David fled from the **p** at Ramah,
Psa 23:2 makes me lie down in green **p**.
65:12 The **p** in the desert overflow
65:13 The **p** are covered with flocks.
Isa 30:23 your cattle will graze in large **p**.
32:14 wild donkeys and **p** for flocks
49:9 and they will find **p** on every
Jer 6:2 people Zion are like lovely **p**.
9:10 sing a funeral song for the **p**
23:10 **P** in the wilderness have dried
25:37 The peaceful **p** are destroyed
33:12 there will once again be **p**
35:9 vineyards, **p**, or grainfields.
50:19 people of Israel back to their **p**.
Lam 2:2 of Jacob's **p** without any pity.
Eze 34:14 and they will feed on the best **p**
45:15 the well-watered **p** of Israel.
48:15 be left for cities, homes, and **p**.
Joe 1:19 Fire has burned up the open **p**.
1:20 Fire has burned up the open **p**.
2:22 The **p** in the wilderness have
Amo 1:2 The **p** of the shepherds are
Mic 7:14 alone in the woods, in fertile **p**.
Zec 11:3 their rich **p** are destroyed.

Patara (2)

Act 21:1 and from there to the city of **P**.
21:2 In **P**, we found a ship that was

patch (5)

Lev 13:42 But if there is a pink **p** on the
Mat 9:16 When the **p** shrinks,
Mar 2:21 Otherwise, the new **p** will
Luk 5:36 of cloth from a new coat to **p**
5:36 Besides, the **p** from the new

patched (1)

Jos 9:4 were old, split, and **p**.

patches (2)

Mat 9:16 "No one **p** an old coat with a
Mar 2:21 "No one **p** an old coat with a

paternal (1)

Lev 18:12 She is your **p** aunt.

path (63)

Gen 49:17 snake on a road, a viper on a **p**,
1Sm 25:20 mountain **p** when she met
2Sm 22:37 You make a wide **p** for me to
Job 16:22 I will take the **p** of no return.
Job 18:10 trap is on his **p** ⌊to catch⌋ him.
19:8 "God has blocked my **p** so that
22:3 you follow the **p** of integrity?
22:15 "Are you following the old **p**
22:28 and light will shine on your **p**.
23:11 I have stayed on his **p** and did
30:13 they remove all traces of my **p**
31:7 steps have left the ⌊proper⌋ **p**,
38:20 may know the **p** to its home?
38:25 and a **p** for the thunderstorms
41:32 It leaves a shining **p** behind it
Psa 1:1 take the **p** of sinners,
16:11 You make the **p** of life known
18:36 You make a wide **p** for me to
25:10 Every **p** of the LORD is ⌊one
25:12 will teach which **p** to choose.
27:11 Lead me on a level **p** because I
35:6 Let their **p** be dark and slippery
37:34 for the LORD, and follow his **p**,
44:18 Our feet never left your **p**.
77:19 Your **p** went through raging
78:50 He cleared a **p** for his anger.
85:13 him and make a **p** for his steps.
101:2 to understand the **p** to integrity.
119:35 Lead me on the **p** of your
119:101 ⌊from walking⌋ on any evil **p**
119:104 That is why I hate every **p** that
119:105 for my feet and a light for my **p**.
139:24 See whether I am on an evil **p**.
139:24 lead me on the everlasting **p**.
142:3 for me on the **p** where I walk.
Pro 1:15 Do not even set foot on their **p**,
4:14 Do not stray onto the **p** of
4:18 But the **p** of righteous people is
4:26 Carefully walk a straight **p**,
5:6 even think about the **p** of life.
6:23 from discipline are the **p** of life
12:26 but the **p** of wicked people
12:28 Eternal death is not along its **p**.
15:10 who leaves the ⌊right⌋ **p**.
15:19 The **p** of lazy people is like a
15:24 The **p** of life for a wise person
16:29 and leads him on a **p** that is not
Isa 26:7 The **p** of the righteous is level.
26:8 ⌊as we follow⌋ the **p** of your
30:11 Stop blocking our **p**!
41:3 marching by safely on a **p** his
43:16 The LORD makes a **p** through
49:9 They will graze along every **p**,
Jer 18:15 the way, on the ancient **p**.
31:9 on a level **p** where they will
Hos 9:8 are set on every prophet's **p**,
Nah 1:3 winds and storms mark his **p**,
Mal 2:8 turned from the ⌊correct⌋ **p**
Act 2:28 You make the **p** of life known
2Pe 2:10 their corrupt nature along the **p**
2:15 teachers have left the straight **p**
2:15 off to follow the **p** of Balaam,
Jud 1:11 have followed the **p** of Cain.

pathetic (2)

Job 16:2 You are all **p** at comforting me.
Psa 74:3 steps toward these **p** ruins.

pathless (2)

Job 12:24 about in a **p** wilderness.
Psa 107:40 stumble around in a **p** desert.

Pathros (4)

Jer 44:1 Tahpanhes, Noph, and **P**.
44:15 all the people who lived at **P**
Eze 29:14 captives and return them to **P**,
30:14 I will destroy **P**, set fire to

Pathrusites (2)

Gen 10:14 **P**, Casluhites (from whom the
1Ch 1:12 **P**, Casluhites (from whom the

paths (32)

Jdg 5:20 Sisera from their heavenly **p**.
Job 3:23 whose **p** have been hidden,
19:8 He has made my **p** dark.
24:13 They do not stay on its **p**.
28:26 and set **p** for the thunderstorms
33:11 stocks and watches all my **p**.'
Psa 17:5 have remained firmly in your **p**.
Psa 23:3 He guides me along the **p** of
25:4 and teach me your **p**.
119:128 I follow the straight **p** of your
Pro 2:8 in order to guard those on **p** of
2:13 from those who abandon the **p**
2:15 Their **p** are crooked.
2:19 do they ever reach the **p** of life.
2:20 on the **p** of righteous people.
3:6 and he will make your **p**
3:17 and all its **p** lead to peace.
4:11 guided you along decent **p**.
7:25 Do not wander onto her **p**,
8:20 on the **p** of justice,
Isa 42:16 I will lead them on unfamiliar **p**.
59:8 They've made their **p** crooked.
Jer 6:16 Ask which **p** are the old,
6:16 paths are the old, reliable **p**.
23:12 will become like slippery **p**
Lam 3:9 and made my **p** crooked.
Hab 3:6 The ancient **p** belong to him.
Mat 3:3 Make his **p** straight!'"
Mar 1:3 Make his **p** straight!'"
Luk 3:4 Make his **p** straight!
14:23 'Go to the roads and **p**!
Heb 12:13 Keep walking along straight **p**

pathway (1)

Psa 119:128 I hate every **p** that leads to

patience (14)

Pro 25:15 With **p** you can persuade a
Isa 7:13 that you try the **p** of mortals?
7:13 you also try the **p** of my God?
Mic 6:3 How have I tried your **p**?
Mal 2:17 You have tried the **p** of the
2:17 "How have we tried his **p**?"
Rom 3:25 In his **p** God waited to deal
2Co 6:6 purity, knowledge, **p**, kindness,
Gal 5:22 peace, **p**, kindness, goodness,
1Ti 1:16 to demonstrate his **p**.
1:16 This **p** serves as an example
2Ti 3:10 my faith, my **p**, my love,
Heb 6:12 promises through faith and **p**.
2Pe 3:15 Think of our Lord's **p** as an

patient (31)

Exo 34:6 and merciful God, **p**,
Num 14:18 **p**, forever loving .... He forgives
Neh 9:17 **p**, and always ready to forgive.
9:30 You were **p** with them for many
Job 36:2 "Be **p** with me a little longer,
Psa 86:15 You are **p**, always faithful and
103:8 **p**, and always ready to forgive.
145:8 **p**, and always ready to forgive.
Pro 14:29 of great understanding is **p**,
19:11 A person with good sense is **p**,
Ecc 7:8 It is better to be **p** than arrogant
Isa 48:9 For my name's sake I'll be **p**.
Jer 15:15 Be **p**, and don't take me away.
Joe 2:13 merciful and compassionate, **p**,
Jnh 4:2 and compassionate God, **p**,
Nah 1:3 The LORD is **p** and has great
Mat 18:26 feet and said, 'Be **p** with me,
18:29 and begged him, 'Be **p** with me,
Rom 9:22 But can't he be extremely **p**
12:12 confidence, be **p** in trouble,
15:1 have a strong ⌊faith⌋ must be **p**
1Co 13:4 Love is **p**. Love is kind. Love
13:7 Love never stops being **p**,
Eph 4:2 Be **p** with each other and
Col 3:12 kind, humble, gentle, and **p**.
1Th 5:14 and be **p** with everyone.
2Ti 4:2 Be very **p** when you teach.
Jas 5:7 Brothers and sisters, be **p** until
5:8 You, too, must be **p**.
5:10 They were **p** when they
2Pe 3:9 Rather, he is **p** for your sake.

patiently (11)

Psa 37:7 and wait **p** for him.
40:1 I waited **p** for the LORD.
Mat 10:22 But the person who **p** endures
Act 26:3 So I ask you to listen **p** to me.
Rom 2:4 and deals **p** with you?
2Co 12:12 While I was among you I **p** did
Col 1:11 need to **p** endure everything

Heb 6:15 because he waited **p** for it.
13:22 to listen **p** to my encouraging
Jas 5:7 They wait **p** for fall and spring
1Pe 3:20 God waited **p** while Noah built

Patmos (1)

Rev 1:9 ⌊exiled⌋ on the island of **P**

Patrobas (1)

Rom 16:14 Phlegon, Hermes, **P**, Hermas,

patrol (3)

Zec 1:10 LORD has sent to **p** the earth."
6:7 they were eager to **p** the earth.
6:7 He said, "Go, **p** the earth!"

patrolled (2)

Zec 1:11 "We have **p** the earth.
6:7 And they **p** the earth.

pattern (2)

2Ti 1:13 be the **p** of accurate teachings.
Heb 8:5 serve at a place that is a **p**,

Pau (1)

Gen 36:39 name of his capital city was **P**.

Paul (275)

Act 13:9 But Saul, also known as **P**,
13:13 **P** and his men took a ship from
13:14 **P** and Barnabas left Perga and
13:15 message⌋ to **P** and Barnabas.
13:16 Then **P** stood up, and said,
13:42 As **P** and Barnabas were
13:43 followed **P** and Barnabas.
13:43 **P** and Barnabas talked with
13:45 to contradict whatever **P** said.
13:46 **P** and Barnabas told them
13:50 people started to persecute **P**
13:51 **P** and Barnabas shook the dust
14:1 **P** and Barnabas went into the
14:3 **P** and Barnabas stayed in the
14:5 In the meantime, **P** and
14:9 listened to what **P** was saying.
14:9 **P** observed him closely and
14:10 So **P** said in a loud voice,
14:11 The crowds who saw what **P**
14:12 as Zeus and **P** as Hermes
14:12 as Hermes because **P** did most
14:13 sacrifice ⌊to **P** and Barnabas⌋.
14:14 and **P** heard what was
14:18 Although **P** and Barnabas said
14:19 They tried to stone **P** to death
14:20 The next day **P** and Barnabas
14:22 **P** and Barnabas told them,
15:2 **P** and Barnabas had a fierce
15:2 So **P** and Barnabas and some
15:3 The church sent **P** and
15:4 spiritual leaders welcomed **P**
15:4 **P** and Barnabas reported
15:12 to Barnabas and **P** tell about all
15:22 of their men to send with **P**
15:25 with our dear Barnabas and **P**.
15:26 Barnabas and **P** have
15:35 **P** and Barnabas stayed in
15:36 After a while **P** said to
15:38 However, **P** didn't think it was
15:39 **P** and Barnabas disagreed so
15:40 **P** chose Silas and left after the
15:41 **P** went through the provinces
16:1 **P** arrived in the city of Derbe
16:3 **P** wanted Timothy to go with
16:6 **P** and Silas went through the
16:9 During the night **P** had a vision
16:9 The man urged **P**, "Come to
16:10 As soon as **P** had seen the
16:14 to pay attention to what **P** said.
16:17 used to follow **P** and shout,
16:18 **P** became annoyed,
16:18 As **P** said this, the evil spirit
16:19 they grabbed **P** and Silas and
16:22 the attack against **P** and Silas.
16:22 officials tore the clothes off **P**
16:23 After they had hit **P** and Silas
16:24 followed these orders and put **P**
16:25 Around midnight **P** and Silas
Act 16:28 But **P** shouted as loudly as he
16:29 he knelt in front of **P** and Silas.
16:30 Then he took **P** and Silas
16:33 the jailer washed **P** and Silas'
16:34 He took **P** and Silas upstairs
16:36 this order to **P** by saying,
16:37 But **P** told the guards,
16:38 to the officials what **P** had said.
16:38 Roman officials heard that **P**
16:39 and apologized to **P** and Silas.
16:39 As the officials escorted **P** and
16:40 After **P** and Silas left the jail,
17:1 **P** and Silas traveled through
17:2 **P** went into the synagogue.
17:4 persuaded to join **P** and Silas,
17:5 home and searched it for **P**
17:6 they didn't find **P** and Silas,
17:10 the believers sent **P** and Silas
17:10 When **P** and Silas arrived in
17:11 to see if what **P** said was true.
17:13 out that **P** was also spreading
17:14 believers immediately sent **P**
17:15 The men who escorted **P** took
17:15 Timothy to join **P** as soon as
17:16 While **P** was waiting for Silas
17:18 things because **P** was telling
17:19 Then they brought **P** to the city
17:22 **P** stood in the middle of the
17:33 this response, **P** left the court.
18:1 After this, **P** left Athens and
18:2 **P** went to visit them,
18:4 On every day of worship, **P**
18:5 **P** devoted all his time to
18:6 So **P** shook the dust from his
18:8 Many Corinthians who heard **P**
18:9 One night the Lord said to **P** in
18:11 **P** lived in Corinth for a year and
18:12 They attacked **P** and brought
18:14 **P** was about to answer when
18:18 **P** left ⌊for Ephesus⌋.
18:19 where **P** left Priscilla and
18:19 **P** went into the synagogue and
18:21 **P** took a boat from Ephesus
18:23 **P** went through the regions of
19:1 was in Corinth, **P** traveled
19:3 **P** asked them, "What kind of
19:4 **P** said, "John's baptism was a
19:6 When **P** placed his hands on
19:8 For three months **P** would go
19:11 unusual miracles through **P**.
19:13 whom **P** talks about."
19:15 and I'm acquainted with **P**,
19:21 **P** decided to go to Jerusalem
19:26 hear what this man **P** has done.
19:29 who traveled with **P**,
19:30 **P** wanted to go into the crowd,
20:1 **P** sent for the disciples,
20:3 When **P** was going to board a
20:4 of Asia accompanied **P**.
20:7 **P** was discussing ⌊Scripture⌋
20:9 As **P** was talking on and on,
20:10 **P** went to him, took him into
20:11 **P** talked with the people for a
20:13 we were going to pick up **P**.
20:14 When **P** met us in Assos,
20:16 **P** had decided to sail past
20:17 From Miletus **P** sent
20:36 When **P** had finished speaking,
20:37 arms around **P** and kissed him.
20:38 The thought of not seeing **P**
20:38 Then they took **P** to the ship.
21:4 had the disciples tell **P** not
21:12 who lived there begged **P** not
21:13 Then **P** replied, "Why are you
21:14 When **P** could not be
21:18 The next day **P** went with us
21:19 After greeting them, **P** related
21:20 They said to **P**, "You see,
21:26 The next day, **P** took the men
21:27 the province of Asia saw **P**
21:27 whole crowd and grabbed **P**.
21:29 and thought **P** had taken him
21:30 The mob grabbed **P** and
21:31 the people were trying to kill **P**,
21:32 they stopped beating **P**.
21:33 Then the officer went to **P**,
Act 21:33 The officer asked who **P** was
21:34 so he ordered **P** to be taken
21:35 When **P** came to the stairs of
21:37 were about to take **P** into
21:37 The officer replied to **P**,
21:39 **P** answered, "I'm a Jew,
21:40 The officer gave **P** permission
21:40 So **P** stood on the stairs of the
21:40 When the mob was silent, **P**
22:2 Then **P** continued,
22:24 the soldiers to take **P** into
22:24 to question **P** as they whipped
22:24 were yelling at **P** like this.
22:25 But when the soldiers had **P**
22:25 **P** asked the sergeant who was
22:27 The officer went to **P** and
22:27 **P** answered, "Yes."
22:28 **P** replied, "But I was born a
22:29 question **P** stepped away from
22:30 the Jews had against **P**.
22:30 So the officer released **P** the
22:30 Then the officer brought **P** and
23:1 **P** stared at the Jewish council
23:2 the men standing near **P**
23:3 Then **P** said to him,
23:4 The men standing near **P** said
23:5 **P** answered, "Brothers, I didn't
23:6 When **P** saw that some of them
23:7 After **P** said that, the Pharisees
23:10 they would tear **P** to pieces.
23:10 his soldiers to drag **P** back
23:11 The Lord stood near **P** the next
23:12 before they had killed **P**.
23:14 any food before we've killed **P**.
23:15 need more information from **P**.
23:16 entered the barracks and told **P**.
23:17 Then **P** called one of the
23:18 "The prisoner **P** called me.
23:20 planned to ask you to bring **P**
23:21 ⌊that you will bring **P**⌋."
23:24 Provide an animal for **P** to ride,
23:31 They took **P** to the city of
23:32 on horseback travel with **P**.
23:33 in the city of Caesarea with **P**,
23:33 and handed **P** over to him.
23:34 he asked **P** which province he
23:34 When he found out that **P** was
23:35 orders to keep **P** under guard
24:1 their charges against **P**.
24:2 When **P** had been summoned,
24:10 motioned for **P** to speak.
24:10 **P** responded, "I know that you
24:23 ordered the sergeant to guard **P**
24:24 He sent for **P** and listened to
24:25 As **P** discussed the subjects of
24:26 Felix was hoping that **P** would
24:26 Felix would send for **P** rather
24:27 he left **P** in prison.)
25:2 about their charges against **P**.
25:3 the favor of having **P** brought
25:3 a plan to ambush and kill **P** as
25:4 soon and would keep **P** there.
25:6 in court and summoned **P**.
25:7 When **P** entered the room,
25:8 **P** defended himself by saying,
25:9 So he asked **P**, "Are you
25:10 **P** said, "I am standing in the
25:12 advisers and then replied to **P**,
25:19 But **P** claimed that Jesus is
25:20 So I asked **P** if he would like to
25:21 But **P** appealed his case.
25:23 Festus gave the order, and **P**
26:1 Agrippa said to **P**, "You're free
26:1 **P** acknowledged King Agrippa
26:24 As **P** was defending himself in
26:24 shouted, "**P**, you're crazy!
26:25 **P** replied, "I'm not crazy,
26:28 Agrippa said to **P**, "Do you
26:29 **P** replied, "I wish to God that
27:1 **P** and some other prisoners
27:3 Julius treated **P** kindly and
27:9 so **P** advised them,
27:11 said and not by what **P** said.
27:21 **P** stood among them and said,
27:24 told me, 'Don't be afraid, **P**!
27:31 **P** told the officer and the

Act 27:33 Just before daybreak **P** was
27:35 After **P** said this, he took some
27:43 the officer wanted to save **P**,
28:3 **P** gathered a bundle of
28:5 **P** shook the snake into the fire
28:8 **P** went to him, prayed,
28:9 people on the island went to **P**
28:15 When **P** saw them,
28:16 After our arrival, **P** was allowed
28:17 After three days **P** invited the
28:21 The Jewish leaders told **P**,
28:23 the place where **P** was staying.
28:23 From morning until evening, **P**
28:25 left after **P** had quoted this
28:30 **P** rented a place to live for two
Rom 1:1 From **P**, a servant of Jesus
1Co 1:1 From **P**, called to be an apostle
1:12 "I follow **P**," or "I follow
1:13 Was **P** crucified for you?
3:4 "I follow **P**" and others say,
3:5 Who is **P**? They are servants
3:22 Whether it is **P**, Apollos,
16:21 I, **P**, am writing this greeting
2Co 1:1 From **P**, an apostle of Christ
10:1 I, **P**, make my appeal to you
Gal 1:1 From **P** — an apostle ⌊chosen⌋
5:2 I, **P**, can guarantee that if you
Eph 1:1 From **P**, an apostle of Christ
3:1 This is the reason I, **P**,
Php 1:1 From **P** and Timothy,
Col 1:1 From **P**, an apostle of Christ
1:23 which I, **P**, became a servant.
4:18 I, **P**, am writing this greeting
1Th 1:1 From **P**, Silas, and Timothy.
2:18 I, **P**, wanted to visit you twice
2Th 1:1 From **P**, Silas, and Timothy.
3:17 I, **P**, am writing this greeting
1Ti 1:1 From **P**, an apostle of Christ
2Ti 1:1 From **P**, an apostle of Christ
Tit 1:1 From **P**, a servant of God and
Phm 1:1 From **P**, who is a prisoner for
1:9 I, **P**, as an old man and now a
1:19 I, **P**, promise to pay it back.
2Pe 3:15 This is what our dear brother **P**
3:16 believe distort what **P** says

Paul's (7)

Act 19:12 aprons that had touched **P** skin
19:31 **P** friends sent messengers
21:11 During his visit he took **P** belt
23:16 But **P** nephew heard about the
25:14 told the king about **P** case.
28:3 The snake bit **P** hand and
1Co 1:13 Were you baptized in **P** name

pavement (9)

Exo 24:10 something like a **p** made out
2Ch 7:3 down with their faces on the **p**.
Est 1:6 couches were on a mosaic **p**
Jer 43:9 and bury them under the brick **p**
Eze 40:17 I saw rooms there and **p** all
40:17 rooms along the edge of the **p**.
40:18 The **p** in the lower courtyard
42:3 and opposite the **p** of the outer
Jon 19:13 seat in a place called Stone **P**.

paws (2)

Lev 11:27 that walk on their **p** are unclean
Job 39:21 It **p** in strength and finds joy in

pay (267)

Gen 23:13 I will **p** you the price of the
30:28 your wages, and I'll **p** them."
34:12 Set the price I must **p** for the
34:12 I'll **p** exactly what you tell me.
38:16 She asked, "What will you **p** to
42:22 we must **p** for this bloodshed."
50:15 What if he decides to **p** us
Exo 2:9 him for me, and I will **p** you."
4:8 "If they won't believe you or **p**
15:26 if you **p** attention to his
21:19 He must **p** the injured man for
21:22 the offender must **p** whatever
21:23 the offender must **p** a life for a
21:32 its owner must **p** 12 ounces of
21:34 He must **p** money to the
Exo 22:3 must be sold ⌊as a slave⌋ to **p**
22:16 he must **p** the bride-price and
22:17 he must **p** an amount of money
23:21 **P** attention to him,
29:36 for sin on the altar in order to **p**
30:12 each person must **p** the LORD
30:16 and use it to **p** the expenses of
35:21 to **p** other expenses,
Lev 5:16 **P** for whatever holy things you
6:5 **P** it back in full plus one-fifth
16:32 his father's place will **p** for sins.
19:13 Never keep the **p** you owe a
19:20 He will only **p** a fine because
22:16 must make those people **p**
25:16 you will **p** more for it.
25:16 you will **p** less for it because
25:27 Then he will **p** what is left to
27:8 the person who is too poor to **p**
27:13 you must **p** its full value plus
27:15 you must **p** its full value plus
27:19 you must **p** its full value plus
27:23 You will **p** its value on that day
Num 5:7 **p** in full for what you did wrong,
20:19 any of your water, we'll **p** for it.
22:7 taking money with them to **p**
Dtr 2:6 You must **p** them in silver for
2:28 We'll **p** you in silver for the food
7:10 But he sends destruction to **p**
7:10 He never takes long to **p** back
15:2 your neighbor or relative **p** you,
15:3 may demand that a foreigner **p**,
24:14 Don't withhold **p** from hired
24:15 **P** them each day before sunset
24:15 they are poor and need their **p**.
32:41 enemies and **p** back those who
32:46 he said to them, "**P** attention to
Jos 23:14 "**P** attention, because I will
1Sm 4:20 But she didn't answer or **p**
30:24 Besides, who is going to **p**
2Sm 12:6 And he must **p** back four times
1Ki 2:23 me dead if Adonijah doesn't **p**
2:44 The LORD is going to **p** you
5:6 I will **p** you whatever wages
5:9 You can **p** me by providing
8:28 please **p** attention to my prayer
20:39 If he gets away, you will **p** for
21:2 I will **p** you a fair price for it."
22:28 **P** attention to this,
2Ki 3:4 ⌊Each year⌋ he had to **p** the
4:7 "Sell the oil, and **p** your debt.
9:26 I will **p** you back in this field,'
10:24 you will **p** for their lives with
12:11 used it to **p** the carpenters,
18:14 I'll **p** whatever penalty you give
18:14 of Judah **p** 22,500 pounds
23:35 he had to tax the country to **p**
2Ch 6:19 please **p** attention to my prayer
7:15 and my ears will **p** attention to
18:27 **P** attention to this,
19:6 He told the judges, "**P** attention
20:15 "**P** attention to me,
33:10 they wouldn't even **p** attention.
Ezr 4:13 Jews will no longer **p** taxes,
6:4 The king's palace will **p** for it.
7:20 may use the king's treasury to **p**
7:24 temple of this God **p** any taxes,
Neh 1:6 Open your eyes, and **p** close
1:11 Lord, please **p** attention to my
5:4 had to borrow money to **p**
9:34 They didn't **p** attention to your
Est 3:9 For this I will **p** 750,000
4:7 Haman had promised to **p** into
Job 7:2 he eagerly looks for his **p**.
11:11 doesn't he **p** attention to it?
13:6 and **p** attention to my plea.
21:19 God should **p** back that person
21:29 But you didn't **p** attention to
21:31 Who will **p** him back for what
33:31 "**P** attention, Job! Listen to me!
35:13 even **p** attention to them.
35:14 Although you say that you **p**
Psa 5:2 **P** attention to my cry for help,
10:17 You **p** close attention to them
17:1 **P** attention to my cry.
28:4 **P** them back for what they
28:4 **P** them back for what their
Psa 35:12 because they **p** me back
38:20 They **p** me back with evil
41:10 up so that I can **p** them back
49:7 back another person or **p** God
54:5 **P** them back with evil.
55:2 **P** attention to me, and answer
61:1 **P** attention to my prayer.
69:4 I am forced to **p** back what I did
79:12 **P** each one of our neighbors
86:6 **P** attention when I plead for
94:7 doesn't even **p** attention to it."
94:8 **P** attention, you stupid people!
107:43 they are wise **p** attention
142:6 **P** attention to my cry for help
Pro 2:2 if you **p** close attention to
4:1 and **p** attention in order to gain
4:20 **p** attention to my words.
5:1 **p** attention to my wisdom.
7:1 **p** attention to my words.
7:24 **P** attention to the words from
11:18 righteousness earns honest **p**.
13:8 does not **p** attention to threats.
13:13 words will **p** the penalty,
19:19 has a hot temper will **p** for it.
22:27 If you have no money to **p** back
23:1 **p** close attention to what is in
24:12 Won't he **p** back people for
24:29 I'll **p** him back for what he has
27:23 and **p** close attention to your
Ecc 9:17 One should **p** more attention to
Isa 1:2 Listen, heaven, and **p** attention,
1:10 **P** attention to the teachings
5:12 Yet, they don't **p** attention to
10:30 **P** attention, you people in
28:23 **P** attention, and hear me!
32:3 who can hear will **p** attention.
34:1 **P** attention, you people.
42:23 Is there anyone who will **p**
43:4 will be the price I **p** for your life.
49:1 **P** attention, you people far
51:4 **P** attention to me, my people.
55:1 You don't have to **p**;
58:3 if you don't **p** attention?
59:18 He will **p** them back according
59:18 He will **p** back his opponents
59:18 He will **p** back the people who
63:16 us and Israel doesn't **p** attention
65:7 so I will be the first to **p** them
66:2 I will **p** attention to those who
66:15 He will **p** them back with his
Jer 6:8 **P** attention to my warning,
6:10 they aren't able to **p** attention.
6:17 **P** attention to the sound of the
6:17 that you wouldn't **p** attention.
6:19 because they won't **p** attention
7:24 But they didn't obey me or **p**
7:26 But you didn't obey me or **p**
11:8 But they didn't obey me or **p**
13:15 Listen, and **p** attention!
16:18 First, I will have them **p** twice
17:23 did not obey me or **p** attention
18:18 **P** no attention to anything he
18:19 **P** attention to me, O LORD,
22:13 for nothing and doesn't **p** them
25:14 and I will **p** them back for what
44:5 wouldn't listen or **p** attention.
50:29 **P** the people of Babylon back
51:6 He will **p** the people of Babylon
51:24 "In your presence I will **p** back
Lam 3:64 **P** them back, O LORD,
5:4 We have to **p** to drink our own
5:4 We have to **p** to chop our own
Eze 7:4 I will **p** you back for the way
7:9 I will **p** you back for the way
11:21 I will **p** them back for what they
16:34 You **p** them, and you don't
16:41 and you will no longer **p** others.
16:43 So I will **p** you back for what
23:49 and they will **p** for their sin of
24:8 so that I would **p** that city back,
29:19 That will be the **p** for his army.
29:20 I have given him Egypt as **p** for
40:4 **P** close attention to everything
44:5 "Son of man, **p** close attention.
44:5 **P** close attention to everyone
Dan 9:19 **P** attention, and act.

Dan 10:11 **P** attention to my words.
Hos 4:9 wicked ways and **p** them back
5:1 **P** attention, nation of Israel!
8:11 build to make offerings to **p**
9:7 The time for them to **p** for their
12:2 He will **p** them back for what
12:12 took care of sheep to **p** for her.
12:14 The Lord will **p** them back for
Joe 3:4 I will quickly **p** you back for
3:7 I will **p** you back for what you
Mic 1:2 **P** attention, earth and all who
1:7 will again **p** for prostitutes.
Zec 1:4 But they didn't listen or **p**
7:11 people refused to **p** attention.
11:12 with you, **p** me my wages.
Mat 5:26 get out until you **p** every penny
16:27 Then he will **p** back each
17:24 your teacher **p** the temple tax?"
18:25 Because he could not **p** off the
18:25 to be sold to **p** off the account.
18:28 '**P** what you owe!' he said.
20:2 After agreeing to **p** the workers
22:17 Is it right to **p** taxes to the
22:19 me a coin used to **p** taxes."
26:15 He asked, "What will you **p** me
Mar 4:24 He went on to say, "**P** attention
12:14 Is it right to **p** taxes to the
12:14 Should we **p** taxes or not?"
Luk 3:14 "Be satisfied with your **p**,
7:42 When they couldn't **p** it back,
8:18 "So **p** attention to how you
10:7 the worker deserves his **p**.
10:35 I'll **p** you on my return trip.'
12:59 get out until you **p** every penny
14:14 have any way to **p** you back.
18:6 The Lord added, "**P** attention to
19:8 I'll **p** four times as much as I
20:22 Is it right for us to **p** taxes to
Act 2:14 so **p** attention to what I say.
4:29 **p** attention to their threats now,
16:14 made her willing to **p** attention
20:28 **P** attention to yourselves and
21:24 and **p** the expenses to shave
Rom 2:6 He will **p** all people back for
4:4 When people work, their **p** is
8:3 sinners have and to **p** for sin.
11:35 which the Lord must **p** back?
12:17 Don't **p** people back with evil
12:19 I will **p** back, says the Lord."
13:6 is also why you **p** your taxes.
13:7 **P** everyone whatever you owe
13:7 If you owe taxes, **p** them.
13:7 If you owe tolls, **p** them.
13:8 **P** your debts as they come due.
1Co 4:18 you think I won't **p** you a visit.
2Co 11:8 churches by taking **p** from them
Gal 4:5 God sent him to **p** for the
Php 3:17 and **p** attention to those who
Col 4:2 **P** attention when you offer
2Th 1:9 They will **p** the penalty by
3:12 Lord Jesus Christ to **p** attention
1Ti 5:18 "The worker deserves his **p**."
5:19 Don't **p** attention to an
2Ti 2:16 People who ⌊**p**⌋ attention to
4:14 The Lord will **p** him back for
Tit 1:14 They shouldn't **p** attention to
Phm 1:19 I, Paul, promise to **p** it back.
Heb 2:1 For this reason we must **p**
5:11 become too lazy to **p** attention,
10:30 I will **p** back." God also said,
12:5 **p** attention when the Lord
Jas 4:13 **P** attention to this!
5:1 **P** attention to this if you're rich.
5:4 The wages you refused to **p**
1Pe 3:9 Don't **p** people back with evil
2Pe 1:19 Continue to **p** attention as you
Rev 1:3 of this prophecy and **p** attention
6:6 "A quart of wheat for a day's **p**
6:6 quarts of barley for a day's **p**.
22:12 with me to **p** all people based

paying (16)

Exo 21:2 without **p** for his freedom.
21:11 without **p** any money for her
21:30 his life by **p** whatever price is
Rut 2:10 Why are you **p** attention to me?
2Sm 16:8 The LORD is **p** you back for all
2Ch 20:11 They are now **p** us back by
Job 4:20 without anyone **p** attention.
31:39 eaten its produce without **p**
Isa 66:6 It is the sound of the LORD **p**
Joe 3:4 Are you **p** me back for
3:4 If you are **p** me back,
Mat 10:8 you received them without **p**.
Luk 23:2 He keeps them from **p** taxes to
Rom 13:8 one debt you can never finish **p**
2Th 3:8 anyone's food without **p** for it.
2Pe 1:19 You're doing well by **p** attention

payment (27)

Gen 47:14 in Egypt and in Canaan as **p**
Exo 32:30 I will be able to make a **p**
Lev 14:29 in order to make a **p** for him.
23:27 a special day for the **p** for sins.
23:28 a special day for the **p** for sins.
25:9 the special day for the **p** for sin,
27:27 The **p** will be its full value plus
Num 5:8 be no heir to whom the **p** can
5:8 In that case, the **p** for what you
5:8 This **p** is in addition to the ram
35:31 "Never accept a cash **p** in
35:32 Don't accept a cash **p** to allow
Dtr 15:2 don't collect **p** on the debt your
15:3 but don't collect **p** on the debt
Jdg 3:15 people sent him with their tax **p**
3:17 Then he brought the tax **p** to
3:18 had finished delivering the **p**,
1Sm 18:25 'The king doesn't want any **p**
2Sm 3:14 I made a **p** of 100 Philistine
Ezr 6:8 Full **p** should be made to these
Isa 45:13 my exiles go free without any **p**
Eze 16:34 and you don't accept **p**.
27:15 you ivory and ebony as **p**.
1Pe 1:18 you from your ancestors by a **p**
1:19 Rather, the **p** that freed you
1Jn 2:2 He is the **p** for our sins,
4:10 his Son to be the **p** for our sins.

payments (4)

Dtr 15:2 the ⌊time⌋ for suspending **p**
15:9 seventh year — the year when **p**
2Ki 17:3 to make annual **p** to him.
17:4 had stopped making annual **p**

pays (12)

Job 24:12 but God **p** no attention to their
Psa 31:23 but he **p** back in full those who
137:8 blessed is the one who **p** you
Pro 13:18 but whoever **p** attention to
17:4 An evildoer **p** attention to
17:13 Whoever **p** back evil for good —
29:3 but one who **p** prostitutes
29:12 If a ruler **p** attention to lies,
Jer 23:18 Who **p** attention and listens to
Eze 33:15 **p** back everything he stole,
Mal 2:13 he no longer **p** attention
1Th 5:15 Make sure that no one ever **p**

peace (343)

Gen 15:15 But you will die in **p** and be
26:29 good to you and let you go in **p**.
32:20 "He thought, "I'll make **p** with
44:17 can go back to your father in **p**."
Exo 29:33 through which they made **p**
29:36 bull as an offering to make **p**
29:37 seven days at the altar make **p**
30:10 a year Aaron must make **p**
30:10 placed on the altar to make **p**
30:15 contribution is given to make **p**
30:16 the Israelites give to make **p**
32:30 for your sin and make **p**
33:14 and I will give you **p**."
Lev 1:4 to make **p** with the LORD.
4:20 So the priest will make **p** with
4:26 So the priest will make **p** with
4:31 So the priest will make **p** with
4:35 So the priest will make **p** with
5:6 Then the priest will make **p**
5:10 So the priest will make **p** with
5:13 So the priest will make **p** with
5:16 for the guilt offering to make **p**
5:18 The priest will make **p** with the
Lev 6:7 So the priest will make **p** with
6:30 in the tent of meeting to make **p**
7:7 to make **p** with the LORD.
8:15 it to make **p** with the LORD.
8:34 commanded me to make **p**
9:7 and a burnt offering to make **p**
9:7 to make **p** with the LORD for
10:17 the congregation and to make **p**
12:7 the LORD's presence to make **p**
12:8 So the priest will make **p** with
14:18 So he will make **p** with the
14:19 the offering for sin to make **p**
14:20 So the priest will make **p** with
14:21 present it to make **p** with the
14:31 presence the priest will make **p**
14:53 He will make **p** with the LORD
15:15 the priest will make **p** with the
15:30 presence the priest will make **p**
16:6 By doing this, he will make **p**
16:10 to Azazel in order to make **p**
16:11 By doing this he will make **p**
16:16 So he will make **p** with the
16:17 Aaron will make **p** with the
16:18 LORD's presence and make **p**
16:20 "When he finishes making **p**
16:24 and for the people to make **p**
16:27 into the holy place to make **p**
16:30 On this day Aaron will make **p**
16:33 and will make **p** with the LORD
16:33 He will make **p** with the LORD
16:34 law tells you how to make **p**
17:11 this blood to you to make **p**
17:11 is needed to make **p** with me.
19:22 priest will use them to make **p**
23:28 It is a time when you make **p**
26:6 "I will bring **p** to your land.
Num 5:8 which makes **p** with the LORD.
6:11 The priest will make **p** with the
6:26 you with favor and give you **p**.'
8:12 These sacrifices will make **p**
8:19 They will make **p** with the
8:21 to the LORD and made **p**
15:25 The priest will make **p** with the
15:28 offer the sacrifice to make **p**
16:46 into the community to make **p**
16:47 the incense burner to make **p**
25:12 making a promise of **p** to him.
25:13 up for his God and he made **p**
28:22 sin to make **p** with the LORD.
28:30 goat to make **p** with the LORD.
29:5 sin to make **p** with the LORD.
29:11 offering for sin to make **p**
31:50 to make **p** with the LORD."
35:33 committed can never make **p**
Dtr 2:26 with the following offer of **p**:
12:10 He will give you **p** from all your
20:12 they won't accept your offer of **p**
21:8 make **p** with your people Israel,
21:8 Then there will be **p** with the
23:6 Never offer them **p** or friendship
25:19 God gives you **p** from all your
28:65 nations you will find no **p**,
32:43 with his enemies and make **p**
Jos 9:15 So Joshua made **p** with them
10:1 people of Gibeon had made **p**
10:4 Gibeon because it has made **p**
11:19 Not one city had made a **p**
11:23 So the land had **p**.
14:15 So the land had **p**.
21:44 LORD allowed them to have **p**
22:4 God has given your relatives **p**,
23:1 the LORD gave the Israelites **p**
Jdg 3:11 So there was finally **p** in the
3:30 So there was finally **p** in the
5:31 So the land had **p** for 40 years.
8:28 So the land had **p** for 40 years
18:6 The priest told them, "Go in **p**.
21:13 Rock and offered them **p**.
1Sm 1:17 Eli replied, "Go in **p**,
3:14 will ever ⌊be able to⌋ make **p**
7:14 There was also **p** between
16:4 "May **p** be with you."
20:42 "Go in **p**!" Jonathan told David.
25:35 and told her, "Go home in **p**.
2Sm 7:1 the LORD gave him **p** with all
7:11 So I will give you **p** with all

2Sm 10:19 they made **p** with Israel and
15:9 "Go in **p**," the king told him.
17:3 all the people will have **p**."
21:3 should I ⌊give you⌋ to make **p**
1Ki 2:5 When there was **p**,
2:33 receive **p** from the LORD."
4:24 So he lived in **p** with all the
5:4 God has surrounded me with **p**.
5:12 There was **p** between Hiram
20:18 come out to make **p** or to fight."
22:17 Let each one go home in **p**."
22:44 Jehoshaphat made **p** with the
2Ki 5:19 Elisha told Naaman, "Go in **p**."
18:31 Assyria says: Make **p** with me!
20:19 "Isn't it enough if there is **p** and
22:20 to bring you to your grave in **p**,
1Ch 19:19 they made **p** with David and
22:9 I will give him **p** from all the
22:9 His name will be Solomon [**P**],
22:9 I will give Israel **p** and quiet.
22:18 Hasn't he given you **p** with all
2Ch 14:1 the land had **p** for ten years.
14:5 was at **p** during his reign.
14:6 Judah because the land had **p**.
14:6 the LORD gave him a time of **p**.
14:7 he has surrounded us with **p**.
15:5 no one could come and go in **p**,
15:15 LORD surrounded them with **p**.
18:16 Let each one go home in **p**.'"
20:30 his God surrounded him with **p**.
29:24 for sin at the altar to make **p**
32:22 The LORD gave them **p** with
34:28 to bring you to your grave in **p**,
Ezr 4:17 I wish you **p** and prosperity!
5:7 We wish you **p** and prosperity
7:12 I wish you **p** and prosperity!
9:12 and never seek **p** or trade with
Neh 10:33 offerings for sin that make **p**
Est 9:30 official documents granting **p**
Job 3:26 I have no **p**! I have no quiet! I
5:23 animals will be at **p** with you.
5:24 "You will know **p** in your tent.
15:21 While he enjoys **p**,
20:20 He will never know **p** in his
22:21 in harmony and at **p** with God.
25:2 He establishes **p** in his high
Psa 4:8 I fall asleep in **p** the moment I
28:3 troublemakers who speak of **p**
29:11 will bless his people with **p**.
34:14 Seek **p**, and pursue it!
35:20 They do not talk about **p**.
35:27 happy when his servant has **p**."
37:11 land and will enjoy unlimited **p**.
38:3 There is no **p** in my bones
55:18 With ⌊his⌋ **p**, he will rescue
72:3 May the mountains bring **p** to
72:7 May there be unlimited **p** until
85:8 because he promises **p** to his
85:10 and **p** have kissed.
94:13 You give him **p** and quiet from
116:7 Be at **p** again, my soul,
119:165 There is lasting **p** for those
120:6 too long with those who hate **p**.
120:7 I am for **p**, but when I talk about
122:6 Pray for the **p** of Jerusalem:
122:7 May there be **p** inside your
125:5 Let there be **p** in Israel!
128:6 Let there be **p** in Israel!
147:14 He is the one who brings **p** to
Pro 3:2 long life, good years, and **p**.
3:17 and all its paths lead to **p**.
12:20 belongs to those who advise **p**.
16:6 **p** is made with the LORD.
16:7 enemies to be at **p** with him.
16:14 a wise man makes **p** with him.
17:1 of dry bread ⌊eaten⌋ in **p** than
29:9 but there is no **p** and quiet.
29:17 and he will give you **p** of mind.
Ecc 3:8 a time for war and a time for **p**.
4:6 One handful of **p** and quiet is
Sos 8:10 me to be one who has found **p**.
Isa 9:6 Everlasting Father, Prince of **P**.
9:7 His government and **p** will
26:3 With perfect **p** you will protect
26:12 you will establish **p** for us,
27:5 Let them make **p** with me.
Isa 27:5 Yes, let them make **p** with me.
32:17 will bring about **p**,
33:7 Messengers of **p** cry bitterly.
36:16 Assyria says: Make **p** with me!
38:17 bitter experience turns into **p**.
39:8 He added, "Just let there be **p**
48:18 Your **p** would be like a river
48:22 "There is no **p** for the wicked,"
53:5 so that we could have **p**,
54:10 My promise of **p** will never
54:13 children will have unlimited **p**.
55:12 out with joy and be led out in **p**.
57:2 When **p** comes, everyone who
57:19 "Perfect **p** to those both far and
57:21 "There is no **p** for the wicked,"
59:8 They don't know the way of **p**.
59:8 on them will never know **p**.
60:17 I will appoint **p** as your
66:12 I will offer you **p** like a river and
Jer 8:15 We hoped for **p**, but nothing
12:1 people have **p** and quiet?
14:13 you lasting **p** in this place.'"
14:19 We hope for **p**, but no good
16:5 I'm taking my **p**, love,
28:9 **p** was recognized as
29:11 They are plans for **p** and not
30:5 cries of panic, not cries of **p**.
30:10 will again have **p** and security,
33:6 I will give them **p** and security.
46:26 Afterward, they will live in **p** as
46:27 will again have undisturbed **p**,
Lam 3:17 has been kept from enjoying **p**.
Eze 7:25 People will look for **p**,
16:42 I will be at **p**. I will no longer be
16:49 of food and had **p** and security.
34:25 "'I will promise them **p**.
37:26 I will promise them **p**.
43:20 and make **p** with the LORD.
43:26 days the priests should make **p**
45:15 fellowship offerings to make **p**
45:17 fellowship offerings to make **p**
45:20 So you must make **p** with the
Dan 4:1 I wish you **p** and prosperity.
6:25 I wish you **p** and prosperity.
11:6 to the northern king to make **p**.
Oba 1:7 The people who are at **p** with
Mic 5:5 This man will be their **p**.
Hag 2:9 this place I will give ⌊them⌋ **p**,
Zec 1:11 whole world is at rest and in **p**."
8:16 fair verdicts for **p** in your courts.
8:19 So love truth and **p**.
9:10 He will announce **p** to the
Mal 2:5 "I promised Levi life and **p**.
2:6 He lived with me in **p** and
Mat 5:9 Blessed are those who make **p**.
5:24 First go away and make **p** with
5:25 "Make **p** quickly with your
10:34 that I came to bring **p** to earth.
10:34 come to bring **p** but conflict.
Mar 5:34 Go in **p**! Be cured from your
9:50 and live in **p** with one another."
Luk 1:79 will guide us into the way of **p**."
2:14 and on earth **p** to those who
2:29 to leave in **p** as you promised.
7:50 faith has saved you. Go in **p**!"
8:48 has made you well. Go in **p**!"
10:5 'May there be **p** in this house.'
12:51 think I came to bring **p** to earth?
14:32 to ask for terms of **p** while
16:25 Now he has **p** here,
19:38 **P** in heaven, and glory in the
19:42 today what would bring you **p**!
24:36 said to them, "**P** be with you!"
Jon 14:27 "I'm leaving you **p**.
14:27 I'm giving you my **p**.
14:27 I don't give you the kind of **p**
16:33 I've told you this so that my **p**
20:19 said to them, "**P** be with you!"
20:21 to them again, "**P** be with you!
20:26 them and said, "**P** be with you!"
Act 7:26 tried to make **p** between them.
9:31 and Samaria had **p**.
10:36 of **p** through Jesus Christ.
12:20 to ask Herod for terms of **p**.
24:2 leadership we have lasting **p**
Rom 1:7 Good will and **p** from God our
Rom 2:10 and **p** for every person who
3:17 have not learned to live in **p**.
5:1 we have **p** with God because
8:6 attitude leads to life and **p**.
12:18 live in **p** with everyone.
14:17 of God's approval and **p**,
14:19 those things which bring **p**
15:13 fill you with joy and **p** through
15:33 May the God of **p** be with you
16:20 The God of **p** will quickly
1Co 1:3 Good will and **p** from God our
7:15 God has called you to live in **p**.
14:33 God of disorder but a God of **p**.
2Co 1:2 Good will and **p** from God our
2:13 But I didn't have any **p** of mind,
13:11 the same attitude and live in **p**.
13:11 The God of love and **p** will be
Gal 1:3 Good will and **p** are yours from
5:22 joy, **p**, patience, kindness,
6:16 **P** and mercy will come to rest
Eph 1:2 Good will and **p** from God our
2:14 So he is our **p**. In his body he
2:15 in himself. So he made **p**.
2:17 came with the Good News of **p**
4:3 Through the **p** that ties you
6:15 the Good News that gives **p**.
6:23 give our brothers and sisters **p**
Php 1:2 Good will and **p** from God our
4:7 Then God's **p**, which goes
4:9 Then the God who gives this **p**
Col 1:2 Good will and **p** from God our
1:20 He did this by making **p**
3:15 Also, let Christ's **p** control you.
3:15 God has called you into this **p**
1Th 1:1 Good will and **p** are yours!
5:13 Live in **p** with each other.
5:23 May the God who gives **p**
2Th 1:2 Good will and **p** from God our
3:16 May the Lord of **p** give you his
3:16 give you his **p** at all times
1Ti 1:2 Good will, mercy, and **p** from
2Ti 1:2 Good will, mercy, and **p** from
2:22 Pursue faith, love, and **p**
3:3 refuse to make **p** with anyone.
Tit 1:4 Good will and **p** from God the
Phm 1:3 Good will and **p** from God our
Heb 2:17 in God's presence and make **p**
7:2 Salem (which means king of **p**).
12:11 have **p** that comes from
13:20 The God of **p** brought the great
13:21 May this God of **p** prepare you
Jas 3:18 the **p** planted by peacemakers.
1Pe 1:2 good will and **p** fill your lives!
3:11 must seek **p** and pursue it.
5:14 **P** to all of you who are in
2Pe 1:2 May good will and **p** fill your
3:14 effort to have him find you at **p**,
2Jn 1:3 and **p** will be with us.
3Jn 1:15 **P** be with you! Your friends here
Jud 1:2 May mercy, **p**, and love fill your
Rev 1:4 Good will and **p** to you from the
6:4 the power to take **p** away from

peaceful (19)

Dtr 20:10 its people a **p** way to surrender.
Jdg 4:17 Heber's family were on **p** terms.
18:7 They were **p** and secure.
18:27 They attacked a **p** and secure
2Sm 20:19 We are **p** and faithful Israelites.
1Ch 4:40 The land was vast, **p**,
22:9 a son who will be a **p** man.
2Ch 20:30 Jehoshaphat's kingdom was **p**,
Psa 23:2 He leads me beside **p** waters.
35:20 they scheme against the **p**
Isa 14:7 The whole earth rests and is **p**.
32:18 people will live in a **p** place,
33:20 see Jerusalem as a **p** place.
Jer 25:37 The **p** pastures are destroyed
Eze 38:11 I will attack **p** people who live
Zec 6:13 **p** understanding between them.
Luk 10:6 If a **p** person lives there,
1Ti 2:2 a quiet and **p** life always lived
Jas 3:17 Then it is **p**, gentle, obedient,

peacefully (14)

Gen 26:31 on their way, and they left **p**.

Jdg 11:13 Now give it back **p**."
1Sm 29:7 So leave **p** without doing
2Sm 3:21 dismissed Abner, who left **p**.
3:23 him, and Abner left **p**."
15:27 "Go back to the city **p**,
1Ki 2:6 old man go to his grave **p**.
Job 3:13 I would now be sleeping **p**.
21:13 and they go **p** to the grave.
Jer 34:5 You will die **p**. People will burn
43:12 He will leave Egypt **p**.
49:31 nation living **p** and securely,
Act 16:36 So you can leave **p** now."
Heb 12:14 Try to live **p** with everyone,

peacemaker (1)
Psa 37:37 because the **p** has a future.

peacemakers (1)
Jas 3:18 from the peace planted by **p**.

peacetime (1)
Zec 8:12 Seeds will thrive in **p**.

peak (3)
Job 39:28 Its fortress is on a jagged **p**.
Psa 48:2 Its beautiful **p** is the joy of the
Sos 4:8 will travel with me from the **p**

peaks (5)
Psa 42:6 on the **p** of Hermon,
68:15 is the mountain with many **p**.
68:16 you mountains with many **p**,
95:4 and the mountain **p** are his.
Sos 4:8 from the mountain **p** in Senir

pearl (2)
Mat 13:46 When he found a valuable **p**,
Rev 21:21 Each gate was made of one **p**.

pearl-like (1)
Est 1:6 **p** stone, and black marble.

pearls (8)
Sos 1:10 your neck with strings of **p**.
Mat 7:6 to dogs or throw your **p** to pigs.
13:45 who was searching for fine **p**.
1Ti 2:9 styles or the gold jewelry, **p**,
Rev 17:4 gold jewelry, gems, and **p**.
18:12 **p**, fine linen, purple cloth, silk,
18:16 gold jewelry, gems, and **p**.
21:21 The 12 gates were 12 **p**.

pebble (2)
2Sm 17:13 valley so that not even a **p** will
Amo 9:9 Not one **p** will fall to the ground.

pebbles (1)
Job 22:24 Ophir among the **p** in the rivers,

Pedahel (1)
Num 34:28 **P**, son of Ammihud, the leader

Pedahzur (5)
Num 1:10 of Ephraim; Gamaliel, son of **P**,
2:20 is Gamaliel, son of **P**.
7:54 Manasseh, Gamaliel, son of **P**,
7:59 gifts from Gamaliel, son of **P**.
10:23 Gamaliel, son of **P**,

Pedaiah (7)
2Ki 23:36 daughter of **P** from Rumah.
1Ch 3:18 then Malchiram, **P**,
27:20 of Manasseh: Joel, son of **P**
Neh 3:25 After him **P**, Parosh's son,
8:4 **P**, Mishael, Malchiah, Hashum,
11:7 who was the son of **P**,
13:13 the scribe, and **P** the Levite,

Pedaiah's (1)
1Ch 3:19 **P** sons were Zerubbabel and

pedestal (1)
1Ki 7:31 formed like a pedestal,

peeking (1)
Sos 2:9 **p** through the window,

peeled (2)
Gen 30:37 and plane trees and **p** the bark
30:38 He placed the **p** branches in

peels (1)
Job 30:30 My skin turns dark and **p**.

peeped (1)
Isa 10:14 a wing, opened its mouth, or **p**."

peer (1)
Psa 73:7 Their eyes **p** out from their fat

peered (1)
Jdg 5:28 and cried as she **p** through

peg (8)
Jdg 4:21 took a tent **p** and walked
4:21 She hammered the tent **p**
4:22 the tent **p** through his temples.
5:26 She reached for a tent **p** with
Isa 22:23 him firmly in place like a **p**,
22:25 "On that day the **p** which I
Eze 15:3 Do they make a **p** from it to
Zec 10:4 from them a tent **p**,

pegs (14)
Exo 26:17 with two identical **p**.
26:19 of each frame for the two **p**.
27:19 including all the **p** for the tent
35:18 the **p** for the tent and the
36:22 with two identical **p**.
36:24 of each frame for the two **p**.
38:20 All the **p** for the tent and the
38:31 all the **p** for the tent,
38:31 and all the **p** for the surrounding
39:40 the ropes and **p** — all the
Num 3:37 the bases, **p**, and ropes.
4:32 the bases, **p**, and ropes.
Isa 33:20 Its tent **p** will never be pulled
54:2 and drive in the tent **p**.

Pekah (13)
2Ki 15:25 His officer **P**, son of Remaliah,
15:25 **P** attacked Pekahiah,
15:25 **P** killed him and succeeded
15:27 of Judah, **P**, son of Remaliah,
15:29 In the days of King **P** of Israel,
15:30 son of Elah, plotted against **P**,
15:31 Everything else about **P** —
15:32 In the second year that King **P**,
15:37 use King Rezin of Aram and **P**,
16:1 **P**, son of Remaliah, was in his
16:5 King Rezin of Aram and King **P**,
2Ch 28:6 In one day **P**, son of Remaliah,
Isa 7:1 King Rezin and Israel's King **P**,

Pekahiah (5)
2Ki 15:22 and his son **P** succeeded him
15:23 Menahem's son **P** began to
15:23 **P** was king of Israel in Samaria
15:25 Pekah attacked **P**,
15:26 Everything else about **P** —

Pekod (2)
Jer 50:21 and the people who live in **P**.
Eze 23:23 men from **P**, Shoa, and Koa,

Pelaiah (3)
1Ch 3:24 **P**, Akkub, Johanan, Delaiah,
Neh 8:7 and **P** — explained the
10:10 Hodiah, Kelita, **P**, Hanan,

Pelaliah (1)
Neh 11:12 who was the son of **P**,

Pelatiah (5)
1Ch 3:21 sons were **P** and Jeshaiah.
4:42 Ishi's sons **P**, Neariah,
Neh 10:22 **P**, Hanan, Anaiah,
Eze 11:1 and Benaiah's son **P**.
11:13 Benaiah's son **P** died.

Peleg (8)
Gen 10:25 of the one was **P** [Division],
11:16 he became the father of **P**.
11:17 After he became the father of **P**,
11:18 **P** was 30 years old when he
11:19 **P** lived 209 years and had
1Ch 1:19 of the one was **P** [Division],
1:25 Eber, **P**, Reu,
Luk 3:35 of Reu, son of **P**, son of Eber,

Pelet (2)
1Ch 2:47 **P**, Ephah, and Shaaph.
12:3 Azmaveth's sons Jeziel and **P**,

Peleth (2)
Num 16:1 and On (son of **P**) dared to
1Ch 2:33 sons were **P** and Zaza.

Pelethites (7)
2Sm 8:18 of the Cherethites and the **P**.
15:18 the Cherethites, all the **P**, Ittai,
20:7 Joab's men, the Cherethites, **P**,
20:23 of the Cherethites and **P**.
1Ki 1:38 and the **P** put Solomon on King
1:44 and the **P** with him.
1Ch 18:17 of the Cherethites and the **P**.

pelicans (4)
Lev 11:18 barn owls, **p**, ospreys,
Dtr 14:17 **p**, ospreys, cormorants,
Isa 34:11 **P** and herons will take
Zep 2:14 Even **p** and herons will nest on

Pelonite (3)
1Ch 11:27 from Harod, Helez the **P**,
11:36 the Mecherathite, Ahijah the **P**,
27:10 Helez, a **P** from the

pen (13)
Psa 45:1 My tongue is a **p** for a skillful
Isa 8:1 and write on it with a **p**:
Jer 17:1 sin is written with an iron **p**.
Eze 9:2 who was carrying paper and **p**.
9:3 who was carrying paper and **p**.
9:11 carrying paper and **p** reported,
Mic 2:12 them together like sheep in a **p**,
Hab 3:17 even if the sheep **p** is empty
Jon 10:1 enter the sheep **p** through
10:3 and leads them out of the **p**.
10:9 Those who enter the sheep **p**
10:9 of the sheep **p** and find food.
10:16 sheep that are not from this **p**.

penalty (13)
Lev 22:16 make those people pay the **p**
Num 35:31 has been given the death **p**.
Dtr 19:6 he didn't deserve the death **p**,
1Ki 20:40 "That's your own **p**.
2Ki 18:14 I'll pay whatever **p** you give
Pro 13:13 ⌊God's⌋ words will pay the **p**,
Eze 16:38 I will give you the death **p** in
Mat 26:66 "He deserves the death **p**!"
Luk 23:15 to deserve the death **p**.
23:22 man deserving of the death **p**.
Act 25:11 for which I deserve the death **p**,
25:25 to deserve the death **p**.
2Th 1:9 They will pay the **p** by being

pendants (3)
Exo 35:22 earrings, signet rings, and **p**.
Num 31:50 signet rings, earrings, and **p**.
Isa 3:19 **p**, bracelets, scarfs,

Peniel (1)
Gen 32:30 So Jacob named that place **P**

Peninnah (5)
1Sm 1:2 named Hannah, the other **P**.
1:2 **P** had children, but Hannah had
1:4 give portions of it to his wife **P**
1:6 her rival ⌊**P**⌋ tormented her
1:7 **P** would make her miserable,

penis (3)
Lev 15:2 has a discharge from his **p**,
15:3 of the discharge from his **p**.
Dtr 23:1 crushed or whose **p** is cut off

penny (3)
Mat 5:26 you pay every **p** of your fine.
10:29 two sparrows sold for a **p**?
Luk 12:59 you pay every **p** of your fine."

pens (6)
1Sm 24:3 He came to some sheep **p**
Psa 50:9 a single male goat from your **p**.
68:13 you stayed among the sheep **p**,
78:70 He took him from the sheep **p**.
Isa 44:13 They mark them with **p**.
Jer 8:8 The scribes have used their **p**

Pentecost (3)
Act 2:1 When **P**, the fiftieth day after
20:16 to Jerusalem for the day of **P**,
1Co 16:8 here in Ephesus until **P**.

Penuel (6)
Gen 32:31 The sun rose as he passed **P**.
Jdg 8:8 Then Gideon went to **P** and
8:17 he tore down the tower of **P**
1Ki 12:25 he left that place and built **P**.
1Ch 4:4 **P** was the father of Gedor,
8:25 Iphdeiah, and **P**.

Peor (9)
Num 23:28 Balaam to the top of Mount **P**,
25:3 worshiping the god Baal of **P**,
25:5 worshiping the god Baal of **P**."
25:18 incident that took place at **P**.
25:18 caused by the incident at **P**."
31:16 incident that took place at **P**.
Dtr 4:3 god Baal while you were at **P**.
Jos 22:17 committed at **P** mean nothing
Psa 106:28 god Baal while they were at **P**,

Perazim (1)
Isa 28:21 will rise as he did on Mount **P**.

perceive (1)
Mar 4:12 'They see clearly but don't **p**.

percent (3)
Eze 45:13 seventeen **p** of your wheat and
45:13 and seventeen **p** of your barley.
45:14 You must give one **p** of your

perch (1)
Eze 32:4 I will make birds **p** on you,

perched (1)
Eze 31:13 All the birds **p** on the fallen tree,

perches (1)
Job 39:28 It **p** for the night on a cliff.

Peresh (1)
1Ch 7:16 and she named him **P**.

Perez (17)
Gen 38:29 was named **P** [Bursting Into].
46:12 Onan, Shelah, **P**, and Zerah.
46:12 The sons of **P** were Hezron
Num 26:20 of Shelah, the family of **P**,
26:21 The descendants of **P** were the
Rut 4:12 become like the family of **P**,
4:18 This is the account of **P** and
4:18 **P** was the father of Hezron.
1Ch 2:4 to Judah's sons **P** and Zerah.
4:1 Judah's descendants were **P**,
9:4 From the descendants of **P**,
27:3 He was a descendant of **P**,
Neh 11:4 who was the son of **P**;
11:6 All the descendants of **P** who
Mat 1:3 and mother of **P** and Zerah.
1:3 **P** was the father of Hezron,
Luk 3:33 Hezron, son of **P**, son of Judah,

Perez's (1)
1Ch 2:5 **P** sons were Hezron and

Perez Uzzah (2)
2Sa 6:8 is still called **P** [The Striking of
1Ch 13:11 is still called **P** [The Striking of

perfect (36)
Num 19:2 to bring you a red cow that is **p**,
Dtr 32:4 What he does is **p**.
2Sm 22:31 God's way is **p**! The promise of
22:33 His **p** way sets me free.
Psa 18:30 God's way is **p**! The promise of
18:32 strength and makes my way **p**.
19:7 teachings of the LORD are **p**.
64:6 They search for the **p** crime
Sos 5:2 my sister, my dove, my **p** one.
6:9 is unique, my dove, my **p** one.
Isa 26:3 With **p** peace you will protect
57:19 I'll create praise on their lips: "**P**
Eze 15:5 the vine was in **p** condition,
16:14 Your beauty was **p** because I
27:3 you used to brag about your **p**
27:4 builders made your beauty **p**.
27:11 making your beauty **p**.
28:12 You were the **p** example,
28:12 full of wisdom and **p** in beauty.
28:15 Your behavior was **p** from the
40:47 It was a **p** square — 175 feet
Mat 5:48 That is why you must be **p** as
5:48 as your Father in heaven is **p**.
19:21 "If you want to be **p**,
Rom 12:2 what is good, pleasing, and **p**.
Eph 1:4 be holy and **p** in his presence.
Php 3:6 keeping Jewish laws, I was **p**.
Heb 7:11 Levitical priests had been **p**,
9:11 more **p** tent that was not made
10:1 make those who worship **p**.
10:2 have made the worshipers **p**,
Jas 1:17 Every good present and every **p**
1:25 God's **p** teachings that make
3:2 he speaks, he would be **p**.
1Jn 4:18 Rather, **p** love gets rid of fear,
4:18 in fear doesn't have **p** love.

perfected (3)
Psa 64:6 "We have **p** a foolproof
1Jn 2:5 in whom God's love is **p**.
4:12 and his love is **p** in us.

perfection (1)
Psa 50:2 from Zion, the **p** of beauty.

perform (33)
Exo 15:11 your splendor. You **p** miracles.
34:10 I will **p** miracles that have
34:10 are that I will **p** for you.
Jos 3:5 Joshua told the people, "**P** the
1Sm 16:5 **P** the ceremonies to make
1Ch 15:12 You and your relatives must **p**
26:8 had the ability to **p** the service.
2Ch 29:5 **P** the ceremonies to make the
30:24 of priests were able to **p**
31:16 went to the LORD's temple to **p**
35:6 Slaughter the Passover lamb, **p**
Neh 11:23 they should **p** day by day.
Psa 88:10 Will you **p** miracles for those
Isa 28:21 work, and **p** his deeds,
Jer 21:2 Maybe the LORD will **p**
Mat 14:2 the power to **p** these miracles."
Mar 6:14 the power to **p** these miracles."
8:11 him by demanding that he **p**
Luk 23:8 hoped to see him **p** some kind
Jon 2:11 Jesus began to **p** miracles.
3:2 No one can **p** the miracles you
3:2 miracles you **p** unless God is
5:36 these tasks which I **p**,
6:30 are you going to **p** so that we
7:31 will he **p** more miracles than
9:16 a sinner **p** miracles like these?"
10:41 "John didn't **p** any miracles,
12:37 Jesus **p** so many miracles,
Act 5:12 The people saw the apostles **p**
14:3 will by having them **p** miracles
1Co 12:28 then those who **p** miracles,
12:29 Do all of them **p** miracles
Heb 9:6 part of the tent to **p** their duties.

performed (44)
Num 8:21 The Levites **p** the ceremonies
1Sm 16:5 He **p** the ceremonies for Jesse
1Ki 13:5 sign the man of God **p** at
1Ch 6:32 They **p** their duties according
16:12 Remember the miracles he **p**,
25:1 of the men who **p** this service:
2Ch 5:11 priests who were present had **p**
29:15 gathered their relatives and **p**
29:17 and for eight days they **p** the
30:3 not enough priests had **p**
30:15 so they **p** the ceremonies to
31:2 based on the service he **p**:
35:3 who instructed all Israel and **p**
Neh 4:15 Each person **p** his own job.
9:10 You **p** miraculous signs and
9:17 the miracles you **p** for them.
Psa 44:1 told us about the miracle you **p**
78:12 In front of their ancestors he **p**
78:43 when he **p** his miraculous
105:2 on all the miracles he has **p**.
105:5 Remember the miracles he **p**,
107:8 He **p** his miracles for Adam's
107:15 He **p** his miracles for Adam's
107:21 He **p** his miracles for Adam's
107:24 the miracles he **p** in the depths
107:31 He **p** his miracles for Adam's
Jer 32:20 You **p** miraculous signs and
Joe 2:26 who has **p** miracles for you.
Mat 21:15 saw the amazing miracles he **p**
Jon 2:23 saw the miracles that he **p**.
4:54 miracle that Jesus **p** after
6:2 miracles that he **p** for the sick.
6:14 saw the miracle Jesus **p**,
7:21 them, "I **p** one miracle,
12:18 that Jesus had **p** this miracle,
20:30 Jesus **p** many other miracles
Act 4:16 Clearly, they've **p** a miracle that
4:17 that they have **p** will not spread
6:8 He did amazing things and **p**
8:6 and saw the miracles that he **p**.
18:25 only about the baptism John **p**.
Col 2:11 It was not a circumcision **p** by
2:11 in the circumcision **p** by Christ.
Heb 10:11 Every day each priest **p** his

performing (3)
Jos 7:13 'Get ready for tomorrow by **p**
Jon 11:47 This man is **p** a lot of miracles.
Act 4:30 power by healing, **p** miracles,

performs (2)
Psa 77:14 are the God who **p** miracles.
Rev 13:13 beast **p** spectacular signs.

perfume (26)
Exo 30:33 Whoever prepares a **p** like this
Rut 3:3 Freshen up, put on some **p**,
Neh 3:8 a **p** maker, made repairs.
Pro 27:9 **P** and incense make the heart
Ecc 7:1 is better than expensive **p**,
10:1 will make a bottle of **p** stink,
Sos 1:12 my **p** fills the air with its
4:10 of your **p** than any spice.
Isa 3:20 blouses, **p** boxes, charms,
3:24 Instead of the smell of **p**,
57:9 oils and put on plenty of **p**.
Mat 26:7 a bottle of very expensive **p**
26:12 She poured this **p** on my body
Mar 14:3 expensive **p** made from pure
14:3 and poured the **p** on his head.
14:4 was the **p** wasted like this?
14:5 This **p** could have been sold
14:8 She came to pour **p** on my
Luk 7:37 So she took a bottle of **p**
7:38 and poured the **p** on them.
7:46 she has poured **p** on my feet.
Jon 11:2 was the woman who poured **p**
12:3 expensive **p** made from pure
12:3 of the **p** filled the house.
12:5 "Why wasn't this **p** sold for a
Rev 18:13 cinnamon, spices, incense, **p**,

perfumed (3)
Exo 30:32 Never make any **p** oil using
Sos 3:6 She is **p** with myrrh and
Isa 57:9 to the king with **p** oils

perfumer (3)
Exo 30:25 Have a **p** make these into a

Exo 30:35 Have a **p** make it into fragrant
37:29 He also had a **p** make the holy

perfumes (4)

1Sm 8:13 and have them make **p**,
2Ch 16:14 full of spices and blended **p**.
Est 2:12 myrrh and six months using **p**
Luk 23:56 city and prepared spices and **p**.

Perga (3)

Act 13:13 from Paphos and arrived in **P**,
13:14 Paul and Barnabas left **P** and
14:25 the message in the city of **P**

Pergamum (2)

Rev 1:11 Smyrna, **P**, Thyatira, Sardis,
2:12 messenger of the church in **P**,

Perida (1)

Neh 7:57 of Sotai, Sophereth, **P**,

period (24)

Gen 13:15 for an indefinite **p** of time.
31:35 to greet you; I'm having my **p**."
Lev 12:2 is unclean for her monthly **p**.
12:5 be unclean as in her monthly **p**.
15:19 a woman has her monthly **p**,
15:20 on during her **p** will be unclean.
15:24 with her while she has her **p**,
15:25 days other than her monthly **p**,
15:25 If her **p** lasts longer than usual,
15:25 a discharge. It is like her **p**.
15:26 on is unclean. It is like her **p**.
15:33 for any woman who has her **p**,
18:19 unclean during her monthly **p**.
20:18 while she has her monthly **p**,
Num 6:12 The first time **p** won't count.
2Sm 11:4 herself after her monthly **p**.)
1Ch 9:25 for a **p** of seven days.
Jer 2:24 find you during your monthly **p**.
Eze 18:6 while she is having her **p**.
36:17 as a woman's menstrual **p**.
Dan 1:18 end of the three-year training **p**,
7:12 allowed to live for a **p** of time.
Mat 5:18 neither a **p** nor a comma will
1Pe 1:20 known in the last **p** of time.

periods (17)

Eze 22:10 having their **p** and are unclean.
Dan 2:21 changes times and **p** of history.
4:16 like this for seven time **p**.
4:23 wild animals for seven time **p**.'
4:25 And seven time **p** will pass
4:32 And seven time **p** will pass
4:34 At the end of the seven time **p**,
9:24 "Seventy sets of seven time **p**
9:24 These time **p** will serve to
9:25 seven sets of seven time **p**
9:25 sets of seven time **p** will pass.
9:26 sixty-two sets of seven time **p**,
9:27 for one set of seven time **p**.
9:27 the middle of the seven time **p**,
9:27 until ⌊those time **p**⌋ come
Act 1:7 to know about times or **p** that
2Ti 3:1 there will be violent **p** of time.

Perizzites (23)

Gen 13:7 (Canaanites and **P** were also
15:20 the Hittites, the **P**, the Rephaim,
34:30 the Canaanites and the **P**,
Exo 3:8 **P**, Hivites, and Jebusites live.
3:17 **P**, Hivites, and Jebusites,
23:23 Hittites, **P**, Canaanites, Hivites,
33:2 **P**, Hivites, and Jebusites.
34:11 Canaanites, Hittites, **P**, Hivites,
Dtr 7:1 Canaanites, **P**, Hivites,
20:17 Canaanites, **P**, Hivites,
Jos 3:10 **P**, Girgashites, Amorites,
9:2 **P**, Hivites, and Jebusites.)
11:3 west, the Amorites, Hittites, **P**,
12:8 Canaanites, **P**, Hivites,
17:15 there in the land of the **P**
24:11 **P**, Canaanites, Hittites,
Jdg 1:4 the Canaanites and **P** over
1:5 defeated the Canaanites and **P**.
3:5 **P**, Hivites, and Jebusites.
1Ki 9:20 The Amorites, Hittites, **P**,
2Ch 8:7 The Hittites, **P**, Hivites,
Ezr 9:1 **P**, Jebusites, Ammonites,
Neh 9:8 Hittites, Amorites, **P**, Jebusites,

permanent (68)

Gen 17:8 as your **p** possession.
23:4 "I'm a stranger with no **p** home.
48:4 as a **p** possession.'
Exo 12:14 This is a **p** law for generations
12:17 This is a **p** law for future
12:24 They are a **p** law for you and
27:21 This is a **p** law among the
28:43 "This is a **p** law for him and his
29:9 to be priests; this is a **p** law.
29:28 It is a **p** law that the Israelites
30:21 This will be a **p** law for him
31:16 to come as a **p** reminder
31:17 It will be a **p** sign between me
32:13 It will be their **p** possession.'"
40:15 Their anointing will begin a **p**
Lev 3:17 This is a **p** law for generations
6:18 It is a **p** law for generations to
6:22 This is a **p** law of the LORD:
7:34 This is a **p** law for generations
7:36 This is a **p** law for generations
10:9 This is a **p** law for generations
10:15 This will be a **p** law,
16:29 "This will be a **p** law for you:
16:31 yourselves. It is a **p** law.
16:34 "This **p** law tells you how to
17:7 This is a **p** law for the people
23:14 It is a **p** law for generations to
23:21 It is a **p** law for generations to
23:31 It is a **p** law for generations to
23:41 This is a **p** law for generations
24:3 It is a **p** law for generations to
24:9 by fire. This is a **p** law."
25:23 are strangers without **p** homes.
25:34 because it is their **p** property.
25:35 as a stranger without a **p** home.
25:46 descendants as **p** property.
25:47 without a **p** home among you
Num 10:8 This will be a **p** law for you
15:15 It is a **p** law for future
18:23 This is a **p** law for future
19:10 This will be a **p** law for the
19:21 This will be a **p** law for them.
24:21 "You have a **p** place to live.
Jos 4:7 These stones are a **p** reminder
14:9 on will be a **p** inheritance
1Sm 3:13 down a **p** judgment against his
1Ki 11:38 I will build a **p** dynasty for you
1Ch 29:15 foreigners without **p** homes.
2Ch 13:5 forever in a **p** promise?
Job 41:4 can take it as your **p** slave?
Isa 30:8 in the future as a **p** witness.
32:14 will become **p** caves.
56:5 I will give them a **p** name that
Jer 5:22 a **p** barrier that it cannot cross.
25:12 I will turn Babylon into a **p**
49:33 It will become a **p** wasteland.
50:5 They will go there to make a **p**
51:26 You will become **p** ruins,"
51:62 and it will become a **p** ruin.'
Eze 35:9 turn you into a **p** wasteland.
Mat 12:45 and take up **p** residence there.
Luk 11:26 and take up **p** residence there.
Act 7:46 that he might provide a **p** place
1Co 9:25 do it to win one that will be **p**.
Heb 10:34 better and more **p** possession.
11:10 the city with **p** foundations.
11:13 with no **p** home on earth.
13:14 We don't have a **p** city here on

permanently (25)

Lev 25:23 "Land must never be sold **p**,
Num 25:13 descendants will be priests **p**
1Sm 1:22 and he'll stay there **p**."
13:13 your kingdom over Israel **p**.
1Ki 8:13 a home for you to live in **p**."
2Ki 5:27 you and your descendants **p**!"
1Ch 6:31 the ark was placed there **p**.
22:10 of his kingdom **p** over Israel.'"
28:4 chose me to be king of Israel **p**.
2Ch 6:2 a home for you to live in **p**."
9:8 he has established them **p** and
20:7 your friend Abraham to have **p**?
Psa 37:29 inherit the land and live there **p**.
Isa 34:17 They will possess it **p** and live
59:21 **p**," says the LORD.
60:21 they will possess the land **p**.
64:6 acts are like **p** stained rags.
Jer 7:7 in the land that I gave **p** to your
25:5 the land that the LORD **p** gave
25:9 and something **p** ruined.
49:13 All its cities will lie in ruins **p**.
Eze 37:25 grandchildren will live in it **p**.
37:26 my holy place among them **p**.
37:28 place will be among them **p**.'"
Dan 7:26 be completely and **p** destroyed.

permission (13)

Gen 41:44 do anything without your **p**."
Ezr 5:3 "Who gave you **p** to rebuild this
5:9 "Who gave you **p** to rebuild this
5:13 Cyrus gave **p** for God's temple
5:17 whether King Cyrus gave **p**
Neh 13:6 I asked the king for **p** to return.
Est 4:8 The decree gave **p** to
8:11 that the king had given **p** for the
Dan 1:8 asked the chief-of-staff for **p** not
2:49 With the king's **p**, Meshach,
Mat 10:29 ground without your Father's **p**.
Jon 19:38 Pilate gave him **p** to remove
Act 21:40 officer gave Paul **p** to speak.

permit (7)

Dtr 29:26 the LORD didn't **p** them to have.
1Sm 20:29 If you will **p** it, please let me go
27:5 to Achish, "If you will **p** me,
1Ch 16:21 He didn't **p** anyone to oppress
Job 6:29 Don't **p** any injustice.
Psa 105:14 He didn't **p** anyone to oppress
Mat 23:13 and you don't **p** others to enter

permits (1)

Heb 6:3 If God **p**, we will do this.

permitted (5)

Ezr 9:13 than we deserve and have **p**
Est 8:12 ⌊This was **p**⌋ on one day in all
Lam 5:5 worn out ⌊and⌋ not **p** to rest.
Dan 2:44 No other people will be **p** to
Mar 2:24 doing something that is not **p**

persecute (21)

Dtr 30:7 those who hate you and **p** you.
Job 19:28 "You say, 'We will **p** him!
Psa 31:15 from those who **p** me.
69:26 They **p** the one you have
119:84 those who **p** me to justice?
119:86 Those people **p** me with lies.
Jer 15:15 revenge on those who **p** me.
20:11 That is why those who **p** me
Hos 8:3 The enemy will **p** them.
Mat 5:11 people insult you, **p** you, lie,
5:44 and pray for those who **p** you.
10:23 So when they **p** you in one city,
23:34 synagogues and **p** from city
Luk 11:49 and apostles and **p** others.'
21:12 people will arrest and **p** you.
Jon 5:16 The Jews began to **p** Jesus
15:20 they will also **p** you.
Act 7:52 prophet your ancestors didn't **p**
13:50 These people started to **p** Paul
Rom 12:14 Bless those who **p** you.
1Co 4:12 When people **p** us,

persecuted (15)

Psa 119:161 Influential people have **p** me for
Mat 5:10 Blessed are those who are **p**
5:12 you were **p** in these ways.
Jon 15:20 If they **p** me, they will also
Act 22:4 I **p** people who followed the
1Co 15:9 because I **p** God's church.
2Co 4:9 We're **p**, but we're not
Gal 1:13 You heard how I violently **p**
1:23 "The man who **p** us is now
4:29 conceived in a natural way **p**
5:11 why am I still being **p**?
1Th 2:15 and who have **p** us severely.

1Ti 1:13 In the past I cursed him, **p** him,
2Ti 3:12 in Christ Jesus will be **p**.
Rev 12:13 it **p** the woman who had given

persecutes (1)
Psa 55:3 me and a wicked person **p** me.

persecuting (7)
Isa 14:6 **p** them without restraint.
Act 9:4 Why are you **p** me?"
9:5 "I'm Jesus, the one you're **p**.
22:7 Why are you **p** me?'
22:8 Nazareth, the one you're **p**.'
26:14 Why are you **p** me?
26:15 'I am Jesus, the one you're **p**.

persecution (8)
Mat 13:21 When suffering or **p** comes
Mar 4:17 When suffering or **p** comes
Act 8:1 On that day widespread **p**
Rom 8:35 Can trouble, distress, **p**,
2Co 12:10 mistreatment, hardship, **p**,
Gal 6:12 Their only aim is to avoid **p**
1Th 3:3 that we're destined to suffer **p**.
3:4 that we were going to suffer **p**.

persecutions (5)
Mar 10:30 and fields, along with **p**.
1Th 2:14 You suffered the same **p** from
2Th 1:4 endurance and faith in all the **p**
2Ti 3:11 also know about the kind of **p**
3:11 I endured those **p**, and the Lord

persecutor (1)
Php 3:6 I was a **p** of the church.

persecutors (2)
Psa 119:157 I have many **p** and opponents,
Jer 17:18 Put my **p** to shame,

perseverance (1)
Rom 8:25 we eagerly wait for it with **p**.

Persia (24)
2Ch 36:22 in Cyrus' first year as king of **P**.
36:23 is what King Cyrus of **P** says:
Ezr 1:1 in Cyrus' first year as king of **P**.
1:2 is what King Cyrus of **P** says:
1:8 King Cyrus of **P** put the
3:7 Cyrus of **P** had authorized them
4:3 as King Cyrus of **P** ordered us
4:5 reign of King Cyrus of **P** until
4:5 the reign of King Darius of **P**.
4:7 Artaxerxes was king of **P**.
4:9 **P**, Erech, Babylon, Susa,
4:24 second year as king of **P**.
6:14 (the kings of **P**) had ordered.
7:1 reign of King Artaxerxes of **P**,
9:9 he has made the kings of **P**
Est 1:18 the wives of the officials in **P**
Eze 27:10 People from **P**, Lud, and Put
38:5 **P**, Sudan, and Put will be with
Dan 1:21 first year of King Cyrus ⌊of **P**⌋.
8:20 the kingdoms of Media and **P**.
10:1 In Cyrus' third year as king of **P**,
10:13 left alone with the kings of **P**.
10:20 to fight the commander of **P**.
11:2 Three more kings will rule **P**.

Persian (4)
2Ch 36:20 until the **P** Empire began
Neh 12:22 until the reign of Darius the **P**.
Dan 6:28 and the reign of Cyrus the **P**.
10:13 The commander of the **P**

Persians (10)
Ezr 5:6 and his group (the **P** west
6:6 and those of your group (the **P**
Est 1:3 officers of the **P** and Medes,
1:14 These seven officials of the **P**
1:19 decrees of the **P** and Medes,
10:2 the kings of the Medes and **P**.
Dan 5:28 and given to the Medes and **P**."
6:8 the Medes and **P** no one could
6:12 to the law of the Medes and **P**
6:15 the Medes and **P** have a law

Persis (1)
Rom 16:12 Greet dear **P**, who has worked

persisted (1)
Jon 8:7 When they **p** in asking him

persisting (1)
Rom 2:7 and immortality by **p** in doing

persists (1)
Dtr 25:8 If he **p** in saying that he doesn't

personal (9)
Gen 34:23 their livestock, their **p** property,
Jdg 2:10 They had no **p** experience with
2Sm 13:17 Then he called his **p** servant
2Ki 12:8 from the people ⌊for **p** use⌋ nor
1Ch 29:3 I have a **p** treasury of gold and
Est 2:2 So the king's **p** staff said to
6:3 The king's **p** staff replied,
Jer 26:21 Jehoiakim and all his **p** troops
Php 2:25 You sent him as your **p**

personally (6)
Exo 9:14 that will affect you **p** as well as
33:11 would speak to Moses **p**,
Gal 1:18 to become **p** acquainted
1:22 in Judea didn't know me **p**.
2Jn 1:12 and talk things over with you **p**.
3Jn 1:14 Then we can talk things over **p**.

persuade (6)
Jdg 19:3 her husband went to **p** her to
2Ch 32:15 deceive you or **p** you like this.
Pro 25:15 With patience you can **p** a ruler,
Act 23:21 Don't let them **p** you to do this.
26:28 you think you can quickly **p** me
2Co 5:11 fear the Lord, we try to **p** others.

persuaded (10)
Jos 15:18 she **p** him to ask her father for a
Jdg 1:14 she **p** him to ask her father for a
9:3 They were **p** to follow
2Ch 18:2 And Ahab **p** Jehoshaphat to
Psa 141:4 Do not let me be **p** to do
Mat 27:20 the chief priests and leaders **p**
Luk 16:31 they won't be **p** even if
Act 17:4 Some of the Jews were **p** to
21:14 When Paul could not be **p**,
27:11 However, the officer was **p** by

persuades (1)
Pro 7:21 seductive charms, she **p** him.

persuading (2)
Act 13:43 with them and were **p** them
18:13 They said, "This man is **p**

persuasive (2)
1Co 1:20 Where is the **p** speaker of our
2:4 with **p** intellectual arguments.

Peruda (1)
Ezr 2:55 of Sotai, Hassophereth, **P**,

perversion (9)
Rom 1:24 by sexual **p** with each other.
1:27 they deserve for their **p**.
6:19 to sexual **p** and disobedience.
2Co 12:21 they think and act about the **p**,
Gal 5:19 illicit sex, **p**, promiscuity,
Eph 4:19 practice every kind of sexual **p**
5:3 let sexual sin, **p** of any kind,
5:5 is involved in sexual sin, **p**,
Col 3:5 sexual sin, **p**, passion, lust,

pervert (4)
Exo 23:2 don't side with the majority to **p**
Dtr 16:19 Never **p** justice. Instead, be
Job 34:12 and the Almighty will never **p**
Mic 3:9 You despise justice and **p**

perverted (8)
Lev 18:17 are related. Doing this is **p**.
Lev 19:29 be filled with people who are **p**.
20:14 they have done a **p** thing.
20:14 Never do this **p** thing.
Jdg 20:6 citizens of Gibeah did this **p**
Ezr 9:11 been polluted by its **p** people
Hab 1:4 justice is carried out, it's **p**.
Zep 3:5 who are **p** are shameless.

pester (1)
Pro 6:3 and **p** your neighbor.

pestered (1)
Jdg 16:16 She **p** him until he wished he

pestilence (1)
Dtr 32:24 by famines and ravaged by **p**

pestle (1)
Pro 27:22 fool in a mortar with a **p** along

petals (6)
Exo 25:31 and **p** must be hammered out of
25:33 blossoms, with buds and **p**.
25:34 blossoms, with buds and **p**.
37:17 and **p** were hammered out of
37:19 blossoms, with buds and **p**.
37:20 each with a bud and **p**.

Peter (222)
Mat 4:18 Simon (called **P**) and Andrew.
10:2 Simon (who is called **P**) and
14:28 **P** answered, "Lord, if it is you,
14:29 So **P** got out of the boat and
15:15 **P** said to him, "Explain this
16:16 Simon **P** answered,
16:18 You are **P**, and I can guarantee
16:22 **P** took him aside and objected
16:23 But Jesus turned and said to **P**,
17:1 After six days Jesus took **P**,
17:4 **P** said to Jesus, "Lord,
17:24 of the temple tax came to **P**.
17:25 **P** went into the house.
17:26 other people," **P** answered.
18:21 Then **P** came to Jesus and
19:27 Then **P** replied to him,
26:33 **P** said to him, "Even if
26:34 Jesus replied to **P**,
26:35 **P** told him, "Even if I have to
26:37 He took **P** and Zebedee's two
26:40 He said to **P**, "Couldn't you
26:58 **P** followed at a distance until
26:69 **P** was sitting in the courtyard.
26:70 But **P** denied it in front of them
26:72 Again **P** denied it and swore
26:73 there approached **P** and said,
26:74 Then **P** began to curse and
26:75 **P** remembered what Jesus had
26:75 Then **P** went outside and cried
Mar 3:16 Simon (whom Jesus named **P**),
5:37 no one to go with him except **P**
8:29 **P** answered him, "You are the
8:32 **P** took him aside and objected
8:33 and objected to what **P** said.
9:2 six days Jesus took only **P**,
9:5 **P** said to Jesus, "Rabbi,
9:6 (**P** didn't know how to respond.
10:28 Then **P** spoke up,
11:21 **P** remembered ⌊what Jesus
13:3 buildings, **P**, James, John,
14:29 **P** said to him, "Even if
14:30 Jesus said to **P**, "I can
14:31 But **P** said very strongly,
14:33 He took **P**, James, and John
14:37 He said to **P**, "Simon, are you
14:54 **P** followed him at a distance
14:66 **P** was in the courtyard.
14:67 saw **P** warming himself.
14:68 But **P** denied it by saying,
14:70 **P** again denied it. After a little
14:70 standing there said to **P** again,
14:71 Then **P** began to curse and
14:72 **P** remembered that Jesus said
14:72 Then **P** began to cry very hard.
16:7 Go and tell his disciples and **P**
Luk 5:8 When Simon **P** saw this,
6:14 Simon (whom Jesus named **P**)

Luk 8:45 him, **P** said, "Teacher,
8:51 one to go with him except **P**,
9:20 **P** answered, "You are the
9:28 said this, Jesus took **P**, John,
9:32 **P** and the men with him were
9:33 **P** said to Jesus, "Teacher,
9:33 **P** didn't know what he was
12:41 **P** asked, "Lord, did you use
18:28 Then **P** said, "We've left
22:8 Jesus sent **P** and John and
22:33 But **P** said to him, "Lord,
22:34 Jesus replied, "**P**, I can
22:54 **P** followed at a distance.
22:55 **P** sat among them.
22:57 But **P** denied it by saying,
22:58 someone else saw **P** and said,
22:58 But **P** said, "Not me!"
22:60 But **P** said, "I don't know what
22:61 turned and looked directly at **P**.
22:61 **P** remembered what the Lord
22:62 Then **P** went outside and cried
24:12 But **P** got up and ran to the
Jon 1:42 be Cephas" (which means "**P**").
1:44 hometown of Andrew and **P**.)
6:68 Simon **P** answered Jesus,
13:6 When Jesus came to Simon **P**,
13:6 Peter, **P** asked him, "Lord,
13:7 Jesus answered **P**,
13:8 **P** told Jesus, "You will never
13:8 Jesus replied to **P**,
13:9 Simon **P** said to Jesus,
13:10 Jesus told **P**, "People who
13:24 Simon **P** motioned to that
13:36 Simon **P** asked him,
13:37 **P** said to Jesus, "Lord,
18:10 Simon **P** had a sword.
18:11 Jesus told **P**, "Put your sword
18:15 Simon **P** and another disciple
18:16 **P**, however, was standing
18:16 brought **P** into the courtyard.
18:17 The gatekeeper asked **P**,
18:17 **P** answered, "No, I'm not!"
18:18 **P** was standing there,
18:25 Simon **P** continued to stand
18:25 **P** denied it by saying,
18:26 man whose ear **P** had cut off,
18:27 **P** again denied it, and just then
20:2 So she ran to Simon **P** and the
20:3 So **P** and the other disciple
20:4 other disciple ran faster than **P**
20:6 Simon **P** arrived after him and
21:2 Simon **P**, Thomas (called
21:3 Simon **P** said to the others,
21:7 whom Jesus loved said to **P**,
21:7 When Simon **P** heard that it
21:11 Simon **P** got into the boat and
21:15 Jesus asked Simon **P**,
21:15 **P** answered him, "Yes, Lord,
21:16 **P** answered him "Yes,
21:17 **P** felt sad because Jesus had
21:17 So **P** said to him, "Lord,
21:19 of death **P** would bring glory
21:19 After saying this, Jesus told **P**,
21:20 **P** turned around and saw the
21:21 When **P** saw him, he asked
21:22 Jesus said to **P**, "If I want him
Act 1:13 city, **P**, John, James, Andrew,
1:15 **P** got up and spoke to them.
2:14 Then **P** stood up with the
2:37 They asked **P** and the other
2:38 **P** answered them,
2:40 **P** said much more to warn
2:41 Those who accepted what **P**
3:1 **P** and John were going to the
3:3 When the man saw that **P** and
3:4 **P** and John stared at him.
3:4 "Look at us!" **P** said.
3:6 However, **P** said to him,
3:7 **P** took hold of the man's right
3:8 He went with **P** and John into
3:11 wouldn't let go of **P** and John.
3:12 When **P** saw this, he said to
4:1 Sadducees approached **P**
4:2 **P** and John were teaching the
4:3 they put **P** and John in jail until
4:7 They made **P** and John stand
Act 4:8 Then **P**, because he was filled
4:13 After they found out that **P** and
4:14 standing with **P** and John,
4:15 So they ordered **P** and John to
4:18 They called **P** and John and
4:19 **P** and John answered them,
4:21 any way to punish **P** and John.
4:23 When **P** and John were
5:3 **P** asked, "Ananias, why did
5:5 Ananias heard **P** say this,
5:8 So **P** asked her, "Tell me,
5:9 Then **P** said to her,
5:10 she dropped dead in front of **P**.
5:29 **P** and the other apostles
8:14 they sent **P** and John to them.
8:15 **P** and John went to Samaria
8:17 Then **P** and John placed their
8:18 he offered **P** and John money
8:20 **P** told Simon, "May your
9:32 When **P** was going around to
9:33 In Lydda **P** found a man named
9:34 **P** said to him, "Aeneas,
9:38 the disciples heard that **P** was
9:38 They begged **P**, "Hurry to
9:39 So **P** went with them.
9:39 were crying and showing **P**
9:40 **P** made everyone leave the
9:40 her eyes, saw **P**, and sat up.
9:41 **P** took her hand and helped her
9:43 **P** stayed in Joppa for a number
10:5 man whose name is Simon **P**.
10:9 **P** went on the roof to pray.
10:13 A voice told him, "Get up, **P**!
10:14 **P** answered, "I can't do that,
10:17 While **P** was puzzled by the
10:18 if Simon **P** was staying there.
10:19 **P** was still thinking about the
10:21 So **P** went to the men.
10:23 **P** asked the men to come into
10:23 The next day **P** left with them.
10:25 When **P** was about to enter
10:25 down, and worshiped **P**.
10:26 But **P** made him get up.
10:27 As **P** talked, he entered
10:32 man whose name is Simon **P**.
10:34 Then **P** said, "Now I
10:44 While **P** was still speaking,
10:45 come with **P** were amazed that
10:46 praising God. Then **P** said,
10:48 So **P** ordered that they should
10:48 Then they asked **P** to stay with
11:2 when **P** went to Jerusalem,
11:4 Then **P** began to explain to
11:7 a voice telling me, 'Get up, **P**!
11:13 man whose name is Simon **P**.
12:3 the Jews, he arrested **P** too.
12:4 After capturing **P**, Herod had
12:4 Herod wanted to bring **P** to trial
12:5 So **P** was kept in prison,
12:6 was going to bring **P** to trial,
12:6 **P** was sleeping between two
12:7 from the Lord stood near **P**,
12:8 **P** did this. Then the angel told
12:9 **P** followed the angel out of the
12:10 The angel suddenly left **P**.
12:11 When **P** came to his senses,
12:12 When **P** realized what had
12:13 **P** knocked on the door of the
12:14 "**P** is standing at the door!"
12:15 But she insisted that **P** was at
12:16 But **P** kept knocking.
12:17 **P** motioned with his hand to
12:18 over what had happened to **P**.
12:19 Herod searched for **P** but
15:7 **P** stood up and said to them,
Gal 2:7 as **P** had been entrusted
2:8 The one who made **P** an
1Pe 1:1 From **P**, an apostle of Jesus
2Pe 1:1 From Simon **P**, a servant and

Peter's (8)

Mat 8:14 When Jesus went to **P** house,
8:14 he saw **P** mother-in-law in bed
Jon 1:40 Andrew, Simon **P** brother, was
6:8 was Simon **P** brother, told him,
Act 5:15 at least **P** shadow might fall
Act 12:7 The angel nudged **P** side,
12:7 the chains fell from **P** hands
12:14 When she recognized **P** voice,

Pethahiah (4)

1Ch 24:16 the nineteenth for **P**,
Ezr 10:23 Kelita), **P**, Judah, and Eliezer
Neh 9:5 and **P** — said, "Stand up,
11:24 **P**, son of Meshezabel, one of

Pethor (2)

Num 22:5 son of Beor, who was at **P**,
Dtr 23:4 from **P** in Aram Naharaim,

Pethuel (1)

Joe 1:1 LORD said to Joel, son of **P**.

petitions (1)

1Ti 2:1 I encourage you to make **p**,

petrified (1)

Exo 15:16 they will be **p** until your people

Peullethai (1)

1Ch 26:5 (the seventh), **P** (the eighth).

Phanuel (1)

Luk 2:36 She was a descendant of **P**

Pharaoh (224)

Gen 12:15 they raved about her to **P**,
12:17 However, the LORD struck **P**
12:18 Then **P** called for Abram.
12:20 **P** gave his men orders
40:2 **P** was angry with his chief
40:7 these officials of **P** who were
40:13 In the next three days **P** will
40:14 Mention me to **P**, and get me
40:17 all kinds of baked goods for **P**,
40:19 In the next three days **P** will
40:20 **P** had a special dinner
41:1 After two full years **P** had a
41:4 cows. Then **P** woke up.
41:7 Then **P** woke up. It was only a
41:8 **P** told them his dreams,
41:9 the chief cupbearer spoke to **P**,
41:10 Some time ago when **P** was
41:13 **P** restored me to my position,
41:14 Then **P** sent for Joseph,
41:14 he came in front of **P**.
41:15 **P** said to Joseph, "I had a
41:16 Joseph answered **P**,
41:16 but God can give **P** the answer
41:17 Then **P** said to Joseph,
41:25 Then Joseph said to **P**,
41:25 "**P** had the same dream twice.
41:25 God has told **P** what he's going
41:28 "It's just as I said to **P**.
41:28 God has shown **P** what he's
41:32 The reason **P** has had a
41:33 "**P** should look for a wise and
41:37 **P** and all his servants liked the
41:38 So **P** asked his servants,
41:39 Then **P** said to Joseph,
41:40 only because I'm **P**."
41:41 Then **P** said to Joseph,
41:42 Then **P** took off his signet ring
41:43 **P** put Joseph in charge of
41:44 "Even though I am **P**,
41:45 **P** named Joseph
41:46 the service of **P** (the king
41:46 He left **P** and traveled all
41:55 the people cried to **P** for food.
41:55 But **P** said to all the Egyptians,
42:15 as surely as **P** lives,
42:16 as surely as **P** lives,
44:18 although you are equal to **P**.
45:8 made me like a father to **P**,
45:16 **P** and his officials were
45:17 So **P** said to Joseph,
45:21 for their trip as **P** had ordered.
46:5 in the wagons **P** had sent
46:31 "I'm going to **P** to tell him,
46:33 when **P** calls for you and asks,
47:1 Joseph went and told **P**,
47:2 he presented them to **P**.

Gen 47:3 **P** asked the brothers,
47:3 They answered **P**,
47:5 Then **P** said to Joseph,
47:7 and had him stand in front of **P**.
47:7 of Pharaoh. Jacob blessed **P**.
47:8 **P** asked him, "How old are
47:9 Jacob answered **P**,
47:10 Then Jacob blessed **P** and left.
47:11 As **P** had ordered, Joseph had
47:20 all the land in Egypt for **P**.
47:22 received an income from **P**,
47:23 bought you and your land for **P**,
47:24 one-fifth of the produce to **P**.
47:26 (of the produce) belongs to **P**.
47:26 of the priests didn't belong to **P**.
50:4 "Please speak directly to **P**.
50:6 **P** replied, "Go and bury your
Exo 1:11 as supply cities for **P**.
1:19 The midwives answered **P**,
1:22 Then **P** commanded all his
2:15 When **P** heard what Moses had
2:15 But Moses fled from **P** and
3:10 I am sending you to **P** so that
3:11 "Who am I that I should go to **P**
4:21 see that you show **P** all the
4:22 Then tell **P**, 'This is what the
5:1 and Aaron went to **P** and said,
5:2 **P** asked, "Who is the LORD?
5:5 Then **P** added, "Look how
5:6 That same day **P** gave these
5:10 "This is what **P** says:
5:15 foremen complained to **P**.
5:17 **P** answered. "That's why you
5:20 As they left **P**, they found
5:21 You have made **P** and his
5:23 Ever since I went to **P** to speak
6:1 you will see what I will do to **P**.
6:11 "Go tell **P** (the king of Egypt) to
6:12 Why would **P** listen to me?
6:13 the Israelites and **P** (the king
6:27 and Aaron — told **P** (the king
6:29 Tell **P** (the king of Egypt)
6:30 "Why would **P** listen to me?"
7:1 "I have made you a god to **P**,
7:2 and he must tell **P** to let the
7:3 But I will make **P** stubborn.
7:4 **P** will not listen to you.
7:7 was 83 when they talked to **P**.
7:9 "When **P** says to you,
7:9 throw it down in front of **P**,' and
7:10 Moses and Aaron went to **P**
7:10 his staff down in front of **P**
7:11 Then **P** sent for his wise men
7:13 Yet, **P** continued to be stubborn
7:14 "**P** is being stubborn.
7:15 In the morning meet **P** when
7:20 In front of **P** and his officials,
7:22 So **P** continued to be stubborn
7:23 **P** turned and went back to his
8:1 Moses, "Go to **P**, and tell him,
8:8 **P** sent for Moses and Aaron
8:9 Moses answered **P**,
8:10 "Pray for me tomorrow," **P** said.
8:12 After Moses and Aaron left **P**,
8:12 the frogs he had brought on **P**.
8:15 When **P** saw that the plague
8:19 So the magicians said to **P**,
8:19 Yet, **P** continued to be stubborn
8:25 **P** called for Moses and Aaron
8:28 **P** said, "I will let you go,
8:30 Moses left **P** and prayed to the
8:31 The swarms of flies left **P**,
8:32 Yet, this time, too, **P** was
9:1 Moses, "Go to **P**, and tell him,
9:7 **P** found out that not one of the
9:7 Yet, **P** continued to be stubborn
9:8 up in the air as **P** watches.
9:10 a kiln and stood in front of **P**.
9:12 the LORD made **P** stubborn,
9:13 go to **P** and say to him,
9:27 Then **P** sent for Moses and
9:33 As soon as he left **P** and went
9:34 When **P** saw that the rain,
9:35 **P** was stubborn and would not
10:1 LORD said to Moses, "Go to **P**.
10:3 So Moses and Aaron went to **P**
Exo 10:6 Moses turned and left **P**.
10:8 Aaron were brought back to **P**.
10:10 **P** said to them, "The LORD
10:16 Then **P** quickly called for
10:18 Moses left **P** and prayed to the
10:20 the LORD made **P** stubborn,
10:24 Then **P** called for Moses and
10:27 the LORD made **P** stubborn,
10:28 **P** said to Moses, "Get out of
11:1 more plague on **P** and Egypt.
11:5 from the firstborn of **P** who
11:8 with anger, Moses left **P**.
11:9 "**P** will not listen to you.
11:10 Moses and Aaron showed **P**
11:10 the LORD made **P** stubborn,
12:29 the firstborn son of **P** who ruled
12:30 **P**, all his officials, and all the
12:31 **P** called for Moses and Aaron
13:15 When **P** was too stubborn to let
13:17 When **P** let the people go,
14:3 **P** will think, 'The Israelites are
14:4 I will make **P** so stubborn that
14:4 because of what I do to **P**
14:5 When **P** (the king of Egypt)
14:6 So **P** prepared his chariot and
14:8 The LORD made **P** (the king of
14:10 As **P** approached, the Israelites
14:17 because of what I will do to **P**,
14:18 I am honored for what I did to **P**,
18:8 the LORD had done to **P**
18:10 from the Egyptians and their **P**
Dtr 6:22 Egypt, **P**, and his whole family.
7:8 from slavery under **P** (the king
7:18 the LORD your God did to **P**
11:3 he did in Egypt to **P** (the king
29:2 the LORD did in Egypt to **P**,
34:11 amazing things in Egypt to **P**,
1Sm 6:6 Egyptians and their **P** were?
1Ki 3:1 the son-in-law of **P** (the king
11:18 they went to **P** (the king of
11:18 **P** gave Hadad a home,
11:19 **P** approved of Hadad.
11:20 presented the boy to **P**
11:21 army, had died, he said to **P**,
11:22 **P** asked him, "What don't you
2Ki 17:7 from the power of **P** (the king
18:21 This is what **P** (the king of
23:29 In Josiah's days **P** Necoh (the
23:29 When **P** saw him at Megiddo,
23:29 him at Megiddo, **P** killed him.
23:33 **P** Necoh made him a prisoner
23:34 Then **P** Necoh made Josiah's
23:35 Jehoiakim gave **P** the silver
23:35 pay the silver **P** had demanded.
23:35 the land and give it to **P** Necoh.
Neh 9:10 and did amazing things to **P**
Psa 135:9 the heart of Egypt against **P**
136:15 He swept **P** and his army into
Isa 19:11 How can you tell **P**,
36:6 This is what **P** (the king of
Jer 25:19 **P** king of Egypt, his servants,
44:30 I'm going to hand **P** Hophra,
46:2 about the army of **P** Neco,
46:17 There they will cry, '**P**,
46:25 I will also punish **P**,
46:25 and whoever trusts **P**.
47:1 before **P** defeated Gaza.
Eze 17:17 **P** will not be able to help him
29:2 "Son of man, turn to **P**,
29:3 against you, **P**, king of Egypt.
30:21 I have broken the arm of **P**,
30:22 I'm against **P**, king of Egypt.
30:24 **P** will groan like a person who
31:2 "Son of man, say to **P**,
31:18 "This tree is you, **P**,
32:2 sing a funeral song for **P**,
32:21 warriors will say to **P** from
32:31 "**P** and his army will see these
32:32 **P** and all his soldiers will be
Act 7:10 in the presence of **P** (the king
7:13 and **P** learned about Joseph's
Rom 9:17 Scripture says to **P**,

Pharaoh's (59)

Gen 12:15 When **P** officials saw her,
12:15 so Sarai was taken to **P** palace
37:36 one of **P** officials and captain
39:1 Potiphar, one of **P** Egyptian
40:11 **P** cup was in my hand,
40:11 I put the cup in **P** hand.
40:13 You will put **P** cup in his hand
40:21 cupbearer put the cup in **P** hand
41:35 store up grain under **P** control,
45:2 and **P** household heard about it.
45:16 When **P** household heard the
47:14 Then he took it to **P** palace
47:19 Then we will be **P** slaves and
47:20 The land became **P**.
47:25 we are willing to be **P** slaves.
50:4 spoke to the **P** palace staff.
50:7 All **P** officials, the leaders in
Exo 2:5 While **P** daughter came to the
2:6 **P** daughter opened the basket,
2:7 asked **P** daughter, "Should
2:9 **P** daughter said to the woman,
2:10 she brought him to **P** daughter,
2:10 **P** daughter named him Moses
5:14 **P** slave drivers had placed
8:20 stand in **P** way when he's
8:24 of flies came into **P** palace
9:20 Those members of **P** court who
10:7 Then **P** officials asked him,
10:11 were thrown out of **P** palace
11:3 highly respected by **P** officials
14:9 **P** army, including all his
14:23 and all **P** horses, chariots,
14:28 and covered **P** entire army,
15:4 He has thrown **P** chariots and
15:4 **P** best officers were drowned
15:19 When **P** horses, chariots,
18:4 He saved me from **P** death
Dtr 6:21 "We were **P** slaves in Egypt,
1Sm 2:27 were under **P** control in Egypt.
1Ki 3:1 After marrying **P** daughter,
7:8 like this for his wife, **P** daughter
9:24 **P** daughter moved from the
11:1 in addition to **P** daughter.
11:20 in the palace among **P** children
2Ch 8:11 Solomon brought **P** daughter
Sos 1:9 to a mare among **P** stallions
Isa 19:11 The wisest of **P** counselors
30:2 for shelter under **P** protection
30:3 But **P** protection will be their
30:4 Although **P** officials are in
Jer 37:5 **P** army had come from Egypt,
37:7 '**P** army has come out to help
37:11 because **P** army was coming.
43:9 at the entrance to the **P** palace
Eze 30:24 but I will break **P** arms.
30:25 but **P** arms will fall.
Act 7:10 Egypt and of **P** whole palace.
7:21 **P** daughter adopted him and
Heb 11:24 known as a son of **P** daughter

Pharisee (13)

Luk 7:39 The **P** who had invited Jesus
11:37 After Jesus spoke, a **P** invited
11:38 The **P** was surprised to see
14:1 at the home of a prominent **P**.
18:10 One was a **P**, and the other
18:11 The **P** stood up and prayed,
18:14 approval, but the **P** didn't.
Jon 3:1 Nicodemus was a **P** and a
7:48 ruler or any **P** believed in him?
Act 5:34 But a **P** named Gamaliel stood
23:6 I'm a **P** and a descendant of
26:5 know that I lived my life as a **P**.
Php 3:5 up to standards, I was a **P**.

Pharisee's (2)

Luk 7:36 Jesus went to the **P** house and
7:37 was eating at the **P** house.

Pharisees (93)

Mat 3:7 But when he saw many **P** and
5:20 than the scribes and **P**,
9:11 The **P** saw this and asked his
9:14 "Why do we and the **P** fast
9:34 But the **P** said, "He forces
12:2 When the **P** saw this,
12:14 The **P** left and plotted to kill
12:24 When the **P** heard this,

Mat 12:38 Then some scribes and **P** said,
15:1 Then some **P** and scribes
15:12 "Do you realize that when the **P**
16:1 The **P** and Sadducees came to
16:6 yeast of the **P** and Sadducees!"
16:11 yeast of the **P** and Sadducees!"
16:12 of the **P** and Sadducees.
19:3 Some **P** came to test him.
19:7 The **P** asked him, "Why, then,
21:45 the **P** heard his illustrations,
22:15 Then the **P** went away and
22:34 When the **P** heard that Jesus
22:41 While the **P** were still gathered,
23:2 "The scribes and the **P** teach
23:13 it will be for you, scribes and **P**!
23:15 it will be for you, scribes and **P**!
23:23 it will be for you, scribes and **P**!
23:25 it will be for you, scribes and **P**!
23:26 You blind **P**! First clean the
23:27 it will be for you, scribes and **P**!
23:29 it will be for you, scribes and **P**!
27:62 the chief priests and **P**
Mar 2:16 When the scribes who were **P**
2:18 and the **P** were fasting.
2:24 The **P** asked him, "Look!
3:6 The **P** left, and with Herod's
7:1 The **P** and some scribes who
7:3 (The **P**, like all other Jewish
7:5 The **P** and the scribes asked
8:11 The **P** went to Jesus and
8:15 Watch out for the yeast of the **P**
10:2 Some **P** came to test him.
12:13 The leaders sent some of the **P**
Luk 5:17 some **P** and experts in Moses'
5:21 The scribes and the **P** thought,
5:30 The **P** and their scribes
5:33 so do the disciples of the **P**.
6:2 Some of the **P** asked,
6:7 The scribes and the **P** were
6:11 The scribes and **P** were furious
7:30 But the **P** and the experts in
7:36 One of the **P** invited Jesus to
11:39 The Lord said to him, "You **P**
11:42 horrible it will be for you **P**!
11:43 horrible it will be for you **P**!
11:53 the scribes and the **P** held a
12:1 out for the yeast of the **P**.
13:31 At that time some **P** told Jesus,
14:3 Jesus reacted by asking the **P**
15:2 But the **P** and the scribes
16:14 The **P**, who love money,
17:20 The **P** asked Jesus when the
19:39 Some of the **P** in the crowd
Jon 1:24 who had been sent were **P**.
4:1 Jesus knew that the **P** had
7:32 The **P** heard the crowd saying
7:32 So the chief priests and the **P**
7:45 chief priests and **P** asked them,
7:47 The **P** asked the temple
7:50 of those **P** was Nicodemus,
8:3 The scribes and the **P** brought
8:9 the scribes and **P** left.
8:12 Jesus spoke to the **P** again.
8:13 The **P** said to him,
8:19 The **P** asked him, "Where is
8:21 Jesus spoke to the **P** again.
9:13 who had been blind to the **P**.
9:15 So the **P** asked the man again
9:15 The man told the **P**,
9:16 Some of the **P** said,
9:16 Other **P** asked, "How can a
9:16 So the **P** were divided in their
9:40 Some **P** who were with Jesus
11:46 But some of them went to the **P**
11:47 So the chief priests and the **P**
11:57 (The chief priests and the **P**
12:19 The **P** said to each other,
12:42 the **P** would have thrown
18:3 from the chief priests and **P**
Act 15:5 from the party of the **P** stood up
23:6 Sadducees and others were **P**,
23:6 and a descendant of **P**.
23:7 After Paul said that, the **P** and
23:8 The **P** believe in all these
23:9 Some of the scribes were **P**

Pharisees' (1)

Mar 2:18 and the **P** disciples fast,

Pharpar (1)

2Ki 5:12 The Abana and **P** Rivers in

Phicol (3)

Gen 21:22 accompanied by **P**,
21:32 Beersheba, Abimelech and **P**,
26:26 his friend Ahuzzath, and **P**,

Philadelphia (2)

Rev 1:11 Sardis, **P**, and Laodicea."
3:7 messenger of the church in **P**,

Philemon (2)

Phm 1:1 To our dear coworker **P**,
1:4 ⌊**P**,⌋ I always thank my God

Philetus (1)

2Ti 2:17 Hymenaeus and **P** are like that.

Philip (39)

Mat 10:3 **P** and Bartholomew;
14:3 the wife of his brother **P**.
Mar 3:18 Andrew, **P**, Bartholomew,
Luk 3:1 and his brother **P** ruled Iturea
6:14 James, John, **P**, Bartholomew,
Jon 1:43 He found **P** and told him,
1:44 (**P** was from Bethsaida,
1:45 **P** found Nathanael and told
1:46 Nathanael said to **P**,
1:46 **P** told him, "Come and see!"
1:48 fig tree before **P** called you."
6:5 coming to him, he said to **P**,
6:7 **P** answered, "We would need
12:21 They went to **P** (who was from
12:22 **P** told Andrew, and they told
14:8 **P** said to Jesus, "Lord,
14:9 Don't you know me yet, **P**?
Act 1:13 **P**, Thomas, Bartholomew,
6:5 and they chose **P**,
8:5 **P** went to the city of Samaria
8:6 close attention to what **P** said.
8:12 However, when **P** spread the
8:13 he became devoted to **P**.
8:26 angel from the Lord said to **P**,
8:27 So **P** went. An Ethiopian man
8:29 The Spirit said to **P**,
8:30 **P** ran to the carriage and could
8:30 **P** asked him, "Do you
8:31 So he invited **P** to sit with him
8:34 The official said to **P**,
8:35 Then **P** spoke. Starting with
8:35 Starting with that passage, **P**
8:36 The official said to **P**,
8:38 He and **P** stepped into the
8:38 and **P** baptized him.
8:39 the Lord suddenly took **P** away.
8:39 his way and didn't see **P** again.
8:40 **P** found himself in the city of
21:9 **P** had four unmarried daughters

Philippi (5)

Act 16:12 there we went to the city of **P**.
16:12 **P** is a leading city in that part
20:6 we boarded a ship at **P**.
Php 1:1 To God's people in the city of **P**
1Th 2:2 and insulting treatment in **P**.

Philippians (1)

Php 4:15 You **P** also know that in the

Philip's (2)

Mar 6:17 used to be his brother **P** wife.
Act 21:8 next day we went to **P** home

Philistia (9)

Exo 15:14 The people of **P** will be in
Psa 60:8 I will shout in triumph over **P**."
83:7 Gebal, Ammon, and Amalek, **P**,
87:4 and Babylon as well as **P**,
108:9 I will shout in triumph over **P**."
Isa 11:14 swoop down on the slopes of **P**
Jer 25:20 land of Uz; all the kings of **P**,
Joe 3:4 Sidon and all the regions of **P**?
Oba 1:19 will take possession of **P**.

Philistine (96)

Exo 13:17 on the road through **P** territory,
Jos 13:3 even though there are five **P**
Jdg 14:1 he saw a young **P** woman.
14:2 "I've seen a **P** woman at
16:5 The **P** rulers came to her and
16:8 The **P** rulers brought her seven
16:18 sent a message to the **P** rulers,
16:18 So the **P** rulers arrived with the
16:23 Now, the **P** rulers gathered
16:27 All the **P** rulers were there.
1Sm 5:8 called together all the **P** rulers.
5:11 called together all the **P** rulers.
6:1 in **P** territory seven months
6:4 gold mice for the ⌊five⌋ **P** rulers
6:18 number of **P** cities belonging
7:7 the **P** rulers came to attack
7:7 heard ⌊about the **P** plan⌋
13:3 Jonathan defeated the **P** troops
13:4 have defeated the **P** troops,
13:17 Raiding parties left the **P** camp
13:23 Now, **P** troops had gone out to
14:1 "Let's go to the **P** military post
14:4 to attack the **P** military post.
14:11 themselves to the **P** troops.
14:16 ⌊in the **P** camp⌋ dispersing
14:19 the confusion in the **P** camp
14:20 They found **P** soldiers killing
17:4 The **P** army's champion came
17:8 Am I not a **P**, and aren't you
17:10 The **P** added, "I challenge the
17:11 heard what this **P** said,
17:16 the **P** came forward and made
17:23 to them, the **P** champion,
17:25 coming ⌊from the **P** lines⌋?
17:25 man who kills this **P** very rich.
17:26 for the man who kills this **P**
17:26 Who is this uncircumcised **P**
17:32 I will go and fight this **P**."
17:33 "You can't fight this **P**.
17:36 and this uncircumcised **P** will
17:37 will save me from this **P**."
17:40 he approached the **P**.
17:41 The **P**, preceded by the man
17:42 When the **P** got a good look at
17:43 The **P** asked David,
17:43 So the **P** called on his gods to
17:44 "Come on," the **P** told David,
17:45 David told the **P**, "You come to
17:46 the dead bodies of the **P** army
17:48 When the **P** moved closer in
17:48 battle line to attack the **P**.
17:49 and struck the **P** in the
17:50 to be stronger than the **P**.
17:50 struck down and killed the **P**,
17:51 David ran and stood over the **P**.
17:51 and made certain the **P** was
17:53 all the goods in the **P** camp.
17:55 David going out against the **P**,
17:57 returned from killing the **P**,
18:25 except 100 **P** foreskins so that
18:30 The **P** generals still went out
19:5 his life and killed the **P** Goliath,
21:9 "The sword of Goliath the **P**,
22:10 the sword of Goliath the **P**."
23:3 to Keilah against the **P** army?"
27:1 sure that I escape to **P** territory.
27:7 David stayed in **P** territory for
27:11 long as he lived in **P** territory.
28:5 Saul looked at the **P** army,
29:2 The **P** leaders were marching
29:3 The **P** officers asked,
29:3 Achish asked the **P** officers,
29:4 But the **P** officers were angry
29:4 the **P** officers told him.
29:7 to displease the **P** rulers."
29:9 However, the **P** officers said,
29:11 his men returned to **P** territory,
30:16 so much loot from **P** territory
31:9 sent men throughout **P** territory
2Sm 3:14 of 100 **P** foreskins for her."
5:24 of you to defeat the **P** army."
8:1 of the main **P** city from them.

2Sm 21:17 He attacked the **P** and killed
23:13 from the **P** army was camping
23:14 **P** troops were at Bethlehem.
23:16 men burst into the **P** camp
1Ki 15:27 assassinated him in the **P** city
16:15 near the **P** city of Gibbethon.
2Ki 8:2 family went to live in **P** territory
8:3 the woman came home from **P**
1Ch 10:9 men throughout **P** territory
11:16 **P** troops were in Bethlehem.
11:18 So the three burst into the **P**
14:15 of you to defeat the **P** army."
14:16 and his men defeated the **P**
Jer 47:4 Sidon any **P** who might have

Philistine's (2)

1Sm 17:54 David took the **P** head and
17:57 David had the **P** head in his

Philistines (199)

Gen 10:14 (from whom the **P** came),
21:32 went back to the land of the **P**.
21:34 a long time in the land of the **P**.
26:1 Abimelech of the **P** in Gerar.
26:8 King Abimelech of the **P**
26:14 the **P** became jealous of him.
26:15 So the **P** filled in all the wells
26:18 The **P** had filled them in after
Jos 13:2 belong to the **P** and Geshur.
Jdg 3:3 He left the five rulers of the **P**,
3:31 He killed 600 **P** with a sharp
10:6 and the gods of the **P**.
10:7 So he used the **P** and
10:11 the Ammonites, the **P**,
13:1 them over to the **P** for 40 years.
13:5 Israel from the power of the **P**."
14:3 woman from those godless **P**?"
14:4 to do something to the **P**.
14:4 time the **P** were ruling Israel.)
15:3 when I get even with the **P**,
15:6 Some **P** asked, "Who did this?"
15:6 So the **P** burned Samson's wife
15:9 The **P** came, camped in Judah,
15:10 The **P** answered, "We've come
15:11 you know that the **P** rule us?
15:12 up and hand you over to the **P**."
15:14 When he came to Lehi, the **P**
15:20 years during the time of the **P**.
16:9 the **P** are attacking!"
16:12 the **P** are attacking!"
16:14 the **P** are attacking!"
16:20 the **P** are attacking!"
16:21 The **P** grabbed him.
16:25 When all the **P** were enjoying
16:28 Let me get even with the **P** for
16:30 me die with the **P**," he said.
16:30 So he killed more **P** when he
1Sm 4:1 went to fight against the **P**
4:1 while the **P** camped at Aphek.
4:2 The **P** organized their troops to
4:2 As the battle spread, the **P**
4:3 "Why has the LORD used the **P**
4:6 As the **P** heard the noise,
4:6 The **P** found out that the
4:9 Be strong, **P**, and act like men,
4:10 The **P** fought and defeated
4:17 "Israel fled from the **P**," the
5:1 After the **P** had captured the ark
6:2 when the **P** called for priests
6:2 The **P** asked, "What should we
6:4 The **P** asked, "What kind of
6:12 The rulers of the **P** followed
6:16 the five rulers of the **P** saw this,
6:17 which the **P** sent as
6:21 "The **P** have brought back the
7:3 he will rescue you from the **P**."
7:7 When the **P** heard that the
7:8 Ask him to save us from the **P**!"
7:10 the **P** came to fight against
7:10 LORD thundered loudly at the **P**
7:11 left Mizpah, pursued the **P**,
7:13 power of the **P** was crushed,
7:13 The LORD restrained the **P** as
7:14 which the **P** took from Israel
7:14 by these cities from the **P**.
9:16 will save my people from the **P**
1Sm 10:5 where the **P** have a military
12:9 of the army of Hazor, to the **P**,
13:3 and the **P** heard about it.
13:4 become offensive to the **P**!"
13:5 The **P** assembled to fight
13:11 and the **P** were assembling at
13:12 So I thought, 'Now, the **P** will
13:16 the **P** camped at Michmash.
13:19 In this way the **P** kept the
13:20 in Israel had to go to the **P**
14:8 we'll cross over to the **P** and
14:11 The **P** said, "Look,
14:13 Jonathan struck down the **P**.
14:21 had been with the **P** before this
14:22 heard that the **P** were fleeing,
14:22 also pursued the **P** in battle.
14:30 We would have killed more **P**."
14:31 down the **P** from Michmash
14:36 "Let's attack the **P** tonight and
14:37 "Should I attack the **P**?
14:46 Saul stopped pursuing the **P**.
14:46 So the **P** returned to their own
14:47 the kings of Zobah, and the **P**.
14:52 warfare with the **P** as long as
17:1 The **P** assembled their armies
17:2 a battle line to fight the **P**.
17:3 The **P** were stationed on a hill
17:19 the Elah Valley fighting the **P**."
17:21 Israel and the **P** formed their
17:23 from the battle lines of the **P**.
17:51 When the **P** saw their hero had
17:52 and pursued the **P** as far as
17:52 Wounded **P** lay on the road to
17:53 back from their pursuit of the **P**,
18:6 from a campaign against the **P**.
18:17 Let the **P** do that.")
18:21 and the **P** will get him."
18:25 fall into the hands of the **P**.
18:27 out and struck down 200 **P**.
19:8 David went to fight the **P**.
23:1 "Did you know that the **P** are
23:2 I go and attack these **P**?"
23:2 told David, "attack the **P**,
23:4 you the power to defeat the **P**."
23:5 went to Keilah, fought the **P**,
23:27 The **P** are raiding the country."
23:28 David and went to fight the **P**.
24:1 back from ⌊fighting⌋ the **P**,
28:1 At that time the **P** had gathered
28:4 The **P** assembled and camped
28:15 The **P** are at war with me,
28:19 you and Israel over to the **P**.
28:19 Israel's army over to the **P**."
29:1 The **P** assembled their whole
29:11 while the **P** went to Jezreel.
31:1 When the **P** were fighting
31:1 the men of Israel fled from the **P**
31:2 The **P** caught up to Saul and
31:7 So the **P** came to live in these
31:8 The next day, when the **P**
31:11 heard what the **P** had done
2Sm 1:20 or the daughters of the **P** will
3:18 my people Israel from the **P**
5:17 When the **P** heard that David
5:18 The **P** had come and overrun
5:19 "Should I attack the **P**?
5:19 hand the **P** over to you."
5:20 and defeated the **P** there.
5:21 The **P** left their idols there,
5:22 The **P** again attacked and
5:25 and defeated the **P** from Geba
8:1 defeated and crushed the **P**.
8:12 Moab, Ammon, the **P**, Amalek,
19:9 and saved us from the **P**,
21:12 where the **P** had hung them the
21:15 battle between the **P** and Israel.
21:15 and his men went to fight the **P**,
21:18 battle with the **P** at Gob.
21:19 broke out with the **P** at Gob,
23:9 when the **P** gathered there
23:10 he attacked and killed **P** until
23:11 The **P** had gathered at Lehi,
23:11 the troops fled from the **P**,
23:12 and defended it by killing **P**.
1Ki 4:21 River to the country of the **P**
2Ki 18:8 He conquered the **P** from the
1Ch 1:12 (from whom the **P** came),
10:1 When the **P** fought against
10:1 the men of Israel fled from the **P**
10:2 The **P** caught up to Saul and
10:7 So the **P** came to live in these
10:8 The next day, when the **P**
10:11 everything the **P** had done
11:13 when the **P** gathered there
11:13 the troops fled from the **P**,
11:14 and defended it by killing **P**.
11:15 the army of the **P** was camping
12:19 David when he went with the **P**
12:19 David didn't help the **P**
14:8 When the **P** heard that David
14:9 The **P** had come and raided the
14:10 "Should I attack the **P**?
14:11 defeated the **P** at Baal Perazim
14:12 The **P** left their gods there,
14:13 The **P** again raided the valley.
18:1 defeated and crushed the **P**.
18:11 Ammon, the **P**, and Amalek.
20:4 broke out with the **P** at Gezer.
20:4 and the **P** were defeated.
20:5 fighting broke out with the **P**,
2Ch 9:26 River to the country of the **P**
17:11 Some of the **P** brought gifts and
21:16 The LORD prompted the **P** and
26:6 to wage war against the **P**.
26:6 and elsewhere among the **P**.
26:7 him when he attacked the **P**,
28:18 The **P** had raided the foothills
Isa 2:6 are fortunetellers like the **P**,
9:12 from the east and the **P** from
14:29 All you **P**, don't rejoice that the
14:31 Be frightened, all you **P**!
Jer 47:1 the **P** before Pharaoh defeated
47:4 has come to destroy all the **P**,
47:4 The LORD will destroy the **P**
Eze 16:27 to your greedy enemies, the **P**,
16:57 The daughters of the **P** also
25:15 The **P** have taken revenge with
25:16 to use my power against the **P**,
Amo 1:6 The **P** have taken all the
1:8 The rest of the **P** will die.
6:2 go to Gath, the city of the **P**.
9:7 Didn't I bring the **P** from Crete
Zep 2:5 you, Canaan, the land of the **P**:

Philistines' (3)

Jdg 15:5 the foxes in the **P** grain fields.
1Sm 14:32 troops seized the **P** belongings.
Zec 9:6 I will cut off the **P** arrogance

Philologus (1)

Rom 16:15 Greet **P** and Julia,

philosophers (2)

Act 17:18 Some Epicurean and Stoic **p**
17:18 The **p** said these things

philosophy (1)

Col 2:8 a shallow and misleading **p**.

Phinehas (28)

Exo 6:25 She gave birth to **P**.
Num 25:7 **P**, son of Eleazar and grandson
25:11 "**P**, son of Eleazar and
25:12 So tell **P** that I'm making a
31:6 from each tribe along with **P**,
31:6 **P** took with him the holy
Jos 22:13 The Israelites sent **P**,
22:30 When the priest **P**,
22:31 Then **P**, son of the priest
22:32 Then **P** (son of the priest
24:33 had been given to his son **P**
Jdg 20:28 (**P**, son of Eleazar and
1Sm 1:3 Eli's two sons, Hophni and **P**,
2:12 Eli's sons, ⌊Hophni and **P**,⌋
2:34 your two sons, Hophni and **P**,
4:4 Eli's two sons, Hophni and **P**,
4:11 Eli's sons, Hophni and **P**, died.
4:17 Your two sons, Hophni and **P**,
14:3 who was the son of **P** and the
1Ch 6:4 Eleazar was the father of **P**.
6:4 **P** was the father of Abishua.
6:50 Eleazar's son was **P**.

1Ch 9:20 (**P**, Eleazar's son, had been the
Ezr 7:5 who was the son of **P**,
8:2 from the family of **P**:
8:33 well as Eleazar, the son of **P**.
Psa 106:30 Then **P** stood between God
106:31 Because of this, **P** was

Phinehas' (2)
1Sm 4:19 **P** wife, was pregnant.
1Ch 6:50 **P** son was Abishua.

Phlegon (1)
Rom 16:14 Greet Asyncritus, **P**,

Phoebe (1)
Rom 16:1 this letter I'm introducing **P**

Phoenicia (4)
Mar 7:26 to be Greek, born in **P** in Syria.
Act 11:19 death went as far as **P**,
15:3 going through **P** and Samaria,
21:2 a ship that was going to **P**,

Phoenix (2)
Act 27:12 to reach the city of **P** somehow
27:12 (**P** is a harbor that faces the

phony (2)
Dan 2:9 to make up a **p** explanation
2Ti 3:13 But evil people and **p**

phrases (1)
Ecc 1:8 these sayings are worn-out **p**.

Phrygia (3)
Act 2:10 **P**, Pamphylia, Egypt, and the
16:6 went through the regions of **P**
18:23 the regions of Galatia and **P**,

Phygelus (1)
2Ti 1:15 including **P** and Hermogenes.

physical (22)
Lev 21:17 generations) has a **p** defect,
21:18 Indeed, no one who has a **p**
21:21 the priest Aaron has a **p** defect,
21:23 since he has a **p** defect.
22:20 Never bring any animal with a **p**
22:25 castration is a **p** defect."
Dtr 34:7 and he never lost his **p**
Jon 1:13 been born in a **p** way — from
6:63 Your **p** existence doesn't
Rom 6:12 never let sin rule your **p** body
1Co 4:12 ourselves out doing **p** labor.
15:44 It is planted as a **p** body.
15:44 As there is a **p** body,
15:46 but the **p** and then the spiritual.
Gal 6:12 deal out of a **p** thing are trying
Php 3:3 any confidence in **p** things,
3:4 in my **p** qualifications.
3:4 he can trust in something **p**,
Col 1:22 to God by dying in his **p** body.
Jas 2:16 for that person's **p** needs,
1Jn 2:16 world offers — **p** gratification,
Jud 1:19 are concerned about **p** things,

physically (8)
Nah 1:12 the people of Nineveh are **p** fit
1Co 5:3 Although I'm not **p** present with
2Co 12:2 to him **p** or spiritually.
12:4 to him **p** or spiritually.
Eph 2:11 once you were not Jewish **p**.
Col 2:5 Although I'm absent from you **p**
1Pe 4:1 Since Christ has suffered **p**,
4:1 has suffered **p** no longer sins.)

physician (1)
Col 4:14 My dear friend Luke, the **p**,

physicians (1)
Job 13:4 All of you are worthless **p**.

pick (41)
Exo 12:21 He said to them, "**P** out a lamb
Lev 19:10 time or **p** up fallen grapes.
25:11 grows by itself or **p** grapes from
Dtr 23:25 you may **p** grain by hand.
24:21 When you **p** the grapes in your
24:21 don't **p** all of them.
Jos 4:3 Order them to **p** up 12 stones
6:6 "**P** up the ark of the promise,
Jdg 1:7 cut off used to **p** up food under
2Ki 5:7 understand that he's trying to **p**
6:7 Elisha said, "**P** it up."
1Ch 21:11 the LORD says: 'Take your **p**:
Job 24:6 They **p** the leftover grapes in
30:4 They **p** saltwort from the
30:22 You **p** me up and let the wind
Pro 27:16 He can even **p** up olive oil with
Isa 10:15 stick cannot **p** up a person.
Jer 6:9 Thoroughly **p** through the
10:17 **P** up your bags. You are being
49:9 people come to **p** your grapes,
Lam 4:5 clothes now **p** through piles
Eze 29:5 No one will **p** you up or bury
Oba 1:5 people come to **p** your grapes,
Mat 7:16 "People don't **p** grapes from
9:6 **p** up your stretcher,
12:1 were hungry and began to **p**
16:24 **p** up their crosses,
Mar 2:9 up, **p** up your cot, and walk'?
2:11 **p** up your cot, and go home!"
2:23 they began to **p** the heads of
8:34 **p** up their crosses,
16:18 They will **p** up snakes,
Luk 5:24 **p** up your stretcher,
6:44 You don't **p** figs from thorny
9:23 **p** up their crosses every day,
Jon 2:16 sold pigeons, "**P** up this stuff,
5:8 up, **p** up your cot, and walk."
5:11 me well told me to **p** up my cot
5:12 is the man who told you to **p**
Act 9:34 Get up, and **p** up your cot."
20:13 we were going to **p** up Paul.

picked (33)
Gen 22:10 Next, Abraham **p** up the knife
42:24 Then he **p** Simeon and had him
Exo 10:19 It **p** up the locusts and blew
12:34 So the people **p** up their bread
Jos 8:3 Joshua **p** 30,000 of his best
Jdg 8:2 the grapes that Ephraim **p**
15:15 He **p** it up and killed 1,000 men
Rut 2:18 She **p** it up and went into the
1Sm 9:24 So the cook **p** up the leg and
17:40 He took his stick with him, **p**
2Sm 4:4 His nurse **p** him up and fled ⌊to
23:6 they cannot be **p** by hand.
1Ki 8:3 the priests **p** up the LORD's ark.
13:29 The old prophet **p** up the body
14:7 I **p** you out of the people and
2Ki 2:13 Then he **p** up Elijah's coat
4:20 The servant **p** him up and
6:7 reached for it and **p** it up.
13:16 So the king **p** up the bow.
2Ch 5:4 the Levites **p** up the ark.
Neh 2:1 I **p** up the cup of wine and gave
Psa 102:10 because you have **p** me up
Mat 14:20 When they **p** up the leftover
15:37 The disciples **p** up the leftover
Mar 2:12 immediately **p** up his cot,
6:43 When they **p** up the leftover
8:8 The disciples **p** up the leftover
Luk 5:25 up in front of them and **p** up
9:17 When they **p** up the leftover
Jon 5:9 well, **p** up his cot, and walked.
8:59 Then some of the Jews **p** up
Act 20:9 was dead when they **p** him up.
Rev 18:21 Then a powerful angel **p** up a

picking (4)
Psa 80:12 All who pass by are **p** its fruit.
Jer 6:9 Like someone **p** grapes,
Mic 7:1 like those **p** grapes.
Luk 6:1 His disciples were **p** the heads

picks (4)
Num 35:17 If any of you **p** up a stone as a
35:18 Or if any of you **p** up a piece of
Pro 31:16 "She **p** out a field and buys it.
Jer 6:9 Israel like someone **p** through

picture (2)
Lam 2:14 They painted a good **p** of you.
Eze 40:26 one **p** on each side.

pictures (11)
Eze 23:14 She saw **p** of men carved on
40:16 **P** of palm trees were carved on
40:22 and palm tree **p** were the same
40:26 **P** of palm trees were carved on
40:31 **P** of palm trees were carved on
40:34 **P** of palm trees were carved on
40:37 **P** of palm trees were carved on
41:18 there were **p** of angels and
41:19 These **p** were carved all
41:20 **P** of angels and palm trees
41:25 **P** of angels and palm trees

piece (58)
Gen 33:19 Then he bought the **p** of land
38:28 The midwife took a **p** of red
Exo 15:25 showed him a **p** of wood.
25:19 of mercy out of one **p** of gold.
25:31 hammered out of one **p** of gold.
25:36 be hammered out of the same **p**
27:2 out of one **p** ⌊of wood⌋ covered
30:2 made out of one **p** ⌊of wood⌋.
37:8 of mercy out of one **p** ⌊of gold⌋.
37:17 out of one **p** ⌊of gold⌋.
37:22 hammered out of the same **p**
37:25 made out of one **p** ⌊of wood⌋.
38:2 out of one **p** ⌊of wood⌋ covered
Lev 6:28 Any **p** of pottery in which the
11:33 falls into a **p** of pottery,
13:47 or red area on a **p** of clothing
13:52 He must burn the **p** of clothing
Num 5:17 will take holy water in a **p**
35:18 Or if any of you picks up a **p** of
Dtr 33:21 Indeed, a commander's **p** of
1Sm 2:5 themselves out for a **p** of bread,
2:36 so that I may eat a **p** of bread.'"
1Ki 17:11 bring me a **p** of bread too."
2Ki 3:19 to ruin every good **p** of land."
6:6 Elisha cut off a **p** of wood.
Job 2:8 Job took a **p** of broken pottery
33:6 was formed from a **p** of clay.
Psa 31:12 like a **p** of broken pottery.
Pro 28:21 on you even for a **p** of bread.
Isa 29:16 Can a **p** of pottery say about
30:14 No **p** will be big enough to
Lam 4:4 one will break off a **p** for them.
Eze 24:6 Empty the meat out of it **p** by
24:6 by **p** without choosing any
24:6 choosing any particular **p**.
Hos 4:12 A **p** of wood tells them what to
10:7 will be carried away like a **p**
Amo 3:12 rescues two legs or a **p**
3:12 of a bed or a **p** of a couch.
Hab 2:19 one who says to a **p** of wood,
Mat 7:3 So why do you see the **p** of
7:4 'Let me take the **p** of sawdust
7:5 will see clearly to remove the **p**
9:16 an old coat with a new **p**
Mar 2:21 an old coat with a new **p**
Luk 5:36 "No one tears a **p** of cloth from
6:41 "Why do you see the **p** of
6:42 let me take the **p** of sawdust
6:42 will see clearly to remove the **p**
24:42 gave him a **p** of broiled fish.
Jon 4:5 Sychar was near the **p** of land
6:7 for each of them to have a **p**."
13:26 one to whom I will give this **p**
13:27 after Judas took the **p** of bread,
13:30 Judas took the **p** of bread and
19:23 been woven in one **p** from top
Act 1:18 he bought a **p** of land where he
1:19 They even call that **p** of land

pieces (90)
Gen 15:17 passed between the animal **p**.
33:19 of Shechem, for 100 **p** of silver.
37:33 must have been torn to **p**!"
44:28 "He must have been torn to **p**!"
45:22 gave Benjamin three hundred **p**
Exo 29:17 Cut the ram into **p**,
29:17 with the other **p** and the head.

Lev 1:6 burnt offering, and cut it into **p**.
1:8 will also lay the **p**,
1:12 Then cut it into **p**. The priest
2:6 Break it into **p** and pour olive
6:21 Offer baked **p** of the grain
6:28 cooked must be broken into **p**.
8:20 When the ram was cut into **p**,
8:20 with the other **p** and the fat.
9:13 which was cut in **p** and
9:24 the burnt offering and the **p**
Dtr 32:26 I said that I would cut them in **p**
Jos 24:32 of Shechem, for 100 **p** of silver.
Jdg 5:30 and two **p** of colorful,
9:4 So they gave him 70 **p** of silver
16:5 will give you 1,100 **p** of silver."
17:2 were upset about the 1,100 **p**
17:3 So Micah gave the 1,100 **p** of
17:4 she took 200 **p** of the silver and
17:10 I'll give you ten **p** of silver a
19:29 cut her limb from limb into 12 **p**.
19:29 Then he sent the **p** throughout
20:6 concubine and cut her into **p**.
20:6 Then I sent the **p** throughout
1Sm 2:10 the LORD are broken into **p**.
11:7 a pair of oxen, cut them in **p**,
15:33 And Samuel cut Agag in **p** in
2Sm 16:1 100 **p** of ripened fruit,
1Ki 11:30 garment and tore it into 12 **p**.
11:31 He told Jeroboam, "Take 10 **p**
13:26 It tore him to **p** and killed him
13:28 nor had it torn the donkey to **p**.
18:23 cut it into **p**, lay it on the wood,
Job 34:24 He breaks mighty people into **p**
41:30 Its underside is like sharp **p** of
Psa 2:9 smash them to **p** like pottery."
7:2 a lion they will tear me to **p**
22:15 My strength is dried up like **p** of
27:2 closed in on me to tear me to **p**.
50:22 Otherwise, I will tear you to **p**,
68:30 humbles itself with **p** of silver.
Isa 7:23 vines (worth 1,000 **p** of silver),
24:12 Its gate is battered to **p**.
51:9 Didn't you cut Rahab into **p** and
Jer 5:6 the cities will be torn to **p**,
34:18 two and passed between its **p**.
34:19 between the **p** of the calf.
Lam 3:11 road I was taking, torn me to **p**,
Eze 13:11 stormy winds will break it to **p**.
13:19 of barley and a few **p** of bread.
16:40 you into **p** with their swords.
22:25 lions who tear their prey into **p**.
22:27 that tear their prey into **p**.
23:34 You will break it into **p** and tear
24:4 Cut the meat into **p**,
24:4 meat into pieces, all the best **p**,
30:16 Thebes will be broken into **p**,
Dan 11:4 kingdom will be broken into **p**
Hos 6:1 though he has torn us to **p**,
8:6 It will be smashed to **p**.
Mic 1:7 its idols will be smashed to **p**.
3:3 You break their bones to **p**
4:13 many nations into small **p**.
5:8 victims⌋ and tears ⌊them⌋ to **p**,
Nah 2:12 The lion tore its prey to **p** to
Zec 11:10 called Favor and broke it in **p**,
11:12 me my wages — 30 **p** of silver.
11:13 So I took the 30 **p** of silver.
11:13 I gave the **p** of silver to the
11:14 second staff, called Unity, in **p**,
Mat 7:6 them and then tear you to **p**.
14:20 they picked up the leftover **p**,
15:37 picked up the leftover **p**
Mar 6:41 He also gave **p** of the two fish
6:43 they picked up the leftover **p**,
8:8 picked up the leftover **p**
8:19 did you fill with leftover **p**?"
8:20 did you fill with leftover **p**?"
Luk 9:17 they picked up the leftover **p**,
Jon 6:12 "Gather the leftover **p** so that
6:13 gathered the leftover **p**
Act 23:10 that they would tear Paul to **p**.
27:41 of the ship was broken to **p** by
27:44 or some other **p** ⌊of wood⌋ from

pierce (10)

Exo 21:6 or the doorframe and **p** his ear
Num 24:8 and **p** them with arrows.
Dtr 15:17 Then take an awl and **p** it
Job 20:24 a bronze bow will **p** him.
40:24 Can anyone blind its eyes or **p**
41:2 through its nose or **p** its jaw
41:26 sword may strike it but not **p** it.
Psa 37:15 own swords will **p** their hearts,
Hab 3:14 You **p** the leader of his gang
Luk 2:35 And a sword will **p** your heart."

pierced (3)

Jdg 5:26 shattered and **p** his temples.
Psa 22:16 They have **p** my hands and
Rev 1:7 even those who **p** him.

pierces (2)

Job 30:17 At night God **p** my bones.
Pro 7:23 until an arrow **p** his heart,

pigeon (3)

Gen 15:9 a mourning dove, and a **p**."
Lev 1:14 sacrifice a mourning dove or **p**.
12:6 lamb for a burnt offering and a **p**

pigeons (13)

Lev 5:7 mourning doves or two **p** as
5:11 two mourning doves or two **p**,
12:8 two mourning doves or two **p**.
14:22 doves or two **p** (whatever
14:30 doves or **p** (whichever
15:14 two mourning doves or two **p**
15:29 two mourning doves or two **p**
Num 6:10 mourning doves or two young **p**
Mat 21:12 the chairs of those who sold **p**.
Mar 11:15 the chairs of those who sold **p**.
Luk 2:24 doves or two young **p**."
Jon 2:14 and **p** in the temple courtyard.
2:16 He told those who sold **p**,

pig's (2)

Pro 11:22 ⌊Like⌋ a gold ring in a **p** snout,
Isa 66:3 someone who ⌊offers⌋ **p** blood.

pigs (20)

Lev 11:7 You must never eat **p**.
11:7 (Because **p** have completely
Dtr 14:8 Also, you may not eat **p**.
Mat 7:6 dogs or throw your pearls to **p**.
8:30 A large herd of **p** was feeding
8:31 send us into that herd of **p**."
8:32 came out and went into the **p**.
8:33 Those who took care of the **p**
Mar 5:11 A large herd of **p** was feeding
5:12 "Send us into the **p**!
5:13 of the man and went into the **p**.
5:13 two thousand **p** rushed down
5:14 took care of the **p** ran away.
5:16 man and the **p**.
Luk 8:32 A large herd of **p** was feeding
8:32 Jesus to let them enter those **p**.
8:33 of the man and went into the **p**.
8:34 care of the **p** saw what had
15:15 was sent to feed **p** in the fields.
15:16 eaten what the **p** were eating.

Pi Hahiroth (4)

Exo 14:2 and set up their camp facing **P**
14:9 up their camp by the sea at **P**
Num 33:7 and turned back to **P**, east of
33:8 They moved from **P** and went

Pilate (76)

Mat 27:2 and handed him over to **P**,
27:11 in front of the governor, ⌊**P**⌋.
27:13 Then **P** asked him,
27:17 gathered, **P** asked them,
27:18 **P** knew that they had handed
27:19 While **P** was judging the case,
27:22 **P** asked them, "Then what
27:23 **P** asked, "Why? What has he
27:24 **P** saw that he was not getting
27:24 So **P** took some water and
27:26 Then **P** freed Barabbas for the
27:58 He went to **P** and asked for the
27:58 **P** ordered that it be given to
27:62 together and went to **P**.
27:65 **P** told them, "You have the
Mar 15:1 and hand him over to **P**.
15:2 **P** asked him, "Are you the king
15:4 So **P** asked him again,
15:5 so **P** was surprised.
15:6 At every Passover festival, **P**
15:8 The crowd asked **P** to do for
15:9 **P** answered them,
15:10 **P** knew that the chief priests
15:11 so that **P** would free Barabbas
15:12 So **P** again asked them,
15:14 **P** said to them, "Why?
15:15 **P** wanted to satisfy the people,
15:44 **P** wondered if Jesus had
15:45 **P** let Joseph have the corpse.
Luk 3:1 Pontius **P** was governor of
13:1 whom **P** had executed while
23:1 stood up and took him to **P**.
23:3 **P** asked him, "Are you the king
23:4 **P** said to the chief priests and
23:6 When **P** heard that,
23:7 When **P** found out that he was,
23:11 on him and sent him back to **P**.
23:12 So Herod and **P** became
23:13 Then **P** called together the
23:20 But because **P** wanted to free
23:22 A third time **P** spoke to them.
23:23 But the crowd pressured **P**.
23:24 **P** decided to give in to their
23:52 He went to **P** and asked for the
Jon 18:29 So **P** came out to them and
18:30 The Jews answered **P**,
18:31 **P** told the Jews, "Take him,
18:33 **P** went back into the palace,
18:35 **P** answered, "Am I a Jew?
18:37 **P** asked him, "So you are a
18:38 **P** said to him, "What is truth?"
18:38 After **P** said this, he went out to
19:1 Then **P** had Jesus taken away
19:4 **P** went outside again and told
19:5 **P** said to the Jews,
19:6 **P** told them, "You take him and
19:7 The Jews answered **P**,
19:8 When **P** heard them say that,
19:10 So **P** said to Jesus,
19:11 Jesus answered **P**,
19:12 When **P** heard what Jesus
19:13 When **P** heard what they said,
19:14 **P** said to the Jews,
19:15 **P** asked them, "Should I
19:16 Then **P** handed Jesus over to
19:19 **P** wrote a notice and put it on
19:21 of the Jewish people told **P**,
19:22 **P** replied, "I have written what
19:31 So they asked **P** to have the
19:38 the city of Arimathea asked **P**
19:38 **P** gave him permission to
Act 3:13 You handed Jesus over to **P**.
3:13 even though **P** had decided to
4:27 Pontius **P** made plans together
13:28 they asked **P** to have him
1Ti 6:13 testimony in front of Pontius **P**,

Pilate's (2)

Mar 15:43 boldly went to **P** quarters
Act 3:13 **P** presence, even though Pilate

Pildash (1)

Gen 22:22 Kesed, Hazo, **P**, Jidlaph,

pile (40)

Gen 31:46 took stones, put them into a **p**,
31:46 ate there by the **p** of stones.
31:47 it Jegar Sahadutha [Witness **P**],
31:48 Laban said, "This **p** of stones
31:51 "Here is the **p** of stones,
31:52 This **p** of stones and this
31:52 that I will not go past the **p**
31:52 that you will not go past the **p**
Lev 26:30 and **p** your dead bodies on top
Jos 7:26 They made such a large **p** of
8:29 of the city and made a large **p**
8:29 That **p** is still there today.
Rut 3:7 lay at the edge of a **p** of grain.
Ezr 6:11 be turned into a **p** of rubble.
Job 8:17 weave through a **p** of stones.

Isa 3:6 This **p** of ruins will be under
17:1 It will become a **p** of rubble.
17:11 will become a ⌊rotting⌋ **p**
25:10 is trampled in a **p** of manure.
30:1 They **p** sin on top of sin.
Jer 9:11 Jerusalem into a **p** of rubble,
22:5 will become a **p** of rubble.
26:9 and this city will become a **p**
26:18 will become a **p** of rubble,
46:19 a **p** of rubble where no one
49:2 It will become a **p** of rubble.
49:13 will become a **p** of rubble.
50:26 **p** up their corpses like piles of
Eze 24:5 **P** wood under the pot.
24:9 I, too, will **p** the wood high.
24:10 **P** it high, and light the fire.
29:9 a wasteland and a **p** of rubble.
29:10 turn Egypt into a **p** of rubble.
Mic 1:6 turn Samaria into a **p** of rubble,
1:7 will be turned into a **p** of rubble.
3:12 will become a **p** of rubble,
Nah 3:3 Dead bodies **p** up!
Hag 2:16 When anyone came to a **p** of
Zec 12:6 of Judah like a fire on a **p**
Luk 14:35 the ground or for the manure **p**.

piled (11)

Exo 8:14 They were **p** into countless
15:8 your nostrils, the water **p** up.
Jos 7:25 bodies and **p** stones over them.
Jdg 9:49 They **p** the brushwood on top
2Sm 18:17 and **p** a large heap of stones
2Ch 31:6 They **p** these holy things in
Ezr 9:6 Our sins have **p** up over our
Neh 13:15 They **p** the loads on donkeys
Isa 30:33 deep and wide and **p** high
Zec 9:3 It **p** up silver like dust and gold
Rev 18:5 Her sins are **p** as high as

piles (14)

Jdg 15:16 I've made two **p** of them.
2Ki 10:8 Jehu said, "Put them in two **p**
19:25 fortified cities into **p** of rubble.
Job 15:28 are doomed to be **p** of rubble.
27:16 like dust and **p** up clothing like
27:17 people will wear what he **p** up,
Isa 25:2 fortified cities into **p** of rubble,
37:26 fortified cities into **p** of rubble.
Jer 50:26 up their corpses like **p** of grain,
51:37 will become **p** of rubble.
Lam 4:5 now pick through **p** of garbage.
Dan 2:5 will be turned into **p** of rubble.
3:29 will be turned into **p** of rubble.
Hos 12:11 their altars will become like **p**

pilgrimage (5)

Exo 10:9 For us it's a **p** festival in the
12:14 this day as a **p** festival
13:6 The seventh day will be a **p**
23:14 you must celebrate a **p** festival
Num 28:17 this same month is a **p** festival.

Pilha (1)

Neh 10:24 Hallohesh, **P**, Shobek,

piling (1)

2Ch 31:7 month they started **p** them up,

pillar (14)

1Sm 14:5 One cliff stood like a **p** on the
1Ki 7:21 He set up the **p** on the right and
7:21 Then he set up the **p** on the left
2Ki 11:14 standing by the **p** according
23:3 The king stood beside the **p**
25:17 One **p** was 27 feet high and
25:17 The second **p** and its filigree
2Ch 3:15 and the capital on each **p** was
23:13 king was standing by the **p** at
Jer 1:18 an iron **p**, and a bronze wall.
52:21 One **p** was 27 feet high and 18
52:22 The second **p** was the same.
1Ti 3:15 the **p** and foundation of the
Rev 3:12 who wins the victory a **p**

pillars (40)

1Sm 2:8 "The **p** of the earth are the
1Ki 7:2 **p** supporting cedar beams.
7:3 supported by 45 **p** (15 per row).
7:6 Solomon made the Hall of **P** 75
7:6 was an entrance hall with **p**.
7:15 He made two bronze **p**.
7:16 bronze to put on top of the **p**.
7:18 After he made the **p**,
7:18 which were above the **p**.
7:19 The capitals on top of the **p** in
7:20 on the capitals on both **p**.
7:21 Hiram set up the **p** in the
7:22 capitals at the top of the **p**.
7:22 He finished the work on the **p**.
7:41 2 **p**, the bowl-shaped capitals
7:41 capitals on top of the 2 **p**,
7:41 capitals on top of the **p**,
7:42 bowl-shaped capitals on the **p**),
2Ki 25:13 broke apart the bronze **p**
25:16 The bronze from the two **p**,
1Ch 18:8 used it to make the pool, **p**,
2Ch 3:15 He made two **p** for the front of
3:17 He set up the **p** in front of the
4:12 2 **p**, bowl-shaped capitals on
4:12 capitals on top of the 2 **p**,
4:12 capitals on top of the **p**,
4:13 bowl-shaped capitals on the **p**),
Est 1:6 and marble **p** by cords made
Job 9:6 its place, and its **p** tremble.
26:11 The **p** of heaven tremble and
Pro 9:1 has carved out her seven **p**.
Jer 3:9 standing stones and wood **p**.
27:19 But he didn't take the **p**,
52:17 broke apart the bronze **p**
52:20 The bronze from the 2 **p**,
Eze 26:11 and your strong **p** will fall to the
40:49 **P** stood by the recessed walls,
42:6 They didn't have **p** like the
42:6 didn't have pillars like the **p**
Amo 9:1 Strike the tops of the **p** so that

pilot (1)

Act 27:11 was persuaded by what the **p**

pilots (1)

Jas 3:4 Yet, by using small rudders, **p**

Piltai (1)

Neh 12:17 Miniamin, from Moadiah, **P**;

pim (1)

1Sm 13:21 The price was a **p** for plow

pine (4)

Eze 27:5 all your boards from **p** trees
27:6 They made your deck from **p**
31:8 The **p** trees couldn't equal its
Hos 14:8 I am like a growing **p** tree.

pink (5)

Lev 13:19 is a white sore or a **p** area,
13:24 flesh of the burn turns into a **p**
13:42 But if there is a **p** patch on the
13:43 in back or in front is **p** like
Lam 4:7 bodies were more **p** than coral.

pinned (1)

Num 22:25 it moved over and **p** Balaam's

Pinon (2)

Gen 36:41 Oholibamah, Elah, **P**,
1Ch 1:52 Oholibamah, Elah, **P**,

pins (1)

Exo 35:22 **p**, earrings, signet rings,

pipes (1)

Zec 4:12 two golden **p** that are pouring

Piram (1)

Jos 10:3 King **P** of Jarmuth,

Pirathon (5)

Jdg 12:13 from **P** judged Israel.
12:15 he was buried in **P**,
2Sm 23:30 Benaiah from **P**, Hiddai from
1Ch 11:31 in Benjamin, Benaiah from **P**,
27:14 of the tribe of Ephraim from **P**,

Pisgah (8)

Num 21:20 Mount **P** overlooks Jeshimon.
23:14 of Zophim on top of Mount **P**,
Dtr 3:17 is near Mount **P** on the east.
3:27 Go to the top of Mount **P**,
4:49 foot of the slopes of Mount **P**.
34:1 He went to the top of **P**,
Jos 12:3 to the foot of the slopes of **P**.
13:20 Beth Peor, the slopes of **P**,

Pishon (1)

Gen 2:11 The name of the first river is **P**.

Pisidia (3)

Act 13:14 in Antioch, a city near **P**.
14:21 and Antioch (which is in **P**).
14:24 After they had gone through **P**,

Pispa (1)

1Ch 7:38 were Jephunneh, **P**, and Ara.

pistachio (1)

Gen 43:11 myrrh, **p** nuts, and almonds.

pit (72)

2Sm 18:17 threw him into a huge **p** in the
23:20 He also went into a **p** and
Job 9:31 plunge me into a muddy **p**,
17:14 if I say to the **p**, 'You are my
33:18 He keeps their souls from the **p**
33:22 Their souls approach the **p**.
33:24 them from going into the **p**.
33:28 my soul from going into the **p**,
33:30 turn their souls away from the **p**
Psa 7:15 He digs a **p** and shovels it out.
9:15 into the **p** they have made.
28:1 be like those who go into the **p**.
30:1 have pulled me out ⌊of the **p**⌋
30:3 those who had gone into the **p**.
30:9 blood is shed, if I go into the **p**?
35:7 reason they hid their net in a **p**.
35:7 they dug the **p** ⌊to trap me⌋.
35:8 their own **p** and be destroyed.
40:2 He pulled me out of a horrible **p**,
49:9 forever and never see the **p**.
55:23 people⌋ into the deepest **p**.
57:6 They dug a **p** to trap me,
69:15 or the **p** close its mouth over
88:4 with those who go into the **p**.
88:6 put me in the bottom of the **p**—
94:13 of trouble while a **p** is dug
103:4 rescues your life from the **p**,
140:10 Let them be thrown into a **p**,
143:7 be like those who go into the **p**.
Pro 1:12 good health who go into the **p**.
22:14 adulterous woman is a deep **p**.
23:27 A prostitute is a deep **p**.
26:27 Whoever digs a **p** will fall into
28:10 into evil will fall into his own **p**,
Ecc 10:8 Whoever digs a **p** may fall into
Isa 14:15 to the deepest part of the **p**.
14:19 down to the stones of the **p** like
24:18 of a disaster will fall into a **p**.
24:18 Whoever climbs out of that **p**
38:17 and kept me from the rotting **p**.
38:18 Those who go down to the **p**
Jer 18:20 They dig a **p** to take my life.
18:22 because they dug a **p** to catch
48:44 from a disaster will fall into a **p**.
48:44 Whoever climbs out of the **p**
Lam 3:53 They threw me alive into a **p**
3:55 your name from the deepest **p**,
Eze 19:4 caught him in their **p**,
19:8 him and caught him in their **p**.
28:8 They will throw you into a **p**,
31:14 died and gone down to the **p**.
31:16 who had gone down to the **p**.
32:18 who have gone down to the **p**.
32:23 in the deepest parts of the **p**.
32:24 who have gone down to the **p**.
32:25 who have gone down to the **p**.
32:29 who have gone down to the **p**.
32:30 those who went down to the **p**.
Jnh 2:6 brought me back from the **p**,

Zec 9:11 free from the waterless **p**
Mat 12:11 If it falls into a **p** on a day of
15:14 both will fall into the same **p**."
Luk 6:39 Won't both fall into the same **p**?
8:31 to go into the bottomless **p**.
Rev 9:1 to the shaft of the bottomless **p**.
9:2 the shaft of the bottomless **p**,
9:11 angel from the bottomless **p**.
11:7 bottomless **p** will fight them,
17:8 come from the bottomless **p**
20:1 the key to the bottomless **p**
20:3 threw it into the bottomless **p**.
20:3 shut and sealed the **p** over

pitch (6)

Exo 2:3 and coated it with tar and **p**.
Isa 13:20 Arabs won't **p** their tents there.
Jer 6:3 **p** their tents all around them,
Eze 25:4 camps and **p** their tents among
Dan 11:45 He will **p** his royal tents
Amo 5:20 It is **p** black, with no light.

pitch-black (2)

Job 3:4 "That day — let it be **p**.
28:3 the limit of the gloomy, **p** rock.

pitched (1)

Gen 26:25 He also **p** his tent in that place,

pitcher (1)

Ecc 12:6 the **p** is smashed near the

pitchers (6)

Exo 25:29 as well as **p** and bowls to be
37:16 and **p** to be used for pouring
Num 4:7 and **p** for the wine offerings.
1Ch 28:17 gold for the forks, bowls, and **p**,
Jer 35:5 Then I set cups and **p** filled
48:12 of its jars and to smash its **p**.

pitfalls (1)

Lam 3:47 Panic and **p** have found us,

Pithom (1)

Exo 1:11 They built **P** and Rameses as

Pithon (2)

1Ch 8:35 Micah's sons were **P**,
9:41 Micah's sons were **P**,

pitiful (1)

Rev 3:17 **p**, poor, blind, and naked.

pits (10)

Gen 14:10 of Siddim was full of tar **p**.
14:10 they fell because of the tar **p**,
1Sm 13:6 rocks, in **p**, and in cisterns.
Psa 119:85 Arrogant people have dug **p** to
Isa 24:17 Disasters, **p**, and traps are in
42:22 They are all trapped in **p** and
Jer 2:6 through a wasteland and its **p**,
48:43 Disasters, **p**, and traps are in
Lam 4:20 was caught in their **p**.
Zep 2:9 salt **p**, and ruins forever.

pity (59)

Dtr 7:16 Have no **p** on them,
13:8 Have no **p** on them.
19:13 They must have no **p** on him.
19:21 Have no **p** on him:
25:12 off her hand. Have no **p** on her.
28:50 the old and no **p** for the young.
Jdg 21:22 tell them, 'Have **p** on them,
2Sm 12:4 man thought it would be a **p**
12:6 he did this and had no **p**."
Job 19:21 "Have **p** on me, my friends!
19:21 Have **p** on me because God's
33:24 then he will have **p** on them
Psa 4:1 Have **p** on me, and hear my
6:2 Have **p** on me, O LORD,
9:13 Have **p** on me, O LORD.
25:16 Turn to me, and have **p** on me.
26:11 Rescue me, and have **p** on me.
27:7 Have **p** on me, and answer me.
30:10 and have **p** on me!
31:9 Have **p** on me, O LORD,
Psa 41:4 I said, "O LORD, have **p** on me!
41:10 Have **p** on me, O LORD!
51:1 Have **p** on me, O God,
56:1 Have **p** on me, O God,
57:1 Have **p** on me, O God.
57:1 Have **p** on me, because my
59:5 Have no **p** on any traitors.
67:1 May God have **p** on us and
72:13 He will have **p** on the poor and
86:3 Have **p** on me, O Lord,
86:16 and have **p** on me.
102:14 and they **p** its rubble.
109:12 Let no one show any **p** to his
119:132 Turn toward me, and have **p** on
123:2 our God until he has **p** on us.
123:3 Have **p** on us, O LORD.
123:3 Have **p** on us because we
140:6 your ears to hear my plea for **p**.
Pro 19:17 Whoever has **p** on the poor
Isa 13:18 they look with **p** on children.
26:10 the wicked are shown **p**,
27:11 Creator won't have **p** on them.
30:19 The LORD will certainly have **p**
33:2 O LORD, have **p** on us.
Jer 13:14 I will have no **p**, mercy,
15:5 No one will take **p** on you,
16:13 I will no longer have **p** on you.'
20:16 the LORD destroyed without **p**.
Lam 2:2 Jacob's pastures without any **p**.
2:17 tore you down without any **p**,
2:21 them without any **p**.
3:43 You killed without **p**.
Eze 24:14 I will not ignore you, **p** you,
Dan 4:27 and have **p** on the poor.
Joe 2:18 and he had **p** on his people.
Amo 5:15 God of Armies will have **p**
Zec 11:5 will have no **p** on them.
11:6 "I will no longer have **p** on
1Co 15:19 we deserve more **p** than any

plague (56)

Exo 5:3 may kill us with a **p** or a war."
8:2 I will bring a **p** of frogs on your
8:15 saw that the **p** was over,
9:3 the LORD will bring a terrible **p**
9:15 with a **p** that would have
10:17 this deadly **p** away from me."
11:1 "I will bring one more **p** on
30:12 Then no **p** will happen to them
Num 8:19 Then no **p** will strike the
11:33 struck them with a severe **p**.
14:12 I'll strike them with a **p**,
14:36 in front of the LORD from a **p**.
16:46 his anger; a **p** has started."
16:47 because the **p** had already
16:48 and the **p** stopped.
16:49 Still, 14,700 died from the **p** in
16:50 the **p** had stopped.
25:8 Because of this, the **p** that the
25:9 24,000 people died from that **p**.
25:18 on the day of the **p** caused by
26:1 After the **p** the LORD said to
31:16 experienced a **p** at that time.
Dtr 28:21 The LORD will send one **p**
28:61 of sickness and **p** not written
Jos 22:17 of that sin there was a **p**
1Sm 4:8 every kind of **p** in the desert.
6:4 rulers suffer from the same **p**.
2Sm 24:13 or should there be a three-day **p**
24:15 So the LORD sent a **p** among
24:21 Then the **p** on the people will
24:25 and the **p** on Israel stopped.
1Ki 8:37 During every **p** or sickness
1Ch 21:7 so he struck Israel ⌊with a **p**⌋.
21:12 days of the LORD's sword — a **p**
21:14 So the LORD sent a **p** on Israel,
21:17 punish your people with a **p**."
21:22 Then the **p** on the people will
2Ch 6:28 During every **p** or sickness
20:9 form of war, flood, **p**, or famine,
Job 27:15 him will be buried by a **p**,
Psa 78:50 He let the **p** take their lives.
106:29 and a **p** broke out among them.
106:30 and the **p** was stopped.
Isa 19:22 will strike Egypt with a **p**.
Jer 21:6 They will die from a terrible **p**.
Jer 21:7 in this city who survives the **p**,
21:9 will die in the war, famine, or **p**.
Eze 14:19 "Suppose I send a **p** into that
28:23 I will send a **p** against you and
Hos 13:14 Death, I want to be a **p** to you.
Zec 14:12 This will be the **p** the LORD
14:15 A similar **p** will also affect
14:18 The **p** the LORD uses to strike
Rev 11:6 the earth with any **p** as often as
16:21 cursed God because the **p**
16:21 of hail was such a terrible **p**.

plagued (3)

Dtr 28:27 boils that **p** the Egyptians.
Psa 73:5 They are not **p** ⌊with
73:14 I'm **p** ⌊with problems⌋ all day

plagues (49)

Gen 12:17 his household with terrible **p**
Exo 9:14 Now I will send **p** that will
Lev 26:25 I will send **p** on you and you
Dtr 4:34 He did this using **p**,
7:19 your own eyes the terrible **p**,
28:59 with unimaginable **p**.
28:59 will be terrible and continuing **p**
29:3 You also saw those terrible **p**,
29:22 see the **p** that have happened
Jos 24:5 and I struck Egypt with **p**.
Psa 91:3 traps and from deadly **p**.
91:6 **p** that roam the dark,
Jer 14:12 with wars, famines, and **p**."
24:10 send wars, famines, and **p** until
27:8 by wars, famines, and **p**,
27:13 die in wars, famines, and **p**?
28:8 and **p** against many countries
29:17 them wars, famines, and **p**.
29:18 with wars, famines, and **p**.
32:24 of wars, famines, and **p**,
32:36 and **p** it will be handed over to
34:17 "I will free you to die in wars, **p**,
38:2 will die in wars, famines, or **p**.
42:17 die in wars, famines, and **p**.
42:22 or **p** in the place where you
44:13 with wars, famines, and **p**.
Eze 5:12 One-third of you will die in **p**
5:17 I will send **p**, violence,
6:11 die in wars, famines, and **p**.
6:12 **P** will kill those who are far
7:15 and inside are **p** and famines.
7:15 be devoured by famines and **p**.
12:16 from wars, famines, and **p**.
14:21 famines, wild animals, and **p**.
33:27 and caves will die from **p**.
38:22 punish Gog with **p** and death.
Amo 4:10 I sent **p** on you as I did to
Hab 3:5 **P** follow after him.
Rev 6:8 people using wars, famines, **p**,
9:18 These three **p** — the fire,
9:20 survived these **p** still did not
15:1 with the last seven **p** which are
15:6 with the seven **p** came out
15:8 the temple until the seven **p**
16:9 has the authority over these **p**.
18:4 and suffer from any of her **p**.
18:8 For this reason her **p** of death,
21:9 full of the last seven **p** came
22:18 God will strike him with the **p**

plain (34)

Gen 11:2 they found a **p** in Shinar
13:10 Jordan **P** was well-watered like
13:11 the whole Jordan **P** for himself.
13:12 lived among the cities of the **p**,
19:17 and don't stop on the **p**.
19:25 those cities, the whole **p**,
19:28 and all the land in the **p**,
19:29 destroyed the cities on the **p**,
Exo 5:17 ⌊Just **p**⌋ lazy!" Pharaoh
Dtr 34:3 the Negev, and the Jordan **P** —
Jos 5:10 at Gilgal in the Jericho **p**.
2Sm 16:22 concubines in **p** sight of Israel.
1Ki 20:23 if we fight them on the **p**,
20:25 Then, if we fight them on the **p**,
2Ki 25:4 the road to the **p** ⌊of Jericho⌋.
25:5 up with him in the **p** of Jericho.
Neh 6:2 Hakkephirim on the **p** of Ono."

Isa 65:10 The Sharon **P** will be a pasture
Jer 21:13 on the rock in the **p**," declares
39:4 the road to the **p** of Jericho.
39:5 Zedekiah in the **p** of Jericho.
48:8 and the **p** will be laid waste as
48:21 come to all the cities on the **p**:
52:7 the road to the **p** of Jericho.
52:8 up with him in the **p** of Jericho.
Eze 3:22 said, "Get up, and go to the **p**.
3:23 I got up and went to the **p**.
Zec 4:7 you will become a **p**.
12:11 Rimmon in the **p** of Megiddo.
Jon 16:25 about the Father in **p** words.
16:29 "Now you're talking in **p** words
Rom 3:21 approval has been made **p**
2Co 10:7 Look at the **p** facts!
2Ti 3:9 stupidity will be **p** to everyone.

plainly (3)

Num 12:8 **p** and not in riddles.
Jon 10:24 you are the Messiah, tell us **p**."
11:14 Then Jesus told them **p**,

plains (37)

Num 22:1 on the **p** of Moab east of the
26:3 spoke to the Israelites on the **p**
26:63 number of Israelites on the **p**
31:12 of Israel at the camp on the **p**
33:48 and set up camp on the **p**
33:49 They set up camp on the **p** of
33:50 LORD said to Moses on the **p**
35:1 LORD spoke to Moses on the **p**
36:13 through Moses on the **p**
Dtr 1:1 River, on the **p**, near Suph,
1:7 go to everyone living on the **p**,
2:8 the road that goes through the **p**
3:17 Their land included the **p**
3:17 Sea of the **P** (the Dead Sea),
4:49 It included all the **p** on the east
11:30 who live on the **p** facing Gilgal,
34:1 Mount Nebo from the **p** of Moab
34:8 mourned for Moses in the **p**
Jos 3:16 the Sea of the **P** (the Dead Sea)
4:13 in front of the LORD to the **p**
8:14 They rushed out toward the **p**
11:2 the **p** south of Chinneroth,
11:16 of Goshen, the foothills, the **p**,
12:1 and all the eastern **p**.
12:3 It included the eastern **p** from
12:3 the Sea of the **P** (the Dead Sea)
12:8 foothills, **p**, slopes, desert,
13:32 Moses distributed on Moab's **p**,
18:18 side of the slope facing the **p**
18:18 the plains and down into the **p**.
1Sm 23:24 in the **p** south of Jeshimon.
2Sm 2:29 through the **p** all that night.
4:7 all night along the road to the **p**.
2Ch 26:10 herds in the foothills and the **p**.
Job 24:5 The **p** provide food for their
Jer 47:5 you people left on the **p**?
Zec 14:10 become like the **p** from Geba

plan (66)

Gen 11:6 Now nothing they **p** to do will
Num 14:41 Your **p** won't work!
Jdg 19:30 Form a **p**, and speak out!"
1Sm 7:7 heard about the Philistine **p**
2Sm 17:4 of Israel approved this **p**.
17:6 "Ahithophel has told us his **p**.
20:22 all the people with her clever **p**.
1Ch 28:19 the details of the **p** clear to me."
2Ch 30:4 assembly considered their **p**
Est 9:25 that the evil **p** Haman had
Job 21:16 (The **p** of the wicked is foreign
22:18 (The **p** of the wicked is foreign
Psa 21:11 Although they scheme and **p**
33:11 The LORD's **p** stands firm
35:4 Let those who **p** my downfall
56:5 thought is an evil **p** against me.
62:4 They **p** to force him out of his
83:5 agree completely on their **p**.
140:2 They **p** evil things in their
Pro 3:29 Do not **p** to do something
10:23 when he carries out an evil **p**,
12:20 in the heart of those who **p** evil,
14:22 Don't those who stray **p** what is
Pro 14:22 and faithful **p** what is good?
16:9 A person may **p** his own
Isa 5:19 Let the **p** of the Holy One of
14:26 This is the **p** determined for the
32:6 and their minds **p** evil in order
44:26 of his servant and fulfills the **p**
46:10 saying, "My **p** will stand,
46:11 I will call someone for my **p**
48:14 the LORD's **p** against Babylon.
Jer 18:23 know that they **p** to kill me.
19:2 there the things I **p** to do.
26:3 Then I'll change my **p** about the
26:13 LORD will change his **p** about
26:19 So the LORD changed his **p**
36:3 about all the disasters that I **p**
48:2 will **p** Moab's destruction.
51:11 of the Medes because his **p** is
Eze 11:2 these are the men who **p** evil
Dan 7:25 and **p** to change the appointed
11:27 The two kings will both **p** to do
Hos 7:15 Yet, they **p** evil against me.
Joe 2:14 reconsider and change his **p**
Mic 4:12 the LORD or understand his **p**.
Mat 22:18 Jesus recognized their evil **p**,
28:12 the leaders and agreed on a **p**.
Luk 7:30 rejected God's **p** for them.
Act 2:23 to death by a **p** that God had
5:38 I can guarantee that if the **p**
20:27 telling you the whole **p** of God.
23:15 Here's our **p**: You and the
25:3 The Jews had a **p** to ambush
27:13 thought their **p** would work.
27:42 The soldiers had a **p** to kill the
27:43 from carrying out their **p**.
Rom 8:28 has called according to his **p**.
9:11 so that God's **p** would remain
Eph 1:9 the mystery of his **p** to us.
1:11 Christ according to his **p**,
3:11 This was God's **p** for all of
1Ti 1:4 rather than promoting God's **p**,
2Ti 1:9 of his own **p** and kindness.
Heb 6:17 God wouldn't change his **p**.
8:5 everything based on the **p**

plane (2)

Gen 30:37 and **p** trees and peeled the bark
Eze 31:8 The **p** trees couldn't measure

planks (3)

1Ki 6:9 rows of cedar beams and **p**.
6:15 of the temple with cypress **p**.
Act 27:44 ordered the rest to follow on **p**

planned (46)

Gen 50:20 Even though you **p** evil against
50:20 God **p** good to come out of it.
Num 33:56 Then I will do to you what I **p**
Dtr 19:19 then do to him what he **p** to do
1Sm 18:25 enemies.'" In this way Saul **p**
2Sm 21:5 He **p** to wipe us out to keep us
2Ki 7:12 the Arameans had **p** for them.
19:25 I **p** it in the distant past.
1Ch 28:13 He **p** all the work done for
29:19 to build the palace I have **p**."
Est 2:21 became angry and **p** to kill
3:6 So Haman **p** to wipe out
Psa 10:2 in the schemes that he **p**.
Isa 7:5 and Remaliah's son have **p**
14:24 It will turn out exactly as I've **p**.
14:27 The LORD of Armies has **p** it.
23:8 Who **p** such a thing against
23:9 The LORD of Armies **p** this in
37:26 I **p** it in the distant past.
46:11 I have **p** it, and I will do it.
63:4 I **p** the day of vengeance.
Jer 2:33 You carefully **p** ways to look
4:28 I have spoken, and I have **p** it.
13:25 the destiny I have **p** for you,"
18:8 my plans about the disaster I **p**
Lam 2:8 The LORD **p** to destroy the
2:17 what he had **p** to do.
Mic 6:5 King Balak of Moab **p** to do
Hab 2:10 You have **p** disgrace for your
Zec 1:6 done to us what he had **p** to do.
Mat 22:2 of heaven is like a king who **p**
22:15 the Pharisees went away and **p**
Luk 22:22 the way it has been **p** for him.
Jon 11:53 Jewish council **p** to kill Jesus.
12:10 The chief priests **p** to kill
Act 9:23 the Jews **p** to murder Saul,
14:5 people with their rulers **p**
20:13 since he had **p** to walk
23:20 "The Jews have **p** to ask you
Rom 1:13 that I often **p** to visit you.
1Co 2:7 which God had **p** for our glory
2Co 1:16 Then from Macedonia I had **p**
Eph 1:10 He **p** to bring all of history to its
1:12 He **p** all of this so that we who
2Ti 1:9 Before the world began, God **p**
Heb 11:40 God **p** to give us something

planning (12)

Gen 27:42 himself by **p** to kill you.
Exo 32:12 'He was **p** all along to kill them
1Sm 23:9 David learned that Saul was **p**
Neh 6:2 They were **p** to harm me.
6:6 and the Jews are **p** to rebel.
Est 9:2 to kill those who were **p**
Job 18:7 and his own **p** trips him up.
Ecc 9:10 there is no work, **p**, knowledge,
Isa 19:12 of Armies is **p** against Egypt.
19:17 LORD of Armies is **p** against it.
Mic 2:3 I'm **p** a disaster to punish your
Act 23:21 More than forty of them are **p** to

plans (101)

Exo 21:14 becomes so angry that he **p**
25:9 furnishings exactly like the **p**
25:40 to the **p** you were shown
26:30 to the **p** you were shown
1Sm 20:13 If my father **p** to harm you and I
23:22 Please make more **p**,
2Sm 14:14 He never **p** to keep a banished
15:11 nothing about Absalom's **p**.
1Ki 6:38 to all its **p** and specifications.
2Ki 16:10 the altar and a set of detailed **p**.
1Ch 28:11 gave his son Solomon the **p**
28:12 He gave him **p** for the
28:18 He also gave Solomon the **p**
2Ch 2:14 and follow any set of **p** that will
32:3 and his military staff made **p** to
Ezr 4:5 carrying out their **p** throughout
Neh 4:15 their **p** from being successful,
Job 5:12 carrying out their **p** so that they
5:13 The **p** of schemers prove to be
10:3 you favor the **p** of the wicked?
17:11 My **p** are broken. My dreams
42:2 that your **p** are unstoppable.
Psa 2:2 Rulers make **p** together against
20:4 desire and carry out all your **p**.
31:13 made **p** together against me.
33:10 The LORD blocks the **p** of the
40:5 made many wonderful **p** for us.
50:19 Your tongue **p** deceit.
64:5 one another in their evil **p**.
83:3 They make **p** in secret against
90:13 Change your **p** about us,
106:45 rich mercy, he changed his **p**.
140:8 Do not let their evil **p** succeed,
146:4 On that day their **p** come to an
Pro 6:18 a mind devising wicked **p**,
15:22 Without advice **p** go wrong,
16:1 The **p** of the heart belong to
16:3 and your **p** will succeed.
19:21 Many **p** are in the human heart,
20:18 **P** are confirmed by getting
21:5 The **p** of a hard-working person
24:8 Whoever **p** to do evil will be
Isa 8:10 Make **p** for battle, but they will
19:3 I will unravel their **p**.
25:1 out your **p** from long ago.
29:15 who try to hide their **p** from
30:1 They carry out **p**, but not mine.
32:7 They devise wicked **p** in order
47:13 are worn out by your many **p**.
59:7 Their **p** are evil. Ruin and
65:2 They followed their own **p**.
Jer 4:14 Don't continue making evil **p**.
4:28 I won't change my **p**,
7:24 They followed their own **p** and
18:8 Then I will change my **p** about
18:10 Then I will change my **p** about

Jer	18:11	and make **p** against you.
	19:7	I will smash the **p** of Judah and
	29:11	I know the **p** that I have for you,
	29:11	They are **p** for peace and not
	29:11	**p** to give you a future filled with
	32:19	You make wise **p** and do
	42:10	I will change my **p** about the
	49:20	Listen to the **p** that the LORD is
	49:30	has made **p** against you
	50:45	Listen to the **p** that the LORD is
	51:12	The LORD will carry out his **p**
	51:29	The LORD carries out his **p**
Eze	16:43	Didn't you make wicked **p** in
	24:14	you, pity you, or change my **p**.
	38:10	and you will make wicked **p**.
	43:10	Let them study the **p**.
Hos	10:6	be ashamed because of its **p**.
	11:6	and put an end to their **p**.
	13:14	even think of changing my **p**."
Joe	2:13	to change his **p** about disaster.
Amo	1:3	I will not change my **p**.
	1:6	I will not change my **p**.
	1:9	I will not change my **p**.
	1:11	I will not change my **p**.
	1:13	I will not change my **p**.
	2:1	I will not change my **p**.
	2:4	I will not change my **p**.
	2:6	I will not change my **p**.
	7:3	changed his **p** about this.
	7:6	changed his **p** about this.
Jnh	3:9	God may reconsider his **p** and
Mic	2:1	invent trouble and work out **p**
	2:1	they carry out their **p** because
Nah	1:11	a person who **p** evil against the
Zec	8:14	I made **p** to destroy you,
	8:14	and I didn't change my **p**.
	8:15	So now I have again made **p**,
Mat	26:4	They made **p** to arrest Jesus in
Act	4:26	Rulers make **p** together against
	4:27	Pontius Pilate made **p** together
	4:27	They made their **p** against your
2Co	1:16	My **p** had been to go from the
	1:17	that I made these **p** lightly,
	1:17	you think that when I make **p**,
Jas	4:15	will live and carry out our **p**."

plant (112)

Gen	1:29	"I have given you every **p** with
	9:20	the first person to **p** a vineyard.
	47:23	**P** crops in the land.
Exo	9:22	and every **p** in the fields of
	9:25	and every **p** in the fields and
	10:12	Egypt and eat up every **p**
	10:15	tree or **p** anywhere in Egypt.
	12:22	Take the branch of a hyssop **p**,
	15:17	You will bring them and **p** them
	23:10	"For six years you may **p**
	23:16	harvested from whatever you **p**
Lev	19:19	Never **p** two kinds of crops in
	19:23	into the land and **p** all kinds
	25:3	Then, for six years you may **p**
	25:4	Don't **p** crops in your fields or
	25:11	Don't **p** or harvest what grows
	25:20	the seventh year if we do not **p**
	25:22	You will **p** ⌊again⌋ in the
	26:16	You will **p** your crops and get
Num	20:5	This is no place to **p** crops.
Dtr	6:11	and olive trees that you didn't **p**.
	11:10	There you used to **p** your seed,
	14:22	whatever you **p** in your fields.
	16:21	never **p** beside it any tree
	22:9	Never **p** anything between the
	28:30	You will **p** a vineyard,
	28:38	You will **p** many crops in your
	28:39	You will **p** vineyards and take
2Sm	7:10	people Israel and **p** them there.
1Ki	8:37	**P** diseases, heat waves,
	19:4	He sat down under a broom **p**
	19:5	and slept under the broom **p**.
2Ki	19:29	year you will **p** and harvest,
	19:29	plant and harvest, **p** vineyards,
1Ch	17:9	people Israel and **p** them there.
2Ch	6:28	**P** diseases, heat waves,
Neh	10:31	we won't **p** the fields or collect
Job	8:16	He is like a well-watered **p** in
	14:9	and grow branches like a **p**.
Job	30:4	of the broom **p** are their food.
Psa	107:37	They **p** in fields and vineyards
	126:5	Those who cry while they **p**
Ecc	3:2	a time to **p** and a time to pull
	11:4	watches the wind will never **p**.
	11:6	**P** your seed in the morning,
Isa	17:11	On the day you **p**, you will
	28:24	every day so he can **p**?
	28:25	cumin seed and **p** cumin?
	28:25	Doesn't he **p** wild wheat in
	30:23	you rain for the seed that you **p**
	32:20	Blessed are those who **p**
	37:30	year you will **p** and harvest,
	37:30	plant and harvest, **p** vineyards,
	41:19	I will **p** cedar, acacia, myrtle,
	44:14	Then they **p** cedars,
	65:21	They will **p** vineyards and eat
	65:22	They will not **p** and have
Jer	1:10	You will build and **p**."
	4:3	and don't **p** among thorns.
	12:2	You **p** them, and they take root.
	18:9	I may promise to build and **p**
	24:6	I will **p** them and not uproot
	29:5	**P** gardens, and eat what they
	29:28	**P** gardens, and eat what they
	31:5	Once again you will **p**
	31:5	Those who **p** them will enjoy
	31:27	"when I will **p** the nations of
	31:28	to build them up and to **p** them,"
	32:41	and soul I will faithfully **p** them
	35:7	Never build any houses or **p**
	42:10	I will **p** you and not uproot you.
	50:16	in Babylon to **p** or harvest.
Eze	16:7	I made you grow like a **p** in the
	17:6	The **p** sprouted and grew into a
	17:22	break off the highest twig and **p**
	17:23	I will **p** it on a high mountain in
	28:26	build homes and **p** vineyards.
Hos	2:23	I will **p** my people in the land.
	8:7	people of Israel **p** the wind,
	10:12	**P** righteousness, and harvest
Amo	5:11	You **p** beautiful vineyards,
	7:2	had finished eating every **p**
	9:14	They will **p** vineyards and
	9:14	They will **p** gardens and eat
	9:15	I will **p** the people of Israel in
Jnh	4:6	The LORD God made a **p** grow
	4:6	was very happy with the **p**.
	4:7	a worm to attack the **p** so that
	4:9	have to be angry over this **p**?"
	4:10	The LORD replied, "This **p**
	4:10	You didn't **p** it or make it grow.
	4:10	Yet, you feel sorry for this **p**.
Mic	6:15	You will **p**, but you won't
Zep	1:13	They will **p** vineyards,
Mat	6:26	They don't **p**, harvest, or gather
	13:3	A farmer went to **p** seed.
	13:27	didn't you **p** good seed in your
	15:13	He answered, "Any **p** that my
	15:13	did not **p** will be uprooted.
Mar	4:3	A farmer went to **p** seed.
Luk	8:5	"A farmer went to **p** his seeds.
	12:24	They don't **p** or harvest.
	17:6	and **p** yourself in the sea!'
1Co	9:7	Does anyone **p** a vineyard and
	15:36	The seed you **p** doesn't come
	15:37	What you **p**, whether it's wheat
	15:37	the form that the **p** will have.
	15:38	God gives the **p** the form he
Gal	6:7	Whatever you **p** is what you'll
	6:8	If you **p** in ⌊the soil of⌋ your
	6:8	But if you **p** in ⌊the soil of⌋
Rev	9:4	green **p**, or tree on the earth.

planted (101)

Gen	2:8	The LORD God **p** a garden in
	21:33	Abraham **p** a tamarisk tree at
	26:12	Isaac **p** ⌊crops⌋ in that land.
	26:12	times as much as he had **p**
Lev	11:37	fall on seed that is to be **p**,
	27:16	be based on the seed **p** on it.
	27:16	Ground **p** with 2 quarts of
Num	24:6	like aloes **p** by the LORD,
Dtr	20:6	If you have **p** a vineyard and
	21:4	land hasn't been plowed or **p**.
	22:9	This includes the crop you **p**
Dtr	29:23	Nothing will be **p**. Nothing will
Jos	24:13	olive groves that you hadn't **p**.
Jdg	6:3	Whenever Israel **p** crops,
Job	4:8	wickedness and **p** misery,
	31:8	else eat what I have **p**,
Psa	1:3	He is like a tree **p** beside
	44:2	but you **p** our ancestors
	80:8	forced out the nations and **p** it.
	80:15	care of what your right hand **p**,
	92:13	They are **p** in the LORD's
	104:16	cedars in Lebanon which he **p**,
	141:7	so our bones will be **p** at the
Ecc	2:4	I **p** vineyards for myself.
	2:5	I **p** every kind of fruit tree in
	3:2	a time to pull out what was **p**,
Isa	5:2	**p** it with the choicest vines,
	17:10	Instead, you have **p** the best
	19:7	and all the fields **p** beside the
	40:24	They have hardly been **p**.
	60:21	will be the seedling I have **p**,
Jer	2:21	I **p** you like a choice grapevine
	11:17	The LORD of Armies **p** you.
	12:13	My people **p** wheat,
	17:8	be like a tree that is **p** by water.
	45:4	I have **p** throughout the earth.
Eze	17:4	It **p** the twig in a city of
	17:5	from that country and **p**
	17:5	The eagle **p** the seedling like a
	17:7	from the garden where it was **p**.
	17:8	It was **p** in good soil beside
	17:10	It might be **p** again,
	19:10	that was **p** near water.
	19:13	Now it is **p** in the desert,
	31:4	the place where the tree was **p**.
	36:9	and you will be plowed and **p**.
	36:36	the ruined places and **p** crops
Hos	9:13	**p** in a pleasant place.
	10:13	You have **p** wickedness and
Hag	1:6	You **p** a lot, but you harvested
Mat	13:4	Some seeds were **p** along the
	13:5	Other seeds were **p** on rocky
	13:7	were **p** among thornbushes,
	13:8	But other seeds were **p** on
	13:8	thirty times as much as was **p**.
	13:19	away what was **p** in him.
	13:19	This is what the seed **p** along
	13:20	The seed **p** on rocky ground
	13:22	The seed **p** among
	13:23	But the seed **p** on good ground
	13:23	thirty times as much as was **p**."
	13:24	is like a man who **p** good seed
	13:25	his enemy **p** weeds in the
	13:31	seed that someone **p** in a field.
	13:39	The enemy who **p** them is the
	21:33	A landowner **p** a vineyard.
	25:24	harvest where you haven't **p**
	25:26	that I harvest where I haven't **p**
Mar	4:4	Some seeds were **p** along the
	4:5	Other seeds were **p** on rocky
	4:7	were **p** among thornbushes.
	4:8	But other seeds were **p** on
	4:8	times as much as was **p**."
	4:15	like seeds that were **p** along
	4:15	the word that was **p** in them.
	4:16	are like seeds that were **p**
	4:18	seeds **p** among thornbushes.
	4:20	Others are like seeds **p** on
	4:20	times as much as was **p**."
	4:31	It's like a mustard seed **p** in the
	4:32	However, when **p**,
	12:1	He said, "A man **p** a vineyard.
Luk	8:5	Some seeds were **p** along the
	8:6	Others were **p** on rocky soil.
	8:7	were **p** among thornbushes.
	8:8	Others were **p** on good ground.
	8:8	times as much as was **p**."
	8:12	like seeds that were **p** along
	8:14	The seeds that were **p** among
	8:15	The seeds that were **p** on good
	13:19	a mustard seed that someone **p**
	19:21	harvest grain you haven't **p**.'
	19:22	and harvest grain I haven't **p**.
	20:9	"A man **p** a vineyard,
Jon	12:24	produce anything unless it is **p**
1Co	3:6	I **p**, and Apollos watered,
	9:11	If we have **p** the spiritual seed

1Co 15:42 When the body is **p**,
15:43 When the body is **p**,
15:44 It is **p** as a physical body.
Jas 3:18 the peace **p** by peacemakers.

planting (4)
Gen 8:22 earth exists, **p** and harvesting,
Lev 26:5 grape gathering will last until **p**.
Mic 1:6 a place for **p** vineyards.
Luk 17:28 and selling, **p** and building.

plantings (1)
Isa 61:3 the **P** of the LORD,

plants (44)
Gen 1:11 vegetation: **p** bearing seeds,
1:12 vegetation: **p** bearing seeds,
1:30 I have given all green **p** as food
2:5 Wild bushes and **p** were not on
3:18 and you will eat wild **p**.
9:3 I gave you green **p** as food;
Exo 2:3 a basket made of papyrus **p**
2:3 set it among the papyrus **p** near
2:5 basket among the papyrus **p**
10:15 They ate all the **p** and all the
Dtr 29:23 There will be no **p** in sight.
32:2 like showers on green **p**.
2Ki 19:26 They will be like **p** in the field,
Job 40:21 It lies down under the lotus **p** in
40:22 Lotus **p** provide it with cover.
Psa 37:2 and wither away like green **p**.
105:35 They devoured all the **p** in the
144:12 be like full-grown, young **p**.
Pro 22:8 Whoever **p** injustice will
31:16 She **p** a vineyard from the
Isa 17:10 you have planted the best **p**
37:27 They will be like **p** in the field,
Jer 12:4 How long will the **p** in every
14:6 because they have no green **p**.
Dan 4:15 And let it get its share of the **p**
4:23 Let it get its share of the **p** on
Hos 9:16 of Ephraim are like sick **p**.
Amo 9:13 will catch up to the one who **p**.
Zec 10:1 showers for the **p** in the field.
Mat 13:5 The **p** sprouted quickly
13:32 it is taller than the garden **p**.
13:37 He answered, "The one who **p**
Mar 4:5 The **p** sprouted quickly
4:14 "The farmer **p** the word.
4:32 taller than all the garden **p**.
Luk 6:44 don't pick figs from thorny **p**
8:6 When the **p** came up,
Jon 4:36 So the person who **p** the grain
4:37 saying is true: 'One person **p**,
1Co 3:7 So neither the one who **p** nor
3:8 The one who **p** and the one
2Co 9:6 The farmer who **p** a few seeds
9:6 But the farmer who **p** because
Jas 1:11 scorching heat and dries up **p**.

plaster (5)
Lev 14:41 The **p** dust scraped off the
14:45 and all the **p** — must be torn
Dtr 27:2 stones and cover them with **p**.
27:4 and cover them with **p**,
Dan 5:5 wrote on the **p** wall opposite

plastered (3)
Lev 14:42 and the house must be **p** again.
14:48 in the house after it is **p** again,
Isa 44:18 Their eyes are **p** shut,

plate (13)
Num 7:13 He brought a silver **p** that
7:19 He brought a silver **p** that
7:25 brought his gifts: a silver **p** that
7:31 brought his gifts: a silver **p** that
7:37 brought his gifts: a silver **p** that
7:43 brought his gifts: a silver **p** that
7:49 brought his gifts: a silver **p** that
7:55 brought his gifts: a silver **p** that
7:61 brought his gifts: a silver **p** that
7:67 brought his gifts: a silver **p** that
7:73 brought his gifts: a silver **p** that
7:79 brought his gifts: a silver **p** that
7:85 Each silver **p** weighed 3 ¼

plateau (7)
Dtr 3:10 took all of the cities of the **p**,
4:43 were Bezer on the desert **p**
Jos 13:9 and the whole **p** from Medeba
13:16 and the whole **p** near Medeba.
13:17 and all its cities on the **p**,
13:21 included all the cities of the **p**,
20:8 Bezer on the desert **p** from the

plates (4)
Exo 25:29 Make **p** and dishes for the table
37:16 For the table he made **p**,
Num 4:7 presence and put on it the **p**,
7:84 12 silver **p**, 12 silver bowls,

platform (3)
2Ch 6:13 (Solomon had made a bronze **p**
6:13 He stood on the **p**,
Neh 8:4 on a raised wooden **p** made

platforms (3)
Eze 16:24 you built yourself **p** and illegal
16:31 You build your **p** at the head of
16:39 They will destroy your **p** and

platter (4)
Mat 14:8 of John the Baptizer on a **p**."
14:11 So the head was brought on a **p**
Mar 6:25 the Baptizer on a **p** at once."
6:28 he brought the head on a **p**

play (29)
Gen 4:21 He was the first person to **p** the
1Sm 16:16 us to look for a man who can **p**
16:17 find me a man who can **p** well
16:18 Bethlehem who can **p** well.
2Ki 3:15 me someone to **p** some music."
1Ch 15:16 They were expected to **p**
15:19 appointed to **p** bronze cymbals.
15:20 appointed to **p** harps according
15:21 were appointed to **p** lyres
Job 21:11 little children out ⌊to **p**⌋ like
40:20 and all the wild animals **p**
41:5 Can you **p** with it like a bird or
Psa 33:3 **P** beautifully and joyfully on
47:6 **P** music for him! Make music to
47:6 our king. **P** music for him!
71:22 I will give thanks to you as I **p**
81:2 **P** lyres and harps with their
137:5 hand forget ⌊how to **p** the lyre⌋.
Isa 11:8 Infants will **p** near cobras'
38:20 let us **p** stringed instruments.
Lam 5:14 men no longer **p** their music.
Luk 20:21 Besides, you don't **p** favorites.
Act 10:34 that God doesn't **p** favorites.
Rom 2:11 God does not **p** favorites.
Gal 2:6 since God doesn't **p** favorites.)
Eph 6:9 and he doesn't **p** favorites.
Col 3:25 God does not **p** favorites.
1Ti 5:21 I've told you. Never **p** favorites.
1Pe 1:17 and he doesn't **p** favorites.

played (10)
1Ch 16:5 Asaph **p** the cymbals.
16:6 and Jahaziel **p** trumpets all
16:42 and Jeduthun **p** trumpets,
25:3 the LORD as they **p** lyres.)
25:6 They **p** cymbals, lyres,
2Ch 30:21 They **p** the LORD's instruments
Mat 11:17 'We **p** music for you,
Luk 7:32 'We **p** music for you,
1Co 14:7 tell what tune is being **p**?
Rev 14:2 like the music **p** by harpists.

players (1)
Mat 9:23 He saw flute **p** and a noisy

playing (9)
Jdg 5:16 to the shepherds **p** their flutes?
1Sm 10:5 will be led by men **p** a harp,
2Ki 3:15 While the musician was **p**,
Psa 98:6 with trumpets and the **p** of a
Dan 3:5 and three-stringed harps **p** at
3:10 and three-stringed harps **p** at
3:15 and three-stringed harps **p** at

Zec 8:5 boys and girls **p** in the streets.
2Ti 2:5 prize only when **p** by the rules.

plays (3)
Dtr 10:17 He never **p** favorites and never
Psa 104:26 which you made, **p** in it.
Eze 33:32 musician who **p** an instrument.

plea (11)
1Ki 8:30 Hear the **p** for mercy that your
8:52 your eyes always see my **p**
8:52 people Israel's **p** so that you
2Ch 6:21 Hear the **p** for mercy that your
Job 13:6 and pay attention to my **p**.
Psa 6:9 has heard my **p** for mercy.
17:1 Hear my **p** for justice,
55:1 not hide from my **p** for mercy.
119:170 Let my **p** for mercy come into
140:6 your ears to hear my **p** for pity.
Jer 37:20 and accept my **p** for mercy.

plead (26)
1Ki 8:33 and **p** with you in this temple,
8:47 and **p** with you in the land
2Ch 6:24 and **p** with you in this temple,
6:37 and **p** with you in the land
Job 8:5 If you search for God and **p** for
9:15 I would have to **p** for mercy
16:21 But my witness will **p** for a
16:21 of Man will **p** for his friend!"
41:3 Will it **p** with you for mercy or
Psa 30:8 I will **p** to the Lord for mercy:
35:23 **P** my case, O my God and my
43:1 Judge me, O God, and **p** my
86:6 attention when I **p** for mercy.
119:154 **P** my case ⌊for me⌋,
142:1 I **p** with the LORD for mercy.
Pro 22:23 because the LORD will **p** their
23:11 He will **p** their case against
Isa 1:17 **P** the case of widows."
32:7 needy people **p** for justice.
Jer 7:16 Don't **p** with me, because I will
15:11 certainly make your enemies **p**
42:9 "You sent me to humbly **p** your
Lam 3:58 **P** my case for me,
Hos 2:2 "**P** with your mother;
2:2 with your mother; **p** with her.
Mic 6:1 **P** your case in front of the

pleaded (12)
Gen 42:21 troubled he was when he **p**
Exo 32:11 But Moses **p** with the LORD
Dtr 3:23 Then I **p** with the LORD:
Jdg 13:8 Then Manoah **p** with the LORD,
1Sm 12:19 All the people **p** with Samuel,
2Sm 12:16 David **p** with God for the child;
19:19 He **p** with the king,
2Ki 13:4 Then Jehoahaz **p** with the
Jer 18:20 I stood in your presence and **p**
Dan 9:3 I prayed, **p**, and fasted in
Hos 12:4 Jacob cried and **p** with him.
Heb 5:7 He prayed and **p** with loud

pleading (2)
Jer 3:21 It is the crying and the **p** of the
Dan 6:11 praying and **p** to his God.

pleads (1)
Isa 59:4 and no one **p** his case

pleas (4)
Psa 31:22 But you heard my **p** for mercy
116:1 my voice, my **p** for mercy.
130:2 ears be open to my **p** for mercy.
Isa 1:23 don't notice the widows' **p**.

pleasant (23)
Gen 49:15 is good and that the land is **p**,
2Sm 19:35 How can I tell what is **p** and
Psa 16:6 Your boundary lines mark out **p**
81:2 and harps with their **p** music.
106:24 refused ⌊to enter⌋ the **p** land.
133:1 See how good and **p** it is when
141:6 It will sound **p** ⌊to them⌋.
147:1 It is **p** to sing ⌊his⌋ praise
Pro 2:10 will be **p** to your soul.

Pro 3:17 ⌊Wisdom's⌋ ways are **p** ways,
15:26 but **p** words are pure to him.
16:24 **P** words are ⌊like⌋ honey from
22:18 It is **p** if you keep them in mind
23:8 and spoil your **p** conversation.
24:4 both precious and **p**.
Ecc 10:19 and wine makes life **p**,
Jer 3:19 children and give you a **p** land,
12:10 They've turned my **p** property
31:20 Is he a **p** child? Even though I
31:26 My sleep had been **p**.
Hos 9:13 planted in a **p** place.
Mic 2:9 my people out of their **p** homes
Zec 7:14 They have turned a **p** land into

please (211)

Gen 12:13 **P** say that you're my sister.
13:8 Abram said to Lot, "**P**,
18:3 "**P**, sir," Abraham said,
18:30 "**P** don't be angry if I speak
18:32 "**P** don't be angry if I speak
19:2 He said, "**P**, gentlemen,
19:7 "**P**, my friends, don't be so
24:14 I will ask a girl, 'May I **p** have a
24:17 "**P** give me a drink of water."
24:23 **P** tell me whether there is room
24:42 **p** make my trip successful.
24:43 "**P** give me a drink of water."
27:31 Then he said to his father, "**P**,
30:14 Rachel said to Leah, "**P** give
32:11 **P** save me from my brother
32:29 "**P** tell me your name."
33:10 **p** take the gift I'm giving you,
33:11 **P** take the present I've brought
34:8 **P** let her marry him.
37:6 "**P** listen to the dream I had.
37:16 **P** tell me where they're taking
40:14 and **p** do me a favor.
43:20 "**P**, sir," they said, "we came
44:18 up to Joseph and said, "**P**, sir,
44:33 Sir, **p** let me stay and be your
45:4 "**P** come closer to me,"
47:4 So **p** let us live in Goshen."
47:25 "**P**, sir, we are willing to be
47:29 **P** don't bury me here.
48:9 Then Israel said, "**P** bring them
50:4 "**P** speak directly to Pharaoh.
50:5 **P** let me go there and bury my
50:17 **p** forgive our crime,
Exo 3:18 **P** let us travel three days into
4:10 Moses said to the LORD, "**P**,
4:13 But Moses said, "**P**,
4:18 Moses said to him, "**P** let me
5:3 **P** let us travel three days into
10:17 **P** forgive my sin one more time.
21:8 If she doesn't **p** the master who
32:32 If not, **p** wipe me out of the
33:18 "**P** let me see your glory."
34:9 he said, "Lord, **p** go with us!
Num 10:31 Moses said, "**P** don't leave us.
12:11 So he said to Moses, "**P**,
12:13 the LORD, "**P**, God, heal her!"
14:19 **p** forgive these people's sins,
20:17 **P** let us go through your
22:6 **P** come and curse these
22:17 **P**, come and curse these
23:13 Then Balak said to him, "**P**
27:16 **P** appoint someone over the
32:5 **P** give us this land as our
Dtr 2:28 **P** let us go through,
3:25 **P** let me go over and see the
Jos 2:12 **P** swear by the LORD that
Jdg 4:19 Sisera said to her, "**P** give me
8:5 "**P** give me some food for the
9:2 He said, "**P** ask all citizens of
10:15 But **p** rescue us today!"
11:17 They said, '**P** let us go through
11:19 '**P** let us go through your land
13:8 with the LORD, "**P**, Lord,
13:15 "**P** stay while we prepare a
16:6 So Delilah said to Samson, "**P**
16:28 LORD, **p** remember me!
18:5 They said to him, "**P** find out
19:9 **P** stay another night.
19:23 **P** don't do anything so evil!
Rut 2:2 "**P** let me go to the field of
Rut 2:7 said, '**P** let me gather grain.
4:1 "**P** come over here and sit,
1Sm 2:36 '**P** appoint me to one of the
3:17 "**P** don't hide anything from me.
9:18 "**P** tell me where the seer's
10:15 Saul's uncle said, "**P** tell me
15:25 Now **p** forgive my sin and
15:30 Now **p** honor me in front of the
16:17 Saul told his officials, "**P** find
16:22 "**P** let David stay with me
19:2 **P** be careful tomorrow morning
20:29 David said to me '**P** let me go.
20:29 **p** let me go to see my brothers.'
20:36 "**p** find the arrows I shoot."
22:3 He asked the king of Moab, "**P**
23:11 LORD God of Israel, **p** tell me."
23:22 **P** make more plans,
25:8 **P** give us and your son David
25:24 **P** let me speak with you.
25:24 **P** listen to my words.
25:28 **P** forgive my offense.
26:8 **P** let me nail him to the ground
26:11 But **p** take that spear near his
26:19 **p** listen to my words.
28:8 He said to her, "**P** consult with
28:22 Now **p** listen to me.
30:7 "**P** bring me the priestly ephod."
2Sm 1:4 "**P** tell me." The man answered,
1:9 '**P** stand over me and kill me.
7:29 Now, **p** bless my house so that
13:5 '**P** let my sister Tamar come to
13:6 Amnon asked the king, "**P** let
13:7 "**P** go to your brother Amnon's
13:26 then **p** let my brother Amnon go
14:2 "**P** act like a mourner,
14:11 She said, "Your Majesty, **p**
14:12 The woman said, "**P** let me
14:18 The king said to the woman, "**P**
14:18 "**P** speak, Your Majesty."
17:5 Absalom said, "**P** call Hushai,
19:37 **P** let me go back so that I can
24:10 LORD, **p** forgive me because I
24:14 "**P** let us fall into the LORD's
24:17 **P** let your punishment be
1Ki 2:17 He said, "**P** ask King Solomon
3:26 She said to the king, "**P**,
3:26 **P** don't kill him!" But the other
8:28 Nevertheless, my LORD God, **p**
9:12 However, they didn't **p** him.
13:6 "**P** make an appeal to the
17:10 "**P** bring me a drink of water."
17:11 "**P** bring me a piece of bread
17:21 **p** make this child's life return to
18:43 "**P** go back to ⌊Mount Carmel⌋,
19:20 "**P** let me kiss my father and
20:32 '**P** let me live.'" Ahab asked,
2Ki 1:13 **p** treat my life and the lives of
2:2 Elijah said to Elisha, "**P** stay
2:4 Elijah said, "Elisha, **p** stay
2:6 Elijah said to Elisha, "**P** stay
2:16 **P** let them go and search for
4:22 "**P** send me one of the servants
5:8 **P** let Naaman come to me and
5:15 So **p** accept a present from
5:17 **p** have someone give me as
5:22 **P** give them 75 pounds of
5:23 Naaman replied, "**P** let me give
6:3 "Won't you **p** come with us?"
6:17 Then Elisha prayed, "LORD, **p**
6:18 "**P** strike these people with
7:13 One of his officers replied, "**P**
8:4 He said, "**P** tell me about all
9:12 **P** tell us." Jehu replied, "We
16:18 He did this to **p** the king of
20:3 "**P**, LORD, remember how I've
1Ch 4:10 "**P** bless me and give me more
21:13 "**P** let me fall into the LORD's
2Ch 6:19 Nevertheless, my LORD God, **p**
10:7 and try to **p** them by speaking
Ezr 5:17 Then **p** send us Your Majesty's
6:10 they can offer sacrifices that **p**
Neh 1:8 **P** remember what you told us
1:11 Lord, **p** pay attention to my
1:11 **P** give me success today and
9:37 and they do as they **p** with our
Est 1:8 this rule: Drink as you **p**.
Job 6:29 **P** change your mind.
10:9 **P** remember that you made me
13:6 **P** listen to my argument,
13:20 "**P** don't do two things to me so
17:3 **P** guarantee my bail yourself.
33:1 "**P**, Job, listen to my words and
34:9 do any good to try to **p** God.'
Psa 40:13 O LORD, **p** rescue me!
69:31 This will **p** the LORD more
116:4 LORD: "**P**, LORD, rescue me!"
119:108 **P** accept the praise I gladly
Pro 15:8 prayers of decent people **p** him.
Sos 1:7 **P** tell me, you whom I love,
Isa 29:11 can read, saying, "**P** read this."
29:12 read, saying, "**P** read this."
38:3 "**P**, LORD, remember how I've
38:14 O Lord! **P** help me!
58:13 of worship and doing as you **p**
Jer 10:24 me, O LORD, but **p** be fair.
27:5 I give it to anyone I **p**.
32:8 He said to me, '**P** buy my field
36:15 "**P** sit down, and read it to us."
36:17 Then they asked Baruch, "**P**
37:3 They asked him, "**P** pray to the
37:20 now, Your Majesty, **p** listen,
42:2 "**P** listen to our request,
Lam 1:18 **P** listen, all you people,
Dan 1:12 "**P** test us for ten days.
Hos 9:4 and their sacrifices won't **p** him.
Amo 7:2 "Almighty LORD, **p** forgive us!
7:5 I said, "Almighty LORD, **p** stop!
Jnh 1:14 the LORD for help: "**P**, LORD,
Mat 25:24 that you are a hard person to **p**.
Luk 4:6 and I give it to anyone I **p**.
14:18 I need to see it. **P** excuse me.'
14:19 well they plow. **P** excuse me.'
Act 24:4 **P** listen to us. We will be brief.
Rom 8:8 the corrupt nature can't **p** God.
1Co 7:32 about how he can **p** the Lord.
7:33 about how he can **p** his wife.
7:34 how she can **p** her husband.
10:33 I try to **p** everyone in every
Gal 1:10 Am I trying to **p** people?
1:10 If I were still trying to **p** people,
Eph 5:10 which things **p** the Lord.
6:6 you merely wanted to **p** people.
Php 2:13 desires and actions that **p** him.
Col 1:10 Then you will want to **p** him in
3:22 you merely wanted to **p** people.
1Th 2:4 We don't try to **p** people but
Tit 2:9 Tell them to **p** their masters,
Heb 11:6 No one can **p** God without faith.
13:16 kinds of sacrifices that **p** God.
Jas 2:3 say to him, "**P** have a seat."
1Pe 2:13 governments to **p** the Lord.

pleased (84)

Gen 6:8 the LORD was **p** with Noah.
45:16 and his officials were **p**.
Exo 33:12 and I'm **p** with you.'
33:13 If you really are **p** with me,
33:13 will continue to be **p** with me.
33:16 will anyone ever know you're **p**
33:17 because I am **p** with you,
Lev 26:9 and I will be **p** with you.
Num 14:8 If the LORD is **p** with us,
Dtr 21:14 you are no longer **p** with her,
24:1 her and she no longer **p** him.)
33:11 them with strength and be **p**
1Sm 18:5 This **p** all the people,
18:20 told about it, the news **p** him.
2Sm 15:26 'I'm not **p** with you,'
19:6 I think you would be **p** if
22:20 me because he was **p** with me.
1Ki 3:10 The LORD was **p** that Solomon
10:9 who is **p** with you.
1Ch 17:27 Now, you were **p** to bless my
28:4 my father's sons he was **p**
2Ch 9:8 who is **p** with you.
Neh 12:44 The people of Judah were **p**
Est 1:8 to let everyone do as he **p**.)
2:9 The young woman **p** him and
9:5 and doing whatever they **p** to
Job 22:3 Is the Almighty **p** when you are
33:26 who will be **p** with them.
Psa 18:19 me because he was **p** with me.

Psa 22:8 him since he is **p** with him!"
40:6 You were not **p** with sacrifices
41:11 I know that you are **p** with me.
44:3 because you were **p** with them.
51:16 are not **p** with burnt offerings.
51:19 Then you will be **p** with
147:10 nor is he **p** by brave soldiers.
147:11 The LORD is **p** with those who
Pro 3:12 a son with whom he is **p**.
24:25 But people will be **p** with those
Isa 1:11 I'm not **p** with the blood of bulls,
42:1 with whom I am **p**.
42:21 The LORD is **p** because he
57:6 you think I am **p** with all this?
Jer 6:20 I'm not **p** with your sacrifices.
14:12 I won't be **p** with them.
Dan 4:2 I am **p** to write to you about the
8:4 It did anything it **p** and
Amo 5:21 I'm not **p** with your religious
Mic 6:7 Will the LORD be **p** with
Hag 1:8 I will be **p** with it, and I will be
Mal 1:10 I'm not **p** with you,"
2:17 He is **p** with them,"
Mat 3:17 my Son with whom I am **p**."
11:26 Yes, Father, this is what **p** you.
17:5 I love and with whom I am **p**.
17:12 people treated him as they **p**
Mar 1:11 whom I love. I am **p** with you."
9:13 people treated him as they **p**,
14:11 They were **p** to hear what
Luk 3:22 whom I love. I am **p** with you."
10:21 Yes, Father, this is what **p** you.
12:32 Your Father is **p** to give you the
22:5 They were **p** and agreed to
23:8 Herod was very **p** to see Jesus.
Jon 8:56 Your father Abraham was **p** to
Act 5:4 you could have done as you **p**
6:5 The suggestion **p** the whole
11:23 he arrived there, he was **p**
12:3 he saw how this **p** the Jews,
13:48 who were not Jews were **p**
14:16 all people to live as they **p**.
15:31 they were **p** with the
24:10 So I'm **p** to present my case to
1Co 10:5 Yet, God was not **p** with most
2Co 7:13 we were especially **p** to see
7:16 I'm **p** that I can be confident
Gal 1:15 me by his kindness, was **p**
Php 4:18 and with which he is **p**.
Col 1:19 God was **p** to have all of
1:20 God was also **p** to bring
Heb 10:38 I will not be **p** with him."
11:5 God was **p** with him.
1Pe 2:19 God is **p** if a person is aware of
2:20 God is **p** with you.

pleases (26)

2Sm 23:5 everything that **p** me.
Ezr 5:17 If it **p** Your Majesty,
Neh 2:5 "If it **p** Your Majesty,
2:7 "If it **p** Your Majesty,
Est 1:19 If it **p** you, Your Majesty,
2:4 the young woman who **p** you,
5:4 Esther answered, "If it **p** you,
5:8 and if it **p** you, Your Majesty,
7:3 and if it **p** you, Your Majesty,
8:5 said, "Your Majesty, if it **p** you,
9:13 Esther said, "If it **p** you,
Ecc 2:26 and joy to anyone who **p** him.
2:26 over to the person who **p** God.
7:26 Whoever **p** God will escape
8:3 he can do whatever he **p**.
Isa 56:4 choose what **p** me,
Jer 9:24 This kind of bragging **p** me,
Dan 11:3 a vast empire and do as he **p**.
11:16 The invader will do as he **p**,
11:36 "The king will do as he **p**.
Jon 3:8 The wind blows wherever it **p**.
8:29 I always do what **p** him."
1Ti 2:3 is good and **p** God our Savior.
2Ti 2:4 This **p** his commanding officer.
Heb 12:28 and awe in a way that **p** him.
1Jn 3:22 and do what **p** him.

pleasing (17)

Neh 2:18 another to begin this God-**p** work
Est 8:5 reasonable and if I am **p** to you,
Psa 51:17 The sacrifice **p** to God is a
104:34 May my thoughts be **p** to him.
Pro 11:1 accurate weights are **p** to him.
16:7 When a person's ways are **p** to
Sos 1:16 my beloved, so **p** to me!
Eze 20:41 as if you were a **p** sacrifice.
Mal 3:4 Judah and Jerusalem will be **p**
Rom 12:1 dedicated to God and **p** to him.
12:2 what is good, **p**, and perfect.
14:18 Christ with this in mind is **p**
2Co 5:9 our goal is to be **p** to him.
Col 3:20 This is **p** to the Lord.
1Ti 5:4 This is **p** in God's sight.
1Th 4:1 to excel in living a God-**p** life
Heb 13:21 Christ to do what is **p** to him.

pleasure (21)

Gen 34:19 said because he took such **p**
2Ch 15:15 They took great **p** in looking for
Psa 5:4 who takes **p** in wickedness.
36:8 drink from the river of your **p**.
149:4 because the LORD takes **p** in
Pro 21:17 Whoever loves **p** will become
Ecc 2:1 I want to experiment with **p**
2:2 What does **p** accomplish?"
2:10 myself to have any **p** I wanted,
2:10 since I found **p** in my work.
12:1 "I have found no **p** in them."
Isa 47:8 listen to this, you lover of **p**.
57:8 a deal with those you have **p**
Eze 16:37 lovers with whom you found **p**.
Jon 5:35 you enjoyed the **p** of his light.
Rom 7:22 I take **p** in God's standards in
1Ti 5:6 But the widow who lives for **p**
2Ti 3:4 will love **p** rather than God.
Jas 4:3 wrong reason — for your own **p**.
5:5 You have lived in luxury and **p**
2Pe 2:13 They take **p** in holding wild

pleasures (7)

Psa 16:11 **P** are by your side forever.
Ecc 2:8 singers and the **p** men have
Mat 13:22 of life and the deceitful **p**
Mar 4:19 the deceitful **p** of riches,
Luk 8:14 and **p** of life choke them.
Tit 3:3 to many kinds of lusts and **p**.
Heb 11:25 rather than to enjoy the **p**

pledge (8)

Jos 2:14 "We **p** our lives for your lives.
1Sm 18:3 So Jonathan made a **p** of
22:8 my son entered into a loyalty **p**
23:18 Both of them made a **p** in the
2Ch 29:10 Now I intend to make a **p** to the
Ezr 10:19 They shook hands as a **p** that
Psa 50:5 people who have made a **p**
Pro 6:1 for your neighbor or **p** yourself

pledged (4)

1Ch 29:24 David's sons **p** their loyalty
Psa 119:132 have pity on me as you have **p**
Eze 17:18 and the treaty that he **p** to keep.
Act 5:2 of the money ⌊they had **p**⌋

pledges (4)

Psa 144:8 Their right hands take false **p**.
144:11 Their right hands take false **p**.
Rom 9:4 glory, the **p**, Moses' Teachings,
Eph 2:12 and the **p** ⌊God made in his⌋

Pleiades (3)

Job 9:9 Ursa Major, Orion, and the **P**,
38:31 chains of the ⌊constellation⌋ **P**
Amo 5:8 ⌊constellations⌋ **P** and Orion.

plentiful (6)

Dtr 33:16 and the most **p** crops of the
1Ki 10:27 and he made cedars as **p** as fig
2Ch 1:15 and he made cedars as **p** as fig
9:27 and he made cedars as **p** as fig
Pro 14:4 of an ox produces **p** harvests.
Jon 3:23 Water was **p** there.

plenty (44)

Gen 24:25 We have **p** of straw and feed
27:28 and **p** of fresh grain and new
34:21 Look, there's **p** of room in this
41:29 coming when there will be **p**
41:30 will forget that there was **p**
41:31 that there once was **p**
41:53 seven years when there was **p**
Exo 3:8 that land to a good land with **p**
Num 24:7 their crops will have **p** of water.
Dtr 28:11 will give you **p** of blessings:
1Ch 12:40 There was **p** of flour,
2Ch 2:9 They'll prepare **p** of lumber for
31:5 the Israelites brought **p** of
31:10 wanted to eat and **p** to spare.
32:4 of Assyria find **p** of water?"
32:5 and made **p** of weapons and
Neh 9:25 and **p** of fruit trees.
Est 1:7 The king also provided **p** of
Psa 68:9 watered the land with **p** of rain,
72:16 May there be **p** of grain in the
78:15 He gave them **p** to drink,
78:25 and God sent them **p** of food.
107:9 He gave **p** to drink to those
Pro 12:11 his land will have **p** to eat,
13:11 gathers little by little has **p**.
20:13 and you will have **p** to eat.
20:15 There are gold and **p** of jewels,
28:19 his land will have **p** to eat.
28:19 dreams will have **p** of nothing.
Isa 23:18 LORD so that they will have **p**
30:33 and wide and piled high with **p**
33:16 He will have **p** of food and a
57:9 oils and put on **p** of perfume.
Jer 44:17 We had **p** to eat then,
Eze 16:49 were proud that they had **p**
17:5 where there was **p** of water.
17:8 planted in good soil beside **p**
19:10 because there was **p** of water.
Dan 4:12 beautiful leaves and **p** of fruit,
4:21 beautiful leaves and **p** of fruit,
Hos 2:8 I gave her **p** of silver and gold,
Joe 2:22 There are **p** of figs and grapes.
2:26 You will have **p** to eat,
Jon 6:10 The people had **p** of grass to

plight (1)

Psa 22:24 or been disgusted with the **p**

plot (18)

Gen 37:21 to save Joseph from their **p**.
Jos 24:32 They were placed in the **p** of
24:32 The **p** was inherited by
1Sm 22:13 and Jesse's son **p** against me?
1Ki 16:20 about Zimri and his **p** written
Est 8:3 to undo the evil **p** of Haman,
8:5 orders ⌊concerning⌋ the **p**
Job 21:27 the schemes you **p** against me
Psa 71:10 They watch me as they **p** to
83:3 and **p** together against those
106:43 but they continued to **p**
119:23 influential people **p** against me,
Pro 24:2 their minds **p** violence,
Jer 11:18 The LORD revealed their **p** to
18:18 "Let's **p** against Jeremiah,
Act 9:24 but Saul was told about their **p**.
23:13 forty men took part in this **p**.
23:30 there was a **p** against this man,

plots (11)

Neh 4:15 that we knew about their **p**
Psa 2:1 their people devise useless **p**?
37:12 The wicked person **p** against a
64:2 from the secret **p** of criminals,
119:150 Those who carry out **p** against
Pro 14:17 a person who **p** evil is hated.
16:27 A worthless person **p** trouble,
Jer 6:19 It is the result of their own **p**,
Lam 3:60 all their **p** against me.
3:61 all their **p** against me.
Act 4:25 their people devise useless **p**?

plotted (26)

Gen 37:18 them, they **p** to kill him.
Num 25:18 They **p** to trick you in the
1Ki 15:27 of Issachar, **p** against Nadab.
16:9 Elah's chariots, **p** against him.
16:16 heard that Zimri had **p** ⌊against

2Ki 9:14 of Nimshi, **p** against Joram.
10:9 I **p** against my master and
12:20 His own officials **p** against him
14:19 in Jerusalem **p** against him,
15:10 **p** against Zechariah,
15:25 son of Remaliah, **p** against him.
15:30 son of Elah, **p** against Pekah,
21:23 Amon's officials **p** against him
21:24 who had **p** against King Amon.
2Ch 24:21 But they **p** against Zechariah,
24:25 His own officials **p** against him
25:27 in Jerusalem **p** against him.
33:24 His officials **p** against him and
33:25 who had **p** against King Amon.
Neh 4:8 All of them **p** to attack
Est 6:2 had **p** a rebellion against King
9:24 had **p** against the Jews to
9:25 that the evil plan Haman had **p**
Mat 12:14 left and **p** to kill Jesus.
Mar 3:6 immediately **p** to kill Jesus.
Act 20:19 when the Jews **p** against me.

plotting (7)

1Sm 22:8 All of you are **p** against me,
Psa 31:13 They were **p** to take my life.
Pro 16:30 eye is **p** something devious.
Isa 33:15 to those who are **p** murders.
Jer 11:19 that they were **p** against me.
Amo 7:10 It read, "Amos is **p** against you
Act 20:3 found out that the Jews were **p**

plow (14)

Dtr 22:10 Never **p** with an ox and a
Jdg 14:18 you hadn't used my cow to **p**,
1Sm 8:12 to **p** his ground and harvest his
13:20 to sharpen the blade of his **p**,
13:21 The price was a pim for **p**
Job 39:10 or will it **p** the valleys behind
Psa 129:3 back ⌊like farmers **p** fields⌋.
Pro 13:23 When poor people are able to **p**,
20:4 A lazy person does not **p** in the
Jer 4:3 **P** your unplowed fields,
Hos 10:11 Judah must **p**. Jacob must break
Amo 6:12 Does a farmer **p** the sea with
Luk 9:62 "Whoever starts to **p** and looks
14:19 way to see how well they **p**.

plowblades (3)

Isa 2:4 will hammer their swords into **p**
Joe 3:10 Hammer your **p** into swords
Mic 4:3 will hammer their swords into **p**

plowed (9)

Dtr 21:4 land hasn't been **p** or planted.
Job 4:8 Whenever I saw those who **p**
Psa 65:10 You drench **p** fields ⌊with rain⌋
129:3 They have **p** my back ⌊like
Jer 26:18 Zion will be **p** like a field,
Eze 36:9 and you will be **p** and planted.
36:34 The wasteland will be **p**.
Hos 12:11 piles of rubble beside a **p** field.
Mic 3:12 Zion will be **p** like a field,

plowing (6)

Gen 45:6 years without **p** or harvesting.
Exo 34:21 Even during the time of **p** or
1Ki 19:19 Elisha was **p** behind 12 pairs
Job 1:14 "While the oxen were **p** and
Isa 28:24 Does a farmer go on **p** every
Luk 17:7 has a servant who is **p** fields

plows (3)

Psa 141:7 As someone **p** and breaks up
Amo 9:13 when the one who **p** will catch
1Co 9:10 so that the person who **p**

pluck (1)

Isa 50:6 to those who **p** hairs out

plucked (3)

Gen 8:11 beak was a freshly **p** olive leaf.
Pro 30:17 mother will be **p** out by ravens
Dan 7:4 until its wings were **p** off

plug (1)

Isa 6:10 **P** their ears. Shut their eyes.

plugged (1)

Jer 6:10 Their ears are **p**, and they

plumb (8)

2Ki 21:13 for Samaria and the **p** line used
Isa 28:17 line and righteousness a **p** line.
34:11 line of chaos and the **p** line
Amo 7:7 built with the use of a **p** line,
7:7 and he had a **p** line in his hand.
7:8 I answered, "A **p** line."
7:8 "I'm going to hold a **p** line in the
Zec 4:10 when they see the **p** line

plunder (1)

Gen 49:27 the evening he divides the **p**."

plunge (1)

Job 9:31 then you would **p** me into a

plunged (4)

Jdg 3:21 and **p** it into Eglon's belly.
2Sm 18:14 and **p** them into Absalom's
Psa 107:26 They **p** into the depths.
Rom 1:21 minds were **p** into darkness.

plus (8)

Exo 12:37 **p** all the women and children.
Lev 5:16 you used **p** one-fifth more.
6:5 it back in full **p** one-fifth more.
27:13 its full value **p** one-fifth more.
27:15 its full value **p** one-fifth more.
27:19 its full value **p** one-fifth more.
27:27 its full value **p** one-fifth more.
Neh 5:15 food and wine **p** one pound

p.m. (3)

Mat 20:5 out again about noon and 3 **p**.
20:6 About 5 **p**. he went out and
20:9 who started working about 5 **p**.

Pochereth Hazzebaim (2)

Ezr 2:57 Shephatiah, Hattil, **P**, and Ami.
Neh 7:59 Shephatiah, Hattil, **P**, and

pocket (1)

Luk 6:38 over will be put into your **p**.

pockets (3)

Psa 74:11 Take your hands out of your **p**.
Mat 10:9 or even copper coins in your **p**.
Mar 6:8 or money in their **p**.

poems (2)

Job 27:1 Job continued his **p** and said,
29:1 Job continued his **p** and said,

poets (2)

Num 21:27 This is why the **p** say:
Act 17:28 As some of your **p** have said,

point (26)

1Sm 13:21 set a metal **p** on a cattle-prod.
16:3 for me the one I **p** out to you."
18:23 Saul's officers made it a **p**
1Ki 13:4 But the arm that he used to **p** to
Neh 1:9 be driven to the most distant **p**
3:16 made repairs all the way to a **p**
3:26 as far as a **p** across from Water
Job 20:25 The glittering **p** comes out of
Psa 50:21 I will argue my **p** with you and
Isa 58:9 Don't **p** your finger and say
Jer 17:1 It is engraved with a diamond **p**
Eze 47:20 to a **p** opposite Hamath Pass.
Mar 14:59 did not agree even on this **p**.
Act 11:4 explain to them **p** by point what
11:4 point by **p** what had happened.
22:22 Up to that **p** the mob listened.
26:19 "At that **p** I did not disobey the
1Co 1:26 wise from a human **p** of view.
10:18 Israel from a human **p** of view.
15:34 back to the right **p** of view,
2Co 5:16 from a human **p** of view.
5:16 Christ from a human **p** of view,
Php 2:8 obedient to the **p** of death,
1Ti 4:6 when you **p** these things out
2Ti 4:2 **P** out errors, warn people,
Heb 8:1 The main **p** we want to make

pointed (3)

Dtr 23:13 You must carry a **p** stick as
1Ki 13:4 he **p** to the man across the
Mat 24:1 They proudly **p** out to him the

pointing (4)

Eze 1:11 were spread out, **p** upward.
Mat 12:49 **P** with his hand at his
2Co 8:8 genuine your love is by **p** out
2Ti 3:16 **p** out errors, correcting people,

pointless (46)

Psa 94:11 that people's thoughts are **p**.
Ecc 1:2 "Absolutely **p**!" says the
1:2 "Absolutely **p**! Everything is
1:2 pointless! Everything is **p**."
1:14 It's all **p**. ⌊It's like⌋ trying to
2:1 But even this was **p**.
2:11 I saw that it was all **p**.
2:15 So I thought that even this is **p**.
2:17 Everything was **p**.
2:19 my wisdom. Even this is **p**.
2:21 Even this is **p** and a terrible
2:23 don't rest. Even this is **p**.
2:26 Even this is **p**. ⌊It's like⌋ trying
3:19 over animals. All ⌊of life⌋ is **p**.
4:4 Even this is **p**. ⌊It's like⌋ trying
4:7 at something **p** under the sun:
4:8 Even this is **p** and a terrible
4:16 Even this is **p**. ⌊It's like⌋ trying
5:7 **p** actions, and empty words,
5:10 more income. Even this is **p**.
6:2 This is **p** and is a painful
6:4 A stillborn baby arrives in a **p**
6:9 Even this is **p**. ⌊It's like⌋ trying
6:11 the more **p** they become.
6:12 the brief, **p** days they live?
7:6 under a pot. Even this is **p**.
7:15 I have seen it all in my **p** life:
8:10 such things. Even this is **p**.
8:14 being done on earth that is **p**.
8:14 I say that even this is **p**.
9:9 love, during all your brief, **p** life.
9:9 God has given you your **p** life
11:8 Everything that is coming is **p**.
11:10 childhood and youth are **p**.
12:8 "Absolutely **p**!" says the
12:8 spokesman. "Everything is **p**!"
Isa 59:4 People trust **p** arguments and
Mal 3:14 'It's **p** to serve God.
Mat 15:9 Their worship of me is **p**,
Mar 7:7 Their worship of me is **p**,
1Co 3:20 the thoughts of the wise are **p**."
15:58 you do for the Lord is not **p**.
Gal 2:21 then Christ's death was **p**.
1Ti 6:20 Turn away from **p** discussions
2Ti 2:16 Avoid **p** discussions.
2:16 **p** discussions⌋ will become

points (4)

Psa 78:2 open my mouth to illustrate **p**.
Pro 6:13 ⌊and⌋ **p** with his fingers.
Mat 13:35 open my mouth to illustrate **p**.
1Co 15:3 on to you the most important **p**

poison (12)

Dtr 29:18 source of this kind of bitter **p**.
32:33 the deadly **p** of cobras.
Job 6:4 and my spirit is drinking their **p**.
20:16 person sucks the **p** of snakes.
Jer 8:14 He has given us **p** to drink
9:15 and give them **p** to drink.
23:15 to eat and **p** to drink.
Lam 3:19 the wormwood and **p**.
Amo 5:7 You, Israel, turn justice into **p**
6:12 and what is righteous into **p**.
Mar 16:18 and if they drink any deadly **p**,
Jas 3:8 evil filled with deadly **p**.

poisoned (3)

Dtr 29:23 They will see all the soil **p**
Psa 69:21 They **p** my food, and when I
Act 14:2 and **p** their minds against

poisonous (16)

Num 21:6 So the LORD sent **p** snakes
Dtr 8:15 with **p** snakes and scorpions.
32:24 along with **p** animals that crawl
32:32 Their grapes are **p**,
Psa 58:4 They have **p** venom like
140:3 hide the venom of **p** snakes.
Pro 23:32 and strikes like a **p** snake.
Isa 30:6 Vipers and **p** snakes live there.
59:5 a **p** snake is hatched.
Hos 10:4 spring up like **p** weeds
Mat 3:7 said to them, "You **p** snakes!
12:34 You **p** snakes! How can you
23:33 You **p** snakes! How can you
Luk 3:7 say to them, "You **p** snakes!
Act 28:3 The heat forced a **p** snake out
Rom 3:13 Their lips hide the venom of **p**

poke (2)

1Sm 11:1 He would **p** out everyone's right
11:2 I'll **p** out everyone's right eye

poked (2)

Jdg 16:21 They **p** out his eyes and took
1Sm 11:1 of Ammon had not **p** out.

pole (26)

Gen 40:19 hang your dead body on a **p**.
41:13 but he hung the baker on a **p**."
Num 13:23 They carried it on a **p** between
21:8 a snake, and put it on a **p**.
21:9 bronze snake and put it on a **p**.
Dtr 21:23 body hung on a **p** overnight.
21:23 is hung on a **p** is cursed by
Jos 8:29 king of Ai's ⌊dead body⌋ on a **p**
Jdg 6:25 and cut down the **p** dedicated
6:26 the Asherah **p** that you have
6:28 The Asherah **p** next to it had
6:30 the Asherah **p** that was beside
2Ki 13:6 In addition, the **p** dedicated to
17:16 They made a **p** dedicated to
21:3 to Baal and made a **p** dedicated
23:6 He took the **p** dedicated to the
23:15 the **p** dedicated to Asherah.
2Ch 33:3 and made a **p** dedicated
Est 2:23 and Teresh were hung on a **p**.
5:14 "Have a **p** set up, 75 feet high,
5:14 so he had the **p** set up.
6:4 hanging Mordecai on the **p**
7:9 The 75-foot **p** Haman made for
7:10 ⌊dead body⌋ on the very **p**
8:7 body⌋ was hung on the **p**
Jon 3:14 lifted up the snake ⌊on a **p**⌋

poles (60)

Exo 25:13 Make **p** of acacia wood,
25:14 Put the **p** through the rings on
25:15 The **p** must stay in the rings of
25:27 They are to hold the **p** for
25:28 Make the **p** out of acacia wood,
27:6 "Make **p** out of acacia wood for
27:7 The **p** should be put through
30:4 to hold the **p** for carrying it.
30:5 Make the **p** out of acacia wood,
34:13 and cut down their **p** dedicated
35:12 the ark with its **p**, the throne of
35:13 the table with its **p**,
35:15 the altar for incense with its **p**,
35:16 its **p**, and all its accessories,
37:4 Then he made **p** out of acacia
37:14 close to the rim to hold the **p**
37:15 These **p** were made out of
37:27 to hold the **p** for carrying it.
37:28 He made the **p** out of acacia
38:5 He cast four rings to hold the **p**
38:6 He made the **p** out of acacia
38:7 He put the **p** through the rings
39:35 of God's promise with its **p**
39:39 its **p**, and all its accessories,
40:20 He put the **p** on the ark and
Num 4:6 they will put the **p** in place.
4:8 they will put the **p** in place.
4:11 they will put the **p** in place.
4:14 they will put the **p** in place.
Dtr 7:5 cut down their **p** dedicated to
12:3 burn their **p** dedicated to the
Jos 10:26 bodies on five **p** until evening.
10:27 to take them down from the **p**.
1Ki 8:7 above the ark and its **p**.
8:8 The **p** were so long that their
14:15 River because they dedicated **p**
14:23 up⌋ large stones and Asherah **p**
16:33 Ahab made **p** dedicated to the
2Ki 17:10 sacred stones and **p** dedicated
18:4 and cut down the **p** dedicated
23:14 cut down the **p** dedicated to
1Ch 15:15 They used **p** as Moses had
2Ch 5:8 above the ark and its **p**.
5:9 The **p** were so long that their
14:3 and cut down the **p** dedicated
17:6 of worship and **p** dedicated
19:3 You've burned the Asherah **p** in
24:18 idols and the **p** dedicated
31:1 cut down the **p** dedicated to the
33:19 set up idols and **p** dedicated
34:3 **p** dedicated to the goddess
34:4 He destroyed the Asherah **p**,
34:7 beat the Asherah **p** and idols
Est 9:13 hang Haman's ten sons on **p**."
9:14 hung Haman's ten sons ⌊on **p**⌋.
9:25 hung Haman and his sons on **p**.
Isa 17:8 their hands or to the Asherah **p**
27:9 chalk and no **p** dedicated
Jer 17:2 altars and their **p** dedicated
Mic 5:14 I will pull out your **p** dedicated

polish (1)

Jer 46:4 **P** your spears. Put on your armor.

polished (11)

1Ki 7:45 these utensils out of **p** bronze
2Ch 4:16 Huram made all of them out of **p**
Ezr 8:27 and two utensils of fine **p**
Eze 1:7 and they glittered like **p** bronze.
21:9 a sword is sharpened and **p**,
21:10 It's sharpened to kill and **p** to
21:11 has been handed over to be **p**,
21:11 is being sharpened and **p**
21:15 flash like lightning. It's **p** to kill.
21:28 It's **p** to destroy and flash like
Dan 10:6 His arms and legs looked like **p**

politely (1)

Jer 9:8 People speak **p** to their

political (1)

Jon 18:40 (Barabbas was a **p**

pollute (2)

Num 35:33 "You must not **p** the land where
Dtr 24:4 Don't **p** with sin the land that

polluted (11)

Ezr 9:11 of has been **p** by its perverted
Psa 106:38 The land became **p** with blood.
Pro 25:26 a muddied spring and a **p** well,
Isa 24:5 The earth is **p** by those who
Jer 3:1 would become thoroughly **p**.
3:2 You have **p** the land with your
3:9 she **p** the land and committed
16:18 because they have **p** my land.
Eze 23:38 They have **p** my holy places
Act 15:20 from things **p** by false gods,
Jas 3:11 Do clean and **p** water flow out

pollutes (1)

Num 35:33 Murder is what **p** the land.

Pollux (1)

Act 28:11 the gods Castor and **P** carved

pomegranate (7)

Exo 28:34 a gold bell alternating with a **p**
39:26 A gold bell alternated with a **p**
1Sm 14:2 under a **p** tree at Migron.
Sos 4:3 your veil are like slices of **p**.
6:7 your veil are like slices of **p**.
Joe 1:12 The **p**, palm, and apricot trees,
Hag 2:19 The vine, the fig tree, the **p**,

pomegranates (21)

Exo 28:33 of the robe make **p** of violet,
39:24 the robe they made **p** of violet,
39:25 in between the **p** all around
Num 13:23 also brought some **p** and figs.
20:5 and **p** won't grow here.
Dtr 8:8 grapevines, fig trees, and **p**.
1Ki 7:20 Two hundred **p** in rows were
7:42 400 **p** for the 2 sets of filigree (2
7:42 2 sets of filigree (2 rows of **p**
2Ki 25:17 The filigree and the **p** around
2Ch 3:16 He made 100 **p** and put them
4:13 400 **p** for the 2 sets of filigree (2
4:13 2 sets of filigree (2 rows of **p**
Sos 4:13 are paradise that produces **p**
6:11 and if the **p** were in bloom.
7:12 if the **p** are in bloom.
8:2 juice squeezed from my **p**.
Jer 52:22 with a filigree and **p** around it.
52:22 was the same. It also had **p**.
52:23 There were 96 **p** on the sides.
52:23 The total number of **p** on the

pond (1)

2Sm 4:12 dead bodies by the **p** in Hebron.

ponds (3)

Exo 7:19 of Egypt — its rivers, canals, **p**,
8:5 over the rivers, canals, and **p**.
Isa 42:15 into islands. I will dry up **p**.

Pontius (3)

Luk 3:1 **P** Pilate was governor of
Act 4:27 "In this city Herod and **P** Pilate
1Ti 6:13 testimony in front of **P** Pilate,

Pontus (3)

Act 2:9 **P**, the province of Asia,
18:2 Aquila had been born in **P**,
1Pe 1:1 throughout the provinces of **P**,

pool (49)

2Sm 2:13 groups met at the **p** of Gibeon.
2:13 one group on one side of the **p**
2:13 group on the other side of the **p**.
1Ki 7:23 Hiram made a **p** from cast
7:24 45-foot circumference of the **p**.
7:24 in metal when the **p** was cast.
7:25 The **p** was set on 12 metal
7:25 The **p** was set on them,
7:25 toward the center ⌊of the **p**⌋.
7:26 The **p** was three inches thick.
7:39 He set the **p** on the south side
7:44 1 **p**, 12 bulls under the pool,
7:44 1 pool, 12 bulls under the **p**,
22:38 washed at the **p** of Samaria,
2Ki 16:17 He took the bronze **p** down
18:17 at the channel for the Upper **P**
20:20 acts and how he made the **p**
25:13 and the bronze **p** in the LORD's
25:16 from the two pillars, the **p**,
1Ch 18:8 Solomon used it to make the **p**,
2Ch 4:2 Huram made a **p** from cast
4:3 45-foot circumference of the **p**.
4:3 in metal when the **p** was cast.
4:4 The **p** was set on 12 metal
4:4 The **p** was set on them,
4:4 toward the center ⌊of the **p**⌋.
4:5 The **p** was three inches thick.
4:6 the **p** to wash themselves.
4:10 He set the **p** on the south side
4:15 1 **p** and the 12 bulls under it,
Neh 2:14 I arrived at King's **P**,
3:15 repairs on the wall of the **P**
3:16 tombs of David as far as the **p**
Psa 114:8 He turns a rock into a **p** filled
Isa 7:3 end of the ditch of the Upper **P**
22:9 will store water in the Lower **P**.
22:11 to hold the water of the Old **P**.
35:7 the hot sand will become a **p**,
36:2 at the channel for the Upper **P**
Jer 27:19 the bronze **p**, the stands,
41:12 him at the large **p** in Gibeon.
52:17 and the bronze **p** in the LORD's
52:20 bronze from the 2 pillars, the **p**,

Nah 2:8 Nineveh was like a **p** of water
Jon 5:2 was a **p** called Bethesda
5:7 to put me into the **p** when
5:7 steps into the **p** ahead of me."
9:7 "Wash it off in the **p** of Siloam."
Jas 3:12 In the same way, a **p** of salt

pools (4)

Ecc 2:6 I made **p** to water the forest of
Sos 7:4 eyes are like **p** in Heshbon,
7:4 **p** by the gate of Bath Rabbim.
Isa 14:23 It will become **p** of water.

poor (170)

Exo 6:12 I'm such a **p** speaker."
22:25 to any **p** person among you
23:3 favors to **p** people in court.
23:6 justice to **p** people in court.
23:11 In that way the **p** among your
23:11 eat what the **p** people leave.
30:15 and the **p** must not give less.
Lev 14:21 if the one to be cleansed is **p**
19:10 Leave them for **p** people and
19:15 give special favors to **p** people,
23:22 Leave it for **p** people and
25:25 If your brother becomes **p** and
25:35 "If an Israelite becomes **p** and
25:39 "If an Israelite becomes **p** and
25:47 living with him may be **p**.
25:47 The **p** Israelite may sell
27:8 But the person who is too **p** to
Num 13:20 Is the soil rich or **p**?
Dtr 15:4 there shouldn't be any **p** people
15:7 whenever there are **p** Israelites
15:8 Be generous to these **p** people,
15:9 you might be stingy toward **p**
15:9 The **p** will complain to the
15:11 There will always be **p** people
15:11 Israelites who are **p** and needy.
24:12 If the person is **p**, don't keep
24:14 workers who are **p** and needy,
24:15 sunset because they are **p**
34:7 His eyesight never became **p**,
Jdg 6:6 So the Israelites became very **p**
14:15 invite us ⌊just to make us **p**⌋?"
Rut 3:10 whether rich or **p** — is better
1Sm 2:8 He raises the **p** from the dust.
18:23 a **p** and unimportant person."
2Sm 12:1 and the other was **p**.
12:3 but the **p** man had only one
12:4 So he took the **p** man's lamb
Neh 5:10 money and grain to the **p**.
Est 9:22 especially gifts to the **p**.
Job 5:16 Then the **p** have hope while
20:10 will have to ask the **p** for help.
20:19 crushed and abandoned the **p**.
24:4 All the **p** people of the country
24:5 **p** people go out to do their
24:9 and take a **p** woman's baby as
24:10 ⌊That is why⌋ the **p** go around
24:14 they kill the **p** and needy.
29:12 because I rescued the **p** who
30:25 Didn't my soul grieve for the **p**?
31:16 refused the requests of the **p**
31:19 or a **p** person going naked
34:19 important people over **p** people
34:28 They forced the **p** to cry out to
Psa 34:6 Here is a **p** man who called out.
49:2 rich people and **p** ones.
72:13 He will have pity on the **p** and
82:3 of the oppressed and the **p**.
112:9 He gives freely to **p** people.
113:7 He lifts the **p** from the dust.
Pro 10:15 Poverty ruins the **p**.
13:7 Another pretends to be **p** but
13:8 but the **p** person does not pay
13:23 When **p** people are able to
14:20 A **p** person is hated even by
14:31 Whoever oppresses the **p**
17:5 Whoever makes fun of a **p**
18:23 A **p** person is timid when
19:1 Better to be a **p** person who
19:4 but a **p** person is separated
19:7 The entire family of a **p** person
19:17 Whoever has pity on the **p**
19:22 it is better to be **p** than a liar.
Pro 20:13 love sleep or you will end up **p**.
21:13 ear to the cry of the **p** will call
21:17 loves pleasure will become **p**.
22:2 The rich and the **p** have this in
22:7 A rich person rules **p** people,
22:9 has shared his food with the **p**.
22:16 Oppressing the **p** for profit ⌊or⌋
22:22 Do not rob the **p** because they
22:22 rob the poor because they are **p**
23:21 and a glutton will become **p**.
28:3 A **p** person who oppresses
28:6 Better to be a **p** person who
28:8 for the one who is kind to the **p**.
28:11 but a **p** person with
28:15 ruler is a threat to **p** people.
28:27 gives to the **p** lacks nothing.
28:27 the **p** receives many curses.
29:7 knows the just cause of the **p**.
29:13 A **p** person and an oppressor
29:14 king judges the **p** with honesty,
30:9 or I may become **p** and steal
Ecc 4:13 A young man who is **p** and
5:8 Don't be surprised if you see **p**
6:8 What advantage does a **p**
9:15 A **p**, wise person was found in
9:15 But no one remembered that **p**
9:16 even though that **p** person's
Isa 3:14 with goods stolen from the **p**."
3:15 of the **p** ⌊into the ground⌋?"
10:2 They deprive the **p** of justice.
11:4 He will judge the **p** justly.
14:30 The poorest of the **p** will eat,
25:4 have been a refuge for the **p**,
26:6 the footsteps of the **p**.
32:7 plans in order to ruin **p** people
41:17 "The **p** and needy are looking
58:7 take the **p** and homeless into
Jer 2:34 You have the blood from **p** and
5:4 I thought, "These are **p**,
5:28 don't defend the rights of the **p**.
22:16 the cause of the **p** and needy.
39:10 left some **p** people who had
Eze 16:49 didn't help the **p** and the needy.
18:12 He oppresses the **p** and needy.
18:17 He refuses to hurt the **p**.
22:29 humble people and to **p** people.
Dan 4:27 and have pity on the **p**.
Amo 2:7 They stomp the heads of the **p**
4:1 You women oppress the **p** and
5:11 You trample on the **p** and take
8:6 We can buy the **p** with money
Mic 7:1 **P** me! I am like those gathering
Hab 3:14 who secretly eat up the **p**.
Zep 3:12 a humble and **p** people.
Zec 7:10 foreigners, and **p** people.
Mat 6:2 So when you give to the **p**,
6:3 When you give to the **p**,
11:5 and **p** people hear the Good
19:21 Give the money to the **p**,
26:9 have been given to the **p**."
26:11 always have the **p** with you,
Mar 10:21 Give the money to the **p**,
12:42 A **p** widow dropped in two
12:43 This **p** widow has given more
14:5 have been given to the **p**."
14:7 You will always have the **p**
Luk 4:18 to tell the Good News to the **p**.
6:20 "Blessed are those who are **p**.
7:22 and **p** people hear the Good
11:41 what is inside as a gift to the **p**,
12:33 and give the money to the **p**.
14:13 invite the **p**, the handicapped,
14:21 Bring back the **p**, the blind, and
18:22 Distribute the money to the **p**,
19:8 half of my property to the **p**.
21:2 He noticed a **p** widow drop in
21:3 This **p** widow has given more
Jon 12:5 and the money given to the **p**?"
12:6 because he cared about the **p**
12:8 always have the **p** with you,
13:29 or to give something to the **p**.
Act 9:36 and gave things to the **p**.
10:2 Cornelius gave many gifts to **p**
10:4 prayers and your gifts to the **p**,
10:31 remembered your gifts to the **p**.
24:17 and brought gifts for the **p**
Rom 15:26 up a collection for the **p** among
2Co 8:9 yet for your sake he became **p**
9:9 person gives freely to the **p**.
Gal 2:10 to do was to remember the **p**,
Heb 11:37 Some were **p**, abused,
Jas 2:2 the other man, who is **p**,
2:3 But you say to the **p** man,
2:5 Didn't God choose **p** people in
2:6 show no respect to **p** people.
Rev 2:9 how **p** you are — but you are
3:17 pitiful, **p**, blind, and naked.
13:16 people, rich and **p** people,

poorer (2)

Pro 11:24 what he owes and yet grows **p**.
28:3 A poor person who oppresses **p**

poorest (7)

2Ki 24:14 Only the **p** people of the land
25:12 guard left some of the **p** people
Isa 14:30 The **p** of the poor will eat,
29:19 The **p** of people will find joy in
40:20 The **p** people choose wood
Jer 40:7 some of the country's **p** men,
52:16 left some of the **p** people in the

poorly (1)

1Co 4:11 **p** dressed, roughly treated,

poplar (1)

Gen 30:37 took fresh-cut branches of **p**,

poplars (4)

Lev 23:40 branches of leafy trees and **p**,
Job 40:22 **P** by the stream surround it.
Isa 44:4 the grass as **p** spring up by
Hos 4:13 under oaks, **p**, and other trees.

popular (1)

Est 10:3 respected by, and **p** with,

popularity (1)

1Ki 12:27 will regain **p** if they go to

populated (1)

Gen 9:19 them the whole earth was **p**.

population (9)

Dtr 1:10 made your **p** increase so that
6:3 for you and your **p** will increase
8:1 and your **p** will increase.
13:17 he will make your **p** increase,
30:16 your **p** will increase,
2Ki 25:11 and the rest of the **p**.
Pro 14:28 A large **p** is an honor for a king,
Jer 3:16 and your **p** will increase in the
52:15 and the rest of the **p**.

Poratha (1)

Est 9:8 **P**, Adalia, Aridatha,

porch (3)

Jon 10:23 was walking on Solomon's **p**
Act 3:11 the place called Solomon's **P**.
5:12 as they met on Solomon's **P**.

porches (2)

Jon 5:2 in Hebrew. It had five **p**.
5:3 Under these **p** a large number

Porcius Festus (1)

Act 24:27 Then **P** took Felix's place.

pork (2)

Isa 65:4 They ate **p** and in their pots
66:17 into the garden and devour **p**,

port (3)

Isa 23:1 Your **p** at Tyre is destroyed.
Act 27:8 We finally came to a **p** called
27:8 The **p** was near the city of

portion (13)

Gen 43:34 but Benjamin's **p** was five
Exo 29:28 that the Israelites give this **p**
Num 5:26 grain offering as a memorial **p**

Dtr 21:17 must give that son a double **p**
1Sm 1:5 He would also give one **p** to
9:23 "Bring me the **p** of the
27:10 or "the **p** of the Negev where
27:10 or "the **p** of the Negev where
30:14 We raided the **p** of the Negev
30:14 the **p** of the Negev where Caleb
2Ch 31:19 Men were appointed to give a **p**
Eze 48:12 So they will have a special **p**
Rev 22:19 God will take away his **p** of the

portions (11)

Gen 43:34 Joseph had **p** of food brought to
Jos 17:5 Ten **p** of land went to
17:6 These **p** were distributed
1Sm 1:4 he would give **p** of it to his wife
2:28 ancestors the right to keep **p**
2Ch 31:4 Levites the **p** they were due
Neh 8:10 and send **p** to those who
8:12 to eat and drink and to send **p**.
13:10 had not been given their **p**.
13:13 ⌊the **p**⌋ to their relatives.
Pro 31:15 gives food to her family and **p**

portray (1)

2Sm 14:20 servant Joab has done this to **p**

ports (1)

Act 27:2 The ship was going to stop at **p**

posed (1)

Jos 9:4 They **p** as messengers.

position (58)

Gen 40:13 you and restore you to your **p**.
40:21 the chief cupbearer to his **p**.
41:13 Pharaoh restored me to my **p**,
Jos 8:9 They took their **p** west of Ai,
Jdg 7:21 While each man kept his **p**
20:33 in ambush rushed from their **p**
2Sm 2:25 together and taking their **p**
3:6 Abner strengthened his **p** in
1Ki 15:13 Maacah from the **p**
2Ki 25:28 him a special **p** higher than
2Ch 1:1 strengthened his **p** over the
12:13 Rehoboam strengthened his **p**
15:16 Maacah from the **p**
20:17 ⌊Instead,⌋ take your **p**,
21:4 he strengthened his **p** and then
23:1 Jehoiada strengthened his **p**
Est 1:19 you should give her royal **p** to
3:1 He gave Haman a **p** higher in
4:14 may have gained your royal **p**
5:11 king promoted him to a **p** over
Psa 62:4 to force him out of his high **p**.
109:8 Let someone else take his **p**.
110:1 "Sit in the highest **p** in heaven
Ecc 10:4 don't resign your **p**.
Isa 22:19 office and do away with your **p**.
Jer 52:32 him a special **p** higher than
Mat 22:44 "Take the highest **p** in heaven
26:64 Man in the highest **p** in heaven.
Mar 12:36 "Take the highest **p** in heaven
14:62 Man in the highest **p** in heaven.
16:19 God gave him the highest **p**.
Luk 20:42 "Take the highest **p** in heaven
22:69 be in the highest **p** in heaven."
Jon 11:48 away our **p** and our nation."
Act 1:20 **p**.'" "Therefore, someone must
1:25 since Judas abandoned his **p**
2:33 to give Jesus the highest **p**.
2:34 "Take my highest **p** of power
5:31 Jesus the highest **p** as leader
7:55 and Jesus in the **p** of authority
7:56 and the Son of Man in the **p**
23:9 who argued their **p** forcefully.
Rom 8:34 has the highest **p** in heaven.
Eph 1:20 him the highest **p** in heaven.
2:6 Jesus and has given us a **p**
Col 3:1 Christ holds the highest **p**.
1Ti 2:11 in keeping with her **p**.
Heb 1:3 he received the highest **p**,
1:13 "Sit in the highest **p** in heaven
7:26 has the highest **p** in heaven.
8:1 has received the highest **p**,
10:12 the highest **p** in heaven.
Heb 12:2 the highest **p** in heaven,
Jas 4:10 Then he will give you a high **p**.
1Pe 2:13 holds the highest **p** of authority.
3:22 the highest **p** that God gives.
2Pe 3:17 you won't fall from your firm **p**.
Jud 1:6 angels who didn't keep their **p**

positioned (3)

Jos 8:13 All the troops were **p**.
Neh 4:13 That is why I **p** people by their
Eze 41:18 Palm trees were **p** between

positions (16)

Jdg 20:33 So the men of Israel left their **p**.
1Ki 20:24 all of the kings from their **p**,
1Ch 9:22 appointed them to these **p**
2Ch 35:10 The priests took their **p** with
Psa 3:6 who have taken **p** against me
59:4 hurry to take **p** against me.
Ecc 10:6 people are often given high **p**,
10:6 people are left to fill lower **p**.
Jer 46:4 Take your **p**, and put on your
46:14 Say, 'Take your **p**,
50:9 will take up **p** against Babylon.
50:14 up your **p** around Babylon,
Dan 3:30 and Abednego to higher **p** in
Mat 20:23 these **p** for certain people."
Mar 10:40 Those **p** have already been
1Co 1:26 You were not in powerful **p** or

positive (1)

Gal 4:15 happened to your **p** attitude?

possess (17)

Num 14:24 His descendants will **p** it.
26:53 "The land these people will **p**
Dtr 4:26 from the land you're going to **p**
5:31 which I'm giving them to **p**."
5:33 the land that you are going to **p**.
9:6 giving you this good land to **p**.
1Ch 28:8 Then you will be able to **p** this
2Ch 20:6 You **p** power and might,
Neh 9:23 told their parents to enter and **p**.
Isa 14:2 The nation of Israel will **p**
14:21 be able to rise, **p** the earth,
34:17 They will **p** it permanently and
57:13 But whoever trusts me will **p**
60:21 and they will **p** the land
Eze 25:4 They will **p** your land.
Oba 1:20 They will **p** land as far as
2Co 6:10 although we **p** everything.

possessed (31)

Jos 12:8 and Jebusites ⌊had **p**⌋.
17:11 Manasseh **p** Beth Shean and
1Ki 3:28 because they saw he **p**
1Ch 27:32 educated man who **p** insight,
Pro 8:22 "The LORD already **p** me long
Isa 63:18 Your holy people **p** the land for
Mat 4:24 and people **p** by demons,
8:16 many who were **p** by demons.
8:28 They were **p** by demons and
8:33 about the men **p** by demons.
9:32 because he was **p** by a demon.
12:22 brought Jesus a man **p** by
Mar 1:32 sick and those **p** by demons.
5:15 the man who had been **p** by
5:16 happened to the demon-**p** man
5:18 had been demon-**p** begged him
9:17 He is **p** by a spirit that won't let
Luk 4:33 In the synagogue was a man **p**
8:27 The man was **p** by demons
8:36 Jesus had restored the demon-**p**
13:11 A woman who was **p** by a
Jon 7:20 "You're **p** by a demon!
8:48 and that you're **p** by a demon?"
8:49 Jesus answered, "I'm not **p**.
8:52 "Now we know that you're **p** by
10:20 "He's **p** by a demon!
10:21 "No one talks like this if he's **p**
Act 8:7 of the many people they had **p**.
16:16 She was **p** by an evil spirit that
19:13 spirits out of those who were **p**.
19:16 Then the man **p** by the evil

possessing (1)

1Ti 3:9 clear consciences about **p**

possession (125)

Gen 15:7 so that you will take **p** of it."
15:8 certain that I will take **p** of it?"
17:8 as your permanent **p**.
22:17 Your descendants will take **p**
24:60 May your descendants take **p**
28:4 so that you may take **p**
35:4 they had in their **p** as well as
48:4 descendants as a permanent **p**.'
Exo 6:8 give it to you as your own **p**.
19:5 you will be my own special **p**,
22:4 animal is found alive in his **p**,
23:30 in number to take **p** of the land.
32:13 It will be their permanent **p**."'
Num 13:30 "Let's go now and take **p** of the
18:20 I am your **p** and your property
21:24 them in battle and took **p**
21:35 And they took **p** of his land.
27:11 that relative will take **p** of it.
32:19 We won't take **p** of any land on
32:30 the land they will take **p** of
32:32 but the land we will take **p** of is
33:53 Take **p** of the land and live
Dtr 1:8 Enter, and take **p** of the land
1:21 Take **p** of it, as the LORD God
1:38 help Israel take **p** of the land.
1:39 and they will take **p** of it.
2:24 and take **p** of his country.
2:31 Take **p** of his land."
3:12 At that time we took **p** of this
3:18 so that you can take **p** of it.
3:20 other Israelites until they take **p**
3:28 and he will help them take **p** of
4:1 and be able to enter and take **p**
4:5 the land and taken **p** of it.
4:14 River⌋ and take **p** of the land.
4:22 going to go across and take **p**
4:38 This land is your own **p** today.
4:47 They took **p** of his land and the
6:1 enter the land and take **p** of it.
6:18 and you will enter and take **p** of
7:1 about to enter and take **p** of.
7:6 you to be his own special **p** out
8:1 You will enter and take **p** of the
9:3 You will take **p** of their land
9:4 LORD brought us here to take **p**
9:5 that you're entering to take **p**
9:23 "Go and take **p** of the land I'm
10:9 LORD your God is their only **p**,
10:11 They will enter and take **p** of
11:8 the strength to enter and take **p**
11:10 you're about to enter and take **p**
11:23 Then you will take **p** of ⌊the
11:31 Jordan River to enter and take **p**
11:31 When you take **p** of it and live
12:29 You will take **p** of their land
14:2 you to be his own special **p**.
15:4 he is giving you as your own **p**.
16:20 so that you will live and take **p**
17:14 You will take **p** of it and live
23:20 the land and taken **p** of it.
26:1 Soon you will enter and take **p**
26:18 his own special **p**,
28:21 about to enter and take **p** of.
28:63 about to enter and take **p** of.
30:5 You will take **p** of it,
30:16 about to enter and take **p** of.
30:18 land that you're going to take **p**
31:3 and you will take **p** of their
31:7 help them take **p** of the land.
31:13 that you are going to take **p**
32:9 Jacob was his own **p**.
32:47 that you are going to take **p**
33:23 They will take **p** of the lake
Jos 1:6 will help these people take **p**
1:11 cross the Jordan River to take **p**
1:15 take **p** of the land the LORD
1:15 you may go back and take **p** of
11:23 He gave it to Israel as a **p**,
12:1 Israel also took **p** of their lands
12:6 Then he gave their land as a **p**
12:7 Joshua gave it as a **p** to Israel,

Jos 17:12 was not able to take **p**
21:12 son of Jephunneh, as his **p**.
21:43 They took **p** of it and settled
22:4 to the land that is your own **p**.
22:9 This was their own **p** which
Jdg 1:19 so that they were able to take **p**
2:6 So each family went to take **p**
11:21 Israel defeated them and took **p**
11:24 Shouldn't you take **p** of what
Ezr 9:11 land you are going to take **p**
Neh 9:15 You told them to take **p** of the
9:22 So they took **p** of the land of
9:24 Their children took **p** of the
9:25 They took **p** of houses filled
Psa 2:8 of the earth as your own **p**.
44:3 their swords that they took **p**
69:35 will live there and take **p** of it.
74:2 bought this tribe to be your **p**.
Isa 14:23 "It will become the **p** of herons.
19:25 and my **p** Israel are blessed."
34:11 Pelicans and herons will take **p**
Jer 30:3 and they will take **p** of it."
32:23 They entered and took **p** of it.
37:12 territory of Benjamin to take **p**
49:2 Then Israel will take **p** of its
Eze 7:24 and it will take **p** of people's
35:10 We will take **p** of them."
36:3 You became the **p** of the rest of
36:5 The Edomites have taken **p** of
36:12 They will take **p** of you,
Dan 7:18 of the Most High will take **p**
7:22 people took **p** of the kingdom.
Amo 2:10 years so that you could take **p**
Oba 1:19 from the Negev will take **p**
1:19 foothills will take **p** of Philistia.
1:19 They will take **p** of the lands of
1:19 Benjamin will take **p** of Gilead.
1:20 Israel will take **p** of Canaan.
1:20 who are in Sepharad will take **p**
Hab 1:6 throughout the earth to take **p**
Zep 2:9 my nation will take **p** of them."
Mal 3:17 I will make them my special **p**.
Act 7:45 Joshua's help when they took **p**
Heb 10:34 a better and more permanent **p**.

possessions (37)

Gen 12:5 and all the **p** they had
13:6 They had so many **p** that they
14:11 So the four kings took all the **p**
14:12 nephew Lot and his **p** since
14:16 back his relative Lot and his **p**.
15:14 will come out with many **p**.
31:18 of him and took all the **p** that
36:6 household, his **p**, all his cattle,
36:7 because they had too many **p**
46:6 the **p** they had accumulated
1Sm 14:36 tonight and take their **p** until
14:48 the enemies who looted their **p**.
25:21 Not one of his **p** was missing.
Est 3:13 Their **p** were also to be seized.
9:10 did not seize any of their **p**.
9:15 did not seize any of their **p**.
9:16 did not seize any of their **p**.
Job 15:29 His **p** won't spread out over the
Psa 105:21 palace and the ruler of all his **p**.
Pro 1:13 find all kinds of valuable **p**.
6:31 give up all the **p** in his house.
16:8 Better a few ⌊**p**⌋ gained
Ecc 5:19 some people wealth and **p**,
Eze 29:19 take its prized **p**, and loot it.
38:13 to rob these people of their **p**?
44:28 Don't give them any **p** in Israel.
Oba 1:17 of Jacob will get back their **p**.
Mic 2:4 our people's **p** ⌊to others⌋.
Zec 9:4 The Lord will take away its **p**.
Luk 12:15 having a lot of material **p**."
12:21 a person treasures material **p**
12:33 "Sell your material **p**,
15:13 the younger son gathered his **p**
Act 2:45 sold their property and other **p**
4:32 called any of his **p** his own.
2Co 12:14 I don't want your **p**.
Heb 10:34 though your **p** were stolen,

possessive (1)

Zec 8:2 I am fiercely **p** of it.

possibilities (1)

Mar 9:23 said to him, "As far as **p** go,

possible (26)

Gen 29:31 he made it **p** for her to have
30:22 her prayer and made it **p**
Job 14:4 could become clean! It's not **p**.
Eze 8:17 insult me in the worst **p** way.
Mat 19:26 but everything is **p** for God."
24:24 things to deceive, if **p**,
26:39 and prayed, "Father, if it's **p**,
Mar 9:22 If it's **p** for you, put yourself in
9:23 everything is **p** for the person
10:27 Everything is **p** for God."
13:22 things to deceive, if **p**,
14:35 and prayed that if it were **p**
Luk 4:13 tempting Jesus in every **p** way,
13:33 It's not **p** for a prophet to die
18:27 for people to do are **p**
Act 17:15 to join Paul as soon as **p**.
20:16 day of Pentecost, if that was **p**.
Rom 1:10 God will now at last make it **p**
12:18 As much as it is **p**,
2Co 11:6 clear to you in every **p** way.
Gal 4:15 It's a fact that if it had been **p**,
Col 4:4 this mystery as clear as **p**.
1Th 2:16 commit as many sins as **p**.
2:17 We have made every **p** effort to
2Ti 1:18 well that he did everything **p**
Heb 9:5 things in detail isn't **p** now.)

possibly (5)

Gen 43:7 How could we **p** know he
Jos 24:19 you can't **p** serve him.
Job 7:20 If I sin, what can I ⌊**p**⌋ do to
9:14 "How can I **p** answer God?
1Co 11:20 you can't **p** be eating the Lord's

post (14)

Jos 10:18 and **p** a guard there.
Jdg 7:13 When it got to the command **p**,
1Sm 10:5 Philistines have a military **p**.
14:1 go to the Philistine military **p**
14:4 attack the Philistine military **p**.
14:6 "Let's go to the military **p** of
14:12 the men of the military **p** said to
14:12 me up ⌊to the military **p**⌋
14:15 all the troops in the military **p**.
Isa 21:6 says to me: **P** a watchman.
21:8 I stand guard at my **p**.
Hab 2:1 I will stand at my guard **p**.
Act 17:9 Jason and the others **p** bond,
22:25 ⌊to tie him to the whipping **p**⌋

posted (3)

Isa 62:6 I have **p** watchmen on your
Jer 6:17 I **p** watchmen over you.
Mat 27:66 a seal on the stone and **p**

posts (46)

Exo 26:32 gold hooks to hang it on four **p**
26:37 Make five **p** of acacia wood for
26:37 five bronze bases for the **p**."
27:10 ⌊hung⌋ on 20 **p** ⌊set in⌋ 20
27:10 The hooks and bands on the **p**
27:11 with curtains on 20 **p** set in 20
27:11 The hooks and bands on the **p**
27:12 ⌊hung⌋ on ten **p** ⌊set in⌋ ten
27:14 on⌋ three **p** ⌊set in⌋ three
27:16 ⌊hung⌋ on four **p** ⌊set in⌋ four
27:17 All the **p** around the courtyard
35:11 crossbars, **p**, and sockets,
35:17 for the courtyard, the **p**, bases,
36:36 They made four **p** of acacia
36:36 made gold hooks for the **p**,
36:38 They also made five **p** with
36:38 They covered the tops of the **p**
36:38 but the five bases for the **p**
38:10 ⌊hung⌋ on 20 **p** ⌊set in⌋ 20
38:10 The hooks and bands on the **p**
38:11 also 150 feet long with 20 **p**
38:11 The hooks and bands on the **p**
38:12 ⌊hung⌋ on 10 **p** ⌊set in⌋ 10
38:12 The hooks and bands on the **p**
38:14 on three **p** ⌊set in⌋ three
Exo 38:17 The bases for the **p** were made
38:17 The hooks and bands on the **p**
38:17 The tops of the **p** were covered
38:17 And the bands on all the **p** of
38:19 It was hung on four **p** ⌊set in⌋
38:19 The hooks and bands on the **p**
38:19 The tops of the **p** were covered
38:28 the hooks and bands for the **p**
38:28 coverings for the tops of the **p**.
39:33 frames, crossbars, **p**, sockets,
39:40 for the courtyard, the **p**, bases,
40:18 the crossbars, and set up the **p**.
Num 3:36 tent, the crossbars, **p**, sockets,
3:37 They also took care of the **p** for
4:31 the crossbars, **p**, and sockets,
4:32 the **p** for the surrounding
Jdg 16:3 took hold of the doors, door **p**,
2Ch 7:6 priests were standing at their **p**.
17:2 of Judah and placed military **p**
Neh 7:3 some at their **p** and others in
Sos 3:10 He had its **p** made out of silver,

pot (31)

Gen 25:30 "Let me have the whole **p** of
Num 11:8 They would cook it in a **p** or
Jdg 6:19 in a basket and the broth in a **p**.
1Sm 2:14 he would stick it into the **p**,
2:14 up ⌊from the **p**⌋ belonged
2Ki 4:38 "Put a large **p** on the fire,
4:39 Then he cut them into the **p** of
4:40 "There's death in the **p**,
4:41 He threw it into the **p** and said,
4:41 was nothing harmful in the **p**.
Job 41:20 **p** heated over brushwood.
41:31 the deep sea boil like a **p**.
Psa 58:9 than a cooking **p** is heated by
Pro 26:23 ⌊Like⌋ a clay **p** covered with
Ecc 7:6 of thorns burning under a **p**.
Jer 1:13 I answered, "I see a boiling **p**,
18:4 Whenever a clay **p** he was
18:4 rework it into a new clay **p**
22:28 and broken **p** that no one
Eze 11:3 This city is a cooking **p**,
11:7 and the city is the cooking **p**.
11:11 city will not be your cooking **p**,
24:3 Put the **p** on the fire;
24:4 Fill the **p** with the meatiest
24:5 Pile wood under the **p**.
24:5 Bring the mixture in the **p** to a
24:6 for that tarnished **p**.
24:11 Then set the empty **p** on the
24:12 out trying to clean this **p**.
Mic 3:3 chop them up like meat for a **p**,
Zec 14:21 Yes, every **p** in Jerusalem and

Potiphar (5)

Gen 37:36 Midianites sold Joseph to **P**,
39:1 **P**, one of Pharaoh's Egyptian
39:4 **P** liked Joseph so much that
39:5 was on everything **P** owned
39:19 When **P** heard his wife's story,

Potiphera (3)

Gen 41:45 She was the daughter of **P**,
41:50 by Asenath, daughter of **P**,
46:20 by Asenath, daughter of **P**,

pots (17)

Exo 16:3 There we sat by our **p** of meat
27:3 **p** for taking away the altar's
38:3 **p**, shovels, bowls, forks,
2Sm 17:28 bowls, **p**, wheat, barley, flour,
1Ki 7:40 Hiram also made **p**,
7:45 **p**, shovels, and bowls.
2Ki 25:14 They took the **p**, shovels,
2Ch 4:11 Huram also made the **p**,
4:16 **p**, shovels, and three-pronged
35:13 boiled the holy offerings in **p**,
Isa 45:9 among other earthenware **p**.
65:4 They ate pork and in their **p**
Jer 52:18 They took the **p**, shovels,
52:19 bowls, **p**, lamp stands, dishes,
Lam 4:2 are now treated like clay **p**,
Zec 14:20 And the cooking **p** in the house
Mar 7:4 brass **p**, and dinner tables.)

potsherd (1)

Jer 19:2 at the entrance to **P** Gate.

potter (9)

Isa 29:16 Is the **p** no better than his clay?
29:16 of pottery say about the **p**,
41:25 were treading on clay like a **p**.
64:8 are the clay, and you are our **p**.
Jer 18:6 can't I do with you as this **p**
19:1 Go and buy a clay jar from a **p**.
Zec 11:13 told me, "Give it to the **p**."
11:13 the pieces of silver to the **p** at
Rom 9:21 A **p** has the right to do

potter's (7)

Jer 18:2 "Go to the **p** house.
18:3 I went to the **p** house, and he
18:6 are like the clay in the **p** hands
19:11 this **p** jar was smashed beyond
Lam 4:2 like those made by a **p** hands
Mat 27:7 to use it to buy a **p** field
27:10 the coins to buy a **p** field, as

potters (1)

1Ch 4:23 They were the **p** who lived at

potters' (1)

Dan 2:41 They were partly **p** clay and

pottery (17)

Lev 6:28 Any piece of **p** in which the
11:33 creatures falls into a piece of **p**,
11:33 break the **p** because everything
11:34 If water ⌊from that **p**⌋ touches
11:34 drink from that **p** is unclean.
15:12 has a discharge touches **p**,
Num 5:17 take holy water in a piece of **p**
Job 2:8 Job took a piece of broken **p** to
41:30 like sharp pieces of broken **p**.
Psa 2:9 smash them to pieces like **p**."
22:15 up like pieces of broken **p**.
31:12 like a piece of broken **p**.
Isa 29:16 Can a piece of **p** say about the
30:14 It will break like **p**.
45:9 He is **p** among other
Jer 25:34 and you will break like fine **p**.
Rev 2:27 and shatter them like **p**.

pouch (1)

Sos 1:13 My beloved is a **p** of myrrh that

poultry (1)

Neh 5:18 **P** was prepared for me.

pounce (2)

Dtr 33:22 they **p** ⌊on their enemies⌋."
Job 18:11 "Terrors suddenly **p** on him

pound (4)

Jos 7:21 weighing about one **p** among
Neh 5:15 and wine plus one **p** of silver.
Psa 88:7 make all your waves **p** on me.
Isa 30:32 the LORD will **p** on them.

pounded (2)

Jdg 5:22 Then the horses' hoofs **p**.
19:22 surrounded the house and **p**

pounding (4)

Psa 38:10 My heart is **p**. I have lost my
93:3 The ocean rises with its **p**
Jer 4:19 My heart is **p**! I can't keep quiet
Lam 1:20 My heart is **p** because I've

pounds (116)

Gen 20:16 your brother 25 **p** of silver.
23:15 land is worth ten **p** of silver.
23:16 ten **p** of silver at the current
Exo 25:39 Use 75 **p** of pure gold to make
30:23 12 ½ **p** of powdered myrrh;
30:23 6 ¼ **p** of fragrant cinnamon;
30:23 6 ¼ **p** of fragrant cane;
30:24 12 ½ **p** of cassia — all
37:24 made out of 75 **p** of pure gold.
38:24 place weighed over 2,193 **p**,
Exo 38:25 was taken weighed 7,544 **p**,
38:27 He used 7,500 **p** of silver to
38:27 This was 75 **p** per base.
38:28 He used 44 **p** of silver to make
38:29 to the LORD weighed 5,310 **p**.
Num 3:50 Israelites weighed 34 **p**,
7:13 plate that weighed 3 ¼ **p**
7:13 bowl that weighed 1 ¾ **p**,
7:19 plate that weighed 3 ¼ **p**
7:19 that weighed 1 ¾ **p** using
7:25 plate that weighed 3 ¼ **p**
7:25 that weighed 1 ¾ **p** using
7:31 plate that weighed 3 ¼ **p**
7:31 that weighed 1 ¾ **p** using
7:37 plate that weighed 3 ¼ **p**
7:37 that weighed 1 ¾ **p** using
7:43 plate that weighed 3 ¼ **p**
7:43 that weighed 1 ¾ **p** using
7:49 plate that weighed 3 ¼ **p**
7:49 that weighed 1 ¾ **p** using
7:55 plate that weighed 3 ¼ **p**
7:55 that weighed 1 ¾ **p** using
7:61 plate that weighed 3 ¼ **p**
7:61 that weighed 1 ¾ **p** using
7:67 plate that weighed 3 ¼ **p**
7:67 that weighed 1 ¾ **p** using
7:73 plate that weighed 3 ¼ **p**
7:73 that weighed 1 ¾ **p** using
7:79 plate that weighed 3 ¼ **p**
7:79 that weighed 1 ¾ **p** using
7:85 silver plate weighed 3 ¼ **p**,
7:85 each bowl weighed 1 ¾ **p**.
7:85 the silver dishes weighed 60 **p**,
7:86 gold dishes weighed about 3 **p**.
31:52 weighed about 420 **p**.
Dtr 22:19 They will fine him 2 ½ **p** of
22:29 the girl's father 1 ¼ **p** of silver,
Jos 7:21 from Babylonia, five **p** of silver,
Jdg 8:26 had asked for weighed 40 **p**.
1Sm 17:5 armor scales weighing 125 **p**.
17:7 spear was made of 15 **p** of iron.
2Sm 12:30 (The crown weighed 75 **p** and
14:26 it weighed five **p** according to
18:12 "Even if I felt the weight of 25 **p**
21:16 spear weighing 7 ½ **p** which
24:24 the oxen for 1 ¼ **p** of silver.
1Ki 9:14 Hiram had sent the king 9,000 **p**
9:28 got 31,500 **p** of gold,
10:10 gave the king 9,000 **p** of gold,
10:14 in one year weighed 49,950 **p**,
10:16 using 15 **p** of gold on each
10:17 using four **p** of gold on each
10:29 imported from Egypt for 15 **p**
16:24 from Shemer for 150 **p** of silver.
20:39 life or be fined 75 **p** of silver.'
2Ki 5:5 he took 750 **p** of silver,
5:5 pounds of silver, 150 **p** of gold,
5:22 Please give them 75 **p** of silver
5:23 let me give you 150 **p** of silver."
5:23 Naaman tied up 150 **p** of silver
6:25 a donkey's head sold for two **p**
15:19 Menahem gave Pul 75,000 **p**
18:14 of Judah pay 22,500 **p**
18:14 of silver and 2,250 **p** of gold.
23:33 and fined the country 7,500 **p**
23:33 of silver and 75 **p** of gold.
1Ch 19:6 the Ammonites sent 75,000 **p**
20:2 was found to weigh 75 **p**,
21:25 So David gave Ornan 15 **p** of
22:14 There are 7,500,000 **p** of gold,
22:14 75,000,000 **p** of silver,
29:4 There are 225,000 **p** of gold
29:4 gold from Ophir and 525,000 **p**
29:7 They gave 375,186 **p** of gold,
29:7 750,000 **p** of silver,
29:7 135,000 **p** of bronze,
29:7 and 7,500,000 **p** of iron for the
2Ch 1:17 each chariot from Egypt for 15 **p**
3:8 it with 45,000 **p** of fine gold.
8:18 got 33,750 **p** of gold,
9:9 gave the king 9,000 **p** of gold,
9:13 in one year weighed 49,950 **p**,
9:15 using 15 **p** of gold on each
9:16 using 7 ½ **p** of gold on each
25:6 from Israel for 7,500 **p** of silver.
25:9 should I do about the 7,500 **p**
2Ch 27:5 gave him 7,500 **p** of silver,
36:3 and fined the country 7,500 **p**
36:3 of silver and 75 **p** of gold.
Ezr 2:69 for this work: 1,030 **p** of gold,
2:69 of gold, 5,740 **p** of silver,
7:22 him⌊ up to 7,500 **p** of silver,
8:26 weighing 150 **p** apiece,
8:26 pounds apiece, 7,500 **p** of gold,
8:27 bowls weighing 18 **p** apiece,
Neh 7:70 nearly 18 **p** of gold,
7:71 337 **p** of gold and 3,215 pounds
7:71 of gold and 3,215 **p** of silver.
7:72 contributed 337 **p** of gold,
7:72 of gold, 2,923 **p** of silver,
Est 3:9 For this I will pay 750,000 **p** of
Job 37:1 "My heart **p** because of this
Sos 8:11 Each one was to bring 25 **p** of
8:12 That 25 **p** is yours,
8:12 and 5 **p** go to those who take
Jon 19:39 with Joseph and brought 75 **p**

pour (87)

Exo 4:9 water from the Nile River and **p**
29:7 anointing oil, **p** it on his head,
29:12 **P** the rest of it out at the bottom
30:9 Never **p** a wine offering on it.
Lev 2:1 **P** olive oil on it, and put
2:6 Break it into pieces and **p** olive
4:7 He will **p** the rest of the bull's
4:18 He will **p** the rest of the blood
4:25 He will **p** the rest of the blood
4:30 He will **p** the rest of the blood
4:34 He will **p** the rest of the blood
14:15 take some of the olive oil and **p**
14:26 The priest will **p** some of the
14:29 the priest will **p** the rest of the
17:6 The priest will **p** the blood
17:13 they must **p** out the animal's
Num 5:15 He must not **p** olive oil on the
19:17 Then **p** fresh water on them.
28:7 **P** it out to the LORD in a holy
Dtr 12:16 **P** it on the ground like water.
12:24 **P** it on the ground like water.
15:23 **P** it on the ground like water.
Jdg 6:20 and **p** the broth over them."
1Ki 18:34 **P** the water on the offering and
2Ki 4:4 and **p** oil into all those
9:3 of oil, **p** it on his head, and say,
2Ch 12:7 I will not use Shishak to **p** my
Job 3:24 I **p** out my groaning like water.
10:10 Didn't you **p** me out like milk
38:37 to count the clouds or **p** out
Psa 16:4 I will not **p** out their sacrificial
22:7 Insults **p** from their mouths.
42:4 these things as I **p** out my soul:
62:8 **P** out your hearts in his
69:24 **P** your rage on them.
79:6 **P** your fury on the nations that
119:171 Let my lips **p** out praise
142:2 I **p** out my complaints in his
Pro 1:23 I will generously **p** out my spirit
15:2 but the mouths of fools **p** out a
15:28 mouths of wicked people **p** out
Ecc 11:3 they will let it **p** down on the
Isa 44:3 I will **p** water on thirsty ground
44:3 I will **p** my Spirit on your
45:8 and **p** down righteousness,
46:6 People **p** gold out of their bags
Jer 6:11 "**P** it out on the children in the
7:18 They **p** out wine offerings to
10:25 **P** out your fury on the nations
14:16 I will **p** on them the destruction
18:21 **P** out their ⌊blood⌋ by using
32:29 Baal and to **p** out wine offerings
44:17 and **p** out wine offerings
44:25 and **p** out wine offerings
48:12 "when I will send people to **p**
Lam 2:19 **P** your heart out like water in
Eze 7:8 Soon I will **p** out my fury on
9:8 while you **p** out your anger
13:11 Rain will **p** down, and stormy
13:13 In my anger rain will **p** down,
14:19 that country or **p** out my fury
20:8 So I was going to **p** out my fury
20:13 So I was going to **p** out my fury
20:21 So I was going to **p** out my fury

Exe 20:33 and I will **p** out my fury.
20:34 I will **p** out my fury.
21:31 I will **p** out my fury on you and
22:31 So I will **p** out my anger on you,
24:3 put it on. **P** water in it.
30:15 I will **p** out my fury on Sin,
39:29 because I will **p** out my Spirit
Hos 5:10 I will **p** my fury on them like
9:4 They won't **p** wine offerings to
Joe 2:28 I will **p** my Spirit on everyone.
2:29 In those days I will **p** my Spirit
Amo 5:8 calls for water from the sea to **p**
Zep 3:8 together, and to **p** my rage,
Zec 12:10 "I will **p** out the Spirit of
Mat 9:17 Nor do people **p** new wine into
9:17 Rather, people **p** new wine into
Mar 2:22 People don't **p** new wine into
14:8 She came to **p** perfume on my
Luk 5:37 People don't **p** new wine into
Jon 2:8 Jesus said to them, "**P** some,
Act 2:17 I will **p** my Spirit on everyone.
2:18 In those days I will **p** my Spirit
Rev 16:1 "**P** the seven bowls of God's

poured (89)

Gen 28:18 He set it up as a marker and **p**
31:13 where you **p** olive oil on a
35:14 He **p** a wine offering and olive
Exo 30:32 It must never be **p** on the
Lev 8:12 He also **p** some of the
8:15 He **p** the rest of the blood at the
9:9 Then he **p** out the blood at the
11:38 But if water is **p** on the seed
Dtr 12:27 sacrifices is to be **p** out beside
Jdg 5:4 the sky **p**, the clouds burst,
1Sm 7:6 **p** it out in front of the LORD,
10:1 **p** it on Saul's head,
2Sm 14:14 we are all like water that is **p**
20:10 and his intestines **p** out on the
23:16 He **p** it out ⌊as an offering⌋ to
1Ki 13:3 The ashes on it will be **p** ⌊on
13:5 ashes from the altar were **p** ⌊on
2Ki 7:2 LORD **p** rain through windows
7:19 LORD **p** rain through windows
9:6 The prophet **p** olive oil on his
16:13 **p** out his wine offering,
1Ch 11:18 He **p** it out ⌊as an offering⌋ to
2Ch 34:21 LORD's fierce anger has been **p**
34:25 Therefore, my anger will be **p**
Job 29:6 and the rocks **p** streams of
Psa 22:14 I am **p** out like water,
45:2 Grace is **p** on your lips.
68:8 the earth quaked and the sky **p**
77:17 The clouds **p** out water.
92:10 and soothing lotion is **p** on me.
107:40 He **p** contempt on their
Isa 29:10 The LORD has **p** out on you a
32:15 until the Spirit is **p** on us from
42:25 So he **p** out his burning anger
53:12 because he **p** out his life in
63:6 them drunk and **p** their blood
Jer 1:14 "Disaster will be **p** out from the
7:20 My anger and fury will be **p** out
19:13 and **p** out wine offerings
42:18 anger and my fury were **p** out
42:18 so my fury will be **p** out on you
44:6 my fury and anger were **p** out
44:19 **p** out wine offerings to her,
48:11 They aren't **p** from one jar to
Lam 2:4 He **p** out his fury like fire on the
2:11 My heart is **p** out on the ground
Eze 16:9 I **p** olive oil over you.
20:28 sacrifices and **p** out their wine
22:22 have **p** out my fury on you."
24:7 The blood was **p** on a bare
24:7 It wasn't **p** on the ground where
36:18 So I **p** out my fury on them
36:18 them because they **p** out blood
Zep 1:17 Their blood will be **p** out like
Mat 7:25 Rain **p**, and floods came.
7:27 Rain **p**, and floods came.
26:7 very expensive perfume and **p**
26:12 She **p** this perfume on my body
26:28 It is **p** out for many people so
Mar 2:22 is to be **p** into fresh skins."
6:13 demons out of people and **p** oil
Mar 14:3 She opened the bottle and **p**
14:24 It is **p** out for many people.
Luk 5:38 wine is to be **p** into fresh skins.
7:38 and **p** the perfume on them.
7:46 But she has **p** perfume on my
22:20 He said, "This cup that is **p** out
Jon 2:9 although the servers who had **p**
11:2 (Mary was the woman who **p**
12:3 made from pure nard and **p**
13:5 Then he **p** water into a basin
Act 2:33 also received and has **p** out
10:45 of the Holy Spirit had been **p**
Rom 5:5 because God's love has been **p**
Eph 1:8 He **p** out his kindness by
Php 2:17 My life is being **p** out as a part
2Ti 4:6 now time for me to be **p** out as
Tit 3:6 God **p** a generous amount of
Rev 12:15 The snake's mouth **p** out a river
12:16 the river which had **p** out
14:10 which has been **p** unmixed
16:2 The first angel **p** his bowl over
16:3 The second angel **p** his bowl
16:4 The third angel **p** his bowl over
16:6 drink because they have **p** out
16:8 The fourth angel **p** his bowl on
16:10 The fifth angel **p** his bowl on
16:12 The sixth angel **p** his bowl on
16:17 The seventh angel **p** his bowl

pouring (14)

Gen 7:12 and rain came **p** down on the
8:2 and the rain had stopped **p**.
Exo 9:33 and no more rain came **p** down
25:29 to be used for **p** wine offerings.
37:16 to be used for **p** wine offerings.
Num 20:11 Water came **p** out,
1Sm 1:15 I'm **p** out my heart to the LORD.
2Ki 4:5 to her, and she kept **p**.
Job 30:16 "Now my life is **p** out of me.
37:6 and to the **p** rain, 'Rain harder!'
Pro 25:20 coat on a cold day or **p** vinegar
Jer 44:18 and **p** out wine offerings
Mic 1:4 split apart like water **p** down
Zec 4:12 pipes that are **p** out gold?"

pours (6)

Job 12:21 He **p** contempt on influential
36:28 It **p** down on many people.
41:21 and a flame **p** from its mouth.
Psa 59:7 See what **p** out of their mouths
Amo 9:6 for the water in the sea and **p**
Nah 1:6 He **p** out his rage like fire and

poverty (18)

1Sm 2:7 The LORD causes **p** and
Pro 6:11 Then your **p** will come ⌊to
10:4 Lazy hands bring **p**,
10:15 strong city. **P** ruins the poor.
13:18 **P** and shame come to a person
14:23 but idle talk leads only to **p**.
21:5 in a hurry ends up in **p**.
22:16 to the rich certainly leads to **p**.
24:34 Then your **p** will come like a
28:22 not realizing that **p** is about to
30:8 Don't give me either **p** or riches.
31:7 person drinks and forgets his **p**
Ecc 4:14 though he had been born in **p**
Mar 12:44 But she, in her **p**, has given
Luk 21:4 But she, in her **p**, has given
2Co 8:2 along with their extreme **p**,
8:9 to make you rich through his **p**.
Php 4:12 how to live in **p** or prosperity.

powder (10)

Exo 30:36 Grind some of it into a fine **p**,
32:20 burned it, ground it into **p**,
Dtr 9:21 until it was as fine as **p**.
9:21 Then I threw the **p** into the river
2Sm 22:43 I beat them into a **p** as fine as
2Ki 23:15 crushing it to **p** and burning the
2Ch 34:4 He ground them into **p** and
34:4 and scattered the **p** over
34:7 Asherah poles and idols into **p**,
Psa 18:42 I beat them into a **p** as fine as

powdered (2)

Exo 30:23 12 ½ pounds of **p** myrrh;
Isa 27:9 all the altar stones into **p** chalk

powders (1)

Sos 3:6 from the merchants' scented **p**.

power (424)

Gen 31:29 I have the **p** to harm you.
49:3 first in majesty and first in **p**.
Exo 3:8 come to rescue them from the **p**
3:20 So I will use my **p** to strike
4:21 I have given you the **p** to do.
6:1 I will show him my **p**,
6:1 I will show him my **p**,
7:4 Then I will use my **p** to punish
7:5 when I use my **p** against Egypt
9:15 By now I could have used my **p**
9:16 I want to show you my **p** and
14:31 the Israelites saw the great **p**
15:16 Because of the **p** of your arm,
32:11 your great **p** and mighty hand?
Lev 26:13 I have broken their **p** over you
Num 11:23 there a limit to the LORD's **p**?
14:13 (You used your **p** to take these
14:17 "Lord, let your **p** be as great as
Dtr 4:37 you out of Egypt by his great **p**.
9:3 will use you to crush their **p**.
9:26 You saved them by your great **p**
11:2 his great **p** — his mighty
32:39 one can rescue you from my **p**.
Jos 4:24 world would know his mighty **p**
24:10 So I saved you from his **p**.
Jdg 2:15 the **p** of the LORD brought
3:30 The **p** of Moab was crushed by
4:23 people of Israel to crush the **p**
6:2 Midian's **p** was too strong for
6:9 I rescued you from the **p** of the
6:9 of the Egyptians and from the **p**
8:28 The **p** of Midian was crushed
13:5 from the **p** of the Philistines."
15:18 fall into the **p** of godless men."
1Sm 4:8 Who can save us from the **p** of
7:13 The **p** of the Philistines was
10:18 and rescued you from the **p**
23:4 I'm giving you the **p** to defeat
1Ki 2:12 his **p** was firmly established.
2:46 Solomon's **p** as king was now
18:46 The LORD's **p** was on Elijah.
2Ki 3:15 LORD's **p** came over Elisha.
13:5 they were freed from Aram's **p**.
17:7 ⌊and rescued them⌋ from the **p**
17:36 who used his great **p** and a
1Ch 4:10 May your **p** be with me and free
11:10 who exercised **p** with him in
14:11 David said, "Using my **p** like
16:28 Give to the LORD glory and **p**.
22:18 live in this country under my **p**,
29:11 Greatness, **p**, splendor, glory,
29:12 You hold **p** and strength in your
29:30 about his reign, his **p**,
2Ch 6:41 you and the ark of your **p**.
13:20 Jeroboam never regained **p**
17:5 Jehoshaphat's **p** over
20:6 You possess **p** and might,
25:8 because God has the **p** to help
30:6 of you who escaped from the **p**
32:8 king of Assyria has human **p**
Ezr 8:22 but his **p** and his anger oppose
Neh 1:10 you have saved by your great **p**
5:15 took advantage of their **p** over
Est 6:13 starting to lose **p** to Mordecai.
10:2 All his acts of **p** and might
Job 1:12 "Everything he has is in your **p**,
2:6 told Satan, "He is in your **p**,
5:15 needy from the **p** of the mighty.
9:4 wise in heart and mighty in **p**.
12:6 for those whose god is their **p**.
12:16 "God has **p** and priceless
21:16 their happiness in their own **p**?
24:22 ⌊these⌋ mighty men by his **p**.
26:2 the person who has no **p**
26:12 With his **p** he calmed the sea.
26:14 the thunder of his **p**?"
27:11 "I will teach you about God's **p**.

Job 27:22 He flees from its **p**.
28:9 "Humans exert their **p** on the
29:20 My **p** will be fresh ⌊every day⌋,
35:9 The **p** of mighty people makes
36:22 does great things by his **p**.
37:23 is great in **p** and judgment,
39:21 strength and finds joy in its **p**.
40:9 Do you have **p** like God's?
40:16 the **p** in its stomach muscles.
41:22 and **p** dances in front of it.
Psa 9:19 Do not let mortals gain any **p**.
10:10 fall under ⌊the weight of⌋ his **p**.
17:14 With your **p** rescue me from
21:13 make music to praise your **p**.
29:1 Give to the LORD glory and **p**.
29:11 The LORD will give **p** to his
37:33 him to the wicked person's **p**
44:2 By your **p** you forced nations
49:15 will buy me back from the **p**
59:11 wander aimlessly by your **p**.
62:11 "**P** belongs to God.
63:2 to see your **p** and your glory.
65:6 the one who is clothed with **p**,
66:3 Your **p** is so great that your
68:34 Acknowledge the **p** of God.
68:34 and his **p** is in the skies.
68:35 He gives strength and **p** to his
69:29 Let your saving **p** protect me,
71:18 to tell about your **p** to all who
77:10 makes me feel sick that the **p**
78:4 generation about the LORD's **p**
78:42 They did not remember his **p**—
78:54 mountain that his **p** had won.
78:61 He allowed his **p** to be taken
80:2 Wake up your **p**, and come to
80:17 Let your **p** rest on the man you
81:5 Joseph rose to **p** over Egypt.
81:14 turn my **p** against their foes.
82:4 escape the **p** of wicked people.
88:5 who are cut off from your **p**.
89:48 can set himself free from the **p**
90:11 Who fully understands the **p** of
90:16 children see your glorious **p**.
93:1 he has armed himself with **p**.
96:7 Give to the LORD glory and **p**.
97:10 from the **p** of wicked people.
106:8 make his mighty **p** known.
106:10 He rescued them from the **p** of
106:42 made them subject to their **p**.
107:2 from the **p** of their enemies
111:6 He has revealed the **p** of his
125:3 do not use their **p** to do wrong.
132:8 place with the ark of your **p**.
145:6 People will talk about the **p** of
147:5 Lord is great, and his **p** is great.
Pro 3:27 when you have the **p** to do so.
18:21 The tongue has the **p** of life
31:3 strength to women or your **p**
Ecc 4:1 oppressors have ⌊all⌋ the **p**.
5:19 the **p** to enjoy them,
6:2 Yet, God doesn't give him the **p**
8:4 a king's word has such **p**,
8:8 No one has the **p** to prevent the
Isa 1:25 I will turn my **p** against you.
5:25 and he is ready to use his **p** to
5:25 he is still ready to use his **p**.
8:7 king of Assyria with all his **p**.
9:12 he is still ready to use his **p**.
9:17 he is still ready to use his **p**.
9:21 he is still ready to use his **p**.
10:4 he is still ready to use his **p**.
10:10 My **p** has reached kingdoms
10:16 into a raging fire under his **p**.
10:33 the branches with terrifying **p**.
11:2 the Spirit of advice and **p**,
11:11 the Lord will use his **p** again
14:26 This is how he will use his **p**
14:27 He is ready to use his **p**.
25:10 The LORD's **p** will be on this
26:11 O LORD, your **p** is visible,
40:10 LORD is coming with **p**
40:26 might and the strength of his **p**,
41:20 the LORD's **p** has done this,
43:13 can rescue people from my **p**.
45:1 strip kings of their **p**,
50:2 Don't I have the **p** to rescue

Isa 52:10 The LORD will show his holy **p**
53:1 the LORD's **p** been revealed?
59:16 So with his own **p** he wins a
63:5 So with my own **p** I won a
66:14 The **p** of the LORD will be
Jer 6:12 I will use my **p** against those
10:12 LORD made the earth by his **p**.
15:6 So I will use my **p** against you
15:21 I will rescue you from the **p** of
15:21 free you from the **p** of tyrants.
16:21 This time I will make my **p** and
20:13 from the **p** of wicked people.
27:8 them by Nebuchadnezzar's **p**,
42:11 you and rescue you from his **p**.
51:15 LORD made the earth by his **p**.
51:25 "I will use my **p** against you,
Lam 1:7 when its people fell into the **p**
Eze 1:3 The **p** of the LORD came over
3:14 The strong **p** of the LORD
3:22 The **p** of the LORD came over
6:14 I will use my **p** against them
8:1 The **p** of the Almighty LORD
13:9 I will use my **p** against the
13:21 people from your **p** so that they
13:23 rescue my people from your **p**.
14:9 I will use my **p** against you and
14:13 I will use my **p** against it,
16:27 "'So I used my **p** against you.
16:30 "'You have no will **p**!
17:14 and be unable to regain its **p**.
20:22 But I didn't use my **p** so that my
22:6 used their **p** to murder people.
22:13 "'I will use my **p** against you
25:7 That is why I will use my **p**
25:13 I will use my **p** against Edom.
25:16 I'm going to use my **p** against
30:18 dark when I break Egypt's **p**.
32:30 terrified people with their **p**.
33:22 the **p** of the LORD came over
33:28 will no longer brag about its **p**.
35:3 I will use my **p** against you,
37:1 The **p** of the LORD came over
38:12 I will use my **p** against the
39:21 I will turn my **p** against them
40:1 At that time the LORD's **p** came
Dan 2:23 You gave me wisdom and **p**.
2:37 He has given you **p**,
2:39 will rise to **p** after you.
3:15 can save you from my **p** then?"
3:17 furnace and from your **p**,
4:3 He uses his **p** to do amazing
4:3 His **p** lasts from one generation
4:17 has **p** over human kingdoms.
4:22 Your **p** reaches the most
4:25 has **p** over human kingdoms
4:30 by my own impressive **p**
4:32 has **p** over human kingdoms
4:34 because his **p** lasts forever and
5:19 because God gave him **p**.
5:21 has **p** over human kingdoms.
5:23 who has **p** over your life and
6:26 His **p** lasts to the end ⌊of time⌋.
7:6 It was given **p** to rule.
7:12 The **p** of the rest of the animals
7:14 He was given **p**, honor, and a
7:14 His **p** is an eternal power that
7:14 His power is an eternal **p** that
7:17 that will rise to **p** on the earth.
7:24 will rise to **p** from that kingdom.
7:24 king will rise to **p** after them.
7:26 his **p** will be taken away,
7:27 The kingdom, along with the **p**
8:4 no one could escape from its **p**.
8:7 the ram from the goat's **p**.
8:9 It gained **p** over the south,
8:10 It continued to gain **p** until it
8:23 mysterious things will rise to **p**.
8:25 He will cleverly use his **p** to
8:25 though not by any human **p**.
11:6 She won't hold on to her **p**,
11:16 He will rise to **p** in the beautiful
11:17 will decide to invade with the **p**
11:23 will act deceitfully and rise to **p**
11:25 army he will summon his **p**
11:41 will escape from his **p**.
11:42 He will use his **p** against many

Dan 12:7 When the **p** of the holy people
Hos 2:10 one will rescue her from my **p**.
10:13 You have trusted your own **p**
13:14 "I want to free them from the **p**
Amo 1:8 I will turn my **p** against Ekron.
Mic 3:8 But I am filled with the **p** of the
5:9 You will use your **p** against
Hab 3:4 That is where his **p** is hidden.
Zep 1:4 "I will use my **p** against Judah
2:13 The LORD will use his **p**
Hag 2:22 and destroy the **p** of nations.
Zec 4:6 ⌊succeed⌋ by might or by **p**,
11:6 any of them from their **p**."
Mat 7:22 and do many miracles by the **p**
13:54 man get this wisdom and the **p**
14:2 That's why he has the **p** to
20:25 have absolute **p** over people
22:29 know the Scriptures or God's **p**.
24:30 the sky with **p** and great glory.
Mar 5:30 At that moment Jesus felt **p**
6:14 That's why he has the **p** to
9:1 kingdom of God arrive with **p**."
9:18 they didn't have the **p** to do it."
9:38 out of a person by using the **p**
10:42 have absolute **p** over people
12:24 the Scriptures or God's **p**?
13:26 clouds with great **p** and glory.
16:17 They will use the **p** and
Luk 1:17 the spirit and **p** that Elijah had.
1:35 and the **p** of the Most High will
1:51 "He displayed his mighty **p**.
1:71 our enemies and from the **p**
1:74 from our enemies' **p** so that we
4:6 "I will give you all the **p** and
4:14 The **p** of the Spirit was with
4:36 With authority and **p** he gives
5:17 Jesus had the **p** of the Lord to
6:19 because **p** was coming from
8:46 I know **p** has gone out of me."
9:1 together and gave them **p**
9:1 over every demon and **p**
9:43 to see God's wonderful **p**.
9:49 out of a person by using the **p**
10:17 obey us when we use the **p**
10:19 and to destroy the enemy's **p**.
11:20 with the help of God's **p**,
12:5 afraid of the one who has the **p**
21:27 a cloud with **p** and great glory.
21:36 Pray so that you have the **p** to
22:25 "The kings of nations have **p**
24:49 you receive **p** from heaven."
Jon 3:35 and has put everything in his **p**.
12:38 the Lord's **p** been revealed?"
14:30 of this world has no **p** over me.
17:11 keep them safe by the **p** of your
17:12 I kept them safe by the **p** of
Act 1:8 But you will receive **p** when
2:24 death had no **p** to hold him.
2:33 God used his **p** to give Jesus
2:34 "Take my highest position of **p**
3:6 Through the **p** of Jesus Christ
3:12 by our own **p** or godly life?
3:16 Through his **p** alone this man,
4:7 "By what **p** or in whose name
4:10 healthy body because of the **p**
4:12 we can be saved only by the **p**
4:28 Through your will and **p**,
4:30 Show your **p** by healing,
4:30 amazing things through the **p**
4:33 With great **p** the apostles
5:31 God used his **p** to give Jesus
6:8 filled with God's favor and **p**.
8:10 "This man is the **p** of God,
8:10 and that **p** is called great."
8:19 and said, "Give me this **p** so
9:28 He spoke boldly with the **p** and
10:38 with the Holy Spirit and with **p**.
10:38 who was under the devil's **p**.
11:21 The Lord's **p** was with his
26:12 I had the **p** and authority of the
Rom 1:16 It is God's **p** to save everyone
1:20 his eternal **p** and divine nature,
3:9 of being under the **p** of sin,
6:4 death to life by the glorious **p**
6:9 no longer has any **p** over him.
6:10 died once and for all to sin's **p**.

Rom 6:11 yourselves dead to sin's p
6:11 God in the p Christ Jesus gives
6:13 any part of your body to sin's p.
6:14 Certainly, sin shouldn't have p
7:1 that laws have p over people
9:17 to demonstrate my p through
9:22 his anger and reveal his p,
13:1 obey the government in p.
15:13 overflow with hope by the p
15:19 by the p of miraculous and
15:19 and by the p of God's Spirit,
1Co 1:18 but it is God's p to us who are
1:24 God's p and God's wisdom.
2:4 with a show of spiritual p
2:5 human wisdom but on God's p.
2:6 of this world who are in p today
4:19 saying and what p they have.
4:20 kingdom is not just talk, it is p.
5:4 our Lord Jesus, and with his p,
6:14 and by his p God will also
10:13 beyond your p to resist.
15:17 and sin still has you in its p.
15:24 every ruler, authority, and p.
15:56 God's standards give sin its p.
2Co 4:7 This shows that the superior p
6:7 and the presence of God's p.
12:9 My p is strongest when you are
12:9 in order that Christ's p will live
13:3 he makes his p felt among you.
13:4 but by God's p he lives.
13:4 but by God's p we will live for
Gal 3:22 is controlled by the p of sin.
Eph 1:19 unlimited greatness of his p as
1:20 He worked with that same p in
3:7 when his p worked ⌊in me⌋.
3:16 and p through his Spirit.
3:20 whose p is at work in us.
3:20 By this p he can do infinitely
6:10 Finally, receive your p from the
Php 3:10 Faith knows the p that his
3:21 Through his p to bring
Col 1:11 might with all the p you need
1:13 God has rescued us from the p
1:29 his mighty p works in me.
2:12 through faith in the p of God,
2:15 and authorities ⌊of their p⌋
1Th 1:5 with words but also with p,
2Th 1:9 and from his glorious p.
1:11 also pray that through ⌊his⌋ p
2:9 will come with the p of Satan.
2:9 He will use every kind of p,
1Ti 6:16 Honor and p belong to him
2Ti 1:7 cowardly spirit but a spirit of p,
1:8 Instead, by God's p,
3:5 will not let its p change them.
3:15 They have the p to give you
Heb 2:14 one who had p over death (that
7:16 but because he has p that
1Pe 1:5 by God's p through faith
4:11 Glory and p belong to Jesus
5:6 Be humbled by God's p so that
5:11 P belongs to him forever.
2Pe 1:3 God's divine p has given us
1:3 This p was given to us through
2:11 who have more strength and p
Jud 1:25 for eternity glory, majesty, p,
Rev 1:5 Glory and p forever and ever
1:10 I came under the Spirit's p on
4:2 I came under the Spirit's p.
4:11 and p because you created
5:12 slain deserves to receive p,
5:13 and p forever and ever."
6:4 Its rider was given the p to take
6:8 They were given p over
7:12 wisdom, thanks, honor, p,
9:3 and they were given p like the
9:3 like the p of earthly scorpions.
9:10 They had the p to hurt people
9:19 The p of these horses is in
11:17 you have taken your great p
12:10 p, kingdom of our God,
13:2 The serpent gave its p,
15:8 from the glory of God and his p.
17:3 angel carried me by his p into
17:13 one purpose — to give their p
18:1 He had tremendous p,
Rev 19:1 and p belong to our God.
20:6 death has no p over them.
21:10 He carried me by his p away to

powerful (103)

Gen 26:16 become more p than we are."
Exo 6:6 I will rescue you with my p
15:15 The p men of Moab will
Dtr 3:24 me how great and p you are.
4:34 his mighty hand and p arm
5:15 his mighty hand and p arm
7:1 larger and more p than you.
7:19 He used his mighty hand and p
9:29 your great strength and p arm
10:17 p, and awe-inspiring God.
11:2 his mighty hand and p arm.
26:5 then they became a great, p,
26:8 his mighty hand and p arm
Jos 17:17 an important and very p people.
23:9 important and p nations out
1Sm 9:1 Kish was a p man.
2Sm 5:10 David continued to grow more p
1Ki 8:41 name, mighty hand, and p arm.
2Ki 10:6 with the city's most p men.
10:11 all the most p men,
1Ch 11:9 David continued to grow more p
29:25 made Solomon extremely p,
2Ch 1:1 with him and made him very p.
6:32 name, mighty hand, and p arm.
17:12 became more and more p.
26:8 because he became very p.
26:13 They were a p force that could
26:15 support until he became p.
26:16 But when he became p,
27:6 Jotham grew p because he
Ezr 4:20 Jerusalem has had p kings
7:28 and all the king's p officials
Est 9:4 becoming more and more p.
Job 21:7 and even become more p?
Psa 20:6 mighty deeds of his p hand.
21:8 Your p hand will find all who
29:4 The voice of the LORD is p.
60:5 Save ⌊us⌋ with your p hand,
68:33 his voice heard, his p voice.
79:11 With your p arm rescue those
108:6 Save ⌊us⌋ with your p hand,
110:2 The LORD will extend your p
117:2 His mercy toward us is p.
136:12 with a mighty hand and a p
136:17 the one who defeated p kings —
Pro 18:18 ⌊issues⌋ between p people.
24:5 knowledge is even more p.
Ecc 9:14 and a p king came to attack it.
Isa 8:7 the raging and p floodwaters
8:11 the LORD said with his p hand
10:13 this with my own two p hands.
27:1 will use his fierce and p sword
28:2 has one who is strong and p.
31:3 the LORD uses his p hand,
63:1 I am p enough to save ⌊you⌋."
63:12 is the one who sent his p arm
Jer 5:27 is why they become p and rich.
10:6 You are great. Your name is p.
21:5 and rage with my p hand and
27:5 my great strength and my p arm
32:17 your great strength and p arm.
32:21 a mighty hand and a p arm,
Eze 20:33 a mighty hand and a p arm,
20:34 my mighty hand and p arm.
31:6 All the p nations lived in its
32:29 They used to be p,
Dan 2:10 no matter how great and p,
2:20 because he is wise and p.
8:8 But when the goat became p,
8:24 He will destroy those who are p
Jnh 1:4 The storm was so p that the
Mic 7:3 P people dictate what they
Zec 8:22 Many people and p nations will
Mat 3:11 after me is more p than I.
28:2 there was a p earthquake.
Mar 1:7 after me is more p than I.
Luk 3:16 But the one who is more p than
24:19 He was a p prophet in what he
Act 9:22 Saul grew more p,
13:17 He used his p arm to bring
18:24 use the Scriptures in a p way.
Act 19:20 In this p way the word of the
27:14 Soon a p wind (called a
Rom 1:4 This was shown in a p way
1Co 1:26 You were not in p positions or
2Co 10:4 they are p weapons from God.
10:10 that my letters are p and strong,
2Th 2:11 send them a p delusion so that
Heb 1:3 together through his p words.
2:4 amazing things, other p acts,
11:34 They were p in battle and
2Pe 1:16 told you about the p coming
Rev 5:2 I saw a p angel calling out in a
6:12 A p earthquake struck.
6:15 the generals, the rich, the p,
10:1 I saw another p angel come
11:13 moment a p earthquake struck.
16:18 and a p earthquake.
16:18 There has never been such a p
18:2 He cried out in a p voice,
18:8 Lord God, who judges her, is p.
18:10 the p city Babylon!
18:21 Then a p angel picked up a

powerfully (2)

Exo 15:13 P, you will guide them to your
Job 40:23 the river flows p against it,

powerless (3)

Job 14:10 But a human dies and is p.
Isa 16:14 will be very few and p."
Gal 4:9 you turn back again to the p

powers (10)

Dan 7:27 All other p will serve and obey
Mat 24:29 and the p of the universe will
Mar 13:25 and the p of the universe will
Luk 21:26 Indeed, the p of the universe
Rom 8:39 or p in the world above or in the
Eph 1:21 all rulers, authorities, p, lords,
6:12 the p who govern this world of
Col 1:16 rulers or p — everything has
Heb 6:5 of God's word and the p
1Pe 3:22 Angels, rulers, and p have

practice (17)

Dtr 18:10 them alive, p black magic,
18:14 to those who p black magic.
1Sm 17:39 never had any p doing this."
27:11 This was his p as long as he
Psa 37:3 and p being faithful.
Mic 3:7 Those who p witchcraft will be
Mat 23:3 they don't p what they preach.
Act 8:9 of Samaria with his p of magic.
8:11 a long time with his p of magic.
16:21 or p as Roman citizens."
Rom 3:13 Their tongues p deception.
Eph 4:19 They p every kind of sexual
Php 4:9 P what you've learned and
1Ti 4:15 P these things. Devote your life
Heb 5:14 whose minds are trained by p
Jas 2:1 My brothers and sisters, p your
1Pe 4:7 Therefore, p self-control,

practiced (5)

1Sm 17:39 but he had never p doing this.
2Ki 17:17 They p black magic and cast
2Ch 33:6 cast evil spells, p witchcraft,
Job 29:14 I p justice, and it was my robe
Isa 47:12 You have p them ever since

practices (20)

Exo 23:24 their gods or follow their p.
Lev 18:24 By these p all the nations
20:23 Never follow the p of the
Dtr 18:9 disgusting p of those nations.
18:12 because of their disgusting p.
Jdg 2:19 their evil p and stubborn ways.
1Ki 14:24 did all the disgusting p done by
2Ch 36:14 followed all the disgusting p
Ezr 6:21 themselves from the unclean p
9:1 and from the disgusting p
9:11 disgusting p that have filled
Est 9:31 and their descendants the p
9:32 established these p of Purim,
Pro 10:17 Whoever p discipline is on the
Jer 10:2 Don't learn the p of the nations.

Eze 16:43 to all your disgusting **p**?
23:36 them about their disgusting **p**?
Dan 6:5 we find it in his religious **p**."
Mic 6:16 kept Omri's laws and all the **p**
1Th 2:3 corrupt **p**, or deception.

practicing (2)

Isa 47:12 Keep **p** your spells and your
Rev 9:21 **p** witchcraft, sinning sexually,

praise (271)

Gen 9:26 **P** the LORD, the God of Shem!
24:27 He said, "**P** the LORD,
29:35 "This time I will **p** the LORD."
29:35 So she named him Judah [**P**].
49:8 your brothers will **p** you.
Exo 15:2 is my God, and I will **p** him,
Lev 19:24 holy offering of **p** to the LORD.
Dtr 10:8 and to **p** his name,
26:19 He will give you **p**,
Jos 7:19 give honor and **p** to the LORD
Jdg 5:2 **P** the LORD! Men in Israel
5:9 who volunteered. **P** the LORD!
9:27 Then they made an offering of **p**
Rut 4:14 said to Naomi, "**P** the LORD,
2Sm 22:50 make music to **p** your name.
1Ki 1:48 and said, '**P** the LORD God of
8:33 turn to you, **p** your name, pray,
8:35 toward this place, **p** your name,
1Ch 16:4 and **p** to the LORD God of
16:9 Make music to **p** him.
16:35 and make your **p** our glory.'
23:5 and 4,000 were appointed to **p**
23:30 to stand to give thanks and **p**
29:13 and **p** your wonderful name.
29:20 "**P** the LORD your God!"
2Ch 5:13 they sang in **p** to the LORD:
6:24 people turn, **p** your name, pray,
6:26 toward this place, **p** your name,
7:6 and which he used to offer **p**.
20:19 stood up to **p** the LORD God of
20:21 to sing to the LORD and **p** him
29:30 the leaders told the Levites to **p**
Ezr 3:10 their places with cymbals to **p**
3:11 people shouted, "**P** the LORD,"
Neh 9:5 high above all blessing and **p**.
12:24 one another to sing hymns of **p**
12:46 ⌊in singing⌋ the songs of **p**
Job 36:24 that you should **p** his work.
40:14 Then even I will **p** you
Psa 7:17 I will make music to **p** the
9:2 make music to **p** your name,
9:11 Make music to **p** the LORD,
16:7 I will **p** the LORD, who advises
18:49 make music to **p** your name.
21:13 make music to **p** your power.
22:22 I will **p** you within the
22:23 All who fear the LORD, **p** him!
22:25 My **p** comes from you while I
22:26 look to the LORD will **p** him.
26:12 I will **p** the LORD with the
27:6 make music to **p** the LORD.
30:4 Make music to **p** the LORD,
30:12 so that my soul may **p** you with
34:1 My mouth will always **p** him.
34:3 **P** the LORD's greatness with
35:18 I will **p** you in a crowd ⌊of
35:28 about your **p** all day long.
40:3 a song of **p** to our God.
42:5 because I will still **p** him.
42:11 because I will still **p** him.
43:5 because I will still **p** him.
44:8 All day long we **p** our God.
47:6 Make music to **p** God.
47:6 Make music to **p** our king.
48:10 Like your name, O God, your **p**
49:18 alive (and they **p** you when you
51:15 my mouth will tell about your **p**.
56:4 I **p** the word of God.
56:10 I **p** the word of God.
56:10 I **p** the word of the LORD.
57:9 I want to make music to **p** you
59:17 I will make music to **p** you!
61:8 Then I will make music to **p**
63:3 My lips will **p** you because
63:5 sing ⌊your⌋ **p** with joyful lips.
Psa 66:2 Make music to **p** the glory of
66:2 Make his **p** glorious.
66:4 It will make music to **p** you.
66:4 make music to **p** your name."
66:8 Make the sound of his **p** heard.
66:17 High **p** was on my tongue.
68:4 make music to **p** his name.
68:32 Make music to **p** the Lord.
69:30 I want to **p** the name of God
69:30 I want to **p** its greatness with a
69:34 that moves in them, **p** him.
71:6 My songs of **p** constantly
71:8 My mouth is filled with your **p**,
71:14 I will **p** you more and more.
71:16 I will **p** your righteousness,
71:22 music with a harp to **p** you,
71:23 when I make music to **p** you.
72:15 May ⌊they⌋ **p** him all day long.
74:21 and needy people **p** your name.
75:9 I will make music to **p** the God
76:10 Even angry mortals will **p** you.
79:13 We will **p** you throughout every
89:5 O LORD, the heavens **p** your
89:15 who know how to **p** you.
92:1 to make music to **p** your name,
96:2 **P** his name! Day after day
100:4 his courtyards with a song of **p**.
100:4 thanks to him; **p** his name.
101:1 I will make music to **p** you.
102:18 to be created may **p** the LORD:
102:21 in Zion and his **p** in Jerusalem
103:1 **P** the LORD, my soul!
103:1 **P** his holy name, all that is
103:2 **P** the LORD, my soul,
103:20 **P** the LORD, all his angels,
103:21 **P** the LORD, all his armies,
103:22 **P** the LORD, all his creatures
103:22 **P** the LORD, my soul!
104:1 **P** the LORD, my soul! O LORD
104:33 I will make music to **p** my God
104:35 **P** the LORD, my soul!
105:2 Make music to **p** him.
106:2 for which he is worthy of **p**?
106:12 what he said. They sang his **p**.
106:47 and make your **p** our glory.
107:32 Let them **p** him in the company
108:3 I want to make music to **p** you
109:1 O God, whom I **p**, do not turn a
109:30 I will **p** him among many
111:10 His **p** continues forever.
113:1 servants of the LORD, **p** him.
113:1 **P** the name of the LORD.
115:17 are dead do not **p** the LORD,
117:1 **P** the LORD, all you nations!
117:1 **P** him, all you people of the
119:108 Please accept the **p** I gladly
119:164 Seven times a day I **p** you for
119:171 Let my lips pour out **p** because
119:175 new life so that it can **p** you.
134:1 **P** the LORD, all you servants
134:2 holy place, and **p** the LORD.
135:1 **P** the name of the LORD.
135:1 **P** him, you servants of the
135:3 **P** the LORD because he is
135:3 Make music to **p** his name
135:19 of Israel, **p** the LORD.
135:19 of Aaron, **p** the LORD.
135:20 of Levi, **p** the LORD.
135:20 fear the LORD, **p** the LORD.
138:1 I will make music to **p** you in
145:1 I will highly **p** you,
145:2 I will **p** your name forever and
145:4 One generation will **p** your
145:10 and your faithful ones will **p**
145:21 My mouth will speak the **p** of
145:21 and all living creatures will **p**
146:1 **P** the LORD, my soul!
146:2 I want to **p** the LORD
146:2 I want to make music to **p** my
147:1 It is pleasant to sing ⌊his⌋ **p**
147:12 **P** the LORD, Jerusalem!
147:12 Jerusalem! **P** your God, Zion!
148:1 **P** the LORD from the heavens.
148:1 **P** him in the heights above.
148:2 **P** him, all his angels.
148:2 **P** him, his entire heavenly
Psa 148:3 **P** him, sun and moon.
148:3 **P** him, all shining stars.
148:4 **P** him, you highest heaven and
148:5 Let them **p** the name of the
148:7 **P** the LORD from the earth.
148:7 **P** him, large sea creatures and
148:13 Let them **p** the name of the
149:1 Sing his **p** in the assembly of
149:3 Let them **p** his name with
150:1 **P** God in his holy place.
150:1 **P** him in his mighty heavens.
150:2 **P** him for his mighty acts.
150:2 **P** him for his immense
150:3 **P** him with sounds from horns.
150:3 **P** him with harps and lyres.
150:4 **P** him with tambourines and
150:4 **P** him with stringed
150:5 **P** him with loud cymbals.
150:5 **P** him with crashing cymbals.
150:6 that breathes **p** the LORD!
Pro 27:2 **P** should come from another
27:21 tested⌋ by the **p** given to him.
28:4 teachings **p** wicked people,
31:31 and let her achievements **p** her
Sos 1:4 We will **p** your expressions of
Isa 12:1 will say, "I will **p** you, O LORD.
12:4 you will say, "**P** the LORD.
12:5 Make music to **p** the LORD.
24:16 we hear songs of **p** that honor
25:1 I will **p** your name.
38:18 Death doesn't **p** you!
38:19 Those who are living **p** you as
41:16 will find joy in the LORD and **p**
42:8 glory to anyone else or the **p**
42:10 Sing his **p** from the ends of the
42:11 the settlements of Kedar **p** him.
42:12 his **p** on the coastlands.
43:21 for myself. They will **p** me.
45:25 and they will **p** the LORD.
57:19 I'll create **p** on their lips:
60:18 Salvation and your gates **P**.
61:3 and clothes of **p** instead of a
61:11 righteousness and **p** spring up
62:7 object of **p** throughout the earth
62:9 will eat it and **p** the LORD.
Jer 13:11 **p**, and honor to me. However,
17:14 You are the one I **p**.
20:13 **P** the LORD! He has rescued the
30:19 live there will sing songs of **p**,
31:7 Shout, sing **p**, and say,
33:9 my source of joy, **p**, and honor.
48:2 People will no longer **p** Moab.
Dan 2:20 He said, "**P** God's name from
2:23 ancestors, I thank and **p** you.
3:28 "**P** the God of Shadrach,
4:37 Now I, Nebuchadnezzar, will **p**,
Hos 14:2 Then we'll **p** you with our lips.
Joe 2:26 You will **p** the name of the
Hab 3:3 His **p** fills the earth.
Zec 11:5 them will say, "**P** the LORD!
Mat 5:16 that you do and **p** your Father
11:25 Jesus said, "I **p** you, Father,
21:16 you have created **p**'?"
Luk 1:64 and he began to **p** God.
1:68 "**P** the Lord God of Israel!
10:21 Jesus said, "I **p** you,
17:18 foreigner came back to **p** God."
19:37 of disciples began to **p** God
Jon 5:41 "I don't accept **p** from humans.
5:44 when you accept each other's **p**
5:44 look for the **p** that comes from
Act 16:25 and singing hymns of **p** to God.
Rom 1:21 They knew God but did not **p**
2:29 That person's **p** will come from
13:3 what is right, and it will **p** you.
14:11 and everyone will **p** God."
15:6 you will **p** the God and Father
15:9 People who are not Jewish **p**
15:11 And again, "**P** the Lord,
15:11 **P** him, all you people of the
1Co 4:5 person will receive **p** from God.
11:2 I **p** you for always thinking
11:17 I have no **p** for you as I instruct
11:22 Should I **p** you? I won't praise
11:22 I won't **p** you for this.
14:16 Otherwise, if you **p** God only

2Co 1:3 **P** the God and Father of our
8:18 whom all the churches **p**
Eph 1:3 **P** the God and Father of our
1:12 our hope on Christ would **p** him
1:14 God receives **p** and glory for
Php 1:11 then bring glory and **p** to God.
4:8 whatever is right or deserves **p**:
1Th 2:6 We didn't seek **p** from people,
Heb 2:12 I will **p** you within the
3:3 Jesus deserves more **p** than
13:15 bring God a sacrifice of **p**,
Jas 3:9 With our tongues we **p** our Lord
3:10 **P** and curses come from the
1Pe 1:3 **P** the God and Father of our
1:7 the test, it gives **p**, glory,
1:8 with joy and **p** that can hardly
2:12 they will **p** God on the day he
2:14 wrong and to **p** those who do
4:16 but **p** God for being called that
Rev 5:12 strength, honor, glory, and **p**."
5:13 the throne and to the lamb be **p**,
7:12 **P**, glory, wisdom, thanks,
15:4 won't fear and **p** your name?
19:5 It said, "**P** our God,

praised (70)

Gen 24:48 I **p** the LORD, the God of my
Num 23:21 is with them, **p** as their king.
Jos 22:33 So they **p** God and didn't talk
Jdg 16:24 saw him, they **p** their god.
2Sm 14:25 Now, no one in all Israel was **p**
18:28 "May the LORD your God be **p**.
22:4 The LORD should be **p**.
1Ki 5:7 "May the LORD be **p** today.
1Ch 16:25 He should be highly **p**.
16:36 said amen and **p** the LORD.
22:5 magnificent, large, famous, **p**,
25:3 They thanked and **p** the LORD
29:10 he **p** the LORD while the whole
29:10 David said, "May you be **p**,
29:20 So the whole assembly **p** the
2Ch 2:12 the LORD God of Israel be **p**.
5:13 the trumpeters and singers **p**
7:3 worshiped and **p** the LORD,
30:21 day the Levites and priests **p**
31:8 they **p** the LORD and his
Ezr 3:11 As they **p** and gave thanks to
Neh 5:13 said amen and **p** the LORD.
9:5 your glorious name is **p**
Job 1:21 the name of the LORD be **p**."
Psa 18:3 The LORD should be **p**.
48:1 He should be highly **p**.
65:1 You are **p** with silence in Zion,
96:4 He should be highly **p**.
113:3 name of the LORD should be **p**.
145:3 and he should be highly **p**.
Pro 12:8 A person will be **p** based on
31:30 fear of the LORD should be **p**.
Ecc 8:10 They were **p** in the city for
Sos 6:9 concubines saw her and **p** her.
Isa 52:13 He will be respected, **p**,
64:11 where our ancestors **p** you,
Jer 51:41 the city that the whole world **p**,
Dan 2:19 So Daniel **p** the God of heaven.
4:34 I thanked the Most High, and I **p**
5:4 They drank the wine and **p**
5:23 You **p** your gods made of silver,
6:10 He had always **p** God this way.
Zep 3:19 I will make them **p** and famous
3:20 I will make you famous and **p**
Mat 6:2 in order to be **p** by people.
9:8 they were filled with awe and **p**
15:31 So they **p** the God of Israel.
Mar 2:12 was amazed and **p** God,
Luk 2:20 they glorified and **p** God for
2:28 his arms and **p** God by saying,
4:15 and everyone **p** him.
5:26 was amazed and **p** God.
7:16 struck with fear and **p** God.
13:13 stood up straight and **p** God.
16:8 "The master **p** the dishonest
17:15 he turned back and **p** God in a
18:43 He followed Jesus and **p** God.
18:43 saw this, and they, too, **p** God.
23:47 he **p** God and said,
24:53 where they **p** God.
Act 2:47 At the same time, they **p** God
11:18 They **p** God by saying,
13:48 with what they heard and **p**
21:20 about everything, they **p** God.
1Co 12:26 If one part is **p**, all the others
2Co 6:8 as we are **p** and dishonored,
11:31 Lord Jesus, who is **p** forever,
Gal 1:24 So they **p** God for what had
Eph 1:6 would be **p** and given glory.
Heb 3:3 of a house is **p** more than

praises (16)

Jdg 11:40 would go out to sing the **p**
2Ch 20:22 As they started to sing **p**,
29:30 They joyfully sang **p**,
Neh 6:19 nobles were singing Tobiah's **p**
Psa 6:5 In the grave, who **p** you?
9:14 so that I may recite your **p** one
22:3 enthroned on the **p** of Israel.
149:6 Let the high **p** of God be in their
Pro 31:28 In addition, he sings her **p**,
Ecc 7:5 than to fools who sing your **p**.
Isa 42:21 He **p** the greatness of his
60:6 will sing the **p** of the LORD.
63:7 and ⌊sing⌋ the **p** of the LORD,
Luk 1:46 soul **p** the Lord's greatness!
Rom 15:9 and I will sing **p** to your name."
1Co 13:4 It doesn't sing its own **p**.

praiseworthy (1)

Psa 148:14 someone **p** for his faithful ones,

praising (13)

1Ch 23:5 David had made for **p** God.
2Ch 7:6 which King David made for **p**
8:14 ⌊The Levites⌋ were to lead in **p**
23:12 people running and **p** the king,
31:2 or **p** within the gates of the
Psa 33:1 **P** ⌊the LORD⌋ is proper for
84:4 They are always **p** you.
Luk 2:13 They were **p** God by saying,
5:25 **P** God, he went home.
Act 3:8 walking, jumping, and **p** God.
3:9 saw him walking and **p** God.
4:21 Since all the people were **p**
10:46 in other languages and **p** God.

pray (155)

Gen 20:7 He will **p** for you, and you will
Exo 8:8 "**P** that the LORD will take the
8:9 when I should **p** for you,
8:10 "**P** for me tomorrow,"
8:28 God in the desert and **p** for me."
8:29 I will **p** to the LORD.
9:28 **P** to the LORD. We've had
10:17 **P** to the LORD your God to
Num 21:7 **P** to the Lord so that he will
Dtr 4:7 to us whenever we **p** to him?
1Sm 2:25 who will **p** for him?"
7:5 and I will **p** to the LORD for
12:19 "**P** to the LORD your God for us
12:23 LORD by failing to **p** for you.
2Sm 14:11 please **p** to the LORD your God
1Ki 8:28 cry for help as I **p** to you today.
8:29 to me as I **p** toward this place.
8:30 Israel and I **p** toward this place.
8:30 us ⌊when we **p**⌋ to heaven,
8:33 to you, praise your name, **p**,
8:35 and they **p** toward this place,
8:42 to **p** facing this temple,
8:44 send them) and they **p** to you,
8:48 if they **p** to you toward the land
13:6 and **p** for me so that I can use
18:42 down on the ground to **p**.
2Ki 19:4 **P** for the few people who are
1Ch 17:25 ⌊the courage⌋ to **p** to you.
2Ch 6:12 stretched out his hands ⌊to **p**⌋.
6:19 to my cry for help as I **p** to you.
6:20 to me as I **p** toward this place.
6:21 Israel and I **p** toward this place.
6:24 turn, praise your name, **p**,
6:26 and they **p** toward this place,
6:32 come to **p** facing this temple,
6:34 you may send them) and they **p**
6:38 if they **p** to you toward the land
7:14 themselves, **p**, search for me,
Ezr 6:10 the God of heaven and **p**
Neh 1:4 I continued to fast and **p** to the
Job 11:13 your heart right, then **p** to him.
21:15 do we gain if we **p** to him?'
22:27 You will **p** to him, and he will
33:26 They will **p** to God,
42:8 My servant Job will **p** for you.
Psa 5:2 because I **p** only to you.
32:6 reason let all godly people **p**
44:20 our hands to **p** to another god,
63:4 my hands ⌊to **p**⌋ in your name.
72:15 May ⌊the people⌋ **p** for him
109:4 accuse me, but I **p** for them.
119:5 I **p** that my ways may become
122:6 **P** for the peace of Jerusalem:
Isa 16:12 come into the holy place to **p**,
37:4 **P** for the few people who are
44:17 They **p** to them, saying,
45:14 will bow to you and **p** to you,
45:20 carry wooden idols and **p**
Jer 7:16 don't **p** for these people.
7:16 Don't cry or **p** for them.
11:14 don't **p** for these people.
11:14 Don't cry or **p** for them.
14:11 The LORD said to me, "Don't **p**
29:7 and **p** to the LORD for that city.
29:12 You will come and **p** to me,
31:9 They will **p** as I bring them
37:3 They asked him, "Please **p** to
42:2 and **p** to the LORD your God for
42:4 I will **p** to the LORD your God
42:20 '**P** to the LORD our God for us,
Dan 9:20 I continued to **p**, confessing my
Hos 7:14 They don't **p** to me sincerely,
Jnh 1:6 Get up, and **p** to your God.
Mat 5:44 and **p** for those who persecute
6:5 "When you **p**, don't be like
6:5 corners to **p** so that everyone
6:6 When you **p**, go to your room
6:6 **P** privately to your Father who
6:7 "When you **p**, don't ramble like
6:9 "This is how you should **p**:
14:23 up a mountain to **p** by himself.
19:13 him bless them and **p** for them.
24:20 **P** that it will not be winter or a
26:36 while I go over there and **p**."
26:41 Stay awake, and **p** that you
Mar 1:35 where he could be alone to **p**.
6:46 he went up a mountain to **p**.
11:24 received whatever you **p** for,
11:25 Whenever you **p**, Then your
13:18 **P** that it will not be in winter.
14:32 "Stay here while I **p**."
14:38 Stay awake, and **p** that you
Luk 6:12 Jesus went to a mountain to **p**.
6:28 **P** for those who insult you.
9:28 and went up a mountain to **p**.
11:1 teach us to **p** as John taught
11:2 Jesus told them, "When you **p**,
18:1 them that they need to **p** all
18:10 into the temple courtyard to **p**.
21:36 **P** so that you have the power
22:40 "**P** that you won't be tempted."
22:46 Get up, and **p** that you won't be
Jon 17:9 "I **p** for them. I'm not praying for
17:21 I **p** that all of these people
17:21 I **p** that they may be united with
Act 8:24 Simon answered, "**P** to the
10:9 Peter went on the roof to **p**.
Rom 1:10 every time I **p**. I ask that
8:26 we don't know how to **p**
10:14 But how can people **p** to him if
12:12 in trouble, and **p** continually.
15:30 my struggle. **P** to God for me
15:31 **P** that God's people in
15:32 Also **p** that by the will of God I
1Co 11:13 Is it proper for a woman to **p** to
14:13 in another language should **p**
14:14 If I **p** in another language,
14:15 It means that I will **p** with my
14:15 and I will **p** with my mind.
2Co 1:11 to help us when you **p** for us.
9:14 With deep affection they will **p**
13:7 We **p** to God that you won't do
Eph 1:17 I **p** that the glorious Father,
3:16 I **p** that he would give you inner

Eph 3:17 I also **p** that love may be the
6:18 **P** in the Spirit in every
6:19 Also **p** that God will give me
6:20 So **p** that I speak about this
Php 1:4 Every time I **p** for all of you,
1:9 I **p** that your love will keep on
Col 4:3 At the same time also **p** for us.
4:3 **P** that God will give us an
4:4 **P** that I may make this mystery
1Th 3:10 We **p** very hard night and day
3:11 We **p** that God our Father and
3:12 We also **p** that the Lord will
5:25 Brothers and sisters, **p** for us.
2Th 1:11 With this in mind, we always **p**
1:11 We also **p** that through ⌊his⌋
3:1 Finally, brothers and sisters, **p**
3:2 Also **p** that we may be rescued
1Ti 2:2 **P** for these people so that we
2Ti 4:16 I **p** that it won't be held against
Phm 1:6 I **p** that you may come to have
Heb 13:18 **P** for us. We are sure that our
Jas 4:2 because you don't **p** for them.
4:3 When you **p** for things,
5:13 of you are having trouble, **p**.
5:14 Have them **p** for you and anoint
5:16 and **p** for each other so that you
1Pe 4:7 minds clear so that you can **p**.
1Jn 5:16 you should **p** that God would
5:16 not telling you to **p** about that.
3Jn 1:2 I **p** that you're doing well in
Jud 1:20 **P** with the Holy Spirit's help.

prayed (84)

Gen 20:17 Abraham **p** to God,
24:12 Then he **p**, "LORD, God of my
24:42 I came to the spring today, I **p**,
25:21 Isaac **p** to the LORD for his
32:9 Then Jacob **p**, "God of my
Exo 8:12 Moses **p** to the LORD about the
8:30 left Pharaoh and **p** to the LORD.
10:18 left Pharaoh and **p** to the LORD.
Num 11:2 Moses **p** to the LORD,
21:7 So Moses **p** for the people.
Dtr 9:20 But at that time I **p** for Aaron,
9:26 I **p** to the LORD and said,
1Sm 1:10 she **p** to the LORD while she
1:26 next to you and **p** to the LORD.
1:27 I **p** for this child, and the LORD
2:1 Hannah **p** out loud,
8:6 So Samuel **p** to the LORD.
15:11 and he **p** to the LORD all night.
22:10 Ahimelech **p** to the LORD for
22:13 him bread and a sword and **p**
22:15 Is this the first time I have **p** to
28:6 He **p** to the LORD,
2Sm 15:31 So David **p**, "LORD,
1Ki 8:59 these words which I have **p**
2Ki 4:33 and **p** to the LORD.
6:17 Then Elisha **p**, "LORD,
6:18 Elisha **p** to the LORD,
17:16 They **p** to the entire army of
19:15 and **p** to the LORD,
19:20 You **p** to me about King
20:2 to the wall and **p** to the LORD,
21:21 way and worshiped and **p**
1Ch 4:10 Jabez **p** to the God of Israel,
4:10 God gave him what he **p** for.
2Ch 30:18 Hezekiah **p** for them:
32:20 **p** about this and called to
32:24 He **p** to the LORD,
33:13 He **p** to the LORD,
Neh 2:4 So I **p** to the God of heaven,
4:4 ⌊Nehemiah **p**,⌋ "Our God,
4:9 But we **p** to our God and set
6:14 ⌊Nehemiah **p**,⌋ "My God,
13:14 ⌊Nehemiah **p**,⌋ "Remember me
13:22 ⌊Nehemiah **p**,⌋ "Remember me
13:29 **p**,⌋ "Remember them,
13:31 ⌊Nehemiah **p**,⌋ "Remember me,
Job 42:10 After Job **p** for his friends,
Psa 99:6 among those who **p** to him.
Isa 37:15 and **p** to the LORD,
37:21 You **p** to me about King
38:2 to the wall and **p** to the LORD.
43:22 Jacob, you have not **p** to me.
Jer 32:16 son of Neriah, I **p** to the LORD.
Jer 32:16 I prayed to the LORD. I **p**,
Dan 6:10 got down on his knees and **p**
9:3 I **p**, pleaded, and fasted in
9:4 I **p** to the LORD my God.
Jnh 2:1 From inside the fish Jonah **p** to
2:2 Jonah **p**: "I called to the LORD
4:2 So he **p** to the LORD,
Mat 26:39 his face to the ground and **p**,
26:42 away a second time and **p**,
26:44 he went away and **p** the same
Mar 14:35 he fell to the ground and **p** that
14:39 He went away again and **p** the
Luk 18:11 The Pharisee stood up and **p**,
22:32 But I have **p** for you,
22:41 throw, knelt down, and **p**,
22:44 So he **p** very hard in anguish.
Act 1:24 Then they **p**, "Lord, you know
4:24 united and loudly **p** to God,
6:6 who **p** and placed their hands
8:15 went to Samaria and **p** that
9:40 He knelt and **p**. Then he turned
10:2 people and always **p** to God.
20:36 he knelt down and **p** with all of
21:5 We knelt on the beach, **p**,
27:29 from the back of the ship and **p**
28:8 Paul went to him, **p**,
2Co 1:11 because many people **p** for us.
Heb 5:7 life on earth, Jesus **p** to God,
5:7 He **p** and pleaded with loud
Jas 5:17 when he **p** that it wouldn't rain,
5:18 Then he **p** again. It rained, and

prayer (108)

Gen 25:21 The LORD answered his **p**,
30:6 He has heard my **p** and has
30:17 God answered Leah's **p**.
30:22 God answered her **p** and made
47:31 Then Israel bowed down in **p**
Exo 9:29 out my hands to the LORD in **p**.
9:33 out his hands to the LORD in **p**.
2Sm 7:27 courage to offer this **p** to you.
1Ki 8:28 pay attention to my **p** for mercy.
8:38 ⌊hear⌋ every **p** for mercy,
8:45 then hear their **p** for mercy in
8:49 hear their **p** for mercy.
8:54 Solomon finished praying this **p**
9:3 "I have heard your **p** for mercy
2Ki 16:15 I will use the bronze altar for **p**."
20:5 David says: I've heard your **p**.
2Ch 6:19 pay attention to my **p** for mercy.
6:29 ⌊hear⌋ every **p** for mercy made
6:35 then hear their **p** for mercy in
6:39 hear their **p** for mercy.
7:12 "I have heard your **p** and have
7:14 will hear ⌊their **p**⌋ from heaven,
33:13 and the LORD accepted his **p**
33:18 Manasseh — including his **p**
33:19 His **p** and how God accepted it
Ezr 8:23 and he answered our **p**.
9:5 to the LORD my God in **p**,
Neh 1:11 please pay attention to my **p**
11:17 who led the **p** of thanksgiving.
Job 6:8 "How I wish that my **p** would
16:17 and my **p** is sincere.
42:8 Then I will accept his **p** not to
42:9 the LORD accepted Job's **p**.
Psa 4:1 pity on me, and hear my **p**!
6:9 The LORD accepts my **p**.
17:1 Open your ears to my **p**,
21:2 You did not refuse the **p** from
28:2 Hear my **p** for mercy when I
28:6 He has heard my **p** for mercy!
35:13 my **p** returned unanswered,
39:12 Listen to my **p**, O LORD.
42:8 night his song is with me — a **p**
54:2 O God, hear my **p**,
55:1 Open your ears to my **p**,
61:1 Pay attention to my **p**.
66:19 He has paid attention to my **p**.
66:20 who has not rejected my **p** or
68:31 out its hands to God ⌊in **p**⌋.
69:13 May my **p** come to you at an
77:2 in **p** without growing tired.
80:4 against the **p** of your people?
84:8 of armies, hear my **p**.
86:6 Open your ears to my **p**,
Psa 88:2 Let my **p** come into your
88:9 out my hands to you ⌊in **p**⌋.
88:13 and in the morning my **p** will
102:1 O LORD, hear my **p**,
109:7 Let his **p** be considered sinful.
119:48 I lift my hands ⌊in **p**⌋ because
141:2 Let my **p** be accepted as
141:2 the lifting up of my hands in **p**
141:5 because my **p** is directed
143:1 O LORD, listen to my **p**.
143:6 out my hands to you in **p**.
Pro 28:9 Surely the **p** of someone who
Isa 1:15 stretch out your hands ⌊in **p**⌋,
38:5 David says: I've heard your **p**.
56:7 them happy in my house of **p**.
56:7 a house of **p** for all nations.
Lam 2:19 Lift up your hands to him ⌊in **p**⌋
3:8 he shuts out my **p**.
3:44 so that no **p** could get through
Dan 9:17 listen to my **p** and request.
10:12 come in response to your **p**.
Jnh 2:7 My **p** came to you in your holy
Hab 3:1 A **p** of the prophet Habakkuk;
Mat 21:13 a house of **p**,' but you're turning
21:22 whatever you ask for in **p**."
26:27 and spoke a **p** of thanksgiving.
26:44 prayed the same **p** a third time.
Mar 9:29 can be forced out only by **p**."
11:17 will be called a house of **p**
14:23 spoke a **p** of thanksgiving,
14:39 prayed the same **p** as before.
Luk 1:13 God has heard your **p**.
5:16 where he could be alone for **p**.
6:12 the whole night in **p** to God.
19:46 house of **p**,' but you have turned
22:17 and spoke a **p** of thanksgiving.
22:19 and spoke a **p** of thanksgiving.
22:45 When Jesus ended his **p**,
Jon 18:1 After Jesus finished his **p**,
Act 1:14 they devoted themselves to **p**.
2:42 the breaking of bread, and to **p**.
3:1 courtyard for the three o'clock **p**
10:31 God has heard your **p** and has
14:23 and with **p** and fasting they
16:13 Jewish people gathered for **p**.
16:16 were going to the place of **p**,
Rom 10:1 my heart's desire and **p** to God
1Co 7:5 time to devote yourselves to **p**.
11:24 and spoke a **p** of thanksgiving.
14:16 to your **p** of thanksgiving?
14:17 Your **p** of thanksgiving may be
Eph 6:18 Use every kind of **p** and
1Ti 2:8 hands in **p** after putting aside
4:5 The word of God and **p** set it
1Pe 3:12 His ears hear their **p**.

prayers (46)

2Sm 21:14 answered the **p** for the land.
24:25 So the LORD heard the **p** for
1Ch 5:20 and he answered their **p**
16:4 of the LORD's ark by offering **p**,
2Ch 6:40 ears attentive to the **p** ⌊offered⌋
7:15 to those **p** at this place.
30:27 and their **p** went to God's holy
Neh 1:11 to my prayer and to the **p**
Job 24:12 pays no attention to their **p**.
Psa 65:2 You are the one who hears **p**.
72:20 The **p** by David, son of Jesse,
102:17 will turn his attention to the **p**
102:17 He will not despise their **p**.
Pro 15:8 but the **p** of decent people
15:29 hears the **p** of righteous people.
31:2 What, son of my **p**?
Isa 1:15 Even though you offer many **p**,
19:22 to their **p** and heal them.
Jer 36:7 Maybe their **p** will come into
Hos 2:21 will answer your ⌊**p**⌋," declares
Mar 12:40 houses and then say long **p**
Luk 5:33 frequently fast and say **p**,
20:47 houses and then say long **p**
Act 10:4 "God is aware of your **p** and
2Co 9:12 also produces more and more **p**
Eph 1:16 always remember you in my **p**.
Php 1:19 I will be set free through your **p**
4:6 God know what you need in **p**
Col 1:3 Jesus Christ, in our **p** for you.

Col 4:2 you offer **p** of thanksgiving.
1Th 1:2 as we remember you in our **p**.
1Ti 2:1 petitions, **p**, intercessions,
2:1 and **p** of thanks for all people,
2:8 men to offer **p** everywhere.
4:3 food to be received with **p**
4:4 it is received with **p** of thanks.
2Ti 1:3 remember you in my **p** night
Phm 1:4 when I mention you in my **p**
1:22 I hope that, because of your **p**,
Heb 13:19 I especially ask for your **p** so
Jas 5:15 (**P** offered in faith will save
5:16 **P** offered by those who have
1Pe 3:7 will interfere with your **p**.
Rev 5:8 the **p** of the God's holy people.
8:3 He offered it with the **p** of all of
8:4 with the **p** of God's people.

praying (39)

Gen 24:15 Before he had finished **p**,
24:45 "Before I had finished **p**,
1Sm 1:12 While Hannah was **p** a long
1:13 She was **p** silently.
1:16 I was **p** like this because I've
1Ki 8:54 When Solomon finished **p** this
2Ch 7:1 When Solomon finished **p**,
Ezr 10:1 While Ezra was **p**,
Neh 1:6 to what I, your servant, am **p**.
1:6 I am **p** to you day and night
Dan 6:11 as a group and found Daniel **p**
9:21 While I was **p**, the man
Hos 7:14 cuts on their bodies while **p**
Luk 1:10 All the people were **p** outside
2:37 day and night by fasting and **p**.
3:21 baptized. While he was **p**,
9:18 Once when Jesus was **p**
9:29 While Jesus was **p**,
11:1 Once Jesus was **p** in a certain
11:1 When he stopped **p**,
Jon 17:9 I'm not **p** for the world but for
17:20 "I'm not **p** only for them.
17:20 I'm also **p** for those who will
Act 4:31 the apostles had finished **p**,
6:4 we will devote ourselves to **p**
9:11 from the city of Tarsus. He's **p**.
10:30 days ago I was **p** at home.
11:5 "I was **p** in the city of Joppa
12:5 but the church was **p** very hard
12:12 at her home and were **p**.
13:3 After fasting and **p**,
16:25 midnight Paul and Silas were **p**
22:17 While I was **p** in the temple
2Co 13:9 also **p** for your improvement.
Eph 3:19 I am **p** this so that you may be
Col 1:9 reason we have not stopped **p**
4:2 Keep **p**. Pay attention when you
1Th 5:17 Never stop **p**.
1Ti 5:5 her confidence in God by **p**

prays (10)

Psa 145:18 near to everyone who **p** to him,
145:18 faithful person who **p** to him.
Dan 6:13 He **p** three times each day."
Rom 10:12 to everyone who **p** to him.
10:13 So then, "Whoever **p** in the
1Co 11:4 covers his head when he **p**
11:5 Every woman who **p** or speaks
14:14 another language, my spirit **p**,
Col 4:12 He always **p** intensely for you.
4:12 He **p** that you will continue to

preach (8)

Pro 12:23 but foolish minds **p** stupidity.
Eze 20:46 **p** against the south,
21:2 **p** against the holy places.
Mic 2:11 "We will **p** to you about wine
Zec 1:4 the earlier prophets **p** to them,
1:6 servants the prophets to **p**,
Mat 23:3 they don't practice what they **p**.
Rom 2:21 As you **p** against stealing,

preached (1)

Dtr 13:5 because he **p** rebellion against

preacher (1)

Mic 2:11 be just the type of **p** you want.

preachers (1)

2Ti 3:13 But evil people and phony **p**

preaching (2)

Amo 7:16 and stop **p** against the
Gal 5:11 if I am still **p** that circumcision

preceded (2)

1Sm 17:41 The Philistine, **p** by the man
Jer 28:8 Long ago, the prophets who **p**

precedes (2)

Pro 16:18 Pride **p** a disaster,
16:18 and an arrogant attitude **p** a fall.

precious (49)

Exo 25:7 onyx stones, and other **p**
28:17 Fasten four rows of **p** stones
35:9 onyx stones, and other **p**
35:27 onyx stones and other **p** stones
39:10 They fastened four rows of **p**
2Sm 12:30 and contained a **p** stone.)
1Ki 10:2 quantity of gold, and **p** stones.
10:10 of spices, and **p** stones.
10:11 and **p** stones from Ophir.
2Ki 1:13 of yours as something **p**.
1:14 treat my life as something **p**."
1Ch 20:2 and in it was a **p** stone.)
29:8 Whoever happened to have **p**
2Ch 9:1 quantity of gold, and **p** stones.
9:9 of spices, and **p** stones.
9:10 sandalwood and **p** stones.
32:27 gold, **p** stones, spices, shields,
Ezr 8:27 bronze that were as **p** as gold.
Job 28:10 Their eyes see every **p** thing.
28:16 or with **p** onyx or sapphire.
Psa 35:17 Rescue my **p** life from the lions.
36:7 Your mercy is so **p**,
72:14 blood will be **p** in his sight.
116:15 **P** in the sight of the LORD is
139:17 How **p** are your thoughts
Pro 3:15 is more **p** than jewels,
20:15 but the lips of knowledge are **p**
24:4 both **p** and pleasant.
Sos 4:16 and let him eat his own **p** fruit.
7:13 our door are all kinds of **p** fruits.
Isa 28:16 been tested, a **p** cornerstone,
43:4 Since you are **p** to me,
44:9 Their **p** treasures are worthless
54:11 rebuild your city with **p** stones.
54:12 and all your walls with **p**
Lam 4:2 "Zion's **p** children,
Eze 22:25 treasures and **p** belongings.
27:22 the finest spices, **p** stones,
28:13 with every kind of **p** stone:
Dan 11:8 their gods and their **p** utensils
11:38 With gold, silver, **p** stones,
Hos 13:15 The wind will destroy every **p**
1Co 3:12 **p** stones, wood, hay, or straw.
Jas 5:7 See how farmers wait for their **p**
1Pe 1:7 Your faith is more **p** than gold,
1:19 that freed you was the **p** blood
2:4 but was chosen as **p** by God.
2:6 "I am laying a chosen and **p**
3:4 which God considers **p**.

predecessor (1)

1Ch 17:13 him my love as I did to your **p**.

predecessors (4)

2Ch 32:13 what I and my **p** have done
32:14 My **p** claimed and destroyed
Ezr 4:15 the official records of your **p**.
Dan 11:24 that none of his **p** ever did.

predict (4)

Dtr 13:1 may **p** a miraculous sign or an
Ecc 7:14 mortals cannot **p** their future.
Isa 44:7 Then let him **p** what will
Eze 13:9 visions and **p** things that don't

predicted (29)

Gen 21:7 Who would have **p** to Abraham
Exo 7:13 as the LORD had **p**.
7:22 as the LORD had **p**.
8:15 as the LORD had **p**.
8:19 as the LORD had **p**.
9:12 as the LORD had **p** to Moses.
9:35 LORD had **p** through Moses.
Dtr 34:5 As the LORD had **p**,
1Ki 22:38 as the LORD had **p**.
2Ki 1:17 the LORD had **p** through Elijah.
4:44 as the LORD had **p**.
7:16 as the LORD had **p**.
7:17 as the man of God had **p** when
9:26 into the field as the LORD **p**."
14:25 of Israel **p** through his servant
24:2 had **p** through his servants
24:13 As the LORD had **p**,
1Ch 22:11 your God as he **p** you would.
Isa 45:21 this in the distant past and **p**
Eze 13:7 visions and **p** things that don't
Jon 18:32 In this way what Jesus had **p**
Act 1:16 the Holy Spirit **p** through David
3:18 God had **p** these sufferings
7:52 They killed those who **p** that a
11:28 Through the Spirit Agabus **p**
Rom 9:29 This is what Isaiah **p**:
1Co 15:3 our sins as the Scriptures **p**.
15:4 third day as the Scriptures **p**.
1Pe 1:11 he **p** Christ's sufferings

prediction (2)

Psa 105:19 fiery trials until his **p** came true.
Dan 4:33 Just then the **p** about

predictions (4)

Jer 14:14 Their **p** are worthless.
Eze 13:6 and their **p** don't come true.
13:8 LORD says: Your **p** are false,
13:23 see false visions or make **p**.

predicts (1)

Dtr 13:2 What he **p** may even take

prefer (10)

1Ki 21:2 Or if you **p**, I will pay you a fair
Job 7:15 My body would **p** death to
34:19 or **p** important people over
Psa 52:3 You **p** evil to good.
52:3 You **p** lying to speaking the
1Co 4:21 would you **p** that I punish you
2Co 5:8 We are confident and **p** to live
Php 1:22 I don't know which I would **p**.
Phm 1:9 However, I would **p** to make an
2Jn 1:12 I would **p** not to write a letter.

preference (1)

Lev 19:15 and never show **p** to important

prefers (1)

Eze 16:32 wife who **p** strangers

pregnancies (1)

Hos 9:11 There will be no more **p**,

pregnant (73)

Gen 4:1 She became **p** and gave birth
4:17 She became **p** and gave birth
16:4 and she became **p**.
16:4 Hagar realized that she was **p**,
16:5 but now that she's **p**,
16:11 LORD said to her, "You are **p**,
19:36 became **p** by their father.
21:2 So she became **p**,
25:21 his wife Rebekah became **p**.
29:32 Leah became **p** and gave birth
29:33 She became **p** again and gave
29:34 She became **p** again and gave
29:35 She became **p** again and gave
30:5 Bilhah became **p**, and she
30:7 slave Bilhah became **p** again
30:17 She became **p** and gave birth
30:19 She became **p** again and gave
30:23 So she became **p** and gave
38:3 She became **p** and gave birth
38:4 She became **p** again and gave
38:5 Then she became **p** again and
38:18 and she became **p**.
38:24 because of it she's **p**."
38:25 "I'm **p** by the man who owns

Exo 2:2 The woman became **p** and had
21:22 and injure a **p** woman so that
Jdg 13:3 but now you will become **p**
13:5 You're going to become **p** and
13:7 'You're going to become **p** and
Rut 4:13 her the ability to become **p**.
1Sm 1:20 Hannah became **p** and gave
2:21 She became **p** ⌊five times⌋
4:19 Phinehas' wife, was **p**.
2Sm 11:5 The woman had become **p**.
11:5 to tell David that she was **p**.
2Ki 4:17 But the woman became **p** and
8:12 and rip open their **p** women."
15:16 ripped open all its **p** women.
1Ch 7:23 and she became **p**.
Job 39:2 count the months they are **p**
Psa 7:14 conceives evil, is **p** with harm,
Isa 7:14 A virgin will become **p** and
8:3 She became **p** and gave birth
26:17 we are like **p** women ready to
26:18 We were **p**; we writhed with
33:11 You will be **p** with hay.
Jer 20:17 would have always been **p**.
31:8 return together with **p** women
Hos 1:3 She became **p** and had a son.
1:6 Gomer became **p** again and
1:8 she became **p** again and had a
2:5 The woman who became **p**
13:16 and their **p** women will be
Amo 1:13 open **p** women in Gilead.
Mat 1:18 Mary realized that she was **p**
1:20 She is **p** by the Holy Spirit.
1:23 "The virgin will become **p** and
24:19 be for the women who are **p**
Mar 13:17 be for the women who are **p**
Luk 1:7 Elizabeth couldn't become **p**.
1:24 his wife Elizabeth became **p**
1:26 after Elizabeth had become **p**,
1:31 You will become **p**,
1:36 is six months **p** with a son in
2:5 to him in marriage and was **p**.
2:21 before his mother became **p**.
21:23 it will be for women who are **p**
23:29 the women who couldn't get **p**,
Rom 9:10 Rebekah became **p** by our
Gal 4:27 women who cannot get **p**,
1Th 5:3 pains come to a **p** woman.
Jas 1:15 Then desire becomes **p** and
Rev 12:2 She was **p**. She cried out from

prematurely (2)

Exo 21:22 so that she gives birth **p**.
1Sm 4:19 she went into labor **p** and gave

preoccupied (3)

Psa 37:1 Do not be **p** with evildoers.
37:7 Do not be **p** with ⌊an evildoer⌋
37:8 Do not be **p**. It only leads to evil.

preparation (1)

Jon 19:42 day was the Jewish day of **p**

preparations (2)

1Ch 22:14 my troubles I've made **p**
28:2 and I have made **p** to build it.

prepare (84)

Gen 27:4 **P** a good-tasting meal for me,
27:7 and **p** a good-tasting meal for
27:9 I'll **p** them as a good-tasting
43:16 an animal, and **p** a meal,
Exo 12:16 except to **p** your own meals.
12:39 Egypt and had no time to **p** food
16:5 when they **p** what they bring
Lev 6:21 **P** it in a frying pan with olive
6:22 his place as priest will **p** it.
26:26 only one oven to **p** your food.
Num 23:1 and **p** seven bulls and seven
23:29 and **p** seven bulls and seven
Dtr 24:6 wouldn't be able to **p** food
Jdg 13:15 "Please stay while we **p** a
2Sm 12:4 of his own sheep or cattle to **p**
13:5 She can **p** a meal in front of me
13:7 "and **p** some food for him."
1Ki 17:12 I'm going to **p** something for
17:13 Then **p** something for yourself
18:25 **P** yours first, because there are
18:44 tell Ahab, '**P** ⌊your chariot⌋,
2Ki 3:6 left Samaria to **p** Israel's army
1Ch 22:5 I'll **p** ⌊the building materials⌋
2Ch 2:9 They'll **p** plenty of lumber for
31:11 Then Hezekiah told them to **p**
35:6 and **p** ⌊the lambs⌋ for the other
Est 5:8 to a dinner I will **p** for you.
Job 30:12 They trip my feet and then **p**
37:19 We are unable to **p** ⌊a case⌋
Psa 23:5 You **p** a banquet for me while
65:9 Indeed, you even **p** the ground.
78:19 "Can God **p** a banquet in the
132:17 I will **p** a lamp for my anointed
Pro 24:27 **P** your work outside,
Isa 8:9 **P** for battle, but be terrified.
8:9 **P** for battle, but be terrified.
14:21 **P** a place to slaughter their
21:5 **P** your shields for battle!
25:6 the LORD of Armies will **p**
57:14 **P** the way! Remove every
62:10 **P** a way for the people!
66:17 holy and **p** themselves
Jer 6:4 ⌊The shepherds say,⌋ '**P**
10:3 of craftsmen **p** them with axes.
12:3 **P** them for the day of slaughter.
18:11 I'm going to **p** a disaster and
33:18 and to **p** daily sacrifices."
51:12 **P** ambushes. The LORD will
51:27 **P** nations to attack Babylon.
51:28 **P** nations to attack Babylon.
51:28 **P** the king of the Medes,
51:39 When they are excited, I will **p**
Eze 45:17 He must **p** offerings for sin,
45:22 At that time the prince must **p**
45:23 he must **p** burnt offerings for
45:25 He must **p** the same offerings
46:2 Then the priests must **p** the
46:13 "'**P** a year-old lamb that has no
46:14 Also, **p** a grain offering with it
46:15 **P** the lamb, the grain offering,
Dan 11:10 "Then his sons will **p** for war.
11:25 who will **p** for war with a large,
Joe 2:16 **P** them for a holy meeting.
3:9 **P** yourselves for war.
Amo 4:12 **P** to meet your God.
Nah 1:14 I will **p** your grave because you
2:1 **P** for battle! Be very courageous
Mat 3:3 '**P** the way for the Lord!
11:10 messenger ahead of you to **p**
26:17 "Where do you want us to **p** the
Mar 1:2 messenger ahead of you to **p**
1:3 '**P** the way for the Lord!
14:12 "Where do you want us to **p** the
Luk 1:17 In this way he will **p** the
1:76 ahead of the Lord to **p** his way.
3:4 '**P** the way for the Lord!
7:27 messenger ahead of you to **p**
22:8 **p** the Passover lamb for us to
22:9 "Where do you want us to **p** it?"
Jon 12:7 She has done this to **p** me for
14:2 have told you that I'm going to **p**
14:3 If I go to **p** a place for you,
Eph 4:12 purpose is to **p** God's people,
Heb 13:21 May this God of peace **p** you to

prepared (90)

Gen 14:8 Zoar) marched out and **p** for
18:7 to his servant, who **p** it quickly.
19:3 He **p** a special dinner for them,
26:30 Isaac **p** a special dinner for
27:14 She **p** a good-tasting meal,
27:17 meal and the bread she had **p**.
27:31 He, too, **p** a good-tasting meal
32:13 Then he **p** a gift for his brother
40:20 Pharaoh had a special dinner **p**
46:29 Joseph **p** his chariot and went
Exo 14:6 So Pharaoh **p** his chariot and
23:20 bring you to the place I have **p**.
Lev 2:5 If your grain offering is **p** in a
2:7 If your grain offering is **p** in a
2:8 the LORD the grain offering **p**
2:11 LORD must be **p** without yeast.
7:9 whether baked in an oven or **p**
Jdg 6:19 went into ⌊his house⌋ and **p**
2Sm 12:4 the poor man's lamb and **p** her
13:10 Tamar took the bread she had **p**
1Ki 5:18 Gebal quarried the stone and **p**
6:19 He **p** the inner room of the
18:26 took the bull he gave them, **p** it,
2Ki 6:23 So the king **p** a great feast for
1Ch 9:30 Some of the priests' sons **p** the
12:38 who were **p** for battle,
15:1 he **p** a place for God's ark and
15:3 ark to the place he had **p** for it.
15:12 of Israel to the place I **p** for it.
22:3 David **p** a large quantity of iron
22:3 He also **p** so much bronze that
22:5 So David **p** many materials ⌊for
22:14 I've also **p** wood and stones,
2Ch 1:4 to a place he had **p** for it.
3:1 There David had **p** the site on
4:6 The priests rinsed the meat **p**
13:3 Abijah **p** for battle with an army
16:14 him in the tomb that he had **p**
26:14 entire army Uzziah **p** shields,
31:11 After they had **p** them,
32:27 He **p** storerooms for himself to
35:10 So the service was **p**.
35:14 Later, they **p** ⌊the animals⌋ for
35:14 So the Levites **p** ⌊the animals⌋
35:15 **p** ⌊animals⌋ for them.
Neh 5:18 Poultry was **p** for me.
Est 5:4 to a dinner I have **p** for you."
5:5 to the dinner that Esther had **p**.
5:12 king to the dinner she had **p**.
6:4 on the pole he had **p** for him.
6:14 to the dinner Esther had **p**.
7:10 pole he had **p** for Mordecai.
Job 13:18 I have **p** my case. I know that I
Pro 9:2 She has **p** her meat.
Isa 30:33 Topheth was **p** long ago.
45:13 I **p** Cyrus for my righteous
65:11 You have **p** a table for the god
Eze 38:7 "'Be **p**! Be prepared, you and all
38:7 Be **p**, you and all the soldiers
Dan 9:14 So you were **p** to bring this
Joe 2:5 like a mighty army **p** for battle.
Zep 1:7 The LORD has **p** a sacrifice.
Mat 8:15 So she got up and **p** a meal for
20:23 My Father has already **p** these
22:4 had been invited, 'I've **p** dinner.
25:34 Inherit the kingdom **p** for you
25:41 into everlasting fire that was **p**
26:19 them and **p** the Passover.
Mar 1:31 and she **p** a meal for them.
10:40 been **p** for certain people."
14:16 So they **p** the Passover.
Luk 2:31 which you have **p** for all people
4:39 She got up immediately and **p**
22:13 told them and **p** the Passover.
23:56 back to the city and **p** spices
24:1 the spices that they had **p**.
Jon 12:2 Dinner was **p** for Jesus in
Act 9:37 Her body was **p** for burial and
10:10 While the food was being **p**,
13:48 Everyone who had been **p** for
Rom 9:23 who he had already **p** for glory?
1Co 2:9 the things that God has **p**
2Co 5:5 God has **p** us for this and has
Eph 2:10 with good works that he has **p**
2Ti 2:21 **p** to do good things.
3:17 so that they are completely **p**
Heb 10:5 but you **p** a body for me.
11:16 He has **p** a city for them.
Rev 9:7 looked like horses **p** for battle.
12:6 wilderness where God had **p**

prepares (7)

Exo 30:33 Whoever **p** a perfume like this
30:38 Whoever **p** anything like it for
Psa 7:13 He **p** his deadly weapons and
Ecc 10:10 But wisdom **p** the way for
Isa 42:13 He **p** himself for battle like a
Eze 46:12 When the prince **p** a freewill
Nah 2:3 on the day he **p** for battle.

preparing (9)

Gen 25:29 Once, Jacob was **p** a meal
1Ch 9:31 entrusted with **p** the flat bread.
Neh 5:18 **P** one ox and six choice
Jer 6:22 A great nation is **p** itself in the

Eze 39:17 the sacrifice that I'm **p** for you.
39:19 the sacrifice that I am **p** for you.
Amo 7:1 He was **p** swarms of locusts
Mat 4:21 their father Zebedee **p** their nets
Mar 1:19 They were in a boat **p** their

presence (402)

Gen 4:16 Then Cain left the LORD's **p**
17:1 Live in my **p** with integrity.
27:7 so that I will bless you in the **p**
31:32 In the **p** of our relatives,
48:15 in whose **p** my grandfather
Exo 10:3 to humble yourself in my **p**?
16:9 'Come into the LORD's **p**.
16:33 and put it in the LORD's **p** to be
18:12 Moses' father-in-law in God's **p**.
23:15 into my **p** without an offering.
23:17 your men must come into the **p**
25:30 Put the bread of the **p** on this
27:21 the LORD's **p** from evening until
28:12 as a reminder in the LORD's **p**.
28:29 reminder in the LORD's **p**.
28:30 he comes into the LORD's **p**.
28:30 whenever he's in the LORD's **p**,
28:35 and goes out of the LORD's **p**
29:11 the bull in the LORD's **p** at
29:23 bread which is in the LORD's **p**,
29:25 aroma in the LORD's **p**,
29:42 ⌊made⌋ in the LORD's **p** at
30:8 constantly in the LORD's **p**.
30:16 Israelites in the LORD's **p** that
33:14 "My **p** will go ⌊with you,⌋
33:15 "If your **p** is not going ⌊with
34:2 and stand in my **p** on the top of
34:20 into my **p** without an offering.
34:23 your men must come into the **p**
34:34 Moses went into the LORD's **p**
35:13 the dishes, the bread of the **p**,
39:36 the dishes, the bread of the **p**,
40:23 on the table in the LORD's **p**,
40:25 up the lamps in the LORD's **p**,
Lev 1:5 the bull in the LORD's **p**.
1:11 Slaughter it in the LORD's **p** on
3:1 of cattle in the LORD's **p**,
4:4 the bull into the LORD's **p** at
4:4 the bull in the LORD's **p**.
4:6 times in the LORD's **p** facing
4:7 incense in the LORD's **p**
4:15 the bull's head in the LORD's **p**.
4:15 slaughter it in the LORD's **p**.
4:17 LORD's **p** facing the canopy.
4:18 of the altar in the LORD's **p**
4:24 it in the LORD's **p** where
6:14 must bring it into the LORD's **p**
6:25 be slaughtered in the LORD's **p**
8:26 which was in the LORD's **p**.
9:2 Sacrifice them in the LORD's **p**.
9:4 oil to sacrifice in the LORD's **p**.
9:5 and stood in the LORD's **p**.
9:24 came out from the LORD's **p**
10:1 Then in the LORD's **p** they
10:2 they died in the **p** of the LORD.
10:19 burnt offering in the LORD's **p**,
12:7 will offer them in the LORD's **p**
14:11 offerings into the LORD's **p** at
14:16 seven times in the LORD's **p**.
14:18 for that person in the LORD's **p**.
14:23 tent of meeting in the LORD's **p**.
14:27 seven times in the LORD's **p**.
14:29 In the LORD's **p**, the priest will
14:31 So in the LORD's **p** the priest
15:14 and come into the LORD's **p** at
15:15 So in the LORD's **p**,
15:30 So in the LORD's **p** the priest
16:1 into the LORD's **p** and died.
16:7 bring them into the LORD's **p** at
16:10 for Azazel into the LORD's **p**.
16:12 which is in the LORD's **p**,
16:13 on the fire in the LORD's **p**.
16:18 the altar that is in the LORD's **p**
16:30 all your sins in the LORD's **p**.
19:22 In the LORD's **p** the priest will
22:3 must be excluded from my **p**.
23:40 and celebrate in the **p** of the
24:3 the LORD's **p** from evening until
24:4 lamp stand lit in the LORD's **p**.
Lev 24:6 the gold table in the LORD's **p**.
24:8 the bread in the LORD's **p**.
Num 3:4 and Abihu died in the LORD's **p**
3:4 unauthorized fire in his **p**
4:7 cloth over the table of the **p**
4:7 in the LORD's **p** will also
5:16 and stand in the LORD's **p**.
5:18 the woman into the LORD's **p**
5:30 his wife stand in the LORD's **p**,
8:10 the Levites into the LORD's **p**,
8:22 at the tent of meeting in the **p**
10:10 a reminder for you in God's **p**.
16:7 in them in the LORD's **p**.
16:16 must come into the LORD's **p**.
17:7 put the staffs in the LORD's **p**
17:9 out the staffs from the LORD's **p**
18:19 promise of salt in the LORD's **p**
19:3 camp and slaughtered in his **p**.
20:3 Israelites died in the LORD's **p**!
20:9 of ⌊the tent in⌋ the LORD's **p** as
25:4 broad daylight in the LORD's **p**.
26:61 fire in the LORD's **p**.
27:19 him his instructions in their **p**.
27:21 decisions in the LORD's **p**.
31:54 brought it into the LORD's **p** at
32:13 evil in the LORD's **p** was gone.
32:20 In the LORD's **p** have all your
32:22 own property in the LORD's **p**.
32:27 But in the LORD's **p** we will all
32:29 ready for battle in the LORD's **p**
32:32 armed troops in the LORD's **p**,
Dtr 6:25 obey all these laws in the **p**
10:8 to stand in the LORD's **p** when
12:7 in the **p** of the LORD your God,
12:12 Enjoy yourselves in the **p** of
12:18 cities must eat these in the **p**
12:18 There in the **p** of the LORD
14:23 and goats in the **p** of the LORD
14:26 enjoy yourselves there in the **p**
15:20 must eat these animals in the **p**
16:11 Enjoy yourselves in the **p** of
16:16 your men must come into the **p**
16:16 But no one may come into the **p**
18:7 do their work in the LORD's **p**.
19:17 must stand in the LORD's **p**,
24:4 be disgusting in the LORD's **p**.
24:13 done the right thing in the **p**
25:9 must go up to him in the **p**
26:5 this formal statement in the **p**
26:10 will place the basket in the **p**
27:7 and enjoy yourselves in the **p**
29:10 are standing here today in the **p**
29:15 here with us today in the **p**
31:7 Joshua and said to him in the **p**
31:11 Israelites will come into the **p**
Jos 2:9 Your **p** terrifies us.
4:14 LORD honored Joshua in the **p**
7:23 laid it out in the **p** of the LORD.
18:6 draw lots for you here in the **p**
18:8 I will draw lots for you in the **p**
18:10 drew lots for them in the **p**
19:51 They did this in Shiloh in the **p**
22:27 that we may worship in the **p**
Jdg 5:5 the mountains shook in the **p**
5:5 in the **p** of the LORD God of
11:11 things in the **p** of the LORD.
20:1 united in the **p** of the LORD.
20:23 went and cried in the **p**
20:26 sat there and cried in the **p**
21:2 to Bethel and sat there in the **p**
21:5 part in the assembly in the **p**
21:5 had not come into the **p**
21:8 that did not come into the **p**
Rut 4:4 Buy it in the **p** of these men
4:4 men sitting here and in the **p**
1Sm 2:28 and to wear the ephod in my **p**.
2:30 would always live in my **p**.
10:17 people to ⌊come into the **p** of⌋
11:15 and there in the LORD's **p**,
12:17 the LORD's **p** when you asked
15:33 cut Agag in pieces in the **p**
16:6 here in the LORD's **p** is his
16:13 oil and anointed David in the **p**
21:6 bread of the **p** which had been
21:6 been taken from the LORD's **p**
21:7 stay in the LORD's **p** was there.
1Sm 21:13 ⌊when he was⌋ in their **p**
23:18 made a pledge in the LORD's **p**.
26:20 away from the LORD's **p**.
2Sm 6:5 celebrating in the LORD's **p**
6:14 David danced in the LORD's **p**
6:16 and dancing in the LORD's **p**,
6:17 offerings in the LORD's **p**.
6:21 I will celebrate in the LORD's **p**,
7:16 will remain in my **p** forever.
7:26 will be established in your **p**.
7:29 may continue in your **p** forever.
21:6 in the LORD's **p** at Saul's town
21:9 the mountain in the LORD's **p**.
1Ki 3:6 He lived in your **p** with truth,
7:48 the bread of the **p** was placed,
8:22 In the **p** of the entire assembly
9:25 altar that was in the LORD's **p**.
11:36 a lamp in my **p** in Jerusalem,
21:29 is humbling himself in my **p**?
21:29 he's humbling himself in my **p**,
2Ki 20:3 and sincerely in your **p**.
25:29 meals in the king's **p** as long as
1Ch 13:8 were celebrating in God's **p**
13:10 He died in God's **p**.
16:1 fellowship offerings in God's **p**.
16:11 Always seek his **p**.
16:27 and majesty are in his **p**.
16:30 Tremble in his **p**, all the earth!
16:33 forest will sing with joy in the **p**
17:24 will be established in your **p**.
17:27 may continue in your **p** forever.
22:8 so much bloodshed in my **p**.
24:6 recorded their names in the **p**
2Ch 1:6 In the LORD's **p** Solomon went
2:4 incense in his **p**,
2:6 as a place to sacrifice in his **p**?
4:19 the bread of the **p** was placed,
6:12 In the **p** of the entire assembly
Ezr 4:18 read word for word in my **p**.
8:21 humble ourselves in the **p**
9:15 in your **p** because of this."
Neh 2:1 I had never been sad in his **p**
10:33 for rows of the bread of the **p**,
Est 1:16 Memucan spoke up in the **p**
2:23 was written up in the king's **p**
4:11 summoned to enter the king's **p**
5:9 up nor trembling in his **p**,
7:6 became panic-stricken in the **p**
8:15 Mordecai went out from the **p** of
Job 1:12 Then Satan left the LORD's **p**.
2:7 Satan left the LORD's **p** and
26:6 Sheol is naked in God's **p**,
30:11 no longer restrained in my **p**.
31:23 In the **p** of his majesty I can do
Psa 4:6 Let the light of your **p** shine on
9:3 will stumble and die in your **p**.
9:19 the nations be judged in your **p**.
16:11 Complete joy is in your **p**.
21:6 him glad with the joy of your **p**.
22:25 I will fulfill my vows in the **p** of
31:20 place of your **p** from those who
39:1 wicked people are in my **p**."
41:12 and you set me in your **p**
44:3 and the light of your **p** ⌊that did
44:16 because of the **p** of the enemy
51:11 not force me away from your **p**,
52:9 In the **p** of your godly people,
56:13 so that I could walk in your **p**,
61:7 May he sit enthroned in the **p** of
62:8 Pour out your hearts in his **p**.
68:2 melt in God's **p** like wax next
68:3 Let them celebrate in God's **p**.
68:4 Celebrate in his **p**.
68:8 and the sky poured in the **p**
68:8 in the **p** of the God of Israel.
73:22 like a dumb animal in your **p**.
76:7 Who can stand in your **p** when
79:11 of prisoners come into your **p**.
86:9 have made will bow in your **p**,
88:2 Let my prayer come into your **p**.
88:13 prayer will come into your **p**.
89:15 They walk in the light of your **p**,
89:36 will be in my **p** like the sun.
90:8 sins in the light of your **p**.
95:2 Let's come into his **p** with a
96:6 and majesty are in his **p**.

Psa 96:9 Tremble in his **p**, all the earth!
96:13 in the LORD's **p** because he is
97:5 melt like wax in the **p**
97:5 in the **p** of the Lord of the whole
98:6 Shout happily in the **p** of the
98:9 in the LORD's **p** because he is
100:2 Come into his **p** with a joyful
101:7 lies will not remain in my **p**.
102:28 will be secure in your **p**."
105:4 Always seek his **p**.
114:7 tremble in the **p** of the Lord,
114:7 in the **p** of the God of Jacob.
116:9 I will walk in the LORD's **p** in
116:14 my vows to the LORD in the **p**
116:18 my vows to the LORD in the **p**
119:46 written instructions in the **p**
119:169 cry for help come into your **p**,
119:170 for mercy come into your **p**.
140:13 people will live in your **p**.
141:2 incense in your **p**.
142:2 pour out my complaints in his **p**
143:2 who is righteous in your **p**.
Pro 17:18 a loan in the **p** of his friend.
18:16 him into the **p** of great people.
25:5 wicked person away from the **p**
Ecc 5:2 eager to speak in the **p** of God.
5:6 Don't say in the **p** of a ⌊temple⌋
8:2 of the oath you took in God's **p**.
Isa 1:12 When you appear in my **p**,
2:10 of the LORD's terrifying **p**
2:19 of the LORD's terrifying **p**
2:21 of the LORD's terrifying **p**
3:8 are defiant in his honored **p**.
9:3 It will be happy in your **p** like
18:4 My **p** will be like scorching
19:1 idols will tremble in his **p**.
23:18 to those who live in the **p**
24:23 He will be glorious in the **p** of
38:3 and sincerely in your **p**.
40:17 amount to nothing in his **p**.
48:19 be cut off or wiped out in my **p**.
49:16 Your walls are always in my **p**.
53:2 He grew up in his **p** like a
55:12 into songs of joy in your **p**,
57:16 would grow faint in my **p**.
64:1 would quake at your **p**.
64:2 nations will tremble in your **p**.
64:3 mountains quaked in your **p**.
66:22 will continue in my **p**," declares
66:22 will also continue in my **p**.
Jer 1:17 Don't be terrified in their **p**,
1:17 ⌊even more⌋ terrified in their **p**.
4:31 in the **p** of murderers!"
5:22 "Don't you tremble in my **p**?
7:10 Then you stand in my **p** in the
12:11 Devastated, it mourns in my **p**.
15:9 these people to death in the **p**
15:19 you will stand in my **p**.
18:20 how I stood in your **p**
18:23 Make them stumble in your **p**.
23:39 I will throw you out of my **p**
30:20 will be established in my **p**,
31:36 stop being a nation in my **p**.
32:12 I did this in the **p** of my cousin
32:12 signed the deed and in the **p**
32:31 remove this city from my **p**.
33:18 to have a descendant in my **p**
34:15 you made a promise in my **p**,
34:18 made in my **p** when they cut
36:7 will come into the LORD's **p**,
36:9 to fast in the LORD's **p**.
49:37 the people of Elam in the **p**
49:37 in the **p** of those who want to
51:24 "In your **p** I will pay back
52:33 meals in the king's **p** as long as
Lam 2:19 heart out like water in the **p**
3:35 deny people their rights in the **p**
Eze 2:6 Don't be terrified in their **p**,
3:9 Don't be terrified in their **p**,
5:14 nations around you and in the **p**
16:18 olive oil and incense in their **p**.
16:41 houses and punish you in the **p**
28:18 ashes on the ground in the **p**
38:20 on earth will tremble in my **p**.
41:22 that is in the **p** of the LORD."
44:3 sit there and eat food in the **p**
Eze 44:15 and they may stand in my **p**.
46:3 the door of the gateway in the **p**
46:9 will enter the LORD's **p** at
Hos 6:2 us so that we may live in his **p**.
7:2 Their sins are in my **p**.
Joe 2:6 People are terrified in their **p**.
2:10 The earth quakes in their **p**,
Mic 6:6 when I come into the LORD's **p**,
7:17 They will turn away from your **p**
Nah 1:5 The earth draws back in his **p**.
1:6 Who can stand in the **p** of his
Hab 2:20 earth should be silent in his **p**.
Zep 1:7 Be silent in the **p** of the
Zec 2:13 "Everyone be silent in the **p** of
6:5 going out after standing in the **p**
Mal 3:16 A book was written in his **p** to
Mat 12:4 God and ate the bread of the **p**?
Mar 2:26 and ate the bread of the **p**?
Luk 1:8 As he served in God's **p**,
1:19 I stand in God's **p**.
6:4 ate the bread of the **p**,
Jon 5:45 that I will accuse you in the **p**
8:38 I have seen in my Father's **p**.
14:3 Then I will bring you into my **p**
17:5 give me glory in your **p** with the
Act 2:28 In your **p** there is complete joy.'
3:13 You rejected him in Pilate's **p**,
4:10 that this man stands in your **p**
7:10 When Joseph stood in the **p** of
10:33 All of us are here now in the **p**
Rom 4:17 when he stood in the **p**
1Co 1:29 no one can brag in God's **p**.
12:7 The evidence of the Spirit's **p**
2Co 2:10 I did in the **p** of Christ for your
2:17 spokesmen and in God's **p**,
3:4 about you in God's **p**.
6:6 the Holy Spirit's **p** ⌊in our
6:7 and the **p** of God's power.
13:13 and the Holy Spirit's **p** be with
Eph 1:4 to be holy and perfect in his **p**.
3:14 I kneel in the **p** of the Father
Col 1:22 come into God's **p** without sin,
1Th 1:3 In the **p** of our God and Father,
2:19 that we can brag about in the **p**
3:9 us as we rejoice in God's **p**.
3:13 you will be blameless in the **p**
2Th 1:9 separated from the Lord's **p**
2Ti 4:1 I solemnly call on you in the **p**
Heb 2:17 a faithful chief priest in God's **p**
9:2 and the bread of the **p** were in
9:24 appear in God's **p** on our behalf.
Jas 4:10 yourselves in the Lord's **p**.
1Jn 1:2 eternal life that was in the **p**
2:1 come into the **p** of the Father.
3:19 we will be reassured in his **p**.
Jud 1:24 in his glorious **p** without fault.
Rev 2:13 who was killed in your **p**,
3:5 will acknowledge them in the **p**
8:2 angels who stand in God's **p**,
11:4 lamp stands standing in the **p**
11:16 on their thrones in God's **p**,
12:10 them day and night in the **p**
13:12 of the first beast in its **p**.
14:10 tortured by fiery sulfur in the **p**
20:11 and the sky fled from his **p**,

present (86)

Gen 30:20 me with a beautiful **p**.
33:11 Please take the **p** I've brought
Exo 22:14 dies while the owner is not **p**,
29:26 and **p** it to the LORD.
Lev 7:30 Take the breast and **p** it to the
10:15 that is to be burned and **p** them
14:12 the quart of olive oil and **p** them
14:21 **p** it to make peace with the
14:24 the quart of olive oil and **p** them
23:11 He will **p** it to the LORD so that
23:11 He will **p** it on the day after
23:12 On the day you **p** the bundle,
23:17 of bread from your homes to **p**
23:20 The priest must **p** them along
Num 5:25 was holding, **p** it to the LORD,
6:20 The priest will **p** them as an
8:11 Aaron will **p** the Levites to the
8:13 and **p** them as an offering to the
Jos 20:4 and **p** his case to the leaders of
1Sm 1:22 Then I'll bring him and **p** him to
9:7 There's no **p** we can bring the
2Sm 11:8 and the king sent a **p** to him.
1Ki 9:16 wife, as a wedding **p**.)
15:19 I'm sending you a **p** of silver
18:1 "**P** yourself to Ahab.
18:2 So Elijah went to **p** himself to
18:15 I will **p** myself to Ahab."
2Ki 5:15 So please accept a **p** from me."
8:8 king told Hazael, "Take a **p**,
8:9 He took with him a **p** and all
16:8 to the king of Assyria as a **p**.
20:12 sent letters and a **p** to
2Ch 5:11 All the priests who were **p** had
35:7 offerings for all who were **p**.
35:12 The laypeople could then **p**
35:17 The Israelites who were **p**
Est 7:9 Harbona, one of the eunuchs **p**
Job 5:8 seek God's help and **p** my case
23:4 I would **p** ⌊my⌋ case to him.
33:5 **P** your case to me,
Psa 75:1 You are **p**, and your miracles
Pro 25:9 **P** your argument to your
Ecc 3:15 ⌊in the past⌋ is **p** now.
Isa 39:1 letters and a **p** to Hezekiah.
41:21 "**P** your case," says the LORD.
45:21 Speak and **p** your case.
Jer 40:5 Jeremiah some food and a **p**
Hos 10:6 will be carried to Assyria as a **p**
Luk 2:22 They took Jesus to **p** him to
5:17 in Moses' Teachings were **p**.
Act 4:6 the chief priest's family were **p**.
16:14 A woman named Lydia was **p**.
21:18 All the spiritual leaders were **p**.
22:1 listen as I now **p** my case to
24:10 So I'm pleased to **p** my case to
24:18 No crowd or noisy mob was **p**.
25:24 and everyone who is **p** with us!
27:24 You must **p** your case to the
Rom 3:26 his approval at the **p** time.
7:21 Evil is **p** with me even when I
8:18 I consider our **p** sufferings
8:22 of childbirth up to the **p** time.
8:38 by anything in the **p** or anything
1Co 3:22 life or death, **p** or future things,
5:3 I'm not physically **p** with you,
5:3 as though I were **p** with you.
7:26 Because of the **p** crisis I
7:31 It is clear that this world in its **p**
14:28 But if an interpreter isn't **p**,
2Co 4:14 He will **p** us to God together
5:2 In our **p** tent-like existence we
8:14 At the **p** time, your surplus fills
Gal 1:4 to free us from this **p** evil world,
Eph 1:21 not only in this **p** world but also
2:2 You followed the ways of this **p**
5:27 Then he could **p** it to himself
Col 1:6 This Good News is **p** with you
1:28 We want to **p** everyone as
2Ti 2:15 Do your best to **p** yourself to
4:10 He fell in love with this **p** world
Tit 2:12 and godly lives in this **p** world.
Heb 2:8 However, at the **p** time we still
9:9 is an example for the **p** time.
Jas 1:17 Every good **p** and every perfect
2Pe 1:9 If these qualities aren't **p** in
3:7 By God's word, the **p** heaven

presentable (3)

Lev 15:31 keeps them from being **p** to me.
1Co 12:23 parts are made more **p**.
12:24 However, our **p** parts don't need

presented (27)

Gen 30:20 Leah said, "God has **p** me with
43:15 they **p** themselves to Joseph.
47:2 he **p** them to Pharaoh.
Exo 38:24 of gold from the offerings **p**
38:29 The bronze from the offerings **p**
Lev 7:34 the breast that was **p** ⌊to me⌋
8:27 Moses **p** all these things to the
8:29 of the ordination offering and **p**
9:21 and the right thighs and **p** them
10:14 Also eat the breast **p** ⌊to the
10:15 the breast **p** ⌊to the LORD⌋,
23:15 as an offering **p** to the LORD)

Num 6:20 with the ram's breast that is **p**
7:10 They **p** their gifts in front of the
8:15 them clean and **p** them as
8:21 Aaron **p** them as an offering to
18:11 taken from the offerings **p** by
18:18 and the right thigh that are **p**.
Jos 24:1 and they **p** themselves to God.
Jdg 6:19 Then he went out and **p** them
1Sm 6:15 The people of Beth Shemesh **p**
1Ki 11:20 Tahpenes **p** the boy to Pharaoh
1Ch 16:1 They **p** burnt offerings and
Ezr 7:19 your God's temple must all be **p**
Eze 16:21 children and **p** them as burnt
Dan 7:13 years, and was **p** to him.
Act 9:41 he **p** Tabitha to them.

presently (1)

Zec 8:9 you people who are **p** listening

presents (6)

Gen 24:53 He also gave expensive **p** to
1Sm 10:27 him and wouldn't bring him **p**,
2Ch 32:23 to the LORD and expensive **p**
Psa 72:10 and the islands bring **p**.
Ecc 9:10 Whatever **p** itself for you to do,
Isa 3:14 The LORD **p** his case to the

preserve (8)

Gen 7:3 of each) to **p** animal life all
19:32 we'll be able to **p** our family line
19:34 we'll be able to **p** our family line
Dtr 6:24 live so that he will **p** our lives.
Isa 56:1 **P** justice, and do what is right.
Mal 2:7 lips should **p** knowledge.
Mat 10:39 The person who tries to **p** his
10:39 loses his life for me will **p** it.

preserved (2)

Job 10:12 watchfulness has **p** my spirit.
Isa 49:6 those in Israel whom I have **p**.

preserves (2)

Pro 16:17 his way **p** his own life.
19:16 obeys the law **p** his life,

press (2)

Job 23:6 would **p** charges against me.
24:11 They **p** out olive oil between

pressed (4)

1Sa 13:6 because the army was hard-**p**
Isa 8:21 they are hard-**p** and hungry
Mar 5:24 followed Jesus and **p** him
Luk 6:38 A large quantity, **p** together,

pressing (2)

Mar 5:31 when you see the crowd **p** you
Luk 8:45 you and **p** against you."

pressure (2)

Job 33:7 I won't put too much **p** on you.
2Co 11:28 I have the daily **p** of my

pressured (2)

1Sm 13:12 I felt **p** into sacrificing the burnt
Luk 23:23 But the crowd **p** Pilate.

pretend (4)

Dtr 22:1 don't **p** that you don't see it.
22:3 Don't **p** that you don't know
22:4 don't **p** that you don't see it.
1Ki 14:5 she will **p** to be someone else."

pretended (3)

Jos 8:15 Joshua and all Israel **p** to be
Est 8:17 Then many common people **p**
Act 27:30 the sea and **p** they were going

pretending (1)

1Ki 14:6 Why are you **p** to be someone

pretends (2)

Pro 13:7 One person **p** to be rich but has
13:7 Another **p** to be poor but has

pretext (1)

Act 23:15 officer on the **p** that you need

pretty (1)

2Sm 11:2 and she was very **p**.

prevent (2)

Psa 106:23 stood in his way to **p** him from
Ecc 8:8 No one has the power to **p** the

prevented (2)

1Sm 26:19 They have **p** me from having a
Neh 4:15 that God had **p** their plans from

previously (7)

Gen 28:19 **P**, the name of the city was
Neh 13:5 **P**, this room had been used to
Job 42:11 who had **p** known him came
Pro 22:20 Didn't I write to you **p** with
Jon 7:50 who had **p** visited Jesus.
9:8 who had **p** seen him begging
2Co 1:15 Confident of this, I had **p**

prey (35)

Gen 15:11 When birds of **p** came down
49:27 the morning he devours his **p**.
Num 23:24 lie down until it eats its **p**
Job 4:11 die without any **p** ⌊to eat⌋,
9:26 eagle swooping down on its **p**.
28:7 No bird of **p** knows the way to
29:17 and made him drop the **p** out
38:39 "Can you hunt **p** for the lioness
39:26 make a bird of **p** fly
Psa 17:12 a lion eager to tear ⌊its **p**⌋ apart
104:21 The young lions roar for their **p**
Pro 12:27 hunter does not catch his **p**,
Isa 5:29 growl as they snatch their **p**
5:30 they will roar over their **p** as
8:1 the **P** Will be Easy].
10:2 They **p** on widows and rob
18:6 will be left for the birds of **p**
18:6 The birds of **p** will feed on
31:4 growls over its **p** when a crowd
42:22 They have become **p** with no
46:11 I will call a bird of **p** from the
Jer 12:9 are like a colorful bird of **p**.
12:9 Other birds of **p** surround it.
Eze 22:25 who tear their **p** into pieces.
22:27 that tear their **p** into pieces.
34:8 my sheep have become **p**.
34:22 and they will no longer be **p**.
34:28 They will no longer be **p** to the
36:4 cities that have become **p**
39:4 become food for every bird of **p**
Amo 3:4 roar in the forest if it has no **p**?
Nah 2:12 The lion tore its **p** to pieces to
2:12 It strangled ⌊the **p**⌋ for its
2:13 I will remove your **p** from the
Hab 1:8 that swoops down for its **p**.

price (43)

Gen 23:9 me for its full **p** as my property
23:13 I will pay you the **p** of the field.
34:12 Set the **p** I must pay for the
Exo 21:30 whatever **p** is demanded
22:16 pay the bride-**p** and marry her.
22:17 of money equal to the bride-**p**
Lev 25:50 His sale **p** will be adjusted
25:51 refund from his purchase **p**
25:52 refund from his purchase **p**
Num 18:16 buy them back at the fixed **p**
1Sm 13:21 The **p** was a pim for plow
2Sm 12:6 must pay back four times the **p**
24:24 buy it from you at a ⌊fair⌋ **p**.
1Ki 10:28 them from Kue for a fixed **p**.
10:29 For the same **p** they obtained
21:2 I will pay you a fair **p** for it."
1Ch 21:22 Sell it to me for the full **p**.
21:24 insist on buying it for the full **p**.
2Ch 1:16 them from Kue for a fixed **p**.
1:17 For the same **p** they obtained
Psa 44:12 and at that **p** you have gained
49:8 The **p** to be paid for his soul is
Pro 6:26 A prostitute's **p** is ⌊only⌋ a loaf
Isa 43:3 Sudan and Seba are the **p** I
43:4 Nations will be the **p** I pay for
52:3 but no **p** was paid.
Jer 15:13 and treasures as loot as the **p**
Dan 11:39 and distribute land for a **p**.
Mic 3:11 Your priests teach for a **p**.
Zec 11:13 Such a magnificent **p** was set
Mat 26:9 have been sold for a high **p**,
27:9 the **p** the people of Israel had
Mar 14:5 have been sold for a high **p**,
Jon 12:5 this perfume sold for a high **p**
Act 5:8 did you sell the land for that **p**?"
5:8 "Yes, that was the **p**."
Rom 3:24 through the **p** Christ Jesus paid
1Co 6:20 You were bought for a **p**.
7:23 You were bought for a **p**.
Gal 3:13 Christ paid the **p** to free us from
3:14 ⌊Christ paid the **p**⌋ so that the
Col 1:14 His Son paid the **p** to free us,
Heb 9:15 Through his death he paid the **p**

priceless (5)

Job 12:16 "God has power and **p** wisdom.
Psa 119:162 who finds a **p** treasure.
Pro 2:7 He has reserved **p** wisdom for
3:21 Use **p** wisdom and foresight.
8:14 Advice and **p** wisdom are mine.

prices (1)

Rev 18:19 because of that city's high **p**.

prickly (1)

Eze 28:24 no longer be hurt by **p** thorns

pride (22)

2Ch 26:16 his **p** destroyed him.
Psa 47:4 the **p** of Jacob, whom he loved.
Pro 8:13 I hate **p**, arrogance,
16:18 **P** precedes a disaster,
29:23 A person's **p** will humiliate him,
Isa 4:2 fruit of the land will be the **p**
13:11 and humble the **p** of tyrants.
14:11 Your **p** has been brought down
43:14 in the ships that they take **p** in.
60:15 you a source of everlasting **p**,
Eze 32:12 They will shatter the **p** of Egypt
Amo 6:8 I am disgusted with Jacob's **p**,
8:7 sworn an oath by Jacob's **p**:
Zep 2:10 they will get for their sinful **p**,
Zec 10:11 The **p** of Assyria will be
Luk 1:14 He will be your **p** and joy,
Rom 2:8 fury on those who, in selfish **p**,
1Co 11:15 teach you that it is a woman's **p**
15:31 I swear to you on my **p** in you
Php 1:26 even more reason to have **p**
3:3 serve God's Spirit and take **p**
3:19 and they take **p** in the shameful

priest (497)

Gen 14:18 He was a **p** of God Most High.
41:45 **p** from the city of On.
41:50 **p** from the city of On.
46:20 **p** from the city of On.
Exo 2:16 seven daughters of the **p** of
3:1 Jethro, the **p** of Midian,
18:1 Jethro, the **p** of Midian,
28:3 holy when he serves me as **p**.
28:35 wear it when he serves as **p**.
29:30 son who succeeds him as **p** —
30:33 on anyone who is not a **p** must
31:10 the holy clothes for the **p** Aaron
35:19 the holy clothes for Aaron the **p**
38:21 son of the **p** Aaron.
39:26 by Aaron when he serves as **p**.
39:41 the holy clothes for the **p** Aaron
40:13 dedicate him to serve me as **p**.
Lev 1:7 Then the sons of the **p** Aaron
1:9 Then the **p** will burn all of it on
1:12 The **p** will lay the head and the
1:13 Then the **p** will burn all of it on
1:15 The **p** must bring it to the altar.
1:17 Then the **p** will lay the bird on
2:2 The **p** will burn it on the altar
2:8 Offer it to the **p** who will bring
2:9 The **p** will remove part of the
2:16 The **p** will burn the flour,
3:11 Then the **p** will burn the

Lev	3:16	Then the **p** will burn them on
	4:3	"If the anointed **p** does
	4:5	Then the anointed **p** will take
	4:6	The **p** will dip his finger in it
	4:7	Then the **p** will put some of the
	4:10	The **p** will lay them on the altar
	4:16	Then the anointed **p** will bring
	4:17	The **p** will dip his finger in
	4:20	So the **p** will make peace with
	4:25	Then the **p** will take some of
	4:26	So the **p** will make peace with
	4:30	The **p** will take some of the
	4:31	The **p** will burn it on the altar
	4:31	So the **p** will make peace with
	4:34	Then the **p** will take some of
	4:35	Then the **p** will burn it on the
	4:35	So the **p** will make peace with
	5:6	Then the **p** will make peace
	5:8	Bring them to the **p**,
	5:10	So the **p** will make peace with
	5:12	Bring it to the **p**. The priest will
	5:12	The **p** will take a handful of it.
	5:13	So the **p** will make peace with
	5:13	The offering will belong to the **p**
	5:16	Give it to the **p**. So the priest
	5:16	So the **p** will use the ram
	5:18	You must bring the **p** a ram that
	5:18	The **p** will make peace with
	6:6	in money. Bring it to the **p**.
	6:7	So the **p** will make peace with
	6:10	"The **p** must put on his linen
	6:12	The **p** will burn wood on it
	6:22	his place as **p** will prepare it.
	6:23	grain offering made by a **p** must
	6:26	The **p** who makes the offering
	7:2	⌊A **p**⌋ will throw the blood
	7:5	The **p** will burn them on the
	7:7	Both offerings belong to the **p**
	7:8	to the **p** who sacrifices it.
	7:9	belongs to the **p** who offers it.
	7:14	It will belong to the **p** who
	7:31	"The **p** will burn the fat on the
	7:32	You will also give the **p** the
	7:34	I have given them to the **p**
	12:6	She must bring them to the **p** at
	12:7	The **p** will offer them in the
	12:8	So the **p** will make peace with
	13:2	he must be taken to the **p**
	13:3	The **p** will examine the
	13:3	When the **p** has examined him,
	13:4	the **p** must put him in isolation
	13:5	On the seventh day the **p** will
	13:5	the **p** must put him in isolation
	13:6	On the seventh day the **p** will
	13:6	the **p** must declare him clean.
	13:7	he has shown himself to the **p**
	13:7	he must show himself to the **p**
	13:8	The **p** will examine him one
	13:8	the **p** must declare him
	13:9	he must be taken to the **p**.
	13:10	The **p** will examine him.
	13:11	the **p** must declare him unclean
	13:12	to foot (so far as the **p** can see),
	13:13	the **p** will examine him.
	13:13	the **p** must declare the
	13:15	The **p** will examine the raw
	13:16	he must go to the **p**.
	13:17	The **p** will examine him again,
	13:17	the **p** must declare the
	13:19	it must be shown to the **p**.
	13:20	The **p** will examine it.
	13:20	the **p** must declare the person
	13:21	But if the **p** examines the
	13:21	the **p** must put him in isolation
	13:22	If the area has spread, the **p**
	13:23	The **p** must declare him clean.
	13:25	the **p** will examine it.
	13:25	The **p** must declare him
	13:26	But if the **p** examines it and the
	13:26	the **p** must put him in isolation
	13:27	On the seventh day the **p** will
	13:27	If the area has spread, the **p**
	13:28	The **p** must declare him clean,
	13:30	the **p** will examine the disease.
	13:30	the **p** must declare the person
	13:31	But if the **p** examines the
Lev	13:31	the **p** must put the person with
	13:32	On the seventh day the **p** will
	13:33	The **p** will put the person with
	13:34	On the seventh day the **p** will
	13:34	the **p** must declare him clean.
	13:36	the **p** will make another
	13:36	the **p** does not have to look for
	13:37	The person is clean, so the **p**
	13:39	the **p** will make an
	13:43	The **p** will examine him.
	13:44	The **p** must declare him
	13:49	It must be shown to the **p**.
	13:50	The **p** will examine the mildew
	13:53	But if the **p** sees that the area
	13:55	The **p** will examine the area
	13:56	If the **p** sees that the area is
	14:2	He must be taken to the **p**.
	14:3	The **p** will go outside the camp
	14:4	the **p** will order someone to get
	14:5	Then the **p** will order someone
	14:6	The **p** will take the living bird,
	14:11	The **p** who will declare him
	14:12	The **p** will take one of the male
	14:13	for sin, belongs to the **p**.
	14:14	Then the **p** will take some of
	14:15	The **p** will also take some of
	14:17	The **p** will put some of the oil
	14:18	The **p** will put the rest of the oil
	14:19	The **p** will also sacrifice the
	14:20	The **p** will sacrifice the burnt
	14:20	So the **p** will make peace with
	14:23	day he will take them to the **p**
	14:24	The **p** will take the lamb for the
	14:25	Then the **p** will take some of
	14:26	The **p** will pour some of the
	14:28	The **p** will put some of the oil
	14:29	In the LORD's presence, the **p**
	14:31	the **p** will make peace
	14:35	come and tell the **p** that there is
	14:36	"Before the **p** examines the
	14:36	Then the **p** will go inside to
	14:38	the **p** will go out to the door of
	14:39	On the seventh day the **p** will
	14:40	the **p** must order the stones that
	14:44	the **p** will examine it one more
	14:48	But if the **p** comes and makes
	14:48	the **p** must declare the house
	14:49	"The **p** must take two birds,
	15:14	will give these birds to the **p**.
	15:15	The **p** will sacrifice one as an
	15:15	the **p** will make peace with the
	15:29	and bring them to the **p** at
	15:30	The **p** will offer one as an
	15:30	the **p** will make peace
	16:32	The **p** who is anointed and
	16:32	ordained to serve as chief **p**
	17:5	They must bring them to the **p**
	17:6	The **p** will pour the blood
	19:22	In the LORD's presence the **p**
	21:7	because a **p** is God's holy
	21:10	"The **p** who is anointed with
	21:13	"The anointed **p** must marry a
	21:21	If a descendant of the **p** Aaron
	22:10	even if they are visiting a **p** or
	22:11	But if a **p** buys a slave,
	22:14	another holy offering to the **p**
	23:10	bring the **p** a bundle of the first
	23:20	The **p** must present them along
	24:8	Every day of worship ⌊a **p**⌋
	27:8	must stand in front of the **p**.
	27:8	The **p** will determine the
	27:11	bring it in front of the **p**.
	27:12	The **p** will determine what its
	27:12	will be whatever the **p** decides.
	27:14	the **p** will determine what its
	27:14	will be whatever the **p** decides.
	27:18	the **p** will estimate its value
	27:21	become the property of the **p**.
	27:23	The **p** must figure out the field's
Num	3:6	stand in front of the **p** Aaron
	3:32	son of the **p** Aaron.
	4:16	"Eleazar, son of the **p** Aaron,
	4:28	Ithamar, son of the **p** Aaron,
	4:33	Ithamar, son of the **p** Aaron,
	5:8	to the LORD for the **p** ⌊to use⌋.
	5:9	bring to the **p** will belong
Num	5:9	the priest will belong to the **p**.
	5:10	but whatever is given to the **p**
	5:10	the priest will belong to the **p**."
	5:15	take his wife to the **p** along
	5:16	"The **p** will have the woman
	5:17	Then the **p** will take holy water
	5:18	The **p** will bring the woman
	5:18	The **p** will hold in his hands
	5:19	"Then the **p** will say to her,
	5:21	"Then the **p** will administer the
	5:23	"The **p** will write these curses
	5:25	The **p** will take the grain
	5:26	The **p** will take a handful of the
	5:30	and the **p** will do everything
	6:10	two young pigeons to the **p** at
	6:11	The **p** will sacrifice one as an
	6:11	The **p** will make peace with
	6:16	"The **p** will bring these
	6:19	"Then the **p** will take one of the
	6:20	The **p** will present them as an
	6:20	are holy and belong to the **p**,
	7:8	son of the **p** Aaron.
	15:25	The **p** will make peace with
	15:28	The **p** will offer the sacrifice to
	16:37	son of the **p** Aaron,
	16:39	So the **p** Eleazar took the
	18:28	contribution to the **p** Aaron.
	19:3	Give it to the **p** Eleazar.
	19:4	The **p** Eleazar will take some
	19:6	The **p** will take some cedar
	19:7	The **p** must then wash his
	25:7	and grandson of the **p** Aaron,
	25:11	and grandson of the **p** Aaron,
	26:1	son of the **p** Aaron,
	26:3	So Moses and the **p** Eleazar
	26:63	Moses and the **p** Eleazar
	26:64	and the **p** Aaron had counted
	27:2	him, the **p** Eleazar, the leaders,
	27:19	Make him stand in front of the **p**
	27:21	stand in front of the **p** Eleazar,
	27:22	stand in front of the **p** Eleazar
	31:6	son of the **p** Eleazar.
	31:12	to Moses, the **p** Eleazar,
	31:13	Moses, the **p** Eleazar,
	31:21	Then the **p** Eleazar said to the
	31:26	"You, the **p** Eleazar,
	31:29	and give them to the **p** Eleazar
	31:31	Moses and the **p** Eleazar did
	31:41	LORD's taxes to the **p** Eleazar,
	31:51	Moses and the **p** Eleazar took
	31:54	Moses and the **p** Eleazar took
	32:2	came to Moses, the **p** Eleazar,
	32:28	about them to the **p** Eleazar,
	33:38	At the LORD's command the **p**
	34:17	the **p** Eleazar and Joshua,
	35:25	of the high **p** who was anointed
	35:28	until the death of the high **p**.
	35:32	before the death of the high **p**.
Dtr	10:6	Eleazar succeeded him as **p**.
	17:12	disobeys the **p** (who serves
	20:2	Before the battle starts, a **p**
	26:3	Go to the **p** who is serving at
	26:4	Then the **p** will take the basket
Jos	14:1	The **p** Eleazar, Joshua (son of
	17:4	They came to the **p** Eleazar,
	19:51	The **p** Eleazar, Joshua son of
	20:6	whoever is chief **p** at that time
	21:1	of Levi came to the **p** Eleazar,
	21:4	These descendants of the **p**
	21:13	descendants of Aaron, the **p**.
	22:13	son of the **p** Eleazar,
	22:30	When the **p** Phinehas,
	22:31	son of the **p** Eleazar,
	22:32	Then Phinehas (son of the **p**
Jdg	17:5	one of his sons to be his **p**.
	17:10	Be a father and a **p** to me.
	17:12	the young man became his **p**
	17:13	I have a Levite for my **p**."
	18:4	so I became his **p**."
	18:6	The **p** told them, "Go in peace.
	18:17	The **p** stood at the entrance to
	18:18	metal idol, the **p** asked them,
	18:19	with us and be our father and **p**.
	18:19	Is it better for you to be a **p** for
	18:20	The **p** was content.
	18:24	gods I made as well as my **p**.

Jdg 18:27 the man who had become his **p**
1Sm 1:9 (The **p** Eli was sitting on a
2:11 the LORD under the **p** Eli.
2:14 the pot⌋ belonged to the **p**.
2:15 "Give the meat to the **p** to roast.
2:28 of Israel to serve as my **p**,
2:35 Then I will appoint a faithful **p**
14:3 the LORD's **p** at Shiloh.
14:19 Saul was talking to the **p**,
14:19 Then Saul said to the **p**,
14:36 But the **p** said, "Let's consult
14:41 ⌊let the **p**⌋ draw Urim.
21:1 David went to the **p** Ahimelech
21:2 answered the **p** Ahimelech,
21:4 the chief **p** answered David.
21:5 David answered the **p**,
21:6 So the **p** gave him holy
21:9 The chief **p** answered,
22:11 king sent for the **p** Ahimelech,
23:9 he told the **p** Abiathar,
30:7 David told the **p** Abiathar,
2Sm 15:27 the king asked Zadok the **p**.
20:26 of Jair, was a **p** to David.
1Ki 1:7 and with the **p** Abiathar,
1:8 But the **p** Zadok, Benaiah (son
1:19 the king's sons, Abiathar the **p**,
1:25 and the **p** Abiathar ⌊to his
1:26 But he didn't invite me or the **p**
1:32 "Summon the **p** Zadok,
1:34 Have the **p** Zadok and the
1:38 Then the **p** Zadok,
1:39 The **p** Zadok took the container
1:42 son of the **p** Abiathar,
1:44 The king has sent the **p** Zadok,
1:45 The **p** Zadok and the prophet
2:22 The **p** Abiathar and Joab
2:26 The king told the **p** Abiathar,
2:27 Abiathar as the LORD's **p**
2:35 Abiathar with the **p** Zadok.
4:2 was the ⌊chief⌋ **p**.
2Ki 11:9 as the **p** Jehoiada had ordered
11:9 and came to the **p** Jehoiada.
11:15 Then the **p** Jehoiada ordered
11:15 (The **p** had said, "She must not
11:18 and killed Mattan, the **p** of Baal,
11:18 Next, the **p** appointed officials
12:2 the **p** Jehoiada instructed him.
12:9 Then the **p** Jehoiada took a
12:10 the king's scribe and the chief **p**
16:10 So King Ahaz sent the **p** Urijah
16:15 this command to the **p** Urijah:
16:16 The **p** Urijah did what King
22:4 "Go to the chief **p** Hilkiah.
22:8 The chief **p** Hilkiah told the
22:10 "The **p** Hilkiah has given me a
22:12 gave an order to the **p** Hilkiah,
22:14 So the **p** Hilkiah, Ahikam,
23:4 king ordered the chief **p** Hilkiah
23:24 book that the **p** Hilkiah found
25:18 guard took the chief **p** Seraiah,
25:18 the second **p** Zephaniah,
1Ch 6:10 was the one who served as **p**
24:6 king, the princes, the **p** Zadok,
27:5 son of the **p** Jehoiada.
29:22 leader and Zadok to be the **p**.
2Ch 13:9 as a **p** of nonexistent gods.
15:3 without a **p** who taught
19:11 Now, the chief **p** Amariah will
22:11 and wife of Jehoiada the **p**.
23:8 the **p** Jehoiada had ordered
23:14 Then the **p** Jehoiada brought
23:14 (The **p** had said, "Don't kill her
23:17 and killed Mattan, the **p** of Baal,
24:2 long as the **p** Jehoiada lived.
24:6 called for the chief **p** Jehoiada
24:20 son of the **p** Jehoiada,
24:25 the son of the **p** Jehoiada.
26:17 The **p** Azariah went in after him
26:20 When the chief **p** Azariah and
31:2 Each **p** or Levite was put in a
31:10 The chief **p** Azariah from
34:9 They came to the chief **p**
34:14 the **p** Hilkiah found the book of
34:18 "The **p** Hilkiah has given me a
Ezr 2:63 most holy food until a **p** could
7:5 the son of Aaron (the first **p**).
Ezr 7:11 gave Ezra the **p** and scribe,
7:12 king of kings To: Ezra the **p**,
7:21 to do exactly what Ezra the **p**,
7:24 are forbidden to make any **p**,
8:33 son of the **p** Uriah,
10:10 Ezra the **p** stood up and said to
10:16 Ezra the **p** chose men who
Neh 3:1 The chief **p** Eliashib and his
3:20 house of the chief **p** Eliashib.
3:28 Each **p** made repairs across
7:65 most holy food until a **p** could
8:2 Then Ezra the **p** brought the
8:9 Ezra the **p** and scribe,
10:38 A **p** — one of Aaron's
12:26 and of Ezra the **p** and scribe.
13:4 before this, the **p** Eliashib,
13:13 storerooms: Shelemiah the **p**,
13:28 the son of the chief **p** Eliashib.)
Psa 110:4 "You are a **p** forever,
110:4 the way Melchizedek was a **p**."
Isa 8:2 the **p** Uriah and Zechariah (son
Jer 20:1 Now the **p**, Immer's son
21:1 and the **p** Zephaniah,
29:25 to the **p** Zephaniah,
29:26 The LORD made you **p** instead
29:29 The **p** Zephaniah read this
37:3 and the **p** Zephaniah (son
52:24 guard took the chief **p** Seraiah,
52:24 the second **p** Zephaniah,
Eze 1:3 his word to the **p** Ezekiel,
44:25 "'A **p** must not make himself
44:25 But a **p** may become unclean if
44:26 After a **p** is made clean,
45:19 The **p** must take some blood
Amo 7:10 Then Amaziah, the **p** at Bethel,
Hag 1:1 to the chief **p** Joshua (who was
1:12 the chief **p** Joshua (who was
1:14 the chief **p** Joshua (who was
2:2 the chief **p** Joshua (who is the
2:4 "Chief **P** Joshua (son of
Zec 3:1 me Joshua, the chief **p**,
3:8 "Listen, Chief **P** Joshua and
6:11 on the head of Chief **P** Joshua,
6:13 He will be a **p** on his throne.
Mat 8:4 Instead, show yourself to the **p**.
26:3 palace of the chief **p** Caiaphas.
26:57 him to Caiaphas, the chief **p**,
26:62 The chief **p** stood up and said
26:63 Then the chief **p** said to him,
26:65 Then the chief **p** tore his robes
Mar 1:44 Instead, show yourself to the **p**.
2:26 God when Abiathar was chief **p**
14:53 men took Jesus to the chief **p**.
14:60 So the chief **p** stood up in the
14:61 The chief **p** asked him again,
14:63 The chief **p** tore his clothes ⌊in
Luk 1:5 was a **p** named Zechariah,
5:14 Instead, show yourself to the **p**.
10:31 "By chance, a **p** was traveling
Jon 11:49 who was chief **p** that year,
11:51 As chief **p** that year,
18:13 Caiaphas, the chief **p** that year,
18:15 was well-known to the chief **p**.
18:19 The chief **p** questioned Jesus
18:22 how you answer the chief **p**?"
18:24 Jesus to Caiaphas, the chief **p**.
Act 4:6 The chief **p** Annas,
5:17 The chief **p** and the whole
5:21 The chief **p** and those who
5:27 The chief **p** questioned them.
7:1 the chief **p** asked Stephen,
9:1 He went to the chief **p**
14:13 The **p** of the god Zeus brought
14:13 The **p** and the crowd wanted to
19:14 of Sceva, a Jewish chief **p**,
22:5 The chief **p** and the entire
23:2 The chief **p** Ananias ordered
23:4 "You're insulting God's chief **p**!"
23:5 know that he is the chief **p**.
24:1 Five days later the chief **p**
Rom 15:16 I serve as a **p** by spreading the
Heb 2:17 could serve as a faithful chief **p**
3:1 the apostle and chief **p** about
4:14 We have a superior chief **p**
4:15 We have a chief **p** who is able
5:1 Every chief **p** is chosen from
Heb 5:2 The chief **p** can be gentle with
5:5 of being a chief **p** for himself.
5:6 "You are a **p** forever,
5:6 the way Melchizedek was a **p**."
5:10 God appointed him chief **p** in
5:10 the way Melchizedek was a **p**.
6:20 He has become the chief **p**
6:20 the way Melchizedek was a **p**.
7:1 was king of Salem and **p**
7:3 continues to be a **p** forever.
7:11 speak about another kind of **p**.
7:11 speak about another kind of **p**,
7:11 a **p** like Melchizedek,
7:11 not a Levitical **p** like Aaron.
7:13 The **p** whom we are talking
7:13 ever served as a **p** at the altar.
7:15 when a different **p** who is like
7:16 That person is a **p**,
7:17 "You are a **p** forever,
7:17 the way Melchizedek was a **p**."
7:21 but Jesus became a **p** when
7:21 You are a **p** forever."
7:23 priests because when a **p** died
7:24 so he serves as a **p** forever.
7:26 We need a chief **p** who is holy,
7:27 We need a **p** who doesn't have
8:1 We do have this kind of chief **p**.
8:1 This chief **p** has received the
8:2 He serves as **p** of the holy
8:3 Every chief **p** is appointed to
8:3 Therefore, this chief **p** had to
8:4 he would not even be a **p**.
9:7 But only the chief **p** went into
9:11 But Christ came as a chief **p** of
9:25 Every year the chief **p** went
10:11 Every day each **p** performed
10:12 However, this chief **p** made
10:21 We have a superior **p** in charge
13:11 The chief **p** brings the blood of

priesthood (5)

Exo 40:15 will begin a permanent **p**
Heb 7:11 the Levitical **p** based
7:12 kind of **p** is established,
1Pe 2:5 that is being built into a holy **p**.
2:9 people, a royal **p**, a holy nation,

priestly (16)

Num 20:26 Take off Aaron's **p** clothes,
20:28 Moses took off Aaron's **p**
1Sm 2:36 to one of the **p** classes so that
14:3 was wearing the **p** ephod.
14:18 "Bring the **p** ephod,"
21:9 in a cloth behind the **p** ephod.
22:18 men wearing the linen **p** ephod.
23:6 brought a **p** ephod with him.
30:7 "Please bring me the **p** ephod."
1Ch 16:39 David left Zadok and his **p**
24:19 These were their **p** groups
2Ch 23:8 not dismissed the **p** divisions.
31:19 all the males in the **p** families
Neh 13:29 have contaminated the **p** office
Luk 1:9 he was chosen by **p** custom to
Heb 8:6 Jesus has been given a **p** work

priest's (25)

Exo 25:7 to be set in the ⌊chief **p**⌋ ephod
28:4 the chief **p** turban, and a cloth
35:9 **p**⌋ ephod and breastplate.
35:27 **p**⌋ ephod and breastplate.
39:28 also made the chief **p** turban
Lev 21:9 When a **p** daughter dishonors
21:10 the chief **p** clothes is chief over
22:11 household may eat the **p** food
22:12 However, if a **p** daughter
22:13 If a **p** daughter is widowed or
1Sm 2:13 the **p** servant would come with
2Ch 24:11 the chief **p** officer would empty
Isa 61:10 bridegroom with a **p** turban,
Mal 2:7 "A **p** lips should preserve
Mat 26:51 off the ear of the chief **p** servant
26:58 came to the chief **p** courtyard.
Mar 14:47 off the ear of the chief **p** servant
14:54 went into the chief **p** courtyard.
14:66 One of the chief **p** female
Luk 22:50 right ear of the chief **p** servant

Luk 22:54 him away to the chief **p** house.
Jon 18:10 attacked the chief **p** servant,
18:15 Jesus into the chief **p** courtyard
18:26 One of the chief **p** servants, a
Act 4:6 the chief **p** family were present.

priests (486)

Gen 47:22 land because the **p** received
47:26 Only the land of the **p** didn't
Exo 19:6 You will be my kingdom of **p**
19:22 Even the **p** who are allowed to
19:24 But the **p** and the people must
28:1 They will serve me as **p**.
28:4 so that they can serve me as **p**.
28:41 them apart to serve me as **p**.
28:43 near the altar to serve as **p**
29:1 sons apart to serve me as **p**:
29:9 They alone are to be **p**;
29:44 holy duties of serving me as **p**.
30:20 near the altar to serve as **p**
30:30 holy duties of serving me as **p**.
31:10 his sons when they serve as **p**,
32:29 are ordained as the LORD's **p**.
35:19 sons when they serve as **p**."
39:41 worn when serving as **p**
39:41 for his sons when serving as **p**.
40:15 Anoint them to serve me as **p**,
Lev 1:5 Aaron's sons, the **p**,
1:8 Aaron's sons, the **p**,
1:11 Aaron's sons, the **p**,
2:2 bring it to Aaron's sons, the **p**.
3:2 Then Aaron's sons, the **p**,
6:29 Any male among the **p** may eat
7:6 Any male among the **p** may eat
7:35 them to serve the LORD as **p**.
8:15 declared it holy so that **p** could
13:2 one of his sons who are also **p**.
16:33 peace with the LORD for the **p**
21:1 "Tell the **p**, Aaron's sons:
22:9 The **p** must do what I order,
22:15 **P** must not dishonor the holy
23:20 will belong to the LORD's **p**.
Num 3:3 of Aaron's sons, the anointed **p**,
3:3 were ordained to serve as **p**.
3:4 and Ithamar served as **p** during
3:10 and his sons to serve as **p**.
10:8 The sons of Aaron, the **p**,
16:10 but now you demand to be **p**.
18:1 commit when you work as **p**.
18:7 work of **p** — everything done
18:7 You may serve me as **p**.
25:13 will be **p** permanently
Dtr 10:8 when they serve him as **p**,
17:9 Go to the Levitical **p** and the
17:18 he should have the Levitical **p**
18:1 The Levitical **p** — in fact,
18:3 the **p** whenever they sacrifice
19:17 in front of the **p** and judges who
21:5 The **p**, the descendants of
21:5 chosen them to serve him as **p**
24:8 as the Levitical **p** instruct you.
27:9 Then Moses and the Levitical **p**
31:9 to the Levitical **p** who carried
Jos 3:3 and the Levitical **p** who carry it,
3:6 Joshua also told the **p**,
3:8 Order the **p** who carry the ark
3:13 The **p** who carry the ark of the
3:14 The **p** who carried the ark of
3:15 When the **p** who were carrying
3:17 The **p** who carried the ark of
4:9 where the **p** who carried the ark
4:10 The **p** who carried the ark
4:11 the **p** with the LORD's ark
4:16 "Order the **p** who carry the ark
4:17 So Joshua ordered the **p**,
4:18 The **p** who carried the ark of
6:4 Seven **p** will carry rams' horns
6:4 while the **p** blow their horns.
6:6 son of Nun, summoned the **p**.
6:6 and have seven **p** carry seven
6:8 the seven **p** carrying the seven
6:9 men went ahead of the **p**,
6:9 the ark while the **p** continued
6:12 The **p** carried the LORD's ark.
6:13 The seven **p** carrying the
6:13 The **p** blew their horns as they
Jos 6:16 the **p** blew their rams' horns.
8:33 They faced the Levitical **p** who
8:33 Moses had commanded the **p**
18:7 is to serve the LORD as **p**.
21:19 were given to the **p**,
Jdg 18:30 and his descendants were **p**
1Sm 1:3 served there as **p** of the LORD.
2:12 were good-for-nothing **p**;
2:13 Now, this was how the **p** dealt
2:14 This is what the **p** did in Shiloh
5:5 This is why the **p** of Dagon and
6:2 the Philistines called for **p**
6:3 The **p** answered, "If you're
6:4 The **p** answered, "Five gold
22:11 family who were the **p** in Nob.
22:17 "Turn and kill the LORD's **p**
22:17 refused to attack the LORD's **p**.
22:18 "You turn and attack the **p**."
22:18 turned and attacked the **p**,
22:19 people of Nob, the city of the **p**.
22:21 Saul had killed the LORD's **p**.
2Sm 8:17 son Ahimelech were **p**.
8:18 And David's sons were **p**.
15:35 The **p** Zadok and Abiathar will
15:35 it to the **p** Zadok and Abiathar.
17:15 Then Hushai told the **p** Zadok
19:11 ⌊this message⌋ to the **p** Zadok
20:25 Zadok and Abiathar were **p**.
1Ki 4:4 Zadok and Abiathar were **p**.
8:3 the **p** picked up the LORD's ark.
8:4 The **p** and the Levites carried
8:6 The **p** brought the ark of the
8:10 When the **p** left the holy place,
8:11 The **p** couldn't serve because
12:31 descended from Levi to be **p**.
12:32 He appointed **p** from the illegal
13:2 Josiah will sacrifice the **p** from
13:33 once again made some men **p**
13:33 and appointed them to be **p** at
13:34 Appointing illegal **p** became
2Ki 10:11 powerful men, friends, and **p**.
10:19 servants, and **p** of Baal.
12:4 Joash told the **p**, "⌊Collect⌋ all
12:5 Each of the **p** should receive it
12:6 the **p** still had not repaired the
12:7 for Jehoiada and the other **p**
12:8 The **p** agreed neither to receive
12:9 The **p** who guarded the
12:16 It belonged to the **p**.
17:27 "Bring one of the **p** you
17:28 So one of the **p** who had been
17:32 kinds of people to serve as **p**
19:2 and the leaders of the **p**,
23:2 Jerusalem, the **p**, the prophets,
23:4 the **p** who served under Hilkiah
23:5 He got rid of the pagan **p** whom
23:8 He brought all the **p** out of the
23:8 those **p** sacrificed unclean.
23:9 The **p** of the illegal worship
23:20 He slaughtered all the **p** of the
1Ch 9:2 Israelites, the **p**, the Levites,
9:10 From the **p** were Jedaiah,
9:12 Also from the **p** were Adaiah
13:2 region of Israel and to the **p**
15:11 David called for the **p** Zadok
15:14 So the **p** and the Levites made
15:24 The **p** Shebaniah, Joshaphat,
16:6 The **p** Benaiah and Jahaziel
18:16 son Abimelech were **p**.
23:2 of Israel and the **p** and Levites.
24:2 and Ithamar served as **p**.
24:6 leaders of the **p** and Levites.
24:31 families of the **p** and Levites.
28:13 the divisions of **p** and Levites.
28:21 are also the divisions of the **p**
2Ch 4:6 The **p** rinsed the meat prepared
5:5 The **p** and the Levites carried
5:7 The **p** brought the ark of the
5:11 All the **p** who were present had
5:12 were 120 **p** blowing trumpets.
5:12 When the **p** left the holy place,
5:14 The **p** couldn't serve because
6:41 Clothe your **p**, LORD God,
7:2 The **p** couldn't go into the
7:6 The **p** were standing at their
7:6 The **p** were opposite the
2Ch 8:14 he set up the divisions of **p** for
8:14 beside the **p** by doing whatever
8:15 the king's orders to the **p**
11:13 The **p** and Levites in every
11:14 The **p** abandoned their land
11:14 rejected them as the LORD's **p**.
11:15 appointed ⌊his own⌋ **p**
11:16 Israel followed the Levitical **p**
13:9 You forced out the LORD's **p**
13:9 you could appoint your own **p**,
13:10 The **p** who serve the LORD are
13:12 His **p** will sound their trumpets
13:14 the **p** blew the trumpets,
17:8 the **p** Elishama and Jehoram.
19:8 appointed some Levites, **p**,
22:12 Joash was with the **p**.
23:4 the **p** and Levites who are on
23:6 LORD's temple except the **p**
23:18 direction of the **p** and Levites.
24:5 He gathered the **p** and the
26:17 80 of the LORD's courageous **p**.
26:18 That right belongs to the **p**,
26:19 While he was angry with the **p**,
26:19 This happened in front of the **p**
26:20 and all the **p** turned toward him,
29:4 He brought the **p** and Levites
29:16 The **p** entered the LORD's
29:21 Hezekiah told the **p**,
29:22 and the **p** sprinkled the blood
29:24 The **p** slaughtered the goats
29:26 and the **p** had the trumpets.
29:34 But the **p** needed more help to
29:34 the **p** could make themselves
29:34 holy than the **p** were.
30:3 not enough **p** had performed
30:15 The **p** and Levites were
30:16 The **p** sprinkled the blood they
30:21 Each day the Levites and **p**
30:24 So a large number of **p** were
30:25 from Judah, the **p**, the Levites,
30:27 Then the Levitical **p** blessed
31:2 Hezekiah assigned the **p** and
31:4 in Jerusalem to give the **p**
31:9 Hezekiah asked the **p** and the
31:15 in the cities belonging to the **p**.
31:17 to the **p** who were enrolled
31:18 The **p** and Levites were
31:18 The **p** and Levites had to be
31:19 **p** who lived in the pasturelands
34:5 He burned the bones of the **p**
34:30 Jerusalem, the **p**, the Levites,
35:2 Josiah appointed the **p** to their
35:8 people, **p**, and Levites. Hilkiah,
35:8 gave the **p** 2,600 sheep and
35:10 The **p** took their positions with
35:11 The **p** sprinkled the blood with
35:14 for themselves and for the **p**
35:14 **p** (Aaron's descendants) were
35:14 for themselves and the **p**.
35:18 as Josiah celebrated it with **p**,
36:14 All the officials, the **p**,
Ezr 1:5 of Judah and Benjamin, the **p**,
2:36 These **p** returned from exile:
2:61 These descendants of the **p**
2:62 contaminated and couldn't be **p**.
2:69 and 100 robes for the **p**.
2:70 The **p**, the Levites, some of the
3:2 and his relatives ⌊who were⌋ **p**
3:8 of the Jews, (the **p**, Levites,
3:10 Then the **p** who were dressed
3:12 But many of the **p**,
6:9 Also, whatever the **p** in
6:16 Then the people of Israel, the **p**,
6:18 The **p** were assigned to their
6:20 Since the **p** and Levites had
6:20 for the rest of the **p**,
7:7 Some Israelites (including **p**,
7:13 includes the **p** and Levites.
7:16 by the people and the **p**.
8:15 I noticed laypeople and **p** there,
8:24 leaders from the **p** — Sherebiah
8:29 Do this in front of the chief **p**,
8:30 So the **p** and the Levites took
9:1 including the **p** and Levites,
9:7 Our kings and our **p** have been
10:5 made the leaders, **p**, Levites,

Ezr 10:18 the descendants of the **p**,
Neh 2:16 I hadn't yet told the Jews, the **p**,
3:1 and his relatives, the **p**,
3:22 After him the **p** who lived in
3:28 Horse Gate the **p** made repairs.
5:12 Then I called the **p** and made
7:39 These **p** returned from exile:
7:63 These **p** couldn't prove they
7:64 contaminated and couldn't be **p**.
7:70 and 530 robes for the **p**.
7:72 and 67 robes for the **p**.
7:73 The **p**, Levites, the singers,
8:13 including the **p** and the Levites,
9:32 leaders, **p**, prophets, ancestors,
9:34 Our kings, leaders, **p**,
9:38 Our leaders, Levites, and **p** are
10:8 These were the **p**.
10:28 These people included the **p**,
10:34 We **p**, Levites, and laypeople
10:36 and our flocks to the **p** serving
10:37 and olive oil to the **p**,
10:39 are and where the **p** who serve
11:3 Some Israelites, **p**,
11:10 These were the **p**:
11:20 The rest of the Israelites, **p**,
12:1 These are the **p** and Levites
12:7 These were the leaders of the **p**
12:12 these were the **p** who were the
12:22 of the Levites and the **p** at
12:30 The **p** and the Levites
12:35 So did some **p** with trumpets:
12:41 these **p** stood in God's temple:
12:44 by Moses' Teachings for the **p**
12:44 ministry of the **p** and Levites.
13:5 The contributions for the **p** had
13:29 you made to the **p** and Levites."
13:30 duties to the **p** and Levites.
Job 12:19 He leads **p** away barefoot and
Psa 78:64 His **p** were cut down with
78:64 The widows of his **p** could
99:6 and Aaron were among his **p**.
132:9 your **p** with righteousness.
132:16 will clothe its **p** with salvation.
Isa 24:2 will happen to people and **p**,
28:7 **P** and prophets stagger from
37:2 and the leaders of the **p**,
43:27 and your **p** rebelled against me.
61:6 You will be called the **p** of the
66:21 some of them **p** and Levites,"
Jer 1:1 He was one of the **p** at
1:18 kings, its officials, its **p**,
2:8 The **p** didn't ask, "Where is the
2:26 Their kings, princes, **p**,
4:9 The **p** will be stunned.
5:31 **P** rule under the prophets'
6:13 All of them, from prophets to **p**,
8:1 the bones of the **p** and the
8:10 All of them, from prophets to **p**,
13:13 throne, the **p**, the prophets,
14:18 Prophets and **p** wander through
18:18 because the teachings of the **p**,
19:1 some of the leaders of the **p**.
23:11 prophets and **p** are godless.
23:33 the prophets, or the **p** ask you,
23:34 Suppose the prophets, the **p**,
26:7 The **p**, the prophets, and all the
26:8 him to say, the **p**, the prophets,
26:11 Then the **p** and the prophets
26:16 said to the **p** and prophets,
27:16 spoke this message to the **p**
28:1 He said to me in front of the **p**
28:5 Hananiah in front of the **p**
29:1 He also sent it to the **p**,
29:25 of Maaseiah, and to all the **p**.
31:14 I will satisfy the **p** with rich
32:32 their **p** and prophets,
33:18 The Levitical **p** will never fail
33:21 the Levitical **p** could also
34:19 the palace officials, the **p**,
48:7 with all its **p** and officials.
49:3 with its **p** and officials.
Lam 1:4 Its **p** are groaning. Its young
1:19 My **p** and leaders breathed their
2:6 He expelled kings and **p**
2:20 Should **p** and prophets be
4:13 and the crimes of its **p**,
Lam 4:16 They no longer respected the **p**,
Eze 7:26 The teachings of **p** and the
22:26 Your **p** violate my teachings
40:38 This is the room where the **p**
40:42 On these tables the **p** laid the
40:45 south is for the **p** who serve
40:46 north is for the **p** who serve at
40:46 These **p** are Zadok's
42:13 These rooms are where the **p**
42:13 the **p** keep the holiest offerings
42:14 Once the **p** enter the holy
42:14 The **p** must put on other
43:19 Give a young bull to the **p** as
43:19 These **p** are Zadok's
43:24 The **p** must throw salt on them
43:26 For seven days the **p** should
43:27 the **p** must sacrifice burnt
44:13 near me and serve me as **p**.
44:15 "'But the **p** who are Levites and
44:21 None of the **p** may drink wine
44:22 nation of Israel or widows of **p**.
44:24 In all disputes the **p** must act
44:28 "'The **p** will have no
44:28 The **p** belong to me.
44:30 The **p** should have the best of
44:30 contributions must go to the **p**.
44:30 of your dough must go to the **p**.
44:31 The **p** must never eat any bird
45:4 will belong to the **p** who serve
45:4 the **p** who come near to serve
46:2 Then the **p** must prepare the
46:19 rooms were reserved for the **p**.
46:20 "This is the place where the **p**
48:10 holy area will belong to the **p**.
48:11 to the **p** who are descendants
48:13 the land belonging to the **p** will
Hos 4:4 My case is against you **p**.
4:6 I will refuse to let you be my **p**.
4:7 The more **p** there are,
4:9 So the **p** will be punished like
5:1 "Listen to this, you **p**!
6:9 The **p** are like gangs of robbers
10:5 The **p** will cry loudly because
Joe 1:9 The **p**, the LORD's servants,
1:13 sackcloth and mourn, you **p**.
2:17 The **p** who serve the LORD cry
Mic 3:11 Your **p** teach for a price.
Zep 1:4 the names of the pagan **p** along
1:4 pagan priests along with my **p**.
3:4 Its **p** contaminate what is holy.
Hag 2:11 Ask the **p** for a decision.
2:12 The **p** answered, "No."
2:13 The **p** answered, "That makes
Zec 7:3 They asked the **p** from the
7:5 people of the land and the **p**,
Mal 1:6 You **p** despise my name.
2:1 "And now, you **p**, this warning
Mat 2:4 called together all the chief **p**
12:4 Only the **p** have that right.
12:5 that on the day of worship the **p**
16:21 leaders, chief **p**, and scribes.
20:18 to the chief **p** and scribes.
21:15 When the chief **p** and the
21:23 The chief **p** and the leaders of
21:45 When the chief **p** and the
26:3 Then the chief **p** and the
26:14 went to the chief **p**.
26:47 They were from the chief **p** and
26:59 The chief **p** and the whole
27:1 in the morning all the chief **p**
27:3 back to the chief **p** and leaders.
27:6 The chief **p** took the money
27:12 While the chief **p** and leaders
27:20 But the chief **p** and leaders
27:41 The chief **p** together with the
27:62 the chief **p** and Pharisees
28:11 They told the chief **p**
28:12 The chief **p** gathered together
Mar 2:26 Only the **p** have that right.
8:31 the chief **p**, and the scribes.
10:33 will be betrayed to the chief **p**
11:18 When the chief **p** and scribes
11:27 the chief **p**, the scribes,
14:1 The chief **p** and the scribes
14:10 to the chief **p** to betray Jesus.
14:43 They were from the chief **p**,
Mar 14:53 All the chief **p**, leaders,
14:55 The chief **p** and the whole
15:1 Early in the morning the chief **p**
15:3 The chief **p** were accusing him
15:10 Pilate knew that the chief **p**
15:11 The chief **p** stirred up the
15:31 The chief **p** and the scribes
Luk 1:5 of **p** named after Abijah.
1:8 on duty with his division of **p**.
3:2 were chief **p** that God spoke
6:4 Only the **p** have that right."
9:22 the chief **p**, and the scribes.
17:14 "Show yourselves to the **p**."
19:47 The chief **p**, the scribes,
20:1 The chief **p**, scribes,
20:19 The scribes and the chief **p**
22:2 The chief **p** and the scribes
22:4 Judas went to the chief **p** and
22:52 Then Jesus said to the chief **p**,
22:66 the chief **p** and the scribes,
23:4 Pilate said to the chief **p** and
23:5 The **p** and the crowd became
23:10 Meanwhile, the chief **p** and the
23:13 called together the chief **p**,
24:20 Our chief **p** and rulers had him
Jon 1:19 answer when the Jews sent **p**
7:32 So the chief **p** and the
7:45 the chief **p** and Pharisees
11:47 So the chief **p** and the
11:57 (The chief **p** and the Pharisees
12:10 The chief **p** planned to kill
18:3 and the guards from the chief **p**
18:35 the chief **p** handed you over
19:6 When the chief **p** and the
19:15 The chief **p** responded,
19:21 The chief **p** of the Jewish
Act 4:1 Some **p**, the officer in charge of
4:23 told them everything the chief **p**
5:24 and the chief **p** heard this,
6:7 number of **p** accepted the faith.
9:14 with authority from the chief **p**
9:21 to the chief **p** in Jerusalem?"
22:30 day and ordered the chief **p**
23:14 They went to the chief **p** and
25:2 The chief **p** and the other
25:15 the chief **p** and the Jewish
26:10 I received from the chief **p**,
26:12 and authority of the chief **p**.
Heb 7:5 who become **p** must receive
7:5 The **p** collect it from their own
7:8 **P** receive a tenth of everything,
7:11 If the work of the Levitical **p**
7:12 for those **p** are different.
7:14 about **p** coming from that
7:20 become **p** without an oath,
7:23 was a long succession of **p**
7:27 sacrifices as those chief **p** did.
7:28 as chief **p** even though they
8:4 On earth other **p** offer gifts by
9:6 The **p** always went into the
Rev 1:6 **p** for God his Father.
5:10 made them a kingdom and **p**
20:6 They will continue to be **p** of

priests' (11)

Gen 47:22 But he didn't buy the **p** land
Lev 8:2 the **p** clothes, the anointing oil,
22:16 have eaten the **p** holy offerings.
Num 3:10 tries to do the **p** duties must
Jos 4:3 where the **p** feet stood firmly.
2Ki 10:22 of the **p** robes, "Bring out
1Ch 9:30 Some of the **p** sons prepared
2Ch 4:9 He also made the **p** courtyard
Eze 41:10 and the **p** rooms. It was 35 feet
Heb 8:6 superior to the Levitical **p** work.
9:1 had rules for the **p** service.

prime (4)

1Sm 2:33 will die in the **p** of life.
Job 21:23 One person dies in his **p** and
29:4 If only I were in the **p** of my life
Isa 38:10 I thought that in the **p** of my life

prince (48)

Gen 49:26 of the **p** among his brothers.
1Ki 22:26 of the city, and to Joash, the **p**.

1Ch 5:2 than his brothers and the **p** was
11:6 be made a general and a **p**."
2Ch 1:2 and battalions, judges, every **p**,
6:5 man to be **p** over my people
11:22 as family head and **p** among
18:25 of the city, and to Joash, the **p**.
Ezr 1:8 for **P** Sheshbazzar of Judah.
Job 31:37 and approach him like a **p**.
Psa 82:7 humans and fall like any **p**."
Pro 25:7 in front of a **p** whom your eyes
Isa 9:6 Everlasting Father, **P** of Peace.
Eze 12:10 about the **p** from Jerusalem
12:12 The **p** who is among you will
12:12 The **p** will cover his face so
21:25 and wicked **p** of Israel,
30:13 A **p** will never rise again in
34:24 servant David will be their **p**.
37:25 David will always be their **p**.
38:2 He is the chief **p** of ⌊the
38:3 chief **p** of Meshech and Tubal.
39:1 the chief **p** of Meshech and
44:3 Only the **p** may sit there and
45:7 "The **p** will have all the land
45:8 will belong to the **p** in Israel.
45:16 contribution to the **p** in Israel.
45:17 Then the **p** is responsible to
45:22 At that time the **p** must prepare
46:2 The **p** must enter from the
46:4 The **p** must offer to the LORD
46:5 be whatever the **p** can bring.
46:7 must be whatever the **p** wants
46:8 When the **p** enters,
46:10 The **p** must be among them.
46:11 But with the lambs, the **p** may
46:12 When the **p** prepares a freewill
46:16 Suppose the **p** offers one of his
46:17 But suppose the **p** offers a gift
46:17 the gift will go back to the **p**.
46:18 The **p** must not take any of the
48:21 property will belong to the **p**.
48:21 These areas belong to the **p**,
48:22 boundaries will belong to the **p**.
Dan 9:25 until the anointed **p** comes,
9:26 be destroyed with the **p** who is
11:22 including the **p** of the promise.
Luk 19:12 He said, "A **p** went to a distant

prince's (2)

Eze 46:2 prepare the **p** burnt offerings
48:22 will be between the **p** part

princes (48)

Gen 17:20 He will be the father of 12 **p**,
Num 21:18 the well dug by **p**, dug out by
22:8 So the **p** of Moab stayed with
22:13 he said to Balak's **p**,
22:14 So the Moabite **p** went back to
22:15 of more highly respected **p**.
22:21 and left with the Moabite **p**.
22:35 Balaam went with Balak's **p**.
22:40 to Balaam and the **p** who were
23:6 offering with all the **p** of Moab.
23:17 offering with the **p** of Moab.
Dtr 33:16 people who are like **p** in Israel.
Jos 13:21 They were **p** of Sihon,
Jdg 5:3 Open your ears, you **p**!
2Sm 10:3 the Ammonite **p** asked their
1Ch 19:3 the Ammonite **p** asked Hanun,
24:6 king, the **p**, the priest Zadok,
2Ch 28:21 the royal palace, and the **p**,
Job 3:15 I would be with **p** who had
29:9 **P** held back ⌊their⌋ words and
34:19 not grant special favors to **p**
Psa 45:16 You will make them **p** over the
122:5 It consists of ⌊**p** who are⌋
Pro 8:16 Through me **p** rule,
19:10 much less a slave ruling **p**.
Isa 23:8 Its merchants are **p**.
34:12 All of its **p** have disappeared.
49:7 **P** will see ⌊you⌋ and bow.
Jer 2:26 Their kings, **p**, priests,
17:25 then the kings and **p** who sit
17:25 They and their **p** will ride in
24:1 of Judah), the **p** of Judah,
24:8 King Zedekiah of Judah, his **p**,
Lam 4:7 Zion's **p** were purer than snow,
Eze 7:27 and **p** will give up hope.
19:1 funeral song for the **p** of Israel.
21:12 and against all the **p** of Israel.
21:12 I will throw the **p** and my
22:6 "'See how all the **p** of Israel
22:25 Your **p** are like roaring lions
26:16 Then the **p** from the coast will
32:29 is there with its kings and its **p**.
39:18 and drink the blood of the **p**
45:8 Then my **p** will no longer
45:9 enough of you, you **p** of Israel.
Hos 8:4 They chose their own **p**,
8:4 own princes, **p** I didn't know.
8:10 the burdens of kings and **p**.

princess (5)

Gen 17:15 Instead, her name is Sarah [**P**].
Isa 47:1 virgin **p** of Babylon!
47:1 **p** of the Babylonians!
47:5 **p** of the Babylonians!
Lam 1:1 Once it was a **p** among the

princesses (1)

1Ki 11:3 He had 700 wives who were **p**

principle (1)

Gal 6:16 all those who conform to this **p**.

principles (32)

Job 2:3 And he still holds on to his **p**.
2:9 you still holding on to your **p**?
Psa 103:18 to follow his guiding **p**.
111:7 his guiding **p** are trustworthy.
111:10 who follows ⌊God's guiding **p**⌋.
119:4 guiding **p** be carefully followed.
119:15 to reflect on your guiding **p**
119:27 your guiding **p** so that
119:40 I long for your guiding **p**.
119:45 I sought out your guiding **p**.
119:56 I have obeyed your guiding **p**.
119:63 who follows your guiding **p**.
119:69 ⌊yet⌋ I obey your guiding **p**
119:78 I reflect on your guiding **p**.
119:87 did not abandon your guiding **p**.
119:93 will never forget your guiding **p**,
119:94 searched for your guiding **p**.
119:100 I have obeyed your guiding **p**.
119:104 From your guiding **p** I gain
119:110 away from your guiding **p**.
119:128 straight paths of your guiding **p**.
119:134 that I may obey your guiding **p**.
119:141 I never forget your guiding **p**.
119:159 I have loved your guiding **p**!
119:168 I have followed your guiding **p**
119:173 ⌊to follow⌋ your guiding **p**.
Isa 26:8 the path of your guiding **p**.
26:9 When your guiding **p** are on
Gal 4:3 slaves to the **p** of this world.
4:9 the powerless and bankrupt **p**
2Pe 2:7 of people who had no **p**
3:17 of people who have no **p**.

Prisca (3)

Rom 16:3 Greet **P** and Aquila,
1Co 16:19 Aquila and **P** and the church
2Ti 4:19 Give my greetings to **P** and

Priscilla (4)

Act 18:2 named Aquila and his wife **P**.
18:18 **P** and Aquila went with him.
18:19 where Paul left **P** and Aquila.
18:26 When **P** and Aquila heard him,

prison (106)

Gen 39:20 put him in the same **p** where
39:20 While Joseph was in **p**,
39:22 prisoners who were in that **p**.
40:3 He put them in the **p** of the
40:7 were with him in his master's **p**,
40:14 and get me out of this **p**.
41:10 to the captain of the guard's **p**.
42:16 while the rest of you stay in **p**.
42:19 of your brothers stay here in **p**.
Jdg 16:21 and took him to the **p** in Gaza.
16:25 Samson was called from the **p**,
1Ki 22:27 king says: Put this man in **p**,
2Ki 17:4 arrested him and put him in **p**.
25:27 King Jehoiakin of Judah from **p**.
25:29 no longer wore **p** clothes,
2Ch 16:10 Hanani that he put Hanani in **p**.
18:26 king says: Put this man in **p**,
Job 12:14 When he puts someone in **p**,
Psa 68:6 He leads prisoners out of **p** into
69:33 despise his own who are in **p**.
142:7 Release my soul from **p** so that
Ecc 4:14 A young man came out of **p** to
Isa 24:22 in a jail and locked in **p**.
51:14 They will not die in **p**.
Jer 20:2 put him in **p** at Upper Benjamin
20:3 Pashhur took Jeremiah out of **p**,
29:26 a prophet in **p** and in shackles.
32:2 up in the courtyard of the **p**.
32:2 This **p** was in the palace of the
32:8 to me in the courtyard of the **p**.
32:12 sitting in the courtyard of the **p**.
33:1 held in the courtyard of the **p**,
37:4 hadn't put him in **p** yet.
37:15 they beat him and put him in **p**
37:15 which had been turned into a **p**.
37:16 Jeremiah went into a **p** cell,
37:18 Why have you put me in **p**?
37:21 put in the courtyard of the **p**.
37:21 stayed in the courtyard of the **p**.
38:6 It was in the courtyard of the **p**.
38:13 stayed in the courtyard of the **p**.
38:28 in the courtyard of the **p** until
39:14 out of the courtyard of the **p**
39:15 in the courtyard of the **p**,
52:11 to Babylon and put him in a **p**,
52:31 Judah and released him from **p**.
52:33 no longer wore **p** clothes,
Eze 19:9 They put him in **p** so that his
Mat 4:12 that John had been put in **p**,
5:25 who will throw you into **p**.
11:2 When John was in **p**,
14:3 tied him up, and put him in **p**.
14:10 He had John's head cut off in **p**.
18:30 had that servant put into **p** until
25:36 I was in **p**, and you visited me.'
25:39 you sick or in **p** and visit you?'
25:43 I was sick and in **p**,
25:44 need of clothes or sick or in **p**
Mar 1:14 After John had been put in **p**,
6:17 tied him up, and put him in **p**.
6:27 guard cut off John's head in **p**.
15:7 a man named Barabbas in **p**.
Luk 3:20 he locked John in **p**.
12:58 who will throw you into **p**.
22:33 I'm ready to go to **p** with you
23:19 had been thrown into **p**
23:25 who had been put in **p** for
Jon 3:24 John had not yet been put in **p**.)
Act 5:19 cell and led them out of the **p**.
5:21 They also sent men to the **p** to
5:22 temple guards arrived at the **p**,
5:23 "We found the **p** securely
5:25 "The men you put in **p** are
8:3 another and threw them into **p**.
9:14 who calls on your name in **p**."
12:4 Herod had him thrown into **p**
12:5 So Peter was kept in **p**,
12:6 They were watching the **p**.
12:17 the Lord had taken him out of **p**.
16:27 up and saw the **p** doors open.
22:4 put them into **p** until they were
23:29 to die or to be put into **p**.
24:27 Jews a favor, he left Paul in **p**.)
25:14 "Felix left a man here in **p**.
25:21 He asked to be held in **p** and to
25:21 So I ordered him to be held in **p**
26:10 I locked many Christians in **p**.
26:31 deserves to die or be put in **p**."
Rom 11:32 has placed all people into the **p**
2Co 11:23 been in **p** many more times,
Eph 6:20 representative, I am in **p**.
Php 1:7 whether I'm in **p** or defending
1:13 that I am in **p** because of Christ.
1:14 So through my being in **p**,
1:17 up trouble for me while I'm in **p**.
2Ti 2:9 I have even been put into **p**
Phm 1:10 his spiritual father here in **p**.
1:13 in your place while I am in **p**

Heb 11:36 were chained and put in **p**.
13:3 Remember those in **p** as if you
13:3 as if you were in **p** with them.
1Pe 3:19 victory to the spirits kept in **p**.
Rev 2:10 some of you into **p** so that you
13:10 taken prisoner, he must go to **p**.
18:2 She is a **p** for every evil spirit,
20:7 Satan will be freed from his **p**.

prisoner (28)

Gen 40:3 place where Joseph was a **p**.
Exo 12:29 the firstborn son of the **p** in jail,
1Ki 20:39 around and brought a **p** to me.
20:39 He said, 'Guard this **p**.
2Ki 17:28 taken **p** from Samaria went
23:33 Pharaoh Necoh made him a **p**
1Ch 3:17 The descendants of the **p**
Isa 22:3 found were taken **p** before any
Lam 3:34 crush any **p** on earth underfoot,
Mat 27:15 would free one **p** whom
27:16 there was a well-known **p** by
Mar 15:6 Pilate would free one **p** whom
Act 23:18 "The **p** Paul called me.
25:27 I find it ridiculous to send a **p** to
26:21 this reason the Jews took me **p**
26:29 as I am (except for being a **p**)."
28:17 Yet, I'm a **p** from Jerusalem,
Eph 3:1 am the **p** of Christ Jesus for
4:1 I, a **p** in the Lord,
Col 4:3 of this mystery that I am a **p**.
4:10 Aristarchus, who is a **p** like me,
4:18 Remember that I'm a **p**.
2Ti 1:8 or be ashamed of me, his **p**.
1:16 wasn't ashamed that I was a **p**.
Phm 1:1 who is a **p** for Christ Jesus,
1:9 and now a **p** for Christ Jesus,
1:23 Epaphras, who is a **p** because
Rev 13:10 If anyone is taken **p**,

prisoners (51)

Gen 31:26 off my daughters like **p** of war.
39:20 where the king's **p** were kept.
39:22 in charge of all the **p** who were
40:5 both **p** — the cupbearer and the
Num 14:3 will be taken as **p** of war!
14:31 would be taken as **p** of war.
21:1 and took some of them as **p**.
21:29 he let his daughters become **p**
24:22 Assyria takes you as **p** of war."
31:9 and children as **p** of war.
31:12 and brought the **p** of war,
31:19 You and your **p** of war must
Dtr 28:41 they will be taken as **p** of war.
Jdg 5:12 Take your **p**, son of Abinoam.
1Sm 30:2 and other **p**⌋ and gone away.
2Ki 24:14 all the soldiers (10,000 **p**),
2Ch 28:5 defeated him, captured many **p**,
28:11 Return these **p** you have
28:13 "Don't bring the **p** here.
28:14 So the army left the **p** and the
28:15 by name took charge of the **p**
28:15 to all the **p** who were naked.
28:17 defeated Judah and captured **p**.
29:9 wives are **p** because of this.
Neh 4:4 in the land where they are **p**.
Psa 68:6 He leads **p** out of prison into
68:18 You took **p** captive.
79:11 Let the groans of **p** come into
102:20 He heard the groans of the **p**
107:10 shadow were **p** in misery.
146:7 The LORD sets **p** free.
Isa 10:4 left but to crouch among **p**
14:17 who didn't let his **p** go home?"
24:22 They'll be gathered like **p** in a
42:7 bring **p** out of prisons,
49:9 You will say to the **p**,
49:24 away from mighty men or **p**
49:25 This is what the LORD says: **P**
51:14 Chained **p** will be set free.
60:11 with their kings led as **p**.
61:1 set free and **p** will be released.
Hab 1:9 They will gather **p** like sand.
Luk 4:18 announce forgiveness to the **p**
21:24 carried off into all nations as **p**.
Act 9:21 to take these worshipers as **p**
16:25 The other **p** were listening to
16:27 Thinking the **p** had escaped,
27:1 Paul and some other **p** were
27:42 soldiers had a plan to kill the **p**
Rom 16:7 They are **p** like me and are
Heb 10:34 You suffered with **p**.

prisoners' (1)

Act 16:26 all the **p** chains came loose.

prisons (3)

Isa 42:7 bring prisoners out of **p**,
42:22 trapped in pits and hidden in **p**.
Luk 21:12 and put you into their **p**.

private (14)

Gen 43:30 He went into his **p** room and
1Sm 18:22 "Talk to David in **p**.
1Ki 1:15 went to the king in his **p** room.
7:8 His own **p** quarters were in a
7:8 Solomon also built **p** quarters
Sos 1:4 brought me into his **p** rooms.
Isa 48:16 I have spoken nothing in **p**.
Mat 6:4 Father sees what you do in **p**.
6:6 Father sees what you do in **p**.
6:18 Father who is with you in **p**.
6:18 Father sees what you do in **p**.
Luk 10:23 He turned to his disciples in **p**
12:3 have whispered in **p** rooms will
Gal 2:2 I did this in a **p** meeting with

privately (12)

1Sm 8:21 he reported it **p** to the LORD.
2Sm 3:27 gateway as if to talk to him **p**.
Isa 45:19 I haven't spoken **p** or in some
Jer 37:17 and the king asked him **p** in the
Mat 6:4 Give your contributions **p**.
6:6 Pray **p** to your Father who is
17:19 came to Jesus **p** and asked,
20:17 aside and said to them **p**,
24:3 came to him **p** and said,
Mar 9:28 his disciples asked him **p**,
13:3 and Andrew asked him **p**,
Luk 9:18 when Jesus was praying **p**

privilege (4)

Rom 1:5 God's kindness and the **p**
Php 1:29 God has given you the **p** not
Rev 2:7 I will give the **p** of eating from
19:8 She has been given the **p** of

privileged (1)

Job 22:8 A **p** person lives in it.

prize (11)

Isa 53:12 and he will divide the **p** with
Jer 50:10 Babylonians will become the **p**.
Eze 26:5 will become a **p** for the nations.
Hab 2:7 Then you will become their **p**.
1Co 9:24 but only one runner gets the **p**?
Php 3:14 win the **p** that God's heavenly
Col 2:18 you that you don't deserve a **p**.
1Th 2:19 Who is our hope, joy, or **p** that
2Ti 2:5 wins the **p** only when playing
4:8 The **p** that shows I have God's
4:8 will give me that **p** on that day.

prized (1)

Eze 29:19 take its **p** possessions,

prizes (3)

Jer 49:32 camels will be taken as **p**.
Eze 7:21 most evil people on earth as **p**.
26:12 and take your goods as **p**.

probed (1)

Psa 17:3 You have **p** my heart.

problem (9)

Jdg 18:23 said to Micah, "What's your **p**?
18:24 say to me, 'What's your **p**?'"
Ezr 2:63 and Thummim ⌊to settle the **p**⌋.
Neh 7:65 and Thummim ⌊to settle the **p**⌋.
Job 19:28 The root of the **p** is found in
Mat 27:4 do we care? That's your **p**."
Act 6:3 put them in charge of this **p**.
2Co 12:7 to deal with a recurring **p**.
12:7 That **p**, Satan's messenger,

problems (8)

Lev 26:16 from eye **p** and depression.
Dtr 1:12 How can I take care of your **p**,
Jdg 9:23 to cause **p** between Abimelech
Rut 2:15 Don't give her any **p**.
Psa 73:5 plagued ⌊with **p**⌋ like others.
73:14 I'm plagued ⌊with **p**⌋ all day
Dan 5:12 solve riddles, and untangle **p**.
5:16 such things and untangle **p**.

procedures (2)

Lev 5:10 Then, following the proper **p**,
9:16 Following the proper **p**,

proceeded (1)

Neh 4:14 I looked them over and **p** to tell

procession (4)

Neh 12:31 to give thanks and march in **p**.
Psa 42:4 the crowd and lead it in a **p**
118:27 March in a festival **p** with
Luk 7:12 he met a funeral **p**.

processions (2)

Psa 68:24 Your festival **p**, O God, can be
68:24 They are the **p** for my God,

Prochorus (1)

Act 6:5 **P**, Nicanor, Timon, Parmenas,

proclaim (4)

Lev 25:10 and **p** liberty to everyone living
Dtr 32:3 I will **p** the name of the LORD.
Jer 3:12 Go and **p** these things to the
1Pe 3:19 In it he also went to **p** his

proclaimed (2)

Dtr 15:2 payments on debts has been **p**
Jdg 9:6 and **p** Abimelech king.

proclamation (2)

2Ch 24:9 Then they issued a **p** in Judah
Ezr 10:7 Then he sent a **p** throughout

produce (113)

Gen 1:11 "Let the earth **p** vegetation:
1:24 Then God said, "Let the earth **p**
3:19 you will **p** food to eat until you
38:8 and **p** a descendant for your
47:24 one-fifth of the **p** to Pharaoh.
47:26 One-fifth ⌊of the **p**⌋ belongs to
Exo 8:18 The magicians also tried to **p**
22:5 field was expected to **p**.
23:16 first **p** harvested from whatever
23:19 the first **p** harvested from your
34:26 of the **p** harvested from your
Lev 19:25 Do this to make the trees **p**
25:3 and gather what they **p**.
25:21 so that the land will **p** enough
26:4 The land will **p** its crops,
26:4 in the field will **p** their fruit.
26:20 your land will **p** no crops
26:20 and the trees will **p** no fruit.
Num 18:12 you the first of the **p** they give
18:13 The first of all **p** harvested in
18:30 will be considered to be **p** from
28:26 the first **p** harvested from your
Dtr 7:13 He will bless your land with **p**:
18:4 give them the first **p** harvested:
26:2 take some of the first **p**
26:10 So now I've brought the first **p**
28:11 Your soil will **p** many crops in
30:9 Your soil will **p** many crops.
32:13 earth and fed them with the **p**
33:14 the best **p** of each month,
Jos 5:11 they ate some of the **p** of the
2Ki 19:30 again take root and **p** crops.
1Ch 15:16 and cymbals to **p** joyful music
2Ch 31:5 offerings from the first of their **p**
Neh 9:36 they could eat its **p** and
10:35 bring the first **p** harvested
10:37 of the **p** from our fields,
10:37 one-tenth of the **p** from all our
12:44 the first **p** harvested,

Neh 13:31 times and for bringing the first **p**
Job 15:35 Their wombs **p** deception."
31:39 If I have eaten its **p** without
Psa 78:46 and their **p** to locusts.
85:12 and our land will **p** crops.
107:37 and vineyards that **p** crops.
Pro 8:19 What I **p** is better than gold,
12:12 of righteous people **p** fruit.
29:15 and a warning **p** wisdom,
Isa 5:2 waited for it to **p** good grapes,
5:4 I waited for it to **p** good grapes,
5:4 why did it **p** only sour,
5:10 A ten-acre vineyard will **p** only
5:10 and two quarts of seed will **p**
7:22 because they will **p** so much
37:31 again take root and **p** crops.
54:16 and to **p** useful weapons.
Jer 2:7 land to eat its fruit and its **p**.
12:2 They grow, and they **p** fruit.
20:5 This will include all its **p**,
29:5 and eat what they **p**.
29:28 and eat what they **p**.'"
Eze 17:23 will grow branches and **p** fruit.
34:27 Then the trees in the field will **p**
47:12 and they won't fail to **p** fruit.
47:12 Each month they will **p** fresh
Hos 2:22 and the earth will **p** grain,
2:22 You will **p** many crops,
8:7 ripen will never **p** any grain.
8:7 Even if it did **p** grain,
10:1 like vines that used to **p** fruit.
10:12 that your loyalty will **p** for me."
Hab 3:17 even if the olive tree fails to **p**
Hag 1:10 the earth has withheld its **p**.
Zec 8:12 Vines will **p** their grapes.
8:12 The sky will **p** its dew.
Mal 3:11 They will not destroy the **p** of
Mat 3:10 Any tree that doesn't **p** good
7:16 will know them by what they **p**.
7:18 A good tree cannot **p** bad fruit,
7:18 a rotten tree cannot **p** good fruit
7:19 Any tree that fails to **p** good
7:20 will know them by what they **p**.
13:22 word so that it can't **p** anything.
13:23 They **p** one hundred,
21:34 to collect his share of the **p**.
21:41 him his share of the **p** when
21:43 who will **p** what God wants.
Mar 4:7 and they didn't **p** anything.
4:19 word so that it can't **p** anything.
4:20 and **p** crops — thirty,
Luk 3:9 Any tree that doesn't **p** good
6:43 good tree doesn't **p** rotten fruit,
6:43 a rotten tree doesn't **p** good fruit
8:14 So they don't **p** anything good.
8:15 hearts and **p** what is good
Jon 12:24 doesn't **p** anything unless
12:24 If it dies, it will **p** a lot of grain.
15:2 my branches that doesn't **p** fruit
15:2 every branch that does **p** fruit
15:2 fruit to make it **p** more fruit.
15:4 A branch cannot **p** any fruit by
15:4 In the same way, you cannot **p**
15:5 in me while I live in them will **p**
15:5 can't **p** anything without me.
15:8 glory to my Father when you **p**
15:16 to **p** fruit that will last,
1Co 14:7 like the flute or harp **p** sounds.
2Co 4:15 it will **p** even more
9:11 Your generosity will **p**
Php 1:22 my work will **p** more results.
Jas 3:12 can a fig tree **p** olives?
3:12 Can a grapevine **p** figs?
3:12 of salt water can't **p** fresh water.

produced (26)

Gen 1:12 The earth **p** vegetation:
41:47 years the land **p** large harvests.
Lev 25:22 live on what the land already **p**.
Num 17:8 blossomed and **p** ripe almonds.
Dtr 28:33 and your hard work have **p**.
2Ki 8:6 whatever her property **p** from
19:29 vineyards, and eat what is **p**.
1Ch 7:11 They headed families that **p**
Isa 5:2 but it **p** only sour, wild grapes.
23:8 the city that **p** kings?
Isa 37:30 vineyards, and eat what is **p**.
Hos 10:1 The more fruit they **p**,
10:1 The more their land **p**,
10:13 eaten the fruit that your lies **p**.
Joe 2:22 The trees have **p** their fruit.
Nah 3:16 You have **p** more businessmen
Hag 2:19 and the olive tree still haven't **p**.
Mat 13:8 on good ground and **p** grain.
13:8 They **p** one hundred,
Mar 4:8 sprouted, and **p** thirty, sixty,
Luk 8:8 When they came up, they **p** a
12:16 had land that **p** good crops.
Php 2:16 and that my work **p** results.
Jas 1:17 like the shifting shadows **p** by
5:18 and the ground **p** crops.
Rev 22:2 It **p** 12 kinds of fruit.

produces (36)

Lev 23:39 have gathered what the land **p**,
25:6 Whatever the land **p** during that
25:7 Everything the land **p** will be
25:12 will eat what the field itself **p**.
25:22 until the land **p** more.
Ezr 9:12 eat the good things the land **p**,
Job 15:34 of godless people **p** nothing,
37:10 God's breath **p** ice,
Psa 1:3 streams — a tree that **p** fruit
129:6 that dries up before it **p** a stalk.
Pro 13:10 Arrogance **p** only quarreling,
14:4 of an ox **p** plentiful harvests.
30:33 As churning milk **p** butter and
30:33 and punching a nose **p** blood,
30:33 so stirring up anger **p** a fight.
Sos 4:13 You are paradise that **p**
5:13 a garden that **p** scented herbs.
Isa 55:10 and grow so that it **p** seed
Jer 10:13 the water in the sky **p** a storm.
Hag 1:11 and whatever the ground **p**,
Mat 7:17 every good tree **p** good fruit,
7:17 but a rotten tree **p** bad fruit.
13:23 This type **p** crops.
Mar 4:28 The ground **p** grain by itself.
1Co 12:6 but the same God **p** every gift
2Co 9:12 but also **p** more and more
Gal 5:22 But the spiritual nature **p** love,
Eph 5:9 Light **p** everything that is good,
5:11 useless works that darkness **p**.
Php 1:11 that God's approval **p**.
2:13 It is God who **p** in you the
2Th 1:11 you do everything your faith **p**.
1Ti 6:4 This **p** jealousy, rivalry,
Heb 6:7 So rain often falls on it, and it **p**
6:8 However, if the earth **p** thorns
Jas 1:3 of your faith **p** endurance.

producing (9)

Gen 47:13 Egypt nor Canaan were **p** crops
Jdg 9:9 'Should I stop **p** oil,
9:11 'Should I stop **p** my good,
9:13 'Should I stop **p** my wine,
Jer 17:8 It will not stop **p** fruit.
Eze 17:6 So it became a vine, **p**
2Co 4:17 is light and temporary and is **p**
Col 1:6 It is **p** results and spreading all
1:10 as you grow in **p** every kind

product (1)

Act 17:29 an image that is the **p** of

productive (4)

Psa 68:6 out of prison into **p** lives,
1Co 14:14 but my mind is not **p**.
Tit 3:14 so that they can live **p** lives.
2Pe 1:8 Jesus Christ is living and **p**.

products (12)

Gen 43:11 Put some of the best **p** of the
45:23 carrying Egypt's best **p**
Lev 2:12 as offerings of your first **p**.
25:19 The land will give you its **p**,
1Ki 7:47 Solomon left all the **p**
2Ch 4:18 so many of these **p** that no one
Neh 9:37 The many **p** ⌊from our land⌋ go
10:39 They should bring these **p** to
Isa 45:14 LORD says: The **p** from Egypt,
Jer 14:14 They are the **p** of their own
Eze 27:16 because you had so many **p**.
27:18 because you had so many **p**.

professional (4)

2Ch 13:3 800,000 of the best **p** soldiers.
17:13 and an army of **p** soldiers
26:11 had an army of **p** soldiers.
Amo 5:16 to mourn and on **p** mourners

profit (12)

Lev 25:36 or make any **p** from him.
Psa 30:9 "How will you **p** if my blood is
Pro 3:14 The **p** ⌊gained⌋ from
3:14 than the **p** ⌊gained⌋ from silver.
10:2 Treasures gained dishonestly **p**
22:16 Oppressing the poor for **p** ⌊or⌋
31:18 that she is making a good **p**.
Eze 13:18 of my people for your own **p**.
18:8 or make an excessive **p**.
Act 19:24 His business brought a huge **p**
1Ti 6:5 godly life is a way to make a **p**.
Jud 1:11 into Balaam's error to make a **p**.

profitable (1)

Ecc 11:6 this field or that field will be **p**

profits (14)

1Ki 10:15 the merchants, the traders' **p**,
Job 20:18 joy from the **p** of his business
Pro 31:16 from the **p** she has earned.
Isa 23:18 Her **p** and her earnings will be
Jer 22:17 set on nothing but dishonest **p**.
Eze 18:13 and makes excessive **p**.
18:17 interest or make excessive **p**.
22:12 interest and make excessive **p**.
22:12 You make **p** by mistreating
22:13 excessive **p** you have made
22:27 people to make excessive **p**.
33:31 hearts they chase dishonest **p**.
Amo 3:10 Those who collect **p** in their
1Ti 6:6 A godly life brings huge **p** to

progress (4)

Ezr 5:8 job and making rapid **p**.
6:14 leaders continued to make **p**
Neh 4:7 of Jerusalem was making **p**
1Ti 4:15 that everyone can see your **p**.

progressed (1)

2Ch 24:13 the project **p** under the

progressively (1)

2Ch 16:12 disease that became **p** worse.

project (2)

2Ch 24:13 As the men worked, the **p**
Neh 6:3 "I'm working on an important **p**

projecting (2)

Neh 3:26 the east and the **p** tower.
3:27 from the large **p** tower as far

projects (4)

1Ki 9:23 in charge of Solomon's **p**:
2Ch 8:9 the Israelites slaves for his **p**.
8:10 in charge of King Solomon's **p**:
Neh 3:25 and the upper tower that **p** from

prolong (2)

Job 6:11 that I would want to **p** my life?
Dan 4:27 you can **p** your prosperity."

prominent (9)

2Ki 24:16 all 7,000 of the **p** landowners,
1Ch 5:2 Even though Judah was more **p**
25:5 given to him to make him **p**,
Isa 22:16 have to cut it out in a **p** place?
Dan 8:5 This goat had a **p** horn
Luk 14:1 eat at the home of a **p** Pharisee.
Act 17:4 and the wives of many **p** men.
17:12 of them were **p** Greek men
Rom 16:7 like me and are **p** among

promiscuity (3)

Rom 13:13 sexual immorality, **p**, rivalry,
2Co 12:21 and **p** in which they have been

Gal 5:19 illicit sex, perversion, **p**,

promiscuous (2)

Eph 4:19 they have become **p**.
1Pe 4:3 You were **p**, had sinful desires,

promise (394)

Gen 6:18 "But I will make my **p** to you.
9:9 am going to make my **p** to you,
9:11 I am making my **p** to you.
9:12 "This is the sign of the **p** I am
9:13 be a sign of my **p** to the earth.
9:15 Then I will remember my **p** to
9:16 and remember my everlasting **p**
9:17 "This is the sign of the **p** I am
15:18 At that time the LORD made a **p**
17:2 I will give you my **p**,
17:4 "My **p** is still with you.
17:7 I will make my **p** to you and
17:7 to come as an everlasting **p**.
17:9 come are to be faithful to my **p**.
17:10 you are to be faithful to my **p**:
17:11 That will be the sign of the **p**
17:13 So my **p** will be a sign on your
17:13 on your flesh, an everlasting **p**.
17:14 because he has rejected my **p**."
17:19 I will make an everlasting **p** to
17:21 But I will make my **p** to Isaac.
18:10 The LORD said, "I **p** I'll come
41:9 "I remember a **p** I failed to keep.
Exo 2:24 remembered his **p** to Abraham,
3:17 I **p** I will take you away from
6:4 I even made a **p** to give them
6:5 and I have remembered my **p**.
16:34 in front of the words of God's **p**
19:5 are faithful to the terms of my **p**,
24:7 took the Book of the LORD's **P**
24:8 blood which seals the **p** that
25:16 ark the words of my **p** which
25:21 ark the words of my **p** which
26:33 the words of my **p** under it.
27:21 where the words of my **p** are,
30:6 containing the words of my **p**.
30:26 containing the words of my **p**,
30:36 containing⌋ the words of my **p**
31:7 containing the words of my **p**
31:16 a permanent reminder of my **p**.
34:10 "I'm making my **p** again.
34:27 of these words I'm making a **p**
34:28 the tablets the words of the **p**,
38:21 tent of the words of God's **p**).
39:35 containing the words of God's **p**
40:3 the words of my **p** inside it,
40:20 He took the words of God's **p**
Lev 2:13 The salt of God's **p** must never
16:13 is over the words of God's **p**,
24:3 where the words of my **p** are,
24:8 of my **p** to the Israelites.
26:9 and I will keep my **p** to you.
26:15 if you reject my **p** by
26:25 for my **p** ⌊that you rejected⌋.
26:42 I will remember my **p** to Jacob,
26:44 reject or cancel my **p** to them,
26:45 I will remember the **p** to their
Num 4:5 the words of God's **p**.
7:89 the words of God's **p**,
9:15 words of God's **p** was set up,
10:11 the tent of the words of God's **p**.
10:33 The ark of the LORD's **p** went
14:44 though the ark of the LORD's **p**
17:4 in front of the words of my **p**.
17:7 the tent of the words of God's **p**.
17:10 in front of the words of my **p**,
18:2 of the tent of the words of my **p**.
18:19 It is an everlasting **p** of salt in
23:19 When he makes a **p**,
25:12 Phinehas that I'm making a **p**
25:13 My **p** is that he and his
30:6 or carelessly **p** that she won't
30:8 cancel the vow or **p** she made.
30:8 free her ⌊from this vow or **p**⌋.
30:9 must keep her vow or her **p**.
Dtr 4:13 you about the terms of his **p**,
4:23 that you don't forget the **p** that
4:31 or forget the **p** to your ancestors
5:2 The LORD our God made a **p**

Dtr 5:3 He didn't make this **p** to our
7:9 who keeps his **p** and is
7:12 LORD your God will keep his **p**
8:18 He's confirming the **p** which he
9:5 LORD wants to confirm the **p**
9:9 the tablets of the **p** that the
9:11 tablets with his **p** on them.
9:15 two tablets with the **p** on them.
10:8 to carry the ark of the LORD's **p**,
17:2 the conditions of the LORD's **p**
29:1 These are the terms of the **p**
29:1 This was in addition to the **p**
29:9 obey the terms of this **p**.
29:12 and conditions of the **p** that
29:13 With this **p** the LORD will
29:14 this **p** and its conditions.
29:19 hear the conditions of this **p**.
29:21 the conditions of the **p** written
29:25 they abandoned the **p**
29:25 He made this **p** to them when
31:9 carried the ark of the LORD's **p**
31:16 abandon me and reject the **p**
31:20 despise me and reject my **p**.
31:25 carried the ark of the LORD's **p**:
31:26 put it next to the ark of the **p**
33:9 faithful to the terms of your **p**.
Jos 3:3 as you see the ark of the **p**
3:6 "Take the ark of the **p**,
3:8 who carry the ark of the **p**,
3:11 Watch the ark of the **p** of the
3:14 the ark of the **p** went ahead
3:17 ark of the LORD's **p** stood firmly
4:7 front of the ark of the LORD's **p**.
4:9 the ark of the **p** had stood.
4:18 ark of the LORD's **p** came out
6:6 "Pick up the ark of the **p**,
6:8 of the LORD's **p** followed them.
8:33 carried the ark of the LORD's **p**.
14:10 LORD made this **p** to Moses.
21:45 Every single good **p** that the
23:14 that not one single **p** which
Jdg 2:1 'I will never break my **p** to you.
2:20 this nation have rejected the **p**
11:35 I made a foolish **p** to the LORD.
11:36 you made a **p** to the LORD.
15:13 They told him, "We **p** we'll only
20:27 In those days the ark of God's **p**
1Sm 2:30 I **p** that I will honor those who
4:3 of the LORD's **p** from Shiloh so
4:4 brought back the ark of the **p**
20:14 But as long as I live, ⌊**p** me
20:23 We have made a **p** to each
2Sm 7:21 great thing because of your **p**
7:25 "Now, LORD God, keep the **p**
15:24 carrying the ark of God's **p**.
22:31 The **p** of the LORD has proven
23:5 he has made a lasting **p** to me,
1Ki 2:4 the LORD will keep the **p**
3:15 front of the ark of the LORD's **p**.
6:12 I will fulfill the **p** I made about
6:19 the ark of the LORD's **p** there.
8:1 the ark of the LORD's **p** from
8:6 brought the ark of the LORD's **p**
8:9 where the LORD made a **p** to
8:15 With his mouth he made a **p** to
8:20 LORD has kept the **p** he made.
8:21 contains the LORD's **p** that
8:23 You keep your **p** of mercy to
8:24 You have kept your **p** to my
8:25 keep your **p** to my father David,
8:26 may the **p** you made to my
12:15 these events to carry out the **p**
2Ki 11:17 Jehoiada made a **p** to the
13:23 because of his **p** to Abraham,
17:15 rejected his decrees, the **p**
17:35 the LORD made a **p** to Israel,
17:38 Never forget the **p** I made to
18:12 the conditions of the **p**
23:2 in the Book of the **P** found
23:3 beside the pillar and made a **p**
23:3 He confirmed the terms of the **p**
23:3 all the people joined in the **p**.
23:21 is written in this Book of the **P**.
1Ch 15:25 LORD's **p** from Obed Edom's
15:26 carried the ark of the LORD's **p**,
15:28 brought the ark of the LORD's **p**

1Ch 15:29 When the ark of the LORD's **p**
16:6 in front of the ark of God's **p**.
16:15 Remember his **p** forever,
16:16 the **p** that he made to Abraham,
16:16 and his sworn **p** to Isaac.
16:17 as an everlasting **p** to Israel,
16:37 front of the ark of the LORD's **p**,
17:1 while the ark of the LORD's **p**
17:23 faithfully keep the **p** you made
22:19 bring the ark of the LORD's **p**
28:2 the ark of the LORD's **p** could
28:18 cover the ark of the LORD's **p**.
2Ch 1:9 you've kept the **p** you made to
5:2 the ark of the LORD's **p** from
5:7 brought the ark of the LORD's **p**
5:10 where the LORD made a **p** to
6:4 With his mouth he made a **p** to
6:10 LORD has kept the **p** he made.
6:11 the LORD's **p** to Israel there."
6:14 You keep your **p** of mercy to
6:15 You have kept your **p** to my
6:16 keep your **p** to my father David,
6:17 may the **p** you made to David,
7:18 royal dynasty as I said in a **p**
10:15 these events to carry out the **p**
13:5 forever in a permanent **p**?
21:7 But the LORD, recalling the **p**
23:16 Jehoiada made a **p** to the
24:6 the words of God's **p**."
34:30 in the Book of the **P** found
34:31 in his place and made a **p**
34:31 by the terms of the **p** written
34:32 join with him ⌊in the **p**⌋.
34:32 lived according to the **p** of God,
36:22 The **p** the LORD had spoken
Ezr 1:1 The **p** the LORD had spoken
10:3 So we must now make a **p** to
Neh 1:5 you faithfully keep your **p** and
5:13 who refuses to keep this **p**.
9:8 You made a **p** to him to give
9:8 You kept your **p** because you
13:29 office and the **p** you made
Job 22:28 When you **p** to do something,
Psa 15:4 The one who makes a **p** and
18:30 The **p** of the LORD has proven
25:10 his **p** and written instructions.
25:14 to them the intent of his **p**.
44:17 We never ignored your **p**.
55:20 He has broken his solemn **p**.
74:20 Consider your **p** because every
77:8 Has his **p** been canceled
78:10 had not been faithful to God's **p**.
78:37 They were not faithful to his **p**.
89:3 ⌊You said,⌋ "I have made a **p**
89:28 My **p** to him is unbreakable.
89:34 I will not dishonor my **p** or alter
89:39 have refused to recognize the **p**
103:18 those who are faithful to his **p**,
105:8 He always remembers his **p**,
105:9 the **p** that he made to Abraham,
105:10 as an everlasting **p** to Israel,
105:19 The LORD's **p** tested him
105:42 He remembered his holy **p** to
106:45 He remembered his **p** to them.
111:5 He always remembers his **p**.
111:9 He has ordered that his **p**
119:11 I have treasured your **p** in my
119:38 Keep your **p** to me so that I can
119:50 Your **p** gave me a new life.
119:82 strained from looking for your **p**
119:103 sweet the taste of your **p** is!
119:123 fulfillment of your righteous **p**.
119:133 steps secure through your **p**,
119:140 Your **p** has been thoroughly
119:158 They have not accepted your **p**.
119:162 I find joy in your **p** like
119:172 my tongue sing about your **p**
132:6 about the ark ⌊of the **p**⌋ being
132:12 If your sons are faithful to my **p**
138:2 your **p** greater than everything.
147:15 He is the one who sends his **p**
Pro 6:2 caught by your own **p**.
Ecc 5:4 When you make a **p** to God,
5:4 doesn't like fools. Keep your **p**.
5:5 It is better not to make a **p** than
5:6 "My **p** was a mistake!"

Isa 24:5 and rejected the everlasting **p**.
42:6 I will appoint you as my **p** to
49:8 I will appoint you as my **p** to
54:10 My **p** of peace will never
55:3 I will make an everlasting **p** to
56:4 observe the conditions of my **p**.
56:6 observe the conditions of my **p**.
59:21 "This is my **p** to them,"
61:8 make an everlasting **p** to them.
Jer 3:16 about the ark of the LORD's **p**.
11:2 "Listen to the terms of this **p**,
11:3 listen to the terms of this **p**.
11:4 I made this **p** to your ancestors
11:6 Listen to the terms of this **p**,
11:8 not keep all the terms of the **p**,
11:10 Judah have rejected the **p** that
14:21 Remember your **p** to us;
18:9 "At another time I may **p** to
22:9 'They rejected the **p** of the
29:10 I will keep my **p** to you and
31:31 "when I will make a new **p** to
31:32 It will not be like the **p** that I
31:32 They rejected that **p**,
31:33 "But this is the **p** that I will
32:40 I will make an eternal **p** to them
33:14 "when I will keep the **p** that I
34:13 I put a condition on the **p** I
34:15 and you made a **p** in my
34:18 who have rejected my **p**.
34:18 terms of the **p** which they made
Eze 16:59 vows and rejected my **p**.
16:60 I will remember the **p** that I
16:60 and I will make it a **p** that will
16:61 not because of my **p** with you.
16:62 I will make my **p** with you,
17:13 and made him **p** to be loyal.
17:16 The king of Judah broke his **p**
17:18 The king of Judah broke the **p**
17:19 punish you for rejecting my **p**
20:5 I made a **p** to them and said,
20:37 you keep the terms of the **p**.
33:13 I may **p** the righteous person
34:25 "'I will **p** them peace.
37:26 I will **p** them peace.
37:26 This **p** will last forever.
44:7 You rejected my **p** so that you
Dan 9:4 You keep your **p** and show
9:27 He will confirm his **p** with
11:22 including the prince of the **p**.
11:28 to fight against the holy **p**.
11:30 Angry at the holy **p**,
11:30 those who abandon the holy **p**.
11:32 those who abandon the **p**.
Hos 6:7 "Like Adam, you rejected the **p**.
8:1 of Israel have rejected my **p**
Hag 2:5 "This is the **p** I made to you
Zec 9:11 blood that sealed my **p** to you.
11:10 to break the **p** that I had made
Mal 2:4 you this warning so that my **p**
2:8 You have corrupted the **p** made
2:10 And why do we dishonor the **p**
3:1 messenger of the **p** will come.
Mat 14:9 The king regretted his **p**.
20:21 She said to him, "**P** that one of
26:28 is my blood, the blood of the **p**.
Mar 6:26 The king deeply regretted his **p**.
14:24 is my blood, the blood of the **p**.
Luk 1:45 Lord would keep his **p** to you."
1:55 This is the **p** he made to our
1:70 He made this **p** through his
1:72 and remembered his holy **p**,
22:20 out for you is the new **p** made
Act 2:39 This **p** belongs to you and to
3:25 heirs of the **p** that God made
7:8 circumcision to confirm his **p**.
7:44 had the tent of God's **p**.
13:33 God has fulfilled the **p** for us,
23:21 you to **p** ⌊that you will
26:6 I expect God to keep the **p** that
26:7 Our twelve tribes expect this **p**
26:7 I expect God to keep his **p**.
Rom 4:13 received the **p** that
4:14 useless and the **p** is worthless.
4:16 Therefore, the **p** is based on
4:16 Consequently, the **p** is
4:20 He didn't doubt God's **p** out of a
Rom 4:20 giving honor to God ⌊for the **p**⌋,
9:8 Instead, children born by the **p**
9:9 this is what the **p** said,
11:27 My **p** to them will be fulfilled
15:8 As a result, he fulfilled God's **p**
1Co 11:25 He said, "This cup is the new **p**
2Co 3:6 us to be ministers of a new **p**,
3:6 a spiritual **p**, not a written one.
3:12 confidence ⌊in the new **p**⌋,
Gal 3:17 put his **p** ⌊to Abraham⌋ into
3:17 cancel the **p** ⌊to Abraham⌋.
3:18 comes to us because of the **p**.
3:18 to Abraham through a **p**.
3:19 whom the **p** was given came.
3:22 Therefore, a **p** based on faith in
4:23 a **p** ⌊made to Abraham⌋.
4:28 are children of the **p** like Isaac.
Eph 2:12 made in his⌋ **p** were foreign
3:6 the same **p** that God made
6:3 commandment with a **p**.
1Ti 4:8 Godly living has the **p** of life
2Ti 1:1 contains Christ Jesus' **p** of life.
Phm 1:19 I, Paul, **p** to pay it back.
Heb 4:1 God's **p** that we may enter his
6:13 God made a **p** to Abraham.
6:17 those who would receive his **p**,
6:18 he takes an oath or makes a **p**.
7:22 the guarantee of a better **p**.
7:28 But God's **p**, which came after
8:6 He also brings a better **p** from
8:7 had been wrong with the first **p**,
8:8 when I will make a new **p** to
8:9 It will not be like the **p** that I
8:9 They rejected that **p**,
8:10 But this is the **p** that I will
8:13 God made this new **p** and
8:13 that the first **p** was outdated.
9:1 The first **p** had rules for the
9:4 and the ark of the Lord's **p**.
9:4 on which the **p** was written.
9:15 able to bring a new **p** from God.
9:15 committed under the first **p**.
9:18 That is why even the first **p**
9:20 that seals the **p** God has made
10:16 "This is the **p** that I will make
10:23 one who made the **p** is faithful.
10:29 blood of the **p** (the blood that
11:9 received the same **p** from God.
11:11 that God would keep his **p**.
12:24 brings the new **p** from God,
13:20 the blood of an eternal **p**.
2Pe 2:19 They **p** these people freedom,
3:3 people will ridicule ⌊God's **p**⌋
3:4 happened to his **p** to return?
1Jn 2:25 given us the **p** of eternal life.
Rev 11:19 and the ark of his **p** was seen
15:5 the words of God's **p** was open

promised (145)

Gen 4:1 the man that the LORD **p**."
18:19 will do what I have **p**
21:1 and did for her what he had **p**.
21:2 at the exact time God had **p**,
28:15 you until I do what I've **p** you."
50:6 as you have **p** him."
Exo 12:25 LORD will give you as he **p**,
33:1 Go to the land I **p** to Abraham,
Num 10:29 going to the place the LORD **p**
10:29 because the LORD has **p** good
11:12 the land you **p** their ancestors
14:16 people into the land he **p** them,
14:22 land which I **p** their ancestors.
14:40 go to the place the LORD **p**."
32:11 will see the land I **p** Abraham,
32:24 but do what you have **p**."
Dtr 1:11 may he bless you as he has **p**.
6:3 God of your ancestors **p** you.
6:18 good land which the LORD **p**
6:23 here and give us this land he **p**
8:1 of the land that the LORD **p**
9:3 them as the LORD **p** you.
9:28 them to the land he **p** them.
10:9 only possession, as he **p** them.
11:25 As the LORD your God **p**,
12:20 ⌊country's⌋ borders as he **p**.
15:6 God will bless you, as he **p**.
Dtr 18:2 their inheritance, as he **p** them.
19:8 borders as he **p** your ancestors
19:8 whole land he **p** to give them.
26:15 as you **p** with an oath to our
26:19 to the LORD your God, as he **p**.
27:3 milk and honey, as he **p** you.
28:9 as he **p** you with an oath.
29:13 and this is what he **p** your
34:4 "This is the land I **p** with an
Jos 1:3 you set foot, as I **p** Moses.
2:14 The men **p** her, "We pledge our
11:23 as the LORD had **p** Moses.
13:14 as the LORD had **p** them.
13:33 inherited, as he had **p** them.
14:10 has kept me alive as he **p**.
14:12 I can force them out, as he **p**."
22:4 relatives peace, as he **p** them.
23:10 for you, as he had **p** you.
23:15 your God has **p** you has come
Jdg 1:20 As Moses had **p**, Hebron was
11:36 Do to me whatever you **p** since
1Sm 19:6 and he **p**, "I solemnly swear,
25:30 LORD does all the good he **p**
2Sm 3:9 what the LORD had **p** him
7:25 house forever. Do as you **p**.
7:28 You **p** me this good thing.
7:29 you, Almighty LORD, have **p** it.
19:23 The king **p** Shimei,
23:5 ⌊He **p**⌋ everything that helps
1Ki 2:24 gave me a dynasty as he **p**.
5:12 Solomon wisdom as he had **p**.
8:20 throne of Israel as the LORD **p**.
8:24 With your mouth you **p** it.
8:53 as you **p** through your servant
8:56 people Israel rest, as he had **p**.
9:5 forever as I **p** your father David
17:16 the LORD had **p** through Elijah.
1Ch 17:23 house forever. Do as you **p**.
17:26 You **p** me this good thing.
25:5 him prominent, as God had **p**.
27:23 because the LORD had **p** that
2Ch 2:15 and wine he **p** the workers.
6:10 throne of Israel as the LORD **p**.
6:15 With your mouth you **p** it.
Neh 5:12 them swear to do what they **p**.
5:13 people did what they had **p**.
6:18 Many in Judah had **p** to support
Est 4:7 of silver that Haman had **p**
Psa 60:6 God has **p** the following
108:7 God has **p** the following
119:25 Give me a new life as you **p**.
119:28 Strengthen me as you **p**.
119:41 Save me as you **p**.
119:57 I **p** to hold on to your words.
119:58 Be kind to me as you **p**.
119:65 me well, O LORD, as you **p**.
119:76 mercy comfort me as you **p**.
119:107 a new life, O LORD, as you **p**.
119:116 Help me God, as you **p**,
119:154 Give me a new life as you **p**.
119:169 Help me understand as you **p**.
119:170 Rescue me as you **p**.
133:3 That is where the LORD **p** the
Isa 55:3 the blessings I **p** to David.
Jer 18:10 plans about the good that I **p**
32:42 blessings that I have **p** them.
34:8 all the people in Jerusalem **p**
34:10 and all the people agreed and **p**
40:3 The LORD did as he **p**
Eze 6:10 that the disaster I **p** was not
16:8 I **p** to love you, and I
20:6 At that time I **p** to bring them
20:15 them into the land that I had **p**
20:23 I **p** to scatter them among the
20:28 brought them to the land that I **p**
20:42 the land that I **p** to give your
30:5 and people from the **p** land will
Joe 2:32 as the LORD has **p**.
Hab 3:9 for the arrows ⌊you⌋ **p**.
Mal 2:5 "I **p** Levi life and peace.
Mat 1:18 His mother Mary had been **p** to
Mar 14:11 what Judas had to say and **p**
Luk 1:27 The angel went to a virgin **p** in
1:71 He **p** to save us from our
1:74 He **p** to rescue us from our
2:5 She had been **p** to him in

Luk 2:29 to leave in peace as you **p**.
22:6 So Judas **p** to do it.
24:49 sending you what my Father **p**.
Act 1:4 there for what the Father had **p**.
2:30 and knew that God had **p**
2:33 Holy Spirit as the Father had **p**,
3:21 as God **p** through his holy
7:5 But God **p** to give this land to
7:17 "When the time that God had **p**
13:23 descendants, as he had **p**.
13:32 What God **p** our ancestors has
13:34 the enduring love **p** to David.'
Rom 1:2 (God had already **p** this Good
4:21 that God would do what he **p**.
2Co 9:5 that you had already **p** to give.
11:2 you're a virgin whom I **p** in
Gal 3:14 price⌋ so that the blessing **p**
3:14 the **p** Spirit through faith.
3:29 and heirs, as God **p**.
Eph 1:13 with the Holy Spirit whom he **p**.
Tit 1:2 God, who never lies, **p** this
Heb 6:15 Abraham received what God **p**
10:36 you can receive what he has **p**.
11:9 the country that God had **p** him.
11:13 the things that God had **p** them,
11:33 and received what God had **p**.
11:39 them received what God had **p**.
12:26 But now he has **p**,
Jas 1:12 the crown of life that God has **p**
2:5 receive the kingdom that he **p**
2Pe 3:9 Lord isn't slow to do what he **p**,
3:13 forward to what God has **p** —

promises (30)

1Ki 8:56 None of the good **p** he made
11:11 you have no respect for my **p**
19:10 have abandoned your **p**,
19:14 have abandoned your **p**,
2Ki 11:17 He made other **p** between the
20:9 that he will do what he **p**.
Neh 9:32 You faithfully keep your **p**.
Psa 12:6 The **p** of the LORD are pure,
50:16 my decrees and mouth my **p**!
85:8 because he **p** peace to his
138:4 have heard the **p** you spoke.
Isa 5:18 along with lies and empty **p**,
38:7 that he will do what he **p**.
Jer 44:25 You and your wives made **p**,
Dan 11:21 the kingdom using false **p**.
Hos 10:4 and they make **p** they don't
Act 1:4 "I've told you what the Father **p**:
Rom 1:31 have any sense, don't keep **p**,
9:4 the true worship, and the **p**.
1Co 1:9 God faithfully keeps his **p**.
10:13 who faithfully keeps his **p**,
2Co 1:20 made God's many **p** come true.
7:1 Since we have these **p**,
Gal 3:16 The **p** were spoken to Abraham
3:21 to Moses contradict God's **p**?
Heb 6:12 are receiving the **p** through faith
7:6 Abraham, who had God's **p**.
11:17 who received the **p** from God,
2Pe 1:4 he has given us his **p** that are
1:4 Through these **p** you will share

promote (4)

Est 6:3 "How did I reward and **p**
Psa 35:26 Let those who **p** themselves at
38:16 do not let them **p** themselves at
Dan 5:19 whomever he wanted to **p**,

promoted (6)

Est 3:1 Later, King Xerxes **p** Haman.
5:11 and all about how the king **p**
10:2 whom the king had **p**,
Dan 2:48 Then the king **p** Daniel and
3:30 Then the king **p** Shadrach,
5:19 He **p** whomever he wanted to

promotes (1)

1Sm 2:7 ⌊people⌋; he also **p** them.

promoting (1)

1Ti 1:4 rather than **p** God's plan,

prompted (1)

2Ch 21:16 The LORD **p** the Philistines

promptly (1)

Ezr 7:26 orders should be **p** exiled,

pronounce (1)

Jdg 12:6 because he couldn't **p** the word

pronounced (7)

Jos 6:26 that time Joshua **p** this curse:
1Ch 16:12 he did and the judgments he **p**,
16:14 are **p** throughout the earth.
Psa 7:6 You have already **p** judgment.
105:5 and the judgments he **p**,
105:7 are **p** throughout the earth.
Jer 11:17 He has **p** disaster on you.

pronounces (2)

Psa 82:1 He **p** judgment among the gods:
Isa 50:8 The one who **p** me innocent is

proof (12)

Gen 21:30 me so that they may be **p** that
Exo 3:12 And this will be the **p** that I
Num 6:18 take the hair as **p** that they had
Jos 2:12 Also give me some **p**
Psa 86:17 Grant me some **p** of your
Mat 8:4 Moses commanded as **p**
Mar 1:44 which Moses commanded as **p**
Luk 1:18 "What **p** is there for this?
5:14 as Moses commanded as **p**
Act 17:31 God has given **p** to everyone
2Co 13:3 Since you want **p** that Christ is
2Th 3:17 this is **p** that I wrote it.

proper (42)

Lev 5:10 following the **p** procedures,
9:16 Following the **p** procedures,
22:29 to the LORD, do it in the **p** way.
Num 15:24 along with the **p** grain and wine
29:6 with their **p** grain offerings
29:18 Along with them bring the **p**
29:21 Along with them bring the **p**
29:24 Along with them bring the **p**
29:27 Along with them bring the **p**
29:30 Along with them bring the **p**
29:33 Along with them bring the **p**
29:37 Along with them bring the **p**
Dtr 33:19 they will offer the **p** sacrifices.
Jdg 6:26 Then, in the **p** way,
1Sm 6:2 to return it to its ⌊**p**⌋ place."
6:3 means return it to its ⌊**p**⌋ place
2Sm 15:3 "Your case is good and **p**,
1Ki 4:28 chariot horses to the **p** places.
8:32 person with the **p** punishment,
8:36 Teach them the **p** way to live.
8:39 Give each person the **p** reply.
2Ch 6:23 person with the **p** punishment,
6:27 Teach them the **p** way to live.
6:30 give each person the **p** reply.
24:13 God's temple to its **p** condition
Ezr 6:5 be returned to their **p** place
Job 31:7 steps have left the ⌊**p**⌋ path,
Psa 33:1 LORD⌋ is **p** for decent people.
145:15 them their food at the **p** time.
Sos 2:7 or arouse love before its **p** time.
3:5 or arouse love before its **p** time.
8:4 or arouse love before its **p** time!
Jer 33:20 wouldn't come at their **p** time.
Mat 3:15 This is the **p** way to do
22:12 without **p** wedding clothes?'
1Co 11:13 Is it **p** for a woman to pray to
11:28 are doing is **p** when they eat
14:40 be done in a **p** and orderly way.
2Co 11:27 without **p** clothes during cold
Gal 6:9 ⌊everlasting life⌋ at the **p** time,
Eph 6:5 earthly masters with **p** respect.
1Ti 2:10 This is what is **p** for women

properly (5)

Lev 19:5 sacrifice it ⌊**p**⌋ so that you will
1Ki 14:13 family who will be ⌊**p**⌋ buried.
Mar 7:3 don't eat unless they have **p**
Gal 2:14 But I saw that they were not **p**
Heb 2:2 disobedience was **p** punished.

property (139)

Gen 23:4 Let me have some of your **p** for
23:9 it to me for its full price as my **p**
23:18 His **p** included the field with
23:20 the Hittites to Abraham as his **p**
34:10 and acquire **p** here."
34:23 their livestock, their personal **p**,
36:43 lived and the **p** they owned.
47:11 He gave them **p** there.
47:19 and our land will be his **p**.
47:27 They acquired **p** there and had
Exo 21:21 The slave is his **p**.
22:9 or any ⌊other⌋ lost **p** which
Lev 25:10 freed in order to return to his **p**
25:13 freed in order to return to his **p**.
25:15 When you buy **p** from your
25:24 the right to buy their **p** back.
25:25 poor and sells some of his **p**,
25:27 and it will be his **p** again.
25:32 the right to buy back their **p**
25:33 are their **p** among the Israelites.
25:34 because it is their permanent **p**.
25:41 and the **p** of their ancestors.
25:45 They will be your **p**.
25:46 descendants as permanent **p**.
27:21 will become the **p** of the priest.
27:22 that was a part of your family **p**)
27:24 to whom it belongs as family **p**.
Num 16:32 of Korah, and all their **p**.
18:20 "You will have no land or **p** of
18:20 your **p** among the Israelites.
18:23 They will own no **p** as the
18:24 'They will own no **p** as the
18:26 which I'm giving you as your **p**.
27:4 Give us **p** among our father's
27:7 You must give them **p** of their
27:7 their father's **p** over to them.
27:8 turn his **p** over to his daughters.
27:9 give his **p** to his brothers.
27:10 If he has no brothers, give his **p**
27:11 If he has no uncles, give his **p**
32:5 give us this land as our **p**.
32:22 This land will be your own **p** in
32:29 them Gilead as their own **p**.
35:2 some cities from their own **p**.
35:8 you give the Levites from the **p**
35:28 to their own **p** only after his
Dtr 2:5 region of Mount Seir as their **p**.
2:9 giving you any of Ar as your **p**.
2:19 descendants of Lot as their **p**."
4:21 land he is giving you as your **p**.
12:9 the **p** the LORD your God is
12:10 is giving you as your own **p**.
18:1 Levi — will receive no land or **p**
19:14 boundary marker on any **p**
20:16 God is giving you as your **p**.
24:4 God is giving you as your **p**.
25:19 he is giving you as your own **p**,
26:1 God is giving you as your **p**.
29:8 tribe of Manasseh as their **p**.
32:9 the LORD's people were his **p**.
32:49 the Israelites as their own **p**.
Jos 22:19 Take some **p** for yourselves
24:28 each to his own **p**.
Jdg 18:7 to take away their **p** by force.
18:21 and **p** in front of them.
Rut 4:4 If you wish to buy back the **p**,
4:4 you can buy back the **p**.
4:4 do not wish to buy back the **p**,
4:4 "I'll buy back the **p**."
4:6 to buy back the **p** for yourself,
4:7 concerning buying back **p**
1Sm 15:9 and all the best ⌊**p**⌋.
1Ki 22:36 Every man to his own **p**!"
2Ki 8:6 including whatever her **p**
17:20 to those who looted their **p**,
21:14 and they will become **p** that
1Ch 9:2 first to settle again on their **p**
27:25 in charge of King David's **p**:
28:1 officials in charge of all the **p**
2Ch 11:14 abandoned their land and **p**
21:14 and all your **p** because you did
31:1 Each person went to his own **p**.
31:3 He set aside part of the king's **p**

2Ch 32:29 God had given him a lot of **p**.
35:7 animals were the king's **p**.)
Ezr 10:8 then they would lose all their **p**
Neh 2:20 You have no **p** or claim or
11:3 They lived on their own **p** in
11:20 lived on his own inherited **p**.
Est 8:1 Xerxes gave the **p** of Haman,
8:2 in charge of Haman's **p**.
8:7 given Haman's **p** to Esther,
Job 17:5 to get their **p** should have his
24:18 Their **p** is cursed in the land.
Pro 15:25 he protects the **p** of widows.
Jer 2:7 They made my **p** disgusting.
2:14 they become someone's **p**?
3:18 their ancestors as their own **p**.
3:19 the most beautiful **p** among the
12:10 They've trampled my **p**.
12:10 pleasant **p** into a wasteland.
16:18 They have filled my **p** with the
37:12 of his **p** there among
Eze 11:15 been given to us as our own **p**.'
38:12 people have cattle and **p**,
38:13 gold and to take cattle and **p**?'"
45:1 lots for the **p** you will inherit.
45:6 43,750 feet long as the city's **p**.
45:7 both sides of the **p** belonging
46:16 of his sons a gift from his **p**.
46:17 prince offers a gift from his **p**
46:17 Only his sons can inherit his **p**.
46:18 not take any of the people's **p**.
46:18 force them to give up their **p**.
46:18 He must give his own **p** as an
46:18 will be separated from their **p**."
48:20 the LORD along with the city **p**.
48:21 area and the city **p** will belong
48:22 So the Levites' **p** and the city's
48:22 property and the city's **p** will
Mic 2:5 will draw lots to divide your **p**.
Mat 12:29 man's house and steal his **p**?
12:29 his house and steal his **p**.
19:22 because he owned a lot of **p**.
24:47 servant in charge of all his **p**.
Mar 3:27 man's house and steal his **p**.
3:27 man's house and steal his **p**.
10:22 because he owned a lot of **p**.
Luk 11:21 his own mansion, his **p** is safe.
12:44 servant in charge of all his **p**.
15:12 give me my share of the **p**.' So
15:12 So the father divided his **p**
16:1 of wasting the rich man's **p**.
16:2 can't manage my **p** any longer.'
19:8 I'll give half of my **p** to the poor.
Act 2:45 they sold their **p** and other
5:1 his wife Sapphira sold some **p**.
28:7 had **p** around the area.
2Co 11:20 your wealth, seizes your **p**,

prophecies (9)

Lam 2:14 you false **p** that misled you.
Eze 12:27 What he **p** will happen in the
13:2 Tell those who make up their **p**,
13:17 your people who make up **p**,
Jon 12:16 know what these **p** meant.
12:16 that these **p** had been written
12:16 had taken part in fulfilling the **p**.
1Ti 1:18 order about the **p** that are still
1:18 Use these **p** in faith and with a

prophecy (19)

1Sm 3:1 In those days a **p** from the
1Ki 22:12 prophets made the same **p**.
2Ki 9:25 revealed this **p** about him:
2Ch 9:29 in the **p** of Ahijah from Shiloh,
15:8 the prophet Oded's words of **p**,
18:11 prophets made the same **p**.
Jer 28:6 May the LORD make your **p**
Eze 14:9 is tricked into giving a **p**,
Mat 13:14 they make Isaiah's **p** come true:
1Co 14:6 **p**, or doctrine to you.
1Ti 4:14 you received through **p** when
2Pe 1:20 No **p** in Scripture is a matter of
1:21 No **p** ever originated from
Rev 1:3 who hear the words of this **p**
19:10 of Jesus is the spirit of **p**!"
22:7 the words of the **p** in this book."
22:10 seal up the words of the **p**
Rev 22:18 who hears the words of the **p**
22:19 any words from this book of **p**,

prophesied (33)

Num 11:25 came to rest on them, they **p**,
11:25 but they never **p** again.
11:26 and they **p** in the camp.
1Sm 10:10 over him. He **p** with them.
10:11 him before saw how he **p**
19:20 so that they also **p**.
19:21 messengers, but they also **p**.
19:21 of messengers, but they also **p**.
19:24 took off his clothes as he **p**
2Ch 20:37 **p** against Jehoshaphat.
Ezr 5:1 **p** to the Jews in Judah and
Jer 2:8 The prophets **p** in the name of
20:6 to whom you **p** these lies."
23:13 The prophets of Samaria **p** by
23:21 didn't speak to them, yet they **p**.
25:13 everything that Jeremiah **p**
26:11 because he **p** against this city
26:18 "Micah from Moresheth **p** at
26:20 He **p** against this city and this
28:8 preceded you and me **p** wars,
28:9 But the prophet who **p** peace
29:31 Shemaiah **p** to you,
Eze 13:16 The prophets of Israel who **p** to
37:7 So I **p** as I was commanded.
37:10 So I **p** as he commanded me,
38:17 They **p** in those days that I
Mat 11:13 and Moses' Teachings **p** up
15:7 was right when he **p** about you:
Mar 7:6 "Isaiah was right when he **p**
Luk 1:67 filled with the Holy Spirit and **p**,
Jon 11:51 As chief priest that year, he **p**
11:52 He **p** that Jesus wouldn't die
Jud 1:14 after Adam, **p** about them.

prophesies (4)

2Ch 18:7 Nothing he **p** about me is good;
Zec 13:3 "If a man still **p**, his father and
13:3 will stab him when he **p**.
13:4 of his vision when he **p**.

prophesy (54)

1Sm 10:6 person while you **p** with them.
18:10 He began to **p** in his house
1Ki 22:8 He doesn't **p** anything good
22:18 "Didn't I tell you he wouldn't **p**
2Ch 18:17 "Didn't I tell you he wouldn't **p**
Neh 6:12 had hired him to **p** against me.
Jer 5:31 Prophets **p** lies. Priests rule
11:21 They say, "Don't **p** in the name
14:15 Yet, they **p** in my name that
14:16 The people they **p** to will be
19:14 the LORD had sent him to **p**.
23:32 I'm against those who **p**
25:30 "That is why you will **p** all
26:9 Why do you **p** in the LORD's
26:12 "The LORD sent me to **p**
27:15 They **p** lies in my name.
29:21 who **p** lies to you in my name:
Eze 4:7 Shake your fist and **p** against it.
6:2 and **p** against them.
11:4 So **p** against them.
11:4 against them. **P**, son of man."
13:2 **p** against the prophets of Israel.
13:17 and **p** against them.
20:46 and **p** against the forest in the
21:2 **P** against the land of Israel.
21:9 "Son of man, **p**. Tell them, 'This
21:14 So **p**, son of man. Clap your
21:28 "Son of man, **p**. Tell them, 'This
21:29 about you and **p** lies about you.
25:2 Ammonites and **p** against them.
28:21 turn to Sidon and **p** against it.
29:2 and **p** against him and against
30:2 "Son of man, **p**. Say, 'This is
34:2 "Son of man, **p** against the
34:2 **P** to these shepherds.
35:2 to Mount Seir, and **p** against it.
36:1 **p** to the mountains of Israel.
36:3 "So **p**. Say, 'This is what the
36:6 "So **p** about Israel.
37:4 "**P** to these bones.
37:9 said to me, "**P** to the breath!
Eze 37:9 **P**, son of man. Tell the breath,
37:12 So **p**. Tell them, 'This is what
38:2 and Tubal. **P** against him.
38:14 "So **p**, son of man. Tell Gog,
39:1 "Son of man, **p** against Gog.
Joe 2:28 Your sons and daughters will **p**.
Amo 7:12 Eat there, and **p** there!
7:13 But don't ⌊ever⌋ **p** again in
7:15 '**P** to my people Israel.'
Mic 2:6 Your prophets say, "Don't **p**!
2:6 Don't **p** such things!
Mat 7:22 didn't we **p** in your name?
Mar 14:65 They said to him, "**P**!"

prophesying (20)

Num 11:27 and Medad are **p** in the camp."
1Sm 10:5 of prophets **p** as they come
10:13 And when he had finished **p**,
19:20 they saw a group of prophets **p**
19:23 He continued his journey, **p**
1Ki 22:10 All the prophets were **p** in front
2Ch 18:9 All the prophets were **p** in front
Jer 20:1 heard Jeremiah **p** these things.
26:20 There was another man **p** in
27:10 They are **p** lies to you.
27:14 They are **p** lies to you.
27:16 They are **p** lies to you.
29:9 These people are **p** lies to you
32:3 asked him, "Why are you **p**?
Eze 11:13 While I was **p**, Benaiah's son
22:28 false visions and by **p** lies.
37:7 While I was **p**, suddenly there
Amo 2:12 the prophets to stop **p**.
3:8 Who can keep from **p**?
7:16 'Stop **p** against Israel,

prophet (243)

Gen 20:7 to him now, because he's a **p**.
Exo 7:1 your brother Aaron is your **p**.
15:20 Then the **p** Miriam,
Dtr 13:1 claiming to be a **p** or to have
13:2 But don't listen to that **p** or
13:5 That **p** or dreamer must be put
18:15 your God will send you a **p**,
18:18 So I will send them a **p**,
18:19 to the words that **p** speaks
18:20 But any **p** who dares to say
18:22 If a **p** speaks in the LORD's
18:22 That **p** has spoken on his own
34:10 There has never been another **p**
Jdg 4:4 wife of Lappidoth, was a **p**.
6:8 the LORD sent a **p** to them.
1Sm 3:20 was the LORD's appointed **p**.
9:9 a person we now call a **p** used
10:12 "But who's the chief **p**?"
22:5 the **p** Gad told David.
2Sm 7:2 the king said to the **p** Nathan,
12:25 message through the **p** Nathan
24:11 spoke his word to the **p** Gad,
1Ki 1:8 the **p** Nathan, Shimei, Rei,
1:10 he didn't invite the **p** Nathan,
1:22 the **p** Nathan arrived.
1:23 "The **p** Nathan is here."
1:32 the **p** Nathan, and Benaiah,
1:34 and the **p** Nathan anoint him
1:38 the priest Zadok, the **p** Nathan,
1:44 the priest Zadok, the **p** Nathan,
1:45 The priest Zadok and the **p**
11:29 The **p** Ahijah from Shiloh met
13:11 An old **p** was living in Bethel.
13:13 The old **p** told his sons,
13:14 The old **p** asked him,
13:15 eat a meal," the old **p** replied.
13:18 The old **p** said, "I'm also a
13:18 said, "I'm also a **p**, like you.
13:18 (But the old **p** was lying.)
13:20 to the old **p** who had brought
13:23 After the old **p** had something
13:23 he saddled the donkey for the **p**
13:25 city where the old **p** was living.
13:26 When the old **p** who had
13:27 Then the old **p** told his sons to
13:29 The old **p** picked up the body
14:2 The **p** Ahijah, who told me I
14:18 his servant, the **p** Ahijah.
16:7 spoke his word to the **p** Jehu,

1Ki 16:12 had spoken through the **p** Jehu.
18:22 "I'm the only surviving **p** of the
18:36 the **p** Elijah stepped forward.
19:16 from Abel Meholah as **p** to take
20:13 Then a **p** came to King Ahab of
20:14 The **p** answered, "This is what
20:14 "You will," the **p** answered.
20:22 Then the **p** came to the king of
20:38 Then the **p**, disguised with a
20:42 The **p** told him, "This is what
22:7 "Isn't there a **p** of the LORD
2Ki 3:11 "Isn't there a **p** of the LORD
5:3 were with the **p** in Samaria.
5:3 Then the **p** could cure him of
5:8 out that there is a **p** in Israel."
5:13 if the **p** had asked you to do
6:12 Elisha, the **p** in Israel,
9:1 The **p** Elisha called one of the
9:4 the servant of the **p**,
9:6 The **p** poured olive oil on his
14:25 the **p** from Gath Hepher and the
17:13 every kind of **p** and seer,
19:2 to the **p** Isaiah, son of Amoz.
20:1 The **p** Isaiah, son of Amoz,
20:11 Then the **p** Isaiah called on the
20:14 Then the **p** Isaiah came to King
22:14 and Asaiah went to talk to the **p**
23:18 bones of the **p** who had come
1Ch 17:1 he said to the **p** Nathan,
25:2 who served as a **p** under the
25:3 by their father, the **p** Jeduthun.
29:29 the seer Samuel, the **p** Nathan,
2Ch 9:29 in the records of Nathan the **p**,
12:5 The **p** Shemaiah came to
12:15 the records of the **p** Shemaiah
13:22 in the history by the **p** Iddo.
15:8 When Asa heard the **p** Oded's
18:6 "Isn't there a **p** of the LORD
21:12 came to him from the **p** Elijah.
25:15 He sent him a **p** who asked
25:16 The **p** stopped. He said, "I know
26:22 is recorded by the **p** Isaiah,
28:9 A **p** of the LORD named Oded
29:25 and the **p** Nathan had ordered.
32:20 Hezekiah and the **p** Isaiah,
32:32 in the vision of the **p** Isaiah,
34:22 talk to the **p** Huldah about this
35:18 during the time of the **p** Samuel
36:12 in front of the **p** Jeremiah,
Ezr 5:1 The **p** Haggai and Zechariah,
6:14 the message from the **p** Haggai
Neh 6:14 Also, remember the female **p**
Isa 8:3 I slept with the **p**. She became
37:2 to the **p** Isaiah, son of Amoz.
38:1 The **p** Isaiah, son of Amoz,
39:3 Then the **p** Isaiah came to King
Jer 1:5 you to be a **p** to the nations."
20:2 Pashhur struck the **p** Jeremiah
23:28 The **p** who has a dream should
25:2 The **p** Jeremiah spoke to all
28:1 the **p** Hananiah, son of Azzur,
28:5 The **p** Jeremiah replied to the
28:5 replied to the **p** Hananiah
28:9 But the **p** who prophesied
28:9 was recognized as a **p** that
28:9 message of the **p** came true."
28:10 Then the **p** Hananiah took the
28:10 off the neck of the **p** Jeremiah
28:11 Then the **p** Jeremiah went on
28:12 After the **p** Hananiah broke the
28:12 off the neck of the **p** Jeremiah,
28:15 Jeremiah told the **p** Hananiah,
28:17 So the **p** Hananiah died in the
29:1 The **p** Jeremiah sent a letter
29:26 any lunatic who acts like a **p**
29:27 he acts like a **p** among you.
29:29 this letter to the **p** Jeremiah.
32:2 The **p** Jeremiah was locked up
34:6 The **p** Jeremiah told all these
36:8 did as the **p** Jeremiah
36:26 Baruch and the **p** Jeremiah.
37:2 spoken through the **p** Jeremiah.
37:3 of Maaseiah) to the **p** Jeremiah.
37:6 his word to the **p** Jeremiah.
37:13 arrested the **p** Jeremiah.
38:9 to the **p** Jeremiah is wrong.
Jer 38:10 and lift the **p** Jeremiah out of
38:14 King Zedekiah sent for the **p**
42:1 came to the **p** Jeremiah.
42:4 The **p** Jeremiah answered
43:6 including the **p** Jeremiah and
45:1 This is the message that the **p**
46:1 to the **p** Jeremiah about
46:13 to the **p** Jeremiah about
47:1 to the **p** Jeremiah about
49:34 to the **p** Jeremiah about Elam.
50:1 through the **p** Jeremiah.
51:59 This is the message that the **p**
Eze 2:5 they will realize that a **p** has
7:26 will ask for a vision from a **p**.
14:4 Suppose he goes to a **p** ⌞to
14:7 If he goes to a **p** to ask for my
14:9 "'If a **p** is tricked into giving a
14:9 I, the LORD, who tricked the **p**.
14:10 The **p** will be as guilty as you
33:33 know that a **p** has been among
Dan 9:2 The LORD had told the **p**
Hos 12:13 The LORD used a **p** to bring
12:13 He used a **p** to take care of
Amo 7:14 Amos responded, "I'm not a **p**,
Hab 1:1 that the **p** Habakkuk saw.
3:1 A prayer of the **p** Habakkuk;
Hag 1:1 his word through the **p** Haggai
1:3 his word through the **p** Haggai.
1:12 the words of the **p** Haggai
2:1 his word through the **p** Haggai.
2:10 spoke his word to the **p** Haggai.
Zec 1:1 his word to the **p** Zechariah,
1:7 his word to the **p** Zechariah,
13:4 "On that day every **p** will be
13:4 people by dressing ⌞like a **p**⌟
13:5 He will say, 'I am not a **p**.
Mal 4:5 "I'm going to send you the **p**
Mat 1:22 through the **p** came true:
2:5 The **p** wrote about this:
2:15 through the **p** came true:
2:17 the **p** Jeremiah came true:
3:3 Isaiah the **p** spoke about this
4:14 So what the **p** Isaiah had said
8:17 So what the **p** Isaiah had said
10:41 The person who welcomes a **p**
10:41 a prophet as a **p** will receive
11:9 A **p**? Let me tell you that he is
11:9 you that he is far more than a **p**.
12:17 So what the **p** Isaiah had said
12:39 get is the sign of the **p** Jonah.
13:35 So what the **p** had said came
13:57 "The only place a **p** isn't
14:5 they thought John was a **p**.
21:4 that what the **p** had said came
21:11 "This is the **p** Jesus from
21:26 people think of John as a **p**."
21:46 who thought he was a **p**.
24:15 "The **p** Daniel said that the
26:68 said, "You Christ, if you're a **p**,
27:9 Then what the **p** Jeremiah had
Mar 1:2 The **p** Isaiah wrote,
6:4 "The only place a **p** isn't
6:15 Still others said, "He is a **p** like
11:32 thought of John as a true **p**.
Luk 1:76 "You, child, will be called a **p**
2:36 Anna, a **p**, was also there.
3:4 As the **p** Isaiah wrote in his
4:17 him the book of the **p** Isaiah.
4:24 A **p** isn't accepted in his
4:27 in Israel in the **p** Elisha's time.
7:16 They said, "A great **p** has
7:26 A **p**? Let me tell you that he is
7:26 you that he is far more than a **p**.
7:39 "If this man really were a **p**,
11:50 the murder of every **p** since
13:33 It's not possible for a **p** to die
20:6 convinced that John was a **p**."
24:19 He was a powerful **p** in what
Jon 1:21 they asked, "Are you the **p**?"
1:23 as the **p** Isaiah said."
1:25 the Messiah or Elijah or the **p**?"
4:19 "I see that you're a **p**!
4:44 Jesus had said that a **p** is not
6:14 "This man is certainly the **p**
7:40 "This man is certainly the **p**."
7:52 that no **p** comes from Galilee."
Jon 9:17 The man answered, "He's a **p**."
12:38 In this way the words of the **p**
Act 2:16 is what the **p** Joel spoke about:
2:30 David was a **p** and knew that
3:22 your God will send you a **p**,
3:23 who won't listen to that **p** will
7:37 'God will send you a **p**,
7:48 built by humans, as the **p** says:
7:52 Was there ever a **p** your
8:28 reading the **p** Isaiah out loud.
8:30 reading the **p** Isaiah out loud.
8:34 "I would like to know who the **p**
13:6 who claimed to be a **p**.
13:20 until the time of the **p** Samuel.
21:10 a **p** named Agabus arrived from
28:25 ancestors through the **p** Isaiah!
2Pe 2:16 voice and wouldn't allow the **p**
Rev 2:20 who calls herself a **p**.
16:13 the beast, and the false **p**.
19:20 The beast and the false **p** who
19:20 By these miracles the false **p**
20:10 where the beast and the false **p**

prophetic (8)

Dtr 13:1 a prophet or to have **p** dreams,
1Ch 15:22 instructed others how to sing **p**
15:27 of the musicians' **p** songs.
Job 33:15 In a dream, a **p** vision at night,
Pro 29:18 Without **p** vision people run
30:1 Agur's **p** revelation.
31:1 of King Lemuel, a **p** revelation,
Zec 12:1 This is the **p** revelation,

prophet's (3)

Dan 9:24 to put a seal on a **p** vision, and
Hos 9:8 traps are set on every **p** path,
Mat 10:41 prophet will receive a **p** reward.

prophets (267)

Num 11:29 all the LORD's people were **p**
12:6 When there are **p** of the LORD
1Sm 10:5 you will meet a group of **p**
10:10 a group of **p** came to meet him,
10:11 how he prophesied with the **p**,
10:11 Is Saul one of the **p**?"
10:12 "Is Saul one of the **p**?"
19:20 But when they saw a group of **p**
19:24 "Is Saul one of the **p**?"
28:6 through dreams, the Urim, or **p**.
28:15 me anymore — either by the **p**
1Ki 18:4 was killing the LORD's **p**,
18:4 had hidden 100 **p** in caves.
18:4 He put 50 **p** in each cave and
18:13 Jezebel killed the LORD's **p**?
18:13 100 of the LORD's **p** in caves?
18:13 I hid 50 **p** in each cave and
18:19 And bring the 450 **p** of Baal and
18:19 450 prophets of Baal and 400 **p**
18:20 and brought the **p** together
18:22 but there are 450 **p** of Baal.
18:23 Let the **p** of Baal choose one
18:25 Elijah told the **p** of Baal,
18:40 "Seize the **p** of Baal.
19:1 how he had executed all the **p**.
19:2 you took the lives of Baal's **p**."
19:10 and executed your **p**.
19:14 and executed your **p**.
20:35 A disciple of the **p** spoke to a
20:41 recognized him as one of the **p**.
22:6 of Israel called 400 **p** together.
22:10 All the **p** were prophesying in
22:12 All the other **p** made the same
22:13 "The **p** have all told the king
22:22 mouths of all of Ahab's **p**.' "The
22:23 into the mouths of all these **p**
2Ki 2:3 Some of the disciples of the **p**
2:5 the disciples of the **p** who were
2:7 Fifty disciples of the **p** stood at
2:15 The disciples of the **p** who
3:13 Go to your father's **p** or your
3:13 prophets or your mother's **p**."
4:1 of a disciple of the **p** called
4:38 while the disciples of the **p**
4:38 stew for the disciples of the **p**."
5:22 men from the disciples of the **p**
6:1 The disciples of the **p** said to

2Ki 9:1 one of the disciples of the **p**.
9:7 the blood of my servants the **p**
10:19 Summon all the **p**,
17:13 you through my servants the **p**.
17:23 through all his servants, the **p**.
21:10 through his servants the **p**:
23:2 in Jerusalem, the priests, the **p**,
24:2 through his servants the **p**.
1Ch 16:22 anointed ones or harm my **p**.'
25:1 to serve as **p** with lyres,
2Ch 18:5 of Israel called 400 **p** together.
18:9 All the **p** were prophesying in
18:11 All the other **p** made the same
18:12 "The **p** have all told the king
18:21 mouths of all of Ahab's **p**.' "The
18:22 put into the mouths of these **p**
20:20 Believe his **p**, and you will
24:19 The LORD sent them **p** to bring
24:19 The **p** warned them,
29:25 from the LORD through his **p**.
36:16 and made fun of his **p** until the
Ezr 5:2 God's **p** were with them and
9:11 us through your servants the **p**,
Neh 6:7 You've appointed **p** to
6:14 the rest of the **p** who have been
9:26 killed your **p** who warned them
9:30 by your Spirit through your **p**.
9:32 leaders, priests, **p**, ancestors,
Psa 74:9 There are no **p** anymore.
105:15 anointed ones or harm my **p**."
Isa 3:2 and soldiers, judges and **p**,
9:15 **P** who teach lies are the tail.
28:7 Priests and **p** stagger from
29:10 (Your eyes are the **p**.)
44:25 I cause the signs of false **p** to
Jer 2:8 The **p** prophesied in the name
2:26 and **p** will also feel ashamed.
2:30 You killed my **p** like a raging
4:9 The **p** will be amazed and
5:13 The **p** are nothing but
5:31 **P** prophesy lies. Priests rule
6:13 All of them, from **p** to priests,
7:25 have sent all my servants the **p**
8:1 bones of the priests and the **p**,
8:10 All of them, from **p** to priests,
13:13 throne, the priests, the **p**,
14:13 **p** are saying to them,
14:14 "These are the lies that the **p**
14:15 "I didn't send these **p**.
14:15 will bring an end to these **p**.
14:18 **P** and priests wander through a
18:18 word of the **p** won't disappear.
23:9 "⌊Say this⌋ about the **p**:
23:11 The **p** and priests are godless.
23:13 this⌋ about the **p** of Samaria:
23:13 The **p** of Samaria prophesied
23:14 this⌋ about the **p** of Jerusalem:
23:14 The **p** of Jerusalem commit
23:15 of Armies says about the **p**:
23:15 The **p** of Jerusalem have
23:16 Don't listen to what the **p** are
23:21 I didn't send these **p**,
23:25 "I've heard the **p** who speak
23:26 How long will these **p** continue
23:30 "I'm against the **p** who steal my
23:31 "I'm against the **p** who speak
23:33 "When these people, the **p**,
23:34 Suppose the **p**, the priests,
23:37 "Jeremiah, say this to the **p**,
25:4 all his servants the **p** to you,
25:5 The **p** said, 'Turn from your evil
26:5 the words of my servants the **p**,
26:7 The priests, the **p**,
26:8 him to say, the priests, the **p**,
26:11 Then the priests and the **p** said
26:16 said to the priests and **p**,
27:9 Don't listen to **p**, mediums,
27:14 Don't listen to the **p** who tell
27:15 and you and the **p** will die."
27:16 Don't listen to the **p** who tell
27:18 If they are **p** and the LORD is
28:8 Long ago, the **p** who preceded
29:1 also sent it to the priests, the **p**,
29:8 Don't let the **p** or the mediums
29:15 has given you **p** in Babylon.
29:19 I sent them my servants the **p**
Jer 32:32 their priests and **p**,
35:15 have sent all my servants the **p**
37:19 Where are the **p** who told you
44:4 I have sent my servants the **p**
50:36 A sword will kill the false **p**.
Lam 2:9 Its **p** can find no visions from
2:14 Your **p** saw misleading visions
2:20 Should priests and **p** be killed
4:13 of the sins of Jerusalem's **p**
Eze 13:2 against the **p** of Israel.
13:3 it will be for the foolish **p**.
13:4 Israel, your **p** are like foxes
13:6 These foolish **p** see false
13:7 **P** of Israel, haven't you seen
13:9 against the **p** who see false
13:10 the **p** cover it up with paint.
13:14 the wall that the **p** covered up
13:16 The **p** of Israel who prophesied
22:28 Your **p** cover up these things
38:17 my servants the **p** of Israel.
Dan 9:6 listened to your servants the **p**,
9:10 us through your servants the **p**.
Hos 4:5 and during the night the **p**
6:5 ⌊you⌋ down by sending the **p**.
9:7 ⌊They think that⌋ **p** are fools
9:8 **P** are God's watchmen over
12:10 I spoke to the **p** and gave them
12:10 I taught lessons through the **p**."
Amo 2:11 I also sent you **p** from among
2:12 the **p** to stop prophesying.
3:7 his secret to his servants the **p**.
7:14 and I'm not a disciple of the **p**.
Mic 2:6 Your **p** say, "Don't prophesy!
3:5 about the **p** who mislead my
3:6 The sun will set on the **p**,
3:11 Your **p** tell the future for money.
Zep 3:4 Its **p** are reckless and
Zec 1:4 who heard the earlier **p** preach
1:5 And the **p** — are they still alive?
1:6 my servants the **p** ⌊to preach⌋,
7:3 of Armies as well as the **p**,
7:7 through the earlier **p**,
7:12 his Spirit through the earlier **p**.
8:9 of the **p** who spoke when
13:2 I will also remove the ⌊false⌋ **p**
Mat 2:23 So what the **p** had said came
5:12 The **p** who lived before you
5:17 Moses' Teachings or the **P**.
7:12 Moses' Teachings and the **P**.
7:15 "Beware of false **p**.
11:13 All the **P** and Moses'
13:17 Many **p** and many of God's
16:14 Jeremiah or one of the **p**."
22:40 Teachings and the **P** depend
23:29 You build tombs for the **p** and
23:30 have helped to murder the **p**.'
23:31 of those who murdered the **p**.
23:34 I'm sending you **p**,
23:37 you kill the **p** and stone to
24:11 Many false **p** will appear and
24:24 christs and false **p** will appear.
26:56 what the **p** have written would
Mar 6:15 prophet like one of the other **p**."
8:28 still others one of the **p**."
13:22 christs and false **p** will appear.
Luk 1:70 through his holy **p** long ago.
6:23 their ancestors treated the **p**.
6:26 ancestors treated the false **p**.
9:8 that one of the **p** from long ago
9:19 that one of the **p** from long ago
10:24 I can guarantee that many **p**
11:47 build the monuments for the **p**.
11:48 They murdered the **p** for whom
11:49 will send them **p** and apostles.
11:49 will murder some of those **p**
13:28 Isaac, Jacob, and all the **p**.
13:34 you kill the **p** and stone to
16:16 "Moses' Teachings and the **P**
16:29 Moses' ⌊Teachings⌋ and the **P**.
16:31 Moses' ⌊Teachings⌋ and the **P**,
18:31 Everything that the **p** wrote
24:25 believe everything the **p** said!
24:27 Moses' Teachings and the **P**
24:44 in Moses' Teachings, the **P**,
Jon 1:45 and whom the **p** wrote about.
6:45 The **p** wrote, 'God will teach
Jon 8:52 Abraham died, and so did the **p**,
8:53 The **p** have also died.
Act 3:18 sufferings through all the **p**.
3:21 through his holy **p** long ago.
3:24 Samuel and all the **p** who
3:25 are the descendants of the **p**
7:42 is written in the book of the **p**:
10:43 In addition, all the **p** testify that
11:27 At that time some **p** came from
13:1 and Saul were **p** and teachers
13:15 Moses' Teachings and the **P**,
13:27 fulfilled what the **p** had said.
13:40 "Be careful, or what the **p** said
15:15 agrees with what the **p** said.
15:32 and Silas, who were also **p**,
24:14 in Moses' Teachings and the **P**.
26:22 I tell them only what the **p** and
26:27 do you believe the **p**?
28:23 Moses' Teachings and the **P**.
Rom 1:2 this Good News through his **p**
3:21 and the **P** tell us this.
11:3 "Lord, they've killed your **p** and
16:26 that what the **p** wrote must
1Co 12:28 apostles, next **p**, third teachers,
12:29 Are all of them **p**? Do all of them
Eph 2:20 of the apostles and **p**.
3:5 it to his holy apostles and **p**.
4:11 He also gave apostles, **p**,
1Th 2:15 killed the Lord Jesus and the **p**
Tit 1:12 Even one of their own **p** said,
Heb 1:1 different ways through the **p**.
11:32 David, Samuel, and the **p**.
Jas 5:10 follow the example of the **p**
1Pe 1:10 The **p** carefully researched and
1:12 God revealed to the **p** that the
1:12 What the **p** had spoken,
2Pe 1:19 So we regard the words of the **p**
2:1 False **p** were among God's
3:2 in the past by the holy **p**
1Jn 4:1 are many false **p** in the world.
Rev 10:7 known to his servants, the **p**."
11:10 two **p** had tormented those
11:18 the **p**, your holy people,
16:6 blood of God's people and **p**.
18:20 God's people, apostles, and **p**.
18:24 "The blood of **p**, God's people,
22:6 the spirits of the **p** has sent his
22:9 with other Christians, the **p**,

prophets' (2)

Jer 5:31 rule under the **p** directions,
Act 13:27 **p** messages, which are read

proportion (2)

Dtr 16:10 Bring a freewill offering in **p** to
16:17 Each man must bring a gift in **p**

proposal (1)

Gen 34:18 Their **p** seemed good to Hamor

propose (1)

1Sm 25:39 behalf⌋ to **p** marriage to Abigail.

propped (2)

1Ki 22:35 and the king was kept **p** up in
2Ch 18:34 and the king **p** himself up in his

prosecutor (1)

Job 31:35 Let the **p** write ⌊his complaint⌋

prosper (18)

Gen 26:22 and we will **p** in this land."
Jos 1:8 then will you **p** and succeed.
1Sm 24:20 the kingdom of Israel will **p**.
25:6 and all you have **p**!
2Ki 25:24 of Babylon, and you will **p**."
2Ch 24:20 You won't **p** that way!
Job 22:23 to the Almighty, you will **p**.
24:22 These people may **p**,
Psa 122:6 "May those who love you **p**.
140:11 Do not let slanderers **p** on earth
Pro 11:10 When righteous people **p**,
28:13 over his sins does not **p**.
Jer 5:28 But they still **p**. They don't
22:30 He won't **p** in his lifetime.
29:7 it prospers, you will also **p**.

Jer 40:9 of Babylon, and you will **p**.
Zec 9:17 Young men will **p** on grain,
9:17 women will **p** on new wine.

prospered (1)

Dan 6:28 This man, Daniel, **p** during the

prospering (1)

Psa 128:5 you may see Jerusalem **p** all

prosperity (21)

Dtr 30:15 Today I offer you life and **p** or
Ezr 4:17 I wish you peace and **p**!
5:7 We wish you peace and **p** in
7:12 I wish you peace and **p**!
Job 8:7 with the great **p** you'll have
20:21 for him to eat. His **p** won't last.
22:21 In this way you will have **p**.
30:15 My **p** vanishes like a cloud.
36:11 they will live out their days in **p**
42:10 the LORD restored Job's **p** and
Psa 73:3 I saw the **p** that wicked people
106:5 so that I may see the **p** of your
122:7 walls and **p** in your palaces."
Pro 21:5 hard-working person lead to **p**,
Jer 33:9 because of all the **p** that
39:16 disaster on it instead of **p**.
Dan 4:1 I wish you peace and **p**.
4:27 Maybe you can prolong your **p**."
6:25 I wish you peace and **p**.
Zec 1:17 will overflow with **p** once more.
Php 4:12 how to live in poverty or **p**.

prosperous (11)

Gen 32:9 and I will make you **p**.'
32:12 'I will make sure that you are **p**
Dtr 6:10 **p** cities that you didn't build.
28:63 to make you **p** and numerous.
30:5 LORD will make you more **p**
30:9 delight in making you as **p** as
Job 12:6 ⌊But⌋ robbers' tents are **p**,
24:24 ⌊Such people⌋ may be **p** for a
Psa 22:29 All **p** people on earth will eat
Jer 22:21 spoke to you when you were **p**,
Dan 4:4 I was **p** while living in my

prospers (5)

Lev 25:26 but if he **p** and earns enough to
Pro 16:20 attention to the LORD's word **p**,
17:8 Wherever he turns, he **p**.
28:25 but whoever trusts the LORD **p**.
Jer 29:7 When it **p**, you will also

prostitute (63)

Gen 34:31 to treat our sister like a **p**?"
38:15 he thought she was a **p**
38:21 "Where's that **p** who was
38:21 'There's no **p** here,"
38:22 'There's no **p** here.'"
38:24 Tamar has been acting like a **p**.
Lev 19:29 daughter by making her a **p**,
20:5 after Molech as if he were a **p**.
21:9 herself by becoming a **p**,
21:14 has lost her virginity, or a **p**.
Dtr 23:17 ever become a temple **p**.
Jos 2:1 the house of a **p** named Rahab
6:17 Only the **p** Rahab and all who
6:25 Joshua spared the **p** Rahab,
Jdg 8:27 it there as though it were a **p**.
11:1 His mother was a **p**.
16:1 There he saw a **p** and slept
16:3 the **p**⌋ only until midnight.
Pro 7:10 She is dressed as a **p**.
23:27 A **p** is a deep pit. A loose
Sos 1:7 or I will be considered a **p**
Isa 1:21 faithful town has become a **p**!
23:15 will be like the **p** in this song:
23:16 in the city, you forgotten **p**.
23:17 back to earning money as a **p**.
23:17 She will become a **p** for all the
Jer 2:20 lay down and acted like a **p**
3:1 "You have acted like a **p** who
3:3 the shameless look of a **p**,
3:6 and she acted like a **p** there.
3:8 She also acted like a **p**.
3:9 about acting like a **p**,
Jer 13:27 you act like a shameless **p**
Eze 16:15 used your fame to become a **p**.
16:16 is where you acted like a **p**.
16:30 a shameless **p** does.
16:34 You are a different kind of **p**.
16:35 to the word of the LORD, you **p**.
20:30 their detestable idols like a **p**?
23:5 Oholah acted like a **p**,
23:7 She became a **p** for all the
23:8 and treated her like a **p**.
23:19 how she had been a **p**
23:44 just as they slept with a **p**.
Hos 1:2 the LORD told him, "Marry a **p**,
1:2 and have children with that **p**.
2:2 Tell her to stop acting like a **p**.
2:4 they are children of a **p**.
2:5 Their mother acted like a **p**.
3:3 Don't be a **p** or offer yourself to
4:15 "Israel, you act like a **p**.
5:3 you are acting like a **p**,
6:10 Ephraim is acting like a **p**,
Amo 7:17 Your wife will become a **p** in
Mic 1:7 All its wages for being a **p** will
1:7 its wages for being a **p**.
1Co 6:16 with a **p** becomes one body
Heb 11:31 Faith led the **p** Rahab to
Jas 2:25 The same is true of the **p**
Rev 17:1 of that notorious **p** who sits
17:15 on which the **p** is sitting,
17:16 beast you saw will hate the **p**.
19:2 the notorious **p** who corrupted

prostitute's (3)

Jos 6:22 "Go to the **p** house.
Pro 6:26 A **p** price is ⌊only⌋ a loaf of
1Co 6:15 make them parts of a **p** body?

prostitutes (42)

Exo 34:15 gods as though they were **p**
34:16 gods as though they were **p**,
Lev 17:7 them as though they were **p**.
20:6 them as though they were **p**.
21:7 You should never marry **p**,
Num 15:39 as if you were chasing after **p**.
Dtr 31:16 gods as though they were **p**.
Jdg 2:17 gods as though they were **p**
8:33 Baals — as though they were **p**.
1Ki 3:16 A short time later two **p** came
14:24 There were even male **p** in the
15:12 He forced the male temple **p**
22:38 where the **p** bathed.
22:46 male temple **p** who were left
2Ki 23:7 of the male temple **p** who were
1Ch 5:25 of the land as if they were **p**.
2Ch 21:11 foreign gods as if they were **p**.
21:13 foreign gods as if they were **p**.
Job 36:14 or they live on as male **p** in the
Psa 106:39 They behaved like **p**.
Pro 29:3 who pays **p** wastes his wealth.
Isa 57:3 of adulterers and **p**!
Jer 5:7 in crowds to the houses of **p**.
Eze 16:31 Yet, you aren't like other **p**,
16:33 All **p** get paid. But you give gifts
23:3 They became **p** in Egypt when
43:7 my holy name by acting like **p**,
43:9 they must stop acting like **p**
Hos 1:2 in this land have acted like **p**
4:10 They will have sex with **p**,
4:11 **P**, old wine, and new wine
4:13 why your daughters become **p**,
4:14 daughters when they become **p**
4:14 The men go to **p** and offer
4:14 offer sacrifices with temple **p**.
4:18 to have sex with the **p**.
Joe 3:3 They traded boys for **p**.
Mic 1:7 money will again pay for **p**.
Mat 21:31 Tax collectors and **p** are going
21:32 collectors and **p** believed him.
Luk 15:30 yours spent your money on **p**,
Rev 17:5 the Mother of **P** and Detestable

prostitution (24)

Lev 19:29 or the country will turn to **p** and
Dtr 23:18 gifts or money earned by **p** into
Jer 3:2 with your **p** and wickedness.
Eze 16:20 Wasn't your **p** enough?
Eze 16:22 you did and all your acts of **p**,
16:25 You increased your acts of **p**.
16:26 You used your **p** to make me
16:29 So you increased your acts of **p**
16:38 that those who are guilty of **p**
16:41 I will put an end to your **p**,
23:8 She continued the **p** that she
23:11 Oholibah's **p** became worse
23:11 worse than her sister's **p**.
23:14 she carried her **p** even further.
23:18 "She carried out her **p** openly,
23:19 she took part in even more **p**.
23:27 to your sinning and to your **p**,
23:29 of your **p** will be revealed.
23:30 Your sinning and your **p** have
23:35 for your sinning and **p**."
Hos 4:12 A spirit of **p** leads them astray.
5:4 They have a spirit of **p**,
Nah 3:4 of Nineveh's constant **p**,
3:4 She used to sell nations her **p**

protect (43)

Exo 23:20 in front of you to **p** you
Num 35:25 the community must **p** you from
Dtr 13:8 Don't feel sorry for them or **p**
23:14 around in your camp to **p** you
Jos 2:13 that you'll **p** my father,
Jdg 6:2 ⌊to **p** themselves⌋ from Midian.
2Sm 18:12 '**P** the young man Absalom for
Neh 4:9 to our God and set guards to **p**
Psa 5:11 **P** them, and let those who love
12:7 O LORD, you will **p** them.
16:1 **P** me, O God, because I take
20:1 of the God of Jacob will **p** you.
25:20 **P** my life, and rescue me!
25:21 Integrity and honesty will **p** me
32:7 You **p** me from trouble.
40:11 and your truth always **p** me.
41:2 The LORD will **p** him and keep
59:1 **P** me from those who attack
61:7 May mercy and truth **p** him.
64:1 **P** my life from a terrifying
69:29 Let your saving power **p** me,
82:3 **P** the rights of the oppressed
86:2 **P** me, because I am faithful ⌊to
91:11 in charge of you to **p** you
91:14 I will **p** you because you know
127:1 If the LORD does not **p** a city,
140:4 **P** me from the hands of wicked
Pro 2:11 Foresight will **p** you.
4:6 Love wisdom, and it will **p** you.
7:2 my teachings just as you **p**
20:28 Mercy and truth **p** a king,
29:10 people seek ⌊to **p**⌋ his life.
Isa 26:3 With perfect peace you will **p**
31:5 He will pass over it and **p** it.
42:6 I will **p** you. I will appoint you
49:8 I will **p** you. I will appoint you
Jer 31:22 A woman will **p** a man.
38:12 under your arms to **p** you from
Eze 25:9 the cities that **p** Moab's borders
Jon 17:15 of the world but to **p** them from
2Th 3:3 you and **p** you against
2Ti 1:12 that he is able to **p** what
1:14 **p** the Good News that has

protected (8)

Dtr 32:10 and **p** them because they were
1Sm 30:23 He has **p** us and handed the
1Ki 15:4 rule after him and **p** Jerusalem.
Pro 14:3 people are **p** by their speech.
Eze 13:5 So Israel will not be **p** in battle
Dan 11:6 and the one who fathered and **p**
Mar 6:20 fair and holy man, so he **p** him.
2Pe 2:5 but he **p** Noah and seven other

protecting (1)

1Sm 25:16 They were a wall **p** us day and

protection (11)

Gen 39:21 love and gave him **p**.
Exo 12:13 will be a sign for your **p**.
Num 14:9 They have no **p**, and the LORD
Rut 2:12 under whose **p** you have come
1Sm 22:23 you will be under my **p**."
Psa 61:4 and to take refuge under the **p**

Psa 143:9 I come to you for **p**.
Pro 30:5 to those who come to him for **p**.
Isa 27:5 else let them come to me for **p**.
30:2 for shelter under Pharaoh's **p**
30:3 But Pharaoh's **p** will be their

protective (4)
Ezr 9:9 its ruins and to give us a **p** wall
Job 1:10 Haven't you put a **p** fence
Psa 105:39 He spread out a cloud as a **p**
2Co 11:2 I'm as **p** of you as God is.

protects (12)
Psa 31:23 The LORD **p** faithful people,
34:22 The LORD **p** the souls of his
116:6 LORD **p** defenseless people.
145:20 The LORD **p** everyone who
146:9 The LORD **p** foreigners.
Pro 13:3 Whoever controls his mouth **p**
13:6 Righteousness **p** the honest
15:25 but he **p** the property of
27:18 and whoever **p** his master is
Ecc 7:12 Wisdom **p** us just as money
7:12 protects us just as money **p** us,
1Jn 5:18 Rather, the Son of God **p** them,

protest (3)
Mat 20:11 they began to **p** to the owner.
Luk 10:11 from our feet in **p** against you!
Act 13:51 In **p** against these people,

protested (3)
Exo 4:1 Moses **p**. "They will say, 'The
6:12 But Moses **p** to the LORD,
Jdg 8:1 strongly **p** Gideon's actions.

proud (24)
Job 10:16 Like a **p**, ferocious lion you
28:8 No **p** beast has ever walked on
38:11 Here your **p** waves will stop'?
Isa 2:12 conceited and all who are **p**
13:19 the **p** beauty of the Chaldeans,
Eze 7:20 They were **p** of their beautiful
7:24 who are strong from feeling **p**,
16:49 She and her daughters were **p**
24:25 It makes them happy and **p**.
28:17 You became too **p** because of
Hab 2:4 "Look at the **p** person.
Zep 3:11 and never again will you act **p**
2Co 1:12 We are **p** that our conscience
1:12 We are **p** of the way that we
1:14 We are your reason to be **p**,
1:14 you will be our reason to be **p**
5:12 an opportunity to be **p** of us.
5:12 can answer those who are **p**
7:4 a lot of reasons to be **p** of you.
8:24 we were right to be **p** of you.
Gal 6:4 Then you can be **p** of your own
Heb 3:6 to have courage and to be **p**
Jas 1:9 Humble believers should be **p**
1:10 Rich believers should be **p**

proudly (5)
Psa 75:5 Don't raise your weapons so **p**
75:10 people will be raised **p**.
Mic 2:3 no longer be able to walk **p**.
Hab 1:8 Their riders will gallop along **p**.
Mat 24:1 They **p** pointed out to him the

prove (29)
Gen 44:16 How can we **p** we're innocent?
Exo 7:9 'Give me a sign to **p** that God
34:12 This will **p** to be a trap to you.
Dtr 13:14 If it is true, and you can **p** that
1Sm 18:17 as your wife if you **p** yourself
2Sm 10:12 Let's **p** ourselves strong for our
1Ch 19:13 Let's **p** ourselves strong for our
Ezr 2:59 but they couldn't **p** they were
2:61 ⌊couldn't **p** their families were
Neh 7:61 but they couldn't **p** they were
7:63 These priests ⌊couldn't **p** they
Job 5:13 of schemers **p** to be hasty.
8:6 and **p** your righteousness by
24:25 "If it isn't so, who can **p** I'm a
36:3 far away and **p** that my Creator
Isa 43:9 witnesses to **p** that they were
43:26 so that you can **p** you are right.
Mat 3:8 Do those things that **p** you
Luk 3:8 Do those things that **p** that you
21:15 be able to oppose or **p** wrong.
Jon 5:36 They **p** that the Father has sent
Act 22:5 of our leaders can **p** that
24:13 These people cannot even **p**
25:7 that they couldn't **p**.
26:20 I told them to do things that **p**
2Co 12:12 and miracles which **p** that I'm
13:7 It's not that we want to **p** that
Col 1:10 kind of lives that **p** you belong
Heb 6:11 We want each of you to **p** that

proved (11)
Jos 7:1 The people of Israel **p** to be
1Sm 17:50 David **p** to be stronger than the
24:18 Today you have **p** how good
Psa 48:3 He has **p** that he is a
Mat 11:19 "Yet, wisdom is **p** right by its
25:21 You **p** that you could be trusted
25:23 You **p** that you could be trusted
Luk 7:35 "Yet, wisdom is **p** right by all
19:17 You **p** that you could be trusted
2Co 7:14 our bragging to Titus has also **p**
Php 2:22 kind of person Timothy **p** to be.

proven (4)
Dtr 17:4 If it's true and it can be **p** that
2Sm 22:31 The promise of the LORD has **p**
Psa 18:30 The promise of the LORD has **p**
Pro 30:5 "Every word of God has **p** to be

proverb (11)
1Sm 10:12 So it became a **p**: "Is Saul one
Psa 44:14 You made our ⌊defeat⌋ a **p**
49:4 I will turn my attention to a **p**.
Pro 1:6 to understand a **p** and a clever
26:7 so is a **p** in the mouths of fools.
26:9 so is a **p** in the mouths of fools.
Eze 12:22 "Son of man, what is this **p**
12:23 put a stop to the use of this **p**.
18:2 when you use this **p** about
18:3 no longer use this **p** in Israel.
Luk 4:23 probably quote this **p** to me,

proverbs (8)
1Ki 4:32 Solomon spoke 3,000 **p** and
Job 13:12 recollections are worthless **p**.
Pro 1:1 The **p** of Solomon,
10:1 The **p** of Solomon:
25:1 These also are Solomon's **p**
Ecc 12:9 and arranged it in many **p**.
Eze 16:44 "'Everyone who uses **p** will
2Pe 2:22 These **p** have come true for

proves (6)
Luk 7:47 Her great love **p** that.
1Co 9:2 You are the seal which **p** that I
Eph 4:1 of life which **p** that God has
1Th 2:12 you should live in a way that **p**
2Th 1:5 Your suffering **p** that God's
3Jn 1:6 trip in a way that **p** you belong

provide (42)
Gen 22:8 answered, "God will **p**
22:14 that place The LORD Will **P**.
45:11 I will **p** for you in Egypt,
49:20 He will **p** delicacies fit for a
50:21 I will **p** for you and your
Dtr 11:15 I will **p** grass in the fields for
19:3 **P** a route to each of these
Jdg 21:7 What will we do to **p** wives for
21:16 "What should we do to **p** wives
21:22 since we didn't **p** a wife for
2Sm 19:33 I'll **p** for you in Jerusalem."
1Ki 4:7 They were to **p** food for the
5:17 blocks of stone in order to **p**
Ezr 1:4 should **p** the people who are
7:20 anything else that you must **p**
Neh 8:10 who cannot **p** for themselves.
Job 24:5 The plains **p** food for their
36:31 is how he uses the rains to **p**
40:22 Lotus plants **p** it with cover.
Psa 10:18 in order to **p** justice for orphans
12:5 "I will **p** safety for those who
51:12 and **p** me with a spirit of willing
65:9 You **p** grain for them.
78:20 he also give us bread or **p** us,
119:29 Graciously **p** me with your
135:14 The LORD will **p** justice for his
Pro 27:26 Lambs ⌊will **p**⌋ you with
Isa 4:1 "We'll eat our own food and **p**
26:1 Its walls and fortifications **p**
43:20 I will **p** water in the desert.
46:13 I'll **p** salvation for Zion and
61:3 ⌊He has sent me⌋ to **p** for all
Jer 33:9 the prosperity that I will **p** for it.
Eze 45:17 responsible to **p** burnt offerings
48:18 It will be used to **p** food for the
Hos 4:13 that these trees **p** good shade.
Act 7:46 David asked that he might **p** a
23:24 **P** an animal for Paul to ride,
Rom 16:2 **P** her with anything she may
2Co 12:14 Children shouldn't have to **p** for
12:14 should **p** for their children.
Jas 2:16 If you don't **p** for that person's

provided (34)
Gen 22:14 of the LORD it will be **p**."
27:37 I've **p** fresh grain and new wine
47:12 Joseph also **p** his father,
Num 1:18 years old **p** his genealogy by
2Sm 19:32 he had **p** the king with food
20:3 He **p** for them but no longer
1Ki 4:27 Each of the governors **p** food
18:13 in each cave and **p** bread
1Ch 12:39 Judah⌋ had **p** enough for them.
2Ch 2:7 men whom my father David **p**
28:15 They **p** clothes for them,
30:24 King Hezekiah of Judah **p**
30:24 The leaders **p** 1,000 bulls and
35:7 Josiah **p** the people with
35:7 In addition, he **p** 3,000 bulls.
Ezr 1:6 were remaining behind⌋ **p** them
6:9 and olive oil — should be **p** for
Neh 9:21 You **p** for them in the desert for
13:5 had **p** a large room for Tobiah.
Est 1:7 The king also **p** plenty of royal
2:9 So he immediately **p** her with
10:3 since he **p** for the good of his
Psa 68:10 you **p** for oppressed people.
128:2 what your own hands have **p**.
Ecc 2:8 I **p** myself with male and
Mat 6:33 these things will be **p** for you.
22:11 clothes ⌊**p** for the guests⌋.
Luk 8:3 They **p** financial support for
12:31 these things will be **p** for you.
Rom 7:8 But sin took the opportunity **p**
7:11 Sin, taking the opportunity **p** by
16:2 because she has **p** help to
Php 4:16 you **p** for my needs twice.
Col 4:11 They have **p** me with comfort.

provider (1)
Psa 54:4 The Lord is the **p** for my life.

provides (10)
Job 38:41 "Who **p** food for the crow when
Psa 111:5 He **p** food for those who fear
147:8 He **p** rain for the ground.
Pro 18:20 A person's speaking ability **p**
18:20 His talking **p** him a living.
Isa 30:23 and the food that the ground **p**
Jer 31:35 The LORD **p** the sun to be a
Jon 6:65 unless the Father **p** the way."
2Co 9:12 do to serve others not only **p**
1Ti 6:17 confidence in God who richly **p**

providing (3)
1Ki 5:9 You can pay me by **p** food for
18:4 and kept them alive by **p** bread
Neh 13:7 Eliashib had done by **p** Tobiah

province (82)
Ezr 2:1 These were the people in the **p**.
4:16 nothing left ⌊of your **p**⌋ west
4:20 have ruled the whole ⌊**p**⌋ west
5:3 Governor Tattenai ⌊from the **p**⌋
5:6 Tattenai ⌊from the **p**⌋ west
5:8 that we went to the **p** of Judah,
6:2 which is in the **p** of Media.

Ezr 6:6 Governor Tattenai ⌊from the **p**⌋
6:8 from the taxes ⌊on the **p**⌋ west
6:13 Tattenai ⌊from the **p**⌋ west
7:16 that you find in the whole **p**
7:21 the treasurers ⌊in the **p**⌋ west
7:25 and live ⌊in the **p**⌋ west
8:36 and governors ⌊in the **p**⌋ west
Neh 1:3 survived captivity are in the **p**.
2:7 the governors ⌊of the **p**⌋ west
2:9 the governors ⌊of the **p**⌋ west
3:7 the governor ⌊from the **p**⌋ west
7:6 These were the people in the **p**.
11:3 officials of the **p** who settled
Est 1:16 in every **p** of King Xerxes.
1:22 to each **p** in its own script and
1:22 and to the people in each **p**
3:12 the governors of every **p**,
3:12 They wrote to each **p** in its
3:12 and to the people in each **p**
3:14 public in a decree to every **p**.
4:3 In every **p** touched by the
8:9 It was written to each **p** in its
8:11 the people and **p** that is hostile
8:13 public in a decree to every **p**
8:17 In every **p** and every city where
9:28 every age, family, **p**, and city.
Dan 2:48 Daniel governor of the whole **p**
2:49 to govern the **p** of Babylon.
3:1 in the wall in the **p** of Babylon.
3:4 "People of every **p**,
3:7 all the people from every **p**,
3:12 to govern the **p** of Babylon:
3:29 I order that people from every **p**
3:30 positions in the **p** of Babylon.
4:1 To the people of every **p**,
5:19 People from every **p**,
6:25 wrote to the people of every **p**,
7:14 People from every **p**,
8:2 of Susa in the **p** of Elam.
Act 2:9 Pontus, the **p** of Asia,
16:6 the word in the **p** of Asia.
16:7 They went to the **p** of Mysia
19:10 and Greeks who lived in the **p**
19:22 stayed longer in the **p** of Asia.
19:26 also throughout the **p** of Asia.
19:31 officials who were from the **p**
20:4 and Trophimus from the **p**
20:16 spending time in the **p** of Asia.
20:18 day I arrived in the **p** of Asia.
21:27 the Jews from the **p** of Asia
23:34 he asked Paul which **p** he was
23:34 Paul was from the **p** of Cilicia,
24:19 But some Jews from the **p** of
25:1 his duties in the **p** of Judea,
27:2 on the coast of the **p** of Asia.
27:5 city of Myra in the **p** of Lycia.
Rom 16:5 He was the first person in the **p**
1Co 16:5 go through the **p** of Macedonia,
16:19 The churches in the **p** of Asia
2Co 1:8 experienced in the **p** of Asia.
1:16 Corinth to the **p** of Macedonia.
2:13 went to the **p** of Macedonia.
7:5 arrived in the **p** of Macedonia,
8:1 in the **p** of Macedonia.
9:2 in the **p** of Macedonia.
11:9 My friends from the **p** of
Php 4:15 when I left the **p** of Macedonia
1Th 1:7 for all the believers in the **p**
1:8 out not only through the **p**
4:10 throughout the **p** of Macedonia.
1Ti 1:3 going to the **p** of Macedonia,
2Ti 1:15 know that everyone in the **p**
4:10 went to the **p** of Galatia,
4:10 Titus went to the **p** of Dalmatia.
Rev 1:4 churches in the **p** of Asia.

provinces (27)

Ezr 4:15 been a threat to kings and **p**.
Est 1:1 who ruled over 127 **p** from India
1:3 the nobles and officials of the **p**
1:22 documents to all the king's **p**,
2:3 And appoint scouts in all the **p**
2:18 that day a holiday in the **p**,
3:8 the nationalities in all the **p**
3:13 documents to all the king's **p**.
4:11 in the king's **p** know that no
8:5 destroy the Jews in all your **p**.
8:9 and officers of the 127 **p** from
8:12 on one day in all the **p**
9:2 their cities throughout all the **p**
9:3 All the officials of the **p**,
9:4 was spreading to all the **p**,
9:12 done in the rest of the king's **p**!
9:16 king's **p** had also assembled
9:20 to all the Jews in all the **p**
9:30 to all the Jews in the 127 **p**
Ecc 2:8 the treasures of kings and **p**.
Lam 1:1 it was a princess among the **p**.
Dan 11:24 invade the richest parts of the **p**
Act 6:9 and Alexandria and the **p**
15:41 Paul went through the **p** of
19:1 traveled through the interior **p**
27:5 sailed along the coast of the **p**
1Pe 1:1 throughout the **p** of Pontus,

provincial (2)

Dan 3:2 and all the other **p** officials to
3:3 and all the other **p** officials

proving (1)

Act 9:22 Damascus by **p** that Jesus was

provisions (2)

Dtr 15:14 Generously give them **p** —
1Ki 20:27 been organized and given **p**,

provoke (5)

Job 2:3 You're trying to **p** me into
12:6 security for those who **p** God,
41:10 is brave enough to **p** Leviathan.
Eze 8:17 continue to **p** me even more.
Gal 5:26 to act arrogantly and to **p**

provoked (3)

Gen 49:23 Archers **p** him, shot at him,
2Sm 24:1 so he **p** David to turn against
Isa 65:3 constantly and openly **p** me.

provoking (2)

1Ch 21:1 to attack Israel by **p** David
Jer 7:19 They aren't really **p** me,"

prowl (3)

Psa 59:6 like dogs. They **p** the city.
59:14 like dogs. They **p** the city.
Pro 7:12 on the **p** at every corner.

prowled (1)

Eze 19:6 and he **p** among the lions.

prowling (1)

1Pe 5:8 Your opponent the devil is **p**

prune (2)

Lev 25:3 in your fields, **p** your vineyards,
25:4 your fields or **p** your vineyards.

pruned (1)

Isa 5:6 It will never be **p** or hoed.

prunes (1)

Jon 15:2 He also **p** every branch that

pruning (4)

Isa 2:4 and their spears into **p** shears.
18:5 he will cut off the shoots with **p**
Joe 3:10 and your **p** shears into spears.
Mic 4:3 and their spears into **p** shears.

psalm (6)

Psa 81:2 Begin a **p**, and strike a
98:5 a lyre and the melody of a **p**,
144:9 I will sing a **p** to you on a
Act 13:33 Scripture says in the second **p**:
13:35 Another **p** says, 'You will not
1Co 14:26 each person has a **p**,

psalms (12)

2Sm 23:1 the singer of Israel's **p**:
Psa 95:2 shout happily to him with **p**.
119:54 Your laws have become like **p**
147:1 It is good to sing **p** to our God.
Luk 20:42 David says in the book of **P**,
24:44 and the **P** had to come true."
Act 1:20 You've read in **P**, 'Let his home
1Co 14:15 I will sing **p** with my spirit,
14:15 and I will sing **p** with my mind.
Eph 5:19 by reciting **p**, hymns,
Col 3:16 Use **p**, hymns, and spiritual
Jas 5:13 If you are happy, sing **p**.

psychic (3)

Lev 20:27 who is a medium or a **p** must
Dan 2:10 any magician, **p**, or astrologer.
2:27 "No wise adviser, **p**, magician,

psychics (13)

Lev 19:31 "Don't turn to **p** or mediums to
20:6 who turn to mediums and **p**
1Sm 28:3 rid the land of mediums and **p**.)
28:9 rid the land of mediums and **p**.
2Ki 21:6 ⌊royal⌋ mediums and **p**.
23:24 **p**, family idols, other idols,
2Ch 33:6 ⌊royal⌋ mediums and **p**.
Dan 1:20 than all the magicians and **p**
2:2 for the magicians, **p**, sorcerers,
4:7 The magicians, **p**,
5:7 The king screamed for the **p**,
5:11 the magicians, **p**, astrologers,
5:15 The wise advisers and the **p**

Ptolemais (2)

Act 21:7 from Tyre to the city of **P**.
21:7 We greeted the believers in **P**

Puah (4)

Exo 1:15 names were Shiphrah and **P**,
Num 26:23 family of Tola, the family of **P**,
Jdg 10:1 who was the son of **P** and
1Ch 7:1 Tola, **P**, Jashub, and Shimron.

public (19)

Dtr 24:5 duty or any other **p** service.
Rut 4:10 relatives or from the **p** records.
2Sm 21:12 stolen them from the **p** square
Est 3:14 of the document was made **p**
8:13 of the document was made **p**
Job 11:2 a good **p** speaker be acquitted?
30:28 I stand up in **p** and call for help.
34:26 he strikes them in **p**,
Pro 1:20 In the **p** squares she raises her
Mat 6:1 not to do your good works in **p**
Luk 1:24 pregnant and didn't go out in **p**
1:25 He has removed my **p**
Jon 2:11 He made his glory **p** there,
7:26 He's speaking in **p**,
Act 16:19 the authorities in the **p** square.
17:5 who hung around the **p** square,
17:17 every day in the **p** square
18:28 In **p** Apollos helped them by
Col 2:15 and made a **p** spectacle

publicly (18)

Lev 20:17 They both must be **p** excluded
Dtr 25:3 he would be **p** humiliated.
Rut 4:7 was **p** approved in Israel.)
Neh 5:1 complained **p** about their
Jer 36:13 Baruch read from the scroll **p**.
36:14 the scroll that you read **p**,
Mat 1:19 did not want to disgrace her **p**.
7:23 Then I will tell them **p**,
Jon 7:4 when he wants to be known **p**.
7:10 He didn't go **p** but secretly.
12:42 they wouldn't admit it **p**
18:20 "I have spoken **p** for everyone
Act 16:37 have had us beaten **p** without
20:20 I didn't avoid teaching you **p**
Rom 16:26 but now is **p** known.
Heb 6:6 again and **p** disgracing him.
10:33 At times you were **p** insulted
1Pe 1:20 but for your good he became **p**

Publius (1)

Act 28:7 A man named **P**, who was the

Pudens (1)

2Ti 4:21 Eubulus, **P**, Linus, Claudia and

Pul (3)
2Ki 15:19 King **P** of Assyria came to
15:19 So Menahem gave **P** 75,000
1Ch 5:26 the God of Israel led King **P**

pull (25)
Lev 1:17 Then **p** on the bird's wings to
1:17 but don't **p** the wings off.
Num 16:14 Do you think you can still **p** the
Jdg 3:22 blade because Ehud didn't **p**
Rut 2:16 Even **p** some grain out of the
2Sm 8:4 so that they couldn't **p** chariots.
1Ki 13:4 so that he couldn't **p** it back.
1Ch 18:4 so that they couldn't **p** chariots.
Job 41:1 "Can you **p** Leviathan out ⌊of
Psa 31:4 You are my refuge, so **p** me out
37:14 Wicked people **p** out their
52:5 He will **p** your roots out of this
Ecc 3:2 a time to plant and a time to **p**
Jer 22:24 I will **p** you off my hand.
38:13 They used the ropes to **p**
Eze 17:9 strength or many people to **p**
29:4 I will **p** you out of your river
Mic 5:14 I will **p** out your poles
Hab 1:15 The Babylonians **p** them all up
Mat 13:28 want us to **p** out the weeds?'
13:29 If you **p** out the weeds,
13:29 you may **p** out the wheat with
Luk 14:5 you **p** him out immediately?"
17:6 '**P** yourself up by the roots,
Jon 21:6 net out and were unable to **p**

pulled (22)
Gen 19:10 **p** Lot into the house with them,
37:28 the brothers **p** Joseph out of the
38:29 As he **p** back his hand,
49:33 he **p** his feet into his bed.
Exo 2:10 named him Moses [**P** Out]
2:10 "I **p** him out of the water."
Jdg 16:3 of the city gate and **p** them out.
1Sm 17:51 **p** it out of its sheath,
2Sm 22:17 He **p** me out of the raging water.
Ezr 9:3 **p** hair from my scalp and my
Neh 13:25 and **p** out their hair.
Psa 18:16 He **p** me out of the raging water.
30:1 because you have **p** me out ⌊of
40:2 He **p** me out of a horrible pit,
Isa 33:20 tent pegs will never be **p** out,
Mat 13:48 they **p** it to the shore.
26:51 one of the men with Jesus **p**
Mar 14:47 One of those standing there **p**
Luk 1:52 He **p** strong rulers from their
Jon 21:11 Peter got into the boat and **p**
Act 11:10 Then everything was **p** back
27:17 The men **p** it up on deck.

pulling (1)
Lev 5:8 neck without **p** its head off.

pulls (2)
Job 20:25 He **p** it out, and it comes out of
Pro 21:22 a city of warriors and **p** down

punch (3)
1Ki 20:35 ⌊The disciple said,⌋ "**P** me,"
20:35 but the man refused to **p** him.
20:37 He said, "**P** me." The man

punched (1)
1Ki 20:37 The man **p** him hard and

punches (1)
1Co 9:27 I toughen my body with **p** and

punching (1)
Pro 30:33 milk produces butter and **p**

punish (128)
Gen 15:14 But I will **p** the nation they
Exo 7:4 my power to **p** Egypt severely,
12:12 I will severely **p** all the gods of
20:5 I **p** children for their parents'
32:34 But when I **p**, I will punish
32:34 I will **p** them for their sin."
Lev 18:25 I will **p** it for its sins.
Lev 26:24 I will **p** you seven times for
Num 12:11 don't **p** us for this foolish sin
Dtr 5:9 I **p** children for their parents'
21:18 Even though they **p** him,
22:18 must take the man and **p** him.
Jos 22:23 let the LORD **p** us.
Jdg 20:10 territory of Benjamin they can **p**
1Sm 15:2 I will **p** Amalek for what they
20:16 the LORD **p** David's house."
25:22 May God **p** me if I leave even
2Sm 7:14 If he sins, I will **p** him with a
13:21 But David didn't **p** his son
1Ki 12:11 I will **p** you with scorpions.'"
12:14 I will **p** you with scorpions."
2Ki 19:4 The LORD your God may **p**
1Ch 21:17 but don't **p** your people with a
2Ch 10:11 I will **p** you with scorpions.'"
Job 35:15 his anger doesn't **p** ⌊anyone⌋
Psa 6:1 O LORD, do not **p** me in your
10:15 **P** his wickedness until you
38:1 O LORD, do not angrily **p** me or
59:5 arise to **p** all the nations.
89:32 then with a rod I will **p** their
94:10 Do you think he can't **p**?
149:7 to **p** the people of the world,
Pro 16:22 but stubborn fools **p**
17:11 will be sent ⌊to **p**⌋ him.
17:26 To **p** an innocent person is not
Isa 10:12 he will **p** the king of Assyria for
13:11 I will **p** the world for its evil and
24:21 On that day the LORD will **p**
26:21 place to **p** those who live
27:1 powerful sword to **p** Leviathan,
29:6 The LORD of Armies will **p**
37:4 The LORD your God may **p**
54:9 to be angry with you or **p** you.
59:18 with wrath and **p** his enemies.
66:15 his burning anger and **p** them
Jer 2:19 your unfaithful ways will **p** you.
5:9 I will **p** them for these things,"
5:9 "I will **p** this nation.
5:29 I will **p** them for these things,"
5:29 "I will **p** this nation.
6:15 brought down when I **p** them,"
8:12 down when I **p** them,'" says
9:9 I will **p** them for these things,
9:9 I will **p** this nation.
9:25 "when I will **p** all who are
9:26 I will **p** Egypt, Judah, Edom,
9:26 I will **p** all who shave the hair
11:22 I'm going to **p** them.
14:10 their crimes and **p** their sins.
15:3 devise four ways to **p** them,"
21:14 "'I will **p** you because of the
23:34 I will **p** them and their families.
25:12 I will **p** the king of Babylon and
27:8 I will **p** those nations by wars,
29:32 The LORD says: I will **p**
29:32 I will also **p** his descendants.
30:20 and I will **p** everyone who
32:18 However, you **p** children for the
36:31 I will **p** him, his descendants,
44:13 I will **p** those living in Egypt as
44:29 'I will **p** you in this place so
46:25 "I'm going to **p** Amon,
46:25 I will also **p** Pharaoh,
49:8 When I **p** them, I will bring
50:18 I am going to **p** the king of
50:31 the time when I will **p** you.
51:44 I will **p** Bel in Babylon.
51:47 when I will **p** Babylon's idols.
51:52 "when I will **p** their idols,
51:56 I will certainly **p** them.
Lam 4:22 People of Edom, he will **p** you
Eze 5:8 and I will **p** you in front of the
5:10 I will **p** you and scatter
5:15 When I **p** you because of my
7:3 and I will **p** you for all the
7:8 and I will **p** you for all the
9:1 who are going to **p** this city.
11:9 to foreigners, and I will **p** you.
15:6 live in Jerusalem to **p** them.
16:38 I will **p** you the same way that
16:41 burn your houses and **p** you
17:19 I will certainly **p** you for
23:24 They will **p** you with their own
Eze 23:45 Righteous people will **p** these
24:14 I will **p** you because of the way
25:11 I will **p** Moab. Then they will
25:17 revenge on them and **p** them
28:22 because I will **p** you and show
28:26 will live in safety when I **p** all
38:22 I will **p** Gog with plagues and
39:21 power against them to **p** them.
Hos 1:4 In a little while I will **p** Jehu's
2:13 I will **p** her for all the times she
4:9 I will **p** them for their wicked
4:14 Yet, I will not **p** your daughters
5:2 So I will **p** all of you.
7:12 I will **p** you for all the evil
8:13 their wickedness and **p** them
9:9 their wickedness and **p** them
10:10 "I will **p** them when I'm ready.
Joe 3:21 I will **p** those who murder."
Amo 3:2 That is why I am going to **p**
3:14 On the day I **p** Israel for its
Mic 2:3 a disaster to **p** your family.
Zep 1:8 sacrifice I will **p** the officials,
1:9 On that day I will **p** all who
1:12 lamps and **p** those who are
Zec 10:3 I will **p** the male goats.
Mal 2:3 going to **p** your descendants.
Mat 24:51 Then his master will severely **p**
Luk 12:46 Then his master will **p** him
Act 4:21 any way to **p** Peter and John.
7:7 God also told him, "I will **p** the
22:5 back to Jerusalem to **p** them.
1Co 4:21 would you prefer that I **p** you or
2Co 7:11 You were ready to **p** the wrong
10:6 We are ready to **p** every act of
1Pe 2:14 has sent to **p** those who do

punishable (1)
Job 19:29 ⌊your anger⌋ is **p** by death.

punished (62)
Gen 19:15 away when the city is **p**."
42:21 "We're surely being **p** for what
Exo 20:7 uses his name will be **p**.
21:19 one who hit him must not be **p**.
21:20 the owner must be **p**.
21:21 the owner must not be **p**.
Lev 5:1 you are sinning and will be **p**.
5:17 your guilt, you must be **p**.
7:18 who eats any of it must be **p**.
19:8 Those who eat it will be **p**
20:17 with his sister and must be **p**.
20:19 with a close relative must be **p**.
24:15 contempt will be **p** for their sin.
Num 32:23 that you will be **p** for your sin.
Dtr 5:11 his name carelessly will be **p**.
Jdg 11:36 has **p** your enemy Ammon."
1Ki 12:11 If my father **p** you with whips,
12:14 If my father **p** you with whips,
2Ki 7:9 when it's light out, we'll be **p**.
2Ch 10:11 If my father **p** you with whips,
10:14 If my father **p** you with whips,
Ezr 9:13 have **p** us far less than we
Pro 21:11 When a mocker is **p**,
Isa 24:6 and its people are **p** for their
24:22 After a long time they'll be **p**.
26:14 You have **p** them, and wiped out
27:8 He **p** Israel by sending it away.
53:4 him, beat him, and **p** him.
53:5 He was **p** so that we could
53:7 He was abused and **p**,
57:17 so I **p** them, hid ⌊from them⌋,
Jer 2:30 "I have **p** your children without
6:6 This city must be **p**.
10:15 jokes. When they are **p**,
11:8 So I **p** them, because they did
23:12 to be **p**," declares the LORD.
30:14 I've **p** you as an enemy would.
44:13 living in Egypt as I **p** Jerusalem
46:21 At that time they will be **p**.
50:18 of Babylon and his land as I **p**
50:27 the time for them to be **p**.
51:18 When they are **p**, they will
Lam 3:39 complain about being **p** for sin?
Eze 16:38 of prostitution and murder are **p**
18:19 'Why isn't the son **p** for his
18:20 A son will not be **p** for his

Eze 18:20 and a father will not be **p** for his
21:10 refused to be disciplined or **p**.
23:10 about how she was **p**.
23:35 So you will be **p** for your
23:49 They will be **p** for their sins,
44:10 They must be **p** for their sins.
44:12 and swore that they would be **p**
Hos 4:9 So the priests will be **p** like the
9:7 time for them to be **p** will come.
10:10 They will be **p** for their many
Mic 7:4 you would be **p** has come.
Zep 3:7 out even though I have **p** them.
Luk 21:23 and its people will be **p**.
Act 26:11 each synagogue, **p** believers,
2Co 6:9 We are **p**, but we are not killed.
Heb 2:2 disobedience was properly **p**.

punishes (5)

Psa 75:7 He **p** one person and rewards
99:8 who **p** their ⌊sinful⌋ deeds.
Jer 51:56 am a God who **p** evil.
Hos 12:2 against Judah and **p** Jacob
1Th 4:6 The Lord is the one who **p**

punishing (4)

Exo 34:7 **p** children and grandchildren
Num 14:18 go unpunished, **p** children ...
Jer 23:2 I will take care of you by **p** you
Eze 7:11 a weapon for **p** wickedness.

punishment (63)

Gen 4:13 "My **p** is more than I can stand!
Lev 26:21 I will increase the **p** for your
Jos 22:31 of Israel from the LORD's **p**."
2Sm 24:17 Please let your **p** be against
1Ki 8:32 guilty person with the proper **p**,
2Ki 19:3 with misery, **p**, and disgrace.
1Ch 21:17 LORD my God, let your **p** be
2Ch 6:23 guilty person with the proper **p**,
Job 21:19 'God saves a person's **p** for his
21:19 he would know that it is a **p**.
24:1 set aside times ⌊for **p**⌋?
Psa 73:14 morning my **p** ⌊begins again⌋.
79:10 the nations learn that there is **p**
81:15 time ⌊for **p**⌋ would last forever.
91:8 to see the **p** of wicked people.
Pro 6:29 who touch her will escape **p**.
17:5 distress will not escape **p**.
28:20 to get rich will not escape **p**.
Isa 37:3 with misery, **p**, and disgrace.
Jer 4:18 This is your **p**. It is bitter. It
10:19 Then I thought that this is my **p**,
11:23 It will be a year of **p**.
48:44 I will bring a year of **p** to Moab,"
Lam 4:6 The **p** for my people's
4:6 been more severe than the **p**
4:22 People of Zion, the **p** for your
5:7 take the **p** for their wickedness.
Eze 4:4 on your left side and take the **p**
4:4 You will bear its **p** as many
4:5 day for each year its **p** will last.
4:5 you will bear the **p** for the sins
4:6 You will bear the **p** for the sins
20:37 Then I will make you suffer **p**
21:25 time for your final **p** has come.
21:29 the time of final **p** has come.
23:24 handed you over to them for **p**.
23:24 you with their own kind of **p**.
30:14 and bring **p** on Thebes.
30:19 I will bring **p** on Egypt.'"
35:5 in trouble during their final **p**.
Dan 2:9 you'll all receive the same **p**.
Hos 5:9 when the time for **p** comes.
5:11 is oppressed — crushed by **p**,
10:2 Now they must take their **p**.
Zec 14:19 This will be ⌊the **p**⌋ for Egypt's
Mat 25:46 will go away into eternal **p**,
Mar 12:40 will receive the most severe **p**."
Luk 12:48 he deserved **p** will receive
20:47 will receive the most severe **p**."
23:41 Our **p** is fair. We're getting what
Rom 1:27 themselves the **p** they deserve
11:9 a snare and a **p** for them.
13:2 will bring **p** on themselves.
2Co 2:6 enough **p** on that person.
3:9 ministry that brings **p** has glory
2Co 3:10 that brings **p** lost its glory
Gal 1:4 Christ took the **p** for our sins,
2:20 me and took the **p** for my sins.
Heb 2:3 So how will we escape **p** if we
10:29 He deserves a much worse **p**.
2Pe 2:9 to hold immoral people for **p**
1Jn 4:18 because fear involves **p**.
Jud 1:7 is an example for us of the **p**

punishments (2)

Pro 19:29 **P** are set for mockers and
Eze 14:21 terrible **p** against Jerusalem.

Punon (2)

Num 33:42 and set up camp at **P**.
33:43 They moved from **P** and set up

pupil (2)

Psa 17:8 Guard me as if I were the **p** in
Pro 7:2 you protect the **p** of your eye.

Pur (3)

Est 3:7 **P** (which means the lot) was
9:24 Haman had the **P** (which
9:26 based on the word **P**.

Purah (2)

Jdg 7:10 take your servant **P** to the
7:11 So Gideon and his servant **P**

purchase (3)

Lev 25:51 he must refund from his **p** price
25:52 He must refund from his **p** price
Jer 32:8 It is your responsibility to **p** it,

purchased (4)

Exo 15:16 until the people you **p** pass by.
Lev 25:33 in the jubilee the **p** house in the
Mar 15:46 Joseph had **p** some linen cloth.
Act 7:16 in the tomb that Abraham **p**

pure (110)

Gen 2:12 (The gold of that land is **p**.
Exo 25:11 Cover it with **p** gold inside and
25:17 the ark out of **p** gold 45 inches
25:24 Cover it with **p** gold,
25:29 for the table out of **p** gold,
25:31 a lamp stand out of **p** gold.
25:36 of the same piece of **p** gold as
25:38 must be made of **p** gold.
25:39 Use 75 pounds of **p** gold to
27:20 the Israelites to bring you **p**,
28:14 and two chains of **p** gold,
28:22 make chains out of **p** gold,
28:36 medallion out of **p** gold,
30:3 Cover all of it with **p** gold — the
30:34 and mix them with one part **p**
30:35 seasoned with salt, **p** and holy.
31:8 the table and the dishes, the **p**
37:2 He covered it with **p** gold
37:6 mercy out of **p** gold 45 inches
37:11 He covered it with **p** gold and
37:16 All of them were made out of **p**
37:17 the lamp stand out of **p** gold.
37:22 of the same piece of **p** gold as
37:23 incense burners out of **p** gold.
37:24 out of 75 pounds of **p** gold.
37:26 He covered all of it with **p** gold
37:29 used for anointing and for the **p**,
39:15 they made chains out of **p** gold,
39:25 They made bells out of **p** gold
39:30 (the holy crown) out of **p** gold
39:37 the **p** ⌊gold⌋ lamp stand with
Lev 24:2 the Israelites to bring you **p**,
24:4 lamps on the **p** gold lamp stand
24:7 Lay **p** incense on top of each
Num 5:28 woman is not unclean and is **p**,
2Sm 22:27 with **p** people you are pure.
22:27 with pure people you are **p**.
1Ki 5:11 120,000 gallons of **p** olive oil.
6:20 and the cedar altar with **p** gold.
6:21 of the temple with **p** gold.
7:49 lamp stands of **p** gold (five on
7:50 incense burners of **p** gold,
2Ki 2:22 To this day the water is still **p**,
1Ch 28:17 the **p** gold for the forks,
2Ch 3:4 its inside walls with **p** gold.
4:20 lamp stands and lamps of **p**
4:21 flowers, lamps, **p** gold tongs,
4:22 incense burners of **p** gold,
9:17 and covered it with **p** gold.
Job 4:17 being be **p** to his maker?'
15:15 heavens are not **p** in his sight,
23:10 I'll come out as **p** as gold.
25:4 anyone born of a woman be **p**?
25:5 the stars aren't **p** in his sight.
25:6 How much less **p** is a mortal —
28:19 for ⌊any amount of⌋ **p** gold.
33:9 ⌊You said,⌋ 'I'm **p** — without
Psa 12:6 promises of the LORD are **p**,
18:26 with **p** people you are pure.
18:26 with pure people you are **p**.
19:9 The fear of the LORD is **p**.
24:4 has clean hands and a **p** heart
73:1 to those whose lives are **p**.
73:13 no reward for keeping my life **p**
119:9 a young person keep his life **p**?
119:127 than gold, more than **p** gold.
Pro 8:19 is better than gold, **p** gold.
10:20 a righteous person is **p** silver.
15:26 pleasant words are **p** to him.
16:2 thinks all his ways are **p**,
20:9 "I've made my heart **p**.
20:11 his deeds are **p** or right.
21:8 of those who are **p** is moral.
22:11 Whoever loves a **p** heart and
30:12 kind of person thinks he is **p**
Sos 5:15 marble set on bases of **p** gold.
6:9 She is **p** to the one who gave
6:10 like the moon, **p** like the sun,
Isa 1:22 Your silver is not **p**.
13:12 harder to find than **p** gold
52:11 Make yourselves **p**,
Dan 7:9 on his head was like **p** wool.
Hab 1:13 Your eyes are too **p** to look at
Zep 3:9 "Then I will give all people **p**
Mal 1:11 Incense and **p** offerings will be
Mat 5:8 those whose thoughts are **p**.
Mar 14:3 perfume made from **p** nard.
Jon 12:3 perfume made from **p** nard
2Co 2:17 we speak the **p** message that
11:3 and **p** devotion to Christ.
Php 1:10 what is best and be **p**
4:8 honorable, fair, **p**, acceptable,
1Th 2:10 God are witnesses of how **p**,
1Ti 1:5 for love to flow from a **p** heart,
5:2 keeping yourself morally **p**.
5:22 Keep yourself morally **p**.
2Ti 2:22 worship the Lord with a **p** heart.
Tit 2:5 and to be morally **p**.
Heb 7:26 **p**, set apart from sinners,
Jas 1:27 **P**, unstained religion,
3:17 from above is first of all **p**.
1Pe 2:2 Desire God's **p** word as
3:2 husbands would see how **p**
1Jn 3:3 in Christ keep themselves **p**,
3:3 themselves pure, as Christ is **p**.
Rev 14:4 These 144,000 virgins are **p**.
19:8 of wearing dazzling, **p** linen."
19:14 heaven, wearing **p**, white linen,
21:18 The city was made of **p** gold,
21:21 of the city was made of **p** gold,

pure-blooded (1)

Php 3:5 I'm a **p** Hebrew. When it comes

purer (1)

Lam 4:7 princes were **p** than snow,

purification (7)

Jon 2:6 were used for Jewish **p** rituals.
3:25 a Jew about **p** ceremonies.
Act 21:24 go through the **p** ceremony
21:26 went through the **p** ceremony
21:26 the time when the **p** would
24:18 gone through the **p** ceremony.
Heb 9:10 used in various **p** ceremonies.

purified (5)

2Ki 2:21 I have **p** this water.
Psa 12:6 in a furnace and **p** seven times.
Dan 12:10 Many will be **p**, made white,

1Pe 1:22 After all, you have **p**
Rev 3:18 I advise you: Buy gold **p** in fire

purifier (1)

Mal 3:3 He will act like a refiner and a **p**

purifies (1)

Pro 17:3 but the one who **p** hearts ⌊by

purify (5)

Psa 51:7 **P** me from sin with hyssop,
Eze 43:26 the altar, **p** it, and consecrate it.
Dan 11:35 be defeated in order to refine, **p**,
Mal 3:3 He will **p** Levi's sons and refine
Jon 11:55 to **p** themselves before

purifying (1)

Mal 3:2 He is like a **p** fire and like a

Purim (5)

Est 9:26 the Jews called these days **P**,
9:28 These days of **P** must not be
9:29 well-known celebration of **P**.
9:31 to establish these days of **P** at
9:32 these practices of **P**,

purity (5)

Job 22:30 will be rescued by your **p**."
1Co 5:8 celebrate it with the bread of **p**
2Co 6:6 ⌊People can see⌋ our **p**,
1Ti 4:12 and **p** an example for other
Tit 2:7 example of moral **p** and dignity.

purple (50)

Exo 25:4 violet, **p**, and bright red yarn,
26:1 Take violet, **p**, and bright red
26:31 "Make a canopy of violet, **p**,
26:36 violet, **p**, and bright red yarn.
27:16 violet, **p**, and bright red yarn,
28:5 They must use gold, violet, **p**,
28:6 Creatively work gold, violet, **p**,
28:15 Make it out of gold, violet, **p**,
28:33 pomegranates of violet, **p**,
35:6 violet, **p**, and bright red yarn,
35:23 Those who had violet, **p**,
35:25 violet, **p**, and bright red yarn,
35:35 **p** and bright red yarn on fine
36:8 violet, **p**, and bright red yarn.
36:35 the canopy out of violet, **p**,
36:37 violet, **p**, and bright red yarn.
38:18 was made of violet, **p**,
38:23 how to embroider violet, **p**,
39:1 From the violet, **p**,
39:2 violet, **p**, and bright red yarn.
39:3 violet, **p**, and bright red yarn,
39:8 violet, **p**, and bright red yarn,
39:24 of violet, **p**, and bright red yarn,
39:29 violet, **p**, and bright red yarn.
Num 4:13 they will spread a **p** cloth over
Jdg 8:26 the **p** clothes worn by the kings
2Ch 2:7 and iron as well as **p**,
2:14 **p**, violet, and dark red cloth,
3:14 made the canopy of violet, **p**,
Est 1:6 made of white and **p** fine linen.
1:6 a mosaic pavement of **p** rock,
8:15 and a **p** outer robe of fine linen.
Pro 31:22 ⌊made of⌋ linen and **p** cloth.
Sos 3:10 its seat out of **p** fabric.
Jer 10:9 for the idols is blue and **p**,
Eze 23:6 and commanders clothed in **p**.
27:7 awnings were violet and **p**.
27:16 **p** cloth, richly woven cloth,
27:24 **p** robes, embroidered cloth,
Dan 5:7 meaning will be dressed in **p**,
5:16 you will be dressed in **p**,
5:29 that Daniel be dressed in **p**
Mar 15:17 They dressed him in **p**,
15:20 they took off the **p** cape and put
Jon 19:2 and put a **p** cape on him.
19:5 crown of thorns and the **p** cape.
Act 16:14 city of Thyatira and sold **p** dye
Rev 17:4 The woman wore **p** clothes,
18:12 **p** cloth, silk, bright red cloth,
18:16 **p** clothes, bright red clothes,

purpose (28)

Gen 31:13 on a stone marker for a holy **p**
Exo 29:37 set the altar apart for its holy **p**.
30:29 dedicate them for their holy **p**.
Lev 7:24 you may use for any other **p**,
11:32 or anything used for any **p**.
1Ch 12:38 came with a single **p** to Hebron
Pro 16:4 made everything for his own **p**,
Isa 10:7 Their **p** is to destroy and put an
23:18 over to the LORD for his holy **p**.
45:13 Cyrus for my righteous **p**.
Jer 1:5 I set you apart for my holy **p**.
32:39 and the same **p** so that they
Lam 4:11 fury has accomplished his **p**.
Eze 11:19 I will give them a single **p** and
38:16 for my holy **p** as they watch.
Zep 3:9 and to serve him with one **p**.
Hag 2:12 meat set aside for a holy **p**
Jon 10:36 God set me apart for this holy **p**
Act 1:14 The apostles had a single **p** as
2:46 The believers had a single **p**
7:57 at Stephen with one **p** in mind,
1Co 12:25 God's **p** was that the body
Gal 3:19 What, then, is the **p** of the laws
Eph 4:12 Their **p** is to prepare God's
Php 2:2 and keeping one **p** in mind.
2Ti 3:10 my **p**, my faith, my patience,
1Pe 1:7 The **p** of these troubles is to
Rev 17:13 They have one **p** — to give their

purposes (1)

Exo 29:44 and the altar for their holy **p**.

purses (1)

Isa 3:22 fine robes, coats, shawls, **p**,

pursue (32)

Exo 14:4 so stubborn that he will **p** them.
15:9 "The enemy said, 'I'll **p** them!
Dtr 19:6 to avenge the death will **p** him.
28:22 They will **p** you until you die.
28:45 They will **p** you and stay close
Jdg 7:23 and all Manasseh to help **p** the
1Sm 30:8 "Should I **p** these troops?
30:8 "**P** them," the LORD told him.
2Sm 20:7 left Jerusalem to **p** Sheba,
24:13 your enemies as they **p** you,
Job 19:22 Why do you **p** me as God
Psa 34:14 Seek peace, and **p** it!
35:3 the way of those who **p** me.
71:11 **P** him and grab him because
83:14 **P** them with your storms,
94:15 are decent will **p** justice.
119:32 I will eagerly **p** your
142:6 Rescue me from those who **p**
Pro 15:9 but he loves those who **p**
Isa 51:1 Listen to me, you people who **p**
Lam 3:66 **P** them in anger, and wipe
Eze 5:12 and I will **p** them with a sword.
12:14 I will **p** them with my sword.
35:6 Murderers will **p** you.
35:6 people, murder will **p** you.
Nah 1:8 He will **p** his enemies with
Rom 14:19 So let's **p** those things which
1Co 14:1 **P** love, and desire spiritual
1Ti 6:11 **P** what God approves of:
2Ti 2:22 **P** what has God's approval.
2:22 **P** faith, love, and peace
1Pe 3:11 They must seek peace and **p** it.

pursued (30)

Gen 14:14 and **p** the four kings all the way
31:23 He and his relatives **p** Jacob
35:5 terrified so that no one **p** them.
Exo 14:8 that he **p** the Israelites,
14:9 The Egyptians **p** the Israelites.
14:23 The Egyptians **p** them,
Dtr 11:4 the Red Sea when they **p** you.
Jos 2:7 The king's men **p** them on the
8:24 desert where they had been **p**.
Jdg 4:16 Barak **p** the chariots and the
8:12 fled as Gideon **p** them.
20:43 and **p** them without stopping.
1Sm 7:11 left Mizpah, **p** the Philistines,
14:22 they also **p** the Philistines in
17:52 and **p** the Philistines as far as
23:25 Saul heard about it and **p** David
25:29 Even though someone **p** you
2Sm 20:10 his brother Abishai **p** Sheba,
20:13 followed Joab and **p** Sheba,
1Ki 20:20 fled, and Israel **p** them.
2Ki 9:27 Jehu **p** him and ordered,
25:5 The Babylonian army **p** King
2Ch 13:19 Abijah **p** Jeroboam and
14:13 Asa and his troops **p** them as
Neh 9:11 those who **p** your people as
Psa 143:3 The enemy has **p** me.
Jer 39:5 The Babylonian army **p** them
52:8 The Babylonian army **p** King
Lam 3:43 yourself with anger and **p** us.
Amo 1:11 The Edomites **p** their relatives

pursues (5)

Jos 20:5 can avenge the death **p** him,
Psa 10:2 The wicked person arrogantly **p**
35:6 of the LORD **p** them.
Pro 11:19 so whoever **p** evil finds his
21:21 Whoever **p** righteousness and

pursuing (12)

Gen 14:15 **p** them all the way to Hobah,
Jos 2:16 the men who are **p** you will not
Jdg 4:22 Barak was still **p** Sisera.
7:25 of Zeeb and kept on **p** Midian.
8:4 but they kept **p** the enemy.
8:5 They're exhausted, and I'm **p**
1Sm 14:46 Saul stopped **p** the Philistines.
23:28 Saul gave up **p** David and went
24:14 Whom are you **p**? A dead dog?
26:18 "Why are you **p** me?"
2Sm 18:16 and the troops returned from **p**
Psa 7:1 me from all who are **p** me.

pursuit (2)

1Sm 17:53 came back from their **p**
30:10 David and 400 men went in **p**,

push (9)

Dtr 33:17 They will use them to **p** away
1Ki 22:11 With these horns you will **p** the
2Ki 4:27 Gehazi went to **p** her away.
2Ch 18:10 With these horns you will **p** the
Psa 36:11 of wicked people **p** me away.
Jer 46:15 the LORD will **p** them down.
Eze 34:21 You fat sheep **p** the skinny
Amo 2:7 They **p** the humble out of the
Luk 5:3 to Simon and asked him to **p** off

pushed (13)

Gen 19:9 They **p** hard against Lot and
Exo 14:21 All that night the LORD **p** back
Jdg 16:29 he **p** hard against them.
16:30 he **p** with all his might,
Psa 36:12 They have been **p** down and
78:41 and they **p** the Holy One of
118:13 They **p** hard to make me fall,
Zec 5:8 and he **p** her back into the
Luk 6:48 the floodwaters **p** against that
6:49 The floodwaters **p** against it,
Act 7:27 one of the men **p** Moses aside.
7:39 Instead, they **p** him aside,
19:33 so the Jews **p** him to the front.

pushes (1)

Isa 59:19 The wind of the LORD **p** him.

Put (7)

Gen 10:6 Cush, Egypt, **P**, and Canaan.
1Ch 1:8 Cush, Egypt, **P**, and Canaan.
Jer 46:9 you warriors from Sudan and **P**
Eze 27:10 People from Persia, Lud, and **P**
30:5 Sudan, **P**, Lud, all the Arabs,
38:5 and **P** will be with you.
Nah 3:9 **P** and the Lybians were her

Puteoli (2)

Act 28:13 later we arrived at the city of **P**.
28:14 In **P** we discovered some

Puthites (1)

1Ch 2:53 Ithrites, the **P**, the Shumathites,

Putiel (1)
Exo 6:25 one of the daughters of **P**.

Puvah (1)
Gen 46:13 were Tola, **P**, Iob, and Shimron.

puzzled (6)
Luk 24:4 While they were **p** about this,
Act 2:12 men were stunned and **p**.
5:24 they were **p** about what could
10:17 While Peter was **p** by the
25:20 about these things left me **p**.
Gal 4:20 I'm completely **p** by what

Pyrrhus (1)
Act 20:4 Sopater (son of **P**) from Berea,

Q

quail (1)
Psa 105:40 and he brought them **q** and

quails (5)
Exo 16:13 That evening **q** came and
Num 11:31 from the sea that brought **q**
11:31 There were **q** on the ground
11:32 went out and gathered the **q**.
11:32 Then they spread the **q** out all

quake (6)
Psa 60:2 You made the land **q**.
99:1 the angels. Let the earth **q**.
Isa 64:1 would **q** at your presence.
Jer 49:21 The earth will **q** at the sound of
50:46 The earth will **q** at the news
Nah 1:5 The mountains **q** because of

quaked (5)
Jdg 5:4 the earth **q**, the sky poured,
2Sm 22:8 Then the earth shook and **q**.
Psa 18:7 Then the earth shook and **q**.
68:8 the earth **q** and the sky poured
Isa 64:3 mountains **q** in your presence.

quakes (3)
Psa 46:2 afraid even when the earth **q**
Joe 2:10 The earth **q** in their presence,
Amo 9:5 It **q**, and all who live on it

qualifications (3)
2Co 3:1 have to show you our **q** again?
5:12 trying to show you our **q** again,
Php 3:4 confidence in my physical **q**.

qualified (14)
Gen 47:6 If they are **q**, put them in charge
Num 4:3 ages of 30 and 50 who are **q**
4:23 ages of 30 and 50 who are **q**
4:30 ages of 30 and 50 who are **q**
4:35 ages of 30 and 50 who were **q**
4:39 ages of 30 and 50 who were **q**
4:43 ages of 30 and 50 who were **q**
4:47 ages of 30 and 50 who were **q**
Jdg 18:2 sent out five **q** men from Zorah
Act 1:23 that two men were **q**.
2Co 2:16 Who is **q** to tell about Christ?
3:5 By ourselves we are not **q** in
3:5 Rather, God makes us **q**.
3:6 He has also **q** us to be

qualities (6)
Rom 1:20 of the world, God's invisible **q**,
1Ti 1:6 Some people have left these **q**
1Pe 2:9 about the excellent **q** of God,
2Pe 1:8 If you have these **q** and they
1:9 If these **q** aren't present in your
1:12 remind you about these **q**,

quantities (2)
Gen 41:49 stored up grain in huge **q** like
2Ch 31:5 They brought large **q**,

quantity (11)
2Sm 8:8 King David also took a large **q**
1Ki 10:2 a very large **q** of gold,
10:10 a very large **q** of spices,
10:10 Never again was such a large **q**
10:11 Ophir also brought a large **q**
1Ch 18:8 David also took a large **q** of
22:3 David prepared a large **q** of iron
2Ch 9:1 spices, a large **q** of gold,
9:9 a very large **q** of spices,
9:9 Never was there such a large **q**
Luk 6:38 A large **q**, pressed together,

quarrel (23)
Gen 26:22 They didn't **q** over this one.
45:24 "Don't **q** on your way back!"
Exo 21:18 you must do whenever men **q**
Lev 24:10 got into a **q** with an Israelite in
2Ch 35:21 "What's your **q** with me,
Job 33:13 Why do you **q** with him since
Pro 3:30 Do not **q** with a person for no
17:14 Starting a **q** is like opening a
17:19 Whoever loves sin loves a **q**.
20:3 Avoiding a **q** is honorable.
26:17 involved in someone else's **q**.
26:20 without gossip a **q** dies down.
Isa 58:4 you **q** and fight and beat your
Mat 12:19 He will not **q** or shout,
Luk 22:24 Then a **q** broke out among the
Jon 6:52 The Jews began to **q** with
Act 23:7 and Sadducees began to **q**,
23:10 The **q** was becoming violent,
1Co 3:3 and **q** among yourselves,
1Ti 6:4 to argue and **q** about words.
2Ti 2:14 of God not to **q** over words.
2:24 servant of the Lord must not **q**.
Jas 4:2 You **q** and fight. You don't have

quarreled (4)
Gen 26:20 The herders from Gerar **q** with
26:21 and they **q** over that one too.
Dtr 33:8 You **q** with them at the oasis of
2Sm 14:6 I had two sons who **q** in the

quarreling (13)
Job 10:2 know why you are **q** with me.
Pro 13:10 Arrogance produces only **q**,
19:13 and a **q** woman is like
21:9 share a home with a **q** woman.
21:19 with a **q** and angry woman.
22:10 **Q** and abuse will stop.
25:24 share a home with a **q** woman.
27:15 a rainy day is like a **q** woman.
Rom 1:29 **q**, deceit, and viciousness.
1Co 1:11 you are **q** among yourselves.
16:11 Without **q**, give him your
Eph 4:31 loud **q**, cursing, and hatred.
2Ti 2:14 **Q** doesn't do any good but only

quarrels (14)
Gen 13:7 **Q** broke out between Abram's
13:8 let's not have any more **q**
Pro 10:12 Hate starts **q**, but love covers
16:28 A devious person spreads **q**.
18:18 Flipping a coin ends **q** and
23:29 Who has **q**? Who has a
Isa 45:9 it will be for the one who **q**
Jer 15:10 I am a man who argues and **q**
Hab 1:3 **Q** and disputes arise.
Act 24:5 He starts **q** among all Jews
1Ti 2:8 their anger and any **q** they have
2Ti 2:23 You know they cause **q**.
Tit 3:9 about genealogies, **q**,
Jas 4:1 fights and **q** among you?

quarrelsome (4)
Psa 31:20 safe from **q** tongues.
Pro 26:21 so a **q** person fuels a dispute.
1Ti 3:3 must not be **q** or love money.
Tit 3:2 shouldn't curse anyone or be **q**,

quarried (4)
1Ki 5:15 70,000 who **q** stone in the
5:18 and men from Gebal **q** the
2Ki 22:6 to buy lumber and **q** stones
2Ch 34:11 They were to buy **q** stones and

quarries (1)
Jos 7:5 gate to the slope of the stone **q**.

quarry (6)
1Ki 5:17 The king commanded them to **q**
6:7 that were finished at the **q**.
2Ch 2:2 80,000 to **q** stones in the
2:18 80,000 of them **q** stone in the
Ecc 10:9 Whoever works in a stone **q**
Isa 51:1 cut and to the **q** from which you

quart (14)
Exo 29:40 cups of flour mixed with one **q**
29:40 wine offering of one **q** of wine.
Lev 14:10 along with a **q** of olive oil.
14:12 of the male lambs and the **q**
14:21 a grain offering, a **q** of olive oil,
14:24 for the guilt offering and the **q**
23:13 Use one **q** of wine for the wine
Num 15:4 mixed with one **q** of olive oil.
15:5 an offering of one **q** of wine.
28:5 cups of flour mixed with one **q**
28:7 bring a wine offering of one **q**
28:14 with each lamb 1 **q** of wine.
Eze 4:11 out two-thirds of a **q** of water,
Rev 6:6 "A **q** of wheat for a day's pay or

quartermaster (6)
1Sm 17:22 behind in the hands of the **q**,
2Ki 18:17 his commander-in-chief, his **q**,
Jer 39:3 in Middle Gate: Nergal (the **q**),
39:3 Nergal (the **q** and the chief
39:13 Nergal (the **q** and the chief
51:59 (Seraiah was the **q**.)

quarters (11)
1Ki 7:8 His own private **q** were in a
7:8 Solomon also built private **q**
1Ch 9:18 gatekeepers for the Levite **q**.
Neh 3:30 repairs across from his living **q**.
Est 2:3 of Susa, to the women's **q**.
2:9 best place in the women's **q**.
2:11 the courtyard of the women's **q**
2:13 with her from the women's **q**
2:14 to the other **q** for women.
Mar 15:43 boldly went to Pilate's **q**
Act 12:20 in charge of the king's living **q**.)

quarts (23)
Exo 16:16 Take two **q** for each person in
16:22 much food, four **q** per person.
16:32 Take two **q** of manna to be
16:33 put two **q** of manna in it,
16:36 measure at that time held 20 **q**.)
30:24 place — and 4 **q** of olive oil.
Lev 23:13 Bring a grain offering of four **q**
23:17 Bake them with four **q** of flour.
24:5 ring will contain four **q** of flour.
27:16 Ground planted with 2 **q** of
Num 15:6 of flour mixed with 1 ¼ **q** of oil
15:7 an offering of 1 ¼ **q** of wine.
15:9 mixed with two **q** of olive oil.
15:10 an offering of two **q** of wine.
28:14 each bull will be 2 **q** of wine,
28:14 with each ram 1 ½ **q** of wine,
Jdg 6:19 bread made with 18 **q** of flour.
1Ki 18:32 a trench that could hold 12 **q**
Isa 5:10 and two **q** of seed will produce
5:10 produce only four **q** of grain."
Eze 46:14 three-and-a-third **q** of grain and
46:14 of grain and one-and-a-third **q**
Rev 6:6 wheat for a day's pay or three **q**

Quartus (1)
Rom 16:23 **Q**, our brother in the Christian

quartz (14)
Exo 28:17 In the first row put red **q**,
28:20 row put beryl, onyx, and gray **q**.
39:10 In the first row they put red **q**,
39:13 put beryl, onyx, and gray **q**.
Eze 28:13 red **q**, topaz, crystal, beryl,
28:13 gray **q**, sapphire, turquoise,
Rev 4:3 sitting there looked like gray **q**

Rev 4:3 like gray quartz and red **q**.
21:11 like gray **q**, as clear as crystal.
21:18 Its wall was made of gray **q**.
21:19 The first foundation was gray **q**,
21:20 the fifth onyx, the sixth red **q**,
21:20 the seventh yellow **q**,
21:20 ninth topaz, the tenth green **q**,

queen (55)

1Ki 10:1 The **q** of Sheba heard about
10:4 When the **q** of Sheba saw all of
10:10 ⌊into Israel⌋ as those that the **q**
10:13 King Solomon gave the **q** of
11:19 the sister of **Q** Tahpenes,
15:13 from the position of **q** mother
2Ki 10:13 of the king and the **q** mother."
2Ch 9:1 The **q** of Sheba heard about
9:3 When the **q** of Sheba saw
9:9 ⌊in Israel⌋ as those that the **q**
9:12 King Solomon gave the **q** of
15:16 from the position of **q** mother
Neh 2:6 Then, while the **q** was sitting
Est 1:9 **Q** Vashti also held a banquet
1:11 to bring **Q** Vashti in front of the
1:12 But **Q** Vashti refused the king's
1:15 what must we do with **Q**
1:16 "**Q** Vashti has done wrong,
1:17 The news of what the **q** has
1:17 'King Xerxes ordered **Q** Vashti
1:18 heard what the **q** did will talk
2:4 will become **q** instead of
2:17 made her **q** instead of Vashti.
2:22 about it and informed **Q** Esther.
4:4 The **q** was stunned.
5:2 When the king saw **Q** Esther
5:3 is troubling you, **Q** Esther?
5:12 **Q** Esther allowed no one
7:1 to have dinner with **Q** Esther.
7:2 is your request, **Q** Esther?
7:3 Then **Q** Esther answered,
7:5 King Xerxes interrupted **Q**
7:6 the presence of the king and **q**.
7:7 But Haman stayed to beg **Q**
7:8 "Is he even going to rape the **q**
8:1 of the Jews, to **Q** Esther.
8:7 King Xerxes said to **Q** Esther
9:12 So the king said to **Q** Esther,
9:29 Abihail's daughter **Q** Esther
9:31 Mordecai the Jew and **Q**
Psa 45:9 The **q** takes her place at your
Isa 47:5 be called the **q** of kingdoms.
47:7 said, "I will always be a **q**."
Jer 7:18 cakes for the **q** of heaven.
44:17 We will burn incense to the **q**
44:18 burning incense to the **q**
44:19 incense to the **q** of heaven,
44:25 We will burn incense to the **q**
Eze 16:13 eventually you became a **q**.
Dan 5:10 brought the **q** herself into
5:10 The **q** said, "Your Majesty,
Mat 12:42 The **q** from the south will stand
Luk 11:31 The **q** from the south will stand
Act 8:27 of **Q** Candace of Ethiopia.
Rev 18:7 'I'm a **q** on a throne,

queens (3)

Sos 6:8 There are 60 **q**, 80 concubines,
6:9 **Q** and concubines saw her and
Isa 49:23 and their **q** will nurse you.

quench (3)

Neh 9:15 flow from a rock to **q** their thirst.
9:20 them water to **q** their thirst.
Psa 104:11 Wild donkeys **q** their thirst.

question (28)

1Sm 9:9 person went to ask God ⌊a **q**⌋,
17:29 "Didn't I ⌊merely⌋ ask a **q**?"
17:30 man and asked the same **q**,
2Sm 3:8 Ishbosheth's **q** made Abner
14:18 refuse to answer the **q** I'm going
1Ki 10:3 No **q** was too difficult for the
2Ki 22:18 you to me to ask the LORD a **q**,
2Ch 9:2 No **q** was too difficult for
34:26 you to me to ask the LORD a **q**,
Ezr 5:9 their leaders the following **q**:
Job 9:3 to answer one **q** in a thousand.
Isa 41:28 When I ask them a **q**,
Jer 38:14 "I'm going to ask you a **q**," the
Dan 2:23 told me the answer to our **q**.
3:16 need to answer your last **q**.
Mat 21:24 them, "I, too, have a **q** for you.
22:46 one dared to ask him another **q**.
Mar 11:29 said to them, "I'll ask you a **q**.
12:34 one dared to ask him another **q**.
Luk 10:29 the man wanted to justify his **q**.
20:3 them, "I, too, have a **q** for you.
20:40 one dared to ask him another **q**.
Jon 6:6 Jesus asked this **q** to test him
9:17 had been born blind another **q**:
18:21 Why do you **q** me?
18:21 **Q** those who heard what I said
Act 22:24 and told them to **q** Paul as they
22:29 going to **q** Paul stepped away

questioned (8)

Jdg 8:14 He **q** him, and the young man
21:9 So they **q** the people,
Jer 38:27 came to Jeremiah and **q** him.
Luk 11:53 They **q** him about many things
23:14 I've **q** him in front of you and
Jon 18:19 The chief priest **q** Jesus about
Act 5:27 The chief priest **q** them.
12:19 So he **q** the guards and gave

questioning (1)

Jer 38:27 So they stopped **q** him,

questions (13)

Gen 43:7 We simply answered his **q**.
Jdg 16:16 his life miserable with her **q**.
1Ki 10:3 Solomon answered all her **q**.
2Ch 9:2 Solomon answered all her **q**.
Job 33:13 since he doesn't answer any **q**?
Luk 2:46 and asking them **q**.
23:9 Herod asked Jesus many **q**,
Jon 8:7 they persisted in asking him **q**,
16:23 you won't ask me any more **q**.
16:30 You don't need to wait for **q** to
1Co 4:3 I don't even ask myself **q**.
2Co 8:23 If any **q** are raised,
1Ti 1:4 a lot of **q** rather than promoting

quick (16)

Gen 18:6 "**Q**," he said, "get three
19:15 angels urged Lot by saying, "**Q**!
27:43 **Q**! Run away to my brother
28:2 **Q**! Go to Paddan Aram. Go to
1Sm 20:38 Jonathan added, "**Q**!
1Ki 20:33 were **q** to take him at his word.
22:9 for an officer and said, "**Q**!
2Ch 18:8 for an officer and said, "**Q**!
Pro 6:18 feet that are **q** to do wrong,
29:20 a person who is **q** to answer?
Ecc 7:9 Don't be **q** to get angry,
Isa 5:28 wheels are as **q** as the wind.
16:5 He is **q** to do what is right.
Mal 3:5 I will be **q** to testify against
Luk 16:6 **Q**! Sit down, and write "four
Jas 1:19 Everyone should be **q** to listen,

quicker (3)

Job 4:19 can be crushed **q** than a moth!
8:12 they would wither **q** than grass.
Hab 1:8 leopards and **q** than wolves

quickly (124)

Gen 18:7 his servant, who prepared it **q**.
19:22 Run there **q**, because I can't do
24:18 She **q** lowered her jar to her
24:20 So she **q** emptied her jar into
24:46 She **q** lowered her jar and said,
27:20 "How did you find it so **q**,
44:11 Each one **q** lowered his sack
Exo 9:20 servants and cattle indoors **q**.
10:16 Then Pharaoh **q** called for
12:33 people to leave the country **q**.
Num 16:46 and go **q** into the community to
Dtr 4:26 you will **q** disappear from the
7:4 you and will **q** destroy you.
7:22 be able to wipe them out **q**.
9:3 land and will **q** destroy them as
Dtr 9:12 They've **q** turned from the way I
9:16 You had **q** turned from the way
11:17 and you'll **q** disappear from this
28:20 destroyed and **q** disappear
32:35 Their doom is coming **q**.
Jos 8:19 and **q** set it on fire.
10:6 Come **q**, and save us. Help us
23:16 Then you will **q** disappear from
Jdg 2:17 They **q** turned from the ways of
2:23 to Joshua or forced them out **q**.
9:21 Then Jotham ran away **q**.
9:33 get up **q** and raid the city.
9:54 He **q** called his armorbearer.
13:10 The woman ran **q** to tell her
20:37 The men in ambush **q** charged
1Sm 4:14 So the man went **q** to tell Eli
17:48 David **q** ran toward the
20:41 rock⌋ and **q** bowed down three
23:27 to Saul and said, "Come **q**!
25:18 So Abigail **q** took 200 loaves of
25:23 When Abigail saw David, she **q**
25:34 you hadn't come to meet me **q**,
25:42 Then Abigail **q** got up and rode
2Sm 9:6 he **q** bowed down with his face
14:22 Joab **q** bowed down with his
17:16 Now send messengers **q** to tell
17:18 So both of them left **q** and
17:21 "Cross the river **q** because this
1Ki 20:41 Then he **q** took the bandage off
2Ki 4:22 I will go **q** to the man of God
13:21 So they **q** put the man into
2Ch 29:36 Everything had happened so **q**.
Est 6:14 arrived and **q** took Haman
8:14 They left **q**, in keeping with the
Job 5:3 but I **q** cursed his house.
9:25 "My days go by more **q** than a
9:26 They pass by **q** like boats
20:25 "Terrors come **q** to the godless
Psa 16:4 Those who **q** chase after other
22:19 Come **q** to help me,
31:2 Rescue me **q**. Be a rock of
37:2 They will **q** dry up like grass
38:22 Come **q** to help me,
40:13 Come **q** to help me,
69:17 face from me. Answer me **q**!
70:1 Come **q** to rescue me,
70:1 Come **q** to help me,
70:5 O God, come to me **q**.
71:12 O my God, come **q** to help me.
81:14 I would **q** defeat their enemies.
94:17 my soul would have **q** fallen
102:2 Answer me **q** when I call.
106:13 They **q** forgot what he did.
141:1 I cry out to you, "Come **q**."
143:7 Answer me **q**, O LORD.
Pro 20:21 An inheritance **q** obtained in
Ecc 8:11 a crime isn't carried out **q**,
Sos 8:14 Come away **q**, my beloved.
Isa 5:19 They say, "Let God hurry and **q**
5:19 of Israel happen **q** so that we
5:26 Look, they are coming very **q**!
8:1 Baz' [The Looting Will Come **Q**;
32:4 stutter will speak **q** and clearly.
52:12 nor will you go away **q**.
58:8 and you will heal **q**.
60:22 will make it happen **q**."
Jer 9:18 They should come **q** and cry
46:8 like a river **q** overflowing its
48:16 disaster is coming **q**.
Dan 6:19 the king got up and **q** went to
10:7 and they **q** hid themselves.
Hos 6:4 It disappears as **q** as the
13:3 morning dew that disappears **q**.
Joe 3:4 I will **q** pay you back for what
Hab 1:11 They will move **q** and pass
2:2 so that anyone can read it **q**.
Zep 1:14 It is near and coming very **q**.
Mat 5:25 "Make peace **q** with your
13:5 The plants sprouted **q** because
14:22 Jesus **q** made his disciples get
21:20 did the fig tree dry up so **q**?"
26:39 a little farther, he **q** bowed
26:49 Then Judas **q** stepped up to
28:7 Then go **q**, and tell his
Mar 1:28 The news about him spread **q**
4:5 The plants sprouted **q** because

Mar 4:37 boat so that it was **q** filling up.
5:22 When he saw Jesus, he **q**
5:33 So she **q** bowed in front of him
6:45 Jesus **q** made his disciples get
14:45 Then Judas **q** stepped up to
Luk 2:16 They went **q** and found Mary
6:49 and that house **q** collapsed and
8:41 arrived and **q** bowed down in
8:47 she **q** bowed in front of him.
17:16 He **q** bowed at Jesus' feet and
18:8 that he will give them justice **q**.
Jon 10:12 the sheep and **q** runs away.
11:29 she got up **q** and went to
11:31 saw her get up **q** and leave.
Act 7:29 After he said that, Moses **q** left
10:16 Then the sheet was **q** taken
26:28 "Do you think you can **q**
26:29 listening to me today would **q**
Rom 3:15 They run **q** to murder people.
16:20 The God of peace will **q** crush
1Co 14:25 and in this way they will **q** bow
Gal 1:6 you're so **q** deserting Christ,
Rev 2:16 or I will come to you **q** and

quiet (56)

Gen 25:27 Jacob remained a **q** man,
34:5 so Jacob kept **q** until they
Num 13:30 Caleb told the people to be **q**
Dtr 27:9 Israel, "Be **q** and listen, Israel.
Jdg 3:19 The king replied, "Keep **q**!"
16:2 They were **q** all night.
18:19 They told him, "Keep **q**!
1Sm 15:16 "Be **q**," Samuel told Saul,
2Sm 13:20 Sister, be **q** for now.
1Ki 19:12 And after the fire there was a **q**,
2Ki 2:3 I know. Be **q**."
2:5 I know. Be **q**."
11:20 But the city was **q** because
1Ch 4:40 and **q** because the Hamites
22:9 I will give Israel peace and **q**.
2Ch 23:21 But the city was **q** because
Job 3:26 I have no **q**! I have no rest! And
13:13 Be **q**, because I want to speak.
31:34 terrified me so that I kept **q**
33:31 Keep **q**, and let me speak.
33:33 Keep **q**, and I'll teach you
34:29 If he keeps **q**, who can
Psa 4:4 this on your bed and remain **q**.
83:1 Do not keep **q**, O God.
89:9 its waves rise, you **q** them.
94:13 You give him peace and **q** from
107:30 were glad that the storm was **q**.
131:2 have kept my soul calm and **q**.
Pro 11:12 has understanding keeps **q**.
29:9 but there is no peace and **q**.
Ecc 3:7 a time to keep **q** and a time to
4:6 One handful of peace and **q** is
12:4 who sing songs become **q**.
Isa 18:4 I will keep **q** and watch from
30:15 You can be strong by being **q**
32:18 homes and **q** places of rest.
42:14 I kept **q** and held myself back.
57:20 It isn't **q**, and its water throws
Jer 4:19 I can't keep **q** because I hear a
12:1 people have peace and **q**?
Eze 33:22 and I was no longer **q**.
Mat 20:31 The crowd told them to be **q**.
Mar 1:25 "Keep **q**, and come out of him!"
10:48 The people told him to be **q**.
Luk 4:35 "Keep **q**, and come out of him!"
18:39 told the blind man to be **q**.
19:39 tell your disciples to be **q**."
19:40 can guarantee that if they are **q**,
Act 12:17 with his hand to **q** them down
19:33 motioned with his hand to **q**
19:36 So you have to be **q** and not do
21:40 his hand for the people to be **q**.
22:2 they became even more **q**.
1Ti 2:2 people so that we can have a **q**
2:12 Instead, she should be **q**.
1Pe 3:4 and **q** attitude which God

quieted (1)

Act 19:35 city clerk finally **q** the crowd.

quietly (5)

Jdg 4:21 took a tent peg and walked **q**
1Sm 24:4 think is right.'" David **q** got up
Job 3:13 I would now be **q** lying down.
29:21 **q** waiting for my advice.
1Th 4:11 make it your goal to live **q**,

quilts (1)

Pro 31:22 She makes **q** for herself.

Quirinius (1)

Luk 2:2 taken while **Q** was governor

quit (4)

Exo 5:5 Do you want them to **q**
Luk 12:29 and **q** worrying about these
Act 13:10 **Q** trying to distort the truth
Eph 4:28 Thieves must **q** stealing and,

quiver (6)

Gen 27:3 equipment, your **q** and bow,
Job 39:23 A **q** of arrows rattles on it along
Psa 127:5 who has filled his **q** with them.
Isa 22:6 Elam takes its **q** of arrows,
49:2 arrow and hid me in his **q**.
Lam 3:13 arrows from his **q** into my heart

quivered (1)

Hab 3:16 At the report my lips **q**.

quivering (1)

Job 16:5 and my **q** lips could ease ⌊your

quivers (2)

Jer 5:16 Their arrow **q** are like open
51:11 Sharpen the arrows; fill the **q**.

quota (1)

1Ki 4:28 They brought their **q** of barley

quote (3)

Psa 50:16 "How dare you **q** my decrees
Eze 12:23 You will no longer **q** it in Israel.'
Luk 4:23 "You'll probably **q** this proverb

quoted (2)

Act 28:25 left after Paul had **q** this
Heb 4:7 David in the passage already

R

Raama (1)

1Ch 1:9 Sabta, **R**, and Sabteca.

Raamah (2)

Gen 10:7 Sabtah, **R**, and Sabteca.
Eze 27:22 from Sheba and **R** traded

Raamah's (1)

Gen 10:7 **R** descendants were Sheba

Raama's (1)

1Ch 1:9 **R** descendants were Sheba

Raamiah (1)

Neh 7:7 **R**, Nahamani, Mordecai,

Rabbah (15)

Dtr 3:11 still in the Ammonite city of **R**.)
Jos 13:25 as far as Aroer, which is by **R**.
15:60 called Kiriath Jearim) and **R**
2Sm 11:1 the Ammonites and attacked **R**,
12:26 against the Ammonite city of **R**
12:27 "I fought against **R** and
12:29 all the troops and went to **R**.
17:27 of Nahash from **R** in Ammon,
1Ch 20:1 the Ammonites and came to **R**
20:1 Joab defeated **R** and tore it
Jer 49:2 sound the battle cry against **R**,
49:3 Cry, people of **R**, put on your
Eze 21:20 take to the Ammonite city of **R**,
25:5 I will turn **R** into a pasture for
Amo 1:14 I will set fire to the walls of **R**

Rabbah's (2)

2Sm 12:30 crown from the head of **R** king
1Ch 20:2 crown from the head of **R** king

Rabbi (15)

Mat 23:7 and to have people call them **R**.
23:8 don't make others call you **R**,
26:25 don't mean me, do you, **R**?"
26:49 to Jesus and said, "Hello, **R**!"
Mar 9:5 Peter said to Jesus, "**R**,
11:21 so he said to Jesus, "**R**, look!
14:45 up to Jesus and said, "**R**!"
Jon 1:38 "**R**" (which means "teacher"),
1:49 Nathanael said to Jesus, "**R**,
3:2 one night and said to him, "**R**,
3:26 to John and asked him, "**R**,
4:31 "**R**, have something to eat."
6:25 "**R**, when did you get here?"
9:2 His disciples asked him, "**R**,
11:8 The disciples said to him, "**R**,

Rabbith (1)

Jos 19:20 **R**, Kishion, Ebez,

rabbits (3)

Lev 11:6 You must never eat **r**.
11:6 (**R** are unclean because they
Dtr 14:7 They include camels, **r**,

Rabboni (1)

Jon 20:16 and said to him in Hebrew, "**R**!"

Racal (1)

1Sm 30:29 **R**, the cities belonging to the

race (12)

Ezr 9:2 They have mixed our holy **r**
Psa 87:5 "Every **r** is born in it.
87:6 "Every **r** ⌊claims that it⌋ was
Pro 8:31 and delighted in the human **r**.
Ecc 9:11 The **r** isn't ⌊won⌋ by fast
Zec 9:6 A mixed **r** will live in Ashdod,
Act 10:28 visit with anyone of another **r**.
20:24 I want to finish the **r** I'm running
1Co 9:24 everyone who runs in a **r** runs
1Th 2:15 enemies of the whole human **r**
2Ti 4:7 I have completed the **r**.
Heb 12:1 We must run the **r** that lies

raced (1)

Jer 12:5 "If you have **r** against others on

Rachel (45)

Gen 29:6 his daughter **R** with the sheep."
29:9 **R** arrived with her father's
29:10 Jacob saw **R**, daughter of his
29:11 kissed **R** and sobbed loudly.
29:12 When Jacob told **R** that he was
29:16 of the younger one was **R**.
29:17 Leah had attractive eyes, but **R**
29:18 Jacob loved **R**. So he offered,
29:18 for your younger daughter **R**."
29:20 seven years in return for **R**,
29:25 I work for you in return for **R**?
29:28 Laban gave his daughter **R**
29:29 to his daughter **R** as her slave.)
29:30 Jacob slept with **R** too.
29:30 He loved **R** more than Leah.
29:31 have children, but **R** had none.
30:1 **R** saw that she could not have
30:2 angry with **R** and asked,
30:6 **R** said, "Now God has judged
30:8 **R** said, "I have had a great
30:14 **R** said to Leah, "Please give
30:15 **R** said, "Very well, Jacob can
30:22 Then God remembered **R**.
30:25 After **R** gave birth to Joseph,
31:4 So Jacob sent a message to **R**
31:14 **R** and Leah answered him,
31:19 **R** stole her father's idols.
31:32 (Jacob didn't know that **R** had
31:34 **R** had taken the idols and had
31:35 **R** said to her father,
33:1 Leah, **R**, and the two slaves.

Gen 33:2 and **R** and Joseph last.
33:7 Finally, Joseph and **R** came
35:16 **R** went into labor and was
35:18 **R** was dying. As she took her
35:19 **R** died and was buried on the
35:24 The sons of **R** were Joseph
44:27 'You know that my wife ⌊**R**⌋
46:19 The sons of Jacob's wife **R**
46:22 of **R** who were born
46:25 Laban gave to his daughter **R**.
48:7 **R** died in Canaan when we
Rut 4:11 your home, like **R** and Leah,
Jer 31:15 **R** is crying for her children.
Mat 2:18 **R** was crying for her children.

Rachel's (5)

Gen 30:7 **R** slave Bilhah became
31:33 Leah's tent and went into **R** tent
35:20 The same marker is at **R** grave
35:25 The sons of **R** slave Bilhah
1Sm 10:2 two men will be at **R** grave on

racing (2)

Sos 2:8 the mountains, **r** over the hills.
Nah 2:4 Chariots are **r** madly through

Raddai (1)

1Ch 2:14 (his fourth son), **R** (his fifth son

radiant (4)

Psa 19:8 The command of the LORD is **r**.
34:5 All who look to him will be **r**.
76:4 You are the **r** one. You are more
Act 10:30 Suddenly, a man dressed in **r**

rafters (3)

1Ki 6:16 boards from the floor to the **r**.
2Ch 3:7 the **r**, the threshold, the walls,
Sos 1:17 The cypress trees will be our **r**.

rafts (2)

1Ki 5:9 have them make them into **r**
2Ch 2:16 Then we will make **r** out of it

rage (25)

Dtr 19:6 Otherwise, in a **r** the relative
2Ki 19:27 and how you **r** against me.
19:28 Since you **r** against me and
2Ch 28:9 You killed them in a **r** that
Est 1:12 and his **r** burned inside him.
Psa 6:1 anger or discipline me in your **r**.
37:8 and leave **r** behind.
38:3 on my body because of your **r**.
59:13 Destroy them in your **r**.
69:24 Pour your **r** on them.
78:49 He sent his burning anger, **r**,
88:7 Your **r** lies heavily on me.
90:7 us. Your **r** terrifies us.
Pro 15:1 A gentle answer turns away **r**,
19:12 The **r** of a king is like the roar
20:2 The **r** of a king is like the roar
Isa 37:28 and how you **r** against me.
37:29 Since you **r** against me and
Jer 21:5 and **r** with my powerful hand
Dan 3:13 Then, in a fit of **r** and anger,
Nah 1:6 stand in the presence of his **r**?
1:6 He pours out his **r** like fire and
Hab 2:15 drink from the bowl of God's **r**,
Zep 3:8 together, and to pour my **r**,
Act 26:11 In my furious **r** against them,

rages (1)

Pro 19:3 his heart **r** against the LORD.

raging (44)

Exo 15:10 They sank like lead in the **r**
24:17 of the LORD looked like a **r** fire
Dtr 4:24 The LORD your God is a **r** fire,
9:3 going ahead of you like a **r** fire.
18:16 our God or see this **r** fire again.
33:2 his right was a **r** fire for them.
2Sm 22:9 and a **r** fire came out of his
22:17 He pulled me out of the **r** water.
Neh 9:11 throws a stone into **r** water.
Est 2:1 Xerxes got over his **r** anger,
7:10 Then the king got over his **r**
Job 3:17 There the wicked stop their **r**.
Psa 18:8 and a **r** fire came out of his
18:16 He pulled me out of the **r** water.
29:3 The LORD shouts over **r** water.
32:6 Then **r** floodwater will not
50:3 him and a **r** storm around him.
55:8 from the **r** wind and storm."
77:19 Your path went through **r** water,
89:9 You rule the **r** sea.
93:4 than the sound of **r** water,
124:5 Then **r** water would have
144:7 and rescue me from **r** waters
Sos 8:7 **R** water cannot extinguish
Isa 8:7 to bring against them the **r**
10:16 A flame will be turned into a **r**
17:13 will make noise like **r** water.
Jer 2:30 You killed my prophets like a **r**
4:13 His chariots are like a **r** wind.
51:55 come roaring in like **r** water.
Lam 2:3 He burned like a **r** fire in ⌊the
Dan 7:11 destroyed and put into a **r** fire.
Hos 7:6 the morning it burns like a **r** fire
Nah 1:3 **R** winds and storms mark his
Hab 3:15 into the mighty **r** waters.
2Co 11:26 I've faced dangers from **r** rivers,
Heb 10:27 judgment and a **r** fire that will
11:34 put out **r** fires, and escaped
Rev 1:15 was like the sound of **r** waters.
14:2 heaven like the noise of **r** water
17:1 prostitute who sits on **r** waters.
18:9 the smoke rise from her **r** fire.
18:18 the smoke rise from her **r** fire,
19:6 like the noise of **r** waters,

rags (4)

Pro 23:21 will dress a person in **r**.
Isa 64:6 are like permanently stained **r**.
Jer 38:11 He took **r** and torn clothes from
38:12 "Put these **r** and torn clothes

Rahab (13)

Jos 2:1 house of a prostitute named **R**
2:3 Jericho sent messengers to **R**,
2:8 **R** went up to them on the roof.
6:17 Only the prostitute **R** and all
6:23 spies went and brought out **R**,
6:25 Joshua spared the prostitute **R**,
Job 26:12 he killed **R** ⌊the sea monster⌋.
Psa 89:10 You crushed **R**; it was like a
Isa 30:7 why I call it, '**R** who sits still.'
51:9 Didn't you cut **R** into pieces
Mat 1:5 Salmon and **R** were the father
Heb 11:31 Faith led the prostitute **R** to
Jas 2:25 the prostitute **R** who welcomed

Rahab's (1)

Job 9:13 Even **R** helpers bow humbly in

Raham (1)

1Ch 2:44 Shema was the father of **R**,

raid (6)

Jdg 9:33 get up quickly and **r** the city.
1Sm 27:8 men went to **r** the Geshurites,
27:10 "Whom did you **r** today?"
2Sm 3:22 were coming home from a **r**
2Ki 6:23 **r** Israel's territory anymore.
Job 1:17 three companies and made a **r**

raided (6)

1Sm 30:1 Amalekites had **r** the Negev,
30:14 We **r** the portion of the Negev
1Ch 14:9 The Philistines had come and **r**
14:13 Philistines again **r** the valley.
2Ch 25:13 couldn't go with him into battle **r**
28:18 The Philistines had **r** the

raiders (2)

Gen 49:19 will be attacked by a band of **r**,
2Ch 22:1 because the **r** who came to the

raiding (8)

1Sm 13:17 **R** parties left the Philistine
14:15 The **r** party also trembled ⌊in
23:27 Philistines are **r** the country."
2Sm 4:2 who were captains of **r** parties.
2Ki 13:20 Moabite **r** parties used to
13:21 man saw one of these **r** parties.
24:2 The LORD sent **r** parties of
1Ch 12:21 They helped David fight **r**

raids (2)

Jdg 11:3 and went out ⌊on **r**⌋ with him.
2Ki 5:2 when the Arameans went on **r**,

railing (1)

Dtr 22:8 put a **r** around the edge of the

rain (100)

Gen 2:5 the LORD God hadn't sent **r**
7:4 In seven days I will send **r** to
7:12 and **r** came pouring down on
8:2 and the **r** had stopped pouring.
19:24 burning sulfur and fire **r** out
Exo 9:33 and no more **r** came pouring
9:34 When Pharaoh saw that the **r**,
16:4 you food from heaven like **r**.
Lev 26:4 "I will give you **r** at the right
26:19 You will have no **r**,
Dtr 11:11 watered by **r** from the sky.
11:14 I will send **r** on your land at the
11:17 the sky so that there'll be no **r**.
28:12 He will send **r** on your land at
32:2 like gentle **r** on grass,
1Sm 12:17 and he'll send thunder and **r**.
12:18 sent thunder and **r** so that all
2Sm 1:21 may there be no dew or **r** on
22:12 the dark **r** clouds his covering.
23:4 The **r** makes the grass grow
1Ki 8:35 the sky is shut and there's no **r**
8:36 Then send **r** on the land,
17:1 there will be no dew or **r** during
17:7 up because no **r** had fallen
17:14 Until the LORD sends **r** on the
18:1 I will allow **r** to fall on the
18:41 like a heavy **r** ⌊is coming⌋."
18:44 leave before the **r** delays you.'"
18:45 and there was a heavy **r**.
2Ki 3:17 You will not see wind or **r**,
7:2 poured **r** through windows
7:19 poured **r** through windows
2Ch 6:26 the sky is shut and there's no **r**
6:27 Then send **r** on the land,
7:13 the sky so that there is no **r**,
Ezr 10:9 because of the heavy **r**.
Job 5:10 He gives **r** to the earth and
20:23 wrath come down on him like **r**.
28:26 when he made rules for the **r**
29:23 to hear me as they were for **r**.
36:27 He distills **r** from his mist,
37:6 and to the pouring **r**,
37:6 to the pouring rain, '**R** harder!'
38:26 to bring **r** on a land where no
38:28 Does the **r** have a father?
Psa 18:11 the dark **r** clouds his covering.
18:12 those **r** clouds passed by with
65:10 drench plowed fields ⌊with **r**⌋
68:9 the land with plenty of **r**,
72:6 May he be like **r** that falls on
105:32 of **r** throughout their land.
147:8 He provides **r** for the ground.
Pro 16:15 is like a cloud bringing spring **r**.
25:23 ⌊As⌋ the north wind brings **r**,
26:1 Like snow in summertime and **r**
28:3 is like a driving **r** that leaves no
Ecc 11:3 If the clouds are full of **r**,
12:2 the clouds come back with **r**.
Sos 2:11 The **r** is over and gone.
Isa 4:6 hiding place from storms and **r**.
5:6 the clouds not to **r** on it.
25:4 a shelter from the **r**,
30:23 The Lord will give you **r** for the
32:2 and a hiding place from the **r**.
44:3 water on thirsty ground and **r**
44:14 and the **r** makes them grow.
45:8 **R** down from above,
55:10 "**R** and snow come down from
55:11 is like the **r** and snow.
Jer 3:3 So the **r** has been withheld,
5:24 He sends **r** at the right time,
5:24 the autumn **r** and the spring
5:24 autumn rain and the spring **r**.

Jer 10:13 lightning flash with the **r**.
14:4 because there has been no **r**
14:22 of the nations can't make it **r**.
51:16 He sends lightning with the **r**.
Eze 13:11 **R** will pour down, and stormy
13:13 In my anger **r** will pour down,
22:24 land that has not had **r** during
34:26 I will send **r** at the right time.
Hos 10:12 he will **r** righteousness on you.
Joe 2:23 He has sent the autumn **r** and
2:23 rain and the spring **r** as before.
Amo 4:7 I stopped the **r** from falling three
4:7 I sent **r** on one city and not on
4:7 One field had **r**. Another field
Zec 10:1 Ask the LORD for **r** in the
10:1 He gives everyone **r** showers
14:17 then **r** won't fall on them.
14:18 then ⌊**r**⌋ won't fall⌊ on them.
Mat 5:45 He lets **r** fall on them whether
7:25 **R** poured, and floods came.
7:27 **R** poured, and floods came.
Act 14:17 He gives you **r** from heaven
28:2 it because of the **r** and the cold.
Heb 6:7 So **r** often falls on it,
Jas 5:17 he prayed that it wouldn't **r**,
5:17 no **r** fell on the ground for
Rev 11:6 to keep **r** from falling during

rainbow (6)

Gen 9:13 I will put my **r** in the clouds to
9:14 a **r** will appear in the clouds.
9:16 Whenever the **r** appears in the
Eze 1:28 all around him looked like a **r**
Rev 4:3 There was a **r** around the
10:1 and there was a **r** over his

raindrops (1)

Dtr 32:2 teachings come down like **r**.

rained (6)

2Sm 21:10 of the harvest until the sky **r**
Psa 78:24 He **r** manna down on them to
78:27 He **r** meat down on them like
Luk 4:25 It had not **r** for three-and-a-half
17:29 fire and sulfur **r** from the sky
Jas 5:18 It **r**, and the ground produced

rains (7)

Job 36:31 This is how he uses the **r** to
38:25 a channel for the flooding **r**
Psa 11:6 He **r** down fire and burning
84:6 The early **r** cover it with
Hos 6:3 come to us like the autumn **r**
6:3 rains and the spring **r** that water
Jas 5:7 patiently for fall and spring **r**.

rainstorm (3)

2Sm 23:4 like the brightness after a **r**.
Isa 25:4 breath is like a **r** against a wall,
Luk 12:54 going to be a **r**,' and it happens.

rainstorms (4)

Job 24:8 They are drenched by the **r** in
Isa 29:6 windstorms, **r**, and fire storms.
30:30 windstorms, **r**, and hailstones.
Eze 38:22 I will send **r**, large hailstones,

rainy (2)

Ezr 10:13 and it's the **r** season.
Pro 27:15 Constantly dripping water on a **r**

raise (43)

Gen 14:22 "I now **r** my hand and solemnly
Exo 14:16 **R** your staff, stretch out your
Dtr 32:40 I **r** my hand toward heaven and
1Sm 24:6 for me to **r** my hand against
24:10 'I will not **r** my hand against
2Sm 12:17 beside him to **r** him up from
18:12 I wouldn't **r** my hand against
2Ki 4:28 I said, 'Don't **r** my hopes.'"
Psa 41:10 **R** me up so that I can pay them
75:4 "Don't **r** your weapons.
75:5 Don't **r** your weapons so
Pro 4:8 It will **r** you up. It will bring you
8:1 not understanding **r** its voice?
Isa 10:24 when they **r** their staff against
10:26 Then the LORD of Armies will **r**
11:12 He will **r** a banner for the
13:2 **R** a banner on the bare
24:14 They **r** their voices.
40:9 **R** your voice without fear.
42:2 will not cry out or **r** ⌊his voice⌋.
42:11 and its cities **r** their voices.
49:22 I will **r** my flag for the people.
52:8 Your watchmen **r** their voices
58:1 **R** your voice like a ram's horn.
62:10 **R** a flag for the people!
Jer 4:6 **R** the flag to signal people to
6:1 **R** the flag over Beth Hakkerem,
22:20 **R** your voice in Bashan!
50:2 **R** a flag, and announce it.
51:12 **R** your battle flag in front of the
51:27 **R** your battle flag throughout
Lam 3:41 Let us **r** our hearts and hands to
Eze 21:22 the order to kill, **r** a battle cry,
26:8 and **r** his shields against you.
36:7 I **r** my hand and swear that the
Dan 11:11 who will **r** a large army that will
11:13 northern king will return and **r**
Hos 6:2 On the third day he will **r** us so
Mat 3:9 I can guarantee that God can **r**
Luk 3:8 I guarantee that God can **r** up
1Co 6:14 his power God will also **r** us.
1Ti 1:4 These myths and genealogies **r**
2:8 They should **r** their hands in

raised (62)

Exo 7:20 Aaron **r** his staff and struck the
Lev 9:22 Then Aaron **r** his hands toward
Num 14:1 community **r** their voices
14:30 I **r** my hand and swore an oath
20:11 Moses **r** his hand and hit the
1Sm 18:11 He **r** the spear and thought,
20:33 Saul **r** his spear to strike him.
2Sm 12:3 He **r** her, and she grew up in
23:1 by the man whom God **r** up,
1Ki 11:14 The LORD **r** up Hadad the
11:23 God also **r** up Rezon,
16:2 He said, "I **r** you from the dust
2Ki 3:4 King Mesha of Moab **r** sheep.
10:6 These men had **r** them.
15:20 Menahem **r** the money from all
Neh 8:4 Ezra the scribe stood on a **r**
8:6 as they **r** their hands and then
Est 2:7 Mordecai had **r** Hadassah,
Job 38:15 and an arm **r** ⌊in victory⌋ is
Psa 27:6 Now my head will be **r** above
60:4 Yet, you have **r** a flag for those
75:10 people will be **r** proudly.
89:19 I have **r** up one chosen from the
112:9 His head is **r** in honor.
Pro 11:11 of decent people a city is **r** up,
Isa 1:2 The LORD has spoken, "I **r**
2:2 of the mountains and **r** above
10:26 of Oreb and **r** his staff over
16:10 No shouts are **r**. No one stomps
23:4 I've **r** no sons. I've brought up
40:4 Every valley will be **r**.
41:2 "Who has **r** up from the east
41:25 "I have **r** up someone from the
49:21 Who **r** these ⌊children for me⌋?
51:18 From all the children she **r**,
Lam 2:17 He **r** the weapons of your
2:22 the children I nursed and **r**."
Eze 11:22 Then the angels **r** their wings,
19:3 One of the cubs she **r** became
19:5 one of her cubs and **r** him into
20:5 I **r** my hand and swore an oath
20:23 I **r** my hand and swore an oath
41:8 I also saw a **r** base all around
44:12 So I **r** my hand and swore that
47:14 I **r** my hand and swore that I
Dan 7:5 It was **r** on one side and had
12:7 He **r** his right hand and left
Mic 4:1 of the mountains and **r** above
Zec 1:21 The nations **r** their horns to
5:7 cover ⌊on the basket⌋ was **r**,
Mat 17:8 As they **r** their heads,
Luk 1:69 He has **r** up a mighty Savior for
24:50 There he **r** his hands and
Act 2:24 But God **r** him from death to life
7:21 adopted him and **r** him as her
22:3 I was born and **r** in the city of
27:13 They **r** the anchor and sailed
27:40 Then they **r** the top sail to
1Co 6:14 God **r** the Lord, and by his
15:32 If the dead are not **r**,
2Co 8:23 If any questions are **r**,
Rev 10:5 and on the land **r** his right hand

raises (6)

1Sm 2:6 and he **r** them up ⌊again⌋.
2:8 He **r** the poor from the dust.
Pro 1:20 public squares she **r** her voice.
Isa 5:26 The LORD **r** up a flag for the
14:9 It **r** all who were kings of the
18:3 Look when someone **r** a flag on

raisin (4)

2Sm 6:19 one date cake, and one **r** cake.
1Ch 16:3 a date cake, and a **r** cake.
Isa 16:7 Mourn and grieve over the **r**
Hos 3:1 gods and love to eat **r** cakes."

raising (2)

Psa 106:26 **R** his hand, he swore that he
1Ti 5:10 **r** children, being hospitable,

raisins (7)

Num 6:3 never eat fresh grapes or **r**.
1Sm 25:18 roasted grain, 100 bunches of **r**,
30:12 fig cake and two bunches of **r**.
2Sm 16:1 of bread, 100 bunches of **r**,
1Ki 14:3 ten loaves of bread, some **r**,
1Ch 12:40 cakes, **r**, wine, olive oil, cattle,
Sos 2:5 Strengthen me with **r** and

Rakem (1)

1Ch 7:16 whose sons were Ulam and **R**.

Rakkath (1)

Jos 19:35 Zer, Hammath, **R**, Chinnereth,

Rakkon (1)

Jos 19:46 Me Jarkon, and **R**,

rallied (2)

1Sm 13:4 All the troops **r** behind Saul at
2Sm 2:25 of Benjamin **r** behind Abner,

rally (1)

Psa 60:4 who fear you so that they can **r**

ram (95)

Gen 15:9 female goat, a three-year-old **r**,
22:13 he saw a **r** behind him caught
22:13 So Abraham took the **r** and
Exo 29:17 Cut the **r** into pieces,
29:18 Then burn the whole **r** on the
29:19 "Take the other **r**. Then Aaron
29:22 "From this ⌊same⌋ **r** take the
29:22 (This is the **r** for the ordination.
29:26 "Take the breast from the **r**
29:27 Both will come from the **r** used
29:31 "Take the **r** used for the
29:32 sons will eat the meat of the **r**
Lev 5:15 It must be a **r** that has no
5:16 So the priest will use the **r**
5:18 You must bring the priest a **r**
6:6 a **r** that has no defects or its
8:18 He brought forward the **r** for the
8:20 When the **r** was cut into pieces,
8:21 Then Moses burned the whole **r**
8:22 brought forward the second **r**
8:29 also took the breast from the **r**
9:2 for sin and a **r** that has no
9:4 a bull and a **r** as a fellowship
9:18 slaughtered the bull and the **r**
9:19 the fat from the bull and the **r**
16:3 as an offering for sin and a **r** as
16:5 as an offering for sin and a **r** as
19:21 He must bring a **r** for his guilt
Num 5:8 to the **r** which makes peace
6:14 and a **r** as a fellowship offering.
6:17 He will sacrifice the **r** as a
6:19 of the shoulders from a boiled **r**,
7:15 a young bull, a **r**, and a
7:21 a young bull, a **r**, and a

Num 7:27 a young bull, a **r**, and a
7:33 a young bull, a **r**, and a
7:39 a young bull, a **r**, and a
7:45 a young bull, a **r**, and a
7:51 a young bull, a **r**, and a
7:57 a young bull, a **r**, and a
7:63 a young bull, a **r**, and a
7:69 a young bull, a **r**, and a
7:75 a young bull, a **r**, and a
7:81 a young bull, a **r**, and a
15:6 "With a **r**, give a grain offering
15:11 Do this for each bull, each **r**,
23:2 a bull and a **r** on each altar.
23:4 a bull and a **r** on each altar."
23:14 a bull and a **r** on each altar.
23:30 a bull and a **r** on each altar.
28:11 of two young bulls, one **r**,
28:12 with each **r** a grain offering of
28:14 with each **r** 1 ½ quarts of
28:19 of two young bulls, one **r**,
28:20 16 cups for each **r**,
28:27 LORD — two young bulls, one **r**,
28:28 16 cups for each **r**,
29:2 bring one young bull, one **r**,
29:3 16 cups for each **r**,
29:8 bring one young bull, one **r**,
29:9 16 cups for each **r**,
29:36 the LORD, bring one bull, one **r**,
29:37 the bull, the **r**, and the lambs.
Rut 4:19 Hezron was the father of **R**.
4:19 **R** was the father of
1Ch 2:9 Jerahmeel, **R**, and Chelubai.
2:10 **R** was the father of
2:25 fathered **R** (his firstborn),
2:27 The sons of **R** (the firstborn son
Ezr 10:19 They sacrificed a **r** from their
Job 32:2 of Buz from the family of **R**,
Pro 7:22 like a **r** hobbling into captivity
Eze 43:23 offer a young bull and a **r** that
43:25 and a **r** from the flock as an
45:24 and a half-bushel for each **r**.
46:4 defects and one **r** that has no
46:5 is to be brought with the **r** must
46:6 and one **r** — all animals that
46:7 each young bull and each **r**
46:11 must be brought with each **r**.
Dan 8:3 I looked up and saw a single **r**
8:3 The **r** had two long horns,
8:4 I saw the **r** charging west,
8:6 toward the two-horned **r** that
8:6 It furiously ran at the **r**.
8:7 I saw it come closer to the **r**.
8:7 was extremely angry with the **r**,
8:7 so it attacked the **r**.
8:7 The **r** didn't have the strength to
8:7 So the **r** was thrown down on
8:7 No one could rescue the **r** from
8:20 "The two-horned **r** that you saw
Nah 2:5 been set up for the battering **r**.
Mat 1:3 Hezron the father of **R**,
1:4 **R** the father of Amminadab,

Ramah (39)

Jos 18:25 villages: Gibeon, **R**, Beeroth,
19:29 Then it turns at **R** and goes on
19:36 Adamah, **R**, Hazor,
Jdg 4:5 Tree of Deborah between **R**
19:13 the night either at Gibeah or **R**."
1Sm 1:19 Then they returned home to **R**.
2:11 Then Elkanah went home to **R**.
7:17 he would return home to **R**.
7:17 And in **R** he built an altar to the
8:4 and came to Samuel at **R**.
15:34 Then Samuel went to **R**,
16:13 Then Samuel left for **R**.
19:18 and went to Samuel at **R**.
19:19 David was in the pastures at **R**,
19:22 Then he went to **R** himself.
19:22 there in the pastures at **R**."
19:23 went toward the pastures at **R**,
19:23 he came to the pastures at **R**.
20:1 fled from the pastures at **R**,
25:1 buried him at his home in **R**.
28:3 buried him in his hometown **R**.
1Ki 15:17 invaded Judah and fortified **R**
15:21 he stopped fortifying **R** and
15:22 the stones and lumber from **R**.
2Ki 8:29 by the Arameans at **R** when
1Ch 27:27 the vineyards: Shimei from **R**
2Ch 16:1 invaded Judah and fortified **R**
16:5 he stopped fortifying **R** and
16:6 took everyone in Judah ⌊to **R**⌋.
16:6 the stones and lumber from **R**.
22:6 by the Arameans at **R** when
Ezr 2:26 of **R** and Geba: 621
Neh 7:30 of **R** and Geba: 621
11:33 Hazor, **R**, Gittaim,
Isa 10:29 The people in **R** tremble;
Jer 31:15 A sound is heard in **R**,
40:1 of the guard, let him go at **R**.
Hos 5:8 Blow the trumpet in **R**.
Mat 2:18 "A sound was heard in **R**,

Ramathaim Zophim (1)

1Sa 1:1 named Elkanah from **R** in the

Ramath Lehi (1)

Jdg 15:17 called that place **R** [Jawbone Hill

Ramath Mizpeh (1)

Jos 13:26 from Heshbon to **R** and Betonim

Ramath Negev (1)

Jos 19:8 Baalath Beer and **R** were also

ramble (2)

Psa 94:4 They **r**. They speak arrogantly.
Mat 6:7 "When you pray, don't **r** like

Rameses (5)

Gen 47:11 part of Egypt, the region of **R**.
Exo 1:11 They built Pithom and **R** as
12:37 The Israelites left **R** to go to
Num 33:3 They moved from **R** on the
33:5 The Israelites moved from **R**

Ramiah (1)

Ezr 10:25 **R**, Izziah, Malchiah, Mijamin,

Ramoth (22)

Dtr 4:43 **R** in Gilead for the tribe of Gad,
Jos 20:8 **R** in Gilead from the tribe of
21:38 **R** in Gilead (a city of refuge for
1Sm 30:27 Bethel, **R** in the Negev, Jattir,
1Ki 22:3 "Do you know that **R** in Gilead
22:4 me to fight at **R** in Gilead?"
22:6 "Should I go to war against **R**
22:6 Lord will hand over **R** to you."
22:12 They said, "Attack **R** in Gilead,
22:15 should we go to war against **R**
22:20 and be killed at **R** in Gilead?'
22:29 of Judah went to **R** in Gilead.
1Ch 6:73 **R** with its pastureland,
6:80 they received **R** in Gilead with
2Ch 18:2 Jehoshaphat to attack **R**
18:3 go with me to **R** in Gilead?"
18:5 "Should we go to war against **R**
18:5 "God will hand over **R** to you."
18:11 They said, "Attack **R** in Gilead,
18:14 should we go to war against **R**
18:19 and be killed at **R** in Gilead?'
18:28 of Judah went to **R** in Gilead.

Ramoth Gilead (6)

1Ki 4:13 was in charge of **R**;
2Ki 8:28 Hazael of Aram at **R**.
9:1 and go to **R**.
9:4 the prophet, went to **R**.
9:14 guarding **R** against King
2Ch 22:5 Hazael of Aram at **R**.

ramp (3)

2Sm 20:15 They put up a dirt **r** against the
Job 19:12 They build a **r** to attack me and
Hab 1:10 and build a dirt **r** to capture it.

ramps (11)

2Ki 19:32 or put up dirt **r** to attack it.
25:1 up camp and built dirt **r** around
Isa 37:33 or put up dirt **r** to attack it.
Jer 32:24 "'See how the dirt **r** have been
33:4 to be used against the dirt **r**
52:4 up camp and built dirt **r** around
Eze 4:2 put up dirt **r** around it,
17:17 the Babylonians put up dirt **r**
21:22 put up **r**, and set up blockades.
26:8 set up blockades, put up dirt **r**,
Dan 11:15 will come, build dirt attack **r**,

ram's (38)

Exo 19:13 ⌊only⌋ when the **r** horn sounds
19:16 from a **r** horn ⌊was heard⌋.
20:18 heard the blast of the **r** horn
Lev 8:18 their hands on the **r** head
8:22 their hands on the **r** head
Num 6:20 along with the **r** breast that is
Jdg 3:27 he blew a **r** horn in the
6:34 So Gideon blew the **r** horn to
1Sm 13:3 With the sounding of the **r** horn
2Sm 2:28 So Joab blew a **r** horn, and all
15:10 the sound of the **r** horn, say,
18:16 Joab blew the **r** horn to stop
20:1 He blew a **r** horn to
20:22 He blew the **r** horn, and
1Ki 1:34 Then blow the **r** horn and say,
1:39 They blew the **r** horn, and all
2Ki 9:13 They blew a **r** horn and said,
Job 39:24 trust the sound of the **r** horn
Psa 47:5 up with the sound of a **r** horn
81:3 Blow the **r** horn on the day of
98:6 and the playing of a **r** horn.
Isa 18:3 a **r** horn, all you inhabitants
27:13 On that day a **r** horn will be
58:1 Raise your voice like a **r** horn.
Jer 4:5 Say, "Blow the **r** horn
4:19 I hear a **r** horn sounding
6:1 Blow the **r** horn in Tekoa.
6:17 to the sound of the **r** horn.
42:14 hear the sound of a **r** horn, or be
51:27 Blow the **r** horn among the
Eze 7:14 They have blown a **r** horn, and
Dan 8:7 It broke both of the **r** horns.
Hos 5:8 "Blow the **r** horn in Gibeah.
8:1 "Sound the alarm on the **r** horn.
Joe 2:1 Blow the **r** horn in Zion.
2:15 Blow the **r** horn in Zion.
Amo 3:6 If a **r** horn sounds an alarm in a
Zec 9:14 LORD will blow the **r** horn

rams (68)

Gen 30:40 Jacob separated the **r** from the
31:38 ate any **r** from your flocks.
Exo 29:1 defects and two **r** that have no
29:3 the young bull and the two **r**.
29:15 "Take one of the **r**.
Lev 8:2 be the offering for sin, the two **r**,
23:18 no defects, one bull, and two **r**.
Num 7:17 and two bulls, five **r**,
7:23 and two bulls, five **r**,
7:29 and two bulls, five **r**,
7:35 and two bulls, five **r**,
7:41 and two bulls, five **r**,
7:47 and two bulls, five **r**,
7:53 and two bulls, five **r**,
7:59 and two bulls, five **r**,
7:65 and two bulls, five **r**,
7:71 and two bulls, five **r**,
7:77 and two bulls, five **r**,
7:83 and two bulls, five **r**,
7:87 was 12 young bulls, 12 **r**,
7:88 24 bulls, 60 **r**, 60 male goats,
23:1 bulls and seven **r** for me."
23:29 bulls and seven **r** for me."
29:13 2 **r**, and 14 one-year-old lambs,
29:14 16 cups for each of the 2 **r**,
29:17 day bring 12 young bulls, 2 **r**,
29:18 each of the bulls, **r**, and lambs.
29:20 the third day bring 11 bulls, 2 **r**,
29:21 each of the bulls, **r**, and lambs.
29:23 fourth day bring 10 bulls, 2 **r**,
29:24 each of the bulls, **r**, and lambs.
29:26 the fifth day bring 9 bulls, 2 **r**,
29:27 each of the bulls, **r**, and lambs.
29:29 the sixth day bring 8 bulls, 2 **r**,
29:30 each of the bulls, **r**, and lambs.
29:32 seventh day bring 7 bulls, 2 **r**,
29:33 each of the bulls, **r**, and lambs.
Dtr 32:14 **r** from the stock of Bashan,

1Sm 15:22 than sacrificing the fat of **r**.
2Ki 3:4 and the wool from 100,000 **r**.
1Ch 15:26 seven bulls and seven **r**.
29:21 bulls, 1,000 **r**, 1,000 lambs,
2Ch 13:9 a young bull and seven **r** can
17:11 7,700 **r** and 7,700 male goats.
29:21 bulls, seven **r**, seven lambs,
29:22 Then they slaughtered the **r**
29:32 70 bulls, 100 **r**, and 200 lambs.
Ezr 6:9 **r**, lambs, wheat, salt, wine,
6:17 bulls, 200 **r**, and 400 lambs.
7:17 to buy bulls, **r**, lambs, grain,
8:35 for all Israel, 96 **r**, 77 lambs,
Job 42:8 seven young bulls and seven **r**.
Psa 66:15 offerings with the smoke from **r**.
114:4 The mountains jumped like **r**.
114:6 what made you jump like **r**?
Isa 1:11 of your burnt offerings of **r**
34:7 young bulls along with **r**.
60:7 The **r** of Nebaioth will serve
Jer 51:40 like lambs, **r**, and male goats.
Eze 4:2 place battering **r** all around it.
21:22 will set up his battering **r** there,
21:22 aim the battering **r** against the
26:9 He will direct his battering **r**
27:21 They traded lambs, **r**,
34:17 between **r** and male goats.
39:18 All of them will be killed like **r**,
45:23 seven **r** that have no defects,
Mic 6:7 be pleased with thousands of **r**

rams' (32)

Exo 25:5 **r** skins dyed red, fine leather,
26:14 Make a cover of **r** skins that
35:7 **r** skins dyed red, fine leather,
35:23 goats' hair, **r** skins dyed red,
36:19 out of **r** skins that had been
39:34 the cover made of **r** skins dyed
Lev 23:24 by the blowing of **r** horns
25:9 sound **r** horns throughout the
Jos 6:4 Seven priests will carry **r** horns
6:6 carry seven **r** horns ahead
6:8 the seven **r** horns ahead
6:13 the seven **r** horns were ahead
6:16 the priests blew their **r** horns.
6:20 heard the blast of the **r** horns,
Jdg 7:8 all the supplies and **r** horns.
7:16 He gave them each **r** horns and
7:18 with me blow our **r** horns, then
7:19 They blew their **r** horns and
7:20 also blew their **r** horns
7:20 their left hands and the **r** horns
7:22 kept on blowing their **r** horns,
2Sm 6:15 joy and the sounding of **r** horns
1Ch 15:28 sounding of **r** horns, trumpets,
2Ch 15:14 blowing of trumpets and **r** horns
Isa 34:6 with the fat of **r** kidneys.
Jer 4:21 and hear the sound of **r** horns
Dan 3:5 the sound of **r** horns, flutes,
3:7 the sound of **r** horns, flutes,
3:10 the sound of **r** horns, flutes,
3:15 the sound of the **r** horns, flutes,
Amo 2:2 and **r** horns are blowing.
Zep 1:16 a day of **r** horns and battle cries

ran (81)

Gen 16:6 Hagar so much that she **r** away.
18:2 saw them, he **r** to meet them,
18:7 Then Abraham **r** to the herd and
24:17 The servant **r** to meet her and
24:20 **r** back to the well to draw more
24:28 The girl **r** and told her mother's
24:30 Immediately, Laban **r** out to the
29:12 she **r** and told her father.
29:13 son Jacob, he **r** to meet him.
33:4 Then Esau **r** to meet Jacob.
39:12 "But he **r** outside and left his
39:15 he **r** outside and left his clothes
39:18 But when I screamed, he **r**
41:43 Men **r** ahead of him and
Exo 4:3 and he **r** away from it.
36:33 so that it **r** from one end
Num 11:27 Then a young man **r** and told
16:34 All the Israelites around them **r**
16:47 and **r** into the middle of the
Jos 7:8 I say after Israel **r** away from its
7:22 and they **r** to the tent.
8:15 They **r** away toward the desert.
10:16 The five kings **r** away and hid
20:6 the city from which he **r** away.'"
Jdg 9:21 Then Jotham **r** away quickly.
9:40 so that he **r** away from him.
13:10 The woman **r** quickly to tell her
1Sm 3:5 He **r** to Eli and said,
4:12 from the tribe of Benjamin **r**
10:23 They **r** and got him from there.
17:22 **r** to the battle line,
17:48 David quickly **r** toward the
17:51 David **r** and stood over the
19:12 and he **r** away to escape.
20:36 The boy **r**, and Jonathan shot
2Sm 18:9 that was under him **r** away.
18:21 in front of Joab and then **r** off.
18:23 So Ahimaaz **r** along the valley
1Ki 18:46 He hiked up his robe and **r**
19:20 oxen, **r** after Elijah, and said,
2Ki 3:9 After seven days they **r** out of
7:7 donkeys and **r** for their lives.)
Psa 48:5 terrified and **r** away in fear.
78:9 turned ˻and **r**˼ on the day of
104:7 Water **r** away at the sound of
114:3 Sea looked at this and **r** away.
Isa 20:6 We **r** ˻to Egypt˼ for help to be
Jer 23:21 yet they **r** ˻with their
41:14 captive at Mizpah turned and **r**
Lam 1:6 They **r** without any strength
Eze 1:14 The living creatures **r** back and
31:4 Streams **r** beside all the other
40:18 the lower courtyard **r** alongside
42:7 There was a wall which **r**
42:7 It **r** alongside the side rooms for
42:12 wall that **r** eastward.
Dan 8:6 It furiously **r** at the ram.
Mat 8:33 who took care of the pigs **r** into
26:56 abandoned him and **r** away.
27:48 One of the men **r** at once,
28:8 with fear and great joy and **r**
Mar 5:6 So he **r** ˻to Jesus˼,
5:14 took care of the pigs **r** away.
6:33 The people **r** from all the cities
6:55 They **r** all over the countryside
9:15 Jesus and **r** to welcome him.
14:50 abandoned him and **r** away.
14:52 behind and **r** away naked.
15:36 Someone **r** and soaked a
16:8 They went out of the tomb and **r**
Luk 8:34 had happened, they **r** away.
15:20 He **r** to his son, put his arms
19:4 So Zacchaeus **r** ahead and
24:12 But Peter got up and **r** to the
Jon 20:2 So she **r** to Simon Peter and
20:4 but the other disciple **r** faster
Act 3:11 and everyone **r** to see them at
8:30 Philip **r** to the carriage and
12:14 she **r** back inside and reported,
19:16 them up so badly that they **r** out
27:41 a sandbar in the water and **r**

rancher (1)

Amo 7:14 I am a **r** and a grower of figs.

random (2)

1Ki 22:34 One man aimed his bow at **r**
2Ch 18:33 One man aimed his bow at **r**

rang (1)

1Sm 4:5 that the earth **r** with echoes.

range (2)

1Sm 31:3 the archers got him in their **r**,
1Ch 10:3 the archers got him in their **r**,

rank (5)

2Sm 23:9 Next in **r** to him was Eleazar,
23:11 Next in **r** to him was Shammah,
1Ch 11:12 Next in **r** to him was Eleazar,
Est 1:5 of Susa, whatever their **r**.
1:14 the king and held the highest **r**

ranked (1)

Est 10:3 Mordecai the Jew was **r**

ranks (4)

2Ki 11:8 tries to break through your **r**.
Isa 14:31 there are no stragglers in its **r**.
Jer 50:37 all the foreigners within their **r**.
Joe 2:8 they do not break their **r**.

ransom (12)

Exo 30:12 person must pay the LORD a **r**
Num 3:49 So Moses took this **r** money
3:51 and his sons this **r** money as
Job 6:23 or '**R** me from a tyrant'?
33:24 into the pit. I have found a **r**.'
Psa 49:7 or pay God a **r** for his life.
Pro 13:8 A person's riches are the **r** for
21:18 Wicked people become a **r** for
Isa 43:3 Egypt is the **r** I exchanged for
Mat 20:28 his life as a **r** for many people."
Mar 10:45 his life as a **r** for many people."
1Co 1:30 our holiness, and our **r** from sin.

ransomed (2)

Isa 35:10 The people **r** by the LORD will
51:11 The people **r** by the LORD will

rant (2)

1Ki 18:29 afternoon they continued to **r**
Pro 29:9 he may **r** and rave,

rape (3)

Jdg 19:24 **R** them, and do with them
2Sm 13:12 "No," she told him, "don't **r** me!
Est 7:8 "Is he even going to **r** the

raped (8)

Gen 34:2 he took her and **r** her.
Dtr 22:29 Since he **r** her, he can never
Jdg 20:5 they **r** my concubine until she
2Sm 13:14 He grabbed his sister and **r** her.
13:32 half brother **r** his sister Tamar.
Isa 13:16 will be looted and their wives **r**.
Lam 5:11 Women in Zion are **r**,
Zec 14:2 looted, and the women **r**.

rapes (2)

Dtr 22:25 But if a man **r** an engaged girl
22:28 you must do when a man **r**

Rapha (1)

1Ch 8:2 and **R** (his fifth son).

Raphah (1)

1Ch 8:37 Binea's son was **R**.

Raphah's (1)

1Ch 8:37 **R** son was Eleasah.

Raphu (1)

Num 13:9 Palti, son of **R**, from the tribe of

rapid (1)

Ezr 5:8 job and making **r** progress.

rapidly (2)

Psa 105:24 LORD made his people grow **r**
2Th 3:1 that we spread the Lord's word **r**

raping (2)

Gen 34:7 family by **r** Jacob's daughter.
2Sm 13:22 Amnon for **r** his sister Tamar.

rare (3)

1Sm 3:1 prophecy from the LORD was **r**;
Isa 13:12 beings more **r** than gold from
Rom 5:7 die for a godly person is **r**.

rash (6)

Lev 13:2 "If anyone has a sore, a **r**,
13:6 It is only a **r**. The person must
13:7 But if the **r** has spread after he
13:8 and if the **r** has spread,
13:39 a **r** has developed on the skin.
14:56 a sore, a **r**, or an irritated area.

rate (1)

Gen 23:16 current merchants' exchange **r**.

rationed (2)

Eze 4:16 People will anxiously eat **r**
4:16 and fearfully drink **r** water.

rattles (1)

Job 39:23 A quiver of arrows **r** on it along

rattling (5)

Job 41:29 and it laughs at a **r** javelin.
Jer 47:3 the **r** of enemy chariots,
Eze 37:7 suddenly there was a **r** noise,
Joe 2:5 they sound like **r** chariots,
Nah 3:2 The sound of **r** wheels!

ravaged (1)

Dtr 32:24 by famines and **r** by pestilence

rave (2)

1Ki 18:29 continued to rant and **r** until
Pro 29:9 fool, he may rant and **r**,

raved (1)

Gen 12:15 they **r** about her to Pharaoh,

raven (2)

Gen 8:7 and sent out a **r**. It kept flying
Sos 5:11 His hair is wavy, black as a **r**.

ravenous (1)

Gen 49:27 "Benjamin is a **r** wolf.

ravens (4)

1Ki 17:4 and I've commanded **r** to feed
17:6 **R** brought him bread and meat
Psa 147:9 and to young **r** when they call
Pro 30:17 mother will be plucked out by **r**

ravine (7)

Jos 8:11 of Ai with the **r** between them
1Sm 17:3 There was a **r** between the two
Isa 15:7 and stored up over Willow **R**.
57:6 the smooth stones in the **r**.
Eze 31:12 broken branches fell in every **r**
47:19 Meribah in Kadesh along the **r**
Zec 1:8 among the myrtle trees in a **r**.

ravines (8)

2Sm 17:9 already hidden in one of the **r**
23:30 Hiddai from the Gaash **r**,
1Ch 11:32 Hurai from the Gaash **r**,
Eze 6:3 hills and to the **r** and valleys:
32:6 **R** will be filled with your dead
35:8 hills and in your valleys and **r**.
36:4 to the **r** and valleys,
36:6 and hills and the **r** and valleys,

raw (9)

Exo 12:9 Don't eat any of it **r** or boiled but
Lev 13:10 and if there is **r** flesh in the
13:14 But if **r** flesh appears,
13:15 The priest will examine the **r**
13:15 The **r** flesh is unclean.
13:16 But if the **r** flesh turns white
13:24 burn on his skin and the **r** flesh
1Sm 2:15 meat from you. He wants it **r**."
Eze 29:18 soldier's shoulder was rubbed **r**.

rays (3)

Job 41:18 are like the first **r** of the dawn.
Psa 139:9 If I climb upward on the **r** of the
Hab 3:4 **R** of light ⌊stream⌋ from his

razor (5)

Num 6:5 no **r** may touch their heads.
1Sm 1:11 A **r** will never be used on his
Psa 52:2 It's like a sharp **r**, you master of
Isa 7:20 the Euphrates River to be a **r**
Eze 5:1 and use it as a barber's **r** to

reach (28)

Gen 3:22 He must not **r** out and take the
Exo 4:4 "**R** out and grab the snake by
Dtr 30:11 hard for you or beyond your **r**.
2Sm 5:8 to defeat the Jebusites must **r**
15:5 Absalom would **r** out,
2Ch 30:8 **R** out for the LORD.
Job 6:9 that he would **r** out to cut me
37:23 The Almighty, whom we can't **r**,
Psa 32:6 floodwater will not **r** them.
79:8 **R** out to us soon with your
119:41 Let your blessings **r** me,
119:77 Let your compassion **r** me so
139:6 It is so high I cannot **r** it.
Pro 2:2 your mind **r** for understanding,
2:19 Nor do they ever **r** the paths of
Ecc 7:23 but it is out of my **r**."
7:24 wisdom may be, it is out of **r**.
Isa 40:28 His understanding is beyond **r**.
59:9 and righteousness doesn't **r** us.
Eze 31:14 longer allowed to **r** the clouds.
Dan 4:11 and tall enough to **r** the sky.
4:20 and tall enough to **r** the sky.
12:12 wait until they **r** 1,335 days.
Mic 1:9 It will **r** the gates of my people
5:4 because his greatness will **r**
Act 17:27 somehow **r** for him,
27:12 They hoped to **r** the city of
Rom 9:31 but they did not **r** their goal.

reached (52)

Gen 8:9 He **r** out and brought the dove
19:10 The men ⌊inside⌋ **r** out,
37:18 Before he **r** them, they plotted
37:23 So when Joseph **r** his brothers,
39:21 The LORD **r** out to him with his
48:14 crossed his hands and **r** out.
Exo 4:4 He **r** out and grabbed it,
Jdg 3:21 Ehud **r** with his left hand,
4:12 The report **r** Sisera that Barak,
5:26 She **r** for a tent peg with one
1Sm 17:49 Then David **r** into his bag,
20:37 When the boy **r** the place
2Sm 6:6 So Uzzah **r** out for the ark of
19:11 What all Israel was saying **r**
22:7 and my cry for help **r** his ears.
22:17 He **r** down from high above and
1Ki 2:28 The news **r** Joab. (He had
2Ki 6:7 The disciple **r** for it and picked
9:18 you sent has **r** them,
9:20 announced, "He has **r** them,
19:28 your boasting has **r** my ears,
1Ch 13:9 So Uzzah **r** out to grab the ark.
Ezr 8:32 When we **r** Jerusalem,
Psa 18:6 and my cry for help **r** his ears.
18:16 He **r** down from high above and
80:11 It **r** out with its branches to the
80:11 shoots **r** the Euphrates River.
Pro 5:14 I almost **r** total ruin in the
Isa 7:2 When word **r** David's family
10:10 My power has **r** kingdoms
16:8 The grapevines ⌊once⌋ **r** as far
30:4 his messengers have **r** Hanes,
37:29 your boasting has **r** my ears,
Jer 48:32 and they **r** as far as the sea of
Eze 10:7 One of the angels **r** into the fire
31:7 Its roots **r** down to many
31:10 and its top **r** the clouds.
Dan 4:22 and mighty until you **r** the sky.
6:24 Before they **r** the bottom of the
8:10 to gain power until it **r**
Jnh 3:6 When the news **r** the king of
Mat 8:3 Jesus **r** out, touched him,
14:31 Immediately, Jesus **r** out,
21:1 Jerusalem and had **r** Bethphage
Mar 1:41 Jesus felt sorry for him, **r** out,
Luk 5:13 Jesus **r** out, touched him,
Jon 6:21 Immediately, the boat **r** the
Act 11:22 After the news about Antioch **r**
1Co 14:36 Are you the only ones it has **r**?
Php 3:12 It's not that I've already **r** the
1Jn 4:17 God's love has **r** its goal in us.
Rev 1:13 wearing a robe that **r** his feet.

reaches (13)

2Ki 10:2 As soon as this letter **r** you,
2Ch 28:9 in a rage that **r** up to heaven.
Ezr 9:6 overwhelming that it **r** heaven.
Neh 12:37 palace and **r** Water Gate
Job 20:6 If his height **r** to the sky and his
Psa 36:5 your mercy **r** to the heavens,
48:10 your praise ⌊**r**⌋ to the ends of
57:10 Your truth **r** the skies.
71:19 Your righteousness **r** to the
108:4 Your truth **r** the skies.
Pro 4:18 and brighter until it **r** midday.
Isa 23:5 When the news **r** Egypt,
Dan 4:22 Your power **r** the most distant

reaching (3)

Gen 28:12 up on the earth with its top **r** up
1Ch 13:10 with Uzzah and killed him for **r**
Psa 146:9 wicked people from **r** their goal.

reacted (2)

Luk 14:3 Jesus **r** by asking the
Jon 2:18 The Jews **r** by asking Jesus,

read (92)

Exo 24:7 of the LORD's Promise and **r**
Dtr 17:19 He must keep it with him and **r**
31:11 **R** these teachings so that they
Jos 8:34 Afterwards, Joshua **r** all the
8:35 Joshua **r** ⌊Moses' Teachings⌋
2Ki 5:6 It **r**, "I'm sending my officer
5:7 the king of Israel **r** the letter,
10:1 in Samaria. The letters **r**,
10:6 It **r**, "If you are on my side and
19:14 from the messengers, **r** them,
22:8 book to Shaphan, who then **r** it.
22:10 And Shaphan **r** it to the king.
22:16 that the king of Judah has **r**.
23:2 Josiah **r** everything written in
2Ch 21:12 It **r**, "This is what the LORD
34:18 And Shaphan **r** it to the king.
34:24 written in the book that was **r**
34:30 He **r** everything written in the
Ezr 4:18 you sent me has been **r** word
Neh 8:3 From daybreak until noon, he **r**
8:8 They **r** the Book of God's
8:8 could understand what was **r**.
8:18 Ezra continued to **r** from the
9:3 of the LORD their God was **r**,
13:1 the Book of Moses was **r** while
Est 6:1 and they were **r** to the king.
Psa 139:2 You **r** my thoughts from far
Isa 29:11 book to someone who can **r**,
29:11 read, saying, "Please **r** this."
29:11 He answers, "I can't **r** it.
29:12 book to someone who can't **r**,
29:12 read, saying, "Please **r** this."
29:12 He answers, "I can't **r**."
34:16 the LORD's book, and **r** it.
37:14 letter from the messengers, **r** it,
Jer 29:29 The priest Zephaniah **r** this
36:6 On a day of fasting, you must **r**
36:6 You must **r** it to the people in
36:6 You must also **r** it to all the
36:8 In the LORD's temple he **r** from
36:10 Then Baruch **r** the scroll
36:10 Baruch **r** it to all the people in
36:11 heard Baruch **r** from the scroll
36:13 he heard Baruch **r** from
36:14 the scroll that you **r** publicly,
36:15 sit down, and **r** it to us."
36:15 So Baruch **r** it to them.
36:21 Jehudi **r** it to the king and all
36:23 As Jehudi **r** three or four
36:24 they heard everything being **r**.
51:61 see that you **r** all this.
Dan 5:8 but they couldn't **r** the writing or
5:15 brought to me to **r** this writing
5:16 If you can **r** the writing and tell
5:17 I'll still **r** the writing for you and
Amo 7:10 It **r**, "Amos is plotting against
Hab 2:2 so that anyone can **r** it quickly.
Mat 12:3 "Haven't you **r** what David did
12:4 Haven't you **r** how he went into
12:5 Or haven't you **r** in Moses'
19:4 Jesus answered, "Haven't you **r**
21:16 Have you never **r**, 'From the
21:42 "Have you never **r** in the
22:31 Haven't you **r** what God told
27:37 It **r**, "This is Jesus, the king of
Mar 2:25 "Haven't you ever **r** what David
2:26 Haven't you ever **r** how he went
2:26 Haven't you ever **r** how he also
12:10 Have you never **r** the Scripture

Mar 12:26 Haven't you **r** in the book of
15:26 It **r**, "The king of the Jews."
Luk 4:16 He stood up to **r** the lesson.
4:17 and found the place where it **r**:
4:21 today when you heard me **r** it."
6:3 "Haven't you **r** what David did
6:4 Haven't you **r** how he went into
10:26 What do you **r** there?"
Jon 19:19 The notice **r**, "Jesus from
19:20 Many Jews **r** this notice,
Act 1:20 You've **r** in Psalms,
13:27 which are **r** every day of
15:21 His teachings are **r** in
15:31 When the people **r** the letter,
23:34 the governor had **r** the letter,
2Co 1:13 already knew before you **r** this.
3:14 veil is still there when they **r**
3:15 Yet, even today, when they **r**
Eph 3:4 When you **r** this,
Col 4:16 After you have **r** this letter,
4:16 **r** it in the church at Laodicea.
4:16 Make sure that you also **r** the
1Th 5:27 I order you to **r** this letter to all

reader (2)

Mat 24:15 see this (let the **r** take note),
Mar 13:14 should not (let the **r** take note),

reading (8)

Neh 8:9 to the **r** of God's Teachings.
Jer 51:63 When you finish **r** this scroll,
Act 8:28 he was **r** the prophet Isaiah out
8:30 and could hear the official **r**
8:30 you understand what you're **r**?"
8:32 that the official was **r**:
13:15 After **r** from Moses' Teachings
1Ti 4:13 there, concentrate on **r** ⌊Scripture⌋

reads (3)

Dan 5:7 "Whoever **r** this writing and
2Co 3:2 that everyone knows and **r**.
Rev 1:3 Blessed is the one who **r**,

ready (151)

Gen 4:7 outside your door **r** to attack.
33:12 Esau said, "Let's get **r** to go,
43:25 They got their gifts **r** for
46:30 you're still alive, I'm **r** to die."
Exo 13:18 The Israelites were **r** for battle
17:4 They're almost **r** to stone me!"
19:10 they have two days to get **r**.
19:11 and be **r** by the day after
19:14 the people, he had them get **r**,
19:15 "Be **r** two days from now.
34:2 Be **r** in the morning.
34:6 always faithful and **r** to forgive.
Num 4:15 and the camp is **r** to move,
8:11 Then they will be **r** to do the
11:18 the people to get **r** for tomorrow
31:3 "Some of your men must get **r**
31:5 of Israel — 12,000 men **r** for war.
32:17 Then we'll be **r** ⌊to march⌋ in
32:20 your armed men get **r** for battle.
32:27 presence we will all get **r**
32:29 tribes of Gad and Reuben get **r**
32:30 If they don't get **r** for battle and
Dtr 1:7 Break camp, and get **r**!
3:18 All your soldiers must be **r** for
29:12 You are **r** to accept the terms
Jos 1:11 'Get your supplies **r**.
7:13 Tell the people, 'Get **r** for
8:4 Everyone must be **r**.
18:8 As the men got **r** to go,
1Sm 6:7 Now get a new cart **r** for two
25:41 "I am **r** to serve," she said.
25:41 "I am **r** to wash the feet of my
2Sm 10:11 my ⌊troops⌋, be **r** to help me.
18:3 It's better for you to be **r** to send
1Ki 20:12 He told his officers to get **r**.
20:12 So they got **r** ⌊to attack⌋ the
2Ki 10:6 "If you are on my side and **r** to
18:20 advice about getting **r** for war.
1Ch 5:18 had 44,760 soldiers **r**
12:35 there were 28,600 **r** for battle.
12:36 soldiers **r** for battle.
1Ch 12:37 there were 120,000 soldiers **r** to
19:12 my ⌊troops⌋, be **r** to help me.
2Ch 26:11 They were **r** to go to war in
35:4 Get yourselves **r** with the
Neh 9:17 and always **r** to forgive.
Est 3:14 people were to be **r** for this day.
8:13 that day the Jews were to be **r**
Job 15:24 him like a king **r** for battle.
32:19 wineskins that are **r** to burst.
38:40 crouch in their dens and lie **r**
Psa 7:12 he makes it **r** ⌊to shoot⌋.
38:17 I am **r** to fall. I am continually
55:21 they are like swords **r** to attack.
86:15 always faithful and **r** to forgive.
89:21 My hand is **r** to help him.
103:8 and always **r** to forgive.
103:20 carry out his orders and are **r**
145:8 and always **r** to forgive.
Pro 21:31 The horse is made **r** for the day
24:27 and get things **r** for yourself in
25:4 and a vessel is **r** for the
Isa 5:25 and he is **r** to use his power to
5:25 and he is still **r** to use his
5:28 all their bows are **r** to shoot.
9:12 and he is still **r** to use his
9:17 and he is still **r** to use his
9:21 and he is still **r** to use his
10:4 and he is still **r** to use his
14:27 He is **r** to use his power.
21:15 from swords **r** to kill,
21:15 from bows **r** to shoot,
22:7 and horsemen will stand **r** in
26:17 we are like pregnant women **r**
30:13 with a bulging crack, **r** to fall.
30:33 It was made **r** for the king.
36:5 advice about getting **r** for war.
51:13 of those who are **r** to destroy
65:1 I was **r** to answer those who
Jer 6:23 They march like soldiers **r** for
46:3 your large and small shields **r**;
46:14 'Take your positions, and get **r**.
49:14 attack Edom. Get **r** for battle."
49:28 says: Get **r**, attack Kedar,
49:31 Get **r**! Attack the nation living
50:42 They are **r** for war,
50:42 ready for war, **r** to attack you,
Eze 4:2 have troops **r** to attack it,
7:14 and everything is **r**.
7:23 "Get the chains **r**! The land is
21:15 It's **r** to flash like lightning.
21:28 a sword is drawn **r** to kill.
Hos 10:10 "I will punish them when I'm **r**.
Joe 2:13 and always **r** to forgive and to
Oba 1:1 the nations to say, "Get **r**!
Jnh 4:2 and always **r** to forgive and to
Hab 3:9 You get your bow **r** for action,
Zec 5:11 When the house is **r**,
Mat 3:10 The ax is now **r** to cut the roots
21:41 of the produce when it is **r**."
22:4 Everything is **r**. Come to the
22:8 'The wedding is **r**,
24:44 Therefore, you, too, must be **r**
25:7 woke up and got their lamps **r**.
25:10 The bridesmaids who were **r**
Mar 3:9 to have a boat **r** so that
4:29 As soon as the grain is **r**,
6:10 stay there until you're **r** to leave
14:15 Get everything **r** for us there."
Luk 3:9 The ax is now **r** to cut the roots
9:4 stay there until you're **r** to leave.
12:35 "Be **r** for action, and have your
12:40 Be **r**, because the Son of Man
12:47 master wanted but didn't get **r**
14:17 Everything is **r** now.'
14:26 come to me and are not **r**
17:8 'Get dinner **r** for me!
22:12 Get things **r** there."
22:33 I'm **r** to go to prison with you
Jon 4:35 the fields are **r** to be harvested.
21:18 you would get **r** to go where
21:18 someone else will get you **r**
Act 12:8 your shoes on, and get **r** to go!"
21:13 I'm **r** not only to be tied up in
21:15 we got **r** to go to Jerusalem.
23:15 We'll be **r** to kill him before he
23:21 They are **r** now and are
Act 23:23 Have them **r** to go to Caesarea
1Co 3:2 because you weren't **r** for it.
3:2 Even now you aren't **r** for it
14:8 who will get **r** for battle?
2Co 7:11 You were **r** to clear yourselves
7:11 You were **r** to punish the wrong
9:2 have been **r** ⌊to send their
9:3 that when we brag that you're **r**,
9:4 find out that you're not **r** after all
10:6 We are **r** to punish every act of
12:14 I'm **r** to visit you for a third time,
Eph 6:15 on your shoes so that you are **r**
2Ti 4:2 Be **r** to spread the word
Tit 3:1 should obey them and be **r**
Phm 1:22 have a guest room **r** for me.
1Pe 1:5 faith for a salvation that is **r**
1:13 must be clear and **r** for action.
3:15 Always be **r** to defend your
4:5 an account to the one who is **r**
Rev 8:6 trumpets got **r** to blow them.
9:15 The four angels who were **r** for
10:7 when the seventh angel is **r**
19:7 His bride has made herself **r**.
21:2 like a bride **r** for her husband.

Reaiah (4)

1Ch 4:2 **R**, son of Shobal, was the
5:5 Micah's son was **R**.
Ezr 2:47 Giddel, Gahar, **R**,
Neh 7:50 **R**, Rezin, Nekoda,

Reaiah's (1)

1Ch 5:5 was Reaiah. **R** son was Baal.

real (16)

Dtr 21:16 for the **r** firstborn (the son
1Ki 18:24 answers by fire is the **r** God."
2Ki 19:18 these gods aren't **r** gods.
Isa 37:19 these gods aren't **r** gods.
Zec 7:9 Administer **r** justice,
Luk 16:11 trust you with wealth that is **r**?
Jon 1:9 The **r** light, which shines on
Col 3:22 out of respect for your **r** master.
3:23 were working for your **r** master
3:24 You know that your **r** master
3:24 It is Christ, your **r** master,
1Th 1:9 from false gods to serve the **r**,
Heb 9:24 go into a model of the **r** thing.
1Jn 5:20 so that we know the **r** God.
5:20 We are in the one who is **r**,
5:20 This Jesus Christ is the **r** God

realize (56)

Exo 10:7 When will you **r** that Egypt is
Lev 5:17 know it — when you **r** your guilt
Num 5:6 When you **r** your guilt,
Dtr 9:3 **R** today that the LORD your
32:29 this and **r** what will happen
Jdg 13:16 (Manoah did not **r** that it was
16:20 (He didn't **r** that the LORD had
20:34 But Benjamin's men didn't **r**
1Sm 12:17 Then you will **r** what a wicked
2Ki 5:7 All of you should **r** and
Job 14:21 and he doesn't **r** it.
Psa 100:3 **R** that the LORD alone is God.
Pro 5:6 and she doesn't **r** it.
7:23 He does not **r** that it will cost
Ecc 2:14 But I have also come to **r** that
3:12 I **r** that there's nothing better for
3:14 I **r** that whatever God does will
11:9 But **r** that God will make you
Jer 14:20 O LORD, we **r** our wickedness
Eze 2:5 they will **r** that a prophet has
12:16 they will **r** that everything they
Dan 4:25 will pass until you **r** that
4:26 as you **r** that heaven rules.
4:32 will pass until you **r** that
Hos 7:2 They don't **r** that I remember all
7:9 your strength, but you don't **r** it.
7:9 old man, but you don't **r** it.
11:3 But they didn't **r** that I had
Mat 15:12 "Do you **r** that when the
20:22 "You don't **r** what you're asking.
24:43 You **r** that if a homeowner had
Mar 10:38 "You don't **r** what you're asking.
Luk 2:49 Didn't you **r** that I had to be in

Luk 10:11 But **r** that the kingdom of God
12:39 "Of course, you **r** that if the
21:20 **r** that the time is near for it to be
Jon 15:18 "If the world hates you, **r** that it
21:4 The disciples didn't **r** that it
Act 12:9 He didn't **r** that what the angel
Rom 2:4 Don't you **r** that it is God's
7:1 Don't you **r**, brothers and
7:15 I don't **r** what I'm doing.
1Co 6:15 Don't you **r** that your bodies are
6:16 Don't you **r** that the person who
9:13 Don't you **r** that those who work
9:24 Don't you **r** that everyone who
11:3 However, I want you to **r** that
2Co 13:6 I hope that you will **r** that we
Gal 5:3 to be circumcised must **r** that
1Ti 1:9 For example, a person must **r**
Jas 5:9 **R** that the judge is standing at
5:20 **R** that whoever brings a sinner
1Pe 1:18 **R** that you weren't set free from
1Jn 3:16 is when we **r** that Christ gave
Rev 3:9 and bow at your feet and **r** that
3:17 Yet, you do not **r** that you are

realized (41)

Gen 3:7 and they both **r** that they were
16:4 When Hagar **r** that she was
28:8 Esau **r** that his father Isaac
29:23 came, he **r** it was Leah.
38:14 (She did this because she **r**
39:13 When she **r** that he had gone
50:15 Joseph's brothers **r** what their
Exo 5:19 The Israelite foremen **r** they
Jdg 6:22 That's when Gideon **r** that this
16:18 When Delilah **r** that he had told
20:36 Then the men of Benjamin **r**
20:41 They **r** that their evil had
1Sm 3:8 Then Eli **r** that the LORD was
5:7 When the people of Ashdod **r**
18:28 Saul **r** that the LORD was with
21:12 When David **r** what they had
26:3 When he **r** Saul had come to
2Sm 5:12 So David **r** that the LORD had
10:6 The Ammonites **r** that they had
12:19 he **r** that the child was dead.
1Ki 3:15 Solomon woke up and **r** it had
3:21 I took a good look at him and **r**
22:33 the chariot commanders **r** that
1Ch 14:2 So David **r** that the LORD had
19:6 The Ammonites **r** that they had
2Ch 18:32 and the chariot commanders **r**
32:26 when they **r** they had become
Neh 6:12 Then I **r** that God hadn't sent
6:16 They **r** we had done this work
Eze 10:20 I **r** that they were angels.
18:28 He **r** what he was doing and
Dan 5:21 This happened until he **r** that
Zec 11:11 who were watching me **r** that
Mat 1:18 Mary **r** that she was pregnant
Luk 1:22 So they **r** that he had seen a
Jon 4:53 Then the boy's father **r** that it
6:15 Jesus **r** that the people
Act 4:13 They **r** that these men had
12:12 When Peter **r** what had
16:19 When her owners **r** that their
1Th 2:13 you **r** it wasn't the word of

realizing (4)

2Sm 10:15 **R** that Israel had defeated them,
1Ch 19:16 **R** that Israel had defeated them,
Job 19:4 I've made a mistake without **r** it,
Pro 28:22 not **r** that poverty is about to

reapers (6)

Rut 2:2 the grain left behind by the **r**."
2:3 the grain left behind by the **r**.
2:4 and he said to his **r**,
2:5 young man in charge of his **r**,
2:7 the bundles behind the **r**.' So
2:14 So she sat beside the **r**,

reaping (1)

Rut 2:9 Watch where my men are **r**,

rear (6)

Num 10:25 As a **r** guard for the whole
Jos 6:9 The **r** guard followed the ark
6:13 and the **r** guard followed the
10:19 Cut off their **r** guard.
1Sm 29:2 marching in the **r** with Achish.
1Ki 6:16 off a 30-foot-long room at the **r**

reason (104)

Gen 41:32 The **r** Pharaoh has had a
Exo 9:16 But I have spared you for this **r**.
Lev 11:44 "Here is the **r**: I am the LORD
11:45 Here is the **r** ⌊again⌋:
Jos 5:4 This is the **r** Joshua
7:26 For this **r** that place is still
Jdg 11:8 "The **r** we've turned to you now
1Sm 19:5 innocent blood for no **r**?"
25:31 you spilled blood for no good **r**
1Ki 1:41 "What's the **r** for the noise in
20:42 For that **r** your life will be taken
2Ki 4:27 has hidden the **r** from me.
2Ch 20:27 The LORD gave them a **r** to
23:19 unclean for any **r** could enter.
Ezr 2:62 For this **r** they were considered
Neh 7:64 For this **r** they were considered
12:43 had given them **r** to rejoice.
Job 1:9 you given Job a **r** to fear God?
2:3 me into ruining him for no **r**."
9:17 and bruise me without a **r**.
22:6 For no **r** you take your brothers'
35:16 opens his mouth for no good **r**
Psa 7:4 rescued someone who has no **r**
32:6 For this **r** let all godly people
35:7 For no **r** they hid their net in a
35:7 For no **r** they dug the pit ⌊to
35:19 hate me for no **r** wink ⌊at me⌋.
38:19 Many hate me for no **r**.
39:6 They are busy for no **r**.
53:5 ⌊but⌋ there was no **r** to panic,
69:4 Those who hate me for no **r**
69:4 They have no **r** to be my
89:47 Adam's descendants for no **r**?
109:3 They fight against me for no **r**.
119:161 have persecuted me for no **r**,
Pro 3:30 quarrel with a person for no **r** if
23:29 Who has wounds for no **r**?
24:28 your neighbor without a **r**,
Ecc 7:25 out wisdom and the **r** for things.
7:27 in order to find a **r** for things.
7:28 I am still seeking a **r** for things,
Isa 29:21 those who, without any **r**,
52:4 oppressed them for no **r**.
52:5 people are taken away for no **r**.
Jer 15:11 rescue you for a good **r**.
Lam 3:21 "The **r** I can ⌊still⌋ find hope is
3:29 Maybe a **r** to hope exists.
3:52 enemies for no **r** hunted me like
Eze 14:23 was done for a **r**," declares
22:29 oppress foreigners for no **r**.
Mal 1:10 light fires on my altar for no **r**.
Mat 5:32 any **r** other than unfaithfulness
19:3 man divorce his wife for any **r**?"
19:9 his wife for any **r** other than her
19:10 "If that is the only **r** a man can
Mar 2:28 For this **r** the Son of Man has
Luk 2:34 "This child is the **r** that many
12:56 But for some **r** you don't know
Jon 8:6 They wanted to find a **r** to bring
8:24 For this **r** I told you that you'll
12:11 Lazarus was the **r** why many
15:25 'They hate me for no **r**.'
18:37 come into the world for this **r**:
Act 13:28 they couldn't find any good **r**
18:14 **r** would demand that I put up
19:40 of rioting today for no **r**.
24:26 For that **r**, Felix would send for
26:16 I have appeared to you for a **r**.
26:21 For this **r** the Jews took me
Rom 1:24 For this **r** God allowed their
1:26 For this **r** God allowed their
2:12 Here's the **r**: Whoever sins
4:2 he would have had a **r** to brag.
9:17 "I put you here for this **r**:
14:9 For this **r** Christ died and came
1Co 11:30 This is the **r** why many of you
2Co 1:14 We are your **r** to be proud,
1:14 as you will be our **r** to be proud
1:20 For that **r**, because of our
2Co 2:3 This is the very **r** I wrote to you.
4:6 For that **r** we bring to light the
Eph 1:15 all of God's people. For this **r**
3:1 This is the **r** I, Paul, am the
3:14 This is the **r** I kneel in the
4:30 give God's Holy Spirit any **r**
6:13 For this **r**, take up all the armor
6:18 For the same **r** be alert.
Php 1:19 for another **r**. I know that I will
1:26 I want to give you even more **r**
2:18 For this same **r** you also
Col 1:9 For this **r** we have not stopped
1Th 2:13 Here is another **r** why we never
2Ti 1:12 For this **r** I suffer as I do.
2:10 For that **r**, I endure everything
Tit 1:13 For this **r**, sharply correct
Heb 2:1 For this **r** we must pay closer
10:5 For this **r**, when Christ came
Jas 4:3 you want them for the wrong **r**
1Jn 3:1 For this **r** the world doesn't
3:8 The **r** that the Son of God
3Jn 1:10 For this **r**, when I come I will
Jud 1:4 in writing for the following **r**:
Rev 12:12 Be glad for this **r**, heavens and
18:8 For this **r** her plagues of death,

reasonable (1)

Est 8:5 you consider my cause to be **r**

reasoned (1)

1Co 13:11 like a child, and **r** like a child.

reasoning (1)

Pro 18:1 He opposes all sound **r**.

reasons (2)

1Sm 28:19 For the same **r** the LORD will
2Co 7:4 and I have a lot of **r** to be proud

reassembled (1)

2Sm 10:15 the Arameans **r** ⌊their troops⌋.

reassure (1)

2Sm 14:17 I thought that you would **r** me.

reassured (4)

Gen 50:21 In this way he **r** them,
Rut 2:13 have comforted me and **r** me,
1Jn 3:19 we will be **r** in his presence.
3:20 we will be **r** that God is greater

Reba (2)

Num 31:8 Evi, Rekem, Zur, Hur, and **R**.
Jos 13:21 Evi, Rekem, Zur, Hur, and **R**.

Rebekah (31)

Gen 22:23 Bethuel is the father of **R**.
24:15 **R** came with her jar on her
24:29 **R** had a brother whose name
24:45 I had finished praying, **R** came
24:51 Here's **R**! Take her and go! She
24:53 clothes and gave them to **R**.
24:58 They called for **R** and asked
24:59 So they let their sister **R** and
24:60 They gave **R** a blessing:
24:61 Then **R** and her maids left.
24:61 The servant took **R** and left.
24:64 When **R** saw Isaac,
24:67 He married **R**. She became his
25:20 years old when he married **R**,
25:21 his wife **R** became pregnant.
25:28 However, **R** loved Jacob.
26:7 place would kill him to get **R**,
26:8 Isaac caressing his wife **R**.
26:35 women brought Isaac and **R**
27:5 **R** was listening while Isaac
27:6 **R** said to her son Jacob,
27:11 Jacob said to his mother **R**,
27:15 Then **R** took her older son
27:42 When **R** was told what her
27:46 **R** said to Isaac, "I can't stand
28:5 the Aramean and brother of **R**.
49:31 Isaac and his wife **R** are buried
Rom 9:10 The same thing happened to **R**.
9:10 **R** became pregnant by our
9:11 **R** was told that the older child

Zec 1:16 will be used to **r** Jerusalem.
6:12 he will **r** the LORD's temple.
6:13 He will **r** the LORD's temple
6:15 are far away will come and **r**
Mal 1:4 but we will **r** the ruins.'
1:4 of Armies says: They may **r**,
Mat 26:61 tear down God's temple and **r**
Jon 2:19 and I'll **r** it in three days."
2:20 you really think you're going to **r**
Gal 2:18 If I **r** something that I've torn

rebuilder (1)

Isa 58:12 You will be called the **R** of

rebuilding (12)

2Ch 24:27 and the **r** of God's temple is in
Ezr 4:12 They are **r** that rebellious and
4:21 So order these men to stop **r**.
4:23 They forced the Jews to stop **r**.
5:11 We are **r** the temple that was
Neh 3:1 started by **r** Sheep Gate.
3:2 The men from Jericho were **r**
4:1 heard we were **r** the wall,
4:17 who were **r** the wall.
6:6 That's why you're **r** the wall.
Job 8:6 righteousness by **r** your home.
Mic 7:11 The day for **r** your walls and

rebuilt (54)

Num 32:34 The tribe of Gad **r** the cities of
32:37 The tribe of Reuben **r** the cities
32:38 they gave the cities they **r**.
Dtr 13:16 mound of ruins and never be **r**.
Jos 19:50 He **r** the city and lived there.
Jdg 18:28 The people of Dan **r** the city
21:23 So they **r** their cities and lived
1Ki 9:17 So Solomon **r** Gezer,
12:25 Jeroboam **r** Shechem in the
16:34 time Hiel from Bethel **r** Jericho.
18:30 He **r** the LORD's altar that had
2Ki 14:22 Azariah **r** Elath and returned it
21:3 He **r** the illegal places of
1Ch 11:8 Joab **r** the rest of the city.
2Ch 8:2 He **r** the cities Huram gave him,
8:4 He **r** Tadmor in the desert and
8:5 He **r** Upper Beth Horon and
8:6 ⌊He also **r**⌋ Baalath and all the
11:6 He **r** Bethlehem, Etam, Tekoa,
26:2 Uzziah **r** Elath and returned it to
32:5 He **r** all the broken sections of
33:3 He **r** the illegal places of
33:14 After this, Manasseh **r** the outer
Ezr 3:3 So they **r** the altar on its
4:13 also know that if this city is **r**
4:16 king to know that if this city is **r**
4:21 Keep this city from being **r** until
5:13 for God's temple to be **r**.
5:17 of God to be **r** in Jerusalem.
6:3 The temple should be **r** as a
Neh 3:1 They **r** as far as the Tower of
3:3 of Hassenaah **r** Fish Gate.
3:13 They **r** it and set its doors,
3:14 He **r** it and set its doors,
3:15 He **r** it, put a roof over it,
4:6 So we **r** the wall, which was
4:6 which was **r** to about half its
6:1 our enemies heard that I had **r**
7:1 duties after the wall had been **r**
Job 12:14 down, it cannot be **r**.
Isa 25:2 into cities that will never be **r**.
44:26 of Judah, "They will be **r**."
44:28 about Jerusalem, "It will be **r**."
Jer 31:4 build you up, and you will be **r**,
31:38 "when the city will be **r** for me
Eze 13:5 the gaps in the wall or **r**
26:14 You will never be **r**.
36:10 and the ruins will be **r**.
36:33 and your ruins will be **r**.
36:36 have **r** the ruined places and
38:8 a land that has been **r** after
Dan 9:25 will be restored and **r**
Zec 1:16 My house will be **r** in it,
8:9 so that the temple might be **r**,

Recah (1)

1Ch 4:12 These were the men from **R**.

recall (2)

Isa 46:8 **R** your rebellious acts.
Lam 1:22 **R** all of their wickedness.

recalled (1)

Isa 45:23 mouth that will not be **r**,

recalling (1)

2Ch 21:7 But the LORD, **r** the promise he

recapture (2)

Jdg 11:26 Why didn't you **r** these cities
Eze 14:5 I will do this to **r** the hearts of

recede (1)

Gen 8:3 The water began to **r** from the

receive (142)

Exo 14:4 his entire army, I will **r** honor,
14:17 I will **r** honor because of what I
Lev 7:18 You will not **r** credit for it.
24:19 injures a neighbor must **r**
24:20 injures another person must **r**
Num 18:28 LORD out of all that you **r** from
18:29 Out of all the gifts you **r**,
18:31 because it's the wages you **r**
26:55 The tribes will **r** their land
Dtr 10:18 orphans and widows **r** justice.
18:1 the whole tribe of Levi — will **r**
18:1 sacrifices will be what they **r**.
29:14 You aren't the only people to **r**
33:3 your feet to **r** your instructions.
Jos 21:2 Moses that we should **r** cities
Rut 2:12 May you **r** a rich reward from
2Sm 15:28 crossings in the desert until I **r**
20:1 We won't **r** an inheritance from
1Ki 2:33 and throne always **r** peace from
12:16 We won't **r** an inheritance from
2Ki 12:5 Each of the priests should **r** it
12:8 The priests agreed neither to **r**
2Ch 10:16 We won't **r** an inheritance from
Job 3:9 Let it hope for light and **r** none.
15:8 on God's council meeting and **r**
27:13 that tyrants **r** from the Almighty
Psa 24:5 ⌊This person⌋ will **r** a blessing
146:5 Blessed are those who **r** help
Pro 14:7 because you will not **r**
Ecc 9:11 necessarily **r** special treatment.
Isa 34:6 The LORD will **r** a sacrifice in
50:11 This is what you will **r** from me:
61:7 You will **r** a double measure of
Jer 22:19 He will **r** a donkey's burial.
Eze 47:23 Foreign residents will **r** their
48:23 what the rest of the tribes will **r**:
Dan 2:9 you'll all **r** the same
Hos 14:2 all our sins, and kindly **r** us.
Zec 6:13 temple and **r** royal honor.
Mat 7:7 "Ask, and you will **r**.
7:8 Everyone who asks will **r**.
10:41 a prophet as a prophet will **r**
10:41 as a righteous person will **r**
19:29 because of my name will **r**
20:10 they expected to **r** more.
21:22 Have faith that you will **r**
Mar 10:15 Whoever doesn't **r** the kingdom
10:30 will certainly **r** a hundred times
10:30 They will certainly **r** homes,
10:30 to come they will **r** eternal life.
10:38 the baptism that I'm going to **r**?"
10:39 the baptism that I'm going to **r**.
12:40 The scribes will **r** the most
Luk 6:38 Give, and you will **r**.
11:9 I tell you to ask, and you will **r**.
11:10 Everyone who asks will **r**.
12:47 to do it will **r** a hard beating.
12:48 he deserved punishment will **r**
18:17 Whoever doesn't **r** the kingdom
18:30 will certainly **r** many times as
18:30 in this life and will **r** eternal life
18:42 Jesus told him, "**R** your sight!
20:47 The scribes will **r** the most
24:49 until you **r** power from heaven."
Jon 3:27 John answered, "People can't **r**
7:39 whom his believers would **r**.
9:10 "How did you **r** your sight?"
11:4 of God will **r** glory through it."
16:24 Ask and you will **r** so that you
20:22 and said, "**R** the Holy Spirit.
Act 1:8 But you will **r** power when the
2:38 Then you will **r** the Holy Spirit
3:5 to **r** something from them.
3:21 Heaven must **r** Jesus until the
8:15 would **r** the Holy Spirit.
8:19 hands on will **r** the Holy Spirit."
10:43 one named Jesus **r** forgiveness
17:11 willing to **r** God's message,
19:2 and asked them, "Did you **r** the
22:13 said, 'Brother Saul, **r** your sight!
26:18 Then they will **r** forgiveness for
27:3 visit his friends and **r** any care
Rom 3:21 Now, the way to **r** God's
3:24 They **r** God's approval freely by
4:25 that we could **r** God's approval.
5:2 that we will **r** glory from God.
5:17 **r** God's overflowing kindness
5:19 humanity will **r** God's approval.
10:3 ⌊how to **r**⌋ God's approval.
10:4 has faith may **r** God's approval.
10:10 believing you **r** God's approval,
1Co 2:12 Now, we didn't **r** the spirit that
3:8 and each will **r** a reward for his
3:14 survives, he will **r** a reward.
4:5 person will **r** praise from God.
9:10 or threshes should expect to **r**
9:11 is it too much if we **r** part of the
2Co 1:5 we can **r** so much comfort from
5:10 Then all people will **r** what
5:21 take our sin so that we might **r**
9:6 received God's blessings will **r**
11:4 When you **r** a spirit that is
Gal 1:12 I didn't **r** it from any person.
2:16 people don't **r** God's approval
2:16 in order to **r** God's approval
2:16 People won't **r** God's approval
2:21 If we **r** God's approval by
3:2 Did you **r** the Spirit by your own
3:14 Jesus Christ and we would **r**
3:21 then certainly we would **r**
3:24 Christ came so that we could **r**
6:9 Certainly, each of us will **r**
Eph 1:14 that we will **r** our inheritance.
6:10 Finally, **r** your power from the
Php 2:19 I can **r** some encouraging news
3:9 This means that I didn't **r** God's
2Th 3:9 didn't have a right to **r** support.
1Ti 6:2 better because those who **r**
2Ti 2:10 may **r** salvation from Christ
Heb 1:14 who are going to **r** salvation.
4:16 of God's kindness to **r** mercy
6:17 those who would **r** his promise,
7:5 who become priests must **r**
7:8 Priests **r** a tenth of everything,
7:9 later his descendants would **r**
10:36 you can **r** what he has
11:8 go to a place that he would **r** as
11:13 They didn't **r** the things that
11:19 Abraham did **r** Isaac back from
12:17 when he wanted to **r** the
12:17 that the firstborn son was to **r**,
Jas 1:7 expect to **r** anything from
1:12 they will **r** the crown of life that
2:5 to become rich in faith and to **r**
2:21 Didn't our ancestor Abraham **r**
1Pe 5:4 you will **r** the crown of glory
1Jn 3:22 and **r** from him anything we
3:22 We **r** it because we obey his
2Jn 1:8 but that you **r** your full reward.
Rev 4:11 you deserve to **r** glory,
5:12 was slain deserves to **r** power,
17:12 They will **r** authority to rule as

received (130)

Gen 4:11 which has **r** the blood of your
43:23 I **r** your money." Then he
47:22 land because the priests **r**
Lev 10:13 That is the command I **r**.
22:25 kind of castrated animal **r** from
Num 23:20 I have **r** a command to bless.
31:36 sheep and goats they **r**,
31:38 Of the 36,000 cattle they **r**,
31:39 Of the 30,500 donkeys they **r**,

Num 31:40 Of the 16,000 people they **r**,
31:43 The community **r** 337,500
32:18 Israelite has **r** his own land.
34:14 have already **r** their land.
34:15 Those two-and-a-half tribes **r**
Jos 13:8 had **r** their inheritance east
15:45 Judah also **r** Ekron with its
15:55 They also **r** another ten cities
16:4 **r** this land as their inheritance.
17:1 had **r** Gilead and Bashan
18:2 who had not yet **r** any land as
18:7 of the tribe of Manasseh have **r**
19:2 In their inheritance they **r** 13
19:9 So Simeon **r** its inheritance
19:49 When they all had finally **r** the
21:4 Aaron the Levite **r** 13 cities from
21:5 descendants **r** 10 cities from
21:6 Gershon's descendants **r** 13
21:7 Merari's descendants **r** 12
Jdg 18:1 Up to that time they had not **r**
1Sm 11:9 men of Jabesh **r** the message,
14:37 But he **r** no answer that day.
1Ki 5:8 "I've **r** the message you sent
21:15 Jezebel **r** the message and
2Ki 9:15 wounds he **r** while fighting King
1Ch 5:2 Joseph **r** the rights as firstborn.)
5:20 and **r** help while fighting them.
6:60 Aaron's descendants **r** Geba
6:61 descendants **r** 10 cities chosen
6:71 Gershom's descendants **r**
6:72 tribe of Issachar, they **r** Kedesh
6:74 From the tribe of Asher, they **r**
6:76 tribe of Naphtali, they **r** Kedesh
6:77 descendants **r** Rimmono
6:78 Merari's descendants **r** land
6:80 From the tribe of Gad, they **r**
2Ch 30:16 blood they **r** from the Levites.
Ezr 5:5 be stopped until Darius **r**
Job 29:13 I **r** a blessing from the dying.
Psa 28:7 heart trusted him, so I **r** help.
68:18 You **r** gifts from people,
73:13 I've **r** no reward for keeping my
109:17 so he never **r** a blessing.
Isa 40:2 It has **r** from the LORD double
53:5 and we **r** healing from his
Hag 1:9 a lot, but you **r** a little.
1:13 of the LORD who had **r**
Mat 10:8 you **r** them without paying.
15:5 you might have **r** from me,'
20:9 and each **r** a day's wages.
20:10 each of them **r** a day's wages.
25:16 "The one who **r** ten thousand
25:18 But the one who **r** two
25:20 The one who **r** ten thousand
25:22 "The one who **r** four thousand
25:24 "Then the one who **r** two
25:27 When I returned, I would have **r**
Mar 11:24 already **r** whatever you pray
Luk 1:2 They **r** their information from
Jon 1:16 Each of us has **r** one gift after
9:11 washed it off, and **r** my sight."
9:15 man again how he **r** his sight.
Act 1:18 With the money he **r** from the
2:33 Jesus has also **r** and has
5:3 of the money you **r** for the land.
7:38 Moses **r** life-giving messages
7:45 After our ancestors **r** the tent,
7:53 who **r** Moses' Teachings,
8:17 the Samaritans **r** the Holy Spirit.
10:47 They have **r** the Holy Spirit in
20:24 to carry out the mission I **r** from
21:31 charge of the Roman soldiers **r**
22:3 Cilicia and **r** my education from
26:10 By the authority I **r** from the
28:21 "We haven't **r** any letters from
Rom 1:5 Through him we have **r** God's
4:13 Abraham or his descendants **r**
5:18 and everyone **r** God's
8:15 You haven't **r** the spirit of
8:15 Instead, you have **r** the spirit of
1Co 2:12 Instead, we **r** the Spirit who
6:11 and you have **r** God's approval
6:19 whom you **r** from God,
11:23 I passed on to you what I had **r**
15:1 I already told you, which you **r**,
15:3 points of doctrine that I had **r**:
2Co 1:4 comfort we have **r** from God.
7:7 the comfort he had **r** while
9:6 he has **r** God's blessings will
11:4 from the Spirit you **r** earlier,
Gal 1:9 from the Good News you **r**,
Php 4:9 you've learned and **r** from me,
4:15 and you **r** what I gave you.
Col 2:6 You **r** Christ Jesus the Lord,
4:10 You have **r** instructions about
1Th 2:13 When you **r** God's word from
2Th 3:6 the tradition you **r** from us.
1Ti 4:3 God created food to be **r** with
4:4 should be rejected if it is **r**
4:14 you **r** through prophecy when
2Ti 1:6 You **r** a gift from God when I
Heb 1:3 he **r** the highest position,
6:15 So Abraham **r** what God
7:6 he **r** a tenth of everything from
7:8 Melchizedek **r** a tenth of
7:11 based on instructions they **r**.
8:1 This chief priest has **r** the
10:12 Then he **r** the highest position
11:4 his faith Abel **r** God's approval,
11:7 world and **r** God's approval that
11:9 who **r** the same promise from
11:17 Abraham, the one who **r** the
11:33 and **r** what God had promised.
11:35 Women **r** their loved ones back
11:39 but none of them **r** what God
12:2 Then he **r** the highest position
Jas 2:25 She **r** God's approval because
2Pe 1:17 eyewitnesses when he **r** honor
1Jn 2:27 The anointing you **r** from Christ
Rev 2:26 I have **r** authority from my
3:3 what you **r** and heard.

receives (17)

Num 24:16 **r** knowledge from the Most
Pro 9:7 corrects a mocker **r** abuse.
28:13 abandons them **r** compassion.
28:27 ignores the poor **r** many curses.
Isa 31:3 and the one who **r** help will fall.
Mar 10:15 of God as a little child **r**
Luk 7:47 But whoever **r** little forgiveness
18:17 of God as a little child **r**
Act 13:39 in Jesus **r** God's approval.
Rom 3:7 that God **r** by showing that
2Co 10:18 who **r** approval,
Gal 3:11 No one **r** God's approval by
Eph 1:14 God **r** praise and glory for this.
3:15 heaven and on earth **r** its name.
Jas 2:24 You see that a person **r** God's
1Pe 4:11 way God **r** glory through Jesus
Rev 2:17 only to the person who **r** it.

receiving (6)

Act 13:38 Sins kept you from **r** God's
20:35 is more satisfying than **r** them.'"
Rom 10:3 God's way for **r** his approval.
10:5 Moses writes about **r** God's
1Th 2:16 at last they are **r** ⌊God's⌋ anger.
Heb 6:12 you will imitate those who are **r**

recently (6)

Dtr 24:5 A man who has **r** been married
Jer 34:15 **R**, you changed and did what I
Mic 2:8 **R**, my people have turned into
Luk 14:20 another said, 'I **r** got married,
24:18 know what has happened **r**?"
Act 18:2 and they had **r** come from Italy

reception (1)

Luk 5:29 Levi held a large **r** at his home

receptive (1)

Mat 10:13 But if it is not **r**, take back your

recessed (19)

Eze 40:9 Its **r** walls were 3 ½ feet thick.
40:10 and the **r** walls on each side
40:16 The guardrooms and **r** walls
40:16 were carved on the **r** walls.
40:21 three guardrooms, its **r** walls,
40:22 Its windows, **r** walls,
40:24 He measured its **r** walls and its
40:26 were carved on the **r** walls,
Eze 40:29 Its guardrooms, **r** walls,
40:31 were carved on the **r** walls,
40:33 Its guardrooms, **r** walls,
40:34 were carved on the **r** walls,
40:36 Its guardrooms, **r** walls,
40:37 Its **r** walls faced the outer
40:37 were carved on the **r** walls,
40:48 and measured its **r** walls.
40:49 Pillars stood by the **r** walls,
41:1 and measured the **r** walls.
Dan 3:1 He set it up in a **r** area in the

Rechab (11)

2Sm 4:2 and the other was named **R**.
4:5 **R** and Baanah, the sons of
4:6 Then **R** and his brother Baanah
4:9 David responded to **R** and his
4:12 who executed **R** and Baanah,
2Ki 10:15 he met Jehonadab, son of **R**,
10:23 Jehu and Jehonadab, son of **R**,
Jer 35:2 "Go to the family of **R** and talk
35:3 sons — the whole family of **R**.
35:5 wine in front of the family of **R**.
35:18 said to the family of **R**,

Rechab's (6)

Neh 3:14 **R** son, the official in charge of
Jer 35:6 **R** son, gave us this order:
35:8 **R** son, in everything he ordered
35:14 Jonadab, **R** son, ordered his
35:16 **R** son, have carried out the
35:19 **R** son, will always serve me."

recite (2)

Dtr 11:29 **r** the blessing from Mount
Psa 9:14 so that I may **r** your praises one

recited (2)

Dtr 31:30 Moses **r** all the words of this
32:44 and **r** all the words of this song

reciting (3)

Dtr 32:45 When Moses had finished **r** all
Jos 1:8 Never stop **r** these teachings.
Eph 5:19 by **r** psalms, hymns,

reckless (5)

Jdg 9:4 hired worthless and **r** men
Isa 32:4 Then those who are **r** will
Hab 1:6 that fierce and **r** nation.
Zep 3:4 Its prophets are **r** and unfaithful.
2Ti 3:4 They will be **r** and conceited.

recklessly (1)

Psa 106:33 him bitter so that he spoke **r**.

reclaim (8)

Isa 50:2 Am I too weak to **r** you?
52:9 He will **r** Jerusalem.
Jer 31:11 of Jacob and **r** them from those
Lam 3:58 O LORD. **R** my life.
Hos 7:13 I want to **r** them, but they tell
13:14 I want to **r** them from death.
Mic 4:10 There the LORD will **r** you from
Mal 4:6 If not, I will come and **r** my land

reclaimed (10)

Isa 35:9 But the people **r** ⌊by the
43:1 because I have **r** you.
44:22 because I have **r** you.
44:23 The LORD has **r** Jacob.
44:24 The LORD **r** you. He formed you
48:20 LORD has **r** his servant Jacob.
51:10 the sea so that the people **r** ⌊by
62:12 Those **R** by the LORD,
63:9 and compassion he **r** them.
Zec 10:8 them because I have **r** them.

reclaiming (1)

Isa 63:4 year for my **r** ⌊you⌋ has come.

reclaims (1)

Isa 49:26 One of Jacob, who **r** you.

recognize (37)

Gen 27:23 He didn't **r** Jacob, because his

Gen 38:25 See if you **r** whose signet ring,
42:8 his brothers, they didn't **r** him.
Exo 7:17 This is the way you will **r** that I
Dtr 18:21 "How can we **r** that the LORD
21:17 Instead, he must **r** the son of
33:9 They didn't **r** their own brothers
1Ki 14:2 that people will not **r** you as my
Job 2:12 they didn't even **r** him.
7:10 doesn't **r** him anymore.
37:7 so that people will **r** his work.
Psa 36:2 not hate or ⌊even⌋ **r** his guilt.
89:39 You have refused to **r** the
Pro 14:33 person. Even fools **r** this.
Isa 29:15 see us" and "No one can **r** us."
43:19 Don't you **r** it? I will clear a way
61:9 Everyone who sees them will **r**
Hos 14:9 person with insight will **r** them.
Mat 5:3 "Blessed are those who **r** they
12:33 A person can **r** a tree by its fruit.
17:12 because they didn't **r** him.
Luk 2:12 This is how you will **r** him:
19:44 because you didn't **r** the time
24:16 they saw him, they didn't **r** him.
Jon 1:10 Yet, the world didn't **r** him.
10:4 him because they **r** his voice.
10:5 because they don't **r** his voice."
10:38 Then you will know and **r** that
Act 2:6 Each person was startled to **r**
27:39 morning they couldn't **r** the land
1Co 1:21 wisdom was unable to **r** God
11:29 he doesn't **r** the Lord's body.
2Co 13:5 Don't you **r** that you are people
2Ti 3:7 but are never able to **r** the truth.
1Jn 3:1 reason the world doesn't **r** us,
3:1 and it didn't **r** him either.
4:2 is how you can **r** God's Spirit:

recognized (24)

Gen 37:33 He **r** it and said, "It is my son's
38:26 Judah **r** them and said,
42:7 saw his brothers, he **r** them.
42:8 though Joseph **r** his brothers,
Jdg 18:3 they **r** the young Levite's voice.
Rut 3:14 early before anyone could be **r**.
1Sm 26:17 Saul **r** David's voice.
1Ki 18:7 Obadiah **r** him and immediately
20:41 The king of Israel **r** him as one
Jer 28:9 prophesied peace was **r** as
Mat 14:35 The men there **r** Jesus and
22:18 Jesus **r** their evil plan,
Mar 6:33 saw them leave and **r** them.
6:54 the people **r** Jesus.
12:15 Jesus **r** their hypocrisy,
Luk 24:31 were opened, and they **r** him.
24:35 how they had **r** Jesus when
Act 12:14 When she **r** Peter's voice,
19:34 But when they **r** that Alexander
Rom 7:7 In fact, I wouldn't have **r** sin if
7:13 by sin so that sin would be **r**
Gal 2:2 those **r** as important people
2:6 Those who were **r** as important
2:9 and John (who were **r** as the

recognizes (3)

Dtr 32:5 He **r** that his people are corrupt.
Psa 138:6 and he **r** arrogant people from a
Lam 4:8 No one **r** them on the streets.

recollections (1)

Job 13:12 "Your **r** are worthless proverbs.

recommend (3)

Ecc 8:15 So I **r** the enjoyment ⌊of life⌋.
2Co 3:1 need letters that **r** us to you or
3:1 from you that **r** us to others?

recommendation (3)

2Co 3:2 You're our letter of **r** written in
4:2 This is our ⌊letter of⌋ **r**.
10:18 own **r** who receives approval,

recommendations (1)

2Co 10:12 enough to make their own **r**.

recommended (1)

2Co 12:11 You should have **r** me to others.

recommends (1)

2Co 10:18 but the person whom the Lord **r**.

reconquered (1)

2Ki 13:25 **r** the cities that Benhadad had

reconsider (4)

Exo 32:12 **R** your decision to bring this
Joe 2:14 He may **r** and change his plan
Jnh 3:9 God may **r** his plans and turn
4:2 to forgive and to **r** your threats

reconsidered (3)

Exo 32:14 So the LORD **r** his threat to
1Ch 21:15 the LORD **r** and changed his
Jnh 3:10 So God **r** his threat to destroy

record (14)

1Ki 3:8 are too numerous to count or **r**.
9:15 This is the **r** of the forced
2Ki 21:25 he did — written in the official **r**
2Ch 24:27 The **r** about his sons,
Ezr 5:10 so that we would have a **r**
Est 2:23 in his official **r** of daily events.
Job 14:16 will not keep ⌊a **r** of⌋ my sins.
Psa 56:8 (You have kept a **r** of my
87:6 The LORD will **r** this in the
109:15 and sin always remain on **r**
130:3 to stand if you kept a **r** of sins?
Hos 13:12 "Ephraim's wickedness is on **r**.
13:12 The **r** of the people's sins is
Rom 5:13 But no **r** of sin can be kept

recorded (22)

Jos 10:13 Isn't this **r** in the Book of
2Sm 1:18 (It is **r** in the Book of Jashar.)
1Ki 2:3 instructions as they are **r**
1Ch 5:17 All these people were **r** in
7:5 of them was **r** in the genealogy.
7:7 22,034 of them were **r**.
7:9 of them were **r** according
7:40 military roster had 26,000 **r** in it.
9:1 All Israel was **r** in the
9:22 Their genealogies were **r** in
24:6 Shemaiah **r** their names in the
2Ch 26:22 is **r** by the prophet Isaiah,
Ezr 8:34 entire weight was **r** at that time.
Neh 12:22 and Jaddua were **r** until the
12:23 heads of the Levites were **r**
Est 1:19 It should be **r** in the decrees of
10:2 are **r** in the history of the kings
Psa 139:16 Every day ⌊of my life⌋ was **r** in
Isa 4:3 everyone who is **r** among the
49:1 mother's womb, he **r** my name.
Eze 13:9 people make decisions or be **r**
Rev 20:12 had done, as **r** in the books.

records (60)

Gen 41:49 finally gave up keeping any **r**
Rut 4:10 relatives or from the public **r**.
1Ki 11:41 written in the **r** of Solomon?
14:19 reign is written in the official **r**
14:29 he did — written in the official **r**
15:7 he did — written in the official **r**
15:23 written in the official **r**
15:31 he did — written in the official **r**
16:5 acts — written in the official **r**
16:14 he did — written in the official **r**
16:20 his plot written in the official **r**
16:27 acts — written in the official **r**
22:39 written in the official **r**
22:45 fought — written in the official **r**
2Ki 1:18 he did — written in the official **r**
8:23 he did — written in the official **r**
10:34 acts — written in the official **r**
12:19 he did — written in the official **r**
13:8 acts — written in the official **r**
13:12 Judah — written in the official **r**
14:15 Judah — written in the official **r**
14:18 Amaziah written in the official **r**
14:28 Israel — written in the official **r**
15:6 he did — written in the official **r**
15:11 is written in the official **r**
15:15 is written in the official **r**
15:21 he did — written in the official **r**
2Ki 15:26 did — is written in the official **r**
15:31 did — is written in the official **r**
15:36 he did — written in the official **r**
16:19 he did — written in the official **r**
20:20 written in the official **r** of the
21:17 written in the official **r**
23:28 he did — written in the official **r**
24:5 he did — written in the official **r**
1Ch 4:22 Lehem (according to ancient **r**).
4:33 had their own genealogical **r**:
5:7 in the genealogical **r** according
5:17 were recorded in genealogical **r**
27:24 in the official **r** of King David.
29:29 first to last is written in the **r**
2Ch 9:29 from first to last written in the **r**
12:15 from first to last written in the **r**
12:15 the prophet Shemaiah and the **r**
20:34 last is written in the **r** of Jehu,
31:16 genealogical **r** did not matter.
32:32 and in the **r** of the kings of
33:18 God of Israel — are in the **r**
33:19 it are written in the **r** of Hozai.
35:4 which are listed in the **r** of King
35:4 of King David of Israel and the **r**
35:27 first to last — are written in the **r**
Ezr 2:62 names in the genealogical **r**,
4:15 you should search the official **r**
4:15 You will find in those official **r**
Neh 4:5 their sins disappear from your **r**.
7:64 names in the genealogical **r**,
Est 6:1 to bring the official daily **r**,
6:2 The **r** showed how Mordecai
Eze 13:9 or be recorded in the **r**

recover (6)

2Ki 1:2 if I will **r** from this injury."
8:8 'Will I **r** from this illness?'"
8:9 he will **r** from this illness."
9:15 had returned to Jezreel to **r** from
Isa 11:11 power again to **r** what remains
Luk 22:32 So when you **r**, strengthen the

recovered (6)

Jos 5:8 in the camp until they **r**.
1Sm 7:14 And Israel **r** the territory
30:22 be given any of the loot we **r**.
2Ki 13:25 three times and **r** those cities
14:28 how he **r** Damascus and
Isa 39:1 had been sick and had **r**.

recovery (1)

Pro 6:15 he will be crushed beyond **r**.

recruit (2)

1Ki 20:25 **R** an army with as many
Mat 23:15 You cross land and sea to **r** a

recurring (2)

Gen 41:32 Pharaoh has had a **r** dream is
2Co 12:7 forced to deal with a **r** problem.

red (120)

Gen 25:25 The first one born was **r**.
25:30 "Let me have the whole pot of **r**
25:30 red stuff to eat — that **r** stuff
38:28 midwife took a piece of **r** yarn,
38:30 brother was born with the **r** yarn
Exo 10:19 and blew them into the **R** Sea.
13:18 the desert toward the **R** Sea.
15:4 were drowned in the **R** Sea.
15:22 Israel away from the **R** Sea into
23:31 your borders from the **R** Sea
25:4 violet, purple, and bright **r** yarn,
25:5 rams' skins dyed **r**,
26:1 violet, purple, and bright **r** yarn,
26:14 skins that have been dyed **r**
26:31 violet, purple, and bright **r** yarn.
26:36 violet, purple, and bright **r** yarn.
27:16 violet, purple, and bright **r** yarn,
28:5 and bright **r** yarn, and fine linen.
28:6 and bright **r** yarn into the fabric.
28:15 and bright **r** yarn and out of fine
28:17 In the first row put **r** quartz,
28:33 and bright **r** yarn with gold bells
35:6 violet, purple, and bright **r** yarn,
35:7 rams' skins dyed **r**,

Exo 35:23 or bright **r** yarn, fine linen,
35:23 rams' skins dyed **r**,
35:25 and bright **r** yarn, and fine linen,
35:35 purple and bright **r** yarn on fine
36:8 violet, purple, and bright **r** yarn.
36:19 skins that had been dyed **r**
36:35 and bright **r** yarn and fine linen
36:37 violet, purple, and bright **r** yarn.
38:18 and bright **r** yarn embroidered
38:23 and bright **r** yarn on fine linen.
39:1 and bright **r** yarn they made
39:2 violet, purple, and bright **r** yarn.
39:3 violet, purple, and bright **r** yarn,
39:8 violet, purple, and bright **r** yarn,
39:10 In the first row they put **r** quartz
39:24 and bright **r** yarn, and fine yarn.
39:29 violet, purple, and bright **r** yarn.
39:34 made of rams' skins dyed **r**,
Lev 13:47 if there is a green or **r** area
14:4 birds, some cedar wood, **r** yarn,
14:6 bird, the cedar wood, the **r** yarn,
14:37 If it is green and **r** in sunken
14:49 two birds, cedar wood, **r** yarn,
14:51 the hyssop sprig, the **r** yarn,
14:52 and the **r** yarn to make the
Num 4:8 They will spread a bright **r**
14:25 road that goes to the **R** Sea."
19:2 to bring you a **r** cow that is
19:6 and some **r** yarn and throw
19:17 ashes from the **r** cow that was
21:4 the road that goes to the **R** Sea,
33:10 and set up camp by the **R** Sea.
33:11 They moved from the **R** Sea
Dtr 1:40 road that goes to the **R** Sea."
2:1 road that goes to the **R** Sea as
11:4 He drowned them in the **R** Sea
32:14 They drank the blood-**r** wine of
Jos 2:10 dried up the water of the **R** Sea
2:18 tie this **r** cord in the window
2:21 let them go and tied the **r** cord
4:23 as he did to the **R** Sea until we
24:6 your ancestors to the **R** Sea.
Jdg 11:16 through the desert to the **R** Sea
2Sm 1:24 you in decorated, **r** clothes,
1Ki 9:26 a fleet near the **R** Sea coast at
2Ki 3:22 It was as **r** as blood.
2Ch 2:7 purple, dark **r**, and violet cloth.
2:14 and dark **r** cloth, and linen.
3:14 and dark **r** cloth and of linen
Neh 9:9 heard them crying at the **R** Sea.
Job 16:16 My face is **r** from crying,
Psa 106:7 rebelled at the sea, the **R** Sea.
106:9 angrily commanded the **R** Sea,
106:22 and terrifying things at the **R**
114:3 The **R** Sea looked at this and
114:5 **R** Sea, why did you run away?
136:13 to one who divided the **R** Sea—
136:15 and his army into the **R** Sea—
Pro 23:31 not look at wine because it is **r**,
Isa 1:18 "Though your sins are bright **r**,
1:18 Though they are dark **r**,
13:8 Their faces will be burning **r**.
15:9 water in Dimon is **r** with blood,
34:3 will be **r** with their blood.
63:1 his clothes stained bright **r**?
63:2 Why are your clothes **r** and
Jer 4:30 Why do you dress in **r** and put
22:14 with cedar, and paints them **r**.
49:21 will be heard at the **R** Sea.
Eze 23:14 men, painted in bright **r**.
28:13 **r** quartz, topaz, crystal, beryl,
Dan 3:19 Abednego that his face turned **r**.
Joe 2:31 and the moon will become as **r**
Nah 2:3 of his warriors are painted **r**.
2:3 His soldiers have **r** uniforms.
2:3 on his chariots flashes fiery **r**,
Zec 1:8 I saw a man riding on a **r** horse.
1:8 Behind him were **r**,
6:2 The first chariot had **r** horses.
Mat 16:2 be fine because the sky is **r**.
16:3 the sky is **r** and overcast.
27:28 and put a bright **r** cape on him.
Act 2:20 and the moon will become as **r**
7:36 in Egypt, at the **R** Sea,
Heb 9:19 with some water, **r** yarn,
11:29 to go through the **R** Sea as if
Rev 4:3 like gray quartz and **r** quartz.
6:4 It was fiery **r**. Its rider was given
6:12 full moon turned as **r** as blood.
9:17 breastplates that were fiery **r**,
12:3 a huge fiery **r** serpent with
17:3 on a bright **r** beast covered
17:4 bright **r** clothes, gold jewelry,
18:12 purple cloth, silk, bright **r** cloth,
18:16 bright **r** clothes, gold jewelry,
21:20 fifth onyx, the sixth **r** quartz,

red-hot (3)

Psa 120:4 sharpened arrows and **r** coals.
Pro 6:28 Can anyone walk on **r** coals
1Ti 4:2 as if branded by a **r** iron.

reduce (5)

1Ki 12:4 **R** the hard work and lighten the
2Ch 10:4 **R** the hard work and lighten the
Jer 10:24 you'll **r** me to nothing.
Mat 24:22 If God does not **r** the number of
Mar 13:20 If the Lord does not **r** that time,

reduced (7)

Exo 5:11 work load will not be **r** one bit."
Psa 102:23 He has **r** ⌊the number of⌋ my
Isa 25:5 silenced like heat that is ⌊**r**⌋ by
41:11 who oppose you will be **r**
41:12 are at war with you will be **r**
Mat 24:22 But those days will be **r**
Mar 13:20 But those days will be **r**

reeds (6)

Gen 41:2 began to graze among the **r**.
41:18 began to graze among the **r**.
Job 9:26 quickly like boats made from **r**,
40:21 place among **r** and swamps.
Isa 18:2 made of **r** ⌊skimming⌋ over
19:6 The **r** and cattails will wither.

Reelaiah (1)

Ezr 2:2 **R**, Mordecai, Bilshan, Mispar,

reeled (1)

Psa 107:27 They **r** and staggered like

reestablished (1)

2Ch 29:35 in the LORD's temple was **r**.

referred (1)

1Sm 24:4 "Today is the day the LORD **r**

referring (3)

Gal 3:16 say, "descendants," **r** to many,
3:16 but "your descendant," **r** to one.
1Pe 1:11 the Spirit of Christ kept **r**

refine (4)

Jer 9:7 I will now **r** them with fire and
Dan 11:35 will be defeated in order to **r**,
Zec 13:9 I will **r** them as silver is refined.
Mal 3:3 He will purify Levi's sons and **r**

refined (11)

1Ch 28:18 and the **r** gold for the altar of
29:4 and 525,000 pounds of **r** silver.
Job 28:1 and a place where gold is **r**.
Psa 12:6 like silver **r** in a furnace and
66:10 You have **r** us in the same way
66:10 us in the same way silver is **r**.
Pro 17:7 **R** speech is not fitting for a
Isa 48:10 I have **r** you, but not like silver.
Dan 12:10 be purified, made white, and **r**.
Zec 13:9 I will refine them as silver is **r**.
Rev 1:15 feet were like glowing bronze **r**

refiner (1)

Mal 3:3 He will act like a **r** and a

refining (4)

Pro 17:3 The crucible is for **r** silver and
27:21 The crucible is for **r** silver and
Jer 6:27 of testing and **r** my people.
6:29 It is useless to go on **r** because

reflect (12)

Psa 48:9 your temple we carefully **r**
77:6 song in the night and **r** ⌊on it⌋.
77:12 I will **r** on all your actions and
119:15 I want to **r** on your guiding
119:23 against me, I **r** on your laws.
119:27 that I may **r** on your miracles.
119:48 I will **r** on your laws.
119:78 ⌊yet⌋ I **r** on your guiding
119:148 hours to **r** on your word.
143:5 I **r** on all that you have done.
2Co 3:18 As all of us **r** the Lord's glory
Php 1:27 Live as citizens who **r** the

reflected (2)

Pro 27:19 As a face is **r** in water,
27:19 so a person is **r** by his heart.

reflection (1)

Heb 1:3 His Son is the **r** of God's glory

reflects (2)

Psa 1:2 teachings of the LORD and **r**
37:30 righteous person **r** on wisdom.

reforms (1)

Act 24:2 lasting peace and **r** that benefit

refrained (1)

Job 32:6 That's why I **r** from speaking

refresh (5)

Sos 2:5 me with raisins and **r** me
Jer 31:25 I will **r** everyone who is filled
Act 3:20 come when the Lord will **r** you.
2Pe 1:13 think it's right to **r** your memory
3:1 I'm trying to **r** your memory.

refreshed (8)

Exo 23:12 and foreigners will also be **r**.
31:17 stopped working and was **r**.'"
Jdg 15:19 Then he was **r** and revived.
Psa 36:8 They are **r** with the rich foods
66:12 you brought us out and **r** us.
68:9 You **r** it when your land was
69:32 who look to God for help be **r**.
Rom 15:32 to you with joy and be **r** when

refreshes (2)

Pro 15:30 Good news **r** the body.
25:13 send him: He **r** his masters.

refreshing (1)

Isa 26:19 because your dew is a **r** dew,

refuge (83)

Num 35:6 the Levites will be cities of **r**.
35:11 certain cities to be places of **r**.
35:12 These cities will be places of **r**
35:13 cities you select as places of **r**,
35:15 will be places of **r** for Israelites,
35:25 back to the city of **r** you fled to.
35:26 outside the city of **r** you fled to.
35:27 finds you outside the city of **r**
35:28 must stay in their city of **r** until
35:32 fled to a city of **r** must never go
Dtr 19:9 more cities of **r** to these three.
32:37 Where is the rock they took **r**
32:38 Let them be your **r**!'
Jos 20:2 the cities of **r** about which
20:3 They will be a place of **r** from
20:7 were chosen as cities of **r**.
20:8 were chosen as cities of **r**
20:9 the cities chosen as cities of **r**
21:13 (a city of **r** for murderers),
21:21 were Shechem (a city of **r**
21:27 Golan in Bashan (a city of **r** for
21:32 (a city of **r** for murderers),
21:38 (a city of **r** for murderers),
2Sm 22:3 my rock in whom I take **r**,
22:3 salvation, my stronghold, my **r**,
22:31 to all those who take **r** in him.
1Ch 6:57 given Hebron as a city of **r**,
6:67 were given these cities of **r**:
Psa 2:12 is everyone who takes **r** in him.

Psa 5:11 But let all who take **r** in you
7:1 I have taken **r** in you.
11:1 I have taken **r** in the LORD.
14:6 because the LORD is their **r**.
16:1 because I take **r** in you.
17:7 O Savior of those who find **r** by
18:2 my rock in whom I take **r**,
18:30 to all those who take **r** in him.
25:20 I have taken **r** in you.
31:1 I have taken **r** in you,
31:2 Be a rock of **r** for me,
31:4 You are my **r**, so pull me out of
31:19 it to those who take **r** in you.
34:8 the person who takes **r** in him.
34:22 All who take **r** in him will never
36:7 that Adam's descendants take **r**
37:40 they have taken **r** in him.
46:1 God is our **r** and strength,
57:1 my soul takes **r** in you.
57:1 I will take **r** in the shadow of
61:3 You have been my **r**,
61:4 tent forever and to take **r** under
62:7 is the rock of my strength, my **r**.
62:8 God is our **r**. Selah
64:10 in the LORD and take **r** in him.
71:1 I have taken **r** in you,
71:7 but you are my strong **r**.
73:28 the Almighty LORD my **r** so that
90:1 our **r** throughout every
91:2 "(You are) my **r** and my
91:4 under his wings you will find **r**.
91:9 You, O LORD, are my **r**!
94:22 God has become my rock of **r**.
104:18 The rocks are a **r** for badgers.
141:8 I have taken **r** in you.
142:5 I say, "You are my **r**,
144:2 the one in whom I take **r**,
Pro 14:26 children will have a place of **r**.
14:32 a righteous person has a **r**.
Isa 4:6 during the day as well as a **r**
14:32 humble people will find **r** in it.
16:4 Be their **r** from the destroyer.
25:4 You have been a **r** for the poor,
25:4 a **r** for the needy in their
28:15 because we have taken **r** in our
28:17 will sweep away your **r** of lies,
30:2 look for **r** in Egypt's shadow.
30:3 and the **r** in Egypt's shadow
Jer 16:19 my **r** in times of trouble.
17:17 You are my **r** on the day of
21:13 Who can enter our places of **r**?"
Joe 3:16 The LORD will be a **r** for his
Zep 3:12 They will seek **r** in the name of
Heb 6:18 Those of us who have taken **r**

refugee (5)

Eze 24:26 On that day a **r** will come to
24:27 and you will talk to the **r**.
33:21 a **r** from Jerusalem came to me.
33:22 evening before the **r** arrived,
33:22 On the morning the **r** arrived,

refugees (10)

Num 21:29 Chemosh let his sons become **r**
Isa 16:3 the fugitives. Don't betray the **r**.
43:14 bring back all the Babylonian **r**
45:20 you **r** from the nations.
Jer 44:14 Only a few **r** will return there.
49:5 No one will gather the **r**.
49:36 nation where Elam's **r** won't go.
50:28 Fugitives and **r** from Babylon
Oba 1:14 at the crossroads to kill their **r**.
1:17 "But **r** will live on Mount Zion.

refund (2)

Lev 25:51 he must **r** from his purchase
25:52 He must **r** from his purchase

refuse (58)

Gen 22:12 because you did not **r** to give
Exo 8:2 If you **r** to let them go,
9:2 If you **r** to let them go and
10:3 How long will you **r** to humble
10:4 If you **r** to let my people go,
16:28 "How long will you **r** to do what
Num 14:11 How long will they **r** to trust me
2Sm 13:13 won't **r** your request to marry
14:18 "Please don't **r** to answer the
1Ki 2:16 Don't **r** me." "What is it?" she
2:17 as my wife. He will not **r** you."
2:20 "Don't **r** me." "Ask, Mother," the
2:20 king told her. "I won't **r** you."
20:7 silver, and gold, I didn't **r** him."
2Ch 25:16 but you **r** to listen to my
Job 6:7 I **r** to touch such things.
Psa 21:2 You did not **r** the prayer from
141:5 My head will not **r** it,
Pro 21:7 drag them away since they **r**
21:25 because his hands **r** to work.
Isa 1:20 But if you **r** and rebel,
30:9 children who **r** to listen to the
58:7 Don't **r** to help your relatives.
Jer 3:3 and you **r** to blush.
5:3 but they **r** to be corrected.
5:3 They **r** to turn back.
8:5 cling to deceit. They **r** to return.
9:6 They **r** to acknowledge me,"
13:10 These wicked people **r** to
19:15 and they **r** to obey me."
25:28 But if they **r** to take the cup
35:16 but you **r** to listen to me.
38:21 But if you **r** to surrender,
50:33 They **r** to let them go.
Eze 3:7 But the people of Israel will **r** to
3:7 to listen to you because they **r**
3:27 and some will **r** to listen.
21:13 What if you **r** to be disciplined
Hos 4:6 so I will **r** to let you be my
Mar 6:26 he didn't want to **r** her.
Jon 1:20 John didn't **r** to answer.
10:38 I'm doing those things and you **r**
20:25 Thomas told them, "I **r** to
Act 10:47 "No one can **r** to baptize these
26:8 Why do all of you **r** to believe
Rom 2:8 **r** to believe the truth and who
15:31 in Judea who **r** to believe.
Eph 2:2 in people who **r** to obey God.
5:6 to those who **r** to obey him.
Col 3:6 on those who **r** to obey him.
2Th 1:8 take revenge on those who **r**
1:8 God and on those who **r**
2Ti 3:3 They will **r** to make peace with
4:4 People will **r** to listen to the
Heb 11:24 faith led him to **r** to be known
12:25 Be careful that you do not **r** to
1Pe 4:17 will be the end for those who **r**
2Jn 1:7 They **r** to declare that Jesus

refused (108)

Gen 22:16 have done this and have not **r**
37:35 but he **r** to be comforted.
39:8 But Joseph **r** and said to her,
39:10 he **r** to go to bed with her or be
48:19 His father **r** and said,
Exo 4:23 But you **r** to let him go.
10:27 so he **r** to let them go.
Num 14:22 ten times and **r** to obey me.
20:21 Since the Edomites **r** to let
22:13 because the LORD has **r** to let
22:14 "Balaam **r** to come with us."
Dtr 1:26 the LORD your God and **r** to go.
23:5 But the LORD your God **r** to
Jos 24:10 But I **r** to listen to Balaam.
Jdg 2:17 They **r** to be like their
3:28 River that led to Moab and **r**
19:10 But the Levite **r** to spend
19:25 But the men **r** to listen to him.
20:13 But the men of Benjamin **r** to
1Sm 8:19 But the people **r** to listen to
15:9 The army **r** to claim them for
22:17 "But the king's men **r** to attack
26:23 but I **r** to attack the LORD's
28:23 But he **r**. "I don't want to eat," he
31:4 But his armorbearer **r** because
2Sm 2:19 He chased Abner and **r** to leave
2:21 But Asahel **r** to turn away from
2:23 But Asahel **r** to turn away.
13:9 But he **r** to eat. "Have everyone
14:29 but Joab **r** to come.
14:29 but he still **r** to come.
23:16 it to David, but he **r** to drink it.
23:17 So he **r** to drink it. These are the
1Ki 12:15 The king **r** to listen to the
12:16 all Israel saw that the king **r**
20:35 but the man **r** to punch him.
21:4 (from everyone), and **r** to eat.
21:15 which Naboth from Jezreel **r**
22:49 But Jehoshaphat **r**.
2Ki 5:16 urged him to take it, but he **r**.
17:14 But they **r** to listen.
17:14 with as their ancestors who **r**
17:40 The people of Israel had **r** to
18:12 This happened because they **r**
18:12 They **r** to obey everything that
24:4 and the LORD **r** to forgive him.
1Ch 10:4 But his armorbearer **r** because
11:18 it to David, but he **r** to drink it.
11:19 So he **r** to drink it. These are the
2Ch 10:15 The king **r** to listen to the
10:16 all Israel saw that the king **r**
15:13 male or female) who **r** to
29:19 and all the utensils King Ahaz **r**
35:22 He **r** to listen to Neco's words,
36:13 to deal with that he **r**
Neh 9:17 They **r** to listen. They forgot the
Est 1:12 But Queen Vashti **r** the king's
4:4 but he **r** to accept it.
Job 31:16 "If I have **r** the requests of the
Psa 52:7 "Look at this person who **r** to
60:10 Isn't it you, O God, who **r** to
77:2 Yet, my soul **r** to be comforted.
78:10 They **r** to follow his teachings.
89:39 You have **r** to recognize the
106:24 They **r** (to enter) the pleasant
108:11 Isn't it you, O God, who **r** to
Pro 1:24 "I called, and you **r** to listen.
1:30 They **r** my advice.
Jer 11:10 ways of their ancestors and **r**
29:19 but they **r** to listen,
32:23 However, they **r** to obey you or
32:33 but they **r** to listen and learn.
34:14 But your ancestors **r** to obey
35:14 but you have **r** to listen to me.
35:15 However, you **r** to listen to me
36:25 he **r** to listen to them.
36:31 They **r** to listen. So I will bring
40:3 have sinned against him and **r**
Eze 20:8 they rebelled against me and **r**
21:10 My son has **r** to be disciplined
Dan 9:11 ignored your teachings and **r**
Hos 4:6 You have **r** to learn,
9:17 will reject them because they **r**
11:5 rule them because they have **r**
Amo 1:11 They **r** to show any
1:11 They **r** to control their fury.
Zec 7:11 "But people **r** to pay attention.
Mat 2:18 She **r** to be comforted because
18:30 But he **r**. Instead, he turned
22:3 but they **r** to come.
27:34 he tasted it, he **r** to drink it.
Luk 7:30 They **r** to be baptized.
18:4 "For a while the judge **r** to do
Act 5:42 they **r** to stop teaching and
7:57 shouted and **r** to listen.
14:2 But the Jews who **r** to believe
18:20 him to stay longer, but he **r**.
19:9 became stubborn, **r** to believe,
2Co 4:2 Instead, we have **r** to use
2Th 2:10 those who **r** to love the truth
1Ti 1:19 Some have **r** to let their faith
Heb 4:11 of those who **r** to obey.
11:31 with those who **r** to obey God.
11:35 were brutally tortured but **r**
12:25 didn't escape when they **r**
Jas 5:4 The wages you **r** to pay the
1Pe 2:8 over the word because they **r**
Rev 12:11 their life so much that they **r**

refuses (18)

Exo 7:14 He **r** to let my people go.
22:17 If her father absolutely **r** to give
Dtr 18:19 Whoever **r** to listen to the
25:7 "My brother-in-law **r** to let his
25:9 what happens to a man who **r**
Neh 5:13 home and work everyone who **r**
Pro 13:24 Whoever **r** to spank his son
28:9 the prayer of someone who **r**
Isa 33:15 getting rich by extortion and **r**

Isa 33:15 He **r** to listen to those who are
Jer 31:15 She **r** to be comforted,
Eze 18:8 He **r** to do evil things,
18:17 He **r** to hurt the poor.
Dan 6:13 **r** to obey your order or the
Hos 2:3 If she **r**, I will strip her. I will
Rom 8:7 It **r** to place itself under the
3Jn 1:10 He also **r** to accept the
Rev 2:21 but she **r** to turn away from her

refusing (1)

Jer 15:18 my wound incurable, **r** to heal?

refute (1)

Job 32:14 not choose his words to **r** me,

refuted (1)

Job 32:12 but none of you **r** Job.

regain (4)

Gen 18:5 so that you can **r** your strength.
1Sm 29:4 Is this man going to try to **r** his
1Ki 12:27 will **r** popularity if they go to
Eze 17:14 and be unable to **r** its power.

regained (1)

2Ch 13:20 Jeroboam never **r** power during

regard (6)

1Ki 5:8 will do everything you want in **r**
2Ch 5:11 holy to God without **r**
Psa 119:80 heart be filled with integrity in **r**
1Pe 5:12 whom I **r** as a faithful brother.
2Pe 1:19 So we **r** the words of the
1Jn 4:17 like him with **r** to love.

regarded (16)

Gen 15:6 and the LORD **r** that faith to be
Lev 25:31 walls are **r** as belonging
Pro 28:23 people will be more highly **r**
Rom 4:3 and that faith was **r** by God to
4:4 their pay is not **r** as a gift but
4:5 faith is **r** as God's approval.
4:9 We say, "Abraham's faith was **r**
4:10 How was his faith **r** as God's
4:11 Abraham's faith was **r** as God's
4:11 is **r** as God's approval of them.
4:19 Through faith he **r** the facts:
4:22 That is why his faith was **r** as
4:23 But the words "his faith was **r**
4:24 Our faith will be **r** as God's
Gal 3:6 and that faith was **r** by God to
Jas 2:23 and that faith was **r** by God to

regarding (3)

Lev 6:18 law for generations to come **r**
11:24 "**R** the creatures mentioned
2Sm 18:5 this order **r** Absalom.

regardless (2)

Est 1:20 husbands, **r** of their status."
Gal 5:10 you will suffer God's judgment **r**

Regem (1)

1Ch 2:47 Jahdai's sons were **R**,

Regem Melech (1)

Zec 7:2 sent Sharezer and **R**

regiment (7)

1Sm 17:18 cheeses to the captain of the **r**.
18:13 He made David captain of a **r**.
22:7 make you all officers over a **r**
1Ch 13:1 commanded a **r** or battalion.
27:1 **r** and battalion commanders,
2Ch 25:5 assigned them by families to **r**
Act 10:1 army officer in the Italian **R**.

regimental (1)

2Ch 17:14 Judah's **r** commanders were

regiments (7)

1Sm 29:2 by with their companies and **r**.
2Sm 18:1 in charge of **r** and battalions.
18:4 out by battalions and **r**.
1Ch 26:26 of **r** and battalions,
1Ch 28:1 of **r** and battalions,
29:6 of **r** and battalions,
2Ch 1:2 of **r** and battalions,

region (85)

Gen 10:30 The **r** where they lived
23:7 the people of that **r**,
23:12 in front of the people of that **r**.
23:13 people of that **r** could hear him.
25:18 lived as nomads from the **r**
35:22 While Israel was living in that **r**,
46:28 arrived in the **r** of Goshen,
46:34 may live in the **r** of Goshen,
47:11 part of Egypt, the **r** of Rameses.
47:27 in Egypt in the **r** of Goshen.
Exo 8:22 But on that day I will treat the **r**
9:26 didn't hail was the **r** of Goshen,
Num 13:17 and then into the mountain **r**.
13:29 Amorites live in the mountain **r**.
14:40 headed into the mountain **r**.
14:44 into the mountain **r** anyway,
22:36 in the **r** of the Arnon Valley,
Dtr 1:7 Go to the mountain **r** of the
1:19 on the way to the mountain **r**
1:20 have come to the mountain **r**
1:41 easily invade the mountain **r**.
1:43 and invaded the mountain **r**.
2:1 around the **r** of Mount Seir.
2:3 around this **r** long enough.
2:5 given Esau's descendants the **r**
3:12 and half of the mountain **r**
11:30 in the **r** of the Canaanites who
Jos 14:12 Now give me this mountain **r**
15:7 turns north to the **r** that faces
17:14 did you give us only one **r**
17:17 One **r** is really not enough for
17:18 The mountain **r** will be yours
18:7 has no separate **r** among you,
18:17 and from there to the **r** opposite
22:10 tribe of Manasseh came to the **r**
22:11 It's in the **r** near the Jordan
Jdg 7:24 to the whole mountain **r**
10:4 They are in the **r** of Gilead.
11:1 a soldier from the **r** of Gilead.
17:1 from the mountain **r** of Ephraim
19:16 He was from the mountain **r** of
1Sm 9:4 mountains of Ephraim and the **r**
9:4 went through the **r** of Shaalim,
13:17 road to Ophrah to the **r** of Shual.
13:18 road toward the **r** that overlooks
17:12 a man named Jesse from the **r**
2Sm 5:6 who lived in that **r**.
8:13 Edomites in the Dead Sea **r** as
17:26 camped in the **r** of Gilead.
1Ki 4:10 and the entire **r** of Hepher.
4:11 had the entire **r** of Dor.
9:13 So he named it the **r** of Cabul
18:10 for you in every **r** and kingdom.
18:10 made that kingdom or **r** take
2Ki 10:33 the entire **r** of Gilead (the
14:7 Edomites in the Dead Sea **r**
1Ch 5:10 the entire **r** east of Gilead.
11:4 Jebusites were living in that **r**.
13:2 rest of our relatives in every **r**
18:12 Edomites in the Dead Sea **r**.
2Ch 11:13 priests and Levites in every **r**
11:23 placed his sons in every **r**
25:11 he came to the Dead Sea **r**,
Ezr 4:4 Then the people of that **r**
Neh 12:29 from Beth Gilgal, and from the **r**
Jer 32:44 in the **r** of Jerusalem,
Eze 19:8 The nations from every **r** came
Mat 4:13 This was in the **r** of Zebulun
9:26 this spread throughout that **r**.
9:31 about him throughout that **r**.
15:21 left that place and went to the **r**
16:13 When Jesus came to the **r** of
Mar 1:28 the surrounding **r** of Galilee.
8:10 went into the **r** of Dalmanutha.
Luk 1:39 city in the mountain **r** of Judah.
1:65 the mountain **r** of Judea,
3:3 John traveled throughout the **r**
4:37 throughout the surrounding **r**.
7:17 Judea and the surrounding **r**.
8:26 They landed in the **r** of the
8:37 people from the surrounding **r**
Act 9:35 city of Lydda and the coastal **r**
13:49 spread throughout the whole **r**.
20:2 He went through that **r** and
Rom 15:23 opportunities for work in this **r**.

region's (1)

Dtr 1:25 They took some of the **r** fruit

regions (8)

Num 32:1 They saw that the **r** of Jazer
Dtr 19:3 God is giving you into three **r**.
Ezr 3:3 the people in the neighboring **r**.
Joe 3:4 Sidon and all the **r** of Philistia?
Act 16:6 and Silas went through the **r**
18:23 Paul went through the **r** of
2Co 10:16 News in the **r** far beyond you.
Gal 1:21 Then I went to the **r** of Syria

register (9)

Num 1:3 You and Aaron must **r**
1:49 "Don't **r** the tribe of Levi or
3:40 The LORD said to Moses, "**R**
4:3 **R** all the men between the
4:23 **R** all the men between the
4:29 "**R** the Merarites by families
4:30 **R** all the men between the
Luk 2:3 All the people went to **r** in the
2:5 went there to **r** with Mary.

registered (25)

Num 1:19 So Moses **r** the men of Israel in
1:22 for the descendants of Simeon **r**
1:45 were **r** by households.
1:47 tribe of Levi were not **r** along
2:33 the Levites were not **r** along
3:16 the LORD said and **r** them as
3:42 So Moses **r** all the firstborn
4:34 the leaders of the community **r**
4:35 They **r** all the men between the
4:36 of those who were **r** was 2,750.
4:37 Moses and **r** the Kohathites.
4:38 The Gershonites were **r** by
4:39 at the tent of meeting were **r**.
4:40 of those who were **r** was 2,630.
4:41 Moses and **r** the Gershonites.
4:42 The Merarites were **r** by
4:43 at the tent of meeting were **r**.
4:44 those who were **r** was 3,200.
4:45 This was the total of those **r** in
4:45 Moses and **r** the Merarites.
4:46 leaders of Israel **r** was 8,580.
4:49 through Moses each man was **r**
4:49 So they were **r** as the LORD
14:29 who were **r** and listed,
1Ch 23:24 families were **r** by name as

regret (2)

1Sm 15:11 "I **r** that I made Saul king.
2Co 7:10 No one can **r** that. But the

regretted (4)

1Sm 15:35 And the LORD **r** that he had
Mat 14:9 The king **r** his promise.
27:3 **r** what had happened when he
Mar 6:26 The king deeply **r** his promise.

regular (15)

Lev 23:7 Don't do any **r** work.
23:8 Don't do any **r** work."
23:21 Don't do any **r** work.
23:25 Don't do any **r** work.
23:35 Don't do any **r** work.
23:36 Don't do any **r** work.
Num 8:26 but they may not do any **r** work.
28:18 Don't do any **r** work.
28:25 You must not do any **r** work.
28:26 you must not do any **r** work.
29:1 You must not do any **r** work.
29:12 You must not do any **r** work.
2Ch 30:3 couldn't celebrate it at the **r** time
30:16 They stood in their **r** places as
Neh 13:31 for delivering wood at **r** times

regularly (5)

Exo 29:38 to offer on the altar **r** every day:
2Ki 4:9 And he **r** travels past our house.

2Ch 19:4 he **r** went to the people
Luk 16:20 Lazarus who was **r** brought
Act 10:7 one of those who served him **r**.

regulation (3)

Psa 119:13 every **r** that ⌊comes⌋ from
Eze 43:12 This is a **r** of the temple:
43:12 Yes, this is a **r** of the temple."

regulations (41)

Num 9:3 Follow all the rules and **r** for
9:14 follow these same rules and **r**.
Dtr 6:17 of the LORD your God and the **r**
6:20 you, "What do these **r**, laws,
1Ch 6:32 according to the **r** set down
23:32 were appointed to follow the **r**
2Ch 19:10 or **r** derived from Moses'
23:6 should follow the LORD's **r**.
33:8 and the **r** ⌊I gave⌋ through
Ezr 7:10 teach their rules and **r** in Israel.
Neh 1:7 or **r** that you gave us through
8:18 in accordance with the **r**.
9:29 sinned by not following your **r**.
10:29 and **r** of the LORD our Lord.
Psa 119:7 thanks to you as I learn your **r**,
119:20 with endless longing for your **r**.
119:30 I have set your **r** in front of me.
119:39 because your **r** are good.
119:43 My hope is based on your **r**.
119:52 I remembered your **r** from long
119:62 to give thanks to you for the **r**,
119:75 I know that your **r** are fair,
119:91 stand today because of your **r**,
119:102 I have not neglected your **r**,
119:106 I took an oath to follow your **r**,
119:108 and teach me your **r**.
119:120 and I am afraid of your **r**.
119:137 O LORD, and your **r** are fair.
119:149 me a new life guided by your **r**.
119:156 me a new life guided by your **r**.
119:160 your righteous **r** endure forever.
119:164 I praise you for your righteous **r**.
119:175 Let your **r** help me.
Isa 10:1 and who make oppressive **r**.
Eze 43:11 them about all its rules and **r**.
44:5 Listen to all the rules and **r** for
44:24 my rules and my **r** at all my
Mal 4:4 the rules and **r** that I gave to
Luk 1:6 commands and **r** perfectly.
Heb 7:12 the **r** for those priests are
7:15 The **r** were different.

Rehabiah (4)

1Ch 23:17 Eliezer's only son was **R**.
23:17 but **R** had many sons.
24:21 descendants⌋ through **R**),
26:25 (Eliezer's son was **R**;

Rehob (10)

Jos 19:28 Abdon, **R**, Hammon, Kanah,
19:30 Umma, Acco, Aphek, and **R**.
21:31 Helkath, and **R**.
Jdg 1:31 Achzib, Helbah, Aphek, or **R**.
2Sm 8:3 King Hadadezer, son of **R**.
8:12 King Hadadezer, son of **R**.
10:8 Arameans from Zobah and **R**
1Ch 6:75 and **R** with its pastureland.
19:9 Arameans from Zobah and **R**
Neh 10:11 Mica, **R**, Hashabiah,

Rehoboam (53)

1Ki 11:43 His son **R** succeeded him as
12:1 **R** went to Shechem because
12:2 When he heard ⌊about **R**⌋,
12:3 of Israel went to speak to **R**.
12:6 King **R** sought advice from the
12:12 came back to **R** two days later,
12:17 But **R** ruled the Israelites who
12:18 Then King **R** sent Adoram to
12:18 So King **R** got on his chariot as
12:21 When **R** came to Jerusalem,
12:21 and return the kingdom to **R**,
12:23 "Speak to Judah's King **R**,
12:27 King **R** of Judah, the former
12:27 and return to King **R** of Judah."
14:21 **R**, son of Solomon,
1Ki 14:27 So King **R** made bronze
14:29 else concerning **R** — everything
14:30 There was war between **R** and
14:31 **R** lay down in death with his
15:6 and **R** throughout their lives.
1Ch 3:10 Solomon's son was **R**.
2Ch 9:31 His son **R** succeeded him as
10:1 **R** went to Shechem because
10:2 When he heard ⌊about **R**⌋,
10:3 all Israel went to speak to **R**.
10:6 King **R** sought advice from the
10:12 came back to **R** two days later,
10:17 But **R** ruled the Israelites who
10:18 Then King **R** sent Hadoram to
10:18 So King **R** got on his chariot as
11:1 When **R** came to Jerusalem,
11:1 and return the kingdom to **R**.
11:3 "Speak to Judah's King **R**,
11:5 **R** lived in Jerusalem and built
11:12 So **R** held on to Judah and
11:13 region of Israel sided with **R**.
11:17 of Judah by supporting **R**,
11:18 **R** married Mahalath,
11:21 **R** loved Maacah, more than all
11:22 **R** appointed Abijah,
11:22 **R** could make him king.
12:1 When **R** had established his
12:5 prophet Shemaiah came to **R**
12:10 So King **R** made bronze
12:12 After **R** humbled himself,
12:13 King **R** strengthened his
12:15 Aren't the events concerning **R**
12:15 There was war between **R** and
12:16 **R** lay down in death with his
13:7 They opposed **R**, son of
13:7 when **R** was too young and
Mat 1:7 Solomon was the father of **R**,
1:7 **R** the father of Abijah,

Rehoboam's (5)

1Ki 14:21 **R** mother was an Ammonite
14:25 In the fifth year of **R** reign, King
1Ch 3:10 **R** son was Abijah.
2Ch 12:2 In the fifth year of **R** reign, King
12:13 (**R** mother was an Ammonite

Rehoboth (3)

Gen 26:22 So he named it **R** [Roomy] and
36:37 Samlah died, Shaul from **R**
1Ch 1:48 Samlah died, Shaul from **R**

Rehoboth Ir (1)

Gen 10:11 and built Nineveh, **R**, Calah,

Rehum (8)

Ezr 2:2 Mispar, Bigvai, **R**, and Baanah.
4:8 **R** the commander and
4:9 At that time, **R** the commander
4:17 To **R** the commander,
4:23 **R** the commander,
Neh 3:17 including **R** (Bani's son),
10:25 **R**, Hashabnah, Maaseiah,
12:3 Shecaniah, **R**, Meremoth,

Rei (1)

1Ki 1:8 the prophet Nathan, Shimei, **R**,

reign (63)

1Ki 1:47 and his **r** greater than your
1:47 reign greater than your **r**.' The
6:1 fourth year of his **r** over Israel.
6:37 the fourth year of Solomon's **r**,
6:38 of the eleventh year ⌊of his **r**⌋,
11:42 The length of Solomon's **r** in
14:19 and his **r** is written in the
14:25 the fifth year of Rehoboam's **r**,
15:1 In the eighteenth year of the **r** of
16:11 At the beginning of Zimri's **r**,
2Ki 11:4 the seventh year of Athaliah's **r**,
18:9 was the seventh year in the **r**
23:23 year of King Josiah's **r**,
23:33 territory of Hamath during his **r**
24:1 During Jehoiakim's **r** King
24:12 In the eighth year of his **r**,
25:1 the ninth year of Zedekiah's **r**,
25:27 in the first year of his **r**,
1Ch 26:31 In the fortieth year of David's **r**,
29:30 includes everything about his **r**,
2Ch 3:2 month of the fourth year of his **r**.
12:2 the fifth year of Rehoboam's **r**,
13:1 year of the **r** of Jeroboam,
14:5 was at peace during his **r**.
15:10 of the fifteenth year of Asa's **r**,
15:19 the thirty-fifth year of Asa's **r**.
16:1 the thirty-sixth year of Asa's **r**,
16:10 the people at that time in his **r**.
16:12 In the thirty-ninth year of his **r**,
16:13 in the forty-first year of his **r**.
17:7 In the third year of his **r**,
23:1 the seventh year of Athaliah's **r**,
29:19 to use during his **r** when
34:3 In the eighth year of his **r**,
34:8 In the eighteenth year of his **r**
35:19 eighteenth year of Josiah's **r**,
Ezr 4:5 out their plans throughout the **r**
4:5 King Cyrus of Persia until the **r**
5:13 in the first year of the **r** of King
6:15 the sixth year of King Darius' **r**.
7:1 After these things, during the **r**
8:1 during the **r** of King Artaxerxes
Neh 5:14 year of King Artaxerxes' **r**
5:14 the thirty-second year of his **r**,
12:22 were recorded until the **r**
13:6 King Artaxerxes' **r** in Babylon,
Est 1:3 in the third year of his **r**.
2:16 in the seventh year of his **r**.
Pro 8:15 Through me kings **r**,
Jer 35:1 during the **r** of Jehoiakim,
36:1 year of the **r** of Jehoiakim,
36:2 time I spoke to you during the **r**
36:9 fifth year of the **r** of Jehoiakim,
52:4 the ninth year of Zedekiah's **r**,
52:31 in the first year of his **r**,
Lam 5:19 and your **r** continues throughout
Dan 1:1 In the third year of the **r** of King
2:1 year of Nebuchadnezzar's **r**,
6:28 prospered during the **r** of Darius
6:28 the reign of Darius and the **r**
9:2 In the first year of his **r**,
Amo 6:3 bring the **r** of violence closer.
Luk 3:1 It was the fifteenth year in the **r**

reigns (1)

Amo 1:1 vision⌋ about Israel during the **r**

reinforce (2)

1Ki 20:22 Israel and said, "**R** your army.
Act 27:17 ropes under the ship to **r** it.

reinforced (3)

Exo 28:32 in the center with a **r** edge (like
2Ch 24:13 to its proper condition and **r** it.
26:9 and the Angle, and he **r** them.

reinforcements (2)

Jdg 20:22 But Israel's troops got **r**.
Isa 43:17 and horses, an army and **r**.

reject (40)

Lev 26:15 if you **r** my laws and look at my
26:15 if you **r** my promise by
26:44 I will not **r** them or look at them
26:44 I will not **r** or cancel my
Dtr 31:16 They will abandon me and **r**
31:20 despise me and **r** my promise.
1Ki 9:7 I will **r** this temple that I
2Ki 23:27 I will **r** Jerusalem, the city that I
23:27 and I will **r** the temple where I
1Ch 28:9 he will **r** you from then on.
2Ch 6:42 do not **r** your anointed one.
7:20 I will **r** this temple that I
Job 8:20 "Certainly, God does not **r** a
Psa 36:4 He does not **r** evil.
44:23 Do not **r** us forever!
71:9 Do not **r** me when I am old or
77:7 Will the Lord **r** ⌊me⌋ for all
88:14 Why do you **r** my soul,
119:118 You **r** all who wander away
132:10 do not **r** your anointed one.
Pro 3:11 Do not **r** the discipline of the
Isa 7:15 until he knows how to **r** evil
7:16 before the boy knows how to **r**

Isa 31:7 all of you will **r** the silver and
Jer 4:30 Your lovers **r** you; they want to
6:19 They **r** my teachings.
31:37 would I ever **r** all of Israel's
33:26 Then I would **r** the
Lam 3:31 not **r** ⌊such⌋ people forever.
Eze 14:8 I will **r** him, and I will make an
Hos 9:17 My God will **r** them because
Luk 2:35 thoughts of those who **r** him.
Jon 12:48 Those who **r** me by not
Act 13:46 Since you **r** the word and
25:11 I don't **r** the idea of dying.
1Co 1:19 I will **r** the intelligence of
Gal 2:21 I don't **r** God's kindness.
4:14 you didn't despise or **r** me.
Heb 2:3 we escape punishment if we **r**
Jud 1:8 **r** the Lord's authority,

rejected (89)

Gen 17:14 because he has **r** my promise."
Lev 26:25 for my promise ⌊that you **r**⌋.
26:43 guilt because they **r** my rules
Num 11:20 This is because they **r** the
14:31 bring them into the land you **r**,
Dtr 32:19 The LORD saw this and **r** them,
Jdg 2:20 the people of this nation have **r**
1Sm 8:7 They haven't **r** you;
8:7 rejected you; they've **r** me.
10:19 But now you have **r** your God,
15:23 Because you **r** the word of the
15:26 with you because you **r** what
16:1 now that I have **r** him as king
16:7 because I have **r** him.
2Ki 17:15 They **r** his decrees,
17:20 So the LORD **r** all of Israel's
2Ch 11:14 and his descendants **r** them as
Job 6:10 because I have not **r** the words
34:33 terms since you have **r** his?
Psa 15:4 The one who despises those **r**
43:2 Why have you **r** me?
44:9 But now you have **r** and
53:5 After all, God has **r** them.
60:1 O God, you have **r** us.
60:10 Isn't it you, O God, who **r** us?
66:20 who has not **r** my prayer or
74:1 have you **r** us forever?
78:59 He completely **r** Israel.
78:67 He **r** the tent of Joseph.
89:38 But you have despised, **r**,
108:11 Isn't it you, O God, who **r** us?
118:22 The stone that the builders **r**
Isa 5:24 They have **r** the teachings of
8:6 "These people have **r** the
14:19 out of your tomb like a **r** branch.
24:5 and **r** the everlasting promise.
30:12 You have **r** this warning,
33:8 Witnesses are **r**. People are no
41:9 I've chosen you; I haven't **r** you.'
49:21 I was exiled and **r**.
53:3 was despised and **r** by people.
54:6 and was **r**," says your God.
Jer 2:37 because the LORD has **r** those
6:30 because the LORD has **r** them."
7:29 in his anger the LORD has **r**
8:9 They have **r** the word of the
11:10 of Israel and Judah have **r**
14:19 Have you completely **r** Judah?
22:9 The answer will be: 'They **r** the
22:28 This Jehoiakin is like a **r** and
31:32 They **r** that promise,
33:24 have said that the LORD has **r**
34:18 people who have **r** my promise.
Lam 2:7 The Lord **r** his altar and
5:22 unless you have completely **r**
Eze 5:6 They have **r** my rules,
16:5 You were **r** when you were
16:45 She **r** her husband and her
16:45 They **r** their husbands and their
16:59 vows and **r** my promise.
20:13 and they **r** my rules.
20:16 They **r** my rules, and they
20:24 and they **r** my laws.
44:7 You **r** my promise so that you
Hos 6:7 "Like Adam, you **r** the promise.
8:1 The people of Israel have **r** my
8:3 they have **r** what is good.
Amo 2:4 The people of Judah have **r** the
Zec 10:6 as though I had never **r** them,
Mat 21:42 'The stone that the builders **r**
Mar 8:31 them that he would be **r** by
12:10 'The stone that the builders **r**
Luk 7:30 Moses' Teachings **r** God's plan
9:22 He would be **r** by the leaders,
10:6 your greeting will be **r**.
17:25 he must suffer a lot and be **r** by
20:17 'The stone that the builders **r**
Act 3:13 You **r** him in Pilate's presence,
3:14 You **r** the man who was holy
4:11 is the stone that the builders **r**,
7:35 the Israelites **r** by saying,
Rom 11:1 "Has God **r** his people Israel?"
11:2 God has not **r** his people whom
1Ti 4:4 Nothing should be **r** if it is
Heb 7:18 The former requirements are **r**
8:9 They **r** that promise,
12:17 son was to receive, he was **r**.
1Pe 2:4 the living stone who was **r** by
2:7 "The stone that the builders **r**

rejecting (7)

Job 10:3 by **r** the work of your hands
Eze 17:19 I will certainly punish you for **r**
Mar 7:9 "You have no trouble **r** the
1Th 4:8 ⌊order⌋ is not **r** human authority
1Ti 5:12 They condemn themselves by **r**
Tit 1:14 who are always **r** the truth.
Heb 10:28 of **r** Moses' Teachings,

rejection (1)

Rom 11:15 If Israel's **r** means that the

rejects (12)

1Sm 15:23 of the LORD, he **r** you as king."
15:26 So the LORD **r** you as king of
Isa 33:15 He **r** getting rich by extortion
Luk 10:16 and the person who **r** you
10:16 person who rejects you **r** me.
10:16 The person who **r** me rejects
10:16 The person who rejects me **r**
Jon 3:36 but whoever **r** the Son will not
1Th 4:8 Therefore, whoever **r** this
1Jn 2:22 Who else but the person who **r**
2:22 The person who **r** the Father
2:23 Everyone who **r** the Son

rejoice (74)

1Sm 2:1 I **r** because you saved ⌊me⌋.
1Ch 16:10 of those who seek the LORD **r**.
16:31 Let the heavens **r** and the earth
16:32 fields and everything in them **r**.
2Ch 6:41 Let your godly ones **r** in what is
20:27 a reason to **r** about ⌊what had
Neh 12:43 had given them reason to **r**.
Psa 2:11 and **r** with trembling.
5:11 let all who take refuge in you **r**.
13:4 My opponents will **r** because I
14:7 of his people, Jacob will **r**.
19:8 They make the heart **r**.
30:1 not let my enemies **r** over me.
31:7 I will **r** and be glad because of
34:2 are oppressed will hear it and **r**.
35:27 innocent joyfully sing and **r**.
40:16 Let all who seek you **r** and be
48:11 glad and the cities of Judah **r**
53:6 of his people, Jacob will **r**.
58:10 Righteous people will **r** when
68:3 But let righteous people **r**.
69:32 people will see ⌊this⌋ and **r**.
70:4 Let all who seek you **r** and be
89:42 made all of his adversaries **r**.
90:14 sing joyfully and **r** all our days.
90:15 Make us **r** for as many days as
96:11 Let the heavens **r** and the earth
96:12 fields and everything in them **r**.
97:1 Let the earth **r**. Let all the
105:3 of those who seek the LORD **r**.
107:42 people will see this and **r**,
109:28 me be ashamed, but let me **r**.
118:24 Let's **r** and be glad today!
119:74 who fear you will see me and **r**,
149:2 people of Zion **r** over their king.
Pro 23:15 my heart will **r** as well.
Pro 23:24 person's father will certainly **r**.
23:25 she who gave birth to you **r**.
29:2 the people ⌊of God⌋ **r**,
Ecc 5:19 and ⌊the ability⌋ to **r** in their
Sos 1:4 will celebrate and **r** with you.
Isa 9:3 harvest or **r** when dividing loot.
14:8 Even the cypresses **r** over you.
14:29 All you Philistines, don't **r** that
22:13 Instead, you will **r**,
25:9 Let us **r** and be glad because
35:1 wilderness will **r** and blossom.
35:2 It will **r** and sing with joy.
44:23 **R**, you deep places of the
49:13 **R**, you earth! Break into shouts
60:5 Then you will see this and **r**,
62:5 so your God will **r** over you.
65:18 Be glad, and **r** forever in what
65:19 I will **r** about Jerusalem and be
66:10 be happy and **r** with her.
66:14 your heart will **r** and you will
Jer 11:15 They **r** when they do evil."
31:13 Then young women will **r** and
51:48 in them will **r** over Babylon,
Lam 4:21 "**R** and be glad, people of
Eze 7:12 Buyers will not **r**, and sellers
21:10 How can we **r**? My son has
Hos 9:1 Israel, don't **r**. Don't celebrate as
Joe 2:21 Be glad and **r**. The LORD has
Amo 6:13 for those who **r** over Lo Debar
Hab 1:15 So they **r** and are happy.
Zep 3:14 Celebrate and **r** with all your
Zec 2:10 Sing for joy and **r**, people of
9:9 **R** with all your heart,
Mat 5:12 **R** and be glad because you
Luk 6:23 **R** then, and be very happy!
Gal 4:27 Scripture says: "**R**,
1Th 3:9 us as we **r** in God's presence.
Rev 19:7 Let us **r**, be happy, and give

rejoiced (13)

1Sm 19:5 When you saw it, you **r**.
1Ki 8:66 They **r** with cheerful hearts for
2Ch 7:10 They **r** with cheerful hearts for
20:27 They **r** while Jehoshaphat led
30:25 and those who lived in Judah **r**.
Neh 12:43 offered many sacrifices and **r**
12:43 women and children **r** as well.
Est 8:15 the city of Susa cheered and **r**.
Psa 35:15 they **r** and gathered together.
66:6 We **r** because of what he did
Pro 8:30 I **r** in front of him all the time,
Eze 25:6 You **r** and felt contempt for the
Heb 11:13 in the distant future and **r**.

rejoices (6)

Psa 16:9 my heart is glad and my soul **r**.
97:8 Zion hears about this and **r**.
Pro 23:16 My heart **r** when you speak
Isa 62:5 As a bridegroom **r** over his
Zep 3:17 He happily **r** over you,
Act 2:26 heart is glad and my tongue **r**.

rejoicing (5)

Gen 31:27 have sent you on your way **r**,
2Ki 11:14 All the people of the land were **r**
2Ch 23:13 All the people of the land were **r**
Neh 12:43 The sound of **r** in Jerusalem
Joe 1:16 Happiness and **r** disappear

Rekem (5)

Num 31:8 Evi, **R**, Zur, Hur, and Reba.
Jos 13:21 Evi, **R**, Zur, Hur, and Reba.
18:27 **R**, Ir Peel, Taralah,
1Ch 2:43 Tappuah, **R**, and Shema.
2:44 **R** was the father of Shammai.

relate (4)

Est 5:11 Then Haman began to **r** in
6:13 There, Haman began to **r** in
Job 12:8 Even the fish will **r** ⌊the story⌋
15:17 I'll **r** what I have seen.

related (11)

Gen 17:12 a foreigner who's not **r** to you.
Lev 18:6 intercourse with anyone **r**
18:8 She is **r** to you through your

Lev 18:10 because she is **r** to you.
18:17 They are **r**. Doing this is
2Ki 8:27 because he was **r** to Ahab's
Neh 13:4 who was **r** to Tobiah and had
Est 8:1 him how Mordecai was **r** to her.
Pro 18:9 Whoever is lazy in his work is **r**
Act 6:4 in ways that are **r** to the word."
21:19 After greeting them, Paul **r**

relations (3)

Mat 1:25 He did not have marital **r** with
Rom 1:26 sexual **r** for unnatural ones.
1:27 have given up natural sexual **r**

relationship (22)

Jos 22:24 'What **r** do you have with the
Act 23:1 my **r** with God has always
Rom 5:10 death of his Son restored our **r**
5:10 because of this restored **r**,
5:11 have this restored **r** with God.
1Co 8:8 will not affect our **r** with God.
2Co 1:21 with you, in a **r** with Christ.
5:18 He has restored our **r** with him
5:19 to restore his **r** with humanity.
Gal 2:19 I live in a **r** with God.
5:6 As far as our **r** to Christ Jesus
6:14 By his cross my **r** to the world
6:14 to the world and its **r**
Eph 4:15 up completely in our **r** to Christ,
5:32 about Christ's **r** to the church.)
Php 3:9 and to have a **r** with him.
4:1 keep your **r** with the Lord firm!
1Th 3:8 as long as you keep your **r**
1Jn 1:3 can have a **r** with us.
1:3 Our **r** is with the Father and
1:6 If we say, "We have a **r** with
1:7 we have a **r** with each other.

relationships (4)

2Co 5:18 us this ministry of restoring **r**.
5:19 of restored **r** to tell others.
6:14 **r** with unbelievers.
Php 2:1 Do you have any spiritual **r**?

relative (50)

Gen 14:16 He also brought back his **r** Lot
24:48 of my master's **r** for his son.
29:15 "Just because you're my **r**
Lev 20:19 a close **r** must be punished.
25:25 responsibility, his nearest **r**,
25:47 and your **r** living with him may
25:49 or some other **r** could also buy
Num 27:11 his property to the nearest **r**
27:11 and that **r** will take possession
35:12 from any **r** who can avenge
35:19 The **r** who can avenge the
35:21 The **r** who can avenge the
35:24 the dead person's **r** can avenge
35:25 must protect you from that **r**.
35:27 If the **r** who can avenge the
35:27 the **r** is not guilty of murder.
36:2 the land of our **r** Zelophehad
Dtr 15:2 that your neighbor or **r** pay you,
19:6 Otherwise, in a rage the **r** who
19:6 too far away, the **r** may catch up
19:12 hand him over to the **r** who has
Jos 20:3 from any **r** who can avenge
20:5 "'If the **r** who can avenge the
20:5 must not hand him over to the **r**
20:9 over to the **r** who can avenge
Jdg 9:3 because he was their **r**.
Rut 2:1 Naomi had a **r**. He was from
2:20 "That man is a **r** of ours.
2:20 He is a close **r**, one of those
3:2 been working with, our **r**?
3:9 you are a close **r** who can take
3:12 true that I am a close **r** of yours,
3:12 but there is a **r** closer than I.
4:1 Just then, the **r** about whom he
4:3 belonged to our **r** Elimelech.
4:4 there is no other **r** except me."
2Sm 19:42 "Because the king is our **r**.
1Ch 6:39 Heman's **r** Asaph stood on his
Pro 7:4 name "my **r**" to understanding
27:10 is better than a **r** far away.
Isa 3:7 When that day comes the **r** will
Jer 9:4 Every **r** cheats. Every neighbor
32:7 because as the closest **r** it is
32:8 rights of the closest **r** belong
Eze 18:18 oppressed others, robbed his **r**,
38:21 use his sword against his **r**.
Amo 6:10 If a **r** or a mortician comes to
Oba 1:10 you did to Jacob, your **r**,
Luk 1:36 "Elizabeth, your **r**, is six
Jon 18:26 a **r** of the man whose ear Peter

relative's (2)

Pro 27:10 Do not go to a **r** home when
Oba 1:12 gloat over your **r** misfortune

relatives (208)

Gen 12:1 your **r**, and your father's home.
13:8 our herders. After all, we're **r**.
16:12 have conflicts with all his **r**."
19:12 or any other **r** in the city?
24:4 you will go to the land of my **r**
24:27 to the home of my master's **r**."
24:38 to my father's home and to my **r**,
24:40 get my son a wife from my **r**
24:41 to me if my **r** are not willing
31:3 of your ancestors and to your **r**,
31:13 go back to the land of your **r**.'"
31:23 He and his **r** pursued Jacob for
31:25 So Laban and his **r** put up their
31:32 In the presence of our **r**,
31:37 Put it here in front of all our **r**.
31:46 Then Jacob said to his **r**,
31:54 He invited his **r** to eat the meal
32:9 back to your land and to your **r**,
Exo 21:8 back by one of her close **r**.
32:27 other, and kill your **r**, friends,
Lev 10:4 "Come and take your **r** away
21:1 one of your **r** who has died.
21:2 one of your nearest **r** dies.
21:2 These **r** include your mother,
25:46 harshly. They are your **r**.
Num 10:30 own country where my **r** are."
27:4 property among our father's **r**."
27:7 their own among their father's **r**.
Dtr 2:4 through the territory of your **r**,
2:8 So we passed by our **r**,
23:7 They're your **r**. Never consider
Jos 1:14 battle formation ahead of your **r**.
1:14 You must help your **r**
6:23 and even all of her **r**.
17:4 inheritance among our male **r**."
17:4 among their father's **r** as
22:3 you have never deserted your **r**.
22:4 God has given your **r** peace,
22:7 tribe their land with their **r** west
22:8 from your enemies with your **r**."
Jdg 1:17 tribe of Simeon, their close **r**.
14:3 there any women among our **r**
16:31 Then his **r** and his father's
18:8 The men went back to their **r** in
18:8 Their **r** asked them,
20:23 wage war against our close **r**,
20:28 wage war against our close **r**,
21:6 Israel felt sorry for their close **r**,
Rut 4:10 will not be cut off from his **r**
1Sm 18:18 "And how important are my **r** or
20:6 because his **r** are offering the
20:29 Our **r** will offer a sacrifice in the
2Sm 2:26 troops from chasing their **r**?"
2:27 chasing their **r** until morning."
3:8 to his **r** and friends,
19:12 You are my **r**, my own flesh
1Ki 12:24 war against your **r** from Israel.
16:11 of Baasha's male **r** or friends.
2Ki 10:13 he found some **r** of King
10:13 "We're Ahaziah's **r**.
1Ch 5:13 Their seven **r** by families were
6:44 one of Heman's **r** descended
6:48 Their **r**, the Levites,
7:5 Their **r** (that is, all of Issachar's
8:32 next to their **r** in Jerusalem.
9:6 of Zerah were Jeuel and their **r**,
9:9 and their **r** according to their
9:13 Their **r** who were heads of their
9:17 Talmon, Ahiman, and their **r**.
9:25 Their **r** had to come from their
9:32 Some of their Kohathite **r** were
1Ch 9:38 next to their **r** in Jerusalem.
12:2 They were Saul's **r**,
12:29 Saul's **r**, there were 3,000 men,
12:32 Their **r** were under their
12:39 because their **r** ⌊in Judah⌋ had
13:2 invitation⌋ to the rest of our **r**
15:5 who came with 120 of his **r**.
15:6 who came with 220 of his **r**.
15:7 who came with 130 of his **r**.
15:8 who came with 200 of his **r**.
15:9 who came with 80 of his **r**.
15:10 who came with 112 of his **r**.
15:12 You and your **r** must perform
15:16 to appoint some of their **r**
15:17 and from his **r** they appointed
15:17 their own **r**, they appointed
15:18 they appointed their **r** from the
16:7 entrusted Asaph and his **r**
16:37 David left Asaph and his **r** to
16:38 and 68 of his **r** ⌊to serve there⌋.
16:39 left Zadok and his priestly **r**
16:41 Zadok and his **r** were Heman,
23:32 holy place and to help their **r**,
24:31 They drew lots as their **r**,
25:7 They, along with their **r**,
25:9 and his **r** — 12 men.
25:10 and his **r** — 12 men.
25:11 and his **r** — 12 men.
25:12 and his **r** — 12 men.
25:13 and his **r** — 12 men.
25:14 and his **r** — 12 men.
25:15 and his **r** — 12 men.
25:16 and his **r** — 12 men.
25:17 and his **r** — 12 men.
25:18 and his **r** — 12 men.
25:19 and his **r** — 12 men.
25:20 and his **r** — 12 men.
25:21 and his **r** — 12 men.
25:22 and his **r** — 12 men.
25:23 and his **r** — 12 men.
25:24 and his **r** — 12 men.
25:25 and his **r** — 12 men.
25:26 and his **r** — 12 men.
25:27 and his **r** — 12 men.
25:28 and his **r** — 12 men.
25:29 and his **r** — 12 men.
25:30 and his **r** — 12 men.
25:31 and his **r** — 12 men.
26:8 They, their sons, and their **r**
26:9 Meshelemiah's sons and **r**
26:11 were 13 sons and **r** of Hosah.
26:12 assigned duties with their **r**
26:25 From his **r** on Eliezer's side of
26:26 He and his **r** were in charge of
26:28 of Shelomith and his **r**.
26:30 male **r** were appointed to serve
26:32 Jeriah's **r** were 2,700 skilled
28:2 my **r** and subjects.
2Ch 5:12 and their **r** — were dressed in
11:4 Don't wage war against your **r**.
19:10 Warn your **r** living in other
19:10 Then your **r** will not become
19:10 angry with you and your **r**.
28:8 girls from their **r** ⌊the Judeans⌋.
28:11 you have captured from your **r**,
29:15 These men gathered their **r** and
29:34 So their **r**, the Levites,
30:7 and your **r** who were unfaithful
30:9 your **r** and children will find
31:15 offerings faithfully to all their **r**,
35:5 the family divisions of your **r**,
35:15 because their **r**, the Levites,
Ezr 3:2 and his **r** ⌊who were⌋ priests
3:2 son Zerubbabel and his **r** built
3:9 Jeshua with his sons and **r**
3:9 family and their sons and **r**,
7:18 You and your **r** may do
8:17 I told them to tell Iddo and his **r**,
8:18 so Iddo and his **r** brought us
8:18 18 of Sherebiah's sons and **r**.
8:19 of Jeshaiah's **r** and their sons,
8:24 Hashabiah, and 10 of their **r**.
Neh 3:1 chief priest Eliashib and his **r**,
3:18 After him their **r** made repairs.
5:1 publicly about their Jewish **r**.
5:5 same flesh and blood as our **r**.

Neh 5:7 on loans made to your own **r**."
5:8 our Jewish **r** who had been
5:8 your Jewish **r** so that we
10:10 and their **r** Shebaniah,
10:29 They joined their **r**,
11:12 From Seraiah's **r** 822 did the
11:13 Adaiah's **r**, the heads of the
11:14 Their **r**, who were warriors,
11:17 among his **r**;
11:19 and their **r** who guarded the
12:7 of the priests and of their **r** at
12:8 who with his **r** was in charge of
12:9 Their **r** Bakbukiah and Unno
12:24 They and their **r** stood in
12:36 these **r** of Zechariah followed:
13:13 ⌊the portions⌋ to their **r**.
Est 4:14 but you and your **r** will die.
8:6 to see the destruction of my **r**."
Job 19:14 My **r** and my closest friends
Psa 38:11 and my **r** stand far away
122:8 the sake of my **r** and friends,
Pro 6:19 who spreads conflict among **r**.
Isa 3:6 of one of his **r** from his father's
41:6 neighbors and say to their **r**,
58:7 Don't refuse to help your **r**.
66:5 Your **r**, who hate you and
66:20 They will bring all your **r** from
Jer 7:15 sight as I forced out all your **r**,
9:4 Don't trust your **r**.
12:6 Even your **r** and members of
23:35 ask their neighbors and their **r**,
29:16 the people who are your **r** and
31:34 neighbors or his **r** by saying,
34:17 freed your **r** and neighbors.
49:10 Their children and **r** will be
Eze 11:15 are talking about your own **r**
Hos 13:15 important among their **r**.
Amo 1:9 their treaty with their **r**.
1:11 pursued their **r** with swords.
Mar 6:4 in his hometown, among his **r**,
Luk 1:58 Her neighbors and **r** heard that
1:61 have any **r** with that name."
2:44 him among their **r** and friends.
14:12 other **r**, or rich neighbors.
21:16 "Even parents, brothers, **r**,
Act 7:3 'Leave your land and your **r**.
7:14 for his father Jacob and his **r**,
10:24 them and had called his **r**
1Ti 5:8 doesn't take care of his own **r**,
5:16 and has **r** who are widows,
Heb 8:11 neighbors or his **r** by saying,

relax (1)

Pro 4:13 Do not **r** your grip on it.

release (11)

Gen 40:13 three days Pharaoh will **r** you
Lev 16:10 He will **r** it in the desert to
16:21 A man will be appointed to **r**
16:22 The man must **r** the goat in the
25:41 Then you will **r** him and his
Psa 105:20 king sent someone to **r** him.
142:7 **R** my soul from prison so that I
Mat 27:20 the crowd to ask for the **r**
Act 16:35 "You can **r** those men now."
16:36 have sent word to **r** you.
Rev 9:14 "**R** the four angels who are held

released (15)

Lev 16:26 "The man who **r** the goat to
25:28 In the jubilee it will be **r**,
25:30 It will not be **r** in the jubilee.
25:31 They will be **r** in the jubilee.
25:33 house in the city will be **r**,
25:54 he and his children will be **r** in
27:21 When the field is **r** in the
Jdg 15:5 He set the torches on fire and **r**
Isa 61:1 set free and prisoners will be **r**.
Jer 52:31 of Judah and **r** him from prison.
Act 4:23 When Peter and John were **r**,
13:3 and **r** them ⌊from their work in
22:30 So the officer **r** Paul the next
Heb 11:35 but refused to be **r** so that they
Rev 9:15 and year were **r** to kill one-third

releases (1)

Job 12:15 When he **r** them, they flood the

reliable (10)

Dtr 32:4 He is honorable and **r**.
Psa 93:5 testimonies are completely **r**.
119:86 (All your commandments are **r**.)
119:142 and your teachings are **r**.
119:151 all your commandments are **r**.
Isa 25:1 You have been completely **r** in
Jer 6:16 paths are the old, **r** paths.
Act 25:26 But I don't have anything **r** to
Heb 2:2 that the angels brought was **r**,
1Jn 1:9 God is faithful and **r**.

relied (3)

Jdg 20:36 The Israelites **r** on those
Job 6:20 are ashamed because they **r**
Rom 9:32 but they **r** on their own efforts.

relief (13)

Gen 5:29 He named him Noah [**R**],
5:29 "This child will bring us **r** from
1Sm 16:23 Saul got **r** ⌊from his terror⌋ and
Neh 9:28 As soon as they felt some **r**,
Job 14:14 I will wait for my **r** to come as
32:20 I must speak to get **r**.
Psa 146:9 The LORD gives **r** to orphans
147:6 The LORD gives **r** to those
Isa 14:3 the LORD will give you **r** from
Lam 3:56 your ears when I cry out for **r**.
Nah 3:19 There is no **r** for your collapse.
2Co 8:13 should have **r** while you have
2Th 1:7 all of us **r** from our suffering.

relieve (3)

Dtr 23:12 you can go ⌊to **r** yourself⌋.
1Sm 24:3 Saul went into ⌊it⌋ to **r** himself
Psa 25:17 **R** my troubled heart,

relieved (2)

Act 20:12 They were greatly **r** that he
Php 2:28 him again and I will feel **r**.

relieving (1)

1Ki 18:27 Maybe he's thinking, **r** himself,

religion (8)

Jer 10:3 The **r** of the people is
Act 25:19 with him about their own **r**
26:5 the strictest party of our **r**.
Gal 1:13 when I followed the Jewish **r**.
1:14 group in following the Jewish **r**.
Col 4:11 the Jewish **r** who are working
Jas 1:26 That person's **r** is worthless.
1:27 Pure, unstained **r**, according to

religious (13)

Gen 1:14 signs and will mark **r** festivals,
Num 29:35 you must hold a **r** assembly.
Dtr 16:8 and on the seventh day hold a **r**
2Ki 11:12 crown and the **r** instructions,
2Ch 23:11 crown and the **r** instructions,
Pro 29:4 but a person who confiscates **r**
Dan 6:5 unless we find it in his **r**
Amo 5:21 I'm not pleased with your **r**
Luk 20:20 to act like sincere **r** people.
Act 4:2 These **r** authorities were
17:22 I see that you are very **r**.
Heb 10:11 priest performed his **r** duty.
Jas 1:26 If a person thinks that he is **r**

religiously (1)

Gal 4:10 You **r** observe days,

rely (11)

Job 39:12 Can you **r** on it to bring your
Psa 20:7 Some ⌊**r**⌋ on chariots and
40:4 in the LORD and does not **r**
44:6 I do not **r** on my bow,
Pro 3:5 and do not **r** on your own
Isa 31:1 for help, who **r** on horses,
Eze 33:26 You **r** on your swords.
Mic 3:11 But they **r** on the LORD when
Rom 2:17 You call yourself a Jew, **r** on
Rom 9:32 They didn't **r** on faith to gain
Gal 3:10 there is a curse on all who **r** on

remain (81)

Gen 13:6 they were unable to **r** together.
Lev 11:11 They must **r** disgusting to you.
11:35 and will **r** unclean for you.
11:36 holding water will **r** clean.
Dtr 13:16 It must **r** a mound of ruins and
21:8 murder **r** among your people
Jos 20:6 The accused person may **r** in
23:4 of the nations that still **r** as
2Sm 7:16 Your royal house will **r** in my
14:7 name or descendants **r**
16:4 "I hope to **r** in your good graces,
1Ch 28:7 forever if he will **r** determined
2Ch 15:7 But you must **r** strong and not
Ezr 1:4 All who ⌊choose to⌋ **r** behind,
9:15 of us continue to **r** as survivors.
Est 4:14 even if you **r** silent now,
Job 29:20 and the bow in my hand will **r**
36:13 have godless hearts **r** angry.
Psa 4:4 this on your bed and **r** quiet.
23:6 and I will **r** in the LORD's
27:4 This I will seek: to **r** in the
28:1 If you **r** silent, I will be like
35:22 Do not **r** silent. O Lord, do not
50:3 will come and will not **r** silent.
79:5 Will you **r** angry forever?
83:1 O God, do not **r** silent.
85:9 ⌊this⌋ glory will **r** in our land.
91:1 shelter of the Most High will **r**
101:7 The one who tells lies will not **r**
102:12 But you, O LORD, **r** forever.
102:27 But you **r** the same,
109:15 Let their guilt and sin always **r**
Pro 2:21 People of integrity will **r** in it.
Ecc 10:4 If you **r** calm, you can make up
11:3 the tree will **r** where it fell.
Isa 7:9 If you don't **r** faithful,
7:9 you won't **r** standing.
10:19 The trees that **r** in the forest
22:18 your splendid chariots will **r**.
62:1 Zion's sake I will not **r** silent.
Jer 8:3 "Then the few who **r** from these
12:4 plants in every field **r** dried up?
40:5 "If you wish to **r**, then go back
Lam 3:28 They should sit alone and **r**
4:22 LORD will not let you **r** in exile.
Eze 17:14 so that it would **r** a humiliated
22:14 Will you **r** strong when I deal
36:34 It will no longer **r** empty for
47:11 become fresh. It will **r** salty.
Dan 4:16 Let it **r** like this for seven time
5:22 You didn't **r** humble,
9:2 that Jerusalem would **r** in ruins.
9:2 that Jerusalem would **r**
Hos 8:5 How long will they **r** unclean?
Zec 12:6 will **r** safe in Jerusalem.
14:10 Jerusalem will rise and **r** on its
Mat 12:5 day of worship yet **r** innocent?
19:5 and mother and will **r** united
Mar 10:7 and mother and will **r** united
Jon 12:34 the Messiah will **r** here forever.
Act 11:23 people to **r** solidly committed
14:22 the disciples to **r** faithful.
Rom 9:11 so that God's plan would **r**
11:20 but you **r** on the tree because
1Co 4:13 are attacked, we **r** courteous.
7:24 you should **r** in whatever
7:26 good for people to **r** as they are.
7:39 A married woman must **r** with
13:13 So these three things **r**:
14:28 those people should **r** silent in
Php 1:24 it's better that I **r** in this life.
1Th 3:1 We thought it best to **r** in
1Ti 5:25 aren't obvious can't **r** hidden.
Heb 1:12 But you **r** the same,
3:14 After all, we will **r** Christ's
6:11 so that you will **r** confident until
12:27 that cannot be shaken will **r**.
Jas 1:27 and to **r** uncorrupted by this
1Pe 5:12 **R** firmly established in it!
Jud 1:21 **R** in God's love as you look for
Rev 17:10 he must **r** for a little while.

remainder (1)

Psa 76:10 will wear the **r** of ⌊their⌋ anger.

remained (34)

Gen 18:22 but Abraham **r** standing in front
22:19 Abraham **r** in Beersheba.
25:27 Jacob **r** a quiet man,
37:7 It **r** standing while your bundles
49:24 and his arms **r** limber because
Exo 17:12 His hands **r** steady until sunset.
Jos 4:10 who carried the ark **r** standing
5:8 they **r** in the camp until they
11:22 of the people of Anak **r** in Israel.
Jdg 5:17 Gilead **r** east of the Jordan
5:17 Asher sat on the seashore and **r**
11:17 the people of Israel **r** at Kadesh.
1Sm 3:15 Samuel **r** in bed until morning.
13:7 But Saul **r** in Gilgal,
26:9 anointed king and **r** free of guilt.
2Sm 10:8 and Maacah **r** by themselves
20:2 But the people of Judah **r** loyal
1Ki 12:20 Only the tribe of Judah **r** loyal
15:14 Asa **r** committed to the LORD
2Ki 13:6 Asherah **r** standing in Samaria.
1Ch 12:29 though most of them **r** loyal to
19:9 who had come **r** by themselves
2Ch 15:17 Asa **r** committed ⌊to the
36:20 They **r** captives until the
Psa 17:5 my steps have **r** firmly in your
39:2 I **r** totally speechless.
39:9 I **r** speechless. I did not open
50:21 you did these things, I **r** silent.
68:12 The women who **r** at home will
Ecc 2:9 Yet, my wisdom **r** with me.
Isa 57:17 hid ⌊from them⌋, and **r** angry.
Jer 48:11 why its flavor has **r** the same,
Luk 1:22 to them but **r** unable to talk.
Act 7:45 This tent **r** here until the time of

remaining (24)

Exo 26:9 set and the **r** six into another
26:12 The **r** half-sheet should hang
28:10 on one stone and the **r** six
36:16 and the **r** six into another set.
1Ki 6:27 Their **r** wings touched each
2Ki 25:22 to govern the **r** people in the
Ezr 1:6 All their neighbors ⌊who were **r**
Neh 11:1 The **r** nine-tenths were
Isa 10:20 At that time the **r** few Israelites,
10:21 A few, the **r** few of Jacob,
11:16 will be a highway for the **r** few
17:3 The **r** few from Aram will share
21:17 The **r** number of archers,
28:5 crown for his few **r** people.
Jer 23:3 "Then I will gather the **r** part of
24:8 the **r** few in Jerusalem who
31:7 the **r** few from Israel."
Eze 5:2 Then scatter the **r** third to the
5:12 I will scatter the **r** third to the
11:13 all the **r** people in Israel?"
Zec 8:6 impossible to the few **r** people
8:11 deal with the few **r** people as
8:12 I will give the few **r** people all
Rev 8:13 because of the **r** trumpet blasts

remains (24)

Num 15:31 completely. He **r** guilty."
2Sm 7:2 the ark of God **r** in the tent."
Neh 9:10 a name which **r** to this day.
Psa 17:14 leave what **r** to their children.
73:26 but God **r** the foundation of my
112:7 His heart **r** secure,
125:1 be shaken. It **r** firm forever.
146:6 The LORD **r** faithful forever.
Pro 10:7 of a righteous person **r** blessed,
11:2 wisdom **r** with humble people.
11:15 the closing of a deal **r** secure.
Isa 4:3 is left in Zion and whoever **r**
11:11 power again to recover what **r**
26:2 the nation that **r** faithful.
Eze 17:21 Anyone who **r** will be scattered
23:25 ears and kill everyone who **r**.
Amo 5:13 That is why a wise person **r**
Hag 2:5 My Spirit **r** with you.
2Co 3:11 that ministry which **r** continue
Col 1:24 I am completing whatever **r**
2Ti 2:13 If we are unfaithful, he **r** faithful
Jas 1:25 free and who **r** committed
1Jn 3:14 doesn't grow in love **r** in death.
Rev 16:15 Blessed is the one who **r** alert

Remaliah (9)

2Ki 15:25 His officer Pekah, son of **R**,
15:27 king of Judah, Pekah, son of **R**,
15:30 against Pekah, son of **R**.
15:32 son of **R**, ruled Israel, Jotham,
15:37 son of **R**, to attack Judah.
16:1 Pekah, son of **R**, was in his
16:5 King Pekah, son of **R** of Israel,
2Ch 28:6 In one day Pekah, son of **R**,
Isa 7:1 Israel's King Pekah, son of **R**,

Remaliah's (4)

Isa 7:4 of Rezin from Aram and **R** son.
7:5 Aram, Ephraim, and **R** son
7:9 the leader of Samaria is **R** son.
8:6 find joy in Rezin and **R** son.

remarkable (2)

Mat 5:47 Are you doing anything **r** if you
2Th 1:3 your faith is showing **r** growth

remarked (1)

Jon 1:47 coming toward him and **r**,

remarks (2)

Luk 16:14 making sarcastic **r** about him.
23:35 rulers were making sarcastic **r**.

remember (209)

Gen 9:15 Then I will **r** my promise to you
9:16 I will see it and **r** my
28:15 **R**, I am with you and will
31:50 **r** that God stands as a witness
40:14 **R** me when things go well for
40:23 chief cupbearer didn't **r** Joseph.
41:9 "I **r** a promise I failed to keep.
41:31 People won't **r** that there once
Exo 12:14 day will be one for you to **r**.
13:3 "**R** this day — the day when you
16:29 **R**: The LORD has given you
20:8 "**R** the day of worship by
32:13 **R** your servants Abraham,
33:13 **R**: This nation is your people."
Lev 26:42 I will **r** my promise to Jacob,
26:42 I will also **r** the land.
26:45 But for their sake, I will **r** the
Num 10:9 Then the LORD your God will **r**
11:5 **R** all the free fish we ate in
15:39 you will **r** all the LORD's
15:40 You will **r** to obey all my
31:16 "**R**, they were the ones who
Dtr 4:39 **R** today, and never forget that
5:15 **R** that you were slaves in
7:18 **R** what the LORD your God did
7:24 earth will even **r** their names.
8:2 **R** that for 40 years the LORD
8:18 But **r** the LORD your God is the
9:27 **R** your servants Abraham,
10:14 **R** that the sky, the highest
11:2 **R** today the discipline you
15:15 **R** that you were slaves in
16:3 you will **r** the day you left
16:12 **R** that you were slaves in
24:9 **R** what the LORD your God did
24:18 **R** that you were slaves in
24:22 **R** that you were slaves in
25:17 **R** what the Amalekites did to
32:7 **R** a time long ago.
Jos 1:13 "**R** what the LORD's servant
Jdg 8:34 The Israelites did not **r** the
9:2 **R**, I'm your own flesh and
16:28 "Almighty LORD, please **r** me!
1Sm 1:11 **r** me, and give me a boy,
25:31 has given you success, **r** me."
2Sm 19:19 "Don't **r** the crime I committed
2Ki 9:25 **R** when you and I were driving
20:3 "Please, LORD, **r** how I've
1Ch 16:12 **R** the miracles he performed,
16:15 **R** his promise forever,
2Ch 6:42 **R** your mercy to your servant
24:22 King Joash did not **r** how kind
Neh 1:8 Please **r** what you told us
4:14 **R** how great and awe-inspiring
5:19 **R** me, my God.
6:14 prayed,⌋ "My God, **r** what Tobiah
6:14 Also, **r** the female prophet
13:14 "**R** me for what I have done,
13:22 "**R** me also for this,
13:29 ⌊Nehemiah prayed,⌋ "**R** them,
13:31 ⌊Nehemiah prayed,⌋ "**R** me,
Job 7:7 **R**, my life is only a breath,
10:9 Please **r** that you made me out
11:16 will forget your misery and **r**
14:13 time for me when you will **r** me.
21:6 When I **r** it, I'm terrified,
36:24 **R** that you should praise his
Psa 8:4 what is a mortal that you **r** him
20:3 He will **r** all your grain offerings
22:27 All the ends of the earth will **r**
25:6 **R**, O LORD, They have existed
25:7 Do not **r** the sins of my youth or
25:7 **R** me, O LORD, in keeping
30:4 **R** his holiness by giving
42:4 I will **r** these things as I pour
42:6 That is why I will **r** you in the
63:6 As I lie on my bed, I **r** you.
74:2 **R** your congregation.
74:18 **R** how the enemy insulted you,
74:18 **R** how an entire nation of
74:22 **R** how godless fools insult you
77:3 I sigh as I **r** God. I begin to lose
77:6 I **r** my song in the night and
77:11 I will **r** the deeds of the LORD.
77:11 I will **r** your ancient miracles.
78:7 to **r** what he has done,
78:42 They did not **r** his power — the
88:5 those whom you no longer **r**,
89:47 **R** how short my life is!
89:50 **R**, O LORD, how your servant
89:50 **R** how I have carried in my
97:12 Give thanks to him as you **r**
103:18 to those who **r** to follow his
105:5 **R** the miracles he performed,
106:4 **R** me, O LORD, when you
106:7 They did not **r** your numerous
109:14 Let the LORD **r** the guilt of his
109:16 because he did not **r** to be kind.
119:49 **R** the word ⌊you gave⌋ me.
119:55 At night I **r** your name,
132:1 O LORD, **r** David and all the
132:2 **R** how he swore an oath to the
137:6 roof of my mouth if I don't **r** you,
137:7 O LORD, **r** the people of Edom.
137:7 **R** what they did the day
143:5 I **r** the days long ago.
145:7 They will announce what they **r**
Pro 31:7 does not **r** his trouble anymore.
Ecc 11:8 But they should also **r** there
12:1 **R** your Creator when you are
12:2 **R** your Creator before the sun,
12:3 **R** your Creator when those who
12:4 **R** your Creator when the doors
12:5 **R** your Creator when someone
12:6 **R** your Creator before the silver
Isa 8:13 **R** that the LORD of Armies is
12:4 Make them **r** that his name is
26:8 We want to **r** you and your
38:3 "Please, LORD, **r** how I've
43:25 will not **r** your sins ⌊anymore⌋.
44:21 **R** these things, Jacob: You are
46:8 **R** this, and take courage.
46:9 **R** the first events, because I
54:4 You won't **r** the disgrace of your
56:4 ⌊I will **r**⌋ the castrated men
56:6 And ⌊I will **r**⌋ the foreigners
64:9 Don't **r** our sin forever.
Jer 2:2 I **r** the unfailing loyalty of your
2:2 I **r** how you followed me into
3:16 They won't **r** it, miss it, or make
14:10 He will **r** their crimes and
14:21 **R** your promise to us;
15:15 **R** me, take care of me,
17:2 Even their children **r** their altars
18:20 **R** how I stood in your presence
31:21 **R** the highway, the road on
44:21 "Doesn't the LORD **r** that you

Jer 51:50 **R** the LORD in a distant land,
Lam 2:1 He didn't ⌊even⌋ **r** his footstool
3:19 **R** my suffering and my
3:20 My soul continues to **r** ⌊these
5:1 "**R**, O LORD, what has
Eze 6:9 Then those who escape will **r**
16:22 you didn't **r** the time when you
16:22 You didn't **r** when you were
16:43 "'You didn't **r** the time when
16:60 I will **r** the promise that I made
16:61 Then you will **r** what you have
16:63 You will **r** and be ashamed.
20:43 There you will **r** the way you
21:24 You make people **r** how sinful
23:27 anymore or **r** Egypt anymore.
29:16 The people of Israel will **r** how
36:31 Then you will **r** your evil ways
43:11 so that they can **r** its design
Dan 6:15 They said to him, "**R**,
Hos 7:2 They don't realize that I **r** all the
8:13 Now I will **r** their wickedness
9:9 God will **r** their wickedness
Amo 1:9 The Tyrians didn't **r** their treaty
Mic 6:5 My people, **r** what King Balak
6:5 **R** ⌊your journey⌋ from Shittim
Hab 3:2 all this chaos, **r** to be merciful.
Zec 10:9 they will **r** me even in faraway
Mal 4:4 "**R** the teachings of my servant
Mat 5:23 the altar and **r** there that another
16:9 Don't you **r** the five loaves for
16:10 Don't you **r** the seven loaves for
27:63 They said, "Sir, we **r** how that
28:20 "And **r** that I am always with
Mar 8:18 blind and deaf? Don't you **r**?
Luk 16:25 "Abraham replied, '**R**,
17:32 **R** Lot's wife!
22:19 up for you. Do this to **r** me."
23:42 Then he said, "Jesus, **r** me
24:6 **R** what he told you while he
Jon 3:26 do you **r** the man you spoke so
15:20 **R** what I told you: 'A servant
16:4 it happens you'll **r** what I've told
16:21 she doesn't **r** the pain anymore
Act 20:31 **R** that I instructed each of you
20:35 We should **r** the words that the
Rom 11:18 **r** that you don't support the root
1Co 4:17 to help you **r** my Christian way
11:24 given for you. Do this to **r** me."
11:25 you drink from it, do it to **r** me."
2Co 8:12 ⌊**r**⌋ that people are accepted if
8:23 If any questions are raised, **r**
9:6 **R** this: The farmer who plants a
Gal 2:10 us to do was to **r** the poor,
Eph 1:16 I always **r** you in my prayers.
2:11 **R** that once you were not
Col 4:18 **R** that I'm a prisoner.
1Th 1:2 God for all of you as we **r** you
2:9 You **r**, brothers and sisters,
2Th 2:5 Don't you **r** that I told you about
2Ti 1:3 I constantly **r** you in my prayers
1:4 I **r** your tears and want to see
Heb 2:6 a mortal that you should **r** him,
10:32 **R** the past, when you first
13:3 **R** those in prison as if you
13:3 **R** those who are mistreated as
13:7 **R** your leaders who have
Jas 1:19 **R** this, my dear brothers and
2Pe 1:15 see that you **r** these things after
3:2 I want you to **r** the words
Jud 1:17 Dear friends, **r** what the
Rev 2:5 **R** how far you have fallen.
3:3 So **r** what you received and

remembered (61)

Gen 8:1 God **r** Noah and all the wild
19:29 on the plain, he **r** Abraham.
30:22 Then God **r** Rachel.
42:9 Then he **r** the dreams he once
Exo 2:24 and he **r** his promise to
6:5 and I have **r** my promise.
20:24 I choose to have my name **r**,
Jos 7:9 your great name ⌊will be **r**⌋?"
Rut 4:14 who has **r** today to give you
1Sm 1:19 and the LORD **r** her.
Est 2:1 he **r** Vashti, what she had done,
9:28 So these days must be **r** and
Psa 9:12 murder has **r** oppressed people.
45:17 I will cause your name to be **r**
78:35 They **r** that God was their rock,
78:39 He **r** that they were only flesh
83:4 of Israel will no longer be **r**."
102:12 **r** throughout every generation.
105:42 He **r** his holy promise to his
106:45 He **r** his promise to them.
112:6 person will always be **r**.
119:52 I **r** your regulations from long
135:13 be **r** throughout every
136:23 He **r** us when we were
137:1 we sat down and cried as we **r**
Ecc 1:11 Nothing from the past is **r**.
1:11 nothing will be **r** by those who
2:16 nor the fool will be **r** for long,
9:15 But no one **r** that poor person.
Isa 17:10 You haven't **r** the rock,
23:16 many songs so that you'll be **r**."
57:11 You haven't **r** me or cared about
63:11 Then his people **r** Moses and
65:17 Past things will not be **r**.
Eze 3:20 things they did will not be **r**.
18:22 things that he did will not be **r**.
18:24 that he has done will not be **r**
21:32 You will no longer be **r**.
23:19 She **r** how she had been a
25:10 longer be **r** among the nations.
33:13 that he has done will be **r**.
33:16 sins that he has done will be **r**.
Hos 12:5 is the name by which he is **r**.
Jnh 2:7 slipping away, I **r** the LORD.
Zec 13:2 They will no longer be **r**.
Mat 26:75 Peter **r** what Jesus had said:
Mar 11:21 Peter **r** ⌊what Jesus had said⌋,
14:72 Peter **r** that Jesus said to him,
Luk 1:54 "He **r** to help his servant Israel
1:72 and **r** his holy promise,
22:61 Peter **r** what the Lord had said:
24:8 Then the women **r** what Jesus
Jon 2:17 His disciples **r** that Scripture
2:22 his disciples **r** that he had said
12:16 the disciples **r** that these
12:16 The disciples **r** that they had
Act 10:4 to the poor, and he has **r** you.
10:31 your prayer and has **r** your gifts
11:16 I **r** that the Lord had said,
Rev 16:19 God **r** to give Babylon the
18:5 and God has **r** her crimes.

remembers (8)

Job 24:20 No one **r** them anymore,
Psa 6:5 In death, no one **r** you.
105:8 He always **r** his promise,
111:5 He always **r** his promise.
Isa 64:5 does right and **r** your ways.
Lam 1:7 Jerusalem **r** all the treasures it
Nah 2:5 He **r** his best fighting men.
2Co 7:15 more as he **r** how obedient all

Remeth (1)

Jos 19:21 **R**, En Gannim, En Haddah,

remind (11)

Num 5:15 for a confession — to **r** someone
16:40 The bronze-covered altar will **r**
Dtr 32:7 Ask your fathers to **r** you,
1Ki 17:18 Did you come here to **r** me of
Isa 43:26 **R** me ⌊of what happened⌋.
Eze 21:23 But the king of Babylon will **r**
Jon 14:26 He will **r** you of everything that
2Ti 2:14 **R** believers about these things,
Tit 3:1 **R** believers to willingly place
2Pe 1:12 Therefore, I will always **r** you
Jud 1:5 I want to **r** you about what you

reminded (4)

Isa 19:17 Whenever they are **r** of Judah,
Jer 11:19 we won't be **r** of him anymore."
2Ti 1:5 I'm **r** of how sincere your faith
Heb 10:3 this yearly cycle of sacrifices **r**

reminder (23)

Exo 13:9 a mark on your hand or a **r**
17:14 "Write this **r** on a scroll,
28:12 names on his shoulders as a **r**
28:29 over his heart as a constant **r**
30:16 It will be a **r** for the Israelites in
31:16 a permanent **r** of my promise.
39:7 straps of the ephod as a **r**
Lev 2:2 will burn it on the altar as a **r**.
2:9 grain offering and burn it as a **r**
2:16 and all the incense as a **r**.
5:12 He will burn it as a **r** on top of
6:15 will burn it on the altar as a **r**.
24:7 on the bread will be a **r**,
24:8 It is a continual **r** of my promise
Num 10:10 The trumpets will be a **r** for you
31:54 meeting as a **r** to the Israelites.
Dtr 6:8 them as headbands as a **r**.
11:18 them as headbands as a **r**.
Jos 4:7 These stones are a permanent **r**
Isa 55:13 This will be a **r** of the LORD's
Zec 6:14 The crown will be a **r** to Helem,
Mal 3:16 written in his presence to be a **r**
Rom 15:15 are rather bold, as a **r** to you.

reminders (1)

Exo 28:12 straps of the ephod as **r**

reminding (1)

2Ti 1:6 Now I'm **r** you to fan that gift

remote (2)

Jdg 19:1 a Levite who lived in a **r** area
19:18 Bethlehem in Judah to a **r** area

removal (1)

Col 2:11 But it was a **r** of the corrupt

remove (74)

Exo 12:15 On the very first day you must **r**
25:15 rings of the ark. Never **r** them.
Lev 1:16 **R** the gizzard with its filth and
2:9 The priest will **r** part of the
3:3 From your offering **r** the fat that
3:9 **R** all the fat from the tail and
3:10 Also **r** the two kidneys with the
3:15 Also **r** the lobe of the liver
4:8 He will **r** all of the fat from the
4:9 He will also **r** the lobe of the
4:19 He will **r** all the fat and burn it
4:31 He will **r** all the fat the same
4:35 He will **r** all the fat the same
6:10 Then he will **r** the ashes left on
6:15 One of them will **r** a handful of
7:4 He will also **r** the lobe of the
26:6 I will **r** dangerous animals,
Jos 7:9 they will surround us and **r**
1Sm 2:33 whom I do not **r** from my altar
14:19 Then Saul said to the priest, "**R**
1Ki 2:31 You can **r** the innocent blood —
20:24 This is what we must do: **R** all
2Ki 24:3 He wanted to **r** the people of
2Ch 29:5 **R** anything that has been
33:8 I will never again **r** Israel from
Job 30:13 Yes, they **r** all traces of my
Psa 25:11 **r** my guilt, because it is great.
39:10 **R** the sickness you laid upon
109:15 Let the LORD **r** every memory
119:22 **R** the insults and contempt that
Pro 4:24 **R** dishonesty from your mouth.
22:15 Spanking will **r** it far from him.
Isa 1:25 I will **r** your impurities with
22:8 On that day the LORD will **r** the
22:19 "I will **r** you from your office
25:7 On this mountain he will **r** the
25:8 and he will **r** the disgrace of his
47:2 **R** your veil. Take off your skirt.
57:14 **R** every obstacle in the way of
Jer 28:16 I'm going to **r** you from the face
32:31 So now I must **r** this city from
Eze 11:18 They will come and **r** all the
11:19 I will **r** their stubborn hearts
26:16 They will **r** their robes and take
34:25 I will **r** the wild animals from
36:26 I will **r** your stubborn hearts
43:20 When you do this, you will **r**
43:22 **R** sin from the altar as you did
45:18 has no defects and **r** sin from
Hos 2:2 Tell her to **r** the lovers from
Nah 1:14 I will **r** the wooden and metal

Nah 2:13 I will **r** your prey from the earth,
Zep 1:3 I will **r** all people from the face
1:4 I will **r** the faithful few of Baal
1:5 I will **r** those who worship all
1:6 I will **r** those who have turned
3:11 Then I will **r** your arrogance
Zec 3:4 "**R** Joshua's filthy clothes.
3:9 "I will **r** this land's sin in a
9:7 I will **r** the blood from their
13:2 I will also **r** the ⌊false⌋
Mat 3:11 am not worthy to **r** his sandals.
7:5 First **r** the beam from your own
7:5 Then you will see clearly to **r**
Luk 6:42 First **r** the beam from your own
6:42 Then you will see clearly to **r**
Jon 19:38 Pilate to let him **r** Jesus' body.
19:38 permission to **r** Jesus' body.
20:15 have put him, and I'll **r** him."
Rom 11:26 will **r** godlessness from Jacob.
1Co 5:7 **R** the old yeast ⌊of sin⌋ so that
5:13 **R** that wicked man from among
2Co 3:14 because only Christ can **r** it.
Heb 9:26 he has appeared once to **r** sin

removed (47)

Exo 30:16 that the sins in their lives are **r**."
Lev 4:10 the same way they were **r** from
4:31 the fat the same way it is **r** from
4:35 way the fat of the lamb is **r** from
Dtr 19:13 person must be **r** from Israel.
Jos 5:9 "Today I have **r** the disgrace of
1Ki 2:27 So Solomon **r** Abiathar as the
15:13 He also **r** his grandmother
2Ki 16:17 ⌊used in the temple⌋ and **r**
16:18 Ahaz **r** the covered walkway
16:18 He also **r** the outer entrance for
17:11 that the LORD had **r** from
17:18 Israel that he **r** them from his
23:11 He **r** the horses that Judah's
1Ch 6:49 holy place and **r** Israel's sins
2Ch 15:16 King Asa also **r** his
34:6 he **r** all their temples,
36:3 The king of Egypt **r** him from
Est 3:10 At that, the king **r** his signet
Psa 30:11 You have **r** my sackcloth and
81:6 "I **r** the burden from his
85:2 You **r** your people's guilt.
103:12 far he has **r** our rebellious acts
Isa 5:2 He dug it up, **r** its stones,
10:27 will be **r** from your shoulders.
10:27 Their yoke will be **r** from your
14:25 Then its yoke will be **r** from my
14:25 will be **r** from their shoulders."
22:25 fastened in place will be **r**.
27:8 He **r** it with a fierce blast from
53:8 thought that he would be **r** from
Jer 6:29 the impurities can't be **r**.
Dan 5:20 he was **r** from the royal throne.
Hos 11:4 I **r** the yokes from their necks.
Nah 1:15 It will be completely **r**.
Mat 8:17 and **r** our diseases."
Luk 1:25 He has **r** my public disgrace."
Jon 13:4 **r** his outer clothes,
19:31 legs broken and their bodies **r**.
19:38 Jesus' body. So Joseph **r** it.
20:1 that the stone had been **r** from
20:2 She told them, "They have **r**
20:13 "They have **r** my Lord,
Act 3:19 ⌊to God⌋ to have your sins **r**.
13:22 God **r** Saul and made David
1Co 5:2 have been **r** from among you.
2Co 3:14 It isn't **r**, because only Christ

removes (3)

Psa 25:15 He **r** my feet from traps.
Dan 2:21 He **r** kings and establishes
Jon 15:2 He **r** every one of my branches

removing (4)

Jer 40:4 Today I'm **r** the chains from
Eze 43:23 When you finish **r** sin,
Luk 6:1 the heads of grain, **r** the husks,
1Pe 3:21 Baptism doesn't save by **r** dirt

renamed (6)

Jos 19:47 They took it, settled there, and **r**
Dan 2:26 (who had been **r** Belteshazzar),
4:8 (He had been **r** Belteshazzar
4:19 Then Daniel (who had been **r**
5:12 This Daniel (who had been **r**
10:1 (who had been **r** Belteshazzar).

renew (6)

Psa 19:7 They **r** the soul. The testimony
51:10 and **r** a faithful spirit within me.
104:30 You **r** the face of the earth.
Isa 57:15 I will **r** the spirit of those who
61:4 They will **r** the ruined cities,
Hab 3:2 In the course of the years, **r** it.

renewal (1)

Tit 3:5 Spirit gives us new birth and **r**.

renewed (4)

Isa 40:31 hope in the LORD will be **r**.
57:10 You've found **r** strength,
2Co 4:16 inwardly we are **r** day by day.
Col 3:10 new person is continually **r**

renews (2)

Psa 23:3 He **r** my soul. He guides me
Zep 3:17 **r** you with his love,

renovate (2)

2Ch 24:4 wanted to **r** the LORD's temple.
24:12 masons and carpenters to **r**

rental (1)

Exo 22:15 the **r** fee covers the loss.

rented (2)

Exo 22:15 If it is **r**, the rental fee covers
Act 28:30 Paul **r** a place to live for two

reopen (1)

Jer 13:19 there will be no one to **r** them.

reopened (1)

Neh 13:19 shut and not to be **r** until after

repair (9)

2Ki 12:14 and they used it to **r** the temple.
22:6 quarried stones to **r** the temple.
2Ch 24:5 money throughout Israel to **r**
24:12 bronze to **r** the LORD's temple.
34:8 to **r** the temple of the LORD his
Neh 4:7 Ashdod heard that the **r** work
Pro 29:1 suddenly be broken beyond **r**.
Jer 19:11 jar was smashed beyond **r**.
Amo 9:11 I will **r** the holes in it.

repaired (13)

Jos 9:5 sandals were worn-out and **r**,
2Ki 12:6 still had not **r** the temple.
2Ch 15:8 He also **r** the LORD's altar in
29:3 the LORD's temple and **r** them.
35:20 when Josiah had **r** the temple,
Neh 3:13 of Zanoah **r** Valley Gate.
3:13 and they **r** 1,500 feet of the
3:14 Gate itself was **r** by Malchiah,
3:15 of Mizpah, **r** Fountain Gate.
3:19 **r** a section across from the
3:27 After him the men from Tekoa **r**
3:30 sixth son, **r** another section.
Eze 13:5 They haven't **r** the gaps in the

repairing (4)

1Ki 11:27 was building the Millo and **r**
2Ki 12:7 "Why aren't you **r** the damage
12:8 be responsible for **r** the temple.
2Ch 34:10 were restoring and **r** the temple.

repairs (38)

2Ki 12:5 the donors and use it to make **r**
12:7 use it to make **r** on the temple."
12:12 wood and cut stones to make **r**
12:12 they needed for the temple **r**.
22:5 the workmen who are making **r**
Neh 3:4 grandson of Hakkoz, made **r**.
3:4 of Meshezabel, made **r**.
3:4 Zadok, son of Baana, made **r**.
3:5 the men from Tekoa made **r**.
Neh 3:6 made **r** on Old Gate.
3:7 made **r** on the wall.
3:8 son, a goldsmith, made **r**.
3:8 a perfume maker, made **r**.
3:9 a district of Jerusalem, made **r**.
3:10 made **r** across from his own
3:10 Hashabneiah's son, made **r**.
3:11 made **r** on a section that
3:12 made **r** with the help of his
3:15 He also made **r** on the wall of
3:16 made **r** all the way to a point
3:17 Rehum (Bani's son), made **r**.
3:17 made **r** for his district.
3:18 After him their relatives made **r**.
3:20 made **r** on a section from the
3:21 made **r** on a section from the
3:22 who lived in that area made **r**.
3:23 made **r** across from their
3:23 made **r** next to his home.
3:24 made **r** on a section from
3:25 Palal, Uzai's son, made **r**
3:26 living on the Ophel made **r**
3:28 Horse Gate the priests made **r**.
3:28 Each priest made **r** across from
3:29 made **r** across from his own
3:29 the guard at East Gate, made **r**.
3:30 made **r** across from his living
3:31 made **r** as far as the building
3:32 and merchants made **r** between

repay (21)

Dtr 32:6 Is this how you **r** the LORD,
Rut 1:9 May the LORD **r** each of you so
1Sm 24:19 The LORD will **r** you
2Sm 3:39 May the LORD **r** this evildoer
1Ki 2:32 The LORD will **r** him for the
2Ch 6:23 **R** the guilty person with the
32:25 so he didn't **r** the LORD for his
Job 34:11 God will **r** humanity for what it
41:11 confront me that I should **r** him?
Psa 37:21 borrows, but he does not **r**.
116:12 How can I **r** the LORD for all
Pro 6:31 he has to **r** it seven times.
19:17 and he will **r** him for his good
Isa 65:6 I will not be silent, but I will **r**.
65:6 I will repay. I will **r** you in full.
65:7 I will **r** you for your sins and for
Joe 2:25 "Then I will **r** you for the years
Mat 18:26 and I will **r** everything!'
18:29 with me, and I will **r** you.'
18:30 until he would **r** what he owed.
18:34 until he would **r** everything that

repaying (1)

1Ti 5:4 own family by **r** their parents.

repeal (1)

Dan 6:8 no one could change it or **r** it."

repealed (2)

Est 1:19 and Medes, never to be **r**,
Dan 6:12 Persians the decree can't be **r**."

repeat (9)

Dtr 6:7 **R** them to your children.
Jdg 5:11 Over and over again they **r** the
Psa 107:2 LORD defended **r** these words.
124:1 (Israel should **r** this.)
129:1 (Israel should **r** this.)
Ecc 10:20 creature may **r** what you say.
Jer 23:38 you not to **r** this saying,
Heb 6:1 We shouldn't **r** the basics about
6:2 We shouldn't **r** the basic

repeated (9)

Gen 44:6 he **r** these words to them.
Exo 19:7 He **r** to them all the words that
Jdg 9:3 His uncles **r** everything he said
11:11 to Mizpah and **r** all these things
1Sm 17:23 He **r** his words, and David
17:27 The soldiers **r** ⌊to David⌋ how
25:9 they **r** all of this to him for
Psa 119:13 With my lips I have **r** every
Luk 2:17 When they saw the child, they **r**

repeatedly (10)

1Sm 20:6 'David **r** begged me to let him
20:28 "David **r** begged me ⌊to let him
1Ki 2:8 He cursed me **r** when I went to
2Ki 6:10 be on their guard. He did this **r**.
2Ch 36:15 **r** sent messages through
Pro 17:20 tongue ⌊**r**⌋ gets into trouble.
Jer 46:16 They have **r** stumbled,
Amo 4:9 Locusts **r** devoured your
Jon 5:18 when he said **r** that God was
Rev 18:18 her raging fire, they **r** cried out,

repeating (1)

Jdg 5:29 But she kept **r** to herself,

repeats (1)

Pro 26:11 ⌊so⌋ a fool **r** his stupidity.

repentance (4)

Mar 1:4 people about a baptism of **r**
Luk 3:3 told people about a baptism of **r**
Act 13:24 in Israel about the baptism of **r**.
19:4 baptism was a baptism of **r**.

Rephael (1)

1Ch 26:7 and Othni's skilled brothers **R**,

Rephah (1)

1Ch 7:25 Beriah's son was **R**.

Rephah's (1)

1Ch 7:25 **R** son was Resheph.

Rephaiah (5)

1Ch 3:21 Jeshaiah's son was **R**.
4:42 sons Pelatiah, Neariah, **R**,
7:2 Tola's sons were Uzzi, **R**,
9:43 Binea's son was **R**.
Neh 3:9 Next to them **R**, Hur's son,

Rephaiah's (2)

1Ch 3:21 **R** son was Arnan. Arnan's son
9:43 **R** son was Eleasah.

Rephaim (17)

Gen 14:5 the **R** at Ashteroth Karnaim,
15:20 Hittites, the Perizzites, the **R**,
Dtr 2:11 They were thought to be **R**,
2:20 as the land of the **R** who used
3:11 (Of the **R** only King Og of
3:13 to be called the land of the **R**.
Jos 12:4 He was the last of the **R**.
13:12 He was the last of the **R**.
15:8 the north end of the valley of **R**.
17:15 land of the Perizzites and **R** if
18:16 the north end of the valley of **R**.
2Sm 5:18 and overrun the valley of **R**.
5:22 and overran the valley of **R**.
23:13 was camping in the valley of **R**.
1Ch 11:15 was camping in the valley of **R**.
14:9 and raided the valley of **R**.
Isa 17:5 gathering grain in the **R** Valley.

Rephan (1)

Act 7:43 the star of the god **R**,

Rephidim (5)

Exo 17:1 They camped at **R**,
17:8 Amalekites fought Israel at **R**.
19:2 Israel had moved from **R** and
Num 33:14 Alush and set up camp at **R**,
33:15 They moved from **R** and set up

replace (11)

Exo 22:1 loss with five head of cattle to **r**
22:1 or four sheep to **r** the sheep.
Lev 24:18 kills an animal must **r** it,
24:21 kills an animal must **r** it.
1Ki 2:35 to **r** Joab as commander of the
14:27 made bronze shields to **r** them
2Ch 12:10 made bronze shields to **r** them
Isa 9:10 but we will **r** them with cedars."
Jer 28:13 but I will **r** it with an iron yoke.
Eze 47:8 it will **r** the salt water there with
Dan 11:7 from her roots to **r** her father.

replaced (4)

Lev 14:42 The stones must be **r**,
1Sm 21:6 from the LORD's presence and **r**
1Ki 2:35 King Solomon also **r** Abiathar
Dan 8:22 broke off, and four horns **r** it.

replaces (3)

Pro 30:23 maid when she **r** her mistress.
Ecc 2:12 what can the man who **r** the
2:18 leave it to the person who **r** me.

replied (201)

Gen 17:19 God **r**, "No! Your wife Sarah
21:26 Abimelech **r**, "I don't know who
24:55 Her brother and mother **r**,
29:4 "We're from Haran," they **r**.
29:8 They **r**, "We can't until all the
30:15 Leah **r**, "Isn't it enough that you
30:27 Laban **r**, "Listen to me.
37:16 Joseph **r**, "I'm looking for my
40:18 is what it means," Joseph **r**.
42:38 Jacob **r**, "My son will not go
44:22 We **r**, 'The boy can't leave his
47:16 Joseph **r**, "If you don't have any
50:6 Pharaoh **r**, "Go and bury your
Exo 3:13 Then Moses **r** to God,
5:3 They **r**, "The God of the
8:10 Moses **r**, "It will be as you say
8:26 Moses **r**, "It wouldn't be right to
9:29 Moses **r**, "As soon as I'm out of
18:17 Moses' father-in-law **r**,
32:18 Moses **r**, "It's not the sound of
Num 12:14 The LORD **r** to Moses,
20:19 The Israelites **r**, "We'll stay on
22:38 Balaam **r**, "Well, I've come to
Jos 10:18 Joshua **r**, "Roll large stones
17:15 Joshua **r**, "If there are so many
24:24 The people **r** to Joshua,
Jdg 3:19 The king **r**, "Keep quiet!"
4:9 Deborah **r**, "Certainly, I'll go
6:16 The LORD **r**, "I will be with
7:14 His friend **r**, "That can only be
8:2 Gideon **r**, "I haven't done
8:6 The generals at Succoth **r**,
8:19 Gideon **r**, "They were my
8:23 Gideon **r**, "I will not rule you
9:36 Zebul **r**, "The shadows of the
11:7 But Jephthah **r** to Gilead's
13:23 But Manoah's wife **r**,
14:16 Samson **r**, "I haven't even told
14:18 Samson **r**, "If you hadn't used
15:11 Samson **r**, "I did to them what
16:13 Samson **r**, "Just weave the
18:9 They **r**, "Get up, let's attack
18:25 The people of Dan **r**,
19:18 The Levite **r**, "We're on our way
Rut 2:13 Ruth **r**, "Sir, may your kindness
3:10 Boaz **r**, "May the LORD bless
3:18 Naomi **r**, "Stay here,
4:6 The man **r**, "In that case I
1Sm 1:17 Eli **r**, "Go in peace, and may
3:5 "I didn't call ⌊you⌋," Eli **r**.
3:10 And Samuel **r**, "Speak.
3:18 Eli **r**, "He is the LORD. May he
9:19 Samuel **r**, "I'm the seer.
9:21 Saul **r**, "I am a man from the
13:11 Saul **r**, "I saw the troops were
14:33 Saul **r**, "You have been
14:39 But not one of the soldiers **r**.
15:16 last night." "Speak," Saul **r**.
15:30 Saul **r**, "I have sinned!
16:5 "Greetings," he **r**, "I have come
17:34 David **r** to Saul, "I am a
18:25 Saul **r**, "Tell David, 'The king
20:5 David **r**, "Tomorrow is the New
2Sm 2:1 "To Hebron," the LORD **r**.
9:4 Ziba **r**, "He is at the home of
12:13 Nathan **r**, "The LORD has
18:23 I'd like to run," ⌊**r** Ahimaaz.⌋
19:21 But Abishai, Zeruiah's son, **r**,
19:34 Barzillai **r**, "I don't have much
1Ki 2:21 She **r**, "Let Abishag from
3:11 God **r**, "You've asked for this
3:27 The king **r**, "Give the living
13:15 eat a meal," the old prophet **r**.
2Ki 1:8 They **r**, "He was hairy and had
5:23 Naaman **r**, "Please let me give
7:2 Elisha **r**, "You will see it with
7:13 One of his officers **r**,
8:10 Elisha **r**, "Tell him that he will
9:12 Jehu **r**, "We talked for a while,
9:18 'Is everything alright?'" Jehu **r**,
9:19 'Is everything alright?'" Jehu **r**,
20:10 Hezekiah **r**, "It's easy for the
2Ch 1:11 God **r** to Solomon,
Neh 2:18 They **r**, "Let's begin to rebuild."
Est 5:5 The king **r**, "Bring Haman right
6:3 The king's personal staff **r**,
Job 4:1 Eliphaz from Teman **r** ⌊to Job⌋,
6:1 Then Job **r** ⌊to his friends⌋,
8:1 Bildad from Shuah **r** ⌊to Job⌋,
9:1 Then Job **r** ⌊to his friends⌋,
11:1 Zophar from Naama **r** ⌊to Job⌋,
12:1 Then Job **r** ⌊to his friends⌋,
15:1 Eliphaz from Teman **r** ⌊to Job⌋,
16:1 Then Job **r** ⌊to his friends⌋,
18:1 Bildad from Shuah **r** ⌊to Job⌋,
19:1 Then Job **r** ⌊to his friends⌋,
20:1 Zophar from Naama **r** ⌊to Job⌋,
21:1 Then Job **r** ⌊to his friends⌋,
22:1 Eliphaz from Teman **r** ⌊to Job⌋,
23:1 Then Job **r** ⌊to his friends⌋,
25:1 Bildad from Shuah **r** ⌊to Job⌋,
26:1 Then Job **r** ⌊to his friends⌋,
32:6 of Buz, **r** ⌊to Job⌋, "I am young,
Isa 6:11 And he **r**, "Until the cities lie in
Jer 28:5 The prophet Jeremiah **r** to the
Dan 2:8 The king **r**, "I'm sure you're
3:25 The king **r**, "But look, I see four
6:13 They **r**, "Your Majesty, Daniel,
12:9 He **r**, "Go, Daniel. These words
Jnh 4:10 The LORD **r**, "This plant grew
Zec 4:6 Then he **r**, "This is the word
Mat 9:15 Jesus **r**, "Can wedding guests
12:48 He **r** to the man speaking to
13:29 "He **r**, 'No. If you pull out the
15:26 Jesus **r**, "It's not right to take
16:17 Jesus **r**, "Simon, son of Jonah,
17:17 Jesus **r**, "You unbelieving and
19:20 The young man **r**, "I have
19:27 Then Peter **r** to him,
20:22 Jesus **r**, "You don't realize
21:16 Jesus **r**, "Yes, I do. Have you
21:29 "His son **r**, 'I don't want to!'
21:30 He **r**, 'I will, sir,' but he didn't go.
22:21 They **r**, "The emperor's."
25:9 "But the wise bridesmaids **r**,
25:21 "His master **r**, 'Good job!
25:23 "His master **r**, 'Good job!
26:25 "Yes, I do," Jesus **r**.
26:34 Jesus **r** to Peter, "I can
27:4 They **r**, "What do we care?
Mar 2:19 Jesus **r**, "Can wedding guests
3:33 He **r** to them, "Who is my
4:11 Jesus **r** to them, "The mystery
6:37 Jesus **r**, "You give them
9:21 The father **r**, "He has been this
10:20 The man **r**, "Teacher,
Luk 3:16 John **r** to all of them,
7:40 Simon **r**, "Teacher, you're free
9:13 Jesus **r**, "You give them
9:49 John **r**, "Master, we saw
10:30 Jesus **r**, "A man went from
11:28 Jesus **r**, "Rather, how blessed
13:2 Jesus **r** to them, "Do you think
13:8 "The gardener **r**, 'Sir, let it
16:6 "The debtor **r**, 'Eight hundred
16:7 "The debtor **r**, 'A thousand
16:25 "Abraham **r**, 'Remember,
16:29 "Abraham **r**, 'They have Moses'
16:30 "The rich man **r**, 'No,
18:21 The official **r**, "I've obeyed all
19:25 "They **r**, 'Sir, he already has
19:40 Jesus **r**, "I can guarantee that if
22:34 Jesus **r**, "Peter, I can guarantee
24:18 One of them, Cleopas, **r**,
Jon 1:21 you the prophet?" John **r**, "No."
1:50 Jesus **r**, You will see greater
2:19 Jesus **r**, "Tear down this
3:3 Jesus **r** to Nicodemus,
3:9 Nicodemus **r**, "How can that

Jon 4:10 Jesus **r** to her, "If you only
4:17 The woman **r**, "I don't have a
5:11 The man **r**, "The man who
5:17 Jesus **r** to them, "My Father is
6:26 Jesus **r** to them, "I can
6:29 Jesus **r** to them, "God wants to
6:70 Jesus **r**, "I chose all twelve of
8:14 Jesus **r** to them, "Even if I
8:19 Jesus **r**, "You don't know me or
8:33 They **r** to Jesus, "We are
8:39 The Jews **r** to Jesus,
8:48 The Jews **r** to Jesus,
9:11 He **r**, "The man people call
9:20 His parents **r**, "We know that
9:27 The man **r**, "I've already told
9:30 The man **r** to them,
9:36 The man **r**, "Sir, tell me who he
10:32 Jesus **r** to them, "I've shown
12:23 Jesus **r** to them, "The time has
12:30 Jesus **r**, "That voice wasn't for
13:8 Jesus **r** to Peter, "If I don't
13:38 Jesus **r**, "Will you give your life
14:9 Jesus **r**, "I have been with all
16:31 Jesus **r** to them, "Now you
18:8 Jesus **r**, "I told you that I am
18:23 Jesus **r** to him, "If I've said
18:34 Jesus **r**, "Did you think of that
18:37 Jesus **r**, "You're correct in
19:22 Pilate **r**, "I have written what
Act 9:5 The person **r**, "I'm Jesus,
9:13 Ananias **r**, "Lord, I've heard a
10:22 The men **r**, "Cornelius,
21:13 Then Paul **r**, "Why are you
21:37 The officer **r** to Paul,
22:28 The officer **r**, "I paid a lot of
22:28 Paul **r**, "But I was born a
25:4 Festus **r** that he would be
25:12 his advisers and then **r** to Paul,
25:16 "I **r** to them, 'That's not the
25:22 Festus **r**, "You'll hear him
26:25 Paul **r**, "I'm not crazy,
26:29 Paul **r**, "I wish to God that you

reply (16)

Jdg 8:8 But they gave him the same **r**
1Ki 8:39 Give each person the proper **r**.
2Ch 6:30 give each person the proper **r**.
Ezr 4:17 Then the king sent this **r**:
5:5 a report and sent a **r** to it.
5:11 This was their **r** to us:
10:12 whole assembly shouted in **r**,
Est 4:15 sent this **r** back to Mordecai,
Dan 9:23 your request, a **r** was sent.
9:23 I have come to give you the **r**
Zec 13:9 They will **r**, 'The LORD is our
Mat 25:37 God's approval will **r** to him,
27:14 absolutely nothing to him in **r**,
Mar 12:17 They were surprised at his **r**.
Jon 5:18 His **r** made the Jews more
Rom 11:4 But what was God's **r**?

replying (1)

Pro 18:23 a rich person is blunt when **r**.

report (35)

Num 13:26 They gave their **r** and showed
22:8 "and I'll **r** to you what the LORD
Dtr 1:22 Have them **r** to us about the
Jos 18:6 seven parts of the land and **r**
22:32 in Canaan and gave them the **r**.
22:33 Israel were satisfied with the **r**.
Jdg 4:12 The **r** reached Sisera that
1Sm 2:24 Sons, the **r** that I hear the
2Sm 11:18 Joab sent a messenger to **r**
15:36 Send them to **r** to me anything
1Ch 27:24 and the **r** from it was never
Ezr 5:5 until Darius received a **r**
5:7 They sent him the following **r**:
Neh 6:6 According to this **r**,
6:7 This **r** will get back to the king.
Est 2:23 When the **r** was investigated
Psa 73:28 so that I may **r** everything that
Pro 22:21 that you can give an accurate **r**
25:10 and his evil **r** about you will
Isa 21:6 Have him **r** whatever he sees.
Jer 4:5 **R** this message in Judah.
Jer 4:15 and a **r** of disaster comes from
10:22 The **r** has arrived.
20:10 **R** him! Let's report him!" All my
20:10 Let's **r** him!" All my closest
Dan 6:2 The satraps were to **r** to these
Mic 1:10 Don't **r** it in Gath. Don't cry
Hab 3:2 I have heard the **r** about you.
3:16 At the **r** my lips quivered.
Mat 2:8 When you have found him, **r** to
Mar 2:1 The **r** went out that he was
Luk 14:21 "The servant went back to **r**
Act 15:27 have sent Judas and Silas to **r**
21:31 received a **r** that all Jerusalem
1Th 1:9 They even **r** how you turned

reported (40)

Gen 24:66 The servant **r** to Isaac
Exo 6:9 Moses **r** this to the Israelites.
Num 13:27 This is what they **r** to Moses:
Dtr 1:25 They **r**, "The land that the
Jos 14:7 I **r** to him exactly what I
Jdg 9:25 This was **r** to Abimelech.
1Sm 8:21 he **r** it privately to the LORD.
17:31 was overheard and **r** to Saul,
19:2 so he **r** to David, "My father
19:19 When it was **r** to Saul that
2Sm 11:22 he **r** to David everything Joab
24:9 Joab **r** the census figures to the
1Ki 2:30 So Benaiah **r** to the king what
2Ki 22:9 Shaphan went to the king and **r**,
22:20 on this place.'" So they **r** this
1Ch 21:5 Joab **r** the census figures to
2Ch 20:2 Some men **r** to Jehoshaphat,
34:16 took the book to the king and **r**,
34:28 who live here.'" So they **r** this
Neh 6:6 In it was written: It has been **r**
Est 9:11 of Susa was **r** to the king.
Eze 9:11 was carrying paper and pen **r**,
Hab 1:5 believe even if it were **r** to you.
Zec 1:11 Then they **r** to the Messenger
Mat 8:33 There they **r** everything,
Mar 5:14 they **r** everything that had
6:30 They **r** to him everything they
Luk 8:34 They **r** everything in the city
13:1 At that time some people **r** to
Jon 12:17 him back to life **r** what they had
Act 5:22 The guards came back and **r**,
12:14 she ran back inside and **r**,
13:41 even if it were **r** to you!'"
14:27 They **r** everything God had
15:4 Paul and Barnabas **r**
16:36 The jailer **r** this order to Paul
16:38 The guards **r** to the officials
22:26 he **r** it to his commanding
24:1 They **r** to the governor their
28:21 who has come to Rome has **r**

reporting (4)

Neh 6:19 Tobiah's praises to me and **r**
1Jn 1:2 We are **r** to you about this
1:3 We are **r** about it to you also so
1:5 from Christ and are **r** to you:

reports (4)

Num 14:15 heard these **r** about you will
1Ki 10:7 But I didn't believe the **r** until I
2Ch 9:6 But I didn't believe the **r** until I
Jer 50:43 has heard **r** about them,

repossessed (1)

Pro 22:27 why should your bed be **r**?

represent (8)

Exo 20:4 or statues that **r** any creature
Dtr 4:16 statues that **r** men or women,
4:23 idols or statues that **r** anything
4:25 idols or statues that **r** anything.
5:8 or statues that **r** any creature
Ezr 10:14 Let our leaders **r** the whole
Jer 40:10 I'm going to live in Mizpah and **r**
Heb 5:1 chosen from humans to **r** them

representative (4)

Exo 18:19 You must be the people's **r** to
Eph 6:20 been doing this as Christ's **r**,
Php 2:25 You sent him as your personal **r**
2Ti 4:12 to the city of Ephesus as my **r**.

representatives (3)

Luk 19:14 They sent **r** to follow him and
2Co 5:20 Therefore, we are Christ's **r**,
8:23 The other men are **r** of the

representing (3)

Num 1:44 each **r** his own family,
2Sm 2:15 (**r** Saul's son Ishbosheth),
2Ch 35:5 Stand in the holy place **r** the

represents (4)

Eze 23:4 Oholah **r** Samaria,
23:4 and Oholibah **r** Jerusalem.
Dan 8:20 two-horned ram that you saw **r**
Rev 19:8 This fine linen **r** the things that

reprimand (5)

Pro 17:10 A **r** impresses a person who
30:6 to his words, or he will **r** you,
Ecc 7:5 to wise people who **r** you than
1Ti 5:20 **R** those leaders who sin.
Jud 1:9 "May the Lord **r** you!"

reprimanded (3)

Neh 13:11 I **r** the leaders. "Why is God's
13:17 I **r** the nobles of Judah and
13:25 So I **r** those Jews,

reprimands (1)

Pro 13:1 a mocker does not listen to **r**.

reptiles (4)

1Ki 4:33 animals, birds, **r**, and fish.
Act 10:12 animals, **r**, and birds.
11:6 wild animals, **r**, and birds.
Jas 3:7 birds, **r**, and sea creatures.

repulsive (4)

Lev 7:18 It is **r** to God. The person who
19:7 it is **r** and will not be accepted.
1Ki 15:13 of the **r** goddess Asherah.
2Ch 15:16 of the **r** goddess Asherah.

reputation (17)

Dtr 22:14 her and ruin her **r** by saying,
22:19 The husband ruined the **r** of an
1Sm 18:30 So David gained a good **r**.
1Ki 10:1 Sheba heard about Solomon's **r**.
10:1 (He owed his **r** to the name of
2Ch 9:1 Sheba heard about Solomon's **r**.
Neh 6:13 they could give me a bad **r**
Est 9:4 Moreover, his **r** was spreading
Job 18:17 and his **r** will not be known on
Psa 106:8 He saved them because of his **r**
Pro 5:9 Either you will surrender your **r**
30:9 the name of my God a bad **r**.
1Ti 3:2 A bishop must have a good **r**.
3:10 Then, if he has a good **r**,
3:13 serve well gain an excellent **r**
Tit 1:6 leader must have a good **r**.
1:7 he must have a good **r**.

reputations (2)

1Co 4:13 When our **r** are attacked,
1Ti 5:7 that widows will have good **r**.

request (37)

Gen 17:20 heard your **r** about Ishmael.
19:21 I will grant you this **r** too.
Num 22:18 whether the **r** was important
24:13 good or bad the **r** might seem
1Sm 1:17 the God of Israel grant your **r**."
1:27 and the LORD granted my **r**.
8:6 it wrong for them to **r**
25:35 you've said and granted your **r**."
28:8 Conjure up the person I **r**."
2Sm 13:13 refuse your **r** to marry me."
1Ki 2:23 pay with his life for this **r**!
7:45 temple at King Solomon's **r**.
17:22 The LORD heard Elijah's **r**,
1Ch 10:13 He asked a medium to **r**
10:14 He didn't **r** information from the
2Ch 1:11 "I know this **r** is from your heart
4:16 temple at King Solomon's **r**.

2Ch 33:13 his prayer and listened to his **r**.
Neh 2:5 you are willing to grant my **r**,
Est 5:6 asked Esther, "What is your **r**?
5:7 Esther answered, "My **r**?
5:8 may you then grant my **r** and
7:2 "What is your **r**, Queen Esther?
7:3 That is my **r**. And spare the life
9:12 Now, what is your **r**?
Jer 42:2 "Please listen to our **r**,
42:4 "I have listened to your **r**.
Dan 9:17 listen to my prayer and **r**.
9:20 I humbly placed my **r** about my
9:23 as you began to make your **r**,
Mic 6:1 and let the hills listen to your **r**.
Mar 6:25 back to the king with her **r**.
2Co 8:17 He accepted my **r** and eagerly
Eph 6:18 kind of prayer and **r** there is.
6:18 effort and make every kind of **r**
2Th 2:1 we have this **r** to make of you
1Pe 3:21 Rather, baptism is a **r** to God

requested (5)

1Ki 15:20 Benhadad did what King Asa **r**.
2Ch 16:4 Benhadad did what King Asa **r**.
Ezr 7:6 king gave Ezra everything he **r**
Est 2:14 desired her and **r** her by name.
Jer 42:4 LORD your God as you have **r**,

requesting (2)

Dan 9:18 We are not **r** this from you
2Jn 1:5 Dear lady, I'm now **r** that we

requests (6)

1Ch 29:19 he will obey your commands, **r**,
Job 31:16 "If I have refused the **r** of the
Psa 20:5 The LORD will fulfill all your **r**.
143:1 your ears to hear my urgent **r**.
Php 4:6 and **r** while giving thanks.
1Jn 5:15 know that he listens to our **r**.

require (5)

2Ki 12:15 They didn't **r** the men who were
22:7 don't **r** them to account for the
2Ch 24:6 "Why didn't you **r** the Levites to
Act 15:1 as Moses' Teachings **r**.
Heb 10:8 Teachings **r** people to offer.)

required (24)

Lev 27:8 to pay the **r** amount must stand
Jos 16:10 but they are **r** to do forced labor.
17:4 relatives as the LORD had **r**.
1Ki 8:31 against another person and is **r**
2Ki 12:4 each person is currently **r**
17:3 became his servant and was **r**
1Ch 16:37 as the daily work **r**.
23:31 the **r** numbers whenever burnt
2Ch 6:22 against another person and is **r**
24:6 and the assembly had **r** Israel
24:9 servant Moses had **r** Israel
30:19 for those who are not clean as **r**
Ezr 3:4 Each day they sacrificed the **r**
Neh 12:45 were doing what their God **r**,
Est 2:12 the **r** 12-month treatment
Dan 1:20 about things that **r** wisdom
Luk 2:22 After the days **r** by Moses'
2:24 also offered a sacrifice as **r** by
2:27 him what Moses' Teachings **r**.
2:39 the Lord's Teachings **r**,
1Co 4:2 are **r** to be trustworthy.
Heb 7:19 everything that God **r**.
7:28 everything that God **r**.
9:10 These ceremonies were **r** for

requirements (7)

Num 6:21 They must fulfill the **r** of these
Jos 7:11 They have ignored the **r** that I
7:15 He has ignored the LORD's **r**
Zec 3:7 to my ways and follow my **r**,
Rom 2:15 They show that some **r** found
Heb 7:16 not because he met human **r**,
7:18 The former **r** are rejected

requires (2)

Mic 6:8 is what the LORD **r** from you:
Mat 3:15 do everything that God **r** of us."

requiring (2)

Isa 43:23 I did not burden you by **r** grain
43:23 you by **r** incense offerings.

rerouted (2)

2Sm 6:10 Instead, he **r** it to the home of
1Ch 13:13 Instead, he **r** it to the home of

rescue (203)

Gen 37:22 Reuben wanted to **r** Joseph
49:18 wait with hope for you to **r** me,
Exo 3:8 I have come to **r** them from the
5:23 nothing at all to **r** your people."
6:6 I will **r** you with my powerful
Num 10:9 you and **r** you from your
Dtr 22:27 but no one was there to **r** her.
25:11 comes to **r** her husband from
28:29 robbed with no one to **r** you.
28:31 and no one will **r** it.
32:39 and no one can **r** you from my
Jdg 2:16 judges to **r** them from those
3:9 LORD sent a savior to **r** them.
3:15 LORD sent a savior to **r** them.
6:14 "You will **r** Israel from Midian
6:15 How can I **r** Israel?
6:36 you would **r** Israel through me.
6:37 then I'll know that you will **r**
10:1 of Dodo, came to **r** Israel.
10:12 Didn't I **r** you from them?
10:13 That's why I won't **r** you again.
10:14 Let them **r** you when you're in
10:15 But please **r** us today!"
12:2 but you didn't **r** me from them.
12:3 I saw that you would not **r** me,
13:5 He will begin to **r** Israel from
18:28 There was no one to **r** them
1Sm 7:3 Then he will **r** you from the
11:1 and allow no one to **r** Israel.
12:10 But **r** us from our enemies now,
12:21 They can't help or **r** you,
26:24 on my life and **r** me from all
30:8 with them and **r** the captives."
2Sm 14:16 the king will listen and **r** me,
22:49 You **r** me from violent people.
2Ki 17:39 and he will **r** you from your
18:29 He can't **r** you from me.
18:30 'The LORD will certainly **r** us,
18:32 'The LORD will **r** us.'
18:33 nations **r** their countries from
18:34 Did they **r** Samaria from my
18:35 those countries **r** them from my
18:35 Could the LORD then **r**
19:12 ancestors destroyed **r** Gozan,
19:19 Now, LORD our God, **r** us from
19:34 "I will shield this city to **r** it for
20:6 I'll **r** you and defend this city
1Ch 16:35 Say, '**R** us, O God our Savior.
2Ch 32:11 'The LORD our God will **r** us
32:13 able to **r** their countries from
32:14 able to **r** their people from
32:14 Is your God able to **r** you from
32:15 God will not **r** you from me!"
32:17 couldn't **r** their people from
32:17 Hezekiah's God cannot **r** his
Neh 9:27 You gave them saviors to **r**
Est 4:14 else will help and **r** the Jews,
Job 5:4 and no one is there to **r** them.
6:23 or '**R** me from an enemy,'
10:7 but there is no one to **r** me from
22:30 He will **r** one who is not
Psa 6:4 **R** me. Save me because of your
7:1 Save me, and **r** me from all
7:2 drag me off with no one to **r** me.
17:13 With your sword **r** my life from
17:14 With your power **r** me from
18:48 You **r** me from violent people.
22:8 Let God **r** him since he is
22:20 **R** my soul from the sword,
25:20 Protect my life, and **r** me!
25:22 **R** Israel, O God, from all its
26:11 **R** me, and have pity on me.
31:2 **R** me quickly. Be a rock of
31:15 **R** me from my enemies,
33:19 to **r** their souls from death and
35:10 You **r** the weak person from the
Psa 35:17 **R** me from their attacks.
35:17 **R** my precious life from the
39:8 **R** me from all my rebellious
40:13 O LORD, please **r** me!
41:1 The LORD will **r** him in times
43:1 **R** me from deceitful and unjust
44:26 **R** us because of your mercy!
50:15 I will **r** you, and you will honor
50:22 and there will be no one left to **r**
51:14 **R** me from the guilt of murder,
55:18 With this peace, he will **r** my
59:1 **R** me from my enemies,
59:2 **R** me from troublemakers.
69:14 **R** me from the mud.
70:1 Come quickly to **r** me,
71:2 **R** me and free me because of
71:11 there is no one to **r** him."
72:12 He will **r** the needy person who
72:14 He will **r** them from oppression
79:9 **R** us, and forgive our sins for
79:11 With your powerful arm **r** those
82:4 **R** weak and needy people.
91:3 He is the one who will **r** you
91:14 you love me, I will **r** you.
97:10 his godly ones will **r** them from
106:47 **R** us, O LORD our God,
109:21 **R** me because of your mercy.
116:4 LORD: "Please, LORD, **r** me!"
119:153 Look at my misery, and **r** me,
119:170 **R** me as you promised.
120:2 O LORD, **r** me from lying lips
130:8 He will **r** Israel from all its sins.
140:1 **R** me from evil people,
142:6 **R** me from those who pursue
143:9 **R** me from my enemies,
144:7 Snatch me, and **r** me from
144:11 Snatch me, and **r** me from
Pro 12:6 the words of decent people **r**.
19:19 If you **r** him, you will have to do
24:11 **R** captives condemned to
Isa 5:29 it off to where no one can **r** it.
19:20 a savior and defender to **r** them.
31:5 He will defend it and **r** it.
35:4 He will come and **r** you."
36:14 deceive you. He can't **r** you.
36:15 'The LORD will certainly **r** us,
36:18 'The LORD will **r** us.'
36:18 nations **r** their countries from
36:19 Did they **r** Samaria from my
36:20 these countries **r** them from my
36:20 Could the LORD then **r**
37:12 ancestors destroyed **r** Gozan,
37:20 Now, LORD our God, **r** us from
37:35 "I will shield this city to **r** it for
38:6 I'll **r** you and defend this city
38:20 The LORD is going to **r** me,
42:22 prey with no one to **r** them.
43:13 No one can **r** people from my
44:17 pray to them, saying, "**R** us,
44:20 They can't **r** themselves or ask
46:7 It can't **r** them from their
47:14 They can't **r** themselves from
50:2 Don't I have the power to **r** you?
Jer 1:8 I am with you, and I will **r** you,"
1:19 I am with you, and I will **r** you,"
2:27 you ask me to come and **r** you.
2:28 Let them come and **r** you when
3:23 the LORD our God will **r** us.
11:12 But these gods will never **r**
15:11 "I will certainly **r** you for a good
15:20 and I will save you and **r** you,
15:21 I will **r** you from the power of
17:14 **R** me, and I will be rescued.
21:12 **R** those who have been robbed
22:3 **R** those who have been robbed
30:10 I'm going to **r** you from a
30:10 I'm going to **r** your descendants
30:11 I am with you, and I will **r** you,"
31:7 say, "O LORD, **r** your people,
39:17 But at that time I will **r** you,
39:18 I will certainly **r** you.
42:11 I will save you and **r** you from
46:27 I'm going to **r** you and your
Lam 5:8 is no one to **r** us from them.
Eze 7:19 and gold won't be able to **r** them
13:21 veils and **r** my people from

Eze 13:23 I will **r** my people from your
14:14 **r** only themselves,"
14:16 and Job could **r** their own sons
14:16 They could **r** only themselves.
14:18 and Job could **r** their sons or
14:18 They could **r** only themselves.
14:20 **r** their sons or daughters.
14:20 They could **r** only themselves.
34:10 I will **r** my sheep from their
34:12 I will **r** them on a cloudy and
34:22 So I will **r** my sheep,
34:27 on their yokes and **r** them from
36:29 I will **r** you from all your
Dan 3:29 No other god can **r** like this."
6:14 everything he could to **r** him.
8:7 No one could **r** the ram from the
Hos 1:7 I will **r** them because I am the
1:7 or horsemen to **r** them."
2:10 and no one will **r** her from my
5:14 and no one will **r** ⌊them⌋.
Mic 2:3 won't be able to **r** yourselves.
5:6 They will **r** us from the
5:8 and there is no one to **r** them.
Hab 1:2 yet you will not come to the **r**.
Zep 1:18 gold will not be able to **r** them
3:19 I will **r** those who are lame.
Zec 9:16 LORD their God will **r** them as
10:6 I will **r** Joseph's people.
11:6 And I won't **r** any of them from
Mat 6:13 Instead, **r** us from the evil one.
27:43 Let God **r** him now if he wants.
Luk 1:74 He promised to **r** us from our
Act 7:34 and have come to **r** them.
12:11 his angel to **r** me from Herod
23:27 I went with my soldiers to **r**
26:17 I will **r** you from the Jewish
Rom 7:24 Who will **r** me from my dying
2Co 1:10 and he will **r** us in the future.
1:10 that he will continue to **r** us,
2Ti 4:18 The Lord will **r** me from all
2Pe 2:9 he knows how to **r** godly

rescued (72)

Gen 48:16 who has **r** me from all evil,
Exo 2:19 They answered, "An Egyptian **r**
18:10 He **r** you from the Egyptians
18:10 and **r** these people from
Jos 9:26 So Joshua **r** them and did not
22:31 Now you have **r** the people of
Jdg 2:18 The LORD **r** them from their
3:31 So he, too, **r** Israel.
6:9 I **r** you from the power of the
8:22 You **r** us from Midian."
8:34 who had **r** them from all the
9:17 his life and **r** you from Midian.
1Sm 10:18 out of Egypt and **r** you from
11:9 you will be **r**.'" When the men
12:11 and Samuel and **r** you from
14:45 troops **r** Jonathan from death.
14:48 He **r** Israel from the enemies
17:35 and **r** the sheep from its mouth.
23:5 So David **r** the people who
30:18 David **r** everything the
2Sm 4:11 The LORD has **r** me from every
12:7 over Israel and **r** you from Saul.
19:9 "The king **r** us from our
22:1 when the LORD **r** him from all
22:18 He **r** me from my strong enemy
22:20 He **r** me because he was
22:44 You **r** me from my conflicts
2Ki 17:7 out of Egypt ⌊and **r** them⌋ from
19:11 destroyed them. Will you be **r**?
Ezr 8:31 God was guiding us, and he **r**
Neh 9:28 You **r** them many times
Job 21:30 day of ⌊God's⌋ anger he is **r**.
22:30 person will be **r** by your purity."
29:12 because I **r** the poor who called
Psa 7:4 with evil or **r** someone who has
18:17 He **r** me from my strong enemy
18:19 He **r** me because he was
18:43 You **r** me from my conflicts
22:4 They trusted, and you **r** them.
31:5 You have **r** me, O LORD,
34:4 He answered me and **r** me from
56:13 You have **r** me from death.
60:5 who are dear to you may be **r**.
Psa 69:14 I want to be **r** from those who
71:23 My soul, which you have **r**,
81:7 called out ⌊to me⌋, and I **r** you.
86:13 You have **r** me from the depths
106:10 He **r** them from the power of the
106:10 He **r** them from the enemy.
106:43 He **r** them many times,
107:6 He **r** them from their troubles.
107:20 He **r** them from the grave.
108:6 who are dear to you may be **r**.
Pro 11:8 person is **r** from trouble,
11:9 people are **r** by knowledge.
Isa 20:6 ⌊to Egypt⌋ for help to be **r** from
37:11 destroyed them. Will you be **r**?
Jer 4:14 your heart so that you may be **r**.
17:14 Rescue me, and I will be **r**.
20:13 He has **r** the lives of needy
30:7 but they will be **r** from it.
41:16 whom he had **r** from Ishmael,
Dan 12:1 written in the book, will be **r**.
Amo 3:12 living in Samaria will be **r**,
Mic 4:10 There you will be **r**.
Act 7:10 and **r** him from all his suffering.
Rom 15:31 that I will be **r** from those
2Co 1:10 He has **r** us from a terrible
Col 1:13 God has **r** us from the power of
2Th 3:2 Also pray that we may be **r**
2Ti 3:11 and the Lord **r** me from all of
2Pe 2:7 Yet, God **r** Lot, a man who had

rescues (14)

Job 36:15 He **r** suffering people through
Psa 33:16 No warrior **r** himself by his own
34:7 who fear him, and he **r** them.
34:17 The LORD hears and **r** them
34:19 but the LORD **r** him from all of
37:40 LORD helps them and **r** them.
37:40 He **r** them from wicked people.
54:7 Your name **r** me from every
103:4 the one who **r** your life from the
Pro 10:2 but righteousness **r** from death.
Dan 6:27 He saves, **r**, and does
Amo 3:12 As a shepherd **r** two legs or a
Rom 7:25 that our Lord Jesus Christ **r** me!
1Th 1:10 Jesus is the one who **r** us from

rescuing (1)

Exo 18:9 done for Israel in **r** them from

researched (2)

1Ch 26:31 was **r** family by family.
1Pe 1:10 The prophets carefully **r** and

Resen (1)

Gen 10:12 and **R**, the great city between

resent (2)

Pro 3:11 and do not **r** his warning,
Mat 20:15 Or do you **r** my generosity

resentful (6)

1Sm 1:10 Though she was **r**,
1Ki 20:43 **R** and upset, the king of Israel
21:4 **R** and upset, Ahab went home
21:5 are you so **r** of everything?
Pro 31:6 and wine to one who feels **r**.
Col 3:21 don't make your children **r**,

resentment (2)

Ecc 5:17 frustration, sickness, and **r**.
Rom 3:14 are full of curses and bitter **r**.

reserve (2)

Gen 41:36 This food will be a **r** supply for
Psa 31:19 You **r** it for those who fear you.

reserved (4)

Dtr 33:21 piece of land was **r** for them.
Job 15:20 Only a few years are **r** for the
Pro 2:7 He has **r** priceless wisdom for
Eze 46:19 These rooms were **r** for the

reserves (1)

2Ch 11:11 put army officers with **r** of food,

reservoir (2)

Isa 22:11 You will build a **r** between the
30:14 or to dip water from a **r**.

reservoirs (1)

Exo 7:19 and all its **r** — so that they turn

reset (1)

Isa 54:11 I will **r** your foundations with

resettle (2)

Isa 14:1 He will **r** them in their own
54:3 and they will **r** deserted cities.

Resheph (1)

1Ch 7:25 Rephah's son was **R**.

Resheph's (1)

1Ch 7:25 **R** son was Telah. Telah's son

residence (3)

2Ki 11:6 You will guard the king's **r**.
Mat 12:45 and take up permanent **r** there.
Luk 11:26 and take up permanent **r** there.

resident (2)

2Sm 1:13 the son of a foreign **r**."
Psa 39:12 for I am a foreign **r** with you,

residents (7)

Dtr 13:12 You may hear that the **r** in one
13:15 you must kill the **r** of that city
Eze 47:22 It will also be for the foreign **r**
47:23 Foreign **r** will receive their
1Pe 1:1 people who are temporary **r** ⌊in
1:17 live your time as temporary **r**
2:11 foreigners and temporary **r** ⌊in

resides (1)

Job 41:22 Strength **r** in its neck,

resign (1)

Ecc 10:4 don't **r** your position.

resin (2)

Exo 30:34 spices (two kinds of gum **r**
Num 11:7 seeds and looked like **r**.

resist (13)

Lev 26:21 "If you **r** and don't listen to me,
26:23 does not help and you still **r**,
26:24 then I, too, will **r** you.
26:27 not listen to me and still **r** me,
26:28 I will fiercely **r** you.
Ecc 4:12 two people can **r** one opponent.
Act 26:14 for ⌊a mortal like⌋ you to **r** God.'
Rom 9:19 Who can **r** whatever God
13:2 Those who **r** will bring
1Co 10:13 beyond your power to **r**.
Jas 4:7 **R** the devil, and he will run
5:6 even though they didn't **r** you.
1Pe 5:9 Be firm in the faith and **r** him,

resistant (1)

Pro 18:19 An offended brother is more ⌊**r**⌋

resists (1)

Rom 13:2 Therefore, whoever **r** the

resourceful (3)

Exo 31:3 making him highly skilled, **r**,
35:31 making him highly skilled, **r**,
1Ki 7:14 Hiram was highly skilled, **r**,

resources (1)

Php 4:17 looking for your **r** to increase.

respect (49)

Lev 19:3 "**R** your mother and father.
19:30 of worship and **r** my holy tent.
19:32 "Show **r** to the elderly,
19:32 In this way you show **r** for your
22:2 and his sons that they must **r**
26:2 of worship and **r** my holy tent.
Dtr 28:50 They will show no **r** for the old

1Sm 2:29 Why do you show no **r** for my
2Sm 6:7 killed him there for his lack of **r**.
1Ki 11:11 your attitude and you have no **r**
2Ki 3:14 notice you if it weren't for my **r**
Job 29:8 up straight out of **r** ⌊for me⌋.
37:24 He does not **r** those who think
Psa 119:117 and I will always **r** your laws.
Pro 11:16 A gracious woman wins **r**,
22:1 **R** is better than silver or gold.
Jer 5:28 They have no **r** for the rights of
5:28 They have no **r** for the rights of
Lam 5:12 older leaders are shown no **r**.
Dan 9:4 you are great and deserve **r** as
Mal 1:6 If I am a master, where is my **r**?
2:5 to him so that he would **r** me.
Mat 21:37 thought, 'They will **r** my son.'
Mar 12:6 thought, 'They will **r** my son.'
Luk 18:2 who didn't fear God or **r** people.
18:4 Although I don't fear God or **r**
20:13 They'll probably **r** him.'
Jon 4:37 In this **r** the saying is true:
Act 10:22 Also, the Jewish people **r** him.
28:10 They showed **r** for us in many
Rom 12:10 in showing **r** for each other.
13:7 If you owe someone **r**,
13:7 someone respect, **r** that person.
1Co 11:10 out of **r** for the angels.
Eph 5:21 authority out of **r** for Christ.
5:33 wives should **r** their husbands.
6:5 earthly masters with proper **r**.
6:9 should also treat them with **r**.
Col 3:22 sincere in your motives out of **r**
1Th 4:12 Then your way of life will win **r**
1Ti 5:4 first learn to **r** their own family
6:1 believe must give complete **r**
6:2 should **r** their masters even
2Ti 3:2 have no **r** for what is holy,
Heb 10:29 think a person who shows no **r**
12:9 disciplined us, and we **r** them.
Jas 2:6 you show no **r** to poor people.
1Pe 2:18 and show them complete **r**.
3:15 defense with gentleness and **r**.

respectable (3)

1Ti 2:9 clothes that are modest and **r**.
2:15 if they lead **r** lives in faith,
3:2 judgment, be **r**, be hospitable,

respected (37)

Exo 11:3 And Moses was highly **r** by
Num 22:15 group of more highly **r** princes.
Jos 4:14 the Israelites **r** him in the same
4:14 same way they had **r** Moses.
1Sm 9:6 God in this city, a highly **r** man.
2Sm 7:26 Your name will be **r** forever
1Ki 3:28 They **r** the king very highly,
8:1 Then Solomon assembled the **r**
21:8 She sent them to the **r** leaders
21:11 men in Naboth's city — the **r**
2Ki 5:1 was **r** and highly honored by
10:1 of Jezreel, the **r** leaders,
10:5 mayor of the city, the **r** leaders,
23:1 Then the king sent for all the **r**
1Ch 17:24 Your name will endure and be **r**
2Ch 5:2 Then Solomon assembled the **r**
34:29 Then the king sent for all the **r**
Est 10:3 He was greatly **r** by,
Job 12:20 the good judgment of **r** leaders.
Psa 105:22 taught his **r** leaders wisdom.
107:32 in the company of **r** leaders.
Isa 3:14 his case to the **r** leaders
9:15 **R** and honored leaders are the
24:23 in the presence of his **r** leaders.
33:8 People are no longer **r**.
52:13 He will be **r**, praised,
Lam 2:10 The **r** leaders of Zion's people
4:16 They no longer **r** the priests,
Dan 9:23 reply because you are highly **r**.
10:11 to me, "Daniel, you are highly **r**.
10:19 You are highly **r**. Everything is
Mal 1:14 the nations my name is **r**.
2:5 He **r** me and stood in awe of
3:16 the LORD and **r** his name.
Act 5:34 He was a highly **r** expert in
10:2 home were devout and **r** God.
Rom 14:18 to God and **r** by people.

respectfully (2)

1Ti 3:4 His children should **r** obey him.
1Pe 3:6 Abraham and spoke to him **r**.

respecting (1)

Lev 25:36 God by **r** other Israelites' lives.

respects (2)

Act 10:22 God's approval and who **r** God.
10:35 Rather, whoever **r** God and

respond (18)

1Sm 10:27 him presents, but he didn't **r**.
2Sm 3:11 Ishbosheth couldn't **r** to a
1Ki 12:6 should I **r** to these people?"
12:9 How should we **r** to these
2Ch 10:6 should I **r** to these people?"
10:9 How should we **r** to these
Pro 29:19 He will not **r**, though he may
Isa 19:22 And he will **r** to their prayers
Jer 2:30 They didn't **r** to correction.
7:27 but they will not **r** to you.
Hos 2:15 Then she will **r** as she did
Mar 9:6 (Peter didn't know how to **r**.
Jon 5:25 the Son of God and those who **r**
10:3 and the sheep **r** to his voice.
10:8 the sheep didn't **r** to them.
10:16 They, too, will **r** to my voice.
10:27 My sheep **r** to my voice,
2Th 1:8 and on those who refuse to **r**

responded (66)

Gen 25:31 Jacob **r**, "First, sell me your
27:13 His mother **r**, "Let any curse on
29:19 Laban **r**, "It's better that I give
30:29 Jacob **r**, "You know how much
37:13 to them." Joseph **r**, "I'll go."
Dtr 1:41 You **r**, "We have sinned
Jos 1:16 The people **r** to Joshua,
9:8 They **r** to Joshua, "We're at
17:16 Joseph's descendants **r**,
24:16 The people **r**, "It would be
Jdg 6:13 Gideon **r**, "Excuse me, sir!
8:7 Gideon **r**, "Alright, then.
9:9 But the olive tree **r**,
9:11 But the fig tree **r**, 'Should I stop
9:13 But the grapevine **r**,
9:15 But the thornbush **r** to the trees
13:16 the Messenger of the LORD **r**,
14:13 They **r**, "Tell us your riddle!
1Sm 1:15 "No, sir," Hannah **r**,
3:4 "Here I am," Samuel **r**.
3:6 "I didn't call ⌊you⌋, son," he **r**.
3:16 he said. "Here I am," he **r**.
9:6 The servant **r**, "There's a man
11:2 Nahash the Ammonite **r**,
14:36 you think is best," they **r**.
14:40 the troops **r** to Saul.
17:33 Saul **r** to David, "You can't fight
22:12 sir?" he **r**.
23:21 Saul **r**, "The LORD bless you
26:22 David **r**, "Here's the king's
28:2 "Very well," David **r** to Achish,
2Sm 4:9 David **r** to Rechab and his
9:11 Ziba **r**, "I will do everything
14:18 The woman **r**, "Please speak,
18:4 what you think best," the king **r**.
19:22 David **r**, "Are you sure we're
24:3 Joab **r** to the king, "May the
1Ki 3:6 Solomon **r**, "You've shown
5:7 Hiram **r**, "May the LORD be
1Ch 21:3 Joab **r**, "May the LORD
2Ch 1:8 Solomon **r** to God,
2:11 Then King Huram of Tyre **r** to
Neh 5:12 They **r**, "We'll return it and not
8:6 All the people **r**, "Amen!
Est 7:9 The king **r**, "Hang him on it!"
Job 40:1 The LORD **r** to Job,
40:6 Then the LORD **r** to Job out of
Jer 21:3 Jeremiah **r** to them,
Amo 7:14 Amos **r**, "I'm not a prophet,
Mic 6:5 Balaam, son of Beor, **r** to him.
Zec 1:13 The LORD **r** to the angel who
Mat 8:8 The officer **r**, "Sir, I don't
12:39 He **r**, "The people of an evil
Mat 15:24 Jesus **r**, "I was sent only to the
16:2 He **r** to them, "In the evening
25:26 "His master **r**, 'You evil and
Luk 16:27 "The rich man **r**, 'Then I ask
20:39 Some scribes **r**, "Teacher,
Jon 6:43 Jesus **r**, "Stop criticizing me!
7:16 Jesus **r** to them, "What I teach
9:25 The man **r**, "I don't know if he's
12:34 The crowd **r** to him,
19:15 The chief priests **r**,
20:28 Thomas **r** to Jesus,
Act 15:13 speaking, James **r**, "Brothers,
24:10 Paul **r**, "I know that you have

response (5)

Job 19:7 but I get no **r**. I call for help, but
33:32 If you have a **r**, answer me.
Dan 10:12 I have come in **r** to your prayer.
Act 17:33 With this **r**, Paul left the court.
Gal 2:2 I went in **r** to a revelation ⌊from

responses (1)

Job 32:5 the three men had no further **r**,

responsibility (13)

Lev 25:25 the one who can assume **r**,
Jos 2:19 We will be free from that **r**.
2:19 But we will take **r** if anyone
Rut 4:5 you will also assume **r** for the
4:6 case I cannot assume **r** for her.
4:6 I cannot assume that **r**."
1Ki 2:33 The **r** for their blood will fall on
2Ch 31:14 His **r** was to distribute the
Jer 32:7 relative it is your **r** to buy it."'
32:8 It is your **r** to purchase it,
Mat 27:25 All the people answered, "The **r**
Gal 6:5 Assume your own **r**.
Eph 3:2 heard how God gave me the **r**

responsible (52)

Gen 19:8 since I'm **r** for them."
39:22 Joseph became **r** for everything
43:9 You can hold me **r** for him.
Num 18:1 and your family will be **r** for any
18:1 and your sons will also be **r**
18:23 They will be **r** for their own
32:15 would be **r** for their destruction.
Dtr 22:8 Then you won't be **r** for a death
Jos 2:19 leaves your house will be **r**
Rut 2:20 one of those **r** for taking care of
1Sm 22:22 I am the one **r** for all the lives of
25:24 let me be held **r** for this wrong.
2Sm 1:16 while David said, "You are **r** for
3:37 of Israel knew the king wasn't **r**
14:9 "Let me be held **r** for the sin,
14:9 Let my father's family be held **r**.
1Ki 2:37 You will be **r** for your own
2Ki 12:8 ⌊for personal use⌋ nor to be **r**
1Ch 9:19 (Korah's descendants) were **r**
9:32 their Kohathite relatives were **r**
23:29 They were also **r** for the rows
23:29 In addition, they were **r** for
2Ch 28:13 You'll make us **r** for this sin
31:16 that each division was **r** for.
Ezr 8:30 They were **r** for bringing these
Neh 13:13 I made them **r** for distributing
Psa 118:23 The LORD is **r** for this,
Pro 9:12 you alone will be held **r**.
19:18 not be the one **r** for his death.
20:16 and hold **r** the person who
23:11 because the one who is **r** for
27:13 and hold **r** the person who
Jer 51:35 be held **r** for our deaths."
Eze 3:18 I will hold you **r** for their deaths.
3:20 I will hold you **r** for their deaths.
18:13 So he must die, and he will be **r**
33:4 they will be **r** for their own
33:5 So they are **r** for their own
33:6 I will hold him **r** for their deaths.
33:8 I will hold you **r** for his death.
45:17 Then the prince is **r** to provide
Jnh 1:7 throw dice to find out who is **r**
1:7 indicated that Jonah was **r**.
1:12 I know that I'm **r** for this violent
1:14 Don't hold us **r** for the death of
Mat 21:42 The Lord is **r** for this,

Luk 11:51 today will be held **r** for this.
Act 18:6 "You're **r** for your own death.
20:26 to you today that I am not **r**
1Co 11:27 an improper way will be held **r**
Heb 1:2 made his Son **r** for everything.
13:17 you because they are **r** for you.

rest (267)

Gen 8:4 the ship came to **r** in the
18:4 stretch out and **r** under the tree.
30:36 care of the **r** of Laban's flocks.
30:40 from the flock and made the **r**
42:16 to get your brother while the **r**
42:19 The **r** of you will go and take
43:9 can blame me the **r** of my life.
44:9 and the **r** of us will become
44:10 and the **r** of you can go free."
44:17 The **r** of you can go back to
44:32 then you can blame me the **r** of
47:30 I want to **r** with my ancestors.
49:26 May these blessings **r** on the
Exo 4:7 again like the **r** of his body.
23:12 your ox and donkey can **r**.
29:12 Pour the **r** of it out at the bottom
29:20 Throw the ⌊**r** of the⌋ blood
Lev 2:3 The **r** of the grain offering will
2:10 The **r** of the grain offering
4:7 He will pour the **r** of the bull's
4:18 He will pour the **r** of the blood
4:25 He will pour the **r** of the blood
4:30 He will pour the **r** of the blood
4:34 He will pour the **r** of the blood
5:9 and the **r** of the blood will be
6:16 and his sons will eat the **r** of it.
8:15 He poured the **r** of the blood at
8:17 He burned the **r** of the bull,
8:24 Moses threw the **r** of the blood
13:3 area looks deeper than the **r**
13:4 does not look deeper than the **r**
13:20 If it looks deeper than the **r** of
13:21 area is not deeper than the **r**
13:25 area looks deeper than the **r**
13:26 area is not deeper than the **r**
13:30 If it looks deeper than the **r** of
13:31 does not look deeper than the **r**
13:32 deeper than the **r** of the skin,
13:34 does not look deeper than the **r**
14:18 The priest will put the **r** of the
14:29 the priest will pour the **r** of the
14:37 deeper than the **r** of the wall,
Num 8:6 "Separate the Levites from the **r**
9:7 LORD at the same time the **r**
10:33 to find them a place to **r**.
11:25 the Spirit came to **r** on them,
11:26 The Spirit came to **r** on them,
16:9 has separated you from the **r**
24:9 His people lie down ⌊and⌋ **r**
31:27 war and the **r** of the community.
32:6 going to stay here while the **r**
32:9 But then they discouraged the **r**
Dtr 3:13 I gave the **r** of Gilead and all of
3:20 Then they will have a place to **r**
5:14 female slaves can **r** as you do.
12:9 haven't come to your place of **r**,
17:20 think he's better than the **r**
18:1 property of their own like the **r**
19:20 When the **r** of the people hear
Jos 1:13 you this land — a place to **r**.'
1:15 Then they will have a place to **r**
8:5 I'll approach the city with the **r**
13:27 the **r** of the kingdom of King
17:2 The land was given to the **r** of
21:5 The **r** of Kohath's descendants
21:20 tribe of Ephraim to give to the **r**
21:26 were given to the **r**
22:9 the tribe of Manasseh left the **r**
22:11 The **r** of the Israelites heard
Jdg 7:6 All the **r** of the men knelt down
7:18 then the **r** of you around the
14:17 cried on his shoulder for the **r**
16:26 him by the hand, "Let me **r**.
20:48 Israel went back to attack the **r**
Rut 3:18 The man won't **r** unless he
1Sm 5:4 The **r** of Dagon's body was
13:2 But the **r** of the people he sent
13:15 The **r** of the people followed
1Sm 15:15 But the **r** they claimed for God
18:30 was more successful than the **r**
22:1 his brothers and all ⌊the **r**⌋
2Sm 10:10 Abishai in charge of the **r**
12:28 Gather the **r** of the troops,
13:27 he let Amnon and all ⌊the **r** of⌋
17:16 'Don't **r** tonight in the river
1Ki 8:56 has given his people Israel **r**,
11:41 Aren't the **r** of Solomon's acts —
12:23 and the **r** of the people.
2Ki 4:7 The **r** is for you and your
7:13 will be no worse off than the **r**
10:17 Jehu killed the **r** of Ahab's
13:7 of Aram had destroyed the **r**.
21:14 I will abandon the **r** of my
22:6 Also, use ⌊the **r** of⌋ the money
23:18 So Josiah said, "Let him **r**.
25:11 and the **r** of the population.
1Ch 6:61 The **r** of Kohath's descendants
6:70 the **r** of Kohath's descendants.
6:77 The **r** of Merari's descendants
8:7 Gera led the **r** of them away as
11:8 Joab rebuilt the **r** of the city.
12:38 The **r** of Israel also had agreed
13:2 send ⌊an invitation⌋ to the **r**
16:41 and the **r** of the Levites who
19:11 Abishai in charge of the **r**
23:25 of Israel has given his people **r**.
2Ch 9:29 Aren't the **r** of Solomon's acts
24:14 they brought the **r** of the money
36:21 The land had its years of **r** and
36:21 ⌊the land had its⌋ 70 years of **r**.
Ezr 3:8 and the **r** of the Jews,
4:3 and the **r** of the heads of
4:7 and the **r** of their group wrote to
4:10 and the **r** of the people whom
4:10 the cities of Samaria and the **r**
4:17 and the **r** of their group living in
6:20 for the **r** of the priests,
7:18 you think is right with the **r**
10:5 and all the **r** of Israel swear to
Neh 2:16 or any of the **r** who would be
4:14 and the **r** of the people,
4:19 and the **r** of the people,
6:1 and the **r** of our enemies heard
6:14 prophet Noadiah and the **r**
7:72 The **r** of the people contributed
7:73 and the **r** of Israel settled in
10:28 The **r** of the people took an
11:1 The **r** of the people drew lots to
11:20 The **r** of the Israelites,
Est 4:13 safer than all the **r** of the Jews.
9:12 must they have done in the **r**
Job 3:17 There the weary are able to **r**.
3:26 I have no **r**! And trouble keeps
11:18 will look around and **r** in safety.
17:16 Will my hope **r** with me in the
30:17 My body doesn't **r**.
Psa 3:8 May your blessing **r** on your
22:2 also at night, but I find no **r**.
33:22 Let your mercy **r** on us,
55:6 I would fly away and find **r**.
78:34 ⌊the **r**⌋ searched for him.
80:17 Let your power **r** on the man
95:11 will never enter my place of **r**!'"
139:3 me when I travel and when I **r**.
Pro 5:9 others and ⌊the **r** of⌋ your years
6:4 Don't let your eyes **r** or your
14:33 Wisdom finds **r** in the heart of
19:20 may be wise the **r** of your life.
19:23 and such a person will **r** easy
21:16 the way of wise behavior will **r**
26:2 curse does not come to **r**.
Ecc 2:23 at night their minds don't **r**.
6:5 the baby finds more **r** than the
11:6 let your hands **r** until evening.
12:5 Mortals go to their eternal **r**,
Isa 9:6 The government will **r** on his
11:2 The Spirit of the LORD will **r**
13:20 won't let their flocks **r** there.
17:6 four or five olives on the **r** of the
23:12 Even there you will find no **r**.
28:12 This is a place of **r** for those
28:12 This is a place for them to **r**."
30:15 You can have **r**. You can be
32:18 homes and quiet places of **r**.
Isa 34:14 Screech owls will **r** there and
38:10 be robbed of the **r** of my life.
38:15 I will be careful the **r** of my life
44:17 But the **r** of the wood they
44:19 Now I am making the **r** of the
57:2 who has lived honestly will **r**
57:18 I'll guide them and give them **r**.
60:13 the place where my feet **r**.
62:1 Jerusalem's sake I will not **r**,
62:6 do not give yourselves any **r**,
62:7 and do not give him any **r** until
63:14 they were given **r** by the
Jer 27:19 and the **r** of the utensils that are
29:1 a letter from Jerusalem to the **r**
31:2 Israel went to find its **r**.
33:12 shepherds can **r** their flocks.
39:3 and all the **r** of the officers of
39:9 and the **r** of the people.
41:10 Then Ishmael took captive the **r**
41:16 with him brought back the **r**
45:3 groaning. I can't find any **r**.'
47:6 scabbard. Stay there and **r**!"
47:7 can the sword of the LORD **r**?
50:34 their cause in order to bring **r**
52:15 and the **r** of the population.
Lam 1:3 the nations; they find no **r**.
2:18 Don't let your eyes **r**.
5:5 out ⌊and⌋ not permitted to **r**.
Eze 16:42 Then I will **r** from my fury
21:17 I will also clap my hands and **r**
34:14 They will **r** on the good land
34:15 of my sheep and lead them to **r**,
34:18 Must you trample the **r** of the
34:18 Must you muddy the **r** of the
36:3 became the possession of the **r**
36:4 prey and are mocked by the **r**
36:5 I have spoken against the **r**
43:7 and the place where my feet **r**.
44:30 a blessing to **r** on your home.
48:18 The **r** of the land borders the
48:23 This is what the **r** of the tribes
Dan 2:18 not be destroyed with the **r**
7:12 The power of the **r** of the
12:13 You will **r**, and you will rise for
Joe 1:7 could eat, threw the **r** away,
Amo 1:8 The **r** of the Philistines will die.
4:2 and the **r** of you on fishhooks.
Mic 2:10 This is not a place to **r**!
5:3 Then the **r** of the LORD's
Nah 3:18 Your best fighting men are at **r**.
Hab 2:8 All the **r** of the people will loot
Zec 1:11 world is at **r** and in peace."
6:8 made my Spirit **r** in the north."
9:1 and will **r** on Damascus
14:2 but the **r** of the people won't be
Mat 11:28 and I will give you **r**.
11:29 you will find **r** for yourselves
12:43 places looking for a place to **r**.
22:6 The **r** grabbed the king's
22:26 and the **r** of the seven brothers.
27:25 for killing him will **r**
Mar 6:31 where we can be alone to **r**
Luk 11:24 places looking for a place to **r**.
Jon 1:39 he was staying and spent the **r**
11:16 said to the **r** of the disciples,
Act 2:3 one came to **r** on each believer.
4:6 and the **r** of the chief priest's
7:5 not even a place to **r** his feet.
7:49 to build for me? Where will I **r**?
13:36 He was laid to **r** with his
19:27 she whom all Asia and the **r**
27:44 Then he ordered the **r** to follow
Rom 1:13 among the **r** of the nations.
11:7 The minds of the **r** of Israel
1Co 7:12 the Lord) say to the **r** of you:
11:32 along with the **r** of the world.
2Co 7:5 of Macedonia, we've had no **r**.
Gal 6:16 Peace and mercy will come to **r**
Php 4:3 along with Clement and the **r**
Heb 3:11 never enter my place of **r**."
3:18 never enter his place of **r**?
3:19 they couldn't enter his place of **r**
4:1 enter his place of **r** still stands.
4:1 you won't enter his place of **r**.
4:3 are entering that place of **r**.
4:3 never enter my place of **r**."

Heb 4:5 will never enter my place of **r**."
4:6 people enter that place of **r**.
4:6 did not enter God's place of **r**
4:7 place of **r**⌋ God spoke about
4:8 Joshua had given the people **r**,
4:9 Therefore, a time of **r** and
4:10 his place of **r** also rested from
4:11 effort to enter that place of **r**.
1Pe 4:2 human desires as you live the **r**
2Pe 3:16 the same way they distort the **r**
Rev 2:24 But the **r** of you in Thyatira
6:11 They were told to **r** a little
11:13 and the **r** were terrified.
14:11 There will be no **r** day or night
14:13 Let them **r** from their hard work
19:21 rider on the horse killed the **r**
20:5 The **r** of the dead did not live

rested (11)

2Sm 12:3 She **r** in his arms and was like
16:14 their destination⌋ and **r** there.
1Ki 8:7 the place where the ark ⌊**r**⌋,
2Ki 4:11 the upstairs room, and **r** there.
2Ch 5:8 place where the ark ⌊**r**⌋ so that
Ezr 8:32 we **r** for three days.
Est 9:17 On the fourteenth they **r** and
9:18 They **r** on the fifteenth and
Luk 23:56 But on the day of worship they **r**
Heb 4:4 "On the seventh day God **r**
4:10 of rest also **r** from their work

resting (14)

Gen 49:15 When he sees that his **r** place
2Ch 6:41 and come to your **r** place,
Psa 132:8 and come to your **r** place with
132:14 will be my **r** place forever.
Isa 11:10 His **r** place will be glorious.
22:16 you have to carve out a **r** place
34:14 find a **r** place for themselves.
65:10 The Achor Valley will be a **r**
66:1 build a house or **r** place for me?
Jer 6:16 Live that way, and find a **r**
50:6 They have forgotten their **r**
Eze 25:5 and I will turn Ammon into a **r**
Zep 2:15 a **r** place for wild animals!
1Pe 4:14 the Spirit of God — is **r** on you.

restless (4)

Psa 42:5 Why are you so **r**?
42:11 Why are you so **r**?
43:5 Why are you so **r**?
55:2 My thoughts are **r**, and I am

restore (42)

Gen 40:13 will release you and **r** you
Num 21:27 Rebuild it! **R** Sihon's city!
Dtr 30:3 he will **r** your fortunes.
2Sm 8:3 When David went to **r** his
2Ki 8:6 he said, "**R** all that is hers,
Ezr 9:9 our God's temple and **r** its ruins
Psa 41:3 You will **r** this person to health
51:12 **R** the joy of your salvation to
60:1 You have been angry. **R** us!
71:20 You **r** me to life again.
80:3 O God, **r** us and smile on us so
80:7 O God, commander of armies, **r**
80:19 commander of armies, **r** us,
85:4 **R** us, O God, our savior.
85:6 Won't you **r** our lives again so
126:4 **R** our fortunes, O LORD,
126:4 as you **r** streams ⌊to dry
Isa 44:26 about their ruins, "I will **r** them.
49:8 You will **r** the land.
58:12 rebuild the ancient ruins and **r**
61:4 They will **r** the places
Jer 30:17 I'll **r** your health and heal your
33:6 "But I will heal this city and **r** it
33:7 I will **r** Judah and Israel and
33:11 I will **r** the fortunes of the land
33:26 However, I will **r** their fortunes
48:47 But I will **r** Moab in the last
Eze 16:53 "'I will **r** the fortunes of Sodom
16:53 I will also **r** your fortune along
Dan 9:25 time the command is given to **r**
Amo 9:11 I will **r** its ruined places.
9:14 I will **r** my people Israel.
Nah 2:2 The LORD will **r** Jacob's glory
Zep 2:7 of them and will **r** their fortunes.
3:20 when I **r** your fortunes right
Mar 9:50 how will you **r** its flavor?
Luk 14:34 how will you **r** its flavor?
Act 1:6 the time when you're going to **r**
9:12 his hands on him to **r** his sight."
15:16 I will **r** its ruined places again.
2Co 5:19 God was using Christ to **r** his
1Pe 5:10 will **r** you, strengthen you,

restored (21)

Gen 40:21 He **r** the chief cupbearer to his
41:13 Pharaoh **r** me to my position,
2Ki 14:25 He **r** Israel's boundaries from
2Ch 24:13 They **r** God's temple to its
29:19 We have **r** them and made
Job 42:10 the LORD **r** Job's prosperity
Psa 85:1 You **r** the fortunes of Jacob.
126:1 When the LORD **r** the fortunes
Isa 49:11 and my highways will be **r**.
Jer 8:22 of my dear people been **r**?
Eze 21:27 It will not be **r** until its rightful
Dan 4:26 your kingdom will be **r** to you
9:25 Jerusalem will be **r** and rebuilt
Mat 20:34 Their sight was **r** at once,
Luk 8:36 the people how Jesus had **r**
Act 3:21 will be **r** as God promised
Rom 5:10 If the death of his Son **r** our
5:10 because of this **r** relationship,
5:11 this **r** relationship with God.
2Co 5:18 He has **r** our relationship with
5:19 this message of **r** relationships

restorer (1)

Isa 58:12 of Broken Walls and the **R**

restores (4)

Job 33:26 joy as he **r** their righteousness.
Psa 14:7 When the LORD **r** the fortunes
53:6 When God **r** the fortunes of his
Isa 49:6 are not just my servant who **r**

restoring (3)

2Ch 34:10 it to the workmen who were **r**
Luk 4:18 to the prisoners of sin and the **r**
2Co 5:18 this ministry of **r** relationships.

restrain (2)

Psa 32:9 bridle in their mouth to **r** them,
Mar 5:3 No one could **r** him any longer,

restrained (4)

1Sm 7:13 The LORD **r** the Philistines as
Job 30:11 are no longer **r** in my presence.
36:16 area where you were not **r**,
Psa 78:38 He **r** his anger many times.

restraint (1)

Isa 14:6 persecuting them without **r**.

restrict (1)

1Co 7:35 for your benefit, not to **r** you.

rests (8)

Gen 49:9 He lies down and **r** like a lion.
2Ki 2:15 "Elijah's spirit **r** on Elisha!"
Psa 16:9 My body **r** securely
121:4 of Israel never **r** or sleeps.
146:5 Their hope **r** on the LORD their
Isa 14:7 The whole earth **r** and is
Hab 2:5 he is arrogant and never **r**.
Act 2:26 My body also **r** securely

result (38)

Gen 30:43 As a **r**, Jacob became very
Lev 18:27 As a **r**, the land has become
1Ki 21:26 many disgusting things as a **r**
2Ch 14:13 As a **r**, the Sudanese army
17:10 As a **r**, they didn't wage war
Est 1:12 As a **r**, the king became very
9:25 As a **r**, they hung Haman and
Pro 12:14 enjoys good things as a **r**
13:2 A person eats well as a **r** of his
Jer 6:19 It is the **r** of their own plots,
Mat 7:27 and the **r** was a total disaster."
23:35 As a **r**, you will be held
Jon 11:4 "His sickness won't **r** in death.
Act 5:15 As a **r**, people carried their sick
8:8 As a **r**, that city was extremely
9:42 the city of Joppa, and as a **r**,
Rom 1:20 As a **r**, people have no excuse.
1:24 As a **r**, they dishonor their
4:18 As a **r**, he became a father of
5:15 If humanity died as the **r** of one
7:4 As a **r**, we can do what God
7:5 they did things that **r** in death.
15:8 As a **r**, he fulfilled God's
1Co 1:29 As a **r**, no one can brag in
9:1 Aren't you the **r** of my work for
2Co 3:3 written as a **r** of our ministry.
4:4 As a **r**, they don't see the light
Gal 2:19 As a **r**, I live in a relationship
5:17 As a **r**, you don't always do
Eph 2:9 It's not the **r** of anything you've
Php 1:13 As a **r**, it has become clear to
1Th 2:16 The **r** is that those Jews
1Ti 3:13 and will have confidence as a **r**
6:2 As a **r**, believers who are
Tit 3:7 As a **r**, God in his kindness
Jas 2:21 receive God's approval as a **r**
1Pe 1:22 As a **r** you have a sincere love
Jud 1:12 As a **r**, they have died twice.

results (15)

1Ch 21:2 Bring me ⌊the **r**⌋ so that I may
Neh 13:18 with the **r** that our God brought
Isa 55:11 not come back to me without **r**,
Jer 2:30 your children without **r**.
17:10 him for the **r** of his actions.
46:11 many medicines without **r**;
Luk 7:35 is proved right by all its **r**."
Rom 1:13 I want is to enjoy some of the **r**
1:13 as I have also enjoyed the **r**
5:21 This **r** in our living forever
6:22 This **r** in a holy life and,
1Co 11:17 it **r** in more harm than good.
Php 1:22 my work will produce more **r**.
2:16 and that my work produced **r**.
Col 1:6 It is producing **r** and spreading

retire (1)

Num 8:25 they must **r** from active service

retreat (7)

Psa 6:10 In a moment they will **r** and be
9:3 When my enemies **r**,
44:10 You make us **r** from the enemy.
56:9 Then my enemies will **r** when I
129:5 hate Zion. Force them to **r**.
Isa 44:25 I make wise men **r** and turn
Jer 21:2 so that Nebuchadnezzar will **r**."

retreated (3)

2Sm 23:9 When the soldiers from Israel **r**,
Jer 37:5 they **r** from Jerusalem.
37:11 The Babylonian army had **r**

retreating (1)

Jer 46:5 They are **r**. Their warriors are

retreats (1)

2Sm 17:13 If he **r** into a city, all Israel will

return (176)

Gen 3:19 produce food to eat until you **r**
3:19 and you will **r** to dust."
28:21 and if I **r** safely to my father's
29:18 "I'll work seven years in **r** for
29:20 seven years in **r** for Rachel,
29:25 I work for you in **r** for Rachel?
30:15 go to bed with you tonight in **r**
38:11 "**R** to your father's home.
43:12 You must **r** the money that was
43:25 ready for Joseph's **r** at noon,
Lev 6:4 **R** what you stole or seized,
16:26 Then he may **r** to the camp.
16:28 Then he may **r** to the camp.
24:19 receive the same injury in **r** —
24:20 receive the same injury in **r**.
25:10 slave will be freed in order to **r**
25:13 in order to **r** to his property.

Num 10:36 he would say, "**R**, O LORD,
18:21 This is in **r** for the work they do
27:21 at his command they will **r**."
32:18 We will not **r** to our homes until
Dtr 17:16 of horses or make the people **r**
23:15 don't **r** him to his master.
30:2 If you and your children **r** to the
30:10 in this Book of Teachings and **r**
Jos 2:16 days until they **r** to Jericho.
18:8 a description of it, and **r** to me.
22:4 So **r** home, to the land that is
22:8 He also said to them, "**R** to
Jdg 11:31 me when I **r** safely from Ammon
20:8 go to his tent or **r** to his house.
1Sm 1:28 In **r**, I am giving him to the
6:2 Tell us how to **r** it to its
6:3 but by all means **r** it to its
7:17 Then he would **r** home to
29:4 "**R** him to the place you
2Sm 1:22 nor did Saul's sword **r** unused.
10:5 and then **r** ⌊to Jerusalem⌋."
14:24 "Absalom should **r** to his own
17:3 I'll **r** all the people to you as a
22:38 I did not **r** until I had ended their
1Ki 12:21 the people of Israel and **r**
12:26 "The kingdom will probably **r** to
12:27 Then they will kill me and **r** to
17:21 make this child's life **r** to him."
2Ki 19:7 that he will hear a rumor and **r**
1Ch 19:5 and then **r** ⌊to Jerusalem⌋."
2Ch 11:1 to fight against Israel and **r** the
18:26 water until I **r** home safely.'"
28:11 **R** these prisoners you have
30:6 **r** to the LORD God of Abraham,
30:6 Then he will **r** to the few of you
30:9 When you **r** to the LORD,
30:9 They will **r** to this land.
30:9 away from you if you **r** to him."
Ezr 3:8 second year following their **r**
Neh 1:9 But if you **r** to me and continue
5:11 You must **r** their fields,
5:11 Also, you must **r** the interest on
5:12 They responded, "We'll **r** it and
13:6 the king for permission to **r**.
Job 1:21 my mother, and naked I will **r**.
10:9 of clay and that you will **r** me
10:22 as darkness. I'll never **r**.'"
15:22 He doesn't believe he'll **r** from
15:31 will get worthless things in **r**.
16:22 I will take the path of no **r**.
22:23 If you **r** to the Almighty,
34:15 and humanity would **r** to dust.
34:26 In **r** for their evil, he strikes
Psa 9:17 forget God, will **r** to the grave.
18:37 I did not **r** until I had ended their
22:27 the earth will remember and **r**
51:13 and sinners will **r** to you.
59:6 They **r** in the evening.
59:14 They **r** in the evening.
78:39 that blows and does not **r**.
90:3 "**R**, descendants of Adam."
90:13 **R**, LORD! How long ...?
104:29 and they die and **r** to dust.
109:4 In **r** for my love, they accuse
146:4 they **r** to the ground.
Isa 1:27 and those who **r** will be
6:10 and **r** and be healed."
10:21 will **r** to the mighty God.
10:22 the seashore, only a few will **r**.
13:14 Everyone will **r** to his own
31:6 You people of Israel, **r** to the
35:10 ransomed by the LORD will **r**.
37:7 that he will hear a rumor and **r**
51:11 ransomed by the LORD will **r**.
55:7 Let them **r** to the LORD,
55:7 Let them **r** to our God,
63:17 **R** for the sake of your servants.
Jer 8:5 to deceit. They refuse to **r**.
8:7 storks know when it's time to **r**.
8:7 am urging them to **r**.
12:15 I will **r** them to their inheritance
15:19 the LORD says: If you will **r**,
15:19 The people will **r** to you,
15:19 but you will not **r** to them.
22:27 You will want to **r** to this land,
31:8 and lame people will **r** together

Jer 31:8 A large crowd will **r** here.
31:9 They will cry as they **r**.
31:16 You will **r** from the land of the
31:17 Your children will **r** to their own
37:8 Then the Babylonians will **r**.
37:20 Don't **r** me to the scribe
42:12 compassion on you and **r** you
44:14 Egypt will survive or **r** to Judah,
44:14 where they long to **r** and live.
44:14 Only a few refugees will **r**
44:28 who escape the wars will **r**
49:6 I will **r** the captives of Ammon,
49:39 I'll **r** the captives of Elam,
Lam 3:40 them and then **r** to the LORD.
Eze 14:6 and don't **r** to any of your
16:55 Samaria and her daughters **r**
16:55 you and your daughters will **r** to
16:61 You will be ashamed when I **r**
18:12 He doesn't **r** the security for a
21:30 "'**R** your sword to its scabbard.
26:20 You will never **r** or take your
29:14 Egyptian captives and **r** them
Dan 10:20 Now I will **r** to fight the
11:9 the southern kingdom and **r**
11:10 They will **r** and wage war all
11:13 "The northern king will **r** and
11:28 The northern king will **r** to his
11:28 He will take action and **r** to his
11:30 promise, he will **r**, take action,
Hos 6:1 Let's **r** to the LORD.
7:16 They don't **r** to the Most High.
9:3 They will **r** to Egypt,
11:5 "They will not **r** to Egypt.
11:5 they have refused to **r** to me.
12:6 **R** to your God. Be loyal and fair,
14:1 Israel, **r** to the LORD your God.
14:2 **R** to the LORD, and say these
Joe 2:12 "**r** to me with all your heart —
2:13 **R** to the LORD your God.
Amo 4:6 And you still didn't **r** to me,
4:8 And you still didn't **r** to me,
4:9 And you still didn't **r** to me,
4:10 And you still didn't **r** to me,
4:11 And you still didn't **r** to me,
Mic 2:8 a care as they **r** from war.
4:8 The kingdom will **r** to the
5:3 rest of the LORD's people will **r**
Zec 1:3 LORD of Armies says: **R** to me,
1:3 of Armies, and I will **r** to you,
8:3 I will **r** to Zion and live in
9:12 **R** to your fortress, you captives
9:12 Today I tell you that I will **r** to
10:9 with their children and then **r**.
Mal 3:7 **R** to me, and I will return to
3:7 and I will **r** to you,"
3:7 "But you ask, 'How can we **r**?'
Mat 13:15 And they never **r** to me for
24:42 on what day your Lord will **r**.
24:44 of Man will **r** when you least
24:50 His master will **r** unexpectedly.
Mar 4:12 They never **r** to me and are
13:35 the owner of the house will **r**.
Luk 10:35 I'll pay you on my **r** trip.'
12:40 because the Son of Man will **r**
12:46 His master will **r** at an
14:12 Otherwise, they will **r** the favor.
15:27 celebrate your brother's safe **r**.'
Act 15:16 'Afterwards, I will **r**.
2Co 1:16 Macedonia I had planned to **r**
9:6 harvest of God's blessings in **r**.
2Pe 3:4 happened to his promise to **r**?
Rev 2:5 **R** to me and change the way
2:16 So **r** to me and change the way

returned (128)

Gen 18:33 he left. Abraham **r** home.
22:19 Then Abraham **r** to his
Exo 14:27 and at daybreak the water **r** to
Num 14:37 They died because they had **r**
Jos 2:22 until the king's men **r** to Jericho.
2:23 and **r** to Joshua, son of Nun.
4:18 the water of the Jordan **r** to its
6:14 once on the second day and **r**
10:15 Then Joshua and all Israel **r** to
10:21 Then the whole army **r** safely
10:43 Then Joshua and all Israel **r** to

Jos 18:9 Then they **r** to Joshua at the
22:9 They **r** to Gilead. This was their
22:32 and the leaders **r** from Reuben
Jdg 3:19 near Gilgal ⌊and **r** to Eglon⌋.
8:13 Gideon, son of Joash, **r** from
17:4 When Micah **r** the silver to his
Rut 3:16 When Ruth **r**, her mother-in-law
1Sm 1:19 Then they **r** home to Ramah.
7:14 took from Israel were **r** to Israel.
14:46 So the Philistines **r** to their own
17:57 When David **r** from killing the
19:7 So David was **r** to his former
25:12 David's young men **r** and told
26:25 while Saul **r** home.
27:9 and clothing and **r** to Achish.
29:11 morning David and his men **r**
2Sm 1:1 After Saul died and David **r**
2:30 Joab **r** from chasing Abner.
3:27 When Abner **r** to Hebron,
6:20 When David **r** to bless his
8:13 region as he **r** ⌊to Jerusalem⌋.
10:14 Ammonites and **r** to Jerusalem.
12:31 all the troops **r** to Jerusalem.
14:24 So Absalom **r** to his house and
17:3 the people to you as a bride is **r**
17:20 servants **r** to Jerusalem.
18:16 troops **r** from pursuing Israel.
23:10 The army **r** to Eleazar,
23:10 but they only **r** to strip the dead.
1Ki 12:2 Rehoboam⌋, he **r** from Egypt.
12:20 heard that Jeroboam had **r**,
12:24 They **r** ⌊home⌋, as the LORD
14:28 the shields and then **r** them
17:22 and the child's life **r** to him.
2Ki 1:5 When the messengers **r**,
2:18 They **r** to Elisha in Jericho,
2:25 Carmel, and **r** to Samaria.
5:15 Then he and all his men **r** to
7:15 The messengers **r** and told the
8:29 King Joram **r** to Jezreel to let
9:15 But King Joram had **r** to Jezreel
14:14 Then he **r** to Samaria.
14:22 Azariah rebuilt Elath and **r** it to
16:11 Ahaz **r** home from Damascus.
19:8 The field commander **r** and
1Ch 19:15 So Joab **r** to Jerusalem.
20:3 all the troops **r** to Jerusalem.
21:4 and **r** to Jerusalem.
2Ch 10:2 Rehoboam⌋, he **r** from Egypt.
12:11 the shields and then **r** them
14:15 Then it **r** to Jerusalem.
19:1 King Jehoshaphat of Judah **r**
20:27 and Jerusalem **r** to Jerusalem.
22:6 Joram **r** to Jezreel to let his
25:10 furious with Judah and **r** home.
25:24 Then he **r** to Samaria.
26:2 Uzziah rebuilt Elath and **r** it to
28:15 Then they **r** to Samaria.
31:1 Then all the Israelites **r** to their
32:21 Humiliated, Sennacherib **r** to
Ezr 2:1 These exiles **r** to Jerusalem
2:36 These priests **r** from exile:
2:40 These Levites **r** from exile:
2:41 These singers **r** from exile:
2:42 gatekeepers **r** from exile:
2:43 temple servants **r** from exile:
2:55 servants **r** from exile:
4:1 people who **r** from exile were
6:5 They should be **r** to their proper
6:16 and the others who had **r** from
6:19 those who had **r** from exile
6:20 people who had **r** from exile,
6:21 Israelites who had **r** from exile
Neh 2:15 entered Valley Gate, and **r**.
7:6 They **r** to Jerusalem and Judah.
7:39 These priests **r** from exile:
7:43 These Levites **r** from exile:
7:44 These singers **r** from exile:
7:45 gatekeepers **r** from exile:
7:46 temple servants **r** from exile:
7:57 servants **r** from exile:
13:6 reign in Babylon, I **r** to the king.
Est 4:9 So Hathach **r** and told Esther
6:12 Mordecai **r** to the king's gate,
7:8 When the king **r** from the
Psa 35:13 When my prayer **r** unanswered,

Isa 9:13 But the people have not **r** to the
37:8 The field commander **r** and
Jer 40:12 So all the Jews **r** from all the
Hag 1:12 and the faithful few who **r** from
1:14 and the faithful few who **r** from
2:2 faithful few who **r** from Babylon.
Zec 1:16 I have **r** to Jerusalem with
4:1 who was speaking with me **r**
Mat 21:18 as Jesus **r** to the city,
25:19 the master of those servants **r**
25:27 When I **r**, I would have
Mar 11:27 his disciples **r** to Jerusalem.
Luk 2:20 As the shepherds **r** to their
2:39 Joseph and Mary **r** to their
2:51 Then he **r** with them to
4:14 Jesus **r** to Galilee.
7:10 the men who had been sent **r**
19:12 appointed king, and then he **r**.
23:48 they cried and **r** to the city.
Jon 4:27 At that time his disciples **r**.
4:46 Jesus **r** to the city of Cana in
4:47 that Jesus had **r** from Judea
6:15 So he **r** to the mountain by
7:45 When the temple guards **r**,
8:2 Early the next morning he **r** to
9:7 blind man washed it off and **r**.
Act 1:12 Then they **r** to Jerusalem from
12:25 they **r** to Antioch from
22:17 "After that, I **r** to Jerusalem.
23:32 They **r** to their barracks the
25:6 most and then **r** to Caesarea.

returning (10)

Num 31:14 who were **r** from battle.
1Sm 6:3 "If you're **r** the ark of the God of
7:3 "If you are **r** to the LORD
18:6 As they arrived, David was **r**
Isa 30:15 You can be saved by **r** to me.
49:18 gathering together and **r** to you.
Jer 8:5 away from me without ever **r**.
Hos 5:4 have done keep them from **r**
Act 25:4 replied that he would be **r**
Heb 7:1 Abraham was **r** from defeating

returns (4)

Jer 8:4 turns away from me, he **r**.
Eze 18:7 He **r** what a borrower gives him
33:15 He **r** the security for a loan,
Luk 12:36 when he **r** from a wedding.

Reu (6)

Gen 11:18 he became the father of **R**.
11:19 After he became the father of **R**,
11:20 **R** was 32 years old when he
11:21 **R** lived 207 years and had
1Ch 1:25 Eber, Peleg, **R**,
Luk 3:35 son of Serug, son of **R**,

Reuben (88)

Gen 29:32 She named him **R** [Here's My
30:14 During the wheat harvest **R**
35:22 **R** went to bed with his father's
35:23 Leah were Jacob's firstborn **R**,
37:21 When **R** heard this,
37:22 **R** wanted to rescue Joseph
37:29 When **R** came back to the
42:22 **R** said to them, "Didn't I tell you
42:37 So **R** said to his father,
46:8 **R** was Jacob's firstborn.
46:9 The sons of **R** were Hanoch,
48:5 mine just as **R** and Simeon are.
49:3 "**R**, you are my firstborn,
Exo 1:2 **R**, Simeon, Levi, and Judah;
6:14 of the families: The sons of **R**,
6:14 the families descended from **R**.
Num 1:5 from the tribe of **R**;
1:20 for the descendants of **R**,
1:21 for the tribe of **R** was 46,500.
2:10 led by **R** will camp under
2:10 for the people of **R** is Elizur,
7:30 leader of the descendants of **R**,
13:4 from the tribe of **R**;
16:1 On were descendants of **R**.)
26:5 **R** was Israel's firstborn.
26:5 The descendants of **R** were the
26:7 These were the families of **R**.
Num 32:1 The tribes of **R** and Gad had a
32:6 asked the tribes of Gad and **R**,
32:16 Then the tribes of Gad and **R**
32:25 Then the tribes of Gad and **R**
32:29 "If the tribes of Gad and **R** get
32:31 tribes of Gad and **R** answered,
32:33 gave the tribes of Gad, **R**,
32:37 The tribe of **R** rebuilt the cities
34:14 households from the tribes of **R**,
Dtr 3:12 I gave the tribes of **R** and Gad
3:16 I gave the tribes of **R** and Gad
3:18 I gave the tribes of **R** and Gad
4:43 desert plateau for the tribe of **R**,
11:6 from the tribe of **R**.
27:13 **R**, Gad, Asher, Zebulun, Dan,
29:8 and gave it to the tribes of **R**,
33:6 "May the tribe of **R** live and not
Jos 1:12 Joshua said to the tribes of **R**
4:12 The men of **R**, Gad, and half of
12:6 a possession to the tribes of **R**
13:8 The tribes of **R** and Gad with
13:15 the tribe of **R** for their families.
15:6 to the Rock of Bohan, son of **R**.
18:7 The tribes of Gad and **R** and
18:17 to the Rock of Bohan, son of **R**.
20:8 plateau from the tribe of **R**,
21:7 families from the tribes of **R**,
21:36 The tribe of **R** also gave them
22:1 summoned the tribes of **R**
22:9 So the tribes of **R** and Gad and
22:10 **R**, Gad, and half of the tribe of
22:11 **R**, Gad, and half of the tribe of
22:13 to the tribes of **R** and Gad and
22:21 Then the tribes of **R** and Gad
22:25 the descendants of **R** and Gad.
22:30 heard what the tribes of **R**,
22:31 said to the tribes of **R**,
22:32 the leaders returned from **R**
22:33 about going to war against **R**
22:34 The tribes of **R** and Gad gave
1Sm 11:1 the tribes of Gad and **R**.
2Ki 10:33 **R**, and Manasseh) from Aroer,
1Ch 2:1 These were Israel's sons: **R**,
5:1 These are the sons of **R**,
5:3 The sons of **R**, were Hanoch,
5:6 He was leader of the tribe of **R**.
5:18 The descendants of **R**,
5:22 **R**, Gad, and half of the tribe of
5:25 But Gad, **R**, and half of the tribe
5:26 Pilneser of Assyria) to take **R**,
6:63 by lot from the tribes of **R**,
6:78 From the tribe of **R**,
11:42 the tribe of **R** (who was leader
11:42 was leader of the tribe of **R**
12:37 the Jordan River, from **R**, Gad,
26:32 or the king for the tribes of **R**,
27:16 Israel: for the tribe of **R**: Eliezer,
Eze 48:6 **R** will have one part of the land
48:7 part of the land and border **R**
48:31 the north side will be **R** Gate,
Rev 7:5 12,000 from the tribe of **R**,

Reuben's (9)

Num 2:16 troops in **R** camp is 151,450.
10:18 **R** descendants broke camp next.
Jos 13:23 The border of **R** territory was
13:23 This was **R** inheritance for its
Jdg 5:15 Among **R** divisions important
5:16 **R** divisions of important men
1Ch 5:8 **R** descendants lived in Aroer
5:11 lived next to **R** descendants
5:20 handed over to **R** descendants.

Reuel (10)

Gen 36:4 and Basemath gave birth to **R**.
36:10 of Esau's wife Adah, and **R**,
36:17 descendants of Esau's son **R**:
36:17 descended from **R** in Edom.
Exo 2:18 came back to their father **R**,
2:20 **R** asked his daughters,
2:21 So **R** gave his daughter
Num 10:29 son of **R** the Midianite,
1Ch 1:35 Esau's sons were Eliphaz, **R**,
9:8 of Shephatiah, grandson of **R**,

Reuel's (2)

Gen 36:13 These were **R** sons: Nahath,
1Ch 1:37 **R** sons were Nahath,

Reumah (1)

Gen 22:24 whose name was **R**,

reunited (1)

2Co 5:20 of Christ to become **r** with God.

reveal (26)

1Sm 16:3 I will **r** to you what you should
Est 2:10 Esther did not **r** her nationality
Psa 17:7 **R** your miraculous deeds of
Pro 25:9 do not **r** another person's secret
Isa 42:9 I will **r** new things before they
48:6 From now on I will **r** to you
Eze 20:41 Through you I will **r** myself as
36:23 I will **r** the holiness of my great
36:23 because I will **r** my holiness
38:23 I will **r** myself to many nations.
Dan 2:47 He can **r** secrets because you
2:47 you were able to **r** this secret."
Hab 3:2 In the course of the years, **r** it.
Mat 11:27 the Son is willing to **r** him.
Luk 2:32 He is a light that will **r**
10:22 the Son is willing to **r** him."
Jon 14:22 that you are going to **r** yourself
Rom 2:5 At that time God will **r** that his
8:19 for God to **r** who his children
9:22 his anger and **r** his power,
9:23 Can't God also **r** the riches of
15:8 Jewish people to **r** God's truth.
1Co 3:13 visible because fire will **r** it.
4:5 the dark and **r** people's motives.
2Co 4:2 As God watches, we clearly **r**
Eph 6:19 I will speak boldly when I **r**

revealed (88)

Gen 35:7 That's where God had **r** himself
Dtr 29:29 But the things that have been **r**
1Sm 2:27 I **r** myself to your ancestors
3:7 had not yet been **r** to him.
3:21 since the LORD **r** himself to
9:15 Now, the LORD had **r** the
2Sm 7:27 have **r** it especially to me,
2Ki 9:25 The LORD **r** this prophecy
1Ch 17:25 You, my God, have **r**
Est 2:20 Esther still had not **r** her family
Job 38:17 to death been **r** to you,
Psa 111:6 He has **r** the power of his
Pro 26:26 will be **r** to the community.
Isa 22:14 The LORD of Armies **r** this to
40:5 Then the LORD's glory will be **r**
41:26 Who **r** this from the beginning
41:26 Who **r** this from the past so that
41:26 No one **r** it. No one announced
43:9 among them could have **r** this?
43:12 I have **r** it to you, I have saved
45:21 Who **r** this in the distant past
46:10 From the beginning I **r** the end.
48:3 From the beginning I **r** to you
48:5 That is why I **r** to you what
48:14 What idol has **r** such things?
53:1 has the LORD's power been **r**?
56:1 righteousness is about to be **r**.
Jer 9:12 To whom has the LORD **r** this
11:18 The LORD **r** their plot to me so
Eze 16:57 before your wickedness was **r**.
23:29 of your prostitution will be **r**.
Dan 2:19 The secret was **r** to Daniel in a
2:30 This secret wasn't **r** to me
2:30 It was **r** so that you could be
10:1 a message was **r** to Daniel
Mat 16:17 No human **r** this to you,
16:17 my Father in heaven **r** it to you.
Mar 4:22 hidden that will not be **r**.
Luk 8:17 hidden that will not be **r**.
17:30 when the Son of Man is **r** will
Jon 12:38 has the Lord's power been **r**?"
Act 2:17 will speak what God has **r**.
2:18 will speak what God has **r**.
19:6 and to speak what God had **r**.
21:9 to speak what God had **r**.
Rom 1:17 God's approval is **r** in this

Rom 1:18 God's anger is **r** from heaven
8:18 glory that will soon be **r** to us.
10:20 I was **r** to those who weren't
1Co 1:7 for our Lord Jesus Christ to be **r**.
2:10 God has **r** those things to us by
11:4 what God has **r** dishonors
11:5 or speaks what God has **r**
12:10 can speak what God has **r**.
13:2 gift to speak what God has **r**,
13:8 of speaking what God has **r**,
13:9 what God has **r** is incomplete.
14:1 of speaking what God has **r**.
14:3 person speaks what God has **r**,
14:4 person speaks what God has **r**,
14:5 could speak what God has **r**.
14:5 God has **r** is more important
14:22 of speaking what God had **r** is
14:24 you speak what God has **r**.
14:29 should speak what God has **r**.
14:31 turns speaking what God has **r**.
14:32 has **r** must control themselves.
14:39 to speak what God has **r**,
Gal 1:12 but Jesus Christ **r** it to me.
3:23 was about to come would be **r**.
Eph 1:9 when he **r** the mystery of his
3:5 The Spirit has now **r** it to his
Col 1:26 but now he has **r** it to his
1Th 5:20 Don't despise what God has **r**.
2Th 1:7 this when the Lord Jesus is **r**,
2:3 sin, the man of destruction, is **r**.
2:6 so that he will be **r** when his
2:8 Then the man of sin will be **r**
2Ti 1:10 Savior Christ Jesus, he has **r** it.
Tit 1:3 God has **r** this in every era by
1Pe 1:5 salvation that is ready to be **r** at
1:12 God **r** to the prophets that the
5:1 share in the glory that will be **r**.
1Jn 1:2 This life was **r** to us.
1:2 of the Father and was **r** to us.
Rev 10:11 must speak what God has **r**
11:3 to speak what God has **r**.
11:6 they speak what God has **r**.

revealing (3)

Mat 11:25 intelligent people and **r** them
Luk 10:21 intelligent people and **r** them
Rom 16:25 He can strengthen you by **r** the

reveals (9)

Num 23:3 tell you whatever he **r** to me."
Psa 25:14 He **r** to them the intent of his
Dan 2:22 He **r** deeply hidden things.
2:28 a God in heaven who **r** secrets.
2:29 The one who **r** secrets told you
Amo 3:7 unless he ⌊first⌋ **r** his secret
4:13 He **r** his thoughts to humans.
Act 7:2 The God who **r** his glory
1Co 14:30 If God **r** something to another

revelation (33)

Pro 16:10 When a divine **r** is on a king's
30:1 Agur's prophetic **r**. This man's
31:1 of King Lemuel, a prophetic **r**,
Isa 13:1 is the divine **r** which Isaiah,
14:28 This was the divine **r** in the
15:1 This is the divine **r** about Moab.
17:1 is the divine **r** about Damascus.
19:1 is the divine **r** about Egypt.
21:1 This is the divine **r** about the
21:11 is the divine **r** about Dumah.
21:13 is the divine **r** about Arabia.
22:1 This is the divine **r** about the
23:1 This is the divine **r** about Tyre.
30:6 This is the divine **r** about the
Jer 23:33 'What **r** has the LORD
23:34 'This is the LORD's **r**!' I
23:36 'This is the LORD's **r**,' because
23:36 person's word becomes the **r**.
23:38 'This is the LORD's **r**!' Then
23:38 "This is the LORD's **r**!"
Eze 12:10 This is the divine **r** about the
Nah 1:1 This is a **r** from the LORD
Hab 1:1 The divine **r** that the prophet
Zec 9:1 This is the divine **r**.
12:1 This is the prophetic **r**,
Mal 1:1 This is a divine **r**. The LORD

1Co 14:6 unless I explained **r**,
14:26 doctrine, **r**, another language,
Gal 2:2 in response to a **r** ⌊from God⌋.
Eph 1:17 of wisdom and **r** as you come
3:3 know this mystery through a **r**.
Rev 1:1 This is the **r** of Jesus Christ.
1:1 He sent this **r** through his angel

revelations (4)

2Ch 24:27 the many divine **r** against him,
Mic 3:6 will have darkness without **r**.
2Co 12:1 to visions and **r** from the Lord.
12:7 number of **r** that I've had.

revenge (47)

Lev 19:18 Never get **r**. Never hold a grudge
26:25 I will bring war on you to get **r**
Dtr 32:35 I will take **r** and be satisfied.
32:41 Then I will take **r** on my
32:43 because he will take **r** for the
Jos 10:13 stopped until a nation got **r**
1Sm 14:24 comes and before I've gotten **r**
18:25 foreskins so that he can get **r**
24:12 May the LORD take **r** on you for
2Sm 4:8 has given Your Royal Majesty **r**
4:11 I'll now seek **r** for his murder
2Ki 9:7 I will get **r** on Jezebel for
2Ch 24:22 the LORD see ⌊this⌋ and get **r**!"
Est 8:13 to take **r** on their enemies.
Psa 58:10 when they see ⌊God⌋ take **r**.
Pro 6:34 no mercy when he takes **r**.
Isa 1:24 horrible it will be when I take **r**
34:8 a year of **r** in defense of Zion.
35:4 with vengeance, with divine **r**.
47:3 I will take **r**. I won't spare
Jer 11:20 want to see you take **r** on them,
15:15 and take **r** on those who
20:10 him and take **r** on him."
20:12 want to see you take **r** on them,
46:10 vengeance when he will take **r**
50:15 take **r** against them.
51:36 up your cause and get **r** for you.
Eze 5:13 against you, and I will get **r**.
5:15 of my anger, fury, and fierce **r**,
25:12 Edom took **r** on the nation of
25:14 people Israel to take **r** on Edom.
25:14 the Edomites will know my **r**,
25:15 The Philistines have taken **r**
25:17 I will take fierce **r** on them and
25:17 I will take **r** on them.
Mic 5:15 I will take **r** with great anger on
Nah 1:2 The LORD takes **r**.
1:2 The LORD takes **r** and is full of
1:2 The LORD takes **r** against his
Act 5:28 You want to take **r** on us for
7:24 He took **r** by killing the
Rom 12:19 Don't take **r**, dear friends.
12:19 "I alone have the right to take **r**.
2Th 1:8 He will take **r** on those who
Heb 10:30 "I alone have the right to take **r**.
Rev 6:10 before you judge and take **r**
19:2 He has taken **r** on her for the

reverence (3)

Psa 5:7 Out of **r** for you, I will bow
1Ti 2:10 who claim to have **r** for God.
3:16 The mystery that gives us our **r**

reverent (2)

1Ti 2:2 lived in a godly and **r** way.
1Pe 3:2 how pure and **r** their lives are.

reversed (1)

Zep 3:15 The LORD has **r** the judgments

review (1)

Dtr 1:5 began to **r** God's teachings.

revive (2)

Isa 26:19 and the earth will **r** the spirits of
Hos 6:2 After two days he will **r** us.

revived (2)

Jdg 15:19 Then he was refreshed and **r**.
1Sm 30:12 After he had eaten, he **r**.

revolt (4)

Pro 28:2 When a country is in **r**,
Isa 59:13 spoken about oppression and **r**.
Act 5:37 appeared and led people in a **r**.
2Th 2:3 unless⌋ a **r** takes place first,

revolution (1)

Act 21:38 who started a **r** not long ago

revolutionary (1)

Jon 18:40 (Barabbas was a political **r**.)

revolutions (1)

Luk 21:9 "When you hear of wars and **r**,

reward (72)

Gen 15:1 Your **r** will be very great."
30:16 "You are my **r** for my son's
30:18 "God has given me my **r**
30:18 she named him Issachar [**R**].
Num 22:37 You knew I'd be able to **r** you."
24:11 I said I'd **r** you richly,
24:11 has made you lose your **r**."
Rut 2:12 May the LORD **r** you for what
2:12 May you receive a rich **r** from
1Sm 26:23 The LORD will **r** any person
2Sm 4:10 I killed him in Ziklag to **r** him
4:11 How much more ⌊should I **r**⌋
19:36 should you give me such a **r**?
Est 6:3 The king asked, "How did I **r**
6:6 whom the king wishes to **r**?"
6:6 king wish to **r** more than me?"
6:9 man whom the king wishes to **r**
6:9 whom the king wishes to **r**.'"
6:11 whom the king wishes to **r**."
Job 20:29 This is the **r** God gives to the
34:33 Should God **r** you on your own
Psa 19:11 is a great **r** in following them.
58:11 people certainly have a **r**.
62:12 You **r** a person based on what
73:13 I've received no **r** for keeping
75:6 The ⌊authority⌋ to **r** someone
109:5 They **r** me with evil instead of
119:112 They offer a **r** that never ends.
127:3 They are a **r** from him.
Pro 10:16 A righteous person's **r** is life.
25:22 and the LORD will **r** you.
31:31 **R** her for what she has done,
Ecc 2:10 This was my **r** for all my hard
4:9 ⌊together⌋ they have a good **r**
9:5 There is no more **r** for the dead
Isa 40:10 His **r** is with him, and the
45:13 without any payment or any **r**,
49:4 and my **r** is with my God."
61:8 I will faithfully **r** my people's
62:11 His **r** is with him, and the
Jer 17:10 I will **r** each person for what he
17:10 I will **r** him for the results of his
32:19 You **r** them for the way they
Eze 29:18 Yet, he and his army got no **r**
Mat 5:12 you have a great **r** in heaven!
5:46 do you deserve a **r**?
6:1 your Father in heaven will not **r**
6:2 That will be their only **r**.
6:4 you do in private. He will **r** you.
6:5 That will be their only **r**.
6:6 you do in private. He will **r** you.
6:16 That will be their only **r**.
6:18 you do in private. He will **r** you.
10:41 will receive a prophet's **r**.
10:41 receive a righteous person's **r**.
10:42 will certainly never lose his **r**."
Mar 9:41 will certainly not lose his **r**."
Luk 6:23 You have a great **r** in heaven.
6:35 Then you will have a great **r**.
Rom 6:23 The **r** for sin is death,
1Co 3:8 and each will receive a **r** for his
3:14 he will receive a **r**.
9:17 News willingly, I'll have a **r**.
9:18 So what is my **r**? It is to spread
Eph 6:8 your heavenly master will **r** all
Col 3:24 you an inheritance as your **r**.
Heb 10:35 It will bring you a great **r**.
11:26 He was looking ahead to his **r**.
2Jn 1:8 but that you receive your full **r**.

Rev 2:23 I will **r** each of you for what you
11:18 to **r** your servants, the prophets,
22:12 I will bring my **r** with me to pay

rewarded (9)

Num 22:17 will make sure you are richly **r**,
2Sm 18:22 "You won't be **r** for this news."
22:21 The LORD **r** me because of my
2Ch 15:7 Your actions will be **r**."
Psa 18:20 The LORD **r** me because of my
Pro 11:31 righteous person is **r** on earth,
13:13 ⌊God's⌋ commands will be **r**.
13:21 people are **r** with good.
Jer 31:16 You will be **r** for your work,

rewards (3)

Psa 75:7 He punishes one person and **r**
109:20 This is how the LORD **r** those
Heb 11:6 and that he **r** those who seek

rework (1)

Jer 18:4 he would **r** it into a new clay

Rezeph (2)

2Ki 19:12 rescue Gozan, Haran, **R**,
Isa 37:12 rescue Gozan, Haran, **R**,

Rezin (10)

2Ki 15:37 the LORD began to use King **R**
16:5 Then King **R** of Aram and King
16:6 At that time King **R** of Aram
16:9 to Kir as captives, and killed **R**.
Ezr 2:48 **R**, Nekoda, Gazzam,
Neh 7:50 Reaiah, **R**, Nekoda,
Isa 7:1 Aram's King **R** and Israel's King
7:4 the fierce anger of **R** from Aram
7:8 the leader of Damascus is **R**.
8:6 joy in **R** and Remaliah's son."

Rezin's (1)

Isa 9:11 set **R** oppressors against Israel

Rezon (4)

1Ki 11:23 God also raised up **R**,
11:23 **R** fled from his master,
11:24 **R** gathered men and became
11:25 **R** was Israel's rival as long as

Rhegium (1)

Act 28:13 and arrived at the city of **R**.

Rhesa (1)

Luk 3:27 son of Joanan, son of **R**,

Rhoda (1)

Act 12:13 named **R** came to answer.

Rhodes (3)

Gen 10:4 Tarshish, Cyprus, and **R**.
1Ch 1:7 Tarshish, Cyprus, and **R**.
Act 21:1 day we sailed to the island of **R**

rib (1)

Gen 2:22 formed a woman from the **r** that

Ribai (2)

2Sm 23:29 Ittai (son of **R**) from Gibeah in
1Ch 11:31 Ithai (son of **R**) from Gibeah in

Riblah (11)

Num 34:11 the border goes down to **R**,
2Ki 23:33 made him a prisoner at **R**
25:6 him to the king of Babylon at **R**,
25:20 to the king of Babylon at **R**.
25:21 of Babylon executed them at **R**
Jer 39:5 King Nebuchadnezzar at **R**
39:6 as Zedekiah watched at **R**.
52:9 king of Babylon at **R** in Hamath,
52:10 all the officials of Judah at **R**.
52:26 to the king of Babylon at **R**.
52:27 of Babylon executed them at **R**

ribs (2)

Gen 2:21 God took out one of the man's **r**
Dan 7:5 on one side and had three **r**

rich (134)

Gen 13:2 Abram was very **r** because he
14:23 able to say, 'I made Abram **r**.'
26:13 successful, becoming very **r**.
49:20 "Asher's food will be **r**.
Exo 30:15 The **r** must not give more than
Lev 25:47 among you may become **r**,
25:49 If he becomes **r**, he could buy
Num 11:8 It tasted like **r** pastry made with
13:20 Is the soil **r** or poor?
Dtr 28:12 his **r** storehouse, for you.
Jdg 5:19 But they didn't carry off any **r**
Rut 2:12 May you receive a **r** reward
3:10 whether **r** or poor — is better
1Sm 17:25 who kills this Philistine very **r**.
25:2 He was a very **r** man.
2Sm 12:1 One was **r**, and the other was
12:2 The **r** man had a very large
12:4 a visitor came to the **r** man.
12:4 The **r** man thought it would be
19:32 Because he was a very **r** man,
2Ki 4:8 where a **r** woman lived.
1Ch 4:40 pasture that was **r** and good.
Neh 8:10 eat **r** foods, drink sweet drinks,
9:25 fortified cities and a **r** land.
Est 5:11 to them how very **r** he was,
Job 15:29 He won't get **r**, and his wealth
27:19 He may go to bed **r**,
27:19 but he'll never be **r** again.
31:25 If I enjoyed being very **r**
36:16 table was covered with **r** foods.
Psa 36:8 They are refreshed with the **r**
49:2 **r** people and poor ones.
49:16 when someone becomes **r**,
62:10 on extortion ⌊to make you **r**⌋.
106:45 In keeping with his **r** mercy,
119:36 getting **r** in underhanded ways.
Pro 10:15 The **r** person's wealth is ⌊his⌋
10:22 blessing that makes a person **r**,
11:25 person will be made **r**,
13:7 One person pretends to be **r** but
14:20 but a **r** person is loved by
18:11 A **r** person's wealth is his
18:23 but a **r** person is blunt when
21:17 food will not become **r**.
22:2 The **r** and the poor have this in
22:7 A **r** person rules poor people,
22:16 giving to the **r** certainly leads
23:4 not wear yourself out getting **r**.
28:6 than to be **r** and double-dealing.
28:11 A **r** person is wise in his own
28:20 but anyone in a hurry to get **r**
28:22 person is in a hurry to get **r**,
Ecc 5:12 But the full stomachs that **r**
6:3 Suppose a **r** person wasn't
6:5 more rest than the **r** person.
6:6 Even if the **r** person lives two
10:6 and **r** people are left to fill lower
10:20 and don't curse **r** people even
Isa 5:17 eat among the ruins of the **r**.
30:23 will be **r** and nourishing.
33:15 He rejects getting **r** by extortion
53:9 He was put there with the **r**
Jer 5:27 they become powerful and **r**.
9:23 Don't let **r** people brag about
17:11 A person who gets **r**
31:14 satisfy the priests with **r** food.
51:13 rivers and are **r** with treasures,
Eze 26:2 I'll get **r** now that it's ruined.'
27:12 because you were so very **r**.
27:33 made the kings of the earth **r**.
28:4 you've made yourself **r**.
Dan 1:5 allowance of the king's **r** food
1:8 by eating the king's **r** food
1:13 who are eating the king's **r** food.
1:15 been eating the king's **r** food.
1:16 took away the king's **r** food
11:26 People who eat the king's **r**
Hos 12:8 of Ephraim say, 'We're **r**.
Mic 6:12 The **r** people in the city are
Hab 1:16 They are **r** and well fed
2:6 the one who makes himself **r**
Zec 11:3 because their **r** pastures are
11:5 I've become **r**!" Even their own
Mat 19:23 It will be hard for a **r** person to
19:24 of a needle than for a **r** person
27:57 In the evening a **r** man named
Mar 10:23 "How hard it will be for **r**
10:25 of a needle than for a **r** person
12:41 Many **r** people put in large
Luk 1:53 He sent **r** people away with
6:24 it will be for those who are **r**.
12:16 He said, "A **r** man had land that
14:12 other relatives, or **r** neighbors.
16:1 "A **r** man had a business
16:1 of wasting the **r** man's property.
16:2 So the **r** man called for his
16:19 "There was a **r** man who wore
16:20 to the gate of the **r** man's house.
16:21 that fell from the **r** man's table.
16:22 The **r** man also died and was
16:27 "The **r** man responded,
16:30 "The **r** man replied,
18:23 because he was very **r**.
18:24 "How hard it is for **r** people to
18:25 of a needle than for a **r** person
19:2 of tax collectors, and he was **r**.
21:1 saw people, especially the **r**,
Rom 11:12 made the world spiritually **r**.
11:12 are not Jewish spiritually **r**.
1Co 1:5 Jesus you have become **r**
4:8 You've already become **r**!
2Co 6:10 make many people spiritually **r**,
8:9 He was **r**, yet for your sake he
8:9 make you **r** through his poverty
9:11 God will make you **r** enough
Eph 2:4 But God is **r** in mercy because
2:7 show his extremely **r** kindness
1Ti 6:9 But people who want to get **r**
6:10 getting **r** have wandered away
Jas 1:10 **R** believers should be proud
1:10 being **r** should make them
1:10 **R** people will wither like
1:11 The same thing will happen to **r**
2:5 people in the world to become **r**
2:6 Don't **r** people oppress you and
5:1 Pay attention to this if you're **r**.
Rev 2:9 poor you are — but you are **r**.
3:17 You say, 'I'm **r**. I'm wealthy. I
3:18 from me so that you may be **r**.
6:15 generals, the **r**, the powerful,
13:16 people, **r** and poor people,
18:3 the merchants of the earth **r**."
18:15 had become **r** by selling these
18:19 who had a ship at sea grew **r**

richer (6)

2Ch 32:27 Hezekiah became **r** and was
Psa 65:9 You make it much **r** than it was.
Pro 11:24 spends freely and yet grows **r**,
Ecc 2:9 So I grew **r** than anyone in
Dan 11:2 who will become much **r** than
Rom 11:12 will make the world even **r**.

riches (51)

Gen 49:26 the oldest mountains and the **r**
1Ki 3:11 for a long life, or **r** for yourself,
3:13 what you haven't asked for — **r**
1Ch 29:12 **R** and honor are in front of you.
2Ch 1:11 You didn't ask for **r**,
1:12 I will also give you **r**,
17:5 and he had a lot of **r** and honor.
Job 20:15 He vomits up the **r** that he
36:18 you are not led astray with **r**.
36:19 Will your **r** save you from
Psa 39:6 They accumulate **r** without
49:6 They trust their **r** and brag
49:10 They leave their **r** to others.
62:10 When **r** increase, do not
112:3 Wealth and **r** will be in his
119:14 than I find joy in all kinds of **r**.
Pro 3:16 left hand are **r** and honor.
8:18 I have **r** and honor,
10:4 but hard-working hands bring **r**.
11:4 **R** are of no help on the day of
11:16 but ruthless men gain **r**.
11:28 Whoever trusts his **r** will fall,
13:8 A person's **r** are the ransom for
22:4 (the fear of the LORD) are **r**
24:4 are filled with every kind of **r**,
30:8 give me either poverty or **r**.

Ecc 4:8 eyes are never satisfied with **r**.
5:13 **R** lead to the downfall of those
5:14 These hoarded **r** were then lost
6:2 God gives one person **r**,
9:11 people don't necessarily have **r**,
Isa 10:14 I've found the **r** of nations as
30:6 They carry their **r** on the backs
33:6 The **r** of salvation are wisdom
60:5 because the **r** of the sea will
Jer 9:23 rich people brag about their **r**.
20:5 I will hand all the **r** of this city
Eze 26:12 His troops will loot your **r** and
Mat 13:22 deceitful pleasures of **r** choke
Mar 4:19 the deceitful pleasures of **r**,
Luk 8:14 as life goes on the worries, **r**,
12:21 and his **r** don't serve God."
Rom 9:23 Can't God also reveal the **r** of
10:12 who gives his **r** to everyone
11:33 God's **r**, wisdom,
Col 1:27 the world to know the glorious **r**
2:2 by all the **r** that come from
1Ti 6:17 Tell those who have the **r** of
6:17 in anything as uncertain as **r**.
Jas 5:2 Your **r** have decayed,
5:3 You have stored up **r** in these

richest (3)

Psa 45:12 people of Tyre, the **r** people,
63:5 my soul with the **r** foods.
Dan 11:24 he will invade the **r** parts of the

rid (74)

Gen 21:10 "Get **r** of this slave and her son,
35:2 "Get **r** of the foreign gods
Num 33:52 Get **r** of all their stone and
Dtr 2:15 the LORD himself who got **r**
13:5 You must get **r** of this evil.
17:7 You must get **r** of this evil.
17:12 You must get **r** of this evil in
19:19 You must get **r** of this evil.
21:9 This is how you will get **r** of
21:21 You must get **r** of this evil.
22:21 You must get **r** of this evil.
22:22 You must get **r** of this evil in
22:24 You must get **r** of this evil.
24:7 You must get **r** of this evil.
Jos 7:13 your enemies until you get **r**
24:14 Get **r** of the gods your
24:23 "Get **r** of the foreign gods that
Jdg 9:29 Then I'd get **r** of Abimelech.
10:16 Then they got **r** of the foreign
20:13 We must put them to death to **r**
1Sm 1:14 "Get **r** of your wine."
7:3 get **r** of the foreign gods you
7:4 So the Israelites got **r** of the
17:26 kills this Philistine and gets **r**
28:3 (Saul had **r** the land of
28:9 "You know that Saul **r** the land
2Sm 4:11 revenge for his murder and **r**
13:17 servant and said, "Get **r** of her.
1Ki 15:12 out of the land and got **r**
22:46 He **r** the land of the male
2Ki 10:28 So Jehu got **r** of Baal worship
18:4 He got **r** of the illegal places of
18:22 and altars Hezekiah got **r** of.
23:5 He got **r** of the pagan priests
23:19 Josiah also got **r** of all the
23:24 Josiah also got **r** of the
2Ch 14:3 He got **r** of the altars of foreign
14:5 He got **r** of the illegal places of
17:6 He also got **r** of the illegal
30:14 Then the people got **r** of the
30:14 They got **r** of all the altars for
32:12 the same Hezekiah who got **r**
33:15 Manasseh got **r** of the foreign
33:15 He got **r** of the altars he had
34:33 Josiah got **r** of all the
Ezr 10:3 a promise to our God to get **r**
10:19 a pledge that they would get **r**
Psa 73:20 As ⌊someone⌋ gets **r** of a
73:20 get **r** of the thought of them
101:8 wicked people in the land to **r**
119:119 You get **r** of all wicked people
Ecc 11:10 Get **r** of what troubles you or
Isa 1:25 I will get **r** of all your impurities.
36:7 and altars Hezekiah got **r** of.
50:1 I give her any to get **r** of her?
50:1 I got **r** of your mother because
58:9 Get **r** of that yoke. Don't point
Jer 4:4 and get **r** of the foreskins of
Eze 20:7 I said to them, "Get **r** of the
20:8 Not one of them got **r** of the
20:38 I will get **r** of rebels and those
21:26 and get **r** of your crown.
Hos 8:5 Get **r** of your calf-shaped idol,
Zec 11:8 I got **r** of three shepherds in one
Rom 13:12 So we should get **r** of the
Gal 4:30 "Get **r** of the slave woman and
Eph 4:25 So then, get **r** of lies.
4:31 Get **r** of your bitterness,
Col 3:8 Also get **r** of your anger,
3:9 You've gotten **r** of the person
Heb 12:1 we must get **r** of everything that
Jas 1:21 So get **r** of all immoral behavior
1Pe 2:1 So get **r** of every kind of evil,
1Jn 4:18 perfect love gets **r** of fear,

ridden (2)

Num 22:30 You've always **r** me.
Est 6:8 and a horse that the king has **r**,

riddle (10)

Jdg 14:12 "Let me tell you a **r**.
14:13 responded, "Tell us your **r**!
14:14 days they couldn't solve the **r**.
14:15 into solving the **r** for us.
14:16 You gave my friends a **r** and
14:17 her friends the answer to the **r**.
14:18 you wouldn't know my **r** now."
14:19 to the men who solved the **r**.
Psa 49:4 I will explain my **r** with the
Eze 17:2 "Son of man, tell this **r**.

riddles (6)

Num 12:8 plainly and not in **r**.
1Ki 10:1 So she came to test him with **r**.
2Ch 9:1 to Jerusalem to test him with **r**.
Pro 1:6 of wise people and their **r**.
Dan 5:12 solve **r**, and untangle problems.
Hab 2:6 clever sayings and **r** at him,

ride (25)

Gen 41:43 He had him **r** in the chariot of
Dtr 32:13 He made them **r** on the heights
Jdg 5:10 You people who **r** on brown
2Sm 16:2 are for the king's family to **r** on,"
19:26 and I'll **r** on it and go with the
2Ki 10:16 had Jehonadab **r** on his chariot.
19:23 "With my many chariots I'll **r** up
Est 6:9 to reward and have him **r**
6:11 robe on Mordecai and had him **r**
Psa 45:4 **R** on victoriously in your
66:12 You let people **r** over our heads.
68:4 Make a highway for him to **r**
Isa 30:16 "We'll **r** on fast horses."
37:24 "With my many chariots I'll **r** up
58:14 I will make you **r** on the heights
Jer 6:23 They **r** on horses. They march
17:25 They and their princes will **r** in
22:4 on David's throne will **r** through
50:42 They will **r** horses.
Eze 23:23 All of them **r** on horses.
38:15 All of you will **r** on horses.
Hos 14:3 We won't **r** on horses anymore.
Hab 3:8 ⌊why⌋ do you **r** your horses,
Zec 10:5 shame those who **r** on horses.
Act 23:24 Provide an animal for Paul to **r**,

rider (9)

Gen 49:17 so that its **r** falls off backwards.
Job 39:18 It laughs at the horse and its **r**
Zec 12:4 and every **r** with madness.
Rev 6:2 and its **r** had a bow.
6:4 Its **r** was given the power to
6:5 and its **r** held a scale.
19:11 and its **r** is named Faithful and
19:19 to wage war against the **r**
19:21 The **r** on the horse killed the

rider's (1)

Rev 6:8 and its **r** name was Death.

riders (18)

Exo 15:1 horses and their **r** into the sea.
15:21 horses and their **r** into the sea."
2Ki 18:23 horses if you can put **r** on them.
Psa 76:6 chariot **r** and horses were put to
Isa 21:7 of horsemen, **r** on donkeys,
21:7 on donkeys, and **r** on camels.
36:8 horses if you can put **r** on them.
Jer 4:29 at the sound of **r** and archers.
51:21 you to crush horses and their **r**.
Eze 38:4 forces, with horses and **r**.
39:20 will be filled with horses and **r**,
Hab 1:8 Their **r** will gallop along
1:8 Their **r** will come from far away.
Hag 2:22 overthrow chariots and their **r**,
2:22 will fall along with their **r**.
Rev 9:17 the horses and their **r** looked
9:17 The **r** had breastplates that
19:18 warriors, horses and their **r**,

rides (4)

Dtr 33:26 He **r** through the heavens to
33:26 he **r** through the clouds.
Psa 68:33 God **r** through the ancient
Zec 9:9 He is humble and **r** on a

ridge (2)

Gen 48:22 mountain **r** than your brothers.
Psa 48:2 Mount Zion is on the northern **r**

ridges (1)

Jos 17:11 last three are on mountain **r**.

ridicule (24)

Exo 32:25 and they became an object of **r**
Dtr 28:37 an example of you and **r** you.
1Ki 9:7 an example and an object of **r**
2Ch 7:20 it an example and an object of **r**
29:8 people and that people **r**,
Psa 44:13 our neighbors and an object of **r**
69:11 but I became the object of **r**.
73:8 They **r**. They speak maliciously.
79:4 an object of **r** and contempt to
102:8 Those who **r** me use my name
123:4 our share of **r** from those who
Isa 43:28 I will set up Israel for **r**.
51:7 Don't be discouraged by their **r**.
Eze 5:14 and an object of **r** among
5:15 that are around you will **r** you
Hos 7:16 in Egypt will **r** them for this.
Joe 2:17 Don't let the nations **r** them.
Hab 2:6 Won't all of them **r** him,
1Ti 5:14 enemy any chance to **r** them.
1Pe 2:12 Then, although they **r** you as if
3:9 or **r** those who ridicule you.
3:9 or ridicule those who **r** you.
2Pe 3:3 people will **r** ⌊God's promise⌋
Jud 1:18 "In the last times people who **r**

ridiculed (14)

2Ch 30:10 But the people **r** them.
Neh 2:19 they made fun of us and **r** us.
Jer 24:9 They will become something **r**
25:9 something terrible, something **r**
25:18 something **r** and cursed,
29:18 cursed, **r**, and hissed at,
42:18 You will become something **r**,
44:8 and be cursed and **r** by all
44:12 cursed, **r**, and disgraced.
48:39 Moab has become something **r**
49:13 horrifying, **r**, ruined, and cursed
Eze 5:15 you will become something **r**
Mic 6:16 Your people will be **r**.
1Pe 3:16 ashamed that they have **r** you.

ridiculing (1)

Neh 5:9 to keep our enemies from **r** us?

ridiculous (1)

Act 25:27 I find it **r** to send a prisoner to

riding (11)

Gen 24:61 **R** on camels, they followed the
Num 22:22 Balaam was **r** on his donkey,
1Sm 25:20 She was **r** on her donkey down

2Sm 18:9 He was **r** on a mule,
Neh 2:12 I had was the one I was **r**.
2:14 I was **r** couldn't get through.
Isa 19:1 The LORD is **r** on a
Zec 1:8 During that night I saw a man **r**
Mat 21:5 He's gentle, **r** on a donkey,
Luk 19:36 As he was **r** along,
Jon 12:15 He is **r** on a donkey's colt."

right (561)

Gen 2:18 make a helper who is **r** for him."
2:20 no helper who was **r** for him.
13:9 you go to the left, I'll go to the **r**,
13:9 and if you go to the **r**,
16:5 May the LORD decide who is **r**
18:19 by doing what is **r** and just.
24:48 The LORD led me in the **r**
31:37 decide which one of us is **r**.
31:42 and last night he made it **r**."
32:18 Jacob is **r** behind us.'"
32:20 'Jacob is **r** behind us,
35:18 Benjamin [Son of My **R** Hand].
42:24 Simeon and had him arrested **r**
42:27 money was **r** inside his sack.
42:28 It's **r** here in my sack!"
45:9 Come here to me **r** away!
47:15 "Do you want us to die **r** in front
47:19 Do you want us to die **r** in front
48:13 both of them, Ephraim on his **r**,
48:13 on his left, facing Israel's **r**,
48:14 He put his **r** hand on Ephraim's
48:17 his father had put his **r** hand
48:18 his father, "That's not **r**, Father!
48:18 Put your **r** hand on his head."
Exo 8:26 "It wouldn't be **r** to do that.
9:27 "The LORD is **r**, and my
10:29 "You're **r**!" Moses answered.
14:22 stood like a wall on their **r**
14:29 stood like a wall on their **r**
15:6 Your **r** hand, O LORD,
15:6 Your **r** hand, O LORD,
15:12 You stretched out your **r** hand.
15:26 and do what he considers **r**,
18:16 I decide which person is **r**,
21:8 He has no **r** to sell her to
23:8 to those who are in the **r**.
29:20 and put it on the **r** ear lobes of
29:20 and his sons, on their **r** thumbs,
29:20 on the big toes of their **r** feet.
29:22 the fat on them, and the **r** thigh.
Lev 7:32 give the priest the **r** thigh as
7:33 the **r** thigh will belong to him as
8:23 and put it on Aaron's **r** ear lobe,
8:23 right ear lobe, on his **r** thumb,
8:23 and on the big toe of his **r** foot.
8:24 of the blood on their **r** ear lobes,
8:24 ear lobes, on their **r** thumbs,
8:24 on the big toes of their **r** feet.
8:25 with their fat, and the **r** thigh.
8:26 He put them on the fat and the **r**
9:21 the breasts and the **r** thighs
14:14 and put it on the **r** ear lobe,
14:14 right ear lobe, on the **r** thumb,
14:14 and on the big toe of the **r** foot
14:16 He will dip his **r** finger in the oil
14:17 in his hand on the **r** ear lobe,
14:17 right ear lobe, on the **r** thumb,
14:17 and on the big toe of the **r** foot
14:25 and put it on the **r** ear lobe,
14:25 right ear lobe, on the **r** thumb,
14:25 and on the big toe of the **r** foot
14:27 With his **r** finger he will
14:28 is in his hand on the **r** ear lobe,
14:28 right ear lobe, on the **r** thumb,
14:28 and on the big toe of the **r** foot
25:24 People must always have the **r**
25:29 year after selling it he has the **r**
25:32 "The Levites always have the **r**
25:48 he has the **r** to be bought back.
26:4 will give you rain at the **r** time.
Num 9:13 to the LORD at the **r** time.
18:18 like the breast and the **r** thigh
20:8 **R** before their eyes,
22:26 room to turn to the **r** or the left.
22:29 in my hand, I'd kill you **r** now."
22:36 **r** on the border of Moab.
Num 25:6 He did this **r** in front of Moses
27:7 "Zelophehad's daughters are **r**.
28:2 me my offerings at the **r** times.
36:5 of Joseph's descendants is **r**.
Dtr 6:18 LORD considers **r** and good.
6:22 **R** before our eyes the LORD
9:4 "Because we've been living **r**,
9:5 because you've been living **r**
9:6 you've been living **r** that
9:12 He told me, "Leave **r** away.
11:14 rain on your land at the **r** time,
12:8 does whatever he considers **r**.
12:25 what the LORD considers **r**.
12:28 your God considers good and **r**.
13:18 and do what he considers **r**.
16:19 to those who are in the **r**.
21:9 what the LORD considers **r**.
24:13 You will have done the **r** thing
25:1 who's **r** and who's wrong.
28:12 rain on your land at the **r** time
33:2 On his **r** was a raging fire for
Jos 8:33 **R** from the beginning,
9:6 Make a treaty with us **r** now."
9:11 Make a treaty with us **r** now."'
9:25 what you think is good and **r**."
23:5 your God will expel them **r**
24:17 signs **r** before our eyes.
Jdg 3:16 He fastened it to his **r** side
3:21 took the dagger from his **r** side,
7:20 horns in their **r** hands so that
10:15 to us whatever you think is **r**.
11:23 So what **r** do you have to take
11:27 whether Israel or Ammon is **r**."
16:29 With his **r** hand on one column
17:6 did whatever he considered **r**.
20:7 Give me your advice **r** now!"
21:25 did whatever he considered **r**.
1Sm 2:28 And I gave your ancestors the **r**
3:18 May he do what he thinks is **r**."
6:12 the road and didn't turn **r** or left.
11:1 He would poke out everyone's **r**
11:1 River whose **r** eye King Nahash
11:2 I'll poke out everyone's **r** eye
11:10 to us whatever you think is **r**."
12:16 going to do **r** before your eyes.
12:23 you the way that is good and **r**.
17:17 brothers in the camp **r** away.
20:31 neither you nor your **r** to be king
24:4 think is **r**.'" David quietly got up
2Sm 8:15 He did what was fair and **r** for
10:12 will do what he considers **r**."
14:17 to distinguish **r** from wrong.
14:19 you are absolutely **r**.
15:14 Let's leave **r** away,
15:26 do to me what he considers **r**."
17:21 "Leave **r** away," they told
19:27 Do what you think is **r**.
19:28 So I no longer have the **r** to
19:37 do for him what you think is **r**."
20:9 Amasa's beard with his **r** hand
24:22 offer whatever you think is **r**.
1Ki 2:19 and she sat at his **r** side.
3:11 so that you can do what is **r**.
3:28 from God to do what was **r**.
7:21 He set up the pillar on the **r** and
8:45 and do what is **r** ⌊for them⌋.
8:49 Do what is **r** for them.
11:33 He did not do what I consider **r**
11:38 and do what I consider **r** by
14:8 doing only what I considered **r**.
14:14 It will happen **r** now.
15:5 what the LORD considered **r**:
15:11 what the LORD considered **r**,
22:19 near him on his **r** and his left.
22:43 what the LORD considered **r**.
2Ki 1:11 Come here **r** away!"
2:8 divided to their left and their **r**,
2:14 it divided to his left and his **r**,
7:9 "What we're doing is not **r**.
10:30 "You did what I consider **r**,
12:2 what the LORD considered **r**,
12:9 and put it at the **r** side of the
14:3 what the LORD considered **r**,
15:3 what the LORD considered **r**,
15:34 what the LORD considered **r**,
16:2 LORD his God considered **r**,
2Ki 17:9 LORD their God that weren't **r**:
18:3 what the LORD considered **r**,
20:3 I've done what you consider **r**.
22:2 what the LORD considered **r**.
1Ch 6:39 relative Asaph stood on his **r**.
12:2 shoot arrows with either their **r**
13:4 considered it the **r** thing to do.
18:14 He did what was fair and **r** for
19:13 will do what he considers **r**."
21:23 and do whatever you think is **r**.
2Ch 3:17 one on the **r** and the other on
3:17 He named the one on the **r**
6:35 and do what is **r** ⌊for them⌋.
6:39 Do what is **r** for them.
12:6 "The LORD is **r**!" they said.
14:2 his God considered good and **r**.
18:18 standing on his **r** and his left.
19:11 LORD be with those who do **r**."
20:32 what the LORD considered **r**.
24:2 what the LORD considered **r**,
25:2 what the LORD considered **r**,
26:4 what the LORD considered **r**,
26:18 you have no **r** to burn incense
26:18 That **r** belongs to the priests,
27:2 what the LORD considered **r**,
28:1 what the LORD considered **r**,
29:2 what the LORD considered **r**,
30:4 their plan to be the **r** thing to do.
31:20 He did what was good and **r**
34:2 what the LORD considered **r**.
Ezr 4:3 It isn't **r** for your people and our
4:14 it isn't **r** for us to watch
7:18 may do whatever you think is **r**
Neh 2:20 or historic **r** in Jerusalem."
4:11 we will be **r** in the middle of
8:4 stood beside him on his **r**.
12:31 One choir went to the **r** on the
Est 4:2 He even went **r** up to the king's
5:5 "Bring Haman **r** away,
Job 5:26 a stack of hay in the **r** season.
6:29 because I am still **r** about this!
6:30 between **r** and wrong?
9:14 How can I find the **r** words ⌊to
9:15 Even if I were **r**, I could not
11:13 "If you want to set your heart **r**,
27:5 for me to admit that you are **r**.
30:12 They have attacked me on my **r**
32:11 until you could find the **r** words.
33:12 You aren't **r** about this!
33:23 to tell people what is **r** for them,
33:27 wrong instead of what was **r**,
33:32 I'd be happy if you were **r**.
34:4 decide for ourselves what is **r**
35:2 "Do you think this is **r** when
38:32 the constellations at the **r** time
40:14 because your **r** hand can save
42:7 speak what is **r** about me as
42:8 you didn't speak what is **r**
Psa 18:35 Your **r** hand supports me.
25:9 humble people to do what is **r**,
26:10 Their **r** hands are full of bribes.
44:3 It was your **r** hand,
45:4 Let your **r** hand teach you
45:7 You have loved what is **r** and
45:9 takes her place at your **r** hand
48:10 Your **r** hand is filled with
51:19 offered in the **r** spirit —
59:3 lie in ambush for me **r** here!
63:8 Your **r** hand supports me.
73:23 You hold on to my **r** hand.
74:11 especially your **r** hand?
75:2 When I choose the **r** time,
80:15 of what your **r** hand planted,
89:13 Your **r** hand is lifted high.
89:25 hand on the sea and his **r** hand
89:42 You held the **r** hand of his
91:7 or ten thousand at your **r** side.
98:1 His **r** hand and his holy arm
99:4 what is fair and **r** for Jacob.
103:6 The LORD does what is **r** and
104:27 them their food at the **r** time.
106:3 and do what is **r** at all times.
110:5 The Lord is at your **r** side.
118:15 The **r** hand of the LORD
118:16 The **r** hand of the LORD is held
118:16 The **r** hand of the LORD

Psa 119:75 and that you were **r** to make me
119:121 I have done what is fair and **r**.
119:144 instructions are always **r**.
121:5 is the shade over your **r** hand.
137:5 let my **r** hand forget ⌞how to
138:7 and your **r** hand saves me.
139:10 me and your **r** hand would hold
142:4 Look to my **r** and see that no
144:8 Their **r** hands take false
144:11 Their **r** hands take false
Pro 2:9 you will understand what is **r**
3:16 life is in ⌞wisdom's⌟ **r** hand.
4:27 Do not lean to the **r** or to the left.
8:6 and my lips will say what is **r**.
8:9 who has understanding and **r**
12:15 his own way the **r** one,
14:2 Whoever lives **r** fears the
14:12 There is a way that seems **r** to
15:10 who leaves the ⌞**r**⌟ path.
16:13 speaks what is **r** is loved.
16:25 There is a way that seems **r** to
17:26 down noble people is not **r**.
18:17 seems **r** ⌞until⌟ his neighbor
20:11 whether his deeds are pure or **r**.
21:2 thinks everything he does is **r**,
21:3 Doing what is **r** and fair is more
23:16 when you speak what is **r**.
23:19 mind going in the **r** direction.
24:6 After all, with the **r** strategy you
25:11 ⌞so⌟ is a word spoken at the **r**
26:1 so honor is not **r** for a fool.
27:16 up olive oil with his **r** hand.
28:11 sees **r** through him.
Ecc 3:11 done everything at the **r** time.
8:5 person will know the **r** time
8:5 time and the **r** way ⌞to act⌟.
8:6 There is a **r** time and a right
8:6 There is a right time and a **r**
10:2 person's heart leads the **r** way.
10:17 high officials eat at the **r** time
12:10 tried to find just the **r** words.
Sos 1:4 How **r** it is that the young
2:6 His **r** hand caresses me.
8:3 His **r** hand caresses me.
Isa 1:7 Your fields are destroyed **r**
5:16 holy when he does what is **r**.
9:20 On the **r**, one gobbles up food
13:16 to death **r** before their eyes.
16:5 He is quick to do what is **r**.
22:16 What **r** do you have to dig a
22:16 What **r** do you have to cut it out
22:16 What **r** do you have to carve
26:9 the world learn to do what is **r**.
26:10 do not learn to do what is **r**.
29:21 to people who are in the **r**.
30:10 visions that tell us what is **r**.
30:21 whether it turns to the **r** or to
33:15 The person who does what is **r**
38:3 I've done what you consider **r**.
40:14 Who taught him the **r** way?
41:10 you with my victorious **r** hand.
41:13 hold your **r** hand and say to
41:26 we could say that he was **r**?
42:6 have called you to do what is **r**.
42:21 because he does what is **r**.
43:9 to prove that they were **r**.
43:26 so that you can prove you are **r**.
44:20 "Isn't what I hold in my **r** hand a
45:1 I have held him by his **r** hand
45:19 what is fair and say what is **r**.
48:13 My **r** hand stretched out the
51:1 people who pursue what is **r**
54:3 will spread out to the **r** and left.
56:1 justice, and do what is **r**.
58:2 a nation that has done what is **r**
60:22 At the **r** time I, the LORD,
62:8 The LORD has sworn with his **r**
63:12 arm to support the **r** hand
64:5 the one who gladly does **r**
Jer 1:12 Then the LORD said to me, "**R**.
4:2 in an honest, fair, and **r** way,
5:1 find anyone who does what is **r**
5:24 He sends rain at the **r** time,
11:15 "What **r** do these people I love
12:1 you would always be **r**.
22:3 Judge fairly, and do what is **r**.

Jer 22:15 drank and did what is fair and **r**.
22:24 the signet ring on my **r** hand,
23:5 do what is fair and **r** in the land.
26:14 you think is good and **r**.
33:15 do what is fair and **r** in the land.
34:15 and did what I consider **r**.
35:15 your evil ways, do what is **r**,
48:30 the LORD, "but it isn't **r**.
Lam 1:18 "The LORD is **r** in what he did,
2:3 He withdrew his **r** hand when
2:4 Like an opponent his **r** hand
Eze 1:10 From the **r**, each one had the
3:20 turn from living the **r** way
3:20 and the **r** things they did will
4:6 this time on your **r** side.
18:5 person does what is fair and **r**.
18:19 son has done what is fair and **r**.
18:21 and does what is fair and **r**.
18:22 He will live because of the **r**
18:24 person turns away from doing **r**
18:24 All the **r** things that he has
18:26 person turns away from doing **r**
18:27 and does what is fair and **r**,
21:16 Sword, cut to the **r**.
21:22 that he should go to the **r**,
33:12 'The **r** things that a righteous
33:13 But if he trusts in the **r** things
33:13 none of the **r** things that he has
33:14 sin and does what is fair and **r**.
33:16 He has done what is fair and **r**.
33:18 turns from the **r** things that
33:19 and does what is fair and **r**,
34:26 I will send rain at the **r** time.
39:3 drop the arrows in your **r** hand.
45:9 and do what is fair and **r**.
Dan 4:27 stop sinning, and do what is **r**.
4:37 he does is true, his ways are **r**,
12:7 He raised his **r** hand and left
Hos 14:9 The LORD's ways are **r**.
Joe 1:16 Food disappears **r** before our
Amo 3:10 don't know how to do what is **r**,
Jnh 4:4 The LORD asked, "What **r** do
4:9 asked Jonah, "What **r** do you
4:9 answered, "I have every **r**
4:11 tell their **r** hand from their
Mic 3:9 and pervert everything that is **r**.
6:8 to do what is **r**, to love mercy,
Hab 2:4 He is not **r** in himself.
2:16 The cup in the LORD's **r** hand
Zep 2:3 Search for what is **r**.
3:20 fortunes **r** before your eyes,"
Hag 1:2 These people say it's not the **r**
Zec 3:1 was standing at Joshua's **r** side
4:3 one on the **r** of the bowl and the
4:11 do these two olive trees at the **r**
11:17 strike his arm and his **r** eye.
11:17 His **r** eye will be completely
12:6 the surrounding nations to the **r**
Mat 5:29 "So if your **r** eye causes you to
5:30 And if your **r** hand leads you to
5:39 slaps you on your **r** cheek,
6:3 what your **r** hand is doing.
11:19 is proved **r** by its actions."
12:2 doing something that is not **r**
12:4 He and his men had no **r** to eat
12:4 Only the priests have that **r**.
12:10 asked Jesus whether it was **r**
12:12 So it is **r** to do good on the day
14:4 "It's not **r** for you to be married
15:7 Isaiah was **r** when he
15:26 Jesus replied, "It's not **r** to take
15:27 She said, "You're **r**,
20:4 I'll give you whatever is **r**.' So
20:21 one of my sons will sit at your **r**
20:23 grant you a seat at my **r** or left.
21:23 "What gives you the **r** to do
21:24 I'll tell you why I have the **r** to
21:25 Did John's **r** to baptize come
21:27 I won't tell you why I have the **r**
22:17 Is it **r** to pay taxes to the
24:45 servants their food at the **r** time.
25:33 He will put the sheep on his **r**
25:34 king will say to those on his **r**,
26:41 You want to do what's **r**,
27:6 "It's not **r** to put it into the
27:29 and put a stick in his **r** hand.

Mat 27:38 one on his **r** and the other on
Mar 2:26 He had no **r** to eat those loaves.
2:26 Only the priests have that **r**.
3:4 Then he asked them, "Is it **r** to
5:15 there dressed and in his **r** mind.
6:18 "It's not **r** for you to be married
7:6 Jesus told them, "Isaiah was **r**
7:27 It's not **r** to take the children's
10:37 "Let one of us sit at your **r** and
10:40 grant you a seat at my **r** or left.
11:28 "What gives you the **r** to do
11:29 then I'll tell you why I have the **r**
11:30 Did John's **r** to baptize come
11:33 I won't tell you why I have the **r**
12:2 "At the **r** time he sent a servant
12:14 Is it **r** to pay taxes to the
14:38 You want to do what's **r**,
15:27 one on his **r** and the other on
16:5 robe and sat on the **r** side.
Luk 1:11 to the **r** of the incense altar,
1:20 will come true at the **r** time."
4:30 But Jesus walked **r** by them
6:2 doing something that is not **r**
6:4 He had no **r** to eat those loaves.
6:4 Only the priests have that **r**."
6:6 A man whose **r** hand was
6:9 "I ask you — what is the **r** thing
7:29 They admitted that God was **r**
7:35 "Yet, wisdom is proved **r** by all
7:43 Jesus said to him, "You're **r**!"
8:35 Dressed and in his **r** mind,
10:5 greet the family **r** away with the
10:28 Jesus told him, "You're **r**!
10:42 Mary has made the **r** choice,
12:42 their share of food at the **r** time?
12:57 judge for yourselves what is **r**?
13:16 Isn't it **r** to free her on the day of
14:3 "Is it **r** to heal on the day of
20:2 what gives you the **r** to do
20:4 did John's **r** to baptize come
20:7 who gave John the **r** to baptize.
20:8 I won't tell you why I have the **r**
20:10 "At the **r** time he sent a servant
20:19 wanted to arrest him **r** there,
20:21 we know that you're **r** in what
20:22 Is it **r** for us to pay taxes to the
22:50 of the disciples cut off the **r** ear
22:70 "You're **r** to say that I am."
23:33 one on his **r** and the other on
Jon 1:12 However, he gave the **r** to
4:17 Jesus told her, "You're **r** when
5:17 "My Father is working **r** now,
5:30 My judgments are **r** because I
7:6 "Now is not the **r** time for me to
7:6 Any time is **r** for you.
7:8 not going to this festival **r** now.
7:8 Now is not the **r** time for me to
8:48 "Aren't we **r** when we say that
13:13 and you're **r** because that's
18:10 and cut off the servant's **r** ear.
21:6 "Throw the net out on the **r** side
Act 3:7 Peter took hold of the man's **r**
6:2 "It's not **r** for us to give up
10:35 does what is **r** is acceptable
15:29 you will be doing what's **r**.
15:38 Paul didn't think it was **r** to take
Rom 2:2 that God's judgment is **r** when
2:18 and distinguish **r** from wrong
5:6 at it this way: At the **r** time,
7:12 is holy, **r**, and good.
7:18 have the desire to do what is **r**,
9:9 "I will come back at the **r** time,
9:21 A potter has the **r** to do
11:20 That's **r**! They were broken off
12:19 "I alone have the **r** to take
13:3 People who do what is **r** don't
13:3 Do what is **r**, and it will praise
13:4 The government has the **r** to
14:21 The **r** thing to do is to avoid
14:22 knows is **r** shouldn't feel guilty.
15:17 So Christ Jesus gives me the **r**
15:25 **R** now I'm going to Jerusalem
1Co 4:13 **R** now we have become
9:4 Don't we have the **r** to eat and
9:5 Don't we have the **r** to take our
9:12 If others have the **r** to expect

1Co 14:29 each person said is **r** or wrong.
14:34 They don't have the **r** to speak.
15:34 Come back to the **r** point of
16:7 **R** now all I could do is visit
2Co 6:2 "At the **r** time I heard you.
6:8 and as we use what is **r** to
6:14 Can **r** and wrong be partners?
8:21 We intend to do what is **r**,
8:24 congregations that we were **r**
13:7 want you to do whatever is **r**,
Gal 4:4 But when the **r** time came,
4:20 I wish I were with you **r** now so
6:9 to get tired of living the **r** way.
Eph 5:4 It's not **r** that dirty stories,
6:1 This is the **r** thing to do.
6:19 God will give me the **r** words
Php 1:7 So it's **r** for me to think this way
4:8 your thoughts on whatever is **r**
1Th 2:7 apostles of Christ we had the **r**
5:14 those who are not living **r**,
2Th 1:3 It's **r** to do this because your
1:5 proves that God's judgment is **r**
1:6 Certainly, it is **r** for God to give
1:7 It is also **r** for God to give all of
2:2 Don't get upset **r** away or
3:9 not as though we didn't have a **r**
3:13 to get tired of doing what is **r**.
1Ti 6:15 At the **r** time God will make
2Ti 4:2 whether or not the time is **r**.
Phm 1:8 to order you to do the **r** thing.
Heb 1:9 You have loved what is **r** and
2:10 it was the **r** time to bring Jesus,
4:16 which will help us at the **r** time.
5:13 to talk about what is **r**.
10:30 "I alone have the **r** to take
12:11 comes from doing what is **r**.
13:10 who serve at the tent have no **r**
Jas 2:8 You are doing **r** if you obey this
3:13 Show this by living the **r** way
4:17 Whoever knows what is **r** but
1Pe 2:14 and to praise those who do **r**.
2:15 people by doing what is **r**.
5:6 so that when the **r** time comes
2Pe 1:13 I think it's **r** to refresh your
1Jn 3:10 who doesn't do what is **r**
Rev 1:16 In his **r** hand he held seven
1:17 Then he laid his **r** hand on me
1:20 stars that you saw in my **r** hand
2:1 the seven stars in his **r** hand,
5:1 I saw a scroll in the **r** hand of
5:7 He took the scroll from the **r**
10:2 He set his **r** foot on the sea and
10:5 raised his **r** hand to heaven.
13:16 to be branded on their **r** hands
22:14 so that they may have the **r**

righteous (214)

Gen 7:1 that you alone are **r** among
1Sm 12:7 LORD and cite all the **r** things
24:17 "You are more **r** than I.
26:23 person who is **r** and faithful.
Job 4:17 'Can ⌊any⌋ mortal be **r** to God?
9:2 a mortal be declared **r** to God?
9:20 If I am **r**, my own mouth would
10:15 Even if I'm **r**, I dare not lift up
12:4 of integrity, a man who is **r**,
13:18 I know that I will be declared **r**.
15:14 of a woman be considered **r**?
17:9 the **r** person clings to his way,
22:3 pleased when you are **r**?
22:19 The **r** saw it and were glad,
25:4 How can a person be **r** to God?
27:17 **r** people will wear what he
32:1 because Job thought he was **r**.
32:2 he was more **r** than God.
34:5 because Job has said, 'I'm **r**,
34:17 the one who is **r** and mighty?
34:19 The one who is **r** and mighty
35:7 If you're **r**, what can you give
36:7 take his eyes off **r** people.
36:8 However, if **r** people are bound
36:11 "If **r** people listen and serve
40:8 me so that you can be **r**?
Psa 1:5 to stand where **r** people gather.
1:6 knows the way of **r** people,
5:12 You bless **r** people,
Psa 7:9 but make the **r** person secure,
7:9 O **r** God who examines
11:3 what can a **r** person do?"
11:5 The LORD tests **r** people,
11:7 The LORD is **r**. He loves a
11:7 He loves a **r** way of life.
14:5 is with the person who is **r**.
15:2 with integrity, does what is **r**,
31:18 since they speak against **r**
32:11 joy in the LORD, you **r** people.
33:1 sing to the LORD, you **r** people.
34:15 LORD's eyes are on **r** people.
34:17 ⌊**R** people⌋ cry out.
34:19 The **r** person has many
34:21 and those who hate **r** people
37:12 person plots against a **r** one
37:16 The little that the **r** person has
37:17 continues to support **r** people.
37:21 A **r** person is generous and
37:25 but I have never seen a **r**
37:29 **R** people will inherit the land
37:30 The mouth of the **r** person
37:32 person watches the **r** person
37:39 The victory for **r** people comes
52:6 **R** people will see ⌊this⌋ and
55:22 never let the **r** person stumble.
58:10 **R** people will rejoice when
58:11 Then people will say, "**R**
64:10 **R** people will find joy in the
68:3 But let **r** people rejoice.
69:28 Do not let them be listed with **r**
72:7 May **r** people blossom in his
75:10 but the weapons of **r** people
92:12 **R** people flourish like palm
94:21 to take the lives of **r** people.
97:11 Light dawns for **r** people and
97:12 joy in the LORD, you **r** people.
106:31 was considered **r** forever,
112:6 A **r** person will always be
116:5 The LORD is merciful and **r**.
118:15 is heard in the tents of **r** people.
118:20 which **r** people will enter.
119:123 the fulfillment of your **r** promise
119:137 You are **r**, O LORD, and your
119:160 **r** regulations endure forever.
119:164 you for your **r** regulations.
125:3 the land set aside for **r** people.
125:3 That is why **r** people do not
129:4 The LORD is **r**. He has cut me
140:13 Indeed, **r** people will give
141:5 A **r** person may strike me or
142:7 **R** people will surround me
143:1 because you are faithful and **r**.
143:2 alive who is **r** in your presence.
143:11 Because you are **r**,
146:8 The LORD loves **r** people.
Pro 2:20 stay on the paths of **r** people.
3:33 but he blesses the home of **r**
4:18 But the path of **r** people is like
9:9 Teach a **r** person, and he will
10:3 The LORD will not allow a **r**
10:6 cover the head of a **r** person,
10:7 The name of a **r** person
10:11 The mouth of a **r** person is a
10:16 A **r** person's reward is life.
10:20 The tongue of a **r** person is
10:21 The lips of a **r** person feed
10:24 grants the desire of **r** people.
10:25 but the **r** person has an
10:28 The hope of **r** people ⌊leads
10:30 A **r** person will never be moved,
10:31 The mouth of a **r** person
10:32 The lips of a **r** person
11:8 A **r** person is rescued from
11:9 but **r** people are rescued by
11:10 When **r** people prosper,
11:21 of **r** people will escape.
11:23 The desire of **r** people ends
11:28 but **r** people will flourish like a
11:30 The fruit of a **r** person is a tree
11:31 If the **r** person is rewarded on
12:3 and the roots of **r** people cannot
12:5 The thoughts of **r** people are
12:7 but the families of **r** people
12:10 A **r** person cares ⌊even⌋ about
12:12 of **r** people produce ⌊fruit⌋.
Pro 12:13 but a **r** person escapes from
12:21 harm comes to a **r** person,
12:26 A **r** person looks out for his
13:5 A **r** person hates lying,
13:9 The light of **r** people beams
13:21 but **r** people are rewarded with
13:22 is stored away for a **r** person.
13:25 A **r** person eats to satisfy his
14:19 bow at the gates of a **r** person.
14:32 but even in his death a **r**
15:6 is in the house of a **r** person,
15:28 The heart of a **r** person
15:29 but he hears the prayers of **r**
16:31 beautiful crown found in a **r** life.
17:15 **r** people is disgusting
18:10 A **r** person runs to it and is safe.
20:7 A **r** person lives on the basis of
21:12 A **r** person wisely considers
21:15 a **r** person is delighted,
21:18 become a ransom for **r** people,
21:26 but a **r** person gives and does
23:24 A **r** person's father will certainly
24:15 at the home of a **r** person.
24:16 A **r** person may fall seven
25:26 ⌊so⌋ is a **r** person who gives in
28:1 but **r** people are as bold as
28:12 When **r** people triumph,
28:28 they die, **r** people increase.
29:2 When **r** people increase,
29:6 but a **r** person runs away from it
29:7 A **r** person knows the just
29:16 but **r** people will witness their
29:27 is disgusting to **r** people.
Ecc 3:17 "God will judge **r** people as
7:15 **R** people die in spite of being
7:15 people die in spite of being **r**.
7:20 Certainly, there is no one so **r**
8:14 **R** people suffer for what the
8:14 people get what the **r** deserve.
9:1 **R** people and wise people,
9:2 whether they are **r**,
Isa 1:26 you will be called the **R** City,
3:10 Tell the **r** that blessings will
5:23 who take away the rights of **r**
24:16 of praise that honor the **R** One.
26:2 and let the **r** nation come in,
26:7 The path of the **r** is level.
26:7 you make the road of the **r**
45:13 Cyrus for my **r** purpose.
45:21 There is no other **r** God and
45:23 A word has gone out from my **r**
45:25 of Israel will be declared **r**,
46:12 people who are far from being **r**.
53:11 My **r** servant will acquit many
57:1 **R** people die, and no one
57:1 **R** people are spared when evil
57:12 I'll tell you about your **r** ways
60:21 Then all your people will be **r**,
64:6 and all our **r** acts are like
Jer 20:12 of Armies examines the **r**.
23:5 "when I will grow a **r** branch for
33:15 I will cause a **r** branch to spring
Lam 4:13 the blood of **r** people within it.
Eze 3:20 If **r** people turn from living the
3:21 But if you warn **r** people not to
13:22 You have discouraged **r** people
18:5 "Suppose a **r** person does what
18:9 This person is **r**. He will
18:20 The righteousness of the **r**
18:24 "But suppose a **r** person turns
18:26 When a **r** person turns away
21:3 scabbard and kill the **r** people
21:4 I'm going to kill the **r** people
23:45 **R** people will punish these
33:12 'The right things that a **r** person
33:12 The **r** person will not live when
33:13 I may promise the **r** person that
33:18 If the **r** person turns from the
Dan 9:7 You, Lord, are **r**. But we — the
9:14 you are **r** in everything you do.
9:16 Lord, since you are very **r**,
9:18 this from you because we are **r**,
Hos 14:9 **R** people live by them.
Amo 2:6 The people of Israel sell the **r**
5:12 You oppress the **r** by taking
6:12 and what is **r** into poison.

Hab 1:4 Wicked people surround **r**
1:13 who are more **r** than they are?
2:4 But the **r** person will live
Zep 3:5 The **r** LORD is in that city.
Zec 9:9 He is **r** and victorious.
Mal 3:18 the difference between **r** people
Mat 10:41 The person who welcomes a **r**
10:41 as a **r** person will receive
10:41 will receive a **r** person's reward.
23:35 from the murder of **r** Abel to
Jon 17:25 **R** Father, the world didn't know
2Co 9:9 Scripture says, "The **r** person
Eph 4:24 to be like God, truly **r** and holy.

righteousness (134)

2Sm 22:21 rewarded me because of my **r**,
22:25 paid me back because of my **r**,
1Ki 3:6 with truth, **r**, and commitment.
10:9 would maintain justice and **r**."
2Ch 9:8 would maintain justice and **r**."
Job 8:3 or does the Almighty distort **r**?
8:6 prove your **r** by rebuilding your
27:6 I cling to my **r** and won't let go.
29:14 I put on **r**, and it was my
33:26 for joy as he restores their **r**.
35:8 Your **r** affects only the
37:23 has more than enough **r**,
Psa 4:1 me when I call, O God of my **r**.
4:5 Offer the sacrifices of **r** by
5:8 O LORD, lead me in your **r**
7:8 O LORD, according to my **r**,
7:17 thanks to the LORD for his **r**.
9:8 alone judges the world with **r**.
18:20 rewarded me because of my **r**,
18:24 paid me back because of my **r**,
22:31 yet to be born about his **r** — that
23:3 guides me along the paths of **r**
24:5 from the LORD and **r** from God,
31:1 Save me because of your **r**.
33:5 The LORD loves **r** and justice.
35:24 Judge me by your **r**,
35:28 my tongue will tell about your **r**,
36:6 Your **r** is like the mountains of
36:10 those who know you and your **r**
37:6 He will make your **r** shine like
40:9 of **r** among those assembled
40:10 I have not buried your **r** deep in
45:4 cause of truth, humility, and **r**.
48:10 Your right hand is filled with **r**.
50:6 The heavens announce his **r**
51:14 sing joyfully about your **r**!
65:5 awe-inspiring acts ⌊done⌋ in **r**,
71:2 and free me because of your **r**.
71:15 My mouth will tell about your **r**,
71:16 I will praise your **r**,
71:19 Your **r** reaches to the heavens,
71:24 My tongue will tell about your **r**
72:1 and the king's son your **r**
72:2 may judge your people with **r**
72:3 the people and the hills bring **r**.
85:10 **R** and peace have kissed.
85:11 and **r** looks down from heaven.
85:13 **R** will go ahead of him and
88:12 that dark place or about your **r**
89:14 **R** and justice are the
89:16 They are joyful in your **r**
96:13 He will judge the world with **r**
97:2 **R** and justice are the
97:6 The heavens tell about his **r**,
98:2 He has uncovered his **r** for the
103:17 His **r** belongs to their children
111:3 His **r** continues forever.
112:3 His **r** continues forever.
112:9 His **r** continues forever.
118:19 Open the gates of **r** for me.
119:7 which are based on your **r**.
119:40 Give me a new life in your **r**.
119:62 which are based on your **r**.
119:106 which are based on your **r**.
119:142 Your **r** is an everlasting
119:142 is an everlasting **r**,
132:9 Clothe your priests with **r**.
145:7 will joyfully sing about your **r**.
Pro 1:3 discipline of wise behavior — **r**
2:13 who abandon the paths of **r**
8:18 lasting wealth and **r**.
Pro 8:20 I walk in the way of **r**,
10:2 but **r** rescues from death.
11:4 but **r** saves from death.
11:5 The **r** of innocent people
11:6 people are saved by their **r**,
11:18 spreads **r** earns honest pay.
11:19 As **r** leads to life, so whoever
12:28 life is on the way of **r**.
13:6 **R** protects the honest way of
14:34 **R** lifts up a nation,
15:9 he loves those who pursue **r**.
16:12 throne is established through **r**.
21:21 Whoever pursues **r** and mercy
21:21 will find life, **r**, and honor.
Ecc 3:16 where **r** should be found.
Isa 1:21 full of justice, and **r** lived in her.
1:27 be pardoned by ⌊the LORD's⌋ **r**.
5:7 for **r** but heard only cries of
9:7 uphold it with justice and **r** now
28:17 justice a measuring line and **r**
32:16 and **r** will be at home in the
32:17 Then an act of **r** will bring
33:5 will fill Zion with justice and **r**.
45:8 and pour down **r**, you skies.
45:8 Let salvation and **r** sprout.
45:24 **r** and strength are found in the
46:13 I'll bring my **r** near;
48:18 Your **r** would be like waves on
51:5 My **r** is near. My salvation is on
51:6 and my **r** will never fail.
51:7 you people who know **r**,
51:8 But my **r** will last forever,
54:14 You will be established in **r**.
56:1 My **r** is about to be revealed.
58:8 Your **r** will go ahead of you,
59:9 and **r** doesn't reach us.
59:14 and **r** stands far away.
59:16 His **r** supports him.
59:17 He puts on **r** like a coat of
60:17 governor and **r** as your ruler.
61:3 They will be called Oaks of **R**,
61:10 wrapped me in the robe of **r** like
61:11 the Almighty LORD will make **r**
62:1 until its **r** shines like the dawn
62:2 The nations will see your **r**.
Jer 9:24 love, **r**, and justice on the earth.
23:6 be given: The LORD Our **R**.
31:23 you, home of **r**, holy mountain."
33:16 be called The LORD Our **R**.
Eze 14:14 country, they would, by their **r**,
14:20 and Job could, by their **r**,
18:20 The **r** of the righteous person
Dan 9:24 to usher in everlasting **r**,
12:3 many people to **r** will shine like
Hos 10:12 Plant **r**, and harvest the fruit
10:12 he will rain **r** on you.
Joe 2:23 given you the Teacher of **R**.
Amo 5:7 and throw **r** on the ground.
5:24 flow like a river and **r** like
Mal 4:2 "The Sun of **R** will rise with
1Co 1:30 from God, our **r**, our holiness,
2Co 9:9 His **r** continues forever."
Heb 7:2 name means king of **r**.

rightful (2)

Jer 30:18 will be built in their **r** place.
Eze 21:27 until its **r** owner comes.

rights (34)

Gen 25:31 sell me your **r** as firstborn."
25:33 and sold him his **r** as firstborn.
25:34 contempt for his **r** as firstborn.
27:36 He took my **r** as firstborn,
Dtr 21:17 The **r** of the firstborn son are
Rut 4:6 Take all my **r** to buy back the
1Sm 8:9 tell them about the **r** of a king."
8:11 "These are the **r** of a king:
1Ch 5:1 his **r** as firstborn were given to
5:2 received the **r** as firstborn.)
Job 27:2 one who has taken away my **r**,
31:13 "If I have abused the **r** of my
34:5 but God has taken away my **r**.
34:6 a liar in spite of my **r**.
Psa 82:3 Protect the **r** of the oppressed
140:12 that the LORD will defend the **r**
Pro 22:22 are poor or trample on the **r**
Pro 31:8 for the **r** of those who are
31:9 and defend the **r** of oppressed
Ecc 5:8 or denied their **r** in any district.
Isa 5:23 away the **r** of righteous people.
10:2 They take away the **r** of the
40:27 and my **r** are ignored by my
Jer 5:28 no respect for the **r** of others.
5:28 no respect for the **r** of orphans.
5:28 don't defend the **r** of the poor.
32:8 because the **r** of the closest
Lam 3:35 deny people their **r** in the
Mal 3:5 deprive foreigners of their **r**.
1Co 9:6 and I who don't have any **r**,
9:12 But we haven't used our **r**.
9:15 I haven't used any of these **r**,
9:18 In that way I won't use the **r**
Heb 12:16 He sold his **r** as the firstborn

rim (15)

Exo 25:25 Make a **r** three inches wide
25:25 put a gold molding around the **r**.
25:27 rings are to be close to the **r**.
37:12 He made a **r** 3 inches wide
37:12 put a gold molding around the **r**.
37:14 rings were put close to the **r**
1Ki 7:24 Under the **r** were two rows of
7:26 Its **r** was like the rim of a cup,
7:26 Its rim was like the **r** of a cup,
2Ch 4:3 Under the **r** were two rows of
4:5 Its **r** was like the rim of a cup,
4:5 Its rim was like the **r** of a cup,
Eze 43:13 was a **r** measuring 9 inches
43:17 It had a **r** all the way around
43:20 and on the **r** all the way around

Rimmon (14)

Jos 15:32 Lebaoth, Shilhim, Ain, and **R**.
19:7 Ain, **R**, Ether, and Ashan.
19:13 and **R**, where it turns to Neah.
Jdg 20:45 fled into the desert to **R** Rock.
20:47 fled into the desert to **R** Rock.
20:47 They stayed at **R** Rock for four
21:13 the men of Benjamin at **R** Rock
2Sm 4:2 They were the sons of **R** from
4:5 the sons of **R** from Beeroth,
4:9 the sons of **R** from Beeroth,
2Ki 5:18 to the temple of **R** to worship,
5:18 to bow down in the temple of **R**.
1Ch 4:32 Ain, **R**, Tochen, and Ashan.
Zec 14:10 like the plains from Geba to **R**,

Rimmono (1)

1Ch 6:77 descendants received **R**

Rimmon Perez (2)

Num 33:19 and set up camp at **R**.
33:20 They moved from **R** and

rims (2)

1Ki 7:33 The axles, **r**, spokes, and hubs
Eze 1:18 The **r** of the wheels were large

ring (39)

Gen 24:22 the man took out a gold nose **r**
24:30 He saw the nose **r** and the
24:47 "I put the **r** in her nose and the
38:18 "Your signet **r**, its cord, and the
38:25 you recognize whose signet **r**,
41:42 Pharaoh took off his signet **r**
Exo 26:24 tightly at the top by a single **r**.
27:4 and make a bronze **r** for ⌊each
28:11 a jeweler engraves a signet **r**.
28:21 stone engraved (like a signet **r**)
28:36 engrave on it (as on a signet **r**):
29:23 a **r** of bread made with olive oil,
36:29 tightly at the top by a single **r**.
39:14 stone engraved (like a signet **r**)
39:30 on it (as on a signet **r**):
Lev 8:26 a **r** of bread made with olive oil,
24:5 Each **r** will contain four quarts
Num 6:19 one **r** of unleavened bread from
15:20 one part of your dough into a **r**
1Sm 3:11 ears of everyone who hears it **r**.
2Ki 21:12 who hears about it will **r**.
Est 3:10 the king removed his signet **r**
3:12 and sealed with the king's **r**.

Est 8:2 the king took off his signet **r**,
8:8 it also with the king's signet **r**,
8:8 signet **r** cannot be canceled."
8:10 with the king's signet **r**.
Job 41:2 Can you put a **r** through its
42:11 him some money and a gold **r**.
Pro 11:22 ⌊Like⌋ a gold **r** in a pig's snout,
25:12 ⌊Like⌋ a gold **r** and a fine gold
Sos 8:6 Wear me as a signet **r** on your
8:6 as a **r** on your hand.
Jer 19:3 who hears about it will **r**.
22:24 are the signet **r** on my right
Eze 16:12 I put a **r** in your nose,
Dan 6:17 using his **r** and the rings of his
Hag 2:23 I will make you like a signet **r**,
Luk 15:22 Put a **r** on his finger and

ringleader (1)
Act 24:5 He's a **r** of the Nazarene sect.

rings (45)
Exo 25:12 Cast four gold **r** for it,
25:12 two **r** on each side.
25:14 Put the poles through the **r** on
25:15 The poles must stay in the **r** of
25:26 Make four gold **r** for it,
25:27 The **r** are to be close to the rim.
26:29 make gold **r** to hold the
27:7 should be put through the **r**
28:23 Make two gold **r** for the
28:24 the two gold ropes to the **r** at
28:26 Make two gold **r**, and fasten
28:27 Make two ⌊more⌋ gold **r**,
28:28 should be fastened by its **r**
28:28 be fastened by its rings to the **r**
29:2 some **r** of bread made with
30:4 Make two gold **r**, and put them
35:22 signet **r**, and pendants.
36:34 with gold and made gold **r**
37:3 He cast four gold **r** for its four
37:3 two **r** on each side.
37:5 He put them through the **r** on
37:13 He cast four gold **r** for it and
37:13 rings for it and fastened the **r**
37:14 The **r** were put close to the rim
37:27 He made two gold **r** and put
38:5 He cast four **r** to hold the poles
38:7 He put the poles through the **r**
39:16 gold settings and two gold **r**
39:16 rings and attached the two **r**
39:17 the two gold ropes to the **r** at
39:19 They made two gold **r** and
39:20 They made two ⌊more⌋ gold **r**
39:21 fastened the breastplate by its **r**
39:21 breastplate by its rings to the **r**
Lev 2:4 it must be **r** of unleavened
7:12 you must also bring **r** of
7:13 In addition to these **r** of bread,
24:5 and bake twelve **r** of bread.
Num 6:15 bread containing some **r**
31:50 bracelets, signet **r**, earrings,
Isa 3:21 signet **r**, nose rings,
3:21 signet rings, nose **r**,
Dan 6:17 using his ring and the **r** of his
Hos 2:13 She put on her **r** and jewelry,
Jas 2:2 One man is wearing gold **r** and

ringworm (1)
Lev 22:22 bones, cuts, warts, scabs, or **r**.

Rinnah (1)
1Ch 4:20 Shimon's sons were Amnon, **R**,

rinsed (3)
Lev 6:28 be scoured and **r** with water.
15:12 bucket he touches must be **r**.
2Ch 4:6 The priests **r** the meat prepared

rinsing (1)
Lev 15:11 without first **r** his hands,

riot (6)
Mat 26:5 may be a **r** among the people."
27:24 Instead, a **r** was breaking out.
Mar 14:2 will be a **r** among the people."
15:7 committed murder during a **r**.
Luk 23:19 in a **r** that had taken
Act 17:5 and started a **r** in the city.

rioting (3)
Luk 23:25 in prison for **r** and murdering,
Act 19:40 risk of being accused of **r** today
21:31 report that all Jerusalem was **r**.

riots (1)
2Co 6:5 beatings, imprisonments, **r**,

rip (7)
2Ki 8:12 and **r** open their pregnant
Job 18:4 Why do you **r** yourself apart in
Eze 23:26 They will **r** off your clothes and
Hos 13:8 I will **r** you open. Like a lion I
Mat 9:16 it will **r** away from the coat,
Mar 2:21 the new patch will shrink and **r**
Jon 19:24 "Let's not **r** it apart.

ripe (11)
Num 17:8 and produced **r** almonds.
2Sm 16:2 "The bread and the **r** fruit are
23:11 there was a field of **r** lentils.
1Ch 11:13 There was a field of **r** barley.
Job 5:26 to your grave at a **r** old age like
Joe 3:13 The harvest is **r**. Stomp on them
Amo 8:1 a basket of **r** summer fruit.
8:2 "A basket of **r** summer fruit,"
8:2 "My people Israel are now **r**.
Mat 21:34 the grapes were getting **r**,
Rev 14:18 because those grapes are **r**."

ripen (5)
Exo 9:32 because they **r** later.)
Num 13:20 grapes were beginning to **r**.)
Sos 2:13 The green figs **r**. The
Jer 24:2 like figs that **r** first.
Hos 8:7 A field of grain that doesn't **r**

ripened (8)
Gen 40:10 Then its clusters **r** into grapes.
2Sm 16:1 100 pieces of **r** fruit,
Isa 16:9 The shouts of joy for your **r**
28:4 will be like figs that **r** early.
Jer 48:32 will destroy your **r** fruits
Eze 44:30 the best of all the first **r** fruits.
Hos 2:9 back my grain when it has **r**
Mic 7:1 grapes to eat or any **r** figs that

ripening (1)
Isa 18:5 grapes are **r** from blossoms,

Riphath (2)
Gen 10:3 Ashkenaz, **R**, and Togarmah.
1Ch 1:6 Ashkenaz, **R**, and Togarmah.

ripped (2)
2Ki 15:16 he attacked it and **r** open all its
Hos 13:16 pregnant women will be **r** open.

ripping (1)
Amo 1:13 by **r** open pregnant women

rise (61)
Exo 33:8 all the people would **r** and
Num 24:17 A scepter will **r** from Israel.
Dtr 28:43 live among you will **r** higher
Jdg 20:38 a big column of smoke **r** from
20:40 of smoke started to **r** from
1Sm 22:13 so that he can **r** up against me
Job 8:6 then he will **r** up on your behalf
9:7 He commands the sun not to **r**.
14:12 lies down and does not **r** until
19:25 he will **r** on the earth.
24:14 At dawn murderers **r**;
25:3 on whom his light does not **r**?
Psa 20:8 but we will **r** and stand firm.
35:23 Wake up, and **r** to my defense.
88:10 Will the spirits of the dead **r**
89:9 When its waves **r**,
102:13 You will **r** and have
107:25 and it made the waves **r** high.
135:7 who makes the clouds **r** from
140:10 into a pit, never to **r** again.
Pro 28:12 but when wicked people **r**,
Pro 28:28 When wicked people **r**,
Ecc 1:5 place where it will **r** ⌊again⌋.
Isa 14:21 They won't be able to **r**,
14:22 "I'll **r** up against them,"
26:14 The spirits of the dead won't **r**.
26:19 Their corpses will **r**.
28:21 The LORD will **r** as he did on
34:3 A stench will **r** from their
47:13 to you, **r** up, and save you.
58:10 then your light will **r** in the dark,
Jer 10:13 He makes clouds **r** from the
46:8 Egypt says, 'I will **r**;
50:41 and many kings will **r** from
51:16 He makes clouds **r** from the
51:42 The sea will **r** over Babylon,
51:64 It will never **r** again because of
Eze 10:16 lifted their wings to **r** from
26:3 you as the waves on the sea **r**.
30:13 A prince will never **r** again in
Dan 2:39 will **r** to power after you.
7:17 are four kingdoms that will **r**
7:24 horns are ten kings that will **r**
7:24 Another king will **r** to power
8:23 things will **r** to power.
11:16 He will **r** to power in the
11:23 he will act deceitfully and **r** to
12:13 You will rest, and you will **r** for
Joe 2:20 A foul odor will **r** from the dead
Amo 5:2 have fallen, never to **r** again.
8:8 The entire land will **r** like the
Hab 2:7 Won't your creditors suddenly **r**
3:10 Its waves **r** up high.
Zec 14:10 Jerusalem will **r** and remain on
Mal 4:2 Sun of Righteousness will **r**
Mat 5:45 He makes his sun **r** on people
Rom 15:12 He will **r** to rule the nations,
Eph 5:14 **R** from the dead, and Christ
2Pe 1:19 morning star to **r** in your hearts.
Rev 18:9 see the smoke **r** from her raging
18:18 When they saw the smoke **r**

risen (6)
Gen 19:23 The sun had just **r** over the
Exo 12:34 their bread dough before it had **r**
12:39 The dough hadn't **r** because
Psa 27:12 witnesses have **r** against me.
Eze 47:5 But the water had **r** so much
Mat 4:16 A light has **r** for those who live

rises (28)
Jos 12:7 Halak which **r** toward Seir.
Jdg 5:31 LORD be like the sun when it **r**
9:33 In the morning, when the sun **r**,
2Sm 23:4 the morning light as the sun **r**,
Neh 12:37 There the wall **r** past David's
Job 16:8 My frail body **r** up and testifies
20:27 Earth **r** up against him.
31:14 what could I do if God **r** up?
41:25 are afraid when Leviathan **r**.
Psa 19:6 It **r** from one end of the
50:1 the earth from where the sun **r**
93:3 The ocean **r**, O LORD.
93:3 The ocean **r** with a roar.
93:3 The ocean **r** with its pounding
104:22 When the sun **r**, they gather
113:3 From where the sun **r** to where
Ecc 1:5 The sun **r**, and the sun sets,
Isa 2:19 honor of his majesty when he **r**
2:21 honor of his majesty when he **r**
13:10 The sun will be dark when it **r**.
30:18 He **r** to have compassion on
30:28 It **r** neck high, sifting the
31:2 He **r** against wicked people
Amo 9:5 All of it **r** like the Nile and sinks
Nah 3:17 The sun **r**, and they scatter in
Zec 8:7 from the land where the sun **r**
Mal 1:11 the nations where the sun **r**
Jas 1:11 The sun **r** with its scorching

rising (15)
Gen 19:28 he saw smoke **r** from the land
Exo 27:13 the east end, facing the **r** sun,
38:13 The east side, facing the **r** sun,
Num 2:3 the east side, facing the **r** sun,
1Sm 28:13 "I see a god **r** from the ground,"
2Ki 3:22 morning as the sun was **r** over

Jer 46:7 is this, **r** like the Nile River,
46:8 Egypt is like the **r** Nile River,
47:2 Water is **r** in the north.
Eze 8:16 east and worshiping the **r** sun.
Hos 13:3 be like smoke **r** from chimneys.
Mat 2:2 We saw his star **r** and have
2:9 The star they had seen **r** led
Luk 3:15 People's hopes were **r** as they
Jon 21:4 As the sun was **r**, Jesus stood

risk (5)

2Sm 17:17 They could not **r** being seen
1Ch 11:19 They had to **r** their lives to get
Lam 5:9 To get our food, we have to **r**
Act 19:31 to urge him not to **r** going into
19:40 At this moment we run the **r** of

risked (9)

Jdg 5:18 and Naphtali **r** his life on the
9:17 He **r** his life and rescued you
12:3 I **r** my life and went to fight the
1Sm 19:5 He **r** his life and killed the
2Sm 23:17 blood of men who **r** their lives!"
1Ch 11:19 of these men who **r** their lives?
Dan 3:28 They disobeyed the king and **r**
Rom 16:4 They **r** their lives to save me.
Php 2:30 He **r** his life and almost died for

Rissah (2)

Num 33:21 Libnah and set up camp at **R**.
33:22 They moved from **R** and set up

Rithmah (2)

Num 33:18 Hazeroth and set up camp at **R**.
33:19 They moved from **R** and set up

ritual (4)

Num 31:19 of war must use the **r** water
31:23 also be put through the **r** water
31:23 be put through the **r** water.
1Ki 18:28 (This is what their **r** called for.)

ritually (1)

Gen 35:2 until you are **r** clean,

rituals (2)

Isa 66:17 themselves for their garden **r**.
Jon 2:6 used for Jewish purification **r**.

rival (6)

Lev 18:18 never marry her sister as a **r**
1Sm 1:6 her **r** ⌊Peninnah⌋ tormented her
1Ki 5:4 I have no **r** and no trouble.
11:14 the Edomite as a **r** to Solomon.
11:23 as a **r** to Solomon.
11:25 Rezon was Israel's **r** as long

rivalry (6)

Ecc 4:4 and skillful effort come from **r**.
Rom 13:13 immorality, promiscuity, **r**,
2Co 12:20 I'm afraid that there may be **r**,
Gal 5:20 idolatry, drug use, hatred, **r**,
1Ti 6:4 This produces jealousy, **r**,
Jas 3:16 there is jealousy and **r**,

rivals (7)

Exo 20:5 a God who does not tolerate **r**.
34:14 a God who does not tolerate **r**.
34:14 he is known for not tolerating **r**.)
Dtr 4:24 a God who does not tolerate **r**.
5:9 a God who does not tolerate **r**.
6:15 a God who does not tolerate **r**.
Jos 24:19 a God who does not tolerate **r**.

river (366)

Gen 2:10 A **r** flowed from Eden to water
2:11 name of the first **r** is Pishon.
2:13 name of the second **r** is Gihon.
2:14 name of the third **r** is Tigris.
2:14 The fourth **r** is the Euphrates.
15:18 This is the land from the **r** of
15:18 the river of Egypt to the great **r**,
31:21 He crossed the Euphrates **R**
32:10 when I crossed the Jordan **R**,
32:22 shallow part of the Jabbok **R**.
36:37 Shaul from Rehoboth on the **r**
Gen 41:1 he was standing by the Nile **R**.
41:2 cows came up from the **r**
41:3 up from the **r** behind them.
41:18 cows came up from the **r**
50:10 the east side of the Jordan **R**,
Exo 2:3 near the bank of the Nile **R**.
2:5 walked along the bank of the **r**.
4:9 some water from the Nile **R**
7:15 for him on the bank of the **r**.
7:18 and the **r** will stink.
7:20 water in the **r** turned into blood.
7:21 drink any water from the **r**.
7:24 any of the water from the **r**.
8:3 The Nile **R** will swarm with
17:5 you used to strike the Nile **R**.
23:31 Desert to the Euphrates **R**.
Num 13:29 and all along the Jordan **R**."
21:12 set up camp at the Zered **R**.
21:24 Arnon Valley to the Jabbok **R**.
22:1 of Moab east of the Jordan **R**.
22:5 on the Euphrates **R**,
24:6 like gardens by a **r**,
26:3 Jordan **R** across from Jericho.
26:63 Jordan **R** across from Jericho.
31:12 Jordan **R** across from Jericho.
32:5 make us cross the Jordan **R**."
32:19 the other side of the Jordan **R**,
32:29 and cross the Jordan **R**
33:48 Jordan **R** across from Jericho.
33:50 Jordan **R** across from Jericho,
33:51 Jordan **R** and entering Canaan.
34:5 Azmon it turns toward the **R**
34:12 goes along the Jordan **R** so that
34:15 Jordan **R** across from Jericho."
35:1 Jordan **R** across from Jericho.
35:10 the Jordan **R** and enter Canaan,
35:14 on the east side of the Jordan **R**
36:13 Jordan **R** across from Jericho.
Dtr 1:1 the desert east of the Jordan **R**,
1:5 were east of the Jordan **R**
1:7 as far as the Euphrates **R**.
2:13 "Now cross the Zered **R**."
2:13 So we crossed the Zered **R**.
2:14 until we crossed the Zered **R**.
2:29 until we cross the Jordan **R** into
2:37 along the bank of the Jabbok **R**
3:8 kings east of the Jordan **R**,
3:16 is the border) to the Jabbok **R**,
3:17 the plains around the Jordan **R**.
3:17 The western border was the **r**,
3:18 cross ⌊the Jordan **R**⌋ ahead
3:20 the other side of the Jordan **R**.
3:21 Jordan **R**⌋ where you're going.
3:25 the Jordan **R** — those beautiful
3:27 will never cross the Jordan **R**.
3:28 people across ⌊the Jordan **R**⌋,
4:14 after you cross ⌊the Jordan **R**⌋
4:21 I wouldn't cross the Jordan **R**
4:22 and not cross the Jordan **R**,
4:26 the other side of the Jordan **R**.
4:41 the east side of the Jordan **R**.
4:46 they were east of the Jordan **R**
4:47 who were east of the Jordan **R**.
4:49 side of the Jordan **R** as far as
9:1 about to cross the Jordan **R**.
9:21 into the **r** that flowed down
11:8 you've crossed ⌊the Jordan **R**⌋.
11:24 from the Euphrates **R** to the
11:31 about to cross the Jordan **R**
12:10 But you will cross the Jordan **R**
21:4 will bring the heifer down to a **r**,
21:4 At the **r** they must break the
27:2 day you cross the Jordan **R**
27:4 After you cross the Jordan **R**,
27:12 After you cross the Jordan **R**,
30:18 when you cross the Jordan **R**.
31:2 I cannot cross the Jordan **R**.
31:3 one who will cross the **r** ahead
31:3 Joshua will also cross the **r**
31:13 when you cross the Jordan **R**."
32:47 when you cross the Jordan **R**."
Jos 1:2 must cross the Jordan **R** into
1:4 to the Euphrates **R** (the country
1:11 you will cross the Jordan **R**
1:14 gave you east of the Jordan **R**.
1:15 land east of the Jordan **R** which
Jos 2:7 place to cross the Jordan **R**.
2:10 who ruled east of the Jordan **R**.
2:23 crossed the Jordan **R**,
3:1 They came to the Jordan **R**,
3:8 into the water of the Jordan **R**,
3:11 ahead of you into the Jordan **R**.
3:14 camp to cross the Jordan **R**.
3:15 to the edge of the Jordan **R**
3:16 **R**⌋ directly opposite Jericho.
3:17 the Jordan **R** on dry ground.
4:1 finished crossing the Jordan **R**.
4:5 to the middle of the Jordan **R**
4:7 'The water of the Jordan **R** was
4:7 the **r** stopped flowing.
4:9 in the middle of the Jordan **R**,
4:13 armed men crossed the **r**
4:16 to come out of the Jordan **R**."
4:19 came out of the Jordan **R**.
4:22 the Jordan **R** on dry ground.
5:1 kings west of the Jordan **R**
5:1 dried up the Jordan **R** so that
7:7 people across the Jordan **R**?
9:1 the Jordan **R** heard about these
12:1 land east of the Jordan **R** that
12:2 Arnon Valley to the Jabbok **R**,
12:7 of the Jordan **R** that Joshua
13:3 It extends from the Shihor **R**,
13:8 east of the Jordan **R**,
13:23 territory was the Jordan **R**.
13:27 The Jordan **R** served as its
13:32 of the Jordan **R** near Jericho.
14:3 east of the Jordan **R**.
15:4 It comes out at the **R** of Egypt
15:5 as the mouth of the Jordan **R**.
15:47 and villages as far as the **R**
16:1 from the Jordan **R** at Jericho
16:7 and ends at the Jordan **R**.
16:8 goes west along the Kanah **R**
17:5 Bashan east of the Jordan **R**.
17:9 southward to the Kanah **R**.
17:9 ⌊southern⌋ border is the **r**,
17:10 What is south ⌊of the **r**⌋
18:7 the east side of the Jordan **R**."
18:19 the south end of the Jordan **R**.
18:20 The Jordan **R** is its eastern
19:11 and the **r** near Jokneam.
19:22 and ends at the Jordan **R**.
19:33 and ends at the Jordan **R**.
20:8 the east side of the Jordan **R**,
22:4 gave you east of the Jordan **R**.
22:10 built an altar by the Jordan **R**.
22:11 the Jordan **R** on Israel's side."
22:25 LORD has made the Jordan **R**
23:4 from the Jordan **R** westward
24:2 other side of the Euphrates **R**
24:3 other side of the Euphrates **R**.
24:8 the east side of the Jordan **R**.
24:11 you crossed the Jordan **R**
24:14 other side of the Euphrates **R**
Jdg 3:28 of the Jordan **R** that led
4:7 troops to you at the Kishon **R**.
4:13 to come to the Kishon **R**.
5:17 remained east of the Jordan **R**.
5:21 The Kishon **R** swept them
5:21 swept them away — that old **r**,
6:33 crossed ⌊the Jordan **R**⌋,
7:24 Beth Barah and the Jordan **R**."
7:24 Beth Barah and the Jordan **R**.
7:25 the other side of the Jordan **R**.
8:4 headed toward the Jordan **R**.
10:8 who lived east of the Jordan **R**
10:9 also crossed the Jordan **R**
11:13 It stretched from the Arnon **R** to
11:13 the Arnon River to the Jabbok **R**
11:13 Jabbok River and the Jordan **R**.
11:18 of Moab — east of the Arnon **R**.
11:18 They did not cross the Arnon **R**
11:22 territory from the Arnon **R**
11:22 the Arnon River to the Jabbok **R**
11:22 from the desert to the Jordan **R**.
11:26 all the cities along the Arnon **R**
12:1 ⌊the Jordan **R**⌋ to Zaphon.
12:5 of the Jordan **R** leading back
12:6 crossings of the Jordan **R**.
1Sm 11:1 of the Jordan **R** whose right eye
13:7 crossed the Jordan **R** into

1Sm 31:7 across the Jordan **R** saw that
2Sm 2:29 They crossed the Jordan **R**
8:3 along the Euphrates **R**,
10:16 from beyond the Euphrates **R**.
10:17 crossed the Jordan **R**,
15:28 I'll wait at the **r** crossings in the
17:16 'Don't rest tonight in the **r**
17:16 make sure you cross ⌊the **r**⌋,
17:21 "Cross the **r** quickly because
17:22 him left to cross the Jordan **R**.
17:22 had crossed the Jordan **R**.
17:24 with him crossed the Jordan **R**.
19:15 came back to the Jordan **R**,
19:15 bring him across the Jordan **R**.
19:17 rushed to the Jordan **R** across
19:18 They crossed the **r** to bring
19:18 going to cross the Jordan **R**.
19:31 with the king to the Jordan **R**
19:33 "Cross the **r** with me.
19:36 cross the Jordan **R** with you.
19:39 troops crossed the Jordan **R**,
19:40 king crossed the **r** to Gilgal,
19:41 and men across the Jordan **R**?"
20:2 from the Jordan **R** to Jerusalem.
24:5 They crossed the Jordan **R**
1Ki 2:8 to meet me at the Jordan **R**,
4:21 kingdoms from the Euphrates **R**
4:24 the Euphrates **R** from Tiphsah
8:65 the border of Hamath and the **R**
14:15 them beyond the Euphrates **R**
17:3 and hide beside the Cherith **R**,
17:3 which is east of the Jordan **R**.
17:5 went to live by the Cherith **R**,
17:5 which is east of the Jordan **R**.
18:40 took them to the Kishon **R**
2Ki 2:6 is sending me to the Jordan **R**."
2:7 Elisha stood by the Jordan **R**.
2:8 crossed ⌊the **r**⌋ on dry ground.
2:13 on the bank of the Jordan **R**.
2:14 and Elisha crossed ⌊the **r**⌋.
5:10 seven times in the Jordan **R**,
5:14 in the Jordan **R** seven times,
6:2 Let's go to the Jordan **R**.
6:4 They came to the Jordan **R**
7:15 them as far as the Jordan **R**
10:33 east of the Jordan **R**:
10:33 which is near the Arnon **R**,
17:6 along the Habor **R** in Gozan,
18:11 along the Habor **R** in Gozan,
23:29 of Assyria at the Euphrates **R**.
24:7 taken all the territory from the **R**
24:7 of Egypt to the Euphrates **R**.
1Ch 1:48 Shaul from Rehoboth on the **r**
5:9 extends to the Euphrates **R**,
5:26 Habor, Hara, and the Gozan **R**.
6:78 land east of the Jordan **R**
12:15 crossed the Jordan **R** when
12:37 the east side of the Jordan **R**,
13:5 from the Shihor **R** near Egypt
18:3 along the Euphrates **R**,
19:16 from beyond the Euphrates **R**.
26:30 Israel west of the Jordan **R**.
2Ch 7:8 of Hamath and the **R** of Egypt.
9:26 the kings from the Euphrates **R**
35:20 Carchemish at the Euphrates **R**.
Ezr 4:10 lands west of the Euphrates **R**.)
4:16 west of the Euphrates **R**.
4:17 others west of the Euphrates **R**:
5:3 west of the Euphrates **R**,
5:6 west of the Euphrates **R**,
5:6 Persians west of that **r**) sent
6:6 (the Persians west of the **r**):
6:13 west of the Euphrates **R**,
7:21 west of the Euphrates **R**
7:25 west of the Euphrates **R**.
8:15 I had this group gather by the **r**
8:21 there at the Ahava **R** so that we
8:31 Then we left the Ahava **R** on
8:36 west of the Euphrates **R**.
Neh 2:7 west of the Euphrates **R**.
2:9 west of the Euphrates **R**
3:7 west of the Euphrates **R**.
Job 14:11 or ⌊as⌋ a **r** dries up completely,
22:16 A **r** washes their foundation
33:18 from crossing the **R** ⌊of Death⌋.
36:12 they will cross the **R** ⌊of
Job 40:23 Though the **r** flows powerfully
Psa 36:8 from the **r** of your pleasure.
46:4 There is a **r** whose streams
65:9 (The **r** of God is filled with
66:6 They crossed the **r** on foot.
72:8 from the Euphrates **R** to the
80:11 reached the Euphrates **R**.
83:9 and Jabin at the Kishon **R**.
105:41 and flowed like a **r** through
114:3 The Jordan **R** turned back.
114:5 Jordan **R**, what made you turn
Isa 7:18 distant branches of the Nile **R**
7:20 from beyond the Euphrates **R**
8:7 of the Euphrates **R**—
9:1 to the land across the Jordan **R**,
11:15 his hand over the Euphrates **R**
16:2 crossings of the Arnon **R**.
19:5 The water in the Nile **R** will be
19:5 and the **r** will be dry and empty.
23:3 The harvest of the Nile **R** is
27:12 stream of the Euphrates **R**
47:2 your legs, and cross the **r**.
48:18 Your peace would be like a **r**
66:12 I will offer you peace like a **r**
Jer 2:18 to drink water from the Nile **R**.
2:18 water from the Euphrates **R**.
12:5 the jungle along the Jordan **R**?
13:4 Go to the Euphrates **R**,
46:2 along the Euphrates **R** during
46:6 in the north by the Euphrates **R**.
46:7 rising like the Nile **R**,
46:8 Egypt is like the rising Nile **R**,
46:8 like a **r** quickly overflowing its
46:10 in the north by the Euphrates **R**.
47:2 It will become an overflowing **r**.
49:19 the Jordan **R** into pastureland.
50:44 the Jordan **R** into pastureland.
51:32 The **r** crossings have been
51:63 the middle of the Euphrates **R**.
Lam 2:18 Let your tears run down like a **r**
Eze 1:1 the exiles by the Chebar **R**,
1:3 in Babylon by the Chebar **R**.
3:15 who lived by the Chebar **R**.
3:23 glory I saw by the Chebar **R**,
10:15 that I saw at the Chebar **R**.
10:20 God of Israel at the Chebar **R**.
10:22 that I saw by the Chebar **R**.
29:3 crocodile lying in the Nile **R**.
29:3 You say, "The Nile **R** is mine.
29:4 the fish in the Nile **R** stick
29:4 I will pull you out of your **r** with
29:9 You said, "The Nile **R** is mine.
29:10 I'm against you and the Nile **R**.
30:12 I will dry up the Nile **R** and sell
43:3 the one I saw by the Chebar **R**.
47:5 much that it became a **r** which
47:5 The **r** was too deep to cross
47:7 back along the bank of the **r**.
47:7 trees on both sides of the **r**.
47:9 Wherever the **r** flows,
47:9 The **r** will make the water in
47:9 Wherever the **r** flows,
47:12 will grow on both sides of the **r**.
47:18 The Jordan **R** will serve as the
Dan 7:10 A **r** of fire flowed. It came from
10:4 I was by the great Tigris **R**.
12:5 man stood on one side of the **r**,
12:6 clothes who was above the **r**,
12:7 clothes who was above the **r**.
Amo 5:24 But let justice flow like a **r** and
8:8 and then sink like Egypt's **r**.
9:5 Nile and sinks like Egypt's **r**.
Mic 7:12 from Egypt to the Euphrates **R**,
Zec 9:10 and from the ⌊Euphrates⌋ **R**
10:11 the deep places of the Nile **R**.
Mat 3:6 baptized them in the Jordan **R**.
3:13 from Galilee to the Jordan **R**
4:15 across the Jordan **R**,
4:25 and from across the Jordan **R**.
19:1 the other side of the Jordan **R**
Mar 1:5 baptized them in the Jordan **R**.
1:9 by John in the Jordan **R**.
3:8 and from across the Jordan **R**,
10:1 the other side of the Jordan **R**.
Luk 3:3 the region around the Jordan **R**.
4:1 Spirit as he left the Jordan **R**.
Jon 1:28 the east side of the Jordan **R**,
3:26 the other side of the Jordan **R**?
10:40 went back across the Jordan **R**
Act 16:13 along the **r** where we thought
Rev 9:14 held at the great Euphrates **R**."
12:15 snake's mouth poured out a **r**
12:16 the **r** which had poured
16:12 bowl on the great Euphrates **R**.
16:12 The water in the **r** dried up to
22:1 The angel showed me a **r** filled
22:2 of the city and the **r** there was

riverbank (1)

Gen 41:3 the first seven cows on the **r**.

riverbed (1)

1Sm 17:40 five smooth stones from the **r**,

riverbeds (4)

Job 6:15 like the seasonal **r** that flood.
6:17 In the heat their **r** dry up.
30:6 They have to live in dry **r**,
Psa 126:4 streams ⌊to dry **r**⌋ in the Negev.

rivers (44)

Gen 2:10 the garden it divided into four **r**.
Exo 7:19 over the waters of Egypt—its **r**,
8:5 'Hold your staff over the **r**,
Num 24:6 Your tents spread out like **r**,
Dtr 8:7 It is a land with **r** that don't dry
10:7 a land with **r** that don't dry up.
2Ki 5:12 The Abana and Pharpar **R** in
5:12 water than any of the **r** in Israel.
Job 6:15 as deceptive as seasonal **r**,
20:17 from the streams or from the **r**
22:24 among the pebbles in the **r**,
28:11 They explore the sources of **r**
Psa 24:2 seas and set it firmly on the **r**.
74:15 You dried up the ever-flowing **r**.
78:16 He made the water flow like **r**.
78:44 He turned their **r** into blood so
89:25 sea and his right hand on the **r**.
98:8 Let the **r** clap their hands and
107:33 He changes **r** into a desert,
137:1 By the **r** of Babylon,
Sos 8:7 and **r** will never wash it away.
Isa 18:1 lies beyond the **r** of Sudan.
18:2 whose land is divided by **r**.
18:7 whose land is divided by **r**.
33:21 by wide **r** and streams.
41:18 I will make **r** flow on bare
42:15 I will turn **r** into islands.
43:2 When you go through **r**,
43:19 I will make **r** on dry land.
43:20 I will make **r** on the dry land for
44:27 So I will dry up your **r**.
50:2 and I turn **r** into deserts.
Jer 51:13 you live beside many **r**
Eze 31:4 **R** flowed around the place
31:15 springs and held back the **r**.
Nah 1:4 He dries up all the **r**.
2:6 The gates of the **r** are opened,
Hab 3:8 LORD is not angry with the **r**,
3:8 If you are angry with the **r**,
3:9 Selah You split the land with **r**.
Zep 3:10 From beyond the **r** of Sudan my
2Co 11:26 I've faced dangers from raging **r**
Rev 8:10 It fell on one-third of the **r** and
16:4 poured his bowl over the **r**

Rizia (1)

1Ch 7:39 were Arah, Hanniel, and **R**.

Rizpah (4)

2Sm 3:7 named **R** (Aiah's daughter).
21:8 the two sons whom **R** (Aiah's
21:10 **R** (Aiah's daughter) took
21:11 **R** (Aiah's daughter) had

road (157)

Gen 38:14 which is on the **r** to Timnah.
38:21 was beside the **r** at Enaim?"
49:17 Dan will be a snake on a **r**,
Exo 13:17 God didn't lead them on the **r**
13:18 on the **r** through the desert
Num 14:25 and follow the **r** that goes to the

Num 20:19 "We'll stay on the main **r**,
21:1 coming on the **r** to Atharim,
21:4 following the **r** that goes to the
21:33 and followed the **r** that goes
22:22 of the LORD stood in the **r**
22:23 of the LORD standing in the **r**
22:23 the donkey turned off the **r** into
22:23 donkey to get it back on the **r**.
22:24 Where the **r** went through the
22:31 who was standing in the **r**
22:34 you were standing there in the **r**
Dtr 1:40 and follow the **r** that goes to the
2:1 following the **r** that goes to the
2:8 We turned off the **r** that goes
2:8 and took the **r** that goes through
2:27 and won't ever leave the **r**.
3:1 and followed the **r** that goes
11:30 beyond the **r** that goes west,
22:4 donkey or ox lying on the **r**,
Jos 2:7 pursued them on the **r** leading
2:22 for them all along the **r**
10:10 He chased them along the **r**
12:3 Sea) and the **r** that goes south
Jdg 5:10 and who walk on the **r** — think.
8:11 went up Tent Dwellers **R**,
9:25 who passed by them on the **r**.
9:37 is coming along the **r** by
14:8 ⌊On his way⌋ he left the **r** to
20:42 in front of Israel toward the **r**
20:42 the cities on the **r** to the desert.
Rut 1:7 began to walk back along the **r**
1Sm 4:13 sitting on a chair beside the **r**,
6:9 If it goes up the **r** to its own
6:12 The cows went straight up the **r**
6:12 they stayed on the **r** and didn't
13:17 One column turned onto the **r** to
13:18 column turned onto the **r**
13:18 And one turned onto the **r**
17:52 Philistines lay on the **r**
24:3 along the **r** where there was
24:7 cave and went out onto the **r**.
26:3 Saul camped by the **r** at the hill
2Sm 2:24 opposite Giah on the **r** from
4:7 night along the **r** to the plains.
13:34 coming down the **r** beside
15:2 early and stand by the **r** leading
15:23 down the **r** toward the desert.
16:13 and his men went along the **r**,
18:23 Ahimaaz ran along the valley **r**
20:12 his blood in the middle of the **r**.
20:12 he carried Amasa from the **r** to
20:13 as he was moved from the **r**,
1Ki 11:29 from Shiloh met him on the **r**.
13:9 go back on the same **r** I took."
13:10 the man of God left on another **r**
13:10 road and didn't go back on the **r**
13:12 "Which **r** did he take?"
13:12 (His sons had seen which **r** the
13:17 drink there or go back on the **r**
13:24 him ⌊as he traveled⌋ on the **r**
13:24 dead body was thrown on the **r**.
13:25 by saw the body lying on the **r**
13:26 back from the **r** heard about it,
13:28 of the man thrown on the **r**.
18:7 Obadiah was on the **r** when he
20:38 waited for the king by the **r**.
2Ki 2:23 As he walked along the **r**,
3:8 "Which **r** should we take?"
3:8 Jehoshaphat answered, "The **r**
7:15 how the whole **r** was littered
9:27 he fled on the **r** leading to Beth
12:20 Millo on the **r** that goes down
18:17 for the Upper Pool on the **r**
25:4 All Judah's soldiers left on the **r**
25:4 the king took the **r** to the plain
Job 23:10 because he knows the **r** I take.
24:4 force needy people off the **r**.
24:18 People do not travel the **r** that
Psa 77:19 Your **r** went through the sea.
84:5 Their hearts are on the **r** ⌊that
107:4 on a deserted **r** without finding
107:7 He led them on a **r** that went
110:7 drink from the brook along the **r**
140:5 set traps for me along the **r**.
Pro 9:6 the **r** to understanding."
11:5 people makes their **r** smooth,
Pro 15:19 but the **r** of decent people is an
26:13 a ferocious lion out on the **r**!
Ecc 12:5 and of dangers along the **r**,
Isa 7:3 ditch of the Upper Pool on the **r**
9:1 he will bring glory to the **r** by
15:5 go up the mountain **r** to Luhith.
26:7 O Upright One, you make the **r**
35:8 It will be called the Holy **R**.
36:2 on the **r** to Laundryman's Field.
43:16 through the sea and a **r** through
51:10 You made a **r** in the depths of
57:14 It will be said: "Build a **r**!
57:14 Build a **r**! Prepare the way!
Jer 6:25 into the field or walk on the **r**.
31:21 Put up **r** signs! Remember the
31:21 the **r** on which you traveled.
39:4 and they took the **r** to the plain
48:5 On the **r** down to Horonaim
48:19 Stand by the **r** in Aroer,
50:5 They will ask which **r** goes to
52:7 they took the **r** to the plain ⌊of
Lam 2:15 who walks along the **r** shakes
3:11 He has forced me off the **r** I
Eze 21:20 Mark the **r** that the king and his
21:20 and mark the **r** that leads to
21:21 where there is a fork in the **r**.
48:1 It will extend from the **r** to
Hos 6:9 murder on the **r** to Shechem.
13:7 wait by the **r** to ambush you.
Amo 8:14 swear as long as there is a **r**
Nah 2:1 Keep a lookout on the **r**!
Mat 2:12 for their country by another **r**.
7:13 the gate and **r** that lead
7:14 But the narrow gate and the **r**
8:28 No one could travel along that **r**
13:4 seeds were planted along the **r**,
13:19 planted along the **r** illustrates.
20:30 blind men were sitting by the **r**.
21:8 spread their coats on the **r**.
21:8 trees and spread them on the **r**.
21:19 When he saw a fig tree by the **r**,
Mar 4:4 seeds were planted along the **r**,
4:15 that were planted along the **r**.
8:3 become exhausted on the **r**.
9:33 you arguing about on the **r**?"
9:34 On the **r** they had argued about
10:17 Jesus was coming out to the **r**,
10:46 was sitting by the **r**.
10:52 and he followed Jesus on the **r**.
11:8 spread their coats on the **r**.
11:8 fields and spread them on the **r**.
Luk 8:5 seeds were planted along the **r**,
8:12 that were planted along the **r**.
9:57 they were walking along the **r**,
10:31 was traveling along that **r**.
18:35 sitting and begging by the **r**.
19:36 spread their coats on the **r**.
19:37 place where the **r** went down
24:32 when he talked with us on the **r**
24:35 what had happened on the **r**
Act 8:26 and take the desert **r** that goes
8:36 As they were going along the **r**,
9:27 Saul had seen the Lord on the **r**
Jas 2:25 sent them away on another **r**.
Rev 16:12 in the river dried up to make a **r**

roads (19)

Lev 26:22 few that your **r** will be deserted.
Jdg 5:6 days of Jael, **r** were deserted.
5:6 who traveled took back **r**.
20:31 in the open country and on the **r**
20:32 lead them from the city to the **r**."
20:45 killed 5,000 more on the **r**.
Pro 8:2 by the wayside where the **r**
Isa 42:16 lead the blind on unfamiliar **r**.
45:13 I will make all his **r** straight.
49:11 turn all my mountains into **r**,
Jer 18:15 They go on side **r** and not on
Lam 1:4 "The **r** to Zion are deserted.
Eze 21:19 "Son of man, mark two **r** that
21:19 Both of these **r** should start
21:19 and put it where the **r** start to
21:21 will stop where the **r** branch off,
Mat 22:9 Go where the **r** leave the city.
Luk 3:5 The rough **r** will be made
14:23 'Go to the **r** and paths!

roadside (2)

Gen 38:16 her by the **r** and said,
Jer 3:2 You sat by the **r** waiting for

roadway (1)

Isa 35:8 A highway will be there, a **r**.

roam (6)

Psa 91:6 plagues that **r** the dark,
Sos 3:2 I will get up now and **r** around
Isa 32:20 let oxen and donkeys **r** freely.
Lam 5:18 Foxes **r** around on Mount Zion,
Amo 8:12 from sea to sea and **r** from
Zec 4:10 eyes of the LORD **r** over all

roar (28)

1Ch 16:32 everything in it **r** like thunder.
Job 4:10 Though the **r** of the lion and the
37:2 Listen to the **r** of God's voice,
37:4 It is followed by the **r** of his
Psa 38:8 I **r** because my heart's in
42:7 sea calls to another at the **r**
65:7 the one who calms the **r** of the
93:3 The ocean rises with a **r**.
96:11 everything in it **r** like thunder.
98:7 who live in it **r** like thunder.
104:21 The young lions **r** for their prey
Pro 19:12 The rage of a king is like the **r**
20:2 The rage of a king is like the **r**
Isa 5:29 They **r** like a lioness.
5:30 On that day they will **r** over
17:12 They will **r** like the roaring sea.
51:15 the sea and makes its waves **r**.
Jer 5:22 Although they **r**, they can't
12:8 They **r** at me, so I hate them.
31:35 up the sea so that its waves **r**.
Eze 19:7 terrified by the sound of his **r**.
19:9 in prison so that his **r** wouldn't
Dan 10:6 sounded like the **r** of a crowd.
Hos 11:10 will follow me when I **r** like
11:10 When I **r**, my children will
Joe 3:16 The LORD will **r** from Zion,
Amo 3:4 Does a lion **r** in the forest if it
Rev 9:9 from their wings was like the **r**

roared (3)

Psa 74:4 Your opponents have **r** inside
Jer 2:15 Young lions have **r** very loudly
Amo 3:8 The lion has **r**. Who isn't afraid?

roaring (14)

Jdg 14:5 a young **r** lion met Samson.
Psa 22:13 me like ferocious, **r** lions.
Pro 28:15 ⌊Like⌋ a **r** lion and a charging
Isa 17:12 They will roar like the **r** sea.
Jer 6:23 They sound like the **r** sea.
51:38 Its people are like **r** lions and
51:42 and its **r** waves will cover it.
51:55 Waves of enemies will come **r**
Eze 22:25 Your princes are like **r** lions
Zep 3:3 Its officials are ⌊like⌋ **r** lions.
Zec 11:3 The young lions are **r**,
Luk 21:25 and confused because of the **r**
1Pe 5:8 prowling around like a **r** lion as
2Pe 3:10 will pass away with a **r** sound.

roars (9)

Psa 46:3 Water **r** and foams,
Isa 5:30 roar over their prey as the sea **r**.
Jer 25:30 'The LORD **r** from above.
25:30 He **r** against his land.
50:42 sound like the sea when it **r**.
51:16 the water in the sky **r**.
Amo 1:2 He said: The LORD **r** from Zion,
Hab 3:10 The deep ocean **r**.
Rev 10:3 in a loud voice as a lion **r**.

roast (4)

Exo 12:9 eat any of it raw or boiled but **r**
Lev 2:14 **r** the cracked grain over fire.
1Sm 2:15 "Give the meat to the priest to **r**.
Isa 44:16 Over this half they **r** meat that

roasted (9)

Exo 12:8 It must be **r** over a fire and

Lev 23:14 Don't eat bread, **r** grain,
Jos 5:11 unleavened bread and **r** grain.
Rut 2:14 he handed her some **r** grain.
1Sm 17:17 "Take this half-bushel of **r** grain
25:18 a bushel of **r** grain,
2Sm 17:28 flour, **r** grain, beans, lentils,
2Ch 35:13 They **r** the Passover lambs
Isa 44:19 I **r** meat and ate it. Now I am

rob (19)

Lev 19:13 oppress or **r** your neighbor.
26:22 They will **r** you of your children,
Psa 44:10 Those who hate us **r** us at will.
Pro 22:22 Do not **r** the poor because they
22:23 the lives of those who **r** them.
24:15 Do not **r** his house.
Isa 10:2 They prey on widows and **r**
Eze 5:17 and they will **r** you of your
18:7 He doesn't **r** anyone.
18:16 He doesn't **r** anyone.
22:29 people oppress and **r** others.
38:12 I will come to **r** them and loot
38:13 "Did you come to **r** these
Hos 7:1 They **r** people in the streets.
Mar 12:40 They **r** widows by taking their
Luk 20:47 They **r** widows by taking their
Act 19:37 brought here don't **r** temples
1Co 6:10 or who **r** people will not inherit
Col 2:8 Be careful not to let anyone **r**

robbed (21)

Dtr 28:29 you will be oppressed and **r**
Jdg 2:14 over to people who **r** them.
2:16 them from those who **r** them.
9:25 They also **r** everyone who
Ezr 9:7 We have been taken captive, **r**,
Neh 4:4 and let them be **r** in the land
Psa 12:5 oppressed people are **r**
76:5 Brave people were **r**.
89:41 who passed by **r** him.
Pro 4:16 and they are **r** of their sleep
17:12 Better to meet a bear **r** of its
Isa 17:14 the destiny of those who **r** us.
38:10 to the gates of Sheol and be **r**
42:22 these people are **r** and looted.
Jer 21:12 Rescue those who have been **r**
22:3 Rescue those who have been **r**
Eze 18:18 oppressed others, **r** his relative,
Hos 4:11 and new wine have **r** them of
Act 19:27 worship will be **r** of her glory."
2Co 11:8 I **r** other churches by taking pay
1Ti 6:5 corrupt minds have been **r**

robber (3)

Pro 23:28 She is like a **r**, lying in
Luk 18:11 I'm not a **r** or a dishonest
Jon 10:1 else is a thief or a **r**.

robbers (8)

Psa 10:3 He blesses **r**, but he curses the
Isa 42:24 and handed Israel over to **r**?
Eze 7:22 **R** will go in and dishonor it.
Hos 6:9 The priests are like gangs of **r**
Luk 10:30 On the way **r** stripped him,
10:36 man who was attacked by **r**?"
Jon 10:8 before I did were thieves or **r**.
2Co 11:26 from **r**, from my own people,

robbers' (1)

Job 12:6 ⌊But⌋ **r** tents are prosperous,

robbery (2)

Psa 62:10 hope to gain anything through **r**.
Isa 61:8 I hate **r** and wrongdoing.

robbing (2)

1Sm 23:1 They are **r** the threshing floors."
Rom 2:22 are you **r** temples?

robe (61)

Gen 37:3 a special **r** with long sleeves.
37:23 his special **r** with long sleeves.
37:31 So they took Joseph's **r**,
37:31 and dipped the **r** in the blood.
37:32 Then they brought the special **r**
37:32 whether it's your son's **r** or not."
Gen 37:33 it and said, "It is my son's **r**!
Exo 28:4 an ephod and the **r** that is worn
28:4 specially woven linen **r**,
28:31 "Make the **r** that is worn with
28:33 All around the hem of the **r**
28:34 all around the hem of the **r**.
28:39 the specially woven inner **r**
29:5 put them on Aaron — the linen **r**
29:5 the ephod and the **r** that is worn
39:22 They made the **r** that is worn
39:23 in the center of the **r** had
39:24 On the hem of the **r** they made
39:25 all around the hem of the **r**.
39:26 the hem of the **r** that is worn
Lev 8:7 He put the linen **r** on Aaron and
8:7 He also dressed him in the **r**
16:4 He must put on a holy linen **r**
Jos 7:21 I saw a fine **r** from Babylonia,
7:24 the silver, the **r**, the bar of gold,
1Sm 2:19 His mother would make him a **r**
15:27 Saul grabbed the hem of his **r**,
24:4 cut off the border of Saul's **r**.
24:5 cut off the border of Saul's **r**.
24:11 The border of your **r** is in my
24:11 I cut off the border of your **r**
28:14 and he's wearing a **r**."
2Sm 13:18 daughters wore this kind of **r**.)
1Ki 18:46 He hiked up his **r** and ran
1Ch 15:27 was dressed in a fine linen **r**,
Est 6:8 should bring a royal **r** that
6:9 Give the **r** and the horse to one
6:9 Put the **r** on the man whom the
6:10 take the **r** and the horse as you
6:11 So Haman took the **r** and the
6:11 He put the **r** on Mordecai and
8:15 the royal violet and white **r**,
8:15 and a purple outer **r** of fine
Job 1:20 tore his **r** ⌊in grief⌋,
29:14 and it was my **r** and my turban.
30:18 seizes me by the collar of my **r**.
Psa 104:2 with light as though it were a **r**.
104:6 an ocean as though it were a **r**.
109:29 shame as though it were a **r**.
Sos 5:7 on the walls took my **r** from me!
Isa 6:1 bottom of his **r** filled the temple.
22:21 I will dress him in your linen **r**
61:10 He has wrapped me in the **r** of
Eze 16:8 So I spread my **r** over you,
Jnh 3:6 took off his **r**, put on sackcloth,
Mar 16:5 He was dressed in a white **r**
Luk 15:22 Bring out the best **r**,
23:11 They put a colorful **r** on him
Jon 19:23 His **r** was left over.
Rev 1:13 He was wearing a **r** that
6:11 the souls was given a white **r**.

robes (31)

Gen 41:42 He had Joseph dressed in **r** of
Exo 28:40 "Also make linen **r**,
29:8 Dress them in their linen **r**,
39:27 They wove inner **r** out of fine
40:14 and dress them in their linen **r**.
Lev 8:13 He put linen **r** on them,
10:5 men were still in their linen **r**.
1Ki 22:10 Judah were dressed in royal **r**
22:30 you should wear your royal **r**."
2Ki 10:22 man in charge of the priests' **r**,
10:22 "Bring out the **r** for all the
10:22 So he brought out **r** for them.
2Ch 18:9 Judah were dressed in royal **r**
18:29 you should wear your royal **r**."
Ezr 2:69 and 100 **r** for the priests.
3:10 in their **r** took their places
Neh 7:70 and 530 **r** for the priests.
7:72 and 67 **r** for the priests.
Est 5:1 day Esther put on her royal **r**.
Psa 45:8 All your **r** are ⌊fragrant⌋ with
133:2 running over the collar of his **r**.
Isa 3:22 fine **r**, coats, shawls, purses,
Eze 26:16 They will remove their **r** and
27:24 purple **r**, embroidered cloth,
Mat 26:65 Then the chief priest tore his **r**
Mar 12:38 like to walk around in long **r**,
Luk 20:46 like to walk around in long **r**
Rev 7:9 They were wearing white **r**,
7:13 these people wearing white **r**,
Rev 7:14 They have washed their **r** and
22:14 who wash their **r** so that they

robs (4)

Psa 35:10 from the one who **r** them."
Pro 28:24 The one who **r** his father or his
Eze 18:10 has a son who **r** and murders.
18:12 He **r**. He doesn't return the

rock (129)

Gen 49:24 of the Shepherd, the **R** of Israel,
Exo 15:5 sank to the bottom like a **r**.
17:6 you there by a **r** at Mount Horeb
17:6 Strike the **r**, and water will
17:12 So Aaron and Hur took a **r**,
21:18 and one hits the other with a **r**
Lev 11:5 You must never eat **r** badgers.
11:5 (**R** badgers are unclean
Num 20:8 tell the **r** to give up its water.
20:8 the community water from the **r**
20:10 the community in front of the **r**
20:10 water out of this **r** for you?"
20:11 his hand and hit the **r** twice
24:21 Your nest is built in a **r**.
Dtr 8:15 come out of solid **r** for you.
14:7 camels, rabbits, and **r** badgers.
32:4 He is a **r**. What he does is
32:13 rocks and olive oil from solid **r**.
32:15 made them and treated the **r**
32:18 (You ignored the **r** who fathered
32:30 Their **r** used these people to
32:31 Their **r** isn't like our rock.
32:31 Their rock isn't like our **r**.
32:37 Where is the **r** they took refuge
Jos 15:6 and goes up to the **R** of Bohan,
18:17 It descends to the **R** of Bohan,
Jdg 6:20 bread, put them on this **r**,
6:21 Fire flared up from the **r** and
7:25 They killed Oreb at the **R** of
13:19 them to the LORD on a **r**
20:45 into the desert to Rimmon **R**.
20:47 into the desert to Rimmon **R**.
20:47 at Rimmon **R** for four months.
21:13 men of Benjamin at Rimmon **R**
1Sm 2:2 There is no **R** like our God.
6:14 and stopped there by a large **r**.
6:15 and put them on the large **r**.)
6:18 The large **r** on which they put
7:12 Then Samuel took a **r** and set
7:12 He named it Ebenezer [**R** of
14:33 Roll a large **r** over to me now."
20:19 occasion, and stay by the **r**.
20:41 from the south side ⌊of the **r**⌋
23:28 place was called Slippery **R**.
2Sm 18:18 Absalom had taken a **r** and set
18:18 He called the **r** by his name,
20:8 were at the large **r** in Gibeon,
21:10 and stretched it out on the **r**
22:2 He said, The LORD is my **r**
22:3 my **r** in whom I take refuge,
22:32 Who is a **r** other than our God?
22:47 Thanks be to my **r**!
22:47 May God, the **r** of my salvation,
23:3 The **r** of Israel told me,
1Ki 1:9 at Zoheleth **R** near En Rogel.
1Ch 11:15 men went down to David's **r** at
Neh 9:15 and made water flow from a **r**
Est 1:6 a mosaic pavement of purple **r**,
Job 19:24 were forever engraved on a **r**
28:3 of the gloomy, pitch-black **r**.
41:24 Its chest is solid like a **r**,
Psa 18:2 The LORD is my **r** and my
18:2 my **r** in whom I take refuge,
18:31 Who is a **r** except our God?
18:46 Thanks be to my **r**!
19:14 my **r** and my defender.
27:5 He sets me high on a **r**.
28:1 O my **r**, do not turn a deaf ear to
31:2 Be a **r** of refuge for me,
31:3 you are my **r** and my fortress.
40:2 He set my feet on a **r** and made
42:9 I will ask God, my **r**,
61:2 Lead me to the **r** that is high
62:2 He alone is my **r** and my savior
62:6 He alone is my **r** and my savior
62:7 God is the **r** of my strength,

Psa 71:3 Be a **r** on which I may live,
71:3 you are my **r** and my fortress.
75:3 its foundations as solid as **r**.
78:16 made streams come out of a **r**.
78:20 True, he did strike a **r**,
78:35 that God was their **r**,
81:16 them with honey from a **r**."
89:26 and the **r** of my salvation.'
91:12 never hit your foot against a **r**.
92:15 He is my **r**. He is never unfair.
94:22 has become my **r** of refuge.
95:1 happily to the **r** of our salvation.
105:41 He opened a **r**, and water
114:8 He turns a **r** into a pool filled
137:9 and smashes them against a **r**.
144:1 Thank the LORD, my **r**,
Pro 30:19 snake making its way over a **r**,
30:26 **R** badgers are not a mighty
Isa 8:14 But he will be a **r** that makes
10:26 he struck down Midian at the **R**
17:10 You haven't remembered the **r**,
22:16 place for yourself in the **r**?
26:4 is an everlasting **r**.
28:16 I am going to lay a **r** in Zion,
28:16 a **r** that has been tested,
30:29 mountain, to the **r** of Israel.
32:2 and the shade of a large **r**
33:16 will be a fortress made of **r**.
44:8 There is no ⌊other⌋ **r**;
48:21 water flow from a **r** for them.
48:21 He split a **r**, and water gushed
51:1 Look to the **r** from which you
Jer 21:13 that is in the valley and on the **r**
23:29 a hammer that shatters a **r**?"
Eze 24:7 blood was poured on a bare **r**.
24:8 blood of its victims on a bare **r**.
26:4 dust and turn Tyre into a bare **r**.
26:14 I will turn you into bare **r**.
Hab 1:12 O **R**, you have destined them
Mat 4:6 never hit your foot against a **r**.'"
7:24 person who built a house on **r**.
7:25 its foundation was on **r**.
16:18 I can guarantee that on this **r**
27:60 which had been cut in a **r**.
Mar 15:46 which had been cut out of **r**,
Luk 4:11 never hit your foot against a **r**.'"
23:53 laid the body in a tomb cut in **r**,
Rom 9:32 over the **r** that trips people.
9:33 "I am placing a **r** in Zion that
9:33 a large **r** that people find
1Co 10:4 They drank from the spiritual **r**
10:4 and that **r** was Christ.
1Pe 2:8 a large **r** that people find

rocks (33)

Dtr 8:9 The land has **r** with iron ore,
32:13 He gave them honey from **r** and
1Sm 13:6 thickets, among **r**, in pits,
24:2 for David and his men on the **R**
1Ki 19:11 and shattered **r** ahead
2Ki 3:19 and use **r** to ruin every good
3:25 each man throwing **r** on every
Job 6:12 Do I have the strength of **r**?
14:18 falls and **r** are dislodged,
24:8 They hug the **r** because they
28:2 and **r** are melted for ⌊their⌋
28:9 exert their power on the flinty **r**
28:10 cut out mineshafts in the **r**.
29:6 and the **r** poured streams of
30:6 in the ground, and among **r**.
Psa 78:15 He split **r** in the desert.
104:18 The **r** are a refuge for badgers.
Pro 30:26 they make their home in the **r**.
Isa 2:10 Go in among the **r** and hide
2:19 will go into caves in the **r**
2:21 They will go into caves in the **r**
57:5 and under the cracks in the **r**.
Jer 4:29 thickets and climb among the **r**.
5:3 They are more stubborn than **r**.
13:4 bury it there in a crack in the **r**."
16:16 and even in the cracks in the **r**.
Lam 3:53 into a pit and threw **r** at me.
Amo 6:12 Do horses run on **r**?
Mat 27:51 and the **r** were split open.
Jon 10:31 Jews had again brought some **r**
Act 27:29 Fearing we might hit **r**,
Rev 6:15 among the **r** in the mountains.
6:16 said to the mountains and **r**,

rocky (13)

Exo 33:21 Stand by this **r** cliff.
Num 23:9 see them from the top of **r** cliffs,
Sos 2:14 hiding places of the **r** crevices,
Jer 18:14 The **r** slopes of Lebanon are
49:16 You live on **r** cliffs and occupy
Oba 1:3 You live on **r** cliffs.
Nah 1:6 fire and smashes the **r** cliffs.
Mat 13:5 were planted on **r** ground,
13:20 The seed planted on **r** ground
Mar 4:5 were planted on **r** ground,
4:16 that were planted on **r** ground.
Luk 8:6 Others were planted on **r** soil.
8:13 people are like seeds on **r** soil.

rod (17)

2Sm 7:14 I will punish him with a **r** and
Job 9:34 God should take his **r** away
21:9 God doesn't use his **r** on them.
Psa 23:4 Your **r** and your staff give me
89:32 then with a **r** I will punish their
Pro 10:13 but a **r** is for the back of one
26:3 and a **r** is for the backs of fools.
Isa 10:5 It is the **r** of my anger.
10:15 A **r** cannot move the person
10:24 when they strike with a **r**
11:4 He will strike the earth with a **r**
14:29 don't rejoice that the **r** of the
28:27 Black cumin is beaten with a **r**
30:31 He will strike them with his **r**.
Jer 48:17 the beautiful **r**, that is broken!'
Lam 3:1 under the **r** of God's fury.
Eze 41:8 full length of the measuring **r**,

rode (12)

Jdg 10:4 Jair had 30 sons who **r** on 30
12:14 sons and 30 grandsons who **r**
1Sm 25:42 Abigail quickly got up and **r**
30:17 men who **r** away on camels.
2Sm 22:11 He **r** on one of the angels as he
2Ki 9:18 So a chariot driver **r** off,
Est 8:10 who **r** special horses bred
8:14 The messengers **r** the king's
Psa 18:10 He **r** on one of the angels as he
Eze 23:6 young men who **r** on horses.
Act 8:28 As the official **r** along in his
Rev 6:2 He was given a crown and **r** off

rods (1)

Est 1:6 were attached to silver **r**

Rogelim (2)

2Sm 17:27 and Barzillai from **R** in Gilead
19:31 came from **R** with the king to

Rohgah (1)

1Ch 7:34 of his brother Shomer were **R**,

role (1)

Act 1:17 an active **r** in this ministry.

roll (11)

Jos 10:18 Joshua replied, "**R** large stones
1Sm 14:33 **R** a large rock over to me now."
Pro 26:27 will have it **r** back on him.
Isa 28:28 wheels of his cart will **r** over it,
Jer 6:26 and **r** around in ashes,
25:34 **R** in the dust, you leaders of
51:25 against you, **r** you off the cliffs,
Mic 1:6 I will **r** its stones down into a
1:10 **R** in the dust of Beth Leaphrah.
Mar 16:3 "Who will **r** away the stone for
2Pe 2:22 washed goes back to **r** around

rolled (17)

Gen 29:3 the stone would be **r** off the
29:8 When the stone is **r** off the
29:10 He came forward and **r** the
1Ki 3:19 son died because she **r** over
2Ki 2:8 Elijah took his coat, **r** it up,
Isa 9:5 of battle and every garment **r**
28:27 wheels aren't **r** over cumin.
34:4 The heavens will be **r** up like a
Isa 38:12 You **r** it up like a shepherd's
38:12 You **r** up my life like a weaver.
Mat 28:2 from heaven, **r** the stone away,
Mar 9:20 He fell on the ground, **r** around,
15:46 and he **r** a stone against the
16:4 that the stone had been **r** away.
Luk 24:2 the stone had been **r** away from
Jon 20:7 linen but was **r** up separately.
Rev 6:14 like a scroll being **r** up.

rolling (2)

Jdg 7:13 a loaf of barley bread **r** around
Mat 27:60 After **r** a large stone against the

rolls (2)

Psa 29:3 The voice of the LORD **r** over
Pro 26:27 Whoever **r** a stone will have it

Romamti Ezer (2)

1Ch 25:4 Giddalti, **R**, Joshbekashah,
25:31 twenty-fourth chose **R**, his sons,

Roman (27)

Mat 8:5 a **R** army officer came to beg
Luk 2:1 a census of the **R** Empire.
7:2 There a **R** army officer's
Act 10:1 He was a **R** army officer in the
10:22 a **R** army officer, sent us.
16:12 and it is a **R** colony.
16:20 In front of the **R** officials,
16:21 or practice as **R** citizens."
16:35 In the morning the **R** officials
16:37 But Paul told the guards, "**R**
16:37 even though we're **R** citizens.
16:38 When the **R** officials heard that
16:38 Paul and Silas were **R** citizens,
21:31 the officer in charge of the **R**
22:25 "Is it legal for you to whip a **R**
22:26 This man is a **R** citizen."
22:27 are you a **R** citizen?"
22:28 money to become a **R** citizen."
22:28 "But I was born a **R** citizen."
22:29 that he had tied up a **R** citizen.
23:15 council must go to the **R** officer
23:27 out that he was a **R** citizen,
25:16 'That's not the **R** way of doing
25:23 **R** army officers and the most
28:17 over to the **R** authorities.
28:18 The **R** authorities
2Co 11:25 three times **R** officials had me

Romans (1)

Jon 11:48 Then the **R** will take away our

Rome (13)

Act 2:10 and visitors from **R**,
18:2 ordered all Jews to leave **R**.
19:21 have been there, I must see **R**."
23:11 tell the truth about me in **R**."
25:25 have decided to send him to **R**.
25:27 to send a prisoner to **R** when
28:15 Believers in **R** heard that we
28:15 finally arrived in the city of **R**.
28:17 the most influential Jews in **R**
28:21 has come to **R** has reported
Rom 1:7 To everyone in **R** whom God
1:15 eager to tell you who live in **R**
2Ti 1:17 When he arrived in **R**,

roof (34)

Gen 6:16 Make a **r** for the ship,
Dtr 22:8 railing around the edge of the **r**.
22:8 home if someone falls off the **r**.
Jos 2:6 (She had taken them up to the **r**
2:8 Rahab went up to them on the **r**.
Jdg 3:20 sat alone in his room on the **r**.
9:51 went up on the **r** of the tower.
16:27 On the **r** there were about three
1Sm 9:25 blankets on the **r** for Saul,
9:26 Samuel called to Saul on the **r**,
2Sm 11:2 bed and walked around on the **r**
11:2 From the **r** he saw a woman
16:22 put up on the **r** for Absalom,
18:24 watchman walked along the **r**
1Ki 7:9 From the foundation to the **r**,
2Ki 4:10 make a small room on the **r**

2Ki 23:12 had made and placed on the **r**
Neh 3:15 He rebuilt it, put a **r** over it,
Job 20:13 holds it on the **r** of his mouth,
Psa 22:15 My tongue sticks to the **r** of my
129:6 Make them be like grass on a **r**,
137:6 Let my tongue stick to the **r** of
Pro 21:9 Better to live on a corner of a **r**
25:24 Better to live on a corner of a **r**
Ecc 10:18 A **r** sags because of laziness.
Eze 3:26 make your tongue stick to the **r**
41:25 There was a wooden **r** hanging
Hab 2:11 A beam in the **r** will answer it.
Mat 24:17 Those who are on the **r** should
Mar 2:4 they made an opening in the **r**
13:15 Those who are on the **r** should
Luk 5:19 So they went up on the **r**.
17:31 on the **r** shouldn't come down
Act 10:9 Peter went on the **r** to pray.

roofed (1)
1Ki 6:9 he **r** the temple with rows of

roofs (9)
2Ki 19:26 green grass on the **r**,
Neh 8:16 Some made booths on their **r**,
Job 29:10 stuck to the **r** of their mouths.
Isa 15:3 On their **r** and in their city
22:1 do all of you go up on the **r**?
37:27 green grass on the **r**,
Jer 32:29 me furious by going up to the **r**
Lam 4:4 of nursing infants stick to the **r**
Eze 41:26 of the temple, and on the **r**.

rooftop (2)
Psa 102:7 I am like a lonely bird on a **r**.
Jer 48:38 in Moab will mourn on every **r**

rooftops (2)
Jer 19:13 and all the **r** of the houses will
Zep 1:5 all the stars in the sky on their **r**

room (108)
Gen 24:23 tell me whether there is **r**
24:25 feed ⌊for your camels⌋ and **r**
26:22 the LORD has made **r** for us,
34:21 Look, there's plenty of **r** in this
43:30 his private **r** and cried there.
Exo 3:8 with plenty of **r** ⌊for everyone⌋.
Lev 26:10 to make **r** for new ones.
Num 22:26 place where there was no **r**
Jdg 3:19 Then all his advisers left the **r**.
3:20 to him as he sat alone in his **r**
3:23 Ehud left the **r**. (He had closed
3:23 the doors of the **r** before he left.
17:10 and your **r** and board."
1Sm 3:2 Eli was lying down in his **r**.
3:9 went and lay down in his **r**.
2Sm 18:33 He went to the **r** above the gate
1Ki 1:15 went to the king in his private **r**.
6:3 hall in front of the main **r**
6:16 He sectioned off a 30-foot-long **r**
6:16 He built it to serve as an inner **r**,
6:17 The 60-foot-long **r** at the front of
6:19 He prepared the inner **r** of the
6:20 The inner **r** was 30 feet long,
6:21 the inner **r** which was covered
6:22 altar in the inner **r** with gold.
6:23 In the inner **r** he made two
6:27 put the angels in the inner **r**
6:27 each other in the center of the **r**.
6:31 the entrance to the inner **r** out
7:49 the north in front of the inner **r**),
7:50 of the inner ⌊**r**⌋ (the most holy
8:6 to its place in the inner **r**
8:8 standing in front of the inner **r**,
14:6 when she came into the **r**.
17:19 carried him to the upstairs **r**
17:23 him down from the upstairs **r**
20:30 to the city and hid in an inner **r**.
22:25 you go into an inner **r** to hide."
2Ki 1:2 window lattice in his upstairs **r**
4:10 Let's make a small **r** on the roof
4:11 went into the upstairs **r**,
4:21 of the man of God, left ⌊the **r**⌋,
4:33 He went into the **r**,
4:35 walked across the **r** and came
2Ki 9:2 Take him into an inner **r**.
23:11 the temple courtyard near the **r**
23:12 on the roof of Ahaz's upstairs **r**,
1Ch 28:11 and the **r** for the throne of
2Ch 3:4 of ⌊the main **r**⌋ was 30 feet
3:16 He made chains for the inner **r**
4:20 directed in front of the inner **r**),
4:22 the gold doors of the inner ⌊**r**⌋
5:7 to its place in the inner **r**
5:9 standing in front of the inner **r**,
18:24 you go into an inner **r** to hide."
Ezr 10:6 and went to the **r** of Jehohanan,
Neh 3:31 far as the upper **r** at the corner.
3:32 repairs between the upper **r** at
13:5 provided a large **r** for Tobiah.
13:5 Previously, this **r** had been
13:7 with a **r** in God's temple.
13:8 household goods out of the **r**.
Est 4:11 **r** without being summoned.
5:1 facing the king's throne **r**.
7:8 garden to the palace dining **r**,
Sos 2:4 He leads me into a banquet **r**
Isa 49:20 Make **r** for me to live here."
Jer 35:4 into the side **r** of the sons of
35:4 It was next to the **r** of the
35:4 above the side **r** of Maaseiah,
36:10 in the LORD's temple in the **r**
36:12 he went down to the scribe's **r**
36:20 they put the scroll in the side **r**
36:21 took the scroll from the side **r**
38:11 to a **r** under the treasury.
Eze 8:12 Each of them is in the **r** where
40:38 There was a **r** with a door that
40:38 This is the **r** where the priests
40:39 tables on each side of the **r**.
40:43 to the wall all around the **r**,
40:44 One **r** was at the side of the
40:44 The other **r** was at the side of
40:45 The man said to me, "This **r**
40:46 The **r** that faces north is for the
41:4 Then he measured the **r** at the
41:5 The width of each side **r**
Dan 6:10 An upper **r** in his house had
Zec 10:10 won't be enough **r** for them."
Mat 6:6 go to your **r** and close the door.
Mar 2:2 There was no **r** left,
4:21 anyone bring a lamp into a **r**
14:14 'Where is my **r** where I can eat
14:15 and show you a large **r**.
14:15 The **r** will be completely
Luk 2:7 because there wasn't any **r**
12:17 I don't have enough **r** to store
14:22 there is still **r** for more people.'
22:11 'Where is the **r** where I can eat
22:12 show you a large furnished **r**.
Jon 21:25 world wouldn't have enough **r**
Act 1:13 second-story **r** where they were
4:15 and John to leave the council **r**
5:41 The apostles left the council **r**.
9:37 and was laid in an upstairs **r**.
9:40 made everyone leave the **r**.
20:8 in the upstairs **r** where we were
25:7 When Paul entered the **r**,
Phm 1:22 thing — have a guest **r** ready

rooms (65)
Gen 6:14 Make **r** in the ship and coat it
1Ki 6:5 containing side **r** all around
6:29 inner and outer **r** of the temple.
6:30 the floor of the inner and outer **r**
7:3 with cedar above the side **r**,
1Ch 9:26 were in charge of the **r**
9:33 They lived in **r** in the temple
23:28 the courtyards and the temple **r**,
28:11 upper **r**, inner rooms,
28:11 upper rooms, inner **r**,
28:12 and for all the **r** around it.
28:12 (These **r** served as treasuries
2Ch 3:9 overlaid the upper **r** with gold.
Neh 10:38 into the **r** of the storehouses
12:44 They stored in those **r** the gifts
13:9 I told them to cleanse the **r**,
Pro 24:4 With knowledge its **r** are filled
Sos 1:4 brought me into his private **r**.
Isa 26:20 My people, go to your **r**,
Jer 22:13 his upper **r** through injustice.
Jer 22:14 for myself with big upper **r**.' He
22:14 panels the **r** with cedar,
35:2 Take them into one of the side **r**
Eze 40:10 All three **r** on each side were
40:17 I saw **r** there and pavement all
40:17 There were 30 **r** along the edge
40:44 the inner courtyard were the **r**
41:6 The **r** were arranged on three
41:6 There were 30 **r** on each story.
41:6 These **r** had supports all the
41:7 The side **r** grew wider all the
41:8 the foundation for the side **r**.
41:9 The outer wall of the side **r**
41:9 between the side **r** connected
41:10 and the priests' **r**. It was 35 feet
41:11 The doors in the side **r** were
41:26 on the side **r** of the temple,
42:1 He brought me to the side **r**
42:4 In front of the side **r** was a
42:4 of these side **r** faced north.
42:5 The side **r** on the third story
42:6 The **r** were in three stories.
42:6 That is why the **r** on the third
42:7 which ran parallel to the side **r**
42:7 It ran alongside the side **r** for 87
42:8 The row of **r** in the outer
42:8 The **r** that faced the temple
42:9 These lower side **r** had an
42:10 There were side **r** parallel to
42:11 that was in front of the side **r**
42:11 These side **r** were as long and
42:11 and as wide as the northern **r**.
42:12 The doors to the south **r** were
42:12 as the doors to the north **r**.
42:13 and southern side **r** that face
42:13 face the open area are holy **r**.
42:13 These **r** are where the priests
42:13 Because these **r** are holy,
44:19 leave their clothes in the side **r**
46:19 to the side **r** that faced north.
46:19 These **r** were reserved for the
46:19 place on the west side of the **r**.
Joe 2:16 Grooms leave their **r**.
Luk 12:3 have whispered in private **r** will
Jon 14:2 My Father's house has many **r**.

roomy (1)
Gen 26:22 it Rehoboth [**R**] and said,

rooster (13)
Pro 30:31 a strutting **r**, a male goat, a king
Mat 26:34 Before a **r** crows tonight,
26:74 Just then a **r** crowed.
26:75 had said: "Before a **r** crows,
Mar 14:30 before a **r** crows twice,
14:68 the entrance. Then a **r** crowed.
14:72 Just then a **r** crowed a second
14:72 "Before a **r** crows twice,
Luk 22:34 I can guarantee that the **r** won't
22:60 was still speaking, a **r** crowed.
22:61 "Before a **r** crows today,
Jon 13:38 I can guarantee this truth: No **r**
18:27 and just then a **r** crowed.

root (22)
2Ki 19:30 again take **r** and produce crops.
Job 5:3 seen a stubborn fool take **r**,
19:28 The **r** of the problem is found in
Psa 80:9 the ground for it so that it took **r**
Isa 11:10 At that time the **r** of Jesse will
14:29 will come from that snake's **r**,
14:30 But I will put your **r** to death
27:6 to come Jacob will take **r**.
37:31 again take **r** and produce crops.
40:24 They have hardly taken **r** in the
53:2 like a **r** out of dry ground.
Jer 12:2 You plant them, and they take **r**.
Mal 4:1 won't leave a single **r** or branch.
Mat 13:21 Since he doesn't have any **r**,
Rom 11:16 If the **r** is holy, the branches are
11:18 that you don't support the **r**,
11:18 the **r** supports you.
15:12 "There will be a **r** from Jesse.
1Ti 6:10 the love of money is the **r** of all
Heb 12:15 so that bitterness doesn't take **r**
Rev 5:5 tribe of Judah, the **R** of David,

Rev 22:16 I am the **r** and descendant of

rooted (1)

Hos 14:5 They will be firmly **r** like

roots (32)

Job 8:17 Its **r** weave through a pile of
14:8 If its **r** grow old in the ground
18:16 His **r** dry up under him.
29:19 My **r** will grow toward the
30:4 and the **r** of the broom plant are
Psa 52:5 He will pull your **r** out of this
Pro 12:3 and the **r** of righteous people
12:12 but the **r** of righteous people
Isa 5:24 in flames, so their **r** will rot,
11:1 branch from its **r** will bear fruit.
Jer 17:8 It will send its **r** down to a
Eze 17:6 but its **r** grew downward.
17:7 Now, the vine stretched its **r**
17:9 to pull the vine up by its **r**.
31:7 Its **r** reached down to many
Dan 4:15 But leave the stump and its **r** in
4:23 But leave the stump and its **r** in
4:26 the stump and the tree's **r** were
11:7 a shoot will grow from her **r**
Hos 9:16 Their **r** are dried up.
Amo 2:9 the ground and their **r** below it.
Zep 2:4 Ekron will be torn out by the **r**.
Mat 3:10 ax is now ready to cut the **r**
13:6 their **r** weren't deep enough.
Mar 4:6 They didn't have any **r**,
4:17 But they don't develop any **r**.
Luk 3:9 ax is now ready to cut the **r**
8:13 but they don't develop any **r**.
17:6 'Pull yourself up by the **r**,
Rom 11:17 get your nourishment from the **r**
Eph 3:17 into which you sink your **r**
Col 2:7 Sink your **r** in him and build on

rope (5)

Jos 2:15 So she let them down by a **r**
2Sm 8:2 and measured them with a **r**.
Job 18:10 A **r** is hidden on the ground for
41:1 or tie its tongue down with a **r**?
Ecc 4:12 A triple-braided **r** is not easily

ropes (51)

Exo 28:14 of pure gold, twisted like **r**,
28:22 out of pure gold, twisted like **r**.
28:24 Then fasten the two gold **r** to
28:25 Fasten the other ends of the **r**
35:18 and the courtyard with their **r**,
39:15 out of pure gold, twisted like **r**.
39:17 They fastened the two gold **r** to
39:18 fastened the other ends of the **r**
39:40 the **r** and pegs — all the
Num 3:26 tent and the altar, and the **r**.
3:37 the bases, pegs, and **r**.
4:26 entrance to the courtyard, the **r**,
4:32 the bases, pegs, and **r**.
Jdg 15:13 they tied him up with two new **r**
15:14 The **r** on his arms became like
16:11 with new **r** that have never
16:12 So Delilah took some new **r**
16:12 But Samson tore the **r** off his
2Sm 17:13 all Israel will bring **r** to that city
22:6 The **r** of the grave had
1Ki 20:31 put **r** around our necks,
20:32 and put **r** around their necks.
Job 4:21 Haven't the **r** of their tent been
36:8 and tangled in **r** of misery,
38:31 Pleiades or untie the **r** of Orion?
39:5 Who unties the **r** of the wild
Psa 2:3 chains and shake off their **r**."
18:4 The **r** of death had become
18:5 The **r** of the grave had
116:3 The **r** of death became tangled
119:61 ⌊Though⌋ the **r** of wicked
129:4 He has cut me loose from the **r**
140:5 have spread out a net with **r**.
Pro 5:22 and he will be caught in the **r** of
Isa 3:24 They will wear **r** instead of
33:20 and none of its **r** will be broken.
33:23 Your **r** hang loose,
54:2 Lengthen your tent **r**,
Jer 10:20 and all my **r** are broken.
Jer 30:8 your necks and tear off your **r**.
38:6 They used **r** to lower Jeremiah
38:11 there and lowered them with **r**
38:12 arms to protect you from the **r**."
38:13 They used the **r** to pull
Eze 3:25 People will tie you up with **r**,
4:8 I will tie you up with **r** so that
Hos 11:4 human kindness, with **r** of love.
Jon 2:15 He made a whip from small **r**
Act 27:17 Then they passed **r** under the
27:32 Then the soldiers cut the **r** that
27:40 time they untied the **r** that held

rose (29)

Gen 7:17 the ship so that it **r** high above
7:18 As the water **r** and became
7:19 The water **r** very high above
7:20 It **r** 23 feet above the
32:31 The sun **r** as he passed
Exo 19:18 Smoke **r** from the mountain like
Dtr 33:2 For his people he **r** from Seir
Jos 3:16 The water **r** up like a dam as
Jdg 3:20 As the king **r** from his throne,
9:35 his troops **r** from their ambush.
1Sm 17:52 of Israel and Judah **r** up,
Psa 76:9 when you **r** to judge,
76:9 when you **r** to save every
81:5 for Joseph when Joseph **r**
104:8 The mountains **r** and the
107:26 The sailors aboard ship **r**
Sos 2:1 I am a **r** of Sharon,
Eze 1:19 When the living creatures **r**
1:19 from the earth, the wheels **r**.
1:20 The wheels **r** with them,
1:21 And whenever the creatures **r**
1:21 the wheels **r** with them,
10:4 The LORD's glory **r** from the
10:15 The angels **r**. These were the
10:17 When the angels **r**,
10:17 the wheels **r** with them.
10:19 lifted their wings and **r** from
Jnh 4:8 When the sun **r**, God made a
Mat 28:1 as the sun **r** Sunday morning,

Rosh (2)

Gen 46:21 **R**, Muppim, Huppim, and Ard.
Isa 66:19 Meshech, **R**, Tubal, Javan,

roster (13)

Num 1:20 The **r** of families and
1:22 The **r** of families and
1:24 The **r** of families and
1:26 The **r** of families and
1:28 The **r** of families and
1:30 The **r** of families and
1:32 The **r** of families and
1:34 The **r** of families and
1:36 The **r** of families and
1:38 The **r** of families and
1:40 The **r** of families and
1:42 The **r** of families and
1Ch 7:40 Their military **r** had 26,000

rot (9)

Job 20:7 he will certainly **r** like his own
Pro 10:7 of wicked people will **r** away.
Isa 5:24 so their roots will **r**,
34:4 All the stars in the sky will **r**.
40:20 choose wood that will not **r**
Hos 5:12 of Judah as **r** destroys wood.
Zec 14:12 Their flesh will **r** while they are
14:12 Their eyes will **r** in their
14:12 tongues will **r** in their mouths.

rotten (13)

Job 41:27 and bronze to be like **r** wood.
Psa 14:3 Together they have become **r**
38:5 My wounds smell **r**.
53:3 Together they have become **r**
Jer 29:17 These people are like **r** figs to
Hab 3:16 A **r** feeling has entered me.
Mat 7:17 but a **r** tree produces bad fruit.
7:18 and a **r** tree cannot produce
12:33 Or make a tree **r**, and then its
12:33 and then its fruit will be **r**.
Luk 6:43 good tree doesn't produce **r** fruit
Luk 6:43 and a **r** tree doesn't produce
Rom 3:12 Together they have become **r**

rotting (4)

Isa 17:11 harvest will become a ⌊**r**⌋ pile
38:17 me and kept me from the **r** pit.
Eze 32:5 the valleys with your **r** corpse.
33:10 and we are **r** away because of

rough (5)

Isa 40:4 **R** places will be made smooth.
42:16 I will make **r** places smooth.
45:2 and smooth out the **r** places.
Luk 3:5 The **r** roads will be made
1Th 2:2 As you know, we suffered **r**

roughly (1)

1Co 4:11 **r** treated, and homeless.

round (14)

Exo 12:39 Egypt, they baked **r**, flat bread.
29:23 take a **r** loaf of bread,
Num 11:8 it in a pot or make **r** loaves
1Ki 7:23 It was **r**, 7 ½ feet high,
7:31 The opening **w** round,
7:31 panels were square, **n** round.
7:35 The top of each stand had a **r**,
2Ch 4:2 It was **r**, 7 ½ feet high,
Job 37:12 the clouds as they churn **r**
37:12 as they churn round and **r** over
Ecc 1:6 **R** and round it blows.
1:6 Round and **r** it blows.
Sos 4:4 A thousand **r** shields belonging
7:2 Your navel is a **r** bowl.

rounds (2)

Sos 3:3 The watchmen making their **r**
5:7 The watchmen making their **r**

route (6)

Exo 13:17 that was the shortest **r**.
Dtr 1:22 us about the **r** we should take
1:33 to show you which **r** to take.
19:3 Provide a **r** to each of these
2Ki 3:9 took an indirect **r** ⌊to Moab⌋.
Job 11:20 Their escape **r** will be closed.

row (14)

Exo 28:17 In the first **r** put red quartz,
28:18 In the second **r** put turquoise,
28:19 In the third **r** put jacinth,
28:20 In the fourth **r** put beryl,
39:10 In the first **r** they put red quartz,
39:11 In the second **r** they put
39:12 In the third **r** they put jacinth,
39:13 In the fourth **r** they put beryl,
39:37 lamp stand with its lamps in a **r**
1Ki 7:3 by 45 pillars (15 per **r**).
Ezr 6:4 of large stones and a **r** of wood.
Eze 27:8 Sidon and Arvad used to **r** you.
42:8 The **r** of rooms in the outer
Jnh 1:13 Instead, the men tried to **r**

rowed (2)

Mar 6:48 in a lot of trouble as they **r**,
Jon 6:19 After they had **r** three or four

rowers (2)

Eze 27:26 Your **r** took you out to the high
27:29 All the **r**, the sailors, and all the

rows (25)

Exo 28:17 Fasten four **r** of precious
39:10 They fastened four **r** of
Dtr 22:9 plant anything between the **r**
1Ki 6:9 he roofed the temple with **r** of
7:2 It had four **r** of cedar pillars
7:4 The windows were in three **r**
7:17 He also made seven **r** of
7:18 he made two **r** ⌊of decorations⌋
7:20 Two hundred pomegranates in **r**
7:24 Under the rim were two **r** of
7:42 for the 2 sets of filigree (2 **r**
1Ch 9:32 the bread out in **r** every day
23:29 responsible for the **r** of bread,
28:16 each table with the **r** of bread,

2Ch 2:4 and have **r** of bread there
4:3 Under the rim were two **r** of
4:13 for the 2 sets of filigree (2 **r**
13:11 sweet-smelling incense and **r**
29:18 the table for the **r** of bread and
Ezr 6:4 with three **r** of large stones and
Neh 10:33 for **r** of the bread of the
Job 24:11 oil between **r** ⌊of olive trees⌋.
41:15 Its back has **r** of scales that are
Isa 28:25 he plant wild wheat in **r**?
Jer 5:10 "Go among Jerusalem's **r** of

royal (140)

Jos 10:2 It was like one of the **r** cities,
13:31 the **r** cities of Og in Bashan.
Jdg 5:25 offered him buttermilk in a **r**
1Sm 26:15 Someone came to kill His **R**
26:17 is my voice, Your **R** Majesty,"
27:5 I live in the **r** city with you?"
2Sm 3:1 As the war between the **r**
3:6 his position in Saul's **r** family.
4:8 given Your **R** Majesty revenge
7:16 Your **r** house will remain in my
8:16 was the **r** historian.
8:17 Seraiah was the **r** scribe.
11:2 on the roof of the **r** palace.
11:8 Uriah left the **r** palace,
11:9 of the **r** palace among his
12:26 and captured its **r** fortress.
14:26 according to the **r** standard.
15:35 hear anything from the **r** palace,
20:24 was the **r** historian.
20:25 Sheva was the **r** scribe.
1Ki 1:46 Solomon is now seated on the **r**
1:47 Furthermore, the **r** officials
4:3 was the **r** historian.
9:1 LORD's temple, the **r** palace,
9:5 then I will establish your **r**
9:10 house and the **r** palace).
10:12 temple and the **r** palace,
10:13 her out of his **r** generosity.
11:14 Hadad was from the Edomite **r**
14:26 temple and the **r** palace.
14:27 by the entrance to the **r** palace,
15:18 LORD's temple and the **r** palace
16:18 the stronghold in the **r** palace
22:10 Judah were dressed in **r** robes
22:30 you should wear your **r** robes."
2Ki 7:9 Let's bring the news to the **r**
7:11 the news to the **r** palace.
11:1 to destroy the entire **r** family.
11:5 must guard the **r** palace.
11:16 the horses enter the **r** palace,
11:19 Guards' Gate to the **r** palace.
11:19 Then Joash sat on the **r** throne.
11:20 with a sword at the **r** palace.
12:18 temple and the **r** palace.
14:14 and in the **r** palace treasury.
15:25 and Arieh in the fortress of the **r**
16:8 in the treasury in the **r** palace
18:15 and in the **r** palace treasury.
18:18 who was the **r** historian and the
18:37 who was the **r** historian and the
21:6 and appointed ⌊**r**⌋ mediums
22:12 and the **r** official Asaiah.
22:14 in charge of the ⌊**r**⌋ wardrobe.
24:13 temple and the **r** palace.
25:9 LORD's temple, the **r** palace,
1Ch 17:14 him in my **r** house forever,
18:15 was the **r** historian.
18:16 Shavsha was the **r** scribe.
27:25 for the **r** treasuries:
27:34 the commander of the **r** army.
29:25 The people of Israel gave him **r**
2Ch 2:1 and a **r** palace for himself.
2:12 LORD's temple and a **r** palace.
7:11 LORD's temple and the **r** palace
7:18 then I will establish your **r**
9:11 temple and the **r** palace,
12:9 temple and the **r** palace.
12:10 by the entrance to the **r** palace,
16:2 temple and the **r** palace.
18:9 Judah were dressed in **r** robes
18:29 you should wear your **r** robes."
21:17 could be found in the **r** palace.
22:10 to destroy the entire **r** family
2Ch 23:5 third must be at the **r** palace.
23:15 Horse Gate of the **r** palace,
23:20 Upper Gate to the **r** palace
23:20 seated the king on the **r** throne.
25:24 and in the **r** palace treasury.
26:21 was in charge of the **r** palace
28:21 the **r** palace, and the princes,
32:9 all his **r** forces were attacking
33:6 and appointed ⌊**r**⌋ mediums
34:8 the **r** historian and son of
34:20 and the **r** official Asaiah.
34:22 in charge of the ⌊**r**⌋ wardrobe.
Est 1:2 King Xerxes sat on the **r** throne
1:7 provided plenty of **r** wine out
1:7 wine out of his **r** generosity.
1:9 for the women at the **r** palace
1:11 wearing her **r** crown.
1:13 in **r** decrees and decisions,
1:15 "According to the **r** decrees,
1:19 Your Majesty, issue a **r** decree.
1:19 you should give her **r** position
2:16 to King Xerxes in his **r** palace
2:17 So he put the **r** crown on her
2:18 out gifts from his **r** generosity.
4:14 you may have gained your **r**
4:16 even if it is against a **r** decree.
5:1 day Esther put on her **r** robes.
5:1 The king was sitting on the **r**
6:8 ⌊The servants⌋ should bring a **r**
6:8 one that has a **r** crest on its
8:15 of the king wearing the **r** violet
Pro 30:28 yet it can even be found in **r**
Sos 7:5 dangling curls are **r** beauty.
Isa 36:3 who was the **r** historian and the
36:22 who was the **r** historian and the
60:16 nations and nurse at **r** breasts.
62:3 a **r** crown in the hand of your
Jer 27:18 in the **r** palace of Judah,
27:21 in the **r** palace of Judah,
38:7 But an official in the **r** palace,
38:8 Ebed Melech left the **r** palace
38:11 him and went to the **r** palace,
39:8 burned down the **r** palace
41:1 a descendant of the **r** family
43:10 his **r** canopy above them.
52:13 LORD's temple, the **r** palace,
Eze 17:13 took someone from the **r** family,
43:13 using **r** measurements.
43:13 (The **r** measuring stick was 21
Dan 1:3 the **r** family, and the nobility.
1:21 Daniel served the **r** palace until
2:14 the captain of the **r** guard,
2:15 He asked Arioch, the **r** official,
4:29 around the **r** palace in Babylon.
4:30 I built the **r** palace by my own
4:36 My **r** honor and glory were also
5:5 the lamp stand of the **r** palace.
5:20 was removed from the **r** throne.
11:20 official go out in **r** splendor.
11:21 He will not be given **r** splendor.
11:45 He will pitch his **r** tents
Hos 5:1 Open your ears, **r** family!
Zec 6:13 temple and receive **r** honor.
Mat 11:8 fine clothes are in **r** palaces.
Luk 7:25 live in luxury are in **r** palaces.
Act 12:21 Herod, wearing his **r** clothes,
1Pe 2:9 a **r** priesthood, a holy nation,

rub (4)

Dtr 28:40 your country but no olive oil to **r**
2Sm 14:2 Don't **r** olive oil on yourself,
Amo 6:6 They **r** the finest oils all over
Mic 6:15 but you won't **r** the oil on your

rubbed (3)

2Sm 1:21 was never **r** with olive oil.
Eze 16:4 You weren't **r** with salt or
29:18 soldier's shoulder was **r** raw.

rubbish (2)

Neh 4:2 the stones out of the **r** heaps,
Psa 119:119 on earth as if they were **r**.

rubble (26)

2Ki 19:25 fortified cities into piles of **r**.
23:12 and dumped their **r** in the
Ezr 6:11 should be turned into a pile of **r**.
Neh 4:10 and there is too much **r**.
Job 15:28 that are doomed to be piles of **r**.
Psa 102:14 stones, and they pity its **r**.
Isa 17:1 It will become a pile of **r**.
25:2 fortified cities into piles of **r**,
37:26 fortified cities into piles of **r**.
Jer 9:11 turn Jerusalem into a pile of **r**,
22:5 palace will become a pile of **r**.
26:9 this city will become a pile of **r**
26:18 will become a pile of **r**,
27:17 this city be turned into **r**?
46:19 a pile of **r** where no one lives.
49:2 It will become a pile of **r**.
49:13 Bozrah will become a pile of **r**.
51:37 Babylon will become piles of **r**.
Eze 29:9 a wasteland and a pile of **r**.
29:10 I will turn Egypt into a pile of **r**.
Dan 2:5 will be turned into piles of **r**.
3:29 will be turned into piles of **r**.
Hos 12:11 become like piles of **r** beside
Mic 1:6 will turn Samaria into a pile of **r**,
1:7 will be turned into a pile of **r**.
3:12 will become a pile of **r**,

rubies (2)

Isa 54:12 I will rebuild your towers with **r**,
Eze 27:16 and **r** for your merchandise.

rudders (1)

Jas 3:4 Yet, by using small **r**,

ruddy (1)

Sos 5:10 My beloved is dazzling yet **r**.

rude (1)

1Co 13:5 It isn't **r**. It doesn't think about

Rufus (2)

Mar 15:21 the father of Alexander and **R**.
Rom 16:13 Greet **R**, that outstanding

rugs (2)

Isa 21:5 Spread the **r** ⌊by the table⌋.
Eze 27:24 and many multicolored **r** with

Ruhamah (1)

Hos 2:1 and call your sisters **R** [Loved].

ruin (41)

Gen 41:30 and the famine will **r** the land.
Exo 22:5 But if he lets them **r** the whole
Lev 26:31 and **r** your sacred places.
Dtr 20:8 Then you won't **r** the morale of
22:14 her and **r** her reputation by
Jdg 6:5 came into the land only to **r** it.
Rut 4:6 I did, I would **r** my inheritance.
2Sm 17:14 defeated in order to **r** Absalom.)
2Ki 3:19 and use rocks to **r** every good
Job 15:23 He knows that his **r** is close at
21:20 His eyes should see his own **r**.
31:29 "If I enjoyed the **r** of my enemy
Psa 52:5 But God will **r** you forever.
73:18 and make them fall into **r**.
Pro 5:14 I almost reached total **r** in the
10:14 of a stubborn fool invites **r**.
10:29 for an innocent person but a **r**
11:3 leads treacherous people to **r**.
11:9 person can **r** his neighbor,
13:3 has a big mouth comes to **r**.
18:7 A fool's mouth is his **r**.
26:28 and a flattering mouth causes **r**.
31:3 power to those who **r** kings.
Sos 2:15 the little foxes that **r** vineyards.
Isa 32:7 plans in order to **r** poor people
59:7 **R** and destruction are on their
Jer 31:28 and to wreck, **r**, and hurt them.
44:6 So they became the desolate **r**
51:62 it will become a permanent **r**.'
Lam 3:48 down from my eyes over the **r**
Dan 11:26 the king's rich food will **r** him.
Amo 6:6 and are not sorry for the **r** ⌊of
8:4 the needy and **r** those who are
Mic 6:13 with heavy blows and to **r** you
6:16 That is why I will **r** you.
Zep 2:13 turn Nineveh into a deserted **r**,

Rom 3:16 There is **r** and suffering
14:20 Don't **r** God's work because of
1Co 15:33 people will **r** decent people.
Eph 4:22 to be will **r** you through desires
1Ti 6:9 them in destruction and **r**.

ruined (63)

Gen 41:36 will not be **r** by the famine."
47:19 Do you want the land to be **r**?
Exo 9:31 (The flax and the barley were **r**,
10:7 you realize that Egypt is **r**?"
32:7 of Egypt have **r** ⌊everything⌋.
Dtr 9:12 of Egypt have **r** ⌊everything⌋.
22:19 The husband **r** the reputation of
28:22 scorching winds, and **r** crops.
28:51 until they've completely **r** you.
2Ch 28:23 But they **r** him and all Israel.
Job 15:28 He lives in **r** cities where no
30:24 one who is **r** when that person
Psa 78:45 bit them and frogs that **r** them.
109:10 help far from their **r** homes.
Pro 14:28 but without people a ruler is **r**.
Isa 24:10 The **r** city lies desolate.
30:22 away like clothing **r** by stains.
60:12 The nations will certainly be **r**.
61:4 They will renew the **r** cities,
64:7 have let us be **r** by our sins.
64:11 All that we valued has been **r**.
Jer 4:7 Your cities will be **r**,
4:20 The whole land is **r**.
4:27 The whole earth will be **r**,
9:12 The land dies; it has been **r**
9:19 "We're **r**! We're very ashamed.
13:7 Now the belt was **r**.
18:4 pot he was working on was **r**,
25:9 and something permanently **r**.
25:11 This whole land will be **r** and
25:38 Their land has been **r** because
33:10 have said that this place is **r**
44:22 land has become something **r**,
49:13 ridiculed, **r**, and cursed.
51:43 Its cities will be **r**. It will
Eze 6:6 the cities will be **r**,
6:6 altars will be **r** and demolished.
25:3 when the land of Israel was **r**,
26:2 I'll get rich now that it's **r**.'
29:12 They will be **r** more than any
30:7 They will be **r** more than other
33:24 those who live in the **r** cities in
33:27 whoever is in the **r** cities will
33:28 will become so **r** that no one
36:35 They were empty and **r**,
36:36 have rebuilt the **r** places and
36:38 Their **r** cities will be filled with
38:8 mountains that have been **r** for
Joe 1:7 They **r** my fig trees.
1:10 Israel's fields are **r**,
1:17 Barns are **r**. The grain has dried
Amo 9:11 I will restore its **r** places.
9:14 They will rebuild the **r** cities
Oba 1:5 You will be **r**! If people come to
Mic 2:4 "We are completely **r**.
Zec 7:14 They left behind a land so **r**
Mat 9:17 and the skins are **r**.
12:25 divided against itself is **r**.
Mar 2:22 wine and the skins will be **r**.
Luk 5:37 and the skins will be **r**.
11:17 divided against itself is **r**.
Act 15:16 I will restore its **r** places again.
2Co 7:2 **r** anyone, or cheated anyone.

ruining (5)

Exo 8:24 All over Egypt the flies were **r**
Job 2:3 trying to provoke me into **r** him
Psa 38:12 out to harm me talk about **r** me.
1Co 8:11 your knowledge is **r** a believer
Tit 1:11 they are **r** whole families by

ruins (65)

Exo 22:6 or standing grain or **r** a field,
Lev 26:33 Your country will be in **r**.
Dtr 13:16 It must remain a mound of **r**
Jos 8:28 made it a deserted mound of **r**.
8:28 It is still in **r** today.
2Ch 36:21 While it lay in **r**, ⌊the land had
Ezr 9:9 God's temple and restore its **r**
Neh 2:3 is in **r** and its gates are burned
2:17 Jerusalem is in **r**, and its gates
Job 3:14 themselves ⌊what are now⌋ **r**.
30:14 They crawl through the **r**.
Psa 9:6 enemy is finished — in **r** forever
74:3 steps toward these pathetic **r**.
79:1 They have left Jerusalem in **r**.
89:40 have laid his fortified cities in **r**.
102:6 like an owl living in the **r**.
Pro 10:15 Poverty **r** the poor.
13:6 but wickedness **r** a sacrifice for
19:13 A foolish son **r** his father,
Isa 3:6 This pile of **r** will be under your
5:17 will eat among the **r** of the rich.
6:11 "Until the cities lie in **r** with no
23:13 and turned these places into **r**.
24:12 The city is left in **r**.
25:2 You have turned cities into **r**,
34:10 will lie in **r** for generations.
44:26 He says about their **r**,
49:19 and your land is in **r**,
51:3 all those who live among its **r**.
52:9 shouts of joy, **r** of Jerusalem.
58:12 people will rebuild the ancient **r**
61:4 They will rebuild the ancient **r**.
Jer 25:18 they became wastelands and **r**,
30:18 Cities will be built on the **r**,
44:2 Today they are deserted **r**.
48:9 cities will become deserted **r**.
49:13 All its cities will lie in **r**
51:26 **r**," declares the LORD.
Lam 5:18 on Mount Zion, which lies in **r**.
Eze 13:4 foxes among the **r** ⌊of a city⌋.
21:27 **R**! Ruins! I will turn this place
21:27 **R**! I will turn this place into
21:27 I will turn this place into **r**!
25:13 I will turn the land into **r** from
26:19 I will turn your city into **r** like
26:20 the earth among the ancient **r**
29:12 years Egypt's cities will lie in **r**.
30:7 and Egypt's cities will lie in **r**.
35:4 I will turn your cities into **r**,
36:3 Your enemies turned you into **r**
36:4 and to the empty **r** and
36:10 and the **r** will be rebuilt.
36:33 and your **r** will be rebuilt.
38:12 against the **r** that people are
Dan 9:2 Jerusalem would remain in **r**.
9:2 would remain in **r** for 70 years.
9:17 which is lying in **r**.
9:18 your eyes and look at our **r**
Amo 5:9 He destroys strongholds and **r**
7:9 places of Israel will be in **r**.
Zep 2:9 weeds, salt pits, and **r** forever.
2:14 The doorway will be in **r**,
Hag 1:4 while this house lies in **r**?
1:9 "It's because my house lies in **r**
Mal 1:4 but we will rebuild the **r**.' "Yet,

rule (179)

Gen 1:16 the larger light to **r** the day and
1:16 the smaller light to **r** the night.
1:26 Let them **r** the fish in the sea,
1:28 **R** the fish in the sea,
3:16 and he will **r** you."
37:8 going to be our king or **r** us?"
Exo 1:8 began to **r** in Egypt.
15:18 The LORD will **r** as king
Lev 24:22 The same **r** applies to every
Num 24:19 He will **r** from Jacob and
27:11 This will be a **r** for the
Dtr 15:6 You will **r** many nations,
15:6 but no nation will ever **r** you.
17:20 So he and his sons will **r** for a
Jos 12:2 His **r** extended from Aroer on
Jdg 8:22 then your grandson, must **r** us.
8:23 "I will not **r** you nor will my son.
8:23 The LORD will **r** you."
9:2 of Jerubbaal's 70 sons to **r** you
9:9 in order to **r** the trees?'
9:11 fruit in order to **r** the trees?'
9:13 in order to **r** the trees?'
10:18 will **r** everyone who lives
15:11 know that the Philistines **r** us?
1Sm 10:1 You will **r** his people and save
11:12 said that Saul shouldn't **r** us?
1Sm 12:12 a king should **r** over us,'
23:17 You will **r** Israel, and I will be
24:20 that you certainly will **r** as king,
30:25 that time on he made this a **r**
2Sm 3:21 and you will **r** everything your
7:11 judges to **r** my people Israel.
19:10 whom we anointed to **r** us,
1Ki 5:7 wise son to **r** this great nation."
8:16 David to **r** my people Israel.'
11:37 can **r** everything you desire.
14:21 years old when he began to **r**.
15:1 Abijam began to **r** Judah.
15:4 descendant to **r** after him
15:9 Asa began to **r** as king of
15:25 began to **r** Israel in Asa's
15:33 began to **r** Israel in Tirzah.
16:8 Elah, son of Baasha, began to **r**
16:23 Omri began to **r** Israel in Asa's
16:29 Ahab, son of Omri, began to **r**
22:42 years old when he began to **r**,
2Ki 8:16 of Judah, began to **r**.
8:17 years old when he began to **r**,
8:22 rebelled against Judah's **r**
8:26 years old when he began to **r**,
11:21 years old when he began to **r**.
12:1 Joash began to **r** in Jehu's
13:1 began to **r** in Samaria as king
13:10 son Jehoash began to **r** Israel
14:1 of Joash of Judah, began to **r**.
14:2 years old when he began to **r**,
14:23 of Israel began to **r** in Samaria.
15:1 son Azariah began to **r** as king
15:2 years old when he began to **r**,
15:17 began to **r** as king of Israel.
15:23 son Pekahiah began to **r**.
15:27 began to **r** Israel in Samaria.
15:30 Hoshea began to **r** as king in
15:32 began to **r** as king of Judah.
15:33 years old when he began to **r**.
16:1 began to **r** as king of Judah.
16:2 years old when he began to **r**.
17:1 began to **r** as king of Israel in
18:1 began to **r** as king.
18:2 years old when he began to **r**,
21:1 years old when he began to **r**,
21:19 years old when he began to **r**,
22:1 8 years old when he began to **r**,
23:36 years old when he began to **r**,
24:8 old when he began to **r** as king.
24:18 years old when he began to **r**,
1Ch 17:10 judges to **r** my people Israel.
28:5 the LORD's kingdom to **r** Israel.
29:12 You **r** everything. You hold
2Ch 6:6 David to **r** my people Israel.'
12:13 years old when he began to **r**.
13:1 Abijah began to **r** Judah.
20:6 You **r** all the kingdoms of the
20:31 years old when he began to **r**,
21:10 rebelled against Judah's **r**
22:2 years old when he began to **r**,
22:9 family was able to **r** as king.
24:1 7 years old when he began to **r**,
25:1 years old when he began to **r**,
26:3 years old when he began to **r**,
27:1 years old when he began to **r**.
27:8 old when he began to **r** as king.
28:1 years old when he began to **r**.
29:1 Hezekiah began to **r** as king
33:1 years old when he began to **r**,
33:21 years old when he began to **r**,
34:1 8 years old when he began to **r**,
36:5 years old when he began to **r**,
36:9 old when he began to **r** as king.
36:11 years old when he began to **r**,
36:20 the Persian Empire began to **r**.
Ezr 4:6 When Xerxes began to **r**,
Est 1:8 The drinking followed this **r**:
Job 34:30 so that godless people cannot **r**
38:33 sky or make them **r** the earth?
Psa 8:6 You have made him **r** what
46:10 I **r** the nations. I rule the earth.
46:10 I rule the nations. I **r** the earth.
49:14 (Decent people will **r** them in
72:8 May he **r** from sea to sea,
89:9 You **r** the raging sea.
110:2 **R** your enemies who surround

Psa 136:8 the sun to **r** the day — because
136:9 the moon and stars to **r** the
Pro 8:16 Through me princes **r**,
Ecc 4:14 came out of prison to **r** as king,
Isa 3:12 Women will **r** them.
14:2 captive and **r** their oppressors.
16:5 He will **r** faithfully.
19:4 A strong king will **r** them,"
24:23 the LORD of Armies will **r**
26:13 are not the only master to **r** us,
28:14 you foolish talkers who **r** the
32:1 A king will **r** with fairness,
32:1 and officials will **r** with justice.
34:12 are no nobles to **r** a kingdom.
40:10 with power to **r** with authority.
Jer 5:31 Priests **r** under the prophets'
9:3 Lies and dishonesty **r** the land.
22:30 throne and **r** Judah again.
23:5 be a king who will **r** wisely.
26:1 son of Josiah, began to **r**.
27:1 Josiah of Judah, began to **r**,
28:1 In that same year, early in the **r**
33:21 not have a descendant to **r**
33:26 any of David's descendants **r**
49:34 Early in the **r** of King Zedekiah
51:28 and all the countries that they **r**.
51:59 the fourth year of Zedekiah's **r**.
52:1 years old when he began to **r**,
Lam 5:8 Slaves **r** us. There is no one to
Eze 20:33 I will **r** you with a mighty hand
29:15 and they will never **r** the
29:15 will never **r** the nations again.
37:22 One king will **r** all of them.
Dan 2:39 that will **r** the whole world.
2:44 people will be permitted to **r** it.
6:1 to **r** throughout the kingdom.
7:6 It was given power to **r**.
11:2 Three more kings will **r** Persia.
11:3 He will **r** a vast empire and do
11:5 than he is and **r** a vast empire.
11:8 He will **r** for more years than
Hos 11:5 Instead, Assyria will **r** them
Oba 1:21 Zion to **r** Esau's mountain.
Mic 4:7 The LORD will **r** them on
5:6 They will **r** Assyria with their
Zec 6:13 He will sit and **r** from his throne.
9:10 He will **r** from sea to sea and
Act 7:18 began to **r** in Egypt.
7:35 sent to free them and to **r** them
Rom 2:29 not just a written **r**.
5:17 the gift of his approval will **r**
5:21 God's kindness would **r** by
6:12 Therefore, never let sin **r** your
15:12 He will rise to **r** the nations,
1Co 9:8 I merely stating some human **r**?
15:25 Christ must **r** until God has put
2Ti 2:12 we endure, we will **r** with him.
4:1 will come to **r** ⌊the world⌋.
Rev 2:27 Those people will **r** the nations
5:10 They will **r** as kings on the
11:15 and he will **r** as king forever
12:5 who is to **r** all the nations with
17:12 who have not yet started to **r**.
17:12 They will receive authority to **r**
19:15 He will **r** them with an iron
20:6 They will **r** with him for 1,000
22:5 They will **r** as kings forever

ruled (123)

Gen 36:31 These were the kings who **r**
36:31 ruled Edom before any king **r**
36:32 Bela, son of Beor, **r** Edom.
Exo 12:29 firstborn son of Pharaoh who **r**
Num 21:34 who **r** in Heshbon."
Dtr 1:4 who **r** in Heshbon,
1:4 who **r** in Ashtaroth and in Edrei.
3:2 who **r** in Heshbon."
3:13 and all of Bashan **r** by Og
4:46 who **r** in Heshbon.
Jos 2:10 who **r** east of the Jordan River.
12:5 He **r** Mount Hermon,
13:12 Og **r** in Ashtaroth and Edrei.
13:21 who **r** in Heshbon.
Jdg 4:2 who **r** at Hazor, to defeat them.
9:22 Abimelech **r** Israel for three
11:19 Sihon **r** from Heshbon.
2Sm 2:10 He **r** for two years,
5:2 in the past when Saul **r** us,
5:4 and he **r** for 40 years.
5:5 In Hebron he **r** Judah for seven
5:5 In Jerusalem he **r** for 33 years
8:15 So David **r** all Israel.
1Ki 2:11 He **r** as king of Israel for 40
2:11 He **r** for 7 years in Hebron and
4:21 Solomon **r** all the kingdoms
11:24 and **r** a kingdom in Damascus.
11:25 He **r** Aram and despised Israel.
12:17 But Rehoboam **r** the Israelites
14:20 Jeroboam **r** for 22 years.
14:21 son of Solomon, **r** Judah.
14:21 He **r** for 17 years in Jerusalem,
15:2 He **r** for three years in
15:10 He **r** 41 years in Jerusalem.
15:25 He **r** for two years.
15:33 in Tirzah. He **r** for 24 years.
16:8 He **r** in Tirzah for two years.
16:15 Zimri **r** for seven days in Tirzah
16:23 He **r** for 12 years, 6 of them in
16:29 He **r** for 22 years in Samaria.
22:42 and he **r** for 25 years in
22:47 in Edom; instead, a deputy **r**.
22:51 Ahaziah **r** Israel for two years.
2Ki 3:1 of Judah. He **r** for 12 years.
8:15 Hazael **r** as king in his place.
8:16 Jehoram **r** while Jehoshaphat
8:17 and he **r** for 8 years in
8:26 and he **r** for one year in
10:36 Jehu **r** as king of Israel in
11:3 while Athaliah **r** the country.
12:1 and he **r** for 40 years in
13:1 of Israel. He **r** for 17 years.
13:9 His son Jehoash **r** as king in
13:10 in Samaria. He **r** for 16 years.
13:22 Israel as long as Jehoahaz **r**.
14:2 and he **r** for 29 years in
14:23 Jeroboam **r** for 41 years.
15:2 and he **r** for 52 years in
15:13 Shallum **r** for an entire month in
15:17 He **r** for 10 years in Samaria.
15:27 in Samaria. He **r** for 20 years.
15:32 of Remaliah, **r** Israel, Jotham,
15:33 He **r** for 16 years in Jerusalem.
16:2 He **r** for 26 years in Jerusalem.
17:1 He **r** for nine years.
18:2 and he **r** for 29 years in
21:1 and he **r** for 55 years in
21:19 and he **r** for 2 years in
24:18 and he **r** for 11 years in
1Ch 1:43 These were the kings who **r**
1:43 ruled Edom before any king **r**
3:4 where he **r** for seven years and
3:4 He **r** for 33 years in Jerusalem.
4:22 Saraph **r** Moab and Jashubi
11:2 "Even in the past when Saul **r**,
18:14 So David **r** all Israel.
26:6 had sons who **r** their families
29:26 son of Jesse, had **r** all Israel.
29:27 He **r** as king of Israel for 40
29:27 He **r** for 7 years in Hebron and
2Ch 1:13 to Jerusalem. And he **r** Israel.
9:26 He **r** all the kings from the
9:30 Solomon **r** in Jerusalem over
10:17 But Rehoboam **r** the Israelites
12:13 his position in Jerusalem and **r**.
12:13 He **r** for 17 years in Jerusalem,
13:2 He **r** for three years in
20:31 Jehoshaphat **r** as king of
20:31 and he **r** for 25 years in
21:5 and he **r** for 8 years in
21:20 and he **r** for 8 years in
22:2 and he **r** for one year in
22:12 while Athaliah **r** the country.
24:1 and he **r** for 40 years in
25:1 and he **r** for 29 years in
26:3 and he **r** for 52 years in
27:1 He **r** for 16 years in Jerusalem.
27:8 He **r** for 16 years in Jerusalem.
28:1 He **r** for 26 years in Jerusalem.
29:1 He **r** for 29 years in Jerusalem.
33:1 and he **r** for 55 years in
33:21 and he **r** for 2 years in
36:5 and he **r** for 11 years in
2Ch 36:11 and he **r** for 11 years in
Ezr 4:20 had powerful kings who have **r**
Est 1:1 who **r** over 127 provinces
Psa 106:41 and those who hated them **r**
Ecc 1:16 ⌊has **r**⌋ Jerusalem before me.
Isa 14:6 They **r** nations in anger,
25:3 and cities **r** by the world's
63:19 like those whom you never **r**,
Jer 34:1 he **r** were attacking Jerusalem
52:1 and he **r** for 11 years in
Eze 26:17 You and your people **r** the sea.
34:4 You have **r** them harshly and
Luk 3:1 Herod **r** Galilee, and his brother
3:1 and his brother Philip **r** Iturea
23:7 Herod **r** Galilee and was in
Rom 5:14 Yet, death **r** from the time of
5:17 It is certain that death **r**
5:21 As sin **r** by bringing death,
Rev 9:11 The king who **r** them was the
20:4 They lived and **r** with Christ for

ruler (65)

Gen 34:2 son of the local **r** Hamor the
45:8 household, and **r** of Egypt.
45:26 Yes, he is **r** of Egypt."
Exo 2:14 made you our **r** and judge?
Jdg 3:25 shocked to see their **r** lying
9:30 Zebul, Shechem's **r**,
9:38 ⌊whose **r**⌋ you despised?
11:8 You will be the **r** of everyone
1Sm 9:16 Anoint him to be **r** of my people
10:1 LORD has anointed you to be **r**
10:1 you to be **r** of his people.
13:14 LORD has appointed him as **r**
25:30 and makes you **r** of Israel,
1Ki 11:34 Instead, I will allow him to be **r**
Est 1:22 "Let every husband be the **r** in
Psa 105:20 The **r** of nations set him free.
105:21 master of his palace and the **r**
125:3 A wicked **r** will not be allowed
Pro 6:7 it has no overseer, officer, or **r**,
14:28 but without people a **r** is ruined.
23:1 you sit down to eat with a **r**,
25:15 patience you can persuade a **r**,
28:15 ⌊so⌋ a wicked **r** is a threat to
29:12 If a **r** pays attention to lies,
29:26 seek an audience with a **r**,
Ecc 9:17 than shouting from a **r** of fools.
10:4 If a **r** becomes angry with you,
Isa 16:1 Send lambs to the **r** of the land.
32:2 Then each **r** will be like a
60:17 and righteousness as your **r**.
Jer 30:21 Their **r** will come from among
51:46 Rumors that one **r** will fight
Eze 28:2 "Son of man, tell the **r** of Tyre,
28:12 a funeral song for the **r** of Tyre.
31:11 So I handed it over to a mighty **r**
Dan 2:38 He has made you **r** of them all.
5:7 third-highest **r** in the kingdom."
5:16 third-highest **r** in the kingdom."
5:29 third-highest **r** in the kingdom.
9:1 was made **r** of the kingdom of
Mic 5:2 Yet, from you Israel's future **r**
Hab 1:14 of sea life that have no **r**.
Mat 9:34 the help of the **r** of demons."
12:24 of Beelzebul, the **r** of demons."
14:1 At that time Herod, **r** of Galilee,
Mar 3:22 the help of the **r** of demons."
Luk 3:1 Lysanias was the **r** of Abilene.
3:19 John spoke out against the **r**
9:7 Herod the **r** heard about
11:15 of Beelzebul, the **r** of demons."
12:58 you to court in front of a **r**,
Jon 7:48 Has any **r** or any Pharisee
12:31 The **r** of this world will be
14:30 The **r** of this world has no
16:11 because the **r** of this world has
Act 7:10 wisdom so that he became **r**
7:27 made you our **r** and judge?
7:35 made you our **r** and judge?'
23:5 evil about a **r** of your people."'
1Co 15:24 Father as he destroys every **r**,
Eph 2:2 present world and its spiritual **r**.
2:2 This **r** continues to work in
Col 2:10 charge of every **r** and authority.
1Ti 6:15 God is the blessed and only **r**.

Rev 1:5 and the **r** over the kings of the

ruler's (1)

Gen 49:10 nor a **r** staff from between his

rulers (75)

Lev 26:17 who hate you will be your **r**.
Num 21:28 the **r** of Arnon's worship sites.
Jos 13:3 are five Philistine **r** over Gaza,
Jdg 3:3 He left the five **r** of the
16:5 The Philistine **r** came to her
16:8 The Philistine **r** brought her
16:18 a message to the Philistine **r**,
16:18 So the Philistine **r** arrived with
16:23 Now, the Philistine **r** gathered
16:27 All the Philistine **r** were there.
16:30 and the building fell on the **r**
1Sm 5:8 together all the Philistine **r**.
5:8 be taken to Gath," the **r** said.
5:11 together all the Philistine **r**.
6:4 mice for the ⌊five⌋ Philistine **r**
6:4 all of you and your **r** suffer from
6:12 The **r** of the Philistines
6:16 After the five **r** of the Philistines
6:18 cities belonging to the five **r**,
7:7 the Philistine **r** came to attack
29:6 But the **r** don't approve of you.
29:7 to displease the Philistine **r**."
1Ch 12:19 because their **r** sent him away
Psa 2:2 **R** make plans together against
2:10 Be warned, you **r** of the earth!
47:9 The **r** of the earth belong to
58:1 Do you **r** really give fair
94:20 Are wicked **r** who use the law
Pro 8:15 and **r** decree fair laws.
28:2 is in revolt, it has many **r**,
31:4 wine or for **r** to crave liquor.
Ecc 7:19 person more than ten **r** can help
10:5 an error often made by **r**.
Isa 1:10 of the LORD, you **r** of Sodom!
1:23 Your **r** are rebels, friends with
14:5 of the wicked, the scepter of **r**.
16:8 **R** of the nations have cut off
40:23 He makes **r** unimportant and
41:25 He will attack **r** as if they were
49:7 by the nation, to the slave of **r**:
52:5 Their **r** are screaming,
Jer 2:8 The **r** rebelled against me.
Eze 32:30 "All the **r** from the north and all
Dan 9:12 do to us and our **r** by bringing
11:39 make them **r** over many people,
Hos 4:18 Their **r** dearly love to act
Mic 3:1 you **r** of the nation of Israel.
3:9 you **r** of the nation of Israel.
Hab 1:10 make fun of kings and treat **r** as
Mat 20:25 "You know that the **r** of nations
Mar 10:42 know that the acknowledged **r**
Luk 1:52 He pulled strong **r** from their
12:11 or in front of **r** and authorities,
23:13 priests, the **r**, and the people.
23:35 But the **r** were making
24:20 Our chief priests and **r** had him
Jon 7:26 Can it be that the **r** really know
12:42 Many **r** believed in Jesus.
Act 3:17 I know that like your **r** you
4:5 The next day the Jewish **r**,
4:8 "**R** and leaders of the people,
4:26 **R** make plans together against
13:27 and their **r** didn't know who
14:5 people with their **r** planned
Rom 8:38 by death or life, by angels or **r**,
1Co 2:6 belong to this world or to the **r**
2:8 Not one of the **r** of this world
Eph 1:21 He is far above all **r**,
3:10 he could let the **r** and
6:12 We are wrestling with **r**,
Col 1:16 **r** or powers — everything has
2:15 He stripped the **r** and
1Ti 2:2 for **r**, and for everyone who has
1Pe 3:22 Angels, **r**, and powers have
5:3 Don't be **r** over the people

rules (112)

Exo 11:5 of Pharaoh who **r** the land,
12:43 "These are the **r** for the
13:10 you must follow these **r** every
15:25 the LORD set down laws and **r**
Lev 18:4 Follow my **r**, and live by my
18:5 my standards, and obey my **r**.
18:26 my standards, and obey my **r**.
19:37 "Obey all my laws and all my **r**,
20:22 obey all my laws and my **r**,
25:18 and carefully follow my **r**.
26:15 and look at my **r** with disgust,
26:43 because they rejected my **r**
26:46 These are the laws, **r**,
Num 9:3 Follow all the **r** and regulations
9:12 You must follow all the **r** for the
9:14 these same **r** and regulations.
9:14 The same **r** will apply to
15:16 The instructions and **r** are the
35:24 community must use these **r**
35:29 "These will be the **r** for future
36:13 These are the commands and **r**
Dtr 4:1 Israel, listen to the laws and **r** I
4:5 I have taught you laws and **r**
4:8 fair laws and **r** as all these
4:14 the laws and **r** you must obey
4:45 and **r** Moses gave the Israelites
5:1 listen to the laws and **r** I'm
5:31 and **r** that you must teach them
6:1 and **r** the LORD your God
6:20 and **r** which the LORD our God
7:11 and **r** I'm giving you today.
7:12 If you listen to these **r** and
8:11 fail to obey his commands, **r**,
11:1 Always obey his laws, **r**,
11:32 all the laws and **r** I'm giving you
12:1 Here are the laws and **r** you
26:16 you to obey these laws and **r**.
26:17 and **r**, and listen to him.
30:16 his commands, laws, and **r**.
33:10 They teach Jacob your **r** and
Jos 24:25 people and set up laws and **r**
2Sm 23:3 'The one who **r** humans with
23:3 rules humans with justice **r**
1Ki 2:3 directions, laws, commands, **r**,
3:3 lived by his father David's **r**.
6:12 live by my laws, follow my **r**,
8:58 his commands, laws, and **r**,
9:4 and keep my laws and **r**,
2Ki 17:37 Faithfully obey the laws, **r**,
17:40 listen and made up their own **r**,
1Ch 16:31 'The LORD **r** as king!'
24:19 Aaron made these **r** for them,
2Ch 7:17 and obey my laws and **r**,
19:10 bloodshed or commands, **r**,
Ezr 7:10 and teach their **r** and
Neh 9:13 You gave them fair **r**,
10:29 all the commandments, **r**,
Job 28:26 when he made **r** for the rain and
Psa 22:28 the LORD and he **r** the nations.
47:8 God **r** the nations. He sits upon
47:9 to God. He **r** everything.
59:13 Then they will know that God **r**
66:7 He **r** forever with his might.
89:30 and do not live by my **r**,
93:1 The LORD **r** as king!
96:10 "The LORD **r** as king!"
97:1 The LORD **r** as king.
99:1 The LORD **r** as king.
103:19 His kingdom **r** everything.
146:10 The LORD **r** as king forever.
146:10 Zion, your God **r** throughout
Pro 22:7 A rich person **r** poor people,
29:2 but when a wicked person **r**,
Isa 29:13 ⌊based on⌋ **r** made by humans.
52:7 tells Zion that its God **r** as king.
Eze 5:6 have rebelled against my **r**
5:6 They have rejected my **r**,
5:7 by my laws or obeyed my **r**.
11:12 and you haven't obeyed my **r**.
11:20 live by my laws and obey my **r**.
18:9 He lives by my **r** and obeys my
18:17 He obeys my **r** and lives by my
18:19 He obeyed my **r** and followed
20:11 my laws and made my **r** known
20:13 and they rejected my **r**.
20:16 They rejected my **r**,
20:18 Don't obey their **r** or dishonor
20:19 Obey my **r** and follow them.
20:21 and they didn't obey my **r** and
Eze 20:24 They didn't follow my **r**,
20:25 no good and **r** by which they
33:15 lives by the **r** of life,
36:27 and you will obey my **r**.
37:24 They will live by my **r**,
43:11 about all its **r** and regulations.
43:11 its design and follow all its **r**.
43:18 These are the **r** for sacrificing
44:5 Listen to all the **r** and
44:24 They must obey my **r** and my
46:14 These **r** are to be followed
Dan 4:26 as you realize that heaven **r**.
Mal 4:4 the **r** and regulations that I gave
Mat 15:9 are **r** made by humans.'"
Mar 7:4 taught to follow many other **r**.
7:7 are **r** made by humans.'
Luk 22:53 when darkness **r**."
Act 22:3 My education was in the strict **r**
Rom 5:20 **R** were added to increase the
2Ti 2:5 only when playing by the **r**.
Heb 9:1 The first promise had **r** for the
13:9 from following **r** about food,
13:9 **r** that don't help those who

ruling (8)

Exo 21:31 this same **r** applies.
Jdg 14:4 the Philistines were **r** Israel.)
Rut 1:1 days when the judges were **r**,
2Ch 7:18 fail to have an heir **r** Israel.'
Pro 19:10 much less a slave **r** princes.
Rev 1:9 I share your suffering, **r**,
11:17 and have begun **r** as king.
17:10 them have fallen, one is **r** now,

Rumah (1)

2Ki 23:36 daughter of Pedaiah from **R**.

rumbled (1)

Psa 77:18 The sound of your thunder **r** in

rumbling (3)

Job 37:2 to the **r** that comes from his
Jer 47:3 and the **r** of their wheels.
Eze 3:13 them as well as a loud **r**.

rummaged (2)

Gen 31:34 Laban **r** through the whole tent
31:37 Now that you've **r** through all

rumor (8)

2Sm 13:30 David heard this **r**:
2Ki 19:7 in him so that he will hear a **r**
Job 28:22 'We've heard a **r** about it.'
Isa 37:7 in him so that he will hear a **r**
Jer 51:46 One **r** comes one year;
51:46 another **r** comes the next year.
Eze 7:26 One **r** will follow another.
Jon 21:23 So a **r** that that disciple

rumors (7)

Exo 23:1 "Never spread false **r**.
1Sm 24:9 "Why do you listen to **r** that I
Jer 51:46 or be afraid when **r** are heard
51:46 **R** of violence are in the land.
51:46 **R** that one ruler will fight
Mat 24:6 will hear of wars and **r** of wars.
Mar 13:7 you hear of wars and **r** of wars,

run (125)

Gen 15:16 will not have **r** its course until
19:17 angels⌋ said, "**R** for your lives!
19:17 **R** for the hills, or you'll be
19:19 I can't **r** as far as the hills.
19:20 Why don't you let me **r** there?
19:22 **R** there quickly, because I can't
27:43 **R** away to my brother Laban in
Exo 26:28 The middle crossbar will **r** from
Lev 26:17 You will **r** away even when no
26:36 leaf will make them **r**.
26:36 They will **r** away and fall,
Num 10:35 who hate you **r** away from you!"
35:11 another person may **r** to them.
Dtr 19:3 Whoever kills someone may **r**
19:4 never hated in the past may **r**
19:5 killed the other person may **r**
28:7 direction but **r** away from you

Dtr 28:25 direction but **r** away from them
Jos 7:12 They will **r** away from their
8:5 we will **r** away from them.
8:6 As we **r** away from them,
20:3 kills someone may **r** to them.
20:4 someone accidentally can **r**
Jdg 7:21 camp began to **r** away,
1Sm 8:11 and make them **r** ahead of his
20:6 me to let him **r** to Bethlehem,
20:36 "**R**," he told the boy,
21:13 let his spit **r** down his beard.
2Sm 15:1 and 50 men to **r** ahead of him.
18:19 "Let me **r** and bring the king the
18:22 I also want to **r** after the
18:23 I'd like to **r**," ⌊replied Ahimaaz.⌋
18:23 "**R**," Joab told him.
1Ki 1:5 and 50 men to **r** ahead of him.
2Ki 4:26 **R** to meet her and ask her how
5:20 As sure as the LORD lives, I'll **r**
Neh 6:11 "Should a man like me **r** away?
Job 31:5 my feet have **r** after deception,
41:28 An arrow won't make it **r** away.
Psa 19:5 it is eager to **r** its course.
31:11 on the street **r** away from me.
55:7 Indeed, I would **r** far away.
68:12 of the armies flee; they **r** away.
73:7 and their imaginations **r** wild.
114:5 Red Sea, why did you **r** away?
139:7 Where can I **r** ⌊to get away⌋
Pro 4:12 Even if you **r**, you will not
29:18 prophetic vision people **r** wild,
Sos 1:4 Let's **r** away. The king has
2:17 **R** like a gazelle or a young
8:14 **R** like a gazelle or a young
Isa 1:23 all love bribes and **r** after gifts.
7:25 loose and letting sheep **r**."
10:3 Where will you **r** for help?
15:6 The Nimrim Brook has **r** dry!
17:13 and they will **r** far away.
19:23 a highway will **r** from Egypt to
31:9 In terror they will **r** to their
40:31 They will **r** and won't become
52:11 **R** away! Run away! Get away
52:11 **R** away! Get away from there!
55:5 that doesn't know you will **r**
59:7 Their feet **r** to do evil.
Jer 2:25 Don't **r** until your feet are bare
6:1 **R** away from Jerusalem!
7:9 and **r** after other gods that you
9:18 Our eyes will **r** with tears.
17:16 I have not **r** away from being
46:21 will turn and **r** away together.
48:6 "**R** away! Run for your lives!
48:6 **R** for your lives! Run like a wild
48:6 **R** like a wild donkey in the
49:3 **R** back and forth between the
49:8 Turn and **r**. Hide in deep caves,
49:30 **R** far away! Find a place to
50:3 People and animals will **r**
50:8 "**R** away from Babylon.
51:6 **R** away from Babylon!
51:6 **R** for your lives! You shouldn't
51:31 Runners **r** to meet runners.
51:45 **R** for your lives! Run from the
51:45 **R** from the burning anger of the
Lam 2:18 Let your tears **r** down like a
3:48 "Streams of tears **r** down from
Eze 24:16 or let tears **r** down your face.
47:15 north side the border will **r** from
47:15 It will **r** through the city of
47:16 It will **r** to Hazer Hatticon,
47:17 So the border will **r** from the
47:18 border will **r** between Hauran
47:19 the border will **r** from Tamar
48:28 of Gad will **r** south from Tamar
48:28 and it will **r** along the Brook of
Dan 4:14 the animals under it **r** away,
Hos 2:7 She will **r** after her lovers,
7:11 You call for Egypt and **r** to
7:13 They have **r** away from me.
13:15 Then their springs will **r** dry,
Joe 1:10 The olive oil has **r** out.
1:20 Streams **r** dry. Fire has burned
2:4 They **r** like war horses.
2:7 They **r** like warriors.
2:9 They **r** along the wall.
Amo 2:16 Brave soldiers will **r** away
6:12 Do horses **r** on rocks?
7:12 "You seer, **r** away to Judah!
9:10 not catch up to us or **r** into us."
Jnh 1:3 Jonah immediately tried to **r**
4:2 That's why I tried to **r** to
Nah 3:7 who sees you will **r** from you,
Zec 2:4 and said to him, "**R**,
Luk 5:37 The wine will **r** out,
14:21 He told his servant, '**R** to every
17:23 Don't **r** after those people.
Jon 10:5 Instead, they will **r** away from a
Act 19:40 At this moment we **r** the risk of
27:26 However, we will **r** aground on
27:39 to try to **r** the ship ashore.
Rom 3:15 They **r** quickly to murder
1Co 9:24 **R** like them, so that you can
9:26 So I **r** — but not without a clear
Php 3:12 But I **r** to win that which Jesus
3:14 I **r** straight toward the goal to
Heb 12:1 We must **r** the race that lies
Jas 4:7 and he will **r** away from you.

run-down (1)

2Ch 34:11 had allowed to become **r**.

runner (3)

2Sm 18:25 The **r** continued to come closer.
Job 9:25 go by more quickly than a **r**.
1Co 9:24 but only one **r** gets the prize?

runners (6)

1Sm 22:17 the king said to the **r** standing
Ecc 9:11 The race isn't ⌊won⌋ by fast **r**,
Jer 51:31 **R** run to meet runners.
51:31 Runners run to meet **r**.
Amo 2:14 **R** will not be able to escape.
2:15 Fast **r** will not be able to

running (18)

Gen 16:8 She answered, "I'm **r** away
Jos 8:6 They'll say, 'They're **r** away
8:20 who had been **r** toward the
2Sm 18:24 he saw a man **r** alone.
18:26 watchman saw another man **r**,
18:26 ⌊another⌋ man **r** alone."
2Ki 5:21 saw Gehazi **r** after him,
2Ch 23:12 Athaliah heard the people **r**
Psa 133:2 **r** down the beard — down
133:2 down Aaron's beard — **r** over
Pro 5:15 cistern and **r** water from your
Lam 1:2 with tears **r** down its cheeks.
Jnh 1:10 They knew that he was **r** away
Mar 9:25 Jesus saw that a crowd was **r**
10:17 a man came **r** to him and knelt
Luk 6:38 and **r** over will be put into your
Jon 20:4 The two were **r** side by side,
Act 20:24 I want to finish the race I'm **r**.

runs (12)

Dtr 19:11 and **r** to one of these cities.
2Sm 18:27 that the first one **r** like Ahimaaz,
Pro 18:10 A righteous person **r** to it and is
20:26 wicked and then **r** them over.
29:6 but a righteous person **r** away
Isa 48:18 like a river ⌊that never **r** dry⌋.
Jer 2:23 that swiftly **r** here and there.
Eze 48:18 the holy area and **r** lengthwise.
Mat 9:17 the skins burst, the wine **r** out,
Jon 10:12 the sheep and quickly **r** away.
1Co 9:24 you realize that everyone who **r**
9:24 who runs in a race **r** to win,

rush (4)

Pro 1:16 because they **r** to do evil and
Isa 33:4 people **r** for your loot.
Dan 11:40 The northern king will **r** at him
Joe 2:9 They **r** into the city.

rushed (13)

Jos 8:14 They **r** out toward the plains to
Jdg 20:33 those waiting in ambush **r** from
2Sm 19:17 **r** to the Jordan River across
2Ch 26:20 They **r** him away. Uzziah was
Mat 8:32 Suddenly, the whole herd **r**
Mar 3:10 everyone with a disease **r** up
Mar 5:13 two thousand pigs **r** down
Luk 8:33 Then the herd **r** down the cliff
Act 7:57 Then they **r** at Stephen with
14:14 They **r** into the crowd
16:29 asked for torches and **r** into
19:29 thought in mind as they **r** into
Jud 1:11 They have **r** into Balaam's error

rushes (5)

Job 8:11 Can **r** grow tall without water?
40:23 the Jordan **r** against its mouth.
Ecc 1:5 and then it **r** back to the place
Isa 19:7 The **r** by the Nile, by the edge
35:7 will become cattails and **r**

rushing (6)

Isa 17:12 be like the noise from **r** water.
59:19 He will come like a **r** stream.
Eze 1:24 was like the noise of **r** water,
43:2 was like the sound of **r** water,
Nah 2:4 **r** this way and that in the city
Rev 9:9 with many horses **r** into battle.

rust (2)

Mat 6:19 where moths and **r** destroy and
6:20 where moths and **r** don't

Ruth (27)

Rut 1:4 son married a woman named **R**.
1:14 but **R** held on to her tightly.
1:16 But **R** answered, "Don't force
1:18 When Naomi saw that **R** was
1:22 **R**, her Moabite daughter-in-law,
2:2 **R**, who was from Moab, said to
2:3 So **R** went. She entered a field
2:8 Boaz said to **R**, "Listen,
2:10 **R** immediately bowed down to
2:13 **R** replied, "Sir, may your
2:17 So **R** gathered grain in the field
2:18 **R** also took out what she had
2:19 So **R** told her mother-in-law
2:21 **R**, who was from Moab,
2:22 told her daughter-in-law **R**,
2:23 So **R** stayed with the young
3:5 **R** answered her, "I will do
3:6 **R** went to the threshing floor
3:9 She answered, "I am **R**.
3:14 So **R** lay at his feet until
3:15 Then Boaz told **R**,
3:16 When **R** returned, "How did
3:16 **R** told Naomi everything the
4:5 responsibility for the Moabite **R**
4:10 as my wife the Moabite **R**,
4:13 Then Boaz took **R** home,
Mat 1:5 Boaz and **R** were the father and

ruthless (9)

Job 15:20 are reserved for the **r** person.
Psa 54:3 **R** people seek my life.
86:14 and a mob of **r** people seeks
Pro 11:16 but **r** men gain riches.
Isa 16:4 **R** people will come to an end.
Eze 28:7 the most **r** foreigners among
30:11 He and his troops, the most **r**
31:12 Foreigners from the most **r**
32:12 All of them will be the most **r**

Ruth's (1)

Rut 3:1 **R** mother-in-law, said to her,

S

sabachthani (2)

Mat 27:46 a loud voice, "Eli, Eli, lema **s**?"
Mar 15:34 voice, "Eloi, Eloi, lema **s**?"

Sabaeans (1)

Isa 45:14 and the important **S** will come

Sabta (1)

1Ch 1:9 **S**, Raama, and Sabteca.

Sabtah (1)

Gen 10:7 **S**, Raamah, and Sabteca.

Sabteca (2)

Gen 10:7 Sabtah, Raamah, and **S**.
1Ch 1:9 Havilah, Sabta, Raama, and **S**.

Sachar (2)

1Ch 11:35 Ahiam (son of **S** the Hararite),
26:4 Joah (the third), **S** (the fourth),

Sachia (1)

1Ch 8:10 Jeuz, **S**, and Mirmah. All of

sack (10)

Gen 42:25 man's money back into his **s**
42:27 one of them opened his **s** to
42:27 money was right inside his **s**.
42:28 It's right here in my **s**!"
42:35 his bag of money in his **s**.
44:1 Put each man's money in his **s**.
44:2 the youngest brother's **s** along
44:11 Each one quickly lowered his **s**
44:12 cup was found in Benjamin's **s**.
Lev 11:32 article, clothing, leather, a **s**,

sackcloth (48)

Gen 37:34 put **s** around his waist,
2Sm 3:31 put on **s**, and mourn for Abner."
21:10 Rizpah (Aiah's daughter) took **s**
1Ki 20:31 Allow us to dress in **s**,
20:32 So they dressed in **s** and put
21:27 ⌊in distress⌋ and dressed in **s**.
21:27 He fasted, lay in **s**,
2Ki 6:30 wearing **s** under his clothes.
19:1 covered himself with **s**,
19:2 of the priests, clothed in **s**,
1Ch 21:16 the leaders were dressed in **s**.
Neh 9:1 this month, they fasted, wore **s**,
Est 4:1 and put on **s** and ashes.
4:2 one could enter it wearing **s**.)
4:3 Many put on **s** and ashes.
4:4 to put on in place of his **s**,
Job 16:15 "I have sewn **s** over my skin,
Psa 30:11 You have removed my **s** and
35:13 when they were sick, I wore **s**.
69:11 I dressed myself in **s**,
Isa 3:24 They will wear **s** instead of
15:3 In their streets they wear **s**.
20:2 "Take off the **s** that you are
22:12 your heads and for wearing **s**.
32:11 and wear **s** around your waists.
37:1 covered himself with **s**,
37:2 of the priests, clothed in **s**,
50:3 and cover them with **s**.
58:5 your bed from **s** and ashes?
Jer 4:8 So put on **s**, mourn, and cry
6:26 Wear **s**, and roll around in
48:37 hand and **s** on every waist.
49:3 put on your **s**, and mourn.
Lam 2:10 dirt on their heads and put on **s**.
Eze 7:18 They will put on **s**,
27:31 because of you and put on **s**.
Dan 9:3 and fasted in **s** and ashes.
Joe 1:8 woman who is dressed in **s**,
1:13 Put on your **s** and mourn,
1:13 Spend the night in **s**,
Amo 8:10 I will put **s** around everyone's
Jnh 3:5 least important, dressed in **s**.
3:6 put on **s**, and sat in ashes.
3:8 and animal must put on **s**.
Mat 11:21 acted long ago in **s** and ashes.
Luk 10:13 ago they would have worn **s**
Rev 6:12 The sun turned as black as **s**
11:3 my two witnesses who wear **s**

sacks (10)

Gen 42:35 As they were emptying their **s**,
43:12 that was put back in your **s**.
43:18 that was put back into our **s**
43:21 for the night, we opened our **s**,
43:22 put our money back in our **s**."
43:23 given you treasure in your **s**.
44:1 "Fill the men's **s** with as much
44:8 in our **s** back from Canaan.
Jos 9:4 They took worn-out **s** on their
1Sm 9:7 since the food in our **s** is gone?

sacred (22)

Exo 23:24 gods and crush their **s** stones.
24:4 and ⌊set up⌋ 12 **s** stones
34:13 crush their **s** stones,
Lev 26:1 up a carved statue or a **s** stone
26:31 and ruin your **s** places.
Dtr 7:5 smash their **s** stones,
12:3 crush their **s** stones,
16:22 Never set up a **s** stone.
2Ki 3:2 He put away the **s** stone that
10:26 brought out the large **s** stone
10:27 They destroyed the **s** stone of
17:10 They set up **s** stones and
18:4 crushed the **s** stones,
23:14 Josiah crushed the **s** stones,
1Ch 16:42 that accompany **s** songs.
2Ch 14:3 broke down the **s** stones,
31:1 They crushed the **s** stones,
Isa 6:13 When a **s** oak or an oak is cut
Lam 4:1 The **s** stones are scattered at
Hos 3:4 without sacrifices or **s** stones,
Mic 5:13 idols and your **s** monuments.
1Ti 1:9 who think nothing is holy or **s**,

sacrifice (194)

Gen 22:2 **S** him there as a burnt offering
22:10 took it in his hand to **s** his son.
31:54 and offered a **s** on the
Exo 8:25 **s** to your God here in this
12:27 'It's the Passover **s** in the
13:12 **s** every firstborn male offspring
13:15 This is why we **s** every
20:24 **S** your burnt offerings and your
23:18 "Never offer the blood of a **s** to
29:36 Each day **s** a young bull as an
29:36 **S** this offering for sin on the
34:15 were prostitutes and **s** to them,
34:25 "Never offer the blood of a **s** to
34:25 No part of the **s** at the Passover
Lev 1:2 If any of you bring a **s** to the
1:14 you must **s** a mourning dove or
3:1 "If your **s** is a fellowship
3:6 "If your **s** is a fellowship
4:14 the congregation must **s** a bull
5:8 and he will **s** the offering for sin
5:10 he will **s** the second bird as a
7:17 over from the **s** must be burned.
7:29 must bring a part of that **s** as
9:2 **S** them in the LORD's
9:4 mixed with olive oil to **s**
9:7 "Come to the altar and **s** an
14:19 The priest will also **s** the
14:20 The priest will **s** the burnt
14:31 and **s** it as an offering for sin.
14:31 He will take the other and **s** it
15:15 The priest will **s** one as an
16:6 "Aaron must **s** the bull as his
16:9 Aaron must **s** the goat chosen
16:24 Then he will come out and **s**
17:5 The people will **s** them as
19:5 **s** it ⌊properly⌋ so that you will
19:6 Eat your **s** on the day you bring
20:2 give one of their children as a **s**
22:22 any of these in a **s** by fire
22:27 may be accepted as a **s** by fire
22:29 "When you **s** a thank offering to
23:8 Bring the LORD a **s** by fire for
23:12 you must **s** a one-year-old male
23:13 This will be a **s** by fire made to
23:18 They will be a **s** by fire,
23:19 Also **s** one male goat as an
23:25 Bring a **s** by fire to the LORD."
23:27 and bring the LORD a **s** by fire.
23:36 days bring a **s** by fire
23:36 Bring the LORD a **s** by fire.
Num 6:11 The priest will **s** one as an
6:17 He will **s** the ram as a
8:12 **S** one of them as an offering for
10:10 blow the trumpets when you **s**
15:3 offerings or any other kind of **s**.
15:5 the burnt offering or any other **s**
15:8 "Suppose you **s** a young bull
15:8 or make any other kind of **s**
Num 15:12 however many you **s**.
15:24 the whole community must **s** a
15:28 The priest will offer the **s** to
Dtr 12:13 Be careful that you don't **s** your
12:14 Instead, **s** them ⌊only⌋ at the
12:27 **S** the meat and the blood of
15:21 other serious defect — never **s**
16:2 flock or herd as the Passover **s**
16:3 bread with the meat from this **s**.
17:1 seriously wrong with it as a **s**
18:3 priests whenever they **s** an ox,
18:10 You must never **s** your sons or
27:6 **S** burnt offerings on it to the
27:7 **S** fellowship offerings,
33:10 to smell and **s** burnt offerings
Jdg 6:26 Take this second bull and **s** it
11:31 I will **s** it as a burnt offering."
13:16 burnt offering, **s** it to the LORD."
16:23 together to offer a great **s**
1Sm 1:3 his own city to worship and **s**
1:4 Whenever Elkanah offered a **s**,
1:21 offer the annual **s** to the LORD.
2:14 Israel who came there ⌊to **s**⌋.
2:19 husband to offer the annual **s**.
2:28 to **s** burnt offerings on my altar,
3:14 No offering or **s** will ever ⌊be
9:12 the people are offering a **s**
9:13 since he blesses the **s**.
10:8 Then I will come to **s** burnt
15:15 the best sheep and cows to **s**
15:21 claimed for God — in order to **s**
15:22 instructions is better than to **s**.
16:2 'I've come to **s** to the LORD.'
16:3 Invite Jesse to the **s**.
16:5 "I have come to **s** to the LORD.
16:5 and come with me to the **s**."
16:5 sons and invited them to the **s**.
20:6 are offering the annual **s** there.'
20:29 Our relatives will offer a **s** in
1Ki 3:4 Solomon went to Gibeon to **s**
12:27 regain popularity if they go to **s**
12:32 went to the altar in Bethel to **s**
13:1 standing at the altar to offer a **s**.
13:2 Here on you Josiah will **s** the
18:29 until the time for the evening **s**.
18:36 When it was time to offer the **s**,
22:44 The people continued to **s** and
2Ki 5:17 From now on I will **s** to the
5:17 not offer any burnt offering or **s**
10:19 because I have a great **s**
17:35 them, serve them, or **s** to them.
17:36 to the LORD, and **s** to him.
21:6 He burned his son as a **s**,
23:5 of Judah had appointed to **s** at
23:10 would never again **s** their sons
1Ch 16:40 They were ordered to **s** burnt
2Ch 2:4 I want to ⌊**s**⌋ burnt offerings
2:6 a place to **s** in his presence?
11:16 priests to Jerusalem to **s**
13:11 They **s** burnt offerings to the
23:18 They were appointed to **s** burnt
28:23 I'll **s** to them so that they will
28:25 he made places of worship to **s**
29:7 and didn't burn incense or **s**
29:21 to **s** the animals on the LORD's
32:12 'Worship and **s** at one altar?'
33:6 He burned his son as a **s** in the
33:17 The people continued to **s** at
Ezr 3:2 it in order to **s** burnt offerings.
9:4 in shock until the evening **s**.
9:5 At the evening **s** I got up from
Job 1:5 morning and **s** burnt offerings
Psa 50:14 ⌊your⌋ thanks to God as a **s**,
50:23 offers thanks as a **s** honors me.
51:16 You are not happy with any **s**.
51:17 The **s** pleasing to God is a
54:6 I will make a **s** to you along
66:15 I will offer you a **s** of fattened
107:22 of thanksgiving as their **s**.
116:17 of thanksgiving to you as a **s**.
141:2 be accepted as an evening **s**.
Pro 13:6 wickedness ruins a **s** for sin.
15:8 A **s** brought by wicked people
21:3 to the LORD than offering a **s**.
21:27 The **s** of wicked people is
Isa 34:6 will receive a **s** in Bozrah,

Isa 53:10 the LORD has made his life a **s**
66:3 Whoever offers a grain **s** is like
Jer 11:13 ⌊in Jerusalem⌋ to **s** to Baal.
14:12 Even if they **s** burnt offerings
32:35 sites for Baal to **s** their sons
33:18 presence to **s** burnt offerings,
Eze 20:41 as if you were a pleasing **s**.
39:17 for the **s** that I'm preparing
39:19 until you are drunk at the **s** that
43:25 seven days you must **s** a goat,
43:27 the priests must **s** burnt
45:15 You must **s** them with grain
46:12 He must **s** burnt offerings and
Dan 9:21 about the time of the evening **s**.
Hos 12:11 They **s** bulls in Gilgal.
Jnh 2:9 But I will **s** to you with songs
Hab 1:16 That is why they **s** to their nets
Zep 1:7 The LORD has prepared a **s**.
1:8 "On the day of the LORD's **s** I
Zec 14:21 All who come to **s** will take
Mal 1:8 you bring a blind animal to **s**,
1:14 that they vow to give ⌊as a **s**⌋.
1:14 But they **s** second-rate ones to
Mat 8:4 Then offer the **s** Moses
Luk 2:24 They also offered a **s** as
5:14 Then offer the **s** as Moses
Act 7:41 They offered a **s** to that false
14:13 wanted to offer a **s** ⌊to Paul
21:26 would be over and the **s** would
Eph 5:2 life for us as an offering and **s**,
Php 2:17 poured out as a part of the **s**
4:18 a **s** that God accepts and with
2Ti 4:6 to be poured out as a **s** to God.
Heb 7:27 Jesus brought the **s** for the sins
9:12 of goats and bulls, for the **s**.
9:12 place and offered this **s** once
9:25 into the holy place to make a **s**
9:25 Christ didn't go into heaven to **s**
9:26 once to remove sin by his **s**.
10:11 He offered the same type of **s**
10:12 priest made one **s** for sins,
10:12 and this **s** lasts forever.
10:14 With one **s** he accomplished
10:18 longer any need to **s** for sins.
10:26 no **s** can take away our sins.
11:4 a better **s** than Cain's sacrifice.
11:4 a better sacrifice than Cain's **s**.
11:17 to offer his only son as a **s**.
13:15 always bring God a **s** of praise,
Jas 2:21 son Isaac as a **s** on the altar?

sacrificed (96)

Gen 22:13 So Abraham took the ram and **s**
Exo 23:18 The fat **s** at my festivals
24:5 and they **s** bulls as burnt
32:6 Early the next day the people **s**
40:29 He **s** burnt offerings and grain
Lev 5:16 So the priest will use the ram **s**
7:25 an animal which they **s** by fire
9:15 He **s** it to take away sins as he
9:16 the burnt offering and **s** it.
9:22 He **s** the offering for sin,
10:19 "Today they **s** their offering for
Num 15:27 female goat must be **s** as
22:40 Balak **s** cattle, sheep,
Dtr 18:1 They will eat what has been **s**
32:17 They **s** to demons that are not
Jos 8:31 and **s** fellowship offerings
Jdg 6:28 the second bull had been **s** as
13:19 and a grain offering and **s** them
20:26 Then they **s** burnt offerings and
21:4 They built an altar there and **s**
1Sm 6:14 up the wood of the cart and **s**
7:9 and **s** it as a burnt offering to
11:15 There they **s** fellowship
13:9 So he **s** the burnt offering.
2Sm 6:13 David **s** a bull and a fattened
6:17 David **s** burnt offerings and
24:25 there and **s** burnt offerings
1Ki 1:9 Adonijah **s** sheep,
1:19 He has **s** many fattened calves,
1:25 he went and **s** many bulls,
3:3 However, he still **s** and burned
3:4 Solomon **s** 1,000 burnt
3:15 He **s** burnt offerings and
8:63 Solomon **s** 22,000 cattle and
1Ki 8:64 He **s** the burnt offerings,
9:25 Three times a year Solomon **s**
10:5 and the burnt offerings that he **s**
11:8 incense and **s** to their gods.
2Ki 3:27 and **s** him on the wall as a
16:3 of Israel and even **s** his son by
16:13 He **s** his burnt offering and
17:11 they **s** in the same way as the
17:17 They **s** their sons and
22:17 they have abandoned me and **s**
23:8 where those priests **s** unclean.
1Ch 15:26 they **s** seven bulls and seven
21:26 there and **s** burnt offerings
29:21 The next day they **s** to the
29:21 They **s** burnt offerings to the
2Ch 1:6 and **s** 1,000 burnt offerings
7:7 He **s** the burnt offerings,
8:12 Then Solomon **s** burnt offerings
8:13 He **s** every day, on weekly
9:4 and the burnt offerings that he **s**
15:11 On that day they **s** to the LORD
24:14 they **s** burnt offerings in the
28:3 Ben Hinnom and **s** his son by
28:23 He **s** to the gods of Damascus,
30:22 **s** fellowship offerings,
33:16 He built the LORD's altar and **s**
33:17 but they **s** only to the LORD
33:22 Amon **s** to all the idols his
34:4 of those who had **s** to them.
34:25 they have abandoned me and **s**
35:7 to be **s** as Passover offerings
35:16 and the burnt offerings were **s**
Ezr 3:3 They **s** burnt offerings on it to
3:4 Each day they **s** the required
3:5 they **s** the daily burnt offerings,
6:17 they **s** 100 bulls, 200 rams,
6:17 They **s** 12 male goats as an
8:35 from captivity **s** burnt offerings
10:19 They **s** a ram from their flock
Psa 106:28 ate what was **s** to the dead.
106:37 They **s** their sons and
106:38 and daughters whom they **s**
Isa 57:6 offerings and **s** grain offerings
60:7 They will be **s** as acceptable
Eze 16:20 and you **s** them as food to
16:36 your children and **s** their blood
20:26 when they **s** all their firstborn
22:9 who live in you eat food **s**
23:37 They have **s** the children they
23:39 When they **s** their children to
Hos 11:2 They **s** to other gods — the
Act 15:29 by keeping away from food **s** to
21:25 that they should not eat food **s**
1Co 5:7 Passover lamb, has been **s**.
10:28 "This was **s** to a god,"
Col 1:20 Christ's blood **s** on the cross.
1Ti 2:6 He **s** himself for all people to
Heb 7:27 and for all when he **s** himself.
9:28 Likewise, Christ was **s** once to
13:10 to eat what is **s** at our altar.
Rev 2:14 them to eat food **s**
2:20 and to eat food **s** to idols.

sacrifices (171)

Gen 46:1 he offered **s** to the God of his
Exo 3:18 days into the desert to offer **s**
5:3 days into the desert to offer **s**
5:8 'Let us go offer **s** to our God.'
5:17 'Let us go offer **s** to the LORD.'
8:8 go to offer **s** to the LORD."
8:26 The **s** we offer to the LORD our
8:26 If they see us offer **s** that they
8:27 days into the desert to offer **s**
8:28 You may offer **s** to the LORD
8:29 go to offer **s** to the LORD."
10:25 to take ⌊our animals⌋ for the **s**
18:12 offering and other **s** to God.
22:20 "Whoever **s** to any god except
32:8 down to it and offered **s** to it.
34:15 the meat from their **s** with them.
Lev 7:8 belongs to the priest who **s** it.
7:19 is clean may eat from these **s**.
7:30 Bring the **s** by fire made to the
7:35 sons from the **s** by fire made
9:6 you to offer these **s** so that you
17:5 must take the **s** they have been
Lev 17:8 make burnt offerings or **s**
18:21 Never give your children as **s**
21:6 Be holy because you bring **s**
21:21 he must never bring **s** by fire to
23:37 for bringing **s** by fire
23:37 grain offerings, other **s**,
26:31 the soothing aroma from your **s**.
Num 8:12 These **s** will make peace with
25:2 who invited the people to the **s**
25:2 people ate the meat from the **s**
Dtr 12:6 him your burnt offerings, your **s**
12:11 your burnt offerings, your **s**,
12:27 The blood of your **s** is to be
12:31 daughters as **s** to their gods.
18:1 These **s** will be what they
32:38 who ate the fat from their **s**
33:19 they will offer the proper **s**.
Jos 13:14 The **s** offered to the LORD God
22:26 not be for burnt offerings or **s**,
22:27 **s**, and fellowship offerings.'
22:28 make it for burnt offerings or **s**
22:29 or **s** in addition to the altar of
Jdg 2:5 They offered **s** there to the
1Sm 2:13 the people who were offering **s**:
2:28 to keep portions of the **s** that
2:29 you show no respect for my **s**
2:29 best of all the **s** offered by my
6:15 presented burnt offerings and **s**
15:22 with burnt offerings and **s** as
2Sm 15:12 While Absalom was offering **s**,
24:24 my God burnt **s** that cost me
1Ki 8:5 countless sheep and cattle **s**
8:62 all Israel offered **s** to the LORD.
13:2 sites who offer **s** on you.
2Ki 10:24 So they went in to offer **s** and
12:3 The people continued to offer **s**
14:4 The people continued to offer **s**
15:4 The people continued to offer **s**
15:35 The people continued to offer **s**
16:4 He offered **s** and burned
16:15 offerings and ⌊other⌋ **s** on it.
1Ch 6:49 and his descendants offered **s**
21:24 and offer burnt **s** that cost me
21:28 the Jebusite, he offered **s** there.
23:13 to offer **s** to the LORD,
29:21 and many **s** for all Israel.
2Ch 5:6 countless sheep and cattle **s**
7:1 burnt offerings and the other **s**,
7:4 people offered **s** to the LORD.
7:5 cattle and 120,000 sheep as **s**
7:12 for myself as a temple for **s**.
25:14 and burned **s** to them.
28:3 He burned **s** in the valley of
28:4 He offered **s** and burned
29:11 be his servants, and burn **s**."
29:31 Come, bring **s** and thank
29:31 The assembly brought **s** and
29:33 as holy **s** were 600 bulls
30:24 bulls and 7,000 sheep as **s**
35:8 and 300 bulls for Passover **s**.
35:9 and 500 bulls as Passover **s**.
Ezr 6:3 be rebuilt as a place to offer **s**.
6:10 Then they can offer **s** that
Neh 4:2 Are they going to offer **s**?
12:43 That day they offered many **s**
Job 1:5 Job offered **s** for them all the
Psa 4:5 Offer the **s** of righteousness by
27:6 I will offer **s** with shouts of joy
40:6 pleased with **s** and offerings.
40:6 for burnt offerings or **s** for sin.
50:5 a pledge to me through **s**."
50:8 am not criticizing you for your **s**
51:19 will be pleased with **s** offered
Ecc 5:1 than to bring the **s** fools bring.
9:2 whether they offer **s** or don't
9:2 offer sacrifices or don't offer **s**.
Isa 1:11 "What do your many animal **s**
19:21 They will worship with **s** and
43:23 or honor me with your **s**.
43:24 me with the best part of your **s**.
56:7 Their burnt offerings and their **s**
57:7 You've gone to offer **s** there.
65:3 They offered **s** in gardens and
66:3 Whoever **s** a lamb is like
Jer 6:20 I'm not pleased with your **s**.
7:21 your burnt offerings to your **s**,

Jer 7:22 about burnt offerings and **s**.
7:31 their sons and daughters as **s**.
11:15 Can the meat from their **s** turn
17:26 **s**, grain offerings, and incense.
19:5 burn their children as **s** to Baal.
33:18 and to prepare daily **s**."
46:10 of Armies will offer them as **s**
Eze 16:19 them sweet and fragrant **s**.
20:28 they made **s** and brought
20:28 There they offered their **s** and
20:31 You offer your children as **s** by
36:38 will be like the sheep for **s**,
40:42 for burnt offerings and **s**.
43:15 The place where the **s** were
44:11 for the burnt offerings and the **s**
46:24 must boil the people's **s**."
Dan 9:27 he will stop the **s** and food
Hos 3:4 without **s** or sacred stones,
4:13 They offer **s** on mountaintops,
4:14 go to prostitutes and offer **s**
4:19 and their **s** will bring them
6:6 I want your loyalty, not your **s**.
8:13 They offer **s** to me and eat the
8:13 to me and eat the meat of **s**,
8:13 do not accept these **s**.
9:4 and their **s** won't please him.
9:4 Their **s** will be like the food
13:2 "They offer human **s** and kiss
Amo 4:4 Bring your **s** every morning.
5:25 Did you bring me **s** and grain
Jnh 1:16 They offered **s** and made vows
Mal 2:3 excrement from your festival **s**.
Mat 9:13 'I want mercy, not **s**.' I've
Mar 1:44 Then offer the **s** which Moses
12:33 all the burnt offerings and **s**."
Act 7:42 'Did you bring me **s** and grain
Rom 12:1 to offer your bodies as living **s**,
1Co 10:18 Don't those who eat the **s** share
10:20 these **s** which people make
Heb 5:1 to offer gifts and **s** for sin.
5:3 he has to offer **s** for his own
7:27 to bring daily **s** as those chief
7:27 First they brought **s** for their
7:27 and then they brought **s** for the
8:3 is appointed to offer gifts and **s**.
9:9 The gifts and **s** that were
9:10 These gifts and **s** were meant
9:23 had to be cleansed by these **s**.
9:23 had to be cleansed by better **s**.
10:1 their yearly cycle of **s** are only
10:2 If these **s** could have made the
10:2 the **s** would have stopped long
10:3 Instead, this yearly cycle of **s**
10:5 did not want **s** and offerings,
10:6 of burnt offerings and **s** for sin.'
10:8 "You did not want **s**,
10:8 burnt offerings, and **s** for sin.
10:8 (These are the **s** that Moses'
10:9 He did away with **s** in order to
10:11 Yet, these **s** could never take
11:4 since God accepted his **s**.
13:16 the kinds of **s** that please God.
1Pe 2:5 So offer spiritual **s** that God

sacrifices' (1)

Mat 12:7 not **s** means, you would not

sacrificial (5)

Lev 7:16 "If your **s** offering is something
1Sm 9:23 "Bring me the portion of the **s**
Psa 16:4 I will not pour out their **s**
Pro 7:14 "I have some **s** meat.
Zec 9:15 They will be filled like a **s**

sacrificing (22)

Lev 17:7 The people must stop **s** to goat
1Sm 2:15 and say to the man who was **s**,
7:10 While Samuel was **s** the burnt
13:10 As he finished **s** the burnt
13:12 into **s** the burnt offering."
15:22 To obey is better than **s** the fat
2Sm 6:18 When David had finished **s** the
1Ki 3:2 The people were still **s** at other
2Ki 16:3 **S** ⌊children⌋ was one of the
23:5 They had been **s** to Baal,
1Ch 16:2 When David had finished **s**
2Ch 29:27 Then Hezekiah ordered the **s** of
31:2 he performed: **s** burnt offerings
31:2 **s** fellowship offerings,
35:14 (Aaron's descendants) were **s**
Ezr 4:2 We have been **s** to him since
Psa 69:31 the LORD more than ⌊**s**⌋
Jer 11:12 gods to whom they've been **s**.
Eze 43:18 These are the rules for **s** burnt
Luk 13:1 while they were **s** animals.
Act 14:18 kept the crowd from **s** to them.
Heb 10:10 him to do by **s** his body once

sad (25)

Gen 45:5 Now, don't be **s** or angry with
1Sm 1:18 She was no longer **s**.
Neh 2:1 I had never been **s** in his
2:2 "Why do you look so **s**?
2:3 "Why shouldn't I look **s** when
8:10 Don't be **s** because the joy you
8:11 is a holy day. Don't be **s**."
Ecc 7:3 in spite of a **s** face,
Joe 1:11 Be **s**, you farmers! Cry loudly,
Mic 2:4 They will sing this **s** song
Mat 6:16 stop looking **s** like hypocrites.
6:16 They put on **s** faces to make it
9:15 "Can wedding guests be **s**
17:23 the disciples became very **s**.
18:31 had happened and felt very **s**.
19:22 he went away **s** because he
Mar 10:22 unhappy and went away **s**,
Luk 8:52 and showing how **s** they were.
18:23 heard this, he became **s**,
24:17 stopped and looked very **s**.
Jon 16:20 You will cry because you are **s**,
21:17 Peter felt **s** because Jesus had
Rom 12:15 Be **s** with those who are sad.
12:15 Be sad with those who are **s**.
2Co 6:10 People think we are **s** although

saddle (6)

Lev 15:9 has a discharge sits on a **s**,
Jdg 5:10 who sit on **s** blankets,
2Sm 19:26 '**S** the donkey for me,
1Ki 13:13 "**S** the donkey for me."
13:27 told his sons to **s** his donkey
Eze 27:20 traded **s** blankets with you.

saddlebag (1)

Gen 31:34 had put them in her camel's **s**

saddlebags (2)

Gen 49:14 lying down between the **s**.
Jdg 5:16 Why did you sit between the **s**?

saddled (9)

Gen 22:3 morning Abraham **s** his donkey
Num 22:21 he **s** his donkey and left with
Jdg 19:10 He had with him two **s**
2Sm 16:1 him with a pair of **s** donkeys.
17:23 followed, he **s** his donkey, left,
1Ki 2:40 so he **s** his donkey and went to
13:13 After they had **s** the donkey for
13:23 he **s** the donkey for the prophet
2Ki 4:24 She **s** the donkey.

Sadducees (15)

Mat 3:7 many Pharisees and **S** coming
16:1 The Pharisees and **S** came to
16:6 yeast of the Pharisees and **S**!"
16:11 yeast of the Pharisees and **S**!"
16:12 of the Pharisees and **S**.
22:23 On that day some **S**,
22:34 that Jesus had silenced the **S**,
Mar 12:18 Some **S**, who say that people
12:28 during the argument with the **S**.
Luk 20:27 Some **S**, who say that people
Act 4:1 and some **S** approached Peter
5:17 whole party of the **S** who were
23:6 saw that some of them were **S**
23:7 the Pharisees and **S** began to
23:8 (The **S** say that the dead won't

sadness (6)

Est 9:31 the practices of fasting with **s**.
Isa 60:20 and your days of **s** will be over.
65:14 you will cry because of your **s**
Mat 11:17 but you didn't show any **s**.'
Luk 22:45 asleep and overcome with **s**.
Jon 16:6 you're filled with **s**.

safe (34)

Num 32:17 **s** from the other people who
Dtr 29:19 "I'll be **s** even if I go my own
1Sm 20:7 then I will be **s**. But if he gets
20:21 You will be **s**, and there will be
Ezr 8:21 God to ask him for a **s** journey
8:23 asked our God for a **s** journey,
Neh 2:7 to grant me **s** conduct until
Job 5:19 He will keep you **s** from six
5:21 lashes out, you will be **s**,
Psa 12:7 You will keep each one **s** from
22:9 the one who made me feel **s** at
31:20 **s** from quarrelsome tongues.
37:28 They will be kept **s** forever,
119:117 Hold me, and I will be **s**,
140:1 Keep me **s** from violent people.
140:4 Keep me **s** from violent people.
Pro 18:10 person runs to it and is **s**.
28:18 lives honestly will be **s**.
29:25 one who trusts the LORD is **s**.
Isa 32:18 in **s** homes and quiet places of
47:10 You feel **s** in your wickedness
Jer 7:10 You think that you're **s** to do all
7:14 the place where you feel so **s**.
12:12 to the other. No one will be **s**.
Zec 8:10 No one who traveled was **s**
12:6 will remain **s** in Jerusalem.
Luk 11:21 own mansion, his property is **s**.
15:27 your brother's **s** return.'
Jon 17:11 Holy Father, keep them **s** by
17:12 I kept them **s** by the power of
Col 1:5 of the hope which is kept **s**
1Th 5:3 "Everything is **s** and sound!"
Jud 1:1 who are kept **s** for Jesus Christ.
Rev 3:10 I will keep you **s** during the

safeguards (1)

1Sm 2:9 He **s** the steps of his faithful

safekeeping (1)

Luk 19:20 I've kept it in a cloth for **s**

safely (30)

Gen 19:16 brought them **s** outside the city.
28:21 and if I return **s** to my father's
33:18 Jacob came **s** to the city of
Jos 10:21 Then the whole army returned **s**
Jdg 11:31 I return **s** from Ammon will
1Sm 20:13 tell you and send you away **s**,
2Sm 19:24 king left until he came home **s**.
19:30 me that you've come home **s**."
1Ki 22:27 water until I come home **s**.'"
22:28 "If you really do come back **s**,
2Ch 18:26 water until I return home **s**.'"
18:27 "If you really do come back **s**,
19:1 of Judah returned **s**
Psa 78:53 He led them **s**. They had no fear
Pro 3:23 Then you will go **s** on your
Isa 41:3 He chases them, marching by **s**
Eze 34:25 so that my sheep can live **s**
34:27 and my sheep will live **s** in
34:28 They will live **s**, and no one
38:8 and all of them live there **s**.
38:11 peaceful people who live **s**.
38:14 my people Israel will live **s**,
39:6 Magog and on those who live **s**
39:26 When they live **s** in a land
Hos 2:18 so people can live **s**.
13:12 people's sins is **s** stored away.
Act 23:24 take him **s** to Governor Felix."
27:44 way everyone got to shore **s**.
28:1 When we were **s** on shore,
2Ti 4:18 all harm and will take me **s**

safer (1)

Est 4:13 you will be any **s** than all

safety (16)

Job 5:11 He lifts those who mourn to **s**.
11:18 will look around and rest in **s**.
18:14 He is dragged from the **s** of his
Psa 12:5 "I will provide **s** for those who

Psa 59:16 my stronghold and a place of **s**
Isa 8:14 He will be a place of **s** for you.
14:30 the needy will lie down in **s**.
26:1 and fortifications provide **s**.
32:17 peace, calm, and **s** forever.
Jer 23:6 and Israel will live in **s**.
Eze 28:26 They will live there in **s**.
28:26 They will live in **s** when I
30:9 those who live in **s** in Sudan.
Mic 5:4 They will live in **s** because his
Act 27:24 God has granted **s** to everyone
Php 3:1 to you, and it's for your **s**.

saffron (1)
Sos 4:14 nard and **s**, calamus,

sagging (1)
Psa 62:3 a leaning wall or a **s** fence?

sags (1)
Ecc 10:18 A roof **s** because of laziness.

Sahar (1)
Eze 27:18 from Helbon and wool from **S**.

sail (15)
Psa 104:26 Ships **s** on it, and Leviathan,
107:23 Those who **s** on the sea in
Isa 33:21 Stately ships won't **s** on them.
33:23 and your **s** isn't spread out.
42:10 you people who **s** on the seas
Act 20:16 Paul had decided to **s** past
27:1 that we should **s** to Italy,
27:2 We set **s** on a ship from the
27:7 we started to **s** for the south
27:12 men decided to **s** from there.
27:15 and we couldn't **s** against the
27:17 they lowered the **s** and were
27:21 my advice not to **s** from Crete.
27:40 Then they raised the top **s** to
28:10 when we were going to set **s**,

sailed (16)
Act 13:4 of Seleucia and from there **s**
15:39 took Mark with him and **s**
16:11 a ship from Troas and **s** straight
16:11 The next day we **s** to the city
20:13 went ahead to the ship and **s**
20:15 We **s** from there. On the
21:1 When we finally left them, we **s**
21:1 The next day we **s** to the
21:2 so we went aboard and **s**
21:3 it on our left and **s** to Syria.
21:7 ended when we **s** from Tyre
27:4 Leaving Sidon, we **s** on the
27:5 We **s** along the coast of the
27:13 They raised the anchor and **s**
28:11 After three months we **s** on an
28:13 We **s** from Syracuse and

sailing (5)
Luk 8:23 As they were **s** along,
Act 27:7 We were **s** slowly for a number
27:8 We had difficulty **s** along the
27:9 **S** was now dangerous,
27:24 to everyone who is **s** with you.'

sailors (16)
2Ch 8:18 servants and his experienced **s**
9:21 to Tarshish with Huram's **s**.
Psa 107:26 The **s** aboard ship rose toward
107:27 skills as **s** became useless.
107:30 The **s** were glad that the storm
Eze 27:8 skilled people were your **s**.
27:9 their **s** docked alongside you
27:27 your mariners and your **s**,
27:28 "'When your **s** cried out,
27:29 All the rowers, the **s**,
Jnh 1:5 The **s** were afraid,
1:7 Then the **s** said to each other,
Act 27:27 About midnight the **s**
27:30 The **s** tried to escape from the
27:31 "If these **s** don't stay on the
Rev 18:17 who traveled by ship, **s**,

sails (1)
Eze 27:7 Your **s** were made out of fine

sake (66)
Gen 18:24 you spare that place for the **s**
18:26 the whole place for their **s**."
18:29 He answered, "For the **s** of the
18:31 destroy it for the **s** of the 20."
18:32 destroy it for the **s** of the 10."
26:24 for my servant Abraham's **s**."
Lev 26:45 But for their **s**, I will remember
1Sm 12:22 For the **s** of his great name,
2Sm 5:12 famous for the **s** of Israel,
9:1 kindness for Jonathan's **s**?"
9:7 for your father Jonathan's **s**.
18:5 man Absalom gently for my **s**."
18:12 young man Absalom for my **s**.'
1Ki 11:13 tribe for my servant David's **s**
11:13 and for the **s** of Jerusalem,
15:4 But for David's **s** the LORD his
2Ki 8:19 But for David's **s** the LORD
19:34 this city to rescue it for my **s**
19:34 it for my sake and for the **s**
20:6 of the king of Assyria for my **s**
20:6 for my sake and for the **s**
1Ch 14:2 made famous for the **s** of Israel,
17:19 done this great thing for my **s**
Neh 10:28 inhabitants of the land for the **s**
Job 18:4 earth be abandoned for your **s**
Psa 23:3 for the **s** of his name.
25:11 For the **s** of your name,
31:3 For the **s** of your name,
69:7 Indeed, for your **s** I have
122:8 For the **s** of my relatives and
122:9 For the **s** of the house of the
132:10 For the **s** of your servant David,
143:11 keep me alive for the **s** of your
Isa 37:35 this city to rescue it for my **s**
37:35 it for my sake and for the **s**
43:14 For your **s** I will send ⌊an
43:25 actions for my own **s**.
45:4 For the **s** of my servant Jacob,
48:9 For my name's **s** I'll be patient.
48:9 For my glory's **s** I'll hold my
62:1 For Zion's **s** I will not remain
62:1 For Jerusalem's **s** I will not
63:17 Return for the **s** of your
66:5 exclude you for my name's **s**,
Jer 14:7 for the **s** of your name,
14:21 For the **s** of your name,
Eze 20:44 I will deal with you for the **s**
36:22 I will not do this for your **s** but
36:22 this for your sake but for the **s**
36:32 that I'm not doing this for your **s**
Dan 9:17 For your own **s**, Lord,
9:19 Do this for your **s**, my God,
Mal 3:11 Then, for your **s**, I will stop
Act 9:16 to suffer for the **s** of my name."
21:13 but also to die there for the **s**
Rom 9:3 and cut off from Christ for the **s**
1Co 4:6 Apollos and myself for your **s**.
9:23 I do all this for the **s** of the
2Co 4:5 We are your servants for his **s**.
4:11 to death for Jesus' **s** so that
4:15 All this is for your **s** so that,
8:9 He was rich, yet for your **s** he
Php 1:24 But for your **s** it's better that I
2Ti 1:8 join me in suffering for the **s** of
2:10 I endure everything for the **s** of
2Pe 3:9 Rather, he is patient for your **s**.

Salamis (1)
Act 13:5 Arriving in the city of **S**,

Salcah (2)
Dtr 3:10 Bashan as far as **S** and Edrei,
1Ch 5:11 in Bashan as far ⌊east⌋ as **S**.

sale (4)
Gen 42:1 that grain was for **s** in Egypt,
42:2 there's grain for **s** in Egypt.
Lev 25:27 must count the years from its **s**.
25:50 His **s** price will be adjusted

Salecah (2)
Jos 12:5 He ruled Mount Hermon, **S**,
13:11 and all of Bashan as far as **S**

Salem (4)
Gen 14:18 Then King Melchizedek of **S**
Psa 76:2 tent is in **S**. His home is in Zion
Heb 7:1 Melchizedek was king of **S**
7:2 He is also called king of **S**

Salim (1)
Jon 3:23 baptizing in Aenon, near **S**.

Sallai (2)
Neh 11:8 and after him, Gabbai ⌊and⌋ **S**.
12:20 from **S**, Kallai; from Amok,

Sallu (3)
1Ch 9:7 of Benjamin were **S** (son
Neh 11:7 descendants of Benjamin: **S**,
12:7 **S**, Amok, Hilkiah, and Jedaiah.

Salma (4)
1Ch 2:11 Nahshon was the father of **S**,
2:11 and **S** was the father of Boaz.
2:51 **S**, who first settled Bethlehem,
2:54 The descendants of **S**,

Salmon (5)
Rut 4:20 Nahshon was the father of **S**.
4:21 **S** was the father of Boaz.
Mat 1:4 Nahshon the father of **S**.
1:5 **S** and Rahab were the father
Luk 3:32 son of **S**, son of Nahshon,

Salmone (1)
Act 27:7 So at Cape **S**, we started to

Salome (2)
Mar 15:40 James and Joseph), and **S**.
16:1 and **S** bought spices to go and

salt (28)
Gen 19:26 and turned into a column of **s**.
Exo 30:35 incense, seasoned with **s**,
Lev 2:13 Also put **s** on each of your
2:13 The **s** of God's promise must
2:13 Put **s** on all your offerings.
Num 18:19 It is an everlasting promise of **s**
Dtr 29:23 soil poisoned with sulfur and **s**.
Jdg 9:45 the city and scattered **s** all over
2Ki 2:20 me a new jar, and put **s** in it."
2:21 spring and threw the **s** into it.
Ezr 6:9 rams, lambs, wheat, **s**, wine,
7:22 and as much **s** as he needs.
Job 6:6 tasteless food eaten without **s**,
39:6 to live in and the **s** flats as its
Psa 107:34 fertile ground into a layer of **s**
Jer 48:9 Put **s** on Moab. It will be
Eze 16:4 You weren't rubbed with **s** or
43:24 The priests must throw **s** on
47:8 it will replace the **s** water there
Zep 2:9 **s** pits, and ruins forever.
Mat 5:13 "You are **s** for the earth.
5:13 But if **s** loses its taste,
Mar 9:50 **S** is good. But if salt loses its
9:50 But if **s** loses its taste,
9:50 Have **s** within you,
Luk 14:34 "**S** is good. But if salt loses its
14:34 But if **s** loses its taste,
Jas 3:12 In the same way, a pool of **s**

salted (1)
Mar 9:49 Everyone will be **s** with fire.

saltwort (1)
Job 30:4 They pick **s** from the

salty (3)
Jer 17:6 in a **s** land where no one can
Eze 47:11 become fresh. It will remain **s**.
Mat 5:13 how will it be made **s** again?

Salu (2)
Num 25:14 woman was Zimri, son of **S**.

Num 25:14 (S was the leader of a family

salvation (81)

Dtr 32:15 the rock of their **s** like a fool.
2Sm 22:3 the strength of my **s**,
22:36 given me the shield of your **s**.
22:47 May God, the rock of my **s**,
2Ch 6:41 priests, LORD God, with **s**.
Job 13:16 This also will be my **s**
Psa 9:14 of Zion and find joy in your **s**.
13:5 My heart finds joy in your **s**.
14:7 If only **s** for Israel would come
18:2 and the strength of my **s**,
18:35 given me the shield of your **s**.
27:1 LORD is my light and my **s**.
32:7 me with joyous songs of **s**.
35:9 and be joyful about his **s**.
40:10 your faithfulness and your **s**.
40:16 love your **s** continually say,
50:23 way see the **s** that comes from
51:12 Restore the joy of your **s** to me,
53:6 If only **s** for Israel would come
62:1 My **s** comes from him.
62:7 My **s** and my glory depend on
67:2 your **s** throughout all nations.
68:19 God is our **s**. Selah
69:13 me with the truth of your **s**.
70:4 love your **s** continually say,
71:15 about your **s** all day long.
85:7 by giving us your **s**.
85:9 Indeed, his **s** is near those who
89:26 and the rock of my **s**.'
95:1 happily to the rock of our **s**.
98:2 LORD has made his **s** known.
106:4 Come to help me with your **s**
111:9 He has sent **s** to his people.
116:13 I will take the cup of **s** and call
132:16 I will clothe its priests with **s**.
Isa 12:3 water from the springs of **s**.
17:10 forgotten the God of your **s**.
26:18 We weren't able to bring **s** to
33:6 The riches of **s** are wisdom
45:8 Let **s** and righteousness sprout.
46:13 My **s** will not be delayed.
46:13 I'll provide **s** for Zion and bring
49:8 In the day of **s** I will help you.
51:5 My **s** is on the way.
51:6 But my **s** will last forever,
51:8 and my **s** will last throughout
52:7 the good news, announces **s**,
52:10 earth will see the **s** of our God.
56:1 My **s** is about to come.
59:11 We hope for **s**, but it's far from
59:17 coat of armor and a helmet of **s**
60:18 You will call your walls S and
61:10 dressed me in the clothes of **s**.
62:1 and its **s** burns brightly like
Hab 3:8 your chariots of **s**?
Luk 2:30 My eyes have seen your **s**,
2:32 He is a light that will reveal ⌊**s**⌋
3:6 will see the **s** that God gives."'
Jon 4:22 because **s** comes from the
Act 28:28 know that God has sent his **s**
Rom 11:11 By Israel's failure, **s** has come
13:11 Our **s** is nearer now than when
2Co 1:6 it brings you comfort and **s**.
6:2 On the day of **s** I helped you."
6:2 Now is the day of **s**!
Eph 6:17 Also take **s** as your helmet and
Php 2:12 continue to work out your **s**
1Th 5:8 and the hope of **s** as a helmet.
5:9 we obtain **s** through our Lord
2Ti 2:10 may receive **s** from Christ
Heb 1:14 who are going to receive **s**.
2:10 the source of their **s**,
5:9 became the source of eternal **s**
1Pe 1:5 faith for a **s** that is ready
1:9 as you obtain the **s** that is the
1:10 and investigated this **s**.
2:2 Then you will grow in your **s**.
Jud 1:3 to you about the **s** we share.
Rev 7:10 "S belongs to our God,
12:10 saying, "Now the **s**, power,
19:1 S, glory, and power belong to

Samaria (126)

1Ki 13:32 in the cities of S will happen."
16:24 hill and built the city of S on it.
16:28 ancestors and was buried in S.
16:29 He ruled for 22 years in S.
16:32 He built the temple of Baal in S
18:2 was particularly severe in S.
20:1 He went to blockade S and
20:10 will be enough dust left from S
20:17 some men had come out of S.
20:34 as my father did in S."
20:43 king of Israel went home to S.
21:1 to the palace of King Ahab of S.
21:18 Ahab of Israel, who lives in S.
22:10 at the entrance to the gate of S.
22:37 was brought to S to be buried.
22:38 was washed at the pool of S,
22:51 became king of Israel in S
2Ki 1:2 lattice in his upstairs room in S
1:3 messengers of the king of S,
2:25 Carmel, and returned to S.
3:1 became king of Israel in S
3:6 King Joram immediately left S
5:3 were with the prophet in S.
5:24 Gehazi came to the Ophel in S,
6:19 So he led them into S.
6:20 When they came into S,
6:20 they were in the middle of S.
6:24 went to S and blockaded it.
6:25 of S became so severe
7:1 of silver in the gateway to S.
7:18 tomorrow in the gateway to S."
10:1 Ahab had 70 male heirs in S.
10:1 of Ahab's descendants in S.
10:12 Then Jehu left for S.
10:17 When they arrived in S,
10:17 member who was left in S.
10:35 ancestors and was buried in S.
10:36 Jehu ruled as king of Israel in S
13:1 began to rule in S as king of
13:6 remained standing in S.
13:9 ancestors and was buried in S.
13:10 began to rule Israel in S.
13:13 with the kings of Israel in S.
14:14 Then he returned to S.
14:16 with the kings of Israel in S.
14:23 of Israel began to rule in S.
15:8 of Israel in S for six months.
15:13 ruled for an entire month in S.
15:14 came from Tirzah to S,
15:17 He ruled for 10 years in S.
15:23 king of Israel in S for two years.
15:25 fortress of the royal palace in S.
15:27 began to rule Israel in S.
17:1 to rule as king of Israel in S.
17:5 He attacked S and blockaded it
17:6 the king of Assyria captured S
17:24 settled them in the cities of S
17:24 They took over S and lived in
17:26 in the cities of S don't know
17:28 taken prisoner from S went
17:29 ⌊that settled in S⌋ continued
17:29 the people of S had made.
18:9 of Assyria attacked S,
18:10 S was taken in Hezekiah's
18:34 they rescue S from my control?
21:13 the measuring line used for S
23:18 prophet who had come from S.
23:19 of worship in the cities of S.
2Ch 18:2 later he went to visit Ahab in S.
18:9 at the entrance to the gate of S.
22:9 him while he was hiding in S.
25:13 the towns in Judah from S
25:24 Then he returned to S.
28:8 Judah and brought them to S.
28:9 the army coming home to S.
28:15 Then they returned to S.
Ezr 4:10 settled them in the cities of S
4:17 rest of their group living in S,
Neh 4:2 his allies and the army from S,
Isa 7:9 The capital of Ephraim is S,
7:9 and the leader of S is
8:4 and the loot from S will
9:9 who live in S will know it.
10:9 Isn't S like Damascus?'
Isa 10:10 statues than Jerusalem or S.
10:11 I've done to S and its idols."
36:19 they rescue S from my control?
Jer 23:13 this⌋ about the prophets of S:
23:13 The prophets of S prophesied
31:5 on the mountains of S.
41:5 from Shechem, Shiloh, and S.
Eze 16:46 "'Your older sister was S.
16:51 "'S didn't commit half the sins
16:53 and S and her daughters.
16:55 and her daughters and S
23:4 Oholah represents S,
23:33 The cup of your sister S will be
23:46 people of S and Jerusalem⌋.
Hos 8:5 rid of your calf-shaped idol, S.
10:5 Those who live in S fear the
10:7 The king of S will be carried
13:16 The people of S are guilty as
Amo 3:9 together on the mountains of S.
3:9 and oppression in S."
3:12 so the Israelites living in S will
4:1 Bashan who live on Mount S.
6:1 secure on the mountain of S,
8:14 the idol of S, and say,
Oba 1:19 of the lands of Ephraim and S,
Mic 1:1 saw about S and Jerusalem.
1:5 Isn't it S? What is Judah's
1:6 So I will turn S into a pile of
1:7 S collected its wages for being
1:9 ⌊The news about S⌋ will come
Luk 17:11 along the border between S
Jon 4:4 Jesus had to go through S.
4:5 at a city in S called Sychar.
4:40 He stayed in S for two days.
4:43 After spending two days in S,
Act 1:8 throughout Judea and S,
8:1 throughout Judea and S.
8:5 Philip went to the city of S and
8:9 He amazed the people of S
8:15 Peter and John went to S and
9:31 Galilee, and S had peace.
15:3 going through Phoenicia and S,

Samaria's (3)

Hos 7:1 sin and S wickedness.
8:6 S calf-shaped idol was made
Mic 1:9 S wounds are incurable.

Samaritan (11)

Mat 10:5 not Jewish or into any S city.
Luk 9:52 They went into a S village to
10:33 "But a S, as he was traveling
10:33 When the S saw him,
10:35 The next day the S took out
17:16 (The man was a S.)
Jon 4:7 A S woman went to get some
4:9 The S woman asked him,
4:9 you ask a S woman like me
8:48 when we say that you're a S
Act 8:25 Good News in many S villages

Samaritans (10)

Jon 4:9 don't associate with S.)
4:21 A time is coming when you S
4:39 Many S in that city believed in
4:40 So when the S went to Jesus,
4:41 Many more S believed
Act 8:14 heard that the S had accepted
8:15 prayed that the S would receive
8:16 had not come to any of the S.
8:17 and the S received the Holy
8:18 Spirit was given to the S when

Samgar Nebo (1)

Jer 39:3 S (the chief officer), Nergal

Samlah (4)

Gen 36:36 After Hadad died, S from
36:37 After S died, Shaul from
1Ch 1:47 After Hadad died, S from
1:48 After S died, Shaul from

Samos (1)

Act 20:15 day we went by the island of S,

Samothrace (1)

Act 16:11 straight to the island of **S**.

Samson (55)

Jdg 13:24 had a son and named him **S**.
14:1 When **S** went to Timnah,
14:3 But **S** told his father,
14:5 **S** went with his father and
14:5 a young roaring lion met **S**.
14:10 the woman, **S** threw a party.
14:12 Then **S** said to them,
14:14 So **S** said to them,
14:16 **S** replied, "I haven't even told
14:18 **S** replied, "If you hadn't used
15:1 **S** went to visit his wife.
15:3 **S** said to him, "This time I
15:4 So **S** caught 300 foxes.
15:6 They were told, "**S**!
15:6 **S** did it because the man at
15:7 **S** said to them, "If that's how
15:10 "We've come to tie up **S** and do
15:11 They said to **S**, "Don't you
15:11 **S** replied, "I did to them what
15:12 **S** said to them, "Swear to me
15:15 **S** found the jawbone from a
15:16 Then **S** said, "With a jawbone
15:18 **S** was very thirsty.
15:19 **S** drank some water.
15:20 **S** judged Israel for 20 years
16:1 **S** went to Gaza. There he saw
16:3 But **S** was in bed ⌊with the
16:6 So Delilah said to **S**,
16:7 **S** told her, "If someone ties me
16:8 She tied **S** up with them.
16:9 Then she said to him, "**S**,
16:9 **S** snapped the bowstrings as a
16:10 Delilah told **S**, "Look,
16:11 **S** told her, "If someone ties me
16:12 Then she said to him, "**S**,
16:12 But **S** tore the ropes off his
16:13 Delilah told **S**, "You're still
16:13 **S** replied, "Just weave the
16:14 Then she said to him, "**S**,
16:14 But **S** woke up and tore his
16:15 Delilah said to **S**, "How can
16:18 (She did this because **S** had
16:19 Delilah put **S** to sleep on her
16:20 She said, "**S**, the Philistines
16:20 **S** woke up. He thought, "I'll get
16:23 They said, "Our god handed **S**,
16:25 "Call **S** in to entertain us."
16:25 **S** was called from the prison,
16:26 **S** told the young man who was
16:27 who watched **S** entertain them.
16:28 Then **S** called to the LORD,
16:29 **S** felt the two middle columns
16:31 They took **S** and buried him
16:31 **S** had judged Israel for 20
Heb 11:32 **S**, Jephthah, David, Samuel,

Samson's (6)

Jdg 14:15 to **S** wife, "Trick your husband
14:16 So **S** wife cried on his
14:20 **S** wife was given to his best
15:6 the man at Timnah took **S** wife
15:6 the Philistines burned **S** wife
16:2 "**S** here!" So they surrounded

Samuel (148)

1Sm 1:20 She named him **S** [God Hears],
1:24 As soon as she had weaned **S**,
2:11 But the boy ⌊**S**⌋ served the
2:18 Meanwhile, **S** continued to
2:21 Meanwhile, the boy **S** grew up
2:26 The boy **S** continued to grow
3:1 The boy **S** was serving the
3:3 and **S** was asleep in the
3:4 Then the LORD called **S**.
3:4 "Here I am," **S** responded.
3:5 So **S** went back and lay down.
3:6 The LORD called **S** again.
3:6 **S** got up, went to Eli, and said,
3:7 **S** had no experience with the
3:8 The LORD called **S** a third
3:8 **S** got up, went to Eli, and said,
1Sm 3:9 "Go, lie down," Eli told **S**.
3:9 "So **S** went and lay down in
3:10 had called the other times: "**S**!
3:10 **S**!" And Samuel replied,
3:10 And **S** replied, "Speak.
3:11 Then the LORD said to **S**,
3:15 **S** remained in bed until
3:15 But **S** was afraid to tell Eli
3:16 Then Eli called **S**.
3:16 "**S**, my son!" he said. "Here I
3:18 So **S** told Eli everything.
3:19 **S** grew up. The LORD was with
3:20 Dan to Beersheba knew **S** was
3:21 the LORD revealed himself to **S**
3:21 And **S** spoke to all Israel.
7:3 **S** told the entire nation of Israel,
7:5 Then **S** said, "Gather all the
7:6 So **S** judged Israel in Mizpah.
7:8 The Israelites said to **S**,
7:9 Then **S** took a lamb,
7:9 **S** cried to the LORD on behalf
7:10 While **S** was sacrificing the
7:12 Then **S** took a rock and set it
7:13 Philistines as long as **S** lived.
7:15 **S** judged Israel as long as he
8:1 When **S** was old, he made his
8:4 and came to **S** at Ramah.
8:6 But **S** considered it wrong for
8:6 So **S** prayed to the LORD.
8:7 The LORD told **S**, "Listen to
8:10 Then **S** told the people who
8:11 **S** said, "These are the rights of
8:19 people refused to listen to **S**.
8:21 When **S** heard everything the
8:22 Then **S** told the people of
9:14 As they entered it, **S** was
9:15 message to **S** one day before
9:17 When **S** noticed Saul,
9:18 Saul approached **S** inside the
9:19 **S** replied, "I'm the seer.
9:22 **S** brought Saul and his servant
9:23 **S** said to the cook,
9:24 **S** said, "This was kept in order
9:24 Saul ate with **S** that day.
9:26 At dawn **S** called to Saul on
9:26 both he and **S** went outside.
9:27 the city limits, **S** told Saul,
10:1 **S** took a flask of olive oil,
10:9 Saul turned around to leave **S**,
10:14 find them, we went to **S**."
10:15 tell me what **S** said to you."
10:16 But Saul didn't tell him what **S**
10:17 **S** called the people to ⌊come
10:20 When **S** had all the tribes of
10:24 **S** asked the people,
10:25 **S** explained the laws
10:25 Then **S** sent the people back to
11:7 Saul and **S** ⌊into battle⌋."
11:12 Then the people asked **S**,
11:14 **S** told the troops, "Come,
12:1 Then **S** said to all Israel,
12:5 **S** told them, "The LORD is a
12:6 **S** told the people, "The LORD
12:11 and **S** and rescued you from
12:18 Then **S** called on the LORD.
12:18 the LORD and **S** very much.
12:19 All the people pleaded with **S**,
12:20 be afraid," **S** told the people.
13:8 seven days, the time set by **S**.
13:8 But **S** had not come to Gilgal,
13:10 the burnt offering, **S** came,
13:11 **S** asked, "What have you
13:13 a foolish thing," **S** told Saul.
13:15 **S** left Gilgal. The rest of the
15:1 **S** told Saul, "The LORD sent
15:10 Then the LORD spoke to **S**:
15:11 **S** was angry, and he prayed to
15:12 **S** was told, "Saul went to
15:13 **S** came to Saul, who said,
15:14 However, **S** asked,
15:16 "Be quiet," **S** told Saul,
15:17 **S** said, "Even though you don't
15:20 obey the LORD," Saul told **S**.
15:22 Then **S** said, "Is the LORD as
15:24 Then Saul told **S**, "I have
15:26 **S** told Saul, "I will not go back
1Sm 15:27 When **S** turned to leave,
15:28 **S** told him, "The LORD has
15:31 Then **S** turned and followed
15:32 King Agag of Amalek," **S** said.
15:33 But **S** said, "As your sword
15:33 And **S** cut Agag in pieces in
15:34 Then **S** went to Ramah,
15:35 **S** didn't see Saul again before
15:35 though **S** mourned over Saul.
16:1 The LORD asked **S**,
16:2 **S** asked. "When Saul hears
16:4 **S** did what the LORD told him.
16:7 But the LORD told **S**,
16:8 Abinadab and brought him to **S**.
16:8 But **S** said, "The LORD has not
16:9 had Shammah come to **S**.
16:9 chosen this one either," **S** said.
16:10 seven ⌊more⌋ of his sons to **S**,
16:10 to Samuel, but **S** told Jesse,
16:11 **S** told Jesse, "Send someone
16:13 **S** took the flask of olive oil and
16:13 Then **S** left for Ramah.
19:18 and went to **S** at Ramah.
19:18 He told **S** everything Saul had
19:18 Then he and **S** went to the
19:20 with **S** serving as their
19:22 "Where are **S** and David?"
19:24 as he prophesied in front of **S**
25:1 **S** died, and all Israel gathered
28:3 Meanwhile, **S** had died,
28:11 "Conjure up **S** for me,"
28:12 When the woman saw **S**,
28:14 Then Saul knew it was **S**.
28:15 **S** asked Saul, "Why did you
28:16 **S** said, "Why are you asking
1Ch 6:33 who was the son of **S**,
9:22 David and the seer **S** appointed
11:3 LORD had spoken through **S**.
26:28 Everything that **S** the seer,
29:29 in the records of the seer **S**,
2Ch 35:18 during the time of the prophet **S**
Psa 99:6 **S** was among those who
Jer 15:1 "Even if Moses and **S** were
Act 3:24 **S** and all the prophets who
13:20 until the time of the prophet **S**.
Heb 11:32 David, **S**, and the prophets.

Samuel's (2)

1Sm 28:20 He was frightened by **S** words.
1Ch 6:28 **S** sons were Joel,

Sanballat (11)

Neh 2:10 But when **S** the Horonite and
2:19 When **S** the Horonite,
4:1 When **S** heard we were
4:3 who was beside **S**,
4:7 When **S**, Tobiah, the Arabs,
6:1 **S**, Tobiah, Geshem the Arab,
6:2 Then **S** and Geshem sent this
6:5 When **S** sent me the same
6:12 Instead, Tobiah and **S** had
6:14 what Tobiah and **S** have done.
13:28 of **S** from Beth Horon.

sanctuary (2)

1Ki 6:5 main building and the inner **s**.
Eze 11:16 I have been their **s** for a little

sand (28)

Gen 22:17 in the sky and the grains of **s**
32:12 be as many as the grains of **s**
41:49 in huge quantities like the **s**
Exo 2:12 death and hid the body in the **s**.
Dtr 33:19 the treasures hidden in the **s**."
Jos 11:4 as numerous as the grains of **s**
Jdg 7:12 the grains of **s** on the seashore.
1Sm 13:5 and as many soldiers as the **s**
2Sm 17:11 they are as numerous as the **s**
1Ki 4:20 were as numerous as the **s**
4:29 as the **s** on the seashore.
Job 6:3 would be heavier than the **s**
29:18 my days as numerous as the **s**.
Psa 78:27 like the **s** on the seashore.
139:18 them than there are grains of **s**.
Pro 27:3 and **s** weighs a lot,
Isa 10:22 ⌊numerous as⌋ the grains of **s**

Isa 35:7 Then the hot **s** will become a
48:19 descendants would be like **s**.
Jer 5:22 I made the **s** a boundary for the
15:8 numerous than the grains of **s**
33:22 cannot be counted and the **s**
Hos 1:10 as numerous as the grains of **s**
Hab 1:9 will gather prisoners like **s**.
Mat 7:26 person who built a house on **s**.
Rom 9:27 as numerous as the grains of **s**
Heb 11:12 the grains of **s** on the seashore.
Rev 20:8 the grains of **s** on the seashore.

sandal (8)

Gen 14:23 won't take a thread or a **s** strap.
Dtr 25:10 Family of the Man Without a **S**.
Rut 4:7 a man would take off his **s** and
4:8 it for yourself," he took off his **s**.
Isa 5:27 loose or their **s** straps broken.
Mar 1:7 down and untie his **s** straps.
Luk 3:16 not worthy to untie his **s** straps.
Jon 1:27 I am not worthy to untie his **s**

sandals (23)

Exo 3:5 Take off your **s** because this
12:11 your **s** on your feet,
Dtr 25:9 She must take off one of his **s**
Jos 5:15 "Take off your **s** because this
9:5 Their **s** were worn-out and
9:13 Our clothes and **s** are also
2Ch 28:15 clothes for them, gave them **s**,
Sos 7:1 beautiful are your feet in their **s**,
Isa 11:15 can walk over it in their **s**.
20:2 and take off your **s**!"
Eze 16:10 dress on you and fine leather **s**
24:17 your turban, and put on your **s**.
24:23 on your heads and your **s**
Amo 2:6 and the needy for a pair of **s**.
8:6 and the needy for a pair of **s**.
Mat 3:11 am not worthy to remove his **s**.
10:10 **s**, or a walking stick. After all,
Mar 6:9 They could wear **s** but could
Luk 10:4 a wallet, a traveling bag, or **s**,
15:22 on his finger and **s** on his feet.
22:35 or **s**, you didn't lack anything,
Act 7:33 Lord told him, 'Take off your **s**.
13:25 good enough to untie his **s**.'

sandalwood (6)

1Ki 10:11 brought a large quantity of **s**
10:12 With the **s** the king made
10:12 Never again was **s** like this
2Ch 2:8 and **s** from Lebanon.
9:10 brought **s** and precious stones.
9:11 With the **s** the king made

sandbank (1)

Act 27:17 they would hit the large **s** off

sandbar (1)

Act 27:41 They struck a **s** in the water

sandstorms (1)

Dtr 28:24 will send dust storms and **s**

sandy (1)

Rev 12:18 The serpent stood on the **s**

sane (2)

Act 26:25 What I'm saying is true and **s**.
2Co 5:13 If we are **s**, it is for you.

sang (26)

Exo 15:1 and the Israelites **s** this song
15:21 Miriam **s** to them: "Sing to the
Num 21:17 Then Israel **s** this song about
Jdg 5:1 son of Abinoam, **s** this song:
1Sm 18:6 They **s** and danced,
18:7 who were celebrating **s**,
2Sm 3:33 The king **s** a funeral song for
22:1 David **s** this song to the LORD
1Ch 25:6 All these ⌊Levites⌋ **s** at the
2Ch 5:13 they **s** in praise to the LORD:
20:21 in front of the troops, they **s**,
29:30 They joyfully **s** praises,
35:25 Jeremiah **s** a funeral song
Ezr 3:11 they **s** antiphonally:
Neh 12:42 The singers **s** under the
Job 38:7 when the morning stars **s**
Psa 42:4 ⌊I **s**⌋ songs of joy and
106:12 They **s** his praise.
Eze 27:32 They **s** a funeral song for you
Mat 11:17 We **s** a funeral song,
26:30 After they **s** a hymn,
Mar 14:26 After they **s** a hymn,
Luk 7:32 We **s** a funeral song,
23:27 cried and **s** funeral songs
Rev 5:9 Then they **s** a new song,
15:3 They **s**, "The things you do are

sank (15)

Exo 15:5 They **s** to the bottom like a
15:10 They **s** like lead in the raging
Jdg 5:27 He **s**. He fell. He lay between
5:27 He **s**. He fell between her feet.
5:27 Where he **s**, he fell dead.
1Sm 17:49 The stone **s** into Goliath's
Psa 104:8 rose and the valleys **s**
Jer 38:6 and Jeremiah **s** in the mud.
Eze 27:27 everyone else on board **s** into
27:34 your whole crew **s** with you.
Jnh 2:6 I **s** to the foot of the mountains.
2:6 I **s** to the bottom, where bars
Luk 5:7 boats until the boats nearly **s**.
Act 27:28 It **s** 120 feet. They waited a little
27:28 This time the line **s** 90 feet.

Sansannah (1)

Jos 15:31 Ziklag, Madmannah, **S**,

Saph (1)

2Sm 21:18 Sibbecai from Hushah killed **S**,

Sapphira (2)

Act 5:1 his wife **S** sold some property.
5:10 they found **S** dead.

sapphire (9)

Exo 24:10 made out of **s** as clear
28:18 put turquoise, **s**, and crystal.
39:11 put turquoise, **s**, and crystal.
Job 28:6 That place's stones are **s**.
28:16 or with precious onyx or **s**.
Eze 1:26 looked like a throne made of **s**.
10:1 looked like a throne made of **s**.
28:13 **s**, turquoise, and emerald.
Rev 21:19 the second **s**, the third agate,

sapphires (3)

Sos 5:14 a block of ivory covered with **s**.
Isa 54:11 reset your foundations with **s**.
Lam 4:7 Their hair was like **s**.

Sarah (36)

Gen 17:15 her name is **S** [Princess].
17:17 Can **S**, a ninety-year-old
17:19 Your wife **S** will give you a
17:21 **S** will give birth to him at this
18:6 hurried into the tent to find **S**.
18:9 "Where is your wife **S**?"
18:10 and your wife **S** will have a
18:10 **S** happened to be listening at
18:11 Abraham and **S** were old.
18:11 **S** was past the age of
18:12 And so **S** laughed to herself,
18:13 "Why did **S** laugh and say,
18:14 and **S** will have a son."
18:15 **S** denied that she had laughed.
20:2 that his wife **S** was his sister.
20:2 of Gerar sent men to take **S**.
20:14 gave his wife **S** back to him.
20:16 He said to **S**, "Don't forget,
20:18 because of Abraham's wife **S**.)
21:1 The LORD came to help **S** and
21:6 **S** said, "God has brought me
21:7 that **S** would nurse children?
21:9 **S** saw that Abraham's son by
21:12 Listen to what **S** says because
23:1 **S** lived to be 127 years old.
23:2 Abraham went to mourn for **S**
23:19 Abraham buried his wife **S** in
24:36 My master's wife **S** gave him a
25:10 was buried with his wife **S**.
Gen 49:31 Abraham and his wife **S** are
Isa 51:2 your ancestor, and to **S**,
Rom 4:19 and **S** was unable to have
9:9 and **S** will have a son."
Heb 11:11 even though he was old and **S**
1Pe 3:6 as **S** did. Sarah obeyed
3:6 **S** obeyed Abraham and spoke

Sarah's (3)

Gen 24:67 took her into his mother **S** tent.
25:12 He was the son of **S** Egyptian
1Pe 3:6 You became **S** daughters by

Sarai (17)

Gen 11:29 name of Abram's wife was **S**,
11:30 **S** was not able to have
11:31 and his daughter-in-law **S**,
12:5 He took along his wife **S**,
12:11 Abram said to his wife **S**,
12:15 so **S** was taken to Pharaoh's
12:17 terrible plagues because of **S**,
16:1 **S**, Abram's wife, was not able
16:2 So **S** said to Abram,
16:2 Abram agreed with **S**.
16:3 Abram's wife **S** took her
16:4 began to be disrespectful to **S**,
16:5 So **S** complained to Abram,
16:6 Abram answered **S**,
16:6 Then **S** mistreated Hagar so
16:8 away from my owner **S**."
17:15 wife by the name **S** anymore.

Sarai's (1)

Gen 16:8 He said, "Hagar, **S** slave,

Saraph (2)

1Ch 4:22 Jokim, Joash, **S**, and the men
4:22 **S** ruled Moab and Jashubi

sarcastic (2)

Luk 16:14 making **s** remarks about him.
23:35 rulers were making **s** remarks.

Sardis (3)

Rev 1:11 Thyatira, **S**, Philadelphia,
3:1 messenger of the church in **S**,
3:4 But you have a few people in **S**

Sargon (1)

Isa 20:1 In the year when King **S** of

Sarid (2)

Jos 19:10 inheritance goes as far as **S**.
19:12 But from **S** it turns directly east

sat (107)

Gen 21:16 arrow can be shot and **s** down.
21:16 So she **s** down and sobbed
37:25 As they **s** down to eat,
38:14 Then she **s** down at the
48:2 his strength and **s** up in bed.
Exo 16:3 There we **s** by our pots of meat
17:12 put it under him, and he **s** on it.
32:6 they **s** down to a feast,
Lev 15:6 Those who sit on anything he **s**
Jdg 3:20 Ehud came up to him as he **s**
5:17 Asher **s** on the seashore and
6:11 of the LORD came and **s** under
19:6 So they both **s** down and ate
19:15 entered Gibeah and **s** down
20:26 They **s** there and cried in the
21:2 went to Bethel and **s** there
Rut 2:7 She just **s** down this minute in
2:14 So she **s** beside the reapers,
4:1 to the city gate and **s** there.
4:1 So the man came over and **s**
4:2 So they also **s** down.
1Sm 20:24 King Saul **s** down to eat the
20:25 He **s** in his usual seat by the
20:25 Abner **s** beside Saul,
28:23 the ground and **s** on the bed.
2Sm 2:13 They **s** down there,
7:18 David went into the tent and **s**
19:8 The king **s** in the gateway.
1Ki 2:12 Solomon **s** on his father
2:19 Then he **s** on his throne.

1Ki 2:19 and she s at his right side.
7:7 where he s on his throne and
19:4 He s down under a broom plant
21:13 came in and s opposite him.
2Ki 4:20 The boy s on her lap until noon,
11:19 Then Joash s on the royal
1Ch 17:16 David went into the tent and s
29:23 Then Solomon s on the
Ezr 9:3 and s down in shock.
9:4 I s in shock until the evening
10:9 all the people s in the courtyard
10:16 They s down on the first day of
Neh 1:4 I s down and cried.
Est 1:2 the time when King Xerxes s
3:15 So the king and Haman s down
Job 2:8 himself as he s in the ashes.
2:13 Then they s down on the
29:25 I s as their leader. I lived like a
Psa 9:4 You s down on your throne as
29:10 The LORD s enthroned over
55:19 The one who has s enthroned
137:1 By the rivers of Babylon, we s
Isa 65:4 They s among the graves and
Jer 3:2 You s by the roadside waiting
15:17 I s alone because your hand
26:10 They s at the entrance of New
39:3 king of Babylon came in and s
Eze 3:15 I s there among them for seven
14:1 came to me and s down
20:1 They s in front of me.
23:41 They s on their fine couches
Dan 7:9 for endless years, s down.
Jnh 3:6 on sackcloth, and s in ashes.
4:5 Jonah left the city and s down
4:5 He s in its shade and waited to
Mat 5:1 up a mountain and s down.
13:1 left the house and s down by
13:2 He s in the boat while the
13:48 Then they s down,
15:29 up a mountain and s there.
26:58 He went inside and s with the
27:36 Then they s there and kept
Mar 3:34 Then looking at those who s in
4:1 so he got into a boat and s in it.
6:40 They s down in groups of
9:35 He s down and called the
11:2 No one has ever s on it.
11:7 their coats on it, and he s on it.
12:41 As Jesus s facing the temple
14:54 He s with the guards and
16:5 dressed in a white robe and s
Luk 4:20 to the attendant, and s down.
5:3 Then Jesus s down and taught
7:15 The dead man s up and began
10:13 worn sackcloth and s in ashes.
10:39 Mary s at the Lord's feet and
19:30 No one has ever s on it.
22:55 As they s together,
22:55 Peter s among them.
22:56 servant saw him as he s facing
Jon 4:6 Jesus s down by the well
6:3 and s with his disciples.
8:2 so he s down and began to
12:14 obtained a donkey and s on it,
19:13 he took Jesus outside and s
Act 6:15 Everyone who s in the council
9:40 her eyes, saw Peter, and s up.
12:21 s on his throne and began
13:14 the synagogue and s down.
16:13 We s down and began talking
1Co 10:7 "The people s down to a feast
Rev 3:21 the victory and have s down
4:4 and on these thrones s 24
14:14 and on the cloud s someone
14:15 a loud voice to the one who s
14:16 The one who s on the cloud
20:4 I saw thrones, and those who s

Satan (51)

1Ch 21:1 S attempted to attack Israel by
Job 1:6 S the Accuser came along with
1:7 The LORD asked S,
1:7 S answered the LORD,
1:8 The LORD asked S,
1:9 S answered the LORD,
1:12 The LORD told S, but you must
Job 1:12 Then S left the LORD's
2:1 S the Accuser came along with
2:2 The LORD asked S,
2:2 S answered the LORD,
2:3 The LORD asked S,
2:4 S answered the LORD,
2:6 The LORD told S, "He is in
2:7 S left the LORD's presence and
Psa 109:6 Let S stand beside him.
Zec 3:1 S the Accuser was standing at
3:2 The LORD said to S,
3:2 "I, the LORD, silence you, S!
Mat 4:10 said to him, "Go away, S!
12:26 If S forces Satan out,
12:26 If Satan forces S out,
16:23 Peter, "Get out of my way, S!
Mar 1:13 where he was tempted by S for
3:23 "How can S force out Satan?
3:23 "How can Satan force out S?
3:26 So if S rebels against himself
4:15 they hear the word, S comes at
8:33 said, "Get out of my way, S!
Luk 10:18 "I watched S fall from heaven
11:18 if S is divided against himself,
13:16 S has kept her in this condition
22:3 Then S entered Judas Iscariot,
22:31 S has demanded to have you
Jon 13:27 piece of bread, S entered him.
Act 5:3 why did you let S fill you with
Rom 16:20 quickly crush S under your feet.
1Co 5:5 hand such a person over to S
7:5 back together so that S doesn't
2Co 2:11 I don't want S to outwit us.
11:14 And no wonder, even S
1Th 2:18 but S made that impossible.
2Th 2:9 will come with the power of S.
1Ti 1:20 whom I have handed over to S
5:15 turned away to follow S.
Rev 2:9 They are the synagogue of S.
2:13 your presence, where S lives.
2:24 called the deep things of S —
12:9 named Devil and S,
20:2 named Devil and S.
20:7 S will be freed from his prison.

Satan's (5)

Act 26:18 to light and from S control
2Co 2:11 not ignorant about S scheming
12:7 That problem, S messenger,
Rev 2:13 S throne is there. You hold on to
3:9 who are in S synagogue come

satisfaction (1)

Ecc 2:24 and find s in their work.

satisfied (37)

Lev 10:20 Moses heard this, he was s.
Dtr 32:35 I will take revenge and be s.
Jos 22:30 Manasseh said, they were s.
22:33 The people of Israel were s
1Sm 26:19 let him be s with an offering.
Neh 9:25 So they ate and were s and
Job 19:22 are you never s with my flesh?
Psa 17:14 Their children are s ⌊with it⌋,
17:15 I will be s ⌊with seeing⌋ you.
37:19 times of famine they will be s.
Pro 11:25 others will himself be s.
13:4 of hard-working people is s.
14:14 person is s with God's ways.
27:20 Hell and decay are never s,
27:20 a person's eyes are never s.
30:9 or I may feel s and deny you
30:15 Three things are never s.
Ecc 4:8 eyes are never s with riches.
5:10 will never be s with money.
5:10 loves wealth will never be s
6:3 Suppose a rich person wasn't s
6:7 but their appetite is never s.
Isa 53:11 He will see and be s because
66:11 You will nurse and be s from
Jer 5:7 even though I s their needs.
9:9 this nation. I still won't be s.
Eze 16:28 because you weren't s.
16:28 You still weren't s.
16:29 Even after that, you weren't s.
Joe 2:19 You will be s with them.
Hab 2:5 He is like death — never s.
Zep 1:12 and punish those who are s
Mat 5:6 approval. They will be s.
Luk 3:14 "Be s with your pay,
6:21 They will be s. Blessed are
1Ti 6:8 and clothes, we should be s.
3Jn 1:10 He's not s with saying

satisfies (2)

Psa 147:14 borders and s your ⌊hunger⌋
Pro 11:25 and whoever s others will

satisfy (23)

Neh 9:15 from heaven to s their hunger
Job 38:39 hunt prey for the lioness and s
Psa 63:5 You s my soul with the richest
81:16 the finest wheat and s them
90:14 S us every morning with your
91:16 I will s you with a long life.
132:15 I will s its needy people with
145:16 You open your hand, and you s
Pro 5:19 Always let her breasts s you.
6:30 he steals to s his appetite,
6:35 The largest bribe will not s him.
13:25 person eats to s his appetite,
Isa 43:24 with ⌊your⌋ money or s me
55:2 on what does not s you?
58:10 hungry and to s ⌊the needs of⌋
58:11 guide you and s you even
Jer 31:14 I will s the priests with rich
Eze 7:19 It will no longer s their hunger
Hos 9:4 food will only s their hunger.
Mar 15:15 Pilate wanted to s the people,
Jon 14:8 and that will s us."
1Co 7:3 Husbands and wives should s
1Pe 1:14 Once you lived to s your

satisfying (2)

Act 20:35 is more s than receiving them.'"
Rom 13:14 and forget about s the desires

satraps (14)

Ezr 8:36 the king's orders to the king's s
Est 3:12 were written to the king's s,
8:9 to the Jews and to the s,
9:3 provinces, the s, the governors,
Dan 3:2 messengers to assemble the s,
3:3 Then the s, governors, mayors,
3:27 The king's s, governors,
6:1 would be good to appoint 120 s
6:2 Over these s were three
6:2 The s were to report to these
6:3 among the other officials and s
6:4 So the other officials and s
6:6 So these officials and s went
6:7 All the officials, governors, s,

saturate (1)

Job 38:27 to s the desolate wasteland in

sauce (1)

Jon 13:26 after I've dipped it in the s."

saucers (1)

1Ki 7:50 dishes, snuffers, bowls, s,

Saul (371)

1Sm 9:2 He had a son named S,
9:2 was more handsome than S.
9:3 Kish were lost, Kish told S,
9:4 Then S and his servant went
9:5 S told his servant who was
9:7 "If we go," S asked his servant,
9:8 The servant again answered S,
9:10 S told his servant,
9:14 So S and his servant went to
9:15 one day before S came:
9:17 When Samuel noticed S,
9:18 S approached Samuel inside
9:21 S replied, "I am a man from the
9:22 Samuel brought S and his
9:24 thigh and laid it in front of S.
9:24 S ate with Samuel that day.
9:25 blankets on the roof for S,
9:26 At dawn Samuel called to S on
9:26 S got up, and both he and

1Sm 9:27 the city limits, Samuel told S,
10:9 When S turned around to leave
10:10 When S came to the hill,
10:11 Is S one of the prophets?"
10:12 "Is S one of the prophets?"
10:14 S answered, "To look for the
10:16 S answered his uncle.
10:16 But S didn't tell him what
10:21 Then S, the son of Kish,
10:26 S also went home to Gibeah.
11:5 Just then S was coming from
11:5 S asked. So they told him the
11:7 S took a pair of oxen,
11:7 of anyone who doesn't follow S
11:7 came out united ⌊behind S⌋.
11:8 When S counted them at
11:11 The next day S arranged the
11:12 "Who said that S shouldn't rule
11:13 But S said, "No one will be
11:15 they confirmed S as their king.
11:15 S and all of Israel's soldiers
13:1 S was ⌊thirty⌋ years old when
13:2 S chose 3,000 men from Israel;
13:2 stationed with S at Michmash
13:3 the land, S announced, "Listen,
13:4 "I, S, have defeated the
13:4 rallied behind S at Gilgal.
13:7 But S remained in Gilgal,
13:9 Then S said, "Bring me the
13:10 and S went to greet him.
13:11 S replied, "I saw the troops
13:13 a foolish thing," Samuel told S.
13:15 rest of the people followed S
13:15 where S counted the troops
13:16 S, his son Jonathan, and the
13:22 who were with S and Jonathan.
13:22 But S and his son Jonathan
14:2 S was staying on the outskirts
14:17 "Look around," S told the
14:18 Then S said to Ahijah,
14:19 While S was talking to the
14:19 Then S said to the priest,
14:20 S and all the troops with him
14:21 who were with S and Jonathan.
14:24 S made the troops swear,
14:33 Some ⌊soldiers⌋ told S,
14:33 S replied, "You have been
14:34 Then S said, "Spread out
14:35 Then S built an altar to the
14:36 S said ⌊to his men⌋,
14:37 Then S asked God,
14:38 So S ordered all the leaders of
14:40 S told all Israel, "You stand on
14:40 the troops responded to S.
14:41 Then S said to the LORD,
14:41 Jonathan and S were chosen,
14:42 and my son Jonathan," S said.
14:43 "Tell me," S asked Jonathan.
14:44 S said, "May God do worse
14:45 The troops asked S,
14:46 Then S stopped pursuing the
14:47 When S had taken over the
14:52 Philistines as long as S lived.
14:52 S would enlist him in the army.
15:1 Samuel told S, "The LORD
15:4 S organized the troops,
15:5 S went to the city of Amalek
15:6 Then S said to the Kenites,
15:7 S attacked the Amalekites from
15:9 S and the army spared Agag
15:11 "I regret that I made S king.
15:12 morning he got up to meet S.
15:12 Samuel was told, "S went to
15:13 Samuel came to S,
15:15 S answered, "The army
15:16 "Be quiet," Samuel told S,
15:16 "Speak," S replied.
15:20 the LORD," S told Samuel.
15:24 Then S told Samuel,
15:26 Samuel told S, "I will not go
15:27 S grabbed the hem of his robe,
15:30 S replied, "I have sinned!
15:31 Samuel turned and followed S,
15:31 and S worshiped the LORD.
15:34 and S went to his home at
15:35 Samuel didn't see S again

1Sm 15:35 Samuel mourned over S.
15:35 he had made S king of Israel.
16:1 going to mourn for S now that
16:2 "When S hears about it,
16:14 the LORD's Spirit had left S,
16:17 S told his officials,
16:19 S sent messengers to Jesse to
16:20 them with his son David to S.
16:21 David came to S and served
16:21 S loved him very much and
16:22 S sent ⌊this message⌋ to
16:23 God's spirit came to S,
16:23 S got relief ⌊from his terror⌋
17:2 So S and the army of Israel
17:11 When S and all the Israelites
17:19 They, along with S and all the
17:31 overheard and reported to S,
17:32 David told S, "No one should
17:33 S responded to David,
17:34 David replied to S,
17:37 "Go," S told David,
17:38 S put his battle tunic on David;
17:39 in these things," David told S.
17:55 As S watched David going out
17:57 Abner brought him to S.
17:58 S asked him, "Whose son are
18:1 David finished talking to S.
18:2 (From that day on S kept David
18:5 wherever S sent him.
18:5 S put him in charge of the
18:6 cities came to meet King S.
18:7 "S has defeated thousands but
18:8 S became very angry because
18:9 From that day on S kept an eye
18:10 evil spirit from God seized S.
18:10 S had a spear in his hand.
18:12 S was afraid of David,
18:12 was with David but had left S.
18:15 S noticed how very successful
18:17 Finally, S said to David,
18:17 (S thought, "I must not lay a
18:18 David asked S. "And how
18:20 When S was told about it,
18:21 S thought, "I'll give her to
18:22 S ordered his officers,
18:24 When the officers told S what
18:25 S replied, "Tell David,
18:25 In this way S planned
18:27 Then S gave him his daughter
18:28 S realized that the LORD was
18:29 Then S was even more afraid
18:29 and so S became David's
19:1 S told his son Jonathan and all
19:2 "My father S is trying to kill
19:4 well of David to his father S.
19:6 S listened to Jonathan,
19:7 Then Jonathan took David to S.
19:9 the LORD came over S while
19:10 S tried to nail David to the wall
19:10 escaping ⌊from S⌋ that night.
19:11 S sent messengers to watch
19:14 When S sent messengers to
19:15 Then S sent the messengers
19:15 S told them, "Bring him here to
19:17 S asked Michal, "Why did you
19:18 He told Samuel everything S
19:19 When it was reported to S that
19:20 S sent messengers to get
19:21 When they told S ⌊about this⌋,
19:21 S even sent a third group of
19:24 "Is S one of the prophets?"
20:24 King S sat down to eat the
20:25 Abner sat beside S,
20:26 S didn't say anything that day,
20:27 S asked his son Jonathan,
20:28 Jonathan answered S,
20:30 Then S got angry with
20:33 S raised his spear to strike him.
21:10 He was ⌊still⌋ fleeing from S
21:11 'S has defeated thousands but
22:6 S heard that David and his men
22:6 S was staying in Gibeah under
22:12 S said, "Listen here, son of
22:13 S asked him, "Why did you
22:16 S said, "Ahimelech, you and
22:21 Abiathar told David that S had

1Sm 22:22 he would be certain to tell S.
23:7 When S was told that David
23:7 David went to Keilah, S said,
23:8 So S called together all the
23:9 When David learned that S
23:10 I have actually heard that S is
23:11 Will S come here as I have
23:12 me and my men over to S?"
23:13 Then S was told, "David has
23:14 S was always searching for
23:15 David was afraid because S
23:17 "my father S won't find you.
23:17 Even my father S knows this."
23:19 Then the men of Ziph went to S
23:21 S responded, "The LORD
23:24 They left for Ziph ahead of S.
23:25 When S and his men came to
23:25 S heard about it and pursued
23:26 S went on one side of the
23:26 hurrying to get away from S,
23:26 and S and his men were going
23:27 messenger came to S and said,
23:28 S gave up pursuing David and
24:1 When S came back from
24:2 Then S took 3,000 of the
24:3 S went into ⌊it⌋ to relieve
24:7 and didn't let them attack S.
24:7 S left the cave and went out
24:8 left the cave, and called to S,
24:8 When S looked back,
24:9 David asked S, "Why do you
24:16 S asked, "Is that you speaking,
24:16 and S cried loudly.
24:22 So David swore to S.
24:22 Then S went home,
25:44 S had given his daughter
26:1 of Ziph came to S at Gibeah.
26:2 S went to the desert of Ziph,
26:3 S camped by the road at the
26:3 When he realized S had come
26:4 to confirm that S had arrived.
26:5 the place where S had camped.
26:5 David saw the place where S
26:5 S was lying in the camp,
26:6 "Who will go with me to S in
26:7 S was lying asleep inside the
26:17 S recognized David's voice.
26:21 "My servant David," S said,
26:25 Then S said, "Blessed are you,
26:25 while S returned home.
27:1 "One of these days S will
27:1 Then S will give up looking all
27:4 When S was told that David
28:3 (S had rid the land of mediums
28:4 S also assembled the whole
28:5 When S looked at the
28:7 S told his officers,
28:8 S left with two men and came
28:9 "You know that S rid the land
28:10 But S took an oath in the
28:12 you deceive me? You're S!"
28:14 Then S knew it was Samuel.
28:14 S knelt down with his face
28:15 Samuel asked S, "Why did you
28:15 S answered, "I'm in serious
28:20 S fell flat on the ground.
28:21 The woman came over to S
28:25 Then she served it to S and his
29:3 the servant of King S of Israel,
29:5 'S has defeated thousands but
31:2 The Philistines caught up to S
31:3 fighting was against S.
31:4 S told his armorbearer,
31:4 So S took the sword and fell on
31:5 saw that S was dead,
31:6 So S, his three sons,
31:7 of Israel had fled and that S
31:8 they found S and his three
31:11 the Philistines had done to S,
31:12 and took the dead bodies of S
2Sm 1:1 After S died and David returned
1:4 S and his son Jonathan are
1:5 "How do you know S and his
1:6 S was there leaning on his
1:12 fasted until evening because S,
1:17 this song of mourning for S

2Sm 1:23 S and Jonathan were loved
1:24 Daughters of Israel, cry over S,
2:4 were the ones who buried S."
2:5 your master S by burying him.
2:7 your master S is dead,
3:1 between the royal families of S
3:6 the families of S and David,
3:7 S had a concubine named
4:4 news about ⌊the death of⌋ S
4:8 the son of your enemy S who
4:8 on S and his descendants."
4:10 who told me that S had died.
5:2 in the past when S ruled us,
7:15 him my love as I did to S,
9:6 and grandson of S) came
9:7 the land of your grandfather S,
9:9 belonged to S and his family.
12:7 Israel and rescued you from S.
16:5 cousin of S came out cursing.
16:8 you spilled in the family of S,
21:1 "It's because of S and his
21:2 them⌋, S, in his eagerness,
21:6 (It was S whom the LORD had
21:7 David and Jonathan, son of S.
21:8 daughter) gave birth to for S,
21:12 went and took the bones of S
21:12 the day they killed S at Gilboa.
21:13 the bones of S and Jonathan,
21:14 they buried the bones of S
22:1 especially from S.
1Ch 8:33 Kish was the father of S.
8:33 S was the father of Jonathan,
9:39 Kish was the father of S.
9:39 S was the father of Jonathan,
10:2 The Philistines caught up to S
10:3 fighting was against S.
10:4 S told his armorbearer,
10:4 So S took the sword and fell on
10:5 saw that S was dead,
10:6 So S, his three sons, and his
10:7 ⌊their army⌋ had fled and that S
10:8 they found S and his sons
10:11 the Philistines had done to S,
10:12 took away the dead bodies of S
10:13 So S died because of his
11:2 "Even in the past when S ruled,
12:1 when he was banished by S,
12:19 with the Philistines to attack S.
12:19 and joins his master S.")
13:3 we ignored while S was king."
26:28 the seer, S (son of Kish),
Act 7:58 with a young man named S.
8:1 S approved of putting Stephen
8:3 S tried to destroy the church.
9:1 S kept threatening to murder
9:2 S wanted to arrest any man or
9:3 As S was coming near the city
9:4 heard a voice say to him, "S!
9:4 S! Why are you persecuting me?
9:5 S asked, "Who are you, sir?"
9:8 S was helped up from the
9:11 and ask for a man named S
9:14 S has come here to Damascus
9:17 After he placed his hands on S,
9:17 "Brother S, the Lord Jesus,
9:18 Then S stood up and was
9:19 S was with the disciples in the
9:22 S grew more powerful,
9:23 the Jews planned to murder S,
9:24 but S was told about their plot.
9:26 After S arrived in Jerusalem,
9:27 Barnabas took an interest in S
9:27 the apostles how S had seen
9:27 how boldly S had spoken about
9:28 Then S went throughout
9:30 they took S to Caesarea and
11:25 the city of Tarsus to look for S.
11:26 After finding S, Barnabas and
11:26 Barnabas and S met with the
11:30 with Barnabas and S
12:25 After Barnabas and S delivered
13:1 and S were prophets and
13:2 "Set Barnabas and S apart for
13:3 their hands on Barnabas and S,
13:4 After Barnabas and S were
13:7 sent for Barnabas and S
Act 13:9 But S, also known as Paul,
13:21 so God gave them S,
13:22 God removed S and made
22:7 heard a voice asking me, 'S!
22:7 S! Why are you persecuting me?
22:13 'Brother S, receive your sight!'
26:14 asking me in Hebrew, 'S, Saul!
26:14 asking me in Hebrew, 'Saul, S!

Saul's (85)

1Sm 9:3 to S father Kish were lost,
10:1 poured it on S head, kissed
10:9 God changed S attitude.
10:14 S uncle asked him and his
10:15 S uncle said, "Please tell me
11:4 came to S town, Gibeah.
11:14 acknowledge ⌊S⌋ kingship.
14:1 One day S son Jonathan said
14:16 S watchmen at Gibeah in
14:49 S sons were Jonathan,
14:50 The name of S wife was
14:50 the son of S uncle Ner.
14:51 Kish (S father) and Ner (Abner's
14:52 S attention, Saul would enlist
16:15 S officials told him,
17:8 and aren't you S servants?
17:12 and in S day he was an old
17:13 three oldest sons joined S army
17:14 The three oldest joined S army
17:15 back and forth from S camp
17:39 David fastened S sword over
18:5 including S officials
18:19 came to give S daughter Merab
18:20 However, S daughter Michal
18:23 When S officers made it a point
18:30 than the rest of S officers.
19:1 But S son Jonathan was very
19:7 to his former status in S court
19:10 and S spear struck the wall.
19:20 over S messengers so that they
21:7 S servants who was obligated
21:7 A foreman for S shepherds, he
22:9 standing with S officials,
23:16 S son Jonathan came to David
24:4 and cut off the border of S robe
24:5 had cut off the border of S robe
26:7 among ⌊S⌋ troops that night.
26:12 the jar of water near S head,
29:10 with S servants who came
31:2 and Malchishua, S sons
2Sm 1:2 day a man came from S camp.
1:21 S shield was never rubbed
1:22 nor did S sword return unused.
2:8 commander of S army, took
2:8 took S son Ishbosheth and
2:10 S son Ishbosheth was 40
2:12 of S son Ishbosheth went from
2:15 S son Ishbosheth),
3:1 and S family became weaker
3:6 his position in S royal family.
3:8 faithful to your father S family,
3:10 the kingship from S family
3:13 S daughter, when you come."
3:14 to S son Ishbosheth
4:1 When S son Ishbosheth heard
4:2 S son had two men who were
4:4 In addition, S son Jonathan
6:16 S daughter Michal looked out
6:20 S daughter Michal came out to
6:23 So S daughter Michal was
9:1 "Is there anyone left in S family
9:2 Now, S family had a servant
9:3 there someone left in S family
9:9 S servant, and said to him,
12:8 I gave you your master S house
16:3 is your master S grandson?"
19:17 the servant of S family, rushed
19:24 Mephibosheth, S grandson,
21:4 silver or gold from S family,"
21:6 presence at S town Gibeah."
21:7 son and S grandson,
21:8 Merab (S daughter) gave birth
21:11 S concubine Rizpah (Aiah's
21:14 in the tomb of S father Kish.
1Ch 5:10 In S day they fought a war
10:2 and Malchishua, S sons
1Ch 12:2 They were S relatives, ⌊from
12:19 had deserted ⌊S army⌋
12:23 Hebron to turn S kingship over
12:29 S relatives, there were 3,000
12:29 them remained loyal to S family
15:29 S daughter Michal looked out
Isa 10:29 the people in S Gibeah flee.
Act 9:18 fish scales fell from S eyes,
9:25 However, S disciples lowered

savage (2)

Isa 33:19 no longer see those **s** people,
Tit 1:12 **s** animals, and lazy gluttons."

save (189)

Gen 32:11 Please **s** me from my brother
37:21 he tried to **s** Joseph from their
45:5 God sent me ahead of you to **s**
45:7 on the earth and to **s** your lives
Exo 14:13 LORD will do to **s** you today.
16:23 S all that's left over,
21:30 the bull's owner may **s** his life
Num 31:18 But **s** for yourselves every girl
Dtr 4:42 of these cities and **s** their lives.
14:22 Every year be sure to **s** a tenth
19:4 one of these cities to **s** his life.
19:5 of these cities and **s** his life.
Jos 2:13 and that you'll **s** us from death."
10:6 Come quickly, and **s** us.
Jdg 6:31 Do you think you should **s** him?
7:7 who lapped water I will **s** you
1Sm 4:3 that he may be with us and **s**
4:8 Who can **s** us from the power
7:8 Ask him to **s** us from the
9:16 He will **s** my people from the
10:1 You will rule his people and **s**
10:27 "How can this man **s** us?"
11:3 And if there's no one to **s** us,
17:37 will **s** me from this Philistine."
17:47 the LORD can **s** without sword
19:11 "If you don't **s** yourself tonight,
23:2 the Philistines, and **s** Keilah."
2Sm 3:18 'I will **s** my people Israel from
22:28 You **s** humble people,
22:42 but there was no one to **s** them.
1Ki 1:12 advice about how to **s** your life
19:3 Elijah fled to **s** his life.
2Ki 13:5 Israelites someone to **s** them,
16:7 Come and **s** me from the kings
1Ch 16:35 Gather us and **s** us from the
2Ch 20:9 and you will hear us and **s** us.'
25:15 Those gods couldn't **s** their
32:15 could **s** his people from
Neh 6:11 go into the temple to **s** his life?
Job 5:20 "In famine he will **s** you from
5:20 and in war he will **s** you from
22:29 he will **s** the humble person.
36:19 Will your riches **s** you from
40:14 your right hand can **s** you.
Psa 3:7 S me, O my God! You have
6:4 S me because of your mercy!
7:1 S me, and rescue me from all
18:27 You **s** humble people,
18:41 but there was no one to **s** them.
22:8 Let the LORD **s** him!
22:21 S me from the mouth of the lion
28:9 S your people, and bless those
31:1 S me because of your
31:2 a strong fortress to **s** me.
31:16 S me with your mercy.
36:6 You **s** people and animals,
44:6 and my sword will never **s** me.
54:1 O God, **s** me by your name,
59:2 S me from bloodthirsty people.
60:5 S ⌊us⌋ with your powerful
69:1 S me, O God! The water is
71:2 your ear toward me, and **s** me.
71:3 You gave the order to **s** me!
72:4 May he **s** the children of needy
72:13 the poor and needy and will **s**
76:9 when you rose to **s** every
78:22 God or trust him to **s** them.
80:2 your power, and come to **s** us.
86:2 S your servant who trusts you.
86:16 S me because I am the son of
91:15 I will **s** you and honor you.

Psa 91:16 I will show you how I will **s**
108:6 **S** ⌊us⌋ with your powerful
109:26 **S** me because of your mercy.
109:31 people to **s** them from those
118:25 We beg you, O LORD, **s** us!
119:41 **S** me as you promised.
119:81 from waiting for you to **s** me.
119:94 **S** me, because I have
119:123 from looking for you to **s** me
119:134 **S** me from human oppression
119:146 **S** me, so that I can obey your
119:154 my case ⌊for me⌋, and **s** me.
119:166 with hope for you to **s** me,
119:174 I have longed for you to **s** me,
Pro 2:12 ⌊Wisdom will⌋ **s** you from the
2:16 ⌊Wisdom will⌋ also **s** you from
20:22 the LORD, and he will **s** you.
23:14 and you will **s** his soul from
Ecc 8:8 Wickedness will not **s** wicked
Isa 25:9 and now he will **s** us.
25:9 be glad because he will **s** us."
45:20 gods that cannot **s** ⌊anyone⌋.
46:4 I'll support you and **s** you.
47:13 to you, rise up, and **s** you.
47:15 and there will be no one to **s**
49:6 you would **s** people all over
49:25 and I will **s** your children.
57:13 your collection of idols **s** you.
59:1 The LORD is not too weak to **s**
63:1 I am powerful enough to **s**
Jer 15:20 I am with you, and I will **s** you
42:11 I will **s** you and rescue you
50:14 Shoot at it; don't **s** any arrows,
Lam 3:26 silently for the LORD to **s** us.
4:17 for a nation that didn't **s** us.
Eze 3:18 ways in order to **s** their lives.
3:19 but you will **s** yourself.
3:21 You will **s** yourself."
13:22 wicked ways to **s** their lives.
33:9 However, you will **s** yourself.
33:12 has done will not **s** him when
Dan 3:15 What god can **s** you from my
3:17 can **s** us from a blazing furnace
6:14 he could think of to **s** Daniel.
6:16 you always worship, **s** you!"
6:20 able to **s** you from the lions?
Hos 13:10 one who is supposed to **s** you?
14:3 Assyria cannot **s** us.
Amo 2:14 Soldiers will not be able to **s**
2:15 Horsemen will not be able to **s**
Mic 6:14 but you won't **s** them.
6:14 Anything you **s** I will destroy.
7:7 I will wait for God to **s** me.
Hab 2:9 and **s** himself from disaster.'
3:13 You go out to **s** your people,
3:13 to **s** your anointed.
Zec 8:7 I am going to **s** my people from
8:13 so I will now **s** you,
12:7 "The LORD will **s** Judah's
Mat 1:21 because he will **s** his people
8:25 **S** us! We're going to die!"
14:30 He shouted, "Lord, **s** me!"
16:25 Those who want to **s** their
19:26 for people ⌊to **s** themselves⌋,
27:40 **S** yourself! If you're the Son of
27:42 but he can't **s** himself.
27:49 Let's see if Elijah comes to **s**
Mar 8:35 Those who want to **s** their
8:35 for the Good News will **s** them.
10:27 for people ⌊to **s** themselves⌋,
10:27 impossible for God to **s** them.
15:30 from the cross, and **s** yourself!"
15:31 but he can't **s** himself.
Luk 1:71 He promised to **s** us from our
7:3 to come and **s** the servant's life.
9:24 Those who want to **s** their
9:24 their lives for me will **s** them.
17:33 Those who try to **s** their lives
17:33 lose their lives will **s** them.
19:10 seek and to **s** people who are
21:19 endurance you will **s** your life.
23:35 let him **s** himself!"
23:37 king of the Jews, **s** yourself!"
23:39 Well, **s** yourself and us!"
Jon 3:17 the world, but to **s** the world.
5:34 I'm telling you this to **s** you.
Jon 12:27 Should I say, 'Father, **s** me
12:47 the world but to **s** the world.
Act 2:40 He urged, "**S** yourselves from
4:12 No one else can **s** us.
11:14 you a message that will **s** you
13:47 you would **s** people all over
27:43 the officer wanted to **s** Paul,
Rom 1:16 It is God's power to **s** everyone
5:9 more certain that Christ will **s**
5:10 the life his Son lived will **s** us.
11:14 jealous and **s** some of them.
16:4 They risked their lives to **s** me.
1Co 1:21 speak to **s** those who believe.
7:16 you will **s** your husband?
7:16 whether you will **s** your wife?
9:22 in order to **s** at least some
16:2 some of your money and **s** it.
2Th 2:10 the truth that would **s** them.
1Ti 1:15 into the world to **s** sinners,
4:16 If you do this, you will **s**
Heb 5:7 who could **s** him from death.
6:9 for you and that they will **s** you.
7:25 able to **s** those who come
9:28 but he will **s** those who eagerly
11:7 and built a ship to **s** his family.
Jas 1:21 This word can **s** you.
2:14 Can this kind of faith **s** him?
4:12 He is able to **s** or destroy you.
5:15 (Prayers offered in faith will **s**
5:20 his ways will **s** him from death,
1Pe 3:21 Baptism doesn't **s** by removing
Jud 1:23 **S** others by snatching them

saved (124)

Gen 19:20 Then my life will be **s**."
27:36 So he asked, "Haven't you **s** a
32:30 but my life was **s**."
47:25 "You have **s** our lives,"
Exo 14:30 That day the LORD **s** Israel
15:13 lead the people you have **s**.
16:24 So they **s** it until the next
18:4 He **s** me from Pharaoh's death
18:8 and how the LORD had **s** them.
Dtr 9:26 You **s** them by your great
33:29 a nation **s** by the LORD?
Jos 24:10 So I **s** you from his power.
Jdg 7:2 brag and say, 'We **s** ourselves.'
1Sm 2:1 I rejoice because you **s** ⌊me⌋.
11:13 because today the LORD **s**
14:23 So the LORD **s** Israel that day.
17:37 who **s** me from the lion and the
2Sm 19:5 "They **s** your life and the lives
19:9 us from our enemies and **s**
22:3 Savior who **s** me from violence.
22:4 and I was **s** from my enemies.
1Ki 1:29 as the LORD who has **s** my life
2Ki 11:2 She **s** him from being killed
14:27 he **s** them through Jeroboam,
1Ch 11:14 So the LORD **s** ⌊them⌋ with an
2Ch 22:11 She **s** him from being killed
32:22 So the LORD **s** Hezekiah and
Neh 1:10 whom you have **s** by your great
Job 26:2 who has no power and **s**
Psa 18:3 and I was **s** from my enemies.
22:5 They cried to you and were **s**.
34:6 The LORD heard him and **s**
44:7 But you **s** us from our enemies.
80:3 on us so that we may be **s**.
80:7 on us so that we may be **s**.
80:19 on us so that we may be **s**.
106:8 He **s** them because of his
107:13 He **s** them from their troubles.
107:19 He **s** them from their troubles.
109:27 are the one who **s** me.
116:6 When I was weak, he **s** me.
116:8 You **s** me from death.
116:8 You **s** my eyes from tears
119:155 people are far from being **s**,
Pro 11:6 Decent people are **s** by their
Ecc 9:15 He **s** the town using his
Sos 7:13 I have **s** new and old things for
Isa 29:22 the LORD, who **s** Abraham,
30:15 You can be **s** by returning to
38:17 You have **s** me and kept me
43:12 revealed it to you, I have **s** you,
45:17 Israel has been **s** by the LORD
Isa 45:22 Turn to me and be **s**,
63:9 the Messenger who **s** them.
64:5 Can we still be **s**?
Jer 8:20 and we haven't been **s**.
23:6 In his lifetime, Judah will be **s**,
33:16 In those days Judah will be **s**
Eze 28:4 You **s** gold and silver in your
33:5 they would have **s** themselves.
Dan 3:28 his angel and **s** his servants,
6:27 He **s** Daniel from the lions.
Joe 2:32 name of the LORD will be **s**.
Mat 9:17 fresh skins, and both are **s**."
10:22 endures to the end will be **s**.
19:25 "Then who can be **s**?"
24:13 endures to the end will be **s**.
24:22 of those days, no one will be **s**.
27:42 "He **s** others, but he can't save
Mar 10:26 other, "Who, then, can be **s**?"
13:13 endures to the end will be **s**.
13:20 that time, no one will be **s**.
15:31 They said, "He **s** others,
16:16 and is baptized will be **s**,
Luk 1:77 that they can be **s** through
2:34 and many others will be **s**.
7:50 "Your faith has **s** you.
8:12 don't believe and become **s**.
13:23 a few people going to be **s**?"
18:26 asked, "Who, then, can be **s**?"
19:9 your family have been **s** today.
23:35 They said, "He **s** others.
Jon 2:10 But you have **s** the best wine
10:9 pen through me will be **s**.
Act 2:21 the name of the Lord will be **s**.'
2:47 Every day the Lord **s** people,
4:12 Indeed, we can be **s** only by
15:1 can't be **s** unless they are
16:17 telling you how you can be **s**."
16:30 what do I have to do to be **s**?"
16:31 you and your family will be **s**."
Rom 8:24 We were **s** with this hope in
9:27 only a few will be **s**.
10:1 people is that they would be **s**.
10:9 him back to life, you will be **s**.
10:10 declaring your faith you are **s**.
10:13 the name of the Lord will be **s**."
11:26 Israel as a whole will be **s**,
1Co 1:18 power to us who are being **s**.
3:15 However, he will be **s**,
5:5 his spiritual nature may be **s**
10:33 people so that they might be **s**.
15:2 In addition, you are **s** by this
2Co 2:15 Christ among those who are **s**
7:10 and act and leads them to be **s**.
Eph 1:13 Good News that he has **s** you.
2:5 (It is God's kindness that **s**
2:8 God **s** you through faith as an
2:8 Being **s** is a gift from God.
Php 1:28 and that you will be **s**.
1Th 2:16 not Jewish how they can be **s**.
2Th 2:13 he chose you to be **s** through
1Ti 2:4 He wants all people to be **s**
2:15 she ⌊and all women⌋ will be **s**
2Ti 1:9 God **s** us and called us to be
3:15 that you can be **s** through faith
Tit 3:5 he **s** us, but not because of
3:5 because of his mercy he **s** us
Heb 2:3 the message that God **s** us?
10:39 those who have faith and are **s**.
1Pe 3:20 eight in all — were **s** by water.
4:18 has God's approval to be **s**,
2Pe 3:15 an opportunity ⌊for us⌋ to be **s**.
Jud 1:5 The Lord once **s** his people

saves (29)

1Sm 10:19 who **s** you from all your
1Ch 16:23 that the LORD **s** his people.
Job 5:15 "But he **s** ⌊other people⌋ from
21:19 "⌊You say,⌋ 'God **s** a person's
Psa 7:10 My shield is God above, who **s**
18:48 He **s** me from my enemies.
34:18 He **s** those whose spirits are
37:40 He **s** them because they have
55:16 and the LORD **s** me.
57:3 his help from heaven and **s** me.
69:35 When God **s** Zion,
96:2 that the LORD **s** his people.

Psa 98:3 seen how our God **s** ⌊them⌋.
138:7 and your right hand **s** me.
140:7 the strong one who **s** me,
145:19 their cries for help and **s** them.
Pro 11:4 but righteousness **s** from death.
14:25 An honest witness **s** lives,
Isa 49:26 that I am the LORD, who **s** you,
Jer 14:8 the one who **s** it in times of
Dan 6:27 He **s**, rescues, and does
Hab 3:18 truly find joy in God, who **s** me.
Zep 3:17 He is a hero who **s** you.
Mat 1:21 will name him Jesus [He **S**],
Act 13:26 that God **s** people was sent
15:11 believe that the Lord Jesus **s**
15:11 way that he **s** them — through
1Pe 3:21 is like that water, now **s** you.
3:21 It **s** you through Jesus Christ,

saving (4)

Gen 19:19 very kind to me by **s** my life,
Psa 69:29 Let your **s** power protect me,
Tit 2:11 After all, God's **s** kindness has
Heb 2:3 the Lord told this **s** message.

savior (71)

Exo 15:2 He is my **S**. This is my God,
Jdg 3:9 The LORD sent a **s** to rescue
3:15 The LORD sent a **s** to rescue
1Sm 14:39 as the LORD and **S** of Israel
2Sm 22:2 rock and my fortress and my **S**,
22:3 and my **S** who saved me from
1Ch 16:35 Say, 'Rescue us, O God our **S**.
Psa 17:7 O **S** of those who find refuge
18:2 rock and my fortress and my **S**,
18:46 May God my **S** be honored.
24:5 righteousness from God, his **s**.
25:5 because you are God, my **s**.
27:9 not abandon me, O God, my **s**!
35:3 Say to my soul, "I am your **s**."
38:22 to help me, O Lord, my **s**.
40:17 You are my help and my **s**.
42:5 He is my **s** and my God.
42:11 He is my **s** and my God.
43:5 He is my **s** and my God.
51:14 guilt of murder, O God, my **s**.
62:2 He alone is my rock and my **s**
62:6 He alone is my rock and my **s**
65:5 in righteousness, O God, our **s**,
70:5 You are my help and my **s**.
79:9 Help us, O God, our **s**,
85:4 Restore us, O God, our **s**.
88:1 O LORD God, my **s**,
106:21 They forgot God, their **s**,
118:14 and my song. He is my **s**.
118:21 answered me. You are my **s**.
144:2 and my **s**, my shield,
Isa 12:2 God is my **S**. I am confident and
12:2 and my song. He is my **S**."
19:20 he will send a **s** and defender
33:2 be our **s** in times of trouble.
33:22 The LORD is our **s**.
43:3 the Holy One of Israel, your **S**.
43:11 and there is no **s** except me.
45:15 are the God of Israel, the **S**!
45:21 God and **S** besides me.
59:20 "Then a **S** will come to Zion,
60:16 that I am the LORD, your **S**,
62:11 'Your **S** is coming.
63:8 So he became their **S**.
Hos 13:4 There is no **s** except me.
Luk 1:47 spirit finds its joy in God, my **S**,
1:69 He has raised up a mighty **S**
2:11 Today your **S**, Christ the Lord,
Jon 4:42 he really is the **s** of the world."
Act 5:31 position as leader and **s**.
13:23 "God had the **S**, Jesus,
Rom 11:26 "The **S** will come from Zion.
Eph 5:23 It is his body, and he is its **S**.
Php 3:20 coming from heaven as our **S**.
1Ti 1:1 by the command of God our **S**
2:3 is good and pleases God our **S**.
4:10 He is the **S** of all people,
2Ti 1:10 coming of our **S** Christ Jesus,
Tit 1:3 by the command of God our **S**.
1:4 Christ Jesus our **S** are yours!
2:10 the teachings about God our **S**
Tit 2:13 glory of our great God and **S**,
3:4 However, when God our **S**
3:6 us through Jesus Christ our **S**.
2Pe 1:1 that comes from our God and **S**,
1:11 of our Lord and **S** Jesus Christ.
2:20 our Lord and **S** Jesus Christ
3:2 and **S** commanded you through
3:18 of our Lord and **S** Jesus Christ.
1Jn 4:14 his Son as the **S** of the world.
Jud 1:25 belong to the only God, our **S**,

saviors (1)

Neh 9:27 You gave them **s** to rescue

savors (1)

Job 20:13 Though he **s** it and won't let go

saw (659)

Gen 1:4 God **s** the light was good.
1:10 God **s** that it was good.
1:12 God **s** that they were good.
1:18 God **s** that it was good.
1:21 God **s** that they were good.
1:25 God **s** that they were good.
1:31 And God **s** everything that he
3:6 The woman **s** that the tree had
6:2 The sons of God **s** that the
6:5 The LORD **s** how evil humans
6:12 God **s** the world and how
8:13 and **s** the surface of the ground.
9:22 **s** his father naked.
12:14 the Egyptians **s** how very
12:15 When Pharaoh's officials **s** her,
13:10 He **s** that the whole Jordan
18:2 and suddenly he **s** three men
18:2 When he **s** them, he ran to
19:1 When Lot **s** them, he got up to
19:28 he **s** smoke rising from the land
21:9 Sarah **s** that Abraham's son by
21:19 Then she **s** a well.
22:4 Two days later Abraham **s** the
22:13 he **s** a ram behind him caught
24:30 He **s** the nose ring and the
24:63 he **s** camels coming.
24:64 When Rebekah **s** Isaac,
26:8 and **s** Isaac caressing his
28:12 He had a dream in which he **s**
28:12 He **s** the angels of God going
29:2 and out in a field he **s** a well
29:10 Jacob **s** Rachel, daughter of
29:31 When the LORD **s** Leah was
30:1 Rachel **s** that she could not
30:9 When Leah **s** that she had
31:10 I looked up and **s** that the male
32:2 When he **s** them, Jacob said,
32:25 When the man **s** that he could
33:1 Jacob **s** Esau coming with 400
33:5 When he **s** the women and
34:2 ruler Hamor the Hivite, **s** her,
37:4 Joseph's brothers **s** that their
37:9 dream: I **s** the sun, the moon,
37:18 They **s** him from a distance.
37:25 As they sat down to eat, they **s**
37:29 cistern and **s** that Joseph was
38:15 When Judah **s** her,
39:3 Joseph's master **s** that the
40:6 he **s** that they were upset.
40:16 The chief baker **s** that the
41:22 second dream I **s** seven good,
42:7 soon as Joseph **s** his brothers,
42:21 We **s** how troubled he was
42:35 When they and their father **s**
43:16 When Joseph **s** Benjamin with
43:29 he **s** his brother Benjamin,
44:13 When they **s** this, they tore
45:27 had said to them and he **s**
46:29 As soon as he **s** his father,
48:8 When Israel **s** Joseph's sons,
48:17 When Joseph **s** that his father
50:11 the Canaanites living there **s**
50:23 He **s** his grandchildren,
Exo 2:2 She **s** how beautiful he was
2:5 She **s** the basket among the
2:6 and **s** it was a boy.
2:11 He **s** a Hebrew, one of his own
2:13 he **s** two Hebrew men fighting.
Exo 2:25 God **s** the Israelites ⌊being
3:4 When the LORD **s** that Moses
8:15 When Pharaoh **s** that the
9:34 When Pharaoh **s** that the rain,
10:6 never **s** anything like this
14:10 the Israelites looked up and **s**
14:30 and Israel **s** the Egyptians
14:31 When the Israelites **s** the great
16:10 Suddenly, they **s** the glory of
16:15 When the Israelites **s** it,
18:14 When Moses' father-in-law **s**
20:18 the thunder and **s** the lightning.
20:18 the blast of the ram's horn and **s**
24:10 They **s** the God of Israel.
24:11 So they **s** God, and then they
32:1 When the people **s** that Moses
32:5 When Aaron **s** this,
32:19 he **s** the calf and the dancing.
32:25 When Moses **s** this,
33:10 When all the people **s** the
34:30 Moses and **s** his face shining,
39:43 all the work and **s** that they had
Lev 5:1 oath and won't tell what you **s**
9:24 When all the people **s** this,
Num 12:10 Aaron turned to her and **s** she
13:28 We even **s** the descendants of
13:32 All the people we **s** there are
13:33 We **s** Nephilim there.
14:10 they all **s** the glory of the LORD
14:22 none of the people who **s** my
16:42 they **s** the smoke covering it,
20:27 The whole community **s** them
20:29 The whole community **s** that
22:2 Balak, son of Zippor, **s** all that
22:23 When the donkey **s** the
22:25 When the donkey **s** the
22:27 When the donkey **s** the
22:33 The donkey **s** me and turned
24:1 When Balaam **s** that the LORD
24:2 looked up, and **s** Israel's camp
24:20 Then Balaam **s** the Amalekites
24:21 Then he **s** the Kenites and
25:7 of the priest Aaron, **s** this.
32:1 They **s** that the regions of
32:9 Eshcol Valley and **s** the land.
Dtr 1:19 and dangerous desert you **s**
1:28 We even **s** the people of Anak
1:30 will fight for you as you **s** him
1:31 There you **s** how the LORD
4:3 With your own eyes you **s**
4:12 a voice speaking but **s** no one.
5:23 from the darkness and **s**
7:19 You **s** with your own eyes the
9:16 Then I **s** that you had sinned
10:21 and awe-inspiring deeds you **s**
11:2 You **s** and experienced his
11:3 You **s** the miraculous signs
11:4 You **s** what he did to the
11:5 You **s** what he did for you in
11:6 You also **s** what he did to
11:7 You **s** with your own eyes all
26:7 He **s** our misery, suffering,
29:3 You also **s** those terrible
29:17 You **s** their disgusting gods
32:19 The LORD **s** this and rejected
Jos 5:13 he looked up and **s** a man
7:21 I **s** a fine robe from Babylonia,
8:14 When the king of Ai **s** the main
8:21 When Joshua and all Israel **s**
24:7 You **s** for yourselves what I did
Jdg 1:24 The spies **s** a man coming out
4:22 He **s** Sisera lying there dead
6:28 they **s** that the Baal altar had
6:28 They **s** that the second bull
9:36 When Gaal **s** the troops,
9:43 He watched and **s** the people
9:55 When the people of Israel **s**
11:34 he **s** his daughter coming out to
11:35 When he **s** her, he tore his
12:3 When I **s** that you would not
13:20 Manoah and his wife **s** this,
14:1 he **s** a young Philistine woman.
14:8 He **s** a swarm of bees and
14:11 When ⌊her family⌋ **s** him,
16:1 There he **s** a prostitute and
16:24 When the people **s** him,

Jdg 18:7 They **s** that the people there
18:9 We **s** the land. It's very good!
18:26 Micah **s** they were stronger
19:17 He **s** the traveler in the city
19:30 Everyone who **s** it said,
20:40 Benjamin turned around and **s**
Rut 1:18 When Naomi **s** that Ruth was
2:18 and her mother-in-law **s** what
1Sm 5:3 of Ashdod **s** that Dagon had
5:4 But the next morning they **s**
6:13 they looked up and **s** the ark,
6:16 rulers of the Philistines **s** this,
10:11 had known him before **s** how
12:12 But when you **s** King Nahash
13:6 When the Israelites **s** they
13:11 "I **s** the troops were scattering.
16:6 he **s** Eliab and thought,
17:24 all the men of Israel **s** Goliath,
17:51 When the Philistines **s** their
19:5 When you **s** it, you rejoiced.
19:20 But when they **s** a group of
22:9 "I **s** Jesse's son when he came
24:10 Today you **s** how the LORD
25:23 When Abigail **s** David,
26:5 David **s** the place where Saul
26:12 No one **s** them, knew about it,
28:12 When the woman **s** Samuel,
28:21 came over to Saul and **s** that
31:5 When the armorbearer **s** that
31:7 across the Jordan River **s** that
2Sm 1:7 he looked back and **s** me,
6:16 and **s** King David leaping
10:9 When Joab **s** he was under
10:14 When the Ammonites **s** that the
10:19 to Hadadezer **s** that Israel had
11:2 From the roof he **s** a woman
12:19 But when David **s** that his
13:34 he **s** many people coming
17:18 But a young man **s** Jonathan
17:23 When Ahithophel **s** that his
18:10 A man who **s** this told Joab,
18:10 "I **s** Absalom hanging in a tree."
18:11 You **s** that!" Joab said to the
18:21 tell the king what you **s**."
18:24 he **s** a man running alone.
18:26 When the watchman **s** another
18:29 Ahimaaz answered, "I **s** a lot of
20:12 When the man **s** that all the
24:17 When David **s** the Messenger
24:20 Araunah looked down and **s**
1Ki 3:28 because they **s** he possessed
4:27 The governors **s** to it that
10:4 When the queen of Sheba **s** all
10:7 the reports until I came and **s**
11:28 Solomon **s** that Jeroboam was
12:16 When all Israel **s** that the king
13:25 People who passed by **s** the
16:18 When Zimri **s** that the city had
18:17 When he **s** Elijah, Ahab said,
18:39 All the people **s** it and
19:6 When he looked, he **s** near his
22:17 So Micaiah said, "I **s** Israel's
22:19 I **s** the LORD sitting on his
22:32 commanders **s** Jehoshaphat,
2Ki 2:12 When Elisha **s** this,
2:15 who were at Jericho **s** him from
2:24 Looking back, he **s** them and
3:22 they **s** the water from a
3:26 When the king of Moab **s** he
4:25 When he **s** her coming at a
5:21 When Naaman **s** Gehazi
6:15 outside, he **s** troops, horses,
6:21 When the king of Israel **s** them,
6:30 the people **s** that he was
7:15 as the Jordan River and **s** how
9:17 Jezreel **s** Jehu's troops coming.
9:22 When Joram **s** Jehu,
9:26 'Just as I **s** the blood of Naboth
9:27 King Ahaziah of Judah **s** this,
11:1 **s** that her son was dead,
12:10 Whenever they **s** a lot of
13:4 heard him because he **s** how
13:21 who were burying a man **s** one
14:26 he **s** how bitterly everyone
16:10 He **s** an altar there in
16:12 from Damascus, he **s** the altar.

2Ki 19:35 they **s** all the corpses.
20:15 Hezekiah answered, "They **s**
23:16 When Josiah turned and **s** the
23:29 When Pharaoh **s** him at
1Ch 10:5 When the armorbearer **s** that
10:7 in the valley **s** that ⌊their army⌋
15:29 and **s** King David dancing
19:10 When Joab **s** he was under
19:15 When the Ammonites **s** that the
19:19 to Hadadezer **s** that Israel had
21:16 When David looked up, he **s**
21:21 Ornan looked up and **s** him.
21:28 At that time, when David **s** the
2Ch 7:3 When all the Israelites **s** the
9:3 of Sheba **s** Solomon's wisdom,
9:6 the reports until I came and **s**
10:16 When all Israel **s** that the king
12:7 When the LORD **s** that they
15:9 when they **s** that Asa's God,
18:16 So Micaiah said, "I **s** Israel's
18:18 I **s** the LORD sitting on his
18:31 commanders **s** Jehoshaphat,
22:10 **s** that her son was dead,
24:11 to the king's officers and they **s**
31:8 and the leaders **s** the heaps,
32:2 When Hezekiah **s** that
Ezr 3:12 eyes began to sob when they **s**
Neh 9:9 You **s** how our ancestors
13:15 In those days I **s** people in
13:15 I **s** them bringing in loads of
13:23 In those days I **s** some Jews
Est 2:15 who **s** Esther liked her.
3:5 When Haman **s** that Mordecai
5:2 When the king **s** Queen Esther
5:9 But when Haman **s** Mordecai at
7:7 because he **s** that the king had
Job 2:12 When they **s** him from a
2:13 to him because they **s** that
3:16 infants who never **s** the light.
4:8 Whenever I **s** those who
8:18 it ⌊and says⌋, 'I never **s** you!'
20:9 Eyes that **s** him will see him
22:19 The righteous **s** it and were
28:27 then he **s** it and announced it.
29:8 young men **s** me and kept out
29:11 ⌊Any⌋ eyes that **s** me spoke
31:26 If I **s** the light shine or the moon
32:5 When Elihu **s** that the three
42:16 He **s** his children, and great-
Psa 48:5 ⌊When⌋ they **s** ⌊Mount Zion⌋,
73:3 of arrogant people when I **s**
77:16 The water **s** you, O God.
77:16 The water **s** you and shook.
106:44 He **s** that they were suffering
139:16 Your eyes **s** me when I was
Pro 7:7 at gullible people when I **s**
24:31 I **s** that it was all overgrown
24:32 I **s** it and learned my lesson.
Ecc 2:11 I **s** that it was all pointless.
2:13 But I **s** that wisdom has an
2:24 I **s** that even this comes from
3:16 I **s** something else under the
3:22 I **s** that there's nothing better
4:4 Then I **s** that all hard work and
4:15 I **s** all living people moving
8:10 Then I **s** wicked people given
8:17 then I **s** everything that God
9:11 I **s** something else under the
Sos 6:9 Her sisters **s** her and blessed
6:9 Queens and concubines **s** her
8:1 If I **s** you on the street,
Isa 1:1 **s** about Judah and Jerusalem
2:1 **s** about Judah and Jerusalem.
5:7 for justice but **s** only slaughter,
6:1 the year King Uzziah died, I **s**
10:15 Can a **s** make itself greater
13:1 son of Amoz, **s** about Babylon.
37:36 they **s** all the corpses.
39:4 Hezekiah answered, "They **s**
Jer 3:7 treacherous sister Judah **s** her.
3:8 Judah **s** that I sent unfaithful
23:13 I **s** something disgusting.
39:4 and all the soldiers **s** them,
41:13 **s** Kareah's son Johanan
44:17 comfortably and **s** no disaster.
Lam 2:14 Your prophets **s** misleading

Eze 1:1 and I **s** visions from God.
1:4 As I looked, I **s** a storm coming
1:5 In the center of the cloud I **s**
1:15 I **s** a wheel on the ground
1:27 Then I **s** what he looked like
1:28 When I **s** it, I immediately
2:9 As I looked, I **s** a hand
3:23 there like the glory I **s** by
8:2 As I looked, I **s** something that
8:4 There I **s** the glory of Israel's
8:4 the vision that I **s** in the valley.
8:5 I **s** the idol that stirs up
8:7 I **s** a hole in the wall.
8:8 through the wall, and I **s** a door.
8:10 I **s** that the walls were covered
10:1 I **s** something that looked like a
10:9 As I looked, I **s** four wheels
10:15 the living creatures that I **s** at
10:20 living creatures that I **s** under
10:22 like the faces that I **s** by
11:1 I **s** among them Azzur's son
11:24 Then the vision I **s** left me.
16:5 No one who **s** you felt sorry
16:6 "'Then I went by you and **s**
16:50 away with them when I **s** this.
19:5 The lioness waited until she **s**
19:11 and everyone **s** it because of
20:28 When they **s** any high hill or
23:11 younger sister Oholibah **s** this,
23:13 I **s** that she was dishonoring
23:14 She **s** pictures of men carved
28:18 the presence of all who **s** you.
37:2 I **s** that there were very many
37:8 As I looked, I **s** that ligaments
40:3 I **s** a man who looked like he
40:5 I **s** a wall that surrounded the
40:17 I **s** rooms there and pavement
40:24 and I **s** a gateway that faced
41:8 I also **s** a raised base all
43:2 I **s** the glory of the God of Israel
43:3 This vision was like the one I **s**
43:3 and like the one I **s** by
43:5 I **s** the LORD's glory fill the
44:4 When I looked, I **s** the LORD's
46:21 I **s** that in each corner of the
47:1 I **s** water flowing from under the
47:7 As I went back, I **s** many trees
Dan 2:31 You **s** a large statue.
2:41 You also **s** the feet and toes.
2:41 As you **s**, iron was mixed with
2:43 As you **s**, iron was mixed with
2:45 This is the stone that you **s** cut
3:27 They **s** that the fire had not
4:10 and I **s** an oak tree in the
4:13 I **s** a guardian, a holy being,
4:20 You **s** an oak tree grow and
4:23 You **s** a guardian, a holy being,
6:23 people **s** that he was
7:1 He **s** a vision while he was
7:2 **s** the four winds of heaven
7:5 I **s** a second animal.
7:6 After this, I **s** another animal.
7:7 After this, I **s** a fourth animal in
7:13 I **s** among the clouds in heaven
7:21 I **s** that horn making war
8:1 as king, I, Daniel, **s** a vision.
8:1 came after the one I **s** earlier.
8:2 In my vision I **s** myself in the
8:2 In my vision I **s** myself at Ulai
8:3 I looked up and **s** a single ram
8:4 I **s** the ram charging west,
8:5 As I was watching closely, I **s**
8:7 I **s** it come closer to the ram.
8:15 I **s** someone who looked like a
8:20 "The two-horned ram that you **s**
10:5 I **s** a man dressed in linen,
10:7 the only one who **s** the vision.
12:5 I **s** two men standing there.
Hos 5:13 "When Ephraim **s** that he was
5:13 Judah **s** his own wounds,
9:10 When I **s** your ancestors,
Amo 1:1 He **s** ⌊a vision⌋ about Israel
9:1 I **s** the Lord standing by the
Jnh 3:10 God **s** what they did.
3:10 He **s** that they turned from their
Mic 1:1 This is the vision that Micah **s**

Hab 1:1 that the prophet Habakkuk **s**.
Hag 2:3 faithful few who **s** this house
Zec 1:8 During that night I **s** a man
1:18 up and **s** four animal horns.
2:1 I looked up and **s** a man with a
5:1 up again and **s** a flying scroll.
5:9 I looked up and **s** two women
6:1 I looked up again and **s** four
Mat 2:2 We **s** his star rising and have
2:11 they **s** the child with his mother
2:16 When Herod **s** that the wise
3:7 But when he **s** many Pharisees
3:16 and he **s** the Spirit of God
4:18 of Galilee, he **s** two brothers,
4:21 he **s** two other brothers,
5:1 When Jesus **s** the crowds,
8:14 he **s** Peter's mother-in-law in
8:18 Now, when Jesus **s** a crowd
8:34 When they **s** him, they begged
9:2 When Jesus **s** their faith,
9:8 When the crowd **s** this,
9:9 he **s** a man sitting in a tax
9:11 The Pharisees **s** this and
9:22 When Jesus turned and **s** her
9:23 He **s** flute players and a noisy
9:36 When he **s** the crowds,
12:2 When the Pharisees **s** this,
14:14 he **s** a large crowd.
14:26 When the disciples **s** him
17:8 they **s** no one but Jesus.
18:31 with him **s** what had happened
20:3 he **s** others standing in the
21:15 chief priests and the scribes **s**
21:19 When he **s** a fig tree by the
21:38 "When the workers **s** his son,
22:11 he **s** a person who was not
26:8 were irritated when they **s** this.
26:71 another female servant **s** him.
27:3 when he **s** that Jesus was
27:24 Pilate **s** that he was not getting
27:54 watching Jesus with him **s**
28:17 When they **s** him, they bowed
Mar 1:10 he **s** heaven split open and the
1:16 he **s** Simon and his brother
1:19 he **s** James and John,
2:5 When Jesus **s** their faith,
2:14 he **s** Levi, son of Alphaeus,
2:16 were Pharisees **s** him eating
3:11 people with evil spirits **s** him,
5:6 The man **s** Jesus at a distance.
5:15 They came to Jesus and **s** the
5:16 Those who **s** this told what
5:22 When he **s** Jesus,
5:38 Jesus **s** a noisy crowd there.
6:33 But many people **s** them leave
6:34 he **s** a large crowd and felt
6:48 Jesus **s** that they were in a lot
6:49 When they **s** him walking on
6:50 All of them **s** him and were
7:2 They **s** that some of his
8:25 and the man **s** clearly.
9:8 they **s** no one with them but
9:14 they **s** a large crowd around
9:20 As soon as the spirit **s** Jesus,
9:25 When Jesus **s** that a crowd
9:38 we **s** someone forcing demons
10:14 When Jesus **s** this,
11:13 In the distance he **s** a fig tree
11:20 they **s** that the fig tree had dried
12:28 He **s** how well Jesus
14:67 **s** Peter warming himself.
14:69 The servant **s** him.
15:39 who stood facing Jesus **s** how
16:4 When they looked up, they **s**
16:5 they **s** a young man.
Luk 2:17 When they **s** the child,
2:48 When his parents **s** him,
5:2 Jesus **s** two boats on the
5:8 When Simon Peter **s** this,
5:12 When the man **s** Jesus,
5:20 When Jesus **s** their faith,
5:27 He **s** a tax collector named
7:13 When the Lord **s** her,
7:39 who had invited Jesus **s** this
8:28 When he **s** Jesus,
8:34 the pigs **s** what had happened,
Luk 8:47 The woman **s** that she couldn't
9:32 When they woke up, they **s**
9:36 they **s** that Jesus was alone.
9:49 John replied, "Master, we **s**
9:54 and John, his disciples, **s** this.
10:31 When he **s** the man,
10:32 When he **s** the man,
10:33 When the Samaritan **s** him,
13:12 When Jesus **s** her,
15:20 his father **s** him and felt sorry
16:23 he **s** Abraham and Lazarus.
17:14 When he **s** them, he told them,
17:15 When one of them **s** that he
18:15 When the disciples **s** this,
18:43 All the people **s** this,
19:7 But the people who **s** this
19:41 he came closer and **s** the city,
20:14 "When the workers **s** him,
20:23 He **s** through their scheme,
21:1 Looking up, Jesus **s** people,
22:49 with Jesus **s** what was going
22:56 A female servant **s** him as he
22:58 A little later someone else **s**
23:47 When an army officer **s** what
23:48 But when all of them **s** what
24:12 down to look inside and **s** only
24:16 Although they **s** him,
Jon 1:14 We **s** his glory. It was the glory
1:29 John **s** Jesus coming toward
1:32 John said, "I **s** the Spirit come
1:36 John **s** Jesus walk by.
1:38 Jesus turned around and **s**
1:47 Jesus **s** Nathanael coming
1:48 Jesus answered him, "I **s** you
1:50 I told you that I **s** you under
2:23 believed in him because they **s**
5:6 Jesus **s** the man lying there
6:2 followed him because they **s**
6:5 As Jesus **s** a large crowd
6:14 When the people **s** the miracle
6:19 they **s** Jesus walking on the
6:24 When the people **s** that neither
6:26 for me because you **s** miracles.
8:56 He **s** it and was happy."
9:1 As Jesus walked along, he **s** a
11:31 Mary in the house **s** her get up
11:32 where Jesus was and **s** him,
11:33 When Jesus **s** her crying,
19:6 priests and the guards **s** Jesus,
19:26 Jesus **s** his mother and the
19:33 came to Jesus and **s** that
19:35 The one who **s** this is an
20:1 She **s** that the stone had been
20:5 He **s** the strips of linen lying
20:6 He **s** the strips of linen lying
20:7 He also **s** the cloth that had
20:8 He **s** and believed.
20:12 She **s** two angels in white
20:14 she turned around and **s** Jesus
20:30 miracles that his disciples **s**.
21:9 When they went ashore, they **s**
21:9 and they **s** a loaf of bread.
21:20 Peter turned around and **s** the
21:21 When Peter **s** him,
Act 1:11 same way that you **s** him go
3:3 When the man **s** that Peter and
3:9 All the people **s** him walking
3:12 When Peter **s** this,
3:16 was healed, as all of you **s**.
4:14 When they **s** the man who was
5:12 The people **s** the apostles
6:15 at him and **s** that his face
7:24 When he **s** an Israelite man
7:26 The next day Moses **s** two
7:31 was surprised when he **s** this.
7:55 into heaven, **s** God's glory,
8:6 They listened to him and **s** the
8:18 Simon **s** that the Spirit was
9:35 of Sharon **s** what had happened
9:40 her eyes, **s** Peter, and sat up.
10:3 He clearly **s** an angel from God
10:11 He **s** the sky open and
11:5 I **s** something like a large linen
11:6 closely and **s** tame animals,
12:3 When he **s** how this pleased
13:12 When the governor **s** what had
Act 13:45 When the Jews **s** the crowds,
14:9 him closely and **s** that
14:11 The crowds who **s** what Paul
16:27 The jailer woke up and **s** the
17:16 he **s** that the city had statues of
21:27 the province of Asia **s** Paul
21:32 When the crowd **s** the officer
22:9 "The men who were with me **s**
22:18 and **s** the Lord. He told me,
23:6 When Paul **s** that some of them
26:13 I **s** a light that was brighter than
26:19 the vision I **s** from heaven,
28:4 who lived on the island **s**
28:6 and **s** nothing unusual happen
28:15 When Paul **s** them,
Gal 1:19 I only **s** James, the Lord's
2:7 In fact, they **s** that I had been
2:14 But I **s** that they were not
3:8 Scripture **s** ahead of time that
Php 1:30 struggle that you **s** me having.
4:9 what you heard and **s** me do.
Heb 11:13 but they **s** these things coming
11:23 They did this because they **s**
12:2 He **s** the joy ahead of him,
Jas 5:11 You **s** that the Lord ended Job's
2Pe 2:8 was like torture to him as he **s**
Rev 1:2 John testified about what he **s**:
1:12 I **s** seven gold lamp stands.
1:17 When I **s** him, I fell down at his
1:20 of the seven stars that you **s**
4:1 After these things I **s** a door
4:2 I **s** a throne in heaven,
5:1 I **s** a scroll in the right hand of
5:2 I **s** a powerful angel calling out
5:6 I **s** a lamb standing in the
6:9 I **s** under the altar the souls of
7:1 After this I **s** four angels
7:2 I **s** another angel coming from
7:9 After these things I **s** a large
8:2 Then I **s** the seven angels who
8:13 I **s** an eagle flying overhead,
9:1 I **s** a star that had fallen to earth
10:1 I **s** another powerful angel
10:5 The angel whom I **s** standing
12:13 When the serpent **s** that it had
13:1 I **s** a beast coming out of the
13:2 The beast that I **s** was like a
13:11 I **s** another beast come from the
14:6 I **s** another angel flying
15:1 I **s** another sign in heaven.
15:2 Then I **s** what looked like a
15:5 and I **s** that the temple of the
16:13 Then I **s** three evil spirits like
17:3 I **s** a woman sitting on a bright
17:6 I **s** that the woman was drunk
17:6 I was very surprised when I **s**
17:8 "You **s** the beast which once
17:12 "The ten horns that you **s** are
17:15 "The waters you **s**,
17:16 and the beast you **s** will hate
17:18 The woman you **s** is the
18:1 After these things I **s** another
18:18 When they **s** the smoke rise
19:11 I **s** heaven standing open.
19:17 I **s** an angel standing in the
19:19 I **s** the beast, the kings of the
20:1 I **s** an angel coming down from
20:4 I **s** thrones, and those who sat
20:4 Then I **s** the souls of those
20:9 I **s** that they spread over the
20:11 I **s** a large, white throne and the
20:12 I **s** the dead, both important and
21:1 I **s** a new heaven and a new
21:2 Then I **s** the holy city,
22:8 heard and **s** these things.

sawdust (6)

Mat 7:3 why do you see the piece of **s**
7:4 'Let me take the piece of **s** out
7:5 of **s** from another believer's
Luk 6:41 "Why do you see the piece of **s**
6:42 let me take the piece of **s** out of
6:42 of **s** from another believer's

sawed (1)

Heb 11:37 were stoned to death, **s** in half,

saws (4)

2Sm 12:31 and put them to work with **s**,
1Ki 7:9 cut to size and trimmed with **s**
1Ch 20:3 and put them to work with **s**,
Isa 10:15 than the person who **s** with it?

sayings (6)

Psa 49:3 My mouth will speak wise **s**,
Pro 24:23 These also are the **s** of wise
31:1 The **s** of King Lemuel,
Ecc 1:8 All of these **s** are worn-out
12:11 Their collected **s** are like nails
Hab 2:6 directing clever **s** and riddles at

says (755)

Gen 21:12 Listen to what Sarah **s**
24:44 If she **s** to me, "Not only may
45:9 is what your son Joseph **s**,
Exo 4:22 'This is what the LORD **s**:
5:1 what the LORD God of Israel **s**:
5:10 "This is what Pharaoh **s**:
7:9 "When Pharaoh **s** to you,
7:17 Here is what the LORD **s**:
8:1 'This is what the LORD **s**:
8:20 'This is what the LORD **s**:
9:1 LORD God of the Hebrews **s**:
9:13 LORD God of the Hebrews **s**:
10:3 LORD God of the Hebrews **s**:
11:4 "This is what the LORD **s**:
32:27 what the LORD God of Israel **s**:
Num 20:14 is what your brother Israel **s**:
22:16 is what Balak, son of Zippor, **s**:
23:19 When he **s** something,
23:26 do whatever the LORD **s**?"
24:13 say only what the LORD **s**.'
30:4 If her father **s** nothing to her
30:14 If he **s** nothing to her about it
Dtr 5:27 that the LORD our God **s**.
13:2 that prophet or dreamer if he **s**,
13:4 listen to what he **s**,
15:16 suppose a male slave **s** to you,
18:22 and what he **s** doesn't happen
22:17 He **s** he found out that my
Jos 7:13 what the LORD God of Israel **s**:
8:8 Do what the LORD **s**.
24:2 what the LORD God of Israel **s**:
Jdg 6:8 what the LORD God of Israel **s**:
11:15 "This is what Jephthah **s**:
1Sm 2:27 "This is what the LORD **s**:
9:6 Everything he **s** is sure to
10:18 what the LORD God of Israel **s**:
12:14 don't rebel against what he **s**,
12:15 if you rebel against what he **s**,
15:2 is what the LORD of Armies **s**:
20:7 If he **s**, 'Good!' then I will be
2Sm 7:5 'This is what the LORD **s**:
7:8 is what the LORD of Armies **s**:
12:7 what the LORD God of Israel **s**:
12:11 "This is what the LORD **s**:
14:10 The king said, "If anyone **s**
15:26 But if he **s**, 'I'm not pleased
17:6 Should we do what he **s**?
24:12 'This is what the LORD **s**:
1Ki 1:36 "The LORD your God **s** so too.
2:30 "The king **s**, 'Come out.'" "No,"
11:31 what the LORD God of Israel **s**:
12:24 This is what the LORD **s**:
13:2 This is what the LORD **s**:
13:21 "This is what the LORD **s**:
14:7 what the LORD God of Israel **s**:
17:14 what the LORD God of Israel **s**:
20:2 "This is what Benhadad **s**:
20:13 "This is what the LORD **s**:
20:14 "This is what the LORD **s**:
20:28 "This is what the LORD **s**:
20:32 "Your servant Benhadad **s**,
20:42 "This is what the LORD **s**:
21:19 'This is what the LORD **s**:
22:11 "This is what the LORD **s**:
22:27 Say, 'This is what the king **s**:
2Ki 1:4 This is what the LORD **s**:
1:6 'This is what the LORD **s**:
1:9 God, the king **s**, 'Come down."
1:11 this is what the king **s**:
1:16 "This is what the LORD **s**:
2Ki 2:21 "This is what the LORD **s**:
3:16 "This is what the LORD **s**:
4:43 "This is what the LORD **s**:
5:22 He **s**, 'Just now two young
7:1 This is what the LORD **s**:
9:3 'This is what the LORD **s**:
9:6 what the LORD God of Israel **s**:
9:11 and the kind of things he **s**."
9:12 'This is what the LORD **s**:
18:19 king, the king of Assyria, **s**:
18:29 This is what the king **s**:
18:31 is what the king of Assyria **s**:
19:3 "This is what Hezekiah **s**:
19:6 'This is what the LORD **s**:
19:20 what the LORD God of Israel **s**:
19:32 "This is what the LORD **s**
20:1 "This is what the LORD **s**:
20:5 God of your ancestor David **s**:
20:17 The LORD **s**, 'The days are
22:15 what the LORD God of Israel **s**:
22:16 'This is what the LORD **s**:
22:18 the LORD God of Israel **s** about
1Ch 17:4 'This is what the LORD **s**:
17:7 is what the LORD of Armies **s**:
21:10 'This is what the LORD **s**:
21:11 "This is what the LORD **s**:
2Ch 11:4 This is what the LORD **s**:
12:5 "This is what the LORD **s**:
18:10 "This is what the LORD **s**:
18:13 him whatever my God **s** to me."
18:26 Say, 'This is what the king **s**:
20:15 is what the LORD **s** to you:
21:12 God of your ancestor David **s**:
24:20 "This is what God **s**:
32:10 King Sennacherib of Assyria **s**:
32:11 hunger and thirst when he **s**,
34:23 what the LORD God of Israel **s**:
34:24 'This is what the LORD **s**:
34:26 the LORD God of Israel **s** about
36:23 is what King Cyrus of Persia **s**:
Ezr 1:2 is what King Cyrus of Persia **s**:
Job 6:26 person **s** to the wind?
8:18 ⌊the ground⌋ denies it ⌊and **s**⌋,
28:14 The deep ocean **s**,
28:14 The sea **s**, 'It isn't with me.'
32:12 has an answer to what he **s**.
33:27 in front of other people and **s**,
34:9 He **s**, 'It doesn't do any good to
34:31 such a person **s** to God,
37:6 "He **s** to the snow,
39:25 horn sounds, the horse **s**, 'Aha!'
Psa 10:4 He turns up his nose ⌊and **s**⌋,
10:6 He **s** to himself, "Nothing can
10:11 He **s** to himself, "God has
12:5 I will now arise," **s** the LORD.
32:8 ⌊The LORD **s**,⌋ "I will instruct
50:16 But God **s** to wicked people,
85:8 to hear what God the LORD **s**,
87:4 ⌊The LORD **s**,⌋ "I will add
Pro 7:13 him and brazenly **s** to him,
9:4 She **s** to a person without
9:16 She **s** to a person without
16:23 what he **s** helps others learn.
20:14 **s** the buyer. Then, as he goes
22:13 A lazy person **s**, "There's a
24:24 Whoever **s** to a guilty person,
26:13 A lazy person **s**, "There's a
26:19 who tricks his neighbor and **s**,
28:24 his father or his mother and **s**,
30:20 eats, wipes her mouth, and **s**,
Ecc 1:2 **s** the spokesman. "Absolutely
12:8 **s** the spokesman. "Everything
Isa 1:18 **s** the LORD. "Though your sins
1:24 the Mighty One of Israel, **s**,
7:7 is what the Almighty LORD **s**:
10:24 Almighty LORD of Armies **s**:
16:14 But now the LORD **s**,
18:4 This is what the LORD **s** to me:
21:6 This is what the Lord **s** to me:
21:16 This is what the Lord **s** to me:
22:14 **s** the Almighty LORD of
22:15 Almighty LORD of Armies **s**:
23:12 He **s**, "You will no longer be
28:16 is what the Almighty LORD **s**:
29:13 The Lord **s**, "These people
29:22 **s** about the descendants of
Isa 30:12 what the Holy One of Israel **s**:
30:15 the Holy One of Israel, **s**:
33:10 The LORD **s**, "Now I will arise.
36:4 king, the king of Assyria, **s**:
36:14 This is what the king **s**:
36:16 is what the king of Assyria **s**:
37:3 "This is what Hezekiah **s**:
37:6 'This is what the LORD **s**:
37:21 what the LORD God of Israel **s**:
37:33 "This is what the LORD **s**
38:1 "This is what the LORD **s**:
38:5 God of your ancestor David **s**:
39:6 The LORD **s**, 'The days are
40:1 Comfort them!" **s** your God.
41:21 your case," **s** the LORD.
41:21 arguments," **s** Jacob's king.
42:5 This is what the LORD God **s**:
43:1 Now, this is what the LORD **s**:
43:14 the Holy One of Israel, **s**:
43:17 This is what the LORD **s**:
44:2 This is what the LORD **s**:
44:6 This is what the LORD **s**:
44:24 This is what the LORD **s**:
44:26 He **s** about Jerusalem,
44:26 He **s** about the cities of Judah,
44:26 He **s** about their ruins,
44:27 He **s** to the deep water,
44:28 He **s** about Cyrus, "He is my
44:28 He **s** about Jerusalem,
44:28 He **s** about the temple,
45:1 what the LORD **s** about Cyrus,
45:10 it will be for the one who **s**
45:11 This is what the LORD **s**:
45:13 **s** the LORD of Armies.
45:14 This is what the LORD **s**:
45:18 This what the LORD **s**:
48:17 **s**: I am the LORD your God.
48:22 for the wicked," **s** the LORD.
49:6 Now, the Lord **s**, "You are not
49:7 This is what the LORD **s** to the
49:8 This is what the LORD **s**:
49:22 is what the Almighty LORD **s**:
49:25 This is what the LORD **s**:
50:1 This is what the LORD **s**:
51:22 This is what your master **s**:
52:3 This is what the LORD **s**:
52:4 is what the Almighty LORD **s**:
52:6 know⌋ that I am the one who **s**,
54:1 married women," **s** the LORD.
54:6 and was rejected," **s** your God.
54:8 **s** the LORD your defender.
54:10 never change," **s** the LORD,
56:1 This is what the LORD **s**:
56:4 This is what the LORD **s**:
57:15 This is what he **s**:
57:19 "I'll heal them," **s** the LORD.
57:21 for the wicked," **s** my God.
59:21 promise to them," **s** the LORD.
59:21 permanently," **s** the LORD.
65:7 your ancestors," **s** the LORD.
65:8 This is what the LORD **s**:
65:13 This is what the LORD God **s**:
65:25 holy mountain," **s** the LORD.
66:1 This is what the LORD **s**:
66:12 This is what the LORD **s**:
Jer 2:2 'This is what the LORD **s**:
2:5 This is what the LORD **s**:
4:3 This is what the LORD **s** to the
4:27 This is what the LORD **s**:
5:14 the LORD God of Armies **s**:
6:6 is what the LORD of Armies **s**:
6:9 is what the LORD of Armies **s**:
6:15 I punish them," **s** the LORD.
6:16 This is what the LORD **s**:
6:21 This is what the LORD **s**:
6:22 This is what the LORD **s**:
7:3 of Armies, the God of Israel, **s**:
7:20 is what the Almighty LORD **s**:
7:21 of Armies, the God of Israel, **s**:
8:4 'This is what the LORD **s**:
8:12 I punish them,'" **s** the LORD.
9:7 is what the LORD of Armies **s**:
9:15 of Armies, the God of Israel, **s**:
9:17 is what the LORD of Armies **s**:
9:22 This is what the LORD **s**:
9:23 This is what the LORD **s**:

Jer	10:2	This is what the LORD **s**:
	10:18	This is what the LORD **s**:
	11:3	the LORD, the God of Israel, **s**:
	11:11	This is what the LORD **s**:
	11:21	This is what the LORD **s**:
	11:22	is what the LORD of Armies **s**:
	13:9	"This is what the LORD **s**:
	13:12	what the LORD God of Israel **s**:
	13:13	'This is what the LORD **s**:
	14:10	This is what the LORD **s** about
	15:2	'This is what the LORD **s**:
	15:19	This is what the LORD **s**:
	16:3	This is what the LORD **s** about
	16:5	"This is what the LORD **s**:
	16:9	of Armies, the God of Israel, **s**:
	17:1	⌊The LORD **s**,⌋ "Judah's sin is
	17:5	"This is what the LORD **s**:
	17:21	This is what the LORD **s**:
	18:11	'This is what the LORD **s**:
	18:13	"This is what the LORD **s**:
	18:18	no attention to anything he **s**."
	19:1	This is what the LORD **s**:
	19:3	of Armies, the God of Israel, **s**:
	19:10	⌊The LORD **s**,⌋ "Then smash
	19:11	is what the LORD of Armies **s**:
	19:15	of Armies, the God of Israel, **s**:
	20:4	This is what the LORD **s**:
	21:4	what the LORD God of Israel **s**:
	21:8	'This is what the LORD **s**:
	21:12	This is what the LORD **s**:
	22:1	This is what the LORD **s**:
	22:3	"This is what the LORD **s**:
	22:6	"This is what the LORD **s**
	22:11	This is what the LORD **s** about
	22:14	He **s**, 'I will build a large house
	22:18	the LORD **s** about Jehoiakim,
	22:30	This is what the LORD **s**:
	23:15	the LORD of Armies **s** about
	23:16	is what the LORD of Armies **s**:
	23:17	despise me, "The LORD **s**,
	23:38	'This is what the LORD **s**:
	24:5	what the LORD God of Israel **s**:
	24:8	"But this is what the LORD **s**
	24:8	The LORD **s**, 'Like these bad
	25:8	is what the LORD of Armies **s**:
	25:27	**s**: Drink, get drunk, vomit,
	25:28	is what the LORD of Armies **s**:
	25:32	is what the LORD of Armies **s**:
	26:2	"This is what the LORD **s**:
	26:4	'This is what the LORD **s**:
	26:18	is what the LORD of Armies **s**:
	27:4	**s**: Say this to your masters,
	27:21	**s** about the utensils that are left
	28:2	of Armies, the God of Israel, **s**:
	28:11	"This is what the LORD **s**:
	28:13	'This is what the LORD **s**:
	28:14	of Armies, the God of Israel, **s**:
	28:16	This is what the LORD **s**:
	29:4	**s** to all those who were taken
	29:8	of Armies, the God of Israel, **s**:
	29:10	This is what the LORD **s**:
	29:16	But this is what the LORD **s**
	29:17	The LORD of Armies **s**:
	29:21	**s** about Kolaiah's son Ahab
	29:24	⌊The LORD **s**,⌋ "Say to
	29:25	of Armies, the God of Israel, **s**:
	29:31	'This is what the LORD **s**
	29:32	The LORD **s**: I will punish
	30:2	what the LORD God of Israel **s**:
	30:5	"This is what the LORD **s**:
	30:12	"This is what the LORD **s**:
	30:18	"This is what the LORD **s**:
	31:2	This is what the LORD **s**:
	31:7	This is what the LORD **s**:
	31:15	This is what the LORD **s**:
	31:16	This is what the LORD **s**:
	31:23	of Armies, the God of Israel, **s**:
	31:35	This is what the LORD **s**:
	31:37	This is what the LORD **s**:
	32:3	'This is what the LORD **s**:
	32:14	of Armies, the God of Israel, **s**:
	32:15	of Armies, the God of Israel, **s**:
	32:28	This is what the LORD **s**:
	32:36	what the LORD God of Israel **s**:
	32:42	"This is what the LORD **s**:
	33:2	This is what the LORD **s**:
Jer	33:4	God of Israel **s** about this:
	33:10	"This is what the LORD **s**:
	33:11	they were before," **s** the LORD.
	33:12	is what the LORD of Armies **s**:
	33:13	their sheep," **s** the LORD.
	33:17	"This what the LORD **s**:
	33:20	"This is what the LORD **s**:
	33:25	"This is what the LORD **s**:
	34:2	what the LORD God of Israel **s**:
	34:2	and tell him, 'The LORD **s**:
	34:4	is what the LORD **s** about you:
	34:13	what the LORD God of Israel **s**:
	34:17	"This is what the LORD **s**:
	35:13	of Armies, the God of Israel, **s**:
	35:17	of Armies, the God of Israel, **s**:
	35:18	of Armies, the God of Israel, **s**:
	35:19	**s**: A descendant of Jonadab,
	36:29	'This is what the LORD **s**:
	36:30	This is what the LORD **s** about
	37:7	what the LORD God of Israel **s**:
	37:9	"'This is what the LORD **s**:
	38:2	"This is what the LORD **s**:
	38:3	"This is what the LORD **s**:
	38:17	of Armies, the God of Israel, **s**:
	39:16	of Armies, the God of Israel, **s**:
	42:4	tell you everything the LORD **s**.
	42:9	what the LORD God of Israel **s**:
	42:15	of Armies, the God of Israel, **s**:
	42:18	of Armies, the God of Israel, **s**:
	42:20	that the LORD our God **s**,
	43:10	of Armies, the God of Israel, **s**:
	44:2	of Armies, the God of Israel, **s**:
	44:7	of Armies, the God of Israel, **s**:
	44:11	of Armies, the God of Israel, **s**:
	44:25	of Armies, the God of Israel, **s**:
	44:26	by my great name,' **s** the LORD,
	44:30	This is what the LORD **s**:
	45:2	LORD God of Israel **s** to you,
	45:4	'This is what the LORD **s**:
	46:8	Egypt **s**, 'I will rise; I will cover
	46:25	**s**, "I'm going to punish Amon,
	47:2	This is what the LORD **s**:
	48:1	God of Israel, **s** about Moab:
	48:40	"This is what the LORD **s**:
	49:1	This is what the LORD **s** about
	49:2	of its inheritance, **s** the LORD.
	49:7	LORD of Armies **s** about Edom:
	49:12	This is what the LORD **s**:
	49:18	will stay there," **s** the LORD.
	49:28	This is what the LORD **s**:
	49:35	is what the LORD of Armies **s**:
	50:18	of Armies, the God of Israel, **s**:
	50:33	is what the LORD of Armies **s**:
	51:1	This is what the LORD **s**:
	51:33	of Armies, the God of Israel, **s**:
	51:35	Jerusalem **s**, "May the people
	51:36	This is what the LORD **s**:
	51:58	is what the LORD of Armies **s**:
Eze	2:4	is what the Almighty LORD **s**.'
	3:11	is what the Almighty LORD **s**.'"
	3:27	the Almighty LORD **s**.' Some
	5:5	is what the Almighty LORD **s**:
	5:7	is what the Almighty LORD **s**:
	5:8	is what the Almighty LORD **s**:
	6:3	is what the Almighty LORD **s**
	6:11	is what the Almighty LORD **s**:
	7:2	is what the Almighty LORD **s**
	7:5	is what the Almighty LORD **s**:
	11:5	"This is what the LORD **s**:
	11:7	is what the Almighty LORD **s**:
	11:16	is what the Almighty LORD **s**:
	11:17	is what the Almighty LORD **s**:
	12:10	is what the Almighty LORD **s**:
	12:19	the Almighty LORD **s** about
	12:23	is what the Almighty LORD **s**:
	12:28	is what the Almighty LORD **s**:
	13:3	is what the Almighty LORD **s**:
	13:8	is what the Almighty LORD **s**:
	13:13	is what the Almighty LORD **s**:
	13:18	is what the Almighty LORD **s**:
	13:20	is what the Almighty LORD **s**:
	14:4	'This is what the LORD **s**:
	14:6	is what the Almighty LORD **s**:
	14:21	is what the Almighty LORD **s**:
	15:6	is what the Almighty LORD **s**:
	16:3	is what the Almighty LORD **s**
Eze	16:36	is what the Almighty LORD **s**:
	16:59	is what the Almighty LORD **s**:
	17:3	is what the Almighty LORD **s**:
	17:9	is what the Almighty LORD **s**:
	17:19	is what the Almighty LORD **s**:
	17:22	is what the Almighty LORD **s**:
	18:29	"But the nation of Israel **s**,
	20:3	is what the Almighty LORD **s**:
	20:5	is what the Almighty LORD **s**:
	20:27	is what the Almighty LORD **s**:
	20:30	is what the Almighty LORD **s**:
	20:39	is what the Almighty LORD **s**:
	20:47	is what the Almighty LORD **s**:
	21:3	'This is what the LORD **s**:
	21:9	'This is what the Lord **s**:
	21:24	is what the Almighty LORD **s**:
	21:26	is what the Almighty LORD **s**:
	21:28	the Almighty LORD **s** about
	22:3	is what the Almighty LORD **s**:
	22:19	is what the Almighty LORD **s**:
	22:28	the Almighty LORD **s**.' Yet,
	23:22	is what the Almighty LORD **s**:
	23:28	is what the Almighty LORD **s**:
	23:32	is what the Almighty LORD **s**:
	23:35	is what the Almighty LORD **s**:
	23:46	is what the Almighty LORD **s**:
	24:3	is what the Almighty LORD **s**:
	24:6	is what the Almighty LORD **s**:
	24:9	is what the Almighty LORD **s**:
	24:21	is what the Almighty LORD **s**:
	25:3	is what the Almighty LORD **s**:
	25:6	is what the Almighty LORD **s**:
	25:8	is what the Almighty LORD **s**:
	25:12	is what the Almighty LORD **s**:
	25:13	is what the Almighty LORD **s**:
	25:15	is what the Almighty LORD **s**:
	25:16	is what the Almighty LORD **s**:
	26:3	is what the Almighty LORD **s**:
	26:7	is what the Almighty LORD **s**:
	26:15	the Almighty LORD **s** to Tyre:
	26:19	is what the Almighty LORD **s**:
	27:3	is what the Almighty LORD **s**:
	28:2	is what the Almighty LORD **s**:
	28:6	is what the Almighty LORD **s**:
	28:12	is what the Almighty LORD **s**:
	28:22	is what the Almighty LORD **s**:
	28:25	is what the Almighty LORD **s**:
	29:3	is what the Almighty LORD **s**:
	29:8	is what the Almighty LORD **s**:
	29:13	is what the Almighty LORD **s**:
	29:19	is what the Almighty LORD **s**:
	30:2	is what the Almighty LORD **s**:
	30:6	"'This is what the LORD **s**:
	30:10	is what the Almighty LORD **s**:
	30:13	is what the Almighty LORD **s**:
	30:22	is what the Almighty LORD **s**:
	31:10	is what the Almighty LORD **s**:
	31:15	is what the Almighty LORD **s**:
	32:3	is what the Almighty LORD **s**:
	32:11	is what the Almighty LORD **s**:
	33:25	is what the Almighty LORD **s**:
	33:27	is what the Almighty LORD **s**:
	34:2	is what the Almighty LORD **s**:
	34:10	is what the Almighty LORD **s**:
	34:11	is what the Almighty LORD **s**:
	34:17	is what the Almighty LORD **s**:
	34:20	the Almighty LORD **s** to them:
	35:3	is what the Almighty LORD **s**:
	35:14	is what the Almighty LORD **s**:
	36:2	is what the Almighty LORD **s**:
	36:3	is what the Almighty LORD **s**:
	36:4	is what the Almighty LORD **s**
	36:6	is what the Almighty LORD **s**:
	36:7	is what the Almighty LORD **s**:
	36:13	is what the Almighty LORD **s**:
	36:22	is what the Almighty LORD **s**:
	36:33	is what the Almighty LORD **s**:
	36:37	is what the Almighty LORD **s**:
	37:5	is what the Almighty LORD **s**
	37:9	is what the Almighty LORD **s**:
	37:12	is what the Almighty LORD **s**:
	37:19	is what the Almighty LORD **s**:
	37:21	is what the Almighty LORD **s**:
	38:3	is what the Almighty LORD **s**:
	38:10	is what the Almighty LORD **s**:
	38:14	is what the Almighty LORD **s**:

Eze	38:17	is what the Almighty LORD **s**:
	39:1	is what the Almighty LORD **s**:
	39:17	is what the Almighty LORD **s**:
	39:25	is what the Almighty LORD **s**:
	43:18	is what the Almighty LORD **s**:
	44:6	is what the Almighty LORD **s**:
	44:9	is what the Almighty LORD **s**:
	45:9	is what the Almighty LORD **s**:
	45:18	is what the Almighty LORD **s**:
	46:1	is what the Almighty LORD **s**:
	46:16	is what the Almighty LORD **s**:
	47:13	is what the Almighty LORD **s**:
Hos	12:7	⌊The LORD **s**,⌋ "The
	14:4	⌊The LORD **s**,⌋ "I will cure
Amo	1:3	This is what the LORD **s**:
	1:6	This is what the LORD **s**:
	1:9	This is what the LORD **s**:
	1:11	This is what the LORD **s**:
	1:13	This is what the LORD **s**:
	2:1	This is what the LORD **s**:
	2:4	This is what the LORD **s**:
	2:6	This is what the LORD **s**:
	3:11	is what the Almighty LORD **s**:
	3:12	This is what the LORD **s**:
	5:3	is what the Almighty LORD **s**:
	5:4	This is what the LORD **s** to the
	5:16	the Almighty God of Armies, **s**:
	5:27	Damascus, **s** the LORD,
	7:11	Amos **s** that Jeroboam will be
	7:17	this is what the LORD **s**:
	9:7	from Sudan, **s** the LORD.
	9:15	**s** the LORD your God.
Oba	1:1	Almighty LORD **s** about Edom:
Mic	2:3	So this is what the LORD **s**:
	3:5	This is what the LORD **s** about
Nah	1:12	This is what the LORD **s**:
Hab	2:19	it will be for the one who **s**
Zep	3:20	before your eyes," **s** the LORD.
Hag	1:2	is what the LORD of Armies **s**:
	1:5	is what the LORD of Armies **s**:
	1:7	is what the LORD of Armies **s**:
	2:6	is what the LORD of Armies **s**:
	2:7	**s** the LORD of Armies.
	2:11	is what the LORD of Armies **s**:
Zec	1:3	is what the LORD of Armies **s**:
	1:3	**s** the LORD of Armies.'
	1:4	is what the LORD of Armies **s**:
	1:14	is what the LORD of Armies **s**:
	1:16	is what the LORD of Armies **s**:
	1:17	is what the LORD of Armies **s**:
	2:8	is what the LORD of Armies **s**:
	3:7	is what the LORD of Armies **s**:
	4:6	**s** the LORD of Armies.
	5:3	The one side of the scroll **s**
	5:3	The other side of the scroll **s**
	6:12	is what the LORD of Armies **s**:
	7:9	is what the LORD of Armies **s**:
	7:13	**s** the LORD of Armies.
	8:2	is what the LORD of Armies **s**:
	8:3	This is what the LORD **s**:
	8:4	is what the LORD of Armies **s**:
	8:6	is what the LORD of Armies **s**:
	8:7	is what the LORD of Armies **s**:
	8:9	is what the LORD of Armies **s**:
	8:14	is what the LORD of Armies **s**:
	8:19	is what the LORD of Armies **s**:
	8:20	is what the LORD of Armies **s**:
	8:23	is what the LORD of Armies **s**:
	11:4	is what the LORD my God **s**:
	12:1	forms the spirit in a person — **s**,
Mal	1:2	"I loved you," **s** the LORD.
	1:4	is what the LORD of Armies **s**:
	1:6	is what the LORD of Armies **s**:
	1:10	**s** the LORD of Armies,
	1:11	**s** the LORD of Armies.
	1:13	**s** the LORD of Armies.
	1:14	**s** the LORD of Armies.
	2:2	**s** the LORD of Armies,
	2:4	**s** the LORD of Armies.
	2:8	**s** the LORD of Armies.
	2:16	**s** the LORD God of Israel.
	2:16	**s** the LORD of Armies.
	3:1	**s** the LORD of Armies.
	3:5	**s** the LORD of Armies.
	3:7	**s** the LORD of Armies.
	3:10	**s** the LORD of Armies.
Mal	3:11	**s** the LORD of Armies.
	3:12	**s** the LORD of Armies.
	3:13	against me," **s** the LORD.
	3:17	**s** the LORD of Armies.
	4:1	**s** the LORD of Armies.
	4:3	**s** the LORD of Armies.
Mat	4:4	Jesus answered, "Scripture **s**,
	4:6	Scripture **s**, 'He will put his
	4:7	to him, "Again, Scripture **s**,
	4:10	Scripture **s**, 'Worship the Lord
	7:21	"Not everyone who **s** to me,
	11:10	one about whom Scripture **s**,
	12:34	Your mouth **s** what comes from
	12:44	Then it **s**, 'I'll go back to the
	21:3	If anyone **s** anything to you,
	21:13	He told them, "Scripture **s**,
	22:43	call him Lord? David **s**,
	24:26	don't believe anyone who **s**,
	26:18	and tell him that the teacher **s**,
	26:31	Scripture **s**, 'I will strike the
Mar	9:13	as Scripture **s** about him."
	11:17	them by saying, "Scripture **s**,
	11:23	what he **s** will happen:
	14:27	Scripture **s**, 'I will strike the
Luk	4:4	answered him, "Scripture **s**,
	4:8	answered him, "Scripture **s**,
	4:10	Scripture **s**, 'He will put his
	5:39	He **s**, 'The old wine is better!'"
	6:26	everyone **s** nice things about
	7:27	one about whom Scripture **s**,
	8:21	and do what God's word **s**."
	11:24	Then it **s**, 'I'll go back to the
	12:10	Everyone who **s** something
	15:6	together and **s** to them,
	15:9	and neighbors together and **s**,
	17:4	to you seven times and **s** that
	19:46	He said to them, "Scripture **s**,
	20:37	He **s** that the Lord is the God of
	20:42	David **s** in the book of Psalms,
	22:37	the Scripture passage which **s**,
	23:2	and he **s** that he is Christ,
	24:46	He said to them, "Scripture **s**
	24:47	Scripture also **s** that by the
Jon	3:32	Yet, no one accepts what he **s**.
	5:32	and I know that what he **s**
	6:31	Scripture **s**, 'He gave them
	6:60	"What he **s** is hard to accept.
	7:36	What does he mean when he **s**,
	7:38	As Scripture **s**, 'Streams of
	8:22	that what he means when he **s**,
	8:47	God understands what God **s**.
	8:55	and I do what he **s**.
	12:14	and sat on it, as Scripture **s**:
	13:18	It **s**, 'The one who eats my
	16:15	Everything the Father **s** is also
	16:18	does he mean when he **s**,
	19:35	What he **s** is true, and he
	19:37	Another Scripture passage **s**,
	21:24	We know that what he **s** is true.
Act	2:17	'In the last days, God **s**,
	7:48	by humans, as the prophet **s**:
	7:49	'The Lord **s**, "Heaven is my
	13:33	This is what Scripture **s** in the
	13:35	Another psalm **s**, 'You will not
	15:15	the prophets said. Scripture **s**,
	21:11	"The Holy Spirit **s**,
	23:5	After all, Scripture **s**,
Rom	1:17	ends with faith as Scripture **s**,
	2:24	As Scripture **s**, "God's name is
	3:4	else is a liar, as Scripture **s**,
	3:10	as Scripture **s**, "Not one person
	4:6	David **s** the same thing when
	4:17	as Scripture **s**: "I have made
	8:36	As Scripture **s**: "We are being
	9:7	However, ⌊as Scripture **s**,⌋
	9:17	Scripture **s** to Pharaoh,
	9:25	As God **s** in Hosea:
	9:27	Isaiah also **s** about Israel:
	9:33	As Scripture **s**, "I am placing a
	10:5	He **s**, "The person who obeys
	10:6	However, Scripture **s** about
	10:11	Scripture **s**, "Whoever believes
	10:15	As Scripture **s**, "How beautiful
	11:2	Don't you know what Elijah **s**
	11:2	to God about Israel? He **s**,
	11:8	as Scripture **s**, "To this day
Rom	11:9	And David **s**, "Let the table set
	11:26	will be saved, as Scripture **s**,
	12:19	After all, Scripture **s**,
	12:19	I will pay back, **s** the Lord."
	14:11	Scripture **s**, "As certainly as I
	14:11	certainly as I live, **s** the Lord,
	15:3	Rather, as Scripture **s**,
	15:10	And Scripture **s** again,
	15:12	Again, Isaiah **s**, "There will be
	15:21	As Scripture **s**, "Those who
1Co	1:19	Scripture **s**, "I will destroy the
	1:31	As Scripture **s**, "Whoever brags
	2:9	But as Scripture **s**:
	3:19	That's why Scripture **s**,
	3:20	Again Scripture **s**, "The Lord
	4:7	Who **s** that you are any better
	6:16	God **s**, "The two will be one."
	10:7	of them did, as Scripture **s**,
	10:28	However, if someone **s** to you,
	12:3	one speaking by God's Spirit **s**,
	12:15	Suppose a foot **s**, "I'm not a
	12:16	Or suppose an ear **s**,
	14:5	he can interpret what he **s**
	14:13	an interpretation of what he **s**.
	14:21	God's word **s**, "Through people
	14:21	not listen to me, **s** the Lord."
	14:27	interpret what each person **s**.
	15:27	When God **s** that everything
	15:45	This is what Scripture **s**:
2Co	6:2	God **s**, "At the right time I heard
	6:17	The Lord **s**, "Get away from
	6:18	The Lord Almighty **s**,
	8:15	This is what Scripture **s**:
	9:9	Scripture **s**, "The righteous
Gal	3:10	standards because Scripture **s**,
	3:13	Scripture **s**, "Everyone who is
	4:22	Scripture **s** that Abraham had
	4:27	Scripture **s**: "Rejoice,
Eph	5:14	That's why it **s**: "Wake up,
2Th	2:8	will destroy him by what he **s**.
1Ti	4:1	The Spirit **s** clearly that in later
	5:18	After all, Scripture **s**,
Heb	2:12	He **s**, "I will tell my people
	2:13	In addition, Jesus **s**,
	2:13	And Jesus **s**, "I am here with
	3:7	As the Holy Spirit **s**,
	3:15	Scripture **s**, "If you hear God
	8:8	days are coming, **s** the Lord,
	8:9	so I ignored them, **s** the Lord.
	8:10	after those days, **s** the Lord:
	10:9	Then Christ **s**, "I have come to
	10:16	after those days, **s** the Lord:
Jas	1:22	Do what God's word **s**.
	1:23	word but doesn't do what it **s**,
	2:23	It **s**, "Abraham believed God,
	4:5	It **s**, "The Spirit that lives in us
	4:6	Scripture **s**, "God opposes
1Pe	1:16	Scripture **s**, "Be holy,
	1:23	That's why ⌊Scripture **s**,⌋
	2:6	That is why Scripture **s**,
2Pe	3:16	they believe distort what Paul **s**
1Jn	2:4	The person who **s**,
	2:5	whoever obeys what Christ **s** is
	4:20	Whoever **s**, "I love God,"
3Jn	1:12	**s** good things about Demetrius.
Rev	1:8	**s** the Lord God, the one who is,
	2:1	the seven gold lamp stands, **s**:
	2:7	ears listen to what the Spirit **s**
	2:8	was dead and became alive, **s**:
	2:11	ears listen to what the Spirit **s**
	2:12	the sharp two-edged sword **s**:
	2:17	ears listen to what the Spirit **s**
	2:18	feet are like glowing bronze, **s**:
	2:29	the Spirit **s** to the churches.
	3:1	spirits and the seven stars **s**:
	3:6	the Spirit **s** to the churches.
	3:7	door⌋ that no one can open, **s**:
	3:13	the Spirit **s** to the churches.
	3:14	the source of God's creation, **s**:
	3:22	the Spirit **s** to the churches."
	14:13	"Yes," **s** the Spirit.
	18:7	She **s** to herself, 'I'm a queen
	22:20	is testifying to these things **s**,

scab (11)

Lev	13:30	It is a **s**, a disease on the head

Lev 13:32 If the **s** has not spread,
13:32 and the **s** does not look deeper
13:33 shave everything except the **s**.
13:33 will put the person with the **s**
13:34 priest will examine the **s** again.
13:34 If the **s** has not spread on the
13:35 But if the **s** spreads after the
13:36 If the **s** has spread on the skin,
13:37 But if he sees that the **s** hasn't
13:37 grows on it, the **s** is healed.

scabbard (7)
2Sm 20:8 it at his hip was a sword in a **s**.
1Ch 21:27 he put his sword back in its **s**.
Jer 47:6 Go back into your **s**.
Eze 21:3 I will take my sword out of its **s**
21:4 my sword will come out of its **s**
21:5 taken my sword from its **s**,
21:30 "Return your sword to its **s**.

scabby (2)
Lev 13:31 But if the priest examines the **s**
13:31 the person with the **s** disease

scabs (2)
Lev 22:22 cuts, warts, **s**, or ringworm.
Job 7:5 is covered with maggots and **s**.

scale (7)
1Ki 22:34 of Israel between his **s** armor
2Ch 18:33 of Israel between his **s** armor
Psa 62:9 all of them are weighed on a **s**,
Isa 40:12 weighed the mountains on a **s**
40:15 to be like dust on a **s**.
Dan 5:27 you have been weighed on a **s**
Rev 6:5 and its rider held a **s**.

scales (22)
Lev 11:9 streams that has fins and **s**.
11:10 have no fins or **s** disgusting.
11:12 without fins or **s** is disgusting
19:36 Use honest **s**, honest weights,
Dtr 14:9 creature that has fins and **s**.
14:10 that doesn't have fins and **s**.
1Sm 17:5 armor **s** weighing 125 pounds.
Job 6:2 could be laid on the **s** with it,
31:6 let God weigh me on honest **s**,
41:15 Its back has rows of **s** that are
Pro 11:1 Dishonest **s** are disgusting to
16:11 Honest balances and **s** belong
20:23 and dishonest **s** are no good.
Isa 46:6 bags and weigh silver on **s**.
Eze 5:1 Take **s** to weigh your hair and
29:4 in the Nile River stick to your **s**.
29:4 in the Nile sticking to your **s**.
45:10 You must have honest **s** and
Hos 12:7 merchants use dishonest **s**.
Amo 8:5 and cheat with dishonest **s**.
Mic 6:11 I cannot tolerate dishonest **s**
Act 9:18 something like fish **s** fell from

scalp (1)
Ezr 9:3 pulled hair from my **s** and my

scan (1)
2Ch 16:9 The LORD's eyes **s** the whole

scandal (2)
Job 31:11 That would be a **s**,
Mat 17:27 so that we don't create a **s**,

scar (2)
Lev 13:23 it is a **s** caused by the boil.
13:28 because it is a **s** caused by the

scare (2)
Lev 26:6 lie down with no one to **s** you.
Dtr 28:26 will be no one to **s** them away.

scarecrows (1)
Jer 10:5 These trees are like **s** in

scared (2)
Jos 7:5 lost heart and were **s** stiff.
Jdg 7:3 'Whoever is **s** or frightened

scarfs (1)
Isa 3:19 pendants, bracelets, **s**,

scarlet (1)
Sos 4:3 Your lips are like **s** thread.

scarred (2)
Isa 3:24 Their beauty will be **s**.
1Ti 4:2 Their consciences have been **s**

scars (2)
Zec 13:6 'What are these **s** on your
Gal 6:17 After all, I carry the **s** of Jesus

scatter (52)
Gen 49:7 Jacob and **s** them among ⌊the
Lev 26:33 I will **s** you among the nations.
Num 10:35 **S** your enemies! Make those
16:37 burners out of the fire and **s**
Dtr 4:27 The LORD will **s** you among
28:64 Then the LORD will **s** you
30:1 the LORD your God will **s** you.
30:3 the world where he will **s** you.
1Sm 13:8 and the troops began to **s**.
1Ki 14:15 He will **s** them beyond the
Neh 1:8 I will **s** you among the nations.
Psa 44:11 be butchered like sheep and **s**
68:30 **S** the people who find joy in
106:27 and **s** them throughout various
144:6 bolts of lightning, and **s** them.
Ecc 3:5 a time to **s** stones and a time to
Isa 24:1 mar the face of the earth and **s**
28:25 doesn't he **s** black cumin seed
33:3 Nations **s** when you attack.
41:16 The windstorm will **s** them.
Jer 8:3 than live where I will **s** them,"
9:16 I will **s** them among nations
13:24 "I will **s** you like straw that is
18:17 Like the east wind I will **s** them
24:9 and cursed wherever I **s** them.
27:10 I'll **s** you, and you will die.
27:15 So I will **s** you, and you and
29:18 all the nations where I **s** them.
40:15 gathered around you would **s**.
49:32 I will **s** to the winds those who
49:36 against Elam and **s** its people
Eze 4:13 the nations where I **s** them."
5:2 Then **s** the remaining third to
5:10 I will punish you and **s**
5:12 I will **s** the remaining third to
6:5 and I will **s** their bones around
10:2 Then **s** them over the city."
12:14 I will **s** in every direction all
12:15 because I will **s** them among
20:23 I promised to **s** them among the
22:15 I will **s** you among the nations
29:12 I will **s** the Egyptians among
30:23 I will **s** the Egyptians among
30:26 I will **s** the Egyptians among
32:5 I will **s** your flesh on the hills
Dan 4:14 **S** its fruit! Make the animals
Nah 2:1 The one who will **s** you is
3:17 and they **s** in every direction.
Hab 3:11 They **s** at the light of your
3:14 like a violent storm to **s** me.
Zec 1:21 nations raised their horns to **s**
7:14 I used a windstorm to **s** them

scattered (89)
Gen 10:18 Later the Canaanite families **s**.
11:4 that we won't become **s** all over
11:8 So the LORD **s** them all over
11:9 From that place the LORD **s**
Exo 5:12 So the people **s** all over Egypt
32:20 it into powder, **s** it on the water,
Dtr 30:4 Even if you are **s** to the most
Jdg 9:45 the city and **s** salt all over
1Sm 11:11 The survivors were so **s** that
2Sm 17:19 and **s** some grain over it so that
20:22 and everyone **s** and withdrew
22:15 He shot arrows and **s** them.
1Ki 1:49 got up and **s** in all directions.
22:17 "I saw Israel's troops **s** in the
2Ch 18:16 "I saw Israel's troops **s** in the
34:4 ground them into powder and **s**
Est 3:8 there is a certain nationality **s**
Job 4:11 the cubs of the lioness are **s**.
18:15 Sulfur is **s** over his home.
38:24 to the place where light is **s**
Psa 18:14 He shot his arrows and **s** them.
53:5 because God has **s** the bones
68:1 His enemies will be **s**.
89:10 strong arm you **s** your enemies.
92:9 and all troublemakers are **s**.
Isa 11:12 and bring together the **s** people
16:2 fluttering birds, like **s** nestlings,
56:8 who gathers the **s** people of
Jer 10:21 and all their flocks will be **s**.
16:15 the lands where he had **s** them.
23:2 You have **s** my sheep and
23:8 the lands where he had **s** them.
25:34 time has come for you to be **s**,
29:14 and places where I've **s** you,
30:11 all the nations where I **s** you,
31:10 Say, 'The one who **s** the
32:37 all the lands where I **s** them
40:12 places where they had been **s**.
43:5 places where they had been **s**.
46:28 all the nations where I **s** you,
49:5 Everyone will be **s**.
50:17 "The people of Israel are like **s**
Lam 2:9 people are ⌊**s**⌋ among
4:1 The sacred stones are **s** at
4:16 The LORD himself has **s** them.
Eze 6:8 be **s** throughout the countries.
11:16 the nations and **s** them among
11:17 the countries where I've **s** them.
17:21 Anyone who remains will be **s**
20:34 countries where I have **s** you
20:41 where you have been **s**,
28:25 the nations where they were **s**,
29:13 where they have been **s**.
31:17 were **s** among the nations.
34:5 So they were **s** because there
34:5 When they were **s**,
34:6 They were **s** throughout the
34:12 when he is with his **s** sheep,
34:12 place where they have been **s**.
34:21 You have **s** them all over.
36:19 and they became **s** among the
Dan 9:7 all the Israelites whom you **s**
Joe 3:2 They **s** the Israelites,
Amo 8:3 be dead bodies **s** everywhere.
Mic 4:6 bring together those who are **s**
Nah 3:18 Your people are **s** on the
Zep 3:10 my worshipers, my **s** people,
3:19 gather those who have been **s**.
Zec 1:19 ⌊of the nations⌋ that **s** Judah,
1:21 He answered, "Those horns **s**
2:6 I've **s** you to the four winds of
10:9 Although I have **s** them among
13:7 and the sheep will be **s**.
Mat 25:24 where you haven't **s** any seeds.
25:26 and gather where I haven't **s**,
26:31 the sheep in the flock will be **s**.'
Mar 14:27 and the sheep will be **s**.'
Luk 1:51 He **s** those who think too
Jon 7:35 the Jews who are **s** among
11:52 bring God's **s** children together
16:32 when all of you will be **s**.
Act 5:36 and all his followers were **s**.
5:37 and all his followers were **s**.
8:1 were **s** throughout Judea and
8:4 The believers who were **s**
11:19 of the believers who were **s** by
1Co 10:5 bodies were **s** over the desert.
Jas 1:1 people who have been **s**.
1Pe 1:1 the world⌋ and are **s** throughout

scattering (3)
1Sm 13:11 "I saw the troops were **s**.
Psa 68:14 the Almighty was still **s** kings
Jer 23:1 who are destroying and **s**

scatters (8)
Job 36:30 Look, he **s** his flashes of
37:11 and **s** his lightning from
Psa 147:16 wool and **s** frost like ashes.
Pro 20:26 A wise king **s** the wicked and
Mat 12:30 doesn't gather with me **s**.
Mar 4:26 God is like a man who **s** seeds

Luk 11:23 doesn't gather with me **s**.
Jon 10:12 sheep away and **s** the flock.

scene (1)
Mar 9:25 a crowd was running to the **s**,

scenes (1)
Sos 3:10 Its inside — with inlaid **s** of love

scent (1)
Job 14:9 merely a **s** of water will make it

scented (3)
Psa 133:2 It is like fine, **s** oil on the head,
Sos 3:6 from the merchants' **s** powders.
5:13 a garden that produces **s** herbs.

scepter (21)
Gen 49:10 A **s** will never depart from
Num 24:17 A **s** will rise from Israel.
Est 4:11 the king holds out the golden **s**
5:2 held out the golden **s** that was
5:2 and touched the top of the **s**.
8:4 held out his golden **s** to Esther,
Psa 2:9 will break them with an iron **s**.
45:6 The **s** in your kingdom is a
45:6 your kingdom is a **s** for justice.
60:7 on my head. Judah is my **s**.
108:8 on my head. Judah is my **s**.
110:2 your powerful **s** from Zion.
Isa 14:5 of the wicked, the **s** of rulers.
Eze 19:14 could be used as a king's **s**.
Amo 1:5 and the one who holds the **s**
1:8 who holds the **s** in Ashkelon.
Zec 10:11 and the **s** of Egypt will depart.
Heb 1:8 The **s** in your kingdom is a
1:8 your kingdom is a **s** for justice.
Rev 12:5 all the nations with an iron **s**.
19:15 He will rule them with an iron **s**

scepters (3)
Num 21:18 people with their **s** and staffs."
Eze 19:11 were used to make **s** for kings.
Rev 2:27 will rule the nations with iron **s**

Sceva (1)
Act 19:14 Seven sons of **S**, a Jewish

schedule (2)
Joe 1:14 **S** a time to fast! Call for an
2:15 **S** a time to fast. Call for an assembly.

scheme (8)
Jos 9:4 they devised a **s**. They posed
Psa 21:11 Although they **s** and plan evil
31:20 from those who **s** against them.
35:20 Instead, they **s** against the
64:6 have perfected a foolproof **s**!"
Pro 30:32 as to honor yourself, or if you **s**,
Mic 7:3 So they **s** together.
Luk 20:23 He saw through their **s**,

schemer (1)
Pro 24:8 to do evil will be known as a **s**.

schemers (1)
Job 5:13 The plans of **s** prove to be

schemes (12)
Job 21:27 I know your thoughts and the **s**
Psa 5:10 Let their own **s** be their
10:2 caught in the **s** that he planned.
26:10 Evil **s** are in their hands.
33:10 He frustrates the **s** of the
37:7 way when he carries out his **s**.
Pro 1:31 will be stuffed with their own **s**.
12:2 condemns everyone who **s**.
Dan 11:25 of the **s** devised against him.
Act 13:10 are full of dirty tricks and **s**,
1Th 2:3 we didn't use unethical **s**,
2:5 we never used flattery or **s** to

scheming (3)
Dtr 32:5 They are devious and **s**.
Pro 24:9 Foolish **s** is sinful,

2Co 2:11 not ignorant about Satan's **s**.

scholar (1)
1Co 1:20 Where is the **s**? Where is the

school (1)
Jon 7:15 when he hasn't gone to **s**?"

schools (1)
Hab 1:14 like **s** of sea life that have no

scolded (1)
Luk 23:40 But the other criminal **s** him:

scorched (8)
Gen 41:6 thin and **s** by the east wind,
41:23 and **s** by the east wind,
41:27 empty heads of grain **s** by
2Ki 19:26 **s** before it sprouted.
Isa 9:19 The land is **s** by the fury of the
Jer 51:25 and make you a **s** mountain.
Mat 13:6 the sun came up, they were **s**.
Mar 4:6 the sun came up, they were **s**.

scorching (8)
Gen 31:40 The **s** heat during the day and
Dtr 28:22 **s** winds, and ruined crops.
Job 6:17 vanish during a **s** summer.
Psa 11:6 from a cup filled with **s** wind.
Isa 11:15 River with his **s** wind
18:4 My presence will be like **s** heat
Hos 13:15 However, the LORD's **s** wind
Jas 1:11 The sun rises with its **s** heat

scorn (5)
Job 16:10 In **s** they slapped my cheeks.
34:7 who drinks **s** like water,
Psa 89:41 the object of his neighbors' **s**.)
Eze 28:26 people who treat them with **s**.
36:5 joy and with complete **s**.

scorned (3)
Psa 22:6 I am **s** by humanity and
Isa 49:7 to the one **s** by the nation,
Eze 23:32 You will be **s** and mocked,

scorpion (1)
Luk 11:12 would you give him a **s**?

scorpion's (1)
Rev 9:5 was like the pain of a **s** sting

scorpions (9)
Dtr 8:15 with poisonous snakes and **s**.
1Ki 12:11 I will punish you with **s**.'"
12:14 I will punish you with **s**."
2Ch 10:11 I will punish you with **s**.'"
10:14 you with whips, I will use **s**."
Eze 2:6 you and you live among **s**.
Luk 10:19 to trample snakes and **s**
Rev 9:3 like the power of earthly **s**.
9:10 had tails and stingers like **s**.

scoundrel (2)
Job 34:18 'You good-for-nothing **s**!' or
Pro 6:12 A good-for-nothing **s** is a

scoundrels (3)
Job 11:11 He knows who the **s** are.
Isa 32:5 **s** be considered gentlemen.
32:7 The tricks of **s** are evil.

scoured (1)
Lev 6:28 for sin is cooked must be **s**

scouts (1)
Est 2:3 And appoint **s** in all the

scraped (4)
Lev 14:41 the entire inside of the house **s**.
14:41 The plaster dust **s** off the walls
Jdg 14:9 He **s** ⌊the honey⌋ into his
14:9 He didn't tell them he had **s** it

scraps (3)
Mat 15:27 But even the dogs eat **s** that
Mar 7:28 eat some of the children's **s**."
Luk 16:21 have eaten any **s** that fell from

scratch (2)
Job 2:8 broken pottery to **s** himself as
3:3 "**S** out the day I was born and

scrawny (1)
Gen 41:19 These cows were **s**,

scream (4)
Gen 39:15 As soon as he heard me **s**,
Dtr 22:24 in a city and didn't **s** for help.
Mat 14:26 and began to **s** because they
Mar 6:49 and they began to **s**.

screamed (6)
Gen 39:14 but I **s** as loud as I could.
39:18 But when I **s**, he ran outside
Dtr 22:27 She may have **s** for help,
Dan 5:7 The king **s** for the psychics,
Mar 9:26 The evil spirit **s**, shook the
Act 8:7 Evil spirits **s** as they came out

screaming (4)
Jdg 7:21 to run away, **s** as they fled.
Isa 52:5 Their rulers are **s**, declares the
65:19 **S** and crying will no longer be
Mar 5:5 and on the mountainsides **s**

screams (1)
Num 16:34 away when they heard their **s**.

screech (1)
Isa 34:14 **S** owls will rest there and find

screen (21)
Exo 26:36 make a **s** out of fine linen yarn,
26:37 posts of acacia wood for the **s**
26:37 Make gold hooks for this **s**.
27:16 have a 30-foot **s** made from fine
35:15 the **s** for the entrance to the
35:17 and the **s** for the entrance to the
36:37 They made a **s** out of fine linen
36:38 hooks for ⌊hanging⌋ the **s**.
38:18 The **s** for the entrance to the
39:38 the **s** for the entrance to the
39:40 and **s** for the entrance to the
40:5 Put up the **s** at the entrance to
40:8 and put up the **s** at the entrance
40:28 Then he put up the **s** at the
40:33 and the altar and put up the **s** at
Num 3:25 the **s** for the entrance to the tent
3:26 the **s** for the entrance to the
3:31 in the holy place, and the **s**.
4:25 the **s** for the entrance to the tent
4:26 the **s** for the entrance to the
Pro 7:6 house I looked through my **s**.

scribbled (1)
1Sm 21:13 He **s** on the doors of the city

scribe (49)
2Sm 8:17 Seraiah was the royal **s**.
20:25 Sheva was the royal **s**.
2Ki 12:10 the king's **s** and the chief priest
18:18 Shebnah the **s**, and Joah,
18:37 Shebna the **s**, and Joah,
19:2 of the palace, Shebna the **s**,
22:3 he sent the **s** Shaphan,
22:8 Hilkiah told the **s** Shaphan,
22:9 The **s** Shaphan went to the
22:10 Then the **s** Shaphan told the
22:12 of Micaiah), the **s** Shaphan,
25:19 the **s** who was in charge of the
1Ch 18:16 Shavsha was the royal **s**.
24:6 The **s** Shemaiah was a son of
2Ch 24:11 the king's **s** and the chief
26:11 organized by the **s** Jeiel
34:15 Hilkiah told the **s** Shaphan,
34:18 Then the **s** Shaphan told the
34:20 (son of Micah), the **s** Shaphan,
Ezr 4:8 the **s** wrote another letter
4:9 and Shimshai the **s** were
4:17 commander, Shimshai the **s**,
4:23 commander, Shimshai the **s**,

Ezr 7:6 As a **s**, Ezra was an expert in
7:11 gave Ezra the priest and **s**,
7:12 a **s** for the Teachings of the
7:21 a **s** for the Teachings of the
Neh 8:1 They told Ezra the **s** to bring
8:4 Ezra the **s** stood on a raised
8:9 Ezra the priest and **s**,
8:13 met with Ezra the **s** to study
12:26 and of Ezra the priest and **s**.
12:36 Ezra the **s** led them.
13:13 the priest, Zadok the **s**,
Isa 36:3 Shebna the **s**, and Joah,
36:22 Shebna the **s**, and Joah,
37:2 of the palace, Shebna the **s**,
Jer 36:10 in the room of the **s** Gemariah,
36:12 The **s** Elishama, Delaiah (son
36:20 side room of the **s** Elishama,
36:21 side room of the **s** Elishama.
36:26 Abdeel) to arrest the **s** Baruch
36:32 and gave it to the **s** Baruch,
37:15 in the **s** Jonathan's house,
37:20 me to the **s** Jonathan's house,
52:25 the **s** who was in charge of the
Mat 8:19 A **s** came to him and said,
13:52 "That is why every **s** who has
Mar 12:32 The **s** said to Jesus,

scribe's (2)

Jer 36:12 he went down to the **s** room
36:23 cut them off with a **s** knife

scribes (72)

1Ki 4:3 the sons of Shisha, were **s**.
1Ch 2:55 and the families of **s** who lived
2Ch 34:13 of the Levites served as **s**,
Est 3:12 the king's **s** were summoned.
8:9 the king's **s** were summoned.
Isa 33:18 Where are the **s**? Where are the
Jer 8:8 The **s** have used their pens to
36:12 where all the **s** were sitting.
Nah 3:17 and your **s** are like swarms of
Mat 2:4 all the chief priests and **s**
5:20 than the **s** and Pharisees,
7:29 Unlike their **s**, he taught them
9:3 Then some of the **s** thought,
12:38 Then some **s** and Pharisees
15:1 Then some Pharisees and **s**
16:21 leaders, chief priests, and **s**.
17:10 "Why do the **s** say that Elijah
20:18 to the chief priests and **s**.
21:15 the chief priests and the **s** saw
23:2 "The **s** and the Pharisees
23:13 be for you, **s** and Pharisees!
23:15 be for you, **s** and Pharisees!
23:23 be for you, **s** and Pharisees!
23:25 be for you, **s** and Pharisees!
23:27 be for you, **s** and Pharisees!
23:29 be for you, **s** and Pharisees!
26:57 where the **s** and the leaders
27:41 chief priests together with the **s**
Mar 1:22 Unlike their **s**, he taught them
2:6 Some **s** were sitting there.
2:16 When the **s** who were
3:22 The **s** who had come from
3:30 Jesus said this because the **s**
7:1 The Pharisees and some **s**
7:5 and the **s** asked Jesus,
8:31 the chief priests, and the **s**.
9:11 So they asked him, "Don't the **s**
9:14 Some **s** were arguing with
9:16 Jesus asked the **s**,
10:33 to the chief priests and the **s**.
11:18 chief priests and **s** heard him,
11:27 the chief priests, the **s**,
12:28 One of the **s** went to Jesus
12:35 "How can the **s** say that the
12:38 "Watch out for the **s**!
12:40 The **s** will receive the most
14:1 The chief priests and the **s**
14:43 **s**, and leaders of the people.
14:53 and **s** had gathered together.
15:1 with the leaders and the **s**.
15:31 The chief priests and the **s**
Luk 5:21 The **s** and the Pharisees
5:30 The Pharisees and their **s**
6:7 The **s** and the Pharisees were
Luk 6:11 The **s** and Pharisees were
9:22 the chief priests, and the **s**.
11:53 When Jesus left, the **s** and the
15:2 and the **s** complained,
19:47 The chief priests, the **s**,
20:1 The chief priests, **s**,
20:19 The **s** and the chief priests
20:39 Some **s** responded,
20:46 "Beware of the **s**! They like to
20:47 The **s** will receive the most
22:2 The chief priests and the **s**
22:66 the chief priests and the **s**,
23:10 the chief priests and the **s**
Jon 8:3 The **s** and the Pharisees
8:9 the **s** and Pharisees left.
Act 4:5 and **s** met in Jerusalem.
6:12 people, the leaders, and the **s**.
23:9 Some of the **s** were Pharisees

script (5)

Ezr 4:7 was written with the Aramaic **s**
Est 1:22 to each province in its own **s**
3:12 to each province in its own **s**
8:9 to each province in its own **s**,
8:9 and to the Jews in their own **s**

Scripture (96)

Mat 4:4 Jesus answered, "S says,
4:6 S says, 'He will put his angels
4:7 said to him, "Again, S says,
4:10 S says, 'Worship the Lord your
11:10 is the one about whom S says,
21:13 He told them, "S says,
26:31 S says, 'I will strike the
Mar 7:6 about you hypocrites in S:
9:13 as S says about him."
11:17 them by saying, "S says,
12:10 you never read the S passage:
14:27 S says, 'I will strike the
Luk 4:4 Jesus answered him, "S says,
4:8 Jesus answered him, "S says,
4:10 S says, 'He will put his angels
7:27 is the one about whom S says,
19:46 He said to them, "S says,
20:17 does this S verse mean:
22:37 I can guarantee that the S
24:46 He said to them, "S says that
24:47 S also says that by the
Jon 2:17 remembered that S said,
2:22 So they believed the S and this
6:31 S says, 'He gave them bread
7:38 As S says, 'Streams of living
7:42 Doesn't S say that the Messiah
12:14 and sat on it, as S says:
13:18 I've made my choice so that S
17:12 became lost. So S came true.
19:24 In this way the S came true:
19:28 He said this so that S could
19:36 This happened so that the S
19:37 Another S passage says,
20:9 They didn't know yet what S
Act 1:16 David in S about Judas had
13:33 This is what S says in the
15:15 the prophets said. S says,
17:2 he had discussions about S
18:4 Paul would discuss ⌊S⌋ in the
20:7 Paul was discussing ⌊S⌋ with
23:5 After all, S says, 'Don't speak
Rom 1:17 and ends with faith as S says,
2:24 As S says, "God's name is
3:4 else is a liar, as S says,
3:10 as S says, "Not one person
4:3 What does S say?
4:17 as S says: "I have made you a
8:36 As S says: "We are being
9:7 However, ⌊as S says,⌋
9:17 S says to Pharaoh,
9:33 As S says, "I am placing a
10:6 However, S says about God's
10:11 S says, "Whoever believes in
10:15 As S says, "How beautiful are
11:2 says in the S passage when
11:8 as S says, "To this day God
11:26 will be saved, as S says,
12:19 After all, S says, "I alone have
14:11 S says, "As certainly as I live,
Rom 15:3 Rather, as S says,
15:10 And S says again,
15:21 As S says, "Those who were
1Co 1:19 S says, "I will destroy the
1:31 As S says, "Whoever brags
2:9 But as S says: "No eye has
3:19 That's why S says,
3:20 Again S says, "The Lord
4:6 go beyond what is written in S.
10:7 some of them did, as S says,
15:45 This is what S says:
15:54 then the teaching of S will
2Co 8:15 This is what S says:
9:9 S says, "The righteous person
Gal 3:8 S saw ahead of time that God
3:8 So S announced the Good
3:10 of standards because S says,
3:13 S says, "Everyone who is
3:16 S doesn't say, "descendants,"
3:22 But S states that the whole
4:22 S says that Abraham had two
4:27 S says: "Rejoice, women who
4:30 But what does S say?
1Ti 4:13 on reading ⌊S⌋ in worship,
5:18 After all, S says, and "The
2Ti 3:16 Every S passage is inspired by
Heb 2:6 declared this somewhere in S:
3:15 S says, "If you hear God speak
4:4 Somewhere in S God has said
5:6 In another place in S,
11:5 S states that before Enoch was
Jas 2:23 The S passage came true.
4:6 S says, "God opposes arrogant
1Pe 1:16 S says, "Be holy, because I
1:23 That's why ⌊S says⌋,
2:6 That is why S says,
2Pe 1:20 No prophecy in S is a matter of

Scriptures (34)

Dan 9:2 learned from the S the number
Mat 21:42 "Have you never read in the S:
22:29 know the S or God's power.
23:34 and teachers of the S.
26:24 is going to die as the S say
26:54 How, then, are the S to be
Mar 12:24 know the S or God's power?
14:21 is going to die as the S say
14:49 But what the S say must come
Luk 24:27 about him throughout the S.
24:32 the meaning of the S for us?"
24:45 their minds to understand the S.
Jon 5:39 You study the S in detail
5:39 These S testify on my behalf.
7:52 Study ⌊the S⌋, and you'll see
10:34 them, "Don't your S say, 'I said,
10:35 The S cannot be discredited.
10:35 people to whom he gave the S),
12:34 "We have heard from the S that
15:25 written in their S has come true:
Act 8:32 This was the part of the S that
17:11 they carefully examined the S
18:24 and knew how to use the S
18:28 from the S that Jesus is
Rom 1:2 his prophets in the Holy S.
9:13 The S say, "I loved Jacob,
15:4 which the S give us.
15:9 This is what the S say,
1Co 15:3 our sins as the S predicted.
15:4 the third day as the S predicted.
Eph 4:8 That's why the S say:
2Ti 3:15 you have known the Holy S.
Heb 7:17 The S say the following about
2Pe 3:16 they distort the rest of the S.

scroll (59)

Exo 17:14 "Write this reminder on a **s**,
Num 5:23 will write these curses on a **s**
Dtr 17:18 copy of these teachings on a **s**.
1Sm 10:25 He wrote the laws on a **s**,
Ezr 6:2 A **s** was found in the palace of
Job 19:23 they were inscribed on a **s**.
31:35 write ⌊his complaint⌋ on a **s**.
Psa 40:7 about me in the **s** of the book.)
Isa 34:4 will be rolled up like a **s**.
Jer 36:2 "Take a **s**, and write on it
36:4 Baruch wrote it all down on a **s**.

Jer 36:6 you must read from the **s** the
36:8 read from the **s** everything that
36:10 Then Baruch read the **s**
36:11 heard Baruch read from the **s**
36:13 Baruch read from the **s** publicly
36:14 "Bring the **s** that you read
36:14 took the **s** and went with him to
36:18 and I wrote it on the **s** in ink."
36:20 After they put the **s** in the side
36:21 king sent Jehudi to get the **s**.
36:21 He took the **s** from the side
36:23 the whole **s** was burned up.
36:25 urged the king not to burn the **s**
36:27 After the king burned up the **s**
36:28 "Take another **s**, and write on it
36:28 on the **s** that King Jehoiakim
36:29 You burned this **s**,
36:32 Then Jeremiah took another **s**
36:32 on the **s** that King Jehoiakim
45:1 on a **s** as Jeremiah dictated
51:60 Jeremiah wrote on a **s** all the
51:63 When you finish reading this **s**,
51:64 'Babylon will sink like this **s**.
Eze 2:9 out toward me. In it was a **s**.
2:10 He spread the **s** in front of me.
3:1 Eat this **s**. Then speak to the
3:2 and he gave me the **s** to eat.
3:3 eat this **s** I'm giving you,
Zec 5:1 up again and saw a flying **s**.
5:2 "I see a flying **s**," I answered.
5:3 The one side of the **s** says that
5:3 The other side of the **s** says
Heb 9:19 and hyssop and sprinkled the **s**
10:7 (It is written about me in the **s**
Rev 1:11 "Write on a **s** what you see,
5:1 I saw a **s** in the right hand of
5:2 "Who deserves to open the **s**
5:3 the earth could open the **s**
5:4 who deserved to open the **s**
5:5 He can open the **s** and the
5:7 He took the **s** from the right
5:8 When the lamb had taken the **s**,
5:9 "You deserve to take the **s** and
6:14 The sky vanished like a **s**
10:2 opened **s** in his hand.
10:8 It said, "Take the opened **s**
10:9 him to give me the small **s**.
10:10 I took the small **s** from the

scrolls (1)

2Ti 4:13 Also bring the **s** and especially

sculptured (1)

2Ch 3:10 place he made two **s** angels

scum (2)

Job 24:18 Such people are like **s** on the
Lam 3:45 You made us the **s** and trash of

sea (366)

Gen 1:10 came together he named **s**.
1:21 created the large **s** creatures,
1:22 increase in number, fill the **s**,
1:26 Let them rule the fish in the **s**,
1:28 Rule the fish in the **s**,
9:2 the fish in the **s** have been put
14:3 of Siddim (that is, the Dead **S**).
Exo 10:19 and blew them into the Red **S**.
13:18 the desert toward the Red **S**.
14:2 between Migdol and the **s**.
14:2 camp facing north — by the **s**.
14:9 camp by the **s** at Pi Hahiroth
14:16 out your hand over the **s**,
14:16 go through the **s** on dry ground.
14:21 out his hand over the **s**.
14:21 the LORD pushed back the **s**
14:21 turned the **s** into dry ground.
14:22 through the middle of the **s**
14:23 followed them into the **s**.
14:26 out your hand over the **s** so that
14:27 stretched his hand over the **s**,
14:27 LORD swept them into the **s**.
14:28 had followed Israel into the **s**.
14:29 had gone through the **s**
15:1 and their riders into the **s**.
15:4 chariots and army into the **s**.
Exo 15:4 were drowned in the Red **S**.
15:8 in the middle of the **s**.
15:10 breath blew the **s** over them.
15:19 and cavalry went into the **s**,
15:19 water of the **s** flow back over
15:19 through the **s** on dry ground.
15:21 and their riders into the **s**."
15:22 Israel away from the Red **S** into
20:11 made heaven, earth, and the **s**,
23:31 your borders from the Red **S**
23:31 Red Sea to the Mediterranean **S**
Num 11:22 all the fish in the **s** were caught
11:31 from the **s** that brought quails
13:29 coast of the Mediterranean **S**
14:25 road that goes to the Red **S**."
21:4 the road that goes to the Red **S**,
33:8 through the middle of the **s** into
33:10 and set up camp by the Red **S**.
33:11 They moved from the Red **S**
34:3 from the end of the Dead **S**
34:5 ends at the Mediterranean **S**.
34:6 of the Mediterranean **S**.
34:7 Mediterranean **S** to Mount Hor,
34:11 slope of the **S** of Galilee.
34:12 so that it ends at the Dead **S**.
Dtr 1:40 road that goes to the Red **S**."
2:1 road that goes to the Red **S** as
3:17 from the **S** of Galilee to the Sea
3:17 from the Sea of Galilee to the **S**
3:17 Sea of the Plains (the Dead **S**),
4:49 River as far as the Dead **S** at
11:4 He drowned them in the Red **S**
11:24 River to the Mediterranean **S**.
30:13 isn't on the other side of the **s**.
30:13 "Who will cross the **s** to get it
34:2 as far as the Mediterranean **S**,
Jos 1:4 Mediterranean **S** on the west.
2:10 dried up the water of the Red **S**
3:16 flowing down toward the **S**
3:16 Dead **S**) was completely cut
4:23 as he did to the Red **S** until we
5:1 the Mediterranean **S** heard that
12:3 the eastern plains from the **S**
12:3 from the Sea of Galilee to the **S**
12:3 Sea of the Plains (the Dead **S**)
13:27 to the end of the **S** of Galilee.
15:2 the south end of the Dead **S**
15:4 ends at the Mediterranean **S**.
15:5 is the Dead **S** as far north
15:5 the north end of the Dead **S** at
15:11 ends at the Mediterranean **S**.
15:12 of the Mediterranean **S**.
15:46 **S** and alongside Ashdod.
15:47 coast of the Mediterranean **S**.
16:3 ends at the Mediterranean **S**.
16:8 ends at the Mediterranean **S**.
17:9 ends at the Mediterranean **S**.
17:10 So the Mediterranean **S** ⌊is its
18:19 northern bay of the Dead **S** at
19:29 ends at the Mediterranean **S**.
23:4 to the Mediterranean **S**.
24:6 you came to the **s**.
24:6 your ancestors to the Red **S**.
24:7 He made the **s** flow back and
Jdg 11:16 through the desert to the Red **S**
2Sm 8:13 in the Dead **S** region as
1Ki 5:9 logs from Lebanon to the **s**,
5:9 make them into rafts to go by **s**
9:26 near the Red **S** coast at Ezion
18:43 and look toward the **s**."
18:44 hand is coming from the **s**."
2Ki 14:7 Edomites in the Dead **S** region
14:25 of Hamath to the Dead **S** as
1Ch 16:32 Let the **s** and everything in it
18:12 Edomites in the Dead **S** region.
2Ch 2:16 them to you in Joppa by **s**.
20:2 the other side of the Dead **S**,
25:11 he came to the Dead **S** region,
Ezr 3:7 would bring by **s** from Lebanon
Neh 9:9 heard them crying at the Red **S**.
9:11 You divided the **s** in front of
9:11 they could walk through the **s**
Est 10:1 and the islands of the **s**.
Job 7:12 "Am I the **s** or a sea monster
7:12 "Am I the sea or a **s** monster
9:8 walks on the waves of the **s**.
Job 11:9 the earth and wider than the **s**.
26:12 his power he calmed the **s**.
26:12 killed Rahab ⌊the **s** monster⌋.
28:14 The **s** says, 'It isn't with me.'
28:25 measured the water ⌊in the **s**⌋,
36:30 and covers the depths of the **s**.
38:8 "Who shut the **s** behind gates
38:16 you gone to the springs in the **s**
41:31 It makes the deep **s** boil like a
41:32 behind it so that the **s** appears
Psa 33:7 He gathers the water in the **s**
42:7 One deep **s** calls to another at
46:2 topple into the depths of the **s**.
65:5 earth and of the most distant **s**,
66:6 He turned the **s** into dry land.
68:22 back from the depths of the **s**
72:8 May he rule from **s** to sea,
72:8 May he rule from sea to **s**,
74:13 You stirred up the **s** with your
74:13 You smashed the heads of **s**
77:16 Even the depths of the **s**
77:19 Your road went through the **s**.
78:13 He divided the **s** and led them
78:53 the **s** covered their enemies.
80:11 to the Mediterranean **S**.
89:9 You rule the raging **s**.
89:25 will put his ⌊left⌋ hand on the **s**
93:4 the foaming waves of the **s**.
95:5 The **s** is his. He made it, and his
96:11 Let the **s** and everything in it
98:7 Let the **s**, everything in it,
104:25 The **s** is so big and wide with
106:7 so they rebelled at the **s**,
106:7 rebelled at the sea, the Red **S**.
106:9 angrily commanded the Red **S**,
106:22 terrifying things at the Red **S**.
107:23 who sail on the **s** in ships,
107:24 in the depths of the **s**.
114:3 The Red **S** looked at this and
114:5 Red **S**, why did you run away?
136:13 to one who divided the Red **S** —
136:15 and his army into the Red **S** —
139:9 distant shore of the **s** where
146:6 who made heaven, earth, the **s**,
148:7 Praise him, large **s** creatures
Pro 8:29 when he set a limit for the **s** so
23:34 down in the middle of the **s**
Ecc 1:7 All streams flow into the **s**,
1:7 but the **s** is never full.
Isa 5:30 over their prey as the **s** roars.
9:1 bring glory to the road by the **s**,
11:9 like water covering the **s**.
11:11 and the islands of the **s**.
11:15 up the gulf of the Egyptian **S**.
16:8 had spread out over the **s**.
17:12 They will roar like the roaring **s**.
18:2 It sends messengers by **s** in
21:1 about the desert by the **s**.
23:2 have crossed the **s**.
23:4 by the **s** has spoken,
23:11 stretched his hand over the **s**
24:14 From the **s** they sing joyfully
27:1 monster which lives in the **s**.
40:12 measured the water of the **s**
43:2 When you go through the **s**,
43:16 makes a path through the **s**
48:18 would be like waves on the **s**.
50:2 I dry up the **s** with my
51:10 Didn't you dry up the **s**,
51:10 in the depths of the **s** so that
51:15 your God who stirs up the **s**
57:20 wicked are like the churning **s**.
60:5 because the riches of the **s**
63:11 who brought them out of the **s**
Jer 5:22 the sand a boundary for the **s**,
6:23 They sound like the roaring **s**.
31:35 He stirs up the **s** so that its
46:18 Carmel by the **s** will come.
48:32 ⌊once⌋ spread as far as the **s**,
48:32 as far as the **s** of Jazer.
49:21 will be heard at the Red **S**.
49:23 They are troubled like a **s** that
50:42 They will sound like the **s**
51:36 I will dry up Babylon's **s** and
51:42 The **s** will rise over Babylon,
Lam 2:13 wounds are as deep as the **s**.

Eze 26:3 you as the waves on the **s** rise.
26:5 It will become a place by the **s**
26:17 have been shattered by the **s**.
26:17 and your people ruled the **s**.
26:18 will terrify the islands in the **s**.
26:19 Mediterranean **S** will cover you.
27:3 the city at the entrance to the **s**.
27:4 Your home is the **s**.
27:9 All the ships on the **s** and their
27:25 filled with heavy cargo in the **s**.
27:26 wind wrecked you in the **s**.
27:27 sank into the **s** when your ship
27:32 the city destroyed in the **s**?"
27:34 Now you are wrecked in the **s**,
27:34 at the bottom of the **s**.
28:2 I sit on God's throne in the **s**."
28:8 will die a violent death in the **s**.
39:11 east of the Dead **S**.
45:7 extend to the Mediterranean **S**.
47:8 and into the Dead **S**.
47:8 water flows into the Dead **S**,
47:9 the water in the Dead **S** fresh.
47:10 standing on the shore of the **s**
47:10 are in the Mediterranean **S**.
47:15 run from the Mediterranean **S**
47:17 run from the Mediterranean **S**
47:18 continue from the Dead **S** down
47:19 ravine to the Mediterranean **S**.
47:20 side the Mediterranean **S** is
48:28 Egypt to the Mediterranean **S**.
Dan 7:2 stirring up the Mediterranean **S**
7:3 the others, came out of the **s**.
Joe 2:20 be forced into the eastern **s**.
2:20 be forced into the western **s**.
Amo 5:8 He calls for water from the **s** to
6:12 a farmer plow the **s** with oxen?
8:12 People will wander from **s** to
8:12 will wander from sea to **s**
9:3 from me at the bottom of the **s**,
9:3 I will command a **s** snake to
9:6 who calls for the water in the **s**
Jnh 1:4 sent a violent wind over the **s**.
1:9 who made the **s** and the land."
1:11 we do with you to calm the **s**?"
1:12 Then the **s** will become calm.
1:15 and the **s** became calm.
2:3 into the depths of the **s**,
2:5 The deep ⌊**s**⌋ covered me
Mic 7:12 Euphrates River, from **s** to sea,
7:12 Euphrates River, from sea to **s**,
7:19 all our sins into the deep **s**.
Nah 1:4 He yells at the **s** and makes it
3:8 The **s** was ⌊her⌋ defense.
Hab 1:14 all people like the fish in the **s**,
1:14 like schools of **s** life that have
2:14 like the water covers the **s**.
3:8 if you are furious with the **s**,
3:15 with your horses into the **s**,
Zep 1:3 in the sky, the fish in the **s**,
Hag 2:6 the **s** and the dry land.
Zec 9:4 will throw its wealth into the **s**
9:10 He will rule from **s** to sea and
9:10 He will rule from sea to **s** and
10:11 pass through a **s** of distress,
10:11 strike the waves in the **s**,
14:8 half of it to the Dead **S** and the
14:8 half to the Mediterranean **S**.
Mat 4:13 the shores of the **S** of Galilee.
4:15 on the way to the **s**,
4:18 walking along the **S** of Galilee,
4:18 were throwing a net into the **s**
8:18 other side of the **S** of Galilee.
8:24 storm came across the **s**.
8:26 an order to the wind and the **s**,
8:26 and the **s** became very calm.
8:27 the wind and the **s** obey him!"
8:28 other side ⌊of the **S** of Galilee⌋,
8:32 rushed down the cliff into the **s**
9:1 got into a boat, crossed the **s**,
13:1 sat down by the **S** of Galilee.
13:47 net that was thrown into the **s**.
14:25 He was walking on the **s**.
14:26 saw him walking on the **s**,
14:34 They crossed the **s** and landed
15:29 went along the **S** of Galilee.
16:5 other side of the **S** of Galilee.
Mat 17:27 go to the **s** and throw in a hook.
18:6 faith to be drowned in the **s**
21:21 and thrown into the **s**,' and
23:15 You cross land and **s** to recruit
Mar 1:16 going along the **S** of Galilee,
1:16 were throwing a net into the **s**
3:7 disciples for the **S** of Galilee.
4:1 teach again by the **S** of Galilee.
4:39 and said to the **s**, "Be still,
4:39 and the **s** became very calm.
4:41 the wind and the **s** obey him!"
5:1 other side of the **S** of Galilee.
5:13 the cliff into the **s** and drowned.
5:21 to the other side of the **S**
6:47 boat was in the middle of the **s**,
6:48 He was walking on the **s**.
6:49 they saw him walking on the **s**,
6:53 They crossed the **s**,
7:31 Ten Cities to the **S** of Galilee.
8:13 other side of the **S** of Galilee.
9:42 faith to be thrown into the **s**
11:23 and thrown into the **s**,' and
Luk 5:1 standing by the **S** of Galilee.
8:24 and the **s** became calm.
17:2 person to be thrown into the **s**
17:6 and plant yourself in the **s**!' and
21:25 the roaring and tossing of the **s**.
Jon 6:1 to the other side of the **S**
6:1 of Galilee (or the **S** of Tiberias).
6:16 his disciples went to the **s**.
6:17 boat and started to cross the **s**
6:18 to blow and stir up the **s**.
6:19 saw Jesus walking on the **s**.
6:22 still on the other side of the **s**.
6:25 him on the other side of the **s**,
21:1 Later, by the **S** of Tiberias,
21:7 taken off and jumped into the **s**.
Act 4:24 the **s**, and everything in them.
7:36 in Egypt, at the Red **S**,
10:6 whose house is by the **s**."
10:32 who lives by the **s**.'
14:15 the **s**, and everything in them.
21:7 Our **s** travel ended when we
27:27 through the Mediterranean **S**.
27:30 let the lifeboat down into the **s**
27:38 dumping the wheat into the **s**.
27:40 free and left them in the **s**.
28:4 may have escaped from the **s**,
1Co 10:1 and they all went through the **s**.
10:2 in the cloud and in the **s**.
2Co 11:25 and I drifted on the **s** for a night
11:26 in the open country, on the **s**,
Heb 11:29 to go through the Red **S** as if
Jas 1:6 the wind and tossed by the **s**.
3:7 birds, reptiles, and **s** creatures.
Jud 1:13 on the wild waves of the **s**.
Rev 4:6 there was something like a **s** of
5:13 under the earth, and on the **s**.
7:1 on the land, the **s**, or any tree.
7:2 allowed to harm the land and **s**,
7:3 "Don't harm the land, the **s**,
8:8 with fire was thrown into the **s**.
8:8 of the **s** turned into blood,
8:9 that were living in the **s** died,
10:2 He set his right foot on the **s**
10:5 whom I saw standing on the **s**
10:6 and the **s** and everything in it.
10:8 angel who is standing on the **s**
12:12 it is for the earth and the **s**
12:18 on the sandy shore of the **s**.
13:1 a beast coming out of the **s**.
14:7 the **s** and springs."
15:2 I saw what looked like a **s**
15:2 were standing on the glassy **s**.
16:3 poured his bowl over the **s**.
16:3 The **s** turned into blood like the
16:3 and every living thing in the **s**
18:17 from the **s** stood far away.
18:19 Everyone who had a ship at **s**
18:21 He threw it into the **s** and said,
20:13 The **s** gave up its dead.
21:1 and the **s** was gone.

seacoast (6)

Isa 23:6 you inhabitants of the **s**!
Jer 25:22 and the kings on the **s**;
Zep 2:5 be for those who live on the **s**,
2:6 The **s** will become pastureland
Luk 6:17 and the **s** of Tyre and Sidon.
Act 17:14 immediately sent Paul to the **s**,

seagulls (2)

Lev 11:16 ostriches, nighthawks, **s**,
Dtr 14:15 ostriches, nighthawks, **s**,

seal (27)

1Ki 21:8 and sealed them with his **s**.
2Ki 3:19 every good tree, **s** all the wells,
Est 8:8 **S** it also with the king's signet
Job 38:14 like clay stamped by a **s**,
Isa 8:16 **S** the teachings among my
Jer 32:44 for money, sign deeds, **s** them,
Dan 6:17 The king put his **s** on the stone,
8:26 **S** the vision, because it is
9:24 to put a **s** on a prophet's vision,
12:4 and **s** the book until the end
Mat 27:66 They placed a **s** on the stone
Jon 6:27 the Father has placed his **s** of
Rom 4:11 mark of circumcision is the **s**
1Co 9:2 You are the **s** which proves
2Co 1:22 In addition, he has put his **s** ⌊of
Eph 4:30 He has put his **s** on you for the
Rev 6:3 the lamb opened the second **s**,
6:5 the lamb opened the third **s**,
6:7 the lamb opened the fourth **s**,
6:9 the lamb opened the fifth **s**,
6:12 as the lamb opened the sixth **s**.
7:2 coming from the east with the **s**
7:3 trees until we have put the **s**
8:1 When he opened the seventh **s**,
9:4 people who do not have the **s**
10:4 "**S** up what the seven thunders
22:10 "Don't **s** up the words of the

sealed (23)

1Ki 21:8 and **s** them with his seal.
2Ki 3:25 They **s** every well and cut
Neh 10:1 people **s** the agreement:
Est 3:12 the name of King Xerxes and **s**
8:8 written in the king's name and **s**
8:10 in King Xerxes' name and **s**
Job 41:15 of scales that are tightly **s**.
Pro 17:28 if he keeps his lips **s**.
Sos 4:12 is locked, a spring that is **s**.
Isa 29:11 in a book that is closed and **s**.
29:11 "I can't read it. It's **s**."
Jer 32:10 I signed the deed, **s** it,
32:11 Then I took the **s** copy of the
32:14 both the **s** and the unsealed
Dan 12:9 are to be kept secret and **s** until
Zec 9:11 of the blood that **s** my promise
Eph 1:13 In him you were **s** with the
Rev 5:1 It was **s** with seven seals.
7:4 I heard how many were **s**:
7:4 Those who were **s** were from
7:5 from the tribe of Judah were **s**,
7:8 the tribe of Benjamin were **s**.
20:3 The angel shut and **s** the pit

seals (9)

Exo 24:8 "Here is the blood which **s** the
Neh 9:38 their **s** on the document."
Pro 10:19 but whoever **s** his lips is wise.
Heb 9:20 "Here is the blood that **s** the
Rev 5:1 It was sealed with seven **s**.
5:2 scroll and break the **s** on it?"
5:5 scroll and the seven **s** on it."
5:9 the scroll and open the **s** on it,
6:1 opened the first of the seven **s**.

seam (3)

Exo 28:27 This will be close to the **s** just
39:20 This was close to the **s** just
Jon 19:23 It didn't have a **s** because it

seamen (1)

1Ki 9:27 ⌊who were⌋ experienced **s**

seams (1)

Eze 27:9 inside you to caulk your **s**.

search (62)

Gen 31:32 s as much as you want through
31:35 Laban had made a thorough s,
44:12 the man made a thorough s.
Dtr 4:29 will find him whenever you s
4:32 S the distant past,
4:32 S from one end of heaven to
1Sm 23:23 I'll s for him among all the
24:2 from all Israel and went to s
26:2 best-trained men to s for David.
26:20 king of Israel has come to s
27:4 he didn't s for him anymore.
1Ki 1:2 let us s for a young woman
2:40 and went to Achish in Gath to s
20:6 my servants to s your palace
2Ki 2:16 Please let them go and s for
1Ch 16:11 S for the LORD and his
2Ch 7:14 themselves, pray, s for me,
Ezr 4:15 that you should s the official
4:19 and a s was made.
5:17 allow someone to s the king's
6:1 King Darius gave the order to s
Est 2:2 "S for attractive young virgins
Job 6:19 from Sheba s for them.
7:21 Then you will s for me,
8:5 If you s for God and plead for
10:6 you look for guilt in me and s
28:3 end to darkness ⌊there⌋ and s
Psa 27:4 at the LORD's beauty and to s
63:1 At dawn I s for you.
64:6 They s for the perfect crime
105:4 S for the LORD and his
119:2 They wholeheartedly s for him.
119:176 S for me, because I have never
Pro 2:4 if you s for wisdom as if it were
Ecc 8:17 hard a person may s for it,
Isa 34:16 S the LORD's book,
40:20 rot and s out skillful craftsmen
41:12 You will s for your enemies,
45:19 "S for me in vain!"
65:10 for my people who s for me.
Jer 5:1 S the city squares.
17:10 s minds and test hearts.
Eze 34:11 I will s for my sheep myself,
39:14 months they will begin their s.
Hos 2:7 She will s for them,
5:6 their sheep and their cattle to s
5:15 Then they will s for me.
Amo 5:4 of Israel: S for me and live!
5:5 But don't s ⌊for me⌋ at Bethel.
5:6 S for the LORD and live!
5:14 S for good instead of evil so
Zep 1:12 "At that time I will s Jerusalem
2:3 S for the LORD, all you humble
2:3 S for what is right.
2:3 S for humility. Maybe you will
Zec 11:16 He will not s for the young.
Mat 2:8 "Go and s carefully for the
2:13 because Herod intends to s for
7:7 S, and you will find. Knock,
Luk 11:9 S, and you will find. Knock,
Act 15:17 may s for the Lord,
Rom 2:7 life to those who s for glory,

searched (24)

Jos 2:22 The king's men had s for them
1Sm 13:14 The LORD has s for a man
14:4 pass where Jonathan s
1Ki 1:3 So they s throughout Israel for
18:10 my master has s for you in
2Ki 2:17 "They sent 50 men who s for
2Ch 15:4 When they s for him,
22:9 He s for Ahaziah, and Jehu's
Ezr 2:62 These people s for their
Neh 7:64 These people s for their
Psa 37:36 I s for him, but he could not be
78:34 ⌊the rest⌋ s for him.
119:10 I wholeheartedly s for you.
119:94 Save me, because I have s for
119:155 they have not s for your laws.
Jer 31:37 of the earth could be s,
Eze 34:6 No one s or looked for them.
34:8 My shepherds haven't s for my
Mar 1:36 Simon and his friends s for him.
Luk 4:42 The crowds s for him.
Act 12:19 Herod s for Peter but couldn't
17:5 attacked Jason's home and s
21:4 In Tyre we s for the disciples.
2Ti 1:17 he s hard for me and found me.

searches (14)

1Ch 28:9 because he s every heart
Psa 24:6 who s for the face of the God of
77:6 My spirit s ⌊for an answer⌋:
Pro 11:27 Whoever eagerly seeks good s
14:6 A mocker s for wisdom without
15:14 understanding s for knowledge,
20:27 It s his entire innermost being.
Isa 16:5 He judges and s for justice.
Mat 7:8 The one who s will find,
Luk 11:10 The one who s will find,
Rom 3:11 No one s for God.
8:27 The one who s our hearts
1Co 2:10 The Spirit s everything,
Rev 2:23 that I am the one who s hearts

searching (7)

1Sm 23:14 Saul was always s for him,
Pro 25:27 and s for honor is not
Amo 8:12 s for the word of the LORD.
Mat 13:45 who was s for fine pearls.
26:59 and the whole council were s
Mar 14:55 whole Jewish council were s
Gal 2:17 the same people who are s for

seas (16)

Lev 11:9 you may eat — anything in the s
11:10 creatures living in the s
Dtr 33:19 by the abundance from the s
Neh 9:6 the s and everything in them.
Job 6:3 heavier than the sand of the s.
37:10 and the s freeze over.
Psa 8:8 swims in the currents of the s.
24:2 He laid its foundation on the s
65:7 who calms the roar of the s,
69:34 Let heaven and earth, the s,
107:23 who do business on the high s,
135:6 on the s or in all the depths of
Pro 30:19 making its way through high s,
Isa 42:10 you people who sail on the s
Eze 27:26 took you out to the high s,
Dan 11:45 his royal tents between the s at

seashore (21)

Gen 22:17 and the grains of sand on the s.
32:12 as the grains of sand on the s.
41:49 like the sand on the s.
Exo 14:30 Egyptians lying dead on the s.
Jos 11:4 as the grains of sand on the s.
Jdg 5:17 Asher sat on the s and
7:12 as the grains of sand on the s.
1Sm 13:5 soldiers as the sand on the s.
2Sm 17:11 numerous as the sand on the s.
1Ki 4:20 numerous as the sand on the s.
4:29 limitless as the sand on the s.
Psa 78:27 birds like the sand on the s.
Isa 10:22 as⌋ the grains of sand on the s,
Jer 15:8 the grains of sand on the s.
33:22 the sand on the s that cannot
Hos 1:10 as the grains of sand on the s.
Mar 2:13 Jesus went to the s again.
5:21 gathered around him by the s.
Rom 9:27 as the grains of sand on the s,
Heb 11:12 as the grains of sand on the s.
Rev 20:8 as the grains of sand on the s.

season (9)

Gen 31:10 "During the mating s I had a
Exo 34:22 Harvest at the end of the s.
Num 13:20 (It was the s when grapes were
Jos 3:15 its banks during the harvest s.)
Ezr 10:13 and it's the rainy s.
Job 5:26 a stack of hay in the right s.
Psa 1:3 a tree that produces fruit in s
Hos 2:9 my new wine when it's in s.
Mar 11:13 because it wasn't the s for figs.

seasonal (3)

Jos 4:18 returned to its s flood level.
Job 6:15 been as deceptive as s rivers,
6:15 like the s riverbeds that flood.

seasoned (1)

Exo 30:35 s with salt, pure and holy.

seasons (5)

Psa 104:19 which marks the s,
Jer 5:24 sure that we have harvest s.'
Act 14:17 heaven and crops in their s.
17:26 He has given them the s of the
Gal 4:10 days, months, s, and years!

seat (13)

1Sm 20:18 missed when your s is empty.
20:25 He sat in his usual s by the
1Ki 10:19 armrests on both sides of the s.
21:9 S Naboth as leader of the
2Ch 9:18 armrests on both sides of the s.
Job 29:7 the city gate and took my s
Psa 7:7 Take your s high above them.
Sos 3:10 its s out of purple fabric.
Mat 20:23 to grant you a s at my right
Mar 10:40 to grant you a s at my right
Jon 19:13 outside and sat on the judge's s
2Co 5:10 in front of Christ's judgment s.
Jas 2:3 "Please have a s."

seated (10)

Gen 43:33 The brothers were s facing him
2Sm 19:28 Instead, you've s me with
1Ki 1:46 Solomon is now s on the royal
21:12 a fast and had Naboth s as
22:10 in royal robes and s on thrones.
2Ch 18:9 in royal robes and s on thrones.
23:20 Gate to the royal palace and s
Psa 113:5 He is s on his high throne.
Isa 46:1 Their statues are s on animals
1Co 14:30 to another person who is s,

seating (2)

1Ki 10:5 his officers' s arrangement,
2Ch 9:4 his officers' s arrangement,

seats (6)

Job 36:7 He s them on thrones with
Psa 113:8 He s them with influential
Mat 23:6 and the front s in synagogues.
Mar 12:39 and to have the front s in
Luk 11:43 You love to sit in the front s in
20:46 to have the front s in the

seaweed (1)

Jnh 2:5 S was wrapped around my

Seba (4)

Gen 10:7 Cush's descendants were S,
1Ch 1:9 Cush's descendants were S,
Psa 72:10 from Sheba and S bring gifts.
Isa 43:3 Sudan and S are the price I

Sebam (1)

Num 32:3 Elealeh, S, Nebo, and Beon,

Secacah (1)

Jos 15:61 Beth Arabah, Middin, S,

second (166)

Gen 1:8 then morning — a s day.
2:13 The name of the s river is
7:11 seventeenth day of the s month
8:14 day of the s month
22:15 Abraham from heaven a s time
30:7 gave birth to a s son for Jacob.
30:12 birth to her s son for Jacob.
32:19 also commanded the s servant,
41:5 again and had a s dream.
41:22 "In my s dream I saw seven
41:52 He named the s son Ephraim
Exo 4:8 they may believe the s.
16:1 day of the s month after they
19:16 On the morning of the s day,
28:18 In the s row put turquoise,
39:11 In the s row they put turquoise,
40:17 first month of the s year ⌊after
Lev 5:10 he will sacrifice the s bird as a
8:22 He brought forward the s ram
19:10 Don't harvest your vineyard a s

Num 1:1 It was the first day of the **s**
1:1 in the **s** year after leaving
1:18 on the first day of the **s** month.
2:16 They will be the **s** group to
7:18 On the **s** day Nethanel,
8:8 You must take a **s** young bull
9:1 In the first month of the **s** year
9:11 day of the **s** month at dusk.
10:6 the trumpets sound a **s** fanfare,
10:11 On the twentieth day of the **s**
10:11 the second month of the **s** year,
29:17 "On the **s** day bring 12 young
Dtr 24:3 If her **s** husband doesn't love
Jos 6:14 the city once on the **s** day
19:1 The **s** lot was drawn for the
Jdg 5:15 important men had **s** thoughts.
5:16 important men had **s** thoughts.
6:26 Take this **s** bull and sacrifice it
6:28 They saw that the **s** bull had
20:24 On the **s** day the Israelite
1Sm 8:2 the name of his **s** son was
17:13 the **s** was Abinadab,
18:21 So he said to David a **s** time,
20:27 But on the **s** day of the month,
20:34 and ate nothing that **s** day
2Sm 3:3 The **s** was Chileab,
14:29 Absalom sent for him a **s** time,
1Ki 6:1 the month of Ziv (the **s** month)
6:6 the **s** story was 9 feet wide,
9:2 appeared to him a **s** time,
15:25 began to rule Israel in Asa's **s**
2Ki 9:19 Then Joram sent out a **s** driver.
10:6 So he wrote them a **s** letter.
14:1 was in his **s** year as king
15:32 In the **s** year that King Pekah,
22:14 in the S Part of Jerusalem.
25:17 The **s** pillar and its filigree
25:18 the **s** priest Zephaniah,
1Ch 2:13 Abinadab (his **s** son),
3:1 The **s** was Daniel,
3:15 the **s** was Jehoiakim,
5:12 from Gad's **s** son Shapham.
6:28 who was his **s** son.
7:15 The name of his **s** son was
8:1 Ashbel (his **s** son),
8:39 firstborn), Jeush (the **s** son),
12:9 The **s** was Obadiah.
15:18 relatives from the **s** division:
16:5 Zechariah was **s**, then Jeiel,
23:11 and Ziza was the **s**.
23:19 his **s** was Amariah;
23:20 his **s** was Isshiah.
24:7 for Jehoiarib, the **s** for Jedaiah,
24:23 Amariah (the **s** of Hebron's
25:9 The **s** chose Gedaliah,
26:2 (the firstborn), Jediael (the **s**),
26:4 Jehozabad (the **s**),
26:11 other sons were Hilkiah (the **s**),
27:4 of the unit during the **s** month.
29:22 For the **s** time they made
2Ch 3:2 He began to build on the **s** day
3:2 the second day in the **s** month
30:2 the Passover in the **s** month.
30:13 Bread in the **s** month.
30:15 fourteenth day of the **s** month.
34:22 in the S Part of Jerusalem.
Ezr 3:8 This happened in the **s** month
3:8 of the **s** year following their
4:24 until Darius' **s** year as king
Neh 8:13 On the **s** day the leaders of the
Est 2:19 virgins were gathered a **s** time,
7:2 On the **s** day, while they were
9:29 to establish with this **s** letter
10:3 the Jew was ranked **s** only
Job 42:14 Jemimah, the **s** Cassia,
Pro 20:25 and later to have **s** thoughts
Ecc 4:15 sided with the **s** young man,
Jer 33:1 spoke his word to him a **s** time.
52:22 The **s** pillar was the same.
52:24 the **s** priest Zephaniah,
Eze 10:14 the **s** was the face of a human,
41:7 first story through the **s** story
42:5 those on the first or **s** stories
42:6 those on the first and **s** stories.
43:22 "On the **s** day bring a male
Dan 2:1 During the **s** year of
7:5 I saw a **s** animal. It looked like
Amo 7:1 when the **s** crop was being
Jnh 3:1 his word to Jonah a **s** time.
Zep 1:10 a howling from the S Part of the
Hag 1:1 month in Darius' **s** year as king,
1:15 month in Darius' **s** year as king.
2:10 month in Darius' **s** year as king,
2:20 his word to Haggai a **s** time
Zec 1:1 In the eighth month of Darius' **s**
1:7 in Darius' **s** year as king,
6:2 The **s** had black horses.
11:14 Then I broke my **s** staff,
Mat 6:24 the first master and love the **s**,
6:24 to the first and despise the **s**.
22:26 The **s** brother also died,
22:39 The **s** is like it: 'Love your
26:42 Then he went away a **s** time
Mar 8:25 on the man's eyes a **s** time,
12:21 The **s** married her and died
12:31 The **s** most important
14:72 then a rooster crowed a **s** time.
Luk 16:13 the first master and love the **s**,
16:13 to the first and despise the **s**.
19:18 "The **s** servant said,
20:30 Then the **s** brother married the
Jon 3:4 back inside his mother a **s** time
4:54 This was the **s** miracle that
21:16 a **s** time, "Simon, son of John,
Act 7:13 On the **s** trip, Joseph told his
10:15 A voice spoke to him a **s** time,
11:9 spoke from heaven a **s** time,
12:10 They passed the first and **s**
13:33 Scripture says in the **s** psalm:
1Co 15:47 The **s** man came from heaven.
15:52 in a split **s** at the sound of the
2Co 13:2 I was with you the **s** time,
Heb 6:6 cannot be led a **s** time to God.
9:3 Behind the **s** curtain was the
9:7 chief priest went into the **s** part
9:28 that he will appear a **s** time.
2Pe 3:1 Dear friends, this is the **s** letter
Rev 2:11 never be hurt by the **s** death.
4:7 the **s** was like a young bull,
6:3 the lamb opened the **s** seal,
6:3 I heard the **s** living creature
6:4 A **s** horse went out.
8:8 When the **s** angel blew his
11:14 The **s** catastrophe is over.
13:12 The **s** beast uses all the
13:12 The **s** beast makes the earth
13:13 The **s** beast performs
13:15 The **s** beast was allowed to
13:16 The **s** beast forces all people —
14:8 Another angel, a **s** one,
16:3 The **s** angel poured his bowl
19:3 A **s** time they said,
20:6 The **s** death has no power over
20:14 (The fiery lake is the **s** death.)
21:8 This is the **s** death."
21:19 the **s** sapphire, the third agate,

secret (39)

Gen 49:6 let me attend their **s** meetings.
Num 5:13 She may have kept it **s** if there
Dtr 27:15 and sets it up in **s** will be
Jdg 3:19 I have a **s** message for you."
Job 15:18 not kept **s** from their ancestors.
Psa 31:20 You hide them in the **s** place of
64:2 Hide me from the **s** plots of
83:3 They make plans in **s** against
90:8 You have put our **s** sins in the
139:15 when I was being made in **s**,
Pro 9:17 and food eaten in **s** is tasty."
11:13 in spirit can keep a **s**.
21:14 A gift given in **s** calms anger,
21:14 and a **s** bribe calms great fury.
25:9 not reveal another person's **s**.
Ecc 12:14 This includes every **s** thing,
Sos 2:14 in the **s** places of the cliffs,
Eze 8:12 nation of Israel are doing in **s**?
28:3 than Daniel and that no **s** can
Dan 2:18 merciful and to explain this **s**
2:19 The **s** was revealed to Daniel
2:27 can tell the king this **s**.
2:30 This **s** wasn't revealed to me
2:47 you were able to reveal this **s**."
4:9 No **s** is too hard for you to
12:4 keep these words **s**,
12:9 These words are to be kept **s**
Amo 3:7 unless he first reveals his **s**
Mat 10:26 Whatever is **s** will be made
24:26 'He's in a **s** place!'
Mar 4:22 There is nothing kept **s** that
7:24 it couldn't be kept a **s**.
Luk 8:17 There is nothing kept **s** that
12:2 Whatever is **s** will be made
Jon 18:20 I haven't said anything in **s**.
Rom 2:16 will judge people's **s** thoughts.
2Co 4:2 we have refused to use **s** and
Eph 5:12 what some people do in **s**.
Php 4:12 I've learned the **s** of how to live

secretly (28)

Gen 31:27 Why did you leave **s** and trick
Dtr 13:6 best friend may **s** tempt you,
27:24 kills another person **s** will
28:57 She will **s** eat them out of dire
Jos 2:1 **s** sent out two men as spies.
Jdg 9:31 He **s** sent messengers to
Rut 3:7 Then she went over to him **s**,
2Sm 12:12 You did this **s**, but I will make
2Ki 17:9 The Israelites **s** did things
Job 4:12 "I was told something **s** and
13:10 you if you **s** favor him?
31:9 or I have **s** waited near my
31:27 that my heart was **s** tempted,
Psa 31:4 net that they have **s** laid for me.
101:5 I will destroy anyone who **s**
Pro 17:23 A wicked person **s** accepts a
Jer 13:17 I will cry **s** over your arrogance.
38:16 So King Zedekiah **s** swore an
40:15 **s** asked Gedaliah at Mizpah,
Hab 3:14 like those who **s** eat up
Mat 1:19 marriage agreement with her **s**.
2:7 Then Herod **s** called the wise
Jon 7:4 No one does things **s** when he
7:10 He didn't go publicly but **s**.
19:38 was a disciple of Jesus but **s**
Act 16:37 they going to throw us out **s**?
26:26 None of this was done **s**.
2Pe 2:1 They will **s** bring in their own

secrets (9)

Job 11:6 would tell you the **s** of wisdom,
11:7 you discover God's hidden **s**,
Psa 44:21 he knows the **s** in our hearts?
Pro 11:13 gossips gives away **s**,
20:19 around as a gossip tells **s**.
Dan 2:28 God in heaven who reveals **s**.
2:29 The one who reveals **s** told
2:47 He can reveal **s** because you
1Co 14:25 The **s** in their hearts will

sect (3)

Act 24:5 a ringleader of the Nazarene **s**.
24:14 which they call a **s**.
28:22 are talking against this **s**."

section (9)

2Ki 14:13 He tore down a 600-foot **s** of
2Ch 25:23 He tore down a 600-foot **s** of
Neh 3:11 made repairs on a **s** that
3:19 repaired a **s** across from the
3:20 made repairs on a **s** from the
3:21 made repairs on a **s** from the
3:24 made repairs on a **s** from
3:27 Tekoa repaired a **s** across from
3:30 repaired another **s**.

sectioned (1)

1Ki 6:16 He **s** off a 30-foot-long room at

sections (3)

2Ch 32:5 He rebuilt all the broken **s** of
Eze 48:8 will be as long as one of the **s**
48:21 are as long as one of the **s**

Secu (1)

1Sm 19:22 as far as the big cistern in S

Secundus (1)

Act 20:4 and S from Thessalonica,

secure (28)

Jdg 18:7 They were peaceful and **s**.
18:10 you will come to a **s** people.
18:27 They attacked a peaceful and **s**
1Sm 20:31 nor your right to be king is **s**.
2Ch 11:12 He made the cities very **s**.
Ezr 9:8 Babylon and to give us a **s** hold
Job 11:15 and you will be **s** and unafraid.
24:22 they will never feel **s** about life.
Psa 7:9 make the righteous person **s**,
40:2 a rock and made my steps **s**.
87:5 The Most High will make it **s**."
102:28 will be **s** in your presence."
112:7 His heart remains **s**,
119:133 Make my steps **s** through your
Pro 4:26 and all your ways will be **s**.
11:15 the closing of a deal remains **s**.
25:5 justice will make his throne **s**.
29:14 his throne will always be **s**.
Isa 33:23 hang loose, your mast isn't **s**,
Dan 4:15 **S** it with an iron and bronze
4:23 **S** it with an iron and bronze
11:21 when people are feeling **s**,
11:24 When people feel **s**,
Amo 6:1 for those who feel **s** on the
Mat 27:64 order to make the tomb **s** until
27:65 Go and make the tomb as **s** as
27:66 So they went to **s** the tomb.
2Pe 1:10 calling and choosing of you **s**.

secured (1)

2Pe 2:4 where he has **s** them with

securely (20)

Lev 25:18 Then you will live **s** in the land.
25:19 all you want and live there **s**.
26:5 want and live **s** in your land.
Dtr 12:10 you so that you will live **s**.
33:12 people will live **s** with him.
33:28 So Israel will live **s**.
1Sm 12:11 side so that you could live **s**.
1Ki 4:25 Dan to Beersheba) lived **s**,
Psa 4:8 enable me to live **s**.
16:9 soul rejoices. My body rests **s**
Pro 10:9 lives honestly will live **s**,
Isa 47:8 You live **s** and say to yourself,
Jer 32:37 and make them live here **s**.
33:16 and Jerusalem will live **s**.
48:11 "Moab has lived **s** ever since it
49:31 nation living peacefully and **s**,
Zep 2:15 this the city that used to live **s**,
Zec 14:11 Jerusalem will live **s**.
Act 2:26 My body also rests **s**
5:23 "We found the prison **s** locked

security (19)

Dtr 24:10 his house to take a **s** deposit.
Rut 1:9 of you so that you may find **s**
2Ki 20:19 there is peace and **s** as long as
Est 9:30 granting peace and **s**
Job 12:6 and there is **s** for those who
22:6 take your brothers' goods as **s**
24:3 the widow's ox as **s** for a loan.
24:9 woman's baby as **s** for a loan.
Pro 21:29 way of life is his own **s**.
Isa 39:8 "Just let there be peace and **s**
Jer 30:10 will again have peace and **s**,
33:6 I will give them peace and **s**.
Eze 16:49 of food and had peace and **s**.
18:7 what a borrower gives him as **s**
18:12 He doesn't return the **s** for a
18:16 He doesn't keep the **s** for a
33:15 He returns the **s** for a loan,
Amo 2:8 out on clothes taken as **s**.
Act 16:23 to keep them under tight **s**.

sedan (1)

Sos 3:7 Solomon's **s** chair!

seduce (4)

Eze 16:25 your beauty to **s** people there.
2Pe 2:14 sin as they **s** people who aren't
2:18 to **s** people by appealing
2:18 They **s** people who have just

seduced (1)

Job 31:9 "If I have been **s** by a woman

seduces (1)

Exo 22:16 "Whenever a man **s** a virgin

seductive (2)

Pro 7:21 With all her **s** charms,
Isa 3:16 making **s** glances,

see (782)

Gen 2:19 them to the man to **s** what
8:8 Next, he sent out a dove to **s** if
9:16 I will **s** it and remember my
9:23 they didn't **s** their father naked.
11:5 The LORD came down to **s** the
12:12 When the Egyptians **s** you,
13:10 of Zoar as far as he could **s**.
13:15 I will give all the land you **s** to
18:16 with them to **s** them off,
18:21 I must go down and **s** whether
24:21 watching her to **s** whether
26:26 came from Gerar to **s** Isaac.
31:12 He said, 'Look up and **s** that all
31:43 Everything you **s** is mine!
31:49 we're unable to **s** each other.
32:20 After that I will **s** him,
37:14 So Israel said, "**S** how your
37:20 Then we'll **s** what happens to
37:32 You better examine it to **s**
38:25 **S** if you recognize whose
42:16 We'll **s** if you're telling the truth.
43:3 'You won't be allowed to **s** me
43:5 'You won't be allowed to **s** me
44:21 me so that I can **s** him myself.'
44:23 be allowed to **s** me again.'
44:26 The man won't **s** us unless our
44:34 bear to **s** my father's misery!"
45:12 and my brother Benjamin can **s**
45:28 I will go and **s** him before I die."
48:1 and Ephraim ⌊to **s** Jacob⌋.
48:2 son Joseph is here to **s** you,"
48:10 and he could hardly **s**.
48:11 never expected to **s** you again,
48:11 has even let me **s** your sons."
Exo 2:4 to **s** what would happen
2:11 Then he went to ⌊**s**⌋ his own
2:12 and when he didn't **s** anyone,
3:3 there and **s** this strange sight."
3:4 Moses had come over to **s** it,
4:14 and he will be very glad to **s**
4:18 I would like to **s** if they're still
4:21 **s** that you show Pharaoh all
5:21 So they said, "May the LORD **s**
6:1 "Now you will **s** what I will do
8:26 If they **s** us offer sacrifices that
10:23 People couldn't **s** each other,
10:28 Don't ever let me **s** your face
10:29 "You'll never **s** my face again."
11:7 This is how you will **s** that the
12:13 When I **s** the blood,
13:17 God said, "If they **s** that they
14:13 Stand still, and **s** what the
14:13 never **s** these Egyptians again.
16:4 In this way I will test them to **s**
16:7 In the morning you will **s** the
16:32 This way they will **s** the food
17:5 to where the people can **s** you.
19:21 ⌊the boundary⌋ to **s** the LORD,
20:26 able to **s** under your clothes."
23:5 Whenever you **s** that the
23:8 bribes blind those who can **s**
33:18 "Please let me **s** your glory."
33:20 But you can't **s** my face,
33:20 no one may **s** me and live."
33:23 and you'll **s** my back,
34:10 All the people around you will **s**
34:35 they would **s** that Moses' face
40:38 way all the Israelites could **s**
Lev 9:6 you may **s** the LORD's glory."
13:12 foot (so far as the priest can **s**),
27:33 You must not look to **s** if it is
Num 5:21 to **s** what happens when
11:23 Now you will **s** whether or not
13:18 **S** what the land is like and
Num 14:22 in Egypt and in the desert will **s**
14:23 treat me with contempt will **s** it!
15:39 and go after whatever you **s**,
22:31 Then the LORD let Balaam **s**
22:41 From there he could **s** the
23:9 I **s** them from the top of rocky
23:9 I **s** a nation that lives by itself,
23:13 where you can **s** the Israelites.
23:13 You will **s** only some of them,
23:23 '**S** what God has done!'
24:17 I **s** someone who is not here
27:13 After you **s** it, you, too, will join
32:11 will **s** the land I promised
32:12 of Nun) will get to **s** the land.
Dtr 1:35 of these evil people will ever **s**
1:36 He will **s** it, and I will give the
3:25 Please let me go over and **s**
3:28 possession of the land you **s**."
4:15 You didn't **s** the LORD the day
4:19 worship and serve what you **s**
4:28 These gods can't **s**,
5:24 our God has let us **s** how great
6:19 You will **s** the LORD expel
11:2 They didn't **s** or experience
18:16 our God or **s** this raging fire
20:1 you may **s** horses,
21:11 If you **s** a beautiful woman
22:1 If you **s** another Israelite's ox or
22:1 don't pretend that you don't **s** it.
22:4 If you **s** another Israelite's
22:4 don't pretend that you don't **s** it.
23:14 the LORD will never **s** anything
28:10 in the world will **s** that you are
28:34 The things you **s** will drive you
28:67 because of the things you'll **s**.
29:4 eyes that **s**, or ears that hear.
29:22 from distant countries will **s**
29:23 They will **s** all the soil
32:39 **S**, I am the only God. There are
32:52 You may **s** the land from a
34:1 He could **s** Gilead as far as
34:4 I have let you **s** it with your
Jos 3:3 "As soon as you **s** the ark of
5:6 not let them **s** this land flowing
8:20 they could **s** the city going up
9:13 **S** how they are splitting!
22:11 about it and said, "**S** there!
Jdg 2:22 with these nations to **s** whether
3:25 They were shocked to **s** their
9:1 went to Shechem to **s** the
13:23 He would not have let us **s** or
14:10 his father went to **s** the woman,
19:3 Her father was thrilled to **s** him.
Rut 3:8 he was surprised to **s** a woman
1Sm 2:32 You will **s** distress in my
3:2 to fail so that he couldn't **s** well.
4:15 had failed so that he couldn't **s**.)
10:24 "Do you **s** whom the LORD has
12:13 **S**, the LORD has put a king
14:16 at Gibeah in Benjamin could **s**
14:17 "and **s** who has left ⌊our
14:29 **S** how my eyes lit up when I
15:35 Samuel didn't **s** Saul again
16:7 God does not **s** as humans
16:7 does not see as humans **s**.
17:18 **S** how your brothers are doing,
17:25 "Did you **s** that man coming
17:28 came here just to **s** the battle."
19:15 back to **s** David themselves.
20:29 let me go to **s** my brothers.'
21:14 Don't you **s** ⌊that he's⌋ insane?
24:11 should know and be able to **s**
25:25 But I didn't **s** the young men
28:13 "What do you **s**?" "I see a god
28:13 "I **s** a god rising from the
2Sm 1:19 **S** how the mighty have fallen!
1:25 **S** how the mighty have fallen
1:27 **S** how the mighty have fallen!
1:27 **S** how the weapons of war
3:13 You can't come to **s** me unless
3:24 Abner came to **s** you.
13:5 your father comes to **s** you,
13:6 and the king came to **s** him.
14:24 He will not **s** me." So Absalom
14:24 his house and didn't **s** the king.
14:32 Let me **s** the king now!

2Sm 15:25 me to come back and **s** both
16:12 Maybe the LORD will **s** my
22:25 because he can **s** that I am
24:3 may Your Majesty ⌊live⌋ to **s** it.
1Ki 1:18 But now, you **s**, Adonijah has
1:48 God of Israel who has let me **s**
8:52 "May your eyes always **s** my
9:12 Hiram left Tyre to **s** the cities
13:3 You will **s** the altar torn apart.
14:4 Ahijah couldn't **s**. His eyesight
20:7 He said, "You can **s** how this
21:29 "Do you **s** how Ahab is
2Ki 2:10 If you **s** me taken from you,
2:12 he couldn't **s** Elijah anymore,
3:17 You will not **s** wind or rain,
6:17 his eyes so that he may **s**."
6:17 servant's eyes and let him **s**.
6:20 of these men, and let them **s**."
6:20 and let them **s** that they were
6:32 "Do you **s** how this murderer
7:2 Elisha replied, "You will **s** it
7:10 and we didn't **s** or hear anyone.
7:19 Elisha answered, "You will **s** it
8:29 Jezreel to **s** Ahab's son Joram,
9:16 of Judah had come to **s** Joram.)
9:17 He said, "I **s** some troops."
10:16 **S** how devoted I am to the
19:16 Open your eyes, LORD, and **s**.
20:15 Isaiah asked, "What did they **s**
22:20 and your eyes will not **s** any of
23:17 is this monument that I **s**?"
1Ch 12:17 may the God of our ancestors **s**
29:17 I've been overjoyed to **s** your
29:25 as all Israel could **s**.
2Ch 20:17 and **s** the victory of the LORD
21:20 No one was sorry to **s** him die.
22:6 Jezreel to **s** Ahab's son Joram,
24:22 "May the LORD **s** ⌊this⌋ and
29:8 as you can **s** with your own
34:28 and your eyes will not **s** any of
Neh 2:17 "You **s** the trouble we're in.
4:11 what is happening or **s** a thing,
9:12 of fire to give them light to **s**
9:19 but it gave them light to **s** the
Est 3:4 So they informed Haman to **s** if
5:13 to me every time I **s** Mordecai
7:4 You **s**, we — my people and I —
8:6 I cannot bear to **s** my people
8:6 And I simply cannot bear to **s**
Job 3:9 Let it not **s** the first light of
4:18 "You **s**, God doesn't trust his
6:21 You **s** something terrifying,
7:7 will my eyes **s** anything good.
7:8 over me will no longer **s** me.
9:11 and I don't even **s** him.
9:25 They don't **s** anything good.
10:4 Do you **s** as a mortal sees?
11:4 'As you can **s**, I'm innocent.'
17:15 Can you **s** any hope left in me?
19:26 I will **s** God in my own flesh.
19:27 I will **s** him with my own eyes,
20:9 Eyes that saw him will **s** him
21:8 They **s** their children firmly
21:8 they get to **s** their descendants.
21:20 His eyes should **s** his own ruin.
21:27 "You **s**, I know your thoughts
22:11 you and you cannot **s**
22:14 him so that he cannot **s**.
23:9 If I turn southward, I can't **s** him
24:1 are close to him **s** his days ⌊of
28:10 eyes **s** every precious thing.
28:24 because he can **s** to the ends
31:4 Doesn't he **s** my ways and
33:26 They will **s** God's face and
33:28 and my life will **s** the light.'
34:29 If he hides his face, who can **s**
34:32 Teach me what I cannot **s**.
35:5 "Look at the heavens and **s**.
39:29 and its eyes **s** it from far away.
Psa 7:14 **S** how that person conceives
10:11 He will never **s** it!"
11:4 His eyes **s**. They examine
11:7 Decent people will **s** his face.
14:2 descendants to **s** if there is
17:15 I will **s** your face when I am
18:24 because he can **s** that my
Psa 22:7 All who **s** me make fun of me.
25:19 **S** how my enemies have
26:3 I **s** your mercy in front of me.
27:13 I believe that I will **s** the
31:11 Those who **s** me on the street
34:8 Taste and **s** that the LORD is
36:9 In your light we **s** light.
37:34 people are cut off, you will **s** it.
40:3 Many will **s** this and worship.
40:12 me so that I can no longer **s**.
42:2 may I come to **s** God's face?
46:8 **s** the works of the LORD,
49:9 live forever and never **s** the pit.
49:10 one can **s** that wise people die,
49:19 who will never **s** light ⌊again⌋.
50:18 When you **s** a thief,
50:21 and lay it all out for you to **s**.
50:23 who continues in my way **s**
52:6 Righteous people will **s** ⌊this⌋
53:2 descendants to **s** if there is
55:9 because I **s** violence and
58:10 they **s** ⌊God⌋ take revenge.
59:4 and help me; **s** ⌊for yourself⌋.
59:7 **S** what pours out of their
63:2 the holy place to **s** your power
64:5 "Who can **s** them?"
66:5 Come and **s** what God has
69:23 clouded so that they cannot **s**.
69:32 Oppressed people will **s** ⌊this⌋
74:9 no longer **s** miraculous signs.
80:14 Look from heaven and **s**!
86:17 that those who hate me may **s**
89:48 go on living and never **s** death?
90:16 **s** what you can do.
90:16 children **s** your glorious power.
91:8 to look with your eyes to **s**
94:7 "The LORD doesn't **s** it.
94:9 Do you think he can't **s**?
97:6 people of the world **s** his glory.
98:2 for the nations to **s**.
106:5 so that I may **s** the prosperity of
107:42 Decent people will **s** this and
115:5 have eyes, but they cannot **s**.
118:7 I will **s** ⌊the defeat of⌋ those
118:23 and it is amazing for us to **s**.
119:18 my eyes so that I may **s**
119:74 Those who fear you will **s** me
119:159 **S** how I have loved your
128:5 may **s** Jerusalem prospering all
128:6 May you live to **s** your
133:1 **S** how good and pleasant it is
135:16 have eyes, but they cannot **s**.
139:24 **S** whether I am on an evil path.
142:4 Look to my right and **s** that no
Pro 17:5 Whoever is happy ⌊to **s**
22:29 Do you **s** a person who is
23:33 Your eyes will **s** strange sights,
24:18 The LORD will **s** it,
25:17 Otherwise, he will **s** too much
Ecc 3:22 Who will allow them to **s** what
5:8 Don't be surprised if you **s** poor
11:7 for one's eyes to **s** the sun.
11:9 you and whatever your eyes **s**.
12:3 of the windows **s** a dim light.
Sos 2:14 let me **s** your figure and hear
6:11 to **s** if the grapevine had
7:12 Let's **s** if the vines have
Isa 3:1 **S** now, the Lord, the LORD of
5:12 is doing or **s** what his hands
5:19 work so that we may **s** what
5:30 they will **s** only darkness and
6:9 you look, you'll never **s**.'
6:10 they may **s** with their eyes,
8:22 at the earth and **s** only distress
9:2 who walk in darkness will **s**
11:3 not judge by what his eyes **s**
14:16 Those who **s** you stare at you;
21:3 I'm terrified by what I **s**.
21:7 He will **s** chariots,
22:9 You will **s** how many places in
22:11 You didn't **s** the one who
26:10 in the upright land and do not **s**
26:11 but they do not **s** it.
26:11 They will **s** how devoted your
28:7 stagger when they **s** visions.
29:15 "No one can **s** us" and "No one
Isa 29:18 The blind will **s** out of their
29:23 When they **s** all their children,
30:10 'Don't **s** ⌊the future⌋.'
30:10 we want to hear. **S** illusions.
30:20 You will **s** your teacher with
32:3 vision of those who can **s** won't
33:17 Your eyes will **s** how
33:17 You will **s** a land that stretches
33:19 You will no longer **s** those
33:20 Your eyes will **s** Jerusalem as
35:2 Everyone will **s** the glory of the
37:17 Open your eyes, LORD, and **s**.
38:11 I thought that I wouldn't **s** the
38:11 I would never **s** another person.
39:4 Isaiah asked, "What did they **s**
40:5 and all people will **s** it together.
40:26 Look at the sky and **s**.
41:20 People will **s** and know.
42:18 blind people, so that you can **s**.
44:9 Their own witnesses do not **s**
44:16 We can **s** the fire!"
44:18 plastered shut, so they can't **s**.
47:3 People will **s** you naked.
47:3 People will **s** your shame.
47:10 "No one can **s** me."
49:7 Kings will **s** ⌊you⌋ and stand.
49:7 Princes will **s** ⌊you⌋ and bow.
52:8 they will **s** it with their own
52:10 All the ends of the earth will **s**
52:15 They will **s** things that they
53:10 he will **s** his descendants for
53:11 He will **s** and be satisfied
58:3 Don't you **s** that on the days
58:4 Don't you **s** that when you fast,
58:7 when you **s** ⌊them⌋ naked.
60:5 Then you will **s** this and
62:2 will **s** your righteousness.
62:2 All kings will **s** your glory.
63:15 Look down and **s** from heaven,
66:5 then we will **s** your joy."
66:14 When you **s** it, your heart will
66:18 They will come and **s** my glory.
Jer 1:11 "Jeremiah, what do you **s**?"
1:11 I answered, "I **s** a branch of an
1:13 and asked, "What do you **s**?"
1:13 I answered, "I **s** a boiling pot,
2:10 to the coasts of Cyprus, and **s**.
2:10 **S** if there has ever been
2:19 You should know and **s** how
2:22 I would still **s** the stains from
3:2 "Look at the bare hills, and **s**.
3:6 "Did you **s** what unfaithful
4:21 How long must I **s** the battle
4:23 I **s** the earth. It's formless and
4:23 I **s** the sky. Its lights are gone.
4:24 I **s** the mountains. They are
4:25 I **s** that there are no people,
4:26 I **s** that the fertile land has
5:1 **S** if you can find anyone who
5:21 have eyes, but you cannot **s**.
6:7 I **s** that it is sick and wounded.
7:12 **S** what I did to Shiloh because
7:17 Don't you **s** what they are doing
11:20 I want to **s** you take revenge on
12:3 You **s** me and test my devotion
13:20 Look up, and **s** those who are
14:13 'You won't **s** wars or famines,
14:18 I **s** those killed because of war.
14:18 If I go to the city, I **s** those sick
16:17 I **s** everything that they do.
16:17 can't be hidden; I can **s** it.
17:6 He will not **s** when something
20:4 and you will **s** it with your own
20:10 are waiting to **s** me stumble.
20:12 I want to **s** you take revenge on
22:10 come back to **s** their homeland.
22:12 he will never **s** this land again.
23:14 I **s** something horrible.
23:24 can hide so that I can't **s** him,"
24:3 "What do you **s**, Jeremiah?"
24:3 I also **s** figs that are very bad,
29:32 He will not **s** the blessings that
30:6 Ask now, and **s**: Can a man
30:6 Why, then, do I **s** every strong
32:19 You **s** everything the
32:24 "'**S** how the dirt ramps have

Jer	32:24	has happened, as you can **s**.
	34:3	You will **s** the king of Babylon
	36:14	went with him to **s** the officers.
	42:2	As you can **s**, there are only a
	42:14	where we won't have to **s** war,
	42:18	You won't **s** this place again.
	46:5	"What do I **s** in them?
	50:23	**S** how desolate Babylon is of
	51:61	**s** that you read all this.
Lam	1:11	'O LORD, look and **s** how
	1:12	Look and **s** if there's any pain
	1:20	"O LORD, **s** the distress I'm in!
	3:36	isn't happy to **s** these things.
	3:51	What I **s** with my eyes disturbs
	5:17	why our eyes **s** less and less.
Eze	8:6	do you **s** what the people of
	8:6	But you will **s** even more
	8:9	me, "Go in, and **s** the wicked,
	8:12	do you **s** what the leaders of
	8:12	'The LORD doesn't **s** me.
	8:13	Then he said to me, "You will **s**
	8:15	"Son of man, do you **s** this?
	8:15	You will **s** even more
	8:17	"Son of man, do you **s** this?
	9:9	the land and that he doesn't **s**.
	12:2	have eyes, but they can't **s**.
	12:3	Let the people **s** you leave in
	12:4	Let them **s** you in the daylight.
	12:4	In the evening let them **s** you
	12:6	Let them **s** you put your bags
	12:6	so that you won't **s** the land.
	12:7	I let the people **s** me as I
	12:12	so that he cannot **s** the land.
	12:13	but he will not **s** it.
	13:6	prophets **s** false visions,
	13:9	prophets who **s** false visions
	13:23	will no longer **s** false visions
	14:22	you will **s** how they live.
	14:23	when you **s** how they live.
	16:37	and they will **s** you naked.
	21:29	People **s** false visions about
	22:6	"'**S** how all the princes of Israel
	26:21	they will never **s** you again,"
	28:17	kings so that they could **s** you.
	32:31	"Pharaoh and his army will **s**
	36:34	for everyone passing by to **s**.
	37:20	let the people **s** them.
	39:15	they go through the land and **s**
	39:21	All the nations will **s** how I will
	39:27	Many nations will **s** that I am
	40:4	of Israel everything that you **s**."
	47:6	"Son of man, do you **s** this?"
Dan	3:25	replied, "But look, I **s** four men.
	5:23	These gods can't **s**,
	10:7	men with me didn't **s** the vision.
	10:8	So I was left alone to **s** this
Hos	7:1	all I can **s** is Ephraim's sin and
Joe	2:28	Your young men will **s** visions.
Amo	3:9	**S** the widespread confusion
	7:8	He asked me, "What do you **s**,
	8:2	He asked, "What do you **s**,
Jnh	2:4	Will I ever **s** your holy temple
	4:5	waited to **s** what would happen
Mic	7:9	and I will **s** his victory.
	7:10	Then my enemies will **s** this,
	7:15	Let us **s** miracles like the time
	7:16	Nations will **s** this and be
Hab	1:3	you make me **s** wrongdoing?
	2:1	I will watch to **s** what he will
	3:7	I **s** trouble in the tents of
	3:7	I **s** trembling in the tents of
Zec	2:2	Jerusalem to **s** how wide
	3:4	"Then he said to Joshua, "**S**,
	4:2	asked me, "What do you **s**?"
	4:2	I answered, "I **s** a solid gold
	4:10	will be delighted when they **s**
	5:2	asked me, "What do you **s**?"
	5:2	"I **s** a flying scroll,"
	5:5	and **s** what's coming."
	9:5	Ashkelon will **s** this and be
	10:2	fortunetellers **s** false visions.
	10:7	Their sons will **s** it and be glad.
Mal	1:5	You will **s** these things with
	3:10	"**S** if I won't open the windows
	3:18	Then you will again **s** the
Mat	2:10	with joy to **s** the star.
Mat	5:8	are pure. They will **s** God.
	5:16	Then they will **s** the good that
	6:5	so that everyone can **s** them.
	7:3	So why do you **s** the piece of
	7:5	Then you will **s** clearly to
	9:30	Then they could **s**.
	11:4	tell John what you hear and **s**:
	11:5	Blind people **s** again,
	11:7	did you go into the desert to **s**?
	11:8	Really, what did you go to **s**?
	11:9	"Really, what did you go to **s**?
	12:22	him so that he could talk and **s**.
	13:13	They **s**, but they're blind.
	13:14	You will **s** clearly but never
	13:15	eyes so that their eyes never **s**.
	13:16	are your eyes because they **s**
	13:17	longed to **s** what you see
	13:17	longed to see what you **s**
	13:17	see what you see but didn't **s** it,
	15:31	The crowd was amazed to **s**
	16:28	here will not die until they **s**
	18:10	angels in heaven always **s**
	21:20	were surprised to **s** this.
	21:42	and it is amazing for us to **s**'?
	22:11	the king came to **s** the guests,
	23:39	you will not **s** me again until
	24:2	"You **s** all these buildings,
	24:15	When you **s** this (let the reader
	24:30	will cry in agony when they **s**
	24:33	when you **s** all these things,
	25:37	when did we **s** you hungry and
	25:37	and feed you or **s** you thirsty
	25:38	When did we **s** you as a
	25:38	you into our homes or **s** you
	25:39	When did we **s** you sick or in
	25:44	when did we **s** you hungry or
	26:58	the guards to **s** how this would
	26:64	that from now on you will **s**
	27:49	Let's **s** if Elijah comes to save
	28:6	Come, **s** the place where he
	28:7	There they will **s** him.
	28:10	There they will **s** me."
Mar	3:2	They wanted to **s** whether he
	4:12	'They **s** clearly but don't
	5:14	came to **s** what had happened.
	5:31	when you **s** the crowd pressing
	5:32	But he kept looking around to **s**
	6:38	Go and **s**." When they found
	8:23	"Can you **s** anything?"
	8:24	up and said, "I **s** people.
	8:25	He could **s** everything clearly
	9:1	here will not die until they **s**
	9:15	were very surprised to **s** Jesus
	10:51	I want to **s** again."
	10:52	At once he could **s** again,
	11:13	He went to **s** if he could find
	12:11	and it is amazing for us to **s**'?"
	13:2	Jesus said to him, "Do you **s**
	13:14	"When you **s** the disgusting
	13:26	"Then people will **s** the Son of
	13:29	In the same way, when you **s**
	14:62	and you will **s** the Son of Man
	15:24	dice to **s** what each one
	15:32	so that we may **s** and believe."
	15:36	The man said, "Let's **s** if Elijah
	16:7	There they will **s** him,
Luk	1:62	to the baby's father to **s** what
	2:15	"Let's go to Bethlehem and **s**
	2:31	prepared for all people to **s**.
	3:6	All people will **s** the salvation
	5:9	was with him was amazed to **s**
	6:7	They wanted to **s** whether he
	6:41	"Why do you **s** the piece of
	6:42	when you don't **s** the beam in
	6:42	Then you will **s** clearly to
	7:22	Blind people **s** again,
	7:24	did you go into the desert to **s**?
	7:25	Really, what did you go to **s**?
	7:26	Really, what did you go to **s**?
	7:44	"You **s** this woman,
	8:10	When they look, they don't **s**,
	8:16	who come in will **s** the light.
	8:19	and his brothers came to **s** him.
	8:20	They want to **s** you."
	8:35	The people went to **s** what had
	9:9	So Herod wanted to **s** Jesus.
Luk	9:27	here will not die until they **s**
	9:43	Everyone was amazed to **s**
	10:23	you are to **s** what you've seen.
	10:24	prophets and kings wanted to **s**
	11:33	who come in will **s** its light.
	11:38	surprised to **s** that Jesus didn't
	12:54	"When you **s** a cloud coming
	12:55	When you **s** a south wind
	13:28	you'll do when you **s** Abraham,
	13:35	you will not **s** me again until
	14:10	Then all the other guests will **s**
	14:18	a field, and I need to **s** it.
	14:19	and I'm on my way to **s** how
	14:28	Then you would **s** if you have
	17:21	You **s**, the kingdom of God is
	17:22	when you will long to **s** one
	17:22	but you will not **s** it.
	18:41	I want to **s** again."
	18:43	Immediately, he could **s** again.
	19:3	He tried to **s** who Jesus was.
	19:3	and he couldn't **s** Jesus
	19:4	climbed a fig tree to **s** Jesus,
	19:42	so you cannot **s** it.
	21:6	these buildings that you **s** —
	21:20	"When you **s** armies camped
	21:27	"Then people will **s** the Son of
	21:31	In the same way, when you **s**
	23:8	was very pleased to **s** Jesus.
	23:8	time he had wanted to **s** him.
	23:8	hoped to **s** him perform some
	23:40	Can't you **s** that you're
	23:48	had gathered to **s** the sight.
	24:24	but they didn't **s** him."
	24:39	and **s** that it's really me.
	24:39	me, and **s** for yourselves.
	24:39	but you can **s** that I do."
Jon	1:33	'When you **s** the Spirit come
	1:39	them, "Come, and you will **s**."
	1:39	So they went to **s** where he
	1:46	Philip told him, "Come and **s**!"
	1:50	You will **s** greater things than
	1:51	You will **s** the sky open and
	3:3	No one can **s** the kingdom of
	3:36	rejects the Son will not **s** life.
	3:36	will **s** God's constant anger."
	4:19	"I **s** that you're a prophet!
	4:35	I'm telling you to look and **s**
	4:48	"If people don't **s** miracles and
	6:30	to perform so that we can **s**
	6:40	Father wants all those who **s**
	6:62	What if you **s** the Son of Man
	7:3	so that your disciples can **s**
	7:4	you should let the world **s** you."
	7:52	and you'll **s** that no prophet
	8:51	what I say will never **s** death."
	8:56	was pleased to **s** that my day
	9:7	and returned. He was able to **s**.
	9:15	washed it off, and now I can **s**."
	9:19	Why can he **s** now?"
	9:25	to be blind, but now I can **s**."
	9:39	who can **s** will become blind."
	9:41	But now you say, 'We **s**,' so
	11:9	because they **s** the light of this
	11:34	him, "Lord, come and **s**."
	11:36	The Jews said, "**S** how much
	11:40	you would **s** God's glory?"
	12:9	So they went there not only to **s**
	12:9	Jesus but also to **s** Lazarus,
	12:40	so that their eyes don't **s**
	14:17	because it doesn't **s** or know
	14:19	the world will no longer **s** me,
	14:19	see me, but you will **s** me.
	16:10	and you won't **s** me anymore.
	16:16	while you won't **s** me anymore.
	16:16	while you will **s** me again."
	16:17	in a little while we won't **s** him.
	16:17	little while we will **s** him again
	16:19	'In a little while you won't **s** me,
	16:19	while you will **s** me again'?
	16:22	But I will **s** you again.
	17:24	I want them to **s** my glory,
	18:26	"Didn't I **s** you with Jesus in
	19:24	Let's throw dice to **s** who will
	20:20	were glad to **s** the Lord.
	20:25	refuse to believe this unless I **s**
Act	1:9	that they could no longer **s** him.

Act 2:17 Your young men will **s** visions.
2:25 'I always **s** the Lord in front of
3:10 to **s** what had happened
3:11 and everyone ran to **s** them at
4:13 they were surprised to **s** how
7:56 So Stephen said, "Look, I **s**
8:13 Simon was amazed to **s** the
8:21 God can **s** how twisted your
8:23 I can **s** that you are bitter with
8:39 way and didn't **s** Philip again.
9:7 the voice but didn't **s** anyone.
9:9 For three days he couldn't **s**
9:17 He wants you to **s** again and to
9:18 and he could **s** again.
11:23 he was pleased to **s** what God
12:16 they were shocked to **s** him.
13:11 unable to **s** the light of day."
13:11 Elymas couldn't **s** a thing.
15:2 were sent to Jerusalem to **s**
15:36 to **s** how they're doing."
17:11 the Scriptures to **s** if what Paul
17:22 I **s** that you are very religious.
19:21 been there, I must **s** Rome."
19:26 and you **s** and hear what this
20:25 of God will **s** me again.
21:3 We could **s** the island of
21:20 They said to Paul, "You **s**,
21:24 Instead, they'll **s** that you
22:13 back and I could **s** Ananias.
22:14 to **s** the one who has God's
25:24 to me about this man you **s**
27:20 a number of days we couldn't **s**
27:39 but they could **s** a bay with a
28:20 That's why I asked to **s** you
28:26 You will **s** clearly but never
28:27 eyes so that their eyes never **s**.
Rom 1:11 I long to **s** you to share a
7:23 However, I **s** a different
8:24 for something we already **s**,
8:25 if we hope for what we don't **s**,
11:8 Their eyes don't **s**,
11:10 clouded so that they cannot **s**.
15:21 never told about him will **s**,
15:24 so I hope to **s** you when I come
1Co 4:9 As I **s** it, God has placed us
13:12 Now we **s** a blurred image in a
13:12 Then we will **s** very clearly.
2Co 2:9 I wanted to **s** if you would be
3:13 want the people of Israel to **s**
4:4 As a result, they don't **s** the
6:6 People can **s** our purity,
6:9 as you **s**, we go on living.
7:7 He told us how you wanted to **s**
7:11 You wanted to **s** us.
7:13 pleased to **s** how happy Titus
13:5 Examine yourselves to **s**
Gal 1:17 Jerusalem to **s** those who were
1:19 I didn't **s** any other apostle.
2:2 people to **s** whether all my
Eph 3:4 When you read this, you'll **s**
5:14 makes everything easy to **s**.
Php 1:8 I long to **s** every one of you.
1:27 Then, whether I come to **s** you
2:23 as soon as I **s** how things are
2:26 He has been longing to **s** all of
Col 2:5 I'm happy to **s** how orderly you
1Th 2:17 we may not be able to **s** you,
2:17 to fulfill our desire to **s** you.
3:5 I wanted to **s** whether the
3:6 of us and want to **s** us,
3:6 as we want to **s** you.
3:10 that we may **s** you again so
1Ti 4:15 everyone can **s** your progress.
6:16 nor can they **s** him.
2Ti 1:4 tears and want to **s** you so that
Heb 2:8 still don't **s** everything under
2:9 but we **s** him crowned with
3:19 So we **s** that they couldn't enter
4:13 and exposed for him to **s**.
7:4 You can **s** how important
10:25 each other even more as we **s**
11:1 of things we cannot **s**.
11:7 in the future that he could not **s**.
11:27 actually **s** the invisible God.
12:14 you will not **s** the Lord.
Jas 2:22 You **s** that Abraham's faith and
Jas 2:24 You **s** that a person receives
5:7 **S** how farmers wait for their
1Pe 1:8 You don't **s** him now,
3:2 Their husbands would **s** how
2Pe 1:15 So I will make every effort to **s**
1Jn 2:11 they can't **s** in the dark.
3:2 him because we will **s** him as
4:1 **S** whether the spirit they have
5:16 If you **s** another believer
Rev 1:7 Every eye will **s** him,
1:11 "Write on a scroll what you **s**,
3:8 **S**, I have opened a door in front
3:18 your eyes so that you may **s**.
9:20 which cannot **s**, hear, or walk.
16:15 "**S**, I am coming like a thief.
16:15 and let others **s** his shame."
17:8 will be surprised when they **s**
18:9 mourn over her when they **s**
21:22 I did not **s** any temple in it,
22:4 and **s** his face. His name will be

seed (41)

Gen 47:19 But give us **s** so that we won't
47:23 for Pharaoh, here is **s** for you.
47:24 will be yours to use as **s**
Lev 11:37 If their dead bodies fall on **s**
11:37 is to be planted, the **s** is clean.
11:38 But if water is poured on the **s**
11:38 the **s** is unclean for you.
27:16 its value will be based on the **s**
Dtr 11:10 There you used to plant your **s**,
Psa 126:6 carrying his bag of **s**,
Ecc 11:6 Plant your **s** in the morning,
Isa 5:10 and two quarts of **s** will
6:13 The holy **s** will be the land's
28:25 he scatter black cumin **s**
30:23 you rain for the **s** that you plant
55:10 and grow so that it produces **s**
61:11 like a garden that makes the **s**
Jer 2:21 grapevine from the very best **s**.
Hag 2:19 Is there any **s** left in the barn?
Mat 13:3 A farmer went to plant **s**.
13:19 This is what the **s** planted
13:20 The **s** planted on rocky ground
13:22 The **s** planted among
13:23 But the **s** planted on good
13:24 who planted good **s** in his field.
13:27 didn't you plant good **s** in your
13:31 **s** that someone planted
17:20 faith is the size of a mustard **s**,
Mar 4:3 A farmer went to plant **s**.
4:31 It's like a mustard **s** planted in
4:31 The mustard **s** is one of the
Luk 8:11 The **s** is God's word.
13:19 It's like a mustard **s** that
17:6 faith the size of a mustard **s**,
1Co 9:11 the spiritual **s** that has been
15:36 The **s** you plant doesn't come
15:37 or something else, is only a **s**.
15:38 Each kind of **s** grows into its
2Co 9:10 God gives **s** to the farmer and
9:10 God will also give you **s** and
1Pe 1:23 not from a **s** that can be

seedling (5)

Isa 17:11 the morning you set out the **s**,
60:21 They will be the **s** I have
Eze 17:5 "Then it took a **s** from that
17:5 that country and planted the **s**
17:5 The eagle planted the **s** like a

seeds (37)

Gen 1:11 vegetation: plants bearing **s**,
1:11 fruit trees bearing fruit with **s**,
1:12 vegetation: plants bearing **s**,
1:12 and trees bearing fruit with **s**,
1:29 given you every plant with **s**
1:29 every tree that has fruit with **s**.
Exo 16:31 It was like coriander **s**.
Num 6:4 not even grape **s** or skins.
11:7 was small like coriander **s**
Joe 1:17 **S** shrivel up in their shells.
Zec 8:12 **S** will thrive in peacetime.
Mat 13:4 Some **s** were planted along the
13:5 Other **s** were planted on rocky
13:7 Other **s** were planted among
Mat 13:8 But other **s** were planted on
13:32 It's one of the smallest **s**.
13:37 one who plants the good **s** is
13:38 The good **s** are those who
25:24 you haven't scattered any **s**.
Mar 4:4 Some **s** were planted along the
4:5 Other **s** were planted on rocky
4:7 Other **s** were planted among
4:8 But other **s** were planted on
4:15 Some people are like **s** that
4:16 Other people are like **s** that
4:18 Other people are like **s** planted
4:20 Others are like **s** planted on
4:26 who scatters **s** on the ground.
4:27 The **s** sprout and grow,
4:31 one of the smallest **s** on earth.
Luk 8:5 "A farmer went to plant his **s**.
8:5 Some **s** were planted along the
8:12 Some people are like **s** that
8:13 Some people are like **s** on
8:14 The **s** that were planted among
8:15 The **s** that were planted on
2Co 9:6 The farmer who plants a few **s**

seeing (12)

Gen 33:10 seen your face as if I were **s**
2Sm 14:28 full years without **s** the king.
Psa 17:15 I will be satisfied with **s** you.
Eze 22:28 these things by **s** false visions
Dan 4:13 "I was **s** these visions as I
Hos 9:10 it was like **s** the first figs of the
Mat 15:31 lame walking, and the blind **s**.
Luk 24:37 thought they were **s** a ghost.
Act 2:33 is what you're **s** and hearing.
12:9 He thought he was **s** a vision.
20:38 The thought of not **s** Paul again
Php 2:28 will have the joy of **s** him again

seek (54)

2Sm 4:11 I'll now **s** revenge for his
2Ki 1:3 'Do you **s** advice from
1:6 Do you send messengers to **s**
1:16 You sent messengers to **s**
1:16 Israel whose word you can **s**?
1Ch 16:10 those who **s** the LORD rejoice.
16:11 Always **s** his presence.
2Ch 11:16 who were determined to **s**
20:4 people of Judah gathered to **s**
Ezr 9:12 and never **s** peace or trade with
Job 5:8 "But I would **s** God's help and
Psa 4:2 what is empty and **s** what is
9:10 those who **s** your help.
27:4 This I will **s**: to remain in the
27:8 When you said, "**S** my face,"
27:8 I will **s** your face."
34:10 but those who **s** the LORD's
34:14 **S** peace, and pursue it!
35:4 Let those who **s** my life be put
38:12 Those who **s** my life lay traps
40:14 Let all those who **s** to end my
40:16 Let all who **s** you rejoice and
54:3 Ruthless people **s** my life.
70:2 Let those who **s** my life be
70:4 Let all who **s** you rejoice and
104:21 their prey and **s** their food from
105:3 those who **s** the LORD rejoice.
105:4 Always **s** his presence.
109:10 Let them **s** help far from their
122:9 I will **s** what is good for you.
Pro 18:15 The ears of wise people **s**
28:5 but those who **s** the LORD
29:10 but decent people **s** to
29:26 Many **s** an audience with a
Ecc 7:25 and to **s** out wisdom and the
Isa 1:17 **S** justice. Arrest oppressors.
31:1 They don't **s** the LORD.
51:1 what is right and **s** the LORD.
55:6 **S** the LORD while he may be
Jer 29:13 When you wholeheartedly **s**
50:4 will cry as they go together to **s**
Hos 10:12 It's time to **s** the LORD!
Nah 1:7 those who **s** shelter in him.
Zep 1:6 and those who no longer **s**
3:12 They will **s** refuge in the name
Zec 8:21 LORD for a blessing and to **s**
8:22 powerful nations will come to **s**

Zec 12:9 "On that day I will **s** to destroy
Mal 2:7 people will **s** instruction from
Luk 19:10 the Son of Man has come to **s**
1Co 7:27 Don't **s** a divorce. Are you
1Th 2:6 We didn't **s** praise from people,
Heb 11:6 he rewards those who **s** him.
1Pe 3:11 They must **s** peace and pursue

seeking (6)

Exo 33:7 Anyone who was **s** the LORD's
1Sm 22:23 The one who is **s** my life is
22:23 my life is ⌊also⌋ **s** your life.
2Sm 17:3 Since you will be **s** the life of
1Ki 12:28 After **s** advice, the king made
Ecc 7:28 I am still **s** a reason for things,

seeks (12)

Job 39:29 From there it **s** food,
Psa 14:2 anyone who **s** help from God.
24:6 This is the person who **s** him,
37:32 person and **s** to kill him.
53:2 anyone who **s** help from God.
86:14 of ruthless people **s** my life.
Pro 11:27 Whoever eagerly **s** good
17:9 forgives an offense **s** love,
31:13 "She **s** out wool and linen
Isa 56:11 Each one **s** his own gain.
Jer 5:1 what is right and **s** the truth.
Lam 3:25 to anyone who **s** help from him.

seem (7)

Num 24:13 bad the request might **s** to me.
Job 8:7 the past will **s** small compared
Amo 8:10 I will make that day **s** like a
Hag 2:3 Doesn't it **s** like nothing to you?'
Zec 8:6 It may **s** impossible to the few
8:6 but will it **s** impossible to me?
2Co 13:7 even if we **s** to have failed.

seemed (10)

Gen 29:20 but the years **s** like only a few
34:18 Their proposal **s** good to
Dtr 1:23 It **s** like a good idea to me.
2Sm 13:2 It **s** impossible for him to be
1Ki 20:27 **s** like two newborn goats.
Ecc 2:17 done under the sun **s** wrong
Mat 25:40 how unimportant ⌊they **s**⌋,
25:45 how unimportant ⌊they **s**⌋,
Luk 24:41 because this **s** too good
Rev 9:7 They **s** to have crowns that

seems (11)

Dtr 23:16 in any of your cities that **s** best
Jdg 9:2 'What **s** best to you?
2Sm 18:27 The watchman said, "It **s** to me
Psa 10:5 He always **s** to succeed.
Pro 14:12 There is a way that **s** right to a
16:25 There is a way that **s** right to a
17:8 A bribe **s** ⌊like⌋ a jewel to the
18:17 The first to state his case **s**
Mat 5:19 command that **s** unimportant
Act 17:18 Others said, "He **s** to be
Heb 12:11 It always **s** to cause more pain

seen (221)

Gen 7:1 I have **s** that you alone
26:28 They answered, "We have **s**
29:32 the LORD has **s** my misery;
30:27 from the signs I've **s** that
31:5 He said to them, "I have **s** that
31:12 because I have **s** everything
31:42 God has **s** my misery and hard
32:30 "I have **s** God face to face,
33:10 because I've **s** your face as if I
41:19 I've never **s** such sickly cows
44:28 I haven't **s** him since.
45:13 about everything you have **s**.
46:30 "Now that I've **s** for myself that
Exo 3:7 The LORD said, "I have **s** the
3:9 I have **s** how the Egyptians are
3:16 you and have **s** what has been
4:31 and that he had **s** their misery,
10:5 so that the ground can't be **s**.
13:7 or yeast should be **s** anywhere
19:4 'You have **s** for yourselves
20:22 You've **s** for yourselves that I
Exo 32:9 "I've **s** these people,
33:23 but my face must not be **s**."
34:3 you or even be **s** anywhere
Num 14:14 that they have **s** you with their
Dtr 3:21 "You have **s** with your own
4:9 the things which you have **s**
5:24 Today we've **s** that people can
8:3 your ancestors had **s** before.
8:16 your ancestors had never **s**.
9:13 "I've **s** these people,
29:2 You've **s** with your own eyes
34:12 deeds that were **s** by all
Jos 23:3 You have **s** for yourselves
Jdg 2:7 outlived him and who had **s** all
5:8 Not a weapon was **s** among
6:22 I have **s** the Messenger of the
9:48 and do what you've **s** me do!"
13:22 die because we have **s** God."
14:2 "I've **s** a Philistine woman at
19:30 thing happened or been **s** from
1Sm 9:16 I've **s** my people's ⌊suffering⌋
23:22 Who has **s** him there?
2Sm 7:17 words and everything he had **s**.
17:17 They could not risk being **s**
22:16 the ocean floor could be **s**.
1Ki 6:18 No stone could be **s**.
8:8 long that their ends could be **s**
8:8 but they couldn't be **s** outside.
10:12 nor has any been **s** ⌊there⌋ to
13:12 (His sons had **s** which road the
20:13 Have you **s** this large army?
2Ki 20:5 I've **s** your tears. Now I'm going
23:24 disgusting gods that could be **s**
1Ch 17:15 words and everything he had **s**.
21:20 around and **s** the Messenger.
2Ch 5:9 long that their ends could be **s**
5:9 but they couldn't be **s** outside.
9:11 No one had ever **s** anything
30:7 shocks people, as you have **s**.
Ezr 3:12 who were old enough to have **s**
Est 9:26 letter — both what they had **s**
Job 5:3 I have **s** a stubborn fool take
13:1 "My eye has certainly **s** all of
15:17 I'll relate what I have **s**.
20:7 Those who have **s** him will
27:12 Certainly, you have all **s** it.
28:7 No hawk's eye has ever **s** it.
31:19 If I have **s** anyone die because
33:21 so thin that it can't be **s**.
33:21 Their bones, not **s** before,
36:25 Every person has **s** it.
38:17 or have you **s** the gateways to
38:22 where snow is stored or **s**
42:5 but now I have **s** you with my
Psa 10:14 You have **s** ⌊it⌋; yes, you have
18:15 the ocean floor could be **s**.
31:7 You have **s** my misery.
35:21 Our own eyes have **s** it."
35:22 You have **s** it, O LORD. Do not
37:13 because he has **s** that his time
37:25 but I have never **s** a righteous
37:35 I have **s** a wicked person
48:8 we have now **s** in the city of
68:24 can be **s** by everyone.
77:19 your footprints could not be **s**.
95:9 although they had **s** what I had
98:3 All the ends of the earth have **s**
107:24 have **s** what the LORD can do,
119:96 I have **s** a limit to everything
119:158 I have **s** traitors, and I am filled
Pro 5:21 person's ways are clearly **s** by
25:7 prince whom your eyes have **s**.
Ecc 1:14 I have **s** everything that is done
3:10 I have **s** mortals weighed down
4:3 He hasn't **s** the evil that is done
5:13 tragedy that I have **s** under
5:18 At last I have **s** what is good
6:1 There is a tragedy that I have **s**
6:5 Though it has never **s** the sun
7:15 I have **s** it all in my pointless
8:9 I have **s** all of this,
9:13 I also have **s** this example of
10:5 There is a tragedy that I've **s**
10:7 I have **s** slaves sitting on
Sos 3:3 "Have you **s** the one I love?"
Isa 6:5 I have **s** the king, the LORD of
Isa 38:5 I've **s** your tears. I'm going to
41:5 The coastlands have **s** him
42:20 You have **s** much,
57:8 You've **s** them naked.
57:18 I've **s** their ⌊sinful⌋ ways,
64:4 and no one has **s** any god
66:8 Who has **s** such things?
66:19 heard of my fame or **s** my glory.
Jer 7:11 I have **s** what you are doing,'"
13:26 and your shame will be **s**.
13:27 I have **s** you commit adultery
13:27 I have **s** you act like a
20:18 All I've **s** is trouble and grief.
44:2 You have **s** all the disasters I
Lam 1:8 They've **s** it naked.
1:10 Jerusalem has **s** the nations
2:16 At last we have **s** it!'
Eze 8:17 things that you have **s** here?
13:3 and they have **s** nothing.
13:7 haven't you **s** false visions
Dan 4:11 be **s** everywhere on earth.
4:20 be **s** everywhere on earth.
7:7 animals that I had **s** before.
8:6 that I had **s** standing beside
9:21 whom I had **s** in the first vision,
Hos 6:10 "I have **s** horrible things in the
9:13 I have **s** Ephraim, like Tyre,
Nah 3:6 I will make you a sight to be **s**.
Zec 9:8 because I have **s** it with my
Mat 2:9 The star they had **s** rising led
4:16 who lived in darkness have **s**
9:33 "We have never **s** anything like
17:9 tell anyone what you have **s**.
21:32 But even after you had **s** that,
Mar 2:12 never **s** anything like this."
9:9 to tell anyone what they had **s**.
16:11 alive and that she had **s** him.
16:14 those who had **s** him alive.
Luk 1:22 So they realized that he had **s**
2:20 they had **s** and heard.
2:26 die until he had **s** the Messiah,
2:30 My eyes have **s** your salvation,
5:26 "We've **s** things today we can
7:22 what you have **s** and heard:
8:36 Those who had **s** this told the
9:36 no one about what they had **s**.
10:23 you are to see what you've **s**.
10:24 hear what you've **s** and heard,
19:37 for all the miracles they had **s**.
24:23 They told us that they had **s**
Jon 1:18 No one has ever **s** God.
1:34 I have **s** this and have declared
3:11 and we confirm what we've **s**.
3:21 do for God may be clearly **s**.
3:32 tells what he has **s** and heard.
4:45 They had **s** everything he had
5:37 and you have never **s** his form.
6:36 told you that you have **s** me.
6:46 that no one has **s** the Father.
6:46 is from God has **s** the Father.
8:38 I'm saying is what I have **s**
8:57 How could you have **s**
9:8 **s** him begging asked,
9:37 Jesus told him, "You've **s** him.
11:45 and had **s** what Jesus had
12:17 to life reported what they had **s**.
12:37 Although they had **s** Jesus
12:41 because he had **s** Jesus' glory
14:7 me⌋ and have **s** him ⌊in me⌋."
14:9 The person who has **s** me has
14:9 has seen me has **s** the Father.
15:24 But now they have **s** and hated
20:18 "I have **s** the Lord."
20:25 "We've **s** the Lord."
20:29 believe because you've **s** me.
20:29 who haven't **s** me but believe."
Act 4:20 about what we've **s** and heard."
7:34 I've **s** how my people are
7:44 He used the model he had **s**.
9:12 In a vision he has **s** a man
9:27 the apostles how Saul had **s**
11:13 "He told us that he had **s** an
16:10 soon as Paul had **s** the vision,
21:29 They had **s** Trophimus from
22:15 what you have **s** and heard.
26:16 witness of what you have **s**

Rom 8:24 Who hopes for what can be **s**?
1Co 2:9 Scripture says: "No eye has **s**,
9:1 Haven't I **s** Jesus our Lord?
2Co 4:18 look for things that can be **s**
4:18 but for things that can't be **s**.
4:18 Things that can be **s** are only
4:18 that can't be **s** last forever.
Col 2:18 details of the visions he has **s**.
1Ti 3:16 by the Spirit, was **s** by angels,
6:16 No one has **s** him,
Heb 3:10 although they had **s** what I had
11:3 This means what can be **s**
11:3 something that could not be **s**.
Jas 4:14 You are a mist that is **s** for a
1Pe 1:8 you have never **s** Christ,
1Jn 1:1 We have **s** it. We observed and
1:2 We have **s** it, and we testify
1:3 is the life we have **s** and heard.
3:6 haven't **s** or known Christ.
4:12 No one has ever **s** God.
4:14 We have **s** and testify to the
4:20 whom they have **s**,
4:20 whom they have not **s**.
3Jn 1:11 does evil has never **s** God.
Rev 1:19 write down what you have **s**,
11:19 was **s** inside his temple.
16:20 could no longer be **s**.
22:8 When I had heard and **s** them,

seer (21)

1Sm 9:9 let's go to the **s**," because a
9:9 prophet used to be called a **s**.)
9:11 asked the girls, "Is the **s** here?"
9:19 Samuel replied, "I'm the **s**.
2Sm 15:27 "Aren't you a **s**?" the king asked
24:11 to the prophet Gad, David's **s**.
2Ki 17:13 every kind of prophet and **s**,
1Ch 9:22 David and the **s** Samuel
21:9 LORD spoke to Gad, David's **s**.
25:5 the sons of the king's **s** Heman.
26:28 Everything that Samuel the **s**,
29:29 in the records of the **s** Samuel,
29:29 prophet Nathan, and the **s** Gad.
2Ch 12:15 and the records of the **s** Iddo
16:7 At that time the **s** Hanani came
16:10 Asa was furious at the **s**.
19:2 Jehu, son of the **s** Hanani,
29:25 as David, the king's **s** Gad,
29:30 of David and the **s** Asaph.
35:15 and the king's **s** Jeduthun had
Amo 7:12 "You **s**, run away to Judah!

seer's (2)

1Sm 9:18 tell me where the **s** house is."
2Ch 9:29 and in Iddo the **s** visions about

seers (4)

2Ch 33:18 and the words that the **s** spoke
Isa 29:10 (Your heads are the **s**.)
30:10 They say to the **s**,
Mic 3:7 **S** will be put to shame.

sees (45)

Gen 44:31 and he **s** that the boy isn't
49:15 When he **s** that his resting
Exo 12:23 When he **s** the blood on the top
Lev 13:37 But if he **s** that the scab hasn't
13:53 But if the priest **s** that the area
13:56 If the priest **s** that the area is
Num 12:8 He even **s** the form of the
23:21 He **s** no misfortune for the
Dtr 32:36 when he **s** that their strength
Job 10:4 Do you see as a mortal **s**?
11:11 And when he **s** sin,
34:21 He **s** all his steps.
Psa 33:13 He **s** all of Adam's
58:8 child who never **s** the sun.
64:8 Everyone who **s** them will
97:4 The earth **s** them and trembles.
112:10 The wicked person **s** this and
138:6 he **s** humble people ⌊close
Pro 20:12 the eye that **s** — the LORD
28:11 **s** right through him.
31:18 She **s** that she is making a
Ecc 7:11 to everyone who **s** the sun.
Isa 21:6 Have him report whatever he **s**.
Isa 28:4 As soon as someone **s** them,
59:15 The LORD **s** it, and he's angry
59:16 He **s** that there's no one to help.
61:9 Everyone who **s** them will
Jer 20:12 He **s** their motives and
23:18 in the LORD's inner circle and **s**
Lam 3:50 looks down from heaven and **s**.
Eze 12:27 'The vision that Ezekiel **s**
18:14 The son **s** all the sins that his
33:3 If he **s** the enemy coming to
33:6 "'But if the watchman **s** the
Dan 1:10 If he **s** that you look worse than
Nah 3:7 Everyone who **s** you will run
Mat 6:4 Your Father **s** what you do in
6:6 Your Father **s** what you do in
6:18 Your Father **s** what you do in
Jon 5:19 He can do only what he **s** the
10:12 When he **s** a wolf coming,
12:45 Whoever **s** me sees the one
12:45 Whoever sees me **s** the one
1Co 8:10 with a weak conscience **s** you,
2Co 12:6 more of me than what he **s**

Segub (3)

1Ki 16:34 cost him his youngest son, **S**.
1Ch 2:21 She gave birth to **S**.
2:22 **S** was the father of Jair,

Seir (38)

Gen 14:6 Horites in the hill country of **S**.
32:3 of him to his brother Esau in **S**,
33:14 pace until I come to you in **S**."
33:16 day Esau started back to **S**.
36:8 lived in the mountains of **S**.
36:9 of Edom in the mountains of **S**.
36:20 were the sons of **S** the Horite,
36:21 were the sons of **S** in Edom.
36:30 tribal leaders in the land of **S**.
Num 24:18 will be conquered, and **S**,
Dtr 1:2 Barnea by way of Mount **S**.)
1:44 chasing you from **S** all the way
2:1 around the region of Mount **S**.
2:4 of Esau, who live in **S**.
2:5 of Mount **S** as their property.
2:8 of Esau, who lived in **S**.
2:12 The Horites used to live in **S**,
2:22 of Esau, who lived in **S**.
2:29 of Esau, who live in **S**,
33:2 For his people he rose from **S**
Jos 11:17 which ascends to **S** as far as
12:7 Halak which rises toward **S**.
15:10 border turns west to Mount **S**
24:4 I gave Esau the mountains in **S**
Jdg 5:4 when you went out from **S**,
1Ch 4:42 male descendants to Mount **S**.
2Ch 20:10 and the people of Mount **S**
20:22 and the people of Mount **S** who
20:23 the people from Mount **S**
20:23 had finished off the people of **S**,
25:11 he killed 10,000 men from **S**.
25:14 the gods of the people of **S**,
Isa 21:11 is calling to me from **S**,
Eze 25:8 LORD says: Moab and **S** said,
35:2 "Son of man, turn to Mount **S**,
35:3 says: I'm against you, Mount **S**.
35:7 I will turn Mount **S** into a barren
35:15 become a wasteland, Mount **S**,

Seirah (1)

Jdg 3:26 stone idols and escaped to **S**.

Seir's (1)

1Ch 1:38 **S** sons were Lotan,

seize (9)

1Ki 18:40 "**S** the prophets of Baal.
Est 8:11 and to **s** their goods.
9:10 But the Jews did not **s** any of
9:15 but they did not **s** any of their
9:16 but they did not **s** any of their
Job 30:16 Days of suffering **s** me.
Isa 13:8 Pain and anguish will **s** them.
Dan 11:21 and he will **s** the kingdom
Mic 2:2 fields, so they **s** them.

seized (13)

Gen 21:25 Abimelech's servants had **s**.
Lev 6:2 stolen or **s** from your neighbor,
6:4 Return what you stole or **s**,
1Sm 14:32 So the troops **s** the Philistines'
18:10 an evil spirit from God **s** Saul.
2Sm 4:10 "I once **s** a man who told me
1Ki 18:40 The people **s** them,
Est 3:13 possessions were also to be **s**.
Job 18:20 in the east are **s** with horror.
Psa 48:6 Trembling **s** them like the
55:4 The terrors of death have **s** me.
73:21 my mind was **s** ⌊with envy⌋,
Act 23:27 The Jews had **s** this man and

seizes (4)

Job 21:6 and shuddering **s** my body.
30:18 He **s** me by the collar of my
Isa 33:14 Trembling **s** the ungodly.
2Co 11:20 your wealth, **s** your property,

seizing (1)

Mat 11:12 forceful people have been **s** it.

seizure (1)

Mar 9:18 the spirit brings on a **s**,

seizures (2)

Job 34:20 People have **s** and pass away.
Mat 17:15 He suffers from **s**. Often he falls

Sela (3)

2Ki 14:7 and took the city of **S** in battle.
Isa 16:1 Send lambs from **S** through the
42:11 Let those who live in **S** sing for

Selah (74)

Jdg 1:36 Pass — from **S** northward.
Psa 3:2 he won't be victorious." **S**
3:4 me from his holy mountain. **S**
3:8 rest on your people. **S**
4:2 and seek what is a lie? **S**
4:4 your bed and remain quiet. **S**
7:5 lay my honor in the dust. **S**
9:16 of his own hands. Higgaion **S**
9:20 that they are ⌊only⌋ mortal. **S**
20:3 favor on your burnt offerings. **S**
21:2 the prayer from his lips. **S**
24:6 face of the God of Jacob. **S**
24:10 Armies is the king of glory! **S**
32:4 in the summer heat. **S**
32:5 you forgave all my sins. **S**
32:7 joyous songs of salvation. **S**
39:5 like a whisper in the wind. **S**
39:11 like a whisper in the wind. **S**
44:8 give thanks to you forever. **S**
46:3 at the surging waves. **S**
46:7 of Jacob is our stronghold. **S**
46:11 of Jacob is our stronghold. **S**
47:4 whom he loved. **S**
48:8 Zion stand firm forever. **S**
49:13 delighted by what they say: **S**
49:15 because he will take me. **S**
50:6 because God is the judge. **S**
52:3 lying to speaking the truth. **S**
52:5 of this world of the living. **S**
54:3 do not think about God. **S**
55:7 I would stay in the desert. **S**
55:19 **S** They never change.
57:3 **S** God sends his mercy and
57:6 but then they fell into it. **S**
59:5 Have no pity on any traitors. **S**
59:13 to the ends of the earth. **S**
60:4 by bows ⌊and arrows⌋. **S**
61:4 protection of your wings. **S**
62:4 in their hearts they curse. **S**
62:8 God is our refuge. **S**
66:4 music to praise your name." **S**
66:7 not be able to oppose him. **S**
66:15 I will offer cattle and goats. **S**
67:1 May he smile on us. **S**
67:4 the nations on the earth. **S**
68:7 marched through the desert, **S**
68:19 God is our salvation. **S**
68:32 music to praise the Lord. **S**

Psa 75:3 as solid as rock. S
76:3 and weapons of war. S
76:9 oppressed person on earth. S
77:3 hope as I think about him. S
77:9 because of his anger? S
77:15 of Jacob and Joseph. S
81:7 at the oasis of Meribah. S
82:2 side with wicked people?" S
83:8 the descendants of Lot. S
84:4 are always praising you. S
84:8 O God of Jacob. S
85:2 You pardoned all their sins. S
87:3 O city of God! S
87:6 that it was born there." S
88:7 your waves pound on me. S
88:10 rise and give thanks to you? S
89:4 every generation."' S
89:45 covered him with shame. S
89:48 the power of the grave? S
140:3 of poisonous snakes. S
140:5 traps for me along the road. S
140:8 they will become arrogant. S
143:6 my soul thirsts for you. S
Hab 3:3 S His splendor covers the
3:9 S You split the land with rivers.
3:13 him bare from head to toe. S

select (4)

Num 35:11 s certain cities to be places of
35:13 There will be six cities you s
2Sm 10:9 he took the s troops of Israel
1Ch 19:10 he took the s troops of Israel

selected (11)

Jos 4:4 whom he had s (one from each
7:15 The man who is s,
7:16 The tribe of Judah was s.
7:17 and the family of Zerah was s.
7:17 man by man, and Zabdi was s.
7:18 and Achan was s.
16:9 the cities and their villages s
1Sm 16:1 Bethlehem because I've s one
1Ch 16:41 of the Levites who had been s,
Ezr 8:24 Then I s 12 leaders from the
Eze 24:5 s from the best sheep.

selects (3)

Jos 7:14 The tribe the LORD s will
7:14 Then the family the LORD s
7:14 and the household the LORD s

Seled (2)

1Ch 2:30 sons were S and Appaim,
2:30 but S died without children.

Seleucia (1)

Act 13:4 they went to the city of S and

self-centered (2)

Jas 3:14 and filled with s ambition,
3:15 It is s and demonic.

self-confidence (1)

Neh 6:16 were afraid and lost their s.

self-control (9)

Pro 25:28 (so) is a person who lacks s.
Act 24:25 s, and the coming judgment,
1Co 7:5 use your lack of s to tempt you.
Gal 5:23 gentleness, and s.
2Ti 3:3 will be slanderous, lack s,
Tit 1:8 be fair and moral, and have s.
1Pe 4:7 Therefore, practice s,
2Pe 1:6 to knowledge add s;
1:6 to s add endurance;

self-controlled (1)

Tit 2:12 desires so that we can live s,

self-destructive (1)

Ecc 10:12 but a fool's lips are s.

self-imposed (1)

Col 2:23 wisdom with their s worship,

selfish (8)

Psa 10:3 boasts about his s desires.
Rom 2:8 fury on those who, in s pride,
2Co 12:20 s ambition, slander, gossip,
Gal 5:20 s ambition, conflict, factions,
Php 1:17 about Christ out of s ambition
2:3 Don't act out of s ambition or be
2Ti 3:2 People will be s and love
Jas 4:1 Aren't they caused by the s

self-reliant (1)

Job 24:23 let them feel confident and s,

sell (46)

Gen 23:9 He should s it to me for its full
25:31 s me your rights as firstborn."
31:15 Not only did he s us,
37:27 Let's s him to the Ishmaelites.
47:22 why they didn't s their land.
Exo 21:8 He has no right to s her to
21:35 they must s the live bull and
Lev 25:14 If you s anything to your
25:15 Your neighbor must s it to you
25:47 The poor Israelite may s
Dtr 14:21 You may also s it to foreigners
21:14 You must never s her or
28:68 There you will try to s
1Ki 21:6 'S me your vineyard.
21:15 from Jezreel refused to s you.
2Ki 4:7 He said, "S the oil,
7:1 24 cups of the best flour will s
7:1 And 48 cups of barley will s for
7:18 cups of barley will s
7:18 cups of the best flour will s
1Ch 21:22 S it to me for the full price.
Neh 10:31 bring merchandise or grain to s
13:20 and those who s all kinds
Job 6:27 you buy and s your friend?
Psa 44:12 You s your people for almost
Pro 23:23 Buy truth (and do not s it),
Isa 50:1 To which of my creditors did I s
Eze 27:27 and the goods you s,
30:12 will dry up the Nile River and s
48:14 They must not s any of it or
Joe 3:8 I will s your sons and
3:8 They will s them to the people
Amo 2:6 The people of Israel s the
8:5 so that we can s more grain?
8:5 so that we can s more wheat?
8:6 We can s the husks mixed in
Nah 3:4 She used to s nations her
Zec 11:5 Those who s them will say,
Mat 19:21 to be perfect, s what you own.
25:9 someone to s you some oil.'
Mar 10:21 S everything you have.
Luk 12:33 "S your material possessions,
18:22 S everything you have.
22:36 have a sword should s his coat
Act 5:8 did you s the land for that
Rev 13:17 no one may buy or s unless

sellers (3)

Isa 24:2 and masters, buyers and s,
Eze 7:12 and s will not mourn,
7:13 S will not live long enough to

selling (15)

Gen 42:6 Joseph was s grain to
Lev 25:16 for it because he is s you only
25:29 for one year after s it he has the
Dtr 18:8 gets from s his family's goods.
Rut 4:3 is s the field that belonged to
Neh 5:8 Now you are s your Jewish
13:15 I warned them about s food on
13:16 They were s them on the day
Mat 21:12 who was buying and s there.
Mar 11:15 who were buying and s there.
Luk 17:28 eating, drinking, buying and s,
19:45 those who were s things there.
Jon 2:14 found those who were s cattle,
2Co 2:17 At least we don't go around s
Rev 18:15 rich by s these things will

sells (7)

Exo 21:7 "Whenever a man s his
22:1 a sheep and butchers it or s it,
Lev 25:25 becomes poor and s some
25:29 "If anyone s a home in a
25:39 becomes poor and s himself
Pro 11:26 the head of the one who s it.
31:24 linen garments and s them

Semachiah (1)

1Ch 26:7 as well as Elihu and S.

Semein (1)

Luk 3:26 son of S, son of Josech,

semen (7)

Gen 38:9 he wasted his s on the ground
Lev 15:16 "If a man has an emission of s,
15:17 clothes or any leather with s
15:18 and has an emission of s,
15:32 emission of s that makes him
22:4 who has an emission of s
Eze 23:20 and whose s was like that

Senaah (2)

Ezr 2:35 of S: 3,630
Neh 7:38 of S: 3,930

send (269)

Gen 6:17 I'm about to s a flood on the
7:4 In seven days I will s rain to
24:7 "God will s his angel ahead of
24:40 The LORD will s his angel
27:45 I'll s for you and get you back.
33:8 "Why did you s this whole
37:13 I'm going to s you to them."
38:17 "I'll s you a young goat from the
38:17 as a deposit until you s it."
38:23 I did s her this young goat,
42:4 Jacob wouldn't s Joseph's
43:8 "S the boy along with me.
43:14 that he will s your other brother
Exo 4:13 Lord, s someone else."
5:22 Why did you s me?
8:21 I will s swarms of flies on you,
9:14 Now I will s plagues that will
9:18 at this time tomorrow I will s
9:19 Now, s (servants) to bring
16:4 "I'm going to s you food from
23:20 "I'm going to s a Messenger in
23:27 "I will s my terror ahead of you
33:2 I will s a Messenger ahead of
Lev 26:22 I will s wild animals among
26:25 I will s plagues on you and you
Num 5:2 "Command the Israelites to s
5:3 S all of these unclean men and
13:2 "S men to explore Canaan,
13:2 S one leader from each of their
31:4 S 1,000 men from each of the
Dtr 1:22 "Let's s men ahead of us to
11:14 I will s rain on your land at the
15:13 s them away empty-handed.
18:15 The LORD your God will s you
18:18 So I will s them a prophet,
19:12 the leaders of your city must s
28:12 He will s rain on your land at
28:20 The LORD will s you curses,
28:21 The LORD will s one plague
28:24 The LORD will s dust storms
28:37 the LORD will s you will make
28:48 the LORD will s against you.
32:24 I will s vicious animals against
33:13 the best gift heaven can s,
Jos 1:16 us and go wherever you s us.
7:3 "You don't need to s all the
18:4 and I will s them out.
Jdg 2:16 Then the LORD would s
1Sm 5:11 "S the ark of the God of Israel
6:3 don't s it away empty,
6:6 didn't they s the Israelites on
6:8 S the cart on its way,
9:16 this time tomorrow I will s you
9:26 time for me to s you away."
11:3 can s messengers throughout
12:17 and he'll s thunder and rain.
16:11 "S someone to get him.
16:19 "S me your son David,
17:10 S out a man so that we can

1Sm 20:12 then I will **s** someone to tell
20:13 tell you and **s** you away safely,
20:21 Then I will **s** out a boy and say,
20:31 **s** some men to bring him to me.
24:19 does he **s** him away
29:4 "**S** the man back,"
2Sm 7:12 I will **s** one of your
11:6 "**S** me Uriah the Hittite."
11:12 and tomorrow I'll **s** you back."
14:29 sent for Joab in order to **s** him
14:32 here because I wanted to **s** you
15:36 **S** them to report to me anything
17:16 Now **s** messengers quickly to
18:3 better for you to be ready to **s**
19:31 to the Jordan River to **s** him
1Ki 8:36 Then **s** rain on the land,
8:44 (wherever you may **s** them)
20:6 I'm going to **s** my servants
22:26 "**S** Micaiah back to Amon,
2Ki 1:6 Do you **s** messengers to seek
2:16 "Don't **s** them ⌊to look⌋."
2:17 disciples kept urging him ⌊to **s**
2:17 So he said, "**S** them.
4:22 "Please **s** me one of the
5:5 I will also **s** a letter to the king
6:9 So the man of God would **s** a
6:10 Then the king of Israel would **s**
6:13 Then I will **s** men to capture
7:13 Let's **s** them to take a look."
8:1 The LORD has decided to **s** a
9:17 **s** him to meet them,
18:27 "Did my master **s** me to tell
18:27 Didn't he **s** me to the men
1Ch 13:2 we will **s** ⌊an invitation⌋ to the
17:11 I will **s** one of your
2Ch 2:7 "**S** me a man who has the skill
2:8 **S** me cedar, cypress,
2:15 Majesty may now **s** the wheat,
2:16 make rafts out of it and **s** them
6:27 Then **s** rain on the land,
6:34 (wherever you may **s** them)
7:13 or **s** an epidemic among my
18:25 "**S** Micaiah back to Amon,
30:5 So they decided to **s** an
Ezr 5:17 Then please **s** us Your
Neh 8:10 and **s** portions to those who
8:12 eat and drink and to **s** portions.
8:15 and **s** this message throughout
Est 9:19 They also **s** gifts of food to one
Job 1:4 They would **s** someone to
1:5 Job would **s** for them in order to
14:20 appearance and **s** him away.
21:11 They **s** their little children out
22:9 You **s** widows away
38:35 Can you **s** lightning flashes so
Psa 20:2 He will **s** you help from his
43:3 **S** your light and your truth.
104:30 You **s** out your Spirit,
Pro 10:26 person to those who **s** him ⌊on
22:21 report to those who **s** you?
25:13 messenger to those who **s** him:
26:6 Whoever uses a fool to **s** a
Isa 6:8 Lord, saying, "Whom will I **s**?
6:8 "Here I am. **S** me!"
6:12 The LORD will **s** his people far
10:6 I **s** them against a godless
10:16 LORD of Armies will **s**
16:1 **S** lambs to the ruler of the land.
16:1 **S** lambs from Sela through the
19:20 he will **s** a savior and defender
36:12 "Did my master **s** me to tell
36:12 Didn't he **s** me to the men
42:19 or deaf like the messenger I **s**?
43:14 For your sake I will **s** ⌊an
55:11 achieve whatever I **s** it to do."
66:19 a sign among them and **s** some
Jer 1:7 You will go wherever I **s** you.
2:10 **S** ⌊someone⌋ to Kedar,
8:17 "I am going to **s** snakes among
9:16 I will **s** armies after them until
9:17 **S** for those who are the most
14:3 Important people **s** their
14:15 "I didn't **s** these prophets.
15:1 **S** them away from me,
15:3 "I will **s** swords to kill,
15:8 At noontime I will **s** a destroyer
Jer 16:16 "I'm going to **s** for many
16:16 I will **s** for many hunters,
17:8 It will **s** its roots down to a
18:22 **s** troops against them,
22:7 I will **s** people to destroy you.
23:21 I didn't **s** these prophets,
23:32 I didn't **s** them or command
24:10 I will **s** wars, famines,
25:9 so I'm going to **s** for all the
25:9 I will also **s** for my servant
25:16 wars that I'm going to **s** them.
25:27 wars that I'm going to **s** you.'
27:3 Then **s** messages to the kings
27:15 I didn't **s** them, declares the
29:9 I didn't **s** them, declares the
29:17 I'm going to **s** them wars,
29:31 "**S** this message to all the
29:31 to you, but I didn't **s** him.
29:32 that I'm going to **s** my people,
38:26 'I asked the king not to **s** me
43:2 The LORD our God didn't **s**
43:10 I'm going to **s** for my servant
48:12 "when I will **s** people to pour
49:37 I'll **s** armies after them until I
51:2 I will **s** people to winnow
Eze 3:6 If I **s** you to those nations,
5:17 I will **s** famines and wild
5:17 I will **s** plagues, violence,
7:3 I will **s** my anger against you.
7:24 So I will **s** the most evil nation,
14:13 its food supply, **s** a famine to it,
14:15 "Suppose I **s** wild animals
14:19 "Suppose I **s** a plague into that
14:21 I will surely **s** four terrible
14:21 I will **s** wars, famines,
28:23 I will **s** a plague against you
30:9 On that day I will **s**
32:18 **S** them down below the earth
34:26 I will **s** rain at the right time.
38:22 I will **s** rainstorms,
39:6 I will **s** fire on Magog and on
Hos 8:14 I will **s** a fire on their cities and
Joe 2:19 "I am going to **s** grain,
3:6 That way you could **s** them far
Amo 1:4 I will **s** a fire on the house of
1:7 I will **s** a fire on the walls of
1:10 I will **s** a fire on the walls of
1:12 I will **s** a fire on Teman and
2:2 I will **s** a fire on Moab and burn
2:5 I will **s** a fire on Judah and burn
5:27 I will **s** you into exile beyond
8:11 when I will **s** a famine
Nah 2:13 "I will **s** your chariots up in
Hab 1:6 am going to **s** the Babylonians,
Zec 5:4 I will **s** out a curse,
Mal 2:2 "then I'll **s** a curse on you,
3:1 "I'm going to **s** my messenger,
4:5 "I'm going to **s** you the prophet
Mat 8:31 **s** us into that herd of pigs."
9:38 gives this harvest to **s** workers
13:41 Son of Man will **s** his angels.
14:15 **S** the crowds to the villages to
15:23 and urged him, "**S** her away.
15:32 I don't want to **s** them away
21:3 person will **s** them at once."
24:31 He will **s** out his angels with a
26:53 Father to **s** more than twelve
Mar 5:10 He begged Jesus not to **s** them
5:12 "**S** us into the pigs!
6:36 **S** the people to the closest
8:3 If I **s** them home before they've
11:3 That person will **s** it here at
12:6 "He had one more person to **s**.
13:27 He will **s** out his angels,
Luk 2:26 whom the Lord would **s**.
4:26 But God didn't **s** Elijah to
9:12 They said to him, "**S** the crowd
10:2 gives this harvest to **s** workers
11:49 'I will **s** them prophets and
14:32 If he can't, he'll **s** ambassadors
16:24 **S** Lazarus to dip the tip of his
16:27 to **s** Lazarus back to my
20:13 I'll **s** my son, whom I love.
20:20 to **s** out some spies.
Jon 13:16 to the people who **s** them.
14:26 whom the Father will **s** in my
Jon 15:26 "The helper whom I will **s** to
16:7 But if I go, I will **s** him to you.
Act 3:20 He will **s** you Jesus,
3:22 'The Lord your God will **s** you
7:37 'God will **s** you a prophet,
7:43 I will **s** you into exile beyond
10:5 **S** messengers now to the city
10:32 So **s** messengers to Joppa,
11:13 '**S** messengers to Joppa,
15:22 choose some of their men to **s**
15:25 should choose men and **s** them
22:21 I'll **s** you on a mission.
24:25 I'll **s** for you again."
24:26 For that reason, Felix would **s**
25:21 in prison until I could **s** him
25:25 have decided to **s** him to Rome.
25:27 I find it ridiculous to **s** a
Rom 16:22 **s** you Christian greetings.
1Co 1:17 Christ didn't **s** me to baptize.
16:3 You can **s** your gift to
16:19 house **s** their warmest Christian
2Co 9:2 ⌊to **s** their collection⌋ since
Php 2:19 will allow me to **s** Timothy
2:23 I hope to **s** him as soon as I
2:25 I feel that I must **s**
2:28 So I'm especially eager to **s**
4:21 are with me **s** greetings to you.
2Th 2:11 That's why God will **s** them a
3:17 In every letter that I **s**,
2Ti 4:21 and sisters **s** you greetings.
Tit 3:12 When I **s** Artemas or Tychicus
Phm 1:24 and Luke **s** you greetings.
Heb 1:6 When God was about to **s** his
1Pe 5:13 my son Mark **s** you greetings.
3Jn 1:10 believers ⌊we **s**⌋ as guests.
1:15 Your friends here **s** you their
Rev 1:11 and **s** it to the seven churches:
11:10 They will celebrate and **s** gifts

sending (53)

Gen 32:20 him this gift that I'm **s** ahead
Exo 3:10 I am **s** you to Pharaoh so that
33:12 know whom you're **s** with me.
Jos 7:3 Don't tire the troops out by **s** all
Jdg 6:14 strength you have. I am **s** you."
1Sm 16:1 I'm **s** you to Jesse in
19:17 "Why did you betray me by **s**
21:2 about this mission I'm **s** you
2Sm 13:16 She said to him, "No, **s** me
1Ki 15:19 I'm **s** you a present of silver
2Ki 2:2 because the LORD is **s** me
2:4 because the LORD is **s** me
2:6 because the LORD is **s** me
5:6 It read, "I'm **s** my officer
1Ch 21:26 him by ⌊**s**⌋ fire from heaven
2Ch 2:11 responded to Solomon by **s**
2:13 And now, I'm **s** a man with skill
16:3 I'm **s** you silver and gold.
Ezr 4:14 So we are **s** this letter to inform
7:14 and my seven advisers are **s**
Neh 6:19 Tobiah kept **s** letters to
Est 9:22 and celebrating and for **s** gifts
Isa 27:8 punished Israel by **s** it away.
Jer 25:15 to whom I'm **s** you drink from
42:6 our God to whom we are **s** you,
Eze 2:3 I am **s** you to the people of
2:4 I am **s** you to these defiant and
3:5 I am not **s** you to people whose
3:5 I am **s** you to Israel.
3:6 I am not **s** you to nations
17:15 Babylon by **s** his messengers
Hos 6:5 ⌊you⌋ down by **s** the prophets.
Mat 10:16 "I'm **s** you out like sheep
11:10 'I'm **s** my messenger ahead of
14:23 After **s** the people away,
23:34 I'm **s** you prophets,
Mar 1:2 "I am **s** my messenger ahead
Luk 7:27 'I am **s** my messenger ahead of
10:3 I'm **s** you out like lambs among
24:49 "I'm **s** you what my Father
Jon 20:21 has sent me, so I am **s** you."
Act 7:34 So now I'm **s** you to Egypt.'
26:17 people to whom I am **s** you.
Eph 6:21 I'm **s** Tychicus to you.
6:22 That's why I'm **s** him to you so
Col 4:7 I'm **s** Tychicus to you.

Col 4:8 I'm **s** him to you so that you
4:9 I'm **s** Onesimus with him.
2Ti 4:12 I'm **s** Tychicus to the city of
Phm 1:12 I am **s** him back to you.
1:12 This is like **s** you a part of
1Pe 5:12 this short letter to you and I'm **s**
1Jn 4:9 us his love by **s** his only Son

sends (18)

Dtr 7:10 But he **s** destruction to pay
1Ki 17:14 Until the LORD **s** rain on the
2Ki 5:7 This man **s** someone to me so
Job 5:10 He gives rain to the earth and **s**
Psa 57:3 He **s** his help from heaven and
57:3 Selah God **s** his mercy and his
147:15 He is the one who **s** his
147:16 He is the one who **s** snow like
147:18 He **s** out his word and melts
Isa 18:2 It **s** messengers by sea in
Jer 5:24 He **s** rain at the right time,
51:16 He **s** lightning with the rain.
Amo 5:3 The city that **s** 1,000 troops off
5:3 The one that **s** 100 troops off to
Act 23:26 Claudius Lysias **s** greetings to
Rom 10:15 Good News if no one **s** them?
Col 4:10 a prisoner like me, **s** greetings.
Tit 3:15 with me **s** you greetings.

Seneh (1)

1Sm 14:4 the name of the other was **S**.

senior (1)

Gen 24:2 So Abraham said to the **s**

Senir (3)

Dtr 3:9 and the Amorites call it **S**.)
1Ch 5:23 Hermon, **S**, and Mount Hermon
Sos 4:8 peaks in **S** and Hermon,

Sennacherib (18)

2Ki 18:13 King **S** of Assyria attacked all
19:9 Now, **S** heard that King
19:9 **S** sent messengers to
19:16 Listen to the message that **S**
19:20 to me about King **S** of Assyria.
19:36 Then King **S** of Assyria left.
2Ch 32:1 King **S** of Assyria came to
32:2 When Hezekiah saw that **S**
32:9 After this, while King **S** of
32:10 "This is what King **S** of
32:17 **S** wrote letters cursing the
32:21 **S** returned to his own country.
32:22 living in Jerusalem from King **S**
Isa 36:1 King **S** of Assyria attacked all
37:9 Now, **S** heard that King
37:17 the entire message that **S** sent
37:21 to me about King **S** of Assyria.
37:37 Then King **S** of Assyria left.

Sennacherib's (2)

2Ch 32:16 **S** officers said more against
32:18 **S** officers shouted loudly in the

sense (27)

Dtr 32:28 people have lost their good **s**.
Job 12:24 He takes away the common **s**
Psa 111:10 Good **s** is shown by everyone
Pro 6:32 with a woman has no **s**.
7:7 without much **s** among youths.
9:4 She says to a person without **s**,
9:16 She says to a person without **s**,
10:13 is for the back of one without **s**.
10:21 die because they have no **s**.
11:12 despises a neighbor has no **s**,
12:11 unrealistic dreams has no **s**.
13:15 Good **s** brings favor,
15:5 a warning shows good **s**.
15:21 fun to the one without much **s**,
17:18 A person without good **s**
19:8 who gains **s** loves himself.
19:11 A person with good **s** is patient,
24:30 to a person without **s**.
Ecc 2:2 "Laughter doesn't make any **s**.
3:11 He has put a **s** of eternity in
10:3 he has no **s** and shows
Mar 9:12 But in what **s** was it written
Luk 24:11 story didn't make any **s**,
Rom 1:31 don't have any **s**, don't keep
1Co 1:23 Jewish people and makes no **s**
Eph 4:19 no longer have any **s** of shame,
Heb 11:19 from the dead in a figurative **s**.

senseless (2)

Jer 5:21 you stupid and **s** people!
Hos 7:11 you are like a silly, **s** dove.

senses (6)

1Ki 8:47 If they come to their **s**,
2Ch 6:37 If they come to their **s**,
Hos 4:11 have robbed them of their **s**.
Luk 15:17 "Finally, he came to his **s**.
Act 12:11 When Peter came to his **s**,
2Ti 2:26 they might come back to their **s**

sensible (12)

1Sm 25:3 She was **s** and beautiful,
Pro 8:5 people, learn how to be **s**.
12:16 but a **s** person hides the insult.
12:23 A **s** person (discreetly) hides
13:16 Any **s** person acts with
14:8 The wisdom of a **s** person
14:15 but a **s** person watches his
14:18 but **s** people are crowned with
19:14 but a **s** wife comes from the
22:3 **S** people foresee trouble and
26:16 people who give a **s** answer.
27:12 **S** people foresee trouble and

sensitive (3)

Dtr 28:54 Even the most tender and **s**
28:56 The most tender and **s** woman
28:56 woman among you — so **s**

sent (668)

Gen 2:5 the LORD God hadn't **s** rain
3:23 So the LORD God **s** the man
3:24 After he **s** the man out,
8:7 and **s** out a raven. It kept flying
8:8 Next, he **s** out a dove to see if
8:10 seven more days and again **s**
8:12 seven more days and **s** out
12:20 They **s** Abram away with his
19:13 so loud that the LORD has **s**
20:2 So King Abimelech of Gerar **s**
21:14 He also gave her the boy and **s**
25:6 He **s** them away from his son
26:27 since you hate me and **s** me
26:31 Then Isaac **s** them on their
27:42 she **s** for her younger son
28:5 Isaac **s** Jacob to Paddan Aram.
28:6 Jacob and had **s** him away
31:4 So Jacob **s** a message to
31:27 I would have **s** you on your
31:42 you would have **s** me away
32:3 Jacob **s** messengers ahead of
32:5 I've **s** (these messengers) to
32:18 This is a gift **s** to you.
32:21 So Jacob **s** the gift ahead of
32:23 After he **s** them across the
32:23 he **s** everything else across.
37:14 Then he **s** Joseph away from
38:20 Judah **s** his friend Hirah to
38:25 As she was brought out, she **s**
41:8 he was so upset that he **s**
41:14 Then Pharaoh **s** for Joseph,
42:16 One of you must be **s** to get
44:3 At dawn the men were **s** on
45:5 God **s** me ahead of you to save
45:7 God **s** me ahead of you to
45:8 It wasn't you who **s** me here,
45:23 He **s** his father ten male
45:24 So Joseph **s** his brothers on
45:27 saw the wagons Joseph had **s**
46:5 in the wagons Pharaoh had **s**
46:28 Israel **s** Judah ahead of him to
50:16 They **s** a messenger to Joseph
Exo 2:5 plants and **s** her slave girl
3:12 will be the proof that I **s** you:
3:13 of your ancestors has **s** me
3:14 'I Am has **s** me to you.'"
3:15 and Jacob, has **s** me to you.
4:28 everything the LORD had **s** him
Exo 7:9 to prove that God has **s** you,'
7:11 Then Pharaoh **s** for his wise
7:16 God of the Hebrews **s** me
8:8 Pharaoh **s** for Moses and Aaron
9:23 the LORD **s** thunder and hail,
9:27 Then Pharaoh **s** for Moses and
15:7 You **s** out your burning anger.
18:2 When Moses had **s** away his
18:6 Jethro had **s** word to Moses,
18:27 Moses **s** his father-in-law on
24:5 Then he **s** young Israelite men,
Lev 10:6 cry over the fire the LORD **s**,
Num 5:4 They **s** these unclean people
11:31 The LORD **s** a wind from the
13:3 Moses **s** these men from the
13:16 the names of the men Moses **s**
13:17 When Moses **s** them to explore
13:27 to the land where you **s** us.
14:36 So the men Moses **s** to explore
16:12 Then Moses **s** for Dathan and
16:28 will know that the LORD **s** me
16:29 then the LORD hasn't **s** me.
20:14 Moses **s** messengers from
20:16 he heard us, **s** a messenger,
21:6 So the LORD **s** poisonous
21:21 Then Israel **s** messengers to
21:32 After Moses **s** spies to Jazer,
22:5 He **s** messengers to summon
22:10 **s** them with this message:
22:15 Balak **s** a larger group of more
22:40 and **s** some of the meat to
24:12 "I told the messengers you **s**
31:6 Then Moses **s** them off to war,
32:8 did when I **s** them from Kadesh
Dtr 2:26 I **s** messengers to King Sihon
9:23 When the LORD **s** you from
29:22 the diseases the LORD **s** here.
34:11 He was the one the LORD **s** to
Jos 2:1 secretly **s** out two men as
2:3 So the king of Jericho **s**
6:17 she hid the messengers we **s**.
6:25 the messengers Joshua had **s**
7:2 Joshua **s** men from Jericho to
7:4 three thousand men were **s**.
7:22 Joshua **s** messengers,
8:3 best soldiers and **s** them out at
8:9 So Joshua **s** them out,
9:22 Joshua **s** for the people of
10:3 of Jerusalem **s** (this message)
10:6 The men of Gibeon **s** this
11:1 So he **s** messengers to King
11:2 He also **s** messengers to the
14:7 Moses **s** me from Kadesh
14:11 I was when Moses **s** me out.
22:6 He **s** them on their way,
22:7 When Joshua **s** them home,
22:13 The Israelites **s** Phinehas,
24:5 "Then I **s** Moses and Aaron,
24:12 I **s** hornets ahead of you to
24:28 Then Joshua **s** the people
Jdg 1:23 They **s** men to spy on Bethel.
2:6 Now, Joshua **s** the people of
3:9 The LORD **s** a savior to rescue
3:15 The LORD **s** a savior to rescue
3:15 The people **s** him with their tax
3:18 he **s** back the men who had
5:15 They were also with Barak, **s**
6:8 the LORD **s** a prophet to them.
6:35 He also **s** messengers
7:8 So Gideon **s** the other men of
7:24 Gideon also **s** messengers to
9:23 Then God **s** an evil spirit to
9:31 He secretly **s** messengers to
11:12 Jephthah **s** messengers to the
11:14 Jephthah again **s** messengers
11:17 The people of Israel **s**
11:17 They also **s** messengers to the
11:19 "Then the people of Israel **s**
11:28 the message Jephthah **s** him.
11:38 and he **s** her off for two months.
13:8 let the man of God you **s** come
16:18 she **s** a message to the
18:2 So all the families of Dan **s** out
18:2 They were **s** to spy throughout
19:29 Then he **s** the pieces
20:6 Then I **s** the pieces throughout

Jdg 20:12 The tribes of Israel s men
21:10 congregation s 12,000 soldiers.
21:13 Then the whole congregation s
Rut 1:13 the LORD has s me so much
1Sm 4:4 The troops s some men who
5:10 So the people of Gath s the ark
6:17 which the Philistines s as
6:21 They s messengers to the
10:25 Then Samuel s the people
11:7 and s them by messengers
12:8 who s Moses and Aaron to
12:11 "Then the LORD s Jerubbaal,
12:18 That day the LORD s thunder
13:2 But the rest of the people he s
14:15 there was a panic s from God.
15:1 told Saul, "The LORD s me
15:18 And the LORD s you on a
15:20 "I went where the LORD s me,
16:12 So Jesse s for him.
16:19 Saul s messengers to Jesse to
16:20 and a young goat and s them
16:22 Saul s ⌊this message⌋ to
17:31 who then s for him.
18:5 wherever Saul s him.
19:11 Saul s messengers to watch
19:14 When Saul s messengers to
19:15 Then Saul s the messengers
19:20 Saul s messengers to get
19:21 he s other messengers,
19:21 Saul even s a third group of
20:22 the LORD has s you away.
22:11 Then the king s for the priest
25:5 So David s ten young men and
25:14 "David s messengers from the
25:25 didn't see the young men you s.
25:32 who s you today to meet me.
25:39 Then David s men ⌊on his
25:40 "David has s us to you so that
26:4 David s spies to confirm that
30:26 he s part of the loot to his
31:9 Then they s men throughout
2Sm 2:5 So David s messengers to the
3:12 Then Abner s messengers to
3:14 Then David s messengers to
3:15 So Ishbosheth s men to take
3:17 Meanwhile, Abner s the
3:26 Joab s messengers after Abner.
5:11 Then King Hiram of Tyre s
8:10 he s his son Joram to greet
9:5 So King David s men to get
10:2 "So David s his servants to
10:3 your father because he s men
10:3 Hasn't David s his men to
10:4 waist down, and s them away.
10:5 he s ⌊someone⌋ to meet them
10:7 he s Joab and all the elite
10:16 Hadadezer s ⌊messengers⌋ to
11:1 David s Joab, his mercenaries,
11:3 David s someone to ask about
11:4 So David s messengers and
11:5 So she s someone to tell David
11:6 Then David s a messenger to
11:6 So Joab s Uriah to David.
11:8 and the king s a present to him.
11:14 to Joab and s it with Uriah.
11:18 Then Joab s ⌊a messenger⌋ to
11:27 David s for her and brought her
12:1 So the LORD s Nathan to
12:25 and s a message through the
12:27 So he s messengers to tell
13:7 David s for Tamar at the
14:2 So Joab s ⌊someone⌋ to
14:29 So Absalom s for Joab in order
14:29 Absalom s for him a second
14:32 Absalom answered Joab, "I s
15:10 But Absalom s his loyal
15:12 he s for Ahithophel,
18:29 when Joab s me away,
19:11 So King David s ⌊this
19:14 So they s the king this
24:13 should give the one who s me."
24:15 So the LORD s a plague
1Ki 1:44 The king has s the priest
1:53 King Solomon s men to take
2:29 Solomon s Benaiah,
5:1 King Hiram of Tyre s his
1Ki 5:2 Solomon s word to Hiram,
5:8 Hiram s men to Solomon to
5:8 the message you s me.
5:14 He s a shift of 10,000 men to
9:14 Hiram had s the king 9,000
9:27 Hiram s his own servants
12:3 ⌊Israel⌋ s for Jeroboam and
12:18 Then King Rehoboam s
12:20 they s men to invite him to the
15:18 King Asa s them to Damascus
15:20 He s his generals and their
18:3 Ahab s for Obadiah,
18:20 Ahab s word to all the
19:2 Then Jezebel s a messenger
20:2 He s messengers into the city
20:5 But Benhadad s messengers
20:5 They said, "Benhadad has s
20:7 When he s for my wives,
20:10 Then Benhadad s Ahab the
20:17 Benhadad had s men ⌊to
21:8 She s them to the respected
21:11 had written in the letters she s.
21:14 Then the leaders s ⌊this
2Ki 1:2 So he s messengers ⌊to
1:6 back to the king who s you.
1:9 The king s an army officer with
1:11 The king s another officer with
1:13 The king s a third officer with
1:16 You s messengers to seek
2:17 "They s 50 men who searched
3:7 He s this message to King
5:8 he s a messenger to the king.
5:10 Elisha s a messenger to him.
5:22 My master has s me.
6:14 So the king s horses and
6:23 and then he s them back to
6:32 The king had s one of his men
6:32 this murderer has s someone
7:14 and the king s them to follow
8:9 Benhadad of Aram has s me
9:18 "The messenger you s has
9:19 Then Joram s out a second
10:5 and the guardians s this
10:7 heads in baskets and s them
10:21 Jehu s messengers to all the
11:4 Jehoiada s for the company
12:18 He s these things to King
14:8 Then Amaziah s messengers
14:9 King Jehoash of Israel s this
14:9 "A thistle in Lebanon s a
14:19 But they s men to Lachish after
16:7 Ahaz s messengers to King
16:8 in the royal palace and s them
16:10 So King Ahaz s the priest
16:11 King Ahaz s from Damascus.
17:4 (Hoshea had s messengers to
17:13 the commands I s to you
17:25 So the LORD s lions to kill
17:26 of that country, so he s lions.
18:14 Then King Hezekiah of Judah s
18:17 s his commander-in-chief,
19:2 Then he s Eliakim,
19:4 s him to defy the living God.
19:9 Sennacherib s messengers to
19:16 message that Sennacherib s
19:20 s a message to Hezekiah,
20:12 s letters and a present to
22:3 he s the scribe Shaphan,
22:15 Tell the man who s you to me,
22:18 "But tell Judah's king who s
23:1 Then the king s for all the
23:16 he s men to take the bones out
24:2 The LORD s raiding parties of
1Ch 10:9 Then they s men throughout
12:19 their rulers s him away after
14:1 King Hiram of Tyre s
18:10 he s his son Hadoram to greet
19:2 "So David s messengers to
19:3 your father because he s men
19:4 waist down, and s them away.
19:5 he s ⌊someone⌋ to meet them
19:6 So Hanun and the Ammonites s
19:8 he s Joab and all the elite
19:16 the kings s ⌊messengers⌋ to
21:12 should give the one who s me."
21:14 So the LORD s a plague on
1Ch 21:15 God also s a Messenger to
2Ch 2:3 Solomon s word to King Huram
2:3 You s him cedar so that he
8:18 Huram s his own servants and
10:3 ⌊Israel⌋ s for Jeroboam and
10:18 Then King Rehoboam s
16:2 He s them to Damascus to
16:4 He s his generals and their
17:7 he s his officers Ben Hail,
24:19 The LORD s them prophets to
24:23 The Arameans s all the loot
25:13 The troops that Amaziah s
25:15 He s him a prophet who asked
25:17 King Amaziah of Judah s
25:18 King Jehoash of Israel s this
25:18 "A thistle in Lebanon s a
25:27 but they s men to Lachish after
28:16 At that time King Ahaz s for
30:1 Hezekiah s a message to all
32:9 he s his officers to King
32:21 The LORD s an angel who
32:31 When the leaders of Babylon s
34:8 Josiah s Shaphan,
34:23 Tell the man who s you to me,
34:26 "Tell Judah's king who s you
34:29 Then the king s for all the
35:21 But Neco s messengers to
36:10 spring King Nebuchadnezzar s
36:15 s messages through his
Ezr 4:11 copy of the letter they s to him:
4:17 Then the king s this reply:
4:18 The letter you s me has been
5:5 Darius received a report and s
5:6 of that river) s to King Darius.
5:7 They s him the following report
8:16 Then I s for Eliezer,
8:17 I s them to Iddo, the leader in
10:7 Then he s a proclamation
Neh 2:9 (The king had s army officers
6:2 Then Sanballat and Geshem s
6:3 I s messengers to tell them,
6:4 They s the same message to
6:5 When Sanballat s me the same
6:8 Then I s someone to tell him,
6:12 I realized that God hadn't s him.
6:17 nobles of Judah s many letters
6:17 and Tobiah s many letters
Est 1:22 He s official documents to all
3:13 Messengers were s with
4:4 She s clothing for Mordecai to
4:13 Mordecai s this answer back to
4:15 Esther s this reply back to
5:10 He went home and s for his
8:10 Then he s them by
9:20 down and s official letters
9:30 Mordecai s official documents
Psa 78:25 and God s them plenty of food.
78:45 He s a swarm of flies that bit
78:49 He s his burning anger,
78:49 He s an army of destroying
105:17 He s a man ahead of them.
105:17 He s Joseph, who was sold as
105:20 The king s someone to release
105:26 He s his servant Moses,
105:26 Moses, and he s Aaron,
105:28 He s darkness and made ⌊their
107:20 He s his message and healed
111:9 He has s salvation to his
135:9 He s miraculous signs and
Pro 9:3 She has s out her servant girls.
17:11 will be s ⌊to punish⌋ him.
Isa 9:8 The LORD s a message
20:1 s his commander-in-chief
23:7 Is this the city that s its people
36:2 Then the king of Assyria s his
37:2 Then he s Eliakim,
37:4 s him to defy the living God.
37:9 When he heard this, he again s
37:17 message that Sennacherib s
37:21 s a message to Hezekiah,
39:1 s letters and a present to
48:16 Now the Almighty LORD has s
57:9 You've s your ambassadors far
57:9 far away and s them down
61:1 He has s me to heal those who
61:2 ⌊He has s me⌋ to announce

Isa	61:3	He has **s** me to provide for
	63:12	Where is the one who **s** his
Jer	3:8	Judah saw that I **s** unfaithful
	7:25	I have **s** all my servants the
	14:14	They claim that I **s** them,
	19:14	where the LORD had **s** him to
	21:1	King Zedekiah **s** Pashhur,
	24:5	whom I **s** away from here to
	25:4	"Even though the LORD has **s**
	25:17	the LORD **s** me drink from
	26:5	whom I **s** to you again and
	26:12	"The LORD **s** me to prophesy
	26:15	The LORD has certainly **s** me
	26:22	King Jehoiakim **s** soldiers to
	28:9	prophet that the LORD **s** only if
	28:15	the LORD hasn't **s** you.
	29:1	The prophet Jeremiah **s** a letter
	29:1	He also **s** it to the priests,
	29:3	He **s** the letter with Shaphan's
	29:3	King Zedekiah of Judah had **s**
	29:19	I **s** them my servants the
	29:20	all you captives who were **s**
	29:25	You **s** letters in your own name
	29:28	That's why Jeremiah **s** this
	35:15	I have **s** all my servants the
	36:14	Then all the officials **s** Jehudi,
	36:21	Then the king **s** Jehudi to get
	37:3	King Zedekiah **s** Jehucal (son
	37:7	who **s** you to get advice from
	37:17	King Zedekiah **s** for Jeremiah,
	38:14	King Zedekiah **s** for the prophet
	39:13	king of Babylon **s** for Jeremiah.
	40:14	the Ammonites has **s** Ishmael,
	42:9	Jeremiah said to them, "You **s**
	42:20	yourselves when you **s** me
	42:21	the LORD your God **s** me
	43:1	the LORD their God **s** him
	44:4	I have **s** my servants the
	49:14	A messenger was **s** among the
Lam	1:13	He **s** fire from above.
Eze	11:16	Although I **s** them far away
	13:6	But the LORD hasn't **s** them.
	17:7	and **s** its branches toward
	23:16	at first sight and **s** messengers
	23:40	"They even **s** messengers to
	27:33	merchandise was **s** overseas.
	39:28	I **s** them into captivity among
Dan	2:2	The king **s** for the magicians,
	2:13	and some men were **s** to find
	3:2	King Nebuchadnezzar **s**
	3:28	He **s** his angel and saved his
	5:24	So he **s** the hand to write this
	6:22	My God **s** his angel and shut
	9:23	your request, a reply was **s**.
	10:11	because I've been **s** to you."
Joe	2:23	He has **s** the autumn rain and
	2:25	(They are the large army that I **s**
Amo	2:11	I also **s** you prophets from
	4:7	I **s** rain on one city and not on
	4:10	I **s** plagues on you as I did to
	7:10	**s** a message to King Jeroboam
Oba	1:1	A messenger was **s** among the
Jnh	1:4	The LORD **s** a violent wind
	1:17	The LORD **s** a big fish to
	3:7	made this announcement and **s**
	4:7	At dawn the next day, God **s** a
Mic	6:4	I **s** Moses, Aaron, and Miriam
Hag	1:12	the LORD their God had **s** him
Zec	1:10	the horses the LORD has **s**
	2:8	the Glory **s** me to the nations
	2:9	the LORD of Armies has **s** me.
	2:11	of Armies has **s** me to you.
	4:9	of Armies has **s** me to you.
	6:15	the LORD of Armies has **s** me
	7:2	the people from Bethel **s**
	7:12	of Armies had **s** by his Spirit
Mal	2:4	Then you will know that I **s**
Mat	2:8	As he **s** them to Bethlehem,
	2:16	He **s** soldiers to kill all the
	10:5	Jesus **s** these twelve out with
	10:40	welcomes the one who **s** me.
	11:2	So he **s** his disciples
	13:36	When Jesus had **s** the people
	14:22	while he **s** the people away.
	14:35	and **s** messengers all around
	15:24	Jesus responded, "I was **s**
Mat	15:39	After he **s** the people on their
	18:32	"Then his master **s** for him and
	20:2	he **s** them to work in his
	21:1	Jesus **s** two disciples ahead of
	21:34	he **s** his servants to the
	21:36	the landowner **s** more servants.
	21:37	"Finally, he **s** his son to them.
	22:3	He **s** his servants to those who
	22:4	He **s** other servants to tell the
	22:7	He **s** his soldiers, killed those
	22:16	They **s** their disciples to him
	23:37	stone to death those **s** to you!
	27:19	his wife **s** him a message.
Mar	1:43	Jesus **s** him away at once and
	3:14	him and to be **s** out by him
	3:31	They stood outside and **s**
	6:7	**s** them out two by two,
	6:17	Herod had **s** men who had
	6:27	Immediately, the king **s** a guard
	6:45	while he **s** the people away.
	8:9	Then he **s** the people on their
	8:26	told him when he **s** him home,
	9:37	not me but the one who **s** me."
	11:1	Jesus **s** two of his disciples
	12:2	"At the right time he **s** a servant
	12:3	and **s** him back with nothing.
	12:4	So the man **s** another servant
	12:5	The man **s** another,
	12:5	Then he **s** many other servants.
	12:6	Finally, he **s** his son to them.
	12:13	The leaders **s** some of the
	14:13	He **s** two of his disciples and
Luk	1:19	God **s** me to tell you this good
	1:26	God **s** the angel Gabriel to
	1:53	He **s** rich people away with
	4:18	He has **s** me to announce
	4:43	That's what I was **s** to do."
	7:3	and **s** some Jewish leaders
	7:6	when the officer **s** friends
	7:10	When the men who had been **s**
	7:19	and **s** them to ask the Lord,
	7:20	"John the Baptizer **s** us to ask
	8:38	But Jesus **s** the man away and
	9:2	He **s** them to spread the
	9:20	whom God has **s**."
	9:48	welcomes the one who **s** me.
	9:52	He **s** messengers ahead of him.
	10:16	me rejects the one who **s** me."
	13:34	stone to death those **s** to you!
	14:4	healed him, and **s** him away.
	14:17	he **s** his servant to tell those
	15:15	in that country and was **s**
	19:14	They **s** representatives to
	19:29	Jesus **s** two of his disciples
	19:32	The men Jesus **s** found it as
	20:10	"At the right time he **s** a servant
	20:10	the servant and **s** him back
	20:11	So he **s** a different servant.
	20:11	and **s** him back with nothing.
	20:12	Then he **s** a third servant.
	22:8	Jesus **s** Peter and John and
	22:35	"When I **s** you out without a
	23:7	he **s** Jesus to Herod.
	23:11	robe on him and **s** him back
	23:15	So he **s** this man back to us.
Jon	1:6	God **s** a man named John to be
	1:19	when the Jews **s** priests
	1:22	back to those who **s** us.
	1:24	had been **s** were Pharisees.
	1:33	But God, who **s** me to baptize
	3:2	we know that God has **s** you
	3:17	God **s** his Son into the world,
	3:28	but I've been **s** ahead of him.'
	3:34	The man whom God has **s**
	4:34	the one who **s** me wants me
	4:38	I have **s** you to harvest a crop
	5:23	honor the Father who **s** him.
	5:24	in the one who **s** me will have
	5:30	what the one who **s** me wants.
	5:33	You **s** people to John the
	5:36	prove that the Father has **s** me.
	5:37	The Father who **s** me testifies
	5:38	believe in the person he has **s**.
	6:29	in the one whom he has **s**."
	6:38	the one who **s** me wants me
	6:39	The one who **s** me doesn't
Jon	6:44	Father who **s** me brings them
	6:57	The Father who has life **s** me,
	7:16	me but from the one who **s** me.
	7:18	glory to the one who **s** him is
	7:28	The one who **s** me is true.
	7:29	I am from him and he **s** me."
	7:32	the Pharisees **s** temple guards
	7:33	Then I'll go to the one who **s**
	8:16	with the Father who **s** me.
	8:18	and so does the Father who **s**
	8:26	But the one who **s** me is true.
	8:29	the one who **s** me is with me.
	8:42	Instead, God **s** me.
	9:4	what the one who **s** me wants
	9:7	(Siloam means "**s**.") The blind
	10:36	holy purpose and has **s** me into
	11:3	So the sisters **s** a messenger
	11:42	me will believe that you **s** me."
	12:44	but also in the one who **s** me.
	12:45	me sees the one who **s** me.
	12:49	Instead, the Father who **s** me
	13:20	me accepts the one who **s** me."
	14:24	from the Father who **s** me.
	15:21	don't know the one who **s** me.
	16:5	I'm going to the one who **s** me.
	17:3	and Jesus Christ, whom you **s**.
	17:8	They have believed that you **s**
	17:18	I have **s** them into the world the
	17:18	the same way you **s** me into
	17:21	believe that you have **s** me.
	17:23	knows that you have **s** me
	17:25	have known that you **s** me.
	18:24	Annas **s** Jesus to Caiaphas,
	20:21	As the Father has **s** me,
Act	3:26	back to life and has **s** him
	5:21	They also **s** men to the prison
	7:12	he **s** our ancestors there.
	7:14	Joseph **s** for his father Jacob
	7:35	This is the one God **s** to free
	8:14	they **s** Peter and John to them.
	9:17	to Damascus, **s** me to you.
	9:30	Caesarea and **s** him to Tarsus.
	9:38	they **s** two men to him.
	10:8	to them and **s** them to Joppa.
	10:17	the men **s** by Cornelius found
	10:20	these men. I have **s** them."
	10:22	a Roman army officer, **s** us.
	10:29	here when you **s** for me.
	10:29	to know why you **s** for me."
	10:33	So I **s** for you immediately.
	10:36	God **s** his word to the people of
	11:11	They had been **s** from
	11:22	Barnabas was **s** to Antioch.
	11:30	The disciples did this and **s**
	12:11	"Now I'm sure that the Lord **s**
	13:4	After Barnabas and Saul were **s**
	13:7	The governor **s** for Barnabas
	13:15	the synagogue leaders **s** a
	13:26	God saves people was **s** to us.
	15:2	and some of the others were **s**
	15:3	The church **s** Paul and
	15:27	We have **s** Judas and Silas to
	15:30	So the men were **s** on their
	15:33	the congregation **s** them back
	15:33	to those who had **s** them.
	16:35	officials **s** guards who told
	16:36	"The officials have **s** word to
	17:10	the believers **s** Paul and Silas
	17:14	The believers immediately **s**
	19:22	So he **s** two of his helpers,
	19:31	Paul's friends **s** messengers
	20:1	Paul **s** for the disciples,
	20:17	From Miletus Paul **s**
	23:30	I immediately **s** him to you.
	24:24	He **s** for Paul and listened to
	28:28	that God has **s** his salvation
Rom	8:3	But God **s** his Son to have a
	11:13	As long as I am an apostle **s** to
1Co	1:17	Instead, he **s** me to spread the
	1:30	our wisdom **s** from God,
	4:17	That's why I've **s** Timothy to
2Co	8:18	With him we have **s** our
	8:22	We have also **s** with them our
	9:3	I've **s** my coworkers so that
	12:17	through any of the men I **s** you?
	12:18	and I **s** my friend with him.

Gal 2:12 **s** ⌊from Jerusalem⌋ arrived.
4:4 God **s** his Son ⌊into the world⌋.
4:5 God **s** him to pay for the
4:6 God has **s** the Spirit of his Son
Php 2:25 You **s** him as your personal
1Th 3:2 we **s** our brother Timothy to
3:5 I **s** ⌊Timothy⌋ to find out about
Tit 1:1 I was **s** to lead God's chosen
Heb 1:14 They are spirits **s** to serve
Jas 2:25 the spies and **s** them away
1Pe 1:12 who was **s** from heaven,
2:14 are people the emperor has **s**
1Jn 4:10 but that he loved us and **s** his
4:14 that the Father **s** his Son as
Rev 1:1 He **s** this revelation through his
5:6 seven spirits of God **s** all over
22:6 of the prophets has **s** his angel
22:16 "I, Jesus, have **s** my angel to

sentence (12)

Exo 18:4 me from Pharaoh's death **s**."
2Ki 25:6 and passed **s** on him.
Est 7:8 Then the king passed **s** on him,
Ecc 8:11 When a **s** against a crime isn't
Jer 1:16 I will pass **s** on my people
4:12 Now, I will pass **s** on them."
39:5 of Babylon passed **s** on him.
52:9 of Babylon passed **s** on him.
Mar 14:64 him with the death **s**.
Rom 9:28 The Lord will carry out his **s** on
13:4 right to carry out the death **s**.
2Co 1:9 feel as if we're under a death **s**.

sentenced (5)

Dtr 17:6 The person can only be **s** to
17:6 but no one should ever be **s** to
Ezr 7:26 be imprisoned or be **s** to die.
Act 25:16 A person can't be **s** as a favor.
25:16 Before he is **s**, he must face

Senuah (1)

Neh 11:9 in charge, and Judah, son of **S**,

Seorim (1)

1Ch 24:8 third for Harim, the fourth for **S**,

separate (32)

Gen 1:6 water in order to **s** the water."
1:14 there be lights in the sky to **s**
1:18 and to **s** the light from the
13:9 Let's **s**. If you go to the left, I'll
25:23 Two nations will go their **s**
30:40 So he made **s** herds for himself
Lev 13:50 put the clothing in a **s** place
13:54 put the clothing in a **s** place
15:31 "You must **s** the Israelites from
20:25 **S** clean and unclean animals
Num 8:6 "**S** the Levites from the rest of
8:14 In this way you will **s** the
Jos 18:7 Levi's tribe has no **s** region
Jdg 7:5 The LORD said to him, "**S**
2Sm 14:6 there was no one to **s** them.
2Ki 15:5 So the king lived in a **s** house.
2Ch 26:21 he lived in a **s** house and was
Ezr 9:1 to keep themselves **s** from
10:11 **S** yourselves from the people
Est 3:8 scattered among — but **s** from
Sos 2:17 on the mountains that **s** us!
Isa 56:3 "The LORD will **s** us from his
Jer 15:7 "I will **s** them with a
Mat 13:49 The angels will go out and **s**
19:6 Therefore, don't let anyone **s**
25:32 He will **s** them as a shepherd
Mar 10:9 Therefore, don't let anyone **s**
Luk 22:31 He wants to **s** you from me as
Rom 8:35 What will **s** us from the love
8:35 or violent death **s** us from his
8:38 that nothing can ever **s**
2Co 6:17 **S** yourselves from them.

separated (25)

Gen 1:4 So God **s** the light from the
1:7 So God made the horizon and **s**
30:40 Jacob **s** the rams from the flock
Lev 20:24 I am the LORD your God who **s**
20:25 I have **s** you from every
20:26 I have **s** you from other people
Num 16:9 God of Israel has **s** you from
Jdg 4:11 Heber the Kenite had **s** from the
Rut 2:17 Then she **s** the grain from its
2Sm 1:23 They were not **s** even when
2Ki 2:11 fiery chariot with fiery horses **s**
Ezr 6:21 all who had **s** themselves from
Neh 4:19 are widely **s** from one another
9:2 of Israel **s** themselves from all
10:28 and all who had **s** themselves
13:3 they **s** the non-Israelites from
Pro 19:4 poor person is **s** from his friend.
Isa 59:2 But your wrongs have **s** you
Eze 42:20 It **s** what was holy from what
43:8 Only a wall **s** me from them.
46:18 will be **s** from their property."
Rom 8:38 We can't be **s** by death or life,
Col 1:21 Once you were **s** from God.
1Th 2:17 we have been **s** from you for a
2Th 1:9 by being **s** from the Lord's

separately (3)

Gen 43:32 He was served **s** from his
43:32 with him were also served **s**,
Jon 20:7 of linen but was rolled up **s**.

separates (6)

Rut 1:17 but death **s** you and me!"
Pro 16:28 A gossip **s** the closest of
17:9 keeps bringing up the issue **s**
Mat 25:32 separate them as a shepherd **s**
Luk 16:26 Besides, a wide area **s** us.
22:31 a farmer **s** wheat from husks.

separating (1)

Rut 3:2 He will be **s** the barley from its

Sephar (1)

Gen 10:30 extended from Mesha toward **S**

Sepharad (1)

Oba 1:20 are in **S** will take possession

Sepharvaim (7)

2Ki 17:24 and **S** and settled them in the
17:31 The people from **S** burned their
17:31 Anammelech, the gods of **S**.
18:34 Where are the gods of **S**,
19:13 and the king of the cities of **S**,
Isa 36:19 Where are the gods of **S**?
37:13 and the king of the cities of **S**,

Serah (3)

Gen 46:17 Their sister was **S**.
Num 26:461 had a daughter named **S**.)
1Ch 7:30 Their sister was **S**.

Seraiah (21)

2Sm 8:17 **S** was the royal scribe.
2Ki 25:18 guard took the chief priest **S**,
25:23 **S** (son of Tanhumeth from
1Ch 4:13 sons were Othniel and **S**.
4:14 **S** was the father of Joab,
4:35 of Joshibiah, grandson of **S**,
6:14 Azariah was the father of **S**.
6:14 **S** was the father of Jehozadak.
Ezr 2:2 **S**, Reelaiah, Mordecai,
7:1 Ezra was the son of **S**,
Neh 10:2 **S**, Azariah, Jeremiah,
11:11 **S**, who was the son of Hilkiah,
12:1 and Jeshua: **S**, Jeremiah, Ezra,
12:12 their families: From **S**, Meraiah;
Jer 36:26 king's son), **S** (son of Azriel),
40:8 **S** (son of Tanhumeth),
51:59 the prophet Jeremiah gave to **S**,
51:59 when **S** went to Babylon with
51:59 (**S** was the quartermaster.)
51:61 Jeremiah said to **S**,
52:24 guard took the chief priest **S**,

Seraiah's (1)

Neh 11:12 From **S** relatives 822 did the

Sered (2)

Gen 46:14 The sons of Zebulun were **S**,
Num 26:26 Zebulun were the family of **S**,

sergeant (5)

Act 22:25 Paul asked the **s** who was
22:26 When the **s** heard this,
22:26 The **s** asked him, "What are
23:18 The **s** took the young man to
24:23 Felix ordered the **s** to guard

sergeants (2)

Act 23:17 Then Paul called one of the **s**
23:23 officer summoned two of his **s**

Sergius Paulus (1)

Act 13:7 **S**, who was the governor of the

serious (24)

Gen 18:20 and their sin is very **s**.
20:9 you would bring such a **s** sin
Exo 32:21 them to commit such a **s** sin?"
32:30 "You have committed a **s** sin.
32:31 have committed such a **s** sin!
Num 5:2 who has a **s** skin disease
Dtr 15:21 has any other **s** defect — never
24:8 outbreaks of **s** skin diseases.
1Sm 2:17 The sin of Eli's sons was a **s**
28:15 answered, "I'm in **s** trouble.
2Ki 17:21 and led them to commit a **s** sin.
2Ch 12:14 not **s** about dedicating himself
Neh 1:3 They are enduring **s** troubles
13:27 commit such a **s** crime against
Ecc 10:4 you can make up for **s**
Jer 6:14 as though they were not **s**,
8:11 as though they were not **s**,
10:19 My wound is **s**. Then I thought
14:17 It will be a very **s** blow."'
Mat 8:2 A man with a **s** skin disease
Mar 1:40 Then a man with a **s** skin
Luk 5:12 covered with a **s** skin disease.
Act 19:23 During that time a **s**
25:7 They made a lot of **s**

seriously (6)

Gen 50:11 ceremonies are taken very **s** by
Exo 9:21 warning **s** left their servants
Dtr 17:1 a defect or anything **s** wrong
1Sm 25:25 this worthless person Nabal **s**.
Luk 1:66 Everyone who heard about it **s**
Rev 3:19 Take this **s**, and change the

serpent (18)

Gen 3:4 the **s** told the woman.
Isa 14:29 will be a flying, fiery **s**.
51:9 into pieces and stab the **s**?
Rev 12:3 a huge fiery red **s** with seven
12:4 The **s** stood in front of the
12:7 had to fight a war with the **s**.
12:7 The **s** and its angels fought.
12:9 The huge **s** was thrown down.
12:13 When the **s** saw that it had
12:17 The **s** became angry with the
12:18 The **s** stood on the sandy
13:2 The **s** gave its power,
13:4 They worshiped the **s** because
13:11 like a lamb. It talked like a **s**.
16:13 out of the mouths of the **s**,
20:2 He overpowered the **s**,
20:2 up the **s** for 1,000 years.
20:3 and sealed the pit over the **s**

serpent's (1)

Rev 12:16 had poured out of the **s** mouth

Serug (6)

Gen 11:20 he became the father of **S**.
11:21 After he became the father of **S**,
11:22 **S** was 30 years old when he
11:23 **S** lived 200 years and had
1Ch 1:26 **S**, Nahor, Terah,
Luk 3:35 son of **S**, son of Reu, son of

servant (363)

Gen 18:7 He gave it to his **s**,
24:2 Abraham said to the senior **s**
24:5 The **s** asked him, "What if the
24:9 So the **s** did as his master
24:10 Then the **s** took ten of his

Gen	24:11	The **s** had the camels kneel
	24:14	have chosen for your **s** Isaac.
	24:17	The **s** ran to meet her and said,
	24:34	"I am Abraham's **s**," he said.
	24:52	When Abraham's **s** heard their
	24:53	The **s** took out gold and silver
	24:59	with Abraham's **s** and his men.
	24:61	The **s** took Rebekah and left.
	24:65	She asked the **s**, "Who is that
	24:65	is my master," the **s** answered.
	24:66	The **s** reported to Isaac
	26:24	for my **s** Abraham's sake."
	30:3	She said, "Here's my **s** Bilhah.
	32:17	He commanded the first **s**,
	32:18	they belong to your **s** Jacob.
	32:19	also commanded the second **s**,
	39:4	that he made him his trusted **s**.
Exo	14:31	in him and in his **s** Moses.
Num	12:7	not the way I treat my **s** Moses.
	12:8	afraid to criticize my **s** Moses?"
	14:24	But because my **s** Caleb has a
Dtr	34:5	the LORD's **s** Moses died in
Jos	1:1	death of the LORD's **s** Moses,
	1:2	"My **s** Moses is dead.
	1:7	my **s** Moses commanded you.
	1:13	"Remember what the LORD's **s**
	1:15	LORD's **s** Moses gave you."
	8:31	This was as the LORD's **s**
	8:33	the LORD's **s** Moses had
	9:24	God commanded his **s** Moses
	11:12	as the LORD's **s** Moses had
	11:15	had commanded his **s** Moses
	12:6	The LORD's **s** Moses and the
	13:8	since the LORD's **s** Moses had
	14:7	the LORD's **s** Moses sent me
	18:7	the LORD's **s** Moses gave them
	22:2	**s** Moses commanded you.
	22:4	It is the land that the LORD's **s**
	22:5	the LORD's **s** Moses gave you.
	24:29	the LORD's **s** Joshua,
Jdg	2:8	The LORD's **s** Joshua,
	7:10	take your **s** Purah to the camp
	7:11	So Gideon and his **s** Purah
	19:3	He took along his **s** and two
	19:9	with his concubine and his **s**.
	19:11	The Levite's **s** said to him,
	19:13	He told his **s**, "Let's go
	19:19	myself, the woman, and my **s**.
1Sm	2:13	the priest's **s** would come with
	2:16	If the man said to the **s**,
	2:16	the **s** would say to him,
	9:4	Then Saul and his **s** went
	9:5	Saul told his **s** who was with
	9:6	The **s** responded, "There's a
	9:7	"If we go," Saul asked his **s**,
	9:8	The **s** again answered Saul,
	9:10	Saul told his **s**, "That's a good
	9:14	So Saul and his **s** went to the
	9:22	Samuel brought Saul and his **s**
	9:27	"Have the **s** go ahead of you."
	10:14	uncle asked him and his **s**,
	17:58	"The son of your **s** Jesse of
	18:2	on Saul kept David ⌊as his **s**⌋
	19:4	a sin against your **s** David,"
	20:38	Jonathan's young **s** gathered
	22:8	has encouraged my **s** David
	24:16	you speaking, my **s** David?"
	26:17	that your voice, my **s** David?"
	26:21	"My **s** David," Saul said,
	26:25	"Blessed are you, my **s** David.
	27:12	He'll be my **s** from now on."
	29:3	the **s** of King Saul of Israel,
2Sm	3:18	enemies through my **s** David.'"
	7:5	"Say to my **s** David,
	7:8	you will say to my **s** David:
	7:26	And the house of your **s** David
	9:2	Now, Saul's family had a **s**
	9:9	Ziba, Saul's **s**, and said to him,
	9:12	became Mephibosheth's **s**.
	13:17	called his personal **s** and said,
	13:18	So his **s** took her out and
	13:34	When the **s** who kept watch
	14:19	Yes, your **s** Joab ordered me
	14:20	Your **s** Joab has done this to
	15:34	'Your Majesty, I'll be your **s**.
	15:34	I was your father's **s** in the past,
2Sm	15:34	but now I'll be your **s**,' then
	16:1	Mephibosheth's **s**,
	17:17	so a **s** girl was to go and tell
	19:17	Ziba, the **s** of Saul's family,
	19:26	"My **s** deceived me,
1Ki	1:2	stay with you and be your **s**.
	1:4	She became the king's **s** and
	1:19	But he hasn't invited your **s**
	1:26	or your **s** Solomon.
	3:6	father David, who was your **s**.
	8:24	to my father David, your **s**.
	8:25	to my father David, your **s**.
	8:26	father David, your **s**, come true.
	8:53	your **s** Moses when you
	8:56	through his **s** Moses has failed
	8:66	LORD had given his **s** David
	11:13	one tribe for my **s** David's sake
	11:32	⌊left⌋ because of my **s** David
	11:34	because of my **s** David whom
	11:36	so that my **s** David will always
	11:38	commands as my **s** David did,
	14:8	have not been like my **s** David.
	14:18	LORD had said through his **s**,
	15:29	his **s** Ahijah from Shiloh.
	18:36	God in Israel and that I'm your **s**
	18:43	He said to his **s**, "Please go
	18:44	the seventh time the **s** said,
	19:3	in Judah and left his **s** there.
	20:32	"Your **s** Benhadad says,
2Ki	4:12	He told his **s** Gehazi,
	4:19	The father told his **s**,
	4:20	The **s** picked him up and
	4:24	Then she told her **s**,
	4:25	he told his **s** Gehazi,
	4:38	meeting with him, he told his **s**,
	4:43	But his **s** asked, "How can I
	4:44	The **s** set it in front of them.
	5:2	the **s** of Naaman's wife.
	5:20	Gehazi, the **s** of Elisha (the
	6:15	When the **s** of the man of God
	6:15	Elisha's **s** asked, "Master,
	7:2	The **s** on whose arm the king
	7:17	The king appointed the **s** on
	7:19	Then the **s** answered the man
	7:20	what happened to the king's **s**:
	8:4	the **s** of the man of God.
	8:9	"Your humble **s** King Benhadad
	9:4	the **s** of the prophet,
	9:36	his **s** Elijah from Tishbe.
	10:10	he said through his **s** Elijah."
	14:25	predicted through his **s** Jonah,
	16:7	to say, "I'm your **s**, your son.
	17:3	who became his **s** and was
	18:12	the LORD's **s**, had commanded.
	19:34	for the sake of my **s** David."
	20:6	for the sake of my **s** David.'"
	21:8	that my **s** Moses gave them."
1Ch	6:49	**s** Moses had commanded.
	16:13	descendants of Israel, his **s**,
	17:4	"Say to David, my **s**,
	17:7	you will say to my **s** David:
	17:24	And the house of David, your **s**,
2Ch	1:3	Moses, the LORD's **s**,
	6:15	to my father David, your **s**.
	6:16	to my father David, your **s**.
	6:17	to David, your **s**, come true.
	6:42	Remember your mercy to your **s**
	13:6	He had been the **s** of David's
	24:6	The LORD's **s** Moses and the
	24:9	(In the desert the LORD's **s**
	32:16	LORD God and his **s** Hezekiah.
Ezr	7:24	Levite, singer, gatekeeper, **s**,
Neh	1:6	to what I, your **s**, am praying.
	1:7	gave us through your **s** Moses.
	1:8	told us through your **s** Moses:
	2:10	the Ammonite **s** heard this,
	2:19	Tobiah the Ammonite **s**,
	4:22	"Every man and his **s** should
	6:5	his **s** held in his hand an
	9:14	and teachings through your **s**
	10:29	given by Moses, God's **s**.
Est	6:1	So he told ⌊a **s**⌋ to bring the
Job	1:8	you thought about my **s** Job?
	2:3	you thought about my **s** Job?
	42:7	me as my **s** Job has done.
	42:8	Go to my **s** Job, and make a
Job	42:8	My **s** Job will pray for you.
	42:8	me as my **s** Job has done."
Psa	19:11	As your **s** I am warned by them.
	35:27	happy when his **s** has peace."
	78:70	He chose his **s** David.
	86:2	Save your **s** who trusts you.
	86:16	strength because I am your **s**.
	86:16	I am the son of your female **s**.
	89:3	I swore this oath to my **s** David:
	89:20	I found my **s** David.
	89:39	recognize the promise to your **s**
	89:50	how your **s** has been insulted.
	105:6	descendants of his **s** Abraham,
	105:26	He sent his **s** Moses,
	105:42	holy promise to his **s** Abraham.
	116:16	O LORD, I am indeed your **s**.
	116:16	I am your **s**, the son of your
	116:16	the son of your female **s**.
	119:125	I am your **s**. Help me understand
	132:10	For the sake of your **s** David,
	136:22	as an inheritance for his **s**
	143:12	because I am your **s**.
	144:10	your **s** David away from
Pro	9:3	She has sent out her **s** girls.
	14:35	A king is delighted with a **s**
	27:27	and to keep your **s** girls alive.
Ecc	7:21	hear your own **s** cursing you.
	10:16	where the king used to be a **s**
Isa	20:3	Then the LORD said, "My **s**
	22:20	I will call my **s** Eliakim,
	37:35	for the sake of my **s** David."
	41:8	"But you are my **s** Israel,
	41:9	I said to you, 'You are my **s**.
	42:1	Here is my **s**, whom I support.
	42:19	Who is blind except my **s** or
	42:19	or blind like the **s** of the LORD?
	43:10	"I have chosen you as my **s** so
	44:1	But now listen, my **s** Jacob,
	44:2	afraid, my **s** Jacob, Jeshurun,
	44:21	Jacob: You are my **s**, Israel.
	44:21	I formed you; you are my **s**.
	44:26	He confirms the word of his **s**
	45:4	For the sake of my **s** Jacob,
	48:20	has reclaimed his **s** Jacob.
	49:3	"You are my **s** Israel.
	49:5	me in the womb to be his **s**
	49:6	"You are not just my **s** who
	50:10	the LORD and obeys his **s**?
	52:13	My **s** will be successful.
	53:11	My righteous **s** will acquit
Jer	25:9	I will also send for my **s** King
	27:6	to my **s** King Nebuchadnezzar
	30:10	"Don't be afraid, my **s** Jacob,"
	33:21	with my **s** David could
	33:22	the descendants of my **s** David
	33:26	of Jacob and of my **s** David.
	43:10	I'm going to send for my **s** King
	46:27	"Don't be afraid, my **s** Jacob.
	46:28	Don't be afraid, my **s** Jacob,"
Eze	28:25	the land I gave to my **s** Jacob.
	34:23	over them, my **s** David,
	34:24	and my **s** David will be their
	37:24	"'My **s** David will be their king,
	37:25	land that I gave my **s** Jacob,
	37:25	My **s** David will always be
	46:17	The gift will belong to the **s**
Dan	6:20	**s** of the living God!
	9:11	the Teachings of your **s** Moses.
Hag	2:23	my **s** Zerubbabel (son of
Zec	3:8	I'm going to bring my **s**,
Mal	1:6	and a **s** honors his master.
	4:4	the teachings of my **s** Moses,
Mat	8:6	The officer said, "Sir, my **s** is
	8:8	and my **s** will be healed.
	8:9	I tell my **s**, 'Do this!' and he
	8:13	that moment the **s** was healed.
	12:18	"Here is my **s** whom I have
	18:24	When he began to do this, a **s**
	18:26	Then the **s** fell at his master's
	18:27	"The master felt sorry for his **s**,
	18:28	But when that **s** went away,
	18:28	he found a **s** who owed him
	18:28	He grabbed the **s** he found and
	18:29	"Then that other **s** fell at his
	18:30	he turned away and had that **s**
	18:32	and said to him, 'You evil **s**!

Mat 18:33 the other **s** as mercifully as
20:26 great among you will be your **s**.
23:11 among you will be your **s**.
24:45 is the faithful and wise **s**?
24:46 That **s** will be blessed if his
24:47 He will put that **s** in charge of
24:48 On the other hand, that **s**,
24:49 The **s** may begin to beat the
25:21 You're a good and faithful **s**!
25:23 You're a good and faithful **s**!
25:26 'You evil and lazy **s**!
25:30 Throw this useless **s** outside
26:51 off the ear of the chief priest's **s**.
26:69 A female **s** came to him and
26:71 another female **s** saw him.
Mar 9:35 and be a **s** to everyone else."
10:43 great among you will be your **s**.
12:2 "At the right time he sent a **s** to
12:3 The workers took the **s**,
12:4 the man sent another **s** to them.
12:4 They hit the **s** on the head and
12:5 and they killed that **s**.
14:47 off the ear of the chief priest's **s**.
14:69 The **s** saw him. Once again she
Luk 1:38 answered, "I am the Lord's **s**.
1:48 favorably on me, his humble **s**.
1:54 to help his **s** Israel forever.
1:69 us in the family of his **s** David.
2:29 you are allowing your **s** to
7:7 and let my **s** be cured.
7:8 I tell my **s**, 'Do this!' and he
7:10 they found the **s** healthy again.
12:43 That **s** will be blessed if his
12:44 He will put that **s** in charge of
12:45 On the other hand, that **s** may
12:45 The **s** may begin to beat the
12:47 "The **s** who knew what his
12:48 But the **s** who didn't know
14:17 he sent his **s** to tell those who
14:21 "The **s** went back to report this
14:21 He told his **s**, 'Run to every
14:22 "The **s** said, 'Sir, what you've
14:23 "Then the master told his **s**,
15:27 "The **s** told him, 'Your brother
16:13 "A **s** cannot serve two masters.
17:7 "Suppose someone has a **s**
17:7 Does he tell his **s** when he
17:8 Instead, he tells his **s**,
17:9 thank the **s** for following orders.
19:16 "The first **s** said, 'Sir, the coin
19:17 You're a good **s**. You proved that
19:18 "The second **s** said,
19:19 "The king said to this **s**,
19:20 "Then the other **s** said,
19:22 by what you've said, you evil **s**!
20:10 "At the right time he sent a **s** to
20:10 But the workers beat the **s** and
20:11 So he sent a different **s**.
20:12 Then he sent a third **s**.
22:26 your leader must be like a **s**.
22:27 who sits at the table or the **s**?
22:27 But I'm among you as a **s**.
22:50 right ear of the chief priest's **s**.
22:56 A female **s** saw him as he sat
Jon 15:15 because a **s** doesn't know
15:20 Remember what I told you: 'A **s**
18:10 attacked the chief priest's **s**,
Act 3:13 has glorified his **s** Jesus.
3:26 God has brought his **s** back to
4:25 who spoke through your **s**
4:27 against your holy **s** Jesus,
4:30 the name of your holy **s** Jesus."
12:13 and a **s** named Rhoda came to
16:16 a female **s** met us.
26:16 I'm appointing you to be a **s**
Rom 1:1 From Paul, a **s** of Jesus Christ,
13:4 The government is God's **s**
13:4 It is God's **s**, an avenger to
14:4 to criticize someone else's **s**?
14:4 his **s** has been successful.
14:4 The **s** will be successful
15:8 Christ became a **s** for the
15:16 to be a **s** of Christ Jesus to
Gal 1:10 I would not be Christ's **s**.
Eph 3:7 I became a **s** of this Good
Php 2:7 by taking on the form of a **s**,
Col 1:7 Epaphras, our dear fellow **s**.
1:23 of which I, Paul, became a **s**.
1:25 I became a **s** of the church
4:12 Epaphras, a **s** of Christ Jesus
4:17 that he started as the Lord's **s**.
1Ti 4:6 You are a good **s** of Christ
2Ti 2:24 A **s** of the Lord must not quarrel
Tit 1:1 From Paul, a **s** of God and an
Heb 3:5 Moses was a faithful **s** in
Jas 1:1 From James, a **s** of God and of
2Pe 1:1 a **s** and apostle of Jesus Christ.
Jud 1:1 From Jude, a **s** of Jesus Christ
Rev 1:1 through his angel to his **s** John.
15:3 and singing the song of God's **s**

servant's (5)

2Ki 6:17 The LORD opened the **s** eyes
Luk 7:3 to come and save the **s** life
22:51 Then he touched the **s** ear and
Jon 18:10 and cut off the **s** right ear.
18:10 (The **s** name was Malchus.)

servants (282)

Gen 12:5 and the **s** they had acquired
21:25 Abimelech's **s** had seized.
22:3 He took with him two of his **s**
22:5 Then Abraham said to his **s**,
22:19 Abraham returned to his **s**,
26:14 so many flocks, herds, and **s**,
26:15 his father's **s** had dug during
26:19 Isaac's **s** dug in the valley and
26:25 and his **s** dug a well there.
26:32 That same day Isaac's **s** came
32:16 He placed **s** in charge of each
32:16 Then he said to his **s**,
39:11 of the household **s** were there.
39:14 she called her household **s**
40:20 dinner prepared for all his **s**.
40:20 Of all his **s** he gave special
41:10 Pharaoh was angry with his **s**,
41:37 and all his **s** liked the idea.
41:38 So Pharaoh asked his **s**,
50:17 because we are **s** of your
Exo 2:5 her **s** walked along the bank of
9:19 Now, send ⌊**s**⌋ to bring your
9:20 LORD's warning brought their **s**
9:21 warning seriously left their **s**
32:13 Remember your **s** Abraham,
Lev 25:42 They are my **s**. I brought them
25:55 Israelites belong to me as **s**.
25:55 They are my **s**. I brought them
Num 22:18 Balaam answered Balak's **s**,
22:22 accompanied by his two **s**.
Dtr 9:27 Remember your **s** Abraham,
32:36 compassion on his **s** when
32:43 revenge for the death of his **s**.
Jos 9:23 You will always be **s**.
Jdg 5:29 Her wisest **s** gave her an
6:27 Gideon took ten of his **s** and
Rut 2:13 not even one of your own **s**."
2:15 Boaz ordered his **s**,
1Sm 2:15 their **s** would come and say to
8:17 In addition, you will be his **s**.
9:3 "Take one of the **s** with you,
17:8 and aren't you Saul's **s**?
21:7 That same day one of Saul's **s**
25:10 Nabal answered David's **s**.
25:10 So many **s** nowadays are
25:40 When David's **s** came to
25:41 the feet of my master's **s**."
25:42 of her female **s** following her.
29:10 with Saul's **s** who came
2Sm 8:7 that belonged to Hadadezer's **s**,
9:10 You, your sons, and your **s**
9:10 (Ziba had 15 sons and 20 **s**.)
10:2 "So David sent his **s** to comfort
10:2 **s** entered Ammonite territory,
13:28 Absalom gave an order to his **s**.
13:29 Absalom's **s** did to Amnon as
13:31 All his **s** were standing beside
14:30 So Absalom said to his **s**,
14:30 So Absalom's **s** set it on fire.
14:30 Joab's **s** came to him ⌊in grief⌋
14:30 "Absalom's **s** have set ⌊your⌋
14:31 "Why did your **s** set my field on
15:15 The king's **s** told him,
2Sm 15:15 we are Your Majesty's **s**."
16:2 ripe fruit are for ⌊your⌋ **s** to eat.
16:6 stones at David and David's **s**,
16:11 told Abishai and all his **s**,
17:20 Absalom's **s** came to the
17:20 The **s** looked for them but did
17:20 **s** returned to Jerusalem.
17:21 After Absalom's **s** left,
19:6 and **s** mean nothing
19:14 "Come back with all your **s**."
19:17 brought his 15 sons and 20 **s**.
1Ki 1:23 The **s** told the king,
3:24 So the king told his **s** to bring
8:23 promise of mercy to your **s**,
8:36 Forgive the sins of your **s**,
9:27 Hiram sent his own **s** ⌊who
9:27 Along with Solomon's **s**
10:2 with a large group of **s**,
10:8 How blessed these **s** of yours
10:13 Then she and her **s** went back
11:11 I will give it to one of your **s**.
11:17 father's Edomite **s** fled to Egypt.
12:7 they will always be your **s**."
20:6 I'm going to send my **s**
22:49 "Let my **s** go with your
22:49 "Let my servants go with your **s**
2Ki 1:13 life and the lives of these 50 **s**
4:22 "Please send me one of the **s**
5:13 But Naaman's **s** went to him
5:23 them to a couple of his own **s**
9:7 for shedding the blood of my **s**
9:7 and all the LORD's ⌊other⌋ **s**.
9:28 His **s** brought him in a chariot
10:5 to Jehu: "We are your **s**.
10:19 Summon all the prophets, **s**,
17:13 you through my **s** the prophets.
17:23 said he would through all his **s**,
19:23 Through your **s** you defy the
21:10 through his **s** the prophets:
24:2 through his **s** the prophets.
1Ch 9:2 the Levites, and the temple **s**.
18:7 that Hadadezer's **s** carried,
19:2 But when David's **s** entered
19:3 Haven't his **s** come to explore,
21:3 aren't they all your **s**?
2Ch 2:8 I know that your **s** are skilled
6:14 promise of mercy to your **s**,
6:27 Forgive the sins of your **s**,
8:18 Huram sent his own **s** and his
8:18 with Solomon's **s** to Ophir,
9:1 arrived with a large group of **s**,
9:7 How blessed these **s** of yours
9:10 Huram's **s** and Solomon's
9:10 Solomon's **s** who brought gold
9:12 Then she and her **s** went back
10:7 they will always be your **s**."
12:8 But they will become his **s** so
29:11 be his **s**, and burn sacrifices."
Ezr 2:43 These temple **s** returned from
2:55 **s** returned from exile:
2:58 The temple **s** and the
2:58 of Solomon's **s** totaled 392.
2:65 female **s** who numbered 7,337,
2:70 and the temple **s** settled in their
4:11 King Artaxerxes, From your **s**,
5:11 "We are the **s** of the God of
7:7 and temple **s**) went to
8:17 the temple **s** in Casiphia,
8:20 and 220 temple **s**. ⌊They were
8:20 from the temple **s** whom David
9:11 us through your **s** the prophets,
Neh 1:6 about your **s** the Israelites.
1:10 These are your **s** and your
1:11 of all your other **s** who want
2:20 "We, his **s**, are going to rebuild.
3:26 and the temple **s** who were
3:31 that housed the temple **s**
4:23 My brothers, my **s**,
5:10 My brothers, my **s**,
5:15 Even the governors' **s** took
7:46 These temple **s** returned from
7:57 **s** returned from exile:
7:60 The temple **s** and the
7:60 of Solomon's **s** totaled 392.
7:67 female **s** who numbered 7,337,
7:73 of the people, the temple **s**,

Neh 9:10 things to Pharaoh and all his **s**
10:28 gatekeepers, singers, temple **s**,
11:3 priests, Levites, temple **s**,
11:3 of Solomon's **s** settled
11:21 But the temple **s** lived on
Est 2:9 and seven suitable female **s**
2:9 Then he moved her and her **s**
4:4 Esther's **s** and eunuchs came
4:12 So Esther's **s** told Mordecai
4:16 My **s** and I will also fast.
6:8 ⌊The **s**⌋ should bring a royal
6:9 The king's **s** are also to shout
7:8 and **s** covered Haman's face.
7:10 So **s** hung Haman's ⌊dead
Job 1:3 and a large number of **s**.
1:15 livestock and massacred the **s**.
1:16 burned your flocks and **s**.
1:17 camels and massacred the **s**.
4:18 God doesn't trust his own **s**,
31:13 have abused the rights of my **s**,
Psa 34:22 protects the souls of his **s**.
69:35 His **s** will live there and take
69:36 The descendants of his **s** will
79:2 given the dead bodies of your **s**
79:10 shedding the blood of your **s**.
90:13 your plans about ⌊us,⌋ your **s**.
90:16 Let ⌊us,⌋ your **s**, see what you
102:14 Your **s** value Zion's stones,
102:28 The children of your **s** will go
103:21 his **s** who carry out his will.
104:4 winds and your **s** flames of fire.
105:25 dealt treacherously with his **s**.
113:1 You **s** of the LORD,
119:91 since they are all your **s**.
123:2 As **s** depend on their masters,
134:1 all you **s** of the LORD,
135:1 Praise him, you **s** of the LORD
135:14 and have compassion on his **s**.
Pro 29:12 all his **s** become wicked.
Isa 37:24 Through your **s** you defy the
54:17 the inheritance of the LORD's **s**.
56:6 LORD's name, and to be his **s**.
61:6 You will be called the **s** of our
63:17 Return for the sake of your **s**.
65:8 I will do this for my **s**:
65:9 My **s** will live there.
65:13 LORD God says: My **s** will eat,
65:13 My **s** will drink, but you will be
65:13 My **s** will be glad, but you will
65:14 My **s** will sing because of the
65:15 and call his **s** by another name.
66:14 will be made known to his **s**,
Jer 7:25 I have sent all my **s** the
25:4 the LORD has sent all his **s**
25:19 his **s**, officials, all his people,
26:5 the words of my **s** the prophets,
29:19 I sent them my **s** the prophets
33:21 The arrangement with my **s** the
35:15 I have sent all my **s** the
44:4 I have sent my **s** the prophets
Eze 38:17 about long ago through my **s**
46:17 his property to one of his **s**.
46:24 where the temple **s** must boil
Dan 3:26 and Abednego — **s** of the Most
3:28 sent his angel and saved his **s**,
5:3 So the **s** brought the gold
9:6 listened to your **s** the prophets,
9:10 us through your **s** the prophets.
Joe 1:9 The priests, the LORD's **s**,
1:13 Cry loudly, you **s** of the altar.
1:13 in sackcloth, you **s** of my God.
2:29 days I will pour my Spirit on **s**,
Amo 3:7 his secret to his **s** the prophets.
Zec 1:6 which I've commanded my **s**
Mat 18:23 to settle accounts with his **s**.
18:31 "The other **s** who worked with
21:34 he sent his **s** to the workers to
21:35 The workers took his **s** and
21:36 So the landowner sent more **s**.
22:3 He sent his **s** to those who had
22:4 He sent other **s** to tell the
22:6 The rest grabbed the king's **s**,
22:8 "Then the king said to his **s**,
22:10 The **s** went into the streets and
22:13 Then the king told his **s**,
24:45 giving the other **s** their food at
Mat 24:49 may begin to beat the other **s**
25:14 He called his **s** and entrusted
25:19 the master of those **s** returned
Mar 12:5 Then he sent many other **s**.
13:34 he put his **s** in charge.
14:66 of the chief priest's female **s**
Luk 1:2 had been eyewitnesses and **s**
12:36 Be like **s** waiting to open the
12:37 Blessed are those **s** whom the
12:42 of giving the other **s** their share
12:45 may begin to beat the other **s**
15:22 "The father said to his **s**,
15:26 He called to one of the **s** and
17:10 'We're worthless **s**.
19:13 he called ten of his **s** and gave
19:13 He said to his **s**, 'Invest this
19:15 Then he said, 'Call those **s** to
Jon 4:51 his **s** met him and told him that
4:52 His **s** told him, "The fever left
12:26 My **s** will be with me wherever
15:15 I don't call you **s** anymore,
18:18 The **s** and the guards were
18:26 One of the chief priest's **s**,
Act 2:18 I will pour my Spirit on my **s**,
10:7 called two of his household **s**
16:17 "These men are **s** of the Most
Rom 13:6 are God's **s** while they do
1Co 3:5 They are **s** who helped you
4:1 People should think of us as **s**
2Co 4:5 We are your **s** for his sake.
4:6 We are his **s** because the
6:4 that we are God's **s**.
6:7 that we are God's **s**
11:15 So it's not surprising if his **s**
11:15 as **s** who have God's
11:23 Are they Christ's **s**?
Php 1:1 and Timothy, **s** of Christ Jesus.
2Ti 3:17 They equip God's **s** so that
Heb 1:7 He makes his **s** flames of fire."
Rev 1:1 gave it to him to show his **s**
2:20 teaches and misleads my **s**
7:3 foreheads of the **s** of our God."
10:7 Good News known to his **s**,
11:18 to reward your **s**, the prophets,
19:2 on her for the blood of his **s**."
22:3 His **s** will worship him
22:6 sent his angel to show his **s**

servants' (1)

1Ki 20:6 your palace and your **s** houses.

serve (270)

Gen 15:14 I will punish the nation they **s**,
25:23 the older will **s** the younger."
27:29 May nations **s** you.
27:37 made all his brothers **s** him.
27:40 and you will **s** your brother.
43:31 when he said, "**S** the food."
Exo 14:12 have been better for us to **s**
20:5 Never worship them or **s** them,
23:24 Never worship or **s** their gods
23:25 You must **s** the LORD your
28:1 They will **s** me as priests.
28:4 that they can **s** me as priests.
28:41 them apart to **s** me as priests.
28:43 near the altar to **s** as priests
29:1 sons apart to **s** me as priests:
29:30 into the tent of meeting to **s**
30:20 near the altar to **s** as priests
31:10 sons when they **s** as priests,
35:19 sons when they **s** as priests."
40:13 dedicate him to **s** me as priest.
40:15 Anoint them to **s** me as priests,
Lev 7:35 day Moses ordained them to **s**
8:35 night for seven days and **s** as
16:32 ordained to **s** as chief priest
25:53 During those years he should **s**
Num 3:3 were ordained to **s** as priests.
3:10 and his sons to **s** as priests.
4:23 and 50 who are qualified to **s** at
4:30 and 50 who are qualified to **s** at
4:39 50 who were qualified to **s** at
4:43 50 who were qualified to **s** at
8:24 old or older are eligible to **s** at
16:9 of the community to **s** them.
18:2 and help you and your sons **s**
Num 18:7 You may **s** me as priests.
Dtr 4:19 to worship and **s** what you see
5:9 Never worship them or **s** them,
6:13 fear the LORD your God, **s** him,
8:19 and if you **s** them and bow
10:8 when they **s** him as priests,
11:13 and **s** him with all your heart
13:2 worship and **s** other gods."
13:4 **s** him, and be loyal to him.
18:7 and may **s** in the name of the
20:11 to do forced labor and **s** you.
21:5 them to **s** him as priests
28:14 Never worship other gods or **s**
28:47 You didn't **s** the LORD your
28:48 So you will **s** your enemies,
28:48 You will **s** them even though
28:64 There you will **s** gods made of
Jos 9:27 They still **s** today.
18:7 their inheritance is to **s**
22:5 Be loyal to him, and **s** him with
23:7 Don't ever **s** their gods or bow
23:16 **s** them and bow down to them,
24:14 "Fear the LORD, and **s** him
24:14 and **s** only the LORD.
24:15 if you don't want to **s** the LORD,
24:15 choose today whom you will **s**.
24:15 and I will still **s** the LORD."
24:16 the LORD to **s** other gods.
24:18 We, too, will **s** the LORD,
24:19 you can't possibly **s** him.
24:20 the LORD and **s** foreign gods,
24:21 We will ⌊only⌋ **s** the LORD!"
24:22 have chosen to **s** the LORD."
24:24 "We will **s** the LORD our God
Jdg 2:11 They began to **s** other gods —
2:13 They abandoned the LORD to **s**
9:28 that we should **s** him?
9:28 **S** the descendants of Hamor,
9:28 Why should we **s** Abimelech?
9:38 that we should **s** him?'
10:6 They began to **s** other gods
10:6 the LORD and did not **s** him.
1Sm 2:18 Samuel continued to **s** in front
2:28 of Israel to **s** as my priest,
2:35 appoint a faithful priest to **s** me.
4:9 or else you will **s** the Hebrews
7:3 to the LORD, and **s** only him.
8:11 make them **s** on his chariots
11:1 treaty with us, and we'll **s** you."
12:10 and we will **s** you.'
12:14 If you fear the LORD, **s** him,
12:20 **s** the LORD wholeheartedly.
12:24 and **s** him sincerely.
17:9 will be our slaves and **s** us."
25:41 "I am ready to **s**," she said.
26:19 'Go and **s** other gods,'
28:22 I will **s** you something to eat.
2Sm 15:8 I will **s** the LORD.'"
16:19 And besides, whom should I **s**?
16:19 your father, so I'll **s** you."
19:13 Joab's place to **s** me always as
22:44 A people I did not know will **s**
24:9 able-bodied men who could **s**
1Ki 6:16 He built it to **s** as an inner room,
8:11 The priests couldn't **s** because
9:6 and follow and **s** other gods
12:4 and we will **s** you."
12:7 They told him, "If you will **s**
12:32 worship sites ⌊to **s**⌋ in Bethel.
17:1 God of Israel whom I **s** lives,
18:15 of Armies whom I **s** lives,
2Ki 3:14 of Armies whom I **s** lives,
5:16 as the LORD whom I **s** lives,
10:18 but Jehu will **s** him a lot.
17:32 kinds of people to **s** as priests
17:35 **s** them, or sacrifice to them.
18:7 and wouldn't **s** him anymore.
25:24 **s** the king of Babylon,
1Ch 9:25 They would come to **s** under
15:2 his ark and to **s** him forever.
15:16 relatives to **s** as musicians.
16:4 appointed some Levites to **s**
16:37 his relatives to **s** continually
16:38 68 of his relatives ⌊to **s** there⌋.
16:39 and his priestly relatives to **s**
21:5 1,100,000 men who could **s**

1Ch 21:5 who could **s** in the army.
23:13 to the LORD, to **s** him,
23:28 Aaron's descendants to **s**
23:28 and to **s** in God's temple.
24:19 groups when they went to **s** at
25:1 and Jeduthun to **s** as prophets
26:12 duties with their relatives to **s**
26:30 were appointed to **s** Israel west
28:9 **S** the LORD wholeheartedly
2Ch 5:14 The priests couldn't **s** because
7:19 and follow and **s** other gods
8:14 ⌊the LORD⌋ and to **s** beside
10:4 and we will **s** you."
13:10 The priests who **s** the LORD
17:16 who volunteered to **s** the LORD
19:11 The Levites will **s** as officers
29:11 of him, **s** him, be his servants,
30:8 **S** the LORD your God,
30:22 had the skills to **s** the LORD.
31:13 and Benaiah to **s** under
33:16 And he told Judah to **s** the
34:33 all people found in Israel **s**
35:2 and encouraged them to **s**
35:3 **S** the LORD your God and his
Ezr 8:17 should bring us men who can **s**
Neh 9:35 they didn't **s** you or turn away
10:39 and where the priests who **s**
Est 4:5 eunuchs appointed to **s** her.
Job 12:19 those who **s** in a temple.
21:15 Almighty that we should **s** him?
36:11 "If righteous people listen and **s**
39:9 the wild ox agree to **s** you,
Psa 2:11 **S** the LORD with fear,
18:43 A people I did not know will **s**
22:30 be descendants who **s** him,
72:11 May all nations **s** him.
100:2 **S** the LORD cheerfully.
101:6 lives with integrity will **s** me.
Pro 22:29 He will **s** kings. He will not
22:29 He will not **s** unknown people.
Isa 28:20 is too narrow to **s** as a cover.
60:7 rams of Nebaioth will **s** you.
60:10 and their kings will **s** you.
60:12 kingdoms that do not **s** you will
Jer 5:19 So you will **s** foreigners in a
13:10 other gods in order to **s** them
15:14 I will make you **s** your enemies
16:13 There you will **s** other gods
17:4 I will make you **s** your enemies
25:6 Don't follow other gods to **s**
25:11 These nations will **s** the king
27:6 even made wild animals **s** him.
27:7 All nations will **s** him,
27:8 nations or kingdoms won't **s**
27:9 who tell you that you'll never **s**
27:12 **s** him and his people,
27:13 the nations that don't **s**
27:14 who tell you that you'll never **s**
27:17 Instead, **s** the king of Babylon,
28:14 will **s** King Nebuchadnezzar
28:14 They will **s** him! I will even
28:14 make wild animals **s** him."
30:8 no longer make you **s** them.
30:9 You will **s** the LORD your God
33:22 and the Levites who **s** me like
35:15 other gods in order to **s** them.
35:19 will always **s** me."
40:9 be afraid to **s** the Babylonians.
40:9 **s** the king of Babylon,
44:3 incense and **s** other gods that
Eze 20:32 You want to **s** wood and stone.
20:39 **S** your disgusting idols.
40:45 the priests who **s** in the temple.
40:46 north is for the priests who **s** at
40:46 near the LORD and **s** him."
43:19 who can come near me and **s**
44:13 near me and **s** me as priests.
44:15 may come near me and **s** me,
44:16 come near my table to **s** me,
44:17 no wool on them while they **s**
44:27 courtyard of the holy place to **s**
45:4 will belong to the priests who **s**
45:4 who come near to **s** the LORD.
45:5 belong to the Levites who **s**
47:18 The Jordan River will **s** as the
Dan 1:4 and able to **s** in the king's
Dan 1:5 they were to **s** the king.
7:14 and language were to **s** him.
7:27 powers will **s** and obey them."
9:24 These time periods will **s** to
Joe 2:17 The priests who **s** the LORD
Zep 3:9 worship the LORD and to **s** him
Mal 3:14 'It's pointless to **s** God.
3:18 and the one who doesn't **s** him.
Mat 4:10 Lord your God and **s** only him.'"
6:24 "No one can **s** two masters.
6:24 You cannot **s** God and wealth.
20:28 so that others could **s** him.
20:28 He came to **s** and to give his
Mar 8:6 his disciples to **s** to the people.
10:45 so that others could **s** him.
10:45 He came to **s** and to give his
Luk 1:74 we could **s** him without fear
4:8 Lord your God and **s** only him.'"
10:8 eat whatever they **s** you.
11:6 and I don't have anything to **s**
12:21 and his riches don't **s** God."
12:37 down at the table, and **s** them.
16:13 servant cannot **s** two masters.
16:13 You cannot **s** God and wealth."
17:8 After you **s** me my dinner,
Jon 12:26 Those who **s** me must follow
12:26 If people **s** me, the Father will
Act 1:20 be added to our number to **s**
7:7 the people whom they will **s**.
24:14 This means that I **s** our
27:23 and whom I **s** stood by me
Rom 1:9 I **s** God by spreading the Good
1:25 ungodly and **s** what is created
9:11 told that the older child would **s**
12:11 Use your energy to **s** the Lord.
15:16 I **s** as a priest by spreading the
1Co 9:7 Does a soldier ever **s** in the
2Co 6:3 to find fault with how we **s**.
9:12 What you do to **s** others not
11:8 taking pay from them to **s** you.
Gal 5:13 **s** each other through love.
Eph 4:12 to prepare God's people, to **s**,
6:7 **S** eagerly as if you were
Php 3:3 because we **s** God's Spirit
1Th 1:9 from false gods to **s** the real,
1Ti 3:13 Those deacons who **s** well
6:2 should **s** their masters even
2Ti 1:3 whom I **s** with a clear
Heb 1:14 They are spirits sent to **s** those
2:17 like them so that he could **s** as
7:23 died he could no longer **s**.
8:5 They **s** at a place that is a
9:14 Now we can **s** the living God.
12:28 we must **s** God with fear and
13:10 Those who **s** at the tent have
1Pe 2:16 use your freedom to **s** God.
4:10 God has given you to **s** others.
4:11 Whoever serves must **s** with
5:2 but out of a desire to **s**.
5:5 Furthermore, all of you must **s**
3Jn 1:7 they went on their trip to **s** the
Rev 7:15 They **s** him day and night in
18:6 **S** her a drink in her own cup
19:5 all who **s** and fear him,

served (100)

Gen 43:32 He was **s** separately from his
43:32 him were also **s** separately,
Exo 38:8 given by the women who **s** at
Num 3:4 So only Eleazar and Ithamar **s**
4:37 the Kohathite families who **s** at
31:27 between the soldiers who **s**
31:28 From the soldiers who **s** in the
31:36 of it went to the soldiers who **s**
Jos 9:27 They **s** the LORD's altar,
13:27 The Jordan River **s** as its
24:2 River and **s** other gods.
24:14 rid of the gods your ancestors **s**
24:15 the gods your ancestors **s**
24:31 Israel **s** the LORD as long as
Jdg 2:7 The people **s** the LORD
2:19 They followed, **s**, They never
3:6 Israel also **s** their gods.
3:7 their God and **s** other gods
3:8 So Israel **s** Cushan Rishathaim
3:14 The Israelites **s** King Eglon of
Jdg 10:10 our God and **s** other gods —
10:13 me and **s** other gods.
10:16 gods they had and **s** the LORD.
20:28 of Aaron, **s** in front of it.)
1Sm 1:3 **s** there as priests of the LORD.
2:11 But the boy ⌊Samuel⌋ **s** the
2:22 with the women who **s** at
4:9 the Hebrews as they **s** you.
7:4 Astarte and **s** only the LORD.
12:10 the LORD and **s** other gods
16:21 David came to Saul and **s** him.
28:25 Then she **s** it to Saul and his
2Sm 13:9 Then she took the pan and **s**
16:19 As I **s** your father, so I'll serve
1Ki 6:17 at the front of the temple **s** as
7:7 on his throne and **s** as judge.
9:9 gods, worshiped, and **s** them.
12:6 who had **s** his father Solomon
16:31 then **s** and worshiped Baal.
19:10 I have eagerly **s** you.
19:14 I have eagerly **s** you.
22:53 Ahaziah **s** Baal, and made the
2Ki 10:18 He said, "Ahab **s** Baal a little,
17:12 They **s** idols, although the
17:33 but also **s** their own gods
17:41 but also **s** their own idols.
21:3 worshiped and **s** the entire
23:4 the priests who **s** under Hilkiah,
1Ch 6:10 (He was the one who **s** as
6:32 They **s** as musicians in the
6:33 These are the men who **s** (their
6:33 (their descendants also **s**):
9:13 They **s** in God's temple and
23:24 Everyone who **s** in the LORD's
23:32 as they **s** in the LORD's temple.
24:2 and Ithamar **s** as priests.
25:2 who **s** as a prophet under the
26:16 One squad of guards **s** its
26:21 ⌊Those who **s**⌋ for Ladan,
26:29 They **s** as officials and judges
26:30 and they **s** the king.
28:1 the army units that **s** the king,
28:12 (These rooms **s** as treasuries
2Ch 7:22 gods, worshiped, and **s** them.
10:6 who had **s** his father Solomon
17:19 These were the men who **s** the
31:15 and Shecaniah **s** under him in
31:16 The six men who **s** under Kore
31:17 way they **s** in their divisions.
33:3 worshiped and **s** the entire
34:13 of the Levites **s** as scribes,
35:13 and pans and immediately **s**
Est 1:10 who **s** under King Xerxes,
Jer 5:19 me and **s** foreign gods
8:2 loved, **s**, gone after, sought,
16:11 gods, **s** them, worshiped them,
22:9 other gods and **s** them.'"
34:14 When they have **s** you for six
Eze 42:14 that they wore as they **s**.
44:11 They could have **s** in my holy
44:11 They could have **s** in the
44:11 front of the people and **s** them.
44:12 But they **s** the people by
44:19 that they wore as they **s**.
Dan 1:19 So these four men **s** the king.
1:21 Daniel **s** the royal palace until
7:10 and thousands **s** him.
Mar 8:7 should also be **s** to the people.
Luk 1:8 As he **s** in God's presence,
Jon 12:2 Martha **s** the dinner,
Act 10:7 of those who **s** him regularly.
17:25 and he isn't **s** by humans as if
20:19 I humbly **s** the Lord,
20:19 I **s** the Lord during the difficult
1Co 12:5 and yet the same Lord is **s**.
Gal 3:24 Moses' laws **s** as our guardian.
Phm 1:13 Then he could have **s** me in
Heb 3:2 when he **s** in God's house.
7:13 No one from that tribe ever **s** as
Rev 18:6 large as the drink she **s** others.

servers (5)

Jon 2:5 His mother told the **s**,
2:7 Jesus told the **s**, "Fill the jars
2:7 The **s** filled the jars to the brim.
2:8 "The **s** did as they were told.

Jon 2:9 although the **s** who had poured

serves (18)

Exo 28:3 holy when he **s** me as priest.
28:35 wear it when he **s** as priest.
39:26 by Aaron when he **s** as priest.
Dtr 17:12 disobeys the priest (who **s**
Jer 27:11 the king of Babylon and **s** him.
Mal 3:17 spares his own son who **s** him.
3:18 between the one who **s** God
Jon 2:10 "Everyone **s** the best wine first.
2:10 the host **s** cheap wine.
Rom 14:18 The person who **s** Christ with
1Co 10:27 eat anything he **s** you without
Gal 3:6 Abraham **s** as an example.
1Th 3:2 He **s** God by spreading the
1Ti 1:16 This patience **s** as an example
2Ti 2:4 Whoever **s** in the military
Heb 7:24 so he **s** as a priest forever.
8:2 He **s** as priest of the holy place
1Pe 4:11 Whoever **s** must serve with the

service (29)

Gen 41:46 old when he entered the **s**
50:2 ordered the doctors in his **s**
Exo 39:40 the equipment needed for the **s**
Num 8:25 they must retire from active **s**
Dtr 24:5 duty or any other public **s**.
Jdg 5:2 and people volunteered for **s**.
1Sm 25:27 young men who are in your **s**.
2Ki 25:14 utensils used in the temple **s**.
1Ch 24:3 descendants into groups for **s**.
25:1 the men who performed this **s**:
26:8 had the ability to perform the **s**.
2Ch 8:14 divisions of priests for their **s**
24:14 and silver utensils for the **s**
31:2 based on the **s** he performed:
31:16 the daily **s** that each division
35:10 So the **s** was prepared.
Neh 13:11 them back in their places of **s**.
Ecc 8:3 in a hurry to leave the king's **s**.
Jer 52:18 utensils used in the temple **s**.
Eze 38:8 time you will be called to **s**.
Luk 1:23 the days of his **s** were over,
Rom 16:3 in the **s** of Christ Jesus.
16:8 dear friend in the **s** of the Lord.
16:9 our coworker in the **s** of Christ,
2Co 9:13 through this genuine act of **s**
Php 2:17 of the sacrifice and **s** ⌊I offer
Heb 9:1 had rules for the priests' **s**.
Jas 2:2 men come to your worship **s**.
Rev 2:19 I know your love, faith, **s**,

services (2)

Num 22:7 them to pay for Balaam's **s**.
1Sm 28:7 I'll go to her and ask for her **s**."

serving (54)

Exo 14:12 Let us go on **s** the Egyptians'?
23:33 and trap you into **s** their gods."
29:44 holy duties of **s** me as priests.
30:30 holy duties of **s** me as priests.
39:41 clothes worn when **s** as priests
39:41 for his sons when **s** as priests.
Num 4:47 qualified to do the work of **s**
Dtr 17:9 the judge who is **s** at that time.
18:5 to do the work of **s**
19:17 judges who are **s** at that time.
26:3 Go to the priest who is **s** at that
1Sm 3:1 The boy Samuel was **s** the
8:8 leaving me and **s** other gods.
19:20 with Samuel **s** as their leader,
1Ki 12:8 up with him and were **s** him.
1Ch 9:19 for **s** as watchmen at
15:13 dedicated our lives to **s** him
22:19 your hearts and lives to **s**
27:1 and officers who were **s** the
28:9 you dedicate your life to **s** him,
2Ch 10:8 up with him and were **s** him.
12:8 the difference between **s** me
12:8 me and **s** foreign kings."
12:14 himself to **s** the LORD.
14:4 to dedicate their lives to **s**
14:7 have dedicated our lives to **s**
15:2 dedicate your lives to **s** him,
15:12 to dedicate their lives to **s**
2Ch 17:3 his life to **s** other gods —
19:3 dedicated your life to **s** God."
22:8 nephews) who were **s** Ahaziah,
22:9 dedicated his life to **s**
25:15 do you dedicate your life to **s**
26:5 He dedicated his life to **s** God
26:5 his life to **s** the LORD,
30:19 dedicating their lives to **s** God.
31:2 offerings, **s**, giving thanks,
31:21 and dedicated his life to **s** God.
34:3 began to dedicate his life to **s**
Ezr 8:22 who dedicates his life to **s** him,
Neh 10:36 and our flocks to the priests **s**
Jon 16:2 will think that they are **s** God.
Act 6:4 ourselves to praying and to **s**
13:36 After doing God's will by **s** the
Rom 7:6 effect on us so that we are **s**
12:7 If your gift is **s**, then devote
12:7 then devote yourself to **s**.
16:18 People like these are not **s**
16:18 They are **s** their own desires.
1Co 12:5 There are different ways of **s**,
16:15 itself to **s** God's people.
Eph 6:7 Serve eagerly as if you were **s**
6:7 not merely **s** human masters.
Col 3:24 real master, whom you are **s**.

session (1)

Job 11:10 and then calls a court into **s**,

set (532)

Gen 2:3 blessed the seventh day and **s**
8:21 from birth their hearts are **s**
11:31 They **s** out together from Ur of
12:5 Abram **s** out for Canaan.
15:12 As the sun was just about to **s**,
18:8 and **s** these in front of them.
21:28 Then Abraham **s** apart seven
21:29 lambs you have **s** apart?"
22:3 he **s** out for the place that God
26:17 He **s** up his tents in the Gerar
28:12 which he saw a stairway **s** up
28:18 He **s** it up as a marker and
28:22 This stone that I have **s** up as
31:45 Jacob took a stone and **s** it up
31:51 that I have **s** up between you
33:20 He **s** up an altar there and
34:8 son Shechem has his heart **s**
34:12 **S** the price I must pay for the
35:14 So Jacob **s** up a memorial,
35:20 Then Jacob **s** up a stone as a
49:21 "Naphtali is a doe **s** free that
Exo 2:3 She put the baby in it and **s** it
9:5 The LORD **s** a definite time.
13:2 "**S** apart every firstborn male
14:2 to go back and **s** up their camp
14:2 **S** up your camp facing north —
15:25 There the LORD **s** down laws
19:2 They had **s** up camp there in
19:10 They must **s** themselves apart
19:22 must **s** themselves apart as
20:11 his work and **s** this day apart
21:13 to a place I will **s** aside for you.
24:4 mountain and ⌊**s** up⌋ 12 sacred
24:13 Moses **s** out with his assistant
25:7 other precious stones to be **s**
25:37 "Make seven lamps, and **s**
26:4 of the end sheet in each **s**,
26:9 the sheets together into one **s**
26:9 remaining six into another **s**.
26:10 of the end sheet in each **s**.
26:30 "**S** up the inner tent according
27:10 ⌊hung⌋ on 20 posts ⌊**s** in⌋ 20
27:11 with curtains on 20 posts **s** in
27:12 on ten posts ⌊**s** in⌋ ten bases.
27:14 three posts ⌊**s** in⌋ three bases.
27:16 on four posts ⌊**s** in⌋ four bases.
28:3 These clothes will **s** him apart
28:41 and **s** them apart to serve me
29:1 you must do in order to **s** Aaron
29:27 **S** apart as holy the breast that
29:37 peace with the LORD and **s**
29:44 I will **s** Aaron and his sons
30:30 In this way you will **s** them
31:5 He knows how to cut and **s**
33:7 used to take a tent and **s**
Exo 35:9 other precious stones to be **s**
35:27 other precious stones to be **s**
35:33 He knows how to cut and **s**
36:11 of the end sheet in each **s**,
36:16 were sewn together into one **s**,
36:16 remaining six into another **s**.
36:17 of the end sheet in each **s**.
38:10 ⌊hung⌋ on 20 posts ⌊**s** in⌋ 20
38:12 on 10 posts ⌊**s** in⌋ 10 bases.
38:14 three posts ⌊**s** in⌋ three bases.
38:19 It was hung on four posts ⌊**s**
40:2 "**S** up the tent (the tent of
40:4 and **s** up the lamps.
40:8 **S** up the surrounding courtyard
40:17 So the tent was **s** up on the
40:18 When Moses **s** up the tent,
40:18 and **s** up the posts.
40:25 He **s** up the lamps in the
40:33 He **s** up the courtyard around
Lev 2:3 It is very holy, **s** apart from the
2:10 It is very holy, **s** apart from the
8:12 and anointed him to **s** him apart
21:8 I **s** you apart as holy.
21:15 **s** him apart as holy."
21:23 **s** them apart as holy."
22:2 which the Israelites **s** apart
22:3 offerings the Israelites **s** apart
22:7 When the sun has **s**,
24:9 It is very holy, **s** apart from the
25:10 **S** apart the fiftieth year as holy,
26:1 make worthless idols or **s** up
27:25 "All values will be **s** using the
27:26 it cannot be **s** apart as holy.
Num 1:51 we camp, they will **s** it up.
2:34 They **s** up camp under their
3:13 I **s** apart as holy every firstborn
4:26 and all the equipment used to **s**
8:2 When you **s** up the seven
8:3 So Aaron **s** up the lamps on the
8:17 I **s** them apart as holy to me.
9:15 of God's promise was **s** up,
9:17 the Israelites would **s** up camp.
9:18 they would **s** up camp.
9:20 they would **s** up camp,
9:23 command they **s** up camp,
10:21 would already be **s** up.
10:31 You know where we can **s** up
11:18 They must be **s** apart as holy.
12:16 from Hazeroth and **s** up camp
16:3 Why do you **s** yourselves
21:10 The Israelites moved and **s** up
21:11 from Oboth and **s** up camp at
21:12 From there they moved and **s**
21:13 They moved from there and **s**
22:1 moved and **s** up camp across
23:4 "I have **s** up seven altars,
33:1 the Israelites **s** up camp after
33:5 Rameses and **s** up camp at
33:6 from Succoth and **s** up camp at
33:7 and **s** up camp near Migdol.
33:8 they **s** up camp at Marah.
33:9 so they **s** up camp there.
33:10 They moved from Elim and **s**
33:11 the Red Sea and **s** up camp
33:12 Desert of Sin and **s** up camp at
33:13 from Dophkah and **s** up camp at
33:14 They moved from Alush and **s**
33:15 from Rephidim and **s** up camp
33:16 of Sinai and **s** up camp at
33:17 Hattaavah and **s** up camp at
33:18 from Hazeroth and **s** up camp at
33:19 from Rithmah and **s** up camp at
33:20 Perez and **s** up camp at
33:21 They moved from Libnah and **s**
33:22 They moved from Rissah and **s**
33:23 Kehelathah and **s** up camp at
33:24 Shepher and **s** up camp at
33:25 from Haradah and **s** up camp at
33:26 Makheloth and **s** up camp at
33:27 They moved from Tahath and **s**
33:28 They moved from Terah and **s**
33:29 from Mithcah and **s** up camp at
33:30 Hashmonah and **s** up camp at
33:31 Moseroth and **s** up camp at
33:32 Bene Jaakan and **s** up camp at
33:33 Haggidgad and **s** up camp at

Num 33:34 Jotbathah and **s** up camp at
33:35 from Abronah and **s** up camp at
33:36 Ezion Geber and **s** up camp at
33:37 from Kadesh and **s** up camp at
33:41 Mount Hor and **s** up camp at
33:42 Zalmonah and **s** up camp at
33:43 They moved from Punon and **s**
33:44 They moved from Oboth and **s**
33:45 They moved from Iyim and **s**
33:46 Dibon Gad and **s** up camp at
33:47 Diblathaim and **s** up camp
33:48 Mountains and **s** up camp
33:49 They **s** up camp on the plains
Dtr 1:36 give the land that he **s** his feet
4:41 Then Moses **s** aside three
7:7 The LORD **s** his heart on you
10:8 At that time the LORD **s** apart
10:15 The LORD **s** his heart on your
11:24 place on which you **s** foot.
15:10 you work for and **s** out to do.
16:22 Never **s** up a sacred stone.
19:2 When all this is done, **s** aside
19:7 you to **s** aside three cities
20:12 **s** up a blockade around the
21:11 and have your heart **s** on her,
23:9 When you're at war and have **s**
26:4 take the basket from you and **s**
27:2 **s** up some large stones and
27:4 **s** up these stones on Mount
27:8 on the stones you **s** up."
31:21 their hearts are **s** on doing,
32:8 he **s** up borders for the tribes
32:22 the earth and its crops and **s**
Jos 1:3 place on which you **s** foot,
3:15 of the Jordan River and **s** foot in
4:3 and **s** them down where you
4:8 camp and **s** them down there.
4:9 Joshua also **s** 12 stones in the
4:20 At Gilgal Joshua **s** up the 12
6:26 him his youngest son to **s** up
8:2 **S** an ambush behind the city."
8:4 "**S** an ambush behind the city.
8:8 captured the city, **s** it on fire.
8:19 and quickly **s** it on fire.
10:7 best warriors, **s** out from Gilgal.
10:13 the sun was in no hurry to **s**.
18:1 gathered at Shiloh and **s** up
24:25 for the people and **s** up laws
24:26 he took a large stone and **s**
Jdg 1:8 killed everyone there and **s**
4:11 near Kedesh and **s** up his tent.
6:18 I want to bring my gift and **s** it
9:25 So citizens of Shechem **s**
9:32 **S** an ambush ⌊for them⌋ in the
9:34 **s** ambushes around Shechem.
9:43 and **s** an ambush in the fields.
9:49 on top of the basement and **s**
15:5 He **s** the torches on fire and
15:5 So he **s** fire to all their grain,
17:10 of silver a year, a **s** of clothes,
18:30 The people of Dan **s** up the
18:31 So they **s** up for themselves
1Sm 2:8 He has **s** the world on them.
7:12 Then Samuel took a rock and **s**
9:24 I **s** it aside for you."
13:8 the time **s** by Samuel.
13:21 silver to sharpen a mattock or **s**
15:5 to the city of Amalek and **s**
15:12 "Saul went to Carmel to **s** up a
24:15 matter and **s** me free from
2Sm 6:17 The men carrying the ark **s** it in
14:30 Go and **s** it on fire."
14:30 So Absalom's servants **s** it on
14:30 "Absalom's servants have **s**
14:31 "Why did your servants **s** my
15:24 They **s** down the ark of God
18:18 had taken a rock and **s**
24:18 **s** up an altar for the LORD at
1Ki 2:24 The LORD **s** me on my father
7:21 Hiram **s** up the pillars in the
7:21 He **s** up the pillar on the right
7:21 Then he **s** up the pillar on the
7:25 The pool was **s** on 12 metal
7:25 The pool was **s** on them,
7:28 had side panels **s** in frames.
7:29 On the panels **s** in frames were

1Ki 7:39 He **s** the pool on the south side
8:17 father David had his heart **s**
8:18 'Since you had your heart **s** on
8:53 After all, you, LORD God, **s**
14:12 The moment you **s** foot in the
15:3 sinful example his father had **s**
15:15 his father had **s** apart as holy.
16:32 of Baal in Samaria and **s** up
18:23 on the wood, but not **s** it on fire.
18:25 but don't **s** the wood on fire."
20:34 You may **s** up trading centers
22:43 example his father Asa had **s**
2Ki 3:2 stone that his father had **s** up
4:4 When one is full, **s** it aside."
4:43 "How can I **s** this in front of a
4:44 The servant **s** it in front of them.
8:12 You will **s** their fortresses on
16:10 altar and a **s** of detailed plans.
16:17 bulls that were under it and **s**
17:10 They **s** up sacred stones and
21:3 He **s** up altars dedicated to
21:7 Then he **s** it up in the temple,
25:1 They **s** up camp and built dirt
1Ch 6:32 regulations **s** down for them.
15:1 a place for God's ark and **s** up
16:1 The men carrying the ark **s** it
21:18 Gad to tell David to go and **s** up
22:7 "I had my heart **s** on building a
28:2 I had my heart **s** on building the
2Ch 2:14 of engravings and follow any **s**
3:17 He **s** up the pillars in front of
4:4 The pool was **s** on 12 metal
4:4 The pool was **s** on them,
4:10 He **s** the pool on the south side
6:7 father David had his heart **s**
6:8 'Since you had your heart **s** on
8:14 he **s** up the divisions of priests
8:14 Solomon also **s** up divisions of
13:13 But Jeroboam had **s** an
14:10 and the two armies **s** up their
15:18 his father had **s** apart as holy.
20:22 the LORD **s** ambushes against
20:32 example his father Asa had **s**
20:33 still didn't have their hearts **s**
25:14 **s** them up as his gods,
30:19 those who have their hearts **s**
31:3 He **s** aside part of the king's
32:1 He **s** up camp ⌊to attack⌋ the
33:3 He **s** up altars dedicated to
33:7 Then he **s** it up in God's
33:8 from the land that I **s** aside
33:19 worship sites and **s** up idols
35:12 They **s** aside the burnt
Ezr 10:14 At a **s** time, everyone who has
Neh 3:1 They dedicated it and **s** its
3:3 laid its beams and **s** its doors,
3:6 laid its beams and **s** its doors,
3:13 They rebuilt it and **s** its doors,
3:14 He rebuilt it and **s** its doors,
3:15 over it, and **s** its doors, locks,
4:9 But we prayed to our God and **s**
4:22 in Jerusalem so that we can **s**
9:35 fertile land which was **s** in front
12:47 They **s** aside holy gifts for ⌊the
12:47 and the Levites **s** aside holy
Est 5:14 "Have a pole **s** up,
5:14 so he had the pole **s** up.
Job 7:12 a sea monster that you have **s**
11:13 "If you want to **s** your heart
14:5 and you **s** his limit,
14:13 **S** a specific time for me when
16:12 He **s** me up as his target,
24:1 "Why doesn't the Almighty **s**
28:4 where no one has **s** foot.
28:26 rules for the rain and **s** paths
34:23 He doesn't have to **s** a time for
38:10 when I **s** a limit for it and put up
Psa 8:3 stars that you have **s** in place —
9:7 He has **s** up his throne for
11:2 They **s** their arrows against the
19:4 He has **s** up a tent in the
21:3 blessings of good things and **s**
24:2 foundation on the seas and **s**
31:8 You have **s** my feet in a place
40:2 He **s** my feet on a rock and
41:12 and you **s** me in your presence

Psa 44:2 but you **s** our ancestors free.
53:5 those who **s** up camp against
65:6 the one who **s** the mountains in
69:18 **S** me free because of my
69:22 Let the table **s** for them become
74:4 They have **s** up their own
74:16 You **s** the moon and the sun in
81:5 are the instructions God **s**
83:15 and flames **s** mountains on fire.
89:19 "I **s** a boy above warriors.
89:48 Who can **s** himself free from
90:8 You have **s** our sins in front of
93:1 The world was **s** in place;
93:2 Your throne was **s** in place a
102:20 prisoners and **s** free those who
103:19 The LORD has **s** his throne in
104:5 You **s** the earth on its
104:9 cross the boundary you **s**
104:19 which knows when to **s**.
105:20 The ruler of nations **s** him free.
118:5 me ⌊and⌋ **s** me free ⌊from
119:30 I have **s** your regulations in
119:90 You **s** the earth in place,
119:110 Wicked people have **s** a trap
125:3 to govern the land **s** aside
132:11 "I will **s** one of your own
140:5 They have **s** traps for me along
141:3 **s** a guard at my mouth.
141:9 me away from the trap they **s**
141:9 the traps **s** by troublemakers.
148:6 He **s** them in their places
Pro 1:11 Let's **s** an ambush to kill
1:15 Do not even **s** foot on their path,
1:18 But these people **s** an ambush
8:27 "When he **s** up the heavens,
8:29 when he **s** a limit for the sea so
9:2 She has **s** her table.
16:11 made the entire **s** of weights.
19:29 Punishments are **s** for mockers
22:17 and **s** your mind on the
22:25 you will learn his ways and **s**
22:28 that your ancestors **s** in place.
25:17 Do not **s** foot in your neighbor's
30:4 Who has **s** up the earth from
Sos 5:12 His eyes are **s** like doves
5:14 disks of gold **s** with emerald.
5:15 legs are columns of marble **s**
Isa 7:6 and **s** up Tabeel's son as its
9:11 The LORD will **s** Rezin's
14:13 "I'll go up to heaven and **s** up
16:5 Then the LORD will **s** up a
17:10 the best plants and have **s** out
17:11 On the morning you **s** out the
21:5 **S** the table. Spread the rugs ⌊by
23:13 Assyria **s** up battle towers,
27:4 fight them in battle and **s** all
29:3 I will **s** up war camps all
33:12 They will be **s** on fire like dry
40:20 craftsmen to **s** up idols that
42:4 until he has **s** up justice
43:28 I will **s** up Israel for ridicule.
45:18 He **s** it up. He did not create it to
46:7 They **s** the idol in its place,
50:7 I have **s** my face like a flint.
51:14 prisoners will be **s** free.
57:8 You've **s** up your idols beside
61:1 that captives will be **s** free
66:19 I will **s** up a sign among them
Jer 1:5 Before you were born, I **s** you
1:15 and they will **s** up their thrones
2:3 Israel was **s** apart for the
4:7 destroyer of nations has **s** out.
5:26 They **s** traps and catch people.
7:30 "They **s** up their detestable
9:8 of ways to **s** traps for them.
10:12 He **s** up the world by his skill.
10:20 There's no one to **s** up my tent
11:13 You have **s** up many altars ⌊in
11:16 He will **s** fire to you with a
17:27 I will **s** its gates on fire.
22:17 your eyes and your mind are **s**
24:1 me two baskets of figs **s**
26:4 follow my teachings that I **s**
31:21 **S** up landmarks! Put up road
31:29 children's teeth are **s** on edge.'
31:30 have his own teeth **s** on edge.

Jer 32:29 will break in, **s** this city on fire,
32:34 They **s** up their detestable
33:2 formed it, and **s** it in place.
34:10 So they **s** them free.
34:14 you must **s** them free.'
34:16 slaves that you had **s** free
35:5 Then I **s** cups and pitchers
43:10 I will **s** his throne over these
43:12 He will **s** fire to the temples of
49:27 "I will **s** fire to the walls of
49:38 I'll **s** my throne in Elam and
50:24 I will **s** traps for you,
50:29 **S** up blockades around it.
51:15 He **s** up the world by his
51:30 Their buildings are **s** on fire.
51:58 its high gates will be **s** on fire.
52:4 They **s** up camp and built dirt
Eze 4:2 **S** up a blockade against it,
4:3 Then take an iron pan, and **s** it
4:10 of food every day at **s** times.
4:11 and drink it at **s** times.
11:12 followed the standards **s** by
11:21 as for those whose minds are **s**
17:17 dirt ramps and **s** up blockades
18:2 children's teeth are **s** on edge'?
20:20 **S** apart certain holy days to
20:47 I am about to **s** fire to you to
21:22 So he will **s** up his battering
21:22 and **s** up blockades.
24:11 Then **s** the empty pot on the
25:4 They will **s** up their camps and
26:8 He will **s** up blockades,
27:6 of Cyprus. It had ivory **s** in it.
28:18 So I **s** fire to you to burn you up.
30:8 because I will **s** fire to Egypt
30:14 destroy Pathros, **s** fire to Zoan,
30:16 I will **s** fire to Egypt.
37:28 have **s** Israel apart as holy,
39:9 They will **s** fire to weapons
39:15 they will **s** up a marker beside
40:2 God brought me to Israel and **s**
42:6 story were **s** farther back than
45:1 **S** aside an area 43,750 feet
48:8 The land that you **s** aside as a
48:9 This special land that you **s**
48:11 This land that has been **s** apart
Dan 3:1 He **s** it up in a recessed area in
3:2 the statue he had **s** up.
3:3 Nebuchadnezzar had **s** up.
3:5 Nebuchadnezzar has **s** up.
3:7 Nebuchadnezzar had **s** up.
3:12 the statue that you **s** up."
3:14 the gold statue that I **s** up?
3:18 the gold statue that you **s** up."
7:9 I watched until thrones were **s**
9:27 promise with many for one **s**
11:31 and **s** up the disgusting thing
12:11 that causes destruction is **s** up,
Hos 5:1 You **s** traps at Mizpah and
6:11 "Yet, Judah, I have **s** a harvest
9:8 Yet, traps are **s** on every
10:1 the more stone markers they **s**
Amo 1:14 I will **s** fire to the walls of
9:11 On that day I will **s** up David's
Oba 1:7 eat food with you will **s** traps
Mic 3:6 The sun will **s** on the prophets,
Nah 2:5 The shield has been **s** up for
Hab 2:9 in order to **s** his nest up
Hag 2:12 a person carries meat **s** aside
Zec 3:9 "Look at the stone I have **s** in
5:11 they will **s** the basket there on
9:11 I will **s** your captives free from
11:13 Such a magnificent price was **s**
Mat 5:17 to **s** aside Moses' Teachings
5:17 I didn't come to **s** them aside
16:19 And whatever you **s** free,
16:19 you set free, God will **s** free."
18:18 And whatever you **s** free,
18:18 you set free, God will **s** free.
Mar 1:32 when the sun had **s**,
Luk 1:68 his people and to **s** them free.
2:23 "Every firstborn boy is to be **s**
2:38 for Jerusalem to be **s** free.
21:28 you will be **s** free is near."
23:16 have him whipped and **s** free."
23:22 have him whipped and **s** free."

Jon 8:32 and the truth will **s** you free."
8:33 you say that we will be **s** free?"
10:36 God **s** me apart for this holy
Act 13:2 "**S** Barnabas and Saul apart for
15:16 I will **s** up David's fallen tent
15:16 again. I will **s** it up again
17:31 He has **s** a day when he is
26:32 "This man could have been **s**
27:2 We **s** sail on a ship from the
28:10 when we were going to **s** sail,
Rom 3:24 the price Christ Jesus paid to **s**
8:2 have **s** you free from the
8:21 that it would also be **s** free from
10:3 So they try to **s** up their own
11:9 David says, "Let the table **s**
1Co 7:5 you agree to do so for a **s** time
16:2 of you should **s** aside some
Gal 2:16 according to a **s** of standards,
2:16 according to a **s** of standards.
3:2 efforts to live according to a **s**
3:10 efforts to live according to a **s**
4:2 until the time **s** by his father.
Eph 1:7 we are **s** free from our sins.
1:14 guarantee until we are **s** free
4:17 are **s** on worthless things.
4:30 the day you will be **s** free ⌊from
Php 1:19 I know that I will be **s** free
3:19 minds are **s** on worldly things.
2Th 3:9 Rather, we wanted to **s** an
1Ti 4:5 The word of God and prayer **s**
6:10 Some people who have **s** their
2Ti 2:21 They will be **s** apart for the
Tit 2:7 Always **s** an example by doing
2:14 He gave himself for us to **s** us
3:14 should also learn how to **s**
Heb 4:7 So God **s** another day.
7:26 **s** apart from sinners,
8:2 and of the true tent **s** up by
9:2 A tent was **s** up. The first part of
9:6 two parts of the tent were **s** up.
9:15 the price to **s** people free from
10:10 We have been **s** apart as holy
Jas 3:5 A large forest can be **s** on fire
3:6 and is itself **s** on fire from hell.
1Pe 1:18 Realize that you weren't **s** free
Rev 10:2 He **s** his right foot on the sea
20:3 After that it must be **s** free for a

Seth (9)

Gen 4:25 birth to a son and named him **S**,
4:26 A son was also born to **S**,
5:3 own image. He named him **S**.
5:4 Adam became the father of **S**,
5:6 When **S** was 105 years old,
5:7 **S** lived 807 years and had
5:8 **S** lived a total of 912 years;
1Ch 1:1 Adam, **S**, Enosh,
Luk 3:38 son of Enos, son of **S**,

Sethur (1)

Num 13:13 **S**, son of Michael, from the

sets (40)

Exo 26:6 Use them to link the ⌊two **s** of⌋
36:13 the ⌊two **s** of⌋ sheets together
Lev 20:8 I am the LORD who **s** you apart
22:9 who **s** them apart as holy.
22:16 who **s** them apart as holy."
22:32 who **s** you apart as holy.
Dtr 25:13 Never carry two **s** of weights,
27:15 and **s** it up in secret will be
2Sm 22:33 His perfect way **s** me free.
1Ki 7:41 and 2 **s** of filigree to cover the 2
7:42 400 pomegranates for the 2 **s** of
2Ki 5:5 and 10 **s** of clothing with him.
5:22 of silver and two **s** of clothing.'"
5:23 bags with two **s** of clothing.
2Ch 4:12 and 2 **s** of filigree to cover the 2
4:13 400 pomegranates for the 2 **s** of
Job 41:21 Its breath **s** coals on fire,
Psa 27:3 Even though an army **s** up
27:5 He **s** me high on a rock.
50:1 the sun rises to where it **s**.
113:3 sun rises to where the sun **s**,
139:9 of the sea where the sun **s**,
146:7 The LORD **s** prisoners free.

Pro 29:25 A person's fear **s** a trap ⌊for
Ecc 1:5 The sun rises, and the sun **s**,
Isa 9:18 It **s** the underbrush in the forest
Dan 9:24 "Seventy **s** of seven time
9:25 seven **s** of seven time periods
9:25 time periods and sixty-two **s**
9:26 But after the sixty-two **s** of
Amo 9:6 heaven and **s** their foundation
Nah 1:11 evil against the LORD **s** out.
Zec 8:7 from the land where the sun **s**.
Mal 1:11 to the nations where the sun **s**,
Mat 5:19 So whoever **s** aside any
Jon 8:36 So if the Son **s** you free,
Rom 7:23 with the standards my mind **s**
1Ti 3:1 If anyone **s** his heart on being a
3:7 insults that the devil **s** as traps
Jas 3:6 The tongue **s** our lives on fire,

setting (14)

Gen 50:21 **s** their minds at ease.
Exo 14:9 as they were **s** up their camp
Num 7:1 When Moses finished **s** up the
22:5 and are **s** up their camp
1Ki 16:34 **S** up the city doors cost him
1Ch 9:32 relatives were responsible for **s**
Psa 64:5 They talk about **s** traps and
Pro 12:12 A wicked person delights in **s**
Isa 30:33 of burning sulfur, **s** it on fire.
Zec 2:13 He is waking up and **s** out from
Luk 4:40 When the sun was **s**,
Tit 3:8 in God can concentrate on **s**
Heb 6:2 **s** people apart for holy tasks,
10:14 the work of **s** them apart

settings (12)

Exo 28:11 Mount them in gold **s**,
28:13 Make gold **s**
28:14 fasten these chains to the **s**.
28:20 Mount them in gold **s**.
28:25 ends of the ropes to the two **s**
39:6 the onyx stones in gold **s**,
39:13 stones were mounted in gold **s**.
39:16 They made two gold **s** and two
39:18 ends of the ropes to the two **s**
1Ch 29:2 onyx stones and **s**,
Pro 25:11 golden apples in silver **s**,
Eze 28:13 Your **s** and your sockets were

settle (24)

Exo 16:35 until they came to a place to **s**.
18:22 **s** disagreements among
18:22 but they should **s** all minor
Lev 26:32 will be shocked as they **s** in it.
Dtr 12:10 cross the Jordan River and **s**
2Sm 20:18 That's the way they **s** matters.'
1Ch 4:12 was the first to **s** Beth Rapha.
7:14 Machir was the first to **s**
9:2 The first to **s** again on their
Ezr 2:63 Thummim ⌊to **s** the problem⌋.
Neh 7:65 Thummim ⌊to **s** the problem⌋.
Isa 2:4 **s** arguments between many
7:19 All of them will come and **s** in
23:7 its people to **s** in distant lands?
Jer 48:11 Its people are like wine left to **s**
Hos 11:11 I will **s** them in their own
Mic 4:3 **s** arguments between many
Nah 3:17 like swarms of locusts that **s**
Mat 18:23 king who wanted to **s** accounts
Luk 12:58 do your best to **s** with him
Act 19:39 you must **s** the matter in a legal
1Co 6:1 how dare you go to court to **s**
6:1 Why don't you **s** it in front of
6:5 **s** disagreements between

settled (76)

Gen 11:2 Shinar [Babylonia] and **s** there.
19:30 He and his two daughters **s** in
20:1 Negev and **s** between Kadesh
25:11 who **s** near Beer Lahai Roi.
47:27 So the Israelites **s** in Egypt in
Exo 2:15 Moses fled from Pharaoh and **s**
18:23 disagreements **s** so that they
18:26 **s** disagreements among
18:26 but they **s** all minor ones
22:11 them must be **s** by swearing

Exo 24:16 The glory of the LORD **s** on
40:35 because the smoke **s** on it and
Num 15:2 Once you're **s** in the land I'm
21:31 So Israel **s** in the land of the
Dtr 19:15 Cases must be **s** based on the
26:1 When you have **s** there,
Jos 19:47 They took it, **s** there,
21:43 possession of it and **s** there.
Jdg 5:14 Those who had **s** in Amalek's
1Sm 12:8 The LORD **s** them in this place.
30:14 of the Negev where Caleb **s**,
2Sm 2:3 and they **s** in the towns around
1Ki 11:24 went to Damascus, **s** there,
17:1 who was from Tishbe but had **s**
2Ki 17:6 He **s** them in Halah,
17:24 and Sepharvaim and **s** them in
17:26 you took as captives and **s**
17:29 But each group ⌊that **s** in
1Ch 2:21 the man who first **s** Gilead.
2:23 the man who first **s** Gilead.
2:24 who first **s** Tekoa.
2:42 son Mesha, who first **s** Ziph,
2:42 who first **s** Hebron.
2:44 who first **s** Jorkeam.
2:45 who first **s** Beth Zur.
2:49 who first **s** Madmannah,
2:49 who first **s** Machbenah and
2:50 who first **s** Kiriath Jearim,
2:51 Salma, who first **s** Bethlehem,
2:51 who first **s** Beth Gadar.
2:52 who first **s** Kiriath Jearim,
2:54 ⌊who first **s**⌋ Bethlehem,
2:54 ⌊who first **s**⌋ Beth Joab,
2:55 They first **s** Beth Rechab.
4:4 who first **s** Bethlehem.
4:5 Ashhur, who first **s** Tekoa,
4:12 who first **s** the city of Nahash.
4:14 who first **s** the valley of
4:17 who first **s** Eshtemoa.
4:18 who first **s** Gedor, Heber,
4:18 Gedor, Heber, who first **s** Soco,
4:18 who first **s** Zanoah.
4:19 first **s** Keilah of the Garmites
4:21 Er, who first **s** Lecah, Laadah,
4:21 who first **s** Mareshah,
6:54 the places where they **s** in the
7:31 who first **s** Birzaith.
8:29 Jeiel, who first **s** Gibeon,
9:3 Jerusalem was **s** by
9:13 temple and **s** in Jerusalem.
9:35 Jeiel, who first **s** Gibeon,
Ezr 2:70 and the temple servants **s** in
2:70 All the other Israelites **s** in their
3:1 had already **s** in their cities.)
4:10 (Assurbanipal **s** them in the
Neh 7:73 and the rest of Israel **s** in their
11:1 of the people **s** in Jerusalem.
11:3 province who **s** in Jerusalem.
11:3 of Solomon's servants **s**
11:4 of Benjamin **s** in Jerusalem.
11:6 descendants of Perez who **s**
11:30 So they **s** in the land from
Psa 68:10 Your flock **s** there.
78:55 He **s** the tribes of Israel in their
Pro 8:25 before the mountains were **s**
Mat 25:19 and **s** accounts with them.

settlement (1)

Exo 21:30 However, if only a cash **s** is

settlements (8)

Gen 25:16 their names listed by their **s**
Num 31:10 Midianites lived and all their **s**.
32:41 captured the **s** in Gilead.
32:41 them Havvoth Jair [S of Jair].
Dtr 3:14 The **s** in Bashan he named
Jos 13:30 Og of Bashan) and all 60 **s**
1Ki 4:13 he had the **s** of Jair,
Isa 42:11 Let those who live in the **s** of

settlers (1)

1Ch 4:3 These were the first **s** in Etam:

settles (3)

Rut 3:18 unless he **s** this matter today."
Psa 107:36 There he **s** those who are
Pro 18:18 **s** ⌊issues⌋ between powerful

settling (1)

Exo 18:13 The next day Moses was **s**

seventh (114)

Gen 2:2 By the **s** day God had finished
2:2 On the **s** day he stopped the
2:3 Then God blessed the **s** day
8:4 day of the **s** month,
Exo 12:15 first day through the **s** day must
12:16 day and another one on the **s**.
13:6 The **s** day will be a pilgrimage
16:26 on six days, but on the **s** day,
16:27 On the **s** day some people
16:29 On the **s** day you may not
16:30 never worked on the **s** day
20:10 The **s** day is the day of
20:11 He didn't work on the **s** day.
21:2 In the **s** year he may leave as a
23:11 but in the **s** year you must
23:12 but on the **s** day you must not
24:16 and on the **s** day the LORD
31:15 but the **s** day is a day of
31:17 and on the **s** day he stopped
34:21 but on the **s** day you must not
35:2 but the **s** day is a holy day of
Lev 13:5 On the **s** day the priest will
13:6 On the **s** day the priest will
13:27 On the **s** day the priest will
13:32 On the **s** day the priest will
13:34 On the **s** day the priest will
13:51 On the **s** day he will examine
14:9 On the **s** day he must shave off
14:39 On the **s** day the priest will go
16:29 On the tenth day of the **s** month
23:3 But the **s** day is a day of
23:8 On the **s** day there will be a
23:16 until the day after the **s** week.
23:24 On the first day of the **s** month
23:27 the tenth day of this **s** month is
23:34 The fifteenth day of this **s**
23:39 the fifteenth day of the **s** month,
23:41 Celebrate this festival in the **s**
25:4 However, the **s** year will be a
25:9 the tenth day of the **s** month,
25:20 'What will we eat in the **s** year
Num 7:48 On the **s** day the leader of the
19:12 on the third day and the **s** day
19:12 on the third day and the **s** day,
19:19 on the third day and the **s** day.
19:19 On the **s** day the clean person
28:25 On the **s** day you must have a
29:1 "On the first day of the **s** month
29:7 "On the tenth day of the **s**
29:12 "On the fifteenth day of the **s**
29:32 "On the **s** day bring 7 bulls,
31:19 water on the third and **s** days
31:24 On the **s** day wash your
Dtr 5:14 The **s** day is the day of
15:9 When the **s** year — the year
15:12 In the **s** year you must let them
16:8 and on the **s** day hold a
31:10 "At the end of every **s** year you
Jos 6:4 But on the **s** day you must
6:15 On the **s** day they got up at
6:16 they went around the **s** time,
19:40 The **s** lot was drawn for the
Jdg 14:17 Finally, on the **s** day he told
14:18 before sundown on the **s** day,
2Sm 12:18 On the **s** day the child died.
1Ki 8:2 month of Ethanim, the **s** month.
18:44 After the **s** time the servant
20:29 and on the **s** day the battle
2Ki 11:4 In the **s** year of Athaliah's reign,
12:1 Joash began to rule in Jehu's **s**
18:9 as king (which was the **s** year
25:8 On the **s** day of the fifth month
25:25 In the **s** month Ishmael (son of
1Ch 2:15 and David (his **s** son).
12:11 was Attai. The **s** was Eliel.
24:10 the **s** for Hakkoz, the eighth for
25:14 The **s** chose Jesarelah,
26:3 Eliehoenai (the **s**).
26:5 (the sixth), Issachar (the **s**),
27:10 was in charge of the **s** unit
1Ch 27:10 unit during the **s** month.
2Ch 5:3 ⌊of Booths⌋ in the **s** month.
7:10 twenty-third day of the **s** month,
23:1 In the **s** year of Athaliah's reign,
31:7 in the **s** month they finished.
Ezr 3:1 When the **s** month came,
3:6 on the first day of the **s** month,
7:7 in Artaxerxes' **s** year as king.
Neh 7:73 When the **s** month came,
8:1 ⌊When the **s** month came,⌋
8:2 on the first day of the **s** month.
8:14 during a festival in the **s** month.
10:31 During the **s** year, we won't
Est 1:10 On the **s** day when the king
2:16 in the **s** year of his reign.
Job 5:19 and when the **s** one comes,
Jer 28:17 Hananiah died in the **s** month
41:1 In the **s** month Ishmael (son of
52:28 In his **s** year as king,
Eze 20:1 of the fifth month in the **s** year,
30:20 On the **s** day of the first month
45:20 You must do the same on the **s**
45:25 the fifteenth day of the **s** month,
Hag 2:1 twenty-first day of the **s** month,
Zec 7:5 fifth and **s** months these past
8:19 the fast in the **s** month,
Heb 4:4 has said this about the **s** day:
4:4 "On the **s** day God rested from
Jud 1:14 Furthermore, Enoch, from the **s**
Rev 8:1 When he opened the **s** seal,
10:7 In the days when the **s** angel is
11:15 When the **s** angel blew his
16:17 The **s** angel poured his bowl
21:20 the **s** yellow quartz,

severe (29)

Gen 12:10 because the famine was **s**.
35:16 and was having **s** labor pains.
41:31 the coming famine will be so **s**.
41:56 the famine was **s** in Egypt.
41:57 since the famine was so **s** all
43:1 The famine was **s** in the land.
43:3 "The man gave us a **s** warning:
47:4 The famine is so **s** in Canaan
47:13 The famine was so **s** that there
47:20 because the famine was so **s**.
Num 11:33 struck them with a **s** plague.
Dtr 28:35 and legs with **s** boils that can't
28:59 and **s** and lingering diseases.
1Ki 18:2 was particularly **s** in Samaria.
2Ki 6:25 of Samaria became so **s** that
6:33 He said to Elisha, "This **s**
25:3 in the city became so **s** that
Jer 52:6 in the city became so **s** that
Lam 4:6 has been more **s** than
Mat 8:24 a **s** storm came across the sea.
Mar 12:40 the most **s** punishment."
Luk 4:25 and the famine was **s**
15:14 He had nothing left when a **s**
20:47 the most **s** punishment."
Act 11:28 that a **s** famine would affect
27:20 It was so **s** that we finally
Rom 11:22 Look at how kind and how **s**
11:22 He is **s** to those who fell,
2Co 2:6 a **s** enough punishment

severed (1)

Jdg 7:25 Then they brought the **s** heads

severely (14)

Exo 7:4 my power to punish Egypt **s**,
12:12 I will **s** punish all the gods of
1Sm 11:1 King Nahash of Ammon was **s**
Psa 62:2 I cannot be **s** shaken.
118:18 The LORD disciplined me **s**,
Zec 12:3 try to lift it will be **s** injured.
Mat 24:51 Then his master will **s** punish
Luk 12:46 his master will punish him **s**
2Co 8:2 While they were being **s** tested
11:23 been beaten more **s**,
1Th 2:15 and who have persecuted us **s**.
Heb 12:6 He **s** disciplines everyone he
Jas 3:1 teach will be judged more **s**.
Rev 16:9 They were **s** burned.

sew (3)

Exo 26:9 S five of the sheets together
Ecc 3:7 apart and a time to s together,
Eze 13:18 women who s magic charms

sewed (1)

Gen 3:7 They s fig leaves together and

sewn (6)

Exo 26:3 the sheets must be s together,
26:3 five must also be s together.
36:10 of the sheets were s together,
36:10 and the other five were also s
36:16 Five of the sheets were s
Job 16:15 "I have s sackcloth over my

sex (29)

Gen 19:5 that we can have s with them."
19:8 who have never had s.
Exo 21:10 first wife of food, clothes, or s.
Num 25:1 to have s with Moabite women
Dtr 21:14 you've already had s with her.
22:21 She had s before marriage,
22:24 must die because he had s
28:30 man will have s with her.
Jdg 19:22 that we can have s with him."
19:25 They had s with her and
2Sm 3:7 "Why did you have s with my
Pro 2:19 None who have s with her
6:29 So it is with a man who has s
Jer 3:2 You have had s with men in
Eze 16:15 You had s with everyone who
16:26 You had s with your lustful
16:28 "'You had s with the Assyrians
16:33 directions to have s with you.
22:10 Men have s with their father's
22:10 They have s with women
22:11 men who live in you have s
23:43 continued to have s with her.
Hos 4:10 will have s with prostitutes,
4:18 they continue to have s with
9:1 You have sold s on every
Gal 5:19 obvious: illicit s, perversion,
Rev 17:2 of the earth had s with her,
18:3 of the earth had s with her.
18:9 kings of the earth who had s

sexual (98)

Gen 24:16 No man had ever had s
Exo 19:15 by having s intercourse."
22:16 anyone and has s intercourse
22:19 "Whoever has s intercourse
Lev 15:18 "When a man has s intercourse
15:24 If a man has s intercourse with
15:33 or for any man who has s
18:6 "Never have s intercourse with
18:7 "Never have s intercourse with
18:7 have s intercourse with her.
18:8 Never have s intercourse with
18:9 Never have s intercourse with
18:10 Never have s intercourse with
18:11 Never have s intercourse with
18:12 Never have s intercourse with
18:13 Never have s intercourse with
18:14 Never have s intercourse with
18:15 Never have s intercourse with
18:15 have s intercourse with her.
18:16 Never have s intercourse with
18:17 Never have s intercourse with
18:18 have s intercourse with her.
18:19 "Never have s intercourse with
18:20 Never have s intercourse with
18:22 Never have s intercourse with
18:23 Never have s intercourse with
18:23 to an animal for s intercourse.
19:20 "If a man has s intercourse
20:11 Whoever has s intercourse
20:12 If a man has s intercourse with
20:13 When a man has s intercourse
20:15 A man who has s intercourse
20:17 and has s intercourse does a
20:17 He has had s intercourse with
20:18 If a man has s intercourse with
20:18 both of them have had s
20:19 Never have s intercourse with
Lev 20:19 Whoever has s intercourse
20:20 Whoever has s intercourse
Num 5:13 and may have had s
5:19 'If no other man has had s
5:20 and have had s intercourse
Dtr 22:22 If a man is caught having s
22:23 when a man has s intercourse
22:29 the man who had s intercourse
27:20 "Whoever has s intercourse
27:21 "Whoever has s intercourse
27:22 "Whoever has s intercourse
27:23 "Whoever has s intercourse
1Sm 21:4 had s intercourse ⌊today⌋."
Eze 18:6 wife or have s intercourse
Mat 15:19 ⌊other⌋ s sins, stealing, lying,
Mar 7:21 Evil thoughts, s sins,
Luk 1:34 I've never had s intercourse."
Act 15:20 by false gods, from s sins,
15:29 animals, and from s sins.
21:25 They also should not commit s
Rom 1:24 they dishonor their bodies by s
1:26 exchanged natural s relations
1:27 given up natural s relations
1:29 filled with of all kinds of s sins,
6:19 body as slaves to s perversion
13:13 s immorality, promiscuity,
1Co 5:1 aware that there is s sin going
5:9 who continue to commit s sins.
5:10 who commit s sins,
5:11 Christian faith but live in s sin,
6:9 who continue to commit s sins,
6:13 However, the body is not for s
6:18 Stay away from s sins.
6:18 the same way s sins do.
7:2 But in order to avoid s sins,
7:3 satisfy each other's ⌊s⌋ needs.
7:9 than to burn ⌊with s desire⌋.
2Co 12:21 about the perversion, s sins,
Eph 4:19 They practice every kind of s
5:3 Don't let s sin, perversion of
5:5 who is involved in s sin,
Col 3:5 your s sin, perversion, passion,
1Th 4:3 you keep away from s sin as
1Ti 1:10 for people involved in s sins,
Heb 12:16 sure that no one commits s sin
13:4 those who commit s sins,
2Pe 2:2 follow them in their s freedom
2:7 and lived in s freedom.
2:18 by appealing to their s desires,
2:18 especially to s freedom.
Jud 1:4 as an excuse for s freedom
1:7 because they committed s sins
Rev 2:21 to turn away from her s sins.
2:22 Those who commit s sins with
14:8 wine of her passionate s sins."
17:2 on the wine of her s sins."
17:4 and evil things from her s sins.
18:3 of the wine of her s sins.
19:2 the world with her s sins.
21:8 s sinners, sorcerers, idolaters,
22:15 s sinners, murderers, idolaters,

sexually (9)

Lev 20:16 When a woman offers herself s
Eze 22:9 on the hills, and they sin s.
22:11 Some men s dishonor their
1Co 6:18 People who sin s sin against
10:8 We shouldn't sin s as some of
1Th 4:7 God didn't call us to be s
Rev 2:14 sacrificed to idols and to sin s.
2:20 misleads my servants to sin s
9:21 sinning s, or stealing.

Shaalabbin (1)

Jos 19:42 S, Aijalon, Ithlah,

Shaalbim (2)

Jdg 1:35 at Har Heres, Aijalon, and S.
1Ki 4:9 of Makaz, S, Beth Shemesh,

Shaalbon (2)

2Sm 23:32 Elihba from S, Bene Jashen,
1Ch 11:33 from Bahurim, Eliahba from S,

Shaalim (1)

1Sm 9:4 went through the region of S,

Shaaph (2)

1Ch 2:47 Geshan, Pelet, Ephah, and S.
2:49 Also, she was the mother of S,

Shaaraim (3)

Jos 15:36 S, Adithaim, Gederah,
1Sm 17:52 Philistines lay on the road to S
1Ch 4:31 Hazar Susim, Beth Biri, and S.

Shaashgaz (1)

Est 2:14 the care of the king's eunuch S,

Shabbethai (3)

Ezr 10:15 Meshullam and S,
Neh 8:7 S, Hodiah, Maaseiah, Kelita,
11:16 S and Jozabad, Levite leaders,

shabby (1)

Jas 2:2 is wearing s clothes.

shack (3)

Job 27:18 like a s that a watchman
Isa 1:8 like a s in a cucumber field,
24:20 like a drunk and sway like a s

shackles (9)

2Ki 25:7 They put him in bronze s and
2Ch 33:11 put him in bronze s,
36:6 and put him in bronze s
Job 13:27 You put my feet in s.
Psa 105:18 They hurt his feet with s,
149:8 and their leaders in iron s,
Jer 29:26 a prophet in prison and in s.
39:7 put him in bronze s,
52:11 and put him in bronze s.

shade (13)

Jdg 9:15 come and take shelter in my s.
Job 7:2 Like a slave, he longs for s.
Psa 80:10 Its s covered the mountains.
121:5 The LORD is the s over your
Isa 25:4 and s from the heat.
32:2 on parched ground and the s
Eze 31:6 powerful nations lived in its s.
31:12 out from under its s and left.
Dan 4:12 Wild animals found s under it.
Hos 4:13 that these trees provide good s.
Jnh 4:5 He sat in its s and waited to
4:6 up beside Jonah to give him s
Mar 4:32 that birds can nest in its s."

shaded (1)

Eze 31:3 fine branches that s the forest.

shadow (44)

2Ki 9:30 She put on eye s, fixed her
20:9 Do you want the s to go
20:10 "It's easy for the s to extend
20:11 and the LORD made the s that
Job 8:9 on earth are only a fleeting s.
14:2 He is like a fleeting s;
17:7 Now all my limbs are like a s.
34:22 There's no darkness or deep s
Psa 17:8 Hide me in the s of your wings.
36:7 refuge in the s of your wings.
39:6 who walks around is like a s.
44:19 covered us with the s of death.
57:1 I will take refuge in the s of
63:7 In the s of your wings,
91:1 remain in the s of the Almighty.
102:11 My days are like a s that is
107:10 in death's s were prisoners in
107:14 out of the dark, out of death's s.
109:23 fade away like a lengthening s.
144:4 life span is like a fleeting s.
Ecc 6:12 Mortals pass by like a s.
Sos 2:3 I want to sit in his s.
Isa 9:2 live in the land of death's s.
16:3 At high noon make your s as
25:5 ⌊reduced⌋ by the s of a cloud.
30:2 and look for refuge in Egypt's s.
30:3 and the refuge in Egypt's s will
34:15 will gather their young in the s
38:8 The sun made a s that went
38:8 I'm going to make the s go

Jer 2:6 of drought and the s of death.
4:30 Why do you wear eye s?
13:16 the LORD will turn it into the s
48:45 exhausted in the s of Heshbon.
Lam 4:20 king's s among the nations."
Eze 31:17 All who lived in its s were
Hos 14:7 They will live again in God's s.
Luk 1:79 live in the dark and in death's s.
Act 5:15 that at least Peter's s might fall
1Co 9:26 not as if I were just s boxing.
Col 2:17 These are a s of the things to
2:17 casts the s⌋ belongs to Christ.
Heb 8:5 a s, of what is in heaven.
10:1 cycle of sacrifices are only a s

shadows (10)

Jdg 9:36 Zebul replied, "The s of the
1Ch 29:15 Our days are as fleeting as s
Job 3:5 Let the darkness and long s
10:22 to a dismal land of long s and
16:16 and dark s encircle my eyes,
Ecc 8:13 Their lives are like s,
Sos 2:17 a cooling breeze and the s flee,
4:6 a cool breeze and the s flee,
Jer 6:4 The day is passing, and the s
Jas 1:17 like the shifting s produced by

Shadrach (15)

Dan 1:7 Hananiah he gave the name S.
2:49 Daniel appointed S,
3:12 S, Meshach, and Abednego.
3:13 Nebuchadnezzar summoned S,
3:14 "S, Meshach, and Abednego,
3:16 S, Meshach, and Abednego
3:19 so filled with anger toward S,
3:20 from his army to tie up S,
3:22 hot that the men who carried S,
3:23 So these three men — S,
3:26 furnace and said, "S, Meshach,
3:26 S, Meshach, and Abednego
3:28 "Praise the God of S,
3:29 slanderous about the God of S,
3:30 Then the king promoted S,

shaft (11)

Exo 25:31 lamp stand, its base, and its s,
37:17 lamp stand, its base, and its s,
1Sm 17:7 The s of his spear was like the
2Sm 5:8 hate me by using the water s."
21:19 (The s of Goliath's spear was
23:7 them uses iron ⌊tools⌋ or the s
1Ch 20:5 (The s of Lahmi's spear was
Job 28:4 ⌊In this s⌋ men dangle and
Rev 9:1 star was given the key to the s
9:2 It opened the s of the
9:2 and smoke came out of the s

Shage (1)

1Ch 11:34 (son of S the Hararite),

Shaharaim (1)

1Ch 8:8 S divorced his wives Hushim

Shaharaim's (1)

1Ch 8:10 All of S sons became heads of

Shahazimah (1)

Jos 19:22 The border touches Tabor, S,

shake (45)

Dtr 2:25 tremble and s because of you."
Jdg 16:20 as usual and s myself free."
1Ki 14:15 Israel like cattails which s
2Ki 19:21 My people in Jerusalem s their
Job 16:4 against you and s my head at
38:13 edges and s wicked people out
Psa 2:3 chains and s off their ropes."
6:2 my bones s with terror.
10:6 "Nothing can s me.
22:7 They s their heads and say,
44:14 so that people s their heads at
46:3 and mountains s at the surging
64:8 Everyone who sees them will s
69:23 Let their thighs continually s.
82:5 the foundations of the earth s.
109:25 look at me and s their heads.
Isa 10:32 They s their fist at the
19:16 of Armies will s his fist at
23:11 over the sea to s kingdoms.
24:18 foundations of the earth will s.
24:19 The earth will s back and forth
37:22 My people in Jerusalem s their
52:2 S the dust from yourselves.
54:10 and the hills may s,
Jer 18:16 will be stunned and s his head.
22:10 Don't s your heads at them.
48:27 about them you s your heads
Lam 2:15 They hiss and s their heads at
Eze 4:7 S your fist and prophesy
12:18 s as you eat your food.
21:21 He will s some arrows,
26:10 and chariots will s your walls
26:15 who live on the coast will s
Dan 10:10 made my hands and knees s.
Joe 3:16 The sky and the earth will s.
Amo 9:1 so that the foundations s.
Hab 2:7 are going to s you wake up?
Hag 2:6 I am going to s the sky and the
2:7 I will s all the nations,
2:21 'I am going to s the heavens
Zec 2:9 I'm going to s my fist at the
Mat 10:14 and s its dust off your feet.
Mar 6:11 leave and s the dust from your
Luk 9:5 and s its dust off your feet as a
Heb 12:26 "Once more I will s not only

shaken (26)

2Sm 18:33 The king was s ⌊by the news⌋.
Job 31:21 If I have s my fist at an orphan
Psa 6:3 has been deeply s with terror.
6:10 shame and deeply s with terror.
13:4 rejoice because I have been s.
15:5 these things will never be s.
30:6 "I will never be s."
62:2 I cannot be severely s.
62:6 my stronghold. I cannot be s.
104:5 so that it can never be s.
109:23 I have been s off like a
125:1 which can never be s.
Isa 7:2 king and his people were s as
7:2 of the forest are s by the wind.
13:13 and the earth will be s from its
24:13 an olive tree which has been s
33:9 Bashan and Carmel are s.
Nah 3:12 When s, the figs fall into the
Mat 24:29 of the universe will be s.
Mar 13:25 of the universe will be s.
Luk 6:38 pressed together, s down,
21:26 of the universe will be s.
Heb 12:27 are the things that can be s.
12:27 that cannot be s will remain.
12:28 a kingdom that cannot be s.
Rev 6:13 from a fig tree when it is s by

shakes (4)

Job 9:6 He s the earth from its place,
Lam 2:15 who walks along the road s
Joe 2:10 their presence, and the sky s.
Hab 3:6 He stands and s the earth.

shaking (2)

Isa 21:4 I'm s with terror. The twilight
Jer 4:24 They are s, and the hills are

Shalisha (1)

1Sm 9:4 the region of S without finding

Shallecheth (1)

1Ch 26:16 for the west side with S Gate at

shallow (7)

Gen 32:22 and crossed at the s part
Jos 2:7 on the road leading to a s place
Jdg 3:28 and captured the s crossings
12:5 captured the s crossings
12:6 and kill him at the s crossings
Isa 16:2 at the s crossings of the Arnon
Col 2:8 you ⌊of this faith⌋ through a s

Shallum (29)

2Ki 15:10 S, son of Jabesh, attacked him
15:13 S, son of Jabesh, became king
15:13 S ruled for an entire month in
15:14 attacked S (son of Jabesh),
15:15 Everything else about S — all
22:14 She was the wife of S,
22:14 S was in charge of the ⌊royal⌋
1Ch 2:40 Sismai was the father of S.
2:41 S was the father of Jekamiah.
3:15 and the fourth was S.
4:25 Shaul's son was S.
6:12 Zadok was the father of S.
6:13 S was the father of Hilkiah.
7:13 Jahziel, Guni, Jezer, and S.
9:17 The gatekeepers were S,
9:17 (S was in charge.)
9:19 S (son of Kore, grandson of
9:31 the firstborn son of S,
2Ch 28:12 son of S, and Amasa,
34:22 She was the wife of S,
34:22 S was in charge of the ⌊royal⌋
Ezr 2:42 the descendants of S,
7:2 who was the son of S,
10:24 gatekeepers: S, Telem, and Uri
10:42 S, Amariah, and Joseph
Neh 3:12 Next to them S, an official in
7:45 the descendants of S,
Jer 22:11 about King Josiah's son S,
32:7 your cousin Hanamel, son of S,

Shallum's (2)

1Ch 4:25 S son was Mibsam.
Jer 35:4 S son, the doorkeeper.

Shallun (1)

Neh 3:15 S, Col Hozeh's son, the official

Shalmai (2)

Ezr 2:46 Hagab, S, Hanan,
Neh 7:48 Lebanah, Hagabah, S,

Shalman (1)

Hos 10:14 the time S destroyed Beth Arbel

Shalmaneser (2)

2Ki 17:3 King S of Assyria defeated
18:9 son of Elah of Israel) King S of

Shama (1)

1Ch 11:44 Uzzia from Ashteroth, S and

shame (102)

Dtr 32:5 To their s they are no longer
1Sm 20:30 You have no s. ⌊You act⌋ as if
Job 8:22 hate you will be clothed with s,
11:3 make fun of us without any s?
Psa 6:10 All my enemies will be put to s
6:10 they will retreat and be put to s.
14:6 of oppressed people to s
25:2 Do not let me be put to s.
25:3 for you will ever be put to s,
25:3 are unfaithful will be put to s.
25:20 Do not let me be put to s.
31:1 Never let me be put to s.
31:17 so do not let me be put to s,
31:17 Let wicked people be put to s.
34:5 will never be covered with s.
35:4 life be put to s and disgraced.
35:26 put to s and confused.
35:26 be clothed with s and disgrace.
37:19 They will not be put to s in
40:14 life be confused and put to s.
40:15 be stunned by their own s.
44:7 You put to s those who hate us.
44:15 front of me. S covers my face
53:5 You put them to s.
69:6 with hope for you be put to s
69:19 put to s, and humiliated.
70:2 life be confused and put to s.
70:3 back because of their own s.
71:1 Never let me be put to s.
71:24 been disgraced and put to s.
83:16 Let their faces blush with s,
83:17 Let them be put to s and
86:17 me may see it and be put to s.
89:45 youth and covered him with s.
97:7 false gods will be put to s.
109:29 Let them be wrapped in their s

Psa 119:31 do not let me be put to s.
119:78 Let arrogant people be put to s
119:80 so that I will not be put to s.
127:5 He will not be put to s when he
129:5 Put to s all those who hate
132:18 will clothe his enemies with s,
Pro 10:5 sleeps at harvest time brings s.
11:2 comes, then comes s,
13:5 behaves with s and disgrace.
13:18 Poverty and s come to a
19:26 mother brings s and disgrace.
Isa 26:11 and they will be put to s.
30:3 protection will be their s,
30:5 people of Judah will be put to s
30:5 can only offer s and disgrace."
42:17 be turned away and put to s.
44:9 so they will be put to s.
44:11 with the gods will be put to s.
47:3 People will see your s.
49:23 hope for me will not be put to s.
50:7 know that I will not be put to s.
54:4 because you won't be put to s.
54:4 You'll forget the s you've had
61:7 of wealth instead of your s.
66:5 But they will be put to s.
Jer 2:36 You will be put to s by Egypt
2:36 you were put to s by Assyria.
3:25 We must lie down in our s and
7:19 themselves to their own s.
8:9 Wise people are put to s,
10:14 Metalsmiths are put to s by
13:26 and your s will be seen.
17:13 abandon you will be put to s.
17:18 Put my persecutors to s,
17:18 but do not let me be put to s.
20:11 Their eternal s will not be
20:18 I will finish my days in s.
23:40 eternal disgrace and s on you.
31:19 I hung my head in s.
46:12 nations have heard of your s;
46:24 people of Egypt will be put to s.
48:1 Kiriathaim will be put to s;
48:1 will be put to s and torn down.
48:39 Moab turns away in s!' Moab
50:2 Bel will be put to s.
50:2 statues will be put to s.
51:17 Metalsmiths are put to s by
51:47 whole country will be put to s,
51:51 We have been put to s,
51:51 S covers our faces,
Eze 7:18 faces will be covered with s,
23:29 The s of your prostitution will
39:26 they will forget their s and all
Hos 4:7 So I will turn their glory into s.
4:19 sacrifices will bring them s.
Oba 1:10 you will be covered with s.
Mic 3:7 Seers will be put to s.
7:10 they will be covered with s,
Zec 10:5 They will put to s those who
Mar 16:14 He put them to s for their
1Co 1:27 to put wise people to s.
1:27 weak to put what is strong to s.
Eph 4:19 no longer have any sense of s,
1Jn 2:28 we won't turn from him in s.
Jud 1:13 Their s is like the foam on the
Rev 16:15 naked and let others see his s."

shameful (16)

Lev 20:17 intercourse does a s thing.
Psa 71:13 accuse me come to a s end.
Pro 18:13 he listens is stupid and s.
Jer 3:24 the s worship of Baal has
29:23 They have done s things in
Hos 2:5 with them did s things.
9:10 Peor and worshiped s idols.
Rom 1:26 God allowed their s passions
1Co 14:35 It's s for a woman to speak in
2Co 4:2 to use secret and s ways.
Eph 5:12 It is s to talk about what some
Php 3:19 and they take pride in the s
1Ti 3:8 They must not use s ways to
Tit 1:7 He must not use s ways to
1:11 This is the s way they make
Rev 3:18 so that you may keep your s,

shamefully (6)

Pro 14:35 is furious with one who acts s.
17:2 master over a son who acts s,
Hos 4:18 Their rulers dearly love to act s.
Mar 9:12 suffer a lot and be treated s?
12:4 on the head and treated him s.
Luk 20:11 beat him, treated him s,

shameless (6)

Jer 3:3 Yet, you have the s look of a
13:27 I have seen you act like a s
Eze 16:30 everything a s prostitute does.
Zep 2:1 gather together, you s nation,
3:5 those who are perverted are s.
Mar 7:22 cheating, s lust, envy, cursing,

Shamgar (2)

Jdg 3:31 After Ehud came S,
5:6 In the days of S, son of Anath,

Shamhuth (1)

1Ch 27:8 S, Izrah's descendant,

Shamir (4)

Jos 15:48 their villages: S, Jattir, Socoh,
Jdg 10:1 from Issachar and lived in S
10:2 Tola died and was buried in S.
1Ch 24:24 S (for Uzziel's descendants

Shamma (1)

1Ch 7:37 Bezer, Hod, S, Shilsha, Ithran,

Shammah (8)

Gen 36:13 Nahath, Zerah, S, and Mizzah.
36:17 Nahath, Zerah, S, and Mizzah.
1Sm 16:9 Then Jesse had S come to
17:13 was Abinadab, the third was S,
2Sm 23:11 Next in rank to him was S,
23:25 S from Harod, Elika from Harod
23:33 (son of S the Hararite),
1Ch 1:37 Nahath, Zerah, S, and Mizzah.

Shammai (3)

1Ch 2:28 Onam's sons were S and Jada.
2:44 Rekem was the father of S.
4:17 wife gave birth to Miriam, S,

Shammai's (3)

1Ch 2:28 S sons were Nadab and
2:32 The sons of Jada (S brother)
2:45 S son was Maon, who first

Shammoth (1)

1Ch 11:27 S from Harod, Helez the

Shammua (5)

Num 13:4 These are their names: S,
2Sm 5:14 S, Shobab, Nathan, Solomon,
1Ch 14:4 S, Shobab, Nathan, Solomon,
Neh 11:17 Abda who was the son of S,
12:18 from Bilgah, S; from Shemaiah,

Shamsherai (1)

1Ch 8:26 Jeroham's sons were S,

shape (6)

Num 15:20 S one part of your dough into a
1Ki 6:25 measurements and the same s.
7:37 identical in size and s.
Isa 44:12 Blacksmiths s iron into tools.
44:12 them over the coals and s them
Jer 10:9 and goldsmiths s these metals.

shaped (12)

Exo 25:33 cups s like almond blossoms,
25:34 cups s like almond blossoms,
37:19 cups s like almond blossoms,
37:20 cups s like almond blossoms,
1Ki 7:26 rim of a cup, s like a lily's bud.
2Ch 4:3 rows of figurines s like bulls all
4:5 rim of a cup, s like a lily's bud.
Isa 2:8 what their hands have s
42:5 He s the earth and all that
Jer 25:6 the idols your hands have s.
25:7 the idols your hands have s

Eze 1:5 They were s like humans,

shapes (1)

Isa 45:9 the clay ask the one who s it,

Shapham (1)

1Ch 5:12 from Gad's second son S.

Shaphan (29)

2Ki 22:3 he sent the scribe S,
22:8 priest Hilkiah told the scribe S,
22:8 Hilkiah gave the book to S,
22:9 The scribe S went to the king
22:10 Then the scribe S told the king,
22:10 And S read it to the king.
22:12 to Ahikam (son of S),
22:12 (son of Micaiah), the scribe S,
22:14 Hilkiah, Ahikam, Achbor, S,
25:22 of Ahikam and grandson of S,
2Ch 34:8 Josiah sent S, son of Azaliah,
34:15 Hilkiah told the scribe S,
34:15 Hilkiah gave the book to S.
34:16 S took the book to the king and
34:18 Then the scribe S told the king,
34:18 And S read it to the king.
34:20 Ahikam (son of S),
34:20 (son of Micah), the scribe S,
Jer 26:24 Ahikam, son of S, So Jeremiah
36:10 the scribe Gemariah, son of S,
36:11 and the grandson of S,
36:12 Gemariah (son of S),
39:14 of Ahikam and grandson of S,
40:5 of Ahikam and grandson of S,
40:9 of Ahikam and grandson of S,
40:11 of Ahikam and grandson of S,
41:2 of Ahikam and grandson of S,
43:6 of Ahikam and grandson of S,
Eze 8:11 Jaazaniah, son of S,

Shaphan's (1)

Jer 29:3 He sent the letter with S son

Shaphat (8)

Num 13:5 S, son of Hori, from the tribe of
1Ki 19:16 And anoint Elisha, son of S,
19:19 Elijah found Elisha, son of S.
2Ki 3:11 "Elisha, the son of S, is here.
6:31 if the head of Elisha, son of S,
1Ch 3:22 Igal, Bariah, Neariah, and S.
5:12 sons Janai and S in Bashan.
27:29 in the valleys: S, son of Adlai

Shaphir (1)

Mic 1:11 and ashamed, inhabitants of S.

Sharai (1)

Ezr 10:40 Machnadebai, Shashai, S,

Sharar (1)

2Sm 23:33 Ahiam (son of S the Hararite),

share (100)

Gen 14:24 and Mamre take their s."
21:10 this slave's son must never s
Exo 12:4 next door can s one animal.
29:26 This will be your s.
Lev 6:17 given it to them as their s from
7:33 will belong to him as his s.
7:35 "This is the s for Aaron and his
8:29 It was Moses' s, as the LORD
Num 10:32 If you come with us, we will s
18:8 from the Israelites as your s.
Dtr 28:57 She won't s with them the
Jos 14:4 The Levites were not given a s
15:13 a s of land among the people of
1Sm 26:19 prevented me from having a s
30:24 Certainly, the s of those who
30:24 go into battle must be like the s
30:24 They will all s alike."
2Sm 20:1 "We have no s in David's
1Ki 12:16 "What s do we have in David's
2Ki 2:9 inherit a double s of your spirit."
1Ch 16:18 It is your s of the inheritance.'
2Ch 10:16 "What s do we have in David's
Job 8:10 Won't they s their thoughts with
32:11 I listened for you to s your

Psa 105:11 It is your s of the inheritance."
123:3 more than our s of contempt.
123:4 have suffered more than our s
123:4 have suffered more than our s
Pro 5:17 do not s them with strangers.
14:10 and no stranger can s its joy.
16:19 people than to s stolen goods
17:2 and he will s the inheritance
17:17 and a brother is born to s
21:9 on a corner of a roof than to s
25:24 on a corner of a roof than to s
Ecc 9:2 All people will s the same
Isa 17:3 from Aram will s Israel's honor,"
53:12 So I will give him a s among
58:7 S your food with the hungry,
Eze 47:23 residents will receive their s
Dan 4:15 And let it get its s of the plants
4:23 Let it get its s of the plants on
Mat 21:34 to collect his s of the produce.
21:41 who will give him his s
25:21 and s your master's happiness.'
25:23 and s your master's happiness.'
Mar 12:2 to collect from them a s
Luk 3:11 has two shirts should s
3:11 has food should s it too."
12:13 tell my brother to give me my s
12:42 giving the other servants their s
15:12 give me my s of the property.'
20:10 workers to obtain from them a s
22:17 He said, "Take this, and s it.
Jon 19:23 each soldier could have a s.
Act 8:21 You won't have any s in this
26:18 and a s among God's people
Rom 1:11 I long to see you to s a spiritual
8:17 If we s in Christ's suffering in
8:17 suffering in order to s his glory,
8:21 slavery to decay in order to s
12:13 S what you have with God's
1Co 9:10 to receive a s of the crop.
9:13 who help at the altar get a s
9:23 in order to s what it offers.
10:17 All of us s one loaf.
10:18 eat the sacrifices s what is
12:26 the other parts s its suffering.
12:26 the others s in its happiness.
2Co 1:7 that as you s our sufferings,
1:7 you also s our comfort.
6:15 Can a believer s life with an
13:11 S the same attitude and live in
Gal 4:30 the slave woman must never s
6:6 word should s all good things
Eph 3:6 belong to the same body and s
4:4 you were called to s one hope.
4:28 that they'll have something to s
Php 1:7 Together we s God's favor,
2:17 and I s that joy with all of you.
2:18 be filled with joy and s that joy
3:10 it means to s his suffering.
4:14 kind of you to s my troubles.
4:15 you were the only church to s
Col 1:12 made you able to s the light,
1Th 2:8 that we were determined to s
1Ti 6:18 to be generous, and to s.
2Ti 2:6 have the first s of the crops.
Tit 1:4 genuine child in the faith we s.
Phm 1:6 As you s the faith you have in
Heb 13:16 others and to s what you have
1Pe 3:7 s God's life-giving kindness
4:13 as you s Christ's sufferings.
5:1 Christ's sufferings and will s
2Pe 1:4 these promises you will s
2Jn 1:1 I love because we s the truth.
3Jn 1:1 I love because we s the truth.
Jud 1:3 you about the salvation we s.
1:12 at the special meals you s
Rev 1:9 I s your suffering, ruling,

shared (10)

Lev 7:10 will be s equally by all of
1Ki 2:26 because you s all my father's
Pro 22:9 because he has s his food
Luk 1:58 and they s her joy.
Act 2:44 and they s everything with
2:46 other's homes and s their food.
4:32 Instead, they s everything.
20:32 the inheritance that is s by all
Rom 15:27 and Greeks have s
Heb 6:4 the heavenly gift and s

shares (8)

1Sm 30:27 There were s for those in
Psa 19:2 One night s knowledge with
Ecc 9:3 Everyone s the same destiny.
Luk 9:26 he comes in the glory that he s
Jon 1:14 was the glory that the Father s
1Co 16:16 anyone else who s their labor
2Th 3:2 since not everyone s our faith.
2Jn 1:11 Whoever greets him s the evil

Sharezer (3)

2Ki 19:37 Adrammelech and S
Isa 37:38 Adrammelech and S,
Zec 7:2 people from⌊ Bethel sent S

sharing (4)

Rom 12:8 If it is s, be generous. If it is
1Co 10:16 the cup of blessing aren't we s
10:16 we break the bread aren't we s
2Co 9:13 because of your generosity in s

Sharon (9)

Jos 12:18 king of Aphek, the king of S,
1Ch 5:16 in the entire pastureland of S
27:29 for the herds grazing in S:
27:29 Shitrai from S for the herds in
Sos 2:1 I am a rose of S, a lily
Isa 33:9 S has become like a
35:2 the majesty of Carmel and S.
65:10 The S Plain will be a pasture
Act 9:35 region of S saw what had

sharp (19)

Jdg 3:31 Philistines with a s stick used
2Sm 18:14 He took three s sticks and
Job 41:30 Its underside is like s pieces of
Psa 45:5 Your arrows are s in the heart
52:2 It's like a s razor, you master of
57:4 Their tongues are s swords.
140:3 They make their tongues as s
Pro 5:4 as s as a two-edged sword.
25:18 and a sword and a s arrow,
Isa 41:15 a new threshing sledge with s,
49:2 He made my tongue like a s
Eze 5:1 "Son of man, take a s blade,
28:24 thorns or s briars from
Rev 1:16 and out of his mouth came a s,
2:12 the s two-edged sword says:
14:14 on his head and a s sickle
14:17 He, too, had a s sickle.
14:18 to the angel with the s sickle,
19:15 A s sword comes out of his

sharpen (5)

Dtr 32:41 I will s my flashing sword and
1Sm 13:20 had to go to the Philistines to s
13:21 of an ounce of silver to s
Psa 64:3 They s their tongues like
Jer 51:11 S the arrows; fill the quivers.

sharpened (7)

Psa 120:4 He will give you a warrior's s
Ecc 10:10 ax is blunt and the edge isn't s,
Isa 5:28 Their arrows are s;
49:2 He made me like a s arrow and
Eze 21:9 a sword is s and polished,
21:10 It's s to kill and polished to
21:11 The sword is being s and

sharpens (3)

Psa 7:12 not change, God s his sword.
Pro 27:17 ⌊As⌋ iron s iron, so one person
27:17 so one person s the wits of

sharper (2)

Mic 7:4 person is s than thornbushes.
Heb 4:12 It is s than any two-edged

sharply (3)

Job 16:9 My opponent looked s at me.
Act 15:39 disagreed so s that they parted
Tit 1:13 For this reason, s correct

Sharuhen (1)

Jos 19:6 Beth Lebaoth, and S.

Shashai (1)

Ezr 10:40 Machnadebai, S, Sharai,

Shashak (1)

1Ch 8:14 brothers were S and Jeremoth.

Shashak's (1)

1Ch 8:22 S sons were Ishpan,

shatter (2)

Eze 32:12 They will s the pride of Egypt
Rev 2:27 and s them like pottery.

shattered (18)

Jdg 5:26 She s and pierced his temples.
1Ki 19:11 mountains and s rocks ahead
Job 4:20 morning to evening, they are s.
8:14 His confidence is easily s.
16:12 I was at ease, and he s me.
17:11 My dreams ⌊are s⌋.
Psa 44:2 You s many groups of people,
107:16 He s bronze gates and cut iron
Isa 7:8 Ephraim will be s within 65
20:5 Then the people will be s and
21:9 worship lie s on the ground."
30:31 the people of Assyria will be s.
Jer 50:23 whole earth is broken and s.
51:8 will suddenly fall and be s.
Lam 2:9 ⌊The LORD⌋ destroyed and s
Eze 26:17 You have been s by the sea.
Dan 12:7 people has been completely s,
Luk 4:18 those who have been s by sin,

shattering (2)

2Sm 22:39 I ended their lives by s them.
Psa 42:10 With a s blow to my bones,

shatters (2)

Jer 23:29 or like a hammer that s a rock?"
Dan 2:40 smashes and s everything.)

Shaul (9)

Gen 36:37 After Samlah died, S from
36:38 After S died, Baal Hanan,
46:10 Ohad, Jakin, Zohar, and S,
Exo 6:15 Ohad, Jachin, Zohar, and S,
Num 26:13 and the family of S.
1Ch 1:48 After Samlah died, S from
1:49 After S died, Baal Hanan,
4:24 Jamin, Jarib, Zerah, and S.
6:24 Uzziah's son was S.

Shaul's (1)

1Ch 4:25 S son was Shallum.

shave (21)

Lev 13:33 the person will s everything
14:8 s off all his hair, and wash.
14:9 On the seventh day he must s
19:27 "Never s the hair on your
Num 6:9 Seven days later he must s his
6:18 "Then the Nazirites will s their
8:7 Make them s their whole
Dtr 21:12 She must s her head,
Jdg 16:19 She called for a man to s off
Isa 7:20 River to be a razor to s
Jer 9:26 I will punish all who s the hair
16:6 own body or s his own head
25:23 and all who s the hair on their
47:5 Gaza will s its head in
49:32 to the winds those who s
Eze 5:1 a barber's razor to s your head
44:20 "They must not s their heads
Amo 8:10 waist and s everyone's head.
Mic 1:16 S your head in mourning for the
Act 21:24 the expenses to s their heads.
1Co 11:6 to cut off her hair or s her head,

shaved (13)

Gen 41:14 After he had s and changed his
Num 6:19 after they have s off their hair.
Jdg 16:17 If my hair is ever s off,

Jdg 16:22 back as soon as it was **s** off.
2Sm 10:4 **s** off half of each man's beard,
1Ch 19:4 took David's men, **s** them,
Job 1:20 robe ⌊in grief⌋, and **s** his head.
Isa 15:2 Every head is **s** bald,
Jer 41:5 Their beards were **s** off,
48:37 "Every head is **s**, and every
Eze 7:18 and every head will be **s**.
27:31 They **s** their heads because of
1Co 11:5 woman who has her head **s**.

Shaveh (1)

Gen 14:17 him in the S Valley (that is,

Shaveh Kiriathaim (1)

Gen 14:5 at Ham, the Emim at S,

shaving (4)

Lev 21:5 "You should never mourn by **s**
21:5 **s** the edges of your beards,
Dtr 14:1 yourselves or **s** bald spots
Isa 22:12 for **s** your heads and for

Shavsha (1)

1Ch 18:16 S was the royal scribe.

shawl (1)

Dtr 22:12 corners of the **s** you wear over

shawls (2)

Isa 3:22 fine robes, coats, **s**,
Mat 23:5 and the tassels on their **s** long.

Sheal (1)

Ezr 10:29 Jashub, S, and Jeremoth

Shealtiel (9)

1Ch 3:17 Jeconiah were his son S,
Hag 1:1 (who was the son of S
1:12 (who was the son of S),
1:14 (who was the son of S
2:2 (who is the son of S
2:23 servant Zerubbabel (son of S),
Mat 1:12 became the father of S.
1:12 S was the father of Zerubbabel,
Luk 3:27 son of S, son of Neri,

Shealtiel's (4)

Ezr 3:2 priests and S son Zerubbabel
3:8 Zerubbabel (who was S son),
5:2 who was S son, and Jeshua,
Neh 12:1 back with Zerubbabel (S son)

shear (4)

Gen 31:19 Laban went to **s** his sheep,
38:13 way to Timnah to **s** his sheep,
Dtr 15:19 and never **s** a firstborn sheep.
18:4 wool you **s** from your sheep.

sheared (1)

Sos 4:2 a flock of sheep about to be **s**,

shearers (1)

1Sm 25:11 meat that I butchered for my **s**

Sheariah (2)

1Ch 8:38 S, Obadiah, and Hanan.
9:44 S, Obadiah, and Hanan.

shearing (3)

Gen 38:12 the men were **s** Judah's sheep.
1Sm 25:2 And he was **s** his sheep in
25:4 that Nabal was **s** his sheep.

Shear Jashub (1)

Isa 7:3 Go out with your son S to meet

shears (4)

Isa 2:4 and their spears into pruning **s**.
18:5 off the shoots with pruning **s**
Joe 3:10 and your pruning **s** into spears.
Mic 4:3 and their spears into pruning **s**.

sheath (1)

1Sm 17:51 pulled it out of its **s**,

Sheba (34)

Gen 10:7 were S and Dedan.
10:28 Obal, Abimael, S,
25:3 was the father of S and Dedan.
Jos 19:2 Beersheba (S), Moladah,
2Sm 20:1 man by the name of S,
20:2 of Israel left David to follow S,
20:6 David then told Abishai, "S,
20:7 left Jerusalem to pursue S,
20:10 his brother Abishai pursued S,
20:13 followed Joab and pursued S,
20:14 S passed through all the tribes
20:21 of Ephraim by the name of S,
1Ki 10:1 The queen of S heard about
10:4 When the queen of S saw all of
10:10 queen of S gave King Solomon.
10:13 of S anything she wanted,
1Ch 1:9 were S and Dedan.
1:22 Ebal, Abimael, S,
1:32 sons were S and Dedan.
5:13 S, Jorai, Jacan, Zia, and Eber.
2Ch 9:1 The queen of S heard about
9:3 When the queen of S saw
9:9 queen of S gave King Solomon.
9:12 of S anything she wanted,
Job 1:15 men from S attacked.
6:19 from S search for them.
Psa 72:10 May the kings from S and Seba
72:15 May the gold from S be given
Isa 60:6 Everyone from S will come.
Jer 6:20 Incense that comes from S is
Eze 27:22 The merchants from S and
27:23 the merchants from S,
38:13 "'S, Dedan, the merchants from
Joe 3:8 sell them to the people of S,

Shebaniah (7)

1Ch 15:24 The priests S, Joshaphat,
Neh 9:4 Jeshua, Bani, Kadmiel, S,
9:5 S, and Pethahiah — said,
10:4 Hattush, S, Malluch,
10:10 and their relatives S,
10:12 Zaccur, Sherebiah, S,
12:14 Malluchi, Jonathan; from S,

Sheba's (1)

2Sm 20:22 They cut off S head and threw

Shebat (1)

Zec 1:7 eleventh month (the month of S

Sheber (1)

1Ch 2:48 the mother of S and Tirhanah.

Shebna (7)

2Ki 18:37 Hilkiah, S the scribe, and Joah,
19:2 of the palace, S the scribe,
Isa 22:15 LORD of Armies says: Go to S,
36:3 Hilkiah, S the scribe, and Joah,
36:11 Then Eliakim, S, and Joah
36:22 Hilkiah, S the scribe, and Joah,
37:2 of the palace, S the scribe,

Shebnah (2)

2Ki 18:18 Hilkiah, S the scribe, and Joah,
18:26 Eliakim (son of Hilkiah), S,

Shebuel (3)

1Ch 23:16 Gershom's only son was S.
25:4 S, Jerimoth, Hananiah, Hanani,
26:24 there was S, a descendant of

Shecaniah (8)

1Ch 3:21 Obadiah's son was S.
24:11 ninth for Jeshua, the tenth for S,
2Ch 31:15 and S served under him in the
Ezr 8:3 son of S from the family of
8:5 from the family of Zattu: S,
10:2 Then S, son of Jehiel, one of
Neh 6:18 he was the son-in-law of S,
12:3 S, Rehum, Meremoth,

Shecaniah's (2)

1Ch 3:22 S son was Shemaiah.
Neh 3:29 S son, the guard at East Gate,

Shechem (68)

Gen 12:6 tree belonging to Moreh at S.
33:18 to the city of S in Canaan.
33:19 the sons of Hamor, father of S,
34:2 When S, son of the local ruler
34:4 So S said to his father Hamor,
34:5 Jacob heard that S had
34:7 because S had committed such
34:8 "My son S has his heart set on
34:11 Then S said to Dinah's father
34:13 Then Jacob's sons gave S and
34:18 good to Hamor and his son S.
34:20 So Hamor and his son S went
34:24 with Hamor and his son S.
34:26 including Hamor and his son S.
34:31 "Should S have been allowed
35:4 under the oak tree near S.
37:12 care of their father's flocks at S.
37:13 taking care of the flocks at S.
37:14 When Joseph came to S,
Num 26:31 family of Asriel, the family of S,
Jos 17:2 S, Hepher, and Shemida.
17:7 Michmethath, which faces S.
20:7 S in the mountains of Ephraim,
21:21 pasturelands were S (a city
24:1 the tribes of Israel together at S.
24:25 up laws and rules for them at S.
24:32 from Egypt, were buried at S.
24:32 the sons of Hamor, father of S,
Jdg 8:31 His concubine at S also gave
9:1 went to S to see the uncles on
9:2 "Please ask all citizens of S,
9:3 he said to all citizens of S.
9:6 All the citizens from S and
9:6 tree that was still standing in S
9:7 to me, you citizens of S,
9:18 king over the citizens of S just
9:20 and burn up citizens of S
9:20 let fire come out of citizens of S
9:23 Abimelech and citizens of S.
9:23 of S turned against Abimelech.
9:24 to Abimelech and citizens of S.
9:24 Citizens of S had helped
9:25 So citizens of S set ambushes
9:26 and his brothers moved into S.
9:26 Citizens of S trusted him.
9:28 who are we, the people of S,
9:31 his brothers have come to S.
9:32 them⌋ in the fields ⌊around S⌋.
9:34 to set ambushes around S.
9:39 Then Gaal led citizens of S out
9:41 would not let them live in S.
9:42 The next day the people ⌊of S⌋
9:57 also paid back the men of S
21:19 going from Bethel to S,
1Ki 12:1 Rehoboam went to S because
12:1 all Israel had gone to S
12:25 Jeroboam rebuilt S in the hills
1Ch 6:67 S with its pastureland in the
7:19 Shemida's sons were Ahian, S,
7:28 S and its villages,
2Ch 10:1 Rehoboam went to S because
10:1 all Israel had gone to S
Psa 60:6 I will divide S. I will measure
108:7 I will divide S. I will measure
Jer 41:5 80 men arrived from S,
Hos 6:9 They murder on the road to S.
Act 7:16 They were taken to S for burial
7:16 in S from Hamor's sons.

Shechem's (6)

Gen 34:6 So S father Hamor came to
34:26 Dinah from S home and left.
Jdg 9:28 of Hamor, S father!
9:30 Zebul, S ruler, heard what Gaal
9:46 All the citizens of S Tower
9:49 So all the people in S Tower

shed (13)

Gen 9:6 by humans his blood will be **s**,
Lev 17:4 He has **s** blood and must be
1Ki 2:5 When there was peace, he **s**
2:31 blood which Joab **s** — from me
2Ki 24:4 the innocent blood he had **s**.
Psa 30:9 will you profit if my blood is **s**,

Psa 79:3 They have s the blood of your
106:38 They s innocent blood,
Pro 1:16 to do evil and hurry to s blood.
Isa 26:21 earth will uncover the blood s
59:7 They hurry to s innocent blood.
Heb 9:22 because if no blood is s,
Rev 6:10 on earth who s our blood?"

shedding (3)

1Sm 19:5 Why then should you sin by s
2Ki 9:7 get revenge on Jezebel for s
Psa 79:10 that there is punishment for s

Shedeur (5)

Num 1:5 will help you: Elizur, son of S,
2:10 of Reuben is Elizur, son of S.
7:30 of Reuben, Elizur, son of S,
7:35 the gifts from Elizur, son of S.
10:18 Elizur, son of S, was in

sheds (2)

Gen 9:6 Whoever s human blood,
2Ch 32:28 He made s to store his

sheep (292)

Gen 12:16 and he was given s,
13:5 also had his own s,
20:14 Then Abimelech took s,
21:27 Abraham took some s and
24:35 has given him s and cattle,
29:2 Three flocks of s were lying
29:3 of the well so that the s could
29:6 daughter Rachel with the s."
29:7 Water the s. Then let them
29:8 we can water the s."
29:9 arrived with her father's s,
29:10 with his uncle Laban's s.
29:10 watered his uncle Laban's s.
30:32 every speckled or spotted s,
30:40 the rest of the s face any that
31:19 Laban went to shear his s,
31:38 Your s and goats never
32:5 and donkeys, s and goats,
32:7 the s and goats, the cattle,
32:14 200 female s and 20 male
32:14 female sheep and 20 male s,
34:28 They took the s and goats,
38:12 men were shearing Judah's s.
38:13 way to Timnah to shear his s,
47:17 s, goats, cattle, and donkeys.
Exo 2:16 troughs to water their father's s.
2:17 and then watered their s.
2:19 water for us and watered the s."
3:1 Moses was taking care of the s
3:1 As he led the s to the far side
9:3 camels, cattle, s, and goats.
12:38 along with large numbers of s,
13:13 It will cost you a s or a goat to
20:24 your s, goats, and cattle on it.
22:1 someone steals a bull or a s
22:1 to replace the bull or four s
22:1 or four sheep to replace the s.
22:4 it's a bull, donkey, or a s,
22:9 a s, an article of clothing,
22:10 neighbor a donkey, a bull, a s,
22:30 with your cattle and your s.
34:19 whether cattle, s, or goats.
34:20 It will cost you a s or a goat to
Lev 1:2 from your cattle, s, or goats.
1:10 "If your offering is a s or goat,
3:6 is a fellowship offering of s
5:6 It must be a female s or goat as
5:7 "Now, if you cannot afford a s,
7:23 any fat from bulls, s, or goats.
17:3 who slaughters a bull, s,
22:19 no defects from your cattle, s,
22:21 Whether it is from the cattle, s,
22:23 You may use a bull or a s with
22:28 Never slaughter a cow or a s
27:26 Whether it is a bull or a s,
27:32 Every tenth head of cattle or s
Num 15:3 They may be cattle, s,
15:5 With each s or goat for the
15:11 and each s or goat.
18:17 ox, s, or goat. They are holy.
22:40 Balak sacrificed cattle, s,
Num 27:17 be like s without a shepherd."
31:28 cattle, donkeys, s, and goats.
31:30 cattle, donkeys, s, goats,
31:32 675,000 s and goats,
31:36 Of the 337,500 s and goats
31:43 received 337,500 s and goats,
Dtr 12:6 of your cattle, s, and goats.
12:17 of your cattle, s, or goats;
14:4 you may eat: oxen, s, goats,
14:5 antelope, and mountain s.
14:23 the firstborn of your cattle, s,
14:26 want: cattle, s, goats, wine,
15:14 provisions — s from your flocks
15:19 and never shear a firstborn s.
17:1 Never offer an ox or a s that
18:3 ox, a s, or a goat: the shoulder,
18:4 wool you shear from your s.
22:1 Israelite's ox or s is out where
32:14 drank milk from s and goats.
Jos 6:21 well as cattle, s, and donkeys.
7:24 his cattle, his donkeys, his s,
Jdg 6:4 for Israel to live on — not one s,
1Sm 14:32 They took s, cows, and calves,
14:34 bring me your ox or your s,
15:3 and children, cows and s,
15:9 Agag and the best s and cows,
15:14 "But what is this sound of s in
15:15 They spared the best s and
15:21 of their belongings — the best s
16:11 "He's tending the s."
16:19 who is with the s."
17:20 someone else watch ⌊the s⌋.
17:28 did you leave those few s
17:34 am a shepherd for my father's s.
17:34 carried off a s from the flock,
17:35 and rescued the s from its
22:19 infants, cows, donkeys, and s.
24:3 He came to some s pens along
25:2 He had 3,000 s and 1,000
25:2 was shearing his s in Carmel.
25:4 that Nabal was shearing his s.
25:16 were watching the s near them.
25:18 2 full wineskins, 5 butchered s,
27:9 He also took s, cattle, donkeys,
30:20 He took all the s and the cattle.
2Sm 7:8 you followed s so that you
12:2 large number of s and cows,
12:4 a pity to take one of his own s
17:29 honey, buttermilk, s,
24:17 What have these s done?
1Ki 1:9 Adonijah sacrificed s,
1:19 fattened calves, bulls, and s.
1:25 bulls, fattened calves, and s.
4:23 and 100 s in addition to deer,
8:5 Israel were offering countless s
8:63 s as fellowship offerings
22:17 in the hills like s without
22:17 'These ⌊s⌋ have no master.
2Ki 3:4 King Mesha of Moab raised s.
5:26 vineyards, s, cattle, or slaves?
1Ch 5:21 250,000 s and goats,
12:40 wine, olive oil, cattle, and s,
17:7 you followed s so that you
21:17 What have these s done?
2Ch 5:6 Israel were offering countless s
7:5 and 120,000 s as sacrifices
14:15 captured many s and camels.
15:11 700 cattle and 7,000 s.
18:2 Ahab slaughtered many s and
18:16 in the hills like s without
18:16 'These s have no master.
29:33 were 600 bulls and 3,000 s.
30:24 bulls and 7,000 s as sacrifices
30:24 1,000 bulls and 10,000 s
31:6 a tenth of their cattle and s
32:29 he had many s and cattle.
35:7 the people with 33,000 s
35:8 gave the priests 2,600 s and
35:9 gave the Levites 5,000 s and
Neh 3:1 started by rebuilding S Gate.
3:32 room at the corner and S Gate.
5:18 choice s was necessary every
12:39 the Hundred, as far as S Gate.
Job 1:3 He owned 7,000 s and goats,
31:20 or the wool from my s didn't
42:12 He had 14,000 s and goats,
Psa 8:7 all the s and cattle,
44:11 us over to be butchered like s
44:22 of as s to be slaughtered.
49:14 Like s, they are driven to hell
68:13 you stayed among the s pens,
74:1 against the s in your care?
78:52 led his own people out like s
78:70 He took him from the s pens.
80:1 descendants of Joseph like s,
100:3 people and the s in his care.
144:13 May our s give birth to
Sos 4:2 Your teeth are like a flock of s
4:2 s that come up from the
6:6 Your teeth are like a flock of s,
6:6 s that come up from the
Isa 7:21 alive a young cow and two s.
7:25 oxen loose and letting s run."
13:14 like hunted gazelle and like s
17:2 These cities will be used for s,
17:2 be no one to disturb those s.
22:13 slaughter cattle, and butcher s.
40:11 helps the s and their lambs.
43:23 You did not bring me s for your
53:6 We have all strayed like s.
53:7 He was like a s that is silent
Jer 12:3 Drag them away like s to be
13:20 given to you — your beautiful s?
23:1 destroying and scattering the s
23:2 You have scattered my s and
23:4 My s will no longer be afraid or
33:13 count their s," says the LORD.
50:6 My people have been lost s.
50:17 like scattered s that lions have
Eze 24:5 selected from the best s.
25:5 into a resting place for s.
34:2 shepherds take care of the s?
34:3 You eat the best parts of the s,
34:3 and butcher the finest s.
34:3 you don't take care of the s.
34:6 My s wandered over all the
34:8 my s have become prey.
34:8 My s have become food for
34:8 haven't searched for my s.
34:8 of only themselves, not my s.
34:10 that they hand over my s.
34:10 take care of my s anymore,
34:10 I will rescue my s from their
34:10 and my s will no longer be their
34:11 I will search for my s myself,
34:12 he is with his scattered s,
34:12 so I will look after my s.
34:15 I will take care of my s and
34:16 I will take care of my s fairly.
34:17 "'As for you, my s,
34:17 between one s and another,
34:19 Must my s eat what your feet
34:20 disputes between the fat s
34:20 the fat sheep and the skinny s.
34:21 You fat s push the skinny
34:21 fat sheep push the skinny s
34:21 you knock down all the sick s
34:22 So I will rescue my s,
34:22 between one s and another.
34:25 so that my s can live safely
34:27 and my s will live safely in
34:31 You, my s, are the sheep in my
34:31 are the s in my pasture.
36:37 make them as numerous as s.
36:38 will be like the s for sacrifices,
36:38 like the s in Jerusalem during
45:15 You must take one s out of
Hos 5:6 They go with their s and their
12:12 he took care of s to pay for her.
Joe 1:18 Even flocks of s are suffering.
Amo 1:1 one of the s farmers from
Jnh 3:7 people, animals, cattle, and s.
Mic 2:12 will gather them together like s
5:8 a young lion among flocks of s.
7:14 the s that belong to you.
Hab 3:17 even if the s pen is empty and
Zep 2:6 and fenced-off places for s.
2:7 There they will graze their s.
3:13 They will graze their s and lie
Zec 10:2 people wander around like s.
11:4 Take care of the s that are
11:7 the shepherd of the s that were

Zec 11:7 and also of the oppressed **s**.
11:7 And I took care of the **s**.
11:8 I became impatient with the **s**,
11:11 and the oppressed among the **s**
11:17 who abandoned the **s**.
13:7 and the **s** will be scattered.
Mat 7:15 come to you disguised as **s**,
9:36 like **s** without a shepherd.
10:6 Instead, go to the lost **s** of the
10:16 you out like **s** among wolves.
12:11 "Suppose one of you has a **s**.
12:12 is more valuable than a **s**!
15:24 "I was sent only to the lost **s** of
18:12 Suppose a man has 100 **s** and
18:12 Won't he leave the 99 **s** in the
25:32 separates the **s** from the goats.
25:33 He will put the **s** on his right
26:31 and the **s** in the flock will be
Mar 6:34 They were like **s** without a
14:27 and the **s** will be scattered.'
Luk 15:4 "Suppose a man has 100 **s**
15:4 Doesn't he leave the 99 **s**
15:4 and look for the lost **s** until
15:5 He puts that **s** on his shoulders
15:6 I've found my lost **s**!'
17:7 is plowing fields or watching **s**.
Jon 2:14 who were selling cattle, **s**,
2:15 and threw everyone with their **s**
5:2 Near S Gate in Jerusalem was
10:1 doesn't enter the **s** pen through
10:3 and the **s** respond to his voice.
10:3 He calls his **s** by name and
10:4 he has brought out all his **s**,
10:4 The **s** follow him because they
10:7 I am the gate for the **s**.
10:8 the **s** didn't respond to them.
10:9 Those who enter the **s** pen
10:9 They will go in and out of the **s**
10:10 But I came so that my **s** will
10:11 gives his life for the **s**.
10:12 and doesn't own the **s**.
10:12 he abandons the **s** and quickly
10:12 So the wolf drags the **s** away
10:13 to get paid and not about the **s**.
10:14 I know my **s** as the Father
10:14 My **s** know me as I know the
10:15 So I give my life for my **s**.
10:16 I also have other **s** that are not
10:26 because you're not my **s**.
10:27 My **s** respond to my voice,
21:16 "Take care of my **s**."
21:17 Jesus told him, "Feed my **s**.
Act 8:32 He was like a **s** that is silent
Rom 8:36 of as **s** to be slaughtered."
1Co 9:7 and not drink milk from the **s**?
Heb 11:37 wore the skins of **s** and goats.
13:20 the great shepherd of the **s**,
1Pe 2:25 You were like lost **s**.
Rev 18:13 cattle, **s**, horses, wagons,

sheepshearers (3)

1Sm 25:7 I hear that your **s** are with you.
2Sm 13:23 Two years later Absalom had **s**
13:24 king and said, "Since I have **s**,

Sheerah (1)

1Ch 7:24 Beriah's daughter was S,

sheet (17)

Exo 26:2 Each **s** will be 42 feet long and
26:4 edge of the end **s** in each set,
26:9 Fold the sixth **s** in half ⌊to
26:10 edge of the end **s** in each set.
36:9 Each **s** was 42 feet long and 6
36:11 edge of the end **s** in each set,
36:17 edge of the end **s** in each set.
2Sm 20:12 field and threw a **s** over him.
Mar 14:51 He had nothing on but a linen **s**.
14:52 but he left the linen **s** behind
Act 5:6 wrapped his body in a **s**,
10:11 large linen **s** being lowered by
10:12 In the **s** were all kinds of
10:16 Then the **s** was quickly taken
11:5 large linen **s** being lowered by
11:5 The **s** came near me.
11:6 I looked into the **s** very closely

sheets (18)

Exo 26:1 "Make the inner tent with ten **s**
26:3 Five of the **s** must be sewn
26:6 ⌊two sets of⌋ **s** together so that
26:7 "Make 11 **s** of goats' hair to
26:8 Each of the 11 **s** will be 45 feet
26:9 Sew five of the **s** together into
26:13 the length of the outer tent's **s**.
36:8 tent with ten **s** made from fine
36:10 Five of the **s** were sewn
36:13 ⌊two sets of⌋ **s** together so that
36:14 They made 11 **s** of goats' hair
36:15 Each of the 11 **s** was 45 feet
36:16 Five of the **s** were sewn
39:3 hammered the gold into thin **s**
Num 4:25 They will carry the **s** that are
16:38 Hammer them into thin metal **s**
16:39 hammered into thin metal **s**
Pro 7:16 colored **s** of Egyptian linen.

Sheházriah (1)

1Ch 8:26 were Shamsherai, S, Athaliah,

shekel (1)

Eze 45:12 One **s** must weigh 20 gerahs.

shekels (1)

Eze 45:12 One mina must weigh 60 **s**.

Shelah (19)

Gen 10:24 was the father of S,
10:24 and S was the father of Eber.
11:12 he became the father of S.
11:13 After he became the father of S,
11:14 S was 30 years old when he
11:15 S lived 403 years and had
38:5 whom she named S.
38:11 Live as a widow until my son S
38:14 realized that S was grown up
38:26 I haven't given her my son S."
46:12 Er, Onan, S, Perez, and Zerah.
Num 26:20 Judah were the family of S,
1Ch 1:18 was the father of S,
1:18 and S was the father of Eber.
1:24 Shem, Arpachshad, S,
2:3 sons were Er, Onan, and S.
4:21 The descendants of S,
Neh 3:15 on the wall of the Pool of S by
Luk 3:35 of Peleg, son of Eber, son of S,

Shelemiah (9)

1Ch 26:14 S was chosen for the east side.
Ezr 10:39 S, Nathan, Adaiah,
10:41 Azarel, S, Shemariah,
Neh 13:13 S the priest, Zadok the scribe,
Jer 36:14 the grandson of S,
36:26 and S (son of Abdeel) to arrest
37:3 sent Jehucal (son of S)
37:13 son of S and grandson of
38:1 of Pashhur), Jucal (son of S),

Shelemiah's (1)

Neh 3:30 S son, and Hanun,

Sheleph (2)

Gen 10:26 S, Hazarmaveth, Jerah,
1Ch 1:20 S, Hazarmaveth, Jerah,

Shelesh (1)

1Ch 7:35 Zophah, Imna, S, and Amal.

shells (2)

Exo 30:34 resin and aromatic mollusk **s**),
Joe 1:17 Seeds shrivel up in their **s**.

Shelomi (1)

Num 34:27 Ahihud, son of S, the leader of

Shelomith (9)

Lev 24:10 A man, whose mother was S
1Ch 3:19 and S was their sister.
23:9 Shimei had three sons: S,
23:18 Izhar's only son was S.
26:25 side of the family was S.
26:25 his grandson was S.)
26:28 of S and his relatives.
2Ch 11:20 to Abijah, Attai, Ziza, and S.
Ezr 8:10 from the family of Bani: S,

Shelomoth (1)

1Ch 24:22 Izhar's descendants through S),

shelter (19)

Dtr 33:12 The LORD will **s** them all day
33:27 The eternal God is your **s**,
Jdg 9:15 then come and take **s** in my
Rut 2:7 sat down this minute in the **s**."
2:12 you have come for **s**."
Job 24:8 rocks because they can't find **s**.
Psa 27:5 He hides me in his **s** when
31:20 You keep them in a **s**,
55:8 I would hurry to find **s** from the
91:1 Whoever lives under the **s** of
Isa 4:6 It will be a **s** from the heat
10:31 who live in Gebim take **s**.
25:4 their distress, a **s** from the rain,
30:2 They look for **s** under
32:2 Then each ruler will be like a **s**
Eze 17:23 a home in the **s** of its branches.
Jnh 4:5 He made himself a **s** there.
Nah 1:7 those who seek **s** in him.
Zep 2:3 Maybe you will find **s** on the

sheltered (2)

Isa 51:16 words in your mouth and **s** you
Act 27:16 As we drifted to the **s** side of a

shelters (3)

Gen 33:17 moved on to Succoth [S],
33:17 a house for himself and made **s**
2Sm 11:11 and Judah are in temporary **s**,

Shelumiel (5)

Num 1:6 S, son of Zurishaddai, from the
2:12 for the people of Simeon is S,
7:36 Simeon, S, son of Zurishaddai,
7:41 These were the gifts from S,
10:19 S, son of Zurishaddai,

Shem (18)

Gen 5:32 he became the father of S,
6:10 He had three sons: S,
7:13 day Noah and his sons S,
9:18 were S, Ham, and Japheth.
9:23 S and Japheth took a blanket
9:26 Praise the LORD, the God of S!
9:27 May he live in the tents of S.
10:1 the account of Noah's sons S,
10:1 S, Ham and Japheth had
10:21 S, Japheth's older brother,
10:21 ⌊S was⌋ the ancestor of all the
11:10 This is the account of S and
11:10 flood when S was 100 years
11:11 S lived 500 years and had
1Ch 1:4 Noah: S, Ham, and Japheth.
1:17 descendants of S were Elam,
1:24 S, Arpachshad, Shelah,
Luk 3:36 son of S, son of Noah,

Shema (6)

Jos 15:26 Amam, S, Moladah,
1Ch 2:43 Tappuah, Rekem, and S.
2:44 S was the father of Raham,
5:8 (son of Azaz, grandson of S,
8:13 Beriah and S were the heads of
Neh 8:4 Mattithiah, S, Anaiah, Uriah,

Shemaah (1)

1Ch 12:3 the sons of S from Gibeah),

Shemaiah (42)

1Ki 12:22 But God spoke his word to S,
1Ch 3:22 Shecaniah's son was S.
4:37 a descendant of Shimri and S).
5:4 Joel's son was S. Shemaiah's
9:14 from Merari were S (son
9:16 Obadiah (son of S,
15:8 descendants was S,
15:11 Joel, S, Eliel, and Amminadab.
24:6 The scribe S was a son of
24:6 S recorded their names in the

1Ch 26:4 Edom's sons S (the firstborn),
26:6 His son S had sons who ruled
2Ch 11:2 But God spoke his word to S,
12:5 The prophet S came to
12:5 S said to them, "This is what
12:7 he spoke his word to S:
12:15 in the records of the prophet S
17:8 With them were the Levites S,
29:14 were S and Uzziel.
31:15 Eden, Miniamin, Jeshua, S,
35:9 his brothers S and Nethanel,
Ezr 8:13 Eliphelet, Jeuel, and S,
8:16 Then I sent for Eliezer, Ariel, S,
10:21 Elijah, S, Jehiel, and Uzziah
10:31 Isshiah, Malchiah, S, Shimeon,
Neh 3:29 After him S, Shecaniah's son,
6:10 day, I went to the home of S,
6:10 S who was confined to his
10:8 Maaziah, Bilgai, and S.
11:15 These were the Levites: S who
12:6 S, Joiarib, Jedaiah,
12:18 from Bilgah, Shammua; from S,
12:34 Judah, Benjamin, S,
12:35 who was the son of S,
12:36 S, Azarel, Milalai, Gilalai,
12:42 and Maaseiah, S, Eleazar,
Jer 26:20 His name was Uriah, son of S,
29:24 "Say to S from Nehelam,
29:31 says about S from Nehelam:
29:31 S prophesied to you,
29:32 I will punish S from Nehelam.
36:12 Delaiah (son of S),

Shemaiah's (3)

1Ch 3:22 S six sons were Hattush,
5:4 S son was Gog. Gog's son was
26:7 S sons were Othni,

Shemariah (4)

1Ch 12:5 Eluzai, Jerimoth, Bealiah, S,
2Ch 11:19 sons: Jeush, S, and Zaham.
Ezr 10:32 Benjamin, Malluch, and S
10:41 Azarel, Shelemiah, S,

Shemeber (1)

Gen 14:2 King S of Zeboiim,

Shemed (1)

1Ch 8:12 and S (who built Ono,

Shemer (3)

1Ki 16:24 Omri bought a hill from S for
16:24 city after its former owner, S.
1Ch 6:46 who was the son of S,

Shemida (2)

Num 26:32 the family of S, and the family
Jos 17:2 Shechem, Hepher, and S.

Shemida's (1)

1Ch 7:19 S sons were Ahian,

sheminith (1)

1Ch 15:21 play lyres and to conduct the s.

Shemiramoth (4)

1Ch 15:18 S, Jehiel, Unni, Eliab, Benaiah,
15:20 Zechariah, Jaziel, S,
16:5 S, Jehiel, Mattithiah, Eliab,
2Ch 17:8 S, Jehonathan, Adonijah,

Shem's (2)

Gen 10:22 S descendants were Elam,
10:31 These were S descendants by

Shemuel (2)

Num 34:20 S, son of Ammihud, from the
1Ch 7:2 Jeriel, Jahmai, Ibsam, and S.

Shen (1)

1Sm 7:12 it up between Mizpah and S.

Shenazzar (1)

1Ch 3:18 then Malchiram, Pedaiah, S,

Sheol (11)

Job 14:13 I wish you would hide me in S
26:6 S is naked in God's presence,
Psa 88:11 tell about your mercy in S
Pro 15:11 If S and Abaddon lie open in
Isa 14:9 S below wakes up to meet you
14:11 been brought down to S along
14:15 you've been brought down to S,
38:10 go down to the gates of S
38:18 S doesn't thank you!
57:9 away and sent them down to S.
Amo 9:2 if they dig their way into S,

Shepham (3)

Num 34:10 extends from Hazar Enan to S.
34:11 From S the border goes down
1Ch 27:27 the vineyards: Zabdi from S

Shephatiah (13)

2Sm 3:4 The fifth was S, whose mother
1Ch 3:3 The fifth was S, born to
9:8 and Meshullam (son of S,
12:5 and S from Haruph,
27:16 of Simeon: S, son of Maacah
2Ch 21:2 Azariahu, Michael, and S.
Ezr 2:4 of S: 372
2:57 S, Hattil, and Ami.
8:8 from the family of S:
Neh 7:9 of S: 372
7:59 S, Hattil, and Amon.
11:4 who was the son of S,
Jer 38:1 S (son of Mattan), Jucal (son of

Shepher (2)

Num 33:23 and set up camp at Mount S.
33:24 They moved from Mount S and

shepherd (56)

Gen 4:2 Abel was a s, and Cain was a
29:9 because she was a s.
48:15 who has been my s all my life
49:24 because of the name of the S,
Num 27:17 not be like sheep without a s."
1Sm 17:34 "I am a s for my father's sheep.
2Sm 5:2 'You will be s of my people
1Ki 22:17 the hills like sheep without a s.
1Ch 11:2 'You will be s of my people
2Ch 18:16 the hills like sheep without a s.
Psa 23:1 The LORD is my s.
28:9 Be their s, and carry them
49:14 to hell with death as their s.
77:20 Like a s, you led your people.
78:71 so that David could be the s
78:72 devotion David became their s.
80:1 Open your ears, O S of Israel,
Ecc 12:11 They come from one s.
Isa 40:11 Like a s he takes care of his
44:28 says about Cyrus, "He is my s.
Jer 17:16 not run away from being your s,
31:10 them as a s watches over his
43:12 Egypt as his coat as a s puts
Eze 34:5 because there was no s.
34:8 because there is no s,
34:12 As a s looks after his flock
34:23 I will place one s over them,
34:23 care of them and be their s.
37:24 and all of them will have one s.
Amo 3:12 As a s rescues two legs or a
Mic 5:4 The child will become the s of
Zec 10:2 troubled because there is no s.
11:7 So I became the s of the sheep
11:7 I took two s staffs and named
11:9 So I said, "I won't be your s.
11:15 equipment of a foolish s again.
11:16 I'm about to place a s in the
11:17 the foolish s who abandoned
13:7 "Arise, sword, against my s,
13:7 "Strike the s, and the sheep
Mat 2:6 He will s my people Israel."
9:36 like sheep without a s.
25:32 He will separate them as a s
26:31 says, 'I will strike the s,
Mar 6:34 were like sheep without a s.
14:27 says, 'I will strike the s,
Jon 10:2 enters through the gate is the s.
10:11 "I am the good s. The good
10:11 The good s gives his life for
10:12 A hired hand isn't a s and
10:14 "I am the good s. I know my
10:16 will be one flock with one s.
Heb 13:20 of peace brought the great s
1Pe 2:25 you have come back to the s
5:4 when the chief s appears,
Rev 7:17 near the throne will be their s.

shepherd's (11)

Gen 32:10 I only had a s staff when I
38:18 and the s staff that's in your
38:25 and s staff these are."
Exo 4:2 He answered, "A s staff.
4:17 Take that s staff with you,
7:9 'Take your s staff and throw it
12:11 and your s staff in your hand.
1Sm 17:40 and put them in his s bag.
2Ki 4:29 take my s staff in your hand,
Isa 38:12 You rolled it up like a s tent.
Mic 7:14 With your s staff, take care of

shepherds (59)

Gen 46:32 The men are s. They take care
46:34 because all s are disgusting to
47:3 answered Pharaoh, "We are s,
Exo 2:17 But some s came and chased
2:19 rescued us from some s.
Num 14:33 Your children will be s in the
Jdg 5:16 Was it to listen to the s playing
1Sm 21:7 A foreman for Saul's s,
25:7 Your s have been with us,
2Sm 7:7 of Israel whom I ordered to be s
2Ki 10:12 he came to Beth Eked of the S,
1Ch 17:6 of Israel whom I ordered to be s
Job 24:2 flocks and tend them as s.
Isa 13:20 S won't let their flocks rest
31:4 when a crowd of s is called
56:11 They are the s, but they don't
61:5 come forward and become s
63:11 them out of the sea with the s
Jer 3:15 I will give you s after my own
3:15 They will be s who feed you
6:3 s will come to them,
6:4 'The s say,' Let's attack at
10:21 The s are foolish. They don't
12:10 Many s have destroyed my
22:22 wind will blow away all your s,
23:1 "How horrible it will be for the s
23:2 said to the s who take care of
23:4 I will put s over them.
23:4 Those s will take care of them.
25:34 Mourn, you s, and cry. Roll in
25:35 be no place for the s to flee,
25:36 The s are crying and the
31:24 Farmers and s will also live
33:12 pastures where s can rest their
33:13 s will once again count their
50:6 Their s have led them astray.
51:23 I will use you to crush s and
Eze 34:2 against the s of Israel.
34:2 Prophesy to these s.
34:2 How horrible it will be for the s
34:2 Shouldn't s take care of the
34:7 "'So, you s, listen to the word
34:8 My s haven't searched for my
34:9 So, you s, listen to the word of
34:10 I am against the s.
Amo 1:2 The pastures of the s are
Mic 5:5 with seven s and eight leaders.
Nah 3:18 Your s, king of Assyria,
Zep 2:6 with meadows for s
Zec 10:3 anger is directed against the s.
11:3 The s are crying, because their
11:5 Even their own s will have no
11:8 I got rid of three s in one month.
Luk 2:8 S were in the fields near
2:15 The s said to each other,
2:20 As the s returned to their flock,
Act 20:28 placed you as bishops to be s
1Pe 5:2 Be s over the flock God has
Jud 1:12 They are s who care only for

shepherds' (2)

Sos 1:8 young goats near the s tents

Luk 2:18 Everyone who heard the **s** story

Shephi (1)
1Ch 1:40 Manahath, Ebal, S, and Onam.

Shepho (1)
Gen 36:23 Manahath, Ebal, S, and Onam.

Shephuphan (1)
1Ch 8:5 Gera, S, and Huram.

Sherebiah (8)
Ezr 8:18 us someone competent, S,
8:24 12 leaders from the priests — S,
Neh 8:7 The Levites — Jeshua, Bani, S,
9:4 Shebaniah, Bunni, S, Bani,
9:5 S, Hodiah, Shebaniah,
10:12 Zaccur, S, Shebaniah,
12:8 S, Judah, and Mattaniah,
12:24 the Levites were Hashabiah, S,

Sherebiah's (1)
Ezr 8:18 us 18 of S sons and relatives.

Sheresh (1)
1Ch 7:16 His brother's name was S,

Sheshach (2)
Jer 25:26 Last of all, the king of S will
51:41 "S has been captured.

Sheshai (3)
Num 13:22 Ahiman, S, and Talmai lived.
Jos 15:14 Caleb forced out S,
Jdg 1:10 There they killed S,

Sheshan (3)
1Ch 2:31 and Ishi's son was S,
2:34 S had no sons, but he had
2:35 S let Jarha marry one of his

Sheshan's (1)
1Ch 2:31 and S son was Ahlai.

Sheshbazzar (4)
Ezr 1:8 of them for Prince S of Judah.
1:11 S took all these utensils with
5:14 gave them to a man named S,
5:16 Then S laid the foundation of

Sheth (1)
Num 24:17 and destroy all the people of S.

Shethar (1)
Est 1:14 S, Admatha, Tarshish, Meres,

Shethar Bozenai (4)
Ezr 5:3 Euphrates River, S,
5:6 S Bozenai and his group (the
6:6 of the Euphrates, S Bozenai,
6:13 Euphrates River, S Bozenai,

Sheva (2)
2Sm 20:25 S was the royal scribe.
1Ch 2:49 settled Madmannah, and of S,

Shibah (1)
Gen 26:33 So he named it S [Oath].

shibboleth (1)
Jdg 12:6 tell him, "Say the word **s**."

shield (40)
Gen 15:1 I am your **s**. Your reward will be
Dtr 33:29 He is a **s** that helps you and a
1Sm 17:7 The man who carried his **s**
17:41 by the man carrying his **s**,
2Sm 1:21 Saul's **s** was never rubbed with
22:3 in whom I take refuge, my **s**,
22:31 He is a **s** to all those who take
22:36 You have given me the **s** of
1Ki 10:16 15 pounds of gold on each **s**.
10:17 four pounds of gold on each **s**.
2Ki 19:32 hold a **s** in front of it,
19:34 "I will **s** this city to rescue it for
2Ch 9:15 15 pounds of gold on each **s**.
9:16 7 ½ pounds of gold on each **s**.
25:5 could handle a spear and a **s**.
Job 15:26 charges at him with a thick **s**.
Psa 3:3 are a **s** that surrounds me.
5:12 Like a large **s**, you surround
7:10 My **s** is God above,
18:2 in whom I take refuge, my **s**,
18:30 He is a **s** to all those who take
18:35 You have given me the **s** of
28:7 LORD is my strength and my **s**.
33:20 He is our help and our **s**.
59:11 Bring them down, O Lord, our **s**
84:9 Look at our **s**, O God.
84:11 The LORD God is a sun and **s**.
89:18 Our **s** belongs to the LORD.
91:4 His truth is your **s** and armor.
115:9 He is your helper and your **s**.
115:10 He is your helper and your **s**.
115:11 He is your helper and your **s**.
119:114 are my hiding place and my **s**.
144:2 and my savior, my **s**,
Pro 2:7 He is a **s** for those who walk in
30:5 He is a **s** to those who come to
Isa 37:33 hold a **s** in front of it,
37:35 "I will **s** this city to rescue it for
Nah 2:5 The **s** has been set up for the
Eph 6:16 the Christian faith as your **s**.

shielding (1)
2Sm 16:6 all the warriors were **s** David.

shields (43)
2Sm 1:21 because warriors' **s** were
8:7 David took the gold **s** that
1Ki 10:16 Solomon made 200 large **s**
10:17 He also made 300 small **s** of
14:26 the gold **s** Solomon had made.
14:27 King Rehoboam made bronze **s**
14:28 guards carried the **s** and then
2Ki 11:10 and the **s** that had belonged
1Ch 5:18 fighters who could carry **s**
12:8 able to fight with **s** and spears.
12:24 They carried **s** and spears.
12:34 who fought with **s** and spears.
18:7 David took the gold **s** that
2Ch 9:15 Solomon made 200 large **s**
9:16 He also made 300 small **s** of
11:12 city he stored **s** and spears.
12:9 the gold **s** Solomon had made.
12:10 King Rehoboam made bronze **s**
12:11 guards carried the **s** and then
14:8 who were armed with large **s**
14:8 armed with small **s** and bows.
17:17 armed men with bows and **s**),
23:9 and large **s** that had belonged
26:14 entire army Uzziah prepared **s**,
32:5 made plenty of weapons and **s**.
32:27 **s**, and all kinds of valuables.
Neh 4:16 holding spears, **s**, and bows.
Psa 35:2 Use your **s**, (both) small and
76:3 flaming arrows, **s**, swords,
Sos 4:4 A thousand round **s** belonging
Isa 21:5 Prepare your **s** for battle!
22:6 Kir uncovers its **s**.
Jer 46:3 your large and small **s** ready;
46:9 Sudan and Put who carry **s**,
Eze 23:24 around with small and large **s**
26:8 and raise his **s** against you.
27:10 They hung their **s** and helmets
27:11 They hung their **s** all around
32:27 Their **s** were placed on their
38:4 will carry large and small **s**
38:5 will have **s** and helmets.
39:9 will burn small and large **s**,
Nah 2:3 The **s** of his warriors are

shift (1)
1Ki 5:14 He sent a **s** of 10,000 men to

shifting (1)
Jas 1:17 the **s** shadows produced by

shifts (1)
Ecc 1:6 toward the south and **s** toward

shigionoth (1)
Hab 3:1 Habakkuk; according to **s**.

Shihor (3)
Jos 13:3 It extends from the S River,
1Ch 13:5 from the S River near Egypt
Isa 23:3 The grain of S is on the

Shihor Libnath (1)
Jos 19:26 touches Carmel and S

Shikkeron (1)
Jos 15:11 side of Ekron and turns to S,

Shilah (1)
1Ch 9:5 From the descendants of S

Shilhi (2)
1Ki 22:42 was Azubah, daughter of S.
2Ch 20:31 was Azubah, daughter of S.

Shilhim (1)
Jos 15:32 Lebaoth, S, Ain, and Rimmon.

Shillem (2)
Gen 46:24 Jahzeel, Guni, Jezer, and S.
Num 26:49 and the family of S.

Shiloah (1)
Isa 8:6 the gently flowing water of S

Shiloh (40)
Gen 49:10 between his feet until S comes
Jos 18:1 of Israel gathered at S
18:8 of the LORD here in S."
18:9 to Joshua at the camp at S.
18:10 the presence of the LORD in S.
19:51 They did this in S in the
21:2 at S in Canaan. They said to
22:9 of the Israelites at S in Canaan.
22:12 of Israel gathered at S.
Jdg 18:31 the house of God was at S.
21:12 to the camp at S in Canaan.
21:19 LORD's festival is held at S.
21:19 S is north of Bethel,
21:21 When the young women of S
21:21 of you catch a woman from S
1Sm 1:3 to the LORD of Armies at S.
1:9 something to eat and drink in S,
1:24 to the LORD's house at S while
2:14 is what the priests did in S
3:21 LORD continued to appear in S,
3:21 himself to Samuel in S through
4:3 LORD's promise from S so that
4:12 He went to S that day with his
14:3 the LORD's priest at S.
1Ki 2:27 spoken at S about Eli's family.
11:29 The prophet Ahijah from S met
12:15 son) through Ahijah from S.
14:2 told his wife, "Go to S,
14:4 She left, went to S,
15:29 his servant Ahijah from S.
2Ch 9:29 the prophecy of Ahijah from S,
10:15 son) through Ahijah from S.
Psa 78:60 his dwelling place in S,
Jer 7:12 go to my place that was at S,
7:12 See what I did to S because of
7:13 the people did at S,'" declares
7:14 So what I did to S I will now do
26:6 to this temple what I did to S.
26:9 that this temple will be like S
41:5 Shechem, S, and Samaria.

Shiloni (1)
Neh 11:5 who was the son of S.

Shilsha (1)
1Ch 7:37 Bezer, Hod, Shamma, S,

Shimea (8)
2Sm 13:3 a son of David's brother S.
13:32 the son of David's brother S,
1Ch 2:13 second son), S (his third son),
2:55 people of Tira, S, and Sucah.
3:5 Jerusalem: S, Shobab, Nathan,

1Ch 6:30 Uzzah's son was **S**.
6:39 who was the son of **S**,
20:7 son of David's brother **S**,

Shimeah (1)
1Ch 8:32 who was the father of **S**.

Shimeam (1)
1Ch 9:38 Mikloth was the father of **S**.

Shimea's (1)
1Ch 6:30 **S** son was Haggiah.

Shimeath (2)
2Ki 12:21 son of **S**, and Jehozabad,
2Ch 24:26 an Ammonite woman named **S**,

Shimei (44)
Exo 6:17 their families were Libni and **S**.
Num 3:18 Libni and **S** were the sons of
3:21 descended from Libni and **S**.
2Sm 16:5 His name was **S**, son of Gera.
16:7 **S** cursed and said,
16:13 **S** was walking along the
16:13 **S** cursed, hurled stones,
19:16 **S**, Gera's son from the tribe of
19:18 **S**, Gera's son, bowed down in
19:21 "Shouldn't **S** be put to death for
19:23 The king promised **S**,
21:21 son of David's brother **S**,
1Ki 1:8 the prophet Nathan, **S**, Rei,
2:8 "**S**, son of Gera from Bahurim
2:36 The king summoned **S** and
2:38 "Very well," **S** answered.
2:38 So **S** stayed in Jerusalem for a
2:39 **S** was told that his slaves
2:40 **S** went to Gath and got his
2:41 After Solomon heard that **S** had
2:42 he summoned **S**. Solomon
2:44 **S**, you know in your heart all
2:46 He went to attack and kill **S**.
4:18 **S**, son of Ela, was in charge of
1Ch 3:19 sons were Zerubbabel and **S**.
4:26 Zaccur's son was **S**.
4:27 **S** had 16 sons and 6 daughters.
5:4 was Gog. Gog's son was **S**.
6:17 Gershom's sons: Libni and **S**.
6:29 Libni's son was **S**.
6:42 who was the son of **S**,
23:7 **S** were Gershon's descendants.
23:9 **S** had three sons: Shelomith,
25:3 **S**, Hashabiah, Mattithiah.
25:17 The tenth chose **S**,
27:27 for the vineyards: **S** from
2Ch 29:14 were Jehiel and **S**.
31:12 his brother **S** was his assistant.
31:13 Conaniah and his brother **S**.
Ezr 10:23 From the Levites: Jozabad, **S**,
10:33 Jeremai, Manasseh, and **S**
10:38 the descendants of Binnui: **S**,
Est 2:5 the grandson of **S**,
Zec 12:13 the family of **S** by itself,

Shimei's (6)
1Ki 2:39 two of **S** slaves fled to Gath's
1Ch 5:5 **S** son was Micah.
6:29 **S** son was Uzzah.
8:19 **S** sons were Jakim,
23:10 **S** sons were Jahath,
23:10 They were **S** four sons.

Shimeon (1)
Ezr 10:31 Malchiah, Shemaiah, **S**,

Shimon's (1)
1Ch 4:20 **S** sons were Amnon,

Shimrath (1)
1Ch 8:21 Adaiah, Beraiah, and **S**.

Shimri (4)
1Ch 4:37 of **S** and Shemaiah).
11:45 Jediael (son of **S**) and his
26:10 **S** was the head, although he
2Ch 29:13 descendants were **S** and Jeiel.

Shimrith (1)
2Ch 24:26 of a Moabite woman named **S**.

Shimron (5)
Gen 46:13 were Tola, Puvah, Iob, and **S**.
Num 26:24 and the family of **S**.
Jos 11:1 the kings of **S** and Achshaph.
19:15 **S**, Idalah, and Bethlehem.
1Ch 7:1 Tola, Puah, Jashub, and **S**.

Shimron Meron (1)
Jos 12:20 the king of **S**,

Shimshai (4)
Ezr 4:8 Rehum the commander and **S**
4:9 Rehum the commander and **S**
4:17 the commander, **S** the scribe,
4:23 the commander, **S** the scribe,

shin (1)
1Sm 17:6 On his legs he had bronze **s**

Shinab (1)
Gen 14:2 of Gomorrah, King **S** of Admah,

Shinar (5)
Gen 10:10 and Calneh in **S** [Babylonia].
11:2 they found a plain in **S**
14:1 kings⌋ — King Amraphel of **S**,
14:9 King Amraphel of **S**,
Zec 5:11 a house for it in **S** [Babylonia].

shine (29)
Gen 1:15 will be lights in the sky to **s**
Job 3:4 Let no light **s** on it.
22:28 and light will **s** on your path.
29:3 when he made his lamp **s** on
31:26 If I saw the light **s** or the moon
Psa 4:6 light of your presence **s** on us,
19:8 It makes the eyes **s**.
37:6 make your righteousness **s** like
72:5 moon ⌊**s**⌋ — throughout every
104:15 olive oil to make faces **s**,
112:4 Light will **s** in the dark for a
132:18 on my anointed one will **s**."
Ecc 8:1 Wisdom makes one's face **s**,
Isa 9:2 The light will **s** on those who
13:10 The moon won't **s**.
45:12 all the stars ⌊to **s**⌋.
60:1 **S**! Your light has come, and the
Eze 32:7 and the moon won't **s** anymore.
Dan 12:3 Those who are wise will **s** like
12:3 to righteousness will **s** like
Joe 2:10 and the stars no longer **s**.
3:15 The stars will no longer **s**.
Mat 5:16 In the same way let your light **s**
13:43 have God's approval will **s** like
2Co 4:6 who said that light should **s** out
Eph 5:14 and Christ will **s** on you."
Php 2:15 You will **s** like stars among
Rev 18:23 Light from lamps will never **s** in
22:5 the Lord God will **s** on them.

shined (2)
Hos 6:5 My judgments **s** on you like
Act 26:13 from the sky and **s** around me

shines (10)
Psa 50:2 God **s** from Zion, the perfection
72:7 until the moon no longer ⌊**s**⌋.
72:17 as long as the sun ⌊**s**⌋.
Isa 62:1 until its righteousness **s** like
Mat 5:15 Then its light **s** on everyone in
Jon 1:5 The light **s** in the dark,
1:9 which **s** on everyone,
2Co 4:6 which **s** from Christ's face.
2Pe 1:19 as you would to a light that **s**
Rev 1:16 face was like the sun when it **s**

shining (15)
Exo 34:29 His face was **s** from speaking
34:30 at Moses and saw his face **s**,
34:35 see that Moses' face was **s**.
Num 14:10 the glory of the LORD ⌊**s**⌋ at
2Ki 8:19 his descendants a ⌊**s**⌋ lamp.
2Ch 21:7 his descendants a ⌊**s**⌋ lamp.
Job 41:32 It leaves a **s** path behind it so
Psa 148:3 Praise him, all **s** stars.
Eze 32:8 I will darken all the lights **s** in
43:2 and the earth was **s** because of
Luk 11:36 as bright as a lamp **s** on you."
23:45 The sun had stopped **s**.
2Co 3:7 His face was **s** with glory,
1Jn 2:8 and the true light is already **s**.
Rev 15:6 **s** linen with gold belts around

Shion (1)
Jos 19:19 Hapharaim, **S**, Anaharath,

ship (74)
Gen 6:14 Make yourself a **s** of cypress
6:14 Make rooms in the **s** and coat
6:15 the **s** is to be 450 feet long,
6:16 Make a roof for the **s**,
6:16 Put a door in the side of the **s**.
6:16 Build the **s** with lower,
6:18 sons' wives will go into the **s**.
6:19 every living creature into the **s**
7:1 "Go into the **s** with your whole
7:7 his sons' wives went into the **s**
7:9 came to Noah to go into the **s**
7:13 went into the **s**.
7:15 came to Noah to go into the **s**.
7:17 and lifted the **s** so that
7:18 the **s** floated on top of the
7:23 with him in the **s** were left.
8:1 animals with him in the **s**.
8:4 the **s** came to rest in the
8:6 window he had made in the **s**
8:9 it came back to Noah in the **s**.
8:9 the dove back into the **s**.
8:10 sent the dove out of the **s**.
8:13 Noah opened the top of the **s**,
8:16 "Come out of the **s** with your
8:19 the earth — came out of the **s**,
9:10 all those that came out of the **s**
9:18 who came out of the **s**,
Psa 107:26 The sailors aboard **s** rose
Pro 30:19 a **s** making its way through
Eze 27:25 You were like a **s** filled with
27:27 sea when your **s** was wrecked.
Jnh 1:3 He went to Joppa and found a **s**
1:4 was so powerful that the **s** was
1:6 The captain of the **s** went to
1:13 to row harder to get the **s** back
Mat 24:38 day that Noah went into the **s**.
Luk 17:27 day that Noah went into the **s**.
Act 13:13 Paul and his men took a **s** from
16:11 So we took a **s** from Troas and
20:3 going to board a **s** for Syria,
20:6 we boarded a **s** at Philippi.
20:13 We went ahead to the **s** and
20:38 Then they took Paul to the **s**.
21:2 In Patara, we found a **s** that
21:3 where the **s** was to unload its
21:6 Then we went aboard the **s**,
27:2 We set sail on a **s** from the city
27:2 The **s** was going to stop at
27:6 In Myra the officer found a **s**
27:10 damage to the cargo and the **s**,
27:11 and the owner of the **s** said
27:15 The wind carried the **s** away,
27:17 they passed ropes under the **s**
27:22 Only the **s** will be destroyed.
27:29 anchors from the back of the **s**
27:30 tried to escape from the **s**.
27:30 anchors from the front of the **s**.
27:31 sailors don't stay on the **s**,
27:37 (There were 276 of us on the **s**.)
27:38 they lightened the **s** by
27:39 to try to run the **s** ashore.
27:40 and steered the **s** to the shore.
27:41 water and ran the **s** aground.
27:41 The front of the **s** stuck and
27:41 while the back of the **s** was
27:44 pieces ⌊of wood⌋ from the **s**.
28:11 Alexandrian **s** that had spent
28:11 The **s** had the gods Castor and
1Ti 1:19 destroyed like a wrecked **s**.
Heb 11:7 He obeyed God and built a **s** to
1Pe 3:20 patiently while Noah built the **s**.

1Pe 3:20 In this **s** a few people — eight in
Rev 18:17 everyone who traveled by **s**,
18:19 Everyone who had a **s** at sea

shipbuilders (1)

Eze 27:9 Master **s** from Gebal went

Shiphi (1)

1Ch 4:37 Ziza (son of S, grandson of

Shiphrah (1)

Exo 1:15 names were S and Puah,

Shiphtan (1)

Num 34:24 Kemuel, son of S, the leader of

shipped (2)

2Ki 25:13 They **s** the bronze to Babylon.
Jer 52:17 They **s** all the bronze to

ship's (5)

Pro 23:34 on top of a **s** mast, saying,
Jnh 1:5 overboard to lighten the **s** load.
Act 27:16 got control of the **s** lifeboat
27:19 the **s** equipment overboard.
Rev 18:17 Every **s** captain, everyone who

ships (34)

Gen 49:13 He will have **s** by the coast.
Num 24:24 S will come from the shores of
Dtr 28:68 bring you back to Egypt in **s**
Jdg 5:17 Why did he stay by the **s**?
1Ki 22:48 made Tarshish-style **s**
22:48 because the **s** were wrecked at
22:49 go with your servants in the **s**."
2Ch 8:18 sailors with **s** to Solomon.
9:21 The king had **s** going to
9:21 Tarshish **s** would bring gold,
20:36 joined him in making **s**
20:36 made the **s** in Ezion Geber.
20:37 So the **s** were wrecked and
Psa 48:7 you smash the **s** of Tarshish.
104:26 S sail on it, and Leviathan,
107:23 Those who sail on the sea in **s**,
Pro 31:14 She is like merchant **s**.
Isa 2:16 against all the large **s** of
23:1 Cry loudly, you **s** of Tarshish!
23:1 has come to the **s** from Cyprus.
23:14 Cry loudly, you **s** of Tarshish,
33:21 S with oars won't travel on
33:21 Stately **s** won't sail on them.
43:14 refugees in the **s** that they take
60:9 The **s** from Tarshish are the
Eze 27:9 All the **s** on the sea and their
27:25 "'S from Tarshish carried your
27:29 came down from their **s**
30:9 I will send messengers in **s**
Dan 11:30 S will come from the west to
11:40 chariots, horses, and many **s**.
Jas 3:4 The same thing is true for **s**.
3:4 pilots steer **s** wherever they
Rev 8:9 of the **s** were destroyed.

shipwrecked (1)

2Co 11:25 three times I was **s**,

shirt (4)

Exo 4:6 "Put your hand inside your **s**."
4:7 your hand back inside your **s**,"
Mat 5:40 sue you in order to take your **s**,
Luk 6:29 stop him from taking your **s**.

shirts (2)

Jdg 14:12 I'll give you 30 linen **s** and 30
Luk 3:11 "Whoever has two **s** should

Shisha (1)

1Ki 4:3 the sons of S, were scribes.

Shishak (8)

1Ki 11:40 fled to King S of Egypt.
14:25 King S of Egypt attacked
2Ch 12:2 King S of Egypt attacked
12:3 S had 1,200 chariots,
12:5 in Jerusalem because of S.
12:5 I will hand you over to S."
12:7 I will not use S to pour my
12:9 King S of Egypt attacked

Shitrai (1)

1Ch 27:29 S from Sharon for the herds in

Shittim (5)

Num 25:1 While Israel was staying at S,
Jos 2:1 From S Joshua, son of Nun,
3:1 He and all the Israelites left S.
Joe 3:18 It will water the valley of S.
Mic 6:5 your journey from S

shivering (2)

Rut 3:8 At midnight the man was **s**.
Ezr 10:9 because of this matter and **s**

Shiza (1)

1Ch 11:42 Adina (son of S) from the tribe

Shoa (1)

Eze 23:23 men from Pekod, S, and Koa,

Shobab (4)

2Sm 5:14 S, Nathan, Solomon,
1Ch 2:18 Her other sons were Jesher, S,
3:5 Jerusalem: Shimea, S, Nathan,
14:4 S, Nathan, Solomon,

Shobach (2)

2Sm 10:16 came to Helam with S,
10:18 David struck S dead.

Shobai (2)

Ezr 2:42 Akkub, Hatita, and S: 139
Neh 7:45 Akkub, Hatita, and S: 138

Shobal (8)

Gen 36:20 land: Lotan, S, Zibeon, Anah,
36:23 These were the sons of S:
36:29 Lotan, S, Zibeon, Anah,
1Ch 1:38 Seir's sons were Lotan, S,
2:50 son of Ephrath, were S,
2:52 S, who first settled Kiriath
4:1 Hezron, Carmi, Hur, and S.
4:2 Reaiah, son of S, was the

Shobal's (1)

1Ch 1:40 S sons were Alian,

Shobek (1)

Neh 10:24 Hallohesh, Pilha, S,

Shobi (1)

2Sm 17:27 David came to Mahanaim, S,

shock (4)

Ezr 9:3 and sat down in **s**.
9:4 I sat in **s** until the evening
Psa 143:4 and my heart is in a state of **s**.
Mar 16:8 S and trembling had

shocked (12)

Lev 26:32 will be **s** as they settle
Jdg 3:25 They were **s** to see their ruler
Job 17:8 Decent people are **s** by this,
18:20 People in the west are **s** by
21:5 Look at me, and be **s**,
Isa 52:14 Many will be **s** by him.
Eze 4:17 They will be **s** at the sight of
26:16 constantly and be **s** at you.
32:10 Many people will be **s** by what
Mar 10:32 His disciples were **s** that he
Luk 2:48 parents saw him, they were **s**.
Act 12:16 they were **s** to see him.

shocking (1)

Lam 1:9 Its downfall was **s**.

shocks (2)

2Ch 29:8 He made them something that **s**
30:7 He made them something that **s**

shoe (2)

Psa 60:8 I will throw my **s** over Edom.
108:9 I will throw my **s** over Edom.

shoes (4)

Dtr 29:5 clothes and **s** never wore out.
1Ki 2:5 his waist and the **s** on his feet.
Act 12:8 angel told him, "Put your **s** on,
Eph 6:15 Put on your **s** so that you are

Shoham (1)

1Ch 24:27 S, Zaccur, and Ibri (for Merari's

Shomer (3)

2Ki 12:21 son of S, executed him.
1Ch 7:32 father of Japhlet, S, Hotham,
7:34 of his brother S were Rohgah,

shook (28)

Exo 19:16 people in the camp **s** with fear.
19:18 and the whole mountain **s**
20:18 So they **s** with fear and stood
Jdg 5:5 and the mountains **s** in the
1Sm 14:15 The earth **s**, and there was a
2Sm 22:8 Then the earth **s** and quaked.
22:8 They **s** violently because he
1Ki 1:40 that their voices **s** the ground.
Ezr 10:19 They **s** hands as a pledge that
Job 4:14 and all my bones **s**.
Psa 18:7 Then the earth **s** and quaked.
18:7 They **s** violently because he
77:16 The water saw you and **s**.
77:18 The earth trembled and **s**.
Isa 6:4 Their voices **s** the foundations
14:16 who **s** the kingdoms,
Mat 27:39 They **s** their heads
27:51 The earth **s**, and the rocks
28:4 afraid of him that they **s**.
Mar 9:26 **s** the child violently,
15:29 They **s** their heads and said,
Act 4:31 their meeting place **s**.
13:51 Paul and Barnabas **s** the dust
16:26 a violent earthquake **s** the
18:6 So Paul **s** the dust from his
28:5 Paul **s** the snake into the fire
Gal 2:9 So they **s** hands with Barnabas
Heb 12:26 his voice **s** the earth.

shoot (25)

1Sm 20:20 I will **s** three arrows from
20:36 "please find the arrows I **s**."
2Sm 11:20 they would **s** from the wall?
2Ki 9:27 "S him down in his chariot."
13:17 "S," Elisha said, and the king
19:32 into this city, **s** an arrow here,
1Ch 5:18 and swords and **s** arrows.
12:2 could sling stones or **s** arrows
2Ch 26:15 towers and corners to **s** arrows
Job 41:19 Flames **s** from its mouth.
Psa 7:12 he makes it ready to **s**.
11:2 arrows against the strings to **s**
64:4 to **s** at innocent people from
64:4 They **s** at them suddenly,
64:7 But God will **s** them with an
144:6 S your arrows, and throw them
Isa 5:28 all their bows are ready to **s**.
11:1 Then a **s** will come out from
21:15 from bows ready to **s**,
37:33 into this city, **s** an arrow here,
Jer 9:3 like bows that **s** arrows.
50:14 S at it; don't save any arrows,
Eze 5:16 When I **s** my destructive
5:16 at you, I will **s** to kill you.
Dan 11:7 "At that time a **s** will grow from

shooting (1)

Dtr 4:11 was on fire with flames **s** into

shoots (7)

Job 8:16 The **s** spread over his garden.
14:7 Its **s** will not stop sprouting.
Psa 80:11 Its **s** reached the Euphrates
Pro 26:18 madman who **s** flaming arrows,
Isa 16:8 Their **s** had spread out over the
18:5 he will cut off the **s** with
Eze 17:6 branches and growing **s**.

Shophach (2)

1Ch 19:16 S, the commander of

1Ch 19:18 David also killed S.

shore (24)

Psa 139:9 ⌊or⌋ land on the most distant s
Eze 27:28 people on the s trembled.
27:29 their ships and stood on the s.
47:10 will be standing on the s
Jnh 1:13 harder to get the ship back to s,
2:10 and it spit Jonah out onto the s.
Mat 13:2 the entire crowd stood on the s.
13:48 they pulled it to the s.
14:24 now hundreds of yards from s,
Mar 4:1 the entire crowd lined the s.
6:53 came to s at Gennesaret,
Luk 5:2 Jesus saw two boats on the s.
5:3 to push off a little from the s.
5:11 partners brought the boats to s,
8:27 Jesus stepped out on the s,
Jon 6:21 the boat reached the s where
21:4 Jesus stood on the s.
21:8 They weren't far from the s,
Act 27:8 sailing along the s of Crete.
27:13 sailed close to the s of Crete.
27:40 and steered the ship to the s.
27:44 In this way everyone got to s
28:1 When we were safely on s,
Rev 12:18 on the sandy s of the sea.

shores (4)

Num 24:24 will come from the s of Cyprus.
Eze 27:6 pine trees on the s of Cyprus.
Mat 4:13 home in Capernaum on the s
Act 27:17 sandbank off the s of Libya,

short (20)

1Ki 3:16 A s time later two prostitutes
4:27 it that nothing was in s supply.
Est 1:18 There will be contempt and s
Job 10:20 "Isn't my life s enough?
16:22 because in a few s years I will
21:21 number of his months is cut s?
Psa 76:12 He cuts s the lives of
89:45 You cut s the days of his youth
89:47 Remember how s my life is!
Pro 14:29 but a s temper is the height of
27:25 ⌊When⌋ grass is cut s,
Isa 3:16 taking s little steps,
28:20 The bed is too s to stretch out
29:17 In a very s time Lebanon will
Mar 4:17 They last for a s time.
Act 8:33 his life on earth being cut s?"
Rom 3:23 have fallen s of God's glory.
Heb 12:10 For a s time our fathers
13:22 I have written you a s letter.
1Pe 5:12 I've written this s letter to you

shortage (2)

1Sm 21:15 Do I have such a s of lunatics
Psa 107:38 he does not allow a s of cattle.

shortages (1)

2Ki 6:25 The s caused by the blockade

shortened (3)

Job 18:7 "His healthy stride is s,
Pro 10:27 years of wicked people are s.
1Co 7:29 The time has been s.

shorter (1)

1Ki 6:3 the same length as the s side

shortest (1)

Exo 13:17 although that was the s route.

short-lived (3)

Job 14:1 who is born of a woman is s
20:5 the triumph of the wicked is s,
Psa 103:15 Human life is as s as grass.

shortsighted (1)

2Pe 1:9 you're s and have forgotten that

short-tempered (1)

Pro 14:17 A s person acts stupidly,

shot (14)

Gen 21:16 far away as an arrow can be s
49:23 Archers provoked him, s at him,
Exo 19:13 be stoned or s with arrows.
Num 21:30 But we s the Amorites full of
1Sm 20:36 The boy ran, and Jonathan s
2Sm 11:24 The archers on the wall s
22:15 He s arrows and scattered
2Ki 9:24 But Jehu took his bow and s
9:27 They s him at Gur Pass,
13:17 Elisha said, and the king s.
2Ch 35:23 Some archers s King Josiah.
Psa 18:14 He s his arrows and scattered
78:57 They were like arrows s from a
Lam 3:13 He has s the arrows from his

shoulder (24)

Gen 21:14 putting them on her s.
24:15 came with her jar on her s.
24:45 came with her jar on her s.
45:14 who was crying on his s.
46:29 and cried on his s a long time.
Exo 28:7 It will have two s straps
28:12 and fasten them on the s straps
28:25 the two settings on the s straps
28:27 to the bottom of the s straps
39:4 They made two s straps
39:7 fastened them on the s straps
39:18 the two settings on the s straps
39:20 to the bottom of the s straps
Dtr 18:3 goat: the s, jaws, and stomach.
Jos 4:5 must take a stone on his s,
Jdg 9:48 and carried it on his s.
14:16 Samson's wife cried on his s.
14:17 But she cried on his s for the
Neh 9:29 But they gave you the cold s,
Job 31:22 ⌊then⌋ let my s fall out of its
31:36 would certainly carry it on my s
Psa 81:6 removed the burden from his s.
Eze 24:4 best pieces, the thigh and s.
29:18 and every soldier's s was

shoulders (25)

Gen 9:23 blanket and laid it over their s.
Exo 12:34 carried it on their s in bowls,
28:12 carry their names on his s as
Num 6:19 will take one of the s from
7:9 the holy things on their own s.
Jdg 16:3 He carried them on his s to the
2Ki 9:24 and shot Joram between the s.
1Ch 15:15 carried God's ark on their s.
2Ch 35:3 be carried on your s any longer.
Neh 9:26 your teachings over their s
Isa 9:4 the bar that is across their s,
9:6 government will rest on his s.
10:27 will be removed from your s.
14:25 will be removed from their s."
46:7 They lift it on their s and carry
49:22 carry your daughters on their s.
Eze 12:6 you put your bags on your s
12:7 as I carried my bags on my s.
12:12 you will put his bags on his s
29:7 splintered and tore up their s.
34:21 sheep with your sides and s,
Zec 7:11 They shrugged their s at me
Mat 11:29 Place my yoke over your s,
23:4 to carry and lay them on the s
Luk 15:5 He puts that sheep on his s and

shout (58)

Jos 6:5 the troops must s very loudly.
6:10 "Don't s, make any noise,
6:10 your mouth until I tell you to s.
6:10 I tell you to shout. Then s!"
6:16 Joshua said to the troops, "S,
Jdg 7:18 the camp do the same and s,
1Ki 18:27 "S louder, since he is a god.
Est 6:9 servants are also to s ahead
Job 30:5 People s at them in the same
30:5 same way they s at thieves.
33:26 They will see God's face and s
Psa 41:11 and my enemy cannot s in
47:1 S to God with a loud,
47:5 has gone up with a joyful s.
60:8 I will s in triumph over
65:13 All of them s triumphantly.
66:1 S happily to God, all the earth!
81:1 S happily to the God of Jacob.
95:1 Let's s happily to the rock of
95:2 Let's s happily to him with
98:4 S happily to the LORD,
98:6 S happily in the presence of
100:1 S happily to the LORD,
108:9 I will s in triumph over
Isa 12:6 S loudly, and sing with joy,
24:14 They s for joy. From the sea
26:19 dust will wake up and s for joy,
35:6 cannot speak will s for joy.
42:11 Let them s from the tops of the
48:20 S for joy as you tell it and
48:20 S it out to the ends of the earth.
52:8 voices and s together joyfully.
Jer 4:5 S loudly and say, Let's go into
20:8 I have to cry out and s,
31:7 S, sing praise, and say,
31:12 They will come and s for joy
48:20 S loudly, and cry. Tell the
49:29 People will s to them,
50:15 S a war cry against them on
51:14 People will s their victory over
51:39 so that they will s and laugh.
Eze 8:18 Even if they s in my ears,
Zep 3:14 S loudly, Israel! Celebrate and
Zec 9:9 S in triumph, people of
9:15 They will drink and s as if they
Mat 10:27 S from the housetops what you
11:16 and s to other children,
12:19 He will not quarrel or s,
15:22 came ⌊to him⌋ and began to s,
27:23 But they began to s loudly,
Mar 3:11 fall down in front of him and s,
10:47 by⌋, he began to s, "Jesus,
Luk 7:32 sit in the marketplace and s
Act 16:17 She used to follow Paul and s,
19:34 everyone started to s in unison,
22:22 Then they began to s,
25:24 They s that he must not be
Jas 5:4 your fields s ⌊to God⌋ against

shouted (67)

Gen 27:34 he s out a very loud and bitter
41:43 Men ran ahead of him and s,
Exo 14:25 Then the Egyptians s,
Lev 9:24 they s and bowed with their
Jos 6:20 So the troops s very loudly
Jdg 7:20 They s, "A sword for the LORD
9:7 He s to them, "Listen to me,
18:23 They s at them. But the people
20:32 The men of Benjamin s,
1Sm 4:5 all Israel s so loudly that the
10:24 Then all the people s,
17:52 Judah rose up, s a battle cry,
1Ki 18:28 So they s louder. They also cut
2Ki 18:28 commander stood and s loudly
2Ch 13:15 and the men of Judah s.
13:15 When they s, God attacked
32:18 Sennacherib's officers s loudly
Ezr 3:11 Then all the people s,
3:12 Many others s for joy.
10:12 the whole assembly s in reply,
Job 38:7 all the sons of God s for joy?
Isa 36:13 commander stood and s loudly
Dan 4:14 He s loudly, 'Cut down the oak
Mat 8:29 They s, "Why are you
9:27 They s, "Have mercy on us,
14:30 He s, "Lord, save me!"
20:30 by, they s, "Lord, Son of David,
20:31 But they s even louder,
25:6 "At midnight someone s,
Mar 1:23 by an evil spirit. He s,
5:7 and s, "Why are you bothering
5:8 He s this because Jesus said,
10:48 But he s even louder,
15:13 "Crucify him!" they s back.
15:14 But they s even louder,
Luk 4:33 evil demon. He s very loudly,
8:28 When he saw Jesus, he s,
9:38 A man in the crowd s,
11:27 a woman in the crowd s,
12:3 will be s from the housetops.
17:13 and s, "Jesus, Teacher,

Luk 18:38 Then the blind man **s**,
18:39 But he **s** even louder,
19:38 They **s** joyfully, "Blessed is
23:10 and **s** their accusations against
23:18 The whole crowd then **s**,
23:23 They **s** that Jesus had to be
Jon 11:43 he **s** as loudly as he could,
18:40 The Jews **s** again,
19:6 Jesus, they **s**, "Crucify him!
19:12 But the Jews **s**, "If you free this
19:15 Then the Jews **s**, "Kill him!
Act 7:57 But the council members **s** and
7:60 Then he knelt down and **s**,
14:11 who saw what Paul had done **s**
16:28 But Paul **s** as loudly as he
17:6 They **s**, "Those men who have
19:32 Some people **s** one thing while
19:32 while others **s** something else.
21:34 Some of the crowd **s** one thing,
21:34 while others **s** something else.
23:6 he **s** in the council,
24:21 As I stood among them, I **s**,
26:24 Festus **s**, "Paul, you're crazy!
Rev 10:3 Then he **s** in a loud voice as a
10:3 When he **s**, the seven thunders
18:19 their heads and **s** while crying

shouting (29)

Exo 32:17 heard the noise of the people **s**.
32:18 "It's not the sound of winners **s**.
1Sm 4:6 "What's ⌊all⌋ this **s** in the
17:20 to the battle line **s** their war cry.
2Ki 19:22 Against whom are you **s**?
Ezr 3:13 the people were **s** so loudly.
Est 6:11 the city square, **s** ahead of him,
Job 3:18 There they do not hear the **s** of
8:21 and your lips with happy **s**.
39:7 listen to the **s** of its master.
Psa 74:23 Do not forget the **s** of your
Ecc 9:17 from wise people than **s** from
Isa 22:2 You are a city filled with **s**,
37:23 Against whom are you **s**?
Jer 4:16 They are **s** battle cries against
Amo 1:14 its palaces while troops are **s**
2:2 of battle while troops are **s**
Mat 15:23 She keeps **s** behind us."
21:9 and that followed him was **s**,
21:15 he performed and the children **s**
Mar 11:9 who followed him were **s**,
Luk 4:41 **s**, "You are the Son of God!"
Jon 12:13 They were **s**, "Hosanna!
Act 12:22 The people started **s**,
19:28 became furious and began **s**,
21:28 Then they began **s**,
21:36 The mob was behind them **s**,
23:9 The **s** became very loud.
Gal 4:27 Break into **s**, those who feel no

shouts (26)

Jdg 15:14 met him with **s** ⌊of triumph⌋.
2Sm 6:15 the ark of the LORD with **s**
1Ch 15:28 of the LORD's promise with **s**
2Ch 15:14 their oath to the LORD with **s**,
Ezr 3:13 between the joyful **s**
Psa 27:6 I will offer sacrifices with **s** of
29:3 The LORD **s** over raging water.
55:3 because my enemy **s** at me
84:2 My whole body **s** for joy to the
Isa 14:7 It breaks out into **s** of joy.
16:9 The **s** of joy for your ripened
16:10 No **s** are raised. No one stomps
16:10 have put an end to the **s** of joy.
42:13 He **s**, gives the battle cry,
44:23 Break into **s** of joy,
49:13 Break into **s** of joy,
52:9 Break out into **s** of joy,
54:1 Break into **s** of joy,
Jer 25:30 He **s** like those who stomp
25:30 He **s** against all those who live
48:33 stomp on grapes with **s** of joy.
48:33 There will be **s**, but not shouts
48:33 will be shouts, but not **s** of joy.
Joe 2:11 The LORD **s** out orders to his
Zep 3:17 over you with **s** of joy.
Zec 4:7 stone with **s** of 'Blessings,

shoved (1)

Num 35:22 Maybe you **s** him or threw

shovel (3)

Jer 15:7 them with a winnowing **s** at
Mat 3:12 His winnowing **s** is in his hand,
Luk 3:17 His winnowing **s** is in his hand

shovels (11)

Exo 27:3 ashes, also **s**, bowls, forks,
38:3 of bronze: pots, **s**, bowls, forks,
Num 4:14 These are the trays, forks, **s**,
1Ki 7:40 Hiram also made pots, **s**,
7:45 pots, **s**, and bowls.
2Ki 25:14 They took the pots, **s**,
2Ch 4:11 Huram also made the pots, **s**,
4:16 pots, **s**, and three-pronged
Psa 7:15 He digs a pit and **s** it out.
Isa 30:24 winnowed with forks and **s**.
Jer 52:18 They took the pots, **s**,

shoving (1)

Num 35:20 someone you hate by **s** him

show (195)

Gen 12:1 Go to the land that I will **s** you.
21:23 **S** me and the land where
22:2 the mountains that I will **s** you."
24:12 **S** your kindness to Abraham.
24:49 you're going to **s** my master true
37:34 Then, to **s** his grief,
42:20 This will **s** that you've been
Exo 4:21 see that you **s** Pharaoh all the
6:1 I will **s** him my power,
6:1 I will **s** him my power,
9:16 I want to **s** you my power and
18:20 **s** them how to live,
20:6 But I **s** mercy to thousands of
22:28 "Never **s** disrespect for God or
33:13 **s** me your ways so that I can
34:7 He continues to **s** his love to
Lev 10:3 'I will **s** my holiness among
10:3 I will **s** my glory to all the
13:7 he must **s** himself to the priest
19:15 and never **s** preference to
19:32 "**S** respect to the elderly,
19:32 In this way you **s** respect for
22:32 I will **s** my holiness among the
Num 6:7 Nazarites **s** their vow to God
16:5 "In the morning the LORD will **s**
18:5 Then I won't **s** my anger
20:12 You didn't **s** the Israelites how
27:14 You didn't **s** the people how
Dtr 1:33 the day to **s** you which route
3:24 you have ⌊only⌋ begun to **s** me
4:6 This will **s** the people of the
5:10 But I **s** mercy to thousands of
7:2 with them or **s** them any mercy.
13:17 angry and will **s** you mercy.
21:16 This would **s** a total disregard
28:50 They will **s** no respect for the
32:51 You didn't **s** the Israelites how
Jdg 1:24 They told him, "**S** us how we
4:22 I have something to **s** you — the
Rut 4:11 So **s** your strength of character
1Sm 2:29 Why do you **s** no respect for
14:8 and **s** ourselves to them.
14:12 "We have something to **s** you."
20:14 ⌊promise me that you will⌋ **s**
21:15 this man so that he can **s** me
2Sm 2:6 LORD always **s** you kindness.
9:1 to whom I can **s** kindness
9:3 I can **s** God's kindness?"
9:7 "I will certainly **s** you kindness
10:2 David thought, "I will **s**
13:31 clothes torn ⌊to **s** their grief⌋.
15:20 always **s** you kindness."
1Ki 3:6 And you continued to **s** him
2Ki 2:12 tore it in two ⌊to **s** his grief⌋.
1Ch 19:2 David thought, "I will **s**
Neh 1:5 keep your promise and **s** mercy
1:11 **s** me compassion."
Est 1:11 He wanted to **s** the people,
4:8 Hathach was supposed to **s** it
Job 6:24 **S** me where I've been wrong.
Job 11:15 Then you will be able to **s** your
24:21 These men **s** no kindness to
24:25 who can prove I'm a liar and **s**
34:35 His words **s** no insight.'
36:2 and I will **s** you that there is
38:2 do not **s** any knowledge ⌊about
42:6 and I sit in dust and ashes to **s**
Psa 4:6 "Who can **s** us anything good?"
31:19 descendants watch as you **s**
36:10 Continue to **s** your mercy to
85:7 **S** us your mercy, O LORD,
91:16 I will **s** you how I will save
106:4 when you **s** favor to your
109:12 Let no one **s** any pity to his
Pro 6:34 The husband will **s** no mercy
Ecc 3:18 in order to **s** them that they
Isa 5:16 The holy God will **s** himself to
9:17 nor will he **s** compassion for
13:10 won't **s** their light anymore.
49:9 in darkness, "**S** yourselves."
52:10 The LORD will **s** his holy
55:7 and he will **s** compassion to
66:5 "Let the LORD **s** his glory;
Jer 6:10 they **s** contempt for it and
18:17 I will **s** them my back,
21:7 **s** them compassion,
30:18 tents and **s** compassion
31:3 continue to **s** you my kindness.
32:18 You **s** mercy to thousands of
36:24 his attendants didn't **s** any fear
Lam 2:13 What parallel can I **s** you,
Eze 21:24 You **s** your sins in everything
27:35 Their faces **s** their fear.
28:22 I will **s** my greatness through
28:22 punish you and **s** you how holy
28:25 I will **s** that I am holy as the
38:23 I will **s** my greatness and my
39:21 "I will **s** my greatness among
40:4 to everything I'm going to **s** you
43:11 Then **s** them the design of the
44:23 They must **s** the people how to
Dan 9:4 You keep your promise and **s**
Hos 2:10 I will **s** her naked body to her
2:19 I will **s** you my love and
Amo 1:11 They refused to **s** any
Mic 7:18 because you would rather **s**
Nah 3:5 I will **s** nations your naked
Zec 1:9 "I will **s** you what they mean."
1:12 how much longer until you **s**
Mat 5:7 are those who **s** mercy.
5:45 In this way you **s** that you are
8:4 Instead, **s** yourself to the priest.
11:17 but you didn't **s** any sadness.'
12:38 we want you to **s** us a
16:1 So they asked him to **s** them a
22:19 **S** me a coin used to pay
Mar 1:44 Instead, **s** yourself to the priest.
4:30 Jesus asked, "How can we **s**
14:15 He will take you upstairs and **s**
Luk 5:14 Instead, **s** yourself to the priest.
6:47 "I will **s** you what everyone
11:16 he **s** them some miraculous
12:5 I'll **s** you the one you should be
17:14 "**S** yourselves to the priests."
18:1 disciples to **s** them that they
20:24 "**S** me a coin. Whose face and
22:12 He will take you upstairs and **s**
Jon 1:31 to baptize with water to **s** him
2:18 "What miracle can you **s** us to
5:20 The Father will **s** him even
9:3 blind so that God could **s** what
12:36 people whose lives **s** the light."
14:8 Jesus, "Lord, **s** us the Father,
14:9 can you say, '**S** us the Father'?
14:21 them and **s** myself to them."
15:8 fruit and therefore **s** that you are
15:13 The greatest love you can **s** is
16:8 to **s** the world what has God's
16:10 He will **s** the world what has
21:19 Jesus said this to **s** by what
Act 1:24 **S** us which of these two you
1:25 **S** us who is to take the place
4:30 **S** your power by healing,
7:3 Go to the land that I will **s** you.'
9:16 I'll **s** him how much he has to
10:40 the third day. God didn't **s** him

Act 26:16 seen and of what I will **s** you.
Rom 1:31 and don't **s** love to their own
2:15 They **s** that some requirements
3:20 Teachings **s** what sin is.
1Co 2:4 with a **s** of spiritual power
4:21 that I punish you or **s** you love
11:10 on her head to **s** she is under
12:31 but I will **s** you the best thing to
14:24 in you will **s** them where they
16:18 Therefore, **s** people like these
2Co 1:11 God for the favor he will **s**
3:1 Do we have to **s** you our
5:12 We are not trying to **s** you our
7:11 You wanted to **s** your concern
7:12 I wanted you to **s** your devotion
8:24 **S** their congregations that we
10:12 they **s** how foolish they are.
11:30 the things that **s** how weak
Gal 1:16 to **s** me his Son. He did this so
Eph 2:7 in order to **s** his extremely rich
Php 3:15 God will **s** you how to think.
4:10 not have an opportunity to **s** it.
1Th 5:12 we ask you to **s** your
2Th 3:5 your lives as you **s** God's love
1Ti 2:9 I want women to **s** their beauty
2Ti 1:9 would **s** us God's kindness.
3:2 their parents, **s** no gratitude,
Tit 2:4 teach young women to **s** love
2:10 Instead, tell slaves to **s** their
2:10 Then they will **s** the beauty of
3:2 and **s** courtesy to everyone.
Heb 9:8 The Holy Spirit used this to **s**
10:24 encourage each other to **s** love
12:27 The words once more **s** clearly
13:2 Don't forget to **s** hospitality to
Jas 2:6 Yet, you **s** no respect to poor
2:13 to those who **s** no mercy
2:18 **S** me your faith apart from the
2:18 I will **s** you my faith by the
3:13 **S** this by living the right way
1Pe 2:18 and **s** them complete respect.
1Jn 3:18 Dear children, we must **s** love
Jud 1:22 **S** mercy to those who have
1:23 **S** mercy to others,
Rev 1:1 God gave it to him to **s** his
4:1 and I will **s** you what must
17:1 I will **s** you the judgment of that
21:9 I will **s** you the bride,
22:6 sent his angel to **s** his servants

showed (61)

Gen 25:34 This is how Esau **s** his
Exo 11:10 Moses and Aaron **s** Pharaoh all
15:25 and the LORD **s** him a piece of
Num 13:26 They gave their report and **s**
17:9 LORD's presence and **s** them
20:13 the LORD and where he **s** them
Dtr 4:36 He **s** you his great fire on earth,
34:1 The LORD **s** him the whole
Jdg 1:25 He **s** them. So they got into the
1Sm 14:11 So both of them **s** themselves
2Sm 2:5 you because you **s** kindness
10:2 father Nahash **s** me kindness.
2Ki 6:6 When he **s** Elisha the place,
11:4 and **s** them the king's son.
20:13 so happy with them that he **s**
20:13 Hezekiah **s** them everything in
20:15 and I **s** them everything in my
1Ch 19:2 father Nahash **s** me kindness.
Est 1:4 He **s** them the enormous
6:2 The records **s** how Mordecai
Psa 99:8 You **s** them that you are a
Isa 39:2 so happy with them that he **s**
39:2 Hezekiah **s** them everything in
39:4 and I **s** them everything in my
47:6 You **s** them no mercy.
64:5 You **s** your anger, We've
Jer 11:18 He **s** me what they were doing.
24:1 After this, the LORD **s** me two
Eze 46:19 He **s** me a place on the west
Amo 7:1 what the Almighty LORD **s** me:
7:4 what the Almighty LORD **s** me:
7:7 This is what he **s** me:
8:1 what the Almighty LORD **s** me:
Zec 1:20 the LORD **s** me four craftsmen.
3:1 Then he **s** me Joshua,
Mat 3:7 Who **s** you how to flee from
4:8 high mountain and **s** him all
21:32 John came to you and **s** you
Luk 3:7 Who **s** you how to flee from
4:5 to a high place and **s** him all
20:37 "Even Moses **s** in the passage
24:40 he **s** them his hands and feet.
Jon 20:20 When he said this, he **s** them
21:1 Jesus **s** himself again to the
21:14 third time that Jesus **s** himself
Act 1:3 After his death Jesus **s** the
10:41 He **s** Jesus to witnesses,
15:8 **s** that he approved of people
15:14 how God first **s** his concern by
17:3 He explained and **s** them that
28:10 They **s** respect for us in many
Rom 3:25 God **s** that Christ is the throne
2Co 8:1 know how God **s** his kindness
Gal 2:2 I **s** them the way I spread the
Eph 3:8 Yet, God **s** me his kindness by
Php 4:10 because you again **s** interest
Col 1:21 you did **s** your hostile attitude.
Heb 8:5 based on the plan I **s** you
8:13 this new promise and **s** that
Rev 21:10 He **s** me the holy city,
22:1 The angel **s** me a river filled

shower (1)

Job 29:23 as if waiting for a spring **s**.

showered (1)

Rom 5:15 have been **s** on humanity.

showers (8)

Dtr 32:2 like **s** on green plants.
Psa 65:10 You soften them with **s** and
72:6 like **s** that water the land.
Jer 3:3 there have been no spring **s**.
14:22 the skies can't give **s**.
Eze 34:26 These **s** will be a blessing to
Mic 5:7 like **s** on the grass.
Zec 10:1 He gives everyone rain **s** for

showing (20)

Exo 25:9 like the plans I am **s** you.
Num 16:46 The LORD is **s** his anger;
2Sm 7:15 But I will never stop **s** him my
1Ch 17:13 And I will never stop **s** him my
Pro 24:23 **S** partiality as a judge is not
28:21 **S** partiality is not good,
Jer 15:6 tired of **s** compassion to you.
Luk 8:52 Everyone was crying and **s**
Act 9:39 They were crying and **s** Peter
18:28 helped them by clearly **s** from
Rom 3:7 God receives by **s** that God is
12:10 Excel in **s** respect for each
12:11 be lazy in **s** your devotion.
1Co 7:35 I'm **s** you how to live a noble
Php 1:28 This is God's way of **s** them
1Th 4:10 In fact, you are **s** love to all the
2Th 1:3 faith is **s** remarkable growth
3Jn 1:5 Dear friend, you are **s** your faith
Rev 3:18 naked body from **s**.
22:8 had been **s** me these things.

shown (53)

Gen 21:23 kindness that I have **s** you."
24:14 This way I'll know that you've **s**
32:10 faithfulness you have **s** me.
41:28 God has **s** Pharaoh what he's
Exo 25:40 you were **s** on the mountain."
26:30 you were **s** on the mountain.
27:8 as you were **s** on the mountain.
Lev 13:7 spread after he has **s** himself
13:19 it must be **s** to the priest.
13:49 It must be **s** to the priest.
Num 8:4 one the LORD had **s** Moses.
Dtr 4:35 You were **s** these things so
Jos 9:14 the evidence they were **s**,
2Sm 12:14 But since you have **s** total
1Ki 3:6 Solomon responded, "You've **s**
2Ki 8:10 although the LORD has **s** me
8:13 "The LORD has **s** me that you
1Ch 17:17 LORD God, you've **s** me the
2Ch 1:8 "You've **s** great love to my
Psa 31:21 He has **s** me the miracle of his
78:11 miracles that he had **s** them.
111:10 Good sense is **s** by everyone
119:14 I find joy in the way ⌊**s** by⌋
Isa 21:2 I was **s** a harsh vision.
26:10 Although the wicked are **s** pity,
Jer 38:21 this is what the LORD has **s**
Lam 5:12 older leaders are **s** no respect.
Eze 11:25 everything the LORD had **s** me.
40:4 here to be **s** these things.
Luk 1:72 He has **s** his mercy to our
19:9 You've **s** that you, too, are one
Jon 10:32 Jesus replied to them, "I've **s**
Act 10:28 But God has **s** me that I should
Rom 1:4 This was **s** in a powerful way
7:7 sin if those laws hadn't **s**
12:3 kindness that God has **s** me,
16:26 the prophets wrote must be **s**
1Co 1:4 Jesus has **s** you God's good
7:25 to whom the Lord has **s** mercy,
2Co 4:10 Jesus is also **s** in our bodies.
4:11 that the life of Jesus is also **s**
9:14 kindness that God has **s** you.
1Ti 2:9 Their beauty will be **s** by what
Heb 6:10 or the love you've **s** for him.
9:16 it must be **s** that the one who
10:28 that person was **s** no mercy as
13:2 believers have **s** hospitality
Jas 2:13 No mercy will be **s** to those
2:20 Do you have to be **s** that faith
2:22 His faith was **s** to be genuine
1Pe 2:10 Once you were not **s** mercy,
2:10 but now you have been **s**
1Jn 4:9 God has **s** us his love by

shows (23)

Exo 11:7 you will see that the LORD **s**
Lev 13:57 However, if it **s** up again,
Jos 18:4 of it which **s** ⌊the borders of⌋
2Sm 22:51 He **s** mercy to his anointed,
Psa 18:50 He **s** mercy to his anointed,
Pro 12:16 he **s** it immediately,
15:5 a warning **s** good sense.
Ecc 10:3 he has no sense and **s**
Isa 9:19 No one **s** concern for others:
Jon 5:20 The Father loves the Son and **s**
Rom 3:5 But if what we do wrong **s** that
3:26 This **s** that he is a God of
8:38 Christ Jesus our Lord **s** us.
16:2 welcome that **s** you are God's
2Co 4:7 This **s** that the superior power
8:19 to the Lord and **s** that we are
1Ti 1:14 love that Christ Jesus **s** people.
6:4 He **s** that he doesn't understand
2Ti 4:8 The prize that **s** I have God's
Tit 2:3 a way that **s** they are dedicated
Heb 10:29 a person who **s** no respect
Jas 4:6 But God **s** us even more
1Pe 5:10 God, who **s** you his kindness

shrewd (3)

Job 5:12 He keeps **s** people from
Dan 2:14 Daniel spoke to him using **s**
Act 7:19 This king was **s** in the way he

shriek (1)

Mar 1:26 came out of him with a loud **s**.

shrieks (1)

Luk 9:39 he **s**, goes into convulsions,

shrine (2)

Jdg 17:5 Micah owned a **s**. He also made
Act 7:43 carried along the **s** of Moloch,

shrines (3)

2Ki 17:32 priests for the **s** at their illegal
Isa 44:13 so the idols can live in **s**.
Act 17:24 live in **s** made by humans,

shrink (4)

Amo 8:5 We can **s** the size of the
Mat 9:16 a new piece of cloth that will **s**.
Mar 2:21 a new piece of cloth that will **s**.
2:21 the new patch will **s**

shrinks (1)
Mat 9:16 When the patch **s**,

shrivel (3)
Job 15:30 A flame will **s** his branches.
Isa 64:6 All of us **s** like leaves,
Joe 1:17 Seeds **s** up in their shells.

shriveled (5)
Job 16:8 You have **s** me up,
30:3 **S** up from need and hunger,
Psa 32:4 My strength **s** in the summer
119:83 I have become like a **s**
Lam 4:8 Their skin has **s** on their bones.

shrivels (1)
Isa 5:24 and dry grass **s** in flames,

shrugged (1)
Zec 7:11 They **s** their shoulders at me

Shua (3)
Gen 38:2 man whose name was S.
38:12 wife, the daughter of S, died.
1Ch 7:32 Hotham, and their sister S.

Shuah (7)
Gen 25:2 Medan, Midian, Ishbak, and S.
1Ch 1:32 Medan, Midian, Ishbak, and S.
Job 2:11 Bildad of S, Zophar of Naama.
8:1 Bildad from S replied ⌊to Job⌋,
18:1 Bildad from S replied ⌊to Job⌋,
25:1 Bildad from S replied ⌊to Job⌋,
42:9 Eliphaz of Teman, Bildad of S,

Shual (2)
1Sm 13:17 to Ophrah to the region of S.
1Ch 4:28 Harnepher, S, Beri, Imrah,

Shubael (2)
1Ch 24:20 descendants through S),
25:20 The thirteenth chose S,

shudder (3)
Isa 23:5 the Egyptians will **s** over the
32:11 S, you pampered women.
Eze 32:10 Their kings will **s** when I

shuddering (1)
Job 21:6 and **s** seizes my body.

shudders (1)
Psa 119:120 My body **s** in fear of you,

Shuhah's (1)
1Ch 4:11 Chelub, S brother, was the

Shuham (2)
Num 26:42 from Dan was the family of S.
26:43 all the family of S was 64,400.

Shulam (2)
Sos 6:13 young woman from S!
6:13 the young woman from S,

Shumathites (1)
1Ch 2:53 the S, and the Mishraites.

Shunem (11)
Jos 19:18 Jezreel, Chesulloth, S,
1Sm 28:4 assembled and camped in S.
1Ki 1:3 They found Abishag from S
1:15 and Abishag from S was taking
2:17 me Abishag from S as my wife.
2:21 "Let Abishag from S be given
2:22 do you ask that Abishag from S
2Ki 4:8 Elisha was traveling through S,
4:12 "Call this S woman."
4:25 "There is the woman from S.
4:36 "Call the S woman.

Shuni (2)
Gen 46:16 S, Ezbon, Eri, Arodi, and Areli.
Num 26:15 family of Haggi, the family of S,

Shupham (1)
Num 26:39 the family of S, and the family

Shuppim (1)
1Ch 26:16 S and Hosah were chosen for

Shuppites (2)
1Ch 7:12 The S and Huppites were Ir's
7:15 a wife from the Huppites and S.

Shur (6)
Gen 16:7 the spring on the way to S.
20:1 settled between Kadesh and S.
25:18 from the region of Havilah to S,
Exo 15:22 Red Sea into the desert of S.
1Sm 15:7 Amalekites from Havilah to S,
27:8 from Telaim to S and Egypt.)

shut (50)
Gen 8:2 and the sky had been **s**,
19:6 Then Lot went outside and **s**
19:10 with them, and **s** the door.
Dtr 11:17 He'll **s** the sky so that there'll
Jos 6:1 was bolted and barred **s**
1Sm 6:10 and **s** the calves in the stall.
23:7 double door ⌊held **s** by⌋ a bar."
1Ki 8:35 "When the sky is **s** and there's
2Ki 4:21 and **s** the door behind her.
6:32 Hold it **s** because the king will
2Ch 6:26 "When the sky is **s** and there's
7:13 I may **s** the sky so that there is
29:7 They also **s** the doors of the
Neh 7:3 they should **s** the doors and bar
13:19 I ordered the doors to be **s** and
Job 3:10 because it did not **s** the doors
7:11 So I won't keep my mouth **s**,
38:8 "Who **s** the sea behind gates
Psa 17:10 They have **s** out all feeling.
63:11 the mouths of liars will be **s**.
88:8 I'm **s** in, and I can't get out.
107:42 people will **s** their mouths.
132:4 get into my bed, **s** my eyes,
Isa 6:10 **S** their eyes. Otherwise, they
22:22 What he opens no one will **s**.
24:10 to every house is barred **s**.
26:20 and **s** the doors behind you.
29:10 He will **s** your eyes.
44:18 Their eyes are plastered **s**,
45:1 that the gates would not be **s**.
52:15 Kings will **s** their mouths
Jer 20:9 me like a burning fire **s** up
Eze 3:24 and **s** yourself inside.
44:1 and the gate was **s**.
44:2 "This gate will stay **s** and will
44:2 through it. It must be kept **s**.
46:12 the gate must be **s** after him.
Dan 6:22 My God sent his angel and **s**
Mic 7:5 Keep your mouth **s** even when
Zec 7:11 at me and **s** their ears so
Mal 1:10 "I wish one of you would **s** the
Mat 13:15 They have **s** their eyes so that
25:10 and the door was **s**.
Act 21:30 doors were immediately **s**.
28:27 They have **s** their eyes so that
Heb 11:33 They **s** the mouths of lions,
Rev 3:7 ⌊a door⌋ that no one can **s**,
3:8 front of you that no one can **s**.
11:6 witnesses have authority to **s**
20:3 The angel **s** and sealed the pit

Shuthelah (4)
Num 26:35 Ephraim were the family of S,
26:36 The descendants of S were the
1Ch 7:20 Ephraim's son was S.
7:21 Zabad's son was S.

Shuthelah's (1)
1Ch 7:20 S son was Bered. Bered's son

shuts (6)
Job 5:16 while wrongdoing **s** its mouth.
Psa 58:4 like a deaf cobra that **s** its ears
Pro 21:13 Whoever **s** his ear to the cry of
Isa 22:22 What he **s** no one will open.
Lam 3:8 he **s** out my prayer.
Rev 3:7 and who **s** ⌊a door⌋ that no one

shuttle (3)
Jdg 16:14 tied his braids to the loom **s**.
16:14 the threads out of the loom **s**.
Job 7:6 go swifter than a weaver's **s**.

Sia (1)
Neh 7:47 Keros, S, Padon,

Siaha (1)
Ezr 2:44 Keros, S, Padon,

Sibbecai (4)
2Sm 21:18 Then S from Hushah killed
1Ch 11:29 S (son of Hushai),
20:4 Then S from Hushah killed
27:11 S, a descendant of Zerah from

sibboleth (1)
Jdg 12:6 If the fugitive would say **s**,

Sibmah (5)
Num 32:38 names were changed), and S.
Jos 13:19 Kiriathaim, S, Zereth Shahar
Isa 16:8 and the vineyards of S wither.
16:9 I will cry for the grapevines of S
Jer 48:32 cry for you, grapevines of S.

Sibraim (1)
Eze 47:16 Berothah and S, which are

sick (98)
Gen 41:19 were scrawny, very **s**, and thin.
41:21 looked just as **s** as before.
Num 11:20 of their ears and they're **s** of it.
1Sm 19:14 David, Michal said, "He's **s**."
20:34 He was worried **s** about David
25:38 LORD made him even more **s**,
30:13 because I got **s** three days ago.
2Sm 12:15 so that the child became **s**.
13:2 Tamar that he made himself **s**.
13:5 Act **s**, and when your father
13:6 Amnon lay down and acted **s**,
1Ki 14:1 Abijah, son of Jeroboam, got **s**.
14:5 you about her son who is **s**.
17:17 who owned the house got **s**.
17:17 He got so **s** that finally no life
2Ki 8:7 of Aram, who was **s**, was told,
8:29 Ahab's son Joram, who was **s**.
20:1 those days Hezekiah became **s**
20:12 that Hezekiah had been **s**.
2Ch 13:20 caused Jeroboam to become **s**,
22:6 Ahab's son Joram, who was **s**.
32:24 those days Hezekiah became **s**
36:17 the old people or the **s** people.
Neh 2:2 You aren't **s**, are you?
Psa 35:13 But when they were **s**,
69:20 broken my heart, and I am **s**.
77:10 I said, "It makes me feel **s** that
Pro 13:12 hope makes one **s** at heart,
Isa 10:18 like a **s** person wasting away.
33:24 ⌊in Zion⌋ will say, "I'm **s**."
38:1 those days Hezekiah became **s**
38:9 Judah wrote this after he was **s**
39:1 had been **s** and had recovered.
Jer 6:7 I see that it is **s** and wounded.
8:18 me. I am **s** at heart!
12:13 worked until they became **s**,
14:18 If I go to the city, I see those **s**
Lam 1:13 He has made me **s** all day long.
1:22 so much and feel so **s** at heart."
5:17 This is why we feel **s**.
Eze 34:4 healed those that were **s**,
34:16 and strengthen those that are **s**.
34:21 and you knock down all the **s**
Dan 8:27 was exhausted and **s** for days.
Hos 5:13 Ephraim saw that he was **s**
9:16 of Ephraim are like **s** plants.
Mal 1:8 you bring a lame or a **s** animal,
1:13 stolen, lame, and **s** animals.
Mat 4:24 him everyone who was **s**,
8:16 cured everyone who was **s**.
9:12 those who are **s** do.
10:8 Cure the **s**, bring the dead back
14:14 them and cured their **s** people.

Mat 14:35 him everyone who was s.
25:36 I was s, and you took care of
25:39 When did we see you s or in
25:43 I was s and in prison,
25:44 or in need of clothes or s
Mar 1:32 to him everyone who was s
1:34 He cured many who were s
2:17 those who are s do.
6:5 his hands on a few s people
6:13 many who were s to cure them.
6:55 and began to carry the s
6:56 people would put their s in the
16:18 hands on the s and cure them."
Luk 2:48 been worried s looking for you!"
4:38 Simon's mother-in-law was s
5:31 those who are s do.
7:2 slave was s and near death.
9:2 of God and to cure the s.
9:6 and cured the s everywhere.
9:11 and cured those who were s.
10:9 Heal the s that are there,
Jon 4:46 His son was s in Capernaum.
5:3 number of s people — people
5:5 who had been s for 38 years,
5:6 and knew that he had been s
5:7 The s man answered Jesus,
6:2 that he performed for the s.
11:1 her sister Martha lived, was s.
11:2 was the one who was s.)
11:3 your close friend is s."
11:6 heard that Lazarus was s,
Act 5:15 people carried their s into the
5:15 might fall on some s people as
5:16 They would bring their s and
9:37 She became s and died.
19:12 skin to those who were s.
28:8 father happened to be s in bed.
28:9 After that had happened, other s
1Co 11:30 many of you are weak and s
Php 2:26 you heard that he was s.
2:27 Indeed, he was so s that he
1Ti 5:23 because you are frequently s.
2Ti 4:20 of Miletus because he was s.
Jas 5:14 If you are s, call for the church
5:15 faith will save those who are s,

sickbed (3)

Psa 41:3 will support him on his s.
41:8 He will never leave his s."
Rev 2:22 I'm going to throw her into a s.

sickbeds (1)

Job 33:19 In pain on their s, they are

sickle (10)

Dtr 23:25 But never use a s to cut your
1Sm 13:20 his plow, his mattock, ax, or s.
Mar 4:29 he cuts it with a s,
Rev 14:14 head and a sharp s in his hand.
14:15 on the cloud, "Swing your s,
14:16 on the cloud swung his s over
14:17 He, too, had a sharp s.
14:18 to the angel with the sharp s,
14:18 sharp sickle, "Swing your s,
14:19 The angel swung his s on the

sickly (5)

Gen 41:3 cows were s and skinny.
41:4 The cows that were s and
41:19 I've never seen such s cows in
41:20 The thin, s cows ate up the
41:27 The seven thin, s cows that

sickness (15)

Exo 23:25 away all s from among you.
Dtr 28:61 also bring you every kind of s
1Ki 8:37 During every plague or s
2Ch 6:28 During every plague or s
21:19 fell out because of his s.
Psa 38:11 far away because of my s.
39:10 Remove the s you laid upon
91:10 No s will come near your
Pro 18:14 A person's spirit can endure s,
Ecc 5:17 frustration, s, and resentment.
Mat 4:23 and s among the people.
9:35 cured every disease and s.
Mat 10:1 to cure every disease and s.
Jon 11:4 "His s won't result in death.
11:4 Instead, this s will bring glory

sicknesses (2)

Luk 7:21 s, and evil spirits. Also,
Act 19:12 Their s would be cured,

Siddim (3)

Gen 14:3 met in the valley of S (that is,
14:8 for battle in the valley of S.
14:10 The valley of S was full of tar

side (317)

Gen 6:16 Put a door in the s of the ship.
23:3 Then Abraham left the s of his
50:10 which is on the east s of the
50:11 why that place on the east s
Exo 3:1 As he led the sheep to the far s
14:20 Neither s came near the other
23:2 don't s with the majority to
25:12 two rings on each s.
25:32 three branches on one s and
26:13 18 inches left over on each s
26:13 part should hang over each s
26:18 Make 20 frames for the south s
26:20 For the north s of the inner tent
26:22 for the far end, the west s.
26:26 five for the frames on one s of
26:27 five for those on the other s,
26:27 of the inner tent, the west s.
26:35 the canopy on the north s
26:35 the table on the south s.
27:9 The south s of the courtyard
27:11 The north s should be the
27:14 Each s ⌊of the entrance⌋ will
32:26 "If you're on the LORD's s,
36:23 made 20 frames for the south s
36:25 For the north s of the inner tent
36:27 for the far end, the west s.
36:31 were for the frames on one s
36:32 were for those on the other s,
36:32 were for the frames on the far s
36:32 of the inner tent, the west s.
37:3 two rings on each s.
37:18 three branches on one s and
38:9 The south s of the courtyard
38:11 The north s was also 150 feet
38:12 The west s was 75 feet long
38:13 The east s, facing the rising
38:14 Each s of the entrance to the
40:22 tent of meeting on the north s
40:24 on the south s of the tent.
Lev 1:11 LORD's presence on the north s
1:15 blood against the s of the altar.
1:16 filth and throw it on the east s
5:9 from the offering for sin on the s
16:14 it with his finger on the east s
Num 2:3 "On the east s, facing the
2:10 "On the south s the armies led
2:18 "On the west s the armies led
2:25 "On the north s the armies led
3:23 their tents on the west s behind
3:29 put up their tents on the south s
3:35 put up their tents on the north s
3:38 put up their tents on the east s
10:5 on the east s will break camp
21:13 and set up camp on the other s
27:10 on his father's s of the family.
32:19 of any land on the other s
34:3 "The southern s includes part
35:5 off 3,000 feet on the east s,
35:5 3,000 feet on the south s,
35:5 3,000 feet on the west s,
35:5 and 3,000 feet on the north s,
35:14 three on the east s of the
36:11 on their father's s of the family.
Dtr 3:20 is giving them on the other s
3:21 the kingdoms on the other s ⌊of
3:25 the beautiful land on the other s
4:26 going to possess on the other s
4:41 aside three cities on the east s
4:49 all the plains on the east s
11:30 mountains are on the west s
30:13 command isn't on the other s
Jos 3:16 crossed from the east s ⌊of
Jos 4:10 people hurried to the other s.
7:7 on the other s of the Jordan!
15:11 the border goes on the north s
18:7 Moses gave them on the east s
18:14 and goes around on the west s,
18:18 it continues on to the north s
20:8 as cities of refuge on the east s
21:44 them to have peace on every s,
22:11 the Jordan River on Israel's s."
24:2 lived on the other s of the
24:3 Abraham from the other s
24:8 who lived on the east s
24:14 ancestors served on the other s
24:15 ancestors served on the other s
Jdg 3:16 to his right s under his clothes.
3:21 took the dagger from his right s
7:25 Zeeb to Gideon on the other s
9:1 the uncles on his mother's s
Rut 2:1 He was from Elimelech's s of
1Sm 12:11 enemies on every s so that you
14:1 military post on the other s."
14:4 There was a cliff on each s of
14:40 "You stand on one s,
14:40 and I will stand on the other s."
14:47 on every s — against Moab,
17:3 stationed on a hill on one s,
17:3 on a hill on the other s.
20:41 came out from the south s ⌊of
23:26 Saul went on one s of the
23:26 his men went on the other s
24:15 He will watch and take my s in
26:13 David went over to the other s
31:7 people of Israel on the other s
2Sm 2:13 one group on one s of the pool
2:13 group on the other s of the pool.
2:16 his sword into his opponent's s,
20:11 David's s should follow Joab."
1Ki 2:19 and she sat at his right s.
6:3 same length as the shorter s
6:5 He built an annex containing s
6:8 first story was on the south s
7:3 with cedar above the s rooms,
7:28 They had s panels set in
7:39 put five stands on the south s
7:39 temple and five on the north s
7:39 He set the pool on the south s
7:49 of pure gold (five on the south s
10:20 on six steps, one on each s.
2Ki 6:16 We have more forces on our s
9:32 "Is anyone on my s?
10:6 It read, "If you are on my s and
11:11 the temple (from the south s
11:11 to the north s of the temple).
11:14 the trumpeters were by his s.
12:9 and put it at the right s of the
16:14 put it on the north s of his altar.
16:17 King Ahaz cut off the s panels
18:25 without the LORD on my s?
1Ch 4:39 on the east s of the valley,
9:18 at the king's gate on the east s.
12:37 From the east s of the Jordan
26:14 was chosen for the east s.
26:14 was chosen for the north s.
26:15 was chosen for the south s,
26:16 were chosen for the west s
26:17 On the east s there were six
26:25 his relatives on Eliezer's s
2Ch 4:6 and put five on the south s
4:6 side and five on the north s.
4:7 five on the south s and five on
4:7 side and five on the north s.
4:8 five on the south s and five on
4:8 side and five on the north s.
4:10 He set the pool on the south s
9:19 on six steps, one on each s.
20:2 against you from the other s
23:10 the temple (from the south s
23:10 to the north s of the temple).
23:13 the trumpeters were by his s.
29:4 on the east s ⌊of the temple⌋.
32:7 Someone greater is on our s.
32:8 has human power on his s,
32:8 the LORD our God is on our s
32:30 underground to the west s
Neh 4:18 his sword fastened to his s.
Job 18:11 pounce on him from every s

Job 19:10 He beats me down on every **s**
30:12 attacked me on my right **s** like
Psa 3:2 "Even with God ⌊on his **s**⌋,
16:8 When he is by my **s**,
16:11 Pleasures are by your **s** forever.
17:7 by your **s** from those who
31:13 terror on every **s** — while they
45:3 strap your sword to your **s** with
56:9 This I know: God is on my **s**.
82:2 How long are you going to **s**
91:7 or ten thousand at your right **s**.
94:16 my **s** against troublemakers?
110:5 The Lord is at your right **s**.
118:6 The LORD is on my **s**.
118:7 The LORD is on my **s** as my
124:1 LORD had not been on our **s** ..."
124:2 on our **s** when people attacked
Sos 3:8 one has his sword at his **s**
Isa 36:10 without the LORD on my **s**?
Jer 18:15 They go on **s** roads and not on
20:11 But the LORD is on my **s** like a
35:2 Take them into one of the **s**
35:4 into the **s** room of the sons of
35:4 officials and above the **s** room
36:20 After they put the scroll in the **s**
36:21 He took the scroll from the **s**
49:32 disaster on them from every **s**,
50:15 cry against them on every **s**.
Lam 2:22 who terrorize me on every **s**,
Eze 4:4 "Then lie on your left **s** and
4:4 many days as you lie on that **s**.
4:6 this time on your right **s**.
4:8 not be able to turn from one **s**
4:9 that you are lying on your **s**.
10:3 were standing on the south **s**
10:16 the wheels didn't leave their **s**.
23:22 them against you from every **s**.
28:23 will attack you from every **s**.
36:3 and crushed you from every **s**.
40:2 On the south **s** of the mountain
40:10 three guardrooms on each **s**
40:10 All three rooms on each **s** were
40:10 recessed walls on each **s** were
40:24 the man led me to the south **s**,
40:26 one picture on each **s**.
40:27 the gateway on the south **s**
40:32 man brought me to the east **s**
40:39 were two tables on each **s**
40:40 On each **s** of the entrance to
40:40 and on the other **s** of the
40:41 were four tables on each **s**
40:44 One room was at the **s** of the
40:44 The other room was at the **s** of
40:48 They were 9 feet on each **s**.
40:48 and the walls on each **s** were 5
40:49 one on each **s** of the entrance
41:1 10 ½ feet wide on each **s**.
41:2 and on each **s** of the entrance
41:5 The width of each **s** room
41:7 The **s** rooms grew wider all the
41:8 the foundation for the **s** rooms.
41:9 The outer wall of the **s** rooms
41:9 the **s** rooms connected
41:11 The doors in the **s** rooms were
41:12 on the west **s** of the temple,
41:14 The eastern **s** of the temple,
41:15 courtyard on the west **s** along
41:19 toward a palm tree on one **s**,
41:19 a palm tree on the other **s**.
41:26 on the **s** rooms of the temple,
42:1 He brought me to the **s** rooms
42:4 In front of the **s** rooms was a
42:4 of these **s** rooms faced north.
42:5 The **s** rooms on the third story
42:7 ran parallel to the **s** rooms
42:7 It ran alongside the **s** rooms for
42:9 These lower **s** rooms had an
42:9 had an entrance on the east **s**.
42:10 There were **s** rooms parallel to
42:10 of the courtyard on the south **s**.
42:11 that was in front of the **s** rooms
42:11 the side rooms on the north **s**.
42:11 These **s** rooms were as long
42:13 "The northern and southern **s**
42:16 He measured the east **s** with a
42:17 He measured the north **s**.
Eze 42:18 He measured the south **s**.
42:19 He came around to the west **s**
44:19 their clothes in the **s** rooms
46:19 to the **s** rooms that faced
46:19 on the west **s** of the rooms.
47:1 was flowing under the south **s**
47:2 down the south **s** of the gate.
47:15 On the north **s** the border will
47:17 This is the north **s**.
47:18 On the east **s** the border will
47:18 This is the east **s**.
47:19 On the south **s** the border will
47:20 On the west **s** the
47:20 This is the west **s**.
48:10 On the north **s** it will be 43,750
48:10 On the west **s** it will be 17,500
48:10 On the east **s** it will be 17,500
48:10 On the south **s** it will be
48:16 On the north **s** it will be 7,875
48:16 On the south **s** it will be 7,875
48:16 On the east **s** it will be 7,875
48:16 And on the west **s** it will be
48:18 will be 17,500 feet on its east **s**
48:18 and 17,500 feet on its west **s**.
48:21 Whatever is left on the east **s**
48:21 left on the east side and west **s**
48:30 The north **s** will be 7,875 feet
48:31 The three gates on the north **s**
48:32 The east **s** will be 7,875 feet
48:32 The three gates on the east **s**
48:33 The south **s** will be 7,875 feet
48:33 The three gates on the south **s**
48:34 The west **s** will be 7,875 feet
48:34 The three gates on the west **s**
Dan 7:5 It was raised on one **s** and had
12:5 One man stood on one **s** of the
12:5 other one stood on the other **s**.
Zec 3:1 Joshua's right **s** to accuse him.
5:3 The one **s** of the scroll says
5:3 The other **s** of the scroll says
Mat 8:18 to cross to the other **s**
8:28 Gadarenes on the other **s** ⌊of
14:22 and cross to the other **s** ahead
16:5 when they went to the other **s**
19:1 and traveled along the other **s**
Mar 4:35 "Let's cross to the other **s**."
5:1 of the Gerasenes on the other **s**
5:21 again crossed to the other **s**
5:24 and pressed him on every **s**.
8:13 and crossed to the other **s**
10:1 of Judea along the other **s**
16:5 robe and sat on the right **s**.
Luk 8:22 "Let's cross to the other **s** of the
19:43 and close you in on every **s**.
Jon 1:28 in Bethany on the east **s**
3:26 he was with you on the other **s**
6:1 later crossed to the other **s**
6:22 people were still on the other **s**
6:25 they found him on the other **s**
7:51 first hearing that person's **s**
18:1 with his disciples to the other **s**
19:34 of the soldiers stabbed Jesus' **s**
20:4 two were running **s** by side,
20:4 two were running side by **s**,
20:20 them his hands and his **s**.
20:25 and put my hand into his **s**."
20:27 and put it into my **s**.
21:6 the net out on the right **s**
Act 2:25 moved because he is by my **s**.
12:7 The angel nudged Peter's **s**,
27:4 we sailed on the northern **s** of
27:7 started to sail for the south **s**
27:16 As we drifted to the sheltered **s**

sided (3)

1Sm 20:30 "I know you've **s** with Jesse's
2Ch 11:13 of Israel **s** with Rehoboam.
Ecc 4:15 They **s** with the second young

sides (58)

Exo 12:7 of the blood and put it on the **s**
12:22 of the blood on the top and **s**
12:23 sees the blood on the top and **s**
25:14 poles through the rings on the **s**
25:32 are to come out of the **s**,
27:7 put through the rings on both **s**
Exo 29:16 it against the altar on all **s**.
29:20 blood against the altar on all **s**.
30:3 the top, the **s**, and the horns.
30:4 the molding on opposite **s**
32:15 They were written on both **s**,
37:5 them through the rings on the **s**
37:18 Six branches came out of its **s**,
37:26 with pure gold — the top, the **s**,
37:27 the molding on opposite **s**
38:7 poles through the rings on the **s**
Lev 1:5 They will throw it against all **s**
1:11 blood against the altar on all **s**.
3:2 blood against the altar on all **s**.
3:8 blood against the altar on all **s**.
3:13 blood against the altar on all **s**.
7:2 blood against the altar on all **s**.
8:19 blood against the altar on all **s**.
8:24 against all the **s** of the altar.
9:12 it against the altar on all **s**.
9:18 threw against the altar on all **s**.
Num 22:24 with stone walls on both **s**.
33:55 your eyes and thorns in your **s**.
Jos 8:22 Israel attacked them on both **s**.
8:33 were standing on opposite **s**
23:13 a whip laid to your **s**,
Jdg 2:3 will be like thorns in your **s**,
1Ki 6:31 The doorposts had five **s**.
7:4 on opposite **s** ⌊of the palace⌋.
7:5 on opposite **s** ⌊of the palace⌋.
7:30 metal with designs on the **s**.
10:19 There were armrests on both **s**
2Ki 25:4 attacking the city from all **s**,
1Ch 9:24 were on the four **s** (east,
2Ch 9:18 There were armrests on both **s**
Psa 3:6 positions against me on all **s**.
88:17 They surround me on all **s**.
Jer 52:7 attacking the city from all **s**,
52:23 96 pomegranates on the **s**.
Eze 1:8 wings on each of their four **s**.
34:21 with your **s** and shoulders,
40:14 was a courtyard on all **s**.
40:25 hall had windows on all **s** like
41:15 with its corridors on both **s**.
41:22 and its **s** were made of wood.
41:26 and palm trees on both **s**
42:20 So he measured all four **s**.
45:7 will have all the land on both **s**
45:7 of the holy area and on both **s**
47:7 trees on both **s** of the river.
47:12 of fruit trees will grow on both **s**
Mar 5:31 crowd pressing you on all **s**?"
Rev 22:2 a tree of life visible from both **s**.

siding (1)

2Sm 15:12 and the number of people **s**

Sidon (44)

Gen 10:15 was the father of **S** his firstborn,
10:19 from **S** toward Gerar as
49:13 His border will go as far as **S**.
Jos 11:8 chased them as far as Great **S**,
13:4 which belongs to **S** as far as
13:6 Maim and all the people of **S**.
19:28 and as far as Great **S**.
Jdg 1:31 those who lived at Acco or **S**,
10:6 of Aram, **S**, Moab, Ammon,
18:7 were like the people of **S**.
18:7 of **S** and totally independent.
18:28 their city was far from **S**
2Sm 24:6 Dan Jaan and around toward **S**.
1Ki 5:6 lumberjacks like those from **S**."
11:1 Moab, Ammon, Edom, and **S**.
16:31 daughter of King Ethbaal of **S**.
17:9 (which belongs to **S**),
1Ch 1:13 was the father of **S** his firstborn,
22:4 The men of **S** and Tyre brought
Ezr 3:7 and olive oil to the men from **S**
Isa 23:2 you merchants from **S**.
23:4 Be ashamed, **S**, because the
23:12 my dear abused people **S**."
Jer 25:22 all the kings of Tyre and **S**,
27:3 Moab, Ammon, Tyre, and **S**,
47:4 to cut off from Tyre and **S** any
Eze 27:8 "People from **S** and Arvad
28:21 "Son of man, turn to **S** and
28:22 LORD says: I'm against you, **S**.

Eze 32:30 all the people from **S** are there.
Joe 3:4 Tyre and **S** and all the regions
Zec 9:2 borders on it, and Tyre and **S**,
Mat 11:21 been worked in Tyre and **S**,
11:22 for Tyre and **S** than for you.
15:21 to the region of Tyre and **S**.
Mar 3:8 Tyre and **S** followed him.
7:31 He went through **S** and the
Luk 4:26 Zarephath in the territory of **S**.
6:17 the seacoast of Tyre and **S**.
10:13 been worked in Tyre and **S**,
10:14 for Tyre and **S** than for you.
Act 12:20 with the people of Tyre and **S**.
27:3 day we arrived at the city of **S**.
27:4 Leaving **S**, we sailed on the

Sidonians (6)

Dtr 3:9 (The **S** call Mount Hermon by
Jdg 3:3 all the Canaanites, the **S**,
10:12 the **S**, the Amalekites, and the
1Ki 11:5 Astarte (the goddess of the **S**)
11:33 Astarte (the goddess of the **S**),
2Ki 23:13 disgusting goddess of the **S**),

siege (1)

Nah 3:14 Store water for the **s**!

sieve (2)

Isa 30:28 nations with a **s** of destruction,
Amo 9:9 nations as if I were using a **s**.

sift (1)

Amo 9:9 I will **s** the nation of Israel out

sifting (1)

Isa 30:28 It rises neck high, **s** the nations

sifts (1)

Pro 20:8 throne to judge **s** out every evil

sigh (8)

Job 3:24 my food is in front of me, I **s**.
Psa 77:3 I **s** as I remember God.
90:9 out our years like one ⌊long⌋ **s**.
Isa 19:8 their nets on the water will **s**.
Eze 9:4 the foreheads of those who **s**
Mar 8:12 With a deep **s** he asked,
2Co 5:2 tent-like existence we **s**,
5:4 While we are in this tent, we **s**.

sighed (1)

Mar 7:34 he looked up to heaven, **s**,

sighing (1)

Job 23:2 I try hard to control my **s**.

sight (90)

Gen 6:11 world was corrupt in God's **s**
33:18 He camped within **s** of the city.
43:30 Deeply moved at the **s** of his
Exo 3:3 there and see this strange **s**."
4:11 Who gives them **s** or makes
10:28 to Moses, "Get out of my **s**!
Lev 21:20 who has defective **s**,
Dtr 29:23 There will be no plants in **s**.
1Sm 19:2 into hiding, and stay out of **s**.
2Sm 16:22 concubines in plain **s** of Israel.
2Ki 17:18 he removed them from his **s**.
23:27 "I will put Judah out of my **s** as
23:27 sight as I put Israel out of my **s**.
24:3 the people of Judah from his **s**
24:20 threw the people out of his **s**.
1Ch 28:8 I order you⌋ in the **s** of Israel
Job 15:15 heavens are not pure in his **s**,
25:5 the stars aren't pure in his **s**.
29:8 men saw me and kept out of **s**.
41:9 Doesn't the **s** of it overwhelm
Psa 5:5 brag cannot stand in your **s**.
31:22 have been cut off from your **s**."
72:14 blood will be precious in his **s**.
90:4 Indeed, in your **s** a thousand
116:15 Precious in the **s** of the LORD
146:8 The LORD gives **s** to blind
Pro 1:17 a net within the **s** of any bird.
3:4 and much success in the **s**
3:21 do not lose **s** of these things.
Pro 4:21 Do not lose **s** of these things.
4:25 look straight ahead and your **s**
29:13 LORD gives both of them **s**.
Isa 1:16 your evil deeds out of my **s**.
30:11 One of Israel out of our **s**.'"
31:9 will be frightened at ⌊the **s** of⌋
42:7 You will give **s** to the blind,
Jer 4:1 disgusting idols out of my **s**
7:15 I will force you out of my **s** as I
15:4 these people a horrifying **s**
18:23 wipe their sins out of your **s**.
24:9 I will make them a horrifying **s**
29:18 I will make them a horrifying **s**
51:42 What a horrifying **s** Babylon
52:3 threw the people out of his **s**.
Eze 4:17 They will be shocked at the **s**
22:16 You will be dishonored in the **s**
23:16 fell in love with them at first **s**
Jnh 2:4 been banished from your **s**.
Nah 3:6 I will make you a **s** to be seen.
Mat 20:34 Their **s** was restored at once,
Mar 8:25 His **s** was normal again.
Luk 4:18 of sin and the restoring of **s**
7:21 Also, he was giving back **s** to
18:42 told him, "Receive your **s**!
20:38 In God's **s** all people are
23:48 had gathered to see the **s**.
24:19 in what he did and said in the **s**
24:31 But he vanished from their **s**.
Jon 9:10 "How did you receive your **s**?"
9:11 and received my **s**."
9:14 dirt and gave the man **s** was
9:15 again how he received his **s**.
9:17 the man who gave you **s**?"
9:18 blind and had been given **s**.
9:21 we don't know how he got his **s**
9:24 who gave you **s** is a sinner."
9:26 How did he give you **s**?"
9:30 Yet, he gave me **s**.
9:32 ever heard of anyone giving **s**
9:39 Blind people will be given **s**,
10:21 a demon give **s** to the blind?"
11:37 blind man **s** keep Lazarus from
Act 9:12 hands on him to restore his **s**."
22:13 Saul, receive your **s**!' At
22:13 At that moment my **s** came
24:16 a clear conscience in the **s**
1Co 3:19 world is nonsense in God's **s**.
4:13 and trash in the **s** of all people.
2Co 5:7 are guided by faith, not by **s**.
7:12 your devotion to us in God's **s**.
8:21 not only in the **s** of the Lord,
8:21 but also in the **s** of people.
12:19 as Christ's people in God's **s**.
1Ti 5:4 This is pleasing in God's **s**.
5:21 call on you in the **s** of God,
6:13 In the **s** of God, who gives life
6:13 and in the **s** of Christ Jesus,
2Ti 2:14 and warn them in the **s** of God
Heb 12:21 The **s** was so terrifying that
Rev 3:2 completed in the **s** of my God.

sights (2)

Pro 23:33 Your eyes will see strange **s**,
Luk 21:11 Terrifying **s** and miraculous

sign (80)

Gen 4:15 The LORD gave Cain a **s** so
9:12 God said, "This is the **s** of the
9:13 rainbow in the clouds to be a **s**
9:17 "This is the **s** of the promise I
17:11 That will be the **s** of the
17:13 So my promise will be a **s** on
Exo 4:8 to the first miraculous **s**,
7:9 'Give me a **s** to prove that God
8:23 **s** will happen tomorrow.'"
12:13 on your houses will be a **s**
31:13 This will be a **s** between me
31:17 It will be a permanent **s**
Num 16:38 will be a **s** to the Israelites."
17:10 and keep it there as a **s** to warn
Dtr 13:1 may predict a miraculous **s** or
28:46 These curses will be a **s** and
Jos 4:6 This will be a **s** for you.
Jdg 6:17 give me a **s** that it is really you
1Sm 2:34 Phinehas, will be a **s** to you:
1Sm 10:1 This will be the **s** that the
14:10 because that will be our **s** that
1Ki 13:3 gave ⌊them⌋ a miraculous **s**,
13:3 "This is the **s** that the LORD
13:5 This was the miraculous **s** the
20:33 men, watching for a good **s**,
2Ki 4:31 there was no sound or **s** of life.
19:29 "'And this will be a **s** for you,
20:8 "What is the **s** that the LORD
20:9 Isaiah said, "This is your **s**
2Ch 32:24 and gave him a miraculous **s**.
32:31 **s** that had happened
Psa 103:16 there is no longer any **s** of it.
Isa 7:11 the LORD your God for a **s**.
7:14 himself will give you this **s**:
19:20 These objects will be a **s** and
20:3 naked for three years as a **s**
37:30 "'And this will be a **s** for you,
38:22 Hezekiah asked, "What is the **s**
38:7 ⌊Isaiah said,⌋ "This is your **s**
55:13 an everlasting **s** that will never
66:19 I will set up a **s** among them
Jer 32:44 for money, **s** deeds, seal them,
44:29 I will give you this **s**,' declares
Eze 4:3 This is a **s** for the people of
12:6 I've made you a **s** to warn the
12:11 'I am your warning **s**.
20:12 to worship me as a **s** between
20:20 This will be a **s** between me
21:19 Make a **s**, and put it where the
24:24 Ezekiel is a **s** to you.
24:27 You will be a **s** to them.
Dan 6:8 issue this decree, and **s** it.
6:12 ⌊They asked,⌋ "Didn't you **s** a
Zec 3:8 These men are a **s** of things to
Mat 12:38 to show us a miraculous **s**."
12:39 era look for a miraculous **s**.
12:39 But the only **s** they will get is
12:39 only sign they will get is the **s**
16:1 a miraculous **s** from heaven.
16:4 people look for a miraculous **s**.
16:4 But the only **s** they will be
24:3 What will be the **s** that you are
24:30 "Then the **s** of the Son of Man
Mar 8:11 a miraculous **s** from heaven.
8:12 do these people demand a **s**?
8:12 If these people are given a **s**,
13:4 What will be the **s** when all
Luk 2:34 He will be a **s** that will expose
11:16 miraculous **s** from heaven.
11:29 They look for a miraculous **s**.
11:29 But the only **s** they will get is
11:29 they will get is the **s** of Jonah.
11:30 Jonah became a miraculous **s**
11:30 of Man will be a miraculous **s**
21:7 What will be the **s** when all
1Co 14:22 is a **s** for unbelievers,
14:22 revealed is a **s** for believers,
Rev 12:1 A spectacular **s** appeared in
12:3 Another **s** appeared in the sky:
15:1 I saw another **s** in heaven.

signal (10)

Num 10:2 and as a **s** to break camp.
10:6 fanfare is the **s** to break camp.
Jdg 20:38 smoke rise from the city as a **s**.
Pro 6:13 makes a **s** with his foot,
Isa 13:2 **S** them with your hand to enter
49:22 lift my hand ⌊to **s**⌋ the nations.
Jer 4:6 Raise the flag to **s** people to go
Zec 10:8 I will **s** them with a whistle and
Mat 26:48 the traitor had given them a **s**.
Mar 14:44 the traitor had given them a **s**.

signaled (1)

Luk 5:7 So they **s** to their partners in

signals (1)

Isa 5:26 With a whistle he **s** those at

signature (1)

Job 31:35 Look, here is my **s**!

signed (8)

1Ki 21:8 **s** them with Ahab's name,
Est 3:12 The orders were **s** in the name

Est 8:5 He **s** ⌊the order⌋ to destroy the
Jer 32:10 I **s** the deed, sealed it,
32:12 and the witnesses who had **s**
Dan 6:9 So Darius **s** the written decree.
6:10 that the document had been **s**,
6:13 order or the decree that you **s**.

signet (19)

Gen 38:18 "Your **s** ring, its cord, and the
38:25 if you recognize whose **s** ring,
41:42 Then Pharaoh took off his **s**
Exo 28:11 a jeweler engraves a **s** ring.
28:21 each stone engraved (like a **s**
28:36 engrave on it (as on a **s** ring):
35:22 earrings, **s** rings, and pendants.
39:14 each stone engraved (like a **s**
39:30 engraved on it (as on a **s** ring):
Num 31:50 **s** rings, earrings, and pendants.
Est 3:10 At that, the king removed his **s**
8:2 the king took off his **s** ring,
8:8 it also with the king's **s** ring,
8:8 with the king's **s** ring cannot
8:10 with the king's **s** ring.
Sos 8:6 Wear me as a **s** ring on your
Isa 3:21 **s** rings, nose rings,
Jer 22:24 are the **s** ring on my right hand,
Hag 2:23 I will make you like a **s** ring,

significant (1)

2Ki 8:13 dog like me do such a **s** thing?"

signing (2)

Jer 32:10 had people witness the **s** of the
32:44 and have people witness the **s**

signpost (1)

Isa 30:17 of a mountain, like a **s** on a hill.

signs (53)

Gen 1:14 They will be **s** and will mark
30:27 I've learned from the **s** I've seen
Exo 4:9 believe these two miraculous **s**
4:17 use it to do the miraculous **s**."
4:28 to say and all the miraculous **s**
4:30 the miraculous **s** for the people,
7:3 I will do many miraculous **s**
10:1 miraculous **s** among them.
10:2 and what miraculous **s**
Num 14:11 in spite of all the miraculous **s**
14:22 my glory and the miraculous **s**
Dtr 4:34 miraculous **s**, amazing things,
6:22 the LORD did miraculous **s**
7:19 plagues, the miraculous **s**,
11:3 You saw the miraculous **s** and
26:8 deeds, miraculous **s**,
29:3 those miraculous **s**,
34:11 sent to do all the miraculous **s**
Jos 24:17 He did these spectacular **s**
1Sm 10:7 When these **s** happen to you,
10:9 That day all these **s** happened.
Neh 9:10 You performed miraculous **s**
Psa 65:8 in awe of your miraculous **s**.
74:9 We no longer see miraculous **s**.
78:43 his miraculous **s** in Egypt,
105:27 his miraculous **s** among them
135:9 He sent miraculous **s** and
Isa 8:18 We are **s** and symbols in Israel
44:25 I cause the **s** of false prophets
Jer 10:2 Don't be frightened by the **s** in
31:21 Put up road **s**! Remember the
32:20 You performed miraculous **s**
32:21 from Egypt with miraculous **s**
Dan 4:2 to you about the miraculous **s**
4:3 miraculous **s** are impressive.
6:27 and does miraculous **s** and
Mat 16:3 interpret the **s** of the times.
24:24 miraculous **s** and do wonderful
Mar 13:22 They will work miraculous **s**
16:17 "These are the miraculous **s**
16:20 **s** that accompanied it.
Luk 21:11 miraculous **s** will come from
21:25 "Miraculous **s** will occur in the
Act 2:19 miracles in the sky and give **s**
2:22 amazing things, and gave **s**.
2:43 miraculous **s** happened through
Rom 15:19 of miraculous and amazing **s**,
1Co 1:22 Jews ask for miraculous **s**,
2Co 12:12 among you I patiently did the **s**,
2Th 2:9 miraculous and wonderful **s**.
Heb 2:4 they said through miraculous **s**,
Rev 13:13 beast performs spectacular **s**.
13:14 living on earth with the **s** that

Sihon (37)

Num 21:21 say to King **S** of the Amorites,
21:23 **S** wouldn't let Israel pass
21:23 **S** gathered all his troops and
21:26 Heshbon was the city of King **S**
21:29 of King **S** of the Amorites.
21:34 to him what you did to King **S**
32:33 the kingdoms of King **S** of the
Dtr 1:4 after he had defeated King **S**
2:24 to hand King **S** of Heshbon,
2:26 I sent messengers to King **S** of
2:30 But King **S** of Heshbon
2:31 "I have begun to give you **S**
2:32 **S** and all his troops came out
2:33 LORD our God gave **S** to us,
3:2 to him what you did to King **S**
3:6 we did to King **S** of Heshbon.
4:46 in the land of King **S** of the
29:7 King **S** of Heshbon and King
31:4 nations what he did to King **S**
Jos 2:10 what you did to **S** and Og,
9:10 King **S** of Heshbon and King
12:2 **S** was the Amorite king who
12:5 border of King **S** of Heshbon.
13:10 included all the cities of King **S**
13:21 the whole kingdom of King **S** of
13:21 They were princes of **S**,
13:27 kingdom of King **S** of Heshbon.
Jdg 11:19 sent messengers to King **S**
11:19 **S** ruled from Heshbon.
11:20 But **S** did not trust the Israelites
11:20 **S** assembled all his troops.
11:21 LORD God of Israel handed **S**
1Ki 4:19 the territory of King **S** the
Neh 9:22 possession of the land of **S**,
Psa 135:11 King **S** of the Amorites,
136:19 King **S** of the Amorites —
Jer 48:45 of Heshbon and a flame from **S**.

Sihon's (4)

Num 21:23 When **S** troops came to Jahaz,
21:27 Rebuild it! Restore **S** city
21:28 flames from **S** city.
Jos 13:10 **S** capital was Heshbon.

Sikkuth (1)

Amo 5:26 of ⌊the god⌋ **S** as your king

Silas (31)

Act 15:22 (called Barsabbas) and **S**,
15:27 We have sent Judas and **S** to
15:32 Judas and **S**, who were also
15:33 After Judas and **S** had stayed
15:40 Paul chose **S** and left after the
16:6 Paul and **S** went through the
16:19 they grabbed Paul and **S** and
16:22 the attack against Paul and **S**.
16:22 tore the clothes off Paul and **S**
16:23 had hit Paul and **S** many times,
16:24 and **S** into solitary confinement
16:25 Around midnight Paul and **S**
16:29 he knelt in front of Paul and **S**.
16:30 Then he took Paul and **S**
16:34 He took Paul and **S** upstairs
16:38 and **S** were Roman citizens,
16:39 and apologized to Paul and **S**.
16:39 escorted Paul and **S** out
16:40 After Paul and **S** left the jail,
17:1 Paul and **S** traveled through the
17:4 persuaded to join Paul and **S**,
17:5 and searched it for Paul and **S**
17:6 they didn't find Paul and **S**,
17:10 the believers sent Paul and **S**
17:10 When Paul and **S** arrived in the
17:14 but **S** and Timothy stayed in
17:15 they took instructions back to **S**
17:16 While Paul was waiting for **S**
18:5 But when **S** and Timothy
1Th 1:1 From Paul, **S**, and Timothy.
2Th 1:1 From Paul, **S**, and Timothy.

Silas' (1)

Act 16:33 washed Paul and **S** wounds.

silence (15)

Gen 20:16 This is to **s** any criticism
Num 17:5 In this way I will **s** the frequent
Job 11:3 Should your empty talk **s**
Psa 8:2 against your opponents to **s**
65:1 You are praised with **s** in Zion,
115:17 go into the **s** ⌊of the grave⌋.
Isa 47:5 Go into the dark, and sit in **s**,
Jer 51:55 He will **s** the loud noise
Dan 11:18 But a commander will **s** the
Zec 3:2 **s** you, Satan! I, the LORD,
3:2 has chosen Jerusalem, **s** you!
Rom 16:25 the mystery that was kept in **s**
1Ti 2:11 A woman must learn in **s**,
1Pe 2:15 God wants you to **s** the
Rev 8:1 there was **s** in heaven for about

silenced (10)

1Sm 2:9 but wicked people are **s** in
Job 23:17 But I am not **s** by the dark or by
Isa 16:9 and your harvest will be **s**.
25:5 The song of tyrants is **s** like
Jer 48:2 You will be **s**, city of Madmen.
49:26 its soldiers will be **s** that day,"
50:30 soldiers will be **s** that day,"
Mat 22:34 Jesus had **s** the Sadducees,
2Co 11:10 not be **s** anywhere in Greece.
Tit 1:11 They must be **s** because they

silent (48)

2Ki 18:36 But the people were **s** and
Est 4:14 even if you remain **s** now,
7:4 I would have kept **s** because
Job 6:24 Teach me, and I'll be **s**.
13:5 I wish you would keep **s**.
13:19 could, I'd be **s** and die.
41:12 "I will not be **s** about
Psa 28:1 If you remain **s**, I will be like
30:12 you with music and not be **s**.
31:17 Let them be **s** in the grave.
32:3 When I kept **s** ⌊about my sins⌋,
35:22 Do not remain **s**. O Lord, do not
39:2 I kept **s**, although it did me no
50:3 come and will not remain **s**.
50:21 did these things, I remained **s**.
76:8 The earth was fearful and **s**
83:1 O God, do not remain **s**.
94:17 quickly fallen **s** ⌊in death⌋.
Pro 17:28 to be wise if he keeps **s**.
Isa 23:2 Be **s**, you inhabitants of the
36:21 They were **s** and didn't say
41:1 "Be **s** and listen to me,
42:14 I have been **s** for a long time.
53:7 He was like a sheep that is **s**
57:11 I've been **s** for a long time.
62:1 Zion's sake I will not remain **s**.
62:6 They will never be **s** day or
64:12 Will you be **s** and make us
65:6 I will not be **s**, but I will repay.
Lam 3:28 should sit alone and remain **s**
Eze 24:27 speak and not be **s** anymore.
Dan 10:15 touching the ground and was **s**.
Amo 5:13 remains **s** at such times,
Hab 1:13 Why are you **s** when wicked
2:20 should be **s** in his presence.
Zep 1:7 Be **s** in the presence of the
Zec 2:13 "Everyone be **s** in the presence
Mat 26:63 But Jesus was **s**. Then the
Mar 3:4 let him die?" But they were **s**.
9:34 They were **s**. On the road they
14:61 But he was **s**. The chief priest
Act 8:32 He was like a sheep that is **s**
15:12 The whole crowd was **s**.
18:9 afraid to speak out! Don't be **s**!
21:40 When the mob was **s**,
1Co 14:28 should remain **s** in church.
14:30 the first speaker should be **s**.
14:34 the women must keep **s**.

silently (5)

Gen 24:21 The man was **s** watching her

1Sm 1:13 She was praying **s**.
Lam 2:10 leaders of Zion's people sit **s**
3:26 to continue to hope and wait **s**
Eze 24:17 Groan **s**. Don't grieve for the

silk (3)

Eze 16:10 linen and covered you with **s**.
16:13 **s**, and embroidered clothes.
Rev 18:12 purple cloth, **s**, bright red cloth,

Silla (1)

2Ki 12:20 the road that goes down to **S**.

silly (2)

Dtr 32:6 you foolish and **s** people?
Hos 7:11 Ephraim, you are like a **s**,

Siloam (4)

Luk 13:4 died when the tower at **S** fell
Jon 9:7 "Wash it off in the pool of **S**."
9:7 (**S** means "sent.") The blind
9:11 me, 'Go to **S**, and wash it off.'

Silvanus (2)

2Co 1:19 **S**, and Timothy told you about,
1Pe 5:12 to you and I'm sending it by **S**,

silver (343)

Gen 13:2 he had livestock, **s**, and gold.
20:16 your brother 25 pounds of **s**.
23:15 land is worth ten pounds of **s**.
23:16 ten pounds of **s** at the current
24:35 sheep and cattle, **s** and gold,
24:53 The servant took out gold and **s**
33:19 for 100 pieces of **s**.
37:28 for eight ounces of **s**.
44:2 Then put my **s** cup in the
44:8 So why would we steal any **s**
45:22 three hundred pieces of **s**
Exo 3:22 woman living in her home for **s**
11:2 for **s** and gold jewelry."
12:35 for gold and **s** jewelry
20:23 Never make any gods of **s** or
21:32 owner must pay 12 ounces of **s**
22:7 someone gives his neighbor **s**
25:3 from them: gold, **s**, and bronze,
26:19 Then make 40 **s** sockets at the
26:21 and 40 **s** sockets, two at the
26:25 eight frames with 16 **s** sockets,
26:32 standing in four **s** sockets.
27:10 the posts should be made of **s**.
27:11 the posts should be made of **s**.
27:17 courtyard should have **s** bands,
27:17 **s** hooks, and bronze bases.
30:13 one-fifth of an ounce of **s** using
30:13 This one-fifth of an ounce of **s**
30:15 than one-fifth of an ounce of **s**,
31:4 with gold, **s**, and bronze.
35:5 the LORD: gold, **s**, and bronze,
35:24 Those who could give **s** or
35:32 with gold, **s**, and bronze.
36:24 Then they made 40 **s** sockets
36:26 and 40 **s** sockets, two at the
36:30 eight frames with 16 **s** sockets,
36:36 they cast four **s** bases for them.
38:10 on the posts were made of **s**.
38:11 on the posts were made of **s**.
38:12 on the posts were made of **s**.
38:17 on the posts were made of **s**.
38:17 the posts were covered with **s**.
38:17 the courtyard were made of **s**.
38:19 on the posts were made of **s**.
38:19 the posts were covered with **s**.
38:25 The **s** collected when the
38:27 He used 7,500 pounds of **s** to
38:28 He used 44 pounds of **s** to
Lev 5:15 value in **s** weighed according
27:3 60 years old is 20 ounces of **s**.
27:6 give 2 ounces of **s** and for a girl
27:16 will be worth 20 ounces of **s**.
Num 3:47 It will cost you two ounces of **s**
3:48 Give the **s** to Aaron and his
3:50 The **s** Moses collected for the
7:13 He brought a **s** plate that
7:13 and a **s** bowl that weighed
7:19 He brought a **s** plate that
Num 7:19 and a **s** bowl that weighed
7:25 brought his gifts: a **s** plate that
7:25 and a **s** bowl that weighed
7:31 brought his gifts: a **s** plate that
7:31 and a **s** bowl that weighed
7:37 brought his gifts: a **s** plate that
7:37 and a **s** bowl that weighed
7:43 brought his gifts: a **s** plate that
7:43 and a **s** bowl that weighed
7:49 brought his gifts: a **s** plate that
7:49 and a **s** bowl that weighed
7:55 brought his gifts: a **s** plate that
7:55 and a **s** bowl that weighed
7:61 brought his gifts: a **s** plate that
7:61 and a **s** bowl that weighed
7:67 brought his gifts: a **s** plate that
7:67 and a **s** bowl that weighed
7:73 brought his gifts: a **s** plate that
7:73 and a **s** bowl that weighed
7:79 brought his gifts: a **s** plate that
7:79 and a **s** bowl that weighed
7:84 12 **s** plates, 12 silver bowls,
7:84 12 silver plates, 12 **s** bowls,
7:85 Each **s** plate weighed 3 ¼
7:85 Together all the **s** dishes
10:2 trumpets out of hammered **s**.
18:16 fixed price of two ounces of **s**,
22:18 palace filled with **s** and gold,
24:13 palace filled with **s** and gold,
31:22 Any gold, **s**, bronze, iron, tin,
Dtr 2:6 You must pay them in **s** for the
2:28 We'll pay you in **s** for the food
7:25 Don't ever long for the **s** and
8:13 herds and flocks, **s** and gold,
14:25 tenth part of your income for **s**.
14:25 Take the **s** with you,
14:26 Use the **s** to buy whatever you
17:17 never own a lot of gold and **s**.
22:19 will fine him 2 ½ pounds of **s**
22:29 girl's father 1 ¼ pounds of **s**,
29:17 of wood, stone, **s**, and gold.
Jos 6:19 All the **s** and gold and
6:24 But they put the **s** and gold and
7:21 Babylonia, five pounds of **s**,
7:21 tent with the **s** beneath them."
7:22 inside with the **s** beneath it.
7:24 the **s**, the robe, the bar of gold,
22:8 livestock, **s**, gold, bronze, iron,
24:32 for 100 pieces of **s**.
Jdg 9:4 gave him 70 pieces of **s** from
9:4 With the **s**, Abimelech hired
16:5 give you 1,100 pieces of **s**."
17:2 pieces of **s** that were taken
17:2 Here's the **s**. I took it!" His
17:3 the 1,100 pieces of **s** back
17:3 "I dedicate this **s** to the LORD
17:3 I'm giving the **s** back to you."
17:4 When Micah returned the **s** to
17:4 she took 200 pieces of the **s**
17:10 give you ten pieces of **s** a year,
1Sm 9:8 one-tenth of an ounce of **s**.
13:21 and one-tenth of an ounce of **s**
2Sm 8:10 of gold, **s**, and bronze with him.
8:11 along with the **s** and gold he
18:11 four ounces of **s** and a belt."
18:12 the weight of 25 pounds of **s**
21:4 "We do not want **s** or gold from
24:24 the oxen for 1 ¼ pounds of **s**.
1Ki 7:51 to his father David — the **s**,
10:21 (Nothing was **s**, because it
10:22 **s**, ivory, apes, and monkeys.
10:25 articles of **s** and gold,
10:27 The king made **s** as common
10:29 from Egypt for 15 pounds of **s**
10:29 each horse for 6 ounces of **s**.
15:15 into the LORD's temple the **s**,
15:18 Then Asa took all the **s** and
15:19 you a present of **s** and gold.
16:24 Shemer for 150 pounds of **s**.
20:3 Your **s** and gold are mine.
20:5 to you: 'Your **s**, gold, wives,
20:7 **s**, and gold, I didn't refuse him."
20:39 life or be fined 75 pounds of **s**.'
2Ki 5:5 he took 750 pounds of **s**,
5:22 give them 75 pounds of **s**
5:23 me give you 150 pounds of **s**."
2Ki 5:23 urged him ⌊to take the **s**⌋.
5:23 tied up 150 pounds of **s**
5:26 How could you accept **s**,
6:25 head sold for two pounds of **s**
6:25 manure for two ounces of **s**.
7:1 will sell for half an ounce of **s**
7:1 will sell for half an ounce of **s**."
7:8 and carried off the **s**,
7:16 flour sold for half an ounce of **s**,
7:16 sold for half an ounce of **s**,
7:18 will sell for half an ounce of **s**.
7:18 will sell for half an ounce of **s**.
12:13 But no **s** bowls, snuffers,
12:13 or any other gold and **s**
14:14 He took all the gold, **s**,
15:19 gave Pul 75,000 pounds of **s**
15:20 Each gave 20 ounces of **s** for
16:8 Ahaz took the **s** and gold he
18:14 Judah pay 22,500 pounds of **s**
18:15 Hezekiah gave him all the **s**
20:13 the **s**, gold, balsam,
23:33 the country 7,500 pounds of **s**
23:35 Jehoiakim gave Pharaoh the **s**
23:35 the **s** Pharaoh had demanded.
23:35 so that he could get the **s**
25:15 that were made of gold or **s**.
1Ch 18:11 **s**, and bronze to the LORD,
18:11 along with the **s** and gold he
19:6 sent 75,000 pounds of **s**
22:14 75,000,000 pounds of **s**,
22:16 The gold, **s**, bronze, and iron
28:15 the weight of **s** for each silver
28:15 the weight of silver for each **s**
28:16 and the **s** for the silver tables,
28:16 and the silver for the **s** tables,
28:17 the weight of each **s** bowl,
29:2 **s** for silver objects,
29:2 silver for **s** objects,
29:3 of gold and **s** that I'm giving
29:4 525,000 pounds of refined **s**.
29:5 make gold objects, **s** objects,
29:7 750,000 pounds of **s**,
2Ch 1:15 The king made **s** and gold as
1:17 from Egypt for 15 pounds of **s**
1:17 each horse for 6 ounces of **s**.
2:7 to work with gold, **s**, bronze,
2:14 **s**, bronze, iron, stone, wood,
5:1 to his father David — the **s**,
9:14 brought gold and **s** to Solomon.
9:20 (**S** wasn't considered valuable
9:21 **s**, ivory, apes, and monkeys.
9:24 articles of **s** and gold,
9:27 The king made **s** as common
15:18 brought into God's temple the **s**,
16:2 Then Asa brought out all the **s**
16:3 I'm sending you **s** and gold.
17:11 brought gifts and **s** as taxes.
21:3 gave them many gifts: **s**, gold,
24:14 dishes and gold and **s** utensils
25:6 Israel for 7,500 pounds of **s**
25:9 do about the 7,500 pounds of **s**
25:24 ⌊He took⌋ all the gold, **s**,
27:5 gave him 7,500 pounds of **s**,
32:27 for himself to hold **s**,
36:3 the country 7,500 pounds of **s**
Ezr 1:4 people who are leaving with **s**,
1:6 articles made from **s** and gold,
1:9 30 **s** dishes: 1,000 knives: 29
1:10 gold bowls: 30 other **s** bowls:
1:11 The gold and **s** utensils totaled
2:69 5,740 pounds of **s**,
5:14 and **s** utensils that belonged
6:5 and **s** utensils that belonged
7:15 Also, you must take the **s** and
7:16 Take any **s** and gold that you
7:18 with the rest of the **s** and gold.
7:22 him⌋ up to 7,500 pounds of **s**,
8:25 I weighed for them the **s**,
8:26 about 24 tons of **s**,
8:26 100 **s** utensils weighing 150
8:28 The **s** and gold are freewill
8:30 Levites took charge of the **s**,
8:33 fourth day we weighed the **s**,
Neh 5:15 and wine plus one pound of **s**.
7:71 of gold and 3,215 pounds of **s**.
7:72 2,923 pounds of **s**,

Neh 10:32 of an ounce of **s** every year
Est 1:6 were attached to **s** rods
1:6 Gold and **s** couches were on a
3:9 I will pay 750,000 pounds of **s**
3:11 "You can keep your **s** and do
4:7 amount of **s** that Haman had
Job 3:15 who filled their homes with **s**.
22:25 gold and your large supply of **s**.
27:16 Though he collects **s** like dust
27:17 the **s** ⌊among themselves⌋.
28:1 "There is a place where **s** is
28:15 or buy it for any amount of **s**.
Psa 12:6 like **s** refined in a furnace and
17:3 You have tested me like **s**,
66:10 in the same way **s** is refined.
68:13 of a dove covered with **s**,
68:30 humbles itself with pieces of **s**.
105:37 Israel out with **s** and gold,
115:4 idols are made of **s** and gold.
119:72 me than thousands in gold or **s**.
135:15 nations are made of **s** and gold.
Pro 3:14 than the profit ⌊gained⌋ from **s**.
8:10 Take my discipline, not **s**,
8:19 I yield is better than fine **s**.
10:20 of a righteous person is pure **s**.
16:16 should be chosen over **s**.
16:31 **S** hair is a beautiful crown
17:3 The crucible is for refining **s**
20:29 of older people is their **s** hair.
22:1 Respect is better than **s** or gold.
25:4 Take the impurities out of **s**,
25:11 golden apples in **s** settings,
26:23 clay pot covered with cheap **s**,
27:21 The crucible is for refining **s**
Ecc 2:8 I also gathered **s** and gold for
12:6 before the **s** cord is snapped,
Sos 1:11 with **s** beads for you.
3:10 He had its posts made out of **s**,
8:9 we will build a **s** barrier around
8:11 was to bring 25 pounds of **s**
Isa 1:22 Your **s** is not pure.
2:7 land is filled with **s** and gold,
2:20 to the moles and the bats the **s**
7:23 vines (worth 1,000 pieces of **s**),
13:17 They don't care for **s** and aren't
31:7 all of you will reject the **s** and
39:2 the **s**, gold, balsam,
40:19 make **s** chains for them.
46:6 bags and weigh **s** on scales.
48:10 have refined you, but not like **s**.
60:9 Their **s** and their gold comes
60:17 I will bring **s** instead of iron,
Jer 6:30 will call them useless **s**
10:4 Craftsmen decorate them with **s**
10:9 Hammered **s** is brought from
32:9 field cost seven ounces of **s**.
32:10 and paid out the **s**.
52:19 that were made of gold or **s**.
Eze 7:19 They will throw their **s** and
7:19 Their **s** and gold won't be able
7:19 Their **s** and gold caused them
16:13 you wore gold and **s** jewelry.
16:17 gold and **s** jewelry that
22:18 like the impurities left from **s**.
22:20 People gather **s**, copper, iron,
22:22 in the city like **s** that is melted
27:12 They exchanged **s**,
28:4 gold and **s** in your treasuries.
38:13 carry away large amounts of **s**
Dan 2:32 and arms were made of **s**.
2:35 **s**, and gold were smashed.
2:45 iron, bronze, clay, **s**, and gold.
5:2 gold and **s** utensils which his
5:4 **s**, bronze, iron, wood, or stone.
5:23 praised your gods made of **s**,
11:8 and their precious utensils of **s**
11:38 With gold, **s**, precious stones,
11:43 He will control gold and **s**
Hos 2:8 I gave her plenty of **s** and gold,
3:2 I bought her for 23 ounces of **s**
8:4 idols with their own **s** and gold.
9:6 will grow over their **s** treasures.
13:2 idols from **s** for themselves.
Joe 3:5 You took my **s** and my gold.
Nah 2:9 Steal the **s**! Steal the gold!
Hab 2:19 It's covered with gold and **s**,
Zep 1:18 Their **s** and their gold will not
Hag 2:8 The **s** is mine, and the gold is
Zec 6:11 Take the **s** and gold,
9:3 It piled up **s** like dust and gold
11:12 me my wages — 30 pieces of **s**.
11:13 So I took the 30 pieces of **s**.
11:13 I gave the pieces of **s** to the
13:9 will refine them as **s** is refined.
14:14 amount of gold, **s**, and clothes.
Mal 3:3 like a refiner and a purifier of **s**.
3:3 and refine them like gold and **s**.
Mat 10:9 "Don't take any gold, **s**,
26:15 They offered him 30 **s** coins.
27:3 He brought the 30 **s** coins back
27:9 "They took the 30 **s** coins,
Luk 7:41 owed him five hundred **s** coins,
10:35 Samaritan took out two **s** coins
Act 17:29 made from gold, **s**, or stone,
19:19 were worth 50,000 **s** coins.
19:24 business of making **s** models
20:33 "I never wanted anyone's **s**,
1Co 3:12 **s**, precious stones, wood, hay,
2Ti 2:20 objects made of gold and **s**,
Jas 5:3 Your gold and **s** are corroded,
1Pe 1:18 ancestors by a payment of **s**
Rev 9:20 **s**, bronze, stone, and wood,
18:12 **s**, gems, pearls, fine linen,

silver-plated (1)

Isa 30:22 Then you will dishonor your **s**

silversmith (3)

Jdg 17:4 of the silver and gave it to a **s**.
Pro 25:4 is ready for the **s** to mold.
Act 19:24 Demetrius, a **s**, was in the

silversmiths (1)

Isa 40:19 **S** make silver chains for them.

silvery (1)

Job 41:32 the sea appears to have **s** hair.

Simeon (52)

Gen 29:33 So she named him **S** [Hearing].
34:25 **S** and Levi, Dinah's brothers,
34:30 Then Jacob said to **S** and Levi,
34:31 **S** and Levi asked,
35:23 then **S**, Levi, Judah, Issachar,
42:24 Then he picked **S** and had him
42:36 **S** is no longer with us,
43:23 Then he brought **S** out to them.
46:10 The sons of **S** were Jemuel,
48:5 mine just as Reuben and **S** are.
49:5 "**S** and Levi are brothers.
Exo 1:2 Reuben, **S**, Levi, and Judah;
6:15 The sons of **S** were Jemuel,
6:15 the families descended from **S**.
Num 1:6 from the tribe of **S**;
1:22 the descendants of **S** registered
1:23 for the tribe of **S** was 59,300.
2:12 to them will be the tribe of **S**.
2:12 the people of **S** is Shelumiel,
7:36 leader of the descendants of **S**,
10:19 commanded the army of **S**.
13:5 from the tribe of **S**;
25:14 the leader of a family from **S**.)
26:12 The families descended from **S**
26:14 These were the families of **S**.
34:20 from the tribe of **S**;
Dtr 27:12 **S**, Levi, Judah, Issachar,
Jos 19:1 for the families of the tribe of **S**.
19:8 of the tribe of **S** for its families.
19:9 So **S** received its inheritance
21:4 of Judah, **S**, and Benjamin.
21:9 from the tribes of Judah and **S**
Jdg 1:3 of Judah said to the tribe of **S**,
1:3 "So the tribe of **S** went along
1:17 to fight along with the tribe of **S**,
1Ch 2:1 **S**, Levi, Judah, Issachar,
6:65 of Judah, **S**, and Benjamin.
27:16 son of Zichri for the tribe of **S**:
2Ch 15:9 Ephraim, Manasseh, and **S**.
34:6 **S**, and as far as Naphtali,
Eze 48:24 **S** will have one part of the land
48:25 part of the land and border **S**
48:33 the south side will be **S** Gate,
Luk 2:25 A man named **S** was in
2:25 The Holy Spirit was with **S**
2:27 Moved by the Spirit, **S** went
2:28 Then **S** took the child in his
2:34 Then **S** blessed them and said
3:30 son of **S**, son of Judah, son of
Act 13:1 Barnabas, **S** (called the Black),
13:3 After fasting and praying, **S**,
Rev 7:7 12,000 from the tribe of **S**,

Simeon's (6)

Jos 19:9 **S** inheritance was a part of
1Ch 4:24 **S** sons were Nemuel,
4:28 **S** descendants lived in
4:42 and Uzziel led 500 of **S** male
4:43 **S** descendants still live there
12:25 From **S** descendants there

similar (10)

1Ki 7:8 but they were **s** in design.
Jer 36:32 They added many **s** messages.
Eze 41:21 holy place was something **s**.
Zec 14:15 A **s** plague will also affect
Act 19:25 and others who did **s** work.
Col 3:8 language, and all **s** sins.
1Pe 3:1 Wives, in a **s** way,
3:7 Husbands, in a **s** way,
5:5 Young people, in a **s** way,
Jud 1:8 Yet, in a **s** way, the people

Simon (81)

Mat 4:18 **S** (called Peter) and Andrew.
10:2 **S** (who is called Peter) and his
10:4 **S** the Zealot and Judas
13:55 James, Joseph, **S**, and Judas?
16:16 **S** Peter answered,
16:17 Jesus replied, "**S**, son of
17:25 him, "What do you think, **S**?
26:6 in Bethany in the home of **S**,
27:32 they found a man named **S**.
Mar 1:16 he saw **S** and his brother
1:29 to the house of **S** and Andrew.
1:36 **S** and his friends searched for
3:16 **S** (whom Jesus named Peter),
3:18 Thaddaeus, **S** the Zealot,
6:3 James, Joseph, Judas, and **S**?
14:3 in Bethany at the home of **S**,
14:37 He said to Peter, "**S**,
15:21 A man named **S** from the city of
Luk 5:3 into the boat that belonged to **S**
5:4 he finished speaking, he told **S**,
5:5 **S** answered, "Teacher,
5:8 When **S** Peter saw this,
5:9 **S** and everyone who was with
5:10 Jesus told **S**, "Don't be afraid.
5:11 **S** and his partners brought the
6:14 They were **S** (whom Jesus
6:15 **S** (who was called the Zealot),
7:40 Jesus spoke up, "**S**,
7:40 **S** replied, "Teacher, you're free
7:43 **S** answered, "I suppose the
7:44 to the woman, he said to **S**,
22:31 ⌊Then the Lord said,⌋ "**S**,
22:31 Lord said,⌋ "Simon, **S**, listen!
22:32 But I have prayed for you, **S**,
23:26 they grabbed a man named **S**,
23:26 **S** was coming into Jerusalem.
24:34 to life and has appeared to **S**."
Jon 1:40 Andrew, **S** Peter's brother,
1:41 at once found his brother **S**
1:42 Andrew brought **S** to Jesus.
1:42 Jesus looked at **S** and said,
1:42 said, "You are **S**, son of John.
6:8 who was **S** Peter's brother,
6:68 **S** Peter answered Jesus,
6:71 meant Judas, son of **S** Iscariot.
13:2 of Judas, son of **S** Iscariot.
13:6 When Jesus came to **S** Peter,
13:9 **S** Peter said to Jesus,
13:24 **S** Peter motioned to that
13:26 it to Judas, son of **S** Iscariot.
13:36 **S** Peter asked him,
18:10 **S** Peter had a sword.
18:15 **S** Peter and another disciple
18:25 **S** Peter continued to stand and
20:2 So she ran to **S** Peter and the

Jon 20:6 S Peter arrived after him and
21:2 S Peter, Thomas (called
21:3 S Peter said to the others,
21:7 When S Peter heard that it was
21:11 S Peter got into the boat and
21:15 Jesus asked S Peter,
21:15 Simon Peter, "S, son of John,
21:16 a second time, "S, son of John,
21:17 a third time, "S, son of John,
Act 1:13 of Alphaeus), S the Zealot,
8:9 A man named S lived in that
8:11 They paid attention to S
8:13 Even S believed, and after he
8:13 S was amazed to see the
8:18 S saw that the Spirit was given
8:20 Peter told S, "May your money
8:24 S answered, "Pray to the Lord
9:43 for a number of days with S,
10:5 a man whose name is S Peter.
10:6 He is a guest of S,
10:18 They asked if S Peter was
10:32 a man whose name is S Peter.
10:32 He's a guest in the home of S,
11:13 a man whose name is S Peter.
15:14 S has explained how God first
2Pe 1:1 From S Peter, a servant and

Simon's (6)

Mar 1:30 S mother-in-law was in bed
Luk 4:38 and went to S house.
4:38 S mother-in-law was sick with
5:10 S partners, were also amazed.
6:14 Peter) and S brother Andrew,
Act 10:17 by Cornelius found S house

simply (3)

Gen 43:7 We s answered his questions.
Est 8:6 And I s cannot bear to see the
Mat 5:37 S say yes or no. Anything more

sin (457)

Gen 4:7 But if you don't do well, s is
15:16 because the s of the Amorites
18:20 and their s is very serious.
20:9 would bring such a serious s
26:10 have made us guilty of s."
39:9 thing and s against God?"
42:22 "Didn't I tell you not to s
50:17 the s your brothers committed
Exo 10:17 Please forgive my s one more
16:1 and came to the desert of S,
17:1 of Israelites left the desert of S
20:20 be in awe of him and won't s."
23:33 or they will make you s against
29:14 It is an offering for s.
29:36 Sacrifice this offering for s on
32:21 to commit such a serious s?"
32:30 have committed a serious s.
32:30 to make a payment for your s
32:30 with the LORD for your s."
32:31 committed such a serious s!
32:32 But will you forgive their s?
32:34 I will punish them for their s."
34:7 disobedience, and s.
34:9 forgive our s and the wrong we
Lev 4:3 an offering for s to the LORD.
4:8 the bull that is the offering for s,
4:14 a bull as an offering for s.
4:20 bull used as the offering for s.
4:21 offering for s for the community
4:24 It is an offering for s.
4:25 of the blood of the offering for s
4:32 a lamb as his offering for s,
4:34 the blood from the offering for s
5:6 LORD for the s you committed.
5:6 or goat as an offering for s.
5:7 for the s you committed.
5:7 One will be an offering for s,
5:8 sacrifice the offering for s first.
5:9 the blood from the offering for s
5:9 It is an offering for s.
5:11 for the s you committed.
5:11 because it is an offering for s.
5:12 It is an offering for s.
6:2 "If any of you s against the
6:3 or commit any other s like this,
Lev 6:17 very holy like the offering for s
6:25 for the offering for s.
6:25 The offering for s must be
6:26 makes the offering for s will eat
6:28 offering for s is cooked must
6:28 offering for s is cooked must
6:29 may eat the offering for s.
6:30 Any offering for s must not be
7:7 apply to the offering for s
7:37 grain offering, the offering for s
8:2 that will be the offering for s,
8:14 bull that was the offering for s.
9:2 for yourself as an offering for s
9:3 a male goat as an offering for s,
9:7 and sacrifice an offering for s
9:8 calf as his own offering for s.
9:10 liver from the offering for s as
9:15 for the people's offering for s
9:22 He sacrificed the offering for s,
10:16 to be the offering for s.
10:17 didn't you eat the offering for s
10:19 sacrificed their offering for s
10:19 eaten the offering for s today,
12:6 dove as an offering for s.
12:8 and the other the offering for s.
14:13 he slaughters the offering for s
14:13 like the offering for s,
14:19 also sacrifice the offering for s
14:22 The one will be an offering for s
14:31 sacrifice it as an offering for s.
15:15 one as an offering for s
15:30 offer one as an offering for s
16:3 take a bull as an offering for s
16:5 of Israel as an offering for s
16:6 bull as his own offering for s.
16:9 the LORD as an offering for s.
16:11 it as his own offering for s.
16:15 for the people's offering for s.
16:25 of the offering for s on the altar.
16:27 offering for s whose blood was
17:16 they will be guilty of s."
19:22 peace with the LORD for this s.
19:22 man will be forgiven for this s.
20:20 man and woman are guilty of s.
22:9 or their s will bring them death
23:19 male goat as an offering for s
24:15 will be punished for their s.
25:9 day for the payment for s,
Num 5:7 you must confess your s,
5:15 of a s that was committed.
5:31 the consequences of her s."
6:11 one as an offering for s
6:14 lamb as an offering for s,
6:16 and make the offering for s
7:16 a male goat as an offering for s;
7:22 a male goat as an offering for s;
7:28 a male goat as an offering for s;
7:34 a male goat as an offering for s;
7:40 a male goat as an offering for s;
7:46 a male goat as an offering for s;
7:52 a male goat as an offering for s;
7:58 a male goat as an offering for s;
7:64 a male goat as an offering for s;
7:70 a male goat as an offering for s;
7:76 a male goat as an offering for s;
7:82 a male goat as an offering for s;
7:87 were used as offerings for s.
8:8 young bull as an offering for s.
8:12 one of them as an offering for s
9:13 the consequences for your s.
12:11 don't punish us for this foolish s
15:24 a male goat as an offering for s.
15:25 to the LORD for their s:
15:25 by fire and an offering for s.
15:27 sacrificed as an offering for s.
18:9 grain offering, an offering for s,
18:22 of their s and die.
18:32 the consequences of any s.
19:9 The cow is an offering for s.
19:12 day to take away his s.
19:13 to take away his s makes
19:17 burned as an offering for s into
19:20 doesn't have his s taken away,
27:3 He died for his own s and left
28:15 the LORD as an offering for s.
28:22 male goat as an offering for s
Num 29:5 male goat as an offering for s
29:11 as an offering for s (in addition
29:11 to the ⌊other⌋ offering for s
29:16 male goat as an offering for s
29:19 male goat as an offering for s
29:22 male goat as an offering for s
29:25 male goat as an offering for s
29:28 male goat as an offering for s
29:31 male goat as an offering for s
29:34 male goat as an offering for s
29:38 male goat as an offering for s
31:19 in order to take away your s.
31:23 in order to take away its s.
32:23 you will be punished for your s.
33:11 set up camp in the Desert of S.
33:12 moved from the Desert of S
Dtr 9:18 of the s you committed.
9:27 and s of these people.
15:9 will be condemned for your s.
19:15 or s he may have committed.
20:18 and you will s against the
22:26 She has not committed a s for
23:21 be guilty of a s if you didn't.
24:4 Don't pollute with s the land
24:15 will be condemned for your s.
Jos 22:17 Does the s we committed at
22:17 Because of that s there was a
22:20 who died because of his s."
1Sm 2:17 The s of Eli's sons was a
3:13 about his sons' s — that they
12:23 unthinkable for me to s against
14:34 But don't s against the LORD
14:38 what s was committed today.
14:41 If this s is mine or my son
15:23 The s of black magic is
15:25 Now please forgive my s and
19:4 "You should not commit a s
19:5 Why then should you s by
20:1 What s have I committed
2Sm 12:13 LORD has taken away your s;
14:9 be held responsible for the s,
14:32 If I'm guilty of a s, he should
24:10 "I have committed a terrible s
1Ki 8:35 and turn away from their s
8:46 "They may s against you.
12:30 them became ⌊Israel's⌋ s.
13:34 illegal priests became the s
16:2 You have led my people to s,
16:7 were like ⌊the s of⌋
16:13 They sinned, led Israel to s,
16:19 Jeroboam and led Israel to s.
16:26 He sinned and led Israel to s
17:18 here to remind me of my s
21:22 You led Israel to s."
22:52 son) who led Israel to s.
2Ki 12:16 offerings for s was not brought
17:21 led them to commit a serious s.
21:11 Judah s by ⌊worshiping⌋ his
21:16 In addition to his s that he led
23:15 who had made Israel s.
1Ch 21:3 make Israel guilty of ⌊this⌋ s?"
21:8 "I have committed a terrible s
2Ch 6:26 and turn away from their s
6:36 "They may s against you.
22:3 him advice that led him to s.
28:13 responsible for this s against
28:19 Ahaz had spread s throughout
29:21 male goats as an offering for s
29:23 male goats for the offering for s
29:24 their blood an offering for s at
29:24 and offerings for s should
33:23 Instead, Amon continued to s.
Ezr 6:17 male goats as an offering for s,
8:35 male goats for an offering for s.
10:13 who are involved in this s that
Neh 6:13 doing this so that I would s.
10:33 offerings for s that make peace
13:26 wives led him to s.
Job 1:5 in order to cleanse them from s.
1:22 Through all this Job did not s
7:20 If I s, what can I ⌊possibly⌋ do
7:21 and take away my s?
10:6 in me and search for s in me?
10:14 "If I s, you watch me and will
11:6 know that God forgets your s.
11:11 And when he sees s,

Job 11:14 If you're holding on to **s**,
13:23 of my disobedience and my **s**.
15:5 Your **s** teaches you what to
20:27 Heaven exposes his **s**.
24:19 the grave steals people who **s**.
31:7 my hands are stained ⌊with **s**⌋,
31:33 Adam and kept my **s** to myself,
33:9 I'm clean; I have no **s**.
34:37 He adds disobedience to his **s**.
Psa 4:4 Tremble and do not **s**.
17:3 that my mouth will not **s**.
32:1 and whose **s** is pardoned.
32:2 the LORD never accuses of **s**
38:3 in my bones because of my **s**.
38:18 my guilt. My **s** troubles me.
39:1 my ways so that I do not **s**
40:6 offerings or sacrifices for **s**.
51:2 and cleanse me from my **s**.
51:3 My **s** is always in front of me.
51:7 Purify me from **s** with hyssop,
59:4 or any **s**, or any guilt on my
78:17 continued to **s** against him,
78:32 they continued to **s**,
78:38 He forgave their **s**.
106:43 sink deeper because of their **s**.
109:14 and not wipe out his mother's **s**.
109:15 Let their guilt and **s** always
119:11 so that I may not **s** against you.
119:133 and do not let any **s** control me.
Pro 5:22 in the ropes of his own **s**.
10:16 A wicked person's harvest is **s**.
10:19 **S** is unavoidable when there is
13:6 ruins a sacrifice for **s**.
14:34 but **s** is a disgrace in any
17:19 Whoever loves **s** loves a
20:9 I'm cleansed from my **s**"?
28:14 who is always fearful ⌊of **s**⌋,
29:6 To an evil person **s** is bait in a
Ecc 2:26 the person who continues to **s**,
5:6 talk you into committing a **s**.
7:26 catch whoever continues to **s**.
Isa 6:7 and your **s** has been forgiven."
29:21 make people **s** with words,
30:1 They pile **s** on top of sin.
30:1 They pile sin on top of **s**.
30:13 That is why your **s** will be like
59:3 your fingers are stained with **s**.
64:5 We've continued to **s** for a long
64:9 Don't remember our **s** forever.
Jer 16:18 their wickedness and their **s**,
17:1 ⌊The LORD says,⌋ "Judah's **s**
17:3 and your **s** throughout all your
31:30 person will die for his own **s**.
32:35 I didn't make Judah **s**.
Lam 3:39 about being punished for **s**?
Eze 3:18 will die because of their **s**,
3:19 they will die because of their **s**,
3:20 they will die because of their **s**,
3:21 warn righteous people not to **s**,
3:21 not to sin, and they don't **s**,
4:17 away because of their **s**."
7:19 gold caused them to fall into **s**.
14:3 themselves to fall into **s**.
14:4 allows himself to fall into **s**.
14:7 allowing himself to fall into **s**.
18:18 father will die because of his **s**.
18:19 punished for his father's **s**?' It
18:24 and because of his **s**.
18:30 so that you will not fall into **s**.
22:9 and they **s** sexually.
23:48 be warned not to **s** as they do.
23:49 will pay for their **s** of idolatry.
30:15 I will pour out my fury on **S**,
30:16 **S** will be in much pain.
33:6 must die because of his **s**.
33:8 will die because of his **s**,
33:9 he will die because of his **s**.
33:14 But suppose he turns from his **s**
40:39 burnt offerings, offerings for **s**,
42:13 offerings, the offerings for **s**,
43:19 the priests as an offering for **s**.
43:20 you will remove **s** from the altar
43:21 young bull as an offering for **s**,
43:22 no defects as an offering for **s**.
43:22 Remove **s** from the altar as you
43:23 When you finish removing **s**,
Eze 43:25 the flock as an offering for **s**.
44:12 and by making Israel fall into **s**.
44:27 he must bring his offering for **s**,
44:29 grain offerings, offerings for **s**,
45:17 He must prepare offerings for **s**,
45:18 no defects and remove **s** from
45:19 blood from the offering for **s**
45:22 young bull as an offering for **s**.
45:23 male goat as an offering for **s**.
45:25 the same offerings for **s**,
46:20 offering and the offering for **s**.
Dan 9:24 to stop **s**, to forgive wrongs,
Hos 4:7 the more they **s** against me.
5:2 You are deeply involved in **s**.
7:1 all I can see is Ephraim's **s**
12:8 one will find us guilty of any **s**.'
Amo 4:4 Go to Bethel and **s**.
4:4 Go to Gilgal and **s** even more.
Mic 1:5 of Jacob's crime and Israel's **s**.
1:13 lead the people of Zion into **s**.
6:7 him my young child for my **s**?
7:18 You forgive **s** and overlook the
Zec 3:4 I have taken your **s** away from
3:9 "I will remove this land's **s** in a
13:1 wash away ⌊their⌋ **s** and stain.
14:19 ⌊the punishment⌋ for Egypt's **s**
14:19 for Egypt's sin and for the **s**
Mal 2:6 many people away from **s**.
Mat 5:29 your right eye causes you to **s**,
5:30 your right hand leads you to **s**,
12:31 be forgiven for any **s** or cursing.
13:41 that causes people to **s**
16:23 You are tempting me to **s**.
Mar 3:28 be forgiven for any **s** or curse.
3:29 is guilty of an everlasting **s**."
Luk 4:18 to the prisoners of **s**
4:18 who have been shattered by **s**,
Jon 1:29 takes away the **s** of the world.
8:11 From now on don't **s**."
8:21 you will die because of your **s**.
8:34 a sinful life is a slave to **s**.
8:46 convict me of committing a **s**?
9:2 Did he or his parents **s**?"
9:34 "You were born full of **s**.
15:22 they wouldn't have any **s**.
15:22 they have no excuse for their **s**.
15:24 they wouldn't have any **s**.
16:8 come to convict the world of **s**,
16:9 He will convict the world of **s**,
19:11 to you is guilty of a greater **s**."
Act 7:60 don't hold this **s** against them."
Rom 3:9 of being under the power of **s**,
3:20 Teachings show what **s** is.
3:24 paid to set us free ⌊from **s**⌋.
5:12 So **s** came into the world
5:12 and death came through **s**.
5:13 **S** was in the world before there
5:13 But no record of **s** can be kept
5:14 even over those who did not **s**
5:20 But where **s** increased,
5:21 As **s** ruled by bringing death,
6:1 Should we continue to **s** so
6:2 As far as **s** is concerned,
6:6 with him to put an end to **s**
6:6 we are no longer slaves to **s**.
6:7 has died has been freed from **s**.
6:12 Therefore, never let **s** rule your
6:14 Certainly, **s** shouldn't have
6:15 Should we **s** because we are
6:16 Either your master is **s**,
6:16 Letting **s** be your master leads
6:17 You were slaves to **s**.
6:18 Freed from **s**, you were made
6:20 When you were slaves to **s**,
6:22 you have been freed from **s**
6:23 The reward for **s** is death,
7:7 I wouldn't have recognized **s** if
7:8 But **s** took the opportunity
7:8 Clearly, without laws **s** is dead.
7:9 came, **s** became alive
7:11 **S**, taking the opportunity
7:13 my death was caused by **s** so
7:13 caused by sin so that **s** would
7:13 Through a commandment **s**
7:14 sold as a slave to **s**.
7:17 but **s** that lives in me is doing
Rom 7:20 **S** that lives in me is doing it.
8:2 the standards of **s** and death.
8:3 sinners have and to pay for **s**.
8:3 That way God condemned **s** in
8:10 bodies are dead because of **s**,
8:23 freeing of our bodies ⌊from **s**⌋.
14:23 that is not done in faith is **s**.
1Co 1:30 and our ransom from **s**.
5:1 that there is sexual **s** going
5:1 This kind of **s** is not even
5:7 Remove the old yeast ⌊of **s**⌋
5:7 actually have the yeast ⌊of **s**⌋.
5:8 with the old yeast ⌊of **s**⌋
5:11 faith but live in sexual **s**,
6:13 the body is not for sexual **s** but
6:18 People who **s** sexually sin
6:18 People who sin sexually **s**
8:9 who is weak in faith fall into **s**.
8:12 When you **s** against other
10:8 We shouldn't **s** sexually as
15:17 your faith is nonsense and **s**
15:56 **S** gives death its sting,
15:56 standards give **s** its power.
2Co 5:21 take our **s** so that we might
11:7 Did I commit a **s** when I
Gal 2:17 that Christ encourages us to **s**?
3:22 is controlled by the power of **s**.
Eph 4:30 set free ⌊from the world of **s**⌋.
5:3 Don't let sexual **s**,
5:5 who is involved in sexual **s**,
Col 1:22 into God's presence without **s**,
3:5 you: your sexual **s**, perversion,
1Th 4:3 keep away from sexual **s** as
2Th 2:3 place first, and the man of **s**,
2:7 The mystery of this **s** is
2:8 Then the man of **s** will be
2:9 The man of **s** will come with
1Ti 2:14 and brought **s** into the world.
5:20 those leaders who **s**.
Tit 2:14 us to set us free from every **s**
Heb 3:13 by **s** and become stubborn.
4:15 that we are, but he didn't **s**.
5:1 offer gifts and sacrifices for **s**.
9:26 to remove **s** by his sacrifice.
9:28 time he will not deal with **s**,
10:2 would have been free from **s**.
10:6 offerings and sacrifices for **s**.'
10:8 and sacrifices for **s**.
11:25 than to enjoy the pleasures of **s**
12:1 especially **s** that distracts us.
12:4 You struggle against **s**,
12:16 that no one commits sexual **s**
13:11 holy place as an offering for **s**.
Jas 1:15 pregnant and gives birth to **s**.
1:15 When **s** grows up,
1Pe 2:22 Christ never committed any **s**.
2Pe 2:14 They can't stop looking for **s**
1Jn 1:7 cleanses us from every **s**.
2:1 to you so that you will not **s**.
2:1 Yet, if anyone does **s**,
3:4 **S** is disobedience.
3:8 has been committing **s** since
5:16 committing a **s** that doesn't lead
5:16 There is a **s** that leads to death.
5:17 Every kind of wrongdoing is **s**,
Jud 1:8 their bodies with **s**,
Rev 2:14 to idols and to **s** sexually.
2:20 my servants to **s** sexually

Sinai (40)

Exo 16:1 which is between Elim and **S**.
19:1 they came to the desert of **S**.
19:2 had come into the desert of **S**.
19:11 come down on Mount **S** as all
19:18 All of Mount **S** was covered
19:20 came down on top of Mount **S**
19:23 people can't come up Mount **S**,
23:31 Sea and from the **S** Desert
24:16 the LORD settled on Mount **S**.
31:18 speaking to Moses on Mount **S**.
34:2 Then come up on Mount **S**,
34:4 he went up on Mount **S**,
34:29 came down from Mount **S**,
34:32 the LORD told him on Mount **S**.
Lev 7:38 On Mount **S** the LORD gave
7:38 offerings to him in the **S** Desert.

Lev 25:1 spoke to Moses on Mount **S**,
26:46 through Moses on Mount **S**.
27:34 on Mount **S** for the Israelites.
Num 1:1 of meeting in the Desert of **S**.
1:19 of Israel in the Desert of **S** as
3:1 spoke to Moses on Mount **S**.
3:4 his presence in the Desert of **S**.
3:14 to Moses in the Desert of **S**,
9:1 to Moses in the Desert of **S**.
9:5 they were in the Desert of **S**.
10:12 moved from the Desert of **S**
26:64 had counted in the Desert of **S**.
28:6 was established on Mount **S**.
33:15 set up camp in the Desert of **S**.
33:16 moved from the Desert of **S**
Dtr 33:2 "The LORD came from **S**.
Jdg 5:5 of the LORD God of **S**,
Neh 9:13 came from heaven to Mount **S**
Psa 68:8 in the presence of the God of **S**,
68:17 ⌊The God of⌋ **S** is in his holy
Act 7:30 bush in the desert of Mount **S**.
7:38 to him on Mount **S** were there
Gal 4:24 arrangement made on Mount **S**.
4:25 Hagar is Mount **S** in Arabia.

sincere (16)

1Ki 9:4 your father David was (with a **s**
Job 16:17 and my prayer is **s**.
Isa 48:1 but you are not honest or **s**.
Dan 11:34 who are not **s** will join them.
Luk 20:20 to act like **s** religious people.
Jon 1:47 is a true Israelite who is **s**."
2Co 6:6 ⌊in our lives⌋, our **s** love,
11:3 be lured away from your **s**
Eph 6:5 Be as **s** as you are when you
Col 3:22 Be **s** in your motives out of
1Ti 1:5 conscience, and from a **s** faith.
2Ti 1:5 I'm reminded of how **s** your
Heb 10:22 to come ⌊to him⌋ with a **s** heart
Jas 3:17 good deeds, impartial, and **s**.
1Pe 1:22 As a result you have a **s** love
1Jn 3:18 love through actions that are **s**,

sincerity (4)

Jdg 9:16 "If you acted with **s** and
9:19 So if you are now acting with **s**
Psa 51:6 Yet, you desire truth and **s**.
2Co 1:12 a God-given holiness and **s**,

sinful (51)

Dtr 9:21 I took that **s** calf you made and
1Ki 15:3 He followed the **s** example his
1Ch 21:7 considered the census to be **s**,
Job 2:10 lips did not utter one **s** word.
Psa 66:18 thought about doing anything **s**,
99:8 who punishes their ⌊**s**⌋ deeds.
109:7 Let his prayer be considered **s**.
Pro 12:13 is trapped by his own **s** talk,
24:9 Foolish scheming is **s**,
Isa 5:18 whose lives are **s**.
6:5 passes through my lips is **s**.
6:5 I live among people with **s** lips.
31:7 that your **s** hands have made.
57:17 angry because of their **s** greed,
57:17 But they continued to be **s**.
57:18 I've seen their ⌊**s**⌋ ways,
Eze 21:24 remember how **s** you are
23:21 So she longed to do the **s**
23:44 slept with those **s** women,
Amo 9:8 my eyes on this **s** kingdom.
Zep 2:10 they will get for their **s** pride,
Mar 8:38 this unfaithful and **s** generation,
Luk 5:8 Lord! I'm a **s** person!"
7:37 A woman who lived a **s** life in
13:2 were more **s** than other people
13:4 were more **s** than other people
24:7 be handed over to **s** people,
Jon 8:34 Whoever lives a **s** life is a
Rom 4:8 the Lord never considers **s**."
5:19 humanity became **s**,
7:5 **s** passions were at work
7:7 Are Moses' laws **s**?
7:7 are **s** if Moses' Teachings
7:13 sin became more **s** than ever.
13:14 the desires of your **s** nature.
1Co 3:4 aren't you acting like ⌊**s**⌋
2Co 1:17 I make them in a **s** way?
12:21 many who formerly led **s** lives
13:2 formerly led **s** lives as well
Col 2:18 Such a person, whose **s** mind
3:7 You used to live that kind of **s**
1Pe 4:2 guided by **s** human desires as
4:3 had **s** desires, got drunk,
2Pe 1:4 the corruption that **s** desires
1Jn 1:8 If we say, "We aren't **s**" we are
3:4 Those who live **s** lives are
3:5 take away our sins. He isn't **s**.
3:8 The person who lives a **s** life
3:9 born from God don't live **s** lives.
3:9 and they can't live **s** lives.
Jud 1:23 be stained by their **s** lives.

sinfully (1)

Job 31:30 (even though I didn't speak **s**

sinfulness (1)

Job 8:4 the consequences of their **s**.

sing (125)

Exo 15:1 "I will **s** to the LORD.
15:21 sang to them: "**S** to the LORD.
Num 21:17 water spring up! **S** to the well,
Dtr 31:19 and have them **s** it.
32:43 Joyfully **s** with the LORD's
Jdg 5:3 I will **s** a song to the LORD.
11:40 girls in Israel would go out to **s**
1Sm 21:11 He's the one they used to **s**
29:5 of whom people **s** in dances:
1Ch 15:22 instructed others how to **s**
16:9 **S** to him. Make music to praise
16:23 "**S** to the LORD, all the earth!
16:33 the trees in the forest will **s**
2Ch 20:21 he appointed people to **s** to the
20:22 As they started to **s** praises,
29:28 singers began to **s**,
35:25 still **s** funeral songs about
Neh 12:24 from one another to **s** hymns
Job 21:12 They **s** with the tambourine
29:13 the widow's heart **s** for joy.
Psa 5:11 Let them **s** with joy forever.
13:6 I will **s** to the LORD because
20:5 We will joyfully **s** about your
21:13 We will **s** and make music to
26:7 so that I may loudly **s** a hymn
27:6 I will **s** and make music to
32:11 **S** with joy, all whose motives
33:1 Joyfully **s** to the LORD,
33:3 **S** a new song to him.
35:27 innocent joyfully **s** and rejoice.
51:14 Let my tongue **s** joyfully about
57:7 I want to **s** and make music.
59:16 But I will **s** about your strength.
59:16 In the morning I will joyfully **s**
63:5 My mouth will **s** ⌊your⌋ praise
63:7 of your wings, I **s** joyfully.
65:8 and evening sunset **s** joyfully.
65:13 triumphantly. Indeed, they **s**.
67:4 Let the nations be glad and **s**
68:4 **S** to God; make music to
68:32 of the world, **s** to God.
71:23 My lips will **s** with joy when I
71:23 also will **s** joyfully.
81:1 **S** joyfully to God, our strength.
87:7 Singers and dancers will **s**,
89:1 I will **s** forever about the
89:12 Hermon **s** your name joyfully.
90:14 so that we may **s** joyfully
92:4 I will **s** joyfully about the works
95:1 let's **s** joyfully to the LORD.
96:1 **S** to the LORD a new song!
96:1 **S** to the LORD, all the earth!
96:2 **S** to the LORD! Praise his
96:12 trees in the forest will **s** joyfully
98:1 **S** a new song to the LORD
98:8 and the mountains **s** joyfully
101:1 I will **s** about mercy and
104:12 They **s** among the branches.
104:33 I will **s** to the LORD throughout
105:2 **S** to him. Make music to praise
108:1 I want to **s** and make music
119:172 Let my tongue **s** about your
126:5 joyfully **s** while they harvest.
Psa 132:9 Let your godly ones **s** with joy.
132:16 Then its godly ones will **s**
137:3 us demanded that we **s**.
137:3 "**S** a song from Zion for us!"
137:4 How could we **s** the LORD's
138:5 They will **s** this about the
144:9 I will **s** a new song to you.
144:9 I will **s** a psalm to you on a
145:7 **s** about your righteousness.
147:1 It is good to **s** psalms to our
147:1 to **s** ⌊his⌋ praise beautifully.
147:7 **S** to the LORD a song of
149:1 **S** a new song to the LORD.
149:1 **S** his praise in the assembly of
149:5 Let them **s** for joy on their beds.
Ecc 7:5 to fools who **s** your praises.
12:4 who **s** songs become quiet.
Isa 5:1 Let me **s** a lovesong to my
12:6 Shout loudly, and **s** with joy,
23:16 **S** many songs so that you'll be
24:9 longer drink wine when they **s**.
24:14 From the sea they **s** joyfully
27:2 On that day **s** about a
30:29 You will **s** a song like the song
30:29 sing a song like the song you **s**
35:2 It will rejoice and **s** with joy.
42:10 **S** a new song to the LORD.
42:10 **S** his praise from the ends of
42:11 those who live in Sela **s** for joy.
44:23 **S** with joy, you heavens,
49:13 **S** with joy, you heavens!
54:1 **S** with joy, you childless
60:6 They will **s** the praises of the
61:7 You will **s** about your wealth
63:7 and ⌊**s**⌋ the praises of the
65:14 My servants will **s** because of
Jer 7:29 **S** a song of mourning on the
9:10 I will **s** a funeral song for the
20:13 **S** to the LORD! Praise the
30:19 who live there will **s** songs
31:7 **S** a happy song about Jacob.
31:7 **S** joyfully for the leader of the
31:7 Shout, **s** praise, and say,
Eze 19:1 **S** a funeral song for the princes
26:17 Then they will **s** this funeral
27:2 **s** a funeral song about Tyre.
28:12 "Son of man, **s** a funeral song
32:2 **s** a funeral song for Pharaoh,
32:16 the nations will **s** this song.
32:16 They will **s** it as they mourn for
Amo 5:1 funeral song that I **s** about you,
Mic 2:4 They will **s** this sad song
Zep 2:14 A bird will **s** in a window.
3:14 **S** happily, people of Zion!
Zec 2:10 **S** for joy and rejoice,
Rom 15:9 the nations and I will **s** praises
1Co 13:4 It doesn't **s** its own praises.
14:15 I will **s** psalms with my spirit,
14:15 and I will **s** psalms with my
Eph 5:19 **S** and make music to the Lord
Col 3:16 **S** to God in your hearts.
Jas 5:13 If you are happy, **s** psalms.

singed (1)

Dan 3:27 hair on their heads wasn't **s**,

singer (3)

2Sm 23:1 the **s** of Israel's psalms:
Ezr 7:24 Levite, **s**, gatekeeper, servant,
Eze 33:32 you are nothing more than a **s**

singers (32)

1Ki 10:12 and lyres and harps for the **s**.
1Ch 15:27 the ⌊Levites who were⌋ **s**,
2Ch 5:13 the trumpeters and **s** praised
9:11 and lyres and harps for the **s**.
23:13 The **s** were leading the
29:28 the ground, **s** began to sing,
35:15 The **s** (Asaph's descendants)
35:25 All the male and female **s** still
Ezr 2:41 These **s** returned from exile:
2:65 had 200 male and female **s**.
2:70 people, the **s**, the gatekeepers,
7:7 Levites, **s**, gatekeepers,
10:24 From the **s**: Eliashib From the
Neh 7:1 The gatekeepers, the **s**,

Neh 7:44 These s returned from exile:
7:67 had 245 male and female s.
7:73 the s, some of the people,
10:28 s, temple servants,
10:39 the gatekeepers and the s are.
11:22 descendants who were the s
12:28 So the groups of s came
12:29 The s had built villages for
12:42 The s sang under the direction
12:45 The s and the gatekeepers did
12:46 had been directors for the s
12:47 for the daily support of the s
13:5 Levites, s, and gatekeepers.
13:10 So each of the Levites and s,
Psa 68:25 The s are in front. The
87:7 S and dancers will sing,
Ecc 2:8 myself with male and female s
Eze 40:44 were the rooms for the s

singing (23)

Jdg 5:11 Listen to the voices of those s
2Sm 19:35 Can I still hear the s of men
1Ch 15:16 to produce joyful music for s.
16:7 with the task of s songs
16:41 ⌞by s,⌟ "His mercy endures
2Ch 15:14 to the LORD with shouts, s,
23:18 with joy and s as David had
Neh 6:19 The nobles were s Tobiah's
12:46 for the singers to lead ⌞in s⌟
Job 3:7 Let no joyful s be heard in it.
Psa 98:4 Break out into joyful s,
118:15 The sound of joyful s and
126:6 will come home s,
Pro 25:20 so is s songs to one who has
Isa 35:10 will come to Zion s with joy.
51:3 and the sound of s.
51:11 will come to Zion s with joy.
Act 16:25 were praying and s hymns
Rev 4:8 day or night they were s,
5:12 In a loud voice they were s,
5:13 creature in those places was s,
14:3 They were s a new song in
15:3 and s the song of God's

single (49)

Gen 14:24 I won't take one s thing except
41:5 were growing on a s stalk.
41:22 of grain growing on a s stalk.
Exo 26:6 so that the tent is a s unit.
26:11 inner tent together as a s unit.
26:24 tightly at the top by a s ring.
36:13 that the inner tent was a s unit.
36:18 inner tent together as a s unit.
36:29 tightly at the top by a s ring.
Num 26:64 Among them there wasn't a s
Dtr 29:21 And the LORD will s him out
Jos 10:21 Not a s person dared to speak
21:45 Every s good promise that the
23:14 that not one s promise which
23:14 Every s word has come true.
Rut 1:13 they grew up and stay s just
1Sm 14:45 not a s hair of his head will fall
27:11 He did not bring a s man or
2Sm 3:11 couldn't respond to a s word,
13:30 and not a s one is left."
1Ch 12:38 came with a s purpose to
Est 3:13 and children — on a s day,
Job 34:29 it is a nation or a s person?
Psa 50:9 or a s male goat from
90:4 years are like a s day,
119:43 Do not take so much as a s
139:4 Even before there is a ⌞s⌟
Sos 4:9 You have charmed me with a s
4:9 with a s strand of your
Isa 15:1 In a s night Ar in Moab is laid
15:1 In a s night Kir in Moab is laid
40:16 enough for a s burnt offering.
Jer 26:2 Don't leave out a s word.
Eze 11:19 I will give them a s purpose
Dan 8:3 I looked up and saw a s ram
Zep 3:6 Not a s person will be left.
Zec 3:9 this land's sin in a s day.
Mal 4:1 won't leave a s root or branch.
Mat 6:27 "Can any of you add a s hour to
23:15 and sea to recruit a s follower,
Jon 12:24 I can guarantee this truth: A s
Act 1:14 The apostles had a s purpose
2:46 The believers had a s purpose
1Co 7:8 good for you to stay s like me.
7:11 If she does, she should stay s
Gal 2:6 people didn't add a s thing
5:14 summarized in a s statement,
Heb 12:16 the firstborn son for a s meal.
Rev 18:8 starvation will come in a s day.

singles (1)

Psa 4:3 Know that the LORD s out

sings (5)

Job 33:27 Each one s in front of other
Pro 1:20 Wisdom s her song in the
8:3 entrance ⌞wisdom⌟ s its song,
31:28 In addition, he s her praises,
Eze 33:32 voice who s love songs

Sinim (1)

Isa 49:12 will come from the land of S.

Sinites (2)

Gen 10:17 the Hivites, the Arkites, the S,
1Ch 1:15 the Hivites, the Arkites, the S,

sink (12)

Dtr 28:43 living⌟ will s lower and lower.
Psa 20:8 They will s to their knees and
69:14 Do not let me s ⌞into it⌟.
106:43 against him and to s deeper
124:6 who did not let them s their
Jer 51:64 'Babylon will s like this scroll.
Eze 21:15 gates so that their hearts will s
Amo 8:8 and then s like Egypt's river.
Hab 3:6 The ancient hills s.
Mat 14:30 became afraid and started to s.
Eph 3:17 into which you s your roots
Col 2:7 S your roots in him and build

sinking (1)

Psa 69:2 I am s in deep mud.

sinks (2)

Pro 2:18 Her house s down to death.
Amo 9:5 the Nile and s like Egypt's river.

sinless (4)

1Ki 8:46 (No one is s.) You may become
2Ch 6:36 (No one is s.) You may become
Jon 8:7 "The person who is s should
2Co 5:21 God had Christ, who was s,

sinned (86)

Gen 20:9 How have I s against you that
Exo 9:27 "This time I have s," he told
9:34 had stopped, he s again.
10:16 "I have s against the LORD
Num 14:40 They said, "We have s.
16:38 burners of these men who s
21:7 "We s when we criticized the
22:34 of the LORD, "I've s.
Dtr 1:41 "We have s against the LORD.
9:16 Then I saw that you had s
Jos 7:11 Israel has s. They have ignored
7:20 I have s against the LORD God
Jdg 10:10 "We have s against you.
10:15 said to the LORD, "We have s.
11:27 I haven't s against you.
1Sm 7:6 "We have s against the LORD."
12:10 LORD and said, 'We have s.
15:24 "I have s by not following the
15:30 Saul replied, "I have s!
19:4 "He hasn't s against you.
24:11 I haven't s against you,
26:21 David," Saul said, "I have s.
2Sm 12:13 "I have s against the LORD."
19:20 I know I've s. Today I've come
24:17 he said to the LORD, "I've s.
1Ki 8:33 they have s against you.
8:47 captives, saying, 'We have s.
8:50 who have s against you.
16:13 They s, led Israel to sin,
16:26 He s and led Israel to sin with
2Ki 17:7 The Israelites s against the
1Ch 9:1 captives because they had s.
1Ch 21:17 I am the one who s and did
2Ch 6:24 they have s against you.
6:37 captives, saying, 'We have s.
6:39 who have s against you.
28:13 because we have already s."
Neh 9:29 They s by not following your
13:26 that King Solomon of Israel s?
Job 1:5 "My children may have s and
8:4 If your children s against him,
33:27 'I s and did wrong instead of
35:6 If you've s, what effect can you
Psa 41:4 because I have s against you."
51:4 I have s against you,
106:6 We have s, and so did our
Isa 42:24 against whom we have s?
43:27 Your first ancestor s,
64:5 your anger, because we've s.
Jer 2:35 because I haven't s.'
3:25 we and our ancestors have s
8:14 we have s against the LORD.
14:7 and have s against you.
14:20 We have s against you.
16:10 How have we s against the
40:3 Israelites have s against him
44:23 s against the LORD,
50:7 They have s against the LORD,
50:7 They have s against the LORD,
50:14 have s against the LORD.
Lam 1:8 Jerusalem has s so much that
5:7 Our ancestors s. Now they are
5:16 Because we have s,
Eze 28:16 to be violent, and you s.
37:23 turned away from me and s.
Dan 9:5 We have s, done wrong,
9:8 we have s against you,
9:11 We s against you.
9:15 We have s and done evil
Hos 9:7 They have s a lot,
10:9 Israel, you have s ever since
Mic 7:9 I have s against the LORD.
Zep 1:17 because they have s against
Mat 27:4 He said, "I've s by betraying an
Luk 15:18 I've s against heaven and you.
15:21 I've s against heaven and you.
Jon 9:3 this man nor his parents s.
Rom 3:23 Because all people have s,
5:12 because everyone s.
5:16 ⌞God's⌟ gift and the one who s.
1Co 7:28 do get married, you have not s.
7:28 gets married, she has not s.
Heb 3:17 He was angry with those who s
Jas 5:15 If you have s, you will be
2Pe 2:4 God didn't spare angels who s.
1Jn 1:10 If we say, "We have never s,"

sinner (17)

Psa 51:5 I was a s when my mother
Pro 11:31 the wicked person and the s!
Ecc 2:26 The s must turn his wealth
8:12 A s may commit a hundred
9:18 but one s can destroy much
Isa 65:20 years old will be cursed as a s.
Luk 7:39 is touching him. She's a s."
18:13 'God, be merciful to me, a s!'
19:7 went to be the guest of a s."
Jon 9:16 "How can a man who is a s
9:24 who gave you sight is a s."
9:25 "I don't know if he's a s or not.
Rom 3:7 why am I still judged as a s?
1Ti 1:15 and I am the foremost s.
1:16 could use me, the foremost s,
Jas 5:20 Realize that whoever brings a s
1Pe 4:18 will happen to the godless s?

sinners (56)

Num 32:14 You're a bunch of s trying to
1Sm 15:18 He said, 'Claim those s,
Psa 1:1 people, take the path of s,
1:5 in the judgment and s will not
25:8 That is why he teaches s the
26:9 my soul along with hardened s
51:13 and s will return to you.
104:35 May s vanish from the world.
Pro 1:10 My son, if s lure you,
13:21 Disaster hunts down s,
13:22 but the wealth of s is stored

Pro 23:17 Do not envy **s** in your heart.
Ecc 9:2 Good people are treated like **s**.
Isa 1:28 Rebels and **s** will be crushed
13:9 He will destroy its **s**.
33:14 The **s** in Zion are terrified.
35:8 **S** won't travel on it.
53:12 and he was counted with **s**.
Amo 9:10 All the **s** among my people are
Zep 1:3 together with the **s**.
Mat 9:10 Many tax collectors and **s**
9:11 eat with tax collectors and **s**?"
9:13 I've come to call **s**,
11:19 and **s**!' "Yet, wisdom is proved
26:45 of Man to be handed over to **s**.
Mar 2:15 Many tax collectors and **s** who
2:16 saw him eating with **s**
2:16 eat with tax collectors and **s**?"
2:17 I've come to call **s**,
14:41 of Man to be handed over to **s**.
Luk 5:30 with tax collectors and **s**?"
5:32 I've come to call **s** to change
6:32 Even **s** love those who love
6:33 thanks for that? **S** do that too.
6:34 **S** also lend to sinners to get
6:34 Sinners also lend to **s** to get
7:34 a friend of tax collectors and **s**!'
15:1 All the tax collectors and **s**
15:2 "This man welcomes **s** and
Jon 9:31 that God doesn't listen to **s**.
9:41 you wouldn't be **s**.
9:41 so you continue to be **s**.
Rom 5:8 for us while we were still **s**.
8:3 have a human nature as **s** have
1Co 14:24 convince them that they are **s**.
Gal 2:15 not **s** from other nations.
2:17 approval in Christ, are still **s**,
1Ti 1:9 for ungodly people and **s**,
1:15 came into the world to save **s**,
Tit 3:11 They are **s** condemned by their
Heb 7:26 innocent, pure, set apart from **s**,
12:3 who endured opposition from **s**,
Jas 4:8 Clean up your lives, you **s**,
Jud 1:15 to convict all these ungodly **s**
Rev 21:8 sexual **s**, sorcerers, idolaters,
22:15 sexual **s**, murderers, idolaters,

sinning (31)

Gen 20:6 I kept you from **s** against me.
Lev 5:1 you are **s** and will be punished.
6:2 you are **s** and will be guilty.
6:4 you are **s** and will be guilty.
19:17 be guilty of **s** along with him.
Num 32:23 you will be **s** against the
1Sm 14:33 "The troops are **s** against the
1Ki 8:35 they are **s** against you,
2Ch 6:26 because they are **s** against you
28:10 But aren't you also guilty of **s**
Job 35:3 and, 'What would I gain by **s**?'
Psa 19:13 Keep me from **s**. Do not let
Eze 23:27 I will put a stop to your **s** and to
23:30 Your **s** and your prostitution
23:35 for your **s** and prostitution."
23:48 So I will put a stop to the **s** in
Dan 4:27 best advice is that you stop **s**,
Hos 8:11 more places they have for **s**.
13:2 They keep on **s** more and more.
Jon 5:14 Stop **s** so that something
1Co 7:36 he isn't **s** by letting her get
8:12 you are **s** against Christ.
15:34 right point of view, and stop **s**.
Eph 4:26 Be angry without **s**.
Heb 10:26 If we go on **s** after we have
Jas 2:9 person over another, you're **s**,
4:17 is right but doesn't do it is **s**.
1Jn 3:6 who live in Christ don't go on **s**.
3:6 Those who go on **s** haven't
5:18 born from God don't go on **s**.
Rev 9:21 **s** sexually, or stealing.

sin's (6)

Rom 6:2 we still live under **s** influence
6:10 once and for all to **s** power.
6:11 yourselves dead to **s** power
6:13 part of your body to **s** power.
7:23 to **s** standards which still exist
7:25 I am obedient to **s** standards

sins (342)

Gen 13:13 terrible **s** against the LORD.)
Exo 20:5 children for their parents' **s**
29:36 the altar in order to pay for its **s**.
30:16 the LORD's presence that the **s**
32:33 book whoever **s** against me.
34:7 for their parents' **s**
Lev 5:5 you are guilty of any of these **s**,
8:15 and cleansed the altar from **s**.
9:7 peace with the LORD for your **s**
9:7 LORD for your sins and the **s**
9:15 He sacrificed it to take away **s**
10:17 given to you to take away the **s**
16:16 with the LORD for all the **s**
16:16 These **s** happened because
16:17 with the LORD for his own **s**,
16:17 for his own sins, his family's **s**,
16:17 and the **s** of the entire
16:18 there for the **s** committed.
16:21 He will confess over it all the **s**,
16:22 The goat will take all their **s**
16:24 with the LORD for his own **s**
16:24 sins and the **s** of the people.
16:27 peace with the LORD for **s**.
16:30 will be clean from all your **s**
16:32 his father's place will pay for **s**.
16:34 LORD once a year for all the **s**
18:25 I will punish it for its **s**.
23:27 day for the payment for **s**.
23:28 day for the payment for **s**.
26:18 you seven times for your **s**.
26:21 for your **s** seven times.
26:24 you seven times for your **s**.
26:28 you seven times for your **s**.
26:39 enemies because of their **s**
26:39 and the **s** of their ancestors.
26:40 "But if they confess their **s** and
26:40 confess their sins and the **s**
Num 8:7 with water to take away their **s**.
8:21 to take away their **s**
14:18 for their parents' **s** to the third
14:19 please forgive these people's **s**,
14:34 day — you will suffer for your **s**
16:22 If one man **s**, will you be angry
16:26 away because of all their **s**."
18:1 responsible for any **s** against
18:1 for any **s** you commit when
18:23 be responsible for their own **s**.
19:19 will finish taking away their **s**.
Dtr 5:9 children for their parents' **s**
Jos 24:19 your rebellious acts and **s**.
1Sm 2:25 If one person **s** against another,
2:25 However, when a person **s**
3:14 peace for the **s** that Eli's family
12:19 to all our other **s** by asking
2Sm 7:14 If he **s**, I will punish him with a
1Ki 8:31 "If anyone **s** against another
8:34 forgive the **s** of your people
8:36 Forgive the **s** of your servants,
14:16 Israel because of Jeroboam's **s**,
14:16 the **s** which he led Israel to
14:22 Their **s** made him more angry
15:26 leading Israel into the same **s**.
15:30 was because of Jeroboam's **s**
15:30 sins and the **s** which
15:30 Those **s** made the LORD God
15:34 into committing the ⌊same⌋ **s**.
16:2 and their **s** make me furious.
16:13 This was for all the **s**
16:19 because of the **s** he had
16:31 same **s** as Jeroboam (Nebat's
2Ki 3:3 But he would not give up the **s**
3:3 not turn away from those **s**.
10:29 the **s** that Jeroboam (Nebat's
10:31 He didn't turn away from the **s**
13:2 He continued to commit the **s**
13:2 gave up committing those **s**.
13:6 away from the **s** that Jeroboam
13:6 continued to commit those **s**.
13:11 the **s** that Jeroboam led
14:24 of the **s** that Jeroboam (Nebat's
15:9 He didn't turn away from the **s**
15:18 the **s** that Jeroboam (Nebat's
15:24 He didn't turn away from the **s**
15:28 He did not turn away from the **s**
2Ki 17:22 The Israelites followed all the **s**
21:17 the **s** he committed — written in
24:3 of Manasseh's **s** — everything
1Ch 6:49 place and removed Israel's **s**
2Ch 6:22 "If anyone **s** against another
6:25 forgive the **s** of your people
6:27 Forgive the **s** of your servants,
7:14 from heaven, forgive their **s**,
28:13 you intend to add to all our **s**?
30:22 and confessed their **s** to the
33:19 This includes all his **s** and
Ezr 9:6 Our **s** have piled up over our
9:7 still are today because of our **s**.
10:1 confessing ⌊these **s**⌋,
Neh 1:6 I confess the **s** that we
1:6 as well as the **s** that my father's
4:5 and don't let their **s** disappear
9:2 confessed their **s** as well as
9:3 they confessed their **s** and
9:18 They committed outrageous **s**.
9:26 They committed outrageous **s**.
9:37 This is because of our **s**.
Job 13:23 How many crimes and **s** have I
13:26 me suffer for the **s** of my youth.
14:16 not keep ⌊a record of⌋ my **s**.
14:17 and you will cover over my **s**.
Psa 25:7 Do not remember the **s** of my
25:18 and forgive all my **s**.
32:3 I kept silent ⌊about my **s**⌋,
32:5 I made my **s** known to you,
32:5 Then you forgave all my **s**.
40:12 My **s** have caught up with me
51:9 Hide your face from my **s**,
59:12 ⌊because of⌋ the **s** from their
65:3 Various **s** overwhelm me.
78:34 They turned from their **s** and
79:9 Rescue us, and forgive our **s**
85:2 You pardoned all their **s**.
90:8 You have set our **s** in front of
90:8 You have put our secret **s** in
94:23 them because of their **s**.
103:3 the one who forgives all your **s**,
103:10 us as we deserve for our **s**
130:3 stand if you kept a record of **s**?
130:8 will rescue Israel from all its **s**.
Pro 8:36 Whoever **s** against me harms
14:21 despises his neighbor **s**,
21:4 lamps of wicked people, are **s**.
28:13 Whoever covers over his **s**
Ecc 7:20 does what is good and never **s**.
Isa 1:4 it will be for a nation that **s**.
1:18 "Though your **s** are bright red,
3:9 They boast about their **s**.
26:21 who live on earth for their **s**.
27:9 turn from their **s** — when they
33:24 The **s** of its inhabitants will be
38:17 thrown all my **s** behind you.
40:2 the LORD double for all its **s**."
43:24 you burdened me with your **s**
43:25 I will not remember your **s**
44:22 a thick cloud and your **s** like
50:1 were sold because of your **s**.
53:5 He was crushed for our **s**.
53:6 LORD has laid all our **s** on him.
53:11 will carry their **s** as a burden.
53:12 He carried the **s** of many.
58:1 of Jacob about their **s**.
59:2 and your **s** have made him hide
59:12 Our **s** testify against us.
64:6 and our **s** carry us away like
64:7 have let us be ruined by our **s**.
65:7 I will repay you for your **s** and
65:7 you for your sins and for the **s**
66:2 humble and sorry ⌊for their **s**⌋
Jer 5:25 Your **s** have kept good things
13:22 because you have so many **s**.
14:7 even though our **s** testify
14:10 their crimes and punish their **s**.
15:13 price for all the **s** that you have
18:23 Don't wipe their **s** out of your
30:14 and you have many **s**.
30:15 and you have many **s**.
31:34 hold their **s** against them."
33:8 from all the **s** that they have
33:8 I will forgive them for all the **s**
36:3 their wickedness and their **s**."

Jer 50:20 They will look for Judah's **s**,
Lam 4:6 punishment for the **s** of Sodom.
4:13 got through, because of the **s**
4:22 He will expose your **s**."
Eze 4:5 bear the punishment for the **s**
4:6 bear the punishment for the **s**
7:13 Because of their **s**,
7:16 will moan because of their **s**.
14:10 of you will suffer for your **s**.
14:11 dishonor me with all their **s**.
14:13 suppose a country **s** against
16:51 didn't commit half the **s** you did.
16:52 Yet, your **s** are more disgusting
18:4 The person who **s** will die.
18:14 The son sees all the **s** that his
18:17 He won't die for his father's **s**.
18:20 The person who **s** will die.
18:20 be punished for his father's **s**,
18:20 not be punished for his son's **s**.
18:21 turns away from all the **s** that
21:23 will remind them of their **s**,
21:24 You show your **s** in everything
23:49 will be punished for their **s**,
28:18 places because of your many **s**
33:10 "Our wickedness and our **s**
33:12 person will not live when he **s**.'
33:16 None of the **s** that he has done
39:24 their uncleanness and their **s**,
43:10 be ashamed because of their **s**.
44:10 must be punished for their **s**.
44:12 would be punished for their **s**,
Dan 9:16 around us because of our **s**
9:20 confessing my **s** and the sins
9:20 confessing my sins and the **s**
Hos 4:8 They feed on the **s** of my
5:5 stumble because of their **s**,
7:2 Now their **s** surround them.
7:2 Their **s** are in my presence.
8:11 offerings to pay for their **s**,
8:13 punish them because of their **s**.
9:7 to pay for their **s** will come.
9:9 punish them because of their **s**.
10:8 Israel **s** there. Thorns and
10:10 be punished for their many **s**.
13:12 The record of the people's **s** is
14:1 stumbled because of your **s**.
14:2 to him: "Forgive all our **s**,
Amo 3:2 to punish you for all your **s**.
5:12 numerous and your **s** are many.
Mic 3:8 nation of Israel about its **s**.
6:13 to ruin you because of your **s**.
7:19 You will throw all our **s** into the
Zep 1:3 and the **s** that make people fall,
Zec 1:6 away from their **s** and said,
5:6 "This is what the people's **s**
Mat 1:21 save his people from their **s**."
3:6 As they confessed their **s**,
9:2 Your **s** are forgiven."
9:5 'Your **s** are forgiven,'
9:6 authority on earth to forgive **s**."
15:19 other sexual **s**, stealing,
26:28 people so that **s** are forgiven.
Mar 1:4 for the forgiveness of **s**.
1:5 As they confessed their **s**,
2:5 your **s** are forgiven."
2:7 besides God can forgive **s**?"
2:9 'Your **s** are forgiven,'
2:10 authority on earth to forgive **s**."
7:21 Evil thoughts, sexual **s**,
Luk 1:77 the forgiveness of their **s**.
3:3 for the forgiveness of **s**.
5:20 your **s** are forgiven."
5:21 besides God can forgive **s**?"
5:23 'Your **s** are forgiven,'
5:24 authority on earth to forgive **s**."
7:47 her many **s** have been forgiven.
7:48 "Your **s** have been forgiven."
7:49 this man who even forgives **s**?"
17:3 "If a believer **s**, correct him.
24:47 think and act so that their **s** will
Jon 8:24 you'll die because of your **s**.
8:24 you'll die because of your **s**."
20:23 Whenever you forgive **s**,
Act 2:38 Jesus Christ so that your **s** will
3:19 God to have your **s** removed.
5:31 and to forgive their **s**.
Act 10:43 for their **s** through him."
13:38 that through Jesus your **s** can
13:38 **S** kept you from receiving
15:20 by false gods, from sexual **s**,
15:29 and from sexual **s**.
21:25 should not commit sexual **s**."
22:16 Be baptized, and have your **s**
26:18 receive forgiveness for their **s**
Rom 1:29 with of all kinds of sexual **s**,
2:12 Here's the reason: Whoever **s**
2:12 laws from God and still **s** will
3:25 to deal with **s** committed
4:7 and whose **s** are pardoned.
11:27 when I take away their **s**."
1Co 5:9 continue to commit sexual **s**.
5:10 who commit sexual **s**,
6:9 continue to commit sexual **s**,
6:18 Stay away from sexual **s**.
6:18 Other **s** that people commit
6:18 the same way sexual **s** do.
7:2 But in order to avoid sexual **s**,
15:3 Christ died to take away our **s**
2Co 12:21 about the perversion, sexual **s**,
Gal 1:4 took the punishment for our **s**,
2:20 took the punishment for my **s**.
Eph 1:7 we are set free from our **s**.
2:1 because of your failures and **s**.
5:6 It is because of **s** like these
Col 1:14 means that our **s** are forgiven.
3:6 It is because of these **s** that
3:8 language, and all similar **s**.
1Th 2:16 commit as many **s** as possible.
1Ti 1:10 for people involved in sexual **s**,
2:6 people to free them from their **s**.
5:22 participate in the **s** of others.
5:24 The **s** of some people are
5:24 The **s** of others follow them
2Ti 3:6 who are burdened with **s**
Heb 1:3 cleansed people from their **s**,
2:17 peace with God for their **s**.
5:3 to offer sacrifices for his own **s**
5:3 he does for the **s** of his people.
7:27 sacrifices for their own **s**,
7:27 they brought sacrifices for the **s**
7:27 brought the sacrifice for the **s**
8:12 hold their **s** against them."
9:15 the **s** they committed under
9:22 no **s** can be forgiven.
9:28 to take away the **s** of humanity,
10:3 reminded people of their **s**.
10:4 and goats cannot take away **s**.)
10:11 could never take away **s**.
10:12 priest made one sacrifice for **s**,
10:17 "I will no longer hold their **s**
10:18 When **s** are forgiven,
10:18 any need to sacrifice for **s**.
10:26 sacrifice can take away our **s**.
13:4 those who commit sexual **s**,
Jas 5:16 So admit your **s** to each other,
5:20 and many **s** will be forgiven.
1Pe 2:24 Christ carried our **s** in his body
2:24 cross so that freed from our **s**,
3:18 Christ suffered for our **s** once.
4:1 physically no longer **s**.)
4:8 because love covers many **s**.
2Pe 1:9 cleansed from your past **s**.
1Jn 1:9 If we confess our **s**,
2:2 He is the payment for our **s**,
2:2 and not only for our **s**,
2:2 but also for the **s** of the whole
2:12 because your **s** are forgiven
3:5 in order to take away our **s**.
4:10 Son to be the payment for our **s**.
5:16 who commit **s** that don't lead
5:17 yet there are **s** that don't lead to
Jud 1:7 they committed sexual **s**
Rev 1:5 freed us from our **s** by his blood
2:21 to turn away from her sexual **s**.
2:22 Those who commit sexual **s**
14:8 of her passionate sexual **s**."
17:2 on the wine of her sexual **s**."
17:4 evil things from her sexual **s**.
18:3 of the wine of her sexual **s**.
18:4 you do not participate in her **s**
18:5 Her **s** are piled as high as
19:2 the world with her sexual **s**.

Siphmoth (1)

1Sm 30:28 Aroer, **S**, Eshtemoa,

Sippai (1)

1Ch 20:4 Sibbecai from Hushah killed **S**,

Sirah (1)

2Sm 3:26 of **S** without David knowing

Sirion (2)

Dtr 3:9 Mount Hermon by the name **S**,
Psa 29:6 like a calf and Mount **S** like

Sisera (24)

Jdg 4:2 of King Jabin's army was **S**,
4:7 I will lead **S** (the commander of
4:9 will use a woman to defeat **S**."
4:12 report reached **S** that Barak,
4:13 So **S** summoned all his
4:14 day the LORD will hand **S** over
4:15 The LORD threw **S**,
4:15 **S** got down from his chariot
4:17 Meanwhile, **S** fled on foot
4:17 **S** did this because King Jabin
4:18 out of her tent, she met **S**.
4:19 **S** said to her, "Please give me
4:21 When **S** had fallen sound
4:21 into the ground. So **S** died.
4:22 Barak was still pursuing **S**.
4:22 He saw **S** lying there dead with
5:20 They fought against **S** from
5:25 **S** asked for water.
5:26 She struck **S**. She crushed his
5:30 colorful clothes for **S**,
1Sm 12:9 So he handed them over to **S**,
Ezr 2:53 Barkos, **S**, Temah,
Neh 7:55 Barkos, **S**, Temah,
Psa 83:9 to **S** and Jabin at the Kishon

Sisera's (2)

Jdg 4:16 So **S** whole army was killed in
5:28 **S** mother looked through her

Sismai (2)

1Ch 2:40 Eleasah was the father of **S**.
2:40 **S** was the father of Shallum.

sister (100)

Gen 4:22 Tubalcain's **s** was Naamah.
12:13 Please say that you're my **s**.
12:19 'She's my **s**' and allow me to
20:2 that his wife Sarah was his **s**.
20:5 'She's my **s**,' and didn't she
20:12 Besides, she is my **s** — my
24:59 So they let their **s** Rebekah and
24:60 a blessing: "May you, our **s**,
25:20 from Paddan Aram and **s**
26:7 Isaac answered, "She's my **s**."
26:9 'She's my **s**'?" Isaac
28:9 son Ishmael and **s** of Nebaioth,
30:1 she became jealous of her **s**.
30:8 had a great struggle with my **s**,
34:13 had dishonored their **s** Dinah.
34:14 We can't give our **s** to a man
34:27 their **s** had been dishonored.
34:31 to treat our **s** like a prostitute?"
36:3 of Ishmael and **s** of Nebaioth.
36:22 Lotan's **s** was Timna.
46:17 Their **s** was Serah.
Exo 2:4 The baby's **s** stood at a
2:7 Then the baby's **s** asked
6:20 married his father's **s** Jochebed.
6:23 Amminadab and **s** of Nahshon.
15:20 the prophet Miriam, Aaron's **s**,
Lev 18:11 She is your own **s**.
18:12 intercourse with your father's **s**.
18:13 with your mother's **s**.
18:18 never marry her **s** as a rival
20:17 Whoever takes his **s**,
20:17 sexual intercourse with his **s**
20:19 intercourse with your mother's **s**
20:19 sister or your father's **s**.
21:3 unmarried virgin **s** who is still
Num 6:7 mother, brother, or **s** dies,
25:18 They used their **s** Cozbi,

Num 26:59 and their s Miriam.
Dtr 27:22 sexual intercourse with his s,
Jdg 15:2 her younger s better looking?
2Sm 13:1 the beautiful s of David's son
13:2 with his half s Tamar that
13:4 love with Absalom's s Tamar,"
13:5 'Please let my s Tamar come
13:6 "Please let my s Tamar come
13:14 He grabbed his s and raped her.
13:20 S, be quiet for now. He's your
13:22 Amnon for raping his s Tamar.
13:32 half brother raped his s Tamar.
17:25 the daughter of Nahash and s
1Ki 11:19 the s of Queen Tahpenes,
11:20 Tahpenes' s had a son
2Ki 11:2 daughter of King Jehoram and s
1Ch 1:39 Timna was Lotan's s.
3:9 Tamar was their s.
3:19 and Shelomith was their s.
4:19 Hodiah's wife, the s of Naham,
7:18 Bedan's s Hammolecheth gave
7:30 Their s was Serah.
7:32 Hotham, and their s Shua.
2Ch 22:11 of the king and s of Ahaziah,
22:11 she was also Ahaziah's s,
Job 17:14 'You are my mother and s,'
Pro 7:4 to wisdom, "You are my s."
Sos 4:9 My bride, my s, you have
4:10 of love, my bride, my s!
4:12 my s is a garden that is locked,
5:1 My bride, my s, I will come to
5:2 to me, my true love, my s,
8:8 We have a little s,
8:8 What will we do for our s on
Jer 3:7 treacherous s Judah saw her.
3:8 But treacherous Judah, her s,
3:10 Israel's treacherous s Judah
22:18 it is for my brother and s!"
Eze 16:46 "'Your older s was Samaria.
16:46 Your younger s is Sodom.
16:48 your s Sodom and her
16:49 This is what your s Sodom has
16:56 You didn't mention your s
23:11 "Even though her younger s
23:11 after men more than her s did.
23:18 I had turned away from her s.
23:31 acted the same way as your s.
23:33 The cup of your s Samaria will
44:25 brother, or unmarried s.
Mat 12:50 my brother and s and mother."
Mar 3:35 my brother and s and mother."
Luk 10:39 She had a s named Mary.
10:40 don't you care that my s has
Jon 11:1 Mary and her s Martha lived,
11:5 Jesus loved Martha, her s,
11:28 and whispered to her s Mary,
11:39 Martha, the dead man's s,
19:25 Jesus' mother, her s,
Rom 16:1 She is our s in the Christian
16:15 and his s, and Olympas,
Phm 1:2 our s Apphia, our fellow soldier
1Pe 5:13 Your s church in Babylon,
2Jn 1:13 of your chosen s greet you.

sister-in-law (5)

Lev 18:16 sexual intercourse with your s.
Rut 1:15 Naomi said, "Look, your s has
1:15 Go back with your s."
1Ki 11:19 So he gave Hadad his s,
Luk 3:19 Herod had married his own s,

sister's (5)

Gen 24:30 the bracelets on his s wrists
29:13 news about his s son Jacob,
1Ch 4:3 Their s name was Hazelelponi.
Eze 23:11 worse than her s prostitution
23:32 You will drink from your s cup,

sisters (134)

Jos 2:13 s, and their households,
1Ch 2:16 Their s were Zeruiah and
Job 1:4 someone to invite their three s
42:11 Then all his brothers and s and
Psa 133:1 brothers and s live together
Sos 6:9 Her s saw her and blessed her.
Eze 16:45 You are exactly like your s.
16:51 you make your s look innocent.
16:52 because you accused your s.
16:52 because you have made your s
16:61 older and younger s to you.
22:11 in you have sex with their s,
23:13 Both s acted the same way.
Hos 2:1 call your s Ruhamah [Loved].
Mat 13:56 And aren't all his s here with
19:29 brothers or s, father, mother,
25:40 did for one of my brothers or s,
25:45 do for one of my brothers or s,
Mar 6:3 Aren't his s here with us?"
10:29 s, mother, father, children,
10:30 s, mothers, children and fields,
Luk 14:26 children, brothers, and s,
Jon 11:3 So the s sent a messenger to
20:17 But go to my brothers and s
Act 6:3 So, brothers and s,
15:23 brothers and s in Antioch,
15:23 Dear brothers and s,
Rom 1:13 you to know, brothers and s,
7:1 you realize, brothers and s,
7:4 the same way, brothers and s,
8:12 So, brothers and s,
10:1 Brothers and s, my heart's
11:25 Brothers and s, I want you to
12:1 Brothers and s, because of
15:14 I'm convinced, brothers and s,
15:30 Brothers and s, I encourage
16:14 and the brothers and s who are
16:17 Brothers and s, I urge you to
1Co 1:10 Brothers and s, I encourage all
1:11 Brothers and s, some people
1:26 Brothers and s, consider what
2:1 Brothers and s, when I came to
3:1 Brothers and s, I couldn't talk to
4:6 Brothers and s, I have applied
5:11 call themselves brothers or s
7:24 Brothers and s, you should
7:29 is what I mean, brothers and s:
10:1 you to know, brothers and s,
11:33 Therefore, brothers and s,
12:1 Brothers and s, I don't want
14:6 Brothers and s, it wouldn't do
14:20 Brothers and s, don't think like
14:26 this mean, brothers and s?
14:39 So, brothers and s,
15:1 Brothers and s, I'm making
15:31 Brothers and s, I swear to you
15:50 Brothers and s, this is what I
15:58 So, then, brothers and s,
16:15 encourage you, brothers and s,
16:20 All the brothers and s ⌊here⌋
2Co 1:8 Brothers and s, we don't want
8:1 Brothers and s, we want you to
13:11 With that, brothers and s,
Gal 1:11 you to know, brothers and s,
3:15 Brothers and s, let me use an
4:12 Brothers and s, I beg you to
4:28 Now you, brothers and s,
4:31 Brothers and s, we are not
5:11 Brothers and s, if I am still
5:13 to be free, brothers and s.
6:1 Brothers and s, if a person gets
6:18 with your spirit, brothers and s!
Eph 6:23 give our brothers and s peace
Php 1:12 you to know, brothers and s,
1:14 our brothers and s confidence
3:1 Now then, brothers and s,
3:13 Brothers and s, I can't consider
3:17 Brothers and s, imitate me,
4:1 So, brothers and s,
4:8 Finally, brothers and s,
4:21 The brothers and s who are
Col 1:2 our brothers and s who are
4:15 our brothers and s in Laodicea,
1Th 1:4 Brothers and s, we never forget
2:1 You know, brothers and s,
2:9 You remember, brothers and s,
2:14 You, brothers and s,
2:17 Brothers and s, we have been
3:7 So brothers and s,
4:1 Now then, brothers and s,
4:13 Brothers and s, we don't want
5:1 Brothers and s, you don't need
5:4 But, brothers and s,
1Th 5:12 Brothers and s, we ask you to
5:14 encourage you, brothers and s,
5:25 Brothers and s, pray for us.
5:26 Greet all the brothers and s
5:27 letter to all the brothers and s.
2Th 1:3 God for you, brothers and s.
2:1 Brothers and s, we have this
2:13 God for you, brothers and s.
2:15 Then, brothers and s,
3:1 Finally, brothers and s,
3:6 Brothers and s, in the name of
3:13 Brothers and s, we can't allow
3:15 them like brothers and s.
1Ti 4:6 things out to our brothers and s.
5:2 women as if they were your s,
2Ti 4:21 and s send you greetings.
Heb 2:11 to call them brothers and s.
2:17 like his brothers and s so that
3:1 Brothers and s, you are holy
3:12 Be careful, brothers and s,
10:19 Brothers and s, because of the
13:22 I urge you, brothers and s,
Jas 1:2 My brothers and s,
1:16 My dear brothers and s,
1:19 my dear brothers and s:
2:1 My brothers and s,
2:5 Listen, my dear brothers and s!
2:14 My brothers and s,
3:1 Brothers and s, not many of
3:10 My brothers and s,
3:12 My brothers and s,
4:11 Brothers and s, stop slandering
5:7 Brothers and s, be patient until
5:9 Brothers and s, or you will be
5:10 Brothers and s, follow the
5:12 my brothers and s,
5:19 My brothers and s,
1Pe 2:17 Love your brothers and s in the
2Pe 1:10 Therefore, brothers and s,
1Jn 3:13 Brothers and s, don't be
Rev 12:10 accusing our brothers and s,

sistrums (1)

2Sm 6:5 tambourines, s, and cymbals.

sit (98)

Gen 27:19 S up and eat this meat I've
Exo 18:14 Why do you s here alone,
Lev 15:6 Those who s on anything he
Jdg 4:5 She used to s under the Palm
5:10 who s on saddle blankets,
5:16 Why did you s between the
18:9 "Don't just s there!
Rut 4:1 "Please come over here and s,
4:2 of that city and said, "S here."
1Sm 2:8 heap in order to make them s
9:22 banquet hall and had them s at
20:5 when I should s and eat at the
1Ki 1:13 and that he will s on your
1:17 that he will s on your throne.
1:24 that he will s on your throne,
1:27 without telling me who would s
1:30 He will s on my throne."
1:35 here when he comes to s
3:6 love by giving him a son to s
8:20 and I s on the throne of Israel
21:10 men s opposite him
2Ki 10:30 of your descendants will s
15:12 of your descendants will s
19:27 you ⌊get up⌋ and s down,
1Ch 28:5 he chose my son Solomon to s
2Ch 6:10 and I s on the throne of Israel
Job 30:1 think their fathers were fit to s
42:6 and I s in dust and ashes to
Psa 26:4 I did not s with liars,
26:5 will not s with wicked people.
50:20 You s and talk against your
61:7 May he s enthroned in the
69:12 Those who s at the gate
110:1 The LORD said to my Lord, "S
132:12 their descendants will also s
132:14 Here I will s enthroned
139:2 You alone know when I s
Pro 23:1 When you s down to eat with a
Sos 2:3 I want to s in his shadow.
Isa 3:26 and Zion will s on the ground,

Isa 5:11 who **s** up late until they are
14:13 I'll **s** on the mountain far away
37:28 you ⌊get up⌋ and **s** down,
47:1 Go, **s** in the dirt, virgin princess
47:1 **S** on the ground, not on a
47:5 into the dark, and **s** in silence,
47:14 and no fire for them to **s** by.
Jer 13:13 The kings who **s** on David's
14:2 The people of Judah **s** in
16:8 Don't **s** with them to eat and
17:25 the kings and princes who **s**
22:4 then the kings who **s** on
22:30 They won't **s** on David's throne
36:15 to Baruch, "Please **s** down,
36:30 He will have no one to **s** on
48:18 from your place of honor and **s**
Lam 2:10 of Zion's people **s** silently
3:28 They should **s** alone and
5:19 **s** enthroned forever,
Eze 26:16 they will **s** on the ground.
28:2 I **s** on God's throne in the sea."
33:31 and they **s** down in front of you.
44:3 Only the prince may **s** there
Dan 11:27 They will **s** at the same table
Joe 3:12 There I will **s** to judge all the
Mic 4:4 They will **s** under their
7:8 Although I **s** in the dark,
Zec 3:10 neighbor to **s** under your vine
6:13 He will **s** and rule from his
8:4 and old women will again **s**
Mat 11:16 They are like children who **s** in
14:19 Then he ordered the people to **s**
15:35 He ordered the crowd to **s**
19:28 will also **s** on twelve thrones,
20:21 of my sons will **s** at your right
21:7 on them for Jesus to **s** on.
25:31 he will **s** on his glorious throne.
26:55 I used to **s** teaching in the
Mar 6:39 Then he ordered all of them to **s**
8:6 He ordered the crowd to **s**
10:37 "Let one of us **s** at your right
Luk 7:32 They are like children who **s** in
9:14 "Have them **s** in groups of
11:43 You love to **s** in the front seats
12:37 make them **s** down at the table,
14:28 You would first **s** down and
14:31 He would first **s** down and
16:6 **S** down, and write "four
22:30 You will also **s** on thrones and
Jon 6:10 "Have the people **s** down."
6:10 had plenty of grass to **s** on.
9:8 man who used to **s** and beg?"
Act 3:10 he was the man who used to **s**
8:31 So he invited Philip to **s** with
23:3 You **s** there and judge me by
Heb 1:13 "**S** in the highest position in
Jas 2:3 or "**S** on the floor at my feet."
Rev 3:21 who wins the victory to **s**

site (28)

Num 21:15 valleys that go down to the **s**
1Sm 9:12 a sacrifice on the worship **s**.
9:13 he goes to the worship **s** to eat.
9:14 on his way to the worship **s**.
9:19 ahead of me to the worship **s**.
9:25 Then they left the worship **s** for
10:5 they come from the worship **s**.
10:13 he came to the worship **s**.
22:6 tamarisk tree at the worship **s**
1Ki 6:7 at the temple construction **s**.
11:7 built an illegal worship **s**
2Ki 23:8 He tore down the worship **s** at
23:8 (The worship **s** was to the left
23:15 They burned the worship **s**,
1Ch 17:5 but I've gone from tent **s** to tent
17:5 I've gone from tent site to tent **s**,
21:29 at the worship **s** at Gibeon.
2Ch 3:1 There David had prepared the **s**
Ezr 2:68 God's temple on its ⌊former⌋ **s**.
3:3 rebuilt the altar on its original **s**,
3:8 following their return to ⌊the **s**⌋
5:15 God's temple on its original **s**.'
Isa 16:12 Moab appear at the worship **s**,
Jer 26:18 a worship **s** covered with trees.'
Eze 20:29 "What is this worship **s** you're
20:29 is still called 'worship **s**' today.
Mic 3:12 a worship **s** covered with trees.
Zec 14:10 will rise and remain on its **s**,

sites (48)

Lev 26:30 I will destroy your worship **s**,
Num 21:28 the rulers of Arnon's worship **s**.
Dtr 12:2 destroy all the worship **s**
1Ki 3:2 sacrificing at other worship **s**
3:3 at these other worship **s**.
12:31 built worship **s** on hilltops.
12:32 the illegal worship **s** ⌊to serve⌋
13:2 worship **s** who offer sacrifices
13:32 and all the illegal worship **s**
13:33 priests for the illegal worship **s**.
13:33 to be priests at the worship **s**.
14:23 They built worship **s** for
15:14 Although the illegal worship **s**
22:44 But the illegal worship **s** were
22:44 incense at these worship **s**.
2Ki 12:3 incense at these worship **s**.
14:4 incense at these worship **s**.
15:4 incense at these worship **s**.
15:35 incense at these worship **s**.
16:4 offering at the illegal worship **s**,
23:9 worship **s** had never gone
23:20 priests of the illegal worship **s**
2Ch 11:15 priests for the illegal worship **s**
15:17 Although the illegal worship **s**
20:33 But the illegal worship **s** on the
28:4 offering at the illegal worship **s**,
33:19 where he built illegal worship **s**
Psa 78:58 of their illegal worship **s**.
Isa 15:2 temple, to the worship **s**, to cry.
Jer 7:31 They have built worship **s** at
17:3 this because of your worship **s**
19:5 They have built worship **s** to
32:35 Hinnom they built worship **s**
48:35 Moab who come to worship **s**,
Eze 6:3 and destroy your worship **s**.
6:6 and the worship **s** will be
16:16 made your worship **s** colorful.
16:24 platforms and illegal worship **s**
16:25 You also built worship **s** at the
16:31 place your illegal worship **s**
16:39 down your illegal worship **s**.
18:6 the illegal mountain worship **s**
18:11 the illegal mountain worship **s**.
18:15 the illegal mountain worship **s**
22:9 to idols at the worship **s**
36:2 The ancient worship **s** now
Hos 10:8 The illegal worship **s** of Aven
Amo 7:9 The worship **s** of Isaac will be

Sithri (1)

Exo 6:22 Mishael, Elzaphan, and **S**.

Sitnah (1)

Gen 26:21 So Isaac named it **S**

sits (31)

Lev 15:4 he lies on or **s** on unclean.
15:9 a man who has a discharge **s**
15:20 Everything she lies on or **s** on
15:22 who touch anything she **s**
15:23 the bed or anything she **s** on,
15:26 she lies on or anything she **s**
Est 6:10 for Mordecai the Jew who **s** at
Psa 29:10 The LORD **s** enthroned as king
33:14 place where he **s** enthroned,
47:8 He **s** upon his holy throne.
122:5 The court of justice **s** there.
123:1 who **s** enthroned in heaven.
Pro 9:14 She **s** at the doorway of her
20:8 A king who **s** on his throne to
31:23 at the city gates when he **s**
Isa 30:7 'Rahab who **s** still.'
Jer 29:16 says about the king who **s**
Nah 3:8 which **s** by the streams of the
Mat 19:28 When the Son of Man **s** on his
23:22 throne and the one who **s** on it.
Luk 22:27 the person who **s** at the table or
22:27 Isn't it really the person who **s**
Rev 4:9 and thanks to the one who **s**
4:10 bow in front of the one who **s**
5:1 the right hand of the one who **s**
5:7 of the one who **s** on the throne.
Rev 5:13 "To the one who **s** on the
6:16 from the face of the one who **s**
7:10 who **s** on the throne,
7:15 The one who **s** on the throne
17:1 who **s** on raging waters.

sitting (82)

Gen 18:1 to Mamre as he was **s** at
19:1 in the evening as Lot was **s**
23:10 Ephron was **s** among the
31:34 saddle-bag and was **s** on them.
Exo 2:15 while Moses was **s** by a well,
Dtr 22:6 If the mother bird is **s** on the
Jdg 13:9 to his wife while she was **s** out
Rut 4:4 presence of these men **s** here
1Sm 1:9 (The priest Eli was **s** on a chair
4:13 When he arrived, Eli was **s** on
19:9 came over Saul while he was **s**
24:3 his men were **s** further back
2Sm 18:24 David was **s** between the two
19:8 "The king is **s** in the gateway,"
1Ki 8:25 will never fail to have an heir **s**
13:14 of God and found him **s** under
13:20 When they were **s** at the table,
22:19 I saw the LORD **s** on his
2Ki 1:9 When the officer found Elijah **s**
6:32 Elisha was **s** in his home with
7:3 "Why are we **s** here waiting to
9:5 generals were **s** together.
18:27 Didn't he send me to the men **s**
2Ch 6:16 will never fail to have an heir **s**
18:9 They were **s** on the threshing
18:18 I saw the LORD **s** on his
Neh 2:6 the queen was **s** beside him,
Est 2:19 Mordecai was **s** at the king's
2:21 while Mordecai was **s** at the
5:1 The king was **s** on the royal
5:13 I see Mordecai the Jew **s** at
Pro 3:29 neighbor while he is **s** there
Ecc 10:7 I have seen slaves **s** on horses
Isa 6:1 I saw the Lord **s** on a high and
36:12 Didn't he send me to the men **s**
Jer 8:14 Why are we just **s** here?
22:2 the one **s** on David's throne.
32:12 of all the Jews who were **s**
33:17 fail to have a descendant **s**
36:12 where all the scribes were **s**.
36:22 king was in his winter house **s**
38:7 to be **s** at Benjamin Gate.
Lam 3:63 Whether they are **s** or standing,
Eze 8:1 I was **s** in my home.
8:1 Judah's leaders were **s** in front
8:14 Women were **s** there and
Zec 3:8 and your friends **s** with you.
5:7 a woman was **s** in the basket.
Mat 9:9 he saw a man **s** in a tax office.
20:30 Two blind men were **s** by the
24:3 As Jesus was **s** on the Mount
26:7 While Jesus was **s** there,
26:69 Peter was **s** in the courtyard.
27:61 the other Mary were **s** there,
28:2 stone away, and was **s** on it.
Mar 2:6 Some scribes were **s** there.
2:14 of Alphaeus, **s** in a tax office.
3:32 The crowd **s** around Jesus told
5:15 The man was **s** there dressed
10:46 was **s** by the road.
13:3 As Jesus was **s** on the Mount
14:3 While Jesus was **s** there,
Luk 2:46 He was **s** among the teachers,
5:27 a tax collector named Levi **s**
8:35 he was **s** at Jesus' feet.
18:35 a blind man was **s** and begging
Jon 2:14 found moneychangers **s** there.
6:11 to the people who were **s** there.
20:12 They were **s** where the body of
Act 14:8 He was always **s** because he
20:9 man named Eutychus was **s**
26:30 and the people who were **s**
2Th 2:4 **s** in God's temple and claiming
Rev 4:2 and someone was **s** on it.
4:3 The one **s** there looked like
11:16 who were **s** on their thrones in
17:3 I saw a woman **s** on a bright
17:9 on which the woman is **s**.
17:15 on which the prostitute is **s**,

Rev 19:4 who was **s** on the throne.
20:11 and the one who was **s** on it.
21:5 The one **s** on the throne said,

situation (21)

Jos 22:24 because of the **s** we're in.
2Sm 24:14 "I'm in a desperate **s**," David
1Ki 11:27 This was the **s** when he
1Ch 21:13 "I'm in a desperate **s**," David
Ezr 7:14 sending you to evaluate the **s**
Ecc 8:6 a right way ⌊to act⌋ in every **s**.
Dan 6:17 so that Daniel's **s** could not be
Luk 17:26 the **s** will be like the time of
17:28 "The **s** will also be like the
Jon 16:22 "Now you're in a painful **s**.
Rom 3:9 What, then, is the **s**?
1Co 11:13 Judge your own **s**.
Eph 6:18 Pray in the Spirit in every **s**.
Php 4:6 But in every **s** let God know
4:11 be content in whatever **s** I'm in.
4:12 No matter what the **s**,
1Pe 1:11 tried to find out what time or **s**
Rev 13:10 In this **s** God's holy people
13:18 In this **s** wisdom is needed.
14:12 In this **s** God's holy people,
17:9 "In this **s** a wise mind is

situations (3)

Dtr 1:18 told you how to handle these **s**.
Mat 18:7 **S** that cause people to lose
Luk 17:1 Jesus told his disciples, "**S**

Sivan (1)

Est 8:9 on the twenty-third day of **S**,

sixth (32)

Gen 1:31 then morning — the **s** day.
30:19 birth to her **s** son for Jacob.
Exo 16:5 But on the **s** day when they
16:22 But on the **s** day they gathered
16:29 you enough food on the **s** day
26:9 Fold the **s** sheet in half ⌊to
Lev 25:21 blessing in the **s** year so that
Num 7:42 On the **s** day the leader of the
29:29 "On the **s** day bring 8 bulls,
Jos 19:32 The **s** lot was drawn for the
2Sm 3:5 The **s** was Ithream,
2Ki 18:10 in Hezekiah's **s** year as king
1Ch 2:15 Ozem (his **s** son), and David
3:3 The **s** was Ithream,
12:11 The **s** was Attai. The seventh
24:9 for Malchiah, the **s** for Mijamin,
25:13 The **s** chose Bukkiah,
26:3 Jehohanan (the **s**),
26:5 Ammiel (the **s**), Issachar (the
27:9 was in charge of the **s** unit
27:9 sixth unit during the **s** month.
Ezr 6:15 the month of Adar in the **s** year
Neh 3:30 and Hanun, Zalaph's **s** son,
Eze 8:1 On the fifth day of the **s** month
8:1 of the sixth month in the **s** year,
Hag 1:1 On the first day of the **s** month
1:15 day of the **s** month
Rev 6:12 as the lamb opened the **s** seal.
9:13 When the **s** angel blew his
9:14 The voice said to the **s** angel
16:12 The **s** angel poured his bowl
21:20 the fifth onyx, the **s** red quartz,

Siyon (1)

Dtr 4:48 Valley to Mount **S** (that is,

sizable (1)

2Sm 18:7 and the massacre was **s** that

size (20)

Exo 26:2 6 feet wide — all the same **s**.
36:9 6 feet wide — all the same **s**.
1Ki 7:9 The stone blocks were cut to **s**
7:11 which had been cut to **s**.
7:37 identical in **s** and shape.
Eze 13:18 make magic veils of every **s**
40:10 on each side were the same **s**,
40:10 on each side were the same **s**.
40:21 hall were the same **s** as those
40:22 were the same **s** as those
40:24 They were the same **s** as
40:28 was the same **s** as the others.
40:29 hall were the same **s** as
40:32 was the same **s** as the others.
40:33 halls were the same **s** as those
40:35 was the same **s** as the others.
46:22 the courtyard were the same **s**.
Amo 8:5 We can shrink the **s** of the
Mat 17:20 If your faith is the **s** of a
Luk 17:6 "If you have faith the **s** of a

skies (13)

Dtr 33:28 Dew will drip from Israel's **s**.
Job 37:18 Can you stretch out the **s** with
Psa 36:5 your faithfulness to the **s**.
57:10 Your truth reaches the **s**.
68:34 and his power is in the **s**.
89:6 Who in the **s** can compare with
108:4 Your truth reaches the **s**.
Pro 3:20 and the **s** dropped dew.
8:28 he established the **s** above,
Isa 45:8 down righteousness, you **s**.
Jer 14:22 the **s** can't give showers.
Joe 2:2 a day of clouds and overcast **s**.
Zep 1:15 a day of clouds and overcast **s**,

skill (11)

Exo 28:3 "Tell all those who have the **s**
31:6 craftsman the **s** necessary
35:26 willing and had the **s** spun
2Ch 2:7 "Send me a man who has the **s**
2:13 I'm sending a man with **s** and
Psa 78:72 With **s** he guided them.
Ecc 2:21 wisdom, knowledge, and **s**.
9:10 or **s** in the grave where you're
Jer 10:12 He set up the world by his **s**.
Eze 28:5 of your great **s** in trading,
Act 17:29 of human imagination and **s**.

skilled (44)

Gen 21:20 desert and became a **s** archer.
Exo 31:3 making him highly **s**,
35:10 "Have all the **s** craftsmen
35:25 All the women who were **s** in
35:31 making him highly **s**,
35:35 has made these men highly **s**
36:4 Finally, all the **s** craftsmen
36:8 All the **s** craftsmen among the
1Sm 6:2 called for priests and people **s**
14:52 Whenever any warrior or any **s**
1Ki 5:6 You know we don't have any **s**
7:14 was a **s** bronze craftsman.
7:14 Hiram was highly **s**,
1Ch 5:18 They were **s** fighters who
8:40 sons were soldiers, **s** archers.
15:22 songs because he was **s** at it.
22:15 and men **s** in every kind of
25:7 **s** musicians for the LORD.
25:8 the **s** ⌊musicians⌋ along with
26:7 and Othni's **s** brothers Rephael,
26:8 and their relatives were **s** and
26:9 and relatives were 18 **s** men.
26:30 Hashabiah and his 1,700 **s**,
26:32 relatives were 2,700 **s** men,
28:21 You have with you every **s**
2Ch 2:7 with the **s** men whom my
2:8 are **s** Lebanese lumberjacks.
2:14 ⌊He can work⌋ with your **s**
2:14 workmen and the **s** workmen
34:12 who were **s** musicians,
Ecc 9:11 and **s** people don't necessarily
Sos 3:8 All of them are **s** in using
Isa 3:3 leaders, counselors, **s** workers,
Jer 9:17 for those who are the most **s**.
10:9 all made by **s** workers.
24:1 of Judah, the **s** workers,
50:9 will be like **s** soldiers who don't
Eze 21:31 who are **s** in destruction.
27:8 Your own **s** people were your
Hos 8:6 **S** workers made it.
Mic 7:3 Their hands are **s** in doing evil.
Luk 12:42 **s** manager that the master will
1Co 3:10 As a **s** and experienced
Rev 18:22 **S** craftsman will never be

skillet (2)

Lev 2:7 grain offering is prepared in a **s**,
7:9 in an oven or prepared in a **s**

skillful (3)

Psa 45:1 My tongue is a pen for a **s**
Ecc 4:4 work and **s** effort come from
Isa 40:20 rot and search out **s** craftsmen

skillfully (2)

Psa 139:15 when I was being **s** woven in
Hos 13:2 These idols are **s** made.

skills (6)

Exo 36:1 the necessary **s** and talents.
36:2 the LORD had given these **s**
Jos 24:12 your battle **s** or fighting ability.
2Ch 30:22 to all the Levites who had the **s**
Job 6:13 Haven't my **s** been taken away
Psa 107:27 and all their **s** as sailors

skimming (1)

Isa 18:2 boats made of reeds ⌊**s**⌋ over

skin (116)

Gen 27:11 and my **s** is smooth.
27:12 My father will feel ⌊my **s**⌋ and
27:21 here so that I can feel your **s**,
27:22 Isaac felt ⌊his **s**⌋. "The voice is
Exo 4:6 it had a **s** disease.
29:14 But burn the bull's meat, **s**,
Lev 1:6 **S** the burnt offering,
4:11 will take the entire bull (the **s**,
7:8 The **s** of the burnt offering
8:17 the rest of the bull, its **s**, meat,
9:11 and the **s** outside the camp.
13:2 or an irritated area on his **s** that
13:2 into an infectious **s** disease,
13:3 deeper than the rest of his **s**,
13:3 it is an infectious **s** disease.
13:4 deeper than the rest of the **s**,
13:8 It is an infectious **s** disease.
13:9 has an infectious **s** disease,
13:11 he has a chronic **s** disease.
13:12 If **s** disease develops and
13:15 It is an infectious **s** disease.
13:18 "If a boil on the **s** has healed
13:20 deeper than the rest of the **s**
13:20 An infectious **s** disease has
13:21 not deeper than the rest of the **s**
13:22 him unclean. It is a **s** disease.
13:24 "If anyone has a burn on his **s**
13:25 deeper than the rest of the **s**,
13:25 an infectious **s** disease has
13:25 It is an infectious **s** disease.
13:26 not deeper than the rest of the **s**
13:27 It is an infectious **s** disease.
13:30 deeper than the rest of the **s**
13:31 deeper than the rest of the **s**
13:32 deeper than the rest of the **s**,
13:34 scab has not spread on the **s**
13:34 deeper than the rest of the **s**,
13:36 If the scab has spread on the **s**,
13:38 has white irritated areas of **s**,
13:39 If the irritated areas on the **s** are
13:39 a rash has developed on the **s**.
13:42 a **s** disease is developing in
13:43 a **s** disease somewhere else
13:44 with an infectious **s** disease.
13:44 because of the **s** disease
13:45 with a **s** disease must wear
13:46 as they have the **s** disease,
14:2 person clean after a **s** disease.
14:20 and the person who had the **s**
14:32 has an infectious **s** disease
14:56 and for **s** diseases where there
14:57 These instructions for **s**
16:27 The **s**, meat, and excrement
21:20 defective sight, **s** diseases,
22:4 of Aaron who has a **s** disease
Num 5:2 who has a serious **s** disease
12:10 with an infectious **s** disease.
19:5 Then the entire cow (the **s**,
Dtr 24:8 of serious **s** diseases.
28:40 but no olive oil to rub on your **s**,

2Sm 3:29 oozing sores and **s** diseases,
2Ki 5:1 but he had a **s** disease.
5:3 cure him of his **s** disease."
5:6 Cure him of his **s** disease."
5:7 that I can cure his **s** disease!
5:10 and your **s** will be healthy and
5:11 and heal the **s** disease.
5:14 His **s** became healthy again
5:14 again like a little child's **s**.
5:27 Naaman's **s** disease will cling
5:27 that made his **s** as flaky as
7:3 Four men with **s** diseases
7:8 When the men with **s** diseases
15:5 with a **s** disease that lasted
2Ch 26:19 a **s** disease broke out on his
26:20 a **s** disease was on his
26:21 King Uzziah had a **s** disease
26:21 Since he had a **s** disease,
26:23 "He had a **s** disease."
29:34 needed more help to **s** all
Job 2:4 the LORD, "**S** for skin!
2:4 the LORD, "Skin for **s**!
7:5 My **s** is crusted over with
10:11 Didn't you dress me in **s** and
16:15 sewn sackcloth over my **s**,
18:13 His **s** is eaten away by
19:20 I am **s** and bones, and I have
19:20 only by the **s** of my teeth.
19:26 Even after my **s** has been
30:30 My **s** turns dark and peels.
41:13 Who can **s** its hide?
Psa 102:5 I am nothing but **s** and bones
Isa 17:4 they will become **s** and bones.
Jer 13:23 change the color of their **s**
Lam 3:4 flesh and my **s** waste away.
4:8 Their **s** has shriveled on their
5:10 Our **s** is as hot as an oven from
Eze 37:6 and cover you with **s**.
37:8 and **s** covered them.
Mic 3:2 You strip the **s** off my people
3:3 You strip off their **s**.
6:15 you won't rub the oil on your **s**.
Mat 8:2 A man with a serious **s**
8:3 his **s** disease went away,
10:8 cleanse those with **s** diseases,
11:5 those with **s** diseases are
26:6 had suffered from a **s** disease.
Mar 1:40 Then a man with a serious **s**
1:42 his **s** disease went away,
14:3 had suffered from a **s** disease.
Luk 4:27 many people with **s** diseases
5:12 with a serious **s** disease.
5:13 his **s** disease went away.
7:22 those with **s** diseases are
17:12 ten men with a **s** disease met
Act 19:12 that had touched Paul's **s**

skinks (1)

Lev 11:30 geckos, monitors, lizards, **s**,

skinned (1)

2Ch 35:11 while the Levites **s** the lambs.

skinny (4)

Gen 41:3 These cows were sickly and **s**.
41:4 that were sickly and **s** ate
Eze 34:20 the fat sheep and the **s** sheep.
34:21 You fat sheep push the **s**

skins (19)

Gen 3:21 made clothes from animal **s**
27:16 She put the **s** from the young
Exo 25:5 rams' **s** dyed red, fine leather,
26:14 Make a cover of rams' **s** that
35:7 rams' **s** dyed red, fine leather,
35:23 goats' hair, rams' **s** dyed red,
36:19 out of rams' **s** that had been
39:34 cover made of rams' **s** dyed red,
Num 6:4 not even grape seeds or **s**.
Mat 9:17 If they do, the **s** burst,
9:17 and the **s** are ruined.
9:17 pour new wine into fresh **s**,
Mar 2:22 the wine will make the **s** burst,
2:22 and both the wine and the **s**
2:22 is to be poured into fresh **s**."
Luk 5:37 wine will make the **s** burst.
5:37 and the **s** will be ruined.
5:38 is to be poured into fresh **s**.
Heb 11:37 Some wore the **s** of sheep and

skip (2)

Psa 29:6 He makes Lebanon **s** along
Isa 13:21 and wild goats will **s** about.

skirt (1)

Isa 47:2 Take off your **s**. Uncover your

skull (8)

Jdg 9:53 on the head and cracked his **s**.
2Ki 9:35 any of her body except her **s**,
Job 16:12 the neck and smashed ⌊my **s**⌋.
Isa 48:4 gets through your thick **s**.
Mat 27:33 means "the place of the **s**").
Mar 15:22 means "the place of the **s**").
Luk 23:33 to the place called The **S**,
Jon 19:17 to a location called The **S**.

skulls (2)

Jer 2:16 have cracked your **s**,
48:45 of the people of Moab and the **s**

sky (137)

Gen 1:8 was above⌋ the horizon **s**.
1:9 "Let the water under the **s**
1:14 "Let there be lights in the **s** to
1:15 They will be lights in the **s** to
1:17 God put them in the **s** to give
1:20 fly through the **s** over the earth.
1:26 in the sea, the birds in the **s**,
1:28 in the sea, the birds in the **s**,
1:30 every bird in the **s**,
6:17 under the **s** — every living,
7:11 burst open. The **s** opened,
7:19 everywhere under the **s**.
8:2 The deep springs and the **s**
11:4 a tower with its top in the **s**.
15:5 "Now look up at the **s** and
22:17 numerous as the stars in the **s**
26:4 numerous as the stars in the **s**
27:28 God give you dew from the **s**,
27:39 and the dew from the **s** above.
Exo 9:22 "Lift your hand toward the **s**,
9:23 lifted his staff toward the **s**,
10:21 "Lift your hand toward the **s**,
10:22 lifted his hand toward the **s**,
20:4 represent any creature in the **s**,
24:10 clear and blue as the **s** itself.
32:13 numerous as the stars in the **s**.
Dtr 1:10 numerous as the stars in the **s**.
4:11 with flames shooting into the **s**.
4:19 serve what you see in the **s** —
5:8 represent any creature in the **s**,
10:14 Remember that the **s**,
10:22 numerous as the stars in the **s**.
11:11 watered by rain from the **s**.
11:17 He'll shut the **s** so that there'll
11:21 as there's a **s** above the earth.
28:23 The **s** above will look like
28:24 the **s** until you're destroyed.
28:62 numerous as the stars in the **s**.
Jos 10:13 stopped in the middle of the **s**,
Jdg 5:4 the **s** poured, the clouds burst,
2Sm 21:10 of the harvest until the **s** rained
1Ki 8:35 "When the **s** is shut and there's
18:45 Gradually, the **s** grew darker
2Ki 7:2 rain through windows in the **s**?"
7:19 rain through windows in the **s**?"
1Ch 27:23 numerous as the stars in the **s**.
2Ch 6:26 "When the **s** is shut and there's
7:13 I may shut the **s** so that there is
Neh 9:23 numerous as the stars in the **s**.
Job 20:6 If his height reaches to the **s**
26:13 his wind the **s** was cleared.
35:11 wiser than the birds in the **s**?'
38:33 Do you know the laws of the **s**
Psa 19:1 and the **s** displays what his
68:8 the earth quaked and the **s**
77:17 The **s** thundered. Even your
77:18 your thunder rumbled in the **s**.
107:26 aboard ship rose toward the **s**.
147:8 He covers the **s** with clouds.
148:4 and the water above the **s**.
Pro 23:5 like an eagle flying into the **s**.
30:19 making its way through the **s**,
Isa 13:10 The stars in the **s** and their
24:18 The floodgates in the **s** will be
34:4 All the stars in the **s** will rot.
40:12 of his hand or measured the **s**
40:22 He stretches out the **s** like a
40:26 Look at the **s** and see.
51:6 Look at the **s**. Look at the earth
51:6 The **s** will vanish like smoke.
55:10 snow come down from the **s**.
Jer 4:23 I see the **s**. Its lights are gone.
4:28 and the **s** will grow black.
8:2 and all the stars in the **s**.
10:2 frightened by the signs in the **s**
10:13 and the water in the **s**
51:16 the water in the **s** roars.
Lam 4:19 faster than eagles in the **s**.
Eze 1:1 the Chebar River, the **s** opened,
32:7 I will cover the **s** and darken
32:8 shining in the **s** above you.
Dan 4:11 and tall enough to reach the **s**.
4:15 wet with the dew from the **s**.
4:20 and tall enough to reach the **s**.
4:22 mighty until you reached the **s**.
4:23 wet with the dew from the **s**.
4:25 The dew from the **s** will make
4:33 Dew from the **s** made his body
5:21 wet with dew from the **s**.
Hos 2:21 "I will speak to the **s**,
Joe 2:10 presence, and the **s** shakes.
2:30 I will work miracles in the **s**
3:16 The **s** and the earth will shake.
Nah 3:16 than there are stars in the **s**.
Zep 1:3 put an end to the birds in the **s**,
1:5 worship all the stars in the **s**
Hag 1:10 It is because of you that the **s**
2:6 I am going to shake the **s** and
Zec 5:9 carried the basket into the **s**.
8:12 The **s** will produce its dew.
Mat 16:2 be fine because the **s** is red.
16:3 today because the **s** is red
16:3 the appearance of the **s**,
24:29 the stars will fall from the **s**,
24:30 Son of Man will appear in the **s**.
24:30 coming on the clouds in the **s**
24:31 every direction under the **s**,
Mar 13:25 the stars will fall from the **s**,
13:27 every direction under the **s**,
Luk 12:56 the appearance of earth and **s**.
17:24 one end of the **s** to the other.
17:29 fire and sulfur rained from the **s**
21:11 signs will come from the **s**.
Jon 1:51 You will see the **s** open and
Act 1:10 They were staring into the **s** as
1:11 standing here looking at the **s**?
2:2 blowing wind came from the **s**
2:19 I will work miracles in the **s**
4:24 you made the **s**, the land,
10:11 He saw the **s** open and
10:16 was quickly taken into the **s**.
11:5 by its four corners from the **s**.
11:10 pulled back into the **s** again.
14:15 The living God made the **s**,
26:13 The light came from the **s** and
Heb 11:12 numerous as the stars in the **s**
12:26 only the earth but also the **s**."
Rev 6:13 The stars fell from the **s** to the
6:14 The **s** vanished like a scroll
8:10 like a torch fell from the **s**.
9:1 had fallen to earth from the **s**.
11:6 have authority to shut the **s**
12:1 sign appeared in the **s**:
12:3 Another sign appeared in the **s**:
12:4 one-third of the stars in the **s**
16:21 fell from the **s** on people.
20:11 The earth and the **s** fled from

sky-high (2)

Dtr 1:28 The cities are big with **s** walls!
9:1 with big cities that have **s**

slabs (1)

Jos 8:32 of Israel he wrote on stone **s**

slain (1)

Rev 5:12 "The lamb who was s

slander (15)

Job 5:15 ⌊other people⌋ from their s
Psa 15:3 The one who does not s with
44:16 of those who insult and s us,
50:20 You s your own mother's son.
Pro 10:18 Whoever spreads s is a fool.
30:10 "Do not s a slave to his master.
Eze 22:9 Some of your people s.
Luk 6:22 and s you because you are
Act 6:11 heard him s Moses and God."
Rom 3:8 Some s us and claim that this
2Co 12:20 ambition, s, gossip, arrogance,
Jas 4:11 Those who s and judge other
4:11 and judge other believers s
1Pe 2:1 and every kind of s.
Rev 2:9 who claim to be Jews s you.

slandered (4)

2Ki 19:6 king's assistants s me.
Isa 37:6 king's assistants s me.
65:7 on the mountains and s me
2Co 6:8 as we are s and honored,

slanderers (3)

Psa 49:5 when s surround me with evil?
140:11 Do not let s prosper on earth.
Rom 1:30 s, haters of God, haughty,

slandering (5)

2Ki 19:22 Whom are you defying and s?
Isa 37:23 Whom are you defying and s?
Jer 6:28 They go around s.
9:4 Every neighbor goes around s.
Jas 4:11 and sisters, stop s each other.

slanderous (3)

Pro 17:4 A liar opens his ears to a s
Dan 3:29 who say anything s about
2Ti 3:3 They will be s, be brutal, and

slanders (1)

Psa 101:5 who secretly s his neighbor.

slapped (6)

Job 16:10 In scorn they s my cheeks.
Psa 3:7 You have s all my enemies in
Mat 26:67 and some of them s him.
Mar 14:65 Even the guards took him and s
Jon 18:22 standing near Jesus s his face
19:3 of the Jews!" and s his face.

slaps (2)

Mat 5:39 If someone s you on your right
2Co 11:20 you around, or s your faces,

slash (1)

Lev 19:28 Never s your body to mourn the

slashes (2)

Job 16:13 He s open my kidneys without
Psa 129:3 made long s ⌊like furrows⌋."

slashing (1)

Lev 21:5 your beards, or s your bodies.

slaughter (51)

Exo 12:6 of Israel must s their animals.
29:11 S the bull in the LORD's
29:16 S it, take the blood, and throw
29:20 S it, take some of the blood,
Lev 1:5 Then s the bull in the LORD's
1:11 S it in the LORD's presence on
3:2 Then s it at the entrance to the
3:8 S it in front of the tent of
3:13 S it in front of the tent of
4:4 He will then s the bull in the
4:15 One of them will s it in the
4:24 hand on the goat's head and s
4:29 on the animal's head and s
4:33 on the animal's head and s
14:13 He will s the lamb in the holy
14:19 he will s the burnt offering.
Lev 14:25 He will s the lamb as a guilt
16:11 He will then s it as his own
16:15 "Next, Aaron will s the goat for
22:28 Never s a cow or a sheep and
Dtr 12:15 you may s and eat as much
12:21 you may s an animal from the
16:2 S an animal from your flock or
16:4 morning any of the meat you s
16:5 You're not allowed to s the
16:6 Instead, s your animals for
1Sm 14:14 In their first s Jonathan and his
2Sm 2:26 "Should this s go on forever?
1Ki 2:32 repay him for the s he caused.
2Ch 35:6 S the Passover lamb,
Psa 37:14 to s those who are decent.
Pro 24:11 those staggering toward their s.
Isa 5:7 for justice but saw only s,
14:21 Prepare a place to s their sons
22:13 s cattle, and butcher sheep.
30:25 the day of the great s comes,
34:6 a huge s in the land of Edom.
53:7 He was led like a lamb to the s.
57:5 You s children in the valleys
Jer 7:32 it will be known as S Valley.
11:19 a trusting lamb brought to the s.
12:3 Prepare them for the day of s.
19:6 it will be called S Valley.
Eze 21:15 I have appointed my sword to s
40:42 that were used to s animals
Hab 2:8 will loot you because of the s
2:12 the one who builds a city by s
2:17 will terrify you because of the s
Act 8:32 was led like a lamb to the s.
Jas 5:5 yourselves for the day of s.
Rev 6:4 to make people s one another.

slaughtered (62)

Lev 4:29 for burnt offerings are s.
6:25 The offering for sin must be s
6:25 where the burnt offering is s.
7:2 It must be s in the same place
7:2 where the burnt offering is s.
8:15 When it was s, Moses took the
8:19 Moses s it and threw the blood
8:23 Moses s it, took some of the
9:8 Aaron came to the altar and s
9:12 He s the animal for the burnt
9:15 people's offering for sin and s it.
9:18 He s the bull and the ram for
Num 14:16 so he s them in the desert.'
19:3 camp and s in his presence.
Jdg 15:8 them violently and s them.
20:21 They s 22,000 of Israel's men.
20:25 This time they s 18,000 men
20:35 On that day the Israelites s
20:42 Israel s whoever came out of
1Ki 18:40 Kishon River and s them there.
2Ki 10:7 they s all 70 heirs.
10:14 ⌊Jehu's men⌋ captured and s
23:20 He s all the priests of the
25:7 They s Zedekiah's sons as he
2Ch 18:2 Ahab s many sheep and cattle
29:22 So they s the bulls,
29:22 Then they s the rams and
29:22 After that, they s the lambs and
29:24 The priests s the goats and
30:15 They s the Passover lamb on
35:1 The Passover lamb was s on
35:11 They s the Passover lambs.
Psa 44:22 are thought of as sheep to be s.
78:31 killed their strongest men and s
78:51 He s every firstborn in Egypt,
Pro 7:22 like a steer on its way to be s,
Isa 34:2 has handed them over to be s.
65:12 All of you will bow to be s.
Jer 12:3 them away like sheep to be s.
25:34 time has come for you to be s.
39:6 The king of Babylon s
39:6 He also s all the leaders of
41:7 and his men s them and threw
48:15 Its finest young men will be s,"
50:27 Let them go to be s.
51:40 take them to be s like lambs,
52:10 The king of Babylon s
52:10 He also s all the officials of
Lam 2:21 You s them without any pity.
Eze 16:21 You s my children and
26:15 people are wounded and s.
40:39 tables the animals were s
40:41 on which they s animals.
Hos 1:4 for the people they s at Jezreel.
Oba 1:9 on Esau's mountain will be s.
Zec 11:4 sheep that are about to be s.
11:7 of the sheep that were to be s
Rom 8:36 thought of as sheep to be s."
Rev 5:6 looked like he had been s.
5:9 because you were s.
6:9 souls of those who had been s
13:8 to the lamb who was s before

slaughtering (3)

1Sm 25:33 me from s people today
1Ki 2:9 old man into his grave by s
Eze 44:11 have served in the temple by s

slaughters (4)

Lev 4:24 presence where he s animals
4:33 slaughter it where he s animals
14:13 in the holy place where he s
17:3 Any Israelite who s a bull,

slave (131)

Gen 9:25 be the lowest s to his brothers.
9:26 Canaan will be his s.
9:27 Canaan will be his s."
16:1 an Egyptian s named Hagar.
16:2 don't you sleep with my s?
16:3 Sarai took her Egyptian s Hagar
16:5 I know that I gave my s to you,
16:6 Sarai, "Here, she's your s.
16:8 He said, "Hagar, Sarai's s,
21:10 "Get rid of this s and her son,
21:12 upset about the boy and your s.
25:12 Egyptian s Hagar and Abraham.
29:24 (Laban had given his s Zilpah
29:24 to his daughter Leah as her s.)
29:29 (Laban had given his s Bilhah
29:29 his daughter Rachel as her s.)
30:4 So she gave him her s Bilhah
30:7 Rachel's s Bilhah became
30:9 she took her s Zilpah and gave
30:10 Leah's s Zilpah gave birth to a
30:12 Leah's s Zilpah gave birth to
30:18 reward because I gave my s
35:25 The sons of Rachel's s Bilhah
35:26 The sons of Leah's s Zilpah
39:17 "The Hebrew s you brought
39:19 "This is what your s did to me,"
41:12 a s of the captain of the guard,
44:10 who has the cup will be my s,
44:17 who had the cup will be my s.
44:33 let me stay and be your s
49:15 and will become a s laborer.
Exo 1:11 So the Egyptians put s drivers
2:5 plants and sent her s girl
3:7 out because of the s drivers.
5:6 to the s drivers and foremen:
5:10 The s drivers and foreman
5:13 The s drivers kept hurrying
5:14 Pharaoh's s drivers had placed
5:14 The s drivers beat the foremen
12:44 "Any male s you have bought
20:17 his male or female s,
21:2 you buy a Hebrew s,
21:2 he will be your s for six years.
21:4 and the s must leave by
21:6 Then he will be his s for life.
21:20 owner hits his male or female s
21:20 a stick so that the s dies from
21:21 But if the s gets up in a day or
21:21 The s is his property.
21:26 owner hits his male or female s
21:26 in the eye and the s is blinded,
21:26 he must let the s go free to
21:27 tooth of his male or female s,
21:27 he must let the s go free to
21:32 bull gores a male or female s,
22:3 he must be sold ⌊as a s⌋ to
Lev 19:20 a female s who is engaged
19:20 pay a fine because she is a s.
22:11 But if a priest buys a s,
22:11 the s and anyone born in his

Lev 25:10 Every s will be freed in order to
25:13 "In this jubilee year every s
25:39 don't work him like a s.
Dtr 5:21 his male or female s,
15:16 But suppose a male s says to
15:17 and he will be your s for life.
15:17 Do the same to a female s ⌊if
15:18 If you have to let your s go free,
21:14 mistreat her as if she were a s,
23:15 If a s escapes from his master
24:7 treated the other person like a s
Jdg 9:18 is the son of my father's s girl,
1Sm 30:13 the s of an Amalekite,"
2Sm 6:20 before the eyes of the s girls
6:21 "I didn't dance in front of the s
6:22 I will be honored by these s
1Ki 9:21 drafted them for s labor.
14:10 whether s or freeman in Israel.
21:21 whether s or freeman in Israel.
2Ki 9:8 whether s or freeman in Israel.
14:26 No s or free person could help
1Ch 2:34 an Egyptian s named Jarha.
2Ch 8:8 drafted them for s labor.
Job 3:18 the shouting of the s driver.
3:19 There the s is free from his
7:2 Like a s, he longs for shade.
19:16 I call my s, but he doesn't
41:4 take it as your permanent s?
Psa 105:17 who was sold as a s.
Pro 11:29 that stubborn fool becomes a s
12:9 unimportant and have a s than
12:24 but lazy hands do s labor.
17:2 A wise s will become master
19:10 much less a s ruling princes.
22:7 a borrower is a s to a lender.
29:19 A s cannot be disciplined with
29:21 Pamper a s from childhood,
30:10 "Do not slander a s to his
30:10 The s will curse you,
30:22 a s when he becomes king,
Isa 49:7 by the nation, to the s of rulers:
Jer 2:20 said that you wouldn't be a s.
27:7 kings will make him their s.
34:9 to keep another Jew as a s.
Mat 10:24 Nor is a s better than his owner.
10:25 teacher and a s like his owner.
20:27 among you will be your s.
Mar 10:44 you will be a s for everyone.
Luk 7:2 officer's valuable s was sick
15:29 I've worked like a s for you.
Jon 8:34 lives a sinful life is a s to sin.
8:35 A s doesn't live in the home
Rom 6:16 if you offer to be someone's s,
7:14 nature, sold as a s to sin.
1Co 7:21 Were you a s when you were
7:22 called you when you were a s,
7:22 were called, you are Christ's s.
9:19 I have made myself a s for all
9:27 and make it my s so that
12:13 are Jewish or Greek, s or free,
Gal 4:1 he is no better off than a s,
4:22 one by a woman who was a s
4:23 Now, the son of the s woman
4:30 "Get rid of the s woman and
4:30 because the son of the s
4:31 we are not children of a s
Eph 6:9 Don't threaten a s. You know
Col 3:11 s, or free person. Instead,
Phm 1:16 no longer as a s but better than
1:16 a slave but better than a s — as
2Pe 2:19 A person is a s to whatever he

slavery (25)

Gen 45:4 brother you sold into s in Egypt!
Exo 6:5 whom the Egyptians hold in s,
6:6 and I will free you from s.
9:2 continue to hold them ⌊in s⌋,
13:3 you left Egypt, the land of s.
13:14 to bring us out of s in Egypt.
20:2 brought you out of s in Egypt.
21:7 a man sells his daughter into s,
Dtr 5:6 brought you out of s in Egypt.
6:12 brought you out of s in Egypt.
7:8 He freed you from s under
8:14 brought you out of s in Egypt.
13:5 of Egypt and freed you from s.
Dtr 13:10 brought you out of s in Egypt.
24:18 your God freed you from s.
Jos 24:17 our ancestors out of s in Egypt.
Jdg 6:8 I took you away from s.
Ezr 9:9 hasn't abandoned us in our s.
Neh 9:17 take them back to s ⌊in Egypt⌋.
Isa 14:3 from the hard s you were forced
Jer 2:14 Were they born into s?
Mic 6:4 of Egypt and freed you from s.
Act 7:9 They sold him into s,
Rom 8:21 it would also be set free from s
Gal 4:24 Her children are born into s.

slave's (3)

Gen 21:10 because this s son must never
21:13 Besides, I will make the s son
Exo 21:32 of silver to the s master,

slaves (129)

Gen 12:16 male and female s,
15:13 where they will be s,
20:14 and male and female s and
20:17 and his female s so that they
24:35 male and female s,
30:43 male and female s,
31:33 and into the tent of the two s.
32:5 and male and female s.
32:22 his two s and his eleven
33:1 Leah, Rachel, and the two s.
33:2 He put the s and their children
33:6 Then the s and their children
43:18 our donkeys, and make us s."
44:9 rest of us will become your s."
44:16 Now all of us are your s,
47:19 Then we will be Pharaoh's s
47:25 are willing to be Pharaoh's s."
50:18 "We are your s!" they said.
Exo 1:13 the Israelites to work hard as s.
2:23 groaned because they were s.
11:5 children of female s who
14:5 We've lost our s because
20:10 your male and female s,
21:7 not go free the way male s do.
23:12 The s born in your household
Lev 25:6 your male and female s,
25:42 They must never be sold as s.
25:44 may have male and female s,
25:46 You may work them as s.
26:13 so that you are no longer s
Dtr 5:14 your male and female s,
5:14 male and female s can rest as
5:15 Remember that you were s in
6:21 "We were Pharaoh's s in Egypt,
12:12 male and female s,
12:18 male and female s,
15:12 or women are sold to you as s,
15:12 they will be your s for six
15:15 Remember that you were s in
16:11 male and female s,
16:12 that you were s in Egypt,
16:14 male and female s,
24:18 Remember that you were s in
24:22 that you were s in Egypt.
28:68 will try to sell yourselves as s
32:36 neither s nor free people.
1Sm 8:16 take your male and female s,
17:9 then we will be your s.
17:9 you will be our s and serve us."
1Ki 2:39 two of Shimei's s fled to Gath's
2:39 told that his s were in Gath,
2:40 in Gath to search for his s.
2:40 went to Gath and got his s.
9:21 (They are still ⌊s⌋ today.)
9:22 make any of the Israelites s.
2Ki 4:1 to take my two children as s."
5:26 vineyards, sheep, cattle, or s?
2Ch 8:8 (They are still ⌊s⌋ today.)
8:9 make any of the Israelites s
36:20 executed to Babylon to be s
Ezr 9:8 opportunities while we were s.
9:9 We are s, but our God hasn't
Neh 5:5 and daughters to become s.
5:5 have already become s.
9:36 We're s! In the land you gave
9:36 good things. But now we're s!
Est 7:4 had only been sold as s,
Job 19:15 My female s consider me to be
Pro 31:15 portions of food to her female s.
Ecc 2:7 I bought male and female s.
2:7 s were born in my household.
10:7 I have seen s sitting on horses
10:7 people going on foot like s.
Isa 14:2 nations as male and female s
24:2 male s and masters,
24:2 female s and masters,
Jer 2:14 "Are the people of Israel s?
25:14 and great kings will make s
34:8 promised to free their s.
34:9 supposed to free his Hebrew s,
34:10 to free their male and female s
34:10 not to keep them as s anymore.
34:11 and made them their s again.
34:13 where they were s.
34:16 male and female s that you had
34:16 your male and female s again.
Lam 5:8 S rule us. There is no one to
Eze 27:13 They exchanged s and bronze
34:27 the people who made them s.
Zec 2:9 and their own s will loot them.
Jon 8:33 we've never been anyone's s.
13:16 I can guarantee this truth: S are
Act 7:6 there would make them s
Rom 6:6 this we are no longer s to sin.
6:17 You were s to sin.
6:18 you were made s who do what
6:19 all the parts of your body as s
6:19 of your body as s that do what
6:20 When you were s to sin,
6:22 sin and have become God's s.
8:15 the spirit of s that leads you
1Co 7:23 Don't become anyone's s.
2Co 11:20 When someone makes you s,
Gal 3:28 nor Greeks, s nor free people,
4:3 we were s to the principles of
4:7 So you are no longer s but
4:8 you were s to things which are
4:9 become their s all over again?
4:25 she and her children are s.
5:1 and don't become s again.
Eph 6:5 S, obey your earthly masters
6:6 But obey like s who belong to
6:8 whether we're s or free people.
6:9 Those who own s should also
Col 3:22 S, always obey your earthly
4:1 be just and fair to your s
1Ti 6:1 All s who believe must give
6:2 S whose masters also believe
6:2 As a result, believers who are s
Tit 2:9 Tell s who are believers to
2:10 Instead, tell s to show their
3:3 We were s to many kinds of
Heb 2:15 those who were s all their lives
1Pe 2:18 S, place yourselves under the
2Pe 2:19 themselves are s to corruption.
Rev 6:15 and all the s and free people
13:16 free people and s — to be
18:13 wagons, s (that is, humans).
19:18 and all free people and s,

sledge (3)

Job 41:30 like a threshing s on the mud.
Isa 28:27 cumin isn't threshed with a s,
41:15 a new threshing s with sharp,

sledges (1)

Amo 1:3 with iron-spiked threshing s.

sleep (62)

Gen 2:21 him to fall into a deep s.
15:12 a deep s — a dreadful,
16:2 Why don't you s with my
28:16 Then Jacob woke up from his s
29:21 I want to s with her."
30:3 S with her. She can have
30:16 "You are to s with me,"
31:40 and I lost a lot of s.
38:8 "Go s with your brother's
38:16 "Come on, let's s together!"
38:16 will you pay to s with me?"
Exo 22:27 What else will he s in?
Dtr 21:13 After that, you may s with her.
22:13 marry a woman, s with her,

Dtr 25:5 must marry her and **s** with her.
Jdg 15:1 He said, "I'm going to **s** with
16:19 Delilah put Samson to **s** on her
1Sm 26:12 made them fall into a deep **s**.
2Sm 16:21 Ahithophel told Absalom, "**S**
1Ki 19:6 and went to **s** again.
Est 6:1 That night the king could not **s**.
Job 4:13 when deep **s** falls on people,
14:12 He is not awakened from his **s**.
33:15 when people fall into a deep **s**,
33:15 when they **s** on their beds,
Psa 3:5 I lie down and **s**. I wake up
76:6 riders and horses were put to **s**.
127:2 to those he loves while they **s**.
Pro 3:24 your **s** will be sweet.
4:16 Wicked people cannot **s**
4:16 and they are robbed of their **s**
6:9 will you get up from your **s**?
6:10 "Just a little **s**, just a little
19:15 throws one into a deep **s**,
20:13 Do not love **s** or you will end
24:33 "Just a little **s**, just a little
Ecc 5:12 The **s** of working people is
5:12 have will not allow them to **s**.
8:16 going without **s** day and night),
Sos 5:2 I **s**, but my mind is awake.
7:9 the lips of those about to **s**.
Isa 5:27 None of them slumber or **s**.
29:10 out on you a spirit of deep **s**.
56:10 dreaming; they love to **s**.
Jer 31:26 My **s** had been pleasant.
51:39 They will fall into a deep **s** and
51:57 They will fall into a deep **s** and
Eze 34:25 wilderness and **s** in the woods.
Dan 6:18 He couldn't get to **s**.
Amo 2:7 Father and son **s** with the
6:4 it will be for those who **s**
Jnh 1:6 and asked, "How can you **s**?
Nah 3:18 have fallen into a deep **s**.
Mat 8:20 Son of Man has nowhere to **s**."
26:45 "You might as well **s** now.
Mar 14:41 "You might as well **s** now.
Luk 9:58 Son of Man has nowhere to **s**."
Act 20:9 Finally, overcome by **s**,
Rom 11:8 given them a spirit of deep **s**.
2Co 11:27 I've often gone without **s**,
1Th 5:7 People who **s**, sleep at night;
5:7 People who sleep, **s** at night;

sleeper (1)

Eph 5:14 why it says: "Wake up, **s**!

sleeping (23)

Gen 2:21 While the man was **s**,
1Sm 2:22 all Israel and that they were **s**
2Sm 4:7 house while Ishbosheth was **s**
1Ki 18:27 Maybe he's **s**, and you have to
Job 3:13 I would now be **s** peacefully.
Psa 44:23 Why are you **s**, O Lord?
78:65 up like one who had been **s**,
Isa 51:20 They lie **s** at every street
Dan 12:2 Many **s** in the ground will wake
Zec 4:1 wake up someone who is **s**.
Mat 8:24 Yet, Jesus was **s**.
9:24 She's **s**." But they laughed at
28:13 his body while they were **s**.
Mar 4:38 But he was **s** on a cushion in
5:39 child isn't dead. She's just **s**."
14:37 to Peter, "Simon, are you **s**?
Luk 8:52 She's not dead. She's just **s**."
9:32 men with him were **s** soundly.
22:46 said to them, "Why are you **s**?
Jon 11:11 "Our friend Lazarus is **s**,
11:12 "Lord, if he's **s**, he'll get well."
11:13 meant that Lazarus was only **s**.
Act 12:6 Peter was **s** between two

sleepless (1)

2Co 6:5 **s** nights, and lack of food.

sleeps (4)

Lev 14:47 Whoever **s** or eats in the house
Psa 121:4 of Israel never rests or **s**.
Pro 10:5 Whoever **s** at harvest time
Mar 4:27 He **s** at night and is awake

sleeves (3)

Gen 37:3 a special robe with long **s**.
37:23 of his special robe with long **s**.
37:32 the special robe with long **s**

slept (22)

Gen 6:4 when the sons of God **s** with
16:4 He **s** with Hagar, and she
29:23 Jacob **s** with her. When morning
29:30 Jacob **s** with Rachel too.
30:4 and Jacob **s** with her.
38:2 He married her and **s** with her.
38:9 so whenever he **s** with his
38:18 Then he **s** with her,
Dtr 22:14 But when I **s** with her,
Jdg 16:1 There he saw a prostitute and **s**
Rut 4:13 He **s** with her, and the LORD
1Sm 9:25 roof for Saul, and he **s** there.
2Sm 11:9 But Uriah **s** at the entrance of
16:22 and he **s** with his father's
20:3 them but no longer **s** with them.
1Ki 19:5 Then he lay down and **s** under
1Ch 2:21 Afterwards, Hezron **s** with the
7:23 Then he **s** with his wife,
Isa 8:3 I **s** with the prophet.
Eze 23:44 Men **s** with her. They slept with
23:44 They **s** with those sinful
23:44 just as they **s** with a prostitute.

slice (1)

1Sm 30:12 They gave him a **s** of fig cake

slices (2)

Sos 4:3 veil are like **s** of pomegranate.
6:7 veil are like **s** of pomegranate.

slime (1)

Isa 57:20 its water throws up mud and **s**.

slimy (1)

Psa 58:8 that leaves behind a **s** trail

sling (8)

Jdg 20:16 Each could **s** a stone at a hair
1Sm 17:40 With a **s** in his hand,
17:49 hurled it from his **s**,
17:50 So using ⌊only⌋ a **s** and a
25:29 like stones thrown from a **s**.
1Ch 12:2 with bows and could **s** stones
Job 41:28 Stones from a **s** turn to dust
Pro 26:8 Like tying a stone to a **s**,

slings (3)

2Ki 3:25 attacked it with **s** and stones.
2Ch 26:14 armor, bows, and stones for **s**.
Zec 9:15 trample the stones used in **s**.

slip (6)

Dtr 32:35 In due time their foot will **s**,
2Sm 22:37 on so that my feet do not **s**.
Job 12:5 it is the fate of those who **s** up.
Psa 18:36 on so that my feet do not **s**.
37:31 in his heart. His feet do not **s**.
90:9 Indeed, all our days **s** away

slipped (5)

Psa 17:5 My feet have not **s**.
73:2 They had almost **s**
Gal 2:4 They **s** in as spies to learn
Jud 1:4 Some people have **s** in among
1:8 the people who **s** in among you

slippery (5)

1Sm 23:28 So that place was called **S**
Psa 35:6 Let their path be dark and **s** as
73:18 You put them in **s** places and
Isa 27:1 that **s** snake, Leviathan,
Jer 23:12 way will become like **s** paths

slipping (2)

Psa 94:18 "My feet are **s**," your mercy,
Jnh 2:7 "As my life was **s** away,

slips (1)

Psa 38:16 When my foot **s**, do not let

slithers (1)

Jer 46:22 hiss like a snake as it **s** away.

slope (11)

Num 34:11 continues along the eastern **s**
Jos 7:5 them from the city gate to the **s**
10:10 the road that goes to the **s**
10:11 from the Israelites down the **s**
15:8 of Ben Hinnom to the south **s**
15:10 Seir and over to the north **s**
18:12 goes up the **s** north of Jericho,
18:13 the border goes to the south **s**
18:16 to the south **s** of the city of
18:18 to the north side of the **s** facing
18:19 border continues to the north **s**

slopes (12)

Num 21:15 Arnon and the **s** of the valleys
Dtr 4:49 foot of the **s** of Mount Pisgah.
33:12 lives on the mountain **s**."
Jos 10:40 Negev, the foothills, and the **s**.
12:3 to the foot of the **s** of Pisgah.
12:8 foothills, plains, **s**, desert,
13:20 Beth Peor, the **s** of Pisgah,
2Sm 1:21 dew or rain on you or on your **s**,
2Ki 19:23 up the **s** of Lebanon.
Isa 11:14 They will swoop down on the **s**
37:24 up the **s** of Lebanon.
Jer 18:14 The rocky **s** of Lebanon are

slow (6)

2Ki 4:24 Don't **s** down unless I tell you."
Ecc 5:4 don't be **s** to keep it because
Luk 18:7 Is he **s** to help them?
24:25 You're so **s** to believe
Jas 1:19 be quick to listen, **s** to speak,
2Pe 3:9 The Lord isn't **s** to do what he

slowly (4)

Gen 33:14 I will **s** and gently guide the
Exo 4:10 I speak **s**, and I become
Pro 16:32 Better to get angry **s** than to be
Act 27:7 We were sailing **s** for a number

slows (1)

Heb 12:1 of everything that **s** us down,

slumber (3)

Pro 6:10 a little sleep, just a little **s**,
24:33 a little sleep, just a little **s**,
Isa 5:27 None of them **s** or sleep.

slumped (1)

2Ki 9:24 and he **s** over in his chariot.

sly (1)

Job 15:5 You choose ⌊to talk with⌋ a **s**

small (56)

Gen 19:20 enough to flee to, and it's **s**.
19:20 Isn't it **s**? Then my life will be
19:22 (The city is named Zoar [S].)
Exo 12:4 A household may be too **s** to
Num 11:7 (Manna was ⌊**s**⌋ like coriander
13:33 We felt as **s** as grasshoppers,
26:56 the tribes are large or **s**,
Jdg 9:53 Then a woman threw a **s**
2Sm 7:19 this you consider to be a **s** act,
11:21 throw a **s** millstone at him
1Ki 8:64 in front of the LORD was too **s**
10:17 He also made 300 **s** shields of
17:13 But first make a **s** loaf and
2Ki 4:10 Let's make a **s** room on the roof
6:1 we're staying is too **s** for us.
1Ch 16:19 a **s** group of foreigners living in
17:17 this you consider to be a **s** act,
2Ch 9:16 He also made 300 **s** shields of
14:8 who were armed with **s** shields
23:9 the spears and the **s**
24:24 had come with a **s** number
Job 8:7 the past will seem **s** compared
Psa 35:2 ⌊both⌋ **s** and large.
104:25 living things both large and **s**.
105:12 a **s** group of foreigners living in
Pro 30:24 Four things on earth are **s**,

Ecc 9:14 There was a **s** town with a few
Jer 46:3 your large and **s** shields ready;
Eze 17:24 and I make **s** trees grow tall.
23:24 you from all around with **s**
38:4 They will carry large and **s**
39:9 They will burn **s** and large
40:16 had **s** windows all around.
41:16 The doorposts, the **s** windows,
41:26 There were **s** windows and
Dan 8:9 one of the horns came a **s** horn.
Mic 4:13 many nations into **s** pieces.
5:2 are too **s** to be included among
Mat 15:34 "Seven, and a few **s** fish."
25:21 be trusted with a **s** amount.
25:23 be trusted with a **s** amount.
Mar 1:38 to the **s** towns that are nearby.
8:7 They also had a few **s** fish.
12:42 widow dropped in two **s** coins,
Luk 12:26 If you can't do a **s** thing like
19:3 But Zacchaeus was a **s** man,
21:2 widow drop in two **s** coins.
Jon 2:15 He made a whip from **s** ropes
6:9 bread and two **s** fish is here.
Act 27:16 side of a **s** island called Cauda,
2Co 9:6 will have a very **s** harvest.
Jas 3:4 Yet, by using **s** rudders,
3:5 way the tongue is a **s** part
Rev 10:2 He held a **s**, opened scroll in
10:9 him to give me the **s** scroll.
10:10 I took the **s** scroll from the

smaller (8)

Gen 1:16 to rule the day and the **s** light
Num 26:54 tribes and less land to **s** ones.
33:54 and less land to **s** ones.
35:8 tribes and fewer from **s** tribes."
Dtr 25:14 a larger one and a **s** one.
Eze 46:21 there was a **s** courtyard.
46:22 The **s** courtyards that were in
46:22 All four of the **s** courtyards in

smallest (9)

Dtr 7:7 You were the **s** of all nations.
1Sm 9:21 the **s** tribe of Israel.
2Ki 17:9 from the ⌊**s**⌋ watchtower to the
18:8 from the ⌊**s**⌋ watchtower
Isa 60:22 The **s** of them will become a
Jer 49:15 "Edom, I will make you the **s** of
Oba 1:2 will make you the **s** of nations.
Mat 13:32 It's one of the **s** seeds.
Mar 4:31 is one of the **s** seeds on earth.

smart (2)

Pro 23:4 Be **s** enough to stop.
Hos 13:13 but they are not **s** enough to

smarter (1)

Rom 12:16 Don't think that you are **s** than

smash (15)

Lev 11:35 If it is an oven or a stove, **s** it.
Dtr 7:5 **s** their sacred stones,
2Ki 8:12 **s** their little children,
Psa 2:9 You will **s** them to pieces like
48:7 With the east wind you **s** the
Isa 13:18 But their bows will **s** the youth.
Jer 13:14 Then I will **s** them like bottles
13:14 I will **s** parents and children
19:7 I will **s** the plans of Judah and
19:10 ⌊The LORD says,⌋ "Then **s**
19:11 I will **s** these people and this
48:12 of its jars and to **s** its pitchers.
Dan 2:40 this fourth kingdom will **s** and
2:44 It will **s** all the other kingdoms
Mic 4:13 You will **s** many nations into

smashed (26)

Exo 32:19 down the tablets and **s** them at
34:1 on the first tablets which you **s**.
Dtr 9:17 and **s** them in front of you.
10:2 the first tablets, which you **s**.
Jdg 7:19 blew their rams' horns and **s**
2Ki 11:18 They **s** Baal's altars and his
2Ch 23:17 They **s** Baal's altars and his
Job 16:12 of the neck and **s** ⌊my skull⌋.
Psa 3:7 You have **s** the teeth of wicked
Psa 74:6 They **s** all its carved paneling
74:13 You **s** the heads of sea
105:33 grapevines and fig trees and **s**
Ecc 12:6 the pitcher is **s** near the spring,
Isa 13:16 Their little children will be **s** to
30:14 It will be **s**, and nothing will be
Jer 19:11 potter's jar was **s** beyond repair.
Eze 6:4 your incense burners will be **s**.
6:6 Your idols will be **s** and
Dan 2:34 iron-and-clay feet and **s** them.
2:35 bronze, silver, and gold were **s**.
2:45 It **s** the iron, bronze, clay,
Hos 8:6 It will be **s** to pieces.
10:14 their children were **s** to death.
13:16 their children will be **s** to death,
Mic 1:7 All its idols will be **s** to pieces.
Nah 3:10 Even her little children were **s**

smashes (4)

Exo 15:6 O LORD, **s** your enemies.
Psa 137:9 children and **s** them against
Dan 2:40 (Iron **s** and shatters everything.
Nah 1:6 like fire and **s** the rocky cliffs.

smeared (3)

Psa 119:69 Arrogant people have **s** me
Jon 9:6 Then he **s** it on the man's eyes
9:11 **s** it on my eyes, and told me,

smearing (1)

Job 13:4 But you are **s** me with lies.

smell (11)

Gen 27:27 "The **s** of my son is like the
27:27 smell of my son is like the **s**
Exo 16:24 but it didn't **s** or have worms in
Dtr 4:28 gods can't see, hear, eat, or **s**.
33:10 They burn incense for you to **s**
Psa 38:5 My wounds **s** rotten.
115:6 have noses, but they cannot **s**.
Isa 3:24 Instead of the **s** of perfume,
3:24 there will be the **s** of decay.
Dan 3:27 and they didn't **s** of smoke.
1Co 12:17 were an ear, how could it **s**?

smelled (4)

Gen 8:21 The LORD **s** the soothing
27:27 When Isaac **s** his clothes,
Exo 7:21 and it **s** so bad that the
16:20 it was full of worms and **s** bad.

smells (1)

Job 39:25 and it **s** the battle far away —

smelter (5)

Dtr 4:20 brought out of Egypt, the iron **s**,
1Ki 8:51 from the middle of an iron **s**.
Pro 17:3 silver and the **s** for gold,
27:21 silver and the **s** for gold,
Jer 11:4 which was an iron **s**.

smelting (2)

Eze 22:18 and lead in a **s** furnace.
22:20 and tin together in a **s** furnace

smile (10)

Num 6:25 The LORD will **s** on you and
Job 9:27 change my expression and **s**,'
10:20 me alone. Let me **s** a little
Psa 31:16 **S** on me. Save me with your
39:13 me so that I may **s** again before
67:1 May he **s** on us. Selah
80:3 O God, restore us and **s** on us
80:7 restore us and **s** on us so that
80:19 and **s** on us so that we may be
119:135 **S** on me, and teach me your

smiled (1)

Job 29:24 When I **s** at them, they could

smiles (1)

Pro 31:25 and she **s** at the future.

smiths (2)

2Ki 24:14 and all the craftsmen and **s**.
24:16 1,000 craftsmen and **s**,

smoke (86)

Gen 19:28 he saw **s** rising from the land
19:28 like the thick **s** of a furnace.
Exo 13:21 ahead of them in a column of **s**
13:22 The column of **s** was always
14:19 So the column of **s** moved from
14:20 The ⌊column of⌋ **s** was there
14:24 from the column of fire and **s**
16:10 the LORD in the ⌊column of⌋ **s**.
19:18 Sinai was covered with **s**
19:18 **S** rose from the mountain like
19:18 the mountain like the **s** from
20:18 the mountain covered with **s**.
33:9 the column of **s** would come
33:10 the column of **s** standing at
40:34 Then the ⌊column of⌋ **s**
40:35 because the **s** settled on it and
40:36 whenever the ⌊column of⌋ **s**
40:38 there was fire in the **s** at night.
Lev 16:2 because I appear in the **s**
Num 9:15 the ⌊column of⌋ **s** covered it.
9:15 the **s** over the tent glowed like
9:16 The **s** always glowed this way.
9:16 At night the **s** covering the tent
9:17 Whenever the **s** moved from
9:18 As long as the ⌊column of⌋ **s**
9:19 When the **s** stayed over the
9:20 when the **s** stayed only
9:21 Sometimes the ⌊column of⌋ **s**
9:21 When the **s** moved in the
9:21 or night, when the **s** moved,
9:22 as long as the ⌊column of⌋ **s**
9:22 But when the **s** moved,
10:11 the ⌊column of⌋ **s** left the tent
10:12 until the ⌊column of⌋ **s** stopped
10:34 The LORD's ⌊column of⌋ **s**
11:25 down in the ⌊column of⌋ **s**
12:5 came down in the column of **s**
12:10 When the **s** left the tent,
14:14 that your column of **s** stays
14:14 of them in a column of **s** by day
16:42 they saw the **s** covering it,
Dtr 1:33 and in a column of **s** during
31:15 appeared in a column of **s** at
Jos 8:20 see the city going up in **s**.
8:21 and that it was going up in **s**,
Jdg 20:38 a big column of **s** rise from
20:40 But when the column of **s**
20:40 the whole city going up in **s**.
2Sm 22:9 **S** went up from his nostrils,
Neh 9:12 during the day by a column of **s**
9:19 The column of **s** didn't leave
Job 41:20 **S** comes from its nostrils like a
Psa 18:8 **S** went up from his nostrils,
37:20 They will vanish like **s**.
66:15 offerings with the **s** from rams.
68:2 Blow them away like **s**.
99:7 to them from a column of **s**.
102:3 My days disappear like **s**.
104:32 the mountains, and they **s**.
144:5 the mountains, and they will **s**.
Pro 10:26 to the teeth, like **s** to the eyes,
Sos 3:6 wilderness like clouds of **s**?
Isa 4:5 will create a cloud of **s** during
6:4 and the temple filled with **s**.
9:18 it whirls upward in clouds of **s**.
14:31 **S** comes from the north,
34:10 and **s** will always go up from
51:6 The sky will vanish like **s**.
65:5 They have become like **s** in
Dan 3:27 and they didn't smell of **s**.
Hos 13:3 be like **s** rising from chimneys.
Joe 2:30 blood, fire, and clouds of **s**.
Nah 2:13 will send your chariots up in **s**,
Act 2:19 blood, fire, and clouds of **s**.
Rev 8:4 The **s** from the incense went
9:2 and **s** came out of the shaft like
9:2 out of the shaft like the **s** from
9:2 The **s** darkened the sun and
9:3 Locusts came out of the **s** onto
9:17 Fire, **s**, and sulfur came out of
9:18 three plagues — the fire, **s**,
14:11 The **s** from their torture will go
15:8 The temple was filled with **s**
18:9 they see the **s** rise from her

Rev 18:18 When they saw the **s** rise from
19:3 The **s** goes up from her forever

smoking (3)

Gen 15:17 Suddenly a **s** oven and a
Isa 42:3 will not even put out a **s** wick.
Mat 12:20 He will not even put out a **s**

smolder (3)

Dtr 29:20 anger will **s** against him.
Psa 74:1 Why does your anger **s** against
80:4 how long will you **s** in anger

smoldering (2)

Isa 7:4 These two are **s** logs.'
65:5 like a **s** fire all day long.

smolders (1)

Hos 7:6 All night long their anger **s**,

smooth (17)

Gen 27:11 a hairy man, and my skin is **s**.
1Sm 17:40 picked out five **s** stones from
Psa 5:8 Make your way in front of me **s**.
Pro 2:16 from a loose woman with her **s**
3:6 and he will make your paths **s**.
6:24 evil woman and from the **s** talk
7:5 from a loose woman with her **s**
7:21 With her **s** lips, she makes him
11:5 people makes their road **s**,
26:23 ⌊SO⌋ is **s** talk that covers up an
Isa 26:7 the road of the righteous **s**.
40:4 Rough places will be made **s**.
42:16 I will make rough places **s**.
45:2 and **s** out the rough places.
57:6 Your idols are among the **s**
Luk 3:5 rough roads will be made **s**.
Rom 16:18 By their **s** talk and flattering

smoothed (1)

Isa 28:25 When he has **s** its surface,

smoother (2)

Psa 55:21 His speech is **s** than butter,
Pro 5:3 Her kiss is **s** than oil,

smoothly (2)

Pro 23:31 because it goes down **s**.
Sos 7:9 that goes down **s** to my

smooth-skinned (2)

Isa 18:2 to a tall and **s** people,
18:7 Armies from a tall and **s** people,

smothered (1)

2Ki 8:15 and **s** the king with it.

Smyrna (2)

Rev 1:11 **S**, Pergamum, Thyatira, Sardis,
2:8 messenger of the church in **S**,

snail (1)

Psa 58:8 Let them become like a **s** that

snake (42)

Gen 3:1 The **s** was more clever than all
3:2 The woman answered the **s**,
3:13 "The **s** deceived me,
3:14 So the LORD God said to the **s**,
49:17 Dan will be a **s** on a road,
Exo 4:3 it on the ground, it became a **s**,
4:4 "Reach out and grab the **s** by
7:9 and it will become a large **s**."
7:10 and it became a large **s**.
7:15 the staff that turned into a **s**.
Num 21:8 "Make a **s**, and put it on a pole.
21:9 So Moses made a bronze **s**
21:9 People looked at the bronze **s**
Dtr 32:33 Their wine is **s** venom,
2Ki 18:4 He even crushed the bronze **s**
Neh 2:13 that night toward **S** Fountain
Job 20:14 It becomes **s** venom in his
26:13 hand he stabbed the fleeing **s**.
Psa 58:5 hear the voice of a **s** charmer
Pro 23:32 Later it bites like a **s** and
23:32 and strikes like a poisonous **s**.
Pro 30:19 a **s** making its way over a rock,
Ecc 10:8 wall may be bitten by a **s**.
10:11 If a **s** bites before it has been
10:11 in being a **s** charmer.
Isa 27:1 that slippery **s**, Leviathan,
27:1 Leviathan, that twisting **s**.
59:5 a poisonous **s** is hatched.
Jer 46:22 Egypt will hiss like a **s** as it
Amo 5:19 wall only to be bitten by a **s**.
9:3 command a sea **s** to bite them.
Mat 7:10 would you give him a **s**?
Luk 11:11 would you give him a **s**
Jon 3:14 "As Moses lifted up the **s** ⌊on a
Act 28:3 The heat forced a poisonous **s**
28:3 The **s** bit Paul's hand and
28:4 saw the **s** hanging from his
28:5 Paul shook the **s** into the fire
2Co 11:3 that as the **s** deceived Eve by
Rev 12:9 That ancient **s**, named Devil
12:14 in order to fly away from the **s**
20:2 the serpent, that ancient **s**,

snake's (3)

Psa 140:3 as sharp as a **s** ⌊fang⌋.
Isa 14:29 viper will come from that **s** root,
Rev 12:15 The **s** mouth poured out a river

snakes (24)

Exo 7:12 and they all became large **s**.
Num 21:6 So the LORD sent poisonous **s**
21:7 will take the **s** away from us."
Dtr 8:15 poisonous **s** and scorpions.
Job 20:16 person sucks the poison of **s**.
Psa 58:4 have poisonous venom like **s**.
91:13 will trample young lions and **s**.
140:3 hide the venom of poisonous **s**.
Isa 30:6 and poisonous **s** live there.
65:25 and dust will be food for **s**.
Jer 8:17 am going to send **s** among you,
Mic 7:17 They will lick dust like **s**,
Mat 3:7 "You poisonous **s**!
10:16 So be as cunning as **s** but as
12:34 You poisonous **s**! How can you
23:33 "You **s**! You poisonous snakes!
23:33 You poisonous **s**! How can you
Mar 16:18 They will pick up **s**,
Luk 3:7 "You poisonous **s**!
10:19 you the authority to trample **s**
Rom 1:23 humans, birds, animals, and **s**.
3:13 hide the venom of poisonous **s**.
1Co 10:9 They were killed by **s**.
Rev 9:19 (Their tails have heads like **s**

snapped (6)

Jdg 15:14 and those on his hands **s**.
16:9 Samson **s** the bowstrings as a
1Sm 17:29 David **s** at him. "Didn't I
Job 24:20 wickedness is **s** like a twig.
Ecc 12:6 before the silver cord is **s**,
Mar 5:4 However, he **s** the chains off

snaps (1)

Jdg 16:9 bowstrings as a thread **s** when

snare (7)

Jos 23:13 Instead, they will be a **s** and a
Job 18:9 his heel. A **s** holds him.
Psa 69:22 a trap and a **s** for their friends.
Ecc 9:12 cruel net or birds caught in a **s**,
Isa 8:14 He will be a trap and a **s** for
Rom 11:9 a **s** and a punishment for them.
2Ti 2:26 from the devil's **s** so that they

snares (3)

Job 40:24 eyes or pierce its nose with **s**?
Ecc 7:26 ⌊like⌋ traps and **s** is more bitter
Jer 18:22 catch me and hid **s** for my feet.

snatch (5)

Job 24:9 "⌊People⌋ **s** the ⌊nursing⌋
Psa 144:7 **S** me, and rescue me from
144:11 **S** me, and rescue me from
Isa 5:29 They growl as they **s** their prey
Hos 7:12 I will **s** you out of the air like a

snatched (8)

Job 22:16 They are **s** up before their time.
Psa 136:24 He **s** us from the grasp of our
Amo 4:11 You were like a burning log **s**
Zec 3:2 like a burning log **s** from a fire?"
2Co 12:2 of Christ who was **s** away
12:4 was **s** away to paradise where
2Ti 4:17 I was **s** out of a lion's mouth.
Rev 12:5 Her child was **s** away and

snatches (3)

Job 27:20 A windstorm **s** him away at
Psa 144:10 You are the one who **s** your
Mat 13:19 at once and **s** away what was

snatching (1)

Jud 1:23 Save others by **s** them from the

sneaked (1)

2Sm 19:3 That day the troops **s** into the

sneezed (1)

2Ki 4:35 The boy **s** seven times and

sneezes (1)

Job 41:18 When Leviathan **s**,

sniff (2)

Jer 14:6 They **s** the air like jackals.
Mal 1:13 and you **s** at it in disgust,"

sniffing (1)

Jer 2:24 **s** the wind while in heat.

snorting (2)

Job 39:20 when its **s** causes terror?
Jer 8:16 The **s** of horses can be heard

snout (1)

Pro 11:22 ⌊Like⌋ a gold ring in a pig's **s**,

snow (21)

Exo 4:6 It looked as ⌊flaky as⌋ **s**.
Num 12:10 She was as white as **s**.
2Ki 5:27 made his skin as flaky as **s**.
Job 6:16 They are hidden by **s**.
24:19 and heat steal water from **s**,
37:6 "He says to the **s**, 'Fall to the
38:22 warehouses where **s** is stored
Psa 51:7 and I will be whiter than **s**.
68:14 kings there like **s** falling
147:16 He is the one who sends **s** like
148:8 lightning and hail, **s** and fog,
Pro 25:13 Like the coolness of **s** on a
26:1 Like **s** in summertime and rain
Isa 1:18 will become as white as **s**.
55:10 "Rain and **s** come down from
55:11 is like the rain and **s**.
Jer 18:14 of Lebanon are never without **s**.
Lam 4:7 princes were purer than **s**,
Dan 7:9 His clothes were as white as **s**
Mat 28:3 his clothes were as white as **s**.
Rev 1:14 were white like wool — like **s**.

snowed (2)

2Sm 23:20 and killed a lion on the day it **s**.
1Ch 11:22 and killed a lion on the day it **s**.

snows (1)

Pro 31:21 not fear for her family when it **s**

snuffed (8)

Job 17:1 My days have been **s** out.
18:5 the light of the wicked is **s** out.
18:6 and the lamp above him is **s**
21:17 the lamp of the wicked **s** out?
Pro 13:9 of wicked people will be **s** out.
20:20 father and mother will be **s** out
24:20 of wicked people will be **s** out.
Isa 43:17 They are extinguished and **s**

snuffers (5)

1Ki 7:50 dishes, **s**, bowls, saucers,
2Ki 12:13 But no silver bowls, **s**,
25:14 They took the pots, shovels, **s**,

2Ch 4:22 **s**, basins, dishes, the gold
Jer 52:18 They took the pots, shovels, **s**,

soak (1)
Psa 6:6 I **s** my couch with tears.

soaked (4)
2Ki 8:15 took a blanket, **s** it in water,
Mat 27:48 and **s** it in some vinegar.
Mar 15:36 Someone ran and **s** a sponge
Jon 19:29 So the soldiers put a sponge **s**

soap (3)
Job 9:30 If I wash myself with lye **s** and
Jer 2:22 detergent and use a lot of **s**,
Mal 3:2 fire and like a cleansing **s**.

soar (1)
Isa 40:31 They will **s** on wings like

soared (2)
2Sm 22:11 and he **s** on the wings of the
Psa 18:10 and he **s** on the wings of the

sob (1)
Ezr 3:12 began to **s** when they saw

sobbed (3)
Gen 21:16 So she sat down and **s** loudly.
27:38 And Esau **s** loudly.
29:11 kissed Rachel and **s** loudly.

sobbing (3)
Ezr 3:13 the joyful shouts and the loud **s**
Psa 30:11 changed my **s** into dancing.
Mar 5:38 People were crying and **s**

sober (4)
1Th 5:6 we must stay awake and be **s**.
5:8 to the day, we must be **s**.
1Ti 3:2 wife, be **s**, use good judgment,
Tit 2:2 Tell older men to be **s**.

sobered (1)
Gen 9:24 When Noah **s** up, he found out

sobering (1)
Psa 78:65 like a warrior **s** up from ⌊too

social (3)
1Sm 17:25 marry and elevate the **s** status
Act 13:50 women of high **s** standing
1Co 1:26 or in the upper **s** classes.

society (2)
Pro 14:34 but sin is a disgrace in any **s**.
23:28 unfaithfulness throughout **s**.

socket (4)
Gen 32:25 he touched the **s** of Jacob's hip
32:32 the thigh attached to the hip **s**
32:32 because God touched the **s**
Job 31:22 let my shoulder fall out of its **s**,

sockets (17)
Exo 26:19 Then make 40 silver **s** at the
26:19 two **s** at the bottom of each
26:21 and 40 silver **s**, two at the
26:25 eight frames with 16 silver **s**,
26:32 standing in four silver **s**.
35:11 crossbars, posts, and **s**,
36:24 Then they made 40 silver **s** at
36:24 two **s** at the bottom of each
36:26 and 40 silver **s**, two at the
36:30 eight frames with 16 silver **s**,
39:33 frames, crossbars, posts, **s**,
40:18 he put the **s** in place,
Num 3:36 posts, **s**, and all the equipment.
4:31 the crossbars, posts, and **s**,
1Ki 7:50 the gold **s** for the doors of the
Eze 28:13 Your settings and your **s** were
Zec 14:12 Their eyes will rot in their **s**,

Soco (3)
1Ch 4:18 who first settled S,
2Ch 11:7 Beth Zur, S, Adullam,
2Ch 28:18 S and its villages,

Socoh (5)
Jos 15:35 Jarmuth, Adullam, S,
15:48 their villages: Shamir, Jattir, S,
1Sm 17:1 They assembled at S,
17:1 and camped between S and
1Ki 4:10 was in charge of Arubboth, S,

soda (1)
Pro 25:20 or pouring vinegar on baking **s**,

Sodi (1)
Num 13:10 Gaddiel, son of S,

Sodom (49)
Gen 10:19 far as Gaza and then toward S,
13:10 destroyed S and Gomorrah.)
13:12 moving his tents as far as S.
13:13 (The people who lived in S
14:2 five kings⌋— King Bera of S,
14:8 Then the kings of S,
14:10 As the kings of S and
14:11 of S and Gomorrah,
14:12 since he was living in S.
14:17 the king of S came out to meet
14:21 The king of S said to Abram,
14:22 But Abram said to the king of S,
18:16 they looked toward S.
18:20 The LORD also said, "S and
18:22 turned and went on toward S,
18:26 people inside the city of S,
19:1 The two angels came to S in
19:4 of S surrounded the house.
19:24 of heaven on S and Gomorrah.
19:28 When he looked toward S and
Dtr 29:23 It will be as desolate as S,
32:32 come from the vineyards of S
Isa 1:9 been like S and Gomorrah.
1:10 of the LORD, you rulers of S!
3:9 like ⌊those of the people of⌋ S.
13:19 will be like S and Gomorrah
Jer 23:14 They are all like S to me,
49:18 Edom will be like S,
50:40 Babylon will be like S,
Lam 4:6 punishment for the sins of S.
4:6 S was destroyed instantly,
Eze 16:46 Your younger sister is S.
16:48 your sister S and her daughters
16:49 This is what your sister S has
16:53 "'I will restore the fortunes of S
16:55 When S and her daughters and
16:56 You didn't mention your sister S
Amo 4:11 as I destroyed S and Gomorrah.
Zep 2:9 "Moab will become like S,
Mat 10:15 day will be better for S
11:23 in you had been worked in S,
11:24 be better for S than for you."
Luk 10:12 day will be easier for S than
17:29 But on the day that Lot left S,
Rom 9:29 been like S and Gomorrah."
2Pe 2:6 God condemned the cities of S
2:8 the people of S and Gomorrah.
Jud 1:7 What happened to S and
Rev 11:8 of that city are S and Egypt.

soft (3)
Job 4:16 of my eyes. I heard a **s** voice:
Pro 25:15 and a **s** tongue can break
Isa 47:1 longer be called **s** and delicate.

soften (1)
Psa 65:10 You **s** them with showers and

softer (1)
Job 33:25 Then their flesh will become **s**

soil (28)
Exo 23:19 produce harvested from your **s**
34:26 produce harvested from your **s**
Num 13:20 Is the **s** rich or poor?
Dtr 28:11 Your **s** will produce many
29:23 They will see all the **s**
30:9 Your **s** will produce many
2Ch 26:10 fields because he loved the **s**.
Job 5:6 sorrow doesn't come from the **s**
Job 14:8 and its stump dies in the **s**,
14:19 floods wash away **s** from the
21:33 The **s** in the creekbed is sweet
38:38 and the **s** clings together?
Psa 65:10 and level their clumps of **s**.
Isa 28:24 he continue to break up the **s**
30:24 which work the **s** will eat
34:9 Its **s** will be turned to burning
Eze 17:5 planted the seedling in fertile **s**.
17:8 It was planted in good **s**
26:12 and **s** into the water.
Mat 13:5 where there was little **s**.
13:5 because the **s** wasn't deep.
Mar 4:5 where there wasn't much **s**.
4:5 because the **s** wasn't deep.
Luk 8:6 were planted on rocky **s**.
8:13 are like seeds on rocky **s**.
13:7 should it use up ⌊good⌋ **s**?'
Gal 6:8 If you plant in ⌊the **s** of⌋ your
6:8 But if you plant in ⌊the **s** of⌋

sold (64)
Gen 23:17 east of Mamre, was **s**
23:20 So the field and its cave were **s**
25:33 oath to him and **s** him his rights
37:28 They **s** him to the Ishmaelites
37:36 in Egypt the Midianites **s**
41:56 all the storehouses and **s** grain
45:4 the brother you **s** into slavery in
45:5 with yourselves that you **s** me.
47:20 Every Egyptian **s** his fields
Exo 21:16 whether he has **s** the
22:3 he must be **s** ⌊as a slave⌋ to
Lev 25:23 must never be **s** permanently,
25:25 must buy back what he **s**.
25:27 left to the man to whom he **s** it,
25:28 what he **s** stays in the hands of
25:34 to their cities must not be **s**,
25:42 must never be **s** as slaves.
25:48 After he has **s** himself,
27:20 you don't buy it back and it is **s**
27:27 it must be **s** at the value given
27:28 belongs to you — must not be **s**
Dtr 15:12 Hebrew men or women are **s**
24:7 person like a slave or **s** him.
1Ki 21:20 Because you **s** yourself to do
21:25 At the urging of his wife, he **s**
2Ki 6:25 severe that a donkey's head **s**
7:16 Then 24 cups of the best flour **s**
7:16 and 48 cups of barley **s** for half
17:17 They **s** themselves by doing
Neh 5:8 relatives who had been **s**
Est 7:4 and I — have been **s** so that we
7:4 had only been **s** as slaves,
Psa 105:17 who was **s** as a slave.
Isa 50:1 You were **s** because of your
52:3 the LORD says: You were **s**,
Jer 34:14 Hebrews who **s** themselves
Eze 7:13 to buy back what they have **s**.
Hos 8:9 The people of Ephraim **s**
8:10 Even though they **s**
9:1 You have **s** sex on every
Joe 3:3 They **s** girls so that they could
3:6 You **s** the people of Judah and
3:7 the place where you **s** them.
Mat 10:29 "Aren't two sparrows **s** for a
13:44 **s** everything he had,
13:46 **s** everything he had,
18:25 and all that he had to be **s** to
21:12 chairs of those who **s** pigeons.
26:9 It could have been **s** for a high
Mar 11:15 chairs of those who **s** pigeons.
14:5 perfume could have been **s**
Luk 12:6 "Aren't five sparrows **s** for two
Jon 2:16 He told those who **s** pigeons,
12:5 "Why wasn't this perfume **s** for
Act 2:45 From time to time, they **s** their
4:34 From time to time, people **s**
4:37 He **s** it and turned the money
5:1 wife Sapphira **s** some property.
5:4 After it was **s**, you could have
7:9 They **s** him into slavery,
16:14 of Thyatira and **s** purple dye
Rom 7:14 **s** as a slave to sin.
1Co 10:25 Eat anything that is **s** in the
Heb 12:16 He **s** his rights as the firstborn

soldering (1)

Isa 41:7 They say that their **s** is good.

soldier (17)

Gen 14:13 Then a **s** who had escaped
Num 31:53 Each **s** kept his own loot.
Jos 17:1 Bashan because he was a **s**.
Jdg 5:30 A girl or two for each **s**,
11:1 Jephthah was a **s** from the
1Sm 4:10 Every ⌊Israelite⌋ **s** fled to his
2Sm 17:8 father is an experienced **s**.
1Ki 20:10 to each **s** who follows me."
2Ki 5:1 This man was a good **s**,
Isa 42:13 himself for battle like a **s**.
Jon 19:23 so that each **s** could have
Act 10:7 servants and a devout **s**,
28:16 he had a **s** who guarded him.
1Co 9:7 Does a **s** ever serve in the
Php 2:25 and fellow **s** — back to you.
2Ti 2:3 like a good **s** of Christ Jesus.
Phm 1:2 our fellow **s** Archippus,

soldier's (2)

Eze 29:18 Every **s** head was worn bald,
29:18 and every **s** shoulder was

soldiers (220)

Gen 14:16 including women and **s**.
Num 11:21 with 600,000 foot **s** around me.
31:21 said to the **s** who had gone
31:27 Divide the loot between the **s**
31:28 From the **s** who served in the
31:36 Half of it went to the **s** who
31:42 half of the loot from the **s**.
31:49 we have counted all the **s**
Dtr 2:14 During that time all our **s** from
2:16 the last of these **s** had died,
3:18 All your **s** must be ready for
3:20 Your **s** will go with the other
Jos 1:14 However, all your best **s** must
5:4 All the **s** had died on the way
5:6 until all their **s** who left Egypt
6:3 All the **s** will march around the
8:3 So Joshua and all the **s** started
8:3 picked 30,000 of his best **s**
10:7 with all his **s** and best warriors,
Jdg 5:13 for me against the mighty **s**.
8:10 In the battle, 120,000 **s** died.
20:2 400,000 foot **s** with swords.
20:17 400,000 **s** armed with swords.
21:10 congregation sent 12,000 **s**.
1Sm 4:2 killed about 4,000 **s** in the field.
4:10 30,000 Israelite foot **s** died.
7:11 Israel's **s** left Mizpah,
8:12 officers over 1,000 or over 50 **s**,
10:26 With him went some **s** whose
11:15 Saul and all of Israel's **s**
13:5 and as many **s** as the sand on
13:15 followed Saul to meet the **s**.
14:20 They found Philistine **s** killing
14:20 their fellow **s** in wild confusion.
14:24 Israel's **s** were driven hard that
14:28 Then one of the **s** told him,
14:33 Some ⌊**s**⌋ told Saul,
14:34 So each of the **s** brought his ox
14:39 But not one of the **s** replied.
15:4 200,000 foot **s** and 10,000 men
17:19 with Saul and all the **s** of Israel,
17:27 The **s** repeated ⌊to David⌋ how
17:30 and the other **s** gave him the
17:52 Then the **s** of Israel and Judah
22:7 a regiment or a battalion of **s**?
26:7 Abner and the **s** were lying
2Sm 1:4 and many of the **s** died.
6:1 all the best **s** in Israel,
8:4 and 20,000 foot **s** from him.
10:6 and Zobah (20,000 foot **s**),
17:9 If some of our **s** are killed in the
20:7 and all the **s** went with Abishai.
22:30 you I can attack a line of **s**.
23:9 the **s** from Israel retreated,
23:20 two distinguished **s** from Moab.
1Ki 4:26 He also had 12,000 chariot **s**.
9:22 Instead, they were **s**,
12:21 180,000 of the best **s**,
20:15 he counted all the Israelite **s**.
20:29 Aramean foot **s** in one day.
2Ki 3:25 **S** surrounded Kir Hareseth and
7:6 The Aramean **s** said to one
13:7 and 10,000 foot **s** because the
19:35 out and killed 185,000 ⌊**s**⌋
24:14 all the **s** (10,000 prisoners),
25:4 All Judah's **s** left on the road of
1Ch 5:18 Manasseh had 44,760 **s** ready
5:24 They were **s** who were famous
7:2 They were **s** grouped
7:4 there were 36,000 **s**.
7:40 **s**, and distinguished leaders.
8:40 Ulam's sons were **s**,
9:13 of their families totaled 1,760 **s**.
11:22 two distinguished **s** from Moab.
11:42 had his own group of thirty **s**),
12:1 They were among the **s** who
12:8 They were warriors, trained **s**,
12:9 Ezer was the first of these **s**.
12:33 were 50,000 experienced **s**.
12:36 experienced **s** ready for battle.
12:37 there were 120,000 **s** ready to
12:38 All of these **s**, who were
18:4 and 20,000 foot **s** from him.
19:18 drivers and 40,000 foot **s**.
26:6 families because they were **s**.
28:1 the **s**, and the fighting men.
29:24 All the leaders and **s** and all of
2Ch 8:9 Instead, they were the **s**,
11:1 180,000 of the best **s**,
13:3 army of 400,000 of the best **s**,
13:3 of the best professional **s**.
13:14 When Judah's **s** looked around,
17:13 and an army of professional **s**
17:14 is a breakdown of these **s**.
24:24 Joash's **s** had abandoned
25:6 He also hired 100,000 **s** from
26:11 had an army of professional **s**.
26:13 was an army of 307,500 **s**.
28:6 killed 120,000 **s** in Judah
32:21 who exterminated all the **s**,
Psa 18:29 you I can attack a line of **s**.
55:18 many ⌊**s** fighting⌋ against me.
147:10 nor is he pleased by brave **s**.
Ecc 9:14 a small town with a few **s** in it,
Sos 3:7 Sixty **s** from the army of Israel
4:4 shields belonging to **s** are hung
Isa 3:2 will take their⌋ heroes and **s**,
37:36 out and killed 185,000 ⌊**s**⌋
Jer 6:23 They march like **s** ready for
26:22 Jehoiakim sent **s** to Egypt:
26:22 and other **s** along with him.
38:4 He discourages the **s** who are
39:4 Judah and all the **s** saw them,
41:3 well as the Babylonian **s** that
41:16 back men, women, children, **s**,
46:15 Why should your **s** be cut
46:21 Egypt's hired **s** are like
48:14 'We are **s** and warriors'?
48:41 On that day Moab's **s** will be
49:22 On that day Edom's **s** will be
49:26 and its **s** will be silenced that
50:9 like skilled **s** who don't come
50:29 the archers, the **s** with bows,
50:30 and all their **s** will be silenced
50:36 will kill their **s** and defeat them.
51:4 Babylon's **s** will fall down
51:32 and its **s** are terrified.
51:47 and all its **s** will lie dead.
51:56 its **s** will be captured,
51:57 their governors, officers, and **s**.
52:7 and all Judah's **s** fled.
Eze 17:15 to get horses and many **s**.
27:10 and Put were **s** in your army.
27:27 your **s** and everyone else on
32:22 and the graves of its **s** are all
32:22 All of its **s** are dead.
32:23 All of its **s** are dead.
32:24 "Elam is there with all its **s**,
32:24 and the graves of its **s** are all
32:24 All of its **s** are dead.
32:25 The graves of its **s** are all
32:25 The **s** were godless people.
32:26 Tubal are there with all their **s**,
32:26 and the graves of their **s** are all
Eze 32:26 Their **s** were all godless
32:31 over all the **s** who have been
32:32 Pharaoh and all his **s** will be
38:4 Your **s** will be fully armed.
38:7 Be prepared, you and all the **s**
38:13 Did you assemble all these **s**
39:14 bury the dead **s** that are still
39:20 and **s** of every kind,
Dan 3:20 He told some **s** from his army
Joe 1:6 It has too many **s** to count.
2:4 The **s** look like horses.
2:7 They climb walls like **s**.
2:20 The **s** in front will be forced
2:20 The **s** in back will be forced
3:11 O LORD, bring your **s**.
Amo 2:14 **S** will not be able to save
2:16 Brave **s** will run away naked
Nah 2:3 His **s** have red uniforms.
3:10 **S** tossed dice for her important
3:13 Look at your **s**; they're women!
Hab 3:14 His **s** come like a violent storm
Mat 2:16 He sent **s** to kill all the boys
8:9 and have **s** at my command.
22:7 He sent his **s**, killed those
27:27 Then the governor's **s** took
27:31 After the **s** finished making fun
27:32 The **s** forced him to carry
27:65 "You have the **s** you want for
27:66 and posted the **s** on guard duty.
28:12 They gave the **s** a large
28:15 The **s** took the money and did
Mar 15:16 The **s** led Jesus into the
15:20 After the **s** finished making fun
15:21 the **s** forced him to carry Jesus'
Luk 3:14 Some **s** asked him,
7:8 and have **s** at my command.
14:31 Can he and his 10,000 **s** fight
14:31 against a king with 20,000 **s**?
23:11 Herod and his **s** treated Jesus
23:26 As the **s** led Jesus away,
23:34 Meanwhile, the **s** divided his
23:36 The **s** also made fun of him.
Jon 18:3 So Judas took a troop of **s** and
19:2 The **s** twisted some thorny
19:16 So the **s** took Jesus.
19:18 The **s** crucified Jesus and two
19:23 When the **s** had crucified
19:24 The **s** said to each other,
19:24 So that's what the **s** did.
19:29 So the **s** put a sponge soaked
19:32 The **s** broke the legs of the first
19:33 When the **s** came to Jesus and
19:34 However, one of the **s** stabbed
Act 12:4 into prison with sixteen **s**
12:6 was sleeping between two **s**.
12:18 In the morning the **s** were in an
21:31 charge of the Roman **s** received
21:32 Immediately, he took some **s**
21:32 saw the officer and the **s**,
21:35 was so violent that the **s** had
21:37 As the **s** were about to take
22:24 So the officer ordered the **s** to
22:25 But when the **s** had Paul
22:29 Immediately, the **s** who were
23:10 So the officer ordered his **s** to
23:23 70 **s** on horseback,
23:23 and 200 **s** with spears.
23:27 I went with my **s** to rescue him.
23:32 the next day and let the **s**
23:33 When the **s** arrived in the city
27:31 Paul told the officer and the **s**,
27:32 Then the **s** cut the ropes that
27:42 The **s** had a plan to kill the
27:43 so he stopped the **s** from
Php 1:13 it has become clear to all the **s**
Rev 9:16 The **s** on horses numbered

soldiers' (2)

Num 31:29 all these things from the **s** half
Neh 3:16 as the pool and the **s** barracks

solemn (9)

Gen 24:2 that he owned, "Take a **s** oath.
26:28 'There should be a **s**
50:10 they began a great and **s**
Jdg 21:5 They had taken a **s** oath that

1Sm 14:28 the troops to take a s oath:
Psa 55:20 He has broken his s promise.
95:11 That is why I angrily took this s
Heb 3:11 So I angrily took a s oath that
4:3 "So I angrily took a s oath that

solemnly (50)

Gen 14:22 "I now raise my hand and s
42:15 how you'll be tested: I s swear,
42:16 If not, I s swear, as surely as
Exo 6:8 I will bring you to the land I s
13:19 made the Israelites s swear
Num 14:21 the whole earth, I s swear that
14:28 I s swear I will do everything to
Dtr 32:40 toward heaven and s swear:
Jdg 8:19 I s swear, as the LORD lives,
Rut 3:13 I s swear, as the LORD lives,
1Sm 14:39 I s swear, as the LORD and
14:45 We s swear, as the LORD
17:55 Abner answered, "I s swear,
19:6 "I s swear, as the LORD lives,
20:3 But I s swear, as the LORD
25:26 Now, sir, I s swear,
25:34 But I s swear — as the LORD
26:10 I s swear, as the LORD lives,"
26:16 I s swear, as the LORD lives,
28:10 "I s swear, as the LORD lives,
29:6 "I s swear, as the LORD lives,
2Sm 2:27 Joab answered, "I s swear,
4:11 I s swear, as the LORD lives,
11:11 I s swear, as sure as you're
12:5 "I s swear, as the LORD lives,"
14:11 "I s swear, as the LORD lives,"
14:19 "I s swear on your life,
15:21 answered the king, "I s swear,
1Ki 1:29 He said, "I s swear,
2:24 So I s swear, as the LORD
17:1 said to Ahab, "I s swear,
17:12 She said, "I s swear,
18:10 I s swear, as the LORD your
18:15 Elijah said, "I s swear,
22:14 Micaiah answered, "I s swear,
2Ki 2:2 Elisha answered, "I s swear,
2:4 Elisha answered, "I s swear,
2:6 Elisha answered, "I s swear,
3:14 Elisha answered, "I s swear,
4:30 boy's mother said, "I s swear,
5:16 Elisha said, "I s swear,
2Ch 18:13 Micaiah answered, "I s swear,
Isa 49:18 "I s swear as I live,"
Jer 11:7 I s warned your ancestors
11:7 I s warned them to obey me.
Amo 8:14 and say, "I s swear, Dan,
8:14 "I s swear as long as there is a
Zep 2:9 Therefore, I s swear,
1Ti 5:21 I s call on you in the sight of
2Ti 4:1 I s call on you in the presence

soles (4)

Dtr 28:35 your whole body from the s
Job 2:7 with painful boils from the s
13:27 marks on the s of my feet.
Mal 4:3 they will be ashes under the s

solid (15)

Dtr 8:15 come out of s rock for you.
32:13 rocks and olive oil from s rock.
Job 28:15 You cannot obtain it with s
41:23 They are s and cannot be
41:24 Its chest is s like a rock,
41:24 like a rock, s like a millstone.
Psa 75:3 its foundations as s as rock.
Isa 28:16 cornerstone, a s foundation.
Jer 15:20 I will make you like a s bronze
Zec 4:2 I answered, "I see a s gold
1Co 3:2 I didn't give you s food
Col 1:23 moved from the s foundation
2Ti 2:19 ⌊people⌋ have a s foundation.
Heb 5:12 You need milk, not s food.
5:14 s food is for mature people,

solitary (1)

Act 16:24 and Silas into s confinement

Solomon (260)

2Sm 5:14 Shammua, Shobab, Nathan, S,
12:24 David named him S.
1Ki 1:10 fighting men, or his brother S.
1:13 swear to me that my son S will
1:17 You said that my son S will be
1:19 hasn't invited your servant S.
1:21 Otherwise, my son S and I will
1:26 son, or your servant S.
1:30 Your son S will be king after
1:33 Put my son S on my mule,
1:34 'Long live King S!'
1:37 so may he be with S.
1:37 May S be an even greater king
1:38 and the Pelethites put S on
1:39 oil from the tent and anointed S.
1:39 "Long live King S!"
1:43 King David has made S king.
1:46 S is now seated on the royal
1:50 Adonijah was afraid of S.
1:51 Someone told S, "Adonijah is
1:51 is afraid of you, King S.
1:51 'Make King S swear to me
1:52 S said, "If he will behave like
1:53 King S sent men to take him
1:53 bowed down in front of King S.
1:53 "Go home," S told him.
2:1 he instructed his son S,
2:12 S sat on his father David's
2:17 He said, "Please ask King S to
2:19 Bathsheba went to King S to
2:22 King S then said, "Why do you
2:23 King S took an oath by the
2:25 King S gave this task to
2:27 So S removed Abiathar as the
2:29 After King S heard that Joab
2:29 of the LORD, S sent Benaiah,
2:35 King S also replaced Abiathar
2:41 After S heard that Shimei had
2:42 S asked him, "Didn't I make
2:45 But King S is blessed,
3:1 S became the son-in-law of
3:1 S brought her to the City of
3:3 S loved the LORD and lived by
3:4 King S went to Gibeon to
3:4 S sacrificed 1,000 burnt
3:5 the LORD appeared to S
3:6 S responded, "You've shown
3:10 pleased that S asked for this.
3:15 S woke up and realized it had
4:1 When King S was the king of
4:7 S appointed 12 district
4:21 S ruled all the kingdoms from
4:21 were subject to S as long as
4:25 As long as S lived,
4:26 S had stalls for 40,000 chariot
4:27 month every year for King S
4:29 God gave S wisdom — keen
4:32 S spoke 3,000 proverbs and
5:1 sent his officials to S when
5:1 heard that S had been anointed
5:2 S sent word to Hiram,
5:7 glad to hear what S had said.
5:8 Hiram sent men to S to say,
5:10 So Hiram gave S all the cedar
5:11 S gave Hiram 120,000 bushels
5:11 S paid Hiram this much every
5:12 The LORD gave S wisdom as
5:12 peace between Hiram and S,
5:13 King S forced 30,000 men from
5:15 S had 70,000 men who carried
6:1 S began to build the LORD's
6:2 The temple that King S built for
6:6 S made ledges all around the
6:11 The LORD spoke to S,
6:14 When S had finished building
6:20 S covered it and the cedar altar
6:27 S put the angels in the inner
7:1 S took 13 years to finish
7:6 S made the Hall of Pillars 75
7:8 S also built private quarters
7:13 King S had Hiram brought from
7:14 He came to King S and did all
7:40 finished all the work for King S
7:47 S left all the products
7:48 S made all the furnishings for
7:51 All the work King S did on the
8:1 Then S assembled the
1Ki 8:1 They came to King S in
8:2 gathered around King S at
8:5 while King S with the whole
8:12 Then S said, "The LORD said
8:22 S stood in front of the LORD's
8:54 When S finished praying this
8:63 S sacrificed 22,000 cattle and
8:65 At that time S and all Israel
9:1 S finished building the LORD's
9:10 It took S 20 years to build the
9:11 ⌊When King S had finished,⌋
9:11 (Hiram had supplied S with as
9:12 to see the cities S gave him.
9:15 laborers whom King S drafted
9:17 So S rebuilt Gezer,
9:21 S drafted them for slave labor.
9:22 But S didn't make any of the
9:24 to the palace that S had built
9:25 Three times a year S sacrificed
9:26 King S also built a fleet near
9:28 and brought it to King S.
10:2 When she came to S,
10:3 S answered all her questions.
10:10 queen of Sheba gave King S.
10:13 King S gave the queen of
10:14 The gold that came to S in one
10:16 King S made 200 large shields
10:23 In wealth and wisdom King S
10:24 to the wisdom that God gave S.
10:26 S built up ⌊his army⌋ with
11:1 King S loved many foreign
11:2 But S was obsessed with their
11:5 S followed Astarte (the
11:6 So S did what the LORD
11:7 Then S built an illegal worship
11:9 the LORD became angry with S
11:10 But S did not obey God's
11:11 The LORD told S, I will certainly
11:14 the Edomite as a rival to S.
11:23 son of Eliada, as a rival to S.
11:25 Israel's rival as long as S lived.
11:27 S was building the Millo and
11:28 S saw that Jeroboam was a
11:40 Then S tried to kill Jeroboam,
11:40 He stayed in Egypt until S died.
11:41 written in the records of S?
11:43 S lay down in death with his
12:2 where he had fled from King S.
12:6 had served his father S while
12:21 to Rehoboam, son of S.
12:23 King Rehoboam, son of S,
14:21 Rehoboam, son of S,
14:26 the gold shields S had made.
2Ki 21:7 said to David and his son S,
23:13 King S of Israel had built them
24:13 all the furnishings that King S
25:16 and the stands that S had
1Ch 3:5 and S (the mother of these four
6:10 temple S built in Jerusalem.)
6:32 the tent of meeting until S built
14:4 Shammua, Shobab, Nathan, S,
18:8 (Later⌋ S used it to make the
22:5 David thought, "My son S is
22:5 ⌊for S⌋ before he died.
22:6 He summoned his son S and
22:7 David told his son S,
22:9 His name will be S [Peace],
22:17 of Israel to help his son S.
23:1 made his son S king of Israel.
28:5 many sons) he chose my son S
28:6 "He told me, 'Your son S will
28:9 "And you, my son S,
28:11 Then David gave his son S the
28:18 He also gave S the plans for
28:20 David also told his son S,
29:1 whole assembly, "My son S,
29:19 Make my son S completely
29:22 they made David's son S king.
29:22 LORD's behalf they anointed S
29:23 Then S sat on the LORD's
29:23 S was successful and all
29:24 pledged their loyalty to King S.
29:25 made S extremely powerful,
29:28 Then his son S succeeded him
2Ch 1:1 S, son of David, The LORD his
1:2 S spoke to all Israel — to the

2Ch 1:3 Then S and the entire
1:5 There S and the assembly
1:6 In the LORD's presence S went
1:7 That night God appeared to S.
1:8 S responded to God,
1:11 God replied to S, "I know this
1:13 S went from the tent of meeting
1:14 S built up his army with
2:1 S gave orders to begin building
2:2 S drafted 70,000 men to carry
2:3 S sent word to King Huram of
2:11 responded to S by sending
2:17 S counted all the men who
2:17 S counted 153,600 foreigners.
3:1 S began to build the LORD's
3:3 This is how S laid the
3:14 S made the canopy of violet,
4:11 for King S in God's temple:
4:18 S made so many of these
4:19 S made all the furnishings for
5:1 All the work S did on the
5:2 Then S assembled the
5:6 while King S and the whole
6:1 Then S said, "The LORD said
6:12 S stood in front of the LORD's
6:13 (S had made a bronze platform
7:1 When S finished praying,
7:5 King S offered 22,000 cattle
7:7 S designated the courtyard in
7:8 At that time S and all Israel
7:10 S dismissed the people to their
7:10 David, S, and his people Israel.
7:11 S finished the LORD's temple
7:12 He said to S, "I have heard
8:1 It took S 20 years to build the
8:3 Then S went to Hamath Zobah
8:8 S drafted them for slave labor.
8:9 But S didn't make any of the
8:11 S brought Pharaoh's daughter
8:12 Then S sacrificed burnt
8:14 S also set up divisions of
8:17 Then S went to the coast near
8:18 sailors with ships to S.
8:18 and brought it to King S.
9:1 When she came to S,
9:2 S answered all her questions.
9:2 too difficult for S to answer.
9:9 queen of Sheba gave King S.
9:12 King S gave the queen of
9:13 The gold that came to S in one
9:14 brought gold and silver to S.
9:15 King S made 200 large shields
9:22 In wealth and wisdom King S
9:23 to the wisdom that God gave S.
9:25 S had 4,000 stalls for horses
9:28 Horses were imported for S
9:30 S ruled in Jerusalem over all
9:31 S lay down in death with his
10:2 where he had fled from King S.
10:6 had served his father S while
11:3 King Rehoboam, son of S,
11:17 son of S, for three years.
11:17 the way David and S had lived.
12:9 the gold shields S had made.
13:6 the servant of David's son S.
13:7 opposed Rehoboam, son of S,
30:26 the days of King S of Israel.
33:7 said to David and his son S,
35:3 holy ark in the temple that S,
35:4 and the records of his son S.
Neh 12:45 and his son S had ordered them
13:26 like these that King S
Pro 1:1 The proverbs of S,
10:1 The proverbs of S:
Sos 1:1 The most beautiful song of S.
3:9 King S had a carriage made for
3:11 come out and look at King S!
8:11 S had a vineyard at Baal
8:12 That 25 pounds is yours, S,
Jer 52:20 stands that King S had made
Mat 1:6 were the father and mother of S.
1:7 S was the father of Rehoboam,
6:29 But I say that not even S in all
12:42 someone greater than S is here!
Luk 11:31 someone greater than S is here!
12:27 But I say that not even S in all
Act 7:47 But S was the one who built a

Solomon's (49)

1Ki 1:11 asked S mother Bathsheba,
1:47 'May your God make S name
2:13 went to Bathsheba, S mother.
2:46 S power as king was now
4:11 (S daughter Taphath was his
4:15 (He also married S daughter
4:22 S food supply for one day was
4:30 S wisdom was greater than
5:18 S workmen, Hiram's workmen,
6:37 Ziv of the fourth year of S reign,
7:45 temple at King S request
9:16 S wife, as a wedding present.)
9:23 of S projects: 550 foremen
9:27 Along with S servants
10:1 heard about S reputation.
10:4 of Sheba saw all of S wisdom,
10:21 All King S cups were gold,
10:21 considered valuable in S time.
10:28 S horses were imported from
11:26 He was one of S officers, but
11:31 tear the kingdom out of S hands
11:41 Aren't the rest of S acts —
11:42 The length of S reign in
1Ch 3:10 S son was Rehoboam.
2Ch 1:16 S horses were imported from
4:16 temple at King S request
8:10 of King S projects: 250 foremen
8:14 As S father David had directed,
8:16 All of S work was carried out
8:18 They went with S servants to
9:1 heard about S reputation.
9:3 of Sheba saw S wisdom,
9:10 S servants who brought gold
9:20 All King S cups were gold,
9:20 considered valuable in S time.
9:29 Aren't the rest of S acts from
Ezr 2:55 S servants returned from exile:
2:58 of S servants totaled 392.
Neh 7:57 S servants returned from exile:
7:60 of S servants totaled 392.
11:3 and descendants of S servants
Pro 25:1 These also are S proverbs that
Sos 1:5 Kedar's tents, like S curtains
3:7 S sedan chair! Sixty soldiers
Mat 12:42 of the earth to hear S wisdom.
Luk 11:31 of the earth to hear S wisdom.
Jon 10:23 Jesus was walking on S porch
Act 3:11 at the place called S Porch.
5:12 Jesus as they met on S Porch

solve (4)

Jdg 14:12 If you s it during the seven
14:13 But if you can't s it,
14:14 days they couldn't s the riddle.
Dan 5:12 to interpret dreams, s riddles,

solved (1)

Jdg 14:19 to the men who s the riddle.

solving (1)

Jdg 14:15 "Trick your husband into s the

Son; son (2212)

Gen 4:17 he named it Enoch after his s.
4:22 Zillah also had a s,
4:25 She gave birth to a s and
4:26 A s was also born to Seth,
5:3 he became the father of a s
5:28 he became the father of a s.
9:24 what his youngest s had done
11:31 Terah took his s Abram,
11:31 his grandson Lot (s of Haran),
11:31 wife of his s Abram.
15:4 Your own s will be your heir."
16:11 and you will give birth to a s.
16:15 Hagar gave birth to Abram's s.
17:16 I will also give you a s by her.
17:17 "Can a s be born to a
17:19 wife Sarah will give you a s,
17:23 Abraham took his s Ishmael,
17:25 His s Ishmael was 13 years
17:26 s Ishmael were circumcised.
18:10 your wife Sarah will have a s."
Gen 18:14 and Sarah will have a s."
19:37 The older one gave birth to a s
19:38 daughter also gave birth to a s
21:2 she gave birth to a s for
21:3 Abraham named his newborn s
21:5 old when his s Isaac was born.
21:7 Yet, I have given him a s in his
21:9 Sarah saw that Abraham's s by
21:10 "Get rid of this slave and her s,
21:10 because this slave's s must
21:10 inheritance with my s Isaac."
21:11 this because of his s Ishmael.
21:13 I will make the slave's s into a
22:2 God said, "Take your s,
22:2 your son, your only s Isaac,
22:3 of his servants and his s Isaac.
22:6 and gave it to his s Isaac.
22:7 "Yes, S?" Abraham answered.
22:8 a lamb for the burnt offering, S.
22:9 Then he tied up his s Isaac
22:10 it in his hand to sacrifice his s.
22:12 not refuse to give me your s,
22:12 give me your son, your only s."
22:13 burnt offering in place of his s.
22:16 not refused to give me your s,
22:16 give me your son, your only s,
23:8 Encourage Ephron, s of Zohar,
24:3 earth that you will not get my s
24:4 and get a wife for my s Isaac."
24:5 Should I take your s all the
24:6 do not take my s back there,"
24:7 and you will get my s a wife
24:8 But don't take my s back there."
24:15 of Bethuel, s of Milcah,
24:24 s of Milcah and Nahor.
24:36 wife Sarah gave him a s
24:36 given that s everything he has.
24:37 'Don't get a wife for my s from
24:38 and get my s a wife.'
24:40 You will get my s a wife from
24:44 has chosen for my master's s.'
24:47 s of Nahor and Milcah.'
24:48 of my master's relative for his s.
24:51 the wife of your master's s,
25:6 He sent them away from his s
25:9 s of Zohar the Hittite.
25:11 God blessed his s Isaac,
25:12 of Abraham's s Ishmael.
25:12 He was the s of Sarah's
25:19 account of Abraham's s Isaac
27:1 he called his older s Esau and
27:1 son Esau and said to him, "S!"
27:5 was speaking to his s Esau.
27:6 Rebekah said to her s Jacob,
27:8 Now listen to me, S,
27:13 any curse on you fall on me, S.
27:15 Then Rebekah took her older s
27:15 and put them on her younger s
27:17 Then she gave her s Jacob the
27:18 "Who are you, S?"
27:20 Isaac asked his s,
27:20 did you find it so quickly, S?"
27:21 so that I can feel your skin, S,
27:21 not you really are my s Esau."
27:24 "Are you really my s Esau?"
27:25 it, S, so that I will bless you."
27:26 here and give me a kiss, S."
27:27 "The smell of my s is like the
27:32 "I'm your firstborn s Esau,"
27:37 is left for me to do for you, S?"
27:42 what her older s Esau had said,
27:42 she sent for her younger s
27:43 So now, S, obey me. Quick!
28:5 s of Bethuel the Aramean and
28:9 daughter of Abraham's s
29:12 and that he was Rebekah's s,
29:13 about his sister's s Jacob,
29:32 pregnant and gave birth to a s.
29:32 him Reuben [Here's My S],
29:33 and gave birth to another s.
29:33 he also has given me this s."
29:34 and gave birth to another s.
29:35 and gave birth to another s.
30:5 she gave birth to a s for Jacob.
30:6 prayer and has given me a s."
30:7 birth to a second s for Jacob.

Gen 30:10 gave birth to a **s** for Jacob.
30:12 birth to her second **s** for Jacob.
30:17 birth to her fifth **s** for Jacob.
30:19 birth to her sixth **s** for Jacob.
30:23 pregnant and gave birth to a **s**.
30:24 the LORD give me another **s**."
34:2 When Shechem, **s** of the local
34:8 "My **s** Shechem has his heart
34:18 to Hamor and his **s** Shechem.
34:20 So Hamor and his **s** Shechem
34:24 Hamor and his **s** Shechem.
34:26 Hamor and his **s** Shechem.
35:17 You're having another **s**!"
35:18 she named her **s** Benoni [Son
35:18 she named her son Benoni [**S**
35:18 father named him Benjamin [**S**
36:10 **s** of Esau's wife Adah,
36:10 **s** of Esau's wife Basemath.
36:12 concubine of Esau's **s** Eliphaz.
36:17 descendants of Esau's **s** Reuel:
36:32 Bela, **s** of Beor, ruled Edom.
36:33 **s** of Zerah from Bozrah,
36:35 After Husham died, Hadad, **s** of
36:38 died, Baal Hanan, **s** of Achbor,
36:39 After Baal Hanan, **s** of Achbor,
37:34 mourned for his **s** a long time.
37:35 I will mourn for my **s** until I die."
38:3 and gave birth to a **s** named Er.
38:4 and gave birth to another **s**,
38:5 and gave birth to another **s**,
38:6 a wife for his firstborn **s** Er.
38:11 Live as a widow until my **s**
38:11 He thought that this **s**,
38:26 haven't given her my **s** Shelah."
41:51 Joseph named his firstborn **s**
41:52 He named the second **s**
42:38 "My **s** will not go with you.
43:29 Benjamin, his mother's **s**.
43:29 to you, my **s**," he said.
45:9 is what your **s** Joseph says,
45:28 "My **s** Joseph is still alive.
46:10 the **s** of a Canaanite woman.
46:23 The **s** of Dan was Hushim.
47:29 He called for his **s** Joseph and
48:2 When Jacob was told, "Your **s**
48:14 Ephraim was the younger **s**.
48:19 **S**, I know! Manasseh, too,
49:3 the very first **s** I had,
49:9 come back from the kill, my **s**.
50:23 of Machir, **s** of Manasseh,
Exo 2:2 became pregnant and had a **s**.
2:10 and he became her **s**.
2:22 She gave birth to a **s**.
4:22 Israel is my firstborn **s**.
4:23 I told you to let my **s** go so that
4:23 going to kill your firstborn **s**.'"
6:15 the **s** of a Canaanite woman.
6:25 Eleazar, **s** of Aaron,
11:5 Every firstborn **s** in Egypt will
12:29 in Egypt from the firstborn **s**
12:29 ruled the land to the firstborn **s**
13:13 buy every firstborn **s** back from
13:15 buy every firstborn **s** back from
18:3 The one **s** was named
21:9 if he has chosen her for his **s**,
21:10 If that **s** marries another
21:31 gores someone's **s** or daughter,
22:29 must give me your firstborn **s**.
29:30 The **s** who succeeds him as
31:2 **s** of Uri and grandson of Hur,
31:6 Oholiab, **s** of Ahisamach,
33:11 assistant, Joshua, **s** of Nun,
35:30 **s** of Uri and grandson of Hur,
35:34 and Oholiab, **s** of Ahisamach,
38:21 **s** of the priest Aaron.
38:22 **s** of Uri and grandson of Hur,
38:23 was Oholiab, **s** of Ahisamach,
Lev 6:22 Aaron's **s** who is anointed to
21:2 father, **s**, daughter, or brother,
24:11 The Israelite woman's **s** began
Num 1:5 help you: Elizur, **s** of Shedeur,
1:6 Shelumiel, **s** of Zurishaddai,
1:7 Nahshon, **s** of Amminadab,
1:8 Nethanel, **s** of Zuar,
1:9 Eliab, **s** of Helon, from the tribe
1:10 Elishama, **s** of Ammihud,
Num 1:10 Gamaliel, **s** of Pedahzur,
1:11 Abidan, **s** of Gideoni,
1:12 Ahiezer, **s** of Ammishaddai,
1:13 Pagiel, **s** of Ochran,
1:14 Eliasaph, **s** of Deuel,
1:15 Ahira, **s** of Enan, from the tribe
1:20 Israel's firstborn **s**,
2:3 is Nahshon, **s** of Amminadab.
2:5 Issachar is Nethanel, **s** of Zuar.
2:7 of Zebulun is Eliab, **s** of Helon.
2:10 Reuben is Elizur, **s** of Shedeur.
2:12 is Shelumiel, **s** of Zurishaddai.
2:14 of Gad is Eliasaph, **s** of Deuel.
2:18 is Elishama, **s** of Ammihud.
2:20 is Gamaliel, **s** of Pedahzur.
2:22 is Abidan, **s** of Gideoni.
2:25 **s** of Ammishaddai.
2:27 of Asher is Pagiel, **s** of Ochran.
2:29 of Naphtali is Ahira, **s** of Enan.
3:24 was Eliasaph, **s** of Lael.
3:30 was Elizaphan, **s** of Uzziel.
3:32 **s** of the priest Aaron.
3:35 was Zuriel, **s** of Abihail.
4:16 "Eleazar, **s** of the priest Aaron,
4:28 Ithamar, **s** of the priest Aaron,
4:33 Ithamar, **s** of the priest Aaron,
7:8 **s** of the priest Aaron.
7:12 Nahshon, **s** of Amminadab,
7:17 Nahshon, **s** of Amminadab.
7:18 day Nethanel, **s** of Zuar,
7:23 gifts from Nethanel, **s** of Zuar.
7:24 of Zebulun, Eliab, **s** of Helon,
7:29 the gifts from Eliab, **s** of Helon.
7:30 Reuben, Elizur, **s** of Shedeur,
7:35 gifts from Elizur, **s** of Shedeur.
7:36 Shelumiel, **s** of Zurishaddai,
7:41 Shelumiel, **s** of Zurishaddai.
7:42 of Gad, Eliasaph, **s** of Deuel,
7:47 gifts from Eliasaph, **s** of Deuel.
7:48 Elishama, **s** of Ammihud,
7:53 from Elishama, **s** of Ammihud.
7:54 Gamaliel, **s** of Pedahzur,
7:59 from Gamaliel, **s** of Pedahzur.
7:60 Abidan, **s** of Gideoni,
7:65 gifts from Abidan, **s** of Gideoni.
7:66 Dan, Ahiezer, **s** of Amishaddai,
7:71 from Ahiezer, **s** of Amishaddai.
7:72 of Asher, Pagiel, **s** of Ochran,
7:77 gifts from Pagiel, **s** of Ochran.
7:78 of Naphtali, Ahira, **s** of Enan,
7:83 the gifts from Ahira, **s** of Enan.
10:14 Nahshon, **s** of Amminadab,
10:15 Nethanel, **s** of Zuar,
10:16 Eliab, **s** of Helon,
10:18 Elizur, **s** of Shedeur,
10:19 Shelumiel, **s** of Zurishaddai,
10:20 Eliasaph, **s** of Deuel,
10:22 Elisha, **s** of Ammihud,
10:23 Gamaliel, **s** of Pedahzur,
10:24 Abidan, **s** of Gideoni,
10:25 Ahiezer, **s** of Ammishaddai,
10:26 Pagiel, **s** of Ochran,
10:27 Ahira, **s** of Enan,
10:29 **s** of Reuel the Midianite,
11:28 So Joshua, **s** of Nun,
13:4 names: Shammua, **s** of Zaccur,
13:5 Shaphat, **s** of Hori,
13:6 Caleb, **s** of Jephunneh,
13:7 Igal, **s** of Joseph, from the tribe
13:8 Hoshea, **s** of Nun, from the tribe
13:9 Palti, **s** of Raphu, from the tribe
13:10 Gaddiel, **s** of Sodi,
13:11 Gaddi, **s** of Susi, from the tribe
13:12 Ammiel, **s** of Gemalli,
13:13 Sethur, **s** of Michael,
13:14 Nahbi, **s** of Vophsi,
13:15 Geuel, **s** of Machi,
13:16 **s** of Nun, the name Joshua.
14:6 Joshua (**s** of Nun) and Caleb
14:6 and Caleb (**s** of Jephunneh),
14:30 will enter it except Caleb (**s**
14:30 and Joshua (**s** of Nun).
14:38 only Joshua (**s** of Nun) and
14:38 (**s** of Jephunneh) survived.
16:1 Korah (**s** of Izhar), Dathan and
16:1 and On (**s** of Peleth) dared to
Num 16:37 **s** of the priest Aaron,
18:15 must buy back every firstborn **s**
20:25 Bring Aaron and his **s** Eleazar
20:26 and put them on his **s** Eleazar.
20:28 and put them on his **s** Eleazar.
22:2 Balak, **s** of Zippor,
22:4 At that time Balak, **s** of Zippor,
22:5 **s** of Beor, who was at Pethor,
22:10 **s** of King Zippor of Moab,
22:16 what Balak, **s** of Zippor, says:
23:18 Hear me, **s** of Zippor!
24:3 message of Balaam, **s** of Beor.
24:15 message of Balaam, **s** of Beor.
25:7 Phinehas, **s** of Eleazar and
25:11 "Phinehas, **s** of Eleazar and
25:14 woman was Zimri, **s** of Salu.
26:1 **s** of the priest Aaron,
26:8 Eliab was the **s** of Pallu,
26:33 (Zelophehad, **s** of Hepher,
26:65 only ones left were Caleb (**s**
26:65 and Joshua (**s** of Nun).
27:1 of Zelophehad, **s** of Hepher,
27:1 of Manasseh, **s** of Joseph.
27:4 family because he had no **s**?
27:18 "Take Joshua, **s** of Nun,
31:6 **s** of the priest Eleazar.
31:8 Balaam, **s** of Beor, in battle.
32:12 Only Caleb (**s** of Jephunneh
32:12 the Kenizzite) and Joshua (**s**
32:28 Joshua (**s** of Nun),
32:33 tribe of Manasseh, **s** of Joseph,
32:39 **s** of Manasseh, went to Gilead,
34:17 Eleazar and Joshua, **s** of Nun.
34:19 names: Caleb, **s** of Jephunneh,
34:20 Shemuel, **s** of Ammihud,
34:21 Elidad, **s** of Kislon,
34:22 Bukki, **s** of Jogli, the leader of
34:23 Hanniel, **s** of Ephod,
34:24 Kemuel, **s** of Shiphtan,
34:25 Elizaphan, **s** of Parnach,
34:26 Paltiel, **s** of Azzan,
34:27 Ahihud, **s** of Shelomi,
34:28 Pedahel, **s** of Ammihud,
36:1 **s** of Machir and grandson of
36:12 of Manasseh, **s** of Joseph.
Dtr 1:36 except Caleb, **s** of Jephunneh.
1:38 Joshua, **s** of Nun, will go there.
10:6 and his **s** Eleazar succeeded
13:6 Your own brother, **s**,
21:15 and the firstborn **s** might belong
21:16 he can't treat the **s** of the wife
21:16 wife he loves as if that **s** were
21:16 for the real firstborn (the **s**
21:17 he must recognize the **s** of the
21:17 He must give that **s** a double
21:17 That **s** is the very first son he
21:17 son is the very first **s** he had.
21:17 rights of the firstborn **s** are his.
21:18 rebellious **s** who doesn't obey
21:20 "This **s** of ours is stubborn and
23:4 even hired Balaam, **s** of Beor,
25:5 them dies without having a **s**,
25:6 Then the first **s** she has will
28:56 toward her own **s** or daughter.
31:23 command to Joshua, **s** of Nun:
32:44 came with Hoshea, **s** of Nun,
34:9 Joshua, **s** of Nun, was filled
Jos 1:1 assistant Joshua, **s** of Nun,
2:1 From Shittim Joshua, **s** of Nun,
2:23 returned to Joshua, **s** of Nun.
6:6 Joshua, **s** of Nun, He said to
6:26 It will cost him his firstborn **s** to
6:26 It will cost him his youngest **s**
7:1 Achan, **s** of Carmi,
7:18 of Judah was the **s** of Carmi,
7:19 Joshua said to Achan, "**S**,
7:24 Israel took Achan (**s** of Zerah),
13:22 also killed Balaam, **s** of Beor,
13:31 of Machir, **s** of Manasseh,
14:1 Joshua (**s** of Nun),
14:6 Caleb, **s** of Jephunneh and
14:13 blessed Caleb, **s** of Jephunneh,
14:14 **s** of Jephunneh and grandson
15:6 Rock of Bohan, **s** of Reuben.
15:13 gave Caleb, **s** of Jephunneh,
15:17 **s** of Caleb's brother Kenaz,

Jos 17:2 Joseph's **s** Manasseh listed by
17:3 Zelophehad, **s** of Hepher,
17:4 Joshua (**s** of Nun),
18:17 Rock of Bohan, **s** of Reuben.
19:49 to Joshua, **s** of Nun.
19:51 Eleazar, Joshua **s** of Nun,
21:1 to Joshua (**s** of Nun),
21:12 to Caleb, **s** of Jephunneh,
22:13 **s** of the priest Eleazar,
22:20 Didn't Achan, **s** of Zerah,
22:31 **s** of the priest Eleazar,
22:32 Then Phinehas (**s** of the priest
24:9 **s** of King Zippor of Moab,
24:9 **s** of Beor, to curse you.
24:29 servant Joshua, **s** of Nun, died.
24:33 Aaron's **s** Eleazar also died.
24:33 been given to his **s** Phinehas
Jdg 1:13 Then Othniel, **s** of Caleb's
2:8 servant Joshua, **s** of Nun,
3:9 It was Othniel, **s** of Caleb's
3:11 Then Othniel, **s** of Kenaz,
3:15 (Ehud was the **s** of Gera.)
3:31 came Shamgar, **s** of Anath.
4:6 Barak, **s** of Abinoam,
4:12 that Barak, **s** of Abinoam,
5:1 **s** of Abinoam, sang this song:
5:6 **s** of Anath, in the days of Jael,
5:12 your prisoners, **s** of Abinoam.
6:11 Joash's **s** Gideon was beating
6:29 "Gideon, **s** of Joash, did this."
6:30 told Joash, "Bring your **s** out.
7:14 Gideon, **s** of Joash, from Israel.
8:13 Gideon, **s** of Joash,
8:18 one looked like a king's **s**."
8:20 he told Jether, his firstborn **s**,
8:22 to Gideon, "You, then your **s**,
8:23 will not rule you nor will my **s**.
8:29 Jerubbaal, **s** of Joash,
8:31 Shechem also gave birth to a **s**.
8:31 That **s** was named Abimelech.
8:32 Gideon, **s** of Joash,
9:1 **s** of Jerubbaal [Gideon],
9:5 Jerubbaal's youngest **s**,
9:18 who is the **s** of my father's
9:26 Then Gaal (**s** of Ebed) and his
9:28 Gaal (**s** of Ebed) said,
9:28 Isn't he Jerubbaal's **s**,
9:30 heard what Gaal (**s** of Ebed)
9:31 Gaal (**s** of Ebed) and his
9:35 Gaal (**s** of Ebed) went out and
9:57 **s** of Jerubbaal, came true.
10:1 who was the **s** of Puah and
11:2 You're the **s** of that other
11:25 **s** of King Zippor of Moab,
12:13 After Elon, Abdon, **s** of Hillel,
13:3 become pregnant and have a **s**.
13:5 become pregnant and have a **s**.
13:7 become pregnant and have a **s**.
13:24 So the woman had a **s** and
17:2 "The LORD bless you, my **s**!"
18:29 of their ancestor Dan, Israel's **s**.
18:30 Jonathan (**s** of Gershom and
20:28 (Phinehas, **s** of Eleazar and
Rut 1:4 Each **s** married a woman from
1:4 One **s** married a woman named
1:4 and the other **s** married a
4:12 the **s** whom Tamar gave birth
4:13 So she gave birth to a **s**.
4:17 said, "Naomi has a **s**."
1Sm 1:1 He was the **s** of Jeroham,
1:20 pregnant and gave birth to a **s**.
1:23 and nursed her **s** until she had
3:6 call [you], **s**," he responded.
3:16 "Samuel, my **s**!" he said. "Here I
4:16 "What happened, **s**?"
4:19 and gave birth to a **s**.
4:20 You've given birth to a **s**."
7:1 They gave Abinadab's **s**
8:2 of his firstborn **s** was Joel;
8:2 of his second **s** was Abijah.
9:1 He was a **s** of Abiel,
9:2 He had a **s** named Saul,
10:2 can I do [to find] my **s**?'"
10:11 has happened to the **s** of Kish?
10:21 Then Saul, the **s** of Kish,
13:16 Saul, his **s** Jonathan,

1Sm 13:22 and his **s** Jonathan had them.
14:1 One day Saul's **s** Jonathan
14:3 in addition to Ahijah, the **s** of
14:3 who was the **s** of Phinehas
14:39 even if it is my **s** Jonathan
14:40 and my **s** Jonathan and I will
14:41 sin is mine or my **s** Jonathan's,
14:42 me and my **s** Jonathan,"
14:50 the **s** of Saul's uncle Ner.
16:19 "Send me your **s** David,
16:20 them with his **s** David to Saul.
17:12 David was a **s** of a man named
17:17 Jesse told his **s** David,
17:55 whose **s** is this young man?"
17:56 "Find out whose **s** this young
17:58 "Whose **s** are you,
17:58 "The **s** of your servant Jesse of
19:1 Saul told his **s** Jonathan and
19:1 But Saul's **s** Jonathan was
20:27 Saul asked his **s** Jonathan,
20:27 "Why hasn't Jesse's **s** come to
20:30 "**S** of a crooked and rebellious
20:30 you've sided with Jesse's **s**.
20:30 your mother's **s** but not mine.
20:31 As long as Jesse's **s** lives on
22:7 Will Jesse's **s** give every one
22:8 me when my **s** entered into
22:8 a loyalty pledge with Jesse's **s**.
22:8 that my **s** has encouraged my
22:9 "I saw Jesse's **s** when he
22:9 Ahimelech, Ahitub's **s**, in Nob.
22:11 who was Ahitub's **s**,
22:12 said, "Listen here, **s** of Ahitub!"
22:13 "Why did you and Jesse's **s**
22:20 But Ahimelech, Ahitub's **s**,
22:20 had one **s** who escaped.
23:6 When Ahimelech's **s** Abiathar
23:16 Saul's **s** Jonathan came to
25:8 Please give us and your **s**
25:10 "Who is Jesse's **s**?
25:44 David's wife, to Palti, Laish's **s**,
26:5 where Saul and Ner's **s** Abner,
26:6 who was Zeruiah's **s** and
26:14 the troops and to Ner's **s** Abner.
27:2 Achish of Gath, Moach's **s**.
30:7 priest Abiathar, Ahimelech's **s**,
2Sm 1:4 Saul and his **s** Jonathan are
1:5 and his **s** Jonathan are dead?"
1:12 because Saul, his **s** Jonathan,
1:13 the **s** of a foreign resident."
1:17 for Saul and his **s** Jonathan.
2:8 Ner's **s** Abner, commander of
2:8 took Saul's **s** Ishbosheth and
2:10 Saul's **s** Ishbosheth was 40
2:12 Ner's **s** Abner and the officers
2:12 Saul's **s** Ishbosheth went from
2:13 Zeruiah's **s** Joab and David's
2:15 Saul's **s** Ishbosheth),
3:2 His first **s** was Amnon,
3:14 to Saul's **s** Ishbosheth
3:15 her husband Paltiel, **s** of Laish.
3:23 "Ner's **s** Abner came to the
3:25 know that Ner's **s** Abner came
3:28 the blood of Ner's **s** Abner.
3:37 for killing Ner's **s** Abner.
4:1 When Saul's **s** Ishbosheth
4:2 Saul's **s** had two men who
4:4 In addition, Saul's **s** Jonathan
4:4 Saul's son Jonathan had a **s**
4:8 the **s** of your enemy Saul who
7:14 and he will be my **S**.
8:3 King Hadadezer, **s** of Rehob.
8:10 he sent his **s** Joram to greet
8:12 King Hadadezer, **s** of Rehob.
8:16 Zeruiah's **s** Joab was in charge
8:16 Ahilud's **s** Jehoshaphat was
8:17 Ahitub's **s** Zadok and
8:17 **s** Ahimelech were priests.
8:18 Jehoiada's **s** Benaiah was
9:3 "Jonathan has a **s** who is
9:4 Ammiel's **s**, in Lo Debar."
9:5 the home of Ammiel's **s** Machir
9:6 When Mephibosheth (**s** of
9:12 Mephibosheth had a young **s**
10:1 and his **s** Hanun became king
11:21 Jerubbesheth's **s** Abimelech?

2Sm 11:27 Then she gave birth to a **s**.
12:14 the **s** that is born to you must
12:24 and she later gave birth to a **s**.
13:1 After this, David's **s** Amnon fell
13:1 the beautiful sister of David's **s**
13:3 a **s** of David's brother Shimea.
13:4 "Why are you, the king's **s**,
13:21 didn't punish his **s** Amnon.
13:21 because he was his firstborn **s**.
13:25 "No, **S**," the king answered
13:32 the **s** of David's brother Shimea,
13:37 King Talmai, Ammihud's **s**.
13:37 for his **s** Amnon every day.
14:1 Joab, Zeruiah's **s**, knew the
14:11 more harm by destroying my **s**.
14:16 and my **s** from [our] God-given
15:27 and take your **s** Ahimaaz and
15:27 Abiathar's **s** Jonathan with you.
16:5 name was Shimei, **s** of Gera.
16:8 the kingship to your **s** Absalom.
16:9 Abishai, Zeruiah's **s**,
16:11 all his servants, "My own **s**,
16:19 Shouldn't it be his **s**?
17:25 (Amasa was the **s** of a man
17:27 **s** of Nahash from Rabbah in
17:27 **s** of Ammiel from Lo Debar,
18:2 brother Abishai (Zeruiah's **s**),
18:12 my hand against the king's **s**.
18:18 He said, "I have no **s** to keep
18:19 Then Ahimaaz, Zadok's **s**,
18:20 because the king's **s** is dead."
18:22 Ahimaaz, Zadok's **s**,
18:22 "Now, **s**, why should you
18:27 runs like Ahimaaz, Zadok's **s**."
18:33 "My **s** Absalom!" he said as he
18:33 "My **s**, my son Absalom!
18:33 "My son, my **s** Absalom!
18:33 Absalom, my **s**, my son!"
18:33 Absalom, my son, my **s**!"
19:2 the king was grieving for his **s**.
19:4 cried loudly, "My **s** Absalom!
19:4 Absalom, my **s**, my son!"
19:4 Absalom, my son, my **s**!"
19:16 Shimei, Gera's **s** from the tribe
19:18 Shimei, Gera's **s**, bowed down
19:21 But Abishai, Zeruiah's **s**,
20:1 the name of Sheba, Bichri's **s**,
20:1 an inheritance from Jesse's **s**.
20:2 to follow Sheba, Bichri's **s**.
20:6 Abishai, "Sheba, **s** of Bichri,
20:7 to pursue Sheba, Bichri's **s**.
20:10 pursued Sheba, **s** of Bichri.
20:13 and pursued Sheba, Bichri's **s**.
20:21 the name of Sheba, **s** of Bichri,
20:23 Benaiah, **s** of Jehoiada,
20:24 Jehoshaphat, **s** of Ahilud,
21:7 Jonathan's **s** and Saul's
21:7 David and Jonathan, **s** of Saul.
21:8 **s** of Barzillai from Meholah.
21:12 Saul and of his **s** Jonathan from
21:14 of Saul and his **s** Jonathan
21:17 But Abishai, **s** of Zeruiah,
21:19 **s** of Jaare Oregim from
21:21 **s** of David's brother Shimei,
23:1 **s** of Jesse — the declaration by
23:9 He was the **s** of Dodo and
23:11 the **s** of Agee from Harar.
23:18 brother Abishai, Zeruiah's **s**,
23:20 Benaiah, **s** of Jehoiada,
23:22 Benaiah, **s** of Jehoiada, did.
23:24 leading men were] Elhanan (**s**
23:26 Ira (**s** of Ikkesh) from Tekoa,
23:27 Mebunnai (**s** of Hushai),
23:29 Heleb (**s** of Baanah) from
23:29 Ittai (**s** of Ribai) from Gibeah in
23:33 Jonathan ([**s** of] Shammah the
23:33 Ahiam (**s** of Sharar the Hararite
23:34 Eliphelet (**s** of Ahasbai and
23:34 Eliam (**s** of Ahithophel) from
23:36 Igal (**s** of Nathan) from Zobah,
23:37 armorbearer for Zeruiah's **s**
1Ki 1:5 Adonijah, **s** of Haggith,
1:7 his actions with Joab (**s**
1:8 Benaiah (**s** of Jehoiada),
1:11 Haggith's **s**, has become king,
1:13 to me that my **s** Solomon will

1Ki 1:17 You said that my **s** Solomon
1:21 Otherwise, my **s** Solomon and
1:26 who is Jehoiada's **s**,
1:30 Your **s** Solomon will be king
1:32 and Benaiah, **s** of Jehoiada."
1:33 Put my **s** Solomon on my mule,
1:36 Benaiah, **s** of Jehoiada,
1:38 Benaiah (**s** of Jehoiada),
1:42 **s** of the priest Abiathar,
1:44 Benaiah (**s** of Jehoiada),
2:1 he instructed his **s** Solomon,
2:5 what Joab (Zeruiah's **s**) did
2:5 Abner, **s** of Ner, and Amasa,
2:5 of Ner, and Amasa, **s** of Jether.
2:8 "Shimei, **s** of Gera from
2:13 Then Adonijah, **s** of Haggith,
2:22 **s**) are supporting him."
2:25 task to Benaiah, **s** of Jehoiada.
2:29 **s** of Jehoiada, to kill Joab.
2:32 to kill Abner (who was the **s**
2:32 and Amasa (who was the **s**
2:34 Then Benaiah, **s** of Jehoiada,
2:35 Benaiah, **s** of Jehoiada,
2:39 King Achish, **s** of Maacah.
2:46 to Benaiah, **s** of Jehoiada.
3:6 great love by giving him a **s**
3:17 I gave birth ⌊to a **s**⌋ while she
3:18 also gave birth ⌊to a **s**⌋.
3:19 That night this woman's **s** died
3:20 during the night and took my **s**,
3:20 she laid her dead **s** in my arms.
3:21 in the morning to nurse my **s**,
3:21 that he wasn't my **s** at all!"
3:22 My **s** is alive — your son is
3:22 son is alive — your **s** is dead."
3:22 Your **s** is dead — my son is
3:22 son is dead — my **s** is alive."
3:23 'My **s** is alive — your son is
3:23 son is alive — your **s** is dead,'
3:23 Your **s** is dead — my son is
3:23 son is dead — my **s** is alive."
3:26 Then the woman whose **s** was
4:2 officials: Azariah, **s** of Zadok,
4:3 Jehoshaphat, **s** of Ahilud,
4:4 Benaiah, **s** of Jehoiada,
4:5 Azariah, **s** of Nathan,
4:5 Zabud, **s** of Nathan,
4:6 Adoniram, **s** of Abda,
4:12 Baana, **s** of Ahilud,
4:14 Ahinadab, **s** of Iddo,
4:16 Baana, **s** of Hushai,
4:17 Jehoshaphat, **s** of Paruah,
4:18 Shimei, **s** of Ela, was in charge
4:19 Geber, **s** of Uri, was in charge
5:5 to my father David: 'Your **s**,
5:7 He has given David a wise **s** to
7:14 Hiram was the **s** of a widow
8:19 Instead, your own **s** will build
11:12 away from the hands of your **s**.
11:13 I will give your **s** one tribe for
11:20 had a **s** ⌊named⌋ Genubath.
11:23 raised up Rezon, **s** of Eliada,
11:26 who was the **s** of Nebat and an
11:35 the kingdom away from his **s**
11:36 I will give his **s** one tribe so
11:43 His **s** Rehoboam succeeded
12:2 Jeroboam (Nebat's **s**) was still
12:15 (Nebat's **s**) through Ahijah
12:16 an inheritance from Jesse's **s**.
12:21 to Rehoboam, **s** of Solomon.
12:23 King Rehoboam, **s** of Solomon,
13:2 There will be a **s** born in
14:1 **s** of Jeroboam, got sick.
14:5 you about her **s** who is sick.
14:20 His **s** Nadab succeeded him as
14:21 Rehoboam, **s** of Solomon,
14:31 His **s** Abijam succeeded him
15:1 reign of Jeroboam (Nebat's **s**),
15:8 His **s** Asa succeeded him as
15:18 **s** of Tabrimmon and grandson
15:24 His **s** Jehoshaphat succeeded
15:25 Nadab, **s** of Jeroboam,
15:27 Then Baasha, **s** of Ahijah from
15:33 of Judah, Baasha, **s** of Ahijah,
16:1 Hanani's **s**, against Baasha.
16:3 family of Jeroboam (Nebat's **s**).

1Ki 16:6 His **s** Elah succeeded him as
16:7 to the prophet Jehu, Hanani's **s**,
16:8 Elah, **s** of Baasha,
16:13 by Baasha and his **s** Elah.
16:21 followed Tibni, **s** of Ginath,
16:22 followed Tibni, Ginath's **s**.
16:26 like Jeroboam (Nebat's **s**).
16:28 His **s** Ahab succeeded him as
16:29 Ahab, **s** of Omri, began to rule
16:30 Ahab, **s** of Omri, did what the
16:31 sins as Jeroboam (Nebat's **s**).
16:34 cost him his firstborn **s**,
16:34 doors cost him his youngest **s**,
16:34 this through Joshua, **s** of Nun.
17:12 for myself and my **s** so that we
17:13 for yourself and your **s**.
17:17 Afterwards, the **s** of the woman
17:18 me of my sin and kill my **s**?
17:19 said to her, "Give me your **s**."
17:20 staying with by killing her **s**?"
17:23 "Look! Your **s** is alive."
19:16 Anoint Jehu, **s** of Nimshi,
19:16 anoint Elisha, **s** of Shaphat,
19:19 found Elisha, **s** of Shaphat.
21:22 family of Jeroboam (Nebat's **s**)
21:22 house of Baasha, **s** of Ahijah,
22:8 **s** of Imlah, but I hate him.
22:9 ⌊Get⌋ Micaiah, **s** of Imlah!"
22:11 Zedekiah, **s** of Chenaanah,
22:24 Zedekiah, **s** of Chenaanah,
22:40 His **s** Ahaziah succeeded him
22:41 Jehoshaphat, **s** of Asa,
22:49 Then Ahaziah, **s** of Ahab,
22:50 His **s** Jehoram succeeded him
22:51 Ahaziah, **s** of Ahab,
22:52 (Nebat's **s**) who led Israel
2Ki 1:17 because Ahaziah had no **s**.
3:1 Joram, **s** of Ahab, became king
3:3 Jeroboam (Nebat's **s**) led Israel
3:11 the **s** of Shaphat, is here.
3:27 Then he took his firstborn **s**,
4:6 were full, she told her **s**,
4:14 answered, "Well, she has no **s**,
4:17 and had a **s** at that time
4:28 "I didn't ask you for a **s**.
4:36 to him, he said, "Take your **s**."
4:37 She took her **s** and left.
6:28 told me, 'Give up your **s**.
6:28 We'll eat my **s** tomorrow.'
6:29 So we boiled my **s** and ate him.
6:29 day I told her, 'Give up your **s**.
6:29 but she hid her **s**."
6:31 head of Elisha, **s** of Shaphat,
8:1 had told the woman whose **s**
8:5 and this is her **s** whom Elisha
8:16 Joram (Ahab's **s**) was in his
8:16 **s** of King Jehoshaphat of
8:24 His **s** Ahaziah succeeded him
8:25 Joram (Ahab's **s**) was in his
8:25 **s** Ahaziah became king
8:28 Ahaziah went with Ahab's **s**
8:29 Then Jehoram's **s** Ahaziah
8:29 Jezreel to see Ahab's **s** Joram,
9:2 **s** of Jehoshaphat and grandson
9:9 family of Jeroboam (Nebat's **s**)
9:9 family of Baasha, **s** of Ahijah.
9:14 So Jehu, **s** of Jehoshaphat and
9:29 Ahab's **s**, was king of Israel.)
10:15 met Jehonadab, **s** of Rechab,
10:23 and Jehonadab, **s** of Rechab,
10:29 Jeroboam (Nebat's **s**) led Israel
10:35 His **s** Jehoahaz succeeded
11:1 saw that her **s** was dead,
11:2 took Ahaziah's **s** Joash.
11:4 and showed them the king's **s**.
11:12 brought out the king's **s**,
12:21 **s** of Shimeath, and Jehozabad,
12:21 **s** of Shomer, executed him.
12:21 His **s** Amaziah succeeded him
13:1 Ahaziah's **s** King Joash of
13:1 when Jehoahaz, **s** of Jehu,
13:2 Jeroboam (Nebat's **s**) led Israel
13:3 Hazael's **s** Benhadad as long
13:9 His **s** Jehoash ruled as king in
13:10 Jehoahaz's **s** Jehoash began
13:24 and his **s** Benhadad

2Ki 13:25 Then Jehoash, **s** of Jehoahaz,
14:1 Jehoahaz's **s** King Jehoash
14:1 **s** of Joash of Judah,
14:8 **s** of Jehoahaz and grandson of
14:9 your daughter marry my **s**,' but
14:13 **s** of Joash and grandson of
14:16 His **s** Jeroboam succeeded
14:17 Joash's **s** King Amaziah of
14:17 of Jehoahaz's **s** King Jehoash
14:23 Joash's **s** Amaziah was in his
14:23 Jehoash's **s** King Jeroboam
14:24 Jeroboam (Nebat's **s**) led Israel
14:25 Hepher and the **s** of Amittai.
14:27 Jeroboam, **s** of Jehoash.
14:29 His **s** Zechariah succeeded
15:1 Amaziah's **s** Azariah began to
15:5 The king's **s** Jotham was in
15:7 His **s** Jotham succeeded him
15:8 Jeroboam's **s** Zechariah was
15:9 Jeroboam (Nebat's **s**) led Israel
15:10 Shallum, **s** of Jabesh,
15:13 Shallum, **s** of Jabesh,
15:14 Then Menahem, **s** of Gadi,
15:14 attacked Shallum (**s** of Jabesh),
15:17 of Judah, Menahem, **s** of Gadi,
15:18 Jeroboam (Nebat's **s**) led Israel
15:22 and his **s** Pekahiah succeeded
15:23 Menahem's **s** Pekahiah began
15:24 Jeroboam (Nebat's **s**) led Israel
15:25 officer Pekah, **s** of Remaliah,
15:27 Judah, Pekah, **s** of Remaliah,
15:28 Jeroboam (Nebat's **s**) led Israel
15:30 Hoshea, **s** of Elah,
15:30 against Pekah, **s** of Remaliah.
15:30 year that Azariah, **s** of Jotham,
15:32 **s** of Remaliah, ruled Israel,
15:32 Israel, Jotham, **s** of Azariah,
15:37 **s** of Remaliah, to attack Judah.
15:38 His **s** Ahaz succeeded him as
16:1 Pekah, **s** of Remaliah,
16:1 when King Ahaz, **s** of Jotham,
16:3 sacrificed his **s** by burning him
16:5 **s** of Remaliah of Israel,
16:7 say, "I'm your servant, your **s**.
16:20 His **s** Hezekiah succeeded him
17:1 of Judah, Hoshea, **s** of Elah,
17:21 Jeroboam (Nebat's **s**) king.
18:1 King Hoshea, **s** of Elah,
18:1 **s** of Ahaz of Judah,
18:9 **s** of Elah of Israel) King
18:18 and was the **s** of Hilkiah,
18:18 historian and the **s** of Asaph,
18:26 Then Eliakim (**s** of Hilkiah),
18:37 and was the **s** of Hilkiah,
18:37 historian and the **s** of Asaph,
19:2 the prophet Isaiah, **s** of Amoz.
19:20 Then Isaiah, **s** of Amoz,
19:37 His **s** Esarhaddon succeeded
20:1 The prophet Isaiah, **s** of Amoz,
20:12 At that time Baladan's **s**,
20:21 His **s** Manasseh succeeded
21:6 He burned his **s** as a sacrifice,
21:7 to David and his **s** Solomon,
21:18 His **s** Amon succeeded him as
21:24 They made his **s** Josiah king
21:26 His **s** Josiah succeeded him
22:3 **s** of Azaliah and grandson of
22:12 to Ahikam (**s** of Shaphan),
22:12 Achbor (**s** of Micaiah),
22:14 She was the wife of Shallum, **s**
23:15 made by Jeroboam (Nebat's **s**),
23:30 land took Josiah's **s** Jehoahaz,
23:34 made Josiah's **s** Eliakim king
24:6 and his **s** Jehoiakin succeeded
25:22 **s** of Ahikam and grandson of
25:23 were Ishmael (**s** of Nethaniah),
25:23 Johanan (**s** of Kareah),
25:23 Seraiah (**s** of Tanhumeth from
25:25 the seventh month Ishmael (**s**
1Ch 1:36 Kenaz and Amalek, **s** of Timna.
1:41 Anah's **s** was Dishon.
1:43 of Israel: Bela, **s** of Beor,
1:44 **s** of Zerah from Bozrah,
1:46 died, Hadad, **s** of Bedad,
1:49 died, Baal Hanan, **s** of Achbor,
2:7 Carmi's **s** was Achar,

1Ch 2:8 Ethan's s was Azariah.
2:13 Abinadab (his second s),
2:13 Shimea (his third s),
2:14 Nethanel (his fourth s),
2:14 Raddai (his fifth s),
2:15 Ozem (his sixth s),
2:15 and David (his seventh s).
2:18 Hezron's s was Caleb.
2:18 Azubah had a s named Jerioth.
2:25 Jerahmeel (the firstborn s of
2:27 sons of Ram (the firstborn s
2:31 Appaim's s was Ishi,
2:31 and Ishi's s was Sheshan,
2:31 and Sheshan's s was Ahlai.
2:42 were his firstborn s Mesha,
2:45 Shammai's s was Maon,
2:50 the firstborn s of Ephrath,
3:1 His first s was Amnon,
3:10 Solomon's s was Rehoboam.
3:10 Rehoboam's s was Abijah.
3:10 Abijah's s was Asa.
3:10 Asa's s was Jehoshaphat.
3:11 Jehoshaphat's s was Joram.
3:11 Joram's s was Ahaziah.
3:11 Ahaziah's s was Joash.
3:12 Joash's s was Amaziah.
3:12 Amaziah's s was Azariah.
3:12 Azariah's s was Jotham.
3:13 Jotham's s was Ahaz.
3:13 Ahaz's s was Hezekiah.
3:13 Hezekiah's s was Manasseh.
3:14 Manasseh's s was Amon.
3:14 Amon's s was Josiah.
3:15 firstborn s was Johanan,
3:16 Jehoiakim's s was Jeconiah,
3:16 whose s was Zedekiah.
3:17 Jeconiah were his s Shealtiel,
3:21 Jeshaiah's s was Rephaiah.
3:21 Rephaiah's s was Arnan.
3:21 Arnan's s was Obadiah.
3:21 Obadiah's s was Shecaniah.
3:22 Shecaniah's s was Shemaiah.
4:2 Reaiah, s of Shobal,
4:8 families of Aharhel, s of Harum.
4:15 s of Jephunneh, were Iru, Elah,
4:15 Elah's s was Kenaz.
4:21 of Shelah, s of Judah, were Er,
4:25 Shaul's s was Shallum.
4:25 Shallum's s was Mibsam.
4:25 Mibsam's s was Mishma.
4:26 Mishma's s was Hammuel.
4:26 Hammuel's s was Zaccur.
4:26 Zaccur's s was Shimei.
4:34 Joshah (s of Amaziah),
4:35 Joel, Jehu (s of Joshibiah,
4:37 Ziza (s of Shiphi, grandson of
5:1 genealogy as the firstborn s.
5:4 Joel's s was Shemaiah.
5:4 Shemaiah's s was Gog.
5:4 Gog's s was Shimei.
5:5 Shimei's s was Micah.
5:5 Micah's s was Reaiah.
5:5 Reaiah's s was Baal.
5:6 Baal's s was Beerah.
5:8 and Bela (s of Azaz,
5:12 from Gad's first s Joel.
5:12 from Gad's second s Shapham.
5:14 who was the s of Huri,
5:14 Gilead was the s of Michael,
5:15 Ahi, s of Abdiel and grandson
6:20 Gershom's s was Libni.
6:20 Libni's s was Jahath.
6:20 Jahath's s was Zimmah.
6:21 Zimmah's s was Joah.
6:21 Joah's s was Iddo.
6:21 Iddo's s was Zerah.
6:21 Zerah's s was Jeatherai.
6:22 Kohath's s was Amminadab.
6:22 Amminadab's s was Korah.
6:22 Korah's s was Assir.
6:23 Assir's s was Elkanah.
6:23 Elkanah's s was Ebiasaph.
6:23 Ebiasaph's s was Assir.
6:24 Assir's s was Tahath.
6:24 Tahath's s was Uriel.
6:24 Uriel's s was Uzziah.

1Ch 6:24 Uzziah's s was Shaul.
6:26 Ahimoth's s was Elkanah.
6:26 Elkanah's s was Zophai.
6:26 Zophai's s was Nahath.
6:27 Nahath's s was Eliab.
6:27 Eliab's s was Jeroham.
6:27 Jeroham's s was Elkanah.
6:28 who was his second s.
6:29 Merari's s was Mahli.
6:29 Mahli's s was Libni.
6:29 Libni's s was Shimei.
6:29 Shimei's s was Uzzah.
6:30 Uzzah's s was Shimea.
6:30 Shimea's s was Haggiah.
6:30 Haggiah's s was Asaiah.
6:33 Heman was the s of Joel,
6:33 who was the s of Samuel,
6:34 who was the s of Elkanah,
6:34 who was the s of Jeroham,
6:34 who was the s of Eliel,
6:34 who was the s of Toah,
6:35 who was the s of Zuph,
6:35 who was the s of Elkanah,
6:35 who was the s of Mahath,
6:35 who was the s of Amasai,
6:36 who was the s of Elkanah,
6:36 who was the s of Joel,
6:36 who was the s of Azariah,
6:36 who was the s of Zephaniah,
6:37 who was the s of Tahath,
6:37 who was the s of Assir,
6:37 who was the s of Ebiasaph,
6:37 who was the s of Korah,
6:38 who was the s of Izhar,
6:38 who was the s of Kohath,
6:38 who was the s of Levi,
6:38 who was the s of Israel.
6:39 He was the s of Berechiah,
6:39 who was the s of Shimea,
6:40 who was the s of Michael,
6:40 who was the s of Baaseiah,
6:40 who was the s of Malchiah,
6:41 who was the s of Ethni,
6:41 who was the s of Zerah,
6:41 who was the s of Adaiah,
6:42 who was the s of Ethan,
6:42 who was the s of Zimmah,
6:42 who was the s of Shimei,
6:43 who was the s of Jahath,
6:43 who was the s of Gershom,
6:43 who was the s of Levi.
6:44 Ethan was the s of Kishi,
6:44 who was the s of Abdi,
6:44 who was the s of Malluch,
6:45 who was the s of Hashabiah,
6:45 who was the s of Amaziah,
6:45 who was the s of Hilkiah,
6:46 who was the s of Amzi,
6:46 who was the s of Bani,
6:46 who was the s of Shemer,
6:47 who was the s of Mahli,
6:47 who was the s of Mushi,
6:47 who was the s of Merari,
6:47 who was the s of Levi.
6:50 His s was Eleazar.
6:50 Eleazar's s was Phinehas.
6:50 Phinehas' s was Abishua.
6:51 Abishua's s was Bukki.
6:51 Bukki's s was Uzzi.
6:51 Uzzi's s was Zerahiah.
6:52 Zerahiah's s was Meraioth.
6:52 Meraioth's s was Amariah.
6:52 Amariah's s was Ahitub.
6:53 Ahitub's s was Zadok.
6:53 Zadok's s was Ahimaaz.
6:56 to Caleb, s of Jephunneh.
7:10 Jediael's s was Bilhan.
7:15 his second s was Zelophehad.
7:16 Maacah, Machir's wife, had a s,
7:17 Ulam's s was Bedan.
7:17 of Machir (s of Manasseh).
7:20 Ephraim's s was Shuthelah.
7:20 Shuthelah's s was Bered.
7:20 Bered's s was Tahath.
7:20 Tahath's s was Eleadah.
7:20 Eleadah's s was Tahath.

1Ch 7:21 Tahath's s was Zabad.
7:21 Zabad's s was Shuthelah.
7:23 She gave birth to a s,
7:25 Beriah's s was Rephah.
7:25 Rephah's s was Resheph.
7:25 Resheph's s was Telah.
7:25 Telah's s was Tahan.
7:26 Tahan's s was Ladan.
7:26 Ladan's s was Ammihud.
7:26 Ammihud's s was Elishama.
7:27 Elishama's s was Nun.
7:27 Nun's s was Joshua.
7:29 s of Israel, live in these cities.
8:1 Ashbel (his second s),
8:1 Aharah (his third s),
8:2 Nohah (his fourth s),
8:2 and Rapha (his fifth s).
8:30 His firstborn s was Abdon,
8:34 Jonathan's s was Meribbaal,
8:37 Binea's s was Raphah.
8:37 Raphah's s was Eleasah.
8:37 Eleasah's s was Azel.
8:39 Jeush (the second s),
8:39 and Eliphelet (the third s).
9:4 Perez, s of Judah, was Uthai,
9:4 who was the s of Ammihud,
9:7 were Sallu (s of Meshullam,
9:8 Ibneiah (s of Jeroham),
9:8 Elah (s of Uzzi and grandson of
9:8 Meshullam (s of Shephatiah,
9:11 Azariah was the s of Hilkiah,
9:11 the s of Ahitub (the official in
9:12 were Adaiah (s of Jeroham,
9:12 and Maasai (s of Adiel,
9:12 was Meshillemith, s of Immer).
9:14 were Shemaiah (s of Hasshub,
9:15 Mattaniah (s of Mica,
9:16 Obadiah (s of Shemaiah,
9:16 and Berechiah (s of Asa and
9:19 Shallum (s of Kore,
9:20 (Phinehas, Eleazar's s,
9:21 Zechariah, s of Meshelemiah,
9:31 the firstborn s of Shallum,
9:36 His firstborn s was Abdon,
9:40 Jonathan's s was Meribbaal,
9:43 Binea's s was Rephaiah.
9:43 Rephaiah's s was Eleasah.
9:43 Eleasah's s was Azel.
10:14 over to David, Jesse's s.
11:6 Zeruiah's s Joab was the first
11:11 Jashobeam, s of Hachmon,
11:12 He was the s of Dodo and
11:22 Benaiah, s of Jehoiada,
11:24 Benaiah, s of Jehoiada, did.
11:26 Elhanan (s of Dodo) from
11:28 Ira (s of Ikkesh) from Tekoa,
11:29 Sibbecai (s of Hushai),
11:30 Heled (s of Baanah) from
11:31 Ithai (s of Ribai) from Gibeah in
11:34 Jonathan (s of Shage the
11:35 Ahiam (s of Sachar the
11:35 the Hararite), Eliphal (s of Ur),
11:37 from Carmel, Naari (s of Ezbai),
11:38 Joel (s of Nathan),
11:38 Mibhar (s of Hagri),
11:39 armorbearer for Zeruiah's s
11:41 Zabad (s of Ahlai),
11:42 Adina (s of Shiza) from the tribe
11:43 Hanan (s of Maacah),
11:45 Jediael (s of Shimri) and his
12:1 banished by Saul, s of Kish.
12:18 We are with you, s of Jesse.
15:17 appointed Heman, s of Joel,
15:17 Asaph, Berechiah's s.
15:17 Ethan, s of Kushaiah.
16:38 Obed Edom (Jeduthun's s) and
17:13 and he will be my S.
18:10 he sent his s Hadoram to greet
18:12 Zeruiah's s Abishai killed
18:15 Zeruiah's s Joab was in charge
18:15 Ahilud's s Jehoshaphat was
18:16 Ahitub's s Zadok and
18:16 s Abimelech were priests.
18:17 Jehoiada's s Benaiah was
19:1 and his s became king in his
20:5 Elhanan, s of Jair, killed Lahmi,

1Ch 20:7 **s** of David's brother Shimea,
22:5 David thought, "My **s** Solomon
22:6 He summoned his **s** Solomon
22:7 David told his **s** Solomon,
22:9 You will have a **s** who will be
22:10 He will be my **s**, and I will be
22:11 ⌊David continued,⌋ "Now, **s**,
22:17 of Israel to help his **s** Solomon.
23:1 he made his **s** Solomon king of
23:16 only **s** was Shebuel.
23:17 Eliezer's only **s** was Rehabiah.
23:18 Izhar's only **s** was Shelomith.
23:19 Hebron's first **s** was Jeriah;
23:20 Uzziel's first **s** was Micah;
24:6 The scribe Shemaiah was a **s**
24:6 Ahimelech (**s** of Abiathar),
24:26 and Merari's **s** Jaaziah,
24:27 through his **s** Jaaziah),
25:9 chose Joseph, the **s** of Asaph.
26:1 Meshelemiah, the **s** of Kore,
26:6 His **s** Shemaiah had sons who
26:14 His **s** Zechariah, a counselor
26:24 of Moses' **s** Gershom.
26:25 (Eliezer's **s** was Rehabiah;
26:25 Joram's **s** was Zichri;
26:28 the seer, Saul (**s** of Kish),
26:28 (son of Kish), Abner (**s** of Ner),
26:28 and Joab (**s** of Zeruiah) had
27:2 Jashobeam, **s** of Zabdiel,
27:5 **s** of the priest Jehoiada.
27:6 His **s** was Ammizabad.
27:7 after him was his **s** Zebadiah.
27:9 Ira, the **s** of Ikkesh from Tekoa,
27:16 **s** of Zichri for the tribe of
27:16 Shephatiah, **s** of Maacah
27:17 **s** of Kemuel for the family of
27:18 of Issachar: Omri, **s** of Michael
27:19 **s** of Obadiah for the tribe of
27:19 Naphtali: Jerimoth, **s** of Azriel
27:20 **s** of Azaziah for half of the tribe
27:20 Manasseh: Joel, **s** of Pedaiah
27:21 **s** of Zechariah for the tribe of
27:21 Benjamin: Jaasiel, **s** of Abner
27:22 for the tribe of Dan: Azarel, **s** of
27:24 Joab, **s** of Zeruiah,
27:25 **s** of Adiel for the goods in the
27:25 Jonathan, **s** of Uzziah
27:26 in the fields: Ezri, **s** of Chelub
27:29 the valleys: Shaphat, **s** of Adlai
27:32 and Jehiel, **s** of Hachmoni,
27:34 Jehoiada (**s** of Benaiah) and
28:5 sons) he chose my **s** Solomon
28:6 "He told me, 'Your **s** Solomon
28:6 I have chosen him to be my **s**.
28:9 "And you, my **s** Solomon,
28:11 Then David gave his **s**
28:20 David also told his **s** Solomon,
29:1 assembly, "My **s** Solomon,
29:19 Make my **s** Solomon
29:22 made David's **s** Solomon king.
29:26 David, **s** of Jesse,
29:28 Then his **s** Solomon
2Ch 1:1 Solomon, **s** of David,
1:5 **s** of Uri and grandson of Hur,
2:12 David a wise **s** who has insight
2:14 He was the **s** of a woman from
6:9 Instead, your own **s** will build
9:29 about Jeroboam (**s** of Nebat)?
9:31 His **s** Rehoboam succeeded
10:2 Jeroboam (Nebat's **s**) was still
10:15 (Nebat's **s**) through Ahijah
10:16 an inheritance from Jesse's **s**.
11:3 King Rehoboam, **s** of Solomon,
11:17 **s** of Solomon, for three years.
11:18 (Jerimoth was the **s** of David
11:18 daughter of Eliab, **s** of Jesse.)
11:22 appointed Abijah, **s** of Maacah,
12:16 His **s** Abijah succeeded him as
13:6 But Jeroboam (Nebat's **s**)
13:6 servant of David's **s** Solomon.
13:7 Rehoboam, **s** of Solomon,
14:1 His **s** Asa succeeded him as
15:1 came to Azariah, **s** of Oded.
17:1 Asa's **s** Jehoshaphat
17:16 to him Amasiah, Zichri's **s**,
18:7 **s** of Imla, but I hate him.

2Ch 18:8 ⌊Get⌋ Micaiah, **s** of Imla!"
18:10 Zedekiah, **s** of Chenaanah,
18:23 Zedekiah, **s** of Chenaanah,
19:2 Jehu, **s** of the seer Hanani,
19:11 Zebadiah, who is the **s** of
20:14 (He was the **s** of Zechariah,
20:34 records of Jehu, **s** of Hanani,
20:37 **s** of Dodavahu from Mareshah,
21:1 His **s** Jehoram succeeded him
21:17 The only **s** left was Ahaziah,
21:17 Jehoram's youngest **s**.
22:1 youngest **s** Ahaziah king
22:1 So Jehoram's **s** Ahaziah
22:5 went with Ahab's **s** King Joram
22:6 Then Jehoram's **s** Ahaziah
22:6 Jezreel to see Ahab's **s** Joram,
22:10 saw that her **s** was dead,
22:11 took Ahaziah's **s** Joash.
23:1 **s** of Jeroham, Ishmael,
23:1 **s** of Jehohanan, Azariah,
23:1 Azariah, **s** of Obed, Maaseiah,
23:1 **s** of Adaiah, and Elishaphat,
23:1 and Elishaphat, **s** of Zichri.
23:3 "Here is the king's **s**.
23:11 they brought out the king's **s**,
24:20 **s** of the priest Jehoiada,
24:22 Instead, he killed Jehoiada's **s**.
24:25 against him for murdering the **s**
24:26 **s** of an Ammonite woman
24:26 **s** of a Moabite woman named
24:27 His **s** Amaziah succeeded him
25:17 **s** of Jehoahaz and grandson of
25:18 your daughter marry my **s**,' but
25:23 **s** of Joash and grandson of
25:25 Joash's **s** King Amaziah of
25:25 of Jehoahaz's **s** King Jehoash
26:21 His **s** Jotham was in charge of
26:22 the prophet Isaiah, **s** of Amoz.
26:23 His **s** Jotham succeeded him
27:9 His **s** Ahaz succeeded him as
28:3 sacrificed his **s** by burning him
28:6 one day Pekah, **s** of Remaliah,
28:7 who was the king's **s**,
28:12 Then Azariah, **s** of Jehohan,
28:12 **s** of Meshillemoth,
28:12 **s** of Shallum, and Amasa,
28:12 **s** of Hadlai (some leaders of
28:27 His **s** Hezekiah succeeded him
29:12 Mahath, **s** of Amasai, and Joel,
29:12 Amasai, and Joel, **s** of Azariah.
29:12 Kish, **s** of Abdi, and Azariah,
29:12 and Azariah, **s** of Jehallelel.
29:12 Joah, **s** of Zimmah, and Eden,
29:12 Zimmah, and Eden, **s** of Joah.
31:14 Kore, **s** of Imnah the Levite,
32:20 the prophet Isaiah, **s** of Amoz,
32:32 the prophet Isaiah, **s** of Amoz,
32:33 His **s** Manasseh succeeded
33:6 He burned his **s** as a sacrifice
33:7 to David and his **s** Solomon,
33:20 His **s** Amon succeeded him as
33:25 They made his **s** Josiah king
34:8 **s** of Azaliah, Maaseiah,
34:8 royal historian and **s** of Joahaz,
34:20 Ahikam (**s** of Shaphan),
34:20 Abdon (**s** of Micah),
34:22 She was the wife of Shallum, **s**
35:3 **s** of David and king of Israel,
35:4 the records of his **s** Solomon.
36:1 land took Josiah's **s** Jehoahaz
36:8 His **s** Jehoiakin succeeded
Ezr 3:2 Then Jozadak's **s** Jeshua and
3:2 and Shealtiel's **s** Zerubbabel
3:8 (who was Shealtiel's **s**),
3:8 Jeshua (who was Jozadak's **s**),
5:2 who was Shealtiel's **s**,
5:2 who was Jozadak's **s**,
7:1 Ezra was the **s** of Seraiah,
7:1 who was the **s** of Azariah,
7:1 who was the **s** of Hilkiah,
7:2 who was the **s** of Shallum,
7:2 who was the **s** of Zadok,
7:2 who was the **s** of Ahitub,
7:3 who was the **s** of Amariah,
7:3 who was the **s** of Azariah,
7:3 who was the **s** of Meraioth,

Ezr 7:4 who was the **s** of Zerahiah,
7:4 who was the **s** of Uzzi,
7:4 who was the **s** of Bukki,
7:5 who was the **s** of Abishua,
7:5 who was the **s** of Phinehas,
7:5 who was the **s** of Eleazer,
7:5 who was the **s** of Aaron (the
8:3 **s** of Shecaniah from the family
8:4 **s** of Zerahiah, with 200 males
8:5 **s** of Jahaziel, with 300 males
8:6 **s** of Jonathan, with 50 males
8:7 **s** of Athaliah, with 70 males
8:8 **s** of Michael, with 80 males
8:9 **s** of Jehiel, with 210 males
8:10 **s** of Josiphiah, with 160 males
8:11 **s** of Bebai, with 38 males
8:12 **s** of Hakkatan, with 110 males
8:33 **s** of the priest Uriah,
8:33 the **s** of Phinehas.
8:33 Jeshua's **s** Jozabad,
8:33 and Binnui's **s** Noadiah,
10:2 Then Shecaniah, **s** of Jehiel,
10:6 of Jehohanan, **s** of Eliashib.
10:15 (Only Jonathan, Asahel's **s**,
10:15 Tikvah's **s**, opposed this.
10:18 Jozadak's **s**) and his brothers.
Neh 1:1 of Nehemiah, **s** of Hacaliah:
3:2 Zaccur, **s** of Imri, was next to
3:4 Next to them Meremoth, **s** of
3:4 Next to them Meshullam, **s** of
3:4 **s** of Baana, made repairs.
3:6 Joiada, Paseah's **s**,
3:6 and Meshullam, Besodeiah's **s**,
3:8 Harhaiah's **s**, a goldsmith,
3:9 Next to them Rephaiah, Hur's **s**,
3:10 to them Jedaiah, Harumaph's **s**,
3:10 Hashabneiah's **s**, made repairs.
3:11 Malchiah, Harim's **s**,
3:11 and Hasshub, Pahath Moab's **s**,
3:12 them Shallum, Hallohesh's **s**,
3:14 by Malchiah, Rechab's **s**,
3:15 Shallun, Col Hozeh's **s**,
3:16 After him Nehemiah, Azbuk's **s**,
3:17 including Rehum (Bani's **s**),
3:18 included Binnui, Henadad's **s**,
3:19 Next to him Ezer, Jeshua's **s**,
3:20 After him Baruch, Zabbai's **s**,
3:21 After him Meremoth, **s** of Uriah
3:23 After them Azariah, **s** of
3:24 After him Binnui, Henadad's **s**,
3:25 Palal, Uzai's **s**, made repairs
3:25 After him Pedaiah, Parosh's **s**,
3:29 After them Zadok, Immer's **s**,
3:29 him Shemaiah, Shecaniah's **s**,
3:30 Shelemiah's **s**, and Hanun,
3:30 and Hanun, Zalaph's sixth **s**,
3:30 him Meshullam, Berechiah's **s**,
6:10 **s** of Delaiah and grandson of
6:18 of Shecaniah, Arah's **s**.
6:18 In addition, Tobiah's **s**
6:18 of Meshullam, Berechiah's **s**.
8:17 From the time of Jeshua (**s** of
10:1 Nehemiah (**s** of Hacaliah),
10:9 Jeshua (**s** of Azaniah),
11:4 who was the **s** of Uzziah,
11:4 who was the **s** of Zechariah,
11:4 who was the **s** of Amariah,
11:4 who was the **s** of Shephatiah,
11:4 who was the **s** of Mahalalel,
11:4 who was the **s** of Perez;
11:5 Maaseiah was the **s** of Baruch,
11:5 who was the **s** of Col Hozeh,
11:5 who was the **s** of Hazaiah,
11:5 who was the **s** of Adaiah,
11:5 who was the **s** of Joiarib,
11:5 who was the **s** of Zechariah,
11:5 who was the **s** of Shiloni.
11:7 who was the **s** of Meshullam,
11:7 who was the **s** of Joed,
11:7 who was the **s** of Pedaiah,
11:7 who was the **s** of Kolaiah,
11:7 who was the **s** of Maaseiah,
11:7 who was the **s** of Ithiel,
11:7 who was the **s** of Jeshaiah,
11:9 Joel, **s** of Zichri, was in
11:9 and Judah, **s** of Senuah,

Neh 11:10 Jedaiah (**s** of Joiarib),
11:11 who was the **s** of Hilkiah,
11:11 who was the **s** of Meshullam,
11:11 who was the **s** of Zadok,
11:11 who was the **s** of Meraioth,
11:11 who was the **s** of Ahitub,
11:12 He was the **s** of Jeroham,
11:12 who was the **s** of Pelaliah,
11:12 who was the **s** of Amzi,
11:12 who was the **s** of Zechariah,
11:12 who was the **s** of Pashhur,
11:12 who was the **s** of Malchiah.
11:13 Amashsai was the **s** of Azarel,
11:13 who was the **s** of Ahzai,
11:13 was the **s** of Meshillemoth,
11:13 who was the **s** of Immer.
11:14 was Zabdiel, **s** of Haggedolim.
11:15 who was the **s** of Hasshub,
11:15 who was the **s** of Azrikam,
11:15 who was the **s** of Hashabiah,
11:15 who was the **s** of Bunni.
11:17 Mattaniah was the **s** of Mica,
11:17 who was the **s** of Zabdi,
11:17 who was the **s** of Asaph,
11:17 who was the **s** of Shammua,
11:17 who was the **s** of Galal,
11:17 who was the **s** of Jeduthum.
11:22 who was the **s** of Bani,
11:22 who was the **s** of Hashabiah,
11:22 who was the **s** of Mattaniah,
11:22 who was the **s** of Mica from
11:24 Pethahiah, **s** of Meshezabel,
11:24 of Zerah, Judah's **s**,
12:1 (Shealtiel's **s**) and Jeshua:
12:24 and Jeshua (**s** of Kadmiel).
12:26 days of Joiakim, **s** of Jeshua,
12:35 who was the **s** of Jonathan,
12:35 who was the **s** of Shemaiah,
12:35 who was the **s** of Mattaniah,
12:35 who was the **s** of Micaiah,
12:35 who was the **s** of Zaccur,
12:35 who was the **s** of Asaph.
12:45 and his **s** Solomon had ordered
13:13 **s** of Zaccur and grandson of
13:28 (Joiada was the **s** of the chief
13:28 Joiada's **s** away from me.
Est 2:5 He was the **s** of Jair,
3:1 (Haman was the **s** of
3:10 (Haman was the **s** of
8:5 plot of Haman (who was the **s**
9:10 who was the **s** of Hammedatha
9:24 (Haman was the **s** of
Job 16:21 The **S** of Man will plead for his
18:13 Death's firstborn **s** eats away at
32:2 Then Elihu, **s** of Barachel,
32:6 So Elihu, **s** of Barachel,
Psa 2:7 He said to me: "You are my **S**.
2:12 Kiss the **S**, or he will become
8:4 that you remember him or the **S**
50:20 slander your own mother's **s**.
72:1 the king's **s** your righteousness
72:20 by David, **s** of Jesse, end here.
80:15 the **s** you strengthened for
80:17 the **s** of man you strengthened
86:16 Save me because I am the **s** of
116:16 the **s** of your female servant.
Pro 1:1 David's **s** who was king of
1:8 My **s**, listen to your father's
1:10 My **s**, if sinners lure you, do not
1:15 My **s**, do not follow them in
2:1 My **s**, if you take my words ⌊to
3:1 My **s**, do not forget my
3:11 discipline of the LORD, my **s**,
3:12 even as a father warns a **s** with
3:21 My **s**, do not lose sight of these
4:10 My **s**, listen and accept my
4:20 My **s**, pay attention to my
5:1 My **s**, pay attention to my
5:20 Why should you, my **s**,
6:1 My **s**, if you guarantee a loan
6:3 Do the following things, my **s**,
6:20 My **s**, Obey the command of
7:1 My **s**, pay attention to my
10:1 A wise **s** makes his father
10:1 but a foolish **s** brings grief to
10:5 in the summer is a wise **s**.
Pro 13:1 A wise **s** listens to his father's
13:24 Whoever refuses to spank his **s**
13:24 but whoever loves his **s**
15:20 A wise **s** makes his father
17:2 over a **s** who acts shamefully,
17:25 A foolish **s** is a heartache to
19:13 A foolish **s** ruins his father,
19:18 Discipline your **s** while there is
19:26 A **s** who assaults his father
19:27 listening to instruction, my **s**,
23:15 My **s**, if you have a wise heart,
23:19 My **s**, listen, be wise, and keep
23:22 your father since you are his **s**,
23:24 has a wise **s** will enjoy him.
23:26 My **s**, give me your heart.
24:13 Eat honey, my **s**, because it is
24:21 Fear the LORD, my **s**.
27:11 Be wise, my **s**, and make my
28:7 ⌊God's⌋ teachings is a wise **s**.
29:17 Correct your **s**, and he will give
30:1 The words of Agur, **s** of Jakeh.
30:4 his name or the name of his **s**?
31:2 "What, my **s**? What, son to
31:2 What, **s** to whom I gave birth?
31:2 What, **s** of my prayers?
Ecc 1:1 the **s** of David and the king in
Isa 1:1 which Isaiah, **s** of Amoz,
2:1 which Isaiah, **s** of Amoz,
7:1 When Ahaz, **s** of Jotham and
7:1 King Pekah, **s** of Remaliah,
7:3 "Go out with your **s** Shear
7:4 from Aram and Remaliah's **s**.
7:5 and Remaliah's **s** have planned
7:6 set up Tabeel's **s** as its king.'
7:9 of Samaria is Remaliah's **s**.
7:14 pregnant and give birth to a **s**,
8:2 Zechariah (**s** of Jeberechiah)."
8:3 pregnant and gave birth to a **s**.
8:6 joy in Rezin and Remaliah's **s**."
9:6 A **s** will be given to us.
13:1 **s** of Amoz, saw about Babylon.
14:12 morning star, **s** of the dawn!
20:2 LORD told Isaiah, **s** of Amoz,
22:20 servant Eliakim, **s** of Hilkiah.
36:3 and was the **s** of Hilkiah,
36:3 historian and the **s** of Asaph,
36:22 palace and was **s** of Hilkiah,
36:22 historian and the **s** of Asaph,
37:2 the prophet Isaiah, **s** of Amoz.
37:21 Then Isaiah, **s** of Amoz,
37:38 His **s** Esarhaddon succeeded
38:1 The prophet Isaiah, **s** of Amoz,
39:1 At that time Baladan's **s**,
Jer 1:1 of Jeremiah, **s** of Hilkiah.
1:2 when King Josiah, **s** of Amon,
1:3 when Jehoiakim, **s** of Josiah,
1:3 ⌊another⌋ **s** of Josiah,
15:4 King Manasseh, **s** of Hezekiah,
20:1 Immer's **s** Pashhur,
21:1 sent Pashhur, **s** of Malchiah,
21:1 **s** of Maaseiah, to Jeremiah.
22:11 about King Josiah's **s** Shallum,
22:18 **s** of Judah's King Josiah:
22:24 **s** of Judah's King Jehoiakim,
24:1 of Babylon took Jehoiakin (**s**
25:1 when Jehoiakim, **s** of Josiah,
25:3 time that Josiah, **s** of Amon,
26:1 **s** of Josiah, began to rule.
26:20 was Uriah, **s** of Shemaiah,
26:22 Elnathan (**s** of Achbor) and
26:24 Ahikam, **s** of Shaphan,
27:1 **s** of King Josiah of Judah,
27:7 nations will serve him, his **s**,
27:19 **s** of King Jehoiakim of Judah,
28:1 **s** of Azzur, from Gibeon,
28:4 **s** of King Jehoiakim of Judah,
29:3 letter with Shaphan's **s** Elasah
29:3 and Hilkiah's **s** Gemariah,
29:21 says about Kolaiah's **s** Ahab
29:21 about Maaseiah's **s** Zedekiah,
29:25 Zephaniah, **s** of Maaseiah,
31:20 Is Ephraim my dear **s**?
32:7 cousin Hanamel, **s** of Shallum,
32:12 **s** of Neriah and grandson of
32:16 copies to Baruch, **s** of Neriah,
35:1 **s** of King Josiah of Judah.
Jer 35:3 who was the **s** of Jeremiah and
35:4 (He was Igdaliah's **s**,
35:4 Shallum's **s**, the doorkeeper.
35:6 Rechab's **s**, gave us this order:
35:8 ancestor Jonadab, Rechab's **s**,
35:14 Jonadab, Rechab's **s**,
35:16 of Jonadab, Rechab's **s**,
35:19 of Jonadab, Rechab's **s**,
36:1 **s** of King Josiah of Judah,
36:4 called Baruch, **s** of Neriah.
36:8 Baruch, **s** of Neriah,
36:9 **s** of King Josiah of Judah,
36:10 Gemariah, **s** of Shaphan,
36:11 Micaiah, who was the **s** of
36:12 Delaiah (**s** of Shemaiah),
36:12 Elnathan (**s** of Achbor),
36:12 Gemariah (**s** of Shaphan),
36:12 Zedekiah (**s** of Hananiah),
36:14 who was the **s** of Nethaniah,
36:14 Baruch, **s** of Neriah,
36:26 Jerahmeel (the king's **s**),
36:26 Seraiah (**s** of Azriel),
36:26 and Shelemiah (**s** of Abdeel) to
36:32 the scribe Baruch, **s** of Neriah.
37:1 Zedekiah, **s** of Josiah,
37:1 Jehoiakin, **s** of Jehoiakim.
37:3 King Zedekiah sent Jehucal (**s**
37:3 and the priest Zephaniah (**s**
37:13 **s** of Shelemiah and grandson
38:1 Shephatiah (**s** of Mattan),
38:1 Gedaliah (**s** of Pashhur),
38:1 Jucal (**s** of Shelemiah),
38:1 and Pashhur (**s** of Malchiah)
38:6 of Malchiah, the king's **s**.
39:14 **s** of Ahikam and grandson of
40:5 **s** of Ahikam and grandson of
40:6 went to Gedaliah, **s** of Ahikam,
40:7 Gedaliah, **s** of Ahikam,
40:8 Ishmael (**s** of Nethaniah),
40:8 Seraiah (**s** of Tanhumeth),
40:8 who was the **s** of a man from
40:9 Gedaliah, **s** of Ahikam and
40:11 **s** of Ahikam and grandson of
40:13 Kareah's **s** Johanan and all the
40:14 Nethaniah's **s**, to kill you?"
40:14 Gedaliah, **s** of Ahikam,
40:15 Then Johanan, Kareah's **s**,
40:15 me kill Ishmael, Nethaniah's **s**.
40:16 Gedaliah, **s** of Ahikam,
40:16 Kareah's **s**, "Don't do that!
41:1 the seventh month Ishmael (**s**
41:1 **s** of Ahikam, at Mizpah.
41:2 Ishmael, **s** of Nethaniah,
41:2 **s** of Ahikam and grandson of
41:6 Ishmael, **s** of Nethaniah,
41:6 to Gedaliah, **s** of Ahikam."
41:7 city, Ishmael, **s** of Nethaniah,
41:9 Ishmael, **s** of Nethaniah,
41:10 of Gedaliah, **s** of Ahikam.
41:10 Ishmael, **s** of Nethaniah,
41:11 When Kareah's **s** Johanan and
41:11 **s** of Nethaniah, had done,
41:13 saw Kareah's **s** Johanan
41:14 and ran to Kareah's **s** Johanan.
41:16 Then Kareah's **s** Johanan and
41:16 from Ishmael, **s** of Nethaniah,
41:16 killed Gedaliah, **s** of Ahikam.
42:1 along with Kareah's **s** Johanan
42:1 and Hoshaiah's **s** Jezaniah
42:8 called Kareah's **s** Johanan,
43:2 Azariah (**s** of Hoshaiah),
43:2 Johanan (**s** of Kareah),
43:3 But Baruch, **s** of Neriah,
43:4 So Johanan (**s** of Kareah),
43:5 Johanan (**s** of Kareah) and all
43:6 **s** of Ahikam and grandson of
43:6 and Baruch, **s** of Neriah.
45:1 spoke to Baruch, **s** of Neriah.
45:1 **s** of Josiah, was king of Judah.
46:2 **s** of Josiah, was king of Judah.
51:59 **s** of Neriah and grandson of
Eze 1:3 to the priest Ezekiel, **s** of Buzi,
2:1 He said to me, "**S** of man,
2:3 He said to me, "**S** of man,
2:6 **S** of man, don't be afraid of
2:8 But you, **s** of man,

Eze	3:1	"**S** of man, eat what you find.
	3:3	He said to me, "**S** of man,
	3:4	He said to me, "**S** of man,
	3:10	He also said to me, "**S** of man,
	3:17	"**S** of man, I have made you a
	3:25	tie you up with ropes, **s** of man,
	4:1	⌊The LORD said,⌋ "**S** of man,
	4:16	He also said to me, "**S** of man,
	5:1	⌊The LORD said,⌋ "**S** of man,
	6:2	"**S** of man, look toward the
	7:2	"**S** of man, this is what the
	8:5	God said to me, "**S** of man,
	8:6	He asked me, "**S** of man,
	8:8	He said to me, "**S** of man,
	8:11	Jaazaniah, **s** of Shaphan,
	8:12	God asked me, "**S** of man,
	8:15	He asked me, "**S** of man,
	8:17	He asked me, "**S** of man,
	11:1	I saw among them Azzur's **s**
	11:1	and Benaiah's **s** Pelatiah.
	11:2	LORD said to me, "**S** of man,
	11:4	Prophesy, **s** of man."
	11:13	Benaiah's **s** Pelatiah died.
	11:15	"**S** of man, the people who live
	12:2	"**S** of man, you are living
	12:3	"**S** of man, pack your bags as if
	12:9	"**S** of man, didn't the rebellious
	12:18	"**S** of man, shake as you eat
	12:22	"**S** of man, what is this proverb
	12:27	"**S** of man, the people of Israel
	13:2	"**S** of man, prophesy against
	13:17	"**S** of man, look at the women
	14:3	"**S** of man, these people are
	14:13	"**S** of man, suppose a country
	15:2	"**S** of man, what good is the
	16:2	"**S** of man, make known to the
	17:2	"**S** of man, tell this riddle.
	18:10	this person has a **s** who robs
	18:10	The **s** does all the things
	18:14	suppose this person has a **s**.
	18:14	The **s** sees all the sins that his
	18:19	"But you ask, 'Why isn't the **s**
	18:19	It is because the **s** has done
	18:20	A **s** will not be punished for his
	20:3	"**S** of man, speak to the leaders
	20:4	Will you judge them, **s** of man?
	20:27	to the nation of Israel, **s** of man.
	20:46	"**S** of man, turn to the south,
	21:2	"**S** of man, turn to Jerusalem,
	21:6	"So, **s** of man, groan with a
	21:9	"**S** of man, prophesy.
	21:10	My **s** has refused to be
	21:12	"'Cry and mourn, **s** of man,
	21:14	So prophesy, **s** of man.
	21:19	"**S** of man, mark two roads that
	21:28	"**S** of man, prophesy.
	22:2	"Will you judge, **s** of man?
	22:18	"**S** of man, the people of Israel
	22:24	"**S** of man, tell the city,
	23:2	"**S** of man, there were once two
	23:36	LORD said to me, "**S** of man,
	24:2	"**S** of man, write down today's
	24:16	"**S** of man, with one blow I'm
	24:25	"**S** of man, on that day I will
	25:2	"**S** of man, turn to the
	26:2	"**S** of man, Tyre said this about
	27:2	"**S** of man, sing a funeral song
	28:2	"**S** of man, tell the ruler of Tyre,
	28:12	"**S** of man, sing a funeral song
	28:21	"**S** of man, turn to Sidon and
	29:2	"**S** of man, turn to Pharaoh,
	29:18	"**S** of man, Every soldier's head
	30:2	"**S** of man, prophesy. Say,
	30:21	"**S** of man, I have broken the
	31:2	"**S** of man, say to Pharaoh,
	32:2	"**S** of man, sing a funeral song
	32:18	"**S** of man, cry for the many
	33:2	"**S** of man, speak to your
	33:7	"**S** of man, I have appointed
	33:10	"**S** of man, say to the people of
	33:12	"**S** of man, say to your people,
	33:24	"**S** of man, those who live in
	33:30	"**S** of man, your people are
	34:2	"**S** of man, prophesy against
	35:2	"**S** of man, turn to Mount Seir,
	36:1	⌊The LORD said,⌋ "**S** of man,
Eze	36:17	"**S** of man, when the people of
	37:3	Then he asked me, "**S** of man,
	37:9	Prophesy, **s** of man.
	37:11	also said to me, "**S** of man,
	37:16	"**S** of man, take a stick and
	38:2	"**S** of man, turn to Gog from the
	38:14	"So prophesy, **s** of man.
	39:1	⌊The LORD said,⌋ "**S** of man,
	39:17	"**S** of man, this is what the
	40:4	He said to me, "**S** of man,
	43:7	voice said to me, "**S** of man,
	43:10	"**S** of man, describe this temple
	43:18	the man said to me, "**S** of man,
	44:5	"**S** of man, pay close attention.
	44:25	mother, **s**, daughter, brother,
	47:6	Then he asked me, "**S** of man,
Dan	3:25	one looks like a **s** of the gods."
	7:13	someone like the **S** of Man.
	8:17	He said to me, "**S** of man,
	9:1	Xerxes' **s** Darius, who was a
Hos	1:1	**s** of Beeri, when Uzziah,
	1:1	**s** of Joash, was king of Israel.
	1:3	became pregnant and had a **s**.
	1:8	pregnant again and had a **s**.
	11:1	and I called my **s** out of Egypt.
Joe	1:1	said to Joel, **s** of Pethuel.
Amo	1:1	King Jeroboam, **s** of Joash.
	2:7	Father and **s** sleep with the
Jnh	1:1	his word to Jonah, **s** of Amittai.
Mic	6:5	**s** of Beor, responded to him.
	7:6	A **s** treats his father with
Zep	1:1	who was the **s** of Cushi,
	1:1	of Amariah, **s** of Hezekiah.
	1:1	King Josiah, **s** of Amon.
Hag	1:1	to Zerubbabel (who was the **s**
	1:1	(who was the **s** of Jehozadak).
	1:12	(who was the **s** of Shealtiel),
	1:12	(who was the **s** of Jehozadak),
	1:14	So Zerubbabel (who was the **s**
	1:14	(who was the **s** of Jehozadak),
	2:2	to Zerubbabel (who is the **s**
	2:2	(who is the **s** of Jehozadak),
	2:4	Priest Joshua (**s** of Jehozadak),
	2:23	Zerubbabel (**s** of Shealtiel),
Zec	1:1	who was the **s** of Berechiah
	1:7	who was the **s** of Berechiah
	6:10	of Josiah, **s** of Zephaniah.
	6:11	Priest Joshua, **s** of Jehozadak.
	6:14	and Hen (**s** of Zephaniah) in the
	12:10	as one mourns for an only **s**,
	12:10	as one cries for a firstborn **s**.
Mal	1:6	A **s** honors his father,
	3:17	his own **s** who serves him.
Mat	1:21	She will give birth to a **s**,
	1:23	pregnant and give birth to a **s**,
	1:25	her before she gave birth to a **s**.
	2:15	have called my **s** out of Egypt."
	3:17	heaven said, "This is my **S**,
	3:17	whom I love — my **S** with
	4:3	"If you are the **S** of God,
	4:6	"If you are the **S** of God,
	8:20	but the **S** of Man has nowhere
	8:29	bothering us now, **S** of God?
	9:6	I want you to know that the **S**
	9:27	mercy on us, **S** of David."
	10:3	James (**s** of Alphaeus),
	10:23	the **S** of Man will come.
	10:37	The person who loves a **s** or
	11:19	The **S** of Man came eating and
	11:27	Only the Father knows the **S**.
	11:27	knows the Father except the **S**
	11:27	those to whom the **S** is willing
	12:8	"The **S** of Man has authority
	12:23	this man be the **S** of David?"
	12:32	speaks a word against the **S**
	12:40	so the **S** of Man will be in the
	13:37	the good seeds is the **S** of Man.
	13:41	The **S** of Man will send his
	13:55	Isn't this the carpenter's **s**?
	14:33	"You are truly the **S** of God."
	15:22	mercy on me, Lord, **S** of David!
	16:13	people say the **S** of Man is?"
	16:16	the **S** of the living God!"
	16:17	**s** of Jonah, you are blessed!
	16:27	The **S** of Man will come with
	16:28	will not die until they see the **S**
Mat	17:5	cloud and said, "This is my **S**,
	17:9	Wait until the **S** of Man has
	17:12	to make the **S** of Man suffer."
	17:15	have mercy on my **s**.
	17:22	"The **S** of Man will be betrayed
	19:28	When the **S** of Man sits on his
	20:18	There the **S** of Man will be
	20:28	same way with the **S** of Man.
	20:30	**S** of David, have mercy on us!"
	20:31	**S** of David, have mercy on us!"
	21:9	"Hosanna to the **S** of David!
	21:15	"Hosanna to the **S** of David!"
	21:28	went to the first and said, '**S**,
	21:29	"His **s** replied, 'I don't want to!'
	21:30	"The father went to the other **s**
	21:37	"Finally, he sent his **s** to them.
	21:37	'They will respect my **s**.'
	21:38	"When the workers saw his **s**,
	22:2	planned a wedding for his **s**.
	22:42	Whose **s** is he?" They
	22:45	how can he be his **s**?"
	23:35	of Zechariah, **s** of Barachiah,
	24:27	The **S** of Man will come again
	24:30	"Then the sign of the **S** of Man
	24:30	in agony when they see the **S**
	24:36	heaven and the **S** don't know.
	24:37	"When the **S** of Man comes
	24:39	is how it will be when the **S**
	24:44	must be ready because the **S**
	25:31	"When the **S** of Man comes in
	26:2	At that time the **S** of Man will
	26:24	The **S** of Man is going to die as
	26:24	who betrays the **S** of Man.
	26:45	The time is near for the **S** of
	26:63	the Messiah, the **S** of God?"
	26:64	from now on you will see the **S**
	27:40	If you're the **S** of God,
	27:43	'I am the **S** of God.'"
	27:54	this was the **S** of God!"
	28:19	of the Father, and of the **S**,
Mar	1:1	Jesus Christ, the **S** of God.
	1:11	"You are my **S**, whom I love.
	2:10	I want you to know that the **S**
	2:14	he saw Levi, **s** of Alphaeus,
	2:28	For this reason the **S** of Man
	3:11	"You are the **S** of God!"
	3:18	James (**s** of Alphaeus),
	5:7	**S** of the Most High God?
	6:3	the carpenter, the **s** of Mary,
	8:31	began to teach them that the **S**
	8:38	the **S** of Man will be ashamed
	9:7	"This is my **S**, whom I love.
	9:9	They were to wait until the **S** of
	9:12	sense was it written that the **S**
	9:17	I brought you my **s**.
	9:31	He taught them, "The **S** of Man
	10:33	There the **S** of Man will be
	10:45	same way with the **S** of Man.
	10:46	Bartimaeus, **s** of Timaeus,
	10:47	**S** of David, have mercy on me!"
	10:48	even louder, "**S** of David,
	12:6	That person was his **s**,
	12:6	Finally, he sent his **s** to them.
	12:6	'They will respect my **s**.'
	12:35	that the Messiah is David's **s**?
	12:37	So how can he be his **s**?"
	13:26	"Then people will see the **S** of
	13:32	heaven and the **S** don't know.
	14:21	The **S** of Man is going to die as
	14:21	who betrays the **S** of Man!
	14:41	The time has come for the **S** of
	14:61	the **S** of the Blessed One?"
	14:62	and you will see the **S** of Man
	15:39	this man was the **S** of God!"
Luk	1:13	wife Elizabeth will have a **s**,
	1:31	pregnant, give birth to a **s**,
	1:32	man and will be called the **S**
	1:33	Your **s** will be king of Jacob's
	1:35	you will be called the **S** of God.
	1:36	is six months pregnant with a **s**
	1:57	she gave birth to a **s**.
	2:7	She gave birth to her firstborn **s**
	2:48	His mother asked him, "**S**,
	3:2	**s** of Zechariah, in the desert.
	3:22	"You are my **S**, whom I love.
	3:23	was the **s** of Joseph,

Luk	3:23	the son of Joseph, **s** of Eli,
	3:24	**s** of Matthat, son of Levi, son of
	3:24	son of Matthat, **s** of Levi,
	3:24	**s** of Melchi, son of Jannai,
	3:24	**s** of Jannai, son of Joseph,
	3:24	son of Jannai, **s** of Joseph,
	3:25	**s** of Mattathias, son of Amos,
	3:25	son of Mattathias, **s** of Amos,
	3:25	Amos, **s** of Nahum, son of Esli,
	3:25	**s** of Esli, son of Naggai,
	3:25	son of Esli, **s** of Naggai,
	3:26	**s** of Maath, son of Mattathias,
	3:26	son of Maath, **s** of Mattathias,
	3:26	**s** of Semein, son of Josech,
	3:26	**s** of Josech, son of Joda,
	3:26	son of Josech, **s** of Joda,
	3:27	**s** of Joanan, son of Rhesa,
	3:27	son of Joanan, **s** of Rhesa,
	3:27	son of Rhesa, **s** of Zerubbabel,
	3:27	**s** of Shealtiel, son of Neri,
	3:27	son of Shealtiel, **s** of Neri,
	3:28	**s** of Melchi, son of Addi, son of
	3:28	son of Melchi, **s** of Addi,
	3:28	**s** of Cosam, son of Elmadam,
	3:28	**s** of Elmadam, son of Er,
	3:28	son of Elmadam, **s** of Er,
	3:29	**s** of Joshua, son of Eliezer,
	3:29	son of Joshua, **s** of Eliezer,
	3:29	**s** of Jorim, son of Matthat,
	3:29	Jorim, **s** of Matthat, son of Levi,
	3:29	Jorim, son of Matthat, **s** of Levi,
	3:30	**s** of Simeon, son of Judah,
	3:30	son of Simeon, **s** of Judah,
	3:30	**s** of Joseph, son of Jonam,
	3:30	**s** of Jonam, son of Eliakim,
	3:30	son of Jonam, **s** of Eliakim,
	3:31	**s** of Melea, son of Menna,
	3:31	son of Melea, **s** of Menna,
	3:31	**s** of Mattatha, son of Nathan,
	3:31	**s** of Nathan, son of David,
	3:31	son of Nathan, **s** of David,
	3:32	**s** of Jesse, son of Obed, son of
	3:32	son of Jesse, **s** of Obed,
	3:32	**s** of Boaz, son of Salmon,
	3:32	**s** of Salmon, son of Nahshon,
	3:32	son of Salmon, **s** of Nahshon,
	3:33	**s** of Amminadab, son of Admin,
	3:33	son of Amminadab, **s** of Admin,
	3:33	**s** of Arni, son of Hezron,
	3:33	Arni, **s** of Hezron, son of Perez,
	3:33	**s** of Perez, son of Judah,
	3:33	son of Perez, **s** of Judah,
	3:34	**s** of Jacob, son of Isaac, son of
	3:34	son of Jacob, **s** of Isaac,
	3:34	**s** of Abraham, son of Terah,
	3:34	**s** of Terah, son of Nahor,
	3:34	son of Terah, **s** of Nahor,
	3:35	**s** of Serug, son of Reu, son of
	3:35	son of Serug, **s** of Reu,
	3:35	of Reu, **s** of Peleg, son of Eber,
	3:35	Peleg, **s** of Eber, son of Shelah,
	3:35	Peleg, son of Eber, **s** of Shelah,
	3:36	**s** of Cainan, son of Arphaxad,
	3:36	son of Cainan, **s** of Arphaxad,
	3:36	**s** of Shem, son of Noah,
	3:36	**s** of Noah, son of Lamech,
	3:36	son of Noah, **s** of Lamech,
	3:37	**s** of Methuselah, son of Enoch,
	3:37	son of Methuselah, **s** of Enoch,
	3:37	**s** of Jared, son of Mahalaleel,
	3:37	**s** of Mahalaleel, son of Cainan,
	3:37	son of Mahalaleel, **s** of Cainan,
	3:38	**s** of Enos, son of Seth, son of
	3:38	son of Enos, **s** of Seth,
	3:38	of Seth, **s** of Adam, son of God.
	3:38	of Seth, son of Adam, **s** of God.
	4:3	"If you are the **S** of God,
	4:9	"If you are the **S** of God,
	4:22	"Isn't this Joseph's **s**?"
	4:41	"You are the **S** of God!"
	5:24	I want you to know that the **S**
	6:5	Then he added, "The **S** of Man
	6:15	James (**s** of Alphaeus),
	6:16	Judas (**s** of James),
	6:22	are committed to the **S** of Man.
	7:34	The **S** of Man has come eating
Luk	8:28	**S** of the Most High God?
	9:22	Jesus said that the **S** of Man
	9:26	the **S** of Man will be ashamed
	9:35	cloud and said, "This is my **S**,
	9:38	I beg you to look at my **s**.
	9:41	Bring your **s** here!"
	9:44	The **S** of Man will be betrayed
	9:58	but the **S** of Man has nowhere
	10:22	the Father knows who the **S** is.
	10:22	who the Father is except the **S**
	10:22	those to whom the **S** is willing
	11:30	so the **S** of Man will be a
	12:8	I can guarantee that the **S** of
	12:10	says something against the **S**
	12:40	Be ready, because the **S** of
	12:53	A father will be against his **s**
	12:53	son and a **s** against his father.
	14:5	Jesus asked them, "If your **s** or
	15:12	The younger **s** said to his
	15:13	the younger **s** gathered his
	15:19	to be called your **s** anymore.
	15:20	He ran to his **s**, put his arms
	15:21	Then his **s** said to him,
	15:21	to be called your **s** anymore.'
	15:24	My **s** was dead and has come
	15:25	"His older **s** was in the field.
	15:28	"Then the older **s** became
	15:30	But this **s** of yours spent your
	17:22	one of the days of the **S** of Man,
	17:24	The day of the **S** of Man will be
	17:26	"When the **S** of Man comes
	17:30	The day when the **S** of Man is
	18:8	But when the **S** of Man comes,
	18:31	the prophets wrote about the **S**
	18:38	**S** of David, have mercy on me!"
	18:39	even louder, "**S** of David,
	19:10	Indeed, the **S** of Man has come
	20:13	I'll send my **s**, whom I love.
	20:41	that the Messiah is David's **s**?
	20:44	So how can he be his **s**?"
	21:27	"Then people will see the **S** of
	21:36	stand in front of the **S** of Man."
	22:22	The **S** of Man is going to die
	22:48	do you intend to betray the **S** of
	22:69	But from now on, the **S** of Man
	22:70	"So you're the **S** of God?"
	24:7	He said, 'The **S** of Man must
Jon	1:14	Father shares with his only **S**,
	1:18	God's only **S**, the one who is
	1:34	that this is the **S** of God."
	1:42	"You are Simon, **s** of John.
	1:45	He is Jesus, **s** of Joseph,
	1:49	you are the **S** of God!
	1:51	coming down to the **S** of Man."
	3:13	to heaven except the **S** of Man,
	3:14	so the **S** of Man must be lifted
	3:16	He gave his only **S** so that
	3:17	God sent his **S** into the world,
	3:18	don't believe in God's only **S**.
	3:35	The Father loves his **S** and
	3:36	Whoever believes in the **S** has
	3:36	but whoever rejects the **S** will
	4:5	had given to his **s** Joseph.
	4:46	His **s** was sick in Capernaum.
	4:47	to heal his **s** who was about
	4:50	Your **s** will live." The man
	4:52	at what time his **s** got better.
	4:53	had told him, "Your **s** will live."
	5:19	The **S** cannot do anything on
	5:19	Indeed, the **S** does exactly
	5:20	The Father loves the **S** and
	5:21	the **S** gives life to anyone he
	5:22	judgment entirely to the **S**
	5:23	will honor the **S** as they honor
	5:23	Whoever doesn't honor the **S**
	5:25	will hear the voice of the **S**
	5:26	and he has enabled the **S** to be
	5:27	"He has also given the **S**
	5:27	because he is the **S** of Man.
	6:27	This is the food the **S** of Man
	6:40	wants all those who see the **S**
	6:42	this man Jesus, Joseph's **s**?
	6:53	you don't eat the flesh of the **S**
	6:62	What if you see the **S** of Man
	6:71	**s** of Simon Iscariot.
	8:28	you have lifted up the **S** of Man,
Jon	8:35	the home forever, but a **s** does.
	8:36	So if the **S** sets you free,
	9:19	his parents, "Is this your **s**,
	9:20	"We know that he's our **s** and
	9:35	you believe in the **S** of Man?"
	10:36	'I'm the **S** of God'?
	11:4	bring glory to God so that the **S**
	11:27	are the Messiah, the **S** of God,
	12:23	"The time has come for the **S**
	12:34	So how can you say, 'The **S** of
	12:34	Who is this '**S** of Man'?"
	13:2	**s** of Simon Iscariot.
	13:26	**s** of Simon Iscariot.
	13:31	"The **S** of Man is now glorified,
	13:32	because of the **S** of Man,
	13:32	God will glorify the **S** of Man
	13:32	and he will glorify the **S** of Man
	14:13	given glory because of the **S**.
	17:1	Give your **S** glory so that your
	17:1	so that your **S** can give you
	19:7	he claimed to be the **S** of God."
	19:26	mother, "Look, here's your **s**!"
	20:31	is the Messiah, the **S** of God,
	21:15	Peter, "Simon, **s** of John,
	21:16	**s** of John, do you love me?"
	21:17	**s** of John, do you love me?"
Act	1:13	James (**s** of Alphaeus),
	1:13	and Judas (**s** of James) went to
	7:8	So when Abraham's **s** Isaac
	7:8	did the same to his **s** Jacob,
	7:21	him and raised him as her **s**.
	7:56	I see heaven opened and the **S**
	9:20	that Jesus was the **S** of God.
	13:10	schemes, you **s** of the devil!
	13:21	God gave them Saul, **s** of Kish,
	13:22	found that David, **s** of Jesse,
	13:33	second psalm: 'You are my **S**.
	20:4	Sopater (**s** of Pyrrhus) from
Rom	1:3	Good News is about his **S**,
	1:4	he was declared the **S** of God.
	1:9	the Good News about his **S**.
	5:10	If the death of his **S** restored
	5:10	the life his **S** lived will save us.
	8:3	But God sent his **S** to have a
	8:29	form as the image of his **S**.
	8:29	Therefore, his **S** is the firstborn
	8:32	God didn't spare his own **S** but
	9:9	and Sarah will have a **s**."
1Co	1:9	with his **S** Jesus Christ our
	15:28	the **S** will put himself under
2Co	1:19	God's **S**, Jesus Christ, whom I,
Gal	1:16	to show me his **S**.
	1:16	are not Jewish that his **S** is
	2:20	I live by believing in God's **S**,
	4:4	God sent his **S** into the
	4:6	God has sent the Spirit of his **S**
	4:23	Now, the **s** of the slave woman
	4:23	but the **s** of the free woman
	4:29	Furthermore, at that time the **s**
	4:29	persecuted the **s** conceived
	4:30	of the slave woman and her **s**,
	4:30	because the **s** of the slave
	4:30	share the inheritance with the **s**
Eph	1:6	given us in his dear **S** would
	1:7	Through the blood of his **S**,
	4:13	our knowledge about God's **S**,
Php	2:22	Like a father and **s** we worked
Col	1:13	us into the kingdom of his **S**,
	1:14	His **S** paid the price to free us,
1Th	1:10	and to wait for his **S** to come
	1:10	His **S** is Jesus, whom he
Heb	1:2	has spoken to us through his **S**.
	1:2	God made his **S** responsible
	1:2	His **S** is the one through whom
	1:3	His **S** is the reflection of God's
	1:4	The **S** has become greater than
	1:5	of his angels, "You are my **S**.
	1:5	and he will be my **S**."
	1:6	to send his firstborn **S** into
	1:8	But God said about his **S**,
	2:6	or the **S** of Man that you take
	3:6	But Christ is a faithful **s** in
	4:14	person is Jesus, the **S** of God.
	5:5	God, who said, "You are my **S**.
	5:8	Jesus was the **S** of God,
	6:6	They are crucifying the **S** of

Heb 7:3 Like the **S** of God,
7:28 designated the **S** who forever
10:29 who shows no respect for the **S**
11:17 led him to offer his **s** Isaac.
11:17 offer his only **s** as a sacrifice.
11:24 as a **s** of Pharaoh's daughter.
12:16 sold his rights as the firstborn **s**
12:17 that the firstborn **s** was
Jas 2:21 when he offered his **s** Isaac as
1Pe 5:13 and my **s** Mark send you
2Pe 1:17 words to him: "This is my **S**,
2:15 the path of Balaam, **s** of Beor.
1Jn 1:3 and with his **S** Jesus Christ.
1:7 And the blood of his **S** Jesus
2:22 and the **S** is an antichrist.
2:23 Everyone who rejects the **S**
2:23 acknowledges the **S** also has
2:24 you will also live in the **S** and
3:8 The reason that the **S** of God
3:23 to believe in his **S**,
4:9 love by sending his only **S** into
4:10 that he loved us and sent his **S**
4:14 that the Father sent his **S** as
4:15 that Jesus is the **S** of God,
5:5 that Jesus is the **S** of God?
5:6 This **S** of God is Jesus Christ,
5:9 that he has given about his **S**.
5:10 Those who believe in the **S** of
5:10 that God has given about his **S**.
5:11 and this life is found in his **S**.
5:12 The person who has the **S** has
5:12 person who doesn't have the **S**
5:13 to those who believe in the **S**
5:18 the **S** of God protects them,
5:20 We know that the **S** of God has
5:20 his **S** Jesus Christ.
2Jn 1:3 truth and love is the Father's **S**.
1:9 has both the Father and the **S**.
Rev 1:13 There was someone like the **S**
2:18 Thyatira, write: The **S** of God,
12:5 She gave birth to a **s**,
14:14 who was like the **S** of Man.

song (74)

Exo 15:1 and the Israelites sang this **s**
15:2 LORD is my strength and my **s**.
Num 21:17 Then Israel sang this **s** about
Dtr 31:19 "Write down this **s**,
31:19 This **s** will be a witness for me
31:21 this **s** will testify against them,
31:22 day Moses wrote down this **s**
31:30 recited all the words of this **s**:
32:44 all the words of this **s** as
Jdg 5:1 son of Abinoam, sang this **s**:
5:3 I will sing a **s** to the LORD.
5:12 Get up and create a **s**!
2Sm 1:17 David wrote this **s** of mourning
3:33 king sang a funeral **s** for Abner:
22:1 David sang this **s** to the LORD
2Ch 30:21 priests praised the LORD in **s**.
35:25 sang a funeral **s** about Josiah.
Psa 28:7 I give thanks to him with my **s**.
30:5 but there is a **s** of joy in the
33:3 Sing a new **s** to him.
40:3 He placed a new **s** in my
40:3 a **s** of praise to our God.
42:8 and at night his **s** is with me —
45:1 I will direct my **s** to the king.
47:1 to God with a loud, joyful **s**.
69:30 the name of God with a **s**.
69:30 with a **s** of thanksgiving.
77:6 I remember my **s** in the night
95:2 with a **s** of thanksgiving.
96:1 Sing to the LORD a new **s**!
98:1 Sing a new **s** to the LORD
100:2 his presence with a joyful **s**.
100:4 gates with a **s** of thanksgiving.
100:4 courtyards with a **s** of praise.
105:43 chosen ones with a **s** of joy.
116:17 I will bring a **s** of thanksgiving
118:14 LORD is my strength and my **s**.
137:3 "Sing a **s** from Zion for us!"
137:4 could we sing the LORD's **s**
144:9 I will sing a new **s** to you.
147:7 the LORD a **s** of thanksgiving.
149:1 Sing a new **s** to the LORD.
Pro 1:20 Wisdom sings her **s** in the
8:3 entrance ⌊wisdom⌋ sings its **s**,
Sos 1:1 most beautiful **s** of Solomon.
Isa 12:2 LORD is my strength and my **s**.
23:15 be like the prostitute in this **s**:
25:5 The **s** of tyrants is silenced
26:1 On that day this **s** will be sung
30:29 You will sing a **s** like the song
30:29 You will sing a song like the **s**
42:10 Sing a new **s** to the LORD.
Jer 7:29 Sing a **s** of mourning on the
9:10 I will sing a funeral **s** for the
31:7 Sing a happy **s** about Jacob.
Eze 19:1 Sing a funeral **s** for the princes
19:14 This is a funeral **s**.
19:14 It is to be used as a funeral **s**.
26:17 will sing this funeral **s** for you:
27:2 sing a funeral **s** about Tyre.
27:32 They sang a funeral **s** for you
28:12 "Son of man, sing a funeral **s**
32:2 sing a funeral **s** for Pharaoh,
32:16 "This is a funeral **s**.
32:16 the nations will sing this **s**.
Amo 5:1 this funeral **s** that I sing about
Mic 2:4 will sing this sad **s** about you:
Mat 11:17 We sang a funeral **s**,
Luk 7:32 We sang a funeral **s**,
Rev 5:9 Then they sang a new **s**,
14:3 They were singing a new **s** in
14:3 on earth could learn the **s**.
15:3 and singing the **s** of God's
15:3 God's servant Moses and the **s**

songbird (1)

Sos 2:12 The time of the **s** has arrived.

songs (51)

Gen 31:27 with **s** accompanied by
1Ki 4:32 proverbs and wrote 1,005 **s**.
1Ch 13:8 might, with **s**, with lyres, harps,
15:22 others how to sing prophetic **s**
15:27 of the musicians' prophetic **s**.
16:7 with the task of singing **s**
16:42 that accompany sacred **s**.
2Ch 20:19 God of Israel with very loud **s**.
23:13 **s** accompanied by musical
29:27 the **s** to the LORD started.
29:27 These **s** were accompanied by
35:25 funeral **s** about Josiah today.
35:25 in ⌊the Book of⌋ the Funeral **S**.
Neh 12:27 with **s** and cymbals,
12:46 to lead ⌊in singing⌋ the **s**
Job 30:9 they make fun of me with **s**.
35:10 who inspires **s** in the night,
Psa 32:7 me with joyous **s** of salvation.
42:4 ⌊I sang⌋ **s** of joy and
56:12 keep my vows by offering **s**
69:12 drunkards make up **s** about me.
71:6 My **s** of praise constantly
78:63 his virgins heard no wedding **s**.
107:22 Let them bring **s** of
107:22 Let them tell in joyful **s** what he
126:2 and our tongues with joyful **s**.
Pro 11:10 people die, there are **s** of joy.
25:20 so is singing **s** to one who has
Ecc 12:4 who sing **s** become quiet.
Isa 16:10 No **s** are sung. No shouts are
23:16 Sing many **s** so that you'll be
24:16 the ends of the earth we hear **s**
55:12 and the hills will break into **s**
Jer 9:20 Teach your neighbors funeral **s**.
30:19 live there will sing **s** of praise,
Lam 3:14 make fun of me⌋ with their **s**.
3:63 they make fun of me in their **s**.
Eze 2:10 There were funeral **s**,
2:10 funeral songs, **s** of mourning,
26:13 will put a stop to your noisy **s**,
33:32 voice who sings love **s**
Amo 5:23 Spare me the sound of your **s**.
6:5 who make up **s** as they strum
6:5 all kinds of **s** for themselves.
8:3 On that day the **s** of the temple
8:10 all your **s** into funeral songs.
8:10 all your songs into funeral **s**.
Jnh 2:9 But I will sacrifice to you with **s**
Luk 23:27 and sang funeral **s** for him.
Eph 5:19 and spiritual **s** for your own
Col 3:16 and spiritual **s** to teach and

son-in-law (13)

Jdg 15:6 He's the **s** of the man at
19:5 the woman's father told his **s**,
19:6 woman's father said to his **s**,
1Sm 18:18 that I should be the king's **s**?"
18:21 "You will now be my **s**."
18:22 Become the king's **s**.'"
18:23 easy to become the king's **s**?
18:26 to become the king's **s**.
18:27 could become the king's **s**.
22:14 Your Majesty, he's your **s**,
1Ki 3:1 Solomon became the **s** of
Neh 6:18 he was the **s** of Shecaniah,
13:28 one of Joiada's sons was a **s**

son's (17)

Gen 30:14 me some of your **s** mandrakes.
30:15 **s** mandrakes?" Rachel said,
30:15 in return for your **s** mandrakes.
30:16 my reward for my **s** mandrakes.
37:32 whether it's your **s** robe or not."
37:33 it and said, "It is my **s** robe!
Exo 4:25 cut off her **s** foreskin, and
Lev 18:10 whether she is your **s** daughter
18:15 She is your **s** wife.
Jdg 17:3 to the LORD for my **s** benefit.
2Sm 14:11 "not a hair on your **s** head will
1Ki 1:12 to save your life and your **s** life
21:29 evil on it during his **s** lifetime.
Eze 18:20 not be punished for his **s** sins.
1Co 15:28 under the **S** authority.
Heb 2:8 his **S** control, nothing was left
2:8 everything under his **S** control

sons (763)

Gen 5:4 and had other **s** and daughters.
5:7 and had other **s** and daughters.
5:10 and had other **s** and daughters.
5:13 and had other **s** and daughters.
5:16 and had other **s** and daughters.
5:19 and had other **s** and daughters.
5:22 and had other **s** and daughters.
5:26 and had other **s** and daughters.
5:30 and had other **s** and daughters.
6:2 The **s** of God saw that the
6:4 when the **s** of God slept with
6:10 He had three **s**: Shem, Ham,
6:18 You, your **s**, your wife,
7:7 Noah, his **s**, his wife, and his
7:13 day Noah and his **s** Shem,
8:16 your **s**, and your sons' wives.
8:18 So Noah came out with his **s**,
9:1 God blessed Noah and his **s**
9:8 also said to Noah and his **s**,
9:18 Noah's **s**, who came out of the
9:19 These were Noah's three **s**.
10:1 the account of Noah's **s** Shem,
10:21 the ancestor of all the **s** of Eber.
10:25 Two **s** were born to Eber.
10:29 These were Joktan's **s**.
10:32 of Noah's **s** listed by their
11:11 and had other **s** and daughters.
11:13 and had other **s** and daughters.
11:15 and had other **s** and daughters.
11:17 and had other **s** and daughters.
11:19 and had other **s** and daughters.
11:21 and had other **s** and daughters.
11:23 and had other **s** and daughters.
11:25 and had other **s** and daughters.
19:12 any in-laws, **s**, daughters,
22:23 Milcah had these eight **s** by
25:2 birth to these **s** of Abraham:
25:4 The **s** of Midian were Ephah,
25:6 had given gifts to the **s**
25:9 His **s** Isaac and Ishmael buried
25:13 These are the names of the **s**
25:16 These are the **s** of Ishmael and
27:29 and may the **s** of your mother
29:34 I've given him three **s**."
30:20 I have given him six **s**."
30:35 He had his **s** take charge of
31:1 that Laban's **s** were saying,
33:19 bought it from the **s** of Hamor,

Gen 34:5 His **s** were with his livestock
34:7 Jacob's **s** came in from the
34:13 Then Jacob's **s** gave Shechem
34:25 still in pain, two of Jacob's **s**,
34:27 Then Jacob's **s** stripped the
35:22 heard about it. Jacob had 12 **s**.
35:23 The **s** of Leah were Jacob's
35:24 The **s** of Rachel were Joseph
35:25 The **s** of Rachel's slave Bilhah
35:26 The **s** of Leah's slave Zilpah
35:26 These were Jacob's **s**,
35:29 His **s** Esau and Jacob buried
36:5 These were the **s** of Esau who
36:6 Esau took his wives, his **s**,
36:10 were the names of Esau's **s**:
36:11 The **s** of Eliphaz were Teman,
36:13 These were Reuel's **s**:
36:14 These were the **s** of Esau's
36:15 descendants: The **s** of Eliphaz,
36:20 These were the **s** of Seir the
36:21 Horite tribal leaders were the **s**
36:22 The **s** of Lotan were Hori and
36:23 These were the **s** of Shobal:
36:24 These were the **s** of Zibeon:
36:26 These were the **s** of Dishon:
36:27 These were the **s** of Ezer:
36:28 These were the **s** of Dishan:
37:2 care of the flocks with the **s**
37:3 Joseph more than all his **s**
37:35 All his other **s** and daughters
41:50 Joseph had two **s** by Asenath,
42:1 sale in Egypt, he said to his **s**,
42:5 Israel's **s** left with the others
42:11 We're all **s** of one man.
42:13 **s** of one man in Canaan.
42:32 **s** of the same father.
42:37 "You may put my two **s** to
43:2 Israel said to his **s**,
44:20 only one of his mother's **s** left,
44:27 wife ⌊Rachel⌋ gave me two **s**.
45:21 Israel's **s** did as they were told.
46:5 Israel's **s** put their father Jacob,
46:7 He had brought his **s**,
46:9 The **s** of Reuben were Hanoch,
46:10 The **s** of Simeon were Jemuel,
46:11 The **s** of Levi were Gershon,
46:12 The **s** of Judah were Er,
46:12 The **s** of Perez were Hezron
46:13 The **s** of Issachar were Tola,
46:14 The **s** of Zebulun were Sered,
46:15 of the **s** Leah gave
46:15 The total number of these **s**
46:16 The **s** of Gad were Ziphion,
46:17 The **s** of Asher were Imnah,
46:17 The **s** of Beriah were Heber
46:19 The **s** of Jacob's wife Rachel
46:21 The **s** of Benjamin were Bela,
46:24 The **s** of Naphtali were
46:25 gave birth to these **s** for Jacob.
46:26 include the wives of Jacob's **s**.
46:27 Joseph had two **s** who were
48:1 So he took his two **s**
48:5 "So your two **s**, who were born
48:5 before I came here, are my **s**.
48:8 When Israel saw Joseph's **s**,
48:9 "They are my **s**, whom God
48:10 So Joseph brought his **s** close
48:11 has even let me see your **s**."
49:1 Jacob called for his **s** and said,
49:2 around and listen, **s** of Jacob.
49:7 I will divide them among ⌊the **s**
49:8 Your father's **s** will bow down
49:33 these instructions to his **s**,
50:12 Jacob's **s** did for him what he
50:25 Joseph made Israel's **s** swear
Exo 1:1 These are the names of the **s**
3:22 them on your **s** and daughters.
4:20 So Moses took his wife and **s**,
6:14 the families: The **s** of Reuben,
6:15 The **s** of Simeon were Jemuel,
6:16 These are the names of the **s**
6:17 The **s** of Gershon listed by
6:18 The **s** of Kohath were Amram,
6:19 The **s** of Merari were Mahli and
6:21 The **s** of Izhar were Korah,
6:22 The **s** of Uzziel were Mishael,
Exo 6:24 The **s** of Korah were Assir,
10:9 our **s** and daughters,
18:3 along with her two **s**.
18:5 Jethro brought Moses' **s**
18:6 your wife and her two **s**."
20:10 You, your **s**, your daughters,
21:4 gives birth to **s** or daughters,
28:1 brother Aaron and his **s** Nadab,
28:4 Aaron and his **s** so that they
28:9 the names of the **s** of Israel
28:11 Engrave the names of the **s** of
28:21 correspond to the 12 **s** of Israel,
28:29 be carrying the names of the **s**
28:40 and turbans for Aaron's **s**.
28:41 on your brother Aaron and his **s**
28:43 Aaron and his **s** must wear
29:1 to set Aaron and his **s** apart
29:4 "Then bring Aaron and his **s** to
29:8 "Have his **s** come forward.
29:9 the waists of Aaron and his **s**.
29:9 you will ordain Aaron and his **s**.
29:10 Aaron and his **s** will place their
29:15 Then Aaron and his **s** will
29:19 Then Aaron and his **s** will
29:20 ear lobes of Aaron and his **s**,
29:21 and his clothes and on his **s**
29:21 In this way Aaron, his **s**,
29:24 in the hands of Aaron and his **s**,
29:27 both belong to Aaron and his **s**.
29:28 portion to Aaron and his **s** as
29:32 Aaron and his **s** will eat the
29:35 "Do this with Aaron and his **s**
29:44 I will set Aaron and his **s** apart
30:19 Aaron and his **s** will use it for
30:30 Anoint Aaron and his **s** as well.
31:10 for his **s** when they serve
32:2 to them, "Have your wives, **s**,
32:29 with your own **s** and brothers."
34:16 Then your **s** will end up
34:16 they'll lead your **s** to do the
34:20 back every firstborn of your **s**.
35:19 for his **s** when they serve
39:6 the names of the **s** of Israel.
39:14 to the 12 **s** of Israel,
39:27 of fine linen for Aaron and his **s**.
39:41 for his **s** when serving as
40:12 "Bring Aaron and his **s** to the
40:14 Have his **s** come forward,
40:31 Moses, Aaron, and his **s** used
Lev 1:5 Aaron's **s**, the priests, will offer
1:7 Then the **s** of the priest Aaron
1:8 Aaron's **s**, the priests, will also
1:11 Aaron's **s**, the priests,
2:2 Then bring it to Aaron's **s**,
2:3 will belong to Aaron and his **s**.
2:10 belongs to Aaron and his **s**.
3:2 Then Aaron's **s**, the priests,
3:5 Then Aaron's **s** will lay them
3:8 Then Aaron's **s** will throw the
3:13 Then Aaron's **s** will throw the
6:9 "Command Aaron and his **s**:
6:14 Aaron's **s** must bring it into the
6:16 Aaron and his **s** will eat the
6:20 that Aaron and his **s** must bring
6:25 "Tell Aaron and his **s**:
7:10 equally by all of Aaron's **s**.
7:31 will belong to Aaron and his **s**.
7:33 When any of Aaron's **s** offer the
7:34 to the priest Aaron and his **s**.
7:35 share for Aaron and his **s** from
8:2 "Take Aaron and his **s**,
8:6 Aaron and his **s** come forward,
8:13 had Aaron's **s** come forward.
8:14 Aaron and his **s** placed their
8:18 Aaron and his **s** placed their
8:22 Aaron and his **s** placed their
8:24 also brought Aaron's **s** forward.
8:27 in the hands of Aaron and his **s**.
8:30 and his clothes and on his **s**
8:30 his **s**, and their clothes.
8:31 Moses told Aaron and his **s**:
8:31 'Aaron and his **s** will eat it.'
8:36 So Aaron and his **s** did
9:1 summoned Aaron and his **s**
9:9 Aaron's **s** brought him the
9:12 Aaron's **s** gave him the blood,
Lev 9:18 Aaron's **s** gave him the blood,
10:1 Aaron's **s** Nadab and Abihu
10:4 the **s** of Aaron's uncle,
10:6 Moses told Aaron and his **s**
10:9 "You and your **s** must not drink
10:12 and his surviving **s** Eleazar
10:14 You and your **s** and daughters
10:16 Aaron's surviving **s**.
13:2 or to one of his **s** who are also
16:1 Aaron's two **s** had come into
17:2 "Tell Aaron, his **s**,
21:1 "Tell the priests, Aaron's **s**:
21:24 spoke to Aaron and his **s**
22:2 "Tell Aaron and his **s** that they
22:18 "Tell Aaron, his **s**,
24:9 will belong to Aaron and his **s**.
26:29 bodies of your **s** and daughters.
Num 3:2 The names of Aaron's **s** are
3:3 are the names of Aaron's **s**,
3:9 the Levites to Aaron and his **s**.
3:10 Appoint Aaron and his **s** to
3:17 and Merari were the **s** of Levi.
3:18 Shimei were the **s** of Gershon.
3:19 Uzziel were the **s** of Kohath.
3:20 and Mushi were the **s** of Merari.
3:38 Moses, Aaron, and his **s** put up
3:48 the silver to Aaron and his **s**.
3:51 and his **s** this ransom money
4:5 Aaron and his **s** will go in and
4:15 "When Aaron and his **s** have
4:19 Aaron and his **s** will go into the
4:27 the direction of Aaron and his **s**.
6:23 "Tell Aaron and his **s**,
8:13 in front of Aaron and his **s**,
8:18 the firstborn **s** of the Israelites.
8:19 I give to Aaron and his **s**.
8:22 presence of Aaron and his **s**.
10:8 The **s** of Aaron, the priests,
16:1 Dathan and Abiram (**s** of Eliab),
16:12 Dathan and Abiram, **s** of Eliab.
18:1 said to Aaron, "You, your **s**,
18:1 You and your **s** will also be
18:2 and help you and your **s** serve
18:7 Only you and your **s** may do
18:9 will belong to you and your **s**.
18:11 am giving these to you, your **s**,
18:19 I am giving you, your **s**,
21:29 Chemosh let his **s** become
21:35 him, his **s**, and all his troops,
26:9 and Abiram were the **s** of Eliab.
26:19 Er and Onan were **s** of Judah,
26:33 had no **s** — only daughters.
27:3 for his own sin and left no **s**.
27:8 If a man dies and leaves no **s**,
33:4 burying all their firstborn **s**,
Dtr 2:33 him, his **s**, and all his troops.
5:14 You, your **s**, your daughters,
7:3 let your daughters marry their **s**
7:3 your **s** marry their daughters.
11:6 and Abiram, the **s** of Eliab,
12:12 your God along with your **s**,
12:18 your **s** and daughters,
12:31 They even burn their **s** and
16:11 your God along with your **s**,
16:14 the festival along with your **s**,
17:20 So he and his **s** will rule for a
18:10 You must never sacrifice your **s**
21:16 to give his **s** their inheritance,
28:32 with your own eyes as your **s**
28:41 You will have **s** and daughters,
28:53 the **s** and daughters,
32:8 to the number of the **s** of Israel.
32:19 because his own **s** and
33:24 most blessed of the **s** of Israel.
Jos 5:7 The **s** who took their place had
7:24 his **s** and daughters,
16:4 So Joseph's **s**, Manasseh and
17:3 had no **s** — only daughters.
17:6 an inheritance along with his **s**,
24:2 Terah and his **s** Abraham and
24:4 Jacob and his **s** went to Egypt.
24:32 had bought from the **s** of Hamor
Jdg 1:20 forced out the three **s** of Anak.
3:6 The Israelites allowed their **s**
8:19 my brothers, my mother's **s**.
8:30 Gideon had 70 **s** because he

Jdg 9:2 want all of Jerubbaal's 70 **s**
9:5 his 70 brothers, Jerubbaal's **s**.
9:18 You have executed his 70 **s**.
9:24 Jerubbaal's 70 **s** would happen
10:4 Jair had 30 **s** who rode on 30
11:2 wife also gave birth to **s**.
11:2 When his wife's **s** grew up,
11:34 had no other **s** or daughters.
12:9 He had 30 **s** and 30 daughters.
12:9 His **s** and daughters married
12:14 He had 40 **s** and 30 grandsons
17:5 He ordained one of his **s** to be
17:11 became like one of Micah's **s**.
Rut 1:1 went with his wife and two **s**
1:2 and the names of their two **s**
1:3 was left alone with her two **s**.
1:5 her two **s** or her husband.
1:11 Do I have any more **s** in my
1:12 And even if I gave birth to **s**,
4:15 is better to you than seven **s**,
1Sm 1:3 Eli's two **s**, Hophni and
1:4 and all her **s** and daughters.
1:8 I mean more to you than ten **s**?"
2:12 Eli's **s**, Hophni and
2:15 But in the case of Eli's **s**,
2:17 The sin of Eli's **s** was a
2:21 five times and had three **s**
2:22 that his **s** were doing
2:24 **S**, the report that I hear the
2:29 Why do you honor your **s** more
2:34 going to happen to your two **s**,
4:4 Eli's two **s**, Hophni and
4:11 Both of Eli's **s**, Hophni and
4:17 Your two **s**, Hophni and
8:1 made his **s** judges over Israel.
8:3 The **s** didn't follow their father's
8:5 and your **s** aren't following your
8:11 He will draft your **s**,
12:2 but my **s** are with you.
14:49 Saul's **s** were Jonathan,
14:51 father) were the **s** of Abiel.
16:1 one of his **s** to be king."
16:5 ceremonies for Jesse and his **s**
16:10 more of his **s** to Samuel,
16:11 Are these all the **s** you have?"
16:18 "I know one of Jesse's **s** from
17:12 Jesse had eight **s**,
17:13 Jesse's three oldest **s** joined
28:19 Tomorrow you and your **s** will
30:3 down, and their wives, **s**,
30:6 of their **s** and daughters.
30:19 young or old, **s** or daughters,
31:2 caught up to Saul and his **s**.
31:2 and Malchishua, Saul's **s**.
31:6 So Saul, his three **s**,
31:7 that Saul and his **s** were dead,
31:8 they found Saul and his three **s**
31:12 bodies of Saul and his **s** from
2Sm 2:18 Zeruiah's three **s** were there:
3:2 **S** were born to David while he
3:5 These **s** were born to David
3:39 These men, Zeruiah's **s**,
4:2 They were the **s** of Rimmon
4:5 the **s** of Rimmon from Beeroth,
4:9 the **s** of Rimmon from Beeroth,
5:13 fathered more **s** and daughters.
6:3 Uzzah and Ahio, Abinadab's **s**,
8:18 And David's **s** were priests.
9:10 You, your **s**, and your servants
9:10 had 15 **s** and 20 servants.)
9:11 table as one of the king's **s**.
13:23 He invited all the king's **s**.
13:27 of the king's **s** go with him.
13:29 Then all the king's **s** got up,
13:30 has killed all the king's **s**,
13:32 the young men, all the king's **s**,
13:33 that all the king's **s** are dead,
13:35 "The king's **s** have come.
13:36 the king's **s** arrived and cried
14:6 I had two **s** who quarreled in
14:27 Absalom had three **s** and one
15:36 They have two **s** with them:
16:10 like me at all, **s** of Zeruiah.
19:5 your life and the lives of your **s**,
19:17 his 15 **s** and 20 servants.
19:22 the same family, **s** of Zeruiah?

2Sm 21:8 the two **s** whom Rizpah (Aiah's
21:8 and five **s** whom Merab (Saul's
1Ki 1:9 the king's other **s**,
1:19 He has invited all the king's **s**,
1:25 He invited all the king's **s**,
2:7 "Be kind to the **s** of Barzillai
4:3 the **s** of Shisha, were scribes.
4:31 Calcol, or Darda, Mahol's **s**.
13:11 His **s** told him everything the
13:12 (His **s** had seen which road the
13:13 The old prophet told his **s**,
13:27 Then the old prophet told his **s**
13:31 he said to his **s**, "When I die,
18:31 tribes named after Jacob's **s**.
2Ki 9:26 of Naboth and his **s** yesterday,
11:2 killed with the king's other **s**,
17:17 They sacrificed their **s** and
23:10 never again sacrifice their **s**
25:7 They slaughtered Zedekiah's **s**
1Ch 1:19 Two **s** were born to Eber.
1:23 All these were **s** of Joktan.
1:28 Abraham's **s** were Isaac and
1:31 These were the **s** of Ishmael.
1:32 gave birth to the following **s**:
1:32 Jokshan's **s** were Sheba and
1:33 The **s** of Midian were Ephah,
1:34 Isaac's **s** were Esau and Israel.
1:35 Esau's **s** were Eliphaz,
1:36 Eliphaz's **s** were Teman and
1:37 Reuel's **s** were Nahath,
1:38 Seir's **s** were Lotan,
1:39 Lotan's **s** were Hori and
1:40 Shobal's **s** were Alian,
1:40 Zibeon's **s** were Aiah and
1:41 Dishon's **s** were Hamran,
1:42 Ezer's **s** were Bilhan,
1:42 Dishan's **s** were Uz and Aran.
2:1 These were Israel's **s**:
2:3 Judah's **s** were Er,
2:4 gave birth to Judah's **s** Perez
2:4 Judah had five **s** in all.
2:5 Perez's **s** were Hezron and
2:6 Zerah's **s** were Zimri,
2:9 The **s** born to Hezron were
2:16 Zeruiah's three **s** were Abishai,
2:18 Her other **s** were Jesher,
2:27 The **s** of Ram (the firstborn son
2:28 Onam's **s** were Shammai and
2:28 Shammai's **s** were Nadab and
2:30 Nadab's **s** were Seled and
2:32 The **s** of Jada (Shammai's
2:33 Jonathan's **s** were Peleth and
2:34 Sheshan had no **s**,
2:42 and the **s** of Mareshah,
2:43 Hebron's **s** were Korah,
2:47 Jahdai's **s** were Regem,
2:50 The **s** of Hur, the firstborn son
3:1 These were David's **s** who
3:4 Six **s** were born to him in
3:9 All of these were David's **s**.
3:9 Besides these, there were the **s**
3:19 Pedaiah's **s** were Zerubbabel
3:19 Zerubbabel's **s** were
3:20 There were also five other **s**:
3:21 Hananiah's **s** were Pelatiah
3:22 six **s** were Hattush,
3:23 Neariah's three **s** were Elioenai,
3:24 seven **s** were Hodaviah,
4:4 These were the **s** of Hur,
4:6 These were Naarah's **s**.
4:7 Helah's **s** were Zereth,
4:13 Kenaz's **s** were Othniel and
4:13 The **s** of Othniel were Hathath
4:15 The **s** of Caleb, son of
4:16 Jehallelel's **s** were Ziph,
4:17 Ezrah's **s** were Jether,
4:19 The **s** of Hodiah's wife,
4:20 Shimon's **s** were Amnon,
4:20 Ishi's **s** were Zoheth and Ben
4:24 Simeon's **s** were Nemuel,
4:27 Shimei had 16 **s** and 6
4:42 Ishi's **s** Pelatiah, Neariah,
5:1 These are the **s** of Reuben,
5:1 to his nephews, Joseph's **s**,
5:3 The **s** of Reuben, were Hanoch,
5:12 descended from Gad's **s** Janai

1Ch 5:14 These were the **s** of Abihail,
6:1 Levi's **s** were Gershon,
6:2 Kohath's **s** were Amram,
6:3 Aaron's **s** were Nadab,
6:16 Levi's **s** were Gershom,
6:17 are the names of Gershom's **s**:
6:18 Kohath's **s** were Amram,
6:19 Merari's **s** were Mahli and
6:19 are the descendants of Levi's **s**.
6:25 Elkanah's **s** were Amasai and
6:28 Samuel's **s** were Joel,
7:1 Issachar's four **s** were Tola,
7:2 Tola's **s** were Uzzi,
7:3 and Izrahiah's **s** Michael,
7:6 Benjamin had three **s**:
7:7 Bela's five **s** were Ezbon,
7:8 Becher's **s** were Zemirah,
7:8 These were all of Becher's **s**.
7:10 Bilhan's **s** were Jeush,
7:13 Naphtali's **s** were Jahziel,
7:14 Manasseh's **s** were Asriel and
7:16 whose **s** were Ulam and
7:19 Shemida's **s** were Ahian,
7:21 Ephraim's **s** Ezer and Elead
7:30 Asher's **s** were Imnah,
7:31 Beriah's **s** were Heber and
7:33 Japhlet's **s** were Pasach,
7:33 These were Japhlet's **s**.
7:34 The **s** of his brother Shomer
7:35 brother Helem's **s** were Zophah
7:36 Zophah's **s** were Suah,
7:38 Jether's **s** were Jephunneh,
7:39 Ulla's **s** were Arah,
8:3 Bela's **s** were Addar,
8:6 These were Ehud's **s**,
8:9 Hodesh had the following **s**:
8:10 All of Shaharaim's **s** became
8:12 Elpaal's **s** were Eber,
8:15 Beriah's **s** were Zebadiah,
8:17 Elpaal's **s** were Zebadiah,
8:19 Shimei's **s** were Jakim,
8:22 Shashak's **s** were Ishpan,
8:26 Jeroham's **s** were Shamsherai,
8:35 Micah's **s** were Pithon,
8:38 Azel had six **s**. Their names
8:38 All of these men were Azel's **s**.
8:39 His brother Eshek's **s** were
8:40 Ulam's **s** were soldiers,
8:40 had many **s** and grandsons,
9:5 Asaiah (the firstborn) and his **s**.
9:30 Some of the priests' **s** prepared
9:41 Micah's **s** were Pithon,
9:44 Azel had six **s**. Their names
9:44 All of these men were Azel's **s**.
10:2 caught up to Saul and his **s**.
10:2 and Malchishua, Saul's **s**.
10:6 So Saul, his three **s**,
10:7 that Saul and his **s** were dead,
10:8 they found Saul and his **s** lying
10:12 dead bodies of Saul and his **s**
11:44 Shama and Jeiel (**s** of Hotham
11:46 and Joshaviah (**s** of Elnaam),
12:3 then Joash (they were the **s** of
12:3 Azmaveth's **s** Jeziel and Pelet,
12:7 Jeroham's **s** from Gedor.
14:3 fathered more **s** and daughters.
16:42 Jeduthun's **s** were stationed at
17:11 He will be one of your **s**.
18:17 And David's **s** were his main
21:20 Ornan's four **s** who were with
23:6 on which of Levi's **s** (Gershon,
23:8 Ladan had three **s**:
23:9 Shimei had three **s**:
23:10 Shimei's **s** were Jahath,
23:10 They were Shimei's four **s**.
23:11 and Beriah didn't have many **s**,
23:12 Kohath had four **s**:
23:13 Amram's **s** were Aaron and
23:13 Aaron and his **s** were forever
23:14 The **s** of Moses, the man of
23:15 Moses' **s** were Gershom and
23:17 Eliezer had no other **s**,
23:17 but Rehabiah had many **s**.
23:21 Merari's **s** were Mahli and
23:21 Mahli's **s** were Eleazar and
23:22 died without having any **s**.

1Ch	23:22	Their cousins, the **s** of Kish,
	23:23	Mushi had three **s**:
	24:1	Aaron's **s** were Nadab and
	24:28	Eleazar (who had no **s**,
	25:1	appointed the **s** of Asaph,
	25:2	From the **s** of Asaph were
	25:3	From the **s** of Jeduthun were
	25:4	From the **s** of Heman were
	25:5	(All of them were the **s** of the
	25:5	Heman 14 **s** and 3 daughters.)
	25:9	second chose Gedaliah, his **s**,
	25:10	The third chose Zaccur, his **s**,
	25:11	The fourth chose Izri, his **s**,
	25:12	fifth chose Nethaniah, his **s**,
	25:13	sixth chose Bukkiah, his **s**,
	25:14	chose Jesarelah, his **s**,
	25:15	eighth chose Jeshaiah, his **s**,
	25:16	ninth chose Mattaniah, his **s**,
	25:17	The tenth chose Shimei, his **s**,
	25:18	eleventh chose Azarel, his **s**,
	25:19	chose Hashabiah, his **s**,
	25:20	thirteenth chose Shubael, his **s**,
	25:21	chose Mattithiah, his **s**,
	25:22	fifteenth chose Jeremoth, his **s**,
	25:23	chose Hananiah, his **s**,
	25:24	chose Joshbekashah, his **s**,
	25:25	eighteenth chose Hanani, his **s**,
	25:26	chose Mallothi, his **s**,
	25:27	twentieth chose Eliathah, his **s**,
	25:28	twenty-first chose Hothir, his **s**,
	25:29	chose Giddalti, his **s**,
	25:30	chose Mahazioth, his **s**,
	25:31	chose Romamti Ezer, his **s**,
	26:2	Meshelemiah's **s** were
	26:4	**s** Shemaiah (the firstborn),
	26:6	His son Shemaiah had **s** who
	26:7	Shemaiah's **s** were Othni,
	26:8	They, their **s**, and their
	26:9	Meshelemiah's **s** and relatives
	26:10	of Merari there were Hosah's **s**.
	26:11	Hosah's other **s** were Hilkiah
	26:11	There were 13 **s** and relatives
	26:15	and his **s** were chosen for the
	26:22	⌊and⌋ Jehiel's **s** Zetham and
	26:29	his **s** were assigned duties.
	27:32	were in charge of the king's **s**.
	28:1	belonging to the king and his **s**,
	28:4	From among my father's **s** he
	28:5	And of all my **s** (the LORD has
	28:5	LORD has given me many **s**)
	29:24	David's **s** pledged their loyalty
2Ch	5:12	Heman, Jeduthun, their **s**,
	11:19	gave birth to the following **s**:
	11:21	28 **s** and 60 daughters.)
	11:23	He wisely placed his **s** in
	13:21	fathered 22 **s** and 16 daughters.
	21:2	**s** of Jehoshaphat: Azariah,
	21:2	All were the **s** of King
	21:14	people, your **s**, your wives,
	21:17	took Jehoram's **s** and wives.
	22:1	Arabs had killed all the older **s**.
	22:11	killed with the king's other **s**,
	23:11	and Jehoiada and his **s** made
	24:3	Joash had **s** and daughters.
	24:7	(The **s** of that wicked woman
	24:27	The record about his **s**,
	29:9	in battle, and our **s**, daughters,
	29:11	Don't be negligent, my **s**.
	31:18	with their wives, **s**, daughters,
	32:21	some of his own **s** killed him
	36:20	to be slaves for him and his **s**.
Ezr	3:9	Then Jeshua with his **s** and
	3:9	with his **s** who were Judah's
	3:9	family and their **s** and relatives,
	6:10	for the life of the king and his **s**.
	7:23	the king's empire and his **s**?
	8:18	of Sherebiah's **s** and relatives.
	8:19	Jeshaiah's relatives and their **s**,
	9:2	The Israelites and their **s** have
	9:12	let your daughters marry their **s**
	9:12	or your **s** marry their daughters
Neh	3:3	The **s** of Hassenaah rebuilt
	4:14	Fight for your brothers, your **s**,
	5:5	Yet, we have to force our **s** and
	10:9	Binnui (of the **s** of Henadad),
	10:28	Their wives, **s**, daughters,
Neh	10:30	their daughters to marry our **s**.
	10:36	bring the firstborn of our **s**,
	13:25	our daughters to marry their **s**,
	13:25	daughters to marry us or our **s**."
	13:28	Even one of Joiada's **s** was a
Est	5:11	the many **s** he had,
	9:10	were the ten **s** of Haman,
	9:12	out 500 men and Haman's 10 **s**.
	9:13	hang Haman's ten **s** on poles."
	9:14	Haman's ten **s** ⌊on poles⌋.
	9:25	Haman and his **s** on poles.
Job	1:2	seven **s** and three daughters.
	1:4	His **s** used to go to each other's
	1:6	One day when the **s** of God
	1:13	One day when Job's **s** and
	1:18	"Your **s** and your daughters
	2:1	One day when the **s** of God
	14:21	His **s** are honored,
	38:7	sang together and all the **s**
	42:13	seven **s** and three daughters.
Psa	45:16	Your **s** will take the place of
	69:8	a foreigner to my mother's **s**.
	82:6	You are all **s** of the Most High.
	105:36	He killed all the firstborn **s**,
	106:37	They sacrificed their **s** and
	106:38	the blood of their own **s** and
	132:12	If your **s** are faithful to my
	144:12	May our **s** be like full-grown,
Pro	4:1	**S**, listen to ⌊your⌋ father's
	5:7	But now, **s**, listen to me,
	7:24	Now, **s**, listen to me.
	8:32	"Now, **s**, listen to me.
Isa	14:21	a place to slaughter their **s**
	23:4	I've raised no **s**. I've brought up
	37:38	and Sharezer, his **s**,
	43:6	Bring my **s** from far away and
	49:22	They will bring your **s** in their
	56:5	better than **s** and daughters.
	60:4	Your **s** come from far away.
	62:5	so your **s** will marry you.
Jer	3:24	their **s** and daughters.
	5:17	They will devour your **s** and
	7:31	Hinnom in order to burn their **s**
	11:22	Their **s** and daughters will die
	14:16	their **s**, or their daughters.
	15:9	birth to seven **s** will grow faint
	16:2	Don't have any **s** or daughters
	16:3	the LORD says about the **s**
	19:9	flesh of their **s** and daughters.
	29:6	and have **s** and daughters.
	29:6	Find wives for your **s**,
	29:6	they can have **s** and daughters.
	32:35	sites for Baal to sacrifice their **s**
	35:3	brothers and all his **s** —
	35:4	the side room of the **s** of Hanan.
	35:8	We, along with our wives, **s**,
	39:6	**s** as Zedekiah watched
	40:8	and Jonathan (**s** of Kareah),
	40:8	the **s** of Ephai from Netophah,
	48:46	Your **s** will be taken away into
	52:10	**s** as Zedekiah watched.
Eze	14:16	their own **s** or daughters.
	14:18	rescue their **s** or daughters.
	14:20	rescue their **s** or daughters.
	14:22	Some of your **s** and daughters
	16:20	took your **s** and daughters,
	20:26	all their firstborn **s** as gifts ⌊to
	23:4	gave birth to **s** and daughters.
	23:10	took away her **s** and daughters,
	23:25	They will take your **s** and your
	23:47	The mob will kill their **s** and
	24:21	So the **s** and daughters that
	24:25	away their **s** and daughters.
	46:16	the prince offers one of his **s**
	46:17	Only his **s** can inherit his
	46:18	to his **s** so that none
Dan	11:10	"Then his **s** will prepare for
Joe	2:28	Your **s** and daughters will
	3:8	I will sell your **s** and daughters
Amo	7:17	and your **s** and daughters will
Zep	1:8	the officials, the king's **s**,
Zec	10:7	Their **s** will see it and be glad.
Mal	3:3	He will purify Levi's **s** and
Mat	4:21	and John, the **s** of Zebedee.
	10:2	brother John, the **s** of Zebedee;
	20:20	Then the mother of Zebedee's **s**
Mat	20:20	came to Jesus with her two **s**.
	20:21	"Promise that one of my **s** will
	21:28	A man had two **s**. He went to
	21:31	"Which of the two **s** did what
	26:37	and Zebedee's two **s** with him.
	27:56	and the mother of Zebedee's **s**.
Mar	1:19	and John, the **s** of Zebedee.
	3:17	**s** whom Jesus named
	10:35	James and John, **s** of Zebedee,
Luk	5:10	who were Zebedee's **s** and
	15:11	"A man had two **s**.
	15:12	his property between his two **s**.
Jon	4:12	He and his **s** and his animals
	21:2	Cana in Galilee, Zebedee's **s**,
Act	2:17	Your **s** and daughters will
	7:8	to his twelve **s** (the ancestors
	7:9	"Jacob's **s** were jealous of their
	7:16	in Shechem from Hamor's **s**.
	7:29	In Midian he fathered two **s**.
	19:14	Seven **s** of Sceva,
2Co	6:18	will be my **s** and daughters."
Gal	4:22	says that Abraham had two **s**,
Heb	2:10	God was bringing many **s**
	2:13	"I am here with the **s** and
	2:14	Since all of these **s** and
	11:21	to bless each of Joseph's **s**.
	11:28	would not kill the firstborn **s**.

sons' (5)

Gen	6:18	and your **s** wives will go into
	7:7	and his **s** wives went into the
	8:16	your sons, and your **s** wives
	8:18	sons, his wife, and his **s** wives
1Sm	3:13	about his **s** sin — that they

soot (1)

Lam	4:8	are ⌊now⌋ blacker than **s**.

soothed (2)

Psa	94:19	your assuring words **s** my soul.
Isa	1:6	bandaged, or **s** with oil.

soothing (44)

Gen	8:21	LORD smelled the **s** aroma.
Exo	29:18	It's a burnt offering, a **s** aroma,
	29:25	It's a **s** aroma in the LORD's
	29:41	This is a **s** aroma,
Lev	1:9	a **s** aroma to the LORD.
	1:13	a **s** aroma to the LORD.
	1:17	a **s** aroma to the LORD."
	2:2	a **s** aroma to the LORD.
	2:9	a **s** aroma to the LORD.
	2:12	on the altar to make a **s** aroma.
	3:5	a **s** aroma to the LORD.
	3:16	It is a **s** aroma. All the fat
	4:31	burn it on the altar for a **s** aroma
	6:15	It is a **s** aroma to the LORD.
	6:21	the grain offering as a **s** aroma
	8:21	was a burnt offering, a **s** aroma,
	8:28	a **s** aroma to the LORD.
	17:6	He will burn the fat as a **s**
	23:13	made to the LORD, a **s** aroma.
	23:18	a **s** aroma to the LORD.
	26:31	I will no longer accept the **s**
Num	15:3	or goats — offerings that are a **s**
	15:7	Offer them as a **s** aroma to the
	15:10	a **s** aroma to the LORD.
	15:13	a **s** aroma to the LORD.
	15:14	a **s** aroma to the LORD,
	15:24	a **s** aroma to the LORD,
	18:17	a **s** aroma to the LORD.
	28:2	are offerings by fire, a **s** aroma.
	28:6	This offering is a **s** aroma,
	28:8	a **s** aroma to the LORD.
	28:13	is a burnt offering, a **s** aroma,
	28:24	a **s** aroma to the LORD.
	28:27	Bring a burnt offering as a **s**
	29:2	a **s** aroma to the LORD,
	29:6	They are a **s** aroma,
	29:8	As a burnt offering, a **s** aroma,
	29:13	a **s** aroma to the LORD,
	29:36	a **s** aroma to the LORD,
Psa	55:21	His words are more **s** than oil,
	92:10	and **s** lotion is poured on me.
Pro	15:4	A **s** tongue is a tree of life,
Eph	5:2	sacrifice, a **s** aroma to God.

Php 4:18 Your gifts are a **s** aroma,

Sopater (1)
Act 20:4 **S** (son of Pyrrhus) from Berea,

Sophereth (1)
Neh 7:57 of Sotai, **S**, Perida,

sorcerer (1)
Dtr 18:10 be a fortuneteller, witch, or **s**,

sorcerers (7)
Exo 7:11 sent for his wise men and **s**.
Jer 27:9 or **s** who tell you that you'll
Dan 2:2 for the magicians, psychics, **s**,
Mic 5:12 I will destroy your **s**,
Mal 3:5 be quick to testify against **s**,
Rev 21:8 sexual sinners, **s**, idolaters,
22:15 Outside are dogs, **s**,

sore (7)
Lev 13:2 "If anyone has a **s**,
13:10 If there is a white **s** that has
13:10 if there is raw flesh in the **s**,
13:19 in its place there is a white **s**
13:28 it is only a **s** caused by the
13:43 If the **s** from the disease in the
14:56 diseases where there is a **s**,

Sorek (1)
Jdg 16:4 with a woman in the **S** Valley.

sores (10)
Exo 9:9 boils to break into open **s**
9:10 boils to break into open **s**
Dtr 28:27 strike you with hemorrhoids, **s**,
2Sm 3:29 family who have oozing **s**
Job 7:5 My skin is crusted over with **s**;
Isa 1:6 bruises, **s**, and fresh wounds.
3:17 The Lord will cause **s** ⌊to
Luk 16:21 Lazarus was covered with **s**,
Rev 16:2 Horrible, painful **s** appeared on
16:11 for their pains and their **s**.

sorrow (15)
Gen 35:18 her son Benoni [Son of My **S**],
Job 5:6 **s** doesn't come from the soil,
Psa 13:2 I make decisions alone with **s**
31:10 My life is exhausted from **s**,
107:39 of oppression, disaster, and **s**.
Ecc 7:3 **S** is better than laughter
Isa 35:10 They will have no **s** or grief.
51:11 They will have no **s** or grief.
Jer 8:18 **S** has overwhelmed me.
31:13 them joy in place of their **s**.
31:25 everyone who is filled with **s**."
Eze 23:33 filled with drunkenness and **s**.
Rom 9:2 deep **s** and endless heartache.
1Co 7:30 live as though they have no **s**.
Php 2:27 and kept me from having one **s**

sorrowful (1)
Psa 51:17 despise a broken and **s** heart.

sorrows (3)
Psa 16:4 after other gods multiply their **s**.
Isa 53:3 He was a man of **s**,
53:4 our suffering and carried our **s**,

sorry (43)
Gen 6:6 The LORD was **s** that he had
6:7 I'm **s** that I made them."
Exo 2:6 and she felt **s** for him.
Dtr 13:8 Don't feel **s** for them or protect
Jdg 21:6 The people of Israel felt **s** for
21:15 The congregation felt **s** for the
1Sm 22:8 No one felt **s** for me and
23:21 bless you for feeling **s** for me!
1Ki 8:47 are **s** for what they've done,
2Ch 6:37 are **s** for what they've done,
21:20 No one was **s** to see him die.
Job 42:6 and ashes to show that I am **s**."
Isa 51:19 Who will feel **s** for you?
66:2 humble and **s** ⌊for their sins⌋
Jer 15:1 I would not feel **s** for these
Eze 5:11 for you or feel **s** for you.
7:4 for you or feel **s** for you.
7:9 not have compassion or feel **s**.
8:18 for them or feel **s** for them.
9:5 compassion, and don't feel **s**.
9:10 not have compassion or feel **s**.
16:5 No one who saw you felt **s**
Amo 6:6 over themselves and are not **s**
Jnh 4:10 Yet, you feel **s** for this plant.
4:11 Shouldn't I feel **s** for this
Nah 3:7 Who will feel **s** for her?'
Mal 3:14 or if we walk around feeling **s**
Mat 9:36 the crowds, he felt **s** for them.
14:14 He felt **s** for them and cured
15:32 "I feel **s** for the people.
18:27 "The master felt **s** for his
20:34 Jesus felt **s** for them,
Mar 1:41 Jesus felt **s** for him,
6:34 large crowd and felt **s** for them.
8:2 "I feel **s** for the people.
Luk 7:13 Lord saw her, he felt **s** for her.
10:33 he felt **s** for the man,
15:20 saw him and felt **s** for him.
17:4 times and says that he is **s**,
2Co 7:7 how **s** you are for what you've
7:8 you uncomfortable, I'm not **s**.
7:8 for a while, I was **s**.
9:7 You shouldn't be **s** that you

sort (2)
Luk 7:39 he would know what **s** of
Gal 2:6 (What **s** of people they were

sorts (1)
Neh 9:25 of houses filled with all **s**

Sosipater (1)
Rom 16:21 so do Lucius, Jason, and **S**,

Sosthenes (2)
Act 18:17 governor's officers⌋ took **S**,
1Co 1:1 by the will of God, and from **S**,

Sotai (2)
Ezr 2:55 the descendants of **S**,
Neh 7:57 the descendants of **S**,

sought (13)
1Sm 7:2 Israel mournfully **s** the LORD.
13:12 but I haven't **s** the LORD's
25:29 pursued you and **s** your life,
1Ki 12:6 King Rehoboam **s** advice from
12:8 He **s** advice from the young
2Ch 10:6 King Rehoboam **s** advice from
10:8 He **s** advice from the young
25:20 they had **s** help from Edom's
Psa 119:45 because I **s** out your guiding
Isa 9:13 nor have they **s** the LORD of
62:12 and you will be called **S** After,
Jer 8:2 gone after, **s**, and worshiped.
26:19 feared the LORD and **s**

soul (107)
Dtr 4:29 your heart and with all your **s**.
6:5 all your heart, with all your **s**,
10:12 your heart and with all your **s**.
11:13 your heart and with all your **s**,
13:3 your heart and with all your **s**.
26:16 your heart and with all your **s**.
30:2 your heart and with all your **s**,
30:6 your heart and with all your **s**,
30:10 your heart and with all your **s**.
Jos 22:5 him with all your heart and **s**."
23:14 all your heart and **s** that not one
1Ki 15:29 He did not spare a **s**,
2Ki 23:3 laws with all his heart and **s**.
23:25 all his heart, **s**, and strength,
2Ch 15:12 with all their heart and **s**.
34:31 laws with all his heart and **s**.
Job 7:11 about the bitterness in my **s**."
21:25 dies with a bitter **s**.
30:25 Didn't my **s** grieve for the poor?
33:28 The messenger has freed my **s**
Psa 6:3 My **s** has been deeply shaken
16:9 heart is glad and my **s** rejoices.
16:10 you do not abandon my **s**
19:7 They renew the **s**.
22:20 Rescue my **s** from the sword,
23:3 He renews my **s**. He guides me
25:1 To you, O LORD, I lift my **s**.
26:9 Do not sweep away my **s**
30:12 so that my **s** may praise you
31:7 known the troubles in my **s**.
31:9 My eyes, my **s**, and my body
34:2 My **s** will boast about the
35:3 Say to my **s**, "I am your savior."
35:9 My **s** will find joy in the LORD
41:4 Heal my **s** because I have
42:1 so my **s** longs for you,
42:2 My **s** thirsts for God,
42:4 these things as I pour out my **s**:
42:5 are you discouraged, my **s**?
42:6 My **s** is discouraged.
42:11 are you discouraged, my **s**?
43:5 are you discouraged, my **s**?
49:8 The price to be paid for his **s** is
55:18 he will rescue my **s** from the
57:1 Have pity on me, because my **s**
57:4 My **s** is surrounded by lions.
57:6 (My **s** is bowed down.)
57:8 Wake up, my **s**! Wake up, harp
62:1 My **s** waits calmly for God
62:5 calmly for God alone, my **s**,
63:1 My **s** thirsts for you.
63:5 You satisfy my **s** with the
63:8 My **s** clings to you.
69:18 Come close, and defend my **s**.
71:23 My **s**, which you have rescued,
74:19 Do not hand over the **s** of your
77:2 my **s** refused to be comforted.
84:2 My **s** longs and yearns for the
86:4 because I lift my **s** to you.
88:3 My **s** is filled with troubles,
88:14 Why do you reject my **s**,
94:17 my **s** would have quickly fallen
94:19 assuring words soothed my **s**.
103:1 Praise the LORD, my **s**!
103:2 Praise the LORD, my **s**,
103:22 Praise the LORD, my **s**!
104:1 Praise the LORD, my **s**!
104:35 Praise the LORD, my **s**!
108:1 make music even with my **s**.
116:7 Be at peace again, my **s**,
119:20 My **s** is overwhelmed with
119:81 My **s** is weak from waiting for
119:175 Let my **s** have new life so that
130:5 wait for the LORD, my **s** waits,
130:6 My **s** waits for the LORD more
131:2 Instead, I have kept my **s** calm
131:2 My **s** is content as a weaned
138:3 me bold by strengthening my **s**.
139:14 and my **s** is fully aware of this.
142:7 Release my **s** from prison so
143:6 my **s** thirsts for you.
146:1 Praise the LORD, my **s**!
Pro 2:10 will be pleasant to your **s**.
13:19 desire is sweet to the **s**,
18:7 His lips are a trap to his **s**.
20:27 A person's **s** is the LORD's
23:14 you will save his **s** from hell.
24:12 who guards your **s** know it?
24:14 wisdom is like that for your **s**.
25:25 ⌊Like⌋ cold water to a thirsty **s**,
29:17 He will bring delight to your **s**.
Isa 10:18 will destroy both body and **s**.
16:11 My **s** mourns for Kir Hareseth.
26:9 With my **s** I long for you at
Jer 32:41 With all my heart and **s** I will
Lam 3:17 "My **s** has been kept from
3:20 My **s** continues to remember
3:24 My **s** can say, 'The LORD is
Mat 10:28 the body but cannot kill the **s**.
10:28 destroy both body and **s** in hell.
22:37 all your heart, with all your **s**,
Mar 12:30 all your heart, with all your **s**,
Luk 1:46 Mary said, "My **s** praises the
10:27 all your heart, with all your **s**,
Act 2:27 you do not abandon my **s**
1Th 5:23 your whole being — spirit, **s**,
Heb 4:12 as deep as the place where **s**

souls (14)
Job 26:5 "The **s** of the dead tremble

Job 33:18 He keeps their **s** from the pit
33:22 Their **s** approach the pit.
33:30 to turn their **s** away from the pit
Psa 33:19 to rescue their **s** from death and
34:22 The LORD protects the **s** of his
44:25 Our **s** are bowing in the dust.
Pro 2:18 ways lead to the **s** of the dead.
9:18 But he does not know that the **s**
11:30 and a winner of **s** is wise.
Isa 66:3 and their **s** delight in detestable
Rev 6:9 I saw under the altar the **s** of
6:11 Each of the **s** was given a
20:4 Then I saw the **s** of those

sound (107)

Exo 19:19 As the **s** of the horn grew
28:35 The **s** of the bells must be
32:17 "It's the **s** of war in the camp!"
32:18 Moses replied, "It's not the **s** of
32:18 It's not the **s** of losers crying.
32:18 It's the **s** of a wild celebration
Lev 25:9 **s** rams' horns throughout the
26:36 The **s** of a wind-blown leaf will
Num 10:6 When the trumpets **s** a second
10:9 the trumpets will **s** a fanfare.
29:1 ⌊the trumpets to **s**⌋ a fanfare.
Jdg 4:21 When Sisera had fallen **s**
18:25 "Don't make another **s**,
1Sm 15:14 "But what is this **s** of sheep in
15:14 of sheep in my ears and this **s**
2Sm 5:24 When you hear the **s** of
15:10 "When you hear the **s** of the
1Ki 1:41 When Joab heard the **s** of the
1:45 That is the **s** you heard.
6:7 or any other iron tool made a **s**
18:26 But there wasn't a **s** or an
18:29 But there was no **s**,
2Ki 4:31 but there was no **s** or sign of
1Ch 14:15 As you hear the **s** of marching
2Ch 13:12 His priests will **s** their trumpets
Neh 4:18 man who was supposed to **s**
12:43 The **s** of rejoicing in Jerusalem
Job 6:5 an ox make a **s** over its hay?
39:24 ground and doesn't trust the **s**
Psa 6:8 has heard the **s** of my crying.
19:4 ⌊Yet,⌋ their **s** has gone out into
46:6 melts at the **s** of ⌊God's⌋ voice.
47:5 LORD has gone up with the **s**
66:8 Make the **s** of his praise heard.
77:18 The **s** of your thunder rumbled
93:4 is mighty — mightier than the **s**
104:7 away at the **s** of your thunder.
115:7 make a **s** with their throats.
118:15 The **s** of joyful singing and
141:6 It will **s** pleasant ⌊to them⌋.
Pro 18:1 He opposes all **s** reasoning.
Ecc 12:4 the **s** of the mill is muffled,
12:4 you are startled at the **s** of a
Isa 9:5 warrior's boot marching to the **s**
13:4 It is like the **s** of a large army.
13:4 It is the **s** of kingdoms and
30:31 At the **s** of the LORD,
30:32 To the **s** of tambourines and
51:3 and the **s** of singing.
66:6 Listen to the **s** from the temple.
66:6 It is the **s** of the LORD paying
Jer 3:21 The **s** of crying is heard on the
4:21 and hear the **s** of rams' horns?
4:29 in the city will flee at the **s**
6:17 Pay attention to the **s** of the
6:23 They **s** like the roaring sea.
9:10 No one can hear the **s** of cattle.
9:19 The **s** of crying is heard from
25:10 and grooms, the **s** of mills,
25:31 The **s** is echoing to the ends of
30:19 and the **s** of laughter will be
31:15 A **s** is heard in Ramah,
31:15 the **s** of crying in bitter grief.
42:14 hear the **s** of a ram's horn,
47:3 They will hear the **s** of
48:36 I **s** like a flute for the people of
49:2 when I will **s** the battle cry
49:21 The earth will quake at the **s** of
49:21 The **s** of their crying will be
50:42 They will **s** like the sea when
Eze 1:24 I heard the **s** of their wings.
Eze 1:24 The **s** was like the noise of
10:5 The **s** of the angels' wings was
10:5 It was like the **s** of the
19:7 terrified by the **s** of his roar.
31:16 nations tremble in fear at the **s**
33:5 They heard the **s** of the horn
43:2 His voice was like the **s** of
Dan 3:5 When you hear the **s** of rams'
3:7 As soon as they heard the **s** of
3:10 that everyone who hears the **s**
3:15 When you hear the **s** of the
Hos 5:8 **S** the alarm at Beth Aven,
8:1 "**S** the alarm on the ram's horn.
Joe 2:1 **S** the alarm on my holy
2:5 they **s** like rattling chariots,
Amo 5:23 Spare me the **s** of your songs.
Jnh 1:5 and was lying there **s** asleep.
Nah 3:2 The **s** of the whip!
3:2 The **s** of rattling wheels!
Zep 1:10 and a loud crashing **s** from the
Mat 2:18 "A **s** was heard in Ramah,
2:18 the **s** of crying in bitter grief.
Jon 3:8 You hear its **s**, but you don't
Act 2:2 Suddenly, a **s** like a violently
17:20 Some of the things you say **s**
1Co 14:8 if the trumpet doesn't **s** a clear
15:52 in a split second at the **s** of the
15:52 Indeed, that trumpet will **s**,
Col 2:4 arguments that merely **s** good.
1Th 5:3 "Everything is safe and **s**!"
2Pe 3:10 pass away with a roaring **s**.
Rev 1:15 was like the **s** of raging waters.
14:2 Then I heard a **s** from heaven
14:2 The **s** I heard was like the
18:22 The **s** of harpists, musicians,
18:22 The **s** of a millstone will never

sounded (5)

2Ki 7:6 army hear what **s** like chariots,
Dan 10:6 When he spoke, his voice **s**
Rev 6:6 I heard what **s** like a voice from
19:1 these things I heard what **s** like
19:6 I heard what **s** like the noise

sounding (5)

Num 10:7 will blow without **s** a fanfare.
1Sm 13:3 With the **s** of the ram's horn
2Sm 6:15 of joy and the **s** of rams' horns.
1Ch 15:28 with shouts of joy and the **s**
Jer 4:19 because I hear a ram's horn **s**

soundly (1)

Luk 9:32 men with him were sleeping **s**.

sounds (18)

Exo 19:13 the ram's horn **s** a long blast."
1Ki 18:41 It **s** like a heavy rain ⌊is
Job 12:11 Doesn't the ear distinguish **s**
15:21 Terrifying **s** are in his ears.
39:25 As often as the horn **s**,
Psa 51:8 Let me hear ⌊**s** of⌋ joy and
150:3 Praise him with **s** from horns.
Jer 7:34 I will banish the **s** of joy and
7:34 of joy and happiness and the **s**
16:9 I'm going to put a stop to the **s**
16:9 of joy and happiness and the **s**
25:10 I will take from them the **s** of
25:10 the **s** of brides and grooms,
33:11 the **s** of joy and happiness and
33:11 of joy and happiness and the **s**
51:54 **S** of terrible destruction are
Amo 3:6 If a ram's horn **s** an alarm in a
1Co 14:7 like the flute or harp produce **s**.

sour (7)

Rut 2:14 and dip it into the **s** wine."
Job 20:14 the food in his belly turns **s**.
Isa 5:2 but it produced only **s**,
5:4 why did it produce only **s**,
Jer 31:29 'Fathers have eaten **s** grapes,
31:30 Whoever eats **s** grapes will
Eze 18:2 'Fathers have eaten **s** grapes,

source (20)

Dtr 29:18 that no one among you is the **s**
Psa 68:26 the **s** of Israel, with the choirs.
Psa 80:6 You made us a **s** of conflict to
87:7 "Zion is the **s** of all our
Pro 4:23 because the **s** of your life flows
Isa 22:23 and he will be a **s** of honor for
60:15 But now I will make you a **s** of
Jer 33:9 Jerusalem will be my **s** of joy,
Jon 1:4 He was the **s** of life,
5:26 The Father is the **s** of life,
5:26 the Son to be the **s** of life too.
5:39 you think you have the **s**
6:53 you don't have the **s** of life in
Act 3:15 and you killed the **s** of life.
Rom 15:13 May God, the **s** of hope,
2Ti 2:1 My child, find your **s** of
Heb 2:10 the **s** of their salvation,
5:9 he became the **s** of eternal
12:2 the **s** and goal of our faith.
Rev 3:14 the **s** of God's creation,

sources (4)

Job 28:11 They explore the **s** of rivers so
Eze 31:7 down to many **s** of water.
31:15 many water **s** stopped flowing.
32:13 beside its many water **s**.

sourdough (1)

Exo 13:7 No **s** or yeast should be seen

south (123)

Gen 13:14 to Abram, "Look north, **s**, east,
28:14 to the north and to the **s**.
Exo 26:18 Make 20 frames for the **s** side
26:35 the table on the **s** side.
27:9 The **s** side of the courtyard
36:23 They made 20 frames for the **s**
38:9 The **s** side of the courtyard
40:24 on the **s** side of the tent.
Num 2:10 "On the **s** side the armies led
3:29 put up their tents on the **s** side
10:6 on the **s** will break camp.
34:4 and turns **s** of the Akrabbim
35:5 3,000 feet on the **s** side,
Dtr 3:27 look west, north, **s**, and east.
33:23 of the lake and the land **s** of it."
Jos 1:4 will be the desert ⌊on the **s**⌋,
11:2 the plains **s** of Chinneroth,
12:3 goes **s** from Beth Jeshimoth
13:4 in the **s**. This territory includes
15:1 Their territory extends as far **s**
15:2 border starts from the **s** end
15:3 and goes **s** of the Akrabbim
15:3 then passes Zin and goes up **s**
15:7 Pass, **s** of the valley.
15:8 of Ben Hinnom to the **s** slope
17:7 Then the border goes **s** toward
17:10 What is **s** ⌊of the river⌋
18:5 stay within its territory in the **s**,
18:13 the border goes to the **s** slope
18:13 Addar over the mountains **s**
18:14 **s** of the mountain that faces
18:16 to the **s** slope of the city of
18:19 of the Dead Sea at the **s** end
19:34 It touches Zebulun in the **s**,
Jdg 21:19 and **s** of Lebonah."
1Sm 14:5 the other stood **s** facing Geba.
20:41 David came out from the **s** side
23:19 of Hachilah, **s** of Jeshimon.
23:24 in the plains **s** of Jeshimon.
2Sm 24:5 **s** of the city in the middle of the
1Ki 6:8 the first story was on the **s** side
7:25 three faced west, three faced **s**,
7:39 He put five stands on the **s**
7:39 He set the pool on the **s** side of
7:49 of pure gold (five on the **s** side
2Ki 11:11 and the temple (from the **s** side
1Ch 9:24 sides (east, west, north, and **s**).
26:15 was chosen for the **s** side,
26:17 On the **s** there were four every
2Ch 4:4 three faced west, three faced **s**,
4:6 and put five on the **s** side
4:7 five on the **s** side and five on
4:8 five on the **s** side and five on
4:10 He set the pool on the **s** side in
23:10 and the temple (from the **s** side
Job 9:9 the clusters of stars in the **s**.
37:17 earth is calm under a **s** wind?

Job 39:26 spread its wings toward the s?
Psa 78:26 heavens and guided the s wind
89:12 You created north and s.
107:3 from the north and from the s.
Ecc 1:6 The wind blows toward the s
11:3 If a tree falls north or s,
Sos 4:16 Come, s wind! Blow on my
Isa 43:6 "Give them up," and to the s,
Eze 10:3 were standing on the s side
16:46 She lives s of you with her
20:46 "Son of man, turn to the s,
20:46 preach against the s,
20:47 land from the s to the north.
21:4 from the s to the north.
40:2 On the s side of the mountain
40:24 the man led me to the s side,
40:24 I saw a gateway that faced s.
40:27 had a gateway facing s.
40:27 from the gateway on the s side
40:28 through the s gateway.
40:28 He measured the s gateway.
40:44 It faced s. The other room was
40:44 at the side of the s gateway.
40:45 "This room that faces s is for
41:11 the north and another to the s.
42:10 of the courtyard on the s side.
42:12 The doors to the s rooms were
42:18 He measured the s side.
46:9 must leave through the s gate.
46:9 Those entering through the s
47:1 was flowing under the s side
47:1 of the temple, s of the altar.
47:2 was flowing down the s side
47:19 On the s side the border will
48:2 land and border Dan on the s.
48:3 land and border Asher on the s.
48:4 and border Naphtali on the s.
48:5 and border Manasseh on the s.
48:6 and border Ephraim on the s.
48:7 and border Reuben on the s.
48:8 will border Judah on the s.
48:10 On the s side it will be 43,750
48:16 On the s side it will be 7,875
48:17 4,375 feet on the s,
48:24 and border Benjamin on the s.
48:25 and border Simeon on the s.
48:26 and border Issachar on the s.
48:27 and border Zebulun on the s.
48:28 of Gad will run s from Tamar
48:33 The s side will be 7,875 feet
48:33 The three gates on the s side
Dan 8:4 charging west, north, and s.
8:9 It gained power over the s,
11:29 time he will again invade the s,
Zec 6:6 ones are going toward the s."
9:14 march in the storms from the s.
14:4 half will move toward the s.
14:10 to Rimmon, s of Jerusalem.
Mat 12:42 The queen from the s will
Luk 11:31 The queen from the s will
12:55 you see a s wind blowing,
Act 8:26 that goes s from Jerusalem
27:7 we started to sail for the s side
27:13 began to blow from the s,
28:13 The next day a s wind began
Rev 21:13 three gates on the s,

southeast (2)
1Ki 7:39 of the temple in the s ⌊corner⌋.
2Ch 4:10 south side in the s ⌊corner⌋.

southern (25)
Num 34:3 "The s side includes part of the
34:3 In the east the s border starts
Jos 15:2 The s border starts from the
15:4 This is the s border.
17:9 Manasseh's ⌊s⌋ border is the
18:15 The s border begins just
18:19 This is its s border.
2Ki 23:13 They were on the s part of the
Eze 42:13 "The northern and s side rooms
47:19 This is the s border.
48:28 The s border of Gad will run
Dan 11:5 "The s king will be strong,
11:6 After a few years the s and
11:6 The s king's daughter will go to
Dan 11:9 He will invade the s kingdom
11:11 The s king will be outraged.
11:11 will fall into the s king's hands.
11:12 the s king will become
11:14 will rebel against the s king,
11:15 The s forces will not be able to
11:17 He will give the s king his
11:17 order to destroy the s kingdom.
11:25 and courage against the s king,
11:25 But the s king won't be able to
11:40 "In the end times the s king

southward (2)
Jos 17:9 The border then descends s to
Job 23:9 If I turn s, I can't see him.

southwest (1)
Act 27:12 is a harbor that faces the s

sow (1)
2Pe 2:22 and "A s that has been washed

sown (1)
Isa 40:24 They have hardly been s.

space (9)
1Sm 26:13 was a wide s between them.)
1Ki 7:36 designs in every available s
Job 26:7 out his heavens over empty s.
41:16 there is no s between them.
Isa 54:2 Expand the s of your tent.
Eze 40:7 The s between the guardrooms
41:17 In the s above the door to the
41:20 floor to the s above the door.
42:5 took s away from them.

Spain (3)
Rom 15:24 Now I am on my way to S,
15:24 you will support my trip to S.
15:28 I will visit you on my way to S.

span (3)
Exo 23:26 will let you live a normal life s.
Psa 39:5 My life s is nothing compared
144:4 Their life s is like a fleeting

spank (3)
Pro 13:24 Whoever refuses to s his son
23:13 If you s him, he will not die.
23:14 S him yourself, and you will

spanking (2)
Pro 22:15 S will remove it far from him.
29:15 A s and a warning produce

spare (39)
Gen 18:24 Won't you s that place for the
18:26 I will s the whole place for their
19:16 the LORD wanted to s Lot.
Dtr 20:16 However, you must not s
Jos 22:23 don't s us today. If we built an
1Sm 15:3 Don't s them, but kill men and
25:8 David anything you can ⌊s⌋."
2Sm 21:2 had sworn ⌊to s them⌋,
1Ki 15:29 He did not s a soul,
16:11 He didn't s any of Baasha's
2Ch 31:10 wanted to eat and plenty to s.
36:15 he wanted to s his people
36:17 He didn't s the best men or the
Neh 13:22 for this, my God, and s me,
Est 7:3 you, Your Majesty, s my life.
7:3 And s the life of my people.
Job 2:6 but you must s his life!"
Psa 78:50 He did not s them.
Pro 24:11 and s those staggering toward
Isa 47:3 revenge. I won't s anyone.
Jer 21:7 He won't s them, show them
51:3 Don't s Babylon's young men.
Eze 12:16 However, I will s a few of them
13:19 and you s the lives of people
Joe 2:17 They say, "S your people,
Amo 5:23 S me the sound of your songs.
Mal 3:17 I will s them as a man spares
Mar 12:44 have given what they could s.
Luk 21:4 have given what they could s.
Act 20:29 and they won't s the flock.
Rom 8:32 God didn't s his own Son but
11:21 If God didn't s the natural
11:21 he won't s you, either.
1Co 7:28 I would like to s them from that.
2Co 1:23 because I wanted to s you.
12:6 But I'm going to s you so that
13:2 I visit you again, I won't s you.
2Pe 2:4 God didn't s angels who
2:5 God didn't s the ancient world

spared (12)
Exo 9:16 But I have s you for this reason.
12:27 in Egypt and s our homes when
Num 22:33 you by now but s the donkey."
Jos 6:25 Joshua s the prostitute Rahab,
1Sm 15:9 Saul and the army s Agag and
15:15 They s the best sheep and
24:10 told to kill you, I s you, saying,
2Sm 8:2 one length which was to be s.
21:7 But the king s Mephibosheth,
Job 21:30 the wicked person is s.
Isa 57:1 people are s when evil comes.
Jer 50:20 the faithful few whom I have s.

spares (1)
Mal 3:17 I will spare them as a man s

spark (1)
Isa 1:31 and their work will be the s.

sparkle (1)
Zec 9:16 They will certainly s in his

sparkles (1)
Pro 23:31 because it s in the cup,

sparkling (1)
Isa 54:12 your gates with s stones,

sparks (2)
Job 5:7 as surely as s fly up from
41:19 S of fire fly from it.

sparrow (1)
Pro 26:2 Like a fluttering s, like a darting

sparrows (5)
Psa 84:3 Even s find a home,
Mat 10:29 "Aren't two s sold for a penny?
10:31 are worth more than many s.
Luk 12:6 "Aren't five s sold for two
12:7 are worth more than many s.

speak (327)
Gen 18:30 don't be angry if I s again,"
18:32 "Please don't be angry if I s
24:33 "S up," Laban said.
30:33 My honesty will s for itself
34:6 came to Jacob to s with him.
34:20 went to their city gate to s
37:4 hated Joseph and couldn't s
42:24 When he could s to them again,
44:18 let me s openly with you.
48:20 Israel will s this blessing,
50:4 "Please s directly to Pharaoh.
Exo 4:10 I s slowly, and I become
4:12 Now go, and I will help you s
4:14 I know he can s well.
4:15 You will s to him and tell him
4:15 I will help both of you s,
4:16 Aaron will s to the people for
5:23 I went to Pharaoh to s for you,
19:6 you must s to the Israelites."
20:19 "You s to us, and we'll listen.
20:19 But don't let God s to us,
29:42 I will meet with you to s to you.
33:11 The LORD would s to Moses
34:34 LORD's presence to s with him,
34:35 in again to s with the LORD.
Num 5:12 "S to the Israelites and tell
6:2 "S to the Israelites and tell
7:89 into the tent of meeting to s
8:2 "S to Aaron and tell him:
11:17 I'll come down and s with you
12:2 They asked, "Did the LORD s
12:2 Didn't he also s through us?"

Num	12:6	known to them in visions or **s**
	12:8	I **s** with him face to face,
	15:2	"**S** to the Israelites and tell
	15:18	"**S** to the Israelites and tell
	15:38	"**S** to the Israelites and tell
	17:2	"**S** to the Israelites,
	18:26	"**S** to the Levites and say to
	22:28	the LORD made the donkey **s**,
Dtr	4:33	people ever heard God **s** from
	4:36	and you heard him **s** from the
	5:26	voice of the living God **s** from
	18:21	LORD didn't **s** this message?"
	20:2	must come and **s** to the troops.
	31:1	Moses continued to **s** to all the
	31:28	As they listen, I will **s** these
	32:1	Listen, heaven, and I will **s**.
Jos	10:21	Not a single person dared to **s**
Jdg	19:30	Form a plan, and **s** out!"
1Sm	3:9	"When he calls you, say, '**S**,
	3:10	And Samuel replied, "**S**.
	15:16	last night." "**S**," Saul replied.
	19:3	I'll **s** with my father about you.
	25:24	Please let me **s** with you.
2Sm	3:12	sent messengers to David to **s**
	6:22	these slave girls you **s** about."
	13:13	**S** to the king. He won't refuse
	13:22	Absalom wouldn't **s** at all to
	14:12	else to you." "**S**," he said.
	14:15	'I will **s** to the king about this.
	14:18	"Please **s**, Your Majesty."
1Ki	12:3	Israel went to **s** to Rehoboam.
	12:7	humble yourself, and **s** gently,
	12:23	"**S** to Judah's King Rehoboam,
2Ki	4:13	Maybe she would like us to **s**
	5:21	from his chariot to **s** to him.
	5:26	in his chariot to **s** to you.
	18:26	"**S** to us in Aramaic,
	18:26	Don't **s** to us in the Judean
2Ch	10:3	Israel went to **s** to Rehoboam.
	11:3	"**S** to Judah's King Rehoboam,
Neh	13:24	of Judah well enough to **s** it.
Est	1:22	house and **s** with authority."
Job	7:11	but I will **s** from the distress
	9:14	right words ⌊to **s**⌋ with him?
	9:35	Then I would **s** and not be
	10:1	I will **s** as bitterly as I feel.
	11:5	I only wish God would **s** and
	12:8	Or **s** with the earth,
	12:20	trusted advisers unable to **s**
	13:3	I want to **s** to the Almighty,
	13:13	Be quiet, because I want to **s**.
	13:22	Otherwise, I'll **s**, and you'll
	16:4	I, too, could **s** like you if we
	16:6	If I **s**, my pain is not eased. If I
	21:3	Bear with me while I **s**.
	29:22	they wouldn't **s** again.
	31:30	(even though I didn't **s** sinfully
	32:7	I thought, 'Age should **s**,
	32:11	I waited for you to **s**.
	32:16	I wait because they don't **s**,
	32:18	within me forces me ⌊to **s**⌋.
	32:20	I must **s** to get relief.
	33:3	and I sincerely **s** the
	33:31	Keep quiet, and let me **s**.
	33:32	**S**, because I'd be happy if you
	34:1	Elihu continued to **s** ⌊to Job
	34:33	Tell me what you know. **S**!
	35:1	Elihu continued to **s** ⌊to Job
	36:1	Elihu continued to **s** ⌊to Job⌋,
	37:20	he be told that I want to **s**?
	37:20	Can a person **s** when he is
	41:3	for mercy or **s** tenderly to you?
	42:4	said,⌋ 'Listen now, and I will **s**.
	42:7	you didn't **s** what is right
	42:8	After all, you didn't **s** what is
Psa	12:2	All people **s** foolishly.
	12:2	They **s** with flattering lips.
	16:4	or use my lips to **s** their names.
	28:3	with troublemakers who **s** of
	31:18	since they **s** against righteous
	38:13	like a person who cannot **s**.
	49:3	My mouth will **s** wise sayings,
	50:7	"Listen, my people, and I will **s**.
	51:4	hand down justice when you **s**,
	59:12	they **s** curses and lies.
	71:6	praise constantly **s** about you.
Psa	73:8	They **s** maliciously.
	73:8	**s** arrogantly about oppression.
	75:5	so proudly or **s** so defiantly."
	75:9	But I will **s** ⌊about your
	77:4	I am so upset that I cannot **s**.
	94:4	They **s** arrogantly.
	106:2	Who can **s** about all the mighty
	109:2	They **s** against me with lying
	115:5	mouths, but they cannot **s**.
	119:46	I will **s** about your written
	135:16	mouths, but they cannot **s**.
	144:8	Their mouths **s** lies.
	144:11	Their mouths **s** lies.
	145:21	My mouth will **s** the praise of
Pro	5:2	foresight and **s** with insight.
	21:28	to advice will continue to **s**.
	23:16	when you **s** what is right.
	31:8	"**S** out for the one who cannot
	31:8	out for the one who cannot **s**,
	31:9	**S** out, judge fairly, and defend
Ecc	3:7	keep quiet and a time to **s** out,
	5:2	Don't be eager to **s** in the
Isa	8:20	If people don't **s** these words,
	19:18	in Egypt will have people that **s**
	28:10	They **s** utter nonsense.
	28:11	The LORD will **s** to these
	29:4	you will **s** as you lie on the
	32:4	will **s** quickly and clearly.
	32:6	Godless fools **s** foolishness,
	32:6	They **s** falsely about the LORD.
	35:6	and those who cannot **s** will
	36:11	"**S** to us in Aramaic,
	36:11	Don't **s** to us in the Judean
	40:2	"**S** tenderly to Jerusalem and
	41:1	Let them come near and **s**.
	45:19	I, the LORD, **s** what is fair and
	45:21	**S** and present your case.
	59:3	You **s** lies, and you mutter
	59:4	pointless arguments and **s** lies.
Jer	1:3	The LORD continued to **s** to
	1:6	I do not know how to **s**.
	5:5	important people and **s** to them.
	6:10	Whom can I **s** to? Whom can I
	9:5	train their tongues to **s** lies.
	9:8	They **s** deceitfully.
	9:8	People **s** politely to their
	10:5	They aren't able to **s**.
	12:2	They **s** well of you with their
	15:19	If you will **s** what is worthwhile
	20:8	Each time I **s**, I have to cry out
	20:9	and no longer **s** his name."
	22:1	and **s** this message there:
	23:16	They **s** about visions that they
	23:21	I didn't **s** to them, yet they
	23:25	"I've heard the prophets who **s**
	23:28	should honestly **s** my word.
	23:31	"I'm against the prophets who **s**
	23:31	and say that they **s** for me.
	25:3	the LORD continued to **s** his
	26:2	and **s** to all the people who
	26:15	sent me to **s** all these things
Eze	2:1	and I will **s** to you."
	2:7	**S** my words to them whether
	3:1	Then **s** to the people of Israel."
	3:4	and **s** my words to them.
	3:5	to understand or difficult to **s**.
	3:6	to understand, difficult to **s**,
	3:18	but you don't warn them or **s**
	3:22	I will **s** to you there."
	3:27	But when I **s** to you,
	12:25	I, the LORD, will **s**.
	14:4	"So **s** to them. Tell them, 'This
	16:44	who uses proverbs will **s**
	20:3	**s** to the leaders of Israel.
	20:27	"**S** to the nation of Israel,
	24:27	You will **s** and not be silent
	33:2	"Son of man, **s** to your people.
	33:22	the LORD made me **s**.
Dan	7:25	He will **s** against the Most High
	10:9	I heard the man **s**, and as I
Hos	2:14	I will **s** tenderly to her.
	2:21	"I will **s** to the sky,
	2:21	it will **s** to the earth,
Mic	6:12	who live in the city **s** lies,
	6:12	and their tongues **s** deceitfully.
Hab	2:18	worthless idols that cannot **s**.
Hag	2:2	"Now, **s** to Zerubbabel (who is
Zec	8:16	**S** the truth to each other.
	10:2	The idols **s** lies. The
	10:2	They **s** about false dreams.
	13:3	to live because you **s** lies
Mat	9:33	the man began to **s**.
	13:10	when you **s** to people?"
	13:13	This is why I **s** to them this
	17:25	Before he could **s**,
Mar	1:34	not allow the demons to **s**.
	4:34	He did not **s** to them without
	9:39	turn around and **s** evil of me.
	16:17	They will **s** new languages.
Luk	1:22	he was unable to **s** to them.
	1:64	Zechariah was able to **s**,
	4:41	Jesus ordered them not to **s**.
	7:40	"Teacher, you're free to **s**."
	21:38	get up early to hear him **s**
Jon	7:18	Those who **s** their own
	8:28	I **s** as the Father taught me.
	16:13	He won't **s** on his own.
	16:13	He will **s** what he hears and
	16:25	use examples to **s** to you.
	16:25	Rather, I will **s** to you about the
Act	2:4	the Holy Spirit and began to **s**
	2:4	Spirit gave them the ability to **s**.
	2:17	Your sons and daughters will **s**
	2:18	They will **s** what God has
	4:17	tell them that they must never **s**
	4:29	allow us to **s** your word boldly.
	4:31	Holy Spirit and continued to **s**
	5:40	ordered them not to **s** about the
	11:15	"When I began to **s**,
	13:15	for the people, feel free to **s**."
	13:42	the people invited them to **s** on
	13:46	"We had to **s** the word of God
	15:24	not authorize these men ⌊to **s**⌋.
	18:9	"Don't be afraid to **s** out!
	18:26	He began to **s** boldly in the
	19:6	and to **s** what God had
	19:8	the synagogue and **s** boldly.
	19:17	began to **s** very highly about
	21:9	the ability to **s** what God had
	21:37	"Can you **s** Greek?
	21:40	gave Paul permission to **s**.
	22:2	When the mob heard him **s** to
	22:14	and to hear him **s** to you.
	23:5	Scripture says, 'Don't **s** evil
	24:10	governor motioned for Paul to **s**
	26:1	"You're free to **s** for yourself."
	26:26	I can easily **s** to a king who
	28:20	to see you and **s** with you.
Rom	2:15	Their consciences **s** to them.
	3:4	hand down justice when you **s**,
	11:13	I **s** to you who are not Jewish.
1Co	1:21	of the Good News we **s**
	2:1	I didn't **s** about God's mystery
	2:4	I didn't **s** my message with
	2:6	we do use wisdom to **s** to
	2:7	We **s** about the mystery of
	2:13	We don't **s** about these things
	12:2	gods who couldn't even **s**.
	12:8	the ability to **s** with wisdom.
	12:8	the ability to **s** with knowledge.
	12:10	Another can **s** what God has
	12:10	Another can **s** in different kinds
	12:28	and those who can **s** in a
	12:30	Can all of them **s** in other
	13:1	I may **s** in the languages of
	13:2	I may have the gift to **s** what
	13:9	our ability to **s** what God has
	14:2	he doesn't **s** to people but to
	14:5	I wish that all of you could **s** in
	14:5	but especially that you could **s**
	14:9	In the same way, if you don't **s**
	14:18	I thank God that I **s** in other
	14:21	"Through people who **s** foreign
	14:21	the mouths of foreigners I will **s**
	14:23	in the same place and you **s**
	14:24	Now suppose you **s** what God
	14:27	If people **s** in other languages,
	14:27	or three at the most should **s**.
	14:28	They should only **s** to
	14:29	Two or three people should **s**
	14:32	People who **s** what God has
	14:34	They don't have the right to **s**.

1Co 14:35 for a woman to **s** in church.
14:39 desire to **s** what God has
2Co 2:17 we **s** the pure message that
3:12 promise, we **s** very boldly.
4:13 believe; therefore, we also **s**.
8:7 your faith, your ability to **s**,
12:19 We **s** as Christ's people in
Eph 4:15 as we lovingly **s** the truth,
4:25 **S** the truth to each other,
4:29 Instead, **s** only what is good so
6:19 Then I will **s** boldly when I
6:20 So pray that I **s** about this
Php 1:14 to **s** God's word more
1:20 I will **s** very boldly and honor
Col 4:3 will give us an opportunity to **s**
1Ti 1:7 which they **s** so confidently.
3:7 are not Christians must **s** well
4:2 These people will **s** lies
6:1 In this way no one will **s** evil of
Tit 1:10 They **s** nonsense and deceive
2:5 Then no one can **s** evil of
2:8 **S** an accurate message that
Heb 3:7 "If you hear God **s** today,
3:15 "If you hear God **s** today,
4:7 "If you hear God **s** today,
7:11 we wouldn't need to **s** about
7:11 However, we **s** about another
11:22 faith led him to **s** about the
Jas 1:19 be quick to listen, slow to **s**,
1Pe 4:11 speaks must **s** God's words.
2Pe 1:18 We heard that voice **s** to him
1Jn 4:5 That's why they **s** the thoughts
Rev 10:11 "Again you must **s** what God
11:3 sackcloth to **s** what God has
11:3 They will **s** for 1,260 days."
11:6 the time they **s** what God has
13:5 The beast was allowed to **s**

speaker (8)

Exo 4:10 "Please, Lord, I'm not a good **s**.
4:10 I've never been a good **s**,
6:12 I'm such a poor **s**."
Job 11:2 a good public **s** be acquitted?
Act 18:24 He was an eloquent **s** and
1Co 1:20 Where is the persuasive **s** of
14:30 the first **s** should be silent.
2Co 10:10 I'm a weakling and a terrible **s**.

speaking (110)

Gen 16:13 who had been **s** to her,
17:22 God finished **s** with Abraham,
18:33 LORD finished **s** to Abraham,
27:5 listening while Isaac was **s**
27:6 "I've just heard your father **s** to
42:23 he was **s** through an interpreter.
45:12 I am the one who is **s** to you.
Exo 16:10 While Aaron was **s** to the
19:9 that the people will hear me **s**
19:19 and louder, Moses was **s**,
31:18 The LORD finished **s** to Moses
34:29 His face was shining from **s**
34:33 Moses finished **s** to them,
Num 7:89 he heard the voice **s** to him
Dtr 4:12 You heard a voice **s** but saw
5:22 Then he stopped **s**.
20:9 When the officers finish **s** to
Jdg 6:17 that it is really you **s** to me.
1Sm 24:16 this, Saul asked, "Is that you **s**,
2Sm 13:36 When he finished **s**,
1Ki 1:42 He was still **s** when Jonathan,
22:28 the LORD wasn't **s** through me.
2Ch 10:7 try to please them by **s** gently
18:27 the LORD wasn't **s** through me.
Est 6:14 they were still **s** with him,
Job 1:16 While he was still **s**,
1:17 While he was still **s**,
1:18 While he was still **s**,
32:6 That's why I refrained from **s**
36:4 everything is (**s**) with you.
Psa 34:13 lips from **s** deceitful things.
52:3 You prefer lying to **s** the truth.
Pro 8:6 I am **s** about noble things,
12:14 as a result of his **s** ability.
13:2 well as a result of his **s** ability,
16:21 and **s** sweetly helps others
18:20 A person's **s** ability provides for
Ecc 5:3 Careless **s** comes when there
Isa 28:11 He will mock them by **s** in a
65:24 While they're still **s**,
Jer 3:12 It is the LORD **s**. I will no longer
26:7 heard Jeremiah **s** these things
27:18 and the LORD is **s** to them,
28:7 to this message that I am **s**
38:1 heard that Jeremiah was **s**
Eze 1:28 and I heard someone **s**.
2:2 and I heard him **s** to me.
36:6 I am **s** in my anger and fury
43:6 I heard someone **s** to me from
Dan 7:11 words that the horn was **s**.
8:13 Then I heard a holy one **s**.
8:13 one said to the one who was **s**,
Zec 1:9 The angel who was **s** with me
1:13 the angel who was **s** with me,
1:14 The angel who was **s** with me
1:19 the angel who was **s** with me,
2:3 Then the angel who was **s**
4:1 The angel who was **s** with me
4:4 the angel who was **s** with me,
5:5 The angel who was **s** with me
5:10 the angel who was **s** with me,
6:4 the angel who was **s** with me,
Mat 10:20 not the ones who will be **s**.
10:20 Father will be **s** through you.
12:48 He replied to the man **s** to him,
17:5 He was still **s** when a bright
19:1 When Jesus finished **s**,
26:47 while Jesus was still **s**,
Mar 2:2 Jesus was **s** (God's) word to
5:35 While Jesus was still **s** to her,
13:11 are not the one who will be **s**,
14:43 while Jesus was still **s**,
Luk 5:4 When he finished **s**,
8:49 While Jesus was still **s** to her,
11:27 While Jesus was **s**,
22:47 While he was still **s** to the
22:60 Just then, while he was still **s**,
Jon 4:26 and I am **s** to you now."
7:26 He's **s** in public, and no one is
20:15 it was the gardener **s** to her.
Act 2:7 men who are **s** are Galileans.
2:8 Why do we hear them **s** in our
4:1 they were **s** to the people.
5:41 dishonor for **s** about Jesus.
10:44 While Peter was still **s**,
10:46 these non-Jewish people **s**
15:13 After they finished **s**,
16:6 the Holy Spirit kept them from **s**
17:18 Others said, "He seems to be **s**
20:36 When Paul had finished **s**,
22:9 person who was **s** to me said.
Rom 6:19 I'm **s** in a human way because
7:1 (I'm **s** to people who are
12:6 If your gift is **s** God's word,
1Co 9:10 Isn't he **s** entirely for our
12:3 that no one **s** by God's Spirit
13:8 There is the gift of **s** what God
13:8 There is the gift of **s** in other
14:1 but especially the gift of **s** what
14:2 His spirit is **s** mysteries.
14:6 you any good if I came to you **s**
14:22 So the gift of **s** in other
14:22 The gift of **s** what God had
14:31 All of you can take your turns **s**
14:39 from **s** in other languages.
2Co 6:11 We have been very open in **s**
11:17 say if I were **s** for the Lord.
13:3 that Christ is **s** through me,
1Pe 3:10 lips from **s** deceitful things.
Rev 4:1 voice like a trumpet **s** to me.

speaks (58)

Exo 33:11 as a man **s** to his friend.
Dtr 5:24 can live even if God **s** to them.
8:3 on every word that the LORD **s**.
18:19 to the words that prophet **s**
18:20 command him to say or who **s**
18:22 If a prophet **s** in the LORD's
2Ki 19:21 that the LORD **s** to him,
Job 33:14 "God **s** in one way,
34:35 'Job **s** without knowledge.
Psa 2:5 Then he **s** to them in his anger.
15:2 and **s** the truth within his heart.
Psa 37:30 His tongue **s** what is fair.
41:6 to visit me, he **s** foolishly.
127:5 not be put to shame when he **s**
147:19 He **s** his word to Jacob,
Pro 1:21 to the city she **s** her words,
2:12 person who **s** devious things,
12:17 A truthful witness **s** honestly,
12:17 but a lying witness **s**
16:13 and whoever **s** what is right is
22:11 and whoever **s** graciously has
31:26 "She **s** with wisdom,
Isa 9:17 and every mouth **s** foolishness.
28:13 The LORD **s** utter nonsense to
33:15 who does what is right and **s**
37:22 that the LORD **s** to him,
Jer 6:10 When the LORD **s** his word to
9:5 No one **s** the truth.
10:13 He **s**, and the water in the sky
Eze 10:5 of the Almighty God when he **s**.
Amo 5:10 Israel, you hate anyone who **s**
5:10 by anyone who **s** the truth.
Mat 4:4 but on every word that God **s**.'"
12:32 Whoever **s** a word against the
12:32 But whoever **s** against the Holy
Jon 3:29 is overjoyed when the groom **s**.
3:34 The man whom God has sent **s**
Rom 4:6 thing when he **s** this blessing:
1Co 11:4 he prays or **s** what God has
11:5 Every woman who prays or **s**
11:5 while she **s** dishonors
14:2 When a person **s** in another
14:3 But when a person **s** what God
14:3 he **s** to people to help them
14:4 When a person **s** in another
14:4 But when a person **s** what God
14:5 The person who **s** what God
14:5 than the person who **s**
14:11 a foreigner to the person who **s**
14:13 So the person who **s** in another
14:37 Whoever thinks that he **s** for
Heb 11:4 Through his faith Abel still **s**,
12:5 encouraging words that God **s**
12:24 to the sprinkled blood that **s**
12:25 refuse to listen when God **s**.
Jas 3:2 make any mistakes when he **s**,
1Pe 4:11 Whoever **s** must speak God's
1Jn 2:1 He **s** on our behalf when we

spear (46)

Num 25:7 took a **s** in his hand,
25:8 He drove the **s** through the man
Jos 8:18 "Hold out the **s** in your hand
8:18 So Joshua held out his **s**.
8:26 his hand holding the **s** until
1Sm 13:22 not one sword or **s** could be
17:7 The shaft of his **s** was like the
17:7 The head of his **s** was made of
17:45 with sword and **s** and javelin,
17:47 can save without sword or **s**,
18:10 Now, Saul had a **s** in his hand.
18:11 He raised the **s** and thought,
19:9 sitting in his house with his **s**
19:10 David to the wall with his **s**.
19:10 and Saul's **s** struck the wall.
20:33 Saul raised his **s** to strike him.
21:8 "Don't you have a **s** or a sword
21:8 I didn't take either my **s** or any
22:6 at the worship site with his **s**
26:7 the camp with his **s** stuck
26:8 ground with one stab of the **s**.
26:11 But please take that **s** near his
26:12 David took the **s** and the jar of
26:16 Look at the king's **s** and the jar
26:22 "Here's the king's **s**.
2Sm 1:6 was there leaning on his **s**,
2:23 him with the butt of the **s**.
2:23 The **s** went into his belly and
21:16 who had a bronze **s** weighing 7
21:19 (The shaft of Goliath's **s** was
23:7 iron (tools) or the shaft of a **s**.
23:8 He used a **s** to kill 800 men on
23:18 He used his **s** to kill 300 men.
23:21 The Egyptian had a **s** in his
23:21 grabbed the **s** from him,
1Ch 11:11 He used his **s** to kill 300 men
11:20 He used his **s** to kill 300 men,

1Ch 11:23 The Egyptian had a **s** like a
11:23 grabbed the **s** away from him,
20:5 (The shaft of Lahmi's **s** was
2Ch 25:5 could handle a **s** and a shield.
Job 39:23 with the flashing **s** and javelin.
41:26 Neither will a **s**, lance, or dart.
Psa 35:3 Hold your **s** to block the way of
Hab 3:11 at the bright lightning of your **s**.
Jon 19:34 stabbed Jesus' side with his **s**,

spears (26)

1Sm 13:19 from making swords and **s**.
1Ki 18:28 swords and **s** until their blood
2Ki 11:10 He gave the commanders the **s**
1Ch 12:8 able to fight with shields and **s**.
12:24 They carried shields and **s**.
12:34 who fought with shields and **s**.
2Ch 11:12 city he stored shields and **s**.
14:8 armed with large shields and **s**
23:9 gave the commanders the **s**
26:14 **s**, helmets, armor, bows,
Neh 4:13 with swords, **s**, and bows.
4:16 body armor and holding **s**,
4:21 Half of us held **s** from early
Job 41:7 or its head with fishing **s**?
Psa 46:9 He cuts **s** in two. He burns
57:4 Their teeth are **s** and arrows.
Isa 2:4 and their **s** into pruning shears.
Jer 6:23 take hold of bows and **s**.
46:4 Polish your **s**. Put on your armor
50:42 will take hold of bows and **s**.
Eze 39:9 and war clubs and **s**.
Joe 3:10 and your pruning shears into **s**.
Mic 4:3 and their **s** into pruning shears.
Nah 2:3 so do the **s** when they are
3:3 **S** glitter! Many are killed! Dead
Act 23:23 and 200 soldiers with **s**.

special (56)

Gen 19:3 He prepared a **s** dinner for them,
26:30 Isaac prepared a **s** dinner for
37:3 So he made Joseph a **s** robe
37:23 they stripped him of his **s** robe
37:32 Then they brought the **s** robe
40:5 dream with its own **s** meaning.
40:20 Pharaoh had a **s** dinner
40:20 Of all his servants he gave **s**
49:28 each of them his **s** blessing.
Exo 19:5 will be my own **s** possession,
23:3 Never give **s** favors to poor
25:2 to give me as a **s** contribution.
31:10 the **s** clothes — the holy clothes
35:5 own to give as a **s** contribution
35:19 the **s** clothes worn for official
36:6 to give as their **s** contribution
39:1 and bright red yarn they made **s**
39:41 the **s** clothes worn when
Lev 7:14 LORD as a ⌊**s**⌋ contribution.
19:15 Never give **s** favors to poor
23:27 this seventh month is a **s** day
23:28 It is a **s** day for the payment for
23:37 each one on its **s** day.
25:9 the **s** day for the payment for
27:2 If any of you makes a **s** vow
Num 6:2 or a woman may make a **s** vow
Dtr 7:6 He chose you to be his own **s**
14:2 to be his own **s** possession.
26:18 his own **s** possession,
1Sm 25:8 have come on a **s** occasion.
2Ki 25:28 him a **s** position higher than
Est 8:10 who rode **s** horses bred
Job 34:19 mighty does not grant **s** favors
Psa 135:4 Israel to be his own **s** treasure.
Ecc 9:11 receive **s** treatment.
Isa 22:5 of Armies has chosen a **s** day.
Jer 52:32 him a **s** position higher than
Eze 48:8 that you set aside as a **s** gift
48:9 This **s** land that you set aside
48:12 So they will have a **s** portion
48:20 You must give this land as a **s**
Zep 1:7 He has invited his **s** guests.
Mal 3:17 make them my **s** possession.
Act 4:13 had no education or **s** training,
19:38 we have **s** days and officials to
Rom 9:21 He can make something for a **s**
Rom 14:6 When people observe a **s** day,
1Co 7:7 However, each person has a **s**
12:23 are the ones we give **s** honor.
12:24 together and given **s** honor
Gal 2:9 God had given me this **s** gift.
Php 1:7 You have a **s** place in my heart.
Tit 2:14 can be his **s** people who are
Heb 11:40 us something very **s** so that we
Jas 2:3 Suppose you give **s** attention
Jud 1:12 at the **s** meals you share

species (2)

Pro 30:25 Ants are not a strong **s**,
30:26 badgers are not a mighty **s**,

specific (4)

Neh 2:6 When I gave him a **s** date,
Job 14:13 Set a **s** time for me when you
Ecc 3:1 and there is a **s** time for every
3:17 because there is a **s** time for

specifications (2)

1Ki 6:38 according to all its plans and **s**.
2Ch 4:7 stands according to their **s**

specified (1)

1Ch 28:14 ⌊David **s**⌋ the weight of gold to

specify (2)

1Ki 5:9 go by sea to any place you **s**.
Act 25:27 I can't **s** any charges against

speckled (9)

Gen 30:32 flocks today and take every **s**
30:32 and every spotted or **s** goat.
30:33 Any goat I have that isn't **s** or
30:35 all the **s** and spotted female
30:39 that were striped, **s**, or spotted.
31:8 Whenever he said, 'The **s** ones
31:8 flocks gave birth to **s** young.
31:10 were striped, **s**, or spotted.
31:12 are striped, **s**, or spotted,

specks (2)

Num 23:10 of Jacob are like **s** of dust.
2Ch 1:9 who are as numerous as **s**

spectacle (2)

1Co 4:9 We have become a **s** for
Col 2:15 power⌋ and made a public **s**

spectacular (18)

Dtr 6:22 and amazing things that were **s**
10:21 who did for you these **s** and
11:7 eyes all these **s** things that
26:8 He used **s** and awe-inspiring
29:3 and those **s**, amazing things.
34:12 his mighty hand to do all the **s**
Jos 24:17 He did these **s** signs right
Jdg 2:7 who had seen all the **s** works
Psa 92:5 How **s** are your works,
106:21 one who did **s** things in Egypt,
111:2 The LORD's deeds are **s**.
126:2 has done **s** things for them."
126:3 The LORD has done **s** things
Mat 24:24 They will work **s**, if possible,
Rev 12:1 A **s** sign appeared in the sky:
13:13 second beast performs **s** signs.
15:1 It was **s** and amazing.
15:3 you do are **s** and amazing,

speech (15)

Dtr 1:1 This is the **s** Moses gave in
Psa 55:21 His **s** is smoother than butter,
Pro 4:24 Put deceptive **s** far away from
8:13 evil behavior, and twisted **s**.
14:3 people are protected by their **s**.
16:23 person's heart controls his **s**,
16:27 and his **s** is like a burning fire.
17:7 Refined **s** is not fitting for a
26:24 hate disguises it with his **s**,
Mat 7:28 When Jesus finished this **s**,
Mar 7:32 and who also had a **s** defect.
Jon 6:66 Jesus' **s** made many of his
Act 12:21 and began making a **s** to them.
1Co 1:5 rich in every way — in **s**
1Ti 4:12 Instead, make your **s**,

speeches (3)

Job 15:3 with **s** that don't help
16:3 long-winded **s** never end?
32:14 I won't answer him with your **s**.

speechless (5)

Lev 10:3 to all the people."' Aaron was **s**.
Psa 31:18 Let ⌊their⌋ lying lips be **s**,
39:2 I remained totally **s**.
39:9 I remained **s**. I did not open my
Act 9:7 men traveling with him were **s**.

speed (2)

Est 8:10 rode special horses bred for **s**.
Psa 147:15 His word travels with great **s**.

spell (2)

Num 23:23 No **s** can curse the
Gal 3:1 Who put you under an evil **s**?

spells (13)

Exo 7:11 same thing using their magic **s**.
7:22 same thing using their magic **s**.
8:7 same thing using their magic **s**
8:18 gnats using their magic **s**,
Lev 19:26 "Never cast evil **s**,
Dtr 18:11 cast **s**, ask ghosts or spirits for
2Ki 17:17 black magic and cast evil **s**.
21:6 fortunetellers, cast evil **s**,
2Ch 33:6 fortunetellers, cast evil **s**,
Psa 58:5 or of anyone trained to cast **s**.
Isa 47:9 evil magic and your many **s**.
47:12 Keep practicing your **s** and
Act 19:18 involvement with magical **s**

spend (32)

Gen 19:2 to my home and **s** the night?
19:2 "we'd rather **s** the night in the
24:23 house for us to **s** the night."
24:25 and room for you to **s** the night."
Num 22:8 "**S** the night here,"
Jos 2:1 Rahab to **s** the night there.
Jdg 19:6 "Why don't you **s** the night and
19:10 refused to **s** another night.
19:11 "Let's go **s** the night in Jebus."
19:13 We'll **s** the night either at
19:15 They went to **s** the night there.
19:20 Just don't **s** the night in the city
20:4 in Benjamin to **s** the night.
1Ki 5:14 They would **s** one month in
1Ch 9:27 They would **s** the night
Job 21:13 They **s** their days in happiness,
Ecc 5:17 They **s** their entire lives in
Sos 7:11 Let's **s** the night among the
Isa 21:13 from the people of Dedan will **s**
55:2 Why do you **s** money on what
Joe 1:13 **S** the night in sackcloth,
Hag 1:6 You **s** money as fast as you
Mar 6:37 "Should we go and **s** about a
Luk 10:35 If you **s** more than that,
21:37 called) and **s** the night there.
Act 27:12 a good place to **s** the winter,
27:12 of Phoenix somehow and **s**
28:14 believers who begged us to **s**
1Co 16:6 I might even **s** the winter.
16:7 I hope to **s** some time with you.
2Co 12:15 I will be very glad to **s**
Tit 3:12 decided to **s** the winter there.

spending (4)

Neh 13:21 "Why are you **s** the night in
Jon 4:43 After **s** two days in Samaria,
Act 18:23 After **s** some time in Antioch,
20:16 past Ephesus to avoid **s** time

spends (1)

Pro 11:24 One person **s** freely and yet

spent (26)

Gen 24:54 ate and drank and **s** the night.
31:54 They ate with him and **s** the
Jos 8:9 Joshua **s** the night with the
Jdg 18:2 They **s** the night there.
19:8 So they **s** the time eating until

1Ki 6:38 He **s** seven years building it.
19:9 into a cave and **s** the night.
2Ch 20:25 They **s** three days collecting
Neh 13:20 who sell all kinds of goods **s**
Est 2:12 treatment was **s** as follows:
Job 7:6 They are **s** without hope.
31:32 (The visitor never **s** the night
Isa 65:4 the graves and **s** their nights
Dan 6:18 king went to his palace and **s**
Mat 21:17 Bethany and **s** the night there.
Mar 5:26 and had **s** all her money,
6:34 So he **s** a lot of time teaching
Luk 6:12 He **s** the whole night in prayer
15:30 But this son of yours **s** your
Jon 1:39 where he was staying and **s**
3:22 where he **s** some time with
Act 20:18 "You know how I **s** all my time
21:7 believers in Ptolemais and **s**
28:11 an Alexandrian ship that had **s**
Gal 4:11 Maybe the hard work I **s** on you
1Pe 4:3 You **s** enough time in the past

spice (2)

Sos 4:10 of your perfume than any **s**.
5:1 will gather my myrrh with my **s**.

spiced (3)

Sos 7:2 it always be filled with **s** wine.
8:2 I would give you some **s** wine
Isa 65:11 and offered cups full of **s** wine

spices (30)

Exo 25:6 olive oil for the lamps, **s** for the
30:23 "Take the finest **s**:
30:34 "Take one part fragrant **s** (two
35:8 olive oil for the lamps, **s** for the
35:28 They also brought the **s** and
1Ki 10:2 with camels carrying **s**,
10:10 a very large quantity of **s**,
10:10 of **s** brought ⌊into Israel⌋
10:25 **s**, horses, and mules.
1Ch 9:29 wine, olive oil, incense, and **s**.
9:30 sons prepared the mixture of **s**.
2Ch 9:1 with camels carrying **s**,
9:9 a very large quantity of **s**,
9:9 quantity of **s** ⌊in Israel⌋ as
9:24 **s**, horses, and mules.
16:14 They laid him on a bed full of **s**
32:27 precious stones, **s**, shields,
Psa 75:8 is thoroughly mixed with **s**.)
Sos 4:14 myrrh, aloes, and all the best **s**.
4:16 Let its **s** flow from it.
5:13 cheeks are like a garden of **s**,
6:2 to his garden, to the beds of **s**,
8:14 stag on the mountains of **s**.
Eze 27:22 They traded the finest **s**,
Mar 16:1 and Salome bought **s** to go and
Luk 11:42 mint, **s**, and every garden herb.
23:56 and prepared **s** and perfumes.
24:1 They were carrying the **s** that
Jon 19:40 They laced the strips with **s**.
Rev 18:13 cinnamon, **s**, incense, perfume,

spider's (1)

Job 8:14 His trust is a **s** web

spiderwebs (1)

Isa 59:5 hatch viper eggs and weave **s**.

spies (20)

Gen 42:9 "You're **s**!" he said to them,
42:11 We're honest men, not **s**."
42:14 said to them. "You're **s**!
42:16 as Pharaoh lives, you are **s**!"
42:30 to us and treated us like **s**.
42:31 him, 'We're honest men, not **s**.
42:34 Then I'll know that you're not **s**
Num 21:32 After Moses sent **s** to Jazer,
Jos 2:1 secretly sent out two men as **s**.
2:8 Before the **s** fell asleep,
2:23 Then the two **s** came down out
6:22 But Joshua said to the two **s**,
6:23 The **s** went and brought out
Jdg 1:24 The **s** saw a man coming out
1Sm 26:4 David sent **s** to confirm that
Luk 20:20 opportunity to send out some **s**.
Luk 20:20 The **s** were to act like sincere
Gal 2:4 They slipped in as **s** to learn
Heb 11:31 to welcome the **s** as friends.
Jas 2:25 Rahab who welcomed the **s**

spilled (4)

1Sm 25:31 because you **s** blood
2Sm 3:27 Abner died because he **s** the
16:8 you back for all the blood you **s**
Lam 4:13 who **s** the blood of righteous

spilling (3)

1Sm 25:26 kept you from **s** innocent blood
2Sm 1:16 "You are responsible for **s** your
3:28 and I are forever innocent of **s**

spills (1)

Job 16:13 without mercy and **s** my blood

spin (2)

Mat 6:28 work or **s** yarn for clothes.
Luk 12:27 They never work or **s** yarn for

spindle (2)

2Sm 3:29 who can only work a **s**,
Pro 31:19 and her fingers hold a **s**.

spinning (1)

Exo 35:25 skilled in **s** yarn brought violet,

Spirit; spirit (451)

Gen 1:2 The **S** of God was hovering
6:3 Then the LORD said, "My **S**
41:38 man who has God's **S** in him?"
Exo 31:3 Bezalel with the **S** of God,
35:31 Bezalel with the **S** of God,
Num 11:17 I'll take some of the **S** that is
11:25 He took some of the **S** that was
11:25 When the **S** came to rest on
11:26 The **S** came to rest on them,
11:29 would put his **S** on them."
24:2 The **S** of God entered him,
27:18 a man who has the **S**,
Dtr 34:9 filled with the **S** of wisdom,
Jdg 3:10 When the LORD's **S** came over
6:34 Then the LORD's **S** gave
9:23 Then God sent an evil **s** to
11:29 Then the LORD's **S** came over
13:25 The LORD's **S** began to stir in
14:6 The LORD's **S** came over him.
14:19 When the LORD's **S** came over
15:14 But the LORD's **S** came over
1Sm 10:6 Then the LORD's **S** will come
10:10 and God's **S** came over him.
11:6 God's **S** came over him,
16:13 The LORD's **S** came over
16:14 the LORD's **S** had left Saul,
16:14 and an evil **s** from the LORD
16:15 "An evil **s** from God is
16:16 When the evil **s** from God
16:23 Whenever God's **s** came to
16:23 and the evil **s** left him.
18:10 The next day an evil **s** from
19:9 Then an evil **s** from the LORD
19:20 God's **S** came over Saul's
19:23 God's **S** came over him too.
2Sm 23:2 "The **S** of the LORD spoke
1Ki 18:12 the LORD's **S** will take you
22:21 "Then the **S** stepped forward,
22:22 "The **S** answered,
22:22 'I will go out and be a **s** that
22:23 of yours a **s** that makes them
22:24 "How did the LORD's **S** leave
2Ki 2:9 a double share of your **s**."
2:15 "Elijah's **s** rests on Elisha!"
2:16 Maybe the LORD's **S** lifted him
5:26 "I went with you in **s** when the
19:7 I'm going to put a **s** in him so
1Ch 12:18 Then the **S** gave Amasai,
2Ch 15:1 God's **S** came to Azariah,
18:20 "Then the **S** stepped forward,
18:21 "The **S** answered,
18:21 'I will go out and be a **s** that
18:22 of yours a **s** that makes them
18:23 "Which way did the **S** go when
20:14 Then the LORD's **S** came to
2Ch 24:20 God's **S** gave Zechariah,
Neh 9:20 You gave them your good **S** to
9:30 You warned them by your **S**
Job 4:15 A **s** passed in front of me.
6:4 and my **s** is drinking their
7:11 from the distress that is in my **s**
10:12 has preserved my **s**.
12:10 every living creature and the **s**
17:1 "My **s** is broken. My days have
20:3 but a **s** beyond my
26:4 and whose **s** has spoken
32:8 there is in humans a **S**,
32:18 The **S** within me forces me ⌊to
33:4 "God's **S** has made me.
34:14 withdrew his **S** and his breath,
Psa 31:5 Into your hands I entrust my **s**.
51:10 renew a faithful **s** within me.
51:11 not take your Holy **S** from me.
51:12 with a **s** of willing obedience.
51:17 pleasing to God is a broken **s**.
51:19 offered in the right **s** —
77:6 My **s** searches ⌊for an
104:30 You send out your **S**,
139:7 I go ⌊to get away⌋ from your **S**?
143:7 My **s** is worn out. Do not hide
143:10 May your good **S** lead me on
Pro 1:23 pour out my **s** for you.
11:13 but whoever is trustworthy in **s**
15:4 a deceitful tongue breaks the **s**.
16:24 a honeycomb — sweet to the **s**
18:14 A person's **s** can endure
18:14 but who can bear a broken **s**?
29:23 but a humble **s** gains honor.
Ecc 3:21 Who knows whether a human **s**
3:21 an animal **s** goes downward
8:8 has the power to prevent the **s**
Isa 4:4 from Jerusalem with a **s**
4:4 of judgment and a **s** of burning.
11:2 The **S** of the LORD will rest on
11:2 LORD will rest on him — the **S**
11:2 the **S** of advice and power,
11:2 the **S** of knowledge and fear of
26:9 Yes, with my **s** I eagerly look
28:6 He will give a **s** of justice to
29:10 has poured out on you a **s**
29:24 in **s** will gain understanding,
31:3 are flesh and blood, not **s**.
32:15 until the **S** is poured on us from
34:16 and his **S** will gather them
37:7 I'm going to put a **s** in him so
40:13 Who has directed the **S** of the
42:1 I have put my **S** on him.
44:3 I will pour my **S** on your
48:16 LORD has sent me and his **S**.
57:15 I will renew the **s** of those who
59:21 "My **S**, who is on you, and my
61:1 The **S** of the Almighty LORD is
61:3 instead of a **s** of weakness.
63:10 and offended his Holy **S**.
63:11 who put his Holy **S** in them?
63:14 given rest by the LORD's **S**.
Jer 51:11 The LORD will stir up the **s** of
Eze 1:12 They went wherever their **s**
1:20 Wherever their **s** wanted to go,
1:20 because the **s** of the living
1:21 because the **s** of the living
2:2 spoke to me, the **S** entered me,
3:12 Then the **S** lifted me,
3:14 Then the **S** lifted me and took
3:24 Then the **S** entered me and
8:3 visions from God, the **S** carried
10:17 The **s** of the living creatures
11:1 Then the **S** lifted me and took
11:5 The LORD's **S** came to me and
11:19 and put a new **s** in them.
11:24 In this vision from God's **S**,
11:24 the **S** lifted me and brought me
36:26 heart and put a new **s** in you.
36:27 I will put my **S** in you.
37:1 LORD brought me out by his **S**
37:14 I will put my **S** in you,
39:29 because I will pour out my **S**
43:5 The **S** lifted me and brought me
Dan 4:8 The **s** of the holy gods is in
4:9 I know the **s** of the holy gods is
4:18 because the **s** of the holy gods

Dan 5:11 in your kingdom who has the s
5:12 and an extraordinary s.
5:14 I've heard that you have the s
6:3 was an extraordinary s in him.
Hos 4:12 A s of prostitution leads them
5:4 They have a s of prostitution,
Joe 2:28 I will pour my S on everyone.
2:29 I will pour my S on servants,
Mic 2:7 Has the S of the LORD become
3:8 the power of the LORD's S,
Hag 2:5 My S remains with you.
Zec 4:6 or by power, but by my S,
6:8 the north have made my S rest
7:12 had sent by his S through
12:1 and forms the s in a person —
12:10 "I will pour out the S of
13:2 the unclean s from the land.
Mal 2:15 Your flesh and s belong to him.
Mat 1:18 was pregnant by the Holy S.
1:20 She is pregnant by the Holy S.
3:11 you with the Holy S and fire.
3:16 and he saw the S of God
4:1 Then the S led Jesus into the
10:20 The S of your Father will be
12:18 I will put my S on him,
12:28 out with the help of God's S,
12:31 However, cursing the S will not
12:32 against the Holy S will not
12:43 "When an evil s comes out of a
22:43 guided by the S, call him Lord?
28:19 of the Son, and of the Holy S.
Mar 1:8 baptize you with the Holy S."
1:10 open and the S coming down
1:12 At once the S brought him into
1:23 was controlled by an evil s.
1:25 Jesus ordered the s,
1:26 The evil s threw the man into
3:29 But whoever curses the Holy S
3:30 had said that he had an evil s.
5:2 was controlled by an evil s
5:8 Jesus said, "You evil s,
7:25 an evil s heard about Jesus.
9:17 He is possessed by a s that
9:18 Whenever the s brings on a
9:18 disciples to force the s out,
9:20 As soon as the s saw Jesus,
9:25 he gave an order to the evil s.
9:25 "You s that won't let him talk,
9:26 The evil s screamed,
9:28 "Why couldn't we force the s
9:29 He told them, "This kind of s
12:36 David, guided by the Holy S,
13:11 but the Holy S will.
15:39 saw how he gave up his s,
Luk 1:15 He will be filled with the Holy S
1:17 go ahead of the Lord with the s
1:35 "The Holy S will come to you,
1:41 was filled with the Holy S.
1:47 My s finds its joy in God,
1:67 the Holy S and prophesied,
2:25 The Holy S was with Simeon
2:27 Moved by the S, Simeon went
3:16 you with the Holy S and fire.
3:22 and the Holy S came down to
4:1 was filled with the Holy S as
4:1 The S led him while he was in
4:14 The power of the S was with
4:18 "The S of the Lord is with me.
4:33 was a man possessed by a s,
4:35 Jesus ordered the s,
8:29 Jesus ordered the evil s to
8:29 (The evil s had controlled the
9:39 Whenever a s takes control of
9:39 a struggle, the s goes away,
9:40 your disciples to force the s out
9:42 ordered the evil s to leave.
10:21 In that hour the Holy S filled
11:13 in heaven give the Holy S
11:24 "When an evil s comes out of a
11:26 Then the s goes and brings
12:10 dishonors the Holy S will not
12:12 At that time the Holy S will
13:11 possessed by a s was there.
13:11 The s had disabled her for 18
23:46 into your hands I entrust my s."
Jon 1:32 John said, "I saw the S come
Jon 1:33 'When you see the S come
1:33 who baptizes with the Holy S.'
3:5 being born of water and the S.
3:6 but the S gives birth to things
3:8 is with everyone born of the S."
3:34 gives him the S without limit.
4:23 the Father in s and truth.
4:24 God is a s. Those who worship
4:24 must worship in s and truth."
7:39 Jesus said this about the S,
7:39 The S was not yet evident,
14:17 That helper is the S of Truth.
14:26 the helper, the Holy S,
15:26 This helper, the S of Truth who
16:13 When the S of Truth comes,
20:22 "Receive the Holy S.
Act 1:2 instructions through the Holy S
1:5 will be baptized by the Holy S."
1:8 power when the Holy S comes
1:16 "Brothers, what the Holy S
2:4 were filled with the Holy S
2:4 languages as the S gave them
2:17 I will pour my S on everyone.
2:18 In those days I will pour my S
2:33 has poured out the Holy S as
2:38 receive the Holy S as a gift.
4:8 he was filled with the Holy S,
4:25 You said through the Holy S,
4:31 were filled with the Holy S
5:3 you could deceive the Holy S?
5:9 agree to test the Lord's S?
5:32 and so is the Holy S,
6:5 man full of faith and the Holy S,
6:10 that the S had given him.
7:51 always opposed the Holy S,
7:55 Stephen was full of the Holy S.
7:59 "Lord Jesus, welcome my s."
8:15 would receive the Holy S.
8:16 (Before this the Holy S had not
8:17 received the Holy S.
8:18 Simon saw that the S was
8:19 on will receive the Holy S."
8:29 The S said to Philip,
8:39 the S of the Lord suddenly took
9:17 to be filled with the Holy S."
9:31 and the comfort of the Holy S.
10:19 the vision when the S said
10:38 from Nazareth with the Holy S
10:44 the Holy S came to everyone
10:45 of the Holy S had been poured
10:47 They have received the Holy S
11:12 The S told me to go with them
11:15 the Holy S came to these
11:16 will be baptized by the Holy S.'
11:24 was full of the Holy S and faith.
11:28 Through the S Agabus
13:2 and fasting, the Holy S said,
13:4 Saul were sent by the Holy S,
13:9 was filled with the Holy S.
13:52 to be full of joy and the Holy S.
15:8 by giving them the Holy S as
15:8 as he gave the Holy S to us.
15:28 The Holy S and we have
16:6 the Holy S kept them from
16:7 but the S of Jesus wouldn't
16:16 by an evil s that told fortunes.
16:18 turned to the evil s,
16:18 said this, the evil s left her.
19:2 "Did you receive the Holy S
19:2 even heard of the Holy S."
19:6 the Holy S came to them,
19:15 But the evil s answered them,
19:16 by the evil s attacked them.
20:23 However, the Holy S warns me
20:28 the Holy S has placed you
21:4 The S had the disciples tell
21:11 "The Holy S says,
23:9 Maybe a s or an angel actually
28:25 "How well the Holy S spoke to
28:26 The S said: 'Go to these
Rom 5:5 into our hearts by the Holy S,
8:2 The standards of the S,
8:9 But if God's S lives in you,
8:9 Whoever doesn't have the S of
8:11 Does the S of the one who
8:11 bodies alive by his S who lives
Rom 8:14 by God's S are God's children.
8:15 You haven't received the s of
8:15 you have received the s of
8:16 The S himself testifies with our
8:16 testifies with our s that we are
8:23 We, who have the S as the
8:26 At the same time the S also
8:26 But the S intercedes along with
8:27 hearts knows what the S has
8:27 The S intercedes for God's
9:1 The Holy S, along with my
11:8 day God has given them a s
14:17 the joy that the Holy S gives.
15:13 by the power of the Holy S.
15:16 made holy by the Holy S.
15:19 and by the power of God's S,
15:30 by the love that the S creates,
1Co 2:10 those things to us by his S.
2:10 The S searches everything,
2:11 except that person's own s?
2:11 about God except God's S.
2:12 Now, we didn't receive the s
2:12 Instead, we received the S
2:13 things to those who have the S.
2:14 the teachings of God's S.
3:16 and that God's S lives in you?
4:21 show you love and a gentle s?
5:3 I am with you in s.
5:4 I am with you in s.
6:11 Christ and in the S of our God.
6:17 Lord becomes one s with him.
6:19 that belongs to the Holy S?
6:19 The Holy S, whom you
7:34 may be holy in body and in s.
7:40 I think that I, too, have God's S.
12:3 one speaking by God's S says,
12:3 except by the Holy S.
12:4 but the same S gives them.
12:8 The S gives one person the
12:8 The same S gives another
12:9 To another person the same S
12:9 To another person the same S
12:11 There is only one S who does
12:13 By one S we were all baptized
12:13 gave all of us one S to drink.
14:2 His s is speaking mysteries.
14:14 another language, my s prays,
14:15 that I will pray with my s,
14:15 I will sing psalms with my s,
14:16 praise God only with your s,
15:45 Adam became a life-giving s.
2Co 1:22 us the S as his guarantee.
3:3 not with ink but with the S
3:6 but the S brings life.
3:8 brings the S have even more
3:17 This Lord is the S.
3:17 Wherever the Lord's S is,
3:18 from the Lord, who is the S.
4:13 We have that same s of faith.
5:5 given us his S to guarantee it.
7:1 that contaminates body and s
11:4 When you receive a s that is
11:4 from the S you received earlier,
Gal 3:2 Did you receive the S by your
3:5 God supply you with the S
3:14 the promised S through faith.
4:6 God has sent the S of his Son
6:18 Jesus Christ be with your s,
Eph 1:13 the Holy S whom he promised.
1:14 This Holy S is the guarantee
1:17 would give you a s of wisdom
2:18 can go to the Father in one S.
2:22 are being built in the S together
3:5 The S has now revealed it to
3:16 and power through his S.
4:3 the unity that the S gives.
4:4 There is one body and one S.
4:30 Don't give God's Holy S any
5:18 Instead, be filled with the S
6:17 the sword that the S supplies.
6:18 Pray in the S in every situation.
Php 1:19 from the S of Jesus Christ.
1:27 that you are firmly united in s,
3:3 because we serve God's S
Col 1:8 love that the S has given you.
2:5 physically, I'm with you in s.

1Th 1:5 with power, with the Holy **S**,
1:6 of joy that the Holy **S** gives.
4:8 who gives you his Holy **S**.
5:23 he keep your whole being — **s**,
2Th 2:2 that we said through some **s**,
1Ti 3:16 was approved by the **S**,
4:1 The **S** says clearly that in later
2Ti 1:7 God didn't give us a cowardly **s**
1:7 spirit but a **s** of power,
1:14 With the help of the Holy **S**
Tit 3:5 in which the Holy **S** gives
3:6 a generous amount of the **S**
Heb 2:4 from the Holy **S** as he wanted.
3:7 As the Holy **S** says,
4:12 place where soul and **s** meet,
6:4 gift and shared in the Holy **S**.
9:8 The Holy **S** used this to show
9:14 Through the eternal **S** he
10:15 The Holy **S** tells us the same
10:29 and he insults the **S** that God
Jas 4:5 It says, "The **S** that lives in us
1Pe 1:11 out what time or situation the **S**
1:12 had spoken, the Holy **S**,
3:18 brought to life through his **s**.
4:14 you are blessed because the **S**
4:14 the Spirit of glory — the **S**
2Pe 1:21 it was given by the Holy **S** as
1Jn 3:24 because he has given us the **S**.
4:1 who say that they have the **S**.
4:1 See whether the **s** they have is
4:2 you can recognize God's **S**:
4:2 a human has the **S** that is from
4:3 a human has a **s** that isn't from
4:3 This is the **s** of the antichrist
4:3 That **s** is already in the world.
4:6 That's how we can tell the **S** of
4:6 Spirit of truth from the **s** of lies.
4:13 because he has given us his **S**.
5:6 The **S** is the one who verifies
5:6 because the **S** is the truth.
5:8 the **S**, the water, and the blood.
Rev 2:7 ears listen to what the **S** says
2:11 ears listen to what the **S** says
2:17 ears listen to what the **S** says
2:29 ears listen to what the **S** says
3:6 ears listen to what the **S** says
3:13 ears listen to what the **S** says
3:22 ears listen to what the **S** says
14:13 "Yes," says the **S**.
18:2 She is a prison for every evil **s**,
19:10 of Jesus is the **s** of prophecy!"
22:17 The **S** and the bride say,

Spirit's (9)

1Co 2:13 we use the **S** teachings.
12:7 of the **S** presence is given
2Co 6:6 the Holy **S** presence ⌊in our
13:13 and the Holy **S** presence be
1Th 5:19 Don't put out the **S** fire
1Pe 1:2 with the **S** help so that you
Jud 1:20 Pray with the Holy **S** help
Rev 1:10 I came under the **S** power on
4:2 I came under the **S** power.

spirits (46)

Gen 45:27 him back, his **s** were lifted.
Dtr 18:11 ask ghosts or **s** for help,
Est 5:14 king to the dinner in good **s**."
Psa 34:18 those whose **s** are crushed.
78:8 Their **s** were not faithful to God.
88:10 Will the **s** of the dead rise and
Isa 26:14 The **s** of the dead won't rise.
26:19 will revive the **s** of the dead.
57:16 Otherwise, the **s**, the lives of
Eze 18:31 new hearts and new **s**.
Zec 6:5 "They are the four **s** of heaven.
Mat 8:16 He forced the ⌊evil⌋ **s** out of
10:1 authority to force evil **s** out
12:45 seven other **s** more evil than
Mar 1:27 He gives orders to evil **s**,
3:11 people with evil **s** saw him,
5:13 The evil **s** came out of the man
6:7 gave them authority over evil **s**.
Luk 4:36 power he gives orders to evil **s**,
6:18 tormented by evil **s** were cured.
7:21 sicknesses, and evil **s**.
Luk 8:2 had been cured from evil **s**
10:20 be happy that evil **s** obey you.
11:26 seven other **s** more evil than
Act 5:16 who were troubled by evil **s**,
8:7 Evil **s** screamed as they came
19:12 and evil **s** would leave them.
19:13 to place and force evil **s** out
19:13 Lord Jesus to force evil **s** out
23:8 that angels and **s** don't exist.
Rom 8:10 but your **s** are alive because
1Co 12:10 tell the difference between **s**.
1Ti 4:1 They will follow **s** that deceive,
Heb 1:14 They are **s** sent to serve those
12:9 authority of God, the father of **s**,
12:23 God of all people) and to the **s**
1Pe 3:19 victory to the **s** kept in prison.
Rev 1:4 from the seven **s** who are in
3:1 one who has God's seven **s**
4:5 These are the seven **s** of God.
5:6 which are the seven **s** of God
16:13 Then I saw three evil **s** like
16:14 They are **s** of demons that do
16:14 These **s** go to the kings of the
16:16 The **s** gathered the kings at the
22:6 The Lord God of the **s** of the

spiritual (83)

Hos 9:7 and that **s** people are crazy.
Jon 3:6 gives birth to things that are **s**.
6:63 Life is **s**. Your physical
6:63 that I have spoken to you are **s**.
Act 14:23 each church choose **s** leaders,
15:2 and **s** leaders about this
15:4 and the **s** leaders welcomed
15:6 The apostles and **s** leaders
15:22 the apostles, the **s** leaders,
15:23 the apostles and the **s** leaders,
16:4 that the apostles and **s** leaders
20:17 and called the **s** leaders
20:26 responsible for the ⌊**s**⌋ death
21:18 All the **s** leaders were present.
21:20 When the **s** leaders heard
Rom 1:4 In his **s**, holy nature he was
1:11 I long to see you to share a **s**
2:29 Circumcision is **s**,
7:6 we are serving in a new **s** way,
7:14 that God's standards are **s**,
8:4 nature but by our **s** nature,
8:5 But those who live by the **s**
8:5 have the **s** nature's attitude.
8:6 But the **s** nature's attitude leads
8:9 the control of your **s** nature,
8:13 But if you use your **s** nature to
15:27 have shared the **s** wealth
1Co 2:4 with a show of **s** power
2:13 We explain **s** things to those
2:14 A person who isn't **s** doesn't
2:14 must be **s** to evaluate them.
2:15 **S** people evaluate everything
3:1 I couldn't talk to you as **s**
4:15 don't have many ⌊**s**⌋ fathers.
5:5 nature so that his **s** nature may
9:11 If we have planted the **s** seed
10:3 All of them ate the same **s** food,
10:4 of them drank the same **s** drink.
10:4 They drank from the **s** rock that
12:1 concerning **s** gifts.
12:4 There are different **s** gifts,
14:1 Pursue love, and desire **s** gifts,
14:12 you're eager to have **s** gifts,
15:44 comes back to life as a **s** body.
15:44 so there is also a **s** body.
15:46 The **s** does not come first,
15:46 but the physical and then the **s**.
2Co 3:6 a **s** promise, not a written one.
Gal 3:3 Did you begin in a **s** way only
4:29 the son conceived in a **s** way.
5:5 However, in our **s** nature,
5:16 Live your life as your **s** nature
5:17 to what your **s** nature wants,
5:17 and what your **s** nature wants
5:18 If your **s** nature is your guide,
5:22 But the **s** nature produces love,
5:25 If we live by our **s** nature,
5:25 need to conform to our **s** nature.
6:1 those of you who are **s** should
Gal 6:8 in ⌊the soil of⌋ your **s** nature,
Eph 1:3 every **s** blessing that heaven
2:2 present world and its **s** ruler.
5:19 and **s** songs for your own good.
6:12 and **s** forces that control evil in
Php 2:1 you have any **s** relationships?
Col 1:9 kind of **s** wisdom and insight.
3:16 Use psalms, hymns, and **s**
2Th 2:13 through a life of **s** devotion
1Ti 4:14 when the **s** leaders placed their
5:17 Give double honor to **s** leaders
5:19 against a **s** leader unless
Tit 1:5 be done — appointing **s** leaders
1:6 A **s** leader must have a good
Phm 1:10 I became his **s** father here in
1Pe 2:5 a **s** house that is being built
2:5 So offer **s** sacrifices that God
4:6 live like God in their **s** lives.
5:1 I appeal to your **s** leaders.
5:1 I make this appeal as a **s**
5:5 under the authority of **s** leaders.
2Pe 3:14 ⌊**s**⌋ stains or blemishes.
Jud 1:19 physical things, not **s** things.
Rev 11:8 The **s** names of that city are

spiritually (10)

Mat 5:3 recognize they are **s** helpless.
Luk 1:80 grew and became **s** strong.
Act 6:3 the people know are **s** wise.
Rom 11:12 people made the world **s** rich.
11:12 who are not Jewish **s** rich.
1Co 14:37 is **s** gifted must acknowledge
2Co 6:10 we make many people **s** rich,
12:2 to him physically or **s**.
12:4 to him physically or **s**.
3Jn 1:2 I know that you are **s** well.

spiritually-minded (1)

Luk 16:8 clever than **s** people when

spit (23)

Num 12:14 "If her own father had **s** in her
Dtr 25:9 off one of his sandals and **s**
1Sm 21:13 gate and let his **s** run down his
Job 7:19 to let me swallow my **s**?
15:13 God and **s** these words out
17:6 Now they **s** in my face.
30:10 don't hesitate to **s** in my face.
Isa 50:6 who humiliate me and **s** on me.
Jer 51:34 delicacies. Then he **s** us out.
51:44 I will make Bel **s** out
Jnh 2:10 and it **s** Jonah out onto the
Mat 26:67 Then they **s** in his face,
27:30 After they had **s** on him,
Mar 8:23 He **s** into the man's eyes and
10:34 fun of him, **s** on him, whip him,
14:65 of them began to **s** on him.
Luk 18:32 fun of him, insult him, **s** on him,
Jon 9:6 After Jesus said this, he **s** on
9:6 and mixed the **s** with dirt.
9:11 Jesus mixed some **s** with dirt,
9:14 day when Jesus mixed the **s**
9:15 "He put a mixture of **s** and dirt
Rev 3:16 I'm going to **s** you out of my

spite (25)

Lev 26:27 "If in **s** of this you do not listen
Num 14:11 will they refuse to trust me in **s**
Dtr 1:32 In **s** of this, you didn't trust the
1Sm 2:32 In **s** of the good that I do for
Neh 5:18 Yet, in **s** of all this,
Job 34:6 I'm considered a liar in **s** of my
Psa 17:4 In **s** of what others have done,
78:23 In **s** of that, he commanded the
78:32 In **s** of all this, they continued
Ecc 5:7 In **s** of many daydreams,
7:3 because, in **s** of a sad face,
7:15 Righteous people die in **s** of
7:15 Wicked people go on living in **s**
Isa 16:14 In **s** of their great number,
38:16 people live in **s** of such things,
38:16 the will to live in **s** of them.
47:9 All this will happen to you in **s**
Jer 2:35 In **s** of all this you say,
Amo 9:10 In **s** of this, they will be killed
Mic 7:16 see this and be ashamed in **s**

Rom 2:27 He will condemn you in **s** of
11:24 In **s** of the fact that you have
1Th 1:6 In **s** of a lot of suffering,
2:2 News in **s** of strong opposition.
2Ti 2:19 In **s** of all that, God's ⌊people⌋

spiteful (1)

Eze 25:15 taken revenge with **s** hearts.

spits (3)

Lev 15:8 If a man who has a discharge **s**
15:8 the person he **s** on must wash
Psa 10:5 He **s** at all his opponents.

spitting (3)

Pro 6:19 a dishonest witness **s** out lies,
Mar 7:33 into the man's ears, and after **s**,
15:19 the head with a stick, **s** on him,

splash (1)

Eze 32:2 You **s** around in the water.

splattered (2)

2Ki 9:33 and some of her blood **s** on the
Isa 63:3 Their blood **s** my clothes so all

splendid (3)

Isa 22:18 There your **s** chariots will
Zec 10:3 them like his **s** war horse."
Luk 7:25 Those who wear **s** clothes and

splendor (31)

Exo 15:11 because of your **s**.
1Ch 16:27 **S** and majesty are in his
16:29 the LORD in ⌊his⌋ holy **s**.
29:11 Greatness, power, **s**,
Est 1:4 of his kingdom and the costly **s**
Job 31:26 the moon move along in its **s**
40:10 Clothe yourself in **s** and glory.
Psa 21:5 You place **s** and majesty on
29:2 the LORD in ⌊his⌋ holy **s**.
45:3 side with your **s** and majesty.
89:44 You put an end to his **s** and
96:6 **S** and majesty are in his
96:9 the LORD in ⌊his⌋ holy **s**.
104:1 are clothed with **s** and majesty.
110:3 come to you in holy **s** like dew
Pro 20:29 the **s** of older people is their
Isa 61:6 You will boast in their **s**.
63:1 Who is this dressed in **s**,
Jer 22:18 it is for my master and his **s**!"
Lam 1:6 All **s** has abandoned the
Dan 11:20 a cruel official go out in royal **s**.
11:21 He will not be given royal **s**.
Hab 3:3 Selah His **s** covers the
1Co 15:40 don't all have the same **s**,
15:41 The sun has one kind of **s**,
15:41 the moon has another kind of **s**,
15:41 have still another kind of **s**.
15:41 differs in **s** from another star.
15:43 it doesn't have any **s** and is
15:43 it has **s** and is strong.
Rev 18:14 and your **s** have disappeared.

splintered (1)

Eze 29:7 When Israel grabbed you, you **s**

splinters (2)

Num 33:55 they will be like **s** in your eyes
Psa 29:5 The LORD **s** the cedars of

split (25)

Gen 14:15 He **s** up his men to attack them
Num 16:31 the ground under them **s**,
Jos 9:4 Their wineskins were old, **s**,
Jdg 15:19 So God **s** open the hollow
1Ki 18:6 So they **s** up in order to cover
Job 26:8 ⌊even⌋ **s** under its ⌊weight⌋.
Psa 60:2 You **s** it wide open.
78:15 He **s** rocks in the desert.
106:17 The ground **s** open and
Pro 1:14 We'll **s** the loot equally."
Isa 48:21 He **s** a rock, and water gushed
64:1 If only you would **s** open the
Mic 1:4 Valleys will **s** apart like water
Hab 3:9 Selah You **s** the land with
Zec 14:4 of Olives will be **s** in two,
Mat 27:51 the curtain in the temple was **s**
27:51 and the rocks were **s** open.
Mar 1:10 he saw heaven **s** open and the
15:38 The curtain in the temple was **s**
Luk 23:45 The curtain in the temple was **s**
Act 1:18 His body **s** open, and all his
1Co 1:10 not to **s** into opposing groups.
11:18 church you **s** up into opposing
15:52 in a **s** second at the sound of
Rev 16:19 The important city **s** into three

splits (2)

Psa 29:9 The voice of the LORD **s** the
Ecc 10:9 Whoever **s** wood may be

splitting (1)

Jos 9:13 See how they are **s**!

spoil (1)

Pro 23:8 **s** your pleasant conversation.

spoiled (1)

Ecc 10:1 perfume stink, and then it is **s**.

spoils (1)

Jon 6:27 Don't work for food that **s**.

spoke (403)

Gen 8:15 Then God **s** to Noah,
15:1 Later the LORD **s** his word to
15:4 Suddenly, the LORD **s** his
17:3 and again God **s** to him,
19:14 So Lot went out and **s** to the
22:7 Isaac **s** up and said,
23:3 dead wife and **s** to the Hittites,
23:13 He **s** to Ephron so that the
24:7 He **s** to me and swore this oath:
34:3 the girl and **s** tenderly to her.
41:9 chief cupbearer **s** to Pharaoh,
42:7 didn't know them and **s** harshly
42:30 "The governor of that land **s**
43:19 charge of Joseph's house and **s**
46:2 God **s** to Israel in a vision that
50:4 Joseph **s** to the Pharaoh's
Exo 6:2 God **s** to Moses, "I am the
6:10 Then the LORD **s** to Moses,
6:13 The LORD **s** to Moses and
6:28 At that time the LORD **s** to
13:1 The LORD **s** to Moses,
20:1 Then God **s** all these words:
32:13 descendants all the land I **s** of.
33:9 while the LORD **s** with Moses.
34:31 Then Moses **s** to them.
Lev 1:1 The LORD called Moses and **s**
4:1 The LORD **s** to Moses,
5:14 The LORD **s** to Moses,
6:1 The LORD **s** to Moses,
6:8 The LORD **s** to Moses,
6:19 The LORD **s** to Moses,
6:24 The LORD **s** to Moses,
7:22 The LORD **s** to Moses,
7:28 The LORD **s** to Moses,
8:1 The LORD **s** to Moses,
10:8 The LORD **s** to Aaron,
11:1 The LORD **s** to Moses and
12:1 The LORD **s** to Moses,
13:1 The LORD **s** to Moses and
14:1 The LORD **s** to Moses,
14:33 The LORD **s** to Moses and
15:1 The LORD **s** to Moses and
16:1 The LORD **s** to Moses after
17:1 The LORD **s** to Moses,
18:1 The LORD **s** to Moses,
19:1 The LORD **s** to Moses,
20:1 The LORD **s** to Moses,
21:1 The LORD **s** to Moses,
21:16 The LORD **s** to Moses,
21:24 So Moses **s** to Aaron and his
22:1 The LORD **s** to Moses,
22:17 The LORD **s** to Moses,
22:26 The LORD **s** to Moses,
23:1 The LORD **s** to Moses,
23:9 The LORD **s** to Moses,
23:23 The LORD **s** to Moses,
23:26 The LORD **s** to Moses,
Lev 23:33 The LORD **s** to Moses,
24:1 The LORD **s** to Moses,
24:13 The LORD **s** to Moses,
24:23 Moses **s** to the people of Israel.
25:1 The LORD **s** to Moses on
27:1 The LORD **s** to Moses,
Num 1:1 The LORD **s** to Moses in the
2:1 The LORD **s** to Moses and
3:1 at the time when the LORD **s**
7:89 how the LORD **s** with Moses.
9:1 the LORD **s** to Moses in the
11:25 of⌋ smoke and **s** with him.
11:28 **s** up and said, "Stop them, sir!"
17:6 So Moses **s** to the Israelites.
26:3 Moses and the priest Eleazar **s**
35:1 The LORD **s** to Moses on the
36:1 descendants) came and **s**
Dtr 1:1 He **s** to all the Israelites.
4:12 The LORD **s** to you from the
4:15 see the LORD the day he **s**
5:4 The LORD **s** to you face to
5:22 commandments the LORD **s**
5:22 He **s** in a loud voice from the
5:28 the words that you **s** to me,
9:10 all the words that the LORD **s**
Jos 5:2 time the LORD **s** to Joshua,
10:12 Joshua **s** to the LORD while
14:12 region which the LORD **s**
20:2 cities of refuge about which I **s**
24:27 words which the LORD **s** to us.
Jdg 9:1 He **s** to them and his mother's
9:37 Gaal **s** again, "No, there are
13:11 "Are you the man who **s** to my
18:14 the land around Laish **s** up.
1Sm 3:21 And Samuel **s** to all Israel.
15:10 Then the LORD **s** to Samuel:
19:4 So Jonathan **s** well of David to
28:17 what he **s** through me:
2Sm 2:22 So Abner **s** again to Asahel.
3:19 Abner also **s** specifically to the
7:4 But that same night the LORD **s**
18:22 Zadok's son, **s** to Joab again,
19:43 But the people of Judah **s**
23:2 of the LORD **s** through me.
23:3 The God of Israel **s** to them.
24:11 the LORD **s** his word to the
1Ki 4:32 Solomon **s** 3,000 proverbs and
5:5 LORD my God as the LORD **s**
6:11 The LORD **s** to Solomon,
12:14 He **s** to them as the young men
12:22 But God **s** his word to
13:9 When the LORD **s** to me,
13:17 When the LORD **s** to me,
13:18 An angel **s** the word of the
13:20 the LORD **s** his word to the old
16:1 The LORD **s** his word to Jehu,
16:7 In addition, the LORD **s** his
17:2 Then the LORD **s** his word to
17:8 Then the LORD **s** his word to
18:1 the LORD **s** his word to Elijah:
19:9 Then the LORD **s** his word to
20:35 A disciple of the prophets **s** to
21:17 Then the LORD **s** his word to
21:23 Then the LORD also **s**
21:28 Then the LORD **s** his word to
2Ki 9:36 Jehu said, "The LORD **s**
20:4 when the LORD **s** his word
21:10 Then the LORD **s** through his
1Ch 17:3 But that same night God **s** his
21:9 The LORD **s** to Gad,
21:27 So the LORD **s** to the
22:8 But the LORD **s** his word to me
2Ch 1:2 Solomon **s** to all Israel — to the
10:14 He **s** to them as the young men
11:2 But God **s** his word to
12:7 he **s** his word to Shemaiah:
30:22 Hezekiah **s** encouraging words
32:6 He **s** these words of
32:19 They **s** about the God of
33:10 When the LORD **s** to
33:18 and the words that the seers **s**
36:12 who **s** for the LORD.
Neh 9:13 heaven to Mount Sinai and **s**
13:24 Half their children **s** the
Est 1:16 Then Memucan **s** up in the
4:10 Esther **s** to Hathach and

Est	7:9	who **s** up for the well-being of
	8:3	Esther **s** again to the king.
	10:3	for the good of his people and **s**
Job	6:3	of the seas. I **s** carelessly
	29:11	eyes that saw me **s** well of me,
	32:4	Elihu waited as they **s** to Job
	33:8	"But you **s** directly to me,
	40:5	I **s** once, but I can't answer —
Psa	33:9	He **s**, and it came into being.
	39:3	Then I **s** with my tongue:
	78:19	They **s** against God by saying,
	99:7	He **s** to them from a column of
	105:31	He **s**, and swarms of flies and
	105:34	He **s**, and countless locusts
	106:33	bitter so that he **s** recklessly.
	107:25	He **s**, and a storm began to
	114:1	who **s** a foreign language,
	138:4	have heard the promises you **s**.
Isa	7:10	Again the LORD **s** to Ahaz,
	8:5	The LORD **s** to me again.
	16:13	that the LORD **s** about Moab
	38:4	Then the LORD **s** his word to
	65:12	I **s**, but you didn't listen.
	66:4	I **s**, but they didn't listen.
Jer	1:2	The LORD **s** his word to
	1:3	LORD also **s** when Jehoiakim,
	1:4	The LORD **s** his word to me,
	1:11	Again the LORD **s** his word to
	1:13	Again the LORD **s** his word to
	2:1	The LORD **s** his word to me,
	7:1	The LORD **s** his word to
	7:13	"Although I **s** to you again and
	11:1	that the LORD **s** to Jeremiah.
	13:3	The LORD **s** his word to me
	13:8	Then the LORD **s** his word to
	14:1	The LORD **s** his word to
	14:14	them, and **s** to them.
	16:1	The LORD **s** his word to me.
	18:1	The LORD **s** his word to
	18:5	The LORD **s** his word to me.
	21:1	The LORD **s** his word to
	22:21	I **s** to you when you were
	24:4	The LORD **s** his word to me,
	25:1	The LORD **s** his word to
	25:2	The prophet Jeremiah **s** to all
	26:1	The LORD **s** his word when
	27:1	the LORD **s** his word to
	27:12	I **s** the same message to King
	27:16	I also **s** this message to the
	28:1	**s** to me in the LORD's temple.
	28:12	the LORD **s** his word to
	29:23	neighbors' wives and **s** lies
	29:30	Then the LORD **s** his word to
	30:1	The LORD **s** his word to
	30:4	that the LORD **s** about Israel
	32:1	The LORD **s** his word to
	32:6	"The LORD **s** his word to me.
	32:26	The LORD **s** his word to
	33:1	the LORD **s** his word to him a
	33:19	The LORD **s** his word to
	33:23	Then the LORD **s** his word to
	34:1	The LORD **s** his word to
	34:8	The LORD **s** his word to
	34:12	The LORD **s** his word to
	35:1	The LORD **s** his word to
	35:12	Then the LORD **s** his word to
	36:1	the LORD **s** his word to
	36:2	other nations from the time I **s**
	36:27	the LORD **s** his word to
	37:6	The LORD **s** his word to the
	38:8	left the royal palace and **s**
	39:15	the LORD **s** his word to him.
	40:1	The LORD **s** his word to
	42:7	After ten days the LORD **s** his
	43:8	Then the LORD **s** his word to
	44:1	The LORD **s** his word to
	45:1	prophet Jeremiah **s** to Baruch,
	46:1	The LORD **s** this message to
	46:13	The LORD **s** this message to
	47:1	The LORD **s** this message to
	48:42	because it **s** against the LORD.
	49:34	the LORD **s** his word to the
	50:1	that the LORD **s** about Babylon
Lam	3:37	Who was it who **s** and it came
Eze	1:3	the LORD **s** his word to the
	2:2	As he **s** to me, the Spirit
Eze	3:16	After seven days the LORD **s**
	5:13	**s** to you while I was angry.
	6:1	The LORD **s** his word to me.
	7:1	The LORD **s** his word to me.
	11:14	Then the LORD **s** his word to
	12:1	The LORD **s** his word to me.
	12:8	The next morning the LORD **s**
	12:17	The LORD **s** his word to me.
	12:21	The LORD **s** his word to me.
	12:26	The LORD **s** his word to me.
	13:1	The LORD **s** his word to me.
	14:2	Then the LORD **s** his word to
	14:12	The LORD **s** his word to me.
	15:1	The LORD **s** his word to me.
	16:1	The LORD **s** his word to me.
	17:1	The LORD **s** his word to me.
	17:11	The LORD **s** his word to me.
	18:1	The LORD **s** his word to me.
	20:2	Then the LORD **s** his word to
	20:45	The LORD **s** his word to me.
	21:1	The LORD **s** his word to me.
	21:8	The LORD **s** his word to me.
	21:18	The LORD **s** his word to me.
	22:1	The LORD **s** his word to me.
	22:17	Then the LORD **s** his word to
	22:23	"The LORD **s** his word to me.
	23:1	The LORD **s** his word to me.
	24:1	the LORD **s** his word to me.
	24:15	Then the LORD **s** his word to
	24:18	So I **s** to the people in the
	24:20	"The LORD **s** his word to me.
	25:1	The LORD **s** his word to me.
	26:1	the LORD **s** his word to me.
	27:1	The LORD **s** his word to me.
	28:1	The LORD **s** his word to me.
	28:11	The LORD **s** his word to me.
	28:20	The LORD **s** his word to me.
	29:1	the LORD **s** his word to me.
	29:17	the LORD **s** his word to me.
	30:1	The LORD **s** his word to me.
	30:20	the LORD **s** his word to me.
	31:1	the LORD **s** his word to me.
	32:1	the LORD **s** his word to me.
	32:17	the LORD **s** his word to me.
	33:1	The LORD **s** his word to me.
	33:22	So I **s**, and I was no longer
	33:23	The LORD **s** his word to me.
	34:1	The LORD **s** his word to me.
	35:1	The LORD **s** his word to me.
	35:12	heard all the insults that you **s**
	36:16	The LORD **s** his word to me.
	37:15	The LORD **s** his word to me
	38:1	The LORD **s** his word to me.
	38:17	You are the one I **s** about long
Dan	2:4	The astrologers **s** to the king in
	2:14	Daniel **s** to him using shrewd
	6:12	Then they went and **s** to the
	7:8	mouth that **s** impressive things.
	7:20	mouth that **s** impressive things.
	8:18	As he **s** to me, I fainted
	9:6	who **s** in your name to our
	10:6	When he **s**, his voice sounded
Hos	1:1	The LORD **s** his word to
	1:2	the LORD first **s** to Hosea,
	12:10	I **s** to the prophets and gave
	13:1	When the tribe of Ephraim **s**,
Jnh	1:1	The LORD **s** his word to Jonah,
	2:10	Then the LORD **s** to the fish,
	3:1	Then the LORD **s** his word to
Mic	1:1	The LORD **s** his word to Micah,
Zep	1:1	that the LORD **s** to Zephaniah,
	1:1	The LORD **s** his word in the
Hag	1:1	the LORD **s** his word through
	1:3	Then the LORD **s** his word
	2:1	the LORD **s** his word through
	2:10	the LORD **s** his word to the
	2:20	The LORD **s** his word to
Zec	1:1	the LORD **s** his word to the
	1:7	the LORD **s** his word to the
	4:6	the LORD **s** to Zerubbabel:
	4:8	Then the LORD **s** his word to
	6:9	The LORD **s** his word to me.
	7:1	the LORD **s** his word to
	7:4	Then the LORD of Armies **s** his
	7:8	Then the LORD **s** his word to
	8:1	LORD of Armies **s** his word.
Zec	8:9	of the prophets who **s** when
	8:18	The LORD of Armies **s** his
Mal	1:1	The LORD **s** his word to Israel
	3:16	those who feared the LORD **s**
Mat	3:3	Isaiah the prophet **s** about this
	11:7	As they were leaving, Jesus **s**
	12:41	when Jonah **s** his message.
	22:1	illustrations when he **s** to them.
	26:27	Then he took a cup and **s** a
	28:18	Jesus came near, he **s** to them.
Mar	4:33	Jesus **s** God's word to them
	10:28	Then Peter **s** up, "We've given
	12:1	illustration, Jesus **s** to them.
	14:23	**s** a prayer of thanksgiving,
Luk	1:60	But his mother **s** up,
	2:38	She **s** about Jesus to all who
	3:2	priests that God **s** to John,
	3:19	John **s** out against the ruler
	3:19	He also **s** out against Herod for
	4:22	All the people **s** well of him.
	4:32	because he **s** with authority.
	7:24	Jesus **s** to the crowds about
	7:40	Jesus **s** up, "Simon, I have
	11:32	when Jonah **s** his message,
	11:37	After Jesus **s**, a Pharisee
	12:1	Jesus **s** to his disciples and
	14:7	illustration when he **s** to them:
	15:3	Jesus **s** to them using this
	20:9	Jesus **s** to the people:
	22:17	Then he took a cup and **s** a
	22:19	Then Jesus took bread and **s** a
	23:20	he **s** to the people again.
	23:22	A third time Pilate **s** to them.
	24:44	"These are the words I **s** to you
Jon	1:30	He is the one I **s** about when I
	2:21	But the temple Jesus **s** about
	3:26	man you **s** so favorably about
	8:12	Jesus **s** to the Pharisees again.
	8:20	Jesus **s** these words while he
	8:21	Jesus **s** to the Pharisees again.
	9:29	We know that God **s** to Moses,
Act	1:15	Peter got up and **s** to them.
	2:6	dialect when the disciples **s**.
	2:16	this is what the prophet Joel **s**
	2:31	and he **s** about that before it
	3:24	him **s** about these days.
	4:13	to see how boldly they **s**.
	4:25	who **s** through your servant
	5:13	everyone **s** highly of them.
	6:10	with Stephen because he **s**
	7:38	and the messenger who **s**
	8:35	Then Philip **s**. Starting with that
	9:28	He **s** boldly with the power and
	10:15	A voice **s** to him a second time,
	11:9	"A voice **s** from heaven a
	11:19	They **s** God's word only to
	13:22	God **s** favorably about David.
	14:1	went into the synagogue and **s**
	14:3	They **s** boldly about the Lord,
	14:25	They **s** the message in the city
	15:32	**s** a long time to encourage and
	16:2	and Iconium **s** well of Timothy.
	16:32	They **s** the Lord's word to the
	18:25	way and **s** enthusiastically.
	20:2	that region and **s** many words
	21:40	Paul **s** to them in the Hebrew
	22:12	in Damascus **s** highly of him.
	23:9	or an angel actually **s** to him!"
	28:25	"How well the Holy Spirit **s** to
Rom	10:17	that is heard is what Christ **s**.
1Co	2:4	I **s** my message with a show of
	11:24	and **s** a prayer of thanksgiving.
	13:11	I was a child, I **s** like a child,
2Co	4:13	"I believed; therefore, I **s**."
2Th	2:15	taught you either when we **s**
Heb	1:1	In the past God **s** to our
	4:7	that place of rest, God **s** about
	12:26	When God **s** to your ancestors,
Jas	5:10	example of the prophets who **s**
1Pe	1:10	Long ago they **s** about God's
	2:22	He never **s** deceitfully.
	3:6	Sarah obeyed Abraham and **s**
2Pe	1:17	majestic God **s** these words
	1:21	**s** under God's direction.
	2:16	**s** with a human voice and
Rev	10:3	the seven thunders **s** with

Rev 10:4 When the seven thunders **s**,
10:8 I had heard from heaven **s**

spoken (122)

Gen 35:13 place where he had **s** with him.
35:14 where God had **s** with him.
35:15 the place where God had **s**
Exo 4:10 even though you've **s** to me.
20:22 for yourselves that I have **s**
Num 14:35 I, the LORD, have **s**.
Dtr 10:4 He had **s** these words to you
18:22 That prophet has **s** on his own
30:1 I have **s** about will happen
Rut 4:1 he had **s** was passing by.
2Sm 2:27 as God lives, if you had not **s**,
7:19 You've also **s** about the distant
1Ki 2:27 LORD's word **s** at Shiloh about
13:11 and the exact words he had **s**
15:29 as the LORD had **s** through his
16:12 as the LORD had **s** through the
16:34 The LORD had **s** this through
18:31 (The LORD had **s** his word to
22:23 LORD has **s** evil about you."
2Ki 10:10 LORD **s** about Ahab's family
20:19 word that you have **s** is good."
1Ch 11:3 LORD had **s** through Samuel.
17:17 You've **s** about the distant
2Ch 18:22 LORD has **s** evil about you."
36:21 **s** through Jeremiah would
36:22 The promise the LORD had **s**
Ezr 1:1 The promise the LORD had **s**
Job 15:11 even when gently **s** to you?
21:3 Then after I've **s**, you may go
26:4 have you **s** ⌊these⌋ words,
26:4 spirit has **s** through you?
29:22 After I had **s**, they wouldn't
Psa 17:10 Their mouths have **s** arrogantly
50:1 the only true God, has **s**.
62:11 God has **s** once. I have heard it
66:14 by my lips and **s** by my ⌊own⌋
103:20 are ready to obey his **s** orders.
Pro 4:5 from the words that I have **s**.
25:11 ⌊So⌋ is a word **s** at the right
26:2 so a hastily **s** curse does not
Isa 1:2 The LORD has **s**, "I raised
1:20 by swords." The LORD has **s**.
21:17 The LORD God of Israel has **s**.
22:25 destroyed." The LORD has **s**.
23:4 stronghold by the sea has **s**,
24:3 because the LORD has **s**.
25:8 whole earth. The LORD has **s**.
38:15 I say now that he has **s** to me?
39:8 word that you have **s** is good."
40:5 The LORD has **s**."
45:19 I haven't **s** privately or in some
46:11 I have **s**, and I will bring it
48:15 I alone have **s**. I have called
48:16 From the beginning I have **s**
53:9 violent and had never **s** a lie.
58:14 Jacob. The LORD has **s**.
59:13 We have **s** about oppression
Jer 4:28 I have **s**, and I have planned it.
5:13 LORD hasn't **s** through them,
10:1 that the LORD has **s** to you,
13:15 be arrogant. The LORD has **s**.
25:3 So I have **s** to you again and
26:16 He has **s** to us in the name of
31:20 I have often **s** against him,
32:8 that the LORD had **s** to me.
34:5 I have **s** my word, declares the
35:14 I have **s** to you again and
35:17 I have **s** to them, but they didn't
37:2 what the LORD had **s** through
44:16 to the message that you have **s**
48:26 they have **s** against the LORD.
Eze 3:10 everything I have **s** to you,
5:15 I, the LORD, have **s**.
5:17 I, the LORD, have **s**."
17:21 know that I, the LORD, have **s**.
17:24 I, the LORD, have **s**,
21:17 I, the LORD, have **s**."
21:32 I, the LORD, have **s**.'"
22:14 I, the LORD, have **s**,
22:28 Yet, the LORD hasn't **s**.
23:34 I have **s**, declares the Almighty
24:14 I, the LORD, have **s**.
Eze 26:5 I have **s**, declares the Almighty
26:14 I, the LORD, have **s**,
28:10 I have **s**,'" declares the LORD.
30:12 I, the LORD, have **s**.
34:24 I, the LORD, have **s**.
36:5 In my fiery anger I have **s**
36:36 I, the LORD, have **s**,
37:14 have **s**, and I have done it,
39:8 This is the day I have **s** about.
Joe 3:8 is far away." The LORD has **s**.
Amo 3:1 have **s** against you Israelites,
3:8 The Almighty LORD has **s**.
Oba 1:18 of Esau." The LORD has **s**.
Mic 4:4 The LORD of Armies has **s**.
Mal 3:13 'How have we **s** against you?'
Mat 1:22 what the Lord had **s** through
2:15 What the Lord had **s** through
2:17 Then the words **s** through the
26:13 Wherever this Good News is **s**
Mar 14:9 Wherever the Good News is **s**
Luk 9:36 After the voice had **s**,
Jon 6:63 The words that I have **s** to you
7:46 has ever **s** like this man."
12:41 glory and had **s** about him.
12:48 The words that I have **s** will
12:49 I have not **s** on my own.
15:22 If I hadn't come and **s** to them,
18:20 Jesus answered him, "I have **s**
Act 8:25 After they had boldly **s** about
9:27 and that the Lord had **s** to him.
9:27 how boldly Saul had **s** about
15:17 over whom my name is **s**,
Gal 3:16 The promises were **s** to
Eph 5:26 water along with **s** words.
Heb 1:2 In these last days he has **s** to
4:8 not have **s** about another day.
13:7 leaders who have **s** God's word
1Pe 1:12 the things they had **s** were not
1:12 What the prophets had **s**,
2Pe 3:2 you to remember the words **s**

spokes (1)

1Ki 7:33 The axles, rims, **s**,

spokesman (10)

Exo 4:16 He will be your **s**, and you will
Job 16:20 the **s** for my thoughts.
33:23 them, a **s**, one in a thousand,
Ecc 1:1 The words of the **s**,
1:2 says the **s**. "Absolutely
1:12 I, the **s**, have been king of
7:27 The **s** said, "This is what I've
12:8 says the **s**. "Everything is
12:9 Besides being wise, the **s** also
12:10 The **s** tried to find just the right

spokesmen (1)

2Co 2:17 As Christ's **s** and in God's

sponge (3)

Mat 27:48 the men ran at once, took a **s**,
Mar 15:36 ran and soaked a **s** in vinegar.
Jon 19:29 So the soldiers put a **s** soaked

spot (7)

Lev 13:51 If the **s** is spreading,
Jdg 9:7 he went to a high **s** on Mount
2Sm 2:23 down there and died on the **s**.
Psa 38:3 No healthy **s** is left on my body
38:7 and no healthy **s** is left on my
Pro 25:6 or stand in the **s** that belongs
Isa 1:6 head there is no healthy **s** left

spots (3)

Lev 21:5 never mourn by shaving bald **s**
Dtr 14:1 or shaving bald **s** on your head.
Jer 13:23 or leopards change their **s**?

spotted (10)

Gen 30:32 every speckled or **s** sheep,
30:32 and every **s** or speckled goat.
30:33 I have that isn't speckled or **s**
30:35 the striped and **s** male goats,
30:35 all the speckled and **s** female
30:39 were striped, speckled, or **s**.
31:10 were striped, speckled, or **s**.
Gen 31:12 are striped, speckled, or **s**,
Zec 6:3 the fourth had strong, **s** horses.
6:6 The **s** ones are going toward

spouts (1)

Zec 4:2 There are seven **s** for each

sprang (1)

Dan 3:24 He **s** to his feet. He asked his

sprawl (1)

Amo 6:4 They **s** out on their couches

sprawled (1)

Amo 6:7 The celebrating of those **s**

spread (207)

Gen 8:17 and **s** over the earth."
9:7 **S** over the earth, and increase."
10:5 the coastlands **s** into their own
10:32 the nations **s** over
28:14 You will **s** out to the west and
41:56 When the famine had **s** all over
Exo 1:12 increased in number and **s** out.
9:29 I'll **s** out my hands to the LORD
9:33 Moses **s** out his hands to the
23:1 "Never **s** false rumors.
23:28 I will **s** panic ahead of you to
25:20 have their wings **s** above
37:9 The angels had their wings **s**
40:19 He **s** the outer tent over the
Lev 13:5 looks the same and has not **s**,
13:6 area has faded and not **s**,
13:7 But if the rash has **s** after he
13:8 and if the rash has **s**,
13:22 If the area has **s**, the priest
13:23 if the irritated area has not **s**,
13:27 If the area has **s**, the priest
13:28 If the irritated area does not **s**
13:32 If the scab has not **s**,
13:34 If the scab has not **s** on the
13:36 If the scab has **s** on the skin,
13:37 if he sees that the scab hasn't **s**
13:53 sees that the area has not **s**,
13:55 and the mildew has not **s**,
14:39 in the walls of the house has **s**,
14:48 and the mildew has not **s**
Num 4:6 On top of that they will **s** a
4:7 "They will **s** a violet cloth over
4:8 They will **s** a bright red cloth
4:11 "They will **s** a violet cloth over
4:13 they will **s** a purple cloth over
4:14 They will **s** a covering of fine
11:32 Then they **s** the quails out all
13:32 So they began to **s** lies among
22:5 They've **s** out all over the
24:6 Your tents **s** out like rivers,
Dtr 7:20 The LORD your God will **s**
22:17 Then the girl's parents must **s**
Jos 6:27 his fame **s** throughout the land.
Jdg 7:12 and all of Kedem were **s** out in
8:25 So they **s** out a coat.
20:37 They **s** out in the city and
Rut 3:9 **S** the corner of your garment
1Sm 4:2 As the battle **s**, the Philistines
9:25 They **s** blankets on the roof for
14:34 "**S** out through the troops,
30:16 They were **s** out all over the
2Sm 17:19 **s** it over the top of the cistern,
18:8 The fighting **s** over the whole
22:10 He **s** apart the heavens and
1Ki 4:31 His fame **s** to all the nations
2Ki 19:14 He **s** them out in front of the
1Ch 14:17 David's fame **s** through all
28:18 gold angels with their wings **s**
2Ch 26:8 and his fame **s** to the border of
26:15 Uzziah's fame **s** far and wide
28:19 Ahaz had **s** sin throughout
31:5 As soon as the word **s**,
Est 1:17 what the queen has done will **s**
Job 1:10 His cattle have **s** out over the
8:16 The shoots **s** over his garden.
15:29 His possessions won't **s** out
36:29 understand how clouds **s** out
38:24 wind is **s** across the earth?
39:26 prey fly and **s** its wings toward

Psa 18:9 He **s** apart the heavens and
57:6 ⌊My enemies⌋ **s** out a net to
58:2 and your hands **s** violence.
105:39 He **s** out a cloud as a
136:6 to the one who **s** out the earth
140:5 They have **s** out a net with
Pro 1:17 It does no good to **s** a net
15:7 of wise people **s** knowledge,
Isa 14:11 Maggots are **s** out ⌊like a bed⌋
16:8 Their shoots had **s** out over the
19:8 Those who **s** their nets on the
21:5 **S** the rugs ⌊by the table⌋.
33:23 and your sail isn't **s** out.
37:14 He **s** it out in front of the LORD
44:24 I **s** out the earth all alone.
54:3 You will **s** out to the right and
Jer 8:2 They will be **s** out and
23:15 have **s** godlessness throughout
43:10 and I will **s** his royal canopy
48:32 Your branches ⌊once⌋ **s** as far
48:40 eagles and **s** their wings over
49:22 eagles and **s** their wings over
50:2 the nations, and **s** the news.
Lam 1:13 He **s** a net for my feet.
Eze 1:11 Their wings were **s** out,
1:22 Something like a dome was **s**
2:10 He **s** the scroll in front of me.
5:4 From there a fire will **s**
12:13 I will **s** my net over him,
16:8 So I **s** my robe over you,
17:6 grew into a low vine that **s** over
17:20 I will **s** my net over you to
19:8 They **s** their net over him and
19:14 Fire has **s** from the vine's main
26:5 people **s** their fishing nets.
26:14 a place to **s** fishing nets.
30:13 I will **s** fear throughout Egypt.
32:3 I will **s** my net over you,
32:9 many people troubled when I **s**
47:10 with their fishing nets **s** out.
Hos 5:1 You set traps at Mizpah and **s**
7:12 I will **s** my net over you.
Joe 2:2 A large and mighty army will **s**
Amo 2:8 Beside every altar, they **s**
5:6 If you don't, he will **s** like a fire
Zec 12:1 The LORD — who **s** out the
14:13 the LORD will **s** among them.
Mal 2:3 I'm going to **s** excrement on
Mat 4:23 taught in the synagogues and **s**
4:24 about Jesus **s** throughout Syria.
9:26 this **s** throughout that region.
9:31 But they went out and **s** the
9:35 taught in the synagogues and **s**
10:7 As you go, **s** this message:
21:8 Most of the people **s** their coats
21:8 from the trees and **s** them
24:14 kingdom will be **s** throughout
28:15 Their story has been **s** among
Mar 1:28 The news about him **s** quickly
1:38 I have to **s** ⌊the Good News⌋
1:39 So he went to **s** ⌊the Good
1:45 He **s** his story so widely that
3:14 by him to **s** ⌊the Good News⌋.
7:36 the more they **s** the news.
11:8 Many **s** their coats on the road.
11:8 in the fields and **s** them
13:10 News must be **s** to all nations.
16:20 The disciples **s** ⌊the Good
Luk 4:14 and the news about him **s**
4:37 So news about him **s** to every
4:44 So he **s** his message in the
5:15 about Jesus **s** even more.
7:17 This news about Jesus **s**
8:1 He **s** the Good News about
9:2 He sent them to **s** the message
15:14 **s** throughout that country.
19:36 people **s** their coats on the
Jon 21:23 die **s** among Jesus' followers.
Act 4:17 will not **s** any further among
6:7 word of God continued to **s**,
8:4 where they **s** the word.
8:12 However, when Philip **s** the
8:25 they **s** the Good News in many
8:40 through all the cities and **s**
9:20 He immediately began to **s** the
9:42 The news about this **s**
Act 10:37 began in Galilee after John **s**
11:20 They started to **s** the Good
12:24 But God's word continued to **s**
13:5 they began to **s** God's word in
13:49 The word of the Lord **s**
14:7 They **s** the Good News there.
14:21 They **s** the Good News in that
15:21 Moses' words have been **s** to
15:35 word and **s** the Good News.
15:36 back to every city where we **s**
19:29 The confusion **s** throughout the
26:20 Instead, I **s** the message that I
26:20 I **s** the same message to
26:23 back to life and would **s** light
28:31 He **s** the message about God's
Rom 1:1 an apostle and appointed to **s**
5:12 Death **s** to everyone,
9:17 and to **s** my name throughout
10:8 the message of faith that we **s**.
15:20 My goal was to **s** the Good
1Co 1:17 Instead, he sent me to **s** the
9:14 commanded that those who **s**
9:16 If I **s** the Good News,
9:16 me if I don't **s** the Good News!
9:17 If I **s** the Good News willingly,
9:17 But if I **s** the Good News
9:18 It is to **s** the Good News free of
9:18 to those who **s** the Good News.
9:27 be disqualified after I have **s**
2Co 2:12 gave me an opportunity to **s**
9:13 of your commitment to **s**
Gal 1:11 that the Good News I have **s** is
2:2 I showed them the way I **s** the
Eph 3:8 kindness by allowing me to **s**
6:15 so that you are ready to **s**
Php 1:12 helped to **s** the Good News.
2:22 together to **s** the Good News.
4:3 They fought beside me to **s** the
4:15 the province of Macedonia to **s**
Col 1:23 It has been **s** throughout all
1:28 We **s** the message about Christ
1Th 1:8 From you the Lord's word has **s**
2Th 3:1 pray that we **s** the Lord's word
1Ti 2:7 I was appointed to **s** this Good
2Ti 1:11 and to **s** this Good News.
2:17 they say will **s** like cancer.
4:2 Be ready to **s** the word whether
Heb 11:28 to establish the Passover and **s**
1Pe 1:12 known to you by those who **s**
Rev 7:15 the throne will **s** his tent over
14:6 the everlasting Good News to **s**
20:9 ⌊I saw that⌋ they **s** over the

spreading (30)

Lev 13:51 If the spot is **s**, it is unclean.
14:44 If it is a **s** type of mildew,
Num 14:37 about Moses by **s** lies about
22:11 Egypt and are **s** out all over
1Sm 2:24 of the LORD **s** isn't good!
Est 9:4 Moreover, his reputation was **s**
Job 26:9 He covers his throne by **s** his
Psa 37:35 **s** himself out like a large cedar
Pro 29:5 who flatters his neighbor is **s**
Isa 18:5 and chop off the **s** branches.
Jer 25:32 Disaster is **s** from nation to
Act 4:2 were teaching the people and **s**
14:15 We're **s** the Good News to you
17:13 Paul was also **s** God's word
19:20 was **s** and gaining strength.
Rom 1:8 of your faith is **s** throughout
1:9 I serve God by **s** the Good
2:16 use the Good News that I am **s**
15:16 I serve as a priest by **s** the
15:19 I have finished **s** the Good
2Co 10:16 **s** the Good News in the
Gal 1:23 who persecuted us is now **s**
Col 1:6 It is producing results and **s** all
1Th 2:4 Rather, we are always **s** the
3:2 He serves God by **s** the Good
2Ti 2:9 I'm suffering disgrace for **s** this
4:17 strength so that I could finish **s**
Tit 1:3 this in every era by **s** his word.
Phm 1:13 in prison for **s** the Good News.
3Jn 1:8 with them in **s** the truth.

spreads (13)

Exo 22:6 "Whenever a fire starts and **s**
Lev 13:35 But if the scab **s** after the
Dtr 32:11 **s** its wings to catch them,
Psa 97:3 Fire **s** ahead of him.
Pro 6:14 a twisted mind. He **s** conflict.
6:19 who **s** conflict among relatives.
10:18 Whoever **s** slander is a fool.
11:18 but whoever **s** righteousness
16:28 A devious person **s** quarrels.
23:28 **s** unfaithfulness throughout
Isa 40:22 out the sky like a canopy and **s**
1Co 5:6 that a little yeast **s** through
Gal 5:9 A little yeast **s** through the

sprig (6)

Lev 14:4 and a hyssop **s** to use for the
14:6 and the hyssop **s** and dip them
14:49 and a hyssop **s** and use them
14:51 the hyssop **s**, the red yarn,
Num 19:6 some cedar wood, a hyssop **s**,
19:18 clean will take a **s** of hyssop,

spring (51)

Gen 16:7 of the LORD found her by a **s**
16:7 the **s** on the way to Shur.
24:13 Here I am standing by the **s**,
24:16 She went down to the **s**,
24:30 ran out to the man by the **s**.
24:30 with the camels by the **s**.
24:42 "When I came to the **s** today,
24:43 I'm standing by the **s**.
24:45 She went down to the **s** and
49:22 a fruitful tree by a **s**,
Lev 11:36 However, a **s** or a cistern
Num 21:17 "Make your water **s** up!
Dtr 11:14 both in the fall and in the **s**.
33:28 Jacob's **s** will be ⌊left⌋ alone
Jos 15:9 around to the **s** of Nephtoah.
Jdg 15:19 called the place En Hakkore [**S**
1Sm 29:1 camped at the **s** in Jezreel.
2Sm 11:1 In the **s**, the time when kings
1Ki 18:5 to every **s** and stream.
20:22 When **s** comes, the king of
20:26 **S** came, and Benhadad
2Ki 2:21 He went to the **s** and threw the
4:16 "At this time next **s**,
13:20 to invade the country in the **s**.
1Ch 20:1 In the **s**, the time when kings
2Ch 33:14 of David from west of Gihon **S**
36:10 In the **s** King Nebuchadnezzar
Job 29:23 as if waiting for a **s** shower.
Psa 114:8 flint into a **s** flowing with water.
Pro 5:16 water flow out of your **s**?
16:15 is like a cloud bringing **s** rain.
25:26 ⌊Like⌋ a muddied **s** and a
Ecc 12:6 pitcher is smashed near the **s**,
Sos 4:12 is locked, a **s** that is sealed.
4:15 ⌊You are⌋ a **s** for gardens,
Isa 44:4 They will **s** up with the grass
44:4 as poplars **s** up by streams.
45:8 Let them **s** up. I, the LORD,
58:11 and like a **s** whose water does
61:11 righteousness and praise **s** up
Jer 3:3 there have been no **s** showers.
5:24 the autumn rain and the **s** rain.
33:15 a righteous branch to **s** up
Hos 6:3 rains and the **s** rains that water
10:4 That's why lawsuits **s** up like
Joe 2:23 rain and the **s** rain as before.
3:18 A **s** will flow from the LORD's
Amo 3:5 Does a trap **s** up from the
Jon 4:14 in them a **s** that gushes up
Jas 3:11 water flow out of the same **s**?
5:7 patiently for fall and **s** rains.

spring-fed (1)

Gen 26:19 the valley and found a **s** well.

springing (1)

Act 3:8 **S** to his feet, he stood up and

springs (40)

Gen 7:11 all the deep **s** burst open.
8:2 The deep **s** and the sky had

Gen 36:24 (Anah found the hot **s** in the
49:25 blessings from the deep **s**
Exo 15:27 where there were 12 **s** and 70
Num 33:9 Elim had 12 **s** and 70 palm
Dtr 8:7 There are **s** and underground
33:13 and deep **s** below the ground.
Jos 11:5 kings camped together by the **S**
11:7 troops arrived suddenly at the **S**
15:7 Then the border passes the **S**
15:19 also give me some **s**."
15:19 gave her the upper and lower **s**.
16:1 Jordan River at Jericho to the **s**
18:15 to the **s** of Nephtoah.
Jdg 1:15 also give me some **s**."
1:15 gave her the upper and lower **s**.
2Ch 32:3 flowing out of the **s** outside
32:4 as they stopped all the **s**
Job 38:16 Have you gone to the **s** in the
Psa 74:15 You opened the **s** and brooks.
84:6 they make it a place of **s**.
104:10 water gush from **s** into valleys.
107:33 **s** into thirsty ground,
107:35 lakes and dry ground into **s**.
Pro 8:24 there were **s** filled with water.
Isa 12:3 water from the **s** of salvation.
35:7 and dry ground will have **s**.
41:18 I will make **s** flow through
41:18 I will turn dry land into **s**.
49:10 lead them and guide them to **s**.
Jer 51:36 sea and make its **s** dry.
Eze 31:4 and underground **s** made it tall.
31:15 I covered the underground **s**
Hos 13:15 Then their **s** will run dry,
2Pe 2:17 false teachers are dried-up **s**.
Rev 7:17 He will lead them to **s** filled
8:10 of the rivers and on the **s**.
14:7 and earth, the sea and **s**."
16:4 bowl over the rivers and the **s**.

springtime (1)
Zec 10:1 Ask the LORD for rain in the **s**.

sprinkle (19)
Exo 29:21 and **s** it on Aaron and his
Lev 4:6 dip his finger in it and **s** some
4:17 in some of the blood and **s**
5:9 He will **s** some of the blood
14:7 He will **s** the blood seven
14:16 and with his finger **s** some of
14:27 With his right finger he will **s**
14:51 He must **s** the house seven
16:14 some of the bull's blood and **s**
16:14 Then he will **s** some of the
16:15 and **s** it on the throne of mercy
16:19 With his finger he will **s** some
Num 8:7 **S** them with water to take
19:4 the blood with his finger and **s**
19:18 it in the water, and **s** the tent,
19:18 He must also **s** any person
19:19 A person who is clean will **s**
2Ki 16:15 **S** all the blood of the burnt
Eze 36:25 I will **s** clean water on you and

sprinkled (18)
Exo 24:8 Moses took the blood and **s** it
Lev 8:11 He **s** some of the oil on the
8:30 **s** it on Aaron and his clothes
Num 19:13 uncleanness wasn't **s** on him.
19:20 uncleanness wasn't **s** on him.
2Ki 16:13 and **s** the blood of his
2Ch 29:22 and the priests **s** the blood on
29:22 slaughtered the rams and **s**
29:22 slaughtered the lambs and **s**
30:16 The priests **s** the blood they
35:11 The priests **s** the blood with
Pro 7:17 I've **s** my bed with myrrh,
Heb 9:13 bulls and the ashes of cows **s**
9:19 and hyssop and **s** the scroll
9:21 In the same way, Moses **s**
10:22 We have been **s** ⌊with his
12:24 and to the **s** blood that speaks
1Pe 1:2 to Jesus Christ and are **s**

sprinkles (1)
Num 19:21 "Whoever **s** the water to take

sprinkling (2)
Eze 43:18 burnt offerings and for **s** blood
Zec 9:15 a sacrificial bowl ⌊used for **s**⌋

sprint (1)
Job 9:25 They **s** away. They don't see

sprinting (1)
Sos 2:8 **s** over the mountains,

sprout (13)
Job 5:6 doesn't **s** from the ground.
8:19 and others **s** from the same
14:7 It will **s** again. Its shoots will
14:9 a scent of water will make it **s**
38:27 order to make it **s** with grass?
Psa 90:5 They **s** again in the morning
90:6 morning they blossom and **s**.
92:7 that wicked people **s** like grass
132:17 There I will make a horn **s** up
Isa 17:11 you will make it **s**.
45:8 salvation and righteousness **s**.
55:10 They make it **s** and grow so
Mar 4:27 The seeds **s** and grow,

sprouted (8)
Gen 40:10 Soon after it **s** it blossomed.
41:6 the east wind, **s** behind them.
41:23 the east wind, **s** behind them.
2Ki 19:26 scorched before it **s**.
Eze 17:6 The plant **s** and grew into a
Mat 13:5 The plants **s** quickly because
Mar 4:5 The plants **s** quickly because
4:8 **s**, and produced thirty, sixty,

sprouting (1)
Job 14:7 Its shoots will not stop **s**.

sprouts (3)
Psa 85:11 Truth **s** from the ground,
Mat 24:32 tender and it **s** leaves,
Mar 13:28 tender and it **s** leaves,

spun (1)
Exo 35:26 had the skill **s** the goats' hair.

spurs (1)
Ecc 12:11 from wise people are like **s**.

spy (13)
Jdg 1:23 They sent men to **s** on Bethel.
18:2 They were sent to **s** throughout
18:14 who had gone to **s** throughout
18:17 who had gone to **s** throughout
2Sm 10:3 city, **s** on it, and destroy it?"
2Ki 6:11 tell me who among us is ⌊a **s**⌋
1Ch 19:3 and **s** on the country?"
Psa 5:8 because of those who **s** on me.
27:11 I have enemies who **s** on me.
54:5 My enemies **s** on me.
56:2 day long my enemies **s** on me.
59:10 gloat over those who **s** on me.
92:11 gloat over those who **s** on me.

spying (1)
Job 7:20 you insist on **s** on people?

squad (1)
1Ch 26:16 One **s** of guards served its

squads (1)
Act 12:4 with sixteen soldiers in **s**

square (37)
Gen 19:2 spend the night in the city **s**."
Exo 27:1 It should be 7 ½ feet **s**,
28:16 it in half so that it's 9 inches **s**.
30:2 Make it 18 inches **s** and 36
37:25 It was 18 inches **s** and 36
38:1 out of acacia wood 7 ½ feet **s**
39:9 in half and was 9 inches **s**.
Dtr 13:16 into the middle of the city **s**.
Jdg 19:15 and sat down in the city **s**,
19:17 saw the traveler in the city **s**.
19:20 spend the night in the city **s**."
2Sm 21:12 stolen them from the public **s**
1Ki 6:33 In the same way he made **s**
7:5 doors and doorframes were **s**.
7:27 Each stand was 6 feet **s** and 4
7:31 But the panels **w** square,
2Ch 29:4 and Levites together in the **s**
32:6 the commanders in the **s** by
Est 4:6 out to Mordecai in the city **s**
6:9 ride on the horse in the city **s**.
6:11 and had him ride in the city **s**,
Job 29:7 and took my seat in the town **s**,
Eze 16:24 worship sites in every city **s**.
16:31 illegal worship sites in every **s**.
40:12 guardrooms were 10 ½ feet **s**.
40:47 It was a perfect **s** — 175 feet
41:21 in the holy place were **s**.
43:16 It was **s**, 21 feet wide and 21
43:17 The upper ledge was also **s**.
45:2 An area of 875 feet **s** will be for
48:20 area will be 43,750 feet **s**.
Dan 9:25 and rebuilt with a city **s**
Amo 5:16 be loud crying in every city **s**,
Act 16:19 the authorities in the public **s**.
17:5 who hung around the public **s**,
17:17 every day in the public **s**
Rev 21:16 The city was **s**. It was as wide

squares (5)
Pro 1:20 In the public **s** she raises her
Sos 3:2 city, in the streets, and in the **s**.
Isa 15:3 On their roofs and in their city **s**
Jer 5:1 Search the city **s**. See if you
Nah 2:4 this way and that in the city **s**.

squat (1)
Dtr 23:13 When you go outside to **s**,

squeal (1)
Jer 13:27 adultery and **s** with delight.

squeezed (3)
Gen 40:11 so I took the grapes and **s** them
Jdg 6:38 He **s** out a bowl full of water
Sos 8:2 juice **s** from my pomegranates.

stab (7)
1Sm 26:8 him to the ground with one **s**
31:4 **S** me, or these godless men
31:4 **s** me, and make fun of me."
1Ch 10:4 **S** me, or these godless men
Pro 12:18 Careless words **s** like a sword,
Isa 51:9 into pieces and **s** the serpent?
Zec 13:3 will **s** him when he prophesies.

stabbed (11)
2Sm 3:27 There he **s** Abner in the belly.
4:6 Instead, they **s** him in the belly.
4:7 They **s** him, killed him, and cut
20:10 Joab **s** him in the stomach,
20:10 (He died without being **s** again.)
Job 26:13 hand he **s** the fleeing snake.
Isa 13:15 is found will be **s** to death.
Lam 4:9 Those who were **s** bled to
Zec 12:10 whom they have **s**.
Jon 19:34 However, one of the soldiers **s**
19:37 the person whom they have **s**."

stabs (2)
2Ki 18:21 If you lean on it, it **s** your hand
Isa 36:6 If you lean on it, it **s** your hand

Stachys (1)
Rom 16:9 and my dear friend **S**.

stack (2)
Lev 24:7 pure incense on top of each **s**.
Job 5:26 grave at a ripe old age like a **s**

stacked (2)
Exo 22:6 underbrush so that it burns up **s**
Jdg 15:5 whether it was **s** or in the

stacks (1)
Lev 24:6 Put them in two **s** of six each

stadia (2)

Rev 14:20 as a horse's bridle for 1,600 s.
21:16 It was 12,000 s long.

staff (65)

Gen 32:10 I only had a shepherd's s when
38:18 and the shepherd's s that's in
38:25 and shepherd's s these are."
49:10 nor a ruler's s from between his
50:4 to the Pharaoh's palace s.
50:7 the leaders in his palace s,
Exo 4:2 He answered, "A shepherd's s."
4:4 and it turned back into a s as
4:17 that shepherd's s with you,
4:20 He also brought with him the s
7:9 'Take your shepherd's s and
7:10 Aaron threw his s down in front
7:12 Each of them threw his s down,
7:12 But Aaron's s swallowed theirs.
7:15 Take along the s that turned
7:17 With this s in my hand,
7:19 'Take your s and stretch out
7:20 Aaron raised his s and struck
8:5 'Hold your s over the rivers,
8:6 So Aaron held his s over the
8:16 'Hold out your s and strike the
8:17 Aaron held out the s in his
9:23 When Moses lifted his s
10:13 Moses held his s over the land
12:11 and your shepherd's s in your
14:16 Raise your s, stretch out your
17:5 Take the s you used to strike
17:9 I will hold in my hand the s
Num 17:2 each man's name on his s.
17:3 Write Aaron's name on the s for
17:3 because there must be one s
17:5 The s from the man I choose
17:6 Aaron's s was among them.
17:8 He found that Aaron's s for the
17:9 and each man took his s.
17:10 "Put Aaron's s back in front of
20:8 "Take your s, then you and
20:9 Moses took his s out of ⌊the
20:11 hit the rock twice with the s.
Jdg 6:21 with the tip of the s that was
1Sm 14:27 he stretched out the tip of the s
14:43 a little honey on the tip of the s
2Sm 6:20 girls of his palace s — like
1Ki 22:3 The king of Israel asked his s,
2Ki 4:29 take my shepherd's s in your
4:29 Lay my s on the boy's face."
4:31 ahead of them and put the s
18:21 trusting a broken stick for a s.
2Ch 32:3 and his military s made plans
Est 2:2 So the king's personal s said to
6:3 The king's personal s replied,
6:5 The king's s answered him,
Psa 23:4 and your s give me courage.
Isa 10:5 My fury is the s in the
10:24 raise their s against you as
10:26 of Oreb and raised his s over
14:5 The LORD has broken the s of
36:6 trusting a broken stick for a s.
Jer 48:17 Say, 'Look at the strong s,
Eze 12:14 who are around him — his s
Mic 7:14 With your shepherd's s,
Zec 11:10 Then I took my s called Favor
11:14 Then I broke my second s,
Heb 9:4 Aaron's s that had blossomed,
11:21 of his s and worshiped God.

staffs (6)

Num 17:2 and get 12 s from them,
17:6 Their leaders gave him 12 s,
17:7 Moses put the s in the LORD's
17:9 Moses brought out the s from
21:18 with their scepters and s."
Zec 11:7 I took two shepherd s and

stag (3)

Sos 2:9 is like a gazelle or a young s.
2:17 Run like a gazelle or a young s
8:14 Run like a gazelle or a young s

stagger (12)

Psa 60:3 given us wine that makes us s.
Isa 24:19 violently. The earth will s.
28:7 Priests and prophets s from
28:7 They s from too much liquor
28:7 They s when they see visions.
29:9 You s, but not from liquor.
51:17 the cup that makes people s,
51:22 the cup that makes people s,
Jer 25:16 they will s and go insane
Lam 5:13 and ⌊our⌋ boys s under loads
Nah 3:11 will s like a drunk.
Zec 12:2 all the surrounding people s.

staggered (3)

Psa 107:27 They reeled and s like drunks,
Lam 4:14 My people s blindly through the
Amo 4:8 or three cities s as they walked

staggering (1)

Pro 24:11 those s toward their slaughter.

staggers (2)

Psa 31:10 My strength s under ⌊the
Isa 19:14 like a drunk who s in his vomit.

stain (2)

Zec 13:1 wash away ⌊their⌋ sin and s.
Eph 5:27 without any kind of s or wrinkle

stained (10)

1Ki 2:5 With their blood he s the belt
Job 31:7 or my hands are s ⌊with sin⌋,
Psa 7:3 my hands are s with injustice,
Isa 59:3 Your hands are s with blood,
59:3 and your fingers are s with sin.
63:1 with his clothes s bright red?
63:3 so all my clothing has been s.
64:6 are like permanently s rags.
Hos 6:8 It is s with bloody footprints.
Jud 1:23 you might be s by their sinful

stains (4)

Isa 30:22 away like clothing ruined by s.
Jer 2:22 I would still see the s from your
2Pe 2:13 teachers are s and blemishes.
3:14 ⌊spiritual⌋ s or blemishes.

staircase (1)

1Ki 6:8 A s went up to the middle story

stairs (8)

Exo 20:26 Never use s to go up to my
2Ki 9:13 and laid it on the s below him.
Neh 3:15 as far as the s going down from
9:4 and Chanani stood on the s
12:37 they went straight up the s
Amo 9:6 The one who builds s up to
Act 21:35 When Paul came to the s of the
21:40 So Paul stood on the s of the

stairway (5)

Gen 28:12 in which he saw a s set up
2Ki 20:11 down on Ahaz's s go back up
Isa 38:8 a shadow that went down the s
38:8 So the sun on the s went back
Eze 41:7 A s went from the first story

stalk (3)

Gen 41:5 were growing on a single s.
41:22 of grain growing on a single s.
Psa 129:6 dries up before it produces a s.

stall (4)

1Sm 6:7 and leave them in their s.
6:10 and shut the calves in the s.
Mal 4:2 leap like calves let out of a s.
Luk 13:15 you then take it out of its s

stallions (4)

Sos 1:9 to a mare among Pharaoh's s.
Jer 5:8 They are like well-fed s that
8:16 The neighing of s makes the
50:11 on the grass and neigh like s.

stalls (5)

1Ki 4:26 Solomon had s for 40,000
2Ch 9:25 Solomon had 4,000 s for
32:28 his cattle and s for his flocks.
Amo 6:4 flocks and calves from their s.
Hab 3:17 empty and the s have no cattle

stamped (1)

Job 38:14 The earth changes like clay s

stand (290)

Gen 4:13 is more than I can s!
27:46 "I can't s Hittite women!
31:44 an agreement and let it s as
31:52 this marker s as witnesses that
47:7 his father Jacob and had him s
Exo 1:12 couldn't s them ⌊any longer⌋.
8:20 s in Pharaoh's way when he's
14:13 S still, and see what the LORD
17:9 Tomorrow I will s on top of the
18:14 while all the people s around
25:31 "Make a lamp s out of pure
25:31 The lamp s, its base, and its
25:33 coming out of the lamp s is
25:34 The lamp s itself is to have
25:35 coming out of the lamp s.
25:36 of pure gold as the lamp s.
25:37 and set them on the lamp s so
25:39 of pure gold to make the lamp s
26:35 and put the lamp s opposite the
30:18 with a bronze s for washing.
30:27 the lamp s and all the utensils,
30:28 and the basin with its s.
31:8 the pure ⌊gold⌋ lamp s and all
31:9 the basin with its s,
33:8 all the people would rise and s
33:21 S by this rocky cliff.
34:2 and s in my presence on the
35:14 the lamp s used for the light
35:16 the basin with its s,
37:17 He made the lamp s out of pure
37:17 The lamp s, its base, and its
37:19 of the lamp s had three flower
37:20 The lamp s itself had four
37:21 coming out of the lamp s.
37:22 of pure gold as the lamp s.
37:24 The lamp s and all the utensils
38:8 He made the basin and s out of
39:37 the pure ⌊gold⌋ lamp s with its
39:39 the basin with its s,
40:4 Bring in the lamp s,
40:11 Anoint the basin and s,
40:24 He placed the lamp s in the
Lev 8:11 with its s to dedicate them.
20:23 I cannot s them because they
24:2 virgin olive oil for the lamp s
24:4 on the pure gold lamp s lit
26:37 They will not be able to s up to
27:8 pay the required amount must s
Num 3:6 and have them s in front of the
3:31 the table, the lamp s, the altars,
4:9 cloth and cover the lamp s,
4:10 Then they will put the lamp s
5:16 the woman come forward and s
5:30 He will make his wife s in the
8:2 the seven lamps on the lamp s,
8:3 set up the lamps on the lamp s
8:4 is how the lamp s was made:
8:4 The whole lamp s,
8:13 Make the Levites s in front of
11:16 and have them s with you.
11:24 and had them s around the tent.
11:29 "Do you think you need to s up
16:9 to do the work for his tent and s
21:5 and we can't s this awful food!"
22:3 couldn't s these people.
23:18 "S up, Balak, and listen!
25:11 I didn't have to s up for myself
27:19 Make him s in front of the priest
27:21 He will s in front of the priest
27:22 took Joshua and made him s
Dtr 2:5 land — not even enough to s on.
10:8 to s in the LORD's presence
19:16 a witness takes the s
19:17 two people involved must s

Dtr 27:12 these are the tribes that will **s**
27:13 These are the tribes that will **s**
Jos 3:8 of the Jordan River, **s** there.'"
3:13 will **s** in the water of the
3:13 will stop and **s** up like
10:8 None of them can **s** up to you."
10:12 **s** still over Gibeon,
10:12 **s** still over the valley of
20:4 There he will **s** at the entrance
20:6 in that city until he can **s** trial
22:27 but it will **s** as a witness
22:27 It will **s** as a witness that we
22:28 or sacrifices but to **s** as
23:9 ever been able to **s** up to you.
24:27 "This stone will **s** as a witness
24:27 It will **s** as a witness for you.
Jdg 2:14 They could no longer **s** up
4:20 "**S** at the door of the tent.
5:7 took a **s** — took a stand as a
5:7 took a stand — took a **s** as a
16:25 him **s** between two columns.
1Sm 6:20 "Who can **s** before the LORD,
10:19 Now then, **s** in front of the
12:7 Now, **s** up while I put you on
12:16 Now then, **s** still and watch
14:40 "You **s** on one side,
14:40 my son Jonathan and I will **s**
19:3 I'll go out and **s** beside my
20:38 Don't **s** there!"
2Sm 1:9 'Please **s** over me and kill me.
15:2 used to get up early and **s** by
18:30 "Step aside, and **s** here,"
1Ki 7:27 Each **s** was 6 feet square and
7:30 Each **s** had four bronze wheels
7:32 axles were attached to the **s**.
7:34 four corners of each **s** were part
7:34 each stand were part of the **s**.
7:35 The top of each **s** had a round,
7:35 Above the **s** were supports
19:11 God said, "Go out and **s** in
2Ki 4:10 and lamp **s** there for him.
5:11 ⌊of his house⌋, **s** somewhere,
10:4 "If two kings couldn't **s** up to
10:4 how can we **s** up to him?"
1Ch 23:28 They were appointed to **s**
23:30 They were appointed to **s** to
23:31 They were appointed to **s** in
28:15 weight of gold for each lamp **s**
28:15 of silver for each silver lamp **s**
28:15 of each lamp **s** for worship),
2Ch 13:11 The lamps on the gold lamp **s**
20:9 we will **s** in front of this temple
20:17 take your position, **s** still,
29:11 The LORD has chosen you to **s**
29:25 He had the Levites **s** in the
35:5 **S** in the holy place
Ezr 9:15 None of us can **s** in your
Neh 7:3 men in Jerusalem to **s** guard,
9:5 and Pethahiah — said, "**S** up,
Est 9:2 No one could **s** up against
Job 1:6 the sons of God came to **s**
2:1 the sons of God came to **s**
4:15 It made my hair **s** on end.
19:18 If I **s** up, they make fun of me.
30:20 I **s** up, but you just look at me.
30:28 I **s** up in public and call for
32:16 because they **s** there and don't
33:5 case to me, and take your **s**.
33:6 I **s** in front of God as you do.
38:14 and ⌊parts of it⌋ **s** out like
41:10 Then who can **s** in front of me?
Psa 1:5 people will not be able to **s**
1:5 to **s** where righteous people
5:5 Those who brag cannot **s** in
7:6 **S** up against the fury of my
20:8 but we will rise and **s** firm.
22:23 **S** in awe of him, all you
24:3 Who may **s** in his holy place?
26:12 My feet **s** on level ground.
30:7 have made my mountain **s** firm.
33:8 Let all who live in the world **s**
33:11 His thoughts **s** firm in every
36:12 and are unable to **s** up again.
38:11 and my relatives **s** far away
48:8 God makes Zion **s** firm forever.
69:2 There is nothing to **s** on.
Psa 76:7 Who can **s** in your presence
78:13 He made the waters **s** up like a
84:10 I would rather **s** in the entrance
89:14 Mercy and truth **s** in front of
89:37 his throne will **s** firm forever.
94:16 Who will **s** up for me against
94:16 Who will **s** by my side against
109:6 Let Satan **s** beside him.
119:90 and it continues to **s**.
119:91 All things continue to **s** today
130:3 who would be able to **s** if you
134:1 all who **s** in the house of the
Pro 8:2 ⌊Wisdom⌋ takes its **s** on high
12:3 A person cannot **s** firm on a
12:7 righteous people continue to **s**.
21:30 and no advice ⌊can **s** up⌋
25:6 yourself in front of a king or **s**
31:28 Her children and her husband **s**
Isa 1:13 I can't **s** your evil assemblies.
11:10 time the root of Jesse will **s** as
21:8 The watchman called, "Sir, I **s**
21:8 I **s** guard at my post.
22:7 and horsemen will **s** ready in
28:18 with the grave will not **s**.
29:23 They will **s** in terror of the God
32:8 people act honorably and **s** firm
44:11 all get together and take their **s**.
46:10 saying, "My plan will **s**,
48:13 I call for them, they both **s**.
49:7 Kings will see ⌊you⌋ and **s**.
51:17 **S** up, Jerusalem! You drank
Jer 1:17 **S** up, and say to them
1:18 You will be able to **s** up to the
1:18 You will be able to **s** up to
4:6 Don't just **s** there! I'm bringing
6:16 **S** at the crossroads and look.
7:2 "**S** at the gate of the LORD's
7:10 Then you **s** in my presence in
14:6 Wild donkeys **s** on the bare
15:19 you will **s** in my presence.
17:19 **S** at People's Gate,
17:19 Then **s** at every gate in
26:2 is what the LORD says: **S**
46:15 They can't **s** because the
46:21 They won't **s** their ground.
48:19 **S** by the road in Aroer,
48:45 "Those who flee will **s**
49:19 leader who can **s** up to me?"
50:44 leader who can **s** up to me?
51:50 Don't just **s** there.
Eze 2:1 **s** up, and I will speak to you."
22:30 you who could build walls or **s**
31:14 will ever **s** that tall.
39:25 I will **s** up for my holy name.
44:15 and they may **s** in my
46:2 He must **s** by the doorposts of
Dan 5:5 wall opposite the lamp **s**
7:4 It was made to **s** on two feet
8:4 No other animal could **s** in front
8:7 the strength to **s** up against
8:18 touched me and made me **s** up.
10:11 **S** up, because I've been sent to
12:1 will **s** up on behalf of the
Amo 2:15 Archers will not **s** their ground.
Oba 1:14 Don't **s** at the crossroads to kill
Mic 6:1 the LORD is saying, "**S** up!
Nah 1:6 Who can **s** in the presence of
Hab 2:1 I will **s** at my guard post.
3:11 The sun and the moon **s** still.
3:16 I tremble where I **s**.
Zep 3:8 One day I will **s** up as a
Zec 4:2 "I see a solid gold lamp **s** with
4:11 the left of the lamp **s** mean?"
5:11 set the basket there on a **s**."
11:16 or support those that can still **s**.
14:4 On that day his feet will **s** on
Mat 4:5 into the holy city and had him **s**
5:15 a lamp puts it on a lamp **s**.
6:5 They like to **s** in synagogues
10:13 allow your greeting to **s**.
12:41 The men of Nineveh will **s** up
12:42 The queen from the south will **s**
18:2 and had him **s** among them.
24:15 will cause destruction will **s**
Mar 3:3 "**S** in the center ⌊of the
4:21 Isn't it put on a lamp **s**?
Mar 9:27 hand and helped him to **s** up.
9:36 and had him **s** among them.
13:9 You will **s** in front of governors
Luk 1:19 I **s** in God's presence.
4:9 into Jerusalem and had him **s**
6:8 and **s** in the center ⌊of the
8:16 it on a lamp **s** so that those
9:47 and had him **s** beside him.
11:31 The queen from the south will **s**
11:32 The men of Nineveh will **s** up
11:33 it on a lamp **s** so that those
13:8 let it **s** for one more year.
13:11 over and couldn't **s** up straight.
13:25 You can **s** outside,
21:28 **s** with confidence!
21:36 that is about to happen and to **s**
Jon 8:3 They made her **s** in front of
18:25 Simon Peter continued to **s**
Act 4:7 They made Peter and John **s** in
4:26 Kings take their **s**.
5:20 "**S** in the temple courtyard,
5:27 they made them **s** in front of the
6:6 The disciples had these men **s**
9:41 her hand and helped her **s** up.
10:26 He told him, "**S** up!
14:10 said in a loud voice, "**S** up."
22:30 brought Paul and had him **s**
26:2 I think I'm fortunate today to **s**
26:16 **S** up! I have appeared to you for
26:22 me to this day so that I can **s**
Rom 5:2 we can approach God and **s**
14:10 Everyone will **s** in front of God
Eph 6:11 In this way you can take a **s**
6:13 to take a **s** during these evil
6:13 will be able to **s** your ground.
6:14 So then, take your **s**!
Heb 9:2 The lamp **s**, the table, and the
Jas 2:3 to the poor man, "**S** over there,"
Jud 1:24 you can be full of joy as you **s**
Rev 2:5 take your lamp **s** from its place
8:2 I saw the seven angels who **s**
11:1 I was told, "**S** up and measure
18:10 they will **s** far away and say,
18:15 these things will **s** far away.

standard (37)

Exo 16:36 (Now, the **s** dry measure at that
30:13 of silver using the **s** weight
30:24 all weighed using the **s** weight
38:24 using the **s** weight of the holy
38:25 using the **s** weight of the holy
Lev 27:3 Use the **s** weight of the holy
27:25 will be set using the **s** weight
Num 3:47 per person (using the **s** weight
3:50 using the **s** weight of the holy
7:13 using the **s** weight of the holy
7:19 ¾ pounds using the **s** weight
7:25 ¾ pounds using the **s** weight
7:31 ¾ pounds using the **s** weight
7:37 ¾ pounds using the **s** weight
7:43 ¾ pounds using the **s** weight
7:49 ¾ pounds using the **s** weight
7:55 ¾ pounds using the **s** weight
7:61 ¾ pounds using the **s** weight
7:67 ¾ pounds using the **s** weight
7:73 ¾ pounds using the **s** weight
7:79 ¾ pounds using the **s** weight
7:85 using the **s** weight of the holy
7:86 using the **s** weight of the holy
18:16 using the **s** weight of the holy
Dtr 28:43 The ⌊**s** of living for the⌋
28:43 while your ⌊**s** of living⌋ will
2Sm 14:26 according to the royal **s**.
2Ch 3:3 (They used the old **s**
Pro 20:10 A double **s** of weights and
20:23 A double **s** of weights is
31:5 have decreed and change the **s**
Eze 45:11 The homer must be the **s**
45:14 olive oil using the **s** measure.
Mat 7:2 be judged by the same **s** you
Rom 7:23 However, I see a different **s** ⌊at
Eph 4:13 up to Christ, who is the **s**.
Jas 2:4 a corrupt **s** to make judgments?

standards (33)

Lev 5:15 according to the official **s**

Lev 18:3 Never live by their **s**.
18:4 my rules, and live by my **s**.
18:5 Live by my **s**, and obey my
18:26 Live by my **s**, and obey my
18:30 Don't live by the **s** of the people
Eze 5:7 haven't even lived up to the **s**
11:12 You have followed the **s** set by
Mal 3:14 do we gain if we meet his **s**
Mat 7:2 The **s** you use for others will
Luk 6:38 The **s** you use for others will
Rom 7:14 know that God's **s** are spiritual,
7:16 I agree that God's **s** are good.
7:21 to do what God's **s** say is good.
7:22 I take pleasure in God's **s** in
7:23 It is at war with the **s** my mind
7:23 to sin's **s** which still exist
7:25 So I am obedient to God's **s**
7:25 but I am obedient to sin's **s**
8:2 The **s** of the Spirit,
8:2 have set you free from the **s** of
8:3 to do what God's **s** demand
8:4 are able to meet God's **s**.
8:7 of God's **s** because it can't.
1Co 3:3 nature and living by human **s**?
15:56 and God's **s** give sin its power.
Gal 2:16 to live according to a set of **s**,
2:16 to live according to a set of **s**.
2:19 I tried to obey the law's **s**,
3:2 to live according to a set of **s**
3:10 to live according to a set of **s**
3:11 by obeying the law's **s** since,
Php 3:5 When it comes to living up to **s**,

standing (163)

Gen 18:2 he saw three men **s** near him.
18:22 but Abraham remained **s** in
24:13 Here I am **s** by the spring,
24:30 came to the man, who was **s**
24:31 Why are you **s** out here?
24:43 I'm **s** by the spring.
28:13 The LORD was **s** above it,
37:7 It remained **s** while your
41:1 He dreamed he was **s** by the
41:17 "In my dream I was **s** on the
45:1 who was **s** around him,
Exo 3:5 where you are **s** is holy ground.
10:5 every tree still **s** in the fields.
17:6 I'll be **s** in front of you there by
22:6 it burns up stacked or **s** grain
26:32 **s** in four silver sockets.
33:10 saw the column of smoke **s** at
Num 16:27 had come out and were **s** at
22:23 the Messenger of the LORD **s**
22:31 of the LORD who was **s**
22:34 I didn't know you were **s** there
23:6 found him **s** beside his burnt
23:17 found him **s** beside his burnt
Dtr 29:10 All of you are **s** here today in
29:15 It is for those of you who are **s**
Jos 4:10 who carried the ark remained **s**
5:13 he looked up and saw a man **s**
5:15 place where you are **s** is holy."
8:33 and judges were **s** on opposite
22:19 The LORD's tent is **s** here.
Jdg 6:31 said to everyone **s** around him,
9:6 to the oak tree that was still **s**
1Sm 17:26 the men who were **s** near him,
22:6 all his officials **s** around him.
22:9 **s** with Saul's officials,
22:17 to the runners **s** around him.
2Sm 13:31 All his servants were **s** beside
1Ki 8:8 in the holy place by anyone **s**
8:14 of Israel while they were **s**.
13:1 Jeroboam was **s** at the altar to
13:24 The donkey and the lion were **s**
13:25 on the road and the lion **s** by
13:28 donkey and the lion **s** beside it.
22:19 army of heaven was **s** near him
2Ki 9:17 The watchman **s** on the tower
11:14 She looked, and the king was **s**
13:6 remained **s** in Samaria.
1Ch 21:15 of the LORD was **s** by
21:16 of the LORD **s** between heaven
2Ch 5:9 in the holy place by anyone **s**
6:3 from Israel while they were **s**.
7:6 The priests were **s** at their
2Ch 7:6 while all Israel was **s** ⌊there⌋.
18:18 entire army of heaven was **s**
20:13 and children were **s** in front of
23:13 She looked, and the king was **s**
Neh 7:3 ⌊gatekeepers⌋ are still **s** there,
8:5 Ezra, **s** higher than all the other
8:7 people while they were **s** there.
12:25 and Akkub were gatekeepers **s**
Est 5:2 the king saw Queen Esther **s**
6:5 "Haman happens to be **s** in the
7:9 is still **s** at Haman's house."
Psa 122:2 Our feet are **s** inside your
135:2 who are **s** in the house of the
Isa 6:2 Angels were **s** above him.
7:9 you won't remain **s**.
27:9 or incense altars are left **s**.
Jer 3:9 adultery with **s** stones
15:1 if Moses and Samuel were **s**
28:5 the priests and all the people **s**
36:21 all the officials **s** by the king.
44:15 the women who were **s** there,
Lam 3:63 Whether they are sitting or **s**,
Eze 3:23 The LORD's glory was **s** there
8:11 was **s** with the leaders.
10:3 The angels were **s** on the
43:6 the man was **s** beside me.
44:12 But they served the people by **s**
47:10 to En Eglaim people will be **s**
Dan 7:16 I went to someone who was **s**
8:3 and saw a single ram **s** beside
8:6 ram that I had seen **s** beside
8:15 who looked like a man **s**
10:16 I said to the person **s** in front of
12:5 I saw two men **s** there.
Amo 7:7 The Lord was **s** by a wall built
9:1 I saw the Lord **s** by the altar,
Zec 1:8 He was **s** among the myrtle
1:10 The man **s** among the myrtle
1:11 of the LORD **s** among
3:1 **s** in front of the Messenger of
3:1 Satan the Accuser was **s** at
3:3 filthy clothes and was **s**
3:4 said to those who were **s**
3:5 of the LORD was **s** there.
3:7 to walk among those **s** here.
4:14 ones who are **s** beside
6:5 They are going out after **s** in
14:12 flesh will rot while they are **s**
Mat 12:46 and brothers were **s** outside.
12:47 and your brothers are **s** outside.
16:4 Then he left them **s** there and
16:28 Some people who are **s** here
20:3 he saw others **s** in the
20:6 found some others **s** around.
20:6 'Why are you **s** here all day
26:73 After a little while the men **s**
27:47 When some of the people **s**
Mar 9:1 Some people who are **s** here
11:5 some men **s** there asked them,
13:14 will cause destruction **s** where
14:47 One of those **s** there pulled out
14:69 to those who were **s** around,
14:70 After a little while the men **s**
15:35 When some of the people **s**
Luk 5:1 One day Jesus was **s** by the
8:20 and your brothers are **s** outside.
9:27 Some people who are **s** here
9:32 and the two men **s** with him.
18:13 "But the tax collector was **s** at
Jon 1:26 you don't know is **s** among you.
1:35 The next day John was **s** with
7:37 Jesus was **s** ⌊in the temple
11:42 that the crowd **s** around me will
12:29 The crowd **s** there heard the
18:5 was **s** with the crowd.
18:16 was **s** outside the gate.
18:18 and the guards were **s** around
18:18 Peter was **s** there,
18:22 one of the guards **s** near Jesus
19:25 were **s** beside Jesus' cross.
19:26 whom he loved **s** there.
20:14 around and saw Jesus **s** there.
Act 1:11 from Galilee **s** here looking at
4:14 the man who was healed **s**
5:9 buried your husband are **s** at
5:23 locked and the guards **s** at
Act 5:25 men you put in prison are **s**
7:33 where you're **s** is holy ground.
11:13 us that he had seen an angel **s**
12:14 "Peter is **s** at the door!"
13:50 devout women of high social **s**
22:20 was being killed, I was **s** there.
22:25 the sergeant who was **s** there,
23:2 ordered the men **s** near Paul
23:4 The men **s** near Paul said to
25:10 Paul said, "I am **s** in the
1Co 10:12 So, people who think they are **s**
Jas 5:9 that the judge is **s** at the door.
Rev 3:20 I'm **s** at the door and knocking.
4:1 things I saw a door **s** open
5:6 I saw a lamb **s** in the center
7:1 After this I saw four angels **s** at
7:9 They were **s** in front of the
10:5 The angel whom I saw **s** on
10:8 the hand of the angel who is **s**
11:4 and the two lamp stands **s**
14:1 I looked, and the lamb was **s**
15:2 the number of its name were **s**
19:11 I saw heaven **s** open.
19:17 I saw an angel **s** in the sun.
20:12 **s** in front of the throne.

stands (49)

Gen 31:48 "This pile of stones **s** as a
31:50 remember that God **s** as a
Lev 16:2 he goes up to the canopy and **s**
Jos 20:9 avenge a death before he **s** trial
Jdg 16:26 on which the building **s** so that
1Ki 7:27 He made ten bronze **s**.
7:28 The **s** were made this way:
7:37 is the way he made the ten **s**.
7:38 one basin on each of the ten **s**.
7:39 He put five **s** on the south side
7:43 10 **s** and 10 basins on the
7:43 stands and 10 basins on the **s**,
7:49 lamp **s** of pure gold (five on the
2Ki 16:17 panels of the ⌊bronze⌋ **s** ⌊used
25:13 of the LORD's temple, the **s**,
25:16 and the **s** that Solomon had
1Ch 16:30 "The earth **s** firm; it cannot be
28:15 the weight of the gold lamp **s**
2Ch 4:7 Huram made ten gold lamp **s**
4:14 10 **s** and 10 basins on the
4:14 stands and 10 basins on the **s**,
4:20 lamp **s** and lamps of pure gold
Psa 2:2 Kings take their **s**.
33:11 The LORD's plan **s** firm forever.
87:1 ⌊**S**⌋ on holy mountains.
89:2 Your faithfulness **s** firm in the
96:10 The earth **s** firm; it cannot be
109:7 When he **s** trial, let him be
109:31 because he **s** beside needy
Sos 2:9 There he **s** behind our wall,
5:10 He **s** out among 10,000 men.
Isa 3:13 He **s** to judge his people.
46:7 idol in its place, and it **s** there.
59:14 and righteousness **s** far away.
Jer 27:19 pillars, the bronze pool, the **s**,
52:17 of the LORD's temple, the **s**,
52:19 bowls, pots, lamp **s**, dishes,
52:20 under the **s** that King Solomon
Hab 3:6 He **s** and shakes the earth.
Jon 3:29 who **s** and listens to him,
Act 4:10 understand that this man **s**
Heb 4:1 enter his place of rest still **s**.
Rev 1:12 I saw seven gold lamp **s**.
1:13 Son of Man among the lamp **s**.
1:20 the seven gold lamp **s** is this:
1:20 and the seven lamp **s** are the
2:1 among the seven gold lamp **s**,
2:7 which **s** in the paradise of God,
11:4 and the two lamp **s** standing

star (17)

Num 24:17 A **s** will come from Jacob.
Isa 14:12 from heaven, you morning **s**,
Amo 5:26 as your king and the **s** Kiyyun,
Mat 2:2 We saw his **s** rising and have
2:7 when the **s** had appeared.
2:9 The **s** they had seen rising led
2:10 with joy to see the **s**.
Act 7:43 the **s** of the god Rephan,

1Co 15:41 Even one **s** differs in splendor
15:41 in splendor from another **s**.
2Pe 1:19 day to come and the morning **s**
Rev 2:28 also give them the morning **s**.
8:10 a huge **s** flaming like a torch
8:11 That **s** was named Wormwood.
9:1 I saw a **s** that had fallen to
9:1 The **s** was given the key to the
22:16 I am the bright morning **s**."

stare (3)

Psa 22:17 People **s**. They gloat over me.
Isa 14:16 Those who see you **s** at you;
Hab 2:15 in order to **s** at his nakedness.'

stared (7)

2Ki 8:11 He **s** at him until he became
Luk 22:56 She **s** at him and said,
Act 3:4 Peter and John **s** at him.
6:15 who sat in the council **s** at him
10:4 He **s** at the angel and was
13:9 the Holy Spirit. He **s** at Elymas
23:1 Paul **s** at the Jewish council

stargazers (1)

Isa 47:13 Let your astrologers and your **s**,

staring (3)

Sos 1:6 Stop **s** at me because I am so
Act 1:10 They were **s** into the sky as he
3:12 Why are you **s** at us as though

stars (62)

Gen 1:16 He also made the **s**.
15:5 up at the sky and count the **s**,
22:17 as numerous as the **s**
26:4 as numerous as the **s**
37:9 and 11 **s** bowing down to me."
Exo 32:13 as numerous as the **s**
Dtr 1:10 numerous as the **s** in the sky.
4:19 moon, the **s**, or anything else.
10:22 numerous as the **s** in the sky.
28:62 you were as numerous as the **s**
Jdg 5:20 The **s** fought from heaven.
1Ch 27:23 numerous as the **s** in the sky.
Neh 4:21 dawn until the **s** came out.
9:23 children as numerous as the **s**
Job 3:9 Let its **s** turn dark before dawn.
9:7 He doesn't let the **s** come out.
9:9 the clusters of **s** in the south.
22:12 Look how high the highest **s**
25:5 and the **s** aren't pure in his
38:7 when the morning **s** sang
Psa 8:3 the moon and the **s** that you
33:6 of the LORD and all the **s** by
136:9 the moon and **s** to rule the night
147:4 He determines the number of **s**.
148:3 Praise him, all shining **s**.
Ecc 12:2 and the **s** turn dark,
Isa 13:10 The **s** in the sky and their
14:13 up my throne above God's **s**.
34:4 All the **s** in the sky will rot.
34:4 The **s** will fall like leaves from
40:26 Who brings out the **s** one by
45:12 all the **s** to shine.
Jer 8:2 and all the **s** in the sky.
31:35 He orders the moon and **s** to be
33:22 who serve me like the **s**
Eze 32:7 cover the sky and darken the **s**.
Dan 8:10 of the army of heaven, the **s**,
12:3 like the **s** forever and ever.
Joe 2:10 and the **s** no longer shine.
3:15 The **s** will no longer shine.
Oba 1:4 build your nest among the **s**,
Nah 3:16 businessmen than there are **s**
Zep 1:5 those who worship all the **s**
Mat 24:29 the **s** will fall from the sky,
Mar 13:25 the **s** will fall from the sky,
Luk 21:25 occur in the sun, moon, and **s**.
Act 7:42 worship the sun, moon, and **s**.
27:20 couldn't see the sun or the **s**.
1Co 15:41 and the **s** have still another
Php 2:15 You will shine like **s** among
Heb 11:12 as numerous as the **s**
Jas 1:17 made the sun, moon, and **s**.
Jud 1:13 They are wandering **s** for
Rev 1:16 his right hand he held seven **s**,
1:20 of the seven **s** that you saw
1:20 The seven **s** are the
2:1 The one who holds the seven **s**
3:1 spirits and the seven **s** says:
6:13 The **s** fell from the sky to the
8:12 and one-third of the **s** were
12:1 a crown of 12 **s** on her head.
12:4 swept away one-third of the **s**

start (28)

Exo 14:15 Tell the Israelites to **s** moving.
17:11 the Amalekites would **s** to win.
Lev 1:7 sons of the priest Aaron will **s**
Num 6:12 He has to **s** over from when he
Dtr 2:5 Don't **s** a fight with them,
2:9 bother the people of Moab or **s**
2:19 don't bother them or **s** a fight
2:25 Today I will **s** to make all the
4:32 **S** from the very day God
13:9 You must **s** the execution.
16:9 the time you **s** harvesting grain.
17:7 must **s** the execution,
Jdg 9:32 your men must **s** out tonight.
19:9 Tomorrow you can **s** out early
1Ki 20:14 "Who will **s** the battle?"
1Ch 22:19 **S** building the holy place of the
Psa 140:2 They **s** fights every day.
Pro 9:6 **S** traveling the road to
20:3 any stubborn fool can **s** a fight.
Ecc 1:7 in order to **s** flowing again.
3:6 a time to **s** looking and a time
Isa 44:15 They **s** fires and bake bread.
Jer 21:14 "'I will **s** a fire in your forests,
Eze 9:6 **S** with my holy place."
21:19 Both of these roads should **s**
21:19 and put it where the roads **s** to
Mat 20:8 **S** with the last, and end with
2Co 11:17 What I say as I **s** bragging is

started (67)

Gen 8:1 and the water **s** to go down.
33:16 That day Esau **s** back to Seir.
Exo 2:13 asked the one who **s** the fight,
4:20 and **s** out for Egypt.
22:6 the person who **s** the fire must
Num 10:35 Whenever the ark **s** to move,
11:4 Even the Israelites **s** crying
16:46 his anger; a plague has **s**."
Dtr 32:22 My anger has **s** a fire that will
Jos 8:3 Joshua and all the soldiers **s**
Jdg 4:9 So Deborah **s** out for Kedesh
9:34 Abimelech and all his troops **s**
16:22 But his hair **s** to grow back as
19:7 When the Levite **s** to leave,
19:9 The Levite **s** to leave with his
20:31 They **s** to inflict casualties as
20:40 when the column of smoke **s**
Rut 1:6 and her daughters-in-law **s**
2Sm 21:9 people **s** harvesting barley.
1Ki 18:27 At noon Elijah **s** to make fun of
20:29 on the seventh day the battle **s**.
2Ki 7:5 So they **s** out at dusk to go into
1Ch 27:24 **s** to count them but didn't finish.
2Ch 20:22 As they **s** to sing praises,
29:12 So the Levites **s** to work.
29:17 They **s** on the first day of the
29:27 When the burnt offerings **s**,
29:27 the songs to the LORD **s**.
31:7 In the third month they **s** piling
31:10 "Since the people **s** to bring the
Ezr 3:6 They **s** to bring these burnt
Neh 3:1 **s** by rebuilding Sheep Gate.
Jer 15:14 because my anger has **s** a fire.
Lam 4:11 He **s** a fire in Zion that even
Eze 9:6 So they **s** with the old men in
20:48 that I, the LORD, **s** the fire.
23:8 prostitution that she **s** in Egypt.
Dan 10:7 Yet, they **s** to tremble violently,
Mat 2:9 had heard the king, they **s** out.
14:30 he became afraid and **s** to sink.
20:9 "Those who **s** working about 5
23:32 finish what your ancestors **s**!
Mar 5:42 got up at once and **s** to walk.
Luk 2:44 After traveling for a day, they **s**
8:22 of the lake." So they **s** out.
Luk 8:37 Jesus got into a boat and **s**
9:46 A discussion **s** among them
12:49 I wish that it had already **s**!
14:30 They'll say, 'This person **s** to
23:5 He **s** in Galilee and has come
Jon 6:17 They got into a boat and **s** to
6:18 A strong wind **s** to blow and
Act 3:8 he stood up and **s** to walk.
6:9 provinces of Cilicia and Asia **s**
11:20 They **s** to spread the Good
12:22 The people **s** shouting,
13:50 These people **s** to persecute
15:1 men came from Judea and **s**
17:5 and **s** a riot in the city.
19:34 everyone **s** to shout in unison,
21:5 time was up, we **s** on our way.
21:38 Aren't you the Egyptian who **s**
27:7 So at Cape Salmone, we **s** to
2Co 8:6 way as he had already **s** it.
8:10 but had already **s** to do it.
Col 4:17 all the work that he **s** as
Rev 17:12 who have not yet **s** to rule.

starting (6)

Lev 23:32 Humble yourselves **s** on the
1Ch 11:8 **s** from the Millo and making a
Est 6:13 "You are **s** to lose power to
Psa 74:5 **S** from its entrance,
Pro 17:14 **S** a quarrel is like opening a
Act 8:35 **S** with that passage,

startled (6)

Exo 11:7 not even a dog will be **s** by any
Ecc 12:4 you are **s** at the sound of a bird,
Dan 3:24 Then Nebuchadnezzar was **s**.
Luk 1:29 She was **s** by what the angel
24:22 the women from our group **s** us.
Act 2:6 Each person was **s** to

startles (1)

Hab 3:6 a glance and **s** the nations.

starts (13)

Exo 22:6 "Whenever a fire **s** and spreads
Num 34:3 east the southern border **s** from
Dtr 20:2 Before the battle **s**,
Jos 15:2 The southern border **s** from the
15:5 The northern border **s** from the
18:12 Their northern border **s** at the
19:33 Their border **s** from Heleph at
Jdg 10:18 "Whoever **s** the fight against
Pro 10:12 Hate **s** quarrels, but love
Ecc 10:13 A fool **s** out by talking
Luk 9:62 Jesus said to him, "Whoever **s**
Act 24:5 He **s** quarrels among all Jews
1Pe 4:17 If it **s** with us, what will be the

starvation (4)

Job 5:22 to laugh at destruction and **s**,
Lam 4:9 those who are dying from **s**.
5:10 oven from the burning heat of **s**.
Rev 18:8 and **s** will come in a single

starve (8)

Gen 42:2 us so that we won't **s** to death."
43:8 so that we won't **s** to death.
47:19 give us seed so that we won't **s**
Exo 16:3 desert to let us all **s** to death!"
Psa 34:10 lions go hungry and may **s**,
Pro 10:3 allow a righteous person to **s**,
Isa 5:13 Honored men will **s**,
Jer 38:9 where he'll **s** to death,

starved (1)

Dtr 32:24 They will be **s** by famines and

starving (4)

Gen 42:19 grain back to your **s** families.
42:33 food for your **s** families and go.
2Ki 7:12 He said, "They know we're **s**,
Luk 15:17 while I'm **s** to death here?

state (5)

Psa 143:4 and my heart is in a **s** of shock.
Pro 18:17 The first to **s** his case seems
Isa 43:26 **S** your case so that you can

Dan 6:7 The decree should **s** that for
Act 23:30 to **s** their case against

stated (5)

Gen 23:16 out for Ephron the amount **s**
Job 42:3 Yes, I have **s** things I didn't
Dan 6:12 you sign a decree which **s** that
Mat 26:61 They **s**, "This man said, 'I can
Act 13:34 "God **s** that he brought Jesus

stately (3)

Psa 144:12 May our daughters be like **s**
Isa 33:21 **S** ships won't sail on them.
Zec 11:2 and the **s** trees have been

statement (16)

Exo 21:5 But if he makes this **s**:
Dtr 21:7 they must make this formal **s**:
25:9 She must make this formal **s**:
26:5 You will make this formal **s** in
Jos 22:28 So we thought, if this **s** is
Mat 15:12 your **s** they were offended?"
Jon 2:22 and this **s** that Jesus had
Act 15:6 leaders met to consider this **s**.
Rom 13:9 are summed up in this **s**:
Gal 5:14 are summarized in a single **s**,
1Ti 1:15 This is a **s** that can be trusted
3:1 This is a **s** that can be trusted:
4:9 This is a **s** that can be trusted
2Ti 2:11 This is a **s** that can be trusted:
Tit 1:13 That **s** is true. For this reason,
3:8 This is a **s** that can be trusted.

statements (2)

Mar 14:56 but their **s** did not agree.
Act 15:24 you with **s** that disturb you.

states (2)

Gal 3:22 But Scripture **s** that the whole
Heb 11:5 Scripture **s** that before Enoch

statesmen (1)

Isa 3:2 fortunetellers and **s**,

stating (1)

1Co 9:8 Am I merely **s** some human

station (2)

Jer 51:12 **S** watchmen. Prepare
Hab 2:1 I will **s** myself on the wall.

stationed (22)

1Sm 13:2 2,000 of them were **s** with Saul
13:2 and 1,000 were **s** with
14:21 before this and had been **s**
17:3 The Philistines were **s** on a hill
17:3 and the Israelites were **s** on a
21:2 I've **s** my young men at a
1Ki 10:8 be because they are always **s**
10:26 He **s** ⌊some⌋ in chariot cities
14:27 captains of the guards were **s**.
2Ki 10:24 But Jehu had **s** 80 of his men
11:11 They were **s** around the king
1Ch 9:18 Formerly, they were **s** at the
9:27 They would spend the night **s**
16:42 sons were **s** at the gate.
2Ch 1:14 He **s** ⌊some⌋ in chariot cities
9:7 be because they are always **s**
9:25 He **s** ⌊some⌋ in chariot cities
12:10 captains of the guards were **s**.
23:10 They were **s** around the king
35:15 The gatekeepers were **s** at
Neh 13:19 I **s** some of my men by the
Dan 7:10 times ten thousand were **s**

statue (39)

Exo 32:4 he made it into a **s** of a calf.
32:8 They've made a **s** of a calf for
Lev 26:1 idols or set up a carved **s**
Dtr 9:16 You had made a **s** of a calf for
27:15 has a carved or metal **s**,
1Ki 15:13 mother because she made a **s**
15:13 Asa cut the **s** down and burned
2Ch 15:16 mother because she made a **s**
15:16 Asa cut the **s** down,
Neh 9:18 when they made a metal **s**
Psa 106:19 At Mount Horeb they made ⌊a⌋ **s**
106:20 their glorious God for the **s**
Isa 40:18 To what **s** can you compare
Dan 2:31 You saw a large **s**.
2:31 This **s** was very bright.
2:32 The head of this **s** was made
2:35 But the stone that struck the **s**
3:1 made a gold **s** 90 feet high
3:2 officials to dedicate the **s**
3:3 **s** King Nebuchadnezzar had
3:3 They stood in front of the **s**.
3:5 **s** that King Nebuchadnezzar
3:7 **s** King Nebuchadnezzar had
3:10 down and worship the gold **s**.
3:12 or worship the **s** that you set
3:14 gods or worship the gold **s** that
3:15 and worship the gold **s** I made?
3:18 worship the gold **s** that you set
Hab 2:18 benefit is there in a molded **s**,
Act 19:35 keeper of the **s** that fell down
Rev 13:14 living on earth to make a **s**
13:15 allowed to put breath into the **s**
13:15 Then the **s** of the ⌊first⌋ beast
14:9 worships the beast or its **s**,
14:11 who worship the beast or its **s**,
15:2 the victory over the beast, its **s**,
16:2 the beast and worshiped its **s**.
19:20 the beast and worshiped its **s**.
20:4 not worshiped the beast or its **s**

statue's (1)

Dan 2:34 It struck the **s** iron-and-clay

statues (34)

Exo 20:4 idols or **s** that represent any
Dtr 4:16 Don't make **s** that represent
4:23 or **s** that represent anything
4:25 or **s** that represent anything.
5:8 idols or **s** that represent any
1Sm 7:3 including the **s** of the goddess
7:4 So the Israelites got rid of the **s**
2Ki 11:18 Baal's altars and his **s**
19:18 and stone **s** made by human
2Ch 11:15 sites and the goat and calf **s**
23:17 Baal's altars and his **s**
Isa 10:10 They had more carved **s** than
30:22 idols and your gold-covered **s**.
37:19 and stone **s** made by human
41:29 Their **s** are nothing but air."
42:17 idols and those who say to **s**,
44:15 They make them into carved **s**
44:17 they make into gods, carved **s**
46:1 Their **s** are seated on animals
Jer 2:8 followed **s** that couldn't help
10:14 Their **s** are false ⌊gods⌋.
16:18 my property with the lifeless **s**
50:2 Babylon's **s** will be put to
50:38 **s** that will go crazy with fear.
51:17 Their **s** are false ⌊gods⌋.
Eze 7:20 detestable **s** ⌊of false gods⌋.
30:13 I will destroy the **s** and put an
Dan 11:8 He will take the metal **s** of their
Hos 2:8 she used it to make **s** of Baal.
Amo 5:26 You carried along the **s** of the
Mic 1:7 All its **s** will be turned into a
Act 7:43 and the **s** you made for
17:16 he saw that the city had **s** of
Rom 1:23 God for **s** that looked like

status (3)

1Sm 17:25 the social **s** of his family."
19:7 to his former **s** in Saul's court.
Est 1:20 regardless of their **s**."

statute (2)

Dan 6:7 that the king should make a **s**
6:15 have a law that no decree or **s**

stay (204)

Gen 12:10 Abram went to Egypt to **s**
19:5 came to ⌊s with⌋ you tonight?
19:9 man came here to **s** awhile.
19:30 he was afraid to **s** there.
22:5 "You **s** here with the donkey
24:55 "Let the girl **s** with us ten days
26:2 **S** where I tell you.
27:33 and he will **s** blessed."
27:44 **S** with him awhile,
29:19 to any other man. **S** with me."
38:1 left his brothers and went to **s**
42:16 the rest of you **s** in prison.
42:19 let one of your brothers **s** here
44:33 Sir, please let me **s** and be
47:9 "The length of my **s** on earth
Exo 2:21 Moses decided to **s** with the
9:28 have to **s** here any longer."
10:24 and herds must **s** behind."
16:29 Everyone, **s** where you are."
21:18 him so that he has to **s** in bed.
22:30 They will **s** with their mothers
24:12 **S** there, and I will give you the
25:15 The poles must **s** in the rings
33:9 would come down and **s** at
Lev 8:35 You will **s** at the entrance to
12:4 Then she must **s** at home for
12:5 Then she must **s** at home for
22:27 it must **s** with its mother for
Num 2:17 the Levites will **s** in the middle
9:18 they would **s** in the same
9:22 the Israelites would **s** in the
20:17 We'll **s** on the king's highway
20:19 "We'll **s** on the main road,
21:22 We'll **s** on the king's highway
22:19 why don't you **s** here tonight,
23:3 Balaam said to Balak, "**S** here
23:15 Then Balaam said to Balak, "**S**
31:19 a dead body must **s** outside
32:6 "Are you going to **s** here while
32:26 and all our other animals will **s**
35:28 Accused murderers must **s** in
Dtr 3:19 and livestock must **s** here in
5:31 But you **s** here with me.
23:9 **s** away from anything that will
23:10 outside the camp and **s** there.
23:16 Let him **s** with you ⌊and live⌋
24:5 For one year he is free to **s** at
24:6 prepare food in order to **s** alive.
28:2 will come to you and **s** close
28:15 to you and **s** close to you:
28:45 They will pursue you and **s**
33:18 when you **s** at home.
Jos 1:14 and livestock may **s** in the land
3:4 However, **s** about half a mile
6:18 But **s** away from what has
17:12 determined to **s** in this land.
18:5 Judah will **s** within its territory
18:5 will **s** within their territory
Jdg 2:23 the LORD let these nations **s**.
5:17 Why did he **s** by the ships?
6:18 "I will **s** until you come back,"
13:15 "Please **s** while we prepare a
13:16 LORD responded, "If I **s** here,
17:10 Micah told him, "**S** with me!
19:4 He made the Levite **s** there
19:7 urged him to **s** another night,
19:9 Please **s** another night.
19:9 **S** here, and enjoy yourself.
Rut 1:13 they grew up and **s** single just
1:16 and wherever you **s**,
1:16 and wherever you stay, I will **s**.
2:8 **S** here with my young women.
2:21 '**S** with my younger workers
3:13 **S** here tonight. In the morning if
3:18 Naomi replied, "**S** here,
1Sm 1:14 long are you going to **s** drunk?"
1:22 and he'll **s** there permanently."
5:7 of Israel must not **s** with us,
7:2 ark came to **s** at Kiriath Jearim.
9:27 "But you **s** here, and I will tell
14:9 If they say to us, '**S** where you
14:9 then we'll **s** where we are and
16:22 "Please let David **s** with me
19:2 into hiding, and **s** out of sight.
20:19 occasion, and **s** by the rock.
21:7 who was obligated to **s**
22:3 let my father and mother **s**
22:23 **S** with me. Don't be afraid. The
23:29 From there David went to **s** in
30:24 like the share of those who **s**
2Sm 10:5 The king said to them, "**S** in
11:12 "Then **s** here today,
15:19 and **s** with King Absalom.

2Sm 16:18 be his friend and **s** with him.
18:13 it wouldn't **s** hidden from the
19:7 no one will **s** with you tonight,
1Ki 1:2 She can **s** with you and be
2:36 in Jerusalem, and **s** there.
17:9 belongs to Sidon), and **s** there.
2Ki 2:2 Elijah said to Elisha, "Please **s**
2:4 Elijah said, "Elisha, please **s**
2:6 Elijah said to Elisha, "Please **s**
4:10 He can **s** there whenever he
7:4 But if we **s** here, we'll die.
8:1 **S** wherever you can.
11:8 **S** with the king wherever he
14:10 Enjoy your fame, but **s** home.
1Ch 19:5 The king said to them, "**S** in
2Ch 23:7 **S** with the king wherever he
25:19 **S** home! Why must you invite
Ezr 6:6 You must **s** away from there.
Neh 4:22 his servant should **s** overnight
5:2 are going to eat and **s** alive."
Job 7:1 "Isn't a mortal's **s** on earth
14:2 shadow; he doesn't **s** long.
19:13 "My brothers **s** far away from
24:13 They do not **s** on its paths.
28:28 To **s** away from evil is
37:8 their dens and **s** in their lairs.
39:9 or will it **s** at night beside your
Psa 15:1 who may **s** in your tent?
23:6 goodness and mercy will **s**
55:7 I would **s** in the desert.
59:15 they will **s** all night.
89:28 My mercy will **s** with him
101:7 does deceitful things will not **s**
120:5 a foreigner in Meshech or to **s**
127:1 it is useless for the guard to **s**
Pro 2:20 the way of good people and **s**
5:8 **S** far away from her.
7:11 Her feet will not **s** at home.
14:7 **S** away from a fool,
22:5 Whoever guards himself will **s**
Ecc 8:15 This joy will **s** with them while
Isa 7:4 Say to him, 'Be careful, **s** calm,
16:4 Let the fugitives from Moab **s**
65:5 They said, "**S** away!
Jer 9:2 I wish I had a place to **s** in the
27:11 I will let it **s** in its own land.
27:12 and you will **s** alive.
27:22 to Babylon and **s** there until
32:5 and Zedekiah will **s** there until
38:2 Those who **s** in this city will
42:10 Suppose you **s** in this land.
42:13 'We won't **s** in this land,'
42:14 or be hungry. We'll **s** there.'
43:4 They didn't **s** in Judah.
47:6 scabbard. **S** there and rest!"
49:18 No human will **s** there,"
49:33 No human will **s** there.
50:40 No human will **s** there,"
51:30 They **s** in their fortified cities.
Lam 4:15 'They can't **s** here any longer.'
Eze 44:2 "This gate will **s** shut and will
Hos 9:3 The people of Ephraim won't **s**
Zec 5:4 It will **s** in their houses and
11:9 that are missing **s** missing.
Mat 2:13 **S** there until I tell you,
10:11 **S** with them until you leave
22:14 few of those are chosen to **s**."
25:13 "So **s** awake, because you
26:36 He said to them, "**S** here while
26:38 and **s** awake with me."
26:40 to Peter, "Couldn't you **s** awake
26:41 **S** awake, and pray that you
Mar 5:18 "Let me **s** with you."
6:10 **s** there until you're ready to
14:32 "**S** here while I pray."
14:34 Wait here, and **s** awake."
14:37 Couldn't you **s** awake for one
14:38 **S** awake, and pray that you
Luk 8:27 He would not **s** in a house but
9:4 When you go into a home, **s**
9:12 some food and a place to **s**.
9:52 to arrange a place for him to **s**.
10:7 **S** with the family that accepts
19:5 I must **s** at your house today."
24:29 They urged him, "**S** with us!
24:29 "So he went to **s** with them.
Jon 1:32 from heaven and **s** on him.
1:33 come down and **s** on someone,
4:40 they asked him to **s** with them.
15:4 It has to **s** attached to the vine.
19:31 didn't want the bodies to **s**
Act 8:29 that carriage, and **s** close to it."
10:23 and had them **s** overnight.
10:48 Then they asked Peter to **s**
16:15 she invited us to **s** at her home.
16:15 then **s** at my home."
18:20 Jews asked him to **s** longer,
27:31 "If these sailors don't **s** on the
Rom 16:17 **S** away from them.
1Co 6:18 **S** away from sexual sins.
7:8 for you to **s** single like me.
7:11 If she does, she should **s**
7:20 All people should **s** as they
16:6 I'll probably **s** with you.
Php 1:27 to see you or whether I **s** away,
1Th 5:6 but we must **s** awake and be
1Ti 1:3 I encouraged you to **s** in the
2Ti 2:22 **S** away from lusts which tempt
3:5 **S** away from such people.
Jas 2:16 **S** warm, and make sure you
4:13 into some city, **s** there a year,

stayed (106)

Gen 11:31 as far as Haran, they **s** there.
29:14 Jacob **s** with him for a whole
32:4 Laban and have **s** until now.
32:13 He **s** there that night.
32:21 the gift ahead of him while he **s**
42:13 The youngest brother **s** with
42:32 The youngest brother **s** with
49:24 But his bow **s** steady,
50:22 Joseph and his father's family **s**
Exo 24:18 He **s** on the mountain 40 days
33:11 son of Nun, **s** inside the tent.
40:38 So the LORD's column **s** over
Num 9:18 the column of smoke **s** over
9:19 When the smoke **s** over the
9:20 when the smoke **s** only
9:21 of smoke **s** only from evening
9:22 the column of smoke **s** over
11:26 had **s** in the camp.
11:35 to Hazeroth, and they **s** there.
14:44 and Moses **s** in the camp.
20:1 and they **s** at Kadesh.
22:8 princes of Moab **s** with Balaam.
36:12 So their land **s** in the tribe of
Dtr 1:6 "You have **s** at this mountain
1:46 That's why you **s** in Kadesh as
3:29 So we **s** in the valley near Beth
9:9 I **s** on the mountain 40 days
10:10 I **s** on the mountain 40 days
Jos 2:22 to the mountains and **s** there
6:11 back to the camp and **s** there
7:6 They **s** there until evening.
Jdg 7:8 but the 300 men who **s** kept all
18:31 It **s** there the whole time the
20:47 They **s** at Rimmon Rock for
Rut 2:23 So Ruth **s** with the young
1Sm 1:23 The woman **s** and nursed her
6:12 Continually mooing, they **s** on
13:16 who were with them **s** at Geba
16:13 Spirit came over David and **s**
22:4 and they **s** with him as long as
23:18 David **s** in Horesh,
25:13 men **s** with the supplies.
26:3 but David **s** in the desert.
27:3 David and his men **s** with
27:7 David **s** in Philistine territory
30:10 the Besor Valley **s** behind.
30:21 to go with him and had **s**
2Sm 1:1 David **s** in Ziklag two days.
6:11 The ark of the LORD **s** at the
11:1 while David **s** in Jerusalem.
11:12 So Uriah **s** in Jerusalem that
13:20 So Tamar **s** there at the home
13:38 **s** there three years.
14:28 Absalom **s** in Jerusalem two
15:29 back to Jerusalem and **s** there.
1Ki 2:38 So Shimei **s** in Jerusalem for a
11:16 (Joab and all Israel **s** there six
11:40 He **s** in Egypt until Solomon
2Ki 19:36 home to Nineveh and **s** there.
1Ch 13:14 God's ark **s** at the home of
20:1 while David **s** in Jerusalem.
Est 7:7 But Haman **s** to beg Queen
Job 1:1 and he **s** away from evil.
23:11 I have **s** on his path and did not
Psa 68:13 Though you **s** among the
Isa 37:37 home to Nineveh and **s** there.
Jer 24:8 few in Jerusalem who **s** behind
37:16 and he **s** there a long time.
37:21 So Jeremiah **s** in the courtyard
38:13 Then Jeremiah **s** in the
38:28 Jeremiah **s** in the courtyard of
41:17 When they left Gibeon, they **s**
52:11 where he **s** until he died.
Dan 2:1 was troubled, but he **s** asleep.
2:49 But Daniel **s** at the king's court.
Mat 2:15 He **s** there until Herod died.
24:43 he would have **s** awake.
Mar 1:45 Instead, he **s** in places where
Luk 1:56 Mary **s** with Elizabeth about
2:43 The boy Jesus **s** behind in
Jon 2:12 city of Capernaum and **s** there
4:40 He **s** in Samaria for two days.
7:9 Jesus **s** in Galilee.
10:40 across the Jordan River and **s**
11:6 he **s** where he was for two
11:20 to meet him. Mary **s** at home.
11:54 where he **s** with his disciples.
Act 9:43 Peter **s** in Joppa for a number
12:19 where he **s** for a while.
14:3 Paul and Barnabas **s** in the city
14:28 They **s** for a long time with
15:33 After Judas and Silas had **s** in
15:35 and Barnabas **s** in Antioch.
17:14 Silas and Timothy **s** in Berea.
18:3 he **s** with them and they
19:22 while he **s** longer in the
20:3 and **s** there for three months.
20:6 them in Troas and **s** there
21:4 we **s** there for seven days.
21:8 in Caesarea and **s** with him.
25:6 Festus **s** in Jerusalem for eight
28:12 the city of Syracuse and **s** there
2Co 1:23 that I **s** away from Corinth
Gal 1:18 I **s** with him for fifteen days.
2Ti 4:20 Erastus **s** in the city of Corinth
1Jn 2:19 they would have **s** with us.

staying (29)

Gen 25:27 **s** around the tents.
Num 25:1 While Israel was **s** at Shittim,
Jdg 20:5 where I was **s** that night.
1Sm 14:2 Saul was **s** on the outskirts of
22:6 Saul was **s** in Gibeah under
23:3 "We're afraid of **s** here in Judah.
2Sm 16:3 "He's **s** in Jerusalem,"
19:32 while he was **s** at Mahanaim.
21:5 out to keep us from **s** anywhere
1Ki 17:19 upstairs room where he was **s**,
17:20 misery on the widow I'm **s**
2Ki 6:1 "The place where we're **s** is
10:6 The 70 male heirs were **s** with
2Ch 5:11 regard to **s** in their divisions.
Jer 35:7 in the land where you are **s**.'
Mar 7:24 anyone to know that he was **s**
Luk 1:21 were amazed that he was **s**
Jon 1:38 "where are you **s**?"
1:39 went to see where he was **s**
Act 1:13 room where they were **s**.
2:2 house where they were **s**.
10:18 if Simon Peter was **s** there.
11:11 at the house where we were **s**.
18:18 After **s** in Corinth quite a while
21:16 where we would be **s**.
25:14 Since they were **s** there for a
27:31 you have no hope of **s** alive."
28:23 to the place where Paul was **s**.
1Co 16:8 I will be **s** here in Ephesus

stays (9)

Lev 6:9 for the burnt offering that **s**
25:28 what he sold **s** in the hands of
Num 14:14 column of smoke **s** over them,
19:13 his uncleanness **s** with him.
2Ki 6:31 **s** on his body today."
Job 1:8 and he **s** away from evil."

Job 2:3 and he s away from evil.
Jer 14:8 traveler who s only one night?
1Co 7:40 blessed if she s as she is.

steady (5)

Gen 49:24 But his bow stayed s,
Exo 17:12 hands remained s until sunset.
Psa 112:8 His heart is s, and he is not
Isa 35:3 limp hands. S weak knees.
Lam 2:4 his right hand held the arrow s.

steaks (1)

Pro 15:17 love than juicy s where there is

steal (30)

Gen 31:30 But why did you s my gods?"
44:8 So why would we s any silver
Exo 20:15 "Never s.
Lev 19:11 "Never s, lie, or deceive your
Dtr 5:19 "Never s.
Job 24:2 They s flocks and tend them
24:19 ⌊Just as⌋ drought and heat s
Psa 69:4 to pay back what I did not s.
109:11 Let strangers s what he has
Pro 30:9 or I may become poor and s
Jer 7:9 You s, murder, lie when you
23:30 "I'm against the prophets who s
49:9 won't they s only until they've
Hos 7:1 They break into houses and s.
Oba 1:5 won't they s only until they've
Nah 2:9 S the silver! Steal the gold!
2:9 S the gold! There is no end to
Mat 6:19 and thieves break in and s.
6:20 thieves don't break in and s.
12:29 house and s his property?
12:29 his house and s his property.
19:18 Never s. Never give false
27:64 Otherwise, his disciples may s
Mar 3:27 man's house and s his property.
3:27 man's house and s his property.
10:19 Never s. Never give false
Luk 18:20 Never s. Never give false
Jon 10:10 A thief comes to s,
Rom 13:9 adultery; never murder; never s
Tit 2:10 or s from them. Instead, tell

stealing (7)

Hos 4:2 murdering, s, and adultery.
Mat 15:19 ⌊other⌋ sexual sins, s, lying,
Mar 7:21 Evil thoughts, sexual sins, s,
Rom 2:21 As you preach against s,
2:21 against stealing, are you s?
Eph 4:28 Thieves must quit s and,
Rev 9:21 sinning sexually, or s.

steals (3)

Exo 22:1 "Whenever someone s a bull or
Job 24:19 so the grave s people who sin.
Pro 6:30 thief who is hungry when he s

steep (2)

Isa 40:4 S places will be made level.
Mic 1:4 water pouring down a s hill.

steer (2)

Pro 7:22 follows her like a s
Jas 3:4 pilots s ships wherever they

steered (1)

Act 27:40 top sail to catch the wind and s

steering (1)

Act 27:40 the ropes that held the s oars.

stench (3)

Isa 34:3 A s will rise from their corpses.
Amo 4:10 I made the s from your camps
Jon 11:39 there must already be a s.

step (17)

Dtr 28:56 tender that she wouldn't even s
Jos 3:8 'When you s into the water of
1Sm 5:5 temple in Ashdod still don't s
20:3 only one s away from death."
2Sm 18:30 "S aside, and stand here,"
Job 18:11 chase him every s he takes.
Psa 36:11 let the feet of arrogant people s
56:6 They watch my every s as
89:51 your Messiah every s he took.
91:13 You will s on lions and cobras.
132:3 "I will not s inside my house,
Pro 14:15 sensible person watches his s.
29:5 a net for him to s into.
Ecc 5:1 Watch your s when you go to
Isa 41:2 victory with every s he takes?
Mic 1:3 is going to come down and s
Nah 3:14 S into the claypits and trample

Stephanas (3)

1Co 1:16 I also baptized S and his
16:15 You know that the family of S
16:17 I am glad that S, Fortunatus,

Stephen (16)

Act 6:5 So they chose S, who was a
6:8 S was a man filled with God's
6:9 started an argument with S.
6:10 They couldn't argue with S
6:12 So they went to S,
6:13 stood up and lied about S.
7:1 Then the chief priest asked S,
7:2 S answered, "Brothers and
7:54 council members listened to S,
7:55 But S was full of the Holy
7:56 So S said, "Look, I see heaven
7:57 Then they rushed at S with one
7:59 members were executing S,
8:1 approved of putting S to death.
8:2 Devout men buried S as they
22:20 When S, who witnessed about

Stephen's (1)

Act 11:19 following S death went as far

stepmother (1)

Lev 18:8 sexual intercourse with your s.

stepped (20)

Gen 42:24 He s away from them to cry.
Jos 4:18 When their feet s onto dry land,
2Sm 18:30 He s aside and stood there.
20:8 As he s forward, the sword
1Ki 18:36 the prophet Elijah s forward.
22:21 "Then the Spirit s forward,
2Ch 18:20 "Then the Spirit s forward,
Mat 15:39 Jesus s into the boat and came
26:49 Then Judas quickly s up to
Mar 5:2 As Jesus s out of the boat,
5:18 As Jesus s into the boat,
6:54 As soon as they s out of the
14:45 Then Judas quickly s up to
Luk 5:2 The fishermen had s out of
8:27 When Jesus s out on the shore,
12:1 were so crowded that they s
Jon 6:22 Jesus had not s into that boat
Act 8:38 He and Philip s into the water,
8:39 When they had s out of the
22:29 question Paul s away from him.

steps (40)

1Sm 2:9 He safeguards the s of his
2Sm 6:13 of the LORD had gone six s,
1Ki 10:19 Six s led to the throne.
10:20 Twelve lions stood on six s,
2Ki 20:9 the shadow to go forward ten s
20:9 ten steps or come back ten s?"
20:10 to extend ten ⌊more⌋ s forward.
20:10 No, let it come back ten s."
20:11 stairway go back up ten s.
2Ch 9:18 Six s led to the throne,
9:19 Twelve lions stood on six s,
Job 14:16 Though now you count my s,
29:6 my s were bathed in buttermilk,
31:4 my ways and count all my s?
31:7 "If my s have left the ⌊proper⌋
31:37 tell him the number of my s
34:21 ways. He sees all his s.
Psa 17:5 my s have remained firmly in
37:23 A person's s are directed by the
40:2 a rock and made my s secure.
74:3 Turn your s toward these
85:13 him and make a path for his s.
Psa 119:133 Make my s secure through your
Pro 5:5 Her s lead straight to hell.
5:6 Her s wander, and she doesn't
16:9 but the LORD directs his s.
20:24 one who directs a person's s.
Isa 3:16 taking short little s,
38:8 the shadow go back ten s."
38:8 went back up the ten s
Jer 10:23 not direct their s as they walk.
Eze 40:6 He went up its s and measured
40:22 Seven s went up to it and led
40:26 Seven s went up to it and led
40:31 and eight s led up to each
40:34 and eight s led up to the
40:37 and eight s led up to the
40:49 S led up to it. Pillars stood by
43:17 The s to the altar faced east.
Jon 5:7 someone else s into the pool

stepsister (1)

Lev 18:9 sexual intercourse with your s,

stern (4)

2Sm 22:16 bare at the LORD's s warning,
Psa 18:15 laid bare at your s warning,
39:11 With s warnings you discipline
76:6 At your s warning,

stern-looking (1)

Dan 8:23 a s king who understands

stew (4)

2Ki 4:38 and cook some s for the
4:39 pot of s without knowing what
4:40 As they were eating the s,
Mic 3:3 like s meat for a kettle.

stick (46)

Exo 21:20 or female slave with a s so that
Num 22:27 he hit the donkey with his s.
Dtr 23:13 You must carry a pointed s as
Jdg 3:31 Philistines with a sharp s used
1Sm 2:14 Then he would s it into the pot,
17:40 He took his s with him,
2Ki 18:21 you're trusting a broken s for a
Job 41:23 The folds of its flesh s to each
Psa 137:6 Let my tongue s to the roof of
Pro 18:24 friend can s closer than family.
Isa 9:4 and the s used by their
10:15 A wooden s cannot pick up a
28:27 with a rod and cumin with a s.
36:6 you're trusting a broken s for a
Lam 4:4 tongues of nursing infants s
Eze 3:26 I will make your tongue s to the
29:4 the fish in the Nile River s
29:6 like a ⌊broken⌋ walking s
37:16 take a s and write on it:
37:16 Then take another s and write
37:16 'The s of Ephraim,
37:19 I will take Joseph's s,
37:19 I will put them with Judah's s.
37:19 I will make them into one s.
40:3 measure and a measuring s,
40:5 The man had a measuring s
42:16 east side with a measuring s.
42:16 according to the measuring s.
42:17 according to the measuring s.
42:18 according to the measuring s.
42:19 according to the measuring s.
43:13 (The royal measuring s was 21
Mic 5:1 of Israel on the cheek with a s.
Mat 10:10 sandals, or a walking s.
27:29 and put a s in his right hand.
27:30 they took the s and kept hitting
27:48 Then he put it on a s and
Mar 6:8 on the trip except a walking s.
15:19 him on the head with a s,
15:36 Then he put it on a s and
Luk 9:3 Don't take a walking s,
Jon 19:29 in the vinegar on a hyssop s
Rev 11:1 Then I was given a s like a
11:1 a stick like a measuring s.
21:15 to me had a gold measuring s
21:16 measured the city with the s.

sticking (2)
Isa 57:4 Whom are you **s** out your
Eze 29:4 fish in the Nile **s** to your scales.

sticks (6)
1Sm 17:43 come to ⌊attack⌋ me with **s**?"
2Sm 18:14 He took three sharp **s** and
Psa 22:15 My tongue **s** to the roof of my
Eze 37:17 Then join both **s** together so
37:20 When you hold the **s** in your
Act 16:22 guards⌋ to beat them with **s**.

stiff (2)
Jos 7:5 lost heart and were scared **s**.
Job 40:17 It makes its tail **s** like a cedar.

stillborn (4)
Num 12:12 Don't let her be like a **s** baby
Job 3:16 I would be buried like a **s** baby.
Psa 58:8 trail or like a **s** child who never
Ecc 6:4 A **s** baby arrives in a pointless

sting (3)
1Co 15:55 Death, where is your **s**?"
15:56 Sin gives death its **s**,
Rev 9:5 like the pain of a scorpion's **s**.

stingers (1)
Rev 9:10 had tails and **s** like scorpions.

stingy (5)
Dtr 15:9 you might be **s** toward poor
28:54 become **s** toward his brother,
28:56 an ant — will become **s** toward
Pro 23:6 eat the food of one who is **s**,
28:22 A **s** person is in a hurry to get

stink (7)
Exo 7:18 and the river will **s**.
8:14 began to **s** because of them.
Job 19:17 I **s** to my own children.
Ecc 10:1 will make a bottle of perfume **s**,
Isa 19:6 The canals will **s**.
50:2 Their fish **s** because there is
Joe 2:20 They will **s**." He has done great things!

stir (15)
Jdg 13:25 The LORD's Spirit began to **s**
2Sm 12:11 I will **s** up trouble against you
Isa 9:11 Israel and will **s** up its enemies
13:17 I'm going to **s** up the Medes
Jer 50:9 I am going to **s** up an alliance
51:1 I will **s** up a destructive wind
51:11 The LORD will **s** up the spirit
Eze 23:22 I'm going to **s** up your lovers
24:8 In order to **s** up my fury so that I
24:10 meat thoroughly, **s** the mixture,
32:2 You **s** up the water with your
32:13 the hoofs of animals won't **s** up
Zec 9:13 I will **s** up your people,
Jon 6:18 to blow and **s** up the sea.
Php 1:17 ambition in order to **s** up trouble

stirred (9)
Psa 74:13 You **s** up the sea with your
Jer 17:4 do this because you have **s** up
Mar 15:11 The chief priests **s** up the
Jon 5:7 the pool when the water is **s**.
Act 6:12 The liars **s** up trouble among
13:50 But Jews **s** up devout women
14:2 to believe **s** up some people
21:27 They **s** up the whole crowd
Rom 7:5 **S** up by Moses' laws,

stirring (5)
Pro 30:33 so **s** up anger produces a fight.
Eze 7:6 It is **s** itself up against you.
Dan 7:2 saw the four winds of heaven **s**
Act 16:20 "These men are **s** up a lot of
24:12 in the temple courtyard or **s** up

stirs (13)
Dtr 32:11 Like an eagle that **s** up its nest,
Job 17:8 and it **s** up the innocent against
Job 41:31 It **s** up the ocean like a boiling
Pro 15:1 but a harsh word **s** up anger.
15:18 A hothead **s** up a fight,
28:25 A greedy person **s** up a fight,
29:22 An angry person **s** up a fight,
Isa 51:15 I am the LORD your God who **s**
Jer 31:35 He **s** up the sea so that its
Eze 8:3 That was where an idol that **s**
8:5 idol that **s** up ⌊God's⌋ anger.
Luk 23:2 "We found that he **s** up trouble
23:5 They said, "He **s** up the people

stock (1)
Dtr 32:14 rams from the **s** of Bashan,

stockpiles (1)
Isa 45:3 from dark places and hidden **s**.

stocks (1)
Job 33:11 He puts my feet in the **s** and

Stoic (1)
Act 17:18 Some Epicurean and **S**

stole (6)
Gen 31:19 Rachel **s** her father's idols.
Exo 22:3 a slave⌋ to pay for what he **s**.
Lev 6:4 Return what you **s** or seized,
2Sm 15:6 So Absalom **s** the hearts of the
Jer 30:16 Those who **s** from you in war
Eze 33:15 pays back everything he **s**,

stolen (22)
Gen 30:33 black will be considered **s**."
31:32 that Rachel had **s** the gods.)
31:39 any of the flock was **s** during
Exo 22:3 make up for what he has **s**.
22:4 But if the **s** animal is found
22:7 and they are **s** from that
22:12 But if the animal was **s** from
Lev 6:2 or if you lie about something **s**
Dtr 28:31 as your donkey is **s** from you,
Jos 7:11 They have not only **s**,
7:15 because he has ⌊**s**⌋ what
2Sm 17:8 bear whose cubs have been **s**.
21:12 They had **s** them from the
Pro 1:13 We'll fill our homes with **s**
9:17 "**S** waters are sweet,
16:19 people than to share **s** goods
Isa 3:14 with goods **s** from the poor."
Jer 30:16 will have things **s** from them.
Nah 3:1 full of lies and **s** goods — never
Mal 1:13 "You bring **s**, lame, and sick
Mat 28:13 night and had **s** his body while
Heb 10:34 your possessions were **s**,

stomach (24)
Num 5:21 uterus drop and your **s** swell.'
5:22 body and make your **s** swell
5:27 Her **s** will swell, her uterus will
Dtr 18:3 goat: the shoulder, jaws, and **s**.
2Sm 20:10 Joab stabbed him in the **s**,
Job 15:2 endless details and fill his **s**
20:14 snake venom in his **s**.
20:15 God forces them out of his **s**.
21:24 His **s** is full of milk,
40:16 the power in its **s** muscles.
Pro 18:20 ability provides for his **s**.
Jer 30:6 every strong man holding his **s**
Lam 1:20 My **s** is churning. My heart is
2:11 My **s** is churning. My heart is
Eze 3:3 and fill your **s** with it."
Dan 2:32 Its **s** and hips were made of
Nah 2:10 Every **s** becomes upset.
Mat 15:17 into the mouth goes into the **s**
Mar 7:19 into his thoughts but into his **s**
1Co 6:13 Food is for the **s**, and the
6:13 and the **s** is for food,
1Ti 5:23 drink a little wine for your **s**
Rev 10:9 It will be bitter in your **s**,
10:10 it was bitter in my **s**.

stomachs (3)
Job 31:31 we had never filled ⌊our **s**⌋
Ecc 5:12 But the full **s** that rich people
Eze 7:19 their hunger or fill their **s**.

stomp (9)
Dtr 33:29 and you will **s** on their backs."
2Ki 13:18 "**S** on them," he told the king of
Job 24:11 They **s** on grapes in wine vats,
Jer 25:30 like those who **s** grapes.
48:33 No one will **s** on grapes with
Eze 6:11 **s** your feet, and say, "Oh no!"
Joe 3:13 **S** on them as you would stomp
3:13 as you would **s** on grapes.
Amo 2:7 They **s** the heads of the poor

stomped (5)
2Sm 22:43 I crushed them and **s** on them
2Ki 13:18 The king **s** three times and
13:19 "You should have **s** five or six
Isa 63:3 In my wrath I **s** on them.
Eze 25:6 your hands and **s** your feet.

stomping (1)
Neh 13:15 I saw people in Judah **s** grapes

stomps (2)
Isa 16:10 No one **s** on grapes in the
Amo 9:13 and the one who **s** on grapes

stone (181)
Gen 28:18 next morning Jacob took the **s**
28:22 This **s** that I have set up as a
29:2 saw a well with a large **s** over
29:3 the **s** would be rolled off the
29:3 Then the **s** would be put back
29:8 When the **s** is rolled off the
29:10 forward and rolled the **s** off
31:13 poured olive oil on a **s** marker
31:45 Jacob took a **s** and set it up as
35:14 set up a memorial, a **s** marker,
35:20 Then Jacob set up a **s** as a
Exo 7:19 even in the wooden and **s**
8:26 won't they **s** us to death?
17:4 They're almost ready to **s** me!"
20:25 make it with cut **s** blocks.
24:12 and I will give you the **s**
28:10 six of their names on one **s**
28:21 each **s** engraved (like a signet
31:18 **s** tablets inscribed by God
34:1 "Cut two ⌊more⌋ **s** tablets like
34:4 So Moses cut two ⌊more⌋ **s**
34:4 carrying the two **s** tablets.
39:14 each **s** engraved (like a signet
Lev 20:2 people must **s** them to death.
24:14 must **s** him to death.
24:16 The whole congregation must **s**
26:1 or a sacred **s** for yourselves.
26:1 Never cut figures in **s** to
Num 15:35 outside the camp and **s** him."
22:24 with **s** walls on both sides.
32:16 "Allow us to build **s** fences for
32:24 for your families and **s** fences
32:36 They also built **s** fences for
33:52 Get rid of all their **s** and metal
35:17 If any of you picks up a **s** as a
35:23 Or suppose you drop a big **s**,
Dtr 4:13 Then he wrote them on two **s**
4:28 wooden and **s** gods made by
5:22 on two **s** tablets
9:9 mountain to get the **s** tablets,
9:10 the two **s** tablets inscribed by
9:11 the LORD gave me the two **s**
10:1 "Cut two ⌊more⌋ **s** tablets like
10:3 I cut two ⌊more⌋ **s** tablets like
13:10 **S** them to death because they
16:22 Never set up a sacred **s**.
17:5 and **s** that person to death.
21:21 All the men of the city should **s**
22:21 The men of her city must **s** her
22:24 the gate of the city and **s** them
28:36 gods made of wood and **s**.
28:64 of wood and **s** that neither you
29:17 of wood, **s**, silver, and gold.
Jos 4:5 Each man must take a **s** on his
7:5 to the slope of the **s** quarries.
8:32 of Israel he wrote on **s** slabs
24:26 Then he took a large **s** and set
24:27 "This **s** will stand as a witness
Jdg 3:19 Ehud turned around at the **s**

Jdg 3:26 He went past the **s** idols and
20:16 Each could sling a **s** at a hair
1Sm 17:49 into his bag, took out a **s**,
17:49 The **s** sank into Goliath's
17:50 using (only) a sling and a **s**,
2Sm 12:30 and contained a precious **s**.)
1Ki 5:15 quarried **s** in the mountains,
5:17 expensive blocks of **s** in order
5:17 of cut **s** for the temple.
5:18 men from Gebal quarried the **s**
5:18 and prepared the logs and **s**
6:7 The temple was built with **s**
6:18 No **s** could be seen.
7:9 built with high-grade **s** blocks.
7:9 The **s** blocks were cut to size
7:11 and high-grade **s** blocks,
7:12 had three layers of cut **s** blocks
8:9 the two **s** tablets Moses put
21:10 Then **s** him to death outside
2Ki 3:2 He put away the sacred **s** that
10:26 brought out the large sacred **s**
10:27 They destroyed the sacred **s** of
16:17 under it and set it on a **s** base.
19:18 They're only wooden and **s**
1Ch 20:2 and in it was a precious **s**.)
2Ch 2:14 iron, **s**, wood, purple, violet,
2:18 80,000 of them quarry **s** in the
Neh 4:3 "Even a fox would make their **s**
9:11 throws a **s** into raging water.
Est 1:6 pearl-like **s**, and black marble.
Job 8:17 They cling to a **s** house.
14:19 (so) water wears away **s**,
38:30 The water hardens like a **s**,
Psa 80:12 Why did you break down the **s**
118:22 The **s** that the builders rejected
Pro 24:31 and its **s** fence was torn down.
26:8 Like tying a **s** to a sling,
26:27 Whoever rolls a **s** will have it
27:3 A **s** is heavy, and sand weighs
Ecc 10:8 Whoever breaks through a **s**
10:9 Whoever works in a **s** quarry
Isa 19:19 and a **s** marker for the LORD
37:19 They're only wooden and **s**
60:17 and iron instead of **s**.
Jer 2:27 You call **s** your mother.
51:63 tie a **s** to it and throw it into the
Eze 3:9 as a diamond, harder than **s**.
16:40 They will **s** you and cut you
20:32 You want to serve wood and **s**.
23:47 Then the mob will **s** them and
28:13 with every kind of precious **s**:
40:42 were four tables made of cut **s**
46:23 four courtyards were **s** walls,
Dan 2:34 watching, a **s** was cut out,
2:35 But the **s** that struck the statue
2:45 This is the **s** that you saw cut
5:4 silver, bronze, iron, wood, or **s**.
5:23 gold, bronze, iron, wood, or **s**.
6:17 A **s** was brought and placed
6:17 The king put his seal on the **s**,
Hos 10:1 the more **s** markers they set up
10:2 and destroy their **s** markers.
Hab 2:11 A **s** in the wall will cry out.
2:19 and to a **s** that cannot talk,
Hag 2:15 were before one **s** was laid
Zec 3:9 "Look at the **s** I have set in
3:9 That one **s** has seven eyes.
4:7 He will bring out the topmost **s**
5:4 and destroy the timber and **s**."
12:3 make Jerusalem a **s** too heavy
Mat 7:9 would any of you give him a **s**?
18:6 with a large **s** hung around his
21:42 'The **s** that the builders
21:44 Anyone who falls on this **s** will
21:44 If the **s** falls on anyone,
23:37 you kill the prophets and **s** to
27:60 After rolling a large **s** against
27:66 They placed a seal on the **s**
28:2 from heaven, rolled the **s** away,
Mar 9:42 with a large **s** hung around his
12:10 'The **s** that the builders
15:46 and he rolled a **s** against the
16:3 "Who will roll away the **s** for us
16:4 they saw that the **s** had been
16:4 It was a very large **s**.
Luk 4:3 tell this **s** to become a loaf of
Luk 13:34 you kill the prophets and **s** to
17:2 with a large **s** hung around his
19:44 One **s** will not be left on top of
20:6 everyone will **s** us to death.
20:17 'The **s** that the builders
20:18 Everyone who falls on that **s**
20:18 If that **s** falls on anyone,
24:2 They found that the **s** had been
Jon 2:6 Six **s** water jars were there.
8:5 Moses ordered us to **s** women
8:7 be the first to throw a **s** at her."
10:31 rocks to **s** Jesus to death.
10:32 do you want to **s** me to death?"
10:33 "We're going to **s** you to death,
11:8 ago the Jews wanted to **s** you
11:38 with a **s** covering the entrance.
11:39 Jesus said, "Take the **s** away."
11:41 So the **s** was moved away
19:13 in a place called **S** Pavement.
20:1 She saw that the **s** had been
Act 4:11 He is the **s** that the builders
4:11 the **s** that has become the
5:26 that the people would **s** them
7:58 they began to **s** him to death.
14:5 them and **s** them to death.
14:19 They tried to **s** Paul to death
17:29 made from gold, silver, or **s**,
2Co 3:3 letter written not on tablets of **s**
3:7 death was inscribed on **s**.
11:25 Once people tried to **s** me to
1Pe 2:4 the living **s** who was rejected
2:7 "The **s** that the builders
2:8 a **s** that people trip over,
Rev 2:17 give each person a white **s**
9:20 silver, bronze, **s**, and wood,
18:21 picked up a **s** that was like

stonecutters (3)

2Ki 12:12 masons, and **s**. They also used
1Ch 22:15 **s**, masons, carpenters,
Ezr 3:7 money to the **s** and carpenters.

stoned (17)

Exo 19:13 They must be **s** or shot with
21:28 the bull must be **s** to death,
21:29 then the bull must be **s** and its
21:32 and the bull must be **s**.
Lev 20:27 They must be **s** to death
24:23 There they **s** him to death as
Num 15:36 outside the camp and **s** him
Jos 7:25 And all Israel **s** Achan and his
1Sm 30:6 bitterness said he should be **s**.
1Ki 12:18 but they **s** him to death.
21:13 So the people **s** him to death
21:14 "Naboth has been **s** to death."
2Ch 10:18 but they **s** him to death.
24:21 and by the king's order they **s**
Mat 21:35 and **s** a third to death.
Heb 11:37 Some were **s** to death,
12:20 it must be **s** to death."

stonemasons (1)

2Sm 5:11 cedarwood, carpenters, and **s**.

stone's (1)

Luk 22:41 about a **s** throw, knelt down,

stones (149)

Gen 11:3 They used bricks as **s** and tar
28:11 He took one of the **s** from that
31:46 his relatives, "Gather some **s**."
31:46 They took **s**, put them into a
31:46 and ate there by the pile of **s**.
31:48 Laban said, "This pile of **s**
31:51 "Here is the pile of **s**,
31:52 This pile of **s** and this marker
31:52 I will not go past the pile of **s**
31:52 will not go past the pile of **s**
Exo 20:25 an altar for me made out of **s**,
23:24 gods and crush their sacred **s**.
24:4 and (set up) 12 sacred **s**
25:7 onyx **s**, and other precious
25:7 and other precious **s** to be set
28:9 Take two onyx **s**, and engrave
28:11 the sons of Israel on the two **s**
28:17 four rows of precious **s** on it.
Exo 28:21 The **s** correspond to the 12
31:5 He knows how to cut and set **s**
34:13 crush their sacred **s**,
35:9 onyx **s**, and other precious
35:9 and other precious **s** to be set
35:27 The leaders brought onyx **s**
35:27 stones and other precious **s**
35:33 He knows how to cut and set **s**
39:6 They mounted the onyx **s** in
39:10 four rows of precious **s** on it.
39:13 The **s** were mounted in gold
Lev 14:40 the priest must order the **s** that
14:42 The **s** must be replaced,
14:45 The house — **s**, wood, and all
Dtr 7:5 smash their sacred **s**,
12:3 crush their sacred **s**,
27:2 set up some large **s** and cover
27:3 of these teachings on the **s**.
27:4 set up these **s** on Mount Ebal,
27:5 Build an altar of **s** there
27:5 use an iron chisel on the **s**.
27:6 You must use uncut **s** to build
27:8 teachings on the **s** you set up."
Jos 4:3 Order them to pick up 12 **s** from
4:3 Take the **s** along with you,
4:6 'What do these **s** mean to you?'
4:7 These **s** are a permanent
4:8 They took 12 **s**, one for each of
4:9 Joshua also set 12 **s** in the
4:9 The **s** are still there today.
4:20 set up the 12 **s** they had taken
4:21 'What do these **s** mean?'
7:25 bodies and piled **s** over them.
7:26 a large pile of **s** over Achan that
8:29 made a large pile of **s** over it.
8:31 He built an altar with uncut **s**
10:18 Joshua replied, "Roll large **s**
10:27 hiding and put large **s** over
10:27 These **s** are still there today.
1Sm 17:40 picked out five smooth **s** from
25:29 enemies like **s** thrown from
2Sm 16:6 He threw **s** at David and
16:13 Shimei cursed, hurled **s**,
18:17 a large heap of **s** over him.
1Ki 6:36 with three courses of finished **s**
7:10 high-grade **s** (some 12 feet
10:2 of gold, and precious **s**.
10:10 of spices, and precious **s**.
10:11 and precious **s** from Ophir.
10:27 as common in Jerusalem as **s**,
14:23 and (put up) large **s**
15:22 He made them carry the **s** and
18:31 Elijah took 12 **s**, one for each
18:32 the LORD's name with those **s**.
18:38 burnt offering, wood, **s**, and dirt
19:6 some bread baked on hot **s**
2Ki 3:25 Only the **s** (in the walls) of Kir
3:25 attacked it with slings and **s**.
12:12 used it to buy wood and cut **s**
17:10 They set up sacred **s** and
18:4 crushed the sacred **s**,
22:6 to buy lumber and quarried **s**
23:14 Josiah crushed the sacred **s**,
1Ch 12:2 with bows and could sling **s**
22:2 some of them to cut **s**
22:14 I've also prepared wood and **s**,
29:2 onyx **s** and settings,
29:2 stones and settings, black **s**,
29:2 **s** of different colors,
29:8 to have precious **s** gave them
2Ch 1:15 as common in Jerusalem as **s**,
2:2 80,000 to quarry **s** in the
9:1 of gold, and precious **s**.
9:9 of spices, and precious **s**.
9:10 sandalwood and precious **s**.
9:27 as common in Jerusalem as **s**,
14:3 broke down the sacred **s**,
16:6 He made them carry the **s** and
26:14 armor, bows, and **s** for slings.
26:15 shoot arrows and hurl large **s**.
31:1 They crushed the sacred **s**,
32:27 precious **s**, spices, shields,
34:11 They were to buy quarried **s**
Ezr 5:8 is being built with large **s**
6:4 with three rows of large **s** and a
Neh 4:2 Will they get the **s** out of the

Neh 4:2 burned as these s are,
Job 5:23 a binding agreement with the s
8:17 roots weave through a pile of s.
28:6 That place's s are sapphire.
41:28 S from a sling turn to dust
Psa 102:14 Your servants value Zion's s,
Ecc 3:5 a time to scatter s and a time to
Isa 5:2 He dug it up, removed its s,
9:10 we will rebuild with hand-cut s.
14:19 You go down to the s of the pit
27:9 the altar s into powdered chalk
54:11 your city with precious s.
54:12 your gates with sparkling s,
54:12 all your walls with precious s."
57:6 idols are among the smooth s
62:10 Clear away the s! Raise a flag
Jer 3:9 standing s and wood pillars.
43:9 "Take some large s,
43:10 set his throne over these s that
51:26 People won't find any s in you
51:26 They won't find any s in you to
Lam 3:9 has blocked my way with cut s
4:1 The sacred s are scattered at
Eze 26:12 They will throw your s,
27:22 the finest spices, precious s,
28:14 You walked among fiery s.
28:16 forced you out from the fiery s.
Dan 11:38 With gold, silver, precious s,
Hos 3:4 without sacrifices or sacred s,
Amo 5:11 build houses from hand-cut s,
Mic 1:6 I will roll its s down into a
Zec 9:15 destroy and trample the s used
Mat 3:9 for Abraham from these s.
4:3 tell these s to become loaves
24:2 Not one of these s will be left
Mar 5:5 and cutting himself with s.
13:1 look at these huge s and these
13:2 Not one of these s will be left
Luk 3:8 for Abraham from these s.
19:40 the s will cry out."
21:5 that it was built with fine s
21:6 when not one of these s will
Jon 8:59 some of the Jews picked up s
1Co 3:12 silver, precious s, wood, hay,
1Pe 2:5 You come to him as living s,

stoning (1)

Num 14:10 of Israel talked about s Moses

stood (214)

Gen 18:8 Then he s by them under the
19:27 to the place where he had s
37:7 and suddenly mine s up.
41:3 They s behind the first seven
Exo 2:4 The baby's sister s at a
9:10 took ashes from a kiln and s
14:19 Israelites and s behind them
14:22 The water s like a wall on their
14:29 ground while the water s like
15:8 The waves s up like a dam.
18:13 The people s around Moses
19:17 and they s at the foot of the
20:18 with fear and s at a distance.
32:26 he s at the entrance to the
34:5 down in a cloud and s there
Lev 9:5 congregation came and s
Num 12:5 the column of smoke and s at
16:18 and s with Moses and Aaron at
16:48 He s between those who had
22:22 the Messenger of the LORD s
22:24 of the LORD s there.
22:26 the LORD moved ahead and s
25:11 Since he s up for me,
25:13 permanently because he s up
27:2 to Moses and s in front of him,
Dtr 4:10 Never forget the day you s in
4:11 So you came and s at the foot
5:5 I s between the LORD and you
Jos 3:17 of the LORD's promise s firmly
4:3 where the priests' feet s firmly.
4:9 the ark of the promise had s.
4:10 They s there until everything
10:13 The sun s still, and the moon
21:44 Not one of their enemies s up
Jdg 9:35 (son of Ebed) went out and s at
16:29 on which the building s.
Jdg 18:16 The 600 armed men from Dan s
18:17 The priest s at the entrance to
20:1 The congregation s united in
20:8 All the people s united,
20:11 They s united against the city.
1Sm 1:26 I'm the woman who s here next
3:10 The LORD came and s there.
9:2 He s a head taller than
10:23 As he s among the people,
14:5 One cliff s like a pillar on the
14:5 the other s south facing Geba.
17:8 Goliath s and called to the
17:51 David ran and s over the
20:25 by the wall, while Jonathan s.
26:13 over to the other side and s
2Sm 1:10 "So I s over him and killed him,
12:17 in his palace s beside him
13:31 The king s up, tore his clothes,
18:4 So the king s by the gate while
18:13 would you have s by me?
18:30 He stepped aside and s there.
20:11 One of Joab's young men s
20:15 and it s level with the outer
23:12 he s in the middle of the field
1Ki 1:28 So she s in front of him,
3:15 He went to Jerusalem and s in
3:16 came to the king and s
8:22 Solomon s in front of the
8:54 he s in front of the LORD's altar,
8:55 Then he s and in a loud voice
10:19 lions s beside the armrests.
10:20 Twelve lions s on six steps,
18:21 Elijah s up in front of all the
19:13 and s at the entrance of the
22:21 s in front of the LORD,
2Ki 2:7 Fifty disciples of the prophets s
2:7 as Elijah and Elisha s by
2:13 and s on the bank of the Jordan
3:21 They s at the border.
4:12 and she s in front of him.
4:15 and she s in the doorway.
5:15 Naaman s in front of Elisha and
5:25 He went and s in front of his
8:9 He s in front of Elisha and said,
10:9 In the morning he s there.
11:11 The guards s with their
13:21 came back to life and s up.
18:17 They came there and s at the
18:28 Then the field commander s
23:3 The king s beside the pillar
1Ch 6:39 Heman's relative Asaph s on
11:14 they s in the middle of the field
28:2 David s in front of them and
2Ch 3:13 They s on their feet and faced
5:12 dressed in fine linen and s east
6:12 Solomon s in front of the
6:13 He s on the platform,
9:18 lions s beside the armrests.
9:19 Twelve lions s on six steps,
13:4 Then Abijah s on Mount
18:20 s in front of the LORD,
20:5 Jehoshaphat s in front of the
20:19 s up to praise the LORD God of
23:10 All the troops s with their
24:20 Zechariah s in front of the
29:26 The Levites s with David's
30:16 They s in their regular places
34:31 The king s in his place and
Ezr 10:10 Ezra the priest s up and said to
Neh 4:16 The leaders s behind all the
8:4 Ezra the scribe s on a raised
8:4 and Maaseiah s beside him on
8:4 and Meshullam s beside him
8:5 all the people s up.
9:2 They s and confessed their
9:3 They s in their places,
9:4 and Chanani s on the stairs
12:9 and Unno s across from them
12:24 They and their relatives s in
12:40 So both choirs s in God's
12:41 these priests s in God's temple:
Est 5:1 She s in the courtyard of the
8:4 and Esther got up and s in front
Job 1:20 Job s up, tore his robe in
4:16 Something s there.
29:8 Old men s up straight out of
Psa 33:9 gave the order, and there it s.
104:6 Water s above the mountains
106:23 s in his way to prevent him
106:30 Then Phinehas s between God
Isa 36:2 He s at the channel for the
36:13 Then the field commander s
Jer 18:20 Remember how I s in your
19:14 He s in the courtyard of the
Eze 1:21 Whenever the creatures s still,
1:21 stood still, the wheels s still.
1:24 When the creatures s still,
1:25 over their heads as they s still
2:2 entered me, s me on my feet,
3:24 the Spirit entered me and s me
8:11 In front of these drawings s 70
9:2 The men came in and s by the
10:6 the person went in and s
10:17 When the angels s still,
10:17 stood still, the wheels s still.
10:18 entrance and s over the angels.
10:19 The angels s at the door to the
27:29 their ships and s on the shore.
37:10 Then they came to life and s
40:3 and he s in a gateway.
40:49 Pillars s by the recessed walls,
44:11 They could have s in front of
Dan 2:31 It s in front of you, and it looked
3:3 They s in front of the statue.
10:11 When he said this to me, I s up,
12:5 One man s on one side of the
12:5 and the other one s on the other
Oba 1:11 While you s there doing
Mal 2:5 He respected me and s in awe
Mat 13:2 the entire crowd s on the shore.
26:62 The chief priest s up and said
27:11 Jesus s in front of the governor,
Mar 3:31 They s outside and sent
14:57 Then some men s up and gave
14:60 So the chief priest s up in the
15:39 When the officer who s facing
Luk 4:16 He s up to read the lesson.
5:25 The man immediately s up in
6:8 The man got up and s there.
6:17 the mountain with them and s
10:25 in Moses' Teachings s up
13:13 and she immediately s up
17:12 They s at a distance
18:11 The Pharisee s up and prayed,
19:8 Later, at dinner, Zacchaeus s
22:28 "You have s by me in the
23:1 Then the entire assembly s up
23:10 priests and the scribes s there
23:35 The people s there watching.
23:49 s at a distance and watched
24:4 suddenly s beside them.
24:36 Jesus s among them.
Jon 11:56 As they s in the temple
20:11 Mary, however, s there and
20:19 Jesus s among them and said
20:26 Jesus s among them and said,
21:4 Jesus s on the shore.
Act 1:10 in white clothes s near them.
2:14 Then Peter s up with the
3:8 he s up and started to walk.
5:34 Pharisee named Gamaliel s up.
6:13 Some witnesses s up and lied
7:10 When Joseph s in the
9:18 Then Saul s up and was
9:39 All the widows s around him.
10:30 dressed in radiant clothes s
12:7 from the Lord s near Peter,
13:16 Then Paul s up, motioned with
15:5 the party of the Pharisees s up
15:7 Peter s up and said to them,
17:22 Paul s in the middle of the
21:40 So Paul s on the stairs of the
22:13 He came to me, s beside me,
23:11 The Lord s near Paul the next
24:20 I was charged with when I s
24:21 As I s among them,
25:18 When his accusers s up,
27:21 Paul s among them and said,
27:23 and whom I serve s by me last
Rom 4:17 Abraham believed when he s
2Ti 4:16 At my first hearing no one s up
4:17 However, the Lord s by me and

Rev 7:11 All the angels **s** around the
8:3 a gold incense burner and **s** at
11:11 and they **s** on their feet.
12:4 The serpent **s** in front of the
12:18 The serpent **s** on the sandy
18:17 living from the sea **s** far away.

stool (1)

1Ch 28:2 This temple would be a **s** for

stoop (1)

Isa 46:2 These gods **s** low and bow

stooped (1)

Ecc 12:3 strong men are **s** over,

stoops (1)

Isa 46:1 the god Nebo **s** low.

stop (166)

Gen 8:22 day and night will never **s**."
18:3 "**s** by to visit me for a while.
19:17 and don't **s** on the plain.
Exo 8:29 But you must **s** tricking us by
9:29 The thunder will **s**,
Lev 17:7 The people must **s** sacrificing
Num 11:28 up and said, "**S** them, sir!"
17:10 Then you will **s** their
22:22 stood in the road to **s** him.
22:32 I've come here to **s** you
22:34 there in the road to **s** me.
Dtr 5:32 Never **s** living this way.
7:24 No one will be able to **s** you.
11:25 No one will be able to **s** you.
13:17 Then the LORD will **s** being
25:11 If she tries to **s** the fight by
Jos 1:8 Never **s** reciting these
3:13 flowing from upstream will **s**
10:19 But don't **s**. Chase your
22:25 So your descendants would **s**
Jdg 9:9 'Should I **s** producing oil,
9:11 'Should I **s** producing my good,
9:13 'Should I **s** producing my wine,
15:7 get even with you before I **s**."
20:28 Or should we **s**?" The LORD
1Sm 3:13 but he didn't try to **s** them.
7:8 Don't **s** crying to the LORD our
9:5 or my father will **s** worrying
20:15 never **s** being kind to my
2Sm 2:22 "**S** following me," he said.
7:15 But I will never **s** showing him
18:16 ram's horn to **s** their ⌊fighting⌋,
24:21 plague on the people will **s**."
2Ki 4:29 don't **s** to greet him.
4:29 don't **s** to answer him.
1Ch 17:13 And I will never **s** showing him
21:22 plague on the people will **s**."
2Ch 25:16 **S**! Do you want me to have you
32:3 military staff made plans to **s**
34:33 they didn't **s** following the
35:21 God is with me, so **s** now or
35:22 Josiah would not **s** his attack.
Ezr 4:21 order these men to **s** rebuilding.
4:23 They forced the Jews to **s**
Neh 5:10 must **s** charging them interest.
6:3 Why should the work **s** while I
Job 3:17 There the wicked **s** their raging.
7:19 Why don't you **s** looking at me
9:12 ⌊but⌋ who can **s** him?
10:20 So **s** ⌊this⌋, and leave me
11:10 into session, who can **s** him?
13:21 **S** oppressing me. Don't let your
14:7 Its shoots will not **s** sprouting.
16:6 If I **s** talking, how much of it
31:16 eyes **s** ⌊looking for help⌋,
33:17 and to **s** being arrogant.
34:31 I will **s** my immoral behavior.
37:14 **S** and consider God's miracles.
38:11 Here your proud waves will **s**'?
Pro 9:6 **S** being gullible and live.
17:14 so **s** before the argument gets
19:27 If you **s** listening to instruction,
22:10 Quarreling and abuse will **s**.
23:4 Be smart enough to **s**.
Ecc 3:5 a time to hug and a time to **s**
3:6 looking and a time to **s** looking,
Ecc 12:3 the women at the mill **s**
12:12 People never **s** writing books.
Sos 1:6 **S** staring at me because I am
Isa 1:16 out of my sight. **S** doing evil.
2:22 **S** trusting people. Their life is in
14:6 with blows that didn't **s**.
14:27 Who can **s** it? He is ready to
28:22 Now **s** laughing, or your chains
30:11 **S** blocking our path!
33:8 Travelers **s** traveling.
47:11 You won't be able to **s** it.
58:11 water does not **s** flowing.
58:13 If you **s** trampling on the day of
Jer 16:9 I'm going to put a **s** to the
17:8 It will not **s** producing fruit.
31:16 the LORD says: **S** your crying,
31:36 Only if these laws **s** working,
31:36 will Israel's descendants **s**
32:40 I will never **s** blessing them.
38:5 I won't do anything to **s** you."
44:5 wouldn't **s** burning incense as
48:33 I will **s** the wine flowing from
48:35 I will **s** those in Moab who
Lam 2:18 Don't let them **s**. Don't let your
Eze 7:24 I will **s** those who are strong
12:23 I will put a **s** to the use of this
16:42 and I will **s** being angry.
18:31 **S** all the rebellious things that
21:21 The king of Babylon will **s**
23:27 I will put a **s** to your sinning
23:48 So I will put a **s** to the sinning
26:13 "I will put a **s** to your noisy
43:9 Now they must **s** acting like
45:9 **S** your violence and looting,
45:9 **S** evicting my people,
Dan 4:27 advice is that you **s** sinning,
4:27 **S** committing the same errors,
8:12 it was given an army to put a **s**
9:24 to **s** sin, to forgive wrongs,
9:27 he will **s** the sacrifices and
Hos 2:2 Tell her to **s** acting like a
Amo 2:12 the prophets to **s** prophesying.
6:7 around the banquet table will **s**.
7:5 "Almighty LORD, please **s**!
7:16 '**S** prophesying against Israel,
7:16 and **s** preaching against the
Nah 2:8 "**S**! Stop!" But no one turns
2:8 **S**!" But no one turns around.
Mal 3:11 Then, for your sake, I will **s**
Mat 3:14 But John tried to **s** him and
6:16 **s** looking sad like hypocrites.
6:19 "**S** storing up treasures for
6:25 "So I tell you to **s** worrying
7:1 "**S** judging so that you will not
19:14 Jesus said, "Don't **s** children
Mar 4:39 ordered the wind to **s**,
9:38 We tried to **s** him because he
9:39 Jesus said, "Don't **s** him!
10:14 He told them, "Don't **s** the
Luk 6:29 don't **s** him from taking your
6:37 "**S** judging, and you will never
6:37 **S** condemning, and you will
8:24 the wind and the waves to **s**.
9:49 We tried to **s** him because he
9:50 Jesus said to him, "Don't **s** him!
10:4 and don't **s** to greet anyone on
12:22 "So I tell you to **s** worrying
18:16 "Don't **s** the children from
22:51 But Jesus said, "**S**!
Jon 2:16 **S** making my Father's house a
5:14 **S** sinning so that something
6:43 responded, "**S** criticizing me!
7:24 **S** judging by outward
20:27 **S** doubting, and believe."
Act 4:20 We cannot **s** talking about
5:39 you won't be able to **s** them.
5:42 they refused to **s** teaching and
8:38 ordered the carriage to **s**.
27:2 The ship was going to **s** at
Rom 14:13 So let's **s** criticizing each other.
1Co 6:9 **S** deceiving yourselves!
13:8 but it will **s** by itself.
15:34 point of view, and **s** sinning.
2Co 1:9 we would **s** trusting ourselves
6:14 **S** forming inappropriate
Eph 1:16 I never **s** thanking God for you.
1Th 2:13 why we never **s** thanking God:
5:17 Never **s** praying.
1Ti 1:3 to **s** teaching false doctrine
4:3 They will try to **s** others from
5:23 **S** drinking only water.
2Ti 2:21 Those who **s** associating with
Heb 6:1 With this in mind, we should **s**
10:25 We should not **s** gathering
Jas 4:11 **s** slandering each other.
5:9 Brothers and sisters, **s**
2Pe 2:14 They can't **s** looking for sin as
3Jn 1:10 He even tries to **s** others who
Rev 5:5 leaders said to me, "**S** crying!
16:11 However, they would not **s**

stopped (95)

Gen 2:2 On the seventh day he **s** the
2:3 because on that day he **s** all
8:2 and the rain had **s** pouring.
11:8 and they **s** building the city.
18:5 since this is why you **s** by to
28:11 he **s** for the night because the
29:35 Then she **s** having children.
30:9 that she had **s** having children,
42:27 At the place where they **s** for
43:21 When we **s** for the night,
Exo 4:24 Along the way they **s** for the
9:33 The thunder and the hail **s**,
9:34 and the thunder had **s**,
20:11 blessed the day he **s** his work
31:17 and on the seventh day he **s**
36:4 holy place **s** what they were
36:6 the people **s** bringing gifts.
Num 9:17 break camp, and wherever it **s**,
10:12 until the ⌊column of⌋ smoke **s**
10:36 And whenever it **s**,
16:48 still alive, and the plague **s**.
16:50 of meeting, the plague had **s**.
21:24 ⌊They **s** at⌋ the border of the
25:8 Israelites were experiencing **s**.
Dtr 5:22 Then he **s** speaking.
Jos 3:16 the water, the water **s** flowing
4:7 the river **s** flowing.
5:12 The day after that, the manna **s**.
10:13 and the moon **s** until a nation
10:13 The sun **s** in the middle of the
Jdg 18:3 So they **s** to ask him,
18:15 So they **s** and entered Micah's
Rut 2:20 The LORD hasn't **s** being kind
1Sm 6:14 Beth Shemesh and **s** there by
14:46 Then Saul **s** pursuing the
24:7 So David **s** his men by saying
2Sm 2:23 Asahel fell and died **s** there.
2:27 the men would not have **s**
2:28 and all the troops **s**.
10:14 So Joab **s** his campaign
15:17 they **s** at the last house.
20:12 all the troops **s** as they came
24:25 and the plague on Israel **s**.
1Ki 15:21 he **s** fortifying Ramah and lived
2Ki 4:6 So the olive oil **s** flowing.
4:8 was in the area, he **s** in to eat.
5:9 his horses and chariot and **s** at
13:18 stomped three times and **s**.
17:4 had **s** making annual payments
22:2 his ancestor David and never **s**.
2Ch 16:5 he **s** fortifying Ramah and
20:20 Jehoshaphat **s** and said,
25:16 The prophet **s**. He said, "I know
32:4 crowd gathered as they **s** all
32:30 Hezekiah was the one who **s**
34:2 and never **s** living this way.
Ezr 4:24 temple in Jerusalem was **s**.
5:5 They couldn't be **s** until Darius
Neh 12:39 The choir **s** at Guard's Gate.
Job 16:18 let my cry ⌊for justice⌋ be **s**.
19:14 closest friends have **s** coming.
32:1 These three men **s** answering
Psa 36:3 He has **s** doing what is wise
106:30 and the plague was **s**.
Isa 10:32 This day they **s** at Nob.
Jer 38:27 So they **s** questioning him,
44:18 But since we **s** burning
51:30 of Babylon have **s** fighting.
Lam 5:14 ⌊Our⌋ older leaders have **s**
Eze 11:23 middle of the city and **s** above

Eze 31:15 many water sources **s** flowing.
Amo 4:7 I **s** the rain from falling three
Mat 2:9 rising led them until it **s** over
14:32 the wind **s** blowing.
20:32 Jesus **s** and called them.
Mar 4:39 The wind **s** blowing,
5:29 Her bleeding **s** immediately.
6:51 and the wind **s** blowing.
10:49 Jesus **s** and said, "Call him!"
Luk 7:14 the men who were carrying it **s**.
7:45 she has not **s** kissing my feet.
8:24 The wind **s**, and the sea
8:44 and her bleeding **s** at once.
11:1 When he **s** praying,
18:40 Jesus **s** and ordered them to
23:45 The sun had **s** shining.
24:17 They **s** and looked very sad.
Act 21:32 they **s** beating Paul.
27:43 so he **s** the soldiers from
28:12 We **s** at the city of Syracuse
28:31 Jesus Christ. No one **s** him.
Gal 5:7 Who **s** you from being
Col 1:9 For this reason we have not **s**
Heb 10:2 would have **s** long ago.
Rev 9:20 If they had, they would have **s**

stopping (6)

Jdg 20:43 and pursued them without **s**.
1Ki 19:20 answered him. "I'm not **s** you."
Psa 35:15 tore me apart without **s**.
Jer 14:17 tears day and night without **s**
Lam 3:49 flowing without **s** for a moment
Rev 4:8 Without **s** day or night they

stops (12)

Lev 15:13 "When a man's discharge **s**,
15:28 "When her discharge **s**,
Job 18:5 The flame of his fire **s** glowing.
Ecc 10:14 He never **s** talking.
Isa 24:8 Joyful tambourine music **s**.
24:8 Joyful harp music **s**.
28:28 but the grinding eventually **s**.
44:19 No one **s** to think. No one has
Act 6:13 They said, "This man never **s**
1Co 13:7 Love never **s** being patient,
13:7 patient, never **s** believing,
13:7 never **s** hoping, never gives up.

storage (5)

1Ki 9:19 all the **s** cities that he owned.
2Ch 8:4 built all the **s** cities in Hamath.
8:6 Baalath and all the **s** cities that
16:4 and all the **s** cities in the
Jer 40:10 and put them in **s** jars.

store (18)

Gen 6:21 food that can be eaten and **s** it.
41:35 years and **s** up grain under
Dtr 14:28 and **s** it in your cities.
26:12 is the year when you will **s**
2Ch 32:28 He made sheds to **s** his
Neh 13:5 been used to **s** grain offerings,
Pro 10:14 who are wise **s** up knowledge,
30:25 yet they **s** their food in summer.
Isa 10:28 They **s** their equipment at
22:9 You will **s** water in the Lower
24:17 and traps are in **s** for those who
Jer 48:43 and traps are in **s** for those who
Nah 3:14 **S** water for the siege!
Mat 6:20 Instead, **s** up treasures for
Luk 12:17 enough room to **s** my crops.'
12:18 so that I can **s** all my grain
1Ti 6:19 By doing this they **s** up a
Heb 6:9 that better things are in **s**

stored (21)

Gen 41:49 Joseph **s** up grain in huge
Dtr 26:12 year distribute what you have **s**
26:13 have distributed all that was **s**,
26:13 is left of the holy offering **s**
32:34 Isn't this what I've **s** under lock
2Ki 20:17 your ancestors have **s** up
2Ch 11:12 In each city he **s** shields and
17:12 supplies were **s** in Judah.
Ezr 6:1 the archives were **s** in Babylon.
Neh 12:44 They **s** in those rooms the gifts
13:5 priests had also been **s** there.
Job 38:22 warehouses where snow is **s**
38:23 that I have **s** up for the time of
Pro 13:22 but the wealth of sinners is **s**
Isa 15:7 earned and **s** up over Willow
23:18 It won't be **s** or hoarded.
39:6 your ancestors have **s** up
Hos 13:12 people's sins is safely **s** away.
Nah 2:9 There is no end to what is **s**
Luk 12:19 "You've **s** up a lot of good
Jas 5:3 You have **s** up riches in these

storehouse (2)

Dtr 28:12 the heavens, his rich **s**, for you.
Mal 3:10 income into the **s** so that there

storehouses (10)

Gen 41:56 Joseph opened all the **s** and
Dtr 32:34 under lock and key in my **s**?
Neh 10:38 into the rooms of the **s** there.
12:25 guard at the **s** by the gates.
Psa 33:7 and puts the oceans in his **s**.
Jer 10:13 He brings wind out of his **s**.
50:26 from a distance, open their **s**,
51:16 He brings wind out of his **s**.
Hos 13:15 every precious thing in their **s**.
Joe 1:17 **S** are destroyed. Barns are

storeroom (1)

Luk 12:24 They don't even have a **s** or a

storerooms (16)

1Ki 7:51 utensils — and put them in the **s**
2Ki 12:18 that could be found in the **s**
1Ch 26:15 his sons were chosen for the **s**.
26:17 At the **s** there were four,
28:11 its **s**, upper rooms, inner rooms,
2Ch 5:1 them in the **s** of God's temple.
31:11 Hezekiah told them to prepare **s**
32:27 He prepared **s** for himself to
Ezr 8:29 In Jerusalem, inside the **s** of
Neh 10:37 olive oil to the priests, to the **s**.
10:39 into the **s** their contributions
12:44 men were put in charge of the **s**
13:4 had been put in charge of the **s**
13:12 and olive oil to the **s**.
13:13 men to be in charge of the **s**:
Psa 135:7 who brings wind out of his **s**.

stores (1)

Pro 6:8 in summertime it **s** its food

stories (19)

Jos 9:9 We heard **s** about him and
1Ki 10:7 wealth surpass the **s** I've heard.
2Ch 9:6 surpassed the **s** I've heard.
Eze 20:49 say that I'm only telling **s**."
41:6 arranged on three different **s**.
41:16 of all three **s** were paneled.
42:3 facing corridors on all three **s**.
42:5 those on the first or second **s**
42:6 The rooms were in three **s**.
42:6 those on the first and second **s**.
Mat 13:3 Then he used **s** as illustrations
13:10 "Why do you use **s** as
22:1 Again Jesus used **s** as
Mar 4:2 He used **s** as illustrations to
4:10 they asked him about the **s**.
4:11 on the outside, it is given in **s**:
4:13 you understand any of the **s**
Luk 8:10 But it is given to others in **s**.
Eph 5:4 It's not right that dirty **s**,

storing (3)

1Ch 27:27 Shimei from Ramah for **s** wine
27:28 from Gedor for **s** olive oil:
Mat 6:19 "Stop **s** up treasures for

stork (1)

Zec 5:9 had wings like those of a **s**.

storks (4)

Lev 11:19 **s**, all types of herons, hoopoes,
Dtr 14:18 **s**, all types of herons, hoopoes,
Psa 104:17 **S** makes their homes in fir
Jer 8:7 Even **s** know when it's time to

storm (45)

Exo 9:24 This was the worst **s** in all the
19:9 "I am coming to you in a **s**
Job 1:19 when suddenly a great **s** swept
9:17 would knock me down with a **s**
21:18 that the **s** sweeps away?
30:22 You toss me around with a **s**.
36:33 The **s** announces his angry
37:9 A **s** comes out of its chamber.
37:13 he makes the **s** appear.
38:1 answered Job out of the **s**.
40:6 responded to Job out of a **s**,
Psa 50:3 him and a raging **s** around him.
55:8 from the raging wind and **s**."
107:25 and a **s** began to blow,
107:29 He made the **s** calm down,
107:30 The sailors were glad that the **s**
Pro 1:27 strikes you like a violent **s**,
1:27 strikes you like a wind **s**,
10:25 When the **s** has passed,
25:14 ⌊Like⌋ a dense fog or a dust **s**,
Isa 17:13 dust being blown by a **s**.
21:1 Like a **s** sweeping through the
Jer 10:13 water in the sky produces a **s**.
11:16 set fire to you with a mighty **s**,
23:19 The **s** of the LORD will come
25:32 A great **s** is brewing from the
30:23 The **s** of the LORD will come
Eze 1:4 As I looked, I saw a **s** coming
13:13 In my fury I'll cause a **s** to
38:9 You will attack like a **s** and
Dan 11:40 at him like a **s** with chariots,
Hos 8:7 but they harvest a **s**.
Amo 1:14 are howling on the day of the **s**.
Jnh 1:4 The **s** was so powerful that the
1:11 The **s** was getting worse.
1:12 responsible for this violent **s**."
1:13 The **s** was getting worse.
Hab 3:14 soldiers come like a violent **s**
Mat 8:24 Suddenly, a severe **s** came
16:3 say that there will be a **s** today
Luk 8:23 A violent **s** came across the
Act 27:18 so violently by the **s** that
27:20 The **s** wouldn't let up.
Heb 12:18 to darkness, to gloom, to a **s**,
2Pe 2:17 are a mist blown around by a **s**.

storm-ravaged (1)

Isa 54:11 suffering, comfortless, **s** city!

storms (8)

Dtr 28:24 The LORD will send dust **s**
Psa 57:1 until destructive **s** pass by.
83:14 Pursue them with your **s**,
Isa 4:6 hiding place from **s** and rain.
29:6 rainstorms, and fire **s**.
30:30 anger, with fire **s**, windstorms,
Nah 1:3 Raging winds and **s** mark his
Zec 9:14 march in the **s** from the south.

stormy (1)

Eze 13:11 and **s** winds will break it to

story (42)

Gen 39:17 Then she told him the same **s**:
39:19 Potiphar heard his wife's **s**,
1Ki 6:6 The ⌊interior of⌋ the lowest **s**
6:6 the second **s** was 9 feet wide,
6:6 and the third **s** was 10 ½ feet
6:8 The entrance to the first **s** was
6:8 went up to the middle **s**
6:8 story and then to the third **s**.
6:10 He built ⌊each **s** of the⌋ annex
2Ki 8:6 she told him the **s**.
Job 12:8 Even the fish will relate ⌊the **s**⌋
Psa 19:2 One day tells a **s** to the next.
Eze 24:3 these rebellious people a **s**.
41:6 were 30 rooms on each **s**.
41:7 as they went up, **s** after story.
41:7 as they went up, story after **s**.
41:7 structure went from **s**
41:7 went from story to **s** all around
41:7 A stairway went from the first **s**
41:7 first story through the second **s**
41:7 the second story to the third **s**.

Eze 42:5 The side rooms on the third s
42:6 on the third s were set farther
Mat 13:18 "Listen to what the s about the
13:34 without illustrating it with a s.
18:31 told their master the whole s.
24:32 "Learn from the s of the fig tree.
28:15 Their s has been spread
Mar 1:45 He spread his s so widely that
4:13 "Don't you understand this s?
13:28 "Learn from the s of the fig tree.
Luk 2:18 the shepherds' s was amazed.
8:4 used this s as an illustration:
8:9 asked him what this s meant.
8:11 "This is what the s illustrates:
21:29 Then Jesus used this s as an
24:11 the women's s didn't make any
Jon 7:51 that person's side of the s?
9:27 you want to hear the s again?
Act 15:3 they told the whole s of how
15:3 This s brought great joy to all
20:9 he fell from the third s and was

stove (1)

Lev 11:35 If it is an oven or a s,

stragglers (1)

Isa 14:31 and there are no s in its ranks.

straight (37)

Dtr 2:27 we'll go s through and won't
Jos 6:5 Then the troops must charge s
6:20 The troops charged s ahead
1Sm 6:12 The cows went s up the road
Neh 12:37 At Fountain Gate they went s
Job 29:8 Old men stood up s out of
33:3 My words are s from the heart,
Psa 107:7 led them on a road that went s
119:128 I follow the s paths of your
Pro 4:25 Let your eyes look s ahead
4:26 Carefully walk a s path,
5:5 Her steps lead s to hell.
15:21 understanding forges s ahead.
24:26 Giving a s answer is ⌊like⌋ a
Isa 40:3 Make a s highway in the
45:13 I will make all his roads s.
Jer 31:39 line will stretch from there s
Eze 1:7 Their legs were s,
1:9 The creatures went s ahead,
1:12 of the creatures went s ahead.
1:23 that were stretched out s,
10:22 Each one went s ahead.
Joe 2:7 They march s ahead.
Mat 3:3 Make his paths s!'"
Mar 1:3 Make his paths s!'"
Luk 3:4 for the Lord! Make his paths s!
3:5 crooked ways will be made s.
13:11 over and couldn't stand up s.
13:13 stood up s and praised God.
20:17 Then Jesus looked s at them
Jon 1:23 the way for the Lord s,' as
Act 9:11 Go to Judas' house on S Street,
16:11 a ship from Troas and sailed s
21:1 we sailed s to the island of
Php 3:14 I run s toward the goal to win
Heb 12:13 Keep walking along s paths so
2Pe 2:15 teachers have left the s path

straighten (2)

Ecc 1:15 No one can s what is bent.
7:13 Who can s what God has bent?

straightened (3)

Gen 24:31 I have s up the house and
Jon 8:7 questions, he s up and said,
8:10 Then Jesus s up and asked

straightens (2)

Psa 145:14 He s ⌊the backs⌋ of those who
146:8 The LORD s ⌊the backs⌋ of

strain (2)

Dtr 28:32 You will s your eyes looking
Mat 23:24 You s gnats ⌊out of your wine⌋,

strained (3)

Psa 69:3 My eyes are s ⌊from⌋ looking
119:82 My eyes have become s from
119:123 My eyes are s from looking for

straining (1)

Lam 4:17 "We are still s our eyes,

strand (2)

Exo 39:3 creatively worked into each s
Sos 4:9 a single s of your necklace.

strands (1)

Eze 5:3 Take a few s of hair,

strange (7)

Exo 3:3 over there and see this s sight."
Jdg 7:13 man said, "I had a s dream.
Psa 81:9 Never keep any s god among
Pro 23:33 Your eyes will see s sights,
Hos 8:12 these things s and foreign.
Act 17:20 things you say sound s to us.
1Pe 4:12 something s is happening

stranger (18)

Gen 23:4 "I'm a s with no permanent
Lev 25:35 He must live with you as a s
Job 15:19 and no s passed through their
19:15 slaves consider me to be a s.
Psa 39:12 a s like all my ancestors.
69:8 I have become a s to my
Pro 6:1 for a s with a handshake,
14:10 and no s can share its joy.
27:2 from a s and not from your own
Ecc 6:2 Instead, a s enjoys them.
Jer 14:8 Why should you be like a s in
Hos 5:3 and Israel isn't a s to me.
Mat 25:35 I was a s, and you took me into
25:38 When did we see you as a s
25:43 I was a s, and you didn't take
25:44 you hungry or thirsty or as a s
Jon 10:5 They won't follow a s.
10:5 they will run away from a s

stranger's (3)

Pro 11:15 Whoever guarantees a s loan
20:16 one who guarantees a s loan,
27:13 one who guarantees a s loan,

strangers (15)

Lev 25:23 s without permanent homes.
Num 35:15 foreigners, and s among you.
Job 19:13 friends are complete s to me.
29:16 cases brought by s.
Psa 54:3 S have attacked me.
58:3 wicked people are s ⌊to God⌋.
109:11 Let s steal what he has worked
Pro 5:10 or s will benefit from your
5:17 so do not share them with s.
Jer 3:13 You have given yourself to s
Lam 5:2 has been turned over to s.
Eze 16:32 who prefers s to her husband.
Oba 1:11 s carried off Jacob's wealth.
Mat 27:7 a potter's field for the burial of s.
Heb 11:13 that they were living as s

strangled (4)

Nah 2:12 It s ⌊the prey⌋ for its mates.
Act 15:20 eating the meat of s animals,
15:29 eating the meat of s animals,
21:25 or the meat of s animals.

strap (4)

Gen 14:23 take a thread or a sandal s.
Psa 45:3 O warrior, s your sword to your
Jer 27:2 and s the yoke on your neck.
Jon 1:27 worthy to untie his sandal s."

strapped (1)

2Sm 20:8 and s over it at his hip was a

straps (14)

Exo 28:7 It will have two shoulder s
28:12 fasten them on the shoulder s
28:25 two settings on the shoulder s
28:27 to the bottom of the shoulder s
39:4 They made two shoulder s
39:7 them on the shoulder s
39:18 two settings on the shoulder s
39:20 to the bottom of the shoulder s
Isa 5:27 loose or their sandal s broken.
58:6 untie the s of the yoke,
Jer 27:2 Make leather s and a
Mar 1:7 down and untie his sandal s.
Luk 3:16 worthy to untie his sandal s.
Act 22:25 the whipping post⌋ with the s,

strategies (2)

Eph 4:14 who use cunning and clever s
6:11 a stand against the devil's s.

strategy (1)

Pro 24:6 After all, with the right s you

straw (33)

Gen 24:25 We have plenty of s and feed
24:32 unloaded and given s and feed.
Exo 5:7 give the people any more s
5:7 Let them gather their own s,
5:10 I'm no longer giving you s.
5:11 Get your own s wherever you
5:12 Egypt to gather stubble for s.
5:13 just as when you had s."
5:16 We're given no s, and yet we're
5:18 You won't be given any s,
15:7 It burned them up like s.
Jdg 19:19 We have s and fodder for our
1Ki 4:28 their quota of barley and s
Job 21:18 How often are they like s in the
41:27 It considers iron to be like s
Isa 5:24 As flames burn up s and dry
11:7 Lions will eat s like oxen.
25:10 him like s that is trampled
33:11 You will give birth to s.
40:24 sweeps them away like s.
41:2 he turns them into s blown by
41:15 You will turn the hills into s.
47:14 They are like s. Fire burns
65:25 lions will eat s like oxen,
Jer 13:24 "I will scatter you like s that is
23:28 does grain have to do with s?"
Hos 13:3 They will be like s blown
Joe 2:5 like crackling fire burning up s,
Oba 1:18 of Esau will be like s.
Nah 1:10 burned up like very dry s.
Zec 12:6 torch among freshly cut s.
Mal 4:1 all evildoers will be ⌊like⌋ s.
1Co 3:12 stones, wood, hay, or s.

stray (6)

Exo 22:5 and they s and graze in another
Psa 95:10 whose hearts continue to s.
Pro 4:14 Do not s onto the path of
14:22 Don't those who s plan what is
19:27 you will s from the words of
Heb 3:10 'Their hearts continue to s,

strayed (6)

Isa 16:8 as far as Jazer and s out into
53:6 We have all s like sheep.
Eze 34:4 brought back those that s away
34:16 back those that have s away,
Mat 18:12 to look for the one that has s?
18:13 about the 99 that have not s.

strays (2)

Pro 10:17 whoever ignores a warning s.
Mat 18:12 100 sheep and one of them s.

streaks (3)

2Sm 22:15 He flashed s of lightning and
Psa 18:14 He flashed s of lightning and
77:18 S of lightning lit up the world.

stream (23)

Gen 32:23 After he sent them across the s,
Jdg 7:22 and as far as the bank of the s
2Sm 17:20 "They've crossed the s."
1Ki 17:4 You can drink from the s,
17:6 And he drank from the s.
17:7 But after some time the s dried
18:5 to every spring and s.
Job 40:22 Poplars by the s surround it.
Psa 124:4 An ⌊overflowing⌋ s would

Pro 18:4 of wisdom is an overflowing **s**.
Isa 2:2 All the nations will **s** to it.
27:12 his threshing from the flowing **s**
30:28 breath is like an overflowing **s**.
32:20 those who plant beside every **s**
59:19 He will come like a rushing **s**.
66:12 nations like an overflowing **s**.
Jer 15:18 Will you disappoint me like a **s**
17:8 will send its roots down to a **s**.
31:12 They will **s** to it to enjoy the
51:44 will no longer **s** to Babylon,
Amo 5:24 like an ever-flowing **s**.
Mic 4:1 People will **s** to it.
Hab 3:4 Rays of light ⌊**s**⌋ from his hand.

streams (42)

Lev 11:9 in the seas and **s** that has fins
11:10 the seas or the **s** that have no
Dtr 8:7 underground **s** flowing through
2Ki 19:24 I'll dry up all the **s** of Egypt with
Job 6:20 because they relied on the **s**.
20:17 won't be able to drink from the **s**
29:6 and the rocks poured **s** of olive
Psa 1:3 is like a tree planted beside **s**—
42:1 As a deer longs for flowing **s**,
46:4 There is a river whose **s** bring
78:16 He made **s** come out of a rock.
78:20 and the **s** did overflow.
78:44 could not drink from their **s**.
104:12 The birds live by the **s**.
119:136 **S** of tears flow from my eyes
126:4 as you restore **s** ⌊to dry
Pro 5:16 Why should your **s** flow into
21:1 king's heart is like **s** of water.
Ecc 1:7 All **s** flow into the sea,
1:7 to the place where the **s** began
Isa 11:15 it into seven **s** so that people
19:6 Egypt's **s** will be emptied and
30:25 There will be brooks and **s** on
32:2 They will be like **s** on parched
33:21 by wide rivers and **s**.
34:9 Edom's **s** will be turned to tar.
35:6 and **s** will gush out into the
37:25 I'll dry up all the **s** of Egypt with
44:4 as poplars spring up by **s**.
Jer 18:14 cool mountain **s** never dry up.
31:9 I will lead them beside **s** on a
46:7 like **s** that flow swiftly?
48:34 Even the **s** of Nimrim will dry
Lam 3:48 "**S** of tears run down from my
Eze 31:4 **S** ran beside all the other trees
32:2 You make the **s** muddy.
32:14 and make its **s** flow like oil,
34:13 mountains of Israel, by the **s**,
Joe 1:20 **S** run dry. Fire has burned up
Mic 6:7 of rams or with endless **s**
Nah 3:8 which sits by the **s** of the Nile
Jon 7:38 As Scripture says, '**S** of living

street (28)

2Ki 11:16 her as she came to the **s** where
11:19 They went down the **s** that
Job 18:17 not be known on the **s** corner.
Psa 31:11 Those who see me on the **s**
Pro 7:8 He was crossing a **s** near her
7:12 moment she is out on the **s**,
Ecc 12:4 the doors to the **s** are closed,
Sos 8:1 If I saw you on the **s**,
Isa 51:20 lie sleeping at every **s** corner.
51:23 like the ground and like a **s**
59:14 Truth has fallen in the **s**,
Jer 6:11 it out on the children in the **s**
37:21 day from the bakers' **s** until all
48:38 on every rooftop and in every **s**.
Lam 2:19 from hunger at every **s** corner."
4:1 are scattered at every **s** corner.
Eze 16:25 sites at the head of every **s**.
16:31 platforms at the head of every **s**
Amo 5:16 and people will say in every **s**,
Nah 3:10 to death at every **s** corner.
Mat 6:5 synagogues and on **s** corners
Mar 11:4 the young donkey in the **s**.
Luk 14:21 'Run to every **s** and alley in the
Act 9:11 to Judas' house on Straight **S**,
12:10 they went outside and up the **s**.
Rev 11:8 dead bodies will lie on the **s**
21:21 The **s** of the city was made of
22:2 Between the **s** of the city and

streets (60)

2Sm 1:20 the victory in the **s** of Ashkelon,
22:43 on them like the dirt on the **s**.
Psa 18:42 though they were dirt on the **s**.
55:11 and fraud never leave the **s**.
144:14 be no cries of distress in our **s**.
Pro 1:20 sings her song in the **s**.
1:21 At the corners of noisy **s** she
5:16 your streams flow into the **s**?
22:13 I'll be murdered in the **s**!"
26:13 There's a lion loose in the **s**!"
Ecc 12:5 and mourners go out in the **s**.
Sos 3:2 in the **s**, and in the squares.
Isa 5:25 bodies lie like garbage in the **s**.
10:6 on them like mud in the **s**.
15:3 In their **s** they wear sackcloth.
24:11 People in the **s** call for wine.
33:7 Heroes cry in the **s**.
42:2 make his voice heard in the **s**.
58:12 of **S** Where People Live.
Jer 5:1 around the **s** of Jerusalem.
7:17 and in the **s** of Jerusalem?
7:34 and in the **s** of Jerusalem,
9:21 cut down the children in the **s**
11:6 and in the **s** of Jerusalem:
11:13 as there are **s** in Jerusalem.
14:16 out into the **s** of Jerusalem.
33:10 The cities of Judah and the **s**
44:6 and on the **s** of Jerusalem.
44:9 and on the **s** of Jerusalem?
44:17 and on the **s** of Jerusalem.
44:21 the cities of Judah and on the **s**
49:26 its young men will die in the **s**,
50:30 young men will die in the **s**,
51:4 down badly wounded in their **s**.
Lam 1:20 In the **s** swords kill my
2:11 and infants faint in the city **s**.
2:12 wounded people in the city **s**.
2:21 old lie on the ground in the **s**.
4:5 are now destitute in the **s**.
4:8 one recognizes them on the **s**.
4:14 staggered blindly through the **s**.
4:18 couldn't even go out into the **s**.
Eze 7:19 gold into the **s** like garbage.
11:6 have filled its **s** with corpses.
26:11 hoofs he will trample all your **s**.
28:23 and make blood flow in your **s**.
Hos 7:1 They rob people in the **s**.
Mic 7:10 are trampled like mud in the **s**.
Nah 2:4 are racing madly through the **s**,
Zep 3:6 I will demolish their **s**.
Zec 8:4 again sit in the **s** of Jerusalem.
8:5 boys and girls playing in the **s**.
9:3 dust and gold like mud in the **s**.
10:5 the enemy in the mud on the **s**.
Mat 6:2 in the synagogues and on the **s**
12:19 one will hear his voice in the **s**.
22:10 The servants went into the **s**
Luk 10:10 Announce in its **s**,
13:26 and you taught in our **s**.'
Act 5:15 carried their sick into the **s**.

strength (194)

Gen 18:5 so that you can regain your **s**.
48:2 Israel gathered his **s** and sat
49:3 my **s**, the very first son I had,
Exo 15:2 The LORD is my **s** and my
Num 23:22 them out of Egypt has the **s**
24:8 them out of Egypt has the **s**
Dtr 6:5 and with all your **s**.
8:17 of my own ability and **s**."
9:29 You used your great **s** and
11:8 Then you will have the **s** to
32:36 he sees that their **s** is gone
33:11 LORD, bless them with **s** and
33:25 May your **s** last as long as you
34:7 he never lost his physical **s**.
Jdg 5:21 I must march on with **s**!
6:14 Midian with the **s** you have.
6:34 LORD's Spirit gave Gideon **s**.
16:17 my **s** will leave me.
16:19 him because his **s** had left him.
16:28 give me **s** just one more time!
Jdg 19:5 something to keep up your **s**
19:8 something to keep up your **s**!"
Rut 3:11 woman who has **s** of character.
4:11 So show your **s** of character in
1Sm 2:4 who stumble are armed with **s**.
2:9 cannot succeed by their own **s**.
2:10 He gives **s** to his King and lifts
2:31 when I will break your **s**
2:31 break your strength and the **s**
28:20 He also had no **s** left,
28:22 will have **s** when you leave."
30:4 have the **s** to cry anymore.
30:6 But David found **s** in the LORD
2Sm 22:3 the **s** of my salvation,
22:33 God arms me with **s**.
22:40 You armed me with **s** for battle.
1Ki 7:21 named it Boaz [In Him Is S].
2Ki 19:3 but doesn't have the **s** to do it.
23:25 with all his heart, soul, and **s**,
1Ch 12:18 the **s** ⌊to say⌋, "We are yours,
16:11 Search for the LORD and his **s**.
16:27 **S** and joy are where he is.
29:12 You hold power and **s** in your
2Ch 3:17 on the left Boaz [In Him Is S].
20:12 We don't have the **s** to face this
24:20 son of the priest Jehoiada, **s**.
Neh 4:2 and give them new **s**?"
8:10 have in the LORD is your **s**."
Job 4:4 were weak, you gave them **s**.
6:11 What **s** do I have ⌊left⌋ that I
6:12 Do I have the **s** of rocks?
6:12 my body have the **s** of bronze?
9:19 If it is a matter of **s**,
12:13 God has wisdom and **s**.
16:15 I have thrown my **s** in the dust.
18:12 Hunger undermines his **s**.
30:2 Of what use to me was the **s** of
30:2 their hands? Their **s** is gone.
30:18 With great **s** he grabs my
36:19 Will all your mighty **s** help you?
39:19 "Can you give **s** to a horse or
39:21 It paws in **s** and finds joy in its
40:16 Look at the **s** in its back
41:12 limbs, its **s**, or its graceful form.
41:22 **S** resides in its neck,
Psa 18:1 I love you, O LORD, my **s**.
18:2 and the **s** of my salvation,
18:32 God arms me with **s** and
18:39 You armed me with **s** for battle.
21:1 The king finds joy in your **s**,
21:13 Arise, O LORD, in your **s**.
22:15 My **s** is dried up like pieces of
22:19 quickly to help me, O my **s**.
28:7 The LORD is my **s** and my
28:8 The LORD is the **s** of his
31:10 My **s** staggers under ⌊the
32:4 My **s** shriveled in the summer
33:16 himself by his own great **s**.
33:17 Their great **s** cannot help
38:10 I have lost my **s**. Even the light
44:3 gain victory with their own **s**.
46:1 God is our refuge and **s**,
59:9 O my **s**, I watch for you! God is
59:16 But I will sing about your **s**.
59:17 O my **s**, I will make music to
60:12 God we will display great **s**.
61:3 a tower of **s** against the enemy.
62:7 God is the rock of my **s**,
65:6 mountains in place with his **s**,
68:28 Display your **s**, O God, as you
68:35 He gives **s** and power to his
71:9 abandon me when I lose my **s**.
71:18 what your **s** has accomplished,
74:13 up the sea with your own **s**.
77:14 You have made your **s** known
81:1 Sing joyfully to God, our **s**.
84:5 are those who find **s** in you.
84:7 Their **s** grows as they go along
86:16 Give me your **s** because I am
88:4 I am like a man without any **s**—
89:17 you are the glory of their **s**.
89:21 My arm will also give him **s**.
96:6 **S** and beauty are in his holy
99:4 The king's **s** is that he loves
102:23 He has weakened my **s** along
105:4 Search for the LORD and his **s**.

Psa 108:13 God we will display great s.
118:14 The LORD is my s and my
118:15 hand of the LORD displays s.
118:16 hand of the LORD displays s.
Pro 5:10 will benefit from your s
8:14 I, Understanding, have s.
11:7 his confidence in s vanishes.
12:4 A wife with s of character is
14:4 but the s of an ox produces
17:22 but depression drains one's s.
20:29 glory of young men is their s,
24:5 man knows how to use his s,
31:3 Don't give your s to women or
31:17 She puts on s like a belt and
31:25 dresses with s and nobility,
Ecc 9:16 "Wisdom is better than s,"
10:10 then one has to use more s.
10:17 at the right time in order to get s
Isa 12:2 because the LORD is my s
28:6 He will give s to those who
33:2 Be our s in the morning.
37:3 but doesn't have the s to do it.
40:26 of his might and the s
40:29 He gives s to those who grow
40:29 grow tired and increases the s
40:31 Yet, the s of those who wait
41:1 Let the people gain new s.
44:12 get hungry, and their s fails.
45:24 righteousness and s are found
48:14 his s against the Babylonians.
49:4 I have used my s, but I didn't
49:5 my God has become my s.)
51:9 Clothe yourself with s,
52:1 Clothe yourself with s,
57:10 You've found renewed s,
63:1 going forward with great s?
Jer 9:23 people brag about their s.
16:19 The LORD is my s and my
16:21 my power and my s known
17:5 makes flesh and blood his s
23:10 and they use their s to do the
27:5 'I used my great s and my
32:17 and earth by your great s
49:35 important weapon of their s.
51:30 Their s has failed.
Lam 1:6 They ran without any s ahead
2:3 anger he cut off all of Israel's s.
3:18 I said, 'I've lost my s ⌊to live⌋
Eze 17:9 It won't take much s or many
24:21 that my holy place gives you s.
30:6 Egypt's s will disappear.
Dan 2:37 He has given you power, s,
8:7 The ram didn't have the s to
8:24 but not by his own s.
10:8 I had no s left in me.
10:17 I have no s left, and the wind
Hos 7:9 Foreigners are using up your s,
Amo 2:14 will find that their s is useless.
Mic 3:8 Spirit, with justice, and with s.
5:4 ⌊He will lead them⌋ with the s
7:16 ashamed in spite of all their s.
Nah 1:3 is patient and has great s.
3:9 and Egypt were her endless s.
Hab 1:11 their own s is their god.
3:19 The LORD Almighty is my s.
Mar 12:30 and with all your s.'
12:33 understanding, with all your s,
Luk 10:27 all your soul, with all your s,
22:43 to him and gave him s.
Act 9:19 his s came back to him.
19:20 was spreading and gaining s.
1Co 1:8 He will continue to give you s
1:25 is stronger than human s.
2Co 11:21 Timothy and I don't have the s
Eph 1:19 works with might and s for us,
3:16 that he would give you inner s
6:10 the Lord and from his mighty s.
1Ti 1:12 me to do his work with the s
2Ti 2:1 My child, find your source of s
4:17 by me and gave me s so that
Heb 11:34 They found s when they were
13:9 Gaining inner s from God's
13:9 This s does not come from
1Pe 4:11 with the s God supplies so
2Pe 2:11 Angels, who have more s and
Rev 3:8 You only have a little s,
5:12 s, honor, glory, and praise."
7:12 and s be to our God forever and

strengthen (30)

Dtr 3:28 Encourage and s him,
2Sm 11:25 S your attack against the city,
2Ki 15:19 his support and help s his hold
2Ch 16:9 to him and to s them.
Psa 104:15 and bread to s human hearts.
119:28 S me as you promised.
Sos 2:5 S me with raisins and refresh
Isa 35:3 S limp hands. Steady weak
41:10 I will s you. I will help you. I
45:5 I will s you, although you don't
58:11 He will s your bones.
Jer 51:12 S the guards. Station
Eze 30:25 I will s the arms of the king of
34:16 and s those that are sick.
Nah 3:14 S your defenses! Step into the
Zec 10:6 "I will s the people of Judah.
10:12 "I will s them in the LORD.
Luk 22:32 s the other disciples."
Act 15:32 encourage and s the believers.
Rom 16:25 God can s you by the Good
16:25 He can s you by revealing the
Col 1:11 We ask him to s you by his
1Th 3:2 His mission was to s and
3:13 Then he will s you to be holy.
5:11 encourage each other and s
2Th 2:17 may he encourage and s you to
3:3 Lord is faithful and will s you
Heb 12:12 S your tired arms and weak
1Pe 5:10 you, s you, make you strong,
Rev 3:2 Be alert, and s the things that

strengthened (22)

1Sm 23:16 He s David's ⌊faith⌋ in the
2Sm 3:6 Abner s his position in Saul's
1Ki 19:8 S by that food, he traveled for
2Ch 1:1 Solomon, son of David, s his
11:11 He s them and put army
11:17 So they s the kingdom of
12:13 King Rehoboam s his position
17:1 Jehoshaphat s himself ⌊to
21:4 he s his position and then
23:1 Jehoiada s his position by
32:5 s the Millo in the City of David,
Psa 80:15 the son you s for yourself.
80:17 son of man you s for yourself.
Eze 34:4 You have not s those that were
Dan 10:19 came to say. You have s me."
11:1 I s and defended Michael."
Act 14:22 They s the disciples in these
15:41 and Cilicia and s the churches.
16:5 So the churches were s in the
18:23 where he s ⌊the faith of⌋ all the
Rom 1:11 with you so that you will be s.
Col 2:7 Be s by the faith that you were

strengthening (2)

2Ch 28:20 Instead of s Ahaz,
Psa 138:3 made me bold by s my soul.

strengthens (1)

Php 4:13 through Christ who s me.

stretch (28)

Gen 18:4 you can s out and rest under
Exo 7:19 'Take your staff and s out your
10:12 The LORD said to Moses, "S
14:16 s out your hand over the sea,
14:26 "S out your hand over the sea
Rut 3:15 Then Boaz told Ruth, "S out
1Ki 8:38 who s out their hands toward
2Ch 6:29 who s out their hands toward
Job 1:11 But now s out your hand,
2:5 But s out your hand,
30:24 "But God doesn't s out his
37:18 Can you s out the skies with
Psa 68:31 Sudan will s out its hands to
88:9 I s out my hands to you ⌊in
104:2 You s out the heavens as
138:7 You s out your hand,
143:6 I s out my hands to you in
144:7 S out your hands from above.
Isa 1:15 So when you s out your hands
25:11 The Moabites will s out their
25:11 who s out their hands
28:20 The bed is too short to s out on.
34:11 He will s the measuring line of
54:2 S out the curtains of your tent,
Jer 25:33 the LORD will s from one end
31:39 A measuring line will s from
Jon 21:18 you will s out your hands,
Act 22:25 soldiers had Paul s out ⌊to tie

stretched (35)

Exo 14:21 Then Moses s out his hand
14:27 Moses s his hand over the sea,
15:12 You s out your right hand.
Jos 8:19 as soon as he s out his hand.
Jdg 11:13 It s from the Arnon River to the
1Sm 14:27 So he s out the tip of the staff
2Sm 21:10 daughter) took sackcloth and s
24:16 But when the Messenger s out
1Ki 8:22 He s out his hands toward
8:54 his hands s out toward heaven.
17:21 Then Elijah s himself over the
1Ch 21:16 had a sword in his hand and s
2Ch 6:12 He s out his hands ⌊to pray⌋.
6:13 and s out his hands toward
Ezr 9:5 s out my hands to the LORD
Job 38:5 Who s a measuring line over it?
Psa 44:20 of our God or s out our hands
77:2 At night I s out my hands in
Pro 1:24 I s out my hands to you,
Isa 23:11 The LORD has s his hand over
42:5 the heavens and s them out.
44:24 I s out the heavens by myself.
45:12 I s out the heavens with my
48:13 My right hand s out the
51:13 He s out the heavens and laid
51:16 I s out the heavens,
65:2 I s out my hands all day long to
Jer 1:9 Then the LORD s out his hand
10:12 He s out the world by his
51:15 He s out heaven by his
Eze 1:23 wings that were s out straight,
2:9 I saw a hand s out toward me.
8:3 It s out what looked like a hand
17:7 Now, the vine s its roots
Rom 10:21 "All day long I have s out my

stretcher (6)

Mat 9:2 him a paralyzed man on a s.
9:6 pick up your s, and go home."
Luk 5:18 a paralyzed man on a s.
5:19 the man down on his s among
5:24 pick up your s, and go home."
5:25 of them and picked up the s

stretchers (1)

Act 5:15 They placed them on s and

stretches (7)

Job 9:8 He s out the heavens by
15:25 He s out his hand against God
26:7 "He s out his heavens over
41:30 It s out like a threshing sledge
Pro 31:20 people and s them out
Isa 33:17 a land that s into the distance.
40:22 He s out the sky like a canopy

stretching (1)

Jer 4:31 They are s out their hands,

strict (3)

Act 5:28 He said, "We gave you s
22:3 My education was in the s
1Co 9:25 contest goes into s training.

strictest (1)

Act 26:5 that I followed the s party of our

strictly (2)

Ezr 7:26 Whoever will not s follow your
Mat 16:20 Then he s ordered the

stride (3)

Job 18:7 "His healthy s is shortened,
Pro 4:12 your s will not be hampered.
Php 3:13 look back, I lengthen my s, and

strife (1)

Pro 17:1 than a family feast filled with **s**.

strike (74)

Gen 49:19 but he will **s** back at their
Exo 3:20 I will use my power to **s** Egypt.
7:17 I'm going to **s** the Nile,
8:16 'Hold out your staff and **s** the
12:13 or destroy you when I **s** Egypt.
17:5 you used to **s** the Nile River.
17:6 **S** the rock, and water will
Num 8:19 Then no plague will **s** the
14:12 I'll **s** them with a plague,
Dtr 7:15 He will not **s** you with any of
7:15 Instead, he will **s** all those who
28:22 The LORD will **s** you with
28:27 The LORD will **s** you with the
28:27 He will **s** you with hemorrhoids,
28:28 The LORD will **s** you with
28:59 If so, the LORD will **s** you and
Rut 1:17 May the LORD **s** me down if
1Sm 3:17 May God **s** you dead if you
17:46 I will **s** you down and cut off
20:33 Saul raised his spear to **s** him.
26:10 "the LORD will **s** him.
2Sm 3:9 May God **s** me dead unless I
3:35 "May God **s** me dead if I taste
18:11 "Why didn't you **s** him to the
19:13 May God **s** me dead unless
1Ki 2:23 "May God **s** me dead if
14:15 "The LORD will **s** Israel like
19:2 She said, "May the gods **s** me
20:10 "May the gods **s** me dead if
2Ki 6:18 "Please **s** these people with
6:31 He said, "May God **s** me dead
2Ch 21:14 The LORD will **s** a great blow
Job 1:11 and **s** everything he has.
2:5 and **s** his flesh and bones.
41:26 A sword may **s** it but not pierce
Psa 9:20 **S** them with terror,
78:20 True, he did **s** a rock,
78:48 He let the hail **s** their cattle and
78:48 of lightning **s** their livestock.
81:2 and **s** a tambourine.
91:6 epidemics that **s** at noon.
141:5 A righteous person may **s** me
Pro 17:26 To **s** down noble people is not
19:25 **S** a mocker, and a gullible
23:35 "They **s** me, but I feel no pain.
Isa 3:11 Disaster will **s** them.
5:25 use his power to **s** them down.
10:24 of the Assyrians when they **s**
11:4 He will **s** the earth with a rod
19:22 The LORD will **s** Egypt with a
30:31 He will **s** them with his rod.
47:11 Disaster will **s** you.
49:10 or the burning, hot wind **s** them.
Jer 5:3 You **s** these people,
Eze 21:14 Let the sword **s** again and
30:25 He will **s** Egypt with it.
Amo 9:1 **S** the tops of the pillars so that
Mic 5:1 Enemies will **s** the judge of
6:13 I have begun to **s** you with
Zec 10:11 **s** the waves in the sea,
11:17 A sword will **s** his arm and his
12:4 "On that day I will **s** every
12:4 but I will **s** all the horses of the
13:7 "**S** the shepherd, and the sheep
14:12 the LORD will use to **s** all
14:18 The plague the LORD uses to **s**
Mat 26:31 'I will **s** the shepherd,
Mar 14:27 'I will **s** the shepherd,
Act 23:2 standing near Paul to **s** him
23:3 "God will **s** you, you hypocrite!
23:3 by ordering these men to **s** me!"
1Th 5:3 will suddenly **s** them.
Rev 11:6 to turn water into blood and to **s**
22:18 God will **s** him with the

strikes (15)

Exo 21:12 "Whoever **s** someone and kills
Job 34:26 he **s** them in public,
Psa 29:7 The voice of the LORD **s** with
Pro 1:26 fun of you when panic **s** you,
1:27 when panic **s** you like a
Pro 1:27 when calamity **s** you like a
23:32 Later it bites like a snake and **s**
Ecc 9:12 when it suddenly **s** them.
Isa 19:22 When he **s** them, he will also
Jer 22:23 will groan when pain **s** you,
Lam 3:30 cheeks to the one who **s** them
Oba 1:13 of my people when disaster **s**
1:13 their misery when disaster **s**.
1:13 their wealth when disaster **s**.
Luk 6:29 If someone **s** you on the cheek,

striking (4)

1Sm 5:6 He destroyed them by **s** the
2Sm 6:8 Uzzah [The **S** of Uzzah] today.)
1Ch 13:11 Uzzah [The **S** of Uzzah] today.)
2Co 8:13 it's a matter of **s** a balance.

string (2)

Job 16:4 I could **s** words together
Isa 5:18 for those who **s** people along

stringed (5)

Psa 33:3 and joyfully on **s** instruments.
45:8 of **s** instruments delights you.
150:4 with **s** instruments and flutes.
Isa 38:20 so let us play **s** instruments.
Hab 3:19 choir director; on **s** instruments

strings (4)

Jdg 15:14 his arms became like **s** burned
16:12 arms as though they were **s**.
Psa 11:2 set their arrows against the **s**
Sos 1:10 your neck with **s** of pearls.

strip (14)

Exo 3:22 This way you will **s** Egypt of
1Sm 31:8 Philistines came to **s** the dead,
2Sm 23:10 only returned to **s** the dead.
1Ch 10:8 Philistines came to **s** the dead,
Job 22:6 security for a loan and **s** them
Isa 45:1 **s** kings of their power,
Jer 49:10 Yet, I will **s** the descendants of
51:2 to winnow it and **s** its land
Eze 48:15 A **s** of land, 8,750 feet wide by
Dan 4:14 **S** off its leaves! Scatter its fruit!
Hos 2:3 If she refuses, I will **s** her.
Amo 3:11 **s** you of your defenses,
Mic 3:2 You **s** the skin off my people
3:3 You **s** off their skin.

striped (7)

Gen 30:35 same day Laban took out the **s**
30:39 gave birth to young that were **s**,
30:40 the sheep face any that were **s**
31:8 And whenever he said, 'The **s**
31:8 all the flocks gave birth to **s**
31:10 which were mating were **s**,
31:12 goats which are mating are **s**,

stripped (18)

Gen 34:27 Then Jacob's sons **s** the
37:23 they **s** him of his special robe
Exo 12:36 So the Israelites **s** Egypt of its
1Sm 31:9 They cut off his head and **s** off
2Ki 18:16 At that time Hezekiah **s** ⌊the
24:13 Nebuchadnezzar **s** the gold off
1Ch 10:9 They **s** him and took his head
Job 19:9 He has **s** me of my honor.
19:26 Even after my skin has been **s**
Isa 23:13 battle towers, **s** palaces bare,
24:3 be completely laid waste and **s**
Lam 2:6 He **s** his own booth as if it
Eze 12:19 Their country will be **s** of
23:10 They **s** her naked,
Joe 1:7 They **s** off what they could eat,
Nah 2:7 has determined: "It will be **s**.
Luk 10:30 On the way robbers **s** him,
Col 2:15 He **s** the rulers and authorities

stripping (2)

Jer 25:36 the LORD is **s** their pasture.
Hab 3:13 **s** him bare from head to toe.

strips (12)

Gen 30:37 the bark on them in **s** of white,
Job 12:18 He loosens kings' belts and **s**
Psa 29:9 the oaks and **s** ⌊the trees of⌋
Luk 2:7 She wrapped him in **s** of cloth
2:12 will find an infant wrapped in **s**
24:12 and saw only the **s** of linen.
Jon 11:44 **S** of cloth were wound around
19:40 and bound it with **s** of linen.
19:40 They laced the **s** with spices.
20:5 He saw the **s** of linen lying
20:6 He saw the **s** of linen lying
20:7 It wasn't lying with the **s** of

strive (1)

Dtr 16:20 **S** for nothing but justice so that

striving (1)

Rom 11:7 what it has been **s** for.

strong (201)

Gen 49:14 "Issachar is a **s** donkey,
Exo 1:7 so numerous and **s** that
1:20 in number and became very **s**.
10:19 the wind to a very **s** west wind.
14:21 the sea with a **s** east wind
15:6 wins glory because it is **s**.
Num 11:4 the Israelites had a **s** craving
11:34 had a **s** craving ⌊for meat⌋.
13:18 living there are **s** or weak,
13:28 the people who live there are **s**,
13:31 They're too **s** for us!"
22:6 because they are too **s** for me.
Dtr 2:10 These people were as **s**,
2:21 These people were as **s**,
9:2 Their people are tall and **s**.
31:6 Be **s** and courageous.
31:7 "Be **s** and courageous.
31:23 "Be **s** and courageous,
Jos 1:6 Be **s** and courageous,
1:7 "Only be **s** and very
1:9 'Be **s** and courageous!
1:18 Just be **s** and courageous!"
10:25 Be **s** and courageous,
17:13 Israelites became **s** enough,
17:18 even though they are **s** and
23:6 Now you must be very **s** to
Jdg 1:28 the Israelites were **s** enough,
6:2 power was too **s** for Israel.
9:51 Now, there was a **s** tower
14:14 From the **s** one came
16:5 find out what makes him so **s**.
16:6 tell me what makes you so **s**.
16:9 found out why he was so **s**.
16:15 told me what makes you so **s**."
1Sm 4:9 Be **s**, Philistines, and act like
2Sm 2:7 Now, be **s** and courageous.
10:11 "If the Arameans are too **s** for
10:11 And if the Ammonites are too **s**
10:12 Be **s**! Let's prove ourselves
10:12 Let's prove ourselves **s** for our
13:28 Be **s** and courageous."
22:18 He rescued me from my **s**
22:18 they were too **s** for me.
1Ki 2:2 this world. Be **s** and mature.
2Ki 2:16 "There are 50 **s** men here with
1Ch 19:12 "If the Arameans are too **s** for
19:12 And if the Ammonites are too **s**
19:13 Be **s**! Let's prove ourselves
19:13 Let's prove ourselves **s** for our
22:13 Be **s** and courageous.
28:10 holy place. Be **s**, and do it."
28:20 "Be **s** and courageous,
29:12 can make anyone great and **s**.
2Ch 12:1 kingdom and made himself **s**,
13:21 But Abijah became **s**.
14:11 who are not **s** so that they
15:7 But you must remain **s** and not
19:11 Be **s**, and do your job. May the
26:15 because he had **s** support until
32:7 "Be **s** and courageous.
Ezr 9:12 Then you will be **s**,
10:4 so be **s** and take action."
Neh 1:10 great power and your **s** hand.
6:9 But God made me **s**.
Job 4:3 were weak, you made them **s**.
21:24 his bones are **s** and healthy.
22:8 A **s** person owns the land.

Job 26:2 and saved the arm that isn't s.
37:9 It is cold because of the s
39:11 trust it just because it's so s
Psa 18:17 He rescued me from my s
18:17 they were too s for me.
22:12 S bulls from Bashan have
24:8 The LORD, s and mighty!
27:14 Be s, and let your heart be
31:2 a s fortress to save me.
31:24 Be s, all who wait with hope
35:10 from the one who is too s
52:7 became s through his greed."
68:28 God has decided you will be s.
71:7 but you are my s refuge.
89:10 With your s arm you scattered
89:13 Your hand is s. Your right hand
92:10 But you make me as s as a
112:2 His descendants will grow s
140:7 the s one who saves me,
142:6 because they are too s for me.
147:10 He finds no joy in s horses,
147:13 the bars across your gates s.
148:8 s winds that obey his
148:14 given his people a s leader,
Pro 10:15 person's wealth is ⌞his⌟ s city.
14:26 LORD there is s confidence,
18:10 name of the LORD is a s tower.
18:11 A rich person's wealth is his s
18:19 more ⌞resistant⌟ than a s city,
21:22 and pulls down the s defenses
23:11 is responsible for them is s.
24:5 A s man knows how to use his
30:25 Ants are not a s species,
31:10 find a wife with a s character?
Ecc 12:3 s men are stooped over,
Isa 1:31 S people will become tinder for
18:2 a s and aggressive nation,
18:7 a s and aggressive nation,
19:4 A s king will rule them,"
25:3 That is why s people will
26:1 of Judah: We have a s city.
28:2 has one who is s and powerful.
30:15 You can be s by being quiet
30:26 sun will be seven times as s,
31:1 depend on very s war horses.
43:16 a road through the s currents.
44:12 working them with their s arms.
44:14 They let them grow s among
53:12 will divide the prize with the s,
Jer 9:23 Don't let s people brag about
14:9 like a s man who cannot help?
30:6 Why, then, do I see every s
48:17 Say, 'Look at the s staff,
50:9 up an alliance of s nations from
50:34 Their defender is s.
Eze 3:14 The s power of the LORD
7:24 I will stop those who are s from
19:11 Its branches were s.
19:12 Its s branches broke off.
19:14 It no longer has any s
22:14 Will you remain s when I deal
26:11 and your s pillars will fall to the
29:21 the people of Israel s again,
30:18 Egypt's s army will be
30:21 so it can't heal and be s
30:24 arms of the king of Babylon s.
34:16 destroy those that are fat and s.
Dan 2:40 It will be as s as iron.
2:42 Part of the kingdom will be s,
4:11 The tree grew, and it became s
4:20 grow and become s enough
4:22 You grew and became s and
7:7 dreadful, extraordinarily s,
8:22 but they won't be as s as the
8:24 He will become very s,
9:15 out of Egypt with your s hand
10:19 Be s! Be strong!" As he talked
10:19 Be s!" As he talked to me, I
11:2 As he becomes s through his
11:5 "The southern king will be s,
11:12 he will not always be s.
11:15 troops will not be s enough.
11:25 for war with a large, s army.
11:32 God will be s and take action.
11:39 he will deal with s fortresses.
Hos 7:15 trained them and made them s.
Joe 1:6 A s nation attacked my land.
Amo 2:9 as cedars and as s as oaks.
2:14 S men will find that their
6:13 "We were s enough to capture
8:13 women and s young men will
Mic 4:7 forced away into a s nation."
6:2 you s foundations of the earth.
Hag 2:4 be s," declares the LORD.
2:4 (son of Jehozadak), be s.
2:4 be s," declares the LORD.
Zec 6:3 And the fourth had s,
6:7 When these s horses went out,
8:9 Be s so that the temple might
12:5 who live in Jerusalem are s
Mat 12:29 How can anyone go into a s
12:29 First he must tie up the s man.
14:30 But when he noticed how s the
15:28 her, "Woman, you have s faith!
Mar 3:27 "No one can go into a s man's
3:27 First he must tie up the s man.
3:27 Then he can go through the s
Luk 1:52 He pulled s rulers from their
1:80 grew and became spiritually s.
2:40 The child grew and became s.
11:21 "When a s man, fully armed,
11:22 in which the s man trusted
16:3 I'm not s enough to dig,
Jon 6:18 A s wind started to blow and
Act 3:7 feet and ankles became s.
13:17 them a s nation while they
Rom 4:20 he became s because of faith
15:1 So those of us who have a s
15:1 whose ⌞faith⌟ is not so s.
1Co 1:27 to put what is s to shame.
4:10 We are weak, but you are s.
15:43 it has splendor and is s.
16:13 Be courageous and s.
2Co 10:10 my letters are powerful and s,
12:10 clear that when I'm weak, I'm s.
13:9 we are weak and you are s.
1Th 2:2 News in spite of s opposition.
Heb 6:19 as a sure and s anchor
10:22 with a sincere heart and s faith.
Jas 3:4 big and are driven by s winds.
1Pe 5:10 strengthen you, make you s,
1Jn 2:14 because you are s and God's
Rev 6:13 when it is shaken by a s wind.
12:8 But it was not s enough,

stronger (40)

Gen 25:23 One nation will be s than the
30:41 Whenever the s of the flocks
30:42 Laban and the s ones to Jacob.
Exo 1:9 and they are s then we are.
Num 14:12 larger and s than they are."
Dtr 1:28 are taller and s than we are.
4:38 He forced nations greater and s
9:1 that are larger and s than you,
9:14 larger and s than they are."
11:23 people taller and s than you.
Jdg 1:35 the tribes of Joseph became s,
3:12 Eglon of Moab s than Israel,
4:24 The Israelites became s and
4:24 and s until they destroyed
14:18 What is s than a lion?"
18:26 Micah saw they were s than he
1Sm 17:50 David proved to be s than the
2Sm 1:23 than eagles and s than lions.
3:1 family became s and stronger,
3:1 family became stronger and s,
15:12 the conspiracy grew s,
1Ki 16:22 followed Omri was s than
20:23 That is why they were s than
20:23 we will be s than they are.
20:25 we will be s than they are."
Job 17:9 one with clean hands grows s.
Psa 38:19 mortal enemies are growing s.
105:24 and s than their enemies.
Ecc 6:10 the one who is s than they.
Jer 4:12 It will be a s wind than that.
31:11 those who are s than they are.
Dan 1:15 looked healthier and s than
10:18 touched me, and I became s.
10:19 As he talked to me, I became s.
11:5 his officers will become s than
Luk 11:22 But a s man than he may
Luk 11:22 Then the s man will take away
1Co 1:25 is s than human strength.
10:22 Are we s than he is?
1Ti 5:11 become s than their devotion

strongest (2)

Psa 78:31 He killed their s men and
2Co 12:9 My power is s when you are

stronghold (27)

1Sm 23:25 So he went to his mountain s
2Sm 22:3 my salvation, my s, my refuge,
1Ki 16:18 he went into the s in the royal
2Ki 10:25 and attendants came to the s
Psa 9:9 The LORD is a s for the
9:9 a s in times of trouble.
18:2 strength of my salvation, my s.
46:7 The God of Jacob is our s.
46:11 The God of Jacob is our s.
48:3 He has proved that he is a s.
59:9 God is my s, my merciful God!
59:16 You have been my s and a
59:17 God is my s, my merciful God!
62:2 my rock and my savior — my s.
62:6 my rock and my savior — my s.
94:22 The LORD has become my s.
144:2 fortress, my s, and my savior,
Isa 17:10 remembered the rock, your s.
23:4 because the s by the sea has
31:9 In terror they will run to their s,
33:16 His s will be a fortress made of
Jer 48:1 Its s will be put to shame and
Eze 24:25 on that day I will take their s
Dan 11:7 enter the s of the northern king,
11:10 wage war all the way to the s.
Joe 3:16 He will be a s for the people of
Mic 4:8 s of the people of Zion,

strongholds (5)

Jdg 6:2 and mountain s to protect
Isa 13:22 will howl in Babylon's s,
Jer 51:53 They might fortify their s.
Lam 2:5 He destroyed its s.
Amo 5:9 destroys s and ruins fortresses.

struck (73)

Gen 12:17 However, the LORD s Pharaoh
19:11 Then they s all the men who
Exo 7:20 raised his staff and s the Nile.
7:25 after the LORD s the Nile.
8:17 out the staff in his hand and s
9:23 and lightning s the earth.
9:25 It s down people, animals,
Num 11:33 with the people and s them
Jos 24:5 and I s Egypt with plagues.
Jdg 5:26 She s Sisera. She crushed his
1Sm 4:8 These are the gods who s the
5:9 He s all the important and
5:12 didn't die were s with tumors.
6:9 it wasn't his hand that s us,
6:19 God s down some of the
6:19 He s down 70 people.
6:19 because the LORD s them
14:13 Jonathan s down the
14:31 That day they s down the
17:35 I went after it, s it, and rescued
17:35 of its mane, s it, and killed it.
17:49 and s the Philistine in the
17:50 David s down and killed the
18:27 out and s down 200 Philistines.
19:10 and Saul's spear s the wall.
2Sm 2:23 So Abner s him with the butt of
6:8 had s Uzzah so violently.
10:18 David s Shobach dead.
11:15 that he'll be s down and die."
12:15 The LORD s the child that
1Ki 22:24 went to Micaiah and s him on
2Ki 2:8 and s the water with it.
2:14 He took the coat and s the
2:14 As he s the water,
6:18 The LORD s them with
1Ch 13:11 had s Uzzah so violently.
15:13 the LORD our God s us.
21:7 so he s Israel ⌞with a plague⌟.
2Ch 18:23 went to Micaiah and s him on
21:18 After this, the LORD s Jehoram

Job 1:19 swept across the desert and **s**
2:7 the LORD's presence and **s** Job
19:21 God's hand has **s** me down.
Psa 38:2 Your arrows have **s** me.
38:2 Your hand has **s** me hard.
39:10 My life is over because you **s**
52:6 see ⌊this⌋ and be **s** with fear.
64:7 Suddenly, they will be **s** dead.
69:26 persecute the one you have **s**,
78:66 He **s** his enemies from behind
105:33 He **s** their grapevines and fig
Sos 5:7 They **s** me! They wounded me!
Isa 9:13 returned to the one who **s** them,
10:20 depend on the one who **s** them.
10:26 As he **s** down Midian at the
14:6 They **s** the people with fury,
14:29 of the one who **s** you is broken,
60:10 In my anger I **s** you,
66:16 Many people will be **s** dead by
Jer 2:3 and disaster **s** them,'" declares
14:19 Why have you **s** us so hard
18:21 men will be **s** down in battle.
20:2 Pashhur **s** the prophet
Dan 2:34 It **s** the statue's iron-and-clay
2:35 But the stone that **s** the statue
Amo 4:9 I **s** your ⌊crops⌋ with blight and
Hag 2:17 with blight and mildew and **s**
Mat 7:27 Winds blew and **s** that house.
Luk 7:16 Everyone was **s** with fear and
Act 27:41 They **s** a sandbar in the water
Rev 6:12 A powerful earthquake **s**.
8:12 stars were **s** so that one-third
11:13 a powerful earthquake **s**.

structure (2)
Eze 41:7 The surrounding **s** went from
41:7 The **s** grew wider as it went

struggle (10)
Gen 6:3 "My Spirit will not **s** with
30:8 "I have had a great **s** with my
30:8 named him Naphtali [My **S**].
Job 41:8 Think of the **s**! Don't do it again!
Luk 9:39 After a **s**, the spirit goes away,
Rom 15:30 to join me in my **s**.
Php 1:30 You are involved in the same **s**
Col 1:29 I work hard and **s** to do this
1Ti 4:10 Certainly, we work hard and **s**
Heb 12:4 You **s** against sin,

struggled (4)
Gen 32:28 because you have **s** with God
Hos 12:3 became a man, he **s** with God.
12:4 He **s** with the Messenger and
2Th 3:8 Instead, we worked hard and **s**

struggles (4)
Gen 32:28 but Israel [He **S** With God],
Psa 37:18 The LORD knows the daily ⌊**s**⌋
Ecc 2:22 hard work and **s** under the sun?
Heb 12:4 but your **s** haven't killed you.

struggling (1)
Gen 25:22 the children inside her were **s**

strum (2)
1Sm 16:16 comes to you, he'll **s** a tune,
Amo 6:5 up songs as they **s** a harp.

strummed (2)
1Sm 16:23 took the lyre and **s** a tune.
18:10 in his house while David **s**

strumming (1)
1Sm 19:9 David was **s** a tune.

strutting (1)
Pro 30:31 a **s** rooster, a male goat, a king

stubble (2)
Exo 5:12 over Egypt to gather **s** for straw.
Job 41:29 It considers clubs to be like **s**,

stubborn (86)
Exo 4:21 But I will make him **s** so that
7:3 But I will make Pharaoh **s**.
7:13 Yet, Pharaoh continued to be **s**
7:14 "Pharaoh is being **s**.
7:22 So Pharaoh continued to be **s**
8:15 he became **s** and would not
8:19 Yet, Pharaoh continued to be **s**
8:32 Pharaoh was **s** and did not let
9:7 Yet, Pharaoh continued to be **s**
9:12 But the LORD made Pharaoh **s**,
9:34 his officials continued to be **s**.
9:35 Pharaoh was **s** and would not
10:1 him and his officials **s** so that
10:20 But the LORD made Pharaoh **s**,
10:27 But the LORD made Pharaoh **s**,
11:10 the LORD made Pharaoh **s**,
13:15 When Pharaoh was too **s** to let
14:4 I will make Pharaoh so **s** that
14:8 (the king of Egypt) so **s** that
14:17 I am making the Egyptians so **s**
Dtr 2:30 LORD your God made him **s**
21:18 Parents might have a **s** and
21:20 son of ours is **s** and rebellious.
29:19 even if I go my own **s** way.
Jos 11:20 made their enemies **s** enough
Jdg 2:19 their evil practices and **s** ways.
1Sm 6:6 Why should you be as **s** as the
2Ch 36:13 But Zedekiah became so **s**
Neh 9:16 They became **s** and wouldn't
9:17 They became **s** and appointed
Job 5:2 Certainly, anger kills a **s** fool,
5:3 I have seen a **s** fool take root,
5:5 What a **s** fool gathers,
Psa 32:9 Don't be **s** like a horse or mule.
78:8 a **s** and rebellious generation.
81:12 So I let them go their own **s**
95:8 "Do not be **s** like ⌊my people
Pro 1:7 **S** fools despise wisdom and
10:14 mouth of a **s** fool invites ruin.
10:21 but **s** fools die because they
11:29 and that **s** fool becomes a
12:15 A **s** fool considers his own
12:16 When a **s** fool is irritated,
14:3 Because of a **s** fool's words a
14:9 **S** fools make fun of guilt,
15:5 A **s** fool despises his father's
16:22 but **s** fools punish themselves
17:28 Even a **s** fool is thought to be
20:3 any **s** fool can start a fight.
24:7 beyond the grasp of a **s** fool.
27:3 but annoyance caused by a **s**
27:22 If you crush a **s** fool in a mortar
29:9 goes to court with a **s** fool,
Isa 46:12 Listen to me, you **s** people who
48:4 I know that you are **s**.
63:17 and become so **s** that we are
65:2 hands all day long to **s** people.
Jer 3:17 no longer follow their own **s**,
5:3 They are more **s** than rocks.
5:23 people are **s** and rebellious.
7:24 their own plans and their **s**,
9:14 They followed their own **s**
11:8 They followed their own **s**,
13:10 They go their own **s** ways and
16:12 you are following your own **s**,
18:12 We'll go our own **s**,
23:17 who live by their own **s** ways,
Lam 3:65 Make them **s**. Let your curse be
Eze 2:4 to these defiant and **s** children.
3:7 are very **s** and hardheaded.
3:8 Yet, I will make you as **s** and
11:19 I will remove their **s** hearts and
36:26 I will remove your **s** hearts and
Hos 4:16 "The people of Israel are as **s**
Mar 16:14 and because they were too **s**
Act 7:51 "How **s** can you be?
19:9 when some people became **s**,
Rom 2:5 Since you are **s** and don't want
9:18 he wants to make someone **s**,
Tit 1:7 He must not be a **s** or irritable
Heb 3:7 God speak today, don't be **s**.
3:8 Don't be **s** like those who
3:13 deceived by sin and become **s**.
3:15 God speak today, don't be **s**.
3:15 Don't be **s** like those who
4:7 God speak today, don't be **s**."

stubbornly (1)
Job 15:26 He **s** charges at him with a

stubbornness (2)
Dtr 9:27 Disregard the **s**, wickedness,
Eph 4:18 of their ignorance and **s**.

stuck (8)
Jdg 3:22 The blade **s** out in back.
1Sm 26:7 the camp with his spear **s**
2Sm 2:16 **s** his sword into his opponent's
23:10 until his hand got tired and **s**
Job 29:10 and their tongues **s** to the roofs
Pro 26:9 ⌊Like⌋ a thorn **s** in a drunk's
Jer 38:22 Your feet are **s** in the mud,
Act 27:41 The front of the ship **s** and

student (4)
Isa 50:4 will wake me to listen like a **s**.
Mat 10:24 "A **s** is not better than his
10:25 It is enough for a **s** to become
Luk 6:40 A **s** is no better than his

students (1)
1Ch 25:8 ⌊musicians⌋ along with the **s**.

studied (3)
Job 5:27 "We have **s** all of this
Psa 111:2 They should be **s** by all who
Ecc 12:9 carefully thought about it, **s** it,

studies (1)
Jas 1:24 **s** his features, goes away,

study (12)
Ezr 7:10 Ezra was determined to **s** the
Neh 8:13 met with Ezra the scribe to **s**
Psa 119:6 I **s** all your commandments.
119:15 principles and **s** your ways.
Ecc 1:13 all my heart I used wisdom to **s**
7:25 I turned my attention to **s**,
8:16 considered how to **s** wisdom
Eze 43:10 Let them **s** the plans.
Dan 9:23 So **s** the message,
Jon 5:39 You **s** the Scriptures in detail
7:52 **S** ⌊the Scriptures⌋,
Jas 1:25 the person who continues to **s**

studying (2)
Ecc 12:12 Too much **s** will wear out your
2Ti 3:7 These women are always **s**

stuff (4)
Gen 25:30 me have the whole pot of red **s**
25:30 that red **s** — I'm exhausted."
1Sm 25:21 "I guarded this man's **s** in the
Jon 2:16 sold pigeons, "Pick up this **s**,

stuffed (2)
Dtr 32:15 You were **s**! You were gorged!)
Pro 1:31 They will be **s** with their own

stumble (44)
Lev 19:14 of blind people to make them **s**.
26:37 They will **s** over each other,
1Sm 2:4 but those who **s** are armed with
Job 12:24 and makes them **s** about
12:25 he makes them **s** like drunks.
Psa 9:3 they will **s** and die in your
55:22 let the righteous person **s**.
107:40 and made them **s** around
119:165 can make those people **s**.
Pro 4:12 Even if you run, you will not **s**.
4:16 unless they make someone **s**.
4:19 not know what makes them **s**.
5:23 lack of discipline and **s** around
Isa 5:27 None of them grow tired or **s**.
8:15 Many will **s**. They will fall and
24:20 The earth will **s** like a drunk
31:3 the one who gives help will **s**,
40:30 and young men will **s** and fall.
59:10 We **s** at noon as if it were
63:13 in the wilderness, they didn't **s**.
Jer 6:21 and children will **s** over them.
12:5 If you **s** in open country,

Jer 13:16 before your feet s on the
18:15 and they s along the way,
18:23 Make them s in your presence.
20:10 friends are waiting to see me s.
20:11 those who persecute me will s.
31:9 path where they will not s.
46:6 They s and fall in the north by
46:12 One warrior will s over another,
50:32 arrogant people will s and fall,
Eze 3:20 I will make them s,
33:12 done will not make him s when
Dan 11:19 own country, but he will s, fall,
Hos 4:5 During the day you s,
4:5 night the prophets s with you.
5:5 Israel and Ephraim s because
14:9 Rebellious people s over them.
Nah 2:5 They s over themselves as
Zec 12:8 so that even those who s will
Mal 2:8 many to s over my teachings.
Jon 11:9 walk during the day don't s,
11:10 those who walk at night s
1Co 10:32 Don't cause others to s,

stumbled (12)
2Sm 6:6 threshing floor, the oxen s.
1Ch 13:9 threshing floor, the oxen s.
Job 4:4 When someone s,
Psa 27:2 and enemies s and fell.
35:15 Yet, when I s, they rejoiced
73:2 But my feet had almost s.
105:37 and no one among his tribes s.
Isa 3:8 Jerusalem has s, and Judah
Jer 46:16 They have repeatedly s,
Hos 14:1 You have s because of your
Rom 9:32 They s over the rock that trips
11:11 So I ask, "Has Israel s so

stumbles (2)
Pro 24:17 and do not feel glad when he s.
Hos 5:5 and Judah s with them.

stumbling (4)
Psa 56:13 You have kept my feet from s
116:8 tears ⌊and⌋ my feet from s.
Isa 8:14 people trip and a s block
Jer 6:21 I'm going to lay s blocks in

stump (7)
Job 14:8 old in the ground and its s dies
Isa 6:13 an oak is cut down, a s is left.
6:13 holy seed will be the land's s."
11:1 come out from the s of Jesse,
Dan 4:15 But leave the s and its roots in
4:23 But leave the s and its roots in
4:26 Since I said that the s and the

stunned (15)
Gen 45:26 Jacob was s and didn't believe
Est 4:4 The queen was s.
Psa 40:15 be s by their own shame.
Jer 4:9 The priests will be s.
18:16 who will pass by it will be s
19:8 who goes by it will be s
Eze 3:15 them for seven days. I was s.
Dan 4:19 was momentarily s.
Mar 1:27 Everyone was s. They said to
10:24 The disciples were s by his
Luk 2:47 answers s everyone who heard
4:36 Everyone was s. They said to
Act 2:7 S and amazed, the people in
2:12 men were s and puzzled.
3:10 The people were amazed and s

stunted (1)
Lev 22:23 with a deformity or one that is s

stupid (19)
Job 18:3 we considered s in your eyes?
Psa 49:10 that foolish and s people meet
73:22 I was s, and I did not
92:6 A s person cannot know and a
94:8 Pay attention, you s people!
Pro 14:1 but a s one tears it down with
18:13 he listens is s and shameful.
Ecc 7:25 I learned that wickedness is s
Isa 19:11 counselors gives s advice.
Jer 4:22 They are s people.
5:21 you s and senseless people!
10:14 Everyone is s and ignorant.
31:19 because of all the s things I
51:17 Everyone is s and ignorant.
Gal 3:1 You s people of Galatia!
3:3 Are you that s? Did you begin in
1Ti 6:9 They are trapped by many s
2Ti 2:23 with foolish and s arguments.
Tit 3:3 Indeed, we, too, were once s,

stupidity (25)
Psa 38:5 They fester because of my s.
69:5 O God, you know my s,
85:8 must not go back to their s.
Pro 5:23 around because of his great s.
9:13 The woman S is loud,
12:23 but foolish minds preach s.
13:16 but a fool displays s.
14:8 but the s of fools misleads
14:18 people are gifted with s,
14:24 The s of fools is just that —
14:24 of fools is just that — s!
14:29 short temper is the height of s.
15:2 of fools pour out a flood of s.
15:14 the mouths of fools feed on s.
15:21 S is fun to the one without
16:22 punish themselves with their s.
17:12 fool ⌊carried away⌋ with his s.
19:3 The s of a person turns his life
26:4 answer a fool with his own s,
26:5 Answer a fool with his own s,
26:11 ⌊so⌋ a fool repeats his s.
27:22 ⌊even then⌋ his s will not
Ecc 1:17 as well as madness and s.
2Ti 3:9 Like the s of Jannes and
3:9 their s will be plain to

stupidly (1)
Pro 14:17 A short-tempered person acts s,

stutter (1)
Isa 32:4 and those who s will speak

styles (1)
1Ti 2:9 not by their hair s or the gold

stylus (1)
Job 19:24 a rock with an iron s and lead.

Suah (1)
1Ch 7:36 Zophah's sons were S,

subject (19)
Gen 14:4 had been s to Chedorlaomer,
2Sm 10:19 When all the kings who were s
14:15 will do something for me, his s.
14:16 listen and rescue me, his s,
1Ki 4:21 paid taxes and were s
2Ki 24:1 and Jehoiakim became s to
1Ch 19:19 When all the kings who were s
Ezr 6:3 as king From: King Cyrus S:
Psa 106:42 made them s to their power.
Isa 11:14 of Ammon will be s to them.
Act 13:42 them to speak on the same s
1Co 2:2 with only one s — Jesus Christ,
2:15 evaluate everything but are s
9:20 I became s to Moses'
9:20 Teachings for those who are s
9:20 I'm not s to Moses' Teachings.
9:21 really s to Christ's teachings.
Gal 5:18 you are not s to Moses' laws.
2Pe 3:16 He talks about this s in all his

subjected (2)
Rom 8:20 Creation was s to frustration
8:20 The one who s it to frustration

subjects (11)
2Sm 8:2 the Moabites became David's s
8:6 the Arameans became his s
8:14 the Edomites were David's s.
10:19 with Israel and became their s.
1Ch 18:2 the Moabites became David's s
18:6 the Arameans became his s
18:13 its people became David's s.
19:19 with David and became his s.
28:2 my relatives and s.
Dan 1:4 knowledgeable in all s,
Act 24:25 As Paul discussed the s of

submit (1)
Dtr 22:15 the leaders of the city are and s

substitute (3)
Lev 27:10 Don't exchange or s animals,
27:33 both the first animal and its s
1Ki 20:24 and s governors for them.

substitutes (7)
Num 3:12 I have taken the Levites to be s
3:41 Take the Levites for me to be s
3:41 animals of the Levites to be s
3:45 "Take the Levites to be s for all
3:45 animals of the Levites to be s
8:16 taken them to be mine as s
8:18 I have taken the Levites as s

Sucah (1)
1Ch 2:55 people of Tira, Shimea, and S.

succeed (35)
Jos 1:7 you will s wherever you go.
1:8 then will you prosper and s.
1Sm 2:9 humans cannot s by their own
26:25 things and certainly will s."
1Ki 1:20 to tell them who should s you
2:3 Then you'll s in everything you
2:4 ⌊You'll s⌋ because the LORD
5:1 anointed king to s his father.
5:5 will put on your throne to s you,
22:22 'You will s in deceiving him.
1Ch 22:13 Then you will s if you will
2Ch 13:12 your ancestors. You won't s."
18:21 'You will s in deceiving him.
20:20 his prophets, and you will s."
Job 22:28 to do something, you will s,
Psa 10:5 He always seems to s.
21:11 against you, they will not s.
140:8 Do not let their evil plans s,
Pro 15:22 but with many advisers they s.
16:3 and your plans will s.
Isa 8:10 but they will never s.
47:12 You may s. You may cause terror
48:15 bring him here, and he will s.
53:10 of the LORD will s through him.
54:17 to be used against you will s.
Jer 10:21 That is why they won't s,
12:1 Why do wicked people s?
20:11 very ashamed that they can't s.
22:30 None of his descendants will s
Eze 17:15 Will the king of Judah s?
Dan 11:17 But this will not s or help him.
11:27 But they will not s,
11:36 He will s until God's anger is
Zec 4:6 You won't ⌊s⌋ by might or by
Luk 13:24 try to enter, but they won't s.

succeeded (68)
Gen 36:33 from Bozrah, s him as king.
36:34 of the Temanites s him as king.
36:35 son of Bedad s him as king.
36:36 from Masrekah s him as king.
36:37 on the river s him as king.
36:38 son of Achbor, s him as king.
36:39 Hadar s him as king,
Dtr 10:6 his son Eleazar s him as priest.
2Sm 16:8 whom you s as king.
1Ki 11:43 son Rehoboam s him as king.
14:20 His son Nadab s him as king.
14:31 His son Abijam s him as king.
15:8 His son Asa s him as king.
15:24 Jehoshaphat s him as king.
15:28 Baasha s Nadab as king of
16:6 His son Elah s him as king.
16:10 Zimri s Elah as king ⌊of
16:28 His son Ahab s him as king.
22:40 His son Ahaziah s him as king.
22:50 His son Jehoram s him as king.
2Ki 1:17 Joram s him as king because
3:27 who would have s him as king,
8:24 His son Ahaziah s him as king.

2Ki 10:35 son Jehoahaz **s** him as king.
12:21 son Amaziah **s** him as king.
13:24 son Benhadad **s** him as king.
14:16 son Jeroboam **s** him as king.
14:29 son Zechariah **s** him as king.
15:7 His son Jotham **s** him as king.
15:10 and **s** him as king.
15:14 and **s** him as king.
15:22 son Pekahiah **s** him as king.
15:25 killed him and **s** him as king.
15:38 His son Ahaz **s** him as king.
16:20 son Hezekiah **s** him as king.
18:7 He **s** in everything he tried:
19:37 son Esarhaddon **s** him as king.
20:21 son Manasseh **s** him as king.
21:18 His son Amon **s** him as king.
21:26 His son Josiah **s** him as king.
24:6 son Jehoiakin **s** him as king.
1Ch 1:44 from Bozrah, **s** him as king.
1:45 of the Temanites **s** him as king.
1:46 country of Moab, **s** him as king,
1:47 from Masrekah **s** him as king.
1:48 on the river **s** him as king.
1:49 son of Achbor, **s** him as king.
1:50 Hadad **s** him as king,
27:34 and Abiathar **s** Ahithophel.
29:28 his son Solomon **s** him as king.
2Ch 9:31 son Rehoboam **s** him as king.
12:16 His son Abijah **s** him as king.
14:1 His son Asa **s** him as king.
17:1 Asa's son Jehoshaphat **s** him
21:1 His son Jehoram **s** him as king.
24:27 son Amaziah **s** him as king.
26:23 His son Jotham **s** him as king.
27:9 His son Ahaz **s** him as king.
28:27 son Hezekiah **s** him as king.
31:21 did wholeheartedly, and he **s**.
32:30 Hezekiah **s** in everything he
32:33 son Manasseh **s** him as king.
33:20 His son Amon **s** him as king.
36:8 son Jehoiakin **s** him as king.
Isa 37:38 son Esarhaddon **s** him as king.
Jer 22:11 who **s** his father as king of
37:1 Zedekiah **s** Jehoiakin,
Mat 2:22 had **s** his father Herod

succeeds (3)

Exo 29:30 The son who **s** him as priest —
Psa 1:3 He **s** in everything he does.
37:7 with ⌊an evildoer⌋ who **s**

success (10)

1Sm 25:31 the LORD has given you **s**,
1Ch 12:18 **S**, success to you! Success to
12:18 Success, **s** to you!
12:18 **S** to those who help you,
2Ch 26:5 the LORD gave him **s**.
Neh 1:11 Please give me **s** today and
2:20 God of heaven will give us **s**,"
Psa 118:25 beg you, O LORD, give us **s**!
Pro 3:4 you will find favor and much **s**
Ecc 10:10 wisdom prepares the way for **s**.

successful (28)

Gen 24:12 Abraham, make me **s** today.
24:21 the LORD had made his trip **s**.
24:40 with you to make your trip **s**.
24:42 please make my trip **s**.
24:56 the LORD has made my trip **s**.
26:13 He continued to be **s**,
39:2 so he became a **s** man.
39:3 made everything he did **s**.
39:23 and made whatever he did **s**.
Dtr 28:29 You won't be **s** in anything you
29:9 Then you will be **s** in
Jdg 18:5 God if our journey will be **s**."
1Sm 18:5 David was **s** wherever Saul
18:14 He was **s** in everything he
18:15 Saul noticed how very **s** he
18:30 David was more **s** than the rest
1Ch 22:11 You will be **s**, and you will
29:23 Solomon was **s** and all Israel
Neh 4:15 their plans from being **s**,
Est 8:16 cheerful, happy, joyful, and **s**.
Psa 90:17 Make us **s** in everything we do.
90:17 make us **s** in everything we do.

Isa 52:13 My servant will be **s**.
Dan 8:12 The horn was **s** in everything it
8:24 destruction and will be **s**
Rom 14:4 his servant has been **s**.
14:4 The servant will be **s** because
14:4 because the Lord makes him **s**.

succession (1)

Heb 7:23 There was a long **s** of priests

successive (1)

2Sm 21:1 was a famine for three **s** years,

successor (2)

Ecc 4:15 young man, the king's **s**.
4:16 will not be happy with the **s**.

successors (1)

Dan 5:22 are one of Nebuchadnezzar's **s**.

Succoth (17)

Gen 33:17 moved on to **S** [Shelters],
33:17 is why the place is named **S**.
Exo 12:37 left Rameses to go to **S**.
13:20 They moved from **S** and
Num 33:5 and set up camp at **S**.
33:6 They moved from **S** and set up
Jos 13:27 Beth Nimrah, **S**, and Zaphon,
Jdg 8:5 Gideon said to the men of **S**,
8:6 The generals at **S** replied,
8:8 reply that the men of **S** gave.
8:14 captured a young man from **S**.
8:14 77 officials and leaders of **S**.
8:15 went to the men of **S** and said,
1Ki 7:46 between **S** and Zarethan.
2Ch 4:17 Valley between **S** and Zeredah.
Psa 60:6 I will measure the valley of **S**.
108:7 I will measure the valley of **S**.

Succoth Benoth (1)

2Ki 17:30 from Babylon made **S**.

sucks (1)

Job 20:16 The godless person **s** the

Sudan (33)

Gen 2:13 one that winds throughout **S**.
Num 12:1 married to a woman from **S**.
2Sm 18:21 Joab said to a man from **S**,
2Ki 19:9 King Tirhakah of **S** was coming
2Ch 14:9 Then Zerah from **S** came with
21:16 people of **S** to attack Jehoram.
Est 1:1 127 provinces from India to **S**.
8:9 127 provinces from India to **S**.
Psa 68:31 **S** will stretch out its hands to
87:4 and **S** to the list of those who
Isa 11:11 **S**, Elam, Babylonia, Hamath,
18:1 lies beyond the rivers of **S**.
20:3 as an omen to Egypt and **S**.
20:4 from Egypt and exiles from **S**.
20:5 because **S** was their hope
37:9 King Tirhakah of **S** was coming
43:3 **S** and Seba are the price I paid
45:14 the merchandise from **S**,
Jer 38:7 Ebed Melech from **S**,
38:10 Melech from **S** this command:
38:12 Ebed Melech from **S** said to
39:16 "Say to Ebed Melech from **S**,
46:9 you warriors from **S** and Put
Eze 29:10 all the way to the border of **S**.
30:5 **S**, Put, Lud, all the Arabs,
30:9 those who live in safety in **S**.
30:9 The people of **S** will be in
38:5 Persia, **S**, and Put will be with
Dan 11:43 Libya and **S** will surrender to
Amo 9:7 are like the people from **S**,
Nah 3:9 **S** and Egypt were her endless
Zep 2:12 "Even you, the people from **S**,
3:10 the rivers of **S** my worshipers,

Sudanese (10)

2Sm 18:22 to run after the **S** messenger."
18:23 got ahead of the **S** messenger.
18:31 Then the **S** messenger came.
18:32 The **S** messenger answered,
2Ch 12:3 Sukkites, and **S** from Egypt.

2Ch 14:12 The LORD attacked the **S** army
14:12 and Judah. The **S** army fled.
14:13 Many of the **S** died in battle.
14:13 the **S** army couldn't fight again.
16:8 Weren't the **S** and Libyans a

sue (2)

Job 23:6 Would he **s** me and hide
Mat 5:40 If someone wants to **s** you in

suffer (118)

Gen 4:15 Anyone who kills Cain will **s**
Exo 15:26 I will never make you **s** any of
15:26 I made the Egyptians **s**,
Lev 26:16 You will **s** from eye problems
Num 5:31 but the woman will **s** the
9:13 You must **s** the consequences
14:33 They will **s** for your
14:34 year for each day — you will **s**
18:22 Otherwise, they'll **s** the
18:32 you won't **s** the consequences
30:15 he will **s** the consequences."
Dtr 8:3 So he made you **s** from hunger
28:53 will make you **s** during
28:55 will make you **s** during
28:57 will make you **s** during
Jdg 2:15 he made them **s** a great deal.
10:16 to have Israel **s** any longer.
1Sm 6:4 all of you and your rulers **s** from
1Ki 8:35 sin because you made them **s**,
11:39 David's descendants **s** for this,
2Ki 17:20 descendants, made them **s**,
2Ch 6:26 sin because you made them **s**,
21:15 You will **s** from a chronic
Ezr 4:22 I, the king, **s** any more harm?
Neh 9:27 who made them **s**.
9:27 When they began to **s**,
Est 8:6 to see my people **s** such evil.
Job 8:4 he allowed them to **s** the
9:28 dread everything I must **s**.
13:26 You make me **s** for the sins of
30:11 my cord and has made me **s**,
34:28 hears the cry of those who **s**.
36:19 save you from having to **s**?
Psa 9:13 Look at what I **s** because of
73:4 They **s** no pain. Their bodies
90:15 days as you have made us **s**,
94:5 those who belong to you **s**.
119:67 Before you made me **s**,
119:71 It was good that I had to **s** in
119:75 you were right to make me **s**.
Pro 13:20 associates with fools will **s**.
22:3 and **s** ⌊the consequence⌋.
27:12 people go ahead ⌊and⌋ **s**.
Ecc 4:1 that make people **s** under
4:1 at the tears of those who **s**!
4:1 one can comfort those who **s**.
8:14 Righteous people **s** for what
Isa 47:8 I won't **s** the loss of children."
51:23 of those who made you **s**.
64:12 and make us **s** more than we
Jer 14:17 will **s** massive destruction.
31:12 and they will never **s** again.
Lam 1:4 young women are made to **s**.
1:5 The LORD made Zion **s** for its
1:12 the pain that he has made me **s**
3:32 Even if he makes us **s**,
Eze 14:10 Both of you will **s** for your sins.
16:52 You will have to **s** disgrace
16:52 of yourself and **s** disgrace,
16:54 You will have to **s** disgrace
16:58 You must **s** because of all the
20:37 Then I will make you **s**
32:24 Now they **s** disgrace with
32:25 Now they **s** disgrace with
32:30 They **s** disgrace with those
34:29 and they will no longer **s** the
36:15 You will no longer **s** the
36:30 no longer **s** disgrace among
44:13 They must **s** disgrace because
Hos 8:10 They will **s** for a while under
Mat 16:21 There he would have to **s** a lot
17:12 to make the Son of Man **s**."
Mar 8:31 of Man would have to **s** a lot.
9:12 that the Son of Man must **s**
14:35 not have to **s** what was ahead

Luk 9:22 of Man would have to **s** a lot.
12:50 and I will **s** until it is over.
16:25 has peace here, while you **s**.
17:25 But first he must **s** a lot and be
21:23 the land will **s** very hard times,
22:15 Passover with you before I **s**.
24:26 Didn't the Messiah have to **s**
24:46 says that the Messiah would **s**
Act 5:41 worthy to **s** dishonor
9:16 him how much he has to **s**
14:22 "We must **s** a lot to enter the
17:3 them that the Messiah had to **s**,
26:23 said that the Messiah would **s**
1Co 3:15 he will **s** ⌊the loss⌋.
2Co 1:4 He comforts us whenever we **s**.
1:4 why whenever other people **s**,
1:6 Besides, if we **s**, it brings you
7:4 Even as we **s**, I'm encouraged
7:5 we **s** in a number of ways.
Gal 3:4 Did you **s** so much for nothing?
5:10 **s** God's judgment regardless
Eph 3:13 by the troubles I **s** for you.
Php 1:29 in Christ but also to **s** for him.
Col 1:24 I am happy to **s** for you now.
1Th 3:3 we're destined to **s** persecution.
3:4 were going to **s** persecution.
2Th 1:6 to those who cause you to **s**.
2Ti 1:12 For this reason I **s** as I do.
2:24 He must be willing to **s** wrong.
Heb 9:26 he would have had to **s** many
11:25 He chose to **s** with God's
Jas 1:27 and widows when they **s**
1Pe 1:6 even though you have to **s**
3:14 But even if you **s** for doing
3:17 it's better to **s** for doing good
4:15 If you **s**, you shouldn't suffer for
4:15 If you suffer, you shouldn't **s** for
4:16 If you **s** for being a Christian,
4:19 Those who **s** because that is
5:10 and support you as you **s** for a
Rev 2:10 of what you are going to **s**.
2:22 sins with her will also **s** a lot,
18:4 in her sins and **s** from any

suffered (33)

Gen 41:52 in the land where he had **s**.
Jdg 10:9 So Israel **s** a great deal.
1Sm 4:17 "Our troops **s** heavy casualties.
Neh 9:9 how our ancestors **s** in Egypt,
Psa 107:17 Fools **s** because of their
119:107 I have **s** so much. Give me a
123:3 we have **s** more than our
123:4 We have **s** more than our share
123:4 We have **s** more than our share
Isa 38:14 I've **s** miserably, O Lord!
Nah 3:19 Who hasn't **s** from your endless
Mat 4:24 those who **s** from any kind of
26:6 a man who had **s** from a skin
Mar 14:3 a man who had **s** from a skin
2Co 1:5 Because Christ **s** so much for
1:9 But we **s** so that we would
12:10 and difficulties **s** for Christ.
1Th 2:2 As you know, we **s** rough and
2:14 You **s** the same persecutions
Heb 2:9 and honor because he **s** death.
2:18 temptation when he **s**,
10:34 You **s** with prisoners.
13:12 That is why Jesus **s** outside
13:12 He **s** to make the people holy
Jas 5:10 They were patient when they **s**
1Pe 2:21 because Christ **s** for you.
2:23 When he **s**, he didn't make any
3:18 This is true because Christ **s**
3:18 but he **s** for guilty people so
4:1 Since Christ has **s** physically,
4:1 (A person who has **s**
Jud 1:7 The people of these cities **s**
Rev 2:3 **s** trouble because of my name,

suffering (85)

Exo 2:11 them **s** under forced labor.
3:7 I know how much they're **s**.
Dtr 26:7 He saw our misery, **s**,
1Sm 9:16 I've seen my people's ⌊**s**⌋
2Sm 1:9 I'm alive, but I'm **s**.'
2Ki 14:26 everyone in Israel was **s**.
2Ch 6:29 all who know **s** or pain,
24:25 they left him **s** from many
Job 30:16 Days of **s** seize me.
36:15 He rescues **s** people through
36:15 suffering people through their **s**
36:21 have chosen evil instead of **s**.
Psa 25:18 Look at my misery and **s**,
44:24 do you forget our **s** and misery?
69:29 I am **s** and in pain.
88:9 grow weak because of my **s**.
88:15 I have been **s** and near death.
106:44 He saw that they were **s** when
107:41 lifts needy people high above **s**
116:10 when I said, "I am **s** terribly."
Pro 19:23 will rest easy without **s** harm.
Isa 14:3 you relief from your pain and **s**,
48:10 tested you in the furnace of **s**.
53:3 man of sorrows, familiar with **s**.
53:4 has taken upon himself our **s**
53:10 will to crush him with **s**.
53:11 be satisfied because of his **s**.
53:11 he has learned ⌊through **s**⌋.
54:11 "You **s**, comfortless,
Lam 1:3 has been exiled after ⌊much⌋ **s**
1:7 during its **s** and oppression,
1:9 'O LORD, look at my **s**,
3:1 who has experienced **s** under
3:19 Remember my **s** and my
3:33 He does not willingly bring **s** or
Joe 1:18 Even flocks of sheep are **s**.
Mat 9:20 She had been **s** from chronic
13:21 When **s** or persecution comes
26:39 let this cup ⌊of **s**⌋ be taken
Mar 4:17 When **s** or persecution comes
5:25 been **s** from chronic bleeding
14:36 Take this cup ⌊of **s**⌋ away
Luk 4:40 everyone who had friends **s**
8:43 A woman who had been **s** from
16:24 my tongue. I am **s** in this fire.'
22:42 take this cup ⌊of **s**⌋ away from
Jon 12:27 save me from this time ⌊of **s**⌋'?
12:27 I came for this time of **s**.
18:11 Shouldn't I drink the cup ⌊of **s**⌋
Act 7:10 and rescued him from all his **s**.
7:11 and Canaan brought a lot of **s**.
20:23 imprisonment and **s** are waiting
28:8 He was **s** from fever and
Rom 2:9 There will be **s** and distress for
3:16 is ruin and **s** wherever they go.
5:3 We also brag when we are **s**.
5:3 know that **s** creates endurance,
8:17 If we share in Christ's **s** in order
1Co 12:26 all the other parts share its **s**.
2Co 1:8 about the **s** we experienced
4:17 Our **s** is light and temporary
6:4 things: **s**, distress, anxiety,
8:2 being severely tested by **s**,
Gal 4:19 My children, I am **s** birth pains
Php 3:10 what it means to share his **s**.
1Th 1:6 In spite of a lot of **s**,
2Th 1:4 and **s** you are experiencing.
1:5 Your **s** proves that God's
1:6 it is right for God to give **s** to
1:7 give all of us relief from our **s**.
1Ti 5:10 believers' needs, helping the **s**,
2Ti 1:8 join me in **s** for the sake of the
2:3 Join me in **s** like a good soldier
2:9 I'm **s** disgrace for spreading
4:5 Endure **s**. Do the work of a
Heb 2:10 the end of his work through **s**.
Jas 5:11 saw that the Lord ended Job's **s**
1Pe 2:19 enduring the pains of unjust **s**.
2:20 But if you endure **s** for doing
2:21 God called you to endure **s**
5:9 through the same kind of **s**.
Rev 1:9 I share your **s**, ruling,
2:9 I know how you are **s**,
2:10 Your **s** will go on for ten days.
7:14 are coming out of the terrible **s**.

sufferings (12)

1Ki 2:26 you shared all my father's **s**."
Act 3:18 But in this way God made the **s**
3:18 God had predicted these **s**
Rom 8:18 I consider our present **s**
2Co 1:6 the same **s** that we endure.
2Co 1:7 know that as you share our **s**,
Col 1:24 whatever remains of Christ's **s**.
2Ti 3:11 and **s** which happened
Heb 5:8 to be obedient through his **s**.
1Pe 1:11 he predicted Christ's **s**
4:13 happy as you share Christ's **s**.
5:1 who also witnessed Christ's **s**

suffers (2)

Mat 17:15 He **s** from seizures.
1Co 12:26 If one part of the body **s**,

sugar (3)

Isa 43:24 You did not buy me any **s** cane
Jer 6:20 **S** cane that comes from a
Eze 27:19 and **s** cane for your goods.

suggest (2)

2Sm 19:43 Weren't we the first to **s**
Mat 19:11 everyone can do what you **s**.

suggested (2)

Est 1:21 so the king did as Memucan **s**.
Mat 19:12 If anyone can do what you've **s**,

suggestion (3)

Est 2:4 The king liked the **s**,
Act 6:5 The **s** pleased the whole group.
1Co 7:6 as a command but as a **s**.

suitable (1)

Est 2:9 and seven **s** female servants

Sukkites (1)

2Ch 12:3 **S**, and Sudanese from Egypt.

sulfur (14)

Gen 19:24 Then the LORD made burning **s**
Dtr 29:23 soil poisoned with **s** and salt.
Job 18:15 **S** is scattered over his home.
Psa 11:6 burning **s** upon wicked people.
Isa 30:33 will be like a flood of burning **s**,
34:9 soil will be turned to burning **s**.
Eze 38:22 and burning **s** on his troops and
Luk 17:29 fire and **s** rained from the sky
Rev 9:17 and **s** came out of their mouths.
9:18 and **s** which came out of their
14:10 he will be tortured by fiery **s**
19:20 into the fiery lake of burning **s**.
20:10 thrown into the fiery lake of **s**,
21:8 in the fiery lake of burning **s**.

summarized (1)

Gal 5:14 All of Moses' Teachings are **s**

summed (1)

Rom 13:9 other commandment are **s** up

summer (20)

Gen 8:22 cold and heat, **s** and winter,
Job 6:17 vanish during a scorching **s**.
Psa 32:4 strength shriveled in the **s** heat.
74:17 You created **s** and winter.
Pro 10:5 Whoever gathers in the **s** is a
30:25 yet they store their food in **s**.
Isa 18:6 prey will feed on them in the **s**,
Jer 8:20 is past, the **s** has ended,
17:8 not be afraid in the heat of **s**.
40:10 Gather grapes, **s** fruit,
40:12 harvest of grapes and **s** fruit.
Dan 2:35 husks on a threshing floor in **s**.
Amo 3:15 houses as well as **s** houses.
8:1 a basket of ripe **s** fruit.
8:2 "A basket of ripe **s** fruit,"
Mic 7:1 I am like those gathering **s** fruit,
Zec 14:8 will continue in **s** and in winter.
Mat 24:32 you know that **s** is near.
Mar 13:28 you know **s** is near.
Luk 21:30 being told that **s** is near.

summertime (3)

Pro 6:8 in **s** it stores its food supply.
26:1 Like snow in **s** and rain at
Jer 15:18 like a stream that dries up in **s**?

summon (14)

Num 22:5 sent messengers to **s** Balaam,
22:20 these men have come to **s** you,
Dtr 25:8 leaders of the city must **s** him
Jdg 3:27 of Ephraim ⌊to **s** the troops⌋.
6:34 ram's horn to **s** Abiezer's family
6:35 throughout Manasseh to **s**
1Ki 1:32 "**S** the priest Zadok,
2Ki 10:19 **S** all the prophets,
Isa 55:5 You will **s** a nation that you
Dan 11:25 "With a large army he will **s** his
Act 10:5 and **s** a man whose name is
10:22 A holy angel told him to **s** you
10:32 and **s** a man whose name is
11:13 and **s** a man whose name is

summoned (33)

Lev 9:1 On the eighth day Moses **s**
Num 22:37 didn't you come when I **s** you?
23:7 The king of Moab **s** me from
24:10 "I **s** you to curse my enemies,
Dtr 5:1 Moses **s** all Israel and said to
29:2 Moses **s** all the people of Israel
Jos 6:6 son of Nun, **s** the priests.
22:1 Joshua **s** the tribes of Reuben
24:9 He **s** Balaam, son of Beor,
Jdg 4:6 Deborah **s** Barak, son of
4:13 So Sisera **s** all his chariots
6:35 and Naphtali were also **s** to
7:23 of Israel were **s** from Naphtali,
7:24 of Ephraim were also **s** to help.
10:17 of Ammon were **s** to fight,
12:1 men of Ephraim were **s** to fight.
2Sm 9:2 He was **s** to ⌊come to⌋ David.
11:13 David **s** him, ate and drank
1Ki 2:36 The king **s** Shimei and said to
2:42 he **s** Shimei. Solomon asked
1Ch 22:6 He **s** his son Solomon and
2Ch 30:5 They **s** everyone to come to
Est 3:12 the king's scribes were **s**.
4:11 throne room without being **s**.
4:11 I, myself, have not been **s** to
8:9 the king's scribes were **s**.
Psa 50:1 He has **s** the earth from where
Dan 3:13 Nebuchadnezzar **s** Shadrach,
Mar 15:44 So he **s** the officer to ask him if
Act 23:23 Then the officer **s** two of his
24:2 When Paul had been **s**,
25:6 his place in court and **s** Paul.
25:17 convened court and **s** the man.

summons (1)

Psa 50:4 He **s** heaven and earth to judge

sun (155)

Gen 15:12 As the **s** was just about to set,
15:17 The **s** had gone down,
19:23 The **s** had just risen over the
28:11 because the **s** had gone down.
32:31 The **s** rose as he passed
37:9 dream: I saw the **s**, the moon,
Exo 16:21 When the **s** was hot,
27:13 facing the rising **s**,
38:13 facing the rising **s**,
Lev 22:7 When the **s** has set,
Num 2:3 facing the rising **s**,
Dtr 4:19 you see in the sky — the **s**,
16:6 evening as the **s** goes down.
17:3 to other gods, the **s**, the moon,
33:2 he rose from Seir ⌊like the **s**⌋.
33:14 the best gift the **s** can give,
Jos 8:29 When the **s** went down,
10:12 "**S**, stand still over Gibeon,
10:13 The **s** stood still, and the moon
10:13 The **s** stopped in the middle of
10:13 and for nearly a day the **s** was
10:27 When the **s** went down,
Jdg 5:31 the LORD be like the **s** when
9:33 the morning, when the **s** rises,
19:25 go when the **s** was coming up.
1Sm 11:9 by the time the **s** gets hot,
2Sm 2:24 When the **s** went down,
3:35 else before the **s** goes down."
23:4 the morning light as the **s** rises,
2Ki 3:22 as the **s** was rising over
2Ki 23:5 Baal, the **s** god, the moon god,
23:11 had dedicated to the **s** god at
23:11 the chariots of the **s** god,
Job 9:7 He commands the **s** not to rise.
11:17 be brighter than the noonday **s**.
30:28 I walk in the dark without the **s**.
37:21 People can't look at the **s** when
Psa 19:4 a tent in the heavens for the **s**,
37:6 just cause like the noonday **s**.
50:1 the earth from where the **s** rises
58:8 child who never sees the **s**.
72:5 they fear you as long as the **s**
72:17 as long as the **s** ⌊shines⌋.
74:16 moon and the **s** in their places.
84:11 LORD God is a **s** and shield.
89:36 be in my presence like the **s**.
104:19 marks the seasons, and the **s**,
104:22 When the **s** rises, they gather
113:3 From where the **s** rises to
113:3 sun rises to where the **s** sets,
121:6 The **s** will not beat down on
136:8 the **s** to rule the day — because
139:9 rays of the morning **s** ⌊or⌋ land
139:9 of the sea where the **s** sets,
148:3 Praise him, **s** and moon.
Ecc 1:3 all their hard work under the **s**?
1:5 The **s** rises, and the sun sets,
1:5 The sun rises, and the **s** sets,
1:9 is nothing new under the **s**.
1:14 that is done under the **s**.
2:11 accomplishments⌋ under the **s**.
2:17 under the **s** seemed wrong
2:18 worked so hard under the **s**,
2:19 over everything under the **s**
2:20 worked so hard under the **s**.
2:22 and struggles under the **s**?
3:16 something else under the **s**:
4:1 make people suffer under the **s**.
4:3 evil that is done under the **s**.
4:7 pointless under the **s**:
4:15 moving about under the **s**.
5:13 that I have seen under the **s**:
5:18 hard work under the **s** during
6:1 that I have seen under the **s**.
6:5 Though it has never seen the **s**
6:12 about their future under the **s**?
7:11 to everyone who sees the **s**.
8:9 the **s** whenever one person
8:15 better to do under the **s** than
8:15 has given them under the **s**.
8:17 work that is done under the **s**.
9:3 that happens under the **s**:
9:6 that happens under the **s**.
9:9 your pointless life under the **s**.
9:9 work that you do under the **s**.
9:11 something else under the **s**.
9:13 of wisdom under the **s**,
10:5 that I've seen under the **s**,
11:7 for one's eyes to see the **s**.
12:2 your Creator before the **s**,
Sos 1:6 The **s** has tanned me.
6:10 like the moon, pure like the **s**,
Isa 13:10 The **s** will be dark when it
24:23 The **s** will be ashamed,
30:26 will be like the light of the **s**.
30:26 The light of the **s** will be seven
38:8 The **s** made a shadow that
38:8 So the **s** on the stairway went
49:10 nor will the **s** or the burning,
58:10 as bright as the noonday **s**.
60:19 The **s** will no longer be your
60:20 Your **s** will no longer go down,
Jer 8:2 out and exposed to the **s**,
31:35 The LORD provides the **s** to be
Eze 8:16 and worshiping the rising **s**.
32:7 I will cover the **s** with clouds,
Joe 2:10 The **s** and the moon turn dark,
2:31 The **s** will become dark,
3:15 The **s** and the moon will turn
Amo 8:9 I will make the **s** go down at
Jnh 4:8 When the **s** rose, God made a
4:8 The **s** beat down on Jonah's
Mic 3:6 The **s** will set on the prophets,
Nah 3:17 The **s** rises, and they scatter in
Hab 3:11 The **s** and the moon stand still.
Zec 8:7 from the land where the **s** rises
Zec 8:7 from the land where the **s** sets.
Mal 1:11 "From the nations where the **s**
1:11 to the nations where the **s** sets,
4:2 "The **S** of Righteousness will
Mat 5:45 He makes his **s** rise on people
13:6 But when the **s** came up,
13:43 approval will shine like the **s**
17:2 face became as bright as the **s**
20:12 hard all day under a blazing **s**.'
24:29 the **s** will turn dark,
28:1 as the **s** rose Sunday morning,
Mar 1:32 when the **s** had set,
4:6 When the **s** came up,
13:24 the **s** will turn dark,
16:2 early when the **s** had just come
Luk 4:40 When the **s** was setting,
21:25 signs will occur in the **s**,
23:45 The **s** had stopped shining.
Jon 21:4 As the **s** was rising,
Act 2:20 The **s** will become dark,
7:42 and let them worship the **s**,
26:13 that was brighter than the **s**.
27:20 of days we couldn't see the **s**
1Co 15:41 The **s** has one kind of splendor,
Jas 1:11 The **s** rises with its scorching
1:17 the Father who made the **s**,
1:17 by the **s** and the moon.
Rev 1:16 His face was like the **s** when it
6:12 The **s** turned as black as
7:16 Neither the **s** nor any burning
8:12 his trumpet, one-third of the **s**,
9:2 darkened the **s** and the air.
10:1 His face was like the **s**,
12:1 who was dressed in the **s**,
16:8 angel poured his bowl on the **s**.
16:8 The **s** was allowed to burn
19:17 saw an angel standing in the **s**.
21:23 The city doesn't need any **s** or
22:5 any light from lamps or the **s**

sun-baked (1)

Isa 58:11 satisfy you even in **s** places.

Sunday (8)

Mat 28:1 as the sun rose **S** morning,
Mar 16:2 On **S** they were going to the
16:9 came back to life early on **S**,
Luk 24:1 Very early on **S** morning the
Jon 20:1 Early on **S** morning,
20:19 That **S** evening, the disciples
Act 20:7 On **S** we met to break bread.
1Co 16:2 Every **S** each of you should set

sundown (4)

Jdg 14:18 So before **s** on the seventh day,
1Ki 22:36 At **s** a cry went through the
2Ch 18:34 until evening. At **s** he died.
Dan 6:14 Until **s** he did everything he

sung (4)

Job 36:24 People have **s** about it.
Psa 8:1 glory is **s** above the heavens.
Isa 16:10 No songs are **s**. No shouts are
26:1 On that day this song will be **s**

sunk (3)

Job 38:6 On what were its footings **s**?
Psa 9:15 The nations have **s** into the pit
Lam 2:9 "⌊Zion's⌋ gates have **s** into the

sunken (1)

Lev 14:37 If it is green and red in **s** areas

sunlight (2)

Job 5:14 and grope in the **s** as if
Hab 3:4 His brightness is like the **s**.

sunrise (5)

Gen 38:30 He was named Zerah [**S**].
Exo 22:3 But if it happens after **s**,
Psa 65:8 The lands of the morning **s** and
Mar 1:35 In the morning, long before **s**,
Act 20:11 long time, until **s**, and then left.

sunset (7)

Exo 17:12 hands remained steady until **s**.

Exo 22:26 give it back to him by **s**.
Dtr 23:11 and at **s** he may come back to
24:13 you bring it back to him at **s**.
24:15 Pay them each day before **s**
Jdg 19:14 It was **s** by the time they
Psa 65:8 and evening **s** sing joyfully.

sunshine (3)

Dtr 33:2 He appeared like **s** from Mount
Job 8:16 a well-watered plant in the **s**.
Isa 18:4 be like scorching heat in the **s**,

super-apostles (2)

2Co 11:5 I'm inferior in any way to your **s**.
12:11 inferior in any way to your **s**.

superior (10)

Jon 3:31 from above is **s** to everyone.
3:31 from heaven is **s** to everyone
13:16 Slaves are not **s** to their
13:16 and messengers are not **s** to
2Co 3:10 its glory because of the **s** glory
4:7 This shows that the **s** power of
Heb 1:4 given a name that is **s** to theirs.
4:14 We have a **s** chief priest who
8:6 given a priestly work that is **s**
10:21 We have a **s** priest in charge of

superior's (2)

2Sm 11:9 among his **s** mercenaries.
11:13 bed among his **s** mercenaries.

superiors (1)

Isa 3:5 people will make fun of their **s**.

supervise (3)

Num 3:32 It was Eleazar's duty to **s** those
1Ch 23:4 24,000 were appointed to **s** the
2Ch 2:18 and 3,600 of them **s** the work

supervised (1)

2Ch 34:13 also **s** the workers and directed

supervision (4)

1Ch 9:25 serve under the gatekeepers' **s**
26:28 donated — was under the **s**
2Ch 34:12 their work faithfully under the **s**
Ezr 8:33 them under the **s** of Meremoth,

supervisor (8)

Neh 2:8 the **s** of Your Majesty's forest.
11:11 who was the **s** of God's temple.
Dan 1:11 The chief-of-staff put a **s** in
1:11 Daniel said to the **s**,
1:14 The **s** listened to them about
1:16 So the **s** took away the king's
Mat 20:8 of the vineyard told the **s**,
Tit 1:7 Because a bishop is a **s**

supervisors (3)

Gen 41:34 arrangements to appoint **s** over
2Ch 34:17 it to the **s** and the workmen."
Neh 3:5 themselves to work under **s**.

Suph (1)

Dtr 1:1 River, on the plains, near **S**,

Suphah (1)

Num 21:14 Waheb in **S** and the valleys,

supper (7)

Exo 2:20 Go, invite him to **s**."
Luk 22:20 When **s** was over,
Jon 13:2 While **s** was taking place,
21:20 chest at the **s** and asked,
1Co 11:20 possibly be eating the Lord's **S**.
11:21 Each of you eats his own **s**
11:25 When **s** was over,

supplied (4)

Gen 47:17 During that year he **s** them with
Num 31:5 from each tribe were **s** from
1Ki 9:11 (Hiram had **s** Solomon with as
2Co 11:9 of Macedonia **s** everything

supplies (18)

Gen 42:25 into his sack and gave them **s**
45:21 gave them wagons and **s**
Lev 26:10 You will clear out old food **s** to
Jos 1:11 the people, 'Get your **s** ready.
Jdg 7:8 men who stayed kept all the **s**
20:10 from the tribes of Israel to get **s**
1Sm 17:22 David left the **s** behind in the
25:13 hundred men stayed with the **s**.
30:24 of those who stay with the **s**.
2Sm 17:28 brought ⌊**s**⌋ and food for David
2Ch 17:12 and cities where **s** were stored
17:13 He had large **s** of food in the
Ezr 1:4 with silver, gold, **s**, livestock,
1:6 silver and gold, **s**, livestock,
Eph 6:11 Put on all the armor that God **s**.
6:13 up all the armor that God **s**.
6:17 as the sword that the Spirit **s**.
1Pe 4:11 with the strength God **s** so that

supply (22)

Gen 41:36 This food will be a reserve **s**
Exo 1:11 as **s** cities for Pharaoh.
Lev 26:26 I will destroy your food **s**.
2Sm 12:27 fortress guarding its water **s**.
1Ki 4:7 Each one had to **s** food for one
4:22 Solomon's food **s** for one day
4:27 to it that nothing was in short **s**.
Neh 5:18 Once every ten days a **s** of
9:25 They enjoyed the vast **s** of
Est 2:9 treatment, a daily **s** of food,
Job 22:25 gold and your large **s** of silver.
Psa 105:16 He took away their food **s**.
Pro 6:8 summertime it stores its food **s**.
Isa 3:1 of support and their entire **s**
33:16 and a dependable **s** of water.
Jer 50:38 will diminish their water **s**,
Eze 4:16 off the bread **s** in Jerusalem.
5:16 and I will cut off your food **s**.
14:13 against it, cut off its food **s**,
Act 12:20 on Herod for their food **s**.
Gal 3:5 Does God **s** you with the Spirit
1Th 3:10 we can **s** whatever you still

support (53)

Lev 25:35 poor and cannot **s** himself,
Dtr 33:27 and his everlasting arms **s** you.
Rut 4:15 bring you a new life and **s** you
1Sm 20:3 certainly knows that you **s** me,
22:17 priests because they **s** David,"
2Sm 3:12 "I'll **s** you and bring all Israel to
16:21 with you will **s** you even more."
17:9 'The troops that **s** Absalom
2Ki 15:19 pounds of silver to gain his **s**
18:20 Whom, then, do you trust for **s**
1Ch 26:27 battle to **s** the LORD's temple.)
2Ch 26:13 a powerful force that could **s**
26:15 because he had strong **s** until
Ezr 8:36 officials then gave their **s**
Neh 6:18 had promised to **s** Tobiah
12:47 were giving gifts for the daily **s**
12:47 holy gifts for ⌊the daily **s** of⌋
12:47 for **s** of Aaron's descendants.
Job 8:15 it will not **s** his weight.
Psa 3:5 the LORD continues to **s** me.
20:2 holy place and **s** you from Zion.
37:17 to **s** righteous people.
41:3 The LORD will **s** him on his
89:43 and failed to **s** him in battle.
Isa 3:1 and Judah every kind of **s**
36:5 Whom, then, do you trust for **s**
41:10 I will **s** you with my victorious
42:1 Here is my servant, whom I **s**.
46:4 your hair turns gray, I'll **s** you.
46:4 I'll **s** you and save you.
63:5 that there was no ⌊outside⌋ **s**.
63:12 who sent his powerful arm to **s**
Jer 23:14 They **s** those who do evil so
Dan 10:21 No one will **s** me when I fight
Mic 1:11 It will take its **s** away from you.
Zec 11:16 their legs or **s** those that can
Mat 15:5 whatever **s** you might have
Luk 8:3 They provided financial **s** for
Act 20:34 You know that I worked to **s**
Rom 11:18 that you don't **s** the root,
15:24 I hope that you will **s** my trip to
1Co 9:6 except to find work to **s**
16:6 Then you can give me your **s**
16:11 give him your **s** for his trip so
2Co 1:16 Corinth and have you **s** my trip
Eph 4:16 and unites it through the **s**
Col 2:19 through **s** and unity given by
2Th 3:9 didn't have a right to receive **s**.
3:12 so they can **s** themselves.
Tit 3:13 lawyer and Apollos your best **s**
1Pe 5:10 and **s** you as you suffer for a
3Jn 1:6 You will do well to **s** them on
1:8 We must **s** believers who go

supported (13)

1Ki 1:7 priest Abiathar, so they **s** him.
2:28 (He had **s** Adonijah,
2:28 although he hadn't **s** Absalom.)
7:3 which were **s** by 45 pillars (15
Ezr 5:2 were with them and **s** them.
6:22 change his mind so that he **s**
10:15 **s** Jonathan and Jahzeiah.)
Isa 63:5 won a victory. My anger **s** me.
Jer 26:24 son of Shaphan, **s** Jeremiah.
Mat 27:55 Galilee and had always **s** him.
Mar 15:41 They had followed him and **s**
Act 24:9 The Jews **s** Tertullus'
1Ti 5:19 leader unless it is **s** by two

supporters (1)

2Sm 15:10 But Absalom sent his loyal **s** to

supporting (4)

1Ki 2:22 Joab (Zeruiah's son) are **s** him."
7:2 of cedar pillars **s** cedar beams.
2Ch 11:17 of Judah by **s** Rehoboam,
Rom 3:31 we are **s** Moses' Teachings.

supports (15)

1Ki 7:30 axles and four **s** beneath
7:30 The **s** were made of cast metal
7:34 The four **s** at the four corners of
7:35 Above the stand were **s** which
7:36 space on the **s** and panels.
10:12 sandalwood the king made **s**
Job 16:7 destroyed everyone who **s** me.
Psa 18:35 Your right hand **s** me.
63:8 Your right hand **s** me.
145:14 The LORD **s** everyone who
Isa 59:16 His righteousness **s** him.
Eze 41:6 These rooms had **s** all the way
41:6 but these **s** were not fastened
Rom 9:1 my own thoughts, **s** me in this.
11:18 support the root, the root **s** you.

suppose (78)

Exo 3:13 Then Moses replied to God, "**S**
Num 9:10 **S** you or any of your
15:8 "**S** you sacrifice a young bull
15:14 "**S** foreigners are visiting you or
15:22 "**S** you unintentionally do
35:22 "But **s** you accidentally kill
35:23 Or **s** you drop a big stone,
36:3 **S** they marry men from the
Dtr 15:16 But **s** a male slave says to you,
19:5 **S** two people go into the
19:11 **S** someone hates another
2Ki 18:22 **S** you tell me, "We're trusting
Job 34:31 "But **s** such a person says to
Ecc 6:3 **S** a rich person wasn't satisfied
6:3 **S** he had a hundred children
Isa 36:7 **S** you tell me, "We're trusting
Jer 7:5 "'**S** you really change the way
7:6 **S** you do not oppress
7:6 And **s** you do not follow other
12:16 **S** they learn carefully the ways
12:16 **S** they take an oath in my
12:17 But **s** they don't listen.
18:8 But **s** the nation that I
18:10 But **s** that nation does what I
23:34 **S** the prophets, the priests,
23:38 **S** they say, 'This is the
26:4 **S** you don't listen to me and
26:5 **S** you don't listen to the words
27:8 "'**S** nations or kingdoms won't
27:11 But **s** a nation surrenders to the

Jer 33:20 **S** you could break
33:25 is what the LORD says: **S**
42:10 **S** you stay in this land.
42:13 "But **s** you say, 'We won't stay
42:15 **S** you're determined to go to
Eze 3:18 **S** I tell you that wicked people
3:19 But **s** you warn the wicked
14:4 **S** an Israelite is devoted to
14:4 **S** he goes to a prophet ⌊to ask
14:7 **S** an Israelite or a foreigner
14:13 "Son of man, **s** a country sins
14:15 "**S** I send wild animals through
14:17 "**S** I bring a war against that
14:17 **S** I destroy the people and the
14:19 "**S** I send a plague into that
18:5 "**S** a righteous person does
18:10 "But **s** this person has a son
18:14 "But **s** this person has a son.
18:21 "But **s** a wicked person turns
18:24 "But **s** a righteous person turns
33:2 '**S** I bring war on this country,
33:8 **S** I say to a wicked person,
33:14 But **s** he turns from his sin and
43:11 **S** they are ashamed of
46:16 **S** the prince offers one of his
46:17 But **s** the prince offers a gift
Hag 2:12 **S** a person carries meat set
2:13 Haggai asked, "**S** a person
Mat 12:11 "**S** one of you has a sheep.
18:12 **S** a man has 100 sheep and
Luk 7:43 Simon answered, "I **s** the one
11:5 "**S** one of you has a friend.
11:5 **S** you go to him at midnight
14:28 "**S** you want to build a tower.
14:31 "Or **s** a king is going to war
15:4 "**S** a man has 100 sheep and
15:8 "**S** a woman has ten coins and
17:7 "**S** someone has a servant who
Jon 21:25 I **s** the world wouldn't have
Act 2:15 men are not drunk as you **s**.
1Co 8:10 For example, **s** someone with
12:15 **S** a foot says, "I'm not a hand,
12:16 Or **s** an ear says, "I'm not an
14:23 **S** the whole congregation
14:24 Now **s** you speak what God
Jas 2:3 **S** you give special attention to
2:15 **S** a believer, whether a man or
1Jn 3:17 Now, **s** a person has enough to

supposed (18)

Gen 4:9 "Am I **s** to take care of my
Exo 5:19 each day than you're **s** to."
15:24 "What are we **s** to drink?"
Lev 6:2 about something you were **s**
6:4 what you were **s** to take care
10:16 to the male goat that was **s**
Num 4:5 When the camp is **s** to move,
4:27 everything they're **s** to carry.
Neh 4:18 The man who was **s** to sound
11:1 remaining nine-tenths were **s**
Est 4:8 Hathach was **s** to show it to
Jer 34:9 Everyone was **s** to free his
34:9 No one was **s** to keep another
43:11 death to those who are **s** to die.
43:11 He will capture those who are **s**
43:11 kill in battle those who are **s**
Hos 13:10 the one who is **s** to save you?
Mat 2:4 the Messiah was **s** to be born.

suppress (1)

Rom 1:18 thing people do as they try to **s**

Sur (1)

2Ki 11:6 third must be at **S** Gate.

sure (87)

Gen 15:13 "You can know for **s** that your
24:6 "Make **s** that you do not take
32:12 But you did say, 'I will make **s**
32:20 And be **s** to add, 'Jacob is right
45:7 you to make **s** that you would
46:4 and I will make **s** you come
50:25 So be **s** to carry my bones
Exo 17:14 and make **s** that Joshua hears
20:7 The LORD will make **s** that
22:23 you can be **s** that I will hear
Exo 23:4 be **s** to take it back to him.
23:5 Be **s** to help him with his
25:40 Be **s** to make them according
31:13 "Say to the Israelites, 'Be **s** to
Lev 19:17 Be **s** to correct your neighbor
Num 22:17 I will make **s** you are richly
28:2 Be **s** to bring me my offerings
32:23 You can be **s** that you will be
35:19 avenge the death must make **s**
Dtr 5:11 The LORD will make **s** that
6:17 Be **s** to obey the commands of
10:18 He makes **s** orphans and
12:23 be **s** you never eat blood,
12:28 Be **s** you obey all these
12:32 Be **s** to do everything I
14:22 Every year be **s** to save a tenth
15:10 Be **s** to give to them without
17:15 Be **s** to appoint the king the
21:23 Be **s** to bury him that same day,
22:1 Make **s** you take it back.
22:4 Make **s** you help him get it
22:7 but make **s** you let the mother
23:23 Make **s** you do what you said
24:8 Make **s** you do what I
24:13 Make **s** you bring it back to him
26:18 But you must be **s** to obey his
28:66 will never feel **s** of your life.
29:18 Make **s** there is no man,
29:18 Make **s** that no one among you
1Sm 1:26 Hannah said, "as **s** as you live,
8:9 Listen to them now, but be **s** to
9:6 he says is **s** to happen.
20:7 then you'll know for **s** that he
20:9 If I knew for **s** that my father
27:1 for me to do is to make **s** that
2Sm 11:11 as **s** as you're living,
15:4 and I would make **s** that he got
17:16 but make **s** you cross ⌊the
19:22 David responded, "Are you **s**
20:18 'Be **s** to ask at Abel ⌊before
22:34 a deer and gives me **s** footing
2Ki 5:20 As **s** as the LORD lives,
10:10 You can be **s** that the word of
10:19 Make **s** no one is missing
10:23 "Make **s** that there are no
Ezr 6:9 Make **s** that nothing is omitted.
Neh 13:19 gates to make **s** that no loads
Psa 18:33 a deer and gives me **s** footing
Jer 1:12 I am watching to make **s** that
5:24 He makes **s** that we have
Dan 2:8 The king replied, "I'm **s** you're
Hos 6:3 He will come to us as **s** as the
Zec 9:10 He will make **s** there are no
Mar 13:36 Make **s** he doesn't come
Luk 18:9 who were **s** that God approved
21:34 "Make **s** that you don't become
Jon 17:8 and they know for **s** that I came
Act 12:11 "Now I'm **s** that the Lord sent
26:26 I'm **s** that none of these things
Rom 12:6 make **s** what you say agrees
1Co 1:16 Beyond that, I'm not **s** whether I
16:10 If Timothy comes, make **s** that
2Co 11:1 I'm **s** that you will.
13:11 Make **s** that you improve.
Php 2:29 Make **s** you honor people like
Col 4:16 Make **s** that you also read the
1Th 5:15 Make **s** that no one ever pays
Heb 6:19 We have this confidence as a **s**
8:5 "Be **s** to make everything
12:15 Make **s** that everyone has
12:16 Make **s** that no one commits
13:18 We are **s** that our consciences
Jas 2:16 and make **s** you eat enough."
2Pe 2:14 seduce people who aren't **s**
3:16 people and people who aren't **s**
1Jn 2:3 We are **s** that we know Christ if
2:24 Make **s** that the message you

surface (10)

Gen 2:6 water the entire **s** of the ground.
8:8 gone from the **s** of the ground.
8:13 and saw the **s** of the ground.
Job 24:18 people are like scum on the **s**
26:10 He marks the horizon on the **s**
38:30 and the **s** of the ocean freezes
Pro 8:27 horizon on the **s** of the ocean,
Ecc 11:1 Throw your bread on the **s** of
Isa 18:2 of reeds ⌊skimming⌋ over the **s**
28:25 When he has smoothed its **s**,

surging (1)

Psa 46:3 shake at the **s** waves.

surpass (1)

1Ki 10:7 Your wisdom and wealth **s** the

surpassed (2)

2Ch 9:6 You've **s** the stories I've heard.
Pro 31:29 but you have **s** them all!'

surplus (2)

2Co 8:14 At the present time, your **s** fills
8:14 so that their **s** may fill your

surprise (8)

Lev 10:16 To his **s**, it had already been
Jos 10:9 from Gilgal and took them by **s**.
Psa 35:8 Let destruction **s** them.
89:22 No enemy will take him by **s**.
Jer 14:9 be like someone taken by **s**,
Luk 21:34 could suddenly catch you by **s**
21:35 That day will **s** all people who
1Th 5:4 That day won't take you by **s**

surprised (25)

Jdg 3:24 They were **s** that the doors
Rut 3:8 When he turned over, he was **s**
Ecc 5:8 Don't be **s** if you see poor
Mat 21:20 The disciples were **s** to see
22:22 They were **s** to hear this.
27:14 so the governor was very **s**.
Mar 9:15 All the people were very **s** to
12:17 They were **s** at his reply.
15:5 anything, so Pilate was **s**.
Luk 11:38 The Pharisee was **s** to see
20:26 His answer **s** them,
Jon 3:7 Don't be **s** when I tell you that
4:27 They were **s** that he was
5:28 Don't be **s** at what I've just said.
7:15 The Jews were **s** and asked,
7:21 and all of you are **s** by it.
Act 4:13 they were **s** to see how boldly
7:31 Moses was **s** when he saw
Gal 1:6 I'm **s** that you're so quickly
1Pe 4:4 because they are **s** that you no
4:12 Dear friends, don't be **s** by the
1Jn 3:13 Brothers and sisters, don't be **s**
Rev 17:6 I was very **s** when I saw her.
17:7 asked me, "Why are you **s**?
17:8 will be **s** when they see the

surprising (1)

2Co 11:15 So it's not **s** if his servants also

surrender (16)

Dtr 20:10 its people a peaceful way to **s**.
1Sm 11:3 one to save us, we'll **s** to you."
11:10 "Tomorrow we'll **s** to you,
Psa 27:12 Do not **s** me to the will of my
37:7 **S** yourself to the LORD,
Pro 5:9 Either you will **s** your
Jer 21:9 Those of you who go out and **s**
27:8 or kingdoms won't serve or **s**
27:12 "**S** to the king of Babylon,
38:2 But those who **s** to the
38:17 If you **s** to the officers of the
38:18 But if you don't **s** to the officers
38:21 But if you refuse to **s**,
50:15 They'll **s**. Their towers will fall
Dan 8:13 the **s** of the holy place,
11:43 Libya and Sudan will **s** to him.

surrendered (4)

2Ki 24:12 and eunuchs **s** to the king of
25:11 those who **s** to the king of
Jer 39:9 those who **s** to him,
52:15 those who **s** to the king of

surrenders (1)

Jer 27:11 But suppose a nation **s** to the

surround (30)

Jos 7:9 they will s us and remove
2Sm 12:28 s the city, and capture it.
2Ki 11:8 S the king. Each man should
2Ch 23:7 The Levites should s the king.
Job 22:14 Thick clouds s him so that he
40:22 Poplars by the stream s it.
Psa 5:12 you s them with your favor.
17:9 from my deadly enemies who s
27:6 above my enemies who s me.
32:7 You s me with joyous songs of
49:5 slanderers s me with evil?
88:17 They s me on all sides.
89:7 than those who s him.
97:2 Clouds and darkness s him.
97:3 It burns his enemies who s
109:3 They s me with hateful words.
110:2 Rule your enemies who s you.
125:2 the mountains s Jerusalem,
140:9 Let the heads of those who s
142:7 Righteous people will s me
Sos 3:7 from the army of Israel s it.
Isa 21:2 S them, Media! I will put an
Jer 4:17 They s them like men guarding
12:9 Other birds of prey s it.
Eze 36:7 the nations which s you will
Hos 7:2 Now their sins s them.
Amo 3:11 An enemy will s your land,
Hab 1:4 Wicked people s righteous
Luk 19:43 will build a wall to s you
2Ti 4:3 own desires and s themselves

surrounded (44)

Gen 19:4 citizens of Sodom s the house.
Jdg 16:2 So they s the place and waited
19:22 worthless men from the city s
20:5 They s the house ⌊where I
2Sm 18:15 armorbearers s Absalom,
22:5 The waves of death had s me.
22:6 ropes of the grave had s me.
22:12 He s himself with darkness.
1Ki 5:3 my father David was s by war.
5:4 But the LORD my God has s
2Ki 3:25 Soldiers s Kir Hareseth and
6:14 came at night and s the city.
8:21 chariot commanders s him,
2Ch 14:7 and he has s us with peace.
15:15 the LORD s them with peace.
18:31 So they s him in order to fight
20:30 his God s him with peace.
21:9 chariot commanders s him,
Job 16:13 and his archers s me.
19:6 God has wronged me and s me
41:14 Its teeth are s by terror.
Psa 17:11 They have s me. They have
18:5 ropes of the grave had s me.
22:12 Many bulls have s me.
22:16 Dogs have s me. A mob has
40:12 Countless evils have s me.
57:4 My soul is s by lions.
65:12 The hills are s with joy.
118:10 All the nations s me,
118:11 They s me. Yes, they
118:11 Yes, they s me, ⌊but armed⌋
Ecc 9:14 He s it and blockaded it.
Isa 33:21 in a place s by wide rivers
Lam 3:5 He has attacked me and s me
Eze 1:4 with flashing lightning s by
1:27 A bright light s him.
24:2 The king of Babylon has s
40:5 I saw a wall that s the temple.
Jnh 2:3 of the sea, and water s me.
2:5 "Water s me, threatening my
Jon 10:24 The Jews s him. They asked
Act 25:7 come from Jerusalem s him.
Heb 12:1 Since we are s by so many
Rev 20:9 expanse of the earth and s

surrounding (33)

Exo 38:20 and the s courtyard were made
38:31 and all the pegs for the s
40:8 Set up the s courtyard,
Num 3:37 of the posts for the s courtyard,
4:32 the posts for the s courtyard,
32:33 with its cities and its s territory.
Jos 18:20 These are the borders s the
2Ki 6:15 and chariots s the city.
9:37 in the fields s Jezreel so that
1Ch 18:1 and its s villages from them.
Neh 5:17 came to us from the s nations.
6:16 all the s nations were afraid
9:30 to the people in the s nations.
Jer 25:9 and all these s nations.
52:23 on the s filigree was 100.
Eze 5:6 laws more than the s nations.
28:26 all the s people who treat
36:4 by the rest of the s nations:
36:36 The s nations that are left will
41:7 The s structure went from story
Joe 3:12 There I will sit to judge all the s
Nah 3:8 of the Nile with water s her?
Zec 7:7 when Jerusalem and its s
12:2 makes all the s people stagger.
12:6 They will burn up all the s
14:14 The wealth of all the s nations
Mar 1:28 the s region of Galilee.
Luk 4:14 throughout the s country.
4:37 place throughout the s region.
7:17 Judea and the s region.
8:37 Then all the people from the s
Act 14:6 and to the s territory.
Rev 5:11 and the leaders s the throne.

surrounds (9)

Num 3:26 entrance to the courtyard that s
Job 22:11 ⌊That is why⌋ darkness s you
Psa 3:3 are a shield that s me.
32:10 but mercy s those who trust the
89:8 even your faithfulness s you.
125:2 so the LORD s his people now
Eze 21:14 It's the sword that s them.
Hos 11:12 "Ephraim s me with lies.
11:12 The nation of Israel s me with

survey (2)

Jos 18:4 They will s the land and write
18:8 He said, "Go s the land.

surveyed (2)

Jos 18:9 The men s the land.
Amo 7:17 Your land will be s and divided

surveys (1)

Pro 5:21 and he s all his actions.

survive (15)

2Sm 1:10 since I knew he couldn't s after
Ezr 9:13 have permitted a few of us to s.
Job 27:15 Those who s him will be
Pro 27:4 but who can s jealousy?
28:26 walks in wisdom will s.
Isa 17:6 Only a few people will s.
Jer 42:17 No one will s or escape the
44:14 who went to live in Egypt will s
Eze 7:16 Those who s will escape to
14:22 But some people will s.
17:14 The country could only s by
Amo 7:2 ⌊the descendants of⌋ Jacob s?
7:5 ⌊the descendants of⌋ Jacob s?
Mal 3:2 Who will be able to s on the
Act 27:34 Eating will help you s,

survived (16)

Exo 14:28 Not one of them s.
Num 14:38 Caleb (son of Jephunneh) s.
Jos 8:22 None of them s or escaped.
8:24 all to death; not one person s.
10:20 But some who s got back into
11:11 Not one person s. Joshua also
11:14 destroyed. Not one person s.
Jdg 4:16 in combat. Not one man s.
9:5 son, s because he hid.
21:17 "Benjamin's men who s must
Neh 1:2 the Jews who had s captivity
1:3 They told me, "Those who s
Psa 106:11 Not one Egyptian s.
Jer 31:2 The people who s the wars
Lam 2:22 No one escaped or s on the
Rev 9:20 The people who s these

survives (2)

Jer 21:7 in this city who s the plague,
1Co 3:14 If what a person has built s,

surviving (3)

Lev 10:12 Moses told Aaron and his s
10:16 and Ithamar, Aaron's s sons.
1Ki 18:22 "I'm the only s prophet of the

survivor (1)

Job 18:19 his people or any s where

survivors (31)

Num 21:35 and all his troops, leaving no s.
Dtr 2:34 and children. There were no s.
3:3 We defeated him, leaving no s.
Jos 10:28 There were no s. He did the
10:30 There were no s. He did the
10:33 his troops. There were no s.
10:37 There were no s, the same as
10:39 There were no s. He did the
10:40 There were no s. He claimed
11:8 in the east. There were no s.
1Sm 11:11 The s were so scattered that
1Ki 20:30 The s fled to Aphek,
2Ki 10:14 They didn't leave any s.
Ezr 9:8 leave us a few s from Babylon
9:14 destroy us and no s are left.
9:15 of us continue to remain as s.
Isa 1:9 of Armies hadn't left us a few s,
4:2 the pride and joy of Israel's s.
10:20 the s of Jacob's descendants
14:22 the name of the s from Babylon,
14:30 with famine and kill off your s.
15:9 Moab and the s from Adamah.
16:14 the s will be very few and
66:19 them and send some of their s
Jer 11:23 There will be no s.
15:9 I will put s from these people to
40:11 king of Babylon had left a few s
Joe 2:32 Among the s will be those
Amo 9:12 They will capture the few s of
Oba 1:14 Don't hand over their s when
Act 15:17 so that the s and all the people

Susa (22)

Ezr 4:9 S, (that is, those of Elam),
Neh 1:1 while I was in the fortress at S,
Est 1:2 royal throne in the fortress of S,
1:5 all people in the fortress of S,
2:3 bring them to the fortress of S,
2:5 In the fortress of S there was a
2:8 and brought to the fortress of S.
3:15 also issued at the fortress of S.
3:15 but the city of S was in turmoil.
4:8 decree that was issued in S.
4:16 "Assemble all the Jews in S.
8:14 issued also in the fortress of S.
8:15 city of S cheered and rejoiced.
9:6 In the fortress of S the Jews
9:11 in the fortress of S was reported
9:12 "In the fortress of S the Jews
9:13 allow the Jews in S to do
9:14 issuing a decree in S.
9:15 The Jews in S also assembled
9:15 Adar and killed 300 men in S,
9:18 But the Jews in S had
Dan 8:2 I saw myself in the fortress of S

Susanna (1)

Luk 8:3 S; and many other women.

Susi (1)

Num 13:11 Gaddi, son of S, from the tribe

suspect (1)

Num 5:14 a fit of jealousy and s his wife,

suspected (1)

Act 27:27 About midnight the sailors s

suspecting (1)

Pro 3:29 there with you and s nothing.

suspending (1)

Dtr 15:2 because the ⌊time⌋ for **s**

suspense (1)

Jon 10:24 long will you keep us in **s**?

suspicion (1)

1Ti 6:4 jealousy, rivalry, cursing, **s**,

suspicious (1)

Num 5:30 has a fit of jealousy and is **s**

swallow (15)

Num 16:32 the earth opened up to **s** them,
16:34 the ground would **s** them,
2Sm 20:19 Why should you **s** up what
20:20 I don't wish to **s** ⌊it⌋ up or
Job 7:19 enough to let me **s** my spit?
Psa 21:9 The LORD will **s** them up in
69:15 Do not let the ocean **s** me up,
73:10 wickedness and **s** their words.
Pro 1:12 We'll **s** them alive like the
19:28 of wicked people **s** up trouble.
26:2 sparrow, like a darting **s**,
Isa 25:8 He will **s** up death forever.
Jnh 1:17 sent a big fish to **s** Jonah.
Hab 1:13 wicked people **s** those who are
Mat 23:24 your wine⌋, but you **s** camels.

swallowed (20)

Gen 41:7 The thin heads of grain **s** the
41:24 The thin heads of grain **s** the
Exo 7:12 But Aaron's staff **s** theirs.
15:12 right hand. The earth **s** them.
Num 26:10 The ground opened up and **s**
Dtr 11:6 ground opened up and **s** them,
Job 20:15 vomits up the riches that he **s**.
Psa 35:25 "We have **s** him up."
106:17 ground split open and **s** Dathan.
124:3 then they would have **s** us
Pro 18:8 of a gossip are **s** greedily,
26:22 of a gossip are **s** greedily,
Jer 51:34 He has **s** us like a monster.
51:44 spit out everything that it has **s**.
Lam 2:2 The Lord **s** up all of Jacob's
2:5 He **s** up Israel. He swallowed
2:5 He **s** up all of its palaces.
2:8 hand away until he had **s** it up.
2:16 They say, 'We've **s** it up.
Hos 8:8 Israel will be **s** up.

swallowing (1)

Rev 12:16 by opening its mouth and **s**

swallows (4)

Num 16:30 **s** them and everything that
Psa 84:3 and **s** find a nest for
Isa 38:14 I chirped like **s** and cranes.
Jer 8:7 Mourning doves, **s**,

swamp (1)

Job 8:11 grow up where there is no **s**?

swamps (2)

Job 40:21 place among reeds and **s**.
Eze 47:11 But the water in the **s** and

swarm (12)

Gen 1:20 God said, "Let the water **s**
Exo 8:3 The Nile River will **s** with frogs.
Lev 11:21 winged insects that **s** if they
Dtr 1:44 chased you like a **s** of bees.
28:42 Crickets will **s** all over your
Jdg 7:12 in the valley like a **s** of locusts.
14:8 He saw a **s** of bees and some
Psa 78:45 He sent a **s** of flies that bit
105:30 He made their land **s** with frogs,
Jer 12:12 Looters **s** all over the bare hills
51:14 They will **s** like locusts.
51:27 up horses like a **s** of locusts.

swarmed (1)

Psa 118:12 They **s** around me like bees,

swarming (8)

Lev 5:2 **s** creature — and then ignore
11:10 you must consider all **s**
11:20 "Every **s**, winged insect that
11:29 "The following **s** creatures that
11:31 Among all the **s** creatures that
22:5 an unclean **s** creature or an
Dtr 14:19 Every **s**, winged insect is also
Isa 33:4 Like **s** locusts, people rush for

swarms (16)

Gen 7:21 and everything that **s** over the
Exo 8:21 I will send **s** of flies on you,
8:24 Dense **s** of flies came into
8:29 Tomorrow the **s** of flies will go
8:31 The **s** of flies left Pharaoh,
10:14 all over the country in great **s**.
Lev 11:41 "Any creature that **s** on the
11:42 or any creature that **s** on the
11:43 by eating anything that **s**
11:44 by touching anything that **s**
11:46 creature that **s** on the ground.
Jdg 6:5 Like **s** of locusts, they came
Psa 105:31 He spoke, and **s** of flies and
Pro 30:27 them divide into **s** by instinct.
Amo 7:1 He was preparing **s** of locusts
Nah 3:17 and your scribes are like **s** of

sway (1)

Isa 24:20 stumble like a drunk and **s** like

swaying (3)

Jer 4:24 and the hills are **s**.
Mat 11:7 Tall grass **s** in the wind?
Luk 7:24 Tall grass **s** in the wind?

swear (106)

Gen 14:22 raise my hand and solemnly **s**
21:23 Now, **s** an oath to me here in
21:24 Abraham said, "I so **s**."
24:3 I want you to **s** by the LORD
24:8 from this oath that you **s** to me.
24:37 master made me **s** this oath:
25:33 "First, **s** an oath," Jacob said.
42:15 you'll be tested: I solemnly **s**,
42:16 If not, I solemnly **s**,
47:29 "I want you to **s** that you love
47:31 "**S** to me," he said. So Joseph
50:5 'My father made me **s** an oath.
50:25 made Israel's sons **s** an oath.
Exo 13:19 made the Israelites solemnly **s**
Lev 19:12 "Never **s** by my name in order
Num 14:21 whole earth, I solemnly **s** that
14:28 I solemnly **s** I will do
14:35 I **s** I will do these things to all
30:3 that she will do something or **s**
30:10 that she will do something or **s**
Dtr 32:40 toward heaven and solemnly **s**:
Jos 2:12 Please **s** by the LORD that
2:17 the oath which you made us **s**,
2:20 the oath which you made us **s**."
23:7 the names of their gods or **s**
Jdg 8:19 I solemnly **s**, as the LORD
15:12 Samson said to them, "**S** to me
Rut 3:13 care of you, then, I solemnly **s**,
1Sm 14:24 Saul made the troops **s**,
14:39 I solemnly **s**, as the LORD and
14:45 We solemnly **s**, as the LORD
17:55 Abner answered, "I solemnly **s**,
19:6 and he promised, "I solemnly **s**,
20:3 But I solemnly **s**, as the LORD
20:21 I **s** it, as the LORD lives.
24:21 **S** an oath to the LORD for me
25:26 Now, sir, I solemnly **s**,
25:34 But I solemnly **s** — as the
26:10 I solemnly **s**, as the LORD
26:16 I solemnly **s**, as the LORD
28:10 LORD's name, "I solemnly **s**,
29:6 and told him, "I solemnly **s**,
2Sm 2:27 Joab answered, "I solemnly **s**,
4:11 I solemnly **s**, as the LORD
11:11 I solemnly **s**, as sure as you're
12:5 "I solemnly **s**, as the LORD
14:11 "I solemnly **s**, as the LORD
14:19 "I solemnly **s** on your life,
2Sm 15:21 the king, "I solemnly **s**,
19:7 I **s** to you by the LORD that if
1Ki 1:13 didn't you **s** to me that my son
1:29 He said, "I solemnly **s**,
1:51 'Make King Solomon **s** to me
2:24 So I solemnly **s**, as the LORD
17:1 said to Ahab, "I solemnly **s**,
17:12 She said, "I solemnly **s**,
18:10 I solemnly **s**, as the LORD your
18:15 Elijah said, "I solemnly **s**,
22:14 answered, "I solemnly **s**,
2Ki 2:2 answered, "I solemnly **s**,
2:4 answered, "I solemnly **s**,
2:6 answered, "I solemnly **s**,
3:14 answered, "I solemnly **s**,
4:30 mother said, "I solemnly **s**,
5:16 Elisha said, "I solemnly **s**,
2Ch 18:13 answered, "I solemnly **s**,
36:13 had made Zedekiah **s**
Ezr 10:5 and all the rest of Israel **s** to do
Neh 5:12 the priests and made them **s**
13:25 I made them **s** by God:
Job 27:2 "I **s** an oath by God,
Sos 2:7 Young women of Jerusalem, **s**
3:5 Young women of Jerusalem, **s**
5:8 Young women of Jerusalem, **s**
5:9 that you make us **s** this way?
8:4 Young women of Jerusalem, **s**
Isa 19:18 of Canaan and **s** allegiance
45:23 tongue will **s** ⌊allegiance⌋."
49:18 "I solemnly **s** as I live,"
54:9 So now I **s** an oath not to be
65:16 an oath in the land will **s** by
Jer 44:26 'I **s** by my great name,'
Eze 36:7 I raise my hand and **s** that the
Amo 8:14 for⌋ those who **s** by Ashimah,
8:14 and say, "I solemnly **s**, Dan,
8:14 "I solemnly **s** as long as there
Zep 2:9 Therefore, I solemnly **s**,
Mat 5:34 But I tell you don't **s** an oath at
5:34 Don't **s** an oath by heaven,
5:36 And don't **s** an oath by your
23:16 You say, 'To **s** an oath by the
23:16 But to **s** an oath by the gold in
23:18 Again you say, 'To **s** an oath
23:18 But to **s** an oath by the gift on
23:20 To **s** an oath by the altar is to
23:20 an oath by the altar is to **s** by
23:21 To **s** an oath by the temple is
23:21 an oath by the temple is to **s** by
23:22 And to **s** an oath by heaven is
23:22 heaven is to **s** by God's throne
26:63 "**S** an oath in front of the living
26:74 Peter began to curse and **s**
Mar 5:7 **S** to God that you won't torture
14:71 Peter began to curse and **s**
1Co 15:31 Brothers and sisters, I **s** to you
Heb 3:18 Who did God **s** would never

swearing (4)

Exo 22:11 them must be settled by **s**
32:13 You took an oath, **s** on yourself.
Zep 1:5 those who worship by **s** loyalty
1:5 the LORD while also **s** loyalty

swears (2)

Num 30:2 that he will do something or **s**
Isa 65:16 Whoever **s** an oath in the land

sweat (3)

Gen 3:19 By the **s** of your brow,
Eze 44:18 anything that makes them **s**.
Luk 22:44 His **s** became like drops of

sweaty (1)

Job 37:17 whose clothes are hot and **s**,

sweep (17)

Gen 18:23 "Are you really going to **s** away
18:24 really going to **s** them away?
Dtr 29:19 ⌊the LORD would never⌋ **s**
1Sm 27:1 days Saul will **s** me away.
Job 20:28 A flood will **s** away his house,
Psa 26:9 Do not **s** away my soul along
58:9 Let ⌊God⌋ **s** them away faster
69:15 not let floodwaters **s** me away.

Psa 90:5 You **s** mortals away.
Isa 8:8 It will **s** through Judah.
14:23 I'll **s** it with the broom of
28:17 Hail will **s** away your refuge of
43:2 they will not **s** you away.
Eze 26:4 Then I will **s** up the dust and
Hos 11:6 War will **s** through their cities,
Luk 15:8 she light a lamp, **s** the house,
Rev 12:15 woman in order to **s** her away.

sweeping (2)

Psa 69:2 A flood is **s** me away.
Isa 21:1 Like a storm **s** through the

sweeps (3)

Job 21:18 husks that the storm **s** away?
27:21 It **s** him from his place.
Isa 40:24 and a windstorm **s** them away

sweet (28)

Exo 15:25 and the water became **s**.
Jdg 9:11 **s** fruit in order to rule the trees?
14:14 strong one came something **s**."
Rut 1:20 "Don't call me Naomi [S].
Neh 8:10 eat rich foods, drink **s** drinks,
Job 20:12 "Though evil is **s** in his mouth
21:33 soil in the creekbed is **s** to him.
Psa 119:103 How **s** the taste of your
Pro 3:24 your sleep will be **s**.
9:17 "Stolen waters are **s**,
13:19 A fulfilled desire is **s** to the
16:24 honey from a honeycomb — **s**
20:17 gained dishonestly tastes **s**
24:13 from the honeycomb tastes **s**.
27:7 even bitter food tastes **s**.
Ecc 5:12 sleep of working people is **s**,
11:7 Light is **s**, and it is good for
Sos 2:3 His fruit tastes **s** to me.
2:14 Your voice is **s**, and your figure
5:16 His mouth is **s** in every way.
Isa 5:20 what is bitter into something **s**
5:20 what is **s** into something bitter.
23:16 Make **s** music. Sing many
Eze 3:3 So I ate it, and it tasted as **s** as
16:19 You also offered them **s** and
Act 2:13 "They're drunk on **s** wine."
Rev 10:9 but it will be as **s** as honey in
10:10 It was as **s** as honey in my

sweeter (3)

Jdg 14:18 "What is **s** than honey?
Psa 19:10 They are **s** than honey,
119:103 It tastes **s** than honey.

sweetly (1)

Pro 16:21 speaking **s** helps others learn.

sweetness (1)

Pro 27:9 but the **s** of a friend is a fragrant

sweet-smelling (15)

Exo 25:6 oil and for the **s** incense,
30:7 "Aaron must burn **s** incense on
31:11 the anointing oil, and the **s**
35:8 oil and for the **s** incense,
35:15 the anointing oil, the **s** incense,
35:28 and the **s** incense.
37:29 and for the pure, **s** incense.
39:38 the anointing oil, the **s** incense,
40:27 He burned **s** incense on it,
Lev 4:7 horns of the altar for **s** incense
16:12 of finely ground, **s** incense.
Num 4:16 oil for the lamps, the **s** incense,
2Ch 2:4 burn **s** incense in his presence,
13:11 They offer **s** incense and rows
Psa 141:2 Let my prayer be accepted as **s**

swell (6)

Num 5:21 and your stomach **s**.' "Then
5:22 body and make your stomach **s**
5:27 Her stomach will **s**,
Dtr 8:4 and your feet didn't **s** these
Neh 9:21 and their feet didn't **s**.
Act 28:6 were waiting for him to **s** up

swept (19)

Gen 19:15 or you'll be **s** away when the
19:17 or you'll be **s** away!"
Exo 14:27 but the LORD **s** them into the
Num 16:26 or you'll be **s** away because of
Jdg 5:21 The Kishon River **s** them away
1Sm 26:10 or he'll go into battle and be **s**
Job 1:19 when suddenly a great storm **s**
Psa 42:7 on your waves have **s** over me.
73:19 completely **s** away by terror!
88:16 burning anger has **s** over me.
124:4 would have **s** us away.
136:15 He **s** Pharaoh and his army into
Pro 13:23 but a person is **s** away where
Jnh 2:3 on your waves have **s** over me.
Mat 12:44 **s** clean, and in order.
24:39 until the flood came and **s** all
Luk 11:25 it finds the house **s** clean and
Gal 2:13 was **s** along with them.
Rev 12:4 Its tail **s** away one-third of the

swerve (1)

Isa 28:7 They **s** as they judge.

swift (2)

Isa 18:2 Go, **s** messengers,
2Pe 2:1 bring themselves **s** destruction.

swifter (2)

2Sm 1:23 They were **s** than eagles and
Job 7:6 My days go **s** than a weaver's

swiftly (2)

Jer 2:23 a young camel that **s** runs here
46:7 like streams that flow **s**?

swim (3)

Isa 25:11 stretch out their hands to **s**.
Act 27:43 He ordered those who could **s**
27:43 overboard first and **s** ashore.

swimmers (1)

Isa 25:11 manure like **s** who stretch out

swimming (3)

Gen 1:20 water swarm with **s** creatures,
Eze 47:5 too deep to cross except by **s**.
Act 27:42 from **s** away and escaping.

swims (3)

Gen 1:21 every type of creature that **s**
Lev 11:46 and every living creature that **s**
Psa 8:8 the birds, the fish, whatever **s**

swing (4)

Job 28:4 dangle and **s** back and forth.
Eze 32:10 shudder when I **s** my sword
Rev 14:15 on the cloud, "**S** your sickle,
14:18 sharp sickle, "**S** your sickle,

swinging (1)

Isa 30:32 fight them in battle, **s** his fists.

swings (1)

Dtr 19:5 As one of them **s** the ax to cut

swirl (3)

Psa 88:17 They **s** around me all day long
Jer 23:19 Like a windstorm, it will **s**
30:23 Like a driving wind, it will **s**

swollen (1)

Luk 14:2 A man whose body was **s** with

swoop (4)

Dtr 28:49 The nation will **s** down on you
Isa 11:14 They will **s** down on the
Jer 48:40 The enemy will **s** down like
49:22 The enemy will **s** down like

swooping (1)

Job 9:26 like an eagle **s** down on its

swoops (2)

Hos 8:1 The enemy **s** down on the
Hab 1:8 fly like an eagle that **s** down

sword (162)

Gen 3:24 and a flaming **s** that turned
27:40 You will use your **s** to live,
48:22 with my own **s** and bow."
Exo 15:9 I'll use my **s**! I'll take all they
32:27 Each of you put on your **s**.
Num 22:23 in the road with his **s** drawn,
22:29 If I had a **s** in my hand,
22:31 in the road with his **s** drawn.
Dtr 32:41 I will sharpen my flashing **s**
32:42 My **s** will cut off the heads of
33:29 you and a **s** that wins your
Jos 5:13 standing in front of him with a **s**
11:10 He killed its king with a **s**.
Jdg 7:14 can only be the **s** of Gideon,
7:20 They shouted, "A **s** for the
8:20 But Jether didn't draw his **s**.
9:54 "Take your **s** and kill me!
1Sm 13:22 not one **s** or spear could be
15:33 But Samuel said, "As your **s**
17:39 David fastened Saul's **s** over
17:45 "You come to me with **s** and
17:47 can save without **s** or spear,
17:50 didn't have a **s** in his hand.
17:51 He took Goliath's **s**,
18:4 his **s**, his bow, and his belt.
21:8 you have a spear or a **s** here?
21:9 "The **s** of Goliath the Philistine,
21:9 Let me have the **s**."
22:10 and gave him food and the **s**
22:13 You gave him bread and a **s**
22:19 Using ⌊his⌋ **s**, he killed men
25:13 including David, put on his **s**.
31:4 his armorbearer, "Draw your **s**!
31:4 So Saul took the **s** and fell on
31:5 he also fell on his **s** and died
2Sm 1:22 nor did Saul's **s** return unused.
2:16 stuck his **s** into his opponent's
11:25 because a **s** can kill one
20:8 over it at his hip was a **s**
20:8 the **s** dropped ⌊into his hand⌋.
20:10 on his guard against the **s**
23:10 got tired and stuck to his **s**.
1Ki 2:32 He used his **s** to kill Abner
3:24 his servants to bring him a **s**.
19:17 escapes from Hazael's **s**,
19:17 anyone escapes from Jehu's **s**,
2Ki 11:15 Use your **s** to kill anyone who
11:20 had killed Athaliah with a **s** at
1Ch 10:4 his armorbearer, "Draw your **s**!
10:4 So Saul took the **s** and fell on
10:5 he also fell on the **s** and died.
21:12 or three days of the LORD's **s** —
21:16 The Messenger had a **s** in his
21:27 and he put his **s** back in its
21:30 he was frightened by the **s**
2Ch 23:14 Use your **s** to kill anyone who
23:21 had killed Athaliah with a **s**.
32:21 own sons killed him with a **s**.
Neh 4:18 and each builder had his **s**
Job 5:20 he will save you from the **s**.
15:22 ⌊to be killed⌋ with a **s**.
40:19 maker approaches it with his **s**.
41:26 A **s** may strike it but not pierce
Psa 7:12 God sharpens his **s**.
17:13 With your **s** rescue my life from
22:20 Rescue my soul from the **s**,
44:6 and my **s** will never save me.
45:3 O warrior, strap your **s** to your
89:43 You even took his **s** out of his
144:10 David away from a deadly **s**.
Pro 5:4 as sharp as a two-edged **s**.
12:18 Careless words stab like a **s**,
25:18 ⌊Like⌋ a club and a **s** and a
Sos 3:8 Each one has his **s** at his side
Isa 27:1 use his fierce and powerful **s**
34:5 When my **s** is covered ⌊with
34:6 The LORD's **s** is covered with
41:2 With his **s** he turns them into
49:2 made my tongue like a sharp **s**
66:16 will judge all people with his **s**.
Jer 4:10 but a **s** is held at their throats."
6:25 The enemy has a **s**.
12:12 The LORD's **s** destroys them

Jer 18:21 their ⌊blood⌋ by using your **s**.
46:10 His **s** will devour until it has
46:16 and escape our enemy's **s**.'
47:6 You cry out, "**S** of the LORD,
47:7 How can the **s** of the LORD
50:21 killing them with a **s**," declares
50:35 "A **s** will kill the Babylonians
50:35 "A **s** will kill their officials and
50:36 A **s** will kill the false prophets.
50:36 A **s** will kill their soldiers and
50:37 A **s** will kill their horses,
50:37 A **s** will destroy their treasures,
51:50 who escaped from the **s**,
Eze 5:2 and I will draw a **s** and go after
5:12 and I will pursue them with a **s**.
6:3 am going to attack you with a **s**
12:14 I will pursue them with my **s**.
21:3 I will take my **s** out of its
21:4 That is why my **s** will come
21:5 have taken my **s** from its
21:9 is what the Lord says: A **s**,
21:9 a **s** is sharpened and polished,
21:11 The **s** has been handed over to
21:11 The **s** is being sharpened and
21:12 because the **s** will be used
21:12 and my people on the **s**.
21:14 Let the **s** strike again and
21:14 It's the **s** for killing.
21:14 It's the **s** for killing many
21:14 It's the **s** that surrounds them.
21:15 I have appointed my **s** to
21:16 **S**, cut to the right. Cut to the left
21:19 of Babylon and his **s** can take.
21:20 that the king and his **s** can take
21:28 and their insults: A **s**,
21:28 a **s** is drawn ready to kill.
21:29 The **s** will be placed on the
21:30 "'Return your **s** to its scabbard.
23:10 and killed her with a **s**.
29:8 going to attack you with a **s**.
30:21 be strong enough to hold a **s**.
30:22 I will make the **s** fall from his
30:24 I will put my **s** in his hand,
30:25 because I will put my **s** in the
32:10 shudder when I swing my **s**
32:11 The **s** of the king of Babylon
32:20 A **s** has been drawn.
38:21 use his **s** against his relative.
Amo 7:9 Jeroboam's heirs with my **s**."
7:11 will be killed with a **s**
9:1 I will kill with a **s** all who are
9:4 I will command a **s** to kill them.
Nah 2:13 and a **s** will kill your young
3:15 A **s** will cut you down.
Zep 2:12 you will also die by my **s**."
Zec 9:13 I will use you like a warrior's **s**.
11:17 A **s** will strike his arm and his
13:7 "Arise, **s**, against my shepherd,
Mat 26:51 with Jesus pulled out his **s**
26:52 said to him, "Put your **s** away!
26:52 All who use a **s** will be killed
26:52 a sword will be killed by a **s**.
Mar 14:47 standing there pulled out his **s**
Luk 2:35 And a **s** will pierce your heart."
22:36 doesn't have a **s** should sell his
Jon 18:10 Simon Peter had a **s**.
18:11 told Peter, "Put your **s** away.
Act 16:27 he drew his **s** and was about to
Eph 6:17 the word of God as the **s** that
Heb 4:12 sharper than any two-edged **s**
Rev 1:16 came a sharp, two-edged **s**.
2:12 the sharp two-edged **s** says:
2:16 them with the **s** from my mouth.
6:4 So he was given a large **s**.
13:10 If anyone is killed with a **s**,
13:10 with a **s** he must be killed.
13:14 wounded by a **s** and yet lived.
19:15 A sharp **s** comes out of his
19:21 rest with the **s** that came out

swords (93)

Gen 34:25 took their **s** and boldly attacked
49:5 Their **s** are weapons of
Dtr 13:15 the residents of that city with **s**
20:13 man in that city with your **s**.
Jos 6:21 With their **s** they killed men
10:11 hailstones than from Israelite **s**.
10:28 its people and king with **s**.
11:11 by destroying them with **s**.
Jdg 18:27 killed them all with **s**,
20:2 400,000 foot soldiers with **s**.
20:15 with **s** came from Benjamin's
20:17 400,000 soldiers armed with **s**.
20:25 Israel who were armed with **s**.
20:35 who were armed with **s**.
20:46 armed with **s** were killed that
1Sm 13:19 from making **s** and spears.
25:13 "Each of you put on your **s**!"
1Ki 18:28 also cut themselves with **s**
2Ki 10:25 So they used **s** to kill the Baal
1Ch 5:18 and **s** and shoot arrows.
21:12 away when their **s** catch up
Neh 4:13 The people were armed with **s**,
Est 9:5 Then with their **s**, the Jews
Job 27:14 many children, **s** will kill them,
39:22 and doesn't back away from **s**.
Psa 37:14 Wicked people pull out their **s**
37:15 ⌊But⌋ their own **s** will pierce
44:3 It was not with their **s** that they
55:21 they are like **s** ready to attack.
57:4 Their tongues are sharp **s**.
59:7 their mouths — **s** from their lips
63:10 They will be cut down by **s**.
64:3 sharpen their tongues like **s**.
76:3 **s**, and weapons of war. Selah
78:62 He let **s** kill his people.
78:64 priests were cut down with **s**.
149:6 and two-edged **s** in their hands
Pro 30:14 whose teeth are like **s** and
Sos 3:8 of them are skilled in using **s**,
Isa 1:20 you will be destroyed by **s**."
2:4 They will hammer their **s** into
21:15 They flee from **s**, from swords
21:15 from **s** ready to kill,
22:2 people weren't killed with **s**.
31:8 be killed with **s** not made by
31:8 **S** not made by human hands
Jer 5:17 With their **s** they will destroy
15:3 "I will send **s** to kill,
19:7 I will cut them down with **s** in
20:4 Their enemies' **s** will kill them,
20:4 to Babylon or kill them with **s**.
21:7 will kill them with **s**.
41:2 with him got up, drew their **s**,
46:14 **S** will kill those around you.'
48:10 who keep their **s** from killing.
50:16 because of the enemies' **s**.
Lam 1:20 In the streets **s** kill my children.
2:21 and men are cut down by **s**.
4:9 Those who were killed with **s**
Eze 7:15 "Outside are **s**, and inside are
11:8 You are afraid of **s**,
11:8 so I will bring **s** to attack you,
16:40 cut you into pieces with their **s**.
23:47 them and kill them with **s**.
28:7 They will draw their **s** against
28:23 People with **s** will attack you
30:11 They will draw their **s** to attack
32:12 people with the **s** of warriors.
32:27 Their **s** were placed under their
33:26 You rely on your **s**.
38:4 shields and be able to use **s**.
Dan 11:33 be defeated by **s** and flames.
Hos 1:7 I won't use bows, **s**,
2:18 I will destroy all the bows, **s**,
Joe 3:10 Hammer your plowblades into **s**
Amo 1:11 pursued their relatives with **s**.
4:10 With **s** I killed your best young
7:17 daughters will be killed with **s**.
9:10 they will be killed with **s**.
Mic 4:3 They will hammer their **s** into
5:6 will rule Assyria with their **s**
5:6 country of Nimrod with drawn **s**
Nah 3:3 **S** flash! Spears glitter! Many are
Hag 2:22 will kill one another with **s**.
Mat 26:47 A large crowd carrying **s** and
26:55 "Have you come out with **s**
Mar 14:43 A crowd carrying **s** and clubs
14:48 "Have you come out with **s**
Luk 21:24 **S** will cut them down,
22:38 Here are two **s**!" Then Jesus
22:49 should we use our **s** to fight?"
Luk 22:52 "Have you come out with **s**
Heb 11:37 in half, and killed with **s**.

swordsmen (1)

2Ki 3:26 he took 700 **s** to try to break

swore (75)

Gen 21:31 both of them **s** an oath there.
24:7 He spoke to me and **s** this oath:
24:9 Abraham commanded and **s**
25:33 So Esau **s** an oath to him and
26:3 I will keep the oath that I **s** to
31:53 So Jacob **s** this oath by the
47:31 So Joseph **s** to him.
50:24 out of this land to the land he **s**
Exo 6:8 you to the land I solemnly **s**
13:5 The LORD **s** to your ancestors
13:11 as he **s** to you and your
Lev 6:5 it was that you **s** falsely about.
Num 14:30 I raised my hand and **s** an oath
32:10 became angry and **s** this oath,
Dtr 1:8 of the land the LORD **s**
1:35 ever see the good land that I **s**
4:31 that he **s** he would keep.
6:10 as he **s** to your ancestors
7:8 you and kept the oath he **s**
7:12 as he **s** to your ancestors.
7:13 as he **s** to your ancestors.
8:18 the promise which he **s**
9:5 to confirm the promise he **s**
10:11 as I **s** to their ancestors."
11:9 time in the land the LORD **s**
11:21 in this land that the LORD **s**
13:17 as he **s** to your ancestors.
26:3 as he **s** to our ancestors."
28:11 as he **s** to your ancestors.
30:20 you in the land that the LORD **s**
31:7 as he **s** to their ancestors.
31:20 bring them into the land that I **s**
31:21 the land that I **s** to give them."
31:23 Israelites into the land that I **s**
Jos 1:6 take possession of the land I **s**
5:6 The LORD **s** that he would not
6:22 as you **s** you would do for her."
9:15 leaders of the congregation **s**
9:20 because of the oath we **s**."
14:9 On that day Moses **s** this oath:
Jdg 2:1 of Egypt into the land that I **s**
21:7 We **s** to the LORD that we
1Sm 20:17 Once again Jonathan **s** an oath
24:22 So David **s** to Saul.
2Sm 19:23 and the king **s** to it.
21:17 Then David's men **s** an oath,
1Ki 1:29 and he **s** an oath. He said, "I
1:30 I will do today exactly what I **s**
2Ki 25:24 Gedaliah **s** an oath to them and
2Ch 15:14 Asa and the people **s** their oath
Neh 9:15 land that you **s** you would give
Psa 89:3 I **s** this oath to my servant
89:49 You **s** an oath to David on ⌊the
106:26 Raising his hand, he **s** that he
132:2 Remember how he **s** an oath to
132:11 The LORD **s** an oath to David.
Isa 54:9 when I **s** an oath that Noah's
Jer 32:22 gave them the land that you **s**
38:16 So King Zedekiah secretly **s**
40:9 **s** an oath to them and their
Eze 20:5 I raised my hand and **s** an oath
20:15 I also **s** an oath to them in the
20:15 I **s** that I would not bring them
20:23 I raised my hand and **s** an oath
44:12 So I raised my hand and **s** that
47:14 I raised my hand and **s** that I
Dan 9:11 brought on us the curses you **s**
12:7 and left hand to heaven and **s**
Mic 7:20 mercy on Abraham as you **s** by
Mat 5:33 but give to the Lord what you **s**
14:7 he **s** he would give her
26:72 Again Peter denied it and **s**
Mar 6:23 He **s** an oath to her:
Luk 1:73 the oath that he **s** to our
Rev 10:6 He **s** an oath by the one who

sworn (12)

Dtr 2:14 as the LORD had **s** they would.
Jos 5:6 milk and honey which he had **s**

Jos 9:18 of the congregation had **s**
9:19 "We have **s** an oath about them
21:43 Israel the whole land he had **s**
21:44 as he had **s** with an oath to
2Sm 21:2 Although the Israelites had **s**
1Ch 16:16 and his **s** promise to Isaac.
Psa 105:9 and his **s** oath to Isaac.
Isa 62:8 The LORD has **s** with his right
Amo 6:8 The Almighty LORD has **s** an
8:7 The LORD has **s** an oath by

swung (4)
Eze 26:2 and its doors are **s** open to me.
41:24 were double doors that **s** open.
Rev 14:16 The one who sat on the cloud **s**
14:19 The angel **s** his sickle on the

Sychar (2)
Jon 4:5 at a city in Samaria called **S**.
4:5 **S** was near the piece of land

Syene (2)
Eze 29:10 a wasteland, from Migdol to **S**,
30:6 will die in war from Migdol to **S**,

symbolizes (1)
Num 2:2 the flag that **s** its household.

symbols (2)
Psa 74:4 set up their own emblems as **s**.
Isa 8:18 We are signs and **s** in Israel

sympathetic (3)
Eph 4:32 Be kind to each other, **s**,
Col 3:12 be **s**, kind, humble, gentle,
1Pe 3:8 harmony, be **s**, love each other,

sympathize (2)
Job 2:11 they would go together to **s**
Heb 4:15 a chief priest who is able to **s**

sympathized (1)
Job 42:11 him at his house, **s** with him,

sympathy (2)
Psa 69:20 I looked for **s**, but there was
Php 2:1 have any **s** and compassion?

synagogue (60)
Mat 9:18 A ⌊**s**⌋ leader came to Jesus
9:23 came to the ⌊**s**⌋ leader's house.
12:9 on from there and went into a **s**.
13:54 and taught the people in the **s**
Mar 1:21 Jesus went into the **s** and
1:23 in the **s** who was controlled
1:29 After they left the **s**,
3:1 Jesus went into a **s** again.
3:3 "Stand in the center ⌊of the **s**⌋."
5:22 A **s** leader named Jairus also
5:35 came from the **s** leader's home.
5:35 They told the **s** leader,
5:36 he told the **s** leader,
5:38 to the home of the **s** leader,
6:2 he began to teach in the **s**.
Luk 4:16 As usual he went into the **s** on
4:20 in the **s** watched him closely.
4:28 Everyone in the **s** became
4:33 In the **s** was a man possessed
4:35 down in the middle of the **s**
4:38 Jesus left the **s** and went to
6:6 Jesus went into a **s** to teach.
6:8 stand in the center ⌊of the **s**⌋!"
7:5 and built our **s** at his own
8:41 man named Jairus, a **s** leader,
8:49 came from the **s** leader's home.
8:50 he told the **s** leader,
13:10 Jesus was teaching in a **s** on
13:14 The **s** leader was irritated with
Jon 6:59 teaching in a **s** in Capernaum.
9:22 was the Christ out of the **s**.
9:34 they threw him out ⌊of the **s**⌋.
9:35 thrown the man out ⌊of the **s**⌋.
12:42 have thrown them out of the **s**.
Act 6:9 **s** called Freedmen's Synagogue.
6:9 called Freedmen's **S**.
9:2 of authorization to the **s** leaders
13:14 went into the **s** and sat down.
13:15 the **s** leaders sent ⌊a
13:42 Barnabas were leaving the **s**,
13:43 the meeting of the **s** broke up,
14:1 and Barnabas went into the **s**
17:1 where there was a **s**.
17:2 As usual, Paul went into the **s**.
17:2 Scripture with the **s** members.
17:10 they entered the **s**.
17:17 He held discussions in the **s**
18:4 discuss ⌊Scripture⌋ in the **s**.
18:7 Then he left the **s** and went to
18:7 house was next door to the **s**.
18:8 The **s** leader Crispus and his
18:17 took Sosthenes, the **s** leader,
18:19 Paul went into the **s** and had a
18:26 began to speak boldly in the **s**.
19:8 Paul would go into the **s**
22:19 here know that I went from **s**
22:19 that I went from synagogue to **s**
26:11 I even went to each **s**,
Rev 2:9 They are the **s** of Satan.
3:9 who are in Satan's **s** come

synagogues (22)
Mat 4:23 He taught in the **s** and spread
6:2 is what hypocrites do in the **s**
6:5 They like to stand in **s** and on
9:35 He taught in the **s** and spread
10:17 courts and whip you in their **s**.
23:6 dinners and the front seats in **s**.
23:34 Others you will whip in your **s**
Mar 1:39 News⌋ in the **s** all over Galilee,
12:39 and to have the front seats in **s**
13:9 courts and whip you in their **s**.
Luk 4:15 He taught in the **s**,
4:44 his message in the **s** of Judea.
11:43 to sit in the front seats in the **s**
12:11 "When you are put on trial in **s**
20:46 to have the front seats in the **s**
21:12 will hand you over to their **s**
Jon 16:2 You will be thrown out of **s**.
18:20 I have always taught in **s** or in
Act 9:20 word in their **s** that Jesus was
13:5 to spread God's word in the **s**.
15:21 His teachings are read in **s** on
24:12 in the **s** throughout the city.

Syntyche (1)
Php 4:2 I encourage both Euodia and **S**

Syracuse (2)
Act 28:12 We stopped at the city of **S**
28:13 We sailed from **S** and arrived at

Syria (14)
2Ch 16:7 you depended on the king of **S**
Eze 27:16 "People from **S** traded with
Hos 12:12 Jacob fled to the country of **S**.
Mat 4:24 Jesus spread throughout **S**.
Mar 7:26 born in Phoenicia in **S**.
Luk 2:2 Quirinius was governor of **S**.
4:27 one except Naaman from **S**."
Act 14:26 to the city of Antioch ⌊in **S**⌋.
15:23 in Antioch, **S**, and Cilicia.
15:41 went through the provinces of **S**
18:18 they took a boat headed for **S**
20:3 was going to board a ship for **S**,
21:3 it on our left and sailed to **S**.
Gal 1:21 to the regions of **S** and Cilicia.

Syzugus (1)
Php 4:3 Yes, I also ask you, **S**,

T

Taanach (7)
Jos 12:21 the king of **T**, the king of
17:11 people living in Dor, En Dor, **T**,
21:25 **T** and Gath Rimmon.
Jdg 1:27 of Beth Shean, **T**, Dor, Ibleam,
5:19 They fought at **T** by the waters
1Ki 4:12 Baana, son of Ahilud, had **T**,
1Ch 7:29 **T** and its villages,

Taanath Shiloh (1)
Jos 16:6 turns east to **T** and passes east

Tabbaoth (2)
Ezr 2:43 of Ziha, Hasupha, **T**,
Neh 7:46 of Ziha, Hasupha, **T**,

Tabbath (1)
Jdg 7:22 stream at Abel Meholah near **T**.

Tabbur Haares (1)
Jdg 9:37 troops coming down from **T**.

Tabeel (1)
Ezr 4:7 Bishlam, Mithredath, **T**,

Tabeel's (1)
Isa 7:6 and set up **T** son as its king.'

Taberah (2)
Num 11:3 That place was called **T** [Fire]
Dtr 9:22 made the LORD angry at **T**,

Tabitha (4)
Act 9:36 A disciple named **T** lived in the
9:40 the body and said, "**T**, get up!"
9:40 **T** opened her eyes,
9:41 he presented **T** to them.

table (77)
Gen 43:34 food brought to them from his **t**,
Exo 25:23 "Make a **t** of acacia wood 36
25:27 hold the poles for carrying the **t**.
25:28 and use them to carry the **t**.
25:29 plates and dishes for the **t** out
25:30 of the presence on this **t** so that
26:35 "Place the **t** outside the canopy
26:35 the lamp stand opposite the **t**
30:27 the **t** and all the dishes,
31:8 the **t** and the dishes,
35:13 the **t** with its poles,
37:10 He made the **t** out of acacia
37:14 hold the poles for carrying the **t**.
37:16 For the **t** he made plates,
39:36 the **t** with all the dishes,
40:4 Bring in the **t**, and arrange
40:22 Moses put the **t** in the tent of
40:23 He arranged the bread on the **t**
40:24 tent of meeting opposite the **t**,
Lev 24:6 stacks of six each on the gold **t**
Num 3:31 the **t**, the lamp stand, the altars,
4:7 spread a violet cloth over the **t**
4:8 cloth over everything on the **t**.
Jdg 1:7 to pick up food under my **t**.
1Sm 20:5 sit and eat at the king's ⌊**t**⌋.
20:34 Jonathan got up from the **t** very
2Sm 9:7 you will always eat at my **t**."
9:10 will always eat at my **t**."
9:11 Mephibosheth ate at David's **t**
9:13 He always ate at the king's **t**.
19:28 with those who eat at your **t**.
1Ki 2:7 Let them eat at your **t**.
4:27 and all who ate at his **t**.
7:48 the gold **t** on which the bread of
10:5 the food on his **t**, his officers'
13:20 When they were sitting at the **t**,
18:19 who eat at Jezebel's **t**."
2Ki 4:10 the roof and put a bed, **t**, chair,
1Ch 28:16 the weight of gold for each **t**
2Ch 9:4 the food on his **t**, his officers'
13:11 rows of bread on the clean **t**.
29:18 the **t** for the rows of bread and
Job 36:16 and your **t** was covered with
Psa 69:22 Let the **t** set for them become a
128:3 young olive trees around your **t**.
Pro 9:2 her wine. She has set her **t**.
Sos 1:12 While the king is at his **t**,
Isa 21:5 Set the **t**. Spread the rugs ⌊by
21:5 Spread the rugs ⌊by the **t**⌋.
65:11 You have prepared a **t** for the
Eze 39:20 At my **t** you will be filled with
41:22 "This is the **t** that is in the
44:16 come near my **t** to serve me,
Dan 11:27 They will sit at the same **t** and

Amo 6:7 around the banquet **t** will stop.
Mal 1:7 the LORD's **t** may be despised.
1:12 you say that the Lord's **t** may
Mat 26:20 Jesus was at the **t** with the
Mar 7:28 even the dogs under the **t** eat
14:18 While they were at the **t** eating,
Luk 7:36 house and was eating at the **t**.
12:37 make them sit down at the **t**,
16:21 that fell from the rich man's **t**.
22:14 and the apostles were at the **t**.
22:21 betray me is with me on the **t**.
22:27 the person who sits at the **t** or
22:27 the person who sits at the **t**?
22:30 You will eat and drink at my **t**
24:30 he was at the **t** with them,
Jon 13:4 So he got up from the **t**,
13:12 he took his place at the **t** again.
13:23 was near him at the **t**.
13:28 No one at the **t** knew why
Rom 11:9 And David says, "Let the **t** set
1Co 10:21 You cannot participate at the **t**
10:21 the Lord and at the **t** of demons.
Heb 9:2 The lamp stand, the **t**,

tables (20)

1Ch 28:16 and the silver for the silver **t**,
2Ch 4:8 He made ten **t** and put them in
4:19 the gold **t** on which the bread of
Isa 28:8 All the **t** are covered with vomit
Eze 23:41 sat on their fine couches with **t**
23:41 and my olive oil on their **t**.
40:39 of the gateway there were two **t**
40:39 On these **t** the animals were
40:40 north gateway there were two **t**,
40:40 the gateway there were two **t**.
40:41 So there were four **t** on each
40:41 of the gateway, eight **t** in all,
40:42 There were four **t** made of cut
40:42 On these **t** the priests laid the
40:43 and the **t** were for the meat of
Mat 15:27 that fall from their masters' **t**."
21:12 the moneychangers' **t**
Mar 7:4 jars, brass pots, and dinner **t**.)
11:15 the moneychangers' **t**
Jon 2:15 coins and knocked over their **t**.

tablet (6)

Pro 3:3 them on the **t** of your heart.
7:3 them on the **t** of your heart.
Isa 8:1 "Take a large writing **t**,
30:8 Now, write this on a **t** for them,
Jer 17:1 with a diamond point on the **t**
Luk 1:63 asked for a writing **t** and wrote,

tablets (34)

Exo 24:12 and I will give you the stone **t**
31:18 Then he gave him the two **t**
31:18 stone **t** inscribed by God
32:15 the mountain carrying the two **t**
32:16 The **t** were the work of God,
32:16 God's writing inscribed on the **t**.
32:19 anger Moses threw down the **t**
34:1 "Cut two ⌊more⌋ stone **t** like
34:1 the first **t** which you smashed.
34:4 cut two ⌊more⌋ stone **t** like
34:4 carrying the two stone **t**.
34:28 He wrote on the **t** the words of
34:29 carrying the two **t** with God's
Dtr 4:13 he wrote them on two stone **t**.
5:22 commandments on two stone **t**
9:9 the mountain to get the stone **t**,
9:9 the **t** of the promise that the
9:10 two stone **t** inscribed by God
9:11 LORD gave me the two stone **t**
9:15 I was carrying the two **t** with
9:17 I took the two **t**, threw them
10:1 "Cut two ⌊more⌋ stone **t** like
10:2 I will write on the **t** the same
10:2 words that were on the first **t**,
10:3 I cut two ⌊more⌋ stone **t** like
10:3 the two **t** up the mountain.
10:4 The LORD wrote on these **t** the
10:5 the mountain and put the **t**
1Ki 8:9 the two stone **t** Moses put there
2Ch 5:10 the two **t** Moses placed there
Hab 2:2 Make it clear on **t** so that
2Co 3:3 a letter written not on **t** of stone
3:3 stone but on **t** of human hearts.
Heb 9:4 and the **t** on which the promise

Tabor (10)

Jos 19:22 The border touches **T**,
Jdg 4:6 'Gather troops on Mount **T**.
4:12 had come to fight at Mount **T**.
4:14 came down from Mount **T**
8:18 kind of men did you kill at **T**?"
1Sm 10:3 you come to the oak tree at **T**.
1Ch 6:77 with its pastureland and **T**
Psa 89:12 Mount **T** and Mount Hermon
Jer 46:18 "someone who is like Mount **T**
Hos 5:1 spread out nets on Mount **T**.

Tabrimmon (1)

1Ki 15:18 son of **T** and grandson of

Tadmor (2)

1Ki 9:18 Baalath, **T** in the desert (inside
2Ch 8:4 He rebuilt **T** in the desert and

Tahan (2)

Num 26:35 and the family of **T**.
1Ch 7:25 Telah's son was **T**.

Tahan's (1)

1Ch 7:26 **T** son was Ladan.

Tahash (1)

Gen 22:24 Gaham, **T**, and Maacah."

Tahath (6)

Num 33:26 and set up camp at **T**.
33:27 They moved from **T** and set up
1Ch 6:24 Assir's son was **T**.
6:37 who was the son of **T**,
7:20 Bered's son was **T**.
7:20 Eleadah's son was **T**.

Tahath's (3)

1Ch 6:24 **T** son was Uriel. Uriel's son was
7:20 **T** son was Eleadah.
7:21 **T** son was Zabad.

Tahkemon's (1)

2Sm 23:8 from **T** family was leader

Tahpanhes (7)

Jer 2:16 People from Noph and **T** have
43:7 They went as far as **T**.
43:8 his word to Jeremiah in **T**.
43:9 to the Pharaoh's palace in **T**.
44:1 Migdol, **T**, Noph, and Pathros.
46:14 it known in Memphis and in **T**.
Eze 30:18 At **T** the day will turn dark

Tahpenes (2)

1Ki 11:19 the sister of Queen **T**,
11:20 **T** presented the boy to Pharaoh

Tahpenes' (1)

1Ki 11:20 **T** sister had a son ⌊named⌋

Tahtim Hodshi (1)

2Sa 24:6 went to Gilead and to **T** and then

tail (12)

Exo 4:4 out and grab the snake by its **t**."
29:22 take the fat, the fat from the **t**,
Lev 3:9 Remove all the fat from the **t**
7:3 all the fat, the fat from the **t**,
8:25 took the fat, the fat from the **t**,
9:19 and the ram (the fat from the **t**,
Dtr 28:13 make you the head, not the **t**.
28:44 and you will be the **t**.
Job 40:17 It makes its **t** stiff like a cedar.
Isa 9:14 off from Israel both head and **t**,
9:15 who teach lies are the **t**.
Rev 12:4 Its **t** swept away one-third of

tails (6)

Jdg 15:4 them together in pairs by their **t**.
15:4 a torch between their **t**.
Rev 9:10 They had **t** and stingers like
Rev 9:10 with their **t** for five months.
9:19 is in their mouths and their **t**.
9:19 (Their **t** have heads like

take (1071)

Gen 2:15 farm the land and to **t** care of it.
3:22 He must not reach out and **t** the
4:9 "Am I supposed to **t** care of my
6:21 **T** every kind of food that can
7:2 **T** with you seven pairs of
7:3 Also, **t** seven pairs of every
12:19 my sister' and allow me to **t** her
12:19 your wife! **T** her and go! "
14:23 that I won't **t** a thread or a
14:23 I won't **t** anything that is yours
14:24 I won't **t** one single thing
14:24 and Mamre **t** their share."
15:7 that you will **t** possession of it."
15:8 that I will **t** possession of it?"
19:15 **T** your wife and your two
20:2 of Gerar sent men to **t** Sarah.
21:18 **T** him by the hand,
22:2 God said, "**T** your son,
22:17 Your descendants will **t**
23:13 **T** it from me so that I can bury
24:2 he owned, "**T** a solemn oath.
24:5 Should I **t** your son all the way
24:6 "Make sure that you do not **t**
24:8 But don't **t** my son back there."
24:51 **T** her and go! She will become
24:60 May your descendants **t**
27:3 Now **t** your hunting equipment,
27:10 Then **t** it to your father to eat so
28:4 so that you may **t** possession
30:2 "Can I **t** the place of God,
30:15 Are you also going to **t** my
30:32 today and **t** every speckled
30:35 had his sons **t** charge of them.
30:36 Jacob continued to **t** care of the
31:31 I thought you would **t** your
31:32 and **t** what is yours."
33:10 please **t** the gift I'm giving you,
33:11 Please **t** the present I've
33:13 are frail and that I have to **t** care
34:9 and **t** ours for yourselves.
34:16 daughters to you and **t** yours
34:17 we'll **t** our daughter and go."
37:12 His brothers had gone to **t** care
37:25 on their way to **t** them to Egypt.
41:34 supervisors over the land to **t**
42:19 The rest of you will go and **t**
42:33 **T** food for your starving
42:36 now you want to **t** Benjamin.
42:37 Let me **t** care of him,
43:11 then **t** the man a gift.
43:11 **T** a little balm, a little honey,
43:12 **T** twice as much money with
43:13 **T** your brother, and go back to
43:16 "**T** these men to my house.
43:18 overpower us, **t** our donkeys,
44:29 If you **t** this one away from me
45:18 **T** your father and your families,
45:19 "Give them this order: '**T**
46:32 They **t** care of livestock.
47:19 **T** us and our land in exchange
47:30 **T** me out of Egypt,
50:19 I can't **t** God's place.
50:24 God will definitely **t** care of you
50:24 take care of you and **t** you out
50:25 He said, "God will definitely **t**
Exo 2:5 came to the Nile to **t** a bath,
2:9 "**T** this child, nurse him for me,
3:5 **T** off your sandals because
3:17 I promise I will **t** you away from
4:9 **t** some water from the Nile
4:9 The water you **t** from the Nile
4:17 **T** that shepherd's staff with
4:20 the staff God had told him to **t**.
7:9 '**T** your shepherd's staff and
7:15 **T** along the staff that turned
7:19 '**T** your staff and stretch out
8:8 "Pray that the LORD will **t** the
9:8 "**T** a handful of ashes from a
9:21 But those who didn't **t** the
10:10 ever let you **t** your women
10:17 Pray to the LORD your God to **t**

Exo 10:25 "You must allow us to **t** our
12:3 of this month each man must **t**
12:6 **T** care of it until the fourteenth
12:7 They must **t** some of the blood
12:22 **T** the branch of a hyssop plant,
12:32 **T** your flocks and herds,
12:42 LORD kept watch to **t** them out
12:46 Never **t** any of the meat outside
13:19 **t** my bones with you."
15:9 I'll **t** all I want! I'll use my sword!
15:9 my sword! I'll **t** all they have!'
16:16 **T** two quarts for each person in
16:32 **T** two quarts of manna to be
16:33 Moses said to Aaron, "**T** a jar,
17:5 **T** the staff you used to strike
17:9 staff God told me to **t** along."
20:17 "Never desire to **t** your
20:17 "Never desire to **t** your
21:14 you must **t** him away from my
22:11 that the neighbor did not **t**
22:22 "Never **t** advantage of any
22:26 If you **t** any of your neighbor's
23:4 be sure to **t** it back to him.
23:8 Never **t** a bribe, because bribes
23:25 I will **t** away all sickness from
23:29 and wild animals would **t** over.
23:30 in number to **t** possession
24:14 **T** all your disagreements to
26:1 **T** violet, purple, and bright red
28:9 **T** two onyx stones,
29:1 "**T** a young bull that has no
29:5 **T** the clothes, and put them on
29:7 **T** the anointing oil,
29:12 **T** some of the bull's blood,
29:13 "Then **t** all the fat that covers
29:15 "**T** one of the rams.
29:16 Slaughter it, **t** the blood,
29:19 "**T** the other ram. Then Aaron
29:20 it, **t** some of the blood,
29:21 **T** some of the blood that is on
29:22 this ⌊same⌋ ram **t** the fat,
29:23 **t** a round loaf of bread,
29:25 Then **t** them from their hands,
29:26 "**T** the breast from the ram used
29:31 "**T** the ram used for the
29:35 **T** seven days to ordain them.
30:12 "When you **t** a census of the
30:16 **T** the money the Israelites give
30:23 "**T** the finest spices:
30:34 The LORD said to Moses, "**T**
32:2 and daughters **t** off the gold
32:24 So I told them to **t** off any gold
33:5 Now **t** off your jewelry,
33:7 Now, Moses used to **t** a tent
33:23 Then I will **t** my hand away,
34:24 No one will want to **t** away
40:9 **T** the anointing oil,
Lev 2:2 **T** from this a handful of flour
3:9 Then **t** the fat from the
4:5 Then the anointed priest will **t**
4:11 Then he will **t** the entire bull
4:21 Then he will **t** the bull outside
4:25 Then the priest will **t** some of
4:30 The priest will **t** some of the
4:34 Then the priest will **t** some of
5:4 "If you hastily **t** a vow about
5:12 The priest will **t** a handful of it.
6:2 you were supposed to **t** care
6:4 you were supposed to **t** care of,
6:11 Then he will **t** off these clothes
6:11 He will **t** the ashes to a clean
6:22 is anointed to **t** his place as
7:30 **T** the breast and present it to
8:2 "**T** Aaron and his sons,
8:31 **T** the meat and the bread in the
8:33 It will **t** seven days to ordain
9:2 He told Aaron, "**T** a calf that
9:3 Also tell the Israelites: '**T** a
9:15 He sacrificed it to **t** away sins
10:4 He told them, "Come and **t** your
10:4 **T** them outside the camp."
10:12 "**T** the grain offering left over
10:17 and was given to you to **t** away
14:6 The priest will **t** the living bird,
14:10 "On the eighth day he must **t**
14:10 He must also **t** eight cups of

Lev 14:12 The priest will **t** one of the
14:14 Then the priest will **t** some of
14:15 The priest will also **t** some of
14:21 he must **t** one male lamb,
14:21 He will **t** only eight cups of
14:23 On the eighth day he will **t**
14:24 The priest will **t** the lamb for
14:25 Then the priest will **t** some of
14:30 one to be cleansed must **t** one
14:31 He will **t** the other and sacrifice
14:49 "The priest must **t** two birds,
14:51 He must **t** the cedar wood,
15:14 On the eighth day he must **t**
15:29 On the eighth day she must **t**
16:3 He must **t** a bull as an offering
16:5 He will **t** two male goats from
16:7 He must **t** the two male goats
16:12 He will **t** an incense burner full
16:14 He will **t** some of the bull's
16:15 He will **t** the blood inside,
16:18 He will **t** some of the blood
16:22 The goat will **t** all their sins
16:23 **t** off the linen clothes he had
16:27 He must **t** the bull and the goat
17:5 that the people of Israel must **t**
20:24 you that you will **t** their land.
23:40 On the first day **t** the best fruits,
24:5 "Also **t** flour and bake twelve
25:14 don't **t** advantage of him.
25:15 **t** into account the number of
25:17 Never **t** advantage of each
25:50 Then he and his buyer must **t**
25:52 he must **t** them into account.
Num 1:2 "**T** a census of the whole
1:50 They will **t** care of the tent and
1:51 the Levites will **t** it down.
3:8 They will **t** care of all the
3:41 **T** the Levites for me to be
3:41 Also **t** the animals of the
3:45 "**T** the Levites to be substitutes
4:2 "**T** a census of the Levites who
4:4 They will **t** care of the most
4:5 his sons will go in and **t** down
4:9 "They will **t** a violet cloth and
4:12 "They will **t** all the articles that
4:13 "After they **t** the ashes away,
4:22 "Also **t** a census of the
4:32 They must **t** care of all this
5:15 He must then **t** his wife to the
5:17 Then the priest will **t** holy
5:25 The priest will **t** the grain
5:26 The priest will **t** a handful of
6:18 **t** the hair as proof that they had
6:19 "Then the priest will **t** one of
8:7 Sprinkle them with water to **t**
8:8 Next, they must **t** a young bull
8:8 You must **t** a second young
8:21 ceremonies to **t** away their sins
11:14 I can't **t** care of all these people
11:16 **T** them to the tent of meeting,
11:17 I'll **t** some of the Spirit that is on
11:17 They will help you **t** care of the
11:17 You won't have to **t** care of the
13:30 Caleb said, "Let's go now and **t**
14:13 (You used your power to **t**
15:35 The whole community must **t**
16:6 **T** incense burners,
16:17 Each man will **t** his incense
16:37 to **t** the incense burners out of
16:46 "**T** your incense burner,
18:26 You will **t** one-tenth of the
19:4 The priest Eleazar will **t** some
19:6 The priest will **t** some cedar
19:12 seventh day to **t** away his sin.
19:13 use this water to **t** away his sin
19:18 A person who is clean will **t** a
19:20 The water to **t** away
19:21 to **t** away uncleanness must
20:8 "**T** your staff, then you and your
20:26 **T** off Aaron's priestly clothes,
21:7 Pray to the Lord so that he will **t**
23:27 let me **t** you to another place.
25:4 "**T** all the leaders of the people,
26:2 "**T** a census of the whole
26:4 "**T** a census of those at least
27:11 and that relative will **t**

Num 27:12 and **t** a look at the land I will
27:18 Moses, "**T** Joshua, son of Nun,
31:19 in order to **t** away your sin.
31:23 water in order to **t** away its sin.
32:8 them from Kadesh Barnea to **t**
32:19 We won't **t** possession of any
32:30 the land they will **t** possession
32:32 but the land we will **t**
33:53 **T** possession of the land and
34:18 You must also **t** one leader
35:8 **T** more cities from larger tribes
35:25 They must **t** you back to the
Dtr 1:8 Enter, and **t** possession of the
1:9 "I'm not able to **t** care of you by
1:12 How can I **t** care of your
1:21 **T** possession of it,
1:22 us about the route we should **t**
1:33 to show you which route to **t**.
1:38 because he will help Israel **t**
1:39 and they will **t** possession of it.
2:24 Fight him, and **t** possession of
2:31 **T** possession of his land."
3:4 There wasn't a city we didn't **t**.
3:18 so that you can **t** possession
3:20 until they **t** possession
3:28 and he will help them **t**
4:1 able to enter and **t** possession
4:2 or **t** anything away from it.
4:14 Jordan River⌋ and **t** possession
4:22 to go across and **t** possession
4:34 to come and **t** one nation away
5:21 "Never desire to **t** your
6:1 the land and **t** possession of it.
6:6 **T** to heart these words that I
6:13 and **t** your oaths only in his
6:18 and you will enter and **t**
7:1 to enter and **t** possession of.
7:25 and gold on these idols or **t** any
8:1 You will enter and **t**
9:3 You will **t** possession of their
9:4 the LORD brought us here to **t**
9:5 you're entering to **t** possession
9:23 "Go and **t** possession of the
10:11 They will enter and **t**
10:20 and **t** your oaths in his name.
11:8 to enter and **t** possession
11:10 about to enter and **t** possession
11:18 **T** these words of mine to heart
11:23 Then you will **t** possession of
11:31 River to enter and **t** possession
11:31 When you **t** possession of it
12:19 Don't forget to **t** care of the
12:26 **T** the holy things and the
12:29 You will **t** possession of their
12:32 Never add anything to it or **t**
13:2 he predicts may even **t** place.
13:17 Don't ever **t** any of the things
14:25 **T** the silver with you,
14:27 Never forget to **t** care of the
15:17 Then **t** an awl and pierce it
16:19 Never **t** a bribe, because bribes
16:20 you will live and **t** possession
17:8 **T** this case to the place that
17:14 You will **t** possession of it and
19:6 up with him and **t** his life even
19:12 They must **t** him from that city
19:21 ⌊**T**⌋ a life for a life,
20:14 But **t** the women and children,
21:10 you may **t** them captive.
21:19 His father and mother must **t**
22:1 Make sure you **t** it back.
22:2 **t** the animal home with you.
22:6 never **t** her with the chicks.
22:7 You may **t** the chicks,
22:18 The leaders of that city must **t**
22:21 they must **t** the girl to the
22:24 **t** them to the gate of the city
24:10 house to **t** a security deposit.
24:17 And never **t** widows' clothes to
25:9 She must **t** off one of his
26:1 Soon you will enter and **t**
26:2 **t** some of the first produce
26:4 Then the priest will **t** the
28:21 to enter and **t** possession of.
28:39 You will plant vineyards and **t**
28:63 to enter and **t** possession of.

Dtr 28:68 I said you would never **t** again.
30:1 **T** them to heart when you are
30:5 You will **t** possession of it,
30:16 to enter and **t** possession of.
30:18 you're going to **t** possession
31:3 and you will **t** possession of
31:7 You will help them **t**
31:13 you are going to **t** possession
31:26 "**T** this Book of Teachings,
32:35 I will **t** revenge and be
32:41 sword and **t** justice into my
32:41 Then I will **t** revenge on my
32:43 because he will **t** revenge for
32:47 you are going to **t** possession
32:49 **T** a look at the land of Canaan
33:23 They will **t** possession of the
Jos 1:6 help these people **t** possession
1:11 Jordan River to **t** possession
1:15 **t** possession of the land the
1:15 you may go back and **t**
2:19 But we will **t** responsibility if
3:6 "**T** the ark of the promise,
4:3 **T** the stones along with you,
4:5 Each man must **t** a stone on
5:15 "**T** off your sandals because
6:18 If you **t** anything that is
8:1 **T** all the troops with you,
8:2 However, you may **t** its loot
8:29 Joshua gave the order to **t** his
9:11 **T** what you need for the trip,
10:27 Joshua gave the order to **t** them
17:12 But Manasseh was not able to **t**
20:4 Then they will **t** him into their
22:19 **T** some property for yourselves
23:5 You will **t** their land as the
Jdg 1:19 they were able to **t** possession
2:6 So each family went to **t**
4:6 **T** 10,000 men from Naphtali
5:12 **T** your prisoners, son of
6:20 "**T** the meat and the
6:25 "**T** a bull from your father's herd
6:26 **T** this second bull and
7:10 But if you're afraid to go, **t** your
9:15 then come and **t** shelter in my
9:54 "**T** your sword and kill me!
11:9 Jephthah told them, "If you **t**
11:15 The people of Israel didn't **t**
11:23 right do you have to **t** it back?
11:24 Shouldn't you **t** possession of
11:24 Shouldn't we **t** everything the
18:7 to **t** away their property
18:9 Go at once and **t** the land.
19:15 because no one offered to **t**
19:18 but no one has offered to **t** me
19:20 Let me **t** care of your needs.
20:10 We'll **t** one-tenth of all the men
20:36 to **t** back some ground.
21:5 from Israel that did not **t** part
21:21 of Shiloh come out to **t** part
Rut 3:9 relative who can **t** care of me."
3:13 if he will agree to **t** care
3:13 He can **t** care of you.
3:13 But if he does not wish to **t**
3:13 I will **t** care of you myself.
4:6 **T** all my rights to buy back the
4:7 a man would **t** off his sandal
4:14 you someone who will **t** care
1Sm 1:16 Don't **t** me to be a
2:16 then **t** as much as you want,"
2:16 it to me now, or I'll **t** it by force."
2:25 God will **t** care of him.
6:7 **T** their calves away,
6:8 **T** the ark of the LORD,
6:21 Come and **t** it back with you."
7:1 men of Kiriath Jearim came to **t**
8:13 He will **t** your daughters and
8:14 He will **t** the best of your fields,
8:15 He will **t** a tenth of your grain
8:16 He will **t** your male and female
8:17 He will **t** a tenth of your flocks.
9:3 "**T** one of the servants with
12:3 Did I **t** anyone's ox?
12:3 Did I **t** anyone's donkey?
12:3 Did I **t** a bribe from anyone to
12:4 or **t** anything from anyone."
14:27 forced the troops to **t** an oath.
1Sm 14:28 father forced the troops to **t**
14:36 and **t** their possessions until
16:2 "**T** a heifer with you and say,
17:17 Jesse told his son David, "**T**
17:17 **T** them to your brothers in the
17:18 And **t** these ten cheeses to the
20:40 "**T** them back into town."
21:8 I didn't **t** either my spear or any
21:9 If you want to **t** it, take it.
21:9 If you want to take it, **t** it.
24:11 ambush me in order to **t** my life.
24:12 May the LORD **t** revenge on
24:15 He will watch and **t** my side in
25:11 Should I **t** my bread,
25:25 You shouldn't **t** this worthless
25:40 us to you so that we can **t** you
26:11 But please **t** that spear near his
30:15 He answered, "**T** an oath in
30:22 Each of them should **t** only his
2Sm 1:14 "Why weren't you afraid to **t** it
2:21 and **t** his weapon."
3:15 So Ishbosheth sent men to **t**
12:4 it would be a pity to **t** one
12:11 own eyes I will **t** your wives
14:8 "I will order someone to **t** care
15:5 out, **t** hold of him, and kiss him.
15:16 the king left behind to **t** care
15:20 Go back, and **t** your
15:25 "**T** God's ark back to the city.
15:27 and **t** your son Ahimaaz and
16:21 whom he left to **t** care
17:25 Absalom appointed Amasa to **t**
19:30 "Let him **t** it all," "It's enough for
20:6 **T** my men and go after him,
20:6 find some fortified cities and **t**
22:3 my rock in whom I **t** refuge,
22:31 He is a shield to all those who **t**
24:22 Araunah said to David, "**T** it,
1Ki 1:33 "**T** my officials with you.
1:33 and **t** him to Gihon.
1:53 King Solomon sent men to **t**
2:42 "Didn't I make you **t** an oath by
8:1 King Solomon in Jerusalem to **t**
8:31 person and is required to **t**
8:31 to take an oath and comes to **t**
8:32 **t** action, and make a decision.
8:39 Forgive ⌊them⌋, and **t** action.
11:31 He told Jeroboam, "**T** 10
11:34 "I will not **t** the whole kingdom
11:35 But I will **t** the kingdom away
13:12 "Which road did he **t**?"
14:3 **T** ten loaves of bread,
18:10 made that kingdom or region **t**
18:12 the LORD's Spirit will **t** you
19:2 time tomorrow I don't **t** your life
19:4 "**T** my life! I'm no better than my
19:10 and they're trying to **t** my life."
19:14 and they're trying to **t** my life."
19:16 as prophet to **t** your place.
20:6 They will **t** anything that you
20:9 left to **t** back his answer.
20:18 He said, "**T** them alive,
20:33 were quick to **t** him at his word.
22:3 and we are doing nothing to **t** it
22:16 many times must I make you **t**
2Ki 2:1 When the LORD was going to **t**
2:3 is going to **t** your master from
2:5 is going to **t** your master from
3:8 "Which road should we **t**?"
3:23 let's **t** their goods!"
4:1 Now a creditor has come to **t**
4:29 **t** my shepherd's staff in your
4:36 to him, he said, "**T** your son."
5:16 Naaman urged him to **t** it,
5:17 Naaman said, "If you won't **t** it,
5:23 urged him ⌊to **t** the silver⌋.
6:22 Do you kill everyone you **t**
7:13 "Please let some men **t** five of
7:13 Let's send them to **t** a look."
8:8 king told Hazael, "**T** a present,
9:1 **T** this flask of olive oil,
9:2 **T** him into an inner room.
9:3 **T** the flask of oil, pour it on his
9:15 escape from the city to **t**
9:17 "**T** a chariot driver,
9:25 attendant Bidkar, "**T** him away,
2Ki 9:26 Now **t** him and throw him into
9:34 Then he said, "**T** care of this
10:32 LORD began to **t** away some
11:15 "**T** her out of the temple.
12:7 Don't **t** any more money from
13:16 "**T** the bow in your hand."
13:18 Elisha said, "**T** the arrows."
14:10 defeat and **t** Judah with you?"
18:32 Then I will come and **t** you
19:30 who escape will again **t** root
23:4 and the doorkeepers to **t** out of
23:16 he sent men to **t** the bones out
1Ch 5:26 of Assyria) to **t** Reuben,
6:15 Nebuchadnezzar to **t** Judah
7:21 they came to **t** their livestock.
21:11 the LORD says: '**T** your pick:
21:23 Ornan said to David, "**T** it,
21:24 I won't **t** what is yours for the
22:12 he commands you to **t** charge
2Ch 2:16 You can **t** it ⌊from there⌋ to
5:2 They came to Jerusalem to **t**
6:22 person and is required to **t**
6:22 to take an oath and comes to **t**
6:23 **t** action, and make a decision.
14:14 there were many things to **t**.
18:15 many times must I make you **t**
20:17 ⌊Instead,⌋ **t** your position,
20:25 his troops came to **t** the loot,
23:14 "**T** her out of the temple.
25:19 defeat and **t** Judah with you?"
31:14 at East Gate and had to **t** care
35:23 The king told his officers, "**T**
36:6 shackles to **t** him to Babylon.
Ezr 5:15 told him, '**T** these utensils.
7:15 Also, you must **t** the silver and
7:16 **T** any silver and gold that you
7:16 province of Babylon when you **t**
9:11 'The land you are going to **t**
10:4 It's your duty to **t** action.
10:4 so be strong and **t** action."
10:13 We can't **t** care of this outside.
Neh 9:15 You told them to **t** possession
9:17 a leader to **t** them back
10:32 Also, we **t** upon ourselves the
Est 2:13 Anything she wanted to **t** with
6:10 The king told Haman, "Hurry, **t**
8:13 were to be ready to **t** revenge
Job 3:6 let the blackness **t** it away.
5:3 seen a stubborn fool **t** root,
5:5 They **t** it even from among the
7:21 and **t** away my sin?
8:19 same ground to ⌊**t** its place⌋.
9:32 'Let's **t** our case to court.'
9:34 God should **t** his rod away from
10:18 "'Why did you **t** me out of the
11:20 hope is to **t** their last breath."
16:22 in a few short years I will **t**
22:6 For no reason you **t** your
22:7 and you **t** food away from
23:10 because he knows the road I **t**.
24:3 They **t** the widow's ox as
24:9 orphan from a breast and **t**
24:21 These men **t** advantage of
33:5 case to me, and **t** your stand.
36:7 He doesn't **t** his eyes off
39:12 it to bring your grain back and **t**
41:4 with you so that you can **t**
42:6 That is why I **t** back what I
42:8 So **t** seven young bulls and
Psa 1:1 **t** the path of sinners,
2:2 Kings **t** their stands.
5:11 But let all who **t** refuge in you
7:7 **T** your seat high above them.
8:4 of Man that you **t** care of him?
9:13 You **t** me away from the gates
15:5 collect interest on a loan or **t**
16:1 because I **t** refuge in you.
18:2 my rock in whom I **t** refuge,
18:30 He is a shield to all those who **t**
27:10 the LORD will **t** care of me.
31:13 They were plotting to **t** my life.
31:19 it to those who **t** refuge in you.
34:22 All who **t** refuge in him will
36:7 that Adam's descendants **t**
45:16 Your sons will **t** the place of
49:15 of hell because he will **t** me.

Psa 49:17 He will not **t** anything with him
51:11 and do not **t** your Holy Spirit
55:15 suddenly **t** ⌊wicked people⌋!
55:22 and he will **t** care of you.
56:6 step as they wait to **t** my life.
57:1 I will **t** refuge in the shadow of
58:10 they see ⌊God⌋ **t** revenge.
59:4 They hurry to **t** positions
61:4 forever and to **t** refuge under
64:10 joy in the LORD and **t** refuge
65:9 You **t** care of the earth,
69:35 there and **t** possession of it.
71:10 They watch me as they plot to **t**
73:24 the end you will **t** me to glory.
74:11 **T** your hands out of your
77:20 You had Moses and Aaron **t**
78:50 He let the plague **t** their lives.
80:15 **T** care of what your right hand
83:12 They said, "Let's **t** God's
89:22 No enemy will **t** him by
89:33 But I will not **t** my mercy away
94:21 They join forces to **t** the lives
102:24 I said, "My God, don't **t** me now
104:29 You **t** away their breath,
109:8 someone else **t** his position.
109:11 Let a creditor **t** everything he
116:13 I will **t** the cup of salvation and
119:39 **T** away insults, which I dread,
119:43 Do not **t** so much as a single
119:109 I always **t** my life into my own
132:11 is a truth he will not **t** back:
143:2 Do not **t** me to court for
144:2 the one in whom I **t** refuge,
144:8 right hands **t** false pledges.
144:11 right hands **t** false pledges.
149:7 to **t** vengeance on the nations,
Pro 2:1 My son, if you **t** my words ⌊to
3:18 of life for those who **t** firm hold
8:10 **T** my discipline, not silver,
13:10 who **t** advice gain wisdom.
21:18 and treacherous people will **t**
22:23 will plead their case and will **t**
24:12 one who weighs hearts **t** note
25:4 **T** the impurities out of silver,
25:5 **T** a wicked person away from
Ecc 4:13 who won't **t** advice any longer.
5:15 They won't even be able to **t** a
7:2 is alive should **t** this to heart!
7:21 Don't **t** everything that people
8:3 Don't **t** part in something evil,
9:2 People who **t** oaths are treated
9:2 those who are afraid to **t** oaths.
9:6 They will never again **t** part in
Sos 1:4 **T** me with you. Let's run away.
7:8 "I will climb the palm tree and **t**
8:12 and 5 pounds go to those who **t**
Isa 1:24 "How horrible it will be when I **t**
3:1 is going to **t** from Jerusalem
3:2 ⌊He will **t** their⌋ heroes and
3:18 On that day the Lord will **t**
4:1 **T** away our disgrace."
5:23 who **t** away the rights of
7:7 It won't **t** place; it won't happen.
8:1 "**T** a large writing tablet,
10:2 They **t** away the rights of the
10:6 the people to **t** their belongings,
10:31 those who live in Gebim **t**
14:2 People will **t** them and bring
14:2 They will **t** their captors
20:2 "**T** off the sackcloth that you
20:2 and **t** off your sandals!"
23:16 "**T** your lyre. Go around in the
27:6 times to come Jacob will **t** root.
28:19 time it passes by it will **t** you.
31:2 He doesn't **t** back his words.
32:11 **T** off your clothes,
33:15 and refuses to **t** bribes.
34:11 Pelicans and herons will **t**
36:17 Then I will come and **t** you
37:31 who escape will again **t** root
38:21 Then Isaiah said, "**T** a fig cake,
42:6 I will **t** hold of your hand.
42:25 but they did not **t** it to heart.
43:14 in the ships that they **t** pride in.
44:11 get together and **t** their stand.
44:15 So they **t** some of them and

Isa 46:4 you're old, I'll **t** care of you.
46:8 Remember this, and **t** courage.
47:2 **T** millstones and grind flour.
47:2 **T** off your skirt. Uncover your
47:3 I will **t** revenge. I won't spare
48:1 You **t** oaths by the name of the
51:18 there was no one to **t** her by the
54:3 Your descendants will **t** over
57:13 A breath will **t** them away.
58:7 **t** the poor and homeless into
Jer 3:14 I will **t** you, one from every city
4:1 if you **t** your disgusting idols
4:2 if you **t** the oath, "As the LORD
4:6 **T** cover! Don't just stand there!
5:2 they lie when they **t** this oath.
6:1 "**T** cover, people of Benjamin!
6:23 Its people **t** hold of bows and
7:9 lie when you **t** oaths,
11:20 I want to see you **t** revenge on
12:2 You plant them, and they **t** root.
12:14 all my evil neighbors who **t**
12:16 Suppose they **t** an oath in my
12:16 as they taught my people to **t**
13:4 "**T** the belt that you bought,
15:5 No one will **t** pity on you,
15:15 Remember me, **t** care of me,
15:15 and **t** revenge on those who
15:15 patient, and don't **t** me away.
15:19 will return, I will **t** you back.
18:20 They dig a pit to **t** my life.
19:1 **T** along some of the leaders of
20:4 He will **t** the people away as
20:5 will loot them, **t** them away,
20:10 him and **t** revenge on him."
20:12 I want to see you **t** revenge on
21:4 I'm going to **t** your weapons
22:5 I will **t** an oath on myself,"
23:2 said to the shepherds who **t**
23:2 so now I will **t** care of you by
23:4 Those shepherds will **t** care of
25:10 I will **t** from them the sounds of
25:15 **T** from my hand this cup filled
25:28 But if they refuse to **t** the cup
27:19 But he didn't **t** the pillars,
27:22 I will **t** them from there and
30:3 they will **t** possession of it."
31:4 you will **t** your tambourines,
32:5 Nebuchadnezzar will **t**
32:14 **T** both of these documents,
35:2 **T** them into one of the side
36:2 "**T** a scroll, and write on it
36:28 "**T** another scroll, and write on
36:29 this land and **t** away people
37:12 of Benjamin to **t** possession
38:10 "**T** 30 men from here,
39:12 "**T** him, and look after him.
39:14 of Shaphan, to **t** him home.
43:3 Then they will kill us or **t** us as
43:9 "**T** some large stones,
43:12 and **t** their gods captive.
44:12 I will **t** away from Judah those
44:26 call on my name and **t** the oath,
46:4 **T** your positions, and put on
46:10 when he will **t** revenge
46:14 Say, '**T** your positions,
49:2 Then Israel will **t** possession
49:13 I **t** an oath on myself,
50:9 Those nations will **t** up
50:14 "**T** up your positions around
50:15 **t** revenge against them.
50:34 He will certainly **t** up their
50:42 They will **t** hold of bows and
51:36 I am going to **t** up your cause
51:40 I will **t** them to be slaughtered
Lam 2:8 He didn't **t** his hand away until
3:30 who strikes them and **t** their fill
4:21 You'll get drunk and **t** off all
5:1 **T** a look at our disgrace!
5:7 ⌊but⌋ we have to **t** the
Eze 3:10 **t** to heart everything I have
4:1 **t** clay, put it in front of you,
4:3 Then **t** an iron pan,
4:4 "Then lie on your left side and **t**
4:9 "Then **t** wheat, barley, beans,
5:1 "Son of man, **t** a sharp blade,
5:1 **T** scales to weigh your hair

Eze 5:2 **T** another third, and cut it up
5:3 **T** a few strands of hair,
5:4 Later, **t** some of them,
7:24 and it will **t** possession of
8:18 So I will **t** action because I'm
10:6 in linen to **t** burning coals from
15:6 so I will **t** the people who live
16:39 **t** away your beautiful jewelry,
17:9 It won't **t** much strength or
17:20 I will **t** you to Babylon and
17:22 will **t** hold of the top of a cedar
21:3 I will **t** my sword out of its
21:7 It will surely **t** place!'
21:19 of Babylon and his sword can **t**.
21:20 the king and his sword can **t**
21:26 LORD says: **T** off your turban,
22:12 Other people **t** bribes to murder
22:25 They eat people and **t** their
23:25 They will **t** your sons and your
23:26 and **t** away your beautiful
23:29 and **t** away everything that
24:12 Even the fire can't **t** away its
24:16 with one blow I'm going to **t**
24:25 "Son of man, on that day I will **t**
24:25 I will also **t** away their sons
25:14 I will use my people Israel to **t**
25:17 I will **t** fierce revenge on them
25:17 I will **t** revenge on them.
26:12 your riches and **t** your goods as
26:16 and **t** off their embroidered
26:20 You will never return or **t** your
29:19 **t** its prized possessions,
30:4 People will **t** away Egypt's
32:15 I will **t** everything in the land,
34:2 Shouldn't shepherds **t** care of
34:3 you don't **t** care of the sheep.
34:10 I won't let them **t** care of my
34:10 and they will no longer **t** care of
34:13 I will **t** care of them on the
34:15 I will **t** care of my sheep and
34:16 I will **t** care of my sheep fairly.
34:23 and he will **t** care of them.
34:23 He will **t** care of them and be
35:10 We will **t** possession of them."
36:12 They will **t** possession of you,
36:12 You will no longer **t** their
36:13 you devour your people and **t**
36:14 longer devour your people or **t**
36:15 You will never again **t** the
36:24 "'I will **t** you from the nations
37:12 I will open your graves and **t**
37:16 **t** a stick and write on it:
37:16 Then **t** another stick and write
37:19 I will **t** Joseph's stick,
37:21 I will **t** the Israelites out of the
38:13 and to **t** cattle and property?"'
43:9 acting like prostitutes and **t**
43:20 **T** some of the bull's blood,
43:21 Then **t** a young bull as an
44:8 You didn't **t** care of my holy
44:16 and **t** care of everything I gave
44:19 they must **t** off the clothes that
45:15 You must **t** one sheep out of
45:18 **t** a young bull that has no
45:19 The priest must **t** some blood
46:18 The prince must not **t** any of
Dan 2:24 **T** me to the king, and I'll
7:18 the Most High will **t** possession
8:13 of the army — **t** place?"
11:8 He will **t** the metal statues of
11:20 "Another king will **t** his place.
11:21 person will **t** his place.
11:28 He will **t** action and return to
11:30 promise, he will return, **t** action,
11:31 **t** away the daily burnt offering,
11:32 God will be strong and **t** action.
Hos 2:9 That is why I will **t** back my
2:9 I will **t** away the wool and the
4:15 Don't **t** the oath, 'As the LORD
9:12 I will **t** those children away
10:2 they must **t** their punishment.
10:4 They lie when they **t** oaths,
12:1 with Assyria and **t** olive oil
12:13 a prophet to **t** care of them.
13:13 are not smart enough to **t** it.
14:8 I will answer them and **t** care of

Amo 2:3 I will **t** their judges away from
2:10 so that you could **t** possession
5:11 You trample on the poor and **t**
6:10 or a mortician comes to **t**
9:2 my hand will **t** them from there.
9:3 I will look for them and **t** them
Oba 1:8 Edom and **t** wisdom away from
1:13 Don't **t** their wealth when
1:19 "People from the Negev will **t**
1:19 People from the foothills will **t**
1:19 They will **t** possession of the
1:19 will **t** possession of Gilead.
1:20 Exiles from Israel will **t**
1:20 in Sepharad will **t** possession
Jnh 4:3 So now, LORD, **t** my life.
Mic 1:11 It will **t** its support away from
2:2 houses, so they **t** them.
2:8 You **t** coats from those who
2:9 homes and **t** my glory away
5:15 I will **t** revenge with great anger
7:14 **t** care of your people,
Hab 1:6 the earth to **t** possession
Zep 2:7 The LORD their God will **t** care
2:9 will **t** possession of them."
Hag 2:23 LORD of Armies, I will **t** you,
Zec 5:4 houses of those who **t** oaths
6:10 "**T** an offering from the exiles
6:11 **T** the silver and gold,
8:23 among the nations will **t** hold
9:4 The Lord will **t** away its
11:4 **T** care of the sheep that are
11:16 He will not **t** care of those that
14:21 All who come to sacrifice will **t**
Mat 1:20 don't be afraid to **t** Mary as your
2:13 **t** the child and his mother,
2:20 **t** the child and his mother,
4:11 angels came to **t** care of him.
5:40 sue you in order to **t** your shirt,
7:4 'Let me **t** the piece of sawdust
10:9 "Don't **t** any gold, silver,
10:10 Don't **t** a traveling bag for the
10:13 **t** back your greeting.
10:38 Whoever doesn't **t** up his cross
12:11 wouldn't you **t** hold of it and lift
12:45 They enter and **t** up permanent
15:26 Jesus replied, "It's not right to **t**
16:5 The disciples had forgotten to **t**
17:27 **T** the first fish that you catch.
18:16 But if he does not listen, **t** one
20:14 **T** your money and go!
22:44 'The Lord said to my Lord, "**T**
24:15 see this (let the reader **t** note),
24:34 until all these things **t** place.
25:3 but they didn't **t** any extra oil.
25:28 **T** the two thousand dollars
25:38 as a stranger and **t** you into our
25:43 and you didn't **t** me into your
25:43 and you didn't **t** care of me.'
26:2 that the Passover will **t** place
26:26 and said, "**T** this, and eat it.
28:7 **T** note that I have told you."
28:14 hears about it, we'll **t** care of it,
Mar 4:19 desires for other things **t** over.
6:8 He instructed them to **t** nothing
6:8 They were not to **t** any food,
6:9 sandals but could not **t** along
7:27 It's not right to **t** the children's
8:14 The disciples had forgotten to **t**
9:35 most important person must **t**
12:36 "**T** the highest position in
13:11 When they **t** you away to hand
13:14 not (let the reader **t** note),
13:30 until all these things **t** place.
14:15 He will **t** you upstairs and
14:22 it to them, and said, "**T** this.
14:36 **T** this cup ⌊of suffering⌋ away
14:44 closely as you **t** him away."
15:23 but he wouldn't **t** it.
15:36 if Elijah comes to **t** him down."
Luk 1:68 He has come to **t** care of his
5:4 "**T** the boat into deep water,
5:18 They tried to **t** him into the
6:42 let me **t** the piece of sawdust
9:3 He told them, "Don't **t** anything
9:3 Don't **t** a walking stick,
10:35 the innkeeper, '**T** care of him.

Luk 11:22 Then the stronger man will **t**
11:26 They enter and **t** up permanent
12:19 **T** life easy, eat, drink,
13:15 Don't you then **t** it out of its stall
14:8 don't **t** the place of honor.
14:9 you would have to **t** the place
14:10 **t** the place of least honor.
16:6 '**T** my master's ledger.
16:7 told him, '**T** the ledger,
19:17 **T** charge of ten cities.'
19:19 'You **t** charge of five cities.'
19:21 You **t** what isn't yours and
19:22 You knew that I **t** what isn't
19:24 told his men, '**T** his coin away,
20:42 "**T** the highest position in
22:12 He will **t** you upstairs and
22:17 He said, "**T** this, and share it.
22:36 bag should **t** them along.
22:42 "Father, if it is your will, **t** this
23:18 then shouted, "**T** him away!
Jon 1:22 Tell us so that we can **t** an
2:8 and **t** it to the person in charge.
6:15 intended to **t** him by force
10:17 life in order to **t** it back again.
10:18 and I have the authority to **t** my
11:39 said, "**T** the stone away."
11:48 Then the Romans will **t** away
16:15 That is why I said, 'He will **t**
16:22 and no one will **t** that
17:15 I'm not asking you to **t** them out
18:31 Pilate told the Jews, "**T** him,
19:6 "You **t** him and crucify him.
20:27 **T** your hand, and put it into my
21:16 "**T** care of my sheep."
21:18 you ready to **t** you where you
Act 1:20 and 'Let someone else **t** his
1:25 Show us who is to **t** the place
2:34 "**T** my highest position of
4:26 Kings **t** their stand.
5:28 You want to **t** revenge on us for
7:33 '**T** off your sandals.
8:26 and **t** the desert road that goes
9:21 Didn't he come here to **t** these
15:37 wanted to **t** John Mark along.
15:38 Paul didn't think it was right to **t**
18:15 you'll have to **t** care of that
19:12 People would **t** handkerchiefs
21:24 **T** these men, go through the
21:37 As the soldiers were about to **t**
22:5 they even gave me letters to **t**
22:24 the soldiers to **t** Paul into
23:17 "**T** this young man to the
23:24 and **t** him safely to Governor
24:23 and to let his friends **t** care
Rom 7:22 I **t** pleasure in God's standards
7:23 sets and tries to **t** me captive
11:3 and they're trying to **t** my life."
11:27 when I **t** away their sins."
12:19 Don't **t** revenge, dear friends.
12:19 let God's anger **t** care of it.
12:19 have the right to **t** revenge.
13:12 that belong to the dark and **t** up
15:26 they have decided to **t** up a
1Co 6:15 Should I **t** the parts of Christ's
7:21 a chance to become free, **t** it.
9:5 Don't we have the right to **t** our
9:7 Does anyone **t** care of a flock
14:31 All of you can **t** your turns
14:34 They must **t** their place as
15:3 Christ died to **t** away our sins
2Co 5:4 because we don't want to **t** off
5:21 **t** our sin so that we might
8:10 you were not only willing ⌊to **t**
10:5 We **t** every thought captive so
10:7 he should **t** note that we also
10:11 those things should **t** note
11:12 This will **t** away the
11:16 But if you do, then **t** me for a
12:8 begged the Lord three times to **t**
12:17 Did I **t** advantage of you
12:18 Did Titus **t** advantage of you?
Eph 2:15 so that he could **t** Jewish
6:11 In this way you can **t** a stand
6:13 For this reason, **t** up all the
6:13 Then you will be able to **t** a
6:14 So then, **t** your stand!

Eph 6:16 In addition to all these, **t** the
6:17 Also **t** salvation as your helmet
Php 2:6 he did not **t** advantage of this
3:3 serve God's Spirit and **t** pride
3:19 and they **t** pride in the shameful
1Th 4:6 No one should **t** advantage of
5:4 That day won't **t** you by
2Th 1:8 He will **t** revenge on those who
3:14 **T** note of them and don't
1Ti 1:10 who lie when they **t** an oath,
3:5 how can he **t** care of God's
5:8 If anyone doesn't **t** care of his
6:7 and we can't **t** anything out of it.
6:12 **T** hold of everlasting life to
6:19 In this way they **t** hold of what
2Ti 4:18 all harm and will **t** me safely
Heb 2:6 of Man that you **t** care of him?
5:5 So Christ did not **t** the glory of
6:16 When people **t** oaths,
9:16 In order for a will to **t** effect,
9:28 Christ was sacrificed once to **t**
10:4 and goats cannot **t** away sins.)
10:11 could never **t** away sins.
10:26 sacrifice can **t** away our sins.
10:30 have the right to **t** revenge.
12:15 so that bitterness doesn't **t** root
13:17 They **t** care of you because
Jas 1:27 is to **t** care of orphans and
5:12 do not **t** an oath on anything in
5:12 Do not **t** any oath. If you mean
1Pe 4:1 **t** the same attitude that he had.
2Pe 2:13 They **t** pleasure in holding wild
1Jn 3:5 in order to **t** away our sins.
2Jn 1:10 don't **t** him into your home or
Jud 1:16 in order to **t** advantage of them.
Rev 2:5 I will come to you and **t** your
3:19 **T** this seriously, and change
5:9 "You deserve to **t** the scroll and
6:4 the power to **t** peace away from
6:10 before you judge and **t** revenge
10:8 It said, "**T** the opened scroll
10:9 He said to me, "**T** it and eat it.
22:17 who want the water of life **t**
22:19 God will **t** away his portion of

taken (286)

Gen 2:22 from the rib that he had **t** from
2:23 because she was **t** from man."
3:19 because you were **t** from it.
12:15 was **t** to Pharaoh's palace.
20:3 of the woman that you've **t**!
27:35 and has **t** away your blessing."
27:36 and now he's **t** my blessing."
30:23 "God has **t** away my disgrace."
31:1 "Jacob has **t** everything that
31:9 So God has **t** away your
31:34 Rachel had **t** the idols and had
39:1 Joseph had been **t** to Egypt.
39:1 who had **t** him there.
46:34 you must answer, 'We have **t**
47:2 Since he had **t** five of his
50:11 are **t** very seriously by
Exo 18:2 father-in-law Jethro had **t** her in,
38:25 was **t** weighed 7,544 pounds,
Lev 7:34 I have **t** the breast that was
13:2 he must be **t** to the priest Aaron
13:9 he must be **t** to the priest.
14:2 He must be **t** to the priest.
14:36 he will order everything **t** out of
14:45 must be torn down and **t**
22:12 she must never eat the food **t**
24:14 ⌊my name⌋ must be **t** outside
24:23 the LORD's name was **t** outside
Num 3:12 of all the Israelites, I have **t**
8:16 I have **t** them to be mine as
8:18 So I have **t** the Levites as
10:17 tent ⌊of meeting⌋ was **t** down,
14:3 children will be **t** as prisoners
14:31 would be **t** as prisoners
16:15 I haven't **t** anything from them,
18:11 that come as gifts **t** from
19:3 It must be **t** outside the camp
19:20 doesn't have his sin **t** away,
21:26 of Moab and had **t** all his land
36:3 Their land will be **t** away from
Dtr 4:5 the land and **t** possession of it.

Dtr 23:20 the land and t possession of it.
24:6 or even part of a handmill — be t
28:41 they will be t as prisoners
32:42 who were killed and t captive.
Jos 2:4 But the woman had already t
2:6 (She had t them up to the roof
4:20 they had t from the Jordan.
7:11 They have t what I claimed for
8:12 Joshua had t about five
Jdg 17:2 of silver that were t from you.
18:24 Micah answered, "You've t
18:30 in that land were t captive.
21:1 The men of Israel had t this
21:5 They had t a solemn oath that
21:18 The people of Israel have t an
1Sm 3:14 That is why I have t an oath
5:8 of Israel must be t to Gath,"
6:15 (The Levites had already t
14:47 When Saul had t over the
15:19 Why have you t their
20:42 "We have both t an oath in the
21:6 which had been t from
30:2 Instead, they had t the women
30:3 and daughters had been t
30:16 they had t so much loot
30:18 the Amalekites had t,
30:19 else they had t with them.
30:26 for you from the loot t from
2Sm 3:35 But David had t an oath:
8:12 and from the goods t from
12:13 "The LORD has t away your
18:18 Absalom had t a rock and set it
1Ki 5:9 There I will have them t apart,
8:20 I have t my father David's
13:10 on the road he had t to Bethel.
13:12 man of God from Judah had t.)
20:42 that reason your life will be t
2Ki 2:9 for you before I'm t from you?"
2:10 If you see me t from you,
13:25 Benhadad had t from his father
17:23 So the people of Israel were t
17:28 been t prisoner from Samaria
18:10 Samaria was t in Hezekiah's
20:17 will be t away to Babylon.
20:18 descendants will be t away.
22:9 "We have t the money donated
24:7 the king of Babylon had t all
1Ch 6:15 Jehozadak was t captive when
8:6 who were t away as captives
9:1 The Israelites were t away to
18:11 gold he had t from other nations
26:27 had donated some of the loot t
2Ch 6:10 I've t my father David's place,
15:17 sites in Israel were not t down,
21:4 After Jehoram had t over his
Ezr 1:7 Nebuchadnezzar had t these
2:1 the exiles had been t captive.
2:1 of Babylon had t them
5:14 (Nebuchadnezzar had t them
6:5 (Nebuchadnezzar had t them
9:7 We have been t captive,
10:13 in this sin that it can't be t care
Neh 7:6 the exiles had been t captive.
7:6 of Babylon had t them captive.
Est 2:6 (Kish had been t captive from
2:8 Esther also was t to the king's
2:16 So Esther was t to King
8:2 which he had t from Haman,
Job 1:21 and the LORD has t away!
6:13 skills been t away from me?
19:9 He has t the crown off my head.
20:19 He has t by force a house that
22:15 that wicked people have t?
27:2 the one who has t away my
28:2 Iron is t from the ground,
34:5 but God has t away my rights.
34:20 Mighty people are t away but
Psa 3:6 have t positions against me
7:1 I have t refuge in you.
10:14 you have t note of trouble and
11:1 I have t refuge in the LORD.
25:20 I have t refuge in you.
31:1 I have t refuge in you,
37:40 they have t refuge in him.
66:20 my prayer or t away his mercy
71:1 I have t refuge in you,

Psa 78:61 He allowed his power to be t
88:8 You have t my friends far away
88:18 You have t my loved ones and
89:35 On my holiness I have t an
110:4 The LORD has t an oath and
139:16 before one of them had t place.
141:8 I have t refuge in you.
Ecc 3:14 and nothing can be t away from
Sos 1:6 I have not even t care of my
5:3 I have t off my clothes!
Isa 1:7 Your fields are devastated and t
6:6 burning coal that he had t from
6:7 Your guilt has been t away,
14:24 LORD of Armies has t an oath:
22:3 were t prisoner before any
28:4 they will be t and eaten.
28:9 To those just t from their
28:15 because we have t refuge in
39:6 will be t away to Babylon.
39:7 descendants will be t away.
40:24 They have hardly t root in the
41:9 I have t you from the ends of
46:3 I've t care of you from the time
49:20 The children t from you will
49:24 Can loot be t away from mighty
49:25 Loot will be t away from
52:5 My people are t away for no
53:4 He certainly has t upon himself
53:8 He was arrested, t away,
57:1 Loyal people are t away,
Jer 1:3 were t away into captivity
3:24 has t everything our ancestors
6:11 A man and his wife will be t
8:1 lived in Jerusalem will be t out
8:13 given them will be t away.'"
13:17 LORD's flock will be t captive.
13:19 All the people of Judah will be t
14:9 be like someone t by surprise,
22:10 for those who are t away,
22:12 place where he was t captive,
23:2 You have not t care of them,
25:33 be mourned, t away, or buried.
27:10 They will cause you to be t far
27:18 to be t away to Babylon.
27:22 They will be t to Babylon and
29:4 says to all those who were t
29:7 where I've t you as captives,
29:16 weren't t away as captives:
30:16 and all your enemies will be t
40:1 who were being t to Babylon.
40:7 not been t away to Babylon.
40:10 Live in the cities you have t
41:14 had t captive at Mizpah
46:19 because you will be t away as
48:41 The cities will be t,
48:46 Your sons will be t away into
48:46 will be t away into captivity.
49:1 then, has the god Milcom t over
49:3 Milcom will be t away into
49:29 tents and their flocks will be t.
49:32 camels will be t as prizes.
49:32 large herds will be t as loot.
51:14 The LORD of Armies has t an
51:32 river crossings have been t.
51:41 has been t captive.
52:30 4,600 people were t away.
Eze 6:9 where they are t captive.
15:6 As a vine is t from among the
21:5 have t my sword from its
21:24 So you will be t captive.
25:15 The Philistines have t revenge
33:5 If they had t the warning,
34:8 They have t care of only
36:5 The Edomites have t
Dan 4:31 kingdom has been t from you.
5:2 Nebuchadnezzar had t from
5:3 had been t from God's temple
5:13 So Daniel was t to the king.
5:20 His honor was t away from him.
6:23 overjoyed and had Daniel t out
6:23 When Daniel was t out of the
7:12 rest of the animals was t away,
7:14 power that will not be t away.
7:26 his power will be t away,
12:11 daily burnt offering is t away
Hos 10:5 will be t away into captivity.

Joe 1:5 has been t away from you.
Amo 1:6 The Philistines have t all the
2:8 out on clothes t as security.
4:2 The Almighty LORD has t an
4:2 come when you will be t away
7:11 avoid being t from its land
7:17 Israel cannot avoid being t from
Mic 1:16 children will be t from you into
Zec 3:4 I have t your sin away from
14:1 when the loot you have t will
14:2 people won't be t from the city.
Mat 9:15 will be t away from them.
13:12 will be t away from them.
16:7 they had not t any bread along.
21:43 of God will be t away from you
24:40 One will be t, and the other one
24:41 One will be t, and the other one
25:29 But everything will be t away
26:39 let this cup of suffering be t
26:42 if this cup cannot be t away
Mar 2:20 will be t away from them.
4:25 will be t away from them."
16:19 the Lord was t to heaven,
Luk 1:1 what had t place among us.
2:2 This was the first census t
5:35 will be t away from them.
7:16 and "God has t care of his
8:18 will be t away from them."
8:34 When those who had t care of
9:51 for Jesus to be t to heaven.
10:42 will not be t away from her."
11:52 You have t away the key that
17:34 one will be t and the other one
17:35 One will be t, and the other one
19:26 But everything will be t away
23:19 in a riot that had t place
24:51 left them and was t to heaven.
Jon 12:16 remembered that they had t part
18:28 Jesus was t from Caiaphas'
19:1 Jesus t away and whipped.
19:30 After Jesus had t the vinegar,
21:7 on the clothes that he had t off
Act 1:2 the day he was t to heaven.
1:2 Before he was t to heaven,
1:9 he was t to heaven.
1:11 who was t from you to heaven,
1:22 day that Jesus was t from us."
5:34 apostles should be t outside
7:9 and he was t to Egypt.
7:16 They were t to Shechem for
9:39 he arrived, he was t upstairs.
10:16 was quickly t into the sky.
12:17 how the Lord had t him out
18:18 since he had t a vow.
21:29 and thought Paul had t him into
21:34 Paul to be t into the barracks.
26:10 killed every time a vote was t.
2Co 3:16 to the Lord, the veil is t away.
5:1 on earth is ever t down like
1Th 4:17 we who are still alive will be t
1Ti 3:16 and was t to heaven in glory.
Heb 1:12 They will be t off like a coat.
6:18 Those of us who have t refuge
7:21 "The Lord has t an oath and
11:5 Faith enabled Enoch to be t
11:5 because God had t him.
11:5 states that before Enoch was t,
Rev 5:8 When the lamb had t the scroll,
11:17 because you have t your great
12:5 child was snatched away and t
12:6 her so that she might be t care
12:14 where she could be t care of for
13:10 If anyone is t prisoner,
19:2 He has t revenge on her for the

takes (61)

Exo 30:7 every morning when he t care
Lev 20:17 Whoever t his sister,
Num 19:9 water that t away uncleanness.
19:13 because the water that t away
24:22 when Assyria t you as
Dtr 1:2 (It t 11 days to go from Mount
7:10 He never t long to pay back
10:17 favorites and never t a bribe.
19:11 for him, attacks him, t his life,
19:16 must do whenever a witness t

1Ki 8:46 over to an enemy who t them
2Ch 6:36 over to an enemy who t them
19:7 He is impartial and never t
Job 9:12 He t something away,
12:20 unable to speak and t away
12:24 He t away the common sense
18:11 and chase him every step he t.
27:8 when God t away his life?
Psa 2:12 everyone who t refuge in him.
5:4 You are not a God who t
34:8 the person who t refuge in him.
45:9 The queen t her place at your
57:1 because my soul t refuge in
63:11 Everyone who t an oath by
82:1 God t his place in his own
149:4 because the LORD t pleasure
Pro 1:19 Greed t away his life.
6:34 no mercy when he t revenge.
8:2 ⌞Wisdom⌟ t its stand on high
11:8 a wicked person t his place.
27:18 Whoever t care of a fig tree can
Isa 3:13 The LORD t his place in the
22:6 Elam t its quiver of arrows,
40:11 Like a shepherd he t care of his
41:2 victory with every step he t?
Jer 12:11 but no one t this to heart.
Eze 33:4 the enemy comes and t them,
Mic 2:4 He t them from us.
7:9 endure his fury until he t up my
Nah 1:2 The LORD t revenge.
1:2 The LORD t revenge and is full
1:2 The LORD t revenge against
Zec 5:3 scroll says that everyone who t
10:3 The LORD of Armies t care of
Mar 4:15 Satan comes at once and t
Luk 6:29 If someone t your coat,
6:30 If someone t what is yours,
8:12 He t the word away from them
9:39 Whenever a spirit t control of
21:32 disappear until all this t place.
Jon 1:29 This is the Lamb of God who t
10:18 No one t my life from me.
15:1 and my Father t care of the
Eph 5:29 he feeds and t care of it,
5:29 as Christ t care of the church.
Php 2:20 He t a genuine interest in your
2Th 2:3 unless⌟ a revolt t place first,
Heb 5:4 No one t this honor for himself.
6:18 God cannot lie when he t an
Rev 3:11 so that no one t your crown.
22:19 If anyone t away any words

taking (54)

Gen 22:16 and said, "I am t an oath on my
24:10 t with him all of his master's
30:31 then I'll go back to t care of and
36:24 the desert while he was t care
37:13 "Your brothers are t care of the
37:16 Please tell me where they're t
42:38 to him on the trip you're t,
Exo 3:1 Moses was t care of the sheep
10:9 We'll be t our young and old,
27:3 pots for t away the altar's
Lev 25:15 sell it to you t into account
Num 15:18 enter the land where I'm t you
19:19 will finish t away their sins.
22:7 t money with them to pay for
22:32 because the trip you're t is evil.
Dtr 2:35 t the cattle and goods.
3:7 t all of the cattle and goods.
Jdg 5:28 "Why is his chariot t so long?
Rut 2:20 responsible for t care of us."
1Sm 20:8 Why bother t me to your
26:2 t with him 3,000 of Israel's
2Sm 2:25 banding together and t their
4:5 was t his midday nap
1Ki 1:15 from Shunem was t care of him.
11:18 T some men from Paran with
1Ch 2:7 for Israel by t goods that were
Neh 5:15 the people by t from them food
13:6 While all of this was t place,
Job 13:14 than I can chew and t my life
Pro 25:20 ⌞Like⌟ t off a coat on a cold
Isa 3:16 glances, t short little steps,
51:22 I'm t from your hand the cup
Jer 16:5 I'm t my peace, love,
Lam 3:11 forced me off the road I was t,
Eze 34:2 of Israel who have been t care
Amo 5:12 the righteous by t bribes.
Jnh 1:14 don't let us die for t this man's
Zec 5:10 "Where are they t the basket?"
Mar 12:40 They rob widows by t their
Luk 2:8 They were t turns watching
6:29 don't stop him from t your shirt.
8:23 The boat was t on water,
12:45 may think that his master is t
16:3 My master is t my job away
20:47 They rob widows by t their
Jon 13:2 While supper was t place,
Act 15:14 by t from non-Jewish people
22:23 was yelling, t off their coats,
Rom 7:11 Sin, t the opportunity provided
2Co 11:8 I robbed other churches by t
Php 2:7 he emptied himself by t
Col 1:7 He is t your place here as a
1Th 2:7 like a mother t care of her
1Ti 5:10 t care of believers' needs,

talents (1)

Exo 36:1 the necessary skills and t.

talitha (1)

Mar 5:41 her, "T, koum!" which means,

talk (114)

Exo 4:11 Who makes humans unable to t
Dtr 3:26 Don't t to me anymore about
6:7 T about them when you're at
11:19 and t about them when you're
25:8 must summon him and t to him.
28:67 You'll t this way because of the
32:47 think these words are idle t.
Jos 22:33 didn't t anymore about going
Jdg 14:7 Then he went to t to the young
1Sm 18:22 "T to David in private.
25:17 that it's useless to t to him."
2Sm 3:27 aside in the gateway as if to t
20:16 here so that I can t to him."
1Ki 2:18 "I will t to the king for you."
2:19 went to King Solomon to t
22:24 Spirit leave me to t to you?"
2Ki 22:14 and Asaiah went to t to the
2Ch 18:23 go when he left me to t to you?"
34:22 and the king's officials went to t
Neh 6:7 So let's t about this.
Est 1:18 what the queen did will t back
Job 4:2 "If someone tries to t to you,
11:3 Should your empty t silence
11:5 open his mouth ⌞to t⌟ to you.
13:7 "Will you t wickedly for God
13:7 for God and t deceitfully
15:5 You choose ⌞to t with⌟ a sly
18:2 it through, and then we'll t.
Psa 35:20 They do not t about peace.
38:12 Those who are out to harm me t
50:20 You sit and t against your own
55:14 We used to t to each other in
64:5 They t about setting traps and
69:26 and they t about the pain of
71:10 My enemies t about me.
71:17 and I still t about the miracles
73:15 "I will continue to t like that,"
120:7 but when I t about it,
120:7 they only t about war.
145:4 Each generation will t about
145:6 People will t about the power
145:11 Everyone will t about the glory
Pro 2:16 woman with her smooth t,
6:22 you wake up, they will t to you
6:24 woman and from the smooth t
7:5 woman with her smooth t.
10:19 when there is much t,
11:9 With his t a godless person
12:13 is trapped by his own sinful t,
14:23 but idle t leads only to poverty.
18:21 and those who love to t will
23:9 Do not t directly to a fool,
24:2 and their lips t trouble.
26:23 ⌞so⌟ is smooth t that covers up
Ecc 5:2 Don't be in a hurry to t.
5:6 Don't let your mouth t you into
Jer 3:16 "People will no longer t about
Jer 12:1 Yet, I want to t to you about
23:32 with their lies and their wild t.
32:4 He will t to Nebuchadnezzar in
34:3 and he will t to you face to
35:2 family of Rechab and t to them.
48:27 Whenever you t about them
Eze 3:26 of your mouth so that you can't t
24:27 and you will t to the refugee.
36:3 and people began to t and
Dan 10:16 my mouth and began to t.
10:17 How can I t to you,
Hab 2:19 and to a stone that cannot t,
Mat 6:7 they'll be heard if they t a lot.
9:32 The man was unable to t
12:22 the man blind and unable to t.
12:22 him so that he could t and see.
12:46 They wanted to t to him.
12:47 They want to t to you."
15:30 disabled, those unable to t,
Mar 1:45 he began to t freely.
2:7 "Why does he t this way?
7:35 man could hear and t normally.
7:37 the deaf hear and the mute t."
9:17 by a spirit that won't let him t.
9:25 "You spirit that won't let him t,
Luk 1:20 you will be unable to t until the
1:22 them but remained unable to t.
7:15 man sat up and began to t,
10:39 Lord's feet and listened to him t.
11:14 had made the man unable to t.
11:14 the man began to t.
11:45 when you t this way,
Jon 3:31 and that's all I can t about.
7:13 Yet, no one would t openly
14:30 But he's coming, so I won't t
Act 8:33 Who from his generation will t
17:32 "We'll hear you t about this
19:6 and they began to t in other
21:39 you to let me t to the people."
24:24 and listened to him t about faith
Rom 9:20 Who do you think you are to t
16:18 By their smooth t and flattering
1Co 3:1 Brothers and sisters, I couldn't t
4:20 God's kingdom is not just t,
2Co 6:13 to you as I would t to children.
Gal 1:16 When this happened, I didn't t
Eph 5:4 right that dirty stories, foolish t,
5:12 It is shameful to t about what
1Th 1:9 They t about how you
1Ti 5:1 but t to him as if he were your
5:1 T to younger men as if they
Heb 5:13 experience to t about what is
Jas 2:12 T and act as people who are
2Pe 2:16 which normally can't t,
2Jn 1:12 Instead, I hope to visit and t
3Jn 1:14 can t things over personally.
Rev 13:15 of the ⌞first⌟ beast could t

talked (33)

Gen 4:8 Cain t to his brother Abel.
45:15 that his brothers t with him.
Exo 7:7 was 83 when they t to Pharaoh.
Num 14:10 of Israel t about stoning Moses
2Sm 12:18 child was alive, we t to him,
1Ki 10:2 she t to him about everything
13:25 They t about it in the city
21:6 "I t to Naboth from Jezreel.
2Ki 9:12 Jehu replied, "We t for a while,
2Ch 9:1 she t to him about everything
Jer 5:14 Because you've t like this,
Eze 3:24 He t to me. He said, "Go into
35:13 and continually t against me.
Dan 1:19 The king t to them and found
10:19 As he t to me, I became
Hos 12:4 and he t with him there.
Luk 1:65 people t about everything that
9:11 He welcomed them, t to them
20:5 They t about this among
20:14 they t it over among
24:32 "Weren't we excited when he t
Jon 9:18 Until they t to the man's
10:6 used this illustration as he t
12:29 said that an angel had t to him.
18:16 The other disciple t to the
Act 1:3 days he appeared to them and t
9:29 He t and argued with

Act 10:27 As Peter **t**, he entered
13:43 Paul and Barnabas **t** with them
17:3 the person he **t** about,
20:11 Paul **t** with the people for a
25:24 Jerusalem and Caesarea have **t**
Rev 13:11 like a lamb. It **t** like a serpent.

talkers (1)

Isa 28:14 you foolish **t** who rule the

talking (75)

Gen 19:21 destroy the city you're **t** about.
29:9 While he was still **t** to them,
Dtr 11:2 (I'm not **t** to your children.
1Sm 14:19 While Saul was **t** to the priest,
17:23 While he was **t** to them,
17:28 heard David **t** to the men.
18:1 David finished **t** to Saul.
2Sm 19:10 Why is no one **t** about bringing
19:29 "Why do you keep **t** about it?
1Ki 1:14 And while you're still there **t** to
1:22 While she was still **t** to the
2Ki 2:11 they continued walking and **t**,
6:33 While he was still **t** to them,
8:4 The king was **t** to Gehazi,
2Ch 25:16 As he was **t**, the king asked
Job 2:10 "You're **t** like a godless fool.
4:2 But who can keep from **t**?
16:6 If I stop **t**, how much of it will
Psa 19:3 without **t**, without words,
Pro 18:6 By **t**, a fool gets into an
18:20 His **t** provides him a living.
Ecc 10:13 A fool starts out by **t**
10:14 He never stops **t**. No one knows
Isa 58:13 you want, and by not **t** idly,
Jer 38:25 out that I've been **t** with you.
Eze 11:15 Jerusalem are **t** about your own
33:30 "Son of man, your people are **t**
Mat 9:18 came to Jesus while he was **t**
12:46 While Jesus was still **t** to the
15:31 amazed to see mute people **t**,
16:11 you understand that I wasn't **t**
17:3 to them and were **t** with Jesus.
17:13 that he was **t** about John
21:45 knew that he was **t** about them.
26:70 "I don't know what you're **t**
Mar 9:4 to them and were **t** with Jesus.
14:68 what you're **t** about."
14:71 "I don't know this man you're **t**
16:19 After **t** with the apostles,
Luk 9:30 and Elijah were **t** with him.
12:1 I'm **t** about their hypocrisy.
21:5 Some of the disciples were **t**
22:60 don't know what you're **t** about!"
24:14 They were **t** to each other
24:15 While they were **t**,
24:36 While they were **t** about what
Jon 3:11 We know what we're **t** about,
4:27 were surprised that he was **t**
4:27 or "Why are you **t** to her?"
8:27 Jews didn't know that he was **t**
9:37 person who is now **t** with you."
13:18 "I'm not **t** about all of you.
13:24 "Ask Jesus whom he's **t**
16:18 We don't understand what he's **t**
16:29 "Now you're **t** in plain words
Act 4:20 We cannot stop **t** about what
8:34 who the prophet is **t** about.
8:34 Is he **t** about himself or
14:12 because Paul did most of the **t**.
16:13 We sat down and began **t** to
20:7 he kept **t** until midnight.
20:9 As Paul was **t** on and on,
28:22 people are **t** against this sect."
1Co 10:15 I'm **t** to intelligent people.
10:29 I'm not **t** about your conscience
14:9 You will be **t** into thin air.
2Co 6:13 I'm **t** to you as I would talk to
11:6 I know what I'm **t** about.
Eph 5:32 I'm **t** about Christ's relationship
1Ti 1:7 understand what they're **t** about
Heb 2:5 (about which we are **t**) under
3:18 He was **t** about those who
7:13 The priest whom we are **t**
Rev 1:12 the voice which was **t** to me,
21:15 The angel who was **t** to me

talks (8)

Job 35:16 mouth for no good reason and **t**
Pro 10:8 but the one who **t** foolishly will
10:10 The one who **t** foolishly will be
19:1 to be one who **t** dishonestly
26:25 When he **t** charmingly,
Jon 10:21 Others said, "No one **t** like this
Act 19:13 whom Paul **t** about."
2Pe 3:16 He **t** about this subject in all

tall (26)

Num 13:32 people we saw there are very **t**.
Dtr 2:10 and as **t** as the people of Anak.
2:21 and as **t** as the people of Anak.
9:2 Their people are **t** and strong.
1Sm 16:7 his appearance or how **t** he is,
17:4 from Gath. He was ten feet **t**.
2Sm 21:20 there was a **t** man who had a
1Ch 20:6 there was a **t** man who had 24
Job 8:11 rushes grow **t** without water?
Psa 92:12 like palm trees and grow **t** like
Isa 18:2 Go, swift messengers, to a **t**
18:7 to the LORD of Armies from a **t**
Eze 17:24 I cut down **t** trees, and I make
17:24 and I make small trees grow **t**.
19:11 It grew to be **t** with many
31:3 It was very **t**. Its top was among
31:4 underground springs made it **t**.
31:10 The tree grew very **t**,
31:10 arrogant because it was so **t**.
31:14 will ever stand that **t**.
Dan 4:10 of the earth. It was very **t**.
4:11 strong enough and **t** enough
4:20 strong enough and **t** enough
Amo 2:9 although the Amorites were as **t**
Mat 11:7 **T** grass swaying in the wind?
Luk 7:24 **T** grass swaying in the wind?

taller (8)

Dtr 1:28 'The people there are **t** and
11:23 land belonging to people **t**
1Sm 9:2 a head **t** than everyone else.
10:23 a head **t** than everyone else.
2Ch 32:5 made the towers **t**,
Eze 31:5 That is why it grew **t** than all
Mat 13:32 it is **t** than the garden plants.
Mar 4:32 it comes up and becomes **t**

tallest (3)

2Ki 19:23 I'll cut down its **t** cedars and its
Isa 10:33 The **t** ones will be brought
37:24 I'll cut down its **t** cedars and its

Talmai (6)

Num 13:22 Ahiman, Sheshai, and **T** lived.
Jos 15:14 out Sheshai, Ahiman, and **T**,
Jdg 1:10 killed Sheshai, Ahiman, and **T**.
2Sm 3:3 of King **T**) from Geshur.
13:37 fled to Geshur's King **T**,
1Ch 3:2 of King **T**) from Geshur.

Talmon (5)

1Ch 9:17 **T**, Ahiman, and their relatives.
Ezr 2:42 **T**, Akkub, Hatita, and Shobai:
Neh 7:45 **T**, Akkub, Hatita, and Shobai:
11:19 the gatekeepers: Akkub, **T**,
12:25 Obadiah, Meshullam, **T**,

Tamar (28)

Gen 38:6 son Er. Her name was **T**.
38:11 said to his daughter-in-law **T**,
38:11 So **T** went to live in her father's
38:13 As soon as **T** was told that her
38:24 "Your daughter-in-law **T** has
38:27 The time came for **T** to give
Rut 4:12 the son whom **T** gave birth to
2Sm 13:1 son Amnon fell in love with **T**,
13:2 with his half sister **T** that
13:4 sister **T**," he answered.
13:5 'Please let my sister **T** come to
13:6 "Please let my sister **T** come
13:7 David sent for **T** at the palace.
13:8 So **T** went to her brother
13:10 Amnon told **T**, "Bring the food
13:10 **T** took the bread she had
2Sm 13:11 said, "Come to bed with me, **T**!
13:19 **T** put ashes on her head,
13:20 So **T** stayed there at the home
13:22 Amnon for raping his sister **T**.
13:32 half brother raped his sister **T**.
14:27 His daughter **T** was a beautiful
1Ch 2:4 **T**, Judah's daughter-in-law,
3:9 **T** was their sister.
Eze 47:18 from the Dead Sea down to **T**.
47:19 side the border will run from **T**
48:28 of Gad will run south from **T**
Mat 1:3 Judah and **T** were the father

tamarisk (3)

Gen 21:33 Abraham planted a **t** tree at
1Sm 22:6 in Gibeah under the **t** tree at
31:13 and buried them under the **t** tree

tambourine (5)

Exo 15:20 took a **t** in her hand.
1Sm 10:5 a harp, a **t**, a flute, and a lyre.
Job 21:12 They sing with the **t** and lyre,
Psa 81:2 Begin a psalm, and strike a **t**.
Isa 24:8 Joyful **t** music stops.

tambourines (12)

Gen 31:27 accompanied by **t** and lyres.
Exo 15:20 All the women, dancing with **t**,
Jdg 11:34 She was dancing with **t** in her
1Sm 18:6 accompanied by **t**,
2Sm 6:5 **t**, sistrums, and cymbals.
1Ch 13:8 **t**, cymbals, and trumpets.
Psa 68:25 beating **t** are between them.
149:3 music to him with **t** and lyres,
150:4 Praise him with **t** and dancing.
Isa 5:12 **t** and flutes, and wine. Yet,
30:32 To the sound of **t** and lyres,
Jer 31:4 again you will take your **t**,

tame (4)

Lev 5:2 dead body of a wild or **t** animal
Job 11:12 when a wild donkey is born **t**.
Act 11:6 closely and saw **t** animals,
Jas 3:8 Yet, no one can **t** the tongue.

tamed (1)

Jas 3:7 People have **t** all kinds of

Tammuz (1)

Eze 8:14 there and crying for the god **T**.

tamper (1)

Ezr 6:12 king and nation who tries to **t**

tampers (1)

Ezr 6:11 a decree that if anyone **t**

tangled (6)

2Sm 18:9 and the mule went under the **t**
Job 18:8 His own feet get him **t** in a net
36:8 are bound in chains and **t**
Psa 18:4 death had become **t** around me.
116:3 of death became **t** around me.
Nah 1:10 of Nineveh will be like **t** thorns

Tanhumeth (2)

2Ki 25:23 (son of **T** from Netophah),
Jer 40:8 Seraiah (son of **T**),

tanned (1)

Sos 1:6 The sun has **t** me.

tape (1)

Eze 40:3 The man was holding a linen **t**

Taphath (1)

1Ki 4:11 daughter **T** was his wife.)

Tappuah (6)

Jos 12:17 the king of **T**, the king of
15:34 Zanoah, En Gannim, **T**,
16:8 At **T** the border goes west
17:8 (The land of **T** belongs to
17:8 to Manasseh, but **T** itself,
1Ch 2:43 Hebron's sons were Korah, **T**,

tar (7)
Gen 6:14 coat it inside and out with t.
11:3 as stones and t as mortar.
14:10 of Siddim was full of t pits.
14:10 they fell because of the t pits,
Exo 2:3 and coated it with t and pitch.
Isa 34:9 streams will be turned to t.
34:9 Its land will become blazing t.

Taralah (1)
Jos 18:27 Rekem, Ir Peel, T,

Tarea (2)
1Ch 8:35 Pithon, Melech, T, and Ahaz.
9:41 were Pithon, Melech, and T.

target (7)
1Sm 20:20 from beside it toward a t.
Job 6:4 have found their t in me,
7:20 Why do you make me your t?
16:12 He set me up as his t,
36:32 and orders it to hit the t.
Psa 58:7 let their arrows miss the t.
Lam 3:12 made me the t for his arrows.

tarnish (3)
Eze 24:6 Its t will not come off.
24:11 and its t will burn off.
24:12 fire can't take away its thick t.

tarnished (3)
2Sm 1:21 warriors' shields were t there.
Lam 4:1 how the gold has become t!
Eze 24:6 city of murderers, for that t pot.

Tarpel (1)
Ezr 4:9 T, Persia, Erech, Babylon,

Tarshish (28)
Gen 10:4 T, Cyprus, and Rhodes.
1Ki 10:22 king had a fleet headed for T
10:22 Once every three years the T
22:48 Jehoshaphat made T-style ships
1Ch 1:7 T, Cyprus, and Rhodes.
7:10 Zethan, T, and Ahishahar.
2Ch 9:21 The king had ships going to T
9:21 Once every three years the T
20:36 him in making ships to go to T.
20:37 wrecked and couldn't go to T.
Est 1:14 Admatha, T, Meres, Marsena,
Psa 48:7 wind you smash the ships of T.
72:10 May the kings from T and the
Isa 2:16 against all the large ships of T
23:1 Cry loudly, you ships of T!
23:6 Travel to T! Cry loudly, you
23:10 like the Nile, people of T.
23:14 Cry loudly, you ships of T,
60:9 The ships from T are the first to
66:19 to T, Put and Lud, Meshech,
Jer 10:9 silver is brought from T
Eze 27:12 "People from T traded with
27:25 "Ships from T carried your
38:13 the merchants from T,
Jnh 1:3 from the LORD by going to T.
1:3 and found a ship going to T.
1:3 He wanted to go to T to get
4:2 That's why I tried to run to T in

Tarsus (5)
Act 9:11 named Saul from the city of T.
9:30 to Caesarea and sent him to T.
11:25 Antioch to go to the city of T
21:39 well-known city of T in Cilicia.
22:3 born and raised in the city of T

Tartak (1)
2Ki 17:31 from Avva made Nibhaz and T.

task (3)
1Ki 2:25 gave this t to Benaiah,
1Ch 16:7 and his relatives with the t
2Ch 26:18 who have been given the holy t

tasks (4)
Psa 104:23 to do their t until evening.
Jon 5:36 The t that the Father gave me
5:36 these t which I perform,
Heb 6:2 setting people apart for holy t,

tassel (2)
Num 15:38 with violet threads in each t.
15:39 you look at the threads in the t,

tassels (3)
Num 15:38 to come they must wear t
Dtr 22:12 Make t on the four corners of
Mat 23:5 their headbands large and the t

taste (16)
2Sm 3:35 "May God strike me dead if I t
19:35 Can I t what I eat or drink?
Job 12:11 sounds and the tongue t food?
Psa 34:8 T and see that the LORD is
119:103 How sweet the t of your
141:4 Do not let me t their delicacies.
Pro 11:22 woman who lacks good t.
Sos 7:9 May your mouth t like the best
Isa 3:10 They will t the fruit of their
Mat 5:13 But if salt loses its t,
Mar 9:50 But if salt loses its t,
Luk 14:24 invited earlier will t any food at
14:34 But if salt loses its t,
Jon 8:52 what I say will never t death.'
Act 23:14 curse us if we t any food before
Col 2:21 Don't t or touch that!"

tasted (11)
Exo 15:23 the water because it t bitter.
16:31 It was white and t like wafers
Num 11:8 It t like rich pastry made with
1Sm 14:24 none of his troops t any food.
14:29 how my eyes lit up when I t
14:43 So Jonathan told him, "I t a
Job 21:25 never having t happiness,
Eze 3:3 So I ate it, and it t as sweet as
Mat 27:34 When he t it, he refused to
Jon 2:9 The person in charge t the
1Pe 2:3 Certainly you have t that the

tasteless (1)
Job 6:6 Is t food eaten without salt,

tastes (7)
Job 34:3 words like the tongue t food.
Psa 119:103 It t sweeter than honey.
Pro 20:17 Food gained dishonestly t
24:13 from the honeycomb t sweet.
27:7 even bitter food t sweet.
Sos 2:3 His fruit t sweet to me.
Isa 24:9 Liquor t bad to its drinkers.

tasting (1)
Dan 5:2 As they were t the wine,

tasty (1)
Pro 9:17 and food eaten in secret is t."

Tattenai (4)
Ezr 5:3 At the same time, Governor T
5:6 of the letter Governor T from
6:6 Governor T from the
6:13 Then Governor T from the

tattered (1)
Jos 9:5 and their clothes were t.

tattoo (1)
Lev 19:28 the dead, and never get a t.

taught (77)
Dtr 4:5 I have t you laws and rules as
4:44 This is what Moses t the
31:22 wrote down this song and t
Jdg 8:16 leaders of the city and t them
2Ki 17:28 He t them how to worship the
2Ch 15:3 a priest who t correctly,
17:9 They t in Judah. They had the
17:9 with them when they t
26:5 who t him to fear God.
Neh 8:9 and the Levites who t the
9:14 You t them about your holy day
Psa 71:17 O God, you have t me ever
105:22 and t his respected leaders
119:102 because you have t me.
Pro 4:2 After all, I have t you well.
4:11 I have t you the way of
Ecc 12:9 the spokesman also t the
Isa 40:14 Who t him the right way?
40:14 Who t him knowledge?
54:13 All your children will be t by
Jer 2:33 You t your ways to wicked
9:14 as their ancestors t them."
12:16 as they t my people to take an
13:23 when you're t to do wrong?
31:19 After I was t a lesson,
32:33 I t them again and again,
Dan 1:4 They were to be t the language
Hos 11:3 I was the one who t the people
12:10 I t lessons through the
Mat 4:23 He t in the synagogues and
7:29 he t them with authority.
9:35 He t in the synagogues and
13:54 went to his hometown and t
Mar 1:22 he t them with authority.
2:13 came to him, and he t them.
4:33 could understand what he t.
6:6 around to the villages and t.
6:30 everything they had done and t.
7:4 They have been t to follow
7:5 traditions t by our ancestors?
8:31 He t them that he would be
9:31 He t them, "The Son of Man
10:1 and he t them as he usually
11:17 Then he t them by saying,
12:38 As he t, he said, "Watch out for
Luk 4:15 He t in the synagogues,
4:31 and t them on a day of worship.
5:3 Then Jesus sat down and t the
11:1 to pray as John t his disciples."
13:22 Then Jesus traveled and t in
13:26 and you t in our streets.'
19:47 Jesus t in the temple courtyard
Jon 7:19 of you does what Moses t you.
8:28 I speak as the Father t me.
18:20 I have always t in synagogues
Act 11:26 Antioch for a whole year and t
15:35 They and many others t people
18:11 for a year and a half and t
18:25 He accurately t about Jesus
28:31 and t very boldly about
Rom 2:18 have been t Moses' Teachings.
1Co 15:2 hold on to the doctrine I t you,
Gal 1:12 I wasn't t it, but Jesus Christ
6:6 The person who is t God's
Eph 4:21 and have been t his ways.
4:22 You were t to change the way
4:23 However, you were t to have a
4:24 You were also t to become a
Col 2:7 by the faith that you were t,
1Th 4:1 Do this the way we t you.
4:9 God has t you to love each
4:15 are telling you what the Lord t.
2Th 2:15 traditions we t you either when
1Jn 2:27 live in Christ as he t you to do.
2Jn 1:9 what Christ t doesn't have God.
1:9 to teach what Christ t has both
Rev 2:14 follow what Balaam t Balak.

taunt (1)
Psa 42:10 to my bones, my enemies t me.

taverns (1)
Act 28:15 of Appius' Market and Three T

tax (34)
Num 31:28 Collect a t for the LORD.
Jdg 3:15 The people sent him with their t
3:17 Then he brought the t payment
2Ki 23:35 But he had to t the country to
Est 10:1 King Xerxes levied a t on the
Isa 33:18 Where are the t collectors?
Mat 5:46 Even the t collectors do that!
9:9 saw a man sitting in a t office.
9:10 Many t collectors and sinners
9:11 with t collectors and sinners?"
10:3 and Matthew the t collector;
11:19 a friend of t collectors and

Mat 17:24 the collectors of the temple **t**
17:24 your teacher pay the temple **t**?"
18:17 a heathen or a **t** collector.
21:31 **T** collectors and prostitutes are
21:32 The **t** collectors and prostitutes
Mar 2:14 sitting in a **t** office.
2:15 Many **t** collectors and sinners
2:16 with sinners and **t** collectors,
2:16 with **t** collectors and sinners?"
Luk 3:12 Some **t** collectors came to be
5:27 He saw a **t** collector named
5:27 named Levi sitting in a **t** office.
5:29 A huge crowd of **t** collectors
5:30 with **t** collectors and sinners?"
7:29 including **t** collectors,
7:34 of **t** collectors and sinners!'
15:1 All the **t** collectors and sinners
18:10 and the other was a **t** collector.
18:11 I'm not even like this **t** collector.
18:13 "But the **t** collector was
18:14 "I can guarantee that this **t**
19:2 was the director of **t** collectors,

taxed (1)

2Ki 23:35 He **t** each person according to

taxes (28)

Num 31:37 675 went to the LORD as **t**.
31:38 72 went to the LORD as **t**.
31:39 61 went to the LORD as **t**.
31:40 32 went to the LORD as **t**.
31:41 Moses gave the LORD's **t** to
2Sm 8:2 subjects and paid **t** ⌊to him⌋.
8:6 subjects and paid **t** ⌊to him⌋.
1Ki 4:21 These kingdoms paid **t** and
1Ch 18:2 subjects and paid **t** ⌊to him⌋.
18:6 subjects and paid **t** ⌊to him⌋.
2Ch 17:11 brought gifts and silver as **t**.
26:8 Ammonites paid **t** to Uzziah,
Ezr 4:13 the Jews will no longer pay **t**,
4:20 **T**, fees, and tolls were paid to
6:8 own money from the **t** ⌊on
7:24 temple of this God pay any **t**,
Neh 5:4 money to pay the king's **t**
Pro 28:16 **t** ⌊his people⌋ heavily,
Amo 5:11 take their wheat from them for **t**
Mat 17:25 of the world collect fees or **t**?
22:17 Is it right to pay **t** to the emperor
22:19 Show me a coin used to pay **t**."
Mar 12:14 Is it right to pay **t** to the emperor
12:14 Should we pay **t** or not?"
Luk 20:22 Is it right for us to pay **t** to the
23:2 He keeps them from paying **t** to
Rom 13:6 is also why you pay your **t**.
13:7 If you owe **t**, pay them. If you

teach (152)

Exo 4:12 you speak and will **t** you what
4:15 and I will **t** you both what to do.
35:34 of Dan the ability to **t** others.
Lev 10:10 **T** them the difference between
10:11 Also **t** the Israelites all the
Dtr 4:1 and rules I am about to **t** you.
4:9 **T** them to your children and
4:10 and they will **t** their children the
4:14 also commanded me to **t** you
5:31 and rules that you must **t** them
6:1 God commanded me to **t** you.
8:3 He did this to **t** you that a
11:19 **T** them to your children,
20:18 Otherwise, they will **t** you to
31:19 **t** it to the Israelites,
33:10 They **t** Jacob your rules and
Jdg 3:2 The LORD left them to **t** Israel's
13:8 Let him **t** us what we must do
2Sm 1:18 He said, "**T** this kesheth to the
1Ki 8:36 **T** them the proper way to live.
2Ki 17:27 Let him go back to **t** them the
2Ch 6:27 **T** them the proper way to live.
17:7 and Micaiah to **t** in the cities of
Ezr 7:10 and **t** their rules and regulations
7:25 In addition, you will **t** anyone
Neh 9:20 them your good Spirit to **t** them.
Job 6:24 **T** me, and I'll be silent.
8:10 Won't their words **t** you?
12:7 and they will **t** you.
Job 12:8 with the earth, and it will **t** you.
21:22 anyone **t** God knowledge?
27:11 "I will **t** you about God's power.
32:7 and experience should **t**
33:33 and I'll **t** you wisdom."
34:32 **T** me what I cannot see.
37:19 **T** us what we should say to
38:3 will ask you, and you will **t** me.
40:7 will ask you, and you will **t** me.
42:4 and you will **t** me.'
Psa 25:4 and **t** me your paths.
25:5 Lead me in your truth and **t** me
25:12 the LORD will **t** which path
27:11 **T** me your way, O LORD.
32:8 I will **t** you the way that you
34:11 I will **t** you the fear of the
39:4 "**T** me, O LORD, about the end
39:4 **T** me about the number of days
45:4 **t** you awe-inspiring things.
51:6 inside me you **t** me wisdom.
51:13 ⌊Then⌋ I will **t** your ways to
86:11 **T** me your way, O LORD,
90:12 **T** us to number each of our
119:12 O LORD. **T** me your laws.
119:26 me. **T** me your laws.
119:33 **T** me, O LORD, how to live by
119:64 fills the earth. **T** me your laws.
119:66 **T** me ⌊to use⌋ good judgment
119:68 good things. **T** me your laws.
119:108 and **t** me your regulations.
119:124 and **t** me your laws.
119:135 and **t** me your laws.
119:171 because you **t** me your laws.
132:12 instructions that I will **t** them,
143:10 **T** me to do your will,
Pro 4:4 they used to **t** me and say to
9:9 **T** a righteous person,
22:21 in order to **t** you the words of
Isa 2:3 He will **t** us his ways so that
9:15 Prophets who **t** lies are the tail.
28:26 and his God will **t** him.
48:17 I **t** you what is best for you.
50:4 The Almighty LORD will **t** me
Jer 9:20 **T** your daughters how to cry.
9:20 **T** your neighbors funeral songs.
16:21 That is what I will **t** them.
31:34 No longer will each person **t**
Eze 22:26 They don't **t** the difference
44:23 They must **t** my people the
Mic 3:11 Your priests **t** for a price.
4:2 He will **t** us his ways so that
Hab 2:19 up!" Can that thing **t** ⌊anyone⌋?
Mat 4:19 I will **t** you how to catch people
5:2 and he began to **t** them:
11:1 he moved on from there to **t** his
21:23 courtyard and began to **t**.
22:16 you tell the truth and that you **t**
23:2 **t** with Moses' authority.
28:20 **T** them to do everything I have
Mar 1:17 I will **t** you how to catch people
1:21 the synagogue and began to **t**.
4:1 Jesus began to **t** again by the
4:2 to **t** them many things.
6:2 he began to **t** in the synagogue.
8:31 Then he began to **t** them that
12:14 you **t** the way of God truthfully.
14:49 I used to **t** in the temple
Luk 6:6 went into a synagogue to **t**.
11:1 **t** us to pray as John taught his
12:12 At that time the Holy Spirit will **t**
20:21 right in what you say and **t**.
20:21 you **t** the way of God truthfully.
21:37 During the day Jesus would **t**
Jon 6:45 'God will **t** everyone.'
7:14 courtyard and began to **t**.
7:16 "What I **t** doesn't come from me
7:17 know if what I **t** is from God
7:17 God or if I **t** my own thoughts.
7:35 and that he'll **t** the Greeks?
8:2 so he sat down and began to **t**
9:34 Do you think you can **t** us?"
14:26 will **t** you everything.
Act 1:1 what Jesus began to do and **t**.
4:18 them never to **t** about Jesus
5:21 courtyard and began to **t**.
5:28 Jesus' name when you **t**.
Act 15:1 to **t** believers that people
21:21 have been told that you **t** all
Rom 2:21 As you **t** others, are you failing
2:21 are you failing to **t** yourself?
15:4 long ago was written to **t**
1Co 2:16 the Lord so that he can **t** him?"
4:17 my Christian way of life as I **t**
11:14 Doesn't nature itself **t** you that it
11:15 Doesn't it **t** you that it is a
12:29 Do all of them **t**? Do all of them
14:19 in order to **t** others in church,
Col 1:28 as we instruct and **t** everyone
3:16 and spiritual songs to **t** and
1Ti 1:20 to Satan in order to **t** them not
2:7 an apostle to **t** people who are
2:12 I don't allow a woman to **t** or to
3:2 be hospitable, and be able to **t**.
4:11 Insist on these things and **t**
6:1 of God's name and what we **t**.
6:2 **T** and encourage people to do
2Ti 2:2 will be competent to **t** others.
2:15 worker who isn't ashamed to **t**
3:8 the faith they **t** is counterfeit.
4:2 Be very patient when you **t**.
Tit 1:9 the trustworthy message we **t**.
1:11 teaching what they shouldn't **t**.
2:4 In this way they will **t** young
2:5 Also, tell them to **t** young
2:7 When you **t**, be an example of
3:10 continue to **t** false doctrine after
Heb 5:12 you still need someone to **t**
8:11 No longer will each person **t**
Jas 3:1 You know that we who **t** will
1Jn 2:27 You don't need anyone to **t** you
2Jn 1:9 continue to **t** what Christ taught
1:9 The person who continues to **t**
Rev 2:15 follow what the Nicolaitans **t**.

teacher (65)

Job 36:22 Is there any **t** like him?
Sos 8:2 (She is the one who was my **t**.)
Isa 30:20 But your **t** will no longer be
30:20 You will see your **t** with your
Joe 2:23 you the **T** of Righteousness.
Hab 2:18 in a molded statue, a **t** of lies,
Mat 8:19 came to him and said, "**T**,
9:11 "Why does your **t** eat with tax
10:24 student is not better than his **t**.
10:25 a student to become like his **t**
12:38 and Pharisees said, "**T**,
17:24 asked him, "Doesn't your **t** pay
19:16 came to Jesus and said, "**T**,
22:16 They said to him, "**T**,
22:24 "**T**, Moses said, 'If a man dies
22:36 "**T**, which commandment is the
23:8 because you have only one **t**,
26:18 and tell him that the **t** says,
Mar 4:38 him up and said to him, "**T**,
5:35 Why bother the **t** anymore?"
9:17 "**T**, I brought you my son.
9:38 John said to Jesus, "**T**,
10:17 He asked Jesus, "Good **T**,
10:20 The man replied, "**T**,
10:35 They said to him, "**T**,
10:51 The blind man said, "**T**,
12:14 came to him, they said, "**T**,
12:19 "**T**, Moses wrote for us, 'If a
12:32 The scribe said to Jesus, "**T**,
13:1 of his disciples said to him, "**T**,
14:14 tell the owner that the **t** asks,
Luk 3:12 They asked him, "**T**,
5:5 Simon answered, "**T**,
6:40 A student is no better than his **t**.
6:40 is well-trained will be like his **t**.
7:40 Simon replied, "**T**,
8:45 touching him, Peter said, "**T**,
8:49 Don't bother the **t** anymore."
9:33 "**T**, it's good that we're here.
9:38 man in the crowd shouted, "**T**,
10:25 He asked, "**T**, what must I do
11:45 "**T**, when you talk this way,
12:13 in the crowd said to him, "**T**,
17:13 and shouted, "Jesus, **T**,
18:18 official asked Jesus, "Good **T**,
19:39 in the crowd said to Jesus, "**T**,
20:21 They asked him, "**T**,

Luk 20:28 "**T**, Moses wrote for us, 'If a
20:39 Some scribes responded, "**T**,
21:7 The disciples asked him, "**T**,
22:11 of the house that the **t** asks,
Jon 1:38 "Rabbi" (which means "**t**"),
3:2 that God has sent you as a **t**.
3:10 "You're a well-known **t** of Israel.
7:18 the one who sent him is a true **t**
8:4 and asked Jesus, "**T**,
11:28 her sister Mary, "The **t** is here,
13:13 You call me **t** and Lord,
13:14 So if I, your Lord and **t**,
20:16 (This word means "**t**.")
Rom 2:20 and a **t** of children because you
Gal 6:6 share all good things with his **t**.
2Ti 1:11 to be an apostle and **t**
2:24 He must be a good **t**.
Jas 4:12 There is only one **t** and judge.

teachers (18)

Psa 119:99 have more insight than all my **t**,
Pro 5:13 I didn't listen to what my **t** said
Mat 23:34 and **t** of the Scriptures.
Luk 2:46 He was sitting among the **t**,
Act 13:1 and Saul were prophets and **t**
1Co 12:28 apostles, next prophets, third **t**,
Eph 4:11 as well as pastors and **t** as
2Ti 3:14 You know who your **t** were.
4:3 with **t** who tell them
Heb 5:12 By now you should be **t**.
Jas 3:1 many of you should become **t**.
2Pe 2:1 as false **t** will be among you.
2:10 These false **t** are bold and
2:11 and power than these **t**,
2:12 These false **t** insult what they
2:13 These false **t** are stains and
2:15 These false **t** have left the
2:17 These false **t** are dried-up

teaches (12)

Job 15:5 Your sin **t** you what to say.
35:11 who **t** us more than he teaches
35:11 who teaches us more than he **t**
Psa 25:8 That is why he **t** sinners the
25:9 and he **t** them his way.
94:10 He **t** people. Do you think he
Mat 5:19 seems unimportant and **t** others
5:19 But whoever does and **t** what
Act 21:28 This is the man who **t**
1Ti 6:3 Whoever **t** false doctrine and
1Jn 2:27 Instead, Christ's anointing **t**
Rev 2:20 She **t** and misleads my

teaching (38)

1Sm 12:23 I will go on **t** you the way that
2Sm 7:19 this is the **t** about the man.
Neh 13:3 After the people heard this **T**,
Job 11:4 'My **t** is morally correct,'
Hab 1:4 That is why your **t** is numbed,
Mal 2:6 The **t** that came from his mouth
Mat 22:33 the crowds who heard his **t**.
26:55 I used to sit **t** in the temple
Mar 1:27 This is a new **t** that has
4:2 While he was **t** them,
6:34 So he spent a lot of time **t** them.
9:31 he was **t** his disciples.
11:18 all the crowds with his **t**.
12:35 While Jesus was **t** in the
Luk 5:17 One day when Jesus was **t**,
13:10 Jesus was **t** in a synagogue on
20:1 One day Jesus was **t** the
Jon 6:59 Jesus said this while he was **t**
7:22 Moses gave you the **t** about
7:28 Then, while Jesus was **t** in the
8:20 these words while he was **t**
Act 4:2 Peter and John were **t** the
5:25 They're **t** the people."
5:42 they refused to stop **t** and
17:19 these new ideas that you're **t**?
18:5 Paul devoted all his time to **t**
20:20 and I didn't avoid **t** you publicly
Rom 12:7 If it is **t**, devote yourself to
12:7 devote yourself to **t**.
16:17 faith⌋ by **t** doctrine that is
1Co 15:54 then the **t** of Scripture will
1Ti 1:3 people to stop **t** false doctrine
4:13 messages, and **t** people.
4:16 Focus on your life and your **t**.
5:17 true if they work hard at **t**
2Ti 3:16 All of them are useful for **t**,
Tit 1:11 by **t** what they shouldn't
Rev 2:24 don't hold on to Jezebel's **t**,

teachings (342)

Exo 13:9 on your forehead that the **t**
18:20 them in the laws and the **t**,
24:12 you the stone tablets with the **t**
Num 19:2 the LORD's **t** have commanded:
31:21 "This is what the LORD's **t** told
Dtr 1:5 Moses began to review God's **t**.
4:8 laws and rules as all these **t**
17:18 a copy of these **t** on a scroll.
17:19 found in these **t** and laws.
27:3 words of these **t** on the stones.
27:8 all the words of these **t**
27:26 obey every word of these **t** will
28:58 word of the **t** that are written
28:61 not written in this Book of **T**.
29:21 written in this Book of the **T**.
29:29 been revealed in these **t** belong
29:29 obey every word of these **t**.
30:10 are written in this Book of **T**
31:9 Moses wrote down these **t** and
31:11 Read these **t** so that they can
31:12 obey every word of these **t**.
31:13 who don't know these **t**,
31:24 the words of these **t** in a book.
31:26 "Take this Book of **T**,
32:2 Let my **t** come down like
32:46 obey every word of these **t**.
33:4 Moses gave us these **t**.
33:10 rules and give Israel your **t**.
Jos 1:7 in the **t** that my servant
1:8 Never stop reciting these **t**.
8:31 Israel in the book of Moses' **T**.
8:32 copy of the **T** which Moses had
8:34 Joshua read all the **T** — the
8:35 Joshua read ⌊Moses' **T**⌋ in
22:5 follow the commands and **t** that
23:6 written in the Book of Moses' **T**.
24:26 things in the Book of God's **T**.
1Ki 2:3 they are recorded in Moses' **T**.
2Ki 10:31 didn't wholeheartedly obey the **t**
14:6 written in the Book of Moses' **T**:
17:13 your ancestors in all my **t**,
17:34 live by the decrees, customs, **t**,
17:37 obey the laws, rules, **t**,
21:8 and all the **T** that my servant
22:8 found the book of Moses' **T**
22:11 what the book of the **T** said,
23:24 the words of the **T** written
23:25 as directed in Moses' **T**.
1Ch 16:40 as written in the LORD's **T** that
22:12 of Israel and to follow the **T**
2Ch 12:1 Israel abandoned the LORD's **t**.
14:4 follow his **t** and commands.
15:3 and without Moses' **T**.
17:9 had the Book of the LORD's **T**
19:10 derived from Moses' **T**.
23:18 as it is written in Moses' **T**.
25:4 written in the Book of Moses' **T**:
30:16 as instructed by Moses' **T**.
31:3 as it is written in the LORD's **T**.
31:4 themselves to the LORD's **T**.
31:21 incorporated Moses' **T**
33:8 all the **t**, the ordinances,
34:14 LORD's **T** written by Moses.
34:15 "I have found the book of the **T**
34:19 the king heard what the **T** said,
35:26 is written in the LORD's **T**
Ezr 3:2 directions⌋ written in Moses' **T**.
7:6 was an expert in Moses' **T**,
7:10 to study the LORD's **T**,
7:12 a scribe for the **T** of the God of
7:14 on the basis of your God's **T**,
7:21 a scribe for the **T** of the God of
7:25 God's wisdom — the **T** you hold
7:25 people who know your God's **T**
7:25 who doesn't know the **T**.
7:26 not strictly follow your God's **T**
10:3 must do what Moses' **T** tell us.
Neh 8:1 to bring the Book of Moses' **T**,
Neh 8:2 Ezra the priest brought the **T**
8:3 to the Book of Moses' **T**.
8:7 and Pelaiah — explained the **T**
8:8 They read the Book of God's **T**
8:9 to the reading of God's **T**.
8:13 to study the words of God's **T**.
8:14 They found written in the **T**
8:18 read from the Book of God's **T**.
9:3 listened as⌋ the Book of the **T**
9:13 them fair rules, trustworthy **t**,
9:14 and **t** through your servant
9:26 They threw your **t** over their
9:29 to bring them back to your **t**,
9:34 ancestors didn't obey your **t**.
10:28 land for the sake of God's **T**.
10:29 follow God's **t** given by Moses,
10:34 to the directions in the **T**.
10:36 the directions in the **T**,
12:44 gifts designated by Moses' **T**
Psa 1:2 Rather, he delights in the **t** of
1:2 reflects on his **t** day and night.
19:7 The **t** of the LORD are perfect.
37:31 The **t** of his God are in his
40:8 Your **t** are deep within me.
78:1 Open your ears to my **t**,
78:5 He gave his **t** to Israel.
78:10 They refused to follow his **t**.
89:30 his descendants abandon my **t**
94:12 and instruct from your **t**.
105:45 obey his laws and follow his **t**.
119:1 who follow the **t** of the LORD.
119:18 the miraculous things in your **t**.
119:29 provide me with your **t**.
119:34 so that I can follow your **t**.
119:44 follow your **t** forever and ever.
119:51 not turned away from your **t**.
119:53 who abandon your **t**.
119:55 and I follow your **t**.
119:61 I never forget your **t**.
119:70 ⌊yet⌋ I am happy with your **t**.
119:72 The **t** ⌊that come⌋ from your
119:77 your **t** make me happy.
119:85 to trap me in defiance of your **t**.
119:92 If your **t** had not made me
119:97 Oh, how I love your **t**!
119:109 but I never forget your **t**.
119:113 people, but I love your **t**.
119:126 people have abolished your **t**,
119:136 others do not follow your **t**.
119:142 and your **t** are reliable.
119:150 they are far away from your **t**.
119:153 I have never forgotten your **t**.
119:163 disgusted with it. I love your **t**.
119:165 for those who love your **t**.
119:174 and your **t** make me happy.
Pro 1:8 do not neglect your mother's **t**,
1:9 because discipline and **t** are a
3:1 My son, do not forget my **t**,
4:2 Do not abandon my **t**.
6:20 disregard the **t** of your mother.
6:23 is a lamp, the **t** are a light,
7:2 Follow my **t** just as you protect
13:14 The **t** of a wise person are a
28:4 Those who abandon ⌊God's⌋ **t**
28:4 **t** oppose wicked people.
28:7 Whoever follows ⌊God's⌋ **t** is
28:9 to ⌊God's⌋ **t** is disgusting.
29:18 are those who follow ⌊God's⌋ **t**.
Isa 1:10 Pay attention to the **t** from our
2:3 The **t** will go out from Zion.
5:24 They have rejected the **t** of the
8:16 Seal the **t** among my disciples.
8:20 They should go to the **t** and to
24:5 disobeyed the LORD's **t**,
30:9 refuse to listen to the LORD's **t**.
42:4 coastlands will wait for his **t**.
42:21 praises the greatness of his **t**
42:24 They didn't obey his **t**.
51:4 My **t** will go out from me.
51:7 you people who have my **t** in
Jer 2:8 Those who deal with my **t**
6:19 to my words. They reject my **t**.
8:8 that you have the LORD's **t**?
8:8 pens to turn these **t** into lies.
9:13 "They've abandoned my **t** that I
16:11 They didn't obey my **t**.

Jer 18:18 because the **t** of the priests,
26:4 to me and don't follow my **t** that
31:33 "I will put my **t** inside them,
31:33 and I will write those **t** on their
32:23 to obey you or to follow your **t**.
44:10 me or lived your lives by my **t**
44:23 You didn't live by his **t**,
Lam 2:9 instruction ⌊from Moses' **T**⌋.
Eze 7:26 The **t** of priests and the advice
22:26 Your priests violate my **t** and
Dan 9:10 you or lived by the **t** you gave
9:11 All Israel has ignored your **t**
9:11 the curses written in the **T** of
9:13 as it was written in Moses' **T**.
Hos 4:6 You have forgotten the **t** of your
8:1 and rebelled against my **t**.
8:12 many things for them in my **t**,
Amo 2:4 have rejected the LORD's **T**
2:4 have been led astray by false **t**,
Mic 4:2 The **t** will go out from Zion.
Zep 3:4 They violate the **t**.
Zec 7:12 they couldn't hear the LORD's **t**,
Mal 2:8 many to stumble over my **t**.
2:9 unfair when ⌊applying⌋ my **t**."
4:4 "Remember the **t** of my servant
Mat 5:17 I came to set aside Moses' **T**
5:18 Moses' **T** before everything has
7:12 of⌋ Moses' **T** and the Prophets.
7:28 crowds were amazed at his **t**.
11:13 All the Prophets and Moses' **T**
12:5 Or haven't you read in Moses' **T**
15:9 because their **t** are rules made
16:12 but to watch out for the **t** of the
22:35 an expert in Moses' **T**,
22:36 is the greatest in Moses' **T**?"
22:40 All of Moses' **T** and the
23:23 important things in Moses' **T**.
Mar 1:22 people were amazed at his **t**.
7:7 because their **t** are rules made
Luk 2:22 the days required by Moses' **T**
2:23 was written in the Lord's **T**:
2:24 as required by the Lord's **T**:
2:27 for him what Moses' **T** required.
2:39 the Lord's **T** required,
4:32 people were amazed at his **t**
5:17 in Moses' **T** were present.
7:30 in Moses' **T** rejected God's plan
10:25 Then an expert in Moses' **T**
10:26 "What is written in Moses' **T**?
11:45 One of the experts in Moses' **T**
11:46 be for you experts in Moses' **T**!
11:52 be for you experts in Moses' **T**!
14:3 and the experts in Moses' **T**,
16:16 "Moses' **T** and the Prophets
16:17 drop a comma from Moses' **T**.
16:29 'They have Moses' ⌊**T**⌋ and
16:31 they won't listen to Moses' ⌊**T**⌋
23:5 throughout Judea with his **t**.
24:27 Then he began with Moses' **T**
24:44 written about me in Moses' **T**,
Jon 1:17 The **T** were given through
1:45 Moses wrote about in his **t**
7:19 Didn't Moses give you his **t**?
7:23 of worship to follow Moses' **T**,
7:49 it doesn't know Moses' **T**."
7:51 "Do Moses' **T** enable us to
8:5 In his **t**, Moses ordered us to
8:17 Your own **t** say that the
18:19 about his disciples and his **t**.
Act 2:23 don't acknowledge Moses' **T**,
2:42 disciples were devoted to the **t**
5:28 filled Jerusalem with your **t**.
5:34 respected expert in Moses' **T**.
6:13 the holy place and Moses' **T**.
7:53 people who received Moses' **T**,
7:53 you haven't obeyed those **t**."
13:12 The Lord's **t** amazed him.
13:15 After reading from Moses' **T**
13:38 approval through Moses' **T**.
15:1 as Moses' **T** require.
15:5 ordered to follow Moses' **T**."
15:21 His **t** are read in synagogues
18:13 that are against Moses' **T**."
18:15 words, names, and your own **t**,
21:20 deeply committed to Moses' **T**.
21:24 you carefully follow Moses' **T**.
Act 21:28 Moses' **T**, and this temple.
22:12 person who followed Moses' **T**.
23:3 and judge me by Moses' **T**
23:3 break those **t** by ordering these
23:29 with disputes about Jewish **t**.
24:14 in Moses' **T** and the Prophets.
28:23 Moses' **T** and the Prophets.
Rom 2:14 things that Moses' **T** contain,
2:15 found in Moses' **T** are written
2:17 rely on the laws in Moses' **T**,
2:18 have been taught Moses' **T**.
2:20 and truth in Moses' **T**.
2:23 about the laws in Moses' **T**,
2:23 God by ignoring Moses' **T**?
2:26 does what Moses' **T** demand,
2:27 Moses' **T** say will condemn
2:27 and have Moses' **T** in writing.
3:19 is in Moses' **T** applies
3:20 by following Moses' **T**.
3:20 Moses' **T** show what sin is.
3:21 in a way other than Moses' **T**.
3:21 Moses' **T** and the Prophets tell
3:31 Are we abolishing Moses' **T** by
3:31 we are supporting Moses' **T**.
4:13 obeying Moses' **T** that Abraham
4:14 If those who obey Moses' **T** are
4:15 The laws in Moses' **T** bring
4:16 by obeying Moses' **T**
6:17 to the **t** which you were
7:1 are familiar with Moses' **T**.)
7:4 Moses' **T** through Christ's body
7:7 sinful if Moses' **T** hadn't said,
7:12 So Moses' **T** are holy,
9:4 Moses' **T**, the true worship,
9:31 approval by obeying Moses' **T**,
10:4 of Moses' **T** so that everyone
13:8 person has fulfilled Moses' **T**.
13:10 love fulfills Moses' **T**.
1Co 2:13 things using **t** that are based
2:13 Instead, we use the Spirit's **t**.
2:14 spiritual doesn't accept the **t**
9:8 Don't Moses' **T** say the same
9:9 Moses' **T** say, "Never muzzle
9:20 I became subject to Moses' **T**
9:20 I'm not subject to Moses' **T**.
9:21 who does not have Moses' **T**
9:21 those who don't have those **t**.
9:21 even though I have God's **t**.
9:21 I'm really subject to Christ's **t**.
14:34 their place as Moses' **T** say.
Gal 3:10 written in Moses' **T** is cursed."
4:21 to what Moses' **T** say?
5:3 everything Moses' **T** demand.
5:14 All of Moses' **T** are
6:2 way you will follow Christ's **t**.
Eph 2:15 found in Moses' **T** so that
4:14 all kinds of **t** that change like
4:20 you learned from Christ's **t**.
1Ti 1:7 want to be experts in Moses' **T**.
1:8 We know that Moses' **T** are
1:10 else is against accurate **t**.
1:11 Moses' **T** were intended to be
4:1 will believe the **t** of demons.
4:6 the excellent **t** which you have
6:3 Lord Jesus Christ and godly **t**
2Ti 1:13 to be the pattern of accurate **t**.
3:10 But you know all about my **t**,
4:3 will not listen to accurate **t**.
Tit 1:9 he can use these accurate **t**
2:1 that goes along with accurate **t**.
2:10 beauty of the **t** about God our
3:9 and fights about Moses' **T**.
Heb 6:2 We shouldn't repeat the basic **t**
7:5 Moses' **T** say that members of
7:19 Moses' **T** couldn't accomplish
7:28 Moses' **T** designated mortals
7:28 which came after Moses' **T**,
8:10 I will put my **t** inside them,
8:10 and I will write those **t** on their
9:19 As Moses' **T** tell us,
9:22 As Moses' **T** tell us,
10:1 Moses' **T** with their yearly
10:8 that Moses' **T** require people
10:16 'I will put my **t** in their hearts
10:28 someone of rejecting Moses' **T**,
13:9 by all kinds of unfamiliar **t**.
Jas 1:25 perfect **t** that make people
1:25 they actually do what God's **t**
4:11 slander and judge God's **t**.
4:11 If you judge God's **t**,
2Pe 2:1 bring in their own destructive **t**.
2Jn 1:10 to you and doesn't bring these **t**,

tear (81)

Exo 34:13 But **t** down their altars,
Lev 1:17 pull on the bird's wings to **t**
13:56 he will **t** it out of the clothing or
Dtr 7:5 **T** down their altars,
12:3 **T** down their altars,
33:20 They can **t** off an arm or a head.
Jdg 2:2 You must **t** down their altars.'
6:25 **T** down your father's altar
8:9 I'll **t** down this tower."
2Sm 3:31 with him, "**T** your clothes,
16:9 over there and **t** off his head."
20:15 destroy the wall and **t** it down.
1Ki 11:11 I will certainly **t** the kingdom
11:12 I will **t** it away from the hands
11:13 However, I will not **t** the whole
11:31 I am going to **t** the kingdom out
2Ki 5:8 "Why did you **t** your clothes?
6:32 sent someone to **t** off my head?
Psa 7:2 Like a lion they will **t** me to
17:12 a lion eager to **t** ⌊its prey⌋ apart
27:2 Evildoers closed in on me to **t**
28:5 The LORD will **t** them down
50:22 I will **t** you to pieces,
137:7 They said, "**T** it down!
137:7 **T** it down to its foundation."
Ecc 3:3 a time to **t** down and a time to
3:7 a time to **t** apart and a time to
Isa 5:5 I will **t** away its hedge so that it
5:5 devoured and **t** down its wall
7:6 march against Judah, **t** it apart,
22:10 You will **t** down those houses
Jer 1:10 You will uproot and **t** down.
13:26 I will also **t** off your clothes,
18:7 one time I may threaten to **t** up,
24:6 them up and not **t** them down.
30:8 your necks and **t** off your ropes.
31:28 to **t** them down, and to wreck,
36:24 show any fear or **t** their clothes
42:10 you up and not **t** you down.
45:4 I will **t** down what I have built.
Eze 13:14 I will **t** down the wall that the
13:20 I will **t** them from your arms and
13:21 I will **t** off your magic veils and
16:39 and **t** down your illegal
16:39 They will **t** off your clothes,
17:9 eagle uproot it and **t** off its fruit?
19:3 He learned to **t** apart the
19:6 He learned to **t** apart the
22:25 lions who **t** their prey into
22:27 like wolves that **t** their prey into
23:34 pieces and **t** your breasts off
26:4 of Tyre and **t** down its towers.
26:12 and **t** down your delightful
Hos 10:2 God will **t** down their altars and
13:8 a wild animal I will **t** you apart.
Joe 2:13 **T** your hearts, not your clothes.
Amo 3:15 I will **t** down winter houses as
Mic 5:11 in your land and **t** down all your
Nah 1:13 off of you and **t** its chains from
Zec 11:16 fat animals and **t** off their hoofs.
Mal 1:4 but I will **t** it down.
Mat 5:29 **t** it out and throw it away.
7:6 them and then **t** you to pieces.
9:16 and the **t** will become worse.
18:9 **t** it out and throw it away.
26:61 'I can **t** down God's temple and
27:40 and said, "You were going to **t**
Mar 2:21 and the **t** will become worse.
9:47 you to lose your faith, **t** it out!
14:58 "We heard him say, 'I'll **t** down
15:29 You were going to **t** down
Luk 5:6 of fish that their nets began to **t**.
5:36 the new cloth will **t** the old.
12:18 I'll **t** down my barns and build
Jon 2:19 "**T** down this temple,
10:28 and no one will **t** them away
10:29 and no one can **t** them away
Act 23:10 afraid that they would **t** Paul

Gal 2:18 that I was wrong to **t** it down.
Rev 7:17 wipe every **t** from their eyes."
21:4 He will wipe every **t** from their

tearing (5)

Exo 28:32 all around it to keep it from **t**.
39:23 all around it to keep it from **t**.
Lev 10:6 uncombed or **t** your clothes.
21:10 uncombed or by **t** his clothes.
Isa 22:5 ⌊a day of⌋ **t** down walls and

tears (46)

Jdg 6:31 someone **t** down his altar."
6:32 "When someone **t** down Baal's
2Ki 20:5 I've seen your **t**. Now I'm going
Job 12:14 When he **t** ⌊something⌋ down,
16:20 My eyes drip ⌊with **t**⌋ to God
Psa 6:6 I soak my couch with **t**.
39:12 Do not be deaf to my **t**,
42:3 My **t** are my food day and night.
56:8 Put my **t** in your bottle.
80:5 You made them eat **t** as food.
80:5 made them drink ⌊their own⌋ **t**.
102:9 I eat ashes like bread and my **t**
116:8 You saved my eyes from **t**
119:28 I am drowning in **t**.
119:136 Streams of **t** flow from my eyes
Pro 14:1 but a stupid one **t** it down with
15:25 The LORD **t** down the house of
29:4 contributions **t** it down.
Ecc 4:1 Look at the **t** of those who
Isa 16:9 I will drench you with my **t**,
25:8 wipe away **t** from every face,
38:5 I've seen your **t**. I'm going to
61:3 oil of joy instead of ⌊**t** of⌋ grief,
Jer 9:1 were a fountain of **t** so that
9:18 Our eyes will run with **t**.
13:17 and my eyes will flow with **t**
14:17 'My eyes flow with **t** day and
31:16 and wipe away your **t**.
Lam 1:2 at night with **t** running down its
1:16 My eyes — my eyes flow with **t**.
2:11 My eyes are worn out with **t**.
2:18 Let your **t** run down like a river
3:48 "Streams of **t** run down from my
Eze 24:16 or let **t** run down your face.
Mic 5:8 it tramples ⌊its victims⌋ and **t**
Mal 2:13 cover the LORD's altar with **t**.
Luk 5:36 "No one **t** a piece of cloth from
7:38 and washed his feet with her **t**.
7:44 has washed my feet with her **t**
Act 20:19 often with **t** in my eyes.
20:31 at times with **t** in my eyes.
1Co 7:30 eyes filled with **t** should live as
2Co 2:4 In fact, I had **t** in my eyes when
Php 3:18 and now tell you with **t** in my
2Ti 1:4 I remember your **t** and want to
Heb 5:7 pleaded with loud crying and **t**,

Tebah (1)

Gen 22:24 children: **T**, Gaham, Tahash,

Tebaliah (1)

1Ch 26:11 (the second), **T** (the third),

Tebeth (1)

Est 2:16 royal palace in the month of **T**,

teeth (32)

Gen 49:12 His **t** are whiter than milk.
Job 4:10 have had their **t** knocked out.
16:9 He gritted his **t** at me.
19:20 only by the skin of my **t**.
29:17 I broke the **t** of the wicked
41:14 Its **t** are surrounded by terror.
Psa 3:7 the **t** of wicked people.
35:16 they grit their **t** at me.
37:12 one and grits his **t** at him.
57:4 Their **t** are spears and arrows.
58:6 knock the **t** out of their mouths.
58:6 Break the young lions' **t**,
112:10 grits his **t** and disappears.
124:6 not let them sink their **t** into us.
Pro 10:26 Like vinegar to the **t**,
30:14 whose **t** are like swords and
Sos 4:2 Your **t** are like a flock of sheep
Sos 6:6 Your **t** are like a flock of sheep,
Isa 41:15 with sharp, double-edged **t**.
Jer 31:29 and their children's **t** are set on
31:30 have his own **t** set on edge.
Lam 2:16 They hiss and grit their **t**.
3:16 He has ground my **t** with gravel.
Eze 18:2 and their children's **t** are set on
Dan 7:5 ribs in its mouth between its **t**.
7:7 and had large iron **t**.
7:19 very terrifying and had iron **t**
Joe 1:6 They have **t** like lions.
Zec 9:7 things from between their **t**.
Mar 9:18 at the mouth, grinds his **t**,
Rev 9:8 hair and **t** like lions' teeth.
9:8 hair and teeth like lions' **t**.

Tehinnah (1)

1Ch 4:12 the father of Paseah and **T**,

Tekoa (14)

2Sm 14:2 So Joab sent ⌊someone⌋ to **T**
14:4 The woman from **T** came to the
14:9 The woman from **T** said to the
23:26 Ira (son of Ikkesh) from **T**,
1Ch 2:24 who first settled **T**.
4:5 Ashhur, who first settled **T**,
11:28 Ira (son of Ikkesh) from **T**,
27:9 Ira, the son of Ikkesh from **T**,
2Ch 11:6 He rebuilt Bethlehem, Etam, **T**,
20:20 and went to the desert of **T**.
Neh 3:5 the men from **T** made repairs.
3:27 After him the men from **T**
Jer 6:1 Blow the ram's horn in **T**.
Amo 1:1 of the sheep farmers from **T**.

Tel Abib (1)

Eze 3:15 I went to **T**, to the exiles

Telah (1)

1Ch 7:25 Resheph's son was **T**.

Telah's (1)

1Ch 7:25 **T** son was Tahan.

Telaim (2)

1Sm 15:4 and he counted them at **T**:
27:8 territory which extends from **T**

Telassar (2)

2Ki 19:12 people of Eden who were in **T**?
Isa 37:12 people of Eden who were in **T**?

Telem (2)

Jos 15:24 Ziph, **T**, Bealoth,
Ezr 10:24 Shallum, **T**, and Uri

Tel Harsha (2)

Ezr 2:59 from Tel Melah, **T**, Cherub,
Neh 7:61 from Tel Melah, **T**, Cherub,

tell (718)

Gen 12:18 "Why didn't you **t** me that she's
20:5 Didn't he **t** me himself,
21:26 You didn't **t** me, and I didn't
24:23 Please **t** me whether there is
24:30 wrists and heard her **t** what
24:49 **T** me whether or not you're
26:2 Stay where I **t** you.
27:8 and do what I **t** you.
29:15 **T** me what your wages should
31:27 You didn't even **t** me you were
32:5 to **t** you ⌊this news⌋
32:29 "Please **t** me your name."
34:12 I'll pay exactly what you **t** me.
37:16 Please **t** me where they're
40:8 "but there's no one to **t** us what
40:8 who can **t** what they mean?"
40:8 "Why don't you **t** me all about
41:8 but no one could **t** him what
41:15 and no one can **t** me what it
41:21 no one could **t** they had eaten
41:24 but no one could **t** me what it
42:22 Reuben said to them, "Didn't I **t**
45:13 **T** my father how greatly
46:31 "I'm going to Pharaoh to **t** him,
49:1 and let me **t** you what will
Gen 50:4 directly to Pharaoh. **T** him,
Exo 3:13 What should I **t** them?"
4:15 You will speak to him and **t**
4:22 Then **t** Pharaoh, 'This is what
6:6 "**T** the Israelites, 'I am the
6:11 "Go **t** Pharaoh (the king of
6:29 **T** Pharaoh (the king of Egypt)
6:29 of Egypt) everything I **t** you."
7:2 **T** your brother Aaron
7:2 and he must **t** Pharaoh to let
7:9 that God has sent you,' **t** Aaron,
7:16 the Hebrews sent me to **t** you,
7:19 said to Moses, "**T** Aaron,
8:1 "Go to Pharaoh, and **t** him,
8:5 said to Moses, "**T** Aaron,
8:16 said to Moses, "**T** Aaron,
9:1 "Go to Pharaoh, and **t** him,
10:2 You will be able to **t** your
12:3 **T** the whole community of
13:8 On that day **t** your children,
13:14 you what this means, **t** them,
14:2 "**T** the Israelites to go back and
14:12 Didn't we **t** you in Egypt,
14:15 **T** the Israelites to start moving.
16:9 Moses said to Aaron, "**T** the
16:12 **T** them, 'At dusk you will eat
18:16 and I **t** them God's laws and
18:20 and **t** them what to do.
19:3 of Jacob. **T** the Israelites,
19:10 and **t** them they have two days
19:12 and **t** them not to go up the
25:2 "**T** the Israelites to choose
28:3 "**T** all those who have the skill
33:5 to Moses, "**T** the Israelites,
Lev 1:2 "**T** the Israelites: If any of you
4:2 "**T** the Israelites: If a person
5:1 oath and won't **t** what you saw
6:25 "**T** Aaron and his sons:
7:23 "**T** the Israelites: Never eat any
7:29 "**T** the Israelites: Anyone who
9:3 Also **t** the Israelites:
11:2 "**T** the Israelites: Here are the
12:2 "**T** the Israelites: When a
14:35 of that house must come and **t**
15:2 "**T** the Israelites: If a man has a
16:2 The LORD said, "**T** your
17:2 "**T** Aaron, his sons, and all the
17:8 "**T** them: If Israelites or
18:2 "**T** the Israelites: I am the
19:2 "**T** the whole congregation of
20:2 "**T** the Israelites: If Israelites or
21:1 "**T** the priests, Aaron's sons:
21:17 "**T** Aaron: If any of your
22:2 "**T** Aaron and his sons that
22:3 "**T** them: In future generations if
22:18 "**T** Aaron, his sons, and all the
23:2 "**T** the Israelites: These are the
23:10 "**T** the Israelites: When you
23:24 "**T** the Israelites: On the first
23:34 "**T** the Israelites: The fifteenth
24:15 "Also **t** the Israelites:
25:2 "**T** the Israelites: When you
27:2 "**T** the Israelites: If any of you
Num 4:19 place and **t** each man what
4:32 **T** each man by name the
5:6 "**T** the Israelites: If you do
5:12 to the Israelites and **t** them:
5:29 They **t** you what to do when a
5:30 They also **t** you what to do
5:30 these instructions **t** him to do.
6:2 to the Israelites and **t** them:
6:23 "**T** Aaron and his sons,
8:2 "Speak to Aaron and **t** him:
9:9 to Moses, "**T** the Israelites:
11:18 **T** the people to get ready for
14:14 What if the Egyptians **t** the
14:28 So **t** them, 'As I live,
15:2 to the Israelites and **t** them:
15:18 to the Israelites and **t** them:
15:38 to the Israelites and **t** them:
16:24 "**T** the community:
16:37 "**T** Eleazar, son of the priest
18:30 "Also **t** them: When you
19:2 **T** the Israelites to bring you a
20:8 **t** the rock to give up its water.
22:19 the LORD may have to **t** me."

Num 22:20 but do only what I **t** you."
22:35 but say only what I **t** you."
23:3 I will **t** you whatever he reveals
23:26 Balaam answered, "Didn't I **t**
24:14 I'll **t** you what these people will
25:12 So **t** Phinehas that I'm making
27:8 "**T** the Israelites: If a man dies
33:51 "**T** the Israelites, 'You will be
35:2 "**T** the Israelites to give the
35:10 "**T** the Israelites: When you
Dtr 1:3 had commanded him to **t** them.
1:42 "**T** them, 'Don't go and fight,
5:5 the LORD and you to **t** you
5:27 Then **t** us whatever the LORD
5:30 "**T** the people to go back to
6:21 **T** them, "We were Pharaoh's
17:10 Do what they **t** you.
17:11 and do what they **t** you to do in
17:11 Do exactly what they **t** you to
18:18 He will **t** them everything I
20:3 He should **t** them, "Listen,
20:5 The officers should **t** the troops,
20:8 should also **t** the troops,
22:16 girl's father will **t** the leaders,
26:3 serving at that time, and **t** him,
30:18 If you do, I **t** you today that you
32:7 and your leaders to **t** you.
33:27 out of your way and **t** you
Jos 1:11 **T** the people, 'Get your
1:16 "We'll do everything you **t** us
2:14 If you don't **t** anyone what we're
2:17 if you **t** anyone what we're
2:20 If you **t** anyone what we're
4:10 LORD had ordered Joshua to **t**
5:14 what do you want to **t** me?"
6:10 out of your mouth until I **t** you
7:13 **T** the people, 'Get ready for
7:19 **T** me what you have done.
9:11 **T** them, "We're at your mercy.
20:2 "**T** the people of Israel,
Jdg 4:20 a man around here, **t** them no."
9:29 I would **t** him, 'Get yourself a
12:6 they would **t** him, "Say the
13:6 woman went to **t** her husband.
13:6 and he didn't **t** me his name.
13:10 ran quickly to **t** her husband.
14:6 He didn't **t** his parents what he
14:9 He didn't **t** them he had scraped
14:12 "Let me **t** you a riddle.
14:13 responded, "**T** us your riddle!
14:16 friends a riddle and didn't **t** me
14:16 so why should I **t** you?"
16:6 "Please **t** me what makes you
16:10 **t** me how you can be tied up."
16:13 **T** me how you can be tied up."
20:3 The people of Israel said, "**T**
20:7 **t** me what you think.
21:22 to us to complain, we'll **t** them,
Rut 4:4 to buy back the property, **t** me.
1Sm 3:15 But Samuel was afraid to **t** Eli
3:17 "What did the LORD **t** you?"
4:13 went into the city to **t** the news.
4:14 went quickly to **t** Eli the news.
6:2 **T** us how to return it to its
8:9 but be sure to warn them and **t**
9:6 Maybe he'll **t** us which way we
9:8 Then he'll **t** us where to find the
9:18 "Please **t** me where the seer's
9:19 let you go after I **t** you all that's
9:27 and I will **t** you God's word."
10:2 They'll **t** you, 'We've found the
10:8 days until I come to **t** you what
10:15 Saul's uncle said, "Please **t** me
10:16 But Saul didn't **t** him what
14:1 But Jonathan didn't **t** his father
14:34 and **t** them, 'Each of you,
14:43 "**T** me," Saul asked Jonathan.
15:16 "and let me **t** you what the
18:22 **T** him, 'The king likes you,
18:25 Saul replied, "**T** David,
19:3 If I find out anything, I'll **t** you."
20:6 father really misses me, **t** him,
20:10 Then David asked, "Who will **t**
20:12 then I will send someone to **t**
20:13 to harm you and I fail to **t** you
20:21 Now, if I **t** the boy,
1Sm 20:22 But if I **t** the boy, 'The arrows
22:22 he would be certain to **t** Saul.
23:11 God of Israel, please **t** me."
25:8 and let them **t** you.
25:19 But she didn't **t** her husband
25:36 so she didn't **t** him anything
26:19 serve other gods,' they **t** me.
27:11 He thought, "They could **t**
28:15 So I've called on you to **t** me
31:9 Philistine territory to **t**
2Sm 1:4 "Please **t** me." The man
1:20 Don't **t** the news in Gath.
3:19 to **t** him everything Israel
7:11 I, the LORD, **t** you that I will
11:5 So she sent someone to **t**
12:18 were afraid to **t** him that
12:18 How can we **t** him the child is
12:27 he sent messengers to **t** David,
13:4 Won't you **t** me?" "I'm in love
13:28 wine, I'll **t** you, 'Attack Amnon.'
14:3 to the king, and **t** him this ...."
14:32 "I sent someone to **t** you to
15:13 Someone came to **t** David,
15:35 **t** it to the priests Zadok and
17:6 do what he says? If not, **t** us."
17:16 messengers quickly to **t** David,
17:17 girl was to go and **t** them,
17:17 were to go and **t** King David.
17:19 that no one could **t** it was there.
18:21 **t** the king what you saw."
18:25 "he has good news to **t**."
19:13 And **t** Amasa, 'Aren't you my
19:35 How can I **t** what is pleasant
20:16 **T** Joab to come here so that I
24:12 "Go and **t** David, 'This is what
1Ki 1:20 to **t** them who should succeed
3:9 I can judge your people and **t**
12:10 is what you should **t** them:
14:3 He will **t** you what will happen
14:7 **T** Jeroboam, 'This is what the
18:8 "**T** your master that Elijah is
18:11 "Now you say, '**T** your master
18:12 I'll **t** Ahab, but he won't be able
18:14 Now you say that I should **t** my
18:16 So Obadiah went to **t** Ahab.
18:44 Elijah said, "Go and **t** Ahab,
20:9 messengers, "**T** His Majesty,
21:19 **T** him, 'This is what the LORD
21:19 Then **t** him, 'This is what the
22:14 I will **t** him whatever the LORD
22:16 LORD's name to **t** me nothing
22:18 "Didn't I **t** you he wouldn't
22:23 a spirit that makes them **t** lies.
2Ki 1:6 **T** him, 'This is what the LORD
2:18 "Didn't I **t** you not to go?"
4:2 **T** me, what do you have in
4:24 Don't slow down unless I **t**
6:11 "Won't you **t** me who among us
8:4 He said, "Please **t** me about all
8:10 "**T** him that he will get better,
9:5 "I have something to **t** you,
9:12 Please **t** us." Jehu replied, "We
10:5 We'll do everything you **t** us.
18:19 He said to them, "**T** Hezekiah,
18:22 Suppose you **t** me,
18:27 "Did my master send me to **t**
19:10 "**T** King Hezekiah of Judah,
22:15 **T** the man who sent you to me,
22:18 ⌊Huldah added,⌋ "But **t** Judah's
1Ch 10:9 Philistine territory to **t** their
16:24 **T** people about his glory.
16:24 **T** all the nations about his
17:10 I even **t** you that I, the LORD,
21:10 "Go and **t** David, 'This is what
21:18 Messenger told Gad to **t** David
2Ch 10:10 is what you should **t** them:
18:13 I will **t** him whatever my God
18:15 LORD's name to **t** me nothing
18:17 "Didn't I **t** you he wouldn't
18:22 a spirit that makes them **t** lies.
34:23 **T** the man who sent you to me,
34:26 ⌊Huldah added,⌋ "**T** Judah's
Ezr 8:17 I told them to **t** Iddo and his
10:3 what Moses' Teachings **t** us.
Neh 2:7 In the letters **t** them to grant me
4:14 and proceeded to **t** the nobles,
Neh 6:3 I sent messengers to **t** them,
6:8 Then I sent someone to **t** him,
Job 1:15 one who has escaped to **t** you."
1:16 one who has escaped to **t** you."
1:17 one who has escaped to **t** you."
1:19 one who has escaped to **t** you."
4:16 I couldn't **t** what it was.
6:30 or is my mouth unable to **t** the
11:6 He would **t** you the secrets of
12:7 and they will **t** you.
15:17 "I'll **t** you; listen to me! I'll relate
15:18 I'll **t** you what wise people
21:31 Who will **t** him to his face how
31:37 I would **t** him the number of my
32:6 and was afraid to **t** you what
32:10 Let me **t** you what I know.'
32:17 I'll **t** you what I know.
33:23 to **t** people what is right for
34:33 **T** me what you know.
36:23 Who can **t** him which way he
38:4 **T** me if you have ⌊such⌋
38:18 **T** me, if you know all of this!
Psa 5:6 You destroy those who **t** lies.
9:1 I will **t** about all the miracles
22:22 I will **t** my people about your
22:31 They will **t** people yet to be
26:7 and **t** about all your
30:9 Will it **t** about your truth?"
35:28 Then my tongue will **t** about
40:5 I will **t** others about your
41:6 ⌊Then⌋ he leaves to **t** others.
48:13 you can **t** the next generation,
50:12 were hungry, I would not **t** you,
51:15 mouth will **t** about your praise.
66:16 and I will **t** you what he has
71:15 My mouth will **t** about your
71:18 Let me live to **t** the people of
71:18 to **t** about your power to all who
71:24 My tongue will **t** about your
78:4 We will **t** the next generation
78:6 will grow up and **t** their children
88:11 Will anyone **t** about your mercy
89:1 I will **t** about your faithfulness
96:3 **T** people about his glory.
96:3 **T** all the nations about his
97:6 The heavens **t** about his
107:22 Let them **t** in joyful songs what
118:17 die, but I will live and **t** what
142:2 and **t** him my troubles.
145:6 I will **t** about your greatness.
145:11 glory of your kingdom and will **t**
Pro 3:28 do not **t** your neighbor,
Ecc 6:12 Who will **t** them about their
8:7 So who can **t** them how things
Sos 1:7 Please **t** me, you whom I love,
1:7 ⌊**T** me,⌋ or I will be considered
5:8 find my beloved you will **t** him
Isa 3:10 **T** the righteous that blessings
5:5 Now then, let me **t** you what I
6:9 "Go and **t** these people,
14:32 ⌊**T** them that⌋ the LORD has
19:11 How can you **t** Pharaoh,
19:12 Let them **t** you. Let them explain
30:10 'Don't have visions that **t** us
30:10 **T** us what we want to hear.
35:4 **T** those who are terrified,
36:4 He said to them, "**T** Hezekiah,
36:7 Suppose you **t** me,
36:12 "Did my master send me to **t**
37:10 "**T** King Hezekiah of Judah,
40:9 **T** the good news! Call out with
40:9 **T** the good news! Raise your
40:9 **T** the cities of Judah:
41:22 ⌊your idols⌋ so they can **t**
41:22 **T** us about future events.
41:23 **T** us what's going to happen so
41:27 I was the first to **t** Zion,
44:7 Let him **t** me what happened
48:20 Shout for joy as you **t** it and
57:12 I'll **t** you about your righteous
58:1 **T** my people about their
62:11 "**T** my people Zion,
66:19 They will **t** about my glory
Jer 1:17 and say to them whatever I **t**
5:20 "**T** this to the descendants of
7:22 I did not **t** them anything about

Jer	7:23	But I did **t** them this,
	10:11	**T** them this: These gods will
	11:2	and **t** them to the people of
	14:14	up the visions they **t** you.
	16:10	"When you **t** the people all
	17:20	**T** everyone: "Listen to the word
	23:17	for you."' They **t** all who live
	23:27	They **t** each other the dreams
	23:28	a dream should **t** his dream.
	23:32	"They **t** the dreams they made
	26:2	**T** them everything that I
	26:2	that I command you to **t** them.
	27:9	or sorcerers who **t** you that
	27:14	prophets who **t** you that you'll
	27:16	to the prophets who **t** you that
	28:13	"**T** Hananiah, 'This is what the
	30:2	a book everything that I **t** you.
	31:10	**T** it to the distant islands.
	33:3	I will **t** you great and
	34:2	and **t** him, 'The LORD says:
	35:13	**T** the people of Judah and
	36:16	must **t** the king everything."
	36:17	"Please **t** us how you wrote all
	38:25	**T** us what you said to the king
	42:3	Let the LORD your God **t** us
	42:4	and I will **t** you everything the
	42:20	and **t** us everything that the
	42:21	your God sent me to **t** you.
	43:1	their God sent him to **t** them.
	43:2	our God didn't send you to **t**
	44:4	again and again to **t** you not
	46:14	"**T** this in Egypt; announce this
	48:20	**T** the news in Arnon that Moab
	50:28	are coming to Zion to **t** about
	51:27	**T** the kingdoms of Ararat,
Eze	2:4	**T** them, 'This is what the
	3:11	they listen or not, **t** them,
	3:18	Suppose I **t** you that wicked
	3:27	You will **t** them, 'This is what
	11:16	"So **t** them, 'This is what the
	11:17	"So **t** them, 'This is what the
	12:10	"**T** them, 'This is what the
	12:11	"**T** them, 'I am your warning
	12:19	"**T** the people of this land,
	12:23	"**T** the people, 'This is what
	12:23	Instead, **t** them, 'The time is
	12:28	"**T** them, 'This is what the
	13:2	**T** those who make up their
	13:11	**T** those who cover up the wall
	13:18	"**T** them, 'This is what the
	14:4	**T** them, 'This is what the
	14:6	"So **t** the nation of Israel,
	16:3	**T** them, 'This is what the
	17:2	"Son of man, **t** this riddle.
	17:9	"**T** the nation of Israel,
	17:12	**T** them, 'The king of Babylon
	20:3	**T** them, 'This is what the
	20:4	**T** them about the disgusting
	20:5	**T** them, 'This is what the
	20:27	**T** them, 'This is what the
	20:30	"**T** the nation of Israel,
	20:47	**T** the forest in the Negev,
	21:3	**T** the land of Israel,
	21:9	**T** them, 'This is what the Lord
	21:28	**T** them, 'This is what the
	22:2	Then **t** it about all the
	22:3	**T** it, 'This is what the Almighty
	22:24	"Son of man, **t** the city,
	23:36	Oholibah and **t** them about their
	24:3	**T** these rebellious people a
	24:3	**T** them, 'This is what the
	24:19	The people asked me, "**T** us,
	24:21	'**T** the nation of Israel,
	24:26	come to you to **t** you the news.
	25:3	**T** the Ammonites, 'Listen to the
	28:2	"Son of man, **t** the ruler of Tyre,
	28:12	**T** him, 'This is what the
	28:22	**T** it, 'This is what the Almighty
	29:3	**T** him, 'This is what the
	32:2	**T** him, 'You think you are like a
	32:19	"**T** them, 'Are you more
	33:2	**T** them, 'Suppose I bring war
	33:11	"**T** them, 'As I live,
	33:25	So **t** them, 'This is what the
	33:27	"**T** them, 'This is what the
	34:2	**T** them, 'This is what the
Eze	35:3	**T** it, 'This is what the Almighty
	36:1	**T** them, 'Mountains of Israel,
	36:6	**T** the mountains and hills and
	36:22	"So **t** the people of Israel,
	37:4	**T** them, 'Dry bones, listen to
	37:9	**T** the breath, 'This is what the
	37:12	**T** them, 'This is what the
	37:18	'**T** us what you mean by this.'
	37:21	"Then **t** them, 'This is what the
	38:3	**T** him, 'This is what the
	38:14	**T** Gog, 'This is what the
	38:19	In my fiery anger I **t** you this.
	39:1	**T** it, 'This is what the Almighty
	39:17	**T** every kind of bird and every
	40:4	**T** the nation of Israel
	43:11	**T** them about all its rules and
	44:5	to everything I'm going to **t** you.
	44:6	**T** the rebellious people of
	44:23	must show the people how to **t**
Dan	2:2	so that they could **t** him what
	2:4	**T** us the dream, and we'll
	2:5	If you don't **t** me the dream and
	2:6	But if you **t** me the dream and
	2:6	Now **t** me the dream and its
	2:7	"Your Majesty, **t** us the dream,
	2:7	and we'll **t** you its meaning."
	2:9	If you don't **t** me the dream,
	2:9	So **t** me the dream.
	2:10	"No one on earth can **t** the king
	2:11	No one can **t** what you
	2:26	"Can you **t** me the dream I had
	2:27	or fortuneteller can **t** the king
	2:28	He will **t** King Nebuchadnezzar
	2:36	Now we'll **t** you its meaning.
	4:6	to be brought to me to **t** me
	4:7	they couldn't **t** me its meaning.
	4:9	**T** me the meaning of the
	4:18	Now you, Belteshazzar, **t** me
	4:18	advisers in my kingdom can't **t**
	5:8	couldn't read the writing or **t**
	5:12	Now, call Daniel, and he will **t**
	5:15	writing and **t** me its meaning.
	5:15	they couldn't **t** me its meaning.
	5:16	If you can read the writing and **t**
	5:17	for you and **t** you its meaning.
	7:16	there and asked him to **t** me
	8:19	He said, "I will **t** you what will
	10:19	**t** me what you came to say.
	10:21	However, I will **t** you what is
	11:2	"What I am about to **t** you is the
	11:27	sit at the same table and **t** lies.
Hos	2:2	**T** her to stop acting like a
	2:2	**T** her to remove the lovers from
	7:3	happy with the lies they **t**.
	7:13	but they **t** lies about me.
Joe	1:3	**T** your children about it.
	1:3	your children **t** their children.
	1:3	grandchildren **t** their children.
Jnh	1:8	They asked him, "**T** us,
	4:11	These people couldn't **t** their
Mic	3:8	So I will **t** the descendants
	3:11	Your prophets **t** the future for
Zep	3:13	Israel will not do wrong, **t** lies,
Zec	1:3	**T** the people, 'This is what the
	7:5	"**T** all the people of the land
	9:12	Today I **t** you that I will return
Mat	2:13	Stay there until I **t** you,
	4:3	**t** these stones to become
	4:17	Jesus began to **t** people,
	5:34	But I **t** you don't swear an oath
	5:39	But I **t** you not to oppose an
	5:44	But I **t** you this: Love your
	6:25	"So I **t** you to stop worrying
	7:23	Then I will **t** them publicly,
	8:4	"Don't **t** anyone about this!
	8:9	I **t** one of them, 'Go!' and he
	8:9	I **t** my servant, 'Do this!' and he
	10:27	**T** in the daylight what I say to
	10:33	But I will **t** my Father in heaven
	11:4	and **t** John what you hear and
	11:9	Let me **t** you that he is far more
	12:16	He also ordered them not to **t**
	13:3	to **t** them many things.
	13:30	When the grain is cut, I will **t**
	13:34	Jesus used illustrations to **t** the
	13:34	He did not **t** them anything
Mat	13:35	I will **t** what has been hidden
	14:12	Then they went to **t** Jesus.
	16:20	disciples not to **t** anyone that
	17:9	"Don't **t** anyone what you have
	18:17	If he ignores these witnesses, **t**
	18:22	Jesus answered him, "I **t** you,
	21:3	**t** him that the Lord needs them.
	21:5	"**T** the people of Zion,
	21:24	If you answer it for me, I'll **t** you
	21:27	Jesus told them, "Then I won't **t**
	22:4	He sent other servants to **t** the
	22:16	we know that you **t** the truth
	22:17	So **t** us what you think.
	23:3	to do everything they **t** you.
	24:3	"**T** us, when will this happen?
	26:18	and **t** him that the teacher says,
	26:63	front of the living God and **t** us,
	26:68	a prophet, **t** us who hit you."
	28:7	Then go quickly, and **t** his
	28:8	joy and ran to **t** his disciples.
	28:10	**t** my followers to go to Galilee.
Mar	1:30	did was to **t** Jesus about her.
	1:44	"Don't **t** anyone about this!
	3:12	He gave them orders not to **t**
	5:19	and **t** them how much the Lord
	5:20	He began to **t** how much Jesus
	7:36	the people not to **t** anyone.
	8:30	them not to **t** anyone about him.
	9:9	Jesus ordered them not to **t**
	10:32	He began to **t** them what was
	11:24	That's why I **t** you to have faith
	11:29	Answer me, and then I'll **t** you
	11:33	Jesus told them, "Then I won't **t**
	12:14	we know that you **t** the truth.
	13:4	"**T** us, when will this happen?
	14:14	When he goes into a house, **t**
	16:7	Go and **t** his disciples and
	16:15	and **t** everyone the Good News.
Luk	1:19	God sent me to **t** you this good
	4:3	**t** this stone to become a loaf of
	4:18	He has anointed me to **t** the
	4:43	But he said to them, "I have to **t**
	5:14	ordered him, "Don't **t** anyone.
	6:27	"But I **t** everyone who is
	6:46	Lord but don't do what I **t** you?
	7:6	officer sent friends to **t** Jesus,
	7:8	I **t** one of them, 'Go!' and he
	7:8	I **t** my servant, 'Do this!' and he
	7:22	and **t** John what you have seen
	7:26	Let me **t** you that he is far more
	8:39	"Go home to your family, and **t**
	8:56	Jesus ordered them not to **t**
	9:21	them not to **t** this to anyone.
	9:60	You must go everywhere and **t**
	9:61	let me **t** my family goodbye."
	10:9	that are there, and **t** the people,
	10:40	by myself? **T** her to help me."
	11:9	"So I **t** you to ask, and you will
	12:9	people who **t** others that they
	12:13	**t** my brother to give me my
	12:22	"So I **t** you to stop worrying
	13:27	But he will **t** you, 'I don't know
	13:32	Jesus said to them, "**T** that fox
	14:10	comes, he will **t** you, 'Friend,
	14:17	he sent his servant to **t** those
	17:7	Does he **t** his servant when he
	19:39	**t** your disciples to be quiet."
	20:2	They asked him, "**T** us,
	20:3	have a question for you. **T** me,
	20:8	Jesus told them, "Then I won't **t**
	22:11	**T** the owner of the house that
	22:64	"**T** us who hit you."
	22:67	"**T** us, are you the Messiah?"
	22:67	Jesus said to them, "If I **t** you,
Jon	1:22	**T** us so that we can take an
	2:25	and didn't need anyone to **t** him
	3:7	Don't be surprised when I **t** you
	3:12	If you don't believe me when I **t**
	3:12	me when I **t** you about things
	4:25	he will **t** us everything."
	8:26	So I **t** the world exactly what
	8:45	me because I **t** the truth.
	9:36	The man replied, "Sir, **t** me
	10:24	are the Messiah, **t** us plainly."
	11:3	sent a messenger to **t** Jesus,
	11:40	Jesus said to her, "Didn't I **t**

Jon 11:57 was should **t** them so that
14:28 You heard me **t** you,
16:4 I didn't **t** you this at first,
16:12 "I have a lot more to **t** you,
16:13 and will **t** you about things
16:14 because he will **t** you what I
16:15 take what I say and **t** it to you.'
18:23 wrong, **t** me what it was.
18:34 or did others **t** you about me?"
20:15 **t** me where you have put him,
20:17 brothers and sisters and **t** them,
Act 2:11 own languages as they **t** about
2:29 "Brothers, I can **t** you
4:17 Let's **t** them that they must
5:8 So Peter asked her, "**T** me,
5:20 and **t** the people everything
9:13 I've heard a lot of people **t**
12:17 He added, "**T** James and the
15:12 Barnabas and Paul **t** about all
16:10 that God had called us to **t**
17:19 "Could you **t** us these new
17:21 looked for opportunities to **t**
18:27 disciples in Greece to **t** them
21:4 The Spirit had the disciples **t**
21:21 They claim that you **t** them not
22:15 and will **t** everyone what you
22:27 to Paul and asked him, "**T** me,
23:11 Now you must **t** the truth about
23:17 He has something to **t** him."
23:18 he has something to **t** you."
23:19 "What do you have to **t** me?"
23:22 him not to **t** this information
24:20 are accusing me should **t** what
26:22 I **t** them only what the prophets
Rom 1:15 That's why I'm eager to **t** you
2:22 As you **t** others not to commit
3:21 and the Prophets **t** us this.
10:15 How can people **t** the Good
15:18 I'm bold enough to **t** you only
16:25 message I **t** about Jesus Christ.
1Co 5:10 I didn't **t** you that you could not
11:26 you **t** about the Lord's death
12:10 Another can **t** the difference
14:7 how can a person **t** what tune
2Co 2:16 is qualified to **t** about Christ?
4:3 So if the Good News that we **t**
5:19 relationships to **t** others.
9:2 I **t** them, "The people of Greece
11:4 whom we didn't **t** you about,
Gal 1:16 He did this so that I would **t**
2:7 as Peter had been entrusted to **t**
4:21 laws should **t** me something.
Eph 4:17 So I **t** you and encourage you
6:21 He will **t** you everything that is
Php 1:15 Some people **t** the message
1:15 Others **t** the message about
1:16 Those who **t** the message
1:17 They **t** the message about
3:18 I have often told you, and now **t**
Col 2:18 of angels **t** you that you
2:20 why do you let others **t** you
2:21 People will **t** you, Don't taste or
4:3 the word so that we may **t**
4:7 He will **t** you everything that is
4:9 They will **t** you about
4:17 **T** Archippus to complete all the
1Th 2:2 the courage to **t** you his Good
1Ti 4:7 myths that old women like to **t**.
5:10 People should **t** about the good
6:17 **T** those who have the riches of
6:18 **T** them to do good,
2Ti 1:8 So never be ashamed to **t**
2:8 This is the Good News that I **t**
4:3 teachers who **t** them what they
Tit 2:1 **T** believers to live the kind of
2:2 **T** older men to be sober.
2:2 **T** them to be men of good
2:3 **T** older women to live their
2:3 **T** them not to be gossips or
2:5 Also, **t** them to teach young
2:9 **T** slaves who are believers to
2:9 **T** them to please their masters,
2:10 Instead, **t** slaves to show their
2:15 **T** these things to the believers.
Heb 2:12 He says, "I will **t** my people
9:19 As Moses' Teachings **t** us,
Heb 9:22 As Moses' Teachings **t** us,
11:32 I don't have enough time to **t**
1Pe 2:9 You were chosen to **t** about the
1Jn 4:6 That's how we can **t** the Spirit
Rev 17:7 I will **t** you the mystery of the

telling (72)

Gen 31:20 Laban the Aramean by not **t** him
42:16 We'll see if you're **t** the truth.
42:20 that you've been **t** the truth.
43:6 you made trouble for me by **t**
44:5 that he uses for **t** the future?
Exo 23:7 Avoid **t** lies. Don't kill innocent
33:12 "You've been **t** me to lead
Num 4:27 You are in charge of **t** them
Dtr 5:1 listen to the laws and rules I'm **t**
Jdg 7:13 he heard a man **t** his friend a
16:10 making fun of me by **t** me lies.
16:13 making fun of me by **t** me lies.
1Sm 20:2 does nothing without **t** me,
2Sm 11:19 "When you finish **t** the king
1Ki 1:27 without **t** me who would
2Ki 7:9 and we're not **t** anyone about it.
8:5 While Gehazi was **t** the king
Neh 2:12 men without **t** anyone what my
Jer 14:14 the lies that the prophets are **t**
38:4 people by **t** them such things.
38:20 LORD by doing what I'm **t** you.
43:1 So Jeremiah finished **t** all the
Eze 20:49 say that I'm only **t** stories."
Mat 14:4 John had been **t** Herod,
Mar 1:4 in the desert **t** people about
2:11 "I'm **t** you to get up,
5:41 I'm **t** you to get up!"
6:18 John had been **t** Herod,
13:37 I'm **t** everyone what I'm telling
13:37 telling everyone what I'm **t** you:
Luk 7:14 I'm **t** you to come back to life!"
7:47 That's why I'm **t** you that her
16:9 Jesus continued, "I'm **t** you
16:16 people have been **t** the Good
20:1 the temple courtyard and **t** them
Jon 4:35 I'm **t** you to look and see that
5:34 I'm **t** you this to save you.
8:46 If I'm **t** the truth, why don't you
13:19 I'm **t** you now before it happens.
13:29 thought that Jesus was **t** him
13:33 I'm **t** you what I told the Jews.
14:10 What I'm **t** you doesn't come
14:29 "I'm **t** you this now before it
16:7 However, I am **t** you the truth:
16:26 I'm **t** you that I won't have to
19:35 and he knows that he is **t** the
Act 5:42 refused to stop teaching and **t**
11:7 I also heard a voice **t** me,
13:32 We are **t** you the Good News:
13:38 "So, brothers, I'm **t** you that
15:20 we should write a letter **t** them
16:16 for her owners by **t** fortunes.
16:17 They're **t** you how you can be
17:18 things because Paul was **t**
17:23 I'm **t** you about the unknown
20:20 I didn't avoid **t** you anything
20:27 I didn't avoid **t** you the whole
Rom 9:1 a Christian, I'm **t** you the truth.
1Co 4:15 in the Christian life by **t** you
15:51 I'm **t** you a mystery.
2Co 11:4 When someone comes to you **t**
11:7 I humbled myself by **t** you
12:6 Instead, I would be **t** the truth.
Gal 1:9 I'm now **t** you again what we've
2:7 that I had been entrusted with **t**
4:16 your enemy for **t** you the truth?
5:21 the past and I'm **t** you again that
Col 1:25 me the work of **t** you his entire
1Th 2:16 keep us from **t** people who are
4:15 We are **t** you what the Lord
1Ti 2:7 I'm **t** you the truth. I'm not lying.
1Jn 5:16 I'm not **t** you to pray about that.

tells (47)

Gen 41:55 Do what he **t** you!"
Lev 8:35 and serve as the LORD **t** you.
16:34 "This permanent law **t** you how
Num 22:8 to you what the LORD **t** me."
22:38 say what God **t** me to say."
Num 23:12 what the LORD **t** me to say."
23:19 He **t** no lies. He is not like
Dtr 5:27 the LORD our God **t** you.
1Ki 22:14 him whatever the LORD **t** me."
22:22 be a spirit that **t** lies through
2Ki 6:12 Elisha, the prophet in Israel, **t**
2Ch 18:21 be a spirit that **t** lies through
Job 36:9 he **t** them what they've done
Psa 19:2 One day **t** a story to the next.
101:7 The one who **t** lies will not
Pro 14:25 one who **t** lies is dangerous.
19:5 One who **t** lies will not escape.
19:9 One who **t** lies will die.
20:19 around as a gossip **t** secrets.
23:7 does: He **t** you, "Eat and drink,"
Isa 52:7 and **t** Zion that its God rules as
Jer 42:5 the LORD your God **t** us to do.
Dan 5:7 writing and **t** me its meaning
Hos 4:12 A piece of wood **t** them what to
Mat 10:33 the person who **t** others that
15:5 But you say that whoever **t** his
24:23 don't believe anyone who **t** you,
24:26 So if someone **t** you,
Mar 7:11 But you say, 'If a person **t** his
13:21 don't believe anyone who **t** you,
Luk 17:8 Instead, he **t** his servant,
Jon 2:5 "Do whatever he **t** you."
3:32 and **t** what he has seen and
8:44 Whenever he **t** a lie,
16:17 He **t** us that in a little while we
16:17 Then he **t** us that in a little
Act 3:22 Listen to everything he **t** you.
19:26 He **t** people that gods made by
20:32 to his message that **t** how kind
Rom 10:14 if no one **t** the Good News?
2Co 8:18 the way he **t** the Good News.
11:4 When someone **t** you good
Gal 1:8 Whoever **t** you good news that
1:9 If anyone **t** you good news that
Heb 10:15 The Holy Spirit **t** us the same
Jas 2:16 and one of you **t** that person,
Rev 13:14 It **t** those living on earth to

Tel Melah (2)

Ezr 2:59 people came from **T**, Tel Harsha
Neh 7:61 people came from **T**, Tel Harsha

Tema (5)

Gen 25:15 Hadad, **T**, Jetur, Naphish,
1Ch 1:30 Dumah, Massa, Hadad, **T**,
Job 6:19 Caravans from **T** look for them.
Isa 21:14 you inhabitants of the land of **T**.
Jer 25:23 Dedan, **T**, Buz, and all who

Temah (2)

Ezr 2:53 Barkos, Sisera, **T**,
Neh 7:55 Barkos, Sisera, **T**,

Teman (18)

Gen 36:11 The sons of Eliphaz were **T**,
36:15 were **T**, Omar, Zepho, Kenaz,
36:42 Kenaz, **T**, Mibzar,
1Ch 1:36 sons were **T** and Omar,
1:53 Kenaz, **T**, Mibzar,
Job 2:11 from his home — Eliphaz of **T**,
4:1 from **T** replied to Job,
15:1 from **T** replied to Job,
22:1 from **T** replied to Job,
42:7 LORD said to Eliphaz from **T**,
42:9 Then Eliphaz of **T**,
Jer 49:7 no longer any wisdom in **T**?
49:20 to do to those who live in **T**.
49:20 of the people who live in **T**.
Eze 25:13 land into ruins from **T** to Dedan.
Amo 1:12 I will send a fire on **T** and burn
Oba 1:9 "**T**, your warriors will be
Hab 3:3 God comes from **T**.

Temanites (2)

Gen 36:34 Husham from the land of the **T**
1Ch 1:45 Husham from the land of the **T**

Temeni (1)

1Ch 4:6 Hepher, **T**, and Haahashtari.

temper (4)

Pro 14:29 but a short t is the height of
15:18 holds his t calms disputes.
19:19 A person who has a hot t will
22:24 a friend of one who has a bad t,

tempers (5)

Est 1:18 will be contempt and short t.
2Co 12:20 hot t, selfish ambition, slander,
Eph 4:31 Get rid of your bitterness, hot t,
Col 3:8 Also get rid of your anger, hot t,
1Ti 3:11 but they must control their t

temple (804)

Dtr 23:17 ever become a t prostitute.
Jdg 9:4 70 pieces of silver from the t
9:27 an offering of praise in the t
9:46 basement of the t of El Berith.
1Sm 1:9 chair by the door of the Lord's t.
3:3 The lamp in God's t hadn't
3:3 and Samuel was asleep in the t
5:2 They brought it into the t of
5:5 else who comes into Dagon's t
31:10 They put his armor in the t of
2Sm 22:7 He heard my voice from his t,
1Ki 3:2 other worship sites because a t
5:3 He couldn't build a t for the
5:5 Now I'm thinking of building a t
5:5 will build a t for my name.'
5:17 foundation of cut stone for the t.
5:18 logs and stone to build the t.
6:1 the LORD's t 480 years after
6:2 The t that King Solomon built
6:3 of the main room of the t was
6:3 as the shorter side of the t.
6:3 15 feet in front of the t.
6:4 latticed windows for the t.
6:5 side rooms all around the t.
6:6 all around the t so that this
6:6 fastened to the walls of the t.
6:7 The t was built with stone
6:7 sound at the t construction site.
6:8 was on the south side of the t.
6:9 he roofed the t with rows of
6:10 feet high alongside the entire t.
6:10 beams were attached to the t.
6:12 "This concerns the t you are
6:15 to line the inside walls of the t
6:15 He paneled the inside of the t
6:15 of the t with cypress planks.
6:16 room at the rear of the t
6:17 at the front of the t served as
6:18 the cedar paneling inside the t.
6:19 prepared the inner room of the t
6:21 He covered the inside of the t
6:22 entire inside of the t with gold.
6:27 in the inner room of the t.
6:29 inner and outer rooms of the t.
6:30 outer rooms of the t with gold.
6:37 of the LORD's t was laid.
6:38 the t was finished according to
7:12 inner courtyard of the LORD's t
7:39 on the south side of the t
7:39 five on the north side of the t.
7:39 pool on the south side of the t
7:40 King Solomon on the LORD's t:
7:45 the LORD's t at King Solomon's
7:48 the furnishings for the LORD's t:
7:50 and the doors of the t.
7:51 on the LORD's t was finished.
7:51 the storerooms of the LORD's t.
8:4 the holy utensils in it ⌞to the t⌟.
8:6 room of the t (the most holy
8:10 a cloud filled the LORD's t.
8:11 The LORD's glory filled his t.
8:13 have built you a high t,
8:16 of Israel as a place to build a t
8:17 had his heart set on building a t
8:18 your heart set on building a t
8:19 But you must not build the t.
8:19 will build the t for my name.'
8:20 I've built the t for the name of
8:27 then how can this t that I have
8:29 day may your eyes be on this t,
8:31 in front of your altar in this t,
1Ki 8:33 and plead with you in this t,
8:38 out their hands toward this t.
8:42 to pray facing this t,
8:43 and learn also that this t which
8:44 city you have chosen and the t
8:48 and the t I have built for your
8:63 Israel dedicated the LORD's t.
8:64 in front of the LORD's t as
9:1 finished building the LORD's t,
9:3 I have declared that this t
9:7 I will reject this t that I declared
9:8 Everyone passing by this t,
9:8 things to this land and this t?'
9:25 And he finished the t.
10:5 he sacrificed at the LORD's t,
10:12 made supports for the LORD's t
12:27 in the LORD's t in Jerusalem.
14:26 the treasures from the LORD's t
14:28 the king went into the LORD's t,
15:12 He forced the male t prostitutes
15:15 into the LORD's t the silver,
15:18 in the treasuries of the LORD's t
16:32 He built the t of Baal in
22:46 He rid the land of the male t
2Ki 5:18 when my master goes to the t
5:18 bow down in the t of Rimmon.
10:21 They went into the t of Baal
10:23 went into the t of Baal and said
10:25 the stronghold in the t of Baal.
10:26 the large sacred stone of the t
10:27 sacred stone of Baal and the t
11:3 hidden with her in the LORD's t
11:4 come to him in the LORD's t.
11:4 under oath in the LORD's t,
11:7 guard the king at the LORD's t.
11:10 but were now in the LORD's t.
11:11 around the altar and the t (from
11:11 side to the north side of the t).
11:13 she went into the LORD's t,
11:15 "Take her out of the t.
11:15 not be killed in the LORD's t.")
11:18 people of the land went to the t
11:18 to be in charge of the LORD's t.
11:19 the king from the LORD's t.
12:4 are brought into the LORD's t—
12:4 voluntarily to the LORD's t.
12:5 repairs on the t where they are
12:6 still had not repaired the t.
12:7 repairing the damage in the t?
12:7 use it to make repairs on the t."
12:8 responsible for repairing the t.
12:9 one comes into the LORD's t.
12:9 to the LORD's t in the box.
12:10 was donated in the LORD's t.
12:11 to work on the LORD's t.
12:12 to make repairs on the LORD's t
12:12 they needed for the t repairs.
12:13 were made for the LORD's t
12:14 and they used it to repair the t.
12:16 not brought into the LORD's t.
12:18 the storerooms of the LORD's t
14:14 he found in the LORD's t
15:35 the Upper Gate of the LORD's t.
16:8 gold he found in the LORD's t
16:14 It had been in front of the t
16:14 his altar and the LORD's t.
16:17 stands ⌞used in the t⌟
16:18 had been built in the t.
16:18 for the king from the LORD's t.
18:15 could be found in the LORD's t
18:16 and doorposts of the LORD's t.
19:1 and went into the LORD's t.
19:14 and went to the LORD's t.
19:37 he was worshiping in the t
20:5 you will go to the LORD's t.
20:8 and that I'll go to the LORD's t
21:4 He built altars in the LORD's t,
21:5 two courtyards of the LORD's t,
21:7 Then he set it up in the t,
21:7 "I have chosen this t and
22:3 t with these instructions:
22:4 been brought into the LORD's t,
22:5 are in charge of the LORD's t.
22:5 making repairs on the LORD's t.
22:6 quarried stones to repair the t.
22:8 Teachings in the LORD's t."
2Ki 22:9 the money donated in the t
22:9 are in charge of the LORD's t."
23:2 and old) went to the LORD's t.
23:2 in the LORD's t so that they
23:4 to take out of the LORD's t all
23:6 the goddess Asherah from the t
23:7 the male t prostitutes who were
23:7 who were in the LORD's t,
23:11 at the entrance of the LORD's t.
23:11 They were in the t courtyard
23:12 two courtyards of the LORD's t.
23:24 Hilkiah found in the LORD's t.
23:27 and I will reject the t where I
24:13 all the treasures in the LORD's t
24:13 had made for the LORD's t.
25:9 He burned down the LORD's t,
25:13 bronze pillars of the LORD's t,
25:13 the bronze pool in the LORD's t.
25:14 utensils used in the t service.
25:16 LORD's t couldn't be weighed.
1Ch 6:10 as priest in the t Solomon built
6:31 the music in the LORD's t after
6:32 built the LORD's t in Jerusalem.
9:2 and the t servants.
9:11 official in charge of God's t).
9:13 They served in God's t and
9:26 rooms and treasures in God's t
9:27 night stationed around God's t
9:33 They lived in rooms in the t
10:10 They put his armor in the t of
10:10 his head to the t of Dagon.
18:8 and utensils ⌞for the t⌟.)
22:1 the LORD God's t will be.
22:2 to cut stones to build God's t.
22:5 and the t that will be built for
22:6 commanded him to build a t
22:7 had my heart set on building a t
22:8 You must not build a t for my
22:10 He will build a t for my name.
22:11 and you will build the t of the
22:14 preparations for the LORD's t.
22:19 holy utensils into the t that will
23:4 the work on the LORD's t,
23:24 in the LORD's t was at least
23:28 to serve in the LORD's t.
23:28 the courtyards and the t rooms,
23:28 and to serve in God's t.
23:32 as they served in the LORD's t.
24:19 went to serve at the LORD's t.
25:6 sang at the LORD's t under
25:6 and harps for worship in God's t
26:12 to serve in the LORD's t.
26:20 of the treasuries in God's t
26:22 the treasuries in the LORD's t.
26:27 battle to support the LORD's t.)
26:29 judges outside ⌞the t⌟ in Israel.
28:2 set on building the t where
28:2 This t would be a stool for our
28:3 'You must not build the t for my
28:6 son Solomon will build my t
28:10 you to build the t as his holy
28:11 for the entrance hall and the t,
28:12 the courtyards of the LORD's t
28:12 served as treasuries for God's t
28:13 for worship in the LORD's t.
28:13 for worship in the LORD's t.
28:20 on the LORD's t is finished.
28:21 type of worship in God's t.
29:2 ⌞the materials⌟ for the t
29:3 I delight in the t of my God.
29:3 that I'm giving to my God's t
29:3 else I gathered for the holy t.
29:7 of iron for the work on God's t.
29:8 for the treasury of the LORD's t.
29:16 that we gathered to build a t
2Ch 2:1 orders to begin building the t
2:4 I want to build the t for the
2:5 The t I am building will be
2:6 But who is able to build him a t
2:6 Who am I to build him a t
2:9 because the t I want to build
2:12 and can build the LORD's t
3:1 began to build the LORD's t
3:3 the foundation to build God's t.
3:4 (the same as the width of the t)
3:8 was as long as the t was wide,

2Ch 3:15 two pillars for the front of the **t**.
3:17 up the pillars in front of the **t**,
4:7 and put them in the **t**,
4:8 ten tables and put them in the **t**,
4:11 for King Solomon in God's **t**:
4:16 the LORD's **t** at King Solomon's
4:19 all the furnishings for God's **t**:
4:22 the gold entrance to the **t**,
4:22 and the gold doors of the **t**.
5:1 on the LORD's **t** was finished.
5:1 in the storerooms of God's **t**.
5:5 the holy utensils in it ⌊to the **t**⌋.
5:7 room of the **t** (the most holy
5:13 Then the LORD's **t** was filled
5:14 The LORD's glory filled God's **t**.
6:2 But I have built you a high **t**,
6:5 of Israel as a place to build a **t**
6:7 had his heart set on building a **t**
6:8 your heart set on building a **t**
6:9 But you must not build the **t**.
6:9 will build the **t** for my name.'
6:10 I've built the **t** for the name of
6:18 then how can this **t** that I have
6:20 may your eyes be on this **t**,
6:22 in front of your altar in this **t**,
6:24 and plead with you in this **t**,
6:29 out their hands toward this **t**.
6:32 they come to pray facing this **t**,
6:33 and learn that this **t** which
6:34 city you have chosen and the **t**
6:38 and the **t** I have built for your
7:1 the LORD's glory filled the **t**.
7:2 couldn't go into the LORD's **t**
7:2 glory had filled the LORD's **t**.
7:3 and the LORD's glory on the **t**,
7:5 the people dedicated God's **t**.
7:7 in front of the LORD's **t** as
7:11 Solomon finished the LORD's **t**
7:11 he had in mind for the LORD's **t**
7:12 for myself as a **t** for sacrifices.
7:16 and declared this **t** holy so that
7:20 I will reject this **t** that I declared
7:21 by this impressive **t** will
7:21 things to this land and this **t**?'
8:16 of the LORD's **t** was laid until
8:16 LORD's **t** was ⌊now⌋ finished.
9:4 he sacrificed at the LORD's **t**,
9:11 made gateways to the LORD's **t**
12:9 the treasures from the LORD's **t**
12:11 the king went into the LORD's **t**,
15:18 brought into God's **t** the silver,
16:2 in the treasuries of the LORD's **t**
20:5 new courtyard at the LORD's **t**,
20:8 lived in it and built a holy **t**
20:9 we will stand in front of this **t**
20:9 because your name is in this **t**.
20:28 to the LORD's **t** in Jerusalem.
22:12 He was hidden in God's **t** for
23:3 with the king in God's **t**.
23:5 the courtyards of the LORD's **t**.
23:6 come into the LORD's **t** except
23:7 who tries to come into the **t**.
23:9 David but were now in God's **t**.
23:10 around the altar and the **t** (from
23:10 side to the north side of the **t**).
23:12 she went into the LORD's **t**,
23:14 of the army out ⌊of the **t**⌋.
23:14 "Take her out of the **t**.
23:14 "Don't kill her in the LORD's **t**.")
23:17 all the people went to the **t**
23:18 in charge of the LORD's **t** under
23:18 in divisions for the LORD's **t**.
23:19 gates of the LORD's **t** so that no
23:20 the king from the LORD's **t**.
24:4 to renovate the LORD's **t**.
24:5 throughout Israel to repair the **t**
24:7 had broken into God's **t**
24:7 the LORD's **t** ⌊to worship⌋ other
24:8 the gate of the LORD's **t**.
24:12 were working on the LORD's **t**,
24:12 to renovate the LORD's **t**.
24:12 bronze to repair the LORD's **t**.
24:13 They restored God's **t** to its
24:14 make utensils for the LORD's **t**.
24:14 burnt offerings in the LORD's **t**.
24:16 done in Israel for God and the **t**.

2Ch 24:18 They abandoned the **t** of the
24:21 in the courtyard of the LORD's **t**.
24:27 and the rebuilding of God's **t** is
25:24 the utensils he found in God's **t**
26:16 He went into the LORD's **t** to
26:19 in the LORD's **t** as Uzziah was
26:21 was barred from the LORD's **t**.
27:2 ⌊illegally⌋ enter the LORD's **t**.
27:3 the Upper Gate of the LORD's **t**
28:21 of the things from the LORD's **t**,
28:24 the utensils in God's **t**,
28:24 the doors to the LORD's **t**.
29:3 the LORD's **t** and repaired them.
29:4 on the east side ⌊of the **t**⌋.
29:5 the ceremonies to make the **t**
29:15 LORD's word and entered the **t**
29:16 priests entered the LORD's **t**
29:16 that they found in the LORD's **t**.
29:17 to make the LORD's **t** holy.
29:18 made all of the LORD's **t** clean.
29:20 city and went to the LORD's **t**.
29:25 in the LORD's **t** with cymbals,
29:31 offerings to the LORD's **t**."
29:35 LORD's **t** was reestablished.
30:1 them to come to the LORD's **t**
30:15 burnt offerings to the LORD's **t**.
31:10 the offerings to the LORD's **t**,
31:11 storerooms in the LORD's **t**.
31:13 who was in charge of God's **t**,
31:16 who went to the worship in the LORD's **t**
31:21 did for the worship in God's **t**,
32:21 When he went into the **t** of his
33:4 He built altars in the LORD's **t**,
33:5 two courtyards of the LORD's **t**,
33:7 Then he set it up in God's **t**,
33:7 "I have chosen this **t** and
33:15 and the idol in the LORD's **t**.
33:15 of the altars he had built in the **t**
34:8 the land and the **t** clean,
34:8 to repair the **t** of the LORD his
34:9 had been brought to God's **t**,
34:10 were in charge of the LORD's **t**.
34:10 restoring and repairing the **t**.
34:14 been deposited in the LORD's **t**,
34:15 the Teachings in the LORD's **t**."
34:17 was donated in the LORD's **t**
34:30 old) went up to the LORD's **t**.
34:30 in the LORD's **t** so that they
35:2 them to serve in the LORD's **t**.
35:3 holy ark in the **t** that Solomon,
35:8 the men in charge of God's **t**,
35:20 when Josiah had repaired the **t**,
36:7 of the LORD's **t** to Babylon.
36:10 utensils from the LORD's **t**.
36:14 the LORD had made the **t**
36:14 they made the **t** unclean.
36:17 best young men in their holy **t**.
36:18 of the utensils from God's **t**,
36:18 the treasures from the LORD's **t**,
36:19 They burned God's **t**,
36:23 Then he ordered me to build a **t**
Ezr 1:2 Then he ordered me to build a **t**
1:3 is in Judah) and build a **t**
1:4 used in God's **t** in Jerusalem.
1:5 the LORD's **t** in Jerusalem.
1:7 belonging to the LORD's **t**.
1:7 Jerusalem and put them in the **t**
2:43 These **t** servants returned from
2:58 The **t** servants and the
2:68 to the LORD's **t** in Jerusalem,
2:68 offerings to help rebuild God's **t**
2:70 and the **t** servants settled in
3:6 of the LORD's **t** had not yet
3:8 began to rebuild the **t**.
3:10 the foundation of the LORD's **t**.
3:12 enough to have seen the first **t**
3:12 saw the foundation of this **t**.
4:1 from exile were building a **t**
4:3 and our people to build a **t**
4:24 Then the work on God's **t** in
5:2 to rebuild God's **t** in Jerusalem.
5:3 you permission to rebuild this **t**
5:8 to the **t** of the great God.
5:8 The **t** is being built with large
5:9 you permission to rebuild this **t**
5:11 We are rebuilding the **t** that

Ezr 5:12 destroyed this **t**
5:13 for God's **t** to be rebuilt.
5:14 In addition, Cyrus took out of a **t**
5:14 that belonged to God's **t**.
5:14 had taken them out of God's **t**
5:14 them into a **t** in Babylon.)
5:15 them in the **t** in Jerusalem.
5:15 Rebuild God's **t** on its original
5:16 of God's **t** in Jerusalem.
5:16 The **t** has been under
5:17 Cyrus gave permission for the **t**
6:3 God's **t** in Jerusalem.
6:3 The **t** should be rebuilt as a
6:5 In addition, Cyrus took out of a **t**
6:5 that belonged to God's **t**.
6:5 had taken them out of God's **t**
6:5 them into a **t** in Babylon.)
6:5 place in the **t** in Jerusalem.
6:5 should put each one in God's **t**.
6:7 with the work on God's **t**.
6:7 leaders of Judah rebuild God's **t**
6:8 Jewish leaders rebuild God's **t**:
6:12 orders or tries to destroy the **t**
6:15 This **t** was finished on the third
6:16 at the dedication of God's **t**.
6:17 At the dedication of God's **t**,
6:22 in their work on the **t** of God,
7:7 and **t** servants) went to
7:15 God whose **t** is in Jerusalem.
7:16 contributed these gifts for the **t**
7:17 wine to offer on the altar of the **t**
7:19 be used in your God's **t** must all
7:20 must provide for your God's **t**.
7:23 be carried out in detail for the **t**
7:24 or worker in the **t** of this God
7:27 **t** in Jerusalem beautiful.
8:17 the **t** servants in Casiphia,
8:17 who can serve in our God's **t**.
8:20 and 220 **t** servants.
8:20 from the **t** servants whom David
8:25 had contributed for our God's **t**.
8:29 the storerooms of the LORD's **t**,
8:30 for bringing these items to the **t**
8:33 and the utensils in our God's **t**.
8:36 to the people and the **t** of God.
9:9 to rebuild our God's **t**
10:1 himself down in front of God's **t**,
10:6 Ezra left the front of God's **t**
10:9 sat in the courtyard of God's **t**.
Neh 2:8 gates of the fortress near the **t**,
3:26 and the **t** servants who were
3:31 that housed the **t** servants
6:10 the house of God, inside the **t**,
6:10 and close the **t** doors.
6:11 a man like me go into the **t**
7:46 These **t** servants returned from
7:60 The **t** servants and the
7:73 of the people, the **t** servants,
8:16 in the courtyards of God's **t**,
10:28 singers, **t** servants,
10:32 year for worship in our God's **t**:
10:33 other work in the **t** of our God.
10:34 bring wood to our God's **t**
10:35 tree each year to the LORD's **t**.
10:36 priests serving in our God's **t**.
10:38 of these tenths to our God's **t**,
10:39 We won't neglect our God's **t**.
11:3 priests, Levites, **t** servants,
11:11 was the supervisor of God's **t**.
11:12 822 did the work in the **t**.
11:12 Also, Adaiah worked in the **t**.
11:16 of the work outside God's **t**.
11:21 But the **t** servants lived on
11:22 in charge of worship in God's **t**.
12:40 So both choirs stood in God's **t**,
12:41 these priests stood in God's **t**:
13:4 of the storerooms of our God's **t**,
13:7 Tobiah with a room in God's **t**.
13:9 there the utensils from God's **t**,
13:10 the worship ⌊in the **t**⌋,
13:11 is God's **t** being neglected?"
13:14 that I have done for your **t**
Job 12:19 those who serve in a **t**.
Psa 5:7 I will bow toward your holy **t**.
11:4 The LORD is in his holy **t**.
18:6 He heard my voice from his **t**,

Psa 27:4 to search for an answer in his t.
29:9 Everyone in his t is saying,
48:9 Inside your t we carefully
65:4 your house, from your holy t.
66:13 I will come into your t with
68:29 of your t high above Jerusalem.
74:3 everything in the holy t.
79:1 have dishonored your holy t.
138:2 I will bow toward your holy t.
Ecc 5:6 presence of a ⌞t⌟ messenger,
Isa 6:1 bottom of his robe filled the t.
6:4 and the t filled with smoke.
15:2 The people of Dibon go to the t,
37:1 and went into the LORD's t.
37:14 and went to the LORD's t.
37:38 he was worshiping in the t
38:22 that I'll go to the LORD's t?"
38:20 live our lives in the LORD's t.
44:28 He says about the t,
52:11 the utensils for the LORD's t.
60:7 So I will honor my beautiful t.
64:11 Our holy and beautiful t,
66:6 Listen to the sound from the t.
66:20 in clean dishes to the LORD's t.
Jer 7:4 "This is the LORD's t,
7:4 LORD's temple, the LORD's t,
7:4 LORD's temple, the LORD's t!"
17:26 thank offerings to the LORD's t.
19:14 in the courtyard of the LORD's t
20:1 the chief officer of the LORD's t,
20:2 Gate that was in the LORD's t.
23:11 Even in my t I've found them
24:1 figs set in front of the LORD's t.
26:2 in the courtyard of the LORD's t,
26:2 to worship in the LORD's t.
26:6 Then I will do to this t what I
26:7 these things in the LORD's t.
26:9 the LORD's name that this t will
26:9 Jeremiah in the LORD's t.
26:10 king's palace to the LORD's t.
26:10 of New Gate to the LORD's ⌞t⌟.
26:12 heard me say against this t
26:18 and the t mountain will become
27:16 the utensils of the LORD's t will
27:18 that are left in the LORD's t,
27:21 that are left in the LORD's t,
28:1 spoke to me in the LORD's t.
28:3 t that King Nebuchadnezzar
28:5 standing in the LORD's t.
28:6 the utensils of the LORD's t
29:26 be officials for the LORD's t.
32:34 idols in the t that is called
33:11 offerings to the LORD's t say,
34:15 in the t that is called by my
35:2 the side rooms in the LORD's t,
35:4 brought them into the LORD's t,
36:5 allowed to go to the LORD's t.
36:6 it to the people in the LORD's t.
36:8 In the LORD's t he read from
36:10 to all the people in the LORD's t
36:10 of New Gate of the LORD's t.
38:14 third entrance in the LORD's t.
41:5 and incense to the LORD's t.
50:28 the vengeance for his t.
51:11 The LORD will avenge his t.
51:51 the holy places of the LORD's t.
52:13 He burned down the LORD's t,
52:17 bronze pillars of the LORD's t,
52:17 the bronze pool in the LORD's t.
52:18 utensils used in the t service.
52:20 LORD's t couldn't be weighed.
Lam 2:7 noise in the LORD's t as though
Eze 8:3 of the inner courtyard of the t.
8:14 the north gate of the LORD's t.
8:16 inner courtyard of the LORD's t.
8:16 at the entrance to the LORD's t,
8:16 backs turned to the LORD's t.
9:6 the old men in front of the t.
9:7 said to them, "Dishonor the t!
10:3 on the south side of the t as
10:4 angels to the entrance of the t,
10:4 the cloud filled the t,
10:19 to the east gate of the LORD's t,
11:1 to the east gate of the LORD's t.
23:39 is what they've done in my t.
40:5 a wall that surrounded the t.
Eze 40:7 hall of the t was 10 ½
40:9 It extended 14 feet from the t.
40:9 entrance hall faced the t.
40:45 the priests who serve in the t.
40:47 the altar was in front of the t.
40:48 me to the entrance hall of the t
41:1 me into the holy place in the t
41:5 the man measured the t wall.
41:5 room around the t was 7 feet.
41:6 all the way around the t wall,
41:6 were not fastened to the t wall.
41:7 story to story all around the t.
41:8 a raised base all around the t.
41:9 side rooms connected to the t
41:10 wide and went all around the t.
41:12 on the west side of the t,
41:13 Then the man measured the t.
41:14 The eastern side of the t,
41:19 were carved all around the t.
41:26 on the side rooms of the t,
42:8 The rooms that faced the t
42:15 the inner part of the t area,
43:4 glory came into the t through
43:5 I saw the LORD's glory fill the t.
43:6 to me from inside the t while
43:10 "Son of man, describe this t to
43:11 show them the design of the t,
43:12 This is a regulation of the t:
43:12 this is a regulation of the t."
43:21 the place appointed near the t,
44:4 the north gate in front of the t.
44:4 LORD's glory fill the LORD's t.
44:5 regulations for the LORD's t.
44:5 to everyone who enters the t
44:7 You dishonored my t when you
44:8 put foreigners in charge of my t.
44:11 have guarded the gates of the t.
44:11 They could have served in the t
44:14 the less important work in the t.
44:17 the inner courtyard and in the t.
45:5 the Levites who serve in the t.
45:19 put it on the doorposts of the t,
45:20 peace with the LORD for the t.
46:24 where the t servants must boil
47:1 me back to the door of the t.
47:1 the entrance of the t toward
47:1 (The t faced east.)
47:1 under the south side of the t,
48:21 with the holy place of the t will
Dan 1:2 some utensils from God's t over
1:2 took the utensils to the t
1:2 and put them in the t treasury.
5:2 had taken from the t
5:3 from God's t in Jerusalem.
5:23 You had the utensils from his t
Hos 4:14 sacrifices with t prostitutes.
8:1 down on the LORD's t like
9:4 an offering⌟ to the LORD's t.
9:8 are hostile in the t of their God.
9:15 I will force them out of my t
Joe 1:9 longer brought to the LORD's t.
1:13 are withheld from your God's t.
1:14 Bring them to the t of the LORD
1:16 disappear from our God's t.
2:17 altar and the entrance to the t.
3:18 will flow from the LORD's t.
Amo 8:3 On that day the songs of the t
Jnh 2:4 Will I ever see your holy t
2:7 came to you in your holy t.
Mic 1:2 be a witness from his holy t.
3:12 and the t mountain will become
Nah 1:14 and metal idols from the t
Hab 2:20 The LORD is in his holy t.
Hag 2:15 on another in the t of the LORD.
Zec 3:7 you will govern my t and watch
6:12 he will rebuild the LORD's t.
6:13 He will rebuild the LORD's t
6:14 of Zephaniah) in the LORD's t.
6:15 come and rebuild the LORD's t.
8:9 Be strong so that the t might be
Mal 3:1 for will suddenly come to his t.
Mat 4:5 on the highest part of the t.
12:5 priests in the t do things they
12:6 greater than the t is here.
17:24 the collectors of the t tax came
17:24 "Doesn't your teacher pay the t
Mat 21:12 Jesus went into the t courtyard
21:14 came to him in the t courtyard,
21:15 shouting in the t courtyard,
21:23 Then Jesus went into the t
23:16 'To swear an oath by the t
23:16 oath by the gold in the t means
23:17 the gold or the t that made the
23:21 To swear an oath by the t is to
23:35 between the t and the altar.
24:1 As Jesus left the t courtyard
24:1 out to him the t buildings.
26:55 I used to sit teaching in the t
26:61 'I can tear down God's t and
27:5 he threw the money into the t,
27:6 right to put it into the t treasury,
27:40 were going to tear down God's t
27:51 Suddenly, the curtain in the t
Mar 11:11 and went into the t courtyard,
11:15 Jesus went into the t courtyard
11:16 anything across the t courtyard.
11:27 was walking in the t courtyard,
12:35 was teaching in the t courtyard,
12:41 sat facing the t offering box,
13:1 As Jesus was going out of the t
13:3 of Olives facing the t buildings,
14:49 I used to teach in the t
14:58 'I'll tear down this t made by
14:58 in three days I'll build another t,
15:29 were going to tear down God's t
15:38 The curtain in the t was split in
Luk 1:9 into the Lord's t to burn incense
1:21 he was staying in the t so long.
1:22 he had seen a vision in the t.
1:59 they went ⌞to the t⌟ to
2:27 went into the t courtyard.
2:37 Anna never left the t courtyard
2:46 found him in the t courtyard.
4:9 on the highest part of the t.
11:51 between the altar and the t.
18:10 "Two men went into the t
19:45 Jesus went into the t courtyard
19:47 Jesus taught in the t courtyard
20:1 the people in the t courtyard
21:1 their gifts into the t offering box
21:5 talking about the t complex.
21:37 would teach in the t courtyard.
21:38 him speak in the t courtyard.
22:4 chief priests and the t guards
22:52 to the chief priests, t guards,
22:53 I was with you in the t
23:45 The curtain in the t was split in
24:53 They were always in the t,
Jon 2:14 and pigeons in the t courtyard.
2:15 and cattle out of the t courtyard.
2:19 replied, "Tear down this t,
2:20 forty-six years to build this t.
2:21 But the t Jesus spoke about
5:14 Jesus met the man in the t
7:14 Jesus went to the t courtyard
7:28 was teaching in the t courtyard,
7:32 and the Pharisees sent t guards
7:37 standing ⌞in the t courtyard⌟.
7:45 When the t guards returned,
7:46 The t guards answered,
7:47 Pharisees asked the t guards,
8:2 he returned to the t courtyard.
8:20 treasury area of the t courtyard.
8:59 and he left the t courtyard.
10:22 Dedication of the T took place
10:23 porch in the t courtyard.
11:56 As they stood in the t courtyard,
18:20 or in the t courtyard,
Act 2:46 and went to the t every day.
3:1 were going to the t courtyard
3:2 man at a gate in the t courtyard.
3:8 and John into the t courtyard.
4:1 officer in charge of the t guards,
4:3 So the t guards arrested them.
5:20 "Stand in the t courtyard,
5:21 the apostles went into the t
5:22 When the t guards arrived at
5:24 When the officer of the t guards
5:25 are standing in the t courtyard.
5:26 Then the officer of the t guards
5:42 Every day in the t courtyard
6:14 from Nazareth will destroy the t

Act 14:13 Zeus’ t was at the entrance to
14:13 their necks to the t gates.
19:24 models of the t of Artemis.
19:27 that people will think that the t
19:35 Ephesians is the keeper of the t
21:26 Then he went into the t
21:27 saw Paul in the t courtyard.
21:28 Moses’ Teachings, and this t.
21:28 Greeks into the t courtyard
21:29 taken him into the t courtyard.
21:30 him out of the t courtyard.
22:17 I was praying in the t courtyard,
24:6 He also entered the t courtyard
24:12 with anyone in the t courtyard
24:18 My accusers found me in the t
25:8 against the t or the emperor."
26:21 me prisoner in the t courtyard
1Co 3:16 you know that you are God’s t
3:17 If anyone destroys God’s t,
3:17 him because God’s t is holy.
3:17 You are that holy t!
6:19 your body is a t that belongs
8:10 eating in the t of a false god.
9:13 who work at the t get their food
9:13 temple get their food from the t?
2Co 6:16 Can God’s t contain false
6:16 we are the t of the living God.
Eph 2:21 grow into a holy t in the Lord.
2Th 2:4 sitting in God’s t and claiming
Rev 3:12 wins the victory a pillar in the t
7:15 him day and night in his t.
11:1 "Stand up and measure the t of
11:2 do not measure the t courtyard.
11:19 God’s t in heaven was opened,
11:19 promise was seen inside his t.
14:15 Another angel came out of the t.
14:17 came out of the t in heaven.
15:5 and I saw that the t of the tent
15:6 out of the t wearing clean,
15:8 The t was filled with smoke
15:8 No one could enter the t until
16:1 I heard a loud voice from the t
16:17 came from the throne in the t,
21:22 I did not see any t in it,
21:22 Almighty and the lamb are its t.

temple’s (10)

1Sm 5:4 were lying⌋ on the t threshold.
5:5 still don’t step on the t threshold
1Ki 6:14 finished building the t ⌊frame⌋,
6:33 of olive wood for the t entrance
7:21 the pillars in the t entrance hall.
2Ch 8:15 including the ⌊t⌋ finances
29:7 doors of the ⌊t⌋ entrance hall,
Eze 9:3 it had been, to the t entrance.
10:18 of the LORD left the t entrance
Act 3:10 and beg at the t Beautiful Gate.

temples (17)

Jdg 4:21 the tent peg through his t into
4:22 with the tent peg through his t.
5:26 She shattered and pierced his t.
1Sm 31:9 this good news in their idols’ t.
1Ki 14:24 even male prostitutes in the t
2Ki 23:19 Josiah also got rid of all the t at
2Ch 34:6 he removed all their t,
Job 36:14 prostitutes in the t of idols.
Sos 4:3 Your t behind your veil are like
6:7 Your t behind your veil are like
Jer 43:12 He will set fire to the t of
43:12 He will burn down the t and
43:13 down the t of Egypt’s gods.'"
Joe 3:5 my finest treasures to your t.
Amo 2:8 In the t of their gods,
Act 19:37 you brought here don’t rob t
Rom 2:22 with disgust, are you robbing t?

temporary (8)

2Sm 11:11 and Judah are in t shelters,
Psa 39:4 I may know how t my life is.
1Co 9:25 They do it to win a t crown,
2Co 4:17 Our suffering is light and t and
4:18 that can be seen are only t.
1Pe 1:1 people who are t residents ⌊in
1:17 live your time as t residents on
2:11 since you are foreigners and t

tempt (7)

Dtr 13:6 best friend may secretly t you,
1Ki 11:2 They will surely t you to follow
Mat 4:7 ‘Never t the Lord your God.'"
Luk 4:12 ‘Never t the Lord your God.'"
1Co 7:5 lack of self-control to t you.
2Ti 2:22 lusts which t young people.
Jas 1:13 and God doesn’t t anyone.

temptation (4)

1Co 10:13 There isn’t any t that you have
10:13 to endure the t as your way
1Ti 6:9 to get rich keep falling into t.
Heb 2:18 Because Jesus experienced t

tempted (24)

Dtr 4:19 Don’t let yourselves be t to
11:16 Be careful, or you’ll be t to turn
12:30 be careful you aren’t t to follow
30:17 You might be t to bow down to
1Ki 11:4 In his old age, his wives t him
Job 31:27 so that my heart was secretly t,
Mat 4:1 the desert to be t by the devil.
6:13 Don’t allow us to be t.
26:41 and pray that you won’t be t.
Mar 1:13 where he was t by Satan for 40
14:38 and pray that you won’t be t.
Luk 4:2 where he was t by the devil for
11:4 Don’t allow us to be t.'
22:40 "Pray that you won’t be t."
22:46 and pray that you won’t be t."
1Co 10:13 will not allow you to be t
10:13 But when you are t,
Gal 6:1 so that you also are not t.
1Th 3:5 tempter had in some way t you,
Heb 2:18 to help others when they are t.
4:15 He was t in every way that we
Jas 1:13 When someone is t,
1:13 God can’t be t by evil,
1:14 Everyone is t by his own

tempter (2)

Mat 4:3 The t came to him and said,
1Th 3:5 I wanted to see whether the t

tempting (3)

Mat 16:23 You are t me to sin.
Luk 4:13 After the devil had finished t
Jas 1:13 shouldn’t say that God is t him.

tend (2)

Job 24:2 and t them as shepherds.
Jer 6:3 of them will t his own flock.

tended (2)

1Sm 17:15 where he t his father’s flock.
2Sm 19:24 He had not t to his feet,

tender (8)

Dtr 28:54 Even the most t and sensitive
28:56 The most t and sensitive
28:56 and t that she wouldn’t
Pro 4:3 when I was a t and only child
27:25 the t growth appears,
31:26 and on her tongue there is t
Mat 24:32 When its branch becomes t
Mar 13:28 When its branch becomes t

tenderly (4)

Gen 34:3 the girl and spoke t to her.
Job 41:3 for mercy or speak t to you?
Isa 40:2 "Speak t to Jerusalem and
Hos 2:14 I will speak t to her.

tending (2)

1Sm 16:11 "He’s t the sheep."
Psa 78:71 He brought him from t the ewes

tendons (1)

Job 10:11 me together with bones and t?

tens (11)

Dtr 33:2 He came with t of thousands of
33:17 The t of thousands from the
1Sm 18:7 but David t of thousands!"
18:8 they credit t of thousands,"
21:11 but David t of thousands.'"
29:5 but David t of thousands’?"
Psa 3:6 I am not afraid of the t of
144:13 t of thousands in our fields.
Dan 11:12 Although he will dominate t of
11:41 and t of thousands will be
Heb 12:22 You have come to t of

tent (431)

Gen 9:21 and lay naked inside his t.
12:8 and he put up his t — with
13:3 where his t had been originally,
18:1 at the entrance of his t during
18:6 So Abraham hurried into the t
18:9 "Over there, in the t."
18:10 at the entrance of the t,
24:67 her into his mother Sarah’s t.
26:25 He also pitched his t in that
31:33 So Laban went into Jacob’s t,
31:33 into Jacob’s tent, into Leah’s t,
31:33 and into the t of the two slaves.
31:33 He came out of Leah’s t and
31:33 tent and went into Rachel’s t.
31:34 the whole t but found nothing.
35:21 up his t beyond Migdal Eder.
Exo 16:16 for each person in your t.'"
18:7 they went into the t.
25:9 Make the t and all its
26:1 "Make the inner t with ten
26:6 sheets together so that the t is
26:7 hair to form an outer t over
26:7 an outer tent over the inner t.
26:9 half ⌊to hang⌋ in front of the t.
26:11 to link the inner t together as
26:12 over the back of the inner t.
26:13 in order to cover the inner t.
26:14 been dyed red for the outer t.
26:15 of acacia wood for the inner t.
26:17 for the inner t the same way.
26:18 for the south side of the inner t.
26:20 of the inner t ⌊make⌋ 20 frames
26:23 at the far end of the inner t.
26:26 on one side of the inner t,
26:27 on the far end of the inner t,
26:30 "Set up the inner t according to
26:35 on the north side of the inner t,
26:36 "For the entrance of the outer t,
27:9 "Make a courtyard for the t.
27:19 "All the things for the t,
27:19 including all the pegs for the t
27:21 In the t of meeting outside the
28:43 them when they go into the t
29:4 the entrance of the t of meeting,
29:10 to the front of the t of meeting.
29:11 the entrance to the t of meeting.
29:30 the one who goes into the t
29:32 the entrance to the t of meeting,
29:42 the entrance to the t of meeting.
29:44 I will dedicate the t of meeting
30:16 expenses of the t of meeting.
30:18 Put it between the t of meeting
30:20 they go into the t of meeting,
30:26 it to anoint the t of meeting,
30:36 my promise in the t of meeting,
31:7 the t of meeting, the ark
31:7 the ⌊other⌋ furnishings for the t,
33:7 Now, Moses used to take a t
33:7 He called it the t of meeting.
33:7 the camp to the t of meeting.
33:8 Moses went out to the t,
33:9 soon as Moses went into the t,
33:9 at the entrance to the t while
33:10 at the entrance to the t,
33:11 stayed inside the t.
35:11 the inner t, the outer tent,
35:11 the inner tent, the outer t,
35:15 screen for the entrance to the t,
35:18 the pegs for the t and the
35:21 to construct the t of meeting,
36:8 the workers made the inner t
36:13 together so that the inner t was
36:14 hair to form an outer t over
36:14 an outer tent over the inner t.
36:18 to link the inner t together as
36:19 been dyed red for the outer t,

Exo	36:20	of acacia wood for the inner **t**.
	36:22	for the inner **t** this same way.
	36:23	for the south side of the inner **t**.
	36:25	For the north side of the inner **t**
	36:28	at the far end of the inner **t**.
	36:31	on one side of the inner **t**,
	36:32	on the far side of the inner **t**,
	36:37	for the entrance to the outer **t**.
	38:8	the entrance to the **t** of meeting.
	38:20	All the pegs for the **t** and the
	38:21	that was used for the **t** (the tent
	38:21	that was used for the tent (the **t**
	38:30	the entrance to the **t** of meeting,
	38:31	all the pegs for the **t**,
	39:32	So all the work on the inner **t**
	39:32	the work on the inner tent (the **t**
	39:33	to Moses — the inner **t**,
	39:33	the outer **t** and all its
	39:38	screen for the entrance to the **t**,
	39:40	service of the inner **t** (the tent
	39:40	inner tent (the **t** of meeting) —
	40:2	"Set up the **t** (the tent of
	40:2	"Set up the tent (the **t** of
	40:5	screen at the entrance to the **t**.
	40:6	the entrance to the **t** of meeting.
	40:7	Put the basin between the **t** of
	40:9	and anoint the **t** and everything
	40:12	the entrance of the **t** of meeting,
	40:17	So the **t** was set up on the first
	40:18	When Moses set up the **t**,
	40:19	He spread the outer **t** over the
	40:19	the outer tent over the inner **t**
	40:21	he brought the ark into the **t**
	40:22	Moses put the table in the **t** of
	40:22	of the **t** outside the canopy.
	40:24	placed the lamp stand in the **t**
	40:24	on the south side of the **t**.
	40:26	Moses put the gold altar in the **t**
	40:28	screen at the entrance to the **t**.
	40:29	at the entrance to the **t** (the tent
	40:29	to the tent (the **t** of meeting).
	40:30	He put the basin between the **t**
	40:32	whenever they went into the **t**
	40:33	up the courtyard around the **t**
	40:34	covered the **t** of meeting,
	40:34	glory of the LORD filled the **t**.
	40:35	couldn't go into the **t** of meeting,
	40:35	glory of the LORD filled the **t**.
	40:36	of⌋ smoke moved from the **t**,
	40:38	column stayed over the **t** during
Lev	1:1	to him from the **t** of meeting.
	1:3	Offer it at the entrance to the **t**
	1:5	the entrance to the **t** of meeting.
	3:2	the entrance to the **t** of meeting.
	3:8	it in front of the **t** of meeting.
	3:13	it in front of the **t** of meeting.
	4:4	the entrance to the **t** of meeting.
	4:5	bring it into the **t** of meeting.
	4:7	presence in the **t** of meeting.
	4:7	the entrance to the **t** of meeting.
	4:14	it in front of the **t** of meeting.
	4:16	blood into the **t** of meeting.
	4:18	presence in the **t** of meeting.
	4:18	the entrance to the **t** of meeting.
	6:16	courtyard of the **t** of meeting.
	6:26	courtyard of the **t** of meeting.
	6:30	into the holy place in the **t**
	8:3	entrance to the **t** of meeting."
	8:4	the entrance to the **t** of meeting.
	8:10	the anointing oil to anoint the **t**
	8:31	the entrance to the **t** of meeting.
	8:33	not leave the entrance to the **t**
	8:35	will stay at the entrance to the **t**
	9:5	them in front of the **t** of meeting.
	9:23	went into the **t** of meeting.
	10:7	not leave the entrance to the **t**
	10:9	you go into the **t** of meeting,
	12:6	the entrance to the **t** of meeting.
	14:8	days he will live outside his **t**.
	14:11	the entrance to the **t** of meeting.
	14:23	at the entrance to the **t**
	15:14	the entrance to the **t** of meeting.
	15:29	the entrance to the **t** of meeting.
	15:31	die because they make my **t**,
	16:7	the entrance to the **t** of meeting.
	16:16	He will do the same for the **t** of
Lev	16:17	No one may be in the **t** of
	16:20	the **t** of meeting, and the altar,
	16:23	will go to the **t** of meeting,
	16:33	the **t** of meeting, and the altar.
	17:4	the entrance of the **t** of meeting.
	17:4	LORD in front of the LORD's **t**.
	17:5	the entrance to the **t** of meeting.
	17:6	the entrance to the **t** of meeting.
	17:9	them to the entrance of the **t**
	19:21	the entrance to the **t** of meeting.
	19:30	worship and respect my holy **t**.
	20:3	made my holy **t** unclean,
	21:12	He must not leave the holy **t** of
	24:3	In the **t** of meeting,
	26:2	worship and respect my holy **t**.
	26:11	"I will put my **t** among you,
Num	1:1	LORD spoke to Moses in the **t**
	1:50	the Levites in charge of the **t**
	1:50	the equipment for the **t**
	1:50	else having to do with the **t**.
	1:50	The Levites will carry the **t** and
	1:50	They will take care of the **t** and
	1:51	When the **t** has to be moved,
	1:51	else who comes near the **t** will
	1:53	will camp all around the **t**
	1:53	charge of the **t** of God's words."
	2:2	tents around the **t** of meeting,
	2:17	"When the **t** of meeting is
	3:7	in front of the **t** of meeting,
	3:7	needs to be done for the inner **t**.
	3:8	of all the furnishings in the **t**
	3:8	needs to be done for the inner **t**.
	3:23	side behind the **t** of meeting.
	3:25	At the **t** of meeting the
	3:25	were in charge of the inner **t**,
	3:25	the outer **t** and cover,
	3:25	the entrance to the **t** of meeting,
	3:26	that surrounds the inner **t**
	3:29	south side of the **t** of meeting.
	3:35	north side of the **t** of meeting.
	3:36	of the framework of the inner **t**,
	3:38	side in front of the **t** of meeting.
	4:3	to work at the **t** of meeting.
	4:4	will do in the **t** of meeting:
	4:15	the things from the **t** of meeting.
	4:16	He is in charge of the whole **t**
	4:23	to serve at the **t** of meeting.
	4:25	that are part of the inner **t**
	4:25	inner tent and the **t** of meeting.
	4:25	inner cover for the **t** of meeting,
	4:25	the entrance to the **t** of meeting,
	4:26	for the courtyard around the **t**
	4:28	families in the **t** of meeting.
	4:30	to serve at the **t** of meeting.
	4:31	they work at the **t** of meeting:
	4:31	the framework for the inner **t**,
	4:33	they work at the **t** of meeting.
	4:35	to work at the **t** of meeting.
	4:37	who served at the **t** of meeting.
	4:39	were qualified to serve at the **t**
	4:41	who worked at the **t** of meeting.
	4:43	were qualified to serve at the **t**
	4:47	who carried the **t** of meeting.
	5:17	the floor of the **t** into the water.
	6:10	the entrance to the **t** of meeting.
	6:13	the entrance of the **t** of meeting.
	6:18	the entrance to the **t** of meeting,
	7:1	Moses finished setting up the **t**,
	7:3	brought them in front of the **t**.
	7:5	work done for the **t** of meeting.
	7:89	Moses went into the **t**
	8:9	to the front of the **t** of meeting,
	8:15	their work at the **t** of meeting.
	8:19	Israelites at the **t** of meeting.
	8:22	came and did their work at the **t**
	8:24	to serve at the **t** of meeting.
	8:26	their duties at the **t** of meeting,
	9:15	On the day the **t** of the words of
	9:15	over the **t** glowed like fire.
	9:16	covering the **t** glowed like fire.
	9:17	the smoke moved from the **t**,
	9:18	of⌋ smoke stayed over the **t**,
	9:19	the smoke stayed over the **t**
	9:20	only a few days over the **t**:
	9:22	of⌋ smoke stayed over the **t**,
	10:3	the entrance to the **t** of meeting.
Num	10:11	⌊column of⌋ smoke left the **t**
	10:17	Then the **t** ⌊of meeting⌋ was
	10:21	By the time they arrived, the **t**
	11:16	Take them to the **t** of meeting,
	11:24	had them stand around the **t**.
	11:26	hadn't gone with them to the **t**.
	12:4	you come to the **t** of meeting."
	12:5	stood at the entrance to the **t**.
	12:10	When the smoke left the **t**,
	14:10	⌊shining⌋ at the **t** of meeting.
	16:9	himself to do the work for his **t**
	16:18	the entrance to the **t** of meeting.
	16:19	the entrance to the **t** of meeting,
	16:42	turned toward the **t** of meeting,
	16:43	to the front of the **t** of meeting.
	16:50	the entrance to the **t** of meeting,
	17:4	Put them in the **t** of meeting
	17:7	in the LORD's presence in the **t**
	17:8	next day Moses went into the **t**.
	17:13	near the LORD's **t** will die!
	18:2	your sons serve in front of the **t**
	18:3	is necessary for the whole **t**.
	18:4	necessary for the **t** of meeting,
	18:4	the maintenance work for the **t**.
	18:6	necessary at the **t** of meeting.
	18:21	they do at the **t** of meeting.
	18:22	come near the **t** of meeting.
	18:23	do the work at the **t** of meeting.
	18:31	your work at the **t** of meeting.
	19:4	the front of the **t** of meeting.
	19:13	makes the LORD's **t** unclean.
	19:14	for when a person dies in a **t**:
	19:14	Everyone who goes into the **t**
	19:14	everyone who is in the **t** will
	19:18	in the water, and sprinkle the **t**,
	19:18	people who were in the **t** ⌊with
	20:6	the entrance of the **t** of meeting.
	20:9	took his staff out of ⌊the **t** in⌋
	25:6	the entrance to the **t** of meeting.
	25:8	and went into the **t** after the
	27:2	the entrance to the **t** of meeting.
	31:30	the work done at the LORD's **t**."
	31:47	the work done at the LORD's **t**.
	31:54	the LORD's presence at the **t**
Dtr	31:14	of you come to the **t** of meeting,
	31:14	came to the **t** of meeting.
	31:15	smoke at the entrance to the **t**.
Jos	7:14	by tribes ⌊to the **t** of meeting⌋.
	7:21	find them buried inside my **t**
	7:22	and they ran to the **t**.
	7:23	They took the loot from the **t**
	7:24	and his **t** — everything he had
	18:1	at Shiloh and set up the **t**
	19:51	the entrance of the **t** of meeting.
	22:19	The LORD's **t** is standing here.
	22:29	our God that is in front of his **t**."
Jdg	4:11	near Kedesh and set up his **t**.
	4:17	fled on foot toward the **t** of Jael,
	4:18	When Jael came out ⌊of her **t**⌋,
	4:18	Come into my **t**. Don't be afraid.
	4:18	So he went into her **t**,
	4:18	and she hid him under a **t**
	4:20	"Stand at the door of the **t**.
	4:21	took a **t** peg and walked quietly
	4:21	She hammered the **t** peg
	4:22	When Jael came out ⌊of her **t**⌋,
	4:22	So Barak went into her **t**.
	4:22	dead with the **t** peg through his
	5:24	blessed woman living in a **t**.
	5:26	She reached for a **t** peg with
	7:13	the loaf of bread hit that **t** so
	7:13	so hard that the **t** collapsed,
	8:11	went up **T** Dwellers Road,
	20:8	"None of us will go to his **t** or
1Sm	2:22	at the gate of the **t** of meeting.
	4:10	⌊Israelite⌋ soldier fled to his **t**.
	17:54	he kept Goliath's armor in his **t**.
2Sm	6:17	place inside the **t** David had put
	7:2	the ark of God remains in the **t**."
	7:6	Instead, I moved around in a **t**,
	7:6	the **t** ⌊of meeting⌋.
	7:18	King David went into the **t** and
	16:22	So a **t** was put up on the roof
	20:1	Everyone to his own **t**,
1Ki	1:39	container of olive oil from the **t**
	1:50	went ⌊to the **t** of meeting,⌋

1Ki	2:28	So Joab fled to the LORD's **t**
	2:29	had fled to the altar in the **t**
	2:30	When Benaiah came to the **t** of
	8:4	the ark, the **t** of meeting,
	20:16	when Benhadad was in his **t**
2Ki	7:8	of the camp, they went into a **t**,
	7:8	and clothes they found in that **t**.
	7:8	went into another **t**,
1Ch	6:32	in the courtyard in front of the **t**
	6:48	all the other duties in the **t**,
	9:19	at the entrances to the **t**,
	9:21	the entrance to the **t** of meeting.
	9:23	LORD's house, that is, the **t**.
	15:1	God's ark and set up a **t** for it.
	16:1	set it inside the **t** David had put
	16:39	to serve in the LORD's **t** at
	17:1	LORD's promise is inside a **t**."
	17:5	but I've gone from **t** site to tent
	17:5	I've gone from tent site to **t** site,
	17:5	moving the **t** ⌊of meeting⌋ from
	17:16	Then King David went into the **t**
	21:29	The LORD's **t** that Moses made
	23:26	no longer have to carry the **t**
	23:32	follow the regulations for the **t**
2Ch	1:3	in Gibeon because God's **t**
	1:3	had made the **t** in the desert.
	1:4	He had put up a **t** for it in
	1:5	was in front of the LORD's **t**.
	1:6	the bronze altar in front of the **t**
	1:13	Solomon went from the **t** of
	5:5	the ark, the **t** of meeting,
	10:16	Everyone to his own **t**,
	24:6	for the use of the **t** containing
	29:6	turned away from the LORD's **t**
Job	4:21	ropes of their **t** been loosened?
	5:24	"You will know peace in your **t**.
	8:22	and the **t** of the wicked will
	11:14	don't let injustice live in your **t**.
	18:6	The light in his **t** becomes dark,
	18:14	dragged from the safety of his **t**
	18:15	Fire lives in his **t**. Sulfur is
	19:12	me and camp around my **t**.
	20:26	is left in his **t** will be devoured.
	21:28	Where is the **t** where wicked
	22:23	put wrongdoing out of your **t**,
	29:4	God was an adviser in my **t**.
	31:31	who were in my **t** had said,
Psa	15:1	who may stay in your **t**?
	19:4	He has set up a **t** in the
	27:5	He keeps me hidden in his **t**.
	27:6	with shouts of joy in his **t**.
	52:5	you and drag you out of your **t**.
	61:4	to be a guest in your **t** forever
	76:2	His **t** is in Salem. His home is in Zion.
	78:60	the **t** where he had lived among
	78:67	He rejected the **t** of Joseph.
Isa	16:5	He is from the **t** of David.
	33:20	It is a **t** that can't be moved.
	33:20	Its **t** pegs will never be pulled
	38:12	rolled it up like a shepherd's **t**.
	40:22	spreads it out like a **t** to live in.
	54:2	Expand the space of your **t**.
	54:2	out the curtains of your **t**,
	54:2	Lengthen your **t** ropes,
	54:2	and drive in the **t** pegs.
Jer	10:20	My **t** is destroyed, and all my
	10:20	There's no one to set up my **t**
	10:20	again or put up my **t** curtains.
	49:29	Their **t** curtains, utensils,
Lam	2:4	fire on the **t** of Zion's people.
Amo	9:11	I will set up David's fallen **t**.
Zec	10:4	cornerstone, from them a **t** peg,
Act	7:44	desert our ancestors had the **t**
	7:44	Moses built this **t** exactly as
	7:45	our ancestors received the **t**,
	7:45	This **t** remained here until the
	15:16	set up David's fallen **t** again.
2Co	5:1	is ever taken down like a **t**,
	5:4	While we are in this **t**,
	5:4	we don't want to take off the **t**,
Heb	8:2	place and of the true **t** set up by
	8:5	was about to make the **t**,
	9:2	A **t** was set up. The first part of
	9:2	The first part of this **t** was
	9:2	were in this part of the **t**.
Heb	9:3	was the part of the **t** called
	9:6	two parts of the **t** were set up.
	9:6	went into the first part of the **t**
	9:7	into the second part of the **t**.
	9:8	not open while the **t** was still
	9:9	The first part of the **t** is an
	9:11	more perfect **t** that was not
	9:21	Moses sprinkled blood on the **t**
	13:10	Those who serve at the **t** have
Rev	7:15	will spread his **t** over them.
	13:6	to insult his name and his **t**—
	15:5	the temple of the **t** containing

tenth (36)

Gen	8:5	decreasing until the **t** month.
	8:5	On the first day of the **t** month,
Exo	12:3	On the **t** ⌊day⌋ of this month
Lev	16:29	On the **t** day of the seventh
	23:27	"In addition, the **t** day of this
	25:9	On the **t** day of the seventh
	27:32	Every **t** head of cattle or sheep
Num	7:66	On the **t** day the leader of the
	29:7	"On the **t** day of the seventh
Dtr	14:23	Eat the **t** of your grain,
	14:25	If so, exchange the **t** part of
Jos	4:19	On the **t** day of the first month,
2Ki	25:1	On the **t** day of the tenth month
	25:1	On the tenth day of the **t** month
1Ch	12:13	The **t** was Jeremiah.
	24:11	the **t** for Shecaniah,
	25:17	The **t** chose Shimei,
	27:13	was in charge of the **t** unit
	27:13	tenth unit during the **t** month.
Ezr	10:16	on the first day of the **t** month
Neh	10:38	Levites when they collect the **t**.
Est	2:16	month of Tebeth, the **t** month,
Jer	32:1	Zedekiah's **t** year as king
	39:1	In the **t** month of Zedekiah's
	52:4	On the **t** day of the tenth month
	52:4	On the tenth day of the **t** month
	52:12	On the **t** day of the fifth month
Eze	20:1	On the **t** day of the fifth month
	24:1	On the **t** day of the tenth month
	24:1	On the tenth day of the **t** month
	29:1	On the twelfth day of the **t**
	29:1	of the tenth month in the **t** year,
	33:21	On the fifth day of the **t** month
	40:1	It was the **t** day of the month in
Zec	8:19	and the fast in the **t** month will
Rev	21:20	ninth topaz, the **t** green quartz,

tenths (1)

Neh	10:38	bring one-tenth of these **t**

tent-like (1)

2Co	5:2	In our present **t** existence we

tent's (1)

Exo	26:13	the length of the outer **t** sheets.

tents (73)

Gen	4:20	to live in **t** and have livestock.
	9:27	May he live in the **t** of Shem.
	13:5	his own sheep, cattle, and **t**.
	13:12	moving his **t** as far as Sodom.
	13:18	So Abram moved his **t** and
	25:27	staying around the **t**.
	26:17	He set up his **t** in the Gerar
	31:25	Jacob had put up his **t** in the
	31:25	and his relatives put up their **t**
	33:19	on which he had put up his **t**.
Exo	33:8	stand at the entrances to their **t**
	33:10	at the entrance to their own **t**.
Num	2:2	Israelites will put up their **t**
	2:2	They will put their **t** around the
	3:23	from Gershon put up their **t**
	3:29	from Kohath put up their **t**
	3:35	They put up their **t** on the north
	3:38	and his sons put up their **t** on
	11:10	crying at the entrance to their **t**.
	16:24	Move away from the **t** of Korah,
	16:26	"Move away from the **t** of these
	16:27	away from the **t** of Korah,
	16:27	at the entrances to their **t**
	24:5	How beautiful are your **t**,
	24:6	Your **t** spread out like rivers,
Dtr	1:27	complained in your **t** and said,
	5:30	the people to go back to their **t**.
	11:6	them, their families, their **t**,
	16:7	you may go back to your **t**.
Jdg	6:5	with their livestock and their **t**.
1Ki	8:66	the king and went to their **t**.
	12:16	To your own **t**, Israel! Now look
	12:16	Israel went home to their own **t**.
	20:12	allies were drinking in their **t**.
2Ki	7:7	the camp as it was with its **t**,
	7:10	Even the **t** were left exactly as
1Ch	4:41	listed here knocked down **t**
	5:10	and lived in their **t** throughout
2Ch	7:10	dismissed the people to their **t**.
	10:16	Israel went home to their own **t**.
Job	12:6	⌊But⌋ robbers' **t** are prosperous,
	15:34	and fire burns up the **t** of those
Psa	69:25	be deserted and their **t** empty.
	78:51	the ones born in the **t** of Ham
	78:55	tribes of Israel in their own **t**.
	83:6	the **t** from Edom and Ishmael,
	106:25	They complained in their **t**.
	118:15	and victory is heard in the **t**
	120:5	or to stay in the **t** of Kedar.
Pro	14:11	but the **t** of decent people will
Sos	1:5	dark and lovely like Kedar's **t**,
	1:8	goats near the shepherds' **t**.
Isa	13:20	Arabs won't pitch their **t** there.
Jer	4:20	My **t** are suddenly destroyed.
	6:3	pitch their **t** all around them,
	30:18	the captives back to Jacob's **t**
	35:7	You must always live in **t** so
	35:10	We live in **t**, and we have
	37:10	wounded men left in their **t**,
	49:29	Their **t** and their flocks will be
Eze	25:4	and pitch their **t** among you.
Dan	11:45	He will pitch his royal **t**
Hos	9:6	Thorns will grow over their **t**.
	12:9	I will make you live in **t** again
Hab	3:7	I see trouble in the **t** of Cushan.
	3:7	see trembling in the **t** of Midian.
Zec	12:7	"The LORD will save Judah's **t**
Mal	2:12	he exclude them from Jacob's **t**
Mat	17:4	If you want, I'll put up three **t**
Mar	9:5	Let's put up three **t**— one for
Luk	9:33	Let's put up three **t**— one for
Act	18:3	and because they made **t** for a
Heb	11:9	He lived in **t**, as did Isaac and

Terah (13)

Gen	11:24	he became the father of **T**.
	11:25	After he became the father of **T**,
	11:26	**T** was 70 years old when he
	11:27	This is the account of **T** and
	11:27	**T** was the father of Abram,
	11:28	While his father **T** was still
	11:31	**T** took his son Abram,
	11:32	**T** lived 205 years and died in
Num	33:27	Tahath and set up camp at **T**.
	33:28	They moved from **T** and set up
Jos	24:2	**T** and his sons Abraham and
1Ch	1:26	Serug, Nahor, **T**,
Luk	3:34	son of **T**, son of Nahor,

Teresh (3)

Est	2:21	the king's gate, Bigthan and **T**,
	2:23	of Bigthan and **T** were hung
	6:2	him that Bigthan and **T**,

terms (24)

Gen	23:16	Abraham agreed to Ephron's **t**.
	37:4	speak to him on friendly **t**.
	39:21	on good **t** with the warden.
Exo	19:5	obey me and are faithful to the **t**
Dtr	4:13	The LORD told you about the **t**
	29:1	These are the **t** of the promise
	29:9	Faithfully obey the **t** of this
	29:12	You are ready to accept the **t**
	33:9	faithful to the **t** of your promise.
Jdg	4:17	family were on peaceful **t**.
2Ki	23:3	He confirmed the **t** of the
2Ch	34:31	He said he would live by the **t**
Job	34:33	on your own **t** since you have
Jer	11:2	"Listen to the **t** of this promise,
	11:3	listen to the **t** of this promise.
	11:6	Listen to the **t** of this promise,

Jer 11:8 they did not keep all the **t**
11:8 the **t** that I commanded them to
32:11 containing the **t** and conditions,
34:18 They have not kept the **t** of the
Eze 20:37 you keep the **t** of the promise.
Luk 14:32 send ambassadors to ask for **t**
Act 12:20 to ask Herod for **t** of peace.
1Co 1:21 unable to recognize God in **t**

terrible (45)

Gen 12:17 his household with **t** plagues
13:13 They committed **t** sins against
Exo 9:3 the LORD will bring a **t** plague
Num 20:5 and bring us into this **t** place?
Dtr 6:22 spectacular but **t** for Egypt,
7:15 the **t** diseases you experienced
7:19 your own eyes the **t** plagues,
28:59 They will be **t** and continuing
29:3 You also saw those **t** plagues,
31:17 and many **t** disasters will
31:21 When many **t** disasters happen
Jdg 15:3 to do something **t** to them."
1Sm 26:21 a fool and made a **t** mistake."
2Sm 24:10 "I have committed a **t** sin by
1Ki 14:6 told to give you some **t** news.
1Ch 21:8 "I have committed a **t** sin by
Est 7:7 saw that the king had a **t** end
Job 2:11 about all the **t** things that had
10:15 How **t** it will be for me if I'm
Psa 41:5 My enemies say **t** things about
71:20 me endure many **t** troubles.
Pro 15:10 Discipline is a **t** ⌊burden⌋ to
15:15 Every day is a **t** day for a
Ecc 1:13 down with a **t** burden that God
2:21 Even this is pointless and a **t**
4:8 Even this is pointless and a **t**
6:1 It is a **t** one for mortals.
8:6 Yet, a **t** human tragedy hangs
Jer 21:6 They will die from a **t** plague.
25:9 and turn them into something **t**,
30:7 How **t** that day will be!
44:7 Why do you bring this **t**
51:54 Sounds of **t** destruction are
Eze 9:9 nations of Israel and Judah is **t**.
14:21 I will surely send four **t**
27:36 You have come to a **t** end,
28:19 You have come to a **t** end,
Joe 1:15 This will be a **t** day!
Mat 8:6 home paralyzed and in **t** pain."
Luk 11:53 held a **t** grudge against him.
21:11 There will be **t** earthquakes,
2Co 1:10 has rescued us from a **t** death,
10:10 but that I'm a weakling and a **t**
Rev 7:14 coming out of the **t** suffering.
16:21 of hail was such a **t** plague.

terrified (97)

Gen 9:2 will fear you and be **t** of you.
20:8 all of this, and they were **t**.
32:7 Jacob was **t** and distressed.
35:5 all around them **t** so that no
Exo 14:10 **T**, the Israelites cried out to the
15:15 tribal leaders of Edom will be **t**.
Dtr 1:21 Don't be afraid or **t**."
2:25 people under heaven **t** of you.
9:19 I was **t** of the LORD's anger
11:25 he will make people **t** of you
31:8 So don't be afraid or **t**."
Jos 1:9 Don't tremble or be **t**,
8:1 "Don't be **t** or afraid.
10:25 "Don't be afraid or **t**!
1Sm 11:7 So the people became **t** by the
17:24 from him because they were **t**.
21:12 he was **t** of King Achish of
28:5 he was very afraid — **t**.
28:21 to Saul and saw that he was **t**.
31:4 refused because he was **t**.
1Ch 10:4 refused because he was **t**.
22:13 Don't be afraid or **t**.
28:20 Don't be afraid or **t**.
2Ch 20:15 Don't be frightened or **t** by this
20:17 Don't be frightened or **t**.
32:7 Don't be frightened or **t** by the
Est 8:17 they were **t** of the Jews.
9:2 all the people were **t** of them.
9:3 they were **t** of Mordecai.
Job 21:6 When I remember it, I'm **t**,
23:15 That is why I'm **t** of him.
31:34 the ⌊local⌋ mobs **t** me so that
33:7 don't need to be **t** of me.
Psa 30:7 you hid your face, I was **t**.
36:1 He is not **t** of God.
48:5 They were **t** and ran away in
83:17 be put to shame and **t** forever.
104:29 hide your face, and they are **t**.
105:38 The Egyptians were **t** of Israel,
Pro 21:15 but troublemakers are **t**.
Isa 8:9 Be **t**. Listen, all you distant parts
8:9 Prepare for battle, but be **t**.
8:9 Prepare for battle, but be **t**.
8:13 and the one you should be **t** of.
13:8 They'll be **t**. Pain and anguish
19:16 They will tremble and be **t**
19:17 they will be **t** of it because of
21:3 I'm **t** by what I see.
33:14 The sinners in Zion are **t**.
35:4 Tell those who are **t**,
44:8 Don't be **t** or afraid.
Jer 1:17 Don't be **t** in their presence,
1:17 more⌋ **t** in their presence.
17:18 but do not let me be **t**.
23:4 will no longer be afraid or **t**,
30:10 Don't be **t**, Israel. I'm going to
46:5 They are **t**. They are retreating.
46:27 Don't be **t**, Israel. I'm going to
51:32 and its soldiers are **t**.
Eze 2:6 Don't be **t** in their presence,
3:9 Don't be **t** in their presence,
12:19 their food and **t** as they drink
19:7 everyone living in it were **t** by
20:26 I **t** them so that they would
26:17 All your people **t** those who
32:23 They once **t** people in the land
32:24 They once **t** people in the land
32:25 in battle because they **t** others
32:26 in battle because they **t** others
32:27 bones because they **t** others
32:30 because they **t** people
32:32 I **t** people in the land of the
Dan 4:5 I had a dream that **t** me.
5:9 King Belshazzar was **t**,
5:19 trembled and were **t** by him,
7:28 I, Daniel, was **t** by my thoughts,
8:17 I was **t** and immediately knelt
Joe 2:6 People are **t** in their presence.
Oba 1:9 "Teman, your warriors will be **t**.
Jnh 1:10 Then the men were **t**.
1:16 The men were **t** of the LORD.
Mat 14:26 on the sea, they were **t**.
17:6 The disciples were **t** when
27:54 They were **t** and said,
Mar 6:50 All of them saw him and were **t**.
9:6 He and the others were **t**.)
Luk 2:9 area with light, and they were **t**.
8:37 to leave because they were **t**.
21:9 wars and revolutions, don't be **t**!
24:5 The women were **t** and bowed
24:37 They were **t**, and thought they
Jon 6:19 and they became **t**.
Act 5:5 heard about his death was **t**.
5:11 what had happened were **t**.
10:4 stared at the angel and was **t**.
Rom 3:18 They are not **t** of God."
Rev 11:13 and the rest were **t**.

terrifies (7)

Jos 2:9 Your presence **t** us.
2Ch 29:8 that shocks and **t** people
Job 31:23 "A disaster from God **t** me.
33:16 ears and **t** them with warnings.
Psa 2:5 anger he **t** them by saying,
76:12 He **t** the kings of the earth.
90:7 consumes us. Your rage **t** us.

terrify (23)

Dtr 28:67 of the things that will **t** you
2Ch 32:18 They tried to frighten and **t** the
Job 3:5 hang over it. Let the gloom **t** it.
7:14 dreams and **t** me with visions.
9:34 and he should not **t** me.
13:11 Doesn't his majesty **t** you?
15:24 Distress and anguish **t** him like
Psa 10:18 mere mortal will **t** them again.
83:14 and **t** them with your
Isa 2:19 when he rises to **t** the earth.
2:21 when he rises to **t** the earth.
7:16 the land of the two kings who **t**
8:12 they fear. Don't let it **t** you."
19:17 of Judah will **t** the Egyptians.
Jer 17:18 **T** them, but do not let me be
20:4 I'm going to make you **t**
Eze 26:18 Your end will **t** the islands in
30:9 in ships to **t** those who live
Nah 2:11 about with no one to **t** them?
Hab 2:17 done to the animals will **t** you
Zep 2:11 The LORD will **t** them,
3:13 and there will be no one to **t**
Zec 1:21 craftsmen have come to **t** them,

terrifying (28)

Job 6:21 You see something **t**,
15:21 **T** sounds are in his ears.
37:22 A **t** majesty is around God.
Psa 64:1 Protect my life from a **t** enemy.
89:7 God is **t** in the council of the
106:22 and **t** things at the Red Sea.
111:9 His name is holy and **t**.
145:6 the power of your **t** deeds,
Isa 2:10 of the LORD's **t** presence
2:19 of the LORD's **t** presence
2:21 of the LORD's **t** presence
10:33 trim the branches with **t** power.
21:1 from the desert, from a **t** land.
Jer 20:11 is on my side like a **t** warrior.
32:37 in my anger, fury, and **t** wrath.
36:7 with his **t** anger and fury."
Dan 2:31 in front of you, and it looked **t**.
7:7 It was **t**, dreadful, and had large
7:19 It was very **t** and had iron teeth
Joe 2:11 day of the LORD is extremely **t**.
2:31 as red as blood before the **t** day
Hab 1:7 They will be **t** and fearsome.
Mal 4:5 Elijah before that very **t** day
Luk 21:11 **T** sights and miraculous signs
Act 2:20 as red as blood before the **t** day
Heb 10:27 All that is left is a **t** wait for
10:31 of the living God is a **t** thing.
12:21 The sight was so **t** that even

territories (5)

Jos 10:42 all these kings and their **t**
Jdg 1:18 and Ekron with their **t**.
19:29 throughout the **t** of Israel.
1Ch 12:40 as far as the **t** of Issachar,
2Ch 30:10 went from city to city in the **t**

territory (142)

Gen 9:27 God expand the **t** of Japheth.
14:7 and they conquered the whole **t**
Exo 13:7 be seen anywhere in your **t**.
13:17 on the road through Philistine **t**,
Num 20:16 a city on the edge of your **t**.
20:17 we've passed through your **t**."
20:21 to let Israel go through their **t**,
21:13 that extends into Amorite **t**.
21:22 we've passed through your **t**."
21:23 let Israel pass through his **t**.
32:33 its cities and its surrounding **t**.
Dtr 2:4 going to pass through the **t**
3:4 60 cities — the whole **t** of Argob,
3:13 (The whole **t** of Argob in
3:14 took the whole **t** of Argob as far
34:2 the **t** of Ephraim and Manasseh,
34:2 all the **t** of Judah as far as the
Jos 12:4 The **t** of King Og of Bashan
13:3 is considered to be Canaanite **t**,
13:4 This **t** includes all the land of
13:11 It also included Gilead, the **t** of
13:16 Their **t** extended from Aroer on
13:23 The border of Reuben's **t** was
13:25 Their **t** included Jazer,
13:30 Their **t** extended from
15:1 Their **t** extends as far south as
15:1 extends as far south as the **t**
16:1 The border of Joseph's **t** goes
16:5 This is the **t** for the families
16:9 for Ephraim in Manasseh's **t**.
18:5 Judah will stay within its **t** in

Jos 18:5 stay within their t in the north.
18:11 Their t lies between Judah's
19:18 Their t included Jezreel,
19:25 Their t included Helkath,
19:29 The t includes Meheleb,
19:41 The t of their inheritance
19:49 also gave land within their t as
21:41 Within the t owned by the
23:4 I have given you the t of the
23:4 This includes the t of all the
23:7 with the nations left in your t.
Jdg 1:3 "Come with us into the t given
1:3 we'll go with you into your t.
1:36 The t of the Amorites extended
2:6 of the t they had inherited.
2:9 at Timnath Heres within the t
11:20 to let them go through his t.
11:22 Israel took all the Amorite t
12:12 he was buried in Aijalon in the t
12:15 in the t of Ephraim,
20:6 throughout the t of Israel.
20:10 the troops go to Gibeah in the t
20:48 the rest of the t of Benjamin.
21:21 go back to the t of Benjamin.
Rut 1:2 Bethlehem in the t of Judah.
1:7 along the road to the t of Judah.
1Sm 6:1 in Philistine t seven months
7:13 didn't come into Israel's t again.
7:14 And Israel recovered the t
9:4 The men went through the t of
9:5 they came to the t of Zuph,
9:16 a man from the t of Benjamin.
11:3 throughout the t of Israel.
11:7 by messengers throughout the t
13:7 the Jordan River into the t
27:1 that I escape to Philistine t.
27:7 David stayed in Philistine t for
27:8 (They lived in the t which
27:9 Whenever David attacked the t,
27:11 long as he lived in Philistine t.
29:11 his men returned to Philistine t,
30:14 Cherethites live, the t of Judah,
30:16 so much loot from Philistine t
31:9 sent men throughout Philistine t
2Sm 8:3 his control ⌊over the t⌋ along
10:2 servants entered Ammonite t,
21:5 staying anywhere in Israel's t.
1Ki 4:13 He ⌊also⌋ had the t of Argob in
4:19 the t of King Sihon the Amorite
4:19 only one governor in that t.)
4:24 He controlled all the t west of
8:65 had come from ⌊the t between⌋
9:19 or the entire t that he governed.
15:20 with the entire t of Naphtali.
2Ki 6:23 didn't raid Israel's t anymore.
8:2 in Philistine t for seven years.
8:3 came home from Philistine t
10:32 to take away some of Israel's t.
10:32 army throughout Israel's t
10:33 the entire region of Gilead (the t
15:16 everyone there, and its t.
15:29 and the entire t of Naphtali.
18:8 all the way to Gaza and its t.
23:33 him a prisoner at Riblah in the t
24:7 Babylon had taken all the t from
24:7 This t had belonged to the king
25:21 at Riblah in the t of Hamath.
1Ch 4:10 bless me and give me more t.
6:54 they settled in the t chosen
6:55 were given Hebron in the t
10:9 sent men throughout Philistine t
18:3 his control ⌊over the t⌋ along
19:2 Ammonite t to comfort Nahash,
2Ch 7:8 had come from ⌊the t between⌋
8:6 or the entire t that he governed.
16:4 cities in the t of Naphtali.
34:33 idols throughout Israelite t.
Job 38:20 so that you may lead it to its t,
Psa 105:31 gnats infested their whole t.
105:33 smashed the trees in their t.
Jer 1:1 Anathoth in the t of Benjamin.
15:13 committed throughout your t.
17:3 your sin throughout all your t.
17:26 from the t of Benjamin,
31:17 will return to their own t.
32:8 Anathoth in the t of Benjamin.
Jer 32:44 happen in the t of Benjamin,
33:13 in the t of Benjamin,
37:12 leave Jerusalem and go to the t
39:5 at Riblah in the t of Hamath.
52:27 at Riblah in the t of Hamath.
Eze 45:7 His t will be as large as the
45:7 territory will be as large as the t
Amo 1:13 The Ammonites enlarged their t
6:2 Is their t larger than yours?
Mic 5:6 our land and walk within our t.
Zep 2:8 and bragged about their t.
Mat 8:28 When he arrived in the t of the
8:34 begged him to leave their t.
15:22 A Canaanite woman from that t
15:39 and came to the t of Magadan.
19:1 Jordan River to the t of Judea.
Mar 5:1 They arrived in the t of the
5:10 not to send them out of the t.
5:17 to beg Jesus to leave their t.
7:24 place and went to the t of Tyre.
7:31 went through Sidon and the t
10:1 left there and went into the t
Luk 4:26 at Zarephath in the t of Sidon.
Act 13:50 and threw them out of their t.
14:6 and to the surrounding t.

terror (42)

Exo 15:16 T and dread will fall on them.
23:27 "I will send my t ahead of you
Dtr 28:66 You will live in t day and night.
1Sm 16:23 Saul got relief ⌊from his t⌋ and
Job 13:21 Don't let your t frighten me.
23:16 Almighty has filled me with t.
25:2 "Authority and t belong to God.
39:20 when its snorting causes t?
41:14 Its teeth are surrounded by t.
Psa 6:2 my bones shake with t.
6:3 has been deeply shaken with t.
6:10 and deeply shaken with t.
9:20 Strike them with t,
31:13 whispering of many people — t
73:19 completely swept away by t!
78:33 their years to an end in t.
119:161 words that fill my heart with t.
Pro 3:25 Do not be afraid of sudden t or
Isa 17:14 evening there will be sudden t.
21:4 I'm shaking with t.
28:19 this message brings only t.
29:23 They will stand in t of the God
31:9 In t they will run to their
47:12 succeed. You may cause t.
Jer 6:25 has a sword. T is all around.
8:15 of healing, but there's only t.
8:21 I mourn; t grips me.
14:19 of healing, but there's only t.
15:8 bring anguish and t to them.
20:3 but he calls you T Everywhere.
20:10 whispering, "T is everywhere!
32:21 powerful arm, and with great t.
36:16 they turned to each other in t.
46:5 T is all around them,"
49:5 I am going to bring t on you
49:29 to them, "T is all around!"
50:2 Marduk will be filled with t.
50:2 Its idols will be filled with t.'
Eze 23:46 Hand them over to t and looting.
26:16 Dressed in t, they will sit on
26:21 I will turn you into a t,
Dan 6:26 people should tremble with t

terrorists (1)

Act 21:38 four thousand t into the desert?"

terrorize (3)

Lev 26:16 I will t you with disease and
Jer 17:17 Do not t me. You are my refuge
Lam 2:22 You have invited those who t

terrors (13)

Job 6:4 God's t line up in battle against
18:11 "T suddenly pounce on him
18:14 and marched off to the king of t.
20:25 "T come quickly to the godless
24:17 with the t of deep darkness.
27:20 T overtake him like a flood.
30:15 T are directed toward me.
Psa 55:4 The t of death have seized me.
88:15 I have endured your t,
88:16 Your t have destroyed me.
91:5 You do not need to fear t of the
Sos 3:8 against the t of the night.
Isa 33:18 will be thinking of the t ⌊in

Tertius (1)

Rom 16:22 I, T, who wrote this letter,

Tertullus (3)

Act 24:1 and an attorney named T.
24:2 T began to accuse him.
24:9 that everything T said was true.

Tertullus' (1)

Act 24:9 Jews supported T accusations

test (50)

Exo 16:4 In this way I will t them to see
20:20 God has come only to t you,
Dtr 6:16 Never t the LORD your God as
8:2 order to humble you and t you.
8:16 order to humble you and t you.
Jdg 2:22 I will t the people of Israel with
3:1 the LORD left behind to t all
3:4 were left to t the Israelites,
6:39 Let me make one more t with
7:4 and I will t them for you there.
1Ki 10:1 she came to t him with riddles.
2Ch 9:1 So she came to Jerusalem to t
32:31 God did this to t him,
Psa 26:2 me, O LORD, and t me.
139:23 T me, and know my thoughts.
Ecc 3:18 "God is going to t humans in
7:23 I used wisdom to t all of this.
Jer 6:27 will know how to t their ways.
9:7 refine them with fire and t them.
11:20 you judge fairly and t motives
12:3 You see me and t my devotion
17:10 search minds and t hearts.
Dan 1:12 "Please t us for ten days.
Zec 13:9 I will t them as gold is tested.
Mal 3:10 T me in this way,"
3:15 they even t God and get away
Mat 16:1 Sadducees came to t Jesus.
19:3 Some Pharisees came to t him.
22:18 "Why do you t me,
Mar 10:2 Some Pharisees came to t him.
12:15 "Why do you t me?
Luk 10:25 Teachings stood up to t Jesus.
11:16 Others wanted to t Jesus and
Jon 6:6 Jesus asked this question to t
8:6 They asked this to t him.
Act 5:9 and your husband agree to t
1Co 10:9 put the Lord to the t as some
2Co 2:9 had also written to you to t you.
13:5 T yourselves! Don't you
13:5 it be that you're failing the t?
13:6 that we haven't failed the t.
13:7 prove that we've passed the t.
1Th 2:4 this because we passed his t.
5:21 Instead, t everything.
Jas 1:12 When they pass the t,
1Pe 1:7 troubles is to t your faith as
1:7 and by passing the t,
4:12 are coming in order to t you.
1Jn 4:1 Instead, t them. See whether the
Rev 3:10 whole world to t those living

tested (37)

Gen 22:1 Later God t Abraham and
42:15 This is how you'll be t:
Exo 15:25 and there he t them.
17:7 and because they t the LORD,
Num 14:22 They have t me now ten times
Dtr 33:8 You t your people at Massah.
Job 34:36 let Job be thoroughly t for
Psa 17:3 You have t me like silver,
66:10 You have t us, O God.
78:18 They deliberately t God by
78:41 Again and again they t God,
78:56 They t God Most High and
81:7 I t your ⌊loyalty⌋ at the oasis of
95:9 challenged me and t me there,
105:19 The LORD's promise t him

Psa 106:14 In the desert they t God.
119:140 promise has been thoroughly t,
Pro 27:21 but a person is t by the
Isa 28:16 a rock that has been t,
48:10 I have t you in the furnace of
Eze 21:13 Won't you be t? declares the
Dan 1:14 about this matter and t them
Zec 13:9 I will test them as gold is t.
Mat 22:35 t Jesus by asking,
Mar 8:11 They t him by demanding that
Luk 8:13 but when their faith is t,
22:28 in the troubles that have t me.
2Co 8:2 being severely t by suffering,
8:22 brother whom we have often t
Heb 3:8 those who rebelled and t me
3:9 That is where your ancestors t
11:17 When God t Abraham,
Jas 1:2 you are t in different ways.
1:12 who endure when they are t.
2Pe 2:9 godly people when they are t.
Rev 2:2 You have t those who call
2:10 prison so that you may be t.

testicles (3)

Lev 21:20 skin diseases, or crushed t.
22:24 crushed, torn out, or cut out t.
Dtr 23:1 A man whose t are crushed or

testified (6)

Dtr 19:18 witness lied when he t against
Jos 24:22 "You have t that you have
2Sm 1:16 You t against yourself when
Jon 5:33 and he t to the truth.
1Co 15:15 about God because we t that
Rev 1:2 John t about what he saw:

testifies (8)

Job 16:8 body rises up and t against me.
16:19 and the one who t for me is
Hos 5:5 arrogance t against them.
7:10 your arrogance t against you,
Jon 5:32 Someone else t on my behalf,
5:36 But I have something that t
5:37 The Father who sent me t on
Rom 8:16 The Spirit himself t with our

testify (40)

Exo 20:16 you t about your neighbor.
23:2 When you t in court,
Dtr 5:20 you t about your neighbor.
31:21 this song will t against them,
31:28 and earth to t against them.
1Sm 12:3 T against me in front of the
Job 15:6 Your lips t against you.
Psa 50:7 and I will t against you:
Pro 24:28 Do not t against your neighbor
29:24 He will not t under oath.
Isa 8:2 these dependable witnesses t:
59:12 Our sins t against us.
Jer 14:7 though our sins t against us.
Amo 3:13 Listen, and t against the
Mal 3:5 be quick to t against sorcerers,
3:5 I will also t against those who
Mat 10:18 front of governors and kings to t
23:31 So you t against yourselves
26:62 what these men t against you?"
Mar 13:9 front of governors and kings to t
14:60 what these men t against you?"
Luk 21:13 be your opportunity to t to them
Jon 5:31 "If I t on my own behalf,
5:36 which I perform, t on my behalf.
5:39 Scriptures t on my behalf.
8:13 "You t on your own behalf,
8:14 "Even if I t on my own behalf,
8:18 I t on my own behalf,
10:25 Father's name t on my behalf.
18:37 for this reason: to t to the truth.
Act 1:8 be my witnesses to t about me
4:33 the apostles continued to t that
10:39 We can t to everything Jesus
10:43 In addition, all the prophets t
26:5 me for a long time and can t,
26:22 day so that I can stand and t
1Pe 5:12 you and to t that this is
1Jn 1:2 have seen it, and we t about it.
4:14 We have seen and t to the fact

Rev 17:6 of those who t about Jesus.

testifying (3)

Act 13:31 are now witnesses and are t
20:24 Lord Jesus — the mission of t
Rev 22:20 The one who is t to these

testimonies (1)

Psa 93:5 Your written t are completely

testimony (46)

Exo 23:1 people by giving false t.
Num 35:30 as a murderer only on the t
35:30 one can be put to death on the t
Dtr 17:6 be sentenced to death on the t
17:6 be sentenced to death on the t
19:15 must be settled based on the t
Jos 4:16 who carry the ark of the t
Psa 19:7 The t of the LORD is
Pro 25:18 false t against his neighbor.
Zec 8:17 Don't enjoy false t.
Mat 19:18 Never give false t.
24:14 throughout the world as a t
26:59 were searching for false t
26:60 came forward with false t.
Mar 10:19 Never give false t.
14:55 for some t against Jesus
14:56 Many gave false t against him,
14:57 and gave false t against him.
14:59 But their t did not agree even
Luk 18:20 Never give false t.
22:71 "Why do we need any more t?
Jon 5:34 But I don't depend on human t.
5:36 on my behalf than John's t.
8:13 so your t isn't true."
8:14 my t is true because I know
8:17 own teachings say that the t
Act 22:18 won't accept your t about me.'
2Th 1:10 believed the t we gave you.
1Ti 6:12 about which you made a good t
6:13 who gave a good t in front of
1Jn 5:9 We accept human t.
5:9 God's t is greater because it is
5:9 greater because it is the t that
5:10 in the Son of God have the t
5:10 They haven't believed the t
5:11 This is the t: God has given us
Rev 1:2 and the t about Jesus Christ.
1:9 word and the t about Jesus.
6:9 word and the t they had given
11:7 the witnesses finish their t,
12:11 the lamb and the word of their t.
12:17 and hold on to the t of Jesus.
19:10 who hold on to the t of Jesus.
19:10 Worship God, because the t of
20:4 because of their t about Jesus
22:16 sent my angel to give this t

testing (11)

Exo 17:2 Why are you t the LORD?"
17:7 named that place Massah [T]
Dtr 13:3 The LORD your God is t you to
Isa 7:12 I wouldn't think of t the LORD."
Jer 6:27 I have put you in charge of t
Eze 21:13 T will surely come.
Act 15:10 So why are you t God?
2Co 8:8 but I'm t how genuine your love
Jas 1:3 You know that such t of your
1:4 Endure until your t is over.
Rev 3:10 the time of t which is coming

tests (5)

Job 23:10 When he t me, I'll come out as
34:3 The ear t words like the tongue
Psa 11:5 The LORD t righteous people,
1Th 2:4 who t our motives.
1Pe 1:7 faith as fire t how genuine gold

Thaddaeus (2)

Mat 10:3 (son of Alphaeus), and T;
Mar 3:18 T, Simon the Zealot,

thank (64)

Exo 18:10 He said, "T the LORD!
Lev 7:12 If you offer it as a t offering,
22:29 "When you sacrifice a t offering

Dtr 8:10 t the LORD your God for the
2Sm 16:4 "I sincerely t you,"
1Ki 10:9 T the LORD your God,
1Ch 29:13 "Our God, we t you and praise
2Ch 9:8 T the LORD your God,
20:21 "T the LORD because his
29:31 Come, bring sacrifices and t
29:31 sacrifices and t offerings,
33:16 offerings and t offerings
Neh 9:5 and t the LORD your God:
Psa 28:6 T the LORD! He has heard my
31:21 T the LORD! He has shown me
34:1 I will t the LORD at all times.
41:13 T the LORD God of Israel
63:4 So I will t you as long as I live.
66:8 T our God, you nations.
68:26 T God, the Lord, the source of
72:18 T the LORD God, the God of
89:52 T the LORD forever.
113:2 T the name of the LORD now
115:18 But we will t the LORD now
124:6 T the LORD, who did not let
135:21 T the LORD in Zion.
135:21 T the one who lives in
144:1 T the LORD, my rock,
Isa 38:18 Sheol doesn't t you!
Jer 17:26 They will also bring t offerings
33:11 You will hear those who bring t
Dan 2:23 ancestors, I t and praise you.
Amo 4:5 Burn bread as a t offering.
Luk 2:38 Joseph and began to t God.
17:9 He doesn't t the servant for
18:11 I t you that I'm not like other
Jon 11:41 I t you for hearing me.
Act 10:33 T you for coming. All of us are
24:3 we want to t you very much.
Rom 1:8 First, I t my God through Jesus
1:21 but did not praise and t him
6:17 But I t God that you have
7:25 I t God that our Lord Jesus
1Co 1:4 I always t God for you because
1:14 I t God that I didn't baptize any
14:18 I t God that I speak in other
15:57 T God that he gives us the
2Co 1:11 Then many people will t God
2:14 But I t God, who always leads
8:16 I t God for making Titus as
9:15 I t God for his gift that words
Eph 5:20 Always t God the Father for
Php 1:3 I t my God for all the memories
Col 1:3 We always t God,
1:4 We t God because we have
1:12 You will also t the Father,
1Th 1:2 We always t God for all of you
3:9 We can never t God enough for
2Th 1:3 We always have to t God for
2:13 We always have to t God for
2:13 by the Lord and we t God that
1Ti 1:12 I t Christ Jesus our Lord that he
2Ti 1:3 night and day when I t God,
Phm 1:4 Philemon, I always t my

thanked (8)

1Ch 25:3 They t and praised the LORD
2Ch 5:13 and singers praised and t
20:26 Because they t the LORD there,
Neh 8:6 Ezra t the LORD, the great
Dan 4:34 I t the Most High, and I praised
Luk 17:16 bowed at Jesus' feet and t him.
Act 27:35 t God in front of everyone,
28:15 he t God and felt encouraged.

thankful (4)

Rom 16:4 I'm t to them and so are all the
Col 3:15 you into one body. Be t.
Heb 12:28 Therefore, we must be t that
12:28 Because we are t,

thanking (2)

Eph 1:16 I never stop t God for you.
1Th 2:13 why we never stop t God:

thanks (113)

2Sm 22:47 T be to my rock! May God, the
22:50 That is why I will give t to you,
1Ki 8:15 "T be to the LORD God of

1Ki 8:56 "T be to the LORD!
1Ch 16:4 ark by offering prayers, t,
16:7 singing songs of t to the LORD:
16:8 "Give t to the LORD.
16:34 "Give t to the LORD because
16:35 nations so that we may give t
16:36 T be to the LORD God of Israel
16:41 to give t to the LORD ⌊by
23:30 appointed to stand to give t
2Ch 6:4 "T be to the LORD God of
20:26 in the valley of Beracah [T].
31:2 offerings, serving, giving t,
Ezr 3:11 As they praised and gave t to
7:27 ⌊I, Ezra, said:⌋ T be to the
Neh 12:31 two large choirs to give t
Psa 7:17 I will give t to the LORD for his
9:1 I will give ⌊you⌋ t,
18:46 T be to my rock! May God my
18:49 That is why I will give t to you,
28:7 I give t to him with my song.
30:4 his holiness by giving t.
30:9 ⌊of my body⌋ give t to you?
30:12 I will give t to you forever.
33:2 Give t with a lyre to the LORD.
35:18 I will give you t in a large
43:4 and I will give t to you on the
44:8 We give t to you forever.
45:17 is why the nations will give t
50:14 Bring ⌊your⌋ t to God as a
50:23 Whoever offers t as a sacrifice
52:9 I will give t to you forever for
54:6 I will give t to your good name,
57:9 I want to give t to you among
66:20 T be to God, who has not
67:3 Let everyone give t to you,
67:3 Let everyone give t to you.
67:5 Let the people give t to you,
67:5 Let all the people give t to you.
68:19 T be to the Lord, who daily
68:35 to his people. T be to God!
71:22 even I will give t to you as I
72:19 T be to his glorious name
75:1 We give t to you, O God;
75:1 to you, O God; we give t.
79:13 will give t to you forever.
86:12 I will give t to you with all my
88:10 the dead rise and give t to you?
92:1 It is good to give t to the LORD,
97:12 Give t to him as you remember
99:3 Let them give t to your great
100:4 Give t to him; praise his name.
105:1 Give t to the LORD.
106:1 Give t to the LORD because he
106:47 nations so that we may give t
106:48 T be to the LORD God of Israel
107:1 Give t to the LORD because he
107:8 Let them give t to the LORD
107:15 Let them give t to the LORD
107:21 Let them give t to the LORD
107:31 Let them give t to the LORD
108:3 I want to give t to you among
109:30 my mouth I will give many t
111:1 I will give t to the LORD with
118:1 Give t to the LORD because he
118:19 them ⌊and⌋ give t to the LORD.
118:21 I give t to you, because you
118:28 and I give t to you.
118:29 Give t to the LORD because he
119:7 I will give t to you as I learn
119:12 T be to you, O LORD.
119:62 At midnight I wake up to give t
122:4 it is a law in Israel to give t
136:1 Give t to the LORD because he
136:2 Give t to the God of gods
136:3 Give t to the Lord of lords
136:4 Give t to the only one who
136:10 Give t to the one who killed the
136:13 Give t to one who divided the
136:16 Give t to the one who led his
136:17 Give t to the one who defeated
136:26 Give t to the God of heaven
138:1 I will give t to you with all my
138:2 I will give t to your name
138:4 of the earth will give t to you,
139:14 I will give t to you because I
140:13 righteous people will give t to
Psa 142:7 from prison so that I may give t
145:10 have made will give t to you,
Jer 33:11 'Give t to the LORD of Armies
Mat 15:36 and the fish and gave t to God.
Mar 8:6 loaves and gave t to God.
Luk 6:32 do you deserve any t for that?
6:33 do you deserve any t for that?
6:34 do you deserve any t for that?
Jon 6:11 Jesus took the loaves, gave t,
6:23 the bread after the Lord gave t.
Rom 14:6 since they give t to God.
14:6 and they, too, give t to God.
15:9 "That is why I will give t to you
1Co 10:30 If I give t to God for the food I
Eph 5:4 Instead, give t ⌊to God⌋.
Php 4:6 and requests while giving t.
Col 3:17 giving t to God the Father
1Th 5:18 Whatever happens, give t,
1Ti 2:1 and prayers of t for all people,
4:3 with prayers of t by those who
4:4 it is received with prayers of t.
Rev 4:9 and t to the one who sits on the
7:12 Praise, glory, wisdom, t,
11:17 and said, "We give t to you,

thanksgiving (30)

Lev 7:13 your fellowship offering of t.
7:15 fellowship offering of t must
Neh 11:17 leader who led the prayer of t.
12:8 was in charge of the t hymns.
12:24 and t antiphonally as David,
12:27 joyfully with hymns of t,
12:46 praise and hymns of t to God.
Psa 26:7 I may loudly sing a hymn of t
42:4 ⌊I sang⌋ songs of joy and t
56:12 by offering songs of t to you.
69:30 its greatness with a song of t.
95:2 his presence with a song of t.
100:4 Enter his gates with a song of t.
107:22 Let them bring songs of t as
116:17 I will bring a song of t to you
147:7 Sing to the LORD a song of t.
Isa 51:3 t and the sound of singing.
Jnh 2:9 sacrifice to you with songs of t.
Mat 26:27 a cup and spoke a prayer of t.
Mar 14:23 spoke a prayer of t,
Luk 22:17 a cup and spoke a prayer of t.
22:19 bread and spoke a prayer of t.
1Co 11:24 and spoke a prayer of t.
14:16 to your prayer of t?
14:17 Your prayer of t may be very
2Co 4:15 it will produce even more t to
9:11 Your generosity will produce t
9:12 and more prayers of t to God.
Col 2:7 and overflow with t.
4:2 when you offer prayers of t.

theater (3)

Act 19:29 mind as they rushed into the t.
19:29 two men into the t with them.
19:31 him not to risk going into the t.

Thebes (4)

Jer 46:25 who is the god of T.
Eze 30:14 and bring punishment on T.
30:15 and I will kill many people in T.
30:16 T will be broken into pieces,

Thebez (2)

Jdg 9:50 Then Abimelech went to T,
2Sm 11:21 Didn't a woman on the wall of T

Theophilus (2)

Luk 1:3 for Your Excellency, T.
Act 1:1 In my first book, T,

Thessalonica (10)

Act 17:1 and came to the city of T,
17:6 the world are now here in T,
17:11 than the people of T.
17:13 But when the Jews in T found
20:4 and Secundus from T,
27:2 Macedonian from the city of T,
Php 4:16 Even while I was in T,
1Th 1:1 To the church at T united with
2Th 1:1 To the church at T united with
2Ti 4:10 world and went to the city of T.

Theudas (1)

Act 5:36 Some time ago T appeared.

thick (24)

Gen 19:28 from the land like the t smoke
Exo 10:21 and a darkness ⌊so t⌋ that it
1Ki 7:26 The pool was three inches t.
2Ch 4:5 The pool was three inches t.
Job 15:26 charges at him with a t shield.
22:14 T clouds surround him so that
23:17 or by the t darkness that covers
26:8 holds the water in his t clouds,
37:11 Yes, he loads the t clouds with
Isa 5:30 will be darkened by t clouds.
21:15 and from the t of battle.
44:22 acts disappear like a t cloud
48:4 nothing gets through your t
60:2 and t darkness covers the
Jer 2:31 a land of t darkness,
51:58 The t walls of Babylon will be
52:21 was three inches t and hollow.
Eze 24:12 fire can't take away its t tarnish.
40:5 It was 10 ½ feet t and 10 ½
40:7 the guardrooms was 9 feet t.
40:9 walls were 3 ½ feet t.
41:3 It was 3 ½ feet t. The entrance
41:9 of the side rooms was 9 feet t.
41:12 of the building was 9 feet t all

thickened (1)

Exo 15:8 The deep water t in the middle

thickets (2)

1Sm 13:6 in thorny t, among rocks,
Jer 4:29 They will go off into the t and

thick-leaved (1)

Neh 8:15 and other t branches — to make

thief (20)

Exo 22:2 "If anyone catches a t breaking
22:3 "A t must make up for what he
22:7 house: If the t is caught,
22:8 If the t is not caught,
Psa 50:18 When you see a t,
Pro 6:30 People do not despise a t who
Jer 2:26 "As a t feels ashamed when
Zec 5:3 the scroll says that every t will
Mat 24:43 of the night a t was coming,
24:43 He would not have let the t
Luk 12:39 at what hour the t was coming,
Jon 10:1 else is a t or a robber.
10:10 A t comes to steal,
12:6 poor but because he was a t.
1Th 5:2 will come like a t in the night.
5:4 you by surprise as a t would.
1Pe 4:15 t, criminal, or troublemaker.
2Pe 3:10 of the Lord will come like a t.
Rev 3:3 not alert, I'll come like a t.
16:15 "See, I am coming like a t.

thief's (1)

Pro 29:24 Whoever is a t partner hates

thieves (18)

Job 24:14 At night they become t.
30:5 the same way they shout at t.
Isa 1:23 rulers are rebels, friends with t.
Jer 7:11 become a gathering place for t.
48:27 Were they caught among t?
49:9 If t come during the night,
Joe 2:9 enter through windows like t.
Oba 1:5 "If t or looters come to you
Zec 5:4 and it will enter the houses of t
Mat 6:19 and rust destroy and t break
6:20 don't destroy and t don't break
21:13 it into a gathering place for t!"
Mar 11:17 it into a gathering place for t."
Luk 12:33 In heaven t and moths can't get
19:46 it into a gathering place for t."
Jon 10:8 before I did were t or robbers.
1Co 6:10 or t, those who are greedy or
Eph 4:28 T must quit stealing and,

thigh (16)

Gen 32:32 eat the muscle of the **t** attached
32:32 hip at the muscle of the **t**.)
Exo 29:22 the fat on them, and the right **t**.
29:27 to the LORD and the **t** that is
Lev 7:32 the right **t** as a contribution.
7:33 the right **t** will belong to him as
7:34 ⌊to me⌋ and the **t** from
8:25 with their fat, and the right **t**.
8:26 them on the fat and the right **t**.
10:14 and the **t** that was given
10:15 They will bring the **t** given as a
Num 6:20 and the **t** that is given.
18:18 the right **t** that are presented.
1Sm 9:24 cook picked up the leg and **t**
Eze 24:4 the **t** and shoulder.
Rev 19:16 On his clothes and his **t** he has

thighs (5)

Exo 28:42 to cover them down to their **t**.
Lev 9:21 took the breasts and the right **t**
Job 40:17 of its **t** are intertwined.
Psa 69:23 Let their **t** continually shake.
Sos 7:1 The curves of your **t** are like

thin (14)

Gen 41:6 Seven other heads of grain, **t**
41:7 The **t** heads of grain
41:19 were scrawny, very sick, and **t**.
41:20 The **t**, sickly cows ate up the
41:23 heads of grain, withered, **t**,
41:24 The **t** heads of grain
41:27 The seven **t**, sickly cows that
Exo 16:14 was covered with a **t** layer
39:3 They hammered the gold into **t**
Lev 13:30 skin and there is **t** yellow hair
Num 16:38 Hammer them into **t** metal
16:39 hammered into **t** metal sheets
Job 33:21 Their flesh becomes so **t** that it
1Co 14:9 You will be talking into **t** air.

think (248)

Gen 27:12 skin⌋ and **t** I'm mocking him.
31:15 Doesn't he **t** of us as
44:7 We would never **t** of doing
44:17 "I would never **t** of doing that!
Exo 14:3 Pharaoh will **t**, 'The Israelites
Num 11:29 asked him, "Do you **t** you need
16:14 Do you **t** you can still pull the
22:34 If you still **t** this trip is evil,
Dtr 15:9 Be careful not to **t** these
17:20 Then he won't **t** he's better than
29:19 He may **t** that he is so blessed
32:7 **T** about all the past
32:47 Don't **t** these words are idle
Jos 1:8 You must **t** about them night
9:25 Do to us what you **t** is good
Jdg 2:2 What do you **t** you're doing?
5:10 and who walk on the road — **t**.
6:31 Do you **t** you should save him?
10:15 Do to us whatever you **t** is right.
18:14 What do you **t** we should do?"
19:30 **T** about it! Form a plan, and
20:7 tell me what you **t**.
1Sm 1:23 "Do what you **t** is best,"
11:10 to us whatever you **t** is right."
14:36 "Do whatever you **t** is best,"
14:40 "Do whatever you **t** is best,"
18:23 "Do you **t** it's easy to become
23:3 ⌊afraid⌋ do you **t** we'll be⌋ if
24:4 whatever you **t** is right.'" David
2Sm 10:3 "Do you **t** David is honoring
13:32 don't **t** that all the young men,
16:10 "You don't **t** like me at all,
18:4 "I'll do what you **t** best,"
19:6 I **t** you would be pleased if
19:19 it against me or even **t** about it,
19:27 Do what you **t** is right.
19:37 do for him what you **t** is right."
24:13 **T** it over, and decide what
24:22 offer whatever you **t** is right.
2Ki 1:3 because ⌊you **t**⌋ there is no
1:6 because ⌊you **t**⌋ there is no
1:16 Is this because ⌊you **t**⌋ there is
10:5 Do what you **t** is best."
1Ch 19:3 "Do you **t** David is honoring
21:23 and do whatever you **t** is right.
Ezr 7:18 may do whatever you **t** is right
Neh 4:2 miserable Jews **t** they're doing?
Est 8:8 You write what you **t** is best for
Job 4:7 "Now **t** about this: Find me a
6:26 Do you **t** my words need
6:26 Do you **t** they're what a
18:2 **T** it through, and then we'll talk.
18:3 Why do you **t** of us as cattle?
23:15 When I **t** of it, I'm afraid of him.
30:1 I didn't **t** their fathers were fit to
35:2 "Do you **t** this is right when you
37:24 those who **t** they're wise."
41:8 **T** of the struggle! Don't do it
Psa 4:4 **T** about this on your bed and
35:25 or **t**, "Aha, just what we
38:12 All day long they **t** of ways to
40:17 May the Lord **t** of me.
41:7 They **t** evil things about me
50:21 ⌊That⌋ made you **t** I was like
54:3 They do not **t** about God.
59:7 ⌊They **t**,⌋ "Who will hear us?"
63:6 hours of the night, I **t** about you.
77:3 to lose hope as I **t** about him.
77:12 actions and **t** about what you
86:14 They **t** nothing of you.
94:9 Do you **t** he can't hear?
94:9 Do you **t** he can't see?
94:10 Do you **t** he can't punish?
94:10 Do you **t** he doesn't know
107:43 Let those who ⌊**t**⌋ they are
144:3 that you should **t** about them?
145:5 I will **t** about the glorious honor
Pro 5:6 She doesn't even **t** about the
26:5 or he will **t** he is wise.
Ecc 7:4 of wise people **t** about funerals,
7:4 of fools **t** about banquets.
Isa 5:21 for those who **t** they are wise
7:12 I wouldn't **t** of testing the
44:19 No one stops to **t**. No one has
57:6 Do you **t** I am pleased with all
57:10 You didn't **t** that it was
Jer 5:1 and **t** about these things.
7:10 You **t** that you're safe to do all
9:8 but they **t** of ways to set traps
12:4 They **t** that God doesn't know
20:9 I **t** to myself, "I can forget the
22:15 Do you **t** you're a better king
25:29 Do you **t** you'll go unpunished?
26:14 Do with me whatever you **t** is
31:20 I still **t** fondly of him.
44:19 do you **t** our husbands didn't
49:4 You **t**, "Who would attack me?"
51:50 and **t** about Jerusalem.
Eze 9:9 They **t** that the LORD has
14:6 Change the way you **t** and act!
18:30 "Change the way you **t** and act.
18:32 the way you **t** and act!"
20:32 You **t** that you want to be like
28:2 although you **t** you are a god.
28:3 You **t** that you are wiser than
28:6 You **t** you are wise like God.
32:2 Tell him, 'You **t** you are like a
33:11 Change the way you **t** and act!
47:22 **T** of them as Israelites.
Dan 6:14 He tried every way he could **t**
Hos 4:13 They **t** that these trees provide
9:7 ⌊They **t** that⌋ prophets are
13:14 I won't even **t** of changing my
Amo 6:3 it will be for those who **t** that
Nah 1:9 What do you **t** about the LORD?
Zep 1:12 who **t** that the LORD won't do
2:15 the city that used to **t** to itself,
Zec 1:15 the nations who **t** they are at
7:10 And don't even **t** of doing evil to
8:17 Don't even **t** of doing evil to
12:5 Then the leaders of Judah will **t**
Mat 3:2 change the way you **t** and act,
3:8 changed the way you **t** and act.
3:9 Don't **t** you can say,
3:11 change the way you **t** and act.
4:17 change the way you **t** and act,
5:17 "Don't ever **t** that I came to set
6:7 like heathens who **t** they'll
9:13 not people who **t** they don't
Mat 10:34 "Don't **t** that I came to bring
16:23 thinks but the way humans **t**."
17:25 him, "What do you **t**, Simon?
18:12 "What do you **t**? Suppose a man
21:26 All those people **t** of John as a
21:28 "What do you **t** about this?
22:17 So tell us what you **t**.
22:42 "What do you **t** about the
24:48 may **t** that it will be a long time
26:53 Don't you **t** that I could call on
Mar 1:15 Change the way you **t** and act.
2:17 not people who **t** they don't
6:12 change the way they **t** and act.
8:33 thinks but the way humans **t**."
Luk 1:51 He scattered those who **t** too
3:8 changed the way you **t** and act.
5:32 change the way they **t** and act,
5:32 not to call people who **t** they
7:42 Now, who do you **t** will love
8:18 Even what they **t** they
10:36 who do you **t** was a neighbor to
12:45 that servant may **t** that his
12:51 "Do you **t** I came to bring peace
13:2 Do you **t** that this happened
13:3 change the way you **t** and act,
13:4 Do you **t** that they were more
13:5 change the way you **t** and act,
14:31 sit down and **t** things through.
16:30 change the way they **t** and act.'
24:47 God and change the way they **t**
Jon 2:20 Do you really **t** you're going to
5:39 detail because you **t** you have
5:45 "Don't **t** that I will accuse you
8:53 Who do you **t** you are?"
9:34 Do you **t** you can teach us?"
9:40 "Do you **t** we're blind?"
11:56 "Do you **t** that he'll avoid
16:2 murder you will **t** that they are
18:34 "Did you **t** of that yourself,
Act 2:38 change the way you **t** and act,
3:19 change the way you **t** and act,
5:31 change the way they **t** and act,
11:18 they can change the way they **t**
13:25 'Who do you **t** I am?
15:38 However, Paul didn't **t** it was
17:29 we shouldn't **t** that the divine
17:30 change the way they **t** and act.
19:27 a danger that people will **t** that
20:21 to change the way they **t**
25:25 However, I don't **t** that he has
26:2 "King Agrippa, I **t** I'm fortunate
26:9 "I used to **t** that I had to do a lot
26:28 Agrippa said to Paul, "Do you **t**
28:22 would like to hear what you **t**.
Rom 1:30 They **t** up new ways to be
2:3 do you **t** you will escape God's
2:4 change the way you **t** and act?
2:5 change the way you **t** and act,
9:20 Who do you **t** you are to talk
12:2 Instead, change the way you **t**.
12:3 I ask you not to **t** of yourselves
12:16 Don't **t** that you are smarter than
15:1 must not **t** only of ourselves.
15:3 Christ did not **t** only of himself.
1Co 3:18 If any of you **t** you are wise in
4:1 People should **t** of us as
4:18 become arrogant because you **t**
7:40 is my opinion, and I **t** that I,
8:2 Those who **t** they know
10:12 So, people who **t** they are
10:33 I don't **t** about what would be
12:22 The parts of the body that we **t**
12:23 The parts of the body that we **t**
13:5 It doesn't **t** about itself.
14:20 don't **t** like children.
14:20 but **t** like mature people.
16:4 If I **t** it's worthwhile for me to go
2Co 1:17 You don't **t** that I made these
1:17 Do you **t** that when I make
5:16 So from now on we don't **t** of
5:16 If we did **t** of Christ from a
6:10 People **t** we are sad although
7:9 change the way you **t** and act.
7:10 to change the way they **t**
10:2 some people **t** that we are
10:9 I don't want you to **t** that I'm

2Co 10:15 you will t enough of us to give
11:5 I don't t I'm inferior in any way
11:12 because they t they're like us.
11:16 Again I say that no one should t
12:6 you so that no one may t more
12:21 not changed the way they t
Php 1:7 So it's right for me to t this way
2:3 Instead, humbly t of others as
3:8 It's because of him that I t of
3:15 mature faith should t this way.
3:15 And if you t differently,
3:15 God will show you how to t.
1Th 5:13 We ask you to love them and t
1Ti 1:9 for those who t nothing is holy
6:5 They t that a godly life is a
2Ti 2:8 Always t about Jesus Christ.
2:25 them to change the way they t
Phm 1:17 If you t of me as your partner,
Heb 4:1 We are afraid that some of you t
10:29 What do you t a person who
12:3 T about Jesus, who endured
13:7 T about how their lives turned
Jas 4:5 Do you t this passage means
2Pe 1:13 As long as I'm still alive, I t it's
3:9 he promised, as some people t.
3:9 change the way they t and act.
3:11 So t of the kind of holy and
3:15 T of our Lord's patience as an
Rev 2:5 change the way you t and act,
2:16 change the way you t and act,
3:3 change the way you t and act.
3:19 change the way you t and act.
16:9 not change the way they t

thinking (41)

Gen 18:12 t, "Now that I've become old,
20:10 "What were you t when you did
37:11 father kept t about these things.
Dtr 1:41 t you could easily invade the
1Sm 20:26 didn't say anything that day, t,
30:6 (They were t of their sons and
2Sm 14:1 king was still t about Absalom.
1Ki 5:5 Now I'm t of building a temple
18:27 Maybe he's t, relieving himself,
2Ki 7:12 They're t, 'When they've left the
Neh 5:7 After t it over, I confronted the
Job 21:16 is foreign to my way of t.)
22:18 is foreign to my way of t.)
Psa 115:12 who is ⌊always⌋ t about us,
Isa 33:18 Your mind will be t of the
Jer 37:9 Don't deceive yourselves by t
Eze 8:12 and each one of them is t,
Dan 4:19 What he was t frightened him.
7:8 While I was t about the horns,
Amo 9:10 sinners among my people are t,
Mat 9:4 Jesus knew what they were t.
9:4 "Why are you t evil things?
12:25 Jesus knew what they were t,
16:23 You aren't t the way God thinks
Mar 2:8 inwardly what they were t.
8:33 You aren't t the way God thinks
Luk 5:22 Jesus knew what they were t.
5:22 said to them, "What are you t?
6:8 Jesus knew what they were t.
9:47 Jesus knew what they were t.
11:17 Jesus knew what they were t,
Act 8:21 can see how twisted your t is.
8:22 will forgive you for t like this.
10:19 Peter was still t about the
16:27 T the prisoners had escaped,
1Co 11:2 I praise you for always t about
15:2 you believed it without t it over.
2Co 12:19 Have you been t all along that
Heb 11:15 If they had been t about the
Jas 1:8 A person who has doubts is t
Rev 9:20 the way they were t and acting.

thinks (21)

1Sm 3:18 May he do what he t is right."
Job 12:5 He t it is the fate of those who
Pro 16:2 A person t all his ways are
21:2 A person t everything he does
26:12 Have you met a person who t
26:16 A lazy person t he is wiser
30:12 A certain kind of person t he is
Sos 6:9 Her mother t she is unique.
Mat 16:23 aren't thinking the way God t
Mar 8:33 aren't thinking the way God t
Luk 15:7 God and changes the way he t
15:10 the way he t and acts."
17:3 changes the way he t and acts,
Rom 11:34 "Who knows how the Lord t?
14:14 to a person who t it is.
1Co 2:14 He t they're nonsense.
14:37 Whoever t that he speaks for
Gal 6:3 So if any one of you t you're
Php 3:4 If anyone else t that he can
Jas 1:26 If a person t that he is religious
Rev 2:21 change the way she t and acts,

third (116)

Gen 1:13 then morning — a t day.
2:14 The name of the t river is
32:19 the second servant, the t,
42:18 On the t day Joseph said to
Exo 20:5 for their parents' sins to the t
28:19 In the t row put jacinth,
34:7 to the t and fourth generation."
39:12 In the t row they put jacinth,
Lev 7:17 However, on the t day any
7:18 offering is eaten on the t day.
19:6 On the t day burn whatever is
19:7 If you eat any of it on the t day,
Num 2:24 They will be the t group to
7:24 On the t day the leader of the
14:18 for their parents' sins to the t
19:12 use this water on the t day
19:12 use this water on the t day
19:19 of unclean people on the t day
29:20 "On the t day bring 11 bulls,
31:19 use the ritual water on the t
Dtr 5:9 for their parents' sins to the t
14:28 At the end of every t year bring
26:12 Every t year is the year when
Jos 19:10 The t lot was drawn for the
Jdg 20:30 On the t day the men of Israel
1Sm 3:8 LORD called Samuel a t time.
17:13 the t was Shammah,
19:21 Saul even sent a t group of
2Sm 1:2 On the t day a man came from
3:3 The t was Absalom,
1Ki 6:6 and the t story was 10 ½ feet
6:8 story and then to the t story.
15:28 in Asa's t year as king
15:33 In Asa's t year as king of
18:1 A while later in the t year of the
18:34 Then he said, "Do it a t time,"
18:34 and they did it a t time.
22:2 In the t year King Jehoshaphat
2Ki 1:13 The king sent a t officer with
1:13 The officer of the t group went
19:29 But in the t year you will plant
1Ch 2:13 Shimea (his t son),
3:2 The t was Absalom,
3:15 the t was Zedekiah,
8:1 Aharah (his t son),
8:39 and Eliphelet (the t son).
12:9 Obadiah. The t was Eliab.
23:19 his t was Jahaziel;
24:8 the t for Harim, the fourth for
24:23 Jahaziel (the t⌋ of Hebron's
25:10 The t chose Zaccur,
26:2 (the second), Zebadiah (the t),
26:4 Joah (the t), Sachar (the fourth)
26:11 (the second), Tebaliah (the t),
27:5 The t commander of the army
27:5 the t month was Benaiah,
2Ch 15:10 In the t month of the fifteenth
17:7 In the t year of his reign,
31:7 In the t month they started
Ezr 6:15 was finished on the t day
Est 1:3 he held a banquet in the t year
5:1 On the t day Esther put on her
8:9 day of Sivan, the t month,
Job 42:14 and the t Keren Happuch.
Isa 37:30 But in the t year you will plant
Jer 38:14 brought him to the t entrance
Eze 10:14 the t was the face of a lion,
31:1 On the first day of the t month
41:7 the second story to the t story.
42:5 The side rooms on the t story
42:6 That is why the rooms on the t
Dan 1:1 In the t year of the reign of King
2:39 Then there will be a t kingdom,
8:1 In Belshazzar's t year as king,
10:1 In Cyrus' t year as king of
Hos 6:2 On the t day he will raise us so
Zec 6:3 The t had white horses.
13:9 I will bring this t⌊ of the
Mat 16:21 He would be killed, but on the t
17:23 They will kill him, but on the t
20:19 But on the t day he will be
21:35 and stoned a t to death.
22:26 also died, as well as the t,
26:44 the same prayer a t time.
27:64 the tomb secure until the t day.
Mar 9:31 They will kill him, but on the t
12:21 having children. So did the t.
14:41 He came back a t time and
Luk 9:22 He would be killed, but on the t
13:32 I will finish my work on the t
18:33 But on the t day he will come
20:12 Then he sent a t servant.
20:31 and so did the t. In the same
23:22 A t time Pilate spoke to them.
24:7 and come back to life on the t
24:21 What's more, this is now the t
24:46 come back to life on the t day.
Jon 21:14 This was the t time that Jesus
21:17 Jesus asked him a t time,
21:17 Jesus had asked him a t time,
Act 10:40 him back to life on the t day.
20:9 he fell from the t story and was
27:19 On the t day they threw the
1Co 12:28 next prophets, t teachers,
15:4 back to life on the t day as
2Co 12:2 to the t heaven fourteen years
12:14 ready to visit you for a t time,
13:1 This is the t time that I'll be
Rev 4:7 the t had a face like a human,
6:5 the lamb opened the t seal,
6:5 I heard the t living creature say,
8:10 When the t angel blew his
11:14 The t catastrophe will soon be
14:9 Another angel, a t one,
16:4 The t angel poured his bowl
21:19 the t agate, the fourth emerald,

thirst (14)

Exo 17:3 and our livestock die of t?"
Jdg 15:18 But now I'll die from t and fall
2Ch 32:11 to die from hunger and t when
Neh 9:15 from a rock to quench their t.
9:20 them water to quench their t.
Psa 104:11 Wild donkeys quench their t.
Isa 5:13 people will be parched with t."
29:8 lightheaded and parched with t.
41:17 tongues are parched with t.
50:2 and people die of t.
Lam 4:4 their mouths because of their t.
Hos 2:3 and she will die of t.
Amo 8:13 will faint because of their t.
Mat 5:6 are those who hunger and t

thirsts (3)

Psa 42:2 My soul t for God, for the living
63:1 My soul t for you. My body
143:6 parched land, my soul t for you.

thirsty (43)

Exo 17:3 But the people were t for water
Dtr 8:15 vast and dangerous desert — a t
28:48 are already hungry, t, naked,
Jdg 4:19 I'm t." But instead she gave him
15:18 Samson was very t.
Rut 2:9 When you're t, go to the jars
2Sm 16:2 tired and t in the desert."
17:29 are hungry, exhausted, and t."
23:15 When David became t,
1Ch 11:17 David was t and said,
Job 5:5 and t people pant after his
24:11 in wine vats, yet they are t.
Psa 69:21 my food, and when I was t,
107:5 They were hungry and t.
107:9 to drink to those who were t.
107:33 springs into t ground,
Pro 25:21 some food to eat, and if he is t,
25:25 ⌊Like⌋ cold water to a t soul,

Isa 21:14 Bring water for the **t**,
29:8 They will be like **t** people who
32:6 withhold water from **t** people.
44:3 I will pour water on **t** ground
48:21 They weren't **t** when he led
49:10 They will never be hungry or **t**,
55:1 Whoever is **t**, come to the
65:13 will drink, but you will be **t**.
Hag 1:6 You drink, but you're still **t**.
Mat 25:35 I was **t**, and you gave me
25:37 and feed you or see you **t**
25:42 I was **t**, and you gave me
25:44 did we see you hungry or **t**
Jon 4:13 this water will become **t** again.
4:14 will never become **t** again.
4:15 Then I won't get **t** or have to
6:35 in me will never become **t**.
7:37 He said loudly, "Whoever is **t**
19:28 been finished, he said, "I'm **t**."
Rom 12:20 If he is **t**, give him a drink.
1Co 4:11 are hungry, **t**, poorly dressed,
2Co 11:27 been hungry and **t**,
Rev 7:16 will never be hungry or **t** again.
21:6 water of life to anyone who is **t**.
22:17 Let those who are **t** come!

thistle (4)

2Ki 14:9 "A **t** in Lebanon sent a
14:9 came along and trampled the **t**.
2Ch 25:18 "A **t** in Lebanon sent a
25:18 came along and trampled the **t**.

thistles (9)

Gen 3:18 will grow thorns and **t** for you,
Jdg 8:7 thorns and **t** from the desert."
8:16 thorns and **t** from the desert.
Job 31:40 ⌊then⌋ let it grow **t** instead of
Pro 24:31 that it was all overgrown with **t**.
Isa 34:13 fortresses have nettles and **t**.
Eze 2:6 even though thorns and **t** are
Mat 7:16 from thornbushes or figs from **t**,
Heb 6:8 the earth produces thorns and **t**

Thomas (13)

Mat 10:3 Philip and Bartholomew; **T** and
Mar 3:18 **T**, James (son of Alphaeus),
Luk 6:15 Matthew, **T**, James (son of
Jon 11:16 **T**, who was called Didymus,
14:5 **T** said to him, "Lord, we don't
20:24 **T**, one of the twelve apostles,
20:25 **T** told them, "I refuse to believe
20:26 and **T** was with them.
20:27 Then Jesus said to **T**,
20:28 **T** responded to Jesus,
20:29 Jesus said to **T**, "You believe
21:2 **T** (called Didymus),
Act 1:13 **T**, Bartholomew, Matthew,

thorn (1)

Pro 26:9 ⌊Like⌋ a **t** stuck in a drunk's

thornbush (4)

Jdg 9:14 Then all the trees said to the **t**,
9:15 But the **t** responded to the trees,
9:15 fire will come out of the **t** and
Luk 6:44 thorny plants or grapes from a **t**.

thornbushes (18)

Job 30:7 and huddle together under **t**.
Psa 118:12 extinguished like burning **t**.
Isa 7:19 cracks in the cliffs, on all the **t**,
10:17 the weeds and **t** in one day.
33:12 will be set on fire like dry **t**.
55:13 Cypress trees will grow where **t**
Hos 2:6 why I will block her way with **t**
Mic 7:4 decent person is sharper than **t**.
Mat 7:16 "People don't pick grapes from **t**
13:7 seeds were planted among **t**,
13:7 and the **t** grew up and choked
13:22 The seed planted among **t** ⌊is⌋
Mar 4:7 seeds were planted among **t**.
4:7 The **t** grew up and choked
4:18 are like seeds planted among **t**.
Luk 8:7 Others were planted among **t**.
8:7 The **t** grew up with them and
8:14 among **t** are people who

thorns (30)

Gen 3:18 The ground will grow **t** and
Num 33:55 like splinters in your eyes and **t**
Jos 23:13 and **t** in your eyes until none of
Jdg 2:3 They will be like **t** in your
8:7 I'll whip your bodies with **t** and
8:16 taught them a lesson using **t**
2Sm 23:6 "Worthless people are like **t**.
Job 5:5 take it even from among the **t**,
Pro 22:5 A devious person has **t** and
Ecc 7:6 the crackling of **t** burning under
Sos 2:2 Like a lily among **t**,
Isa 5:6 **T** and weeds will grow in it,
7:23 there will be briars and **t**.
7:24 will be filled with briars and **t**.
7:25 will be filled with briars and **t**.
9:18 It burns up briars and **t**.
27:4 If only **t** and briars would
32:13 for my people's land where **t**
34:13 Its palaces are covered with **t**.
Jer 4:3 and don't plant among **t**.
12:13 but they harvested **t**.
Eze 2:6 Don't be afraid, even though **t**
28:24 no longer be hurt by prickly **t**
Hos 9:6 **T** will grow over their tents.
10:8 **T** and weeds will grow over
Nah 1:10 Nineveh will be⌋ like tangled **t**
Mat 27:29 They twisted some **t** into a
Mar 15:17 twisted some **t** into a crown,
Jon 19:5 He was wearing the crown of **t**
Heb 6:8 However, if the earth produces **t**

thorny (4)

1Sm 13:6 in **t** thickets, among rocks,
Pro 15:19 of lazy people is like a **t** hedge,
Luk 6:44 You don't pick figs from **t** plants
Jon 19:2 The soldiers twisted some **t**

thorough (5)

Gen 31:35 Laban had made a **t** search,
44:12 Then the man made a **t** search.
Dtr 13:14 Then make a **t** investigation.
19:18 must make a **t** investigation.
Ezr 7:11 a man with a **t** knowledge of

thought (159)

Gen 17:17 He laughed as he **t** to himself,
19:14 But they **t** he was joking.
20:11 Abraham said, "I **t** that because
26:7 He **t** that the men of that place
26:9 Isaac answered him, "I **t** I
26:28 So we **t**, 'There should be a
31:31 I **t** you would take your
32:8 He **t**, "If Esau attacks the one
32:20 "He **t**, "I'll make peace with him
38:11 He **t** that this son, too,
38:15 When Judah saw her, he **t** she
43:18 They **t**, "We've been brought
50:15 So they **t**, "What if Joseph
Exo 2:14 Then Moses was afraid and **t**
3:3 So he **t**, "Why isn't this bush
Num 16:34 They **t** the ground would
Dtr 1:39 Although you **t** the little
2:11 They were **t** to be Rephaim,
2:20 This land was **t** of as the land
Jos 14:7 reported to him exactly what I **t**.
22:24 We **t** sometime in the future
22:28 So we **t**, if this statement is
Jdg 15:2 father said, "I **t** you hated her.
16:2 They **t**, "We'll kill him at dawn."
16:20 He **t**, "I'll get out of this as
Rut 3:14 that moment Boaz **t** to himself,
1Sm 1:13 Eli **t** she was drunk.
2:30 I certainly **t** that your family and
13:12 So I **t**, 'Now, the Philistines
16:6 he saw Eliab and **t**,
18:11 He raised the spear and **t**,
18:17 (Saul **t**, "I must not lay a hand
18:21 Saul **t**, "I'll give her to David.
25:21 David had **t**, "I guarded this
27:11 He **t**, "They could tell Achish
27:12 Achish **t**, "He has definitely
2Sm 4:10 He **t** he was bringing good
10:2 David **t**, "I will show kindness
12:4 The rich man **t** it would be a
12:18 They **t**, "While the child was
12:22 I **t**, 'Who knows? The LORD
14:15 So I **t**, 'I will speak to the king
14:17 I **t** that you would reassure me.
16:23 **t** that Ahithophel's advice
17:29 these things because they **t**,
2Ki 5:11 He said, "I **t** he would at least
5:20 of Elisha (the man of God), **t**,
1Ch 19:2 David **t**, "I will show kindness
22:5 David **t**, "My son Solomon is
28:9 every **t** ⌊we have⌋.
2Ch 28:23 He **t**, "The gods of the kings of
Neh 6:9 They **t** we would give up and
Est 3:6 he **t** it beneath himself to kill
6:6 Haman **t** to himself,
7:8 The king **t**, "Is he even going to
Job 1:5 Job **t**, "My children may have
1:8 "Have you **t** about my servant
2:3 "Have you **t** about my servant
29:18 "I **t**, 'I may die in my own
32:1 Job **t** he was righteous.
32:2 angry with Job because Job **t**
32:7 I **t**, 'Age should speak,
34:14 If he **t** only of himself and
Psa 10:4 His every **t** ⌊concludes⌋,
39:2 While I was deep in **t**,
44:22 We are **t** of as sheep to be
56:5 Their every **t** is an evil plan
66:18 If I had **t** about doing anything
73:20 get rid of the **t** of them when
106:7 they gave no **t** to your miracles.
119:59 I have **t** about my life,
Pro 17:28 Even a stubborn fool is **t** to be
Ecc 1:16 I **t** to myself, "I have grown
2:1 I **t** to myself, "Now I want to
2:2 I **t**, "Laughter doesn't make any
2:15 I **t** to myself, "⌊If⌋ the destiny
2:15 So I **t** that even this is
3:17 I **t** to myself, "God will judge
3:18 I **t** to myself, "God is going to
5:20 people won't give much **t**
9:1 I have carefully **t** about all this,
12:9 He very carefully **t** about it,
Sos 7:8 I **t**, "I will climb the palm tree
Isa 14:13 You **t**, "I'll go up to heaven and
38:10 I **t** that in the prime of my life I
38:11 I **t** that I wouldn't see the LORD
38:11 I **t** I would never see another
53:4 but we **t** that God had wounded
53:8 Who would have **t** that he
65:20 be a hundred years old will be **t**
Jer 3:7 I **t** that after she had done all
3:19 I **t** that you would call me
5:4 I **t**, "These are poor,
10:19 Then I **t** that this is my
13:21 people you **t** were your friends
31:19 changed the way I **t** and acted.
34:17 world horrified at the **t** of you.
Lam 1:9 It gave no **t** to its future.
3:54 my head. I **t** I was finished.
4:20 We had **t** that we would live in
Dan 4:30 The king **t**, "Look how great
6:3 The king **t** about putting him in
Jnh 2:4 "Then I **t**, 'I have been
Mic 7:4 The day you **t** you would be
Mat 9:3 Then some of the scribes **t**,
9:21 She **t**, "If I only touch his
11:20 the way they **t** and acted.
11:21 have changed the way they **t**
12:41 and changed the way they **t**
14:5 because they **t** John was
21:37 He **t**, 'They will respect my
21:46 who **t** he was a prophet.
Mar 2:6 were sitting there. They **t**,
6:49 on the sea, they **t**, "It's a ghost!"
11:32 All the people **t** of John as a
12:6 He **t**, 'They will respect my
Luk 1:3 So I **t** it would be a good idea
1:66 who heard about it seriously **t**
2:19 heart and always **t** about them.
2:44 They **t** that he was with the
3:23 Jesus, so people **t**,
5:21 scribes and the Pharisees **t**,
7:39 invited Jesus saw this and **t**,
7:49 The other guests **t**,
10:13 the way they **t** and acted.

Luk 11:32 and changed the way they **t**
12:17 He **t**, 'What should I do? I don't
16:3 "The manager **t**, 'What should I
18:4 But then he **t**, 'This widow
18:6 to what the dishonest judge **t**.
19:11 and the people **t** that the
24:11 The apostles **t** that the
24:37 and **t** they were seeing a ghost.
Jon 11:13 but the disciples **t** Jesus meant
11:31 They **t** that she was going to
12:43 concerned about what people **t**
12:43 than about what God **t** of them.
13:29 So some **t** that Jesus was
20:15 Mary **t** it was the gardener
Act 7:25 Moses **t** his own people would
8:20 because you **t** you could buy
12:9 He **t** he was seeing a vision.
14:19 out of the city when they **t** that
16:13 we **t** Jewish people gathered
18:12 the Jews had one **t** in mind.
19:29 and the people had one **t** in
20:38 The **t** of not seeing Paul again
21:29 city earlier and **t** Paul had taken
26:20 to change the way they **t**
27:13 the men **t** their plan would
Rom 1:28 And because they **t** it was
8:36 We are **t** of as sheep to be
1Co 13:11 like a child, **t** like a child,
2Co 9:5 So I **t** that I should encourage
10:5 We take every **t** captive so that
Col 4:6 be kind and well **t** out so that
1Th 3:1 We **t** it best to remain in Athens
Heb 11:26 He **t** that being insulted for
12:10 disciplined us as they **t** best.

thoughts (71)

Gen 6:5 All day long their deepest **t**
Dtr 15:9 not to think these worthless **t**.
Jdg 5:15 important men had second **t**.
5:16 of important men had second **t**.
1Ch 29:18 over your people's deepest **t**.
Job 4:13 With disturbing **t** from visions
8:10 they share their **t** with you?
16:20 the spokesman for my **t**.
20:2 "My disturbing **t** make me
21:27 "You see, I know your **t** and the
Psa 5:1 Consider my innermost **t**.
7:9 who examines **t** and emotions.
19:14 mouth and the **t** from my heart
32:2 sin and who has no deceitful **t**.
33:11 His **t** stand firm in every
55:2 My **t** are restless, and I am
92:5 How very deep are your **t**!
94:11 that people's **t** are pointless.
104:34 May my **t** be pleasing to him.
119:97 They are in my **t** all day long.
119:99 written instructions are in my **t**.
139:2 You read my **t** from far away.
139:17 are your **t** concerning me,
139:23 Test me, and know my **t**.
Pro 1:2 to understand deep **t**,
12:5 The **t** of righteous people are
15:26 The **t** of evil people are
20:25 second **t** about those vows.
Ecc 7:26 I find that a woman whose **t** are
10:20 curse the king even in your **t**,
Isa 55:7 Let evil people abandon their **t**.
55:8 "My **t** are not your thoughts,
55:8 "My thoughts are not your **t**,
55:9 and my **t** are higher than your
55:9 thoughts are higher than your **t**.
66:18 of their actions and their **t**,
Jer 11:20 fairly and test motives and **t**.
20:12 He sees their motives and **t**.
23:31 prophets who speak their own **t**
Lam 3:62 The words and **t** of those who
Dan 2:29 **t** about what would happen in
2:30 would know your innermost **t**.
5:6 and his **t** frightened him.
5:10 Don't let your **t** frighten you,
7:28 I, Daniel, was terrified by my **t**,
Amo 4:13 He reveals his **t** to humans.
Mic 4:12 They don't know the **t** of the
Mat 5:8 are those whose **t** are pure.
15:19 Evil **t**, murder, adultery,
Mar 2:8 "Why do you have these **t**?
Mar 7:19 It doesn't go into his **t** but into
7:21 Evil **t**, sexual sins, stealing,
Luk 2:35 the **t** of those who reject him.
Jon 7:17 from God or if I teach my own **t**.
7:18 Those who speak their own **t**
Act 1:24 you know everyone's **t**.
8:22 So change your wicked **t**,
15:8 God, who knows everyone's **t**,
Rom 1:21 their **t** were total nonsense,
2:15 Their **t** accuse them on one
2:16 will judge people's secret **t**.
9:1 along with my own **t**,
12:3 Instead, your **t** should lead you
12:17 Focus your **t** on those things
1Co 3:20 "The Lord knows that the **t** of
Eph 2:3 corrupt desires and **t** wanted
Php 4:7 will guard your **t** and emotions
4:8 keep your **t** on whatever is right
1Th 2:17 you're always in our **t**.
Heb 4:12 a person's **t** and intentions.
1Jn 4:5 That's why they speak the **t** of

thousands (34)

Gen 24:60 mother of many **t** of children.
Exo 20:6 But I show mercy to **t** of
34:7 his love to **t** of generations,
Num 10:36 to the countless **t** of Israel!"
Dtr 5:10 But I show mercy to **t** of
7:9 his promise and is merciful to **t**
33:2 He came with tens of **t** of holy
33:17 The tens of **t** from the tribe of
33:17 tribe of Ephraim and the **t** from
1Sm 18:7 "Saul has defeated **t** but David
18:7 thousands but David tens of **t**!"
18:8 they credit tens of **t**," he said,
21:11 'Saul has defeated **t** but David
21:11 thousands but David tens of **t**.'"
29:5 'Saul has defeated **t** but David
29:5 thousands but David tens of **t**?"
Psa 3:6 I am not afraid of the tens of **t**
68:17 in number, **t** upon thousands.
68:17 in number, thousands upon **t**.
119:72 are worth more to me than **t**
144:13 sheep give birth to **t** of lambs,
144:13 tens of **t** in our fields.
Jer 32:18 show mercy to **t** of generations.
Dan 7:10 **T** and thousands served him.
7:10 Thousands and **t** served him.
11:12 dominate tens of **t** of people,
11:41 and tens of **t** will be defeated.
Mic 6:7 the LORD be pleased with **t**
Luk 12:1 **t** of people had gathered.
Act 21:20 how many **t** of Jews are now
Heb 12:22 You have come to tens of **t** of
Jud 1:14 Lord has come with countless **t**
Rev 5:11 and **t** times thousands.
5:11 and thousands times **t**.

thread (5)

Gen 14:23 that I won't take a **t** or a sandal
Dtr 28:66 will always be hanging by a **t**.
Jdg 16:9 bowstrings as a **t** snaps when
Sos 4:3 Your lips are like scarlet **t**.
Jer 51:13 The **t** of your life has been cut

threads (5)

Exo 39:3 They twisted the gold into **t**,
Num 15:38 with violet **t** in each tassel.
15:39 Whenever you look at the **t** in
Jdg 16:13 with the other **t** in the loom."
16:14 and tore his braids and the **t** out

threat (10)

Exo 32:14 So the LORD reconsidered his **t**
Jdg 8:28 Midian never again became a **t**.
Ezr 4:15 rebellious and has been a **t**
Psa 104:7 and fled because of your **t**.
Pro 28:15 ruler is a **t** to poor people.
Jer 39:16 I'm going to carry out my **t**
40:3 He has carried out his **t**.
Lam 2:17 He carried out the **t** he
Eze 6:10 I promised was not an empty **t**.
Jnh 3:10 So God reconsidered his **t** to

threaten (7)

Psa 68:30 **T** the beast who is among the
119:21 You **t** arrogant people,
Isa 30:17 you will flee when five **t** you.
Jer 16:10 'Why does the LORD **t** us with
18:7 "At one time I may **t** to tear up,
Act 4:17 So let's **t** them. Let's tell them
Eph 6:9 Don't **t** a slave. You know that

threatened (14)

Jdg 18:7 There was no one around who **t**
Jer 18:8 But suppose the nation that I **t**
19:15 its towns the disasters that I **t**.
25:13 on that land all the disasters I **t**
27:13 The LORD has **t** the nations
32:24 What you have **t** to do has
35:17 all the disasters that I **t**.
36:7 The LORD has **t** these people
36:31 all the disasters that I have **t**.'"
40:2 "The LORD your God **t** to bring
48:8 laid waste as the LORD has **t**.
51:62 Then say, 'LORD, you have **t**
Zec 14:11 will never be **t** with destruction.
Act 4:21 The authorities **t** them even

threatening (3)

Psa 80:16 Let them be destroyed by the **t**
Jnh 2:5 surrounded me, **t** my life.
Act 9:1 Saul kept **t** to murder the Lord's

threatens (1)

Isa 30:17 flee when one person **t** them,

threats (8)

Psa 52:2 Your tongue makes up **t**.
140:9 me be covered with their own **t**.
Pro 13:8 does not pay attention to **t**.
Jer 44:29 so that you will know that my **t**
Jnh 4:2 reconsider your **t** of destruction
Luk 3:14 and never use **t** or blackmail to
Act 4:29 pay attention to their **t** now,
1Pe 2:23 he didn't make any **t** but left

thresh (3)

Isa 41:15 You will **t** the mountains and
Hos 10:11 trained calf that loves to **t** grain.
Mic 4:13 Get up and **t**, people of Zion.

threshed (3)

Isa 21:10 have been **t** and winnowed.
28:27 Black cumin isn't **t** with a
28:28 It will be **t**. The wheels of his

threshers (2)

2Sm 24:22 and there are **t** and oxen yokes
1Ch 21:23 the burnt offering, **t** for firewood

threshes (1)

1Co 9:10 who plows or **t** should expect

threshing (46)

Gen 50:10 When they came to the **t** floor
50:11 funeral ceremonies at the **t** floor
Lev 26:5 **T** time will last until grape
Num 15:20 you make from the **t** floor.
18:27 to be grain from the **t** floor
18:30 from the **t** floor or winepress.
Dtr 15:14 grain from your **t** floor,
16:13 the grain from your **t** floor
25:4 Never muzzle an ox when it's **t**
Jdg 6:37 place some wool on the **t** floor.
Rut 3:2 its husks on the **t** floor tonight.
3:3 and go down to the **t** floor.
3:6 Ruth went to the **t** floor and did
3:14 this woman came to the **t** floor."
1Sm 23:1 They are robbing the **t** floors."
2Sm 6:6 they came to Nacon's **t** floor,
24:16 of the LORD was at the **t** floor
24:18 Araunah the Jebusite's **t** floor."
24:21 David answered, "To buy the **t**
24:24 So David bought the **t** floor and
1Ki 22:10 They were on the **t** floor at the
2Ki 6:27 you something from the **t** floor
1Ch 13:9 they came to Chidon's **t** floor,
21:15 was standing by the **t** floor
21:18 at Ornan the Jebusite's **t** floor.
21:20 but Ornan kept on **t** the wheat.
21:21 So he left the **t** floor and bowed

1Ch 21:22 "Let me have the land this **t**
21:28 had answered him at the **t** floor
2Ch 3:1 prepared the site on the **t** floor
18:9 They were sitting on the **t** floor
Job 39:12 back and take it to your **t** floor?
41:30 It stretches out like a **t** sledge
Isa 27:12 the LORD will begin his **t** from
41:15 make you into a new **t** sledge
Jer 51:33 of Babylon are like a **t** floor at
Dan 2:35 They became like husks on a **t**
Hos 9:1 You have sold sex on every **t**
13:3 straw blown away from **t** floors.
Joe 2:24 The **t** floors will be filled with
Amo 1:3 with iron-spiked **t** sledges.
Mic 4:12 like cut grain on the **t** floor.
Mat 3:12 and he will clean up his **t** floor.
Luk 3:17 his hand to clean up his **t** floor.
1Co 9:9 an ox when it is **t** grain."
1Ti 5:18 an ox when it is **t** grain,"

threshold (4)

1Sm 5:4 were lying on the temple's **t**.
5:5 still don't step on the temple's **t**.
1Ki 14:17 When she walked across the **t**
2Ch 3:7 the rafters, the **t**, the walls,

threw (105)

Gen 33:4 **t** his arms around him,
45:14 He **t** his arms around his
46:29 he **t** his arms around him and
50:1 Joseph **t** himself on his father,
Exo 4:3 When Moses **t** it on the ground,
7:10 Aaron **t** his staff down in front
7:12 Each of them **t** his staff down,
9:10 Moses **t** the ashes up in the air,
14:24 column of fire and smoke and **t**
15:25 He **t** it into the water,
24:6 and he **t** the other half against
32:19 In a burst of anger Moses **t**
32:24 I **t** it into the fire, and out came
Lev 8:19 Moses slaughtered it and **t** the
8:24 Moses **t** the rest of the blood
9:12 and he **t** it against the altar on
9:18 which he **t** against the altar on
Num 35:22 Maybe you shoved him or **t**
Dtr 9:17 the two tablets, **t** them down,
9:18 Once again I **t** myself down in
9:21 Then I **t** the powder into the
9:25 I **t** myself down in front of the
Jos 8:29 They **t** it in the entrance of the
10:10 The LORD **t** the enemy into
10:11 the LORD **t** huge hailstones on
10:27 Then they **t** them into the cave
Jdg 4:15 The LORD **t** Sisera,
9:41 Zebul **t** Gaal and his brothers
9:53 Then a woman **t** a small
11:2 they **t** Jephthah out.
14:10 the woman, Samson **t** a party.
15:17 he **t** the jawbone away.
1Sm 5:9 the LORD **t** the city into a great
7:10 Philistines and **t** them into such
2Sm 16:6 He **t** stones at David and
16:13 and **t** dirt at David.
18:17 They took Absalom, **t** him into
20:12 from the road to the field and **t**
20:22 They cut off Sheba's head and **t**
22:15 and **t** them into confusion.
2Ki 2:21 He went to the spring and **t** the
4:41 He **t** it into the pot and said,
6:6 He **t** it into the water at that
9:33 They **t** her down, and some of
10:25 the Baal worshipers and **t** out
23:6 and **t** its ashes on the tombs of
24:20 Jerusalem and Judah and **t**
2Ch 25:12 and **t** them off the top of the cliff
Neh 9:1 and **t** dirt on their heads.
9:11 You **t** into deep water those
9:26 They **t** your teachings over
13:8 So I **t** all of Tobiah's household
Job 2:12 They **t** dust on their heads.
16:11 to unjust people and **t** me into
31:27 and I **t** them a kiss with my
Psa 18:14 and **t** them into confusion.
18:42 I **t** them out as though they
Jer 26:23 The king executed Uriah and **t**
38:6 So they took Jeremiah and **t**
Jer 41:7 them and **t** them into
41:9 the cistern where Ishmael **t** all
52:3 Jerusalem and Judah and **t**
Lam 3:53 They **t** me alive into a pit and
3:53 into a pit and **t** rocks at me.
Eze 28:16 So I **t** you down from God's
28:17 So I **t** you to the ground and left
31:12 cut it down and **t** it away.
Dan 5:1 King Belshazzar **t** a large
8:10 It **t** some of the army of heaven,
8:12 It **t** truth on the ground.
Joe 1:7 they could eat, **t** the rest away,
3:3 They **t** dice for my people.
Oba 1:11 entered his gates and **t** dice
Jnh 1:7 So they **t** dice, and the dice
1:15 Jonah and **t** him overboard,
2:3 You **t** me into the deep,
Mat 13:48 and **t** the bad ones away.
21:12 and **t** out everyone who
21:39 **t** him out of the vineyard,
27:5 So he **t** the money into the
Mar 1:26 The evil spirit **t** the man into
9:20 it **t** the boy into convulsions.
10:50 The blind man **t** off his coat,
12:8 and **t** him out of the vineyard.
Luk 4:35 The demon **t** the man down in
9:42 and **t** him into convulsions.
20:12 But they injured this one and **t**
20:15 So they **t** him out of the
Jon 2:15 small ropes and **t** everyone
9:34 Then they **t** him out of the
19:24 They **t** dice for my clothing."
21:6 So they **t** the net out and were
Act 8:3 another and **t** them into prison.
13:50 and Barnabas and **t** them out
16:23 they **t** them in jail and ordered
27:19 On the third day they **t** the
27:28 So they **t** a line with a weight
Php 3:8 I **t** it all away in order to gain
2Pe 2:4 He **t** them into hell,
Rev 8:5 and **t** it on the earth.
12:4 in the sky and **t** them down
14:19 He **t** them into the winepress of
18:19 Then they **t** dust on their heads
18:21 He **t** it into the sea and said,
20:3 He **t** it into the bottomless pit.

thrilled (3)

Jdg 19:3 Her father was **t** to see him.
Isa 60:5 your heart will be **t** with joy,
Act 16:34 He and his family were **t** to be

thrive (1)

Zec 8:12 Seeds will **t** in peacetime.

throat (3)

Job 7:15 My **t** would rather be choked.
Psa 69:3 My **t** is hoarse. My eyes are
Pro 23:2 and put a knife to your **t** if you

throats (6)

Psa 5:9 Their **t** are open graves.
115:7 make a sound with their **t**.
149:6 high praises of God be in their **t**
Jer 2:25 feet are bare and your **t** are dry.
4:10 but a sword is held at their **t**."
Rom 3:13 Their **t** are open graves.

throbbed (1)

Sos 5:4 the keyhole. My heart **t** for him.

throne (189)

Exo 17:16 was lifted against the LORD's **t**,
25:17 "Make a **t** of mercy to cover the
25:18 the two ends of the **t** of mercy,
25:19 Form the angels and the **t** of
25:20 spread above the **t** of mercy,
25:20 looking at the **t** of mercy.
25:21 place the **t** of mercy on top.
25:22 I will be above the **t** of mercy
26:34 Put the **t** of mercy that is on the
30:6 with you there in front of the **t**
31:7 words of my promise with the **t**
35:12 the ark with its poles, the **t** of
37:6 He made the **t** of mercy out of
37:7 the two ends of the **t** of mercy,
Exo 37:8 He formed the angels and the **t**
37:9 spread above the **t** of mercy,
37:9 looking at the **t** of mercy.
39:35 its poles and the **t** of mercy,
40:20 on the ark and placed the **t**
Lev 16:2 and stands in front of the **t**
16:2 smoke above the **t** of mercy.
16:13 will cover the **t** of mercy,
16:14 the east side of the **t** of mercy.
16:14 times in front of the **t** of mercy.
16:15 and sprinkle it on the **t** of mercy
Num 7:89 to him from above the **t**
Jdg 3:20 As the king rose from his **t**,
1Sm 2:8 make them inherit a glorious **t**.
2Sm 3:10 establish David's **t** over Israel
7:13 and I will establish the **t** of his
7:16 Your **t** will be established
14:9 and your **t** are innocent."
1Ki 1:13 and that he will sit on your **t**?
1:17 and that he will sit on your **t**.
1:20 should succeed you on your **t**.
1:24 and that he will sit on your **t**,
1:27 who would sit on your **t** next?"
1:30 He will sit on my **t**."
1:35 when he comes to sit on my **t**.
1:46 is now seated on the royal **t**.
1:48 let me see the heir to my **t**.'"
2:4 have an heir on the **t** of Israel.'
2:12 sat on his father David's **t**,
2:19 Then he sat on his **t**.
2:19 He had a **t** brought for his
2:24 set me on my father David's **t**
2:33 and **t** always receive peace
3:6 him a son to sit on his **t** today.
5:5 whom I will put on your **t** to
7:7 where he sat on his **t** and
8:20 and I sit on the **t** of Israel as the
8:25 sitting in front of me on the **t**
9:5 have an heir on the **t** of Israel.'
10:9 has put you on the **t** of Israel.
10:18 king also made a large ivory **t**
10:19 Six steps led to the **t**.
10:19 Carved into the back of the **t**
16:11 as soon as he was on his **t**,
22:19 I saw the LORD sitting on his **t**,
2Ki 10:3 and put him on Ahab's **t**.
10:30 will sit on the **t** of Israel."
11:19 Then Joash sat on the royal **t**.
13:13 Then Jeroboam claimed the **t**.
15:12 will sit on the **t** of Israel."
1Ch 17:12 and I will establish his **t**
17:14 and his **t** will be established
22:10 I will establish the **t** of his
28:5 my son Solomon to sit on the **t**
28:11 and the room for the **t** of mercy.
29:23 sat on the LORD's **t** as king
2Ch 6:10 and I sit on the **t** of Israel as the
6:16 sitting in front of me on the **t**
9:8 He has put you on his **t** to be
9:17 king also made a large ivory **t**
9:18 Six steps led to the **t**,
18:18 I saw the LORD sitting on his **t**,
23:20 seated the king on the royal **t**.
Est 1:2 King Xerxes sat on the royal **t**
4:11 king in the **t** room without being
5:1 facing the king's **t** room.
5:1 was sitting on the royal **t** inside
Job 26:9 He covers his **t** by spreading
Psa 9:4 You sat down on your **t** as a
9:7 has set up his **t** for judgment.
11:4 The LORD's **t** is in heaven.
45:6 Your **t**, O God, is forever and
47:8 He sits upon his holy **t**.
89:4 I built your **t** to last throughout
89:14 are the foundations of your **t**.
89:29 endure forever and his **t** like
89:36 His **t** will be in my presence
89:37 Like the moon his **t** will stand
89:44 and hurled his **t** to the ground.
93:2 Your **t** was set in place a long
97:2 are the foundations of his **t**.
103:19 LORD has set his **t** in heaven.
113:5 He is seated on his high **t**.
132:11 own descendants on your **t**.
132:12 will also sit on your **t** forever."
Pro 16:12 a **t** is established through

Pro 20:8 A king who sits on his **t** to
20:28 with mercy he maintains his **t**.
25:5 and justice will make his **t**
29:14 his **t** will always be secure.
Isa 6:1 sitting on a high and lofty **t**.
9:7 David's **t** and kingdom.
14:13 set up my **t** above God's stars.
47:1 Sit on the ground, not on a **t**,
66:1 LORD says: Heaven is my **t**.
Jer 3:17 they will call Jerusalem the **t**
13:13 The kings who sit on David's **t**,
14:21 Don't dishonor your glorious **t**.
17:12 Our holy place is a glorious **t**,
17:25 on David's **t** will come through
22:2 the one sitting on David's **t**.
22:4 sit on David's **t** will ride through
22:30 They won't sit on David's **t** and
29:16 the king who sits on David's **t**
33:17 sitting on the **t** of Israel.
33:21 a descendant to rule on his **t**.
36:30 have no one to sit on David's **t**,
43:10 I will set his **t** over these
49:38 I'll set my **t** in Elam and destroy
Eze 1:26 that looked like a **t** made
1:26 On the **t** was a figure that
10:1 like a **t** made of sapphire.
28:2 I sit on God's **t** in the sea."
43:7 this is the place where my **t** is
Dan 5:20 was removed from the royal **t**.
7:9 His **t** was fiery flames,
Jnh 3:6 he got up from his **t**,
Zec 6:13 He will sit and rule from his **t**.
6:13 He will be a priest on his **t**.
Mat 5:34 by heaven, which is God's **t**,
19:28 of Man sits on his glorious **t**
23:22 heaven is to swear by God's **t**
25:31 he will sit on his glorious **t**.
Luk 1:32 Lord God will give him the **t**
Act 2:30 David's descendants on his **t**.
7:49 Lord says, "Heaven is my **t**.
12:21 sat on his **t** and began making
Rom 3:25 God showed that Christ is the **t**
Heb 1:8 about his Son, "Your **t**, O God,
4:16 we can go confidently to the **t**
8:1 the **t** of majesty in heaven.
9:5 overshadowing the **t** of mercy.
12:2 the one next to the **t** of God.
Rev 1:4 spirits who are in front of his **t**,
2:13 Satan's **t** is there. You hold on to
3:21 victory to sit with me on my **t**,
3:21 down with my Father on his **t**.
4:2 I saw a **t** in heaven,
4:3 around the **t** which looked like
4:4 Around that **t** were 24 other
4:5 and thunder came from the **t**.
4:5 were burning in front of the **t**.
4:6 In front of the **t**, there was
4:6 In the center near the **t** and
4:6 around the **t** were four living
4:9 to the one who sits on the **t**,
4:10 of the one who sits on the **t**
4:10 crowns in front of the **t** and say,
5:1 of the one who sits on the **t**.
5:6 standing in the center near the **t**
5:7 of the one who sits on the **t**.
5:11 the leaders surrounding the **t**.
5:13 "To the one who sits on the **t**
6:16 of the one who sits on the **t**
7:9 were standing in front of the **t**
7:10 to our God, who sits on the **t**,
7:11 the angels stood around the **t**
7:11 They bowed in front of the **t**
7:15 they are in front of the **t** of God.
7:15 The one who sits on the **t** will
7:17 in the center near the **t** will
8:3 on the gold altar in front of the **t**.
12:5 and taken to God and to his **t**.
14:3 a new song in front of the **t**,
16:10 angel poured his bowl on the **t**
16:17 A loud voice came from the **t** in
18:7 'I'm a queen on a **t**,
19:4 who was sitting on the **t**.
19:5 A voice came from the **t**.
20:11 I saw a large, white **t** and the
20:12 standing in front of the **t**.
21:3 a loud voice from the **t** say,
Rev 21:5 The one sitting on the **t** said,
22:1 It was flowing from the **t** of God
22:3 The **t** of God and the lamb will

thrones (16)

1Ki 22:10 in royal robes and seated on **t**.
2Ch 18:9 in royal robes and seated on **t**.
Job 36:7 He seats them on **t** with kings
Isa 14:9 kings of the nations from their **t**.
Jer 1:15 and they will set up their **t** at
13:18 "Come down from your **t**,
Eze 26:16 will come down from their **t**.
Dan 7:9 I watched until **t** were set up
Hag 2:22 I will overthrow the **t** of
Mat 19:28 will also sit on twelve **t**,
Luk 1:52 pulled strong rulers from their **t**
22:30 You will also sit on **t** and judge
Rev 4:4 that throne were 24 other **t**,
4:4 and on these **t** sat 24 leaders
11:16 who were sitting on their **t** in
20:4 I saw **t**, and those who sat on

throw (98)

Gen 37:20 **t** him into one of the cisterns,
Exo 1:22 all his people to **t** into
4:3 "**T** it on the ground."
6:1 and he will **t** them out of his
7:9 your shepherd's staff and **t**
9:8 and have Moses **t** them up in
22:31 countryside. **T** it to the dogs."
23:27 of you and **t** any nation you
29:16 and **t** it against the altar on all
29:20 **T** the ⸤rest of the⸥ blood
Lev 1:5 They will **t** it against all sides
1:11 Aaron's sons, the priests, will **t**
1:16 the gizzard with its filth and **t**
3:2 will **t** the blood against the altar
3:8 Then Aaron's sons will **t** the
3:13 Then Aaron's sons will **t** the
7:2 ⸤A priest⸥ will **t** the blood
16:8 Then Aaron must **t** lots for the
Num 18:17 **T** the blood from these animals
19:6 and some red yarn and **t** them
Dtr 7:23 over to you and will **t** them into
Jdg 11:7 Didn't you **t** me out of my
2Sm 11:21 woman on the wall of Thebez **t**
2Ki 9:25 and **t** him into the field that
9:26 Now take him and **t** him into
9:33 He said, "**T** her down."
Job 6:27 Would you also **t** dice for an
15:33 a vine and **t** off his blossoms
Psa 5:10 **T** them out for their many
22:18 They **t** dice for my clothing.
55:23 But you, O God, will **t** ⸤wicked
60:8 I will **t** my shoe over Edom.
108:9 I will **t** my shoe over Edom.
144:6 and **t** them into confusion.
Ecc 3:6 a time to keep and a time to **t**
10:16 the high officials **t** parties
11:1 **T** your bread on the surface of
Isa 2:20 On that day people will **t** to the
22:17 The LORD will **t** you out.
22:18 He will **t** you far away into
25:12 and **t** them into the dust on the
28:2 He will **t** them to the ground
30:22 You will **t** them away like
Jer 7:29 "Cut off your hair and **t** it away.
10:18 I am going to **t** out those who
16:13 So I will **t** you out of this land
22:7 finest cedar trees and **t** them
22:26 I will **t** you and your mother into
23:39 I will **t** you out of my presence
36:23 a scribe's knife and **t** them into
51:63 tie a stone to it and **t** it into the
Lam 2:10 They **t** dirt on their heads and
Eze 5:4 Later, take some of them, and **t**
7:19 They will **t** their silver and gold
21:12 I will **t** the princes and my
26:12 They will **t** your stones,
28:8 They will **t** you into a pit,
32:4 I will **t** you on the ground and
43:24 The priests must **t** salt on them
Dan 3:24 "Didn't we **t** three men into the
Amo 5:7 turn justice into poison and **t**
Jnh 1:5 They began to **t** the cargo
1:7 "Let's **t** dice to find out who is
Jnh 1:12 He told them, "**T** me overboard.
Mic 7:19 You will **t** all our sins into the
Nah 3:6 I will **t** filth on you.
Zec 1:21 to **t** down the horns of the
9:4 He will **t** its wealth into the sea
Mat 5:25 who will **t** you into prison.
5:29 tear it out and **t** it away.
5:30 cut it off and **t** it away.
7:6 is holy to dogs or **t** your pearls
13:42 The angels will **t** them into a
13:50 Then the angels will **t** the evil
15:26 to take the children's food and **t**
17:27 go to the sea and **t** in a hook.
18:8 cut it off and **t** it away.
18:9 tear it out and **t** it away.
22:13 and **t** him outside into the
25:30 **T** this useless servant outside
Mar 7:27 to take the children's food and **t**
11:15 and began to **t** out those who
Luk 4:29 They intended to **t** him off of it.
12:5 has the power to **t** you into hell
12:49 "I have come to **t** fire on the
12:58 who will **t** you into prison.
14:35 People **t** it away. "Let the
19:45 and began to **t** out those who
22:41 from them about a stone's **t**,
Jon 8:7 sinless should be the first to **t**
8:59 picked up stones to **t** at Jesus.
19:24 Let's **t** dice to see who will get
21:6 He told them, "**T** the net out on
Act 16:37 Now are they going to **t** us out
27:18 began to **t** the cargo overboard.
3Jn 1:10 attempts to **t** those people out
Rev 2:10 The devil is going to **t** some of
2:22 I'm going to **t** her into a sickbed.

throwing (10)

Num 35:20 deliberately **t** something at him,
2Ki 3:25 each man **t** rocks on every
Ezr 10:1 and **t** himself down in front of
Psa 17:11 focused their attention on **t** me
Mat 4:18 They were **t** a net into the sea
27:35 among themselves by **t** dice.
Mar 1:16 They were **t** a net into the sea
15:24 among themselves by **t** dice
Luk 23:34 among themselves by **t** dice.
Act 22:23 and **t** dirt into the air.

thrown (94)

Exo 10:11 Then Moses and Aaron were **t**
12:39 risen because they'd been **t** out
15:1 He has **t** horses and their riders
15:4 He has **t** Pharaoh's chariots
15:21 He has **t** horses and their riders
Lev 14:40 to be torn out and **t** outside
1Sm 25:29 like stones **t** from a sling.
2Sm 20:21 "His head will be **t** to you from
23:6 All of them are **t** away,
1Ki 13:24 His dead body was **t** on the
13:28 He found the body of the man **t**
2Ki 7:15 that the Arameans had **t** away
19:18 They have **t** the gods from
Est 3:7 Pur (which means the lot) was **t**
9:24 means the lot) **t** ⸤in order
Job 16:15 and I have **t** my strength in the
Psa 37:24 When he falls, he will not be **t**
89:39 and have **t** his crown into
102:10 picked me up and **t** me away.
102:26 and they will be **t** away.
140:10 Let them be **t** into a pit,
141:6 When their judges are **t** off a
Pro 10:8 will be **t** down headfirst.
10:10 will be **t** down headfirst.
14:32 A wicked person is **t** down by
16:33 The dice are **t**, but the LORD
Isa 14:19 But you are **t** out of your tomb
34:3 Their dead bodies will be **t** out.
37:19 They have **t** the gods from
38:17 You have **t** all my sins behind
Jer 14:16 prophesy to will be **t** out into
22:19 He will be dragged off and **t**
22:28 his descendants will be **t** out
36:30 and his own corpse will be **t**
38:9 They have **t** him into the
51:34 He has **t** us into confusion.
Lam 2:1 He has **t** down Israel's beauty

Eze 15:4 It is only **t** into the fire as fuel.
16:5 But you were **t** into an open
19:12 in anger it was uprooted and **t**
Dan 3:6 will immediately be **t** into
3:11 down and worship will be **t** into
3:15 you will immediately be **t** into a
3:20 so that they could be **t** into
3:21 Then the three men were **t** into
6:7 will be **t** into a lions' den.
6:12 will be **t** into a lions' den?"
6:16 was brought to him and **t** into
6:24 and their children were **t** into
8:7 So the ram was **t** down on the
Amo 4:3 You will be **t** into a garbage
Mat 3:10 be cut down and **t** into a fire.
5:13 for anything except to be **t** out
5:29 than to have all of it **t** into hell.
6:30 and tomorrow it's **t** into an
7:19 is cut down and **t** into a fire.
8:12 kingdom will be **t** outside into
13:47 is like a net that was **t** into
14:24 was being **t** around by the
18:8 and be **t** into everlasting fire.
18:9 two eyes and be **t** into hellfire.
21:21 'Be uprooted and **t** into the sea,'
Mar 9:22 The demon has often **t** him into
9:42 of them to lose faith to be **t** into
9:45 have two feet and be **t** into hell.
9:47 two eyes and be **t** into hell.
11:23 'Be uprooted and **t** into the sea,'
Luk 3:9 be cut down and **t** into a fire."
12:28 and tomorrow it's **t** into an
13:28 of God, but you'll be **t** out.
17:2 best for that person to be **t** into
23:19 (Barabbas had been **t** into
Jon 9:35 heard that the Jews had **t**
12:31 of this world will be **t** out now.
12:42 would have **t** them out
15:6 Whoever doesn't live in me is **t**
15:6 **t** into a fire, and burned.
16:2 You will be **t** out of
Act 7:58 and after they had **t** him out of
12:4 Herod had him **t** into prison
16:37 without a trial and have **t**
Rev 8:7 and were **t** on the earth.
8:8 burning with fire was **t** into
12:9 The huge serpent was **t** down.
12:9 was **t** down to earth.
12:9 Its angels were **t** down with it.
12:10 of our God, has been **t** out.
12:13 saw that it had been **t** down
18:21 city Babylon will be **t** down
19:20 Both of them were **t** alive into
20:10 was **t** into the fiery lake of
20:10 the false prophet were also **t**.
20:14 Death and hell were **t** into the
20:15 in the Book of Life were **t** into

throws (11)

Lev 7:14 It will belong to the priest who **t**
Neh 9:11 your people as someone **t**
Job 20:23 ⌊God⌋ **t** his burning anger at
30:19 He **t** me into the dirt so that I
Psa 147:17 He is the one who **t** his
Pro 19:15 Laziness **t** one into a deep
21:12 He **t** wicked people into
Isa 26:5 He levels it to the ground and **t**
34:17 He is the one who **t** dice for
57:20 It isn't quiet, and its water **t** up
Mar 9:18 it **t** him to the ground.

thumb (5)

Lev 8:23 right ear lobe, on his right **t**,
14:14 the right ear lobe, on the right **t**,
14:17 the right ear lobe, on the right **t**,
14:25 the right ear lobe, on the right **t**,
14:28 the right ear lobe, on the right **t**,

thumbs (4)

Exo 29:20 and his sons, on their right **t**,
Lev 8:24 right ear lobes, on their right **t**,
Jdg 1:6 and cut off his **t** and big toes.
1:7 "Seventy kings who had their **t**

Thummim (6)

Exo 28:30 Put the Urim and **T** into the
Lev 8:8 it he placed the Urim and **T**.
Dtr 33:8 "Your **T** and Urim belong to
1Sm 14:41 ⌊let him⌋ draw **T**."
Ezr 2:63 use the Urim and **T** ⌊to settle
Neh 7:65 use the Urim and **T** ⌊to settle

thunder (29)

Exo 9:23 the LORD sent **t** and hail,
9:28 had enough of God's **t** and hail.
9:29 The **t** will stop, and there will
9:33 The **t** and the hail stopped,
9:34 and the **t** had stopped,
19:16 there was **t** and lightning with a
20:18 All the people heard the **t** and
1Sm 12:17 and he'll send **t** and rain.
12:18 That day the LORD sent **t** and
1Ch 16:32 and everything in it roar like **t**.
Job 26:14 understand the **t** of his power?"
36:33 The **t** announces his coming.
37:4 back when his **t** is heard.
40:9 Can you **t** with a voice like his?
Psa 77:18 The sound of your **t** rumbled in
81:7 I was hidden in **t**, but I
96:11 and everything in it roar like **t**.
98:7 those who live in it roar like **t**.
104:7 ran away at the sound of your **t**.
Isa 29:6 Armies will punish you with **t**,
Eze 1:24 like the **t** of the Almighty,
Joe 3:16 his voice will **t** from Jerusalem.
Rev 4:5 and **t** came from the throne.
6:1 say with a voice like **t**,
8:5 Then there was **t**, noise,
11:19 There was lightning, noise, **t**,
14:2 water and the noise of loud **t**.
16:18 There was lightning, noise, **t**,
19:6 like the noise of loud **t**,

thunderbolts (1)

Mar 3:17 which means "**T**"),

thundered (5)

1Sm 7:10 On that day the LORD **t** loudly
2Sm 22:14 The LORD **t** from heaven.
Psa 18:13 The LORD **t** in the heavens.
77:17 The sky **t**. Even your arrows
Jon 12:29 the voice and said that it had **t**.

thundering (2)

Job 39:25 battle far away — the **t** ⌊orders⌋
Eze 3:12 me I heard a loud **t** voice say,

thunders (12)

1Sm 2:10 He **t** at them from the heavens.
Job 36:29 or how he **t** from his dwelling
37:4 He **t** with his majestic voice.
37:5 God's voice **t** in miraculous
Psa 29:3 The God of glory **t**.
Jer 25:30 He **t** from his holy dwelling
51:16 When he **t**, the water in the sky
Amo 1:2 and his voice **t** from Jerusalem.
Rev 10:3 When he shouted, the seven **t**
10:4 When the seven **t** spoke,
10:4 up what the seven **t** have said,
10:11 The seven **t** told me,

thunderstorm (2)

Isa 28:2 He is like a **t**, an overwhelming
66:15 and with his chariots like a **t**.

thunderstorms (4)

Job 28:26 the rain and set paths for the **t**,
38:25 rains and a path for the **t**
Psa 135:7 who makes lightning for the **t**,
Zec 10:1 The LORD makes **t**.

Thyatira (4)

Act 16:14 to Judaism from the city of **T**
Rev 1:11 **T**, Sardis, Philadelphia,
2:18 messenger of the church in **T**,
2:24 But the rest of you in **T** — all

Tiberias (3)

Jon 6:1 Sea of Galilee (or the Sea of **T**).
6:23 Other boats from **T** arrived near
21:1 Later, by the Sea of **T**,

Tiberius (1)

Luk 3:1 in the reign of the Emperor **T**.

Tibhath (1)

1Ch 18:8 of bronze from **T** and Cun,

Tibni (3)

1Ki 16:21 Half of the army followed **T**,
16:22 than the half which followed **T**,
16:22 **T** died, and Omri became king.

Tidal (2)

Gen 14:1 and King **T** of Goiim —
14:9 of Elam, King **T** of Goiim,

tie (28)

Gen 49:11 He will **t** his donkey to a
Exo 28:37 Fasten a violet cord to it, and **t**
29:5 Use the belt to **t** it on him
29:9 **T** belts around the waists of
Dtr 6:8 and⌋ **t** them around your wrist,
11:18 **t** them around your wrist,
Jos 2:18 When we invade your land, **t**
Jdg 15:10 "We've come to **t** up Samson
15:12 "We've come to **t** you up and
15:13 "We promise we'll only **t** you
16:5 We want to **t** him up in order to
16:9 waiting for her ⌊to **t** him up⌋.
Job 41:1 a fishhook or **t** its tongue down
Pro 7:3 **T** them on your fingers.
Isa 8:16 **T** up the written instructions.
Jer 51:63 **t** a stone to it and throw it into
Eze 3:25 People will **t** you up with ropes,
4:8 I will **t** you up with ropes so
24:17 **T** on your turban, and put on
Dan 3:20 from his army to **t** up Shadrach,
Mat 12:29 First he must **t** up the strong
13:30 the weeds first and **t** them
22:13 '**T** his hands and feet,
Mar 3:27 First he must **t** up the strong
15:1 council decided to **t** Jesus up,
Act 21:11 the Jews in Jerusalem will **t** up
22:5 I was going there to **t** up
22:25 had Paul stretch out ⌊to **t** him

tied (37)

Gen 22:9 Then he **t** up his son Isaac and
38:28 yarn, **t** it on his wrist, and said,
Exo 39:31 fastened a violet cord to it and **t**
Jos 2:21 So she let them go and **t** the
Jdg 15:4 He **t** them together in pairs by
15:13 So they **t** him up with two new
16:6 How can you be **t** up so that
16:8 She **t** Samson up with them.
16:10 tell me how you can be **t** up."
16:12 some new ropes and **t** him up
16:13 Tell me how you can be **t** up."
16:14 So Delilah **t** his braids to the
16:21 They **t** him up with double
2Sm 3:34 Your hands were not **t**.
2Ki 5:23 Naaman **t** up 150 pounds of
7:10 and donkeys were still **t** up.
Psa 119:61 wicked people are **t** around me,
129:4 wicked people **t** around me.
Lam 1:14 They were **t** together by God's
1:14 They were **t** around my neck.
Dan 3:23 They were still **t** up.
Mat 14:3 **t** him up, and put him in prison.
21:2 You will find a donkey **t** there
27:2 They **t** him up, led him away,
Mar 6:17 **t** him up, and put him in prison.
11:2 find a young donkey **t** there.
11:4 It was **t** to the door of a house.
Luk 19:30 find a young donkey **t** there.
Jon 13:4 and **t** it around his waist.
13:5 that he had **t** around his waist.
18:12 Jesus. They **t** Jesus up
18:24 Jesus was still **t** up.
Act 21:11 Paul's belt and **t** his own feet
21:13 I'm ready not only to be **t** up in
21:33 and ordered him to be **t** up with
22:4 I **t** up men and women and put
22:29 he found out that he had **t** up

ties (4)

Jdg 16:7 Samson told her, "If someone **t**
16:11 Samson told her, "If someone **t**
Eph 4:3 the peace that **t** you together,
Col 3:14 **t** everything together perfectly.

tight (3)

Rut 3:15 you're wearing and hold it **t**."
3:15 So she held it **t** while he
Act 16:23 to keep them under **t** security.

tightened (1)

Isa 28:22 or your chains will be **t**,

tight-fisted (1)

Dtr 15:8 hard-hearted and **t** with them.

tightly (8)

Exo 26:24 at the bottom and held **t** at
29:5 Use the belt to tie it on him **t**.
36:29 at the bottom and held **t** at
Jdg 16:11 "If someone ties me up **t** with
Rut 1:14 but Ruth held on to her **t**.
Job 41:15 of scales that are **t** sealed.
Psa 119:31 I have clung **t** to your written
Isa 22:18 He will wrap you up **t** like a

Tiglath Pileser (3)

2Ki 15:29 of Israel, King **T** of Assyria
16:7 messengers to King **T** of Assyria
16:10 to meet King **T** of Assyria

Tiglath Pilneser (2)

1Ch 5:6 King **T** of Assyria took him away
5:26 Pul of Assyria (King **T** of Assyria

Tigris (2)

Gen 2:14 The name of the third river is **T**.
Dan 10:4 I was by the great **T** River.

Tikvah (1)

2Ki 22:14 son of **T** and grandson of

Tikvah's (1)

Ezr 10:15 **T** son, opposed this.

tiles (1)

Luk 5:19 They made an opening in the **t**

Tillegath Pilneser (1)

2Ch 28:20 King **T** of Assyria attacked Ahaz

Tilon (1)

1Ch 4:20 Rinnah, Ben Hanan, and **T**.

tilted (1)

Jer 1:13 and its top is **t** away from the

Timaeus (1)

Mar 10:46 named Bartimaeus, son of **T**,

timber (1)

Zec 5:4 and destroy the **t** and stone."

time (836)

Gen 2:4 at the **t** when the LORD God
4:26 At that **t** people began to
6:9 among the people of his **t**.
12:6 At that **t** the Canaanites were in
13:15 for an indefinite period of **t**.
14:1 At that **t** ⌊four kings⌋ — King
15:18 At that **t** the LORD made a
17:21 birth to him at this **t** next year."
18:10 back to you next year at this **t**,
18:14 back to you next year at this **t**,
18:32 one more **t**," Abraham said.
21:2 and at the exact **t** God had
21:22 At that **t** Abimelech,
21:34 Abraham lived a long **t** in the
22:15 from heaven a second **t**
25:24 When the **t** came for her to give
26:1 earlier one during Abraham's **t**.
26:8 he had been there a long **t**,
27:41 Esau said to himself, "The **t** to
29:7 "It isn't **t** yet to gather the
Gen 29:21 "The **t** is up; give me my wife!
29:35 "This **t** I will praise the LORD."
30:20 This **t** my husband will honor
34:19 young man didn't waste any **t**
37:34 mourned for his son a long **t**.
38:1 About that **t** Judah left his
38:12 After a long **t** Judah's wife,
38:27 The **t** came for Tamar to give
39:5 From that **t** on the LORD
40:4 had been confined for some **t**,
41:10 Some **t** ago when Pharaoh was
43:18 back into our sacks the first **t**.
46:29 cried on his shoulder a long **t**.
47:24 Every **t** you harvest,
50:3 in the usual **t** — 40 days.
50:4 When the **t** of mourning for
Exo 2:11 In the course of **t** Moses grew
2:23 After a long **t** passed,
4:7 and when he took it out this **t**,
4:26 that she said at that **t**,
6:28 At that **t** the LORD spoke to
8:32 Yet, this **t**, too, Pharaoh was
9:5 The LORD set a definite **t**.
9:18 So, at this **t** tomorrow I will
9:27 "This **t** I have sinned,"
10:6 this from the **t** they first came
10:17 forgive my sin one more **t**.
12:39 out of Egypt and had no **t**
13:10 these rules every year at this **t**.
16:36 at that **t** held 20 quarts.)
20:12 so that you may live for a long **t**
21:19 injured man for the loss of his **t**
23:15 Do this at the appointed **t** in the
23:18 at the same **t** you offer anything
25:30 it will be in front of me all the **t**.
33:5 I might destroy you at any **t**.
34:18 seven days at the appointed **t**
34:21 Even during the **t** of plowing or
34:25 at the same **t** you offer anything
Lev 7:38 offerings at the same **t** that
13:8 will examine him one more **t**,
14:44 will examine it one more **t**.
14:46 goes into the house any **t**
16:17 meeting from the **t** Aaron enters
19:10 your vineyard a second **t**
23:28 It is a **t** when you make peace
25:29 buy it back only within that **t**.
26:4 will give you rain at the right **t**.
26:5 Threshing **t** will last until grape
26:34 "Then the land will enjoy its **t**
26:34 joyfully celebrate its **t** ⌊to honor
26:35 it will celebrate the **t** ⌊to honor
26:43 will enjoy its **t** to honor the
Num 3:1 descendants at the **t** when
6:5 During the entire **t** that they are
6:12 the same length of **t** as before.
6:12 The first **t** period won't count.
9:2 at the same **t** every year.
9:7 to the LORD at the same **t**
9:13 to the LORD at the right **t**.
9:19 stayed over the tent for a long **t**,
10:13 This was the first **t** they moved,
10:21 By the **t** they arrived,
14:6 At the same **t**, two of those
14:15 all these people at the same **t**,
14:19 them from the **t** they left Egypt
16:50 By the **t** Aaron came back to
22:4 At that **t** Balak, son of Zippor,
31:16 experienced a plague at that **t**.
Dtr 1:9 At that **t** I said to you,
1:16 Also at that **t** I gave these
2:1 For a long **t** we traveled around
2:14 from the **t** we left Kadesh
2:14 During that **t** all our soldiers
2:34 At that **t** we captured all his
3:4 At that **t** we captured all of his
3:12 At that **t** we took possession of
4:32 distant past, long before your **t**.
4:40 You will live for a long **t** in the
5:16 Then you will live for a long **t**,
5:33 and you will live for a long **t** in
6:2 and you will live a long **t**.
9:20 But at that **t** I prayed for Aaron,
10:1 At that **t** the LORD said to me,
10:8 At that **t** the LORD set apart the
10:10 and 40 nights as I did the first **t**.
Dtr 11:9 you will also live for a long **t**
11:14 rain on your land at the right **t**,
11:21 children will live for a long **t**
15:2 because the ⌊**t**⌋ for suspending
16:6 This is the same **t** you did it
16:9 Count seven weeks from the **t**
17:9 judge who is serving at that **t**.
17:20 will rule for a long **t** in Israel.
19:17 who are serving at that **t**.
20:19 you blockade a city for a long **t**
22:7 and you will live for a long **t**.
25:15 Then you will live for a long **t**
26:3 priest who is serving at that **t**,
28:12 rain on your land at the right **t**
28:62 At one **t** you were as numerous
28:63 At one **t** the LORD was more
29:5 During that **t** your clothes and
30:18 You will not live for a long **t** in
31:10 At that **t**, during the Festival of
31:14 "The **t** of your death is coming
32:7 Remember a **t** long ago.
32:35 In due **t** their foot will slip,
32:47 will be able to live for a long **t**
34:8 Then the **t** of mourning for him
Jos 5:2 At that **t** the LORD spoke to
6:16 they went around the seventh **t**,
6:26 At that **t** Joshua pronounced
8:5 attack us as they did the first **t**,
8:6 from us just like the first **t**.' As
8:30 At that **t** Joshua built an altar
10:33 At that **t** King Horam of Gezer
11:6 About this **t** tomorrow they will
11:18 with all these kings for a long **t**.
11:21 At that **t** Joshua also wiped out
18:3 going to waste **t** conquering
20:6 is chief priest at that **t** dies.
22:3 All this **t**, to this day, you have
23:1 A long **t** afterward,
24:7 lived in the desert for a long **t**.
Jdg 3:29 At that **t** they killed about ten
4:4 was the judge in Israel at that **t**.
11:26 these cities during that **t**?
12:6 At that **t** 42,000 men from
13:7 dedicated to God from the **t**
14:4 (At that **t** the Philistines were
15:3 Samson said to him, "This **t** I
15:20 during the **t** of the Philistines.
16:28 me strength just one more **t**!
18:1 Up to that **t** they had not
18:31 It stayed there the whole **t** the
19:8 So they spent the **t** eating until
19:11 By the **t** they were near Jebus,
19:14 It was sunset by the **t** they
19:30 or been seen from the **t**
20:25 This **t** they slaughtered 18,000
21:14 Benjamin came back at that **t**.
21:24 At that **t** the people of Israel left.
Rut 2:14 When it was **t** to eat,
2:16 Don't give her a hard **t** about it."
1Sm 1:12 Hannah was praying a long **t**
2:31 The **t** is coming when I will
3:8 LORD called Samuel a third **t**.
7:2 A long **t** passed after the ark
9:16 "About this **t** tomorrow I will
9:26 ⌊It's **t** for⌋ me to send you
11:9 by the **t** the sun gets hot,
13:8 the **t** set by Samuel.
14:35 it was the first **t** he had built an
18:19 But when the **t** came to give
18:21 So he said to David a second **t**,
18:26 Before the **t** was up,
20:16 At that **t**, if Jonathan's name is
22:15 Is this the first **t** I have prayed
26:10 Either his **t** will come when
28:1 At that **t** the Philistines had
29:8 you learned about me from the **t**
30:3 By the **t** David and his men
30:25 From that **t** on he made this a
30:31 his men visited from **t** to time.
30:31 his men visited from time to **t**.
2Sm 3:17 "For some **t** now you've
4:5 home at the hottest **t**
7:12 "When the **t** comes for you to
11:1 In the spring, the **t** when kings
14:2 for the dead for a long **t**.
14:29 sent for him a second **t**,

2Sm 17:7 "This **t** Ahithophel's advice is
17:24 to Mahanaim by the **t** Absalom
18:14 "I shouldn't waste **t** with you
21:1 In the **t** of David, there was a
23:13 At harvest **t** three of the thirty
24:15 from that morning until the **t**
1Ki 2:26 but I won't kill you at this **t**
2:38 in Jerusalem for a long **t**.
3:16 A short **t** later two prostitutes
8:65 At that **t** Solomon and all Israel
9:2 appeared to him a second **t**,
10:21 valuable in Solomon's **t**.)
11:17 was a young boy at the **t**.
11:29 At that **t** Jeroboam left
14:1 At that **t** Abijah, son of
16:34 In Ahab's **t** Hiel from Bethel
17:7 But after some **t** the stream
17:15 her family had food for a long **t**.
18:29 to rant and rave until the **t**
18:34 Then he said, "Do it a third **t**,"
18:34 and they did it a third **t**.
18:36 When it was **t** to offer the
18:44 After the seventh **t** the servant
19:2 me dead if by this **t** tomorrow
20:6 At this **t** tomorrow I'm going to
20:9 messengers told me the first **t**,
22:46 who were left there from the **t**
2Ki 3:20 At the **t** of the grain offering,
4:16 "At this **t** next spring,
4:17 had a son at that **t** next year,
7:1 About this **t** tomorrow 24 cups
7:18 This will happen about this **t**
8:20 During Jehoram's **t** Edom
8:22 At that **t** Libnah also rebelled.
10:6 Jezreel about this **t** tomorrow."
12:17 At this **t** King Hazael of Aram
16:6 At that **t** King Rezin of Aram
18:4 had made because up to that **t**
18:16 At that **t** Hezekiah stripped ⌊the
20:12 At that **t** Baladan's son,
21:15 from the **t** their ancestors left
23:22 celebrated like this during the **t**
23:22 Israel or during the entire **t**
24:10 At that **t** the officers of King
1Ch 7:22 Ephraim mourned a long **t**,
9:25 their villages from **t** to time.
9:25 their villages from time to **t**.
15:13 you weren't there the first **t**,
16:6 played trumpets all the **t**
16:7 For the first **t** David entrusted
17:11 "'When the **t** comes for you to
20:1 In the spring, the **t** when kings
21:28 At that **t**, when David saw the
22:9 and in his **t** I will give Israel
27:1 they came for a month at a **t**
29:22 For the second **t** they made
2Ch 7:8 At that **t** Solomon and all Israel
9:20 valuable in Solomon's **t**.)
13:18 were humbled at that **t**,
13:20 power during Abijah's **t**.
14:1 In Asa's **t** the land had peace
14:6 LORD gave him a **t** of peace.
15:3 For a long **t** Israel was without
16:7 At that **t** the seer Hanani came
16:10 the people at that **t** in his reign.
21:8 During Jehoram's **t** Edom
21:10 At the same **t** Edom rebelled,
28:16 At that **t** King Ahaz sent for
30:3 celebrate it at the regular **t**
32:26 on them during Hezekiah's **t**.
35:17 the Passover at that **t**.
35:18 celebrated in Israel during the **t**
Ezr 4:2 sacrificing to him since the **t**
4:9 At that **t**, Rehum the
5:3 At the same **t**, Shethar Bozenai,
5:16 from that **t** until now,
8:34 weight was recorded at that **t**.
10:14 At a set **t**, everyone who has
Neh 4:22 At that **t** I told the people,
6:1 been left in it (although at that **t**
6:5 me the same message a fifth **t**,
7:3 not be opened at the hottest **t**
7:5 who came back the first **t**.
8:17 From the **t** of Jeshua (son of
9:32 and all your people from the **t** of
12:7 relatives at the **t** of Jeshua.
Neh 12:12 At the **t** of Joiakim,
12:22 the priests at the **t** of Eliashib,
12:23 until the **t** of Johanan,
12:46 Long ago in the **t** of David and
12:47 At the **t** of Zerubbabel and
Est 1:2 At the **t** when King Xerxes sat
2:12 The **t** of beauty treatment was
2:19 were gathered a second **t**,
4:14 royal position for a **t** like this."
5:13 is worth nothing to me every **t**
8:9 At that **t** on the twenty-third day
9:27 and at their appointed **t**.
9:31 of Purim at the appointed **t**.
Job 1:5 sacrifices for them all the **t**.
14:13 Set a specific **t** for me when
15:32 happen before his **t** has come,
20:4 from the **t** humans were placed
22:16 are snatched up before their **t**.
34:23 He doesn't have to set a **t** for a
38:21 and have lived such a long **t**!
38:23 stored up for the **t** of trouble,
38:32 the constellations at the right **t**
39:1 "Do you know the **t** when the
39:2 or know the **t** when they'll give
Psa 37:13 has seen that his **t** is coming.
69:13 come to you at an acceptable **t**,
75:2 When I choose the right **t**,
77:7 the Lord reject ⌊me⌋ for all **t**?
78:69 he made to last for a long **t**.
81:15 and their **t** ⌊for punishment⌋
93:2 was set in place a long **t** ago.
95:8 like the **t** at Massah in the
102:13 because it is **t** to grant a favor
102:13 the appointed **t** has come.
104:27 them their food at the right **t**.
119:126 It is **t** for you to act,
129:1 "From the **t** I was young,
129:2 "From the **t** I was young,
145:15 them their food at the proper **t**.
Pro 1:28 "They will call to me at that **t**,
6:8 At harvest **t** it gathers its food.
6:14 He devises evil all the **t** with a
8:30 rejoiced in front of him all the **t**,
10:5 at harvest **t** brings shame.
21:6 wealth by lying are wasting **t**.
25:11 is a word spoken at the right **t**.
25:19 person in a ⌊**t** of⌋ crisis.
26:1 and rain at harvest **t**,
28:2 knowledge will it last a long **t**.
Ecc 2:3 During all that **t**, I was able to
3:1 Everything has its own **t**,
3:1 and there is a specific **t** for
3:2 a **t** to be born and a time to die,
3:2 a time to be born and a **t** to die,
3:2 a **t** to plant and a time to pull
3:2 a time to plant and a **t** to pull
3:3 a **t** to kill and a time to heal,
3:3 a time to kill and a **t** to heal,
3:3 a **t** to tear down and a time to
3:3 to tear down and a **t** to build up,
3:4 a **t** to cry and a time to laugh,
3:4 a time to cry and a **t** to laugh,
3:4 a **t** to mourn and a time to
3:4 time to mourn and a **t** to dance,
3:5 a **t** to scatter stones and a time
3:5 a time to scatter stones and a **t**
3:5 a **t** to hug and a time to stop
3:5 to hug and a **t** to stop hugging,
3:6 a **t** to start looking and a time to
3:6 a time to start looking and a **t** to
3:6 a **t** to keep and a time to throw
3:6 to keep and a **t** to throw away,
3:7 a **t** to tear apart and a time to
3:7 a time to tear apart and a **t** to
3:7 a **t** to keep quiet and a time to
3:7 keep quiet and a **t** to speak out,
3:8 a **t** to love and a time to hate,
3:8 a time to love and a **t** to hate,
3:8 a **t** for war and a time for peace.
3:8 a time for war and a **t** for peace.
3:11 done everything at the right **t**.
3:11 the beginning to the end ⌊of **t**⌋.
3:17 because there is a specific **t**
7:14 God has made the one **t** as
7:17 you die before your **t** is up?
8:5 person will know the right **t**
Ecc 8:6 There is a right **t** and a right
9:11 But **t** and unpredictable events
9:12 knows when his **t** will come.
10:17 high officials eat at the right **t**
Sos 2:7 arouse love before its proper **t**.
2:12 The **t** of the songbird has
3:5 arouse love before its proper **t**.
8:4 arouse love before its proper **t**!
Isa 1:1 Judah and Jerusalem at the **t**
1:28 will be crushed at the same **t**,
7:17 and your ancestor's family a **t**
10:20 At that **t** the remaining few
10:27 At that **t** their burden will be
11:10 At that **t** the root of Jesse will
11:11 At that **t** the Lord will use his
12:1 At that **t** you will say,
12:4 At that **t** you will say,
13:13 At that **t** he will be very angry.
13:22 Its **t** has almost come.
17:5 That **t** will be like harvesting
18:7 At that **t** gifts will be brought to
19:16 At that **t** Egyptians will act like
20:2 At that **t** the LORD told Isaiah,
24:22 a long **t** they'll be punished.
28:19 Each **t** it passes by it will take
29:17 In a very short **t** Lebanon will
39:1 At that **t** Baladan's son,
40:2 and announce to it that its **t**
42:14 I have been silent for a long **t**.
46:3 of you from the **t** you were born.
48:16 From the **t** it took place,
49:8 In the **t** of favor I will answer
57:11 I've been silent for a long **t**.
60:22 At the right **t** I, the LORD,
64:5 continued to sin for a long **t**.
66:17 same **t**," declares the LORD.
Jer 3:17 At that **t** they will call
4:11 At that **t** it will be said to these
5:15 nation that has lasted a long **t**.
5:24 He sends rain at the right **t**,
7:25 From the **t** that your ancestors
8:1 The LORD declares, "At that **t**
8:7 know when it's **t** to return.
8:7 know when it's **t** to migrate.
8:15 We hoped for a **t** of healing,
10:18 who live in the land at this **t**
14:19 We hope for a **t** of healing,
16:21 This **t** I will make my power
18:7 "At one **t** I may threaten to tear
18:9 "At another **t** I may promise to
20:8 Each **t** I speak, I have to cry
23:8 At that **t** they will live in their
23:12 It is **t** for them to be punished,"
25:3 from the **t** that Josiah,
25:34 The **t** has come for you to be
25:34 The **t** has come for you to be
26:18 Moresheth prophesied at the **t**
29:28 You will be captives a long **t**.
30:7 It will be a **t** of calamity for the
31:1 "At that **t**," declares the LORD,
32:2 At that **t** the army of the king of
32:14 so that they will last a long **t**.
33:1 his word to him a second **t**.
33:15 In those days and at that **t**,
33:20 wouldn't come at their proper **t**.
35:7 so that you may live for a long **t**
36:2 all the other nations from the **t**
36:9 a **t** for fasting was called.
36:9 It was a **t** for all the people in
37:16 and he stayed there a long **t**.
39:10 At that **t** he gave them
39:16 At that **t** these things will
39:17 But at that **t** I will rescue you,
46:21 At that **t** they will be punished.
47:4 The **t** has come to destroy all
50:4 "In those days and at that **t**,"
50:20 In those days and at that **t**,"
50:27 for them when their **t** has come,
50:27 the **t** for them to be punished.
50:31 the **t** when I will punish you.
51:6 This is the **t** for the vengeance
51:33 are like a threshing floor at the **t**
51:33 Their harvest **t** will come soon.
Lam 3:6 like those who died a long **t**
4:18 Our **t** was up. Our end had come
5:20 us for such a long **t**?

Eze 4:6 this t on your right side.
4:14 From the t I was young until
7:7 The t is coming. The day is
7:12 The t is coming. The day is
11:3 'It's almost t to rebuild homes.
12:23 Instead, tell them, 'The t is
12:27 sees won't happen for a long t.
16:22 you didn't remember the t when
16:43 "'You didn't remember the t
16:47 It only took you a little t to be
20:6 At that t I promised to bring
21:25 the t for your final punishment
21:29 for whom the t of final
22:3 Your t has come. You dishonor
28:15 from the t you were created,
30:3 a t of trouble for the nations.
34:26 I will send rain at the right t.
38:8 After a long t you will be called
38:8 have been ruined for a long t.
38:10 At that t ideas will enter your
38:14 At that t my people Israel will
40:1 At that t the LORD's power
45:22 At that t the prince must
46:9 the LORD's presence at the t
Dan 2:8 sure you're trying to buy some t
2:16 king to give him some t so that
2:44 "At the t of those kings,
3:5 harps playing at the same t
3:10 harps playing at the same t
3:15 harps playing at the same t
4:16 like this for seven t periods.
4:23 animals for seven t periods.'
4:25 And seven t periods will pass
4:32 And seven t periods will pass
4:34 the end of the seven t periods,
6:26 power lasts to the end ⌊of t⌋.
7:12 allowed to live for a period of t.
7:22 The t came when the holy
7:25 be handed over to him for a t,
7:25 for a time, times, and half of a t.
8:19 ⌊the t of God's⌋ anger,
8:19 the end t has been determined.
9:21 came to me about the t of the
9:22 He informed me, "Daniel, this t
9:24 "Seventy sets of seven t
9:24 These t periods will serve to
9:25 and understand that from the t
9:25 seven sets of seven t periods
9:25 of seven t periods will pass.
9:26 sets of seven t periods,
9:27 for one set of seven t periods.
9:27 middle of the seven t periods,
9:27 until ⌊those t periods⌋ come
11:7 "At that t a shoot will grow from
11:27 must wait until the appointed t.
11:29 "At the appointed t he will
11:29 but this t will be different from
11:33 But for some t they will be
11:35 But the appointed t is still to
12:1 continued,⌋ "At that t Michael,
12:1 It will be a t of trouble unlike
12:1 from the t there have been
12:1 have been nations until that t.
12:1 But at that t your people,
12:7 He said, "It will be for a t,
12:7 for a time, times, and half of a t.
12:11 From the t the daily burnt
12:13 your inheritance at the end of t."
Hos 3:3 "You must wait for me a long t.
3:4 the Israelites will wait a long t
5:9 a wasteland when the t
6:11 I have set a harvest t for you
9:7 The t for them to be punished
9:7 The t for them to pay for their
10:12 It's t to seek the LORD!
10:14 the t Shalman destroyed Beth
Joe 1:14 Schedule a t to fast!
2:15 Schedule a t to fast.
3:1 "In those days and at that t,
Amo 2:3 all their officials at the same t.
4:2 the t is going to come when
9:11 them as they were a long t ago.
Jnh 3:1 his word to Jonah a second t.
Mic 2:3 This will be a t of disaster.
3:4 hide his face from you at that t
5:3 will abandon Israel until the t
Mic 7:4 Now is the t you will be
7:15 Let us see miracles like the t
Hab 1:12 Didn't you exist before t began,
2:3 still happen at the appointed t.
Zep 1:12 "At that t I will search
3:19 At that t I will deal with all who
3:20 At that t I will bring you
3:20 Yes, at that t I will gather you
Hag 1:2 people say it's not the right t
1:4 "Is it t for you to live in your
2:20 his word to Haggai a second t
Zec 8:10 Before that t there was no
8:15 but this t to do good to
14:5 did from the earthquake at the t
Mal 3:7 Since the t of your ancestors
Mat 1:11 They lived at the t when the
2:16 This matched the exact t he
4:2 At the end of that t,
8:29 here to torture us before it is t?"
9:15 The t will come when the
10:19 When the t comes,
11:12 From the t of John the Baptizer
11:13 prophesied up to the t of John.
11:25 At that t Jesus said,
12:41 will stand up with you at the t
12:42 the south will stand up at the t
13:40 so it will be at the end of t.
13:49 will happen at the end of t.
14:1 At that t Herod, ruler of Galilee,
16:21 From that t on Jesus began to
18:1 At that t the disciples came to
22:46 and from that t on no one dared
23:30 'If we had lived at the t of our
24:21 will be a lot of misery at that t,
24:23 "At that t don't believe anyone
24:40 "At that t two men will be
24:43 had known at what t
24:45 servants their food at the right t.
24:48 may think that it will be a long t
25:19 "After a long t the master of
26:2 At that t the Son of Man will be
26:18 the teacher says, 'My t is near.
26:42 away a second t and prayed,
26:44 the same prayer a third t.
26:45 The t is near for the Son of Man
26:55 At that t Jesus said to the
27:16 At that t there was a
27:38 At that t they crucified two
28:20 with you until the end of t."
Mar 1:9 At that t Jesus came from
1:15 He said, "The t has come,
1:23 At that t there was a man in the
2:20 But the t will come when the
4:17 They last for a short t.
4:29 because harvest t has come."
6:34 spent a lot of t teaching them.
8:1 About that t there was once
8:25 on the man's eyes a second t,
12:2 "At the right t he sent a servant
13:11 don't worry ahead of t about
13:11 you to say when the t comes.
13:19 It will be a t of misery that has
13:20 the Lord does not reduce that t,
13:21 "At that t don't believe anyone
13:33 You don't know the exact t.
14:41 He came back a third t and
14:41 The t has come for the Son of
14:72 a rooster crowed a second t.
Luk 1:20 will come true at the right t."
1:57 When the t came for Elizabeth
2:1 At that t the Emperor Augustus
2:6 the t came for Mary to have her
2:27 into the courtyard at the same t.
3:2 It was at the t when Annas and
4:13 the devil left him until another t.
4:25 widows in Israel in Elijah's t.
4:27 Israel in the prophet Elisha's t.
5:35 The t will come when the
5:35 At that t they will fast."
6:12 At that t Jesus went to a
7:21 At that t Jesus was curing
8:27 not worn clothes for a long t.
8:29 controlled the man for a long t.
9:36 and for some t they told no one
9:51 The t was coming closer for
11:31 the south will stand up at the t
Luk 11:32 of Nineveh will stand up at the t
12:12 At that t the Holy Spirit will
12:42 their share of food at the right t?
12:45 his master is taking a long t
12:46 will return at an unexpected t.
12:56 don't know how to judge the t
13:1 At that t some people reported
13:31 At that t some Pharisees told
14:17 When it was t for the banquet,
16:16 ⌊in force⌋ until the t of John.
16:16 Since that t, people have been
17:22 "The t will come when you will
17:26 will be like the t of Noah.
17:28 will also be like the t of Lot.
18:1 that they need to pray all the t
19:37 By this t he was coming near
19:43 The t will come when enemy
19:44 the t when God came
20:10 "At the right t he sent a servant
20:40 From that t on, no one dared to
21:6 you see — the t will come when
21:8 and 'The t is near.'
21:20 realize that the t is near for it to
21:22 This will be a t of vengeance.
21:28 The t when you will be set free
22:14 When it was t to eat the
22:53 to arrest me. But this is your t,
23:7 and was in Jerusalem at that t.
23:8 For a long t he had wanted to
23:22 A third t Pilate spoke to them.
23:29 The t is coming when people
Jon 2:4 My t has not yet come."
3:4 inside his mother a second t
3:22 where he spent some t with
4:6 The t was about six o'clock in
4:21 A t is coming when you
4:23 Indeed, the t is coming,
4:27 At that t his disciples returned.
4:52 them at what t his son got
4:53 was the same t that Jesus had
5:6 he had been sick for a long t.
5:25 "I can guarantee this truth: A t
5:28 A t is coming when all the
5:35 For a t you enjoyed the
6:4 The t for the Jewish Passover
6:17 By this t it was dark,
6:34 give us this bread all the t."
7:2 The t for the Jewish Festival of
7:6 "Now is not the right t for me to
7:6 Any t is right for you.
7:8 Now is not the right t for me to
7:30 because his t had not yet
8:20 because his t had not yet
9:32 Since the beginning of t,
12:23 Jesus replied to them, "The t
12:27 me from this t ⌊of suffering⌋'?
12:27 I came for this t of suffering.
13:1 Jesus knew that the t had
14:9 been with all of you for a long t.
16:2 Certainly, the t is coming when
16:21 A woman has pain when her t
16:25 The t is coming when I won't
16:32 The t is coming, and is already
17:1 and said, "Father, the t is here.
19:14 The t was about six o'clock in
19:27 From that t on she lived with
21:14 This was the third t that Jesus
21:16 him again, a second t, "Simon,
21:17 Jesus asked him a third t,
21:17 Jesus had asked him a third t,
Act 1:6 is this the t when you're going
1:15 At a t when about 120
1:21 Jesus with us the entire t that
1:22 us from the t that John was
2:45 From t to time, they sold their
2:45 From time to t, they sold their
2:47 At the same t, they praised
3:2 At the same t, a man who had
3:21 until the t when everything will
4:34 From t to time, people sold
4:34 From time to t, people sold
5:36 Some t ago Theudas appeared.
5:37 at the t of the census,
6:1 At that t, as the number of
7:17 "When the t that God had
7:20 "At that t Moses was born,

Act 7:41 That was the t they made a
7:45 here until the t of David,
8:11 had amazed them for a long t
10:15 voice spoke to him a second t,
10:30 It was at this same t,
11:9 spoke from heaven a second t,
11:26 called Christians for the first t
11:27 At that t some prophets came
12:1 About that t King Herod
13:20 his people judges until the t
13:36 by serving the people of his t,
14:3 the city of Iconium for a long t.
14:28 a long t with these disciples.
15:7 what happened some t ago.
15:32 spoke a long t to encourage
15:33 stayed in Antioch for some t,
17:32 talk about this some other t."
18:5 Paul devoted all his t to
18:23 spending some t in Antioch,
19:23 During that t a serious
20:11 with the people for a long t,
20:16 Ephesus to avoid spending t
20:18 "You know how I spent all my t
21:5 When our t was up,
21:26 to announce the t when
24:25 When I find t, I'll send for you
24:26 At the same t, Felix was
26:5 They've known me for a long t
26:10 to have them killed every t
27:9 We had lost so much t that the
27:28 This t the line sank 90 feet.
27:40 At the same t they untied the
28:6 after they had waited a long t
Rom 1:10 every t I pray. I ask that
2:5 At that t God will reveal that
3:26 his approval at the present t.
4:10 he uncircumcised at that t?
5:6 at it this way: At the right t,
5:14 Yet, death ruled from the t of
5:14 time of Adam to the t of Moses,
7:9 At one t I was alive without
8:22 of childbirth up to the present t.
8:26 At the same t the Spirit also
9:9 "I will come back at the right t,
13:11 It's t for you to wake up.
16:25 kept in silence for a very long t
1Co 1:20 persuasive speaker of our t?
4:5 anything before the appointed t.
7:5 you agree to do so for a set t
7:29 The t has been shortened.
11:25 Every t you drink from it,
11:26 Every t you eat this bread and
12:2 every t you were led to
14:27 They should do it one at a t,
15:6 than 500 believers at one t.
16:7 hope to spend some t with you.
16:12 He didn't want to at this t.
2Co 6:2 "At the right t I heard you.
6:2 now is God's acceptable t!
8:14 At the present t, your surplus
12:14 ready to visit you for a third t,
13:1 This is the third t that I'll be
13:2 I was with you the second t,
Gal 3:8 Scripture saw ahead of t that
3:8 to Abraham ahead of t when
4:2 trustees until the t set by his
4:4 But when the right t came,
4:13 You know that the first t I
4:29 Furthermore, at that t the son
6:1 At the same t watch yourself
6:9 life⌋ at the proper t,
Eph 1:11 God also decided ahead of t to
2:12 Also, at that t you were without
3:21 Jesus for all t and eternity!
Php 1:4 Every t I pray for all of you,
Col 1:5 Some t ago you heard about
1:6 At that t you came to know
4:3 At the same t also pray for us.
1Th 2:1 that our t with you was not
3:4 we told you ahead of t that we
2Th 2:6 be revealed when his t comes.
1Ti 5:13 At the same t, they learn to go
6:15 At the right t God will make
2Ti 3:1 will be violent periods of t.
4:2 whether or not the t is right.
4:3 A t will come when people will
2Ti 4:6 and it is now t for me to be
Tit 2:13 At the same t we can expect
Heb 2:8 However, at the present t we
2:10 it was the right t to bring Jesus,
4:9 Therefore, a t of rest and
4:16 which will help us at the right t.
6:6 be led a second t to God.
9:9 is an example for the present t.
9:28 that he will appear a second t.
9:28 This t he will not deal with sin,
10:13 Since that t, he has been
11:32 I don't have enough t to tell you
12:10 For a short t our fathers
Jas 1:8 different things at the same t
1Pe 1:5 to be revealed at the end of t.
1:11 So they tried to find out what t
1:17 live your t as temporary
1:20 known in the last period of t.
4:3 You spent enough t in the past
4:17 The t has come for the
5:6 so that when the right t comes
2Pe 3:5 and earth existed a long t ago.
1Jn 2:18 Children, it's the end of t.
2:18 how we know it's the end of t.
Jud 1:3 God's holy people once for all t.
1:25 Before t began, now, and for
Rev 1:3 in it because the t is near.
2:21 I gave her t to turn to me and
3:10 I will keep you safe during the t
9:6 At that t people will look for
11:6 during the t they speak what
11:18 The t has come for the dead to
12:12 knowing that he has little t left."
12:14 could be taken care of for a t,
12:14 of for a time, times, and half a t.
14:7 because the t has come for him
14:15 The t has come to gather it,
19:3 A second t they said,
19:7 give him glory because it's t
20:5 This is the first t that people
20:6 the first t that people come
22:10 this book because the t is near.

timely (1)

Pro 15:23 and a t word — oh, how good!

times (187)

Gen 4:15 suffer vengeance seven t over."
4:24 If Cain is avenged 7 t,
4:24 7 times, then Lamech, 77 t."
26:12 a hundred t as much as
31:7 has changed my wages ten t.
31:41 you changed my wages ten t.
33:3 of them and bowed seven t
43:34 was five t more than any
Exo 23:14 "Three t a year you must
23:17 "These are the three t each
34:23 "Three t a year all your men
34:24 land while you're gone three t
Lev 4:6 some of the blood seven t
4:17 blood and sprinkle it seven t
8:11 of the oil on the altar seven t
14:7 will sprinkle the blood seven t
14:16 sprinkle some of the oil seven t
14:27 sprinkle some of the oil seven t
14:51 sprinkle the house seven t.
16:14 blood with his finger seven t
16:19 some of the blood on it seven t.
23:4 announce at their appointed t.
25:8 seven of these years seven t
26:18 you seven t for your sins.
26:21 for your sins seven t.
26:24 you seven t for your sins.
26:28 you seven t for your sins.
Num 14:22 They have tested me now ten t
19:4 and sprinkle it seven t toward
22:28 to make you hit me three t?"
22:32 your donkey three t like this?
22:33 away from me these three t.
24:10 you have blessed them three t.
28:2 me my offerings at the right t.
Dtr 1:11 a thousand t more numerous,
16:16 Three t a year all your men
Jos 6:4 around the city seven t while
6:15 around the city seven t
6:15 they marched around it seven t.
Jdg 16:15 made fun of me three t now,
1Sm 2:21 She became pregnant ⌊five t⌋
3:10 as he had called the other t:
20:41 quickly bowed down three t
2Sm 12:6 And he must pay back four t
19:43 "We have ten t your interest in
24:3 the people a hundred t over,
1Ki 9:25 Three t a year Solomon
17:21 himself over the boy three t
18:43 Seven t Elijah told him,
22:16 "How many t must I make you
2Ki 4:35 The boy sneezed seven t and
5:10 said, "Wash yourself seven t
5:14 in the Jordan River seven t,
13:18 stomped three t and stopped.
13:19 have stomped five or six t!"
13:19 defeat the Arameans three t."
13:25 defeated Benhadad three t
1Ch 12:32 leaders who understood the t
21:3 his people a hundred t over.
2Ch 15:5 At those t no one could come
18:15 "How many t must I make you
Neh 4:12 us ten t that our enemies
6:4 the same message to me four t,
9:28 You rescued them many t
10:34 t every year according
13:31 for delivering wood at regular t
Est 1:14 wise men who knew the t,
Job 19:3 have insulted me ten t now.
20:4 you know that from ancient t,
24:1 set aside t ⌊for punishment⌋?
27:10 Can he call on God at all t?
33:29 this two or three t with people
Psa 9:9 a stronghold in t of trouble.
10:1 hide yourself in t of trouble?
12:6 a furnace and purified seven t.
20:1 will answer you in t of trouble.
34:1 I will thank the LORD at all t.
37:19 not be put to shame in trying t.
37:19 Even in t of famine they will be
37:39 is their fortress in t of trouble.
41:1 will rescue him in t of trouble.
46:1 ever-present help in t of trouble.
49:5 should I be afraid in t of trouble,
50:15 Call on me in t of trouble.
59:16 a place of safety in t of trouble.
62:8 Trust him at all t, you people.
78:38 He restrained his anger many t.
79:12 neighbors back with seven t
94:13 give him peace and quiet from t
106:3 and do what is right at all t.
106:43 He rescued them many t,
118:5 During t of trouble I called on
119:164 Seven t a day I praise you for
Pro 6:31 he has to repay it seven t.
24:16 person may fall seven t,
Ecc 7:14 When t are good, be happy.
7:14 But when t are bad,
7:22 you have cursed others many t.
Isa 9:1 and Naphtali in earlier t.
27:6 In t to come Jacob will take
30:26 sun will be seven t as strong,
33:2 be our savior in t of trouble.
Jer 11:14 to me for help in t of trouble.
14:8 one who saves it in t of trouble.
15:11 enemies plead with you in t
15:11 of disaster and in t of distress.
16:19 my refuge in t of trouble.
Lam 1:7 treasures it had from ancient t,
Eze 4:10 of food every day at set t.
4:11 and drink it at set t.
37:23 I will forgive them for all the t
Dan 1:20 he found that they knew ten t
2:21 He changes t and periods of
3:19 seven t hotter than normal.
6:10 Three t each day he got down
6:11 One of those t the men came in
6:13 He prays three t each day."
7:10 Ten thousand t ten thousand
7:25 the appointed t and laws.
7:25 for a time, t, and half of a time.
8:17 the vision is about the end t."
9:25 during the troubles of those t.
10:14 vision is about t still to come."
11:14 In those t many people will
11:35 them white until the end t.

Dan 11:40 "In the end **t** the southern king
12:4 seal the book until the end **t**.
12:7 He said, "It will be for a time, **t**,
12:9 and sealed until the end **t**.
Hos 2:13 I will punish her for all the **t**
Amo 5:13 person remains silent at such **t**,
5:13 because those **t** are so evil.
Zec 8:11 people as I did in earlier **t**,
Mat 13:8 or thirty **t** as much as was
13:23 or thirty **t** as much as was
16:3 interpret the signs of the **t**.
18:21 who wrongs me? Seven **t**?"
18:22 "I tell you, not just seven **t**,
18:22 but seventy **t** seven.
19:29 will receive a hundred **t** more
26:34 you will say three **t** that you
26:75 you will say three **t** that you
Mar 4:8 or one hundred **t** as much as
4:20 or one hundred **t** as much as
10:30 a hundred **t** as much here
14:30 you will say three **t** that you
14:72 you will say three **t** that you
Luk 8:8 they produced a hundred **t** as
16:25 you had a life filled with good **t**,
17:4 Even if he wrongs you seven **t**
17:4 and comes back to you seven **t**
18:30 will certainly receive many **t**
19:8 I'll pay four **t** as much as I owe
19:16 me has earned ten **t** as much.'
19:18 has made five **t** as much.'
21:23 the land will suffer very hard **t**,
21:24 Jerusalem until the **t** allowed
21:36 Be alert at all **t**. Pray so that you
22:34 you say three **t** that you don't
22:61 you will say three **t** that you
Jon 13:38 you say three **t** that you don't
Act 1:7 "You don't need to know about **t**
3:20 Then **t** will come when the
10:16 This happened three **t**.
11:10 This happened three **t**.
16:23 had hit Paul and Silas many **t**,
17:30 "God overlooked the **t** when
20:19 the Lord during the difficult **t**
20:31 at **t** with tears in my eyes.
Rom 13:11 You know the **t** in which we
2Co 11:23 been in prison many more **t**,
11:24 Five **t** the Jewish leaders had
11:25 three **t** Roman officials had me
11:25 three **t** I was shipwrecked,
12:8 I begged the Lord three **t** to take
1Th 5:1 write to you about **t** and dates.
2Th 3:16 give you his peace at all **t**
1Ti 4:1 in later **t** some believers will
Heb 1:1 ancestors at many different **t**
9:26 have had to suffer many **t** since
10:33 At **t** you were publicly insulted
10:33 At **t** you associated with
Jud 1:18 "In the last **t** people who
Rev 5:11 They numbered ten thousand **t**
5:11 and thousands **t** thousands.
9:16 numbered 20,000 **t** 10,000.
12:14 of for a time, **t**, and half a time.

timid (1)

Pro 18:23 poor person is **t** when begging,

Timna (6)

Gen 36:12 **T** was a concubine of Esau's
36:22 Lotan's sister was **T**.
36:40 and name: **T**, Alvah, Jetheth,
1Ch 1:36 Kenaz and Amalek, son of **T**.
1:39 **T** was Lotan's sister.
1:51 tribal leaders of Edom were **T**,

Timnah (13)

Gen 38:12 from Adullam went to **T** where
38:13 was on his way to **T**
38:14 which is on the road to **T**.
Jos 15:10 to Beth Shemesh and on to **T**.
15:57 Kain, Gibeah, and **T**.
19:43 Elon, **T**, Ekron,
Jdg 14:1 When Samson went to **T**,
14:2 seen a Philistine woman at **T**.
14:5 with his father and mother to **T**.
14:5 coming to the vineyards of **T**,
15:6 the son-in-law of the man at **T**.
Jdg 15:6 man at **T** took Samson's wife
2Ch 28:18 **T** and its villages,

Timnath Heres (1)

Jdg 2:9 buried at **T** within the territory

Timnath Serah (2)

Jos 19:50 **T** in the mountains of Ephraim
24:30 buried on his own land at **T** in

Timon (1)

Act 6:5 **T**, Parmenas, and Nicolaus,

Timothy (33)

Act 16:1 a disciple named **T** lived.
16:2 and Iconium spoke well of **T**.
16:3 Paul wanted **T** to go with him.
17:14 Silas and **T** stayed in Berea.
17:15 back to Silas and **T**
17:16 for Silas and **T** in Athens,
18:5 But when Silas and **T** arrived
19:22 **T** and Erastus, to Macedonia,
20:4 Gaius from Derbe, **T**,
Rom 16:21 **T** my coworker greets you;
1Co 4:17 That's why I've sent **T** to you to
4:17 **T** is my dear child,
16:10 If **T** comes, make sure that he
2Co 1:1 and from **T** our brother.
1:19 and **T** told you about,
11:6 **T** and I have made this clear to
11:21 I'm ashamed to admit it, but **T**
Php 1:1 From Paul and **T**, servants of
2:19 Jesus will allow me to send **T**
2:20 I don't have anyone else like **T**.
2:22 what kind of person **T** proved
Col 1:1 and from our brother **T**.
1Th 1:1 From Paul, Silas, and **T**.
3:2 we sent our brother **T** to you.
3:5 I sent **T** to find out about
3:6 But **T** has just now come back
2Th 1:1 From Paul, Silas, and **T**.
1Ti 1:2 To **T**, a genuine child in faith.
1:18 **T**, my child, I'm giving you this
6:20 **T**, guard the Good News which
2Ti 1:2 To **T**, my dear child. Good will,
Phm 1:1 Christ Jesus, and our brother **T**.
Heb 13:23 You know that **T**, our brother,

Timothy's (2)

Act 16:1 **T** mother was a Jewish
16:3 knew that **T** father was Greek.

tin (4)

Num 31:22 Any gold, silver, bronze, iron, **t**,
Eze 22:18 All of them are like copper, **t**,
22:20 and **t** together in a smelting
27:12 They exchanged silver, iron, **t**,

tinder (1)

Isa 1:31 Strong people will become **t** for

tip (9)

Jdg 6:21 meat and the bread with the **t**
1Sm 14:27 So he stretched out the **t** of the
14:43 "I tasted a little honey on the **t**
1Ki 6:24 The distance from the **t** of one
6:24 from the tip of one wing to the **t**
Job 33:2 are on the **t** of my tongue.
Psa 10:7 are on the **t** of his tongue.
Pro 22:18 will be on the **t** of your tongue,
Luk 16:24 Send Lazarus to dip the **t** of his

Tiphsah (2)

1Ki 4:24 of the Euphrates River from **T**
2Ki 15:16 Then Menahem attacked **T**,

Tira (1)

1Ch 2:55 families were the people of **T**,

Tiras (2)

Gen 10:2 Javan, Tubal, Meshech, and **T**.
1Ch 1:5 Javan, Tubal, Meshech, and **T**.

tire (1)

Jos 7:3 Don't **t** the troops out by

tired (27)

Dtr 25:18 attacked you when you were **t**
2Sm 16:2 wine is for those who become **t**
17:2 him while he's **t** and weak,
23:10 Philistines until his hand got **t**
Job 22:7 You don't even give a **t** person
Psa 77:2 in prayer without growing **t**.
Isa 1:14 and I'm **t** of putting up with
5:27 None of them grow **t** or stumble
28:12 of rest for those who are **t**.
38:14 My eyes were **t** from looking up
40:28 doesn't grow **t** or become
40:29 strength to those who grow **t**
40:30 Even young people grow **t** and
40:31 will walk and won't grow **t**.
43:22 Israel, you have grown **t** of me.
57:10 You've **t** yourself out with many
Jer 2:24 All who look for you won't get **t**.
6:11 I am **t** of holding it in.
12:5 and they have **t** you out,
15:6 I'm **t** of showing compassion to
Hab 2:13 Armies that people grow **t** only
Mat 11:28 "Come to me, all who are **t** from
Jon 4:6 he was **t** from traveling.
Gal 6:9 can't allow ourselves to get **t**
2Th 3:13 can't allow ourselves to get **t**
Heb 12:3 you don't become **t** and give up.
12:12 Strengthen your **t** arms and

Tirhakah (2)

2Ki 19:9 Sennacherib heard that King **T**
Isa 37:9 Sennacherib heard that King **T**

Tirhanah (1)

1Ch 2:48 the mother of Sheber and **T**.

Tiria (1)

1Ch 4:16 Ziph, Ziphah, **T**, and Asarel.

Tirzah (17)

Num 26:33 Noah, Hoglah, Milcah, and **T**.)
27:1 Noah, Hoglah, Milcah, and **T**.
36:11 Mahlah, **T**, Hoglah, Milcah,
Jos 12:24 king of **T**. The total was 31 kings
17:3 Noah, Hoglah, Milcah, and **T**.
1Ki 14:17 wife got up, left, and went to **T**.
15:21 fortifying Ramah and lived in **T**.
15:33 began to rule Israel in **T**.
16:6 ancestors and was buried in **T**.
16:8 He ruled in **T** for two years.
16:9 Elah was getting drunk in **T** at
16:9 in charge of the palace in **T**.)
16:15 Zimri ruled for seven days in **T**
16:17 left Gibbethon and attacked **T**.
16:23 for 12 years, 6 of them in **T**.
2Ki 15:14 came from **T** to Samaria,
Sos 6:4 like **T**, lovely like Jerusalem,

Tishbe (6)

1Ki 17:1 Elijah, who was from **T** but had
21:17 his word to Elijah from **T**:
21:28 his word to Elijah from **T**:
2Ki 1:3 the LORD said to Elijah from **T**,
1:8 from **T**," the king answered.
9:36 his servant Elijah from **T**.

Titius Justus (1)

Act 18:7 home of a man named **T**,

title (2)

Exo 3:15 **t** throughout every generation.
Isa 45:4 I have given you a **t** of honor,

Titus (13)

2Co 2:13 because I couldn't find **T**,
7:6 comforted us when **T** arrived.
7:13 to see how happy **T** was.
7:14 our bragging to **T** has also
8:6 This led us to urge **T** to finish
8:16 I thank God for making **T** as
8:23 remember that **T** is my partner
12:18 I encouraged **T** to visit you,
12:18 Did **T** take advantage of you?
Gal 2:1 I also took **T** along.
2:3 **T** was with me, and although

2Ti 4:10 and T went to the province of
Tit 1:4 To T, a genuine child in the

Tizite (1)

1Ch 11:45 and his brother Joha the T,

Toah (1)

1Ch 6:34 who was the son of T,

toast (1)

Est 3:15 Haman sat down to drink a t,

Tob (5)

Jdg 11:3 He went to live in the land of T.
11:5 get Jephthah from the land of T.
2Sm 10:6 and the men of T (12,000 men).
10:8 and Rehob and the men from T
2Ch 17:8 Adonijah, Tobijah, T Adonijah,

Tob Adonijah (1)

2Ch 17:8 Adonijah, Tobijah, T, and the

Tobiah (16)

Ezr 2:60 the descendants of Delaiah, T,
Neh 2:10 Sanballat the Horonite and T
2:19 T the Ammonite servant,
4:3 T the Ammonite, who was
4:7 When Sanballat, T,
6:1 Sanballat, T, Geshem the
6:12 Instead, T and Sanballat had
6:14 remember what T and
6:17 of Judah sent many letters to T,
6:17 and T sent many letters back
6:18 had promised to support T
6:19 T kept sending letters to
7:62 the descendants of Delaiah, T,
13:4 who was related to T and had
13:5 had provided a large room for T.
13:7 had done by providing T

Tobiah's (3)

Neh 6:18 In addition, T son Jehohanan
6:19 nobles were singing T praises
13:8 So I threw all of T household

Tobijah (3)

2Ch 17:8 Adonijah, T, Tob Adonijah,
Zec 6:10 exiles Heldai, T, and Jedaiah,
6:14 reminder to Helem, T, Jedaiah,

Tochen (1)

1Ch 4:32 Ain, Rimmon, T, and Ashan.

today (308)

Gen 4:14 have forced me off this land t.
7:1 among the people of t.
19:37 ancestor of the Moabites of t.
19:38 ancestor of the Ammonites of t.
21:26 and I didn't hear about it until t."
22:14 It is still said t, "On the
24:12 make me successful t.
24:42 "When I came to the spring t,
26:33 of the city is still Beersheba t.
30:32 go through all of your flocks t
31:43 Yet, what can I do t for my
31:48 between you and me t."
32:32 (Therefore, even t the people of
35:20 marker is at Rachel's grave t.
40:7 do you look so unhappy t?"
47:26 in Egypt which is still in force t:
Exo 2:18 you come home so early t?"
5:14 ordered to make yesterday or t.
13:4 T, in the month of Abib, you are
14:13 the LORD will do to save you t.
16:25 "Eat it t," Moses said,
16:25 "because t is a day of worship
16:25 find anything on the ground t.
32:29 Moses said, "T you are
32:29 God gave you a blessing t
34:11 Do everything that I command t
Lev 8:34 I did t what the LORD
9:4 LORD will appear to you t.'"
10:19 Aaron answered Moses, "T
10:19 I had eaten the offering for sin t,
Dtr 2:18 "T you are going to pass by the
2:22 descendants are still there t.
Dtr 2:25 T I will start to make all the
3:14 This is still their name t.)
4:4 your God and are still alive t.
4:8 teachings I am giving you t?
4:20 own people as you still are t.
4:25 as witnesses against you t:
4:38 land is your own possession t.
4:39 Remember t, and never forget
4:40 which I'm giving you t.
5:1 laws and rules I'm telling you t.
5:3 to all of us who are alive here t.
5:24 T we've seen that people can
6:6 these words that I give you t.
6:24 our lives. It's still true t.
7:11 and rules I'm giving you t.
8:1 every command I give you t.
8:11 and laws that I'm giving you t.
8:18 ancestors. It's still in effect t.
8:19 I warn you t that if you forget
9:3 Realize t that the LORD your
10:8 his name, as they still do t.
10:13 and laws that I'm giving you t
10:15 of this, t he chooses you,
11:2 Remember t the discipline you
11:8 the commands I'm giving you t.
11:13 commands that I'm giving you t,
11:26 T I'm giving you the choice of a
11:27 your God that I'm giving you t.
11:28 I'm commanding you to live t,
11:32 laws and rules I'm giving you t.
12:8 way that it's being done here t,
13:18 commands that I'm giving you t,
15:5 commands I'm giving you t.
15:15 I'm giving you this command t.
20:3 t you're going into battle
26:3 "I declare t to the LORD your
26:16 T the LORD your God is
26:17 T you have declared that the
26:18 T the LORD has declared that
27:1 command I'm giving you t.
27:4 the command I'm giving you t.
27:9 T you have become the people
27:10 laws which I'm giving you t."
28:1 commands that I'm giving you t.
28:13 your God that I am giving you t.
28:14 I'm commanding you t.
28:15 and laws that I am giving you t.
29:10 All of you are standing here t in
29:12 LORD your God is giving you t.
29:13 will confirm t that you are
29:15 who are standing here with us t
29:15 for those who are not here t.
29:18 or tribe among you t who turns
29:28 where they still are t."
30:2 everything I command you t,
30:8 commands that I'm giving you t.
30:11 This command I'm giving you t
30:15 T I offer you life and prosperity
30:16 is what I'm commanding you t:
30:18 If you do, I tell you t that you
30:19 and earth as witnesses t that
32:46 these warnings I've given you t.
34:6 Even t no one knows where
Jos 3:7 "T I will begin to honor you in
4:9 The stones are still there t.
5:9 The LORD said to Joshua, "T I
5:9 the name it still has t.
6:25 She still lives in Israel t
7:25 will bring disaster on you t!"
7:26 over Achan that it is still there t.
7:26 still called the valley of Achor t.
8:28 of ruins. It is still in ruins t.
8:29 That pile is still there t.
9:27 to put it. They still serve t.
10:27 These stones are still there t.
13:13 So they still live in Israel t.
14:10 So now look at me t.
15:63 live with Judah in Jerusalem t.
16:10 still live in Ephraim t,
22:16 T you have turned away from
22:16 T you have rebelled against
22:18 T you rebel against the LORD,
22:23 don't spare us t. If we built an
22:29 or to turn back t from following
22:31 "T we know the LORD is
24:15 then choose t whom you will
Jdg 1:21 of Benjamin in Jerusalem t.
1:26 The city still has that name t.
9:18 But t you have attacked my
10:15 But please rescue us t!"
11:27 will decide t whether Israel
12:3 come to fight against me t?"
15:19 It is still there at Lehi t.
18:12 Dan [The Camp of Dan] t.
19:30 Israel came out of Egypt until t.
21:3 tribe be missing t in Israel?"
21:6 They said, "T one tribe has
Rut 2:19 "Where did you gather grain t?
2:19 worked with t is named Boaz."
3:18 unless he settles this matter t."
4:9 "T you are witnesses that I
4:10 T you are witnesses."
4:14 who has remembered t to give
1Sm 4:3 the Philistines to defeat us t?
4:16 I fled from the front line t."
6:18 It is still there t in the field of
9:12 He ⌊just⌋ went into the city t
9:19 You will eat with me t.
10:2 When you leave me t,
11:13 "No one will be killed t,
11:13 because t the LORD saved
12:5 is a witness t that you've found
12:17 the wheat being harvested t?
14:28 anyone who eats food t.'" Now,
14:30 which they found t.
14:38 out what sin was committed t.
14:41 why didn't you answer me t?
14:45 done this with God's help t."
15:28 kingdom of Israel from you t.
17:10 the Israelite battle line t.
17:46 T the LORD will hand you over
20:27 the meal either yesterday or t?"
21:4 had sexual intercourse ⌊t⌋."
21:5 will their bodies be holy t?"
24:4 David's men told him, "T is the
24:10 T you saw how the LORD
24:18 T you have proved how good
24:19 for what you did for me t.
25:32 who sent you t to meet me.
25:33 me from slaughtering people t
26:8 Abishai said to David, "T God
26:21 because you valued my life t.
26:23 LORD handed you over to me t,
26:24 great value on your life t,
27:6 to the kings of Judah t.)
27:10 "Whom did you raid t?"
28:18 The LORD is doing this to you t
2Sm 3:38 "Don't you know that t a leader,
3:39 T I'm weak, though I'm the
4:3 They still live there t.
4:8 "T the LORD has given Your
6:8 [The Striking of Uzzah] t.)
6:20 dignified Israel's king was t!
11:12 to Uriah, "Then stay here t,
14:22 He said, "T I know that you
16:3 "He said, 'T the house of Israel
16:12 curse into a blessing for me t."
18:18 called Absalom's Monument t.)
18:20 the man carrying good news t.
18:20 You must not deliver the news t
18:31 "T the LORD has freed you
19:5 "T you have made all your men
19:5 wives, and concubines t.
19:6 T, you have made it clear that
19:20 T I've come as the first of all
19:22 You are my enemies t.
19:22 anyone in Israel be killed t?
1Ki 1:25 because t he went and
1:30 I will do t exactly what I swore
1:51 Solomon swear to me t that
2:24 Adonijah will be put to death t."
3:6 him a son to sit on his throne t.
5:7 "May the LORD be praised t.
8:8 (They are still there t.)
8:24 hand you carried it out as it is t.
8:28 cry for help as I pray to you t.
8:61 his commands as you have t."
9:13 (They're ⌊still⌋ called ⌊that⌋ t.)
9:21 (They are still ⌊slaves⌋ t.)
12:7 you will serve these people t,
14:14 This will happen t.
18:36 make known t that you are God

1Ki 20:13 I will hand it over to you **t**.
2Ki 2:3 to take your master from you **t**?"
2:5 to take your master from you **t**?"
4:23 "Why are you going to him **t**?
6:28 Let's eat him **t**. We'll eat my son
6:31 stays on his ⌊body⌋ **t**."
8:22 rule and is still independent **t**.
10:27 It is still a latrine **t**.
14:7 which is still its name **t**.
16:6 to Elath and still live there **t**.
17:23 and they are still there **t**.
17:34 **T** they are still following their
19:3 **T** is a day filled with misery,
1Ch 4:41 (Even **t** no Meunites live there.)
4:43 descendants still live there **t**.
5:26 They are still there **t**.
13:11 [The Striking of Uzzah] **t**.)
28:7 and laws, as he is doing **t**.'
29:5 himself to the LORD **t**?"
2Ch 5:9 (They are still there **t**.)
6:15 hand you carried it out as it is **t**.
8:8 (They are still ⌊slaves⌋ **t**.)
20:26 called the valley of Beracah **t**.
21:10 rule and is still independent **t**.
35:25 funeral songs about Josiah **t**.
Ezr 9:7 as we still are **t** because of our
Neh 1:11 Please give me success **t** and
5:11 orchards, and their homes **t**.
8:10 **T** is a holy day for the Lord.
8:11 **T** is a holy day. Don't be sad."
Est 1:18 **T** the wives of the officials in
5:4 come **t** with Haman to a dinner
9:13 what was decreed for **t**.
Job 23:2 "My complaint is bitter again **t**.
Psa 2:7 **T** I have become your Father.
95:7 only you would listen to him **t**!
118:24 Let's rejoice and be glad **t**!
119:91 All things continue to stand **t**
Pro 7:14 **T** I kept my vows.
22:19 **T** I have made them known to
Isa 37:3 **T** is a day filled with misery,
38:19 are living praise you as I do **t**.
48:7 heard about them before **t**,
56:12 And tomorrow will be like **t**,
58:4 The way you fast **t** keeps you
Jer 1:10 **T** I have put you in charge of
1:18 **T** I have made you like a
11:5 you still have **t**.""" I answered,
11:7 warning still applies to you **t**.
25:3 year as king of Judah until **t**,
25:18 ridiculed and cursed, until **t**.
36:2 the reign of Josiah until **t**.
40:4 **T** I'm removing the chains from
42:19 know that I am warning you **t**.
42:21 I have told you **t**, but you won't
44:2 **T** they are deserted ruins.
44:6 the desolate ruin that they are **t**.
44:22 No one lives in that land **t**.
44:23 met with this disaster as it is **t**."
Eze 20:29 it is still called 'worship site' **t**.)
Dan 9:15 made yourself famous even **t**.
Zec 9:12 **T** I tell you that I will return to
Mat 6:11 Give us our daily bread **t**.
6:30 **T** it's alive, and tomorrow it's
11:23 it would still be there **t**.
16:3 say that there will be a storm **t**
21:28 go to work in the vineyard **t**.'
27:19 I've been very upset **t** because
Luk 2:11 **T** your Savior, Christ the Lord,
4:21 "This passage came true **t**
5:26 "We've seen things **t** we can
11:29 "The people living **t** are evil.
11:30 sign to the people living **t**.
11:31 with the men who live **t**.
11:32 with the people living **t**.
11:32 condemn the people living **t**.
11:51 The people living **t** will be held
12:28 **T** it's alive, and tomorrow it's
13:32 heal people **t** and tomorrow.
13:33 But I must be on my way **t**,
19:5 I must stay at your house **t**."
19:9 your family have been saved **t**.
19:42 "If you had only known **t** what
22:61 "Before a rooster crows **t**,
23:43 **T** you will be with me in
Jon 5:10 not allowed to carry your cot **t**."
Act 4:9 **t** you are cross-examining us
13:33 **T** I have become your Father.'
19:40 of being accused of rioting **t**
20:26 Therefore, I declare to you **t**
22:3 to God as all of you are **t**.
26:2 I think I'm fortunate **t** to stand in
26:29 listening to me **t** would quickly
1Co 2:6 in power **t** and gone tomorrow.
2Co 3:15 Yet, even **t**, when they read the
Gal 4:25 She is like Jerusalem **t**
Heb 1:5 **T** I have become your Father."
3:7 "If you hear God speak **t**,
3:15 "If you hear God speak **t**,
4:7 That day is **t**. Many years after
4:7 "If you hear God speak **t**,
5:5 **T** I have become your Father."
13:8 same yesterday, **t**, and forever.
Jas 4:13 You're saying, "**T** or tomorrow

today's (1)

Eze 24:2 "Son of man, write down **t** date.

toddlers (1)

Isa 11:8 **T** will put their hands into

toe (7)

Lev 8:23 and on the big **t** of his right foot.
14:14 and on the big **t** of the right foot
14:17 and on the big **t** of the right foot
14:25 and on the big **t** of the right foot
14:28 and on the big **t** of the right foot
2Sm 14:25 had no blemish from head to **t**.
Hab 3:13 him bare from head to **t**.

toes (10)

Exo 29:20 and on the big **t** of their right
Lev 8:24 and on the big **t** of their right
Jdg 1:6 cut off his thumbs and big **t**.
1:7 thumbs and big **t** cut off used
2Sm 21:20 had a total of 24 fingers and **t**:
21:20 fingers on each hand and six **t**
1Ch 20:6 man who had 24 fingers and **t**:
20:6 fingers on each hand and six **t**
Dan 2:41 You also saw the feet and **t**.
2:42 The **t** were partly iron and

Togarmah (3)

Gen 10:3 Ashkenaz, Riphath, and **T**.
1Ch 1:6 Ashkenaz, Riphath, and **T**.
Eze 38:6 and with the nation of **T** from

Tohu (1)

1Sm 1:1 great-grandson of **T**,

Toi (2)

2Sm 8:9 When King **T** of Hamath heard
8:10 between Hadadezer and **T**.)

toilet (3)

Jdg 3:24 must be using the **t**," they said.
Mat 15:17 the stomach and then into a **t**?
Mar 7:19 his stomach and then into a **t**."

Tokhath (1)

2Ch 34:22 son of **T** and grandson of

Tola (8)

Gen 46:13 The sons of Issachar were **T**,
Num 26:23 Issachar were the family of **T**,
Jdg 10:1 After Abimelech, **T**,
10:1 **T** was from Issachar and lived
10:2 **T** died and was buried in
10:3 After **T**, Jair from Gilead
1Ch 7:1 Issachar's four sons were **T**,
7:2 were heads of the families of **T**.

Tolad (1)

1Ch 4:29 Bilhah, Ezem, **T**,

Tola's (1)

1Ch 7:2 **T** sons were Uzzi,

told (1066)

Gen 3:4 the serpent **t** the woman.
3:11 God asked, "Who **t** you that
9:22 outside and **t** his two brothers.
Gen 12:4 as the LORD had **t** him,
14:13 had escaped came and **t** Abram
17:23 that day, as God had **t** him.
20:2 Abraham **t** everyone that his
20:8 He **t** them about all of this,
22:3 place that God had **t** him about.
22:9 place that God had **t** him about,
22:20 Later Abraham was **t**,
24:28 The girl ran and **t** her mother's
26:32 servants came and **t** him about
27:19 I've done what you **t** me.
27:42 When Rebekah was **t** what her
29:12 When Jacob **t** Rachel that he
29:12 she ran and **t** her father.
29:13 Then Jacob **t** Laban all that
31:16 Now do whatever God has **t**
31:22 Two days later Laban was **t**
34:8 Hamor **t** them. "My son
37:2 Joseph **t** his father about the
37:5 and when he **t** his brothers,
37:9 and he **t** it to his brothers.
37:10 When he **t** his father and his
38:13 As soon as Tamar was **t** that
38:24 three months later Judah was **t**,
39:17 Then she **t** him the same story:
40:9 So the chief cupbearer **t**
41:8 Pharaoh **t** them his dreams,
41:12 We **t** him our dreams,
41:12 and he **t** each of us what they
41:13 What he **t** us happened:
41:15 that when you are **t** a dream,
41:24 I **t** this to the magicians,
41:25 God has **t** Pharaoh what he's
42:14 "It's just as I **t** you,"
42:29 they **t** him all that had
43:27 Then he said, "You **t** me about
43:29 the one you **t** me about?"
44:2 He did what Joseph **t** him.
44:23 Then you **t** us, 'If your
44:24 we **t** him what you had said.
45:1 Joseph **t** his brothers who
45:21 Israel's sons did as they were **t**.
45:26 They **t** him, "Joseph is still
45:27 Yet, when they **t** their father
47:1 Joseph went and **t** Pharaoh,
48:1 Later Joseph was **t**,
48:2 When Jacob was **t**,
50:12 him what he had **t** them to do.
Exo 1:15 Then the king of Egypt **t** the
4:20 the staff God had **t** him to take.
4:23 I **t** you to let my son go so that
4:27 Meanwhile, the LORD had **t**
4:28 Moses **t** Aaron everything the
4:30 Aaron **t** them everything the
5:16 and yet we're **t** to make bricks.
5:19 in trouble when they were **t**,
6:27 Aaron — **t** Pharaoh (the king
8:17 When Moses **t** him,
8:27 our God, as he **t** us to do."
9:27 time I have sinned," he **t** them.
12:35 did what Moses had **t** them
14:5 (the king of Egypt) was **t** that
16:22 to Moses and **t** him about it.
17:9 in my hand the staff God **t** me
17:10 Joshua did as Moses **t** him and
18:8 Moses **t** his father-in-law
19:9 Moses **t** the LORD what the
19:25 down to the people and **t** them.
23:13 ⌊to do⌋ everything I **t** you.
24:3 Moses went and **t** the people
24:3 the LORD has **t** us to do."
32:13 You **t** them, 'I will make your
32:24 So I **t** them to take off any gold
32:28 Levites did what Moses **t** them,
32:34 to the place I **t** you about.
34:32 do everything the LORD **t** him
34:34 Whenever he came out and **t**
Lev 4:23 When he is **t** about what he
4:28 When he is **t** about what he
8:5 Moses **t** the congregation,
8:31 Moses **t** Aaron and his sons:
9:2 He **t** Aaron, "Take a calf that
9:7 Moses **t** Aaron, "Come to the
10:4 He **t** them, "Come and take
10:5 the camp, as Moses **t** them.
10:6 Moses **t** Aaron and his sons

Lev	10:12	Moses **t** Aaron and his
	20:24	I have **t** you that you will take
	23:44	So Moses **t** the Israelites about
	24:12	until the LORD **t** them what
Num	4:49	man was registered and **t** what
	5:4	did as the LORD had **t** Moses.
	9:4	So Moses **t** the Israelites to
	11:24	Moses went out and **t** the
	11:27	a young man ran and **t** Moses,
	13:17	to explore Canaan, he **t** them,
	13:30	Caleb **t** the people to be quiet
	14:39	When Moses **t** these things to
	16:47	burner, as Moses **t** him,
	22:7	They came to Balaam and **t**
	23:2	Balak did what Balaam **t** him,
	23:5	The LORD **t** Balaam,
	23:16	came to Balaam and **t** him,
	23:30	Balak did what Balaam **t** him,
	24:12	Balaam answered Balak, "I **t**
	27:23	as the LORD had **t** him.
	29:40	Moses **t** the Israelites
	31:21	teachings **t** Moses to do:
	32:29	Moses **t** them, "If the tribes of
Dtr	1:3	Moses **t** the Israelites
	1:18	So I **t** you how to handle these
	1:21	God of your ancestors **t** you.
	1:43	I **t** you, but you wouldn't listen.
	2:1	Sea as the LORD had **t** me.
	4:13	The LORD **t** you about the
	9:12	He **t** me, "Leave right away.
	17:4	When you are **t** about it,
	17:16	The LORD has **t** you,
	18:17	The LORD **t** me, "What they've
	26:18	possession, as he **t** you.
	27:1	leaders of Israel **t** the people,
	29:13	This is what he **t** you,
	31:2	Besides, the LORD has **t** me
	31:3	as the LORD **t** you.
Jos	2:1	He **t** them, "Go, look at that
	2:2	The king of Jericho was **t**,
	2:3	to Rahab, who **t** her,
	2:16	She **t** them, "Go to the
	2:17	The men **t** her, "We will be free
	2:23	They **t** him everything that had
	2:24	They **t** Joshua, "The LORD
	3:3	They **t** the people,
	3:5	Joshua **t** the people,
	3:6	Joshua also **t** the priests,
	3:6	They did as they were **t**.
	4:1	The LORD had **t** Joshua,
	4:8	as the LORD had **t** Joshua.
	4:10	was as Moses had **t** Joshua.
	4:12	did as Moses had **t** them.
	4:22	the children should be **t** that
	5:15	So Joshua did as he was **t**.
	6:7	He **t** the troops, "March around
	7:3	back to Joshua and **t** him,
	9:6	They **t** Joshua and the men of
	9:11	who lives in our country **t** us,
	9:24	"We were **t** that the LORD your
	10:8	The LORD **t** Joshua,
	10:14	The LORD did what a man **t**
	10:17	Someone **t** Joshua,
	10:24	He **t** the officers who had gone
	10:25	Joshua **t** them, "Don't be afraid
	11:6	The LORD **t** Joshua,
	11:9	as the LORD had **t** him.
	15:13	Judah as the LORD had **t** them.
	23:5	as the LORD your God **t** you.
	24:27	Joshua **t** all the people,
Jdg	1:24	They **t** him, "Show us how we
	3:28	He **t** them, "Follow me!
	4:6	She **t** him, "The LORD God of
	4:18	She **t** him, "Sir, come in here!
	6:13	our ancestors have **t** us about?
	6:20	Messenger of the LORD **t** him,
	6:27	did what the LORD had **t** him
	6:30	the men of the city **t** Joash,
	8:9	So he **t** them, "When I come
	8:20	Then he **t** Jether, his firstborn
	9:7	When Jotham was **t** about this,
	9:42	Abimelech was **t** about it.
	9:47	When Abimelech was **t** that
	9:48	He **t** his men, "Hurry and do
	9:54	He **t** him, "Take your sword
	11:2	They **t** him, "You'll get no
Jdg	11:9	Jephthah **t** them, "If you take
	13:7	He **t** me, 'You're going to
	13:13	to do everything I **t** her to do.
	14:2	He went ⌊home⌋ and **t** his
	14:3	But Samson **t** his father,
	14:16	"I haven't even **t** my father and
	14:17	Finally, on the seventh day he **t**
	14:17	Then she **t** her friends the
	15:6	They were **t**, "Samson!
	15:12	So the men from Judah **t** him,
	15:13	They **t** him, "We promise we'll
	16:2	The people of Gaza were **t**,
	16:7	Samson **t** her, "If someone ties
	16:10	Delilah **t** Samson, "Look,
	16:11	Samson **t** her, "If someone ties
	16:13	Delilah **t** Samson, "You're still
	16:15	but you still haven't **t** me what
	16:17	Finally, he **t** her the truth.
	16:17	He **t** her, "Because I'm a
	16:18	that he had **t** her everything,
	16:18	Samson had **t** her everything.)
	16:26	Samson **t** the young man who
	17:2	He **t** his mother, "You were
	17:9	The man **t** him, "I'm a Levite
	17:10	Micah **t** him, "Stay with me!
	18:2	They were **t**, "Go and explore
	18:4	The Levite **t** them what Micah
	18:6	The priest **t** them, "Go in
	18:19	They **t** him, "Keep quiet!
	19:5	woman's father **t** his son-in-law,
	19:12	The Levite **t** him, "We'll never
	19:13	He **t** his servant, "Let's go
	19:22	They **t** the old man,
	19:23	He **t** them, "No, my friends!
	21:20	So they **t** the men of Benjamin,
Rut	2:2	the reapers." Naomi **t** her, "Go,
	2:11	"People have **t** me about
	2:11	They **t** me how you left your
	2:11	They also **t** me how you came
	2:14	to eat, Boaz **t** her, "Come here.
	2:19	So Ruth **t** her mother-in-law
	2:20	Then Naomi **t** her, "That man is
	2:21	who was from Moab, **t** her,
	2:22	Naomi **t** her daughter-in-law
	3:15	Then Boaz **t** Ruth,
	3:16	Ruth **t** Naomi everything the
	3:17	of barley and **t** me not
1Sm	1:22	She **t** her husband,
	1:23	her husband Elkanah **t** her.
	3:9	"Go, lie down," Eli **t** Samuel.
	3:13	I **t** him that I would hand down
	3:17	anything he **t** you from me."
	3:18	So Samuel **t** Eli everything.
	4:16	The man **t** Eli, "I'm the one who
	7:3	Samuel **t** the entire nation of
	8:5	They **t** him, "You're old,
	8:7	The LORD **t** Samuel,
	8:10	Then Samuel **t** the people who
	8:22	The LORD **t** him, "Listen to
	8:22	Then Samuel **t** the people of
	9:3	Kish were lost, Kish **t** Saul,
	9:5	Saul **t** his servant who was
	9:10	Saul **t** his servant,
	9:17	noticed Saul, the LORD **t** him,
	9:17	"There's the man I **t** you about.
	9:23	meat that I gave you and **t** you
	9:27	the city limits, Samuel **t** Saul,
	11:3	The leaders of Jabesh **t** him,
	11:4	When they **t** the people the
	11:5	So they **t** him the news about
	11:9	They **t** the messengers who
	11:14	Samuel **t** the troops,
	12:5	Samuel **t** them, "The LORD is
	12:6	Samuel **t** the people,
	12:12	to attack you, you **t** me, 'No,
	12:20	Samuel **t** the people.
	13:13	a foolish thing," Samuel **t** Saul.
	14:12	Jonathan **t** his armorbearer,
	14:17	"Look around," Saul **t** the
	14:28	Then one of the soldiers **t** him,
	14:33	Some ⌊soldiers⌋ **t** Saul,
	14:40	Saul **t** all Israel, "You stand on
	14:43	So Jonathan **t** him,
	15:1	Samuel **t** Saul, "The LORD
	15:12	Samuel was **t**, "Saul went to
	15:16	"Be quiet," Samuel **t** Saul,
1Sm	15:16	what the LORD **t** me last night."
	15:20	the LORD," Saul **t** Samuel.
	15:24	Then Saul **t** Samuel,
	15:26	Samuel **t** Saul, "I will not go
	15:26	rejected what the LORD **t** you.
	15:28	Samuel **t** him, "The LORD has
	16:4	did what the LORD **t** him.
	16:7	But the LORD **t** Samuel,
	16:10	but Samuel **t** Jesse,
	16:11	Samuel **t** Jesse, We won't
	16:15	Saul's officials **t** him,
	16:17	Saul **t** his officials,
	17:17	Jesse **t** his son David,
	17:32	David **t** Saul, "No one should
	17:37	"Go," Saul **t** David,
	17:39	in these things," David **t** Saul.
	17:44	the Philistine **t** David,
	17:45	David **t** the Philistine,
	18:20	When Saul was **t** about it,
	18:24	When the officers **t** Saul what
	18:26	When his officers **t** David this,
	19:1	Saul **t** his son Jonathan and all
	19:7	Jonathan **t** David all of this.
	19:15	Saul **t** them, "Bring him here to
	19:17	Michal answered, "He **t** me,
	19:18	He **t** Samuel everything Saul
	19:21	When they **t** Saul ⌊about this⌋,
	19:22	He was **t**, "Over there in the
	20:9	I would have **t** you about it."
	20:18	Festival," Jonathan **t** him,
	20:36	"Run," he **t** the boy,
	20:40	He **t** the boy, "Take them back
	20:42	Jonathan **t** David. "We have
	21:2	priest Ahimelech, "and he **t** me,
	22:5	the prophet Gad **t** David.
	22:21	Abiathar **t** David that Saul had
	22:22	David **t** Abiathar, "I knew that
	23:2	"Go," the LORD **t** David,
	23:3	David's men **t** him,
	23:7	When Saul was **t** that David
	23:9	he **t** the priest Abiathar,
	23:13	Then Saul was **t**, "David has
	23:17	"Don't be afraid," he **t** David,
	23:22	I'm **t** he's very clever.
	23:25	David was **t** the news.
	24:1	he was **t** "Now David is in the
	24:4	David's men **t** him,
	24:10	Although I was **t** to kill you,
	24:17	He **t** David, "You are more
	25:5	sent ten young men and **t** them,
	25:12	men returned and **t** him all this.
	25:13	David **t** his men. And everyone,
	25:14	One of the young men **t** Abigail,
	25:19	she **t** her young men,
	25:35	what she brought him and **t** her,
	25:37	his wife **t** him what had
	25:40	to Abigail at Carmel, they **t** her,
	26:9	David **t** Abishai. "No one has
	27:4	When Saul was **t** that David
	28:2	"Very well," Achish **t** David,
	28:7	Saul **t** his officers,
	28:7	His officers **t** him, "There is a
	28:9	The woman **t** him,
	28:21	"I listened to you," she **t** him,
	28:21	when I did what you **t** me to do.
	29:4	the Philistine officers **t** him.
	29:6	Then Achish called David and **t**
	30:7	David **t** the priest Abiathar,
	30:8	"Pursue them," the LORD **t** him.
	31:4	Saul **t** his armorbearer,
2Sm	1:15	of ⌊his⌋ young men and **t** him,
	2:4	They **t** David, "The people of
	2:21	Abner **t** him, "Leave me alone!
	3:16	"Go home," Abner **t** him.
	3:21	Abner **t** David, "I must go now
	3:23	with the whole army, he was **t**,
	3:31	David **t** Joab and all the people
	4:8	to kill you," they **t** the king.
	4:10	"I once seized a man who **t** me
	5:6	The Jebusites **t** David,
	6:12	King David was **t**, "The LORD
	7:3	Nathan **t** the king, because the
	7:17	Nathan **t** David all these words
	9:7	"Don't be afraid," David **t** him,
	10:5	After David was **t** ⌊what had
	10:17	David was **t** ⌊about this⌋,

2Sm	11:10	When they **t** David,
	11:22	everything Joab **t** him to say.
	12:7	Nathan **t** David. "This is what
	13:5	Then Jonadab **t** him,
	13:10	Amnon **t** Tamar, "Bring the food
	13:12	"No," she **t** him, "don't rape me!
	13:15	"Get out of here," he **t** her.
	13:35	Then Jonadab **t** the king,
	14:2	He **t** her, "Please act like a
	14:3	Then Joab **t** her exactly what
	14:8	the king **t** the woman.
	14:19	He **t** me to say exactly what I
	14:21	Then the king **t** Joab,
	14:33	went to the king and **t** him this.
	15:2	After the person had **t** him
	15:9	"Go in peace," the king **t** him.
	15:14	David **t** all his men who were
	15:15	The king's servants **t** him,
	15:22	So David **t** Ittai, "Go ahead and
	15:25	The king **t** Zadok, "Take God's
	15:31	Then David was **t**,
	15:33	David **t** him, "If you go with me,
	16:4	The king **t** Ziba, "In that case
	16:10	If the LORD has **t** him,
	16:11	David **t** Abishai and all his
	16:11	since the LORD has **t** him to
	16:21	Ahithophel **t** Absalom,
	17:6	"Ahithophel has **t** us his plan.
	17:15	Then Hushai **t** the priests
	17:18	and Ahimaaz and **t** Absalom.
	17:21	and went and **t** King David.
	17:21	right away," they **t** David.
	18:10	A man who saw this **t** Joab,
	18:11	said to the man who **t** him.
	18:12	But the man **t** Joab,
	18:20	But Joab **t** him, "You won't be
	18:23	"Run," Joab **t** him.
	19:1	Joab was **t**, "The king is crying
	19:8	When all the troops were **t**,
	19:27	He **t** you lies about me,
	19:30	Mephibosheth **t** the king.
	19:33	The king **t** Barzillai,
	20:4	The king **t** Amasa,
	20:6	David then **t** Abishai,
	20:17	what I have to say," she **t** him.
	20:21	fine," the woman **t** Joab.
	21:11	When David was **t** what Saul's
	23:3	The rock of Israel **t** me,
	24:13	he **t** David this and asked,
	24:14	situation," David **t** Gad.
	24:19	David went as Gad had **t** him
1Ki	1:2	His officials **t** him,
	1:23	The servants **t** the king,
	1:51	Someone **t** Solomon,
	1:53	"Go home," Solomon **t** him.
	2:20	"Ask, Mother," the king **t** her.
	2:26	The king **t** the priest Abiathar,
	2:30	he **t** Joab, "The king says,
	2:39	Shimei was **t** that his slaves
	3:24	So the king **t** his servants to
	10:6	She **t** the king, "What I heard in
	10:7	I wasn't even **t** half of it.
	11:10	⌊He **t** him⌋ not to follow other
	11:11	The LORD **t** Solomon,
	11:31	He **t** Jeroboam, "Take 10
	12:7	They **t** him, "If you will serve
	12:24	as the LORD **t** them.
	13:7	The king **t** the man of God,
	13:8	The man of God **t** the king,
	13:11	His sons **t** him everything the
	13:11	When they **t** their father,
	13:13	The old prophet **t** his sons,
	13:17	he **t** me not to eat or drink there
	13:22	place about which he **t** you,
	13:26	word of the LORD had **t** him."
	13:27	Then the old prophet **t** his sons
	14:2	Jeroboam **t** his wife,
	14:2	The prophet Ahijah, who **t** me I
	14:5	the LORD had **t** Ahijah,
	14:5	He also **t** Ahijah what to say to
	14:6	I've been **t** to give you some
	17:5	word of the LORD ⌊had **t** him⌋.
	17:13	Then Elijah **t** her, "Don't be
	17:15	She did what Elijah had **t** her.
	18:5	Ahab **t** Obadiah, "Let's go
	18:22	So Elijah **t** the people,
1Ki	18:25	Elijah **t** the prophets of Baal,
	18:40	Elijah **t** them, "Seize the
	18:41	Then Elijah **t** Ahab,
	18:43	Seven times Elijah **t** him,
	19:1	Ahab **t** Jezebel everything
	19:15	The LORD **t** him, "Go back to
	20:2	They **t** Ahab, "This is what
	20:8	and all the people **t** him,
	20:9	**t** Benhadad's messengers,
	20:9	your messengers **t** me
	20:12	He **t** his officers to get ready.
	20:23	King Benhadad of Aram **t** him,
	20:31	His officers **t** him, "We have
	20:34	Benhadad **t** him, "I will give
	20:35	word of the LORD had **t** him.
	20:40	The king of Israel **t** him,
	20:42	The prophet **t** him,
	21:2	Ahab **t** Naboth, "Give me your
	21:3	Naboth **t** Ahab, "The LORD has
	21:4	Naboth from Jezreel had **t** him.
	21:6	He **t** her, "I talked to Naboth
	22:4	Jehoshaphat **t** the king of
	22:8	king of Israel **t** Jehoshaphat,
	22:13	who went to call Micaiah **t** him,
	22:13	"The prophets have all **t** the
	22:30	king of Israel **t** Jehoshaphat,
	22:34	Ahab **t** his chariot driver,
2Ki	1:2	He had **t** them, "Go ask
	1:6	They **t** him that a man came to
	1:7	the man who **t** you this like?"
	1:9	a hill, he **t** Elijah, "Man of God,
	1:15	The angel of the LORD **t** Elijah,
	1:16	Elijah **t** the king, "This is what
	2:19	of the city ⌊of Jericho⌋ **t** Elisha,
	4:6	were full, she **t** her son,
	4:6	He **t** her, "There are no more
	4:7	She went and **t** the man of God.
	4:9	She **t** her husband,
	4:12	He **t** his servant Gehazi,
	4:17	as Elisha had **t** her.
	4:19	The father **t** his servant,
	4:24	Then she **t** her servant,
	4:25	he **t** his servant Gehazi,
	4:27	from me. He hasn't **t** me."
	4:29	The man of God **t** Gehazi,
	4:31	Gehazi **t** him, "The boy didn't
	4:38	with him, he **t** his servant,
	5:3	The girl **t** her mistress,
	5:4	to his master and **t** him what
	5:19	Elisha **t** Naaman, "Go in
	6:10	the man of God **t** him about.
	6:13	The king was **t**, "He is in
	6:19	Elisha **t** them, "This isn't the
	6:28	"This woman **t** me,
	6:29	The next day I **t** her,
	7:10	city gatekeepers and **t** them,
	7:12	So the king got up at night and **t**
	7:14	the Aramean army and **t** them
	7:15	The messengers returned and **t**
	7:18	as the man of God **t** the king,
	8:1	Elisha had **t** the woman whose
	8:2	did what the man of God **t** her.
	8:6	she **t** him the story.
	8:7	of Aram, who was sick, was **t**,
	8:8	The king **t** Hazael,
	8:14	Hazael answered, "He **t** me
	8:19	The LORD had **t** David that he
	9:6	olive oil on his head and **t** him,
	9:36	They came back and **t** him.
	10:8	A messenger **t** him,
	10:9	He **t** the people, "You are
	10:17	as the LORD had **t** Elijah.
	10:22	Then Jehu **t** the man in charge
	12:4	Joash **t** the priests,
	13:15	Elisha **t** him, "Get a bow and
	13:16	Then Elisha **t** the king of Israel,
	13:18	he **t** the king of Israel.
	15:12	as the LORD had **t** Jehu:
	18:22	He **t** Judah and Jerusalem,
	18:37	They **t** him the message from
	22:8	The chief priest Hilkiah **t** the
	22:10	the scribe Shaphan **t** the king,
	22:15	She **t** them, "This is what the
1Ch	10:4	Saul **t** his armorbearer,
	11:5	They **t** David, "You will never
	12:17	He **t** them, "If you've come to
1Ch	13:2	Then he **t** the whole assembly
	15:16	David **t** the Levite leaders to
	17:2	Nathan **t** David, "Do everything
	17:15	Nathan **t** David all these words
	19:5	After people **t** David ⌊what had
	19:17	David was **t** ⌊about this⌋,
	21:13	situation," David **t** Gad.
	21:18	The LORD's Messenger **t** Gad
	21:19	David went as Gad had **t** him
	21:24	"No," King David **t** Ornan,
	22:7	David **t** his son Solomon,
	28:3	But God **t** me, 'You must not
	28:6	"He **t** me, 'Your son Solomon
	28:20	David also **t** his son Solomon,
2Ch	9:5	She **t** the king, "What I heard in
	9:6	I wasn't even **t** about half of the
	10:7	They **t** him, "If you are good to
	14:4	He **t** the people of Judah to
	14:7	So Asa **t** Judah, "Let's build
	18:3	Jehoshaphat **t** the king of
	18:7	king of Israel **t** Jehoshaphat,
	18:12	who went to call Micaiah **t** him,
	18:12	"The prophets have all **t** the
	18:29	king of Israel **t** Jehoshaphat,
	18:33	Ahab **t** the chariot driver,
	19:6	He **t** the judges, "Pay attention
	21:7	The LORD had **t** David that he
	29:21	Hezekiah **t** the priests,
	29:30	Hezekiah and the leaders **t**
	31:4	He **t** the people living in
	31:11	Then Hezekiah **t** them to
	32:12	worship and altars and **t** Judah
	33:16	And he **t** Judah to serve the
	34:15	Hilkiah **t** the scribe Shaphan,
	34:16	doing everything you **t** us to do.
	34:18	the scribe Shaphan **t** the king,
	34:23	She **t** them, "This is what the
	35:3	He **t** the Levites, "Put the holy
	35:21	God **t** me to hurry. God is with
	35:23	The king **t** his officers,
Ezr	2:63	The governor **t** them not to eat
	4:2	They **t** them, "We want to help
	4:3	of Israel's families **t** them,
	5:15	Cyrus **t** him, 'Take these
	8:17	I **t** them to tell Iddo and his
	8:22	We had already **t** the king,
	8:28	I **t** them, "You and the utensils
Neh	1:3	They **t** me, "Those who
	1:8	Please remember what you **t**
	2:16	I hadn't yet **t** the Jews,
	2:17	Then I **t** them, "You see the
	2:18	Then I **t** them that my God had
	2:18	me and what the king had **t** me.
	4:19	I **t** the nobles, the leaders,
	4:22	At that time I **t** the people,
	5:7	I **t** them, "You are charging
	5:8	Then I **t** them, "We have done
	7:3	I **t** them, "The gates of
	7:65	The governor **t** them not to eat
	8:1	They **t** Ezra the scribe to bring
	8:9	who taught the people **t** them,
	8:10	Then he **t** them, "Go, eat rich
	9:15	You **t** them to take possession
	9:23	into the land you **t** their parents
	13:9	Then I **t** them to cleanse the
	13:22	Then I **t** the Levites to cleanse
Est	2:20	did whatever Mordecai **t** her,
	2:22	Then Esther **t** the king,
	3:4	since Mordecai had **t** them that
	3:8	Now, Haman **t** King Xerxes,
	3:11	The king **t** Haman,
	3:15	hurried out as the king **t** them.
	4:7	He **t** him the exact amount of
	4:9	So Hathach returned and **t**
	4:12	So Esther's servants **t**
	6:1	So he **t** ⌊a servant⌋ to bring the
	6:7	So Haman **t** the king,
	6:10	The king **t** Haman,
	6:13	and his wife Zeresh **t** him,
	8:1	Esther had **t** him how Mordecai
Job	1:12	The LORD **t** Satan,
	2:6	The LORD **t** Satan,
	4:12	"I was **t** something secretly
	22:17	They **t** God, 'Leave us alone!
	28:28	So he **t** humans, 'The fear of
	37:20	Should he be **t** that I want to

Job 42:9 did what the LORD had **t** them
Psa 22:30 that will be **t** about the Lord.
44:1 Our ancestors have **t** us about
78:3 things that our parents have **t**
106:34 as the LORD had **t** them.
119:26 I **t** you what I have done,
Pro 25:7 because it is better to be **t**,
Isa 8:3 The LORD **t** me, "Name him
20:2 At that time the LORD **t** Isaiah,
36:7 Hezekiah **t** Judah and
36:22 They **t** him the message from
40:21 Haven't you been **t** from the
41:22 that your idols **t** you about so
46:10 From long ago I **t** you things
48:5 I **t** you about them before they
52:15 that they had never been **t**.
Jer 7:23 Live the way I **t** you to live so
11:4 and do everything that I have **t**
13:2 as the LORD had **t** me,
13:5 as the LORD had **t** me.
13:6 and get the belt from where I **t**
14:14 Then the LORD **t** me,
17:22 as I **t** your ancestors.
28:15 Then Jeremiah **t** the prophet
32:25 Yet you, Almighty LORD, **t** me
34:6 The prophet Jeremiah **t** all
35:18 did exactly what he **t** you to do.
36:4 that the LORD had **t** him,
36:5 Jeremiah **t** Baruch,
36:13 Micaiah **t** them everything he
36:20 courtyard and **t** him everything.
37:19 Where are the prophets who **t**
38:27 He **t** them exactly what the
38:27 exactly what the king had **t** him
40:16 **t** Johanan, Kareah's son,
42:19 "The LORD has **t** you people
42:21 I have **t** you today,
43:1 He **t** them everything the LORD
Lam 3:57 You **t** me not to be afraid.
Eze 11:5 Spirit came to me and **t** me
11:25 I **t** the exiles everything the
24:20 I **t** them, "The LORD spoke his
41:22 Then the man **t** me,
Dan 1:3 The king **t** Ashpenaz,
1:10 The chief-of-staff **t** Daniel,
2:17 Then Daniel went home and **t**
2:18 He **t** them to ask the God of
2:23 You **t** me the answer to our
2:23 You **t** us what the king wants
2:24 Daniel **t** him, "Don't destroy
2:25 He **t** the king, "I've found one of
2:29 The one who reveals secrets **t**
2:30 revealed so that you could be **t**
2:45 The great God has **t** you what
3:20 He **t** some soldiers from his
4:7 I **t** them the dream,
4:8 is in him. I **t** him the dream:
4:19 I **t** him, "Belteshazzar, don't let
5:7 He **t** these wise advisers of
5:17 Daniel **t** the king, "Keep your
6:16 The king **t** Daniel, "May your
7:5 It was **t**, "Get up, and eat as
7:16 So he **t** me what all this meant.
8:14 He **t** me, "For 2,300 evenings
9:2 The LORD had **t** the prophet
10:12 He **t** me, "Don't be afraid,
Hos 1:2 to Hosea, the LORD **t** him,
1:4 The LORD **t** Hosea,
1:6 The LORD **t** Hosea,
1:10 Wherever they were **t**,
1:10 not my people,' they will be **t**,
3:1 Then the LORD **t** me,
3:3 Then I **t** her, "You must wait for
Jnh 1:10 because he had **t** them.
1:12 He **t** them, "Throw me
3:3 to Nineveh as the LORD **t** him.
Mic 6:8 You mortals, the LORD has **t**
Zep 3:16 that day Jerusalem will be **t**,
Zec 11:13 The LORD **t** me, "Give it to the
Mat 2:5 They **t** him, "In Bethlehem in
8:13 Jesus **t** the officer,
8:20 Jesus **t** him, "Foxes have
8:22 But Jesus **t** him, "Follow me,
12:47 Someone **t** him, "Your mother
13:28 "He **t** them, 'An enemy did this.'
14:17 They **t** him, "All we have here
Mat 17:20 He **t** them, "Because you have
17:22 in Galilee, Jesus **t** them,
18:31 They **t** their master the whole
19:13 But the disciples **t** the people
20:8 of the vineyard **t** the supervisor,
20:22 "We can," they **t** him.
20:31 The crowd **t** them to be quiet.
20:33 They **t** him, "Lord, we want you
21:13 He **t** them, "Scripture says,
21:23 Who **t** you that you could do
21:27 Jesus **t** them, "Then I won't tell
21:30 went to the other son and **t** him
22:13 Then the king **t** his servants,
22:31 Haven't you read what God **t**
24:25 I've **t** you this before it happens.
26:1 these things, he **t** his disciples,
26:13 she has done will also be **t**
26:35 Peter **t** him, "Even if I have to
26:71 She **t** those who were there,
27:65 Pilate **t** them, "You have the
28:7 Take note that I have **t** you."
28:11 They **t** the chief priests
28:13 and **t** them to say that Jesus'
28:15 money and did as they were **t**.
28:16 where Jesus had **t** them to go.
Mar 1:14 Jesus went to Galilee and **t**
1:37 they found him, they **t** him,
3:3 So he **t** the man with the
3:5 Then he **t** the man,
3:9 Jesus **t** his disciples to have a
3:32 sitting around Jesus **t** him,
5:9 He **t** Jesus, "My name is
5:16 Those who saw this **t** what
5:19 Instead, he **t** the man,
5:33 bowed in front of him and **t** him
5:34 Jesus **t** her, "Daughter,
5:35 They **t** the synagogue leader,
5:36 he **t** the synagogue leader,
5:43 He also **t** them to give the little
6:4 But Jesus **t** them, "The only
6:10 He **t** them, "Whenever you go
6:12 So the apostles went and **t**
6:22 The king **t** the girl,
6:38 they found out, they **t** him,
7:6 Jesus **t** them, "Isaiah was right
8:19 They **t** him, "Twelve."
8:26 Jesus **t** him when he sent him
8:32 He **t** them very clearly what he
9:29 He **t** them, "This kind of spirit
9:35 He **t** them, "Whoever wants to
10:13 But the disciples **t** the people
10:14 He **t** them, "Don't stop the
10:21 He **t** him, "You're still missing
10:39 "We can," they **t** him.
10:39 Jesus **t** them, "You will drink
10:48 The people **t** him to be quiet.
10:49 They called the blind man and **t**
10:52 Jesus **t** him, "Go, your faith
11:6 them as Jesus had **t** them.
11:28 Who **t** you that you could do
11:33 Jesus **t** them, "Then I won't tell
12:16 They **t** him, "The emperor's."
12:32 You've **t** the truth that there is
12:34 man answered, he **t** the man,
13:23 I have **t** you everything before it
14:9 she has done will also be **t**
14:13 two of his disciples and **t** them,
14:16 as Jesus had **t** them.
16:7 just as he **t** them."
16:10 She went and **t** his friends,
16:13 went back and **t** the others,
Luk 1:4 that what you've been **t** is true.
1:30 The angel **t** her, "Don't be
2:15 what the Lord has **t** us about."
2:17 they had been **t** about him.
2:20 the way the angel had **t** them.
2:26 and had **t** him that he wouldn't
3:3 He **t** people about a baptism of
3:13 He **t** them, "Don't collect more
3:14 He **t** them, "Be satisfied with
3:18 he **t** the Good News to the
5:4 finished speaking, he **t** Simon,
5:10 Jesus **t** Simon, "Don't be afraid.
6:8 So he **t** the man with the
7:18 John's disciples **t** him about all
8:20 Someone **t** Jesus,
Luk 8:36 Those who had seen this **t** the
8:38 sent the man away and **t** him,
8:39 city and **t** people how much
8:47 she **t** why she touched him and
8:48 Jesus **t** her, "Daughter,
8:50 he **t** the synagogue leader,
9:3 He **t** them, "Don't take anything
9:6 to village, **t** the Good News,
9:10 The apostles came back and **t**
9:14 Then he **t** his disciples,
9:36 and for some time they **t** no one
9:58 Jesus **t** him, "Foxes have
9:59 He **t** another man, "Follow me!"
9:60 But Jesus **t** him, "Let the dead
10:2 He **t** them, "The harvest is
10:28 Jesus **t** him, "You're right!
10:35 He **t** the innkeeper,
10:37 Jesus **t** him, "Go and imitate
11:2 Jesus **t** them, "When you pray,
12:9 But God's angels will be **t** that I
12:15 He **t** the people, "Be careful to
13:14 The leader **t** the crowd,
13:31 time some Pharisees **t** Jesus,
14:12 Then he **t** the man who had
14:21 He **t** his servant, 'Run to every
14:23 "Then the master **t** his servant,
15:27 "The servant **t** him,
16:6 "The manager **t** him,
16:7 "The manager **t** him,
17:1 Jesus **t** his disciples,
17:14 When he saw them, he **t** them,
17:19 Jesus **t** the man, "Get up,
17:37 Jesus **t** them, "Vultures will
18:15 they **t** the people not to do that.
18:37 The people **t** him that Jesus
18:39 at the front of the crowd **t**
18:42 Jesus **t** him, "Receive your
19:24 The king **t** his men,
19:32 sent found it as he had **t** them.
20:2 Who **t** you that you could do
20:8 Jesus **t** them, "Then I won't tell
21:30 you know without being **t** that
22:8 sent Peter and John and **t** them,
22:10 He **t** them, "Go into the city,
22:13 everything as Jesus had **t** them
23:14 He **t** them, "You brought me
24:6 Remember what he **t** you while
24:8 what Jesus had **t** them.
24:9 They **t** everything to the eleven
24:10 They **t** the apostles everything.
24:23 They **t** us that they had seen
24:35 Then the two disciples **t** what
24:44 I **t** you that everything written
24:47 of Jesus people must be **t**
24:47 This must be **t** to people from
Jon 1:20 He **t** them clearly, "I'm not the
1:33 to baptize with water, had **t** me,
1:39 Jesus **t** them, "Come, and you
1:41 his brother Simon and **t** him,
1:43 He found Philip and **t** him,
1:45 found Nathanael and **t** him,
1:46 Philip **t** him, "Come and see!"
1:50 "You believe because I **t** you
2:5 His mother **t** the servers,
2:7 Jesus **t** the servers,
2:8 servers did as they were **t**.
2:16 He **t** those who sold pigeons,
3:10 Jesus **t** Nicodemus,
4:15 The woman **t** Jesus,
4:16 Jesus **t** her, "Go to your
4:17 Jesus **t** her, "You're right when
4:18 You've **t** the truth."
4:21 Jesus **t** her, "Believe me.
4:26 Jesus **t** her, "I am he, and I am
4:28 into the city. She **t** the people,
4:29 and meet a man who **t** me
4:32 Jesus **t** them, "I have food to
4:34 Jesus **t** them, "My food is to do
4:39 "He **t** me everything I've ever
4:42 They **t** the woman,
4:48 Jesus **t** the official,
4:50 Jesus **t** him, "Go home.
4:50 The man believed what Jesus **t**
4:51 his servants met him and **t** him
4:52 His servants **t** him,
4:53 time that Jesus had **t** him,

Jon 5:8 Jesus **t** the man, "Get up,
5:10 So the Jews **t** the man who
5:11 "The man who made me well **t**
5:12 "Who is the man who **t** you to
5:14 the temple courtyard and **t** him,
5:15 the Jews and **t** them that Jesus
6:8 Simon Peter's brother, **t** him,
6:12 Jesus **t** his disciples,
6:20 Jesus **t** them, "It's me. Don't be
6:35 Jesus **t** them, "I am the bread
6:36 I've **t** you that you have seen
6:53 Jesus **t** them, "I can guarantee
6:65 So he added, "That is why I **t**
7:3 So Jesus' brothers **t** him,
7:6 Jesus **t** them, "Now is not the
8:24 For this reason I **t** you that
8:25 Jesus **t** them, "I am whom I
8:26 exactly what he has **t** me."
8:28 So Jesus **t** them, "When you
8:39 Jesus **t** them, "If you were
8:40 I am a man who has **t** you the
8:42 Jesus **t** them, "If God were
8:52 The Jews **t** Jesus,
8:58 Jesus **t** them, "I can guarantee
9:7 and **t** him, "Wash it off in the
9:11 eyes, and **t** me, 'Go to Siloam,
9:15 The man **t** the Pharisees,
9:24 They **t** him, "Give glory to God.
9:27 "I've already **t** you,
9:37 Jesus **t** him, "You've seen him.
9:41 Jesus **t** them, "If you were
10:25 answered them, "I've **t** you,
11:11 said this, he **t** his disciples,
11:14 Then Jesus **t** them plainly,
11:21 Martha **t** Jesus, "Lord, if you
11:23 Jesus **t** Martha, "Your brother
11:39 man's sister, **t** Jesus, "Lord,
11:44 Jesus **t** them, "Free Lazarus,
11:46 and **t** them what Jesus
11:49 chief priest that year, **t** them,
12:21 Bethsaida in Galilee) and **t** him,
12:22 Philip **t** Andrew, and they told
12:22 told Andrew, and they **t** Jesus.
12:49 the Father who sent me **t** me
12:50 is what the Father **t** me to say."
13:8 Peter **t** Jesus, "You will never
13:10 Jesus **t** Peter, "People who
13:27 So Jesus **t** him, "Hurry!
13:33 telling you what I **t** the Jews.
14:2 would I have **t** you that I'm
14:25 "I have **t** you this while I'm still
14:26 that I have ever **t** you.
15:3 because of what I have **t** you.
15:11 I have **t** you this so that you
15:20 Remember what I **t** you:
16:4 But I've **t** you this so that when
16:4 you'll remember what I've **t** you.
16:6 But because I've **t** you this,
16:33 I've **t** you this so that my peace
17:6 They did what you **t** them.
18:5 Jesus **t** them, "I am he." Judas,
18:6 When Jesus **t** them,
18:8 "I **t** you that I am he.
18:11 Jesus **t** Peter, "Put your sword
18:23 But if I've **t** the truth,
18:31 Pilate **t** the Jews, "Take him,
18:38 to the Jews again and **t** them,
19:4 outside again and **t** the Jews,
19:6 Pilate **t** them, "You take him
19:21 of the Jewish people **t** Pilate,
20:2 She **t** them, "They have
20:13 Mary **t** them, "They have
20:17 Jesus **t** her, "Don't hold on to
20:18 to the disciples and **t** them,
20:18 She also **t** them what he had
20:25 The other disciples **t** him,
20:25 Thomas **t** them, "I refuse to
21:3 They **t** him, "We're going with
21:6 He **t** them, "Throw the net out
21:10 Jesus **t** them, "Bring some of
21:12 Jesus **t** them, "Come,
21:15 Jesus **t** him, "Feed my lambs."
21:16 Jesus **t** him, "Take care of my
21:17 Jesus **t** him, "Feed my sheep.
21:19 After saying this, Jesus **t** Peter,
Act 1:4 Jesus said to them, "I've **t** you
Act 1:7 Jesus **t** them, "You don't need
4:23 apostles and **t** them everything
5:20 The angel **t** them, "Stand in the
5:25 Then someone **t** them,
6:2 disciples together and **t** them,
7:3 God **t** him, 'Leave your land
7:6 God **t** Abraham that his
7:7 God also **t** him, "I will punish
7:13 On the second trip, Joseph **t**
7:33 The Lord **t** him, 'Take off your
7:37 Moses who **t** the Israelites,
7:40 They **t** Aaron, 'We don't know
7:44 tent exactly as God had **t** him.
8:5 of Samaria and **t** people about
8:20 Peter **t** Simon, "May your
8:35 Philip **t** the official the Good
9:6 Go into the city, and you'll be **t**
9:11 The Lord **t** him, "Get up! Go to
9:15 The Lord **t** Ananias,
9:24 but Saul was **t** about their plot.
9:27 Barnabas **t** the apostles how
9:27 Barnabas also **t** them how
10:13 A voice **t** him, "Get up, Peter!
10:22 A holy angel **t** him to summon
10:26 He **t** him, "Stand up! I'm only a
11:12 The Spirit **t** me to go with them
11:13 "He **t** us that he had seen an
11:13 The angel **t** him, and summon a
12:8 The angel **t** him, "Put your
12:8 Then the angel **t** him,
12:15 The people **t** her, But she
12:17 them down and **t** them how
13:24 John (the Baptizer) **t** everyone
13:46 and Barnabas **t** them boldly,
14:22 Paul and Barnabas **t** them,
15:3 they **t** the whole story of how
16:4 they **t** people about the
16:16 by an evil spirit that **t** fortunes.
16:35 sent guards who **t** the jailer,
16:37 But Paul **t** the guards,
18:6 from his clothes and **t** them,
18:21 As he left, he **t** them,
19:4 John **t** people to believe in
19:18 spells and **t** all the details.
20:25 that none of you whom I **t** about
21:21 But they have been **t** that you
21:24 they've been **t** about you isn't
21:25 We **t** them that they should not
22:8 "The person **t** me, 'I'm Jesus
22:10 "The Lord **t** me, 'Get up!
22:10 and you'll be **t** everything I've
22:18 He **t** me, 'Hurry! Get out of
22:21 "But the Lord **t** me,
22:24 into the barracks and **t** them
23:11 You've **t** the truth about me in
23:16 He entered the barracks and **t**
23:17 one of the sergeants and **t** him,
23:23 of his sergeants and **t** them,
24:22 He **t** them, "When the officer
25:5 He **t** them, "Have your
25:14 Festus **t** the king about Paul's
25:22 Agrippa **t** Festus, "I would like
26:20 spread the message that I first **t**
26:20 I **t** them to do things that prove
26:32 Agrippa **t** Festus, "This man
27:24 The angel **t** me, 'Don't be
27:25 will turn out as he **t** me.
27:31 Paul **t** the officer and the
28:21 The Jewish leaders **t** Paul,
Rom 4:18 nations, as he had been **t**:
9:11 Rebekah was **t** that the older
9:26 Wherever they were **t**,
15:21 "Those who were never **t** about
1Co 5:9 In my letter to you I **t** you not to
15:1 News which I already **t** you,
15:12 If we have **t** you that Christ has
2Co 1:19 and Timothy **t** you about,
7:3 I've already **t** you that you are
7:7 He **t** us how you wanted to see
7:14 Since everything we **t** you was
12:9 But he **t** me: "My kindness is
Gal 1:9 you again what we've **t** you
2:14 So I **t** Cephas in front of
5:21 I've **t** you in the past and I'm
Php 1:18 people are **t** the message about
3:18 I have often **t** you, and now tell
Col 1:8 and has **t** us about the love that
1Th 3:4 we **t** you ahead of time that we
3:6 back to us from you and has **t**
3:6 He also **t** us that you always
4:6 We've already **t** you and
2Th 2:5 Don't you remember that I **t** you
2:14 News which we **t** you so that
1Ti 4:16 Continue to do what I've **t** you.
5:21 you follow what I've **t** you.
Heb 2:3 the Lord **t** this saving message.
3:5 He **t** (the people) what God
7:8 but we are **t** that he lives.
9:19 Moses **t** all the people every
1Pe 1:25 Good News that was **t** to you.
4:6 After all, the Good News was **t**
4:6 It was **t** to them so that they
2Pe 1:16 When we apostles **t** you about
2:5 Noah was his messenger who **t**
2:21 the holy life God **t** them to live.
3Jn 1:3 some believers came and **t**
1:6 These believers have **t** the
Jud 1:17 Jesus Christ **t** you to expect:
Rev 6:11 They were **t** to rest a little
7:14 Then he **t** me, "These are the
9:4 They were **t** not to harm any
10:11 The seven thunders **t** me,
11:1 I was **t**, "Stand up and measure
14:5 They've never **t** a lie.
19:9 banquet.'" He also **t** me,
19:10 But he **t** me, "Don't do that! I am
22:9 He **t** me, "Don't do that! I am

tolerate (11)

Exo 20:5 a God who does not **t** rivals.
34:14 is a God who does not **t** rivals.
Dtr 4:24 a God who does not **t** rivals.
5:9 a God who does not **t** rivals.
6:15 is a God who does not **t** rivals.
Jos 24:19 is a God who does not **t** rivals.
Est 3:8 is not in your interest to **t** them,
Psa 101:5 I will not **t** anyone with a
Mic 6:11 I cannot **t** dishonest scales and
Rev 2:2 you cannot **t** wicked people.
2:20 You **t** that woman Jezebel,

tolerated (1)

Est 3:4 Mordecai's actions would be **t**,

tolerating (1)

Exo 34:14 he is known for not **t** rivals.)

tolls (4)

Ezr 4:13 longer pay taxes, fees, and **t**.
4:20 and **t** were paid to them.
7:24 God pay any taxes, fees, or **t**.
Rom 13:7 If you owe **t**, pay them. If you

tomb (78)

Gen 23:4 of your property for a **t** so that
23:6 us will withhold from you his **t**
23:9 to be used as a **t** among you."
23:20 his property to be used as a **t**.
47:30 and bury me in their **t**."
49:30 Ephron the Hittite to use as a **t**.
50:5 Bury me in the **t** I bought for
50:13 Abraham had bought this **t** from
Jdg 8:32 He was buried in the **t** of his
16:31 Zorah and Eshtaol in the **t**
2Sm 2:32 in his father's **t** in Bethlehem.
4:12 buried it in Abner's **t** in Hebron.
17:23 and was buried in his father's **t**.
21:14 in the **t** of Saul's father Kish.
1Ki 13:22 in the **t** of your ancestors."
13:30 of the man of God in his own **t**
13:31 bury me in the **t** where the man
2Ki 9:28 They buried him in a **t** with his
13:21 put the man into Elisha's **t**.
21:26 He was buried in his **t** in the
23:17 "It's the **t** of the man of God
23:30 They buried Josiah in his **t**.
2Ch 16:14 They buried him in the **t** that he
Job 10:19 carried from the womb to the **t**.
Isa 14:18 with honor, each in his own **t**.
14:19 But you are thrown out of your **t**
14:20 be joined by the kings in the **t**,
22:16 you have to dig a **t** for yourself?

Isa 53:9 He was placed in a **t** with the
Mat 26:12 body before it is placed in a **t**.
27:60 he laid it in his own new **t**,
27:60 stone against the door of the **t**,
27:61 were sitting there, facing the **t**.
27:64 give the order to make the **t**
27:65 Go and make the **t** as secure
27:66 So they went to secure the **t**.
28:1 other Mary went to look at the **t**.
28:8 They hurried away from the **t**
Mar 6:29 for his body and laid it in a **t**.
14:8 body before it is placed in a **t**.
15:46 Then he laid the body in a **t**,
15:46 stone against the door of the **t**.
16:2 going to the **t** very early when
16:3 us from the entrance to the **t**?
16:5 As they went into the **t**,
16:8 They went out of the **t** and ran
Luk 23:53 Then he laid the body in a **t** cut
23:53 a **t** in which no one had ever
23:55 They observed the **t** and how
24:1 the women went to the **t**.
24:2 been rolled away from the **t**.
24:9 The women left the **t** and went
24:12 Peter got up and ran to the **t**.
24:22 went to the **t** early this morning
24:24 Some of our men went to the **t**
Jon 11:17 had been in the **t** for four days.
11:31 she was going to the **t** to cry.
11:38 Jesus went to the **t**.
11:41 away from the entrance of the **t**.
12:7 the day I will be placed in a **t**.
12:17 he called Lazarus from the **t**
19:41 In that garden was a new **t** in
19:42 Nicodemus put Jesus in that **t**,
19:42 and since the **t** was nearby.
20:1 from Magdala went to the **t**.
20:2 removed the Lord from the **t**,
20:3 other disciple headed for the **t**.
20:4 Peter and came to the **t** first.
20:5 over and looked inside the **t**.
20:6 after him and went into the **t**.
20:8 who arrived at the **t** first,
20:11 cried as she looked at the **t**.
Act 2:29 buried and that his **t** is here
7:16 in the **t** that Abraham purchased
13:29 the cross and placed him in a **t**.
Rom 6:4 were placed into the **t** with him.
1Co 15:4 He was placed in a **t**.
Col 2:12 when you were placed in the **t**

tomb's (1)

Jon 20:1 removed from the **t** entrance

tombs (21)

Gen 23:6 your dead in one of our best **t**.
2Ki 23:6 and threw its ashes on the **t** of
23:16 Josiah turned and saw the **t**
23:16 to take the bones out of the **t**
2Ch 21:20 but not in the **t** of the kings.
24:25 bury him in the **t** of the kings.
26:23 field containing **t** that belonged
28:27 they didn't put him into the **t**
32:33 He was buried in the upper **t** of
34:4 scattered the powder over the **t**
35:24 He died and was buried in the **t**
Neh 3:16 way to a point across from the **t**
Mat 8:28 and had come out of the **t**.
23:29 You build **t** for the prophets and
27:52 The **t** were opened,
27:53 They came out of the **t** after he
Mar 5:2 a man came out of the **t** and
5:3 and lived among the **t**.
5:5 and day he was among the **t**
Luk 8:27 in a house but lived in the **t**.
Jon 5:29 they will come out of their **t**.

tomorrow (63)

Gen 19:2 Then early **t** morning you can
Exo 8:10 "Pray for me **t**," Pharaoh said.
8:23 sign will happen **t**.'"
8:29 **T** the swarms of flies will go
9:5 He said, "**T** I will do this."
9:18 So, at this time **t** I will send the
10:4 **t** I will bring locusts into your
16:23 **T** is a day of worship,
Exo 16:23 and keep it until **t** morning."
17:9 **T** I will stand on top of the hill.
19:11 and be ready by the day after **t**.
32:5 "**T** there will be a festival in the
Num 11:18 the people to get ready for **t**.
14:25 **T** you must turn around,
16:6 your followers must do this **t**:
16:16 Moses said to Korah, "**T** you
Jos 3:5 yourselves holy because **t**
7:13 Tell the people, 'Get ready for **t**
11:6 About this time **t** they will all
22:18 and **t** he will be angry with the
Jdg 19:9 **T** you can start out early to go
20:28 **T** I will hand them over to you."
1Sm 9:16 "About this time **t** I will send
11:9 the men of Jabesh Gilead: '**T**,
11:10 "**T** we'll surrender to you,
19:2 Please be careful **t** morning.
19:11 tonight, you'll be dead **t**!"
20:5 "**T** is the New Moon Festival,
20:18 "**T** is the New Moon Festival,"
20:19 The day after **t** you will be
28:19 **T** you and your sons will be
2Sm 11:12 and **t** I'll send you back."
1Ki 12:5 and come back the day after **t**."
19:2 strike me dead if by this time **t**
20:6 At this time **t** I'm going to send
2Ki 6:28 We'll eat my son **t**.'
7:1 About this time **t** 24 cups of the
7:18 will happen about this time **t**
10:6 me in Jezreel about this time **t**."
20:5 The day after **t** you will go to
20:8 LORD's temple the day after **t**?"
2Ch 10:5 "Come back the day after **t**."
20:16 **T** go into battle against them.
20:17 **T** go out to face them.
Est 5:8 And **t** I will answer you,
5:12 And again **t** I am her invited
9:13 allow the Jews in Susa to do **t**
Pro 3:28 Come back **t**. I'll give you
27:1 Do not brag about **t**,
Isa 22:13 "Let's eat and drink because **t**
56:12 And **t** will be like today,
Mat 6:30 Today it's alive, and **t** it's
6:34 "So don't ever worry about **t**.
6:34 all, **t** will worry about itself.
Luk 12:28 Today it's alive, and **t** it's
13:32 and heal people today and **t**.
13:33 way today, **t**, and the next day.
Act 23:20 Paul to the Jewish council **t**.
25:22 "You'll hear him **t**."
1Co 2:6 are in power today and gone **t**.
15:32 "Let's eat and drink because **t**
Jas 4:13 You're saying, "Today or **t** we
4:14 don't know what will happen **t**.

tone (1)

Gal 4:20 so that I could change the **t**

tongs (6)

Exo 25:38 The **t** and incense burners
37:23 made the seven lamps, the **t**,
Num 4:9 as well as the lamps, **t**, trays,
1Ki 7:49 room), flowers, lamps, gold **t**,
2Ch 4:21 flowers, lamps, pure gold **t**,
Isa 6:6 had taken from the altar with **t**.

tongue (61)

2Sm 23:2 His words were on my **t**.
Job 5:21 "When the **t** lashes out,
6:30 Is there injustice on my **t**,
12:11 sounds and the **t** taste food?
15:5 choose ⌊to talk with⌋ a sly **t**.
20:12 and he hides it under his **t** ....
27:4 and my **t** will not mumble
33:2 words are on the tip of my **t**.
34:3 words like the **t** tastes food.
41:1 with a fishhook or tie its **t** down
Psa 10:7 are on the tip of his **t**.
12:3 lip and every bragging **t**
15:3 does not slander with his **t**,
22:15 My **t** sticks to the roof of my
34:13 Keep your **t** from saying evil
35:28 Then my **t** will tell about your
37:30 His **t** speaks what is fair.
39:1 so that I do not sin with my **t**.
Psa 39:3 Then I spoke with my **t**:
45:1 My **t** is a pen for a skillful
50:19 Your **t** plans deceit.
51:14 Let my **t** sing joyfully about
52:2 Your **t** makes up threats.
52:4 accusation, you deceitful **t**!
66:17 High praise was on my **t**.
71:24 My **t** will tell about your
119:172 Let my **t** sing about your
120:2 lying lips and from a deceitful **t**.
120:3 You deceitful **t**, what can the
137:6 Let my **t** stick to the roof of my
139:4 is a ⌊single⌋ word on my **t**,
Pro 6:17 arrogant eyes, a lying **t**,
10:20 The **t** of a righteous person is
10:31 but a devious **t** will be cut off.
15:4 A soothing **t** is a tree of life,
15:4 a deceitful **t** breaks the spirit.
16:1 but an answer on the **t** comes
17:4 his ears to a slanderous **t**.
17:20 and one with a devious **t**
18:21 The **t** has the power of life and
21:23 and his **t** keeps himself out
22:18 they will be on the tip of your **t**,
25:15 and a soft **t** can break bones.
25:23 **t** brings angry looks.
26:28 A lying **t** hates its victims,
28:23 the one who flatters with his **t**.
31:26 and on her **t** there is tender
Sos 4:11 and milk are under your **t**.
Isa 30:27 His **t** is like a devouring flame.
45:23 **t** will swear ⌊allegiance⌋."
49:2 He made my **t** like a sharp
57:4 are you sticking out your **t** at?
Eze 3:26 I will make your **t** stick to the
Mar 7:33 he touched the man's **t**.
Luk 16:24 finger in water to cool off my **t**.
Act 2:26 heart is glad and my **t** rejoices.
Jas 1:26 religious but can't control his **t**,
3:5 In the same way the **t** is a
3:6 The **t** is that kind of flame.
3:6 The **t** sets our lives on fire,
3:8 Yet, no one can tame the **t**.

tongues (29)

Jdg 7:5 water with their **t** like dogs from
Job 29:10 and their **t** stuck to the roofs of
Psa 5:9 They flatter with their **t**.
12:4 "We will overcome with our **t**.
31:20 safe from quarrelsome **t**.
57:4 Their **t** are sharp swords.
64:3 sharpen their **t** like swords.
64:8 They will trip over their own **t**.
68:23 your feet in blood and the **t**
78:36 and lied to him with their **t**.
109:2 speak against me with lying **t**.
126:2 filled with laughter and our **t**
140:3 They make their **t** as sharp as
Pro 15:2 The **t** of wise people give good
Isa 41:17 Their **t** are parched with thirst.
Jer 9:3 They use their **t** like bows that
9:5 My people train their **t** to speak
9:8 Their **t** are like deadly arrows.
Lam 4:4 The **t** of nursing infants stick to
Mic 6:12 and their **t** speak deceitfully.
Zep 3:13 or use their **t** to deceive others.
Zec 14:12 and their **t** will rot in their
Act 2:3 **T** that looked like fire appeared
2:3 The **t** arranged themselves so
Rom 3:13 Their **t** practice deception.
Jas 3:9 With our **t** we praise our Lord
3:9 Yet, with the same **t** we curse
1Pe 3:10 keep their **t** from saying evil
Rev 16:10 gnawed on their **t** in anguish

tongue-tied (1)

Exo 4:10 and I become **t** easily."

tonight (22)

Gen 19:5 came to ⌊stay with⌋ you **t**?
19:34 give him wine to drink again **t**.
30:15 Jacob can go to bed with you **t**
Num 22:19 Now, why don't you stay here **t**,
Jos 2:2 have entered the city **t**.
4:3 down where you will camp **t**."
Jdg 9:32 and your men must start out **t**.

Rut 1:12 And if I had a husband **t** ....
3:2 husks on the threshing floor **t**.
3:13 Stay here **t**. In the morning if he
1Sm 14:36 "Let's attack the Philistines **t**
19:11 "If you don't save yourself **t**,
2Sm 17:1 choose 12,000 men and leave **t**
17:8 will not camp with the troops **t**.
17:16 'Don't rest **t** in the river
19:7 no one will stay with you **t**,
Mat 26:31 "All of you will abandon me **t**.
26:34 Before a rooster crows **t**,
Mar 14:30 "I can guarantee this truth: **T**,
Luk 12:20 demand your life from you **t**!
22:34 won't crow **t** until you say
Act 23:23 to Caesarea at nine o'clock **t**.

tons (1)

Ezr 8:26 about 24 **t** of silver,

took (743)

Gen 2:15 Then the LORD God **t** the man
2:21 the LORD God **t** out one of the
3:6 So she **t** some of the fruit and
5:24 was gone because God **t** him.
9:23 Shem and Japheth **t** a blanket
11:31 Terah **t** his son Abram,
12:5 He **t** along his wife Sarai,
14:11 So the four kings **t** all the
14:12 They also **t** Abram's nephew
15:5 He **t** Abram outside and said,
16:3 Abram's wife Sarai **t** her
17:23 So Abraham **t** his son Ishmael,
18:7 ran to the herd and **t** one
18:8 Abraham **t** cheese and milk,
20:14 Then Abimelech **t** sheep,
21:14 next morning Abraham **t** bread
21:27 Abraham **t** some sheep and
22:3 He **t** with him two of his
22:6 Then Abraham **t** the wood for
22:10 picked up the knife and **t**
22:13 So Abraham **t** the ram and
24:7 "The LORD God of heaven **t**
24:10 Then the servant **t** ten of his
24:22 the man **t** out a gold nose ring
24:53 The servant **t** out gold and
24:61 The servant **t** Rebekah and left.
24:65 Then she **t** her veil and
24:67 Isaac **t** her into his mother
25:8 Then he **t** his last breath,
25:17 Then he **t** his last breath and
27:15 Then Rebekah **t** her older son
27:36 He **t** my rights as firstborn,
28:11 He **t** one of the stones from that
28:18 Early the next morning Jacob **t**
29:23 In the evening he **t** his daughter
30:9 she **t** her slave Zilpah and
30:15 enough that you **t** my husband?
30:35 that same day Laban **t** out
30:37 Then Jacob **t** fresh-cut
31:16 all the wealth that God **t** away
31:18 livestock ahead of him and **t** all
31:18 He **t** his own livestock that he
31:45 Jacob **t** a stone and set it up as
31:46 They **t** stones, put them into a
33:11 So Esau **t** it because Jacob
34:2 he **t** her and raped her.
34:19 because he **t** such pleasure
34:25 **t** their swords and boldly
34:26 They **t** Dinah from Shechem's
34:28 They **t** the sheep and goats,
35:18 As she **t** her last breath,
35:29 when he **t** his last breath and
36:6 Esau **t** his wives, his sons,
37:2 He **t** care of the flocks with the
37:24 Then they **t** him and put him
37:28 The Ishmaelites **t** him to Egypt.
37:31 So they **t** Joseph's robe,
38:7 So the LORD **t** away his life.
38:10 the LORD **t** away Onan's life
38:14 she **t** off her widow's clothes,
38:19 After she got up and left, she **t**
38:28 The midwife **t** a piece of red
40:4 and he **t** care of them.
40:11 so I **t** the grapes and squeezed
41:42 Then Pharaoh **t** off his signet
43:15 The men **t** the gifts,
Gen 43:17 did as Joseph said and **t** them
43:24 The man **t** the brothers into
46:6 They also **t** their livestock and
47:14 Then he **t** it to Pharaoh's
48:1 So he **t** his two sons
48:12 Joseph **t** them off his father's
48:13 Then Joseph **t** both of them,
48:17 So he **t** his father's hand in
48:22 I **t** it from the Amorites with my
49:33 He **t** his last breath and joined
50:10 Joseph **t** seven days to mourn
Exo 2:3 she **t** a basket made of papyrus
2:9 She **t** the child and nursed him.
4:6 and when he **t** his hand out,
4:7 and when he **t** it out this time,
4:20 So Moses **t** his wife and sons,
4:25 Then Zipporah **t** a flint knife,
9:10 They **t** ashes from a kiln and
13:19 Moses **t** the bones of Joseph
14:6 his chariot and **t** his army
14:7 He **t** 600 of his best chariots as
15:20 **t** a tambourine in her hand.
17:12 So Aaron and Hur **t** a rock,
22:8 he **t** his neighbor's valuables.
24:6 Moses **t** half of the blood and
24:7 Then he **t** the Book of the
24:8 Moses **t** the blood and
32:3 So all the people **t** off their gold
32:13 You **t** an oath, swearing on
32:20 Then he **t** the calf they had
34:34 he **t** off the veil until he came
35:22 They **t** these gifts of gold and
40:20 He **t** the words of God's
Lev 8:10 Moses **t** the anointing oil to
8:15 Moses **t** the blood and put it on
8:16 Moses **t** all the fat that was on
8:23 **t** some of the blood,
8:25 He **t** the fat, the fat from the tail,
8:26 He **t** a loaf of unleavened bread,
8:28 Then he **t** them from their
8:29 Moses also **t** the breast from
8:30 Moses **t** some of the anointing
9:5 So they **t** the things Moses
9:15 He **t** the male goat for the
9:17 He **t** a handful of grain and
9:21 However, he first **t** the breasts
10:1 sons Nadab and Abihu each **t**
10:5 So they came and **t** them away
Num 1:17 Moses and Aaron **t** the men
3:26 They **t** care of all these things.
3:31 They **t** care of all these things.
3:36 They **t** care of all these things.
3:37 They also **t** care of the posts
3:49 So Moses **t** this ransom money
7:6 Moses **t** the wagons and the
7:9 because they **t** care of the holy
11:25 He **t** some of the Spirit that was
15:36 So the whole community **t** him
16:18 So each man **t** his incense
16:39 So the priest Eleazar **t** the
16:47 Aaron **t** his incense burner,
17:9 and each man **t** his staff.
20:9 Moses **t** his staff out of the
20:28 Moses **t** off Aaron's priestly
21:1 he fought them and **t** some of
21:24 them in battle and **t** possession
21:25 Israel **t** all those Amorite cities,
21:35 And they **t** possession of his
22:41 The next morning Balak **t**
23:14 So he **t** him to the Field of
23:28 So Balak **t** Balaam to the top of
25:7 **t** a spear in his hand,
25:18 the incident that **t** place at Peor.
27:22 He **t** Joshua and made him
31:6 Phinehas **t** with him the holy
31:9 The Israelites **t** the Midianite
31:9 They also **t** all their animals,
31:11 Then they **t** everything as loot,
31:16 the incident that **t** place at Peor.
31:32 everything that the troops **t**:
31:42 Moses **t** the Israelites' half of
31:51 Moses and the priest Eleazar **t**
31:54 Moses and the priest Eleazar **t**
Dtr 1:15 So I **t** the heads of your tribes
1:25 They **t** some of the region's fruit
1:34 he was angry and **t** this oath:
Dtr 2:8 to Elath and Ezion Geber and **t**
2:12 them out, and **t** their place,
2:21 their land and **t** their place.
2:22 their land and **t** their place.
2:23 them out and **t** their place.
3:8 We **t** the land of the two
3:10 We **t** all of the cities of the
3:12 At that time we **t** possession of
3:14 **t** the whole territory of Argob as
4:21 So the LORD your God **t** an
4:47 They **t** possession of his land
9:17 I **t** the two tablets, threw them
9:21 I **t** that sinful calf you made and
24:12 don't keep the coat you **t** as a
29:8 We **t** their land and gave it to
32:10 guarded them, **t** care of them,
32:37 is the rock they **t** refuge in?
Jos 4:8 They **t** 12 stones, one for each
4:8 They **t** them from the middle of
5:7 The sons who **t** their place had
7:1 **t** something that had been
7:21 I wanted them, so I **t** them.
7:23 They **t** the loot from the tent
7:24 Joshua and all Israel **t** Achan
8:9 They **t** their position west of Ai,
8:27 Israel **t** the loot and the
9:4 They **t** worn-out sacks on their
10:9 Gilgal and **t** them by surprise.
11:14 The people of Israel **t** all the
11:16 Joshua **t** all this land,
12:1 Israel also **t** possession of their
19:47 They **t** it, settled there,
21:43 They **t** possession of it and
24:3 But I **t** your ancestor Abraham
24:8 So you **t** their land,
24:26 Then he **t** a large stone and set
Jdg 3:21 **t** the dagger from his right side,
3:25 So they **t** the key and opened
4:21 **t** a tent peg and walked quietly
5:6 who traveled **t** back roads.
5:7 **t** a stand — took a stand as a
5:7 took a stand — **t** a stand as a
6:8 I **t** you away from slavery.
6:27 Gideon **t** ten of his servants
7:5 So Gideon **t** the men down to
8:16 So Gideon **t** the leaders of the
8:21 Then he **t** the half-moon
8:25 Each man **t** the earrings from
9:43 So he **t** his troops,
9:48 Abimelech **t** an ax,
11:13 left Egypt, they **t** my land.
11:21 Israel defeated them and **t**
11:22 Israel **t** all the Amorite territory
11:24 your god Chemosh **t** for you?
11:24 the LORD our God **t** for us?
13:19 So Manoah **t** a young goat and
14:19 He **t** their clothes and gave
15:1 He **t** a young goat along for her.
15:6 man at Timnah **t** Samson's wife
16:3 **t** hold of the doors,
16:12 So Delilah **t** some new ropes
16:21 They poked out his eyes and **t**
16:31 They **t** Samson and buried him
17:2 I **t** it!" His mother said, "The
17:4 she **t** 200 pieces of the silver
18:17 They **t** the carved idol,
18:18 entered Micah's house and **t**
18:20 He **t** the ephod, the household
18:27 The people of Dan **t** what
19:1 He **t** a woman from Bethlehem
19:3 He **t** along his servant and two
19:3 She **t** her husband into her
19:21 So he **t** the Levite to his house
19:29 He **t** his concubine and cut her
20:2 all Israel's tribes **t** their places
20:6 So I **t** my concubine and cut
Rut 2:18 Ruth also **t** out what she had
4:8 he **t** off his sandal.
4:13 Then Boaz **t** Ruth home,
4:16 Naomi **t** the child, held him on
1Sm 1:24 she **t** him with her.
5:3 So they **t** Dagon and put him
5:8 So the people **t** the ark of the
6:10 They **t** two dairy cows,
7:9 Then Samuel **t** a lamb,
7:12 Then Samuel **t** a rock and set

1Sm 7:14 Philistines **t** from Israel were
8:3 They **t** bribes and denied
8:8 they've done since I **t** them out
10:1 Samuel **t** a flask of olive oil,
11:7 Saul **t** a pair of oxen,
14:32 They **t** sheep, cows,
15:21 The army **t** some of their
16:13 Samuel **t** the flask of olive oil
16:20 Jesse **t** six bushels of bread,
16:23 David **t** the lyre and strummed
17:20 He **t** ⌊the food⌋ and went,
17:35 I **t** hold of its mane,
17:39 So David **t** all those things off.
17:40 He **t** his stick with him,
17:49 into his bag, **t** out a stone,
17:51 He **t** Goliath's sword,
17:54 David **t** the Philistine's head
18:4 Jonathan **t** off the coat he had
19:7 Then Jonathan **t** David to Saul.
19:13 Then Michal **t** some idols,
19:24 He even **t** off his clothes as he
20:3 But David **t** an oath,
24:2 Then Saul **t** 3,000 of the
25:18 So Abigail quickly **t** 200 loaves
26:12 David **t** the spear and the jar of
27:9 He also **t** sheep, cattle,
28:10 But Saul **t** an oath in the
28:21 "and I **t** my life in my hands
28:24 She **t** flour, kneaded it,
30:11 in the open country and **t** him
30:20 He **t** all the sheep and the
31:4 So Saul **t** the sword and fell on
31:12 men marched all night and **t**
31:13 They **t** the bones and buried
2Sm 1:10 And I **t** the crown that was on
2:3 David **t** his men and their
2:8 **t** Saul's son Ishbosheth and
2:32 They **t** Asahel and buried him
3:27 Joab **t** him aside in the
4:7 They **t** his head and traveled
4:12 Then they **t** Ishbosheth's head
7:6 house from the day I **t** Israel out
7:8 I **t** you from the pasture where
7:15 whom I **t** out of your way.
8:1 He **t** control of the main
8:4 David **t** 1,700 horsemen and
8:7 David **t** the gold shields that
8:8 King David also **t** a large
10:4 So Hanun **t** David's men,
10:9 he **t** the select troops of Israel
11:4 sent messengers and **t** her.
12:4 So he **t** the poor man's lamb
12:9 You **t** his wife as your wife.
12:10 you despised me and **t**
12:30 He **t** the gold crown from the
12:30 David also **t** a lot of goods from
13:8 She **t** dough, kneaded it,
13:9 Then she **t** the pan and served
13:10 Tamar **t** the bread she had
13:18 So his servant **t** her out and
14:7 because he **t** his brother's life.
15:29 So Zadok and Abiathar **t** the
17:19 The man's wife **t** a cover,
18:14 He **t** three sharp sticks and
18:17 They **t** Absalom, threw him into
20:3 he **t** the ten concubines he had
20:5 but he **t** longer to do it than
20:9 He **t** hold of Amasa's beard
21:8 The king **t** Armoni and
21:10 Rizpah (Aiah's daughter) **t**
21:12 David went and **t** the bones of
22:17 from high above and **t** hold
1Ki 1:4 the king's servant and **t** care
1:17 "Sir," she answered, "You **t** an
1:39 The priest Zadok **t** the
1:50 and **t** hold of the horns of the
2:8 I **t** an oath by the LORD and
2:23 King Solomon **t** an oath by the
3:20 during the night and **t** my son,
3:21 I **t** a good look at him and
7:1 Solomon **t** 13 years to finish
9:10 It **t** Solomon 20 years to build
11:30 Ahijah **t** his new garment and
13:9 go back on the same road I **t**."
13:17 on the road I **t** to get there."
13:33 He **t** all who were willing and
1Ki 14:26 He **t** the treasures from the
14:26 He **t** them all. He took all the
14:26 He **t** all the gold shields
15:18 Then Asa **t** all the silver and
17:19 Elijah **t** him from her arms,
17:23 Elijah **t** the child, brought him
18:26 They **t** the bull he gave them,
18:31 Elijah **t** 12 stones,
18:40 and Elijah **t** them to the Kishon
19:2 take your life the way you **t**
19:19 Elijah **t** off his coat and put it
19:21 Elisha left him, **t** two oxen,
20:25 He **t** their advice and followed
20:34 my father **t** from your father.
20:41 Then he quickly **t** the bandage
2Ki 2:8 Elijah **t** his coat, rolled it up,
2:14 He **t** the coat and struck the
3:9 and the king of Edom **t** an
3:26 he **t** 700 swordsmen to try to
3:27 Then he **t** his firstborn son,
4:21 She **t** him upstairs and laid him
4:27 she **t** hold of his feet.
4:37 She **t** her son and left.
5:5 he **t** 750 pounds of silver,
5:24 he **t** these things and put them
7:14 So they **t** two chariots with
8:9 He **t** with him a present and all
8:15 next day Hazael **t** a blanket,
8:21 Jehoram **t** all his chariots to
9:13 them immediately **t** off his coat
9:24 But Jehu **t** his bow and shot
11:2 **t** Ahaziah's son Joash.
11:9 Each commander **t** his men
11:19 He **t** the company commanders
12:9 the priest Jehoiada **t** a box,
12:18 So King Joash of Judah **t** all
13:18 So the king **t** them.
14:7 in the Dead Sea region and **t**
14:14 He **t** all the gold, silver, and all
14:14 He also **t** hostages.
14:21 the people of Judah **t** Azariah,
15:29 Tiglath Pileser of Assyria **t** Ijon,
15:29 He also **t** the people away to
16:8 Ahaz **t** the silver and gold he
16:9 **t** the people to Kir as captives,
16:17 He **t** the bronze pool down from
17:6 Assyria captured Samaria and **t**
17:24 They **t** over Samaria and lived
17:26 "The people you **t** as captives
18:11 The king of Assyria **t** the
19:14 Hezekiah **t** the letters from the
23:6 He **t** the pole dedicated to the
23:30 Then the people of the land **t**
23:34 He **t** Jehoahaz away to Egypt,
24:13 He also **t** away all the
24:15 He **t** Jehoiakin to Babylon as a
24:15 He also **t** the king's mother,
25:4 the king **t** the road to the plain
25:7 shackles and **t** him to Babylon.
25:14 They **t** the pots, shovels,
25:15 The captain of the guard **t** all of
25:18 The captain of the guard **t** the
25:19 From the city he also **t** an army
25:20 **t** them and brought them to the
1Ch 5:6 of Assyria **t** him away as
9:28 in and when they **t** them out.
10:4 So Saul **t** the sword and fell on
10:9 They stripped him and **t** his
10:12 all the fighting men came and **t**
17:7 I **t** you from the pasture where
18:1 He **t** Gath and its surrounding
18:4 David **t** 1,000 chariots,
18:7 David **t** the gold shields that
18:8 David also **t** a large quantity of
19:4 So Hanun **t** David's men,
19:10 he **t** the select troops of Israel
20:2 He **t** the gold crown from the
20:2 David also **t** a lot of goods from
2Ch 8:1 It **t** Solomon 20 years to build
12:9 Egypt attacked Jerusalem and **t**
12:9 He **t** them all. He took the gold
12:9 He **t** the gold shields Solomon
15:15 since they **t** the oath
15:15 They **t** great pleasure in
16:6 Then King Asa **t** everyone in
21:9 Jehoram **t** all his chariot
2Ch 21:17 and **t** away everything that
21:17 They even **t** Jehoram's sons
22:11 **t** Ahaziah's son Joash.
23:8 Each **t** his men who were
23:20 He **t** the company commanders,
24:23 all the loot they **t** from Judah
25:12 **t** them to the top of a cliff,
25:13 They killed 3,000 people and **t**
25:24 ⌊He **t**⌋ all the gold,
25:24 He also **t** hostages.
26:1 the people of Judah **t** Uzziah,
28:8 They also **t** a lot of goods from
28:15 mentioned by name **t** charge
28:21 Ahaz **t** some of the things from
29:16 Then the Levites **t** the unclean
30:6 Messengers **t** letters from the
33:11 They **t** Manasseh captive,
34:16 Shaphan **t** the book to the king
34:17 We **t** the money that was
35:10 The priests **t** their positions
35:24 His officers **t** him out of the
36:1 Then people of the land **t**
36:4 Neco **t** Jehoahaz away to
36:20 The king of Babylon **t** those
Ezr 1:11 Sheshbazzar **t** all these
2:61 and **t** that ⌊family⌋ name).
3:10 in their robes **t** their places
3:10 descendants **t** their places
5:14 In addition, Cyrus **t** out of a
6:5 In addition, Cyrus **t** out of a
8:30 So the priests and the Levites **t**
10:5 had said. So they **t** an oath.
Neh 5:15 Even the governors' servants **t**
6:15 The wall **t** 52 days to finish.
7:63 and **t** that ⌊family⌋ name).
8:2 This **t** place on the first day of
9:7 chose Abram and **t** him from Ur
9:18 'This is your god who **t** you out
9:22 So they **t** possession of the
9:24 Their children **t** possession of
9:25 They **t** possession of houses
10:28 The rest of the people **t** an oath.
10:28 of understanding also **t** an oath.
Est 1:1 the following events **t** place.
6:11 So Haman **t** the robe and the
6:14 arrived and quickly **t** Haman
8:2 Then the king **t** off his signet
Job 1:4 (Each brother **t** his turn having
1:15 They **t** the livestock and
1:17 They **t** the camels and
2:8 Job **t** a piece of broken pottery
29:7 the city gate and **t** my seat
Psa 18:16 from high above and **t** hold
44:3 swords that they **t** possession
68:18 You **t** prisoners captive.
71:6 You **t** me from my mother's
78:70 He **t** him from the sheep pens.
80:9 the ground for it so that it **t** root
89:43 You even **t** his sword out of his
89:51 your Messiah every step he **t**.
95:11 That is why I angrily **t** this
105:16 He **t** away their food supply.
116:3 The horrors of the grave **t** hold
119:106 I **t** an oath, and I will keep it.
119:106 I **t** an oath to follow your
Pro 7:20 He **t** lots of money with him.
24:32 I observed ⌊this⌋, I **t** it to heart.
Ecc 8:2 oath you **t** in God's presence.
Sos 5:7 Those watchmen on the walls **t**
Isa 37:14 Hezekiah **t** the letter from the
48:16 From the time it **t** place,
Jer 5:7 They **t** godless oaths.
20:3 The next day when Pashhur **t**
24:1 of Babylon **t** Jehoiakin (son
25:17 So I **t** the cup from the LORD's
26:23 Uriah from Egypt and **t** him
27:19 Nebuchadnezzar **t** Jehoiakin,
28:3 of Babylon **t** from this place
28:10 Then the prophet Hananiah **t**
29:1 **t** away as captives
31:32 ancestors when I **t** them by
32:11 Then I **t** the sealed copy of the
32:23 They entered and **t** possession
34:11 they changed their minds and **t**
35:3 I **t** Jaazaniah, who was the son
35:3 and I **t** Jaazaniah's brothers

Jer 36:14 Baruch, son of Neriah, **t** the
36:21 He **t** the scroll from the side
36:32 Then Jeremiah **t** another scroll
37:14 Irijah arrested Jeremiah and **t**
38:6 So they **t** Jeremiah and threw
38:11 So Ebed Melech **t** the men with
38:11 He **t** rags and torn clothes from
39:4 and they **t** the road to the plain
39:7 and **t** him to Babylon.
39:14 They **t** Jeremiah out of the
40:2 The captain of the guard **t**
41:10 Then Ishmael **t** captive the rest
41:10 Ishmael, son of Nethaniah, **t**
41:12 they **t** all their men and went to
43:5 all the army commanders **t** all
43:6 They **t** men, women, children,
43:6 They **t** every person whom
52:7 they **t** the road to the plain of
52:11 The king of Babylon **t** him to
52:18 They **t** the pots, shovels,
52:19 of the guard also **t** pans,
52:19 The captain of the guard **t** all of
52:24 The captain of the guard **t** the
52:25 From the city he also **t** an army
52:26 **t** them and brought them to the
52:28 Nebuchadnezzar **t** captive:
52:28 year as king, he **t** 3,023 Jews.
52:29 Nebuchadnezzar **t** 832 people
52:30 of the guard, **t** away 745 Jews.
Eze 3:14 Spirit lifted me and **t** me away.
8:3 He **t** me to Jerusalem,
8:7 Then he **t** me to the entrance of
10:7 angels and **t** out some coals.
10:7 The person **t** them and left.
11:1 Then the Spirit lifted me and **t**
16:16 You **t** some of your clothes and
16:17 You **t** your beautiful gold and
16:18 You **t** off your embroidered
16:20 "'You **t** your sons and
16:27 I **t** away some of your land,
16:47 It only **t** you a little time to be
17:3 It **t** hold of the top of a cedar
17:5 "'Then it **t** a seedling from that
17:13 Then he **t** someone from the
17:13 He **t** away the leading citizens
19:5 Then she **t** another one of her
23:10 **t** away her sons and daughters,
23:19 So she **t** part in even more
25:12 Edom **t** revenge on the nation
27:5 They **t** cedar trees from
27:26 Your rowers **t** you out to the
36:5 out the people and **t** their land.'
42:5 the corridors **t** space away from
43:1 Then the man **t** me to the east
44:1 Then the man **t** me back to the
44:15 descendants of Zadok **t** care
46:21 outer courtyard and **t** me past
47:1 Then the man **t** me back to the
48:11 They **t** care of my holy place.
Dan 1:2 Nebuchadnezzar **t** the utensils
1:16 So the supervisor **t** away the
2:25 Arioch immediately **t** Daniel to
5:31 Darius the Mede **t** over the
7:22 the holy people **t** possession
8:11 of the army so that it **t**
Hos 11:3 I **t** them by the hand.
12:12 Israel worked to get a wife; he **t**
13:5 I **t** care of you in the desert,
13:11 and I **t** him away when I was
Joe 3:5 You **t** my silver and my gold.
Amo 7:15 But the LORD **t** me away from
Jnh 1:15 Then they **t** Jonah and threw
3:3 It **t** three days to walk through
3:6 **t** off his robe, put on sackcloth,
Zec 11:7 I **t** two shepherd staffs and
11:7 And I **t** care of the sheep.
11:10 Then I **t** my staff called Favor
11:13 So I **t** the 30 pieces of silver.
Mat 1:18 The birth of Jesus Christ **t**
1:24 He **t** Mary to be his wife.
2:14 **t** the child and his mother,
2:21 **t** the child and his mother,
4:5 Then the devil **t** him into the
4:8 Once more the devil **t** him to a
8:17 "He **t** away our weaknesses
8:33 Those who **t** care of the pigs

Mat 9:25 Jesus went in, **t** her hand,
13:57 So they **t** offense at him.
14:11 who **t** it to her mother.
14:19 After he **t** the five loaves and
15:36 He **t** the seven loaves and the
16:22 Peter **t** him aside and objected
17:1 After six days Jesus **t** Peter,
20:11 Although they **t** it, they began
20:17 he **t** the twelve apostles aside
21:35 The workers **t** his servants and
25:1 They **t** their oil lamps and went
25:3 bridesmaids **t** their lamps,
25:4 **t** along extra oil for their lamps.
25:35 and you **t** me into your home.
25:36 and you **t** care of me.
26:26 Jesus **t** bread and blessed it.
26:27 Then he **t** a cup and spoke a
26:37 He **t** Peter and Zebedee's two
26:50 came forward, **t** hold of Jesus,
26:57 who had arrested Jesus **t** him
27:6 The chief priests **t** the money
27:9 "They **t** the 30 silver coins,
27:24 So Pilate **t** some water and
27:27 Then the governor's soldiers **t**
27:28 They **t** off his clothes and put a
27:30 they had spit on him, they **t**
27:31 they **t** off the cape and put his
27:48 men ran at once, **t** a sponge,
27:59 Joseph **t** the body and wrapped
28:9 and **t** hold of his feet.
28:15 The soldiers **t** the money and
Mar 1:13 and the angels **t** care of him.
1:31 Jesus went to her, **t** her hand,
4:36 Leaving the crowd, they **t**
5:14 Those who **t** care of the pigs
5:40 Then he **t** the child's father,
5:41 Jesus **t** the child's hand and
6:3 So they **t** offense at him.
6:41 After he **t** the five loaves and
7:33 Jesus **t** him away from the
8:6 He **t** the seven loaves and
8:23 Jesus **t** the blind man's hand
8:32 Peter **t** him aside and objected
9:2 six days Jesus **t** only Peter,
9:27 Jesus **t** his hand and helped
9:36 Then he **t** a little child and had
10:32 Once again he **t** the twelve
12:3 The workers **t** the servant,
12:8 So they **t** him, killed him,
14:22 Jesus **t** bread and blessed it.
14:23 Then he **t** a cup, spoke a
14:33 He **t** Peter, James, and John
14:46 Some men **t** hold of Jesus and
14:53 The men **t** Jesus to the chief
14:65 Even the guards **t** him and
15:20 they **t** off the purple cape and
15:22 They **t** Jesus to Golgotha
15:46 He **t** the body down from the
Luk 2:22 They **t** Jesus to present him to
2:28 Then Simeon **t** the child in his
4:5 The devil **t** him to a high place
4:9 Then the devil **t** him into
7:14 to the open coffin, **t** hold of it,
7:37 So she **t** a bottle of perfume
8:54 But Jesus **t** her hand and
9:10 He **t** them with him to a city
9:16 Then he **t** the five loaves and
9:28 said this, Jesus **t** Peter, John,
9:47 So he **t** a little child and had
10:34 him to an inn, and **t** care of him.
10:35 The next day the Samaritan **t**
14:4 So Jesus **t** hold of the man,
18:31 Jesus **t** the twelve apostles
22:17 Then he **t** a cup and spoke a
22:19 Then Jesus **t** bread and spoke
23:1 stood up and **t** him to Pilate.
23:53 After he **t** it down from the
24:30 he **t** bread and blessed it.
24:43 He **t** it and ate it while they
24:50 Then Jesus **t** them to a place
Jon 2:1 Three days later a wedding **t**
2:20 The Jews said, "It **t** forty-six
6:11 Jesus **t** the loaves,
10:22 of the Temple **t** place
12:3 Mary **t** a bottle of very
12:13 So they **t** palm branches and

Jon 13:4 his outer clothes, **t** a towel,
13:12 he **t** his place at the table
13:27 after Judas **t** the piece of bread,
13:30 Judas **t** the piece of bread and
18:3 So Judas **t** a troop of soldiers
18:13 and **t** him first to Annas,
19:13 he **t** Jesus outside and sat on
19:16 So the soldiers **t** Jesus.
19:23 they **t** his clothes and divided
19:40 These two men **t** the body of
21:13 Jesus **t** the bread, gave it to
Act 3:7 Peter **t** hold of the man's right
5:17 jealous. So they **t** action
5:40 The council **t** his advice.
6:12 went to Stephen, **t** him by force,
7:19 in the way he **t** advantage
7:20 His parents **t** care of him for
7:24 He **t** revenge by killing the
7:45 help when they **t** possession
8:39 Lord suddenly **t** Philip away.
9:27 Then Barnabas **t** an interest in
9:30 they **t** Saul to Caesarea and
9:41 Peter **t** her hand and helped her
13:13 Paul and his men **t** a ship from
13:29 they **t** him down from the cross
14:26 From Attalia they **t** a boat and
15:39 Barnabas **t** Mark with him and
16:11 So we **t** a ship from Troas and
16:30 Then he **t** Paul and Silas
16:34 He **t** Paul and Silas upstairs
17:5 They **t** some low-class
17:15 The men who escorted Paul **t**
17:15 they **t** instructions back to
18:17 officers, **t** Sosthenes,
18:18 From Cenchrea they **t** a boat
18:21 Paul **t** a boat from Ephesus
18:26 they **t** him (home) with them
19:9 He **t** his disciples and held
20:10 **t** him into his arms,
20:12 The people **t** the boy home.
20:14 we **t** him on board and went to
20:38 Then they **t** Paul to the ship.
21:11 During his visit he **t** Paul's belt
21:16 They **t** us to Mnason's home,
21:26 The next day, Paul **t** the men
21:32 Immediately, he **t** some
23:13 More than forty men **t** part in
23:18 The sergeant **t** the young man
23:19 The officer **t** the young man by
23:28 So I **t** him to their Jewish
23:31 They **t** Paul to the city of
24:27 Porcius Festus **t** Felix's place.
25:1 Three days after Festus **t** over
25:6 The next day Festus **t** his
26:21 For this reason the Jews **t** me
27:35 said this, he **t** some bread,
Rom 7:8 But sin **t** the opportunity
1Co 11:23 the Lord Jesus **t** bread
Gal 1:4 Christ **t** the punishment for our
2:1 I also **t** Titus along.
2:20 who loved me and **t** the
Eph 4:8 he **t** captive those who had
Col 2:14 He **t** the charges away by
2Ti 1:16 He often **t** care of my needs
Heb 2:14 Jesus **t** on flesh and blood to
3:11 So I angrily **t** a solemn oath
4:3 As God said, "So I angrily **t** a
6:17 his promise, so he **t** an oath.
7:21 a priest when God **t** an oath.
8:9 ancestors when I **t** them by
9:19 Then he **t** the blood of calves
1Pe 4:3 and **t** part in the forbidden
Rev 5:7 He **t** the scroll from the right
8:5 The angel **t** the incense burner,
10:10 I **t** the small scroll from the

tool (2)

Exo 32:4 worked on the gold with a **t**,
1Ki 6:7 or any other iron **t** made a

tools (3)

Gen 4:22 who made bronze and iron **t**.
2Sm 23:7 touches them uses iron (**t**)
Isa 44:12 Blacksmiths shape iron into **t**.

tooth (11)

Exo 21:24 eye for an eye, a t for a tooth,
21:24 eye for an eye, a tooth for a t,
21:27 If the owner knocks out the t of
21:27 to make up for the loss of the t.
Lev 24:20 eye for an eye, a t for a tooth.
24:20 eye for an eye, a tooth for a t.
Dtr 19:21 eye for an eye, a t for a tooth,
19:21 eye for an eye, a tooth for a t,
Pro 25:19 ⌊Like⌋ a broken t and a lame
Mat 5:38 for an eye and a t for a tooth.'
5:38 for an eye and a tooth for a t.'

top (112)

Gen 6:16 18-inch-high opening at the t.
7:18 ship floated on t of the water.
8:13 Noah opened the t of the ship,
11:4 ourselves and a tower with its t
22:9 his son Isaac and laid him on t
28:12 the earth with its t reaching up
28:18 and poured olive oil on t of it.
40:17 The t basket contained all
Exo 12:22 put some of the blood on the t
12:23 he sees the blood on the t
17:9 Tomorrow I will stand on t of
17:10 and Hur went to the t of the hill.
19:20 The LORD came down on t of
19:20 Sinai and called Moses to the t
24:17 raging fire on t of the mountain.
25:21 place the throne of mercy on t.
26:24 and held tightly at the t by
28:7 at the ⌊t⌋ corners so that
28:23 Attach them to the two ⌊t⌋
28:24 to the rings at the ⌊t⌋ corners
29:25 and burn them on the altar on t
30:3 all of it with pure gold — the t,
34:2 on the t of the mountain.
36:29 and held tightly at the t by
37:26 all of it with pure gold — the t,
39:4 at the ⌊t⌋ corners so that
39:16 two rings to the ⌊t⌋ two corners
39:17 to the rings at the ⌊t⌋ corners
39:31 a violet cord to it and tied it on t
40:19 tent and put the cover on t.
40:20 throne of mercy on t of the ark.
Lev 1:8 and the fat on t of the wood
3:5 Aaron's sons will lay them on t
5:12 will burn it as a reminder on t
8:28 hands and burned them on t
9:14 and the legs and laid them on t
24:7 Lay pure incense on t of each
26:30 and pile your dead bodies on t
Num 4:6 On t of that they will spread a
8:4 lamp stand, from t to bottom,
20:28 Aaron died there on t of the
23:9 I see them from the t of rocky
23:14 him to the Field of Zophim on t
23:28 So Balak took Balaam to the t
Dtr 3:27 Go to the t of Mount Pisgah,
28:13 You will always be at the t,
28:35 your feet to the t of your head.
34:1 He went to the t of Pisgah,
Jos 15:8 It then goes to the t of the
15:9 From the t of that mountain the
Jdg 6:26 altar to the LORD your God on t
9:25 ambushes for Abimelech on t
9:49 They piled the brushwood on t
16:3 them on his shoulders to the t
1Sm 26:13 to the other side and stood on t
2Sm 2:25 their position on t of a hill.
15:32 When David came to the t ⌊of
16:1 David had gone over the t ⌊of
17:19 spread it over the t of the
1Ki 3:19 she rolled over on t of him.
7:16 of cast bronze to put on t
7:19 The capitals on t of the pillars
7:22 lily-shaped capitals at the t
7:31 to the circular frame o top.
7:35 The t of each stand had a
7:41 the bowl-shaped capitals on t
7:41 capitals on t of the pillars,
18:42 Elijah went to the t of Carmel
2Ki 1:9 officer found Elijah sitting on t
2Ch 4:12 bowl-shaped capitals on t of
4:12 capitals on t of the pillars,
2Ch 25:12 took them to the t of a cliff,
25:12 and threw them off the t of the
Neh 4:3 wall collapse if it walked on t
Est 5:2 touched the t of the scepter.
Job 2:7 of his feet to the t of his head.
Psa 7:16 comes down on t of him.
55:10 night they go around on ⌊t of⌋
Pro 23:34 like someone lying down on t
Sos 3:10 out of silver, its t out of gold,
Isa 1:6 the bottom of your feet to the t
14:14 I'll go above the t of the clouds.
17:6 or three olives are left at the t
30:1 They pile sin on t of sin.
30:17 be left alone like a flagpole on t
Jer 1:13 and its t is tilted away from the
22:6 like the t of Lebanon.
31:12 will come and shout for joy on t
Eze 17:3 It took hold of the t of a cedar
17:22 will take hold of the t of a cedar
31:3 Its t was among the clouds.
31:10 and its t reached the clouds.
40:13 the gateway from the t
40:13 top of one guardroom to the t
43:12 area all the way around the t
Amo 1:2 and the t of ⌊Mount⌋ Carmel is
9:3 Even if they hide on t of Mount
Zep 2:14 and herons will nest on t
Zec 4:2 lamp stand with a bowl on t
4:2 for each lamp that is on t of it.
5:8 the lead cover down on t of it.
Mat 24:2 will be left on t of another.
27:51 split in two from t to bottom.
Mar 6:21 gave a dinner for his t officials,
13:2 will be left on t of another.
15:38 split in two from t to bottom.
Luk 19:44 will not be left on t of another,
21:6 will be left on t of another.
Jon 19:23 in one piece from t to bottom.
Act 27:40 Then they raised the t sail to
Php 2:27 one sorrow on t of another.
Heb 11:21 He leaned on the t of his staff

topaz (5)

Exo 28:17 In the first row put red quartz, t,
39:10 put red quartz, t, and emerald.
Job 28:19 T from Ethiopia cannot equal
Eze 28:13 quartz, t, crystal, beryl, onyx,
Rev 21:20 the eighth beryl, the ninth t,

Tophel (1)

Dtr 1:1 between Paran and T,

Topheth (10)

2Ki 23:10 Josiah also made T in the
Isa 30:33 T was prepared long ago.
Jer 7:31 have built worship sites at T
7:32 will no longer be known as T
7:32 They will bury ⌊people⌋ at T
19:6 place will no longer be called T
19:11 They will bury ⌊the dead⌋ in T
19:12 I will make this city like T.
19:13 will be unclean like this city T.
19:14 Then Jeremiah left T,

topics (1)

Heb 6:1 about Christ and move on to t

topmost (1)

Zec 4:7 He will bring out the t stone

topple (2)

Psa 46:2 quakes or the mountains t into
46:6 are in turmoil, and kingdoms t.

topples (1)

Job 9:5 and he t them in his anger.

tops (12)

Gen 8:5 the t of the mountains
Exo 12:7 and put it on the sides and t
36:38 They covered the t of the posts
38:17 The t of the posts were
38:19 The t of the posts were
38:28 coverings for the t of the posts.
2Sm 5:24 the sound of marching in the t
1Ch 14:15 the sound of marching in the t
Psa 72:16 the breeze⌋ on the mountain t,
Isa 42:11 from the t of the mountains.
Eze 31:14 and their t were no longer
Amo 9:1 Strike the t of the pillars so that

torch (5)

Gen 15:17 a flaming t passed between
Jdg 15:4 fastened a t between their tails.
Isa 62:1 salvation burns brightly like a t.
Zec 12:6 a burning t among freshly cut
Rev 8:10 a huge star flaming like a t fell

torches (11)

Jdg 7:16 horns and jars with t inside.
7:20 They held the t in their left
15:5 He set the t on fire and
Isa 50:11 arm yourselves with flaming t.
50:11 and among the t you have lit.
Eze 1:13 looked like burning coals and t.
Dan 10:6 His eyes were like flaming t.
Nah 2:4 They look like t, like lightning,
Jon 18:3 They were carrying lanterns, t,
Act 16:29 The jailer asked for t and
Rev 4:5 Seven flaming t were burning

tore (66)

Gen 37:29 he t his clothes in grief.
37:34 Jacob t his clothes,
44:13 they t their clothes in grief.
Num 14:6 t their clothes in despair.
Jos 7:6 leaders of Israel t their clothes
Jdg 8:17 Then he t down the tower of
9:45 He also t down the city and
11:35 When he saw her, he t his
14:6 With his bare hands, he t the
16:12 But Samson t the ropes off his
16:14 But Samson woke up and t his
1Sm 15:27 the hem of his robe, and it t.
2Sm 1:11 clothes and t them ⌊in grief⌋.
13:19 Tamar put ashes on her head, t
13:31 king stood up, t his clothes,
1Ki 11:30 took his new garment and t
13:26 It t him to pieces and killed him
14:8 I t the kingdom away from
19:11 a fierce wind t mountains and
21:27 he t his clothes ⌊in distress⌋
2Ki 2:12 grabbed his own garment and t
2:24 came out of the woods and t 42
3:25 Then Israel t down the cities,
5:7 he t his clothes ⌊in distress⌋.
6:30 he t his clothes ⌊in distress⌋.
11:14 As Athaliah t her clothes ⌊in
11:18 temple of Baal and t it down.
14:13 He t down a 600-foot section of
17:21 When he t Israel away from the
19:1 he t his clothes in grief,
22:11 he t his clothes ⌊in distress⌋.
22:19 You also t your clothes ⌊in
23:7 He t down the houses of the
23:8 He t down the worship site at
23:12 The king t them down from
23:15 He also t down the altar at
23:15 He t down both the altar and
25:10 the captain of the guard t down
1Ch 20:1 defeated Rabbah and t it down.
2Ch 23:13 As Athaliah t her clothes ⌊in
23:17 temple of Baal and t it down.
25:23 He t down a 600-foot section of
26:6 He t down the walls of Gath,
31:1 and t down the illegal places of
34:7 t down the altars, beat the
34:19 he t his clothes ⌊in distress⌋.
34:27 t your clothes ⌊in distress⌋,
36:19 t down Jerusalem's walls,
Ezr 9:3 I t my clothes ⌊in distress⌋,
Est 4:1 he t his clothes and put on
Job 1:20 t his robe ⌊in grief⌋,
2:12 and each of them t his own
16:9 "God's anger t me ⌊apart⌋ and
Psa 35:15 Unknown attackers t me apart
Isa 14:17 a desert and t down its cities,
37:1 he t his clothes in grief,
Jer 2:20 off your yoke, t off your chains,
39:8 and they t down the walls of
52:14 the captain of the guard t down
Lam 2:2 He t down the fortified cities of

Lam 2:17 He **t** you down without any pity,
Eze 29:7 you splintered and **t** up their
Nah 2:12 The lion **t** its prey to pieces to
Mat 26:65 Then the chief priest **t** his
Mar 14:63 The chief priest **t** his clothes
Act 16:22 Then the officials **t** the clothes

torment (4)

Job 19:2 "How long will you **t** me and
Psa 143:12 and destroy all who **t** me,
Isa 29:2 I will **t** Ariel, and the city will
29:7 against it, blockade it, and **t** it.

tormented (10)

Jdg 2:18 who were **t** and oppressed.
Rut 1:21 when the LORD has **t** me
1Sm 1:6 her rival ⌊Peninnah⌋ **t** her
1:16 I've been troubled and **t**."
16:14 evil spirit from the LORD **t** him.
2Ch 15:6 God had **t** them with every kind
Isa 50:11 receive from me: You will be **t**.
Mat 15:22 My daughter is **t** by a demon."
Luk 6:18 Those who were **t** by evil
Rev 11:10 two prophets had **t** those living

tormenting (1)

1Sm 16:15 "An evil spirit from God is **t**

torments (1)

2Co 12:7 **t** me to keep me from being

torn (68)

Gen 37:33 must have been **t** to pieces!"
44:28 must have been **t** to pieces!"
Lev 13:45 disease must wear **t** clothes
14:40 that have the mildew to be **t** out
14:45 and all the plaster — must be **t**
22:24 **t** out, or cut out testicles.
Dtr 28:63 You will be **t** out of the land
Jdg 6:28 the Baal altar had been **t** down.
6:30 He has **t** down the Baal altar
1Sm 4:12 that day with his clothes **t**
15:28 "The LORD has **t** the kingdom
28:17 The LORD has **t** the kingship
2Sm 1:2 His clothes were **t**,
13:31 their clothes **t** ⌊to show their
15:32 His clothes were **t**,
1Ki 13:3 You will see the altar **t** apart.
13:5 The altar was **t** apart,
13:28 nor had it **t** the donkey to
15:14 worship sites were not **t** down,
18:30 altar that had been **t** down.
19:10 **t** down your altars,
19:14 **t** down your altars,
22:44 worship sites were not **t** down.
2Ki 5:8 king of Israel had **t** his clothes,
12:3 of worship weren't **t** down.
14:4 worship were still not **t** down.
15:4 worship were still not **t** down.
15:35 of worship were not **t** down.
18:37 with their clothes **t** in grief.
2Ch 20:33 on the hills were not **t** down.
33:3 his father Hezekiah had **t** down.
34:4 the various Baal gods **t** down.
Ezr 6:11 on a beam **t** from his own
9:5 and with my clothes **t**,
Pro 2:22 people will be **t** from it.
11:11 of wicked people, it is **t** down.
24:31 and its stone fence was **t**
Isa 10:27 The yoke will be **t** away
36:22 with their clothes **t** in grief.
Jer 4:20 curtains are **t** in an instant.
4:26 and all its cities are **t** down
5:5 yokes and **t** off their chains.
5:6 the cities will be **t** to pieces,
9:19 our homes have been **t** down."
13:22 Your clothes have been **t** off
31:40 be uprooted or **t** down again."
33:4 of Judah have been **t** down
38:11 He took rags and **t** clothes from
38:12 "Put these rags and **t** clothes
41:5 their clothes were **t**,
48:1 be put to shame and **t** down.
50:15 and their walls will be **t** down.
Lam 3:11 I was taking, **t** me to pieces,
Eze 30:4 and its foundations will be **t**
38:20 The mountains will be **t** down,
Dan 2:5 you will be **t** limb from limb,
3:29 and Abednego will be **t** limb
Hos 6:1 Even though he has **t** us to
Nah 2:12 It used to fill its caves with **t**
2:12 and its dens with **t** flesh.
Zep 2:4 and Ekron will be **t** out by the
Mat 24:2 Each one will be **t** down."
Mar 13:2 Each one will be **t** down."
Luk 21:6 Each one will be **t** down."
Jon 21:11 with 153 large fish, it was not **t**.
Rom 11:3 and **t** down your altars.
Gal 2:18 something that I've **t** down,
4:15 you would have **t** out your eyes

torrents (2)

2Sm 22:5 The **t** of destruction had
Psa 18:4 The **t** of destruction had

torture (16)

Jdg 16:5 to tie him up in order to **t** him.
16:6 so that someone could **t** you?"
16:19 Then she began to **t** him
Jer 38:19 and they will **t** me."
Mat 8:29 Did you come here to **t** us
24:9 you over to those who will **t**
Mar 5:7 Swear to God that you won't **t**
Luk 8:28 I beg you not to **t** me!"
16:28 won't end up in this place of **t**.'
2Pe 2:8 Each day was like **t** to him as
Rev 9:5 They were only allowed to **t**
9:5 Their **t** was like the pain of a
14:11 The smoke from their **t** will go
18:7 her just as much **t** and misery.
18:10 Frightened by her **t**,
18:15 "Frightened by her **t**,

tortured (5)

Job 15:20 "The wicked person is **t** all his
Luk 16:23 where he was constantly **t**.
Heb 11:35 Other believers were brutally **t**
Rev 14:10 Then he will be **t** by fiery sulfur
20:10 They will be **t** day and night

torturers (1)

Mat 18:34 handed him over to the **t** until

toss (4)

Job 30:22 You **t** me around with a storm.
Psa 50:17 You **t** my words behind you.
Jer 5:22 the waves **t** continuously,
Eze 32:4 on the ground and **t** you into

tossed (5)

Amo 8:8 rise like the Nile, be **t** about,
Nah 3:10 Soldiers **t** dice for her important
Act 27:18 We continued to be **t** so
Eph 4:14 **t** and carried about by all kinds
Jas 1:6 by the wind and **t** by the sea.

tossing (2)

Job 7:4 from **t** about until dawn.
Luk 21:25 of the roaring and **t** of the sea.

total (100)

Gen 5:5 Adam lived a **t** of 930 years;
5:8 Seth lived a **t** of 912 years;
5:11 Enosh lived a **t** of 905 years;
5:14 Kenan lived a **t** of 910 years;
5:17 Mahalalel lived a **t** of 895
5:20 Jared lived a **t** of 962 years;
5:23 Enoch lived a **t** of 365 years.
5:27 Methuselah lived a **t** of 969
5:31 Lamech lived a **t** of 777 years;
9:29 Noah lived a **t** of 950 years;
46:15 The **t** number of these sons
46:18 for Jacob. The **t** was 16.
46:22 born to Jacob. The **t** was 14.
46:25 sons for Jacob. The **t** was 7.
46:26 The **t** number of Jacob's direct
46:27 The grand **t** of people in
47:28 so he lived a **t** of 147 years.
Exo 1:5 The **t** number of Jacob's
10:22 Egypt there was **t** darkness
38:24 The **t** amount of gold from the
Lev 23:16 This is a **t** of fifty days.
25:8 seven times for a **t** of 49 years.
Num 1:21 The **t** for the tribe of Reuben
1:23 The **t** for the tribe of Simeon
1:25 The **t** for the tribe of Gad was
1:27 The **t** for the tribe of Judah was
1:29 The **t** for the tribe of Issachar
1:31 The **t** for the tribe of Zebulun
1:33 The **t** for the tribe of Ephraim
1:35 The **t** for the tribe of Manasseh
1:37 The **t** for the tribe of Benjamin
1:39 The **t** for the tribe of Dan was
1:41 The **t** for the tribe of Asher was
1:43 The **t** for the tribe of Naphtali
1:45 The grand **t** of men who were
2:4 The **t** number of men in his
2:6 The **t** number of men in his
2:8 The **t** number of men in his
2:9 "The grand **t** of all the troops in
2:11 The **t** number of men in his
2:13 The **t** number of men in his
2:15 The **t** number of men in his
2:16 "The grand **t** of all the troops in
2:19 The **t** number of men in his
2:21 The **t** number of men in his
2:23 The **t** number of men in his
2:24 "The grand **t** of all the troops in
2:26 The **t** number of men in his
2:28 The **t** number of men in his
2:30 The **t** number of men in his
2:31 "The grand **t** of all the men in
2:32 This is the **t** number of
2:32 The grand **t** of all the troops in
3:22 The **t** number of all the males
3:34 The **t** number of all the males
3:39 The grand **t** of Levites that
3:43 The **t** of all the firstborn males
4:36 The **t** of those who were
4:37 This was the **t** of all those in
4:40 The **t** of those who were
4:41 This was the **t** of all those in
4:44 The **t** of all those who were
4:45 This was the **t** of those
4:46 The grand **t** of all the Levites
7:87 The **t** number of animals for the
7:88 The **t** number of animals for
26:7 The **t** number of men was
26:14 The **t** number of men was
26:18 The **t** number of men was
26:22 The **t** number of men was
26:25 The **t** number of men was
26:27 The **t** number of men was
26:34 The **t** number of men was
26:37 The **t** number of men was
26:41 The **t** number of men was
26:43 The **t** number of men in all the
26:47 The **t** number of men was
26:50 The **t** number of men was
26:51 The **t** number of Israelite men
26:62 The **t** number of all the
26:63 Eleazar added up the **t** number
35:7 So you will give a **t** of 48 cities
Dtr 3:4 We captured a **t** of 60 cities —
21:16 This would show a **t** disregard
Jos 12:24 The **t** was 31 kings.
2Sm 12:14 But since you have shown **t**
19:14 of Judah were in **t** agreement.
21:20 was a tall man who had a **t**
1Ch 6:60 There was a **t** of 13 cities for
7:5 A **t** of 87,000 of them was
9:9 A **t** of 956 of them lived in
2Ch 26:12 The **t** number of family heads
Job 20:26 **T** darkness waits in hiding for
38:17 the gateways to **t** darkness?
Pro 5:14 I almost reached **t** ruin in the
20:20 be snuffed out in **t** darkness.
Jer 52:23 The **t** number of pomegranates
Eze 40:15 The **t** length of the gateway
Mat 7:27 and the result was a **t** disaster."
Rom 1:21 their thoughts were **t** nonsense,

totaled (16)

Jdg 20:17 **t** 400,000 soldiers armed
1Ch 9:13 their families **t** 1,760 soldiers.
9:22 at the entrances **t** 212.
2Ch 29:32 by the assembly **t** 70 bulls,
Ezr 1:11 gold and silver utensils **t** 5,400.

Ezr 2:58 of Solomon's servants **t** 392.
2:60 These people **t** 652.
2:64 The whole assembly **t** 42,360.
Neh 7:60 of Solomon's servants **t** 392.
7:62 These people **t** 642.
7:66 The whole assembly **t** 42,360.
11:8 descendants⌋ **t** 928.
11:13 the heads of the families, **t** 242.
11:14 who were warriors, **t** 128.
11:18 All the Levites in the holy city **t**
11:19 who guarded the gates **t** 172.

totally (9)

Num 16:30 does something **t** new — if
24:24 will be **t** destroyed."
Jdg 18:7 of Sidon and **t** independent.
18:28 from Sidon and **t** independent.
2Ki 19:11 how they **t** destroyed them.
Psa 39:2 I remained **t** speechless.
Isa 37:11 how they **t** destroyed them.
Amo 9:8 But I won't **t** destroy the
1Co 6:7 You are already **t** defeated

totals (2)

Num 1:44 own family, added up these **t**.
26:54 Use the **t** ⌊from the census⌋ in

Tou (2)

1Ch 18:9 When King **T** of Hamath heard
18:10 between Hadadezer and **T**.)

touch (43)

Gen 3:3 'You must never eat it or **t** it.
20:6 That's why I didn't let you **t** her.
Exo 12:13 Nothing will **t** or destroy you
19:12 go up the mountain or even **t** it.
19:12 Those who **t** the mountain
19:13 No one should **t** them.
Lev 5:2 "If you **t** anything unclean — the
7:21 Those who **t** anything unclean,
11:8 animals or **t** their dead bodies.
12:4 She must not **t** anything holy or
15:5 Those who **t** his bed must
15:7 Those who **t** a man who has a
15:19 Those who **t** her will be
15:21 Those who **t** her bed must
15:22 Those who **t** anything she sits
15:27 Those who **t** these things are
Num 4:15 They must never **t** the holy
6:5 no razor may **t** their heads.
16:26 Don't **t** anything that belongs to
Dtr 14:8 meat or **t** their dead bodies.
Jos 9:19 so we cannot **t** them now.
Jdg 16:26 Let me **t** the columns on which
Rut 2:9 my young men not to **t** you.
1Ch 16:22 'Do not **t** my anointed ones or
Job 5:19 no harm will **t** you:
6:7 I refuse to **t** such things.
Psa 105:15 "Do not **t** my anointed ones or
144:5 **T** the mountains, and they will
Pro 6:29 None who **t** her will escape
Isa 52:11 Do not **t** anything unclean.
65:5 Don't **t** me! I'm holier than you
Lam 4:14 no one would **t** their clothes.
4:15 Don't **t** anyone.' When they fled
Hag 2:12 If his clothes **t** bread,
Mat 9:21 "If I only **t** his clothes,
14:36 They begged him to let them **t**
Mar 3:10 up to him in order to **t** him.
5:28 "If I can just **t** his clothes,
6:56 They begged him to let them **t**
8:22 They begged Jesus to **t** him.
Luk 6:19 The entire crowd was trying to **t**
24:39 **T** me, and see for yourselves.
Col 2:21 Don't taste or **t** that!"

touched (53)

Gen 26:29 since we have not **t** you.
32:25 he **t** the socket of Jacob's hip
32:32 the hip socket because God **t**
Exo 4:25 and **t** Moses' feet ⌊with it⌋.
Lev 15:11 the person he **t** must wash his
Num 6:11 the LORD for the person who **t**
9:7 "We are unclean because we **t**
19:18 sprinkle any person who has **t**
19:18 who has **t** someone who has
Num 31:19 who killed a person or **t**
Jdg 6:21 the Messenger of the LORD **t**
1Sm 10:26 whose hearts God had **t**.
1Ki 6:27 the wing of one of the angels **t**
6:27 and the wing of the other **t** the
6:27 Their remaining wings **t** each
19:5 An angel **t** him and said,
2Ki 13:21 the body **t** Elisha's bones,
2Ch 3:11 was 7 ½ feet long and **t**
3:11 7 ½ feet long and **t** one wing
3:12 was 7 ½ feet long and **t**
3:12 wing was 7 ½ feet long and **t**
Est 4:3 In every province **t** by the
5:2 Esther went up to him and **t** the
Isa 6:7 He **t** my mouth with it and said,
6:7 "This has **t** your lips.
Jer 1:9 out his hand and **t** my mouth.
Eze 1:9 Their wings **t** each other.
1:11 with which they **t** each other.
Dan 8:18 but he **t** me and made me stand
10:10 Then a hand **t** me and made
10:16 looked like a human **t** my lips.
10:18 who looked like a human **t** me,
Mat 8:3 Jesus reached out, **t** him,
8:15 Jesus **t** her hand, and the fever
9:20 came up behind Jesus and **t**
9:29 He **t** their eyes and said,
14:36 Everyone who **t** his clothes
17:7 But Jesus **t** them and said,
20:34 for them, so he **t** their eyes.
Mar 1:41 **t** him, and said, "I'm willing.
5:27 in the crowd and **t** his clothes.
5:30 "Who **t** my clothes?"
5:31 "How can you ask, 'Who **t** me,'
6:56 Everyone who **t** his clothes
7:33 he **t** the man's tongue.
Luk 5:13 Jesus reached out, **t** him,
8:44 **t** the edge of his clothes,
8:45 Jesus asked, "Who **t** me?"
8:46 Jesus said, "Someone **t** me.
8:47 she told why she **t** him and
22:51 Then he **t** the servant's ear and
Act 19:12 aprons that had **t** Paul's skin
1Jn 1:1 We observed and **t** it.

touches (41)

Gen 26:11 "Anyone who **t** this man or his
Exo 29:37 Anything that **t** the altar will
30:29 and anything that **t** them will
Lev 6:18 Everyone who **t** it will become
6:27 Anything that **t** its meat will be
7:19 "Meat that **t** anything unclean
11:24 Whoever **t** their dead bodies
11:26 Whoever **t** them is unclean.
11:27 Whoever **t** their dead bodies
11:31 Whoever **t** their dead bodies
11:34 ⌊from that pottery⌋ **t** any food,
11:36 But anyone who **t** their dead
11:39 whoever **t** its dead body will be
15:11 If a man who has a discharge **t**
15:12 who has a discharge **t** pottery,
15:12 bucket he **t** must be rinsed.
15:23 If her blood **t** anything on the
22:4 of semen or **t** a dead body,
Num 19:11 "Whoever **t** the dead body of
19:13 Whoever **t** the dead body of a
19:16 "Whoever is outdoors and **t**
19:16 died naturally or anyone who **t**
19:21 And whoever **t** this water will
19:22 person **t** becomes unclean,
19:22 and the person who **t** it will be
Jos 16:7 Ataroth and Naarah, **t** Jericho,
19:11 to Maralah and **t** Dabbesheth
19:22 The border **t** Tabor,
19:26 The border **t** Carmel and Shihor
19:27 to Beth Dagon and **t** Zebulun
19:34 It **t** Zebulun in the south,
Jdg 16:9 as a thread snaps when it **t** fire.
2Sm 23:7 A person who **t** them uses iron
Job 4:5 It **t** you, and you panic.
20:6 sky and his head **t** the clouds,
Psa 104:32 He **t** the mountains,
Amo 9:5 The Almighty LORD of Armies **t**
Hag 2:13 If he **t** any of these things,
Zec 2:8 Whoever **t** you touches the
2:8 Whoever touches you **t** the
Heb 12:20 even an animal **t** the mountain,

touching (63)

Gen 17:3 with his face **t** the ground,
17:17 with his face **t** the ground.
18:2 with his face **t** the ground.
19:1 with his face **t** the ground.
23:7 with his face **t** the ground.
24:26 with his face **t** the ground.
33:3 seven times with his face **t**
42:6 with their faces **t** the ground.
43:26 with their faces **t** the ground.
44:14 with their faces **t** the ground.
48:12 with his face **t** the ground.
Exo 4:31 with their faces **t** the ground.
12:27 with their faces **t** the ground.
18:7 Moses bowed with his face **t**
33:10 would all bow with their faces **t**
34:8 with his face **t** the ground.
Lev 5:3 "If you become unclean by **t**
9:24 with their faces **t** the ground.
11:44 Never become unclean by **t**
21:1 become unclean by **t** one
Num 5:2 is unclean from **t** a dead body.
9:6 had become unclean from **t**
9:10 descendants is unclean from **t**
14:5 Aaron bowed with their faces **t**
16:4 with his face **t** the ground.
16:22 they bowed with their faces **t**
16:45 with their faces **t** the ground.
19:17 who become unclean from **t**
20:6 with their faces **t** the ground,
22:31 with his face **t** the ground.
Jos 5:14 Joshua bowed with his face **t**
Jdg 13:20 with their faces **t** the ground.
1Sm 20:41 with his face **t** the ground.
24:8 with his face **t** the ground.
25:23 with her face **t** the ground.
25:41 with her face **t** the ground.
28:14 with his face **t** the ground.
2Sm 1:2 with his face **t** the ground.
9:6 with his face **t** the ground.
14:4 with her face **t** the ground.
14:22 with his face **t** the ground,
14:33 with his face **t** the ground.
18:21 bowed down with his face **t**
24:20 bowed down with his face **t**
1Ki 1:31 bowed down with her face **t**
2Ki 2:15 with their faces **t** the ground.
1Ch 21:16 with their faces **t** the ground.
21:21 bowed down with his face **t**
2Ch 20:18 with his face **t** the ground.
24:17 with their faces **t** the ground.
29:28 with their faces **t** the ground,
Est 3:2 with their faces **t** the ground,
Isa 49:23 with their faces **t** the ground.
Lam 4:6 without one human hand **t** it.
Eze 1:23 out straight, **t** one another.
3:13 living creatures **t** one another
Dan 8:5 the whole earth without **t** it.
10:15 I bowed down with my face **t**
Hag 2:13 unclean by **t** a corpse.
Luk 7:39 what sort of woman is **t** him.
8:45 After everyone denied **t** him,
1Co 14:25 with their faces **t** the ground,
Rev 7:11 with their faces **t** the ground,

tough (2)

Luk 19:21 You're a **t** person to get along
19:22 You knew that I was a **t** person

toughen (1)

1Co 9:27 Rather, I **t** my body with

towel (2)

Jon 13:4 his outer clothes, took a **t**,
13:5 feet and dry them with the **t** that

tower (31)

Gen 11:4 a city for ourselves and a **t**
11:5 to see the city and the **t** that
Jdg 8:9 I'll tear down this **t**."
8:17 Then he tore down the **t** of
9:46 All the citizens of Shechem's **T**
9:49 in Shechem's **T** died too.
9:51 Now, there was a strong **t**

Jdg 9:51 and went up on the roof of the **t**.
9:52 Abimelech came to the **t**.
9:52 went near the entrance of the **t**
2Ki 9:17 watchman standing on the **t**
Neh 3:1 They rebuilt as far as the **T** of
3:1 then as far as the **T** of Hananel.
3:11 included the **T** of the Ovens.
3:25 the upper **t** that projects from
3:26 the east and the projecting **t**.
3:27 the large projecting **t** as far as
12:38 past the **T** of the Ovens,
12:39 and by the **T** of Hananel and
12:39 the Tower of Hananel and the **T**
Psa 61:3 You have been my refuge, a **t**
Pro 18:10 name of the LORD is a strong **t**.
18:19 the locked gate of a castle **t**.
Sos 4:4 David's beautifully-designed **t**.
7:4 Your neck is like an ivory **t**.
7:4 a Lebanese **t** facing Damascus.
Isa 2:15 against every high **t** and every
Jer 31:38 will be rebuilt for me from the **T**
Zec 14:10 and from the **T** of Hananel to
Luk 13:4 died when the **t** at Siloam fell
14:28 "Suppose you want to build a **t**.

towering (2)

Isa 2:13 against all the **t** and mighty
26:5 who live high in the **t** city.

towers (20)

2Ch 14:7 make walls around them with **t**
26:9 Uzziah built **t** in Jerusalem at
26:10 He built **t** in the desert.
26:15 machines were placed on the **t**
27:4 and he built forts and **t** in the
32:5 of the wall, made the **t** taller,
Psa 48:12 Go around it. Count its **t**.
Sos 8:10 and my breasts are like **t**.
Isa 23:13 Assyria set up battle **t**,
29:3 I will blockade you with **t**.
30:25 slaughter comes, **t** will fall.
33:18 are those who counted the **t**?
54:12 I will rebuild your **t** with rubies,
Jer 50:15 Their **t** will fall and their walls
Lam 2:8 He made the **t** and walls mourn.
Eze 26:4 of Tyre and tear down its **t**.
26:9 cut down your **t** with his axes.
27:11 from Gammad guarded your **t**.
Zep 1:16 and against the high corner **t**.
3:6 Their **t** will be destroyed.

town (22)

Jdg 9:51 was a strong tower inside the **t**.
9:51 and leaders of the **t** fled to it.
Rut 1:19 the whole **t** was excited about
2:18 picked it up and went into the **t**,
3:11 The whole **t** knows that you
3:15 her ⌊back⌋ and went into the **t**.
1Sm 11:4 messengers came to Saul's **t**,
20:40 "Take them back into **t**."
30:3 and his men came to the **t**,
2Sm 19:16 Benjamin and the **t** of Bahurim,
21:6 presence at Saul's **t** Gibeah."
Job 29:7 took my seat in the **t** square,
Ecc 9:14 There was a small **t** with a few
9:15 person was found in that **t**.
9:15 He saved the **t** using his
10:15 don't even know the way to **t**.
Isa 1:21 How the faithful **t** has become
1:26 Righteous City, the Faithful **T**."
22:2 a **t** filled with noise and
Mic 1:14 The **t** of Achzib will betray the
Hab 2:12 and founds a **t** by crime.'
Act 21:22 certainly hear that you're in **t**.

town's (1)

1Ki 17:10 As he came to the **t** entrance, a

towns (11)

Jdg 10:4 He also had 30 **t** that are still
20:14 of Benjamin went from their **t**
1Sm 27:5 in one of the outlying **t** so that
2Sm 2:3 settled in the **t** around Hebron.
1Ki 20:34 "I will give back the **t** my father
1Ch 2:22 who had 23 **t** in Gilead.
2Ch 25:13 with him into battle raided the **t**
Est 9:19 and in the unwalled **t** make
Jer 19:15 bring on this city and on all its **t**
Mat 9:35 went to all the **t** and villages.
Mar 1:38 to the small **t** that are nearby.

toyed (1)

1Sm 6:6 After he **t** with the Egyptians,

trace (3)

Psa 37:10 but there will be no **t** of him.
37:36 and now there is no **t** of him.
Dan 2:35 and not a **t** of them could be

traced (2)

Pro 8:27 When he **t** the horizon on the
8:29 when he **t** the foundations of

traces (1)

Job 30:13 Yes, they remove all **t** of my

Trachonitis (1)

Luk 3:1 Philip ruled Iturea and **T**.

track (2)

1Ch 23:29 the ingredients and keeping **t**
1Co 13:5 It doesn't keep **t** of wrongs.

tracked (1)

Psa 17:11 They have **t** me down.

tracking (1)

Lam 4:18 ⌊The enemy⌋ kept **t** us down,

tracks (2)

Sos 1:8 follow the **t** of the flocks,
Jer 4:11 will blow in the desert on the **t**

trade (6)

Ezr 9:12 seek peace or **t** with them.
Job 16:4 like you if we could **t** places.
Lam 1:11 They **t** their treasures for food
Eze 27:9 alongside you to **t** with you.
28:18 many sins and dishonest **t**.
48:14 They must not sell any of it or **t**

traded (18)

Psa 106:20 They **t** their glorious God for
Eze 27:12 "'People from Tarshish **t** with
27:13 and Meshech **t** with you.
27:15 People from Dedan **t** goods
27:15 You **t** with many people on the
27:16 "'People from Syria **t** with you
27:17 Judah and Israel **t** with you.
27:18 People from Damascus **t** with
27:19 and Greeks from Uzal **t**
27:20 Dedan **t** saddle blankets with
27:21 the officials of Kedar **t** with you.
27:21 They **t** lambs, rams, and male
27:22 Sheba and Raamah **t** with you.
27:22 They **t** the finest spices,
27:23 and Kilmad **t** with you.
27:24 In your marketplace they **t** for
28:16 You **t** far and wide.
Joe 3:3 They **t** boys for prostitutes.

traders (5)

1Ki 10:28 The king's **t** bought them from
2Ch 1:16 The king's **t** bought them from
9:14 the merchants and **t** brought.
Job 41:6 Will **t** bargain over it and divide
Isa 23:8 Its **t** are among the honored

traders' (1)

1Ki 10:15 the **t** profits, all the Arab kings,

trades (6)

Exo 31:3 and knowledgeable in all **t**.
31:5 He's an expert in all **t**.
35:31 and knowledgeable in all **t**.
35:33 He's an expert in all **t**.
35:35 men highly skilled in all **t**.
35:35 They can do all kinds of **t**.

trading (2)

1Ki 20:34 You may set up **t** centers in
Eze 28:5 Because of your great skill in **t**,

tradition (6)

2Ch 35:25 This became a **t** in Israel.
Est 9:23 So the Jews accepted as **t**
9:27 the Jews established a **t** for
9:27 The **t** was that a person should
Act 24:6 in a way that violates our **t**.
2Th 3:6 follow the **t** you received from

traditions (13)

Mat 15:2 do your disciples break the **t**
15:3 of God because of your **t**?
15:6 Because of your **t** you have
Mar 7:3 follow the **t** of their ancestors.
7:5 follow the **t** taught by our
7:8 of God to follow human **t**."
7:9 in order to keep your own **t**!
7:13 Because of your **t** you have
Jon 9:16 because he doesn't follow the **t**
1Co 11:2 for carefully following the **t** that
Gal 1:14 for the **t** of my ancestors.
Col 2:8 Such a person follows human **t**
2Th 2:15 firmly hold on to the **t** we taught

traffic (1)

Neh 13:19 of Jerusalem were cleared of **t**,

tragedy (11)

1Ch 7:23 Ephraim named him Beriah [**T**],
7:23 because **t** had come to his
Ecc 2:21 this is pointless and a terrible **t**.
4:8 this is pointless and a terrible **t**.
5:13 There is a painful **t** that I have
5:16 This also is a painful **t**:
6:1 There is a **t** that I have seen
6:2 is pointless and is a painful **t**.
8:6 human **t** hangs over people.
9:3 This is the **t** of everything that
10:5 There is a **t** that I've seen under

tragic (1)

Ecc 4:10 But how **t** it is for the one who

trail (2)

Job 13:27 You follow my **t** by engraving
Psa 58:8 that leaves behind a slimy **t**

train (5)

Pro 22:6 **T** a child in the way he should
Isa 2:4 they will never **t** for war again.
Jer 9:5 My people **t** their tongues to
Mic 4:3 they will never **t** for war again.
1Ti 4:7 **t** yourself to live a godly life.

trained (12)

Gen 14:14 he armed his 318 **t** men,
1Sa 24:2 Saul took 3,000 of the best-**t** men
26:2 3,000 of Israel's best-**t** men to
1Ch 12:8 They were warriors, **t** soldiers,
25:7 with their relatives, were **t**,
Psa 58:5 or of anyone **t** to cast spells.
105:22 Joseph **t** the king's officers the
144:1 who **t** my hands to fight and my
Dan 1:5 They were to be **t** for three
Hos 7:15 I **t** them and made them strong.
10:11 "Ephraim is like a **t** calf that
Heb 5:14 whose minds are **t** by practice

training (5)

Dan 1:18 end of the three-year **t** period,
Act 4:13 had no education or special **t**,
1Co 9:25 contest goes into strict **t**.
1Ti 4:8 **T** the body helps a little,
2Ti 3:16 and **t** them for a life that has

trains (3)

2Sm 22:35 He **t** my hands for battle so that
Psa 18:34 He **t** my hands for battle so that
Tit 2:12 It **t** us to avoid ungodly lives

traitor (7)

2Ki 17:4 Assyria found Hoshea to be a **t**.
Isa 21:2 The **t** betrays. The destroyer
33:1 horrible it will be for you, you **t**,
33:1 When you've finished being a **t**,
Mat 26:48 the **t** had given them a signal.

Mar 14:44 the **t** had given them a signal.
Luk 6:16 Iscariot (who became a **t**).

traitors (5)

Psa 59:5 Have no pity on any **t**.
119:158 I have seen **t**, and I am filled
Isa 24:16 **T** continue to betray,
Jer 9:2 are all adulterers, a mob of **t**.
2Ti 3:4 They will be **t**. They will be

trample (28)

2Ki 13:7 them like dust that people **t**.
Job 39:15 or a wild animal may **t** them.
Psa 7:5 Let him **t** my life into the
44:5 With your name we can **t** those
60:12 He will **t** our enemies.
91:13 You will **t** young lions and
108:13 He will **t** our enemies.
Pro 22:22 poor because they are poor or **t**
Isa 1:12 you to **t** on my courtyards?
10:6 and **t** on them like mud in the
14:25 I'll **t** it underfoot on my
26:6 Feet **t** it, the feet of the
63:2 like those who **t** grapes
Eze 26:11 With his horses' hoofs he will **t**
34:18 Must you **t** the rest of the
Dan 7:23 It will devour, **t**, and crush the
Amo 5:11 You **t** on the poor and take their
8:4 Listen to this, those who **t** on
Mic 5:5 our land and **t** our palaces,
Nah 3:14 into the claypits and **t** the clay!
Hab 3:12 You **t** the nations in anger.
Zec 9:15 They will destroy and **t** the
10:5 they will be like warriors who **t**
Mal 4:3 You will **t** on wicked people,
Mat 7:6 Otherwise, they will **t** them and
Luk 10:19 you the authority to **t** snakes
21:24 Nations will **t** Jerusalem until
Rev 11:2 and they will **t** the holy city for

trampled (29)

2Ki 7:17 But the people **t** him to death in
7:20 The people **t** him to death in
9:33 the horses. The horses **t** her.
14:9 came along and **t** the thistle.
2Ch 25:18 came along and **t** the thistle.
Isa 5:5 its wall so that it can be **t**.
14:19 stones of the pit like a **t** corpse.
25:10 Moab will be **t** beneath him like
25:10 beneath him like straw that is **t**
28:3 of Ephraim will be **t** underfoot.
28:18 passes by, you will be **t** by it.
63:3 "I have **t** alone in the
63:3 In my anger I **t** on people.
63:6 In my anger I **t** on people.
63:18 Our enemies have **t** on your
Jer 12:10 They've **t** my property.
51:33 threshing floor at the time it is **t**.
Lam 1:15 The LORD **t** the people of
3:16 He has **t** me into the dust.
Eze 34:19 sheep eat what your feet have **t**
Dan 7:7 and **t** whatever was left.
7:19 and **t** whatever was left.
8:7 down on the ground and **t**.
8:10 down on the ground and **t** them.
Hos 4:14 These foolish people will be **t**.
Mic 7:10 They are **t** like mud in the
Mat 5:13 thrown out and **t** on by people.
Luk 8:5 planted along the road, were **t**,
Rev 14:20 The grapes were **t** in the

tramples (2)

Isa 16:4 The one who **t** others will be
Mic 5:8 When a lion hunts, it **t** ⌊its

trampling (5)

2Ki 19:24 of Egypt with the **t** of my feet."
Isa 22:5 will be a day of confusion and **t**
37:25 of Egypt with the **t** of my feet."
58:13 If you stop **t** on the day of
Dan 8:13 and the **t** of the army — take

trance (5)

Num 24:4 and falls ⌊into a **t**⌋ with his
24:16 and falls ⌊into a **t**⌋ with his
Act 10:10 being prepared, he fell into a **t**.
11:5 of Joppa when I fell into a **t**.
22:17 temple courtyard, I fell into a **t**

tranquil (1)

Pro 14:30 A **t** heart makes for a healthy

transfer (4)

Lev 16:21 He will **t** them to the goat's
2Sm 3:10 'I, the LORD, will **t** the kingship
Eze 44:19 clothes so that they do not **t**
46:20 This way they won't **t** holiness

translated (1)

Ezr 4:7 the Aramaic script and **t** into

trap (49)

Exo 23:33 me and **t** you into serving
34:12 This will prove to be a **t** to you.
Dtr 7:16 they will be a **t** for you.
7:25 It might be a **t** for you.
Jos 23:13 will be a snare and a **t** for you,
Jdg 2:3 gods will become a **t** for you.'"
8:27 It became a **t** for Gideon and
1Sm 18:21 She will **t** him, and the
28:9 Why are you trying to **t** me and
2Ki 9:23 to Ahaziah, "It's a **t**, Ahaziah!"
Job 18:9 A **t** catches his heel.
18:10 A **t** is on his path ⌊to catch⌋
34:30 so that they cannot **t** people.
Psa 9:15 they have hidden ⌊to **t** others⌋.
35:7 they dug the pit ⌊to **t** me⌋.
57:6 They dug a pit to **t** me,
69:22 table set for them become a **t**
94:13 a pit is dug to **t** wicked people.
106:36 which became a **t** for them.
119:85 people have dug pits to **t** me
119:110 people have set a **t** for me,
124:7 like a bird caught in a hunter's **t**.
124:7 The **t** was broken,
140:5 people have laid a **t** for me.
141:9 Keep me away from the **t** they
142:3 ⌊My enemies⌋ have hidden a **t**
Pro 7:23 like a bird darting into a **t**.
12:12 person delights in setting a **t**
18:7 His lips are a **t** to his soul.
20:25 It is a **t** for a person to say
22:25 ways and set a **t** for yourself.
29:6 an evil person sin is bait in a **t**,
29:25 person's fear sets a **t** ⌊for him⌋,
Isa 8:14 He will be a **t** and a snare for
24:18 of that pit will be caught in a **t**.
Jer 48:44 of the pit will be caught in a **t**.
Eze 13:18 You want to **t** people.
13:20 you use to **t** people like birds.
17:20 over you to catch you in my **t**.
Amo 3:5 Does a bird land in a **t** on the
3:5 Does a **t** spring up from the
Mic 7:2 They **t** each other with nets.
Mat 22:15 planned to **t** Jesus into saying
Mar 12:13 They wanted to **t** him into
Luk 11:54 and watched him closely to **t**
21:35 like a **t** that catches a bird.
Rom 11:9 table set for them become a **t**
2Co 11:29 When anyone is caught in a **t**,
Jas 1:14 they lure him away and **t** him.

trapped (18)

1Sm 23:7 He has **t** himself by going into
Psa 9:16 The wicked person is **t** by the
59:12 Let them be **t** by their own
66:11 You have **t** us in a net.
Pro 5:22 A wicked person will be **t** by
6:2 you are **t** by the words of your
11:6 but treacherous people are **t** by
12:13 An evil person is **t** by his own
Ecc 9:12 humans are **t** by a disaster
Isa 8:15 They will be **t** and caught.
28:13 That is why they will be hurt, **t**,
42:22 They are all **t** in pits and
Jer 8:9 put to shame, confused, and **t**.
Eze 13:20 free the people that you have **t**.
2Co 12:16 Was I a clever person who **t**
Gal 6:1 a person gets **t** by wrongdoing,
1Ti 6:9 They are **t** by many stupid and
Rev 2:14 Balak **t** the people of Israel by

traps (19)

Job 22:10 That is why **t** are all around
Psa 25:15 He removes my feet from **t**.
38:12 who seek my life lay **t** for me.
64:5 talk about setting **t** and say,
91:3 will rescue you from hunters' **t**
140:5 They have set **t** for me along
141:9 from the **t** set by troublemakers.
Pro 22:5 person has thorns and **t** ahead
Ecc 7:26 whose thoughts are ⌊like⌋ **t**
Isa 24:17 Disasters, pits, and **t** are in
29:21 those who lay **t** for judges,
Jer 5:26 They set **t** and catch people.
9:8 think of ways to set **t** for them.
48:43 Disasters, pits, and **t** are in
50:24 I will set **t** for you, Babylon.
Hos 5:1 You set **t** at Mizpah and spread
9:8 Yet, **t** are set on every prophet's
Oba 1:7 food with you will set **t** for you,
1Ti 3:7 that the devil sets as **t** for him.

trash (3)

1Sm 2:8 He lifts the needy from the **t**
Lam 3:45 the scum and **t** of the nations.
1Co 4:13 in the eyes of the world and **t**

travel (34)

Gen 20:13 my father's home and **t** around,
Exo 3:18 Please let us **t** three days into
5:3 Please let us **t** three days into
8:27 We need to **t** three days into
13:21 light so that they could **t** by day
Num 2:31 They will **t** under their own
Dtr 2:27 "If you allow us to **t** through
Job 24:18 People do not **t** the road that
Psa 139:3 You watch me when I **t** and
Sos 4:8 You will **t** with me from the
Isa 23:6 **T** to Tarshish! Cry loudly, you
23:10 **T** through your country like the
23:12 Get up, and **t** to Cyprus.
30:6 "My people **t** through lands
33:21 with oars won't **t** on them.
34:10 No one will ever **t** through it.
35:8 Sinners won't **t** on it.
Jer 9:10 that no one can **t** through them.
9:12 so that no one can **t** through it.
Eze 33:28 that no one will **t** through them.
39:11 It will block those who **t**
Dan 12:4 Many will **t** everywhere,
Amo 5:5 Don't **t** to Beersheba.
Mic 2:13 Their king will **t** in front of them.
Zec 7:14 no one is able to **t** through it.
Mat 8:28 No one could **t** along that road
Luk 10:1 They were to **t** in pairs.
Jon 7:1 He didn't want to **t** in Judea
Act 18:27 Apollos wanted to **t** to Greece,
19:13 Some Jews used to **t** from
21:7 Our sea **t** ended when we
23:32 on horseback **t** with Paul.
1Co 16:6 can give me your support as I **t**,
2Co 8:19 the churches elected him to **t**

traveled (41)

Gen 12:6 and Abram **t** through the land to
13:3 He **t** from place to place.
24:10 He **t** to Aram Naharaim,
28:10 Beersheba and **t** toward Haran.
30:36 He **t** three days away from
41:45 Joseph **t** around Egypt.
41:46 Pharaoh and **t** all around Egypt.
Exo 15:22 For three days they **t** in the
17:1 desert of Sin and **t** from place
Num 2:34 and each person **t** with his own
10:12 Desert of Sinai and **t** from place
10:33 the mountain of the LORD and **t**
33:2 where they went as they **t**.
33:8 After they **t** for three days in the
Dtr 1:19 We **t** through all that vast and
2:1 For a long time we **t** around the
2:3 "You've **t** around this region
2:7 you as you **t** through this vast
Jdg 5:6 Those who **t** took back roads.
19:10 He left and **t** as far as Jebus
2Sm 4:7 They took his head and **t** all
1Ki 13:24 A lion found him ⌊as he **t**⌋ on

1Ki 19:4 Then he **t** through the
19:8 Strengthened by that food, he **t**
Isa 41:3 his feet have never **t** before.
Jer 5:7 They **t** in crowds to the houses
31:21 the road on which you **t**.
Zec 8:10 No one who **t** was safe from
Mat 19:1 he left Galilee and **t** along the
Luk 3:3 John **t** throughout the region
8:1 After this, Jesus **t** from one city
13:22 Then Jesus **t** and taught in one
17:11 Jesus **t** along the border
Jon 7:1 later **t** throughout Galilee.
Act 8:40 He **t** through all the cities and
17:1 Paul and Silas **t** through the
19:1 Paul **t** through the interior
19:29 Macedonians who **t** with Paul,
25:3 kill Paul as he **t** to Jerusalem.
2Co 11:26 Because I've **t** a lot,
Rev 18:17 everyone who **t** by ship,

traveler (5)
Jdg 19:17 He saw the **t** in the city square.
2Sm 12:4 to prepare a meal for the **t**.
12:4 lamb and prepared her for the **t**.
Job 31:32 I opened my door to the **t**.)
Jer 14:8 like a **t** who stays only one

travelers (5)
Job 6:19 **T** from Sheba search for them.
21:29 Haven't you asked **t**?
Isa 21:13 You caravan of **t** from the
33:8 **T** stop traveling. Agreements
Eze 39:11 It will be in **T** Valley,

traveling (24)
Gen 13:5 who had been **t** with Abram,
Dtr 22:6 Whenever you're **t** and find a
1Ki 18:27 thinking, relieving himself, or **t**!
2Ki 4:8 Elisha was **t** through Shunem,
Pro 9:6 Start **t** the road to
Isa 33:8 Travelers stop **t**. Agreements
Mat 10:10 Don't take a **t** bag for the trip,
17:22 While they were **t** together in
Mar 6:8 not to take any food, a **t** bag,
Luk 2:44 others who were **t** with them.
2:44 After **t** for a day, they started to
9:3 stick, **t** bag, any food, money,
10:4 Don't carry a wallet, a **t** bag,
10:31 a priest was **t** along that road.
10:33 as he was **t** along,
10:38 As they were **t** along,
14:25 crowds were **t** with Jesus.
22:35 a wallet, **t** bag, or sandals,
22:36 wallet and a **t** bag should take
Jon 4:6 because he was tired from **t**.
Act 9:7 Meanwhile, the men **t** with him
19:21 by **t** through Macedonia
26:13 Majesty, at noon, while I was **t**,
27:4 we were **t** against the wind.

travels (8)
Exo 40:36 In all their **t**, whenever the
40:38 the column throughout their **t**.
2Ki 4:9 he regularly **t** past our house.
Job 34:8 who **t** with troublemakers and
Psa 147:15 His word **t** with great speed.
Jer 2:6 No one lives there or **t** there."
51:43 lives and where no human **t**.
Eze 14:15 wasteland that no one **t** through

trays (3)
Num 4:9 as well as the lamps, tongs, **t**,
4:14 These are the **t**, forks, shovels,
Jer 52:19 of the guard took all of the **t**

treacherous (19)
Lev 26:40 the **t** things they did
2Sm 18:13 I had done something **t** to him,
Psa 35:19 Do not let my **t** enemies gloat
78:57 They were disloyal and **t** like
Pro 2:22 from the land and **t** people will
11:3 leads **t** people to ruin.
11:6 but **t** people are trapped by their
12:5 advice of wicked people is **t**.
13:2 of **t** people ⌊craves⌋ violence.
13:15 but the way of **t** people is
Pro 21:18 and **t** people will take the place
22:12 the words of a **t** person.
Jer 3:7 and her **t** sister Judah saw her.
3:8 But **t** Judah, her sister,
3:10 Even after all this, Israel's **t**
3:11 was less guilty than **t** Judah.
12:1 Why do **t** people have peace
Hab 1:13 you keep watching **t** people?
2:5 Also because wine is **t** he is

treacherously (2)
Psa 105:25 they dealt **t** with his servants.
Isa 48:8 I know that you've acted very **t**

treachery (1)
Isa 24:16 and their **t** grows worse and

tread (1)
Rev 19:15 them with an iron scepter and **t**

treading (1)
Isa 41:25 as if he were **t** on clay like a

treason (5)
2Ki 11:14 she cried, "**T**, treason!"
11:14 she cried, "Treason, **t**!"
2Ch 23:13 she said, "**T**, treason!"
23:13 she said, "Treason, **t**!"
Ezr 4:19 are guilty of **t** and rebellion.

treasure (29)
Gen 43:23 must have given you **t** in your
Job 3:21 dig for it more than for buried **t**?
20:26 waits in hiding for his **t**.
Psa 17:14 You fill their bellies with your **t**.
49:12 continue here with what they **t**.
49:20 Mortals, with what they **t**,
83:3 together against those you **t**.
119:162 who finds a priceless **t**.
135:4 Israel to be his own special **t**.
Pro 2:1 and **t** my commands within
2:4 hunt for it as if it were hidden **t**,
7:1 **T** my commands that are
15:6 Great **t** is in the house of a
15:16 LORD than great **t** and turmoil.
21:20 Costly **t** and wealth are in the
Isa 33:6 fear of the LORD is ⌊your⌋ **t**.
Mat 2:11 Then they opened their **t**
6:21 Your heart will be where your **t**
13:44 of heaven is like a **t** buried
13:52 old things out of his **t** chest."
19:21 and you will have **t** in heaven.
Mar 10:21 and you will have **t** in heaven.
Luk 12:33 Make a **t** for yourselves in
12:33 close enough to destroy your **t**.
12:34 Your heart will be where your **t**
18:22 and you will have **t** in heaven.
2Co 4:7 yet we have the **t** of the Good
4:7 superior power of this **t** belongs
1Ti 6:19 By doing this they store up a **t**

treasured (5)
Job 23:12 I have **t** his words in my heart.
Psa 119:11 I have **t** your promise in my
Eze 7:22 will dishonor my **t** place.
Luk 2:19 Mary **t** all these things in her
2:51 His mother **t** all these things in

treasurer (2)
Ezr 1:8 King Cyrus of Persia put the **t**
Rom 16:23 Erastus, the city **t**,

treasurers (5)
Ezr 7:21 order all the **t** ⌊in the province⌋
Est 3:9 pounds of silver to your **t**
9:3 and the king's **t** assisted the
Dan 3:2 advisers, **t**, judges, officers,
3:3 advisers, **t**, judges, officers,

treasures (35)
Dtr 33:19 from the seas and the **t** hidden
1Ki 14:26 He took the **t** from the LORD's
2Ki 24:13 He also took away all the **t** in
1Ch 9:26 in charge of the rooms and **t**
2Ch 12:9 Jerusalem and took the **t** from
36:18 the **t** from the LORD's temple,
2Ch 36:18 and the **t** of the king and his
Job 28:11 that they bring hidden **t** to light.
Pro 10:2 **T** gained dishonestly profit no
Ecc 2:8 I gathered the **t** of kings and
Isa 2:7 and there is no end to their **t**.
30:6 of young donkeys and their **t**
44:9 Their precious **t** are worthless.
45:3 I will give you **t** from dark
Jer 15:13 your wealth and **t** as loot as
17:3 wealth and all your **t** into loot.
20:5 and all the **t** of the kings of
48:7 the things you do and your **t**,
49:4 You trust your **t**. You think,
50:37 A sword will destroy their **t**,
51:13 many rivers and are rich with **t**,
Lam 1:7 Jerusalem remembers all the **t**
1:10 their hands on all of the city's **t**.
1:11 They trade their **t** for food to
Eze 22:25 They eat people and take their **t**
Dan 11:43 He will control gold and silver **t**
Hos 9:6 will grow over their silver **t**.
Joe 3:5 my finest **t** to your temples.
Oba 1:6 your hidden **t** will be looted.
Mat 6:19 "Stop storing up **t** for
6:20 Instead, store up **t** for
Luk 12:21 person **t** material possessions
Act 8:27 official in charge of all the **t**
Col 2:3 God has hidden all the **t** of
Heb 11:26 than having the **t** of Egypt.

treasuries (13)
1Ki 15:18 and gold that was left in the **t**
1Ch 26:20 was in charge of the **t** in God's
26:20 in God's temple and the **t**
26:22 They were in charge of the **t** in
26:24 official in charge of the **t**.
26:26 were in charge of all the **t**
27:25 for the royal **t**: Azmaveth,
28:12 (These rooms served as **t** for
2Ch 16:2 and gold that was left in the **t**
Pro 8:21 who love me and to fill their **t**.
Isa 10:13 I've looted **t**. I've brought down
Eze 28:4 saved gold and silver in your **t**.
Dan 11:43 treasures and all Egypt's **t**.

treasury (22)
Jos 6:19 must go into the LORD's **t**."
6:24 and iron into the LORD's **t**.
2Ki 14:14 and in the royal palace **t**.
16:8 the LORD's temple and in the **t**
18:15 and in the royal palace **t**.
20:13 and everything in his **t**.
20:15 them everything in my **t**."
1Ch 29:3 I have a personal **t** of gold and
29:8 for the **t** of the LORD's temple.
2Ch 25:24 Edom and in the royal palace **t**.
Ezr 2:69 as much as they could to the **t**
7:20 You may use the king's **t** to pay
Neh 7:70 the following to the **t**:
7:71 the families contributed to the **t**
Est 3:9 treasurers to be put in your **t**."
4:7 promised to pay into the king's **t**
Isa 39:2 and everything in his **t**.
39:4 them everything in my **t**."
Jer 38:11 to a room under the **t**.
Dan 1:2 and put them in the temple **t**.
Mat 27:6 right to put it into the temple **t**,
Jon 8:20 he was teaching in the **t** area

treat (49)
Gen 18:25 to **t** the innocent and the guilty
19:9 We're going to **t** you worse than
34:31 been allowed to **t** our sister like
Exo 8:22 But on that day I will **t** the
21:9 he must **t** her like a daughter.
30:32 and you must **t** it as holy.
30:36 You must **t** it as most holy.
30:37 **T** it as holy to the LORD.
Lev 24:15 Those who **t** their God with
25:43 Do not **t** them harshly.
25:46 do not **t** the Israelites harshly.
25:53 buyer should not **t** him harshly.
Num 11:15 this is how you're going to **t** me,
12:7 But this is not the way I **t** my
14:11 "How long will these people **t**
14:23 None of those who **t** me with

Num 25:17 "T the Midianites as your
Dtr 21:16 he can't t the son of the wife he
Jos 2:14 we'll t you kindly and honestly
Jdg 1:24 and we'll t you kindly."
2Sm 18:5 "T the young man Absalom
2Ki 1:13 please t my life and the lives of
1:14 But t my life as something
Ezr 7:28 powerful officials t me kindly.
9:9 the kings of Persia t us kindly.
Neh 13:17 How dare you t the day of
Job 6:14 "A friend should t a troubled
30:21 You have begun to t me cruelly.
42:8 prayer not to t you as godless
Psa 83:11 T their influential people as
83:11 T all their leaders like Zebah
119:124 T me with kindness,
Pro 24:29 "I'll t him as he treated me.
Isa 29:23 They will t the Holy One of
Jer 3:19 "I wanted to t you like children
6:14 They t my people's wounds as
7:5 you really t each other fairly.
8:11 They t my dear people's
Eze 23:29 They will t you hatefully and
28:26 surrounding people who t them
Dan 1:13 Decide how to t us on the
Hos 11:8 How can I t you like Zeboim?
Hab 1:10 fun of kings and t rulers as
Rom 2:22 As you t idols with disgust,
1Co 16:11 so no one should t him with
2Co 6:13 T us the same way we've
Eph 6:9 own slaves should also t them
2Th 3:15 Yet, don't t them like enemies,
1Pe 3:16 Then those who t the good

treated (60)

Gen 16:5 "I'm being t unfairly!
42:30 to us and t us like spies.
Exo 5:23 he has t your people cruelly,
10:2 grandchildren exactly how I t
18:11 who t Israel with contempt.
21:8 since he has t her unfairly.
Num 16:30 know that these men have t
25:18 because they t you as
Dtr 24:7 whether he t the other person
26:6 So the Egyptians t us cruelly,
32:15 the God who made them and t
Jdg 9:16 If you t Jerubbaal and his
9:16 if you t him as he deserved,
1Sm 17:27 who kills Goliath would be t.
24:17 You t me well while I treated
24:17 me well while I t you badly.
1Ki 1:21 my son Solomon and I will be t
2Ki 25:28 He t him well and gave him a
1Ch 24:31 of the oldest brother were t
Job 27:7 "Let my enemy be ⌊t⌋ like
27:7 be ⌊t⌋ like unrighteous people.
31:18 my birth I t the widow kindly.)
Psa 83:11 influential people as you t Oreb
103:10 He has not t us as we deserve
119:65 You have t me well,
Pro 24:29 "I'll treat him as he t me.
Ecc 9:2 Good people are t like sinners.
9:2 People who take oaths are t
Jer 52:32 He t him well and gave him a
Lam 1:15 The Lord has t all the warriors
2:20 Have you ever t anyone like
4:2 are now t like clay pots,
Eze 23:8 and t her like a prostitute.
Oba 1:15 Edom, you will be t as you
1:15 be treated as you have t others.
Mat 5:7 They will be t mercifully.
17:12 Yet, people t him as they
18:33 Shouldn't you have t the other
18:33 as mercifully as I t you?'
20:12 Yet, you've t us all the same,
21:36 But the workers t them the
Mar 9:12 a lot and be t shamefully?
9:13 people t him as they pleased,
12:4 the head and t him shamefully.
Luk 6:23 their ancestors t the prophets.
6:26 ancestors t the false prophets.
20:11 beat him, t him shamefully,
23:11 Herod and his soldiers t Jesus
Act 7:24 Israelite man being t unfairly by
27:3 Julius t Paul kindly and
28:7 welcomed us and t us kindly,
1Co 4:11 roughly t, and homeless.
2Co 6:8 We are t as dishonest although
6:13 us the same way we've t you.
7:2 We haven't t anyone unjustly,
12:13 How were you t worse than the
1Th 2:11 You know very well that we t
1Ti 1:13 However, I was t with mercy
1:16 However, I was t with mercy
Heb 10:33 people who were t this way.

treaties (3)

Dtr 7:2 Don't make any t with them or
Eze 21:23 this because they have made t
Hos 12:1 They make t with Assyria and

treating (7)

Exo 5:15 "Why are you t us this way?
Lev 24:11 cursing the LORD's name and t
1Sm 2:17 because these men were t the
Neh 9:10 they were t our ancestors.
13:18 more angry with Israel by t
Mat 20:13 I'm not t you unfairly.
Act 7:26 are you t each other unfairly?'

treatment (11)

Est 2:3 they will have their beauty t.
2:9 provided her with the beauty t,
2:12 required 12-month t for women.
2:12 The time of beauty t was spent
Psa 137:8 with the same t you gave us.
Ecc 9:11 necessarily receive special t.
Isa 66:4 So I will choose harsh t for
Lam 1:3 ⌊much⌋ suffering and harsh t.
1Co 12:24 parts don't need this kind of t.
Col 2:23 and harsh t of the body.
1Th 2:2 rough and insulting t in Philippi.

treatments (1)

Est 2:12 and other t for women.

treats (4)

Exo 31:14 Whoever t it like any other day
Hos 2:2 She no longer t me like her
Mic 7:6 A son t his father with
1Th 2:11 the way a father t his children.

treaty (30)

Gen 21:32 they made the t at Beersheba,
Exo 23:32 Never make a t with them and
34:12 Be careful not to make a t with
34:15 Be careful not to make a t with
Jos 9:6 Make a t with us right now."
9:7 be able to make a t with you."
9:11 Make a t with us right now."'
9:15 making a t which allowed them
9:16 days after the t was made,
11:19 one city had made a peace t
Jdg 2:2 You must never make a t with
1Sm 11:1 "Make a t with us,
11:2 "I'll make a t with you on this
2Sm 3:21 They will make a t with you,
1Ki 5:12 they made a t with one another.
15:19 He said, "There's a t between
15:19 Now break your t with King
20:34 "If you will put this into a t,
20:34 So Ahab made a t with
2Ch 16:3 He said, "There's a t between
16:3 Now break your t with King
Isa 28:15 You say, "We made a t with
28:18 Your t with death will be wiped
Eze 17:13 made a t with him,
17:14 only survive by keeping the t.
17:15 break a t and go unpunished.
17:16 broke his promise and his t
17:18 broke the promise and the t that
17:19 my promise and hating my t.
Amo 1:9 their t with their relatives.

tree (187)

Gen 1:29 earth and every t that has fruit
2:9 The t of life and the tree of the
2:9 The tree of life and the t of the
2:16 to eat from any t in the garden.
2:17 you must never eat from the t
3:1 the fruit of any t in the garden'?"
3:2 the fruit from any t in the garden
Gen 3:3 except the t in the middle of
3:6 The woman saw that the t had
3:11 Did you eat fruit from the t I
3:12 gave me some fruit from the t,
3:17 wife and ate fruit from the t,
3:22 out and take the fruit from the t
3:24 to guard the way to the t of life.
12:6 the land to the oak t belonging
18:4 stretch out and rest under the t.
18:8 by them under the t as they ate.
21:33 Abraham planted a tamarisk t
35:4 under the oak t near Shechem.
35:8 under the oak t outside Bethel.
35:8 Jacob called it the T of Crying.
49:22 "Joseph is a fruitful t,
49:22 a fruitful t by a spring,
Exo 9:25 destroyed every t in the fields.
10:5 including every t still standing
10:15 Nothing green was left on any t
Dtr 12:2 and under every large t
16:21 never plant beside it any t
19:5 swings the ax to cut down a t,
Jos 19:33 at the oak t at Zaanannim.
24:26 and set it up under the oak t at
Jdg 4:5 used to sit under the Palm T
4:11 as the oak t at Zaanannim near
6:11 came and sat under the oak t
6:19 of the LORD under the oak t.
9:6 They went to the oak t that
9:8 They said to the olive t,
9:9 But the olive t responded,
9:10 Then the trees said to the fig t,
9:11 But the fig t responded,
9:37 road by the Fortunetellers' T."
1Sm 10:3 you come to the oak t at Tabor.
14:2 a pomegranate t at Migron.
22:6 Gibeah under the tamarisk t at
31:13 under the tamarisk t in Jabesh.
2Sm 18:9 tangled branches of a large t.
18:9 head became caught in the t.
18:10 "I saw Absalom hanging in a t."
18:14 while he was still alive in the t.
1Ki 4:25 under his own vine and fig t.
13:14 him sitting under an oak t.
14:23 hill and under every large t.
2Ki 3:19 You will cut down every good t,
3:25 and cut down every good t.
6:5 of them was cutting down a t,
16:4 on hills and under every large t.
17:10 hill and under every large t.
18:31 his own grapevine and fig t
1Ch 10:12 under the oak t in Jabesh.
2Ch 28:4 on hills and under every large t.
Neh 10:35 first fruit from every t each year
10:37 fruit from every t, new wine,
Job 14:7 There is hope for a t when it is
15:33 off his blossoms like an olive t
19:10 He uproots my hope like a t.
Psa 1:3 He is like a t planted beside
1:3 streams—a t that produces fruit
37:35 himself out like a large cedar t.
52:8 But I am like a large olive t in
Pro 3:18 ⌊Wisdom⌋ is a t of life for
11:30 a righteous person is a t of life,
13:12 a fulfilled longing is a t of life.
15:4 A soothing tongue is a t of life,
27:18 Whoever takes care of a fig t
Ecc 2:5 every kind of fruit t in them.
11:3 If a t falls north or south,
11:3 the t will remain where it fell.
12:5 the almond t blossoms,
Sos 2:3 Like an apple t among the trees
7:7 your figure is like a palm t,
7:8 thought, "I will climb the palm t
8:5 Under the apple t I woke you
Isa 17:6 They will be like an olive t that
24:13 They will be like an olive t
34:4 like green figs from a fig t.
36:16 his own grapevine and fig t
44:23 you forests and every t in them.
53:2 in his presence like a young t,
57:5 trees and under every large t.
Jer 1:11 "I see a branch of an almond t."
2:20 hill and under every large t.
3:6 and under every large t,
3:13 to strangers under every large t.

Jer 8:13 There are no figs on the **t**,
11:16 a large olive **t** that has beautiful
11:19 "Let's destroy the **t** with its fruit.
17:8 He will be like a **t** that is
Eze 6:13 and under every large **t** and
15:2 the wood from a **t** in the forest?
17:3 took hold of the top of a cedar **t**.
17:22 take hold of the top of a cedar **t**.
17:23 become a magnificent cedar **t**.
20:28 saw any high hill or any leafy **t**,
31:4 Water made the **t** grow,
31:4 place where the **t** was planted.
31:7 So the **t** was big and beautiful
31:9 This **t** was the envy of all the
31:10 The **t** grew very tall,
31:13 birds perched on the fallen **t**,
31:14 So no **t**, even if it is
31:14 Every **t** is going to die and go
31:15 When the **t** went down to the
31:15 I made Lebanon mourn for the **t**
31:16 I brought the **t** down to the
31:17 They had gone down with the **t**
31:18 "This **t** is you, Pharaoh,
31:18 No **t** in Eden has ever been as
40:22 and palm **t** pictures were the
41:19 was turned toward a palm **t**
41:19 was turned toward a palm **t**
Dan 4:10 and I saw an oak **t** in the
4:11 The **t** grew, and it became
4:14 'Cut down the oak **t**!
4:20 You saw an oak **t** grow and
4:22 You are that **t**, Your Majesty.
4:23 He said, 'Cut down the oak **t**!
Hos 14:8 I am like a growing pine **t**.
Hab 3:17 Even if the fig **t** does not bloom
3:17 even if the olive **t** fails to
Hag 2:19 The vine, the fig **t**,
2:19 and the olive **t** still haven't
Zec 3:10 to sit under your vine and fig **t**."
Mat 3:10 Any **t** that doesn't produce good
7:17 In the same way every good **t**
7:17 but a rotten **t** produces bad fruit.
7:18 A good **t** cannot produce bad
7:18 and a rotten **t** cannot produce
7:19 Any **t** that fails to produce good
12:33 "Make a **t** good, and then its
12:33 Or make a **t** rotten,
12:33 can recognize a **t** by its fruit.
13:32 It becomes a **t** that is large
21:19 When he saw a fig **t** by the
21:19 he went up to the **t** and found
21:19 He said to the **t**, "May fruit
21:19 At once the fig **t** dried up.
21:20 They asked, "How did the fig **t**
21:21 able to do what I did to the fig **t**.
24:32 "Learn from the story of the fig **t**
Mar 11:13 he saw a fig **t** with leaves.
11:14 Then he said to the **t**,
11:20 saw that the fig **t** had dried up.
11:21 The fig **t** you cursed has dried
13:28 "Learn from the story of the fig **t**
Luk 3:9 Any **t** that doesn't produce good
6:43 "A good **t** doesn't produce
6:43 and a rotten **t** doesn't produce
6:44 Each **t** is known by its fruit.
13:6 "A man had a fig **t** growing in
13:6 He went to look for fruit on the **t**
13:7 to look for figs on this fig **t**
13:19 It grew and became a **t**,
17:6 could say to this mulberry **t**,
19:4 ran ahead and climbed a fig **t**
19:5 When Jesus came to the **t**,
21:29 "Look at the fig **t** or any other
21:29 at the fig tree or any other **t**.
23:31 If people do this to a green **t**,
Jon 1:48 "I saw you under the fig **t**
1:50 that I saw you under the fig **t**.
Rom 11:17 from the roots of the olive **t**.
11:19 I could be grafted onto the **t**."
11:20 but you remain on the **t**
11:22 will be cut off ⌊from the **t**⌋.
11:23 will be grafted onto the **t** again,
11:24 been cut from a wild olive **t**,
11:24 onto the olive **t** they belong to?
Gal 3:13 who is hung on a **t** is cursed."
Jas 3:12 can a fig **t** produce olives?
Rev 2:7 of eating from the **t** of life,
6:13 figs dropping from a fig **t** when
7:1 on the land, the sea, or any **t**.
9:4 green plant, or **t** on the earth.
22:2 city and the river there was a **t**
22:2 The leaves of the **t** will heal
22:14 they may have the right to the **t**
22:19 take away his portion of the **t**

tree's (2)

Eze 31:16 fear at the sound of the **t** crash.
Dan 4:26 the stump and the **t** roots were

trees (175)

Gen 1:11 and fruit **t** bearing fruit with
1:12 and **t** bearing fruit with seeds,
2:9 The LORD God made all the **t**
2:9 These **t** were nice to look at,
3:8 God among the **t** in the garden.
13:18 to live by the oak **t** belonging
14:13 He was living next to the oak **t**
18:1 Abraham by the oak **t** belonging
23:18 in it as well as all the **t** inside
30:37 and plane **t** and peeled the bark
Exo 10:15 and all the fruit on the **t** that
15:27 were 12 springs and 70 palm **t**.
Lev 19:23 and plant all kinds of fruit **t**,
19:25 Do this to make the **t** produce
23:40 branches of leafy **t** and poplars,
26:4 and the **t** in the field will
26:20 crops and the **t** will produce no
Num 13:20 Does the land have **t** or not?
23:3 place where there were no **t**.
33:9 had 12 springs and 70 palm **t**,
Dtr 6:11 and olive **t** that you didn't
8:8 fig **t**, and pomegranates.
8:8 honey and olive **t** for olive oil.
11:30 next to the oak **t** of Moreh.)
20:19 Don't harm any of its fruit **t** with
20:19 Never cut those **t** down,
20:19 because the **t** of the field are
20:20 You may destroy **t** that you
20:20 that you know are not fruit **t**.
24:20 you harvest olives from your **t**,
28:40 You will have olive **t**
28:40 the olives will fall off the **t**.
28:42 will swarm all over your **t**
Jdg 9:8 "The **t** went to anoint someone
9:9 in order to rule the **t**?'
9:10 Then the **t** said to the fig tree,
9:11 sweet fruit in order to rule the **t**?
9:12 Then the **t** said to the
9:13 in order to rule the **t**?'
9:14 Then all the **t** said to the
9:15 thornbush responded to the **t**,
2Sm 5:23 at them in front of the balsam **t**.
5:24 in the tops of the balsam **t**,
1Ki 4:33 He described and classified **t**—
6:29 He carved angels, palm **t**,
6:32 He carved angels, palm **t**,
6:32 onto the angels and the palm **t**.
6:35 angels, palm **t**, and flowers.
7:36 engraved angels, lions, palm **t**,
10:27 plentiful as fig **t** in the foothills.
2Ki 6:4 River and began to cut down **t**.
18:32 a country with olive **t**,
1Ch 14:14 at them in front of the balsam **t**.
14:15 in the tops of the balsam **t**,
16:33 Then the **t** in the forest will
27:28 for the olive and fig **t** in the
2Ch 1:15 plentiful as fig **t** in the foothills.
3:5 the form of palm **t** and chains.
9:27 plentiful as fig **t** in the foothills.
Neh 9:25 olive **t**, and plenty of fruit trees.
9:25 and plenty of fruit **t**.
Job 24:11 oil between rows ⌊of olive **t**⌋.
Psa 29:9 the oaks and strips ⌊the **t** of⌋
78:47 hail and their fig **t** with frost.
84:6 a valley where balsam **t** grow,
92:12 people flourish like palm **t**
96:12 Then all the **t** in the forest will
104:16 The LORD's **t**, the cedars in
104:17 makes their homes in fir **t**.
105:33 struck their grapevines and fig **t**
105:33 smashed the **t** in their territory.
128:3 young olive **t** around your table.
Psa 137:2 We hung our lyres on willow **t**.
148:9 fruit **t** and all cedar trees,
148:9 fruit trees and all cedar **t**,
Ecc 2:6 to water the forest of growing **t**.
Sos 1:17 The cypress **t** will be our
2:3 Like an apple tree among the **t**
Isa 7:2 people were shaken as the **t**
9:10 Fig **t** have been cut down,
10:19 The **t** that remain in the forest
10:33 The highest **t** will be cut down.
40:16 All the **t** in Lebanon are not
41:19 and wild olive **t** in the desert.
41:19 and cypress **t** together in the
44:14 Then they choose fir **t** or oaks.
44:14 them grow strong among the **t**
44:15 These **t** become fuel for
44:15 also make gods from these **t**
55:12 and all the **t** will clap their
55:13 Cypress **t** will grow where
55:13 Myrtle **t** will grow where briars
56:3 "We're only dead **t**!"
57:5 You burn with lust under oak **t**
60:13 and cypress **t** will come to
65:22 people will live as long as **t**,
Jer 5:17 your grapevines and your fig **t**.
6:6 of Armies says: Cut down its **t**.
7:20 and on **t** and crops.
10:3 Woodcutters cut down **t** from
10:5 These **t** are like scarecrows in
17:2 beside large **t** on high hills
22:7 cut down your finest cedar **t**
26:18 a worship site covered with **t**.'
Eze 15:6 vine is taken from among the **t**
17:24 Then all the **t** in the field will
17:24 I cut down tall **t**, and I make
17:24 and I make small **t** grow tall.
17:24 I dry up green **t**, and I make dry
17:24 and I make dry **t** grow.
20:47 you to destroy all your green **t**
20:47 green trees and all your dry **t**.
27:5 all your boards from pine **t**
27:5 They took cedar **t** from
27:6 made your deck from pine **t**
31:4 beside all the other **t** around it.
31:5 it grew taller than all the other **t**
31:8 The cedar **t** in God's garden
31:8 The pine **t** couldn't equal its
31:8 The plane **t** couldn't measure
31:8 All the **t** in God's garden
31:9 the envy of all the **t** in Eden,
31:14 Then all the other **t** growing by
31:15 and all the **t** in the field fainted
31:16 Then all the **t** in Eden,
31:16 choicest and best **t** of Lebanon,
31:16 and all the **t** that were
31:18 the earth with the **t** of Eden.
34:27 Then the **t** in the field will
36:30 I will make fruit grow on the **t**
39:10 from the field or cut down **t**
40:16 Pictures of palm **t** were carved
40:26 Pictures of palm **t** were carved
40:31 Pictures of palm **t** were carved
40:34 Pictures of palm **t** were carved
40:37 Pictures of palm **t** were carved
41:18 pictures of angels and palm **t**.
41:18 Palm **t** were positioned
41:20 Pictures of angels and palm **t**
41:25 Pictures of angels and palm **t**
41:26 small windows and palm **t**
47:7 As I went back, I saw many **t**
47:12 All kinds of fruit **t** will grow on
Hos 2:12 her grapevines and fig **t**.
4:13 oaks, poplars, and other **t**.
4:13 They think that these **t** provide
14:6 will be beautiful like olive **t**.
Joe 1:7 They ruined my fig **t**.
1:12 The fig **t** are withered.
1:12 palm, and apricot **t**,
1:12 as well as all the **t** in the
1:19 Flames have burned up all the **t**
2:22 The **t** have produced their fruit.
Amo 4:9 vineyards, fig **t**, and olive trees.
4:9 vineyards, fig trees, and olive **t**.
Mic 3:12 a worship site covered with **t**.
4:4 their grapevines and their fig **t**,
Nah 3:12 your defenses will be like fig **t**

Zec 1:8 standing among the myrtle t
1:10 among the myrtle t explained,
1:11 standing among the myrtle t,
4:3 are also two olive t beside it,
4:11 "What do these two olive t at
4:12 branches from the olive t next
11:2 Cry, cypress t, because the
11:2 stately t have been destroyed.
11:2 Cry, oak t of Bashan,
Mat 3:10 ready to cut the roots of the t.
21:8 Others cut branches from the t
Mar 8:24 look like t walking around."
Luk 3:9 ready to cut the roots of the t.
Jud 1:12 uprooted t without any fruit.
Rev 7:3 or the t until we have put the
8:7 one-third of the t was burned
11:4 witnesses are the two olive t

treetops (1)

Psa 72:16 its fruit like ⌊the t of⌋ Lebanon.

tremble (52)

Exo 15:14 People will hear of it and t.
15:15 powerful men of Moab will t.
Dtr 1:29 Then I said to you, "Don't t.
2:25 they will t and shake because
20:3 alarmed or t because of them.
31:6 Don't t! Don't be afraid of them!
Jos 1:9 Don't t or be terrified,
1Ch 16:30 T in his presence,
Ezr 10:3 ⌊Ezra⌋ and the others who t at
Job 9:6 from its place, and its pillars t.
13:25 trying to make a fluttering leaf t
26:5 "The souls of the dead t
26:11 The pillars of heaven t and are
Psa 4:4 T and do not sin. Think about
18:45 and they will t when they come
29:8 LORD makes the wilderness t.
29:8 the wilderness of Kadesh t.
96:9 T in his presence,
99:1 Let the people t. He is enthroned
114:7 t in the presence of the Lord,
Pro 30:21 things cause the earth to t,
Ecc 12:3 those who guard the house t,
Isa 5:25 The hills t, and dead bodies lie
10:29 The people in Ramah t;
13:13 I will make heaven t,
14:16 the man who made the earth t,
19:1 Egypt's idols will t in his
19:16 They will t and be terrified
21:4 hours I longed for make me t.
32:10 overconfident women will t,
32:11 T, you overconfident women.
41:5 The ends of the earth t.
64:2 nations will t in your presence.
66:2 sins⌋ and who t at my word.
66:5 all who t at his word.
Jer 5:22 "Don't you t in my presence?
8:16 makes the whole land t.
23:9 All my bones t. I am like a
33:9 They will be afraid and t
Eze 12:18 T and be worried as you drink
26:16 They will t constantly and be
26:18 people who live by the coast t.
31:16 I made the nations t in fear at
32:10 When you die, all of them will t
38:20 and every person on earth will t
Dan 6:26 of my kingdom people should t
10:7 Yet, they started to t violently,
Joe 2:1 who lives in the land should t,
Amo 8:8 The land will t because of this.
Hab 3:16 I t where I stand. I wait for the
Act 7:32 Moses began to t and didn't
Jas 2:19 and they t with fear.

trembled (12)

Gen 42:28 They t and turned to each other
1Sm 13:7 who followed him t ⌊in fear⌋.
14:15 raiding party also t ⌊in fear⌋.
2Sm 22:8 foundations of the heavens t.
Ezr 9:4 gathered around me there t at
Psa 18:7 foundations of the mountains t.
77:16 Even the depths of the sea t.
77:18 The earth t and shook.
Eze 27:28 people on the shore t.
Dan 5:19 and language t and were
Hos 13:1 of Ephraim spoke, people t.
Mar 5:33 The woman t with fear.

trembles (4)

Psa 97:4 The earth sees them and t.
104:32 He looks at the earth, and it t.
Jer 10:10 The earth t when he is angry.
51:29 The earth t and writhes in pain.

trembling (26)

Gen 27:33 T violently all over,
1Sm 15:32 Agag came to him t.
16:4 leaders of the city, t with fear,
21:1 Ahimelech was t as he went to
Ezr 10:9 They were t because of this
Est 5:9 neither getting up nor t in his
Job 4:14 fear and t came over me,
Psa 2:11 with fear, and rejoice with t.
48:6 T seized them like the
48:6 seized them like the t that
55:5 Fear and t have overcome me.
Isa 21:3 That is why my body is full of t.
33:14 T seizes the ungodly.
Dan 10:11 he said this to me, I stood up, t.
Hos 3:5 They will come t to the LORD
11:10 will come t from the west.
11:11 They will come t like birds
Mic 7:17 out of their hiding places t.
Hab 3:7 I see t in the tents of Midian.
3:16 so there's t within me.
Mar 16:8 Shock and t had overwhelmed
Luk 8:47 T, she quickly bowed in front
Act 16:29 He was t as he knelt in front of
2Co 7:15 welcomed him with fear and t.
Php 2:12 your salvation with fear and t.
Heb 12:21 said he was t and afraid.

tremendous (2)

Jer 10:22 A t uproar is coming from the
Rev 18:1 He had t power, and his glory

trench (3)

1Ki 18:32 He also made a t that could
18:35 and even the t was filled with
18:38 up the water that was in the t.

trial (17)

Num 35:12 have to die until he has had a t
Jos 20:6 in that city until he can stand t
20:9 a death before he stands t
1Sm 12:7 stand up while I put you on t in
Psa 37:33 him when he is brought to t.
109:7 When he stands t,
Eze 20:35 I will put you on t face to face.
20:36 I will put you on t as I put your
20:36 trial as I put your ancestors on t
Luk 12:11 "When you are put on t in
Act 12:4 Herod wanted to bring Peter to t
12:6 was going to bring Peter to t,
16:37 us beaten publicly without a t
22:25 citizen who hasn't had a t?"
23:6 I'm on t because I expect that
24:22 so he adjourned the t.
26:6 "I'm on t now because I expect

trials (1)

Psa 105:19 fiery t until his prediction

triangles (1)

1Sm 18:6 joyful music, and t.

tribal (17)

Gen 36:15 These were the t leaders
36:16 These were the t leaders
36:17 These were the t leaders
36:17 These were the t leaders
36:18 These were the t leaders
36:18 These were the t leaders
36:19 who were t leaders.
36:21 These Horite t leaders were the
36:29 were the Horite t leaders:
36:30 These were the Horite t leaders
36:40 These were the names of the t
36:43 These were the t leaders of
Exo 15:15 The t leaders of Edom will be
Num 7:2 those t leaders who helped
Num 36:7 Every Israelite must keep the t
1Ch 1:51 The t leaders of Edom were
1:54 were the t leaders of Edom.

tribe (320)

Exo 31:2 from the t of Judah.
31:6 from the t of Dan, to help him.
35:30 from the t of Judah.
35:34 from the t of Dan the ability to
38:22 from the t of Judah,
38:23 Ahisamach, from the t of Dan.
Lev 24:10 from the t of Dan in Israel) and
Num 1:4 One man from each t will help
1:5 from the t of Reuben;
1:6 from the t of Simeon;
1:7 from the t of Judah;
1:8 from the t of Issachar;
1:9 from the t of Zebulun;
1:10 from the t of Ephraim;
1:10 from the t of Manasseh;
1:11 from the t of Benjamin;
1:12 from the t of Dan;
1:13 from the t of Asher;
1:14 son of Deuel, from the t of Gad;
1:15 from the t of Naphtali."
1:21 The total for the t of Reuben
1:23 The total for the t of Simeon
1:25 The total for the t of Gad was
1:27 The total for the t of Judah was
1:29 The total for the t of Issachar
1:31 The total for the t of Zebulun
1:33 The total for the t of Ephraim
1:35 The total for the t of Manasseh
1:37 The total for the t of Benjamin
1:39 The total for the t of Dan was
1:41 The total for the t of Asher was
1:43 The total for the t of Naphtali
1:47 But the households from the t
1:49 "Don't register the t of Levi or
2:5 them will be the t of Issachar.
2:7 ⌊will be⌋ the t of Zebulun.
2:12 to them will be the t of Simeon.
2:14 "Then ⌊will be⌋ the t of Gad.
2:20 them will be the t of Manasseh.
2:22 ⌊will be⌋ the t of Benjamin.
2:27 to them will be the t of Asher.
2:29 ⌊will be⌋ the t of Naphtali.
3:6 "Bring the t of Levi,
4:18 from Levi's t be destroyed.
7:12 from the t of Judah.
7:18 leader from the t of Issachar,
13:4 from the t of Reuben;
13:5 from the t of Simeon;
13:6 from the t of Judah;
13:7 from the t of Issachar;
13:8 from the t of Ephraim;
13:9 from the t of Benjamin;
13:10 from the t of Zebulun;
13:11 from the t of Joseph (that is,
13:11 the t of Manasseh);
13:12 of Gemalli, from the t of Dan;
13:13 from the t of Asher;
13:14 from the t of Naphtali;
13:15 son of Machi, from the t of Gad.
17:3 one staff for the head of each t.
17:8 found that Aaron's staff for the t
18:2 Levites from your ancestor's t
26:54 in giving land to each t.
31:5 So 1,000 men from each t were
31:6 1,000 men from each t along
32:33 and half of the t of Manasseh,
32:34 The t of Gad rebuilt the cities
32:37 The t of Reuben rebuilt the
34:14 and half of the t of Manasseh
34:18 take one leader from each t
34:19 from the t of Judah;
34:20 from the t of Simeon;
34:21 from the t of Benjamin;
34:22 the leader of the t of Dan;
34:23 the leader of the t of Manasseh;
34:24 the leader of the t of Ephraim;
34:25 the leader of the t of Zebulun;
34:26 the leader of the t of Issachar;
34:27 the leader of the t of Asher;
34:28 the leader of the t of Naphtali."
35:8 amount of land each t owns.

Num 36:3 the land of the t they marry into.
36:4 to that of the t they married into.
36:4 our ancestors' t will be gone."
36:5 "The t of Joseph's
36:6 a family of their ancestor's t.
36:7 will pass from one t to another.
36:8 any family in her ancestor's t.
36:9 may pass from one t to another.
36:9 Each Israelite t must keep the
36:12 So their land stayed in the t of
Dtr 1:23 of your men, one from each t.
3:13 Og to half of the t of Manasseh.
3:18 and Gad and half of the t
4:43 plateau for the t of Reuben,
4:43 in Gilead for the t of Gad,
4:43 Bashan for the t of Manasseh.
10:8 time the LORD set apart the t
10:9 This is why the t of Levi has
11:6 from the t of Reuben.
18:1 the whole t of Levi — will
29:8 and half of the t of Manasseh
29:18 or t among you today who turns
33:6 "May the t of Reuben live and
33:7 This is what he said about the t
33:8 About the t of Levi he said,
33:12 About the t of Benjamin he
33:17 tens of thousands from the t
33:17 and the thousands from the t
33:18 About the t of Zebulun he said,
33:20 About the t of Gad he said,
33:22 About the t of Dan [He Judges]
33:23 About the t of Naphtali he said,
33:24 About the t of Asher he said,
33:24 they be the Israelites' favorite t
Jos 1:12 and half of the t of Manasseh,
4:4 had selected (one from each t).
4:5 one for each t of Israel.
4:12 and half of the t of Manasseh
7:1 and a member of the t of Judah,
7:14 The t the LORD selects will
7:16 The t of Judah was selected.
7:18 Achan from the t of Judah was
12:6 and half of the t of Manasseh.
13:7 and half of the t of Manasseh."
13:8 and Gad with half of the t
13:14 an inheritance to the t of Levi.
13:15 land as an inheritance to the t
13:24 land as an inheritance to the t
13:29 to half of the t of Manasseh.
13:29 the families of that half of the t.
13:33 an inheritance to the t of Levi.
14:3 as an inheritance to Levi's t,
15:1 the families of the t of Judah.
15:20 the families of the t of Judah.
15:21 they gave the t of Judah 29
16:8 the families of the t of Ephraim
17:1 drawn for the t of Manasseh,
18:4 Choose three men from each t,
18:7 Levi's t has no separate region
18:7 and Reuben and half of the t
18:11 families of the t of Benjamin.
18:21 villages that belong to the t
19:1 the families of the t of Simeon.
19:8 This is the inheritance of the t
19:23 the families of the t of Issachar.
19:24 for the families of the t of Asher.
19:31 for the families of the t of Asher.
19:32 from the t of Naphtali.
19:39 the families of the t of Naphtali.
19:40 for the families of the t of Dan.
19:48 for the families of the t of Dan.
20:8 plateau from the t of Reuben,
20:8 in Gilead from the t of Gad,
20:8 and Golan in Bashan from the t
21:5 and half of the t of Manasseh.
21:6 and half of the t of Manasseh in
21:10 of Kohath in the t of Levi.
21:17 The t of Benjamin also gave
21:20 were chosen by lot from the t
21:23 The t of Dan gave them four
21:25 Half of the t of Manasseh gave
21:27 who were in the t of Levi,
21:27 from half of the t of Manasseh:
21:28 to them from the t of Issachar:
21:30 to them from the t of Asher:
21:32 to them from the t of Naphtali:
Jos 21:34 who were from the t of Levi,
21:34 the t of Zebulun gave four
21:36 The t of Reuben also gave
21:38 The t of Gad also gave them
22:1 and half of the t of Manasseh.
22:7 the other half of the t their land
22:9 and Gad and half of the t
22:10 Reuben, Gad, and half of the t
22:11 Reuben, Gad, and half of the t
22:13 and Gad and half of the t
22:14 one from each t in Israel,
22:21 and Gad and half of the t
Jdg 1:3 The t of Judah said to the tribe
1:3 Judah said to the t of Simeon,
1:3 "So the t of Simeon went along
1:17 The t of Judah went to fight
1:17 fight along with the t of Simeon,
1:21 Jebusites still live with the t
1:27 Now, the t of Manasseh did not
1:29 The t of Ephraim did not force
1:30 The t of Zebulun did not force
1:31 The t of Asher did not force out
1:32 So the t of Asher continued to
1:33 The t of Naphtali did not force
1:34 The Amorites forced the t of
3:15 man from the t of Benjamin.
12:11 After Ibzan, Elon from the t of
18:1 And in those days the t of Dan
18:11 So 600 men from the t of Dan
18:19 for one man's house or for a t
18:30 were priests for Dan's t until
19:14 belonged to the t of Benjamin.)
19:16 were from the t of Benjamin.
20:12 throughout the t of Benjamin.
21:3 Why should one t be missing
21:6 They said, "Today one t has
21:17 No t of Israel should be wiped
21:24 man went to his t and family.
1Sm 1:1 Zuph from the t of Ephraim.
4:12 A man from the t of Benjamin
9:1 There was a man from the t of
9:21 a man from the t of Benjamin,
9:21 the smallest t of Israel.
9:21 families of the t of Benjamin.
10:20 the t of Benjamin was chosen.
10:21 When he had the t of Benjamin
2Sm 2:4 to be king over the t of Judah.
2:7 the t of Judah has anointed me
2:10 He ruled for two years, but the t
2:11 David was king over the t
2:15 Twelve were from the t of
3:19 Israel and the entire t
4:2 Beeroth from the t of Benjamin.
15:2 the person had told him which t
19:11 'Why should you be the last ⌊t⌋
19:16 Shimei, Gera's son from the t of
20:1 from the t of Benjamin
23:36 Bani from the t of Gad,
1Ki 7:14 a widow from the t of Naphtali.
11:13 I will give your son one t for my
11:32 He will have one t ⌊left⌋
11:36 I will give his son one t so that
12:20 Only the t of Judah remained
12:21 of Judah and the t of Benjamin,
15:27 of Ahijah from the t of Issachar,
2Ki 17:18 Only the t of Judah was left.
1Ch 5:6 was leader of the t of Reuben.
5:18 and half of the t of Manasseh
5:22 Reuben, Gad, and half of the t
5:23 Half of the t of Manasseh lived
5:23 The t members were numerous.
5:25 and half of the t of Manasseh
5:26 and half of the t of Manasseh
6:60 From the t of Benjamin,
6:61 of half of the t of Manasseh.
6:62 and ⌊the part of⌋ the t of
6:66 by lot from the t of Ephraim.
6:70 From half of the t of Manasseh,
6:71 of half of the t of Manasseh.
6:72 From the t of Issachar,
6:74 From the t of Asher,
6:76 From the t of Naphtali,
6:77 from the t of Zebulun.
6:78 From the t of Reuben,
6:80 From the t of Gad,
11:42 Adina (son of Shiza) from the t
1Ch 11:42 (who was leader of the t
12:2 ⌊from the t of⌋ Benjamin.
12:31 From half of the t of Manasseh
12:37 and half the t of Manasseh,
23:14 were counted with the t of Levi.
26:32 and half of the t of Manasseh.
27:12 Abiezer, a member of the t of
27:14 Benaiah, a member of the t of
27:16 for the t of Reuben:
27:16 of Zichri for the t of Simeon:
27:17 for the t of Levi: Hashabiah,
27:18 for the t of Judah: Elihu, one of
27:18 brothers for the t of Issachar:
27:19 for the t of Zebulun:
27:19 of Obadiah for the t of Naphtali:
27:20 for the t of Ephraim:
27:20 for half of the t of Manasseh:
27:21 Zechariah for the t of Benjamin:
27:22 for the t of Dan: Azarel, son of
28:4 He had chosen the t of Judah
2Ch 2:14 of a woman from the t of Dan,
11:16 People from every t of Israel
19:11 and the leader of the t of Judah,
Est 2:5 there was a Jew from the t
Psa 74:2 You bought this t to be your
74:2 This t is Mount Zion,
78:67 did not choose the t of Ephraim,
78:68 but he chose the t of Judah,
Jer 10:16 and Israel is the t that belongs
49:28 This is about the t of Kedar and
51:19 and Israel is the t that belongs
Eze 43:19 men from the t of Levi,
45:8 They will give land to each t of
47:23 of the t among whom they
Hos 13:1 When the t of Ephraim spoke,
Mic 6:9 you t assembled in the city.
Zec 9:7 for our God like a t in Judah,
Luk 2:36 of Phanuel from the t of Asher.
Act 13:21 from the t of Benjamin.
Rom 11:1 from the t of Benjamin.
Php 3:5 I'm from the t of Benjamin.
Heb 7:5 say that members of the t
7:6 was not from the t of Levi,
7:13 was a member of a different t.
7:13 No one from that t ever served
7:14 Lord came from the t of Judah.
7:14 priests coming from that t.
7:20 The men from the t of Levi may
Rev 1:7 Every t on earth will mourn
5:5 The Lion from the t of Judah,
5:9 They are from every t,
7:4 were sealed were from every t
7:5 12,000 from the t of Judah were
7:5 12,000 from the t of Reuben,
7:5 12,000 from the t of Gad,
7:6 12,000 from the t of Asher,
7:6 12,000 from the t of Naphtali,
7:6 12,000 from the t of Manasseh,
7:7 12,000 from the t of Simeon,
7:7 12,000 from the t of Levi,
7:7 12,000 from the t of Issachar,
7:8 12,000 from the t of Zebulun,
7:8 12,000 from the t of Joseph,
7:8 12,000 from the t of Benjamin
7:9 nation, t, people, and language.
13:7 given authority over every t,
14:6 nation, t, language, and people.

tribes (165)

Gen 25:16 camps — 12 leaders of their t.
49:7 them among ⌊the t of⌋ Israel.
49:16 people as one of the t of Israel.
49:28 These are the 12 t of Israel and
Exo 24:4 stones for the 12 t of Israel.
28:21 the name of one of the 12 t.
39:14 the name of one of the 12 t.
Num 1:16 the leaders of their ancestors' t,
2:17 The t will move out in the
10:5 the t that are camped on the
10:6 the t that are camped on the
13:2 from each of their ancestors' t."
17:2 the leader of each of their t.
17:6 the leader of each of their t.
24:2 saw Israel's camp grouped by t.
25:15 of a family from the Midianite t.)
26:54 Give more land to larger t and

Num 26:55 The t will receive their land
26:56 Whether the t are large or small
30:1 to the heads of the t of Israel,
31:4 from each of the t of Israel."
32:1 The t of Reuben and Gad had
32:6 Moses asked the t of Gad and
32:16 Then the t of Gad and Reuben
32:25 Then the t of Gad and Reuben
32:28 family heads of the t of Israel.
32:29 Moses told them, "If the t of
32:31 The t of Gad and Reuben
32:33 So Moses gave the t of Gad,
33:54 it among your ancestors' t.
34:13 given to the nine-and-a-half t.
34:14 from the t of Reuben,
34:15 Those two-and-a-half t
35:8 Take more cities from larger t
35:8 tribes and fewer from smaller t."
36:3 men from the other t of Israel.
36:8 who inherits land in any of the t
Dtr 1:13 From each of your t,
1:15 So I took the heads of your t
1:15 them officers for each of your t.
3:12 I gave the t of Reuben and Gad
3:16 I gave the t of Reuben and Gad
3:18 I gave the t of Reuben and Gad
5:23 heads of your t came to me.
10:9 of their own as the other t have.
12:5 choose a place out of all your t
12:14 will choose in one of your t.
16:18 judges and officers for your t
18:5 Out of all your t, the LORD your
27:12 these are the t that will stand
27:13 These are the t that will stand
29:8 and gave it to the t of Reuben,
29:10 The heads of your t,
29:21 will single him out from all the t
31:28 all the leaders of your t
32:8 he set up borders for the t
33:5 together with all the t of Israel.
33:13 About the t of Joseph he said,
33:16 come to the t of Joseph.
Jos 1:12 Next, Joshua said to the t of
3:12 from each of the 12 t of Israel.
4:2 one man from each of the 12 t.
4:8 one for each of the t of Israel.
7:14 morning come forward by t to
7:16 had Israel come forward by t.
11:23 dividing it among the t.
12:6 land as a possession to the t
12:7 dividing it among the t.
13:7 be an inheritance for the nine t
13:8 The t of Reuben and Gad with
14:1 and the heads of Israel's t
14:2 t was determined by
14:3 t their inheritance east
14:4 and Ephraim, formed two t.
17:17 the t of Ephraim and
18:2 There were still seven t in
18:7 The t of Gad and Reuben and
18:10 the land among the t of Israel.
19:51 This is the land that the t of
21:1 families of the other Israelite t
21:4 13 cities from the t of Judah,
21:5 cities from the families of the t
21:6 the families of the t of Issachar,
21:7 families from the t of Reuben,
21:9 names of the cities from the t
21:13 The nine cities from those two t
22:1 Joshua summoned the t of
22:9 So the t of Reuben and Gad
22:13 to the t of Reuben and Gad and
22:21 Then the t of Reuben and Gad
22:30 heard what the t of Reuben,
22:31 said to the t of Reuben,
22:34 The t of Reuben and Gad gave
23:4 as an inheritance for your t.
24:1 Joshua gathered all the t of
Jdg 1:35 But when the t of Joseph
4:10 Barak called the t of Zebulun
6:35 The t of Asher, Zebulun,
10:9 River to fight the t of Judah,
18:1 as an inheritance among the t
20:2 The leaders of all Israel's t took
20:10 of all the men from the t
20:12 The t of Israel sent men
Jdg 21:15 the unity of the t of Israel.
1Sm 2:28 your ancestors out of all the t
10:19 by your t and family groups."
10:20 When Samuel had all the t of
11:1 was severely oppressing the t
15:17 you were the head of Israel's t.
2Sm 5:1 All the t of Israel came to David
15:10 his loyal supporters to all the t
19:9 All the people in all the t of
20:14 Sheba passed through all the t
24:2 "Go throughout the t of Israel
1Ki 8:1 all the heads of the t,
8:16 choose any city in any of the t
11:28 labor from the t of Joseph.
11:31 hands and give ten t to you.
11:32 chosen from all the t of Israel.
11:35 from his son and give you ten t.
14:21 chose from all the t of Israel,
18:31 one for each of the t named
2Ki 21:7 from all the t of Israel.
1Ch 6:62 by lot from the t of Issachar,
6:63 by lot from the t of Reuben,
6:65 by name from the t of Judah,
26:32 or the king for the t of Reuben,
27:16 were in charge of the t of Israel:
27:22 the commanders of Israel's t.
28:1 of Israel — the leaders of the t,
29:6 the leaders of the t of Israel,
2Ch 5:2 all the heads of the t,
6:5 didn't choose any city from the t
12:13 chose from all the t of Israel,
30:1 Judah and wrote letters to the t
33:7 from all the t of Israel.
34:9 had collected from the t
34:9 from everyone in the t of Judah
Ezr 6:17 goat for each of the t of Israel.
Psa 78:55 He settled the t of Israel in their
105:37 and no one among his t
122:4 All of the LORD's t go to that
Isa 19:13 of its t mislead the Egyptians.
49:6 my servant who restores the t
63:17 They are the t that belong to
Eze 37:19 and the t of Israel associated
45:7 as the territory of one of the t.
47:13 among the 12 t of Israel.
47:21 for each of the t of Israel.
47:22 among the t of Israel.
48:1 These are the names of the t.
48:8 as one of the sections of the t.
48:19 City workers from all the t in
48:21 as one of the sections of the t.
48:23 the rest of the t will receive:
48:29 among the t of Israel,
48:31 be named after the t of Israel.
Hos 5:9 known among the t of Israel.
Zec 9:2 of humanity and of all the t
Mat 19:28 judging the twelve t of Israel.
Luk 22:30 judge the twelve t of Israel."
Act 7:8 sons (the ancestors of our t).
26:7 Our twelve t expect this
Rev 11:9 of the people, t, languages,
21:12 The names of the 12 t of Israel

trick (7)

Gen 31:27 you leave secretly and t me?
Num 25:18 They plotted to t you in the
Jdg 14:15 "T your husband into solving
16:5 came to her and said, "T him,
Job 13:9 Will you try to t him as one
Jer 29:8 who are among you t you.
2Co 12:16 who trapped you by some t?

tricked (5)

Gen 31:20 Jacob also t Laban the
Jer 20:10 They say, "Maybe he will be t.
Eze 14:9 "'If a prophet is t into giving a
14:9 I, the LORD, who t the prophet.
Mat 2:16 that the wise men had t him,

tricking (2)

Gen 31:26 "What have you done by t me?
Exo 8:29 But you must stop t us by not

tricks (7)

Job 5:13 the wise with their own t.
13:9 him as one mortal t another?
Pro 26:19 so is the person who t his
Isa 32:7 The t of scoundrels are evil.
Act 13:10 are full of dirty t and schemes,
2Co 4:2 We don't use t, and we don't
11:3 snake deceived Eve by its t,

tried (76)

Gen 37:21 When Reuben heard this, he t
39:14 He came in and t to go to bed
39:17 you brought here came in and t
Exo 2:15 he t to have him killed.
4:24 met Moses and t to kill him.
8:18 The magicians also t to
14:27 The Egyptians t to escape,
Lev 10:16 Moses t to find out what had
Num 3:38 Anyone else who t to do the
Dtr 4:34 Or has any god ever t to come
1Sm 17:39 over his clothes and t to walk,
19:10 Saul t to nail David to the wall
2Sm 3:35 That entire day all the people t
4:8 son of your enemy Saul who t
15:2 a case to be t by King David,
15:4 had a case to be t could come
21:2 t to destroy them for Israel and
1Ki 7:47 No one t to determine how
11:40 Then Solomon t to kill
2Ki 9:23 his chariot around and t to flee,
18:7 succeeded in everything he t.
1Ch 7:22 his brothers t to comfort him.
2Ch 4:18 of these products that no one t
32:18 They t to frighten and terrify the
Est 8:7 hung on the pole because he t
Psa 73:16 But when I t to understand this,
Ecc 12:10 The spokesman t to find just
Eze 24:13 I t to clean you of your filthy
25:15 They have t to destroy their
Dan 6:4 the other officials and satraps t
6:14 He t every way he could think
8:15 watched the vision and t to
9:13 LORD our God, we never t to
Jnh 1:3 Jonah immediately t to run
1:13 Instead, the men t to row harder
4:2 That's why I t to run to
Mic 6:3 How have I t your patience?
Mal 2:17 You have t the patience of the
2:17 "How have we t his patience?"
Mat 2:4 chief priests and scribes and t
2:20 Those who t to kill the child
3:14 But John t to stop him and said,
Mar 9:38 We t to stop him because he
14:51 They t to arrest him,
15:23 They t to give him wine mixed
Luk 1:29 by what the angel said and t
4:42 they t to keep him from leaving.
5:18 They t to take him into the
9:49 We t to stop him because he
18:36 he t to find out what was
19:3 He t to see who Jesus was.
Jon 7:30 The Jews t to arrest him but
10:39 The Jews t to arrest Jesus
Act 7:26 and he t to make peace
8:3 Saul t to destroy the church.
9:26 he t to join the disciples.
9:29 but they t to murder him.
13:8 opposed them and t to distort
13:11 He t to find people to lead him.
14:19 They t to stone Paul to death
16:7 to the province of Mysia and t
18:4 He t to win over Jews and
19:13 They t to use the name of the
24:21 'I'm being t in front of you
25:9 to go to Jerusalem to be t there
25:10 court where I must be t.
26:21 courtyard and t to murder me.
27:30 The sailors t to escape from
Rom 9:31 The people of Israel t to gain
1Co 16:12 I t hard to get him to visit you
2Co 11:25 Once people t to stone me to
Gal 1:13 God's church and t to destroy it.
1:23 faith that he once t to destroy."
2:19 When I t to obey the law's
Heb 11:29 The Egyptians also t this,
1Pe 1:11 So they t to find out what time

tried-and-true (1)

2Ti 2:15 to God as a t worker who isn't

tries (12)

Num 3:10 Anyone else who t to do the
Dtr 25:11 If she t to stop the fight by
2Ki 11:8 Kill anyone who t to break
18:32 listen to Hezekiah when he t
2Ch 23:7 Kill anyone who t to come into
Ezr 6:12 of each king and nation who t
6:12 to tamper with my orders or t
Job 4:2 "If someone t to talk to you,
Isa 64:7 No one calls on your name or t
Mat 10:39 The person who t to preserve
Rom 7:23 standards my mind sets and t
3Jn 1:10 He even t to stop others who

trim (1)

Isa 10:33 Almighty LORD of Armies will t

trimmed (3)

2Sm 19:24 to his feet, t his mustache,
1Ki 7:9 blocks were cut to size and t
Eze 44:20 keep the hair on their heads t.

trip (51)

Gen 24:21 had made his t successful.
24:27 The LORD has led me on this t
24:40 you to make your t successful.
24:42 please make my t successful.
24:56 has made my t successful.
28:20 and will watch over me on my t
29:1 Jacob continued on his t and
42:25 gave them supplies for their t.
42:38 to him on the t you're taking,
43:10 made this t twice by now."
45:21 for their t as Pharaoh had
45:23 and food for his father's t.
Exo 12:39 no time to prepare food for the t.
23:20 of you to protect you on your t
Num 9:10 body or is away on a long t.
9:13 if you are clean and not on a t
21:4 became impatient on the t
22:32 because the t you're taking is
22:34 If you still think this t is evil,
Dtr 23:4 and water on your t from Egypt.
24:9 to Miriam on your t from Egypt.
25:17 did to you on your t from Egypt.
Jos 9:11 'Take what you need for the t,
Job 30:12 They t my feet and then
Psa 64:8 They will t over their own
140:4 people. They try to t me.
Pro 7:19 He has gone on a long t.
Isa 8:14 be a rock that makes people t
Jnh 1:3 He paid for the t and went on
Nah 3:3 People t over corpses
Mat 10:10 take a traveling bag for the t,
21:33 workers and went on a t.
25:14 is like a man going on a t.
25:15 Then the man went on his t.
Mar 6:8 nothing along on the t except
12:1 workers and went on a t.
13:34 is like a man who went on a t.
Luk 9:3 take anything along on the t.
10:35 I'll pay you on my return t.'
11:6 A friend of mine on a t has
20:9 and went on a long t.
Act 7:12 That was their first t.
7:13 On the second t, Joseph told
Rom 9:33 rock in Zion that people t over,
15:24 you will support my t to Spain.
1Co 16:11 give him your support for his t
2Co 1:16 you support my t to Judea.
Tit 3:13 support for their t so that they
1Pe 2:8 a stone that people t over,
3Jn 1:6 well to support them on their t
1:7 After all, they went on their t to

tripped (1)

1Pe 2:8 The people t over the word

trips (3)

Job 18:7 and his own planning t him up.
Rom 9:32 over the rock that t people.
3Jn 1:8 who go on t like this so

triumph (14)

Jdg 15:14 met him with shouts ⌊of t⌋.
Job 20:5 the t of the wicked is
Psa 5:11 who love your name t in you.
13:2 long will my enemy t over me?
25:2 not let my enemies t over me.
41:11 cannot shout in t over me.
60:6 through his holiness: "I will t!
60:8 I will shout in t over Philistia."
94:3 will wicked people t?
108:7 through his holiness: "I will t!
108:9 I will shout in t over Philistia."
149:5 Let godly people t in glory.
Pro 28:12 When righteous people t,
Zec 9:9 Shout in t, people of

triumphant (1)

Psa 28:7 My heart is t; I give thanks to

triumphantly (2)

Psa 65:13 All of them shout t.
112:8 he will look t at his enemies.

triumphed (1)

Lam 1:9 because my enemies have t.'

triumphs (2)

Isa 13:3 They find joy in my t.
Jas 2:13 Mercy t over judgment.

Troas (7)

Act 16:8 Mysia and went to the city of T.
16:11 So we took a ship from T and
20:5 and were waiting for us in T.
20:6 days later we joined them in T
2Co 2:12 When I went to the city of T,
2:13 said goodbye to the people in T
2Ti 4:13 left with Carpus in the city of T.

troop (5)

2Sm 23:13 cave of Adullam when a t from
1Ki 11:24 the leader of a t of warriors.
Mat 27:27 the whole t around him.
Mar 15:16 and called together the whole t.
Jon 18:3 So Judas took a t of soldiers

troop's (1)

2Ki 9:20 The t leader is driving like a

troops (248)

Num 2:9 "The grand total of all the t in
2:16 "The grand total of all the t in
2:24 "The grand total of all the t in
2:32 The grand total of all the t in
20:20 with many well-armed t.
21:23 Sihon gathered all his t and
21:23 When Sihon's t came to Jahaz,
21:33 King Og of Bashan and all his t
21:34 I'll hand him, all his t,
21:35 him, his sons, and all his t,
31:32 from everything that the t took:
32:32 will enter Canaan as armed t
Dtr 2:32 Sihon and all his t came out to
2:33 him, his sons, and all his t.
3:1 King Og of Bashan and all his t
3:2 I'll hand him, all his t,
3:3 Og of Bashan and all his t over
20:2 must come and speak to the t.
20:5 The officers should tell the t,
20:8 officers should also tell the t,
20:9 officers finish speaking to the t,
Jos 6:5 all the t must shout very loudly.
6:5 Then the t must charge straight
6:7 He told the t, "March around the
6:8 had given orders to the t,
6:10 Joshua ordered the t,
6:16 Joshua said to the t,
6:20 So the t shouted very loudly
6:20 The t charged straight ahead
7:3 don't need to send all the t.
7:3 Don't tire the t out by sending
7:3 There are only a few t in Ai."
7:5 Israel's t lost heart and were
8:1 Take all the t with you,
8:5 the city with the rest of the t.
8:9 spent the night with the t.
8:10 morning and assembled the t.
8:11 All the t with him marched until
Jos 8:13 All the t were positioned.
8:13 and the other t were hiding
8:14 he and all his t got up early in
8:14 didn't know there were t behind
8:16 All the t in the city were called
10:33 But Joshua killed him and his t.
11:4 Their t were as numerous as
11:7 Joshua and all his t arrived
Jdg 1:2 "Judah's t will go first.
1:4 Judah's t went into battle,
1:6 Judah's t chased him,
1:7 Judah's t brought Adoni Bezek
1:11 From there Judah's t went to
3:27 of Ephraim ⌊to summon the t⌋.
3:27 So the t of Israel came down
4:6 'Gather t on Mount Tabor.
4:7 and t to you at the Kishon
4:13 his t from Harosheth Haggoyim
5:14 came with its t after Ephraim.
7:1 Gideon) and all the t with him
7:3 Announce to the t,
7:23 to help pursue the t of Midian.
9:34 Abimelech and all his t started
9:35 Then Abimelech and his t rose
9:36 When Gaal saw the t,
9:36 t are coming down from the
9:37 there are t coming down from
9:38 Aren't these the t ⌊whose ruler⌋
9:43 So he took his t, divided them
9:49 So all his t also cut brushwood
10:17 The t of Ammon were
11:20 Sihon assembled all his t.
20:10 Israel to get supplies for the t.
20:10 When the t go to Gibeah in the
20:16 Out of all these t, the best 700
20:22 Israel's t got reinforcements.
20:24 t advanced against Benjamin.
20:26 men of Israel and all the t went
20:29 Then Israel placed t in ambush
20:31 went out to attack Israel's t
1Sm 4:2 Philistines organized their t
4:3 When the t came back to the
4:4 The t sent some men who
4:17 "Our t suffered heavy
11:8 there were 300,000 t from Israel
11:8 Israel and 30,000 t from Judah.
11:14 Samuel told the t, "Come,
11:15 Then all the t went to Gilgal,
13:3 the Philistine t at Geba,
13:4 have defeated the Philistine t,
13:4 All the t rallied behind Saul at
13:8 and the t began to scatter.
13:11 "I saw the t were scattering.
13:15 where Saul counted the t who
13:16 and the t who were with them
13:22 found among all the t who were
13:23 Now, Philistine t had gone out
14:3 The t didn't know Jonathan had
14:11 themselves to the Philistine t.
14:12 has handed the t over to Israel."
14:15 army in the field and all the t
14:17 "Look around," Saul told the t
14:20 Saul and all the t with him
14:24 Saul made the t swear,
14:24 none of his t tasted any food.
14:26 When the t entered the woods,
14:26 because the t were afraid of
14:27 heard that his father forced the t
14:28 "Your father forced the t to take
14:30 If only the t had eaten some of
14:31 t were thoroughly exhausted.
14:32 So the t seized the Philistines'
14:32 The t ate the meat with blood
14:33 "The t are sinning against the
14:34 "Spread out through the t,
14:38 ordered all the leaders of the t,
14:40 the t responded to Saul.
14:45 The t asked Saul, That would
14:45 So the t rescued Jonathan from
15:4 Saul organized the t,
18:13 David led the t out ⌊to battle⌋
23:8 So Saul called together all the t
26:5 and the t were camped around
26:7 among ⌊Saul's⌋ t that night.
26:14 Then David called to the t and
30:8 "Should I pursue these t?

1Sm 30:15 "Will you lead me to these t?"
30:15 and I'll lead you to these t."
30:23 and handed the t that attacked
2Sm 2:26 call off your t from chasing their
2:28 and all the t stopped.
2:30 When he had gathered all the t,
8:6 David put t in the Aramean
8:14 He put t everywhere in Edom,
10:7 he sent Joab and all the elite t.
10:9 he took the select t of Israel
10:10 in charge of the rest of the t.
10:11 are too strong for my ⌊t⌋,
10:11 are too strong for your ⌊t⌋,
10:13 Then Joab and his t advanced
10:15 reassembled ⌊their t⌋.
10:17 David's ⌊t⌋ and fought him.
11:7 him how Joab and the t were
12:28 Gather the rest of the t,
12:29 So David gathered all the t and
12:31 He brought out the t who were
12:31 all the t returned to Jerusalem.
15:17 As the king and his t were
15:23 as all the t were passing by.
15:24 all the t had withdrawn from
15:30 And all of the t with him
16:15 Absalom and all Israel's t came
17:8 He will not camp with the t
17:9 'The t that support Absalom
17:11 to gather all Israel's t from Dan
17:16 or Your Majesty and all the t
17:22 David and all the t with him left
17:28 and food for David and his t:
17:29 "The t in the desert are hungry,
18:1 David called together the t that
18:2 David put a third of the t under
18:2 the king said to the t.
18:3 going ⌊with us⌋," the t said.
18:4 while all the t marched out by
18:5 All the t heard him give all the
18:6 So the t went out to the country
18:16 the t returned from pursuing
19:2 because all the t heard that
19:3 That day the t sneaked into the
19:8 When all the t were told,
19:39 All the t crossed the Jordan
19:40 All the t from Judah and half of
19:40 half of the t from Israel brought
20:12 When the man saw that all the t
20:15 All the t with Joab were trying
23:11 When the t fled from the
23:14 Philistine t were at Bethlehem.
1Ki 16:16 the Israelite t in the camp made
16:17 Omri and the Israelite t with
20:19 and the t followed them.
20:27 When the Israelite ⌊t⌋ had
22:4 My t will do what your troops
22:4 troops will do what your t do.
22:17 "I saw Israel's t scattered in the
22:34 and get me away from these t.
2Ki 3:7 My t will do what your troops
3:7 troops will do what your t do.
6:15 went outside, he saw t, horses,
6:23 After this, Aramean t didn't raid
8:21 and his t fled home.
9:17 in Jezreel saw Jehu's t coming.
9:17 He said, "I see some t."
1Ch 11:13 When the t fled from the
11:16 Philistine t were in Bethlehem.
12:18 made them officers over his t.
18:6 David put t in the Aramean
18:13 He put t in Edom, and all its
19:8 he sent Joab and all the elite t.
19:10 he took the select t of Israel
19:11 in charge of the rest of the t.
19:12 are too strong for my ⌊t⌋,
19:12 are too strong for your ⌊t⌋,
19:14 Then Joab and his t advanced
20:3 He brought out the t who were
20:3 all the t returned to Jerusalem.
2Ch 14:13 Asa and his t pursued them as
17:2 He put t in all the fortified cities
18:3 My t will do what your troops
18:3 troops will do what your t do.
18:3 ⌊We will join⌋ your t in battle.
18:16 "I saw Israel's t scattered in the
18:33 and get me away from these t.
2Ch 20:21 As they went in front of the t,
20:25 When Jehoshaphat and his t
23:10 All the t stood with their
25:9 silver I gave the t from Israel?"
25:10 Then Amaziah dismissed the t
25:11 courageously led his t.
25:13 The t that Amaziah sent back
32:6 military commanders over the t
32:18 language to the t who were
32:18 and terrify the t so that they
Job 19:12 His t assemble against me.
25:3 ⌊limit to the⌋ number of his t?
29:25 I lived like a king among his t,
Jer 4:16 "Hostile t are coming from a
18:22 suddenly send t against them,
26:21 and all his personal t
Eze 4:2 have t ready to attack it,
12:14 him — his staff and all his t.
17:21 The best of your t will die in
23:24 and with a large number of t.
26:7 many people, and many t.
26:12 His t will loot your riches and
30:11 He and his t, the most ruthless
30:11 the most ruthless t among the
38:6 Gomer will come with all its t
38:9 Your t and the many armies
38:22 and burning sulfur on his t and
39:4 mountains of Israel with your t
39:11 be called the valley of Gog's t.
39:15 bone in the valley of Gog's t.
Dan 11:15 Even their best t will not be
Joe 2:11 The t that carry out his
Amo 1:14 its palaces while t are shouting
2:2 of battle while t are shouting
5:3 The city that sends 1,000 t off
5:3 The one that sends 100 t off to
Mic 5:1 Now, gather your t,
5:1 gather your troops, you city of t.

Trophimus (3)

Act 20:4 and Tychicus and T from the
21:29 They had seen T from
2Ti 4:20 in the city of Corinth and I left T

trouble (151)

Gen 34:30 "You have caused me a lot of t!
42:21 That's why we're in t now."
43:6 "Why have you made t for me
Exo 5:19 they were in t when they were
5:22 "Why have you brought this t
Num 11:11 have you brought me this t?
11:15 I can't face this t anymore."
23:21 He doesn't want any t for the
Jdg 10:14 rescue you when you're in t."
11:7 to me now when you're in t?"
Rut 1:13 LORD has sent me so much t."
1Sm 4:8 We're in t now! Who can save
9:20 Don't t yourself about the
13:6 Israelites saw they were in t
14:29 "My father has brought t to the
20:21 and there will be no t.
22:2 Then everyone who was in t,
26:24 life and rescue me from all t."
28:15 answered, "I'm in serious t.
2Sm 4:11 has rescued me from every t.
11:25 'Don't let this thing t you,
12:11 I will stir up t against you
16:8 Now you're in t because you're
19:7 worse than all the t you've had
1Ki 1:29 saved my life from all t lives,
5:4 I have no rival and no t.
11:25 In addition to the t that Hadad
20:7 how this man is looking for t.
2Ki 4:13 she has gone to a lot of t for us.
1Ch 2:7 who caused t for Israel by
2Ch 15:4 But when they were in t,
15:6 them with every kind of t.
28:20 Pilneser made t for him.
28:22 When he had this t,
Neh 2:17 "You see the t we're in.
Job 3:10 I came⌋ or hide my eyes from t.
3:26 And t keeps coming!"
4:5 But t comes to you,
5:6 and t doesn't sprout from the
5:7 But a person is born for t as
14:1 is short-lived and is full of t.
Job 15:35 They conceive t and give birth
27:9 cry when t comes upon him?
36:16 away from the jaws of t into
38:23 have stored up for the time of t,
Psa 9:9 a stronghold in times of t.
10:1 you hide yourself in times of t?
10:6 I'll never face any t."
10:7 T and wrongdoing are on the
10:14 you have taken note of t and
20:1 will answer you in times of t.
22:11 T is near, and there is no one
27:5 in his shelter when there is t.
32:7 You protect me from t.
36:3 ⌊nothing but⌋ t and deception.
36:4 He invents t while lying on his
37:39 He is their fortress in times of t.
41:1 will rescue him in times of t.
46:1 ever-present help in times of t.
49:5 should I be afraid in times of t,
50:15 Call on me in times of t.
54:7 name rescues me from every t.
55:10 T and misery are everywhere.
59:16 a place of safety in times of t.
66:14 ⌊own⌋ mouth when I was in t.
69:17 I am in t, so do not hide your
77:2 On the day I was in t,
81:7 When you were in t,
86:7 When I am in t, I call out to you
90:10 of them ⌊bring⌋ t and misery.
91:15 be with you when you are in t.
94:13 and quiet from times of t while
102:2 face from me when I am in t.
118:5 During times of t I called on the
119:143 T and hardship have found me,
120:1 When I was in t, I cried out to
138:7 I walk into the middle of t,
143:11 are righteous, lead me out of t.
Pro 1:27 when t and anguish come to
11:8 person is rescued from t,
11:15 a stranger's loan will get into t,
11:29 Whoever brings t upon his
12:13 person escapes from t.
12:21 wicked people have lots of t.
13:17 messenger gets into t,
15:6 but t comes along with the
15:27 greedy for unjust gain brings t
16:4 wicked people for the day of t.
16:27 A worthless person plots t,
17:17 and a brother is born to share t.
17:20 tongue ⌊repeatedly⌋ gets into t.
19:28 of wicked people swallow up t.
21:23 tongue keeps himself out of t.
22:3 Sensible people foresee t and
22:8 plants injustice will harvest t,
23:29 Who has t? Who has misery?
24:2 and their lips talk t.
27:10 home when you are in t.
27:12 people foresee t and hide.
31:7 not remember his t anymore.
Ecc 8:5 his commands will avoid t.
12:1 before the days of t come and
Isa 26:16 people have come to you in t.
33:2 Yes, be our savior in times of t.
43:23 offerings or t you by requiring
59:4 They conceive t and give birth
Jer 2:27 But when you're in t,
2:28 rescue you when you're in t.
10:18 land at this time and cause t
11:12 rescue them when they're in t.
11:14 call to me for help in times of t.
14:8 one who saves it in times of t.
16:19 my refuge in times of t.
20:18 All I've seen is t and grief.
51:2 every direction on the day of t.
Eze 5:7 you have caused more t than
30:3 a time of t for the nations.
30:9 in anguish when Egypt is in t.
30:16 Memphis will be in t every day.
35:5 they were in t during their final
Dan 12:1 It will be a time of t unlike any
Mic 2:1 it will be for those who invent t
Nah 1:7 is⌋ a fortress in the day of t.
1:9 This t will never happen again.
Hab 3:7 I see t in the tents of Cushan.
3:16 I wait for the day of t to come to
Zep 1:15 a day of t and distress,

Mat 6:34 day has enough **t** of its own.
7:14 road that lead to life are full of **t**.
Mar 6:48 were in a lot of **t** as they rowed,
7:9 He added, "You have no **t**
Luk 23:2 "We found that he stirs up **t**
Jon 16:33 In the world you'll have **t**.
Act 6:12 The liars stirred up **t** among the
11:19 scattered by the **t** that broke out
15:19 **t** non-Jewish people who
16:20 men are stirring up a lot of **t**
17:6 "Those men who have made **t**
Rom 8:35 Can **t**, distress, persecution,
12:12 your confidence, be patient in **t**,
1Co 7:28 these people will have **t**,
10:25 letting your conscience **t** you.
10:27 letting your conscience **t** you.
Gal 6:17 don't make any **t** for me!
Php 1:17 ambition in order to stir up **t**
3:1 It's no **t** for me to write the
1Th 3:7 us in all our distress and **t**.
Heb 12:15 to cause **t** that corrupts many
Jas 5:13 If any of you are having **t**,
1Pe 1:6 to suffer different kinds of **t**
Rev 2:3 suffered **t** because of my name,

troubled (32)

Gen 35:3 answered me when I was **t**
42:21 We saw how **t** he was when
1Sm 1:16 I've been **t** and tormented."
25:31 you shouldn't have a **t**
2Sm 7:10 place and not be **t** anymore.
24:10 his conscience **t** him.
1Ki 18:18 answered, "I haven't **t** Israel.
1Ch 17:9 place and not be **t** anymore.
Neh 2:2 must be **t** about something."
Job 6:14 should treat a **t** person kindly,
Psa 25:17 Relieve my **t** heart,
Isa 43:24 me with your sins and **t** me
63:9 In all their troubles he was **t**,
Jer 49:23 They are **t** like a sea that can't
Eze 32:9 "'I will make many people **t**
Dan 2:1 He was **t**, but he stayed
2:3 "I had a dream, and I'm **t** by it.
7:15 I, Daniel, was deeply **t**,
Zep 3:18 those among you who are **t**
Zec 10:2 They are **t** because there is no
Mat 9:36 They were **t** and helpless like
Luk 1:12 Zechariah was **t** and overcome
21:25 of the earth will be deeply **t**
Jon 11:33 he was deeply moved and **t**.
12:27 "I am too deeply **t** now to know
13:21 Jesus was deeply **t**.
14:1 "Don't be **t**. Believe in God, and
14:27 So don't be **t** or cowardly.
Act 5:16 who were **t** by evil spirits,
2Co 2:4 I was deeply **t** and anguished.
4:8 In every way we're **t**,
Php 2:26 to see all of you and is **t**

troublemaker (3)

1Ki 18:17 "Is that you, you **t** of Israel?"
Act 24:5 have found this man to be a **t**.
1Pe 4:15 a murderer, thief, criminal, or **t**.

troublemakers (23)

Job 34:8 who travels with **t** and
34:22 deep shadow where **t** can hide.
Psa 5:5 in your sight. You hate all **t**.
6:8 Get away from me, all you **t**,
14:4 Are all those **t**, those who
28:3 with **t** who speak of peace with
36:12 Look at the **t** who have fallen.
53:4 Are all those **t**, those who
59:2 Rescue me from **t**.
64:2 of criminals, from the mob of **t**.
92:7 all **t** blossom ⌊like flowers⌋,
92:9 and all **t** are scattered.
94:4 All **t** brag about themselves.
94:16 stand by my side against **t**?
101:8 to rid the LORD's city of all **t**.
125:5 will lead them away with **t**.
141:4 with people who are **t**.
141:9 me and from the traps set by **t**.
Pro 10:29 but a ruin to those who are **t**.
21:15 is delighted, but **t** are terrified.
Isa 31:2 and against those who help **t**.

Hos 6:8 Gilead is a city filled with **t**.
Gal 5:12 **t** would castrate themselves.

troubles (37)

Gen 41:51 God helped him forget all his **t**
Num 11:1 loud to the LORD about their **t**.
Dtr 1:12 care of your problems, your **t**,
1Sm 10:19 from all your **t** and distresses.
1Ch 22:14 "Despite my **t** I've made
2Ch 20:9 We will cry out to you in our **t**,
Neh 1:3 They are enduring serious **t**
Job 3:18 the captives have no **t** at all.
5:19 will keep you safe from six **t**,
15:24 "The day of darkness **t** him.
Psa 4:1 You have freed me from my **t**.
25:22 Israel, O God, from all its **t**!
31:7 have known the **t** in my soul.
34:6 and saved him from all his **t**.
34:17 rescues them from all their **t**.
34:19 righteous person has many **t**,
38:18 confess my guilt. My sin **t** me.
71:20 me endure many terrible **t**.
88:3 My soul is filled with **t**,
107:6 He rescued them from their **t**.
107:13 He saved them from their **t**.
107:19 He saved them from their **t**.
107:28 He led them from their **t**.
142:2 his presence and tell him my **t**.
Ecc 11:10 Get rid of what **t** you or wears
Isa 30:20 may give you **t** and hardships.
63:9 In all their **t** he was troubled,
65:16 Past **t** are forgotten.
Dan 9:25 during the **t** of those times.
Luk 22:28 "You have stood by me in the **t**
2Co 4:8 but we aren't crushed by our **t**.
Eph 3:13 to become discouraged by the **t**
3:13 In fact, my **t** bring you glory.
Php 4:14 was kind of you to share my **t**.
1Th 3:3 so that these **t** don't disturb any
1Pe 1:7 The purpose of these **t** is to
4:12 don't be surprised by the fiery **t**

troubling (2)

Est 5:3 "What is **t** you, Queen Esther?
7:4 enemy is not worth **t** you about,

trough (3)

Gen 24:20 emptied her jar into the water **t**,
Job 39:9 at night beside your feeding **t**?
Pro 14:4 the feeding **t** is empty,

troughs (3)

Gen 30:38 branches in the **t** directly
30:41 would lay the branches in the **t**
Exo 2:16 They drew water and filled the **t**

true (193)

Gen 18:21 whether these complaints are **t**.
24:49 my master **t** kindness so that
Num 5:21 the curse of this oath comes **t**:
11:23 or not my words come **t**."
15:23 you through Moses holds as **t**
Dtr 6:24 our lives. It's still **t** today.
13:14 If it is **t**, and you can prove that
17:4 If it's **t** and it can be proven that
18:22 says doesn't happen or come **t**,
22:20 But if the charge is **t**,
Jos 7:20 Achan answered Joshua, "It's **t**.
21:45 the nation of Israel came **t**.
22:22 LORD is ⌊the only **t**⌋ God!
22:22 The LORD is ⌊the only **t**⌋ God!
22:34 the LORD Is ⌊the Only **T**⌋ God.
23:14 you has ever failed to come **t**.
23:14 Every single word has come **t**.
23:15 you has come **t** for you.
Jdg 9:57 son of Jerubbaal, came **t**.
13:12 "When your words come **t**,
13:17 When your words come **t**,
Rut 3:12 It is **t** that I am a close relative
2Sm 22:31 of the LORD has proven to be **t**.
1Ki 8:26 David, your servant, come **t**.
8:56 Moses has failed to come **t**.
10:6 words and your wisdom is **t**!
17:24 the LORD from your mouth is **t**."
2Ki 19:17 It is **t**, LORD, that the kings of
2Ch 6:17 to David, your servant, come **t**.

2Ch 9:5 words and your wisdom is **t**!
15:3 Israel was without the **t** God,
31:20 what was good and right and **t**
36:22 Jeremiah was about to come **t**
Ezr 1:1 Jeremiah was about to come **t**
Neh 6:8 of your accusations are **t**.
Est 2:23 investigated and found to be **t**,
Job 9:2 "Yes, I know that this is **t**.
11:6 because ⌊**t**⌋ wisdom is twice
19:4 Even if it were **t** that I've made
Psa 18:30 of the LORD has proven to be **t**.
19:9 decisions of the LORD are **t**.
50:1 The LORD, the only **t** God,
78:20 **T**, he did strike a rock,
105:19 until his prediction came **t**.
Pro 30:5 word of God has proven to be **t**.
Sos 1:9 My **t** love, I compare you to a
1:15 You are beautiful, my **t** love!
2:2 so is my **t** love among the
2:10 up, my **t** love, my beautiful one,
2:13 Get up, my **t** love, my beautiful
4:1 You are beautiful, my **t** love.
4:7 in every way, my **t** love.
5:2 Open to me, my **t** love,
6:4 You are beautiful, my **t** love,
Isa 16:6 but their boasts aren't **t**.
37:18 It is **t**, LORD, that the kings of
42:9 I said in the past has come **t**.
43:9 Then they will say that it is **t**.
Jer 1:12 sure that my words come **t**."
28:6 make your prophecy come **t**
28:9 of the prophet came **t**."
33:10 It's **t**! The cities of Judah and
42:5 "May the LORD be a **t** and
44:28 whose words have come **t**,
50:7 the LORD, their **t** pasture.
Eze 12:23 when every vision will come **t**.
13:6 their predictions don't come **t**.
13:6 that their message will come **t**.
13:7 things that don't come **t**?
13:9 predict things that don't come **t**.
33:33 When all your words come **t** —
33:33 will come **t** — these people
Dan 2:45 The dream is **t**, and you can
3:14 is it **t** that you don't honor my
3:24 "That's **t**, Your Majesty,"
4:33 about Nebuchadnezzar came **t**.
4:37 Everything he does is **t**,
6:12 The king answered, "That's **t**.
8:26 that was explained to you is **t**.
10:1 The message was **t**.
10:21 is inscribed in the **t** writings.
Hos 2:20 I will be **t** to you, my wife.
Mal 2:6 came from his mouth was **t**.
Mat 1:22 through the prophet came **t**:
2:15 through the prophet came **t**:
2:17 the prophet Jeremiah came **t**:
2:23 the prophets had said came **t**:
4:14 prophet Isaiah had said came **t**:
5:17 aside but to make them come **t**.
5:18 before everything has come **t**.
8:17 prophet Isaiah had said came **t**:
12:17 prophet Isaiah had said came **t**:
13:14 make Isaiah's prophecy come **t**:
13:35 the prophet had said came **t**:
21:4 the prophet had said came **t**:
26:56 have written would come **t**."
27:9 Jeremiah had said came **t**,
Mar 11:32 thought of John as a **t** prophet.
14:49 Scriptures say must come **t**."
Luk 1:4 that what you've been told is **t**.
1:20 Everything will come **t** at the
4:21 "This passage came **t** today
18:31 the Son of Man will come **t**.
21:22 is written about it will come **t**.
22:37 written about me will come **t**."
24:41 this seemed too good to be **t**.
24:44 and the Psalms had to come **t**."
Jon 1:47 "Here is a **t** Israelite who is
3:21 But people who do what is **t**
4:23 when the **t** worshipers will
4:37 In this respect the saying is **t**:
5:31 own behalf, what I say isn't **t**.
5:32 what he says about me is **t**.
6:32 you the **t** bread from heaven.
6:55 My flesh is **t** food, and my

Jon 6:55 and my blood is t drink.
7:18 one who sent him is a t teacher
7:28 The one who sent me is t.
8:13 so your testimony isn't t."
8:14 my testimony is t because I
8:17 testimony of two people is t.
8:26 But the one who sent me is t.
10:41 John said about this man is t."
12:38 of the prophet Isaiah came t:
13:18 so that Scripture will come t:
14:2 If that were not t, would I have
15:1 Jesus said,⌋ "I am the t vine,
15:25 in their Scriptures has come t:
17:3 to know you, the only t God,
17:12 So Scripture came t.
18:9 what Jesus had said came t:
18:32 how he would die came t.
19:24 this way the Scripture came t:
19:35 What he says is t,
19:36 that the Scripture would come t:
21:24 know that what he says is t.
Act 1:16 about Judas had to come t.
3:18 of his Messiah come t.
7:1 asked Stephen, "Is this t?"
17:11 to see if what Paul said was t.
21:24 been told about you isn't t.
24:8 him that our accusations are t."
24:9 everything Tertullus said was t.
26:25 What I'm saying is t and sane.
Rom 5:15 it is certainly t that God's
8:29 This is t because he already
9:4 Teachings, the t worship,
16:10 Greet Apelles, a t Christian.
1Co 12:22 The opposite is t. The parts of
14:5 This is t unless he can
15:15 But if it's t that the dead don't
15:54 of Scripture will come t:
2Co 1:17 something is t when it isn't?
1:18 to you isn't false; it's t.
1:19 told you about, was t not false.
1:19 our message was always t.
1:20 God's many promises come t.
2:17 The opposite is t. As Christ's
7:14 everything we told you was t,
7:14 to Titus has also proved to be t.
Eph 5:9 God's approval, and that is t.
5:13 the t character of everything
Php 3:3 We are the ⌊t⌋ circumcised
3:9 The opposite is t! I have God's
4:3 ask you, Syzugus, my t partner,
4:8 things that are t, honorable, fair,
4:17 The opposite is t. I'm looking for
1Ti 5:17 This is especially t if they
2Ti 3:14 have learned and found to be t.
Tit 1:13 That statement is t.
Heb 8:2 place and of the t tent set up
Jas 2:23 The Scripture passage came t.
2:25 The same is t of the prostitute
3:4 The same thing is t for ships.
3:14 that you are wise when it isn't t.
1Pe 3:18 This is t because Christ
2Pe 2:10 This is especially t of those
2:22 proverbs have come t for them:
1Jn 2:8 and the t light is already
2:27 His anointing is t and contains
5:16 This is t for those who commit
3Jn 1:12 know that what we say is t.
Rev 1:7 of him. This is t. Amen.
3:7 The one who is holy, who is t,
3:14 witness who is faithful and t,
6:10 "Holy and t Master,
15:3 way you do them is fair and t,
16:7 your judgments are t and fair."
19:2 His judgments are t and fair.
19:9 "These are the t words of God."
19:11 rider is named Faithful and T.
21:5 words are faithful and t.'"
22:6 words are trustworthy and t.

trumpet (23)

Num 10:4 If only one t blows,
10:5 When they hear the t fanfare,
Neh 4:18 to sound the t alarm was
4:20 When you hear the t,
Hos 5:8 Blow the t in Ramah.
Mat 6:2 don't announce it with t fanfare.
Mat 24:31 his angels with a loud t call,
1Co 14:8 For example, if the t doesn't
15:52 at the sound of the last t.
15:52 Indeed, that t will sound,
1Th 4:16 and with the t ⌊call⌋ of God.
Rev 1:10 a loud voice behind me like a t,
4:1 I heard the first voice like a t
8:7 When the first angel blew his t,
8:8 the second angel blew his t,
8:10 When the third angel blew his t,
8:12 the fourth angel blew his t,
8:13 because of the remaining t
9:1 When the fifth angel blew his t,
9:13 the sixth angel blew his t,
9:14 the sixth angel who had the t,
10:7 angel is ready to blow his t,
11:15 the seventh angel blew his t,

trumpeters (4)

2Ki 11:14 The commanders and the t
2Ch 5:13 the t and singers praised and
23:13 The commanders and the t
Rev 18:22 and t will never be heard in it

trumpet's (1)

Heb 12:19 to a t blast, and to a voice.

trumpets (34)

Num 10:2 "Make two t out of hammered
10:3 When you blow both t,
10:6 When the t sound a second
10:7 the t will blow without
10:8 the priests, will blow the t.
10:9 the t will sound a fanfare.
10:10 blow the t when you sacrifice
10:10 The t will be a reminder for you
29:1 It is a day for ⌊the t to sound⌋ a
31:6 articles and the t for the fanfare.
2Ki 11:14 were rejoicing and blowing t.
12:13 bowls, snuffers, dishes, t,
1Ch 13:8 tambourines, cymbals, and t.
15:24 and Eliezer blew t in front of
15:28 t, cymbals, harps, and lyres.
16:6 and Jahaziel played t all
16:42 Heman and Jeduthun played t,
2Ch 5:12 were 120 priests blowing t.
5:13 Accompanied by t,
7:6 blowing t while all Israel
13:12 His priests will sound their t to
13:14 the priests blew the t,
15:14 blowing of t and rams' horns.
20:28 and t to the LORD's temple in
23:13 were rejoicing and blowing t.
29:26 and the priests had the t.
29:27 songs were accompanied by t
29:28 and the t blew until the burnt
Ezr 3:10 robes took their places with t,
Neh 12:35 So did some priests with t:
12:41 and Hananiah with t,
Psa 98:6 with t and the playing of a
Rev 8:2 and they were given seven t.
8:6 who had the seven t got ready

trust (85)

Exo 18:21 who fear God, men you can t,
Num 14:11 How long will they refuse to t
20:12 and Aaron, "You didn't t me!
Dtr 1:32 you didn't t the LORD your God,
28:52 fortified walls in which you t
Jdg 11:20 But Sihon did not t the
1Sm 22:14 officials can you t like David?
2Ki 17:14 their ancestors who refused to t
18:20 Whom, then, do you t for
18:21 When you t Egypt,
18:24 officers when you t Egypt
18:30 Don't let Hezekiah get you to t
19:10 'Don't let the god whom you t
2Ch 20:20 T the LORD your God,
Job 4:18 God doesn't t his own servants,
8:14 His t is a spider's web.
15:15 If God doesn't t his holy ones,
15:16 how much less will he t the
15:31 He shouldn't t in worthless
31:24 or said to fine gold, 'I t you' ....
39:11 Can you t it just because it's
39:24 eats up the ground and doesn't t
Psa 9:10 who know your name t you,
13:5 But I t your mercy.
25:2 I t you, O my God. Do not let
31:6 to false gods, but I t the LORD.
31:14 I t you, O LORD. I said,
32:10 those who t the LORD.
33:21 In his holy name we t.
37:3 T the LORD, and do good
37:5 T him, and he will act ⌊on your
40:3 They will t the LORD.
49:6 They t their riches and brag
52:8 I t the mercy of God forever and
55:23 half their days. But I will t you.
56:3 when I am afraid, I still t you.
56:4 I t God. I am not afraid. What
56:11 I t God. I am not afraid. What
62:8 T him at all times,
78:7 to t God, to remember what he
78:22 did not believe God or t him
91:2 my God in whom I t."
115:9 Israel, t the LORD.
115:10 of Aaron, t the LORD.
115:11 you fear the LORD, t the LORD.
118:8 on the LORD than to t mortals.
118:9 than to t influential people.
119:42 insults me since I t your word.
125:1 Those who t the LORD are like
143:8 in the morning, because I t you.
146:3 Do not t influential people,
Pro 3:5 T the LORD with all your heart,
21:22 defenses in which they t.
22:19 so that your t may be in the
26:25 do not t him because of the
Isa 26:3 because they t you.
26:4 T the LORD always,
36:5 Whom, then, do you t for
36:6 When you t Egypt,
36:9 officers when you t Egypt
36:15 Don't let Hezekiah get you to t
37:10 'Don't let the god whom you t
42:17 Then those who t idols and
42:19 blind like the one who has my t
50:10 in darkness and have no light t
59:4 People t pointless arguments
Jer 2:37 LORD has rejected those you t.
5:17 destroy the fortified cities you t.
7:4 Do not t the words of this
9:4 Don't t your relatives.
12:6 Don't t them when they say
48:7 Since you t the things you do
49:4 You t your treasures.
49:11 Your widows can t me."
Eze 29:16 Israel will never t Egypt again.
Dan 2:45 true, and you can t that this is
Mic 7:5 Don't t your neighbors.
Zep 3:2 It does not t the LORD.
Luk 16:11 who will t you with wealth that
Jon 5:45 Moses, the one you t,
Act 27:25 I t God that everything will turn
2Co 1:9 ourselves and learn to t God,
Php 3:4 else thinks that he can t
2Ti 1:12 I know whom I t. I'm convinced
Heb 2:13 Jesus says, "I will t him."

trusted (42)

Gen 39:4 that he made him his t servant.
Dtr 32:20 children who can't be t.
Jdg 9:26 Citizens of Shechem t him.
2Ki 18:5 Hezekiah t the LORD God of
1Ch 5:20 prayers because they t him.
2Ch 13:18 of Judah won because they t
Neh 13:13 Since they could be t,
Job 12:20 He makes t advisers unable to
Psa 22:4 Our ancestors t you.
22:4 They t, and you rescued them.
22:5 They t you and were never
26:1 I have t you without wavering.
28:7 My heart t him, so I received
41:9 my closest friend whom I t,
52:7 Instead, he t his great wealth
Isa 16:5 the LORD will set up a t king.
30:12 t oppression and deceit,
Jer 13:25 forgotten me and t false gods.
38:22 These women will say: 'Your t
39:18 your life because you t me,
48:13 was ashamed when it t Bethel.

Eze 16:15 "'But you t your beauty,
Dan 3:28 saved his servants, who t him.
6:23 because he t his God.
Hos 10:13 You have t your own power
Mat 25:21 You proved that you could be t
25:23 You proved that you could be t
27:43 He t God. Let God rescue him
Luk 11:22 in which the strong man t
16:10 Whoever can be t with very
16:10 with very little can also be t
16:11 Therefore, if you can't be t with
16:12 If you can't be t with someone
19:17 You proved that you could be t
1Co 7:25 shown mercy, so I can be t.
1Ti 1:12 Jesus our Lord that he has t me
1:15 is a statement that can be t
3:1 is a statement that can be t:
4:9 is a statement that can be t
2Ti 2:11 is a statement that can be t:
Tit 3:8 is a statement that can be t.
Heb 11:11 Abraham t that God would

trustees (1)

Gal 4:2 control of guardians and t until

trusting (11)

2Ki 18:21 When you trust Egypt, you're t
18:22 "We're t the LORD our God."
Psa 4:5 righteousness by t the LORD.
Isa 2:22 Stop t people. Their life is in
30:15 by being quiet and by t me.
36:6 When you trust Egypt, you're t
36:7 "We're t the LORD our God."
Jer 7:8 "'You are t the words of a
11:19 I was like a t lamb brought to
Act 13:43 to continue t God's good will.
2Co 1:9 that we would stop t ourselves

trusts (21)

Gen 39:8 He t me with everything he
2Ki 18:21 is like for everyone who t him.
Psa 21:7 Indeed, the king t the LORD,
84:12 blessed is the person who t
86:2 Save your servant who t you.
115:8 So does everyone who t them.
135:18 So does everyone who t them.
Pro 11:28 Whoever t his riches will fall,
16:20 is the person who t the LORD.
28:25 whoever t the LORD prospers.
28:26 Whoever t his own heart is a
29:25 but one who t the LORD is
31:11 Her husband t her with ⌊all⌋
Isa 36:6 is like for everyone who t him.
57:13 But whoever t me will possess
Jer 17:5 is the person who t humans,
17:7 is the person who t the LORD.
46:25 and whoever t Pharaoh.
Eze 33:13 But if he t in the right things
Hab 2:18 The one who formed it t
1Th 2:4 God t us to do this because we

trustworthy (19)

2Sm 7:28 and your words are t.
1Ch 9:22 positions because they were t.
Neh 7:2 Hananiah was a t man,
9:13 them fair rules, t teachings,
Psa 33:4 and everything he does is t.
111:7 All his guiding principles are t.
Pro 11:13 but whoever is t in spirit can
14:5 A t witness does not lie,
20:6 someone who is ⌊really⌋ t?
25:13 ⌊so⌋ is a t messenger to those
28:20 A t person has many blessings,
Dan 6:4 wrong because he was t.
1Co 4:2 Managers are required to be t.
Col 1:7 here as a t deacon for Christ
4:7 He is our dear brother, t deacon,
1Ti 3:11 tempers and be t in every way.
Tit 1:9 He must be devoted to the t
Rev 1:5 Christ, the witness, the t one,
22:6 "These words are t and true.

truth (254)

Gen 42:16 We'll see if you're telling the t.
42:20 that you've been telling the t.
Dtr 5:20 "Never avoid the t when you
Jdg 16:17 Finally, he told her the t.
1Ki 3:6 lived in your presence with t,
22:16 to tell me nothing but the t?"
2Ch 18:15 to tell me nothing but the t?"
Psa 15:2 speaks the t within his heart.
25:5 Lead me in your t and teach me
25:10 LORD is ⌊one of⌋ mercy and t
26:3 I walk in the light of your t.
30:9 Will it tell about your t?"
31:5 rescued me, O LORD, God of t.
36:1 There is an inspired t about the
40:10 your t from those assembled
40:11 and your t always protect me.
43:3 Send your light and your t.
45:4 your majesty for the cause of t,
51:6 Yet, you desire t and sincerity.
52:3 prefer lying to speaking the t.
54:5 Destroy them with your t!
57:3 God sends his mercy and his t!
57:10 Your t reaches the skies.
61:7 May mercy and t protect him.
69:13 me with the t of your salvation.
85:10 Mercy and t have met.
85:11 T sprouts from the ground,
86:11 so that I may live in your t.
89:14 Mercy and t stand in front of
89:33 away from him or allow my t
91:4 His t is your shield and armor.
96:13 and its people with his t.
108:4 Your t reaches the skies.
111:7 are done with t and justice.
111:8 carried out with t and decency.
119:43 single word of t from my mouth.
119:160 There is nothing but t in your
132:11 This is a t he will not take
138:2 because of your mercy and t.
Pro 3:3 not let mercy and t leave you.
8:7 My mouth expresses the t,
12:19 The word of t lasts forever,
20:28 Mercy and t protect a king,
22:21 you the words of t so that you
23:23 Buy t (and do not sell it),
Ecc 12:10 the words of t very carefully.
Isa 33:15 right and speaks the t will live.
59:14 T has fallen in the street,
59:15 T is missing. Those who turn
65:16 be blessed by the God of T.
65:16 will swear by the God of T.
Jer 5:1 what is right and seeks the t.
5:3 LORD, your eyes look for the t.
7:28 T has disappeared and
9:5 No one speaks the t.
Dan 7:16 to tell me the t about all this.
7:19 Then I wanted to know the t
8:12 It threw t on the ground.
9:13 dedicating ourselves to your t.
11:2 I am about to tell you is the t.
Hos 5:9 I will make the t known among
Amo 5:10 by anyone who speaks the t.
Zec 8:3 will be called the City of T.
8:16 Speak the t to each other.
8:19 So love t and peace.
Mat 5:18 I can guarantee this t:
5:26 I can guarantee this t:
6:2 I can guarantee this t:
6:5 I can guarantee this t:
6:16 I can guarantee this t:
8:10 "I can guarantee this t:
10:15 I can guarantee this t:
10:23 I can guarantee this t:
10:42 I can guarantee this t:
11:11 "I can guarantee this t:
13:17 I can guarantee this t:
16:28 I can guarantee this t:
17:20 I can guarantee this t:
18:3 "I can guarantee this t:
18:13 I can guarantee this t:
18:18 I can guarantee this t:
19:23 "I can guarantee this t:
19:28 "I can guarantee this t:
21:21 "I can guarantee this t:
21:31 "I can guarantee this t:
22:16 we know that you tell the t and
22:16 and that you teach the t about
23:36 I can guarantee this t:
24:2 I can guarantee this t:
Mat 24:34 "I can guarantee this t:
24:47 I can guarantee this t:
25:40 'I can guarantee this t:
25:45 'I can guarantee this t:
26:13 I can guarantee this t:
26:21 "I can guarantee this t:
26:34 "I can guarantee this t:
Mar 3:28 "I can guarantee this t:
5:33 of him and told him the whole t.
8:12 I can guarantee this t:
9:1 "I can guarantee this t:
9:41 I can guarantee this t:
10:15 I can guarantee this t:
10:29 "I can guarantee this t:
11:23 I can guarantee this t:
12:14 we know that you tell the t.
12:32 You've told the t that there is
12:43 "I can guarantee this t:
13:30 "I can guarantee this t:
14:9 I can guarantee this t:
14:18 "I can guarantee this t:
14:25 "I can guarantee this t:
14:30 "I can guarantee this t:
Luk 4:24 "I can guarantee this t:
4:25 "I can guarantee this t:
9:27 "I can guarantee this t:
11:51 Yes, I can guarantee this t:
12:37 I can guarantee this t:
12:44 I can guarantee this t:
18:17 I can guarantee this t:
18:29 "I can guarantee this t:
21:3 He said, "I can guarantee this t:
21:32 "I can guarantee this t:
23:43 "I can guarantee this t:
Jon 1:7 John came to declare the t
1:8 to declare the t about the light.
1:14 a glory full of kindness and t.
1:15 (John declared the t about him
1:17 but kindness and t came into
1:51 "I can guarantee this t:
3:3 "I can guarantee this t:
3:5 "I can guarantee this t:
3:11 I can guarantee this t:
4:18 husband. You've told the t."
4:23 the Father in spirit and t.
4:24 must worship in spirit and t."
5:19 "I can guarantee this t:
5:24 I can guarantee this t:
5:25 "I can guarantee this t:
5:33 and he testified to the t.
6:26 "I can guarantee this t:
6:32 "I can guarantee this t:
6:47 I can guarantee this t:
6:53 "I can guarantee this t:
8:32 You will know the t,
8:32 and the t will set you free."
8:34 "I can guarantee this t:
8:40 man who has told you the t that
8:44 He doesn't know what the t is.
8:45 believe me because I tell the t.
8:46 If I'm telling the t, why don't you
8:51 I can guarantee this t:
8:58 "I can guarantee this t:
10:1 "I can guarantee this t:
10:7 "I can guarantee this t:
12:24 I can guarantee this t:
13:16 I can guarantee this t:
13:20 "I can guarantee this t:
13:21 "I can guarantee this t:
13:38 I can guarantee this t:
14:6 am the way, the t, and the life.
14:12 "I can guarantee this t:
14:17 That helper is the Spirit of T.
15:26 This helper, the Spirit of T who
15:26 will declare the t about me.
15:27 You will declare the t,
16:7 However, I am telling you the t:
16:13 When the Spirit of T comes,
16:13 he will guide you into the full t.
16:20 I can guarantee this t:
16:23 I can guarantee this t:
17:17 "Use the t to make them holy.
17:17 them holy. Your words are t.
17:19 will use the t to be holy.
18:23 But if I've told the t,
18:37 this reason: to testify to the t.

Jon 18:37 belongs to the **t** listens to me."
18:38 Pilate said to him, "What is **t**?"
19:35 he is telling the **t** so that you,
21:18 I can guarantee this **t**:
Act 13:10 Quit trying to distort the **t** about
20:30 and say things that distort the **t**.
23:11 You've told the **t** about me in
23:11 Now you must tell the **t** about
Rom 1:18 suppress the **t** by their immoral
1:25 have exchanged God's **t**
2:8 refuse to believe the **t** and who
2:20 and **t** in Moses' Teachings.
7:21 So I've discovered this **t**:
9:1 I'm telling you the **t**.
15:8 people to reveal God's **t**.
1Co 5:8 bread of purity and **t** that has no
13:6 but it is happy with the **t**.
2Co 4:2 clearly reveal the **t** to everyone.
6:8 is wrong and to defend the **t**.
11:10 As surely as I have Christ's **t**,
12:6 Instead, I would be telling the **t**.
13:8 can't do anything against the **t**
13:8 the truth but only to help the **t**.
Gal 2:5 so that the **t** of the Good News
2:14 not properly following the **t**
4:16 enemy for telling you the **t**?
5:7 from being influenced by the **t**?
Eph 1:13 and believed the message of **t**,
4:15 as we lovingly speak the **t**,
4:21 his ways. The **t** is in Jesus.
4:25 Speak the **t** to each other,
6:14 Fasten **t** around your waist like
Php 1:7 defending and confirming the **t**
Col 1:5 which is the message of **t**.
2Th 2:10 those who refused to love the **t**
2:12 who did not believe the **t**,
2:13 devotion and faith in the **t**.
1Ti 2:4 to be saved and to learn the **t**.
2:7 not Jewish about faith and **t**.
2:7 I'm telling you the **t**.
3:15 pillar and foundation of the **t**.
4:2 will speak lies disguised as **t**.
4:3 who believe and know the **t**.
6:5 have been robbed of the **t**.
2Ti 2:15 to teach the word of **t** correctly.
2:18 They have abandoned the **t**.
2:25 and lead them to know the **t**.
3:7 never able to recognize the **t**.
3:8 so these men oppose the **t**.
4:4 will refuse to listen to the **t**
Tit 1:1 knowledge of the **t** that leads
1:14 who are always rejecting the **t**.
Heb 2:1 won't drift away from the **t**.
10:26 after we have learned the **t**,
10:32 when you first learned the **t**.
Jas 1:18 us life through the word of **t**
5:19 one of you wanders from the **t**,
1Pe 1:22 yourselves by obeying the **t**.
2Pe 1:12 in the **t** that you now
2:2 others to dishonor the way of **t**.
1Jn 1:8 and the **t** is not in us.
2:4 The **t** isn't in that person.
2:8 It's a **t** that exists in Christ and
2:21 to you because you know the **t**,
2:21 because you don't know the **t**.
2:21 no lie ever comes from the **t**.
3:19 know that we belong to the **t**
4:6 we can tell the Spirit of **t** from
5:6 because the Spirit is the **t**.
2Jn 1:1 I love because we share the **t**.
1:1 knows the **t** also loves you.
1:2 We love you because of the **t**
1:3 who in **t** and love is the
1:4 your children living in the **t** as
3Jn 1:1 I love because we share the **t**.
1:3 are living according to the **t**.
1:4 are living according to the **t**.
1:8 with them in spreading the **t**.
1:12 Everyone, including the **t** itself,

truthful (6)

Psa 5:9 Nothing in their mouths is **t**.
Pro 12:17 A **t** witness speaks honestly,
Jon 3:33 I have affirmed that God is **t**.
8:44 He has never been **t**.
Rom 3:7 by showing that God is **t**,
1Jn 1:6 we're lying. We aren't being **t**.

truthfully (3)

Isa 59:4 and no one pleads his case **t**.
Mar 12:14 you teach the way of God **t**.
Luk 20:21 you teach the way of God **t**.

truthfulness (1)

2Co 6:7 **t**, and the presence of God's

truths (2)

Heb 5:12 to teach you the elementary **t**
6:1 the elementary **t** about Christ

try (55)

Num 20:18 If you **t**, we'll come out and
Dtr 28:68 There you will **t** to sell
Rut 3:1 shouldn't I **t** to look for a home
1Sm 3:13 but he didn't **t** to stop them.
29:4 Is this man going to **t** to regain
2Sm 15:6 king to have him **t** their case.
1Ki 18:21 "How long will you **t** to have it
2Ki 3:26 he took 700 swordsmen to **t** to
2Ch 10:7 are good to these people and **t**
Neh 5:12 "We'll return it and not **t** to get it
Job 11:19 and many people will **t** to gain
13:9 Will you **t** to trick him as one
17:10 all of you, come and **t** again!
23:2 I **t** hard to control my sighing.
34:9 do any good to **t** to please God.'
Psa 38:20 they accuse me because I **t**
62:3 How long will you **t** to murder
63:9 But those who **t** to destroy my
139:18 If I **t** to count them,
140:4 people. They **t** to trip me.
Pro 19:6 Many **t** to win the kindness of
Isa 7:13 "Isn't it enough that you **t** the
7:13 Must you also **t** the patience of
22:4 Don't **t** to comfort me because
29:15 it will be for those who **t**
Hos 12:1 The people of Ephraim **t** to
12:1 try to catch the wind and **t**
Zec 12:3 All who **t** to lift it will be
Mal 1:8 **T** offering it to your governor.
1:9 "Now **t** asking God to be kind
Mat 13:13 don't even **t** to understand.
15:10 "Listen and **t** to understand!
23:13 others to enter when they **t**.
Mar 7:14 and **t** to understand!
Luk 13:24 "**T** hard to enter through the
13:24 that many will **t** to enter,
16:15 So Jesus said to them, "You **t**
17:33 Those who **t** to save their lives
22:53 every day and you didn't **t**
Jon 5:30 are right because I don't **t**
18:31 and **t** him by your law."
Act 27:39 So they decided to **t** to run the
Rom 1:18 thing people do as they **t**
10:3 So they **t** to set up their own
1Co 10:33 I **t** to please everyone in every
14:12 **t** to excel in them so that you
2Co 5:11 we **t** to persuade others.
Gal 5:4 Those of you who **t** to earn
1Th 2:4 We don't **t** to please people but
2:16 because they **t** to keep us from
5:15 Instead, always **t** to do what is
1Ti 4:3 They will **t** to stop others from
2Ti 3:12 Those who **t** to live a godly life
Heb 12:14 **T** to live peacefully with
12:14 and **t** to live holy lives,

trying (60)

Gen 19:11 so that they gave up **t**
Num 32:14 You're a bunch of sinners **t** to
35:23 and you weren't **t** to harm him.
Dtr 13:5 He was **t** to lead you away
13:10 to death because they were **t**
1Sm 19:2 "My father Saul is **t** to kill you.
20:1 against your father that he's **t**
23:26 and his men, **t** to capture them.
24:9 rumors that I am **t** to harm you?
24:11 but you are **t** to ambush me in
25:26 enemies and those who are **t**
28:9 Why are you **t** to trap me and
2Sm 16:11 flesh and blood, is **t** to kill me.
20:15 All the troops with Joab were **t**
2Sm 20:19 Are you **t** to destroy a mother
1Ki 19:10 and they're **t** to take my life."
19:14 and they're **t** to take my life."
2Ki 5:7 and understand that he's **t**
1Ch 21:3 Why are you **t** to do this?
Neh 6:9 They were all **t** to intimidate us.
6:14 have been **t** to intimidate me."
Job 2:3 You're **t** to provoke me into
13:25 Are you **t** to make a fluttering
13:25 a fluttering leaf tremble or **t**
19:5 If you are **t** to make yourselves
Psa 37:19 not be put to shame in **t** times.
Ecc 1:14 ⌊It's like⌋ **t** to catch the wind.
1:17 I know that this is ⌊like⌋ **t**
2:11 ⌊It was like⌋ **t** to catch the
2:17 ⌊It was like⌋ **t** to catch the
2:26 ⌊It's like⌋ **t** to catch the wind.
4:4 ⌊It's like⌋ **t** to catch the wind.
4:6 handfuls of hard work and of **t**
4:16 ⌊It's like⌋ **t** to catch the wind.
6:9 ⌊It's like⌋ **t** to catch the wind.
Jer 38:4 This man is not **t** to help these
38:4 he's **t** to hurt them."
Lam 4:17 **t** in vain to find help.
Eze 24:12 "'I have worn myself out **t** to
Dan 2:8 "I'm sure you're **t** to buy some
Luk 6:19 The entire crowd was **t** to
16:16 and everyone is **t** to force their
Jon 5:7 While I'm **t** to get there,
16:19 So he said to them, "Are you **t**
Act 13:10 Quit **t** to distort the truth about
17:18 is this babbling fool **t** to say?"
21:31 As the people were **t** to kill
28:23 He was **t** to convince them
Rom 2:4 it is God's kindness that is **t**
9:30 people who were not **t**
11:3 and they're **t** to take my life."
1Co 10:22 Are we **t** to make the Lord
2Co 5:12 We are not **t** to show you our
10:9 don't want you to think that I'm **t**
12:19 thinking all along that we're **t**
Gal 1:10 Am I **t** to please people?
1:10 If I were still **t** to please people,
6:12 out of a physical thing are **t**
2Pe 3:1 In both letters I'm **t** to refresh
1Jn 2:26 those who are **t** to deceive you.

Tryphaena (1)

Rom 16:12 Greet **T** and Tryphosa,

Tryphosa (1)

Rom 16:12 Greet Tryphaena and **T**,

Tubal (8)

Gen 10:2 Javan, **T**, Meshech, and Tiras.
1Ch 1:5 Javan, **T**, Meshech, and Tiras.
Isa 66:19 Lud, Meshech, Rosh, **T**, Javan,
Eze 27:13 People from Greece, **T**,
32:26 "Meshech and **T** are there with
38:2 nations of⌋ Meshech and **T**.
38:3 chief prince of Meshech and **T**.
39:1 chief prince of Meshech and **T**.

Tubalcain (1)

Gen 4:22 Zillah also had a son, **T**,

Tubalcain's (1)

Gen 4:22 **T** sister was Naamah.

tubes (1)

Job 40:18 Its bones are bronze **t**.

tumbleweeds (1)

Psa 83:13 blow them away like **t**,

tumors (5)

1Sm 5:6 in the vicinity of Ashdod with **t**.
5:9 and they were covered with **t**.
5:12 didn't die were struck with **t**.
6:4 "Five gold **t** and five gold mice
6:5 Make models of your **t** and your

tune (5)

1Sm 16:16 comes to you, he'll strum a **t**,
16:23 took the lyre and strummed a **t**.
18:10 while David strummed a **t**

1Sm 19:9 David was strumming a **t**.
1Co 14:7 tell what **t** is being played?

tunic (2)

1Sm 17:38 Saul put his battle **t** on David;
18:4 to David along with his battle **t**,

tunnel (1)

2Ki 20:20 how he made the pool and **t**

turban (16)

Exo 28:4 the chief priest's **t**,
28:37 it so that it's on the front of the **t**.
28:39 Make the **t** of fine linen,
29:6 Put his **t** on him, and fasten the
39:28 also made the chief priest's **t**
39:31 to it and tied it on top of the **t**.
Lev 8:9 He put the **t** on him and
8:9 crown) to the front of the **t** as
16:4 He must wear a linen belt and **t**.
Job 29:14 and it was my robe and my **t**.
Isa 22:18 will wrap you up tightly like a **t**.
61:10 a bridegroom with a priest's **t**,
Eze 21:26 LORD says: Take off your **t**,
24:17 Tie on your **t**, and put on your
Zec 3:5 "Put a clean **t** on his head."
3:5 They put a clean **t** on his head

turbans (7)

Exo 28:40 and **t** for Aaron's sons.
29:9 and put **t** on them. Tie belts
39:28 and the other beautiful **t** out
Lev 8:13 and put **t** on them as the LORD
Eze 23:15 their waists and flowing **t**
24:23 Leave your **t** on your heads and
44:18 They must wear linen **t** on their

turmoil (6)

2Ch 15:5 living in the land had a lot of **t**.
Est 3:15 but the city of Susa was in **t**.
Psa 38:8 I roar because my heart's in **t**.
46:6 Nations are in **t**, and kingdoms
55:4 My heart is in **t**. The terrors of
Pro 15:16 LORD than great treasure and **t**.

turn (346)

Exo 4:9 from the Nile will **t** into blood
7:17 and the water will **t** into blood.
7:19 so that they **t** into blood.
8:16 the dust will **t** into gnats.'"
Lev 19:4 "Don't **t** to worthless gods or
19:29 or the country will **t** to
19:31 "Don't **t** to psychics or
20:6 "I will condemn people who **t**
Num 14:25 Tomorrow you must **t** around,
22:26 where there was no room to **t**
25:4 This will **t** the LORD's anger
27:7 **T** their father's property over to
27:8 **t** his property over to his
32:15 If you **t** away from him,
Dtr 1:40 **T** around, go back into the
7:4 These people will **t** your
11:16 or you'll be tempted to **t** away
11:28 if you **t** from the way I'm
17:17 or he will **t** away ⌊from God⌋.
23:14 you and **t** away from you.
30:17 But your hearts might **t** away,
31:17 I will abandon them and **t** away
31:18 On that day I will certainly **t**
31:20 they will **t** to other gods and
31:29 thoroughly corrupt and **t** from
32:20 He said, "I will **t** away from
Jos 1:7 Don't **t** away from them.
22:29 LORD or to **t** back today from
23:6 Don't **t** away from them.
23:12 "But if you **t** away and go along
24:20 he will **t** and bring disaster on
24:23 **T** yourselves entirely over to
Jdg 20:39 Then the men of Israel would **t**
Rut 1:16 Don't make me **t** back from
1Sm 6:3 he would not **t** his anger away
6:12 on the road and didn't **t** right
7:8 "Don't **t** a deaf ear to us!
12:20 But don't **t** away from the
12:21 Don't **t** away to follow other
22:17 "**T** and kill the LORD's priests
1Sm 22:18 "You **t** and attack the priests."
2Sm 1:22 Jonathan's bow did not **t** away,
2:21 refused to **t** away from him.
2:23 But Asahel refused to **t** away.
5:6 could **t** you away" (meaning
16:12 my misery and **t** his curse into
22:41 You made my enemies **t** their
24:1 David to **t** against Israel.
1Ki 8:33 But when your people **t** to you,
8:35 and **t** away from their sin
9:6 dare to **t** away from me
17:3 "Leave here, **t** east,
22:34 his chariot driver, "**T** around,
2Ki 3:3 Joram would not **t** away from
10:29 But Jehu did not **t** away from
10:31 He didn't **t** away from the sins
13:6 But they didn't **t** away from the
14:24 He didn't **t** away from any of the
15:9 He didn't **t** away from the sins
15:24 He didn't **t** away from the sins
15:28 He did not **t** away from the sins
17:13 "**T** from your evil ways,
19:16 **T** your ear toward me,
19:25 you will **t** fortified cities into
23:26 the LORD still didn't **t** his hot,
1Ch 12:23 Hebron to **t** Saul's kingship over
2Ch 6:24 But when your people **t**,
6:26 and **t** away from their sin
7:14 and **t** from their evil ways,
7:19 descendants **t** away from me
18:33 the chariot driver, "**T** around,
29:10 that he may **t** his burning anger
30:8 and he will **t** his burning anger
30:9 He will not **t** his face away
36:13 with that he refused to **t** back
Neh 4:4 **T** their insults back on them,
9:26 who warned them to **t** back
9:35 they didn't serve you or **t** away
Est 2:12 Each young woman had her **t**
2:15 When Esther's **t** came to go to
9:25 against the Jews should **t** back
Job 1:4 (Each brother took his **t** having
3:9 Let its stars **t** dark before dawn.
5:1 of the holy ones will you **t**?
15:13 when you **t** against God and
23:9 If I **t** southward, I can't see him.
23:11 on his path and did not **t** from it.
33:17 ⌊He warns them⌋ to **t** away
33:30 to **t** their souls away from the
36:10 them to **t** away from wrong.
36:18 Don't let a large bribe **t** you ⌊to
36:21 Don't **t** to evil, because you
41:28 Stones from a sling **t** to dust
Psa 17:6 **T** your ear toward me.
18:40 You made my enemies **t** their
21:12 They **t** their backs ⌊and flee⌋
25:16 **T** to me, and have pity on me.
27:9 Do not angrily **t** me away.
28:1 do not **t** a deaf ear to me.
31:2 **T** your ear toward me.
34:14 **T** away from evil, and do good.
45:10 **T** your ear ⌊toward me⌋.
49:4 I will **t** my attention to a
55:22 **T** your burdens over to the
69:16 unlimited compassion, **t** to me.
71:2 **T** your ear toward me,
73:10 That is why God's people **t** to
74:3 **T** your steps toward these
78:1 **T** your ears to the words from
80:18 Then we will never **t** away
81:14 I would **t** my power against
83:1 Do not **t** a deaf ear to me.
86:1 **T** your ear ⌊toward me⌋,
86:16 **T** toward me, and have pity on
88:2 **T** your ear to hear my cries.
90:3 You **t** mortals back into dust
102:2 **T** your ear toward me.
102:17 He will **t** his attention to the
109:1 do not **t** a deaf ear to me.
114:5 what made you **t** back?
119:29 **T** me away from a life of lies.
119:37 **T** my eyes away from
119:79 Let those who fear you **t** to me
119:116 Do not **t** my hope into
119:132 **T** toward me, and have pity on
139:11 the light around me **t** into night,
Pro 1:23 "**T** to me when I warn you.
3:7 and **t** away from evil.
4:5 Do not **t** away from the words
4:15 **T** away from it, and keep on
5:7 and do not **t** away from what I
9:4 "Whoever is gullible **t** in here!"
9:16 "Whoever is gullible **t** in here!"
13:14 of life to **t** ⌊one⌋ away from
14:27 of life to **t** ⌊one⌋ away from
15:24 in order to **t** him away from
22:6 is old he will not **t** away from it.
24:18 and he will **t** his anger away
28:21 because some people will **t** on
29:8 but wise people **t** away anger.
Ecc 2:21 Yet, he must **t** over his estate
2:26 The sinner must **t** his wealth
7:7 Oppression can **t** a wise
8:7 tell them how things will **t** out?
11:6 them will ⌊**t** out⌋ equally well.
12:2 and the stars **t** dark,
Sos 2:17 flee, **t** around, my beloved.
6:1 Where did your beloved **t**?
6:5 **T** your eyes away from me.
Isa 1:15 I will **t** my eyes away from you.
1:25 I will **t** my power against you.
5:20 who **t** darkness into light and
5:20 who **t** what is bitter into
14:24 It will **t** out exactly as I've
14:27 Who can **t** it back?
19:2 "I will **t** one Egyptian against
19:3 They will **t** to idols,
22:4 That is why I say, "**T** away
24:1 The LORD is going to **t** the
27:9 This is the way they will **t** from
27:9 from their sins — when they **t** all
29:16 You **t** things upside down!
29:22 Jacob's face will no longer **t**
37:17 **T** your ear toward me,
37:26 you will **t** fortified cities into
41:15 You will **t** the hills into straw.
41:18 I will **t** deserts into lakes.
41:18 I will **t** dry land into springs.
42:15 I will **t** rivers into islands.
42:16 I will **t** darkness into light in
44:25 I make wise men retreat and **t**
45:22 **T** to me and be saved,
49:11 I will **t** all my mountains into
50:2 and I **t** rivers into deserts.
50:5 nor will I **t** away ⌊from him⌋.
50:6 I will not **t** my face away from
53:3 from whom people **t** their faces,
59:15 Those who **t** away from evil
59:20 in Jacob who **t** from rebellion,"
Jer 2:35 God will **t** his anger from me,
3:19 and wouldn't **t** away from me.
4:28 and I won't **t** back.
5:3 They refuse to **t** back.
6:8 or I will **t** away from you.
8:6 They don't **t** away from their
8:8 pens to **t** these teachings into
9:11 I will **t** Jerusalem into a pile of
11:15 sacrifices **t** disaster away from
13:16 but the LORD will **t** it into the
17:3 I will **t** your wealth and all your
17:8 Its leaves will **t** green.
17:13 Those who **t** away from you
18:11 **T** from your evil ways,
18:20 in order to **t** your anger away
22:6 I will certainly **t** it into a desert,
23:20 the LORD will not **t** back until
25:5 The prophets said, '**T** from your
25:9 I'm going to destroy them and **t**
25:12 I will **t** Babylon into a
26:3 and they'll **t** from their evil
26:6 I will **t** this city into something
30:24 anger will not **t** back until
31:13 I will **t** their mourning into joy.
31:18 **T** me, and I will be turned,
31:39 and then it will **t** to Goah.
32:40 they will never **t** away from me.
35:15 "**T** from your evil ways,
36:3 and they will **t** from their
36:7 and they will **t** from their evil
44:5 You wouldn't **t** from your
46:21 They will **t** and run away
49:8 **T** and run. Hide in deep caves,

Jer 49:24 They t to flee, but panic grips
50:5 which road goes to Zion and t
50:16 Everyone will t to his own
Lam 1:13 He made me t back.
3:30 They should t their cheeks to
Eze 1:9 they did not t as they moved.
1:12 and they didn't t as they moved.
3:19 and they don't t from their
3:20 If righteous people t from living
4:3 T your face toward the city as
4:7 T your face toward the
4:8 not be able to t from one side
5:14 I will t you into a wasteland
7:22 I will t my face away from the
13:22 not to t from their wicked
14:6 T away from your idols,
14:15 they make it childless and t
15:7 I will t against the people of
15:7 because I will t against them.
15:8 I will t the country into a
18:23 "I want them to t from their evil
18:30 T away from all the rebellious
20:46 "Son of man, t to the south,
21:2 "Son of man, t to Jerusalem,
21:27 I will t this place into ruins!
22:25 They t many women into
25:2 "Son of man, t to the
25:5 I will t Rabbah into a pasture
25:5 and I will t Ammon into a
25:13 I will t the land into ruins from
26:4 up the dust and t Tyre into
26:14 I will t you into bare rock.
26:19 I will t your city into ruins like
26:21 I will t you into a terror,
28:21 "Son of man, t to Sidon and
29:2 "Son of man, t to Pharaoh,
29:10 I will t Egypt into a pile of
30:18 At Tahpanhes the day will t
32:15 I will t Egypt into a wasteland.
33:9 person to t from his ways
33:9 and he doesn't t from them,
33:11 Rather, I want them to t from
33:11 T from your wicked ways!
33:28 I will t the land into a barren
35:2 "Son of man, t to Mount Seir,
35:4 I will t your cities into ruins,
35:7 I will t Mount Seir into a barren
35:9 I will t you into a permanent
35:14 will be glad when I t you into
36:9 I will t to you, and you will be
38:2 "Son of man, t to Gog from the
38:4 I will t you around and put
39:2 I will t you around and lead
39:21 how I will t my power against
Dan 5:10 frighten you, and don't t pale.
9:16 t your anger and fury away from
11:2 he will t everyone against the
11:18 Then he will t his attention to
11:19 He will t back toward the
11:30 will be discouraged and t back.
Hos 2:3 I will t her into a dry and barren
2:12 I will t her vineyards into a
3:5 After that, the Israelites will t
4:7 So I will t their glory into
7:10 you don't t to the LORD your
11:7 My people are determined to t
Joe 2:10 The sun and the moon t dark,
3:15 sun and the moon will t dark.
Amo 1:8 I will t my power against Ekron.
5:7 You, Israel, t justice into
8:10 I will t your festivals into
Oba 1:16 so all nations will drink in t.
Jnh 3:8 T from your wicked ways and
3:9 his plans and t from his burning
Mic 1:6 So I will t Samaria into a pile of
3:6 and the day will t dark for them.
7:17 They will t away from your
Zep 2:13 He will t Nineveh into a
Zec 1:4 T from your evil ways and your
13:7 Then I will t my hand against
Mat 3:2 "T to God and change the way
4:17 "T to God and change the way
5:39 t your other cheek to him as
5:42 Don't t anyone away who
10:35 I came to t a man against his
24:18 in the field should not t back
Mat 24:29 the sun will t dark,
26:58 to see how this would t out.
Mar 6:12 told people that they should t
9:39 in my name can t around
13:16 in the field should not t back
13:24 the sun will t dark,
Luk 13:3 But if you don't t to God and
13:5 But if you don't t to God and
16:30 they will t to God and change
17:31 are in the field shouldn't t back.
24:47 Jesus people must be told to t
Jon 6:37 I will never t away anyone who
12:40 And they never t to me for
16:20 your pain will t to happiness.
Act 2:38 "All of you must t to God and
3:19 and t to God to have your
11:18 people who are not Jewish to t
13:46 we are now going to t to
14:15 News to you to t you away from
17:30 everyone everywhere to t
21:28 everywhere to t against
26:18 You will open their eyes and t
26:20 and acted and to t to God.
27:25 I trust God that everything will t
28:27 And they never t to me for
1Co 9:15 have anyone t my bragging into
15:23 to each person in his own t.
Gal 4:9 So how can you t back again
5:13 Don't t this freedom into an
6:1 that person t away from doing
Php 2:23 things are going to t out for me.
1Ti 6:20 T away from pointless
2Ti 4:4 to the truth and t to myths.
Heb 10:39 belong with those who t back
12:25 escape if we t away from God,
Jas 4:9 T your laughter into mourning
1Pe 3:11 They must t away from evil
5:7 T all your anxiety over to God
2Pe 2:21 to know it and t their backs
3:9 to have an opportunity to t
1Jn 1:10 we t God into a liar and his
2:28 and when he comes we won't t
Rev 2:21 I gave her time to t to me and
2:21 but she refuses to t away from
2:22 unless they t away from what
9:20 these plagues still did not t
9:21 They did not t away from
11:6 They have authority to t water

turned (295)

Gen 3:24 and a flaming sword that t
9:23 They t their faces away so that
11:9 because there the LORD t the
18:22 From there the men t and went
19:26 Lot's wife looked back and t
42:28 They trembled and t to each
Exo 4:4 and it t back into a staff as he
7:15 the staff that t into a snake.
7:20 water in the river t into blood.
7:23 Pharaoh t and went back to his
8:17 It t into gnats that bit people
8:17 in Egypt t into gnats.
10:6 Moses t and left Pharaoh.
14:21 with a strong east wind and t
32:6 which t into an orgy.
32:8 They've already t from the way
32:15 Moses t and went down the
36:3 Moses t over to them all the
Lev 13:3 the diseased area has t white,
13:4 and the hair has not t white,
13:10 there is a white sore that has t
13:13 His body has t white.
13:17 the diseased area has t white,
13:20 skin and its hair has t white,
13:25 on the affected area has t white
Num 12:10 Aaron t to her and saw she
14:43 Now that you have t away from
16:42 When they t toward the tent of
20:21 the Israelites t around and went
21:33 Then they t and followed the
22:23 the donkey t off the road into a
22:33 The donkey saw me and t
22:33 If it had not t away from me,
24:1 He t toward the desert,
25:11 t my fury away from the
33:7 They moved from Etham and t
Dtr 2:8 We t off the road that goes
3:1 Next we t and followed the
9:12 They've quickly t from the way
9:15 So I t and went down the
9:16 You had quickly t from the way
23:5 Instead, he t Balaam's curse
Jos 8:20 had now t back on them.
8:21 they t and attacked the men of
11:10 Then Joshua t back and
22:16 Today you have t away from
22:18 You have t away from
Jdg 2:17 They quickly t from the ways
3:19 However, Ehud t around at the
6:14 The LORD t to him and said,
7:13 t upside down, and fell flat."
9:23 Shechem t against Abimelech.
9:31 They have t the city against
11:8 "The reason we've t to you
18:23 But the people of Dan t around
18:26 so he t around and went home.
20:40 the men of Benjamin t around
20:41 Then the men of Israel t around,
20:42 They t in front of Israel toward
20:45 The others t and fled into the
20:47 But 600 men t and fled into the
Rut 3:8 When he t over, he was
1Sm 8:3 their father's example but t
10:9 When Saul t around to leave
13:17 One column t onto the road to
13:18 Another column t onto the road
13:18 And one t onto the road toward
14:47 Wherever he t, he was
15:11 He t away from me and did not
15:27 When Samuel t to leave,
15:31 Then Samuel t and followed
17:30 He t to face another man and
22:18 Doeg from Edom t and attacked
25:39 The LORD has t Nabal's own
26:8 "Today God has t your enemy
26:19 If the LORD has t you against
26:19 But if mere mortals have t you
28:15 and God has t against me and
28:16 the LORD has t against you
2Sm 14:7 the entire family t against me.
18:31 you from all who t against you."
18:32 and all who t against you
19:2 The victory of that day was t
22:22 not wickedly t away from my
22:23 and I have not t away from his
1Ki 2:15 But the kingship has been t
8:14 Then the king t around and
11:9 because his heart had t from
14:9 You made me furious and t
15:18 royal palace and t them over
20:39 A man t around and brought a
21:4 t his face from everyone,
22:32 So they t to fight him.
22:33 They t away from him.
2Ki 5:12 So he t around and left in anger.
5:26 in spirit when the man t around
9:23 As Joram t his chariot around
13:23 he hasn't t away from them.
15:18 During his entire life he never t
17:20 and finally t away from Israel.
17:22 and never t away from them.
17:23 Finally, the LORD t away from
18:6 and never t away from him.
20:2 Hezekiah t to the wall and
21:13 wiped out and t upside down.
23:16 When Josiah t and saw the
23:25 No king before Josiah had t to
24:1 Then Jehoiakim t against him
1Ch 10:14 So the LORD killed him and t
21:20 Now, Ornan had t around and
2Ch 6:3 Then the king t around and
11:4 They t back from their attack
15:4 they t to the LORD God of
18:32 Then they t away from him.
20:10 The Israelites t away from
25:27 After Amaziah t away from the
26:20 and all the priests t toward him,
29:6 They t away from the LORD's
29:6 LORD's tent and t their backs
Ezr 6:11 and his house should be t into
10:14 burning anger has t away from
Neh 2:15 Then I t back, entered Valley

Neh 13:2 But our God t the curse into a
Est 9:22 In that month their grief t to joy
Job 10:8 then you t to destroy me.
19:19 Those I love have t against me.
34:27 because they t away from
Psa 14:3 Everyone has t away.
18:21 not wickedly t away from my
18:22 and I have not t away from his
35:4 be t back in confusion.
40:1 He t to me and heard my cry for
40:14 be t back and disgraced.
44:18 Our hearts never t away.
66:6 He t the sea into dry land.
70:2 be t back and disgraced.
70:3 be t back because of their own
78:9 t ⌊and ran⌋ on the day of battle.
78:34 They t from their sins and
78:44 He t their rivers into blood so
85:3 You t away from your burning
94:23 He has t their own wickedness
105:29 He t their water into blood and
106:32 Things t out badly for Moses
114:3 The Jordan River t back.
119:51 yet I have not t away from your
119:157 ⌊yet⌋ I have not t away from
Pro 7:25 Do not let your heart be t to her
Ecc 2:11 But when I t to look at all that I
2:12 Then I t ⌊my attention⌋ to
4:1 Next, I t to look at all the acts
4:7 Next, I t to look at something
7:25 I t my attention to study,
Sos 5:6 but my beloved had t away.
Isa 1:4 They have t their backs on him.
10:16 A flame will be t into a raging
12:1 you t your anger away from me,
23:13 and t these places into ruins.
23:18 and her earnings will be t over
25:2 You have t cities into ruins,
29:17 time Lebanon will be t into
32:15 Then the wilderness will be t
34:9 Edom's streams will be t to tar.
34:9 Its soil will be t to burning
38:2 Hezekiah t to the wall and
42:17 "You are our gods" will be t
53:6 Each one of us has t to go his
56:11 All of them have t to go their
59:13 We have t away from our God.
59:14 Justice is t back, Truth has
63:10 So he t against them as their
Jer 2:15 Young lions have t the land
2:21 Now you have t against me
2:27 You've t your backs,
4:8 anger hasn't t away from us.
5:23 They have t aside and
5:25 Your wickedness has t these
6:12 and their wives will be t over to
8:5 The people of Jerusalem t
12:8 My people have t on me like a
12:10 They've t my pleasant property
15:6 "You have t your back on me.
23:22 They would have t back from
27:17 this city be t into rubble?
30:6 Why has every face t pale?
31:18 Turn me, and I will be t,
31:19 After I was t around,
32:33 have t their backs,
36:16 they t to each other in terror.
37:15 which had been t into a prison.
41:14 had taken captive at Mizpah t
43:3 But Baruch, son of Neriah, has t
51:34 He has t us into empty jars.
Lam 5:2 we inherited has been t over
5:2 have been t over to foreigners.
5:15 dancing has t into mourning.
Eze 6:9 which t away from me,
8:16 25 men who had their backs t
17:6 Its branches t upward toward
17:7 The vine t away from the
18:28 was doing and t away from all
19:7 He destroyed fortresses and t
21:16 left or wherever your blade is t.
23:17 she t away from them in
23:18 I t away from her in disgust as I
23:18 as I had t away from her
23:22 They are the lovers you t away
23:28 and to those you t away from
Eze 23:35 You have forgotten me and t
28:18 I t you into ashes on the ground
29:16 they were whenever they t
36:3 Your enemies t you into ruins
37:23 the times they t away from me
41:19 the face of a man, which was t
41:19 which was t toward a palm tree
Dan 2:5 and your houses will be t into
3:19 Abednego that his face t red.
3:29 Their houses will be t into
5:6 Then the king t pale,
5:9 and his face t pale.
7:28 by my thoughts, and I t pale.
9:3 So I t to the Lord God and
9:5 and t away from your
10:8 My face t deathly pale,
Hos 3:1 even though they have t to
7:14 They have t against me.
Joe 2:22 in the wilderness have t green.
Amo 6:12 Yet, you have t justice into
Jnh 3:10 He saw that they t from their
Mic 1:7 All its statues will be t into a
2:8 my people have t into enemies.
Zep 1:6 I will remove those who have t
Zec 1:6 Then your ancestors t away
7:14 They have t a pleasant land
8:10 I t every person against his
Mal 1:3 I t his mountains into a
2:6 and t many people away
2:8 "But you have t from the
3:7 you have t away from my
Mat 3:8 things that prove you have t
9:22 When Jesus t and saw her he
11:27 "My Father has t everything
12:41 because they t to God and
16:23 But Jesus t and said to Peter,
18:30 Instead, he t away and had that
Mar 5:30 He t around in the crowd and
8:33 Jesus t, looked at his
11:17 but you have t it into a
Luk 3:8 that prove that you have t
7:9 He t to the crowd following him
9:55 But he t and corrected them.
10:22 "My Father has t everything
10:23 He t to his disciples in private
11:32 Since the men of Nineveh t to
14:25 He t to them and said,
15:7 99 people who already have t
17:15 he t back and praised God in a
19:46 but you have t it into a
22:61 Then the Lord t and looked
23:28 Jesus t to them and said,
Jon 1:38 Jesus t around and saw them
13:18 my bread has t against me.'
20:14 After she said this, she t
20:16 Mary t around and said to him
21:20 Peter t around and saw the
Act 4:37 He sold it and t the money over
5:2 had pledged⌋ and t only part
7:39 hearts they t back to Egypt.
7:42 "So God t away from them and
9:35 had happened to Aeneas and t
9:40 Then he t toward the body and
11:21 believed and t to the Lord.
16:18 t to the evil spirit, and said,
27:1 other prisoners were t over
Rom 3:12 Everyone has t away.
15:28 and I have officially t
1Co 1:20 Hasn't God t the wisdom of the
10:7 to a feast which t into an orgy."
15:54 "Death is t into victory!
2Co 11:26 and from believers who t out to
1Th 1:9 They even report how you t
1Ti 1:6 have t to useless discussions.
5:15 Some of them have already t
Heb 13:7 about how their lives t out,
Rev 1:12 I t toward the voice which was
1:12 talking to me, and when I t,
6:12 The sun t as black as
6:12 The full moon t as red as blood.
8:8 of the sea t into blood,
8:11 of the water t into wormwood,
8:11 water because it had t bitter.
8:12 so that one-third of them t dark.
16:3 The sea t into blood like the
16:4 the springs. They t into blood.
Rev 16:10 Its kingdom t dark.

turning (15)

Dtr 31:18 they've done in t to other gods.
Pro 1:32 because of their t away.
13:19 but t from evil is disgusting to
Isa 7:25 It will be a place for t oxen
Eze 1:17 without t as they moved.
10:11 without t as they moved.
10:11 faced without t as they moved.
Dan 9:13 your favor by t from our wrongs
Amo 1:2 of the shepherds are t brown,
Mat 21:13 but you're t it into a gathering
Luk 7:44 Then, t to the woman,
Act 3:26 God did this to bless you by t
15:3 people were t to God.
15:19 people who are t to God.
Heb 6:1 the basics about t away from

turns (73)

Lev 13:2 area on his skin that t into
13:16 if the raw flesh t white again,
13:24 the raw flesh of the burn t into
Num 34:4 and t south of the Akrabbim
34:5 From Azmon it t toward the
Dtr 29:18 or tribe among you today who t
Jos 15:7 goes up to Debir and t north
15:10 From Baalah the border t west
15:11 of Ekron and t to Shikkeron,
16:6 The border then t east to
18:14 The border t and goes around
18:17 Then it t north and goes to En
19:12 But from Sarid it t directly east
19:13 where it t to Neah.
19:14 There the border t north to
19:27 Then it t east to Beth Dagon
19:29 Then it t at Ramah and goes on
19:29 The border then t to Hosah and
19:34 The border t west to Aznoth
Rut 3:18 until you know how it t out.
2Sm 22:29 The LORD t my darkness into
Job 17:5 (Whoever t in friends to get
20:14 the food in his belly t sour.
30:30 My skin t dark and peels.
Psa 7:13 and t them into flaming
10:4 He t up his nose ⌊and says⌋,
18:28 My God t my darkness into
114:8 He t a rock into a pool filled
114:8 filled with water and t flint into
116:2 because he t his ear toward
Pro 14:14 A heart that t ⌊from God⌋
14:16 A wise person is cautious and t
15:1 A gentle answer t away rage,
16:17 The highway of decent people t
17:8 Wherever he t, he prospers.
19:3 The stupidity of a person t his
21:1 He t them in any direction he
26:14 ⌊As⌋ a door t on its hinges,
26:14 so the lazy person t on his bed.
30:30 which t away from nothing,
Ecc 9:2 Everything t out the same way
Isa 30:21 Follow it, whether it t to the
38:17 bitter experience t into peace.
41:2 With his sword he t them into
41:2 With his bow he t them into
46:4 Even when your hair t gray,
Jer 8:4 When someone t away from
17:5 and whose heart t away from
18:8 I threatened t away from doing
23:14 so that no one t back from his
48:39 Moab t away in shame!'
Lam 1:8 Jerusalem groans and t away.
Eze 18:21 wicked person t away from all
18:24 person t away from doing
18:26 When a righteous person t
18:27 When a wicked person t away
33:12 he t from his wickedness.
33:14 But suppose he t from his sin
33:18 If the righteous person t from
33:19 If the wicked person t from his
Joe 2:6 presence. Every face t pale.
Amo 5:8 He t deep darkness into dawn.
5:8 He t day into night.
Nah 2:8 But no one t around.
2:10 upset. Every face t pale.
Luk 2:8 They were taking t watching

Luk 15:7 heaven over one person who **t**
15:10 happy about one person who **t**
23:14 me this man as someone who **t**
1Co 14:31 All of you can take your **t**
2Co 3:16 But whenever a person **t** to the
Heb 3:12 unbelieving heart that **t** away
10:38 But if he **t** back, I will not be

turquoise (3)

Exo 28:18 In the second row put **t**,
39:11 In the second row they put **t**,
Eze 28:13 sapphire, **t**, and emerald.

twice (31)

Gen 27:36 He's cheated me **t** already:
41:25 had the same dream **t**.
41:52 [Blessed **T** with Children],
43:10 have made this trip **t** by now."
43:12 Take **t** as much money with
43:15 the gifts, **t** as much money,
Exo 16:5 it should be **t** as much as they
16:22 they gathered **t** as much food,
Num 20:11 his hand and hit the rock **t**
Dtr 15:18 It would have cost you **t** as
1Sm 18:11 But David got away from him **t**.
26:8 I won't have to do it **t**!"
1Ki 11:9 who had appeared to him **t**.
Neh 13:20 Once or **t** merchants and those
Job 11:6 because ⌊true⌋ wisdom is **t**
40:5 but I can't answer — **t**,
42:10 and gave him **t** as much ⌊as
Psa 62:11 I have heard it ⌊said⌋ **t**:
Isa 51:19 **T** as many disasters have
Jer 16:18 First, I will have them pay **t** as
Mat 23:15 you make that person **t** as fit for
Mar 14:30 before a rooster crows **t**,
14:72 "Before a rooster crows **t**,
Luk 18:12 I fast **t** a week, and I give you
2Co 1:15 you so that you could benefit **t**.
Php 4:16 you provided for my needs **t**.
1Th 2:18 wanted to visit you **t** already,
Tit 3:10 have warned them once or **t**.
Jud 1:12 As a result, they have died **t**.
Rev 18:6 Give her **t** as much as she
18:6 in her own cup **t** as large as

twig (4)

Job 24:20 is snapped like a **t**.
Eze 17:4 It broke off the highest **t** and
17:4 It planted the **t** in a city of
17:22 I will break off the highest **t**

twigs (1)

Psa 58:9 pot is heated by burning **t**.

twilight (5)

Job 24:15 Adulterers watch for **t**.
Pro 7:9 in the **t**, in the evening, in the
Isa 21:4 The **t** hours I longed for make
59:10 stumble at noon as if it were **t**.
Jer 13:16 on the mountains in the **t**.

twin (2)

Gen 38:27 and she had **t** boys.
Sos 4:5 like **t** gazelles grazing among

twinkle (1)

Pro 15:30 A **t** in the eye delights the heart.

twins (4)

Gen 25:24 for her to give birth, she had **t**.
Sos 4:2 All of them bear **t**, and not one
6:6 All of them bear **t**, and not one
7:3 like two fawns, **t** of a gazelle.

twist (2)

Psa 56:5 long my enemies **t** my words.
Jer 23:36 They will **t** the words of the

twisted (14)

Exo 28:14 of pure gold, **t** like ropes,
28:22 out of pure gold, **t** like ropes.
39:3 They **t** the gold into threads,
39:15 out of pure gold, **t** like ropes.
Pro 6:14 evil all the time with a **t** mind.
8:8 and there is nothing **t** or
Pro 8:13 evil behavior, and **t** speech.
12:8 but whoever has a **t** mind will
17:20 A **t** mind never finds happiness,
Eze 27:24 rugs with woven and **t** cords.
Mat 27:29 They **t** some thorns into a
Mar 15:17 **t** some thorns into a crown,
Jon 19:2 The soldiers **t** some thorny
Act 8:21 can see how **t** your thinking is.

twisting (1)

Isa 27:1 snake, Leviathan, that **t** snake.

two-faced (2)

Psa 119:113 I hate **t** people, but I love your
1Ti 3:8 They must not be **t** or addicted

Tychicus (5)

Act 20:4 and **T** and Trophimus from the
Eph 6:21 I'm sending **T** to you.
Col 4:7 I'm sending **T** to you.
2Ti 4:12 I'm sending **T** to the city of
Tit 3:12 I send Artemas or **T** to you,

tying (2)

Gen 37:7 We were **t** grain into bundles
Pro 26:8 Like **t** a stone to a sling,

type (24)

Gen 1:11 each according to its own **t**,
1:11 each according to its own **t**."
1:12 each according to its own **t**,
1:12 each according to its own **t**.
1:21 every **t** of creature that swims
1:21 around in the water and every **t**
1:24 "Let the earth produce every **t**
1:24 every **t** of domestic animal,
1:25 God made every **t** of wild
1:25 every **t** of domestic animal,
1:25 and every **t** of creature that
6:20 Two of every **t** of bird,
6:20 every **t** of domestic animal,
6:20 and every **t** of creature that
7:14 They had with them every **t** of
7:14 every **t** of domestic animal,
7:14 every **t** of creature that crawls
7:14 and every **t** of bird (every
8:20 made a burnt offering of each **t**
Lev 14:44 If it is a spreading **t** of mildew,
1Ch 28:21 priests and Levites for every **t**
Mic 2:11 They would be just the **t** of
Mat 13:23 This **t** produces crops.
Heb 10:11 He offered the same **t** of

types (11)

Lev 11:14 kites, all **t** of buzzards,
11:15 all **t** of crows,
11:16 seagulls, all **t** of falcons,
11:19 storks, all **t** of herons,
11:29 and all **t** of lizards:
Num 19:19 is clean will sprinkle these **t**
Dtr 14:13 buzzards, all **t** of kites,
14:14 all **t** of crows,
14:15 seagulls, all **t** of falcons,
14:18 storks, all **t** of herons,
1Co 12:6 There are different **t** of work to

typical (1)

Ecc 7:9 because anger is **t** of fools.

Tyrannus (1)

Act 19:9 in the lecture hall of **T**.

tyrant (3)

Job 6:23 or 'Ransom me from a **t**'?
Psa 37:35 person ⌊acting like⌋ a **t**,
Isa 14:4 "How the **t** has come to an end!

tyrant's (1)

Isa 25:4 (A **t** breath is like a rainstorm

tyrants (7)

Job 27:13 the inheritance that **t** receive
Isa 13:11 and humble the pride of **t**.
25:3 by the world's **t** will fear you.
25:5 The song of **t** is silenced like
29:20 **T** will be gone. Mockers will be
Isa 49:25 Loot will be taken away from **t**.
Jer 15:21 free you from the power of **t**.

Tyre (65)

Jos 19:29 goes on to the fortified city of **T**.
2Sm 5:11 Then King Hiram of **T** sent
24:7 went to the fortified city of **T**
1Ki 5:1 King Hiram of **T** sent his
7:13 had Hiram brought from **T**.
7:14 His father, a native of **T**,
9:11 he gave King Hiram of **T** 20
9:12 Hiram left **T** to see the cities
1Ch 14:1 King Hiram of **T** sent
22:4 The men of Sidon and **T**
2Ch 2:3 to King Huram of **T** by saying,
2:11 Then King Huram of **T**
2:14 and his father is a native of **T**.
Ezr 3:7 oil to the men from Sidon and **T**
Neh 13:16 People from **T** who lived in
Psa 45:12 The people of **T**, the richest
83:7 along with those who live in **T**.
87:4 as well as Philistia, **T**,
Isa 23:1 is the divine revelation about **T**.
23:1 Your port at **T** is destroyed.
23:3 of the Nile River is brought to **T**.
23:3 **T** became the marketplace for
23:5 shudder over the news about **T**.
23:8 planned such a thing against **T**,
23:15 **T** will be forgotten for 70 years,
23:15 At the end of the 70 years, **T**
23:17 the LORD will come to help **T**.
Jer 25:22 all the kings of **T** and Sidon,
27:3 Moab, Ammon, **T**, and Sidon,
47:4 to cut off from **T** and Sidon any
Eze 26:2 **T** said this about Jerusalem:
26:3 says: I am against you, **T**.
26:4 will destroy the walls of **T**
26:4 up the dust and turn **T** into
26:7 of Babylon against you, **T**.
26:15 the Almighty LORD says to **T**:
26:17 for you: **T**, you famous city,
27:2 sing a funeral song about **T**.
27:3 **T** is the city at the entrance to
27:3 Say to **T**, 'This is what the
27:3 the Almighty LORD says: **T**,
27:32 loud crying: "Who is like **T**,
28:2 "Son of man, tell the ruler of **T**,
28:12 a funeral song for the ruler of **T**.
29:18 his army fight hard against **T**.
29:18 hard-fought battle against **T**.
Hos 9:13 I have seen Ephraim, like **T**,
Joe 3:4 **T** and Sidon and all the regions
Amo 1:9 Because **T** has committed
1:10 send a fire on the walls of **T**
Zec 9:2 borders on it, and **T** and Sidon,
9:3 **T** built itself a fortress.
Mat 11:21 been worked in **T** and Sidon,
11:22 day will be better for **T**
15:21 to the region of **T** and Sidon.
Mar 3:8 and from around **T** and Sidon
7:24 and went to the territory of **T**.
7:31 then left the neighborhood of **T**.
Luk 6:17 the seacoast of **T** and Sidon.
10:13 been worked in **T** and Sidon,
10:14 day will be better for **T**
Act 12:20 with the people of **T** and Sidon.
21:3 We landed at the city of **T**,
21:4 In **T** we searched for the
21:7 ended when we sailed from **T**

Tyrians (2)

Amo 1:9 The **T** have handed all the
1:9 The **T** didn't remember their

U

Uel (1)

Ezr 10:34 of Bani: Maadai, Amram, **U**,

Ulai (2)

Dan 8:2 In my vision I saw myself at **U**
8:16 I heard a man in **U** ⌊Gate⌋ call

Ulam (2)

1Ch 7:16 sons were **U** and Rakem.
8:39 sons were **U** (the firstborn),

Ulam's (2)

1Ch 7:17 **U** son was Bedan.
8:40 **U** sons were soldiers,

Ulla's (1)

1Ch 7:39 **U** sons were Arah,

ulterior (1)

Pro 7:10 A woman with an **u** motive

umbilical (1)

Eze 16:4 your **u** cord wasn't cut.

Umma (1)

Jos 19:30 **U**, Acco, Aphek, and Rehob.

unable (31)

Gen 13:6 they were **u** to remain together.
31:49 you and me when we're **u**
Exo 4:11 Who makes humans **u** to talk
22:3 If he is **u** to do so, he must be
23:26 your land will miscarry or be **u**
1Sm 1:6 the LORD had made her **u**
2Sm 22:39 They were **u** to get up.
Neh 5:8 They were **u** to say anything.
Job 6:30 or is my mouth **u** to tell the
12:20 He makes trusted advisers **u** to
37:19 We are **u** to prepare ⌊a case⌋
Psa 18:38 them so badly that they were **u**
36:12 been pushed down and are **u**
Isa 49:21 I was childless and **u** to have
56:10 are like dogs that are **u** to bark.
63:17 so stubborn that we are **u**
66:9 to deliver and then make her **u**
Eze 17:14 a humiliated country and be **u**
Hos 9:14 or else make them **u** to nurse
Mat 9:32 The man was **u** to talk
12:22 the man blind and **u** to talk.
15:30 blind, disabled, those **u** to talk,
Luk 1:20 you will be **u** to talk until the
1:22 he was **u** to speak to them.
1:22 to them but remained **u** to talk.
11:14 had made the man **u** to talk.
Jon 21:6 threw the net out and were **u**
Act 13:11 **u** to see the light of day."
28:25 **u** to agree among themselves,
Rom 4:19 Sarah was **u** to have children.
1Co 1:21 world with its wisdom was **u**

unacceptable (4)

Exo 20:25 you will make it **u** to me.
Rom 14:14 and conviction that no food is **u**
14:14 But it is **u** to a person who
1Co 7:14 children would be **u** ⌊to God⌋,

unafraid (2)

Job 11:15 and you will be secure and **u**.
Isa 12:2 I am confident and **u**,

unanimous (1)

Act 15:25 So we have come to a **u**

unanswered (1)

Psa 35:13 When my prayer returned **u**,

unauthorized (4)

Exo 30:9 "Never burn any **u** incense on
Lev 10:1 they offered this **u** fire.
Num 3:4 because they offered **u** fire
26:61 died because they offered **u** fire

unavoidable (1)

Pro 10:19 Sin is **u** when there is much

unaware (2)

Ecc 5:1 Fools are **u** that they are doing
Eze 45:20 something wrong and is **u** of it.

unbearable (1)

Ecc 2:23 and their work is **u**.

unbelief (4)

Mar 6:6 Their **u** amazed him.
16:14 He put them to shame for their **u**
Rom 11:23 do not continue in their **u**,
1Ti 1:13 I acted ignorantly in my **u**.

unbeliever (5)

1Co 7:12 to a woman who is an **u**,
7:13 married to a man who is an **u**,
10:27 If an **u** invites you ⌊to his
2Co 6:15 a believer share life with an **u**?
1Ti 5:8 faith and is worse than an **u**.

unbelievers (14)

1Co 5:1 is not even heard of among **u** —
5:10 with **u** who commit sexual
6:6 and this happens in front of **u**.
12:2 know that when you were **u**,
14:22 other languages is a sign for **u**,
14:22 is a sign for believers, not for **u**.
14:23 When outsiders or **u** come in,
14:24 When **u** or outsiders come in
2Co 6:14 relationships with **u**.
6:17 "Get away from **u**.
Tit 1:15 nothing is clean to corrupt **u**.
1Pe 2:12 Live decent lives among **u**.
4:3 in the past doing what **u** like
4:4 **U** insult you now because they

unbelieving (7)

Mat 17:17 "You **u** and corrupt generation!
Mar 9:19 "You **u** generation!
Luk 9:41 "You **u** and corrupt generation!
1Co 7:14 Actually, the **u** husband is
7:14 and an **u** wife is made holy
7:15 But if the **u** partners leave,
Heb 3:12 **u** heart that turns away from the

unbreakable (1)

Psa 89:28 My promise to him is **u**.

unbuckles (1)

Job 12:21 on influential people and **u**

uncertain (1)

1Ti 6:17 in anything as **u** as riches.

unchanging (1)

Gen 39:21 out to him with his **u** love

uncircumcised (20)

Gen 17:14 Any **u** male must be excluded
34:14 our sister to a man who is **u**.
Exo 12:48 But no **u** males may ever eat
Lev 26:41 Then, if they humble their **u**
Dtr 10:16 So circumcise your **u** hearts,
1Sm 14:6 military post of these **u** people.
17:26 Who is this **u** Philistine that he
17:36 and this **u** Philistine will be
Jer 9:26 all Israel has **u** hearts."
Act 11:3 went to visit men who were **u**,
Rom 2:26 circumcised even if he is **u**?
2:27 The **u** man who carries out
3:30 faith and **u** people through this
4:9 or are **u** people blessed as
4:10 or was he **u** at that time?
4:11 approval while he was still **u**.
1Co 7:18 Any man who was **u** when he
Eph 2:11 their bodies called you "the **u**."
Col 2:13 and your **u** corrupt nature.
3:11 circumcised or **u**, barbarian,

uncircumcision (1)

Rom 2:25 circumcision amounts to **u**.

uncivilized (1)

Col 3:11 **u** person, slave, or free person.

uncle (14)

Gen 28:2 the daughters of your **u** Laban.
29:10 daughter of his **u** Laban,
29:10 with his **u** Laban's sheep.
29:10 watered his **u** Laban's sheep.
Lev 10:4 the sons of Aaron's **u**,
25:49 His **u**, his cousin, or some
1Sm 10:14 Saul's **u** asked him and his
10:15 Saul's **u** said, "Please tell me
10:16 Saul answered his **u**.
14:50 the son of Saul's **u** Ner.
2Ki 24:17 Jehoiakin's **U** Mattaniah king
1Ch 27:32 David's **u** Jonathan,
2Ch 36:10 Jehoiakin's **u** Zedekiah king
Est 2:15 of Abihail, Mordecai's **u**.

unclean (249)

Gen 7:2 every kind of **u** animal (a male
7:8 Clean and **u** animals,
Lev 5:2 "If you touch anything **u** — the
5:2 unclean — the **u** dead body
5:2 animal or the body of an **u**,
5:2 you are **u** and will be guilty.
5:3 "If you become **u** by touching
7:19 "Meat that touches anything **u**
7:20 offering while **u** must
7:21 Those who touch anything **u**,
10:10 what is clean and what is **u**.
11:4 (Camels are **u** because they
11:5 (Rock badgers are **u** because
11:6 (Rabbits are **u** because they
11:7 their cud, they are also **u**.)
11:8 They are **u** for you.
11:24 is how you would become **u**:
11:24 bodies will be **u** until evening.
11:25 He will be **u** until evening.
11:26 chew their cud are **u** for you.
11:26 Whoever touches them is **u**.
11:27 on their paws are **u** for you.
11:27 bodies will be **u** until evening.
11:28 and will be **u** until evening.
11:28 These animals are **u** for you.
11:29 that move on the ground are **u**
11:31 these are **u** for you.
11:31 bodies will be **u** until evening.
11:32 that thing will be **u**.
11:32 and will be **u** until evening.
11:33 because everything in it is **u**.
11:34 touches any food, the food is **u**.
11:34 you drink from that pottery is **u**.
11:35 their dead bodies fall is **u**.
11:35 It is **u** and will remain unclean
11:35 and will remain **u** for you.
11:36 their dead bodies will be **u**.
11:38 the seed is **u** for you.
11:39 body will be **u** until evening.
11:40 and will be **u** until evening.
11:40 and will be **u** until evening.
11:43 to become **u** because of them.
11:44 Never become **u** by touching
11:47 between clean and **u**,
12:2 she will be **u** for seven days.
12:2 same number of days she is **u**
12:5 she will be **u** as in her monthly
12:5 she will be **u** for two weeks.
13:3 he must declare him **u**.
13:8 the priest must declare him **u**.
13:11 the priest must declare him **u**
13:11 him unclean because he is **u**.
13:14 raw flesh appears, he will be **u**.
13:15 raw flesh and declare him **u**.
13:15 The raw flesh is **u**.
13:20 must declare the person **u**.
13:22 the priest must declare him **u**.
13:25 The priest must declare him **u**.
13:27 the priest must declare him **u**.
13:30 must declare the person **u**.
13:36 yellow hair. The person is **u**.
13:44 He is **u**. The priest must declare
13:44 The priest must declare him **u**
13:45 lips and call out, '**U**, unclean!'
13:45 lips and call out, 'Unclean, **u**!'
13:46 the skin disease, they are **u**.
13:51 If the spot is spreading, it is **u**.
13:55 has not spread, it is still **u**.
13:59 leather article is clean or **u**."
14:36 in the house will become **u**.
14:40 outside the city in an **u** place.
14:41 dumped in an **u** place outside
14:44 type of mildew, the house is **u**.
14:45 and taken to an **u** place outside
14:46 up will be **u** until evening.
14:57 what is clean and what is **u**."

Lev 15:2 his discharge is **u**.
15:3 He is **u** because of the
15:3 no difference; he is still **u**.
15:4 he lies on or sits on **u**.
15:5 They will be **u** until evening.
15:6 They will be **u** until evening.
15:7 They will be **u** until evening.
15:8 He will be **u** until evening.
15:9 sits on a saddle, it becomes **u**.
15:10 They will be **u** until evening.
15:11 He will be **u** until evening.
15:16 He will be **u** until evening.
15:17 It will be **u** until evening.
15:18 They will be **u** until evening.
15:19 she will be **u** for seven days.
15:19 her will be **u** until evening.
15:20 on during her period will be **u**.
15:21 They will be **u** until evening.
15:22 They will be **u** until evening.
15:23 it will be **u** until evening.
15:24 he will be **u** for seven days.
15:24 bed he lies on will become **u**.
15:25 her monthly period, she is **u**.
15:25 she will be **u** as long as she
15:26 on or anything she sits on is **u**.
15:27 who touch these things are **u**
15:27 They will be **u** until evening.
15:30 who had an **u** discharge.
15:31 tent, which is among them, **u**.
15:32 of semen that makes him **u**,
15:33 with a woman when she is **u**."
16:16 because the Israelites were **u**
16:16 which is among an **u** people.
16:19 the Israelites made it **u**,
17:15 They will be **u** until evening.
18:19 she is **u** during her monthly
18:20 wife and become **u** with her.
18:23 animal and become **u** with it.
18:24 "Do not become **u** in any of
18:24 of your way have become **u**.
18:25 The land has become **u**.
18:27 the land has become **u**.
18:28 If you make the land **u**,
18:30 Never become **u** that way.
19:31 That will make you **u**.
20:3 made my holy tent **u**,
20:21 marriage and does an **u** thing.
20:25 Separate clean and **u** animals
20:25 you from every **u** thing.
21:1 None of you should become **u**
21:2 you are allowed to become **u**
21:4 you should never become **u**.
21:11 any dead bodies or become **u**,
22:3 of your descendants, while **u**,
22:5 an **u** swarming creature or an
22:5 creature or an **u** person
22:6 will be **u** until evening.
22:8 It will make him **u**.
27:11 If it is an **u** animal that cannot
27:27 But if it is an **u** animal,
Num 5:2 anyone who is **u** from touching
5:3 Send all of these **u** men and
5:3 where I live among you **u**."
5:4 They sent these **u** people
5:27 If she has become **u** by being
5:28 But if the woman is not **u** and
5:29 to her husband and becomes **u**.
6:7 themselves **u** by going near
6:9 and make the Nazirite's hair **u**.
6:12 over from when he became **u**.
9:6 had become **u** from touching
9:7 and said, "We are **u** because
9:10 descendants is **u** from touching
18:15 firstborn male of any **u** animal.
19:7 But he will be **u** until evening.
19:8 He, too, will be **u** until evening.
19:10 He will be **u** until evening.
19:11 being will be **u** for seven days.
19:12 The **u** person must use this
19:13 sin makes the LORD's tent **u**.
19:13 He is **u**; his uncleanness stays
19:14 tent will be **u** for seven days.
19:15 without a lid fastened on it is **u**.
19:16 grave will be **u** for seven days.
19:17 who become **u** from touching
19:19 these types of **u** people
Num 19:20 becomes **u** doesn't have his
19:20 the holy place of the LORD **u**.
19:20 sprinkled on him. He is **u**.
19:21 water will be **u** until evening.
19:22 Anything that an **u** person
19:22 person touches becomes **u**,
19:22 it will be **u** until evening."
35:34 the land where you and I live **u**.
Dtr 12:15 Clean and **u** people may eat it
12:22 Clean and **u** people may eat it
14:7 They are **u** for you.)
14:10 fins and scales. It is **u** for you.
14:19 winged insect is also **u** for you.
15:22 Clean and **u** people may eat
21:23 you must never become **u**.
23:9 anything that will make you **u**.
23:10 If one of your men becomes **u**
24:4 She has become **u**.
26:14 any of it while I was **u**.
Jos 22:19 If your land is **u**, come over
Jdg 13:4 wine or liquor or eat any **u** food.
13:7 wine or liquor or eat any **u** food
13:14 or liquor, or eat any **u** food.
1Sm 20:26 happened to him so that he's **u**.
20:26 he's unclean. He must be **u**."
2Ki 23:8 those priests sacrificed **u**.
23:10 of Ben Hinnom **u** so that people
23:13 of worship east of Jerusalem **u**.
23:16 them on the altar to make it **u**.
2Ch 23:19 so that no one who was **u**
29:16 every **u** thing that they
29:16 Then the Levites took the **u**
36:14 they made the temple **u**.
Ezr 6:21 from the **u** practices
Job 14:4 "If only an **u** person could
Ecc 9:2 wicked, or good, clean or **u**,
Isa 52:11 Do not touch anything **u**.
64:6 We've all become **u**,
65:4 pots made broth from **u** foods.
Jer 2:7 came and made my land **u**.
7:30 They have made it **u**.
19:13 houses will be **u** like this city
Lam 4:15 You're **u**,' people yelled at them.
Eze 4:13 the people of Israel will eat **u**
4:14 No **u** meat has ever entered my
22:10 having their periods and are **u**.
22:24 'You are an **u** land that has not
22:26 what is clean and what is **u**.
36:17 Their ways were as **u** as a
36:25 make you clean instead of **u**.
44:23 what is clean and what is **u**.
44:25 make himself **u** by going near
44:25 But a priest may become **u** if
Hos 5:3 like a prostitute, and Israel is **u**.
6:10 like a prostitute, and Israel is **u**.
8:5 How long will they remain **u**?
9:3 they will eat **u** food in Assyria.
9:4 All who eat this food will be **u**.
Amo 7:17 and you will die in an **u** land.
Hag 2:13 "Suppose a person becomes **u**
2:13 does that make them **u**?"
2:13 "That makes them **u**."
2:14 that these people are **u**,
2:14 offering they bring is **u**.
Zec 13:2 prophets and the **u** spirit from
Mat 15:11 mouth doesn't make him **u**.
15:11 mouth that makes a person **u**."
15:18 that's what makes a person **u**.
15:20 things that make a person **u**.
15:20 doesn't make a person **u**."
Mar 7:2 some of his disciples were **u**
7:5 They are **u** because they don't
7:15 the outside can make him **u**.
7:15 of a person that makes him **u**.
7:18 the outside can't make him **u**?
7:20 of a person that makes him **u**.
7:23 within and make a person **u**."
Jon 18:28 They didn't want to become **u**,
Act 10:14 anything that is impure or **u**."
10:28 longer call anyone impure or **u**.
11:8 impure or **u** into my mouth.'
21:28 has made this holy place **u**."
2Co 6:17 nothing to do with anything **u**.
Heb 9:13 on **u** people made their
Rev 18:2 every evil spirit, every **u** bird,
18:2 and every **u** and hated beast.
Rev 21:27 Nothing **u**, no one who does

uncleanness (10)

Lev 5:3 unclean by touching human **u**
7:21 or any other disgusting **u** and
Num 19:9 in the water that takes away **u**.
19:13 takes away **u** wasn't sprinkled
19:13 his **u** stays with him.
19:20 The water to take away **u**
19:21 to take away **u** must wash his
Eze 22:15 I will put an end to your **u**.
36:29 will rescue you from all your **u**.
39:24 I paid them back for their **u** and

uncle's (3)

Lev 20:20 his **u** wife violates his uncle's
20:20 wife violates his **u** marriage.
Est 2:7 his **u** daughter, because she

uncles (4)

Num 27:10 give his property to his **u** on his
27:11 If he has no **u**, give his property
Jdg 9:1 went to Shechem to see the **u**
9:3 His **u** repeated everything he

unclouded (2)

Mat 6:22 So if your eye is **u**,
Luk 11:34 When your eye is **u**,

uncombed (3)

Lev 10:6 mourn by leaving your hair **u**
13:45 clothes and leave their hair **u**.
21:10 mourn by leaving his hair **u**

uncomfortable (6)

2Co 2:2 After all, if I had made you **u**,
2:2 me up when you were **u**?
2:4 I didn't write to make you **u** but
7:8 If my letter made you **u**,
7:8 since my letter did make you **u**
7:9 not because I made you **u**,

uncontrollable (1)

Jas 3:8 It is an **u** evil filled with deadly

uncontrolled (1)

Mat 23:25 are full of greed and **u** desires.

uncorrupted (1)

Jas 1:27 and to remain **u** by this world.

uncover (6)

Rut 3:4 Then **u** his feet, and lie down
Psa 119:18 **U** my eyes so that I may see
Isa 26:21 The earth will **u** the blood shed
47:2 **U** your legs, and cross the
Eze 16:37 I will **u** your body for them,
Dan 4:9 is too hard for you ⌊to **u**⌋.

uncovered (8)

Gen 44:16 God has **u** our guilt.
Rut 3:7 **u** his feet, and lay down.
Psa 98:2 He has **u** his righteousness for
Isa 57:8 You've **u** yourself to the idols.
Eze 16:36 You exposed yourself and **u**
1Co 11:5 her head **u** while she speaks
11:13 to pray to God with her head **u**?
Heb 4:13 Everything is **u** and exposed

uncovering (1)

Gen 30:37 **u** the white which was on the

uncovers (2)

Job 12:22 He **u** mysteries ⌊hidden⌋ in the
Isa 22:6 horsemen. Kir **u** its shields.

uncut (2)

Dtr 27:6 You must use **u** stones to build
Jos 8:31 He built an altar with **u** stones

undependable (2)

Psa 116:11 "Everyone is **u**."
Pro 13:17 An **u** messenger gets into

underbrush (4)

Exo 22:6 and spreads into the **u** so that

Job 30:4 They pick saltwort from the **u**,
Isa 9:18 It sets the **u** in the forest on fire,
10:34 He will cut down the **u** of the

underfoot (3)

Isa 14:25 I'll trample it **u** on my
28:3 of Ephraim will be trampled **u**.
Lam 3:34 crush any prisoner on earth **u**,

undergarments (5)

Exo 28:42 "Make linen **u** to cover them
39:28 They made the **u** and belt out
Lev 6:10 including his linen **u**.
16:4 linen robe and wear linen **u**.
Eze 44:18 on their heads and linen **u**.

underground (7)

Gen 2:6 Instead, **u** water would come
Dtr 8:7 There are springs and **u**
2Ch 32:30 channeled the water directly **u**
Psa 139:15 woven in an **u** workshop.
Isa 2:10 in among the rocks and hide **u**
Eze 31:4 and **u** springs made it tall.
31:15 I covered the **u** springs and

undergrowth (1)

Isa 17:9 like abandoned woods and **u**.

underhanded (3)

Psa 119:36 than getting rich in **u** ways.
Mat 26:4 to arrest Jesus in an **u** way
Mar 14:1 were looking for some **u** way

undermined (1)

Psa 11:3 the foundations ⌊of life⌋ are **u**,

undermines (1)

Job 18:12 Hunger **u** his strength.

underside (1)

Job 41:30 Its **u** is like sharp pieces of

understand (177)

Gen 11:7 that they won't **u** each other."
42:23 that Joseph could **u** them,
Dtr 9:6 So **u** this: It's not because
28:49 whose language you won't **u**.
32:28 They are not able to **u**.
32:29 were wise enough to **u** this
2Ki 5:7 All of you should realize and **u**
18:26 to us in Aramaic, since we **u** it.
Neh 8:2 who could **u** what they heard.
8:3 and ⌊children⌋ who could **u** it.
8:8 people could **u** what was read.
13:24 but they couldn't **u** the
Job 5:9 great things that ⌊we⌋ cannot **u**
15:9 What do you **u** that we don't?
17:4 minds so that they cannot **u**.
23:5 I want to **u** the things he would
26:14 Who can **u** the thunder of his
32:9 They don't **u** what justice is
34:16 "If you **u**, listen to this.
36:29 Can anyone really **u** how
37:5 great things that we cannot **u**.
42:3 I have stated things I didn't **u**,
Psa 71:15 it is more than I can **u**.
73:16 But when I tried to **u** this,
73:17 ⌊finally⌋ **u** what would happen
73:22 I was stupid, and I did not **u**.
81:5 I heard a message I did not **u**:
82:5 do not know or **u** anything.
92:6 know and a fool cannot **u**
101:2 I want to **u** the path to integrity.
107:43 may **u** the LORD's blessings.
119:27 Help me **u** your guiding
119:34 Help me **u** so that I can follow
119:73 Help me **u** so that I may learn
119:95 to **u** your written instructions.
119:125 Help me **u** so that I may come
119:130 and it helps gullible people **u**.
119:144 Help me **u** ⌊them⌋ so that I will
119:169 Help me **u** as you promised.
Pro 1:2 to **u** deep thoughts,
1:6 to **u** a proverb and a clever
2:5 then you will **u** the fear of the
2:9 Then you will **u** what is right
Pro 20:24 can anyone **u** his own way?
28:5 Evil people do not **u** justice,
28:5 seek the LORD **u** everything.
29:7 A wicked person does not **u**
29:19 not respond, though he may **u**.
30:18 even four that I cannot **u**:
Ecc 1:8 can express, comprehend, or **u**.
1:17 I've used my mind to **u** wisdom
11:5 you also don't **u** how God,
Isa 1:3 don't **u** ⌊who feeds them⌋.
5:13 they don't **u** what I'm doing.
5:19 quickly so that we may **u** what
6:9 you listen, you'll never **u**.
6:10 **u** with their minds,
27:11 people don't **u** ⌊these things⌋.
29:16 the potter, "He doesn't **u**"?
32:4 are reckless will begin to **u**,
33:19 language that you can't **u**.
36:11 to us in Aramaic, since we **u** it.
40:21 Don't you **u** the foundations of
41:20 they will consider and **u** that
42:25 in flames, but they did not **u**.
43:10 and believe in me and **u** that
44:18 They don't know or **u** anything.
44:18 are closed, so they can't **u**.
52:15 They will **u** things that they
56:11 the shepherds, but they don't **u**.
Jer 4:22 They don't **u**. They are experts
5:15 You can't **u** what its people
9:12 one is wise enough to **u** this.
9:24 they should brag that they **u**
11:18 plot to me so that I would **u**.
15:15 O LORD, you **u**. Remember me,
17:9 No one can **u** how deceitful it
23:20 days you will **u** this clearly.
30:24 days you will **u** this clearly.
Eze 3:5 whose language is hard to **u**
3:6 whose language is hard to **u**,
3:6 or whose words you cannot **u**.
12:3 Maybe they will **u**,
Dan 1:17 and the ability to **u** all kinds of
1:17 Daniel could also **u** all kinds of
8:15 the vision and tried to **u** it,
8:17 He said to me, "Son of man, **u**
8:27 me because I couldn't **u** it.
9:23 the message, and **u** the vision.
9:25 Learn, then, and **u** that from the
10:12 that you could learn to **u** things.
11:33 are wise will help many to **u**.
12:8 I heard him, but I did not **u**.
12:10 and none of them will **u**.
12:10 Only wise people will **u**.
Hos 14:9 people will **u** these things.
Mic 4:12 of the LORD or **u** his plan.
Mat 13:12 Those who **u** ⌊these
13:12 don't **u** ⌊these mysteries⌋.
13:12 Even what they **u** will be taken
13:13 They don't even try to **u**.
13:14 will hear clearly but never **u**.
13:15 Their minds never **u**.
13:19 the kingdom but doesn't **u** it.
15:10 "Listen and try to **u**!
15:16 Jesus said, "Don't you **u** yet?
16:9 Don't you **u** yet? Don't you
16:11 Why don't you **u** that I wasn't
Mar 4:12 They hear clearly but don't **u**.
4:13 "Don't you **u** this story?
4:13 How, then, will you **u** any of
4:25 Those who **u** ⌊these
4:25 don't **u** ⌊these mysteries⌋.
4:25 Even what they **u** will be taken
4:33 people could **u** what he taught.
6:52 (They didn't **u** what had
7:14 to me, all of you, and try to **u**!
7:18 said to them, "Don't you **u**?
8:17 Don't you **u** yet? Don't you catch
9:32 The disciples didn't **u** what he
14:68 and I don't **u** what you're
Luk 2:50 they didn't **u** what he meant.
8:10 when they hear, they don't **u**.
8:18 Those who **u** ⌊these
8:18 don't **u** ⌊these mysteries⌋.
8:18 Even what they think they **u**
9:45 them so that they didn't **u** it.
18:34 But they didn't **u** any of this.
24:45 their minds to **u** the Scriptures.
Jon 3:10 of Israel. Can't you **u** this?
8:43 Why don't you **u** the language I
8:43 Is it because you can't **u** the
8:47 You don't **u** because you don't
10:6 but they didn't **u** what he meant.
12:40 see and their minds don't **u**.
13:7 I'm doing. You will **u** later."
13:12 "Do you **u** what I've done for
13:17 If you **u** all of this, you are
16:18 We don't **u** what he's talking
Act 2:14 You must **u** this, so pay
4:10 of Israel must **u** that this man
7:25 people would **u** that God was
7:25 freedom. But they didn't **u**.
8:30 "Do you **u** what you're reading?
8:31 "How can I **u** unless someone
10:28 He said to them, "You **u** how
10:34 Then Peter said, "Now I **u** that
13:27 They didn't **u** the prophets'
22:9 saw the light but didn't **u** what
28:26 will hear clearly but never **u**.
28:27 Their minds never **u**.
Rom 10:3 They don't **u** ⌊how to receive⌋
10:19 "Didn't Israel **u** ⌊that message⌋?"
10:19 about a nation that doesn't **u**."
11:25 I want you to **u** this mystery so
11:33 his decisions or to **u** his ways.
15:21 those who never heard will **u**."
1Co 2:14 He can't **u** them because a
13:2 and I may **u** all mysteries and
2Co 1:13 I hope you will **u** this as long
1:14 even though you now **u** it only
Gal 3:7 You must **u** that people who
Eph 3:4 you'll see that I **u** the mystery
3:18 you will be able to **u** how wide,
4:18 They can't **u** because they are
5:17 but **u** what the Lord wants.
1Ti 1:7 However, they don't **u** what
6:4 that he doesn't **u** anything.
2Ti 2:7 **U** what I'm saying.
2:7 will help you **u** all these things.
3:1 You must **u** this: In the last
2Pe 1:20 First, you must **u** this:
2:12 insult what they don't **u**.
3:3 First, you must **u** this:
3:16 in his letters are hard to **u**.
1Jn 3:16 We **u** what love is when we
Jud 1:10 Whatever these people don't **u**,

understanding (88)

1Ki 3:11 Instead, you've asked for **u** so
3:12 I'm giving you a wise and **u**
1Ch 22:12 will give you insight and **u** as
Neh 10:28 who is capable of **u** also took
Job 11:12 person will gain **u** when
20:3 my **u** gives me answers.
28:12 Where does **u** live?
28:20 Where does **u** live?
28:28 To stay away from evil is **u**.'"
32:8 Almighty, that gives them **u**.
32:11 to share your **u** until you could
34:10 "You people who have **u**,
34:34 "People of **u**, the wise people
36:26 great that he is beyond our **u**.
38:36 the heart or gave **u** to the mind?
39:17 and did not give it any **u**.
39:26 "Does your **u** make a bird of
Psa 10:5 judgments are beyond his **u**.
49:20 they treasure, still don't have **u**.
119:32 you continue to increase my **u**.
119:104 your guiding principles I gain **u**.
136:5 made the heavens by his **u** —
147:5 There is no limit to his **u**.
Pro 1:5 and an **u** person will gain
2:2 and let your mind reach for **u**,
2:3 if you ask aloud for **u**,
2:6 mouth come knowledge and **u**.
2:11 protect you. **U** will guard you.
3:5 and do not rely on your own **u**.
3:13 and the one who obtains **u**.
3:19 By **u** he established the
4:1 pay attention in order to gain **u**.
4:5 Acquire **u**. Do not forget. Do not
4:7 Acquire **u** with all that you
5:1 Open your ears to my **u**
7:4 the name "my relative" to **u**

Pro 8:1 Does not **u** raise its voice?
8:5 fools, get a heart that has **u**.
8:9 is clear to a person who has **u**
8:14 I, U, have strength.
9:6 Start traveling the road to **u**."
9:10 of the Holy One is **u**.
10:13 the lips of a person who has **u**,
10:23 wisdom to a person who has **u**.
11:12 person who has **u** keeps quiet.
14:6 easily to a person who has **u**.
14:29 A person of great **u** is patient,
14:33 rest in the heart of an **u** person.
15:14 a person who has **u** searches
15:21 has **u** forges straight ahead.
15:32 who listens to warning gains **u**.
16:16 and the gaining of **u** should be
16:21 who is truly wise is called **u**,
16:22 **U** is a fountain of life to the one
17:10 a person who has **u** more than
17:24 directly in front of an **u** person,
17:27 who has **u** is even-tempered.
18:2 A fool does not find joy in **u** but
18:15 has **u** acquires knowledge.
19:8 guards **u** finds something good.
19:25 Warn an **u** person,
20:5 person who has **u** draws it out.
21:30 No wisdom, no **u**, and no
23:23 buy wisdom, discipline, and **u**.
24:3 With **u** it is established.
28:2 only with a person who has **u**
28:11 but a poor person with **u** sees
28:16 A leader without **u** taxes ⌊his
30:2 I don't ⌊even⌋ have human **u**.
Isa 11:2 the Spirit of wisdom and **u**,
28:19 **U** this message brings only
29:24 wayward in spirit will gain **u**,
40:14 Who gave him **u**? Who taught
40:14 him about the way to **u**?
40:28 His **u** is beyond reach.
44:19 enough knowledge or **u** to say,
Jer 10:12 out the world by his **u**.
51:15 stretched out heaven by his **u**.
Eze 28:4 Because you are wise and **u**,
Zec 6:13 be a peaceful **u** between them.
Mat 13:12 they will excel ⌊in **u** them⌋.
Mar 12:33 all your heart, with all your **u**,
Luk 2:47 His **u** and his answers stunned
Rom 3:11 No one has **u**. No one searches
1Co 1:10 united in your **u** and opinions.
Col 2:2 from a complete **u** of Christ.
1Pe 3:7 live with your wives with **u**
1Jn 5:20 and has given us **u** so that we

understands (11)

Dtr 29:4 hasn't given you a mind that **u**,
1Ch 28:9 heart and **u** every thought ⌊we
Job 28:23 "God **u** the way to it.
Psa 33:15 hearts **u** everything they do.
90:11 Who fully **u** the power of your
90:11 when he better **u** your fury.
Isa 57:1 are taken away, and no one **u**.
Dan 8:23 a stern-looking king who **u**
Mat 13:23 who⌋ hears and **u** the word.
Jon 8:47 to God **u** what God says.
1Co 14:2 No one **u** him. His spirit is

understood (14)

1Sm 20:39 but Jonathan and David **u**.
2Sm 3:36 Then all the people **u** and
1Ch 12:32 there were 200 leaders who **u**
Neh 8:12 celebration because they **u**
Job 13:1 My ear has heard and **u** it.
Isa 28:9 will they make the message **u**?
Dan 10:1 Daniel **u** the message because
Mat 13:51 "Have you **u** all of this?"
16:12 Then they **u** that he didn't say
17:13 Then the disciples **u** that he
Jon 2:24 these believers. He **u** people
1Co 14:9 speak in a way that can be **u**,
14:19 that can be **u** than ten thousand
Gal 2:9 It was **u** that we would work

undertook (1)

1Sm 18:14 successful in everything he **u**

underwear (1)

Isa 3:23 mirrors, **u**, headdresses,

undisciplined (1)

Pro 29:15 but an **u** child disgraces his

undisturbed (2)

Jer 46:27 will again have **u** peace,
Zec 7:7 cities were inhabited and **u**

undo (4)

Est 8:3 him to have mercy and to **u**
Job 40:8 "Would you **u** my justice?
Isa 43:13 I do something, who can **u** it?"
1Co 7:18 shouldn't **u** his circumcision.

undoing (1)

2Sm 15:34 me by⌋ **u** Ahithophel's advice.

undying (1)

Eph 6:24 everyone who has an **u** love

unending (1)

Jer 15:18 Why is my pain **u** and my

unethical (1)

1Th 2:3 we didn't use **u** schemes,

unexpected (2)

Isa 28:21 He will do his work, his **u** work,
Luk 12:46 master will return at an **u** time.

unexpectedly (2)

Isa 29:5 of this will happen suddenly, **u**.
Mat 24:50 His master will return **u**.

unexpressed (1)

Pro 27:5 Open criticism is better than **u**

unfailing (1)

Jer 2:2 I remember the **u** loyalty of your

unfair (13)

Psa 92:15 He is my rock. He is never **u**.
Pro 28:8 wealthy through ⌊**u**⌋ loans
Eze 18:25 'The Lord's way is **u**.' Listen,
18:25 Isn't it your ways that are **u**?
18:29 'The Lord's way is **u**.' Isn't
18:29 Isn't it your ways that are **u**?
33:17 'The Lord's way is **u**.' Yet, their
33:17 Yet, their ways are **u**.
33:20 'The Lord's way is **u**.' I
Mal 2:9 You have been **u** when
Rom 3:5 Is God **u** when he vents his
9:14 can we say — that God is **u**?
1Pe 2:18 but also those who are **u**.

unfairly (6)

Gen 16:5 "I'm being treated **u**!
Exo 21:8 since he has treated her **u**.
Psa 82:2 long are you going to judge **u**?
Mat 20:13 I'm not treating you **u**.
Act 7:24 Israelite man being treated **u** by
7:26 are you treating each other **u**?'

unfaithful (66)

Num 5:6 you have been **u** to the LORD.
5:12 wife may have been **u** to him
5:14 she was actually **u** or not.
5:19 you and you haven't been **u**
5:20 If, in fact, you have been **u** and
5:27 become unclean by being **u**
5:29 what to do when a woman is **u**
31:16 caused the Israelites to be **u**
Dtr 32:51 is because both of you were **u**
Jos 22:22 is rebellious or **u** to the LORD,
22:31 did not commit an **u** act against
Jdg 19:2 But she was **u** to him.
1Sm 14:33 Saul replied, "You have been **u**.
1Ch 5:25 of the tribe of Manasseh were **u**
2Ch 26:16 He was **u** to the LORD his God.
26:18 because you have been **u**.
28:19 Judah and was **u** to the LORD.
28:22 became more **u** to the LORD.
29:6 Our ancestors were **u** and did
2Ch 29:19 his reign when he was **u**.
30:7 and your relatives who were **u**
36:14 people became increasingly **u**
Ezr 9:2 have led the way in being **u**."
9:4 the former exiles had been **u**,
10:2 "We have been **u** to our God by
10:6 former exiles had been so **u**.
10:10 "You have been **u** by marrying
Neh 1:8 servant Moses: 'If you are **u**,
13:27 and be **u** to him by marrying
Psa 25:3 but all who are **u** will be put to
73:27 destroy all who are **u** to you.
101:3 I hate what **u** people do.
Pro 25:19 ⌊so⌋ is confidence in an **u**
Jer 2:19 and your **u** ways will punish
3:6 "Did you see what **u** Israel did?
3:8 Judah saw that I sent **u** Israel
3:11 Then the LORD said to me, "U
3:12 north: "'Come back, **u** Israel.
3:22 I will forgive you for being **u**."
5:6 they become more and more **u**.
5:11 Israel and Judah are **u** to me,"
14:7 We have been **u** and have
31:22 wander around, you **u** people?
49:4 fertile valleys, you **u** people?
Eze 14:13 against me by being **u** to me.
15:8 they have been **u**," declares
20:27 because they were **u** to me.
39:26 and all the **u** things they have
Dan 9:7 we have been **u** to you.
Hos 5:7 They have been **u** to the LORD,
6:7 You were **u** to me.
9:1 You have been **u** to your God.
Zep 3:4 Its prophets are reckless and **u**.
Mal 2:10 Why are we **u** to each other?
2:11 Judah has been **u**!
2:14 to whom you have been **u**.
2:15 So be careful not to be **u** to the
2:16 "Be careful not to be **u**."
Mat 12:39 "The people of an evil and **u**
16:4 "Evil and **u** people look for a
Mar 8:38 of me and what I say in this **u**
Luk 12:46 him a place with **u** people.
Rom 3:3 What if some of them were **u**?
2Ti 2:13 If we are **u**, he remains faithful
Jas 4:4 You **u** people! Don't you know
Rev 21:8 But cowardly, **u**, murderers,

unfaithfulness (9)

Num 14:33 They will suffer for your **u** until
1Ch 10:13 So Saul died because of his **u**
2Ch 33:19 This includes all his sins and **u**
Pro 23:28 spreads **u** throughout society.
Eze 18:24 remembered because of his **u**
Hos 14:4 "I will cure them of their **u**.
Mat 5:32 other than **u** makes her look
19:9 her **u** is committing adultery
Rom 3:3 **u** cancel God's faithfulness?

unfamiliar (3)

Isa 42:16 I will lead the blind on **u** roads.
42:16 I will lead them on **u** paths.
Heb 13:9 by all kinds of **u** teachings.

unfit (1)

Tit 1:16 and **u** to do anything good.

unforgettable (1)

Psa 111:4 He has made his miracles **u**.

unfulfilled (1)

1Sm 3:19 didn't let any of his words go **u**.

ungodly (17)

Psa 43:1 my case against an **u** nation.
Isa 32:6 plan evil in order to do **u** things.
33:14 Trembling seizes the **u**.
Rom 1:18 from heaven against every **u**
1:25 So they have become **u** and
4:5 one who approves **u** people,
5:6 Christ died for **u** people.
6:13 ever be used to do any **u** thing.
1Ti 1:9 for **u** people and sinners,
2Ti 2:16 will become more **u**,
Tit 2:12 It trains us to avoid **u** lives
2Pe 2:5 flood on the world of **u** people,

2Pe 2:6 cities an example to **u** people
3:7 kept until the day **u** people will
Jud 1:15 to convict all these **u** sinners
1:15 for all the **u** things they have
1:18 They will follow their own **u**

ungrateful (1)

Pro 29:21 and later he will be **u**.

unhappy (2)

Gen 40:7 "Why do you look so **u** today?"
Mar 10:22 he looked **u** and went away

unharmed (4)

1Sm 24:19 does he send him away **u**?
Psa 141:10 own nets, while I escape **u**.
Dan 3:25 in the middle of the fire, and **u**.
6:23 saw that he was completely **u**

unhealthy (1)

1Ti 6:4 Rather, he has an **u** desire to

unholy (9)

Lev 10:10 what is holy and what is **u**,
21:4 That would make you **u**.
Neh 13:17 treat the day of worship as **u**!
13:18 the day of worship as **u**."
Isa 56:2 of worship from becoming **u**
56:6 of worship from becoming **u**
Eze 22:26 what is holy and what is **u**.
42:20 was holy from what was **u**.
44:23 what is holy and what is **u**.

uniform (1)

2Sm 20:8 Joab wore a military **u**,

uniforms (4)

1Ki 10:5 officials and the **u** they wore,
2Ch 9:4 officials and the **u** they wore,
9:4 his cupbearers and their **u**,
Nah 2:3 His soldiers have red **u**.

unimaginable (1)

Dtr 28:59 descendants with **u** plagues.

unimportant (20)

1Sm 5:9 all the important and **u** people
18:23 I am a poor and **u** person."
Neh 9:32 have been going through as **u**.
Job 3:19 There ⌞you find⌟ both the **u**
14:21 Or they become **u**,
Psa 119:141 I am **u** and despised,
Pro 12:9 Better to be **u** and have a slave
Isa 19:15 important or **u** — can do
40:23 He makes rulers **u** and makes
Jer 30:19 and they won't be considered **u**.
Eze 21:26 Those who are **u** will become
21:26 are important will become **u**.
Mat 5:19 any command that seems **u**
5:19 others to do the same will be **u**
25:40 matter how **u** ⌞they seemed⌟,
25:45 matter how **u** ⌞they seemed⌟,
Act 26:22 to important and **u** people.
Rev 11:18 matter if they are important or **u**
13:16 important and **u** people,
20:12 both important and **u** people,

unintentional (3)

Num 15:24 If it was **u** and no one else
15:25 because the wrongdoing was **u**
15:26 involved in the **u** wrongdoing.

unintentionally (16)

Lev 4:2 person **u** does something wrong
4:13 Israel **u** does something wrong,
4:22 "When a leader **u** does
4:27 "If a common person **u** does
5:15 by **u** doing something wrong
5:18 you did **u** (although you didn't
Num 15:22 "Suppose you **u** do something
15:27 "If one person **u** does
15:29 who does something wrong **u**,
35:11 Anyone who **u** kills another
35:15 Anyone who **u** kills another
Dtr 4:42 Those who **u** killed someone
19:4 A person who **u** kills someone
Jos 20:3 who **u** kills someone may
Eze 45:20 who **u** does something wrong
Heb 9:7 that the people did wrong **u**.

union (1)

Dtr 23:2 A man born from an illicit **u**

unique (2)

Sos 6:9 but she is **u**, my dove,
6:9 Her mother thinks she is **u**.

unison (2)

2Ch 5:13 and thanked the LORD in **u**.
Act 19:34 everyone started to shout in **u**,

unit (32)

Exo 26:6 so that the tent is a single **u**.
26:11 tent together as a single **u**.
36:13 the inner tent was a single **u**.
36:18 tent together as a single **u**.
2Ki 6:14 and a large fighting **u** there.
1Ch 27:1 Each **u** consisted of 24,000
27:2 was in charge of the first **u**,
27:2 In his **u** there were 24,000.
27:4 was in charge of the **u** during
27:4 It was his **u**. (Mikloth was one of
27:4 In Dodai's **u** there were 24,000.
27:5 and in his **u** there were 24,000.
27:6 the thirty as well as his own **u**.
27:7 was in charge of the fourth **u**
27:7 In his **u** there were 24,000.
27:8 was commander of the fifth **u**
27:8 In his **u** there were 24,000.
27:9 was in charge of the sixth **u**
27:9 In his **u** there were 24,000.
27:10 was in charge of the seventh **u**
27:10 In his **u** there were 24,000.
27:11 was in charge of the eighth **u**
27:11 In his **u** there were 24,000.
27:12 was in charge of the ninth **u**
27:12 In his **u** there were 24,000.
27:13 was in charge of the tenth **u**
27:13 In his **u** there were 24,000.
27:14 was in charge of the eleventh **u**
27:14 In his **u** there were 24,000.
27:15 the twelfth **u** was commanded
27:15 In his **u** there were 24,000.
1Co 12:12 For example, the body is one **u**

unite (1)

Isa 14:1 Foreigners will join them and **u**

united (32)

Gen 2:24 father and mother and will be **u**
Jos 10:6 mountains have **u** against us."
Jdg 9:6 Shechem and Beth Millo **u**.
20:1 The congregation stood **u** in
20:8 All the people stood **u**,
20:11 They stood **u** against the city.
1Sm 11:7 they came out **u** ⌞behind Saul⌟.
2Ch 30:12 people of Judah so that they **u**
Job 16:10 They **u** against me.
Psa 73:28 Being **u** with God is my
122:3 a city where the people are **u**.
Mat 19:5 and mother and will remain **u**
Mar 10:7 and will remain **u** with his wife,
Jon 17:21 I pray that they may be **u** with
17:22 I did this so that they are **u** in
17:23 So they are completely **u**.
Act 4:24 they were **u** and loudly prayed
Rom 6:5 If we've become **u** with him in
6:5 certainly we will also be **u** with
1Co 1:10 I want you to be **u** in your
10:2 They were all **u** with Moses by
Eph 1:1 and faithful people who are **u**
4:13 to continue until all of us are **u**
5:31 his father and mother and be **u**
Php 1:1 who is **u** with Christ Jesus.
1:27 that you are firmly **u** in spirit,
1:27 **u** in fighting for the faith that
Col 1:2 brothers and sisters who are **u**
2:2 Because they are **u** in love,
1Th 1:1 the church at Thessalonica **u**
2:14 of God in Judea that are **u**
2Th 1:1 the church at Thessalonica **u**

unites (3)

1Co 6:16 that the person who **u** himself
6:17 However, the person who **u**
Eph 4:16 whole body fit together and **u**

units (4)

1Ki 9:22 of his chariot and cavalry **u**.
1Ch 27:1 the king in all the army's **u**.
28:1 the leaders of the army **u** that
2Ch 8:9 of his chariot and cavalry **u**.

unity (7)

Jdg 21:15 the LORD had broken the **u**
Zec 11:7 one Favor and the other U.
11:14 staff, called U, in pieces,
Jon 17:11 so that their **u** may be like ours.
17:21 people continue to have **u**
Eph 4:3 do your best to maintain the **u**
Col 2:19 through support and **u** given by

universe (7)

Mat 24:29 powers of the **u** will be shaken.
Mar 13:25 powers of the **u** will be shaken.
Luk 21:26 powers of the **u** will be shaken.
Act 17:24 The God who made the **u** and
Heb 1:2 through whom God made the **u**.
2Pe 3:10 Everything that makes up the **u**
3:12 Everything that makes up the **u**

unjust (12)

2Ch 19:7 The LORD our God is never **u**.
Job 16:11 God handed me over to **u**
Psa 43:1 Rescue me from deceitful and **u**
71:4 of one who is cruel and **u**.
Pro 1:19 who is greedy for **u** gain.
15:27 Whoever is greedy for **u** gain
28:16 but those who hate **u** gain will
29:27 An **u** person is disgusting to
Isa 10:1 be for those who make **u** laws
Mal 2:6 Nothing **u** was found on his
Mat 5:45 them whether they are just or **u**.
1Pe 2:19 the pains of **u** suffering.

unjustly (2)

2Co 7:2 We haven't treated anyone **u**,
Jas 5:10 patient when they suffered **u**.

unkind (2)

1Sm 29:10 Don't worry about the **u** words,
Mar 14:5 said some very **u** things to her.

unknown (6)

1Ki 18:12 you away to some **u** place.
Psa 35:15 U attackers tore me apart
Pro 22:29 He will not serve **u** people.
Act 17:23 this written on it: 'To an **u** god.'
17:23 about the **u** god you worship.
2Co 6:9 as **u** although we are

unlawful (1)

Psa 94:20 use the law to do **u** things able

unleash (10)

1Sm 28:18 to him or **u** his burning anger
Job 40:11 U your outbursts of anger.
Isa 10:25 Very soon I will **u** my fury,
Eze 5:13 "I will **u** my anger.
6:12 This is how I will **u** my anger.
7:8 my fury on you and **u** my anger
13:15 I will **u** my fury on the wall and
20:8 fury on them and **u** my anger
20:21 fury on them and **u** my anger
24:13 You will never be clean until I **u**

unleashed (2)

Lam 4:11 He **u** his burning anger.
Eze 5:13 When my fury is **u** against you,

unleavened (54)

Gen 19:3 baked some **u** bread,
Exo 12:8 with bitter herbs and **u** bread.
12:15 days you must eat **u** bread.
12:17 the Festival of U Bread
12:18 day you must eat **u** bread.
12:20 you must eat ⌞only⌟ **u** bread."

Exo 13:6 days you must eat **u** bread.
13:7 Only **u** bread should be eaten
23:15 the Festival of **U** Bread:
23:15 days you must eat **u** bread,
29:23 From the basket of **u** bread
34:18 the Festival of **U** Bread.
34:18 you must eat **u** bread for seven
Lev 2:4 it must be rings of **u** bread
2:4 oil or wafers of **u** bread brushed
2:5 will be **u** bread made of flour
6:16 They will eat **u** bread in a holy
7:12 you must also bring rings of **u**
7:12 wafers of **u** bread brushed with
8:2 and the basket of **u** bread.
8:26 He took a loaf of **u** bread,
8:26 basket of **u** bread which was
10:12 Make **u** bread, and eat it next
23:6 LORD's Festival of **U** Bread.
23:6 For seven days you must eat **u**
Num 6:15 of **u** bread containing some
6:15 and wafers of **u** bread brushed
6:17 offer the basket of **u** bread
6:19 one ring of **u** bread from the
6:19 and one wafer of **u** bread and
9:11 animal along with **u** bread
28:17 you must eat only **u** bread.
Dtr 16:3 for seven days you must eat **u**
16:8 For six days eat **u** bread,
16:16 at the Festival of **U** Bread,
Jos 5:11 **u** bread and roasted grain.
Jdg 6:19 a young goat and **u** bread made
6:20 the meat and the **u** bread,
1Sm 28:24 and baked some **u** bread.
2Ki 23:9 Instead, they ate their **u** bread
1Ch 23:29 the **u** bread wafers,
2Ch 8:13 (the Festival of **U** Bread,
30:13 the Festival of **U** Bread
30:21 the Festival of **U** Bread
35:17 the Festival of **U** Bread
Ezr 6:22 the Festival of **U** Bread
Eze 45:21 days when **u** bread is eaten.
Mat 26:17 day of the Festival of **U** Bread,
Mar 14:1 and the Festival of **U** Bread.
14:12 day of the Festival of **U** Bread.
Luk 22:1 The Festival of **U** Bread,
22:7 the Festival of **U** Bread when
Act 12:3 during the days of **U** Bread.
20:6 After the Festival of **U** Bread,

unlike (5)

2Ch 27:2 But **u** his father, he didn't
Isa 7:17 a time **u** any since Ephraim
Dan 12:1 It will be a time of trouble **u**
Mat 7:29 **U** their scribes, he taught them
Mar 1:22 **U** their scribes, he taught them

unlimited (11)

Exo 15:7 With your **u** majesty,
Psa 37:11 land and will enjoy **u** peace.
51:1 with your **u** compassion,
69:16 Out of your **u** compassion,
72:7 May there be **u** peace until the
130:7 with him there is **u** forgiveness.
Isa 9:7 and peace will have **u** growth.
54:7 but I will bring you back with **u**
54:13 and your children will have **u**
63:7 compassion and his **u** mercy.
Eph 1:19 You will also know the **u**

unload (1)

Act 21:3 the ship was to **u** its cargo.

unloaded (1)

Gen 24:32 The camels were **u** and given

unlocks (1)

Luk 11:52 the key that **u** knowledge.

unloved (4)

Gen 29:31 the LORD saw Leah was **u**,
29:33 the LORD has heard that I'm **u**,
Pro 30:23 a woman who is **u** when she
Hos 1:6 "Name her Lo Ruhamah [**U**].

unmarked (1)

Luk 11:44 You are like **u** graves.

unmarried (8)

Lev 21:3 and especially an **u** virgin
Num 30:6 "An **u** woman might make a
Jdg 21:12 found 400 **u** women who had
2Ch 36:17 the best men or the **u** women,
Eze 44:25 daughter, brother, or **u** sister.
Act 21:9 Philip had four **u** daughters
1Co 7:32 An **u** man is concerned about
7:34 An **u** woman or a virgin is

unmixed (1)

Rev 14:10 which has been poured **u** into

unnatural (2)

Lev 18:23 for sexual intercourse. It is **u**.
Rom 1:26 sexual relations for **u** ones.

Unni (2)

1Ch 15:18 **U**, Eliab, Benaiah, Maaseiah,
15:20 Jehiel, **U**, Eliab, Maaseiah,

Unno (1)

Neh 12:9 and **U** stood across from

unnoticed (1)

Jud 1:4 have slipped in among you **u**.

unoccupied (1)

Mat 12:44 it finds the house **u**,

unplowed (2)

Exo 23:11 leave the land **u** and unused.
Jer 4:3 Plow your **u** fields,

unplugged (1)

Isa 35:5 the ears of the deaf will be **u**.

unpredictable (1)

Ecc 9:11 But time and **u** events overtake

unpresentable (1)

1Co 12:23 So our **u** parts are made more

unproductive (1)

Psa 68:6 people must live in an **u** land.

unprofitable (1)

Jer 16:19 worthless and **u** gods."

unprotected (3)

Gen 42:9 find out where our country is **u**.
42:12 find out where our country is **u**.
Jos 8:17 So the city was left **u** as they

unpunished (17)

Exo 34:7 He never lets the guilty go **u**,
Num 14:18 He never lets the guilty go **u**,
1Ki 2:9 Now, don't let him go **u**.
Pro 11:21 an evil person will not go **u**,
16:5 ⌊such a person⌋ will not go **u**.
19:5 A lying witness will not go **u**.
19:9 A lying witness will not go **u**.
Jer 25:29 Do you think you'll go **u**?
25:29 You will not go **u**! I'm declaring
30:11 I won't let you go entirely **u**.
46:28 I won't let you go entirely **u**."
49:12 why should you go **u**?
49:12 You won't go **u**. You must drink
Eze 17:15 can't break a treaty and go **u**.
17:18 these things, and he can't go **u**.
Nah 1:3 will never let the guilty go **u**.
Zec 11:5 them will kill them and go **u**.

unquestioned (1)

1Ch 12:33 Their loyalty was **u**.

unravel (1)

Isa 19:3 I will **u** their plans.

unrealistic (2)

Pro 12:11 but the one who chases **u**
28:19 Whoever chases **u** dreams will

unreasonable (1)

Psa 106:14 They had an **u** desire ⌊for

unrecognizable (2)

Isa 33:19 people with an **u** language,
Jer 19:4 They have made this place **u**

unreliable (1)

Job 6:21 "So you are as **u** to me ⌊as

unrest (1)

Jer 50:34 rest to the land of Israel and **u**

unrighteous (1)

Job 27:7 me be ⌊treated⌋ like **u** people.

unripened (2)

Job 15:33 He will drop his **u** grapes like a
Mal 3:11 will not lose their **u** grapes,"

unsealed (3)

Neh 6:5 held in his hand an **u** letter.
Jer 32:11 as well as an **u** copy.
32:14 both the sealed and the **u**

unsearchable (3)

Job 9:10 He does great things that are **u**
Psa 145:3 His greatness is **u**.
Pro 25:3 so the mind of kings is **u**.

unselfish (1)

Psa 78:72 With **u** devotion David became

unsettled (1)

Dtr 28:65 LORD will give you an **u** mind,

unsolved (2)

Dtr 21:8 Don't let the guilt of this **u**
21:9 guilt of an **u** murder by doing

unstained (1)

Jas 1:27 Pure, **u** religion, according to

unstoppable (2)

Job 42:2 and that your plans are **u**.
Amo 1:11 Their anger was **u**.

unsuspecting (2)

Jdg 8:11 defeated the **u** Midianite army.
Rom 16:18 words they deceive **u** people.

untamed (1)

Gen 16:12 free and wild as an **u** donkey.

untangle (2)

Dan 5:12 solve riddles, and **u** problems.
5:16 such things and **u** problems.

unthankful (1)

Luk 6:35 he is kind to **u** and evil people.

unthinkable (30)

Gen 18:25 It would be **u** for you to do such
18:25 That would be **u**! Won't the
Jos 22:29 It would be **u** for us to rebel
24:16 "It would be **u** for us to
1Sm 12:23 It would be **u** for me to sin
14:45 That would be **u**! We solemnly
20:2 Jonathan answered, "That's **u**!
20:9 Jonathan answered, "That's **u**!
24:6 "It would be **u** for me to raise
26:11 It would be **u** for me to attack
2Sm 20:20 Joab answered, "That's **u**!
23:17 "It's **u** that I would do this,
1Ch 11:19 "It's **u** that I would do this,
Job 27:5 It's **u** for me to admit that you
34:10 It is **u** that God would ever do
Luk 20:16 who heard him said, "That's **u**!"
Rom 3:4 That would be **u**! God is honest,
3:6 That's **u**! Otherwise, how would
3:31 That's **u**! Rather, we are
6:2 That's **u**! As far as sin is
6:15 by God's favor? That's **u**!
7:7 That's **u**! In fact, I wouldn't have
7:13 That's **u**! Rather, my death was
9:14 that God is unfair? That's **u**!
11:1 That's **u**! Consider this. I'm an
11:11 That's **u**! By Israel's failure,

1Co 6:15 a prostitute's body? That's **u**!
Gal 2:17 us to sin? That's **u**!
3:21 That's **u**! If those laws could
6:14 But it's **u** that I could ever brag

untie (9)

Job 38:31 ⌊constellation⌋ Pleiades or **u**
Isa 58:6 **u** the straps of the yoke,
Mat 21:2 **U** them, and bring them to me.
Mar 1:7 down and **u** his sandal straps.
11:2 ever sat on it. **U** it, and bring it.
Luk 3:16 I am not worthy to **u** his sandal
19:30 ever sat on it. **U** it, and bring it.
Jon 1:27 worthy to **u** his sandal strap."
Act 13:25 good enough to **u** his sandals.'

untied (3)

Job 30:11 Because God has **u** my cord
Dan 3:25 They're **u**, walking in the
Act 27:40 At the same time they **u** the

unties (1)

Job 39:5 Who **u** the ropes of the wild

untimely (1)

Job 4:7 ⌊ever⌋ died ⌊an **u** death⌋?

untrained (1)

Jer 31:18 I was like a young, **u** calf.

untrue (2)

Act 25:11 But if their accusations are **u**,
2Ti 2:13 he cannot be **u** to himself.

untying (5)

Mar 11:4 of a house. As they were **u** it,
11:5 "Why are you **u** that donkey?
Luk 19:31 asks you why you are **u** it,
19:33 While they were **u** the young
19:33 "Why are you **u** the donkey?"

unused (2)

Exo 23:11 leave the land unplowed and **u**.
2Sm 1:22 nor did Saul's sword return **u**.

unusual (4)

Act 17:21 or hear something new and **u**.
19:11 **u** miracles through Paul.
28:6 time and saw nothing **u** happen
1Co 10:13 which is **u** for humans.

unusually (1)

Act 28:2 lived on the island were **u** kind

unwalled (4)

Dtr 3:5 a large number of **u** villages.
Est 9:19 and in the **u** towns make
Eze 38:11 attack a land with **u** villages.
Zec 2:4 be inhabited like an **u** village

unweighed (1)

1Ki 7:47 Solomon left all the products **u**

unwilling (1)

2Sm 12:17 from the ground, but he was **u**.

unwillingly (1)

1Co 9:17 if I spread the Good News **u**,

unwise (1)

Pro 20:1 under their influence is **u**.

unworthy (1)

Act 13:46 and consider yourselves **u**

unyielding (1)

Sos 8:6 Devotion is as **u** as the grave.

Uphaz (2)

Jer 10:9 from Tarshish and gold from **U**.
Dan 10:5 of gold from **U** around his waist.

upheld (1)

Job 36:17 A fair judgment will be **u**.

uphold (1)

Isa 9:7 He will **u** it with justice and

upper (32)

Gen 6:16 lower, middle, and **u** decks.
Lev 13:45 They must cover their **u** lips
Jos 15:19 her the **u** and lower springs.
16:5 Ataroth Addar to **U** Beth Horon.
Jdg 1:15 her the **u** and lower springs.
2Ki 15:35 Jotham built the **U** Gate of the
18:17 at the channel for the **U** Pool
1Ch 7:24 who built **U** and Lower Beth
19:6 Arameans in **U** Mesopotamia,
28:11 **u** rooms, inner rooms,
2Ch 3:9 overlaid the **u** rooms with gold.
8:5 He rebuilt **U** Beth Horon and
23:20 They went through **U** Gate to
27:3 Jotham built the **U** Gate of the
32:30 from flowing from the **u** outlet
32:33 He was buried in the **u** tombs
Neh 3:25 and the **u** tower that projects
3:31 and as far as the **u** room at
3:32 repairs between the **u** room at
Isa 7:3 end of the ditch of the **U** Pool
11:11 **U** and Lower Egypt,
36:2 at the channel for the **U** Pool
38:8 stairway of Ahaz's **u** palace.
Jer 20:2 prison at **U** Benjamin Gate that
22:13 his **u** rooms through injustice.
22:14 for myself with big **u** rooms.'
36:10 in the **u** courtyard at the
Eze 9:2 came from the **u** north gate.
43:14 the lower ledge to the **u** ledge
43:17 The **u** ledge was also square.
Dan 6:10 An **u** room in his house had
1Co 1:26 or in the **u** social classes.

upright (3)

1Ki 9:4 (with a sincere and **u** heart),
Isa 26:7 O **U** One, you make the road of
26:10 They do what is wrong in the **u**

uprisings (1)

Ezr 4:19 long history of **u** against kings.

uproar (10)

Psa 65:7 and the **u** of the nations.
74:23 Do not forget the **u** made by
83:2 Look, your enemies are in an **u**.
Pro 29:8 Mockers create an **u** in a city,
Isa 25:5 You calm the **u** of foreigners.
66:6 Listen to the **u** from the city.
Jer 10:22 A tremendous **u** is coming from
Mat 21:10 the whole city was in an **u**.
Act 12:18 were in an **u** over what had
20:1 When the **u** was over,

uproot (12)

1Ki 14:15 He will **u** Israel from this good
2Ch 7:20 then I will **u** Israel from the land
Job 31:12 It would **u** my entire harvest.
Jer 1:10 You will **u** and tear down.
12:14 I am going to **u** those neighbors
12:14 I will also **u** the people of
12:17 Then I will **u** that nation and
24:6 I will plant them and not **u**
31:28 I watched over them to **u** them,
42:10 I will plant you and not **u** you.
45:4 I will **u** what I have planted
Eze 17:9 Won't the first eagle **u** it and

uprooted (14)

Dtr 29:28 the LORD **u** these people from
Job 8:18 But when it is **u** from its place,
31:8 and let my crops be **u**.
Psa 9:6 You have **u** their cities.
Jer 12:15 After I've **u** them, I will have
31:40 It will never be **u** or torn down
Eze 19:12 But in anger it was **u** and
Dan 7:8 It **u** three of the other horns.
11:4 since it will be **u** and given to
Amo 9:15 and they won't be **u** again from
Mat 15:13 Father did not plant will be **u**.
21:21 'Be **u** and thrown into the sea,'
Mar 11:23 'Be **u** and thrown into the sea,'

Jud 1:12 **u** trees without any fruit.

uproots (1)

Job 19:10 He **u** my hope like a tree.

upset (26)

Gen 21:11 Abraham was **u** by this
21:12 "Don't be **u** about the boy and
40:6 he saw that they were **u**.
41:8 In the morning he was so **u**
Jdg 17:2 He told his mother, "You were **u**
1Ki 20:43 Resentful and **u**, the king of
21:4 Resentful and **u**, Ahab went
Neh 2:10 they were very **u** that someone
Job 20:2 and because of them I am **u**.
Psa 77:4 I am so **u** that I cannot speak.
Pro 24:19 not get overly **u** with evildoers.
Jnh 4:1 Jonah was very **u** about this,
Nah 2:10 Every stomach becomes **u**.
Mat 27:19 I've been very **u** today because
Luk 10:40 But Martha was **u** about all the
18:13 Instead, he became very **u**,
Act 2:37 they were deeply **u**.
14:14 happening, they were very **u**.
17:8 were **u** when they heard
17:13 they went there to **u** and
17:16 gods everywhere. This **u** him.
1Co 5:2 have been more **u** about this.
5:2 If you had been **u**, the man who
Eph 4:30 any reason to be **u** with you.
2Th 2:2 Don't get **u** right away or
1Pe 3:14 want to harm you. Don't get **u**.

upside (4)

Jdg 7:13 turned **u** down, and fell flat."
2Ki 21:13 wiped out and turned **u** down.
Pro 19:3 a person turns his life **u** down,
Isa 29:16 You turn things **u** down!

upstairs (13)

1Ki 17:19 carried him to the **u** room where
17:23 brought him down from the **u**
2Ki 1:2 a window lattice in his **u** room
4:11 went into the **u** room,
4:21 She took him **u** and laid him on
23:12 on the roof of Ahaz's **u** room,
Mar 14:15 He will take you **u** and show
Luk 22:12 He will take you **u** and show
Act 9:37 and was laid in an **u** room.
9:39 he arrived, he was taken **u**.
16:34 He took Paul and Silas **u** into
20:8 (Many lamps were lit in the **u**
20:11 Then Eutychus went **u** again,

upstream (2)

Jos 3:13 Then the water flowing from **u**
3:16 water stopped flowing from **u**.

upward (6)

Psa 139:9 If I climb **u** on the rays of the
Pro 15:24 of life for a wise person leads **u**
Ecc 3:21 whether a human spirit goes **u**
Isa 9:18 and it whirls **u** in clouds of
Eze 1:11 were spread out, pointing **u**.
17:6 Its branches turned **u** toward

Ur (5)

Gen 11:28 Haran died in **U** of the
11:31 They set out together from **U** of
15:7 who brought you out of **U** of the
1Ch 11:35 the Hararite), Eliphal (son of **U**)
Neh 9:7 Abram and took him from **U**

Urbanus (1)

Rom 16:9 Greet **U** our coworker in the

urge (8)

2Sm 13:25 Absalom continued to **u** him,
Luk 14:23 **U** the people to come to my
Act 19:31 sent messengers to **u** him not
Rom 16:17 Brothers and sisters, I **u** you to
2Co 2:8 That is why I **u** you to assure
6:1 we **u** you not to let God's
8:6 This led us to **u** Titus to finish
Heb 13:22 I **u** you, brothers and sisters,

urged (11)

Gen 19:15 the angels **u** Lot by saying,
Jdg 19:7 his father-in-law **u** him to stay
2Sm 13:27 But when Absalom **u** him,
2Ki 5:16 Naaman **u** him to take it,
5:23 Naaman **u** him ⌊to take the
Jer 36:25 and Gemariah **u** the king not to
Mat 14:8 **U** by her mother, she said,
15:23 came to him and **u** him,
Luk 24:29 They **u** him, "Stay with us!
Act 2:40 He **u**, "Save yourselves from
16:9 The man **u** Paul, "Come to

urgent (4)

1Sm 21:8 the king's business was **u**."
Psa 143:1 ears to hear my **u** requests.
Dan 3:22 The king's order was so **u** and
Tit 3:14 things when **u** needs arise so

urging (6)

1Sm 28:23 and the woman kept **u** him until
1Ki 21:25 At the **u** of his wife,
2Ki 2:17 But the disciples kept **u** him
Jer 8:7 am **u** them to return.
Jon 4:31 the disciples were **u** him,
Act 25:2 against Paul. They were **u**

Uri (8)

Exo 31:2 son of **U** and grandson of Hur,
35:30 son of **U** and grandson of Hur,
38:22 son of **U** and grandson of Hur,
1Ki 4:19 Geber, son of **U**, was in charge
1Ch 2:20 Hur was the father of **U**,
2:20 Hur was the father of Uri, and **U**
2Ch 1:5 son of **U** and grandson of Hur,
Ezr 10:24 Shallum, Telem, and **U**

Uriah (35)

2Sm 11:3 Eliam and wife of **U** the Hittite."
11:6 "Send me **U** the Hittite."
11:6 So Joab sent **U** to David.
11:7 When **U** arrived, David asked
11:8 "Go home," David said to **U**,
11:8 **U** left the royal palace,
11:9 But **U** slept at the entrance of
11:10 "**U** didn't go home,"
11:10 go home," David asked **U**,
11:11 **U** answered David,
11:12 David said to **U**, "Then stay
11:12 So **U** stayed in Jerusalem that
11:13 But that evening **U** went to lie
11:14 letter to Joab and sent it with **U**.
11:15 In the letter he wrote, "Put **U** on
11:16 he put **U** at the place where he
11:17 died — including **U** the Hittite.
11:21 'Your man **U** the Hittite is also
11:24 Your man **U** the Hittite also is
11:26 that her husband **U** was dead,
12:9 You had **U** the Hittite killed in
12:10 me and took the wife of **U**
23:39 **U** the Hittite — 37 in all.
1Ki 15:5 matter concerning **U** the Hittite
1Ch 11:41 **U** the Hittite, Zabad (son of
Ezr 8:33 son of the priest **U**,
Neh 3:4 son of **U** and grandson of
3:21 After him Meremoth, son of **U**
8:4 Mattithiah, Shema, Anaiah, **U**,
Isa 8:2 the priest **U** and Zechariah (son
Jer 26:20 His name was **U**, son of
26:21 and officials heard what **U** said,
26:21 But **U** heard about it and fled in
26:23 They brought **U** from Egypt and
26:23 The king executed **U** and

Uriah's (3)

2Sm 11:26 When **U** wife heard that her
12:15 child that **U** wife had given birth
Mat 1:6 David and **U** wife ⌊Bathsheba⌋

Uriel (4)

1Ch 6:24 Tahath's son was **U**.
15:5 Kohath's descendants was **U**,
15:11 Abiathar and for the Levites **U**,
2Ch 13:2 daughter of **U** from Gibeah.

Uriel's (1)

1Ch 6:24 **U** son was Uzziah.

Urijah (4)

2Ki 16:10 So King Ahaz sent the priest **U**
16:11 **U** built an altar exactly like the
16:15 this command to the priest **U**:
16:16 The priest **U** did what King

Urim (8)

Exo 28:30 Put the **U** and Thummim into
Lev 8:8 he placed the **U** and Thummim.
Num 27:21 who will use the **U** to make
Dtr 33:8 "Your Thummim and **U** belong
1Sm 14:41 ⌊let the priest⌋ draw **U**.
28:6 dreams, the **U**, or prophets.
Ezr 2:63 until a priest could use the **U**
Neh 7:65 until a priest could use the **U**

urine (2)

2Ki 18:27 drink their own **u** with you?"
Isa 36:12 drink their own **u** with you?"

Ursa Major (2)

Job 9:9 ⌊the constellations⌋ **U**, Orion,
38:32 or guide **U** with its cubs

use (264)

Gen 27:40 You will **u** your sword to live,
47:24 Four-fifths will be yours to **u** as
49:30 the Hittite to **u** as a tomb.
Exo 3:20 So I will **u** my power to strike
4:17 and **u** it to do the miraculous
7:4 Then I will **u** my power to
7:5 when I **u** my power against
10:26 We'll have to **u** some of them
11:5 slaves who **u** their handmills,
15:9 I'll **u** my sword! I'll take all they
20:7 "Never **u** the name of the LORD
20:25 If you **u** a chisel on it,
20:26 Never **u** stairs to go up to my
25:28 and **u** them to carry the table.
25:39 **U** 75 pounds of pure gold to
26:6 **U** them to link the ⌊two sets
26:32 **U** gold hooks to hang it on four
28:5 They must **u** gold,
29:2 **U** the finest wheat flour,
29:5 **U** the belt to tie it on him tightly.
30:16 and **u** it to pay the expenses of
30:19 Aaron and his sons will **u** it for
30:26 "**U** it to anoint the tent of
Lev 5:16 So the priest will **u** the ram
6:17 Don't **u** yeast in baking the
7:24 by wild animals you may **u**
8:15 it holy so that priests could **u**
11:21 that swarm if they **u** their legs
12:8 she must **u** two mourning
14:4 sprig to **u** for the cleansing.
14:21 and **u** it for his guilt offering.
14:49 and a hyssop sprig and **u** them
14:52 So he must **u** the bird's blood,
19:22 presence the priest will **u** them
19:36 **U** honest scales, and honest
22:23 You may **u** a bull or a sheep
23:13 **U** one quart of wine for the
27:3 **U** the standard weight of the
Num 5:8 the LORD for the priest ⌊to **u**⌋.
6:27 "So whenever they **u** my name
7:5 these gifts from them to **u**
7:5 Give them to the Levites to **u**
10:2 **U** them to call the community
19:12 The unclean person must **u**
19:12 But if he doesn't **u** this water on
19:13 being and doesn't **u** this water
26:54 **U** the totals ⌊from the census⌋
27:21 who will **u** the Urim to make
31:3 The LORD will **u** them to get
31:19 your prisoners of war must **u**
35:24 Then the community must **u**
Dtr 5:11 "Never **u** the name of the LORD
9:3 wipe them out and will **u** you
14:26 **U** the silver to buy whatever
15:19 Never **u** a firstborn ox for work,
20:20 You may cut them down and **u**
23:25 But never **u** a sickle to cut your
Eze 25:15 **U** accurate and honest weights
27:5 Don't **u** an iron chisel on the
27:6 You must **u** uncut stones to
32:21 So I will **u** those who are not
32:23 I will **u** up all my arrows on
33:17 They will **u** them to push away
Jdg 4:9 because the LORD will **u** a
9:9 which people **u** to honor gods
1Sm 8:16 your donkeys for his own **u**.
1Ki 2:6 **U** your wisdom. Don't let that
5:9 and you can **u** them.
13:6 and pray for me so that I can **u**
13:6 and the king was able to **u** his
2Ki 3:19 and **u** rocks to ruin every good
11:15 **U** your sword to kill anyone
12:5 receive it from the donors and **u**
12:7 the donors ⌊for your own **u**⌋.
12:7 Instead, **u** it to make repairs on
12:8 the people ⌊for personal **u**⌋ nor
15:37 LORD began to **u** King Rezin
16:15 I will **u** the bronze altar for
22:6 Also, **u** ⌊the rest of⌋ the money
1Ch 28:15 its lamps (according to the **u**
2Ch 10:14 I will **u** scorpions."
12:7 I will not **u** Shishak to pour my
23:14 **U** your sword to kill anyone
24:6 to give contributions for the **u**
25:8 God will **u** the enemy to defeat
29:19 refused to **u** during his reign
Ezr 2:63 holy food until a priest could **u**
7:17 You must **u** this money to buy
7:20 You may **u** the king's treasury
Neh 7:65 holy food until a priest could **u**
Job 7:3 given months that are of no **u**,
21:9 and God doesn't **u** his rod on
22:2 "Can a human be of any **u** to
23:5 to know the words he would **u**
30:2 Of what **u** to me was the
Psa 16:4 offerings of blood or **u** my lips
35:2 **U** your shields, ⌊both⌋ small
94:20 Are wicked rulers who **u** the
102:8 Those who ridicule me **u** my
104:3 You **u** the clouds for your
104:14 vegetables for humans to **u**
119:66 Teach me ⌊to **u**⌋ good
125:3 people do not **u** their power
Pro 3:21 **U** priceless wisdom and
24:5 knows how to **u** his strength,
Ecc 10:10 one has to **u** more strength.
Isa 5:25 and he is ready to **u** his power
5:25 he is still ready to **u** his power.
9:12 he is still ready to **u** his power.
9:17 he is still ready to **u** his power.
9:21 he is still ready to **u** his power.
10:4 he is still ready to **u** his power.
11:11 At that time the Lord will **u** his
14:26 This is how he will **u** his
14:27 He is ready to **u** his power.
27:1 On that day the LORD will **u**
48:14 He will **u** his strength against
Jer 2:22 you wash with detergent and **u**
6:12 I will **u** my power against those
9:3 They **u** their tongues like bows
15:6 So I will **u** my power against
22:15 because you **u** more cedar?
23:10 The people are evil, and they **u**
29:22 are in Babylon will **u** this curse:
31:23 they will once again **u** this
46:9 Lydia who **u** bows and arrows.
51:20 I will **u** you to crush nations.
51:20 I will **u** you to destroy
51:21 I will **u** you to crush horses and
51:21 I will **u** you to crush chariots
51:22 I will **u** you to crush men and
51:22 I will **u** you to crush the old and
51:22 I will **u** you to crush young men
51:23 I will **u** you to crush shepherds
51:23 I will **u** you to crush farmers
51:23 I will **u** you to crush governors
51:25 "I will **u** my power against you,
51:26 find any stones in you to **u** as
51:26 find any stones in you to **u**
Eze 4:9 Put them in a container, and **u**
4:15 He said to me, "I will let you **u**
5:1 and **u** it as a barber's razor to
5:13 I will **u** my fury against you,

Eze 6:14 I will **u** my power against them
12:23 I will put a stop to the **u** of this
13:9 I will **u** my power against the
13:20 the magic charms that you **u**
14:9 I will **u** my power against you
14:13 I will **u** my power against it,
15:3 Do people **u** it to make
18:2 when you **u** this proverb about
18:3 you will no longer **u** this
20:22 But I didn't **u** my power so that
22:13 "'I will **u** my power against you
25:7 That is why I will **u** my power
25:13 I will **u** my power against
25:14 I will **u** my people Israel to take
25:16 I'm going to **u** my power
30:10 I will **u** King Nebuchadnezzar
35:3 I will **u** my power against you,
35:12 and handed over to us to **u** up."
38:4 and be able to **u** swords.
38:12 I will **u** my power against the
38:12 I will **u** it against the people
38:16 I will **u** you for my holy
38:21 Each person will **u** his sword
45:4 They will **u** this place for their
Dan 8:25 He will cleverly **u** his power to
11:42 He will **u** his power against
Hos 1:7 I won't **u** bows, swords, wars,
12:7 merchants **u** dishonest scales.
Amo 7:7 by a wall built with the **u**
Mic 5:9 You will **u** your power against
6:10 people who **u** their money
6:10 evil and **u** inaccurate weights
Zep 1:4 "I will **u** my power against
2:13 The LORD will **u** his power
3:13 or **u** their tongues to deceive
Zec 9:13 and I will **u** you like a warrior's
11:15 Then the LORD said to me, "**U**
14:12 be the plague the LORD will **u**
Mat 7:2 by the same standard you **u**
7:2 The standards you **u** for others
13:10 "Why do you **u** stories as
19:10 is the only reason a man can **u**
26:52 All who **u** a sword will be
26:59 testimony to **u** against Jesus
27:7 So they decided to **u** it to buy a
Mar 4:13 the stories I **u** as illustrations?
16:17 They will **u** the power and
Luk 3:14 and never **u** threats or
6:38 The standards you **u** for others
10:17 demons obey us when we **u**
12:41 Peter asked, "Lord, did you **u**
13:7 should it **u** up ⌊good⌋ soil?'
16:9 you should **u** it to make friends
22:49 should we **u** our swords to
Jon 4:11 you don't have anything to **u** to
8:43 understand the language I **u**?
8:43 can't understand the words I **u**?
16:25 when I won't **u** examples
17:17 "**U** the truth to make them holy.
17:19 will **u** the truth to be holy.
Act 7:25 that God was going to **u** him
17:31 and he will **u** a man he has
18:24 speaker and knew how to **u**
19:13 They tried to **u** the name of the
Rom 2:16 He will **u** the Good News that I
6:13 **U** them to do everything that
8:13 But if you **u** your spiritual
9:21 something for everyday **u** from
12:3 you to **u** good judgment based
12:11 **U** your energy to serve the Lord
15:27 So they are obligated to **u** their
1Co 1:17 I didn't **u** intellectual arguments
1:21 So God decided to **u** the
2:6 However, we do **u** wisdom to
2:13 we **u** the Spirit's teachings.
5:11 **u** abusive language,
6:10 who **u** abusive language,
6:20 in the way you **u** your body.
7:5 that Satan doesn't **u** your lack
7:17 guideline I **u** in every church.
7:31 Those who **u** the things in this
9:15 this in order to **u** them now.
9:18 In that way I won't **u** the rights
2Co 4:2 Instead, we have refused to **u**
4:2 We don't **u** tricks, and we don't
6:8 and as we **u** what is right to
2Co 10:4 The weapons we **u** in our fight
Gal 3:15 Brothers and sisters, let me **u**
4:24 I'm going to **u** these historical
5:20 idolatry, drug **u**, hatred, rivalry,
Eph 4:14 by people who **u** cunning
6:18 **U** every kind of prayer and
6:18 **U** every kind of effort and make
Col 3:16 **U** psalms, hymns, and spiritual
1Th 2:3 we didn't **u** unethical schemes,
2Th 2:9 He will **u** every kind of power,
2:10 He will **u** everything that God
1Ti 1:16 that Christ Jesus could **u** me,
1:18 **U** these prophecies in faith and
3:2 be sober, **u** good judgment,
3:8 They must not **u** shameful
5:1 Never **u** harsh words when you
6:20 false knowledge that people **u**
2Ti 2:21 be set apart for the master's **u**,
3:2 and **u** abusive language.
Tit 1:7 He must not **u** shameful ways
1:8 what is good, **u** good judgment,
1:9 Then he can **u** these accurate
2:2 to **u** good judgment,
2:5 to **u** good judgment,
2:6 young men to **u** good judgment.
Heb 9:8 while the tent was still in **u**.
1Pe 2:16 **u** your freedom to serve God.
4:10 you as a good manager must **u**
2Pe 1:10 **u** more effort to make God's
2:3 In their greed they will **u**
2:18 They arrogantly **u** nonsense to
Jud 1:4 They **u** God's kindness as an
1:10 they **u** whatever they know to
1:20 **u** your most holy faith to grow.
Rev 9:19 which they **u** to hurt people.)

used (285)

Gen 10:9 That's why people **u** to say,
11:3 They **u** bricks as stones and
23:9 price as my property to be **u** as
23:20 his property to be **u** as a tomb.
31:15 but he has **u** up the money that
40:13 cup in his hand as you **u**
Exo 5:14 make as many as you **u** to?"
9:15 By now I could have **u** my
13:3 The LORD **u** his mighty hand
13:9 Because the LORD **u** his
13:14 'The LORD **u** his mighty hand
13:16 because the LORD **u** his
14:31 power the LORD had **u** against
17:5 Take the staff you **u** to strike
21:1 to be **u** by the Israelites:
25:29 as pitchers and bowls to be **u**
27:19 no matter how they're **u**,
29:26 "Take the breast from the ram **u**
29:27 Both will come from the ram **u**
29:31 "Take the ram **u** for the
30:25 **u** only for anointing.
30:25 be the holy oil **u** for anointing.
30:31 my holy oil **u** only for anointing.
33:7 Now, Moses **u** to take a tent
33:7 was seeking the LORD's will **u**
35:14 the lamp stand **u** for the light
35:21 The gifts were **u** to construct
35:24 acacia wood that could be **u**
35:29 brought these items to be **u**
36:13 They **u** them to link the ⌊two
37:16 and pitchers to be **u** for pouring
37:29 make the holy oil to be **u**
38:21 amount of material that was **u**
38:24 presented to the LORD **u**
38:27 He **u** 7,500 pounds of silver to
38:28 He **u** 44 pounds of silver to
40:31 Moses, Aaron, and his sons **u**
Lev 4:10 were removed from the bull **u**
4:20 that he did with the bull **u** as
5:16 you **u** plus one-fifth more.
11:32 or anything **u** for any purpose.
18:3 You **u** to live in Egypt.
Num 3:31 the utensils **u** in the holy place,
4:9 for the olive oil **u** in the lamps.
4:12 take all the articles that are **u**
4:14 will put all the accessories **u** at
4:26 and all the equipment **u** to set
5:15 an offering **u** for a confession —
5:18 hands he will put the offering **u**
Num 7:87 Twelve male goats were **u** as
14:13 (You **u** your power to take
19:9 the community of Israel and **u**
25:18 They **u** their sister Cozbi,
Dtr 2:10 The Emites **u** to live there.
2:12 The Horites **u** to live in Seir,
2:20 the land of the Rephaim who **u**
3:13 territory of Argob in Bashan **u**
4:34 The LORD your God **u** his
5:15 your God **u** his mighty hand
6:21 but the LORD **u** his mighty
7:8 So he **u** his mighty hand to
7:19 He **u** his mighty hand and
9:26 power and **u** your mighty hand
9:29 You **u** your great strength and
11:10 There you **u** to plant your seed,
26:8 Then the LORD **u** his mighty
26:8 He **u** spectacular and
32:30 Their rock **u** these people to
34:12 Moses **u** his mighty hand to do
Jos 8:31 no iron chisels had been **u**.
11:6 that they cannot be **u** in battle.
13:22 who **u** black magic.
23:10 One of you **u** to chase a
Jdg 1:7 thumbs and big toes cut off **u**
2:14 He also **u** their enemies around
3:8 He **u** King Cushan Rishathaim
3:31 Philistines with a sharp stick **u**
4:2 So the LORD **u** King Jabin of
4:5 She **u** to sit under the Palm
4:23 So on that day, God **u** the
6:4 The enemy **u** to camp on the
8:27 Then Gideon **u** the gold to
9:34 He **u** four companies to set
10:7 So he **u** the Philistines and
13:19 to the LORD on a rock he **u** as
14:10 is what young men **u** to do.)
14:18 Samson replied, "If you hadn't **u**
16:11 ropes that have never been **u**,
Rut 4:7 (This is the way it **u** to be in
1Sm 1:11 will never be **u** on his head."
4:3 "Why has the LORD **u** the
9:9 person we now call a prophet **u**
17:7 like the beam **u** by weavers.
20:13 the LORD be with you as he **u**
21:11 He's the one they **u** to sing
24:13 It's like people **u** to say long
2Sm 7:10 oppress them as they **u** to do
12:9 You **u** the Ammonites to kill
14:26 At the end of every year, he **u**
15:2 Absalom **u** to get up early and
21:19 like a beam **u** by weavers.)
23:8 He **u** a spear to kill 800 men on
23:18 He **u** his spear to kill 300 men.
1Ki 2:32 He **u** his sword to kill Abner
7:47 so much bronze was **u**.
13:4 But the arm that he **u** to point to
15:22 King Asa **u** the materials to
2Ki 3:11 He **u** to be Elijah's assistant."
7:17 the servant on whose arm he **u**
10:25 So they **u** swords to kill the
12:11 They **u** it to pay the carpenters,
12:12 They also **u** it to buy wood and
12:14 and they **u** it to repair the
13:20 Moabite raiding parties **u** to
16:17 of the ⌊bronze⌋ stands ⌊**u**
16:18 the covered walkway **u**
17:36 who **u** his great power and a
21:13 with the measuring line **u**
21:13 Samaria and the plumb line **u**
25:14 and all the bronze utensils **u** in
1Ch 4:40 the Hamites **u** to live there.
6:15 the LORD **u** Nebuchadnezzar
11:11 He **u** his spear to kill 300 men
11:20 He **u** his spear to kill 300 men,
13:6 the ark⌋ where his name is **u**.)
15:15 They **u** poles as Moses had
17:9 frighten them as they **u** to do
18:8 ⌊Later⌋ Solomon **u** it to make
20:5 like a beam **u** by weavers.)
23:26 all the utensils **u** in worship."
28:14 the weight of gold to be **u**
29:4 They are to be **u** to cover the
2Ch 3:3 (They **u** the old standard
3:6 it and **u** gold from Parvaim.
4:6 They **u** the pool to wash

2Ch 7:6 forever" and which he **u**
16:6 Asa **u** the materials to fortify
24:7 into God's temple and **u** all
24:14 who **u** it to make utensils for
Ezr 1:4 and freewill offerings to be **u** in
7:19 to you so that they can be **u**
Neh 13:5 this room had been **u** to store
Job 1:4 His sons **u** to go to each other's
18:19 any survivor where he **u** to live.
29:2 "If only my life could be like it **u**
30:31 So my lyre is **u** for mourning
Psa 42:4 how I **u** to walk with the crowd
55:14 We **u** to talk to each other in
79:12 the number of insults they **u**
119:67 me suffer, I **u** to wander off,
Pro 4:4 they **u** to teach me and say to
31:1 **u** by his mother to discipline
Ecc 1:13 With all my heart I **u** wisdom to
1:17 I've **u** my mind to understand
2:19 so hard and **u** my wisdom.
7:23 I **u** wisdom to test all of this.
8:10 They **u** to go in and out of the
10:16 any country where the king **u**
Isa 7:25 to go to all the hills which **u**
9:4 and the stick **u** by their
17:2 cities will be **u** for sheep,
49:4 I have **u** my strength,
54:17 made to be **u** against you will
59:6 webs can't be **u** for clothes,
65:15 Your name will be **u** as a curse
Jer 2:24 are like a wild donkey that is **u**
8:8 The scribes have **u** their pens
27:5 'I **u** my great strength and my
33:4 been torn down to be **u** against
38:6 They **u** ropes to lower
38:13 They **u** the ropes to pull
38:22 have misled you and **u** you.
46:11 You have **u** many medicines
52:18 and all the bronze utensils **u** in
52:19 and the bowls **u** for wine
Lam 1:8 Everyone who **u** to honor it
2:15 'Is this the city they **u** to call
4:5 Those who **u** to eat delicacies
4:5 Those who **u** to wear
4:10 The children were **u** for food by
Eze 7:20 beautiful jewels and **u** them
13:12 "Where's the paint that you **u** to
15:4 can it be **u** to make anything?
15:5 How can it be **u** to make
15:6 the trees in the forest to be **u**
16:15 and you **u** your fame to become
16:25 You **u** your beauty to seduce
16:26 You **u** your prostitution to make
16:27 "'So I **u** my power against you.
19:11 They were **u** to make scepters
19:14 branches that could be **u** as
19:14 It is to be **u** as a funeral song.
21:4 to be **u** against everyone from
21:12 because the sword will be **u**
22:6 live in you have **u** their power
27:3 you **u** to brag about your perfect
27:8 from Sidon and Arvad **u**
32:29 They **u** to be powerful,
40:42 laid the utensils that were **u**
47:12 leaves will be **u** for healing."
48:18 It will be **u** to provide food for
Hos 2:8 but she **u** it to make statues of
10:1 of Israel are like vines that **u**
12:13 The LORD **u** a prophet to bring
12:13 He **u** a prophet to take care of
Nah 2:12 It **u** to fill its caves with torn
3:4 She **u** to sell nations her
Zep 2:15 Is this the city that **u** to live
2:15 the city that **u** to think to itself,
Zec 1:16 will be **u** to rebuild Jerusalem.
7:14 I **u** a windstorm to scatter them
9:15 trample the stones **u** in slings.
9:15 filled like a sacrificial bowl ⌊**u**
Mal 3:13 "You have **u** harsh words
Mat 13:3 Then he **u** stories as
13:24 Jesus **u** another illustration.
13:31 Jesus **u** another illustration.
13:33 He **u** another illustration.
13:34 Jesus **u** illustrations to tell the
22:1 Again Jesus **u** stories as
22:19 Show me a coin **u** to pay
Mat 26:55 I **u** to sit teaching in the temple
27:10 and **u** the coins to buy a
Mar 3:23 together and **u** this illustration:
4:2 He **u** stories as illustrations to
6:17 (She **u** to be his brother Philip's
7:11 that whatever he might have **u**
14:49 I **u** to teach in the temple
Luk 5:36 He also **u** these illustrations:
8:4 he **u** this story as an
12:16 Then he **u** this illustration.
13:6 Then Jesus **u** this illustration:
14:7 So he **u** this illustration when
16:9 that although wealth is often **u**
16:11 that is often **u** dishonestly,
18:1 Jesus **u** this illustration with
18:9 Jesus also **u** this illustration
19:11 he **u** this illustration.
21:29 Then Jesus **u** this story as an
Jon 2:6 They were **u** for Jewish
5:3 or paralyzed — **u** to lie.
8:6 Jesus bent down and **u** his
9:8 "Isn't this the man who **u** to sit
9:25 I **u** to be blind, but now I can
10:6 Jesus **u** this illustration as he
16:25 "I have **u** examples to illustrate
Act 2:33 God **u** his power to give Jesus
3:10 that he was the man who **u**
5:31 God **u** his power to give Jesus
7:44 He **u** the model he had seen.
13:17 He **u** his powerful arm to bring
13:45 They **u** insulting language to
16:17 She **u** to follow Paul and shout,
19:13 Some Jews **u** to travel from
26:9 "I **u** to think that I had to do a
Rom 6:6 We know that the person we **u**
6:13 of your body should ever be **u**
6:21 You're ashamed of what you **u**
1Co 3:10 I **u** the gift that God gave me to
8:7 Some people are so **u** to
9:12 But we haven't **u** our rights.
9:15 I haven't **u** any of these rights,
13:8 but it will no longer be **u**.
13:8 but it will no longer be **u**.
13:10 incomplete will no longer be **u**.
13:11 I no longer **u** childish ways.
Gal 3:20 A mediator is not **u** when there
Eph 4:22 The person you **u** to be will
Col 2:22 that are only **u** up anyway.
3:7 You **u** to live that kind of sinful
3:9 gotten rid of the person you **u**
3:9 to be and the life you **u** to live,
1Th 2:5 As you know, we never **u**
1Ti 1:8 good if they are **u** as they were
1:8 as they were intended to be **u**.
1:11 were intended to be **u**
2Ti 2:20 are honored when they are **u**;
Heb 9:8 The Holy Spirit **u** this to show
9:10 and items **u** in various
9:12 He **u** his own blood,
9:17 A will is **u** only after a person
9:21 and on everything **u** in worship.
9:22 blood was **u** to cleanse almost
Jas 2:7 name that was **u** to bless you?
5:3 and their corrosion will be **u** as

useful (7)

Job 22:2 person is only **u** to himself?
Isa 54:16 and to produce **u** weapons.
2Ti 3:16 All of them are **u** for teaching,
4:11 He is **u** to me in my work.
Phm 1:10 you for my child Onesimus [U].
1:11 but now he is very **u** to both of
Heb 6:7 it produces **u** crops for farmers.

useless (27)

1Sm 25:17 such a worthless man that it's **u**
2Ki 18:20 You give **u** advice about
Job 13:12 Your answers are absolutely **u**.
Psa 2:1 Why do their people devise **u**
107:27 skills as sailors became **u**.
127:1 it is **u** for the builders to work
127:1 it is **u** for the guard to stay alert.
127:2 It is **u** to work hard for the food
Isa 30:7 Egypt's help is completely **u**.
36:5 You give **u** advice about
Jer 2:25 But you say that it's **u**.
Jer 6:29 It is **u** to go on refining because
6:30 ⌊People⌋ will call them **u**
18:12 "But they will answer, 'It's **u**!
Amo 2:14 will find that their strength is **u**.
Zec 10:2 They give **u** comfort.
Mat 25:30 Throw this **u** servant outside
Act 4:25 Why do their people devise **u**
Rom 4:14 then faith is **u** and the promise
Eph 5:11 Have nothing to do with the **u**
1Ti 1:6 have turned to **u** discussions.
Tit 3:9 This is **u** nonsense.
Phm 1:11 Once he was **u** to you,
Heb 6:1 away from the **u** things we did
7:18 because they are weak and **u**.
9:14 from the **u** things we had
Jas 2:20 faith which does nothing is **u**?

uses (18)

Gen 44:5 drinks from and that he **u**
Exo 20:7 who carelessly **u** his name will
Num 35:16 "But if any of you **u** an iron
35:17 up a stone as a weapon and **u**
35:18 of wood as a weapon and **u**
Dtr 5:11 who **u** his name carelessly
25:16 Everyone who **u** dishonest
2Sm 23:7 A person who touches them **u**
Job 36:31 This is how he **u** the rains to
Pro 26:6 Whoever **u** a fool to send a
Ecc 2:14 A wise person **u** the eyes in
Isa 31:3 When the LORD **u** his powerful
Eze 16:44 "'Everyone who **u** proverbs will
Dan 4:3 He **u** his power to do amazing
Hab 2:9 be for the one who **u** violence
Zec 14:18 The plague the LORD **u** to
2Co 2:14 Wherever we go, God **u** us to
Rev 13:12 The second beast **u** all the

usher (1)

Dan 9:24 to **u** in everlasting

using (90)

Exo 7:11 thing **u** their magic spells.
7:22 thing **u** their magic spells.
8:7 same thing **u** their magic spells
8:18 gnats **u** their magic spells,
30:13 one-fifth of an ounce of silver **u**
30:24 of cassia — all weighed **u**
30:32 any perfumed oil **u** this formula.
30:37 for yourselves **u** this formula.
32:11 out of Egypt **u** your great power
38:24 **u** the standard weight of the
38:25 **u** the standard weight of the
Lev 27:25 "All values will be set **u** the
Num 3:47 ounces of silver per person (**u**
3:50 **u** the standard weight of the
7:13 **u** the standard weight of the
7:19 that weighed 1 ¾ pounds **u**
7:25 that weighed 1 ¾ pounds **u**
7:31 that weighed 1 ¾ pounds **u**
7:37 that weighed 1 ¾ pounds **u**
7:43 that weighed 1 ¾ pounds **u**
7:49 that weighed 1 ¾ pounds **u**
7:55 that weighed 1 ¾ pounds **u**
7:61 that weighed 1 ¾ pounds **u**
7:67 that weighed 1 ¾ pounds **u**
7:73 that weighed 1 ¾ pounds **u**
7:79 that weighed 1 ¾ pounds **u**
7:85 **u** the standard weight of the
7:86 **u** the standard weight of the
18:16 **u** the standard weight of the
26:53 will possess must be divided **u**
Dtr 4:34 He did this **u** plagues,
Jdg 3:24 "He must be **u** the toilet,"
8:16 taught them a lesson **u** thorns
1Sm 17:50 So **u** ⌊only⌋ a sling and a
22:19 **U** ⌊his⌋ sword, he killed men
2Sm 5:8 and the blind who hate me by **u**
1Ki 10:16 **u** 15 pounds of gold on each
10:17 **u** four pounds of gold on each
15:22 Baasha had been **u** those to
19:19 He was **u** the twelfth pair.
19:21 He boiled the meat, **u** the
20:14 by **u** the young officers of the
1Ch 14:11 David said, "**U** my power like
2Ch 9:15 **u** 15 pounds of gold on each
9:16 **u** 7 ½ pounds of gold on each

2Ch 16:6 Baasha had been **u** those to
Ezr 7:25 You, Ezra, **u** your God's
Est 2:12 six months **u** oil of myrrh and
2:12 and six months **u** perfumes
Job 19:5 than me by **u** my disgrace as
Ecc 9:15 saved the town **u** his wisdom.
Sos 3:8 of them are skilled in **u** swords,
Jer 18:21 their blood by **u** your sword.
21:4 You are **u** these weapons to
Eze 4:12 **u** human excrement for fuel."
43:13 **u** royal measurements.
45:14 oil **u** the standard measure.
Dan 2:14 to him **u** shrewd judgment.
6:17 **u** his ring and the rings of his
11:21 the kingdom **u** false promises.
Hos 7:9 Foreigners are **u** up your
Amo 9:9 nations as if I were **u** a sieve.
Zec 1:13 **u** kind and comforting words.
Mat 24:5 Many will come **u** my name.
Mar 4:33 them **u** many illustrations like
4:34 them without **u** an illustration.
9:38 demons out of a person by **u**
12:1 Then, **u** this illustration,
13:6 Many will come **u** my name.
Luk 9:49 demons out of a person by **u**
15:3 to them **u** this illustration:
20:9 Then, **u** this illustration,
21:8 Many will come **u** my name.
Jon 16:29 words and not **u** examples.
Act 2:23 By **u** men who don't
5:26 the apostles without **u** force.
5:26 stone them to death for **u** force.
1Co 2:13 things **u** teachings that are
8:9 But be careful that by **u** your
2Co 1:4 are able to comfort them by **u**
5:19 In other words, God was **u**
13:10 I don't want to be harsh by **u**
Gal 3:19 through angels, **u** a mediator.
Eph 5:26 washing it **u** water along with
Tit 2:15 **u** your full authority.
Jas 2:4 against people and **u**
3:4 Yet, by **u** small rudders,
2Pe 3:15 **u** the wisdom God gave him.
Rev 6:8 the earth to kill people **u** wars,
21:17 which the angel was **u**,

usual (10)

Gen 50:3 completed in the **u** time — 40
Exo 14:27 water returned to its **u** place.
Lev 15:25 If her period lasts longer than **u**,
Jdg 16:20 "I'll get out of this as **u** and
1Sm 20:25 He sat in his **u** seat by the wall,
21:5 away from us as **u** when we go
Mat 20:2 the workers the **u** day's wages,
Luk 2:42 12 years old, they went as **u**.
4:16 As **u** he went into the
Act 17:2 As **u**, Paul went into the

utensils (80)

Exo 25:39 the lamp stand and all the **u**.
27:3 "Make all the **u** for it out of
30:27 the lamp stand and all the **u**,
31:8 gold lamp stand and all its **u**,
35:14 used for the light with its **u**,
37:24 The lamp stand and all the **u**
38:3 He made all the **u** out of bronze:
39:37 its lamps in a row and all its **u**,
40:10 for burnt offerings and all the **u**.
Lev 8:11 and anointed the altar, all the **u**,
Num 3:31 the **u** used in the holy place,
4:10 lamp stand and all its **u** under
7:1 the altar and all the **u**.
1Ki 7:45 Hiram made all these **u** out of
7:51 and **u** — and put them in the
8:4 and all the holy **u** in it to the
10:21 and all the **u** for the hall which
15:15 and the **u** he and his father had
2Ki 12:13 or any other gold and silver **u**
14:14 and all the **u** he found in the
23:4 temple all the **u** that had been
23:4 Josiah burned the **u** outside
25:14 and all the bronze **u** used in the
1Ch 9:28 in charge of the **u** for worship.
9:29 were placed in charge of the **u**,
9:29 the holy **u**, the flour, wine,
18:8 and **u** for the temple.)
1Ch 22:19 promise and God's holy **u** into
23:26 and all the **u** used in worship."
28:13 He designed all the **u** for
28:14 for each of the **u** for worship,
2Ch 5:1 and all the **u** — and put them in
5:5 and all the holy **u** in it to the
9:20 and all the **u** for the hall
15:18 and the **u** he and his father had
24:14 who used it to make **u** for the
24:14 dishes and gold and silver **u**
25:24 and all the **u** he found in God's
28:24 Ahaz collected the **u** in God's
29:18 altar for burnt offerings, all its **u**
29:18 the rows of bread and all its **u**,
29:19 and all the **u** King Ahaz refused
36:7 also brought some of the **u**
36:10 with the valuable **u** from
36:18 of the **u** from God's temple,
Ezr 1:7 King Cyrus brought out the **u**
1:7 taken these **u** from Jerusalem
1:10 silver bowls: 410 other **u**: 1,000
1:11 gold and silver **u** totaled 5,400.
1:11 Sheshbazzar took all these **u**
5:14 gold and silver **u** that belonged
5:15 Cyrus told him, 'Take these **u**.
6:5 gold and silver **u** that belonged
7:19 The **u** that have been given to
8:25 the silver, the gold, and the **u**.
8:26 100 silver **u** weighing 150
8:27 and two **u** of fine polished
8:28 I told them, "You and the **u** are
8:30 the silver, the gold, and the **u**.
8:33 and the **u** in our God's temple.
Neh 10:39 to the place where the **u**
13:5 grain offerings, incense, **u**,
13:9 and I put back in there the **u**
Isa 22:24 and offspring and all the little **u**,
52:11 you Levites who carry the **u** for
Jer 27:16 prophets who tell you that the **u**
27:18 not to allow the **u** that are left
27:19 and the rest of the **u** that are left
27:21 says about the **u** that are left in
28:3 years I will bring back all the **u**
28:6 come true and bring back the **u**
49:29 Their tent curtains, **u**,
52:18 and all the bronze **u** used in the
Eze 40:42 laid the **u** that were used
Dan 1:2 and some **u** from God's temple
1:2 Nebuchadnezzar took the **u** to
5:2 silver **u** which his grandfather
5:3 the gold **u** that had been
5:23 You had the **u** from his temple
11:8 their gods and their precious **u**

uterus (3)

Num 5:21 The LORD will make your **u**
5:22 stomach swell and your **u** drop!'
5:27 will swell, her **u** will drop,

Uthai (2)

1Ch 9:4 of Perez, son of Judah, was **U**,
Ezr 8:14 **U** and Zabbud, with 70 males.

utter (3)

Job 2:10 lips did not **u** one sinful word.
Isa 28:10 They speak **u** nonsense.
28:13 The LORD speaks **u** nonsense

uttered (1)

Isa 59:13 We have conceived and **u** lies

utterly (1)

Sos 8:7 people would **u** despise him.

Uz (8)

Gen 10:23 Aram's descendants were **U**,
22:21 **U** (the firstborn), Buz (his
36:28 sons of Dishan: **U** and Aran.
1Ch 1:17 **U**, Hul, Gether, and Meshech.
1:42 sons were **U** and Aran.
Job 1:1 A man named Job lived in **U**.
Jer 25:20 all the kings of the land of **U**;
Lam 4:21 inhabitants of the country of **U**.

Uzai's (1)

Neh 3:25 Palal, **U** son, made repairs

Uzal (3)

Gen 10:27 Hadoram, **U**, Diklah,
1Ch 1:21 Hadoram, **U**, Diklah,
Eze 27:19 "Danites and Greeks from **U**

Uzza (5)

2Ki 21:18 in the garden of **U**.
21:26 in his tomb in the garden of **U**.
1Ch 8:7 was the father of **U** and Ahihud.
Ezr 2:49 **U**, Paseah, Besai,
Neh 7:51 Gazzam, **U**, Paseah,

Uzzah (11)

2Sm 6:3 **U** and Ahio, Abinadab's sons,
6:6 So **U** reached out for the ark of
6:7 LORD became angry with **U**,
6:8 had struck **U** so violently.
6:8 [The Striking of **U**] today.)
1Ch 6:29 Shimei's son was **U**.
13:7 **U** and Ahio guided the cart.
13:9 So **U** reached out to grab the
13:10 LORD became angry with **U**
13:11 had struck **U** so violently.
13:11 [The Striking of **U**] today.)

Uzzah's (1)

1Ch 6:30 **U** son was Shimea.

Uzzen Sheerah (1)

1Ch 7:24 Lower Beth Horon and **U**.

Uzzi (11)

1Ch 6:5 Bukki was the father of **U**.
6:6 **U** was the father of Zerahiah.
6:51 Bukki's son was **U**.
7:2 Tola's sons were **U**,
7:3 The five descendants of **U**
7:7 five sons were Ezbon, **U**,
9:8 Elah (son of **U** and grandson of
Ezr 7:4 who was the son of **U**,
Neh 11:22 Levites in Jerusalem was **U**,
12:19 Mattenai; from Jedaiah, **U**;
12:42 **U**, Jehohanan, Malchiah, Elam,

Uzzia (1)

1Ch 11:44 **U** from Ashteroth, Shama and

Uzziah (29)

1Ch 6:24 Uriel's son was **U**.
27:25 Jonathan, son of **U**
2Ch 26:1 All the people of Judah took **U**,
26:2 **U** rebuilt Elath and returned it to
26:3 **U** was 16 years old when he
26:6 **U** went to wage war against
26:8 Ammonites paid taxes to **U**,
26:9 **U** built towers in Jerusalem at
26:11 **U** had an army of professional
26:14 entire army **U** prepared shields,
26:18 They opposed King **U**.
26:18 They said to him, "**U**,
26:19 **U**, who held an incense burner
26:19 the LORD's temple as **U** was at
26:20 **U** was in a hurry to get out
26:21 King **U** had a skin disease until
26:22 Everything else about **U**,
26:23 **U** lay down in death with his
27:2 as his father **U** had done.
Ezr 10:21 Shemaiah, Jehiel, and **U**
Neh 11:4 who was the son of **U**,
Isa 1:1 at the time of Kings **U**,
6:1 In the year King **U** died,
7:1 of Jotham and grandson of **U**,
Hos 1:1 Beeri, when **U**, Jotham, Ahaz,
Amo 1:1 the reigns of Judah's King **U**
Zec 14:5 at the time of King **U** of Judah.
Mat 1:8 Joram the father of **U**,
1:9 **U** the father of Jotham,

Uzziah's (2)

1Ch 6:24 Uzziah. **U** son was Shaul.
2Ch 26:15 **U** fame spread far and wide

Uzziel (15)

Exo 6:18 Amram, Izhar, Hebron, and **U**.
6:22 The sons of **U** were Mishael,

Lev 10:4 the sons of Aaron's uncle, **U**.
Num 3:19 and **U** were the sons of Kohath.
3:27 Amram, Izhar, Hebron, and **U**.
3:30 was Elizaphan, son of **U**.
1Ch 4:42 and **U** led 500 of Simeon's
6:2 Amram, Izhar, Hebron, and **U**.
6:18 Amram, Izhar, Hebron, and **U**.
7:7 Uzzi, **U**, Jerimoth, and Iri.
23:12 Amram, Izhar, Hebron, and **U**.
25:4 **U**, Shebuel, Jerimoth,
26:23 Amram, Izhar, Hebron, and **U**,
2Ch 29:14 were Shemaiah and **U**.
Neh 3:8 Next to them **U**, a goldsmith,

Uzziel's (4)

1Ch 15:10 Leading **U** descendants was
23:20 **U** first son was Micah;
24:24 **U** descendants through Micah),
24:25 Zechariah (for ⌊**U**⌋ descendants

Uzzi's (1)

1Ch 6:51 **U** son was Zerahiah.

V

vain (2)

Isa 45:19 "Search for me in **v**!"
Lam 4:17 trying in **v** to find help.

Vaizatha (1)

Est 9:9 Arisai, Aridai, and **V**.

valid (2)

Jon 8:16 my judgment is **v** because I
1Ti 2:6 message is **v** for every era.

valley (171)

Gen 14:3 joined forces and met in the **v**
14:8 for battle in the **v** of Siddim.
14:10 The **v** of Siddim was full of tar
14:17 him in the Shaveh **V** (that is,
14:17 Valley (that is, the King's **V**).
26:17 in the Gerar **V** and lived there.
26:19 Isaac's servants dug in the **v**
37:14 away from the Hebron **V**.
Num 13:23 they came to the Eshcol **V**,
13:24 So they called that **v** Eshcol
21:13 on the other side of the Arnon **V**
21:13 (The Arnon **V** is the border
21:20 and from Bamoth to the **v** in
21:24 of their land from the Arnon **V**
21:26 all his land up to the Arnon **V**.
22:36 in the region of the Arnon **V**,
32:9 went as far as the Eshcol **V**
Dtr 1:24 they came to the Eshcol **V**,
2:24 Cross the Arnon **V**.
2:36 on the edge of the Arnon **V**
2:36 and the city in that **v** as far as
3:8 the Arnon **V** to Mount Hermon.
3:12 north of Aroer near the Arnon **V**
3:16 from the Arnon **V** (the middle
3:16 Valley (the middle of the **v** is
3:29 stayed in the **v** near Beth Peor.
4:46 River in the **v** near Beth Peor,
4:48 on the edge of the Arnon **V**
34:3 and the Jordan Plain — the **v** of
34:6 He was buried in a **v** in Moab,
Jos 7:24 to the **v** of Achor [Disaster].
7:26 still called the **v** of Achor today.
8:13 down into the middle of the **v**.
10:12 still over the **v** of Aijalon!"
11:8 and the **v** of Mizpah in the east.
11:17 Baal Gad in the Lebanon **V** at
12:1 of their lands from the Arnon **V**
12:2 on the edge of the Arnon **V**
12:2 included the middle of the **v**
12:7 from Baal Gad in the **v**
13:9 on the edge of the Arnon **V**,
13:9 the city in the middle of the **v**,
13:16 on the edge of the Arnon **V**,
13:16 the city in the middle of the **v**
13:19 on the mountain in the **v**,
13:27 In the Jordan **V** it included Beth
Jos 15:7 From the **v** of Achor,
15:7 Adummim Pass, south of the **v**.
15:8 It continues up the **v** of Ben
15:8 mountain that overlooks the **v**
15:8 north end of the **v** of Rephaim.
17:16 the Canaanites living in the **v**,
17:16 and in the **v** of Jezreel have
18:16 mountain that overlooks the **v**
18:16 north end of the **v** of Rephaim.
18:16 It descends to the **v** of Hinnom,
19:14 and ends at the **v** of Iphtah El.
19:27 and touches Zebulun and the **v**
Jdg 1:19 living in the **v** who had chariots
1:34 let them come down into the **v**.
5:15 sent into the **v** under his
6:33 and camped in the **v** of Jezreel.
7:1 him at the hill of Moreh in the **v**.
7:8 Midian was below him in the **v**.
7:12 were spread out in the **v** like
16:4 with a woman in the Sorek **V**.
18:28 The city was in the **v** that
1Sm 6:13 were harvesting wheat in the **v**.
13:18 the region that overlooks the **v**
15:5 and set an ambush in the **v**.
17:2 and camped in the Elah **V**.
17:19 Elah **V** fighting the Philistines."
21:9 whom you killed in the Elah **V**,
30:9 600 men went to the Besor **V**,
30:10 the Besor **V** stayed behind.
30:21 and had stayed in the Besor **V**.
31:7 Israel on the other side of the **v**
2Sm 5:18 and overrun the **v** of Rephaim.
5:22 and overran the **v** of Rephaim.
15:23 was crossing the Kidron **V**,
17:13 and drag it into a **v** so that not
18:18 it up for himself in the king's **v**.
18:23 So Ahimaaz ran along the **v**
23:13 camping in the **v** of Rephaim.
24:5 the city in the middle of the **v**.
1Ki 2:37 cross the brook in the Kidron **V**,
7:46 the Jordan **V** between Succoth
15:13 and burned it in the Kidron **V**.
2Ki 3:16 Make this **v** full of ditches.
3:17 but this **v** will be filled with
23:6 Kidron **V** outside Jerusalem.
23:6 He burned it in the Kidron **V**,
23:10 also made Topheth in the **v**
23:12 their rubble in the Kidron **V**.
1Ch 4:14 first settled the **v** of Craftsmen.
4:39 on the east side of the **v**,
10:7 of Israel in the **v** saw that ⌊their
11:15 camping in the **v** of Rephaim.
14:9 and raided the **v** of Rephaim.
14:13 Philistines again raided the **v**.
2Ch 4:17 the Jordan **V** between Succoth
14:10 the Zephathah **V** at Mareshah.
15:16 and burned it in the Kidron **V**.
20:16 find them at the end of the **v**
20:26 day they gathered in the **v**
20:26 called the **v** of Beracah today.
26:9 Wall, **V** Gate, and the Angle,
28:3 He burned sacrifices in the **v** of
30:14 dumping them in the Kidron **V**.
33:6 his son as a sacrifice in the **v**
33:14 west of Gihon Spring in the **v**
35:22 to fight in the **v** of Megiddo.
Neh 2:13 I went through **V** Gate that
2:15 So I went through the **v** that
2:15 entered **V** Gate, and returned.
3:13 of Zanoah repaired **V** Gate.
11:30 Beersheba to the **V** of Hinnom.
11:35 and in the **v** of the Craftsmen.
Psa 23:4 through the dark **v** of death,
60:6 I will measure the **v** of Succoth.
84:6 As they pass through a **v**
108:7 I will measure the **v** of Succoth.
Pro 30:17 plucked out by ravens in the **v**
Sos 6:11 look at the blossoms in the **v**,
Isa 17:5 grain in the Rephaim **V**.
22:1 revelation about the **v** of Vision.
22:5 and trampling in the **v** of Vision,
28:1 to a fertile **v** where they lie
28:4 are at the entrance to a fertile **v**.
28:21 wake up as he did in Gibeon **V**.
40:4 Every **v** will be raised.
63:14 animals going down into a **v**,
Isa 65:10 The Achor **V** will be a resting
Jer 2:23 how you've behaved in the **v**.
7:31 sites at Topheth in the **v**
7:32 be known as Topheth or the **v**
7:32 will be known as Slaughter **V**.
19:2 Go to the **v** of Ben Hinnom at
19:6 be called Topheth or the **v**
19:6 it will be called Slaughter **V**.
21:13 You are the city that is in the **v**
31:40 The whole **v**, filled with its
31:40 the whole area to the Kidron **V**,
32:35 In the **v** of Ben Hinnom they
48:8 The **v** will be destroyed,
Eze 8:4 in the vision that I saw in the **v**.
31:12 the mountains and in every **v**.
37:1 me down in the middle of a **v**.
37:1 The **v** was filled with bones.
37:2 bones at the bottom of the **v**,
39:11 It will be in Travelers **V**,
39:11 who travel ⌊through the **v**⌋.
39:11 be called the **v** of Gog's troops.
39:15 bone in the **v** of Gog's troops.
47:8 down into the Jordan **V**,
Hos 1:5 and arrows in the **v** of Jezreel."
2:15 I will make the **v** of Achor
Joe 3:2 down to the **v** of Jehoshaphat.
3:12 Come to the **v** of Jehoshaphat.
3:14 people in the **v** of decision.
3:14 is near in the **v** of decision.
3:18 It will water the **v** of Shittim.
Amo 1:5 cut off those living in Aven **V**
6:14 of Hamath to the **v** of Arabah.
Mic 1:6 roll its stones down into a **v**
Zec 14:4 forming a very large **v** from east
14:5 Then you will flee to the **v** of
14:5 because this **v** between the
Mat 3:5 whole Jordan **V** went to him.
Luk 3:5 Every **v** will be filled.
Jon 18:1 the other side of the Kidron **V**.

valleys (28)

Num 14:25 Canaanites are living in the **v**.)
21:14 Waheb in Suphah and the **v**,
21:15 Arnon and the slopes of the **v**
Dtr 8:7 flowing through the **v** and hills.
11:11 enter is a land with hills and **v**,
1Ki 20:28 the hills but not a god of the **v**,
2Ki 2:16 of the hills or in one of the **v**."
1Ch 12:15 away all the people in the **v**
27:29 Sharon for the herds in the **v**:
Job 38:16 the sea or walked through the **v**
39:10 will it plow the **v** behind you?
Psa 65:13 The **v** are carpeted with grain.
104:8 The mountains rose and the **v**
104:10 water gush from springs into **v**.
Sos 2:1 a lily ⌊growing⌋ in the **v**.
Isa 7:19 come and settle in the deep **v**,
22:7 Then your fertile **v** will be filled
41:18 make springs flow through **v**.
57:5 You slaughter children in the **v**
Jer 49:4 Why do you brag about your **v**,
49:4 your valleys, your fertile **v**,
Eze 6:3 hills and to the ravines and **v**:
7:16 will moan like doves in the **v**.
32:5 flesh on the hills and fill the **v**
35:8 hills and in your **v** and ravines.
36:4 to the ravines and **v**,
36:6 and hills and the ravines and **v**,
Mic 1:4 **V** will split apart like water

valuable (14)

1Ki 10:21 **v** in Solomon's time.)
20:6 anything that you consider **v**.'"
2Ch 9:20 **v** in Solomon's time.)
36:10 with the **v** utensils from
Ezr 1:6 and **v** gifts besides everything
Job 28:18 Wisdom is more **v** than gems.
Pro 1:13 find all kinds of **v** possessions.
Mat 12:12 Certainly, a human is more **v**
13:46 When he found a **v** pearl,
Luk 7:2 There a Roman army officer's **v**
Rom 2:25 For example, circumcision is **v**
Php 3:7 things that I once considered **v**,
2Pe 1:1 a faith that is as **v** as ours,
Rev 21:11 Its light was like a **v** gem,

valuables (6)

Exo 22:7 his neighbor silver or ⌊other⌋ **v**
22:8 or not he took his neighbor's **v**.
Num 31:9 and their **v** as loot.
2Ch 20:25 a lot of goods, clothes, and **v**.
32:27 shields, and all kinds of **v**.
Jer 20:5 include all its produce, all its **v**,

value (30)

Lev 5:15 ram that has no defects or its **v**
5:18 defects from the flock or its **v**
6:6 no defects or its **v** in money.
27:12 will determine what its **v** is.
27:12 The **v** will be whatever the
27:13 its full **v** plus one-fifth more.
27:14 will determine what its **v** is.
27:14 The **v** will be whatever the
27:15 its full **v** plus one-fifth more.
27:16 its **v** will be based on the seed
27:17 it will have its full **v**.
27:18 the priest will estimate its **v**
27:19 its full **v** plus one-fifth more.
27:23 must figure out the field's **v** until
27:23 You will pay its **v** on that day
27:27 The payment will be its full **v**
27:27 it must be sold at the **v** given it.
1Sm 26:24 As I placed great **v** on your life
26:24 may the LORD place great **v**
2Ch 36:19 and destroyed everything of **v**.
Job 28:17 gold nor glass can equal its **v**.
28:19 Ethiopia cannot equal its **v**.
Psa 102:14 Your servants **v** Zion's stones,
Jer 17:21 If you **v** your lives,
Eze 7:11 and nothing of **v** will be left.
Luk 12:33 heaven that never loses its **v**!
Act 20:24 But I don't place any **v** on my
Rom 3:1 any **v** in being circumcised?
Col 2:23 But they have no **v** for holding
2Pe 1:4 that are of the highest **v**.

valued (2)

1Sm 26:21 because you **v** my life today.
Isa 64:11 All that we **v** has been ruined.

values (1)

Lev 27:25 "All **v** will be set using the

vandal (2)

Pro 18:9 in his work is related to a **v**.
28:24 is a companion to a **v**.

Vaniah (1)

Ezr 10:36 **V**, Meremoth, Eliashib,

vanish (9)

Job 6:17 They **v** during a scorching
18:17 All memory about him will **v**
Psa 37:10 while a wicked person will **v**.
37:20 The LORD's enemies will **v**
37:20 They will **v** like smoke.
104:35 May sinners **v** from the world.
112:10 that wicked people have will **v**.
Isa 11:13 Ephraim's jealousy will **v**,
51:6 The sky will **v** like smoke.

vanished (11)

Psa 10:16 nations have **v** from his land.
12:1 Faithful people have **v** from
Pro 10:25 the wicked person has **v**,
Ecc 9:6 their passions have already **v**.
Isa 16:10 Joy and delight have **v** from the
Jer 7:28 and **v** from their lips.'
49:7 Has their wisdom **v**?
Eze 37:11 and our hope has **v**.
Luk 24:31 But he **v** from their sight.
Rev 6:14 The sky **v** like a scroll being
16:20 Every island **v**, and the

vanishes (3)

Job 30:15 My prosperity **v** like a cloud.
Pro 11:7 of a wicked person, hope **v**.
11:7 his confidence in strength **v**.

vanity (1)

Pro 30:8 Keep **v** and lies far away from

various (12)

1Ki 18:18 and following the **v** Baal gods.
2Ch 34:4 He had the altars of the **v** Baal
34:13 all the workmen on the **v** jobs.
Psa 65:3 **V** sins overwhelm me.
106:27 and scatter them throughout **v**
Mat 24:7 and earthquakes in **v** places.
Mar 1:34 who were sick with **v** diseases
13:8 and famines in **v** places.
Luk 4:40 from **v** diseases brought them
8:2 evil spirits and **v** illnesses.
21:11 dreadful diseases in **v** places.
Heb 9:10 in **v** purification ceremonies.

vary (1)

1Co 7:7 and these gifts **v** from person to

Vashti (10)

Est 1:9 Queen **V** also held a banquet
1:11 to bring Queen **V** in front of the
1:12 But Queen **V** refused the king's
1:15 what must we do with Queen **V**
1:16 "Queen **V** has done wrong,
1:17 'King Xerxes ordered Queen **V**
1:19 that **V** may never again appear
2:1 he remembered **V**,
2:4 become queen instead of **V**."
2:17 made her queen instead of **V**.

vast (11)

Dtr 1:19 We traveled through all that **v**
2:7 traveled through this **v** desert.
8:15 one who led you through that **v**
Jos 22:8 your homes with your **v** wealth,
1Ch 4:40 The land was **v**, peaceful,
Neh 9:25 They enjoyed the **v** supply of
9:35 that you gave them in a **v**,
Psa 103:11 that is how **v** his mercy is
139:17 How **v** in number they are!
Dan 11:3 He will rule a **v** empire and do
11:5 than he is and rule a **v** empire.

vat (2)

Hag 2:16 when anyone came to a wine **v**
Mar 12:1 made a **v** for the winepress,

vats (4)

Job 24:11 stomp on grapes in wine **v**,
Pro 3:10 and your **v** will overflow with
Joe 2:24 The **v** will overflow with new
3:13 The **v** overflow. The nations are

vaults (1)

Pro 7:27 leads to the darkest **v** of death.

vegetable (2)

Dtr 11:10 and you had to water it like a **v**
1Ki 21:2 It will become my **v** garden

vegetables (8)

2Ki 4:39 went into the field to gather **v**
Psa 104:14 grow for cattle and make **v**
Pro 15:17 Better to have a dish of **v**
27:25 and **v** are gathered on the hills.
Dan 1:12 Give us only **v** to eat and water
1:16 and wine and gave them **v**.
Rom 14:2 that they can eat only **v**.
14:3 despise people who eat only **v**.

vegetarians (2)

Rom 14:3 In the same way, the **v** should
14:6 **V** also honor the Lord when

vegetation (4)

Gen 1:11 "Let the earth produce **v**:
1:12 The earth produced **v**:
Isa 15:6 grass dries up, the **v** withers,
42:15 I will dry up all their **v**.

veil (16)

Gen 24:65 took her **v** and covered herself.
38:14 covered her face with a **v**,
38:19 she took off her **v** and put her
Exo 34:33 he put a **v** over his face.
34:34 he took off the **v** until he came
34:35 Then Moses would put the **v**
Sos 4:1 Your eyes behind your **v** are
4:3 Your temples behind your **v** are
6:7 Your temples behind your **v** are
Isa 25:7 mountain he will remove the **v**
47:2 Remove your **v**. Take off your
2Co 3:13 kept covering his face with a **v**.
3:14 In fact, to this day the same **v**
3:15 a **v** covers their minds.
3:16 the **v** is taken away.
4:3 tell others is covered with a **v**,

veils (5)

Isa 3:23 headdresses, and **v**.
Jer 2:32 her jewelry or a bride her **v**.
Eze 13:18 wrists and make magic **v**
13:21 I will tear off your magic **v** and
2Co 3:18 that are not covered with **v**,

vengeance (17)

Gen 4:15 will suffer **v** seven times over."
2Sm 22:48 God gives me **v**! He brings
Psa 18:47 God gives me **v**! He brings
94:1 O LORD, God of **v**,
94:1 O God of **v**, appear!
149:7 to take **v** on the nations,
Isa 34:8 The LORD will have a day of **v**,
35:4 Your God will come with **v**,
59:17 He wears clothes of **v**.
61:2 will and the day of our God's **v**,
63:4 I planned the day of **v**.
Jer 46:10 It is a day of **v** when he will
50:15 Since this is the LORD's **v**,
50:28 to Zion to tell about the **v**
50:28 the **v** for his temple.
51:6 This is the time for the **v** of the
Luk 21:22 This will be a time of **v**.

venom (5)

Dtr 32:33 Their wine is snake **v**,
Job 20:14 snake **v** in his stomach.
Psa 58:4 have poisonous **v** like snakes.
140:3 Their lips hide the **v** of
Rom 3:13 the **v** of poisonous snakes.

vent (1)

2Ch 32:26 So the LORD didn't **v** his anger

vents (2)

Rom 2:5 that day when God **v** his anger.
3:5 Is God unfair when he **v** his

verbally (4)

Psa 73:9 They **v** attack heaven,
1Co 4:12 When people **v** abuse us,
1Pe 2:23 Christ never **v** abused those
2:23 those who **v** abused him.

verdict (10)

Dtr 17:9 and they will give you their **v**
17:11 they tell you to do in their **v**.
Psa 17:2 Let the **v** of my innocence
76:8 heaven you announced a **v**.
Lam 3:59 O LORD. Give me a fair **v**.
Mat 26:66 What's your **v**?" They
Mar 14:64 What's your **v**?" All of them
Rom 5:16 The **v** which followed one
5:18 approval through one **v**.
2Pe 2:3 The **v** against them from long

verdicts (2)

Psa 58:1 Do you rulers really give fair **v**?
Zec 8:16 Give correct and fair **v** for

verified (4)

Mat 18:16 accusation may be **v** by two
1Co 1:6 Christ has been **v** among you.
2Co 13:1 Every accusation must be **v** by
Heb 2:4 God **v** what they said through

verifies (1)

1Jn 5:6 Spirit is the one who **v** this,

verify (1)

Act 24:11 You can **v** for yourself that I

verse (1)

Luk 20:17 does this Scripture **v** mean:

vessel (1)

Pro 25:4 and a **v** is ready for the

vice (1)

1Co 5:8 the yeast of **v** and wickedness.

vicinity (1)

1Sm 5:6 by striking the people in the **v**

vicious (6)

Dtr 32:24 I will send **v** animals against
Est 7:6 Esther answered, "Our **v**
Psa 22:20 my life from **v** dogs.
25:19 how they have hated me with **v**
Jer 6:28 They are all **v** rebels.
Mat 7:15 but in their hearts they are **v**

viciousness (1)

Rom 1:29 quarreling, deceit, and **v**.

victim (6)

Num 23:24 and drinks the blood of its **v**."
Dtr 21:1 do if you find a murder **v** lying
21:6 the murder **v** must wash their
Psa 10:14 The **v** entrusts himself to you.
109:25 I have become the **v** of my
1Ti 3:7 or he might become the **v** of

victims (11)

Psa 10:8 eyes are on the lookout for **v**.
10:10 ⌊His⌋ **v** are crushed.
Pro 7:26 she has brought down many **v**,
26:28 A lying tongue hates its **v**,
Isa 59:15 from evil make themselves **v**.
Jer 14:16 They will be **v** of famines and
Eze 24:8 I put the blood of its **v** on a bare
Dan 7:7 It devoured and crushed its **v**
7:19 It devoured and crushed its **v**,
Mic 5:8 it tramples ⌊its **v**⌋ and tears
Nah 3:1 stolen goods — never without **v**.

victories (13)

Dtr 33:29 and a sword that wins your **v**.
Jdg 5:11 over again they repeat the **v**
5:11 the **v** for his villages in Israel.
2Sm 8:6 the LORD gave him **v**.
8:14 the LORD gave him **v**.
22:51 He gives great **v** to his king.
1Ch 18:6 the LORD gave him **v**.
18:13 the LORD gave him **v**.
Psa 18:50 He gives great **v** to his king.
44:4 You won those **v** for Jacob.
68:20 Our God is the God of **v**.
Eze 27:10 Their **v** made you look good.
Mic 6:5 may know the **v** of the LORD."

victorious (9)

1Sm 14:47 Wherever he turned, he was **v**.
Psa 3:2 ⌊on his side⌋, he won't be **v**."
74:12 been **v** throughout the earth.
89:24 and in my name he will be **v**.
Isa 41:10 you with my **v** right hand.
Dan 11:7 fight against them, and be **v**.
Oba 1:21 Those who are **v** will come
Zec 9:9 He is righteous and **v**.
Mat 12:20 until he has made justice **v**.

victoriously (1)

Psa 45:4 Ride on **v** in your majesty for

victory (77)

Exo 15:1 He has won a glorious **v**.
15:21 He has won a glorious **v**.
Dtr 20:4 your enemies and give you **v**."
32:27 and say, 'We won this **v**!
Jdg 8:9 "When I come back after my **v**,
15:18 have given me this great **v**.
1Sm 14:6 The LORD can win a **v** with a
14:45 has won this great **v** in Israel?
19:5 LORD gave all Israel a great **v**.
25:26 from getting a **v** by your own
25:31 and claimed your own **v**.
1Sm 25:33 and from getting a **v** by my own
2Sm 1:20 Don't announce the **v** in the
19:2 The **v** of that day was turned
23:10 won an impressive **v** that day.
23:12 LORD won an impressive **v**.
1Ki 20:11 'Don't brag about a **v** before
2Ki 5:1 Aram a **v** through Naaman.
13:17 is the arrow of the LORD's **v**,
13:17 the arrow of **v** against Aram.
1Ch 11:14 ⌊them⌋ with an impressive **v**.
2Ch 20:17 and see the **v** of the LORD for
Job 38:15 an arm raised ⌊in **v**⌋ is broken.
Psa 3:8 **V** belongs to the LORD!
20:5 will joyfully sing about your **v**.
20:6 know that the LORD will give **v**
20:9 Give **v** to the king,
21:1 What great joy he has in your **v**!
21:5 Because of your **v** his glory is
28:8 for the **v** of his Messiah.
33:16 No king achieves a **v** with a
33:17 are not a guarantee for **v**.
37:39 The **v** for righteous people
44:3 They did not gain **v** with their
89:17 By your favor you give us **v**.
98:1 holy arm have gained **v** for him.
118:15 of joyful singing and **v** is heard
144:10 the one who gives **v** to kings.
149:4 who are oppressed with **v**.
Pro 11:14 with many advisers there is **v**.
21:31 but the **v** belongs to the LORD.
24:6 with many advisers there is **v**.
Isa 41:2 to whom the LORD gives **v**
54:17 Their **v** comes from me,"
59:16 his own power he wins a **v**.
63:1 I am coming to announce my **v**.
63:5 with my own power I won a **v**.
Jer 51:10 LORD has brought about our **v**.
51:14 will shout their **v** over you."
Eze 39:13 be honored on the day of my **v**,
Jnh 2:9 **V** belongs to the LORD!"
Mic 7:9 and I will see his **v**.
Rom 8:37 us gives us an overwhelming **v**
1Co 15:54 "Death is turned into **v**!
15:55 Death, where is your **v**?
15:57 gives us the **v** through our Lord
2Co 2:14 who always leads us in **v**
Col 2:15 as he celebrated his **v** in Christ.
1Pe 3:19 he also went to proclaim his **v**
1Jn 2:13 because you have won the **v**
2:14 You have won the **v** over the
4:4 So you have won the **v** over
5:4 from God has won the **v** over
5:4 what wins the **v** over the world.
5:5 Who wins the **v** over the world?
Rev 2:7 to everyone who wins the **v**.
2:11 Everyone who wins the **v** will
2:17 to everyone who wins the **v**.
2:26 to everyone who wins the **v**
3:5 Everyone who wins the **v** this
3:12 make everyone who wins the **v**
3:21 allow everyone who wins the **v**
3:21 as I have won the **v** and have
5:5 Root of David, has won the **v**.
12:11 They won the **v** over him
15:2 Those who had won the **v** over
21:7 Everyone who wins the **v** will

view (7)

Num 33:3 Israelites boldly left in full **v**
1Co 1:26 wise from a human point of **v**.
10:18 Israel from a human point of **v**.
15:34 back to the right point of **v**,
2Co 5:16 from a human point of **v**.
5:16 Christ from a human point of **v**,
2Ti 1:10 brought eternal life into full **v**.

vigor (1)

Job 20:11 once full of youthful **v**,

village (21)

Zec 2:4 be inhabited like an unwalled **v**
Mat 10:11 "When you go into a city or **v**,
21:2 "Go into the **v** ahead of you.
Mar 8:23 hand and led him out of the **v**.
8:26 "Don't go into the **v**."
11:2 "Go into the **v** ahead of you.
Luk 5:17 They had come from every **v** in
8:1 from one city and **v** to another.
9:6 apostles went from **v** to village,
9:6 apostles went from village to **v**,
9:52 They went into a Samaritan **v**
9:56 So they went to another **v**.
10:38 Jesus went into a **v**.
13:22 in one city and **v** after another
17:12 As he went into a **v**,
19:30 "Go into the **v** ahead of you.
24:13 going to a **v** called Emmaus.
24:28 When they came near the **v**
Jon 7:42 and from the **v** of Bethlehem,
11:1 the **v** where Mary and her sister
11:30 had not yet come into the **v**

villages (98)

Lev 25:31 However, houses in **v** without
Num 21:25 including Heshbon and all its **v**,
21:32 captured its cities and **v**
32:42 captured Kenath and its **v**.
Dtr 2:23 who lived in **v** as far away
3:5 a large number of unwalled **v**.
Jos 10:37 it and its neighboring **v**
10:39 king and all its neighboring **v**
13:23 It included cities with their **v**.
13:28 It included cities with their **v**.
15:21 of Judah 29 cities with their **v**:
15:33 Judah 14 cities with their **v**:
15:37 16 other cities with their **v**:
15:42 cities with their **v** were given
15:45 Ekron with its cities and **v**.
15:46 with their **v** between Ekron
15:47 with their cities and **v** as far as
15:48 Judah 11 cities with their **v**:
15:52 nine other cities with their **v**:
15:55 another ten cities with their **v**:
15:59 with their **v** that were given
15:60 with their **v** ⌊were given
15:61 given six cities with their **v**:
16:9 with all the cities and their **v**
17:11 Shean and Ibleam with their **v**
17:11 and Megiddo and their **v**.
17:16 in Beth Shean and its **v**,
18:21 cities with their **v** that belong
18:25 14 other cities with their **v**:
19:2 received 13 cities and their **v**:
19:7 four other cities with their **v**:
19:8 All the **v** around these cities as
19:15 were 12 cities with their **v**.
19:16 These cities with their **v** are
19:22 were 16 cities with their **v**.
19:23 These cities with their **v** are
19:30 were 22 cities with their **v**.
19:31 These cities with their **v** are
19:38 were 19 cities with their **v**.
19:39 These cities with their **v** are
19:48 These cities with their **v** are
21:12 gave its fields and **v** to Caleb,
Jdg 1:27 and Megiddo or their **v**.
5:7 **V** in Israel were deserted —
5:11 the victories for his **v** in Israel.
11:26 in Heshbon, Aroer, all their **v**,
1Sm 6:18 walled cities and farm **v**.
1Ch 2:23 with Kenath and its **v** (60 cities
4:33 They also had all the **v** around
5:16 in Bashan and its **v**,
6:56 to the city and its **v** were given
7:28 were in Bethel and its **v**,
7:28 Gezer with its **v** to the west,
7:28 Shechem and its **v**,
7:28 and as far as Gaza and its **v**.
7:29 were Beth Shean and its **v**,
7:29 Taanach and its **v**,
7:29 Megiddo and its **v**,
7:29 its villages, and Dor and its **v**.
8:12 built Ono, Lod, and Lod's **v**).
9:16 who lived in the **v** belonging to
9:22 were recorded in their **v**.
9:25 to come from their **v** from time
18:1 its surrounding **v** from them.
27:25 **v**, and watchtowers: Jonathan,
2Ch 13:19 of his cities: Bethel and its **v**,
13:19 Jeshanah and its **v**,
13:19 and Ephron and its **v**,
28:18 Gederoth, Soco and its **v**,

2Ch 28:18 its villages, Timnah and its **v**,
28:18 and Gimzo and its **v**.
Neh 11:25 Many people lived in **v** that had
11:25 lived in Kiriath Arba and its **v**,
11:25 in Dibon and its **v**,
11:25 in Jekabzeel and its **v**,
11:27 in Beersheba and its **v**,
11:28 and in Meconah and its **v**,
11:30 and Adullam and their **v**,
11:30 and in Azekah and its **v**.
11:31 Aija, Bethel and its **v**,
12:28 from the **v** of Netophah,
12:29 The singers had built **v** for
Est 9:19 why the Jews who live in the **v**
Psa 10:8 He waits in ambush in the **v**.
Jer 49:2 Its **v** will be burned down.
Eze 26:6 The people in the **v** and on the
26:8 He will destroy the **v** on your
30:18 and people from its **v** will go
38:11 attack a land with unwalled **v**.
38:13 and all their **v** will ask you,
Mat 9:35 went to all the towns and **v**.
14:15 Send the crowds to the **v** to
Mar 6:6 around to the **v** and taught.
6:36 to the closest farms and **v**
6:56 Whenever he would go into **v**,
8:27 the **v** around Caesarea Philippi.
Luk 9:12 the crowd to the closest **v**
Act 8:25 News in many Samaritan **v**

vine (29)

Gen 49:11 his colt to the best **v**.
1Ki 4:25 under his own **v** and fig tree.
2Ki 4:39 vegetables and found a wild **v**.
Job 15:33 his unripened grapes like a **v**
Psa 80:8 You brought a **v** from Egypt.
80:12 the stone fences around this **v**?
80:14 Come to help this **v**.
80:16 The **v** has been cut down and
128:3 Your wife will be like a fruitful **v**
Sos 7:8 be like clusters on the **v**.
Jer 2:21 me and have become a wild **v**.
8:13 there are no grapes on the **v**.
Eze 15:2 good is the wood from a **v**?
15:5 When the **v** was in perfect
15:6 As a **v** is taken from among the
17:6 into a low **v** that spread over
17:6 downward. So it became a **v**,
17:7 Now, the **v** stretched its roots
17:7 The **v** turned away from the
17:8 and become a wonderful **v**.'
17:9 Will this **v** live and grow?
17:9 people to pull the **v** up by its
Hag 2:19 The **v**, the fig tree,
Zec 3:10 to sit under your **v** and fig tree."
Jon 15:1 Jesus said, "I am the true **v**,
15:4 It has to stay attached to the **v**.
15:5 "I am the **v**. You are the
Rev 14:18 bunches of grapes from the **v**
14:19 gathered the grapes from the **v**

vinegar (10)

Num 6:3 **v** made from wine or liquor,
Psa 69:21 they gave me **v** to drink.
Pro 10:26 Like **v** to the teeth,
25:20 coat on a cold day or pouring **v**
Mat 27:48 and soaked it in some **v**.
Mar 15:36 ran and soaked a sponge in **v**.
Luk 23:36 go up to him, offer him some **v**,
Jon 19:29 A jar filled with **v** was there.
19:29 put a sponge soaked in the **v**
19:30 After Jesus had taken the **v**,

vine's (1)

Eze 19:14 Fire has spread from the **v** main

vines (12)

Lev 25:5 or harvest grapes from your **v**.
25:11 grapes from the **v** in the land.
Psa 78:47 He killed their **v** with hail and
Sos 7:12 Let's see if the **v** have budded,
Isa 5:2 planted it with the choicest **v**,
7:23 1,000 **v** (worth 1,000 pieces
32:12 for the **v** bearing grapes.
Hos 10:1 The people of Israel are like **v**
Nah 2:2 it and have destroyed its **v**.
Hab 3:17 and the **v** have no grapes,
Zec 8:12 **V** will produce their grapes.
Mal 3:11 The **v** in your fields will not

vineyard (69)

Gen 9:20 the first person to plant a **v**.
Exo 22:5 livestock graze in a field or a **v**,
22:5 the best from his field and **v**.
Lev 19:10 Don't harvest your **v** a second
Dtr 20:6 If you have planted a **v** and not
22:9 between the rows in your **v**.
22:9 and the grapes from the **v**.
23:24 If you go into your neighbor's **v**,
24:21 you pick the grapes in your **v**,
28:30 You will plant a **v**,
1Ki 21:1 Naboth from Jezreel had a **v** in
21:2 told Naboth, "Give me your **v**.
21:2 I will give you a better **v** for it.
21:6 I said to him, 'Sell me your **v**.
21:6 I'll give you another **v** for it.'
21:6 'I won't give you my **v**.'"
21:7 I'll give you the **v** belonging to
21:15 Confiscate the **v** which Naboth
21:16 Ahab went to confiscate the **v**.
21:18 went to confiscate Naboth's **v**.
21:19 just to confiscate a **v**?' Then
2Ch 26:10 He had farmers and **v** workers
Job 24:6 in the wicked person's **v**.
Pro 24:30 the **v** belonging to a person
31:16 She plants a **v** from the profits
Sos 1:6 even taken care of my own **v**.
8:11 Solomon had a **v** at Baal
8:11 entrusted that **v** to caretakers.
8:12 My own **v** is in front of me.
Isa 1:8 Zion are left like a hut in a **v**,
3:14 "You have burned down the **v**!
5:1 to my beloved about his **v**:
5:1 My beloved had a **v** on a fertile
5:3 judge between me and my **v**!
5:4 been done for my **v** than what
5:5 tell you what I will do to my **v**.
5:7 The **v** of the LORD of Armies is
5:10 A ten-acre **v** will produce only
27:2 day sing about a delightful **v**.
Jer 12:10 have destroyed my **v**.
Amo 5:17 will be loud crying in every **v**,
Mat 20:1 to hire workers for his **v**.
20:2 he sent them to work in his **v**.
20:4 He said to them, 'Work in my **v**,
20:7 said to them, 'Work in my **v**.'
20:8 the owner of the **v** told the
21:28 go to work in the **v** today.'
21:33 A landowner planted a **v**.
21:33 Then he leased it to **v** workers
21:39 threw him out of the **v**,
21:40 the owner of the **v** comes,
21:41 Then he will lease the **v** to
Mar 12:1 He said, "A man planted a **v**.
12:1 Then he leased it to **v** workers
12:2 share of the grapes from the **v**.
12:8 and threw him out of the **v**.
12:9 will the owner of the **v** do?
12:9 and give the **v** to others.
Luk 13:6 had a fig tree growing in his **v**.
20:9 "A man planted a **v**,
20:9 leased it to **v** workers,
20:10 share of the grapes from the **v**.
20:12 and threw him out of the **v**.
20:13 "Then the owner of the **v** said,
20:15 So they threw him out of the **v**
20:15 the owner of the **v** do to them?
20:16 and give the **v** to others."
Jon 15:1 my Father takes care of the **v**.
1Co 9:7 Does anyone plant a **v** and not

vineyards (55)

Exo 23:11 with your **v** and olive groves.
Lev 25:3 in your fields, prune your **v**,
25:4 in your fields or prune your **v**.
Num 16:14 us any fields and **v** to own.
20:17 through any of your fields or **v**,
21:22 through any of your fields or **v**
22:24 the road went through the **v**,
Dtr 6:11 that you didn't dig and **v**
28:39 You will plant **v** and take care
32:32 grapevines come from the **v**
Jos 24:13 **v** and olive groves that you
Jdg 9:27 and harvested grapes in the **v**
14:5 coming to the **v** of Timnah,
21:20 of Benjamin, "Hide in the **v** and
21:21 the dances, come out of the **v**.
1Sm 8:14 take the best of your fields, **v**,
22:7 every one of you fields and **v**?
2Ki 5:26 **v**, sheep, cattle, or slaves?
18:32 a country with bread and **v**,
19:29 will plant and harvest, plant **v**,
25:12 in the land to work in the **v**
1Ch 27:27 for the **v**: Shimei from Ramah
27:27 wine that came from the **v**:
Neh 5:3 to mortgage our fields, our **v**,
5:4 taxes on our fields and **v**.
5:5 fields and **v** belong to others."
5:11 their **v**, their olive orchards,
9:25 things, cisterns, **v**, olive trees,
Job 24:18 the road that goes to their **v**.
Psa 107:37 fields and **v** that produce crops.
Ecc 2:4 I planted **v** for myself.
Sos 1:6 made me the caretaker of the **v**.
1:14 flowers in the **v** of En Gedi.
2:15 the little foxes that ruin **v**.
2:15 Our **v** are blooming.
7:12 Let's go to the **v** early.
Isa 16:8 fields of Heshbon and the **v**
36:17 a country with bread and **v**.
37:30 will plant and harvest, plant **v**,
61:5 will work your fields and **v**.
65:21 They will plant **v** and eat fruit
Jer 31:5 Once again you will plant **v** on
32:15 and **v** in this land.'
35:7 houses or plant any fields or **v**.
35:9 to live in, or owned **v**, pastures,
39:10 time he gave them **v** and farms.
52:16 in the land to work in the **v**
Eze 28:26 will build homes and plant **v**.
Hos 2:12 I will turn her **v** into a forest,
2:15 I will give her **v** there.
Amo 4:9 **v**, fig trees, and olive trees.
5:11 You plant beautiful **v**,
9:14 They will plant **v** and drink the
Mic 1:6 a place for planting **v**.
Zep 1:13 They will plant **v**, but they

violate (3)

Psa 89:31 if they **v** my laws and do not
Eze 22:26 Your priests **v** my teachings
Zep 3:4 They **v** the teachings.

violated (3)

Lev 20:11 wife has **v** his father's marriage.
Isa 24:5 LORD's teachings, **v** his laws,
Act 28:17 against the Jewish people or **v**

violates (3)

Lev 20:20 wife **v** his uncle's marriage.
20:21 wife **v** his brother's marriage
Act 24:6 in a way that **v** our tradition.

violating (1)

1Sm 14:26 were afraid of **v** their oath.

violation (1)

Heb 2:2 and every **v** and act of

violence (46)

Gen 6:11 in God's sight and full of **v**.
6:13 the earth is full of their **v**.
49:5 Their swords are weapons of **v**.
Jdg 9:24 **v** committed against Jerubbaal's
2Sm 22:3 Savior who saved me from **v**.
Psa 7:16 His **v** comes down on top of
11:5 and the ones who love **v**.
27:12 They breathe out **v**.
55:9 because I see **v** and conflict in
58:2 and your hands spread **v**.
72:14 them from oppression and **v**.
73:6 and acts of **v** like clothing.
74:20 of the land is filled with **v**.
Pro 4:17 drink wine obtained through **v**.
10:6 but **v** covers the mouths of
10:11 of wicked people conceal **v**.
13:2 treacherous people craves **v**.
21:7 The **v** of wicked people will

Pro 24:2 because their minds plot **v**,
26:6 feet and brings **v** upon himself.
Isa 51:19 **V**, destruction, famine, and war
59:6 have committed acts of **v**.
60:18 No longer will you hear about **v**
Jer 6:7 **V** and destruction can be heard
20:8 "**V** and destruction!"
51:35 "May the **v** done to us be done
51:46 Rumors of **v** are in the land.
Eze 5:17 I will send plagues, **v**,
7:11 **V** has grown into a weapon for
7:23 and the city is filled with **v**.
8:17 they also fill the land with **v**
45:9 Stop your **v** and looting,
Amo 6:3 They bring the reign of **v** closer.
Oba 1:10 "Because of the **v** you did to
Jnh 3:8 ways and your acts of **v**.
Nah 3:1 will be for that city of bloody **v**!
Hab 1:2 I cry out to you, "There's **v**!"
1:3 Destruction and **v** are in front of
1:9 They will all come for **v**.
2:8 of the slaughter and **v** done
2:9 will be for the one who uses **v**
2:17 The **v** done to Lebanon will
2:17 of the slaughter and **v** done
Zep 1:9 house with **v** and deception.
3:1 and corrupt place, the city of **v**.
Mal 2:16 covers himself with **v**," says

violent (30)

Jdg 18:25 or some **v** men will attack you.
2Sm 22:49 You rescue me from **v** people.
Job 16:17 my hands have done nothing **v**,
Psa 18:48 You rescue me from **v** people.
140:1 Keep me safe from **v** people.
140:4 Keep me safe from **v** people.
140:11 Let evil hunt down **v** people
Pro 1:27 strikes you like a **v** storm,
3:31 Do not envy a **v** person.
16:29 A **v** person misleads his
Isa 53:9 although he had done nothing **v**
Eze 12:19 everyone who lives there is **v**.
28:8 and you will die a **v** death in
28:16 You learned to be **v**,
Dan 11:14 and **v** men from your own
Hos 12:1 are very **v** and destructive.
Amo 3:10 in their palaces through **v**
Jnh 1:4 The LORD sent a **v** wind over
1:12 responsible for this **v** storm."
Mic 6:12 rich people in the city are **v**.
Hab 3:14 His soldiers come like a **v**
Mar 4:37 A **v** windstorm came up.
Luk 8:23 A **v** storm came across the
Act 16:26 Suddenly, a **v** earthquake
21:35 the crowd was so **v** that the
23:10 The quarrel was becoming **v**,
Rom 8:35 or **v** death separate us from his
1Ti 3:3 excessively or be a **v** person,
2Ti 3:1 there will be **v** periods of time.
Tit 1:7 too much or be a **v** person.

violently (21)

Gen 27:33 Trembling **v** all over,
Exo 19:18 the whole mountain shook **v**.
19:22 or the LORD will **v** kill them."
19:24 or he will **v** kill them."
Jdg 15:8 So he attacked them **v** and
2Sm 6:8 LORD had struck Uzzah so **v**.
22:8 They shook **v** because he was
1Ch 13:11 LORD had struck Uzzah so **v**.
Psa 17:9 people who **v** attack me,
18:7 They shook **v** because he was
Isa 24:19 will shake back and forth **v**.
31:6 you have so **v** rebelled against.
Jer 22:17 and **v** oppress your people."
Eze 34:4 have ruled them harshly and **v**.
Dan 10:7 Yet, they started to tremble **v**,
Nah 3:7 'Nineveh has been **v** destroyed!
Mar 9:26 screamed, shook the child **v**,
Act 2:2 Suddenly, a sound like a **v**
27:18 We continued to be tossed so **v**
Gal 1:13 You heard how I **v** persecuted
2Ti 4:15 He **v** opposed what we said.

violet (44)

Exo 25:4 **v**, purple, and bright red yarn,
26:1 Take **v**, purple, and bright red
26:4 Make 50 **v** loops along the
26:31 "Make a canopy of **v**,
26:36 embroidered with **v**,
27:16 embroidered with **v**,
28:5 They must use gold, **v**,
28:6 Creatively work gold, **v**,
28:15 Make it out of gold, **v**,
28:28 of the ephod with a **v** cord.
28:31 the ephod entirely of **v** material.
28:33 robe make pomegranates of **v**,
28:37 Fasten a **v** cord to it,
35:6 **v**, purple, and bright red yarn,
35:23 Those who had **v**,
35:25 in spinning yarn brought **v**,
35:35 They know how to embroider **v**,
36:8 from fine linen yarn and **v**,
36:11 Then they made 50 **v** loops
36:35 They made the canopy out of **v**,
36:37 It was embroidered with **v**,
38:18 to the courtyard was made of **v**,
38:23 he knew how to embroider **v**,
39:1 From the **v**, purple, and bright
39:2 **v**, purple, and bright red yarn.
39:3 into each strand of the **v**,
39:8 It was made out of gold, **v**,
39:21 of the ephod with a **v** cord.
39:22 woven entirely of **v** yarn.
39:24 they made pomegranates of **v**,
39:29 belt was embroidered with **v**,
39:31 They fastened a **v** cord to it
Num 4:6 made entirely of **v** material.
4:7 "They will spread a **v** cloth
4:9 "They will take a **v** cloth and
4:11 "They will spread a **v** cloth
4:12 put them in a **v** cloth,
15:38 of their clothes with **v** threads
2Ch 2:7 as purple, dark red, and **v** cloth.
2:14 **v**, and dark red cloth, and linen.
3:14 Solomon made the canopy of **v**,
Est 1:6 had white and **v** linen curtains.
8:15 of the king wearing the royal **v**
Eze 27:7 awnings were **v** and purple.

viper (3)

Gen 49:17 snake on a road, a **v** on a path,
Isa 14:29 because a **v** will come from
59:5 They hatch **v** eggs and weave

viper's (1)

Job 20:16 A **v** fang kills him.

vipers (2)

Isa 30:6 **V** and poisonous snakes live
Jer 8:17 **v** that can't be charmed.

vipers' (1)

Isa 11:8 will put their hands into **v** nests

virgin (29)

Gen 24:16 The girl was a very attractive **v**.
Exo 22:16 "Whenever a man seduces a **v**
27:20 **v** olive oil so that the lamps
29:40 with one quart of **v** olive oil.
Lev 21:3 and especially an unmarried **v**
21:13 anointed priest must marry a **v**.
21:14 He may only marry a **v** from his
24:2 **v** olive oil for the lamp stand so
Num 28:5 with one quart of **v** olive oil.
Dtr 22:14 I found out she wasn't a **v**."
22:15 that their daughter was a **v**.
22:17 out that my daughter wasn't a **v**.
22:19 the reputation of an Israelite **v**.
22:20 the girl was a **v** can be found,
22:23 with a **v** who is engaged
22:28 rapes a **v** who isn't engaged.
Jdg 19:24 Here, let me bring out my **v**
2Sm 13:2 with her because she was a **v**.
13:18 The king's **v** daughters wore
Job 31:1 how can I look with lust at a **v**?
Pro 30:19 man making his way with a **v**.
Isa 7:14 A **v** will become pregnant and
47:1 **v** princess of Babylon!
Mat 1:23 "The **v** will become pregnant
Luk 1:27 The angel went to a **v**
1Co 7:28 If a **v** gets married,
7:34 An unmarried woman or a **v** is
7:36 when his **v** daughter is old
2Co 11:2 After all, you're a **v** whom I

virginity (2)

Lev 21:7 those who have lost their **v**,
21:14 a woman who has lost her **v**,

virgin's (1)

Luk 1:27 The **v** name was Mary.

virgins (10)

Exo 22:17 equal to the bride-price for **v**.
Est 2:2 attractive young **v** for the king.
2:3 gather all the attractive young **v**
2:17 favored her over all the other **v**.
2:19 When the **v** were gathered a
Psa 78:63 so his **v** heard no wedding
Sos 6:8 concubines, and countless **v**,
Eze 44:22 They may marry only **v** from
1Co 7:25 Concerning **v**: Even though I
Rev 14:4 These 144,000 **v** are pure.

virtue (1)

Tit 2:3 but to be examples of **v**.

virtuous (1)

Ecc 7:16 Don't be too **v**, and don't be too

visible (5)

Jos 22:10 was very large and highly **v**.
Isa 26:11 O LORD, your power is **v**,
1Co 3:13 what each one does clearly **v**
Col 1:16 and on earth, **v** and invisible.
Rev 22:2 a tree of life **v** from both sides.

vision (71)

Gen 15:1 spoke his word to Abram in a **v**.
46:2 God spoke to Israel in a **v** that
Num 24:4 has a **v** from the Almighty,
24:16 has a **v** from the Almighty,
1Sm 3:15 afraid to tell Eli about the **v**.
2Ch 32:32 is written in the **v** of the prophet
Job 20:8 away like a **v** in the night.
33:15 a prophetic **v** at night,
Psa 69:23 Let their **v** become clouded so
89:19 Once in a **v** you said to your
Pro 29:18 Without prophetic **v** people run
Isa 1:1 This is the **v** which Isaiah,
21:2 I was shown a harsh **v**.
22:1 revelation about the valley of **V**.
22:5 and trampling in the valley of **V**,
29:7 like a **v** in the night.
32:3 Then the **v** of those who can
Eze 7:26 People will ask for a **v** from a
8:4 God as I did in the **v** that
11:24 In this **v** from God's Spirit,
11:24 Then the **v** I saw left me.
12:22 and every **v** comes to nothing'?
12:23 when every **v** will come true.
12:27 'The **v** that Ezekiel sees won't
43:3 This **v** was like the one I saw
Dan 2:19 revealed to Daniel in a **v** during
2:28 This is your dream, the **v** you
2:31 "Your Majesty, you had a **v**.
7:1 He saw a **v** while he was
7:7 I saw a fourth animal in my **v**
8:1 as king, I, Daniel, saw a **v**.
8:1 This **v** came after the one I
8:2 In my **v** I saw myself in the
8:2 In my **v** I saw myself at Ulai
8:13 long will the things in this **v** —
8:15 as I, Daniel, watched the **v**
8:16 explain the **v** to this man."
8:17 understand that the **v** is about
8:26 The **v** about the 2,300
8:26 Seal the **v**, because it is about
8:27 The **v** horrified me because I
9:21 whom I had seen in the first **v**,
9:23 and understand the **v**.
9:24 to put a seal on a prophet's **v**,
10:1 was given insight during the **v**.
10:7 the only one who saw the **v**.
10:7 men with me didn't see the **v**.
10:8 left alone to see this grand **v**.
10:14 because the **v** is about times

Dan 10:16 of me, "Sir, because of this **v**,
11:14 rebel in keeping with this **v**,
Amo 1:1 He saw ⌊a **v**⌋ about Israel
Oba 1:1 This is the **v** of Obadiah.
Mic 1:1 This is the **v** that Micah saw
Nah 1:1 This book contains the **v** of
Hab 2:2 answered me, "Write the **v**.
2:3 The **v** will still happen at the
Zec 13:4 will be ashamed of his **v** when
Luk 1:22 realized that he had seen a **v**
Act 9:10 The Lord said to him in a **v**,
9:12 In a **v** he has seen a man
10:3 in the afternoon, he had a **v**.
10:17 by the meaning of the **v**,
10:19 still thinking about the **v** when
12:9 He thought he was seeing a **v**.
16:9 During the night Paul had a **v** of
16:10 soon as Paul had seen the **v**,
18:9 the Lord said to Paul in a **v**,
26:19 point I did not disobey the **v**
Rom 11:10 Let their **v** become clouded so
Rev 9:17 In the **v** that I had, the horses

visions (41)

Num 12:6 myself known to them in **v**
1Sm 3:1 was rare; **v** were infrequent.
2Ch 9:29 and in Iddo the seer's **v** about
Job 4:13 With disturbing thoughts from **v**
7:14 dreams and terrify me with **v**.
Isa 28:7 They stagger when they see **v**.
29:11 To you all these **v** will be like
30:10 They say to those who have **v**,
30:10 'Don't have **v** that tell us what
Jer 14:14 They dreamed up the **v** they
23:16 They speak about **v** that they
23:16 These **v** are not from the LORD.
Lam 2:9 can find no **v** from the LORD.
2:14 saw misleading **v** about you.
Eze 1:1 and I saw **v** from God.
7:13 The **v** against that crowd will
8:3 In these **v** from God,
12:24 will no longer be any false **v**
13:6 foolish prophets see false **v**,
13:7 haven't you seen false **v** and
13:8 and your **v** are lies.
13:9 the prophets who see false **v**
13:23 you will no longer see false **v**
21:29 People see false **v** about you
22:28 these things by seeing false **v**
40:2 In **v**, God brought me to Israel
Dan 1:17 all kinds of **v** and dreams.
4:5 The **v** I had while I was asleep
4:9 Tell me the meaning of the **v** I
4:10 These are the **v** I had while I
4:13 "I was seeing these **v** as I was
7:2 In my **v** at night I, Daniel,
7:13 In my **v** during the night,
7:15 and my **v** frightened me.
Hos 12:10 and gave them many **v**.
Joe 2:28 Your young men will see **v**.
Mic 3:6 you will have nights without **v**.
Zec 10:2 The fortunetellers see false **v**.
Act 2:17 Your young men will see **v**.
2Co 12:1 I'll go on to **v** and revelations
Col 2:18 details of the **v** he has seen.

visit (50)

Gen 18:3 "stop by to **v** me for a while.
18:5 why you stopped by to **v** me."
34:1 went out to **v** some of the
Exo 18:6 "I'm coming to ⌊**v**⌋ you,
Jdg 15:1 Samson went to **v** his wife.
1Sm 25:5 **v** Nabal, and greet him for me.
1Ki 2:13 "Is this a friendly **v**?"
22:2 of Judah went to **v**
2Ki 4:10 whenever he comes to **v** us."
2Ch 18:2 A few years later he went to **v**
Psa 41:6 one of them comes to **v** me,
Mat 25:39 sick or in prison and **v** you?'
Act 7:23 he decided to **v** his own
10:28 a Jewish man to associate or **v**
11:3 They said, "You went to **v** men
15:36 We'll **v** the believers to see
18:2 Paul went to **v** them,
18:21 "I'll come back to **v** you if God
21:11 During his **v** he took Paul's belt
Act 21:18 Paul went with us to **v** James.
27:3 allowed him to **v** his friends
Rom 1:10 it possible for me to **v** you.
1:13 that I often planned to **v** you.
15:23 years I have wanted to **v** you.
15:28 I will **v** you on my way to
1Co 4:18 you think I won't pay you a **v**.
4:19 the Lord's will, I'll **v** you soon.
4:21 When I come to **v** you,
16:5 of Macedonia, I'll **v** you.
16:7 all I could do is **v** you briefly,
16:12 I tried hard to get him to **v** you
16:12 However, he will **v** you when
2Co 1:15 I had previously wanted to **v**
2:1 I decided not to **v** you again
2:3 I didn't want to **v** you and be
8:17 eagerly went to **v** you by his
9:5 our coworkers to **v** you before
12:14 I'm ready to **v** you for a third
12:18 I encouraged Titus to **v** you,
13:2 When I **v** you again,
Php 2:24 I will come ⌊to **v** you⌋ soon.
1Th 2:18 We wanted to **v** you.
2:18 wanted to **v** you twice already,
1Ti 3:14 I hope to **v** you soon.
2Ti 4:9 Hurry to **v** me soon.
4:21 Hurry to **v** me before winter
Tit 3:12 hurry to **v** me in the city of
Heb 13:23 both of us will **v** you.
2Jn 1:12 Instead, I hope to **v** and talk
3Jn 1:14 I hope to **v** you very soon.

visited (6)

1Sm 30:31 David and his men **v** from time
2Ki 13:14 King Jehoash of Israel **v** him,
Mat 25:36 I was in prison, and you **v** me.'
Jon 7:50 who had previously **v** Jesus.
11:45 Many Jews who had **v** Mary
Act 11:12 and we **v** Cornelius' home.

visiting (7)

Exo 12:45 "No foreigner **v** you may eat it.
Lev 22:10 even if they are **v** a priest or are
Num 15:14 "Suppose foreigners are **v** you
Dtr 14:21 sell it to foreigners who are **v**.
Luk 1:43 the mother of my Lord is **v** me.
Rom 15:22 so often kept me from **v** you.
2Co 13:1 the third time that I'll be **v** you.

visitor (3)

Lev 25:40 a hired worker or a **v** to you.
2Sm 12:4 a **v** came to the rich man.
Job 31:32 (The **v** never spent the night

visitors (1)

Act 2:10 to Judaism, and **v** from Rome,

vocabulary (1)

Gen 11:1 language with a common **v**.

voice (167)

Gen 27:22 "The **v** is Jacob's,"
Exo 19:19 and the **v** of God answered
24:3 people answered with one **v**,
Num 7:89 he heard the **v** speaking to him
Dtr 4:12 You heard a **v** speaking but
4:12 There was only a **v**.
4:36 He let you hear his **v** from
5:22 He spoke in a loud **v** from the
5:23 But when you heard the **v**
5:24 We've heard his **v** come from
5:25 If we continue to hear the **v** of
5:26 Who has ever heard the **v** of
18:16 "We never want to hear the **v** of
27:14 the people of Israel in a loud **v**:
Jdg 18:3 the young Levite's **v**.
1Sm 1:13 Her **v** couldn't be heard;
26:17 Saul recognized David's **v**.
26:17 "Is that your **v**, my servant
26:17 "It is my **v**, Your Royal
2Sm 22:7 He heard my **v** from his temple,
22:14 The Most High made his **v**
1Ki 8:55 Then he stood and in a loud **v**
19:12 was a quiet, whispering **v**.
19:13 Then the **v** said to him,
Job 4:16 of my eyes. I heard a soft **v**:
Job 37:2 Listen to the roar of God's **v**,
37:4 is followed by the roar of his **v**.
37:4 thunders with his majestic **v**.
37:5 God's **v** thunders in miraculous
40:9 you thunder with a **v** like his?
Psa 5:3 morning, O LORD, hear my **v**.
18:6 He heard my **v** from his temple,
18:13 The Most High made his **v**
29:3 The **v** of the LORD rolls over
29:4 The **v** of the LORD is powerful.
29:4 The **v** of the LORD is majestic.
29:5 The **v** of the LORD breaks the
29:7 The **v** of the LORD strikes with
29:8 The **v** of the LORD makes the
29:9 The **v** of the LORD splits the
46:6 at the sound of ⌊God's⌋ **v**.
55:17 and he listens to my **v**.
58:5 so that it cannot hear the **v** of a
64:1 Hear my **v**, O God, when I
68:33 He makes his **v** heard,
68:33 his voice heard, his powerful **v**.
116:1 LORD because he hears my **v**,
119:149 with your mercy, hear my **v**.
130:2 O Lord, hear my **v**.
Pro 1:20 squares she raises her **v**.
8:1 not understanding raise its **v**?
16:10 he cannot **v** a wrong judgment.
27:14 with a loud **v** — his blessing
Sos 2:8 I hear my beloved's **v**.
2:14 see your figure and hear your **v**.
2:14 Your **v** is sweet, and your
8:13 friends are listening to your **v**,
Isa 6:8 Then I heard the **v** of the Lord,
29:4 Your **v** will come out of the
30:21 You will hear a **v** behind you
30:30 will make his majestic **v** heard.
40:3 A **v** cries out in the desert:
40:6 A **v** called, "Call out!" I asked,
40:9 Call out with a loud **v**,
40:9 Raise your **v** without fear.
42:2 will not cry out or raise ⌊his **v**⌋.
42:2 He will not make his **v** heard in
58:1 Raise your **v** like a ram's horn.
Jer 22:20 Raise your **v** in Bashan!
Eze 1:25 A **v** came from above the dome
3:12 I heard a loud thundering **v** say,
9:1 LORD call out with a loud **v**.
33:32 a beautiful **v** who sings love
43:2 His **v** was like the sound of
43:7 The **v** said to me, "Son of man,
Dan 4:31 a **v** said from heaven,
6:20 to Daniel with anguish in his **v**,
10:6 When he spoke, his **v** sounded
Joe 3:16 and his **v** will thunder from
Amo 1:2 and his **v** thunders from
Mic 6:9 The **v** of the LORD calls out to
Nah 2:13 and no one will ever hear the **v**
Mat 3:3 "A **v** cries out in the desert:
3:17 Then a **v** from heaven said,
12:19 will hear his **v** in the streets.
17:5 Then a **v** came out of the cloud
27:46 Jesus cried out in a loud **v**,
Mar 1:3 "A **v** cries out in the desert:
1:11 A **v** from heaven said,
9:7 A **v** came out of the cloud and
15:34 Jesus cried out in a loud **v**,
15:37 cried out in a loud **v** and died.
Luk 1:42 She said in a loud **v**,
3:4 "A **v** cries out in the desert:
3:22 A **v** from heaven said,
8:28 and said in a loud **v**,
9:35 A **v** came out of the cloud and
9:36 After the **v** had spoken,
17:15 and praised God in a loud **v**.
23:46 Jesus cried out in a loud **v**,
Jon 1:23 "I'm a **v** crying out in the desert,
5:25 when the dead will hear the **v**
5:28 all the dead will hear his **v**,
5:37 You have never heard his **v**,
10:3 and the sheep respond to his **v**.
10:4 because they recognize his **v**.
10:5 they don't recognize his **v**."
10:16 They, too, will respond to my **v**.
10:27 My sheep respond to my **v**,
12:28 A **v** from heaven said,
12:29 standing there heard the **v**

Jon 12:30 Jesus replied, "That **v** wasn't
Act 2:14 In a loud **v** he said to them,
7:31 the **v** of the Lord said to him,
9:4 to the ground and heard a **v** say
9:7 They heard the **v** but didn't see
10:13 A **v** told him, "Get up, Peter!
10:15 A **v** spoke to him a second
11:7 I also heard a **v** telling me,
11:9 "A **v** spoke from heaven a
12:14 When she recognized Peter's **v**,
12:22 "The **v** of a god and not of a
14:10 So Paul said in a loud **v**,
22:7 and heard a **v** asking me,
26:14 and I heard a **v** asking me in
Rom 10:18 "The **v** of the messengers has
Gal 4:20 could change the tone of my **v**.
1Th 4:16 with the **v** of the archangel,
Heb 12:19 to a trumpet's blast, and to a **v**.
12:19 your ancestors heard that **v**,
12:26 his **v** shook the earth.
2Pe 1:17 God the Father and when the **v**
1:18 We heard that **v** speak to him
2:16 spoke with a human **v** and
Rev 1:10 I heard a loud **v** behind me like
1:12 I turned toward the **v** which
1:15 His **v** was like the sound of
3:20 If anyone listens to my **v** and
4:1 I heard the first **v** like a trumpet
5:2 angel calling out in a loud **v**,
5:12 In a loud **v** they were singing,
6:1 say with a **v** like thunder,
6:6 I heard what sounded like a **v**
6:7 I heard the **v** of the fourth living
6:10 They cried out in a loud **v**,
7:2 He cried out in a loud **v** to the
7:10 and crying out in a loud **v**,
8:13 and I heard it say in a loud **v**,
9:13 I heard a **v** from the four horns
9:14 The **v** said to the sixth angel
10:3 Then he shouted in a loud **v** as
10:4 I heard a **v** from heaven say,
10:8 The **v** which I had heard from
11:12 The witnesses heard a loud **v**
12:10 I heard a loud **v** in heaven,
14:7 The angel said in a loud **v**,
14:9 and said in a loud **v**,
14:13 I heard a **v** from heaven saying,
14:15 He cried out in a loud **v** to the
14:18 angel called out in a loud **v**
16:1 I heard a loud **v** from the temple
16:17 A loud **v** came from the throne
18:2 He cried out in a powerful **v**,
18:4 I heard another **v** from heaven
19:5 A **v** came from the throne.
19:17 He cried out in a loud **v** to all
21:3 I heard a loud **v** from the throne

voices (16)

Num 14:1 community raised their **v**
Jdg 5:11 Listen to the **v** of those singing
1Ki 1:40 that their **v** shook the ground.
2Ch 30:27 Their **v** were heard,
Job 29:10 The **v** of nobles were hushed,
Psa 19:3 without their **v** being heard.
Isa 6:4 Their **v** shook the foundations
15:4 Their **v** are heard as far away
24:14 They raise their **v**.
31:4 It isn't frightened by their **v** or
42:11 and its cities raise their **v**.
52:8 Your watchmen raise their **v**
Rev 5:11 Then I heard the **v** of many
10:3 spoke with **v** of their own.
11:15 there were loud **v** in heaven,
18:23 **V** of brides and grooms will

voluntarily (2)

2Ki 12:4 and all the money brought **v**
2Ch 35:8 His officials also **v** gave

volunteer (1)

Psa 110:3 Your people will **v** when you

volunteered (3)

Jdg 5:2 and people **v** for service.
5:9 to those people who **v**.
2Ch 17:16 who **v** to serve the LORD (with

vomit (11)

Lev 18:25 The land will **v** out those who
18:28 it will **v** you out as it has
20:22 you to live in will not **v** you out.
Pro 23:8 You will **v** the little bit you
25:16 you will have too much and **v**.
26:11 As a dog goes back to its **v**,
Isa 19:14 a drunk who staggers in his **v**.
28:8 covered with **v** and excrement.
Jer 25:27 Drink, get drunk, **v**, fall down,
48:26 will wallow in their own **v**,
2Pe 2:22 "A dog goes back to its **v**," and

vomited (1)

Lev 18:28 it will vomit you out as it has **v**

vomits (1)

Job 20:15 He **v** up the riches that he

Vophsi (1)

Num 13:14 Nahbi, son of **V**, from the tribe

vote (1)

Act 26:10 every time a **v** was taken.

voted (1)

Act 26:10 I **v** to have them killed every

vow (51)

Gen 28:20 Then Jacob made a **v**:
31:13 and where you made a **v** to me.
Lev 5:4 "If you hastily take a **v** about
22:21 fellowship offering to fulfill a **v**
22:23 it will not be accepted for a **v**.
27:2 If any of you makes a special **v**
27:9 "If ⌊the **v**⌋ is to give the kind of
Num 6:2 woman may make a special **v**
6:5 as they are under the Nazirite **v**,
6:7 Nazarites show their **v** to God
6:18 proof that they had made this **v**,
15:3 may be offered to fulfill a **v**,
15:8 kind of sacrifice — to keep a **v**
21:2 Then the Israelites made this **v**
30:2 If a man makes a **v** to the
30:3 might make a **v** to the LORD
30:4 her **v** or oath must be kept.
30:5 her **v** or oath doesn't have to be
30:5 LORD will free her ⌊from this **v**
30:6 might make a **v** that she will
30:7 Then her **v** or oath must be
30:8 he can cancel the **v** or promise
30:8 her ⌊from this **v** or promise⌋.
30:9 must keep her **v** or her promise.
30:10 might make a **v** that she will
30:11 Then her **v** or oath must be
30:12 nothing she said in her **v** or
30:12 free her ⌊from this **v** or oath⌋.
30:13 not his wife has to keep any **v**
30:14 she must keep her **v** or oath.
Dtr 12:6 the offerings you **v** to bring,
12:11 and all the best offerings you **v**
12:17 the offerings you **v** to bring;
23:21 If you make a **v** to the LORD
23:22 If you didn't make a **v**,
23:23 said you would do ⌊in your **v**⌋.
23:23 freely chose to make your **v**
Jdg 11:30 Jephthah made a **v** to the
1Sm 1:11 She made this **v**, "LORD of
1:21 To keep his **v**, the man
2Sm 15:7 me go to Hebron and keep the **v**
15:8 I made a **v** while I was living at
Job 22:27 you will keep your **v** to him.
Psa 132:2 to the LORD and made this **v**
Jer 44:25 will certainly do what we **v**.
44:25 and do what you **v**.
Jnh 2:9 I will keep my **v**. Victory
Mal 1:14 in their flocks that they **v**
Act 18:18 since he had taken a **v**.
21:23 who have made a **v** to God.
1Co 7:15 is not bound ⌊by a marriage **v**⌋.

vowed (10)

Lev 7:16 offering is something you **v**
22:18 to the LORD for anything they **v**
Num 6:21 for those who have **v**
Num 6:21 finish whatever they **v** to do."
29:39 the offerings for anything you **v**
Dtr 12:26 offerings you have **v** to bring,
23:18 as an offering you **v** to give.
32:42 of the enemy who **v** to fight.
Jdg 5:2 Men in Israel **v** to fight,
11:39 He did to her what he had **v**,

vows (25)

Lev 23:38 worship, your gifts, all your **v**,
Num 6:13 Nazirites who complete their **v**:
30:1 has commanded ⌊about **v**⌋:
Psa 22:25 I will fulfill my **v** in the
50:14 and keep your **v** to the Most
56:12 I am bound by my **v** to you,
56:12 I will keep my **v** by offering
61:5 O God, you have heard my **v**.
61:8 as I keep my **v** day after day.
65:1 and **v** ⌊made⌋ to you must be
66:13 I will keep my **v** to you,
66:14 the **v** made by my lips and
76:11 Make **v** to the LORD your God,
116:14 I will keep my **v** to the LORD in
116:18 I will keep my **v** to the LORD in
Pro 2:17 her marriage **v** to her God.
7:14 Today I kept my **v**.
20:25 second thoughts about those **v**.
Isa 19:21 They will make **v** to the LORD
Jer 44:25 Keep your **v**, and do what you
Eze 16:8 marriage **v** with you.
16:59 You despised your marriage **v**
Jnh 1:16 and made **v** to the LORD.
Nah 1:15 Keep your **v**! This wickedness
Mal 2:14 the wife of your marriage **v**.

voyage (1)

Act 27:10 and heavy losses on this **v**.

vultures (9)

Lev 11:13 They are eagles, bearded **v**,
11:13 bearded vultures, black **v**,
Dtr 14:12 bearded **v**, black vultures,
14:12 bearded vultures, black **v**,
Pro 30:17 valley and eaten by young **v**.
Isa 34:15 **V** also will gather there,
Mic 1:16 Make yourselves as bald as **v**
Mat 24:28 **V** will gather wherever there is
Luk 17:37 Jesus told them, "**V** will gather

W

wafer (3)

Exo 29:23 made with olive oil, and a **w**.
Lev 8:26 and a **w** from the basket of
Num 6:19 and one **w** of unleavened bread

wafers (6)

Exo 16:31 tasted like **w** made with honey.
29:2 and some **w** brushed with olive
Lev 2:4 flour mixed with olive oil or **w**
7:12 **w** of unleavened bread brushed
Num 6:15 made with olive oil and **w**
1Ch 23:29 the unleavened bread **w**,

wage (21)

Jos 22:12 to **w** war against them.
Jdg 11:6 can **w** war against Ammon."
11:8 us and **w** war against Ammon.
11:12 land and **w** war against me?"
20:23 "Should we continue to **w** war
20:28 "Should we continue to **w** war
1Sm 15:18 **W** war against them until
1Ki 12:24 Don't **w** war against your
2Ki 16:5 came to **w** war against
2Ch 11:4 Don't **w** war against your
13:12 Men of Israel, don't **w** war
17:1 ⌊to **w** war⌋ against Israel.
17:10 they didn't **w** war against
20:1 to **w** war against Jehoshaphat.
26:6 Uzziah went to **w** war against
32:2 to **w** war against Jerusalem,
Pro 24:6 right strategy you can **w** war,
Dan 11:10 They will return and **w** war all

Rev 2:16 and **w** war against them
13:7 It was allowed to **w** war
19:19 and their armies gathered to **w**

waged (4)

Jos 11:18 Joshua **w** war with all these
Jdg 11:4 Ammon **w** war with Israel.
2Ch 20:29 LORD **w** war against Israel's
Psa 55:18 from the war **w** against me,

wages (28)

Gen 29:15 me what your **w** should be."
30:28 So he offered, "Name your **w**,
30:32 They will be my **w**.
30:33 you come to check on my **w**.
31:7 has changed my **w** ten times.
31:8 ones will be your **w**,' all
31:8 striped ones will be your **w**,' all
31:41 you changed my **w** ten times.
Lev 25:50 like the **w** of a hired worker.
Num 18:31 because it's the **w** you receive
1Ki 5:6 I will pay you whatever **w** you
Pro 11:18 person earns dishonest **w**,
20:18 and with guidance one **w** war.
Isa 55:2 cannot nourish you and your **w**
Mic 1:7 All its **w** for being a prostitute
1:7 Samaria collected its **w** for
Zec 11:12 alright with you, pay me my **w**.
11:12 And they paid me my **w** — 30
Mal 3:5 cheat workers out of their **w**
Mat 20:2 the workers the usual day's **w**,
20:8 and give them their **w**.
20:9 and each received a day's **w**.
20:10 of them received a day's **w**.
20:13 agree with me on a day's **w**?
Mar 6:37 go and spend about a year's **w**
Jon 6:7 would need about a year's **w**
Jas 5:4 The **w** you refused to pay the
Rev 19:11 With integrity he judges and **w**

waging (1)

Jdg 11:27 But you have done wrong by **w**

wagon (4)

Num 7:3 one **w** from every two leaders
Isa 28:27 and **w** wheels aren't rolled over
Eze 26:10 from the war horses, **w** wheels,
Amo 2:13 **w** crushes a person.

wagons (11)

Gen 45:19 "Give them this order: 'Take **w**
45:21 Joseph gave them **w** and
45:27 he saw the **w** Joseph had sent
46:5 and their wives in the **w**
Num 7:3 six freight **w** and twelve oxen,
7:6 Moses took the **w** and the
7:7 He gave two **w** and four oxen
7:8 He gave four **w** and eight oxen
Isa 66:20 on horses, in chariots, in **w**,
Eze 23:24 with chariots and **w** and with a
Rev 18:13 **w**, slaves (that is, humans).

Waheb (1)

Num 21:14 **W** in Suphah and the valleys,

wail (3)

Isa 16:7 That is why Moab will **w**.
16:7 Everyone will **w** for Moab.
65:14 of your sadness and **w**

wailing (3)

Est 4:3 fasting, weeping, and **w**.
Isa 15:8 Their **w** echoes as far as
15:8 Their **w** echoes as far as Beer

wails (2)

Isa 15:2 Moab **w** over Nebo and
15:3 squares everyone **w** and cries.

waist (25)

Gen 37:34 put sackcloth around his **w**,
2Sm 10:4 their clothes from the **w** down,
1Ki 2:5 stained the belt around his **w**
2Ki 1:8 a leather belt around his **w**."
1Ch 19:4 their clothes from the **w** down,
Job 15:27 and he is fat around the **w**.
Sos 7:2 Your **w** is a bundle of wheat
Isa 11:5 will be the belt around his **w**.
Jer 13:1 Put it around your **w**.
13:2 and put it around my **w**.
13:11 a belt clings to a person's **w**,
48:37 and sackcloth on every **w**.
Eze 1:27 he looked like from the **w** up.
1:27 From the **w** down,
8:2 From the **w** down its body
8:2 and from the **w** up its body
47:4 The water came up to my **w**.
Dan 10:5 gold from Uphaz around his **w**.
Amo 8:10 sackcloth around everyone's **w**
Mat 3:4 had a leather belt around his **w**.
Mar 1:6 a leather belt around his **w**
Jon 13:4 and tied it around his **w**.
13:5 that he had tied around his **w**.
Eph 6:14 Fasten truth around your **w** like
Rev 1:13 wore a gold belt around his **w**.

waists (5)

Exo 29:9 Tie belts around the **w** of Aaron
Isa 5:27 The belts on their **w** aren't
32:11 wear sackcloth around your **w**.
Eze 23:15 men had belts around their **w**
Rev 15:6 with gold belts around their **w**.

wait (90)

Gen 49:18 "I **w** with hope for you to
Exo 7:15 **W** for him on the bank of the
24:14 He said to the leaders, "**W** here
Lev 15:13 he must **w** seven days to be
15:28 she must **w** seven days.
Num 9:8 Moses answered them, "**W**
Dtr 24:11 **W** outside, and the person to
33:20 They **w** there like a lion.
Rut 1:13 would you **w** until they grew up
1Sm 1:22 "I'll **w** until the boy is weaned.
1:23 "**W** until you've weaned him.
10:8 **W** seven days until I come to
2Sm 15:28 I'll **w** at the river crossings in
2Ki 6:33 Why should I **w** any longer for
7:9 If we **w** until morning when it's
Job 14:14 I will **w** for my relief to come as
32:16 Should I **w** because they don't
35:14 but you'll have to **w** for him.
Psa 5:3 needs in front of you, and I **w**.
25:5 I **w** all day long for you.
25:21 protect me because I **w** for you.
27:14 **W** with hope for the LORD.
27:14 Yes, **w** with hope for the LORD.
31:24 Be strong, all who **w** with hope
33:18 on those who **w** with hope for
33:20 We **w** for the LORD.
33:22 since we **w** with hope for you.
37:7 and **w** patiently for him.
37:9 but those who **w** with hope for
37:34 **W** with hope for the LORD,
38:15 But I **w** with hope for you,
52:9 I will **w** with hope in your good
56:6 watch my every step as they **w**
62:5 **W** calmly for God alone,
69:6 Do not let those who **w** with
106:13 They did not **w** for his advice.
130:5 I **w** for the LORD, my soul
130:5 and with hope I **w** for his word.
147:11 with those who **w** with hope for
Pro 20:22 **W** for the LORD, and he will
Isa 8:17 I will **w** for the LORD,
26:8 we **w** with hope for you,
30:18 are all those who **w** for him.
33:2 We **w** with hope for you.
40:31 the strength of those who **w**
42:4 will **w** for his teachings.
49:23 Those who **w** with hope for me
51:5 and they **w** eagerly for me.
60:9 Certainly, the coastlands **w**
64:4 You help those who **w** for you.
Lam 3:25 is good to those who **w** for him,
3:26 continue to hope and **w** silently
Eze 44:26 he must **w** seven days.
Dan 11:27 because the end must **w** until
12:12 Blessed are those who **w** until
Hos 3:3 Then I told her, "You must **w**
3:3 to any man. I will **w** for you."
3:4 the Israelites will **w** a long time
Hos 12:6 Be loyal and fair, and always **w**
13:7 Like a leopard I will **w** by the
Mic 1:12 **W** anxiously for good,
5:7 in humans or **w** for mortals.
7:7 I will **w** for God to save me.
7:7 I will **w** for my God to listen to
Hab 2:3 If it's delayed, **w** for it.
3:16 I **w** for the day of trouble to
Zep 3:8 The LORD declares, "Just **w**!
Mat 17:9 **W** until the Son of Man has
26:38 **W** here, and stay awake with
Mar 9:9 They were to **w** until the Son of
14:34 **W** here, and stay awake."
Luk 21:26 will faint as they fearfully **w**
24:49 **W** here in the city until you
Jon 16:30 You don't need to **w** for
Act 1:4 leave Jerusalem but to **w** there
Rom 8:23 We groan as we eagerly **w** for
8:25 we eagerly **w** for it with
1Co 1:7 you don't lack any gift as you **w**
4:5 **W** until the Lord comes.
11:33 gather to eat, **w** for each other.
Gal 5:5 faith causes us to **w** eagerly
1Th 1:10 and to **w** for his Son to come
3:1 But, because we couldn't **w**
3:5 when I couldn't **w** any longer,
Heb 9:28 those who eagerly **w** for him.
10:27 All that is left is a terrifying **w**
Jas 5:7 See how farmers **w** for their
5:7 They **w** patiently for fall and
2Pe 1:19 in a dark place as you **w**
3:12 the day of God and eagerly **w**

waited (31)

Gen 8:10 He **w** seven more days and
8:12 He **w** seven more days and
43:10 If we hadn't **w** so long,
Jdg 3:25 They **w** and waited,
3:25 They waited and **w**,
16:2 the place and **w** all night at
1Sm 13:8 He **w** seven days,
25:9 him for David, and then they **w**.
1Ki 20:38 **w** for the king by the road.
Job 30:26 When I **w** for good,
31:9 secretly **w** near my neighbor's
32:4 Elihu **w** as they spoke to Job
32:11 I **w** for you to speak.
Psa 40:1 I **w** patiently for the LORD.
119:95 The wicked people have **w** for
119:166 I have **w** with hope for you to
Isa 5:2 Then he **w** for it to produce
5:4 When I **w** for it to produce good
25:9 we have **w** for him,
25:9 we have **w** for him.
Lam 4:17 We **w** and waited for a nation
4:17 We waited and **w** for a nation
Eze 19:5 The lioness **w** until she saw
Jnh 4:5 He sat in its shade and **w** to
Act 27:28 They **w** a little while and did
27:33 the fourteenth day you have **w**
28:6 But after they had **w** a long
Rom 3:25 In his patience God **w** to deal
3:26 He **w** so that he could display
Heb 6:15 because he **w** patiently for it.
1Pe 3:20 God **w** patiently while Noah

waiters (1)

Est 1:8 (The king had ordered all the **w**

waiting (41)

Exo 5:20 Moses and Aaron **w** for them.
Jos 8:14 behind the city **w** to attack him.
Jdg 3:26 While they had been **w**,
16:9 were hiding in the bedroom **w**
16:12 men were in her bedroom **w**
20:33 Meanwhile, those **w** in
20:36 The Israelites relied on those **w**
20:38 had arranged with those **w**
2Sm 17:17 Jonathan and Ahimaaz were **w**
2Ki 2:18 in Jericho, where he was **w**.
7:3 are we sitting here **w** to die?
Job 17:1 The cemetery is **w** for me.
18:12 Disaster is **w** beside him.
27:13 This is what God has **w** for the
29:21 quietly **w** for my advice.
29:23 their mouths wide as if **w**

Psa 39:7 now, Lord, what am I **w** for?
119:81 My soul is weak from **w** for you
Pro 10:28 but the eager **w** of wicked
Isa 30:18 The LORD is **w** to be kind to
Jer 3:2 You sat by the roadside **w** for
20:10 All my closest friends are **w** to
Lam 2:16 is the day we've been **w** for.
3:10 He is like a bear **w** to ambush
Mar 15:43 was **w** for the kingdom of God.
Luk 1:21 people were **w** for Zechariah.
2:25 He was **w** for the one who
2:38 about Jesus to all who were **w**
12:36 Be like servants **w** to open the
23:51 and he was **w** for the kingdom
Act 17:16 While Paul was **w** for Silas
20:5 men went ahead and were **w**
20:23 and suffering are **w** for me.
22:16 What are you **w** for now?
28:6 The people were **w** for him to
Rom 8:19 All creation is eagerly **w** for
1Co 11:21 his own supper ⌊without **w**
2Ti 4:8 approval is now **w** for me.
4:8 to everyone who is eagerly **w**
Heb 10:13 Since that time, he has been **w**
11:10 Abraham was **w** for the city

waits (11)

Dtr 19:11 **w** in ambush for him,
Job 20:26 Total darkness **w** in hiding for
Psa 10:8 He **w** in ambush in the villages.
25:3 No one who **w** for you will ever
62:1 My soul **w** calmly for God
130:5 I wait for the LORD, my soul **w**,
130:6 My soul **w** for the LORD more
Pro 8:34 **w** by my doorposts.
Ecc 2:14 realize that the same destiny **w**
2:15 "⌊If⌋ the destiny that **w** for the
2:15 destiny that waits for the fool **w**

wake (47)

1Ki 18:27 and you have to **w** him!"
2Ki 4:31 "The boy didn't **w** up."
Job 3:8 how to **w** up Leviathan) curse
14:12 He does not **w** up.
Psa 3:5 I **w** up again because the
7:6 **W** up, my God. You have
17:15 When I **w** up, I will be satisfied
35:23 **W** up, and rise to my defense.
44:23 **W** up! Why are you sleeping, O
57:8 **W** up, my soul! Wake up,
57:8 **W** up, harp and lyre! I want to
57:8 I want to **w** up at dawn.
59:4 **W** up, and help me; see ⌊for
73:20 of them when you **w** up.
80:2 **W** up your power, and come to
108:2 **W** up, harp and lyre! I want to
108:2 I want to **w** up at dawn.
119:62 At midnight I **w** up to give
139:18 When I **w** up, I am still with
Pro 6:22 When you **w** up, they will talk
23:35 Whenever I **w** up, I'm going to
Isa 26:19 lie dead in the dust will **w** up
28:21 He will **w** up as he did in
29:8 that they're eating and **w** up
29:8 that they're drinking and **w** up
50:4 Morning after morning he will **w**
51:9 **W** up! Wake up! Clothe yourself
51:9 **W** up! Clothe yourself with
51:9 **W** up as you did in days long
51:17 **W** up! Wake up! Stand up,
51:17 **W** up! Stand up, Jerusalem! You
52:1 **W** up! Wake up! Clothe yourself
52:1 **W** up! Clothe yourself with
Jer 51:39 sleep and never **w** up again,
51:57 a deep sleep and never **w** up,"
Dan 12:2 in the ground will **w** up.
12:2 Some will **w** up to live forever,
12:2 but others will **w** up to be
Joe 1:5 **W** up and cry, you drunks!
3:9 **W** up the warriors.
3:12 **W** up, you nations. Come to the
Hab 2:7 are going to shake you **w** up?
2:19 to a piece of wood, "**W** up!"
Zec 4:1 one might **w** up someone who
Jon 11:11 and I'm going to Bethany to **w**
Rom 13:11 It's time for you to **w** up.
Eph 5:14 That's why it says: "**W** up,

wakes (4)

Psa 73:20 rid of a dream when he **w** up,
Pro 31:15 She **w** up while it is still dark
Isa 14:9 Sheol below **w** up to meet you
14:9 It **w** up the ghosts of the dead,

waking (1)

Zec 2:13 He is **w** up and setting out from

walk (102)

Gen 13:17 **W** back and forth across the
Exo 21:19 up again and **w** around outside
Lev 11:27 All four-legged animals that **w**
Num 11:31 feet deep as far as you could **w**
Jdg 5:10 and who **w** on the road — think.
11:37 for my friends and me to **w**
Rut 1:7 They began to **w** back along
1Sm 17:39 over his clothes and tried to **w**,
17:39 "I can't **w** in these things,"
2Sm 22:37 make a wide path for me to **w**
Neh 9:11 so that they could **w** through
Est 2:11 Every day Mordecai would **w**
Job 30:28 I **w** in the dark without the sun.
Psa 18:36 make a wide path for me to **w**
23:4 Even though I **w** through the
26:3 I **w** in the light of your truth.
26:6 I will **w** around your altar,
26:11 But I **w** with integrity.
38:6 All day I **w** around in mourning.
42:4 how I used to **w** with the crowd
42:9 Why must I **w** around in
43:2 Why must I **w** around in
44:5 With you we can **w** over our
48:12 **W** around Zion. Go around it.
48:13 **W** through its palaces.
55:14 and **w** into God's house
56:13 stumbling so that I could **w**
82:5 As they **w** around in the dark,
89:15 They **w** in the light of your
115:7 but they cannot **w**.
116:9 I will **w** in the LORD's
119:45 I will **w** around freely because I
138:7 Even though I **w** into the
142:3 for me on the path where I **w**.
Pro 2:7 for those who **w** in integrity
2:13 the paths of righteousness to **w**
2:20 So **w** in the way of good
4:12 When you **w**, your stride will
4:14 Do not **w** in the way of evil
4:15 Do not **w** near it. Turn away
4:26 Carefully **w** a straight path,
4:27 **W** away from evil.
6:22 When you **w** around,
6:28 Can anyone **w** on red-hot coals
8:20 I **w** in the way of
30:29 three things that **w** with dignity,
Isa 3:16 They **w** with their noses in the
9:2 The people who **w** in darkness
11:15 so that people can **w** over
32:11 your clothes, **w** around naked,
35:8 It will be for those who **w** on it.
35:9 ⌊by the LORD⌋ will **w** ⌊on it⌋.
40:31 They will **w** and won't grow
42:5 breath to those who **w** on it.
43:2 When you **w** through fire,
50:10 Let those who **w** in darkness
50:11 So **w** in your own light and
51:23 so that we can **w** over you."
59:9 but we **w** in darkness.
59:9 but we **w** in gloom.
Jer 5:1 **W** around the streets of
6:25 Don't go into the field or **w** on
10:5 because they can't **w**.
10:23 not direct their steps as they **w**.
Lam 3:2 me away and made me **w**
Eze 29:11 or animal will **w** through it,
Hos 11:3 the people of Ephraim to **w**.
Amo 3:3 Do two people ever **w** together
Jnh 3:3 took three days to **w** through it.
Mic 1:8 I will **w** around barefoot and
2:3 no longer be able to **w** proudly.
5:6 land and **w** within our territory.
Hab 3:19 He makes me **w** on the
Zep 1:17 that they will **w** like they are
Zep 3:6 No one will **w** through them.
Zec 3:7 to **w** among those standing
Mal 3:14 or if we **w** around feeling sorry
Mat 9:5 or to say, 'Get up and **w**'?
Mar 2:9 up, pick up your cot, and **w**'?
5:42 got up at once and started to **w**.
12:38 They like to **w** around in long
Luk 5:23 or to say, 'Get up and **w**'?
11:44 People **w** on them without
20:46 They like to **w** around in long
Jon 1:36 John saw Jesus **w** by.
5:8 up, pick up your cot, and **w**."
5:11 me to pick up my cot and **w**."
5:12 told you to pick it up and **w**?"
11:9 Those who **w** during the day
11:10 However, those who **w** at night
12:35 **W** while you have light so that
12:35 Those who **w** in the dark don't
Act 3:6 Christ from Nazareth, **w**!"
3:8 he stood up and started to **w**.
3:12 have made him **w** by our own
14:8 he had never been able to **w**.
14:10 jumped up and began to **w**.
20:13 to **w** overland to Assos.
2Co 6:16 "I will live and **w** among them.
Rev 3:4 They will **w** with me in white
9:20 which cannot see, hear, or **w**.
21:24 The nations will **w** in its light,

walked (38)

Gen 5:22 Enoch **w** with God for 300
5:24 Enoch **w** with God;
6:9 of his time. He **w** with God.
9:23 Then they **w** in backwards and
48:15 and my father Isaac **w**,
Exo 2:5 her servants **w** along the bank
Jos 14:9 'The land your feet **w** on will
Jdg 4:21 took a tent peg and **w** quietly
14:9 hands and ate it as he **w** along.
1Sm 17:7 his shield **w** ahead of him.
2Sm 11:2 up from his bed and **w** around
15:30 his head and **w** barefoot.
18:24 while the watchman **w** along
1Ki 14:17 When she **w** across the
21:27 and **w** around depressed.
2Ki 2:23 As he **w** along the road,
4:35 Elisha got up, **w** across the
Neh 4:3 their stone wall collapse if it **w**
12:38 We **w** on the wall,
Job 28:8 proud beast has ever **w** on it.
29:3 when I **w** through the dark in
31:5 "If I have **w** with lies or my feet
38:16 springs in the sea or **w** through
Psa 26:1 because I have **w** with integrity
35:14 I **w** around as if I were
Isa 20:2 Isaiah did this and **w** around
Eze 16:15 sex with everyone who **w** by.
28:14 You **w** among fiery stones.
Amo 4:8 cities staggered as they **w**
Jnh 3:4 Jonah entered the city and **w**
Mat 12:1 of worship Jesus **w** through
14:29 Peter got out of the boat and **w**
Mar 2:12 and **w** away while everyone
2:23 As the disciples **w** along,
Luk 4:30 But Jesus **w** right by them and
Jon 5:9 well, picked up his cot, and **w**.
9:1 As Jesus **w** along,
11:54 So Jesus no longer **w** openly

walking (41)

Gen 3:8 heard the LORD God **w** around
18:16 As Abraham was **w** with them
2Sm 6:4 with Ahio **w** ahead of the ark.
16:13 Shimei was **w** along the
2Ki 2:11 they continued **w** and talking,
6:26 As the king of Israel was **w** on
6:30 As he was **w** on the city wall,
Psa 119:101 I have kept my feet ⌊from **w**⌋
Pro 4:15 away from it, and keep on **w**.
7:8 corner and **w** toward her house
Ecc 10:3 Even when a fool goes **w**,
Eze 29:6 like a ⌊broken⌋ **w** stick
Dan 3:25 **w** in the middle of the fire,
4:29 Twelve months later, he was **w**
Mat 4:18 As he was **w** along the Sea of
10:10 clothes, sandals, or a **w** stick.

Mat 11:5 lame people are w,
14:25 He was w on the sea.
14:26 When the disciples saw him w
15:31 the disabled cured, the lame w,
24:1 courtyard and was w away,
26:39 After w a little farther,
Mar 6:8 on the trip except a w stick.
6:48 He was w on the sea.
6:49 When they saw him w on the
8:24 They look like trees w around."
10:32 Jesus was w ahead of them.
11:20 and his disciples were w early
11:27 As he was w in the temple
14:35 After w a little farther,
16:12 two disciples as they were w
Luk 6:1 Jesus was w through some
7:22 lame people are w,
9:3 Don't take a w stick,
9:57 As they were w along the road,
24:15 them and began w with them.
Jon 6:19 they saw Jesus w on the sea.
10:23 Jesus was w on Solomon's
Act 3:8 The man was w, jumping,
3:9 saw him w and praising God.
Heb 12:13 Keep w along straight paths so

walks (15)

Lev 11:20 winged insect that w across
11:23 of winged insect that w across
Job 9:8 the heavens by himself and w
18:8 tangled in a net as he w around
22:14 He w above the clouds.'
Psa 15:2 The one who w with integrity,
39:6 Each person who w around is
Pro 13:20 Whoever w with wise people
28:26 Whoever w in wisdom will
Ecc 2:14 but a fool w in the dark.
Isa 59:8 Whoever w on them will never
Lam 2:15 Everyone who w along the
Amo 4:13 He w on the high places of the
Jon 10:4 he w ahead of them.
Rev 2:1 the one who w among the

walkway (5)

2Ki 16:18 Ahaz removed the covered w
16:18 This w had been built in the
Eze 42:4 of the side rooms was a w,
42:11 There was a w in front of them
42:12 end of the w that was parallel

wall (166)

Gen 49:22 branches climbing over a w.
Exo 14:22 The water stood like a w on
14:29 while the water stood like a w
Lev 14:37 deeper than the rest of the w,
Num 22:25 Balaam's foot against the w.
35:4 1,500 feet from the city w.
Jos 2:15 house was built into the city w.
2:15 (She lived in the city w.)
6:5 The w around the city will
6:20 and the w collapsed.
1Sm 18:11 "I'll nail David to the w."
19:10 Saul tried to nail David to the w
19:10 and Saul's spear struck the w.
20:25 sat in his usual seat by the w,
25:16 They were a w protecting us
31:10 corpse to the w of Beth Shan.
31:12 of Saul and his sons from the w
2Sm 11:20 they would shoot from the w?
11:21 Didn't a woman on the w of
11:21 did you go so close to the w?' If
11:24 The archers on the w shot
18:24 the roof of the gate by the w.
20:15 it stood level with the outer w.
20:15 were trying to destroy the w
20:21 be thrown to you from the w."
1Ki 3:1 and the w around Jerusalem.
4:33 hyssop growing out of the w.
6:27 the angels touched the one w,
6:27 the other touched the other w.
11:27 repairing a break in the ⌊w of⌋
20:30 the city where the w fell on
2Ki 3:27 and sacrificed him on the w as
6:26 was walking on the city w,
6:30 he was walking on the city w,
9:33 of her blood splattered on the w
2Ki 14:13 of the w around Jerusalem from
18:26 are people on the w listening."
18:27 sitting on the w who will have
20:2 Hezekiah turned to the w and
2Ch 3:11 ½ feet long and touched the w
3:12 long and touched the other w
25:23 of the w around Jerusalem from
26:9 in Jerusalem at Corner W,
27:3 building of the w at the Ophel.
32:5 the broken sections of the w,
32:5 built another w outside ⌊the
32:5 wall outside ⌊the city w⌋,
32:18 were on the w of Jerusalem.
33:14 Manasseh rebuilt the outer w of
33:14 He made the w go around the
Ezr 9:9 and to give us a protective w
Neh 1:3 The w of Jerusalem has been
2:8 near the temple, for the city w,
2:15 that night and examined the w.
2:17 rebuild the w of Jerusalem,
3:7 made repairs on the w.
3:8 Jerusalem as far as Broad W.
3:13 repaired 1,500 feet of the w,
3:15 He also made repairs on the w
3:24 and to the corner of the w.
3:26 made repairs on the w as far as
3:27 as far as the W of the Ophel.
4:1 we were rebuilding the w,
4:3 make their stone w collapse if
4:6 So we rebuilt the w,
4:10 can't continue to rebuild the w."
4:13 families behind the w where
4:15 back to the work on the w.
4:16 of my men worked on the w,
4:17 who were rebuilding the w.
4:19 from one another on the w.
5:16 effort into the work on this w,
6:1 heard that I had rebuilt the w
6:6 why you're rebuilding the w.
6:15 The w was finished on the
6:15 The w took 52 days to finish.
7:1 after the w had been rebuilt
12:27 When the w of Jerusalem was
12:30 people, the gates, and the w.
12:31 of Judah come up on the w,
12:31 the right on the w to Dung Gate.
12:37 There the w rises past David's
12:38 We walked on the w,
12:38 as far as Broad W,
13:21 the night in front of the w?"
Job 30:14 through a wide hole ⌊in the w⌋.
Psa 62:3 as though he were a leaning w
78:13 the waters stand up like a w.
Pro 18:11 a high w in his imagination.
25:28 into ⌊and⌋ left without a w,
Ecc 10:8 breaks through a stone w may
Sos 2:9 There he stands behind our w,
8:9 If she is a w, we will build a
8:10 I am a w, and my breasts are
Isa 2:15 tower and every fortified w,
5:5 and tear down its w so that
22:9 places in David's w are broken.
25:4 is like a rainstorm against a w,
30:13 your sin will be like a high w
36:11 are people on the w listening."
36:12 sitting on the w who will have
38:2 Hezekiah turned to the w and
59:10 grope like blind men along a w.
Jer 1:18 an iron pillar, and a bronze w.
15:20 make you like a solid bronze w
21:4 blockading you outside the w.
Lam 2:8 LORD planned to destroy the w
2:18 the w of Zion's people.
Eze 4:3 and set it up as a w between
8:7 I saw a hole in the w.
8:8 dig through the w."
8:8 So I dug through the w,
12:5 Dig a hole through the w of
12:7 I dug a hole through the w.
12:12 People will dig holes in the w
13:5 repaired the gaps in the w
13:5 gaps in the wall or rebuilt the w
13:10 someone builds a flimsy w,
13:11 Tell those who cover up the w
13:11 paint that their w will fall down.
13:12 When the w falls down,
Eze 13:12 that you used to cover the w?"
13:13 hailstones will destroy the w.
13:14 I will tear down the w that the
13:14 When the w falls, they will be
13:15 I will unleash my fury on the w
13:15 say to you, "The w is gone,
38:20 and every w will fall to the
40:5 I saw a w that surrounded the
40:5 He measured the w.
40:43 were attached to the w all
41:5 man measured the temple w.
41:6 the way around the temple w,
41:6 not fastened to the temple w.
41:9 The outer w of the side rooms
41:12 The w of the building was 9
42:7 There was a w which ran
42:10 side rooms parallel to the w
42:12 w that ran eastward.
42:20 There was a w all around it.
42:20 The w was 875 feet long and
43:8 Only a w separated me from
Dan 3:1 up in a recessed area in the w
5:5 wrote on the plaster w opposite
Hos 2:6 and build a w so that she
Joe 2:9 They run along the w.
Amo 4:3 city⌋ through breaks in the w,
5:19 puts his hand on the w only
7:7 The Lord was standing by a w
Nah 2:5 They hurry to Nineveh's w.
3:8 The water was her w.
Hab 2:1 I will station myself on the w.
2:11 A stone in the w will cry out.
Zec 2:5 I will be a w of fire around it,
Mat 21:33 He put a w around it,
Mar 12:1 He put a w around it,
Luk 19:43 enemy armies will build a w
Act 9:25 an opening in the w one night.
2Co 11:33 through an opening in the w
Eph 2:14 one by breaking down the w
Rev 21:12 high w with 12 gates.
21:14 The w of the city had 12
21:15 the city, its gates, and its w.
21:17 He measured its w.
21:18 Its w was made of gray quartz.
21:19 The foundations of the city w

walled (5)

Lev 25:29 sells a home in a w city,
Num 32:17 families will live in w cities,
32:36 and Beth Haran as w cities.
1Sm 6:18 including w cities and farm
2Ki 3:19 You will defeat every w city

wallet (3)

Luk 10:4 Don't carry a w, a traveling bag,
22:35 I sent you out without a w,
22:36 the person who has a w and a

wallets (1)

Luk 12:33 Make yourselves w that don't

wallow (1)

Jer 48:26 They will w in their own vomit,

wallowing (1)

2Sm 20:12 Amasa was w in his blood in

walls (123)

Lev 14:37 the mildew area on the w.
14:39 If the mildew in the w of the
14:41 dust scraped off the w must
25:31 houses in villages without w
Num 13:19 Do their cities have w around
13:28 and the cities have w and are
22:24 with stone w on both sides.
Dtr 1:28 cities are big with sky-high w!
2:36 no city had w that could keep
3:5 cities were fortified with high w
9:1 big cities that have sky-high w.
28:52 fortified w in which you trust
1Ki 4:13 60 large cities with w and
6:5 This annex was next to the w
6:6 fastened to the w of the temple.
6:9 he had finished building the w,
6:15 he began to line the inside w of
6:29 and flowers into the w all

1Ki 9:15 the **w** of Jerusalem,
21:23 inside the **w** of Jezreel.
2Ki 3:25 Only the stones ⌊in the **w**⌋ of
9:10 inside the **w** of Jezreel,
9:36 body inside the **w** of Jezreel.
25:1 dirt ramps around the city **w**.
25:4 through the city **w** that night.
25:4 gate between the two **w** beside
25:10 down the **w** around Jerusalem.
1Ch 29:4 to cover the **w** of the buildings,
2Ch 3:4 its inside **w** with pure gold.
3:7 the **w**, and the doors with gold,
3:7 he carved angels into the **w**.
8:5 into cities fortified with **w**,
14:7 cities and make **w** around them
26:6 He tore down the **w** of Gath,
36:19 tore down Jerusalem's **w**,
Ezr 4:12 are close to finishing the **w**.
4:13 is rebuilt and its **w** are finished,
4:16 is rebuilt and its **w** are finished,
5:3 this temple and finish its **w**?"
5:8 wooden beams laid in its **w**.
5:9 this temple and finish its **w**?"
Neh 2:13 the places where the **w**
4:7 that the repair work on the **w**
Psa 51:18 Rebuild the **w** of Jerusalem.
55:10 around on ⌊top of⌋ the city **w**.
89:40 have broken through all his **w**
122:7 there be peace inside your **w**
Sos 1:17 The cedars will be the **w** of our
5:7 Those watchmen on the **w**
Isa 22:5 ⌊a day of⌋ tearing down **w** and
22:10 houses in order to fortify the **w**.
22:11 a reservoir between the two **w**
25:12 down Moab's high fortified **w**,
26:1 Its **w** and fortifications provide
49:16 Your **w** are always in my
54:12 your **w** with precious stones."
56:5 my house and within my **w**,
58:12 the Rebuilder of Broken **W**
60:10 "Foreigners will rebuild your **w**,
60:18 You will call your **w** Salvation
62:6 posted watchmen on your **w**,
Jer 1:15 They will attack all the **w**
39:4 the gate between the two **w**,
39:8 tore down the **w** of Jerusalem.
49:3 back and forth between the **w**.
49:27 "I will set fire to the **w** of
50:15 towers will fall and their **w** will
51:12 flag in front of the **w** of Babylon.
51:44 to Babylon, and its **w** will fall.
51:58 The thick **w** of Babylon will be
52:4 dirt ramps around the city **w**.
52:7 broke through the city **w**,
52:7 gate between the two **w** beside
52:14 down the **w** around Jerusalem.
Lam 1:15 inside my ⌊**w**⌋ with contempt.
2:7 He handed the **w** of Zion's
2:8 made the towers and **w** mourn.
Eze 4:2 build attack **w** around it,
8:10 I saw that the **w** were covered
22:30 among you who could build **w**
22:30 front of me by the gaps in the **w**
23:14 pictures of men carved on **w**.
26:4 They will destroy the **w** of Tyre
26:9 battering rams against your **w**,
26:10 and chariots will shake your **w**
26:12 They will destroy your **w** and
27:11 were guards all around your **w**.
27:11 their shields all around your **w**,
33:30 are talking about you by the **w**
38:11 All of them live without **w**,
40:9 Its recessed **w** were 3 ½ feet
40:10 and the recessed **w** on each
40:16 and recessed **w** inside
40:16 carved on the recessed **w**.
40:21 guardrooms, its recessed **w**,
40:22 Its windows, recessed **w**,
40:24 He measured its recessed **w**
40:26 carved on the recessed **w**,
40:29 Its guardrooms, recessed **w**,
40:31 carved on the recessed **w**,
40:33 Its guardrooms, recessed **w**,
40:34 carved on the recessed **w**,
40:36 Its guardrooms, recessed **w**,
40:37 Its recessed **w** faced the outer
Eze 40:37 carved on the recessed **w**,
40:48 and measured its recessed **w**.
40:48 and the **w** on each side were 5
40:49 stood by the recessed **w**,
41:1 and measured the recessed **w**.
41:2 the entrance the **w** were 9 feet
41:13 with the building and its **w**.
41:16 The **w**, from the floor up to the
41:17 and on the **w** all around it,
41:20 were carved on the **w** from
41:25 of the holy place as on the **w**.
46:23 four courtyards were stone **w**,
46:23 and these **w** were equipped
Joe 2:7 They climb **w** like soldiers.
Amo 1:7 I will send a fire on the **w** of
1:10 I will send a fire on the **w** of
1:14 I will set fire to the **w** of
Mic 7:11 The day for rebuilding your **w**
Heb 11:30 Faith caused the **w** of Jericho

walnut (1)

Sos 6:11 I went to the **w** grove to look at

wander (27)

Num 32:13 he made them **w** in the desert
2Sm 15:20 Should I make you **w** around
2Ki 21:8 again make Israel's feet **w** from
Job 38:41 ones cry to God and **w** around
Psa 59:11 Make them **w** aimlessly by
59:15 They **w** around to find
109:10 Let his children **w** around and
119:10 Do not let me **w** away from
119:21 who are condemned and **w**
119:67 made me suffer, I used to **w** off,
119:118 You reject all who **w** away
Pro 5:6 Her steps **w**, and she doesn't
7:25 Do not **w** onto her paths,
Isa 35:8 fools won't **w** ⌊onto it⌋.
63:17 O LORD, why do you let us **w**
Jer 2:31 that they are free to **w** around
4:1 and you don't **w** away from me,
14:10 these people: They love to **w**.
14:18 Prophets and priests **w** through
31:22 How long will you **w** around,
50:6 They **w** around on the
Eze 14:11 will no longer **w** away from me.
48:11 They didn't **w** away with the
Hos 9:17 They will **w** among the nations.
Joe 1:18 of cattle **w** around confused.
Amo 8:12 People will **w** from sea to sea
Zec 10:2 That is why people **w** around

wandered (16)

Gen 21:14 So she left and **w** around in the
Jos 5:6 For 40 years the Israelites **w**
14:10 been 45 years since Israel **w**
1Ch 16:20 they **w** from nation to nation
Psa 105:13 they **w** from nation to nation,
107:4 They **w** around the desert on a
119:110 but I have never **w** away from
119:176 I have **w** away like a lost lamb.
Jer 5:23 aside and **w** away from me.
Lam 4:15 When they fled and **w** around,
Eze 34:6 My sheep **w** over all the
44:10 from me when Israel **w** off
44:15 the Israelites **w** away from me.
1Ti 6:10 getting rich have **w** away from
Heb 11:38 Some **w** around in deserts and
2Pe 2:15 left the straight path and **w** off

wanderer (2)

Gen 4:12 be a fugitive, a **w** on the earth."
4:14 a fugitive, a **w** on the earth.

wandering (13)

Gen 4:16 lived in Nod [The Land of **W**],
37:15 a man found him **w** around in
Exo 14:3 Israelites are ⌊just⌋ **w** around.
23:4 enemy's ox or donkey **w** loose,
Dtr 26:5 ancestors were **w** Arameans.
Job 1:7 "From **w** all over the earth."
2:2 "From **w** all over the earth."
Pro 27:8 Like a bird **w** from its nest,
27:8 is a husband **w** from his home.
Sos 1:7 a prostitute ⌊**w**⌋ among
Lam 3:19 suffering and my ⌊aimless⌋ **w**,
Hos 8:9 They were like wild donkeys **w**
Jud 1:13 They are **w** stars for whom

wanderings (1)

Psa 56:8 have kept a record of my **w**.

wanders (3)

Job 15:23 He **w** around for food and asks,
Pro 21:16 A person who **w** from the way
Jas 5:19 if one of you **w** from the truth,

want (440)

Gen 21:16 "I don't **w** to watch the boy die."
24:3 I **w** you to swear by the LORD
24:5 "What if the woman doesn't **w**
24:8 If the woman doesn't **w** to
29:21 I **w** to sleep with her."
31:32 search as much as you **w**
33:15 "I only **w** to win your favor,
34:12 give her as high as you **w**.
42:36 and now you **w** to take
47:15 "Do you **w** us to die right in
47:19 Do you **w** us to die right in front
47:19 Do you **w** the land to be ruined?
47:29 "I **w** you to swear that you love
47:30 I **w** to rest with my ancestors.
Exo 5:5 Do you **w** them to quit
9:16 I **w** to show you my power and
12:48 "Foreigners may **w** to celebrate
15:9 I'll take all I **w**! I'll use my
16:8 evening and all the food you **w**
16:12 you will eat all the food you **w**.
16:23 Bake what you **w** to bake,
16:23 and boil what you **w** to boil.
21:5 I don't **w** to leave as a free
33:19 I will be kind to anyone I **w** to.
33:19 I will be merciful to anyone I **w**
34:24 No one will **w** to take away
Lev 25:19 and you will eat all you **w** and
26:5 You will eat all you **w** and live
27:13 If you **w** to buy it back,
27:15 If you **w** to buy it back,
27:19 If you **w** to buy it back,
Num 9:14 living with you may **w**
10:30 I **w** to go back to my own
15:39 you won't do whatever you **w**
20:19 We **w** to pass through on foot.
22:38 But I can't say whatever I **w** to.
23:21 He doesn't **w** any trouble for the
36:6 They may marry anyone they **w**
Dtr 6:11 you have eaten all that you **w**,
8:10 you have eaten all you **w**,
8:12 You will eat all you **w**.
10:12 the LORD your God **w** you
11:15 will be able to eat all you **w**.
12:13 burnt offerings wherever you **w**.
12:15 much meat as you **w** from what
12:20 eat as much meat as you **w**.
12:21 Eat as much as you **w** in your
12:30 We **w** to do what they did."
14:26 silver to buy whatever you **w**:
14:29 may come to eat all they **w**.
15:16 "I don't **w** to leave you,"
15:17 ⌊if she doesn't **w** to leave⌋.
18:16 You said, "We never **w** to hear
25:7 But if the man doesn't **w** to
25:7 He doesn't **w** to do his duty as
25:8 that he doesn't **w** to marry her,
26:12 and they may eat all they **w**.
31:20 they have eaten all they **w**
32:27 But I didn't **w** their enemies to
32:27 I didn't **w** their opponents to
Jos 5:14 what do you **w** to tell me?"
15:18 "What do you **w**?"
24:15 But if you don't **w** to serve the
Jdg 1:14 "What do you **w**?"
6:18 I **w** to bring my gift and set it in
9:2 Do you really **w** all of
9:15 'If you really **w** to anoint me to
9:33 do whatever you **w** to him."
9:54 I don't **w** anyone to say,
11:8 to you now is that we **w** you
14:3 She's the one I **w**!"
16:5 We **w** to tie him up in order to
17:3 I **w** to make a carved idol and a
18:10 have everything you could **w**."

Jdg 19:24 do with them whatever you **w**.
1Sm 2:15 He doesn't **w** boiled meat from
2:16 then take as much as you **w**,"
2:35 He will do everything I **w** him
8:19 They said, "No, we **w** a king!
18:25 'The king doesn't **w** any
21:9 If you **w** to take it, take it.
23:20 Majesty, whenever you **w**.
28:23 "I don't **w** to eat," he said.
2Sm 13:25 David did not **w** to go,
16:18 I **w** to be with the one whom
18:22 I also **w** to run after the
19:38 will do for him whatever you **w**.
21:4 "We do not **w** silver or gold
1Ki 1:16 "What do you **w**?"
2:16 Now I **w** to ask you for one
5:8 I will do everything you **w** in
2Ki 8:19 David's sake the LORD didn't **w**
9:15 "If you **w** me to be king,
13:23 He didn't **w** to destroy the
20:9 Do you **w** the shadow to go
2Ch 2:4 I **w** to build the temple for the
2:4 I **w** to dedicate it to him,
2:4 I **w** to ⌊sacrifice⌋ burnt
2:9 because the temple I **w** to build
21:7 didn't **w** to destroy David's
25:16 Do you **w** me to have you
Ezr 4:2 They told them, "We **w** to help
4:16 We **w** the king to know that if
7:13 who are in my kingdom and **w**
Neh 1:11 all your other servants who **w**
2:4 "What do you **w**?"
6:6 you **w** to become their king.
Job 6:11 goal do I have that I would **w**
7:16 I do not **w** to live forever.
11:13 "If you **w** to set your heart right,
13:3 I **w** to speak to the Almighty,
13:13 Be quiet, because I **w** to speak.
19:6 then I **w** you to know that God
21:14 We don't **w** to know your ways.
23:5 I **w** to know the words he
23:5 I **w** to understand the things he
37:20 he be told that I **w** to speak?
Psa 40:14 Let those who **w** my downfall
45:12 **w** to win your favor with a gift.
50:18 When you see a thief, you **w** to
57:7 I **w** to sing and make music.
57:8 I **w** to wake up at dawn.
57:9 I **w** to give thanks to you
57:9 I **w** to make music to praise
69:4 Those who **w** to destroy me
69:14 I **w** to be rescued from those
69:30 I **w** to praise the name of God
69:30 I **w** to praise its greatness with
70:2 Let those who **w** my downfall
71:13 Let those who **w** my downfall
85:8 I **w** to hear what God the LORD
101:2 I **w** to understand the path to
101:3 people do. I **w** no part of it.
108:1 I **w** to sing and make music
108:2 I **w** to wake up at dawn.
108:3 I **w** to give thanks to you
108:3 I **w** to make music to praise
119:15 I **w** to reflect on your guiding
119:58 With all my heart I **w** to win
119:95 ⌊yet⌋ I **w** to understand your
119:145 I **w** to obey your laws.
132:14 sit enthroned because I **w** Zion.
140:8 wicked people what they **w**.
146:2 I **w** to praise the LORD
146:2 I **w** to make music to praise my
Pro 1:25 You did not **w** me to warn you.
Ecc 2:1 I thought to myself, "Now I **w** to
6:9 to go looking for what you **w**.
7:23 I said, "I **w** to be wise,
Sos 2:3 I **w** to sit in his shadow.
Isa 1:5 "Why do you still **w** to be
7:11 It can be anything you **w**."
26:8 We **w** to remember you and
30:10 Tell us what we **w** to hear.
30:15 But you don't **w** that.
42:24 They didn't **w** to live his way.
44:28 He will do everything I **w** him
55:11 it will accomplish whatever I **w**
58:2 look for me every day and **w**
58:2 They **w** God to be near them.
Isa 58:3 you do what you **w** to do?
58:13 by not going out when you **w**,
Jer 3:1 And now you **w** to come back
4:30 reject you; they **w** to kill you.
8:3 these wicked people will **w**
9:24 If they **w** to brag, they should
11:20 I **w** to see you take revenge on
11:21 The people of Anathoth **w** to
12:1 Yet, I **w** to talk to you about
18:12 We'll live the way we **w** to.
19:7 with the hands of those who **w**
19:9 them when they **w** to kill them."
20:12 I **w** to see you take revenge on
21:7 and to their enemies who **w**
22:25 hand you over to those who **w**
22:27 You will **w** to return to this land,
23:27 because they **w** to make my
30:14 and they don't **w** you anymore.
34:20 over to their enemies who **w**
34:21 over to their enemies who **w**
38:16 these men who **w** to kill you."
40:4 But if you don't **w** to come with
40:4 Go wherever you **w**.
40:5 or go anywhere you **w**."
42:22 in the place where you **w**
44:30 enemies and to those who **w**
46:26 hand them over to those who **w**
49:37 in the presence of those who **w**
50:10 they **w**," declares the LORD.
Eze 13:18 You **w** to trap people.
13:18 You **w** to control the lives of
16:31 because you don't **w** to be paid.
18:23 I don't **w** wicked people to die."
18:23 "I **w** them to turn from their evil
18:31 Why do you **w** to die,
18:32 I don't **w** anyone to die,"
20:32 You think that you **w** to be like
20:32 You **w** to serve wood and
22:9 They **w** to kill people.
33:11 I don't **w** wicked people to die.
33:11 Rather, I **w** them to turn from
33:11 Do you **w** to die, people of
36:32 I **w** you to know that I'm not
Dan 2:3 I **w** to know what the dream
7:5 eat as much meat as you **w**."
Hos 4:8 and they **w** them to do wicked
6:6 I **w** your loyalty, not your
6:6 I **w** you to know me,
7:1 "Whenever I **w** to heal Israel,
7:13 I **w** to reclaim them,
13:14 "I **w** to free them from the
13:14 I **w** to reclaim them from death.
13:14 I **w** to be a plague to you.
13:14 Grave, I **w** to destroy you.
Jnh 1:14 do whatever you **w**."
4:9 so angry that I **w** to die."
Mic 2:11 just the type of preacher you **w**.
7:3 people dictate what they **w**.
Nah 2:9 a person could ever **w**.
Mal 3:1 He is the one you **w**," says the
Mat 1:19 honorable man and did not **w**
7:12 people everything you **w** them
9:6 I **w** you to know that the Son of
9:13 'I **w** mercy, not sacrifices.'
12:7 had known what 'I **w** mercy,
12:38 we **w** you to show us a
12:47 They **w** to talk to you."
13:28 'Do you **w** us to pull out the
15:32 I don't **w** to send them away
16:24 "Those who **w** to come with
16:24 say no to the things they **w**,
16:25 Those who **w** to save their
17:4 If you **w**, I'll put up three tents
18:14 in heaven does not **w** one
19:17 If you **w** to enter into life,
19:21 "If you **w** to be perfect,
20:14 I **w** to give this last worker as
20:15 Can't I do what I **w** with my
20:21 "What do you **w**?"
20:32 "What do you **w** me to do for
20:33 They told him, "Lord, we **w**
21:29 "His son replied, 'I don't **w** to!'
26:17 They asked, "Where do you **w**
26:41 You **w** to do what's right,
26:48 one I kiss is the man you **w**.
27:17 "Which man do you **w** me to
Mat 27:17 Do you **w** me to free Barabbas
27:21 "Which of the two do you **w** me
27:24 this man. Do what you **w**!"
27:65 "You have the soldiers you **w**
Mar 1:24 "What do you **w** with us,
2:10 I **w** you to know that the Son of
6:22 "Ask me for anything you **w**,
6:25 She said, "I **w** you to give me
6:26 he didn't **w** to refuse her.
7:24 He didn't **w** anyone to know
7:27 let the children eat all they **w**.
8:12 far different than what they **w**!"
8:34 He said to them, "Those who **w**
8:34 say no to the things they **w**,
8:35 Those who **w** to save their
9:30 Jesus did not **w** anyone to
10:35 we **w** you to do us a favor."
10:36 "What do you **w** me to do for
10:51 "What do you **w** me to do for
10:51 "Teacher, I **w** to see again."
14:7 help them whenever you **w**.
14:12 "Where do you **w** us to prepare
14:38 You **w** to do what's right,
14:44 one I kiss is the man you **w**.
15:9 "Do you **w** me to free the king
Luk 4:34 What do you **w** with us,
5:12 begged Jesus, "Sir, if you **w** to,
5:13 touched him, and said, "I **w** to.
5:24 I **w** you to know that the Son of
6:31 people everything you **w** them
8:20 They **w** to see you."
9:23 "Those who **w** to come with
9:23 say no to the things they **w**,
9:24 Those who **w** to save their
9:54 They asked, "Lord, do you **w**
11:8 that although he doesn't **w**
14:23 to my house. I **w** it to be full.
14:28 "Suppose you **w** to build a
18:41 "What do you **w** me to do for
18:41 said, "Lord, I **w** to see again."
19:14 'We don't **w** this man to be our
19:15 I **w** to know how much each
19:27 my enemies, who didn't **w** me
22:9 "Where do you **w** us to prepare
Jon 3:20 They don't **w** their actions to be
4:27 "What do you **w** from her?"
5:30 I don't try to do what I **w**
5:40 Yet, you don't **w** to come to me
6:28 "What does God **w** us to do?"
6:38 heaven to do what I **w** to do.
6:39 one who sent me doesn't **w** me
6:67 "Do you **w** to leave me too?
7:1 He didn't **w** to travel in Judea
7:17 Those who **w** to follow the will
7:19 So why do you **w** to kill me?"
7:25 this the man they **w** to kill?
8:37 However, you **w** to kill me
8:40 But now you **w** to kill me.
8:50 I don't **w** my own glory.
9:27 Why do you **w** to hear the story
9:27 Do you **w** to become his
10:32 of these good things do you **w**
11:8 Do you really **w** to go back
14:31 However, I **w** the world to
15:7 then ask for anything you **w**,
16:26 you will ask for what you **w** in
17:24 "Father, I **w** those you have
17:24 I **w** them to see my glory,
18:28 They didn't **w** to become
19:31 the Jews didn't **w** the bodies to
21:18 you where you don't **w** to go."
21:22 Jesus said to Peter, "If I **w** him
21:23 What Jesus said was, "If I **w**
Act 4:9 You **w** to know how he was
5:28 You **w** to take revenge on us
7:28 Do you **w** to kill me as you
10:4 angel, "What do you **w**, sir?"
10:29 I **w** to know why you sent for
13:2 I **w** them to do the work for
13:22 do everything I **w** him to do.'
18:15 I don't **w** to be a judge who
19:39 If you **w** anything else,
20:24 I **w** to finish the race I'm
20:24 I **w** to carry out the mission I
22:10 'What do you **w** me to do,
23:15 make it look as though you **w**

Act 23:20 **w** more accurate information
23:23 "I **w** 200 infantrymen,
24:3 and we **w** to thank you very
24:4 I don't **w** to keep you too long.
Rom 1:13 I **w** you to know, brothers and
1:13 What I **w** is to enjoy some of
2:5 you are stubborn and don't **w**
7:15 I don't do what I **w** to do.
7:16 I don't do what I **w** to do,
7:19 I don't do the good I **w** to do.
7:19 I do the evil that I don't **w** to do.
7:20 when I do what I don't **w** to do,
7:21 present with me even when I **w**
9:15 "I will be kind to anyone I **w** to.
9:15 I will be merciful to anyone I **w**
11:25 Brothers and sisters, I **w** you to
15:20 I didn't **w** to build on a
16:19 I **w** you to do what is good and
1Co 1:10 I **w** you to be united in your
4:8 You already have what you **w**!
7:32 So I don't **w** you to have any
7:36 No father would **w** to do the
7:37 home⌋ because she doesn't **w**
10:1 I **w** you to know, brothers and
10:20 I don't **w** you to be partners
11:3 However, I **w** you to realize
12:1 Brothers and sisters, I don't **w**
12:3 So I **w** you to know that no one
12:31 You ⌊only⌋ **w** the better gifts,
14:35 If they **w** to know anything they
16:1 I **w** you to do as I directed the
16:12 He didn't **w** to at this time.
2Co 1:8 and sisters, we don't **w** you
1:24 It isn't that we **w** to have
1:24 Rather, we **w** to work with you
2:3 I didn't **w** to visit you and be
2:5 extent — although I don't **w**
2:11 I don't **w** Satan to outwit us.
3:13 He didn't **w** the people of Israel
5:4 distressed because we don't **w**
5:4 but we do **w** to put on the
8:1 Brothers and sisters, we **w** you
8:7 the more we **w** you to
8:20 We don't **w** anyone to find fault
10:9 I don't **w** you to think that I'm
11:1 I **w** you to put up with a little
11:12 of those people who **w**
12:14 I don't **w** your possessions.
12:14 Instead, I **w** you. Children
12:20 you different from what I **w** you
12:20 different from what you **w** me
13:3 Since you **w** proof that Christ is
13:7 It's not that we **w** to prove that
13:7 Rather, we **w** you to do
13:10 When I am with you I don't **w** to
Gal 1:7 They **w** to distort the Good
1:11 I **w** you to know, brothers and
3:2 I **w** to learn only one thing from
4:9 Why do you **w** to become their
4:17 They don't **w** you to associate
4:21 Those who **w** to be controlled
6:12 These people who **w** to make
6:13 Yet, they **w** you to be
Php 1:12 I **w** you to know, brothers and
1:26 So by coming to you again, I **w**
Col 1:10 Then you will **w** to please him
1:28 We **w** to present everyone as
2:1 I **w** you to know how hard I
1Th 3:6 fond memories of us and **w**
3:6 as we **w** to see you.
4:13 and sisters, we don't **w** you
4:13 We don't **w** you to grieve like
2Th 3:10 "Whoever doesn't **w** to work
1Ti 1:7 They **w** to be experts in
2:8 I **w** men to offer prayers
2:9 I **w** women to show their
3:15 I **w** you to know how people
5:11 to Christ, they'll **w** to marry.
5:14 So I **w** younger widows to
6:9 But people who **w** to get rich
2Ti 1:4 I remember your tears and **w** to
4:3 tell them what they **w** to hear.
Tit 3:8 I **w** you to insist on these
Phm 1:14 Yet, I didn't **w** to do anything
1:14 I **w** you to do this favor for me
Heb 6:11 We **w** each of you to prove that
Heb 8:1 The main point we **w** to make
10:5 "'You did not **w** sacrifices and
10:7 I have come to do what you **w**,
10:8 "You did not **w** sacrifices,
10:9 have come to do what you **w**."
13:18 are clear because we **w**
Jas 3:4 wherever they **w** them to go.
4:2 You **w** what you don't have,
4:2 but you can't get what you **w**.
4:2 don't have the things you **w**,
4:3 get them because you **w** them
1Pe 1:12 even the angels **w** to look into.
3:10 "People who **w** to live a full life
3:14 Don't be afraid of those who **w**
5:2 but because you **w** to.
2Pe 3:2 I **w** you to remember the words
3:9 He doesn't **w** to destroy anyone
3Jn 1:10 even tries to stop others who **w**
Jud 1:5 I **w** to remind you about what
Rev 2:26 to do what I **w** until the end.
11:6 any plague as often as they **w**.
22:17 Let those who **w** the water of

wanted (171)

Gen 19:16 because the LORD **w** to spare
37:22 Reuben **w** to rescue Joseph
42:28 They **w** to die. They trembled
Exo 4:19 because all the men who **w** to
16:3 meat and ate all the food we **w**!
Num 24:1 Balaam saw that the LORD **w**
Dtr 1:27 He **w** to hand us over to the
8:2 He **w** to know whether or not
9:8 angry that he **w** to destroy you.
9:19 He was so angry he **w** to
9:20 very angry with Aaron and **w**
Jos 7:21 I **w** them, so I took them.
24:13 So you ate all you **w**!
Jdg 13:23 "If the LORD **w** to kill us,
14:7 She was the one he **w**.
Rut 2:14 She ate all she **w** and had
1Sm 2:25 the LORD **w** to kill them.
2Sm 3:17 "For some time now you've **w**
14:22 you have done what I **w**."
14:32 you to come here because I **w**
19:18 to do anything else the king **w**.
21:5 descendants of the man who **w**
1Ki 5:10 cedar and cypress wood he **w**.
9:1 ⌊else⌋ he **w** to build.
9:11 lumber and gold as he **w**.)
9:19 and whatever ⌊else⌋ he **w** to
10:13 of Sheba anything she **w**,
10:24 The whole world **w** to listen to
16:21 and **w** to make him king.
19:4 a broom plant and **w** to die.
2Ki 10:19 He actually **w** to destroy those
10:30 You did everything I **w** done to
17:8 what their kings **w** them to do.
24:3 He **w** to remove the people of
1Ch 26:30 everything the LORD **w** them
2Ch 8:6 and whatever ⌊else⌋ he **w** to
9:12 of Sheba anything she **w**,
9:23 All the kings of the world **w** to
17:6 live the way the LORD **w** him
24:4 After this, Joash **w** to renovate
25:20 this happen because he **w**
27:6 to live as the LORD his God **w**.
31:10 we have had all we **w** to eat
36:15 his messengers because he **w**
Neh 9:24 they **w** with the Canaanites.
Est 1:11 He **w** to show the people,
2:13 Anything she **w** to take with
Psa 35:25 or think, "Aha, just what we **w**!"
71:24 because those who **w** my
78:29 He gave them what they **w**,
78:30 but they still **w** more.
81:11 Israel **w** nothing to do with me.
105:22 the king's officers the way he **w**
137:3 Those who guarded us **w** us to
Ecc 2:10 to have any pleasure I **w**,
Isa 1:29 of the oaks that you **w**
Jer 3:19 "I **w** to treat you like children
18:4 pot the way he **w** to make it.
26:21 the king **w** to put him to death.
37:12 So Jeremiah **w** to leave
44:30 to those who **w** to kill him."'
51:9 We **w** to heal Babylon,
Eze 1:12 wherever their spirit **w** to go,
1:20 Wherever their spirit **w** to go,
Dan 4:36 My advisers and nobles **w** to
5:2 He **w** to drink from them with
5:19 killed whomever he **w** to kill,
5:19 he kept alive whomever he **w**
5:19 whomever he **w** to promote,
5:19 whomever he **w** to demote.
7:19 Then I **w** to know the truth
7:20 I also **w** to know about the ten
Jnh 1:3 He **w** to go to Tarshish to get
4:8 He **w** to die. So he said, "I'd
Mat 12:46 They **w** to talk to him.
14:5 So Herod **w** to kill John.
14:7 would give her anything she **w**.
14:20 of them ate as much as they **w**.
15:28 What you **w** will be done for
15:37 of them ate as much as they **w**.
18:23 of heaven is like a king who **w**
21:31 sons did what the father **w**?"
21:46 They **w** to arrest him but were
23:37 How often I **w** to gather your
27:15 prisoner whom the crowd **w**.
Mar 3:2 They **w** to see whether he
3:13 called those whom he **w**,
6:19 a grudge against John and **w**
6:42 of them ate as much as they **w**.
6:48 He **w** to pass by them.
8:8 people ate as much as they **w**.
12:12 They **w** to arrest him but were
12:13 They **w** to trap him into saying
15:15 Pilate **w** to satisfy the people,
Luk 1:62 baby's father to see what he **w**
6:7 They **w** to see whether he
6:18 They **w** to hear him and be
7:1 had finished everything he **w**
9:9 So Herod **w** to see Jesus.
9:17 of them ate as much as they **w**.
10:24 many prophets and kings **w**
10:29 But the man **w** to justify his
11:16 Others **w** to test Jesus and
11:52 kept out those who **w** to enter."
12:47 who knew what his master **w**
12:48 know ⌊what his master **w**⌋
13:34 How often I **w** to gather your
16:26 direction even if they **w** to.'
20:19 scribes and the chief priests **w**
20:20 They **w** to catch him saying
23:8 For a long time he had **w** to
23:20 But because Pilate **w** to free
23:25 because that's what they **w**.
23:25 them do what they **w** to Jesus.
Jon 1:43 The next day Jesus **w** to go to
6:11 people ate as much as they **w**.
6:26 of those loaves as you **w**.
7:1 Jews there **w** to kill him.
7:44 Some of them **w** to arrest him,
8:6 They **w** to find a reason to
11:8 not long ago the Jews **w** to
16:19 Jesus knew they **w** to ask him
18:28 since they **w** to eat the
19:12 Jesus said, he **w** to free him.
21:18 get ready to go where you **w**.
Act 5:33 they became furious and **w** to
9:2 Saul **w** to arrest any man or
10:10 became hungry and **w** to eat.
12:4 Herod **w** to bring Peter to trial in
12:20 agreed on what they **w** to do:
13:7 and Saul because he **w**
14:13 The priest and the crowd **w** to
15:37 Barnabas **w** to take John Mark
16:3 Paul **w** Timothy to go with him.
18:27 When Apollos **w** to travel to
19:30 Paul **w** to go into the crowd,
19:33 quiet the people because he **w**
20:33 "I never **w** anyone's silver,
22:24 The officer **w** to find out why
22:30 The officer **w** to find out
23:28 I **w** to know what they had
24:27 (Since Felix **w** to do the Jews
25:9 But Festus **w** to do the Jews a
27:21 Since hardly anyone **w** to eat,
27:38 people had eaten all they **w**,
27:43 the officer **w** to save Paul,
28:18 cross-examined me and **w**
Rom 15:23 years I have **w** to visit you.

1Co 12:18 of the body together as he **w** it.
2Co 1:15 I had previously **w** to visit you
1:23 because I **w** to spare you.
2:9 I **w** to see if you would be
7:7 He told us how you **w** to see
7:11 You **w** to see us. You wanted to
7:11 You **w** to show your concern
7:12 Rather, I wrote because I **w**
12:6 If I ever **w** to brag, I wouldn't be
Gal 1:4 what our God and Father **w**.
Eph 2:3 corrupt desires and thoughts **w**
6:6 as if you merely **w** to please
Col 1:27 God **w** his people throughout
3:22 as if you merely **w** to please
1Th 2:18 We **w** to visit you.
2:18 **w** to visit you twice already,
3:5 I **w** to see whether the tempter
2Th 3:9 Rather, we **w** to set an
Phm 1:13 I **w** to keep him here with me.
Heb 2:4 from the Holy Spirit as he **w**.
6:17 He **w** to make this perfectly
10:10 Christ did what God **w** him
12:17 when he **w** to receive the

wants (103)

Gen 4:7 It **w** to control you,
19:9 Now he **w** to be our judge!
24:40 the way the LORD **w** me to.
Lev 16:2 holy place whenever he **w** to.
Num 23:27 Maybe God **w** you to curse
Dtr 9:5 It's also because the LORD **w**
10:12 He **w** you to fear him,
10:13 The LORD **w** you to obey his
11:1 and do what he **w** you to do.
18:6 He may come as often as he **w**
21:14 let her go wherever she **w**.
1Sm 2:15 meat from you. He **w** it raw."
12:22 because the LORD **w** to make
2Sm 5:8 "Whoever **w** to defeat the
14:16 from the man who **w** to cut off
21:4 "And none of us **w** to kill
Ezr 10:11 and do what he **w**.
Job 23:13 He does whatever he **w**!
Psa 34:12 Which of you **w** a full life?
115:3 He does whatever he **w**.
132:13 He **w** it for his home.
135:6 The LORD does whatever he **w**
Pro 18:1 to get what he **w** for himself.
Ecc 6:2 he doesn't lack anything he **w**.
Jer 22:28 and broken pot that no one **w**.
48:38 no one **w**," declares the LORD.
Eze 46:7 whatever the prince **w** to bring.
46:11 bring whatever he **w** to bring.
Dan 2:23 us what the king **w** to know."
Mat 5:40 If someone **w** to sue you in
5:42 Don't turn anyone away who **w**
7:21 what my Father in heaven **w**.
12:50 in heaven **w** is my brother
20:26 Whoever **w** to become great
20:27 Whoever **w** to be most
21:32 you the way that God **w** you
21:43 who will produce what God **w**.
27:43 God rescue him now if he **w**.
Mar 3:35 Whoever does what God **w** is
9:35 He told them, "Whoever **w** to
10:43 Whoever **w** to become great
10:44 Whoever **w** to be most
Luk 5:39 drinking old wine **w** new wine.
13:31 Herod **w** to kill you."
22:31 He **w** to separate you from me
Jon 4:34 the one who sent me **w** me
5:30 what the one who sent me **w**.
6:29 Jesus replied to them, "God **w**
6:38 one who sent me **w** me to do.
6:39 He **w** me to bring them back to
6:40 My Father **w** all those who see
6:40 He **w** me to bring them back to
6:60 Who **w** to listen to him
7:4 things secretly when he **w**
7:18 But the man who **w** to bring
7:20 Who **w** to kill you?"
8:44 to do what your father **w** you
8:50 But there is someone who **w** it,
9:4 what the one who sent me **w**.
9:31 devout and who do what he **w**.
14:10 lives in me, does what he **w**.

Act 4:19 whether God **w** people
9:17 He **w** you to see again and to
13:10 way the Lord **w** people to live.
18:21 to visit you if God **w** me to."
Rom 2:18 know what he **w**,
7:4 we can do what God **w**.
8:12 our corrupt nature **w** us to live.
8:27 people the way God **w** him to.
9:18 if God **w** to be kind to anyone,
9:18 If he **w** to make someone
9:19 resist whatever God **w** to do?"
9:21 the right to do whatever he **w**
9:22 If God **w** to demonstrate his
12:2 what God really **w** — what is
1Co 7:36 If she **w** to get married,
11:16 If anyone **w** to argue about this
12:11 things by giving what God **w**
15:38 gives the plant the form he **w**
Gal 5:16 on what your corrupt nature **w**.
5:17 What your corrupt nature **w** is
5:17 to what your spiritual nature **w**,
5:17 spiritual nature **w** is contrary
5:17 to what your corrupt nature **w**.
Eph 5:17 understand what the Lord **w**.
6:6 to do what God **w** them to do.
Php 4:2 the Lord **w** them to have.
Col 2:19 body grow as God **w** it to,
4:12 of everything that God **w**.
1Ti 2:4 He **w** all people to be saved
Heb 10:9 the obedience that God **w**.
10:36 have done what God **w** you
13:21 to do every good thing he **w**.
Jas 4:4 Whoever **w** to be a friend of
4:5 "The Spirit that lives in us **w**
4:15 "If the Lord **w** us to,
1Pe 2:15 God **w** you to silence the
4:2 by what God **w** you to do.
2Pe 3:9 anyone but **w** all people
1Jn 2:17 does what God **w** lives forever.
Rev 11:5 If anyone **w** to hurt them,
11:5 If anyone **w** to hurt them,
17:17 made them do what he **w** them

war (209)

Gen 14:2 went to **w** against ⌊five kings⌋
31:26 daughters like prisoners of **w**.
Exo 1:10 Then, if **w** breaks out,
5:3 kill us with a plague or a **w**."
13:17 see that they have to fight a **w**,
17:16 he will be at **w** against the
22:10 or is captured in **w**,
32:17 the sound of **w** in the camp!"
Lev 26:6 there will be no **w** in your land.
26:25 I will bring **w** on you to get
26:33 **W** will follow you.
Num 10:9 "When you go to **w** in your own
14:3 will be taken as prisoners of **w**!
14:31 be taken as prisoners of **w**.
24:22 takes you as prisoners of **w**."
31:3 get ready to go to **w** against
31:5 12,000 men ready for **w**.
31:6 Then Moses sent them off to **w**,
31:7 They went to **w** against Midian,
31:9 and children as prisoners of **w**.
31:12 and brought the prisoners of **w**,
31:19 You and your prisoners of **w**
31:27 soldiers who served in the **w**
31:28 served in the **w** collect one out
31:36 soldiers who served in the **w**.
32:6 rest of the Israelites go to **w**?
Dtr 1:39 would be captured in **w**,
1:41 of you armed yourself for **w**,
2:9 of Moab or start a **w** with them.
4:34 signs, amazing things, and **w**.
20:1 When you go to **w** against your
20:12 of peace but declare **w** on you,
20:19 time in order to capture it in **w**.
21:10 When you go to **w** with your
23:9 When you're at **w** and have set
28:41 will be taken as prisoners of **w**.
33:18 yourselves when you go to **w**,
Jos 11:18 Joshua waged **w** with all these
14:11 I'm still as fit to go to **w** now as
22:12 to wage **w** against them.
22:33 going to **w** against Reuben
Jdg 2:15 the Israelites went to **w**,

Jdg 3:1 experienced any **w** in Canaan.
3:2 Israel's descendants about **w**,
3:10 He went out to **w**. The LORD
5:8 **w** broke out inside the city
5:22 The mighty **w** horses galloped
11:4 Ammon waged **w** with Israel.
11:6 can wage **w** against Ammon."
11:8 and wage **w** against Ammon.
11:12 land and wage **w** against me?"
11:27 by waging **w** against me.
18:11 Zorah and Eshtaol armed for **w**.
20:14 at Gibeah to go to **w**
20:20 So the men of Israel went to **w**
20:23 to wage **w** against our close
20:28 to wage **w** against our close
1Sm 8:20 lead us out ⌊to **w**⌋,
15:18 Wage **w** against them until
17:1 assembled their armies for **w**.
17:20 battle line shouting their **w** cry.
19:8 When **w** broke out again,
23:8 all the troops to go to **w**
28:15 Philistines are at **w** with me,
2Sm 1:27 of **w** have been destroyed!"
3:1 As the **w** between the royal
3:6 During the **w** between the
8:10 (There had often been **w**
11:1 and Israel's army ⌊to **w**⌋.
11:7 and how the **w** was going.
1Ki 5:3 David was surrounded by **w**.
8:44 "When your people go to **w**
9:19 cities for his **w** horses,
10:26 with chariots and **w** horses.
10:26 chariots and 12,000 **w** horses.
12:24 Don't wage **w** against your
14:30 There was **w** between
15:6 There was **w** between Abijam
15:7 There was **w** between Abijam
15:16 There was **w** between Asa and
15:32 There was **w** between Asa and
22:1 For three years there was no **w**
22:6 "Should I go to **w** against
22:15 should we go to **w** against
2Ki 3:6 to prepare Israel's army for **w**.
14:8 to declare **w** on Israel.
16:5 to wage **w** against Jerusalem.
18:20 about getting ready for **w**.
24:16 could fight in **w** as captives
1Ch 5:10 In Saul's day they fought a **w**
5:18 soldiers ready to go to **w**.
5:19 They went to **w** against
5:22 because this was God's **w**.
7:11 men who could go to **w**.
11:2 Israel on its campaigns to **w**.
12:23 of the men equipped for **w**.
12:24 6,800 men equipped for **w**.
18:10 (There had often been **w**
20:1 Joab led the army ⌊to **w**⌋.
20:4 After this, **w** broke out with the
2Ch 1:14 with chariots and **w** horses.
1:14 chariots and 12,000 **w** horses.
6:34 "When your people go to **w**
8:6 all the cities for his **w** horses,
9:25 and 12,000 **w** horses.
11:4 Don't wage **w** against your
12:15 There was **w** between
13:2 There was **w** between Abijah
13:12 Men of Israel, don't wage **w**
14:6 There was no **w** during those
15:19 There was no **w** until the
17:1 ⌊to wage **w**⌋ against Israel.
17:10 they didn't wage **w** against
18:5 "Should we go to **w** against
18:14 should we go to **w** against
20:1 wage **w** against Jehoshaphat.
20:9 'If evil comes in the form of **w**,
20:29 **w** against Israel's enemies.
25:17 to declare **w** on Israel.
26:6 Uzziah went to wage **w**
26:11 They were ready to go to **w** in
32:2 to wage **w** against Jerusalem,
35:21 those who are at **w** with me.
Job 5:20 and in **w** he will save you from
38:23 for the day of battle and **w**?
Psa 27:3 Even though a **w** breaks out
55:18 from the **w** waged against me,
55:21 but there is **w** in his heart.

Psa 68:30 the people who find joy in **w**.
76:3 and weapons of **w**.
120:7 they only talk about **w**.
Pro 20:18 with guidance one wages **w**.
24:6 right strategy you can wage **w**,
Ecc 3:8 a time for **w** and a time for
8:8 to avoid the **w** ⌊against death⌋.
9:18 is better than weapons of **w**,
Isa 2:4 and they will never train for **w**
21:2 Go to **w**, Elam! Surround them,
29:3 I will set up **w** camps all
29:7 will go to **w** against Ariel.
29:7 They will go to **w** against it,
31:1 on very strong **w** horses.
36:5 about getting ready for **w**.
41:12 Those who are at **w** with you
42:25 and the horrors of **w** on them.
51:19 and **w** have happened to you.
Jer 4:19 horn sounding the alarm for **w**.
5:12 won't experience **w** or famine.
6:4 yourselves for **w** against Zion.
11:22 men will die because of **w**.
14:18 see those killed because of **w**.
21:7 the plague, **w**, and famine.
21:9 in this city will die in the **w**,
25:29 I'm declaring **w** on all those
30:16 Those who stole from you in **w**
34:4 You will not die in **w**.
39:18 You will not die in **w**.
42:14 where we won't have to see **w**,
47:3 sound of galloping **w** horses,
50:15 Shout a **w** cry against them on
50:42 They are ready for **w**,
51:20 "You are my **w** club and my
Eze 14:17 "Suppose I bring a **w** against
14:17 'I will let a **w** go throughout this
26:7 **w** horses, many people,
26:10 The noise from the **w** horses,
27:14 exchanged horses, **w** horses,
30:4 There will be **w** in Egypt and
30:6 People will die in **w** from
32:27 grave with their weapons of **w**.
33:2 Tell them, 'Suppose I bring **w**
38:8 that has been rebuilt after a **w**.
38:21 I will declare **w** against Gog on
39:9 and **w** clubs and spears.
Dan 7:21 I saw that horn making **w**
9:26 the destructive **w** that has been
10:1 It was about a great **w**.
11:10 his sons will prepare for **w**.
11:10 They will return and wage **w**
11:20 although not in anger or **w**.
11:25 who will prepare for **w** with a
Hos 2:18 and weapons of **w**,
10:9 **W** will overtake the wicked
11:6 **W** will sweep through their
13:16 They will be killed in **w**,
Joe 2:4 They run like **w** horses.
3:9 Prepare yourselves for **w**.
Amo 5:3 troops off to **w** will have ⌊only⌋
5:3 troops off to **w** will have ⌊only⌋
Oba 1:1 Let's go to **w** against Edom."
Mic 2:8 a care as they return from **w**.
3:5 But they declare a holy **w**
4:3 and they will never train for **w**
Zec 9:10 chariots in Ephraim or **w** horses
10:3 like his splendid **w** horse."
14:12 gone to **w** against Jerusalem.
Luk 14:31 to **w** against another king.
Rom 7:23 It is at **w** with the standards my
1Ti 1:18 to fight this noble **w**.
Rev 2:16 and wage **w** against them
12:7 Then a **w** broke out in heaven.
12:7 and his angels had to fight a **w**
13:4 Who can fight a **w** with it?"
13:7 It was allowed to wage **w**
16:14 world and gather them for the **w**
17:14 They will go to **w** against the
19:11 he judges and wages **w**.
19:19 gathered to wage **w** against
20:8 and gather them for **w**.

warden (3)

Gen 39:21 on good terms with the **w**.
39:22 So the **w** placed Joseph in
39:23 The **w** paid no attention to

wardrobe (2)

2Ki 22:14 was in charge of the ⌊royal⌋ **w**.
2Ch 34:22 was in charge of the ⌊royal⌋ **w**.

warehouse (2)

2Ki 20:13 showed the messengers his **w**:
Isa 39:2 showed the messengers his **w**:

warehouses (2)

Job 38:22 Have you been to the **w** where
38:22 is stored or seen the **w** for hail

warfare (2)

1Sm 14:52 There was intense **w** with the
2Sm 12:10 So **w** will never leave your

warm (17)

Jos 9:12 Our bread was **w** when we left
1Sm 21:6 replaced with **w** bread that day.
1Ki 1:1 blankets, he couldn't get **w**.
1:2 in your arms and keep you **w**."
2Ki 4:34 boy's body, and it became **w**.
Job 31:20 my sheep didn't keep him **w** ....)
Ecc 4:11 together, they can keep **w**,
4:11 how can one person keep **w**?
Isa 44:15 of them and **w** themselves
44:16 They also **w** themselves and
44:16 We are **w**. We can see the fire!"
47:14 glowing coals to keep them **w**
Hag 1:6 have enough to keep you **w**.
Jon 18:25 to stand and **w** himself by
2Ti 4:13 When you come, bring the **w**
Jas 2:16 Stay **w**, and make sure you eat
1Pe 1:22 Love each other with a **w** love

warmed (1)

Mar 14:54 He sat with the guards and **w**

warmest (1)

1Co 16:19 their **w** Christian greetings.

warming (3)

Mar 14:67 saw Peter **w** himself.
Jon 18:18 built and were **w** themselves
18:18 and **w** himself with the others.

warmly (3)

Gen 33:10 yet you welcomed me so **w**.
Act 21:17 the believers welcomed us **w**.
1Pe 4:8 Above all, love each other **w**,

warms (1)

Job 39:14 eggs on the ground and **w** them

warn (32)

Exo 19:21 "Go down and **w** the people
Num 17:10 and keep it there as a sign to **w**
Dtr 8:19 I **w** you today that if you forget
28:46 and an amazing thing to **w** you
1Sm 8:9 but be sure to **w** them and tell
1Ki 2:42 Didn't I **w** you that if you left
2Ch 19:10 **W** your relatives living in other
Psa 81:8 my people, and I will **w** you.
Pro 1:23 "Turn to me when I **w** you.
1:25 You did not want me to **w** you.
9:8 Do not **w** a mocker,
9:8 **W** a wise person, and he will
19:25 **W** an understanding person,
Jer 4:16 **W** the nations about these
Eze 3:17 and **w** them for me.
3:18 but you don't **w** them or speak
3:19 But suppose you **w** the wicked
3:20 If you don't **w** them,
3:21 But if you **w** righteous people
12:6 I've made you a sign to **w** the
33:3 blow his horn to **w** the people.
33:6 and doesn't blow his horn to **w**
33:7 and **w** them for me.
33:8 and you say nothing to **w** him
33:9 But if you **w** a wicked person
33:14 I may **w** the wicked person that
Luk 16:28 He can **w** them so that they
Act 2:40 said much more to **w** them.
10:42 He ordered us to **w** the people,
2Ti 2:14 and **w** them in the sight of God
2Ti 4:2 Point out errors, **w** people,
Rev 22:18 I **w** everyone who hears the

warned (32)

Exo 19:23 because you **w** us yourself to
21:29 and the owner has been **w** but
2Ki 6:10 Elisha **w** them so that they
17:13 The LORD had **w** Israel and
1Ch 16:21 He **w** kings about them:
2Ch 24:19 The prophets **w** them,
Neh 4:12 were living near our enemies **w**
9:26 your prophets who **w** them
9:29 You **w** them in order to bring
9:30 You **w** them by your Spirit
13:15 I **w** them about selling food on
13:21 I **w** them. "Why are you
Psa 2:10 Be **w**, you rulers of the earth!
19:11 your servant I am **w** by them.
105:14 He **w** kings about them:
Ecc 12:12 Be **w**, my children,
Isa 8:11 He **w** me not to follow the
Jer 11:7 I solemnly **w** your ancestors
11:7 I solemnly **w** them to obey me.
Eze 23:48 and all the women will be **w**
Mat 2:12 God **w** them in a dream not to
2:22 **W** in a dream, he left for Galilee
9:30 He **w** them, "Don't let anyone
Mar 1:43 him away at once and **w** him,
8:15 Jesus **w** them, "Be careful!
Act 20:21 I **w** Jews and Greeks to
2Co 13:2 I already **w** you when I was
1Th 4:6 told you and **w** you about this.
Tit 3:10 after you have **w** them once
Heb 8:5 to make the tent, God **w** him,
11:7 listen when God **w** him about
12:25 who **w** them on earth.

warning (35)

Gen 43:3 "The man gave us a severe **w**:
Exo 9:20 **w** brought their servants
9:21 LORD's **w** seriously left their
Num 26:10 the 250 men. This was a **w**.
1Sm 2:25 listen to their father's **w**—
2Sm 22:16 laid bare at the LORD's stern **w**,
Job 36:10 He makes them listen to his **w**
Psa 18:15 were laid bare at your stern **w**,
76:6 At your stern **w**, O God of
Pro 1:30 They despised my every **w**.
3:11 and do not resent his **w**,
10:17 but whoever ignores a **w**
15:5 a **w** shows good sense.
15:10 ⌊A⌋nyone who hates a **w** will die.
15:12 does not appreciate a **w**.
15:31 listens to a life-giving **w** will
15:32 to **w** gains understanding.
29:15 and a **w** produce wisdom,
Isa 30:12 You have rejected this **w**,
Jer 6:8 Pay attention to my **w**,
6:10 Whom can I give a **w** to?
11:7 and the **w** still applies to you
42:19 to know that I am **w** you today.
Eze 3:21 because they listened to the **w**.
12:11 "Tell them, 'I am your **w** sign.
33:4 hear the horn and ignore the **w**
33:5 of the horn but ignored its **w**.
33:5 If they had taken the **w**,
Mal 2:1 you priests, this **w** is for you.
2:4 I sent you this **w** so that my
Mar 6:11 from your feet as a **w** to them."
Luk 9:5 off your feet as a **w** to them."
12:5 I'm **w** you to be afraid of him.
1Co 10:11 were written down as a **w**
2Co 13:2 not there now, I'm **w** you again.

warnings (8)

Dtr 32:46 "Pay attention to all these **w**
2Ki 17:15 and the **w** he had given them.
Neh 9:34 or the **w** that you gave
Job 33:16 ears and terrifies them with **w**.
Psa 39:11 With stern **w** you discipline
Pro 6:23 and the **w** from discipline are
29:1 after many **w** will suddenly
Zec 1:6 Didn't my **w** and my laws,

warns (7)

Job 33:17 ⌊He **w** them⌋ to turn away from

Psa 16:7 My conscience **w** me at night.
Pro 3:12 because the LORD **w** the one
3:12 even as a father **w** a son with
9:7 Whoever **w** a wicked person
Act 20:23 However, the Holy Spirit **w** me
Heb 12:25 who **w** us from heaven.

warrior (19)

Gen 10:8 the first mighty **w** on the earth.
Exo 15:3 The LORD is a **w**!
1Sm 14:52 Whenever any **w** or any skilled
16:18 a courageous man and a **w**.
17:33 but he's been a **w** since he
18:17 if you prove yourself to be a **w**
2Sm 17:10 knows that your father is a **w**
1Ch 1:10 the first mighty **w** on the earth.
12:28 and Zadok, a young **w** from
Job 15:25 attacks the Almighty like a **w**.
16:14 He lunges at me like a **w**.
Psa 33:16 No **w** rescues himself by his
45:3 O **w**, strap your sword to your
78:65 like a **w** sobering up from ⌊too
127:4 like arrows in the hand of a **w**.
Isa 42:13 LORD marches out like a **w**.
Jer 20:11 on my side like a terrifying **w**.
46:12 One **w** will stumble over
Rev 6:2 rode off as a **w** to win battles.

warrior-king (1)

Dan 11:3 "Then a **w** will come.

warrior's (3)

Psa 120:4 He will give you a **w** sharpened
Isa 9:5 Every **w** boot marching to the
Zec 9:13 I will use you like a **w** sword

warriors (47)

Jos 6:2 and its **w** over to you.
10:2 All its men were **w**.
10:7 all his soldiers and best **w**,
1Sm 2:4 "The bows of the **w** are broken,
2Sm 1:22 killed and the fat of the **w**,
11:16 knew the experienced **w** were.
16:6 all the **w** were shielding David.
17:8 They are **w** as fierce as a wild
22:26 innocent **w** you are innocent,
1Ki 11:24 the leader of a troop of **w**.
1Ch 12:8 They were **w**, trained soldiers,
12:21 because they were all **w**,
12:25 there were 7,100 **w**.
12:30 20,800 **w** who were famous
26:31 **W** from these families were
2Ch 26:12 among these **w** was 2,600.
Neh 11:14 Their relatives, who were **w**,
Psa 56:1 All day long **w** oppress me.
76:5 None of the **w** were able to lift
89:19 "I set a boy above **w**.
Pro 21:22 A wise man attacks a city of **w**
Isa 3:25 your **w** will die in combat.
Jer 5:16 They are all mighty **w**.
46:5 Their **w** are defeated.
46:6 The **w** can't escape.
46:9 March into battle, you **w**,
46:9 you **w** from Sudan and Put who
46:9 you **w** from Lydia who use
51:30 The **w** of Babylon have
Lam 1:15 The Lord has treated all the **w**
Eze 32:12 people with the swords of **w**.
32:12 be the most ruthless **w** among
32:21 The mightiest **w** will say to
32:27 with the godless **w** who died
39:18 You can eat the meat of **w** and
39:20 **w**, and soldiers of every kind,
Hos 10:13 own power and your many **w**.
Joe 2:7 They run like **w**. They climb
3:9 Wake up the **w**. Have all the
3:9 Have all the **w** come near and
3:10 should say that they are **w**.
Oba 1:9 your **w** will be terrified.
Nah 2:3 The shields of his **w** are
Zep 1:14 **W** will cry out bitterly on the
Zec 10:5 Together they will be like **w**
10:7 Ephraim will be like mighty **w**.
Rev 19:18 **w**, horses and their riders,

warriors' (2)

2Sm 1:21 because **w** shields were
Jer 48:14 'We are soldiers and **w**?

wars (50)

Num 21:14 described in the Book of the **W**
Dtr 32:25 Foreign **w** will kill off their
1Ki 14:19 concerning Jeroboam, his **w**,
22:45 heroic acts he did and ⌊the **w**⌋
1Ch 22:8 and fought in a lot of **w**.
28:3 **w** and caused bloodshed.'
2Ch 16:9 you will have to fight **w**."
27:7 else about Jotham — all his **w**
Psa 46:9 He puts an end to **w** all over
Jer 14:12 destroy these people with **w**,
14:13 'You won't see **w** or famines,
14:15 name that there will be no **w**
14:15 **W** and famines will bring an
14:16 be victims of famines and **w**.
15:2 are destined to die in **w** will die
15:2 to die in wars will die in **w**.
16:4 **W** and famines will bring them
24:10 I will send **w**, famines,
25:16 because of the **w** that I'm going
25:27 because of the **w** that I'm going
27:8 will punish those nations by **w**,
27:13 you and your people die in **w**,
28:8 you and me prophesied **w**,
29:17 I'm going to send them **w**,
29:18 I will chase them with **w**,
31:2 The people who survived the **w**
32:24 Because of **w**, famines,
32:36 city, 'Because of **w**, famines,
34:17 "I will free you to die in **w**,
38:2 stay in this city will die in **w**,
42:16 Then the **w** you fear will catch
42:17 and live in Egypt will die in **w**,
42:22 to know that you will die in **w**,
44:12 will die in **w** or be brought to an
44:13 I punished Jerusalem with **w**,
44:18 nothing but **w** and famines."
44:27 people from Judah will die in **w**
44:28 Those who escape the **w** will
Eze 5:17 violence, and **w** to kill you.
6:11 So they will die in **w**,
6:12 who are near will die in **w**,
12:16 spare a few of them from **w**,
14:21 I will send **w**, famines,
Hos 1:7 I won't use bows, swords, **w**,
Mat 24:6 "You will hear of **w** and rumors
24:6 hear of wars and rumors of **w**.
Mar 13:7 "When you hear of **w** and
13:7 hear of wars and rumors of **w**,
Luk 21:9 you hear of **w** and revolutions,
Rev 6:8 the earth to kill people using **w**,

wartime (1)

1Ki 2:5 he shed blood as if it were **w**.

warts (1)

Lev 22:22 cuts, **w**, scabs, or ringworm.

wary (1)

Jon 2:24 was **w** of these believers.

wash (91)

Gen 18:4 After you **w** your feet,
19:2 ⌊You can⌋ **w** your feet there.
24:32 him and his men to **w** their feet.
35:2 **w** yourselves until you are
43:24 He gave them water to **w** their
49:11 He will **w** his clothes in wine,
Exo 19:10 Have them **w** their clothes
29:4 tent of meeting, and **w** them.
29:17 **w** the internal organs and legs,
30:20 they must **w** so that they will
30:21 they will **w** their hands and feet
40:12 tent of meeting, and **w** them.
40:31 this water to **w** their hands
40:32 They would **w** whenever they
Lev 1:9 **W** the internal organs and legs.
1:13 **W** the internal organs and legs.
6:27 he must **w** them in a holy
11:25 bodies must **w** his clothes.
11:28 animals must **w** their clothes
Lev 11:40 dead body must **w** their clothes
11:40 body away will **w** their clothes
13:6 The person must **w** his clothes
13:58 **w** it again, and it will be clean.
14:8 cleansed must **w** his clothes,
14:8 shave off all his hair, and **w**.
14:9 and he must **w** his clothes and
14:47 the house must **w** his clothes.
15:5 his bed must **w** their clothes
15:6 he sat on must **w** their clothes
15:7 discharge must **w** their clothes
15:8 the person he spits on must **w**
15:10 things must **w** their clothes
15:11 the person he touched must **w**
15:13 He must **w** his clothes and his
15:18 they must **w** themselves.
15:21 her bed must **w** their clothes
15:22 sits on must **w** their clothes
15:27 and must **w** their clothes
16:4 He must **w** his body and put
16:24 He will **w** his body in the holy
16:26 to Azazel must **w** his clothes
16:28 Whoever burns them must **w**
17:15 animal must **w** their clothes
17:16 If they don't **w** their clothes and
Num 5:23 on a scroll and **w** them off into
8:7 bodies and **w** their clothes.
19:7 The priest must then **w** his
19:8 calf must also **w** his clothes
19:10 cow must also **w** his clothes.
19:19 Then they must **w** their clothes
19:21 must **w** his clothes.
31:24 seventh day **w** your clothes,
Dtr 21:6 victim must **w** their hands over
23:11 Toward evening he must **w**,
33:24 favorite tribe and **w** their feet
1Sm 25:41 "I am ready to **w** the feet of my
2Sm 11:8 to Uriah, "and **w** your feet."
2Ki 5:10 He said, "**W** yourself seven
5:12 Couldn't I **w** in them and be
5:13 '**W** and be clean'?"
2Ch 4:6 They used the pool to **w**
Job 9:30 If I **w** myself with lye soap and
14:19 floods **w** away soil from the
Psa 26:6 I will **w** my hands in
51:2 **W** me thoroughly from my guilt,
51:7 **W** me, and I will be whiter than
58:10 They will **w** their feet in the
Sos 8:7 and rivers will never **w** it away.
Isa 1:16 "**W** yourselves! Become clean!
4:4 The Lord will **w** away the filth
28:17 and floodwaters will **w** away
Jer 2:22 Even if you **w** with detergent
4:14 Jerusalem, **w** the evil from your
Dan 10:3 I didn't **w** myself until the entire
Zec 13:1 to **w** away ⌊their⌋ sin
Mat 6:17 When you fast, **w** your face
15:2 They do not **w** their hands
Mar 7:4 they must also **w** their cups,
7:5 they don't **w** their hands before
Luk 7:44 You didn't **w** my feet.
11:38 Jesus didn't **w** before the meal.
Jon 9:7 "**W** it off in the pool of Siloam."
9:11 me, 'Go to Siloam, and **w** it off.'
13:5 into a basin and began to **w**
13:6 are you going to **w** my feet?"
13:8 "You will never **w** my feet."
13:8 to Peter, "If I don't **w** you,
13:9 don't **w** only my feet.
13:9 **W** my hands and my head too!"
13:14 you must **w** each other's feet.
Rev 22:14 "Blessed are those who **w** their

washed (42)

Gen 43:31 Then he **w** his face and came
Exo 19:14 and they **w** their clothes.
Lev 8:6 come forward, and he **w** them.
8:21 He **w** the internal organs and
9:14 He **w** the internal organs and
13:34 When he has **w** his clothes,
13:54 he must order the area to be **w**
13:55 the area again after it is **w**.
13:58 any leather article when it is **w**,
15:17 with semen on it must be **w**.
22:6 unless he has **w** himself.
Num 8:21 their sins and **w** their clothes.

Jdg 19:21 After they **w**, they ate and
2Sm 19:24 or **w** his clothes from the day
1Ki 22:38 His chariot was **w** at the pool
Psa 124:4 stream would have **w** us away.
124:5 water would have **w** us away."
Pro 30:12 pure but is not **w** from his own
Sos 5:3 I have **w** my feet! Why should I
Eze 16:4 You weren't **w** with water to
16:9 and I **w** off your blood.
23:40 they **w** themselves for the men,
40:38 is the room where the priests **w**
Mat 27:24 some water and **w** his hands
Mar 7:3 have properly **w** their hands.
7:4 eat unless they have **w** first.
Luk 6:48 But the house couldn't be **w**
7:38 She was crying and **w** his feet
7:44 But she has **w** my feet with her
Jon 9:7 "sent.") The blind man **w**
9:11 So I went there, **w** it off,
9:15 I **w** it off, and now I can see."
13:10 "People who have **w** are
13:10 need to have only their feet **w**.
13:12 After Jesus had **w** their feet
13:14 and teacher, have **w** your feet,
Act 16:33 the jailer **w** Paul and Silas'
22:16 and have your sins **w** away as
1Co 6:11 But you have been **w** and
Heb 10:22 and our bodies have been **w**
2Pe 2:22 and "A sow that has been **w**
Rev 7:14 They have **w** their robes and

washes (1)

Job 22:16 A river **w** their foundation away.

washing (13)

Exo 30:18 with a bronze stand for **w**.
30:19 will use it for **w** their hands
40:30 altar and put water in it for **w**.
Lev 13:56 that the area is pale after **w**,
2Ch 4:6 also made ten basins for **w**
Psa 73:13 my life pure and **w** my hands
Sos 4:2 sheep that come up from the **w**.
6:6 sheep that come up from the **w**.
Mat 15:20 But eating without **w** one's
Mar 7:2 they ate without **w** their hands.
Luk 5:2 of them and were **w** their nets.
Eph 5:26 **w** it using water along with
Tit 3:5 he saved us through the **w**

washtub (2)

Psa 60:8 Moab is my **w**. I will throw my
108:9 Moab is my **w**. I will throw my

waste (20)

Gen 34:19 The young man didn't **w** any
Lev 26:39 Those who are left will **w**
Jos 18:3 "How long are you going to **w**
2Sm 18:14 Then Joab said, "I shouldn't **w**
Psa 31:9 my body **w** away from grief.
31:10 and my bones **w** away.
73:26 body and mind may **w** away,
Isa 15:1 Moab is laid **w** and destroyed!
15:1 Moab is laid **w** and destroyed!
24:3 earth will be completely laid **w**
24:4 The great leaders of the earth **w**
24:7 and grapevines **w** away.
42:15 I will lay **w** to mountains and
49:17 who destroyed you and laid **w**
Jer 48:8 and the plain will be laid **w** as
Lam 3:4 my flesh and my skin **w** away.
Eze 4:17 They will **w** away because of
24:23 You will **w** away because of
Zep 2:11 the gods of the earth **w** away.
Mat 26:8 "Why did she **w** it like this?

wasted (11)

Gen 38:9 he **w** his semen on the ground
Eze 28:17 You **w** your wisdom because
Mar 14:4 was the perfume **w** like this?
Luk 15:13 There he **w** everything he had
Jon 6:12 so that nothing will be **w**."
1Co 15:10 kindness was not **w** on me.
2Co 6:1 God's kindness be **w** on you.
Gal 2:2 all my efforts have been **w**.
4:11 I spent on you has been **w**.
Php 2:16 Christ that my effort was not **w**
1Th 2:1 our time with you was not **w**.

wasteland (43)

Job 6:18 go into a **w** and disappear.
38:27 to saturate the desolate **w** in
Isa 5:6 I will make it a **w**. It will never
17:9 So it will become a **w**.
24:1 turn the earth into a desolate **w**.
64:10 a desert. Jerusalem is a **w**.
Jer 2:6 through a **w** and its pits,
2:15 have turned the land into a **w**.
7:34 because the land will be a **w**."
12:10 my pleasant property into a **w**.
12:11 They've left it a **w**.
25:11 will be ruined and become a **w**.
25:12 Babylon into a permanent **w**.
32:43 have said that this land is a **w**,
46:19 will become a dreary **w**,
49:33 It will become a permanent **w**.
51:29 to make Babylon a **w** so that no
Eze 5:14 I will turn you into a **w** and an
12:20 the country will become a **w**.
14:15 turn it into such a **w** that no one
14:16 the country would become a **w**.
15:8 I will turn the country into a **w**
29:9 Egypt will become a **w** and a
29:10 It will become a **w**,
32:15 I will turn Egypt into a **w**.
33:28 turn the land into a barren **w**.
33:29 I make the land a barren **w**
35:3 and you will become a **w**.
35:4 and you will become a **w**.
35:7 turn Mount Seir into a barren **w**,
35:9 turn you into a permanent **w**.
35:14 glad when I turn you into a **w**.
35:15 the land of Israel became a **w**.
35:15 You will become a **w**,
36:34 The **w** will be plowed.
36:35 People will say, "This **w** has
Hos 5:9 Ephraim will become a **w**
Joe 3:19 Egypt will become a **w**.
Mic 7:13 The earth will become a **w** for
Zep 2:13 a dried up **w** like the desert.
2:15 What a **w** it is now,
Zec 7:14 a pleasant land into a **w**."
Mal 1:3 I turned his mountains into a **w**

wastelands (2)

Jer 25:18 they became **w** and ruins,
Eze 19:7 and turned cities into **w**.

wastes (4)

Pro 29:3 pays prostitutes **w** his wealth.
Ecc 4:5 A fool folds his hands and **w**
Isa 24:4 The world **w** away and withers.
33:9 country grieves and **w** away.

wasting (5)

Pro 21:6 wealth by lying are **w** time.
Isa 10:18 be like a sick person **w** away.
24:16 But I kept saying, "I'm **w** away!
24:16 I'm **w** away! How horrible it is
Luk 16:1 manager was accused of **w**

watch (103)

Gen 21:16 "I don't want to **w** the boy die."
27:42 Jacob and said to him, "**W** out!
28:15 I am with you and will **w** over
28:20 be with me and will **w** over me
31:49 "May the LORD **w** between
Exo 12:42 That night the LORD kept **w** to
12:42 future generations must keep **w**
19:11 Sinai as all the people **w**.
33:8 to their tents and **w** Moses until
Num 6:24 will bless you and **w** over you.
Dtr 4:9 However, be careful, and **w**
28:31 ox will be butchered as you **w**,
28:31 You will **w** as your donkey is
28:32 You will **w** with your own eyes
Jos 3:11 **W** the ark of the promise of the
Jdg 7:17 He said to them, "**W** me,
7:19 of the midnight **w** just at
9:31 "**W** out! Gaal (son of Ebed) and
21:21 **w**. When the young women of
Rut 2:9 **W** where my men are reaping,
1Sm 6:9 but then **w** where it goes.
1Sm 12:16 Now then, stand still and **w**
17:20 someone else **w** ⌊the sheep⌋.
19:11 Saul sent messengers to **w**
23:22 and **w** where he goes.
23:23 **W** and learn about all the
24:15 He will **w** and take my side in
2Sm 13:5 a meal in front of me as I **w** her,
13:28 "**W** now," he said.
13:34 servant who kept **w** looked up,
1Ki 20:17 had sent men ⌊to **w** the city⌋.
1Ch 26:16 served its **w** after another.
29:18 always **w** over your people's
Ezr 4:14 it isn't right for us to **w**
Job 10:14 "'If I sin, you **w** me and will not
24:15 Adulterers **w** for twilight.
39:1 Do you **w** the does when they
Psa 23:5 for me while my enemies **w**.
31:19 Adam's descendants **w** as you
32:8 you as my eyes **w** over you.
39:1 I said, "I will **w** my ways so
56:6 They **w** my every step as they
59:9 O my strength, I **w** for you!
66:7 His eyes **w** the nations.
71:10 They **w** me as they plot to take
79:10 Let us **w** as the nations learn
130:6 LORD more than those who **w**
130:6 those who **w** for the morning.
139:3 You **w** me when I travel and
141:3 Keep **w** over the door of my
Pro 2:8 paths of justice and to **w** over
4:6 and it will **w** over you.
6:6 **W** its ways, and become wise.
6:22 they will **w** over you.
15:3 They **w** evil people and good
22:12 eyes **w** over knowledge,
Ecc 5:1 **W** your step when you go to
Isa 18:4 I will keep quiet and **w** from my
21:7 Let him **w** carefully,
27:3 I, the LORD, **w** over it.
27:3 I **w** over it day and night so that
49:18 Look up, look around, and **w**!
60:4 "Look up, look around, and **w**.
Jer 16:9 in your lifetime, while you **w**.
17:21 is what the LORD says: **W** out!
24:6 I will **w** over them for their own
29:21 I will kill them as you **w**.
31:10 them and **w** over them as
31:28 Now I will **w** over them to build
39:16 things will happen as you **w**.
43:9 the people of Judah **w** you.
44:27 I am going to **w** over them.
44:27 I am going to **w** over them to
48:19 by the road in Aroer, and **w**.
Eze 12:3 to another place as they **w**.
21:6 crying while the people **w** you.
28:25 that I am holy as the nations **w**.
36:23 holiness among you as they **w**,
38:16 for my holy purpose as they **w**.
Dan 7:11 I continued to **w** because of the
Hab 1:3 why do you **w** wickedness?
1:5 Look among the nations and **w**.
1:13 You can't **w** wickedness.
2:1 I will **w** to see what he will say
Zec 3:7 and **w** over my courtyards.
12:4 I will **w** over the people of
Mat 10:17 **W** out for people who will hand
16:6 **W** out for the yeast of the
16:11 **W** out for the yeast of the
16:12 that he didn't say to **w** out
16:12 but to **w** out for the teachings of
27:36 sat there and kept **w** over him.
Mar 8:15 **W** out for the yeast of the
12:38 "**W** out for the scribes!
13:33 **W**! You don't know the exact
Luk 4:10 of you to **w** over you carefully.
12:1 "**W** out for the yeast of the
17:3 So **w** yourselves! "If a believer
Rom 16:17 I urge you to **w** out for those
Gal 6:1 At the same time **w** yourself so
2Ti 4:15 **W** out for him. He violently
1Pe 5:2 **W** over it as God does:
Rev 2:22 **W** me! I'm going to throw her

watched (40)

Gen 16:13 "This is the place where I **w**
Exo 2:11 and **w** them suffering under

Exo	17:6	the leaders of Israel w him.
Dtr	2:7	He has w over you as you
Jdg	9:43	He w and saw the people
	13:19	While Manoah and his wife w,
	16:27	who w Samson entertain them.
1Sm	17:55	As Saul w David going out
2Ki	25:7	Zedekiah's sons as he w,
1Ch	29:10	while the whole assembly w.
Job	29:2	the days when God w over me,
Jer	31:28	Once I w over them to uproot
	39:6	sons as Zedekiah w at Riblah.
	52:10	sons as Zedekiah w.
Eze	10:2	between the wheels as I w.
	20:14	nations who had w me bring
	20:22	nations who had w me bring
Dan	5:5	The king w as the hand wrote.
	7:4	I w until its wings were
	7:9	I w until thrones were set up
	7:11	I w until the animal was killed.
	8:15	Now as I, Daniel, w the vision
Mar	2:12	away while everyone w.
	12:41	he w how ⌊much⌋ money
	15:47	of Joses) w where Jesus was
Luk	4:20	the synagogue w him closely.
	10:18	Jesus said to them, "I w Satan
	11:54	and w him closely to trap him
	18:24	Jesus w him and said,
	20:20	So they w for an opportunity to
	23:49	stood at a distance and w
	24:43	it and ate it while they w him.
Jon	17:12	I w over them, and none of
Act	3:5	So the man w them closely.
Eph	6:6	them only while you're being w,
Col	3:22	them only while you're being w,
Rev	6:1	I w as the lamb opened the first
	6:12	I w as the lamb opened the
	11:11	Great fear fell on those who w
	11:12	and their enemies w them.

watches (16)

Gen	16:13	Are the God Who W Over Me."
	16:13	⌊the one⌋ who w over me."
	16:14	Living One Who W Over Me].
Exo	9:8	up in the air as Pharaoh w.
Num	19:5	will be burned while he w.
Dtr	11:12	He w over it all year long.
Job	7:8	The eye that w over me will no
	33:11	the stocks and w all my paths.'
Psa	37:32	The wicked person w the
Pro	8:34	w at my door day after day,
	14:15	a sensible person w his step.
	16:17	Whoever w his way preserves
Ecc	11:4	Whoever w the wind will never
Jer	31:10	as a shepherd w over his flock.'
Luk	14:29	everyone who w will make fun
2Co	4:2	As God w, we clearly reveal

watchful (1)

Ezr	5:5	Jews were under God's w eye.

watchfulness (1)

Job	10:12	Your w has preserved my spirit.

watching (31)

Gen	24:21	The man was silently w her to
	30:31	of and w your flocks again.
Jos	10:12	the LORD while Israel was w,
1Sm	1:12	Eli was w her mouth.
	4:13	on a chair beside the road, w.
	25:16	night as long as we were w
1Ki	20:33	The men, w for a good sign,
Job	24:15	They say, 'No one is w us,'
Psa	101:6	My eyes will be w the faithful
Ecc	5:8	authority is w over another,
	5:8	have authorities w over them.
Jer	1:12	I am w to make sure that my
Eze	10:19	I was w them as they left with
	20:9	While other nations were w,
	20:41	holy to the nations that are w.
Dan	2:34	While you were w,
	8:5	As I was w closely,
Hab	1:13	keep w treacherous people?
Zec	11:11	who were w me realized that
Mat	27:54	An army officer and those w
	27:55	Many women were there w
Mar	3:2	people were w Jesus closely.
Mar	15:40	Some women were w from a
Luk	2:8	They were taking turns w their
	6:7	were w Jesus closely.
	14:1	were w Jesus very closely.
	17:7	is plowing fields or w sheep.
	23:35	The people stood there w.
Act	9:24	They were w the city gates
	12:6	They were w the prison.
1Pe	2:12	while they are w you do good

watchman (19)

2Sm	18:24	while the w walked along
	18:25	The w called and alerted the
	18:26	When the w saw another man
	18:26	man running, the w called,
	18:27	The w said, "It seems to me
2Ki	9:17	The w standing on the tower in
	9:18	So the w announced,
	9:20	So the w announced,
Job	27:18	like a shack that a w makes.
Isa	21:6	the Lord says to me: Post a w.
	21:8	The w called, "Sir, I stand on
	21:11	is calling to me from Seir, "W,
	21:11	W, how much of the night is
	21:12	The w answers, "Morning is
Eze	3:17	I have made you a w over the
	33:2	men and make him their w.
	33:6	"'But if the w sees the enemy
	33:6	that w must die because of his
	33:7	I have appointed you as a w

watchmen (12)

1Sm	14:16	Saul's w at Gibeah in
1Ch	9:19	responsible for serving as w at
Sos	3:3	The w making their rounds in
	5:7	The w making their rounds in
	5:7	Those w on the walls took my
Isa	52:8	Your w raise their voices and
	56:10	⌊Israel's⌋ w are blind.
	62:6	I have posted w on your walls,
Jer	6:17	I posted w over you.
	31:6	There will be a day when w on
	51:12	Station w. Prepare ambushes.
Hos	9:8	are God's w over Ephraim.

watchtower (9)

Gen	31:49	and also Mizpah [W],
2Ki	17:9	from the ⌊smallest⌋ w to the
	18:8	from the ⌊smallest⌋ w
2Ch	20:24	people of Judah went to the w
Isa	5:2	choicest vines, built a w in it,
	21:8	I stand on the w every day.
Mic	4:8	You, Jerusalem, w of the flock,
Mat	21:33	a winepress, and built a w.
Mar	12:1	the winepress, and built a w.

watchtowers (2)

1Ch	27:25	villages, and w: Jonathan,
Isa	32:14	Fortresses and w will become

water (546)

Gen	1:2	darkness covered the deep w.
	1:2	God was hovering over the w.
	1:6	a horizon in the middle of the w
	1:6	in order to separate the w."
	1:7	and separated the w above
	1:9	Then God said, "Let the w
	1:10	The w which came together he
	1:20	Then God said, "Let the w
	1:21	that swims around in the w
	2:6	Instead, underground w would
	2:6	come up from the earth and w
	2:10	from Eden to w the garden.
	7:17	The w increased and lifted the
	7:18	As the w rose and became
	7:18	the ship floated on top of the w.
	7:19	The w rose very high above
	8:1	and the w started to go down.
	8:3	The w began to recede from
	8:3	150 days the w had decreased.
	8:5	The w kept decreasing until
	8:7	flying back and forth until the w
	8:8	to see if the w was gone from
	8:9	because the w was still all
	8:11	Then Noah knew that the w
	8:13	the w on the land had dried up.
Gen	9:15	Never again will w become a
	18:4	let someone bring a little w?
	21:14	took bread and a container of w
	21:15	When the w in the container
	21:19	She filled the container with w
	24:11	would go out to draw w.
	24:13	city are coming out to draw w.
	24:14	and I'll also w your camels,'
	24:17	"Please give me a drink of w."
	24:19	"I'll also keep drawing w for
	24:20	her jar into the w trough,
	24:20	to the well to draw more w,
	24:32	Then w was brought for him
	24:43	who comes out to draw w,
	24:43	"Please give me a drink of w."
	24:44	but I will also draw w for your
	24:45	down to the spring and drew w.
	24:46	and I'll w your camels too.'
	26:20	claiming, "This w is ours!"
	26:32	said to him, "We've found w."
	29:7	W the sheep. Then let them
	29:8	we can w the sheep."
	37:24	empty cistern. It had no w in it.
	43:24	He gave them w to wash their
Exo	2:10	"I pulled him out of the w."
	2:16	They drew w and filled the
	2:16	to w their father's sheep.
	2:19	He even drew w for us and
	4:9	take some w from the Nile
	4:9	The w you take from the Nile
	7:17	and the w will turn into blood.
	7:18	to drink any w from the Nile.'"
	7:20	All the w in the river turned into
	7:21	couldn't drink any w from
	7:24	dug along the Nile for w
	7:24	any of the w from the river.
	14:16	over the sea, and divide the w.
	14:21	into dry ground. The w divided,
	14:22	The w stood like a wall on
	14:26	so that the w will flow back
	14:27	and at daybreak the w returned
	14:28	The w flowed back and
	14:29	ground while the w stood like
	15:5	The deep w covered them.
	15:8	your nostrils, the w piled up.
	15:8	The deep w thickened in the
	15:10	sank like lead in the raging w.
	15:19	the LORD made the w of the
	15:22	in the desert without finding w.
	15:23	they couldn't drink the w
	15:25	He threw it into the w,
	15:25	and the w became sweet.
	15:27	They camped there by the w.
	17:1	but there was no w for the
	17:2	"Give us w to drink!"
	17:3	people were thirsty for w there.
	17:6	Strike the rock, and w will
	20:4	sky, on the earth, or in the w.
	23:25	he will bless your food and w.
	30:18	and the altar, and fill it with w.
	32:20	scattered it on the w,
	34:28	40 nights without food or w.
	40:7	and the altar, and put w in it.
	40:30	meeting and the altar and put w
	40:31	and his sons used this w to
Lev	6:28	be scoured and rinsed with w.
	11:9	live in the w which you may
	11:12	Every creature in the w without
	11:32	It should be put in w and will
	11:34	If w ⌊from that pottery⌋ touches
	11:36	a spring or a cistern holding w
	11:38	But if w is poured on the seed
	11:46	creature that swims in the w
	14:5	a clay bowl containing fresh w.
	14:6	was killed over the fresh w.
	14:50	a clay bowl containing fresh w.
	14:51	them in the fresh w containing
	14:52	the fresh w, the living bird,
	15:13	and his body in fresh w.
Num	5:17	Then the priest will take holy w
	5:17	the floor of the tent into the w.
	5:18	the bitter w that can bring
	5:19	This bitter w that can bring a
	5:22	'May this w that can bring a
	5:23	wash them off into the bitter w.
	5:24	drink the bitter w that can bring

Num 5:24 This **w** will go into her ⌊and⌋
5:26 have the woman drink the **w**.
5:27 the **w** that can bring the curse
8:7 Sprinkle them with **w** to take
19:9 used in the **w** that takes away
19:12 person must use this **w**
19:12 But if he doesn't use this **w** on
19:13 being and doesn't use this **w**
19:13 because the **w** that takes away
19:17 Then pour fresh **w** on them.
19:18 sprig of hyssop, dip it in the **w**,
19:20 The **w** to take away
19:21 "Whoever sprinkles the **w** to
19:21 And whoever touches this **w**
20:2 the community was without **w**,
20:5 And there's no **w** to drink!"
20:8 tell the rock to give up its **w**.
20:8 will give the community **w** from
20:10 must we bring **w** out of this
20:11 **W** came pouring out,
20:17 or drink any of the **w** from your
20:19 livestock drink any of your **w**,
21:5 There's no bread or **w**,
21:16 and I will give them **w**."
21:17 "Make your **w** spring up!
21:22 any of the **w** from your wells.
24:6 like cedars by the **w**.
24:7 **W** will flow from their buckets,
24:7 crops will have plenty of **w**.
31:19 of war must use the ritual **w**
31:23 also be put through the ritual **w**
31:23 be put through the ritual **w**.
33:14 where there was no **w** for the
Dtr 2:6 you eat and the **w** you drink.'"
2:28 we eat and the **w** we drink.
4:18 or any fish in the **w**.
5:8 sky, on the earth, or in the **w**.
8:15 He was the one who made **w**
9:9 40 nights without food or **w**.
9:18 I went without food and **w** for
11:10 and you had to **w** it like a
12:16 Pour it on the ground like **w**.
12:24 Pour it on the ground like **w**.
14:9 creature that lives in the **w**:
15:23 Pour it on the ground like **w**.
23:4 didn't greet you with food and **w**
29:11 who cut wood and carry **w**
33:13 bless their land with ⌊**w**,⌋
Jos 2:10 how the LORD dried up the **w**
3:8 'When you step into the **w** of
3:13 will stand in the **w** of the
3:13 Then the **w** flowing from
3:16 the **w**, the water stopped
3:16 the water, the **w** stopped
3:16 The **w** rose up like a dam as
3:16 The **w** flowing down toward
4:7 You should answer, 'The **w** of
4:18 the **w** of the Jordan returned to
9:21 woodcutters and **w** carriers
9:23 You will be woodcutters and **w**
9:27 woodcutters and **w** carriers
Jdg 4:19 give me a little **w** to drink.
5:25 Sisera asked for **w**.
6:38 a bowl full of **w** from the wool.
7:4 Bring them down to the **w**,
7:5 took the men down to the **w**.
7:5 "Separate those who lap **w**
7:6 Three hundred men lapped **w**
7:6 the men knelt down to drink **w**.
7:7 the 300 men who lapped **w**
15:19 and **w** gushed out.
15:19 Samson drank some **w**.
Rut 2:9 and drink some of the **w** that
1Sm 7:6 They drew some **w**,
9:11 met girls coming out to get **w**.
25:11 Should I take my bread, my **w**,
26:11 near his head and that jar of **w**,
26:12 the jar of **w** near Saul's head,
26:16 and the jar of **w** that were near
30:11 him food to eat and **w** to drink.
30:12 eaten any food or drunk any **w**
2Sm 5:8 hate me by using the **w** shaft."
12:27 fortress guarding its **w** supply.
14:14 we are all like **w** that is poured
22:17 pulled me out of the raging **w**.
23:15 I could have a drink of **w** from
2Sm 23:16 camp and drew **w** from
1Ki 14:15 cattails which shake in the **w**.
17:10 "Please bring me a drink of **w**."
18:4 bread and **w** for them.)
18:13 provided bread and **w** for them.
18:34 He said, "Fill four jars with **w**.
18:34 Pour the **w** on the offering and
18:35 The **w** flowed around the altar,
18:35 the trench was filled with **w**.
18:38 The fire even dried up the **w**
19:6 on hot stones and a jar of **w**.
22:27 nothing but bread and **w** until
2Ki 2:8 and struck the **w** with it.
2:8 The **w** divided to their left and
2:14 coat and struck the **w** with it.
2:14 As he struck the **w**,
2:19 But the **w** is bad, and the land
2:21 I have purified this **w**.
2:21 failures will come from this **w**."
2:22 To this day the **w** is still pure,
3:9 seven days they ran out of **w**
3:17 this valley will be filled with **w**.
3:20 **w** flowed from Edom and filled
3:22 the sun was rising over the **w**,
3:22 they saw the **w** from a
5:12 have better **w** than any
6:5 the ax head fell into the **w**.
6:6 He threw it into the **w** at that
6:22 Give them food and **w**.
8:15 took a blanket, soaked it in **w**,
19:24 dig wells and drink foreign **w**.
20:20 pool and tunnel to bring **w** into
1Ch 11:17 I could have a drink of **w** from
11:18 camp and drew **w** from
11:19 to risk their lives to get this **w**."
2Ch 18:26 nothing but bread and **w** until
32:3 to stop the **w** from flowing out
32:4 of Assyria find plenty of **w**?"
32:30 the **w** from flowing from
32:30 He channeled the **w** directly
Ezr 10:6 any food or drink any **w** while
Neh 3:26 across from **W** Gate toward
8:1 the courtyard in front of **W** Gate
8:3 the courtyard in front of **W** Gate
8:16 in the open area by **W** Gate,
9:11 You threw into deep **w** those
9:11 throws a stone into raging **w**.
9:15 hunger and made **w** flow from
9:20 You gave them **w** to quench
12:37 palace and reaches **W** Gate
13:2 the Israelites with food and **w**.
Job 3:24 I pour out my groaning like **w**.
5:10 earth and sends **w** to the fields.
8:11 rushes grow tall without **w**?
11:16 it like **w** that has flowed
14:9 merely a scent of **w** will make
14:11 ⌊As⌋ **w** drains out of a lake,
14:19 ⌊so⌋ **w** wears away stone,
15:16 who drinks wickedness like **w**.
22:7 give a tired person a drink of **w**,
22:11 and a flood of **w** covers you.
24:18 scum on the surface of the **w**.
24:19 and heat steal **w** from snow,
26:5 dead tremble beneath the **w**,
26:8 He holds the **w** in his thick
26:10 on the surface of the **w** at
28:25 measured the **w** ⌊in the sea⌋,
29:19 roots will grow toward the **w**,
34:7 who drinks scorn like **w**,
36:27 He collects drops of **w**.
38:30 The **w** hardens like a stone,
38:34 have a flood of **w** cover you?
38:37 or pour out the **w** jars of heaven
41:1 pull Leviathan out ⌊of the **w**⌋
Psa 18:16 pulled me out of the raging **w**.
22:14 I am poured out like **w**,
29:3 of the LORD rolls over the **w**.
29:3 LORD shouts over raging **w**.
33:7 He gathers the **w** in the sea
46:3 **W** roars and foams,
58:7 Let them disappear like **w** that
63:1 land where there is no **w**.
65:9 care of the earth, and you **w** it.
65:9 river of God is filled with **w**.)
66:12 We went through fire and **w**,
69:1 The **w** is already up to my
Psa 69:2 I am in deep **w**. A flood is
69:14 hate me and from the deep **w**.
72:6 like showers that **w** the land.
74:13 of sea monsters in the **w**.
77:16 The **w** saw you, O God.
77:16 The **w** saw you and shook.
77:17 The clouds poured out **w**.
77:19 path went through raging **w**,
78:15 plenty to drink, an ocean of **w**.
78:16 He made the **w** flow like rivers.
78:20 and **w** did gush out,
79:3 Jerusalem as though it were **w**.
88:17 around me all day long like **w**.
93:4 than the sound of raging **w**,
104:3 beams of your home in the **w**.
104:6 **W** stood above the mountains
104:7 **W** ran away at the sound of
104:9 **W** cannot cross the boundary
104:10 You make **w** gush from springs
104:13 You **w** the mountains from your
105:29 He turned their **w** into blood
105:41 He opened a rock, and **w**
106:9 He led them through deep **w** as
106:11 **W** covered their adversaries.
106:32 They made God angry by the **w**
109:18 cursing entered his body like **w**
114:8 a rock into a pool filled with **w**
114:8 into a spring flowing with **w**.
124:5 Then raging **w** would have
136:6 spread out the earth on the **w**—
147:18 He makes wind blow ⌊and⌋ **w**
148:4 and the **w** above the sky.
Pro 5:15 Drink **w** out of your own cistern
5:15 and running **w** from your own
5:16 Why should **w** flow out of your
8:24 were springs filled with **w**.
19:13 is like constantly dripping **w**.
20:5 the human heart is like deep **w**,
21:1 heart is like streams of **w**.
25:21 give him some **w** to drink.
25:25 ⌊Like⌋ cold **w** to a thirsty soul,
27:15 Constantly dripping **w** on a
27:19 As a face is reflected in **w**,
30:4 Who has wrapped **w** in a
30:16 land that never gets enough **w**,
Ecc 1:7 The **w** goes back to the place
2:6 I made pools to **w** the forest of
11:1 bread on the surface of the **w**,
12:6 and the **w** wheel is broken at
Sos 4:15 living **w** flowing from Lebanon.
8:7 Raging **w** cannot extinguish
Isa 1:30 and like a garden without **w**.
3:1 entire supply of food and **w**.
7:19 and at all the **w** holes.
8:6 rejected the gently flowing **w**
10:26 and raised his staff over the **w**,
11:9 LORD like **w** covering the sea.
12:3 With joy you will draw **w** from
14:23 It will become pools of **w**.
15:9 The **w** in Dimon is red with
17:12 like the noise from rushing **w**.
17:13 will make noise like raging **w**.
18:2 over the surface of the **w**.
19:5 The **w** in the Nile River will be
19:8 their nets on the **w** will sigh.
21:14 Bring **w** for the thirsty,
22:9 You will store **w** in the Lower
22:11 the two walls to hold the **w**
27:3 I **w** it continually. I watch over it
30:14 or to dip **w** from a reservoir.
32:6 withhold **w** from thirsty people.
33:16 and a dependable supply of **w**.
35:6 **W** will gush out into the desert,
37:25 I'll dig wells and drink **w**.
40:12 Who has measured the **w** of
41:17 and needy are looking for **w**,
43:20 I will provide **w** in the desert.
44:3 I will pour **w** on thirsty ground
44:12 If they don't drink **w**,
44:27 He says to the deep **w**,
48:21 He made **w** flow from a rock for
48:21 and **w** gushed out.
50:2 stink because there is no **w**,
51:10 the **w** of the great ocean?
55:1 is thirsty, come to the **w**!
55:10 again until they **w** the earth.

Isa 57:20 It isn't quiet, and its w throws
58:11 spring whose w does not stop
63:12 is the one who divided the w
63:13 led them through the deep w?
64:2 brushwood and makes w boil.
Jer 2:13 the fountain of life-giving w.
2:13 cisterns that can't hold w.
2:18 going to Egypt to drink w from
2:18 going to Assyria to drink w from
6:7 As a well keeps its w fresh,
9:1 my head were ⌊filled with⌋ w
9:18 Our eyelids will flow with w.
10:13 He speaks, and the w in the
14:3 send their assistants out for w.
14:3 but they don't find any w.
17:8 like a tree that is planted by w.
17:13 the fountain of life-giving w.
38:6 There was no w in the cistern,
47:2 W is rising in the north.
50:38 will diminish their w supply,
51:16 the w in the sky roars.
51:55 come roaring in like raging w.
Lam 2:19 Pour your heart out like w in
3:54 W flowed over my head.
5:4 have to pay to drink our own w.
Eze 1:24 like the noise of rushing w,
4:11 out two-thirds of a quart of w,
4:16 and fearfully drink rationed w.
4:17 of the lack of food and w.
7:17 knee will be as weak as w.
12:18 be worried as you drink your w.
12:19 terrified as they drink their w.
16:4 You weren't washed with w to
16:9 "Then I bathed you with w,
17:5 where there was plenty of w.
17:7 so that the eagle could w it.
17:8 soil beside plenty of w so that
19:10 that was planted near w.
19:10 because there was plenty of w.
21:7 will become as weak as w.
24:3 put it on. Pour w in it.
26:12 and soil into the w.
31:4 W made the tree grow,
31:5 long because of so much w.
31:7 down to many sources of w.
31:14 by the w were kept from
31:15 The many w sources stopped
32:2 are like a crocodile in the w.
32:2 You splash around in the w.
32:2 You stir up the w with your feet.
32:13 beside its many w sources.
32:13 won't stir up the w anymore.
32:14 Then I will make its w clear
34:18 You drink clean w.
34:18 the rest of the w with your feet?
36:25 I will sprinkle clean w on you
43:2 like the sound of rushing w,
47:1 I saw w flowing from under the
47:1 The w was flowing under the
47:2 The w was flowing down the
47:3 mile and led me through the w.
47:3 The w came up to my ankles.
47:4 mile and led me through the w.
47:4 The w came up to my knees.
47:4 mile and led me through the w.
47:4 The w came up to my waist.
47:5 But the w had risen so much
47:8 "This w flows through the land
47:8 When the w flows into the
47:8 it will replace the salt w there
47:8 salt water there with fresh w.
47:9 The river will make the w in
47:11 But the w in the swamps and
47:12 fruit because this w flows from
Dan 1:12 to eat and w to drink.
Hos 2:5 They will give me food and w,
5:10 pour my fury on them like w.
6:3 spring rains that w the ground.
10:7 like a piece of wood on w.
Joe 3:18 W will flow in all the brooks of
3:18 It will w the valley of Shittim.
Amo 4:8 city in order to get a drink of w.
5:8 He calls for w from the sea to
9:6 the one who calls for the w in
Jnh 2:3 and w surrounded me.
2:5 "W surrounded me,
Mic 1:4 Valleys will split apart like w
Nah 2:8 Nineveh was like a pool of w
3:8 Nile with w surrounding her?
3:8 The w was her wall.
3:14 Store w for the siege!
Hab 2:14 glory like the w covers the sea.
Zec 14:8 On that day living w will flow
Mat 3:11 I baptize you with w so that
3:16 came up from the w.
8:32 into the sea and died in the w.
10:42 followers a cup of cold w
14:28 me to come to you on the w."
14:29 walked on the w toward Jesus.
17:15 Often he falls into fire or w.
27:24 So Pilate took some w and
Mar 1:8 I have baptized you with w,
1:10 As Jesus came out of the w,
4:1 The boat was in the w while
9:22 thrown him into fire or into w
9:41 Whoever gives you a cup of w
14:13 meet a man carrying a jug of w.
Luk 3:16 "I baptize you with w.
5:4 "Take the boat into deep w,
8:23 The boat was taking on w,
8:25 orders to the wind and the w,
13:15 stall to give it some w to drink?
16:24 to dip the tip of his finger in w
22:10 meet a man carrying a jug of w.
Jon 1:26 them, "I baptize with w.
1:31 I came to baptize with w to
1:33 who sent me to baptize with w,
2:6 Six stone w jars were there.
2:7 "Fill the jars with w."
2:9 tasted the w that had become
2:9 who had poured the w knew.
3:5 being born of w and the Spirit.
3:23 W was plentiful there.
4:7 woman went to get some w.
4:7 "Give me a drink of w."
4:9 like me for a drink of w?"
4:10 have given you living w."
4:11 have anything to use to get w,
4:11 you going to get this living w?
4:12 his animals drank w from it."
4:13 "Everyone who drinks this w
4:14 But those who drink the w that
4:14 In fact, the w I will give them
4:15 Jesus, "Sir, give me this w!
4:15 or have to come here to get w."
4:28 Then the woman left her w jar
4:46 he had changed w into wine.
5:7 the pool when the w is stirred.
7:38 'Streams of living w will flow
13:5 Then he poured w into a basin
19:34 and w immediately came out.
Act 1:5 John baptized with w,
8:36 they came to some w.
8:36 Philip, "Look, there's some w.
8:38 and Philip stepped into the w,
8:39 they had stepped out of the w,
10:47 to baptize these people with w.
11:16 'John baptized with w,
27:28 with a weight on it into the w.
27:41 They struck a sandbar in the w
Eph 5:26 washing it using w along with
1Ti 5:23 Stop drinking only w.
Heb 9:19 goats together with some w,
10:22 been washed with clean w.
Jas 3:11 Do clean and polluted w flow
3:12 a pool of salt w can't produce
3:12 water can't produce fresh w.
1Pe 3:20 eight in all — were saved by w.
3:21 Baptism, which is like that w,
2Pe 3:5 The earth ⌊appeared⌋ out of w
3:5 water and was kept alive by w.
3:6 W also flooded and destroyed
1Jn 5:6 who came by w and blood.
5:6 He didn't come with w only,
5:6 but with w and with blood.
5:8 the Spirit, the w, and the blood.
Rev 7:17 springs filled with the w of life,
8:11 One-third of the w turned into
8:11 many people died from this w
11:6 They have authority to turn w
12:15 poured out a river of w behind
14:2 like the noise of raging w
Rev 16:5 I heard the angel of the w say,
16:12 The w in the river dried up to
21:6 the fountain filled with the w
22:1 a river filled with the w of life,
22:17 Let those who want the w of

watered (11)

Gen 24:46 and she also w the camels.
29:2 flocks were w from that well.
29:3 so that the sheep could be w.
29:10 well and w his uncle Laban's
Exo 2:17 and then w their sheep.
2:19 water for us and w the sheep."
Dtr 11:11 w by rain from the sky.
Psa 68:9 You w the land with plenty of
Isa 1:22 Your wine is w down.
58:11 You will become like a w
1Co 3:6 I planted, and Apollos w,

watering (3)

Gen 30:38 at the w places where the
Jdg 7:24 Capture the w holes as far as
7:24 They captured the w holes as

waterless (2)

Eze 19:13 in a dry and w land.
Zec 9:11 captives free from the w pit

watermelons (1)

Num 11:5 cucumbers, w, leeks, onions,

waters (18)

Exo 7:19 out your hand over the w
8:6 his staff over the w of Egypt.
Jdg 5:19 Taanach by the w of Megiddo.
Job 12:15 When he holds back the w,
Psa 23:2 leads me beside peaceful w.
78:13 He made the w stand up like a
144:7 and rescue me from raging w
Pro 3:20 the deep w were divided,
8:29 so the w would not overstep
9:17 "Stolen w are sweet,
18:4 person's mouth are like deep w.
Hab 3:15 into the mighty raging w.
1Co 3:7 nor the one who w is important
3:8 plants and the one who w have
Rev 1:15 was like the sound of raging w.
17:1 prostitute who sits on raging w.
17:15 said to me, "The w you saw,
19:6 like the noise of raging w,

waterspouts (1)

Psa 42:7 to another at the roar of your w.

watery (1)

Jnh 2:2 From the depths of my ⌊w⌋

wave (5)

2Ki 5:11 w his hand over the ⌊infected⌋
Psa 20:5 We will w our flags in the
72:16 May it w ⌊in the breeze⌋ on the
Isa 11:15 He will w his hand over the
Jas 1:6 doubts is like a w that is blown

waved (1)

Nah 2:3 do the spears when they are w

wavering (1)

Psa 26:1 I have trusted you without w.

waves (32)

Exo 15:8 The w stood up like a dam.
Dtr 28:22 inflammation; heat w, drought,
2Sm 22:5 The w of death had surrounded
1Ki 8:37 Plant diseases, heat w,
2Ch 6:28 Plant diseases, heat w,
Job 9:8 and walks on the w of the sea.
38:11 Here your proud w will stop'?
Psa 42:7 All the whitecaps on your w
46:3 shake at the surging w.
65:7 of the seas, their crashing w,
88:7 You make all your w pound on
89:9 When its w rise, you quiet
93:3 rises with its pounding w.
93:4 than the foaming w of the sea.
107:25 and it made the w rise high.

Psa 107:29 and the **w** became still.
Isa 48:18 would be like **w** on the sea.
51:15 the sea and makes its **w** roar.
Jer 5:22 the **w** toss continuously,
31:35 He stirs up the sea so that its **w**
51:42 and its roaring **w** will cover it.
51:55 **W** of enemies will come
Eze 26:3 nations against you as the **w**
Jnh 2:3 All the whitecaps on your **w**
Hab 3:10 ocean roars. Its **w** rise up high.
Zec 10:11 strike the **w** in the sea,
Mat 8:24 The **w** were covering the boat.
14:24 being thrown around by the **w**
Mar 4:37 The **w** were breaking into the
Luk 8:24 the wind and the **w** to stop.
Act 27:41 to pieces by the force of the **w**.
Jud 1:13 is like the foam on the wild **w**

wavy (1)

Sos 5:11 His hair is **w**, black as a raven.

wax (4)

Psa 22:14 My heart is like **w**.
68:2 in God's presence like **w** next
97:5 The mountains melt like **w** in
Mic 1:4 will melt under him like **w** near

wayside (1)

Pro 8:2 by the **w** where the roads meet,

wayward (1)

Isa 29:24 Then those who are **w** in spirit

weak (62)

Gen 30:42 the flocks in heat were **w**,
Num 13:18 living there are strong or **w**,
1Sm 15:9 that was worthless and **w**
2Sm 3:39 Today I'm **w**, though I'm the
17:2 him while he's tired and **w**,
2Ki 19:26 who live in these cities are **w**,
Job 4:3 When hands were **w**,
4:4 When knees were **w**,
Psa 6:2 me, O LORD, because I am **w**.
35:10 You rescue the **w** person from
35:10 who is too strong for him and **w**
74:21 Let **w** and needy people praise
82:3 Defend **w** people and orphans.
82:4 Rescue **w** and needy people.
88:9 My eyes grow **w** because of
116:6 When I was **w**, he saved me.
119:81 My soul is **w** from waiting for
142:6 for help because I am very **w**.
Pro 24:10 you faint in a crisis, you are **w**.
Sos 2:5 because I am **w** from love.
Isa 14:10 also have become **w** like us!
35:3 limp hands. Steady **w** knees.
37:27 who live in these cities are **w**,
40:29 strength of those who are **w**.
50:2 Am I too **w** to reclaim you?
59:1 The LORD is not too **w** to save
Jer 49:24 people of Damascus are **w**.
Eze 7:17 knee will be as **w** as water.
21:7 will become as **w** as water.
29:14 There they will be a **w**
29:15 I will make them so **w** that they
34:4 those that were **w**,
Mat 26:41 do what's right, but you're **w**."
Mar 14:38 do what's right, but you're **w**."
Act 20:35 like this we should help the **w**.
Rom 14:1 people who are **w** in faith,
14:2 Other people with **w** faith
1Co 1:27 what the world considers **w**
2:3 When I came to you, I was **w**.
4:10 We are **w**, but you are strong.
8:7 because their conscience is **w**.
8:9 make a believer who is **w**
8:10 suppose someone with a **w**
8:11 a believer whose faith is **w**,
8:12 and harm their **w** consciences,
9:22 I became like a person **w** in
9:22 to win those who are **w** in faith.
11:30 reason why many of you are **w**
15:43 have any splendor and is **w**.
2Co 11:29 When anyone is **w**,
11:29 anyone is weak, I'm **w** too.
11:30 things that show how **w** I am.
12:9 is strongest when you are **w**."
12:10 It's clear that when I'm **w**,
13:3 Christ isn't **w** in dealing with
13:4 He was **w** when he was
13:4 We are **w** with him,
13:9 We're glad when we are **w** and
1Th 5:14 are discouraged, help the **w**,
Heb 7:18 they are **w** and useless.
11:34 strength when they were **w**.
12:12 your tired arms and **w** knees.

weak-minded (1)

2Ti 3:6 and mislead **w** women who are

weaken (2)

Psa 32:3 my bones began to **w** because
Rom 4:19 Abraham didn't **w**. Through faith

weakened (2)

Psa 102:23 He has **w** my strength along
Lam 1:14 He has **w** me ⌊with them⌋.

weaker (5)

Gen 30:42 So the **w** ones belonged to
2Sm 3:1 family became **w** and weaker.
3:1 family became weaker and **w**.
1Co 12:22 body that we think are **w** are
1Pe 3:7 since they are **w** than you are.

weakest (3)

Jdg 6:15 It's the **w** one in Manasseh.
Isa 60:22 The **w** of them will become a
Eze 29:15 They will be the **w** kingdom,

weakling (1)

2Co 10:10 but that I'm a **w** and a terrible

weaklings (1)

Joe 3:10 **W** should say that they are

weakness (6)

Isa 61:3 praise instead of a spirit of **w**.
Rom 6:19 a human way because of the **w**
8:3 of the **w** our human nature
8:26 Spirit also helps us in our **w**,
1Co 1:25 and God's **w** is stronger than
2Co 12:10 Therefore, I accept **w**,

weaknesses (8)

Mat 8:17 "He took away our **w** and
Rom 15:1 must be patient with the **w**
2Co 12:5 myself unless it's about my **w**.
12:9 brag even more about my **w**
Heb 4:15 able to sympathize with our **w**.
5:2 because he also has **w**.
5:3 Because he has **w**,
7:28 even though they had **w**.

wealth (96)

Gen 31:1 has gained all his **w** from him."
31:16 Certainly, all the **w** that God
34:29 They carried off all the **w** and
Exo 3:22 you will strip Egypt of its **w**."
12:36 stripped Egypt of its **w**.
Jos 22:8 your homes with your vast **w**,
1Sm 2:7 causes poverty and grants **w**.
1Ki 10:7 Your wisdom and **w** surpass
10:23 In **w** and wisdom King
2Ki 23:35 according to his **w** so that
1Ch 29:16 "LORD, our God, all this **w** that
29:28 life was full of **w** and honor.
2Ch 9:22 In **w** and wisdom King
Est 1:4 showed them the enormous **w**
Job 5:5 thirsty people pant after his **w**.
6:22 'Offer me a bribe from your **w**,'
15:29 and his **w** won't last.
20:10 will have to give back his **w**.
20:22 ⌊Even⌋ with all his **w** the full
22:20 their **w** has been wiped out,
31:25 hand had found great ⌊**w**⌋ ....
Psa 37:16 person has is better than the **w**
49:6 brag about their abundant **w**.
52:7 Instead, he trusted his great **w**
112:3 **W** and riches will be in his
Pro 3:9 Honor the LORD with your **w**
8:18 lasting **w** and righteousness.
10:15 The rich person's **w** is ⌊his⌋
13:7 to be poor but has great **w**.
13:11 **W** ⌊gained⌋ through injustice
13:22 but the **w** of sinners is stored
14:24 of wise people is their **w**.
18:11 A rich person's **w** is his strong
19:4 **W** adds many friends,
19:14 Home and **w** are inherited from
21:6 Those who gather **w** by lying
21:20 Costly treasure and **w** are in
22:1 is more desirable than great **w**.
23:5 a fleeting glimpse of **w** before
27:24 **W** is not forever. Nor does a
29:3 pays prostitutes wastes his **w**.
Ecc 2:26 gathering and collecting ⌊**w**⌋.
2:26 The sinner must turn his **w**
5:10 Whoever loves **w** will never be
5:19 people **w** and possessions,
6:2 gives one person riches, **w**,
Sos 8:7 all his family's **w** for love,
Isa 8:4 the **w** of Damascus and the
10:3 Where will you leave your **w**?
15:7 That is why they carry the **w**
60:5 The **w** of the nations will come
60:11 may bring you the **w** of nations,
61:6 You will consume the **w** of the
61:7 a double measure of **w** instead
61:7 You will sing about your **w**
61:7 have a double measure of **w**
66:12 peace like a river and the **w**
Jer 15:13 I will give away your **w** and
17:3 I will turn your **w** and all your
17:11 he will lose his **w**.
48:36 The **w** they gained has
Eze 7:11 of that crowd, none of their **w**,
27:27 Your **w**, your merchandise,
27:33 many people with your great **w**
28:5 arrogant because of your **w**.
29:19 He will carry off its **w**,
30:4 will take away Egypt's **w**,
Dan 11:2 becomes strong through his **w**,
11:24 He will distribute loot and **w** to
11:28 to his country with a lot of **w**.
Hos 12:8 With all this **w**, no one will find
Oba 1:11 strangers carried off Jacob's **w**.
1:13 their **w** when disaster strikes.
Mic 4:13 their **w** for the Lord of the whole
Zep 1:13 Their **w** will be looted.
Zec 9:4 He will throw its **w** into the sea
14:14 The **w** of all the surrounding
Mat 6:24 You cannot serve God and **w**.
Luk 16:9 "I'm telling you that although **w**
16:11 if you can't be trusted with **w**
16:11 trust you with **w** that is real?
16:12 trusted with someone else's **w**,
16:13 You cannot serve God and **w**."
Rom 15:27 have shared the spiritual **w**
15:27 their earthly **w** to help them.
2Co 11:20 consumes your **w**,
Eph 1:18 glorious **w** that God's people
3:8 News of the immeasurable **w**
3:16 to give you a gift from the **w**
5:5 worshiping **w**) can have any
Col 3:5 same thing as worshiping **w**).
2Pe 1:11 you will also be given the **w**
Rev 5:12 **w**, wisdom, strength, honor,
18:3 Her luxurious **w** has made the
18:17 In one moment all this **w** has
21:26 They will bring the glory and **w**

wealthy (13)

Gen 24:35 and he has become **w**.
30:43 Jacob became very **w**.
Num 24:18 So Israel will become **w**.
Dtr 8:17 "I became **w** because of my
8:18 is the one who makes you **w**.
2Ki 15:20 the money from all the **w** men
2Ch 18:1 Jehoshaphat was **w** and
Psa 73:12 They grow more and more **w**.
Pro 12:27 person becomes **w**.
28:8 Whoever becomes **w** through
Eze 28:5 you've made yourself very **w**.
Hab 2:6 and makes himself **w** on loans.
Rev 3:17 I'm **w**. I don't need anything.'

weaned (9)

Gen 21:8 The child grew and was **w**.
21:8 On the day Isaac was **w**,
1Sm 1:22 "I'll wait until the boy is **w**.
1:23 "Wait until you've **w** him.
1:23 her son until she had **w** him.
1:24 As soon as she had **w** Samuel,
Psa 131:2 My soul is content as a **w** child
Isa 28:9 To children just **w** from milk?
Hos 1:8 Gomer had **w** Lo Ruhamah,

weapon (19)

Num 35:16 if any of you uses an iron **w**
35:17 of you picks up a stone as a **w**
35:18 up a piece of wood as a **w**
Jdg 5:8 Not a **w** was seen among
1Sm 21:8 either my spear or any other **w**
21:9 There's no other **w** here."
2Sm 2:21 young men, and take his **w**."
24:16 "Put down your **w**."
1Ch 12:33 for battle with every kind of **w**.
21:15 "Put down your **w**."
2Ch 23:7 Each man should have his **w**
Job 20:24 person flees from an iron **w**,
Pro 22:8 and this **w** of his own fury will
Isa 54:17 No **w** that has been made to be
Jer 49:35 important **w** of their strength.
51:20 war club and my **w** for battle.
Eze 7:11 Violence has grown into a **w**
9:1 should bring your **w** with you."
9:2 brought a deadly **w** with him.

weapons (39)

Gen 49:5 Their swords are **w** of violence.
1Sm 8:12 and to make **w** and equipment
20:40 Then Jonathan gave his **w** to
2Sm 1:27 See how the **w** of war have
1Ki 10:25 **w**, spices, horses, and mules.
2Ki 10:2 horses, fortified cities, and **w**.
11:8 Each man should have his **w**
11:11 The guards stood with their **w**
1Ch 12:37 to fight with all kinds of **w**.
2Ch 9:24 **w**, spices, horses, and mules.
23:10 All the troops stood with their **w**
32:5 made plenty of **w** and shields.
Neh 4:17 and held their **w** with the other,
4:23 We each kept our **w** at hand.
Psa 7:13 He prepares his deadly **w** and
75:4 "Don't raise your **w**.
75:5 Don't raise your **w** so proudly or
75:10 I will destroy all the **w** of
75:10 but the **w** of righteous people
76:3 shields, swords, and **w** of war.
Ecc 9:18 Wisdom is better than **w** of war,
Isa 13:5 LORD is coming with the **w**
22:8 You will look for **w** in the
54:16 and to produce useful **w**.
Jer 21:4 I'm going to take your **w** away
21:4 You are using these **w** to fight
22:7 They will have their own **w**.
33:4 against the dirt ramps and **w**
50:25 his armory and bring out the **w**
Lam 2:17 raised the **w** of your opponents.
Eze 32:27 to the grave with their **w** of war.
39:9 They will set fire to **w** and burn
39:10 will make fires with the **w**.
Hos 2:18 bows, swords, and **w** of war,
Luk 11:22 man will take away all the **w**
Jon 18:3 lanterns, torches, and **w**.
Rom 13:12 and take up the **w** that belong
2Co 10:4 The **w** we use in our fight are
10:4 they are powerful **w** from God.

wear (73)

Gen 28:20 food to eat and clothes to **w**,
Exo 18:18 people will **w** yourselves out.
28:35 Aaron must **w** it when he
28:43 Aaron and his sons must **w**
29:30 in the holy place — will **w** them
Lev 13:45 disease must **w** torn clothes
16:4 and **w** linen undergarments.
16:4 He must **w** a linen belt and
19:19 Never **w** clothes made from
Num 15:38 to come they must **w** tassels
Dtr 6:8 and **w** them as headbands as a
Dtr 8:4 Your clothes didn't **w** out,
11:18 and **w** them as headbands as a
21:13 and no longer **w** the clothes
22:5 A woman must never **w**
22:5 wear anything men would **w**,
22:5 must never **w** women's clothes.
22:11 Never **w** clothes made of wool
22:12 shawl you **w** over your clothes.
1Sm 2:28 and to **w** the ephod in my
1Ki 22:30 but you should **w** your royal
2Ch 18:29 but you should **w** your royal
Neh 9:21 Their clothes didn't **w** out,
Job 27:17 righteous people will **w** what
Psa 73:6 That is why they **w** arrogance
76:10 You will **w** the remainder of
102:26 They will all **w** out like
109:29 Let those who accuse me **w**
Pro 23:4 Do not **w** yourself out getting
Ecc 9:8 Always **w** clean clothes,
10:15 Fools **w** themselves out with
12:12 studying will **w** out your body.
Sos 8:6 **W** me as a signet ring on your
Isa 3:24 They will **w** ropes instead of
3:24 They will **w** sackcloth instead
15:3 their streets they **w** sackcloth.
16:12 will only **w** themselves out.
32:11 and **w** sackcloth around your
49:18 "you will **w** all of them like
50:9 They will all **w** out like a
51:6 The earth will **w** out like
Jer 4:30 Why do you **w** eye shadow?
6:26 **W** sackcloth, and roll around in
9:5 They **w** themselves out doing
20:9 I **w** myself out holding it in,
51:58 The nations **w** themselves out
Lam 4:5 Those who used to **w**
Eze 44:17 they must **w** linen clothes.
44:18 They must **w** linen turbans on
44:18 They must not **w** anything that
Dan 5:7 **w** a gold chain on his neck,
5:16 **w** a gold chain on your neck,
5:29 be dressed in purple and **w**
Hag 1:6 You **w** clothing, but you never
Mat 6:25 what you will eat, drink, or **w**.
6:31 or 'What are we going to **w**?'
11:8 Those who **w** fine clothes are
25:36 you gave me something to **w**.
25:38 and give you something to **w**?
25:43 didn't give me anything to **w**.
Mar 6:9 They could **w** sandals but
Luk 7:25 Those who **w** splendid clothes
12:22 about what you will eat or **w**.
12:33 wallets that don't **w** out!
1Co 4:12 We **w** ourselves out doing
11:10 Therefore, a woman should **w**
11:15 pride to **w** her hair long?
15:49 we will also **w** the likeness of
1Ti 2:9 or expensive clothes they **w**.
Heb 1:11 They will all **w** out like clothes.
Rev 3:5 this way will **w** white clothes.
3:18 **W** them so that you may keep
11:3 witnesses who **w** sackcloth

wearing (37)

Exo 28:29 He must do this by **w** the
32:2 off the gold earrings they are **w**,
32:24 take off any gold they were **w**.
Dtr 21:13 she was **w** when you captured
Rut 3:15 "Stretch out the cape you're **w**
1Sm 2:18 (already) **w** a linen ephod.
14:3 Ahijah was **w** the priestly
22:18 that day he killed 85 men **w**
28:14 and he's **w** a robe."
2Sm 6:14 **W** a linen ephod, David danced
13:18 (She was **w** a long-sleeved
2Ki 6:30 the people saw that he was **w**
Neh 4:16 and the other half were **w** body
Est 1:11 **w** her royal crown.
4:2 (No one could enter it **w**
8:15 from the presence of the king **w**
Psa 45:14 **W** a colorful gown,
Isa 20:2 the sackcloth that you are **w**,
22:12 heads and for **w** sackcloth.
Jer 13:4 you bought, the one you're **w**.
Dan 3:21 They were **w** their clothes,
Zec 3:3 Joshua was **w** filthy clothes
Jon 19:5 He was **w** the crown of thorns
Act 12:21 Herod, **w** his royal clothes,
28:20 I'm **w** these chains because of
2Co 4:16 outwardly we are **w** out,
Jas 2:2 One man is **w** gold rings and
2:2 is **w** shabby clothes.
2:3 to the man **w** fine clothes
Rev 1:13 He was **w** a robe that reached
4:4 sat 24 leaders **w** white clothes.
7:9 They were **w** white robes,
7:13 these people **w** white robes,
15:6 out of the temple **w** clean,
18:16 city which was **w** fine linen,
19:8 the privilege of **w** dazzling,
19:14 The armies of heaven, **w** pure,

wears (10)

Lev 21:10 who is anointed with oil and **w**
Dtr 24:13 When he **w** his coat to bed
Job 14:19 (so) water **w** away stone,
Psa 45:9 hand and **w** gold from Ophir.
109:19 a belt he always **w**."
Pro 26:15 He **w** himself out as he brings
Ecc 11:10 you or **w** down your body,
Isa 59:17 He **w** clothes of vengeance.
Luk 18:5 to me until she **w** me out.'"
Rev 19:13 He **w** clothes dipped in blood,

weary (11)

Job 3:17 There the **w** are able to rest.
Pro 30:1 This man's declaration: "I'm **w**,
30:1 I'm **w** and worn out,
Isa 32:2 of a large rock in a **w** land.
40:28 doesn't grow tired or become **w**.
40:30 grow tired and become **w**,
40:31 will run and won't become **w**.
46:1 a load for **w** people.
50:4 how to encourage **w** people.
Jer 31:25 I will give those who are **w** all
Rev 2:3 and have not grown **w**.

weather (4)

Mat 16:2 evening you say that the **w** will
16:3 You can forecast the **w** by
Luk 12:56 You can forecast the **w** by
2Co 11:27 proper clothes during cold **w**.

weave (5)

Exo 35:35 They know how to **w** yarn on a
Jdg 16:13 Samson replied, "Just **w** the
Job 8:17 Its roots **w** through a pile of
10:11 and flesh and **w** me together
Isa 59:5 viper eggs and **w** spiderwebs.

weaver (1)

Isa 38:12 You rolled up my life like a **w**.

weaver's (2)

1Ch 11:23 had a spear like a **w** beam
Job 7:6 go swifter than a **w** shuttle.

weavers (5)

1Sm 17:7 was like the beam used by **w**.
2Sm 21:19 was like a beam used by **w**.)
1Ch 20:5 was like a beam used by **w**.)
Isa 19:9 and **w** will be ashamed.
19:10 Egypt's **w** will be crushed.

weaving (1)

2Ki 23:7 women did **w** for Asherah.

web (1)

Job 8:14 His trust is a spider's **w**.

webbing (1)

Job 18:8 as he walks around on its **w**.

webs (1)

Isa 59:6 Their **w** can't be used for

wedding (21)

Gen 29:22 that place and gave a **w** feast.
29:27 Finish the week of **w**
1Ki 9:16 wife, as a **w** present.)
Psa 78:63 so his virgins heard no **w**
Sos 3:11 placed on him on his **w** day,

Mat 9:15 Jesus replied, "Can **w** guests
22:2 who planned a **w** for his son.
22:3 who had been invited to the **w**,
22:4 is ready. Come to the **w**!'
22:8 his servants, 'The **w** is ready,
22:9 everyone you find to the **w**.'
22:10 And the **w** hall was filled with
22:11 in the **w** clothes ⌊provided
22:12 here without proper **w** clothes?'
25:10 went with him into the **w** hall,
Mar 2:19 Jesus replied, "Can **w** guests
Luk 5:34 "Can you force **w** guests to fast
12:36 when he returns from a **w**.
14:8 someone invites you to a **w**,
Jon 2:1 Three days later a **w** took
Rev 19:9 to the lamb's **w** banquet.'"

weeds (17)

Job 31:40 and foul-smelling **w** instead of
Pro 24:31 ground was covered with **w**,
Isa 5:6 Thorns and **w** will grow in it,
10:17 will burn up and devour the **w**
Hos 9:6 **W** will grow over their silver
10:4 spring up like poisonous **w**
10:8 Thorns and **w** will grow over
Zep 2:9 a place of **w**, salt pits,
Mat 13:25 his enemy planted **w** in the
13:26 formed kernels, **w** appeared.
13:27 Where did the **w** come from?'
13:28 you want us to pull out the **w**?'
13:29 If you pull out the **w**,
13:30 the workers to gather the **w** first
13:36 what the illustration of the **w**
13:38 The **w** are those who belong to
13:40 Just as **w** are gathered and

week (8)

Gen 29:27 Finish the **w** of wedding
29:28 He finished the **w** with Leah.
Exo 16:30 on the seventh day of the **w**.
Lev 23:16 the day after the seventh **w**.
Isa 66:23 to the next and from one **w**
Luk 18:12 I fast twice a **w**, and I give you
Jon 20:26 A **w** later Jesus' disciples were
Act 28:14 us to spend a **w** with them.

weekly (10)

1Ch 23:31 made — on **w** worship days,
2Ch 2:4 on **w** worship days,
8:13 on **w** worship days,
31:3 on the **w** worship days,
Neh 10:33 on the **w** days of worship,
Eze 45:17 the **w** days of worship,
46:1 but it must be opened on the **w**
46:3 of the LORD on the **w** days
Hos 2:11 her **w** worship days — all her
Col 2:16 or **w** worship days.

weeks (11)

Exo 34:22 celebrate the Festival of **W**
Lev 12:5 she will be unclean for two **w**.
23:15 "Count seven full **w** from the
Num 28:26 "During the Festival of **W**,
Dtr 16:9 Count seven **w** from the time
16:10 celebrate the Festival of **W**
16:16 Bread, the Festival of **W**,
2Ch 8:13 Bread, the Festival of **W**,
Pro 7:20 be home for a couple of **w**."
Dan 10:2 mourned for three whole **w**.
10:3 the entire three **w** were over.

weep (3)

Psa 78:64 could not even **w** ⌊for them⌋.
Jer 9:10 I will cry and **w** for the
48:31 That is why I will **w** for Moab

weeping (4)

Est 4:3 fasting, **w**, and wailing.
Job 30:31 and my flute for loud **w**.
Psa 30:5 **W** may last for the night,
126:6 The person who goes out **w**,

weigh (9)

1Ch 20:2 was found to **w** 75 pounds,
Ezr 8:29 LORD's temple, **w** these items.
Job 31:6 ⌊then⌋ let God **w** me on
Pro 12:25 anxiety will **w** him down,
Isa 46:6 out of their bags and **w** silver
Eze 5:1 Take scales to **w** your hair and
33:10 and our sins **w** us down,
45:12 One shekel must **w** 20 gerahs.
45:12 One mina must **w** 60 shekels.

weighed (76)

Gen 23:16 So he **w** out for Ephron the
Exo 30:24 12 ½ pounds of cassia — all **w**
38:24 place **w** over 2,193 pounds,
38:25 was taken **w** 7,544 pounds,
38:29 to the LORD **w** 5,310 pounds.
Lev 5:15 its value in silver **w** according
Num 3:50 Israelites **w** 34 pounds,
7:13 He brought a silver plate that **w**
7:13 bowl that **w** 1 ¾ pounds,
7:14 a gold dish that **w** 4 ounces,
7:19 He brought a silver plate that **w**
7:19 silver bowl that **w** 1 ¾ pounds
7:20 a gold dish that **w** 4 ounces,
7:25 a silver plate that **w** 3 ¼
7:25 silver bowl that **w** 1 ¾ pounds
7:26 a gold dish that **w** 4 ounces,
7:31 a silver plate that **w** 3 ¼
7:31 silver bowl that **w** 1 ¾ pounds
7:32 a gold dish that **w** 4 ounces,
7:37 a silver plate that **w** 3 ¼
7:37 silver bowl that **w** 1 ¾ pounds
7:38 a gold dish that **w** 4 ounces,
7:43 a silver plate that **w** 3 ¼
7:43 silver bowl that **w** 1 ¾ pounds
7:44 a gold dish that **w** 4 ounces,
7:49 a silver plate that **w** 3 ¼
7:49 silver bowl that **w** 1 ¾ pounds
7:50 a gold dish that **w** 4 ounces,
7:55 a silver plate that **w** 3 ¼
7:55 silver bowl that **w** 1 ¾ pounds
7:56 a gold dish that **w** 4 ounces,
7:61 a silver plate that **w** 3 ¼
7:61 silver bowl that **w** 1 ¾ pounds
7:62 a gold dish that **w** 4 ounces,
7:67 a silver plate that **w** 3 ¼
7:67 silver bowl that **w** 1 ¾ pounds
7:68 a gold dish that **w** 4 ounces,
7:73 a silver plate that **w** 3 ¼
7:73 silver bowl that **w** 1 ¾ pounds
7:74 a gold dish that **w** 4 ounces,
7:79 a silver plate that **w** 3 ¼
7:79 silver bowl that **w** 1 ¾ pounds
7:80 a gold dish that **w** 4 ounces,
7:85 Each silver plate **w** 3 ¼
7:85 and each bowl **w** 1 ¾ pounds.
7:85 Together all the silver dishes **w**
7:86 with incense **w** 4 ounces each,
7:86 gold dishes **w** about 3 pounds.
31:52 **w** about 420 pounds.
Jdg 8:26 had asked for **w** 40 pounds.
2Sm 12:30 (The crown **w** 75 pounds and
14:26 the hair on his head and **w** it,
14:26 it **w** five pounds according to
1Ki 7:47 how much the bronze **w**.
10:14 in one year **w** 49,950 pounds,
2Ki 12:11 the money that had been **w**
25:16 LORD's temple couldn't be **w**.
1Ch 22:3 bronze that it couldn't be **w**.
22:14 and iron that it can't be **w**.
2Ch 3:9 The gold nails **w** 20 ounces.
4:18 how much the bronze **w**.
9:13 in one year **w** 49,950 pounds,
Ezr 8:25 I **w** for them the silver,
8:26 I **w** ⌊the contributions⌋ for them
8:33 the fourth day we **w** the silver,
8:34 Everything was counted and **w**,
Job 6:2 "If only my grief could be **w**,
Psa 62:9 When all of them are **w** on a
Ecc 1:13 Mortals are **w** down with a
3:10 I have seen mortals **w** down
Isa 40:12 earth in a bushel basket or **w**
Jer 52:20 LORD's temple couldn't be **w**.
Eze 4:10 food that you eat should be **w**.
Dan 5:25 Numbered, **W**, and Divided.
5:27 **W** — you have been weighed
5:27 Weighed — you have been **w**

weighing (7)

Gen 24:22 took out a gold nose ring **w**
24:22 gold bracelets **w** four ounces.
Jos 7:21 and a bar of gold **w** about one
1Sm 17:5 of armor scales **w** 125 pounds.
2Sm 21:16 who had a bronze spear **w** 7
Ezr 8:26 100 silver utensils **w** 150
8:27 20 gold bowls **w** 18 pounds

weighs (6)

1Sm 2:3 and he **w** ⌊our⌋ actions.
Pro 16:2 but the LORD **w** motives.
21:2 but the LORD **w** hearts.
24:12 won't the one who **w** hearts
27:3 is heavy, and sand **w** a lot,
Isa 24:20 Its disobedience **w** heavy on it.

weight (42)

Exo 30:13 of silver using the standard **w**
30:24 weighed using the standard **w**
38:24 using the standard **w** of the
38:25 using the standard **w** of the
Lev 19:35 length, **w**, or measuring liquid.
27:3 Use the standard **w** of the holy
27:25 be set using the standard **w**
Num 3:47 person (using the standard **w**
3:50 using the standard **w** of the
7:13 using the standard **w** of the
7:19 pounds using the standard **w**
7:25 pounds using the standard **w**
7:31 pounds using the standard **w**
7:37 pounds using the standard **w**
7:43 pounds using the standard **w**
7:49 pounds using the standard **w**
7:55 pounds using the standard **w**
7:61 pounds using the standard **w**
7:67 pounds using the standard **w**
7:73 pounds using the standard **w**
7:79 pounds using the standard **w**
7:85 using the standard **w** of the
7:86 using the standard **w** of the
18:16 using the standard **w** of the
2Sm 18:12 "Even if I felt the **w** of 25
1Ch 28:14 ⌊David specified⌋ the **w** of
28:15 the **w** of the gold lamp stands
28:15 the **w** of gold for each lamp
28:15 the **w** of silver for each silver
28:16 the **w** of gold for each table
28:17 the **w** of each gold bowl,
28:17 the **w** of each silver bowl,
Ezr 8:34 and the entire **w** was recorded
Job 8:15 it will not support his **w**.
26:8 ⌊even⌋ split under its ⌊**w**⌋.
35:9 The **w** of oppression makes
Psa 10:10 fall under ⌊the **w** of⌋ his power.
31:10 under ⌊the **w** of⌋ my guilt,
Isa 22:24 will hang on him the whole **w**
40:15 The **w** of the islands is like
Lam 4:2 who are worth their **w** in fine
Act 27:28 So they threw a line with a **w**

weights (11)

Lev 19:36 Use honest scales, honest **w**,
Dtr 25:13 Never carry two sets of **w**,
25:15 and honest **w** and measures.
25:16 who uses dishonest **w**
1Ch 23:29 track of all **w** and measures.
Pro 11:1 but accurate **w** are pleasing to
16:11 He made the entire set of **w**.
20:10 A double standard of **w** and
20:23 A double standard of **w** is
Mic 6:10 inaccurate **w** and measures.
6:11 bags filled with inaccurate **w**.

welcome (29)

Gen 32:20 and he'll **w** me back."
Jdg 19:20 Then the old man said, "**W**!
Neh 13:2 (After all, they didn't **w** the
Job 3:12 Why did knees **w** me?
Mal 1:8 Would he **w** you?"
1:9 Will he **w** you?" asks the LORD
Mat 5:47 if you **w** only your friends?
10:14 If anyone doesn't **w** you or
Mar 6:11 Wherever people don't **w** you or
9:15 to see Jesus and ran to **w** him.

Luk 8:13 They **w** the word with joy
9:5 If people don't **w** you,
9:53 But the people didn't **w** him,
10:8 a city and the people **w** you,
10:10 a city and people don't **w** you,
16:4 that people will **w** me into their
19:6 was glad to **w** Jesus into his
Act 7:59 out, "Lord Jesus, **w** my spirit."
18:27 in Greece to tell them to **w** him.
25:13 city of Caesarea to **w** Festus.
Rom 14:1 **W** people who are weak in
16:2 Give her a Christian **w** that
2Co 6:17 Then I will **w** you."
Php 2:29 Give him a joyful Christian **w**.
Col 4:10 If he comes to you, **w** him.
Phm 1:17 **w** him as you would welcome
1:17 welcome him as you would **w**
Heb 11:31 led the prostitute Rahab to **w**
1Pe 4:9 **W** each other as guests

welcomed (19)

Gen 33:10 and yet you **w** me so warmly.
1Ch 12:18 So David **w** them and made
Psa 21:3 You **w** him with the blessings
Luk 8:40 came back, a crowd **w** him.
9:11 He **w** them, talked to them
10:38 A woman named Martha **w** him
16:9 When life is over, you will be **w**
Jon 4:45 the people of Galilee **w** him.
Act 15:4 and the spiritual leaders **w**
17:7 and Jason has **w** them as his
21:17 the believers **w** us warmly.
28:2 They made a fire and **w** all of
28:7 He **w** us and treated us kindly,
28:30 and **w** everyone who came
2Co 7:15 and how you **w** him with fear
Gal 4:14 Instead, you **w** me as if I were
1Th 1:6 you **w** God's word with the
1:9 They talk about how you **w** us
Jas 2:25 of the prostitute Rahab who **w**

welcomes (17)

Mat 10:40 "The person who **w** you
10:40 who welcomes you **w** me,
10:40 and the person who **w** me
10:40 person who welcomes me **w**
10:41 The person who **w** a prophet
10:41 The person who **w** a righteous
18:5 And whoever **w** a child like
18:5 like this in my name **w** me.
Mar 9:37 "Whoever **w** a child like this in
9:37 like this in my name **w** me.
9:37 Whoever **w** me welcomes not
9:37 Whoever welcomes me **w** not
Luk 9:48 "Whoever **w** this little child in
9:48 little child in my name **w** me.
9:48 Whoever **w** me welcomes the
9:48 Whoever welcomes me **w** the
15:2 "This man **w** sinners and eats

welfare (2)

Est 10:3 his people and spoke for the **w**
Php 2:20 a genuine interest in your **w**.

well (36)

Gen 16:14 This is why the **w** is named
16:14 is named Beer Lahai Roi [W
21:19 Then she saw a **w**.
21:25 **w** which Abimelech's servants
21:30 may be proof that I dug this **w**."
24:11 down outside the city by the **w**.
24:20 ran back to the **w** to draw more
26:19 and found a spring-fed **w**.
26:20 named the **w** Esek [Argument],
26:21 Then they dug another **w**,
26:22 from there and dug another **w**.
26:25 and his servants dug a **w** there.
26:32 him about a **w** they had dug.
29:2 and out in a field he saw a **w**
29:2 were watered from that **w**.
29:3 off the opening of the **w** so that
29:3 over the opening of the **w**.
29:8 rolled off the opening of the **w**,
29:10 stone off the opening of the **w**
Exo 2:15 Moses was sitting by a **w**,
Num 21:16 there they went to Beer [W].
Num 21:16 This is the **w** where the LORD
21:17 sang this song about the **w**:
21:17 water spring up! Sing to the **w**,
21:18 the **w** dug by princes,
2Sm 23:15 a drink of water from the **w** at
23:16 and drew water from the **w**.
Pro 5:15 running water from your own **w**.
23:27 A loose woman is a narrow **w**.
25:26 spring and a polluted **w**,
Sos 4:15 a **w** of living water flowing from
Luk 14:5 son or your ox falls into a **w**
Jon 4:6 Jacob's **W** was there.
4:6 Jesus sat down by the **w**
4:11 and the **w** is deep.
4:12 He gave us this **w**.

well-armed (1)

Num 20:20 attacked with many **w** troops.

well-being (2)

Est 7:9 who spoke up for the **w** of the
Psa 119:122 Guarantee my **w**. Do not let

well-built (1)

Gen 39:6 Joseph was **w** and handsome.

well-equipped (1)

Psa 78:9 **w** with bows ⌊and arrows⌋,

well-fed (7)

Gen 41:2 **w** cows came up from the river
41:4 seven nice-looking, **w** cows.
41:18 **w** cows came up from the river
41:20 cows ate up the seven **w** ones.
1Sm 2:5 Those who were **w** hire
Jer 5:8 They are like **w** stallions that
Luk 6:25 it will be for those who are **w**.

well-grounded (2)

Tit 2:2 and to be **w** in faith,
2Pe 1:12 know about them and are **w**

well-informed (1)

Dan 1:4 in all subjects, **w**, intelligent,

well-known (9)

Num 16:2 **w** leaders of the community,
Est 9:25 he ordered, in the **w** letter,
9:29 the **w** celebration of Purim.
Mat 27:16 At that time there was a **w**
Mar 6:14 Jesus' name had become **w**.
Jon 3:10 "You're a **w** teacher of Israel.
18:15 The other disciple was **w** to
Act 21:39 a citizen from the **w** city of
2Co 6:9 unknown although we are **w**,

well-liked (1)

2Sm 1:23 loved and **w** while they were

wells (10)

Gen 26:15 in all the **w** that his father's
26:18 He dug out the **w** that had been
Num 20:17 any of the water from your **w**.
21:22 any of the water from your **w**.
Dtr 10:6 Israelites moved from the **w**
Jdg 5:11 of those singing at the **w**.
2Ki 3:19 every good tree, seal all the **w**,
19:24 I'll dig **w** and drink foreign
Isa 37:25 I'll dig **w** and drink water.
Hos 13:15 and their **w** will dry up.

well-trained (1)

Luk 6:40 But everyone who is **w** will be

well-watered (7)

Gen 13:10 whole Jordan Plain was **w** like
Dtr 29:19 sweep away **w** ground along
Job 8:16 He is like a **w** plant in the
Jer 31:12 lives will be like **w** gardens,
Eze 31:14 So no tree, even if it is **w**,
31:16 and all the trees that were **w**
45:15 every 200 from the **w** pastures

went (1250)

Gen 7:7 and his sons' wives **w** into the
7:13 **w** into the ship.
Gen 7:16 and a female of every animal **w**
9:22 So he **w** outside and told his
10:11 He **w** from that land to Assyria
12:4 and Lot **w** with him.
12:10 Abram **w** to Egypt to stay
12:16 Everything **w** well for Abram
13:1 and everything he had and **w**
13:3 He **w** from the Negev as far as
13:11 They each **w** their own way.
13:18 Abram moved his tents and **w**
14:2 **w** to war against ⌊five kings⌋—
18:22 there the men turned and **w**
19:3 with him and **w** into his home.
19:6 Then Lot **w** outside and shut
19:14 So Lot **w** out and spoke to the
19:33 Then the older one **w** to bed
19:34 Last night I **w** to bed with my
19:35 Then the younger one **w** to bed
21:16 Then she **w** about as far away
21:32 left and **w** back to the land of
22:6 The two of them **w** on together.
22:8 The two of them **w** on together.
23:2 Abraham **w** to mourn for Sarah
24:16 She **w** down to the spring,
24:32 So the man **w** into the house.
24:45 She **w** down to the spring and
24:63 Toward evening Isaac **w** out
25:22 So she **w** to ask the LORD.
26:1 So Isaac **w** to King Abimelech
26:23 He **w** from there to Beersheba.
27:5 When Esau **w** into the open
27:14 He **w** and got them and brought
27:18 He **w** to his father and said,
27:22 So Jacob **w** over to his father.
27:27 He **w** over and gave him a kiss.
28:5 Jacob **w** to live with Laban,
28:9 So he **w** to Ishmael and
30:14 harvest Reuben **w** out into
30:16 Leah **w** out to meet him.
30:16 "So he **w** to bed with her that
31:18 in Paddan Aram and **w** back
31:19 When Laban **w** to shear his
31:21 Euphrates River and **w** toward
31:33 So Laban **w** into Jacob's tent,
31:33 tent and **w** into Rachel's tent.
31:55 Laban left and **w** back home.
32:1 As Jacob **w** on his way,
32:6 "We **w** to your brother Esau.
33:3 He **w** on ahead of them and
34:1 **w** out to visit some of the
34:20 Hamor and his son Shechem **w**
35:13 Then God **w** up from him at the
35:16 Rachel **w** into labor and was
35:22 Reuben **w** to bed with his
36:6 accumulated in Canaan and **w**
37:17 So Joseph **w** after his brothers
37:30 He **w** back to his brothers and
38:1 Judah left his brothers and **w**
38:11 So Tamar **w** to live in her
38:12 his friend Hirah from Adullam **w**
38:22 So he **w** back to Judah and
39:11 One day he **w** into the house to
42:3 Ten of Joseph's brothers **w** to
43:15 They **w** to Egypt, where they
43:30 He **w** into his private room and
44:13 his donkey and **w** back into
44:18 Then Judah **w** up to Joseph
44:24 When we **w** back to our father,
46:26 direct descendants who **w**
46:27 in Jacob's household who **w**
46:29 prepared his chariot and **w**
47:1 Joseph **w** and told Pharaoh,
50:7 leaders of Egypt **w** with him.
50:8 household also **w** with him.
50:9 and horsemen **w** with him.
50:14 he **w** back to Egypt along with
Exo 2:11 Then he **w** to ⌊see⌋ his own
2:13 When Moses **w** there the next
2:23 their cries for help **w** up to God.
4:18 Then Moses **w** back to his
4:29 Then Moses and Aaron **w** ⌊to
5:1 Later Moses and Aaron **w** to
5:10 drivers and foreman **w** out
5:22 Moses **w** back to the LORD
5:23 Ever since I **w** to Pharaoh to
7:10 Moses and Aaron **w** to Pharaoh

1Sm 9:14 So Saul and his servant **w** to
9:26 and both he and Samuel **w**
9:27 (He **w** ahead.) "But you stay
10:2 the donkeys you **w** looking for.
10:14 find them, we **w** to Samuel."
10:26 Saul also **w** home to Gibeah.
10:26 With him **w** some soldiers
11:15 Then all the troops **w** to Gilgal,
12:8 When your ancestors **w** with
13:10 and Saul **w** to greet him.
13:15 They **w** from Gilgal to Gibeah
14:20 assembled and **w** into battle.
15:5 Saul **w** to the city of Amalek
15:12 Samuel was told, "Saul **w** to
15:12 he left there and **w** to Gilgal."
15:20 "I **w** where the LORD sent me,
15:34 Then Samuel **w** to Ramah,
15:34 and Saul **w** to his home at
17:15 David **w** back and forth from
17:20 He took ⌞the food⌟ and **w**,
17:20 He **w** to the camp as the army
17:35 I **w** after it, struck it,
18:27 David and his men **w** out and
18:30 The Philistine generals still **w**
18:30 But whenever they **w** out ⌞to
19:8 David **w** to fight the Philistines.
19:18 David escaped and **w** to
19:18 Then he and Samuel **w** to the
19:22 Then he **w** to Ramah himself.
19:22 He **w** as far as the big cistern
19:23 As he **w** toward the pastures at
20:11 So they **w** out into the country.
20:35 In the morning Jonathan **w** out
20:42 and Jonathan **w** into the city.
21:1 David **w** to the priest
21:1 was trembling as he **w**
22:1 heard about it, they **w** to him.
22:3 From there David **w** to Mizpah
22:5 So David **w** to the forest of
23:5 David and his men **w** to Keilah,
23:7 told that David **w** to Keilah,
23:13 They **w** wherever they could
23:18 and Jonathan **w** home.
23:19 Then the men of Ziph **w** to
23:25 So he **w** to his mountain
23:26 Saul **w** on one side of the
23:26 and David and his men **w** on
23:28 gave up pursuing David and **w**
23:29 From there David **w** to stay in
24:2 men from all Israel and **w**
24:3 Saul **w** into ⌞it⌟ to relieve
24:7 Saul left the cave and **w** out
24:22 Then Saul **w** home,
24:22 and David and his men **w** to
25:1 Then David **w** to the desert of
25:13 four hundred men **w** with David
25:15 was missing wherever we **w**
25:42 So she **w** with David's
26:2 Saul **w** to the desert of Ziph,
26:5 Then David **w** to the place
26:7 So David and Abishai **w**
26:13 David **w** over to the other side
26:25 So David **w** his way,
27:2 So David **w** with his 600 men
27:8 Then David and his men **w** to
29:11 the Philistines **w** to Jezreel.
30:9 So David and his 600 men **w** to
30:10 and 400 men **w** in pursuit,
2Sm 2:2 David **w** there with his two
2:12 Ishbosheth **w** from Mahanaim
2:23 The spear **w** into his belly and
2:24 When the sun **w** down,
3:16 Her husband **w** with her and
3:16 Abner told him. So he **w** home.
3:19 Then Abner **w** directly to David
3:24 Then Joab **w** to the king and
5:6 The king and his men **w** to
5:17 about it and **w** to the fortress.
5:20 So David **w** to Baal Perazim
6:12 Then David joyfully **w** to get
6:19 Then all the people **w** home.
7:9 was with you wherever you **w**,
7:18 King David **w** into the tent and
8:3 When David **w** to restore his
8:6 Everywhere David **w**,
8:14 Everywhere David **w**,
2Sm 10:14 fled from Abishai and **w** into
11:4 and he **w** to bed with her.
11:4 Then she **w** home.
11:13 But that evening Uriah **w** to lie
12:15 Then Nathan **w** home.
12:20 He **w** into the LORD's house
12:20 Then he **w** home and asked for
12:24 He **w** to bed with her,
12:29 all the troops and **w** to Rabbah.
13:8 So Tamar **w** to her brother
13:19 and **w** away crying.
13:24 Absalom **w** to the king and
14:23 So Joab **w** to Geshur and
14:31 Then Joab immediately **w** to
14:33 Joab **w** to the king and told him
15:9 So he **w** to Hebron.
15:11 Jerusalem **w** with Absalom.
15:11 They **w** innocently,
15:30 David cried as he **w** up the
15:30 heads and cried as they **w**.
15:37 So Hushai, David's friend, **w** to
16:13 As David and his men **w** along
17:18 and they **w** down into it.
17:21 came out of the cistern and **w**
17:23 and **w** home to his own city.
18:6 So the troops **w** out to the
18:9 and the mule **w** under the
18:17 all Israel fled and **w** back
18:33 He **w** to the room above the
18:33 he said as he **w**. "My son, my
19:8 Israel had fled and **w** back to
19:24 **w** to meet the king.
19:39 Then Barzillai **w** back home.
19:40 and Chimham **w** with him.
20:5 Amasa **w** to call Judah
20:7 all the soldiers **w** with Abishai.
20:22 Then the woman **w** to all the
20:22 from the city and **w** home.
20:22 Joab **w** back to the king in
21:12 David **w** and took the bones of
21:15 So David and his men **w** to
22:9 Smoke **w** up from his nostrils,
23:20 He also **w** into a pit and killed
23:21 Benaiah **w** to him with a club,
24:5 Then they **w** to Gad and to
24:6 They **w** to Gilead and to
24:7 They **w** to the fortified city of
24:7 Then they **w** to Beersheba in
24:19 David **w** as Gad had told him
24:20 he **w** out and bowed down with
1Ki 1:15 Bathsheba **w** to the king in his
1:25 because today he **w** and
1:50 **w** ⌞to the tent of meeting,⌟
2:8 when I **w** to Mahanaim.
2:13 of Haggith, **w** to Bathsheba,
2:19 Bathsheba **w** to King Solomon
2:34 **w** and attacked Joab,
2:40 he saddled his donkey and **w**
2:40 Shimei **w** to Gath and got his
2:46 He **w** to attack and kill Shimei.
3:4 King Solomon **w** to Gibeon to
3:15 He **w** to Jerusalem and stood
6:8 A staircase **w** up to the middle
8:66 They blessed the king and **w**
9:28 they **w** to Ophir, got 31,500
10:13 Then she and her servants **w**
11:15 **w** to bury those killed in battle
11:18 left Midian and **w** to Paran.
11:18 they **w** to Pharaoh (the king of
11:24 They **w** to Damascus,
12:1 Rehoboam **w** to Shechem
12:3 the entire assembly of Israel **w**
12:16 So Israel **w** home to their own
12:30 The people **w** as far as Dan to
12:32 He **w** to the altar in Bethel to
12:33 He **w** to his altar in Bethel to
13:14 He **w** after the man of God and
13:19 The man of God **w** back with
14:4 She left, **w** to Shiloh,
14:17 got up, left, and **w** to Tirzah.
14:28 Whenever the king **w** into the
16:18 he **w** into the stronghold in the
17:5 He **w** to live by the Cherith
17:10 He got up and **w** to Zarephath.
18:2 So Elijah **w** to present himself
18:6 Ahab **w** one way by himself,
1Ki 18:6 and Obadiah **w** the other way
18:16 So Obadiah **w** to tell Ahab.
18:16 Ahab **w** to meet Elijah.
18:42 Elijah **w** to the top of Carmel
18:43 He **w** up, looked, and said,
19:6 and **w** to sleep again.
19:9 There he **w** into a cave and
19:13 his face in his coat, **w** out,
20:1 He **w** to blockade Samaria and
20:17 district governors **w** out first.
20:21 The king of Israel **w** out and
20:26 the Aramean army and **w**
20:27 they **w** to meet the enemy.
20:32 They **w** to the king of Israel
20:39 "I **w** to fight in the battle.
20:43 of Israel **w** home to Samaria.
21:4 Resentful and upset, Ahab **w**
21:16 Ahab **w** to confiscate the
21:18 He **w** to confiscate Naboth's
22:2 King Jehoshaphat of Judah **w**
22:13 The messenger who **w** to call
22:24 **w** to Micaiah and struck him on
22:29 King Jehoshaphat of Judah **w**
22:30 himself and **w** into battle.
22:36 At sundown a cry **w** through
2Ki 1:13 The officer of the third group **w**
1:15 So Elijah got up and **w** with
2:2 So they **w** to Bethel.
2:4 So they **w** to Jericho.
2:11 and Elijah **w** to heaven in a
2:13 had fallen off Elijah), **w** back,
2:15 Then they **w** to meet him and
2:21 He **w** to the spring and threw
2:23 From there he **w** to Bethel.
2:25 **w** to Mount Carmel,
3:12 the king of Edom **w** to Elisha.
3:24 Israel **w** after the Moabites and
3:27 So they **w** home to their own
4:7 She **w** and told the man of God.
4:11 **w** into the upstairs room,
4:18 Several years later the boy **w**
4:27 Gehazi **w** to push her away.
4:31 Gehazi **w** ahead of them and
4:33 He **w** into the room,
4:38 When Elisha **w** back to Gilgal,
4:39 One of them **w** into the field to
5:2 Once, when the Arameans **w** on
5:4 Naaman **w** to his master and
5:13 But Naaman's servants **w** to
5:14 So he **w** to dip himself in the
5:21 So Gehazi **w** after Naaman.
5:25 He **w** and stood in front of his
5:26 Then Elisha said to him, "I **w**
6:4 So he **w** with them.
6:15 in the morning and **w** outside,
6:24 They **w** to Samaria and
7:8 of the camp, they **w** into a tent,
7:8 They **w** away and hid them.
7:8 **w** into another tent,
7:8 **w** away, and hid them.
7:10 "We **w** into the Aramean camp,
7:16 So the people **w** out and looted
8:2 She and her family **w** to live in
8:7 Elisha **w** to Damascus.
8:9 Hazael **w** to meet Elisha.
8:14 Hazael left Elisha and **w** to his
8:28 Ahaziah **w** with Ahab's son
8:29 Then Jehoram's son Ahaziah **w**
9:4 **w** to Ramoth Gilead.
9:6 Jehu got up and **w** into the
9:21 and King Ahaziah of Judah **w**
9:34 He **w** inside, ate, and drank.
9:35 But when they **w** out to bury
10:21 They **w** into the temple of Baal
10:23 **w** into the temple of Baal and
10:24 So they **w** in to offer sacrifices
11:13 she **w** into the LORD's temple,
11:18 all the people of the land **w**
11:19 They **w** down the street that
14:13 Shemesh and **w** to Jerusalem.
16:10 Then King Ahaz **w** to
16:12 the altar and **w** up to it.
17:15 They **w** after worthless idols
17:28 taken prisoner from Samaria **w**
18:18 **w** out to the field commander.
18:37 **w** to Hezekiah with their

2Ki	19:1	and **w** into the LORD's temple.
	19:5	Hezekiah's men **w** to Isaiah.
	19:14	and **w** to the LORD's temple.
	19:35	The LORD's angel **w** out and
	19:36	He **w** home to Nineveh and
	22:9	The scribe Shaphan **w** to the
	22:14	and Asaiah **w** to talk to the
	23:2	the people (young and old) **w**
	23:20	He **w** back to Jerusalem.
	23:29	King Josiah **w** to attack Necoh.
	25:23	they **w** to Gedaliah at Mizpah.
	25:25	a descendant of the kings) **w**
1Ch	5:19	They **w** to war against Hagar's
	11:4	David and all Israel **w** to
	11:15	the thirty leading men **w** down
	11:22	He also **w** into a cistern and
	11:23	But Benaiah **w** to him with a
	12:1	the soldiers who **w** into battle
	12:17	David **w** to meet them.
	12:19	army⌋ to join David when he **w**
	12:20	When David **w** to Ziklag,
	13:6	David and all Israel **w** to
	14:8	But David heard about it and **w**
	15:25	army's commanders joyfully **w**
	16:43	Then all the people **w** home.
	16:43	David **w** back to bless his
	17:8	was with you wherever you **w**,
	17:16	Then King David **w** into the
	18:3	When David **w** to establish his
	18:6	Everywhere David **w**,
	18:13	Everywhere David **w**,
	19:15	brother Abishai and **w** into
	21:4	**w** throughout Israel,
	21:19	David **w** as Gad had told him
	24:19	priestly groups when they **w**
2Ch	1:3	and the entire assembly **w**
	1:6	LORD's presence Solomon **w**
	1:13	Solomon **w** from the tent of
	8:3	Then Solomon **w** to Hamath
	8:17	Then Solomon **w** to the coast
	8:18	They **w** with Solomon's
	9:12	Then she and her servants **w**
	10:1	Rehoboam **w** to Shechem
	10:3	Jeroboam and all Israel **w** to
	10:16	So all Israel **w** home to their
	11:14	their land and property and **w**
	12:11	Whenever the king **w** into the
	12:12	So things **w** well in Judah.
	14:7	and everything **w** well.
	14:10	Asa **w** to confront him,
	15:2	Azariah **w** to Asa and said to
	16:12	LORD for help, he **w** to doctors.
	18:2	A few years later he **w** to visit
	18:12	The messenger who **w** to call
	18:23	son of Chenaanah, **w**
	18:28	King Jehoshaphat of Judah **w**
	18:29	himself and **w** into battle.
	19:4	he regularly **w** to the people
	20:20	up early in the morning and **w**
	20:21	As they **w** in front of the troops,
	20:24	The people of Judah **w** to the
	22:5	followed their advice and **w**
	22:6	Then Jehoram's son Ahaziah **w**
	22:7	downfall when he **w** to Joram.
	22:7	He **w** with Joram to meet Jehu,
	23:2	They **w** around Judah,
	23:12	she **w** into the LORD's temple,
	23:17	Then all the people **w** to the
	23:20	They **w** through Upper Gate to
	26:6	Uzziah **w** to wage war against
	26:16	He **w** into the LORD's temple to
	26:17	The priest Azariah **w** in after
	28:9	He **w** to meet the army coming
	29:17	On the eighth day they **w** into
	29:18	Then they **w** to King Hezekiah.
	29:20	the leaders of the city and **w**
	30:10	So the messengers **w** from city
	30:27	and their prayers **w** to God's
	31:1	the Israelites who were there **w**
	31:1	Each person **w** to his own
	31:16	offerings to everyone who **w**
	32:21	When he **w** into the temple of
	32:23	Many people still **w** to
	34:7	Then he **w** back to Jerusalem.
	34:22	and the king's officials **w**
	34:30	people (young and old) **w** up
2Ch	35:20	Josiah **w** to attack him.
	35:22	himself as he **w** into battle.
	35:22	and he **w** to fight in the valley
Ezr	2:1	All of them **w** to their own
	2:2	They **w** with Zerubbabel,
	5:3	and their group **w** to the Jews
	5:8	should know that we **w**
	7:7	and temple servants) **w** to
	10:6	the front of God's temple and **w**
Neh	2:9	I **w** to the governors ⌊of the
	2:11	I **w** to Jerusalem and was there
	2:12	During the night I **w** out with a
	2:13	I **w** through Valley Gate that
	2:15	So I **w** through the valley that
	4:15	we all **w** back to the work on
	6:10	⌊One day⌋ I **w** to the home of
	7:6	All of them **w** to their own
	7:7	They **w** with Zerubbabel,
	8:12	Then all the people **w** to eat
	8:16	So the people **w** to get
	12:27	they **w** to wherever the Levites
	12:31	One choir **w** to the right on the
	12:37	At Fountain Gate they **w**
	12:38	The other choir **w** to the left.
	13:7	I **w** to Jerusalem and
Est	2:14	She never **w** to the king again
	4:1	He **w** into the middle of the city
	4:2	He even **w** right up to the king's
	4:3	the Jews **w** into mourning,
	4:6	So Hathach **w** out to Mordecai
	5:2	Esther **w** up to him and
	5:10	He **w** home and sent for his
	5:12	Haman **w** on to say,
	7:7	got up from dinner and **w** into
	8:15	Mordecai **w** out from the
Job	21:33	Countless others **w** before him.
	29:7	When I **w** through the city gate
	42:9	and Zophar of Naama **w** and
Psa	18:8	Smoke **w** up from his nostrils,
	34:4	I **w** to the LORD for help.
	66:12	We **w** through fire and water,
	68:7	O God, when you **w** in front of
	68:18	You **w** to the highest place.
	77:2	I **w** to the Lord for help.
	77:19	Your road **w** through the sea.
	77:19	Your path **w** through raging
	107:7	He led them on a road that **w**
Sos	6:2	My beloved **w** to his garden,
	6:11	I **w** to the walnut grove to look
	8:5	There your mother **w** into labor
	8:5	There she **w** into labor and
Isa	7:1	**w** to Jerusalem to attack it,
	36:3	**w** out to the field commander.
	36:22	**w** to Hezekiah with their
	37:1	and **w** into the LORD's temple.
	37:5	Hezekiah's men **w** to Isaiah.
	37:14	and **w** to the LORD's temple.
	37:36	The LORD's angel **w** out and
	37:37	He **w** home to Nineveh and
	38:8	The sun made a shadow that **w**
	38:8	So the sun on the stairway **w**
	52:4	In the beginning my people **w**
	66:8	When Zion **w** into labor,
Jer	2:5	me that they **w** so far away
	3:6	She **w** up every high mountain
	7:24	They **w** backward and not
	13:5	So I **w** and buried it by the
	13:7	So I **w** back to the Euphrates
	18:3	I **w** to the potter's house,
	19:10	of the men who **w** with you.
	22:15	Everything **w** well for him.
	22:16	Everything **w** well for him.
	26:10	they **w** from the king's palace
	28:4	of Judah who **w** to Babylon,
	28:11	Jeremiah **w** on his way.
	31:2	Israel **w** to find its rest.
	36:12	Then he **w** down to the scribe's
	36:14	took the scroll and **w** with him
	36:20	they **w** to the king in the
	37:16	Jeremiah **w** into a prison cell,
	38:11	took the men with him and **w**
	40:6	Jeremiah **w** to Gedaliah,
	40:8	are the commanders who **w**
	41:1	and of the king's officers) **w**
	41:6	to meet them, crying as he **w**.
	41:12	they took all their men and **w** to
Jer	43:7	so they **w** to Egypt.
	43:7	They **w** as far as Tahpanhes.
	44:3	They **w** to burn incense and
	44:14	of the people of Judah who **w**
	44:28	all the people of Judah who **w**
	51:59	when Seraiah **w** to Babylon
Eze	1:9	The creatures **w** straight ahead,
	1:12	the creatures **w** straight ahead.
	1:12	They **w** wherever their spirit
	1:20	wanted to go, the creatures **w**.
	3:14	I **w** away feeling bitter and
	3:15	I **w** to Tel Abib, to the exiles
	3:23	I got up and **w** to the plain.
	8:10	So I **w** in and looked.
	8:11	and a cloud of incense **w** up.
	9:3	of the God of Israel **w** up from
	9:7	So they **w** out and killed the
	10:2	So he **w** between the wheels
	10:3	of the temple as the person **w**.
	10:6	the person **w** in and stood
	10:22	Each one **w** straight ahead.
	16:6	"'Then I **w** by you and saw you
	16:8	"'I **w** by you again and looked
	23:8	men **w** to bed with her,
	23:17	Babylon, **w** to bed with her,
	25:3	nation of Judah **w** into exile.
	27:9	from Gebal **w** inside you
	31:15	When the tree **w** down to the
	32:24	They **w** down below the earth
	32:27	warriors who died and **w** down
	32:30	**w** down with the dead.
	32:30	with those who **w** down
	36:20	But wherever they **w** among
	36:21	the nations wherever they **w**.
	39:23	people of Israel **w** into captivity
	40:6	Then the man **w** to the
	40:6	He **w** up its steps and
	40:22	Seven steps **w** up to it and led
	40:26	Seven steps **w** up to it and led
	41:3	Then the man **w** inside and
	41:7	the way around as they **w** up,
	41:7	The surrounding structure **w**
	41:7	grew wider as it **w** higher.
	41:7	A stairway **w** from the first
	41:10	It was 35 feet wide and **w** all
	44:10	"'Some Levites **w** far away
	47:3	the man **w** eastward.
	47:7	As I **w** back, I saw many trees
Dan	2:16	Daniel **w** and asked the king to
	2:17	Then Daniel **w** home and told
	2:24	Then Daniel **w** to Arioch,
	3:26	Then Nebuchadnezzar **w** to the
	6:6	these officials and satraps **w**
	6:10	he **w** to his house.
	6:12	Then they **w** and spoke to the
	6:18	Then the king **w** to his palace
	6:19	the king got up and quickly **w**
	7:16	I **w** to someone who was
Hos	5:13	Ephraim **w** to Assyria to ask
	8:9	people of Israel **w** to Assyria.
	9:10	But they **w** to Baal Peor and
	11:2	the farther they **w** away.
Jnh	1:3	He **w** to Joppa and found a
	1:3	paid for the trip and **w** on board.
	1:6	The captain of the ship **w** to
	3:3	Jonah immediately **w** to
Nah	3:10	Even she **w** into captivity and
Zec	6:7	these strong horses **w** out,
	6:8	Those who **w** to the north have
Mat	2:21	and his mother, and **w** to Israel.
	3:5	whole Jordan Valley **w** to him.
	4:12	he **w** back to Galilee.
	4:21	As Jesus **w** on, he saw two
	4:23	Jesus **w** all over Galilee.
	5:1	he **w** up a mountain and sat
	8:3	his skin disease **w** away,
	8:5	When Jesus **w** to Capernaum,
	8:14	When Jesus **w** to Peter's
	8:15	and the fever **w** away.
	8:23	Jesus' disciples **w** with him as
	8:32	The demons came out and **w**
	8:34	Everyone from the city **w** to
	9:7	So the man got up and **w** home.
	9:25	Jesus **w** in, took her hand,
	9:28	Jesus **w** into a house,
	9:31	But they **w** out and spread the

Mat 9:35 Jesus **w** to all the towns and
12:4 Haven't you read how he **w**
12:9 there and **w** into a synagogue.
13:3 A farmer **w** to plant seed.
13:25 in the wheat field and **w** away.
13:36 he **w** into the house.
13:44 with it that he **w** away,
13:46 a valuable pearl, he **w** away,
13:54 Jesus **w** to his hometown and
14:12 Then they **w** to tell Jesus.
14:13 he left in a boat and **w** to a
14:23 he **w** up a mountain to pray by
15:21 Jesus left that place and **w** to
15:29 on from there and **w** along
15:29 Then he **w** up a mountain and
16:4 standing there and **w** away.
16:5 any bread along when they **w**
17:25 Peter **w** into the house.
18:28 But when that servant **w** away,
19:15 he **w** away from there.
19:22 he **w** away sad because he
20:1 who **w** out at daybreak
20:4 whatever is right.' So they **w**.
20:5 "He **w** out again about noon
20:6 he **w** out and found some
21:9 The crowd that **w** ahead of him
21:12 Jesus **w** into the temple
21:17 He left them and **w** out of the
21:19 he **w** up to the tree and found
21:23 Then Jesus **w** into the temple
21:28 He **w** to the first and said,
21:29 he changed his mind and **w**.
21:30 "The father **w** to the other son
21:33 workers and **w** on a trip.
22:5 paid no attention and **w** away.
22:5 Some **w** to work in their own
22:5 others **w** to their businesses.
22:10 The servants **w** into the streets
22:15 Then the Pharisees **w** away
22:22 Then they left him alone and **w**
24:38 day that Noah **w** into the ship.
25:1 They took their oil lamps and **w**
25:10 bridesmaids who were ready **w**
25:15 Then the man **w** on his trip.
25:18 two thousand dollars **w** off,
26:7 a woman **w** to him with a bottle
26:14 **w** to the chief priests.
26:17 the disciples **w** to Jesus.
26:30 they **w** to the Mount of Olives.
26:36 Then Jesus **w** with the
26:40 When he **w** back to the
26:42 Then he **w** away a second
26:44 After leaving them again, he **w**
26:58 He **w** inside and sat with the
26:71 As he **w** to the entrance,
26:75 Then Peter **w** outside and cried
27:5 **w** away, and hanged himself.
27:53 and they **w** into the holy city
27:58 He **w** to Pilate and asked for
27:60 door of the tomb, he **w** away.
27:62 together and **w** to Pilate.
27:66 So they **w** to secure the tomb.
28:1 Magdala and the other Mary **w**
28:9 They **w** up to him,
28:11 some of the guards **w** into the
28:16 The eleven disciples **w** to the
Mar 1:5 people of Jerusalem **w** to him.
1:14 Jesus **w** to Galilee and told
1:19 As Jesus **w** on a little farther,
1:21 Then they **w** to Capernaum.
1:21 Jesus **w** into the synagogue
1:29 they **w** directly to the house of
1:29 James and John **w** with them.
1:31 Jesus **w** to her, took her hand,
1:31 The fever **w** away,
1:35 Jesus **w** to a place where he
1:39 So he **w** to spread ⌊the Good
1:42 his skin disease **w** away,
2:1 The report **w** out that he was
2:13 Jesus **w** to the seashore again.
2:26 you ever read how he **w** into
3:1 Jesus **w** into a synagogue
3:13 Jesus **w** up a mountain,
3:20 Then Jesus **w** home.
3:21 about it, they **w** to get him.
4:3 A farmer **w** to plant seed.
Mar 4:24 He **w** on to say, "Pay attention
5:13 came out of the man and **w** into
5:24 Jesus **w** with the man.
5:40 disciples and **w** to the child.
6:1 Jesus left that place and **w** to
6:6 Then Jesus **w** around to the
6:12 So the apostles **w** and told
6:24 So she **w** out and asked her
6:32 So they **w** away in a boat to a
6:46 he **w** up a mountain to pray.
7:24 Jesus left that place and **w** to
7:25 She **w** to him and bowed down.
7:30 The woman **w** home and found
7:31 He **w** through Sidon and the
8:10 got into a boat and **w** into
8:11 The Pharisees **w** to Jesus and
8:27 Jesus and his disciples **w**
9:28 When Jesus **w** into a house,
10:1 Jesus left there and **w** into the
10:22 unhappy and **w** away sad,
10:35 sons of Zebedee, **w** to Jesus.
10:50 jumped up, and **w** to Jesus.
11:9 Those who **w** ahead and those
11:11 into Jerusalem and **w** into
11:11 Since it was already late, he **w**
11:13 He **w** to see if he could find
11:15 Jesus **w** into the temple
12:1 workers and **w** on a trip.
12:12 So they left him alone and **w**
12:28 One of the scribes **w** to Jesus
13:34 It is like a man who **w** on a trip.
14:3 a woman **w** to him.
14:10 **w** to the chief priests to betray
14:16 They **w** into the city and found
14:26 they **w** to the Mount of Olives.
14:37 He **w** back and found them
14:39 He **w** away again and prayed
14:54 him at a distance and **w** into
14:68 He **w** to the entrance.
15:43 Joseph boldly **w** to Pilate's
16:5 As they **w** into the tomb,
16:8 They **w** out of the tomb and ran
16:10 She **w** and told his friends,
16:13 They **w** back and told the
Luk 1:23 service were over, he **w** home.
1:27 The angel **w** to a virgin
1:56 months and then **w** back home.
1:59 they **w** ⌊to the temple⌋ to
2:3 All the people **w** to register in
2:4 So Joseph **w** from Nazareth,
2:4 **w** to Bethlehem because David
2:5 Joseph **w** there to register with
2:15 The angels left them and **w**
2:16 They **w** quickly and found
2:22 and Mary **w** to Jerusalem.
2:27 Moved by the Spirit, Simeon **w**
2:42 12 years old, they **w** as usual.
2:45 they **w** back to Jerusalem to
4:16 As usual he **w** into the
4:30 right by them and **w** away.
4:31 Jesus **w** to Capernaum.
4:38 left the synagogue and **w**
4:39 fever to leave, and it **w** away.
4:42 In the morning he **w** to a place
5:13 his skin disease **w** away.
5:19 So they **w** up on the roof.
5:25 Praising God, he **w** home.
6:4 Haven't you read how he **w**
6:6 Jesus **w** into a synagogue to
6:12 At that time Jesus **w** to a
7:1 he **w** to Capernaum.
7:6 Jesus **w** with them.
7:11 Jesus **w** to a city called Nain.
7:11 and a large crowd **w** with him.
7:14 He **w** up to the open coffin,
7:36 Jesus **w** to the Pharisee's
8:5 "A farmer **w** to plant his seeds.
8:24 They **w** to him, woke him up,
8:33 came out of the man and **w** into
8:35 The people **w** to see what had
8:39 He **w** through the whole city
8:42 As Jesus **w**, the people were
8:51 Jesus **w** into the house.
9:6 The apostles **w** from village to
9:28 and James with him and **w** up
9:34 They were frightened as they **w**
Luk 9:52 They **w** into a Samaritan
9:56 So they **w** to another village.
10:30 Jesus replied, "A man **w** from
10:31 When he saw the man, he **w**
10:32 **w** around him and continued on
10:34 **w** to him, and cleaned and
10:38 Jesus **w** into a village.
13:6 He **w** to look for fruit on the tree
14:1 On a day of worship Jesus **w**
14:21 "The servant **w** back to report
15:20 "So he **w** at once to his father.
16:23 He **w** to hell, where he was
17:12 As he **w** into a village,
17:14 As they **w**, they were made
17:27 until the day that Noah **w** into
18:10 He said, "Two men **w** into the
18:14 that this tax collector **w** home
19:7 They said, "He **w** to be the
19:12 He said, "A prince **w** to a
19:37 place where the road **w** down
19:45 Jesus **w** into the temple
20:9 and **w** on a long trip.
22:4 Judas **w** to the chief priests
22:39 Jesus **w** out ⌊of the city⌋ to the
22:45 he got up and **w** to the
22:62 Then Peter **w** outside and cried
23:52 He **w** to Pilate and asked for
23:56 Then they **w** back to the city
24:1 Sunday morning the women **w**
24:3 When they **w** in, they did not
24:9 The women left the tomb and **w**
24:12 of linen. Then he **w** away,
24:22 They **w** to the tomb early this
24:24 Some of our men **w** to the tomb
24:29 "So he **w** to stay with them.
24:33 That same hour they **w** back to
24:52 as they **w** back to Jerusalem.
Jon 1:11 He **w** to his own people,
1:39 So they **w** to see where he
2:12 and disciples **w** to the city of
2:13 so Jesus **w** to Jerusalem.
3:22 Jesus and his disciples **w** to
3:26 So they **w** to John and asked
4:3 and **w** back to Galilee.
4:7 A Samaritan woman **w** to get
4:28 her water jar and **w** back into
4:30 the city and **w** to meet Jesus.
4:40 the Samaritans **w** to Jesus,
4:47 So he **w** to Jesus and asked
5:1 Later, Jesus **w** to Jerusalem for
5:15 The man **w** back to the Jews
6:3 Jesus **w** up a mountain and sat
6:16 his disciples **w** to the sea.
6:24 they got into these boats and **w**
7:10 gone to the festival, Jesus **w**.
7:14 Jesus **w** to the temple
7:53 Then each of them **w** home.
8:1 Jesus **w** to the Mount of
8:2 All the people **w** to him,
9:11 So I **w** there, washed it off,
10:40 He **w** back across the Jordan
10:41 Many people **w** to Jesus.
11:20 she **w** to meet him.
11:28 she **w** back home and
11:29 got up quickly and **w** to Jesus.
11:38 Jesus **w** to the tomb.
11:46 But some of them **w** to the
11:54 Instead, he left Bethany and **w**
12:9 So they **w** there not only to see
12:13 they took palm branches and **w**
12:21 They **w** to Philip (who was
13:30 and immediately **w** outside.
18:1 he **w** with his disciples to the
18:3 priests and Pharisees and **w**
18:4 So he **w** to meet them and
18:15 So that disciple **w** with Jesus
18:33 Pilate **w** back into the palace,
18:38 After Pilate said this, he **w** out
19:3 They **w** up to him,
19:4 Pilate **w** outside again and told
19:5 Jesus **w** outside. He was
19:9 He **w** into the palace again and
19:17 He carried his own cross and **w**
19:39 **w** with Joseph and brought 75
20:1 Mary from Magdala **w** to the
20:6 arrived after him and **w** into

Jon 20:8 at the tomb first, **w** inside.
20:10 So the disciples **w** back home.
20:18 Mary from Magdala **w** to the
21:3 They **w** out in a boat but didn't
21:9 When they **w** ashore,
Act 1:13 and Judas (son of James) **w** to
2:46 had a single purpose and **w**
3:8 He **w** with Peter and John into
4:23 they **w** to the other apostles
5:15 some sick people as he **w** by.
5:21 the apostles **w** into the temple
5:26 officer of the temple guards **w**
6:12 So they **w** to Stephen,
7:15 So Jacob **w** to Egypt,
7:31 As he **w** closer to look at the
8:4 were scattered **w** from place
8:5 Philip **w** to the city of Samaria
8:15 Peter and John **w** to Samaria
8:27 So Philip **w**. An Ethiopian man
9:1 He **w** to the chief priest
9:28 Then Saul **w** throughout
9:39 So Peter **w** with them.
10:9 Peter **w** on the roof to pray.
10:17 house and **w** to the gate.
10:21 So Peter **w** to the men.
10:23 Some disciples from Joppa **w**
10:38 Jesus **w** everywhere and did
11:2 when Peter **w** to Jerusalem,
11:3 They said, "You **w** to visit men
11:12 ⌊from Joppa⌋ **w** with me,
11:19 Stephen's death **w** as far as
12:10 so they **w** outside and up the
12:12 he **w** to the home of Mary,
12:17 he left and **w** somewhere else.
12:19 left Judea and **w** to Caesarea,
13:4 they **w** to the city of Seleucia
13:6 They **w** through the whole
13:13 there and **w** back to Jerusalem.
13:14 On the day of worship they **w**
13:51 the dust off their feet and **w**
14:1 Paul and Barnabas **w** into the
14:20 he got up and **w** back into the
14:21 Then they **w** back to the cities
14:24 they **w** to Pamphylia.
14:25 in the city of Perga and **w**
15:41 Paul **w** through the provinces
16:1 of Derbe and then **w** to Lystra,
16:4 As they **w** through the cities,
16:6 Paul and Silas **w** through the
16:7 They **w** to the province of
16:8 they passed by Mysia and **w**
16:12 and from there we **w** to the city
16:13 On the day of worship we **w**
16:39 So the officials **w** to the jail
16:40 they **w** to Lydia's house.
17:2 Paul **w** into the synagogue.
17:13 they **w** there to upset and
18:1 Paul left Athens and **w** to the
18:2 Paul **w** to visit them,
18:7 he left the synagogue and **w**
18:18 and Aquila **w** with him.
18:19 Paul **w** into the synagogue and
18:22 He **w** ⌊to Jerusalem⌋,
18:22 and **w** back to the city of
18:23 Paul **w** through the regions of
20:2 He **w** through that region and
20:2 Then he **w** to Greece
20:5 All these men **w** ahead and
20:10 Paul **w** to him, took him into
20:11 Eutychus **w** upstairs again,
20:13 We **w** ahead to the ship and
20:14 we took him on board and **w** to
20:15 The next day we **w** by the
20:19 difficult times I **w** through when
21:2 so we **w** aboard and sailed
21:6 Then we **w** aboard the ship,
21:6 the disciples **w** back home.
21:8 The next day we **w** to Philip's
21:16 from Caesarea **w** with us.
21:18 The next day Paul **w** with us
21:26 Paul took the men and **w**
21:26 Then he **w** into the temple
21:33 Then the officer **w** to Paul,
22:19 people here know that I **w** from
22:27 The officer **w** to Paul and
23:14 They **w** to the chief priests and
Act 23:19 **w** where they could be alone,
23:27 I **w** with my soldiers to rescue
24:1 later the chief priest Ananias **w**
24:11 can verify for yourself that I **w**
25:1 he **w** from the city of Caesarea
25:15 When I **w** to Jerusalem,
26:11 I even **w** to each synagogue,
26:12 out these activities when I **w**
27:2 of Thessalonica, **w** with us.
28:8 Paul **w** to him, prayed,
28:9 sick people on the island **w**
28:23 Jews ⌊than expected⌋ **w**
1Co 10:1 and they all **w** through the sea.
10:4 spiritual rock that **w** with them,
2Co 2:12 When I **w** to the city of Troas,
2:13 to the people in Troas and **w**
8:17 my request and eagerly **w**
Gal 1:17 Instead, I **w** to Arabia and then
1:18 Then, three years later I **w** to
1:21 Then I **w** to the regions of Syria
2:1 Then 14 years later I **w** to
2:2 I **w** in response to a revelation
Eph 4:8 "When he **w** to the highest
4:9 mean that he **w** up except that
4:10 gone down also **w** up above all
2Ti 4:10 with this present world and **w**
4:10 Crescens **w** to the province of
4:10 and Titus **w** to the province of
Heb 6:20 where Jesus **w** before us on
9:6 The priests always **w** into the
9:7 But only the chief priest **w** into
9:11 Christ **w** through a better,
9:12 He **w** into the most holy place
9:24 Instead, he **w** into heaven to
9:25 Every year the chief priest **w**
1Pe 3:19 In it he also **w** to proclaim his
4:3 got drunk, **w** to wild parties,
3Jn 1:7 After all, they **w** on their trip to
1:7 the people to whom they **w**.
Rev 6:4 A second horse **w** out.
8:4 The smoke from the incense **w**
10:9 I **w** to the angel and asked him
11:12 They **w** up to heaven in a
12:17 So it **w** away to fight with her

wept (2)

Job 2:12 They cried out loud and **w**,
31:38 and its furrows have **w** ....

west (104)

Gen 12:8 his tent — with Bethel on the **w**
13:14 and **w** of where you are.
28:14 You will spread out to the **w**
Exo 10:19 wind to a very strong **w** wind.
26:22 for the far end, the **w** side.
26:27 of the inner tent, the **w** side.
27:12 "The courtyard on the **w** end
36:27 for the far end, the **w** side.
36:32 of the inner tent, the **w** side.
38:12 The **w** side was 75 feet long
Num 2:18 "On the **w** side the armies led
3:23 their tents on the **w** side behind
21:11 Abarim in the desert **w** of Moab.
32:19 to the **w** and beyond.
35:5 3,000 feet on the **w** side,
Dtr 3:27 and look **w**, north, south,
11:30 (These mountains are on the **w**
11:30 beyond the road that goes **w**,
Jos 1:4 Mediterranean Sea on the **w**.
5:1 All the Amorite kings **w** of the
8:9 took their position **w** of Ai,
8:12 Bethel and Ai, **w** of the city.
8:13 the other troops were hiding **w**
9:1 When all the kings **w** of the
11:2 and Naphoth Dor in the **w**,
11:3 Canaanites from east and **w**,
12:7 are the kings of the land **w**
15:8 the valley of Hinnom to the **w** at
15:10 From Baalah the border turns **w**
16:3 Then it descends **w** to the
16:6 From there the border goes **w**,
16:8 At Tappuah the border goes **w**
18:12 **w** through the mountains,
18:14 and goes around on the **w** side,
18:15 Kiriath Jearim and goes **w**,
19:11 Toward the **w** the border
Jos 19:26 and Shihor Libnath in the **w**.
19:34 The border turns **w** to Aznoth
19:34 in the south, Asher in the **w**,
22:7 their land with their relatives **w**
Jdg 18:12 This is why the place just **w** of
20:33 position to the **w** of Gibeah.
2Sm 13:34 beside the mountain **w** of him.
1Ki 4:24 He controlled all the territory **w**
7:25 faced north, three faced **w**,
1Ch 7:28 with its villages to the **w**,
9:24 (east, **w**, north, and south).
12:15 the valleys to the east and **w**.
26:16 were chosen for the **w** side
26:18 At the courtyard on the **w** there
26:30 appointed to serve Israel **w**
2Ch 4:4 faced north, three faced **w**,
32:30 underground to the **w** side
33:14 wall of the City of David from **w**
Ezr 4:10 and the rest of the lands **w**
4:11 the people **w** of the Euphrates:
4:16 left ⌊of your province⌋ **w**
4:17 and to others **w** of the
4:20 ruled the whole ⌊province⌋ **w**
5:3 Tattenai ⌊from the province⌋ **w**
5:6 Tattenai ⌊from the province⌋ **w**
5:6 and his group (the Persians **w**
6:6 Tattenai ⌊from the province⌋ **w**
6:6 of your group (the Persians **w**
6:8 the taxes ⌊on the province⌋ **w**
6:13 Tattenai ⌊from the province⌋ **w**
7:21 treasurers ⌊in the province⌋ **w**
7:25 and live ⌊in the province⌋ **w**
8:36 governors ⌊in the province⌋ **w**
Neh 2:7 governors ⌊of the province⌋ **w**
2:9 governors ⌊of the province⌋ **w**
3:7 governor ⌊from the province⌋ **w**
Job 18:20 People in the **w** are shocked
23:8 If I go **w**, I can't find him.
Psa 75:6 from the east, from the **w**,
103:12 As far as the east is from the **w**
107:3 from the east and from the **w**,
Isa 9:12 and the Philistines from the **w**.
11:14 the slopes of Philistia in the **w**.
43:5 east and gather you from the **w**.
45:6 so that from the east to the **w**
49:12 from the north and from the **w**,
59:19 The people of the **w** will fear
Eze 41:12 on the **w** side of the temple,
41:15 courtyard on the **w** side along
42:19 He came around to the **w** side
46:19 me a place on the **w** side
47:20 On the **w** side the
47:20 This is the **w** side.
48:10 On the **w** side it will be 17,500
48:16 And on the **w** side it will be
48:17 and 4,375 feet on the **w**.
48:18 and 17,500 feet on its **w** side.
48:21 left on the east side and **w** side
48:34 The **w** side will be 7,875 feet
48:34 The three gates on the **w** side
Dan 8:4 I saw the ram charging **w**,
8:5 a male goat coming from the **w**.
11:30 Ships will come from the **w** to
Hos 11:10 will come trembling from the **w**.
Zec 14:4 large valley from east to **w**.
Mat 24:27 flashes from east to **w**.
Luk 12:54 a cloud coming up in the **w**,
Rev 21:13 and three gates on the **w**.

western (21)

Num 34:6 "The **w** border is the coastline
Dtr 3:17 The **w** border was the river,
Jos 13:27 River served as its **w** border,
15:12 The **w** border is the coastline
17:10 Sea ⌊is its **w** border⌋,
Eze 45:7 From the **w** boundary of the
48:1 from the eastern border to the **w**
48:2 eastern border to the **w** border.
48:3 eastern border to the **w** border.
48:4 eastern border to the **w** border.
48:5 eastern border to the **w** border.
48:6 eastern border to the **w** border.
48:7 eastern border to the **w** border.
48:8 eastern border to the **w** border,
48:21 westward to the **w** border.
48:23 eastern border to the **w** border.

Eze 48:24 eastern border to the **w** border.
48:25 eastern border to the **w** border.
48:26 eastern border to the **w** border.
48:27 eastern border to the **w** border.
Joe 2:20 will be forced into the **w** sea.

westward (2)
Jos 23:4 from the Jordan River **w**
Eze 48:21 and it will extend **w** to the

wet (7)
Sos 5:2 My head is **w** with dew,
Jer 13:1 your waist. Don't let it get **w**."
Dan 4:15 Let it get **w** with the dew from
4:23 Let it get **w** with the dew from
4:25 from the sky will make you **w**.
4:33 made his body **w** until his hair
5:21 and his body became **w** with

wheat (51)
Gen 30:14 During the **w** harvest Reuben
Exo 9:32 Neither the **w** nor the wild grain
29:2 Use the finest **w** flour,
34:22 first grain from your **w** harvest,
Dtr 8:8 The land has **w** and barley,
24:19 do when you're harvesting **w**
24:19 in one of the bundles of **w**,
32:14 male goats, and the best **w**.
Jdg 6:11 son Gideon was beating out **w**
15:1 Later, during the **w** harvest,
Rut 2:23 and the **w** harvest ended.
1Sm 6:13 Shemesh were harvesting **w**
12:17 Isn't the **w** being harvested
2Sm 17:28 **w**, barley, flour, roasted grain,
1Ki 5:11 Hiram 120,000 bushels of **w**
1Ch 21:20 Ornan kept on threshing the **w**.
21:23 and **w** for the grain offering.
2Ch 2:10 120,000 bushels of ground **w**,
2:15 Majesty may now send the **w**,
27:5 60,000 bushels of **w**,
Ezr 6:9 rams, lambs, **w**, salt, wine,
7:22 100 measures of **w**,
Job 31:40 let it grow thistles instead of **w**,
Psa 81:16 feed Israel with the finest **w**
147:14 ⌊hunger⌋ with the finest **w**.
Sos 7:2 bundle of **w** enclosed in lilies.
Isa 28:25 he plant wild **w** in rows?
28:25 and winter **w** at its borders?
Jer 12:13 My people planted **w**,
41:8 We have **w**, barley, olive oil,
Eze 4:9 "Then take **w**, barley, beans,
4:9 lentils, millet, and winter **w**.
27:17 exchanged **w** from Minnith,
45:13 seventeen percent of your **w**
Joe 1:11 Mourn for the **w** and the barley.
Amo 5:11 poor and take their **w** from them
8:5 so that we can sell more **w**?
8:6 husks mixed in with the **w**."
Mat 3:12 He will gather his **w** into a barn,
13:25 planted weeds in the **w** field
13:26 When the **w** came up and
13:29 may pull out the **w** with them.
13:30 them bring the **w** into my barn.'
Luk 3:17 He will gather the **w** into his
16:7 thousand bushels of **w**.' "The
22:31 farmer separates **w** from husks.
Jon 12:24 A single grain of **w** doesn't
Act 27:38 by dumping the **w** into the sea.
1Co 15:37 What you plant, whether it's **w**
Rev 6:6 "A quart of **w** for a day's pay or
18:13 flour, **w**, cattle, sheep, horses,

wheel (10)
1Ki 7:32 Each **w** was two feet high.
Ecc 12:6 and the water **w** is broken at
Jer 18:3 he was working there at his **w**.
Eze 1:15 I saw a **w** on the ground beside
1:16 looked like a **w** within a wheel.
1:16 looked like a wheel within a **w**.
10:9 one **w** beside each of the
10:10 was like a **w** within a wheel.
10:10 was like a wheel within a **w**.
10:12 Each of the angels had a **w**.

wheels (41)
Exo 14:25 He made the **w** of their chariots
1Ki 7:30 Each stand had four bronze **w**
7:32 The four **w** were under the
7:33 The **w** were made like chariot
7:33 were made like chariot **w**.
Isa 5:28 Their chariot **w** are as quick as
28:27 and wagon **w** aren't rolled over
28:28 The **w** of his cart will roll over
Jer 47:3 and the rumbling of their **w**.
Eze 1:16 This is how the **w** looked and
1:16 All four **w** looked the same.
1:18 The rims of the **w** were large
1:19 the **w** moved with them.
1:19 rose from the earth, the **w** rose.
1:20 The **w** rose with them,
1:20 living creatures was in the **w**.
1:21 creatures moved, the **w** moved.
1:21 stood still, the **w** stood still.
1:21 the **w** rose with them,
1:21 living creatures was in the **w**.
3:13 noise of the **w** beside them as
10:2 "Go between the **w** under the
10:2 between the **w** as I watched.
10:6 from between the **w** beside
10:6 and stood beside one of the **w**.
10:9 I saw four **w** beside the angels,
10:9 The **w** looked like beryl.
10:10 All four **w** looked the same.
10:12 and **w** were covered with eyes.
10:13 I heard that the **w** were called
10:13 were called the whirling **w**.
10:16 the **w** moved beside them.
10:16 the **w** didn't leave their side.
10:17 stood still, the **w** stood still.
10:17 the **w** rose with them.
10:17 living creatures was in the **w**.
10:19 left with the **w** beside them.
11:22 with the **w** beside them.
26:10 from the war horses, wagon **w**,
Dan 7:9 and its **w** were burning fire.
Nah 3:2 The sound of rattling **w**!

whim (1)
Gen 49:6 At their **w** they crippled cattle.

whip (16)
Jos 23:13 a **w** laid to your sides,
Jdg 8:7 I'll **w** your bodies with thorns
Pro 14:3 words a **w** is lifted against
26:3 A **w** is for the horse,
Isa 10:26 will raise his **w** against them.
50:6 my back to those who **w** me
Nah 3:2 The sound of the **w**!
Mat 10:17 to the Jewish courts and **w** you
20:19 of him, **w** him, and crucify him.
23:34 Others you will **w** in your
Mar 10:34 on him, **w** him, and kill him.
13:9 to the Jewish courts and **w** you
Luk 18:33 **w** him, and kill him. But on the
Jon 2:15 He made a **w** from small ropes
Act 22:19 and **w** those who believe
22:25 "Is it legal for you to **w** a

whipped (7)
Mat 27:26 But he had Jesus **w** and
Mar 15:15 But he had Jesus **w** and
Luk 23:16 to have him **w** and set free."
23:22 to have him **w** and set free."
Jon 19:1 had Jesus taken away and **w**.
Act 22:24 to question Paul as they **w** him.
Heb 11:36 Some were made fun of and **w**,

whipping (1)
Act 22:25 out ⌊to tie him to the **w** post⌋

whips (5)
1Ki 12:11 my father punished you with **w**,
12:14 my father punished you with **w**,
2Ch 10:11 my father punished you with **w**,
10:14 my father punished you with **w**,
Job 30:8 forced out of the land with **w**.

whirling (2)
Isa 17:13 like **w** dust being blown by a
Eze 10:13 were called the **w** wheels.

whirls (1)
Isa 9:18 and it **w** upward in clouds of

whirring (1)
Isa 18:1 the land of **w** wings which lies

whisper (7)
Job 26:14 We ⌊only⌋ hear a **w** of him!
Psa 39:5 everyone alive is like a **w** in
39:11 Certainly, everyone is like a **w**
62:9 Common people are only a **w**
62:9 are less than a **w** in the wind.
78:33 their days to an end like a **w**
Isa 8:19 who **w** and mutter."

whispered (5)
Job 4:12 heard something **w** in my ear.
Isa 29:4 words will be **w** from the dust.
Mat 10:27 housetops what you hear **w**.
Luk 12:3 Whatever you have **w** in
Jon 11:28 she went back home and **w** to

whispering (5)
2Sm 12:19 saw that his officials were **w**
1Ki 19:12 fire there was a quiet, **w** voice.
Psa 31:13 I have heard the **w** of many
Pro 25:23 so a **w** tongue brings angry
Jer 20:10 I have heard many ⌊people⌋ **w**,

whispers (1)
Psa 41:7 who hates me **w** about me.

whistle (3)
Isa 5:26 With a **w** he signals those at
7:18 On that day the LORD will **w**
Zec 10:8 I will signal them with a **w** and

whistles (1)
Job 27:23 It **w** at him from his own place."

white (59)
Gen 30:35 goats (every one with **w** on it),
30:37 the bark on them in strips of **w**,
30:37 uncovering the **w** which was
40:16 In my dream three baskets of **w**
Exo 16:31 It was **w** and tasted like wafers
Lev 13:3 diseased area has turned **w**,
13:4 But if the irritated area is **w** and
13:4 and the hair has not turned **w**,
13:10 If there is a **w** sore that has
13:10 sore that has turned the hair **w**,
13:13 His body has turned **w**.
13:16 if the raw flesh turns **w** again,
13:17 diseased area has turned **w**,
13:19 and in its place there is a **w**
13:20 skin and its hair has turned **w**,
13:21 area and the hair in it is not **w**
13:24 into a pink or bright **w** area,
13:25 the affected area has turned **w**
13:26 it and the hair in it is not **w**
13:38 "If a man or a woman has **w**
13:39 areas on the skin are pale **w**,
Num 12:10 She was as **w** as snow.
Est 1:6 The garden had **w** and violet
1:6 pillars by cords made of **w**
1:6 **w** marble, pearl-like stone,
8:15 the royal violet and **w** robe,
Job 6:6 any flavor in the **w** of an egg?
Isa 1:18 will become as **w** as snow.
1:18 will become as **w** as wool.
Dan 7:9 His clothes were as **w** as
11:35 and make them **w** until the end
12:10 Many will be purified, made **w**,
Zec 1:8 red, chestnut, and **w** horses.
6:3 The third had **w** horses.
6:6 and the **w** horses are following
Mat 5:36 make one hair black or **w**.
17:2 and his clothes as **w** as light.
28:3 clothes were as **w** as snow.
Mar 9:3 clothes became dazzling **w**,
16:5 He was dressed in a **w** robe
Luk 9:29 clothes became dazzling **w**.
Jon 20:12 saw two angels in **w** clothes.
Act 1:10 Suddenly, two men in **w**
Rev 1:14 His head and his hair were **w**

Rev 2:17 give each person a **w** stone
3:4 They will walk with me in **w**
3:5 this way will wear **w** clothes.
3:18 Buy **w** clothes from me.
4:4 24 leaders wearing **w** clothes.
6:2 and there was a **w** horse,
6:11 the souls was given a **w** robe.
7:9 They were wearing **w** robes,
7:13 these people wearing **w** robes,
7:14 their robes and made them **w**
14:14 and there was a **w** cloud,
19:11 There was a **w** horse,
19:14 heaven, wearing pure, **w** linen,
19:14 follow him on **w** horses.
20:11 I saw a large, **w** throne and the

whitecaps (2)

Psa 42:7 All the **w** on your waves have
Jnh 2:3 All the **w** on your waves have

whiter (4)

Gen 49:12 His teeth are **w** than milk.
Psa 51:7 and I will be **w** than snow.
Lam 4:7 purer than snow, **w** than milk.
Mar 9:3 **w** than anyone on earth could

whitewashed (1)

Mat 23:27 You are like **w** graves that look

wholehearted (1)

Eze 36:5 of my land with **w** joy

wholeheartedly (26)

Num 14:24 and has **w** followed me,
32:11 they didn't **w** follow me.'
32:12 they **w** followed the LORD.
Dtr 1:36 he **w** followed the LORD."
8:2 would **w** obey his commands.
1Sm 7:3 are returning to the LORD **w**,
12:20 Instead, serve the LORD **w**.
1Ki 8:23 servants, who obey you **w**.
11:6 He did not **w** follow the LORD
2Ki 10:31 But Jehu didn't **w** obey the
1Ch 28:9 Serve the LORD **w** and
29:9 gave so generously and **w**
2Ch 6:14 servants, who obey you **w**.
15:15 since they took the oath **w**.
19:3 and you've **w** dedicated your
19:9 He ordered them, "Do this **w**—
25:2 but he did not do it **w**.
31:21 he did **w**, and he succeeded.
Psa 119:2 They **w** search for him.
119:10 I **w** searched for you.
Pro 4:4 "Cling to my words **w**.
Jer 3:10 Judah didn't **w** come back
24:7 because they will **w** come
29:13 When you **w** seek me,
Rom 6:17 you have become **w** obedient
Col 3:23 Whatever you do, do it **w** as

wick (3)

Isa 42:3 not even put out a smoking **w**.
43:17 and snuffed out like a **w**.)
Mat 12:20 even put out a smoking **w** until

wicked (335)

Gen 13:13 lived in Sodom were very **w**.
19:7 don't be so **w**," he said.
39:9 How could I do such a **w** thing
Exo 23:1 Don't join forces with **w** people
Num 14:27 this **w** community that keeps
14:35 whole **w** community who have
16:26 from the tents of these **w** men.
Dtr 9:4 these nations are so **w** that
9:5 these people are so **w** that
13:11 ever do such a **w** thing again.
1Sm 2:9 but **w** people are silenced in
2:23 I hear about your **w** ways from
12:17 Then you will realize what a **w**
24:13 comes from **w** people.'
30:22 Then every **w** and worthless
2Sm 3:34 as one falls in front of **w** men.
4:11 I reward⌋ **w** men who kill
7:10 The **w** will no longer oppress
1Ki 8:47 We have been **w**,'
1Ch 17:9 The **w** will no longer frighten
2Ch 6:37 We have been **w**,'
19:2 "Why do you help **w** people
24:7 (The sons of that **w** woman
Ezr 4:12 that rebellious and **w** city.
Neh 9:2 as the **w** things their ancestors
9:33 but we have been **w**.
9:35 or turn away from their **w** lives.
Est 7:6 enemy is this **w** man Haman!"
Job 3:17 There the **w** stop their raging.
8:20 a helping hand to **w** people.
8:22 and the tent of the **w** will cease
9:22 the man of integrity and the **w**.'
9:24 earth is handed over to the **w**.
10:3 you favor the plans of the **w**?
11:20 But the **w** will lose their
15:20 "The **w** person is tortured all
16:11 me into the hands of **w** people.
18:5 the light of the **w** is snuffed out.
18:21 to the homes of **w** people
20:5 triumph of the **w** is short-lived,
20:29 God gives to the **w** person,
21:7 "Why do the **w** go on living,
21:16 (The plan of the **w** is foreign to
21:17 the lamp of the **w** snuffed out?
21:28 the tent where **w** people live?'
21:30 On the day of disaster the **w**
22:5 "Aren't you really very **w**?
22:15 path that **w** people have taken?
22:18 (The plan of the **w** is foreign to
24:6 in the **w** person's vineyard.
27:7 be ⌊treated⌋ like **w** people.
27:13 has waiting for the **w** person,
29:17 I broke the teeth of the **w**
31:3 Aren't there catastrophes for **w**
34:10 would ever do **w** things.
34:18 or to nobles, 'You **w** people!'
34:36 answers like **w** people do.
36:6 He doesn't allow the **w** person
38:13 edges and shake **w** people out
38:15 **W** people are deprived of their
40:12 Crush **w** people wherever they
Psa 1:1 follow the advice of **w** people,
1:4 **W** people are not like that.
1:5 That is why **w** people will not
1:6 the way of **w** people will end.
3:7 smashed the teeth of **w** people.
7:9 Let the evil within **w** people
9:5 You destroyed **w** people.
9:16 The **w** person is trapped by the
9:17 **W** people, all the nations who
10:2 The **w** person arrogantly
10:3 The **w** person boasts about his
10:13 Why does the **w** person
10:15 Break the arm of the **w** and evil
11:2 **W** people bend their bows.
11:5 but he hates **w** people and the
11:6 burning sulfur upon **w** people.
12:8 **W** people parade around when
17:9 Hide me from **w** people who
17:13 rescue my life from **w** people.
26:5 and will not sit with **w** people.
28:3 drag me away with **w** people,
31:17 Let **w** people be put to shame.
32:10 heartaches await **w** people,
34:21 Evil will kill **w** people,
36:1 about the **w** person who has
36:11 the hands of **w** people push me
37:1 Do not envy those who do **w**
37:10 In a little while a **w** person will
37:12 The **w** person plots against a
37:14 **W** people pull out their swords
37:16 the wealth of many **w** people.
37:17 The arms of **w** people will be
37:20 But **w** people will disappear.
37:21 A **w** person borrows,
37:28 but the descendants of **w**
37:32 The **w** person watches the
37:33 him to the **w** person's power
37:34 When **w** people are cut off,
37:35 I have seen a **w** person ⌊acting
37:38 The future of **w** people will be
37:40 rescues them from **w** people.
39:1 I will bridle my mouth while **w**
50:16 But God says to **w** people,
55:3 and a **w** person persecutes me.
55:15 suddenly take ⌊**w** people⌋!
1Ch 55:23 But you, O God, will throw ⌊**w**
58:3 ⌊Even⌋ inside the womb **w**
58:10 feet in the blood of **w** people.
68:2 Let **w** people melt in God's
71:4 from the hands of a **w** person,
73:3 prosperity that **w** people enjoy.
73:11 Then **w** people ask,
73:12 Look how **w** they are!
75:4 "Don't brag," and to **w** people,
75:8 it, ⌊and⌋ all the **w** people
75:10 all the weapons of **w** people,
82:2 going to side with **w** people?"
82:4 escape the power of **w** people.
82:5 **W** people do not know or
84:10 live inside **w** people's homes.
89:22 No **w** person will mistreat him.
91:8 the punishment of **w** people.
92:7 that **w** people sprout like grass
94:3 will **w** people triumph?
94:13 a pit is dug to trap **w** people.
94:20 Are **w** rulers who use the law
97:10 from the power of **w** people.
101:3 I will not put anything **w** in front
101:8 I will destroy all the **w** people
104:35 no longer be any **w** people.
106:18 Flames burned up **w** people.
107:42 but all the **w** people will shut
109:2 **W** and deceitful people have
112:10 The **w** person sees this and
112:10 The hope that **w** people have
119:53 anger because of **w** people,
119:61 ⌊Though⌋ the ropes of **w**
119:95 The **w** people have waited for
119:110 **W** people have set a trap for
119:119 You get rid of all **w** people on
119:155 **W** people are far from being
125:3 A **w** ruler will not be allowed to
129:4 ropes that **w** people tied around
139:19 that you would kill **w** people,
139:20 They say **w** things about you.
140:4 me from the hands of **w** people,
140:8 O LORD, do not give **w** people
141:10 Let **w** people fall into their own
145:20 but he will destroy all **w**
146:9 But he keeps **w** people from
147:6 He brings **w** people down to
Pro 2:22 But **w** people will be cut off
3:25 destruction of **w** people when
3:33 curses the house of **w** people,
4:14 stray onto the path of **w** people.
4:16 **W** people cannot sleep unless
4:19 The way of **w** people is like
5:22 A **w** person will be trapped by
6:18 a mind devising **w** plans,
9:7 warns a **w** person gets hurt.
10:3 the desires of a **w** person.
10:6 covers the mouths of **w** people.
10:7 but the names of **w** people will
10:11 of **w** people conceal violence.
10:16 A **w** person's harvest is sin.
10:20 of **w** people are worthless.
10:24 That which **w** people dread
10:25 the **w** person has vanished,
10:27 of **w** people are shortened.
10:28 but the eager waiting of **w**
10:30 but **w** people will not continue
10:32 of **w** people are devious.
11:5 but **w** people fall by their own
11:7 At the death of a **w** person,
11:8 and a **w** person takes his
11:10 When **w** people die,
11:11 but by the words of **w** people,
11:18 A **w** person earns dishonest
11:23 but the hope of **w** people ends
11:31 how much more the **w** person
12:5 of **w** people is treacherous.
12:6 The words of **w** people are a
12:7 Overthrow **w** people,
12:10 but the compassion of **w**
12:12 A **w** person delights in setting
12:21 but **w** people have lots of
12:26 but the path of **w** people leads
13:5 but a **w** person behaves with
13:9 but the lamp of **w** people will
13:25 but the bellies of **w** people are
14:11 The houses of **w** people will

Pro 14:19 **W** people will bow at the gates
14:32 A **w** person is thrown down by
15:6 with the income of a **w** person.
15:8 A sacrifice brought by **w**
15:9 The way of **w** people is
15:28 but the mouths of **w** people
15:29 The LORD is far from **w** people,
16:4 even **w** people for the day of
17:4 pays attention to **w** lips.
17:15 Whoever approves of **w** people
17:23 A **w** person secretly accepts a
18:5 to be partial toward a **w** person,
19:28 and the mouths of **w** people
20:26 A wise king scatters the **w** and
21:4 are the lamps of **w** people,
21:7 The violence of **w** people will
21:10 The mind of a **w** person
21:12 the house of a **w** person.
21:12 throws **w** people into disasters.
21:18 **W** people become a ransom for
21:27 The sacrifice of **w** people is
21:29 A **w** person puts up a bold front,
24:15 You **w** one, do not lie in
24:16 in a disaster **w** people fall.
24:19 Do not envy **w** people,
24:20 and the lamps of **w** people will
25:5 Take a **w** person away from
25:26 who gives in to a **w** person.
28:1 A **w** person flees when no one
28:4 teachings praise **w** people,
28:4 teachings oppose **w** people.
28:12 but when **w** people rise,
28:15 ⌊so⌋ a **w** ruler is a threat to
28:28 When **w** people rise,
29:2 but when a **w** person rules,
29:7 A **w** person does not
29:12 all his servants become **w**.
29:16 When **w** people increase,
29:27 is disgusting to **w** people.
Ecc 3:17 people as well as **w** people,
7:15 **W** people go on living in spite
7:15 go on living in spite of being **w**.
7:17 Don't be too **w**, and don't be a
8:8 save **w** people ⌊from dying⌋.
8:10 Then I saw **w** people given an
8:13 But it will not go well for the **w**.
8:14 people suffer for what the **w** do,
8:14 and **w** people get what the
9:2 **w**, or good, clean or unclean,
Isa 3:11 How horrible it will be for the **w**!
11:4 He will kill the **w** with the
13:11 the world for its evil and the **w**
14:5 has broken the staff of the **w**,
14:20 The descendants of the **w** will
26:10 Although the **w** are shown pity,
26:14 The **w** are dead. They are no
31:2 He rises against **w** people and
32:7 They devise **w** plans in order
48:22 for the **w**," says the LORD.
53:9 placed in a tomb with the **w**.
55:7 Let **w** people abandon their
57:20 But the **w** are like the churning
57:21 peace for the **w**," says my God.
58:9 your finger and say **w** things.
59:3 and you mutter **w** things.
Jer 2:33 You taught your ways to **w**
5:26 "**W** people are found among my
8:3 from these **w** people will want
12:1 Why do **w** people succeed?
12:4 because people are **w**.
13:10 These **w** people refuse to
15:21 you from the power of **w** people
20:13 from the power of **w** people.
23:19 down on the heads of the **w**.
25:31 He will kill the **w**, declares the
30:14 You are very **w**, and you have
30:15 You are very **w**, and you have
30:23 down on the heads of the **w**.
36:3 will turn from their **w** ways.
44:5 You wouldn't turn from your **w**
44:9 Have you forgotten the **w**
44:22 could no longer bear the **w**
Eze 3:18 Suppose I tell you that **w**
3:18 they can change their **w** ways
3:18 Then these **w** people will die
3:19 you warn the **w** people,
Eze 3:19 don't turn from their **w** ways.
8:9 to me, "Go in, and see the **w**,
13:22 You encouraged **w** people not
13:22 not to turn from their **w** ways
16:43 Didn't you make **w** plans in
18:20 and the wickedness of the **w**
18:21 "But suppose a **w** person turns
18:23 I don't want **w** people to die."
18:24 things that the **w** person did.
18:27 When a **w** person turns away
18:27 away from the **w** things that
21:3 and the **w** people among you.
21:4 and the **w** people among you.
21:25 "You dishonest and **w** prince of
21:29 necks of dishonest, **w** people,
30:12 and sell the land to **w** people.
33:8 Suppose I say to a **w** person,
33:8 wicked person, 'You **w** person,
33:8 That **w** person will die
33:9 But if you warn a **w** person to
33:11 I don't want **w** people to die.
33:11 Turn from your **w** ways!
33:12 The **w** things that a wicked
33:12 The wicked things that a **w**
33:14 I may warn the **w** person that
33:19 If the **w** person turns from his
36:31 these **w** and disgusting things.
38:10 and you will make **w** plans.
Dan 9:16 and the **w** things our ancestors
12:10 But **w** people will do wicked
12:10 people will do **w** things,
Hos 4:8 and they want them to do **w**
4:9 I will punish them for their **w**
5:4 "The **w** things that the people
7:3 with the **w** things they do.
10:9 the **w** people in Gibeah.
10:15 you have done many **w** things.
Joe 3:13 The nations are very **w**.
Jnh 1:2 the **w** things they have
3:8 Turn from your **w** ways and
3:10 they turned from their **w** ways.
Mic 6:10 I have cursed all the **w** people
Nah 1:11 sets out. His advice is **w**.
Hab 1:4 **W** people surround righteous
1:13 Why are you silent when **w**
3:13 the leader of the **w** household,
Mal 1:4 They will be called 'the **W**
3:18 righteous people and **w** people,
4:3 You will trample on **w** people,
Mat 24:48 hand, that servant, if he is **w**,
Act 8:22 So change your **w** thoughts,
1Co 5:13 Remove that **w** man from
6:1 the matter in front of **w** people.
6:9 Don't you know that **w** people
Heb 3:12 none of you ever develop a **w**,
Jas 1:21 and all the **w** things you do.
Rev 2:2 you cannot tolerate **w** people.

wickedly (4)

2Sm 22:22 I have not **w** turned away from
Job 13:7 "Will you talk **w** for God and
Psa 18:21 I have not **w** turned away from
Dan 9:5 done wrong, acted **w**, rebelled,

wickedness (76)

Dtr 9:27 Disregard the stubbornness, **w**,
1Sm 15:23 **W** and idolatry are arrogance.
24:13 '**W** comes from wicked people.'
25:39 has turned Nabal's own **w** back
Ezr 9:11 filled it with **w** from one end
Job 4:8 I saw those who plowed **w**
15:16 one who drinks **w** like water.
24:20 and **w** is snapped like a twig.
35:8 Your **w** affects only someone
Psa 5:4 God who takes pleasure in **w**.
10:15 Punish his **w** until you find no
73:10 is why God's people turn to **w**
94:23 their own **w** against them.
107:34 a layer of salt because of the **w**
141:4 or to become involved with **w**,
Pro 8:7 and **w** is disgusting to my lips.
11:5 people fall by their own **w**.
12:3 stand firm on a foundation of **w**,
13:6 but **w** ruins a sacrifice for sin.
18:3 When **w** comes, contempt also
20:30 beatings cleanse away **w**.
Pro 26:26 but his **w** will be revealed to
Ecc 3:16 There is **w** where justice
3:16 There is **w** where
7:25 I learned that **w** is stupid and
8:8 **W** will not save wicked people
Isa 9:18 Surely **w** burns like fire.
47:10 feel safe in your **w** and say,
58:6 Loosen the chains of **w**,
Jer 1:16 people because of all their **w**.
2:19 Your own **w** will correct you,
2:22 stains from your **w**," declares
3:2 with your prostitution and **w**.
5:25 Your **w** has turned these things
8:6 turn away from their **w** and ask,
14:20 O LORD, we realize our **w** and
16:17 Their **w** can't be hidden;
16:18 pay twice as much for their **w**
22:22 and disgraced by all your **w**.
23:14 no one turns back from his **w**.
31:34 "because I will forgive their **w**
32:18 you punish children for the **w** of
33:5 from this city because of its **w**.
36:3 forgive their **w** and their sins."
36:31 and his attendants for their **w**.
Lam 1:22 Recall all of their **w**.
4:6 my people's **w** has been more
4:22 punishment for your **w** will end.
4:22 he will punish you for your **w**.
5:7 take the punishment for their **w**.
Eze 7:11 into a weapon for punishing **w**.
9:9 He answered me, "The **w** of
16:23 LORD. After all your **w**,
16:57 before your **w** was revealed.
18:20 and the **w** of the wicked person
31:11 I forced it out because of its **w**.
33:10 "Our **w** and our sins weigh us
33:12 when he turns from his **w**.
33:19 wicked person turns from his **w**
36:33 I cleanse you from all your **w**,
Hos 7:1 Ephraim's sin and Samaria's **w**.
8:13 Now I will remember their **w**
9:9 God will remember their **w** and
9:15 "All Ephraim's **w** began in
9:15 my temple because of their **w**,
10:13 You have planted **w** and
13:12 "Ephraim's **w** is on record.
Mic 3:10 and Jerusalem on **w**.
Nah 1:15 This **w** will never pass your
Hab 1:3 And why do you watch **w**?
1:13 You can't watch **w**.
Zec 5:8 The angel said, "This is **w**,"
Mar 7:22 adultery, greed, **w**,
Rom 1:29 **w**, and greed. They are mean.
1Co 5:8 or with the yeast of vice and **w**.
Heb 8:12 because I will forgive their **w**

wide (119)

Gen 6:15 75 feet **w**, and 45 feet high.
Exo 25:10 45 inches long, 27 inches **w**,
25:17 inches long and 27 inches **w**.
25:23 36 inches long, 18 inches **w**,
25:25 a rim three inches **w** around it,
26:2 42 feet long and 6 feet **w** — all
26:8 be 45 feet long and 6 feet **w**.
26:16 15 feet long and 27 inches **w**,
27:12 west end should be 75 feet **w**
27:13 should also be 75 feet **w**.
27:14 entrance⌋ will be 22 ½ feet **w**
27:18 75 feet **w**, and 7 ½ feet high,
36:9 42 feet long and 6 feet **w** — all
36:15 was 45 feet long and 6 feet **w**.
36:21 15 feet long and 27 inches **w**,
37:1 45 inches long, 27 inches **w**,
37:6 inches long and 27 inches **w**.
37:10 36 inches long, 18 inches **w**,
37:12 He made a rim 3 inches **w**
38:13 rising sun, was 75 feet ⌊**w**⌋.
38:14 the courtyard was 22 ½ feet **w**
Dtr 3:11 than 13 feet long and 6 feet **w**.
Jdg 18:10 The land is **w** open to you.
1Sm 26:13 was a **w** space between them.)
2Sm 22:37 You make a **w** path for me to
1Ki 6:2 30 feet **w**, and 45 feet high.
6:6 of the annex was 7 ½ feet **w**,
6:6 the second story was 9 feet **w**,
6:6 third story was 10 ½ feet **w**.

1Ki 6:20 30 feet **w**, and 30 feet high.
7:2 It was 150 feet long, 75 feet **w**,
7:6 75 feet long and 45 feet **w**.
7:31 and was two **f** ⌊wide⌋.
7:38 Every basin was six feet ⌊**w**⌋.
2Ch 3:3 was 90 feet long and 35 feet **w**.
3:4 was 30 feet **w** (the same as
3:8 as long as the temple was **w**,
3:8 It was also 30 feet **w**.
4:1 30 feet **w**, and 15 feet high.
6:13 7 ½ feet long, 7 ½ feet **w**,
26:15 Uzziah's fame spread far and **w**
Ezr 6:3 be 90 feet high and 90 feet **w**
Job 29:23 They opened their mouths **w**
30:14 They come through a **w** hole
38:18 you ⌊even⌋ considered how **w**
Psa 18:36 You make a **w** path for me to
60:2 You split it **w** open.
81:10 Open your mouth **w**,
104:25 The sea is so big and **w** with
Isa 5:14 It opens its mouth very **w** so
30:33 It was made deep and **w** and
33:21 a place surrounded by **w** rivers
Eze 23:32 a cup that is deep and **w**.
28:16 You traded far and **w**.
40:6 It was 10 ½ feet **w**.
40:7 ½ feet long and 10 ½ feet **w**.
40:7 the temple was 10 ½ feet **w**.
40:11 It was 17 ½ feet **w**,
40:13 It was 44 feet **w** from one door
40:14 It was 35 feet **w**. In front of the
40:18 It was as **w** as it was long.
40:21 87 ½ feet long and 44 feet **w**.
40:25 87 ½ feet long and 44 feet **w**.
40:29 87 ½ feet long and 44 feet **w**.
40:30 all 44 feet long and 9 feet **w**.
40:33 87 ½ feet long and 44 feet **w**.
40:36 87 ½ feet long and 44 feet **w**.
40:42 They were 3 feet long, 3 feet **w**,
40:47 175 feet long and 175 feet **w**.
40:48 gateway was 24 ½ feet **w**,
40:48 on each side were 5 feet **w**.
40:49 was 35 feet long and 21 feet **w**.
41:1 10 ½ feet **w** on each side.
41:2 entrance was 17 ½ feet **w**,
41:2 the walls were 9 feet **w**.
41:2 was 70 feet long and 35 feet **w**.
41:3 10 ½ feet high and 12 feet **w**.
41:4 was 35 feet long and 35 feet **w**.
41:5 It was 10 ½ feet **w**.
41:10 It was 35 feet **w** and went all
41:11 the open area was 9 feet **w** all
41:12 was a building 122 ½ feet **w**.
41:14 was also 175 feet **w**.
41:22 5 feet high and 3 ½ feet **w**.
42:2 175 feet long and 87 ½ feet **w**.
42:3 an area that was 35 feet **w**,
42:4 17 ½ feet **w** and 175 feet long.
42:11 were as long and as **w** as
42:20 875 feet long and 875 feet **w**.
43:13 inches high and 21 inches **w**.
43:13 a rim measuring 9 inches **w**.
43:14 7 feet high and 21 inches **w**.
43:16 21 feet **w** and 21 feet long.
43:17 ½ feet long and 24 ½ feet **w**.
43:17 that was 10 ½ inches **w**.
45:1 feet long and 35,000 feet **w**
45:2 an open area 87 ½ feet **w**.
45:3 feet long and 17,500 feet **w**.
45:5 and 17,500 feet **w** will belong
45:6 designate an area 8,750 feet **w**
46:22 60 feet long and 45 feet **w**.
48:8 It will be 43,750 feet **w**,
48:9 feet long and 17,500 feet **w**.
48:10 side it will be 17,500 feet **w**.
48:10 side it will be 17,500 feet **w**.
48:13 feet long and 17,500 feet **w**.
48:15 A strip of land, 8,750 feet **w** by
48:16 side it will be 7,875 feet **w**.
48:16 side it will be 7,875 feet **w**.
Dan 3:1 90 feet high and 9 feet **w**.
Mic 4:3 many nations far and **w**.
Nah 3:13 The gates of your country are **w**
Zec 2:2 Jerusalem to see how **w**
5:2 "It's 30 feet long and 15 feet **w**."
Mat 7:13 that lead to destruction are **w**.
Mat 7:13 Many enter through the **w** gate.
Luk 16:26 a **w** area separates us.
Eph 3:18 be able to understand how **w**,
Rev 21:16 It was as **w** as it was long.

wide-open (5)

2Sm 22:20 He brought me out to a **w** place.
Neh 7:4 The city was large and **w**.
Job 16:10 gaped at me with **w** mouths.
Psa 18:19 He brought me out to a **w** place.
119:148 My eyes are **w** throughout the

wider (3)

Job 11:9 the earth and **w** than the sea.
Eze 41:7 The side rooms grew **w** all the
41:7 The structure grew **w** as it

widow (40)

Gen 38:8 sleep with your brother's **w**.
38:9 he slept with his brother's **w**,
38:11 Live as a **w** until my son
Exo 22:22 advantage of any **w** or orphan.
Lev 21:14 He must never marry a **w**,
Num 30:9 "But a **w** or a divorced woman
Dtr 25:5 his **w** must not marry outside
25:7 want to marry his brother's **w**,
25:9 his brother's **w** must go up to
Rut 4:5 the dead man's **w**.
4:10 the Moabite Ruth, Mahlon's **w**,
2Sm 14:5 She answered, "I'm a **w**;
1Ki 7:14 Hiram was the son of a **w** from
11:26 His mother Zeruah was a **w**.
17:9 I've commanded a **w** there to
17:10 a **w** was gathering wood.
17:20 misery on the **w** I'm staying
Job 31:18 my birth I treated the **w** kindly.)
Psa 109:9 fatherless and his wife a **w**.
Isa 47:8 I won't live as a **w**.
Lam 1:1 Now it is a **w**. Once it was a
Mat 22:24 his brother should marry his **w**
22:25 he left his **w** to his brother.
Mar 12:19 his brother should marry his **w**
12:42 A poor **w** dropped in two small
12:43 This poor **w** has given more
Luk 2:37 and she had been a **w** for 84
4:26 except a **w** at Zarephath
18:3 In that city there was also a **w**
18:4 'This **w** really annoys me.
20:28 his brother should marry his **w**
20:30 second brother married the **w**,
20:31 seven brothers married the **w**,
21:2 He noticed a poor **w** drop in
21:3 This poor **w** has given more
1Ti 5:4 of a **w** must first learn
5:5 A **w** who has no family has
5:6 But the **w** who lives for
5:9 Any **w** who had only one
Rev 18:7 a queen on a throne, not a **w**.

widowed (1)

Lev 22:13 daughter is **w** or divorced,

widow's (6)

Gen 38:14 she took off her **w** clothes,
38:19 and put her **w** clothes back on.
Job 24:3 They take the **w** ox as security
29:13 I made the **w** heart sing for joy.
31:16 made a **w** eyes stop ⌊looking
Luk 7:12 dead man was a **w** only child.

widows (50)

Exo 22:24 will become **w** and orphans.
Dtr 10:18 orphans and **w** receive justice.
14:29 Foreigners, orphans, and **w**
16:11 and **w** who live among you.
16:14 and **w** who live in your cities.
24:19 for foreigners, orphans, and **w**.
24:20 for foreigners, orphans, and **w**.
24:21 for foreigners, orphans, and **w**.
26:12 and **w** in your cities,
26:13 and **w** as you commanded me.
27:19 or **w** of justice will be cursed."
2Sm 20:3 So they lived like **w** in
Job 22:9 send **w** away empty-handed,
24:21 men show no kindness to **w**.
27:15 and their **w** won't cry ⌊for
Psa 68:5 and the defender of **w**.
78:64 The **w** ⌊of his priests⌋ could
94:6 They kill **w** and foreigners,
146:9 gives relief to orphans and **w**.
Pro 15:25 he protects the property of **w**.
Isa 1:17 Plead the case of **w**."
9:17 for their orphans and **w**.
10:2 prey on **w** and rob orphans.
Jer 7:6 foreigners, orphans, and **w**,
15:8 Their **w** will be more numerous
18:21 will become childless **w**.
22:3 or **w**, and don't oppress them.
49:11 Your **w** can trust me."
Lam 5:3 Our mothers are like **w**.
Eze 22:7 oppress orphans and **w** in you.
22:25 They turn many women into **w**.
44:22 They must not marry **w** or
44:22 nation of Israel or **w** of priests.
Zec 7:10 Don't oppress **w**, orphans,
Mal 3:5 and oppress **w** and orphans.
Mar 12:40 They rob **w** by taking their
Luk 4:25 There were many **w** in Israel in
20:47 They rob **w** by taking their
Act 6:1 that the **w** among them were
9:39 All the **w** stood around him.
9:41 the believers, especially the **w**,
1Co 7:8 not married, especially to **w**:
1Ti 5:3 Honor **w** who have no families.
5:7 Insist on these things so that **w**
5:9 be put on your list ⌊of **w**⌋.
5:11 Don't include younger **w** ⌊on
5:14 So I want younger **w** to marry,
5:16 and has relatives who are **w**,
5:16 and can help **w** who have no
Jas 1:27 and **w** when they suffer

widows' (2)

Dtr 24:17 And never take **w** clothes to
Isa 1:23 They don't notice the **w** pleas

width (5)

2Ch 3:4 feet wide (the same as the **w**
Eze 40:11 Then the man measured the **w**
40:20 measured the length and **w**
41:5 The **w** of each side room
Rev 21:16 Its length, **w**, and height were

wife (339)

Gen 2:24 and will be united with his **w**,
2:25 The man and his **w** were both
3:8 the man and his **w** heard the
3:17 "You listened to your **w** and ate
3:20 Adam named his **w** Eve [Life]
3:21 and his **w** and dressed them.
4:1 Adam made love to his **w** Eve.
4:17 Cain made love to his **w**.
4:25 made love to his **w** again.
6:18 You, your sons, your **w**,
7:7 Noah, his sons, his **w**,
7:13 as well as Noah's **w** and his
8:16 out of the ship with your **w**,
8:18 his **w**, and his sons' wives.
11:29 name of Abram's **w** was Sarai,
11:29 name of Nahor's **w** was Milcah,
11:31 **w** of his son Abram.
12:5 He took along his **w** Sarai,
12:11 Abram said to his **w** Sarai,
12:12 'This is his **w**!' Then
12:14 how very beautiful his **w** was.
12:17 because of Sarai, Abram's **w**.
12:18 you tell me that she's your **w**?
12:19 allow me to take her for my **w**?
12:19 Here's your **w**! Take her and go!
12:20 sent Abram away with his **w**
13:1 Abram left Egypt with his **w**
16:1 Sarai, Abram's **w**, was not able
16:3 Abram's **w** Sarai took her
16:3 her husband Abram to be his **w**.
17:15 "Don't call your **w** by the name
17:19 Your **w** Sarah will give you a
18:9 "Where is your **w** Sarah?"
18:10 and your **w** Sarah will have a
19:15 Take your **w** and your two
19:16 the men grabbed him, his **w**,
19:26 Lot's **w** looked back and turned
20:2 that his **w** Sarah was his

Gen	20:7	Give the man's **w** back to him
	20:11	I'd be killed because of my **w**.
	20:12	She is also my **w**.
	20:14	He also gave his **w** Sarah back
	20:17	God healed Abimelech, his **w**,
	20:18	of Abraham's **w** Sarah.)
	21:21	mother got him a **w** from Egypt.
	23:3	left the side of his dead **w**
	23:4	so that I can bury my dead **w**."
	23:8	are willing to let me bury my **w**,
	23:11	giving it to you. Bury your **w**!"
	23:13	so that I can bury my **w** there."
	23:15	between us? Bury your **w**!"
	23:19	Abraham buried his **w** Sarah
	24:3	will not get my son a **w** from
	24:4	of my relatives and get a **w**
	24:7	will get my son a **w** from there.
	24:15	who was the **w** of Abraham's
	24:36	My master's **w** Sarah gave him
	24:37	'Don't get a **w** for my son from
	24:38	and get my son a **w**.'
	24:40	You will get my son a **w** from
	24:51	She will become the **w** of your
	24:67	She became his **w**,
	25:10	was buried with his **w** Sarah.
	25:21	prayed to the LORD for his **w**
	25:21	**w** Rebekah became pregnant.
	26:7	that place asked about his **w**,
	26:7	He was afraid to say "my **w**."
	26:8	caressing his **w** Rebekah.
	26:9	"So she's really your **w**!
	26:10	easily gone to bed with your **w**,
	26:11	touches this man or his **w** will
	28:2	and get yourself a **w** from there
	28:6	Aram to get a **w** from there.
	29:21	"The time is up; give me my **w**!
	29:28	Rachel to him as his **w**.
	30:4	him her slave Bilhah as his **w**,
	30:9	gave her to Jacob as his **w**.
	34:4	"Get me this girl for my **w**."
	34:12	Give me the girl as my **w**."
	36:10	son of Esau's **w** Adah,
	36:10	son of Esau's **w** Basemath.
	36:12	grandsons of Esau's **w** Adah.
	36:13	of Esau's **w** Basemath.
	36:14	sons of Esau's **w** Oholibamah,
	36:17	of Esau's **w** Basemath.
	36:18	of Esau's **w** Oholibamah:
	36:18	from Esau's **w** Oholibamah,
	38:6	Judah chose a **w** for his
	38:12	After a long time Judah's **w**,
	39:7	After a while his master's **w**
	39:9	because you're his **w**.
	41:45	gave him Asenath as his **w**.
	44:27	'You know that my **w** ⌊Rachel⌋
	46:19	The sons of Jacob's **w** Rachel
	49:31	Abraham and his **w** Sarah are
	49:31	Isaac and his **w** Rebekah are
Exo	2:21	Zipporah to Moses as his **w**.
	4:20	So Moses took his **w** and sons,
	18:2	had sent away his **w** Zipporah,
	18:5	brought Moses' sons and **w**
	18:6	⌊and I'm bringing⌋ your **w** and
	20:17	to take your neighbor's **w**,
	21:3	his **w** may leave with him.
	21:4	If his master gives him a **w**
	21:4	the **w** and her children belong
	21:5	master, my **w**, and my children.
	21:8	who has chosen her as a **w**,
	21:10	not deprive the first **w** of food,
Lev	18:11	of your father and his **w**.
	18:14	sexual intercourse with the **w**
	18:15	She is your son's **w**.
	18:16	She is your brother's **w**.
	18:18	While your **w** is living,
	18:18	marry her sister as a rival **w**
	18:20	with your neighbor's **w**
	20:10	adultery with another man's **w**
	20:10	wife or with his neighbor's **w**,
	20:11	his father's **w** has violated his
	20:11	Both he and his father's **w** must
	20:20	uncle's **w** violates his uncle's
	20:21	**w** violates his brother's
Num	5:12	A man's **w** may have been
	5:14	of jealousy and suspect his **w**,
	5:15	He must then take his **w** to the
Num	5:30	and is suspicious of his **w**.
	5:30	He will make his **w** stand in
	26:59	of Amram's **w** was Jochebed,
	30:13	whether or not his **w** has
Dtr	5:21	neighbor's **w** away from him.
	13:6	or daughter, the **w** you love,
	21:13	will become husband and **w**.
	21:15	son might belong to the **w** that
	21:16	he can't treat the son of the **w**
	21:16	son of the **w** he doesn't love).
	21:17	recognize the son of the **w**
	22:19	She will continue to be his **w**,
	22:24	had sex with another man's **w**.
	22:29	and she will become his **w**.
	22:30	must never marry his father's **w**
	24:1	of divorce, gives it to his **w**,
	24:5	and make his new **w** happy.
	25:11	two men are fighting and the **w**
	27:20	with his father's **w** will
	28:54	his brother, the **w** he loves,
Jos	15:16	my daughter Achsah as a **w**
	15:17	his daughter Achsah as a **w**.
Jdg	1:12	my daughter Achsah as a **w**
	1:13	his daughter Achsah as a **w**.
	4:4	Deborah, **w** of Lappidoth,
	4:17	the **w** of Heber the Kenite.
	4:21	exhaustion, Jael, Heber's **w**,
	5:24	Jael, **w** of Heber the Kenite,
	11:2	Gilead's **w** also gave birth to
	13:2	His **w** was not able to have
	13:9	back to his **w** while she was
	13:11	immediately followed his **w**.
	13:11	the man who spoke to my **w**?"
	13:13	"Your **w** must be careful to do
	13:19	Manoah and his **w** watched,
	13:20	Manoah and his **w** saw this,
	13:21	again to Manoah and his **w**.
	13:22	So Manoah said to his **w**,
	13:23	But Manoah's **w** replied,
	14:15	day they said to Samson's **w**,
	14:16	So Samson's **w** cried on his
	14:20	Samson's **w** was given to his
	15:1	Samson went to visit his **w**.
	15:1	"I'm going to sleep with my **w**
	15:6	at Timnah took Samson's **w**
	15:6	Philistines burned Samson's **w**
	19:27	His **w** (that is, his concubine)
	21:21	from Shiloh to be your **w**.
	21:22	since we didn't provide a **w** for
Rut	1:1	in Judah went with his **w**
	4:10	I have bought as my **w** the
	4:11	May the LORD make this **w**,
	4:13	and she became his **w**.
1Sm	1:4	portions of it to his **w** Peninnah
	1:19	made love to his **w** Hannah,
	2:20	Elkanah (and his **w**) and say,
	4:19	Phinehas' **w**, was pregnant.
	14:50	of Saul's **w** was Ahinoam,
	18:17	I will give her to you as your **w**
	18:27	his daughter Michal as his **w**.
	19:11	But Michal, David's **w**,
	25:14	men told Abigail, Nabal's **w**,
	25:37	his **w** told him what had
	25:40	take you to him to be his **w**."
	25:42	and became his **w**.
	25:44	David's **w**, to Palti, Laish's son,
	27:3	been Nabal's **w**) from Carmel.
	30:5	been Nabal's **w**) from Carmel.
	30:22	of them should take only his **w**
2Sm	2:2	been Nabal's **w**) from Carmel.
	3:3	been Nabal's **w**) from Carmel.
	3:5	⌊born⌋ to David's **w** Eglah.
	3:14	"Give me my **w** Michal.
	11:3	daughter of Eliam and **w** of
	11:11	drink and go to bed with my **w**?
	11:26	When Uriah's **w** heard that her
	11:27	and she became his **w**.
	12:9	You took his **w** as your wife.
	12:9	You took his wife as your **w**.
	12:10	despised me and took the **w**
	12:10	of Uriah the Hittite to be your **w**.
	12:15	that Uriah's **w** had given birth
	12:24	comforted his **w** Bathsheba.
	17:19	The man's **w** took a cover,
1Ki	2:17	from Shunem as my **w**.
	2:21	brother Adonijah as his **w**."
1Ki	4:11	daughter Taphath was his **w**.)
	7:8	quarters like this for his **w**,
	9:16	it to his daughter, Solomon's **w**,
	11:19	Tahpenes, to be Hadad's **w**.
	14:2	Jeroboam told his **w**,
	14:2	not recognize you as my **w**.
	14:4	Jeroboam's **w** did this.
	14:5	"Jeroboam's **w** is coming to
	14:6	You're Jeroboam's **w**.
	14:17	Jeroboam's **w** got up,
	21:5	His **w** Jezebel came to him
	21:7	His **w** Jezebel said to him,
	21:25	At the urging of his **w**,
2Ki	5:2	the servant of Naaman's **w**.
	8:18	because his **w** was Ahab's
	22:14	She was the **w** of Shallum,
1Ch	2:18	Caleb and his **w** Azubah had a
	2:24	Hezron's **w** Abijah gave birth to
	2:26	Jerahmeel had another **w**.
	2:29	of Abishur's **w** was Abihail.
	3:3	⌊born⌋ to David's **w** Eglah.
	4:17	His **w** gave birth to Miriam,
	4:18	His Judean **w** was the mother
	4:19	The sons of Hodiah's **w**
	7:15	He married a **w** from the
	7:16	Maacah, Machir's **w**,
	7:23	Then he slept with his **w**,
	8:9	he and his **w** Hodesh had the
2Ch	8:11	He said, "My **w** will not live in
	21:6	because his **w** was Ahab's
	22:11	of King Jehoram and **w**
	34:22	She was the **w** of Shallum,
Est	5:10	his friends and his **w** Zeresh.
	5:14	Then his **w** Zeresh and all his
	6:13	relate in detail to his **w** Zeresh
	6:13	Then his counselors and his **w**
Job	2:9	His **w** asked him, "Are you still
	19:17	My breath offends my **w**.
	31:10	⌊then⌋ let my **w** grind for
Psa	109:9	fatherless and his **w** a widow.
	128:3	Your **w** will be like a fruitful
Pro	6:29	has sex with his neighbor's **w**.
	12:4	A **w** with strength of character
	12:4	but the **w** who disgraces him is
	18:22	Whoever finds a **w** finds
	19:14	but a sensible **w** comes from
	31:10	"Who can find a **w** with a
Ecc	9:9	Enjoy life with your **w**,
Isa	54:6	were a **w** who was abandoned
	54:6	a **w** who married young and
Jer	3:1	If a man divorces his **w** and
	3:20	But like a **w** who betrays her
	6:11	A man and his **w** will be taken
Eze	16:32	You are an adulterous **w** who
	18:6	dishonor his neighbor's **w**
	18:11	He dishonors his neighbor's **w**.
	18:15	dishonor his neighbor's **w**.
	23:5	although she was my **w**.
	24:18	and in the evening my **w** died.
	33:26	dishonor your neighbor's **w**.
Dan	11:17	king his daughter as a **w**
Hos	2:2	She no longer acts like my **w**.
	2:19	I will make you my **w** forever.
	2:20	I will be true to you, my **w**.
	3:1	"Love your **w** again,
	12:12	Israel worked to get a **w**;
Amo	7:17	Your **w** will become a
Mal	2:14	between you and the **w**
	2:14	the **w** of your marriage vows.
	2:15	to the **w** of your youth.
Mat	1:6	David and Uriah's **w**
	1:20	afraid to take Mary as your **w**.
	1:24	He took Mary to be his **w**.
	5:31	'Whoever divorces his **w** must
	5:32	any man who divorces his **w**
	14:3	the **w** of his brother Philip.
	18:25	him, his **w**, his children,
	19:3	divorce his **w** for any reason?"
	19:5	will remain united with his **w**,
	19:7	order a man to give his **w**
	19:9	that whoever divorces his **w**
	19:10	man can use to divorce his **w**,
	22:28	whose **w** will she be?
	27:19	his **w** sent him a message.
Mar	6:17	to be his brother Philip's **w**.)
	6:18	be married to your brother's **w**."

Mar 10:2 a husband divorce his **w**?"
10:4 allowed a man to give his **w**
10:7 will remain united with his **w**,
10:11 "Whoever divorces his **w** and
10:12 If a **w** divorces her husband
12:19 'If a man dies and leaves a **w**
12:23 whose **w** will she be?
Luk 1:5 Zechariah's **w** Elizabeth was a
1:13 Your **w** Elizabeth will have a
1:18 I'm an old man, and my **w** is
1:24 Later, his **w** Elizabeth became
16:18 "Any man who divorces his **w**
17:32 Remember Lot's **w**!
18:29 his home, **w**, brothers, parents,
20:33 whose **w** will she be?
Jon 19:25 Mary (the **w** of Clopas),
Act 5:1 and his **w** Sapphira sold some
5:7 hours later Ananias' **w** arrived.
18:2 Aquila and his **w** Priscilla.
24:24 arrived with his **w** Drusilla,
1Co 5:1 married to his father's **w**.
7:2 man should have his own **w**,
7:4 A **w** doesn't have authority over
7:4 his own body, but his **w** does.
7:10 A **w** shouldn't leave her
7:11 should not divorce his **w**.
7:14 is made holy because of his **w**,
7:14 and an unbelieving **w** is made
7:16 How do you as a **w** know
7:16 whether you will save your **w**?
7:27 Do you have a **w**?
7:27 Are you divorced from your **w**?
7:33 how he can please his **w**.
11:3 has authority over his **w**,
Eph 5:23 is the head of his **w** as Christ is
5:28 who loves his **w** loves himself.
5:31 and be united with his **w**,
5:33 husband must love his **w** as
1Th 4:4 that finding a husband or **w**
1Ti 3:2 He must have only one **w**,
3:12 deacon must have only one **w**.
Tit 1:6 He must have only one **w** and
Rev 21:9 the **w** of the lamb."

wife's (10)

Gen 25:1 and his **w** name was Keturah.
36:39 His **w** name was Mehetabel,
39:19 **w** story, especially when she
Jdg 11:2 When his **w** sons grew up,
Rut 1:2 his **w** name was Naomi,
1Sm 25:3 and his **w** name was Abigail.
1Ch 1:50 His **w** name was Mehetabel,
7:15 His **w** name was Maacah.
8:29 and his **w** name was Maacah.
9:35 and his **w** name was Maacah.

wild (146)

Gen 1:24 animal, and **w** animal."
1:25 made every type of **w** animal,
2:5 **W** bushes and plants were not
2:19 had formed all the **w** animals
2:20 and all the **w** animals.
3:1 clever than all the **w** animals
3:14 are cursed more than all the **w**
3:18 and you will eat **w** plants.
7:14 them every type of **w** animal,
7:21 domestic and **w** animals,
8:1 remembered Noah and all the **w**
9:2 All the **w** animals and all the
9:10 and all the **w** animals,
16:12 He will be as free and **w** as an
25:28 to eat the meat of **w** animals,
27:3 and hunt some **w** game for me.
27:5 to hunt for some **w** game
27:7 'Bring me some **w** game,
31:39 that was killed by **w** animals.
37:20 and say that a **w** animal has
37:33 A **w** animal has eaten him!
Exo 9:32 Neither the wheat nor the **w**
22:13 If it was killed by a **w** animal,
22:31 been killed by **w** animals out
23:11 and **w** animals may eat what
23:29 and **w** animals would take
32:18 It's the sound of a **w**
Lev 5:2 the unclean dead body of a **w**
7:24 is killed by **w** animals you may
Lev 22:8 or is killed by **w** animals.
25:7 your animals and the **w**
26:22 I will send **w** animals among
Num 23:22 has the strength of a **w** bull.
24:8 has the strength of a **w** bull.
Dtr 7:22 you would be overrun with **w**
14:5 deer, **w** goats, mountain goats,
28:26 for all the birds and **w** animals.
33:17 will be like the horns of a **w** ox.
1Sm 14:20 fellow soldiers in **w** confusion.
17:46 to the birds and the **w** animals.
24:2 on the Rocks of the **W** Goats.
2Sm 2:18 fast on his feet as a **w** gazelle.
17:8 fierce as a **w** bear whose cubs
21:10 or any **w** animals come near
2Ki 4:39 vegetables and found a **w** vine.
4:39 his clothes with **w** gourds.
14:9 but a **w** animal from Lebanon
2Ch 25:18 but a **w** animal from Lebanon
Neh 8:15 branches — olive and **w** olive,
Job 5:22 so do not be afraid of **w**
5:23 and **w** animals will be at peace
6:5 "Does a **w** donkey bray when
11:12 when a **w** donkey is born
24:5 Like **w** donkeys in the desert,
39:4 healthy and grow up in the **w**.
39:5 "Who lets the **w** donkey go
39:5 Who unties the ropes of the **w**
39:9 "Will the **w** ox agree to serve
39:10 Can you guide a **w** ox in a
39:15 or a **w** animal may trample
40:20 all the **w** animals play there.
Psa 8:7 and cattle, the **w** animals,
22:21 and from the horns of **w** oxen.
29:6 and Mount Sirion like a **w** ox.
73:7 and their imaginations run **w**.
74:19 soul of your dove to **w** animals.
80:13 **W** boars from the forest graze
80:13 **W** animals devour it.
92:10 make me as strong as a **w** bull,
104:11 Every **w** animal drinks ⌊from
104:11 **W** donkeys quench their thirst.
104:18 high mountains are for **w** goats.
104:20 when all the **w** animals in the
148:10 **w** animals and all domestic
Pro 29:18 prophetic vision people run **w**,
Isa 5:2 produced only sour, **w** grapes.
5:4 it produce only sour, **w** grapes?
13:21 and **w** goats will skip about.
18:6 mountains and the **w** animals.
18:6 and all the **w** animals on earth
28:25 Doesn't he plant **w** wheat in
32:14 They will be a delight for **w**
34:7 **W** oxen will be killed with
35:9 **W** animals won't go on it.
40:16 Its **w** animals are not enough
41:19 and **w** olive trees in the desert.
43:20 **W** animals, jackals,
Jer 2:21 me and have become a **w** vine.
2:24 You are like a **w** donkey that is
5:8 stallions that are **w** with desire.
14:6 **W** donkeys stand on the bare
23:32 with their lies and their **w** talk.
27:6 made **w** animals serve him.
28:14 make **w** animals serve him."
34:20 food for birds and **w** animals.
48:6 Run like a **w** donkey in the
Lam 4:3 are as cruel as **w** ostriches.
Eze 4:14 was killed by other **w** animals.
5:17 I will send famines and **w**
14:15 "Suppose I send **w** animals
14:21 **w** animals, and plagues.
29:5 you to **w** animals and birds.
31:6 All the **w** animals gave birth to
31:13 and all the **w** animals lived in
32:4 and **w** animals from all over the
33:27 become food for **w** animals.
34:5 they became food for every **w**
34:8 food for every **w** animal.
34:25 I will remove the **w** animals
34:28 and the **w** animals will no
38:20 Fish, birds, **w** animals,
39:4 of prey and for every **w** animal.
39:17 of bird and every **w** animal,
44:31 was killed by other **w** animals.
Dan 2:38 people, **w** animals, and birds,
Dan 4:12 **W** animals found shade under
4:21 **W** animals lived under it,
4:23 the ground with the **w** animals
4:25 and live with the **w** animals.
4:32 and live with the **w** animals.
5:21 He lived with **w** donkeys,
Hos 2:12 and **w** animals will devour
2:18 with the **w** animals,
4:3 **W** animals, birds, and fish are
8:9 They were like **w** donkeys
13:8 Like a **w** animal I will tear you
Joe 1:20 Even **w** animals long for you.
2:22 **W** animals, do not be afraid.
Zep 2:15 a resting place for **w** animals!
Mat 3:4 of locusts and **w** honey.
Mar 1:6 and ate locusts and **w** honey.
1:13 was there with the **w** animals,
Luk 15:13 he had on a **w** lifestyle.
Act 11:6 **w** animals, reptiles, and birds.
Rom 11:17 off, and you, a **w** olive branch,
11:24 been cut from a **w** olive tree,
13:13 **W** parties, drunkenness,
1Co 15:32 If I have fought with **w** animals
Gal 5:21 envy, drunkenness, **w** partying,
Eph 5:18 which leads to **w** living.
Tit 1:6 known for having **w** lifestyles
1Pe 4:3 got drunk, went to **w** parties,
4:4 the same excesses of **w** living.
2Pe 2:13 pleasure in holding **w** parties
Jud 1:13 like the foam on the **w** waves
Rev 6:8 and the **w** animals on the earth.

wilderness (33)

1Sm 17:28 those few sheep in the **w**?
1Ki 19:4 Then he traveled through the **w**
19:15 back to the **w** near Damascus,
1Ch 6:78 Bezer in the **w** with its
Job 12:24 stumble about in a pathless **w**.
Psa 29:8 LORD makes the **w** tremble.
29:8 the **w** of Kadesh tremble.
75:6 or ⌊even⌋ from the **w**.
78:40 rebelled against him in the **w**!
78:52 them like a flock through the **w**.
106:14 desire ⌊for food⌋ in the **w**.
106:26 he would kill them in the **w**,
Sos 3:6 up from the **w** like clouds
8:5 woman coming from the **w**
Isa 32:15 Then the **w** will be turned into
32:16 Then justice will live in the **w**,
33:9 Sharon has become like a **w**.
35:1 and the **w** will rejoice and
35:6 will gush out into the **w**.
40:3 highway in the **w** for our God.
41:19 cypress trees together in the **w**.
51:3 He will make its **w** like the
63:13 Like horses in the **w**,
Jer 5:6 A wolf from the **w** will destroy
9:10 song for the pastures in the **w**.
17:6 He will be like a bush in the **w**.
23:10 Pastures in the **w** have dried
Lam 4:19 and ambushed us in the **w**.
Eze 34:25 sheep can live safely in the **w**
Joe 2:22 The pastures in the **w** have
Rev 12:6 Then the woman fled into the **w**
12:14 the snake to her place in the **w**,
17:3 me by his power into the **w**.

wildly (2)

Jer 4:19 My heart is beating **w**!
46:9 Drive **w**, you chariot drivers.

will (32)

Exo 18:15 come to me to find out God's **w**.
33:7 seeking the LORD's **w** used
Ezr 7:18 conform to the **w** of your God.
Psa 27:12 Do not surrender me to the **w** of
40:8 I am happy to do your **w**,
103:21 servants who carry out his **w**.
143:10 Teach me to do your **w**,
53:10 Yet, it was the LORD's **w** to
Isa 53:10 The **w** of the LORD will
Mat 6:10 Let your **w** be done on earth as
26:42 I drink it, let your **w** be done."
Luk 22:42 "Father, if it is your **w**,
22:42 However, your **w** must be done,
Jon 7:17 who want to follow the **w**

Act 13:36 After doing God's **w** by serving
21:14 "May the Lord's **w** be done."
22:14 has chosen you to know his **w**,
Rom 15:32 Also pray that by the **w** of God
1Co 1:1 Christ Jesus by the **w** of God,
4:19 If it's the Lord's **w**, I'll visit you
2Co 1:1 Christ Jesus by the **w** of God,
8:5 since this was God's **w**.
Gal 3:15 one can cancel a person's **w**
Eph 1:1 of Christ Jesus by God's **w**.
Col 1:1 of Christ Jesus by God's **w**,
1:9 of his **w** through every kind
1Th 4:3 It is God's **w** that you keep
5:18 because it is God's **w** in Christ
2Ti 2:26 so that they can do his **w**.
1Pe 3:17 After all, if it is God's **w**,
4:19 suffer because that is God's **w**
Rev 4:11 created because of your **w**."

willing (49)

Gen 23:8 He said to them, "If you are **w**
24:41 to me if my relatives are not **w**
47:25 "Please, sir, we are **w** to be
Exo 35:5 Let everyone who is **w** bring
35:21 Those who were **w** and whose
35:22 All who were **w** — men and
35:26 All the women who were **w**
35:29 who was **w** brought all these
36:2 these skills and who was **w**
Dtr 29:20 The LORD will never be **w** to
1Ki 13:33 He took all who were **w** and
1Ch 19:19 the Arameans were no longer **w**
29:5 Who else is **w** to make an
2Ch 29:31 was **w** brought burnt offerings.
Neh 2:5 and you are **w** to grant my
2:6 he was **w** to let me go.
Job 6:9 that God would ⌊finally⌋ be **w**
6:28 "But now, if you're **w**,
Psa 51:12 with a spirit of **w** obedience.
Pro 31:13 care⌋ and works with **w** hands.
Isa 1:19 If you are **w** and obedient,
28:12 But they weren't **w** to listen.
Eze 13:19 You lie to my people who are **w**
Mat 8:2 said to Jesus, "Sir, if you're **w**,
8:3 touched him, and said, "I'm **w**.
11:14 If you are **w** to accept their
11:27 the Son is **w** to reveal him.
23:4 However, they are not **w** to lift
23:37 But you were not **w**!
Mar 1:40 and begged Jesus, "If you're **w**,
1:41 touched him, and said, "I'm **w**.
Luk 10:22 the Son is **w** to reveal him."
13:34 But you were not **w**!
Jon 6:21 So they were **w** to help Jesus
Act 7:39 but our ancestors were not **w** to
16:14 because the Lord made her **w**
17:11 They were very **w** to receive
25:9 So he asked Paul, "Are you **w**
26:5 and can testify, if they're **w**,
1Co 7:12 and she is **w** to live with him,
7:13 and he is **w** to live with her,
2Co 8:10 Last year you were not only **w**
8:12 Since you are **w** to do this,
9:2 I know how **w** you are to help,
11:4 you're **w** to put up with it.
11:4 you're also **w** to put up with
11:4 you're **w** to put up with that too.
2Ti 2:24 He must be **w** to suffer wrong.
Heb 11:17 was **w** to offer his only son as

willingly (11)

1Ch 28:9 LORD wholeheartedly and **w**
29:17 With an honest heart I have **w**
29:17 here offering so **w** to you.
Ezr 7:15 and his advisers **w** contributed
7:16 They **w** contributed these gifts
Neh 11:2 everyone who **w** offered
Psa 112:5 who is generous and lends **w**.
Lam 3:33 He does not **w** bring suffering
1Co 9:17 If I spread the Good News **w**,
2Co 8:19 shows that we are doing it **w**.
Tit 3:1 Remind believers to **w** place

willingness (1)

2Co 8:11 Then your **w** will be matched

willow (3)

Psa 137:2 We hung our lyres on **w** trees.
Isa 15:7 and stored up over **W** Ravine.
Eze 17:5 like a **w** where there was

win (41)

Gen 32:5 in order to **w** your favor.'"
32:25 he could not **w** against Jacob,
33:8 He answered, "To **w** your favor,
33:15 "I only want to **w** your favor,
Exo 17:11 up his hands, Israel would **w**,
17:11 Amalekites would start to **w**.
Jdg 4:9 But you won't **w** any honors for
1Sm 14:6 The LORD can **w** a victory
1Ki 22:12 in Gilead, and you will **w**.
22:15 "Attack and you will **w**.
2Ch 18:11 in Gilead, and you will **w**.
18:14 "Attack and you will **w**.
Est 6:13 you will never **w** out over him.
Job 9:4 Who could oppose him and **w**?
Psa 45:12 want to **w** your favor with a gift.
119:58 my heart I want to **w** your favor.
Pro 19:6 Many try to **w** the kindness of
Ecc 10:12 wise person's words **w** favors,
Jer 20:11 They can't **w**. They will be very
32:5 Babylonians, you won't **w**.'"
Hos 2:14 is why I'm going to **w** her back.
Mat 16:26 good will it do for people to **w**
Mar 8:36 good does it do for people to **w**
Luk 9:25 good does it do for people to **w**
Act 12:24 spread and **w** many followers.
18:4 He tried to **w** over Jews and
Rom 3:4 and you **w** your case in court."
1Co 9:19 all people to **w** more of them.
9:20 I did this to **w** them even
9:21 I did this to **w** them even
9:22 in faith to **w** those who are
9:24 who runs in a race runs to **w**,
9:24 so that you can **w**.
9:25 They do it to **w** a temporary
9:25 but we do it to **w** one that will
Gal 1:10 Am I saying this now to **w** the
Php 3:12 But I run to **w** that which Jesus
3:14 straight toward the goal to **w**
1Th 4:12 Then your way of life will **w**
1Pe 3:1 Their wives could **w** these
Rev 6:2 off as a warrior to **w** battles.

wind (146)

Gen 8:1 So God made a **w** blow over
41:6 and scorched by the east **w**,
41:23 and scorched by the east **w**,
41:27 by the east **w** are also seven
Exo 10:13 and the LORD made a **w** from
10:13 By morning the east **w** had
10:19 Then the LORD changed the **w**
10:19 wind to a very strong west **w**.
14:21 the sea with a strong east **w**
Num 11:31 The LORD sent a **w** from the
2Sm 22:11 soared on the wings of the **w**.
1Ki 18:45 grew darker with clouds and **w**,
19:11 a fierce **w** tore mountains and
19:11 But the LORD was not in the **w**.
19:11 After the **w** came an
2Ki 3:17 You will not see **w** or rain,
Job 6:26 person says to the **w**?
15:2 his stomach with the east **w**?
21:18 are they like straw in the **w**
26:13 With his **w** the sky was
27:21 The east **w** carries him away,
28:25 When he gave the **w** its force
30:15 away my dignity like the **w**.
30:22 You pick me up and let the **w**
37:17 earth is calm under a south **w**?
37:21 clouds or after the **w** has blown
38:24 the east **w** is spread across
Psa 1:4 husks that the **w** blows away.
11:6 a cup filled with scorching **w**.
18:10 soared on the wings of the **w**.
18:42 as the dust blown by the **w**.
35:5 like husks blown by the **w** as
39:5 alive is like a whisper in the **w**.
39:11 is like a whisper in the **w**.
48:7 With the east **w** you smash the
55:8 from the raging **w** and storm."
62:9 are only a whisper in the **w**.
62:9 less than a whisper in the **w**.
78:26 He made the east **w** blow in
78:26 the south **w** with his might.
78:33 an end like a whisper in the **w**.
83:13 like husks in the **w**.
103:16 When the **w** blows over the
104:3 move on the wings of the **w**.
135:7 and who brings **w** out of his
147:18 He makes **w** blow ⌊and⌋ water
Pro 1:27 strikes you like a **w** storm,
11:29 his family inherits ⌊only⌋ **w**,
25:23 ⌊As⌋ the north **w** brings rain,
27:16 control her can control the **w**.
30:4 Who has gathered the **w** in the
Ecc 1:6 The **w** blows toward the south
1:14 ⌊It's like⌋ trying to catch the **w**.
1:17 is ⌊like⌋ trying to catch the **w**.
2:11 was like⌋ trying to catch the **w**.
2:17 was like⌋ trying to catch the **w**.
2:26 ⌊It's like⌋ trying to catch the **w**.
4:4 ⌊It's like⌋ trying to catch the **w**.
4:6 and of trying to catch the **w**.
4:16 ⌊It's like⌋ trying to catch the **w**.
5:16 from working so hard for the **w**?
6:9 ⌊It's like⌋ trying to catch the **w**.
11:4 Whoever watches the **w** will
Sos 4:16 Awake, north **w**! Come, south
4:16 Come, south **w**! Blow on my
Isa 5:28 wheels are as quick as the **w**.
7:2 the forest are shaken by the **w**.
11:15 River with his scorching **w**
17:13 being blown by the **w**,
24:20 sway like a shack in the **w**.
26:18 only to give birth to the **w**.
28:2 a hailstorm, a destructive **w**.
29:5 be like husks blown by the **w**.
32:2 will be like a shelter from the **w**
37:27 dried up by the east **w**.
41:2 into straw blown by the **w**.
41:16 The **w** will carry them away.
49:10 the burning, hot **w** strike them.
57:13 A **w** will carry them all away.
59:19 The **w** of the LORD pushes
64:6 sins carry us away like the **w**.
Jer 2:24 sniffing the **w** while in heat.
4:11 "A hot **w** from the heights will
4:11 It will not be a **w** that winnows
4:12 It will be a stronger **w** than that.
4:13 His chariots are like a raging **w**.
10:13 He brings **w** out of his
13:24 is blown away by a desert **w**.
18:17 Like the east **w** I will scatter
22:22 The **w** will blow away all your
30:23 Like a driving **w**, it will swirl
51:1 I will stir up a destructive **w**
51:16 He brings **w** out of his
Eze 5:2 the remaining third to the **w**,
5:10 scatter whoever is left to the **w**.
5:12 the remaining third to the **w**,
17:10 when the east **w** blows
17:21 direction that the **w** blows.
19:12 The east **w** dried up its fruit.
27:26 and an east **w** wrecked you in
Dan 2:35 The **w** carried them away,
10:17 and the **w** has been knocked
Hos 4:19 The **w** will carry them away in
8:7 people of Israel plant the **w**,
12:1 of Ephraim try to catch the **w**
12:1 try to chase the east **w** all day.
13:15 the LORD's scorching **w** will
13:15 The **w** will destroy every
Amo 4:13 mountains and creates the **w**.
Jnh 1:4 The LORD sent a violent **w**
4:8 God made a hot east **w** blow.
Hab 1:11 and pass through like the **w**.
Zec 5:9 women coming forward with **w**
Mat 8:26 gave an order to the **w** and the
8:27 Even the **w** and the sea obey
11:7 Tall grass swaying in the **w**?
14:24 it was going against the **w**.
14:30 noticed how strong the **w** was,
14:32 the **w** stopped blowing.
Mar 4:39 ordered the **w** to stop,
4:39 The **w** stopped blowing,
4:41 Even the **w** and the sea obey

Mar 6:48 they were going against the **w**.
6:51 and the **w** stopped blowing.
Luk 7:24 Tall grass swaying in the **w**?
8:24 he got up and ordered the **w**
8:24 The **w** stopped, and the sea
8:25 He gives orders to the **w** and
12:55 you see a south **w** blowing,
Jon 3:8 The **w** blows wherever it
3:8 but you don't know where the **w**
6:18 A strong **w** started to blow and
Act 2:2 violently blowing **w** came from
2:6 when they heard the **w**.
27:4 were traveling against the **w**.
27:7 because the **w** would not let
27:14 Soon a powerful **w** (called a
27:15 The **w** carried the ship away,
27:15 we couldn't sail against the **w**.
27:15 were carried along by the **w**.
27:17 were carried along by the **w**.
27:40 the top sail to catch the **w**
28:13 The next day a south **w** began
Eph 4:14 that change like the **w**.
Jas 1:6 a wave that is blown by the **w**
Rev 6:13 it is shaken by a strong **w**.

windbag (1)

Jer 46:17 king of Egypt, is a big **w**.

windbags (1)

Jer 5:13 The prophets are nothing but **w**.

windblown (2)

Lev 26:36 The sound of a **w** leaf will
Zep 2:2 the day passes like **w** husks,

window (17)

Gen 8:6 more days Noah opened the **w**
26:8 Philistines looked out of his **w**
Jos 2:15 from her **w** since her house
2:18 tie this red cord in the **w**
2:21 and tied the red cord in the **w**.
Jdg 5:28 mother looked through her **w**
1Sm 19:12 lowered David through a **w**,
2Sm 6:16 Michal looked out of a **w**
2Ki 1:2 Ahaziah fell through a **w** lattice
9:30 looked out of a second-story **w**.
9:32 Looking up at the **w**,
13:17 "Open the **w** that faces east."
1Ch 15:29 Michal looked out of a **w**
Pro 7:6 From a **w** in my house I looked
Sos 2:9 peeking through the **w**,
Zep 2:14 A bird will sing in a **w**.
Act 20:9 Eutychus was sitting in a **w**.

windows (21)

1Ki 6:4 made latticed **w** for the temple.
7:4 The **w** were in three rows
2Ki 7:2 LORD poured rain through **w**
7:19 LORD poured rain through **w**
Ecc 12:3 who look out of the **w** see
Jer 9:21 Death has come through our **w**
22:14 He cuts out **w** in it,
Eze 40:16 had small **w** all around.
40:16 The entrance hall also had **w**
40:22 Its **w**, recessed walls,
40:25 and its entrance hall had **w**
40:25 on all sides like the **w**
40:29 entrance hall had **w** all around.
40:33 entrance hall had **w** all around.
40:36 entrance hall had **w** all around.
41:16 The doorposts, the small **w**,
41:16 from the floor up to the **w**,
41:26 There were small **w** and palm
Dan 6:10 in his house had **w** that opened
Joe 2:9 enter through **w** like thieves.
Mal 3:10 "See if I won't open the **w** of

winds (24)

Gen 2:11 one that **w** throughout Havilah,
2:13 one that **w** throughout Sudan.
Dtr 28:22 scorching **w**, and ruined crops.
Job 37:9 cold because of the strong **w**.
Psa 104:4 You make your angels **w** and
148:8 strong **w** that obey his
Isa 27:8 a fierce blast from the east **w**.
Jer 49:32 I will scatter to the **w** those
49:36 I'll bring the four **w** from the four
Eze 13:11 and stormy **w** will break it to
37:9 Come from the four **w**,
Dan 7:2 saw the four **w** of heaven
8:8 to the four **w** of heaven.
11:4 of the four **w** of heaven.
Amo 1:14 day of battle and **w** are howling
Nah 1:3 Raging **w** and storms mark his
Zec 2:6 you to the four **w** of heaven.
Mat 7:25 **W** blew and beat against that
7:27 **W** blew and struck that house.
Act 27:12 the southwest and northwest **w**
Heb 1:7 "He makes his messengers **w**.
Jas 3:4 big and are driven by strong **w**.
Jud 1:12 clouds blown around by the **w**.
Rev 7:1 were holding back the four **w**

windstorm (8)

2Ki 2:1 to take Elijah to heaven in a **w**,
2:11 Elijah went to heaven in a **w**.
Job 27:20 A **w** snatches him away at
Isa 40:24 and a **w** sweeps them away
41:16 The **w** will scatter them.
Jer 23:19 Like a **w**, it will swirl down on
Zec 7:14 I used a **w** to scatter them
Mar 4:37 A violent **w** came up.

windstorms (3)

Psa 83:14 and terrify them with your **w**
Isa 29:6 noises, with **w**, rainstorms,
30:30 **w**, rainstorms, and hailstones.

windy (1)

Job 8:2 long will your words be so **w**?

wine (293)

Gen 9:21 He drank some **w**,
14:18 Salem brought out bread and **w**.
19:32 Let's give our father **w** to drink.
19:33 gave their father **w** to drink.
19:34 Let's give him **w** to drink again
19:35 night they gave their father **w**
27:25 Jacob also brought him **w**,
27:28 of fresh grain and new **w**.
27:37 fresh grain and new **w** for him.
35:14 He poured a **w** offering and
49:11 He will wash his clothes in **w**,
49:12 His eyes are darker than **w**.
Exo 22:29 withhold your best **w** from me.
25:29 be used for pouring **w** offerings.
29:40 Make a **w** offering of one quart
29:40 wine offering of one quart of **w**.
29:41 grain offering and **w** offering as
30:9 Never pour a **w** offering on it.
37:16 be used for pouring **w** offerings.
Lev 10:9 your sons must not drink any **w**
23:13 Use one quart of **w** for the wine
23:13 Use one quart of wine for the **w**
23:18 bring grain and **w** offerings.
23:37 and **w** offerings — each one on
Num 4:7 and pitchers for the **w** offerings.
6:3 Nazirites must never drink **w**,
6:3 vinegar made from **w** or liquor,
6:15 grain offerings and **w** offerings.
6:17 grain offerings and **w** offerings.
6:20 the Nazirites may drink **w**.
15:5 an offering of one quart of **w**.
15:7 an offering of 1 ¼ quarts of **w**.
15:10 an offering of two quarts of **w**.
15:24 proper grain and **w** offerings,
18:12 of the new **w** and fresh grain.
28:7 Also bring a **w** offering of one
28:7 wine offering of one quart of **w**
28:8 offering and **w** offering as you
28:9 and the **w** offering that goes
28:10 and the **w** offerings that go
28:14 The **w** offering that goes with
28:14 each bull will be 2 quarts of **w**,
28:14 each ram 1 ½ quarts of **w**,
28:14 with each lamb 1 quart of **w**.
28:15 offering with its **w** offering,
28:24 and the **w** offering that goes
28:31 along with their **w** offerings,
29:6 grain offerings and **w** offerings.
29:11 grain offerings and **w** offerings.
29:16 grain offerings and **w** offerings.
Num 29:18 grain offerings and **w** offerings
29:19 grain offerings and **w** offerings.
29:21 grain offerings and **w** offerings
29:22 grain offerings and **w** offerings.
29:24 grain offerings and **w** offerings
29:25 grain offerings and **w** offerings.
29:27 grain offerings and **w** offerings
29:28 grain offerings and **w** offerings.
29:30 grain offerings and **w** offerings
29:31 grain offerings and **w** offerings.
29:33 grain offerings and **w** offerings
29:34 grain offerings and **w** offerings.
29:37 grain offerings and **w** offerings
29:38 grain offerings and **w** offerings.
29:39 offerings, your **w** offerings,
Dtr 7:13 grain, new **w**, and olive oil.
11:14 grain, new **w**, and olive oil.
12:17 grain, new **w**, and olive oil;
14:23 grain, new **w**, and olive oil,
14:26 want: cattle, sheep, goats, **w**,
15:14 and **w** from your winepress.
16:13 floor and made your **w**,
18:4 grain, new **w**, olive oil,
28:39 but you won't drink any **w** or
28:51 grain, no new **w**, no olive oil,
29:6 bread and drank no **w** or liquor.
32:14 the blood-red **w** of grapes.
32:33 Their **w** is snake venom,
32:38 and drank the **w** from their wine
32:38 the wine from their **w** offerings?
33:28 in a land of grain and new **w**.
Jdg 9:13 'Should I stop producing my **w**,
9:27 in the vineyards to make **w**.
13:4 Don't drink any **w** or liquor or
13:7 So don't drink any **w** or liquor or
13:14 drink any **w** or liquor,
19:19 have bread and **w** for myself,
Rut 2:14 and dip it into the sour **w**."
1Sm 1:14 "Get rid of your **w**."
8:15 take a tenth of your grain and **w**
25:37 when the effects of the **w** had
2Sm 13:28 from drinking ⌊too much⌋ **w**,
16:2 The **w** is for those who
2Ki 16:13 poured out his **w** offering,
16:15 and **w** offerings of all the
18:32 country with grain and new **w**,
1Ch 9:29 the flour, **w**, olive oil, incense,
12:40 **w**, olive oil, cattle, and sheep,
27:27 for storing **w** that came from
29:21 rams, 1,000 lambs, **w** offerings,
2Ch 2:10 200,000 gallons of **w**,
2:15 and **w** he promised the
11:11 food, olive oil, and **w** in them.
29:35 **w** offerings that accompanied
31:5 new **w**, fresh olive oil, honey,
32:28 new **w**, and fresh olive oil,
Ezr 6:9 rams, lambs, wheat, salt, **w**,
7:17 and **w** to offer on the altar of the
7:22 of wheat, 600 gallons of **w**,
Neh 2:1 after some **w** was brought for
2:1 I picked up the cup of **w** and
5:11 on the money, grain, new **w**,
5:15 food and **w** plus one pound
5:18 a supply of **w** was ordered.
10:37 fruit from every tree, new **w**,
10:39 of grain, new **w**, and olive oil.
13:5 new **w**, and olive oil.
13:12 all the grain harvested, new **w**,
13:15 them bringing in loads of **w**,
Est 1:7 provided plenty of royal **w** out
1:10 when the king was drunk on **w**,
5:6 While they were drinking **w**,
7:2 while they were drinking **w**,
Job 1:13 were eating and drinking **w**
1:18 and drinking **w** at their oldest
24:11 stomp on grapes in **w** vats,
32:19 My belly is like ⌊a bottle of⌋ **w**
Psa 4:7 their grain and new **w** increase.
60:3 You have given us **w** that
75:8 (Its foaming **w** is thoroughly
78:65 up from ⌊too much⌋ **w**,
104:15 You make **w** to cheer human
Pro 3:10 vats will overflow with fresh **w**.
4:17 **w** obtained through violence.
9:2 She has mixed her **w**.
9:5 and drink the **w** I have mixed.

Pro	20:1	**W** ⌊makes people⌋ mock,
	21:17	Whoever loves **w** and
	23:20	those who drink too much **w**,
	23:30	drink glass after glass of **w**
	23:31	Do not look at **w** because it is
	31:4	It is not for kings to drink **w** or
	31:6	to a person who is dying and **w**
Ecc	2:3	feel better by drinking **w**.
	9:7	and drink your **w** cheerfully,
	10:19	and **w** makes life pleasant,
Sos	1:2	of love are better than **w**,
	1:4	of love more than **w**.
	4:10	expressions of love than **w**
	5:1	I will drink my **w** with my milk.
	7:2	always be filled with spiced **w**.
	7:9	mouth taste like the best **w** ...
	8:2	you some spiced **w** to drink,
Isa	1:22	Your **w** is watered down.
	5:10	produce only six gallons of **w**,
	5:11	late until they are drunk from **w**.
	5:12	tambourines and flutes, and **w**.
	5:22	who are heroes at drinking **w**,
	22:13	You will eat meat, drink **w**,
	24:7	New **w** dries up, All happy
	24:9	People no longer drink **w** when
	24:11	People in the streets call for **w**.
	28:1	where they lie drunk from **w**.
	28:7	and prophets stagger from **w**
	28:7	confused from too much **w**.
	29:9	You are drunk, but not from **w**.
	36:17	country with grain and new **w**,
	49:26	blood as though it were new **w**.
	51:21	who are drunk but not from **w**.
	55:1	Come, buy **w** and milk.
	56:12	"Let me get some **w**,
	57:6	You have given them **w**
	62:8	the new **w** which you made."
	62:9	who gather grapes will drink **w**
	65:8	someone finds juice for new **w**
	65:11	offered cups full of spiced **w**
Jer	7:18	They pour out **w** offerings to
	13:12	will be filled with **w**.' Then
	13:12	bottle will be filled with **w**.'
	19:13	and poured out **w** offerings
	23:9	who has had too much **w**,
	25:15	hand this cup filled with the **w**
	31:12	grain, new **w**, and olive oil,
	32:29	Baal and to pour out **w** offerings
	35:2	and offer them a drink of **w**."
	35:5	cups and pitchers filled with **w**
	35:5	I said to them, "Drink some **w**."
	35:6	"We don't drink **w**,
	35:6	must never drink **w**.
	35:8	We have never drunk **w**,
	35:14	his descendants not to drink **w**.
	35:14	have not drunk any **w**
	44:17	and pour out **w** offerings
	44:18	and pouring out **w** offerings
	44:19	poured out **w** offerings to her,
	44:25	and pour out **w** offerings
	48:11	Its people are like **w** left to
	48:33	I will stop the **w** flowing from
	51:7	The nations drank its **w**.
	52:19	the bowls used for **w** offerings.
Lam	2:12	some bread and **w** as they faint
Eze	20:28	poured out their **w** offerings.
	27:18	They exchanged **w** from
	44:21	None of the priests may drink **w**
	45:17	and **w** offerings at the annual
Dan	1:5	of the king's rich food and **w**.
	1:8	food and drinking the king's **w**.
	1:16	away the king's rich food and **w**
	5:1	nobles and drank **w** with them.
	5:2	As they were tasting the **w**,
	5:4	They drank the **w** and praised
	5:23	concubines drank **w** from them.
	10:3	No meat or **w** entered my
Hos	2:5	wool and linen, olive oil and **w**.'
	2:8	her grain, new **w**, and olive oil.
	2:9	and my new **w** when it's
	2:22	grain, new **w**, and olive oil.
	4:11	Prostitutes, old **w**,
	4:11	and new **w** have robbed them
	4:18	they're done drinking their **w**,
	7:5	officials become drunk from **w**,
	7:14	praying for grain and new **w**.
Hos	9:2	be enough **w** to go around.
	9:4	They won't pour **w** offerings to
Joe	1:5	Cry loudly, you **w** drinkers!
	1:5	New **w** has been taken away
	1:9	Grain offerings and **w** offerings
	1:10	The new **w** has dried up.
	1:13	Grain offerings and **w** offerings
	2:14	grain offerings and **w** offerings
	2:19	new **w**, and olive oil to you.
	2:24	with new **w** and olive oil.
	3:3	that they could buy **w** to drink.
	3:18	On that day new **w** will cover
Amo	2:8	they drink the **w** that they
	2:12	made the Nazirites drink **w**.
	4:1	your husbands, "Get some **w**!
	5:11	but you will not drink their **w**.
	6:6	be for those who drink **w** by
	9:13	New **w** will drip from the
	9:14	and drink the **w** from them.
Mic	2:11	to you about **w** and liquor."
	6:15	You will make new **w**,
Hab	2:5	Also because **w** is treacherous
Zep	1:13	but they won't drink their **w**."
Hag	1:11	grain, the new **w**, the olive oil,
	2:12	food, **w**, oil, or any kind of food,
	2:16	And when anyone came to a **w**
Zec	9:17	women will prosper on new **w**.
	10:7	if they had some **w** ⌊to drink⌋.
	12:2	a cup ⌊of **w**⌋ that makes all
Mat	9:17	Nor do people pour new **w** into
	9:17	the skins burst, the **w** runs out,
	9:17	Rather, people pour new **w** into
	23:24	strain gnats ⌊out of your **w**⌋,
	26:29	drink this **w** again until that
	26:29	that day when I drink new **w**
	27:34	They gave him a drink of **w**
Mar	2:22	People don't pour new **w** into
	2:22	If they do, the **w** will make the
	2:22	and both the **w** and the skins
	2:22	Rather, new **w** is to be poured
	14:25	I won't drink this **w** again until
	14:25	that day when I drink new **w**
	15:23	They tried to give him **w**
Luk	1:15	He will never drink **w** or any
	5:37	People don't pour new **w** into
	5:37	If they do, the new **w** will make
	5:37	The **w** will run out,
	5:38	Rather, new **w** is to be poured
	5:39	old **w** wants new wine.
	5:39	old wine wants new **w**.
	5:39	He says, 'The old **w** is better!'"
	7:33	eating bread nor drinking **w**,
	22:18	now on I won't drink this **w** until
Jon	2:3	When the **w** was gone,
	2:3	"They're out of **w**."
	2:9	the water that had become **w**.
	2:10	serves the best **w** first.
	2:10	the host serves cheap **w**.
	2:10	saved the best **w** for now."
	4:46	he had changed water into **w**.
Act	2:13	"They're drunk on sweet **w**."
Rom	14:21	avoid eating meat, drinking **w**,
Eph	5:18	Don't get drunk on **w**,
1Ti	5:23	Instead, drink a little **w** for your
Rev	6:6	the olive oil and the **w**."
	14:8	all the nations drink the **w**
	14:10	will drink the **w** of God's fury,
	16:19	the cup of **w** from his fierce
	17:2	earth became drunk on the **w**
	18:3	nations fell because of the **w**
	18:13	**w**, olive oil, flour, wheat, cattle,

winepress (17)

Num	18:27	floor or juice from the **w**.
	18:30	from the threshing floor or **w**.
Dtr	15:14	and wine from your **w**.
Jdg	6:11	was beating out wheat in a **w**
	7:25	of Oreb and Zeeb at the **W**
2Ki	6:27	the threshing floor or the **w**."
Isa	5:2	and made a **w** in it.
	63:2	who trample grapes in a **w**?
	63:3	"I have trampled alone in the **w**.
Lam	1:15	the people of Judah in a **w**.
Joe	3:13	The **w** is full. The vats
Mat	21:33	put a wall around it, made a **w**,
Mar	12:1	made a vat for the **w**,
Rev	14:19	them into the **w** of God's anger.
	14:20	were trampled in the **w** outside
	14:20	Blood flowed out of the **w** as
	19:15	an iron scepter and tread the **w**

winepresses (4)

Neh	13:15	stomping grapes in the **w**
Isa	16:10	one stomps on grapes in the **w**,
Jer	48:33	the wine flowing from the **w**.
Zec	14:10	of Hananel to the king's **w**.

wines (3)

Isa	25:6	a banquet with aged **w**,
	25:6	the best foods and the finest **w**.
Hos	14:7	famous as the **w** from Lebanon.

wineskin (5)

1Sm	1:24	a bushel of flour, and a full **w**.
	10:3	one will be carrying a ⌊full⌋ **w**.
	16:20	six bushels of bread, a full **w**,
2Sm	16:1	of ripened fruit, and a full **w**.
Psa	119:83	a shriveled and dried out **w**,

wineskins (8)

Jos	9:4	Their **w** were old, split,
	9:13	These were new **w** when we
1Sm	25:18	2 full **w**, 5 butchered sheep,
Job	13:28	I am like worn-out **w**,
	32:19	like new **w** that are ready to
Mat	9:17	pour new wine into old **w**.
Mar	2:22	don't pour new wine into old **w**.
Luk	5:37	don't pour new wine into old **w**.

wing (11)

1Ki	6:24	Each **w** of the angels was 7
	6:24	distance from the tip of one **w**
	6:27	angels extended so that the **w**
	6:27	and the **w** of the other touched
2Ch	3:11	A **w** of one of the angels was 7
	3:11	Its other **w** was 7 ½ feet long
	3:11	and touched one **w** of the other.
	3:12	The **w** of the other one of the
	3:12	Its other **w** was 7 ½ feet long
	3:12	½ feet long and touched the **w**
Isa	10:14	Not one of them flapped a **w**,

winged (5)

Lev	11:20	"Every swarming, **w** insect
	11:21	However, you may eat **w**
	11:23	Every kind of **w** insect that
Dtr	14:19	Every swarming, **w** insect is
Ecc	10:20	or some **w** creature may repeat

wings (75)

Gen	7:14	of bird (every creature with **w**).
Exo	19:4	how I carried you on eagles' **w**
	25:20	The angels should have their **w**
	37:9	The angels had their **w** spread
Lev	1:17	Then pull on the bird's **w** to tear
	1:17	but don't pull the **w** off.
Dtr	4:17	any creature with **w** that flies,
	32:11	spreads its **w** to catch them,
2Sm	22:11	he soared on the **w** of the wind.
1Ki	6:27	The **w** of the angels extended
	6:27	Their remaining **w** touched
	8:6	under the **w** of the angels.
	8:7	outstretched **w** were over
1Ch	28:18	the gold angels with their **w**
2Ch	3:11	of the angels' **w** was 30 feet.
	5:7	under the **w** of the angels.
	5:8	The angels' outstretched **w**
Job	39:13	the ostrich flap its **w** in joy,
	39:13	or do its **w** lack feathers?
	39:26	spread its **w** toward the south?
Psa	17:8	me in the shadow of your **w**.
	18:10	he soared on the **w** of the wind.
	36:7	refuge in the shadow of your **w**.
	55:6	I said, "If only I had **w** like a
	57:1	your **w** until destructive storms
	61:4	under the protection of your **w**.
	63:7	In the shadow of your **w**,
	68:13	⌊you will be like⌋ the **w** of a
	91:4	and under his **w** you will find
	104:3	You move on the **w** of the wind.
Pro	23:5	It makes **w** for itself like an
Isa	6:2	Each had six **w**: With two they

Isa 8:8 Its outspread **w** will extend
18:1 whirring **w** which lies beyond
34:15 in the shadow of ⌊their **w**⌋.
40:31 will soar on **w** like eagles.
Jer 48:40 and spread their **w** over Moab.
49:22 and spread their **w** over Bozrah.
Eze 1:6 them had four faces and four **w**.
1:8 had human hands under their **w**
1:8 four of them had faces and **w**.
1:9 Their **w** touched each other.
1:11 Their **w** were spread out,
1:11 Each creature had two **w** with
1:11 two **w** covered their bodies.
1:23 each creature had two **w** that
1:23 Each creature had two **w** that
1:24 I heard the sound of their **w**.
1:24 they lowered their **w**.
1:25 stood still with their **w** lowered.
3:13 I also heard the noise of the **w**
10:5 The sound of the angels' **w**
10:8 human hands under their **w**.
10:12 bodies, their backs, hands, **w**,
10:16 When the angels lifted their **w**
10:19 The angels lifted their **w** and
10:21 Each had four faces and four **w**,
10:21 and under their **w** were what
11:22 Then the angels raised their **w**,
17:3 It had large **w** with long,
17:7 large eagle with large **w**
Dan 7:4 but it had **w** like an eagle.
7:4 I watched until its **w** were
7:6 On its back it had four **w**,
7:6 like the **w** of a bird.
Hos 4:19 will carry them away in its **w**,
Zec 5:9 forward with wind in their **w**.
5:9 They had **w** like those of a
Mal 4:2 will rise with healing in his **w**
Mat 23:37 gathers her chicks under her **w**!
Luk 13:34 gathers her chicks under her **w**!
Heb 9:5 ⌊with their **w**⌋ overshadowing
Rev 4:8 four living creatures had six **w**
9:9 The noise from their **w** was
12:14 woman was given the two **w**

wingspan (2)

1Ki 6:25 Both angels had a 15-foot ⌊**w**⌋.
2Ch 3:12 combined **w** was 30 feet.

wink (1)

Psa 35:19 me for no reason **w** ⌊at me⌋.

winks (3)

Pro 6:13 He **w** his eye, makes a signal
10:10 Whoever **w** with his eye
16:30 Whoever **w** his eye is plotting

winner (2)

Pro 11:30 and a **w** of souls is wise.
Php 3:13 I can't consider myself a **w** yet.

winners (1)

Exo 32:18 not the sound of **w** shouting.

winning (2)

1Ki 18:37 you are **w** back their hearts."
Php 3:6 When it comes to **w** God's

winnow (3)

Isa 41:16 You will **w** them. The wind will
Jer 51:2 will send people to **w** Babylon,
51:2 to **w** it and strip its land bare.

winnowed (2)

Isa 21:10 have been threshed and **w**.
30:24 mixture of food that has been **w**

winnowing (3)

Jer 15:7 "I will separate them with a **w**
Mat 3:12 His **w** shovel is in his hand,
Luk 3:17 His **w** shovel is in his hand to

winnows (1)

Jer 4:11 be a wind that **w** or cleanses.

wins (16)

Exo 15:6 **w** glory because it is strong.
Dtr 33:29 a sword that **w** your victories.
Pro 11:16 A gracious woman **w** respect,
Isa 59:16 his own power he **w** a victory.
Mic 7:9 up my cause and **w** my case.
2Ti 2:5 an athletic competition **w**
1Jn 5:4 Our faith is what **w** the victory
5:5 Who **w** the victory over the
Rev 2:7 to everyone who **w** the victory.
2:11 Everyone who **w** the victory
2:17 to everyone who **w** the victory.
2:26 the nations to everyone who **w**
3:5 Everyone who **w** the victory
3:12 I will make everyone who **w**
3:21 I will allow everyone who **w**
21:7 Everyone who **w** the victory

winter (18)

Gen 8:22 cold and heat, summer and **w**,
Psa 74:17 You created summer and **w**.
Sos 2:11 The **w** is past. The rain is over
Isa 18:6 will feed on them in the **w**.
28:25 its own area and **w** wheat at its
Jer 36:22 and the king was in his **w**
Eze 4:9 lentils, millet, and **w** wheat.
Amo 3:15 I will tear down **w** houses as
Zec 14:8 continue in summer and in **w**.
Mat 24:20 Pray that it will not be **w** or a
Mar 13:18 Pray that it will not be in **w**.
Jon 10:22 in Jerusalem during the **w**.
Act 27:12 a good place to spend the **w**,
27:12 and spend the **w** there.
28:11 ship that had spent the **w** at
1Co 16:6 I might even spend the **w**.
2Ti 4:21 to visit me before **w** comes.
Tit 3:12 I have decided to spend the **w**

wipe (42)

Gen 6:7 So he said, "I will **w** off the
6:7 I will **w** out not only humans,
7:4 I will **w** off the face of the earth
Exo 23:23 Jebusites. I will **w** them out.
32:12 the mountains and **w** them off
32:32 If not, please **w** me out of the
32:33 "I will **w** out of my book
Dtr 6:15 with you and will **w** you off
7:22 You won't be able to **w** them
9:3 He will **w** them out and will
9:14 I'll destroy them and **w** their
12:3 and **w** out the names of their
28:63 to destroy you and **w** you out.
1Sm 20:15 The Lord will **w** each of
24:21 will not **w** out my descendants
2Sm 21:5 He planned to **w** us out to keep
2Ki 14:27 not going to **w** out Israel's name
21:13 I will **w** out Jerusalem in the
Neh 13:14 and don't **w** out the good things
Est 3:6 So Haman planned to **w** out
3:13 people were ordered⌋ to **w** out,
8:11 themselves, to **w** out, to kill,
Psa 34:16 in order to **w** out all memory
51:1 **w** out my rebellious acts.
51:9 and **w** out all that I have done
83:4 They say, "Let's **w** out their
109:14 and not **w** out his mother's
143:12 In keeping with your mercy, **w**
Isa 25:8 The Almighty LORD will **w**
43:25 to **w** away your rebellious
Jer 18:23 Don't **w** their sins out of your
31:16 and **w** away your tears.
Lam 3:66 Pursue them in anger, and **w**
Eze 20:13 and completely **w** them out.
20:17 them or completely **w** them out
25:7 I will **w** you out from among the
25:13 I will **w** out people and
Amo 9:8 I will **w** it off the face of the
Mic 5:14 I will **w** out your cities.
Zec 13:2 "I will **w** away the names of
Rev 7:17 and God will **w** every tear from
21:4 He will **w** every tear from their

wiped (33)

Gen 7:23 the face of the earth was **w** out.
7:23 and birds were **w** off the earth.
34:30 my family and I will be **w** out."
Exo 9:15 that would have **w** you off
Dtr 2:12 claimed their land, **w** them out,
Dtr 2:21 But the LORD **w** them out
2:22 he **w** out the Horites so that
2:23 **w** them out and took their
4:26 You'll be completely **w** out.
Jos 11:21 At that time Joshua also **w** out
Jdg 21:17 No tribe of Israel should be **w**
1Sm 12:25 you and your king will be **w**
15:18 them until they're **w** out.'
2Sm 17:16 troops with him will be **w** out.'"
1Ki 13:34 it had to be destroyed and **w** off
2Ki 10:17 He **w** them out, as the LORD
21:13 same way that a dish is **w** out
Est 7:4 sold so that we can be **w** out,
9:6 killed and **w** out 500 men
9:12 have killed and **w** out 500 men
Job 22:20 their wealth has been **w** out,
Psa 9:5 You **w** out their names forever
109:13 their family name be **w** out by
119:87 They almost **w** me off ⌊the
Isa 26:14 and **w** out all memory of them.
28:18 Your treaty with death will be **w**
48:19 would not be cut off or **w** out
Jer 9:16 after them until I've **w** them out.
Lam 2:6 The LORD **w** out the memory
3:22 We were not completely **w** out.
Eze 6:6 you have done will be **w** out.
Zep 3:7 not be **w** out even though
Jon 11:2 on the Lord and **w** his feet

wipes (2)

Dtr 28:21 on you until he **w** you out
Pro 30:20 eats, **w** her mouth, and says,

wiping (1)

Luk 10:11 'We are **w** your city's dust from

wisdom (217)

Dtr 4:6 of the world your **w** and insight.
34:9 was filled with the Spirit of **w**,
1Ki 2:6 Use your **w**. Don't let that
3:28 saw he possessed **w** from God
4:29 God gave Solomon **w** — keen
4:30 Solomon's **w** was greater than
4:30 and all the **w** of the Egyptians.
4:34 from every nation to hear his **w**;
4:34 who had heard about his **w**.
5:12 The LORD gave Solomon **w**
10:4 Sheba saw all of Solomon's **w**,
10:6 your words and your **w** is true!
10:7 Your **w** and wealth surpass the
10:8 listening to your **w**!
10:23 In wealth and **w** King Solomon
10:24 to listen to the **w** that God gave
11:41 he did — and his **w** written
2Ch 1:10 Give me **w** and knowledge so
1:11 Instead, you've asked for **w**
1:12 So **w** and knowledge will be
9:3 of Sheba saw Solomon's **w**,
9:5 your words and your **w** is true!
9:6 half of the extent of your **w**.
9:7 of you and listen to your **w**!
9:22 In wealth and **w** King Solomon
9:23 to listen to the **w** that God gave
Ezr 7:25 You, Ezra, using your God's **w**
Job 4:21 Won't they die without **w**?
11:6 would tell you the secrets of **w**,
11:6 because ⌊true⌋ **w** is twice ⌊as
11:6 is twice ⌊as great as your **w**⌋,
11:8 ⌊God's **w** is⌋ higher than
12:2 and when you die, **w** will die.
12:12 "**W** is with the ancient one.
12:13 God has **w** and strength.
12:16 has power and priceless **w**.
13:5 For you, that would be **w**.
15:8 and receive a monopoly on **w**?
26:3 the person who has no **w**
28:12 "Where can **w** be found?
28:18 **W** is more valuable than gems.
28:20 "Where does **w** come from?
28:28 'The fear of the Lord is **w**!
32:7 experience should teach **w**.'
32:13 So don't say, 'We've found **w**.
33:33 and I'll teach you **w**."
38:36 Who put **w** in the heart or gave
39:17 God has deprived it of **w**
Psa 37:30 righteous person reflects on **w**.

Psa 51:6 inside me you teach me **w**.
90:12 so that we may grow in **w**.
104:24 You made them all by **w**.
105:22 taught his respected leaders **w**.
111:10 LORD is the beginning of **w**.
119:100 I have more **w** than those with
Pro 1:2 to grasp **w** and discipline,
1:7 fools despise **w** and discipline.
1:20 **W** sings her song in the streets.
2:2 if you pay close attention to **w**,
2:4 if you search for **w** as if it were
2:6 The LORD gives **w**.
2:7 He has reserved priceless **w**
2:10 **W** will come into your heart.
2:12 ⌊**W** will⌋ save you from the
2:16 ⌊**W** will⌋ also save you from
3:13 Blessed is the one who finds **w**
3:14 The profit ⌊gained⌋ from ⌊**w**⌋
3:15 ⌊**W**⌋ is more precious than
3:18 ⌊**W**⌋ is a tree of life for those
3:19 By **W** the LORD laid the
3:21 Use priceless **w** and foresight.
4:5 Acquire **w**. Acquire
4:6 Do not abandon **w**,
4:6 Love **w**, and it will protect you.
4:7 The beginning of **w** is to
4:7 of wisdom is to acquire **w**.
4:8 Cherish **w**. It will raise you up. It
4:11 I have taught you the way of **w**.
5:1 My son, pay attention to my **w**.
7:4 Say to **w**, "You are my sister."
8:1 Does not **w** call out?
8:2 ⌊**W**⌋ takes its stand on high
8:3 entrance ⌊**w**⌋ sings its song,
8:11 because **w** is better than
8:12 "I, **W**, live with insight, and I
8:14 and priceless **w** are mine.
9:1 **W** has built her house.
9:10 LORD is the beginning of **w**.
9:12 your **w** will help you.
10:13 **W** is found on the lips of a
10:23 so is **w** to a person who has
10:31 righteous person increases **w**,
11:2 but **w** remains with humble
13:10 those who take advice gain **w**.
14:6 A mocker searches for **w**
14:8 The **w** of a sensible person
14:33 **W** finds rest in the heart of an
15:33 is discipline ⌊leading to⌋ **w**,
16:16 better it is to gain **w** than gold,
17:16 in his hand to buy **w** when
17:24 **W** is directly in front of an
18:4 The fountain of **w** is an
21:30 No **w**, no understanding,
23:9 despise the **w** of your words.
23:23 it), ⌊that is,⌋ buy **w**, discipline,
24:3 With **w** a house is built.
24:7 Matters of **w** are beyond the
24:14 The knowledge of **w** is like
28:26 walks in **w** will survive.
29:3 A person who loves **w** makes
29:15 and a warning produce **w**,
30:3 I haven't learned **w**.
31:26 "She speaks with **w**,
Ecc 1:13 With all my heart I used **w** to
1:16 with **w** and knowledge."
1:17 used my mind to understand **w**
1:18 With a lot of **w** ⌊comes⌋ a lot
2:3 During all that time, **w**
2:9 Yet, my **w** remained with me.
2:12 attention⌋ to experience **w**,
2:13 But I saw that **w** has an
2:19 so hard and used my **w**.
2:21 who had worked hard with **w**,
2:26 God gives **w**, knowledge,
7:10 It isn't **w** that leads you to ask
7:11 **W** is as good as an inheritance.
7:12 **W** protects us just as money
7:12 but the advantage of **w** is that
7:19 **W** will help a wise person
7:23 I used **w** to test all of this.
7:24 Whatever **w** may be,
7:25 and to seek out **w** and the
8:1 **W** makes one's face shine,
8:16 considered how to study **w**
9:13 seen this example of **w** under
Ecc 9:15 He saved the town using his **w**.
9:16 "**W** is better than strength,"
9:16 poor person's **w** was despised,
9:18 **W** is better than weapons of
10:1 outweighs **w** ⌊and⌋ honor.
10:10 But **w** prepares the way for
Isa 10:13 I did this with my **w**,
11:2 Spirit of **w** and understanding,
28:29 and his **w** is great.
29:14 The **w** of their wise people will
33:6 are **w** and knowledge.
47:10 Your **w** and knowledge have
Jer 8:9 They don't really have any **w**.
9:23 wise people brag about their **w**.
49:7 no longer any **w** in Teman?
49:7 Has **w** disappeared from your
49:7 Has their **w** vanished?
51:15 He set up the world by his **w**.
Eze 28:7 swords against your fine **w**
28:12 full of **w** and perfect in beauty.
28:17 You wasted your **w** because of
Dan 1:17 these four men knowledge, **w**,
1:20 that required **w** and insight,
2:21 He gives **w** to those who are
2:23 You gave me **w** and power.
5:11 and **w** like the wisdom of the
5:11 and wisdom like the **w** of the
5:14 and extraordinary **w**.
Oba 1:8 and take **w** away from Esau's
Mic 6:9 (The fear of your name is **w**.)
Mat 11:19 "Yet, **w** is proved right by its
12:42 the earth to hear Solomon's **w**.
13:54 "Where did this man get this **w**
Mar 6:2 Who gave him this kind of **w**
Luk 1:17 so that they will accept the **w**
2:40 He was filled with **w**,
2:52 Jesus grew in **w** and maturity.
7:35 "Yet, **w** is proved right by all its
11:31 the earth to hear Solomon's **w**.
11:49 That's why the **W** of God said,
21:15 I will give you words and **w**
Act 6:10 he spoke with the **w** that
7:10 divine favor and **w** so that
7:22 was educated in all the **w**
Rom 11:33 God's riches, **w**,
1Co 1:19 "I will destroy the **w** of the
1:20 Hasn't God turned the **w** of the
1:21 The world with its **w** was
1:21 God in terms of his own **w**.
1:22 and Greeks look for **w**,
1:24 God's power and God's **w**.
1:25 is wiser than human **w**,
1:30 Jesus has become our **w** sent
2:1 kind of brilliant message or **w**.
2:5 not be based on human **w**
2:6 However, we do use **w** to
2:6 It is a **w** that doesn't belong to
2:7 about the mystery of God's **w**.
2:7 It is a **w** that has been hidden,
3:18 you should give up that **w** in
3:19 The **w** of this world is
4:10 have given up our **w** for Christ,
12:8 the ability to speak with **w**.
2Co 1:12 It was not by human **w** that we
Eph 1:8 us every kind of **w** and insight
1:17 would give you a spirit of **w**
3:10 in heaven know his infinite **w**.
Col 1:9 kind of spiritual **w** and insight.
1:28 with all the **w** there is.
2:3 hidden all the treasures of **w**
2:23 These things look like **w** with
3:16 Let Christ's word with all its **w**
2Ti 3:15 to give you **w** so that you
Jas 1:5 If any of you needs **w** to know
3:13 any of you have **w** and insight?
3:13 the humility that comes from **w**.
3:15 That kind of **w** doesn't come
3:17 However, the **w** that comes
2Pe 3:15 using the **w** God gave him.
Rev 5:12 **w**, strength, honor, glory,
7:12 Praise, glory, **w**, thanks, honor,
13:18 In this situation **w** is needed.

wisdom's (3)

Pro 3:16 Long life is in ⌊**w**⌋ right hand.
3:16 In ⌊**w**⌋ left hand are riches and
Pro 3:17 ⌊**W**⌋ ways are pleasant ways,

wise (190)

Gen 3:6 for making someone **w**.
41:8 all the magicians and **w** men
41:33 "Pharaoh should look for a **w**
41:39 there is no one as **w** and
Exo 7:11 Then Pharaoh sent for his **w**
Dtr 1:13 choose some men who are **w**,
1:15 of your tribes who were **w**
4:6 "What **w** and insightful people
16:19 because bribes blind **w** people
32:29 If only they were **w** enough to
2Sm 14:20 You are as **w** as God's
1Ki 2:9 You are **w** and know what to
3:12 I'm giving you a **w** and
5:7 He has given David a **w** son to
2Ch 2:12 King David a **w** son who has
Ezr 8:16 and Elnathan (who were **w**).
Est 1:14 The king asked these **w** men
Job 5:13 He catches the **w** with their
9:4 "God is **w** in heart and mighty
12:2 "You certainly are ⌊**w**⌋ people,
15:2 "Should a **w** person answer
15:18 I'll tell you what **w** people have
17:10 find one **w** man among you.
22:2 when even a **w** person is only
32:9 People do not become **w**
34:2 to my words, you **w** men.
34:34 the **w** people who listen to me,
37:24 those who think they're **w**."
38:37 Who is **w** enough to count the
Psa 19:7 It makes gullible people **w**.
36:3 doing what is **w** and good.
49:3 mouth will speak **w** sayings,
49:10 one can see that **w** people die,
94:8 When will you become **w**,
107:43 they are **w** pay attention
Pro 1:3 to acquire the discipline of **w**
1:5 a **w** person will listen and
1:6 the words of **w** people and their
3:7 Do not consider yourself **w**.
3:35 **W** people will inherit honor,
6:6 its ways, and become **w**.
8:33 to discipline, and become **w**.
9:8 Warn a **w** person, and he will
9:9 Give ⌊advice⌋ to a **w** person,
9:12 If you are **w**, your wisdom will
10:1 The proverbs of Solomon: A **w**
10:5 in the summer is a **w** son.
10:8 is truly **w** accepts commands,
10:14 Those who are **w** store up
10:19 whoever seals his lips is **w**.
11:29 a slave to the **w** in heart.
11:30 and a winner of souls is **w**.
12:15 who listens to advice is **w**.
12:18 of **w** people bring healing.
13:1 A **w** son listens to his father's
13:14 The teachings of a **w** person
13:20 Whoever walks with **w** people
13:20 with wise people will be **w**,
14:3 but **w** people are protected by
14:16 A **w** person is cautious and
14:24 The crown of **w** people is their
15:2 The tongues of **w** people give
15:7 The lips of **w** people spread
15:12 He will not go to **w** people.
15:20 A **w** son makes his father
15:24 The path of life for a **w** person
15:31 be at home among **w** people.
16:14 but a **w** man makes peace with
16:21 The person who is truly **w** is
16:23 A **w** person's heart controls his
17:2 A **w** slave will become master
17:28 fool is thought to be **w** if
18:15 of **w** people seek knowledge.
19:20 so that you may be **w**
20:26 A **w** king scatters the wicked
21:11 a gullible person becomes **w**,
21:11 and when a **w** person is
21:16 the way of **w** behavior will rest
21:20 are in the home of a **w** person,
21:22 A **w** man attacks a city of
22:17 hear the words of **w** people,
23:15 My son, if you have a **w** heart,
23:19 My son, listen, be **w**,

Pro 23:24 Someone who has a **w** son
24:23 are the sayings of **w** people:
26:5 or he will think he is **w**.
26:12 a person who thinks he is **w**?
27:11 Be **w**, my son, and make my
28:7 ⌊God's⌋ teachings is a **w** son.
28:11 A rich person is **w** in his own
29:8 but **w** people turn away anger.
29:9 When a **w** person goes to court
29:11 but a **w** person controls them.
30:24 yet they are very **w**:
Ecc 2:14 A **w** person uses the eyes in
2:15 is the advantage in being **w**?"
2:16 Neither the **w** person nor the
2:16 Both the **w** person and the fool
2:19 person will be **w** or foolish?
4:13 is poor and **w** is better than
6:8 What advantage does a **w**
7:4 The minds of **w** people think
7:5 It is better to listen to **w** people
7:7 Oppression can turn a **w**
7:16 and don't be too **w**.
7:19 Wisdom will help a **w** person
7:23 I said, "I want to be **w**,
8:1 Who is really **w**? Who knows
8:5 The mind of a **w** person will
8:17 Even though a **w** person
9:1 people and **w** people,
9:11 **W** people don't necessarily
9:15 A poor, **w** person was found in
9:17 from **w** people than shouting
10:2 A **w** person's heart leads the
10:12 A **w** person's words win favors,
12:9 Besides being **w**, He very
12:11 Words from **w** people are like
Isa 5:21 for those who think they are **w**
19:11 "I'm a descendant of **w** men,
19:12 Where are your **w** men now?
29:14 The wisdom of their **w** people
31:2 He is **w** and can bring about
44:25 I make **w** men retreat and turn
Jer 8:8 can you say that you are **w**
8:9 **W** people are put to shame,
9:12 No one is **w** enough to
9:23 Don't let **w** people brag about
10:7 you among all the **w** people
18:18 the advice of **w** people,
32:19 You make **w** plans and do
50:35 their officials and their **w** men.
51:57 their officials and **w** men drunk,
Eze 28:4 you are **w** and understanding,
28:6 You think you are **w** like God.
Dan 2:12 all the **w** advisers in Babylon.
2:13 that the **w** advisers were
2:14 was leaving to kill the **w**
2:18 of the **w** advisers in Babylon.
2:20 because he is **w** and powerful.
2:21 wisdom to those who are **w**
2:24 destroy Babylon's **w** advisers.
2:24 destroy Babylon's **w** advisers.
2:27 king, "No **w** adviser, psychic,
2:48 of all Babylon's **w** advisers.
4:6 So I ordered all the **w** advisers
4:18 because the **w** advisers
5:7 He told these **w** advisers of
5:8 All the king's **w** advisers came,
5:15 The **w** advisers and the
11:33 "People who are **w** will help
11:35 Some of the **w** people will be
12:3 Those who are **w** will shine
12:10 Only **w** people will understand.
Hos 14:9 **W** people will understand
Amo 5:13 That is why a **w** person
Oba 1:8 day I will destroy the **w** people
Zec 9:2 though they are very **w**.
Mat 2:1 After Jesus' birth **w** men from
2:7 secretly called the **w** men
2:16 When Herod saw that the **w**
2:16 he had learned from the **w** men.
7:24 be like a **w** person who built
11:25 for hiding these things from **w**
23:34 sending you prophets, **w** men,
24:45 is the faithful and **w** servant?
25:2 were foolish, and five were **w**.
25:4 The **w** bridesmaids,
25:8 ones said to the **w** ones,
Mat 25:9 "But the **w** bridesmaids replied,
Luk 10:21 for hiding these things from **w**
Act 6:3 people know are spiritually **w**.
24:2 through your **w** leadership we
Rom 1:14 to those who are **w** and those
1:22 While claiming to be **w**,
16:27 God alone is **w**. Glory belongs
1Co 1:19 destroy the wisdom of the **w**.
1:20 Where is the **w** person?
1:26 Not many of you were **w** from a
1:27 nonsense to put **w** people
3:18 If any of you think you are **w** in
3:18 in order to become really **w**.
3:19 the **w** in their cleverness."
3:20 of the **w** are pointless."
6:5 Don't you have at least one **w**
2Co 11:19 You're **w**, so you'll gladly put
Eph 5:15 people but like **w** people.
Col 4:5 Be **w** in the way you act
Jas 3:14 Don't say that you are **w** when
Rev 17:9 "In this situation a **w** mind is

wisely (8)

2Ch 11:23 He **w** placed his sons in every
Psa 2:10 Now, you kings, act **w**.
14:2 if there is anyone who acts **w**,
53:2 if there is anyone who acts **w**,
Pro 14:35 with a servant who acts **w**,
21:12 A righteous person **w**
Jer 23:5 will be a king who will rule **w**.
Mar 12:34 When Jesus heard how **w** the

wiser (9)

1Ki 4:31 He was **w** than anyone,
Job 35:11 who makes us **w** than the birds
Psa 119:98 make me **w** than my enemies,
Pro 9:9 and he will become even **w**.
26:16 A lazy person thinks he is **w**
Ecc 1:16 "I have grown **w** than anyone
Eze 28:3 You think that you are **w** than
Dan 2:30 I'm **w** than anyone else.
1Co 1:25 God's nonsense is **w** than

wisest (3)

Jdg 5:29 Her **w** servants gave her an
Pro 14:1 The **w** of women builds up her
Isa 19:11 The **w** of Pharaoh's counselors

wish (48)

Num 11:29 I **w** all the LORD's people were
Jos 7:7 I **w** we had been content to live
Jdg 9:29 How I **w** I controlled these
Rut 3:13 But if he does not **w** to take
4:4 If you **w** to buy back the
4:4 But if you do not **w** to buy back
2Sm 14:7 In this way they **w** to
15:4 He would add, "I **w** someone
18:33 I **w** I had died in your place!
19:38 Anything you **w** I'll do for you."
20:20 I don't **w** to swallow ⌊it⌋ up or
23:15 "I **w** I could have a drink of
24:3 Your Majesty **w** to do this?"
1Ch 11:17 was thirsty and said, "I **w**
21:3 Why do you **w** to make Israel
Ezr 4:17 I **w** you peace and prosperity!
5:7 We **w** you peace and
7:12 I **w** you peace and prosperity!
Est 6:6 "Whom would the king **w** to
Job 6:8 "How I **w** that my prayer would
10:18 I **w** I had breathed my last
11:5 I only **w** God would speak and
13:3 and I **w** to argue my case in
13:5 I **w** you would keep silent.
14:13 I **w** you would hide me in
19:23 "I **w** now my words were
19:23 I **w** they were inscribed on a
19:24 I **w** they were forever engraved
31:31 'We **w** we had never filled ⌊our
Psa 139:19 I **w** that you would kill wicked
Pro 24:1 Do not envy evil people or **w**
Jer 9:1 "I **w** that my head were ⌊filled
9:2 I **w** I had a place to stay in the
40:5 "If you **w** to remain,
Dan 4:1 I **w** you peace and prosperity.
4:19 I **w** that the dream were about
6:25 I **w** you peace and prosperity.
Mal 1:10 "I **w** one of you would shut the
Mat 14:9 ordered that her **w** be granted.
Luk 12:49 I **w** that it had already started!
Act 26:29 Paul replied, "I **w** to God that
Rom 9:3 I **w** I could be condemned and
1Co 4:8 I **w** you really were kings so
10:27 for dinner⌋, and you **w** to go,
14:5 I **w** that all of you could speak
Gal 4:20 I **w** I were with you right now
5:12 I **w** those troublemakers would
Rev 3:15 I **w** you were cold or hot.

wished (2)

Jdg 16:16 him until he **w** he were dead.
Job 9:3 If he **w** to debate with God,

wishes (10)

Est 6:6 whom the king **w** to reward?"
6:9 on the man whom the king **w**
6:9 whom the king **w** to reward.'"
6:11 whom the king **w** to reward."
Dan 4:17 gives them to whomever he **w**.
4:25 gives them to whomever he **w**.
4:32 gives them to whomever he **w**."
4:35 He does whatever he **w** with
5:21 God puts whomever he **w** in
1Co 7:39 is free to marry anyone she **w**,

witch (2)

Exo 22:18 "Never let a **w** live.
Dtr 18:10 a fortuneteller, **w**, or sorcerer,

witchcraft (5)

2Ki 9:22 continues her idolatry and **w**?"
2Ch 33:6 cast evil spells, practiced **w**,
Mic 3:7 Those who practice **w** will be
Rev 9:21 practicing **w**, sinning sexually,
18:23 were deceived by its **w**.

witches (1)

Isa 57:3 come here, you children of **w**,

withdraw (1)

2Sm 20:21 and I'll **w** from the city."

withdrawn (3)

2Sm 15:24 the troops had **w** from the city.
Jer 34:21 the army that has **w** from you.
Jon 5:13 (Jesus had **w** from the crowd.)

withdrew (6)

Jos 7:26 Then the LORD **w** his burning
2Sm 20:22 and everyone scattered and **w**
2Ch 24:25 When the Arameans **w**,
Job 34:14 only of himself and **w** his Spirit
Lam 2:3 He **w** his right hand when they
Luk 22:41 Then he **w** from them about a

wither (21)

Job 8:12 would **w** quicker than grass.
18:16 His branches **w** over him.
24:24 They **w** like heads of grain.
Psa 1:3 and whose leaves do not **w**.
37:2 grass and **w** away like green
90:6 the evening they **w** and dry up.
102:11 and I **w** away like grass.
Isa 1:30 be like an oak whose leaves **w**
16:8 and the vineyards of Sibmah **w**.
19:6 The reeds and cattails will **w**.
40:7 Grass dries up, and flowers **w**
40:8 Grass dries up, and flowers **w**,
40:24 he blows on them and they **w**,
Eze 17:9 Then it will **w**. All the leaves on
17:9 leaves on its branches will **w**.
17:10 It will **w** completely when the
17:10 It will certainly **w** in the garden
47:12 Their leaves won't **w**,
Nah 1:4 Bashan and Carmel **w**.
1:4 The flowers of Lebanon **w**.
Jas 1:10 Rich people will **w** like flowers.

withered (12)

Gen 41:23 Seven other heads of grain, **w**,
Psa 102:4 My heart is beaten down and **w**
Isa 28:1 beauty is ⌊like⌋ a **w** flower.
28:4 beauty is ⌊like⌋ a **w** flower.

Eze 19:12 They **w** and were burned.
Joe 1:12 The fig trees are **w**.
Jnh 4:7 to attack the plant so that it **w**.
Zec 11:17 His arm will be completely **w**.
Mat 13:6 They **w** because their roots
Mar 4:6 have any roots, so they **w**.
Luk 8:6 they **w** because they had no
Jud 1:12 They are **w**, uprooted trees

withers (4)

Job 14:2 up like a flower; then he **w**.
Isa 15:6 dries up, the vegetation **w**,
24:4 The earth dries up and **w**.
24:4 The world wastes away and **w**.

withheld (4)

Jer 3:3 So the rain has been **w**,
Joe 1:13 offerings are **w** from your God's
Hag 1:10 you that the sky has **w** its dew
1:10 the earth has **w** its produce.

withhold (6)

Gen 23:6 Not one of us will **w** from you
Exo 22:29 "Never **w** your best wine from
Dtr 24:14 Don't **w** pay from hired workers
Psa 40:11 Do not **w** your compassion
Isa 32:6 hungry and **w** water from thirsty
1Co 7:5 Don't **w** yourselves from each

withstand (4)

Psa 147:17 Who can **w** his chilling blast?
Dan 11:15 will not be able to **w** him.
11:16 will be able to **w** his attack.
11:25 king won't be able to **w** him

witness (65)

Gen 31:44 let it stand as a **w** between you
31:47 it Jegar Sahadutha [**W** Pile],
31:48 stands as a **w** between you
31:50 stands as a **w** between you
Lev 5:1 if you are a **w** under oath and
Num 35:30 testimony of more than one **w**.
35:30 on the testimony of only one **w**.
Dtr 17:6 on the testimony of only one **w**.
19:15 One **w** is never enough to
19:16 must do whenever a **w** takes
19:18 If it is found that the **w** lied
21:7 and we didn't **w** it.
31:19 This song will be a **w** for me
31:26 it will be a **w** against you.
Jos 22:27 but it will stand as a **w**
22:27 It will stand as a **w** that we
22:28 to stand as a **w** between us.'
22:34 **W** Between Us That the LORD
24:27 stone will stand as a **w** for us.
24:27 It will stand as a **w** for you.
Jdg 11:10 "The LORD is a **w** between us.
1Sm 6:18 put the ark of the LORD is a **w**.
12:5 "The LORD is a **w** to what
12:5 and his anointed king is a **w**
12:5 "He is a **w**," they answered.
20:12 my **w**⌋," Jonathan continued,
20:23 and the LORD is ⌊a **w**⌋
20:42 'The LORD will be ⌊a **w**⌋
Job 16:8 itself is a **w** ⌊against me⌋.
16:19 My **w** is in heaven,
16:21 But my **w** will plead for a
Psa 89:37 be like a faithful **w** in heaven."
Pro 6:19 a dishonest **w** spitting out lies,
12:17 A truthful **w** speaks honestly,
12:17 a lying **w** speaks deceitfully.
14:5 A trustworthy **w** does not lie,
14:5 a dishonest **w** breathes lies.
14:25 An honest **w** saves lives,
19:5 A lying **w** will not go
19:9 A lying **w** will not go
19:28 A worthless **w** mocks justice,
21:28 A lying **w** will die,
29:16 people will **w** their downfall.
Isa 19:20 will be a sign and a **w** that
30:8 in the future as a permanent **w**.
55:4 I made him a **w** to people,
Jer 29:23 I'm a **w**, declares the LORD.
32:10 had people **w** the signing of the
32:44 and have people **w** the signing
42:5 be a true and faithful **w** against
Mic 1:2 LORD will be a **w** against you.
1:2 The Lord will be a **w** from his
Zep 3:8 One day I will stand up as a **w**.
Mal 2:14 It is because the LORD is a **w**
Act 1:20 us as a **w** that Jesus came
22:15 You will be his **w** and will tell
26:16 you to be a servant and **w**
Rom 1:9 God is my **w** that I always
2Co 1:23 I appeal to God as a **w** on my
Gal 1:20 (God is my **w** that what I'm
Php 1:8 God is my **w** that, with all the
1Th 2:5 to make money. God is our **w**!
Rev 1:5 and from Jesus Christ, the **w**,
2:13 He was my faithful **w** who was
3:14 the **w** who is faithful and true,

witnessed (3)

Act 22:20 Stephen, who **w** about you,
1Pe 5:1 who also **w** Christ's sufferings
2Pe 1:16 Rather, we **w** his majesty with

witnesses (56)

Gen 23:11 My people are **w** that I'm giving
23:18 the official **w** for the agreement.
31:52 and this marker stand as **w** that
Exo 22:10 and there are no **w**.
Num 5:13 kept it secret if there were no **w**
Dtr 4:25 I call heaven and earth as **w**
17:6 the testimony of two or three **w**,
17:7 The **w** must start the
19:15 the testimony of two or three **w**.
30:19 I call on heaven and earth as **w**
Rut 4:9 "Today you are **w** that I have
4:10 Today you are **w**."
4:11 the leaders, said, "We are **w**.
Job 10:17 finding new **w** against me.
Psa 27:12 False **w** have risen against me.
Isa 8:2 these dependable **w** testify:
33:8 **W** are rejected. People are no
43:9 They should bring their **w** to
43:10 "You are my **w**," declares the
43:12 You are my **w** that I am God,"
44:8 You are my **w**. Is there any God
44:9 Their own **w** do not see or
Jer 6:18 you nations, and learn, you **w**,
32:12 and the **w** who had signed
32:25 a field with money and get **w**
Mal 3:5 sorcerers, adulterers, lying **w**,
Mat 18:16 be verified by two or three **w**.
18:17 If he ignores these **w**,
26:65 Why do we need any more **w**?
Mar 14:63 "Why do we need any more **w**?
Luk 11:48 So you are **w** and approve of
24:48 You are **w** to these things.
Jon 3:28 You are **w** that I said,
Act 1:8 Then you will be my **w** to
2:32 We are all **w** to that.
3:15 and we are **w** to that.
5:32 We are **w** to these things,
6:13 Some **w** stood up and lied
7:58 The **w** left their coats with a
10:41 He showed Jesus to **w**,
13:31 These people are now **w** and
1Co 15:15 In addition, we are obviously **w**
2Co 13:1 be verified by two or three **w**.
1Th 2:10 You and God are **w** of how
1Ti 5:19 is supported by two or three **w**.
6:12 testimony in front of many **w**.
2Ti 2:2 it's been confirmed by many **w**.
Heb 10:28 If two or three **w** accused
1Jn 5:7 There are three **w**:
5:8 These three **w** agree.
Rev 11:3 I will allow my two **w** who
11:4 These **w** are the two olive
11:6 These **w** have authority to shut
11:7 When the **w** finish their
11:11 from God entered the two **w**,
11:12 The **w** heard a loud voice from

witnesses' (3)

Rev 11:5 fire comes out of the **w** mouths
11:9 will look at the **w** dead bodies
11:10 will gloat over the **w** death.

wits (1)

Pro 27:17 sharpens the **w** of another.

wives (124)

Gen 4:23 Lamech said to his **w**,
4:23 **W** of Lamech, hear what I say!
6:18 and your sons' **w** will go into
7:7 and his sons' **w** went into the
8:16 your sons, and your sons' **w**.
8:18 his wife, and his sons' **w**.
28:9 in addition to the **w** he had.
30:26 Give me my **w** and my
31:17 children and his **w** on camels.
32:22 got up and gathered his two **w**,
36:2 Esau chose his **w** from the
36:6 Esau took his **w**, his sons,
37:2 and Zilpah, his father's **w**.
45:19 for your children and your **w**.
46:5 and their **w** in the wagons
46:26 include the **w** of Jacob's sons.
Exo 22:24 Then your **w** and children will
32:2 to them, "Have your **w**, sons,
Num 14:3 Our **w** and children will be
16:27 tents with their **w** and children.
30:16 Moses for husbands and **w**,
32:26 Our children, our **w**,
Dtr 3:19 Your **w**, children, and livestock
17:17 have a large number of **w**,
21:15 A man might have two **w** and
21:15 Both **w** might have children,
29:11 Your children, your **w**,
Jos 1:14 Your **w**, children, and livestock
Jdg 8:30 sons because he had many **w**.
21:7 What will we do to provide **w**
21:16 should we do to provide **w**
21:18 any of our daughters as **w**.
21:18 an oath that whoever gives **w**
21:22 give them the **w** yourselves.'"
21:23 They captured the number of **w**
1Sm 1:2 Elkanah had two **w**,
25:43 she and Abigail were his **w**.
27:3 and David had his two **w**,
30:3 down, and their **w**, sons,
30:5 also captured David's two **w**,
30:18 including his two **w**.
2Sm 2:2 went there with his two **w**,
5:13 and **w** from Jerusalem after
12:8 master Saul's house and his **w**.
12:11 own eyes I will take your **w**
12:11 with your **w** in broad daylight.
19:5 **w**, and concubines today.
1Ki 11:3 He had 700 **w** who were
11:3 300 **w** who were concubines.
11:4 In his old age, his **w** tempted
11:8 foreign **w** who burned incense
20:3 Your beloved **w** and children
20:5 gold, **w**, and children are mine.
20:7 When he sent for my **w**,
2Ki 4:1 One of the **w** of a disciple of
24:15 the king's mother, **w**, eunuchs,
1Ch 3:8 Eliphelet (nine ⌊by other **w**⌋).
4:5 had two **w**, Helah and Naarah.
7:4 They had many **w** and children.
8:8 Shaharaim divorced his **w**
14:3 David married more **w** in
2Ch 11:21 all his other **w** and concubines.
11:21 (He had 18 **w** and 60
11:23 and obtained many **w** for them.
13:21 He married 14 **w** and fathered
20:13 from Judah, their infants, **w**,
21:14 your people, your sons, your **w**,
21:17 took Jehoram's sons and **w**.
24:3 Jehoiada got Joash two **w**,
29:9 and **w** are prisoners because of
31:18 were enrolled with their **w**,
Ezr 10:11 land and from your foreign **w**."
10:19 they would get rid of their **w**.
Neh 4:14 your **w**, and your homes."
5:1 the men and their **w**,
10:28 Their **w**, sons, daughters,
13:26 But his non-Israelite **w** led him
Est 1:18 Today the **w** of the officials in
1:20 Then all the **w** will honor their
Isa 13:16 be looted and their **w** raped.
Jer 5:8 neigh for their neighbors' **w**.
6:12 and their **w** will be turned over
8:10 That is why I will give their **w**
14:16 No one will bury them, their **w**,

Jer 18:21 Then their **w** will become
29:6 Find **w** for your sons,
29:23 adultery with their neighbors' **w**
35:8 We, along with our **w**,
38:23 "All your **w** and children will be
44:9 the kings of Judah and their **w**,
44:9 and by you and your **w** in
44:15 their **w** were burning incense
44:25 and your **w** made promises,
Eze 22:10 have sex with their father's **w**.
22:11 things with their neighbors' **w**.
Dan 5:2 his **w**, and his concubines.
5:3 The king, his nobles, **w**,
5:23 You, your nobles, **w**,
6:24 They, their **w**, and their
Zec 12:12 and the **w** by themselves;
12:12 and the **w** by themselves;
12:13 and the **w** by themselves;
12:13 and the **w** by themselves.
12:14 and the **w** by themselves."
Mat 19:8 allowed you to divorce your **w**
Luk 14:26 mothers, **w**, children, brothers,
Act 17:4 to Judaism and the **w**
21:5 All of them with their **w** and
1Co 7:3 Husbands and **w** should
9:5 the right to take our **w** along
Eph 5:22 **W**, place yourselves under
5:24 so **w** are under their husbands'
5:25 Husbands, love your **w** as
5:28 So husbands must love their **w**
5:33 and **w** should respect their
Col 3:18 **W**, place yourselves under
3:19 Husbands, love your **w**,
1Ti 3:11 Their **w** must also be of good
Heb 13:4 so husbands and **w** should be
1Pe 3:1 **W**, in a similar way,
3:1 Their **w** could win these men
3:3 **W** must not let their beauty be
3:7 live with your **w** with
3:7 Honor your **w** as those who

wobble (2)

Isa 28:7 from wine and **w** from too much
28:7 They **w** because of their liquor.

woke (21)

Gen 28:16 Then Jacob **w** up from his
41:4 Then Pharaoh **w** up.
41:7 Then Pharaoh **w** up.
41:21 as sick as before. Then I **w** up.
Jdg 16:14 But Samson **w** up and tore his
16:20 Samson **w** up. He thought, "I'll
1Sm 26:12 them, knew about it, or **w** up.
1Ki 3:15 Solomon **w** up and realized it
19:7 back and **w** him up again.
Psa 78:65 Then the Lord **w** up like one
Sos 8:5 Under the apple tree I **w** you up.
Jer 31:26 I **w** up and looked around.
Zec 4:1 me returned and **w** me up as
Mat 1:24 When Joseph **w** up,
8:25 So they **w** him up,
25:7 Then all the bridesmaids **w** up
Mar 4:38 So they **w** him up and said to
Luk 8:24 They went to him, **w** him up,
9:32 When they **w** up, they saw
Act 12:7 **w** him up, and said, "Hurry!
16:27 The jailer **w** up and saw the

wolf (4)

Gen 49:27 "Benjamin is a ravenous **w**.
Jer 5:6 A **w** from the wilderness will
Jon 10:12 When he sees a **w** coming,
10:12 So the **w** drags the sheep

wolves (9)

Isa 11:6 **W** will live with lambs.
65:25 **W** and lambs will feed together,
Eze 22:27 Your leaders are like **w** that
Hab 1:8 leopards and quicker than **w**
Zep 3:3 Its judges are like **w** in the
Mat 7:15 their hearts they are vicious **w**.
10:16 you out like sheep among **w**.
Luk 10:3 you out like lambs among **w**.
Act 20:29 I know that fierce **w** will come

woman (398)

Gen 2:22 the LORD God formed a **w** from
2:23 She will be named **w** because
3:1 He asked the **w**, "Did God
3:2 The **w** answered the snake,
3:4 the serpent told the **w**.
3:6 The **w** saw that the tree had
3:12 The man answered, "That **w**,
3:13 the LORD God asked the **w**,
3:13 me, and I ate," the **w** answered.
3:15 I will make you and the **w**
3:16 He said to the **w**, "I will
6:2 they married any **w** they chose.
12:11 know that you're a beautiful **w**.
17:17 Can Sarah, a ninety-year-old **w**,
20:3 of the **w** that you've taken!
20:3 She's a married **w**!"
20:18 made it impossible for any **w**
24:5 "What if the **w** doesn't want to
24:8 If the **w** doesn't want to come
24:39 'What if the **w** won't come back
24:43 I'll say to the young **w** who
24:44 let her be the **w** the LORD has
26:7 she was an attractive **w**.
27:46 If Jacob marries a Hittite **w** like
38:20 back his deposit from the **w**,
46:10 the son of a Canaanite **w**.
Exo 2:1 family married a Levite **w**.
2:2 The **w** became pregnant and
2:9 daughter said to the **w**,
3:22 "Every Hebrew **w** should ask
3:22 neighbor and any **w** living
6:15 the son of a Canaanite **w**.
11:2 that each man and **w** must ask
21:10 If that son marries another **w**,
21:22 injure a pregnant **w** so that she
21:28 gores a man or a **w** to death,
21:29 and it kills a man or a **w**,
23:26 No **w** in your land will miscarry
35:29 Every Israelite man and **w** who
36:6 "No man or **w** needs to make
Lev 12:2 When a **w** gives birth to a boy,
12:5 "When a **w** gives birth to a girl,
12:7 for the **w** who gives birth
13:29 "If a man or a **w** has some
13:38 "If a man or a **w** has white
15:18 sexual intercourse with a **w**
15:19 "When a **w** has her monthly
15:25 "If a **w** has a discharge of
15:30 the LORD for the **w** who had
15:33 for any **w** who has her period,
15:33 for any man or **w** who has a
15:33 with a **w** when she is
18:17 sexual intercourse with a **w**
18:17 woman and her daughter or a **w**
18:19 with a **w** while she is
18:22 with a man as with a **w**.
18:23 A **w** must never offer herself to
20:10 both he and the **w** must be put
20:13 with another man as with a **w**,
20:14 When a man marries a **w** and
20:16 When a **w** offers herself
20:16 you must kill both the **w** and
20:18 with a **w** while she has
20:20 That man and **w** are guilty of
20:21 That man and **w** will have no
20:27 "Every man or **w** who is a
21:14 marry a widow, a divorced **w**,
21:14 a **w** who has lost her virginity,
27:4 If it is a **w**, give 12 ounces.
27:7 and for a **w** give 4 ounces.
Num 5:16 "The priest will have the **w**
5:18 The priest will bring the **w** into
5:22 "Then the **w** will say,
5:24 Then he will have the **w** drink
5:26 will have the **w** drink the water.
5:28 But if the **w** is not unclean and
5:29 to do when a **w** is unfaithful
5:31 but the **w** will suffer the
6:2 A man or a **w** may make a
12:1 was married to a **w** from Sudan.
25:6 men brought a Midianite **w**
25:14 with the Midianite **w** was Zimri,
25:15 The name of the Midianite **w**
30:6 "An unmarried **w** might make a
Num 30:9 "But a widow or a divorced **w**
30:10 "A married **w** might make a
31:17 Midianite **w** who has gone
36:8 A **w** who inherits land in any of
Dtr 17:2 there may be a man or **w**
17:5 then bring the man or **w** who
20:7 If you are engaged to a **w** but
21:11 If you see a beautiful **w** among
22:5 A **w** must never wear anything
22:13 A man might marry a **w**,
22:14 by saying, "I married this **w**.
22:22 intercourse with a married **w**,
22:22 that man and the **w** must die.
23:17 No Israelite man or **w** should
28:30 You will be engaged to a **w**,
28:56 and sensitive **w** among you —
29:18 Make sure there is no man, **w**,
Jos 2:4 But the **w** had already taken
6:22 Bring the **w** out, along with
Jdg 4:9 the LORD will use a **w**
5:24 should be the most blessed **w**,
5:24 the most blessed **w** living in a
9:53 Then a **w** threw a small
9:54 'A **w** killed Abimelech.'
11:2 You're the son of that other **w**."
13:6 The **w** went to tell her husband.
13:10 The **w** ran quickly to tell her
13:24 So the **w** had a son and named
14:1 he saw a young Philistine **w**.
14:2 seen a Philistine **w** at Timnah.
14:3 Do you have to marry a **w** from
14:7 he went to talk to the young **w**.
14:10 his father went to see the **w**,
16:4 he fell in love with a **w** in the
19:1 He took a **w** from Bethlehem in
19:19 myself, the **w**, and my servant.
19:26 At daybreak, the **w** came to the
20:4 the husband of the murdered **w**,
21:21 Each of you catch a **w** from
Rut 1:4 son married a **w** from Moab.
1:4 son married a **w** named Orpah,
1:4 son married a **w** named Ruth.
2:5 "Who is this young **w**?"
2:6 "She's a young Moabite **w** who
3:8 he was surprised to see a **w**
3:11 you are a **w** who has strength
3:14 ever know that this **w** came
4:12 give you from this young **w**,
1Sm 1:16 me to be a good-for-nothing **w**.
1:18 Then the **w** went her way and
1:23 The **w** stayed and nursed her
1:26 I'm the **w** who stood here next
2:5 Even the **w** who was childless
2:20 give you children from this **w**
20:30 of a crooked and rebellious **w**!"
27:9 he left no man or **w** alive.
27:11 bring a single man or **w** back
28:7 "Find me a **w** who conjures up
28:7 "There is a **w** at Endor who
28:8 and came to the **w** that night.
28:9 The **w** told him, "You know
28:11 the **w** asked. "Conjure up
28:12 When the **w** saw Samuel,
28:13 the ground," the **w** answered.
28:21 The **w** came over to Saul and
28:23 his officers and the **w** kept
28:24 The **w** immediately butchered
2Sm 3:8 with a crime because of this **w**.
11:2 the roof he saw a **w** bathing,
11:3 someone to ask about the **w**.
11:5 The **w** had become pregnant.
11:21 Didn't a **w** on the wall of
14:2 to get a clever **w** from there.
14:2 but act like a **w** who has been
14:4 The **w** from Tekoa came to the
14:8 "Go home," the king told the **w**.
14:9 The **w** from Tekoa said to the
14:12 The **w** said, "Please let me
14:18 The king said to the **w**,
14:18 The **w** responded,
14:19 The **w** answered, "I solemnly
14:27 Tamar was a beautiful **w**.
17:20 came to the **w** at her home.
17:20 The **w** said, "They've crossed
20:16 Then a clever **w** called from
20:21 "That's fine," the **w** told Joab.

2Sm 20:22 Then the **w** went to all the
1Ki 1:2 let us search for a young **w**
1:3 Israel for a beautiful, young **w**.
1:4 The **w** was very beautiful.
3:17 One **w** said to him,
3:17 this **w** and I live in the same
3:18 Two days later this **w** also
3:22 The other **w** said, "No! My son
3:22 The first **w** kept on saying,
3:26 Then the **w** whose son was
3:26 But the other **w** said,
3:27 the living child to the first **w**.
14:21 Ammonite **w** named Naamah.
14:31 Ammonite **w** named Naamah.)
17:17 Afterwards, the son of the **w**
17:18 The **w** asked Elijah,
17:24 The **w** said to Elijah,
2Ki 4:8 where a rich **w** lived.
4:12 "Call this Shunem **w**."
4:17 But the **w** became pregnant
4:25 "There is the **w** from Shunem.
4:28 The **w** said, "I didn't ask you
4:36 "Call the Shunem **w**.
6:26 a **w** cried to him, "Help me,
6:28 answered, "This **w** told me,
6:30 the king heard the **w** say this,
8:1 Elisha had told the **w** whose
8:2 The **w** did what the man of
8:3 end of seven years, the **w** came
8:5 "Your Majesty, this is the **w**,
8:6 king asked the **w** ⌊about this⌋,
9:34 "Take care of this **w** who had
19:3 We are like a **w** who is about
1Ch 2:3 by Bathshua, a Canaanite **w**.
2Ch 2:14 He was the son of a **w** from the
12:13 Ammonite **w** named Naamah.)
24:7 (The sons of that wicked **w**
24:26 Ammonite **w** named Shimeath,
24:26 of a Moabite **w** named Shimrith.
Ezr 10:14 married a foreign **w** must meet
Est 1:19 to another **w** who is more
2:4 Then the young **w** who
2:7 The young **w** had a beautiful
2:9 The young **w** pleased him and
2:12 Each young **w** had her turn to
2:13 After that, the young **w** would
Job 14:1 "A person who is born of a **w** is
15:14 a **w** be considered righteous?
25:4 anyone born of a **w** be pure?
31:9 "If I have been seduced by a **w**
Psa 48:6 a **w** experiences during labor.
113:9 He makes a **w** who is in a
Pro 2:16 save you from an adulterous **w**,
2:16 from a loose **w** with her smooth
5:3 The lips of an adulterous **w**
5:20 with an adulterous **w**
6:24 to keep you from an evil **w** and
6:24 the smooth talk of a loose **w**.
6:26 but a married **w** hunts for
6:32 with a **w** has no sense.
7:5 yourself from an adulterous **w**,
7:5 from a loose **w** with her smooth
7:10 A **w** with an ulterior motive
9:13 The **w** Stupidity is loud,
11:16 A gracious **w** wins respect,
11:22 ⌊so⌋ is a beautiful **w** who
19:13 and a quarreling **w** is like
21:9 a home with a quarreling **w**.
21:19 with a quarreling and angry **w**.
22:14 The mouth of an adulterous **w**
23:27 A loose **w** is a narrow well.
25:24 a home with a quarreling **w**.
27:15 rainy day is like a quarreling **w**.
30:20 This is the way of a **w** who
30:23 a **w** who is unloved when she
31:30 ⌊but⌋ a **w** who has the fear of
Ecc 7:26 I find that a **w** whose thoughts
7:28 of all these I didn't find one **w**.
Sos 3:6 Who is this young **w** coming
6:10 Who is this young **w**?
6:13 young **w** from Shulam!
6:13 the young **w** from Shulam,
7:7 Young **w**, your figure is like a
8:5 Who is this young **w** coming
8:13 Young **w** living in the gardens,
Isa 13:8 They'll writhe like a **w** giving
Isa 37:3 We are like a **w** who is about
42:14 But like a **w** in childbirth I will
49:15 Can a **w** forget her nursing
62:5 As a young man marries a **w**,
66:7 Before a **w** goes into labor,
Jer 2:32 A young **w** can't forget her
4:31 I hear a **w** in labor.
4:31 I hear the **w** cry with anguish
6:24 and pain like a **w** giving birth
13:21 pain grip you like a **w** in labor?
22:23 pain like a **w** giving birth to a
30:6 in pain like a **w** giving birth
31:22 A **w** will protect a man.
49:24 pain grip them like a **w** in labor.
50:12 The **w** who gave birth to you
50:43 him as pain grips a **w** in labor.
Eze 16:7 and became a young **w**.
18:6 with a **w** while she is
Hos 2:5 The **w** who became pregnant
Joe 1:8 Cry loudly like a young **w** who
Amo 2:7 son sleep with the same **w**.
4:3 one **w** ahead of another.
Mic 4:9 Pain grips you like a **w** in labor.
4:10 and groan like a **w** in labor.
7:5 shut even when a **w** is lying
Zec 5:7 and a **w** was sitting in the
Mal 2:11 has married a **w** who worships
Mat 5:28 that whoever looks at a **w**
5:32 Whoever marries a **w** divorced
9:20 Then a **w** came up behind
9:22 moment the **w** became well.
13:33 like yeast that a **w** mixed into
15:22 A Canaanite **w** from that
15:28 Then Jesus answered her, "**W**,
19:9 if he marries another **w**."
22:27 At last the **w** died.
26:7 a **w** went to him with a bottle of
26:10 "Why are you bothering this **w**?
Mar 5:25 In the crowd was a **w** who had
5:32 to see the **w** who had done
5:33 The **w** trembled with fear.
7:25 A **w** whose little daughter had
7:26 The **w** happened to be Greek,
7:30 The **w** went home and found
10:11 **w** is committing adultery.
12:22 Last of all, the **w** died.
14:3 sitting there, a **w** went to him.
Luk 7:37 A **w** who lived a sinful life in
7:39 he would know what sort of **w**
7:44 Then, turning to the **w**,
7:44 "You see this **w**, don't you?
7:50 Jesus said to the **w**,
8:43 A **w** who had been suffering
8:47 The **w** saw that she couldn't
10:38 A **w** named Martha welcomed
11:27 a **w** in the crowd shouted,
13:11 A **w** who was possessed by a
13:12 to come to him and said, "**W**,
13:21 It's like yeast that a **w** mixed
15:8 "Suppose a **w** has ten coins
16:18 **w** is committing adultery.
16:18 The man who marries a **w**
20:32 Finally, the **w** died.
22:57 saying, "I don't know him, **w**."
Jon 4:7 A Samaritan **w** went to get
4:9 The Samaritan **w** asked him,
4:9 you ask a Samaritan **w** like me
4:11 The **w** said to him,
4:15 The **w** told Jesus,
4:17 The **w** replied, "I don't have a
4:19 The **w** said to Jesus,
4:25 The **w** said to him,
4:27 that he was talking to a **w**.
4:28 Then the **w** left her water jar
4:39 because of the **w** who said,
4:42 They told the **w**, "Our faith is
8:3 brought a **w** who had been
8:4 we caught this **w** in the act of
8:9 was left alone with the **w**.
8:11 The **w** answered, "No one, sir."
11:2 (Mary was the **w** who poured
16:21 A **w** has pain when her time to
18:16 talked to the **w** who was
Act 9:2 any man or **w** who followed
16:14 A **w** named Lydia was present.
17:34 and a **w** named Damaris,
Rom 7:2 For example, a married **w** is
1Co 7:2 and each **w** should have her
7:12 man is married to a **w** who is
7:13 If any Christian **w** is married to
7:15 man or Christian **w** is not bound
7:34 An unmarried **w** or a virgin is
7:34 But the married **w** is concerned
7:39 A married **w** must remain with
11:5 Every **w** who prays or speaks
11:5 She is like the **w** who has her
11:6 So if a **w** doesn't cover her
11:6 If it's a disgrace for a **w** to cut
11:7 The **w**, however, is man's
11:8 man wasn't made from **w** but
11:8 from woman but **w** from man.
11:9 Man wasn't created for **w** but
11:9 for woman but **w** for man.
11:10 Therefore, a **w** should wear
11:12 As a **w** came into existence
11:13 Is it proper for a **w** to pray to
14:35 It's shameful for a **w** to speak
Gal 4:4 A **w** gave birth to him,
4:22 one by a **w** who was a slave
4:22 slave and the other by a free **w**.
4:23 Now, the son of the slave **w**
4:23 but the son of the free **w** was
4:24 The one **w**, Hagar, is the
4:27 Because the deserted **w** will
4:27 children than the **w** who has
4:30 "Get rid of the slave **w** and her
4:30 because the son of the slave **w**
4:30 with the son of the free **w**."
4:31 are not children of a slave **w**
4:31 slave woman but of the free **w**.
1Th 5:3 pains come to a pregnant **w**.
1Ti 2:11 A **w** must learn in silence,
2:12 I don't allow a **w** to teach or to
2:14 It was the **w** who was
5:16 If any **w** is a believer and has
Jas 2:15 whether a man or a **w**,
2Pe 2:14 looking for an adulterous **w**.
Rev 2:20 You tolerate that **w** Jezebel,
12:1 There was a **w** who was
12:4 in front of the **w** who was going
12:6 Then the **w** fled into the
12:13 it persecuted the **w** who had
12:14 The **w** was given the two
12:15 a river of water behind the **w**
12:16 The earth helped the **w** by
12:17 became angry with the **w**.
17:3 I saw a **w** sitting on a bright red
17:4 The **w** wore purple clothes,
17:6 I saw that the **w** was drunk
17:7 tell you the mystery of the **w**
17:9 on which the **w** is sitting.
17:18 The **w** you saw is the

woman's (11)

Exo 21:22 the **w** husband to demand.
Lev 24:11 The Israelite **w** son began
Num 25:8 the man and into the **w** body.
Jdg 19:5 but the **w** father told his
19:6 The **w** father said to his
19:8 The **w** father said,
1Ki 3:19 That night this **w** son died
Job 24:9 take a poor **w** baby as security
Pro 5:20 and fondle a loose **w** breast
Eze 36:17 as a **w** menstrual period.
1Co 11:15 it teach you that it is a **w** pride

womb (28)

Gen 25:23 "Two countries are in your **w**.
49:25 blessings from breasts and **w**.
Rut 1:11 more sons in my **w** who could
Job 3:10 the doors of the **w** ⌊from which
3:11 when I came out of the **w**?
10:18 did you take me out of the **w**?
10:19 carried from the **w** to the tomb.
24:20 The **w** forgets them.
31:15 same God form us in the **w**?
38:8 through and came out of the **w**,
38:29 From whose **w** came the ice,
Psa 22:9 who brought me out of the **w**,
22:10 From my mother's **w** you have
58:3 ⌊Even⌋ inside the **w** the wicked
71:6 took me from my mother's **w**.

Pro 30:16 the grave, a barren w,
Ecc 5:15 from their mother's w naked.
11:5 of a child within its mother's w,
Isa 44:2 formed you in the w,
44:24 He formed you in the w.
49:1 While I was in my mother's w,
49:5 The LORD formed me in the w
49:15 on the child from her w?
Jer 1:5 "Before I formed you in the w,
20:17 killed me while I was in the w.
20:18 Why did I come out of the w?
Hos 12:3 them were in their mother's w.
13:13 come out of its mother's w.

wombs (1)

Job 15:35 Their w produce deception."

women (278)

Gen 4:19 Lamech married two w,
14:16 including w and soldiers.
24:11 It was evening, when the w
26:35 These w brought Isaac and
27:46 "I can't stand Hittite w!
28:1 marry any of the Canaanite w.
28:6 marry any of the Canaanite w.
28:8 disapproved of Canaanite w.
30:13 W will call me blessed."
31:50 marry other w behind my back,
33:5 he saw the w and children,
34:1 visit some of the Canaanite w.
34:29 off all the wealth and all the w
36:2 wives from the w of Canaan:
Exo 1:16 help the Hebrew w in childbirth
1:19 "Hebrew w are not like
1:19 women are not like Egyptian w.
2:7 go and get one of the Hebrew w
10:10 would ever let you take your w
10:24 Even your w and children may
12:37 plus all the w and children.
15:20 All the w, dancing with
35:22 men and w alike — came
35:25 All the w who were skilled in
35:26 All the w who were willing and
38:8 given by the w who served at
Lev 20:14 The man and the two w must
21:7 or divorced w because a priest
26:26 Ten w will need only one oven
Num 5:3 unclean men and w outside
25:1 to have sex with Moabite w
31:9 Israelites took the Midianite w
31:15 did you let all the w live?"
31:35 32,000 w who had never gone
Dtr 2:34 men, w, and children.
3:6 every city, including men, w,
4:16 that represent men or w,
7:14 Your men and w will be able to
15:12 Whenever Hebrew men or w
20:14 But take the w and children,
31:12 Assemble the men, w,
32:25 Young men and young w alike
Jos 6:21 swords they killed men and w,
8:25 Twelve thousand men and w
8:35 of Israel, including w, children,
Jdg 9:49 about a thousand men and w.
9:51 All the men, w, and leaders of
14:3 "Aren't there any w among our
16:27 and w who watched Samson
21:10 including the w and children.
21:12 unmarried w who had never
21:14 These men were given the w
21:14 had not found enough w
21:16 since the w in Benjamin have
21:21 When the young w of Shiloh
21:23 from the w who were dancing
Rut 1:19 can it?" the w asked.
2:8 Stay here with my young w.
2:9 and follow the young w in that
2:22 to the fields with his young w.
2:23 the young w who were working
3:2 Isn't Boaz, whose young w
4:14 The w said to Naomi,
4:17 The w in the neighborhood
1Sm 2:22 with the w who served at
4:20 the w helping her said,
15:3 but kill men and w,
15:33 your sword made w childless,
1Sm 15:33 be made childless among w."
18:6 W from all of Israel's cities
18:7 The w who were celebrating
21:5 "Of course w have been kept
22:19 he killed men and w,
30:2 and old w who were there,
30:2 Instead, they had taken ⌊the w
2Sm 1:26 to me than the love of w.
6:19 both men and w — one loaf of
19:35 hear the singing of men and w?
1Ki 11:1 Solomon loved many foreign w
11:1 He loved Hittite w and women
11:1 women and w from Moab,
2Ki 8:12 and rip open their pregnant w."
15:16 ripped open all its pregnant w.
23:7 where w did weaving for
1Ch 16:3 in Israel — both men and w —
2Ch 28:8 Israelites captured 200,000 w,
28:10 to enslave the men and w
36:17 best men or the unmarried w,
Ezr 9:2 some of these foreign w.
10:1 large crowd of Israelite men, w,
10:2 foreign w who came from
10:3 God to get rid of all foreign w
10:10 by marrying foreign w,
10:17 who had married foreign w.
10:18 were married to foreign w:
10:44 men had married foreign w.
10:44 Some of these w had given
Neh 8:2 This included men, w,
8:3 of Water Gate to the men, w,
12:43 The w and children rejoiced as
13:23 had married w from Ashdod,
13:27 by marrying non-Israelite w?"
Est 1:9 also held a banquet for the w at
1:17 has done will spread to all w,
2:3 the guardian of the w,
2:8 many young w were gathered
2:8 the guardian of the w.
2:12 12-month treatment for w.
2:12 and other treatments for w.
2:14 to the other quarters for w.
2:15 the guardian of the w,
2:17 Esther more than all the other w
3:13 w and children — on a single
7:4 If our men and w had only been
8:11 even w and children,
Job 24:21 take advantage of childless w.
42:15 could be found w who were as
Psa 68:11 The w who announce the good
68:12 The w who remained at home
68:25 The young w beating
148:12 young men and w,
Pro 14:1 The wisest of w builds up her
31:3 Don't give your strength to w or
31:29 'Many w have done noble
Ecc 12:3 the w at the mill stop grinding
Sos 1:3 wonder the young w love you!
1:4 it is that the young w love you!
1:5 Young w of Jerusalem,
1:8 most beautiful of w,
2:2 true love among the young w.
2:7 Young w of Jerusalem,
3:5 Young w of Jerusalem,
3:10 by the young w of Jerusalem.
3:11 Young w of Zion, come out and
5:8 Young w of Jerusalem,
5:9 Most beautiful of w,
5:16 young w of Jerusalem.
6:1 most beautiful of w?
8:4 Young w of Jerusalem,
Isa 3:12 W will rule them. My people,
3:16 "The w of Zion are arrogant.
3:17 on the heads of the w of Zion,
3:25 ⌊W,⌋ your warriors will die in
4:1 When that day comes, seven w
19:16 time Egyptians will act like w.
26:17 we are like pregnant w ready to
27:11 W will come and build a fire
32:9 listen to me, you pampered w.
32:10 overconfident w will tremble,
32:11 Shudder, you pampered w.
32:11 Tremble, you overconfident w.
54:1 Sing with joy, you childless w
54:1 Break into shouts of joy, you w
54:1 children of w who have been
Isa 54:1 of married w," says the LORD.
Jer 2:33 taught your ways to wicked w.
7:18 and w knead dough to make
9:17 Call for the w who cry at
9:20 the word of the LORD, you w,
31:8 return together with pregnant w
31:13 Then young w will rejoice and
34:11 the men and w they had freed
38:22 All the w who are left in the
38:22 These w will say:
40:7 the country's poorest men, w,
41:16 Johanan brought back men, w,
43:6 They took men, w,
44:7 destroying men, w, children,
44:15 all the w who were standing
44:19 The w added, "When we
44:20 all the people, both men and w,
44:24 all the people, including the w,
48:41 will be like w in childbirth.
49:22 will be like w in childbirth.
50:37 They will become w.
51:22 use you to crush men and w.
51:22 you to crush young men and w.
51:30 They have become w.
Lam 1:4 Its young w are made to suffer.
1:18 My young w and young men
2:10 The young w of Jerusalem
2:20 Should w eat their own
2:21 My young w and men are cut
3:51 of all the young w in my city.
4:3 but the w of my people are as
5:11 W in Zion are raped,
Eze 8:14 W were sitting there and crying
9:6 Kill old men, young men, old w,
9:6 women, young w, and children.
13:17 "Son of man, look at the w
13:18 How horrible it will be for w
16:41 you in the presence of many w.
22:10 They have sex with w when
22:10 when the w are having their
22:25 They turn many w into widows.
23:2 there were once two w,
23:10 W gossiped about how she
23:44 They slept with those sinful w,
23:45 people will punish these w
23:45 because these w have
23:48 and all the w will be warned
44:22 widows or w who have been
Dan 11:37 of his ancestors or desire for w.
Hos 9:14 Make the w miscarry,
13:16 and their pregnant w will be
Joe 2:29 on both men and w.
Amo 1:13 open pregnant w in Gilead.
4:1 You w oppress the poor and
8:13 On that day beautiful young w
Mic 2:9 You force the w among my
Nah 2:7 Its young w will be mourning
3:13 Look at your soldiers; they're w!
Zec 5:9 I looked up and saw two w
8:4 Old men and old w will again
9:17 and young w will prosper on
14:2 looted, and the w raped.
Mat 14:21 number does not include the w
15:38 number does not include the w
24:19 be for the w who are pregnant
24:41 Two w will be working at a
27:55 Many w were there watching
28:5 The angel said to the w,
28:11 While the w were on their way,
Mar 13:17 be for the w who are pregnant
15:40 Some w were watching from a
15:41 Many other w who had come to
Luk 1:42 are the most blessed of all w,
8:2 Also, some w were with him.
8:2 These w were Mary,
8:3 and many other w.
17:35 Two w will be grinding grain
21:23 "How horrible it will be for w
23:27 The w in the crowd cried and
23:28 "You w of Jerusalem,
23:29 'Blessed are the w who
23:49 All his friends, including the w
23:55 The w who had come with
24:1 on Sunday morning the w went
24:5 The w were terrified and
24:5 The men asked the w,

Luk 24:8 Then the w remembered what
24:9 The w left the tomb and went
24:10 The w were Mary from
24:10 were also other w with them.
24:22 Some of the w from our group
24:24 as the w had said,
Jon 8:5 Moses ordered us to stone w
Act 1:14 They were joined by some w,
2:18 on both men and w.
5:14 More men and w than ever
8:3 He dragged men and w out of
8:12 men and w believed him and
13:50 But Jews stirred up devout w
16:13 to the w who had gathered
17:12 prominent Greek men and w.
22:4 I tied up men and w and put
Rom 1:26 Their w have exchanged
1:27 natural sexual relations with w
1Co 11:11 Yet, as believers in the Lord, w
11:11 men couldn't exist without w.
11:12 men come into existence by w,
14:34 the w must keep silent.
Gal 4:24 The w illustrate two
4:27 w who cannot get pregnant,
Php 4:3 true partner, to help these w.
1Ti 2:9 I want w to show their beauty
2:10 This is what is proper for w
2:15 However, she ⌊and all w⌋ will
4:7 godless myths that old w like
5:2 older w as if they were your
5:2 and younger w as if they were
2Ti 3:6 w who are burdened
3:7 These w are always studying
Tit 2:3 Tell older w to live their lives
2:4 way they will teach young w
2:5 tell them to teach young w
Heb 11:35 W received their loved ones
1Pe 3:5 After all, this is how holy w

women's (8)

Dtr 22:5 must never wear w clothes.
Est 2:3 of Susa, to the w quarters.
2:9 the best place in the w quarters
2:11 the courtyard of the w quarters
2:13 with her from the w quarters
Eze 23:42 put bracelets on the w wrists
Luk 24:11 that the w story didn't make any
Rev 9:8 They had hair like w hair and

won (38)

Gen 30:8 with my sister, and I have w!"
32:28 with men — and you have w."
Exo 15:1 He has w a glorious victory.
15:21 He has w a glorious victory.
Num 32:4 the land that the LORD w for
Dtr 32:27 'We w this victory!
1Sm 14:45 after he has w this great victory
2Sm 23:10 So the LORD w an impressive
23:12 LORD w an impressive victory.
2Ch 13:18 and the men of Judah w
Est 2:9 him and w his affection.
5:2 the entrance, she w his favor.
Psa 44:4 You w those victories for
78:54 mountain that his power had w.
Ecc 9:11 The race isn't ⌊w⌋ by fast
Isa 40:10 and the people he has w arrive
62:11 and the people he has w arrive
63:5 my own power I w a victory.
Jer 20:7 You overpowered me and w.
Lam 1:16 because my enemies have w."
Hos 12:4 with the Messenger and w.
Mat 18:15 you have w back that believer.
Luk 23:23 and they finally w.
Act 7:46 who w God's favor.
14:19 Iconium arrived in Lystra and w
14:21 that city and w many disciples.
19:26 He has w over a large crowd
Rom 9:30 God's approval w his approval,
1Co 16:15 first family to be w ⌊for Christ⌋
Php 3:12 Christ has already w for me.
1Jn 2:13 because you have w the
2:14 You have w the victory over
4:4 So you have w the victory over
5:4 has been born from God has w
Rev 3:21 as I have w the victory and
5:5 of David, has w the victory.
12:11 They w the victory over him
15:2 Those who had w the victory

wonder (2)

Sos 1:3 No w the young women love
2Co 11:14 And no w, even Satan

wondered (3)

Mar 15:44 Pilate w if Jesus had already
Luk 3:15 they all w whether John was
2Co 1:8 We even w if we could go on

wonderful (15)

2Sm 1:26 Your love was more w to me
7:23 and to do great and w things
1Ch 17:21 and to do great and w things
29:13 you and praise your w name.
Psa 40:5 You have made many w plans
Isa 4:2 LORD will be beautiful and w.
9:6 will be named: W Counselor,
12:5 He has done w things.
28:29 His counsel is w, and his
Eze 17:8 and become a w vine.'
Dan 2:48 and gave him many w gifts.
Mat 24:24 miraculous signs and do w
Mar 13:22 signs and do w things
Luk 9:43 amazed to see God's w power.
2Th 2:9 miraculous and w signs.

wondering (3)

Dtr 18:21 You may be w, "How can we
Luk 24:12 w what had happened.
Jon 13:22 at each other and w which one

wonders (2)

Psa 78:43 his w in the fields of Zoan.
2Co 12:12 you I patiently did the signs, w,

wood (132)

Gen 6:14 yourself a ship of cypress w.
22:3 When he had cut the w for the
22:6 Then Abraham took the w for
22:7 the burning coals and the w,
22:9 altar and arranged the w on it.
22:9 him on top of the w on the altar.
Exo 15:25 showed him a piece of w.
25:5 red, fine leather, acacia w,
25:10 "Make an ark of acacia w 45
25:13 Make poles of acacia w,
25:23 "Make a table of acacia w 36
25:28 the poles out of acacia w,
26:15 a framework out of acacia w
26:26 crossbars out of acacia w:
26:32 four posts of acacia w covered
26:37 Make five posts of acacia w
27:1 "Make an altar out of acacia w.
27:2 ⌊of w⌋ covered with bronze.
27:6 "Make poles out of acacia w
30:1 acacia w for burning incense.
30:2 made out of one piece ⌊of w⌋.
30:5 the poles out of acacia w,
31:5 and how to work with w.
35:7 red, fine leather, acacia w,
35:24 Those who had acacia w that
35:33 and how to work with w.
36:20 a framework out of acacia w
36:31 crossbars out of acacia w.
36:36 made four posts of acacia w
37:1 out of acacia w 45 inches long,
37:4 he made poles out of acacia w
37:10 out of acacia w 36 inches long,
37:15 were made out of acacia w
37:25 made an altar out of acacia w
37:25 made out of one piece ⌊of w⌋.
37:28 made the poles out of acacia w
38:1 out of acacia w 7 ½ feet
38:2 ⌊of w⌋ covered with bronze.
38:6 made the poles out of acacia w
Lev 1:7 altar and lay the w on the fire.
1:8 and the fat on top of the w
1:12 and the fat on the w burning
1:17 lay the bird on the w burning
3:5 burnt offering on the burning w
4:12 He will burn it there on a w fire.
6:12 The priest will burn w on it
14:4 birds, some cedar w, red yarn,
14:6 bird, the cedar w, the red yarn,
14:45 The house — stones, w,
14:49 two birds, cedar w, red yarn,
14:51 He must take the cedar w,
14:52 bird, the cedar w, the hyssop,
Num 15:32 they found a man gathering w
15:33 him gathering w brought him
19:6 priest will take some cedar w,
31:20 of leather, goats' hair, or w."
35:18 of you picks up a piece of w as
Dtr 10:1 Also make an ark out of w.
10:3 I made an ark out of acacia w.
19:5 go into the woods to cut w.
28:36 gods made of w and stone.
28:64 you will serve gods made of w
29:11 and the foreigners who cut w
29:17 gods and idols made of w,
Jdg 6:26 a burnt offering on the w from
1Sm 6:14 The people chopped up the w
2Sm 6:5 made from cypress w
1Ki 5:10 and cypress w he wanted.
6:15 of the temple with w from floor
6:23 angels out of olive w.
6:31 to the inner room out of olive w.
6:32 were ⌊made out of⌋ olive w.
6:33 square doorposts out of olive w
17:10 a widow was gathering w.
17:12 I'm gathering w. I'm going to
18:23 it into pieces, lay it on the w,
18:25 but don't set the w on fire."
18:33 He arranged the w,
18:33 and put it on the w.
18:34 on the offering and on the w."
18:38 offering, w, stones, and dirt.
2Ki 6:6 Elisha cut off a piece of w.
12:12 They also used it to buy w and
1Ch 22:14 also prepared w and stones,
29:2 w for wooden objects,
2Ch 2:14 iron, stone, w, purple, violet,
34:11 to buy quarried stones and w
Ezr 6:4 of large stones and a row of w.
Neh 2:8 letter order him to give me w
10:34 of our families should bring w
13:31 I also arranged for delivering w
Job 41:27 and bronze to be like rotten w.
Pro 26:20 Without w a fire goes out,
26:21 burning coals and w fuels fire,
Ecc 10:9 splits w may be injured.
Sos 3:9 himself from the w of Lebanon.
Isa 40:20 The poorest people choose w
44:13 measure blocks of w
44:16 Half of the w they burn in the
44:17 But the rest of the w they make
44:19 "I burned half of the w in the
44:19 making the rest of the w into
44:19 and bowing to a block of w."
60:17 bronze instead of w,
Jer 2:27 You call w your father.
3:9 standing stones and w pillars.
5:14 These people will be like w.
7:18 Children gather w,
46:22 axes like those who chop w.
Lam 5:4 have to pay to chop our own w.
5:13 boys stagger under loads of w.
Eze 15:2 what good is the w from a
15:2 Is it better than the w from a
20:32 You want to serve w and stone.
24:5 Pile w under the pot.
24:9 I, too, will pile the w high.
26:12 They will throw your stones, w,
39:10 They will not need to get w
41:22 and its sides were made of w.
Dan 5:4 silver, bronze, iron, w, or stone.
5:23 gold, bronze, iron, w, or stone.
Hos 4:12 A piece of w tells them what to
5:12 of Judah as rot destroys w.
10:7 like a piece of w on water.
Hab 2:19 one who says to a piece of w,
Zec 12:6 Judah like a fire on a pile of w
Act 27:44 some other pieces ⌊of w⌋ from
1Co 3:12 stones, w, hay, or straw.
2Ti 2:20 also those made of w and clay.
Rev 9:20 and w, which cannot see, hear,
18:12 all kinds of citron w,
18:12 of ivory and very costly w,

woodcutter (1)

Psa 74:5 away like a **w** in a forest.

woodcutters (4)

Jos 9:21 So they became **w** and water
9:23 You will be **w** and water
9:27 that day Joshua made them **w**
Jer 10:3 **W** cut down trees from the

wooded (1)

2Ch 27:4 forts and towers in the **w** areas.

wooden (20)

Exo 7:19 in the **w** and stone containers.'"
Lev 11:32 It may be a **w** article,
15:12 and any **w** bucket he touches
Dtr 4:28 There you will worship **w** and
2Ki 19:18 They're only **w** and stone
1Ch 29:2 wood for **w** objects,
Ezr 5:8 stones and with **w** beams laid
Neh 8:4 on a raised **w** platform made
Isa 10:15 A **w** stick cannot pick up a
37:19 They're only **w** and stone
45:20 Ignorant people carry **w** idols
Jer 10:8 They learn nonsense from **w**
27:2 ⌊leather⌋ straps and a **w** yoke,
28:13 You have broken the **w** yoke,
Eze 41:22 There was a **w** altar,
41:25 There was a **w** roof hanging
Hos 4:12 My people ask their **w** idols for
Nah 1:14 I will remove the **w** and metal
Mat 7:3 eye and not notice the **w** beam
Luk 6:41 eye and not notice the **w** beam

woods (8)

Dtr 19:5 two people go into the **w**
1Sm 14:26 When the troops entered the **w**,
2Sm 18:8 That day the **w** devoured more
2Ki 2:24 Two bears came out of the **w**
Isa 17:9 abandoned **w** and undergrowth.
Eze 34:25 wilderness and sleep in the **w**.
39:10 field or cut down trees in the **w**.
Mic 7:14 They live alone in the **w**,

wool (26)

Lev 13:48 or knitted from linen or **w**
13:59 or knitted from linen or **w**
Num 16:14 still pull the **w** over our eyes?
Dtr 18:4 and the first **w** you shear from
22:11 Never wear clothes made of **w**
Jdg 6:37 I'll place some **w** on the
6:37 If there is dew on the **w** while
6:38 a bowl full of water from the **w**.
6:39 make one more test with the **w**.
6:39 Let the **w** be dry while all the
6:40 The **w** was dry, but all the
2Ki 3:4 and the **w** from 100,000 rams.
Job 31:20 or the **w** from my sheep didn't
Psa 147:16 one who sends snow like **w**
Pro 31:13 "She seeks out **w** and linen
Isa 1:18 will become as white as **w**.
51:8 Worms will devour them like **w**.
53:7 is silent when its **w** is cut off.
Eze 27:18 from Helbon and **w** from Sahar.
34:3 of the sheep, dress in the **w**,
44:17 They must have no **w** on them
Dan 7:9 on his head was like pure **w**.
Hos 2:5 **w** and linen, olive oil and wine.'
2:9 I will take away the **w** and the
Act 8:32 is silent when its **w** is cut off.
Rev 1:14 were white like **w** — like snow.

Word; word (426)

Gen 15:1 Later the LORD spoke his **w** to
15:4 the LORD spoke his **w** to
Exo 18:6 Jethro had sent **w** to Moses,
Num 15:31 person has despised the **w**
30:2 he must not break his **w**.
Dtr 5:5 LORD and you to tell you the **w**
8:3 bread alone but on every **w** that
9:23 But you rebelled against the **w**
27:26 "Whoever doesn't obey every **w**
28:58 not faithfully obey every **w**
29:29 every **w** of these teachings.
31:12 every **w** of these teachings.
Dtr 32:46 every **w** of these teachings.
33:9 But they obeyed your **w** and
Jos 6:10 or let one **w** come out of your
8:35 He did not leave out one **w**
23:14 Every single **w** has come true.
23:15 "Every good **w** the LORD your
Jdg 12:6 "Say the **w** *shibboleth*."
12:6 pronounce the **w** correctly,
18:19 Don't say a **w**! Come with us
1Sm 1:23 May the LORD keep his **w**."
3:7 because the **w** of the LORD
3:21 Samuel in Shiloh through the **w**
9:27 and I will tell you God's **w**."
15:23 Because you rejected the **w** of
2Sm 3:11 couldn't respond to a single **w**,
7:4 LORD spoke his **w** to Nathan:
12:9 Why did you despise my **w** by
24:11 the LORD spoke his **w** to the
1Ki 2:27 the LORD's **w** spoken at Shiloh
5:2 Solomon sent **w** to Hiram,
12:22 God spoke his **w** to Shemaiah,
12:24 So they obeyed the **w** of the
13:18 An angel spoke the **w** of the
13:20 the LORD spoke his **w** to the
13:26 pieces and killed him as the **w**
16:1 LORD spoke his **w** to Jehu,
16:7 the LORD spoke his **w** to the
17:2 LORD spoke his **w** to Elijah:
17:5 Elijah left and did what the **w**
17:8 LORD spoke his **w** to Elijah:
17:24 a man of God and that the **w**
18:1 LORD spoke his **w** to Elijah:
18:20 Ahab sent **w** to all the
18:21 The people didn't say a **w**.
18:31 had spoken his **w** to Jacob:
19:9 LORD spoke his **w** to Elijah.
20:33 quick to take him at his **w**.
20:35 spoke to a friend as the **w**
21:17 Then the LORD spoke his **w** to
21:28 Then the LORD spoke his **w** to
22:5 find out what the **w** of the
22:19 "Then hear the **w** of the LORD.
2Ki 1:16 Israel whose **w** you can seek?
3:12 "The LORD's **w** is with him."
7:1 "Listen to the **w** of the LORD!
10:10 You can be sure that the **w** of
20:4 the LORD spoke his **w** to him:
20:16 "Hear the **w** of the LORD!
20:19 "The LORD's **w** that you have
23:16 This fulfilled the **w** of the
1Ch 10:13 He did not obey the **w** of the
11:10 to the LORD's **w** to Israel.
16:15 the **w** that he commanded for a
17:3 God spoke his **w** to Nathan:
22:8 But the LORD spoke his **w** to
2Ch 2:3 Solomon sent **w** to King Huram
11:2 God spoke his **w** to Shemaiah,
11:4 So they obeyed the **w** of the
12:7 he spoke his **w** to Shemaiah:
18:4 find out what the **w** of the
18:18 "Then hear the **w** of the LORD.
29:15 king's order from the LORD's **w**
30:12 gave from the LORD's **w**.
31:5 As soon as the **w** spread,
34:21 ancestors did not obey the **w**
Ezr 4:18 you sent me has been read **w**
4:18 word for **w** in my presence.
Est 9:26 based on the **w** Pur.
Job 2:10 lips did not utter one sinful **w**.
2:13 No one said a **w** to him
32:15 don't have another **w** to say.
Psa 17:4 cruelty because of your **w**.
33:4 The **w** of the LORD is correct,
33:6 heavens were made by the **w**
56:4 I praise the **w** of God.
56:10 I praise the **w** of God.
56:10 I praise the **w** of the LORD.
105:8 the **w** that he commanded for a
119:9 do it⌋ by holding on to your **w**.
119:16 I never forget your **w**.
119:17 may live and hold on to your **w**.
119:42 insults me since I trust your **w**.
119:43 not take so much as a single **w**
119:49 Remember the **w** ⌊you gave⌋
119:67 but now I hold on to your **w**.
119:74 my hope is based on your **w**.
Psa 119:81 My hope is based on your **w**.
119:89 O LORD, your **w** is established
119:101 path in order to obey your **w**.
119:105 Your **w** is a lamp for my feet
119:114 My hope is based on your **w**.
119:130 Your **w** is a doorway that lets
119:147 My hope is based on your **w**.
119:148 hours to reflect on your **w**.
119:160 is nothing but truth in your **w**,
130:5 and with hope I wait for his **w**.
139:4 before there is a ⌊single⌋ **w**
147:15 His **w** travels with great speed.
147:18 He sends out his **w** and melts
147:19 He speaks his **w** to Jacob,
Pro 12:19 The **w** of truth lasts forever,
12:25 **w** makes him joyful.
15:1 but a harsh **w** stirs up anger.
15:23 and a timely **w** — oh,
16:20 to the LORD's **w** prospers,
25:11 ⌊so⌋ is a **w** spoken at the right
30:5 "Every **w** of God has proven to
Ecc 8:4 Since a king's **w** has such
Isa 1:10 Listen to the **w** of the LORD,
2:3 The **w** of the LORD will go out
5:24 and have despised the **w**
6:5 Every **w** that passes through
7:2 When **w** reached David's
23:1 **W** has come to the ships from
28:14 So hear the **w** of the LORD,
38:4 LORD spoke his **w** to Isaiah,
39:5 "Hear the **w** of the LORD of
39:8 "The LORD's **w** that you have
40:8 but the **w** of our God will last
44:26 He confirms the **w** of his
45:23 A **w** has gone out from my
55:11 My **w**, which comes from my
66:2 and who tremble at my **w**.
66:5 Listen to the **w** of the LORD,
66:5 all who tremble at his **w**.
Jer 1:2 The LORD spoke his **w** to
1:4 The LORD spoke his **w** to me,
1:11 Again the LORD spoke his **w**
1:13 Again the LORD spoke his **w**
2:1 The LORD spoke his **w** to me,
2:4 Listen to the **w** of the LORD,
2:31 "Consider the **w** of the LORD,
6:10 LORD speaks his **w** to them,
7:1 spoke his **w** to Jeremiah.
7:2 'Listen to the **w** of the LORD,
8:9 They have rejected the **w** of
9:20 Listen to the **w** of the LORD,
13:3 The LORD spoke his **w** to me
13:8 the LORD spoke his **w** to me.
14:1 The LORD spoke his **w** to
16:1 The LORD spoke his **w** to me.
17:15 "Where is the **w** of the LORD?
17:20 "Listen to the **w** of the LORD,
18:1 spoke his **w** to Jeremiah.
18:5 The LORD spoke his **w** to me.
18:18 and the **w** of the prophets won't
19:3 "Listen to the **w** of the LORD,
20:8 The **w** of the LORD has made
20:9 But ⌊his **w**⌋ is inside me like a
21:1 The LORD spoke his **w** to
21:11 'Listen to the **w** of the LORD,
22:2 "Listen to the **w** of the LORD,
22:29 Listen to the **w** of the LORD.
23:18 and sees and hears his **w**?
23:18 attention and listens to his **w**?
23:28 the person who has my **w**
23:28 should honestly speak my **w**.
23:29 "Isn't my **w** like fire or like a
23:36 because each person's **w**
24:4 The LORD spoke his **w** to me,
25:1 The LORD spoke his **w** to
25:3 to speak his **w** to me.
26:1 The LORD spoke his **w** when
26:2 Don't leave out a single **w**.
27:1 spoke his **w** to Jeremiah.
28:12 spoke his **w** to Jeremiah.
29:20 So listen to the **w** of the LORD,
29:30 spoke his **w** to Jeremiah.
30:1 spoke his **w** to Jeremiah.
31:10 listen to the **w** of the LORD.
32:1 The LORD spoke his **w** to
32:6 "The LORD spoke his **w** to me.

Jer 32:26 spoke his **w** to Jeremiah.
33:1 the LORD spoke his **w** to him
33:19 spoke his **w** to Jeremiah.
33:23 spoke his **w** to Jeremiah.
34:1 The LORD spoke his **w** to
34:4 "'Listen to the **w** of the LORD,
34:5 I have spoken my **w**,
34:8 The LORD spoke his **w** to
34:12 spoke his **w** to Jeremiah.
35:1 The LORD spoke his **w** to
35:12 spoke his **w** to Jeremiah.
36:1 spoke his **w** to Jeremiah.
36:27 spoke his **w** to Jeremiah.
37:6 The LORD spoke his **w** to the
39:15 the LORD spoke his **w** to him.
40:1 The LORD spoke his **w** to
42:7 spoke his **w** to Jeremiah.
42:15 listen to the **w** of the LORD,
42:18 You will become a curse **w**.
43:8 Then the LORD spoke his **w** to
44:1 The LORD spoke his **w** to
44:24 "Listen to the **w** of the LORD,
44:26 But listen to the **w** of the LORD,
49:34 the LORD spoke his **w** to the
Lam 1:18 I rebelled against his **w**.
Eze 1:3 the LORD spoke his **w** to the
3:16 the LORD spoke his **w** to me.
6:1 The LORD spoke his **w** to me.
6:3 listen to the **w** of the Almighty
7:1 The LORD spoke his **w** to me.
11:14 the LORD spoke his **w** to me.
12:1 The LORD spoke his **w** to me.
12:8 the LORD spoke his **w** to me.
12:17 The LORD spoke his **w** to me.
12:21 The LORD spoke his **w** to me.
12:26 The LORD spoke his **w** to me.
13:1 The LORD spoke his **w** to me.
13:2 'Listen to the **w** of the LORD.
14:2 the LORD spoke his **w** to me.
14:12 The LORD spoke his **w** to me.
15:1 The LORD spoke his **w** to me.
16:1 The LORD spoke his **w** to me.
16:35 "'Listen to the **w** of the LORD,
17:1 The LORD spoke his **w** to me.
17:11 The LORD spoke his **w** to me.
18:1 The LORD spoke his **w** to me.
20:2 the LORD spoke his **w** to me.
20:45 The LORD spoke his **w** to me.
20:47 'Listen to the **w** of the LORD.
21:1 The LORD spoke his **w** to me.
21:8 The LORD spoke his **w** to me.
21:18 The LORD spoke his **w** to me.
22:1 The LORD spoke his **w** to me.
22:17 the LORD spoke his **w** to me.
22:23 "The LORD spoke his **w** to me.
23:1 The LORD spoke his **w** to me.
24:1 the LORD spoke his **w** to me.
24:15 the LORD spoke his **w** to me.
24:20 "The LORD spoke his **w** to me.
25:1 The LORD spoke his **w** to me.
25:3 'Listen to the **w** of the Almighty
26:1 the LORD spoke his **w** to me.
27:1 The LORD spoke his **w** to me.
28:1 The LORD spoke his **w** to me.
28:11 The LORD spoke his **w** to me.
28:20 The LORD spoke his **w** to me.
29:1 the LORD spoke his **w** to me.
29:17 the LORD spoke his **w** to me.
30:1 The LORD spoke his **w** to me.
30:20 the LORD spoke his **w** to me.
31:1 the LORD spoke his **w** to me.
32:1 the LORD spoke his **w** to me.
32:17 the LORD spoke his **w** to me.
33:1 The LORD spoke his **w** to me.
33:23 The LORD spoke his **w** to me.
33:30 'Let's go and hear the **w** that
34:1 The LORD spoke his **w** to me.
34:7 listen to the **w** of the LORD.
34:9 listen to the **w** of the LORD.
35:1 The LORD spoke his **w** to me.
36:1 listen to the **w** of the LORD.
36:4 listen to the **w** of the Almighty
36:16 The LORD spoke his **w** to me.
37:4 listen to the **w** of the LORD.
37:15 The LORD spoke his **w** to me
38:1 The LORD spoke his **w** to me.
Hos 1:1 LORD spoke his **w** to Hosea,
4:1 Listen to the **w** of the LORD,
Amo 7:16 "Now listen to the **w** of the
8:12 searching for the **w** of the
Jnh 1:1 LORD spoke his **w** to Jonah,
3:1 Then the LORD spoke his **w** to
Mic 1:1 LORD spoke his **w** to Micah,
4:2 The **w** of the LORD will go out
Zep 1:1 This is the **w** that the LORD
1:1 The LORD spoke his **w** in the
2:5 The **w** of the LORD is against
Hag 1:1 the LORD spoke his **w** through
1:3 Then the LORD spoke his **w**
2:1 the LORD spoke his **w** through
2:10 the LORD spoke his **w** to the
2:20 The LORD spoke his **w** to
Zec 1:1 the LORD spoke his **w** to the
1:7 the LORD spoke his **w** to the
4:6 Then he replied, "This is the **w**
4:8 the LORD spoke his **w** to me.
6:9 The LORD spoke his **w** to me.
7:1 spoke his **w** to Zechariah.
7:4 of Armies spoke his **w** to me.
7:8 spoke his **w** to Zechariah.
8:1 LORD of Armies spoke his **w**.
8:18 spoke his **w** to me again.
9:1 The **w** of the LORD is against
11:11 that it was the **w** of the LORD.
12:1 the **w** of the LORD about Israel.
Mal 1:1 The LORD spoke his **w** to
Mat 4:4 on every **w** that God speaks.'"
12:32 Whoever speaks a **w** against
12:36 of every careless **w** they say.
13:19 Someone hears the **w** about
13:20 the person who⌋ hears the **w**
13:21 comes along because of the **w**,
13:22 person who⌋ hears the **w**.
13:22 of riches choke the **w** so that
13:23 hears and understands the **w**.
15:6 the authority of God's **w**.
Mar 2:2 speaking ⌊God's⌋ **w** to them.
4:14 "The farmer plants the **w**.
4:15 Whenever they hear the **w**,
4:15 away the **w** that was planted
4:16 Whenever they hear the **w**,
4:17 comes along because of the **w**,
4:18 thornbushes. They hear the **w**,
4:19 They choke the **w** so that it
4:20 They hear the **w**, accept it,
4:33 Jesus spoke ⌊God's⌋ **w** to
7:13 the authority of God's **w**.
16:20 He confirmed his **w** by the
Luk 1:2 and servants of God's **w** from
5:1 as they listened to God's **w**.
8:11 The seed is God's **w**.
8:12 They hear the **w**, but then the
8:12 He takes the **w** away from
8:13 They welcome the **w** with joy
8:14 are people who hear the **w**,
8:15 people who also hear the **w**.
8:21 and do what God's **w** says."
11:28 who hear and obey God's **w**."
Jon 1:1 the **W** already existed.
1:1 The **W** was with God,
1:1 and the **W** was God.
1:14 The **W** became human and
1:16 because of all that the **W** is.
20:16 (This **w** means "teacher.")
Act 4:29 and allow us to speak your **w**
4:31 to speak the **w** of God boldly.
6:2 right for us to give up God's **w**
6:4 ways that are related to the **w**."
6:7 The **w** of God continued to
8:4 where they spread the **w**.
8:14 had accepted the **w** of God,
9:20 began to spread the **w**
10:36 God sent his **w** to the people of
11:1 Jewish had accepted God's **w**.
11:19 They spoke God's **w** only to
12:24 But God's **w** continued to
13:5 they began to spread God's **w**
13:7 wanted to hear the **w** of God.
13:44 gathered to hear the Lord's **w**.
13:46 "We had to speak the **w** of God
13:46 Since you reject the **w** and
13:48 heard and praised the Lord's **w**.
Act 13:49 The **w** of the Lord spread
15:35 people about the Lord's **w**
15:36 where we spread the Lord's **w**.
16:6 kept them from speaking the **w**
16:32 They spoke the Lord's **w** to the
16:36 "The officials have sent **w** to
17:13 spreading God's **w** in Berea,
18:5 time to teaching the **w** of God.
18:11 and a half and taught the **w**
19:10 of Asia heard the **w** of the Lord.
19:20 In this powerful way the **w** of
Rom 3:2 God entrusted them with his **w**.
9:6 as though God's **w** has failed.
12:6 If your gift is speaking God's **w**,
1Co 14:21 God's **w** says, but even then
14:36 Did God's **w** originate with
2Co 2:17 go around selling an impure **w**
4:2 and we don't distort God's **w**.
Gal 6:6 taught God's **w** should share all
Eph 6:17 as your helmet and the **w**
Php 1:14 to speak God's **w** more boldly
2:16 you hold firmly to the **w** of life.
Col 3:16 Let Christ's **w** with all its
4:3 to speak the **w** so that we
1Th 1:6 you welcomed God's **w** with
1:8 From you the Lord's **w** has
2:13 you received God's **w** from us,
2:13 it wasn't the **w** of humans.
2:13 what it really is — the **w** of God.
2:13 This **w** is at work in you
2Th 3:1 we spread the Lord's **w** rapidly
1Ti 4:5 The **w** of God and prayer set it
5:17 at teaching the **w** ⌊of God⌋.
2Ti 2:9 God's **w** is not imprisoned.
2:15 to teach the **w** of truth correctly.
4:2 Be ready to spread the **w**
Tit 1:3 every era by spreading his **w**.
1:3 I was entrusted with this **w** by
1:9 those who oppose the **w**.
2:5 one can speak evil of God's **w**.
Heb 4:12 God's **w** is living and active.
4:12 God's **w** judges a person's
5:12 elementary truths of God's **w**.
6:5 the goodness of God's **w**
11:3 the world through his **w**.
12:19 not to hear it say another **w**.
13:7 have spoken God's **w** to you.
Jas 1:18 to give us life through the **w**
1:21 Humbly accept the **w** that God
1:21 This **w** can save you.
1:22 Do what God's **w** says.
1:23 If someone listens to God's **w**
1Pe 1:23 but through God's everlasting **w**
1:25 but the **w** of the Lord lasts
1:25 This **w** is the Good News that
2:2 Desire God's pure **w** as
2:8 The people tripped over the **w**
3:1 may not obey God's **w**.
2Pe 3:5 Because of God's **w**,
3:7 By God's **w**, the present
1Jn 1:1 The **W** of life existed from the
1:10 God into a liar and his **W** is not
2:14 are strong and God's **w** lives
Rev 1:2 God's **w** and the testimony
1:9 of Patmos because of God's **w**
3:8 have paid attention to my **w**
6:9 because of God's **w**
12:11 the blood of the lamb and the **w**
19:13 and his name is the **W** of God.
20:4 and because of the **w** of God.

words (352)

Gen 27:34 When Esau heard these **w** from
37:8 more for his dreams and his **w**.
44:6 he repeated these **w** to them.
Exo 16:34 jar of manna in front of the **w**
19:6 These are the **w** you must
19:7 He repeated to them all the **w**
20:1 Then God spoke all these **w**:
24:3 the people all the LORD's **w**
24:4 wrote down all the LORD's **w**.
25:16 you will put into the ark the **w**
25:21 After you put into the ark the **w**
26:33 put the ark containing the **w**
27:21 the canopy where the **w**
30:6 over the ark containing the **w**

Exo 30:26 the w of my promise,
30:36 of ⌊the ark containing⌋ the w
31:7 the ark containing the w of my
31:18 two tablets with his w on them,
32:15 the two tablets with God's w.
34:1 and I will write on them the w
34:27 "Write down these w,
34:27 the basis of these w I'm making
34:28 He wrote on the tablets the w
34:29 tablets with God's w on them.
38:21 for the tent (the tent of the w
39:35 the ark containing the w of
40:3 Place the ark containing the w
40:20 He took the w of God's promise
Lev 16:13 which is over the w of God's
24:3 the canopy where the w
Num 1:50 in charge of the tent of God's w,
1:53 all around the tent of God's w.
1:53 charge of the tent of God's w."
4:5 over the ark containing the w
7:89 on the ark containing the w
9:15 On the day the tent of the w of
10:11 tent of the w of God's promise.
11:23 or not my w come true."
12:6 He said, "Listen to my w:
17:4 in front of the w of my promise.
17:7 tent of the w of God's promise.
17:10 staff back in front of the w
18:2 the tent of the w of my promise.
24:4 one who hears the w of God,
24:16 one who hears the w of God,
Dtr 4:10 and I will let them hear my w.
5:28 When the LORD heard the w
6:6 Take to heart these w that I
9:10 On them were written all the w
10:2 tablets the same w that were
10:4 tablets the same w as before,
10:4 He had spoken these w to you
11:18 Take these w of mine to heart
18:18 I will put my w in his mouth.
18:19 to the w that prophet speaks
27:3 write all the w of these
27:8 clearly and carefully all the w
30:14 No, these w are very near you.
31:24 finished writing all the w
31:28 I will speak these w and call
31:30 recited all the w of this song:
32:1 hear the w from my mouth.
32:2 Let my w drip like dew,
32:44 and recited all the w of this
32:45 reciting all these w to Israel,
32:47 Don't think these w are idle
32:47 By these w you will be able to
Jos 3:9 and listen to the w of the LORD
24:27 It has heard all the w which the
Jdg 13:12 "When your w come true,
13:17 When your w come true,
1Sm 3:19 let any of his w go unfulfilled.
15:1 Now listen to the LORD's w.
16:18 He has a way with w,
17:23 He repeated his w,
25:24 Please listen to my w.
26:19 please listen to my w.
28:20 was frightened by Samuel's w.
29:10 Don't worry about the unkind w
2Sm 7:17 Nathan told David all these w
7:28 and your w are trustworthy.
23:1 These are the last w of David:
23:2 His w were on my tongue.
1Ki 8:59 May these w which I have
10:6 in my country about your w
13:11 that day and the exact w
13:21 You rebelled against the w
13:26 rebelled against the w from
2Ki 19:4 God may have heard all the w
22:13 ask the LORD about the w in
22:18 says about the w you heard:
22:19 heard my w against this place
23:24 He did this to confirm the w of
1Ch 17:15 Nathan told David all these w
2Ch 9:5 in my country about your w
15:8 prophet Oded's w of prophecy,
24:6 the w of God's promise."
29:30 to praise the LORD with the w
30:22 Hezekiah spoke encouraging w
32:6 these w of encouragement:

2Ch 33:18 to his God and the w that
34:21 ask the LORD about the w in
34:26 says about the w you heard:
34:27 heard my w against this place
35:22 refused to listen to Neco's w,
36:16 messengers, despised his w,
36:21 w spoken through Jeremiah
Ezr 9:4 me there trembled at the w
Neh 1:1 These are the w of Nehemiah,
8:12 understood the w that had been
8:13 the w of God's Teachings.
Job 4:4 you lifted him up with your w.
6:10 I have not rejected the w
6:26 think my w need correction?
8:2 long will your w be so windy?
8:10 Won't their w teach you?
9:14 How can I find the right w ⌊to
11:2 answer this flood of w?
13:17 "Listen carefully to my w.
15:3 Should he argue with w that
15:13 God and spit these w out
16:4 I could string w together
18:2 long before your w will end?
19:2 me and depress me with w?
19:23 "I wish now my w were written.
21:2 "Listen carefully to my w,
22:22 and keep his w in your heart.
23:5 I want to know the w he would
23:12 treasured his w in my heart.
24:25 that my w are worthless?"
26:4 have you spoken ⌊these⌋ w,
29:9 Princes held back ⌊their⌋ w
29:22 my w fell gently on them.
31:40 This is the end of Job's w.
32:11 until you could find the right w.
32:14 Job did not choose his w to
32:18 I'm full of w. The Spirit within
33:1 "Please, Job, listen to my w
33:2 The w are on the tip of my
33:3 My w are straight from the
33:8 and I listened to your w.
34:2 "Listen to my w, you wise
34:3 The ear tests w like the tongue
34:16 Open your ears to my w!
34:35 His w show no insight.'
34:37 multiplies his w against God."
36:4 Certainly, my w are not lies.
38:2 my advice with w that do not
Psa 5:1 Open your ears to my w,
19:3 without talking, without w,
19:14 May the w from my mouth and
22:1 from the w of my groaning?
36:3 The w from his mouth are
44:16 because of the w of those who
50:17 You toss my w behind you.
54:2 ears to the w from my mouth.
55:21 His w are more soothing than
56:5 long my enemies twist my w.
59:12 from their mouths and the w
64:3 They aim bitter w like arrows
73:10 and swallow their w.
78:1 ears to the w from my mouth.
94:19 assuring w soothed my soul.
107:2 defended repeat these w.
107:11 had rebelled against God's w
109:3 surround me with hateful w.
119:57 I promised to hold on to your w.
119:139 ⌊for your w⌋ consumes me,
119:139 enemies have forgotten your w.
119:161 but it is only your w that fill my
Pro 1:6 the w of wise people and their
1:21 to the city she speaks her w,
1:23 will make my w known to you.
2:1 My son, if you take my w ⌊to
4:4 "Cling to my w wholeheartedly.
4:5 Do not turn away from the w
4:10 listen and accept my w,
4:20 My son, pay attention to my w.
6:2 you are trapped by the w of
7:1 My son, pay attention to my w.
7:24 to the w from my mouth.
11:11 but by the w of wicked people,
12:6 The w of wicked people are a
12:6 but the w of decent people
12:18 Careless w stab like a sword,
12:18 but the w of wise people bring

Pro 13:13 Whoever despises ⌊God's⌋ w
14:3 Because of a stubborn fool's w
15:26 but pleasant w are pure to him.
16:13 Kings are happy with honest w,
16:24 Pleasant w are ⌊like⌋ honey
17:27 has knowledge controls his w,
18:4 The w of a person's mouth are
18:8 The w of a gossip are
18:21 will have to eat their own w.
19:7 When he chases them with w,
19:27 stray from the w of knowledge.
22:12 but he overturns the w of a
22:17 and hear the w of wise people,
22:21 in order to teach you the w of
23:9 despise the wisdom of your w.
23:12 carefully to w of knowledge.
26:22 The w of a gossip are
29:19 cannot be disciplined with w.
30:1 The w of Agur, son of Jakeh.
30:6 Do not add to his w,
Ecc 1:1 The w of the spokesman,
5:2 limit the number of your w.
5:3 when there are too many w.
5:7 actions, and empty w,
6:11 The more w there are,
9:17 to calm w from wise people
10:12 A wise person's w win favors,
10:20 A bird may carry your w,
12:10 tried to find just the right w.
12:10 He wrote the w of truth very
12:11 W from wise people are like
Isa 8:20 If people don't speak these w,
29:4 Your w will be muffled by the
29:4 Your w will be whispered from
29:11 all these visions will be like w
29:18 the deaf will hear the w written
29:21 who make people sin with w,
31:2 He doesn't take back his w.
37:4 God may have heard the w
41:26 No one heard your w.
48:3 These w came out of my
48:6 You've heard these w.
51:16 I put my w in your mouth and
59:21 and my w that I put in your
Jer 1:1 ⌊These are⌋ the w of Jeremiah,
1:9 I have put my w in your mouth.
1:12 sure that my w come true."
5:14 I'm going to put my w in your
5:14 My w will burn them up.
6:19 won't pay attention to my w.
7:4 Do not trust the w of this
7:8 "'You are trusting the w of a
9:20 open your ears to hear his w.
11:10 and refused to obey my w.
15:16 Your w were found,
15:16 Your w are my joy and my
23:9 of the LORD and his holy w.
23:22 would have announced my w
23:30 steal my w from each other,"
23:36 They will twist the w of the
25:8 You did not listen to my w,
26:5 you don't listen to the w
35:13 your lesson and obey my w?
36:10 containing the w of Jeremiah.
44:28 whose w have come true,
51:64 that I will bring on it.'" The w
Lam 3:62 The w and thoughts of those
Eze 2:7 Speak my w to them whether
3:4 and speak my w to them.
3:6 or whose w you cannot
33:32 They listen to your w,
33:33 When all your w come true —
Dan 4:31 Before the w came out of his
7:11 of the impressive w that
10:9 and as I listened to his w,
10:11 Pay attention to my w.
12:4 keep these w secret,
12:9 These w are to be kept secret
Hos 6:5 I killed you with the w from my
Amo 1:1 These are the w of Amos,
8:11 of hearing the w of the LORD.
Mic 2:7 Are his w good for those who
Hag 1:12 They also obeyed the w of the
Zec 1:13 using kind and comforting w.
7:7 Aren't these the same w that
7:12 the w that the LORD of Armies

Zec 8:9 listening to the w from
Mal 2:17 of the LORD with your w.
3:13 used harsh w against me,"
Mat 2:17 Then the w spoken through the
12:37 By your w you will be declared
12:37 or by your w you will be
24:35 but my w will never disappear.
Mar 10:24 were stunned by his w.
13:31 but my w will never disappear.
Luk 3:18 many other encouraging w,
4:22 the gracious w flowing from his
7:9 officer when he heard these w.
10:5 family right away with the w,
21:15 I will give you w and wisdom
21:33 but my w will never disappear.
24:44 "These are the w I spoke to
Jon 6:63 The w that I have spoken to
6:68 Your w give eternal life.
7:40 heard Jesus say these w,
8:20 Jesus spoke these w while he
8:43 can't understand the w I use?
12:38 In this way the w of the prophet
12:47 If anyone hears my w and
12:48 The w that I have spoken will
16:25 you about the Father in plain w.
16:29 "Now you're talking in plain w
17:17 them holy. Your w are truth.
Act 13:15 if you have any w of
15:21 After all, Moses' w have been
18:15 But since you're disputing w,
20:2 that region and spoke many w
20:35 We should remember the w
Rom 4:23 But the w "his faith was
7:6 old way dictated by written w.
8:26 that cannot be expressed in w.
10:18 the whole world and their w
16:18 w they deceive unsuspecting
1Co 9:15 bragging into meaningless w.
14:19 I would rather say five w that
14:19 w in another language.
2Co 5:19 In other w, God was using
9:15 his gift that w cannot describe.
11:6 though I'm not good with w,
12:4 that can't be expressed in w,
12:4 that humans cannot put into w.
Gal 6:11 the letters ⌊in these w⌋ are
Eph 5:6 you with meaningless w.
5:26 water along with spoken w.
6:19 will give me the right w to say.
1Th 1:5 came to you not only with w
4:18 each other with these w!
1Ti 4:6 you will be nourished by the w
5:1 Never use harsh w when you
6:3 agree with the accurate w
6:4 to argue and quarrel about w.
2Ti 2:14 of God not to quarrel over w.
2:19 These w are engraved on it:
Heb 1:3 through his powerful w.
12:5 w that God speaks
12:27 The w once more show clearly
13:15 w that acknowledge him.
13:22 patiently to my encouraging w.
1Pe 1:8 can hardly be expressed in w
4:11 speaks must speak God's w.
2Pe 1:17 God spoke these w to him:
1:19 So we regard the w of the
1:19 by paying attention to their w.
3:2 I want you to remember the w
1Jn 3:18 not through empty w.
Rev 1:3 well as those who hear the w
15:5 of the tent containing the w
17:17 until God's w are carried out.
19:9 "These are the true w of God."
21:5 'These w are faithful and true.'"
22:6 He said to me, "These w are
22:7 is the one who follows the w
22:9 and those who follow the w in
22:10 "Don't seal up the w of the
22:18 everyone who hears the w
22:19 If anyone takes away any w

wore (26)

Gen 31:40 the cold at night w me down,
Exo 33:4 No one w any jewelry.
33:6 no longer w their jewelry.
Dtr 29:5 clothes and shoes never w out.
Jdg 8:24 Ishmaelites, w gold earrings.)
1Sm 17:5 and he w a bronze coat of
2Sm 13:18 The king's virgin daughters w
20:8 Joab w a military uniform,
21:16 7 ½ pounds which he w
1Ki 10:5 and the uniforms they w,
2Ki 25:29 no longer w prison clothes,
1Ch 15:27 David also w a linen ephod.
2Ch 9:4 and the uniforms they w,
Neh 9:1 they fasted, w sackcloth,
Psa 35:13 they were sick, I w sackcloth.
109:18 He w cursing as though it were
Jer 52:33 no longer w prison clothes,
Eze 16:13 So you w gold and silver
42:14 that they w as they served.
44:19 that they w as they served.
Mat 3:4 John w clothes made from
Mar 1:6 He w a leather belt around his
Luk 16:19 man who w expensive clothes.
Heb 11:37 Some w the skins of sheep
Rev 1:13 He w a gold belt around his
17:4 The woman w purple clothes,

work (415)

Gen 2:2 day God had finished the w
2:2 seventh day he stopped the w
2:3 stopped all his w of creation.
3:17 Through hard w you will eat
5:29 will bring us relief from the w
29:15 that you should w for nothing.
29:18 So he offered, "I'll w seven
29:25 "Didn't I w for you in return for
29:27 But you'll have to w for me
30:26 You know how much w I've
30:29 "You know how much w I've
31:42 seen my misery and hard w,
39:11 into the house to do his w,
46:33 'What kind of w do you do?'
47:3 "What kind of w do you do?"
Exo 1:13 Israelites to w hard as slaves.
1:14 bitter with back-breaking w
1:14 and bricks and every kind of w
5:4 the people from their w?
5:4 their work? Get back to w!"
5:9 Make the w harder for these
5:11 but your w load will not be
5:13 same amount of w each day,
5:18 Now get back to w!
6:9 discouraged by their back w.
12:16 You must not w on these days
18:18 This is too much w for you.
18:23 will be able to continue your w,
20:9 have six days to do all your w.
20:10 never do any w ⌊on that day⌋.
20:11 He didn't w on the seventh day.
20:11 the day he stopped his w
23:12 six days you will do your w,
23:12 seventh day you must not w.
26:1 and creatively w an angel
26:31 Creatively w an angel design
28:6 Creatively w gold,
31:5 and how to w with wood.
31:15 You may w for six days,
31:15 a day when you don't w.
32:16 The tablets were the w of God,
34:21 "You may w six days,
34:21 seventh day you must not w.
34:21 you must not w ⌊on this day⌋.
35:2 You may w for six days,
35:2 a day when you don't w.
35:2 Whoever does any w on this
35:33 and how to w with wood.
35:35 They can do the w of jewelers,
36:1 and Oholiab will do the w as
36:1 will know how to do all the w
36:2 willing to come and do the w.
36:3 Israelites had brought for the w
36:5 than we need for doing the w
39:32 So all the w on the inner tent
39:42 had done all the w following
39:43 Moses inspected all the w and
40:33 Finally, Moses finished the w.
Lev 16:29 They must do no w.
23:3 You may w for six days.
23:3 a day when you don't w,
23:3 Don't do any w. It is the LORD's
Lev 23:7 Don't do any regular w.
23:8 Don't do any regular w."
23:21 Don't do any regular w.
23:25 Don't do any regular w.
23:28 Don't do any w that day.
23:30 who do any w on that day.
23:31 Don't do any w. It is a
23:32 a day when you don't w.
23:35 Don't do any regular w.
23:36 Don't do any regular w.
25:39 don't w him like a slave.
25:40 He may w with you until the
25:46 You may w them as slaves.
26:20 You will w hard for nothing
Num 3:7 They will w for him and the
3:8 in the tent of meeting and w
4:3 50 who are qualified to w at
4:4 "This is the w the Kohathites
4:27 All their w, whatever they carry
4:28 This is the w of the Gershonite
4:31 are their duties as they w at
4:33 families will do as they w at
4:35 50 who were qualified to w at
4:47 who were qualified to do the w
7:5 from them to use in the w done
7:5 need these gifts for their w."
7:7 Gershonites for the w they had
7:8 the Merarites for the w they had
8:11 be ready to do the LORD's w.
8:15 may come and do their w at
8:19 They will w for the Israelites at
8:22 Levites came and did their w at
8:25 service and not w anymore.
8:26 they may not do any regular w.
11:14 This is too much w for me!
14:41 Your plan won't w!
16:9 you near himself to do the w
18:1 commit when you w as priests.
18:3 They will w for you,
18:3 doing whatever w is necessary
18:4 do whatever w is necessary
18:4 all the maintenance w
18:5 be in charge of the w done at
18:6 do whatever w is necessary at
18:7 and your sons may do the w
18:7 place to do this w⌋ must die."
18:21 This is in return for the w they
18:23 Only the Levites will do the w
18:31 you receive for your w at
28:18 Don't do any regular w.
28:25 You must not do any regular w.
28:26 you must not do any regular w.
29:1 You must not do any regular w.
29:7 You must not do any w.
29:12 You must not do any regular w.
29:35 You must not do any daily w.
31:30 are in charge of the w done at
31:47 were in charge of the w done at
Dtr 5:13 have six days to do all your w.
5:14 never do any w ⌊on that day⌋.
14:29 you in whatever w you do.
15:10 bless you in everything you w
15:18 hire someone to do the same w
15:19 Never use a firstborn ox for w,
16:8 Don't do any w that day.
16:15 all your harvest and all your w.
18:5 their descendants to do the w
18:7 other Levites who do their w
21:3 that has never been put to w
26:6 do back-breaking w for them.
28:33 your hard w have produced.
28:48 put a heavy burden of hard w
33:11 be pleased with the w they do.
Jdg 17:8 of Ephraim to carry on his w.
19:16 came into the city from his w
Rut 2:19 Just where did you w?
2Sm 3:29 who can only w a spindle,
12:31 and put them to w with saws,
1Ki 5:6 My workers will w with your
5:13 from all over Israel to w for him.
7:14 and did all his ⌊bronze⌋ w.
7:22 He finished the w on the pillars.
7:40 So Hiram finished all the w for
7:51 All the w King Solomon did on
9:23 for the people who did the w.
12:4 Reduce the hard w and lighten

2Ki 12:11 who had been appointed to **w**
25:12 poorest people in the land to **w**
1Ch 4:23 with the king and did his **w**.
6:49 They did all the **w** in the most
16:37 as the daily **w** required.
20:3 and put them to **w** with saws,
22:15 men skilled in every kind of **w**.
22:16 So get to **w**! May the LORD be
23:4 appointed to supervise the **w**
28:13 He planned all the **w** done for
28:20 and courageous, and do the **w**.
28:20 abandon you before all the **w**
28:21 skilled worker to do all the **w**.
29:1 Yet, the **w** is important
29:6 the king's **w** gave generously.
29:7 iron for the **w** on God's temple.
2Ch 2:7 has the skill to **w** with gold,
2:8 will **w** with your workers.
2:14 knows how to **w** with gold,
2:14 ⌊He can **w**⌋ with your skilled
2:18 supervise the **w** as foremen.
4:11 So Huram finished the **w** for
5:1 All the **w** Solomon did on the
8:10 for the people who did the **w**.
8:16 All of Solomon's **w** was carried
10:4 Reduce the hard **w** and lighten
16:5 and abandoned his **w** on it.
20:37 "The LORD will destroy your **w**
29:12 So the Levites started to **w**.
29:34 helped them until the **w** was
31:18 themselves holy for the holy **w**.
34:12 The men did their **w** faithfully
35:15 didn't need to leave their **w**,
Ezr 2:69 could to the treasury for this **w**:
3:8 20 years old to direct the **w**
4:24 Then the **w** on God's temple in
6:7 Don't interfere with the **w** on
6:8 so that the **w** is not interrupted.
6:22 supported the people in their **w**
8:20 his officials had appointed to **w**
Neh 2:16 rest who would be doing the **w**.
2:18 to begin this God-pleasing **w**.
3:5 to **w** under supervisors.
4:7 Ashdod heard that the repair **w**
4:10 "The **w** crews are worn out,
4:11 and bring the **w** to an end."
4:15 we all went back to the **w** on
4:17 were carrying loads did the **w**
4:19 "So much **w** has to be done in
4:21 So we continued to **w**.
4:22 at night and **w** during the day."
5:13 and **w** everyone who refuses
5:16 I put my best effort into the **w**
5:16 All my men gathered here for **w**.
6:3 Why should the **w** stop while I
6:9 give up and not finish the **w**.
6:16 realized we had done this **w**
7:70 families contributed to this **w**.
7:71 to the treasury for this **w**:
10:33 and for all the other **w** in the
11:12 relatives 822 did the **w**
11:16 of the **w** outside God's temple.
Job 7:1 like a hired hand's daily ⌊**w**⌋?
9:29 Why should I **w** so hard for
10:3 by rejecting the **w** of your
14:6 loves life as a laborer loves **w**.
23:9 go northward, where he is at **w**,
24:5 people go out to do their **w**,
36:24 that you should praise his **w**.
37:7 people will recognize his **w**.
39:16 afraid that its **w** is for nothing
Psa 9:16 person is trapped by the **w**
104:23 Then people go to do their **w**,
107:12 he humbled them with hard **w**.
111:3 His **w** is glorious and majestic.
127:1 for the builders to **w** on it.
127:2 It is useless to **w** hard for the
Pro 5:10 and you will have to **w** hard
10:22 and hard **w** adds nothing to it.
14:23 In hard **w** there is always
16:30 his lips has finished his evil **w**.
18:9 Whoever is lazy in his **w** is
21:25 because his hands refuse to **w**.
22:29 who is efficient in his **w**?
24:27 Prepare your **w** outside,
31:17 belt and goes to **w** with energy.
Pro 31:29 women have done noble **w**,
Ecc 1:3 all their hard **w** under the sun?
2:10 since I found pleasure in my **w**.
2:10 my reward for all my hard **w**.
2:11 and all the hard **w**
2:21 who didn't **w** for it.
2:22 get from all of their hard **w**
2:23 and their **w** is unbearable.
2:24 and find satisfaction in their **w**.
3:13 from every kind of hard **w**.
3:17 and every **w** that is done."
3:22 to do than to enjoy their **w**
4:4 Then I saw that all hard **w** and
4:6 than two handfuls of hard **w**
4:8 end to all the hard **w** they have
4:9 a good reward for their hard **w**.
5:15 with them from all their hard **w**.
5:18 the good in all our hard **w** under
5:19 to rejoice in their own hard **w**.
6:7 Everything that people **w** so
8:15 while they **w** hard during their
8:16 to look at the **w** that is done
8:17 No one is able to grasp the **w**
9:9 get for the hard **w** that you do
9:10 because there is no **w**,
10:15 themselves out with hard **w**,
Sos 7:1 like the **w** of an artist's hands.
Isa 1:31 and their **w** will be the spark.
5:19 quickly do his **w** so that we
10:7 Their minds don't **w** that way.
10:12 the Lord has finished all his **w**
19:10 Those who **w** for money will
19:25 the **w** of my hands Assyria,
28:21 He will do his **w**, and perform
28:21 his unexpected **w**,
30:24 oxen and the donkeys which **w**
41:7 who **w** at their anvils.
44:12 They **w** them over the coals
45:9 Does your **w** say to you,
60:21 the honored **w** of my hands.
61:5 of foreigners will **w** your fields
61:8 faithfully reward my people's **w**.
64:8 We are the **w** of your hands.
65:23 will never again **w** for nothing.
Jer 17:22 Do not do any **w**, but observe
17:24 day by not doing any **w** on it.
22:13 He makes his neighbors **w** for
22:13 doesn't pay them for their **w**.
29:7 **W** for the good of the city
31:16 will be rewarded for your **w**,
48:10 neglect doing the LORD's **w**.
52:16 poorest people in the land to **w**
Lam 5:13 ⌊Our⌋ young men **w** at the mill,
Eze 44:14 less important **w** in the temple.
Hos 13:2 of them are the **w** of craftsmen.
Joe 2:30 I will **w** miracles in the sky and
Mic 2:1 invent trouble and **w** out plans
Hab 3:2 LORD, I fear your **w**.
Hag 1:11 and on all your hard **w**."
2:4 "**W**, because I am with you,"
2:17 I infested all your **w** with blight
Zec 8:13 Let your hands **w** hard.
Mat 6:28 They never **w** or spin yarn for
13:58 He didn't **w** many miracles
20:2 sent them to **w** in his vineyard.
20:3 in the marketplace without **w**.
20:4 '**W** in my vineyard,
20:6 here all day long without **w**?'
20:7 '**W** in my vineyard.'
21:28 go to **w** in the vineyard today.'
22:5 Some went to **w** in their own
24:24 They will **w** spectacular,
Mar 6:5 He couldn't **w** any miracles
13:22 They will **w** miraculous signs
13:34 He assigned **w** to each one
Luk 10:40 upset about all the **w** she had
10:40 me to do the **w** all by myself?
12:27 They never **w** or spin yarn for
13:14 "There are six days when **w**
13:32 I will finish my **w** on the third
Jon 4:34 me to do and to finish the **w**
4:38 people have done the hard **w**,
4:38 have followed them in their **w**."
6:27 Don't **w** for food that spoils.
6:27 Instead, **w** for the food that
17:4 by finishing the **w** you gave me
Jon 17:19 myself to this holy **w** I'm doing
Act 2:19 I will **w** miracles in the sky and
13:2 I want them to do the **w** for
13:3 them ⌊from their **w** in Antioch⌋.
13:25 John was finishing his **w**,
14:26 care for the **w** they had now
15:38 had not gone with them to **w**.
19:25 and others who did similar **w**.
19:27 will discredit our line of **w**,
19:38 Demetrius and the men who **w**
21:19 his **w** with non-Jewish people.
27:13 thought their plan would **w**.
Rom 4:4 When people **w**, their pay is
4:5 However, when people don't **w**
7:5 sinful passions were at **w**
7:23 ⌊at **w**⌋ throughout my body.
8:28 We know that all things **w**
13:6 servants while they do the **w**
14:20 Don't ruin God's **w** because of
15:23 no new opportunities for **w**
1Co 3:8 receive a reward for his own **w**.
3:13 kind of **w** each person has
3:15 If his **w** is burned up,
4:17 he faithfully does the Lord's **w**.
9:1 the result of my **w** for the Lord?
9:6 to find **w** to support ourselves?
9:13 you realize that those who **w** at
12:6 are different types of **w** to do,
12:10 Another can **w** miracles.
15:58 Always excel in the **w** you do
15:58 You know that the hard **w** you
16:9 to do effective **w** here,
16:10 He's doing the Lord's **w** as I am,
16:16 shares their labor and hard **w**.
2Co 1:24 Rather, we want to **w** with you
4:12 Death is at **w** in us,
4:12 but life is at **w** in you.
6:5 riots, hard **w**, sleepless nights,
8:6 us to urge Titus to finish his **w**
8:7 in this **w** of God's kindness.
11:23 I've done much more **w**,
11:27 Because I've had to **w** so hard,
Gal 2:9 that we would **w** among
2:9 **w** among Jewish people.
3:5 and **w** miracles among you
4:11 Maybe the hard **w** I spent on
Eph 1:11 which makes everything **w** the
2:2 This ruler continues to **w** in
3:20 whose power is at **w** in us.
4:27 devil any opportunity ⌊to **w**⌋.
4:28 and, instead, they must **w** hard.
6:21 faithful deacon in the Lord's **w**.
Php 1:6 who began this good **w** in you,
1:22 my **w** will produce more
2:12 In the same way continue to **w**
2:16 that my **w** produced results.
2:30 life and almost died for the **w**
Col 1:10 of good **w** by this knowledge
1:25 when God gave me the **w**
1:29 I **w** hard and struggle to do this
2:1 to know how hard I **w** for you,
2:2 I **w** so that they may be
4:7 and partner in the Lord's **w**.
4:17 to complete all the **w** that
1Th 2:9 our **w** and what we did to earn
2:13 word is at **w** in you believers.
3:5 making our **w** meaningless.
4:11 goal to live quietly, do your **w**,
5:12 leaders who **w** among you
5:13 of the **w** they are doing.
2Th 2:7 of this sin is already at **w**.
2:7 But it cannot **w** effectively until
3:10 "Whoever doesn't want to **w**
3:12 to their own **w** so they can
1Ti 1:12 has appointed me to do his **w**
4:10 Certainly, we **w** hard and
5:17 This is especially true if they **w**
6:2 of their **w** are believers whom
2Ti 4:5 Do the **w** of a missionary.
4:5 yourself completely to your **w**.
4:11 He is useful to me in my **w**.
Heb 2:10 end of his **w** through suffering.
4:3 he had finished his **w** when
4:4 day God rested from all his **w**."
4:10 rested from their **w** as God did
5:9 After he had finished his **w**,

Heb 7:11 If the **w** of the Levitical priests
8:6 a priestly **w** that is superior
8:6 to the Levitical priests' **w**.
10:14 he accomplished the **w**
13:17 that they may do this **w** joyfully
13:21 May he **w** in us through Jesus
3Jn 1:8 this so that we can **w** together
Rev 14:13 Let them rest from their hard **w**
22:9 I **w** with other Christians,

worked (70)

Gen 29:20 Jacob **w** seven years in return
29:30 So he **w** for Laban another
30:26 my children for whom I've **w**,
31:6 You know that I have **w** as
31:41 I **w** for you 14 years for your
39:2 He **w** in the house of his
Exo 16:30 So the people never **w** on the
32:4 After he had **w** on the gold with
36:8 creatively **w** into the fabric.
36:35 creatively **w** into the fabric.
39:3 which they creatively **w** into
Num 4:41 Gershonite families who **w** at
Dtr 12:7 enjoy everything you've **w** for,
12:18 enjoy everything you've **w** for.
Rut 2:19 the person with whom she **w**.
2:19 She said, "The man I **w** with
2Ch 24:12 They also hired men who **w**
24:13 As the men **w**, the project
32:5 Hezekiah **w** hard. He rebuilt all
Neh 4:6 people **w** with determination.
4:16 half of my men **w** on the wall,
11:12 Also, Adaiah **w** in the temple.
Psa 105:44 inherited what others had **w**
109:11 steal what he has **w** for.
Ecc 2:18 for which I had **w** so hard under
2:19 the sun for which I **w** so hard
2:20 for which I had **w** so hard under
2:21 Here is someone who had **w**
Isa 47:15 for those who have **w** with you,
49:4 "I have **w** hard for nothing.
Jer 3:24 everything our ancestors **w** for,
12:13 They **w** until they became sick,
Eze 23:29 everything that you have **w** for.
29:20 and his army **w** for me,
Dan 8:27 Then I got up and **w** for the
Hos 12:12 Israel **w** to get a wife;
Mat 11:20 the cities where he had **w** most
11:21 If the miracles **w** in you had
11:21 worked in you had been **w**
11:23 If the miracles that had been **w**
11:23 in you had been **w** in Sodom,
13:33 the yeast **w** its way through
18:31 "The other servants who **w**
20:12 'These last workers have **w**
20:12 even though we **w** hard all day
Mar 16:20 The Lord **w** with them.
Luk 5:5 we **w** hard all night and caught
10:13 If the miracles **w** in your cities
10:13 in your cities had been **w**
13:21 the yeast **w** its way through
15:29 'All these years I've **w** like a
Jon 4:38 a crop you have not **w** for.
Act 2:22 this man God **w** miracles,
7:36 amazing things and **w** miracles
18:3 with them and they **w** together.
19:11 God **w** unusual miracles
19:24 for the men who **w** for him.
20:34 You know that I **w** to support
Rom 16:6 who has **w** very hard for you.
16:12 who have **w** hard for the Lord.
16:12 Greet dear Persis, who has **w**
1Co 15:10 I **w** harder than all the others.
Eph 1:20 He **w** with that same power in
3:7 me when his power **w** ⌊in me⌋.
Php 2:22 Like a father and son we **w**
1Th 2:9 We **w** night and day so that we
2Th 3:8 Instead, we **w** hard and
Jas 2:22 and what he did **w** together.
2Jn 1:8 don't destroy what we've **w** for,
Rev 2:2 done — how hard you have **w**

worker (14)

Exo 12:45 "No hired **w** may eat it.
Lev 19:13 you owe a hired **w** overnight.
25:40 He will be like a hired **w** or a
Lev 25:50 like the wages of a hired **w**.
25:53 serve his buyer as a hired **w**.
1Ch 28:21 have with you every skilled **w**
Ezr 7:24 or **w** in the temple of this God
Psa 86:10 you are great, a **w** of miracles.
Mat 10:10 After all, the **w** deserves to
20:14 I want to give this last **w** as
Luk 10:7 the **w** deserves his pay.
2Co 8:22 and found to be a dedicated **w**.
1Ti 5:18 and "The **w** deserves his pay."
2Ti 2:15 **w** who isn't ashamed

workers (67)

Exo 36:8 craftsmen among the **w** made
Lev 25:6 female slaves, your hired **w**,
Dtr 24:14 Don't withhold pay from hired **w**
Rut 2:21 'Stay with my younger **w** until
1Ki 5:6 My **w** will work with your
5:6 workers will work with your **w**.
5:6 wages you ask for your **w**.
5:9 My **w** will bring logs from
5:16 who were in charge of the **w**.
2Ki 4:18 who was with the harvest **w**.
12:15 with the money for the **w**
22:6 (These **w** include the
1Ch 4:21 of linen **w** at Beth Ashbea,
22:15 You have many kinds of **w**:
27:26 for the farm **w** in the fields:
2Ch 2:8 My **w** will work with your
2:8 workers will work with your **w**.
2:15 and wine he promised the **w**.
26:10 He had farmers and vineyard **w**
34:11 (These **w** included carpenters
34:13 also supervised the **w** and
Neh 4:17 The **w** who were carrying
Isa 3:3 leaders, counselors, skilled **w**,
16:14 I will count them like **w** count
21:16 I will count it like **w** count the
58:3 You mistreat all your **w**.
58:4 and fight and beat your **w**?
Jer 10:9 all made by skilled **w**.
24:1 princes of Judah, the skilled **w**,
29:2 and metal **w** left Jerusalem.)
Eze 48:18 to provide food for the city **w**.
48:19 City **w** from all the tribes in
Hos 8:6 Skilled **w** made it.
Mal 3:5 and those who cheat **w** out of
Mat 9:37 is large, but the **w** are few.
9:38 gives this harvest to send **w**
13:27 "The owner's **w** came to him
13:28 "His **w** asked him,
13:30 I will tell the **w** to gather the
13:39 The **w** are angels.
20:1 to hire **w** for his vineyard.
20:2 After agreeing to pay the **w** the
20:8 told the supervisor, 'Call the **w**,
20:12 They said, 'These last **w** have
21:33 Then he leased it to vineyard **w**
21:34 he sent his servants to the **w** to
21:35 The **w** took his servants and
21:36 But the **w** treated them the
21:38 "When the **w** saw his son,
21:40 what will he do to those **w**?"
21:41 to other **w** who will give
Mar 12:1 Then he leased it to vineyard **w**
12:2 time he sent a servant to the **w**
12:3 The **w** took the servant,
12:7 "But those **w** said to one
12:9 He will come and destroy the **w**
Luk 10:2 is large, but the **w** are few.
10:2 gives this harvest to send **w**
20:9 leased it to vineyard **w**,
20:10 time he sent a servant to the **w**
20:10 But the **w** beat the servant and
20:11 The **w** beat him, treated him
20:14 "When the **w** saw him,
20:16 He will destroy these **w** and
Act 19:25 He called a meeting of his **w**
19:28 When Demetrius' **w** and the
2Co 11:13 They are dishonest **w**,

working (41)

Exo 5:5 Do you want them to quit **w**?"
31:17 stopped **w** and was refreshed.'"
36:4 skilled craftsmen who were **w**
Lev 22:10 a priest or are **w** for him.
Rut 2:23 women who were **w** for Boaz.
3:2 women you've been **w** with,
2Ch 24:12 to the foremen who were **w**
Ezr 3:9 those **w** on God's house.
5:4 who were **w** on this building.
Neh 6:3 "I'm **w** on an important project
Job 10:16 You keep **w** your miracles
Pro 10:4 but hard-**w** hands bring riches.
12:24 Hard-**w** hands gain control,
12:27 but a hard-**w** person becomes .
13:4 appetite of hard-**w** people is
21:5 plans of a hard-**w** person lead to
Ecc 3:9 What do **w** people gain from
4:8 why they are **w** so hard
5:12 The sleep of **w** people is
5:16 do they gain from **w** so hard
Isa 44:12 **w** them with their strong arms.
Jer 18:3 and he was **w** there at his
18:4 Whenever a clay pot he was **w**
31:36 Only if these laws stop **w**,
Eze 46:1 closed during the six **w** days,
Hag 1:9 while each of you is busy **w**
1:14 returned from Babylon began **w**
Mat 20:9 "Those who started **w** about 5
24:40 "At that time two men will be **w**
24:41 Two women will be **w** at a mill.
Jon 5:17 "My Father is **w** right now,
Act 20:35 that by **w** hard like this
Rom 1:13 the results of **w** among you as
1:13 enjoyed the results of **w** among
13:4 government is God's servant **w**
Col 3:23 as though you were **w**
4:11 the Jewish religion who are **w**
1Th 1:3 your love is **w** hard,
2Th 3:11 You're not **w**, so you go around
2Ti 2:6 hard-**w** farmer should have the
Heb 6:11 prove that you're **w** hard so that

workman's (1)

Jdg 5:26 for a **w** hammer with the other.

workmen (11)

1Ki 5:18 Solomon's **w**, and men from
5:18 workmen, Hiram's **w**,
2Ki 12:14 the money was given to the **w**,
22:5 They should give it to the **w**
22:7 Since the **w** are honest,
22:9 have given it to the **w** who are
2Ch 2:14 can work⌋ with your skilled **w**
2:14 workmen and the skilled **w**
34:10 These foremen gave it to the **w**
34:13 workers and directed all the **w**
34:17 it to the supervisors and the **w**."

works (29)

Exo 31:14 Whoever **w** on that day must
31:15 Whoever **w** on that day must
Jdg 2:7 had seen all the spectacular **w**
13:18 It's a name that **w** miracles."
Ezr 8:22 "Our God **w** things out for the
Psa 46:8 Come, see the **w** of the LORD,
92:4 about the **w** of your hands.
92:5 How spectacular are your **w**,
102:25 are the **w** of your hands.
111:6 revealed the power of his **w**
111:7 His **w** are done with truth and
139:14 Your **w** are miraculous,
Pro 8:22 before any of his **w**.
12:11 Whoever **w** his land will have
16:26 A laborer's appetite **w** to his
28:19 Whoever **w** his land will have
31:13 and **w** with willing hands.
Ecc 10:9 Whoever **w** in a stone quarry
11:5 God, who made everything, **w**.
Isa 59:6 cover themselves with their **w**.
59:6 Their **w** are evil. Their hands
Mat 6:1 careful not to do your good **w**
Mar 9:39 No one who **w** a miracle in my
Eph 1:19 greatness of his power as it **w**
2:10 lives filled with good **w** that
3:9 the way this mystery **w**.
5:11 **w** that darkness produces.
Col 1:29 his mighty power **w** in me.
4:13 I assure you that he **w** hard for

workshop (1)

Psa 139:15 woven in an underground **w**.

world (366)

Gen 6:11 The **w** was corrupt in God's
6:12 God saw the **w** and how
11:1 The whole **w** had one
38:29 this how you burst into the **w**!"
41:57 The whole **w** came to Joseph
41:57 was so severe all over the **w**.
Exo 19:5 though the whole **w** is mine.
34:10 in any other nation in all the **w**.
Dtr 4:6 people of the **w** your wisdom
4:27 you among the people of the **w**,
10:15 out of all the people of the **w**.
28:1 all the other nations in the **w**.
28:10 Then all the people in the **w**
28:25 to all the kingdoms in the **w**.
28:64 among all the people of the **w**,
29:24 other nations in the **w** will ask,
30:3 all the nations of the **w** where
30:4 most distant country in the **w**,
Jos 4:24 in the **w** would know his
1Sm 2:8 He has set the **w** on them.
17:46 The whole **w** will know that
1Ki 2:2 "I'm about to leave this **w**.
8:43 people of the **w** may know your
8:53 from all the people of the **w**
8:60 people of the **w** will know that
9:7 for all the people of the **w**.
10:23 all the ⌊other⌋ kings of the **w**.
10:24 The whole **w** wanted to listen
2Ki 5:15 there's no god in the whole **w**,
19:15 of all the kingdoms of the **w**.
2Ch 6:33 people of the **w** may know your
7:20 for all the people of the **w**.
9:22 all the ⌊other⌋ kings of the **w**.
9:23 All the kings of the **w** wanted
16:9 LORD's eyes scan the whole **w**
36:23 me all the kingdoms of the **w**.
Ezr 1:2 me all the kingdoms of the **w**.
Job 1:8 No one in the **w** is like him!
2:3 No one in the **w** is like him!
3:14 counselors of the **w** who built
18:18 dark and chased out of the **w**.
28:13 be found in this **w** of the living.
34:13 him to be over the whole **w**?
Psa 7:8 judges the people of the **w**.
9:8 the **w** with righteousness.
19:4 has gone out into the entire **w**,
24:1 The **w** and all who live in it are
27:13 LORD in this **w** of the living.
33:8 Let all who live in the **w** stand
33:10 of the people of the **w**.
49:1 all who live in the **w**—
50:12 because the **w** and all that it
52:5 will pull your roots out of this **w**
68:32 You kingdoms of the **w**,
77:18 Streaks of lightning lit up the **w**.
89:11 You made the **w** and
90:2 birth to the earth and the **w**,
93:1 The **w** was set in place;
96:13 He will judge the **w** with
97:4 of lightning light up the **w**.
97:6 people of the **w** see his glory.
98:7 the sea, everything in it, the **w**,
98:9 He will judge the **w** with
104:35 May sinners vanish from the **w**.
116:9 presence in this **w** of the living.
117:1 all you people of the **w**!
119:19 I am a foreigner in this **w**.
142:5 in this **w** of the living."
149:7 to punish the people of the **w**,
Pro 8:26 fields or the first dust of the **w**.
8:31 found joy in his inhabited **w**,
17:24 looking around⌋ all over the **w**.
Isa 10:14 I've gathered the whole **w** as
10:23 destruction throughout the **w** as
11:9 The **w** will be filled with the
13:5 his fury to destroy the whole **w**.
13:11 I will punish the **w** for its evil
14:17 who made the **w** like a desert
18:3 all you inhabitants of the **w**
23:8 the honored people of the **w**.
23:9 all the honored people of the **w**.
Isa 24:4 The **w** wastes away and
26:9 those who live in the **w** learn to
27:6 and fill the whole **w** with fruit.
34:1 The earth, everyone in it, the **w**,
37:16 God of the kingdoms of the **w**.
38:11 see the LORD in this **w**.
38:11 with all the people in the **w**,
45:19 or in some dark corner of the **w**.
49:6 save people all over the **w**."
53:8 would be removed from the **w**?
Jer 10:12 He set up the **w** by his skill.
10:12 out the **w** by his understanding.
11:19 cut Jeremiah off from this **w**
16:19 distant parts of the **w** and say,
34:17 kingdoms of the **w** horrified at
51:7 It made the whole **w** drunk.
51:15 He set up the **w** by his wisdom.
51:27 battle flag throughout the **w**.
51:41 city that the whole **w** praised,
Lam 2:15 the joy of the whole **w**?'
Eze 29:12 most desolate country in the **w**.
30:7 most desolate country in the **w**,
31:12 All the nations in the **w** came
38:12 and they live in the **w**."
Dan 2:35 which filled the whole **w**.
2:39 that will rule the whole **w**.
4:1 and language in the **w**.
4:22 the most distant part of the **w**.
6:25 and language all over the **w**:
7:23 and crush the whole **w**.
9:12 Nowhere in the **w** has anything
Amo 8:4 who are oppressed in the **w**.
Nah 1:5 The **w** and all who live in it
Zep 3:19 and famous in all the **w**.
Zec 1:11 The whole **w** is at rest and in
12:3 All the nations in the **w** will
Mat 4:8 in the **w** and their glory.
5:14 "You are light for the **w**.
8:11 will come from all over the **w**.
10:18 them and to everyone in the **w**.
12:32 forgiven in this **w** or the next.
13:35 hidden since the **w** was made."
13:38 The field is the **w**.
13:39 The harvest is the end of the **w**.
16:26 for people to win the whole **w**
17:25 the kings of the **w** collect fees
18:7 How horrible it will be for the **w**
19:28 throne in the **w** to come,
24:3 and when will the **w** come to
24:14 be spread throughout the **w** as
24:21 beginning of the **w** until now
25:34 you from the creation of the **w**.
26:13 Good News is spoken in the **w**,
Mar 8:36 win the whole **w** yet lose their
10:30 But in the **w** to come they will
14:9 Good News is spoken in the **w**,
16:15 "Go everywhere in the **w**,
Luk 4:5 of the **w** in an instant.
9:25 for people to win the whole **w**
11:50 prophet since the **w** was made.
12:30 Everyone in the **w** is
13:29 will come from all over the **w**
18:30 eternal life in the **w** to come."
20:34 "In this **w** people get married.
20:35 in the next **w** will neither marry
21:26 for what will happen to the **w**.
Jon 1:9 was coming into the **w**.
1:10 He was in the **w**, and the world
1:10 He was in the world, and the **w**
1:10 Yet, the **w** didn't recognize him.
1:29 takes away the sin of the **w**.
3:16 God loved the **w** this way:
3:17 God sent his Son into the **w**,
3:17 not to condemn the **w**,
3:17 the world, but to save the **w**.
3:19 The light came into the **w**.
4:42 he really is the savior of the **w**."
6:14 who is to come into the **w**."
6:33 heaven and gives life to the **w**."
6:51 bring life to the **w** is my flesh."
7:4 you should let the **w** see you."
7:7 The **w** cannot hate you,
8:12 said, "I am the light of the **w**.
8:23 You're from this **w**.
8:23 I'm not from this **w**.
8:26 So I tell the **w** exactly what he
Jon 9:5 As long as I'm in the **w**,
9:5 I'm light for the **w**."
9:39 have come into this **w** to judge:
10:36 and has sent me into the **w**.
11:9 they see the light of this **w**.
11:27 expected to come into the **w**."
12:19 The whole **w** is following him!"
12:25 lives in this **w** will guard them
12:31 "This **w** is being judged now.
12:31 The ruler of this **w** will be
12:46 into the **w** so that everyone
12:47 I didn't come to condemn the **w**
12:47 the world but to save the **w**.
13:1 come for him to leave this **w**
13:1 his own who were in the **w**,
14:17 The **w** cannot accept him,
14:19 In a little while the **w** will no
14:22 to us and not to the **w**?"
14:27 kind of peace that the **w** gives.
14:30 The ruler of this **w** has no
14:31 However, I want the **w** to know
15:18 "If the **w** hates you,
15:19 in common with the **w**,
15:19 the **w** would love you as one of
15:19 in common with the **w**.
15:19 I chose you from the **w**,
15:19 and that's why the **w** hates you.
16:8 come to convict the **w** of sin,
16:8 to show the **w** what has God's
16:8 and to convince the **w** that God
16:9 He will convict the **w** of sin,
16:10 He will show the **w** what has
16:11 He will convince the **w** that
16:11 ruler of this **w** has been judged.
16:20 but the **w** will be happy.
16:21 has been brought into the **w**.
16:28 the Father and came into the **w**.
16:28 I'm going to leave the **w** and go
16:33 In the **w** you'll have trouble.
16:33 I have overcome the **w**."
17:5 with you before the **w** existed.
17:6 They are from this **w**.
17:9 I'm not praying for the **w** but for
17:11 I won't be in the **w** much longer,
17:11 but they are in the **w**,
17:13 I'm still in the **w** so that they
17:14 But the **w** has hated them
17:14 belong to the **w** any more than
17:14 more than I belong to the **w**.
17:15 you to take them out of the **w**
17:16 They don't belong to the **w** any
17:16 more than I belong to the **w**.
17:18 I have sent them into the **w** the
17:18 way you sent me into the **w**.
17:21 so that the **w** will believe that
17:23 In this way the **w** knows that
17:24 me before the **w** was made.
17:25 the **w** didn't know you.
18:36 doesn't belong to this **w**.
18:36 kingdom belonged to this **w**,
18:37 born and have come into the **w**
21:25 I suppose the **w** wouldn't have
Act 11:28 would affect the entire **w**.
13:47 save people all over the **w**.'"
17:6 all over the **w** are now here
17:31 to judge the **w** with justice,
19:27 the rest of the **w** worship will
22:22 The **w** doesn't need a man like
24:5 all Jews throughout the **w**.
Rom 1:8 throughout the whole **w**.
1:20 From the creation of the **w**,
3:6 God be able to judge the **w**?
3:19 The whole **w** is brought under
4:13 that he would inherit the **w**.
5:12 So sin came into the **w** through
5:13 Sin was in the **w** before there
8:39 or powers in the **w** above or in
8:39 world above or in the **w** below,
10:18 has gone out into the whole **w**
11:12 made the **w** spiritually rich.
11:12 will make the **w** even richer.
11:15 that the **w** has been brought
12:2 like the people of this **w**.
15:11 all you people of the **w**!"
1Co 1:20 of the **w** into nonsense?
1:21 The **w** with its wisdom was

1Co 1:27 But God chose what the w
1:27 God chose what the w
1:28 God chose what the w
2:6 that doesn't belong to this w
2:6 to the rulers of this w who are
2:7 our glory before the w began.
2:8 Not one of the rulers of this w
2:12 the spirit that belongs to the w.
3:18 are wise in the ways of this w,
3:19 The wisdom of this w is
3:22 Cephas, the w, life or death,
4:13 garbage in the eyes of the w
5:10 would have to leave this w.
6:2 God's people will judge the w?
6:2 if you're going to judge the w,
7:31 things in this w should do so
7:31 It is clear that this w in its
8:4 gods in this w don't really exist
11:32 along with the rest of the w.
14:10 languages there are in the w,
2Co 1:12 that we have lived in this w.
4:4 The god of this w has blinded
7:10 But the distress that the w
Gal 1:4 free us from this present evil w,
3:8 of the w will be blessed."
3:14 of the w through Jesus Christ
3:22 the whole w is controlled by
4:3 to the principles of this w.
4:4 God sent his Son ⌊into the w⌋.
4:9 bankrupt principles of this w?
6:14 cross my relationship to the w
Eph 1:4 Before the creation of the w,
1:21 not only in this present w but
1:21 but also in the w to come.
2:2 the ways of this present w
2:7 rich kindness in the w to come.
2:12 and were in the w without God.
4:17 like other people in the w.
4:30 be set free ⌊from the w of sin⌋.
6:12 who govern this w of darkness,
6:12 control evil in the heavenly w.
Php 2:10 and in the w below will kneel
2:15 like stars among them in the w
Col 1:6 and spreading all over the w as
1:27 his people throughout the w
1Ti 1:15 Christ Jesus came into the w
2:14 and brought sin into the w.
3:16 was believed in the w,
4:8 life now and in the w to come.
6:7 didn't bring anything into the w,
6:17 have the riches of this w not
2Ti 1:9 Before the w began,
4:1 will come to rule ⌊the w⌋.
4:10 fell in love with this present w
Tit 1:2 eternal life before the w began.
2:12 godly lives in this present w.
Heb 1:6 his firstborn Son into the w,
2:5 He didn't put the w that will
4:3 work when he created the w.
6:5 the powers of the w to come.
9:11 is not part of this created w.
9:26 times since the w was created.
10:5 when Christ came into the w,
11:3 created the w through his word.
11:7 faith Noah condemned the w
11:38 The w didn't deserve these
Jas 1:27 remain uncorrupted by this w.
2:5 choose poor people in the w
3:6 It is a w of evil among the parts
3:15 It belongs to this w.
4:4 this ⌊evil⌋ w is hatred toward
4:4 wants to be a friend of this w is
1Pe 1:1 temporary residents ⌊in the w⌋
1:20 long ago before the w existed,
2:11 temporary residents ⌊in the w⌋,
5:9 the w are going through
2Pe 1:4 sinful desires cause in the w.
2:5 spare the ancient w either.
2:5 He brought the flood on the w
3:4 from the beginning of the w."
3:6 flooded and destroyed that w.
1Jn 2:2 for the sins of the whole w.
2:15 Don't love the w and what it
2:15 Those who love the w don't
2:16 Not everything that the w offers
2:16 It comes from the w,
1Jn 2:17 the w and its evil desires are
3:1 For this reason the w doesn't
3:13 be surprised if the w hates you.
4:1 many false prophets in the w.
4:3 That spirit is already in the w.
4:4 than the one who is in the w.
4:5 These people belong to the w.
4:5 speak the thoughts of the w,
4:5 and the w listens to them.
4:9 only Son into the w so that we
4:14 his Son as the Savior of the w.
4:17 While we are in this w,
5:4 has won the victory over the w.
5:4 wins the victory over the w.
5:5 wins the victory over the w?
5:19 and that the whole w is under
2Jn 1:7 others have gone into the w.
Rev 3:10 is coming to the whole w
5:6 of God sent all over the w.
11:15 "The kingdom of the w has
12:9 the deceiver of the whole w,
13:3 All the people of the w were
13:8 before the creation of the w.
16:14 go to the kings of the whole w
17:8 Life when the w was created,
18:23 the important people of the w,
19:2 prostitute who corrupted the w

worldly (5)

Luk 16:8 W people are more clever than
Php 3:19 Their minds are set on w
Col 3:2 things above, not on w things.
3:5 to death whatever is w in you:
Tit 2:12 filled with w desires so that

world's (6)

Isa 23:17 for all the w kingdoms
25:3 by the w tyrants will fear you.
Col 2:8 traditions and the w way
2:20 died with Christ to the w way
2:20 were still under the w influence
2Pe 2:20 Christ and escape the w filth.

worm (5)

Job 17:14 are my father,' and to the w,
25:6 of Adam — who is only a w!"
Psa 22:6 Yet, I am a w and not a man.
Isa 41:14 Don't be afraid, Jacob, you w.
Jnh 4:7 God sent a w to attack the

worms (9)

Exo 16:20 and it was full of w and
16:24 it didn't smell or have w in it.
Dtr 28:39 because w will eat them.
Job 21:26 and w cover them.
24:20 W feast on them. No one
Isa 14:11 under you, and w cover you.
51:8 W will devour them like wool.
66:24 The w that eat them will not
Mar 9:48 In hell w that eat the body

wormwood (6)

Pro 5:4 in the end she is as bitter as w,
Jer 23:15 I will give them w to eat and
Lam 3:15 He has made me drink w.
3:19 wandering, the w and poison.
Rev 8:11 That star was named W.
8:11 of the water turned into w,

worn (31)

Exo 28:4 and the robe that is w with it,
28:31 "Make the robe that is w with
29:5 and the robe that is w with it,
35:19 the special clothes w for
39:1 they made special clothes w
39:22 They made the robe that is w
39:26 robe that is w by Aaron when
39:41 the special clothes w when
Lev 8:7 him in the robe that is w
Num 19:2 it must never have w a yoke.
Dtr 21:3 to work and never w a yoke.
Jdg 8:26 the purple clothes w by the
1Sm 25:37 effects of the wine had w off,
2Sm 13:4 so w out morning after
Neh 4:10 "The work crews are w out,
Est 6:8 a royal robe that the king has w
Job 16:7 "But now, God has w me out.
Psa 6:6 I am w out from my groaning.
143:7 My spirit is w out. Do not hide
Pro 30:1 I'm weary and w out,
Isa 47:13 You are w out by your many
Jer 45:3 I'm w out from groaning.
Lam 2:11 My eyes are w out with tears.
5:5 We are w out ⌊and⌋ not
Eze 23:43 Then I said, 'She is w out from
24:12 "'I have w myself out trying to
29:18 soldier's head was w bald,
Luk 8:27 demons and had not w clothes
9:39 leaving the child w out.
10:13 Long ago they would have w
1Co 15:49 As we have w the likeness of

worn-out (5)

Jos 9:4 They took w sacks on their
9:5 sandals were w and repaired,
9:13 clothes and sandals are also w
Job 13:28 I am like w wineskins,
Ecc 1:8 these sayings are w phrases.

worried (11)

Jos 22:24 "We were w because of the
1Sm 4:13 He was w about the ark of God.
10:2 Instead, he's w about you.
20:34 He was w sick about David
Job 14:22 He is only w about himself."
Psa 94:19 When I w about many things,
Jer 49:23 "Hamath and Arpad are w
Eze 12:18 Tremble and be w as you drink
12:19 They will be w as they eat
Luk 2:48 Your father and I have been w
21:34 hung over, and w about life.

worries (5)

Ecc 5:3 when there are too many w.
Lam 1:5 Its enemies have no w.
Mat 13:22 But the w of life and the
Mar 4:19 but the w of life, the deceitful
Luk 8:14 but as life goes on the w,

worry (19)

Gen 45:20 Don't w about your belongings
1Sm 9:5 and w about us ⌊instead⌋."
29:10 Don't w about the unkind
Psa 73:12 They never have a w.
Pro 1:33 to me will live without w
Isa 28:16 believes ⌊in him⌋ will not w.
Mat 6:28 "And why w about clothes?
6:31 "Don't ever w and say,
6:34 don't ever w about tomorrow.
6:34 tomorrow will w about itself.
10:19 don't w about what to say or
28:14 and you'll have nothing to w
Mar 13:11 don't w ahead of time about
Luk 10:41 You w and fuss about a lot of
12:11 don't w about how you will
12:26 why w about other things?
21:14 not to w beforehand how you
Act 20:10 his arms, and said, "Don't w!
Php 4:6 Never w about anything.

worrying (6)

1Sm 9:5 or my father will stop w about
Mat 6:25 "So I tell you to stop w about
6:27 a single hour to your life by w?
Luk 12:22 "So I tell you to stop w about
12:25 add an hour to your life by w?
12:29 and quit w about these things.

worse (35)

Gen 19:9 We're going to treat you w than
Rut 1:13 My bitterness is much w than
1Sm 14:19 camp grew w and worse.
14:19 camp grew worse and w.
14:44 Saul said, "May God do w
2Sm 19:7 and that will be w than all the
1Ki 16:30 He was w than all ⌊the kings⌋
22:35 But the battle got w that day,
2Ki 7:13 Those men will be no w off
2Ch 16:12 that became progressively w.
18:34 But the battle got w that day,
Psa 39:2 in thought, my pain grew w.
Isa 24:16 treachery grows w and worse."

Isa 24:16 treachery grows worse and **w**."
Jer 7:26 were **w** than your ancestors.
16:12 You have done **w** than your
Eze 23:11 became **w** than her sister's
Dan 1:10 If he sees that you look **w** than
Jnh 1:11 The storm was getting **w**.
1:13 The storm was getting **w**.
Zec 1:15 but they made things **w**.
Mat 9:16 and the tear will become **w**.
12:45 of that person is **w** than
27:64 will be **w** than the first."
Mar 2:21 and the tear will become **w**.
5:26 Actually, she had become **w**.
Luk 11:26 of that person is **w** than
Jon 5:14 something **w** doesn't happen
1Co 8:8 We are no **w** off if we eat ⌊that
2Co 12:13 How were you treated **w** than
1Ti 5:8 and is **w** than an unbeliever.
2Ti 3:13 from bad to **w** as they mislead
Heb 10:29 He deserves a much **w**
12:13 your injured leg won't get **w**.
2Pe 2:20 they are **w** off than they were

worship (470)

Gen 4:26 people began to **w** the LORD.
22:5 We'll **w**. After that we'll come
Exo 3:12 all of you will **w** God on this
4:23 son go so that he may **w** me.
7:16 "Let my people go to **w** me in
8:1 Let my people go to **w** me.
8:20 Let my people go to **w** me.
9:1 Let my people go to **w** me.
9:13 Let my people go to **w** me.
10:3 Let my people go to **w** me.
10:7 Let the Israelite men go to **w**
10:8 "Go, **w** the LORD your God,"
10:11 men may go to **w** the LORD,
10:24 and said, "Go, **w** the LORD!
12:31 Go, **w** the LORD as you asked.
16:23 Tomorrow is a day of **w**,
16:23 a holy day of **w** dedicated to
16:25 "because today is a day of **w**
16:26 the seventh day, the day of **w**,
16:29 has given you this day of **w**.
20:5 Never **w** them or serve them,
20:8 "Remember the day of **w** by
20:10 day is the day of **w** dedicated
20:23 for yourselves. Never **w** them.
23:24 Never **w** or serve their gods or
24:1 to me and **w** at a distance.
31:13 sure to observe my days of **w**.
31:14 "'Observe the day of **w**
31:15 the seventh day is a day of **w**,
31:16 must observe this day of **w**,
34:14 (Never **w** any other god,
35:2 seventh day is a holy day of **w**,
35:3 your homes on this day of **w**."
Lev 16:31 This is the most important **w**
19:3 Observe my days of **w**.
19:30 "Observe my days of **w** and
23:3 the seventh day is a day of **w**,
23:3 day of **w** wherever you live.
23:24 month hold a **w** festival.
23:32 It is a day of **w**, a day when
23:32 observe the day of **w**."
23:38 to the LORD's days of **w**,
23:39 eighth days will be **w** festivals.
24:8 Every day of **w** ⌊a priest⌋ must
26:1 Never cut figures in stone to **w**
26:2 Observe my days of **w** and
26:30 I will destroy your **w** sites,
Num 15:32 wood on the day of **w**.
21:28 the rulers of Arnon's **w** sites.
28:9 "On the day of **w** offer two
28:10 offering is for every day of **w**
33:52 destroy all their places of **w**.
Dtr 4:19 let yourselves be tempted to **w**
4:28 There you will **w** wooden and
5:9 Never **w** them or serve them,
5:12 "Observe the day of **w** as a
5:14 day is the day of **w** dedicated
5:15 you to observe the day of **w**.
6:14 Never **w** any of the gods
7:4 away from me to **w** other gods.
7:16 and never **w** their gods,
10:12 and **w** him with all your heart

Dtr 10:20 God, **w** him, be loyal to him,
11:16 to turn away and **w** other gods
11:28 and if you **w** other gods you
12:2 Completely destroy all the **w**
12:2 The people you're forcing out **w**
12:4 Never **w** the LORD your God in
12:4 in the way they **w** their gods.
12:5 Go there and **w** him.
12:8 Never **w** in the way that it's
12:30 did these people **w** their gods?
12:31 Never **w** the LORD your God in
12:31 in the way they **w** their gods,
13:2 "Let's **w** and serve other gods."
13:4 **W** the LORD your God,
13:6 "Let's go **w** other gods."
13:13 "Let's **w** other gods."
28:14 Never **w** other gods or serve
28:36 There you will **w** gods made of
29:18 from the LORD our God to **w**
30:17 to other gods and **w** them.
31:20 turn to other gods and **w** them.
Jos 22:27 as a witness that we may **w**
1Sm 1:3 go from his own city to **w**
9:12 a sacrifice on the **w** site.
9:13 before he goes to the **w** site
9:14 them on his way to the **w** site.
9:19 Go ahead of me to the **w** site.
9:25 Then they left the **w** site for the
10:3 their way to **w** God at Bethel:
10:5 as they come from the **w** site.
10:13 he came to the **w** site.
15:25 me so that I may **w** the LORD."
15:30 and let me **w** the LORD your
22:6 the tamarisk tree at the **w** site
1Ki 3:2 still sacrificing at other **w** sites
3:3 incense at these other **w** sites.
3:4 the most important place of **w**.
9:6 serve other gods and **w** them,
11:7 Solomon built an illegal **w** site
12:30 as far as Dan to **w** the one calf.
12:31 Jeroboam built **w** sites on
12:32 the illegal **w** sites ⌊to serve⌋
13:2 the illegal **w** sites who offer
13:32 and all the illegal **w** sites
13:33 priests for the illegal **w** sites.
13:33 to be priests at the **w** sites.
14:23 They built **w** sites for
14:23 stones and Asherah poles to **w**
15:14 Although the illegal **w** sites
19:18 knees have not knelt to **w** Baal
22:44 But the illegal **w** sites were not
22:44 burn incense at these **w** sites.
2Ki 4:23 Moon Festival or a day of **w**."
5:18 to the temple of Rimmon to **w**,
10:28 rid of Baal **w** throughout Israel.
10:29 Israel to commit — ⌊the **w** of⌋
11:5 are on duty on the day of **w**,
11:7 on the day of **w** must guard
11:9 duty on the day of **w** as well as
12:3 But the illegal places of **w**
12:3 burn incense at these **w** sites.
14:4 But the illegal places of **w**
14:4 burn incense at these **w** sites.
15:4 But the illegal places of **w**
15:4 burn incense at these **w** sites.
15:35 But the illegal places of **w**
15:35 burn incense at these **w** sites.
16:4 offering at the illegal **w** sites,
16:18 walkway used on the day of **w**.
17:9 themselves illegal places of **w**
17:11 At all the illegal places of **w**,
17:25 they didn't **w** the LORD.
17:28 them how to **w** the LORD.
17:29 them at the illegal places of **w**,
17:32 at their illegal places of **w**.
17:35 "Never **w** other gods,
17:36 Instead, **w** the LORD,
17:37 'Never **w** other gods.
17:38 Never **w** other gods.
17:39 Instead, **w** the LORD your God,
18:4 rid of the illegal places of **w**,
18:22 the god whose places of **w**
18:22 "**W** at this altar in Jerusalem."'
21:3 places of **w** that his father
23:5 at the illegal places of **w**
23:8 He tore down the **w** site at the

2Ki 23:8 (The **w** site was to the left of
23:9 The priests of the illegal **w**
23:13 the illegal places of **w** east
23:15 place of **w** made by Jeroboam
23:15 the altar and the place of **w**.
23:15 They burned the **w** site,
23:19 at the illegal places of **w**
23:19 done to the **w** places at Bethel.
23:20 the priests of the illegal **w** sites
1Ch 9:28 in charge of the utensils for **w**.
9:32 out in rows every day of **w**.
16:29 **W** the LORD in ⌊his⌋ holy
16:39 at the place of **w** in Gibeon.
21:29 were at the **w** site at Gibeon.
23:26 and all the utensils used in **w**."
23:31 made — on weekly **w** days,
25:6 and harps for **w** in God's
28:13 planned all the work done for **w**
28:13 designed all the utensils for **w**
28:14 for each of the utensils for **w**,
28:15 use of each lamp stand for **w**),
28:21 and Levites for every type of **w**
2Ch 1:3 went to the place of **w**
1:13 of meeting at the place of **w**
2:4 on weekly **w** days,
7:19 serve other gods and **w** them,
8:13 on weekly **w** days,
11:15 priests for the illegal **w** sites
14:5 got rid of the illegal places of **w**
15:17 Although the illegal **w** sites in
17:6 got rid of the illegal places of **w**
20:33 But the illegal **w** sites on the
21:11 made illegal places of **w**
23:4 are on duty on the day of **w**,
23:8 duty on the day of **w** as well as
24:7 temple ⌊to **w**⌋ other gods —
28:4 offering at the illegal **w** sites,
28:25 he made places of **w** to
29:35 So the **w** in the LORD's temple
31:1 down the illegal places of **w**
31:3 on the weekly **w** days,
31:21 and commands into **w**
31:21 Whatever he did for the **w** in
32:12 rid of the LORD's places of **w**
32:12 '**W** and sacrifice at one altar?'
33:3 places of **w** that his father
33:17 at the illegal places of **w**,
33:19 where he built illegal **w** sites
34:3 the illegal places of **w**,
35:16 was arranged that day for the **w**
Ezr 4:2 help you build because we **w**
4:2 worship the same God you **w**.
6:18 to their groups ⌊to lead⌋ the **w**
6:21 the non-Jews in the land to **w**
Neh 1:11 who want to **w** your name.
9:6 and the armies of heaven **w**
9:14 them about your holy day of **w**.
10:31 or grain to sell on the day of **w**,
10:31 from them on the day of **w**
10:32 ounce of silver every year for **w**
10:33 on the weekly days of **w**,
11:22 in charge of **w** in God's temple.
12:9 stood across from them in **w**.
13:10 who conducted the **w** ⌊in the
13:14 and for the **w** that is held
13:15 winepresses on the day of **w**.
13:15 into Jerusalem on the day of **w**.
13:16 selling them on the day of **w**
13:17 How dare you treat the day of **w**
13:18 the day of **w** as unholy."
13:19 Before the day of **w**,
13:19 until after the day of **w**.
13:19 be brought in on the day of **w**.
13:21 longer came on the day of **w**.
13:22 to keep the day of **w** holy.
Psa 22:25 among those assembled for **w**.
22:27 from all the nations will **w** you
22:29 people on earth will eat and **w**.
26:12 the LORD with the choirs in **w**.
29:2 **W** the LORD in ⌊his⌋ holy
40:3 Many will see this and **w**.
40:9 among those assembled for **w**.
40:10 from those assembled for **w**.
45:11 He is your Lord. **W** him.
66:4 The whole earth will **w** you.
67:7 all the ends of the earth **w** him.

Psa 72:11 May all kings **w** him.
78:58 because of their illegal **w** sites.
81:9 Never **w** a foreign god.
95:6 Come, let's **w** and bow down.
96:9 **W** the LORD in ⌊his⌋ holy
102:22 gather to **w** the LORD."
107:32 the people are gathered for **w**.
132:7 Let's **w** at his footstool.
Isa 1:13 Festivals, your days of **w**,
1:29 the oaks that you wanted to **w**
2:8 and they **w** what their hands
2:20 they made for themselves to **w**.
15:2 temple, to the **w** sites, to cry.
16:12 of Moab appear at the **w** site,
19:21 They will **w** with sacrifices
19:23 will **w** with the Assyrians.
21:9 All the idols they **w** lie
27:13 to Egypt will come and **w**
29:13 "These people **w** me with their
29:13 and their **w** of me is ⌊based
36:7 the god whose places of **w**
36:7 Jerusalem, "**W** at this altar.'"
44:15 from these trees and **w** them.
44:17 They bow to them and **w** them.
46:6 They bow down and **w** it.
56:2 day of **w** from becoming unholy
56:4 men who keep my days of **w**,
56:6 joined the LORD to **w** him,
56:6 day of **w** from becoming unholy
58:13 stop trampling on the day of **w**
58:13 if you call the day of **w** a
65:1 to a nation that didn't **w** me.
66:23 all people will come to **w** me,"
Jer 3:23 is the noise of false **w**.
3:24 the shameful **w** ⌊of Baal⌋ has
7:2 these gates to **w** the LORD.
7:31 They have built **w** sites at
10:25 and on people who don't **w** you.
13:10 to serve them and **w** them.
17:3 I will do this because of your **w**
17:21 carry anything on the day of **w**
17:22 of your homes on the day of **w**.
17:22 but observe the day of **w** as a
17:24 of this city on the day of **w**.
17:24 You must observe the day of **w**
17:27 and observe the day of **w** as
17:27 of Jerusalem on the day of **w**.
19:5 They have built **w** sites to burn
25:6 gods to serve and **w** them.
26:2 from the cities of Judah to **w**
26:18 will become a **w** site covered
32:35 Ben Hinnom they built **w** sites
48:35 in Moab who come to **w** sites,
Lam 2:6 festivals and days of **w** in Zion.
Eze 5:11 dishonored my holy **w** place
6:3 and destroy your **w** sites.
6:6 and the **w** sites will be
16:16 and made your **w** sites colorful.
16:24 platforms and illegal **w** sites
16:25 You also built **w** sites at the
16:31 and place your illegal **w** sites
16:39 tear down your illegal **w** sites.
18:6 at the illegal mountain **w** sites
18:11 at the illegal mountain **w** sites.
18:15 at the illegal mountain **w** sites
20:12 them certain days to **w** me as
20:13 dishonored the days to **w** me.
20:16 dishonored the days to **w** me,
20:20 Set apart certain holy days to **w**
20:21 dishonored the days to **w** me.
20:24 dishonored the days to **w** me,
20:29 "What is this **w** site you're
20:29 it is still called '**w** site' today.)
20:40 will **w** me on my holy
22:8 dishonored the day to **w** me.
22:9 to idols at the **w** sites
22:26 They ignore the days to **w** me.
23:38 dishonored the days to **w** me.
36:2 The ancient **w** sites now
44:24 observe holy days to **w** me.
45:17 the weekly days of **w**,
46:1 on the weekly day of **w**.
46:2 He must **w** at the entrance of
46:3 The common people must **w** at
46:3 LORD on the weekly days of **w**
46:4 a burnt offering on the day of **w**.
Eze 46:9 gate to **w** must leave through
46:12 as he does on the day of **w**.
Dan 3:5 bow down and **w** the gold
3:6 down and **w** will immediately
3:10 down and **w** the gold statue.
3:11 doesn't bow down and **w** will
3:12 don't honor your gods or **w**
3:14 you don't honor my gods or **w**
3:15 will you bow down and **w** the
3:15 If you don't **w** it, you will
3:18 never honor your gods or **w**
3:28 to honor or **w** any god except
6:16 whom you always **w**,
6:20 God, whom you always **w**,
Hos 2:11 her weekly **w** days — all her
4:17 have chosen to **w** idols.
10:8 The illegal **w** sites of Aven will
Amo 7:9 The **w** sites of Isaac will be
8:5 When will the day of **w** be over
Jnh 1:9 I **w** the LORD, the God of
Mic 1:3 down and step on the **w** places
1:5 What is Judah's **w** place?
3:12 will become a **w** site covered
5:13 You will no longer **w** what your
Zep 1:5 I will remove those who **w** all
1:5 who **w** by swearing loyalty
3:9 give all people pure lips to **w**
Zec 14:16 come every year to **w** the king,
14:17 go to Jerusalem to **w** the king,
Mat 2:2 and have come to **w** him."
2:8 that I may go and **w** him too."
4:9 you will bow down and **w** me."
4:10 Scripture says, '**W** the Lord
12:1 Then on a day of **w** Jesus
12:2 not right to do on the day of **w**."
12:5 Teachings that on the day of **w**
12:5 day of **w** yet remain innocent?
12:8 authority over the day of **w**."
12:10 heal on a day of **w** so that they
12:11 it falls into a pit on a day of **w**,
12:12 to do good on the day of **w**."
15:9 Their **w** of me is pointless,
24:20 or a day of **w** when you flee.
27:62 which was the day of **w**,
28:1 After the day of **w**,
28:9 bowed down to **w** him,
28:17 they bowed down in **w**,
Mar 1:21 On the next day of **w**,
2:23 Once on a day of **w** Jesus was
2:24 not permitted on the day of **w**?"
2:27 Then he added, "The day of **w**
2:27 not people for the day of **w**.
2:28 authority over the day of **w**."
3:2 on the day of **w** so that they
3:4 or to do evil on the day of **w**,
6:2 When the day of **w** came,
7:7 Their **w** of me is pointless.
15:42 before the day of **w**,
16:1 When the day of **w** was over,
Luk 4:7 So if you will **w** me,
4:8 '**W** the Lord your God and
4:16 the synagogue on the day of **w**.
4:31 and taught them on a day of **w**.
6:1 Once, on a day of **w**,
6:2 not right to do on the day of **w**?"
6:5 authority over the day of **w**."
6:6 On another day of **w**,
6:7 on the day of **w** so that they
6:9 right thing to do on a day of **w**:
13:10 a synagogue on the day of **w**.
13:14 for healing on the day of **w**.
13:14 Don't come on the day of **w**."
13:15 ox or donkey on the day of **w**?
13:16 to free her on the day of **w**?"
14:1 On a day of **w** Jesus went to
14:3 to heal on the day of **w** or not?
14:5 falls into a well on a day of **w**,
23:54 day of **w** was just beginning.
23:56 But on the day of **w** they rested
Jon 4:20 people must **w** in Jerusalem."
4:23 the true worshipers will **w**
4:23 for people like that to **w** him.
4:24 Those who **w** him must
4:24 who worship him must **w**
5:9 That happened on a day of **w**.
5:10 "This is a day of **w**.
Jon 5:16 healing people on the day of **w**.
5:18 the laws about the day of **w**,
7:22 a male on a day of **w**.
7:23 a male on the day of **w**
7:23 entirely well on the day of **w**?
9:14 the man sight was a day of **w**.
9:16 the traditions for the day of **w**."
12:20 those who came to **w** during
19:31 especially important day of **w**,
Act 7:7 that country and **w** me here.'
7:42 them and let them **w** the sun,
7:43 you made for yourselves to **w**.
8:27 come to Jerusalem to **w** was
13:14 On the day of **w** they went into
13:27 which are read every day of **w**.
13:42 subject the next day of **w**.
13:44 On the next day of **w**,
15:21 on every day of **w**."
16:13 On the day of **w** we went out of
17:2 three consecutive days of **w**,
17:23 closely at the objects you **w**,
17:23 about the unknown god you **w**.
18:4 On every day of **w**,
18:13 is persuading people to **w** God
19:27 and the rest of the world **w** will
24:11 to Jerusalem to **w** no more than
26:7 promise to be kept as they **w**
Rom 9:4 the true **w**, and the promises.
11:4 who have not knelt to **w** Baal."
12:1 This kind of **w** is appropriate
14:11 everyone will **w** me,
1Co 5:10 are dishonest, or **w** false gods.
5:11 sin, are greedy, **w** false gods,
6:9 who **w** false gods,
10:7 So don't **w** false gods as some
10:14 get as far away from the **w** of
12:2 every time you were led to **w**
14:25 touching the ground, **w** God,
Col 2:16 or weekly **w** days.
2:18 in ⌊false⌋ humility and the **w**
2:23 with their self-imposed **w**,
1Ti 1:17 **W** and glory belong forever to
4:13 on reading ⌊Scripture⌋ in **w**,
2Ti 2:22 together with those who **w**
Heb 1:6 "All of God's angels must **w**
4:9 Therefore, a time of rest and **w**
9:21 and on everything used in **w**.
10:1 make those who **w** perfect.
10:2 Those who **w** would have
Jas 2:2 men come to your **w** service.
1Pe 4:3 the forbidden **w** of false gods.
Rev 4:10 who sits on the throne and **w**
11:1 Count those who **w** there.
13:8 living on earth will **w** it,
13:12 earth and those living on it **w**
13:15 death whoever would not **w** it.
14:7 **W** the one who made heaven
14:11 day or night for those who **w**
15:4 the nations will come to **w** you
19:10 I bowed at his feet to **w** him.
19:10 **W** God, because the testimony
22:3 His servants will **w** him
22:8 I bowed to **w** at the feet of the
22:9 words in this book. **W** God!"

worshiped (74)

Gen 12:8 LORD there and **w** the LORD.
13:4 There Abram **w** the LORD.
21:33 at Beersheba and **w** the LORD,
26:25 an altar there and **w** the LORD.
Num 25:2 sacrifices and **w** these gods.
Dtr 4:3 everyone among you who **w**
6:14 worship any of the gods **w** by
29:26 They **w** other gods and bowed
32:16 because they **w** foreign gods
32:16 they **w** worthless idols.
32:17 gods your ancestors never **w**.
32:21 because they **w** foreign gods
32:21 they **w** worthless idols.
Jos 5:14 touching the ground and **w**.
Jdg 2:12 They **w** these gods,
2:17 were prostitutes and **w** them.
2:19 served, and **w** other gods.
7:15 interpretation, he **w** the LORD.
1Sm 1:19 and his family got up and **w**
1:28 And they **w** the LORD there.

1Sm 15:31 and Saul w the LORD.
2Sm 12:20 into the LORD's house and w.
15:32 Olives⌋ where people w God,
1Ki 9:9 They adopted other gods, w,
11:33 me and w Astarte (the goddess
16:31 Ahab then served and w Baal.
22:53 Ahaziah served Baal, w him,
2Ki 10:19 to destroy those who w Baal.)
17:7 They w other gods
17:16 army of heaven. They w Baal.
17:33 They w the LORD but also
17:41 These ⌊other⌋ nations w the
21:3 Manasseh, like Ahab, w and
21:21 his father in every way and w
21:21 to the idols his father had w.
2Ch 1:5 and the assembly w the LORD.
7:3 They w and praised the LORD,
7:22 They adopted other gods, w,
24:18 of their ancestors and w idols
29:30 praises, bowed down, and w.
32:19 by human hands and w by
33:3 Manasseh, like Ahab, w and
33:22 had made, and he w them.
Ezr 6:12 May the God whose name is w
Neh 8:6 to the ground and w the LORD.
9:3 confessed their sins and w
Job 1:20 he fell to the ground and w.
Psa 78:58 furious because they w idols.
106:19 They w an idol made of metal.
106:36 and they w their idols,
Jer 1:16 and w what their hands have
8:2 gone after, sought, and w.
16:11 w them, and abandoned me.
22:9 They w other gods and served
Dan 3:7 language bowed down and w
Hos 9:10 Peor and w shameful idols.
9:10 as the things they w.
Mat 2:11 they bowed down and w him.
Luk 2:37 the temple courtyard but w day
24:52 The disciples w him and were
Jon 4:20 Our ancestors w on this
Act 9:21 who destroyed those who w
10:25 bowed down, and w Peter.
2Th 2:4 god or anything that is w
Heb 11:21 the top of his staff and w God.
Rev 5:14 Then the leaders bowed and w.
7:11 touching the ground, w God,
11:16 immediately bowed, w God,
13:4 They w the serpent because it
13:4 They also w the beast and
16:2 of the beast and w its statue.
19:4 creatures bowed and w God,
19:20 of the beast and w its statue.
20:4 They had not w the beast or its

worshiper (2)

1Ki 18:3 was a devout w of the LORD.
Heb 9:9 give the w a clear conscience.

worshipers (13)

Lev 16:33 for the priests and all the w.
2Ki 10:21 All the w of Baal came,
10:22 the robes for all the w of Baal."
10:23 Baal and said to the w of Baal,
10:23 "Make sure that there are no w
10:23 Only the w of Baal should be
10:25 used swords to kill the Baal w
23:9 bread among the other w.
Psa 35:18 praise you in a crowd ⌊of w⌋.
Zep 3:10 the rivers of Sudan my w,
Jon 4:23 when the true w will worship
Act 9:21 to take these w as prisoners
Heb 10:2 could have made the w perfect,

worshiping (26)

Exo 10:26 have to use some of them for w
Num 25:3 Since the Israelites joined in w
25:5 the men who have joined in w
Dtr 17:3 by w and bowing down to other
Jos 22:25 descendants from w the LORD.
1Ki 12:28 He said, "You've been w in
12:30 W them became ⌊Israel's⌋ sin.
21:26 things as a result of w idols as
2Ki 17:32 people were w the LORD,
19:37 While he was w in the temple
21:11 Judah sin by ⌊w⌋ his idols.
2Ch 28:2 metal idols for w other gods —
Psa 106:28 They joined in w the god Baal
Isa 37:38 While he was w in the temple
Jer 11:10 other gods and w them.
Eze 8:16 east and w the rising sun.
Hos 13:1 they became guilty of w Baal,
Jon 4:21 you Samaritans won't be w
4:22 You don't know what you're w.
4:22 ⌊Jews⌋ know what we're w,
Act 13:2 While they were w the Lord
1Co 8:7 Some people are so used to w
12:2 you were w gods who couldn't
Eph 5:5 or greed (which means w
Col 3:5 is the same thing as w wealth).
Rev 9:20 they would have stopped w

worships (6)

Psa 97:7 Everyone who w idols and
Isa 66:3 is like someone who w an idol.
Mal 2:11 a woman who w a foreign god.
Act 2:39 It belongs to everyone who w
2Ti 2:19 and "Whoever w the Lord must
Rev 14:9 "Whoever w the beast or its

worst (3)

Exo 9:18 send the w hailstorm that has
9:24 This was the w storm in all the
Eze 8:17 me in the w possible way.

worth (18)

Gen 23:15 The land is w ten pounds of
Lev 27:16 of barley will be w 20 ounces
2Sm 18:3 But you're w 10,000 of us.
Est 5:13 Yet, all this is w nothing to me
7:4 is not w troubling you about,
Psa 119:72 from your mouth are w more
Pro 31:10 She is w far more than jewels.
Isa 2:22 How can they be w anything?
7:23 1,000 vines (w 1,000 pieces
40:23 earthly judges w nothing.
53:3 consider him to be w anything.
Lam 4:2 who are w their weight in fine
Mat 6:26 Aren't you w more than they?
10:31 You are w more than many
Mar 12:42 w less than a cent.
Luk 12:7 You are w more than many
12:24 You are w much more than
Act 19:19 were w 50,000 silver coins.

worthless (65)

Lev 19:4 "Don't turn to w gods or cast
26:1 "Never make w idols or set up
Dtr 13:13 LORD your God by w people.
15:9 not to think these w thoughts.
32:16 they worshiped w idols.
32:21 they worshiped w idols.
Jdg 9:4 Abimelech hired w and
11:3 W men gathered around
19:22 some w men from the city
20:13 Now hand over those w men in
1Sm 15:9 But everything that was w and
25:17 And he's such a w man that it's
25:25 You shouldn't take this w
30:22 Then every wicked and w man
2Sm 16:7 man! You w person!
23:6 "W people are like thorns.
1Ki 16:13 because of their w idols.
16:26 led Israel to sin with w idols,
2Ki 17:15 They went after w idols and
17:15 idols and became as w as
2Ch 13:7 W, good-for-nothing men
Job 13:4 All of you are w physicians.
13:12 recollections are w proverbs.
15:31 He shouldn't trust in w things
15:31 he will get w things in return.
24:25 show that my words are w?"
30:8 Godless fools and w people
Psa 60:11 human assistance is w.
108:12 human assistance is w.
119:37 my eyes away from w things.
Pro 10:20 hearts of wicked people are w.
16:27 A w person plots trouble,
19:28 A w witness mocks justice,
Isa 1:13 any more w grain offerings.
40:17 them less than nothing and w.
44:9 Their precious treasures are w.
Jer 2:5 They followed w idols and
2:5 and became w themselves.
10:3 The religion of the people is w.
10:15 They are w jokes.
14:14 Their predictions are w.
14:22 The w gods of the nations can't
15:19 worthwhile and not what is w,
16:19 w and unprofitable gods."
18:15 as an offering to w idols,
51:18 They are w jokes.
Eze 22:18 of Israel have become w to me.
22:19 All of you have become w.
Hos 8:8 nations. It has become w.
12:11 They are w. They sacrifice
Jnh 2:8 Those who hold on to w idols
Nah 1:14 your grave because you are w.
Hab 2:18 to make w idols that cannot
Luk 17:10 'We're w servants.
Act 14:15 you away from these w gods
Rom 1:28 because they thought it was w
4:14 useless and the promise is w.
Eph 4:17 Their minds are set on w
Php 3:7 I now consider w for Christ.
3:8 I consider everything else w
3:8 that I think of everything as w.
2Th 3:2 that we may be rescued from w
Heb 6:8 it is w and in danger of being
Jas 1:26 That person's religion is w.
1Pe 1:18 from the w life handed down

worthwhile (2)

Jer 15:19 If you will speak what is w
1Co 16:4 If I think it's w for me to go,

worthy (11)

Gen 32:10 I'm not w of all the love and
Est 1:19 who is more w than she.
Psa 106:2 for which he is w of praise?
Mat 3:11 I am not w to remove his
Mar 1:7 I am not w to bend down and
Luk 3:16 I am not w to untie his sandal
20:35 people who are considered w
Jon 1:27 I am not w to untie his sandal
Act 5:41 to have been considered w
2Th 1:5 considered w of his kingdom.
1:11 that our God will make you w

wound (15)

Exo 21:25 for a bruise, a w for a wound.
21:25 for a bruise, a wound for a w.
Dtr 32:39 I w, and I heal, and no one can
1Ki 22:35 The blood from the w had
Job 16:14 He inflicts w after wound on
16:14 inflicts wound after w on me.
Jer 10:19 My w is serious. Then I thought
15:18 unending and my w incurable,
30:12 Your w is incurable.
30:15 Why do you cry about your w,
Nah 3:19 Your w is fatal. All who hear the
Jon 11:44 Strips of cloth were w around
Rev 13:3 looked like it had a fatal w,
13:3 but its fatal w was healed.
13:12 whose fatal w was healed.

wounded (29)

1Sm 17:52 W Philistines lay on the road to
31:3 he was badly w by them.
2Sm 1:10 survive after he had been w.
1Ki 20:37 punched him hard and w him.
22:34 these troops. I'm badly w."
2Ki 8:28 There the Arameans w Joram.
8:29 (He had been w by the
1Ch 10:3 he was w by them.
2Ch 18:33 these troops. I'm badly w."
22:5 There the Arameans w Joram.
22:6 (He had been w by the
35:23 away because I'm badly w."
Job 24:12 W people cry for help,
34:6 I've been w by a deadly arrow,
Psa 18:38 I w them so badly that they
69:26 the pain of those you have w.
Sos 5:7 They w me! Those watchmen
Isa 53:4 thought that God had w him,
53:5 He was w for our rebellious
Jer 6:7 I see that it is sick and w.
10:19 Oh, I'm w! My wound is serious.

Jer 37:10 only a few badly **w** men left
51:4 soldiers will fall down badly **w**
51:52 and those who are **w** will moan
Lam 2:12 as they faint like **w** people
Eze 26:15 people are **w** and slaughtered.
Hos 6:1 Even though he has **w** us,
Act 19:16 out of that house naked and **w**.
Rev 13:14 for the beast who was **w** by

wounding (1)

Gen 4:23 a young man for **w** me.

wounds (24)

2Ki 8:29 to Jezreel to let his **w** heal.
9:15 to Jezreel to recover from the **w**
2Ch 22:6 to Jezreel to let his **w** heal.
24:25 left him suffering from many **w**.
Psa 38:5 My **w** smell rotten.
147:3 the one who bandages their **w**.
Pro 23:29 Who has **w** for no reason?
27:6 **W** made by a friend are
Isa 1:6 bruises, sores, and fresh **w**.
30:26 and heal the **w** he inflicted.
53:5 received healing from his **w**.
Jer 6:14 They treat my people's **w** as
8:11 They treat my dear people's **w**
30:17 and heal your **w**," declares
49:17 horrified and hiss at all its **w**.
50:13 horrified and hiss at all its **w**.
Lam 2:13 Your **w** are as deep as the sea.
Hos 5:13 when Judah saw his own **w**,
5:13 cure them or heal their **w**.
6:1 he will bandage our **w**.
Mic 1:9 Samaria's **w** are incurable.
Luk 10:34 cleaned and bandaged his **w**.
Act 16:33 washed Paul and Silas' **w**.
1Pe 2:24 His **w** have healed you.

wove (1)

Exo 39:27 They **w** inner robes out of fine

woven (11)

Exo 28:4 another specially **w** linen robe,
28:39 "Make the specially **w** inner
39:22 **w** entirely of violet yarn.
Lev 13:48 that is **w** or knitted from linen or
13:58 the area disappears from the **w**
13:59 mildew in clothing that is **w**
Dtr 22:11 of wool and linen **w** together.
Psa 139:15 when I was being skillfully **w**
Eze 27:16 richly **w** cloth, linen, coral,
27:24 rugs with **w** and twisted cords.
Jon 19:23 a seam because it had been **w**

wrap (2)

Isa 22:18 He will **w** you up tightly like a
Eze 5:3 and **w** them in the hem of your

wrapped (19)

Gen 44:30 "Our father's life is **w** up with
Exo 12:34 **w** up in their clothes.
1Sm 21:9 It is **w** in a cloth behind the
25:29 your life is **w** in the bundle of
1Ki 19:13 he **w** his face in his coat,
Job 38:9 I clothed it with clouds and **w**
Psa 109:29 Let them be **w** in their shame
Pro 30:4 Who has **w** water in a garment?
Isa 61:10 He has **w** me in the robe of
Eze 16:4 rubbed with salt or **w** in cloth.
Jnh 2:5 was **w** around my head.
Mat 27:59 Joseph took the body and **w** it
Mar 15:46 down from the cross and **w**
Luk 2:7 She **w** him in strips of cloth
2:12 You will find an infant **w** in
23:53 from the cross, he **w** it in linen.
Jon 11:44 and his face was **w** with a
Act 5:6 **w** his body in a sheet,
8:23 bitter with jealousy and **w** up

wraps (1)

Isa 59:17 He **w** himself with fury as a

wrath (8)

Job 20:23 and makes his **w** come down
21:20 from the **w** of the Almighty.
36:33 storm announces his angry **w**.
Psa 38:1 me or discipline me in your **w**.
Isa 59:18 pay back his opponents with **w**
63:3 In my **w** I stomped on them.
63:6 In my **w** I made them drunk and
Jer 32:37 my anger, fury, and terrifying **w**.

wreaths (1)

Act 14:13 flowery **w** around their necks

wreck (1)

Jer 31:28 and to **w**, ruin, and hurt them.

wrecked (8)

1Ki 22:48 ships were **w** at Ezion Geber.
2Ch 20:37 So the ships were **w** and
Eze 6:6 the worship sites will be **w**.
27:26 and an east wind **w** you in the
27:27 the sea when your ship was **w**.
27:34 Now you are **w** in the sea,
Dan 8:11 from him and **w** his holy place.
1Ti 1:19 been destroyed like a **w** ship.

wrenched (1)

Eze 29:7 and they **w** their backs.

wrestled (2)

Gen 32:24 Then a man **w** with him until
32:25 it was dislocated as they **w**.

wrestling (2)

Eph 6:12 This is not a **w** match against
6:12 We are **w** with rulers,

wrinkle (1)

Eph 5:27 without any kind of stain or **w**

wrist (3)

Gen 38:28 yarn, tied it on his **w**, and said,
Dtr 6:8 and⌋ tie them around your **w**,
11:18 tie them around your **w**,

wrists (5)

Gen 24:30 the bracelets on his sister's **w**
24:47 and the bracelets on her **w**.
Eze 13:18 magic charms for people's **w**
16:11 I put bracelets on your **w** and a
23:42 put bracelets on the women's **w**

write (83)

Exo 17:14 "**W** this reminder on a scroll,
34:1 and I will **w** on them the words
34:27 "**W** down these words,
Num 5:23 "The priest will **w** these curses
17:2 **W** each man's name on his
17:3 **W** Aaron's name on the staff for
Dtr 6:8 ⌊**W** them down, and⌋ tie them
6:9 **W** them on the doorframes of
10:2 I will **w** on the tablets the same
11:18 ⌊**W** them down,⌋ tie them
11:20 **W** them on the doorframes of
27:3 After you're in that land, **w** all
27:8 **W** clearly and carefully all the
31:19 "**W** down this song,
Jos 18:4 will survey the land and **w**
18:8 Joshua ordered them to **w** a
18:8 **W** a description of it,
Est 8:8 You **w** what you think is best
Job 13:26 You **w** down bitter accusations
31:35 Let the prosecutor **w** ⌊his
Pro 3:3 **W** them on the tablet of your
7:3 **W** them on the tablet of your
22:20 Didn't I **w** to you previously
Isa 8:1 and **w** on it with a pen:
30:8 **w** this on a tablet for them,
44:5 Another will **w** on his hand,
Jer 22:30 **W** this about Jehoiakin:
30:2 **W** in a book everything that I
31:33 and I will **w** those teachings on
36:2 "Take a scroll, and **w** on it
36:28 "Take another scroll, and **w** on
36:29 "Why did you **w** that the king of
Eze 24:2 **w** down today's date.
37:16 take a stick and **w** on it:
37:16 take another stick and **w** on it,
43:11 Then **w** these things down for
Dan 4:2 I am pleased to **w** to you about
Dan 5:24 the hand to **w** this inscription.
Amo 6:5 Like David, they **w** all kinds of
Hab 2:2 answered me, "**W** the vision.
Luk 1:1 Many have attempted to **w**
1:3 it would be a good idea to **w**
16:6 down, and **w** "four hundred!'"
16:7 and **w** "eight hundred!'"
Jon 8:6 his finger to **w** on the ground.
19:21 people told Pilate, "Don't **w**,
19:21 Instead, **w**, 'He said that he is
Act 9:2 and asked him to **w** letters of
15:20 Instead, we should **w** a letter
25:26 reliable to **w** our emperor about
25:26 Then I'll have something to **w**
1Co 14:37 acknowledge that what I **w**
14:38 what I **w** should be ignored.
2Co 2:4 I didn't **w** to make you
7:12 I didn't **w** because of the man
9:1 I don't need to **w** anything
Php 3:1 It's no trouble for me to **w** the
1Th 4:9 You don't need anyone to **w** to
5:1 you don't need anyone to **w** to
Phm 1:21 I am confident as I **w** to you
Heb 8:10 and I will **w** those teachings on
10:16 in their hearts and **w** them
2Jn 1:12 I have a lot to **w** to you.
1:12 I would prefer not to **w** a letter.
3Jn 1:13 I have a lot to **w** to you.
1:13 However, I would rather not **w**.
Jud 1:3 friends, I had intended to **w**
1:3 It demands that I **w** to you and
Rev 1:11 "**W** on a scroll what you see,
1:19 **w** down what you have seen,
2:1 of the church in Ephesus, **w**:
2:8 **w**: The first and the last,
2:12 of the church in Pergamum, **w**:
2:18 Thyatira, **w**: The Son of God,
3:1 of the church in Sardis, **w**:
3:7 **w**: The one who is holy,
3:12 I will **w** on them the name of
3:14 in Laodicea, **w**: The amen,
10:4 I was going to **w** it down.
10:4 and don't **w** it down."
14:13 from heaven saying, "**W** this:
19:9 the angel said to me, "**W** this:
21:5 He said, "**W** this: 'These words

writer (1)

Psa 45:1 tongue is a pen for a skillful **w**.

writes (2)

Dtr 24:1 you must do if a husband **w** out
Rom 10:5 Moses **w** about receiving

writhe (5)

Isa 13:8 They'll **w** like a woman giving
26:17 They **w** and cry out in their
Jer 4:19 I **w** in pain. My heart is beating
Mic 4:10 Daughter of Zion, **w** in pain and
Hab 3:10 They **w** in pain. Floodwaters

writhed (1)

Isa 26:18 We were pregnant; we **w** with

writhes (1)

Jer 51:29 earth trembles and **w** in pain.

writing (40)

Exo 32:16 and the **w** was God's writing
32:16 and the writing was God's **w**
Dtr 31:24 Finally, Moses finished **w** all
2Ch 36:22 kingdom and then to put it in **w**.
Ezr 1:1 kingdom and then to put it in **w**.
Neh 9:38 agreement ⌊and putting it⌋ in **w**
Ecc 12:12 People never stop **w** books.
Isa 8:1 "Take a large **w** tablet,
Eze 2:10 There was **w** on the front and
Dan 5:7 "Whoever reads this **w** and
5:8 but they couldn't read the **w** or
5:15 brought to me to read this **w**
5:16 If you can read the **w** and tell
5:17 I'll still read the **w** for you and
Luk 1:63 Zechariah asked for a **w** tablet
Jon 8:8 and continued **w** on the ground.
Rom 2:27 have Moses' Teachings in **w**.
1Co 4:14 I'm not **w** this to make you feel

1Co 16:21 I, Paul, am **w** this greeting with
2Co 1:13 We are only **w** you what you
13:10 That's why I'm **w** this letter
Gal 1:20 witness that what I'm **w** is not
6:11 are because I'm **w** this myself.
Col 4:18 I, Paul, am **w** this greeting with
2Th 3:17 I, Paul, am **w** this greeting with
1Ti 3:14 However, I'm **w** this to you
Phm 1:19 I'm **w** this with my own hand.
2Pe 3:1 the second letter I'm **w** to you.
1Jn 1:4 We are **w** this so that we can
2:1 My dear children, I'm **w** this to
2:7 it's not as though I'm **w** to give
2:8 On the other hand, I'm **w** to
2:12 I'm **w** to you, dear children,
2:13 I'm **w** to you, fathers,
2:13 I'm **w** to you, young people,
2:21 I'm **w** to you because you
2:26 I'm **w** to you about those who
2Jn 1:5 It's not as though I'm **w** to give
Jud 1:4 ago they were condemned in **w**
Rev 5:1 It had **w** both on the inside and

writings (1)

Dan 10:21 what is inscribed in the true **w**.

written (227)

Gen 5:1 This is the **w** account of Adam
Exo 24:12 the commandments I have **w**
32:15 They were **w** on both sides,
32:32 out of the book you have **w**."
Dtr 9:10 On them were **w** all the words
28:58 of the teachings that are **w**
28:61 of sickness and plague not **w**
29:21 the conditions of the promise **w**
30:10 commands and laws that are **w**
Jos 1:8 do everything **w** in them.
8:32 which Moses had **w** down.
8:34 all been **w** down by Moses.
23:6 to keep and to do everything **w**
1Ki 2:3 and **w** instructions as they are
11:41 he did — and his wisdom **w**
14:19 and his reign is **w** in the official
14:29 everything he did — **w**
15:7 — everything he did — **w**
15:23 and the cities he fortified — **w** in
15:31 — everything he did — **w**
16:5 he did and his heroic acts — **w**
16:14 Elah — everything he did — **w**
16:20 else about Zimri and his plot **w**
16:27 he did and his heroic acts — **w**
21:11 They did just as she had **w** in
22:39 all the cities he fortified — **w**
22:45 and ⌊the wars⌋ he fought — **w**
2Ki 1:18 — the things he did — **w**
8:23 everything he did — **w**
10:34 all his heroic acts — **w** in the
12:19 Joash — everything he did — **w**
13:8 his heroic acts — **w** in the
13:12 King Amaziah of Judah — **w**
14:6 the LORD's command **w**
14:15 King Amaziah of Judah — **w**
14:18 else about Amaziah **w**
14:28 and Hamath for Israel — **w**
15:6 — everything he did — **w**
15:11 else about Zechariah is **w**
15:15 all about his conspiracy — is **w**
15:21 everything he did — **w**
15:26 everything he did — is **w**
15:31 everything he did — is **w**
15:36 — everything he did — **w**
16:19 Ahaz — the things he did — **w**
20:20 **w** in the official records of the
21:17 the sins he committed — **w** in
21:25 Amon — the things he did — **w**
22:13 or do everything **w** ⌊in it⌋."
22:16 here according to everything **w**
23:2 Josiah read everything **w** in the
23:3 the terms of the promise **w**
23:21 the LORD their God as it is **w**
23:24 the words of the Teachings **w**
23:28 Josiah — everything he did — **w**
24:5 everything he did — **w**
1Ch 16:40 as **w** in the LORD's Teachings
28:19 ⌊David said,⌋ "All this was **w**
29:29 David from first to last is **w**
2Ch 9:29 acts from first to last **w**
12:15 Rehoboam from first to last **w**
13:22 lived and what he said — is **w**
16:11 about Asa from first to last is **w**
20:34 from first to last is **w**
23:18 offerings to the LORD as it is **w**
25:4 the LORD's command **w**
25:26 **w** in the Book of the Kings of
27:7 all his wars and his life — is **w**
28:26 from beginning to end — is **w**
30:5 as the **w** instructions said they
30:18 but not in the way the **w**
31:3 as it is **w** in the LORD's
32:32 is **w** in the vision of the prophet
33:19 and how God accepted it are **w**
33:19 himself are also **w** there.
34:14 Teachings **w** by Moses.
34:21 everything **w** in this book."
34:24 here according to the curses **w**
34:30 He read everything **w** in the
34:31 of the promise **w** in this book.
35:12 present them to the LORD as **w**
35:25 They are **w** in ⌊the Book of⌋
35:26 to God by following what is **w**
35:27 acts from first to last — are **w**
36:8 the charges against him — is **w**
Ezr 3:2 ⌊followed the directions⌋ **w**
3:4 Following the **w** directions,
4:7 The letter was **w** with the
6:2 of Media. This was **w** on it:
6:18 by following the directions **w**
Neh 6:6 In it was **w**: It has been
7:5 I found the following **w** in it:
8:14 They found **w** in the Teachings
8:15 to make booths as it is **w**."
Est 2:23 The matter was **w** up in the
3:9 for their destruction be **w**.
3:12 All Haman's orders were **w** to
8:8 because whatever is **w** in the
8:9 Mordecai had ordered was **w**
8:9 It was **w** to each province in its
9:23 as Mordecai had **w** to them.
9:32 and they are **w** in a book.
Job 19:23 "I wish now my words were **w**.
Psa 25:10 his promise and **w** instructions.
40:7 (It is **w** about me in the scroll of
78:5 He established **w** instructions
78:56 They did not obey his **w**
93:5 Your **w** testimonies are
99:7 They obeyed his **w**
102:18 This will be **w** down for a
119:2 who obey his **w** instructions.
119:14 your **w** instructions more than
119:22 obeyed your **w** instructions.
119:24 Indeed, your **w** instructions
119:31 tightly to your **w** instructions.
119:36 Direct my heart toward your **w**
119:46 I will speak about your **w**
119:59 back to your **w** instructions.
119:79 to know your **w** instructions.
119:88 I may obey the **w** instructions.
119:95 understand your **w** instructions.
119:99 because your **w** instructions
119:111 Your **w** instructions are mine
119:119 That is why I love your **w**
119:125 to know your **w** instructions.
119:129 Your **w** instructions are
119:138 issued your **w** instructions.
119:144 Your **w** instructions are always
119:146 so that I can obey your **w**
119:152 Long ago I learned from your **w**
119:157 away from your **w** instructions.
119:167 obeyed your **w** instructions.
119:168 and your **w** instructions,
132:12 and my **w** instructions that
149:9 that is **w** against them.
Isa 8:16 Tie up the **w** instructions.
8:20 and to the **w** instructions.
29:18 the deaf will hear the words **w**
65:6 It is **w** in front of me.
Jer 17:1 "Judah's sin is **w** with an iron
17:13 from you will be **w** in dust,
25:13 everything **w** in this book.
36:27 up the scroll that Baruch had **w**
36:28 on it everything that was **w**
44:23 decrees, or **w** instructions.
Jer 51:60 have been **w** about Babylon.
Eze 2:10 and horrible things **w** on it.
Dan 5:25 This is what has been **w**:
6:9 So Darius signed the **w** decree.
9:11 the curses **w** in the Teachings
9:13 exactly as it was **w** in Moses'
12:1 everyone **w** in the book,
Hos 8:12 I have **w** many things for them
Zec 14:20 "Holy to the LORD" will be **w**
Mal 3:16 A book was **w** in his presence
Mat 5:31 wife must give her a **w** notice.'
19:7 man to give his wife a **w** notice
26:56 have **w** would come true."
27:37 They placed a **w** accusation
Mar 9:12 But in what sense was it **w**
10:4 man to give his wife a **w** notice
15:26 There was a **w** notice of the
Luk 2:23 They did exactly what was **w**
10:20 your names are **w** in heaven."
10:26 "What is **w** in Moses'
21:22 Everything that is **w** about it
22:37 Indeed, whatever is **w** about
23:38 A **w** notice was placed above
24:44 I told you that everything **w**
Jon 12:16 had been **w** about him.
15:25 In this way what is **w** in their
19:20 The notice was **w** in Hebrew,
19:22 "I have **w** what I've written."
19:22 "I have written what I've **w**."
20:30 miracles are not **w** in this book.
20:31 have been **w** so that you
21:25 one of them were **w** down,
21:25 for the books that would be **w**.
Act 7:42 This is **w** in the book of the
13:29 that was **w** about him,
17:23 an altar with this **w** on it:
21:25 have **w** non-Jewish believers
24:14 God and believe everything **w**
Rom 2:15 in Moses' Teachings are **w**
2:29 is spiritual, not just a **w** rule.
4:23 of him" were **w** not only
7:6 not in an old way dictated by **w**
15:4 Everything **w** long ago was
15:4 written long ago was **w**
15:15 However, I've **w** you a letter,
1Co 4:6 beyond what is **w** in Scripture.
9:10 This was **w** for our benefit so
9:15 and I haven't **w** this in order to
10:11 These things were **w** down as
2Co 2:9 I had also **w** to you to test you.
3:2 our letter of recommendation **w**
3:3 **w** as a result of our ministry.
3:3 You are a letter **w** not with ink
3:3 a letter **w** not on tablets of
3:6 spiritual promise, not a **w** one.
3:6 what was **w** brings death,
4:13 The following is **w**,
Gal 3:10 obey everything that is **w**
Eph 3:3 I've already **w** to you about this
Col 2:14 us by the **w** laws God had
Heb 9:4 on which the promise was **w**.
10:7 (It is **w** about me in the scroll of
12:23 names are **w** in heaven).
13:22 I have **w** you a short letter.
1Pe 5:12 I've **w** this short letter to you
5:12 I've **w** to encourage you and to
1Jn 2:14 I've **w** to you, children,
2:14 I've **w** to you, fathers,
2:14 I've **w** to you, young people,
5:13 I've **w** this to those who
Rev 1:3 and pay attention to what is **w**
2:17 stone with a new name **w** on it,
13:8 everyone whose name is not **w**
14:1 name **w** on their foreheads.
17:5 A name was **w** on her forehead.
17:8 whose names were not **w** in
19:12 He has a name **w** on him,
19:16 and his thigh he has a name **w**:
21:12 of Israel were **w** on the gates.
21:14 of the lamb were **w** on them.
21:27 those whose names are **w**
22:18 plagues that are **w** in this book.

wrong (183)

Exo 9:27 and my people and I are **w**.
23:2 follow a crowd in doing **w**.

Exo 28:38 for anything done **w** when
34:9 forgive our sin and the **w** we
Lev 4:2 does something **w** — even one
4:3 priest does something **w**
4:13 does something **w**,
4:14 When the **w** they have done
4:22 does something **w** — even one
4:23 told about what he has done **w**,
4:26 for what the leader did **w**,
4:27 does something **w** — even one
4:28 told about what he has done **w**,
4:28 for what he has done **w**.
4:35 for what that person did **w**,
5:6 the LORD for what you did **w**.
5:10 the LORD for what you did **w**.
5:13 the LORD for what you did **w**,
5:15 doing something **w**
5:16 the LORD for what you did **w**,
5:17 "If any of you do **w** — even one
5:18 the **w** you did unintentionally
16:21 the things the Israelites did **w**.
Num 5:6 If you do something **w** to
5:7 pay in full for what you did **w**,
5:8 the payment for what you did **w**
5:31 isn't guilty of doing anything **w**,
15:22 do something **w** by not obeying
15:27 does something **w**,
15:29 something **w** unintentionally,
15:30 does something **w** insults
Dtr 17:1 defect or anything seriously **w**
25:1 who's right and who's **w**.
25:2 If the person who's in the **w**
27:18 people in the **w** direction will
32:4 a faithful God, who does no **w**.
Jdg 11:27 But you have done **w** by
1Sm 8:6 But Samuel considered it **w** for
25:24 be held responsible for this **w**.
25:39 and kept me from doing **w**.
29:3 I've found nothing **w** with him
29:6 I've never found anything **w**
2Sm 13:16 me away is a greater **w** than
14:17 able to distinguish right from **w**.
24:17 I've done **w**. What have these
1Ki 1:52 But if he does ⌊anything⌋ **w**,
8:47 We have done **w**. We have
18:9 "What have I done **w** to make
2Ki 5:21 "Is something **w**?"
18:14 at Lachish: "I have done **w**.
1Ch 21:17 the one who sinned and did **w**.
2Ch 6:37 We have done **w**. We have
Neh 1:7 We have done you a great **w**.
5:9 "What you're doing is **w**.
Est 1:16 "Queen Vashti has done **w**,
Job 1:22 God for doing anything **w**.
6:24 Show me where I've been **w**.
6:30 between right and **w**?
27:4 lips will not say anything **w**,
31:3 disasters for those who do **w**?
32:3 made it look as if God were **w**.
33:17 to turn away from doing ⌊**w**⌋
33:27 'I sinned and did **w** instead of
34:32 If I've done **w**, I won't do it
36:9 tells them what they've done **w**
36:10 them to turn away from **w**.
36:23 can say to him, 'You did **w**'?
Psa 17:3 but you found nothing **w**.
36:4 chooses to go the **w** direction.
45:7 is right and hated what is **w**.
51:9 wipe out all that I have done **w**.
56:7 With the **w** they do,
103:9 will not always accuse us of **w**
106:6 We have done **w**. We are guilty.
119:3 They do nothing **w**.
125:3 do not use their power to do **w**.
Pro 3:29 Do not plan to do something **w**
4:16 cannot sleep unless they do **w**,
6:18 feet that are quick to do **w**,
10:12 but love covers every **w**.
15:22 Without advice plans go **w**,
16:10 he cannot voice a **w** judgment.
28:24 mother and says, "It isn't **w**!"
29:22 and a hothead does much **w**.
30:20 "I haven't done anything **w**!"
Ecc 2:17 under the sun seemed **w** to me.
10:2 The heart of a fool leads the **w**
Isa 22:14 this **w** will not be forgiven even
Isa 26:10 They do what is **w** in the
29:20 All who look for ways to do **w**
56:2 hands from doing anything **w**.
65:2 chose to go the **w** direction.
Jer 2:5 What did your ancestors find **w**
2:13 have done two things **w**.
3:13 Admit that you've done **w**!
4:22 They are experts in doing **w**,
9:5 wear themselves out doing **w**.
13:23 when you're taught to do **w**?
16:10 What have we done **w**?
18:8 turns away from doing **w**.
23:10 strength to do the **w** things.
38:9 to the prophet Jeremiah is **w**.
Lam 3:59 Look at the **w** that has been
Eze 3:20 living the right way and do **w**,
16:49 your sister Sodom has done **w**.
18:18 and done what is **w** among his
20:38 those who do **w** against me.
20:43 by every **w** thing that you
21:24 are because you openly do **w**.
22:29 They do **w** to humble people
29:16 how **w** they were whenever
39:23 captivity because they did **w**
45:20 does something **w**
Dan 6:4 they couldn't find anything **w**
9:5 We have sinned, done **w**,
Zep 3:5 He does no **w**. He brings his
3:13 few in Israel will not do **w**,
Mal 1:8 to sacrifice, isn't that **w**?
1:8 or a sick animal, isn't that **w**?
Mat 12:10 him of doing something **w**.
18:15 a believer does something **w**,
22:15 Jesus into saying the **w** thing.
27:23 What has he done **w**?"
Mar 3:2 him of doing something **w**.
12:13 him into saying the **w** thing.
15:14 What has he done **w**?"
Luk 6:7 him of doing something **w**.
20:20 him saying the **w** thing so that
20:26 make him say anything **w**
21:15 be able to oppose or prove **w**.
23:22 What has he done **w**?
23:41 man hasn't done anything **w**."
Jon 3:20 People who do what is **w** hate
18:23 "If I've said anything **w**,
Act 1:18 money he received from the **w**
10:28 "You understand how **w** it is for
18:28 and that the Jews were **w**.
23:9 "We don't find anything **w** with
25:5 man has done something **w**."
25:10 I haven't done anything **w** to
25:11 and have done something **w**
Rom 2:8 truth and who follow what is **w**.
2:18 and distinguish right from **w**
3:5 But if what we do **w** shows
7:7 "Never have **w** desires."
7:8 me have all kinds of **w** desires.
13:3 But people who do what is **w**
13:4 But if you do what is **w**,
13:4 anyone who does what is **w**.
13:9 never have **w** desires,"
14:20 food is acceptable, but it's **w**
1Co 6:8 Instead, you do **w** and cheat,
7:36 to do the **w** thing when his
14:24 show them where they are **w**
14:29 each person said is right or **w**.
2Co 6:8 is right to attack what is **w**
6:14 Can right and **w** be partners?
7:11 You were disgusted with the **w**
7:11 You were ready to punish the **w**
7:12 of the man who did the **w**
12:13 Forgive me for this **w**!
13:7 that you won't do anything **w**.
Gal 2:11 because he was completely **w**.
2:18 I admit that I was **w** to tear it
4:12 You didn't do anything **w** to me.
6:1 person turn away from doing **w**.
Col 3:25 The person who does **w** will
3:25 will be paid back for the **w**
1Th 5:15 no one ever pays back one **w**
5:15 one wrong with another **w**.
1Ti 6:14 blamed for doing anything **w**.
2Ti 2:19 the Lord must give up doing **w**."
2:24 He must be willing to suffer **w**.
Heb 1:9 is right and hated what is **w**.
Heb 8:7 If nothing had been **w** with the
8:8 But God found something **w**
9:7 people did **w** unintentionally.
Jas 4:3 want them for the **w** reason —
1Pe 2:12 were doing **w** while they are
2:14 sent to punish those who do **w**
2:20 beating for doing something **w**?
3:17 for doing good than for doing **w**.
1Jn 1:9 from everything we've done **w**.

wrongdoing (22)

Exo 34:7 forgiving **w**, disobedience,
Num 14:18 He forgives **w** and
15:25 the **w** was unintentional
15:26 involved in the unintentional **w**.
Job 5:16 hope while **w** shuts its mouth.
22:5 Is there no end to your **w**?
22:23 If you put **w** out of your tent,
Psa 10:7 Trouble and **w** are on the tip of
Pro 4:17 eat food obtained through **w**
14:32 is thrown down by his own **w**,
16:12 **W** is disgusting to kings
Isa 13:11 evil and the wicked for their **w**.
61:8 I hate robbery and **w**.
Eze 7:10 **W** has blossomed.
9:9 and the city is filled with **w**.
Mic 7:19 You will overcome our **w**.
Hab 1:3 Why do you make me see **w**?
Gal 3:19 added to identify what **w** is.
6:1 if a person gets trapped by **w**,
2Pe 2:13 lose what their **w** earned them.
2:15 loved what his **w** earned him.
1Jn 5:17 Every kind of **w** is sin,

wrongdoings (4)

Isa 27:9 In this way the **w** of the
43:24 and troubled me with your **w**.
53:10 his life a sacrifice for our **w**,
59:12 are with us. We know our **w**.

wronged (4)

Num 5:7 it to the person who was **w**.
Job 19:6 to know that God has **w** me
1Co 6:7 the fact that you have been **w**?
Phm 1:18 If he **w** you in any way or owes

wrongs (12)

1Ki 8:50 ⌊Forgive⌋ all their **w** when
Job 35:6 If you've done many **w**,
Psa 103:10 sins or paid us back for our **w**.
Pro 5:22 will be trapped by his own **w**,
Isa 40:2 over and its **w** have been paid
59:2 But your **w** have separated you
Jer 14:20 and the **w** done by our
Dan 9:13 your favor by turning from our **w**
9:24 to stop sin, to forgive **w**,
Mat 18:21 forgive a believer who **w** me?
Luk 17:4 Even if he **w** you seven times
1Co 13:5 It doesn't keep track of **w**.

wrote (75)

Exo 24:4 So Moses **w** down all the
34:28 He **w** on the tablets the words
Num 33:2 command Moses **w** down
Dtr 4:13 Then he **w** them on two stone
5:22 He **w** the commandments on
10:4 The LORD **w** on these tablets
31:9 Moses **w** down these
31:22 That day Moses **w** down this
Jos 8:32 of the people of Israel he **w**
24:26 Joshua **w** these things in the
Jdg 8:14 and the young man **w** down for
1Sm 10:25 He **w** the laws on a scroll,
2Sm 1:17 David **w** this song of mourning
11:14 In the morning David **w** a letter
11:15 In the letter he **w**, "Put Uriah on
1Ki 4:32 proverbs and **w** 1,005 songs.
21:8 So Jezebel **w** letters,
21:9 In these letters she **w**:
2Ki 10:1 So Jehu **w** letters to the
10:6 So he **w** them a second letter.
17:37 commands that he **w** for you:
2Ch 30:1 Israel and Judah and **w** letters
32:17 Sennacherib **w** letters cursing
Ezr 4:6 of Judah and Jerusalem **w**
4:7 and the rest of their group **w** to

Ezr 4:8 scribe **w** another letter against
Est 3:12 They **w** to each province in its
8:10 Mordecai **w** in King Xerxes'
8:10 bred for speed. ⌊He **w**⌋
9:20 Now, Mordecai **w** these things
9:29 Esther and Mordecai the Jew **w**
Ecc 12:10 He **w** the words of truth very
Isa 38:9 King Hezekiah of Judah **w** this
Jer 36:4 and Baruch **w** it all down on a
36:6 LORD's message that you **w** as
36:17 tell us how you **w** all this.
36:18 and I **w** it on the scroll in ink."
36:32 Jeremiah dictated, Baruch **w**
45:1 Baruch **w** these things on a
51:60 Jeremiah **w** on a scroll all the
51:60 He **w** all these things that have
Dan 5:5 person's hand appeared and **w**
5:5 king watched as the hand **w**.
6:25 Then King Darius **w** to the
7:1 He **w** down the main parts of
Mat 2:5 The prophet **w** about this:
Mar 1:2 The prophet Isaiah **w**,
10:5 Jesus said to them, "He **w** this
12:19 "Teacher, Moses **w** for us,
Luk 1:63 for a writing tablet and **w**,
3:4 As the prophet Isaiah **w** in his
18:31 Everything that the prophets **w**
20:28 "Teacher, Moses **w** for us,
Jon 1:45 the man whom Moses **w** about
1:45 whom the prophets **w** about.
5:46 Moses **w** about me.
5:47 don't believe what Moses **w**,
6:45 The prophets **w**, 'God will
19:19 Pilate **w** a notice and put it on
21:24 these things and **w** them down.
Act 1:1 first book, Theophilus, I **w** about
15:23 They **w** this letter for them to
18:27 They **w** to the disciples in
23:25 The officer **w** a letter to the
Rom 16:22 I, Tertius, who **w** this letter,
16:26 that what the prophets **w** must
1Co 7:1 the things that you **w** about:
2Co 2:3 is the very reason I **w** to you.
2:4 in my eyes when I **w** to you.
7:12 So, when I **w** to you,
7:12 Rather, I **w** because I wanted
10:11 do the things that we **w** about
2Th 3:17 this is proof that I **w** it.
2Pe 3:15 is what our dear brother Paul **w**
3Jn 1:9 I **w** a letter to the congregation.

wrought (1)

Eze 27:19 They exchanged **w** iron,

X

Xerxes (27)

Ezr 4:6 When **X** began to rule,
Est 1:1 In the days of **X** the following
1:1 This was the same **X** who
1:2 At the time when King **X** sat on
1:9 at the royal palace of King **X**.
1:10 who served under King **X**,
1:16 in every province of King **X**.
1:17 They will say, 'King **X** ordered
1:19 again appear in front of King **X**.
2:1 Later, when King **X** got over his
2:12 to go to King **X** after she had
2:16 So Esther was taken to King **X**
2:21 and planned to kill King **X**.
3:1 Later, King **X** promoted Haman.
3:6 in the entire kingdom of **X**.
3:8 Now, Haman told King **X**,
3:12 signed in the name of King **X**
6:2 a rebellion against King **X**.
7:5 Then King **X** interrupted Queen
8:1 On that same day King **X** gave
8:7 King **X** said to Queen Esther
8:12 in all the provinces of King **X**,
9:2 all the provinces of King **X**
9:20 in all the provinces of King **X**,
9:30 provinces of the kingdom of **X**.
10:1 King **X** levied a tax on the
Est 10:3 ranked second only to King **X**.

Xerxes' (4)

Est 1:15 obey King **X** command, which
3:7 In **X** twelfth year as king,
8:10 Mordecai wrote in King **X** name
Dan 9:1 **X** son Darius, who was a Mede

Y

yards (4)

Exo 8:13 in the **y**, and in the fields.
1Sm 14:14 men within about a hundred **y**.
Mat 14:24 now hundreds of **y** from shore,
Jon 21:8 the shore, only about 100 **y**.

yarn (57)

Gen 38:28 midwife took a piece of red **y**,
38:30 brother was born with the red **y**
Exo 25:4 violet, purple, and bright red **y**,
26:1 sheets made from fine linen **y**.
26:1 violet, purple, and bright red **y**,
26:31 violet, purple, and bright red **y**.
26:31 angel design into fine linen **y**.
26:36 a screen out of fine linen **y**,
26:36 violet, purple, and bright red **y**.
27:9 made out of fine linen **y**,
27:16 screen made from fine linen **y**,
27:16 violet, purple, and bright red **y**,
27:18 ⌊curtains⌋ made of fine linen **y**
28:5 and bright red **y**, and fine linen.
28:6 the ephod out of fine linen **y**.
28:6 and bright red **y** into the fabric.
28:15 and bright red **y** and out of fine
28:15 red yarn and out of fine linen **y**.
28:33 and bright red **y** with gold bells
28:39 be embroidered with colored **y**.
35:6 violet, purple, and bright red **y**,
35:23 or bright red **y**, fine linen,
35:25 in spinning **y** brought violet,
35:25 and bright red **y**, and fine linen,
35:35 purple and bright red **y** on fine
35:35 They know how to weave **y** on
36:8 from fine linen **y** and violet,
36:8 violet, purple, and bright red **y**.
36:35 and bright red **y** and fine linen
36:35 bright red yarn and fine linen **y**.
36:37 a screen out of fine linen **y**
36:37 violet, purple, and bright red **y**.
38:9 made out of fine linen **y**,
38:16 were made out of fine linen **y**.
38:18 and bright red **y** embroidered
38:18 ⌊fabric made from⌋ fine linen **y**.
38:23 and bright red **y** on fine linen.
39:1 and bright red **y** they made
39:2 out of fine linen **y** and gold,
39:2 violet, purple, and bright red **y**.
39:3 violet, purple, and bright red **y**,
39:8 violet, purple, and bright red **y**,
39:8 and of fine linen **y**.
39:22 woven entirely of violet **y**.
39:24 and bright red **y**, and fine yarn.
39:24 and bright red yarn, and fine **y**.
39:28 and belt out of fine linen **y**.
39:29 violet, purple, and bright red **y**.
Lev 14:4 birds, some cedar wood, red **y**,
14:6 bird, the cedar wood, the red **y**,
14:49 two birds, cedar wood, red **y**,
14:51 the hyssop sprig, the red **y**,
14:52 and the red **y** to make the
Num 19:6 and some red **y** and throw them
Mat 6:28 work or spin **y** for clothes.
Luk 12:27 work or spin **y** for clothes.
Heb 9:19 with some water, red **y**,

year (305)

Gen 7:11 month of the six hundredth **y**
8:13 Noah's six hundred and first **y**,
14:4 in the thirteenth **y** they rebelled
14:5 In the fourteenth **y**
17:21 birth to him at this time next **y**."
18:10 back to you next **y** at this time,
18:14 I will come back to you next **y**
Gen 26:12 In that same **y** he harvested a
47:17 During that **y** he supplied them
47:18 When that **y** was over,
47:18 they came to him the next **y**.
Exo 12:2 very first month of the **y** for you.
13:10 these rules every **y** at this time.
21:2 In the seventh **y** he may leave
23:11 but in the seventh **y** you must
23:14 "Three times a **y** you must
23:16 end of the **y** when you harvest
23:17 three times each **y** that all your
23:29 them out of your way in one **y**.
30:10 Once a **y** Aaron must make
30:10 Once a **y** — for generations to
34:23 "Three times a **y** all your men
34:24 you're gone three times a **y**
40:2 day of the first month of the **y**.
40:17 month of the second **y** ⌊after
Lev 16:34 peace with the LORD once a **y**
19:24 In the fourth **y** all the fruit will
19:25 In the fifth **y** you may eat the
23:36 This is the last festival of the **y**.
23:41 it for seven days each **y**.
25:2 the land will celebrate a **y** to
25:4 However, the seventh **y** will be
25:4 year will be a festival **y**
25:4 It will be a **y** to honor the
25:5 That **y** will be a festival for the
25:6 land produces during that **y** is
25:10 Set apart the fiftieth **y** as holy,
25:10 This is your jubilee **y**.
25:11 That fiftieth **y** will be your
25:11 year will be your jubilee **y**.
25:12 The jubilee ⌊**y**⌋ will be holy to
25:13 "In this jubilee **y** every slave
25:20 eat in the seventh **y** if we do
25:21 blessing in the sixth **y** so that
25:22 plant ⌊again⌋ in the eighth **y**
25:22 even in the ninth **y**,
25:28 the buyer until the **y** of jubilee.
25:29 for one **y** after selling it he has
25:30 not buy it back during that **y**,
25:40 with you until the **y** of jubilee.
25:50 the number of years from the **y**
25:50 bought until the **y** of jubilee.
25:52 years left until the **y** of jubilee,
25:54 be released in the **y** of jubilee.
27:17 give your field in the jubilee **y**,
27:18 give the field after the jubilee **y**,
27:18 left until the next jubilee **y**.
27:21 is released in the jubilee **y**,
27:23 field's value until the jubilee **y**.
27:24 In the jubilee **y** the field will go
Num 1:1 second **y** after leaving Egypt.
9:1 first month of the second **y** after
9:2 at the same time every **y**.
9:22 was two days, a month, or a **y**,
10:11 second month of the second **y**,
14:34 So for 40 years — one **y** for
28:14 for every month of the **y**.
33:38 fifth month in the fortieth **y** after
36:4 the Israelites' jubilee **y** comes,
Dtr 1:3 in the fortieth **y** ⌊after they had
11:12 He watches over it all **y** long.
14:22 Every **y** be sure to save a tenth
14:28 At the end of every third **y** bring
15:9 When the seventh **y** — the year
15:9 When the seventh year — the **y**
15:12 In the seventh **y** you must let
15:20 Every **y** you and your family
16:16 Three times a **y** all your men
24:5 For one **y** he is free to stay at
26:12 Every third **y** is the year when
26:12 Every third year is the **y** when
26:12 During that **y** distribute what
31:10 "At the end of every seventh **y**
Jos 5:12 That **y** they began to eat the
Jdg 10:8 the people of Israel that **y**.
11:40 that for four days every **y** the
17:10 you ten pieces of silver a **y**,
21:19 Others said, "Every **y** the
1Sm 1:3 Every **y** this man would go
1:7 This happened **y** after year.
1:7 This happened year after **y**.
2:19 to him every **y** when she went
7:16 Every **y** he went around to

1Sm 27:7 for one y and four months.
29:3 with me now for a y or two?
2Sm 14:26 At the end of every y,
1Ki 4:7 food for one month every y.
4:27 food for one month every y
5:11 paid Hiram this much every y.
6:1 second month) of the fourth y
6:37 the month of Ziv of the fourth y
6:38 of the eleventh y ⌊of his reign⌋,
9:25 Three times a y Solomon
10:14 one y weighed 49,950 pounds,
10:25 This happened y after year.
10:25 This happened year after y.
14:25 In the fifth y of Rehoboam's
15:1 In the eighteenth y of the reign
15:9 In Jeroboam's twentieth y as
15:25 in Asa's second y as king
15:28 in Asa's third y as king
15:33 In Asa's third y as king of
16:8 twenty-sixth y as Judah's king.
16:10 Asa's twenty-seventh y as king
16:15 In Asa's twenty-seventh y as
16:23 in Asa's thirty-first y as king
16:29 in Asa's thirty-eighth y as king
18:1 A while later in the third y of
22:2 In the third y King Jehoshaphat
22:41 in Ahab's fourth y as king
22:51 seventeenth y as king
2Ki 3:1 eighteenth y as king
3:4 ⌊Each y⌋ he had to pay the
4:17 had a son at that time next y,
8:16 son) was in his fifth y as king
8:25 was in his twelfth y as king
8:26 he ruled for one y in Jerusalem.
9:29 in the eleventh y that Joram,
11:4 In the seventh y of Athaliah's
12:1 rule in Jehu's seventh y as king
12:6 Joash's twenty-third y as king,
13:1 in his twenty-third y as king
13:10 In Joash's thirty-seventh y as
14:1 was in his second y as king
14:23 was in his fifteenth y as king
15:1 In Jeroboam's twenty-seventh y
15:8 In Azariah's thirty-eighth y as
15:13 Azariah's thirty-ninth y as king
15:17 In Azariah's thirty-ninth y as
15:23 In Azariah's fiftieth y as king of
15:27 In Azariah's fifty-second y as
15:30 in the twentieth y that Azariah,
15:32 In the second y that King
16:1 was in his seventeenth y as
17:1 In Ahaz's twelfth y as king of
17:6 In Hoshea's ninth y as king of
18:9 In Hezekiah's fourth y as king
18:9 king (which was the seventh y
18:10 sixth y as king (which
18:10 was Hoshea's ninth y as king
18:13 fourteenth y as king,
19:29 eat what grows by itself this y
19:29 by itself this year and next y.
19:29 But in the third y you will plant
22:3 In Josiah's eighteenth y as
23:23 But in the eighteenth y of King
24:12 In the eighth y of his reign,
25:1 of the tenth month of the ninth y
25:2 Zedekiah's eleventh y as king.
25:8 nineteenth y as king
25:27 month of the thirty-seventh y
25:27 in the first y of his reign,
1Ch 12:15 In the first month of the y,
26:31 In the fortieth y of David's reign
27:1 Throughout each y they came
2Ch 3:2 of the fourth y of his reign.
9:13 one y weighed 49,950 pounds,
9:24 This happened y after year.
9:24 This happened year after y.
12:2 In the fifth y of Rehoboam's
13:1 In the eighteenth y of the reign
15:10 the third month of the fifteenth y
15:19 the thirty-fifth y of Asa's reign.
16:1 In the thirty-sixth y of Asa's
16:12 In the thirty-ninth y of his reign,
16:13 in the forty-first y of his reign.
17:7 In the third y of his reign,
22:2 he ruled for one y in Jerusalem.
23:1 In the seventh y of Athaliah's
2Ch 24:5 the temple of your God every y.
24:23 At the end of the y,
27:5 That y the Ammonites gave
29:3 first month of his first y as king,
34:3 In the eighth y of his reign,
34:3 In his twelfth y as king,
34:8 In the eighteenth y of his reign
35:19 In the eighteenth y of Josiah's
36:22 true in Cyrus' first y as king
Ezr 1:1 true in Cyrus' first y as king
3:8 second y following their return
4:24 until Darius' second y as king
5:13 "However, in the first y of the
6:3 Cyrus' first y as king From:
6:15 the month of Adar in the sixth y
7:7 Artaxerxes' seventh y as king.
7:8 In that same y in the fifth
Neh 1:1 twentieth y as king,
2:1 twentieth y as king,
5:14 from the twentieth y of King
5:14 reign to the thirty-second y
10:31 During the seventh y,
10:32 of an ounce of silver every y
10:34 times every y according
10:35 first fruit from every tree each y
13:6 In the thirty-second y of King
Est 1:3 he held a banquet in the third y
2:16 in the seventh y of his reign.
3:7 In Xerxes' twelfth y as king,
9:21 they must observe every y.
9:27 these two days every y,
Job 3:6 be included in the days of the y
Psa 65:11 You crown the y with your
Isa 6:1 In the y King Uzziah died,
14:28 in the y King Ahaz died.
20:1 In the y when King Sargon of
21:16 honor will be gone in another y.
29:1 Let y after year go by.
29:1 Let year after y go by.
32:10 In a little less than a y you
34:8 a y of revenge in defense of
36:1 fourteenth y as king,
37:30 eat what grows by itself this y,
37:30 and the next y you will eat
37:30 But in the third y you will plant
61:2 sent me⌋ to announce the y
63:4 The y for my reclaiming ⌊you⌋
Jer 1:2 was in his thirteenth y as king
1:3 in the fifth month of the y.
11:23 It will be a y of punishment.
25:1 was in his fourth y as king.
25:1 (This was the first y that
25:3 was in his thirteenth y as king
28:1 In that same y, early in the rule
28:1 month of his fourth y as king,
28:16 You will die this y because
28:17 in the seventh month of that y.
32:1 Zedekiah's tenth y as king
32:1 eighteenth y as king.)
36:1 In the fourth y of the reign of
36:9 In the ninth month of the fifth y
39:1 of Zedekiah's ninth y as king
39:2 Zedekiah's eleventh y as king,
45:1 the fourth y that Jehoiakim,
46:2 the fourth y that Jehoiakim,
48:44 I will bring a y of punishment to
51:46 One rumor comes one y;
51:46 rumor comes the next y.
51:59 of Judah in the fourth y
52:4 of the tenth month of the ninth y
52:5 Zedekiah's eleventh y as king.
52:12 nineteenth y as king
52:28 In his seventh y as king,
52:29 In his eighteenth y,
52:30 twenty-third y as king,
52:31 month of the thirty-seventh y
52:31 in the first y of his reign,
Eze 1:1 fourth month in the thirtieth y,
1:2 during the fifth y of the exile of
4:5 for each y its punishment will
4:6 one day for each y I have
8:1 the sixth month in the sixth y,
20:1 the fifth month in the seventh y,
24:1 the tenth month in the ninth y,
26:1 of the month in the eleventh y,
29:1 the tenth month in the tenth y,
Eze 29:17 month in the twenty-seventh y,
30:20 first month in the eleventh y,
31:1 third month in the eleventh y,
32:1 twelfth month in the twelfth y,
32:17 of the month in the twelfth y,
33:21 the tenth month in the twelfth y
40:1 beginning of the twenty-fifth y
46:17 only until the y of freedom.
Dan 1:1 In the third y of the reign of
1:21 the royal palace until the first y
2:1 During the second y of
7:1 In Belshazzar's first y as king
8:1 In Belshazzar's third y as king,
9:2 In the first y of his reign,
10:1 In Cyrus' third y as king of
11:1 the Mede's first y as king,
Hag 1:1 in Darius' second y as king,
1:15 in Darius' second y as king.
2:10 in Darius' second y as king,
Zec 1:1 of Darius' second y as king,
1:7 in Darius' second y as king,
7:1 in Darius' fourth y as king,
14:16 Jerusalem will come every y
Luk 2:41 Every y Jesus' parents would
3:1 It was the fifteenth y in the
4:19 to announce the y of the Lord's
13:8 let it stand for one more y.
13:9 Maybe next y it'll have figs.
Jon 11:49 who was chief priest that y,
11:51 As chief priest that y,
18:13 the chief priest that y,
Act 11:26 church in Antioch for a whole y
17:26 them the seasons of the y
18:11 Paul lived in Corinth for a y
2Co 8:10 Last y you were not only
9:2 their collection⌋ since last y,"
Heb 9:7 Once a y he entered and
9:25 Every y the chief priest went
Jas 4:13 into some city, stay there a y,
Rev 9:15 and y were released to kill

yearly (2)

Heb 10:1 Moses' Teachings with their y
10:3 Instead, this y cycle of

yearns (1)

Psa 84:2 My soul longs and y for the

year-old (65)

Gen 15:9 "Bring me a three-y heifer,
15:9 heifer, a three-y female goat,
15:9 a three-y ram, a mourning dove,
17:17 son be born to a hundred-y man
17:17 Can Sarah, a ninety-y woman,
37:2 Joseph was a seventeen-y young
Exo 12:5 animal must be a one-y male
29:38 every day: two one-y lambs.
Lev 9:3 calf and a lamb (each one-y and
12:6 she must bring a one-y lamb for
14:10 and a one-y female lamb that
23:12 you must sacrifice a one-y male
23:18 the bread bring seven one-y
23:19 for sin and two one-y lambs as
Num 6:12 must bring a one-y male lamb
6:14 a one-y male lamb as a burnt
6:14 one-y female lamb as an offering
7:15 a young bull, a ram, and a one-y
7:17 and five one-y male lambs as a
7:21 a young bull, a ram, and a one-y
7:23 and five one-y male lambs as a
7:27 a young bull, a ram, and a one-y
7:29 and five one-y male lambs as a
7:33 a young bull, a ram, and a one-y
7:35 and five one-y male lambs as a
7:39 a young bull, a ram, and a one-y
7:41 and five one-y male lambs as a
7:45 a young bull, a ram, and a one-y
7:47 and five one-y male lambs as a
7:51 a young bull, a ram, and a one-y
7:53 and five one-y male lambs as a
7:57 a young bull, a ram, and a one-y
7:59 and five one-y male lambs as a
7:63 a young bull, a ram, and a one-y
7:65 and five one-y male lambs as a
7:69 a young bull, a ram, and a one-y
7:71 and five one-y male lambs as a

Num 7:75 a young bull, a ram, and a one-y
7:77 and five one-y male lambs as a
7:81 a young bull, a ram, and a one-y
7:83 and five one-y male lambs as a
7:87 12 rams, 12 one-y male lambs,
7:88 and 60 one-y male lambs.
15:27 a one-y female goat must be
28:3 offering two one-y lambs that
28:9 offer two one-y lambs that have
28:11 and seven one-y lambs that have
28:13 with each one-y lamb a grain
28:19 and seven one-y lambs,
28:27 and seven one-y lambs.
29:2 and seven one-y lambs that have
29:8 and seven one-y lambs,
29:13 2 rams, and 14 one-y lambs,
29:15 8 cups for each of the 14 one-y
29:17 and 14 one-y lambs that have no
29:20 and 14 one-y lambs that have no
29:23 and 14 one-y lambs that have no
29:26 and 14 one-y lambs that have no
29:29 and 14 one-y lambs that have no
29:32 and 14 one-y lambs that have no
29:36 and seven one-y lambs that have
1Sm 1:24 She also brought a three-y bull,
Isa 11:6 and y lambs will be together,
Eze 46:13 "'Prepare a y lamb that has no
Mic 6:6 Should I bring him y calves as

year's (4)

Dtr 14:28 year bring a tenth of that y crop,
26:12 that y crops ⌊in your houses⌋.
Mar 6:37 go and spend about a y wages
Jon 6:7 would need about a y wages

years (501)

Gen 1:14 religious festivals, days, and y.
5:3 When Adam was 130 y old,
5:4 he lived 800 y and had other
5:5 Adam lived a total of 930 y;
5:6 When Seth was 105 y old,
5:7 Seth lived 807 y and had other
5:8 Seth lived a total of 912 y;
5:9 When Enosh was 90 y old,
5:10 Enosh lived 815 y and had
5:11 Enosh lived a total of 905 y;
5:12 When Kenan was 70 y old,
5:13 Kenan lived 840 y and had
5:14 Kenan lived a total of 910 y;
5:15 When Mahalalel was 65 y old,
5:16 Mahalalel lived 830 y and had
5:17 Mahalalel lived a total of 895 y;
5:18 When Jared was 162 y old,
5:19 Jared lived 800 y and had other
5:20 Jared lived a total of 962 y;
5:21 When Enoch was 65 y old,
5:22 walked with God for 300 y
5:23 Enoch lived a total of 365 y.
5:25 Methuselah was 187 y old,
5:26 Methuselah lived 782 y and
5:27 lived a total of 969 y;
5:28 When Lamech was 182 y old,
5:30 he lived 595 y and had other
5:31 Lamech lived a total of 777 y;
5:32 When Noah was 500 y old,
6:3 They will live 120 y."
7:6 Noah was 600 y old when the
9:28 Noah lived 350 y after the flood.
9:29 Noah lived a total of 950 y;
11:10 Two y after the flood when
11:10 when Shem was 100 y old,
11:11 Shem lived 500 y and had
11:12 Arpachshad was 35 y old
11:13 Arpachshad lived 403 y and
11:14 Shelah was 30 y old when he
11:15 Shelah lived 403 y and had
11:16 Eber was 34 y old when he
11:17 Eber lived 430 y and had other
11:18 Peleg was 30 y old when he
11:19 Peleg lived 209 y and had
11:20 Reu was 32 y old when he
11:21 Reu lived 207 y and had other
11:22 Serug was 30 y old when he
11:23 Serug lived 200 y and had
11:24 Nahor was 29 y old when he
11:25 Nahor lived 119 y and had
Gen 11:26 Terah was 70 y old when he
11:32 Terah lived 205 y and died in
12:4 Abram was 75 y old when he
14:4 For 12 y they had been subject
15:13 will be oppressed for 400 y.
16:3 had lived in Canaan for ten y,
16:16 Abram was 86 y old when
17:1 When Abram was 99 y old,
17:24 Abraham was 99 y old when
17:25 His son Ishmael was 13 y old
21:5 Abraham was 100 y old when
23:1 Sarah lived to be 127 y old.
25:7 Abraham lived 175 y.
25:17 Ishmael lived 137 y.
25:20 Isaac was 40 y old when he
25:26 Isaac was 60 y old when they
26:34 When Esau was 40 y old,
29:18 So he offered, "I'll work seven y
29:20 Jacob worked seven y in return
29:20 but the y seemed like only a
29:21 ⌊At the end of the seven y⌋
29:27 work for me another seven y."
29:30 for Laban another seven y.
31:38 "I've been with you for 20 y.
31:41 with your household 20 y now.
31:41 I worked for you 14 y for your
31:41 for your two daughters and 6 y
35:28 Isaac was 180 y old
41:1 After two full y Pharaoh had a
41:26 seven good cows are seven y,
41:26 heads of grain are seven y.
41:27 up behind them are seven y.
41:27 the east wind are also seven y.
41:27 Seven y of famine are coming.
41:29 Seven y are coming when
41:30 will come seven y of famine.
41:34 during the seven good y.
41:35 all the food during these good y
41:36 our country during the seven y
41:46 Joseph was 30 y old when he
41:47 During the seven good y the
41:48 in Egypt during those seven y
41:50 Before the y of famine came,
41:53 The seven y when there was
41:54 Then the seven y of famine
45:6 has been in the land for two y.
45:6 There will be five more y
45:11 will be five more y of famine.
47:9 stay on earth has been 130 y.
47:9 The y of my life have been few
47:9 fewer than my ancestors' y."
47:28 Jacob lived in Egypt 17 y,
47:28 so he lived a total of 147 y.
50:22 Joseph lived to be 110 y old.
50:26 died when he was 110 y old.
Exo 6:16 and Merari. Levi lived 137 y.
6:18 Kohath lived 133 y.
6:20 Amram lived 137 y.
7:7 Moses was 80 y old and Aaron
12:40 been living in Egypt for 430 y.
12:41 After exactly 430 y all the
16:35 manna for 40 y until they came
21:2 he will be your slave for six y.
23:10 "For six y you may plant crops
30:14 is at least 20 y old must give
38:26 who was at least 20 y old:
Lev 19:23 the fruit for ⌊the first⌋ three y.
25:3 Then, for six y you may plant
25:8 "Count seven of these y seven
25:8 seven times for a total of 49 y.
25:15 account the number of y since
25:16 If there are still many y ⌊until
25:16 If there are only a few y ⌊until
25:21 will produce enough for three y.
25:27 he must count the y from its
25:50 account the number of y from
25:50 based on the number of y
25:51 If there are many y left,
25:51 an amount equal ⌊to those y⌋.
25:52 If there are only a few y left
25:52 an amount equal to those y.
25:53 During those y he should serve
27:3 a man from 20 to 60 y old is 20
27:5 For a boy from 5 to 20 y old,
27:6 from one month to five y old,
27:7 For a man 60 y or over,
Lev 27:18 on the number of y left until
Num 1:3 who is at least 20 y old.
1:18 Each man at least 20 y old
1:20 who was at least 20 y old
1:22 who was at least 20 y old
1:24 who were at least 20 y old
1:26 who were at least 20 y old
1:28 who were at least 20 y old
1:30 who were at least 20 y old
1:32 who were at least 20 y old
1:34 who were at least 20 y old
1:36 who were at least 20 y old
1:38 who were at least 20 y old
1:40 who were at least 20 y old
1:42 who were at least 20 y old
1:45 men who were at least 20 y old
8:24 Men 25 y old or older are
8:25 But when they're 50 y old,
13:22 (Hebron was built seven y
14:29 you who are at least 20 y old,
14:33 in the desert for 40 y.
14:34 So for 40 y — one year for each
20:15 and we lived there for many y.
26:2 List those who are at least 20 y
26:4 of those at least 20 y old,
32:11 'None of the people 20 y old or
32:13 in the desert for 40 y until
33:39 Aaron was 123 y old when he
Dtr 2:7 For 40 y now the LORD your
2:14 Thirty-eight y passed from the
8:2 Remember that for 40 y the
8:4 didn't swell these past 40 y.
15:1 At the end of every seven y,
15:12 will be your slaves for six y.
15:18 the same work for those six y.
29:5 For 40 y I led you through the
31:2 "I'm 120 y old now,
34:7 Moses was 120 y old when he
Jos 5:6 For 40 y the Israelites
14:7 I was 40 y old when the
14:10 It's been 45 y since Israel
14:10 look at me today. I'm 85 y old.
24:29 He was 110 y old.
Jdg 3:8 Cushan Rishathaim for eight y.
3:11 peace in the land for 40 y.
3:14 King Eglon of Moab for 18 y.
3:30 peace in the land for 80 y.
4:3 oppressed Israel for 20 y.
5:31 So the land had peace for 40 y.
6:1 over to Midian for seven y.
6:25 a bull that is seven y old.
8:28 for 40 y during Gideon's life.
9:22 ruled Israel for three y.
10:2 He judged Israel for 23 y.
10:3 He judged Israel for 22 y.
10:8 For 18 y they oppressed all
11:26 along the Arnon River for 300 y.
12:7 judged Israel for six y.
12:9 He judged Israel for seven y.
12:11 He judged Israel for ten y.
12:14 He judged Israel for eight y.
13:1 over to the Philistines for 40 y.
15:20 Samson judged Israel for 20 y
16:31 had judged Israel for 20 y.
Rut 1:4 They lived there for about ten y.
1Sm 4:15 (Eli was 98 y old, and his
4:18 He had judged Israel for 40 y.
7:2 For 20 y the entire nation of
13:1 Saul was ⌊thirty⌋ y old when
13:1 king of Israel ⌊forty-two⌋ y.
2Sm 2:10 Ishbosheth was 40 y old when
2:10 He ruled for two y,
2:11 for seven y and six months.
4:4 When the boy was five y old,
5:4 David was 30 y old when he
5:4 and he ruled for 40 y.
5:5 he ruled Judah for seven y
5:5 In Jerusalem he ruled for 33 y
13:23 Two y later Absalom had
13:38 stayed there three y.
14:28 two full y without seeing
15:7 Four y later Absalom said to
19:32 was an elderly man, 80 y old.
19:35 I'm 80 y old now. How can I tell
21:1 famine for three successive y,
24:13 "Should seven y of famine

1Ki 2:11 ruled as king of Israel for 40 y.
2:11 He ruled for 7 y in Hebron and
2:11 and for 33 y in Jerusalem.
2:39 But after three y, two of
6:1 temple 480 y after Israel left
6:38 He spent seven y building it.
7:1 Solomon took 13 y to finish
9:10 It took Solomon 20 y to build
10:22 Once every three y the
11:42 over all Israel was 40 y.
14:20 Jeroboam ruled for 22 y.
14:21 He was 41 y old when he
14:21 He ruled for 17 y in Jerusalem,
15:2 ruled for three y in Jerusalem.
15:10 He ruled 41 y in Jerusalem.
15:25 He ruled for two y.
15:33 in Tirzah. He ruled for 24 y.
16:8 He ruled in Tirzah for two y.
16:23 He ruled for 12 y, 6 of them in
16:29 He ruled for 22 y in Samaria.
17:1 during the next few y unless
22:1 For three y there was no war
22:42 Jehoshaphat was 35 y old
22:42 he ruled for 25 y in Jerusalem.
22:51 Ahaziah ruled Israel for two y.
2Ki 3:1 of Judah. He ruled for 12 y.
4:18 Several y later the boy went to
8:1 and it will last seven y."
8:2 Philistine territory for seven y.
8:3 At the end of seven y,
8:17 He was 32 y old when he
8:17 he ruled for 8 y in Jerusalem.
8:26 Ahaziah was 22 y old when he
10:36 of Israel in Samaria for 28 y.
11:3 for six y while Athaliah ruled
11:21 Joash was seven y old when
12:1 he ruled for 40 y in Jerusalem.
13:1 of Israel. He ruled for 17 y.
13:10 in Samaria. He ruled for 16 y.
14:2 Amaziah was 25 y old when
14:2 he ruled for 29 y in Jerusalem.
14:17 of Judah lived 15 y after
14:21 who was 16 y old,
14:23 Jeroboam ruled for 41 y.
15:2 He was 16 y old when he
15:2 he ruled for 52 y in Jerusalem.
15:17 He ruled for 10 y in Samaria.
15:23 of Israel in Samaria for two y.
15:27 in Samaria. He ruled for 20 y.
15:33 He was 25 y old when he
15:33 He ruled for 16 y in Jerusalem.
16:2 Ahaz was 20 y old when he
16:2 He ruled for 26 y in Jerusalem.
17:1 He ruled for nine y.
17:5 and blockaded it for three y.
18:1 three y when King Hezekiah,
18:2 Hezekiah was 25 y old when
18:2 he ruled for 29 y in Jerusalem.
18:10 captured it at the end of three y.
20:6 I'll give you 15 more y to live.
21:1 Manasseh was 12 y old when
21:1 he ruled for 55 y in Jerusalem.
21:19 Amon was 22 y old when he
21:19 he ruled for 2 y in Jerusalem.
22:1 Josiah was 8 y old when he
22:1 was king for 31 y in Jerusalem.
23:31 Jehoahaz was 23 y old when
23:36 Jehoiakim was 25 y old when
23:36 was king for 11 y in Jerusalem.
24:1 subject to him for three y.
24:8 Jehoiakin was 18 y old when
24:18 Zedekiah was 21 y old when
24:18 he ruled for 11 y in Jerusalem.
1Ch 2:21 her when he was 60 y old.
3:4 where he ruled for seven y and
3:4 He ruled for 33 y in Jerusalem.
21:12 either three y of famine,
23:1 old and had lived out his y,
23:3 at least 30 y old was counted.
23:24 temple was at least 20 y old.
23:27 who were at least 20 y old.
27:23 count those under 20 y old,
29:27 ruled as king of Israel for 40 y.
29:27 He ruled for 7 y in Hebron and
2Ch 8:1 It took Solomon 20 y to build
9:21 Once every three y the

2Ch 9:30 over all Israel for 40 y.
11:17 son of Solomon, for three y.
11:17 During ⌊those⌋ three y they
12:13 He was 41 y old when he
12:13 He ruled for 17 y in Jerusalem,
13:2 ruled for three y in Jerusalem.
14:1 the land had peace for ten y.
14:6 was no war during those y
18:2 A few y later he went to visit
20:31 He was 35 y old when he
20:31 he ruled for 25 y in Jerusalem.
21:5 Jehoram was 32 y old when he
21:5 he ruled for 8 y in Jerusalem.
21:19 Two y later, as his life was
21:20 He was 32 y old when he
21:20 he ruled for 8 y in Jerusalem.
22:2 Ahaziah was 42 y old when he
22:12 for six y while Athaliah ruled
24:1 Joash was 7 y old when he
24:1 he ruled for 40 y in Jerusalem.
24:15 old and had lived out his y,
24:15 He was 130 y old when he
25:1 Amaziah was 25 y old when
25:1 he ruled for 29 y in Jerusalem.
25:5 who were at least 20 y old
25:25 of Judah lived 15 y after
26:1 who was 16 y old,
26:3 Uzziah was 16 y old when he
26:3 he ruled for 52 y in Jerusalem.
27:1 Jotham was 25 y old when he
27:1 He ruled for 16 y in Jerusalem.
27:5 same amount for two more y.
27:8 He was 25 y old when he
27:8 He ruled for 16 y in Jerusalem.
28:1 Ahaz was 20 y old when he
28:1 He ruled for 26 y in Jerusalem.
29:1 as king when he was 25 y old.
29:1 He ruled for 29 y in Jerusalem.
31:16 who were at least three y old.
31:17 who were at least 20 y old.
33:1 Manasseh was 12 y old when
33:1 he ruled for 55 y in Jerusalem.
33:21 Amon was 22 y old when he
33:21 he ruled for 2 y in Jerusalem.
34:1 Josiah was 8 y old when he
34:1 was king for 31 y in Jerusalem.
36:2 Jehoahaz was 23 y old when
36:5 Jehoiakim was 25 y old when
36:5 he ruled for 11 y in Jerusalem.
36:9 Jehoiakin was eight y old
36:11 Zedekiah was 21 y old when
36:11 he ruled for 11 y in Jerusalem.
36:21 The land had its y of rest and
36:21 ⌊the land had its⌋ 70 y of rest.
Ezr 3:8 who were at least 20 y old
5:11 originally built many y ago by
Neh 5:14 During the 12 y that I was
9:21 for them in the desert for 40 y,
9:30 patient with them for many y.
Job 10:5 Are your y like a human's
10:5 your years like a human's y?
15:20 Only a few y are reserved for
16:22 because in a few short y I will
36:11 and their y in comfort.
36:26 of his y cannot be counted.
42:12 The LORD blessed the latter y
42:12 life more than the earlier y.
42:16 Job lived 140 y after this.
Psa 31:10 my y from groaning.
61:6 May his y endure throughout
77:5 the days of old, the y long ago.
78:33 He brought their y to an end in
90:4 in your sight a thousand y are
90:9 We live out our y like one
90:10 Each of us lives for 70 y — or
90:15 for as many y as we have
95:10 For 40 y I was disgusted with
102:24 Your y ⌊continue on⌋
119:100 with many y of experience,
Pro 3:2 long life, good y, and peace.
4:10 will multiply the y of your life.
5:9 others and ⌊the rest of⌋ your y
9:11 and y will be added to your life.
10:27 but the y of wicked people are
Ecc 6:3 children and lived for many y.
6:6 y without experiencing anything

Ecc 11:8 people may live for many y,
12:1 come and the y catch up
Isa 7:8 be shattered within 65 y so that
16:14 will be despised within three y.
16:14 like workers count the y left
20:3 and naked for three y as
21:16 it like workers count the y left
23:15 Tyre will be forgotten for 70 y,
23:15 At the end of the 70 y,
23:17 At the end of 70 y the LORD
38:5 to give you 15 more y to live.
65:20 lives to be a hundred y old will
65:20 he is a hundred y old will
Jer 1:3 during the 11 y that Zedekiah,
25:3 "For 23 y, from the time that
25:11 the king of Babylon for 70 y.
25:12 "When the 70 y are over,
28:3 Within two y I will bring back
28:11 of all the nations within two y."
29:10 When Babylon's 70 y are over,
34:14 'Every seven y each of you
34:14 they have served you for six y,
52:1 Zedekiah was 21 y old when
52:1 he ruled for 11 y in Jerusalem.
Eze 22:4 have come to the end of your y.
29:11 no one will live there for 40 y.
29:12 For 40 y Egypt's cities will lie
29:13 After 40 y I will gather the
38:8 In the y to come, you will
39:9 will burn them for seven y.
40:1 fourteen y after Jerusalem was
Dan 1:5 were to be trained for three y.
5:31 the kingdom. He was 62 y old.
7:9 who has lived for endless y,
7:13 who has lived for endless y,
7:22 who has lived for endless y,
9:2 of y that Jerusalem would
9:2 would remain in ruins for 70 y.
11:6 After a few y the southern and
11:8 He will rule for more y than the
11:13 After a few y he will invade
Joe 2:25 "Then I will repay you for the y
Amo 1:1 two y before the earthquake.
2:10 the desert for 40 y so that you
5:25 offerings in the desert for 40 y,
Hab 3:2 In the course of the y,
3:2 In the course of the y,
Zec 1:12 been angry with them for 70 y."
7:3 we have done for so many y?"
7:5 months these past 70 y,
Mal 3:4 as in the past, as in y long ago.
Mat 2:16 to kill all the boys two y old
9:20 chronic bleeding for twelve y.
Mar 5:25 chronic bleeding for twelve y.
5:42 (She was twelve y old.)
Luk 1:18 is beyond her childbearing y."
2:36 Her husband had died seven y
2:37 she had been a widow for 84 y.
2:42 When he was 12 y old,
3:23 Jesus was about 30 y old
4:25 not rained for three-and-a-half y,
8:42 who was about twelve y old,
8:43 bleeding for twelve y was
12:19 lot of good things for y to come.
13:7 'For the last three y I've come
13:11 spirit had disabled her for 18 y.
13:16 her in this condition for 18 y.
15:29 'All these y I've worked like a
Jon 2:20 "It took forty-six y to build this
5:5 who had been sick for 38 y,
8:57 "You're not even fifty y old.
Act 4:22 this miracle was over 40 y old.)
7:6 and mistreat them for 400 y.
7:23 When he was 40 y old,
7:30 "Forty y later, a messenger
7:36 and in the desert for 40 y.
7:42 offerings in the desert for 40 y,
9:33 confined to a cot for eight y.
13:18 for about forty y in the desert.
13:20 about four hundred and fifty y.
13:21 tribe of Benjamin. After forty y
19:10 This continued for two y so
20:31 each of you for three y,
24:10 over this nation for many y.
24:17 After many y I have come back
24:27 Two y passed. Then Porcius

Exo	12:21	"Pick out a lamb or a y goat for
	23:19	"Never cook a y goat in its
	24:5	Then he sent y Israelite men,
	29:1	"Take a y bull that has no
	29:3	the basket along with the y bull
	29:10	"Then bring the y bull to the
	29:36	Each day sacrifice a y bull as
	34:26	"Never cook a y goat in its
Lev	22:28	sheep and its y the same day.
Num	6:10	doves or two y pigeons
	7:15	a y bull, a ram, and a
	7:21	a y bull, a ram, and a
	7:27	a y bull, a ram, and a
	7:33	a y bull, a ram, and a
	7:39	a y bull, a ram, and a
	7:45	a y bull, a ram, and a
	7:51	a y bull, a ram, and a
	7:57	a y bull, a ram, and a
	7:63	a y bull, a ram, and a
	7:69	a y bull, a ram, and a
	7:75	a y bull, a ram, and a
	7:81	a y bull, a ram, and a
	7:87	burnt offerings was 12 y bulls,
	8:8	Next, they must take a y bull
	8:8	You must take a second y bull
	8:12	on the heads of the y bulls.
	11:27	Then a y man ran and told
	11:28	ever since he was a y man,
	15:8	"Suppose you sacrifice a y
	15:9	Offer with the y bull a grain
	15:24	must sacrifice a y bull as
	28:11	a burnt offering of two y bulls,
	28:19	a burnt offering of two y bulls,
	28:27	to the LORD — two y bulls,
	29:2	bring one y bull, one ram,
	29:8	bring one y bull, one ram,
	29:13	LORD, bring 13 y bulls, 2 rams,
	29:17	second day bring 12 y bulls,
	30:3	"A y girl, who still lives in her
	30:16	and for fathers with y daughters
Dtr	1:39	who are still too y to know the
	14:21	Never cook a y goat in its
	28:50	for the old and no pity for the y.
	32:11	up its nest, hovers over its y,
	32:25	Y men and young women alike
	32:25	Young men and y women alike
Jos	6:21	y and old, as well as cattle,
Jdg	6:19	house⌋ and prepared a y goat
	8:14	and captured a y man from
	8:14	He questioned him, and the y
	8:20	because he was only a y man.
	13:15	stay while we prepare a y goat
	13:19	So Manoah took a y goat and a
	14:1	he saw a y Philistine woman.
	14:5	a y roaring lion met Samson.
	14:6	lion apart as if it were a y goat.
	14:7	he went to talk to the y woman.
	14:10	(This is what y men used to
	15:1	He took a y goat along for her.
	16:26	Samson told the y man who
	17:7	There was a y man from
	17:11	The y man became like one of
	17:12	So the y man became his
	18:3	recognized the y Levite's voice.
	18:15	house and greeted the y Levite.
	21:21	When the y women of Shiloh
Rut	2:5	Boaz asked the y man in
	2:5	"Who is this y woman?"
	2:6	The y man answered,
	2:6	"She's a y Moabite woman
	2:8	Stay here with my y women.
	2:9	and follow the y women in that
	2:9	I have ordered my y men not to
	2:9	that the y men have drawn."
	2:22	to the fields with his y women.
	2:23	So Ruth stayed with the y
	3:2	Isn't Boaz, whose y women
	4:12	give you from this y woman,
1Sm	9:2	Saul, a handsome, y man.
	10:3	will be carrying three y goats,
	16:20	and a y goat and sent them
	17:42	After all, David was a y man
	17:55	whose son is this y man?"
	17:56	out whose son this y man is."
	17:58	"Whose son are you, y man?"
	20:35	Jonathan had a y boy with him.
1Sm	20:38	Jonathan's y servant gathered
	21:2	I've stationed my y men at a
	21:4	holy bread for the y men if they
	21:5	The y men's bodies are kept
	25:5	So David sent ten y men and
	25:8	Ask your y men, and let them
	25:8	Be kind to my y men,
	25:9	When David's y men came to
	25:12	David's y men returned and told
	25:14	One of the y men told Abigail,
	25:19	she told her y men,
	25:25	I didn't see the y men you sent.
	25:27	May it be given to the y men
	26:22	One of the y men should come
	30:2	Although they captured the y
	30:13	the y man answered.
	30:17	No one escaped except 400 y
	30:19	Nothing was missing — y or old
2Sm	1:5	David asked the y man who
	1:6	The y man answered,
	1:13	David asked the y man who
	1:13	And the y man answered,
	1:15	called one of ⌊his⌋ y men
	1:15	David's y man executed him
	2:14	"Let's have the y men hold a
	2:21	Catch one of the y men,
	4:12	gave an order to his y men,
	9:12	Mephibosheth had a y son
	13:32	don't think that all the y men,
	14:21	back the y man Absalom."
	17:18	But a y man saw Jonathan and
	18:5	"Treat the y man Absalom
	18:12	'Protect the y man Absalom for
	18:29	"Is the y man Absalom alright?"
	18:32	"Is the y man Absalom alright?"
	18:32	against you be like that y man!"
	20:11	One of Joab's y men stood
1Ki	1:2	let us search for a y woman
	1:3	Israel for a beautiful, y woman.
	3:7	I'm y and inexperienced,
	11:17	Hadad was a y boy at the time.
	12:8	He sought advice from the y
	12:10	The y men who had grown up
	12:14	to them as the y men advised.
	20:14	by using the y officers of the
	20:15	Ahab counted the y officers of
	20:17	The y officers of the district
	20:19	The y officers of the district
2Ki	5:22	He says, 'Just now two y men
	8:12	kill their best y men,
	9:4	The y man, the servant of the
	23:2	and all the people (y and old)
1Ch	12:28	and Zadok, a y warrior from
	22:5	is y and inexperienced,
	29:1	is y and inexperienced.
2Ch	10:8	He sought advice from the y
	10:10	The y men who had grown up
	10:14	to them as the y men advised.
	13:7	when Rehoboam was too y
	13:9	Anyone who has a y bull and
	15:13	All people (y or old,
	31:15	y and old, by their divisions.
	34:30	and all the people (y and old)
	36:17	and execute their best y men
Ezr	6:9	to the God of heaven — y bulls,
Est	2:2	"Search for attractive y virgins
	2:3	all the attractive y virgins
	2:4	Then the y woman who
	2:7	The y woman had a beautiful
	2:8	many y women were gathered
	2:9	The y woman pleased him and
	2:12	Each y woman had her turn to
	2:13	After that, the y woman would
	3:13	all the Jews — y and old,
Job	1:19	It fell on the y people,
	4:10	the y lions have had their teeth
	19:18	Even y children despise me.
	29:8	y men saw me and kept out of
	32:6	Job⌋, "I am y, and you are old.
	36:14	They die while they're y,
	38:41	the crow when its y ones cry
	39:3	to give birth and deliver their y.
	39:4	Their y are healthy and grow
	39:16	It acts harshly toward its y as if
	39:30	Its y ones feed on blood.
	42:8	So take seven y bulls and
Psa	17:12	and like a y lion crouching
	34:10	Y lions go hungry and may
	37:25	I have been y, and now I am
	50:9	⌊another⌋ y bull from your
	51:19	Y bulls will be offered on your
	58:6	Break the y lions' teeth,
	68:25	The y women beating
	71:5	confidence ever since I was y.
	71:17	taught me ever since I was y,
	78:31	the best y men in Israel.
	78:51	Ham when their fathers were y.
	78:63	Fire consumed his best y men,
	84:3	There they hatch their y near
	88:15	Ever since I was y,
	91:13	trample y lions and snakes.
	103:5	that you become y again like
	104:21	The y lions roar for their prey
	105:36	land when their fathers were y.
	110:3	Your y people will come to you
	119:9	How can a y person keep his
	127:4	when he is y are like arrows
	128:3	Your children will be like y
	129:1	"From the time I was y,
	129:2	"From the time I was y,
	144:12	be like full-grown, y plants.
	147:9	and to y ravens when they
	148:12	y men and women,
	148:12	old and y together.
Pro	1:4	and foresight to the y —
	5:18	you married when you were y,
	7:7	I saw a y man without much
	20:29	While the glory of y men is
	30:17	valley and eaten by y vultures.
Ecc	4:13	A y man who is poor and wise
	4:14	A y man came out of prison to
	4:15	sided with the second y man,
	11:9	You y people should enjoy
	11:9	yourselves while you're y.
	11:9	make you happy when you're y.
	12:1	your Creator when you are y,
Sos	1:3	wonder the y women love you!
	1:4	it is that the y women love you!
	1:5	Y women of Jerusalem,
	1:8	and graze your y goats near the
	2:2	so is my true love among the y
	2:3	my beloved among the y men.
	2:7	Y women of Jerusalem,
	2:9	is like a gazelle or a y stag.
	2:17	Run like a gazelle or a y stag
	3:5	Y women of Jerusalem,
	3:6	Who is this y woman coming
	3:10	by the y women of Jerusalem.
	3:11	Y women of Zion, come out
	4:2	and not one has lost its y.
	5:8	Y women of Jerusalem,
	5:16	y women of Jerusalem.
	6:6	and not one has lost its y.
	6:10	Who is this y woman?
	6:13	y woman from Shulam!
	6:13	the y woman from Shulam,
	7:7	Y woman, your figure is like a
	8:4	Y women of Jerusalem,
	8:5	Who is this y woman coming
	8:13	Y woman living in the gardens,
	8:14	Run like a gazelle or a y stag
Isa	3:5	The y will make fun of the old,
	5:29	They growl like a y lion.
	7:21	person will keep alive a y cow
	9:17	isn't happy with their y men,
	11:6	Calves, y lions, and year-old
	11:7	Their y will lie down together.
	20:4	will lead away both the y
	30:6	on the backs of y donkeys
	31:4	to me: A lion, even a y lion,
	31:8	and their y men will be made to
	34:7	y bulls along with rams.
	34:15	They will gather their y in the
	40:30	Even y people grow tired and
	40:30	and y men will stumble and
	47:12	them ever since you were y.
	47:15	you ever since you were y.
	53:2	up in his presence like a y tree,
	54:4	you've had since you were y.
	54:6	a wife who married y and was
	60:6	y camels from Midian and
	62:5	As a y man marries a woman,

Isa 65:20 old will be thought of as y.
65:23 give birth to children who die y,
Jer 2:15 Y lions have roared very loudly
2:15 Y lions have turned the land
2:23 You are like a y camel that
2:32 A y woman can't forget her
3:4 companion ever since I was y.
3:24 Ever since we were y,
3:25 Ever since we were y,
6:11 and on the gangs of y men.
9:21 in the streets and the y men
11:22 The y men will die because of
14:5 give birth and abandon their y
15:8 against the mothers of y men.
16:6 "Old and y alike will die in this
18:21 Their y men will be struck
22:21 been ever since you were y.
31:13 Then y women will rejoice and
31:13 and dance along with y men
31:18 I was like a y, untrained calf.
31:19 I have done ever since I was y.'
32:30 Ever since they were y,
48:11 securely ever since it was y.
48:15 Its finest y men will be
49:26 That is why its y men will die
50:27 Kill all their y bulls.
50:30 That is why their y men will
51:3 Don't spare Babylon's y men.
51:22 you to crush the old and the y.
51:22 to crush y men and women.
Lam 1:4 Its y women are made to suffer.
1:15 an army to defeat my y men.
1:18 My y women and young men
1:18 My young women and y men
2:10 The y women of Jerusalem
2:21 Y and old lie on the ground in
2:21 My y women and men are cut
3:27 endure burdens when they're y.
3:51 because of all the y women
4:3 their breasts to nurse their y,
5:13 ⌊Our⌋ y men work at the mill,
5:14 and ⌊our⌋ y men no longer play
Eze 4:14 the time I was y until now,
9:6 Kill old men, y men,
9:6 y women, and children.
16:7 and became a y woman.
16:22 the time when you were y.
16:43 the time when you were y,
16:60 with you when you were y,
19:3 she raised became a y lion.
19:5 and raised him into a y lion.
19:6 He became a y lion,
23:3 in Egypt when they were y.
23:6 They were all handsome y
23:8 When she was y, men went to
23:12 all of them desirable y men.
23:19 in Egypt when she was y.
23:21 did when she was y in Egypt,
23:21 when y men caressed and
23:23 They are desirable y men,
30:17 The y men from Heliopolis and
31:6 gave birth to their y under it.
43:19 Give a y bull to the priests as
43:21 Then take a y bull as an
43:22 altar as you did with the y bull.
43:23 offer a y bull and a ram that
43:25 must sacrifice a goat, a y bull,
45:18 take a y bull that has no
45:22 the common people a y bull as
45:23 seven y bulls that have no
45:24 a half-bushel for each y bull
46:6 offering must be one y bull,
46:7 With each y bull and each ram
46:11 be brought with each y bull,
Dan 1:4 They were to be y men who
1:6 Among these y men were
1:10 than the other y men your age,
1:13 Then compare us to the y men
1:15 than the y men who had
1:18 the y men to Nebuchadnezzar.
Hos 2:15 as she did when she was y,
5:14 lion to Ephraim and like a y lion
Joe 1:4 What y locusts leave,
1:8 Cry loudly like a y woman who
2:25 and the y locusts ate your
2:28 Your y men will see visions.
Amo 3:4 Does a y lion growl in its den
4:10 With swords I killed your best y
8:13 On that day beautiful y women
8:13 and strong y men will faint
Mic 5:8 like a y lion among flocks of
6:7 Should I give him my y child
Nah 2:7 Its y women will be mourning
2:11 that feeding place for y lions?
2:13 a sword will kill your y lions.
Zec 2:4 and say to that y man,
9:9 on a colt, a y pack animal.
9:17 Y men will prosper on grain,
9:17 and y women will prosper on
11:3 The y lions are roaring,
11:16 He will not search for the y.
Mat 19:20 The y man replied,
19:22 When the y man heard this,
21:5 on a colt, a y pack animal.'"
Mar 11:2 As you enter it, you will find a y
11:4 The disciples found the y
14:51 A certain y man was following
15:40 Mary (the mother of y James
16:5 they saw a y man.
16:6 The y man said to them,
Luk 2:24 doves or two y pigeons."
7:14 He said, "Y man, I'm telling you
19:30 As you enter, you will find a y
19:33 were untying the y donkey,
Jon 21:18 When you were y,
Act 2:17 Your y men will see visions.
5:6 Some y men got up,
5:10 When the y men came back,
7:58 with a y man named Saul.
20:9 A y man named Eutychus was
23:17 "Take this y man to the officer.
23:18 The sergeant took the y man to
23:18 He asked me to bring this y
23:19 The officer took the y man by
23:20 The y man answered,
23:22 The officer dismissed the y
1Ti 4:12 look down on you for being y.
2Ti 2:22 lusts which tempt y people.
Tit 2:4 In this way they will teach y
2:5 Also, tell them to teach y
2:6 Encourage y men to use good
1Pe 5:5 Y people, in a similar way,
1Jn 2:13 I'm writing to you, y people,
2:14 I've written to you, y people,
Rev 4:7 the second was like a y bull,

younger (32)

Gen 19:31 The older daughter said to the y
19:34 daughter said to the y one,
19:35 Then the y one went to bed
19:38 The y daughter also gave birth
25:23 and the older will serve the y."
27:15 put them on her y son Jacob.
27:42 she sent for her y son Jacob
29:16 name of the y one was Rachel.
29:18 for your y daughter Rachel."
29:26 the y daughter ⌊in marriage⌋
44:20 who is old and a y brother born
48:14 Ephraim was the y son.
48:19 Nevertheless, his y brother will
Jdg 1:13 son of Caleb's y brother Kenaz,
3:9 son of Caleb's y brother Kenaz.
15:2 Isn't her y sister better looking?
Rut 2:21 'Stay with my y workers until
3:10 you didn't go after the y men,
1Sm 14:49 and Michal (the y daughter).
Job 30:1 "But now those who are y than
Eze 16:46 Your y sister is Sodom.
16:61 I return your older and y sisters
23:4 and the y girl was named
23:11 "Even though her y sister
Mat 2:16 the boys two years old and y
Luk 15:12 The y son said to his father,
15:13 "After a few days, the y son
Rom 9:11 child would serve the y one.
1Ti 5:1 Talk to y men as if they were
5:2 and y women as if they were
5:11 Don't include y widows ⌊on
5:14 So I want y widows to marry,

youngest (25)

Gen 9:24 he found out what his y son
42:13 The y brother stayed with our
42:15 your y brother comes here.
42:20 must bring me your y brother.
42:32 The y brother stayed with our
42:34 But bring me your y brother.
43:29 "Is this your y brother,
43:33 ages — from the oldest to the y.
44:2 Then put my silver cup in the y
44:12 oldest and ended with the y.
44:23 Then you told us, 'If your y
44:26 We can only go back if our y
44:26 see us unless our y brother is
Jos 6:26 It will cost him his y son to set
Jdg 9:5 But Jotham, Jerubbaal's y son,
1Sm 16:11 "There's still the y one,"
17:14 and David was the y.
1Ki 16:34 city doors cost him his y son,
1Ch 24:31 same way as those of the y.
25:8 the y as well as the oldest,
26:13 y and oldest alike,
2Ch 21:17 was Ahaziah, Jehoram's y son.
22:1 Jehoram's y son Ahaziah king
Psa 68:27 Benjamin, the y, is leading
Luk 22:26 among you must be like the y,

youth (13)

1Sm 12:2 you from my y until this day.
Job 13:26 me suffer for the sins of my y.
31:18 (From my y the orphan grew up
33:25 go back to the days of their y.
Psa 25:7 not remember the sins of my y
89:45 You cut short the days of his y
Pro 2:17 the closest friend of her y,
Ecc 11:10 childhood and y are pointless.
Isa 13:18 their bows will smash the y.
Jer 2:2 the unfailing loyalty of your y,
Mal 2:14 you and the wife of your y,
2:15 unfaithful to the wife of your y.
Act 26:4 I lived the earliest days of my y

youthful (1)

Job 20:11 His bones, once full of y vigor,

youths (3)

2Ki 2:24 and tore 42 of these y apart.
Pro 7:7 without much sense among y.
Amo 2:11 Nazirites from among your y.

Z

Z (3)

Rev 1:8 "I am the A and the Z," says
21:6 I am the A and the Z,
22:13 I am the A and the Z,

Zaanan (1)

Mic 1:11 come out, inhabitants of Z.

Zaanannim (2)

Jos 19:33 Heleph at the oak tree at Z.
Jdg 4:11 the oak tree at Z near Kedesh

Zaavan (2)

Gen 36:27 of Ezer: Bilhan, Z, and Akan.
1Ch 1:42 Ezer's sons were Bilhan, Z,

Zabad (8)

1Ch 2:36 Nathan was the father of Z.
2:37 Z was the father of Ephlal.
7:21 Tahath's son was Z.
11:41 the Hittite, Z (son of Ahlai),
2Ch 24:26 who conspired against him: Z,
Ezr 10:27 Jeremoth, Z, and Aziza
10:33 Z, Eliphelet, Jeremai,
10:43 Z, Zebina, Jaddai, Joel,

Zabad's (1)

1Ch 7:21 Z son was Shuthelah.

Zabbai (1)

Ezr 10:28 Hananiah, Z, and Athlai

Zabbai's (1)
Neh 3:20 After him Baruch, Z son, made

Zabbud (1)
Ezr 8:14 Uthai and Z, with 70 males.

Zabdi (6)
Jos 7:1 son of Carmi, grandson of Z,
7:17 and Z was selected.
7:18 son of Carmi, grandson of Z,
1Ch 8:19 sons were Jakim, Zichri, Z,
27:27 the vineyards: Z from Shepham
Neh 11:17 who was the son of Z,

Zabdiel (2)
1Ch 27:2 Jashobeam, son of Z,
Neh 11:14 man in charge of them was Z,

Zabdi's (1)
Jos 7:18 Then he had Z household

Zabud (1)
1Ki 4:5 Z, son of Nathan, was the

Zaccai (2)
Ezr 2:9 of Z: 760
Neh 7:14 of Z: 760

Zacchaeus (7)
Luk 19:2 A man named Z was there.
19:3 But Z was a small man,
19:4 So Z ran ahead and climbed a
19:5 up and said, "Z, come down!
19:6 Z came down and was glad to
19:8 Z stood up and said to the Lord,
19:9 Then Jesus said to Z,

Zaccur (9)
Num 13:4 names: Shammua, son of Z,
1Ch 4:26 Hammuel's son was Z.
24:27 Shoham, Z, and Ibri (for
25:2 the sons of Asaph were Z,
25:10 The third chose Z,
Neh 3:2 Z, son of Imri, was next to
10:12 Z, Sherebiah, Shebaniah,
12:35 who was the son of Z,
13:13 son of Z and grandson of

Zaccur's (1)
1Ch 4:26 Z son was Shimei.

Zadok (50)
2Sm 8:17 Ahitub's son Z and Abiathar's
15:24 Z and all the Levites with him
15:25 The king told Z, "Take God's
15:27 the king asked Z the priest.
15:29 So Z and Abiathar took the ark
15:35 The priests Z and Abiathar will
15:35 it to the priests Z and Abiathar.
15:36 with them: Z has Ahimaaz,
17:15 told the priests Z and Abiathar,
19:11 to the priests Z and Abiathar:
20:25 Z and Abiathar were priests.
1Ki 1:8 But the priest Z, Benaiah (son
1:26 me or the priest Z or Benaiah,
1:32 "Summon the priest Z,
1:34 Have the priest Z and the
1:38 Then the priest Z, the prophet
1:39 The priest Z took the container
1:44 The king has sent the priest Z,
1:45 The priest Z and the prophet
2:35 Abiathar with the priest Z.
4:2 his officials: Azariah, son of Z,
4:4 Z and Abiathar were priests.
2Ki 15:33 was Jerusha, daughter of Z.
1Ch 6:8 Ahitub was the father of Z.
6:8 Z was the father of Ahimaaz.
6:12 Ahitub was the father of Z.
6:12 Z was the father of Shallum.
6:53 Ahitub's son was Z.
9:11 and great-grandson of Z.
12:28 and Z, a young warrior from
15:11 David called for the priests Z
16:39 David left Z and his priestly
16:41 With Z and his relatives were
18:16 Ahitub's son Z and Abiathar's
24:3 David, Eleazar's descendant Z,
24:6 king, the princes, the priest Z,
24:31 of King David, Z, Ahimelech,
27:17 for the family of Aaron: Z
29:22 Solomon to be leader and Z
2Ch 27:1 was Jerushah, daughter of Z.
Ezr 7:2 who was the son of Z,
Neh 3:4 Next to them Z, son of Baana,
3:29 After them Z, Immer's son,
10:21 Meshezabel, Z, Jaddua,
11:11 who was the son of Z,
13:13 the priest, Z the scribe,
Eze 44:15 and descendants of Z took care
48:11 who are descendants of Z.
Mat 1:14 Azor the father of Z,
1:14 Z the father of Achim,

Zadok's (8)
2Sm 18:19 Then Ahimaaz, Z son, said,
18:22 Z son, spoke to Joab again,
18:27 Z son." "He's a good man,"
1Ch 6:53 Z son was Ahimaaz.
9:11 Z father was Meraioth,
2Ch 31:10 Azariah from Z family said,
Eze 40:46 priests are Z descendants.
43:19 are Z descendants, men from

Zaham (1)
2Ch 11:19 Jeush, Shemariah, and Z.

Zair (1)
2Ki 8:21 took all his chariots to attack Z.

Zalaph's (1)
Neh 3:30 son, and Hanun, Z sixth son,

Zalmon (3)
Jdg 9:48 all his men went to Mount Z.
2Sm 23:28 Z (descendant of Ahohi),
Psa 68:14 like snow falling on Mount Z."

Zalmonah (2)
Num 33:41 Hor and set up camp at Z.
33:42 They moved from Z and set up

Zalmunna (11)
Jdg 8:5 Zebah and King Z of Midian."
8:6 captured Zebah and Z yet."
8:7 LORD hands Zebah and Z over
8:10 Zebah and Z were in Karkor
8:12 Zebah and Z fled as Gideon
8:12 Zebah and King Z of Midian,
8:15 "Here are Zebah and Z!
8:15 you've captured Zebah and Z."'
8:18 He asked Zebah and Z,
8:21 Zebah and Z said,
Psa 83:11 their leaders like Zebah and Z.

Zamzummim (1)
Dtr 2:20 the Ammonites called them Z.

Zanoah (5)
Jos 15:34 Z, En Gannim, Tappuah,
15:56 Jezreel, Jokdeam, Z,
1Ch 4:18 who first settled Z.
Neh 3:13 Hanun and the people of Z
11:30 Z, and Adullam and their

Zaphenathpaneah (1)
Gen 41:45 Pharaoh named Joseph Z and

Zaphon (2)
Jos 13:27 Beth Nimrah, Succoth, and Z,
Jdg 12:1 ⌊the Jordan River⌋ to Z.

Zarephath (4)
1Ki 17:9 "Get up, go to Z (which
17:10 He got up and went to Z.
Oba 1:20 will possess land as far as Z.
Luk 4:26 to anyone except a widow at Z

Zarethan (3)
Jos 3:16 as the city of Adam near Z.
1Ki 4:12 (This was near Z, from Beth
7:46 Valley between Succoth and Z.

Zattu (5)
Ezr 2:8 of Z: 945
8:5 from the family of Z:
10:27 From the descendants of Z:
Neh 7:13 of Z: 845
10:14 Pahath Moab, Elam, Z, Bani,

Zaza (1)
1Ch 2:33 sons were Peleth and Z.

Zealot (4)
Mat 10:4 Simon the Z and Judas
Mar 3:18 Thaddaeus, Simon the Z,
Luk 6:15 Simon (who was called the Z),
Act 1:13 of Alphaeus), Simon the Z,

Zebadiah (9)
1Ch 8:15 Beriah's sons were Z,
8:17 Elpaal's sons were Z,
12:7 and Joelah and Z,
26:2 (the second), Z (the third),
27:7 and after him was his son Z.
2Ch 17:8 Z, Asahel, Shemiramoth,
19:11 Z, who is the son of Ishmael
Ezr 8:8 Shephatiah: Z, son of Michael,
10:20 of Immer: Hanani and Z

Zebah (11)
Jdg 8:5 and I'm pursuing King Z and
8:6 captured Z and Zalmunna yet."
8:7 When the LORD hands Z and
8:10 Z and Zalmunna were in
8:12 Z and Zalmunna fled as
8:12 He captured King Z and King
8:15 "Here are Z and Zalmunna!
8:15 captured Z and Zalmunna."'
8:18 He asked Z and Zalmunna,
8:21 Z and Zalmunna said,
Psa 83:11 leaders like Z and Zalmunna.

Zebedee (6)
Mat 4:21 and John, the sons of Z.
4:21 father Z preparing their nets
10:2 his brother John, the sons of Z;
Mar 1:19 and John, the sons of Z.
1:20 and they left their father Z and
10:35 James and John, sons of Z,

Zebedee's (6)
Mat 20:20 Then the mother of Z sons
26:37 He took Peter and Z two sons
27:56 and the mother of Z sons
Mar 3:17 (Z sons whom Jesus named
Luk 5:10 who were Z sons and Simon's
Jon 21:2 Z sons, and two other

Zebidah (1)
2Ki 23:36 His mother was Z,

Zebina (1)
Ezr 10:43 Z, Jaddai, Joel, and Benaiah

Zeboiim (4)
Gen 10:19 and Z as far as Lasha.
14:2 King Shemeber of Z,
14:8 Admah, Z, and Bela (that is,
Dtr 29:23 Gomorrah, Admah, and Z,

Zeboim (3)
1Sm 13:18 the valley of Z and the desert.
Neh 11:34 Hadid, Z, Neballat,
Hos 11:8 How can I treat you like Z?

Zebul (6)
Jdg 9:28 and isn't Z his officer?
9:30 Z, Shechem's ruler, heard what
9:36 the troops, he said to Z, "Look,
9:36 Z replied, "The shadows of the
9:38 Then Z said to him,
9:41 Z threw Gaal and his brothers

Zebulun (50)
Gen 30:20 So she named him Z [Honor].
35:23 Levi, Judah, Issachar, and Z.
46:14 The sons of Z were Sered,

Gen 49:13 "Z will live by the coast.
Exo 1:3 Issachar, Z, and Benjamin;
Num 1:9 from the tribe of Z;
1:30 for the descendants of Z listed
1:31 for the tribe of Z was 57,400.
2:7 "Then ⌊will be⌋ the tribe of Z.
2:7 for the people of Z is Eliab,
7:24 leader of the descendants of Z,
10:16 commanded the army of Z.
13:10 from the tribe of Z;
26:26 The families descended from Z
26:27 These were the families of Z.
34:25 the leader of the tribe of Z;
Dtr 27:13 Asher, Z, Dan, and Naphtali.
33:18 About the tribe of Z he said,
33:18 Zebulun he said, "People of Z,
Jos 19:10 the families descended from Z.
19:16 the families descended from Z.
19:27 to Beth Dagon and touches Z
19:34 It touches Z in the south,
21:7 tribes of Reuben, Gad, and Z.
21:34 the tribe of Z gave four cities
Jdg 1:30 The tribe of Z did not force out
4:6 from Naphtali and Z with you.
4:10 Barak called the tribes of Z
5:14 The officers from Z also went.
5:18 But Z mocked death,
6:35 The tribes of Asher, Z,
12:11 from the tribe of Z judged Israel.
12:12 in Aijalon in the territory of Z.
1Ch 2:1 Levi, Judah, Issachar, Z,
6:63 tribes of Reuben, Gad, and Z.
6:77 pastureland from the tribe of Z.
12:33 From Z there were 50,000
12:40 as the territories of Issachar, Z,
27:19 for the tribe of Z: Ishmaiah,
2Ch 30:10 and Manasseh, as far as Z.
30:11 and Z humbled themselves
30:18 and Z had not made
Psa 68:27 ⌊then⌋ the leaders of Z,
Isa 9:1 God humbled the lands of Z
Eze 48:26 Z will have one part of the land
48:27 part of the land and border Z
48:33 Issachar Gate, and Z Gate.
Mat 4:13 in the region of Z and Naphtali.
4:15 "Land of Z and land of Naphtali,
Rev 7:8 12,000 from the tribe of Z,

Zechariah (62)

2Ki 14:29 His son Z succeeded him as
15:8 Jeroboam's son Z was king of
15:10 of Jabesh, plotted against Z,
15:11 Everything else about Z is
18:2 mother was Abi, daughter of Z.
1Ch 5:7 The first was Jeiel, then Z
9:21 Z, son of Meshelemiah,
9:37 Gedor, Ahio, Z, and Mikloth.
15:18 Z, Jaaziel, Shemiramoth,
15:20 Z, Jaziel, Shemiramoth, Jehiel,
15:24 Nethanel, Amasai, Z, Benaiah,
16:5 Z was second, then Jeiel,
24:25 and Z (for ⌊Uzziel's⌋
26:2 sons were Z (the firstborn),
26:11 (the third), and Z (the fourth).
26:14 His son Z, a counselor who
27:21 son of Z for the tribe of
2Ch 17:7 Hail, Obadiah, Z, Nethanel,
20:14 (He was the son of Z,
21:2 Jehiel, Z, Azariahu, Michael,
24:20 God's Spirit gave Z,
24:20 Z stood in front of the people
24:21 But they plotted against Z,
24:22 As Z died, he said, "May the
26:5 to serving God in the days of Z,
29:1 was Abijah, daughter of Z.
29:13 were Z and Mattaniah.
34:12 and Z and Meshullam
35:8 Hilkiah, Z, and Jehiel, the men
Ezr 5:1 The prophet Haggai and Z,
6:14 from the prophet Haggai and Z,
8:3 from the family of Parosh: Z,
8:11 from the family of Bebai: Z,
8:16 Jarib, Elnathan, Nathan, Z,
10:26 Z, Jehiel, Abdi, Jeremoth,
Neh 8:4 Hashum, Hashbaddanah, Z,
11:4 who was the son of Z,
Neh 11:5 who was the son of Z,
11:12 who was the son of Z,
12:16 from Iddo, Z; from Ginnethon,
12:35 some priests with trumpets: Z,
12:36 these relatives of Z followed:
12:41 Z, and Hananiah with trumpets,
Isa 8:2 and Z (son of Jeberechiah)."
Zec 1:1 his word to the prophet Z,
1:7 his word to the prophet Z,
7:1 the LORD spoke his word to Z.
7:8 the LORD spoke his word to Z.
Mat 23:35 of righteous Abel to that of Z,
Luk 1:5 there was a priest named Z,
1:6 Z and Elizabeth had God's
1:8 Z was on duty with his
1:12 Z was troubled and overcome
1:13 said to him, "Don't be afraid, Z!
1:18 Z said to the angel,
1:21 the people were waiting for Z.
1:59 to name him Z after his father.
1:63 Z asked for a writing tablet and
1:64 Z was able to speak,
1:67 His father Z was filled with the
3:2 to John, son of Z, in the desert.
11:51 the murders from Abel to Z,

Zechariah's (3)

2Ch 24:22 how kind Z father, Jehoiada,
Luk 1:5 Z wife Elizabeth was a
1:40 She entered Z home and

Zecher (1)

1Ch 8:31 Gedor, Ahio, Z,

Zedad (2)

Num 34:8 of Hamath so that it ends at Z.
Eze 47:15 the city of Z and through

Zedekiah (68)

1Ki 22:11 Z, son of Chenaanah,
22:24 Then Z, son of Chenaanah,
2Ki 24:17 Mattaniah's name to Z.
24:18 Z was 21 years old when he
24:19 Z did what the LORD
24:20 Z rebelled against the king of
25:5 army pursued King Z
25:7 and then they blinded Z.
1Ch 3:15 Jehoiakim, the third was Z,
3:16 whose son was Z.
2Ch 18:10 Z, son of Chenaanah,
18:23 Z, son of Chenaanah, went to
36:10 made Jehoiakin's uncle Z king
36:11 Z was 21 years old when he
36:13 Z also rebelled against King
36:13 Nebuchadnezzar had made Z
36:13 But Z became so stubborn and
Neh 10:1 Nehemiah (son of Hacaliah), Z,
Jer 1:3 and during the 11 years that Z,
21:1 when King Z sent Pashhur,
21:3 is what you should say to Z,
21:7 I will hand over Judah's King Z,
24:8 I will abandon King Z of Judah,
27:1 When Z, son of King Josiah of
27:3 who have come to King Z
27:12 message to King Z of Judah,
28:1 in the rule of King Z of Judah,
29:3 whom King Z of Judah had
29:21 and about Maaseiah's son Z,
29:22 you as he cursed Z and Ahab,
32:3 When King Z of Judah locked
32:3 up Jeremiah, Z asked him,
32:4 King Z of Judah will not
32:5 will take Z to Babylon,
32:5 and Z will stay there until I
34:2 Go to King Z of Judah,
34:4 of the LORD, King Z of Judah.
34:6 told all these things to King Z
34:8 word to Jeremiah after King Z
34:21 I will hand King Z of Judah and
36:12 Z (son of Hananiah),
37:1 of Babylon appointed Z,
37:1 Z succeeded Jehoiakin,
37:2 But Z, his administrators,
37:3 King Z sent Jehucal (son of
37:17 Then King Z sent for Jeremiah,
37:18 Then Jeremiah asked King Z,
Jer 37:21 King Z gave the command to
38:5 King Z answered, "He's in your
38:14 King Z sent for the prophet
38:15 Jeremiah answered Z,
38:16 So King Z secretly swore an
38:17 Jeremiah said to Z,
38:19 King Z answered Jeremiah,
38:24 Z said to Jeremiah,
39:4 When King Z of Judah and all
39:5 them and caught up with Z
39:6 sons as Z watched at Riblah.
39:7 Then he blinded Z,
44:30 just as I handed over King Z of
49:34 in the rule of King Z of Judah,
51:59 went to Babylon with King Z
52:1 Z was 21 years old when he
52:2 Z did what the LORD
52:3 Z rebelled against the king of
52:8 army pursued King Z
52:10 Zedekiah's sons as Z watched.
52:11 Then he blinded Z and put him

Zedekiah's (11)

2Ki 25:1 Z reign, King Nebuchadnezzar
25:2 until Z eleventh year as king.
25:7 They slaughtered Z sons as he
Jer 32:1 during Z tenth year as king
39:1 In the tenth month of Z ninth
39:2 of Z eleventh year as king,
39:6 Z sons as Zedekiah watched
51:59 in the fourth year of Z rule.
52:4 Z reign, King Nebuchadnezzar
52:5 until Z eleventh year as king.
52:10 Z sons as Zedekiah watched.

Zeeb (6)

Jdg 7:25 also captured Oreb and Z,
7:25 at the Rock of Oreb and Z at
7:25 and Zeeb at the Winepress of Z
7:25 severed heads of Oreb and Z
8:3 God handed Oreb and Z,
Psa 83:11 as you treated Oreb and Z.

Zela (2)

Jos 18:28 Z, Eleph, Jebus (now called
2Sm 21:14 in the land of Benjamin, in Z,

Zelek (2)

2Sm 23:37 Z from Ammon, Naharai from
1Ch 11:39 Z from Ammon, Naharai from

Zelophehad (6)

Num 26:33 (Z, son of Hepher, had no sons
27:1 The daughters of Z,
36:2 our relative Z to his daughters.
Jos 17:3 Z, son of Hepher, grandson of
1Ch 7:15 name of his second son was Z.
7:15 Z had only daughters.

Zelophehad's (3)

Num 27:7 "Z daughters are right.
36:6 Z daughters: They may marry
36:10 Z daughters did as the LORD

Zelzah (1)

1Sm 10:2 on the border of Benjamin at Z.

Zemaraim (2)

Jos 18:22 Beth Arabah, Z, Bethel,
2Ch 13:4 Then Abijah stood on Mount Z

Zemarites (2)

Gen 10:18 the Arvadites, the Z,
1Ch 1:16 the Arvadites, the Z,

Zemirah (1)

1Ch 7:8 Becher's sons were Z,

Zenan (1)

Jos 15:37 Z, Hadashah, Migdalgad,

Zenas (1)

Tit 3:13 Give Z the lawyer and Apollos

Zephaniah (10)

2Ki 25:18 the second priest Z,

1Ch 6:36 who was the son of **Z**,
Jer 21:1 of Malchiah, and the priest **Z**,
29:25 in Jerusalem, to the priest **Z**,
29:29 The priest **Z** read this letter to
37:3 and the priest **Z** (son
52:24 the second priest **Z**,
Zep 1:1 word that the LORD spoke to **Z**,
Zec 6:10 the house of Josiah, son of **Z**.
6:14 and Hen (son of **Z**) in the

Zephath (1)
Jdg 1:17 the Canaanites who lived in **Z**

Zephathah (1)
2Ch 14:10 in the **Z** Valley at Mareshah.

Zephi (1)
1Ch 1:36 and Omar, **Z** and Gatam,

Zepho (2)
Gen 36:11 Omar, **Z**, Gatam, and Kenaz.
36:15 were Teman, Omar, **Z**, Kenaz,

Zephon (1)
Num 26:15 from Gad were the family of **Z**,

Zer (1)
Jos 19:35 Ziddim, **Z**, Hammath, Rakkath,

Zerah (26)
Gen 36:13 **Z**, Shammah, and Mizzah.
36:17 **Z**, Shammah, and Mizzah.
36:33 son of **Z** from Bozrah,
38:30 He was named **Z** [Sunrise].
46:12 Onan, Shelah, Perez, and **Z**.
Num 26:13 the family of **Z**, and the family
26:20 and the family of **Z**.
Jos 7:1 great-grandson of **Z**,
7:17 the family of **Z** was selected.
7:17 Then he had the family of **Z**
7:18 and great-grandson of **Z**.
7:24 all Israel took Achan (son of **Z**),
22:20 Didn't Achan, son of **Z**,
1Ch 1:37 Reuel's sons were Nahath, **Z**,
1:44 son of **Z** from Bozrah,
2:4 to Judah's sons Perez and **Z**.
4:24 Jamin, Jarib, **Z**, and Shaul.
6:21 Iddo's son was **Z**. Zerah's son
6:41 who was the son of **Z**,
9:6 And from the descendants of **Z**
27:11 descendant of **Z** from Hushah,
27:13 of **Z** from Netophah,
2Ch 14:9 Then **Z** from Sudan came with
14:9 **Z** got as far as Mareshah.
Neh 11:24 one of the descendants of **Z**,
Mat 1:3 and mother of Perez and **Z**.

Zerahiah (5)
1Ch 6:6 Uzzi was the father of **Z**.
6:6 **Z** was the father of Meraioth.
6:51 Uzzi's son was **Z**.
Ezr 7:4 who was the son of **Z**,
8:4 son of **Z**, with 200 males

Zerahiah's (1)
1Ch 6:52 **Z** son was Meraioth.

Zerah's (2)
1Ch 2:6 **Z** sons were Zimri,
6:21 **Z** son was Jeatherai.

Zered (4)
Num 21:12 and set up camp at the **Z** River.
Dtr 2:13 "Now cross the **Z** River."
2:13 So we crossed the **Z** River.
2:14 until we crossed the **Z** River.

Zeredah (2)
1Ki 11:26 Nebat and an Ephrathite from **Z**.
2Ch 4:17 Valley between Succoth and **Z**.

Zererah (1)
Jdg 7:22 far as Beth Shittah, toward **Z**,

Zeresh (4)
Est 5:10 for his friends and his wife **Z**.
Est 5:14 Then his wife **Z** and all his
6:13 to relate in detail to his wife **Z**
6:13 and his wife **Z** told him,

Zereth (1)
1Ch 4:7 Helah's sons were **Z**,

Zereth Shahar (1)
Jos 13:19 Sibmah, **Z** on the mountain in

Zeri (1)
1Ch 25:3 Gedaliah, **Z**, Jeshaiah, Shimei,

Zeror (1)
1Sm 9:1 a son of Abiel, grandson of **Z**,

Zeruah (1)
1Ki 11:26 His mother **Z** was a widow.

Zerubbabel (22)
1Ch 3:19 sons were **Z** and Shimei.
Ezr 2:2 They went with **Z**,
3:2 priests and Shealtiel's son **Z**
3:8 **Z** (who was Shealtiel's son),
4:2 they approached **Z** and the
4:3 But **Z**, Jeshua, and the rest of
5:2 Then **Z**, who was Shealtiel's
Neh 7:7 They went with **Z**,
12:1 back with **Z** (Shealtiel's son)
12:47 At the time of **Z** and Nehemiah,
Hag 1:1 prophet Haggai to **Z** (who was
1:12 Then **Z** (who was the son of
1:14 So **Z** (who was the son of
2:2 "Now, speak to **Z** (who is the
2:4 "But now, **Z**, be strong,"
2:21 "Say to **Z** (governor of Judah),
2:23 my servant **Z** (son of Shealtiel),
Zec 4:6 the word the LORD spoke to **Z**:
4:7 In front of **Z** you will become a
Mat 1:12 Shealtiel was the father of **Z**,
1:13 **Z** the father of Abiud,
Luk 3:27 son of **Z**, son of Shealtiel,

Zerubbabel's (3)
1Ch 3:19 **Z** sons were Meshullam and
Zec 4:9 "**Z** hands have laid the
4:10 see the plumb line in **Z** hand.

Zeruiah (8)
2Sm 16:10 think like me at all, sons of **Z**.
17:25 and sister of Joab's mother **Z**.)
19:22 the same family, sons of **Z**?
21:17 But Abishai, son of **Z**,
1Ki 1:7 his actions with Joab (son of **Z**)
1Ch 2:16 sisters were **Z** and Abigail.
26:28 and Joab (son of **Z**) had
27:24 Joab, son of **Z**, started to count

Zeruiah's (18)
1Sm 26:6 who was **Z** son and Joab's
2Sm 2:13 **Z** son Joab and David's
2:18 **Z** three sons were there:
3:39 **Z** sons, are too cruel for me.
8:16 **Z** son Joab was in charge of
14:1 Joab, **Z** son, knew the king
16:9 Abishai, **Z** son, asked the king,
18:2 Joab's brother Abishai (**Z** son),
19:21 But Abishai, **Z** son, replied,
23:18 Joab's brother Abishai, **Z** son,
23:37 armorbearer for **Z** son Joab,
1Ki 2:5 "You know what Joab (**Z** son)
2:22 (**Z** son) are supporting him."
1Ch 2:16 **Z** three sons were Abishai,
11:6 **Z** son Joab was the first to go
11:39 armorbearer for **Z** son Joab,
18:12 **Z** son Abishai killed 18,000
18:15 **Z** son Joab was in charge of

Zetham (2)
1Ch 23:8 was the first, then **Z**, and Joel.
26:22 Jehiel's sons **Z** and Joel.

Zethan (1)
1Ch 7:10 **Z**, Tarshish, and Ahishahar.

Zethar (1)
Est 1:10 Abagtha, **Z**, and Carcas,

Zeus (3)
Act 14:12 They addressed Barnabas as **Z**
14:13 The priest of the god **Z** brought
19:35 the statue that fell down from **Z**.

Zeus' (1)
Act 14:13 **Z** temple was at the entrance

Zia (1)
1Ch 5:13 Jorai, Jacan, **Z**, and Eber.

Ziba (16)
2Sm 9:2 a servant whose name was **Z**.
9:2 "Are you **Z**?" the king asked
9:3 who is disabled," **Z** answered.
9:4 **Z** replied, "He is at the home of
9:9 Then the king called for **Z**,
9:10 (**Z** had 15 sons and 20
9:11 **Z** responded, "I will do
16:1 **Z**, Mephibosheth's servant,
16:2 David asked **Z**. "The donkeys
16:2 family to ride on," **Z** answered.
16:3 **Z** answered the king.
16:4 The king told **Z**, "In that case
16:4 "I sincerely thank you," said **Z**.
19:17 And **Z**, the servant of Saul's
19:17 **Z** brought his 15 sons and 20
19:29 I've said that you and **Z** should

Ziba's (1)
2Sm 9:12 Everyone who lived at **Z** home

Zibeon (7)
Gen 36:2 granddaughter of **Z** the Hivite;
36:14 Anah and granddaughter of **Z**.
36:20 land: Lotan, Shobal, **Z**, Anah,
36:24 These were the sons of **Z**:
36:24 that belonged to his father **Z**.)
36:29 Lotan, Shobal, **Z**, Anah,
1Ch 1:38 Shobal, **Z**, Anah, Dishon, Ezer,

Zibeon's (1)
1Ch 1:40 **Z** sons were Aiah and Anah.

Zibia (1)
1Ch 8:9 Jobab, **Z**, Mesha, Malcam,

Zibiah (2)
2Ki 12:1 mother was **Z** from Beersheba.
2Ch 24:1 mother was **Z** from Beersheba.

Zichri (11)
Exo 6:21 were Korah, Nepheg, and **Z**.
1Ch 8:19 Shimei's sons were Jakim, **Z**,
8:23 Abdon, **Z**, Hanan,
8:27 Jaareshiah, Elijah, and **Z**.
9:15 (son of Mica, grandson of **Z**,
26:25 Joram's son was **Z**;
27:16 son of **Z** for the tribe of Simeon:
2Ch 23:1 and Elishaphat, son of **Z**.
28:7 **Z**, a fighting man from Ephraim,
Neh 11:9 Joel, son of **Z**, was in charge,
12:17 from Abijah, **Z**; from Miniamin,

Zichri's (1)
2Ch 17:16 **Z** son, who volunteered to

Ziddim (1)
Jos 19:35 The fortified cities were **Z**,

Ziha (3)
Ezr 2:43 the descendants of **Z**,
Neh 7:46 the descendants of **Z**,
11:21 lived on Mount Ophel with **Z**

Ziklag (15)
Jos 15:31 **Z**, Madmannah, Sansannah,
19:5 **Z**, Beth Marcaboth,
1Sm 27:6 immediately gave him **Z**.
27:6 (This is why **Z** still belongs to
30:1 David and his men came to **Z**,
30:1 raided the Negev, including **Z**.

1Sm 30:1 had attacked **Z** and burned it.
30:14 and we burned down **Z**."
30:26 When David came to **Z**,
2Sm 1:1 David stayed in **Z** two days.
4:10 I killed him in **Z** to reward him
1Ch 4:30 Bethuel, Hormah, **Z**,
12:1 who came to David at **Z** when
12:20 When David went to **Z**,
Neh 11:28 in **Z**, and in Meconah and its

Zillah (3)

Gen 4:19 named Adah and the other **Z**.
4:22 **Z** also had a son, Tubalcain,
4:23 "Adah and **Z**, listen to me!

Zillethai (2)

1Ch 8:20 Elienai, **Z**, Eliel,
12:20 Jozabad, Elihu, and **Z**.

Zilpah (7)

Gen 29:24 (Laban had given his slave **Z**
30:9 she took her slave **Z** and gave
30:10 Leah's slave **Z** gave birth to a
30:12 Leah's slave **Z** gave birth to her
35:26 The sons of Leah's slave **Z**
37:2 with the sons of Bilhah and **Z**,
46:18 were the descendants of **Z**,

Zimmah (3)

1Ch 6:20 Jahath's son was **Z**.
6:42 who was the son of **Z**,
2Ch 29:12 were Joah, son of **Z**, and Eden,

Zimmah's (1)

1Ch 6:21 **Z** son was Joah. Joah's son

Zimran (2)

Gen 25:2 **Z**, Jokshan, Medan, Midian,
1Ch 1:32 **Z**, Jokshan, Medan, Midian,

Zimri (17)

Num 25:14 the Midianite woman was **Z**,
1Ki 16:9 But **Z**, the general who
16:10 **Z** entered Arza's house,
16:10 **Z** succeeded Elah as king ⌊of
16:12 So **Z** destroyed Baasha's entire
16:15 **Z** ruled for seven days in
16:16 When the army heard that **Z**
16:18 When **Z** saw that the city had
16:19 **Z** lived like Jeroboam and led
16:20 Isn't everything else about **Z**
2Ki 9:31 **Z**, murderer of your master?"
1Ch 2:6 Zerah's sons were **Z**,
8:36 of Alemeth, Azmaveth, and **Z**.
8:36 **Z** was the father of Moza.
9:42 of Alemeth, Azmaveth, and **Z**.
9:42 **Z** was the father of Moza.
Jer 25:25 all the kings of **Z**, all the kings

Zimri's (1)

1Ki 16:11 At the beginning of **Z** reign, as

Zin (10)

Num 13:21 the land from the Desert of **Z**
20:1 came into the Desert of **Z**,
27:14 command in the Desert of **Z**.
27:14 at Kadesh in the Desert of **Z**.)
33:36 at Kadesh in the Desert of **Z**.
34:3 part of the Desert of **Z** along
34:4 It then goes past **Z** and ends at
Dtr 32:51 at Kadesh in the Desert of **Z**.
Jos 15:1 of Edom and the desert of **Z**.
15:3 It then passes **Z** and goes up

Zina (1)

1Ch 23:10 Shimei's sons were Jahath, **Z**,

Zion (163)

2Sm 5:7 captured the fortress **Z** (that is,
1Ki 8:1 the City of David (that is, **Z**).
2Ki 19:21 'My dear people in **Z** despise
19:31 escape will go out of Mount **Z**.
1Ch 11:5 captured the fortress **Z** (that is,
2Ch 5:2 the City of David (that is, **Z**).
Psa 2:6 installed my own king on **Z**,
9:11 who is enthroned in **Z**.
Psa 9:14 one by one in the gates of **Z**
14:7 for Israel would come from **Z**!
20:2 place and support you from **Z**.
48:2 Mount **Z** is on the northern
48:5 ⌊When⌋ they saw ⌊Mount **Z**⌋,
48:8 God makes **Z** stand firm
48:11 Let Mount **Z** be glad and the
48:12 Walk around **Z**. Go around it.
50:2 God shines from **Z**,
51:18 Favor **Z** with your goodness.
53:6 for Israel would come from **Z**!
65:1 are praised with silence in **Z**,
69:35 When God saves **Z**,
74:2 This tribe is Mount **Z**,
76:2 is in Salem. His home is in **Z**.
78:68 Mount **Z** which he loved.
84:7 appears in front of God in **Z**.
87:2 The LORD loves the city of **Z**
87:5 But it will be said of **Z**,
87:7 "**Z** is the source of all our
97:8 **Z** hears about this and rejoices.
99:2 The LORD is mighty in **Z**.
102:13 and have compassion on **Z**,
102:16 When the LORD builds **Z**,
102:21 name is announced in **Z**
110:2 your powerful scepter from **Z**.
125:1 the LORD are like Mount **Z**,
126:1 restored the fortunes of **Z**,
128:5 bless you from **Z** so that you
129:5 to shame all those who hate **Z**.
132:13 The LORD has chosen **Z**.
132:14 sit enthroned because I want **Z**.
132:15 certainly bless all that **Z** needs.
134:3 and earth, bless you from **Z**.
135:21 Thank the LORD in **Z**.
137:1 and cried as we remembered **Z**.
137:3 "Sing a song from **Z** for us!"
146:10 **Z**, your God rules throughout
147:12 Praise your God, **Z**!
149:2 Let the people of **Z** rejoice over
Sos 3:11 Young women of **Z**,
Isa 1:8 My people **Z** are left like a hut
1:27 **Z** will be pardoned by ⌊the
2:3 teachings will go out from **Z**.
3:16 "The women of **Z** are arrogant.
3:17 the heads of the women of **Z**,
3:26 The gates of **Z** will cry and
3:26 and **Z** will sit on the ground,
4:3 Then whoever is left in **Z** and
4:5 over the whole area of Mount **Z**
8:18 who lives on Mount **Z**.
10:12 all his work on Mount **Z**
10:24 My people who live in **Z**,
10:32 at the mountain of my people **Z**,
12:6 and sing with joy, people of **Z**!
16:1 desert to my people at Mount **Z**.
18:7 will be brought to Mount **Z**,
24:23 of Armies will rule on Mount **Z**
28:16 I am going to lay a rock in **Z**,
29:8 that fight against Mount **Z**.
30:19 You will live in **Z**, You won't cry
31:4 to fight for Mount **Z** and its hill.
31:9 His fire is in **Z** and his furnace
33:5 He will fill **Z** with justice and
33:14 The sinners in **Z** are terrified.
33:20 Look at **Z**, the city of our
33:24 one who lives ⌊in **Z**⌋ will say,
34:8 year of revenge in defense of **Z**.
35:10 They will come to **Z** singing
37:22 'My dear people in **Z** despise
37:32 will go out from Mount **Z**.
40:9 Go up a high mountain, **Z**.
41:27 I was the first to tell **Z**,
46:13 I'll provide salvation for **Z** and
49:14 But **Z** said, "The LORD has
51:3 So the LORD will comfort **Z**.
51:11 They will come to **Z** singing
51:16 of the earth, and said to **Z**,
52:1 yourself with strength, **Z**!
52:2 captive people of **Z**.
52:7 and tells **Z** that its God rules
52:8 When the LORD brings **Z** back,
59:20 "Then a Savior will come to **Z**,
60:14 you the city of the LORD, **Z**,
61:3 for all those who grieve in **Z**,
62:11 "Tell my people **Z**,
Isa 64:10 **Z** has become a desert.
66:8 When **Z** went into labor,
Jer 3:14 and bring you to **Z**.
4:6 flag to signal people to go to **Z**.
4:31 My people **Z** are gasping for
6:2 "My people **Z** are like lovely
6:4 yourselves for war against **Z**.
6:23 for battle against my people **Z**.
8:19 "Isn't the LORD in **Z**?
9:19 sound of crying is heard from **Z**.
14:19 Do you despise **Z**?
26:18 **Z** will be plowed like a field,
30:17 "People call you an outcast: **Z**,
31:6 Let's go to **Z**, to the LORD our
31:12 shout for joy on top of Mount **Z**.
50:5 will ask which road goes to **Z**
50:28 from Babylon are coming to **Z**
51:10 Let's announce in **Z** what the
51:24 did in **Z**," declares the LORD.
51:35 The people who live in **Z** say,
Lam 1:4 "The roads to **Z** are deserted.
1:4 are made to suffer. **Z** is bitter.
1:5 The LORD made **Z** suffer for its
1:6 has abandoned the people of **Z**.
1:17 **Z** holds out its hands.
2:1 has covered the people of **Z**
2:6 and days of worship in **Z**.
2:13 beloved people of **Z**?
4:11 He started a fire in **Z** that even
4:22 People of **Z**, the punishment for
5:11 Women in **Z** are raped,
5:18 roam around on Mount **Z**,
Joe 2:1 Blow the ram's horn in **Z**.
2:15 Blow the ram's horn in **Z**.
2:23 People of **Z**, be glad and find
2:32 who escape will be on Mount **Z**
3:16 The LORD will roar from **Z**,
3:17 I live on my holy mountain, **Z**.
3:21 The LORD lives in **Z**!
Amo 1:2 The LORD roars from **Z**,
6:1 for those who are at ease in **Z**,
Oba 1:17 refugees will live on Mount **Z**.
1:21 will come from Mount **Z**
Mic 1:13 to lead the people of **Z** into sin.
3:10 You build **Z** on bloodshed and
3:12 **Z** will be plowed like a field,
4:2 teachings will go out from **Z**.
4:7 on Mount **Z** now and forever.
4:8 stronghold of the people of **Z**,
4:10 Daughter of **Z**, writhe in pain
4:11 They say, "Let's dishonor **Z**
4:13 Get up and thresh, people of **Z**.
Zep 3:14 Sing happily, people of **Z**!
3:16 be told, "Do not be afraid, **Z**!
Zec 1:14 jealous about Jerusalem and **Z**,
1:17 The LORD will again comfort **Z**
2:7 Hurry, **Z**! Escape, you
2:10 for joy and rejoice, people of **Z**.
8:2 I am very jealous about **Z**.
8:3 I will return to **Z** and live in
9:9 with all your heart, people of **Z**!
9:13 I will stir up your people, **Z**,
Mat 21:5 "Tell the people of **Z**,
Jon 12:15 "Don't be afraid, people of **Z**!
Rom 9:33 "I am placing a rock in **Z** that
11:26 "The Savior will come from **Z**.
Heb 12:22 you have come to Mount **Z**,
1Pe 2:6 and precious cornerstone in **Z**,
Rev 14:1 lamb was standing on Mount **Z**.

Zion's (14)

Psa 102:14 Your servants value **Z** stones,
133:3 comes down on **Z** mountains.
Isa 4:4 away the filth of **Z** people.
14:32 LORD has laid **Z** foundation,
62:1 For **Z** sake I will not remain
Jer 8:19 Isn't **Z** king still there?"
Lam 2:4 like fire on the tent of **Z** people
2:7 the walls of **Z** palaces over
2:8 to destroy the wall of **Z** people.
2:9 "⌊**Z**⌋ gates have sunk into the
2:10 leaders of **Z** people sit silently
2:18 the wall of **Z** people.
4:2 "**Z** precious children,
4:7 **Z** princes were purer than

Zior (1)

Jos 15:54 (now called Hebron), and Z.

Ziph (11)

Jos 15:24 Z, Telem, Bealoth,
15:55 Maon, Carmel, Z, Juttah,
1Sm 23:14 mountains of the desert of Z.
23:15 at Horesh in the desert of Z.
23:19 Then the men of Z went to
23:24 They left for Z ahead of Saul.
26:1 The people of Z came to Saul
26:2 Saul went to the desert of Z,
1Ch 2:42 who first settled Z,
4:16 Jehallelel's sons were Z,
2Ch 11:8 Gath, Mareshah, Z,

Ziphah (1)

1Ch 4:16 Jehallelel's sons were Ziph, Z,

Ziphion (1)

Gen 46:16 The sons of Gad were Z,

Ziphron (1)

Num 34:9 From there the border goes to Z

Zippor (7)

Num 22:2 Balak, son of Z, saw all that
22:4 At that time Balak, son of Z,
22:10 son of King Z of Moab,
22:16 is what Balak, son of Z, says:
23:18 Hear me, son of Z!
Jos 24:9 son of King Z of Moab,
Jdg 11:25 son of King Z of Moab,

Zipporah (3)

Exo 2:21 So Reuel gave his daughter Z
4:25 Then Z took a flint knife,
18:2 had sent away his wife Z,

Ziv (2)

1Ki 6:1 month of Z (the second month)
6:37 In the month of Z of the fourth

Ziz (1)

2Ch 20:16 will be coming up the Z Pass.

Ziza (3)

1Ch 4:37 Z (son of Shiphi, grandson of
23:11 and Z was the second.
2Ch 11:20 Abijah, Attai, Z, and Shelomith.

Zoan (7)

Num 13:22 seven years before Z in Egypt.)
Psa 78:12 land of Egypt, in the fields of Z.
78:43 his wonders in the fields of Z.
Isa 19:11 The leaders of Z are nothing
19:13 The leaders of Z are acting
30:4 Pharaoh's officials are in Z
Eze 30:14 destroy Pathros, set fire to Z,

Zoar (9)

Gen 13:10 in the direction of Z as far as
14:2 and the king of Bela (that is, Z).
14:8 Z) marched out and prepared
19:22 (The city is named Z [Small].)
19:23 over the land as Lot came to Z.
19:30 Lot left Z because he was
Dtr 34:3 City of Palms) — as far as Z.
Isa 15:5 Its people flee as far as Z at
Jer 48:34 It will be heard from Z to

Zobah (10)

1Sm 14:47 Edom, the kings of Z,
2Sm 8:5 to help King Hadadezer of Z,
10:6 and Z (20,000 foot soldiers),
10:8 while the Arameans from Z
23:36 Igal (son of Nathan) from Z,
1Ki 11:23 King Hadadezer of Z,
11:24 after David killed the men of Z.
1Ch 18:5 to help King Hadadezer of Z,
19:6 Mesopotamia, Maacah, and Z.
19:9 while the Arameans from Z

Zobah's (3)

2Sm 8:3 he defeated Z King Hadadezer,
8:12 taken from Z King Hadadezer,
1Ch 18:9 army of Z King Hadadezer,

Zobebah (1)

1Ch 4:8 was the father of Anub and Z,

zodiac (1)

2Ki 23:5 sun god, the moon god, the z,

Zohar (4)

Gen 23:8 Encourage Ephron, son of Z,
25:9 son of Z the Hittite.
46:10 Ohad, Jakin, Z, and Shaul,
Exo 6:15 Ohad, Jachin, Z, and Shaul,

Zoheleth (1)

1Ki 1:9 and fattened calves at Z Rock

Zoheth (1)

1Ch 4:20 sons were Z and Ben Zoheth.

Zophah (1)

1Ch 7:35 brother Helem's sons were Z,

Zophah's (1)

1Ch 7:36 Z sons were Suah,

Zophai (1)

1Ch 6:26 Elkanah's son was Z.

Zophai's (1)

1Ch 6:26 Z son was Nahath.

Zophar (4)

Job 2:11 Bildad of Shuah, Z of Naama.
11:1 Then Z from Naama replied to
20:1 Then Z from Naama replied to
42:9 and Z of Naama went and did

Zophim (1)

Num 23:14 So he took him to the Field of Z

Zorah (10)

Jos 15:33 villages: Eshtaol, Z, Ashnah,
19:41 of their inheritance included Z,
Jdg 13:2 a man from Z named Manoah.
13:25 between Z and Eshtaol.
16:31 and buried him between Z
18:2 men from Z and Eshtaol.
18:8 their relatives in Z and Eshtaol.
18:11 men from the tribe of Dan left Z
2Ch 11:10 Z, Aijalon, and Hebron.
Neh 11:29 in En Rimmon, Z, Jarmuth,

Zorahites (1)

1Ch 2:53 came the Z and Eshtaolites.

Zorathites (1)

1Ch 4:2 were the families of the Z.

Zorites (1)

1Ch 2:54 half of the Manahathites, the Z,

Zuar (5)

Num 1:8 Nethanel, son of Z,
2:5 Issachar is Nethanel, son of Z.
7:18 second day Nethanel, son of Z,
7:23 gifts from Nethanel, son of Z.
10:15 Nethanel, son of Z,

Zuph (3)

1Sm 1:1 whose father was Z from the
9:5 they came to the territory of Z,
1Ch 6:35 who was the son of Z,

Zur (6)

Num 25:15 was Cozbi, daughter of Z.
25:15 (Z was the head of a family
31:8 Evi, Rekem, Z, Hur, and Reba.
Jos 13:21 Evi, Rekem, Z, Hur, and Reba.
1Ch 8:30 then Z, Kish, Baal, Nadab,
9:36 then Z, Kish, Baal, Nadab,

Zuriel (1)

Num 3:35 and households was Z,

Zurishaddai (5)

Num 1:6 Shelumiel, son of Z,
2:12 Simeon is Shelumiel, son of Z.
7:36 Simeon, Shelumiel, son of Z,
7:41 gifts from Shelumiel, son of Z.
10:19 Shelumiel, son of Z,

Words Omitted in *God's Word* Complete Concordance

Note: Only selected numbers have been concorded. Unconcorded numbers are not listed below.

a
a lot
about
above
absolutely
according
across
actually
addition
after
afterward
afterwards
again
against
ago
ah
aha
ahead
all
almost
along
alongside
already
alright
also
although
am
among
an
and
another
any
anyhow
anymore
anyone
anyone's
anything
anyway
anywhere
apiece
are
aren't
around
as
at
away
awhile
back
backward
backwards
barely
based
be
became
because
become
becomes
becoming
been
before
beforehand
behind
being
below
beneath
beside
besides
between
beyond
both
but
by
came
can
cannot
can't
certainly
clearly
closely
come
comes
completely
consequently
constantly
continually
continuously
could
couldn't
currently
decisively
deeply
definitely
did
didn't
directly
do
does
doesn't
doing
done
don't
down
downward
during
each
earlier
earliest
early
eighteenth
either
eleventh
else
else's
elsewhere
endlessly
enough
enthusiastically
entire
entirely
equally
especially
even
evenly
eventually
every
everybody
everyone
everyone's
everything
everything's
everywhere
except
extraordinarily
extremely
facedown
fact
farewell
fellow
few
fewer
fifty-second
finally
finely
for
formerly
forth
fortieth
forty-first
forward
four-footed
four-legged
frequently
from
front
fully
furthermore
get
gets
getting
got
gradually
great

greatly
had
hadn't
half-baked
half-bushel
half-moon
half-pint
half-sheet
hardly
has
hasn't
have
haven't
having
he
he'll
her
here
hereby
here's
hers
herself
he's
highly
him
himself
his
how
however
I
I'd
if
I'll
I'm
immediately
importantly
impulsively
in
increasingly
indeed
infinite
infinitely
inside
instantly
instead
intensely
into
is
isn't
it
it'll
it's
its
itself
I've
late
later
latter
lengthwise
less
let
let's
lets
letting
like
likewise
many
may
maybe
me
meantime
meanwhile
mere
merely
might
mine
momentarily
more
moreover
much
must
my
myself
near
nearby
nearer
nearest
nearly
neither
never
nevertheless
nineteenth
no
none
nor
not
nothing
nothing's
noticeably
now
nowadays
nowhere
O
obviously
of
off
often
Oh
on
once
one
one's
ones
only
onto
or
other
other's
others
otherwise
our
ours
ourselves
out
outside
over
overly
own
partially
particularly
partly
people
people's
per
perfectly
perhaps
person
person's
place
placed
place's
places
placing
probably
put
puts
putting
quite
rather
really
richly
richness
said
same
say
saying
seventeenth
second-in-command
second-rate
second-story
several
she
she'll
she's
should
shouldn't
since
sincerely
sir
sirs
sixteenth
so
so-called
solidly
some
someday
somehow

someone
someone's
someplace
something
sometime
sometimes
somewhere
soon
specially
specifically
still
strongly
successfully
such
sudden
suddenly
surely
ten-acre
ten-stringed
terribly
than
that
that's
the
their
theirs
them
themselves
then
there
thereby
therefore
there'll
there's
these
they
they'd
they'll
they're
they've
thing
things
third-highest
thirteenth
thirtieth
thirty-eighth
thirty-fifth
thirty-first
thirty-ninth
thirty-second
thirty-seventh
thirty-sixth
this
thoroughly
those
though
three-day
three-pronged
three-stringed
through
throughout
to
together
too
toward
towards
triple-braided
truly
twelfth
twelve-month
twentieth
twenty-fifth
twenty-first
twenty-fourth
twenty-second
twenty-seventh
twenty-sixth
twenty-third
two-horned
two-quart
ultimately
under
unless
until
up
upon
us
usually
vague
very
was
wasn't
way
ways
we
we'd
we'll
we're
we've
well
were
weren't
what
whatever
what's
whatsoever
when
whenever
where
wherever
where's
whether
which
whichever
while
who
whoever
whole
whom
whomever
who's
whose
why
widely
widespread
will
with
within
without
won't
would
wouldn't
yet
you
you'll
you're
you've
your
yours
yourself
yourselves

Archaic Words and Uses in *God's Word* Complete Concordance

The following list of archaic words and their equivalent translations in *God's Word* is not exhaustive, and it does not attempt to include every possible alternate. The purpose of this list is to offer suggestions for words you may remember from another translation but cannot find in *God's Word*.

Word/phrase used in other translations	Word/phrase used in *God's Word*
abomination	disgusting thing
alpha and omega	A and Z
ark	ship (when used with Noah)
ark of the covenant	ark of the promise
ascribe	give
atonement	make acceptable, make peace with, pay, forgive, payment for sins
bath	gallons
blaspheme	curse, dishonor (God), slander
betrothed	promised in marriage
bless the Lord	thank the Lord
censer	incense burner
cloak	coat, clothes
cock	rooster
conceive	become pregnant
consecrate	set apart, set aside, dedicate, holy
covenant	agreement, promise, arrangement, pledge, treaty
covet	desire, greed
cubit	inches, feet
defile	become unclean; dishonor
deliver	rescue, save
dowry	bride price
drachma	pounds, coins
dragon	serpent
drink offering	wine offering
elders	(older, respected) leaders
ephah	bushel
exalt	honor, highly honor
Feast of Tabernacles	Festival of Booths
firstfruits	offerings of the first of your produce, the first grain you harvest
forsake	abandon
fruitful and multiply	fertile and increase
garments	clothes
gentiles	non-Jews
gerah	ounces or pounds
go in to	sleep with, adultery
Gospel	Good News
grace	kindness, good will, favor, care, gift
hardened [someone's] heart	stubborn
harlot	prostitute
heart	mind
hemorrhage	chronic bleeding
holocaust	burnt offering
Holy of Holies	most holy place
homer	gallons
host	armies
hour	a.m., p.m., time, o'clock, moment
house of	family/family line, descendants, tribe(s)
inheritance	possession, those who belong to you, people who belong to you
iniquity	guilt, sin

Word/phrase used in other translations	Word/phrase used in GOD'S WORD
jealous God	a God who does not tolerate rivals
Jehovah	LORD
justify/justification	(receive) God's approval
know	make love to
Law of Moses	Moses' Teachings
leprosy	skin disease
lie with	have sexual intercourse, go to bed with
lineage	descendant
loins	descendant(s), waist, insides
Lord of Hosts	Lord of Armies
mammon	money
mankind	humanity
man-made	made by human hands
Mary Magdalene	Mary from Magdala
my lord	sir
my lord the king	your majesty/your royal majesty
O king	your majesty
overweening	very
parable	story, illustration
paraclete	helper
peace offering	fellowship offering
perish	die, disappear, vanish
pillar of cloud/fire	column of smoke/fire
preach	tell/ spread the Good News/the news/the word/the message, announce
predestine	decide, appoint
presbyter	spiritual leader
pride	arrogance (when used in a negative sense)
proclaim	announce, make an announcement, declare, tell
propitiation/expiation	payment for sins, throne of mercy
prostrated	knelt down with face touching the ground
Redeemer/redeem	defender, relative, buy back, reclaim
reap	harvest
reconcile/reconciliation	restored relationship, brought back to God, make peace with
remission	forgiveness
remnant	faithful few, remaining few, those who are left
repent	change the way you think and act
resurrection	came back to life, brought back to life
right hand	position of authority, highest position
Sabbath	day of worship
sanctify	set apart, set aside, dedicate, holy
Sanhedrin	Jewish council
shekel	ounces or pounds
sow	plant
sower	farmer
statutes	laws, decrees
stiffnecked	impossible to deal with, stubborn
stranger	foreigner
swaddling clothes	strips of cloth
tabernacle	tent of meeting
talent	pounds or dollars
tenants	workers
testament	promise
tithe	tenth
tongues	languages
transfigured	changed

Word/phrase used in other translations	Word/phrase used in *God's Word*
transgression	wrongdoing, sin, failure, disobedience, crime, rebellion
vessel	pottery, clay pot, container, jar
vindicate	take sides, judge favorably, defend, provide justice for
votive offering	freewill offering
wadi	river, brook
wave offering	offering presented to the Lord
whale	fish
with child	pregnant
woe	how horrible, how terrible
wrath	anger, fury, rage
Yahweh	LORD
your handmaid	I, me
your servant(s)	I, me (we, us)